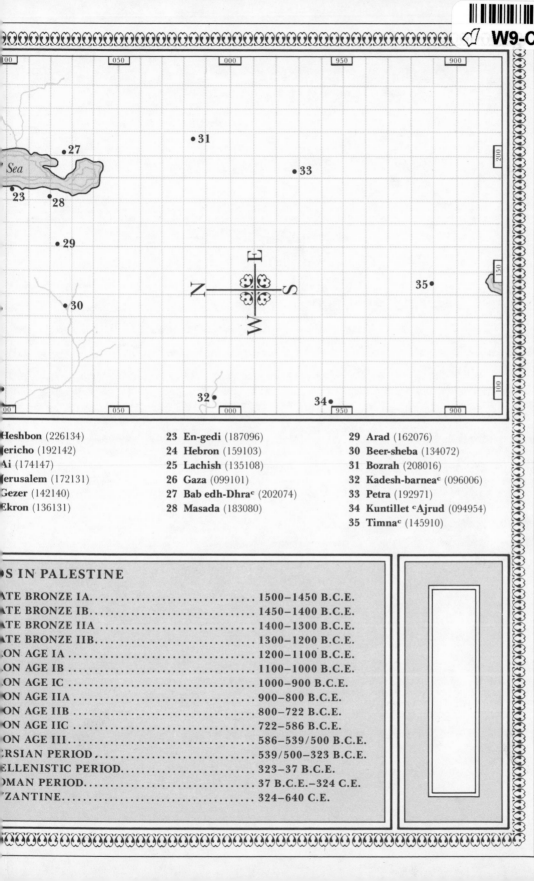

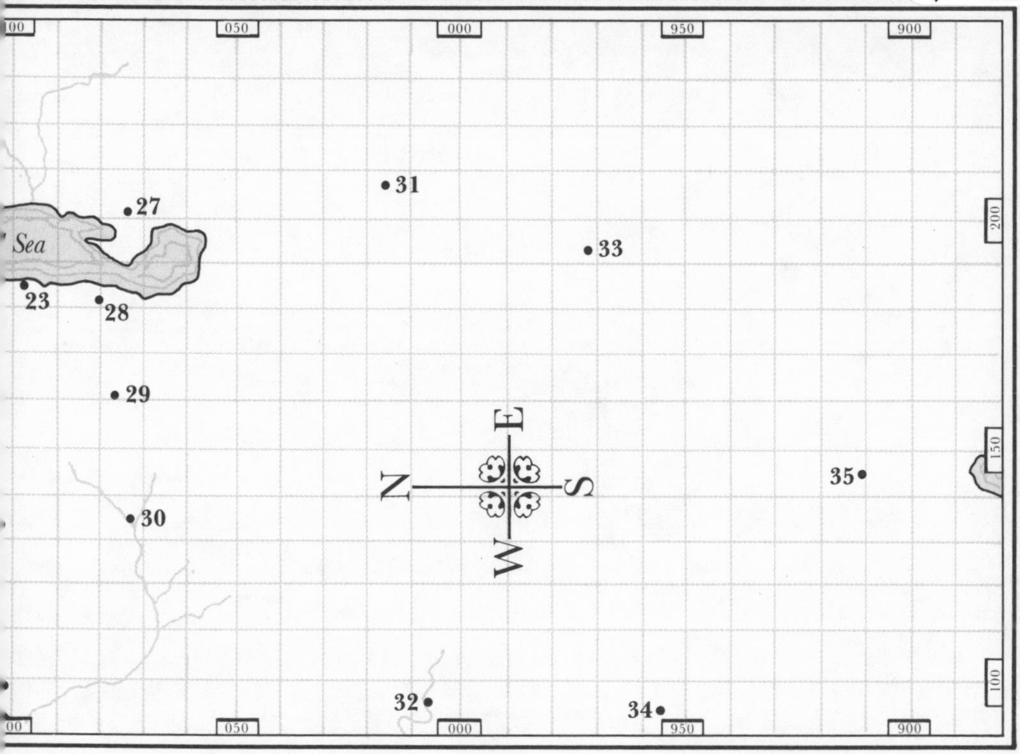

Heshbon (226134)
Jericho (192142)
Ai (174147)
Jerusalem (172131)
Gezer (142140)
Ekron (136131)

23 **En-gedi** (187096)
24 **Hebron** (159103)
25 **Lachish** (135108)
26 **Gaza** (099101)
27 **Bab edh-Dhra**[c] (202074)
28 **Masada** (183080)

29 **Arad** (162076)
30 **Beer-sheba** (134072)
31 **Bozrah** (208016)
32 **Kadesh-barnea**[c] (096006)
33 **Petra** (192971)
34 **Kuntillet** [c]**Ajrud** (094954)
35 **Timna**[c] (145910)

S IN PALESTINE

ATE BRONZE IA	1500–1450 B.C.E.
ATE BRONZE IB	1450–1400 B.C.E.
ATE BRONZE IIA	1400–1300 B.C.E.
ATE BRONZE IIB	1300–1200 B.C.E.
ON AGE IA	1200–1100 B.C.E.
ON AGE IB	1100–1000 B.C.E.
ON AGE IC	1000–900 B.C.E.
ON AGE IIA	900–800 B.C.E.
ON AGE IIB	800–722 B.C.E.
ON AGE IIC	722–586 B.C.E.
ON AGE III	586–539/500 B.C.E.
RSIAN PERIOD	539/500–323 B.C.E.
ELLENISTIC PERIOD	323–37 B.C.E.
OMAN PERIOD	37 B.C.E.–324 C.E.
ZANTINE	324–640 C.E.

THE ANCHOR BIBLE DICTIONARY

THE ANCHOR BIBLE DICTIONARY

VOLUME 5
O–Sh

David Noel Freedman
EDITOR-IN-CHIEF

ASSOCIATE EDITORS
Gary A. Herion • David F. Graf
John David Pleins

MANAGING EDITOR
Astrid B. Beck

ABD

DOUBLEDAY

NEW YORK • LONDON • TORONTO • SYDNEY • AUCKLAND

THE ANCHOR BIBLE DICTIONARY: VOLUME 5
PUBLISHED BY DOUBLEDAY
a division of Bantam Doubleday Dell Publishing Group, Inc.
666 Fifth Avenue, New York, New York 10103

THE ANCHOR BIBLE DICTIONARY, DOUBLEDAY,
and the portrayal of an anchor with the letters ABD
are trademarks of Doubleday,
a division of Bantam Doubleday Dell Publishing Group, Inc.

DESIGN BY Stanley S. Drate/Folio Graphics Company, Inc.

Library of Congress Cataloging-in-Publication Data
Anchor Bible dictionary / David Noel Freedman, editor-in-chief;
associate editors, Gary A. Herion, David F. Graf, John David Pleins;
managing editor, Astrid B. Beck.
—1st ed.
p. cm.
Includes bibliographical references.
1. Bible—Dictionaries. I. Freedman, David Noel, 1922– .
BS440.A54 1992
220.3—dc20 91-8385
CIP

Vol. 1 ISBN 0-385-19351-3
Vol. 2 ISBN 0-385-19360-2
Vol. 3 ISBN 0-385-19361-0
Vol. 4 ISBN 0-385-19362-9
Vol. 5 ISBN 0-385-19363-7
Vol. 6 ISBN 0-385-26190-X

10 9 8 7 6 5 4 3 2 1

FIRST EDITION

CONSULTANTS

HANS DIETER BETZ (Greco-Roman Religion)
Shailer Mathews Professor of NT Studies, University of Chicago

JAMES H. CHARLESWORTH (Apocrypha and Pseudepigrapha)
George L. Collord Professor of NT Language and Literature, Princeton Theological Seminary

FRANK MOORE CROSS (Old Testament)
Hancock Professor of Hebrew and Other Oriental Languages, Harvard University

WILLIAM G. DEVER (Archaeology)
Professor of Near Eastern Archaeology and Anthropology, University of Arizona

A. KIRK GRAYSON (Mesopotamia and Assyriology)
Professor, University of Toronto

PETER MACHINIST (Bible and Ancient Near East)
Professor of Near Eastern Languages and Civilizations, Harvard University

ABRAHAM J. MALHERBE (New Testament)
Buckingham Professor of New Testament Criticism and Interpretation, The Divinity School, Yale University

BIRGER A. PEARSON (Early Christianity)
Professor of Religious Studies, University of California at Santa Barbara

JACK M. SASSON (Bible and Ancient Near East)
Professor in Religious Studies, University of North Carolina

WILLIAM R. SCHOEDEL (Early Christian Literature)
University of Illinois at Urbana-Champaign

EDITORIAL STAFF

EDITOR-IN-CHIEF:
David Noel Freedman

ASSOCIATE EDITORS:
Gary A. Herion
David F. Graf
John David Pleins

MANAGING EDITOR:
Astrid B. Beck

ASSISTANT EDITOR:
Philip C. Schmitz

PRODUCTION EDITOR:
Leslie Barkley

ASSISTANTS TO THE EDITOR:
Mark J. Fretz
Herbert Grether
John Huddlestun
John Kutsko
Dale Manor
Paul Mirecki
James Mueller
David R. Seely
William Ward
Harry Weeks

PRODUCTION ASSISTANTS:
Carol Herion
Dennis Moser

LIST OF ABBREVIATIONS

1 Apoc. Jas.	*First Apocalypse of James* (NHC V,*3*)
1 Chr	1 Chronicles
1 Clem.	*1 Clement*
1 Cor	1 Corinthians
1 En.	*1 Enoch (Ethiopic Apocalypse)*
1 Esdr	1 Esdras
1 John	1 John
1 Kgdms	1 Samuel (LXX)
1 Kgs	1 Kings
1 Macc	1 Maccabees
1 Pet	1 Peter
1 Sam	1 Samuel
1 Thess	1 Thessalonians
1 Tim	1 Timothy
1Q, 2Q, 3Q, etc.	Numbered caves of Qumran, yielding written material; followed by abbreviation of biblical or apocryphal book
1QapGen	*Genesis Apocryphon* of Qumran Cave 1
1QH	*Hōdāyôt (Thanksgiving Hymns)* from Qumran Cave 1
1QIsa$^{a, b}$	First or second copy of Isaiah from Qumran Cave 1
1QM	*Milḥāmāh (War Scroll)*
1QpHab	*Pesher on Habakkuk* from Qumran Cave 1
1QS	*Serek hayyaḥad (Rule of the Community, Manual of Discipline)*
1QSa	Appendix A *(Rule of the Congregation)* to 1QS
1QSb	Appendix B *(Blessings)* to 1QS
1st	first
2 Apoc. Jas.	*Second Apocalypse of James* (NHC V,*4*)
2 Bar.	*2 Baruch (Syriac Apocalypse)*
2 Chr	2 Chronicles
2 Clem.	*2 Clement*
2 Cor	2 Corinthians
2 En.	*2 Enoch (Slavonic Apocalypse)*
2 Esdr	2 Esdras
2 John	2 John
2 Kgdms	2 Samuel (LXX)
2 Kgs	2 Kings
2 Macc	2 Maccabees
2 Pet	2 Peter
2 Sam	2 Samuel
2 Thess	2 Thessalonians
2 Tim	2 Timothy
2d	second
3 Bar.	*3 Baruch (Greek Apocalypse)*
3 Cor.	*3 Corinthians*
3 En.	*3 Enoch (Hebrew Apocalypse)*
3 John	3 John
3 Kgdms	1 Kings (LXX)
3 Macc.	*3 Maccabees*
3d	third
3Q15	Copper Scroll from Qumran Cave 3
4 Bar.	*4 Baruch*
4 Ezra	*4 Ezra*
4 Kgdms	2 Kings (LXX)
4 Macc.	*4 Maccabees*
4QFlor	*Florilegium* (or *Eschatological Midrashim*) from Qumran Cave 4
4QMess ar	Aramaic "Messianic" text from Qumran Cave 4
4QPhyl	Phylacteries from Qumran Cave 4
4QPrNab	Prayer of Nabonidus from Qumran Cave 4
4QTestim	*Testimonia* text from Qumran Cave 4
4QTLevi	*Testament of Levi* from Qumran Cave 4
5 Apoc. Syr. Pss.	*Five Apocryphal Syriac Psalms*
5 Macc.	*5 Maccabees*
11QMelch	*Melchizedek* text from Qumran Cave 11
11QtgJob	*Targum of Job* from Qumran Cave 11
A	Codex Alexandrinus
ÄA	Ägyptologische Abhandlungen
AA	*Archäologischer Anzeiger*, Berlin
AAL	*Afroasiatic Linguistics*, Malibu, CA

AANLM — *Atti dell'Accademia Nazionale dei Lincei, Memorie, Classe di scienze morali, storiche e filologiche,* ser. 8
AANLR — *Atti dell'Accademia Nazionale dei Lincei, Rendiconti, Classe di scienze morali, storiche e filologiche,* ser. 8
AARAS — American Academy of Religion Academy Series
AARASR — American Academy of Religion Aids for the Study of Religion
AARCRS — American Academy of Religion Classics in Religious Studies
AARSR — American Academy of Religion Studies in Religion
AARTT — American Academy of Religion Texts and Translations
AASF — Annales Academiae Scientarum Fennicae, Helsinki
AASOR — Annual of the American Schools of Oriental Research
ÄAT — Ägypten und Altes Testament
AAWLM — *Abhandlungen der Akademie der Wissenschaften und der Literatur Mainz*
AB — Anchor Bible
ABAW — Abhandlungen der Bayerischen Akademie der Wissenschaften
AbB — Altbabylonische Briefe in Umschrift und Übersetzung, ed. F. R. Kraus. Leiden, 1964–
abbr. — abbreviated, abbreviation
ABD — *Anchor Bible Dictionary*
ABIUSJH — *Annual of Bar-Ilan University Studies in Judaica and the Humanities*
ABL — *Assyrian and Babylonian Letters,* 14 vols., ed. R. F. Harper. Chicago, 1892–1914
ABLA — M. Noth. 1971. *Aufsätze zur biblischen Landes- und Altertumskunde,* ed. H. W. Wolff. Neukirchen-Vluyn
ʿAbod. Zar. — *ʿAboda Zara*
ʾAbot — *ʾAbot*
ʾAbot R. Nat. — *ʾAbot de Rabbi Nathan*
Abr — Philo, *De Abrahamo*
ABR — *Australian Biblical Review*
ABRMW — H. Graf Reventlow. 1985. *The Authority of the Bible and the Rise of the Modern World.* Trans. J. Bowden. Philadelphia
AbrN — *Abr-Nahrain*
absol. — absolute
AcApos — *Acta Apostolorum Apocrypha.* 3 vols. Hildesheim, 1959
ACF — *Annuaire du Collège de France,* Paris
ACNT — Augsburg Commentary on the New Testament
AcOr — *Acta orientalia*
AcOrASH — *Acta orientalia Academiae Scientiarum Hungaricae*
ACR — *American Classical Review*
AcSum — *Acta Sumerologica*
act. — active
Acts — Acts (or Acts of the Apostles)
Acts Andr. — *Acts of Andrew*
Acts Andr. Mth. — *Acts of Andrew and Matthias*
Acts Andr. Paul — *Acts of Andrew and Paul*
Acts Barn. — *Acts of Barnabas*
Acts Jas. — *Acts of James the Great*
Acts John — *Acts of John*
Acts John Pro. — *Acts of John (by Prochorus)*
Acts Paul — *Acts of Paul*
Acts Pet. — *Acts of Peter*
Acts Pet. (Slav.) — *Slavonic Acts of Peter*
Acts Pet. 12 Apost. — *Acts of Peter and the Twelve Apostles* (NHC VI,*1*)
Acts Pet. Andr. — *Acts of Peter and Andrew*
Acts Pet. Paul — *Acts of Peter and Paul*
Acts Phil. — *Acts of Philip*
Acts Phil. (Syr.) — *Acts of Philip (Syriac)*
Acts Pil. — *Acts of Pilate*
Acts Thad. — *Acts of Thaddaeus*
Acts Thom. — *Acts of Thomas*
ActSS — *Acta Sanctorum*
ACW — Ancient Christian Writers
A.D. — *anno domini* (year)
ad loc. — *ad locum* (at the place)
ADAIK — Abhandlungen des deutschen archäologischen Instituts, Kairo
ADAJ — *Annual of the Department of Antiquities of Jordan*
Add Dan — Additions to Daniel
Add Esth — Additions to Esther
ADFU — Ausgrabungen der Deutschen Forschungsgemeinschaft in Uruk-Warka
adj. — adjective
ADOG — *Abhandlungen der Deutschen Orient-Gesellschaft,* Berlin
ADPV — Abhandlungen des Deutschen Palästina-Vereins
adv. — adverb
AE — *L'année épigraphique* [cited by year and no. of text]
AEB — *Annual Egyptological Bibliography*
Aeg — *Aegyptus: Revista italiana di egittologia e papirologia*
AEHE IV — *Annuaire de l'École pratique des Hautes Études,* IVᵉ section, Sc. hist. et philol., Paris
AEHE V — *Annuaire de l'École pratique des Hautes Études,* Vᵉ section, Sc. relig., Paris

AEHL — *Archaeological Excavations in the Holy Land,* ed. A. Negev. Englewood Cliffs, NJ, 1980
AEL — M. Lichtheim. 1971–80. *Ancient Egyptian Literature.* 3 vols. Berkeley
AER — *American Ecclesiastical Review*
AESH — B. Trigger, B. J. Kemp, D. O'Connor, and A. B. Lloyd. 1983. *Ancient Egypt: A Social History.* Cambridge
Aet — Philo, *De aeternitate mundi*
Aev — *Aevum: Rassegna di scienze storiche linguistiche e filologiche*
ÄF — Ägyptologische Forschungen
AFER — *African Ecclesiastical Review,* Eldoret, Kenya
AfL — *Archiv für Liturgiewissenschaft,* Regensburg
AFNW — *Arbeitsgemeinschaft für Forschung des Landes Nordrhein-Westfalen,* Cologne
AfO — *Archiv für Orientforschung,* Graz
AfrTJ — *Africa Theological Journal,* Arusha, Tanzania
AgAp — Josephus, *Against Apion (= Contra Apionem)*
ʾAg. Ber. — *ʾAggadat Berešit*
AGJU — Arbeiten zur Geschichte des antiken Judentums und des Urchristentums
Agr — Philo, *De agricultura*
AGSU — Arbeiten zur Geschichte des Spätjudentums und Urchristentums
AH — *An Aramaic Handbook,* ed. F. Rosenthal, 2 vols. Wiesbaden, 1967
Ah. — *Ahiqar*
AHAW — Abhandlungen der Heidelberger Akademie der Wissenschaften
AHG — B. Albrektson. 1967. *History and the Gods.* ConBOT 1. Lund
AHR — *American Historical Review*
AHW — *Akkadisches Handwörterbuch,* ed. W. von Soden. 3 vols. Wiesbaden, 1965–81
AI — Arad Inscription [cited according to Y. Aharoni. 1981. *Arad Inscriptions,* Jerusalem]
AION — *Annali dell'Istituto orientali di Napoli*
AIPHOS — *Annuaire de l'Institut de philologie et d'histoire orientales et slaves*
AIR — *Ancient Israelite Religion: Essays in Honor of Frank Moore Cross,* ed. P. D. Miller, P. D. Hanson, and S. D. McBride. Philadelphia, 1987
AIS — I. Finkelstein. 1988. *The Archaeology of the Israelite Settlement.* Jerusalem
AJA — *American Journal of Archaeology*
AJAS — *American Journal of Arabic Studies*
AJBA — *Australian Journal of Biblical Archaeology*
AJBI — Annual of the Japanese Biblical Institute, Tokyo
AJP — *American Journal of Philology*
AJSL — *American Journal of Semitic Languages and Literatures*
AJT — *American Journal of Theology*
Akk — Akkadian
AKM — *Abhandlungen zur Kunde des Morgenlandes (Leipzig)*
AL — *The Assyrian Laws,* ed. G. R. Driver and J. C. Miles. Oxford, 1935
ALBO — Analecta lovaniensia biblica et orientalia
ALGHJ — Arbeiten zur Literatur und Geschichte des hellenistischen Judentums
Allogenes — *Allogenes* (NHC XI,*3*)
Altertum — *Das Altertum,* Berlin
ALUOS — Annual of Leeds University Oriental Society
Am — *America,* New York
AmBenR — *American Benedictine Review*
AMI — Archäologische Mitteilungen aus Iran
Amos — Amos
AMT — R. C. Thompson. 1923. *Assyrian Medical Texts.* Oxford
AN — J. J. Stamm. 1939. *Die akkadische Namengebung.* MVÄG 44. Berlin
AnBib — Analecta Biblica
AnBoll — *Analecta Bollandiana*
AncIsr — R. de Vaux, 1961. *Ancient Israel: Its Life and Institutions.* Trans. J. McHugh. London. Repr. New York, 1965
ANE — Ancient Near East(ern)
ANEP — *Ancient Near East in Pictures Relating to the Old Testament,* 2d ed. with suppl., ed. J. B. Pritchard, Princeton, 1969
ANET — *Ancient Near Eastern Texts Relating to the Old Testament,* 3d ed. with suppl., ed. J. B. Pritchard, Princeton, 1969
ANF — The Ante-Nicene Fathers
Ang — *Angelicum,* Rome
AnGreg — Analecta Gregoriana
ANHMW — *Annalen des Naturhistorische Museum in Wien*
Anim — Philo, *De animalibus*
Anon. Sam. — *Anonymous Samaritan Text*
AnOr — Analecta orientalia
ANQ — *Andover Newton Quarterly*
ANRW — *Aufstieg und Niedergang der römischen Welt,* ed. H. Temporini and W. Haase, Berlin, 1972–
AnSt — *Anatolian Studies*
Ant — Josephus, *Jewish Antiquities (= Antiquitates Judaicae)*
AntCl — *L'antiquité classique*

ANTF	Arbeiten zur neutestamentlichen Textforschung
ANTJ	Arbeiten zum Neuen Testament und Judentum
Anton	*Antonianum*
Anuario	*Anuario de Filología,* Barcelona
ANVAO	Avhandlinger utgitt av det Norske Videnskaps-Akademi i Oslo
AO	Der Alte Orient
AOAT	Alter Orient und Altes Testament
AOATS	Alter Orient und Altes Testament Sonderreihe
AÖAW	*Anzeiger der Österreichischer Akademie der Wissenschaften,* Vienna
AOB^2	*Altorientalische Bilder zum Alten Testament,* 2d ed., ed. H. Gressman. Berlin and Leipzig, 1927
AOBib	Altorientalische Bibliothek
AoF	*Altorientalische Forschungen*
AOS	American Oriental Series
AOSTS	American Oriental Society Translation Series
AOT^2	*Altorientalische Texte zum Alten Testament,* 2d ed., ed. H. Gressman. Berlin and Leipzig, 1926
AP	*L'année philologique*
Ap. Ezek.	*Apocryphon of Ezekiel*
Ap. Jas.	*Apocryphon of James* (NHC I,*2*)
Ap. John	*Apocryphon of John* (NHC II,*1*; III,*1*; IV,*1*)
APAACS	American Philological Association American Classical Studies
APAPM	American Philological Association Philological Monographs
APAT	*Die Apokryphen und Pseudepigraphen des Alten Testaments,* 2 vols., ed. E. Kautzch. Tübingen, 1900. Repr. 1975
APAW	*Abhandlungen der Preussischen Akademie der Wissenschaft*
APEF	*Annual of the Palestine Exploration Fund*
APNM	H. B. Hoffman. 1965. *Amorite Personal Names in the Mari Texts.* Baltimore
Apoc. Ab.	*Apocalypse of Abraham*
Apoc. Adam	*Apocalypse of Adam* (NHC V,*5*)
Apoc. Dan.	*Apocalypse of Daniel*
Apoc. Dosith.	*Apocalypse of Dositheus*
Apoc. El.	*Apocalypse of Elijah*
Apoc. Ezek.	*Apocalypse of Ezekiel*
Apoc. Messos	*Apocalypse of Messos*
Apoc. Mos.	*Apocalypse of Moses*
Apoc. Paul	*Apocalypse of Paul* (NHC V,*2*)
Apoc. Pet.	*Apocalypse of Peter* (NHC VII,*3*)
Apoc. Sedr.	*Apocalypse of Sedrach*
Apoc. Thom.	*Apocalypse of Thomas*

Apoc. Vir.	*Apocalypses of the Virgin*
Apoc. Zeph.	*Apocalypse of Zephaniah*
Apoc. Zos.	*Apocalypse of Zosimus*
Apocr.	*Apocryphal, Apocrypha*
Apol Jud	Philo, *Apologia pro Iudaeis*
Apos.	Apostolic, Apostles
Apos. Con.	*Apostolic Constitutions and Canons*
APOT	*Apocrypha and Pseudepigrapha of the Old Testament,* 2 vols., ed. R. H. Charles. Oxford, 1913
Ar	Arabic
AR	Archaeological Reports
ʿArak.	*ʿArakin*
Aram	Aramaic
ArbT	*Arbeitzen zur Theologie,* Stuttgart
Arch	*Archaeology*
ArchEleph	B. Porten. 1968. *Archives from Elephantine.* Berkeley
ArchPal	W. F. Albright. 1960. *The Archaeology of Palestine.* 3d rev. ed. Harmondsworth. Repr. Gloucester, MA, 1971
ARE	*Ancient Records of Egypt,* 5 vols., ed. J. H. Breasted. Chicago, 1906. Repr. New York, 1962
ARET	Archivi reali di Ebla, Testi
ARG	*Archiv für Reformationsgeschichte*
ARI	W. F. Albright. 1968. *Archaeology and the Religion of Israel.* 5th ed. Baltimore
Aris. Ex.	*Aristeas the Exegete*
Aristob.	*Aristobulus*
ARM	Archives royales de Mari
ARMT	Archives royals de Mari: transcriptions et traductions
ARNA	*Ancient Records from North Arabia,* ed. F. V. Winnett and W. L. Reed. Toronto, 1970
ArOr	*Archiv orientální*
art.	article
Art.	*Artapanus*
ARW	*Archiv für Religionswissenschaft*
AS	Assyriological Studies
ASAE	*Annales du Service des antiquités de l'Egypte*
ASAW	*Abhandlungen der Sächsischen Akademie der Wissenschaften in Leipzig*
Asc. Jas.	*Ascents of James*
Ascen. Is.	*Ascension of Isaiah*
Asclepius	*Asclepius 21–29* (NHC VI,*8*)
ASNU	Acta seminarii neotestamentici upsaliensis
ASORDS	American Schools of Oriental Research Dissertation Series

ASORMS	American Schools of Oriental Research Monograph Series
ASP	American Studies in Papyrology
ASS	*Acta sanctae sedis*
AsSeign	*Assemblées du Seigneur*
ASSR	*Archives des sciences sociales des religions*
Assum. Mos.	*Assumption of Moses*
Assum. Vir.	*Assumption of the Virgin*
Assur	*Assur,* Malibu, CA
ASTI	*Annual of the Swedish Theological Institute*
ASV	American Standard Version
ATAbh	Alttestamentliche Abhandlungen
ATANT	Abhandlungen zur Theologie des Alten und Neuen Testaments
ATAT	Arbeiten zu Text und Sprache im Alten Testament
ATD	Das Alte Testament Deutsch
ATDan	Acta theologica danica
ATG	*Archivo Teológico Granadino,* Granada
ATJ	*Ashland Theological Journal,* Ashland, OH
ATR	*Anglican Theological Review,* Evanston, IL
Aug	*Augustinianum,* Rome
AulaOr	*Aula Orientalis,* Barcelona
AuS	G. Dalman. 1928–42. *Arbeit und Sitte in Palästina.* 7 vols. BFCT 14, 17, 27, 29, 33, 36, 41. Gütersloh, 1928. Repr. Hildesheim, 1964
AusBR	*Australian Biblical Review*
AUSS	*Andrews University Seminary Studies,* Berrien Springs, MI
Auth. Teach.	*Authoritative Teaching* (NHC VI,*3*)
AUU	Acta universitatis upsaliensis
AV	Authorized Version
AW	*The Ancient World,* Chicago
AWEAT	Archiv für wissenschaftliche Erforschung des Alten Testaments
B	Codex Vaticanus
b. (Talm.)	Babylonian (Talmud) = "Babli"
B. Bat.	*Baba Batra*
B. Meṣ.	*Baba Meṣiᶜa*
B. Qam.	*Baba Qamma*
BA	*Biblical Archaeologist*
Bab.	Babylonian
BAC	Biblioteca de autores cristianos
BAEO	Boletín de la asociación españala des orientalistas
BAfO	*Beihefte zur Archiv für Orientforschung,* Graz
BAGD	W. Bauer, W. F. Arndt, F. W. Gingrich, and F. W. Danker. 1979. *Greek-English Lexicon of the New Testament.* 2d ed. Chicago
BAIAS	*Bulletin of the Anglo-Israel Archaeological Society,* London
BANE	*The Bible in the Ancient Near East,* ed. G. E. Wright. Garden City, NY, 1961. Repr. Winona Lake, IN, 1979
Bar	Baruch
BAR	*Biblical Archaeologist Reader*
Bar.	*Baraita*
BARev	*Biblical Archaeology Review*
BARIS	British Archaeological Reports, International Series
Barn.	*Epistle of Barnabas*
BASOR	*Bulletin of the American Schools of Oriental Research*
BASORSup	BASOR Supplement
BASP	*Bulletin of the American Society of Papyrologists*
BASPSup	Bulletin of the American Society of Papyrologists Supplement
BAss	Beiträge zur Assyriologie und semitischen Sprachwissenschaft
BAT	Die Botschaft des Alten Testaments
BBB	Bonner biblische Beiträge
BBC	Broadman Bible Commentary
BBET	Beiträge zur biblischen Exegese und Theologie
BBLAK	*Beiträge zur biblischen Landes- und Altertumskunde,* Stuttgart
B.C.	before Christ
BC	Biblical Commentary, ed. C. F. Keil and F. Delitzsch. Edinburgh.
B.C.E.	before the common (or Christian) era
BCH	*Bulletin du correspondance hellénique*
BCNHE	Bibliothèque copte de Nag Hammadi Section Études
BCNHT	Bibliothèque copte de Nag Hammadi Section Textes
BCPE	*Bulletin de Centre Protestant d'Études,* Geneva
BDB	F. Brown, S. R. Driver, and C. A. Briggs. 1907. *A Hebrew and English Lexicon of the Old Testament.* Oxford
BDF	F. Blass, A. Debrunner, and R. W. Funk. 1961. *A Greek Grammar of the New Testament and Other Early Christian Literature.* Chicago
BDR	F. Blass, A. Debrunner, and F. Rehkopf. 1984. *Grammatik des neutestamentlichen Griechisch.* 16th ed. Göttingen
BE	*Bulletin epigraphique,* ed. P. Gauthier. Paris
BE	Bibliothèque d'étude (Institut français d'Archéologie orientale)
BEFAR	Bibliothèque des Écoles françaises d'Athènes et de Rome
Bek.	*Bekorot*
Bel	Bel and the Dragon
Bened	*Benedictina,* Rome

BeO	*Bibbia e oriente,* Bornato
Ber.	*Berakot*
Berytus	*Berytus,* Beirut, Lebanon
BES	*Bulletin of the Egyptological Seminar,* Chico, CA
Beṣa	*Beṣa (= Yom Ṭob)*
Beth Mikra	*Beth Mikra,* Jerusalem
BETL	Bibliotheca ephemeridum theologicarum lovaniensium
BEvT	Beiträge zur evangelischen Theologie
BFCT	Beiträge zur Förderung christlicher Theologie
BGBE	Beiträge zur Geschichte der biblischen Exegese
BGU	*Berlin Griechische Urkunden*
BHG	*Bibliotheca Hagiographica Graeca.* Brussels, 1909
BHH	*Biblisch-Historisches Handwörterbuch,* ed. B. Reicke and L. Rost. Göttingen, 1962
BHI	J. Bright. 1981. *A History of Israel.* 3d ed. Philadelphia
BHK	*Biblia hebraica,* 3d ed., ed. R. Kittel
BHNTC	Black's/Harper's New Testament Commentaries
BHS	*Biblia hebraica stuttgartensia*
BHT	Beiträge zur historischen Theologie
BIATC	*Bulletin d'information de l'Académie de Théologie Catholique,* Warsaw
Bib	*Biblica,* Rome
BibAT	*Biblical Archeology Today: Proceedings of the International Congress on Biblical Archaeology, Jerusalem, April 1984.* Jerusalem, 1985
BibB	Biblische Beiträge
BibBh	*Biblebhashyam,* Kerala, India
bibliog.	bibliography
BibOr	Biblica et orientalia
BibS(F)	Biblische Studien (Freiburg, 1895–)
BibS(N)	Biblische Studien (Neukirchen, 1951–)
BICS	Bulletin of the Institute of Classical Studies of the University of London
BIES	*Bulletin of the Israel Exploration Society (= Yediot)*
BIFAO	*Bulletin de l'institute français d'archéologie orientale,* Cairo
Bij	*Bijdragen: Tijdschrift voor Filosofie en Theologie,* Amsterdam
Bik.	*Bikkurim*
BiMes	Bibliotheca Mesopotamica
BIN	*Babylonian Inscriptions in the Collection of James B. Nies,* New Haven, 1917–54
BiOr	*Bibliotheca Orientalis,* Leiden
BIOSCS	*Bulletin of the International Organization for Septuagint and Cognate Studies*
BJPES	*Bulletin of the Jewish Palestine Exploration Society (= Yediot;* later *BIES)*
BJRL	*Bulletin of the John Rylands University Library of Manchester*
BJS	Brown Judaic Studies
BK	*Bibel und Kirche,* Stuttgart
BK	F. Bresciani and M. Kamil. 1966. Le lettere aramaiche di Hermopoli. *AANLM* 12/5: 357–428
bk.	book
Bk. Barn.	*Book of the Resurrection of Christ by Barnabas the Apostle*
Bk. Elch.	*Book of Elchasai*
Bk. Noah	*Book of Noah*
BKAT	Biblischer Kommentar: Altes Testament
BLE	*Bulletin de littérature ecclésiastique,* Toulouse
BLe	H. Bauer and P. Leander. 1918–22. *Historische Grammatik der hebräischen Sprache.* Halle, Repr. Hildesheim, 1962
BLit	*Bibel und Liturgie,* Klosterneuburg
BMAP	E. G. Kraeling. 1953. *The Brooklyn Museum Aramaic Papyri.* New Haven. Repr. 1969
BMMA	*Bulletin of the Metropolitan Museum of Art*
BMQ	*British Museum Quarterly*
BMS	*The Bible in Modern Scholarship,* ed. J. P. Hyatt. Nashville, 1965
BN	*Biblische Notizen,* Bamberg
Bo	Unpublished Boğazköy tablets (with catalog number)
BOSA	*Bulletin on Sumerian Agriculture,* Cambridge
B.P.	before (the) present (time)
BR	*Biblical Research,* Chicago
BRev	*Bible Review*
BRevuo	*Biblia Revuo,* Ravenna
BRL	K. Galling. 1937. *Biblisches Reallexikon.* Tübingen
BRM	*Babylonian Records in the Library of J. Pierpont Morgan,* ed. A. T. Clay, New York, 1912–23
BSac	*Bibliotheca Sacra*
BSAW	*Berichte über die Verhandlungen der Sächsischen Akademie der Wissenschaften zu Leipzig,* phil.-hist. Kl.
BSC	Bible Study Commentary
BSFE	*Bulletin de la Société française d'égyptologie*
BSOAS	*Bulletin of the School of Oriental and African Studies*
BTAVO	Beihefte zum Tübinger Atlas des Vorderen Orients
BTB	*Biblical Theology Bulletin*
BTF	*Bangalore Theological Forum,* Bangalore

BTNT	R. Bultmann. 1955. *Theology of the New Testament.* 2 vols. Trans. K. Grobel. New York and London
BToday	*Bible Today,* Collegeville, MN
BTrans	*Bible Translator,* Aberdeen
BTS	*Bible et terre sainte*
BTZ	*Berliner Theologische Zeitschrift*
BU	Biblische Untersuchungen
BuA	B. Meissner. 1920–25. *Babylonien und Assyrien.* 2 vols. Heidelberg
Burg	*Burgense,* Burgos, Spain
BurH	*Buried History,* Melbourne, Australia
BVC	*Bible et vie chrétienne*
BWANT	Beiträge zur Wissenschaft vom Alten und Neuen Testament
BWL	W. G. Lambert. 1960. *Babylonian Wisdom Literature.* Oxford
ByF	*Biblia y Fe,* Madrid, Spain
BZ	*Biblische Zeitschrift,* Paderborn
BZAW	Beihefte zur *ZAW*
BZNW	Beihefte zur *ZNW*
BZRGG	Beihefte zur *ZRGG*
BZVO	Berliner Beitrage zum Vorderen Orient
C	Codex Ephraemi
C&AH	*Catastrophism and Ancient History,* Los Angeles
ca.	*circa* (about, approximately)
CaByr	*Cahiers de Byrsa*
CAD	*The Assyrian Dictionary of the Oriental Institute of the University of Chicago*
CaE	*Cahiers Evangile,* Paris
CAH	*Cambridge Ancient History*
CahRB	Cahiers de la Revue biblique
CahThéol	Cahiers Théologiques
CaJ	*Cahiers de Josephologie,* Montreal
Cant	Song of Songs (or Canticles)
CaNum	*Cahiers de Numismatique,* Bologna
CAP	A. E. Cowley. 1923. *Aramaic Papyri of the Fifth Century B.C.* Oxford [cited by document number]
CAT	Commentaire de l'Ancient Testament
Cath	*Catholica,* Münster
Cav. Tr.	*Cave of Treasures*
CB	*Cultura biblica*
CBC	Cambridge Bible Commentary on the New English Bible
CBQ	*Catholic Biblical Quarterly,* Washington, DC
CBQMS	Catholic Biblical Quarterly Monograph Series
CBSC	Cambridge Bible for Schools and Colleges
CC	*Cross Currents,* West Nyack, NY
CCath	Corpus Catholicorum
CCER	*Cahiers du Cercle Ernest Renan,* Paris
CChr	Corpus Christianorum
CD	Cairo (Genizah), Damascus Document [= S. Schechter, *Documents of Jewish Sectaries,* vol. 1, *Fragments of a Zadokite Work,* Cambridge, 1910. Repr. New York, 1970]
CdÉ	*Chronique d'Égypte,* Brussels
C.E.	common (or Christian) era
Cerinthus	*Cerinthus*
cf.	*confer,* compare
CGTC	Cambridge Greek Testament Commentary
CGTSC	Cambridge Greek Testament for Schools and Colleges
CH	*Church History*
CH	Code of Hammurabi [cited according to G. R. Driver and J. C. Miles, eds. 1952–55. *The Babylonian Laws.* 2 vols. Oxford]
CHAL	*A Concise Hebrew and Aramaic Lexicon of the Old Testament,* ed. W. L. Holladay. Grand Rapids, 1971
chap(s).	chapter(s)
CHB	*The Cambridge History of the Bible,* 3 vols., ed. P. R. Ackroyd, G. W. M. Lampe, and S. L. Greenslade. Cambridge, 1963–70
CHD	Chicago Hittite Dictionary
Cher	Philo, *De cherubim*
CHI	*Cambridge History of Iran*
CHJ	*The Cambridge History of Judaism,* ed. W. D. Davies and L. Finkelstein. Cambridge, 1984–
CHR	*Catholic Historical Review*
CHSP	*Center for Hermeneutical Studies Protocol Series,* Berkeley, CA
CIG	*Corpus inscriptionum graecarum*
CII	*Corpus inscriptionum indicarum*
CIJ	*Corpvs inscriptionvm ivdaicarvm,* ed. J. B. Frey. Sussidi allo studio delle antichità cristiane, pub. per cura del Pontificio istituto di archeologia cristiana 1, 3. Vatican City, 1936–52
CIL	*Corpus inscriptionum latinarum*
CIS	*Corpus inscriptionum semiticarum*
CiuD	*Ciudad de Dios,* Madrid
CJ	*Concordia Journal,* St. Louis, MO
CJT	*Canadian Journal of Theology*
CL	*Communautés et Liturgies,* Ottignies, Belgium
CL	Code of Lipit-Ishtar [R. R. Steele. 1948. The Code of Lipit-Ishtar. *AJA* 52: 425–50]
Cl. Mal.	*Cleodemus Malchus*
CLA	*Canon Law Abstracts,* Melrose, Scotland
cm	centimeter(s)

CMHE	F. M. Cross. 1973. *Canaanite Myth and Hebrew Epic.* Cambridge, MA
CMIB	*Canadian Mediterranean Institute Bulletin,* Ottawa
CNFI	*Christian News From Israel,* Jerusalem, Israel
CNS	*Cristianesimo nella Storia,* Bologna, Italy
CNT	Commentaire du Nouveau Testament
CO	*Commentationes orientales,* Leiden
Col	Colossians
col(s).	column(s)
Coll	*Collationes,* Brugge, Belgium
Colloquium	*Colloquium,* Auckland/Sydney
ColT	*Collectanea Theologica,* Warsaw
comp.	compiled, compiler
ComViat	*Communio Viatorum,* Prague
ConBNT	Coniectanea biblica, New Testament
ConBOT	Coniectanea biblica, Old Testament
Concilium	Concilium
Conf	Philo, *De confusione linguarum*
Congr	Philo, *De congressu eruditionis gratia*
conj.	conjunction; conjugation
ConNT	*Coniectanea neotestamentica*
constr.	construction; construct
ContiRossini	K. Conti Rossini. 1931. *Chrestomathia Arabica meridionalis ephigraphica,* Rome
COut	Commentaar op het Oude Testament
CP	*Classical Philology*
CPJ	*Corpus papyrorum Judicarum,* ed. A. Tcherikover. 3 vols. Cambridge, MA, 1957–64
CQ	*Church Quarterly*
CQR	*Church Quarterly Review*
CR	*Clergy Review,* London
CRAIBL	*Comptes rendus de l'Académie des inscriptions et belles-lettres*
CRBR	*Critical Review of Books in Religion*
CRINT	Compendia rerum iudaicarum ad novum testamentum
CRRA	*Compte Rendu de . . . Recontre Assyriologique Internationale*
Crux	*Crux,* Vancouver, BC
CS	*Chicago Studies,* Mundelein, IL
CSCO	Corpus scriptorum christianorum orientalium
CSEL	Corpus scriptorum ecclesiasticorum latinorum
CSR	*Christian Scholars Review,* Houghton, NY
CT	*Cuneiform Texts from Babylonian Tablets . . . in the British Museum,* London, 1896–
CT	*The Egyptian Coffin Texts,* ed. A. de Buck and A. H. Gardiner. Chicago, 1935–47
CTA	A. Herdner. 1963. *Corpus des tablettes en cunéiformes alphabétiques découvertes à Ras Shamra-Ugarit de 1929 à 1939.* MRS 10. Paris
CTAED	S. Ahituv. 1984. *Canaanite Toponyms in Ancient Egyptian Documents.* Jerusalem
CTH	E. Laroche. 1971. *Catalogue des textes hittites.* Paris
CThM	Calwer Theologische Monographien
CTJ	*Calvin Theological Journal,* Grand Rapids, MI
CTM	*Concordia Theological Monthly*
CToday	*Christianity Today,* Carol Stream, IL
CTQ	*Concordia Theological Quarterly,* Fort Wayne, IN
CTSAP	*Catholic Theological Society of America Proceedings,* New York
CTSSR	College Theology Society Studies in Religion
CU	Code of Ur-Nammu [J. J. Finkelstein. 1960. The Laws of Ur-Nammu. *JCS* 14: 66–82; F. Yildiz. 1981. A Tablet of Codex Ur-Nammu from Sippar. *Or* 58: 87–97]
CurTM	*Currents in Theology and Mission,* Chicago
D	"Deuteronomic" source; or Codex Bezae
DACL	*Dictionnaire d'archéologie chrétienne et de liturgie*
DAGR	*Dictionnaire des antiquités grecques et romaines d'après les textes et les monuments,* ed. C. Daremberg and E. Saglio. 4 vols. Paris, 1877–1919
Dan	Daniel
DB	*Dictionnaire de la Bible,* 5 vols., ed. F. Vigouroux. Paris, 1895–1912
DBAT	*Dielheimer Blätter zum Alten Testament*
DBM	*Deltion Biblikon Meleton,* Athens
DBSup	*Dictionnaire de la Bible, Supplément,* ed. L. Pirot, A. Robert, H. Cazelles, and A. Feuillet. Paris, 1928–
DBTh	*Dictionary of Biblical Theology,* 2d ed., ed. X. Léon-Dufour. Trans. E. M. Stewart. New York, 1973
DC	*Doctor Communis,* Vatican City
DD	*Dor le Dor,* Jerusalem
DDSR	*Duke Divinity School Review*
Dec	Philo, *De decalogo*
Dem.	*Demetrius (the Chronographer)*
Dem.	*Demai*
Deo	Philo, *De Deo*
Der. Er. Rab.	*Derek Ereṣ Rabba*
Der. Er. Zuṭ.	*Derek Ereṣ Zuṭa*
Deut	Deuteronomy

DH	Deuteronomistic History/Historian
DHRP	Dissertationes ad historiam religionum pertinentes
Diakonia	*Diakonia,* Vienna
Dial. Sav.	*Dialogue of the Savior* (NHC III,5)
Dial. Trypho	Justin, *Dialogue with Trypho*
Did	*Didaskalia,* Portugal
Did.	*Didache*
Diogn.	*Epistle to Diognetes*
Direction	*Direction,* Fresno, CA
Disc. 8–9	*Discourse on the Eighth and Ninth* (NHC VI,6)
DISO	C.-F. Jean and J. Hoftijzer. 1965. *Dictionnaire des inscriptions sémitiques de l'ouest.* Leiden
diss.	dissertation
div.	division
Div	*Divinitas,* Vatican City
DivT	*Divus Thomas,* Piacenza, Italy
DJD	Discoveries in the Judean Desert
DL	*Doctrine and Life,* Dublin
DMOA	Documenta et Monumenta Orientis Antiqui
DN	divine name
DÖAW	*Denkschriften der Österreichischer Akademie der Wissenschaften,* Vienna
DOSA	J. Biella. 1982. *Dictionary of Old South Arabic: Sabaean Dialect.* HSS 25. Chico, CA
DOTT	*Documents from Old Testament Times,* ed. D. W. Thomas. Edinburgh, 1958. Repr. New York, 1961
DRev	*The Downside Review,* Bath
DS	Denzinger-Schönmetzer, *Enchiridion symbolorum*
DTC	*Dictionnaire de théologie catholique*
DTT	*Dansk Teologisk Tidsskrift,* Copenhagen
DunRev	*Dunwoodie Review*
E	east(ern); or "Elohist" source
EA	Tell el-Amarna tablets [cited from J. A. Knudtzon, O. Weber, and E. Ebeling, *Die El-Amarna Tafeln,* 2 vols., VAB 2, Leipzig, 1915; and A. F. Rainey, *El-Amarna Tablets 359–379: Supplement to J. A. Knudtzon, Die El-Amarna Tafeln,* 2d rev. ed., AOAT 8, Kevelaer and Neukirchen-Vluyn, 1970]
EAEHL	*Encyclopedia of Archaeological Excavations in the Holy Land,* 4 vols., ed. M. Avi-Yonah, 1975
EAJET	*East Africa Journal of Evangelical Theology,* Machakos, Kenya
EAJT	*East Asia Journal of Theology,* Singapore
EB	Early Bronze (Age); or Echter Bibel
EBib	Études bibliques
Ebr	Philo, *De ebrietate*
Ec	*The Ecumenist,* New York, NY
Eccl *or* Qoh	Ecclesiastes or Qoheleth
EcR	*The Ecumenical Review,* Geneva
Ecu	*Ecumenismo,* Ravenna, Italy
ed.	editor(s); edition; edited by
ED	Early Dynastic period
ʿEd.	*ʿEduyyot*
EDB	*Encyclopedic Dictionary of the Bible,* ed. and trans. L. F. Hartman. New York, 1963
e.g.	*exempli gratia* (for example)
Eg	Egyptian
ÉgT	*Église et Théologie,* Ottawa
EHAT	Exegetisches Handbuch zum Alten Testament
EHI	R. de Vaux. 1978. *The Early History of Israel.* Trans. D. Smith. Philadelphia
EHS	Einleitung in die Heilige Schrift
EI	*Eretz Israel*
EJ	*Encyclopedia Judaica,* 10 vols., ed. J. Klutzkin and I. Elbogen. Berlin, 1928–34
EKKNT	Evangelisch-katholischer Kommentar zum Neuen Testament
EKL	*Evangelisches Kirchenlexikon*
El. Mod.	*Eldad and Modad*
EM	*Ephemerides Mexicanae,* Mexico City
Emm	*Emmanuel,* New York
EncBib	*Encyclopaedia Biblica,* ed. T. K. Cheyne. London, 1800–1903. 2d ed. 1958
EncBibBarc	*Enciclopedia de la Biblia,* ed. A. Diez Macho and S. Bartina. Barcelona, 1963–65
EncBrit	*Encyclopaedia Britannica*
EnchBib	*Enchiridion biblicum*
EncJud	*Encyclopaedia Judaica* (1971)
EncMiqr	*Entsiqlopēdiā Miqrāʾīt-Encyclopaedia Biblica,* Jerusalem, 1950–
EncRel	*Encyclopedia of Religion,* 16 vols., ed. M. Eliade. New York, 1987
Eng	English
Entr	*Encounter,* Indianapolis, IN
Ep Jer	Epistle of Jeremiah
Ep. Alex.	*Epistle to the Alexandrians*
Ep. Apos.	*Epistle to the Apostles*
Ep. Barn.	*Epistle of Barnabas*
Ep. Chr. Abg.	*Epistle of Christ and Abgar*
Ep. Chr. Heav.	*Epistle of Christ from Heaven*
Ep. Lao.	*Epistle to the Laodiceans*
Ep. Lent.	*Epistle of Lentulus*
Ep. Paul Sen.	*Epistles of Paul and Seneca*

Ep. Pet. Phil.	*Letter of Peter to Philip* (NHC VIII,*2*)
Ep. Pol.	*Epistles of Polycarp*
Ep. Tit. (Apoc.)	*Apocryphal Epistle of Titus*
Eph	Ephesians
Eph.	see *Ign. Eph.*
EphC	*Ephemerides Carmelitica,* Rome
Ephem	M. Lidzbarski. 1900–15. *Ephemeris für semitische Epigraphik.* 3 vols. Giessen
EphLit	*Ephemerides Liturgicae,* Rome
EphMar	*Ephemerides Mariologicae,* Madrid
EPRO	Études préliminaires aux religions orientales dans l'Empire romain
ER	*Epworth Review,* London
ErbAuf	*Erbe und Auftrag*
ERE	*Encyclopaedia of Religion and Ethics,* 12 vols., ed. J. Hastings. Edinburgh and New York, 1908–22
ErFor	Erträge der Forschung
ErfThSt	Erfurter Theologische Studien
ErJb	*Eranos Jahrbuch*
ERT	*Evangelical Review of Theology,* Exeter
ᶜErub.	*ᶜErubin*
Escr Vedat	*Escritos del Vedat,* Torrente
esp.	especially
EspVie	*Esprit et Vie.,* Langres
EstBib	*Estudios Bíblicos,* Madrid
EstEcl	*Estudios Eclesiásticos,* Barcelona
EstFranc	*Estudios Franciscanos,* Barcelona
Esth	Esther
EstTeo	*Estudios Teológicos,* São Leopoldo, Brazil
ET	English translation
et al.	*et alii* (and others)
etc.	*et cetera* (and so forth)
Eth	Ethiopic
ETL	*Ephemerides Theologicae Lovanienses,* Louvain
ETOT	W. Eichrodt. 1961–67. *Theology of the Old Testament.* 2 vols. Trans. J. A. Baker. Philadelphia
ÉTR	*Études théologiques et Religieuses,* Montpellier, France
Études	*Études,* Paris
Eugnostos	*Eugnostos the Blessed* (NHC III,*3*; V,*1*)
EuntDoc	*Euntes Docete,* Rome
Eup.	*Eupolemus*
EV(V)	English version(s)
EvJ	*Evangelical Journal,* Myerstown, PA
EvK	Evangelische Kommentare
EvQ	*Evangelical Quarterly,* Derbyshire
EvT	*Evangelische Theologie,* Munich
EV(V)	English version(s)
EWNT	*Exegetisches Wörterbuch zum Neuen Testament,* ed. H. Balz and G. Schneider
Ex	*Explor,* Evanston, IL
ExB	Expositor's Bible
Exeg. Soul	*Exegesis on the Soul* (NHC II,*6*)
Exod	Exodus
ExpTim	*Expository Times,* Surrey
Ezek	Ezekiel
Ezek. Trag.	*Ezekiel the Tragedian*
Ezra	Ezra
f(f).	following page(s)
FAS	Freiburger Altorientalische Studien
FB	Forschuung zur Bibel
FBBS	Facet Books, Biblical Series
FC	Fathers of the Church
fc.	forthcoming (publication)
fem.	feminine; female
FFNT	Foundations and Facets: New Testament
FGLP	Forschungen zur Geschichte und Lehre des Protestantismus
FGrH	F. Jacoby. *Die Fragmente der griechischen Historiker.* 2d ed. 3 vols. in 10 pts. Leiden, 1957–64 [cited by fragment no.]
FH	*Fides et Historia,* Grand Rapids
fig(s).	figure(s)
FKDG	Forschungen zur Kirchen- und Dogmengeschichte
FKT	*Forum Katholische Theologie,* Aschaffenburg
fl.	*floruit* (flourished)
Flacc	Philo, *In Flaccum*
FoiVie	*Foi et Vie,* Paris
Fond	*Fondamenti,* Bresica
Forum	*Forum,* Bonner, MT
FOTL	Forms of Old Testament Literature
FR	Freiburger Rundbrief
Fran	*Franciscanum,* Bogotá
Frg. Tg.	*Fragmentary Targum*
Frgs. Hist. Wrks.	*Fragments of Historical Works*
Frgs. Poet. Wrks.	*Fragments of Poetic Works*
FRLANT	Forschungen zur Religion und Literatur des Alten und Neuen Testaments
Frm.	*Fragments* (NHC XII,*3*)
FSAC	W. F. Albright. 1957. *From the Stone Age to Christianity.* 2d ed., repr. Garden City, NY
FTS	Freiburger Theologische Studien
FuF	*Forschungen und Fortschritte,* Berlin
Fuga	Philo, *De fuga et inventione*
Fund	*Fundamentum,* Riehen, Switzerland
Furrow	*Furrow,* Maynooth

FWSDFML	*Funk and Wagnall's Standard Dictionary of Folklore, Mythology and Legend*
FZPT	*Freiburger Zeitschrift für Philosophie und Theologie,* Fribourg
GAG	W. von Soden. 1969. *Grundriss der akkadischen Grammatik samt Ergänzungsheft.* AnOr 33/47. Rome
Gaium	Philo, *Legatio ad Gaium*
Gal	Galatians
GARI	A. K. Grayson. 1972. *Assyrian Royal Inscriptions.* RANE. Wiesbaden
GB	D. Baly. 1974. *The Geography of the Bible.* 2d ed. New York
GBS	Guides to Biblical Scholarship
GCS	Griechischen christlichen Schriftsteller
Gem.	*Gemara*
Gen	Genesis
GesB	W. Gesenius. *Hebräisches und aramäisches Handwörterbuch,* 17th ed., ed. F. Buhl. Berlin, 1921
GGR	M. P. Nilsson. *Geschichte der griechische Religion.* 2 vols. 2d ed. Munich, 1961
GHBW	R. R. Wilson. 1977. *Genealogy and History in the Biblical World.* YNER 7. New Haven
Gig	Philo, *De gigantibus*
Giṭ.	*Giṭṭin*
GJV	E. Schürer. 1901–9. *Geschichte des jüdisches Volkes im Zeitalter Jesu Christi.* Leipzig. Repr. Hildesheim, 1970
Gk	Greek
GK	*Gesenius' Hebräische Grammatik,* 28th ed., ed. by E. Kautzsch. Leipzig, 1909. Repr. Hildesheim, 1962
Gk. Apoc. Ezra	*Greek Apocalypse of Ezra*
GKB	G. Bergsträsser. 1918–29. *Hebräische Grammatik mit Benutzung der von E. Kautzsch bearbeiteten 28. Auflage von Wilhelm Gesenius' hebräischer Grammatik.* 2 vols. Leipzig. Repr. Hildesheim, 1962
GKC	*Gesenius' Hebrew Grammar,* 28th ed., ed. E. Kautzsch. Trans. A. E. Cowley. Oxford, 1910
GLECS	*Comptes Rendus du Groupe Linguistique d'Études Chamito-Sémitiques,* Paris
GM	*Göttinger Miszellen*
GN	geographical name
GNB	Good News Bible
GNC	Good News Commentary
GNS	Good News Studies
GNT	Grundrisse zum Neuen Testament
GO	Göttinger Orientforschungen
Gos. Barn.	*Gospel of Barnabas*
Gos. Bart.	*Gospel of Bartholomew*
Gos. Bas.	*Gospel of Basilides*
Gos. Bir. Mary	*Gospel of the Birth of Mary*
Gos. Eb.	*Gospel of the Ebionites*
Gos. Eg.	*Gospel of the Egyptians* (NHC III,*2*; IV,*2*)
Gos. Eve	*Gospel of Eve*
Gos. Gam.	*Gospel of Gamaliel*
Gos. Heb.	*Gospel of the Hebrews*
Gos. Inf.	*Infancy Gospels*
Gos. Inf. (Arab)	*Arabic Gospel of the Infancy*
Gos. Inf. (Arm)	*Armenian Gospel of the Infancy*
Gos. John (Apocr.)	*Apocryphal Gospel of John*
Gos. Marcion	*Gospel of Marcion*
Gos. Mary	*Gospel of Mary*
Gos. Naass.	*Gospel of the Naassenes*
Gos. Naz.	*Gospel of the Nazarenes*
Gos. Nic.	*Gospel of Nicodemus*
Gos. Pet.	*Gospel of Peter*
Gos. Phil.	*Gospel of Philip* (NHC II,*3*)
Gos. Thom.	*Gospel According to Thomas* (NHC II,*2*)
Gos. Trad. Mth.	*Gospel and Traditions of Matthias*
Gos. Truth	*Gospel of Truth* (NHC I,*3*; XII,*2*)
GOTR	*Greek Orthodox Theological Review,* Brookline, MA
GP	F. M. Abel. 1933. *Géographie de la Palestine,* 2 vols. Paris
GRBS	*Greek, Roman and Byzantine Studies,* Durham, NC
Great Pow.	*The Concept of Our Great Power* (NHC VI,*4*)
Greg	*Gregorianum,* Rome
GSAT	*Gesammelte Studien zum Alten Testament,* Munich
GTA	Göttinger theologische Arbeiten
GTJ	*Grace Theological Journal,* Winona Lake, IN
GTT	*Gereformeerd Theologisch Tijdschrift,* Netherlands
GTTOT	J. J. Simons. 1959. *The Geographical and Topographical Texts of the Old Testament.* Francisci Scholten memoriae dedicata 2. Leiden
GuL	*Geist und Leben,* Munich
GVG	C. Brockelmann. 1903–13. *Grundriss der vergleichenden Grammatik der semitischen Sprachen.* 2 vols. Berlin. Repr. 1961
ha.	hectares
Hab	Habakkuk
HAB	*Harper's Atlas of the Bible*
HÄB	Hildesheimer ägyptologische Beiträge
HAD	*Hebrew and Aramaic Dictionary of the OT,* ed. G. Fohrer. Trans W. Johnstone. Berlin, 1973

Hag	Haggai
Ḥag.	*Ḥagiga*
HAIJ	J. M. Miller and J. H. Hayes. 1986. *A History of Ancient Israel and Judah.* Philadelphia
Ḥal.	*Ḥalla*
HALAT	*Hebräisches und aramäisches Lexikon zum Alten Testament,* ed. W. Baumgartner et al.
HAR	*Hebrew Annual Review*
HAT	Handbuch zum Alten Testament
HAW	Handbuch der Altertumswissenschaft
HBC	*Harper's Bible Commentary*
HBD	*Harper's Bible Dictionary,* ed. P. J. Achtemeier. San Francisco, 1985
HBT	*Horizons in Biblical Theology,* Pittsburgh, PA
HDB	*Dictionary of the Bible,* 4 vols., ed. by J. Hastings et al. Edinburgh and New York, 1899–1904. Rev. by F. C. Grant and H. H. Rowley, 1963
HDR	Harvard Dissertations in Religion
HDS	Harvard Dissertation Series
Hdt.	Herodotus
Heb	Hebrew; Epistle to the Hebrews
Heb. Apoc. El.	*Hebrew Apocalypse of Elijah*
Hec. Ab	*Hecataeus of Abdera*
Hel. Syn. Pr.	*Hellenistic Synagogal Prayers*
Hen	*Henoch,* Torino, Italy
Heres	Philo, *Quis rerum divinarum heres*
Herm	*Hermathena,* Dublin, Ireland
Herm. Man.	*Hermas, Mandate*
Herm. Sim.	*Hermas, Similitude*
Herm. Vis.	*Hermas, Vision*
Hermeneia	Hermeneia: A Critical and Historical Commentary on the Bible
Ḥev	Naḥal Ḥever texts
HeyJ	*The Heythrop Journal,* London
HG	J. Friedrich. 1959. *Die hethitischen Gesetze.* DMOA 7. Leiden
HGB	Z. Kallai. 1986. *Historical Geography of the Bible.* Leiden
HHI	S. Herrmann. 1975. *A History of Israel in Old Testament Times.* 2d ed. Philadelphia
HibJ	*Hibbert Journal*
HIOTP	H. Jagersma. 1983. *A History of Israel in the Old Testament Period.* Trans. J. Bowden. Philadelphia
Hist. Eccl.	Eusebius, *Historia ecclesiastica (= Church History)*
Hist. Jos.	*History of Joseph*
Hist. Jos. Carp.	*History of Joseph the Carpenter*
Hist. Rech.	*History of the Rechabites*
Hit	Hittite
HJP^{1}	E. Schürer. *The History of the Jewish People in the Time of Jesus Christ,* 5 vols., trans. J. Macpherson, S. Taylor, and P. Christie. Edinburgh, 1886–90
HJP^{2}	E. Schürer. *The History of the Jewish People in the Age of Jesus Christ,* 3 vols., ed. and trans. G. Vermes et al. Edinburgh, 1973–87
HKAT	Handkommentar zum Alten Testament
HKL	R. Borger. 1967–75. *Handbuch der Keilschriftliteratur.* 3 vols. Berlin
HKNT	Handkommentar zum Neuen Testament
HL	Hittite Laws [*ANET,* 188–97]
HM	*Hamizrah Hehadash/Near East,* Jerusalem
HNT	Handbuch zum Neuen Testament
HNTC	Harper's NT Commentaries
HO	Handbuch der Orientalistik
Hokhma	*Hokhma,* La Sarraz, Switzerland
Hor	*Horizons,* Villanova, PA
Hor.	*Horayot*
Hos	Hosea
HPR	*Homiletic and Pastoral Review,* New York
HPT	M. Noth. 1981. *A History of Pentateuchal Traditions.* Trans. B. Anderson. Chico, CA
HR	*History of Religions,* Chicago
HS	*Hebrew Studies,* Madison, WI
HSAO	*Heidelberger Studien zum Alten Orient.* Wiesbaden, 1967
HSAT	*Die heilige Schrift des Alten Testaments,* 4th ed., ed. E. Kautzsch and A. Bertholet. Tübingen, 1922–23
HSCL	Harvard Studies in Comparative Literature
HSCP	*Harvard Studies in Classical Philology,* Cambridge, MA
HSM	Harvard Semitic Monographs
HSS	Harvard Semitic Studies
HTKNT	Herders theologischer Kommentar zum Neuen Testament
HTR	*Harvard Theological Review*
HTS	Harvard Theological Studies
HUCA	*Hebrew Union College Annual,* Cincinnati
Ḥul.	*Ḥullin*
HUTH	Hermeneutische Untersuchungen zur Theologie
Hymn Dance	*Hymn of the Dance*
Hyp. Arch.	*Hypostasis of the Archons* (NHC II,*4*)
Hypo	Philo, *Hypothetica*
Hypsiph.	*Hypsiphrone* (NHC XI,*4*)
IB	*Interpreter's Bible*

IBC — Interpretation: A Bible Commentary for Teaching and Preaching
ibid. — *ibidem* (in the same place)
IBS — *Irish Biblical Studies,* Belfast
ICC — International Critical Commentary
IDB — *Interpreter's Dictionary of the Bible,* ed. G. A. Buttrick. 4 vols. Nashville, 1962
IDBSup — *Interpreter's Dictionary of the Bible Supplementary Volume,* ed. K. Crim. Nashville, 1976
IEJ — *Israel Exploration Journal,* Jerusalem
IG — *Inscriptiones Graecae*
IGRR — *Inscriptiones Graecae ad res Romanas pertinentes,* ed. R. Cagnat, J. Toutain, et al. 3 vols. Paris, 1901–27. Repr. Rome, 1964
Ign. Eph. — *Ignatius, Letter to the Ephesians*
Ign. Magn. — *Ignatius, Letter to the Magnesians*
Ign. Phld. — *Ignatius, Letter to the Philadelphians*
Ign. Pol. — *Ignatius, Letter to the Polycarp*
Ign. Rom. — *Ignatius, Letter to the Romans*
Ign. Symrn. — *Ignatius, Letter to the Smyrnaeans*
Ign. Trall. — *Ignatius, Letter to the Trallians*
IGLS — Jalabert, L., and Mouterde, R. 1929–. *Inscriptions grecques et latines de la Syrie.* 6 vols. Paris.
IGSK — Inschriften griechischer Städte aus Kleinasien
IJH — *Israelite and Judean History,* ed. J. Hayes and M. Miller. OTL. Philadelphia, 1977
IJT — *Indian Journal of Theology,* Calcutta
IKirZ — *Internationale Kirchliche Zeitschrift,* Bern
ILS — *Inscriptiones Latinae selectae,* ed. H. Dessau. 3 vols. in 5 pts. Berlin, 1892–1916. Repr.
Imm — *Immanuel,* Jerusalem
impf. — imperfect
impv. — imperative
inf. — infinitive
Inf. Gos. Thom. — *Infancy Gospel of Thomas*
INJ — *Israel Numismatic Journal,* Jerusalem
Int — *Interpretation,* Richmond, VA
Interp. Know. — *Interpretation of Knowledge* (NHC XI,*1*)
IOS — *Israel Oriental Studies*
IOTS — B. S. Childs. 1979. *Introduction to the Old Testament as Scripture.* Philadelphia
IPN — M. Noth. 1928. *Die israelitischen Personennamen.* BWANT 3/10. Stuttgart. Repr. Hildesheim, 1966
Iraq — *Iraq*
Irénikon — *Irénikon*
IRT — Issues in Religion and Theology
Isa — Isaiah
ISBE — *International Standard Bible Encyclopedia,* 2d ed., ed. G. W. Bromiley
ISEELA — *Instituto Superior de Estudios Eclesiasticos Libro Anual,* Mexico City
Istina — *Istina,* Paris
ITC — International Theological Commentary
ITQ — *Irish Theological Quarterly,* Maynooth
ITS — *Indian Theological Studies,* Bangalore
IvEph — *Die Inschriften von Ephesos,* ed. H. Wankel. 8 vols. IGSK 11–15
j. (*Talm.*) — Jerusalem (Talmud)
J — "Yahwist" source
JA — *Journal asiatique*
JAAR — *Journal of the American Academy of Religion*
JAC — *Jahrbuch für Antike und Christentum*
Jan. Jam. — *Jannes and Jambres*
JANES — *Journal of the Ancient Near Eastern Society of Columbia University,* New York
JAOS — *Journal of the American Oriental Society,* New Haven
JAOSSup — Journal of the American Oriental Society Supplement
JARCE — *Journal of the American Research Center in Egypt,* Boston
Jas — James
JAS — *Journal of Asian Studies*
JB — Jerusalem Bible
JBC — *The Jerome Biblical Commentary,* ed. R. E. Brown, J. A. Fitzmyer, and R. E. Murphy. 2 vols. in 1. Englewood Cliffs, NJ, 1968
JBL — *Journal of Biblical Literature*
JBR — *Journal of Bible and Religion,* Boston
JCS — *Journal of Cuneiform Studies*
JDAI — *Jahrbuch des deutschen archäologischen Instituts*
JDS — Judean Desert Studies
Jdt — Judith
JEA — *Journal of Egyptian Archaeology,* London
Jeev — *Jeevadhara,* Kottayam, Kerala, India
JEH — *Journal of Ecclesiastical History,* London
JEnc — *The Jewish Encyclopaedia,* 12 vols., ed. I. Singer et al. New York, 1901–6
JEOL — *Jaarbericht Vooraziatisch-Egyptisch Gezelschap "Ex Oriente Lux"*
Jer — Jeremiah
JES — *Journal of Ecumenical Studies,* Philadelphia
JESHO — *Journal of the Economic and Social History of the Orient,* Leiden
JETS — *Journal of the Evangelical Theological Society*
JFA — *Journal of Field Archaeology*

JFSR	*Journal of Feminist Studies in Religion,* Atlanta
JHNES	Johns Hopkins Near Eastern Studies
JHS	*Journal of Hellenic Studies,* London
JIBS	*Journal of Indian and Buddhist Studies*
JIPh	*Journal of Indian Philosophy*
JITC	*Journal of the Interdenominational Theological Center,* Atlanta
JJS	*Journal of Jewish Studies,* Oxford
JLA	*The Jewish Law Annual,* Leiden
JMES	*Journal of Middle Eastern Studies*
JMS	*Journal of Mithraic Studies*
JNES	*Journal of Near Eastern Studies,* Chicago
JNSL	*Journal of Northwest Semitic Languages,* Stellenbosch
Job	Job
Joel	Joel
John	John
Jonah	Jonah
Jos	Philo, *De Iosepho*
Jos. or Joseph.	Josephus
Jos. Asen.	*Joseph and Asenath*
Josh	Joshua
JPOS	*Journal of Palestine Oriental Society,* Jerusalem
JPSV	Jewish Publication Society Version
JPT	*Journal of Psychology and Theology,* La Mirada, CA
JQR	*Jewish Quarterly Review*
JQRMS	Jewish Quarterly Review Monograph Series
JR	*Journal of Religion,* Chicago
JRAI	*Journal of the Royal Anthropological Institute*
JRAS	*Journal of the Royal Asiatic Society*
JRE	*Journal of Religious Ethics*
JRelS	*Journal of Religious Studies,* Cleveland, OH
JRH	*Journal of Religious History*
JRS	*Journal of Roman Studies,* London
JRT	*Journal of Religious Thought,* Washington, DC
JSHRZ	Jüdische Schriften aus hellenistisch-römischer Zeit
JSJ	*Journal for the Study of Judaism,* Leiden
JSNT	*Journal for the Study of the New Testament,* Sheffield
JSNTSup	Journal for the Study of the New Testament Supplement Series
JSOR	*Journal of the Society of Oriental Research*
JSOT	*Journal for the Study of the Old Testament,* Sheffield
JSOTSup	Journal for the Study of the Old Testament Supplement Series
JSP	*Journal for the Study of the Pseudepigrapha*
JSPSup	Journal for the Study of the Pseudepigrapha Supplement
JSS	*Journal of Semitic Studies,* Manchester
JSSEA	*Journal of the Society for the Study of Egyptian Antiquities,* Mississauga, Ontario
JSSR	*Journal for the Scientific Study of Religion*
JTC	*Journal for Theology and the Church*
JTS	*Journal of Theological Studies,* Oxford
JTSoA	*Journal of Theology for Southern Africa,* Cape Town, South Africa
Jub.	*Jubilees*
Judaica	*Judaica: Beiträge zum Verständnis . . .*
Judaism	*Judaism,* New York
Jude	Jude
Judg	Judges
JW	Josephus, *The Jewish War (= Bellum Judaicum)*
JWH	*Journal of World History*
K	Kethib
K	Tablets in the Kouyunjik collection of the British Museum [cited by number]
KAI	*Kanaanäische und aramäische Inschriften,* 3 vols., ed. H. Donner and W. Röllig, Wiesbaden: Otto Harrassowitz, 1962
Kairos	*Kairos,* Salzburg
KAJ	*Keilschrifttexte aus Assur juristischen Inhalts,* ed. E. Ebeling. WVDOG 50. Leipzig, 1927
Kalla	*Kalla*
KAR	*Keilschrifttexte aus Assur religiösen Inhalts,* ed. E. Ebeling. WVDOG 28/34. Leipzig, 1919–23
KAT	Kommentar zum Alten Testament
KAV	*Keilschrifttexte aus Assur verschiedenen Inhalts,* ed. O. Schroeder. WVDOG 35. Leipzig, 1920
KB	*Keilschriftliche Bibliothek,* ed. E. Schrader. Berlin, 1889–1915
KB	L. Koehler and W. Baumgartner. 1953. *Lexicon in Veteris Testamenti libros.* Leiden; *Supplementum ad Lexicon in Veteris Testamenti libros.* Leiden, 1958
KBANT	Kommentare und Beiträge zum Alten und Neuen Testament
KBo	*Keilschrifttexte aus Boghazköi.* WVDOG 30/36/68–70/72– . Leipzig, 1916–23; Berlin, 1954–
KD	*Kerygma und Dogma,* Göttingen
KEHAT	*Kurzgefasstes exegetisches Handbuch zum Alten Testament,* ed. O. F. Fridelin, Leipzig, 1812–96
Kelim	*Kelim*

Ker.	*Keritot*
Ketub.	*Ketubot*
KG	H. Frankfort. 1948. *Kingship and the Gods.* Chicago. Repr. 1978
KHC	*Kurzer Handcommentar zum Alten Testament,* ed. K. Marti. Tübingen
Kil.	*Kil'ayim*
KJV	King James Version
KK	*Katorikku Kenkyu,* Tokyo, Japan
Klosterman	E. Klosterman. 1904. *Eusebius Das Onomastikon der Biblischen Ortsnamen.* Leipzig. Repr. 1966
KlPauly	*Der Kleine Pauly,* ed. K. Zeigler–W. Sontheimer, Stuttgart, 1964
KlSchr	*Kleine Schriften* (A. Alt, 1953–59, 1964 [3d ed.]; O. Eissfeldt, 1963–68; K. Ellinger, 1966)
KlT	Kleine Texte
km	kilometer(s)
KRI	K. Kitchen. 1968– . *Ramesside Inscriptions, Historical and Biographical.* 7 vols. Oxford
KRI	Y. Kaufmann. 1960. *The Religion of Israel.* Trans. M. Greenberg. New York
KTR	*King's Theological Review,* London
KTU	*Keilalphabetischen Texte aus Ugarit,* vol. 1, ed. M. Dietrich, O. Loretz, and J. Sanmartín. AOAT 24. Kevelaer and Neukirchen-Vluyn, 1976
KUB	Staatliche Museen zu Berlin, Voderasiatische Abteilung (later Deutsche Orient-Gesellschaft) *Keilschrifturkunden aus Boghazköi,* 1921–
LÄ	*Lexikon der Ägyptologie,* eds. W. Helck and E. Otto, Wiesbaden, 1972
L. A. B.	*Liber Antiquitatum Biblicarum*
Lad. Jac.	*Ladder of Jacob*
LAE	*The Literature of Ancient Egypt,* ed. W. K. Simpson. New Haven, 1972
L. A. E.	*Life of Adam and Eve*
Lam	Lamentations
Lane	E. W. Lane. 1863–93. *An Arabic-English Lexicon.* 8 vols. London. Repr. 1968
LAPO	Littératures anciennes du Proche-Orient
LAR	D. D. Luckenbill. 1926–27. *Ancient Records of Assyria and Babylonia.* Chicago
LÄS	Leipziger ägyptologische Studien
LAS	D. D. Luckenbill. 1924. *Annals of Sennacherib.* OIP 2. Chicago
LASBF	*Liber Annuus Studii Biblici Franciscani,* Jerusalem
Lat	Latin
Lat	*Lateranum,* Vatican City
Laur	*Laurentianum,* Rome

LavTP	*Laval Théologique et Philosophique,* Quebec
LB	Late Bronze (Age)
LB	*Linguistica Biblica,* Bonn
LBAT	*Late Babylonian Astronomical and Related Texts,* ed. T. G. Pinches and A. Sachs. Providence, RI, 1955
LBHG	Y. Aharoni. 1979. *The Land of the Bible,* 3d ed., rev. and enl. by A. F. Rainey. Philadelphia, 1979
LBS	Library of Biblical Studies
LCC	Library of Christian Classics
LCL	Loeb Classical Library
LD	Lectio divina
LE	Laws of Eshnunna [A. Goetze. 1956. *The Laws of Eshnunna.* AASOR 31. New Haven; *ANET,* 161–63]
LEC	Library of Early Christianity
Leg All I–III	Philo, *Legum allegoriae* I–III
Leš	*Lešonénu*
Let. Aris.	*Letter of Aristeas*
Lev	Leviticus
Levant	*Levant,* London
LexLingAeth	A. Dillmann. 1865. *Lexicon linguae aethiopicae.* Leipzig. Repr. New York, 1955; Osnabruck, 1970
LexSyr	C. Brockelmann. 1928. *Lexicon Syriacum.* 2d ed. Halle. Repr.
LHA	F. Zorrell. 1966. *Lexicon Hebraicum et Aramaicum Veteris Testamenti.* Rome
Life	Josephus, *Life (= Vita)*
List	*Listening: Journal of Religion and Culture,* River Forest, IL
lit.	literally
Liv. Pro.	*Lives of the Prophets*
LL	*The Living Light,* Washington, DC
LLAVT	*Lexicon Linguae aramaicae Veteris Testamenti documentis antiquis illustratum.* E. Vogt. 1971. Rome
loc. cit.	*loco citato* (in the place cited)
Lost Tr.	*The Lost Tribes*
LPGL	G. W. H. Lampe. 1961–68. *A Patristic Greek Lexicon.* Oxford
LQ	*Lutheran Quarterly*
LR	*Lutherische Rundschau*
LS	*Louvain Studies,* Louvain
LSJM	H. G. Liddell and R. Scott. 1968. *A Greek-English Lexicon.* rev. ed., ed. H. S. Jones and R. McKenzie. Oxford
LSS	Leipziger Semitistische Studien
LTJ	*Lutheran Theological Journal,* Adelaide, S. Australia
LTK	*Lexikon für Theologie und Kirche*
LTP	*Laval Théologique et Philosophique*

LTQ	*Lexington Theological Quarterly,* Lexington, KY
LUÅ	Lunds universitets årsskrift
Luc	Lucianic recension
Luke	Luke
LumVie	*Lumière et Vie,* Lyons, France
LumVit	*Lumen Vitae,* Brussels
LW	*Lutheran World*
LXX	Septuagint
m	meter(s)
MA	Middle Assyrian
Maarav	*Maarav,* Santa Monica, CA
Ma^{c}aś.	*Ma^{c}aśerot*
Ma^{c}aś. Š.	*Ma^{c}aśer Šeni*
MABL	*The Moody Atlas of Bible Lands,* ed. B. J. Beitzel. Chicago, 1985
Magn.	see *Ign. Magn.*
MaisDieu	*Maison-Dieu,* Paris
Mak.	*Makkot*
Makš.	*Makširin (= Mašqin)*
Mal	Malachi
MAL	Middle Assyrian Laws
MAMA	*Monumenta Asiae Minoris Antiqua,* vol. 1, ed. W. M. Calder and J. M. R. Cormack. Publications of the American Society for Archaeological Research in Asia Minor. Manchester, 1928. Vol. 3, ed. J. Keil and A. Wilhelm, 1931. Vol. 4, ed. W. H. Buckler, W. M. Calder, W. K. C. Guthrie, 1933. Vol. 5, ed. C. W. M. Cox and A. Cameron, 1937. Vol. 6, ed. W. H. Buckler and W. M. Calder, 1939
Man	*Manuscripta,* St. Louis, MO
MANE	*Monographs on the Ancient Near East,* Malibu, CA
Mansrea	*Mansrea,* Madrid
MAOG	Mitteilungen der Altorientalischen Gesellschaft, Leipzig
Marianum	*Marianum,* Rome
Mark	Mark
Marsanes	*Marsanes* (NHC XI,*1*)
MarSt	*Marian Studies,* Dayton, OH
Mart. Bart.	*Martyrdom of Bartholomew*
Mart. Is.	*Martyrdom of Isaiah*
Mart. Mt.	*Martyrdom of Matthew*
Mart. Paul	*Martyrdom of Paul*
Mat. Pet.	*Martyrdom of Peter*
Mart. Pet. Paul	*Martyrdom of Peter and Paul*
Mart. Phil.	*Martyrdom of Philip*
Mart. Pol.	*Martyrdom of Polycarp*
Mas	Masada texts
MÄS	Münchner Ägyptologische Studien
masc.	masculine
Matt	Matthew
May	*Mayéutica,* Marcilla (Navarra), Spain
MB	Middle Bronze (Age)
MB	*Le Monde de la Bible*
MBA	Y. Aharoni and M. Avi-Yonah. 1977. *The Macmillan Bible Atlas.* Rev. ed. New York
MC	*Miscelánea Comillas,* Madrid
MCBW	R. K. Harrison. 1985. *Major Cities of the Biblical World.* New York, 1985
McCQ	*McCormick Quarterly*
MD	E. S. Drower and R. Macuch. 1963. *Mandaic Dictionary.* Oxford
MDAIK	Mitteilungen des deutschen archäologischen Instituts, Kairo
MDOG	Mitteilungen der deutschen Orient-Gesellschaft
MDP	Mémoires de la délégation en Perse
MedHab	Epigraphic Expedition, *Medinet Habu.* OIP 8 (1930), 9 (1932), Chicago
Meg.	*Megilla*
Me^{c}il.	*Me^{c}ila*
Mek.	*Mekilta*
Melch.	*Melchizedek* (NHC IX,*1*)
Melkon	*Melkon*
MelT	*Melita Theologica,* Rabat, Malta
Mem. Apos.	*Memoria of Apostles*
Menaḥ.	*Menaḥot*
MEOL	*Medeelingen en Verhandelingen van het Vooraziatisch-Egyptisch Gezelschap "Ex Oriente Lux,"* Leiden
Mer	*Merleg,* Munich
MeyerK	H. A. W. Meyer, Kritisch-exegetischer Kommentar über das Neue Testament
MGWJ	*Monatsschrift für Geschichte und Wissenschaft des Judentums*
mi.	mile(s)
Mic	Micah
Mid.	*Middot*
Midr.	*Midraš;* cited with usual abbreviation for biblical book; but *Midr. Qoh.* = *Midraš Qohelet*
MIFAO	Mémoires publiés par les membres de l'Institut français d'archéologie orientale du Caire
Migr	Philo, *De migratione Abrahami*
MIO	*Mitteilungen des Instituts für Orientforschung,* Berlin
Miqw.	*Miqwaʾot*
Mird	Khirbet Mird texts
misc.	miscellaneous

MM	J. H. Moulton and G. Milligan. 1914–30. *The Vocabulary of the Greek Testament Illustrated from the Papyri and other Non-Literary Sources.* London. Repr. Grand Rapids, 1949
MNTC	Moffatt NT Commentary
ModChurch	*Modern Churchman,* Leominster, UK
Moʿed	*Moʿed*
Moʿed Qaṭ.	*Moʿed Qaṭan*
Month	*Month,* London
MPAIBL	*Mémoires présentés à l'Académie des inscriptions et belles-lettres*
MPAT	*A Manual of Palestinian Aramaic Texts,* ed. J. A. Fitzmyer and D. J. Harrington. BibOr 34. Rome, 1978
MRR	*The Magistrates of the Roman Republic,* ed. T. R. S. Broughton and M. L. Patterson. 2 vols. Philological Monographs 15. 1951–52. Suppl., 1960
MRS	Mission de Ras Shamra
ms (pl. mss)	manuscript(s)
MScRel	*Mélanges de science religieuse,* Lille
MSD	Materials for the Sumerian Dictionary
MSL	*Materialen zum sumerischen Lexikon,* Rome, 1937–
MSR	*Mélanges de Science Religieuse,* Lille
MSU	Mitteilungen des Septuaginta-Unternehmens
MT	Masoretic Text
MTS	Marburger Theologische Studien
MTZ	*Münchner theologische Zeitschrift*
Mur	Wadi Murabbaʿat texts
Mus	*Le Muséon: Revue d'Études Orientales,* Paris
MUSJ	*Mélanges de l'Université Saint-Joseph*
Mut	Philo, *De mutatione nominum*
MVAG	Mitteilungen der vorder-asiatisch-ägyptischen Gesellschaft
N	north(ern)
n(n).	note(s)
NA	Neo-Assyrian
NAB	New American Bible
Nah	Nahum
NARCE	*Newsletter of the American Research Center in Egypt*
NASB	New American Standard Bible
Našim	*Našim*
NAWG	*Nachrichten der Akademie der Wissenschaften in Göttingen*
Nazir	*Nazir*
NB	Neo-Babylonian
N.B.	*nota bene* (note well)
NBD	*The New Bible Dictionary,* 2d ed., ed. J. D. Douglas and N. Hillyer. Leicester and Wheaton, IL
NCBC	New Century Bible Commentary
NCCHS	*New Catholic Commentary on Holy Scripture,* ed. R. D. Fuller et al.
NCE	*New Catholic Encyclopedia,* ed. M. R. P. McGuire et al.
NCH	M. Noth. 1986. *The Chronicler's History.* Trans. H. G. M. Williamson. JSOTSup 51. Sheffield [translates chaps. 14–25 of *ÜgS*]
NC1BC	New Clarendon Bible Commentary
NDH	M. Noth. 1981. *The Deuteronomistic History.* Trans. H. G. M. Williamson. JSOTSup 15. Sheffield [translates chaps. 1–13 of *ÜgS*]
NDIEC	*New Documents Illustrating Early Christianity,* ed. G. H. K. Horsley. Macquarie University, 1976– [= 1981–]
NE	northeast(ern)
NE	M. Lidzbarski. 1898. *Handbuch der nordsemitischen Epigraphik.* 2 vols. Weimar
NEB	New English Bible, Oxford, 1961–70
NEBib	Neue Echter Bibel
Ned.	*Nedarim*
NedTTs	*Nederlands Theologisch Tijdschrift,* The Hague
Neg.	*Negaʿim*
Neh	Nehemiah
Neot	*Neotestamentica,* Stellenbosch
NETR	*The Near East School of Theology Theological Review,* Beirut
neut.	neuter
Nez.	*Neziqin*
NFT	New Frontiers in Theology
NGTT	*Nederduits Gereformeerde Teologiese Tydskrif,* Stellenbosch
NHC	Nag Hammadi Codex
NHI	M. Noth. 1960. *The History of Israel.* 2d ed. Trans. S. Godman, rev. P. R. Ackroyd. London
NHL	*The Nag Hammadi Library in English,* 3d ed., ed. J. M. Robinson. San Francisco, 1978
NHS	Nag Hammadi Studies
NHT	S. R. Driver. 1913. *Notes on the Hebrew Text and the Topography of the Books of Samuel.* 2d ed. Oxford
NICNT	New International Commentary on the New Testament
NICOT	New International Commentary on the Old Testament
Nid.	*Niddah*

NIDNTT	*New International Dictionary of New Testament Theology*, 3 vols., ed. C. Brown. Grand Rapids, 1975–78
NIGTC	New International Greek Testament Commentary
NIV	New International Version
NJB	New Jerusalem Bible
NJBC	*New Jerome Bible Commentary*
NJPSV	New Jewish Publication Society Version
NKJV	New King James Version
NKZ	*Neue kirchliche Zeitschrift*
no.	number
Norea	*The Thought of Norea* (NHC IX,*2*)
NorTT	*Norsk Teologisk Tidsskrift*, Oslo, Norway
NovT	*Novum Testamentum*, Leiden
NovTG[26]	*Novum Testamentum Graece*, ed. E. Nestle and K. Aland. 26th ed. Stuttgart, 1979
NovTSup	Novum Testamentum Supplements
NPNF	Nicene and Post-Nicene Fathers
NRSV	New Revised Standard Version
NRT	*La nouvelle revue théologique*
n.s.	new series
NSSEA	*Newsletter of the Society for the Study of Egyptian Antiquities*
NT	New Testament
NTA	*New Testament Abstracts*
NTAbh	Neutestamentliche Abhandlungen
NTApocr	E. Henneke. *New Testament Apocrypha*, ed. W. Schneemelcher. Trans. R. McL. Wilson. 2 vols. Philadelphia, 1963–65
NTC	B. S. Childs. 1985. *The New Testament as Canon: An Introduction*. Philadelphia, 1985
NTCS	*Newsletter for Targumic and Cognate Studies*, Toronto
NTD	Das Neue Testament Deutsch
NTF	Neutestamentliche Forschungen
NTHIP	W. G. Kümmel. 1972. *The New Testament: The History of the Investigation of Its Problems*. Trans. S. M. Gilmour and H. C. Kee. Nashville
NTL	New Testament Library
NTM	New Testament Message
NTOA	Novum Testamentum et Orbis Antiquus
NTS	*New Testament Studies*, Cambridge, MA
NTT	*Nieuw theologisch Tijdschrift*
NTTS	New Testament Tools and Studies
Num	Numbers
Numen	*Numen: International Review for the History of Religions*, Leiden
NV	*Nova et Vetera*, Geneva
NW	northwest(ern)
NWDB	*The New Westminster Dictionary of the Bible*, ed. H. S. Gehman. Philadelphia, 1970
OA	Old Assyrian
OAkk	Old Akkadian
OB	Old Babylonian
Obad	Obadiah
OBO	Orbis biblicus et orientalis
ÖBS	Österreichische biblische Studien
OBT	Overtures to Biblical Theology
OC	*One in Christ*, London
OCA	Orientalia christiana analecta
OCD	*Oxford Classical Dictionary*
OCP	*Orientalia Christiana Periodica*, Rome
Odes Sol.	*Odes of Solomon*
OECT	*Oxford Editions of Cuneiform Texts*, ed. S. Langdon, 1923–
OED	*Oxford English Dictionary*
OG	Old Greek
OGIS	*Orientis graeci inscriptiones selectae*, ed. W. Dittenberger. 2 vols. Leipzig, 1903–5
Ohol.	*Oholot*
OIC	Oriental Institute Communications
OIP	Oriental Institute Publications
OL	Old Latin
OLA	Orientalia Lovaniensia Analecta
OLP	*Orientalia lovaniensia periodica*
OLZ	*Orientalistische Literaturzeitung*, Berlin
OMRO	*Oudheidkundige Medeelingen uit het Rijks-Museum van Oudheden te Leiden*
Onomast.	Eusebius, *Onomasticon*
Op	Philo, *De opificio mundi*
OP	*Occasional Papers on the Near East*, Malibu, CA
op. cit.	*opere citato* ([in] the work cited)
Or	*Orientalia*
ᶜOr.	*ᶜOrla*
OrAnt	*Oriens antiquus*
OrBibLov	Orientalia et biblica lovaniensia
OrChr	*Oriens christianus*
Orig. World	*On the Origin of the World* (NHC II,*5*; XIII,*2*)
OrSyr	*L'orient syrien*
o.s.	old series
OstStud	*Ostkirchliche Studien*, Würzburg
OT	Old Testament
OTA	*Old Testament Abstracts*
OTE	*Old Testament Essays*, Pretoria
OTG	Old Testament Guides

OTG	*The Old Testament in Greek according to the Text of Codex Vaticanus,* ed. A. E. Brooke, N. McLean, and H. St. J. Thackeray. Cambridge, 1906–40
ÖTK	Ökumenischer Taschenbuch-Kommentar
OTL	Old Testament Library
OTM	Old Testament Message
OTP	*Old Testament Pseudepigrapha,* 2 vols., ed. J. Charlesworth. Garden City, NY, 1983–87
OTS	*Oudtestamentische Studiën*
p	Pesher (commentary)
P	"Priestly" source
p(p).	page(s); past
PÄ	*Probleme der Ägyptologie,* Leiden
PAAJR	*Proceedings of the American Academy for Jewish Research,* Philadelphia
Pal.	*Palestinian*
Pal. Tgs.	*Palestinian Targums*
PalCl	*Palestra del Clero*
PAPS	Proceedings of the American Philosophical Society
par(s).	paragraph(s); (gospel) parallel(s)
Para	*Para*
Paraph. Shem	*Paraphrase of Shem* (NHC VII,*1*)
part.	participle
pass.	passive
passim	throughout
PBA	*Proceedings of the British Academy,* Oxford
PBS	University Museum, University of Pennsylvania, *Publications of the Babylonian Section,* Philadelphia
PBSR	*Papers of the British School at Rome*
PCB	*Peake's Commentary on the Bible,* rev. ed., ed. M. Black and H. H. Rowley. New York, 1962
PCPS	*Proceedings of the Cambridge Philosophical Society*
P.E.	Eusebius, *Praeparatio evangelica*
Peʾa	*Peʾa*
PEFA	Palestine Exploration Fund Annual
PEFQS	*Palestine Exploration Fund Quarterly Statement*
PEGLAMBS	*Proceedings of the Eastern Great Lakes and Midwest Biblical Societies*
PEGLBS	*Proceedings of the Eastern Great Lakes Biblical Society*
PEQ	*Palestine Exploration Quarterly,* London
perf.	perfect
Pers	Persian
Pesaḥ.	*Pesaḥim*
Pesiq. R.	*Pesiqta Rabbati*
Pesiq. Rab Kah.	*Pesiqta de Rab Kahana*
PG	J. Migne, *Patrologia graeca*
PGM	*Papyri graecae magicae,* 3 vols., ed. K. Preisendanz. Leipzig, 1928–41
Ph. E. Poet	*Philo the Epic Poet*
PhEW	*Philosophy East and West*
Phil	Philippians
Phil.-hist. Kl.	Philosophische-historische Klasse
Phld.	see *Ign. Phld.*
Phlm	Philemon
PHOE	G. von Rad. 1966. *The Problem of the Hexateuch and Other Essays.* Trans. E. Dicken. Edinburgh and New York
Phoen	Phoenician
PhönWest	*Phönizier im Westen,* ed. H. G. Neimeyer. Madrider Beiträge 8. Mainz, 1982
PhRev	*Philosophical Review*
PI	J. Pedersen. 1926–40. *Israel: Its Life and Culture.* 2 vols. Copenhagen
PIBA	*Proceedings of the Irish Biblical Association,* Dublin
PIOL	Publications de l'Institut orientaliste de Louvain
PIR	*Prosopographia imperii Romani saec. I.II.III,* 3 vols., ed. E. Klebs, H. Dessau, and P. von Rohden. Berlin, 1897–98
PIR^2	*Prosopographia imperii Romani saec. I.II.III,* 2d ed., ed. E. Groag, A. Stein, and L. Petersen. 5 vols. Berlin and Leipzig, 1933–
Pirqe R. El.	*Pirqe Rabbi Eliezer*
P. J.	*Paraleipomena Jeremiou*
PJ	*Palästina-Jahrbuch*
PL	J. Migne, *Patrologia latina*
pl.	plural
pl(s).	plate(s)
Plant	Philo, *De plantatione*
Plato Rep.	*Plato: Republic 588B–589B* (NHC VI,*5*)
PMLA	*Publications of the Modern Language Association of America*
PMR	Charlesworth, J. H. 1976. *The Pseudepigrapha and Modern Research.* SCS 7. Missoula, MT
PN	personal name
PN A	Pottery Neolithic A
PN B	Pottery Neolithic B
PNPI	J. K. Stark. 1971. *Personal Names in Palmyrene Inscriptions.* Oxford
PNPPI	F. Benz. 1972. *Personal Names in the Phoenician and Punic Inscriptions.* Studia Pohl 8. Rome
PNTC	Pelican New Testament Commentaries
PO	Patrologia orientalis
Pol.	see *Ign. Pol.*

Post	Philo, *De posteritate Caini*
POTT	*Peoples of Old Testament Times,* ed. D. J. Wiseman. Oxford, 1973
POuT	De Prediking van het Oude Testament
PPN A	Pre-Pottery Neolithic A
PPN B	Pre-Pottery Neolithic B
Pr Azar	Prayer of Azariah
Pr. Jac.	*Prayer of Jacob*
Pr. Jos.	*Prayer of Joseph*
Pr Man	Prayer of Manasseh
Pr. Mos.	*Prayer of Moses*
Pr. Paul	*Prayer of the Apostle Paul* (NHC I,*1*)
Pr. Thanks.	*The Prayer of Thanksgiving* (NHC VI,*7*)
Praem	Philo, *De praemiis et poeniis*
Praep. Evang.	Eusebius, *Praeparatio evangelica*
Pre. Pet.	*Preaching of Peter*
Presbyterion	*Presbyterion,* St. Louis, MO
Prism	*Prism,* St. Paul, MN
Pro	*Proyección,* Granada, Spain
Prob	Philo, *Probus*
Procl	Proclamation Commentaries
Proof	*Prooftexts: A Journal of Jewish Literary History*
Prot. Jas.	*Protevangelium of James*
Prov	Proverbs
Provid I–II	Philo, *De providentia* I–II
PRS	*Perspectives in Religious Studies,* Macon, GA
PRU	*Le Palais Royal d'Ugarit,* ed. C. F. A. Schaeffer and J. Nougayrol. Paris
Ps(s)	Psalm(s)
Ps-Abd.	*Apostolic History of Pseudo-Abdias*
PSB	*Princeton Seminary Bulletin,* Princeton, NJ
PSBA	*Proceedings of the Society of Biblical Archaeology*
Ps-Clem.	*Pseudo-Clementines*
Ps-Eup.	*Pseudo-Eupolemus*
Ps-Hec.	*Pseudo-Hecataeus*
Ps-Mt.	*Gospel of Pseudo-Matthew*
Ps-Orph.	*Pseudo-Orpheus*
Ps-Philo	*Pseudo-Philo*
Ps-Phoc.	*Pseudo-Phocylides*
Pss. Sol.	*Psalms of Solomon*
PSt	*Process Studies,* Claremont, CA
PSTJ	*Perkins (School of Theology) Journal,* Dallas, TX
PT	*Perspectiva Teológica,* Venda Nova, Brazil
pt.	part
PThS	*Pretoria Theological Studies,* Leiden
PTMS	Pittsburgh Theological Monograph Series
PTU	F. Gröndahl. 1967. *Die Personennamen der Texte aus Ugarit.* Studia Pohl 1. Rome
Pun	Punic
PVTG	Pseudepigrapha Veteris Testamenti graece
PW	A. Pauly–G. Wissowa, *Real-Encyclopädie der classischen Altertumswissenschaft,* Stuttgart, 1839–; supplements, 1903–56, 11 vols.; 2d series, 1914–48
PWCJS	*Proceedings of the . . . World Congress of Jewish Studies*
PWSup	Supplement to PW
Pyr	K. Sethe. 1908–32. *Die altägyptischen Pyramidentexte.* 4 vols. Leipzig. Repr. Hildesheim, 1969
Q	Qere; "Q"-source; Qumran texts (e.g., 4QTestim)
Qad	*Qadmoniot,* Jerusalem
QD	Quaestiones disputatae
QDAP	*Quarterly of the Department of Antiquities in Palestine*
QHBT	*Qumran and the History of the Biblical Text,* ed. F. M. Cross and S. Talmon. Cambridge, MA, 1975
Qidd.	*Qiddušin*
Qinnim	*Qinnim*
QL	Qumran Literature
Qod.	*Qodašin*
Qoh or Eccl	Qoheleth or Ecclesiastes
Quaes Ex I–II	Philo, *Quaestiones et solutiones in Exodum* I–II
Quaes Gen I–IV	Philo, *Quaestiones et solutiones in Genesin* I–IV
Ques. Ezra	*Questions of Ezra*
Quod Det	Philo, *Quod deterius potiori insidiari soleat*
Quod Deus	Philo, *Quod deus immutabilis sit*
Quod Omn	Philo, *Quod omnis probus liber sit*
R	H. C. Rawlinson. 1861–1909. *The Cuneiform Inscriptions of Western Asia.* London
RA	*Revue d'Assyriologie et d'Archéologie orientale,* Paris
RAB	J. Rogerson. 1985. *Atlas of the Bible.* New York
Rab.	*Rabbah* (following abbreviation for biblical book: *Gen. Rab.* = *Genesis Rabbah*)
RAC	*Reallexikon für Antike und Christentum,* 10 vols., ed. T. Klauser, Stuttgart, 1950–78
RANE	Records of the Ancient Near East
RAO	*Recueil d'archéologie orientale*
RÄR	H. Bonnet. 1952. *Reallexikon der ägyptischen Religionsgeschichte.* Berlin
RArch	*Revue archéologique*
RasT	*Rassegna di Teologia,* Naples

RAT	*Revue Africaine de Théologie,* Kinshasa Limete, Zaire
RazFe	*Razón y Fe,* Madrid
RB	*Revue biblique,* Paris
RBén	*Revue bénédictine,* Maredsous
RBI	*Rivista biblica italiana,* Brescia
RBR	*Ricerche Bibliche e Religiose*
RCB	*Revista de Cultura Biblica,* São Paulo, Brazil
RCT	*Revista Catalana de Teología,* Barcelona, Spain
RDAC	*Report of the Department of Antiquities, Cyprus,* Nicosia
RdÉ	*Revue d'égyptologie*
RdM	*Die Religionen der Menschheit,* ed. C. M. Schröder, Stuttgart
RE	*Realencyklopädie für protestantische Theologie und Kirche,* 3d ed., ed. A. Hauck. Leipzig, 1897–1913
REA	*Revue des études anciennes*
REAug	*Revue des études augustiniennes,* Paris
REB	*Revista Eclesiástica Brasileira,* Brazil
RechBib	Recherches bibliques
RefRev	*Reformed Review,* Holland, MI
RefTR	*Reformed Theological Review,* Melbourne
REJ	*Revue des études juives,* Paris
RelArts	Religion and the Arts
RelLond	*Religion,* London, 1971–
RelNY	*Religion,* New York
RelS	*Religious Studies,* London
RelSoc	*Religion and Society*
RelSRev	*Religious Studies Review*
Renovatio	*Renovatio,* Bonn
repr.	reprint, reprinted
RES	*Revue des études sémitiques,* Paris
RES	*Répertoire d'épigraphie sémitique* [cited by number]
ResABib	Die Reste der altlateinische Bibel
ResQ	*Restoration Quarterly,* Abilene, TX
Rev	Revelation
Rev. Ezra	*Revelation of Ezra*
Rev. Steph.	*Revelation of Stephen*
RevExp	*Review and Expositor,* Louisville, KY
RevistB	*Revista Bíblica,* Buenos Aires
RevistEspir	*Revista de Espritualidad,* Madrid
RevQ	*Revue de Qumran,* Paris
RevRef	*La Revue Réformée,* Aix en Provence
RevRel	*Review for Religious,* St. Louis, MO
RevScRel	*Revue des sciences religieuses,* Strasbourg
RevSém	*Revue sémitique*
RevThom	*Revue thomiste,* Toulouse
RGG	*Religion in Geschichte und Gegenwart*
RGTC	*Répertoire géographique des textes cunéiformes,* 8 vols., ed. W. Röllig. BTAVO B7. Wiesbaden
RHA	*Revue hittite et asianique*
RHE	*Revue d'histoire ecclésiastique,* Louvain
RHLR	*Revue d'histoire et de littérature religieuses,* Paris
RhM	*Rheinisches Museum für Philologie*
RHPR	*Revue d'histoire et de philosophie religieuses,* Strasbourg
RHR	*Revue de l'histoire des religions,* Paris
RIC	*The Roman Imperial Coinage,* ed. H. Mattingly et al. London, 1923–81
*RIC*²	*The Roman Imperial Coinage,* 2d ed., ed. C. H. V. Sutherland and R. A. G. Carson. London, 1984–
RIDA	*Revue internationale des droits de l'antiquité*
RIH	J. de Rouge. 1877–78. *Inscriptions hiéroglyphiques copiées en Egypte.* 3 vols. Études égyptologiques 9–11. Paris
RivArCr	*Rivista di archeologia cristiana,* Rome
RivB	*Rivista biblica,* Bologna
RLA	*Reallexikon der Assyriologie,* ed. G. Ebeling et al. Berlin, 1932–
RLT	*Revista Latinoamericana de Teologia,* San Salvador
RNAB	see *RAB*
RNT	Regenesburger Neues Testament
RocTKan	*Roczniki Teologiczno-Kanoniczne,* Lublin
Rom	Romans
Rom.	see *Ign. Rom.*
Roš Hš.	*Roš Haššana*
ROTT	G. von Rad. 1962–65. *Old Testament Theology.* 2 vols. Trans. D. M. G. Stalker. New York
RP	*Revue de philologie*
RQ	*Römische Quartalschrift für christliche Altertumskunde und Kirchengeschichte,* Vatican City
RR	*Review of Religion*
RS	*Ras Shamra*
RSF	*Revista di Studi Fenici*
RSLR	*Rivista di storia letteratura religiosa,* Turin
RSO	*Rivista degli studi orientali*
RSPT	*Revue des sciences philosophiques et théologiques,* Paris
RSR	*Recherches de science religieuse,* Paris
RST	*Religious Studies and Theology,* Edmonton, Alberta
RSV	Revised Standard Version
RT	*Recueil de travaux relatifs à la philologie et à l'archéologie égyptiennes et assyriennes*
RTAM	*Recherches de Theologie Ancienne et Médiévale*

RTL	*Revue théologique de Louvain*
RTP	*Revue de théologie et de philosophie,* Lausanne
RUO	*Revue de l'université d'Ottawa*
Ruth	Ruth
RV	Revised Version
RVV	Religionsgeschichtliche Versuche und Vorarbeiten
Ry	G. Ryckmans. 1927–59. Inscriptions sudarabes I–XVII. *Mus* 40–72 [cited by no. of text]
S	south(ern)
S. ʿOlam Rab.	*Seder ʿOlam Rabbah*
Šabb.	*Šabbat*
SacDoc	*Sacra Doctrina,* Bologna
SacEr	*Sacris Erudiri: Jaarboek voor Godsdienstwetenschappen,* Brugge, Belgium
Sacr	Philo, *De sacrificiis Abelis et Caini*
SAHG	A. Falkenstein and W. von Soden. 1953. *Sumerische und akkadische Hymnen und Gebete.* Zurich
SAK	*Studien zur Altägyptischen Kultur,* Hamburg
Sal	*Salesianum,* Rome
Salman	*Salmanticensis,* Salamanca
Sam. Pent.	Samaritan Pentateuch
Sam. Tg.	*Samaritan Targum*
SamOstr	Samaria Ostracon/Ostraca
SANE	*Sources From the Ancient Near East,* Malibu, CA
Sanh.	*Sanhedrin*
SANT	Studien zum Alten und Neuen Testament
SAOC	Studies in Ancient Oriental Civilization
Sap	*Sapienza,* Naples
SAQ	Sammlung ausgewählter kirchen-und dogmengeschichtlicher Quellenschriften
SAT	*Die Schriften des Alten Testaments in Auswahl,* ed. and trans. H. Gunkel et al. Göttingen
SB	Sources bibliques
SBA	Studies in Biblical Archaeology
SBAW	Sitzungsberichten der (königlichen) bayerischen Akademie der Wissenschaften
SBB	Stuttgarter biblische Beiträge
SBibB	*Studies in Bibliography and Booklore,* Cincinnati, OH
SBJ	La sainte bible de Jérusalem
SBLABS	Society of Biblical Literature Archaeology and Biblical Studies
SBLAS	Society of Biblical Literature Aramaic Studies
SBLASP	Society of Biblical Literature Abstracts and Seminar Papers
SBLBAC	Society of Biblical Literature The Bible in American Culture
SBLBMI	Society of Biblical Literature The Bible and Its Modern Interpreters
SBLBSNA	Society of Biblical Literature Biblical Scholarship in North America
SBLDS	Society of Biblical Literature Dissertation Series
SBLMasS	Society of Biblical Literature Masoretic Studies
SBLMS	Society of Biblical Literature Monograph Series
SBLNTGF	Society of Biblical Literature: The New Testament in the Greek Fathers
SBLRBS	Society of Biblical Literature: Resources for Biblical Study
SBLSBS	Society of Biblical Literature: Sources for Biblical Study
SBLSCS	Society of Biblical Literature: Septuagint and Cognate Studies
SBLSP	*Society of Biblical Literature Seminar Papers*
SBLSS	Society of Biblical Literature: Semeia Studies
SBLTT	Society of Biblical Literature: Texts and Translations
SBLWAW	Society of Biblical Literature: Writings of the Ancient World
SBM	Stuttgarter biblische Monographien
SBS	Stuttgarter Bibelstudien
SBT	Studies in Biblical Theology
SC	Sources chrétiennes
SCCNH	*Studies on the Civilization and Culture of Nuzi and the Hurrians,* 2 vols., ed. D. I. Owen and M. A. Morrison. Winona Lake, IN, 1981–87
ScEccl	*Sciences ecclésiatiques*
ScEs	*Science et esprit,* Montreal
SCHNT	Studia ad corpus hellenisticum novi testamenti
Scr	*Scripture*
SCR	*Studies in Comparative Religion*
ScrB	*Scripture Bulletin*
ScrC	*Scripture in Church,* Dublin
ScrHier	*Scripta Hierosolymitana,* Jerusalem
Scrip	*Scriptorium,* Brussels
Scriptura	*Scriptura,* Stellenbosch
ScrT	*Scripta Theologica,* Barañain/Pamplona
SCS	Septuagint and Cognate Studies
ScuolC	*Scuola Cattolica,* Milan
SD	Studies and Documents

SDB	*Smith's Dictionary of the Bible,* ed. H. B. Hackett. Boston, 1880
SE	southeast(ern)
SE	*Studia Evangelica I, II, III* (= TU 73 [1959], 87 [1964], 88 [1964], etc.)
SEÅ	*Svensk Exegetisk Årsbok*
Search	*Search,* Dublin
Šeb.	*Šebiʿit*
Šebu.	*Šebuʿot*
sec.	section
Sec. Gos. Mk.	*Secret Gospel of Mark*
SecondCent	*Second Century,* Macon, GA
Sef	*Sefarad,* Madrid
SEG	*Supplementum Epigraphicum Graecum,* ed. J. J. E. Hondius. Leiden, 1923–
Sem	*Semitica,* Paris
Ṣem.	*Ṣemaḥot*
Semeia	*Semeia,* Chico, CA
SemiotBib	*Sémiotique et Bible,* Lyon
Semitics	*Semitics,* Pretoria
Sent. Sextus	*Sentences of Sextus* (NHC XII,*1*)
Šeqal.	*Šeqalim*
Seux	J. M. Seux. 1968. *Epithètes Royales Akkadiennes et Sumériennes.* Paris
SGL	A. Falkenstein. 1959. *Sumerische Götterlieder.* Heidelberg
SGV	*Sammlung gemeinverständlicher Vorträge und Schriften aus dem Gebiet der Theologie und Religionsgeschichte,* Tübingen
S.H.A.	Scriptores Historiae Augustae
SHAW	Sitzungsberichte der Heidelberger Akademie der Wissenschaften
Shep. Herm.	*Shepherd of Hermas*
SHIB	R. M. Grant and D. Tracy. 1984. *A Short History of the Interpretation of the Bible.* 2d ed. Philadelphia
Shofar	*Shofar,* West Lafayette, IN
SHR	Studies in the History of Religions
SHT	Studies in Historical Theology
Sib. Or.	*Sibylline Oracles*
SICV	*Sylloge inscriptionum Christianorum veterum musei Vaticani,* ed. H. Zilliacus. Acta instituti Romani Finlandiae 1/1–2. Rome
SIDÅ	Scripta Instituti Donneriana Åboensis, Stockholm
SIDJC	*Service International de Documentation Judéo-chrétienne,* Rome
SIG^3	*Sylloge Inscriptionum Graecarum,* ed. W. Dittenberger. 3d ed. Leipzig
SII	*Studies in Islam,* New Delhi
sing.	singular
Sipra	*Sipra*
Sipre	*Sipre*
Sir	Ecclesiasticus *or* Wisdom of Jesus Ben-Sira
SIRIS	*Sylloge inscriptionum religionis Isiacae et Serapicae,* ed. L. Vidman. RVV 28. Berlin, 1969
SJ	Studia Judaica
SJLA	Studies in Judaism in Late Antiquity
SJOT	*Scandinavian Journal of the Old Testament*
SJT	*Scottish Journal of Theology,* Edinburgh
SkrifK	*Skrif en Kerk,* Pretoria
SLAG	*Schriften der Luther-Agricola-Gesellschaft* (Finland)
SLJT	*Saint Luke's Journal of Theology,* Sewanee, TN
SMEA	*Studi Micenei ed Egeo-Anatolici*
SMS	*Syro-Mesopotamian Studies,* Malibu, CA
SMSR	*Studi e materiali di storia delle religioni*
Smyrn.	see *Ign. Smyrn.*
SNT	Studien zum Neuen Testament
SNTSMS	Society for New Testament Studies Monograph Series
SNTU	*Studien zum Neuen Testament und seiner Umwelt,* Linz
SNVAO	*Skrifter utgitt av det Norske Videnskaps-Akademi i Oslo*
SO	Symbolae osloenses
SÖAW	*Sitzungsberichte der Österreichen Akademie der Wissenschaften*
Sobr	Philo, *De sobrietate*
Somn I–II	Philo, *De somniis* I–II
SonB	Soncino Books of the Bible
Sop.	*Soperim*
Soph. Jes. Chr.	*Sophia of Jesus Christ* (NHC III,*4*)
Soṭa	*Soṭa*
SOTSBooklist	*Society for Old Testament Study Booklist*
SOTSMS	Society for Old Testament Study Monograph Series
Sou	*Soundings,* Nashville
SPap	*Studia papyrologica*
SPAW	Sitzungsberichte der preussischen Akademie der Wissenschaften
SPB	Studia postbiblica
Spec Leg I–IV	Philo, *De specialibus legibus* I–IV
SPhil	*Studia Philonica,* Chicago
SPIB	*Scripta Pontificii Instituti Biblici,* Rome
SpT	*Spirituality Today,* Dubuque, IA
SQAW	Schriften und Quellen der alten Welt
SR	*Studies in Religion/Sciences religieuses,* Waterloo, Ontario
SS	Studi semitici
SSAOI	*Sacra Scriptura Antiquitatibus Orientalibus Illustrata,* Rome

SSEA Society for the Study of Egyptian Antiquities
SSN *Studia Semitica Neerlandica,* Assen
SSS Semitic Study Series
St *Studium,* Madrid
ST *Studia theologica*
STÅ *Svendk teologisk årsskrift*
StadtrChr P. Lampe. 1987. *Die stadtrömischen Christen in den ersten beiden Jahrhunderten.* WUNT 2/18. Tübingen
StANT *Studien zum Alten und Neuen Testament,* Munich
StBT *Studien zu den Boğazköy-Texten,* Wiesbaden
StDI Studia et Documenta ad Iura Orientis Antiqui Pertinenti
STDJ Studies on the Texts of the Desert of Judah
StEb *Studi Eblaiti,* Rome
StEc *Studi Ecumenici,* Verona, Italy
Steles Seth *Three Steles of Seth* (NHC VII,5)
StFS *Studia Francisci Scholten,* Leiden
STK *Svensk teologisk kvartalskrift,* Lund
STL Studia theologica Ludensia
StLtg *Studia Liturgica,* Rotterdam
StMiss *Studia Missionalia,* Rome
StOr *Studia Orientalia,* Helsinki
StOvet *Studium Ovetense,* Oviedo
StPat *Studia Patavina,* Padua, Italy
StPatr *Studia Patristica*
StPhilon *Studia Philonica*
Str *Stromata,* San Miguel, Argentina
Str-B H. L. Strack and P. Billerbeck. 1922–61. *Kommentar zum NT aus Talmud und Midrasch.* 6 vols. Munich
STT *The Sultantepe Tablets,* 2 vols., ed. O. R. Gurney, J. J. Finkelstein, and P. Hulin. Occasional Publications of the British School of Archaeology at Ankara 3, 7. London, 1957–64
StTh *Studia Theologica*
StudBib Studia biblica
StudBT *Studia biblica et theologica,* Guilford, CT
Studium *Studium,* Madrid
StudNeot Studia neotestamentica, Studia
StudOr Studia orientalia
StudPhoen Studia Phoenicia [I–VIII]
STV *Studia theologica varsaviensia*
Sukk. *Sukka*
Sum Sumerian
SUNT Studien zur Umwelt des Neuen Testaments
suppl. supplement
Sus Susanna
SVF *Stoicorum veterum fragmenta,* ed. J. von Arnim. 4 vols. Leipzig, 1903–24. Repr. Stuttgart, 1966; New York, 1986
SVTP Studia in Veteris Testamenti pseudepigrapha
SVTQ *St. Vladimir's Theological Quarterly,* Tuckahoe, NY
SW southwest(ern)
SWBA Social World of Biblical Antiquity
SwJT *Southwestern Journal of Theology,* Fort Worth, TX
SWP *Survey of Western Palestine:*
SWP 1 = C. R. Conder and H. H. Kitchener. 1881. *Galilee.* London.
SWP 2 = C. R. Conder and H. H. Kitchener. 1882. *Samaria.* London.
SWP 3 = C. R. Conder and H. H. Kitchener. 1883. *Judaea.* London.
SWP 4 = E. H. Palmer. 1881. *Arabic and English Name Lists.* London.
SWP 5 = C. Wilson and C. Warren. 1881. *Special Papers.* London.
SWP 6 = C. Warren and C. Warren, 1884. *Jerusalem.* London.
SWP 7 = H. B. Tristram. 1884. *The Fauna and Flora of Palestine.* London.
SymBU Symbolae biblicae upsalienses
Syr Syriac
Syr *Syria: Revue d'Art Oriental et d'Archéologie,* Paris
Syr. Men. *Syriac Menander*
SZ *Stimmen der Zeit,* Munich
T. 12 P. *Testaments of the Twelve Patriarchs*
T. Ab. *Testament of Abraham*
T. Adam *Testament of Adam*
T. Ash. *Testament of Asher*
T. Benj. *Testament of Benjamin*
T. Dan. *Testament of Daniel*
T. Gad *Testament of Gad*
T. Hez. *Testament of Hezekiah*
T. Isaac *Testament of Isaac*
T. Iss. *Testament of Issachar*
T. Jac. *Testament of Jacob*
T. Job *Testament of Job*
T. Jos. *Testament of Joseph*
T. Jud. *Testament of Judah*
T. Levi *Testament of Levi*
T. Mos. *Testament of Moses*
T. Naph. *Testament of Naphtali*
T. Reu. *Testament of Reuben*
T. Sim. *Testament of Simeon*
T. Sol. *Testament of Solomon*
Ṭ. Yom *Ṭebul Yom*

T. Zeb.	*Testament of Zebulun*
TA	*Tel Aviv,* Tel Aviv
Taʿan.	*Taʿanit*
TAD	B. Porten and A. Yardeni. 1986. *Textbook of Aramaic Documents from Ancient Egypt.* Jerusalem *TAD* A = vol. 1, *Letters* *TAD* B = vol. 2, *Contracts* *TAD* C = vol. 3, *Literature and Lists* *TAD* D = vol. 4, *Fragments and Inscriptions*
TAik	*Teologinen Aikakauskirja,* Helsinki
Talm.	*Talmud*
TAM	*Tituli Asiae Minoris*
Tamid	*Tamid*
TAPA	*Transactions of the American Philological Association*
TAPhS	*Transactions of the American Philosophical Society,* Philadelphia
TBC	Torch Bible Commentary
TBei	*Theologische Beiträge,* Wuppertal
TBl	*Theologische Blätter*
TBT	*The Bible Today,* Collegeville, MN
TBü	Theologische Bücherei
TCGNT	B. M. Metzger. 1971. *A Textual Commentary on the Greek New Testament,* United Bible Societies
TCL	*Textes cunéiforms du Musée du Louvre,* Paris, 1910–
TCS	Texts from Cuneiform Sources: TCS 1 = E. Sollberger. 1966. *Business and Administrative Correspondence Under the Kings of Ur.* Locust Valley, NY. TCS 2 = R. Biggs. 1967. *ŠÀ.ZI.GA: Ancient Mesopotamian Potency Incantations.* TCS 3 = Å. Sjöberg, E. Bergmann, and G. Gragg. 1969. *The Collection of the Sumerian Temple Hymns.* TCS 4 = E. Leichty. 1970. *The Omen Series šumma izbu.* TCS 5 = A. K. Grayson. 1975. *Assyrian and Babylonian Chronicles.*
TD	*Theology Digest,* St. Louis, MO
TDNT	*Theological Dictionary of the New Testament,* 10 vols., ed. G. Kittel and G. Friedrich. Trans. G. W. Bromiley. Grand Rapids, 1964–76
TDOT	*Theological Dictionary of the Old Testament,* ed. G. J. Botterweck, H. Ringgren, and H. J. Fabry. Trans. J. T. Willis, G. W. Bromiley, and D. E. Green. Grand Rapids, 1974–
TE	*Theologica Evangelica,* Pretoria
Teach. Silv.	*Teachings of Silvanus* (NHC VII,*4*)
Tem.	*Temura*

Temenos	*Temenos: Studies in Comparative Religion,* Helsinki
Ter	*Teresianum,* Rome
Ter.	*Terumot*
Test	*Testimonianze,* Florence
Testim. Truth	*Testimony of Truth* (NHC IX,*3*)
TEV	Today's English Version
TextsS	Texts and Studies
TF	*Theologische Forschung*
Tg. Esth. I	*First Targum of Esther*
Tg. Esth. II	*Second Targum of Esther*
Tg. Isa.	*Targum of Isaiah*
Tg. Ket.	*Targum of the Writings*
Tg. Neb.	*Targum of the Prophets*
Tg. Neof.	*Targum Neofiti I*
Tg. Onq.	*Targum Onqelos*
Tg. Ps.-J.	*Targum Pseudo-Jonathan*
Tg. Yer. I	*Targum Yerušalmi I*
Tg. Yer. II	*Targum Yerušalmi II*
TGI	K. Galling. 1950. *Textbuch zur Geschichte Israels.* 2d ed. Tübingen
TGl	*Theologie und Glaube,* Paderborn
Thal.	*Thallus*
ThArb	*Theologische Arbeiten,* Berlin
THAT	*Theologisches Handwörterbuch zum Alten Testament,* 2 vols., ed. E. Jenni and C. Westermann. Munich, 1971–76
ThEd	*Theological Educator,* New Orleans
ThEH	*Theologische Existenz Heute,* Munich
Them	*Themelios,* Madison, WI
Theod.	*Theodotus*
Theology	*Theology,* London
THeth	Texte der Hethiter
ThH	*Théologie historique*
THKNT	Theologischer Handkommentar zum Neuen Testament
Thom. Cont.	*Book of Thomas the Contender* (NHC II,7)
Thomist	*Thomist,* Washington, D.C.
ThPh	*Theologie und Philosophie,* Freiburg
ThStud	Theologische Studien
Thund.	*The Thunder: Perfect Mind* (NHC VI,*2*)
ThV	*Theologische Versuche,* Berlin
ThViat	*Theologia Viatorum,* Berlin
TijdTheol	*Tijdschrift voor Theologie,* Nijmegen
Titus	Titus
TJ	*Trinity Journal,* Deerfield, IL
TJT	*Toronto Journal of Theology*
TLZ	*Theologische Literaturzeitung*
TNB	*The New Blackfriars,* Oxford
TNTC	Tyndale New Testament Commentary
Tob	Tobit

Ṭohar.	*Ṭoharot*
TOTC	Tyndale Old Testament Commentary
TP	*Theologie und Philosophie*
TPNAH	J. D. Fowler. 1988. *Theophoric Personal Names in Ancient Hebrew.* JSOTSup 49. Sheffield
TPQ	*Theologisch-Praktische Quartalschrift,* Austria
TQ	*Theologische Quartalschrift*
TR	P. Lucau. *Textes Religieux Égyptiens,* 1, Paris
Trad	*Tradition,* New York
Traditio	*Traditio,* New York
Trall.	see *Ign. Trall.*
TRE	*Theologische Realenzyklopädie*
Treat. Res.	*Treatise on Resurrection* (NHC I,*4*)
Treat. Seth	*Second Treatise of the Great Seth* (NHC VII,*2*)
Treat. Shem	*Treatise of Shem*
TRev	*Theologische Revue*
Tri. Trac.	*Tripartite Tractate* (NHC I,*5*)
Trim. Prot.	*Trimorphic Protennoia* (NHC XIII,*1*)
TRu	*Theologische Rundschau,* Tübingen
TS	*Theological Studies,* Washington, DC
TSK	*Theologische Studien und Kritiken*
TSSI	J. C. L. Gibson. 1971–82. *Textbook of Syrian Semitic Inscriptions.* 3 vols. Oxford
TT	*Teologisk Tidsskrift*
TTKi	*Tidsskrift for Teologie og Kirke,* Oslo, Norway
TTKY	*Türk Tarih Kurumu Kongresi Yayĭnlari.* Ankara
TToday	*Theology Today,* Princeton, NJ
TTS	Trierer Theologische Studien
TTZ	*Trierer theologische Zeitschrift*
TU	Texte und Untersuchungen
TUAT	Texte aus der Umwelt des Alten Testaments
TV	*Teología y Vida,* Santiago, Chile
TvT	*Tijdschrift voor Theologie,* Nijmegen, The Netherlands
TWAT	*Theologisches Wörterbuch zum Alten Testament,* ed. G. J. Botterweck, H. Ringgren, and H. J. Fabry. Stuttgart, 1970–
TWNT	*Theologisches Wörterbuch zum Neuen Testament,* 8 vols., ed. G. Kittel and G. Friedrich. Stuttgart, 1933–69
TynBul	*Tyndale Bulletin*
TZ	*Theologische Zeitschrift,* Basel, Switzerland
UBSGNT	*United Bible Societies Greek New Testament*
UCPNES	University of California Publications in Near Eastern Studies
UCPSP	University of California Publications in Semitic Philology
UET	Ur Excavations: Texts
UF	*Ugarit-Forschungen*
Ug	Ugaritic
UGAÄ	Untersuchungen zur Geschichte und Altertumskunde Aegyptens
ÜgS	M. Noth. 1967. *Überlieferungsgeschichtliche Studien.* 3d ed. Tübingen
UNT	Untersuchungen zum Neuen Testament
ʿUq.	*ʿUqṣin*
Urk. IV	*Urkunden des ägyptischen Altertums.* Abt. IV, *Urkunden der 18. Dynastie,* ed. K. Sethe and W. Helck. 22 fasc. Leipzig, 1903–58
US	*Una Sancta*
USQR	*Union Seminary Quarterly Review,* New York, NY
UT	C. H. Gordon. 1965. *Ugaritic Textbook.* AnOr 38. Rome; suppl. 1967
UUÅ	*Uppsala universitets Årsskrift*
v(v)	verse(s)
VAB	*Vorderasiatische Bibliothek,* Leipzig, 1907–16
Val. Exp.	*A Valentinian Exposition* (NHC XI,*2*)
VAT	Vorderasiatische Abteilung, Thontafelsammlung, Staatliche Musee zu Berlin
VC	*Vigiliae christianae*
VCaro	*Verbum caro*
VD	*Verbum domini*
VE	*Vox Evangilica*
VetChr	*Vetera Christianum,* Bari
VF	*Verkündigung und Forschung*
Vg	Vulgate
Vid	*Vidyajyoti,* Delhi
VigChrist	*Vigiliao Christianae*
VIO	Veröffentlichung der Institut für Orientforschung
Virt	Philo, *De virtutibus*
Vis. Ezra	*Vision of Ezra*
Vis. Is.	*Vision of Isaiah*
Vis. Paul	*Vision of Paul*
Vita	*Vita Adae et Evae*
Vita C	Eusebius, *Vita Constantini*
Vita Cont	Philo, *De vita contemplativa*
Vita Mos I–II	Philo, *De vita Mosis* I–II
VKGNT	*Vollständige Konkordanz zum griechischen Neuen Testament,* ed. K. Aland
VL	Vetus Latina
vol(s).	volume(s)
Vorsokr.	*Fragmente der Vorsokrater,* 4th ed., ed. H. Diels. Berlin, 1922

VR	*Vox Reformata,* Geelong, Victoria, Australia
VS	Vorderasiatische Schriftdenkmäler der königlichen Museen zu Berlin
VSpir	*Vie spirituelle,* Paris
VT	*Vetus Testamentum,* Leiden
VTSup	Vetus Testamentum Supplements
W	west(ern)
WA	["Weimar Ausgabe," =] *D. Martin Luthers Werke: Kritische Gesamtausgabe,* ed. J. K. F. Knaake et al. Weimar, 1883–
Way	*The Way,* London
WbÄS	A. Erman and H. Grapow. 1926–31. *Wörterbuch der ägyptischen Sprache.* 7 vols. Leipzig. Repr. 1963
WBC	World Bible Commentary
WBKL	Wiener Beitrage zur Kulturgeschichte und Linguistik
WbMyth	*Wörterbuch der Mythologie,* ed. H. W. Haussig, Stuttgart, 1961
WC	Westminster Commentaries, London
WD	*Wort und Dienst*
WDB	*Westminster Dictionary of the Bible*
Wehr	H. Wehr. 1976. *A Dictionary of Modern Written Arabic,* 3d ed., ed. J. M. Cowen. Ithaca
WF	Wege der Forschung
WGI	J. Wellhausen. 1878. *Geschichte Israels.* Berlin [see also *WPGI* and *WPHI*]
WHAB	*Westminster Historical Atlas of the Bible*
Whitaker	R. E. Whitaker. 1972. *A Concordance of the Ugaritic Literature.* Cambridge, MA
WHJP	*World History of the Jewish People*
Wis	Wisdom of Solomon
WLSGF	*The Word of the Lord Shall Go Forth: Essays in Honor of David Noel Freedman,* eds. C. L. Meyers and M. O'Connor. Winona Lake, IN, 1983
WMANT	Wissenschaftliche Monographien zum Alten und Neuen Testament
WO	*Die Welt des Orients*
WoAr	*World Archaeology*
Wor	*Worship,* Collegeville, MN
WordWorld	*Word and World,* St. Paul, MN
WPGI	J. Wellhausen. 1895. *Prolegomena zur Geschichte Israels.* 4th ed. Berlin
WPHI	J. Wellhausen. 1885. *Prolegomena to the History of Israel.* 2 vols. Trans. J. S. Black and A. Menzies. Edinburgh. Repr. Cleveland 1957; Gloucester, MA, 1973
WS	*World and Spirit,* Petersham, MA
WTJ	*Westminster Theological Journal,* Philadelphia, PA
WTM	J. Levy. 1924. *Wörterbuch über die Talmudim und Midraschim.* 5 vols. 2d ed., ed. L. Goldschmidt. Leipzig. Repr. 1963
WTS	E. Littmann and M. Höfner. 1962. *Wörterbuch der Tigre-Sprache.* Wiesbaden
WuD	*Wort und Dienst,* Bielefeld
WUNT	Wissenschaftliche Untersuchungen zum Neuen Testament
WUS	J. Aistleitner. 1974. *Wörterbuch der ugaritischen Sprache.* 4th ed., ed. O. Eissfeldt. BSAW 106/3. Berlin
WuW	*Wissenschaft und Weisheit,* Mönchengladbach
WVDOG	*Wissenschaftliche Veröffentlichungen der Deutschen Orient-Gesellschaft*
WW	*Word & World,* Fort Lee, NJ
WZ	*Wissenschaftliche Zeitschrift*
WZKM	*Wiener Zeitschrift für die Kunde des Morgenlandes*
WZKSO	*Wiener Zeitschrift für die Kunde Süd- und Ostasiens*
Yad.	*Yadayim*
Yal.	*Yalqut*
Yebam.	*Yebamot*
Yem. Tg.	*Yemenite Targum*
YES	Yale Egyptological Studies
YGC	W. F. Albright. 1969. *Yahweh and the Gods of Canaan.* Garden City, NY. Repr. Winona Lake, IN, 1990
YJS	*Yale Judaica Series,* New Haven
YNER	Yale Near Eastern Researches
Yoma	*Yoma (= Kippurim)*
YOS	Yale Oriental Series
y. (Talm.)	Jerusalem (Talmud) = "Yerushalmi"
ZA	*Zeitschrift für Assyriologie*
Zabim	*Zabim*
ZAH	*Zeitschrift für Althebräistic*
ZÄS	*Zeitschrift für Ägyptische Sprache und Altertumskunde*
ZAW	*Zeitschrift für die alttestamentliche Wissenschaft,* Berlin
ZB	Zürcher Bibelkommentare
ZDMG	*Zeitschrift der deutschen morgenländischen Gesellschaft*
ZDPV	*Zeitschrift des deutschen Palästina-Vereins*
Zebaḥ.	*Zebaḥim*
Zech	Zechariah
ZEE	*Zeitschrift für evangelische Ethik*
Zeph	Zephaniah
Zer.	*Zeraʿim*
ZHT	*Zeitschrift für historische Theologie*
ZKG	*Zeitschrift für Kirchengeschichte*

ZKT	*Zeitschrift für katholische Theologie,* Innsbruck
ZMR	*Zeitschrift für Missionskunde und Religionswissenschaft*
ZNW	*Zeitschrift für die neutestamentliche Wissenschaft*
Zost.	*Zostrianos* (NHC VIII,*1*)
ZPE	*Zeitschrift für Papyrologie und Epigraphik*
ZPKT	*Zeitschrift für Philosophie und Katholische Theologie*
ZRGG	*Zeitschrift für Religions- und Geistesgeschichte,* Erlangen
ZST	*Zeitschrift für systematische Theologie*
ZTK	*Zeitschrift für Theologie und Kirche*
ZWT	*Zeitschrift für wissenschaftliche Theologie*
ZycMysl	*Zycie i Mysl*

O

OAK OF TABOR (PLACE). See TABOR, OAK OF.

OAK TREE. See FLORA.

OAK, DIVINER'S. See DIVINER'S OAK.

OBADIAH (PERSON) [Heb *ʿōbadyāhû*]. A common Hebrew name meaning "Yahweh's servant."

1. One of the twelve Minor Prophets. See OBADIAH, BOOK OF.

2. The manager of Ahab's household and a devoted follower of Yahweh during the reign of Ahab, king of Israel (1 Kgs 18:1–16). Obadiah is described as "over the house" (Heb *ʾăšer ʿal-habbāyit*) of Ahab. The phrase occurs elsewhere in 1 Kgs 4:6; 16:9; 18:3; 2 Kgs 10:5; 15:5; 18:18 (= Isa 36:3); 18:37 (= Isa 36:22); 19:2 (= Isa 37:2); Isa 22:15; and on a 7th-century B.C. seal. According to Mettinger (1971: 88, 110), it designates the one who supervises the royal estate and who was also probably responsible for royal trade and mining.

Obadiah is noted in 1 Kgs 18:4 as protecting a group of Yahwist prophets during a period of persecution. The Omride dynasty, of which Ahab was the second ruler, arranged diplomatic relations with Ethbaal, king of Sidon (1 Kgs 16:31). This move brought Ethbaal's daughter, Jezebel, into the Omride dynasty and facilitated in Israel the worship of Baal, the Canaanite god of fertility. Conservative forces represented by Yahwist prophets found themselves subjected to persecution by Jezebel. Yet in Obadiah they found a friend who provided secret sanctuary and food for them.

While assisting the king in a search for water during a drought, Obadiah happened upon the prophet Elijah, who commanded him to appear before Ahab with a message concerning the prophet's whereabouts. Fearing for his life, Obadiah balked at the task. He reminded Elijah of how far and wide Ahab had sought him as well as the danger in which he had already placed himself by spiriting Yahweh's prophets into a safe hiding place. He then claimed that when he related Elijah's message to Ahab, the prophet would vanish and thereby place Obadiah's life in even greater danger. Nevertheless, the prophet assured Obadiah of his safety by promising to appear that very day before Ahab. Obadiah delivered the message and was rewarded by Elijah keeping his word.

3. A postexilic descendant of David (1 Chr 3:21). After the name Jeshaiah in v 21, a textual difficulty arises which obscures the verse's sense. Following "Jeshaiah," the MT reads, "the sons of Rephaiah, the sons of Arnan, the sons of Obadiah, the sons of Shecaniah." The MT, therefore, specifies no direct connection between the persons listed. Another possibility is to read *bĕnô* "his son," instead of the MT *bĕnê*, "sons of." According to this emendation, which is supported by the LXX (and accepted by the RSV), Obadiah would be the son of Arnan and the father of Shecaniah. According to the text-critical principle that the more difficult reading is to be preferred, the MT should probably be retained. Nothing can thus be known about Obadiah except that he is from David's family.

4. A descendant of Issachar and son of Izrahiah (1 Chr 7:3). According to the Chronicler, Obadiah would have been roughly contemporary with Moses. This list of Issachar's descendants emphasizes the family's warrior traditions, which correspond with the description of Issachar in Judg 5:15. Obadiah is one of five "chief men" (Heb *roʾšîm*). This title indicates a place of leadership in his family.

5. A son of Azel and a member of the family of Saul (1 Chr 8:38; 9:44). The list in which his name is fixed occurs twice in 1 Chronicles. The first list, in chap. 8, delineates the descendants of Benjamin in relation to the Chronicler's unified Israel theme. The second list, in chap. 9, serves to introduce the story of Saul's death in chap. 10.

6. One of the first exiles to return to Judah (1 Chr 9:16). The list in which his name occurs appears again in Nehemiah 11 but in the latter Obadiah's name does not occur. (For the chronological problem suggested by the two lists, see MESHULLAM.) 1 Chr 9:16 lists Obadiah as a Levite.

7. A member of the tribe of Gad who joined David during his stay in Ziklag (1 Chr 12:9). Obadiah is one of a group of warriors whose skill and prowess underscore the quality of the people who gathered around David. According to v 14, Obadiah was an officer in the army. Verse 15 amplifies the description of Gadite ability already provided in v 8 by stating that these Gadites had crossed the Jordan in its flood stage. The inclusion of the list of Gadites contributes to the Chronicler's theme of Israel united.

8. A member of the tribe of Zebulun and father of Ishmaiah (1 Chr 27:19). Obadiah is here the patronymic for one of the leaders of the tribes during David's reign. The exact bureaucratic task of tribal leaders is not clear, but vv 23 and 24 suggest that they had something to do with census taking.

9. A prince of Judah who was among a group commissioned by Jehoshaphat to teach "the book of the law of Yahweh" to the people of Judah (2 Chr 17:7). That members of the laity are commissioned to perform religious instruction is notable. Myers suggests that the position of members of the laity as teachers is possibly quite old and that the reference to the Levites in 2 Chr 17:8 might be the Chronicler's own addition to an older tradition. According to Myers (*2 Chronicles* AB, 99–100), the "book of the law of Yahweh" could hardly be the Pentateuch as it now exists and might refer instead to a royal law code such as the Code of Hammurabi. Historically, he is certainly correct but from the perspective of the Chronicler, the "book of the law of Yahweh" would most surely have been understood as the Mosaic Torah.

10. A Levite who served as an overseer in the repairing of the temple during the reform of Josiah (2 Chr 34:12). He is noted as a Levite of the lineage of Merari.

11. A priest who accompanied Ezra to Jerusalem (Ezra 8:9 = 1 Esdr 8:35). He bears the patronym "son of Jehiel." In Neh 10:5 Obadiah was among those who set their seal to the covenant renewal under Ezra. If Ezra's journey to Jerusalem took place in 458 B.C., then it is possible that the Obadiah mentioned in Neh 10:5 is the same as in Ezra 8:9 (= 1 Esdr 8:35). However, because of the chronological uncertainty concerning the date of Ezra's mission (see EZRA), an identification of Obadiah in Ezra 8:9 with Obadiah in Neh 10:5 is not certain.

12. A gatekeeper during the priesthood of Joiakim (Neh 12:25). His task was to guard the storehouses of the gates.

Bibliography

Mettinger, T. N. D. 1971. *Solomonic State Officials.* ConBOT 5. Lund.

JAMES M. KENNEDY

OBADIAH, BOOK OF. This prophetic book—only 21 verses, almost entirely in poetic form—stands in the collection of the Twelve after Amos and before Jonah (so MT, EVV): LXX arranges the first six differently.

A. Place in the Canon
B. The Prophet
C. Contents and Plan of the Book
D. Text
  1. Obadiah and Jeremiah 49
  2. Unity and Disunity: Dislocation
  3. Text and Language
E. Historical Context and Interpretation

A. Place in the Canon

The position of Obadiah within the Hebrew canonical order probably implies a belief that the first six books all belonged to one general period. The precise order could be related to possible relationships between the individual books: Obadiah 16–21 could be in some measure based on Amos 9:12, and this could explain why Obadiah follows Amos. Less probably, Obadiah 1–14 could be linked back to Joel 4:19. In the Greek order the first five are of decreasing length, but that tradition perhaps associates Obadiah and Jonah more closely with Nahum, Habakkuk, and Zephaniah, which follow, in order to relate these books to the later Assyrian/Babylonian period. Since Obadiah is so very brief, it may be asked whether its inclusion as a separate unit is linked with the desirability that the last "book" of the Latter Prophets should be made up of twelve prophetic collections.

B. The Prophet

This point may be taken a little further when the name Obadiah is considered. No information is available about the prophet except what may be deduced from the book. No serious question arises of identification with any other biblical character of this name. Later Jewish tradition (*b. Sanh.* 39b: cf. Jerome, *In Abdiam*) associated him with the Obadiah of 1 Kings 18, the controller of the royal household who protected prophets of Yahweh from Jezebel: this is a legend attached to a devout character, showing also the common tendency to identify those who bear the same name. More seriously it may be asked whether here the name Obadiah ("servant" or "worshipper of Yahweh," cf. "Abdiel"), while frequently attested in both biblical and archaeological sources, could, like "Malachi," be a pious invention to identify a prophetic fragment making up the Twelve.

C. Contents and Plan of the Book

The first heading of the book is "vision of Obadiah," an expression used in Isa 1:1 and Nah 1:1 (and elsewhere) in the sense of "prophetic message" rather than narrowly denoting visionary experience. The second heading: "thus says the Lord Yahweh to (concerning) Edom," in effect covers much of what follows, though the content of the book is not so restricted as this phrase may seem to suggest.

The content may be set out briefly:

a. 1b–7: judgment on Edom brought by the nations—divisible into 1b–4 and 5–7;
b. 8–14 (15): the day of doom—within which 10–14 concern Edom and the fate of Jerusalem;
c. (15) 16–21: the day of Yahweh, bringing both judgment and salvation.

These divisions are open to some question. There are markers ("oracle of Yahweh") at the end of 4 and the beginning of 8; there is also a punctuating conclusion ("so Yahweh has spoken") at the end of 18. There are close links of theme between 1–7 and 8–14, but style and content differ. In particular 12–14 show closely structured form: each line begins with a prohibition, and each line (except 14a) ends with an expression descriptive of the day of Yahweh.

Verse 15 is problematic. Most often it is supposed that 15b—a markedly proverbial-style expression—is the true continuation of 14, summing up the warnings or accusations of 12–14 by emphasizing that retribution on Edom will be in exact relation to its own actions. Verse 15a is then seen as the beginning of the salvation oracle or oracles of 16–21. The similarity between the openings of 15b and 16a could have attracted the former away from its correct position. But while this is possible, 15b could be an addition underlining the retributive thought present in the context. 15a broadens the idea of the day of Yahweh to concern all nations, and this could form a fitting conclusion to the Edom oracles, stressing that these oracles, whatever their original reference, are now typical, expressive of a doom which is to come upon the whole world. This is then explained in 16 in terms of a reversal by which Judah, forced to drink the cup of Yahweh's wrath, will now see all nations brought to a comparable judgment (cf. Jeremiah 25, especially 15f).

The emphasis on Edom is clear throughout the book. The major part is an oracle (or oracles) on Edom as a foreign nation, such as may be found in a number of other prophetic books, in most instances as part of a collection of such oracles. The appearance alongside foreign-nation oracles of a message of general judgment ushering in salvation for Israel is also familiar (cf. Zephaniah 3; Isaiah 24–27 as a sequel to 13–23; Jeremiah 25).

The poetry of Obadiah is marked by vivid imagery of a kind frequently to be found in the prophetic books. The contrast between pride and humiliation in 2–4 uses ideas found also in Isaiah 2 and in the poem on the overthrow of Tyre in Ezekiel 28. Being "set among the stars" in 4 (excised as a gloss by some commentators) may echo the mythological theme of the fallen daystar (Isa 14:12–14, AV "Lucifer"; cf. Luke 10:18). The inescapability of divine judgment in 3–4 suggests comparison with Ps 139:7–12. Judgment compared to thieves in 5 (cf. Joel 2:9) was to be developed in the NT (cf. 1 Thess 5:2). The "day of Yahweh" theme, much used here, is especially clear in Amos 5:18–20; Isa 2:12–22; Zephaniah 1. Betrayal of friends or by allies (7, 10, 12–14) is a theme used of Edom in Amos 1:11 (cf. 1:9. Cf. also Ps 41:9; Job 6:14f). The fire motif of 18 may be compared with Isa 10:17f. Inheritance/dispossession (17, 19f) may be seen also in Num 24:18f and often in Deuteronomy (cf 2:12). Direct relationship between such uses is hardly to be posited: the poets draw on a rich heritage of poetic language and image.

D. Text

The text of Obadiah presents some problems.

1. Obadiah and Jeremiah 49. Jer 49:7–22 offers a more substantial oracle against Edom, set in the long series of foreign-nation oracles in Jeremiah 46–51. There are numerous points of similarity between the two texts, most closely in 49:14–16 (cf. Obadiah 1–4) but also in 49:9f (cf. Obadiah 5f). The nature of the relationship between the two texts has been widely discussed but without full agreement being reached. Recent discussions of relationships between such pairs of texts have tended to be cautious of claiming direct dependence of one on the other. The closeness at some points in this particular case suggests a relationship due more probably to the common use of source material or the use of traditional or liturgical material. Close parallels may provide a basis for considering the quality of each text, with consequent proposals for textual emendation where one or the other appears doubtful. More properly, each text needs to be considered in its own right. In such cases, one text may subsequently have influenced the other in the course of transmission, and the versions may similarly have been influenced by the alternative text.

More important is the recognition that Jer 49:7–22 offers a larger and distinctive collection of oracles against Edom and that this collection functions within the whole complex of Jeremiah 46–51, just as the Edom oracle in Amos 1:11f does in Amos 1–2. The Obadiah oracle (or oracles) in 1–14(15) functions differently, being set in the context of the salvation message of (15)16–21; in this respect it comes nearer to the Edom material of Isaiah 34 followed by salvation in Isaiah 35, and of Ezekiel 35 in relation to its sequel in Ezekiel 36–37.

2. Unity and Disunity: Dislocation. The question of the unity of the book has already been raised by the notes on content and the comments on the relation to Jeremiah 49. If, as seems probable, Obadiah 1–4 makes use of an already existing oracle, and possibly some other elements in 1–14 build on earlier material, then the unity of this part of the book is to be seen in the integrating of originally separate elements into a new whole. Such a unity has as much validity as the alternative, still maintained by some, that the whole section is of one piece. Unity is in terms of the total impact of a now-impressive grouping of various types of oracles (noting especially the very different style of 12–14), all gathered around the one theme of doom.

A different type of question is posed by joining (15)16–21 to this material. A division into two units, 16–18 and 19–21, appears proper, though there are verbal links between them which make their association intelligible: to some degree 19–21 provide an exegesis of 16–18. But the extension and reinterpretation of the Edom theme here, precisely picked up by the Esau references of 18, 19, and 21, point to the whole book having a new unity in which the Edom oracles are lifted out of whatever historical context may be postulated for them so as to give them a broader meaning, an application to a situation different from that previous one. The evidence in prophetic books of links with liturgical usage (for example the psalms in Isaiah 12 and Habakkuk 3) invites the possibility that "Obadiah" as the author of the book as we now have it could be understood as a cult prophet, or as one who interpreted existing prophetic material in a cultic context. Attempts at giving greater precision to such a view (for example, Watts, Wolff *Obadja* BKAT) cannot be sufficiently demonstrated.

3. Text and Language. Some of the problems here relate to possible historical references (see below). In addition to proposals for emendation based on the Jeremiah parallels, there are difficulties not easily resolved. Thus the last word of 9 ("by slaughter") should perhaps, with some support from the versions, belong to 10 ("for the slaughter and violence . . ."). In 12 the first "the day of" is probably due to reduplication. The text in 20 is evidently in some disorder: various alternative proposals, all conjectural, may be found in commentaries and modern translation. The curious "there is no understanding of it" or "in it" at the end of 7 could be a marginal note to the last clause of 8 making the comment that Edom's supposed wisdom (from which 1 Kgs 4:30 has sometimes been cited) is in reality nonexistent. Another suggestion, which may be paralleled in ANE scribal practice, is that it is the despairing comment of a copyist who could not understand the text in front of him: certainly the *hapax legomenon* rendered "trap" (RSV) is unclear (cf. the various proposals in commentaries and translations).

E. Historical Context and Interpretation

While it would be proper to determine the historical context of the book or of the prophet before considering interpretation, the two questions interlock. In part, the answer to these questions turns on deciding how far the oracles allude to events already past. Does the doom oracle of 1b–4 refer to a disaster which has already overtaken Edom, or to the future? Or, if it is taken over from an earlier context, does it in effect provide the justification for what has now happened (Jerome, *In Abdiam*)? Do the prohibitions in 12–14 carry their normal sense of "do not . . ." (so NEB, JB), or should they be rendered "you should not have . . ." (so RSV)? Such a difference of interpretation reflects a different understanding of the relation of 12–14 to historical events. Much, indeed, turns on this last point, and has its context in the wider questions of the relationships during the biblical period between Edom and Judah. Since there is evident allusion to a disaster to Judah and Jerusalem here (explicitly in 11), and since Psalm 137 places Babylon and Edom in parallel, it has seemed clear to many that in one way or another Edom was involved in the Judean disaster. Lam 4:21f, often assumed to belong shortly after 587 B.C., has been thought to give added support. Evidence that during the period of Babylonian rule Edomites may have taken over some parts of southern Judean territory would support this. When read as reference to the actualities of the period, 12–14 seem to provide a basis on which more can be said about Edom and its involvement than appears in narrative sources. Some justification must exist for the extreme hostility that is to be found both in the numerous prophetic oracles against Edom and in the Jacob-Esau traditions. At a later period, Judean-Idumaean hostility, particularly in the 2d and 1st centuries B.C., provides indications of the continuing relevance of such older stories and oracles.

The difficulty with this kind of interpretation is that it runs the risk of constructing history largely out of prophetic oracles or poetry. The relationship here, as elsewhere, between historical events, allusions to them in poetic form, and the poetic use of motifs in a nonhistorical manner is very difficult to determine. In respect to Obadiah 12–14 there are possibilities of various kinds. It is entirely intelligible, and may be correct, to see precise allusion; it is also proper to observe that there is no statement here which necessitates a merely historical construction. Underlying the material of these and other Edom oracles there is no doubt the reality of hostile relationships at various periods between the two peoples; but fixing this more precisely always remains open to some question. It is clearly improper to give too definite an answer. It should be noted that 1 Esdr 4:45 adds the gratuitously developed legend that it was Edomites who burnt the temple: such an item cannot be used as if it were historical evidence.

Interpretation is affected by these historical questions. Read with a close linking of the words to historical events, the main part of Obadiah can seem all too much a piece of relentless hostility to one particular people, now rounded off with the hope of a total reversal in which Jerusalem contains a holy refuge, Edom is destroyed, not even a remnant left, and more broadly all the surrounding territories are recovered by Jews returned from exile. The text of 20 may conceal the corrupted name Halah, a place of exile named in 2 Kgs 17:6; "Sepharad" has been variously identified, for example with Sardis in Lydia or Sapardu in Media, possibly to be equated with Sepharvaim (2 Kgs 17:24).

If it is right to see precise references to a particular period for the judgment oracles, then the two favored alternatives are (1) a date shortly after 587 B.C. (cf. Lam 4:21f), the detail of 12–14 being seen as immediate recollection; (2) a 5th-century date, as also for Malachi, on the assumption that the pressures of the Nabataeans represent the experienced or future disaster to Edom. Neither proposal is really adequately based on clear historical or archaeological evidence.

In the light of other Edom oracles, as also of Lam 4:21f and Psalm 137, it is possible to read the Edom references, whatever historical attachment may underlie them, as symbolic of the alien outside world upon which divine judgment ultimately falls and over which in the end-time divine rule is absolutely established. The same themes are to be found in many prophetic passages (for example, Isaiah 11; Zachariah 9, 14) and in psalms which see the eventual subjection of all nations to Yahweh and his anointed king (so Psalms 2; 89; 110). The two styles of interpretation are not mutually exclusive, for the hostilities of centuries, still a factor at the end of the biblical period, can underlie the recognition of a more than historical sense to the book. If the antagonism of Judah and Edom has become of largely antiquarian interest, the confidence in the overthrow of the powers of evil and the establishment of royal rule belonging entirely to God is one that has lasting significance. (For other discussions of various issues see Allen *Obadiah* NICOT; Bewer *Obadiah* ICC; Coggins *Obadiah* ITC; Keller *Abdias* CAT; Rudolph *Obadja* KAT; Watts *Obadiah* CBC; and Wolff *Obadja* BKAT.)

Bibliography

Duval, Y.-M. 1985. Jérôme et les prophètes. VTSup 36: 108–31.
Watts, J. D. W. 1969. *Obadiah.* Grand Rapids.

PETER R. ACKROYD

OBAL (PERSON) [Heb *ʿôbāl*]. Var. EBAL. A son of Joktan and hence the name of a South Arabian tribe (Gen 10:28; 1 Chr 1:22), which, however, hitherto could neither be identified nor localized in a satisfactory way. The forms of the name with an initial *e-* vocalization (e.g., 1 Chr 1:22, RSV Ebal; Samaritan *Ībal;* LXX *Geibal, Gabal*) might have resulted from an assimilation to *ʿêbāl,* which is attested as the name of an Edomite (Gen 36:23; 1 Chr 1:40) and as the name of a mountain near Shechem (Deut 11:29, etc.). The Greek forms with *g* at the beginning of the word could point to a South Arabic *ġbl;* there is, however, no evidence of such a root.

Glaser (1890: 427) considered whether *ʿôbāl* is to be identified with Yemenite *ʿubāl,* a locality on the Wâdī Sihām between Bāğil and Ḥağailah at the border of the Tihāmah toward the highland; if this is correct, one would have to look for *ʿôbāl* in the middle of the Yemenite coastal plain. At the same time, however, Glaser drew attention to the fact that a form like *ʿĀbil* or *ʿAibal* would better correspond to the biblical name. A clan or tribal group *(bnw)* *ᶜblm* is attested several times in the Sabaean inscriptions, especially in votive texts from Mārib. Most of the inscriptions in which the *(bnw) ᶜblm* are mentioned, however, do not give a hint at the provenance of their donors; some, however, indicate that we obviously have to deal with two different groups. The dedicators of the inscription Ja 558 belong to the tribe of Faišān which settled around Mārib, and RES 4387 is the epitaph on a tombstone from Mārib mentioning names of members of the clan *ᶜblm.* On the other hand, the *bnw ᶜblm* of Ja 621 are designated as *ʾʾd̲nn,* i.e., as belonging to the tribe of Maʾd̲in, the territory of which extended in the area NW of Ṣanᶜāʾ. The *bny ᶜblm* of Ja 585, which are counted among the tribe of Ghaimān, were most probably resident in the same region. The donor of the inscription RES 4143, who is identical with the donor of the text Ja 635 and who also belongs to the *ᶜblm,* is supposed to have come from the same district, not far from Ṣanᶜāʾ (cf. Ryckmans 1981: 286). This distinction into two different groups is also supported by the South Arabian tradition. Al-Hamdānī (1966: 106–8, 109) clearly distinguishes between the *D̲ū ᶜIbl* as a clan of Mārib and the tribe *D̲ū ᶜĀbil bin D̲ī Aqyān bin Sabaʾ,* which is itself divided into four branches. Wâdī Ḍahr and the places Kaukabān and T̲ulā are mentioned as the settlement area of the Āl D̲ī Aqyān, and the town of Šibām below the mountain-fortress of Kaukabān is distinguished from the other Yemenite localities of the same name as Šibām Aqyān (Al-Hamdānī 1884: 72). Since an equation of Hebrew *ᶜôbāl* with S Arabic *ᶜĀbil* is worth being advocated, it is quite possible that the biblical name refers to that Sabaean tribal group of the *(bnw) ᶜblm* whose ancient settlement area was likely located in the Yemenite highland approximately between Ṣanᶜāʾ and Šibām Aqyān or Šibām respectively (ca. 45 km NW of Ṣanᶜāʾ). Inscriptions which have been found there enable us to retrace the history of this region to the early time of the Sabaean realm.

Bibliography

Al-Hamdānī. 1884. *Ṣifat Ǧazīrat al-ᶜArab,* ed. D. H. Müller. Leiden.
———. 1966. *Al-Iqlīl,* vol. 2, ed. M. al-Akwaᶜ. Cairo.
Glaser, E. 1890. *Skizze der Geschichte und Geographie Arabiens.* Vol. 2. Berlin.
Rykmans, J. 1981. Un parallèle sud arabe à l'imposition du nom de Jean-Baptiste et de Jésus. In *Al-Hudhud, Festschrift M. Höfner zum 80. Geburtstag,* ed. von R. G. Stiegner. Graz.

W. W. Müller

OBED (PERSON) [Heb *ᶜôbēd*]. Var. EBED. **1.** The son of Ruth and Boaz, the grandfather of King David, ancestor of Jesus Christ (Ruth 4:13, 17, 22; 1 Chr 2:12; Matt 1:5; Luke 3:32). Obed was the son of the Moabite Ruth who had returned with her mother-in-law Naomi to Bethlehem where she married Boaz, a relative of Ruth's deceased husband, Mahlon. See RUTH, BOOK OF; NAOMI. By extension of the Israelite custom of kinship marriage (Deut 25:5–10), Boaz fathered Obed, but he did so in the name of Mahlon. While the narrative indicates that Obed is the son of Mahlon, the genealogy gives the actual lineage of Obed by Boaz. Since the child is Ruth's (4:15) and Naomi's (4:17), the story depicts Obed as heir to Boaz, Mahlon, and Elimelech (Ruth 4:9–10).

The historicity of Obed's kinship to the royal house, however, is often debated. Related to this problem is the legitimacy of the name Obed. The naming of Obed by the women of the city differs from the expected formula for naming a child (4:17). Where the name "Obed" should occur in the formula, only the word *šēm* ("name") appears and there is no connection between the meaning of "Obed" ("worshipper") and the women's explanation: "A son has been born to Naomi." The reconstructed name *ben nōᶜam* ("son of pleasantness") therefore has been suggested for the original name; the lost name has been supplanted by "Obed" in order to tie the narrative to David's genealogy (Eissfeldt 1965: 479). This opinion no longer dominates, however (Sasson 1979: 175). The name Obed is a vocalized participle and derived from *ᶜbd,* meaning "worshipper." It may be a shortened form of "Obadiah" *(ᶜōbadyâ).*

2. Son of Ephlal, descended from Jerahmeel who was the firstborn of Hezron (1 Chr 2:37–38).

3. One of David's "mighty men" (1 Chr 11:47). Obed is among those names added by the Chronicler which are absent in the parallel account of 2 Samuel (*Chronicles* NCBC, 103–4).

4. Son of Shemaiah, a member of the Korahite division of gatekeepers. The four sons of Shemaiah are reported to be leaders as a result of their exceptional ability (1 Chr 26:6–7).

5. Father of the military commander Azariah, who assisted the priest Jehoiada in executing Queen Athaliah and establishing the legitimate rule of King Joash (2 Chr 23:1, 14–15).

6. One of the men who returned with Ezra from Babylon, the son of Jonathan and descendant of Addin (1 Esdr 8:32). In the parallel account of Ezra, the variant name "Ebed" is given (Ezra 8:6).

Bibliography

Eissfeldt, O. 1965. *The Old Testament: An Introduction.* Trans. P. R. Ackroyd. New York.
Sasson, J. M. 1979. *Ruth.* Baltimore.

Kenneth A. Mathews

OBED-EDOM (PERSON) [Heb *ᶜōbēd-ʾĕdôm*]. Four individuals in the OT bear this non-Yahwistic name meaning "Servant of (the god) Edom" (cf. the Phoen personal name *ᶜbdʾdm*). According to Albright (*YGC,* 140 and n. 76), the theophoric element *(ʾĕdōm/ʾādōm?)* names the consort of Resheph, an Underworld deity known from Egypt and Canaan.

1. The "Gittite" (i.e., one from Gath) at whose house David stored the ark of God when the sudden death of Uzzah halted the procession to bring it from Baale-judah (2 Sam 6:2 = Kiriath-jearim, 1 Chr 13:6) to the City of David (2 Sam 6:1–11 = 1 Chr 13:1–14). His name and origins in Gath may well place him among Philistine expatriates loyal to David (2 Sam 15:18–22; 18:2), thus explaining the king's willingness to leave the ark with a foreigner, apparently now a convert to Yahweh (McCarter *2 Samuel* AB, 170). Yahweh blessed Obed-edom and his household because of the ark, prompting David to bring the ark on into the city (2 Sam 6:11–12 = 1 Chr 13:14; cf. 15:25).

2. Son of Jeduthun, named primarily as a gatekeeper (1 Chr 15:18, 24; 16:38) and perhaps performing special service related to the ark (15:24). In the celebration accompanying the ark into the city, he functioned as a musician, appointed by David to lead as one of the lyre players (15:21) and after that to minister with harp and lyre before the ark, along with his 68 brothers (16:5, 38).

3. Son of Korah through Kore (1 Chr 26:1, 19). Obed-edom and his sixty-two descendants, including eight sons, served at the S gate of the temple precinct and the storehouses related to it (26:4–8, 15). The size (26:8; cf. 16:38) and fitness (26:6, 8) of the family for temple service are stressed by the Chronicler.

4. Levitical custodian of temple treasures at the time Joash, king of Israel, sacked Jerusalem following his defeat of Amaziah of Judah (2 Chr 25:24). He presumably served in the gatekeeper tradition of his clan (cf. 1 Chr 26:4–8, 15; and #3 above). Whether Obed-edom was taken captive (LXX, Vg) or (more likely) is simply named keeper of the vessels and precious metals lost to Joash is not clear from the MT. The 2 Kgs 14:14 parallel does not mention him.

The precise relationship between these four remains unclear due to the nature of the Chronicler's work where one or more families of temple servants claiming ties to the Philistine caretaker of the ark are given levitical ancestry.

Bibliography

Williams, H. G. M. 1979. The Origins of the Twenty-Four Priestly Courses. *VTSup* 30: 250–68.

DAVID L. THOMPSON

OBELISK. See MASSEBAH.

OBIL (PERSON) [Heb *ʾôbîl*]. A state official; an Ishmaelite. One of twelve stewards of royal property appointed by David, his specific charge was to oversee the camels (1 Chr 27:30). Of the twelve, he is one of seven identified with a gentilic rather than by paternity, a feature which may underscore his non-Israelite background. Some have argued for the antiquity of the list because of the inclusion of an Ishmaelite; others that it is artificial (and perhaps late) because "Obil" means "camel driver" (see Braun *1 Chronicles* WBC, 263).

RICHARD W. NYSSE

OBLATION [Heb *minḥâ*]. "Oblation" is the word the RSV uses to translate *minḥâ* in 1 Kgs 18:29 and 18:36. *Minḥâ* can refer either to sacrifices in general or to grain offerings specifically. In 1 Kings, it indicates the evening offering, which was one of two daily sacrifices performed in the tabernacle and in the temple. According to Exod 29:39, this offering takes place "between the evenings" *(bên hāʿarĕbāyim)*, that is, after sundown but before all the sun's light has left the sky. Josephus, by contrast, states that the evening offering occurs at the ninth hour, which is about three o'clock in the afternoon (*Ant* 14.4.3). This regular evening sacrifice, as well as the morning one, is described in Exod 29:38–46 and Num 28:1–8 (where the two sacrifices are referred to as *qorbān*). In both offerings, the priests slaughter an unblemished lamb as a burnt offering accompanied by a cereal offering of flour and oil and a drink offering.

PAUL V. M. FLESHER

OBODA (M.R. 128022). A town in the Negeb which was named after a Nabatean king who reigned 30–9 B.C.E.

A. History of Research

U. J. Seetzen passed by Abdeh in 1807 and recognized the preservation of the ancient name of the site. H. Palmer in 1870 drew the first schematic plan of the site, and A. Musil drew a more detailed plan in 1902, recognizing and noting a number of significant features. These investigations were followed by those of A. Jaussen, R. Savignac, and H. L. Vincent in 1904; C. L. Woolley and T. E. Lawrence in 1914; and the German work of T. Wiegand in the same period. The Colt Expedition of 1937 located a building which apparently was a caravansary on the SW end of the plateau. Full-scale excavations at Oboda were conducted by M. Avi-Yonah (1958), A. Negev (1959–61), and A. Negev in collaboration with R. Cohen (1975–77). These investigations have clarified the occupation of the site into the following periods: Early Nabatean (4th–early 1st centuries B.C.E.); Middle Nabatean (30/25 B.C.E.–50/70 C.E.); Late Nabatean (ca. 70–150 C.E.), and Post-Nabatean, including the Late Roman and Byzantine periods. See also NABATEANS.

B. History

Oboda, whose name is preserved in the Arabic form, Abda, is named after the Nabatean king Obodas (apparently the second king by this name), who, according to Stephanus Byzantinus (482.15–16), was buried at the site after his deification. A recently discovered Nabatean inscription and numerous Greek inscriptions in the ruins of the temple at Oboda testify to the persistence of the cult into the 2d and 3d centuries C.E. Ptolemy (Geog. 5.17.4) lists Eboda (= Oboda) among the cities of Arabia Petraea. It is known as Oboda on the Peutinger map along the main road from Aila to Jerusalem. Although the city prospered in the Late Roman and Byzantine periods, it is never mentioned again in historic sources.

The earliest traces of settlement, coins and Hellenistic pottery, are from the late 4th century B.C.E. The wide distribution of the mints from which these coins originate hint of the role of Oboda, with Nessana and Elusa, as a major caravan stop on the network of the international spice trade. No building remains of this period have been found, and it seems that the nomadic Nabateans conducted their trade from tent encampments. The conquest of Gaza by Alexander Jannaeus (ca. 100 B.C.E.) apparently precipitated a brief decline of Oboda. At the beginning of the reign of Obodas II, however, the Nabateans resumed control of the Negeb, establishing at Oboda a major caravan stop. A magnificent temple was built on the W part of the plateau, rising 619 m above sea level. At the N end of the plateau was a military camp, accommodating up to

2,000 soldiers and their camels. The S part of the site was allotted to breeding stock. No private buildings have been discovered for this period and it seems that the civilian population still lived in tents. This period of prosperity encompasses the entire reign of Aretas IV (9 B.C.E.–40 C.E.). By the middle of the 1st century C.E., at the beginning of the reign of Malichus II (40–70 C.E.), Oboda was sacked by Arab tribes who wreaked havoc in all of the Nabatean kingdom, which resulted in the cessation of Nabatean rule at Oboda until ca. 70 C.E., when Rabel II ("He Who Brought Life and Deliverance to His People") ascended the throne. The Nabateans lost their supremacy in commercial trade and turned to agriculture. This transition is attested at Oboda by dedicatory inscriptions on agricultural installations. Rabel's death and the annexation of the Nabatean kingdom to Provincia Arabia had little adverse effect on Oboda, but the building activities that had begun in the 80s of the 1st century continued until ca. 125 C.E. Activities for the remainder of the 2d and 3d centuries can be traced by numismatic evidence. The town extended along part of the W slope of the hill, and in the beginning of the 3d century a new residential quarter was established on the S part of the plateau, with a contemporary cemetery on the W slope. The old Nabatean temple was renovated on the acropolis and dedicated to Aphrodite and to Zeus Oboda, thus perpetuating Oboda's cult. Although the ones dedicating the temple were all of Nabatean descent, the old Aramaic-Nabatean language yielded to Greek, which was the language of the numerous dedications.

With the advent of Diocletian and Constantine, major changes occurred in the E. Some Late Nabatean houses and the old military camp, which had been abandoned since ca. 50 C.E., were plundered for stone to construct a smaller citadel on the E half of the acropolis. During the early Byzantine period, Oboda spread along the entire W slope, with isolated farmhouses along the plateau.

From the 4th century C.E., olive oil and wine production were the basis of the economy. On the plateau and along the slopes, five winepresses, an olive oil press, and several wine cellars were built. Working and storage space was found in the excavation of caves in the back of each of the houses. Numerous cisterns were excavated in and around the city and a bath was supplied with water from a 64-m-deep well. Apparently in the second half of the 4th century, the old Nabatean temple was destroyed and its stones used to build the North Church on the acropolis. A century later the South Church and monastery were built bridging both the North Church and the citadel, making a huge complex.

The latest-dated inscription at Oboda is from 612 C.E. Both churches were discovered full of ash and charred beams from the wooden frame of the roof. This destruction is attributed to 636 C.E., when Oboda was stormed by the Islamic raids, which precipitated the desertion of the site.

Bibliography

Negev, A. 1961a. A Caravan Halt in the Negev. *Archaeology* 14: 122–30.

———. 1961b. Nabatean Inscriptions from Avdat (Oboda). *IEJ* 11: 127–38.

———. 1963. Nabatean Inscriptions from Avdat (Oboda). *IEJ* 13: 113–24.

———. 1965. Stonedressers Marks from A Nabatean Sanctuary at Avdat. *IEJ* 15: 33–37.

———. 1967. Oboda Mampsis and the Provincia Arabia. *IEJ* 17: 46–55.

———. 1974. *Nabatean Potter's Workshop of Oboda.* Bonn.

———. 1976. Eboda. *EAEHL* 2: 345–54.

———. 1981a. House and City Planning in the Ancient Negev and the Provincia Arabia. Pp. 3–32 in *Housing in Arid Lands,* ed. G. Golani. London.

———. 1981b. *Greek Inscriptions from the Negev.* Jerusalem.

———. 1983. *Tempel, Kirchen und Zisternen.* Stuttgart.

AVRAHAM NEGEV

OBOTH (PLACE) [Heb *ʾōbōt*]. An unidentified stage of the Exodus between Mount Hor and the plains of Moab (Num 21:10, 11; 33:43, 44). The encampment at Oboth immediately preceded the people's rest at Iye-abarim.

Oboth has been identified by some with ʿAin el-Weiba on the W edge of the Wâdī ʿArabah, almost 18 miles due W of Feinân (e.g., *GP,* 400–1). Feinân is generally identified with Punon, the encampment preceding Oboth (Num 33:43). See PUNON. However, though ʿAin el-Weiba would be a suitable camping ground, its location produces an inexplicable detour to the W given the general NE direction the Israelites were traveling toward the Transjordanian mountains. Hence other suggestions for Oboth have been offered, including an unspecified location N of Feinân (e.g. Davies 1979: 90) and a position N of Bozrah (*MBA,* 42). The location of Oboth depends largely upon one's reconstruction of the route of the Exodus.

Bibliography

Davies, G. I. 1979. *The Way of the Wilderness.* Cambridge.

ARTHUR J. FERCH

OBSCENE LANGUAGE. See BIBLE, EUPHEMISM AND DYSPHEMISM IN THE.

OCHIEL (PERSON) [Gk *Ochiēlos*]. See JEIEL.

OCHRAN (PERSON) [Heb *ʿokrān*]. The father of the chief (*nāśîʾ*, Num 2:27) Pagiel of the tribe of Asher. Each of the five times that Ochran is mentioned in the OT occurs in a tribal list where his mark of distinction is his status as the father of Pagiel. Under the leadership of Ochran's son Pagiel, the tribe of Asher participated in the census of Israelite fighting men carried out by Moses (Num 1:13, 40–41), presented its offerings on the eleventh day of the twelve-day celebration of the dedication of the altar (Num 7:72, 77), took its proper place on the N side of the tabernacle in the Israelite camp (Num 2:27), and assumed its position in the order of march at the Israelites' departure from Mount Sinai (Num 10:26). The name Ochran seems to mean "the perplexed or afflicted one" (*IPN,* 253).

DALE F. LAUNDERVILLE

OCINA (PLACE) [Gk *Okina*]. A site which is part of a list of towns occurring in the book of Judith (Jdt 2:28). The name Ocina occurs only here in the Bible, where it is part of a list of towns on the seacoast stretching from N to S. It is possible that "Ocina" is a corruption of "Acco," an ancient harbor city N of Mount Carmel. See ACCO (PLACE); PTOLEMAIS (PLACE). This would be the correct geographical location. However, given the genre of the book of Judith, it is also possible that the name is fictitious. See JUDITH, BOOK OF.

SIDNIE ANN WHITE

OCTOPUS. See ZOOLOGY.

ODED (PERSON) [Heb *ʿōdēd, ʿôdēd*]. This name is of uncertain etymology, with BDB (pp. 728–29) deriving it from *ʿûd,* "prob. return, go about, repeat, do again," and KB translating it as *"Orakeldeuter"* (752; cf. also the discussion in Willi 1972: 221–22). There is probably some connection with the name Iddo *(ʿiddô, ʿiddōʾ, ʿiddôʾ).*

1. The first person in the Bible mentioned as having this "name" was an individual in the early 9th or very late 10th century said to be *ʿăzaryāhû ben-ʿōdēd,* a prophet in Judah who preached a word of encouragement to King Asa (2 Chr 15:1). Strangely enough, in 15:8 the prophecy is said to have been given by "Oded the Prophet" *(ʿōdēd hannābîʾ).* The RSV restores "Azariah the son of Oded," a reading at least as old as the Syr Peshitta and some manuscripts of the LXX (specifically the Lucianic recension). Perhaps a clue can be found in the Old Aram inscription of Zakkur, beginning with line 11 (obverse), where we are told by Zakkur, "I lifted up my hands to Baalshamayin and Baalshamayin answered me and Baalshamayin spoke to me through (lit. "by the hand of") seers and prophets *(ʿddn)*" (my translation). Since *(ʿddn)* clearly has the sense of "prophet" in this passage (*DISO,* 204; Degen 1969: 47, 52; Segert 1986: 545; cf. also *ʿdd*—"herald" in Ugaritic, II AB vii, 46 [Gibson 1965: 65]), it is quite likely that *ben-ʿōdēd* referred to a prophetic class in 15:1 (or even a prophetic disciple—cf. the discussion with regard to Amos 7:14 in Wolff *Joel and Amos* Hermeneia, 312–14). Since the term was a rare one for a prophet, *hannābîʾ* was then appended to *ʿōdēd* in 15:8 as an attempt to clarify for the reader the meaning of the term. The term *ʿōdēd* was then later misread as a personal name, resulting in the confusion witnessed by the versions (for a similar explanation, cf. the discussion in Montgomery 1909: 68–69).

2. This individual was also a prophet (!), this time from late-8th-century Samaria, who rebuked Israel for taking 200,000 Judeans captive (2 Chr 28:9). Several Ephraimite tribal leaders joined him and succeeded in dissuading the Israelites to let the Judeans go free, which they did after feeding and clothing them (2 Chr 28:10–15).

Bibliography

Degen, R. 1969. *Altaramäische Grammatik: Der Inschriften des 10–8. Jh. v. Chr.* AKM 38/3. Wiesbaden.
Gibson, J. C. L. 1965. *Canaanite Myths and Legends.* Edinburgh.
Montgomery, J. A. 1909. Some Gleanings from Pognon's ZKR Inscription. *JBL* 28: 57–70.
Segert, S. 1986. *Altaramäische Grammatik.* Leipzig.
Willi, T. 1972. *Die Chronik als Auslegung.* Göttingen.

H. ELDON CLEM

ODOMERA (PERSON) [Gk *Odomēra*]. According to 1 Macc 9:66, Jewish forces under Jonathan the Hasmonean killed Odomera and his brothers along with the sons of Pharison near Bethbasi south of Jerusalem (ca. 160 B.C.E.). Odomera and his brothers were probably a bedouin tribe allied with the Syrian forces under Bacchides. A variant reading, however, would indicate that Jonathan did not slay (Gk *epataxen*) Odomera and his brothers but, rather, commanded or summoned them (Gk *epetaxen* in Codex Venetus and 340). Goldstein (*1 Maccabees* AB, 395) prefers the variant reading, noting its common use in 1 Maccabees. For Goldstein, Jonathan would hardly have slipped out of Bethbasi under Seleucid siege to attack a group of bedouin but would have done so to enlist aid in defeating the Syrian army. Josephus indicates that Jonathan did seek aid to defeat Bacchides, in an account which parallels 1 Maccabees 9 (*Ant* 13.1.5 §28). However, the Josephan account appears to be based on a different tradition in that Jonathan slips out of Bethalaga and not Bethbasi (*Ant* 13.1.5 §26). Zeitlin (1950: 166, n. 66) demurs from using Josephus to argue that these bedouin were allied with the Jews by noting that according to Josippon, who made use of the Hebrew text (unlike Josephus, who probably read the Greek), Jonathan does indeed kill these bedouin allies of Bacchides.

Bibliography

Zeitlin, S. 1950. *The First Book of Maccabees.* Trans. and ed. S. Tedesche and S. Zeitlin. New York.

MICHAEL E. HARDWICK

ODOR [Heb *rêaḥ;* Gk *osmē*]. In the OT odor is not directly related to texts dealing with perfume, except for Cant 1:3 and Jer 25:10 (LXX), "myrrh," or for Cant 1:12, "nard." Odor can be that left by the smell of garments (Gen 27:27) or of fire (Dan 3:27). Most often found is the reference to "a pleasing odor," found 40 times between Gen 8:21 and Num 29:26. Lev 1:3–17 gives the following definition: "it is a burnt offering, an offering by fire upon the altar, a pleasing odor to the Lord." Such a rite is found in the Babylonian narratives that relate to thanksgiving for being rescued from the Flood. God is favorably inclined by the pleasing odor offered by the worshipper; he "acknowledges with his nose," wherewith the breath of life is to be found (Gen 7:22), that odor which restores life. In the biblical Flood Narrative, it is Noah who first presented such an offering: the Lord smelled the pleasing odor and blessed Noah after the Flood (Gen 8:20–22). The Noachian tradition is often referred to during the rite of the burnt offering to the Lord. The only exception is Lev 4:31, which refers to the offering for sin, since in that rite only certain parts are burned, which are never elsewhere termed as producing "a pleasing odor." Another exception is to be found in Ezek 6:13; 16:19; 20:28, which concern idols instead of the Lord.

Odors that conform to divine prescription are efficacious, as in Tob 8:3 where the demon Asmodeus flees from the smell of fish. When angered by his unworthy people, the Lord will not smell the pleasing odors (Lev 26:31). Thus, odors can apparently be tokens of both approval and disapproval.

When quoting LXX, *osmē euōdias* is the translation of *rēaḥ nîḥōaḥ*, and a metaphoric sense of "a pleasing odor" can be discerned (Sir 39:14). The same was asserted about prayer in the Qumran community (1QS 8:9) and later, in the apostolic period, about the praise of the creator (*Ep Barn* 2:10).

The NT usage is exclusively metaphoric. Paul calls the Philippians' offering a pleasing odor, a sacrifice acceptable and pleasing to God (Phil 4:18); the author of Ephesians exhorts his readers to "walk in love, as Christ loved us and gave himself up for us, a pleasing odor and sacrifice to God" (Eph 5:2).

Paul discusses the apostolic ministry of the new covenant in which Christ through the apostle "spreads the fragrance of the knowledge of him everywhere" (2 Cor 2:14–16). This passage expresses a universal apostolate where Paul, Timothy, and Silvanus are a pleasing odor of Christ to God, among those who are being saved and among those who are perishing. This "pleasing odor of Christ" (2 Cor 2:15) is among all people but in a somewhat different fashion. In the Greek text both participles are present tense, "those who *are proceeding* toward perdition and those who *are* by now *proceeding* toward salvation" (2 Cor 2:15). Thus Christ's life is actually the living, present "life of Christ" inspired and conveyed by faith. The "pleasing odor of Christ" is believed to draw to life those who are perishing. Thus God makes use of Paul's apostolic ministry and the work of all Christians in order that Christ may be known by all.

Bibliography

Carrez, M. 1984. Odeur de mort, odeur de vie (à propos de 2 Co 2:16). *RHPR* 64: 135–41.

———. 1987. Parfum. *Dictionnaire encyclopédique de la Bible.* Centre informatique et Bible. Maredsous, France.

———. 1987. Ikanotès: 2 Cor 2:14–17. Pp 79–104 in *Paolo, Ministro del Nuovo Testamento* (2 Cor 2:14–4:6), ed. L. de Lorenzi. Serie Monografica di "Benedictina" 9. Rome.

MAURICE CARREZ

OFFERINGS. See SACRIFICE AND SACRIFICIAL OFFERINGS.

OFFSET [Heb *migrāʿâ*]. Rebatements in the construction of the wall of the temple so that the side chambers could be constructed without actually being attached to the temple (1 Kgs 6:6; cf. Ezek 41:6–7). The distinction of the temple as a separate sacred space is thus preserved. "Offset" is from a root *(grʿ)* meaning "to diminish," and it probably refers to a ledge in the wall created by a reduction in its width at a given point. The second tier of side chambers was thus wider (6 cubits) than the bottom tier (5 cubits); and the uppermost wall was wider still (7 cubits). See also TEMPLE, JERUSALEM.

CAROL MEYERS

OG (PERSON) [Heb *ʿôg*]. King of the land of Bashan in Transjordan (Num 21:33–35). He was defeated and killed by the Israelites as they passed through his territory on the way to the promised land. Og's kingdom is portrayed as a settled region; sixty cities are mentioned in the narrative of the conquest of the area (Deut 3:1–10). Og is also connected with two major cities in the region which are assumed to have been his capitals: Edrei and Ashtaroth (Josh 12:4). After the region had been conquered, the territory of Og was given to the half tribe of Manasseh, which chose to remain east of the Jordan (Josh 13:29–30).

An additional note about Og is found in Deut 3:11, where he is said to be the last survivor of the REPHAIM, a putative race of giants mentioned occasionally in the Hebrew Bible and presumed to have inhabited Canaan in pre-Israelite times (Deut 2:20). The great size of Og was confirmed by a reference to his "iron bedstead" still on display at Rabbah (Deut 3:11). This bedstead was some 6 feet (4 cubits) wide and 13½ feet (9 cubits) long. The Hebrew words translated "bedstead" and "iron" have been much discussed in the secondary literature. The translation "bedstead" is from the Hebrew *ʿereś*, which is usually understood as "couch" or "bed." In Deut 3:11, some take it as a last resting place and so a tomb or sarcophagus (Mayes 1979: 144). In connection with this reference to a sarcophagus, the term *barzel* is understood as "basalt," a dense black stone commonly used in the region (Driver *Deuteronomy* ICC, 54).

The importance of the defeat of Og in Israel's memory is demonstrated by the continued references to the event in various parts of the Hebrew Bible. The Pentateuch refers to the victory over Og in both Numbers and Deuteronomy (Num 21:33; 32:33; Deut 1:4; 3:1–13; 4:47; 29:6—Eng 29:7; 31:4). The Deuteronomistic History picks up this event in Joshua and in 1 Kings (Josh 2:10; 9:10; 12:4; 13:12, 30–31; 1 Kgs 4:19). The summary of Israel's history in Nehemiah 9 includes this event in 9:22. There are also references to Og in Psalms 135:11 and 136:20.

Bibliography

Mayes, A. D. H. 1979. *Deuteronomy.* London.

PHILLIP E. MCMILLION

OHAD (PERSON) [Heb *ʾohad*]. He was the third of the six sons of Simeon (Gen 46:10; Exod 6:15). Ohad was the grandson of Jacob and Leah, and his name is mentioned in the genealogical list of the people who descended with Jacob to Egypt at the invitation of Joseph at the time of a severe famine in the land of Canaan (Gen 46:8–27). Ohad's name does not appear in the parallel genealogical lists of the descendants of Simeon in Num 26:12 and 1 Chr 4:24. Cheyne (*EncBib*, 3460) explained this omission by saying that the name Ohad comes from a dittography of "Zohar," Simeon's fifth son. Keil (1951: 372) explained the omission of Ohad's name in the parallel genealogical lists by saying that Ohad either died without fathering children or did not leave a sufficient number of children to form an independent clan.

Bibliography

Keil, C. F. 1951. *The Pentateuch.* Vol. 1 in *Biblical Commentary on the Old Testament.* Repr. Grand Rapids.

CLAUDE F. MARIOTTINI

OHEL (PERSON) [Heb *ʾōhel*]. The fifth child of Zerubbabel. Ohel is listed second in 1 Chr 3:20, which records a second distinct list of Zerubbabel's children. It has been suggested that these names were grouped separately because they were born after the return to Palestine. It seems unlikely that these names represent the offspring of Meshallum as was previously suggested (Albright 1921: 10; Williamson *Chronicles* NCBC, 57).

Bibliography

Albright, W. F. 1921. The Date and Personality of the Chronicler. *JBL* 40: 110.

RUSSELL FULLER

OHOLIAB (PERSON) [Heb *ʾohŏlîʾāb*]. Ahisamach's son, from the tribe of Dan, and Bezalel's cocraftsman in the tabernacle construction (Exod 38:23—LXX 37:21). Oholiab possessed the necessary skills—traceable to divine inspiration—for fashioning several individual items in accordance with the instructions he received from Moses (31:6). He and Bezalel also taught their special skills to a great host of manual laborers engaged in the work on the tabernacle (35:30–36:7). Yet the two were not architects. When it came to assembling the parts into an integrated whole, not they but Moses personally performed the task (40:1–33). The name Oholiab is unusual but not necessarily an artificial construction since there is evidence of its elements in W Semitic nomenclature. Noth (*IPN*, 158–59), who compares the form with Phoenician *ʾhlbʿl* and *ʾhlmlk* and with Sabaean *ʾhlʾl*, considers it a nominal sentence name, and translates it as "father is a tent (i.e., shelter)" rather than either "family of father" or "tent of father." The name is archaic, not containing the new title YHWH in the function of a formative element. Cole (*Exodus* TOTC, 209) sees no reason to consider it an ungenuine insertion. He adds that it is datable at the latest to the time of the Davidic tent (1 Chr 15:1), since Solomon's artificer had a different name (1 Kgs 7:13). One may therefore accept the possibility that behind the names of both Oholiab and Bezalel, and even behind their assignment to certain Israelite tribes, there stand the historical figures of craftsmen who were at one time involved in the furnishing of the sanctuary (Noth, *Exodus* OTL, 240). Clements (*Exodus* CBC, 199), however, denies an extraordinary instance of survival of tradition and thinks they simply represented famous family guilds of craftsmen well known in ancient Israel—families who were expert in woodcraft and metalcraft and who were employed in making and furnishing the temple.

EDWIN C. HOSTETTER

OHOLIBAMAH (PERSON) [Heb *ʾoholîbāmâ*]. The daughter of Anah, son of Zibon the Horite, and the second wife of Esau (Gen 36:2, 14, 18, 25). Oholibamah was also the mother of Jeush, Jalam, and Korah (vv 5, 14, 18). As such, she (along with Adah and Basemath) was considered one of the Edomite tribal mothers. Originally she probably belonged to the Horitic-Seiritic tribal system. Later (as Esau's wife) she and her three sons were genealogically integrated into the Esauite-Edomite tribal system. Furthermore, she was regarded as her own tribe on the basis of the addendum in Gen 36:40–43, a list of Edomite "tribal leaders" (Heb *ʾallûpîm*) that probably ought to be attributed to the Priestly source (cf. also 1 Chr 1:51b–54, which is a shortened version of that addendum). The meaning of the name is unclear. Perhaps it can be understood as "my (god's) tent (protection, refuge) is with them (*ʾōhel* plus preposition *bĕ-* and 3d person plural suffix?)" or as "my tent (protection) is (divine name)." Another possible meaning could be derived from Arabic *ʾhl*, "people, clan," and mean "people/clan of (a certain) god."

ULRICH HÜBNER

OLD AGE. Aging in the Bible represents a welcomed pilgrimage through the transitions of life. Old age enjoys its own vocabulary and high regard (Lev 19:32). Nevertheless, like other stages of life, it brings mixed blessings.

A. Old Age as Physical Traits

Languages throughout the ANE use "white hair" (wool) to refer to one of optimum age and wisdom. White hair is the primary trait of old age. Akkadian *ši-pa-tu* (wool, gray hair) and *ši-bu* describe those who are old, older, or very old (*AHW* 3: 1228, 1244). Hebrew uses *sêbâ*, "gray head," as a synonym for old age (*BDB*, 966; Gen 15:15; 25:8; Judg 8:32; 1 Chr 29:28). A similar image appears in biblical Aramaic describing the "ancient of days" who sits enthroned with hair like "lamb's wool," *ʿămar nĕqēʾ* (Dan 7:9; Sokoloff 1976).

A second word, "elder," *zāqēn* (Hebrew), and its equivalents *šībtum* (Akkadian), *senator* (Latin), *gerōn* (Greek), and *sheikh* (Arabic), designate both people of advanced age and people of a distinct social grade. Hebrew derives the word from *zaqan*, one who wears a beard, i.e., a fully accredited adult. Though the term defines any person past puberty, it also designates a clan leader, a local official, and an old person. (For discussions of the elders as a distinct social grade or position, see Bornkamm *TDNT* 4: 651–83; Harvey 1974). The feminine form also describes older women (*zĕqēnôt*, Zech 8:4) and old age in general (*ziqnâ*, Gen 24:36). Aged, decrepit persons are designated by a parallel term, *yases* (2 Chr 36:17), and its derivative for the venerable aged, *yasis* (Job 15:10; 32:6; 12:12; 29:8).

B. Old Age as Advanced Years

The Bible also indicates aging by referring to a chronological age. Some texts record a life span in years. Others use idioms to describe longevity as "full of days" or "advanced in years": *ʾōrek yāmîm* ("length of days"); *yāmîm rabbîm* ("many days"); *śĕbaʿ yāmîm* ("sated with days"); *mĕlēʾ yāmîm* ("full of days"); *bāʾ bayyāmîm* ("advanced in years"); and *śêbâ ṭôbâ* ("a ripe old age"). Verbal forms include *haʾărēk yāmîm* ("to lengthen days"); *harbôt yāmîm* ("to increase days"); and *hôsēp yāmîm* ("to add days"). The expression *ʾrkymm* (*ʾōrek yāmîm*) was discovered in a Hebrew inscription at Kuntillet Ajrud dating from the late 9th to the early 8th century B.C.E. Other counterparts of the above phrases have been found in West Semitic languages and in Akkadian (Malamat 1982: 215).

Long life in ancient literatures represents an exceptional achievement. Advanced years indicate importance (Gen

5:1–32) and divine favor. The Bible mentions that Abraham (Gen 25:8), Gideon (Judg 8:33), and David (1 Chr 29:28) lived to a "good (ripe) old age" *(śêbâ ṭôbâ)*. They died prosperous, of natural causes, and were buried in their family tomb, obviously blessed by God (Gen 15:15). The Bible notes one exception: it explains how Enoch walked with God and yet lived only a relatively short time: "God took him" (Gen 5:22–24).

The Bible glorifies some of its heroes by describing their longevity. For example, a Deuteronomic summary praises the good health of Moses at his death (Deut 34:7), and Caleb brags on his extra vigor at 85 years of age (Josh 14:10–11).

A study of fourteen kings from the dynasty of David presents a clearer picture of the average life span during the royal eras of Israel, 926–597 B.C.E. (Wolff 1974: 119–23; *PI* 2: 46). Omitting Jehoiakim, Jehoiachin, and Zedekiah, the age at death of the remaining kings varies between 66 (Manasseh) and 21 (Ahaziah), the average being 44. Premature and unnatural causes of death such as assassination may account for some of these deaths. Nevertheless, in spite of superior diet and medical care, monarchs in stable Judah during this period did not live 70 or 80 years (contra Ps 90:10). Outside of stories about the patriarchs in Genesis, only Moses (120 years), Joshua (110), Job (140), and the high priest Jehoiada (130, 2 Chr 24:15) are said to surpass 100. One passage suggests that only in the eschatological kingdom would people regularly attain 100 years (Isa 65:20). Generally, transitions to old age began earlier than age 65 (see Harris 1987: 11–17).

C. Old Age as the Final Transition

1. Stages of Life. The Bible also describes the aging experience as a sequence of the seasons of life. Such seasons indicate common transitions: childhood, youth, maturity, and elderliness. Akkadian uses a number of words to describe the various age groups: 40 years *(la-lu-tu)*, "prime of life" (CAD 9: 52); 50 years *(umu-ar-ku-tu)*, "short life"; 60 years *(si-pa-tu)*, "wool"; 80 years *(si-bu-tu)*, "old age"; and 90 years *(lit-tu-tu)*, "extreme old age" (CAD 9: 220–21).

Life also is pictured as four seasons (childhood, youth, young marrieds, the elderly; Jer 51:22), or as five stages (small child, youth [maturity begins at age thirteen, Gen 17:25], adult men and women, the elderly *(zāqēn)*, and the aged *(mĕlēʾ yāmîm)*; Jer 6:11). The Bible also defines a maximum life span as the fourth generation of a family, equating it with the life span of 70–80 years mentioned in Ps 90:10 (Malamat 1982: 216–18). Though the fourth-generation position may be an important one, few elderly in fact lived to enjoy it.

2. Adult Responsibilities and Retirement. Life's transitions indicate changes in the work and role patterns of individuals. Twenty-year-old males are considered responsible adults (Num 14:29; 32:11) and liable to enter military service (Num 1:3, 18; 26:2) and to pay taxes (Exod 30:14). According to Num 4:3, the Kohathite branch of Levites were to serve as priests between the ages of 30 and 50. Other texts suggest that (other?) Levites could begin their service as early as age 25 (Num 8:24) or even 20 (1 Chr 23:24). Regardless, Levites would retire at age 50 to assist younger priests (Num 8:24–26). Zechariah, the father of John the Baptist, and also of the priestly division of Abiathar (Luke 1:5; 1 Chronicles 24, esp. v 10) considered his wife and himself "old," yet that did not preclude him from serving in the temple (Luke 1:18–25). Nevertheless, priests at age 50 entered some form of retirement, a common transition of old age.

Life transitions began somewhat earlier in agricultural occupations. The toil was so difficult that parents retired from active farming as soon as children were old enough to work the field. Then they would train their grandchildren and advise the younger generation. A father or mother might also serve as an elder or judge for the clan, the community (wise woman at Abel, 2 Sam 20:14–20), and in some cases a tribe or nation (Deborah, Judg 4:4–5; wise woman of Tekoa, 2 Sam 14:1–7).

A price list associated with payments of vows (Lev 27:1–8) provides values for men and women at different stages of life. Such evaluations apparently estimate the worth of a person's work capacity adjusted to represent the cost of a slave at various times in life (Wenham 1978). These values (calculated in shekels of silver) are as follows:

	Male	Female
1 mo.–5 yrs. old	5	3
5–20 yrs. old	20	10
20–60 yrs. old	50	30
Over 60 yrs. old	15	10

The peak value for a male (20–60 yrs.) may indicate that period when he could be conscripted for military service as given in census instructions (Num 1:3, 20, 22; 26:2, 4; 2 Chr 25:5). After age 60 a female does not decrease in value as much as a male. The comparative worth of an older woman changes from the earlier 3/5 ratio to that of 2/3, perhaps indicating that elderly women lived healthier and more active lives than elderly men. A drop in value of both genders at age 60 suggests that both had retired by then.

D. Old Age as Debilitation and Loss

The Bible also mentions the debilitating losses which accompany old age. A key transition for the woman comes at menopause, when she loses the ability to give birth to children. When a woman can no longer give birth (Gen 18:11; Ruth 1:12; Luke 1:18, 36) or when a man is unable to sire a child for his wife (Gen 18:12), the Bible considers that a sign of advanced age. Failing health (e.g., loss of hearing, sight, or normal vigor) also indicates old age (Gen 27:1–2; 1 Kgs 1:1–4).

To some degree old age brought a loss of income as well as significance. Women especially experienced this dilemma. A widow in the Bible represents the most traumatic example of one who is helpless and yet worthy of support from the community. Without a kinsman-redeemer, or sympathy from a godly leader, or miraculous aid from God, widows possessed little hope (1 Kgs 17:9–24; 2 Kgs 4:1–7). Consequently, the "reproach of widowhood" remained synonymous with suffering and loss (Isa 54:4; Lam 1:1; 5:3–4; Rev 18:7).

An older widow could experience deep bitterness and depression because of her severe losses and inability to recover from them, as in the noteworthy case of Naomi (Ruth 1:20–21). Note also the convincing ruse of the woman of Tekoa (2 Sam 14:1–7). Biblical texts single out older widows as in need of extra help and compassion (1 Tim 5:3–8). Luke–Acts mentions how early Christians organized to care for widows (Acts 6:1–7; 9:39). Jesus praised the widow who gave her remaining money to the temple (Luke 21:1–4), and he showed compassion on a widow whose only son had died (Luke 7:11–16). He angrily denounced those who "devour widows' houses" and then prayed long prayers (Luke 20:47). The epistle of James defines "pure religion" as visiting orphans and widows in their affliction (1:27).

The Bible reveals the God of Israel as the defender of powerless widows (Deut 10:18), commanding the people of the covenant to care for them (Deut 14:29; 24:17, 19–21). Prophets and others condemn violations of these responsibilities (Isa 1:23; 10:2; Mic 2:9; Mal 3:5; Job 22:9; 24:3; 31:16; Ps 94:6).

Aging fathers, likewise, are portrayed as victims in the Bible (often of their children's ambitions). Note how children exploit drunken (old?) fathers in the stories of Noah and Lot. Encouraged by his mother Rebekah, Jacob manipulates his nearly blind father into blessing him instead of his brother Esau (Genesis 27). Absalom temporarily overthrows his aging father David (2 Samuel 15–19). Nathan and Bathsheba exploit David's failing health and memory to establish Solomon as his successor (1 Kings 1).

Prophets condemn disregard for vulnerable parents (Mic 7:6). Intergenerational love remains their ideal (Mal 4:6). The books of Sirach (3:1–16) and Tobit (4:1–4) reinforce these ideals and the benefits of filial support for parents. In the Synoptic Gospels Jesus condemns those who shirk the care of aging parents through a religious vow called "Corban" (Mark 7:5–13). Talmudic rabbis also teach filial reverence and illustrate these laws with examples of obedience (*mora, Qidd.* 31a, 31b, *j. Peʾa* 1:1; 15c).

Aging parents sometimes enter a somewhat dependent and vulnerable stage before death. Qoheleth mentions common debilitating losses of aging in a poem describing death (Eccl 12:1–8). The teacher describes vividly the "coming days of hardship and those years that arrive" as a weakening body which collapses in death. Old age in the Bible signifies more than divine blessing; it also indicates a transition into a weakened social and physical condition which needs respect and protection to compensate for its losses (Prov 19:26; 28:24; Exod 20:12).

Bibliography

Durr, L. 1926. *Die Wertung des Lebens im Alten Testament und im antiken orient.* Munster.

Harris, J. G. 1987. *Biblical Perspectives on Aging: God and the Elderly.* Philadelphia.

Harvey, A. E. 1974. Elders. *JTS* n.s. 25: 318–32.

Maier, J. 1979. Die Wertung des Alters in der judischen Uberlieferung der Spatantike und des fruhen Mittelalters. *Saeculum* 30: 355–64.

Malamat, A. 1982. Longevity: Biblical Concepts and Some Ancient Near Eastern Parallels. *AfO* 19: 215–18.

Prevost, J.-P. 1985. Vieiller ou pas Vieiller? Le Point de Vue de l'Ancien Testament. *ÉgT* 16: 9–23.

Scharbert, J. 1979. Das Alter und die Alten in der Bibel. *Saeculum* 30: 338–54.

Sokoloff, M. 1976. *ʿAmar Neqeʾ*, Lamb's Wool (Dan 7:9). *JBL* 95: 277–79.

Wenham, G. J. 1978. Leviticus 27:28 and the Price of Slaves. *ZAW* 90: 264–65.

Wolff, H. W. 1974. *Anthropology of the Old Testament.* Trans. M. Kohl. London.

J. Gordon Harris

OLD GATE (PLACE) [Heb *šaʿar hayšānâ*]. A gate in the outer defensive wall of Jerusalem on the W side of the Temple Mount above the E slope of the Tyropoeon or Central Valley mentioned by Nehemiah (3:6; 12:39) and possibly by Zechariah (14:10).

Because gates are often identified with some geographic location outside a city to which they lead, it would be natural to think of this gate as having received its name from the village of Yešānâ (i.e., "Jeshanah," identified with Khirbet el-Burj or el-Burj Isana [M.R. 174156]), one of a triangle with Ephron [M.R. 178151] and Bethel [M.R. 172148] guarding the Taiyibe ridge and access to the Benjamin plateau (2 Chr 13:19; Neh 11:25–36; 1 Macc 9:15, *Ant* 14.15.12 § 458). Although this strategic control point on the N frontier of Benjamin was militarily and politically more important than many have realized, the definite article before *yĕšānâ* prevents us from considering *šaʿar hayšānâ* a proper name and associating it with the village of Jeshanah. This coupled with the difference in gender between *šaʿar* (masc) and *yešānâ* (fem) leaves two possibilities: (1) the text needs emending to possibly *šaʿar hammišneh* ("the Mishneh Gate"), associating the gate with the Mishneh quarter of Jerusalem that has been located by some in the Tyropoeon or Central Valley to the W of the Temple Mount; or (2) one should supply a feminine noun such as *hāberēkāh* (the pool) or *hāʿîr* (the city) to read *šaʿar hayšānâ hāʿîr,* "the gate of the old city." Additionally, some have wanted to identify this gate with the Gate of Ephraim in order to resolve (unnecessarily) the absence of the Ephraim Gate in Nehemiah's restoration text (3:7, 8) and the deletion of the Old Gate in the LXX procession text (12:39). Many have reviewed the several possibilities (Avi-Yonah 1954: 242–43; Simons 1952: 276–78, 305–6; Vincent and Steve 1954: 240, 243; Williamson 1984: 81–88), yet the enigma of the Old Gate has not been completely resolved. We know from Nehemiah's restoration and procession texts (3:6; 12:39) that this gate was located to the N of the Ephraim Gate and to the S of the Fish Gate along the rather prominent inclined street (1 Chr 26:18) that ran N–S and led from the inner foundation or Sur Gate to the Fish Gate.

Bibliography

Avi-Yonah, M. 1954. The Walls of Nehemiah—A Minimalist View. *IEJ* 4: 239-48.

Simons, J. 1952. *Jerusalem in the Old Testament.* Leiden.

Vincent, L.-H., and Steve, M.-A. 1954. *Jerusalem de l'Ancien Testament.* Paris.

Williamson, H. G. M. 1984. Nehemiah's Walls Revisited. *PEQ* 116/2: 81–88.

Dale C. Liid

OLD TESTAMENT QUOTATIONS IN THE NT. See NEW TESTAMENT, OT QUOTATIONS IN.

OLIVE OIL. See PERFUMES AND SPICES.

OLIVE TREE. See FLORA.

OLIVES, MOUNT OF (PLACE) [Heb *maʿălē hazzêtîm; har hazzêtîm;* Gk *to oros tōn elaiōn; to oros kaloumenon elaiōn; tou elaiōnos*]. A small ridge of three summits, about two miles long, the highest of which is not quite 3,000 feet above sea level, running N to S across from the Kidron Valley E of Jerusalem and known for its abundance of olive trees.

A. Description
B. Old Testament and Late Judaism
C. New Testament
D. Shrines on the Mount

A. Description

The Mount of Olives belongs to the Central Mountain Range, the main range of mountains which runs through the central and S portions of Palestine from the N to the S. To the W of Olivet lay the Kidron Valley and the city of Jerusalem. Toward the E lay Jericho, the Jordan Valley, and the Dead Sea. There are several undulations along the two-mile ridge separating several high points. The northernmost summit is the highest, which has been reported to be 2,963 feet above Mediterranean Sea level. This summit has been identified with Nob (Isa 10:32) and Mount Scopus (Josephus *JW* 2.19.4, 7; 5.4.1), but there is no certain evidence for these suggestions. This N peak today is called Ras el-Mesharif.

The center of the Mount of Olives is a bit lower (about 2,700 feet) than its N counterpart. It stands opposite the temple area and is about 100 feet higher than Jerusalem itself. To the S and SE one can see the expansive wilderness of Judea; to the E is a spectacular view of the Jordan Valley and the Dead Sea; to the W lies a deeply stirring panorama of the old city of Jerusalem. The S summit, the southernmost part of the ridge, is the smallest of the three. This peak, facing W, overlooks the ancient site of Davidic Jerusalem, just S of the temple area.

The mount itself is composed of cretaceous limestone with a chalklike top layer and was named "Olives" because of its extensive olive groves. The olive tree, one of the hardier trees, was able to thrive in this terrain. Although populous with olive trees, this ancient site was also dotted with pines. The mount, denuded of trees in the time of Titus, contains only a fraction of the tree population it had in ancient times. Today there are major deforested areas and numerous cemeteries. Since Christ often traversed this ridge and spent not a few hours in its groves, there are many commemorative churches honoring this terrain. Some of these sites, however, are questionable.

B. Old Testament and Late Judaism

Surprisingly, in spite of the close proximity of the Mount of Olives to Jerusalem, there are only two explicit references to this mount in the OT. The first reference occurs in 2 Sam 15:30. David, fleeing from Jerusalem after his son Absalom led a successful revolt, took the path which led over the crest of the Mount of Olives as he made his way to his temporary exile in the Transjordan: "David went up the ascent of the Mount of Olives, weeping as he went, barefoot and with his head covered." Interestingly, the text recalls that "David came to the summit where God was worshipped" (2 Sam 15:32). Previously, the OT had not mentioned this "place of worship." However, given the inclination of ancient peoples to worship on mountains, it is not impossible that a sanctuary existed here. It is tempting to identify this place of worship with Nob, but this identification is far from certain (cf. 1 Sam 21:1; 22:9–11). The second explicit reference to the Mount is found in Zechariah's description of the Day of Yahweh: "On that day his feet shall stand on the Mount of Olives and it shall be split in two from east to west by a very wide valley; so that one half of the Mount shall withdraw northward, and the other half southward . . . then the Lord your God will come, and all the holy ones with him" (14:4–5).

Besides these two explicit references there are several probable implicit references. In 1 Kgs 11:7–8 mention is made of high places built by Solomon for all his foreign wives to worship the Moabite god Chemosh and the Ammonite god Molech. These places of worship, the text says, "were east of Jerusalem, to south of the Mount of Corruption" (2 Kgs 23:13). Today the Mount of Offense (variously called Mount of Corruption, Sandal, or Evil Counsel) may well be the place where these abominations occurred, but this identification is by no means certain. Some scholars see a play on words in 2 Kgs 23:13. The Hebrew word "corruption" *(mašḥît)* is very close to the word "anointing" *(māšaḥ)*. Thus the "mount of anointing" (Mount of Olives, from which the sacred anointing oil is produced) has become the "mount of corruption." Though this suggestion is very possible it should be noted that the ascription *Mons Offensionis* (Mount of Offense) can be traced only as far back as Quaresmius of the 17th century A.D.

A second implicit reference is found in Ezekiel. The prophet was enabled to view the glory of God depart from the temple, whereupon it "stood upon the mountain which is on the east side of the city" (Ezek 11:23). Later in the book, Ezekiel reported that he saw the process reversed. In his vision of the new Jerusalem, Ezekiel saw this glory return and enter the eschatological temple (43:2–5). The mountain referred to by Ezekiel is commonly understood as Olivet.

The Mount of Olives has also been associated with the rite of the burning of the red heifer so that its ashes could serve as a purification (Num 19:1–10). According to the Talmud, this purification rite was performed on the Mount of Olives opposite the E gate of the temple (*Para* 3.6–7, 11). Moreover, the Mishnah claims that Jews in Jerusalem announced the new moon to their brethren in Babylonia by means of a chain of fire signals, the first of which began on Olivet. Furthermore, according to tradition, the dove sent forth from the ark by Noah retrieved the olive branch from the Mount of Olives (Gen 8:11; *Gen. Rab.* 33:6).

Tradition also suggests that those faithful Jews who died abroad would be channeled back to Jerusalem through underground caverns and be resurrected and emerge at the sundered Mount of Olives (*m. Ketub.* 111a). Also, when the glory of God departed from the temple it was to have tarried three and a half years on Olivet while eagerly awaiting Israel's repentance (*Lam. Rab.* Proem 25; cf. Ezek 10:18).

C. New Testament

Almost certainly, Jesus traversed this mountain many times to and from feasts and festivals in Jerusalem. Although this route could have been avoided and a route directly N through Samaria followed, the Jewish custom was to head E and then N to avoid stepping on Samaritan soil. Despite the numerous trips using this circuitous route, apart from Jesus' final week of ministry the Mount of Olives is mentioned only infrequently.

The references to the Mount of Olives outside the passion week occur at John 8:1, the pericope of the woman taken in adultery (many scholars seriously question the authenticity of John 7:53–8:11), and Acts 1:12 (cf. Luke 24:50–53), in which Jesus' ascension is described. There may also be several implicit references outside of Jesus' passion week. These references include the visit to Mary and Martha where Mary is affirmed for seeking to be taught (Luke 10:38–42); the raising of Lazarus (John 11); and the feast "six days before the Passover" (John 12:1; cf. Matt 26:6–12; Mark 14:3–9). Although none of these pericopes explicitly mentions the Mount of Olives, nevertheless they all occurred at or near Bethany, which is on the E side of the mountain.

With regard to the passion week, the references to Olivet are numerous. The triumphal entry, which began at Bethany and terminated in Jerusalem, explicitly mentions the Mount of Olives (Matt 21:1–11; Mark 11:1–10; Luke 19:28–39; John 12:12–15). While proceeding into Jerusalem, Jesus paused on Olivet and wept over the unrepentant Jewish nation (Luke 19:41–44); traditionally this site has been marked by the Dominus Flevit chapel, but this identification is by no means certain. Apparently Jesus did not lodge in Jerusalem during his final week, but rather in Bethany, probably at the home of Mary and Martha or perhaps with Simon the leper (cf. Mark 11:11; 14:3; Luke 21:37). The Gospels' description of Bethany suggests an identification with the Arab village of el-Azariyeh. Bethphage was apparently adjacent to Bethany, but nearer the top of the Mount of Olives. Abu-Dis probably corresponds to this city today, although some identify it with the village et-Tur on the very top.

The cursing of the fig tree, occurring the day after the triumphal entry, took place on Jesus' evening return to Bethany (Matt 21:17–19; Mark 11:11–14; 19–20) and probably occurred on this mountain. It is also likely that the Mount of Olives was in view when Jesus taught that the person of faith could say to the mountain, "Be taken up and cast into the sea," and it would occur (Matt 21:21). Also during his passion week, Jesus gave his disciples an eschatological outline (Matthew 24; Mark 13) from "the Mount of Olives opposite the temple" (Mark 13:3; cf. Matt 24:3). Luke informs us that during the evenings of the passion week, Jesus tarried on Mount Olivet (Luke 21:37). The seclusion of the groves was probably heartily welcomed after the rigor of teaching in the temple all day. It is probably from this mountain that Jesus sent his disciples into Jerusalem (Matt 26:18; Luke 22:8) to prepare the Passover. After celebrating this feast in the city, they sang a hymn and went to the Mount of Olives (Matt 26:30; Mark 14:26; Luke 22:39; cf. John 18:1). Jesus' destination on the Mount of Olives was the garden of Gethsemane (Matt 26:36). This garden was probably located on the W side of Olivet, and here Jesus agonized before his Father in prayer (Matt 26:30, 36ff; Mark 14:26, 32ff; Luke 22:30ff; John 18:1ff). It was also in this place that Jesus was betrayed by Judas and seized by the soldiers (John 18:12; cf. Matt 26:47–57; Mark 14:43–50; Luke 22:47–54).

D. Shrines on the Mount

Only the city of Jerusalem would have a greater concentration of shrines than the Mount of Olives. Most of these shrines are related to events named in the NT, but their origin and accuracy are nonetheless problematic. For example, there are three triumphal entry trails, three gardens of Gethsemane, three sites for Jesus' ascension, two Jericho roads, etc. There is even a shrine over the supposed "last footprint of Christ."

A basilica dedicated in the name of Helena, Constantine's mother, was probably the first shrine on Olivet. Located on the S end of the central hill, it was built ca. 325 and is called the Eleona ("Olives"). It was destroyed in the 7th century by the Persians, but became the site upon which the Church of the Pater Noster was built in 1869. Ostensibly the Lord's Prayer was taught on the ground marked by this church and therefore the walls are covered with versions of the Lord's Prayer in no less than sixty different languages. Also on the mount stands a Greek orthodox monastery, *Viri Galilaei,* which reportedly draws its name from Acts 1:11: "Men of Galilee, why do you stand looking into heaven?" Thus the "mountain of Galilee" (Matt 28:15) is dubiously identified with a place on the Mount of Olives. A chapel marking the ascension of Christ is located at the summit of Olivet. Built in 1834, this sanctuary also houses a stone which some have claimed contains the footprints of Jesus.

On the W slope of the Mount of Olives the visitor can choose one of three possible sites for the garden of Gethsemane, commemorated by three different churches. The first one, near the center of the W slope, is the Russian Church of Mary Magdalene. The more celebrated Roman Catholic Church of All Nations, with its Stone of the Agony in front of the altar, lies just below it. The garden, marked by the Church of All Nations, contains olive trees which probably were planted about a millennium ago. Thirdly, the Armenian Gethsemane, with its church built ca. 455, claims to be the site of the burial of Mary. Though not a shrine, the German hospice, Augusta Victoria, built by Kaiser Wilhelm II, located on the N of the Mount of Olives also deserves special mention. In digging its foundation in 1907 an ancient settlement was uncovered. Because of the association of the valley of Jehoshaphat with the Day of the Lord, there is an extensive tradition of religious burials on the Mount of Olives. Included among the burials are James, the Apostle; Mary, the mother of

Jesus; Joachim and Anna, Mary's parents; and Joseph, the husband of Mary.

The Mount of Olives is also important in the Moslem tradition. A Muslim shrine, the Inbomom, built around 375, contains what is claimed to be the last footprint of Christ upon earth. Of greater importance is the Islamic belief that the final judgment will occur in the Kidron Valley between the Mount of Olives and the celebrated Jerusalem shrine, Dome of the Rock. Ibn el-Gaqih summarizes this final cataclysm: "The Mount of Olives faces the Mosque, and between them is the Valley of Ben Hinnom, and from it 'Isa [Jesus] ascended to Heaven. And on the Day of Judgment all souls will be gathered to it and they will cross the bridge over the valley of Jehoshaphat, some to Paradise and some to Gehenham." Additionally, Muslim tradition asserts that Olivet is holy because "Saffiya, the wife of the prophet . . . prayed there."

Bibliography

Baldi, D. 1955. *Enchiridion Locorum Sanctorum.* Jerusalem.
Dalman, G. 1935. *Sacred Sites and Ways.* New York.
Hacohen, M. 1962. *Har Hazeitim.* Jerusalem (in Hebrew).
Hoede, E. 1973. *Guide to the Holy Land.* 7th ed. Jerusalem.
Katsh, A. 1954. *Judaism in Islam.* New York.
Kraeling, E. G. 1956. *Bible Atlas.* New York.
Vincent, H., and Abel, F.-M. 1914–16. *Jérusalem Nouvelle.* Vol. 2. Paris.

WARREN J. HEARD, JR.

OLYMPAS (PERSON) [Gk *Olympas*]. A Roman Christian who received greetings from Paul in Rom 16:15. He was probably a gentile Christian. See NEREUS. The Greek name Olympas was derived from a longer name beginning with the letters "Olymp-" (e.g., Olympiodorus, Olympianus, Olympicus, Olympheius; cf. Patrobas—Patrobius, Epaphras—Epaphroditus). According to the epigraphical and literary sources from the city of Rome, "Olympas" occurs only two times (Lampe *StadtrChr,* 139–41, 149). As the name was not common there, it probably indicates that Olympas had immigrated to Rome.

PETER LAMPE

OLYMPIAN ZEUS, TEMPLE OF [Gk *neās Dios Olympiou*]. The name proposed by Antiochus IV Epiphanes for the temple in Jerusalem (165–164 B.C.E.) in 2 Macc 6:2, when he prohibited the observance of Jewish religious practices. In the language of 2 Maccabees this is the grievous act of Antiochus which parallels the ABOMINATION OF DESOLATION in 1 Macc 1:54 [Gk *bdelygma erēmōseōs*] and Dan 11:31 and 12:11 [Heb *šiqqûṣ měšōmēm*]. Josephus says that the king "compelled them to do reverence to the gods in whom he believed" (*Ant* 12 §253). The strong language reserved for descriptions of this event makes it extremely unlikely that the majority of Jews would have regarded this renaming as somewhat inconsequential or regarded Zeus as almost a common noun for a god in general (cf. Bartlett *Maccabees* CBC, 32; Goldstein *2 Maccabees* AB, 272–73). It is doubtful that Antiochus here was attempting to identify the God of Israel with Zeus in order to transform Judaism into one of the syncretistic religions of the east (cf. Schiffman *HBC,* 905). Nor should Antiochus simply be viewed as an apostle of Hellenism. It is much more likely that he wished to evoke the origins of his dynasty and its first patron, i.e., to establish in Jerusalem a symbol of the Seleucid Empire (Rigsby 1980: 233–38). There is ample evidence of his particular devotion to the Olympian Zeus as patron of the dynasty (Abel *Maccabees* EBib, 360; Habicht *2 Maccabees* JSHRZ, 229). See ANTIOCHUS #4.

Bibliography

Rigsby, K. J. 1980. Seleucid Notes. *TAPA* 110: 233–54.

JOHN KAMPEN

OMAR (PERSON) [Heb *ʾômār*]. The second son of Eliphaz, and therefore Esau's grandson (Gen 36:11, 15; 1 Chr 1:36). Following Gen 36:15, he belonged to Edom's "tribal leaders" (Heb *ʾallûpîm*) and represented a clan within the Esauite-Edomite tribe of Eliphaz. The meaning of the name is not completely clear. It could either be considered an animal name (cf. Heb *ʾimmēr,* "lamb," "sheep"; Assyrian *emāru(m),* Babylonian *imēru(m),* "donkey") or more likely as a shortened form of the theophoric personal name "God NN has spoken" (cf. Heb *ʾamaryāh(û), ʾimrî* (?), *ʾḥyʾmr, ʾmrʾl;* Sabean *ʾlʾmr;* Safaitic/Thamudic *ʾmr(ʾ)l*).

ULRICH HÜBNER

OMEGA. The twenty-fourth and last letter of the Greek alphabet. See also ALPHA AND OMEGA.

OMENS IN THE ANCIENT NEAR EAST. Belief that in omens lies a divine message, and attempts at interpreting this message, are ancient and universal. In the ANE the oldest sources for divinatory practices come from Mesopotamia, where the need to interpret omens gave rise to the extensive and well-attested art of divination and its practitioner, the diviner. Much of the evidence dates from the first half of the 2d millennium.

In Mesopotamia the ominous was found in any deviation from the ordinary, both in nature and among mankind: from the erratic motions of the planets to freak births among humans and beasts; from the behavior of a sacrificial lamb on its way to slaughter to that of a lizard on the wall of a house; from the ominous import of a chance utterance (Akkadian *egirrû,* corresponding to the Greek *kledon;* cf. 1 Sam 14:8–12) to that of one's dreams. All these phenomena were believed to contain divine messages which could be interpreted by the specialist so that appropriate measures could be taken to avert the portended evil, or a course of action leading to disaster could be avoided.

However, the diviner did not depend on natural phenomena alone for clues to the divine will, but commonly created the means whereby the divine response to specific questions could be obtained. This might be accomplished by presenting to the gods the liver of a sacrificial sheep on which they could "write," as it were, their verdicts, or by pouring oil over water and observing the patterns, or by letting smoke rise from a censer and observing its configurations. These three methods of interpreting omens, hepatoscopy, lecanomancy, libanomancy, respectively, are some of the methods of divination attested in ancient Mesopotamia. Of the three, hepatoscopy, i.e., liver divination, or in its more general application, extispicy (since in practice the entire entrails [exta] of the sheep came under scrutiny), was most prevalent in the royal service. Extispicy is attested, in a fully developed form, from early in the 2d millennium B.C. Its practical aspect is represented by the so-called extispicy reports, which are observations on the appearance of the entrails of a sacrificial sheep. Irregularities and abnormalities in the exta were considered ominous, and predictions were derived from them. Such extispicy reports are attested from the first half of the 2d millennium to the 7th century B.C., when this practice was vigorously pursued by the later Sargonid kings of Assyria, Esarhaddon and his son Ashurbanipal. In fact, the extispicy practiced on behalf of these two gave rise to a distinct genre in Mesopotamian omen literature, that of queries to the sun-god, Shamash, co-patron (with Adad) of Mesopotamian divination. Extispicy is also referred to in the inscriptions of Nabonidus (556–539 B.C.) as a means of eliciting a divine response.

The ability of the diviner to elicit a divine response lies in the nature of divination. Of the two types of divination attested, oblativa and impetrita (also referred to as intuitive and inductive, or natural and artificial, divination) it is the latter which enabled the diviner to present to the gods the means whereby a divine decision could be obtained. Oblativa could not serve this purpose, dependent as the Mesopotamians were on the occurrence of natural phenomena. The three divinatory practices mentioned above, extispicy, lecanomancy, and libanomancy, may serve as examples of impetrated omens. To this type belongs also the Israelite method of consulting God through the *ʾûrîm* and *tummîm*. The response appears to have been binary in nature, i.e., "yes" or "no" answers to specific questions, or "favorable" and "unfavorable," as the case might be (*TDOT* 2: 453–54).

Much of the evidence from Mesopotamian divinatory practices (among which are extispicy, lecanomancy, libanomancy, teratomancy [unnatural births], physiognomy, astrology, oneiromancy [dream omina]) and other aspects of Mesopotamian experience considered to be of ominous import is represented by literary omen series. Some omen series date back to the first half of the 2d millennium B.C.; in them the results of centuries of observations have been recorded and eventually systematized in series arranged as conditional statements (i.e., if such-and-such is the case, then such-and-such is the result).

Much of the early evidence that divinatory practices, notably extispicy, played an important role in the everyday life of the people and not just the royal court comes from the city of Mari (dating at the latest from the 18th century B.C.), where accounts of extispicies performed for sundry purposes and their results (favorable or unfavorable) are commonly described in letters.

Other evidence that not only extispicy but astrological omens were popular in the royal courts comes from 7th-century-B.C. Assyria, where aside from diviners in the service of Esarhaddon (681–669 B.C.), scholars who consulted and interpreted the compendiums of astrological omens gained much influence at the court by advising the king of how best to avoid the pitfalls of evil celestial omens, such as eclipses. One way to avert the evil influences of an eclipse was the appointment of a substitute king who was expected to take upon himself any evil consequences; later, he would be executed when the danger was believed to be over.

Some of these practices, notably hepatoscopy, are attested beyond the boundaries of Mesopotamia. Liver models, i.e., clay models of sheeps' livers used by the apprentice diviner to learn his craft, are attested in Boghazkoi, Ugarit, Megiddo, and Hazor (all from the 2d millennium B.C.), indicating the spread of Mesopotamian divinatory practices elsewhere in the Near East and beyond.

In the Bible, the ominous was not found or sought after in deviation from the ordinary, either in nature or in human affairs. Biblical writers, notably in the Wisdom Literature, found the wonders of God's work in the harmony of nature. The Bible, in fact, frowns on most forms of divination, which it proscribes as examples of heathen practices (e.g., Deut 18:10–11).

Nevertheless, procedures for eliciting a divine response to the needs of the people in times of crisis were present in ancient Israel too, and legitimate means to this end were available in the form of the *ûrîm* and *tummîm* and the *ʾēpôd* (Exod 28:30–31; *TDOT* 2:453–54). Other ways of seeking omens were also available, e.g., through dreams and prophecy, which were evidently considered acceptable ways of inquiring of God. Interpretation of dreams is closely associated in the Bible with the careers of Joseph and Daniel, and according to 1 Sam 28:6, God did not answer King Saul through dreams, or the *ʾûrîm* or prophets, on the eve of his final confrontation with the Philistines.

Prophecy was regarded until recent times as a uniquely Israelite institution. However, evidence for it elsewhere in the ANE has come to light in recent years (Wilson 1980). In texts from Mari (pre-18th century B.C.) reference is made to several types of prophets, male and female. They deliver messages, demands, and exhortations from the gods for the last king of Mari, Zimri-Lim. Zakur, an 8th-century-B.C. king of Hamath in Syria, informs us in his inscription that Beʾelshamayn spoke to him "through seers and diviners." In 7th-century-B.C. Assyria, prophets and more commonly prophetesses, who were associated with the cult of Ishtar of Arbela, pronounced oracles for Esarhaddon and Ashurbanipal.

It is clear that in the popular mind, prophets were associated with the foretelling of the future, as indicated by the episode of Saul and his father's lost asses, where it is said (1 Sam 9:9) that formerly a prophet had been known as a "seer" (cf. Amos 7:12).

In Ezek 21:26, there is a description of the king of Babylon standing at the crossroads and trying to determine how to proceed by the oracular means of shaking or tossing arrows (belomancy), consulting the *tĕrāpîm*, and inspecting the liver of a sheep. The omens determined his course of action. Of the three, only the third, hepatoscopy, is not attested in ancient Israel. Of the other two, the *tĕrāphîm* are well-attested and are in some instances associated with the ephod (Judges 17–18 passim; Hos 3:4). Belomancy is also known, e.g., 2 Kgs 13:14–19, which relates an incident involving the prophet Elisha and Joash, the king of Israel. See also PROPHECY.

Bibliography

Starr, I. 1983. *The Rituals of the Diviner.* Malibu.
Wilson, R. R. 1980. *Prophecy and Society in Ancient Israel.* Philadelphia.

IVAN STARR

OMER [Heb *ᶜōmer*]. See WEIGHTS AND MEASURES.

OMICRON. The fifteenth letter of the Greek alphabet.

OMRI (PERSON) [Heb *ᶜomrî*]. The origin of the name Omri is disputed, as is its meaning. Probably it is an abbreviated form of the longer "Omriyahu," following the same pattern as the name Zimri = Zimriyahu = "Yahweh is (my) protection." However, while the first element in the name Zimri[yahu] is known, with the name Omri[yahu] the initial element is questionable; here there is no obvious underlying Hebrew root. A derivation from either Arabic or Amorite is possible. The first hypothesis is somewhat more probable in that the name of the N Israelite king Omri's daughter, Athaliah, can be brought into association with the Arabic language stock. If one goes with the hypothesis of an Arabic verbal root, then the name Omri[yahu] can be rendered: "(The) life (which) Yahweh (has given)" (Gray *I and II Kings* OTL, 365). The chronologically earliest bearer of this name that can be determined with certainty is the Omri who was king of the N kingdom of Israel in the 9th century B.C.E. Those who bear this name in the work of the Chronicler (1 Chr 7:8; 9:4; 27:18), even though they are partly assigned to a historical era somewhat earlier than the time of the N Israelite king Omri, are most likely anachronistic reflections of the linguistic usage of a later time. However, these references in the work of the Chronicler do show that the name Omri came to be incorporated into the onomasticon of Israel and Judah.

1. A king of N Israel and founder of a dynasty. Determinations of the years of his reign differ by several years: 882/878–871 B.C.E. (Begrich; Jepsen); 885/880–874 B.C.E. (Thiele); or 886–875 B.C.E. (Andersen).

1 Kgs 16:15–28 deals with the history of Omri. Here his elevation to the kingship is described in some detail, but very little is said about his actual reign. The name Omri also appears in filiation formulas in 1 Kgs 16:29–30 ("Ahab the son of Omri") and in 2 Kgs 8:26 = 2 Chr 22:2 ("Athaliah the daughter [RSV: granddaughter] of Omri"). "Omri" also appears in a critical retrospect in Mic 6:16. Finally, the name appears in extrabiblical sources, where Omri is the first mentioned king of Israel. He is directly named in lines 4–8 of the inscription of King Mesha of Moab (*ANET,* 320), while he is referred to indirectly in several Assyrian inscriptions.

Omri was the first one in the history of the N Israelite kingdom to succeed in establishing a ruling structure that lasted for any length of time. The Omride dynasty, which encompassed not only the reigns of Omri and his son Ahab but also of his grandsons Ahaziah and Joram, held on to the Israelite throne for a total of 33 years, counting from the beginning of Omri's sole rulership (878–845 B.C.E., following the chronology of A. Jepsen 1979: 204–18). To be sure, the Jehu dynasty, which took over the rulership from the Omrides, considerably outdid its predecessor in length of rule, holding fast to the reins of power for almost a full century (845–747 B.C.E., following the Jepsen chronology). The royal houses of Omri and Jehu were the only two actual dynasties to appear in the history of the N kingdom, a history which otherwise was characterized by constant changes of rulership and usurpations of the throne.

The origins of Omri remain in the dark. The verse which mentions him for the first time (1 Kgs 16:16) neither gives the name of his father nor identifies his tribal or regional affiliation. Only his title is given: "commander of the army." From this one can conclude that the family of Omri was not of Israelite origin and that he himself belonged to that class of foreign mercenaries which, since the time of David, had formed the backbone of the Israelite military. According to whether one associates the name Omri with the Arabic or the Amorite language family, one must correspondingly ascribe to his family an Arabic or a Canaanite line of descent. Since the name Omri is quite likely a shortened form of "Omriyahu" (i.e., a name containing a theophoric element for "Yahweh"), one can further assume that he and his family had adopted the Yahwistic faith and had embraced as their own the traditions of Israel. The name of Omri's daughter, Athaliah (which also contains a theophoric element for "Yahweh"), provides additional evidence for Omri's Yahwistic orientation.

1 Kgs 16:15–22, which rests upon reliable sources, reports the circumstances surrounding Omri's seizing of the Israelite throne. The accession of Omri was preceded by one of the coups d'etat which were so characteristic of the N kingdom. The ruling king, Elah, after a reign of barely two years, had been overthrown in the capital city of Tirzah (Tell el-Farᶜah North) by Zimri, the commander of half of Elah's chariot force. Zimri formed a conspiracy against Elah and seized the opportunity provided by a drinking bout in order to assassinate the king, whose family (the "house of Baasha") Zimri subsequently exterminated when he set himself upon the throne (1 Kgs 16:8–14).

While these events were being played out in Tirzah, the Israelite army, under the command of Omri, was encamped against the Philistine border town of Gibbethon (*ᶜāqir).* These conflicts at Gibbethon (a similar situation is reported for a mere quarter century earlier, and that one also led to a change in the rulership, with Baasha replacing Nadab, cf. 1 Kgs 15:27) had as their chief goal a gaining of clear control over the open countryside leading to the city of Gezer, countryside whose possession was a matter of dispute between the Israelites and the Philistines. As news of the palace revolt and the transfer of power that had taken place in Tirzah reached the military camp at Gibbethon, the warriors gathered there refused to recognize Zimri as their new ruler but rather proclaimed their commander-in-chief, Omri, as king. We can no longer determine whether behind this course of events there might have been some sort of rivalry between the militia and the chariot contingent, perhaps even some deep-seated conflict rooted in the fact that the militia tended to be drawn from the tribes and therefore was oriented toward specifically Israelite traditions whereas the chariot contingent was comprised of professional soldiers who were more strongly oriented toward Canaanite ways.

Omri immediately seized the advantage of the moment, lifted the seige of Gibbethon, and with his army turned against Tirzah. Apparently the forces in support of Zimri proved too weak to be able to mount serious resistance to Omri and the Israelite army. With the final conquest of Tirzah by Omri impending, Zimri burned down a portion of the palace complex over his own head and perished in the blaze. His reign had lasted a mere seven days.

With the conquest of Tirzah, however, the rulership was by no means secured solely in the hands of Omri. As is noted all too briefly (1 Kgs 16:21–22), a portion of the populace raised against Omri another pretender to the throne, Tibni, the son of Ginath. Here the particulars escape us; we can only speculate about the corresponding details. For instance, perhaps certain of the tribes did not concur with the decision of the army encamped before Gibbethon and chose their own candidate for the kingship. Perhaps traditionalist circles opposed the elevation to the throne of a mercenary whose family background was not Israelite. We are just as poorly informed about the regional distribution of the spheres of influence of, respectively, Omri and Tibni. One can imagine that Omri exercised control over the tribes of the central highlands, while Tibni's base of power was Galilee and perhaps also the plain of Jezreel. But all of this remains pure speculation. At the very least, however, one must assume that the Israelite throne was divided for several years—from 882 until 878 B.C.E., according to Begrich and Jepsen, or from 885 until 880 B.C.E., according to Thiele. Andersen's hypothesis that no divided monarchy actually developed, but rather that the reign of Tibni amounted to no more than an episode lasting a few weeks, or at most a few months, during 886–885 B.C.E. must be judged a minority opinion. In the confrontation between these two concurrently ruling monarchs, which hardly ran its course without some military clashes, Omri gained the upper hand. The death of Tibni, which took place under unknown circumstances, finally opened the way for Omri to assume sole rulership over Israel.

Several chronological discrepancies in the OT regarding Omri's accession to the throne and the duration of his reign can be explained by reference to the fact that the throne was divided for several years. In 1 Kgs 16:15 the events which led to both the deaths of Elah and Zimri and the elevation of Omri are said to have fallen in the 27th year of Asa of Judah; according to 16:23, however, Omri did not ascend to the throne until the 31st year of Asa. The difference between these two statements is obviously a reflection of the period of divided rule. Also according to 16:23 Omri reigned for 12 years, whereas according to 16:29 he died in the 38th year of Asa of Judah, which at first glance would seem to ascribe to him a reign of only 7 years. The 12-year ascription actually describes the total time that Omri ruled, including the time that Tibni was his rival, and therefore properly begins with the 27th year of Asa (16:15). The 7-year span between the 31st year of Asa (16:23) and his 38th year (16:29) thus refers to the years when Omri was sole monarch. With some justification one can assume that there were two systems of dating in the N kingdom, one which incorporated the reign of Tibni and the other which ignored it (cf. Noth *Könige I* BK, 351).

The OT conveys very little information regarding the actual reign of Omri (1 Kgs 16:23–28). On the basis of indirect references and extrabiblical sources, however, one can see that Omri must have been one of Israel's greatest, most energetic, and most foresighted kings. He had a new vision for the government of Israel, one which looked beyond the needs of the moment and which went on to become the characteristic Omride policy; it was carried out in exemplary fashion, particularly by his son Ahab, and was continued even by his grandsons Ahaziah and Joram. The guiding principles of his governmental policy were two: treaties without and parity within. Omri introduced a foreign policy in which Israel sought to win the support of certain neighboring states by means of treaties and diplomatic marriages. So, for example, the marriage of the crown prince Ahab to the Phoenician princess Jezebel, which served to guarantee the accord with the Phoenicians, was certainly proposed by Omri and was brought to fruition during his own lifetime. Liekwise the termination of tensions with the neighboring state to the S, Judah, is most probably to be ascribed to the time of Omri, even though the actual marriage between the Judean crown prince Joram and Omri's daughter Athaliah, a marriage which sealed the peaceful relations between the two states, only took place somewhat later. In order to reach agreement with Judah, Omri apparently accepted certain territorial losses; he abandoned efforts to regain portions of the tribal territory of Benjamin that had been annexed to Judah by Asa several decades earlier (1 Kgs 15:22).

This deliberate policy of peaceful alliance was a response to the external state of affairs at the time: it obviously served a defensive purpose in the face of a menacing danger. Since there is no evidence for encroachment by the Assyrians into the Syro-Palestinian area during this time, the opponent against which the policy of Omri was directed can only have been the Aramean state of Damascus. On the basis of their raid into Galilee at the time of King Baasha (1 Kgs 15:16–22), the Arameans had proved themselves a dangerous, militarily effective antagonist. It is quite possible that they had been exerting steady pressure on the N boundaries of Israel, and especially on the N reaches of Israelite Transjordan, ever since. Included in the overall plan of Omri as king was obviously the goal of securing Israel against this constant threat from the N.

Similar intentions can also be recognized as lying behind Omri's domestic policy. With regard to the latter, the primary concern was to reduce tensions within the realm, particularly tensions between the Israelite tribes and the traditionally Canaanite elements of the populace. The sociocultural, and above all religious, differences between these two groups had apparently not been appreciably relaxed since the time of the united monarchy under David and Solomon. In order to eliminate, or at least to reduce, the growing internal tensions that went back to the time of the incorporation of both elements into one state,

Omri initiated a policy of parity, a policy that aimed at equal treatment for both factions of the population. Included within this policy was a recognition, and even fostering, of Canaanite religion on the part of the state. This policy of equal treatment in matters of religion subsequently aroused the opposition of staunchly Yahwistic circles, especially of the prophets Elijah and Elisha and of the prophetic groups that gathered about the latter. In the final analysis, it is also with reference to these Yahwistic opponents and the allies who stood with them that the negative judgment upon Omri and his dynasty in OT traditions is to be explained. So, finally, it must be said that the domestic policy set into effect by Omri did not achieve its desired goal, but that it rather conjured up new tensions, tensions which eventually contributed in no small way to the downfall of the Omride dynasty.

Part of Omri's grand design for the governing of Israel was the building of the new capital city, Samaria (Sebastiya). Up to this point the royal residences of the N kingdom, specifically Shechem (Tell Balatah, 1 Kgs 12:25—the transferring of the capital to Penuel, apparently necessitated by the pharaoh Shishak's invasion, amounted to only a temporary measure) and Tirzah (Tell el-Farᶜah North, 1 Kgs 14:17; 15:33), had been located in territories belonging to the Israelite tribes. For a time Omri continued to use Tirzah as the royal residence after taking it over from Zimri; he had the damage done during the conflict repaired, and he even started to enlarge the city. However, two years after he succeeded in gaining the sole rulership, Omri discontinued the rebuilding of Tirzah and abandoned the city. The excavations at Tell el-Farᶜah North (Stratum III) under the direction of R. de Vaux (*EAEHL* 2: 395–404) have been able to show a destruction of the city, obviously the destruction at the time of Omri's conflict with Zimri, and also a rebuilding of the city that was begun but not finished.

Omri constructed his new capital city of Samaria on a previously unbuilt site. He purchased the hill of Samaria in consonance with Canaanite law—which also suggests that he purchased the land from a Canaanite landowner. The seller is called Shemer (1 Kgs 16:24), but this can hardly be historically correct. Rather, this name must have arisen later as part of an attempt to provide an etiology for the name *šōmrôn,* which in all probability was originally the name of the hill itself. The hill was an advantageous site for the building of a national capital, since it was militarily defensible and also strategically located on the N-S trade route. Since the site had been purchased, the new residence built there fell to the royal family as a private estate. In this way the city acquired a singular juridical position. None of the tribes could lay claim to it as a part of its territory; rather, it stood directly under the jurisdiction of the king. In this way the status of Samaria corresponded to that enjoyed by Jerusalem, the capital city of Judah, since the time that David had conquered it for himself. Finally, the acquisition by Omri of previously unbuilt land offered the advantage that in constructing the new city, no attention needed to be paid to existing structures or to foundations already in place.

Construction work on Samaria lasted until the time of Omri's son Ahab. It is not an easy matter to distinguish between the phases of building activity already completed under Omri from those that were finished only later under Ahab. However, the excavators at Samaria assign—even if not without question—to the time of Omri the weaker, inner walls of the upper city as well as the palace complex (Stratum I). There is no doubt that the palace received its final fitting out only under Ahab, but it is by no means impossible that Omri had already employed Phoenician craftsmen during the palace's basic construction phase.

Omri may have intended from the outset that his capital city, newly erected on formerly Canaanite property and hence not reckoned to any Israelite tribal territory, should be primarily for the benefit of the Canaanite portion of the populace. The hypothesis of A. Alt (*KlSchr* 2: 116–34), namely that under the Omrides Samaria was the capital city for the Canaanite element while Jezreel (Zerᶜin) served as the center for the Israelite element in the population, is admittedly much in dispute. In favor of Alt's thesis, however, is the fact that only during the Omride dynasty—neither before nor after—did Jezreel, which was located in the tribal territory of Issachar, play the role of a secondary royal residence. Whether this duality can be carried back to the time of Omri himself remains open to question, however. Clear attestation for Jezreel as a royal residence does not come until the time of Ahab (1 Kgs 18:45–46; 21:1), and it was not Omri but rather Ahab who built the Baal temple in Samaria (1 Kgs 16:32).

Only an extrabiblical source, the stele of King Mesha of Moab (*ANET,* 320–21), gives information concerning the military successes of Omri. In the retrospect portion of the stele, Mesha reports that "Omri had occupied the land of Medeba" (lines 7–8). Omri therefore did enjoy a certain military success against the Moabites, checked their northward expansion, and pushed them back beyond the Seil Heidan. The area which Omri won back from the Moabites lay between the N tip of the Dead Sea and the Seil Heidan; it was territory traditionally reckoned to the tribe of Gad. Omri restored Israelite settlement to the region and apparently also reaffirmed Israelite hegemony over Moab. Word of further military actions on the part of Omri, which may be hinted at in 1 Kgs 16:27, has not been recorded. However, one can assume that Omri was able to hold and to secure Israel's N boundary against the Arameans. It is historically improbable that he suffered a decisive defeat at the hands of the Aramean state of Damascus and had to accept harsh terms in a peace settlement, despite being presupposed in 1 Kgs 20:34. The whole incident related in 1 Kings 20 probably originally referred to a time during the Jehu dynasty, later in the history of Israel. All in all, there can be little doubt that at the time of his death Omri left behind for his son Ahab an Israelite state that was both strong and well equipped to deal with external threats.

In 845 B.C.E. Jehu overthrew the Omride dynasty and exterminated the Omride royal house. However, the name of Omri outlasted this catastrophe. In Assyrian inscriptions from the time of the Jehu dynasty and even afterward (*ANET,* 280–81, 284–85), not only is Jehu called "son of Omri" *(mār Ḫumrî)* but even the whole of the N kingdom of Israel is referred to as "land of Omri" *(Bīt-Ḫumrî).* The international reputation of the Omride dynasty is reflected in this development from a dynastic appellation to the name of a country. Within the OT, on the other hand, the phrase "house of Omri" never appears; "house of Ahab" is used as a designation for the Omride dynasty.

The Deuteronomistic redactors selected for inclusion in their work only a small amount of the total material which tradition had preserved regarding Omri. Their theological evaluation of him is a negative one (1 Kgs 16:25–26). Their particularly sharp remark that Omri "did more evil than all that were before him" (v 25)—a remark which is then repeated with reference to Omri's son Ahab (v 33)—is not grounded in anything specific, since the reference in the immediately following verse (v 26) to the perpetuation of the "sin of Jeroboam," by which is meant the veneration of the calf images at Bethel and Dan, is a stereotypical charge having nothing uniquely to do with Omri. Perhaps the Deuteronomists derived their particularly negative evaluation of Omri from the fact that he was Ahab's father; in the traditions surrounding the figure of Elijah, Ahab appears as the foremost protagonist of N Israelite idolatry (1 Kgs 16:30-33). An analogous evaluation of Omri and, synonymously, of the "house of Ahab" is also to be found in the Deuteronomically influenced Mic 6:16. Finally, the Chronicler simply passes over the reign of Omri in silence; his name appears only in conjunction with a reference to his daughter Athaliah (2 Chr 22:2). See also *BHH* 2: 1341–42; Eissfeldt *KlSchr* 2: 453–63; Alt *KlSchr* 3: 258–302; *RGG* 4: 1630; *IDB* 3: 600–1.

2. A Benjaminite who appears in the genealogy of the patriarch Benjamin (1 Chr 7:8). It is more likely that he belonged to a postexilic Benjaminite family.

3. A Jerusalemite (1 Chr 9:4), most likely a member of a Judean clan in postexilic Jerusalem.

4. A leader of the tribe of Issachar, ostensibly from the time of David (1 Chr 27:18), but who appears in a list of obviously later origin and in a tradition of questionable historical value (1 Chr 27:16–22).

Bibliography

Andersen, K. T. 1969. Die Chronologie der Könige von Israel und Juda. *ST* 23: 69–114.

Begrich, J. 1929. *Die Chronologie der Konige von Israel und Juda.* BHT 3. Tubingen.

Corney, R. W. 1970. *The Reigns of Omri and Ahab.* Th.D. diss. Union Theological Seminary.

Ishida, T. 1975. "The House of Ahab." *IEJ* 25: 135–37.

Jepsen, A. 1941–44. Israel und Damascus. *AfO* 14: 153–72.

Jepsen, A., ed. 1979. *Von Sinuhe bis Nebukadnezar.* Stuttgart.

Jepsen, A., and Hanhart, R. 1964. *Untersuchungen zur israelitisch-jüdischen Chronologie.* BZAW 88. Berlin.

Miller, J. M. 1964. *The Omride Dynasty in the Light of Recent Literary and Archaeological Research.* Ph.D. diss. Emory.

———. 1968. So Tibni Died (1 Kings XVI 22). *VT* 18: 392–94.

Olivier, J. P. J. 1983. In Search of a Capital for the Northern Kingdom. *JNSL* 11: 117–32.

Schmidt, W. H. 1962. Ein "Haus Omris" bei Samaria? *ZDPV* 78: 30–33.

Soggin, J. A. 1975. Tibni, King of Israel in the First Half of the 9th Century B.C. Pp. 50–55 in *Old Testament and Oriental Studies.* BibOr 29. Rome.

Tadmor, H. 1983. Some Aspects of the History of Samaria during the Biblical Period. *The Jerusalem Cathedra* 3: 1–11.

Thiele, E. R. 1951. *The Mysterious Numbers of the Hebrew Kings.* Chicago.

Timm, S. 1980. Die territoriale Ausdehnung des Staates Israel zur Zeit der Omriden. *ZDPV* 96: 20–40.

———. 1982. *Die Dynastie Omri.* FRLANT 124. Göttingen.

Whitley, C. 1952. The Deuteronomic Presentation of the House of Omri. *VT* 2: 137–52.

WINFRIED THIEL
Trans. Charles Muenchow

ON (PERSON) [Heb *ʾon*]. The son of Peleth, a Reubenite, who participated in a rebellion against Moses along with Korah, Dathan, and Abiram (Num 16:1). There is some question concerning the reliability of this information since this is the only occurrence of the name On. In the account of the rebellion, the names of Korah, Dathan, and Abiram recur, but not On. In addition, Num 26:5–9, which lists the genealogy of Reuben, does not include On. Furthermore, Num 26:8 lists Eliab as the son of Pallu. On this basis, Noth has suggested that two changes be made so that Num 16:11 would read, "he (referring to Eliab) was the son of Pallu" (*Numbers* OTL, 118), rather than, "On was the son of Peleth." Another suggestion involves omitting the name On, and reading, "sons of Eliab, son of Peleth" (Sturdy *Numbers* CBC, 116). There is, however, no manuscript evidence that would support these emendations. Hence, it is wiser to let the enigmatic On stand as the son of Peleth.

CHRISTINA DE GROOT VAN HOUTEN

ON (PLACE). See HELIOPOLIS.

ONAGER. See ZOOLOGY.

ONAM (PERSON) [Heb *ʾônām*]. **1.** A clan name in the genealogical clan list of Seir the Horite. This person is referred to in Gen 36:23 and in the matching genealogy in 1 Chr 1:40 as the fifth son of the clan chief Shobal, and is thus a grandson of Seir. These Horite clans are not to be associated with the Hurrians. They represent the original inhabitants (perhaps as cave dwellers) of the region of Edom, but they lost control of that area to the encroaching "sons of Esau" (Deut 2:12–22). The conquest by the Esau tribes of Edom is matched in the text with the conquest of Canaan by the tribes of Israel.

2. A clan name in the genealogical clan list of Judah in 1 Chr 2:26, 28. Onam is described as the son of Jerameel by his second wife Atarah. Onam, in turn, is the father of Shammai and Jada. Wilson (*GHBW*, 183) suggests that the inclusion of Onam in both the Horite and Judahite lists demonstrates social and/or political contact between these people. Intermarriage might have taken place and economic or political treaties initiated. These agreements in turn may have led the Chronicler to add the Horite genealogies to those of Judah.

VICTOR H. MATTHEWS

ONAN (PERSON) [Heb *ʾônān*]. The second son of Judah and Shua, a Canaanite woman (Gen 38:2–4). He was the brother of Er and Shelah. In the genealogical list of Judah's descendants, Onan is mentioned as the daughter of Bath-shua (1 Chr 2:3).

Judah had arranged a marriage between his firstborn, Er, and a woman named Tamar. Er, however, died an early death, which was attributed to an act of Yahweh because of Er's unmentioned wickedness (Gen 36:7). Because Er had died childless, Tamar was left a widow without a son to continue the family of her deceased husband. According to the custom of levirate marriage, it fell upon Onan to continue the family of his brother by fulfilling the responsibility of the brother-in-law. The meaning of this responsibility is expressed by the Hebrew word *yābām,* "the husband's brother." The Latin translation of the OT rendered the Hebrew word as *levir,* "brother," from which comes the concept of levirate marriage.

The purpose of levirate marriage is expressed by Deut 25:6: "that his name [the name of the dead brother] may not be blotted out of Israel." Thus, in order to comply with the intent of the tradition, Judah commanded Onan to take the wife of his deceased brother in order to raise an offspring for his brother (Gen 38:8). Onan was not required to actually marry Tamar, for in levirate marriage the widow only had the right to a son to preserve her husband's name (Coats 1972: 463). Onan obeyed his father; however, he was unwilling to fulfill his responsibility toward his deceased brother. Whenever he had sexual relations with Tamar he would let the semen fall to the ground (Gen 38:9), thereby avoiding giving a child to Tamar. This action of Onan probably was a reference to coitus interruptus, but Onan's conduct has produced the word "onanism," which has come to be a reference to masturbation.

The reason given in the narrative for Onan's reluctance to provide a son for his brother was that he knew that the offspring to be born of Tamar would not be his son but would belong to his brother and would carry the name of the deceased. It is possible that he refused to provide the heir for his deceased brother because he desired the inheritance of his dead brother for himself (Thompson and Thompson 1968: 9). However, Onan's reluctance to give a child to his sister-in-law may reflect a rejection of this custom already present in society. The regulation of levirate marriage in Deut 25:5–10 shows that the custom had encountered some opposition. The law in Deuteronomy allowing a man to refuse his duty was a concession to the reluctance to comply with the custom. Because of Onan's unwillingness to bear a son for his deceased brother, Yahweh was displeased with Onan and slew him also (Gen 38:10).

The names of Onan and Er are mentioned in the list of the people who descended with Jacob to Egypt (Gen 46:12). Although Onan and Er had died in the land of Canaan, they are counted among the seventy people who migrated to Egypt with Jacob. The marriage of Judah to a Canaanite woman may reflect a political alliance between the tribe of Judah and the Canaanites and consequently be a veiled reference to territorial expansion by the tribe of Judah. Albright (*YGC,* 69) identified the name Onan with the Babylonian clan Awnanum and surmised that the deaths of Er and Onan might reflect the early extinction of two minor clans of Judah. Thompson (1974: 185) has strongly rejected this view.

Bibliography

Coats, G. W. 1972. Widow's Rights: A Crux in the Structure of Genesis 38. *CBQ* 34: 461–66.

Thompson, T. L. 1974. *The Historicity of the Patriarchs.* BZAW 138. Berlin.

Thompson, T., and Thompson, D. 1968. Some Legal Problems in the Book of Ruth. *VT* 18: 79–99.

CLAUDE F. MARIOTTINI

ONESIMUS (PERSON) [Gk *Onēsimos*]. The slave of the addressee of the "Epistle to Philemon" (probably Philemon, also possibly Archippus; Phlm 1–2). Onesimus' name means "useful," representing the type of slave name that expressed what a master wished from his slave. Though his master was Christian and hosted a house-church in Colossae (Phlm 2; Col 4:9, 17), Onesimus himself was still a pagan. Thus, the case differed from others in which a whole household had become Christian (e.g., 1 Cor 1:16; 16:15; cf. Acts 10:2, 44–48; 16:15; 18:8).

The common exegesis of the letter to Philemon is that Onesimus at some time ran away from his master. See also PHILEMON, EPISTLE TO. As a fugitive slave, he went to the imprisoned Paul (e.g., Gnilka *Philemon* HTKNT, 68) after he had embezzled money for his flight (Phlm 18–19; e.g., Gülzow 1969: 31). But this version leaves open why he did not—like other runaway slaves—hide abroad in a robber band or in a big city. Paul's prison (probably in Ephesus) was not a logical place to hide, because fugitive slaves were pursued. Roman legal texts render another solution more probable (Lampe 1985: 135–37). Like many other slaves who had done something wrong (cf. Phlm 18–19) and feared the anger of their master, Onesimus went to a person whom he asked to plead his case with his master. See also SLAVERY. Often, a close friend of the master was chosen by these slaves for this purpose. Asking for intercession, they were not considered fugitive slaves. Their intention was to *return* to the master's house and to continue living there peacefully. (*Digesta* 21:1:17:4, 5, 12; 21:1:43:1; Plinius *Epistulae* 9:21, 24). Exactly what Onesimus' misdeed was we do not know; but it did some damage (Phlm 18–19) so that he needed a mediator. Interestingly enough, the pagan slave asked the Christian apostle for help against his Christian master.

Paul sent Onesimus back with a letter appealing to the master to swallow his anger about the damage Onesimus committed and to accept him again with love. Paul stressed his appeal by pointing out that he had converted Onesimus into a Christian in the meantime (something that the master had not achieved); Onesimus therefore deserved to be welcomed as a "beloved brother" in the master's house church, leaving no more room for anger (Phlm 10, 16, 17).

As a Christian, Onesimus was now "useful" for Paul and his master (v 11). Paul combined his appeal for Onesimus with a request for himself; Paul asked the master to send Onesimus back so that the latter could "serve" the apostle (vv 12–14). The "service" has often been interpreted as a personal one for Paul in prison (e.g., Stuhlmacher *Phile-*

mon EKKNT, 40). It is more probable (Ollrog 1979: 102–6, 122) that Paul asked to have Onesimus as a co-worker in mission for a time in place of the master himself (Phlm 13). This temporary delegation of a co-worker by a single congregation to serve another in mission (cf. Phlm 14) is known elsewhere (2 Cor 8:23; Phil 2:25–30; 1 Cor 16:17; Col 1:7). Through these workers, the congregations shared actively in Paul's mission work. Since Onesimus' master represented a house church (Phlm 2), Paul's wish can be interpreted as such a wish for a congregational delegate. Paul asked for Onesimus to be a mission co-worker as a representative of the master and his house church. Other mission helpers were already present in Ephesus when Paul wrote his letter in prison, and sent their greetings (Phlm 24).

From Col 4:9, it can be concluded that the master indeed released Onesimus for temporary service to Paul's mission. After a while, Paul sent him back to his master together with Tychicus and the letter to the Colossians (Col 4:7). It should be noted, however, that this conclusion from Colossians is based on the assumption that Colossians was written a few weeks later than the letter to Philemon by a co-worker of the apostle (which seems most likely; Schweizer *Colossians* EKKNT, 27–28. Others date Colossians either at exactly the same time as the letter to Philemon or later than Paul's death).

Paul, in the Epistle to Philemon, defined a new relationship between slave and master, but he did not ask to free Onesimus from slavery. Paul never criticized the institution of slavery. (Neither is it clear that in 1 Cor 7:21 he really encouraged the slaves to avail themselves of the opportunity to gain freedom whenever this chance came. Everybody should "remain in whatever state he was called" [7:24].) What mattered to Paul is that the existing social difference between slave and master no longer had relevance in the Christian community (Gal 3:27–28; 1 Cor 12:13), where all should treat each other as equally worthy and with love. Existing worldly social differences should no longer be used to the disadvantage of the (in worldly eyes) lower classes. Paul himself did not care whether his mission co-worker Onesimus was a slave or freeborn. In the Church, "free" and "slave" were no longer relevant social terms; they were transformed into spiritual terms: all Christians were "slaves of Christ" and "free" from sin's power (1 Cor 7:22).

As with almost all slaves in the cities of that time (Alföldy 1981: 359), however, Onesimus was probably freed while he was in his thirties at the latest. That Onesimus later, at the age of over 70 at the beginning of the 2d century, was bishop of Ephesus (*Ign. Eph.* 1:3, 6:2) is only a possibility. For further discussion, see commentaries on Philemon and Colossians in Hermeneia, NCBC, WBC, and BBC.

Bibliography

Alföldy, G. 1981. Die Freilassung von Sklaven und die Struktur der Sklaverei in der römischen Kaiserzeit. Pp. 336–71 in *Sozial- und Wirtschaftsgeschichte der römischen Kaiserzeit*, ed. H. Schneider. Darmstadt.

Bartchy, S. S. 1975. *First-Century Slavery and 1 Corinthians 7:21*. SBLDS 11. Missoula, MT.

Gayer, R. 1976. *Die Stellung des Sklaven in den paulinischen Gemeinden*. Bern.

Gülzow, H. 1969. *Christentum und Sklaverei in den ersten drei Jahrhunderten*. Bonn.

Lampe, P. 1985. Keine "Sklavenflucht" des Onesimus. *ZNW* 76: 135–37.

Laub, F. 1982. *Die Begegnung des frühen Christentums mit der antiken Sklaverei*. SBS 107. Stuttgart.

Lucas, R. C. 1980. *Fullness and Freedom: The Message of Colossians and Philemon*. Basel Studies of Theology. Leicester.

Mayer, B. 1986. *Philipperbrief, Philemonbrief*. Stuttgart.

Ollrog, W.-H. 1979. *Paulus und seine Mitarbeiter*. WMANT 50. Neukirchen.

Petersen, N. R. 1985. *Rediscovering Paul: Philemon and the Sociology of Paul's Narrative World*. Philadelphia.

PETER LAMPE

ONESIPHORUS (PERSON) [Gk *Onēsiphoros*]. Onesiphorus is referred to in 2 Tim 1:16–18 as one who had rendered much service at Ephesus and who later had eagerly searched for and found Paul in his captivity in Rome. This Ephesian, not being "ashamed of [Paul's] chains" (1:16), had often "refreshed" him (1:16)—in contrast to other Asians, e.g. Phygelus and Hermogenes, who had "turned away" from Paul (1:15). 2 Timothy also includes greetings to the household of Onesiphorus (4:19) and a prayer that the Lord might grant mercy to his household because of his service to Paul (1:16). Onesiphorus himself does not seem to be included, suggesting that he was either not envisioned as present among the (alleged) recipients of 2 Timothy, was with Paul, or was already dead. The latter is most likely since the author of 2 Timothy writes: "May the Lord grant him to find mercy from the Lord on that Day" (1:18). If Onesiphorus had indeed died, then this prayer is the earliest one for the dead found in Christian literature. As such it has been cited as clear scriptural support (especially among Roman Catholics) for prayer for the dead. (Jewish precedent for such prayer is found in 2 Macc 12:43–46.) The prayer itself in 1:18 with its double use of "the Lord" is problematic; it raises the question of whether the references are to Christ and/or God (Hanson *Pastoral Epistles* NCBC, 127).

The idea that Onesiphorus searched eagerly for Paul "when he arrived in Rome" (1:17) has been subjected to close scrutiny. The underlying Greek phrase, *genomenos 'en rhōmȩ̄*, literally means "being in Rome" or "having arrived in Rome." Yet, in the interest of reconstructing whatever apparently historical details can be extracted from the Pastoral Epistles—and harmonizing them with what is known about Paul from the authentic letters and Acts—attempts have been made to give a different sense to this phrase. One suggestion had been to take *rhōmȩ̄* as a Greek word for "strength," not the name of a city, and thus read "when he regained his strength." While this removes the necessity of locating Onesiphorus' visit and thus the imprisonment of Paul referred to in 2 Timothy in Rome, it is an improbable reading, for, as Dibelius and Conzelmann (*Pastoral Epistles* Hermeneia, 106) point out, nothing was said previously about Onesiphorus being sick. Paul, and consequently Onesiphorus, must therefore have been envisioned as being in Rome.

Another theory about Onesiphorus, an improbable one because it is too strained, is the attempt to identify him with Onesimus. This is based on the assumption that

Onesimus is a shortened form of Onesiphorus (Lyman *IDB* 3: 602).

Apart from the references in 2 Timothy cited above, Onesiphorus is not mentioned elsewhere in the NT. He is, however, rather prominent in the apocryphal *Acts of Paul* (3.2–7, 15, 23–26, 42). There Onesiphorus is described as a resident of Iconium who, with his wife Lectra and children Simmias and Zeno, welcomes Paul into Iconium and acts as his host. Paul's appreciation of Onesiphorus inspires jealousy in his traveling companions Demas and Hermogenes, who oppose him from that point on. It is in the house of Onesiphorus that the virgin Thecla is inspired by Paul to break her betrothal and follow Paul.

In contrast to 2 Timothy, the apocryphal *Acts* locates Onesiphorus not in Ephesus but in Iconium and names his family members. The document also contrasts him with Demas and Hermogenes, while 2 Timothy contrasts the exemplary Onesiphorus with Phygelus and Hermogenes (2 Tim 1:15), although it refers to Demas later as well (4:10), casting him in an unfavorable light. Apart from these differences, however, both 2 Timothy and *Acts of Paul* share an emphasis on the faithfulness of Onesiphorus and his family to Paul in spite of the desertion of others. While these differences and similarities could be explained as the elaborative dependence of the *Acts of Paul* on 2 Timothy, it remains possible that both are also independent witnesses to a common strand of oral tradition from Asia Minor (MacDonald 1983: 65–66).

Bibliography

MacDonald, D. R. 1983. *The Legend and the Apostle.* Philadelphia.

FLORENCE MORGAN GILLMAN

ONIAS (PERSON) [Gk *Onias*]. The name of four persons of a priestly family in Hellenistic Palestine. "Onias" is the Greek form of the Hebrew name *ḥônĕyû* or *ḥônî*. This form is related to the name John (Heb *y(ĕh)ôḥānan*). The Oniads are traced back to Jehoiada, the high priest who returned from the Babylonian Captivity, and through him to Zadok, who was appointed by King Solomon.

1. Son of Jaddua, who was high priest in Jerusalem at the time of Alexander the Great. He held office about 300 B.C.E., and may have been the Onias who corresponded with a Spartan king named Areus (1 Macc 12:7, 19–23). There is no agreement about who the correspondents were, and various combinations of the four candidates (Onias I or II and Areus I or II) have been proposed. Onias I was father of Simon I.

2. Onias II was the son of the high priest Simon I. On his father's death he was still young, and was substituted temporarily in this office, first by his uncle Eleazar, and then by his grandfather's brother Manasses (*Ant* 12.44, 157). Onias II officiated about the middle of the 3d century B.C.E. He might have been in correspondence with the Spartan king Areus (see #1 above). He came into conflict with Ptolemy III (246–222 B.C.E.), according to Josephus (*Ant* 12.158–59) because of his refusal to pay tribute. But the issue of tribute (and Josephus' characterization of Onias as greedy) cannot serve as a full and satisfactory explanation for the conflict. Political motives may account in part for Onias' behavior. At the accession of Ptolemy III, the third Syrian war began. Onias II sided with the Syrians, perhaps because he believed that direct contact with the Babylonian diaspora accorded better with his interests. But Onias miscalculated the outcome. Ptolemy III was the victor, and Onias II fell into disfavor in the Ptolemaic court. His fall enabled Joseph, the head of the Tobiad family, to strengthen his position in Judea. With this began a power struggle between Tobiads and Oniads that ended eighty years later with the consolidation of Hasmonean power. Nonetheless, under his son Simon II, the high priesthood regained power and prestige.

3. Onias III succeeded his father, the high priest Simon II (known as "the Just"), about 190 B.C.E. At the time he inherited the office of high priest, its influence was at a peak. But the power of the office began to decline, in part because of a severe crisis in Judean society caused by tensions between various political, social, and cultural power groups. Onias III faced opposition from Simon and his supporters.

Simon was the brother of Menelaus and Lysimachus, the leaders of the more extreme hellenizers; he was additionally a member of the priestly order of Bilga (Balgea), who, in cooperation with the Tobiads, contested the hegemony of the Oniads. The confrontation between Simon and Onias III foreshadowed the hellenizers' coup d'état and its consequences for Judea.

Conflict between Simon and Onias III began over supervision of the market in Jerusalem. The main issue was probably pecuniary, although Simon was encroaching on the jurisdiction of the high priest to enlarge his own authority. The incident was a portent of the future of the high priestly office, with increasing interference from the imperial government and greater impetus toward hellenization.

Onias III next faced interference (at Simon's instigation) from Heliodoros, the minister of King Seleucus IV (187–175 B.C.E.), in the fiscal management of the temple (2 Maccabees 3). Heliodoros intended to confiscate deposits entrusted to the temple's treasury, probably because of suspicion sowed by Simon that they belonged to enemies of the Seleucid regime. His intention aroused alarm in Jerusalem. According to the florid account in 2 Maccabees 3, when he approached the treasury office with his bodyguards, a supernatural horseman in golden armor reared against him and two young men beat him nearly to death. The incident was seen by the author of 2 Maccabees as a manifestation of God's power in defense of his sanctuary (2 Macc 3:24). Friends of Heliodoros asked the high priest Onias, who then prayed and offered sacrifice for him with the result that God restored Heliodoros to life. The chastened official returned to Seleucus IV and declared to him the deeds of the supreme God of the temple of Jerusalem. (This story resembles the narrative in Daniel 1–6; see Bickerman 1939–44.)

The "miracle" of Heliodoros' chastisement was not taken at face value, and Simon accused Onias of perpetuating a hoax (2 Macc 4:1–2). Animosity progressed to violence; murders between the factions in Jerusalem and malice on the part of the governor of Coele-Syria and Phoenicia, Appolonius son of Menestheus, convinced Onias that the rivalry had gone too far. Onias traveled in person to meet with the king himself at Antioch.

Jaddua (contemporary of Alexander)

Onias I (ca. 300 B.C.E.)

Manasses (held office for Onias II after death of Eleazar)

Simon I (cf. *Ant* 12.157)

Eleazar (held office for Onias II after death of Simon I)

[Eleazar, see above]

[Manasses, see above]

Onias II (contemporary of Ptolemy III, 246–222, B.C.E.)

Simon II (cf. *m. ʾAbot* 1.2; Sir 50:1)

Onias III

Onias IV (migrated to Egypt)

ONI.01. Genealogical table of the Oniads.

Onias arrived at Antioch (the year is 175 B.C.E.) to find that Seleucus IV had been murdered by his minister Heliodoros. The throne was subsequently occupied by the king's brother, who became Antiochus IV.

Jason, Onias' brother, took advantage of the new situation and bought from the new king the appointment to the high priesthood. Jason held the office for approximately three years and implemented changes in Jerusalem. During that time Onias remained in exile in Antioch (whether voluntarily or under detention is not clear).

At this point the story of Onias dissolves in conflicting accounts. Jason was dethroned by Menelaus, brother of Simon, in the year 172 B.C.E. Menelaus wished to dispose of Onias, the legitimate high priest. To achieve his aim he bribed Andronicus, a regent for Antiochus IV at that time, to murder Onias. Onias took refuge in an asylum at Daphne, near Antioch. He was finally lured out and murdered (2 Macc 4:30–38). The story of the murder of Onias III has a parallel in Diodorus Siculus (30.7.2), where Andronicus is implicated in the murder of Antiochus, son of Seleucus IV, and executed for it. The similarity of the two stories is evident, yet their relationship is unclear.

Josephus records two different accounts of Onias' fate. In *JW* (1.33; 7.423) he states that Onias III was never detained in Antioch and that he founded a Jewish temple in Egypt. But the account of Onias in the *Antiquities* accords with 2 Maccabees 4. For the various critical opinions see Stern (1960).

4. Onias IV was a son of Onias III. The main source about him is *Ant* 13.62–73, to which may be added *Ant* 12.387–88; and 20.236. The narrative in *JW* is erroneous. According to *Ant* 13, Onias had immigrated to Egypt and was living in Alexandria at the time of the Maccabean wars. He requested from the Ptolemaic ruling couple Ptolemy VI Philometor (180–145 B.C.E.) and Queen Cleopatra permission to build a temple to the God of Israel in Egypt. The king and the queen consented to his request, and allotted to him a ruined Egyptian temple in Leontopolis in the nome of Heliopolis. The site was reconstructed as a Jewish temple under Onias as "high priest" and with other priests and Levites. It served mainly as the worship center of the Jewish inhabitants of this region.

There are some problems concerning the date and purpose of Onias' migration to Egypt. According to *Ant* 12.387, this took place in 162 B.C.E., after the execution of Menelaus and the appointment of Alcimus to the high priesthood. His motive for immigrating may have been despair of obtaining the high priesthood in Jerusalem for himself.

The chronology of his activities is not confirmed by *Ant* 13.62, and may be in conflict with *CPJ* 1 no. 132. This papyrus, dated to September 21, 164 B.C.E., is a letter from Heroides to a certain person whose name was restored by Wilcken as *Oni[ai]* (Onias). If the restoration (endorsed by Tcherikover in *CPJ* 1: 244–46) is correct, and the recipient was Onias IV, as seems probable, then Onias IV should have come to Egypt some time before 164 B.C.E. This chronology is in conflict with *Ant* 12.387, but not with *Ant* 13.62, which supposes that a certain time elapsed between Onias IV's arrival at Alexandria and his request to build a temple.

In view of this, we accept Tcherikover's opinion that Onias IV came to Egypt about a decade before he requested permission from Philometor and Cleopatra to build the temple; the temple would then be dated about 160 B.C.E. A reminiscence of Onias as founder of a temple in Egypt is preserved in *b. Menah.* 109:2. There Onias is a son of Simon the Just (Simon II), who founded a temple in Alexandria.

Onias IV also stood at the head of a Jewish army, which was centered in the Heliopolite nome. He and his sons served as generals under the Ptolemies, and played a role in Ptolemaic politics.

Bibliography

Bickerman, E. 1939–44. Héliodore au Temple de Jérusalem. *AIPHOS* 7: 5–40. Repr. pp. 159–91 in *Studies in Jewish and Christian History*, pt. 2, ed. O. Michel; M. Hengel; and P. Schäfer. Leiden, 1980.

Stern, M. 1960. The Death of Onias III. *Zion* 25: 1–16.

URIEL RAPPAPORT

ONION. See FLORA.

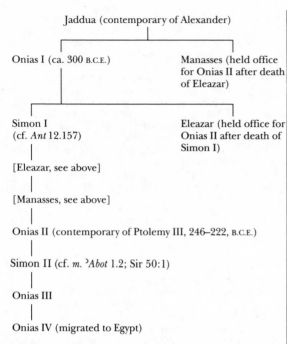

ONO (PLACE) [Heb *ʾônô*]. A settlement in the NW Shephelah (M.R. 137159), first mentioned in a list of locations in Upper Retenu (Palestine and Syria) conquered by Thutmose III (1490–1436 B.C.). Its hieroglyphic representation, as it appears in these annals (Simons 1937: 112, no. 65) carved on the walls of the Sanctuary of Amon at Karnak, is, according to Albright (1934: 35, 46), vocalized as ʾ*U-nu.* Although its location is not precisely fixed, the sequence of towns on the roster provides some geographical perspective (Aharoni *LBHG,* 49): Mahoz, Joppa, Gath, Lod, Ono, Aphek, Socoh, Yaḥam, *hbdn,* Gath, Migdol. Dorsey (1981: 175, 180; fc.: 319) places it at the crossing of the international coastal route (from Gaza to Aphek) with a NW extension (Beth-horon—T. Hadid—Ono—Joppa: the path of a 19th-century-A.D. road) of an alternate branch (between Lod and Beth-horon) of the main road linking Joppa to Beth-horon.

A tradition preserved in 1 Chr 8:12 assigns the building, or rebuilding, of "Ono and Lod and its daughters (i.e., villages, LXX *lōmas*)" to one of the three sons of Elpaal, a Benjaminite. The Greek Codex Vaticanus of this text lacks the words "and Lod." The location of Benjaminite towns so far to the W is problematic. Mazar (*WHJP* 3: 113) believed that during the early settlement, the Benjaminites spread W into the northern coastal plain—to Ono and Lod and elsewhere—to escape the overcrowding of the area bounded by Ephraim, Jerusalem, and the Gibeonite cities. Myers (*1 Chronicles* AB, 60–61) suggests that when the Danites, whose initial allotment included "territory over against Joppa" (Josh 19:46), were removed to Leshem/Laish, their land was absorbed by Judah and Ephraim. Since Judah and Benjamin had, to some extent, merged since the division of the kingdom, Benjaminites, who earlier enjoyed close ties with the Joseph tribes (Gen 35:24; 46:19–21), moved into this territory. Alt (*KlSchr* 2: 283) proposed that following a period of Philistine dominion, probably as part of the state of Ekron, the land N of Ekron to the *Nahr el-ʿAuja* was annexed by Josiah following an overthrow of Ekron.

That Benjaminites were living in Ono during the Persian period is attested by Neh 11:35. Here "Lod and Ono" (see Neubauer 1868: 86) is thought by Simons (*GTTOT,* 390) to be the referent of the apposition "the valley of Craftsmen (*gê haḥărāšîm,* although cf. 1 Chr 4:14 and *b. Meg.* 4a)." Simons (*GTTOT,* 381) believes Lod and Ono formed an "enclave in the territory outlined by the Danite city-list of Josh 19:40–48." Smith (1896: 253, n. 1) understood the area around Lod to be Samaritan. Avi-Yonah (1966: 17–18) suggested that Ono, along with Lod and Hadid, should be considered similar to Judean villages dispersed through Edom which were to be excluded from the Persian province of Judah/Yehud. Both Aharoni (*LBHG,* 416) and Blenkinsopp (*Ezra-Nehemiah* OTL, 268) concur in excluding this region from Judea during the Persian period. On the other hand, Albright (1963: 93) speculated that Lod and its adjoining towns were added to the province of Judah by Nehemiah himself. Stern (1982: 246, 248–49) maintains that the region of the NW Shephelah was part of the Gezer district of the province of Judah during the Persian period.

Ono is also mentioned in the rosters of returnees from exile as the town of origin of some of those who came back to Jerusalem and Judah. In Ezra 2:33 the "sons (i.e., citizens) of Ono" are listed along with those of Lod and Hadid as numbering 725. In Neh 7:37 these same three localities claim 721 of the returnees. In 1 Esdr 5:22 the "sons of Ono" are paired with those of "the other Elam (LXX A *kalamōlalou,* LXX B *kalamōkalou*—a corrupt combination of "Lod and Hadid" according to Turner [*IDB* 1: 482])" and number 725.

Neh 6:2 records a proposal by Nehemiah's enemies to meet him "in the villages *(bakkĕpîrîm)* in the plain of Ono." Although LXX (*kōmais,* cf. LXX 1 Chr 8:12) and the Vulgate read "villages," Myers (*1 Chronicles* AB, 135), Blenkinsopp (*Ezra-Nehemiah* OTL, 267), and others treat *hakkĕpîrîm* as a place-name. Simons (*GTTOT,* 390) suggests that "the plain of Ono" may be the same area referred to as "the valley of Craftsmen." The choice of this location is understandable if, as Blenkinsopp (*ibid.,* 216, 268) suggests, Sanballat's home was nearby in one of the Beth-horons in the Shephelah NW of Jerusalem or if, as Alt (*KlSchr* 2: 343 n. 4) proposes, the territory was a neutral zone between the provinces of Ashdod and Samaria.

Talmudic sources contribute to our knowledge of Ono. It was a walled city in the days of Joshua (*b. Meg.* 4a, *m. ʿArak.* 9:6). It was a part of Judea (*b. ʿArak.* 32a, b). The towns of Lod, Ono, and Ge Haharashim were laid waste in the days of the concubine of Gibeah (Judges 20) and rebuilt by Elpaal; after falling again they were repaired by Asa (*b. Meg.* 4a). The distance from Lod to Ono was three miles (*b. Ketub.* 111b). A Rabbi Ḥanina resided in Ono (*m. Giṭ.* 6:7). Two rabbis spent a Sabbath in Ono on their way to Lydda/Lod (*b. Ḥul.* 56b). The Midrash on Lam 1:17 (also quoted in the Midrashim on Lev 23:5 and Cant 2:2 [section 5]) describes Lydda/Lod and Ono as adversaries.

A late-3d-century-A.D. manumission text (No. 1205) from Oxyrhynchus in Egypt (Hunt 1912: 240) mentions a councillor *(bouleutēs)* of *Oneitai.* If, as Hunt (1912: 241) and Avi-Yonah (1966: 123, n. 43) suggest, this designation refers to Ono (or its inhabitants) it may indicate that Ono was made an independent municipality sometime during the 3d century, maybe as a consequence of the strife with Lod (Avi-Yonah 1966: 123, 158; *EncJud* 12: 1407). Ono appears in 5th- and 6th-century Byzantine town lists as an independent town (Abel *GP* 2: 401; Avi-Yonah *EncJud* 12: 1407).

Bibliography

Albright, W. F. 1934. *Vocalization of the Egyptian Syllabic Orthography.* New Haven.

———. 1963. *Biblical Period from Abraham to Ezra.* New York.

Avi-Yonah, M. 1966. *Holy Land from the Persian to the Arab Conquests.* Grand Rapids.

Dorsey, D. A. 1981. The Roads and Highways of Israel during the Iron Age. Ph.D. diss. Dropsie.

———. fc. *The Roads and Highways of Ancient Israel.* Baltimore.

Hunt, A. S. 1912. *Oxyrhynchus Papyri.* Pt 9. London.

Neubauer, A. 1868. *La Géographie du Talmud.* Paris.

Simons, J. 1937. *Handbook for the Study of Egyptian Topographical Lists relating to Western Asia.* Leiden.

Smith, G. A. 1896. *Historical Geography of the Holy Land.* New York.

Stern, E. 1982. *Material Culture of the Land of the Bible in the Persian Period 538–332 B.C.* Warminster.

RODNEY H. SHEARER

ONYCHA. See PERFUMES AND SPICES.

OPHEL (PLACE) [Heb *ʿōpel*]. The word means "hill," "mound," or "bulge," and in some instances refers to a hill (Isa 32:14; Mic 4:8). With the article, the word refers to a specific hill or mound, such as the hill of Samaria (2 Kgs 5:24; cf. the Mesha Stone from Dhiban, which speaks of the wall of the "citadel" of Qarhoh [the high acropolis of Kerak in Jordan]).

Usually, however, the word *haʿōpel* is used as a proper noun to refer to a section of the SE ridge of ancient Jerusalem, south of the temple platform and just north of the City of David where the ridge widens to join the temple platform, or it may refer to the hill of Zion itself (Kenyon 1967: 14–15). Some of the kings of the divided monarchy initiated various construction programs on the Ophel (Jotham, 2 Chr 27:3; Manasseh, 2 Chr 33:14). After the Exile, the Nethanim (i.e., various temple servants) took their turn in repairing the city walls on the Ophel (Neh 3:26–27; cf. 11:21).

During the Roman period, Josephus calls the area Ophlas, a transliteration into Greek from the Aramaic *apla,* and locates it next to the temple platform. He describes the course of the first old wall of Jerusalem as "passing a spot which they call Ophlas, [which] finally joined the eastern portion of the temple" (*JW* 5.4.2 145). This reference to the Ophlas indicates the external bulge just below and SE of the corner of the present Haram esh-Sharif of the temple platform.

The area was strategically important, and during the Roman siege of Jerusalem, John, one of the Jewish leaders, was able to control the temple area with the "Ophla and the valley called Kedron" (*JW* 5.6.1 §254). Josephus correctly distinguished between the Ophlas, located at the N end of the SE ridge, and the area he called "Akra, that is to say, the lower town" (i.e., farther down the SE ridge) which during the Roman siege was held by another Jewish leader, Simon (*JW* 5.6.1 §253; cf. *JW* 6.6.3 §354; Simons 1952: 60–66; Mazar 1975: 173; Mare 1987: 66).

Bibliography

Kenyon, K. 1967. *Jerusalem.* New York.
Mare, W. H. 1987. *Archaeology of the Jerusalem Area.* Grand Rapids.
Mazar, B. 1975. *Mountain of the Lord.* Garden City.
Simons, J. 1952. *Jerusalem in the Old Testament.* Leiden.

W. HAROLD MARE

OPHIR (PERSON) [Heb *ʾôpir*]. According to the Table of Nations (Gen 10:29) and the parallel genealogy in 1 Chr 1:23, Ophir was a Semite, son of Joktan, born six generations after Noah. His name is also associated with a geographical area. The names of his brothers in the genealogy would seem to place him and his descendants in Arabia. See HAVILAH (PLACE); SHEBA (PERSON) #1. This location is supported by a descriptive note that places the sons of Joktan in the "eastern hill-country" in the region between Mesha and Sephar (Gen 10:30). An exact location is not known, but the S Arabian area around Yemen would fit the evidence. The name itself is recorded in inscriptions coming from the pre-Islamic period (Ryckmans 1934: 298, 339–40).

Bibliography

Ryckmans, G. 1934. *Les noms propres sud-semitiques.* Louvain.

DAVID W. BAKER

OPHIR (PLACE) [Heb *ʾôpîr*]. A maritime nation which was a source of gold from at least the reign of Solomon (1 Kgs 9:28; 22:49; 2 Chr 8:18). It also provided fine wood and precious stones (1 Kgs 10:11; 2 Chr 9:10; Job 28:16). All of these were delivered to Israel by ship through the port of Ezion-geber on the Red Sea. The gold seems to have been of a particularly high quality since in some of the passages it is used in conjunction with more specific Hebrew terms for fine, choice gold (Job 22:24; Ps 45:10[—Eng 45:9]; Isa 13:12). Ophir became so associated with this rare metal that the name Ophir itself, without any further qualifier, is to be understood as "gold" in Job 22:24. Gold from this source is also known from an extra-biblical inscription from Israel (Maisler 1951).

In poetic and prophetic references to the wealth of Ophir, it is not the source or origin but rather the quality of the metal which is stressed. It is said to be precious indeed, but less so than wisdom (Job 28:16), a relationship with God (Job 22:24), or even humanity itself (Isa 13:12).

The geographical location of Ophir is unclear, and the question has raised a multitude of suggestions ranging from southern Africa to India. The popular attraction to the romantic idea of some distant, exotic location of fantastic wealth has undoubtedly fueled the speculation.

Some have suggested that Ophir is strictly a legend, with no historical existence at all. Because of the large amount of gold which is claimed to have been delivered from there (15 tons), some have suggested that it is the mythical equivalent of Eldorado (North 1967: 197–98). Based on other ANE records, however, it is possible to show that this amount of the metal is not implausible.

An issue which has exacerbated the problem of identifying the location of Ophir concerns the possible relationship between the Ophir of the genealogies of Noah (Gen 10:29; 1 Chr 1:23; see OPHIR [PERSON]) and that mentioned above. The former has been fairly certainly located in the Arabian peninsula, leading to the same suggestion as to the location of Ophir in all of its biblical occurrences. A problem with this location has been suggested because it does not lend itself to the production of some of the exotic animal life associated by some with Ophir's gold (1 Kgs 10:22). This argument against an Arabian site is not compelling since the gold mentioned in 1 Kings 10 is not specifically stated to originate in Ophir. Its source is unspecified, and its mass (666 shekels, v 14) exceeds that which is said to have been transported from Ophir (420 shekels; 1 Kgs 9:28). Even if the gold of chap. 10 were from Ophir, it is not stated that the exotic animals were from the same location. They could have come from a different place, with the ships then on-loading the gold en route back to Israel (North 1967: 200). The association of the gold from Ophir with the queen of Sheba (1 Kgs 10:10–12), generally identified with Seba and the Sabeans in SW Arabia, adds to the merit of the Arabian identification of Ophir.

Christidès rejects the identification of the Solomonic Ophir with that of the genealogies on the basis of alternative readings of the name (1970: 242). Most of the non-genealogical texts in their Greek and Latin versions have the place-name with an initial *s* not found in the Hebrew text, i.e., Sōphēr(a) (1 Kgs 9:28; 10:11), Sōpheir(a) (Job 22:24; 28:16; 2 Chr 8:18), Soupheir (1 Chr 29:4; 2 Chr 9:10), and Souphir (Isa 13:12). This distinction from the "Ophir" form of the genealogies he feels sufficient to warrant an interpretation which sees the two as separate entities.

Aside from an Arabian site, one of the two other major contenders for the location of Ophir is India (Schreiden 1953: 587–90). This identification was made by Josephus (*Ant* 8.164) concerning 1 Kgs 9:28, and applied by Jerome to Job 28:16 in his translation of the Latin Vulgate. (S)upara, a site some 40 miles N of Bombay, and mentioned by Ptolemy (*Geog.* 7.1.5), has been suggested (see Christidès 1970: 243), as has Goa (Gray *HDB,* 713). In favor of a location on this subcontinent is a sea trade between India and the Middle East from at least the 2d millennium B.C. Also, the commodities which might be associated in Kings with the biblical Ophir are indigenous to India.

Several have also suggested Africa as the site of Ophir. With the discovery of the wealth of Zimbabwe in southern Africa during the 19th century, some suggested that Ophir had been found (Peters 1895; see North 1967: 200). Albright (*ARI,* 133–34) suggested a location farther N along the African coast in what is now Somalia. This is an area associated with the Egyptian *punt.* See PUT. The commodities associated with Ophir are found in this area. This is especially so if one accepts the possibility that some of the geographical descriptions used for parts of this area extend to both sides of the Red Sea, including East Africa and the W Arabian peninsula (ibid.; also North 1967: 201). This would be a combination of two of the suggestions already mentioned.

None of these possibilities have been compellingly proven. The only extrabiblical reference to Ophir does not shed much geographical light on the subject. A text from Tell Qasile dating from the 8th century B.C. reads "gold of Ophir to Beth-horon. 30 shekels" (Maisler 1951: 266). This could indicate the transfer of the metal from its source to another location. Another possibility is that "Ophir" is a description of the fine quality of the gold, as has already been shown for some OT texts. In neither case are we able to obtain any more geographical precision. Though not conclusive, the Arabian or East African sites seem more likely.

Bibliography

Christidès, V. 1970. L'énigme d'Ophir. *RB* 77: 240–47.
Maisler, B. 1951. Two Hebrew Ostraca from Tell Qasile. *JNES* 10: 265–67.
North, R. 1967. Ophir/Parvaim and Petra/Joktheel. *PWCJS* 4: 197–202.
Peters, C. 1895. *Im Goldenlande des Altertums: Das goldene Ophir Salomo's.* Munich.
Schreiden, R. 1953. Les entreprises navales du roi Salamon. *AIPHOS* 13: 587–90.

DAVID W. BAKER

OPHNI (PLACE) [Heb *ʿopnî*]. A settlement in the E half of Benjamin (Josh 18:23). The text is not explicit regarding its exact location. The fact that it appears in a list that tends to group names according to geographical proximity, in this case neighboring Geba, suggests that it would be located at the modern site of Jifna (M.R. 170152), some 3 miles (5 km) NW of Bethel. If so, the settlement would actually lie in Ephraim rather than Benjamin as suggested by the larger context, leading us to conclude either (1) that the N boundary of Benjamin was in actuality much more irregular than the schematic description of Josh 18:11–20 would suggest, or, as is now more commonly assumed, (2) that the border description and the listing of towns are contradictory, the two deriving from quite different periods in Israel's history.

ELMER H. DYCK

OPHRAH (PERSON) [Heb *ʿoprâ*]. The son of Meonothai in the genealogy of Judah (1 Chr 4:14).

H. C. LO

OPHRAH (PLACE) [Heb *ʿoprāh*]. **1.** A town in the tribal allotment of Benjamin (Josh 18:23). This Ophrah has been identified with modern et-Taiyibeh (M.R. 178151), about 4 miles N of Bethel (Boling *Joshua* AB, 430; McCarter *1 Samuel* AB, 238). It may also be described as lying on the intersection of two lines, one running NE from Jerusalem, the other NW from Jericho. This Ophrah also figures in the story of Jonathan's surprise raid on the Philistines at Michmash, where it is said to be the road (roads at this time being named by their end points) taken by one of three Philistine raiding parties (1 Sam 13:17). The other two roads named are "Beth-Horon" and the "valley of Zeboim." Morton (*IDB* 3: 607) and McCarter (*1 Samuel* AB, 238) equate this Ophrah with the Ephron of 2 Chr 13:17 and, on the basis of evidence from the early Christian father Jerome, with Ephraim of 2 Sam 13:23 and John 11:54 (on the former, see the textual note in McCarter *1 Samuel* AB, 330, who cites manuscripts of the LXX which lend credence to this equation). In addition, Morton (*IDB* 3: 607) cites Aphairema, a district given to Judea from Samaria by Demetrius in 1 Macc 11:34 as identical with the Benjaminite Ophrah.

2. A second Ophrah is associated with the traditions surrounding the judge Gideon (Judg 6:11, 24). This Ophrah is located by these stories in the territory of the tribe Manasseh (that is, to the N of the tribal claim of Benjamin). Judg 6:11 tells us that the Manassite Ophrah belonged to the clan of Abiezer (cf. Josh 17:2, 1 Chr 7:18; see *IDB* 3: 607), and the naming of the place as "the Oak at Ophrah" suggests a place of prophetic activity (cf. the tradition of "Deborah's Palm" in Judg 4:5; see Boling *Judges* AB, 130), though in this case one operating in the Baal cult (cf. Judg 6:25ff). The stories about Gideon continue with no further mention of Ophrah until Judg 8:27 when Gideon makes an ephod there, which the text tells us became a source of apostasy for Gideon and Israel. Upon his death, Gideon is buried in his hometown of Ophrah (Judg 8:32). His son Abimelech killed his brothers there (Judg 9:5), save for Jotham, in a bid to gain sole rule for himself. This Manassite Ophrah has not been located with any certainty, though the location of Gideon traditions in the valley of Jezreel (e.g. Judg 6:35) gives weight to the suggestion of Aharoni (*LBHG,* 263) that this Ophrah should be identified with modern ʿAffuleh (M.R. 177223) in the center of the valley of Jezreel.

JEFFRIES M. HAMILTON

ORACLE. An oracle is information transmitted from the deity to human beings, usually either answers to important questions or revelations about future events. This entry consists of two articles, one surveying the use of the word "oracle" (Heb *maśśāʾ*) in the OT, and the other surveying oracles as an element in ancient Egyptian religion. For other discussions of oracles, see PROPHECY; SIBYLLINE ORACLES; and WOE.

OLD TESTAMENT

Although discussions of prophecy in the OT often use the English word "oracle" as a general term for any speech by a prophet, the RSV and other modern translations use it mostly to translate a single Hebrew word, *maśśāʾ*. *Maśśāʾ* designates a specific type of speech used by ancient Israelite prophets. Thus when translating *maśśāʾ*, "oracle" indicates that a prophetic passage or speech belongs to this specific type.

The OT identifies eighteen passages by means of the Hebrew term *maśśāʾ*. The RSV labels all of them with the term "oracle." These are: 2 Kgs 9:26a; Isa 13:2–14:23; 14:29–32; 15:1b–16:12; 17:1b–11; 19:1b–25; 21:1b–10, 11b–12, 13b–17; 22:1b–14; 23:1b–18; 30:6b–7; Ezek 12:11–16; Nah 1:2–3:19; Hab 1:2–2:20; Zech 9:1–11:3; 12:1b–14:21; Mal 1:2–3:24[—Eng 1:2–4:6].

Jer 23:33–38, Lam 2:14, and 2 Chr 24:27 use the term *maśśāʾ* to refer to unreported speeches of Israelite prophets. In the Lamentations and Chronicles passages the RSV translates *maśśāʾ* with "oracle," but uses "burden" in the Jeremiah passage to show the pun created in Jer 23:33 through the use of a homonym of *maśśāʾ* meaning "burden" (i.e., "You are the burden"). Other passages where translations use the term "oracle" do not contain the term *maśśāʾ*, and in Prov 30:1 and 31:1 *maśśāʾ* is a name. See MASSA [PERSON].

Maśśāʾ has often been thought to designate a specific type of prophetic speech, but a comprehensive definition of the genre has been reconstructed only lately. This definition, developed in a recent study (Weis 1986), indicates that a translation for *maśśāʾ* such as "prophetic exposition of divine revelation" would be preferable to "oracle."

Within ancient Israel the type, or genre, of speech called *maśśāʾ* is found exclusively within the prophetic movement. A *maśśāʾ* responds to a question about a lack of clarity in the relation between divine intention and human reality. Either the divine intention being expressed in some aspect of human experience is unclear, or the divine intention is clear enough, but the human events through which it will gain expression are unclear. In any event, the initiative for a *maśśāʾ* lies not with the deity or the prophet, but with the prophet's community—or a member thereof—which asks the question to which the *maśśāʾ* is a response.

The topic of a *maśśāʾ* is thus always some person, group, situation, or event (e.g., Philistia, the ravaging of Moab, the destruction of Tyre, Babylon, the renovation of postexilic Judah, Nineveh, Jerusalem, King Ahab). The addressee of a *maśśāʾ* is either the prophet's own community or the person or group that is the topic of the passage.

A *maśśāʾ* is based on a particular revelation (given to the prophet) of the divine intention or of a forthcoming divine action. A speech or text belonging to this genre was composed by the prophet in order to expound the way in which the revealed divine action or intention would actually express itself in human affairs. Thus, regardless of the overall formal structure they exhibit, all texts belonging to the genre *maśśāʾ* link descriptions of God's acts or intentions with descriptions of human acts and events in order to present events taking place in the human realm as the manifestation or result of divine initiation (e.g., Isa 13:6–8; 19:1b; 23:11–13; Zech 9:4–5a).

On the basis of this exposition a *maśśāʾ* gives direction for human action in the present or near future, or provides insight into the future. Those texts that give insight into the future are predominantly announcements of future events and conditions (e.g., Isa 17:1b–11; 30:6b–7; Ezek 12:11–16). Those texts that give direction contain commands and/or prohibitions that are justified by reports of past or present events and conditions (e.g., Isa 15:1b–16:12; 21:1b–10; 22:1b–14; 23:1b–18). Commands or prohibitions concerning jubilation and lamentation are addressed to the person or group that is the text's topic (e.g., Isa 23:1b–6, 14). Commands or prohibitions concerning concrete human action apart from jubilation or lamentation are always given to the text's addressee (e.g., Isa 16:3–4a is addressed to officials of Judah, not to the Moabites).

The oldest texts of the OT that belong to this genre (e.g., Isa 14:29–32; 15:1b–16:12; 21:1b–10; 22:1b–14) come from the 8th century B.C.E., and contain within themselves the revelation on which they are based (e.g., Isa 14:32b; 16:6–11, 21:2b [+ 21:9?]; 22:14b). They communicate and expound that revelation for the first time, and respond to a specific inquiry addressed to the prophet about some aspect of the immediate human situation for which the significance is unclear (e.g., Isa 15:1b–16:12 concerns the advisability of giving sanctuary to refugees from an attack on Moab). These examples of the genre *maśśāʾ* usually give direction for action. These texts are produced by prophets who appeal to a living revelatory encounter with the deity, and out of that—through the *maśśāʾ*, which they compose—seek to communicate how the deity is at work in human affairs, and thus how the audience should itself act. The texts are written compositions, but were probably delivered orally. This version of the genre *maśśāʾ* predominates *before* the Exile.

There is some evidence that the prophets who used this type of speech thought of themselves in terms of the metaphor of the lookout on the city wall who watches for dust clouds and other signs of approaching events. These lookouts then had to interpret the significance of the phenomena, or the meaning of the signs that they observed, in order to deliver usable insight or direction—just as the prophets using the genre had to expound the revelation they received in order to give usable insight or direction.

The latest texts of the OT that belong to this genre (e.g.,

Zech 9:1–11:3; 12:1b–14:21; Mal 1:2–3:24—[Eng 1:2–4:6]) come from the late 6th and early 5th centuries B.C.E. Unlike the earliest examples of *maśśāʾ* they refer to a previously communicated revelation that is found outside the *maśśāʾ* (e.g., the previously communicated revelations for the three texts listed above are Haggai 1–2 and Zechariah 1–8, plus Zech 11:4–17 for the last two). Here a *maśśāʾ* is the prophet's response to a generalized complaint that God's intention expressed in the prior communication has not shown itself in human affairs as expected. These examples of the genre tend to give insight into the future rather than direction for action. In other words, they accept the revelatory status of some previous prophetic communication of the divine intention, and in the face of the failure of that intention to appear in human affairs as expected expound how it will actually manifest itself in the near future. These examples of *maśśāʾ* are produced by prophets who derive their authority chiefly from a revelatory text (i.e., earlier prophecy) and only a little (if at all) from a living revelatory encounter with the deity. Although this usage of *maśśāʾ* is a pattern of the postexilic period, there are signs that the shift had begun by the very end of the preexilic period (note the reference to a previously communicated revelation in Hab 2:2–3, although Habakkuk 1–2 otherwise conforms to the preexilic pattern for a *maśśāʾ*).

It is not clear whether the prophets responsible for the postexilic texts conceived of their work under any particular metaphor, but they had become less the originators of new prophecies and more the guardians and interpreters of old prophecies deemed still to have life. The evolution of the genre *maśśāʾ*, in this respect, participates in the evolution currently posited by some for the prophetic movement as a whole. The shift from localizing revelation in a personal encounter with the deity to localizing revelation in a written text, seen in the development of the genre *maśśāʾ*, is also an important step on the road to a religion centered around a canonical Scripture as the source of divine guidance.

Bibliography

Aune, D. E. 1983. *Prophecy in Early Christianity and the Ancient Mediterranean World.* Grand Rapids.

Barton, J. 1986. *Oracles of God: Perceptions of Ancient Prophecy in Israel after the Exile.* London.

Baumgärtel, F. 1961. Die Formel *neʾum jahwe. ZAW* 73: 277–90.

Christensen, D. L. 1975. *Transformation of the War Oracle in Old Testament Prophecy: Studies in the Oracles against the Nations.* HDR 3. Missoula.

Hayes, J. H. 1968. The Usage of Oracles against Foreign Nations in Ancient Israel. *JBL* 87: 81–92.

Porter, J. R. 1981. Ancient Israel. Pp. 191–214 in *Oracles and Divination,* ed. M. Loewe and C. Blacker. Boulder, CO.

Tucker, G. M. 1978. Prophetic Speech. *Int* 32: 31–45.

Weis, R. 1986. *A Definition of the Genre Maśśāʾ in the Hebrew Bible.* Ph.D. diss. Claremont Graduate School.

Westermann, C. 1967. *Basic Forms of Prophetic Speech.* Trans. H. C. White. Philadelphia.

Wilson, R. R. 1980. *Prophecy and Society in Ancient Israel.* Philadelphia.

RICHARD D. WEIS

ANCIENT EGYPT

An oracle is information transmitted from the world of the gods to humans. Different from theological revelations, the term "oracle" is usually reserved for those occasions which relate to the will or knowledge of god with regard to the actions of human beings. Because of this, oracles have often been assumed to reveal a person's destiny, and, therefore, they are indicative of cultures which have a very fatalistic worldview. On analysis, however, this proves to be a highly problematic position.

Oracles can be divided into two categories: the solicited and the unsolicited (Blackman 1925: 249ff.; 1926: 176ff.). The unsolicited oracle, the less common of the two, is a sudden, unexpected message from the divine, often occurring in dreams. We are familiar with such oracles in Egypt in relation to royalty, such as Prince Osorkon (Caminos 1958: 88–89), Pharaoh Merenptah, and on the famous sphinx stele of Tuthmoses IV (Sauneron 1959: 19ff.).

Solicited oracles result from a conscious human attempt to discover the divine will. This attempt usually comes in the form of a question which is phrased either to solicit verification ("yes" or "no") or for specification, the answer to which requires explanation. The former is, of course, the most common type of oracular question (Černý 1935: 41ff.), and it is regularly encountered in Egypt in cases of adjudication where the petitioner presents his case to the god who will, by one means or another, communicate agreement or disagreement (Parker 1962: 44–45). The latter type of question requests much more information from the god; the most common example of this is incubation, creating a situation—usually through an altered state of sleep or deep meditation—wherein one induces the god to communicate the divine will or knowledge (Volten 1942: 40–41). This practice of incubation, or dream invocation, does not seem to occur in the earlier stages of Egyptian history (Ray 1976: 131 ff.), and may be concomitant with the Late Period change in Egyptian thought, which saw a distinct change in the Egyptian acceptance of the power and prominence of fate (Miosi 1982: 69 ff.).

Oracles were made in numerous ways and related to various topics (Roeder 1959: passim). They frequently involved voices which emanated from the recesses of chapels or from statues. These "divine" voices were certainly those of priests who interpreted the will of god. Prophetic messages were also associated with dreams, particularly associated with temple incubation, and they were often transmitted by people who were possessed or in a trance. Oracles could also occur without speech, as was the case for those made during processions of the god in his sacred boat, when he communicated his will by forcing the boat carriers to move in one direction or another or by interpreting the movement of sacred animals (Ray 1976: 131).

Oracles were sought by all classes—from peasants to pharaohs—and they covered all topics; e.g., whether some food was good enough to eat; what was the most effective cure for a disease (Ray 1976: 134); how to ensure conception; matters of commerce; the selection of a high priest or of a pharaoh; and whether professional advancement was likely. Quite often oracles were sought to decide guilt or innocence in legal disputes; usually these were solicited, requiring only a "yes" or "no" response.

The presence of a priest was absolutely essential in oracular matters. Priests sometimes wrote the questions, were usually the vehicle through which a god transmitted an oracle, were responsible for recording oracles, particularly in legal matters (Posener 1968: 99), and were often responsible for interpreting the meaning of oracles. Indeed, there existed at the serapeum at Memphis expert and professional dream interpreters who were available to anyone. Some of these individuals may have been part of the personnel of the main temple, while others worked independently. In the late Ptolemaic and Roman periods, cults and their priesthoods may have been quite competitive in attracting clients for their particular oracular interpretation skills (Ray 1976: 130 ff.).

As mentioned above, there is a tendency to connect too quickly oracles with a fatalistic worldview. However, it can be seen that many oracles, especially those which involved adjudication, refer to *past* events; predictions and fate are certainly not involved with these. Some appeal to god's omniscience and reflect a present circumstance—knowing the most appropriate cure or the whereabouts of someone or something—and again are not associated with fate or predictions. Others merely show a god's preference or favor (e.g., his choice of high priest or pharaoh).

Of course, many oracles do refer to the outcome of future events, but even here we must be wary of automatically linking ability to predict with fate or predestination. Other explanations are possible. An Egyptian's future was not considered fixed and predestined. It was, instead, seen as the result of a dynamic interaction between the individual—with his own desires, motivations, and actions, and his own physical and temporal environment—and the gods. The divine was imminent and was always reacting to man, principally through the process of reward and punishment. When the future was revealed to a person through an oracle, he may simply have been finding out what god wanted him to do or what particular response or reaction god had in store for him based on his position at any given moment within the process of the law of reward and punishment. Divine revelation of some event in a totally static and predestined future is quite different from god's revealing to someone what his future responses will be within a dynamically interactive relationship.

Thus, reference to oracles does not necessarily indicate a belief in a predestined life. Oracles could refer to the past, or to god's omniscience or preference; these are not related to fate. Oracles relating to the future may merely record what deserved rewards or punishments might or will occur, or what questions man feels are beyond his capacity to answer.

Bibliography

Blackman, A. M. 1925. Oracles in Ancient Egypt. *JEA* 11: 249–55.

———. 1926. Oracles in Ancient Egypt. *JEA* 12: 176–85.

Caminos, R. 1958. *Chronicle of Prince Osorkon.* Rome.

Černý, J. 1935. Questions adressees aux oracles. *BIFAO* 35: 41–58.

———. 1962. Egyptian Oracles. Pp. 35–48 in Parker 1962.

Miosi, F. 1982. God, Fate and Free Will in Egyptian Wisdom Literature. Pp. 69–111 in *Studies in Philology in Honour of Ronald J. Williams.* SSEA 3. Toronto.

Parker, R. 1962. *A Saite Oracle Papyrus.* Providence.

Posener, G. 1968. Amenemope 21, 12 et *bi3i.t* au sens d'"oracle." *ZÄS* 90: 99.

Ray, J. D. 1976. *The Archive of Hor.* London.

———. 1981. Ancient Egypt. Pp. 174–90 in *Oracles and Divination,* ed. M. Loewe and C. Blacker. Boulder, CO.

Roeder. 1959. *Kulte und Orakel im alter Aegypten.* Berlin.

Sauneron, S. 1959. *Les songes et leur interpretation.* Sources Orientales 2. Paris.

Volten, A. 1942. *Demotische Traumdeutung.* Copenhagen.

FRANK T. MIOSI

ORAL TRADITION.

This entry consists of two articles. The first deals with the role of oral tradition in the formation of the NT writings. The second deals with the role and importance of oral tradition in early Judaism. For the role of oral tradition in the formation of the OT writings, see FORM CRITICISM (OT); GENESIS, THE NARRATIVE OF; JOSHUA, BOOK OF; JUDGES, BOOK OF; SCANDINAVIAN SCHOOL (OT); TRADITION HISTORY.

NEW TESTAMENT

The oral tradition of the NT developed in a world which had set a high premium on both the written and the spoken word.

On the one hand, early Christianity was in its Jewish and Hellenistic loyalties heir to literate cultures of distinction. In ancient Judaism scrolls were revered as repositories of wisdom and revelation. From the 3d century B.C.E. onward the hellenization of the ANE world accelerated chirographic processes, rapidly increasing the quantity and variety of Hellenistic and Jewish-Hellenistic literature. There had never been in Western history a production of scrolls, papyri, and manuscripts on such a massive scale. The Christian movement, therefore, originated in a Jewish-Hellenistic milieu which highly prized the written word.

On the other hand, the canonization of biblical literature is apt to delude us into thinking of texts as the single most important tool of civilized existence in the ancient world. Orality, which had been humankind's sole or predominant medium for millennia, prevailed long after the introduction of alphabetic writing systems (Ong 1982: 115–16). Despite the growth of a chirographic culture in antiquity, the Hellenistic age remained strongly beholden to oral modes of communication, composition, and education. Mnemonic devices and formulaic modes of expression dominated thought structures. Orators could carry in their minds a vast stock of commonplaces, and rhetoric was one of the most serious and consequential subjects of civilized life. Texts themselves were hearer-friendly. Any text worthy of consideration was meant to be read aloud (Balogh 1926; Hendrickson 1929; Saenger 1982).

As a result of this dual commitment to textuality and orality in late antiquity, Christianity does not possess a tradition transmitted in purely oral fashion over a millennium (like the Hindu Vedas). Texts came early to the Christian movement, and oral proclamation was subject to textualization almost from its inception. But it must likewise be acknowledged that in early Christianity, as elsewhere in the ancient world, speech remained a principal means of communication. There is no rational ground for rejecting the existence of oral tradition altogether (Ellis 1975: 299–315). In early Christian life and worship the oral proclamation was the rule. As is evident from the Pauline letters, this proclamation was saturated with traditional forms and formulas. Even glossolalia was a learned skill which availed itself of fixed sounds and rhythmic utterances. The interaction, moreover, of discourse with texts and vice versa took on many forms, ranging from close partnership to strained relations all the way to textuality's urge to revise antecedent proclamation.

A. Oral Proclamation of Jesus
   1. The Saying
   2. The Parable
   3. Miracle, Exorcism, Apothegm
B. Synoptic Tradition
C. Gospel Composition
D. Paul
E. Commonplace Tradition
F. Rhetoric of the NT

A. Oral Proclamation of Jesus

The oral gospel originated with Jesus himself. In the only canonical passage pertaining to his educational, linguistic background, he is called a man of literary, scriptural knowledge, although without formal rabbinic schooling (John 7:15). In communicating his message, he entrusted himself to the oral medium without—as far as is known—ever committing a word to writing. Insofar as all four canonical Gospels have given us the portrait of an itinerant speaker of authoritative words, surrounded by audiences and engaged in debates, they will have retained genuine features of Jesus the oral performer.

The aphoristic saying *(ho logos)* and the parabolic story *(hē parabolē)* constituted the two formal units of Jesus' proclamation. Both were oral operations, not literary categories, and together they formed the basis of what came to be the gospel tradition. Their formation, moreover, was rooted in Jewish and Greco-Roman culture. Far from being Christian inventions, the saying and the parable presented themselves as ready-made linguistic instruments to Jesus and his early followers.

1. The Saying. Speaking in sayings was a proven way of managing information in antiquity. Teachers and philosophers, prophets and scientists were trained to handle knowledge in aphoristic fashion. Brevity, rhythmic patterning, and appeal to visual imagination were characteristic aspects of ancient sayings, including those of the Jesus tradition. As is true of all generic choices, a commitment to the genre of saying imposed artistic and ideological limitations upon the speaker. An effective operation of the sayings, therefore, depended not only on a rhetorically skilled performance, but on using the genre to its full potential. The latter is well documented by the rich display of varied types of sayings in the gospel tradition: proverbial sayings, wisdom sayings, prophetic sayings, apocalyptic sayings, ethical sayings, curses and beatitudes, among others (Bultmann 1963: 69–166). Within the limitations set by the genre, diversity was desirable in order to achieve maximal rhetorical effects. Irrespective of the literary fixation of Jesus' sayings, the mnemonic structuring, the rhetorical appeal, and the compositional variability of many reminds us of their oral genesis and performance.

2. The Parable. Parable availed itself of story, a chief vehicle in oral teaching. Brevity as well as rhythmic and thematic patterning must once again be viewed as concessions to hearers. Another hallmark of Jesus' parables is their narrative variety; they are not reducible to one single tale (Crossan 1973). The parable, as the saying, functioned like an instrument the effectiveness of which depended on the skills of the performer. In keeping with oral proprieties, Jesus' parables stayed close to the human world. Up to a point hearers could recognize themselves in these stories. But in the course of a parabolic rendition, the narrative realism frequently conflicted with the social experience of the hearers. At this very point the parabolic logic intruded upon hearers' lives, making their engagement in the story inescapable. Remembering, therefore, was not the only, and not even the most important, objective of parables. The tradition has, quite appropriately, furnished some parables with the closing formula: "He who has ears to hear, let him hear." It invited hearers to complete the parable, and to make sense of it in their lives.

a. Plurality of Originals. What was fundamental about the rendition of sayings and parables was their disposition to function as autonomous speech acts. They were not meant to be heard as scattered pieces or fragmented knowledge in need of an explanatory framework. Saying and parable constituted discrete utterances. Each oral performance carried with it its own logic and sense of integrity; each was an authentic act of communication. Our search for *the* one original saying or parable of Jesus is, therefore, not only fraught with technical difficulties, but from the perspective of oral performance meaningless. Multiple oral renditions of a saying or parable produced a plurality of originals, and hence not the one original (Lord 1960).

b. Clustering Processes. If saying and parable constituted the initial phase of proclamation, then their clustering arrangements began to enrich and complicate the tradition. The juxtaposition of sayings and parables resulted in a variety of formations. Two sayings combined into an aphoristic compound. Three or more sayings and parables coalesced into speech complexes (Crossan 1983). Clustering also was at the root of the formation of Jesus' speeches, the best known of which were the Sermon on the Mount (Matthew 5–7), the Sermon on the Plain (Luke 6:20–49), and the Farewell Speech (John 13:31–17:26). Further development of the clustering processes led to sayings collections, arrangements with little or no interest in narrative syntax. A notable example is Q, which was, however, acceptable to the canonizers only by way of Matthean and Lukan mediation. Clustering, moreover, elevated sayings, dialogues, and parables to a gospel in its own right, the sayings gospel or revelation discourse. A prominent example of a sayings gospel was the gospel of Thomas. See THOMAS, GOSPEL OF (NHC II,*2*). Its Jesus functioned as a teacher of wisdom more than as object of faith. Most clustering processes were products of writing: one does not speak in series of sayings. But in seeking to perpetuate the living authority of Jesus as speaker of sayings and parables, the sayings gospel remained committed to oral sensibilities. It displayed, therefore, the competing interests of speech and writing in the tradition.

3. Miracle, Exorcism, Apothegm. In addition to saying and parable other types of oral communication developed which organized and recollected vital information. The miracle (or heroic) story centered on the single, spectacular aspect of Jesus' healings. Simultaneously simplifying and magnifying the dramatic healing action, it created a heroic image of Jesus which conformed to the mnemonic and aesthetic requirements of oral communication. In the exorcism (or polarization) story life was grasped by its opposites and Jesus was profiled as a memorable figure in conflict with evil. Ideological simplicity and adversary relations had obvious imaginative advantages over the monotonous course of daily life. The apothegmatic (or didactic) story enacted a variety of controversy or dialogue scenes which culminated in a saying. In this case the stories served as a mnemonic bridge designed to call attention to the final saying, which carried the tradition's social, cultic, and moral values. What all three types of oral stories had in common was a mnemonic structuring, a high degree of imaginative appeal, and a personalization and actualization of information.

B. Synoptic Tradition

In the 20th century Bultmann (1963), Gerhardsson (1961; 1964; 1979; 1986), and Riesner (1984) developed the most influential models of the precanonical, synoptic tradition. Together with Schmidt (1919) and Dibelius (1934), Bultmann pioneered the school of form criticism. See FORM CRITICISM. Its basic premise was that many of the sayings and brief narrative units in the Gospels had formerly been operating as speech events. This form-critical insight gave rise to the concept of a pre-gospel, oral tradition. Bultmann suggested an active transmission of the tradition along evolutionary lines from oral simplicity to gospel complexity. Gerhardsson and Riesner, questioning many of the assumptions of form criticism, advocated a relatively stable process of transmission. The former appealed to rabbinic transmissional processes, while the latter located a reliable transfer of sayings in circles comprised of Jesus' disciples and sympathizers. It has, however, been questioned as to whether the synoptic tradition submits to a single conceptual model (Kelber 1983). All oral proclamations were discrete acts of speech, separated by intervals of nonspeaking and unconnectable by linear, evolutionary tracts. Nor was the tradition limited to orality. Stories, sayings, and cluster arrangements came to be written down. Once textualized, they were as a rule recycled back into speech. This interplay of text and proclamation ruled out progressive solidification of orality into textuality. While speech was often written down out of preservative instincts, interpretive impulses were built into the tradition from its inception. The parable, for example, always called for interpretation. Prophetic and apostolic figures continued to proclaim Jesus' words, updating them and adding new ones to their repertoire (Beare 1967; Boring 1982). Forgetting and suppression, moreover, were as much part of tradition as remembering and interpretation (Abel 1971). In sum, the synoptic tradition is a catchword used to reify a tangle of transmissional and hermeneutical processes, of recall and revision, of omission and deconstruction, which in their entirety may elude diagrammatic representation.

C. Gospel Composition

According to the two-source hypothesis, the Matthean and Lukan narratives were composed in dependence on Mark and the sayings source Q. Mark in turn had developed out of an orally dominant tradition. The thesis of Griesbach, which has recently been revived in some quarters, presents an alternative model (Farmer 1964). On that hypothesis, Mark wrote after Matthew and Luke, and Luke was dependent on Matthew. The Matthean gospel in turn had developed out of a tradition of early "eyewitnesses." How the ancients were supposed to have proceeded, however, technically and practically, in merging Mark and Q into the Matthean/Lukan syntheses, or in conflating Matthew and Luke into the Markan composition, has remained unexplained and unexplored. What to the modern mind appears to be a skillful juggling of textual sources may in ancient scribality have been a partnership of chirographic activity with an oral memory in possession of multiple traditions.

Whatever the genetic history of the Gospels, their narrative design appeals to the ear more than to the eye. An oral, paratactic style dominates over subordinate, dependent clauses. Multiple kinds of redundancies accommodate listeners to hear their way through these narratives. Single-action scenes, controversies, and speeches make up the backbone of their syntax. Doings and sayings take over narrative functions where the modern reader would expect character development and psychological probing. This is not to suggest that the Gospels are oral traditional literature, e.g., direct transcriptions of the same oral story (Lord 1978). The marks of textuality are unmistakably present in the Gospels. But textual constructions and dependencies notwithstanding, the gospel narratives still operate in the interest of an aesthetics of hearing.

D. Paul

The bulk of the pre-Pauline Christian materials recoverable from the apostolic letters appears in forms fashioned by oral needs and/or designed for oral use in worship: baptismal formula (Gal 3:28), eucharistic formula (1 Cor 11:23–26), acclamation formula (1 Cor 12:3; 16:22), confessional formula (1 Cor 15:3–5; Roman 1:3–4), faith formula (1 Thess 4:14; Rom 10:9b), doxology (Rom 1:25c; 9:5c), and hymn (Phil 2:6–11). In addition, the apostle made use of dominical sayings (1 Cor 7:10–11; 9:14), although with surprising infrequency.

While the degree of Paul's indebtedness to Jewish, Hellenistic, and Jewish-Hellenistic culture has remained controversial, there is growing certainty that his style of argumentation was informed by ancient rhetoric (Wuellner 1979; 1986). The exercise of theology in such a world was primarily a dynamic interpersonal affair. It did not intend to prove truth abstractly, but through persuasion and by soliciting action. Partiality rather than objectivity was desirable. In a number of his letters Paul communicated the nature and terms of the gospel in a disputational, polemical style. This is traditionally understood as a response to historical adversaries but it can also be appreciated as a rhetorically effective communication. Assertion against opposition, rather than dispassionate logic, was a proven rhetorical strategy. In the same vein, Paul communicated by means of popular polarities: Jew/gentile, male/female, master/slave, believer/unbeliever, spirit/flesh, wise/foolish, among others. The best-known example of his rhetorical style is the diatribe (Bultmann 1910; Stowers 1981). In using it, the apostle simulated objections to his argument, or drew false inferences from it, both of which he subsequently refuted (1 Cor 15:35–37; Gal 2:17). In effect the diatribe furnished him with a method of creating dialogues between himself and imaginary interlocutors (Rom 3:27–4:2). The purpose of the diatribe was pedagogical more than polemical. Dialogue enhanced contact with the addressees and the exposition of error sought to deepen their commitment to the gospel. In keeping with the ancient rhetorical tradition, moreover, Paul was in command of an arsenal of fixed topics and popular maxims. The paraenetic section of Galatians (5:25–6:10), for example, is composed of diverse sayings; Galatians 4:12–20 constitutes a collection of maxims focused on the topic of friendship; Romans 12:9–21 contains another series of sayings loosely arranged around the topos of love. Typically, many of these maxims had parallels in Judaism, Hellenism, and Jewish-Hellenistic philosophy. They belonged to a common stock of ancient philosophical, rhetorical wisdom.

In Pauline studies a notable shift is taking place from epistolography to rhetoric (Wuellner 1976). It is based on the premise that the key to the apostle's writings does not lie in theories of literature but rather in theories of argumentation. Work on the rhetorical design of an entire Pauline letter, however, is still in its infancy. The most successful rhetorical interpretation of a Pauline letter has been Betz's commentary on Galatians (*Galatians* Hermeneia). On Betz's reading, Galatians conjures up the situation of a law court, with Paul functioning as the defendant, the addressees as jury, and Paul's opponents as the accusers.

E. Commonplace Tradition

The use of common stock materials was a recurrent feature outside the *corpus Paulinum* as well. The Letter of James, for example, carries clusters of sayings which were occasionally connected by catchwords, but more often lack a discernible connectedness (1:2–27; 3:13–4:12; 5:7–20). Some sayings in James bear a close resemblance to those in the Sermon on the Mount (1:22 = Matt 7:24–27; 5:12 = Matt 5:34–37). But whether or not they originated with Jesus, for James they were *loci communes* in that they belonged to a tradition common to all believers irrespective of individual authorship. The topic of the rules for the household enjoyed special popularity (Col 3:18–4:1; Eph 5:22–6:9; 1 Tim 2:8–15; 6:1–2; Titus 2:1–10; 1 Pet 2:13–3:7). Again, there was little that was specifically Christian in these rules. The ethos they displayed belonged to the common tradition shared by non-Christians and Christians alike.

F. Rhetoric of the NT

The oral tradition of the NT was a phenomenon comprised of a plurality of speech acts and diverse modes of proclamation. Ranging from saying to hymn, and from parable to doxology, it represented a rich world of sound and voices, of shared knowledge and intimacy, of loyalties and polemics, of remembering and participation. Once textualized, each item of proclamation, including its aesthetic, ideological ambience, was subject to revision. In different words, none of the twenty-seven texts was in its entirety the product of orality. The oral tradition of the NT exists only in forms embedded in and overridden by textuality.

A distinction must be made between the primary orality and literary rhetoric. The former entailed acts of speech at specific situations. It was not itself a text, although it could become textualized. At the point of textualization, primary orality was inevitably subject to the norms of the written medium. Literary rhetoric, on the other hand, described the stylistic and argumentative disposition of texts which shared basic objectives with oral proclamation. Not unlike primary orality, literary rhetoric developed strategies appealing to hearers, but owing to its textual identity it had to negotiate rapprochements with the chirographic technology. It may justly be assumed that all twenty-seven texts of the NT, not merely the Pauline letters, represent various degrees of literary rhetoric. The Apocalypse, for example, was constructed less according to a linear plot, but rather as a drama of recapitulation, allowing hearers through successive remembering to immerse themselves in a world of expanding symbols and images (Barr 1987). Even the Letter to the Hebrews, which is distinguished by a polished and educated style, defines itself as a "word of exhortation" (13:22: *logos tēs paraklēseōs*), a discourse designed to prove a case and to move hearers to take appropriate action. Reader-response criticism or reception theory, which has scarcely begun to be employed in biblical studies, is destined to make a crucial contribution to our understanding of the rhetorical nature of the NT texts.

Bibliography

Abel, E. L. 1971. The Psychology of Memory and Rumor Transmission and Their Bearing on Theories of Oral Transmission in Early Christianity. *JR* 51: 270–81.

Balogh, J. 1926. Voces Paginarum. *Philologus* 82: 84–109, 202–40.

Barr, D. L. 1987. The Dawn of a New Day: The Apocalypse of John. Pp. 266–96 in *New Testament Story.* Belmont, CA.

Beare, F. W. 1967. Sayings of the Risen Jesus in the Synoptic Tradition. Pp. 161–81 in *Christian History and Interpretation: Studies Presented to John Knox,* ed. W. R. Farmer; C. F. D. Moule; and R. R. Niebuhr. Cambridge.

Boring, M. E. 1982. *Sayings of the Risen Jesus.* New York.

Bultmann, R. 1910. *Der Stil der Paulinischen Predigt und die kynisch-stoische Diatribe.* Göttingen.

———. 1963. *The History of the Synoptic Tradition.* Trans. J. Marsh. 5th ed. New York.

Crossan, J. D. 1973. *In Parables: The Challenge of the Historical Jesus.* New York.

———. 1983. *In Fragments: The Aphorisms of Jesus.* San Francisco.

Dibelius, M. 1934. *From Tradition to Gospel.* Trans. B. L. Woolf. New York.

Ellis, E. E. 1975. New Directions in Form Criticism. Pp. 299–315 in *Jesus Christus in Historie und Geschichte: Neutestamentliche Fest-*

schrift für Hans Conzelmann zum 60. Geburtstag, ed. G. Strecker. Tübingen.
Farmer, W. R. 1964. *The Synoptic Problem: A Critical Analysis*. New York.
Gerhardsson, B. 1961. *Memory and Manuscript*. ASNU 22. Lund.
———. 1964. *Tradition and Transmission in Early Christianity*. Lund.
———. 1979. *The Origins of the Gospel Traditions*. Philadelphia.
———. 1986. *The Gospel Tradition*. ConBNT 15. Lund.
Hendrickson, G. L. 1929. Ancient Reading. *CJ* 25: 182–96.
Kelber, W. H. 1983. *The Oral and the Written Gospel*. Philadelphia.
Lord, A. B. 1960. *The Singer of Tales*. HSCL 24. Cambridge, MA.
———. 1978. The Gospels as Oral Traditional Literature. Pp. 33–91 in *The Relationships among the Gospels*, ed. W. O. Walker. San Antonio.
Ong, W. J. 1982. *Orality and Literacy*. New Accents Series. London.
Riesner, R. 1984. *Jesus als Lehrer*. WUNT 2/7. 2d ed. Tübingen.
Saenger, P. 1982. Silent Reading: Its Impact on Late Medieval Script and Society. *Viator* 13: 367–414.
Schmidt, K. L. 1919. *Der Rahmen der Geschichte Jesu: Literarkritische Untersuchungen zur Ältesten Jesusüberlieferung*. Berlin. Repr. 1964.
Stowers, S. K. 1981. *The Diatribe and Paul's Letter to the Romans*. SBLDS 57. Chico, CA.
Wuellner, W. 1976. Paul's Rhetoric of Argumentation. *CBQ* 38: 330–51.
———. 1979. Greek Rhetoric and Pauline Argumentation. Pp. 177–88 in *Early Christian Literature and the Classical Intellectual Tradition*, ed. W. R. Schoedel and R. L. Wilken. Paris.
———. 1986. Paul as Pastor: The Function of Rhetorical Questions in First Corinthians. Pp. 49–77 in *L'Apôtre Paul: Personalité, Style et Conception du Ministère*, ed. A. Vanhoye. BETL 73. Leuven.

WERNER H. KELBER

EARLY JUDAISM

According to rabbinic Judaism, "oral tradition" is the authoritative interpretation of the Written Law. Judaism understands the oral tradition to have been given by God to Moses on Sinai and therefore to be equal in authority and holiness to the Written Torah, represented by the Pentateuch.

A. The Concept of Oral Tradition
B. The Character and Antiquity of the Oral Tradition
C. Past Perspectives on the Oral Tradition

A. The Concept of Oral Tradition

Judaism maintains that God's revelation to Moses at Sinai, described in the book of Exodus, contained two distinct parts. One component was the Written Law, embodied in the text of the Pentateuch. This component was transmitted in writing and made accessible to all the people of Israel. The other part was the Oral Law. This aspect of the revelation was formulated for memorization and was transmitted orally by successive generations of sages. Judaism holds that God taught the oral tradition to Moses, who repeated it to Joshua. After Joshua, the chain of tradition lists "elders" and the biblical prophets. Ultimately, the oral materials passed into the hands of rabbinic authorities. To assure that this revelation would not be lost as a result of war, national strife, or other physical or intellectual calamity, beginning in the 2d century C.E., the rabbis codified the oral materials and preserved them in written form.

The first and principal document of the Oral Torah is the Mishnah, a Hebrew-language law code, edited in the land of Israel ca. 200 C.E., but containing statements attributed to rabbis who flourished over the preceding 200 years. Other rabbinic texts, including the Tosefta, Midrashic documents, and the Talmuds of the land of Israel and of Babylonia, are deemed also to embody the originally oral revelation. The Babylonian Talmud, completed in ca. 600 C.E., is the final document considered to be part of the oral tradition. The rabbinic theory of Oral Torah thus holds that statements and principles expressed by sages who lived over a period of close to 600 years preserve teachings that derive from God's original revelation to Moses at Sinai.

In this theory, the Written and Oral Torahs are part of a single, uniform revelation and are, accordingly, of equal authority and importance. When a 2d-century rabbi in the Mishnah or a 5th-century sage in the Midrash or Talmud responds to a discussion or question from his own day, his judgment does not comprise his own thinking and analysis. Rather, it is part and parcel of the divine revelation of Torah at Sinai. Even though the sage's comment is expressed in his own words and responds to a question or issue raised in his own day, it is understood to derive, in detail, from what God told Moses at the time of the original revelation (Neusner 1986: viii). The statement in every respect has the authority of divine revelation.

The first evidence for this concept of Oral Torah is found in Mishnah tractate *ʾAbot*, which dates to early in the 3d century C.E. It begins:

> Moses received Torah at Sinai and passed it on to Joshua, Joshua to elders, and elders to prophets. And prophets handed it on to the men of the great assembly . . .
> (trans. Neusner 1986: 47)

Use of the term "Torah," without the definite article, indicates that the passage does not speak of the Pentateuch, always referred to as "the" Torah. Further, the passage describes Torah's closed transmission to specific individuals and groups. This process does not pertain to the written Scriptures, which were made accessible to all Israelites. The passage thus describes Moses' receiving of a second component of revelation, referred to elsewhere in rabbinic literature as Oral Torah. Developing the theme introduced here, the remainder of the first chapter of *ʾAbot* describes the subsequent transmission of this Oral Torah through generations of Jewish leaders and ultimately to those same rabbis who are cited in the Mishnah.

The notion introduced in *ʾAbot*, of the closed transmission of an esoteric revelation, functions polemically within rabbinic Judaism. The claim to possess an otherwise unknown component of God's revelation legitimates rabbinic authority and promotes the Israelite people's acceptance of rabbinic leadership. The concept of Oral Torah claims that rabbinic leaders are direct successors to Moses, whom these authorities call "our Rabbi," thus designating him the first rabbinic sage. According to the notion of oral tradition, furthermore, only under rabbinic guidance can the Israelite people correctly observe God's will. The Written Torah, available to all of Israel, contains only half of God's revelation. Access to the written Scriptures alone does not provide the people with all the information needed to properly observe the law. Correct observance is possible only under the guidance of rabbinic authorities, who have the revealed key to understanding the written Scripture.

The concept of oral tradition described here is uniquely rabbinic. Other postbiblical Jewish writings know nothing comparable. This is evident, for instance, in Josephus' descriptions of the Pharisees, whom the later rabbis understand to be the direct recipients of the oral tradition. In his first book, *The Jewish War,* Josephus says nothing about the Pharisees' knowledge of inherited traditions. He states only that of the several Jewish philosophical schools, the Pharisees are "considered the more accurate interpreters of the laws" (*JW* 1.97, LCL). Josephus' later work, the *Antiquities,* reworks his earlier descriptions so as to encourage the Roman government to support the Pharisees as leaders of the Jewish people (Smith 1956: 81). To substantiate his case that the Pharisees are the nation's legitimate rulers, Josephus notes that they preserve and follow certain traditions developed in accordance with their distinctive philosophical doctrine:

> They follow the guidance of that which their doctrine has selected and transmitted as good, attaching the chief importance to the observance of those commandments which it has seen fit to dictate to them.
>
> (13.171, LCL)

It is one thing to say that a group preserves and follows some traditions received from past generations. That is what Josephus argues in the passage in *Antiquities.* The same general idea is found in Philo, who focuses upon the Jews' adherence to laws and traditions handed down from Moses, their lawgiver. It is quite another to claim, as the rabbis do, that *all* of the legal and exegetical dicta of a particular group have been passed down by tradition and derive, ultimately, from divine revelation. Outside of the rabbinic writings, such a notion is absent from Jewish discussions of oral tradition.

In sum, the notion of oral tradition legitimates all rabbinic statements about the meaning of Scripture and the content of revelation. Under the theory of Orah Torah, rabbinic interpretations have the authority of the word of God. At the same time, the concept of Oral Torah delegitimizes all interpretations that derive from outside of rabbinic circles. These are viewed as (simply) the work of fallible human intellect. By establishing the rabbis as the only authoritative source for correct practice and understanding of the divine word, the theory of Oral Torah promotes and justifies the rabbis' spiritual and political leadership over the Israelite people.

B. The Character and Antiquity of the Oral Tradition

The nature and content of the documents of rabbinic Judaism lead to conclusions quite different from those suggested by the notion of Oral Torah. What the rabbis conceive of as an oral tradition originating at Sinai takes the concrete form of arguments and discussions among rabbinic sages of the first centuries of the Common Era. The earliest of these discussions, found in the Mishnah, took place for the most part in the aftermath of the destruction of the temple in 70 C.E. and the failed Bar Kokhba revolt of 133–35 C.E. During this decisive period in Jewish history, rabbinic sages studied and interpreted Scripture, working out a program of ritual and legal practice that eventually would shape Judaism according to the rabbis' own ideals and aspirations. By the end of the Mishnaic period, the rabbis came to consider the results of their deliberations to be part of a divinely revealed oral tradition. From the principles, rules, and issues at play in the rabbinic documents, it is apparent, however, that this Oral Torah is substantially the product of the rabbis' own day and of their own distinctive attitudes and philosophies.

To illustrate this point, let us examine Mishnah tractate *Berakot* 1:1, a typical legal discussion:

A. From what time may they recite the Shema-prayer in the evening?
B. From the hour that the priests enter [their homes] to eat their heave offering,
C. "until the end of the first watch"—the words of Rabbi Eliezer.
D. But sages say, "Until midnight."
E. Rabban Gamaliel says, "Until the rise of dawn."
F. There was an incident: His [that is, Gamaliel's] sons returned from a banquet hall [after midnight].
G. They said to him, "We did not [yet] recite the Shema."
H. He said to them, "If the dawn has not yet risen, you are obligated to recite [the Shema].
I. "And [this applies] not only [in] this [case]. Rather, [as regards] all [commandments] which sages said [may be performed] 'Until midnight,' the obligation [to perform them persists] until the rise of dawn."
J. [For example] the offering of the fats and entrails—their obligation [persists] until the rise of dawn [see Lev 1:9, 3:3–5].
K. And all [sacrifices] which must be eaten within one day, the obligation [to eat them persists] until the rise of dawn.
L. If so why did sages [D] say [that these actions may be performed only] until midnight?
M. In order to protect man from sin.

Rabbinic sages discuss the time frame within which a certain obligatory prayer may be recited. As presented here, this issue clearly was live in the period of the discussion's named authorities, the early 2d century C.E. Since the matter is still under dispute, it appears hardly to represent the end product of a tradition of revealed law, intended by God to define exactly how the rules of the Written Torah are to be carried out. The Shema prayer itself is known only from the rabbinic literature. Accordingly, there is no reason to posit a long history of legislation concerning its recitation.

While Eliezer, B-C, suggests temple practice as the guide to the answer to A's question, neither he nor the other cited authorities argue or imply that these positions represent the way things always—or even recently—have been done. Quite to the contrary, L-M explains that the opinion of sages (that is, anonymous rabbinic authorities), D, is not meant to represent the true law at all. These unnamed authorities give an early time—midnight—for completion of the requirement in order to prevent people from becoming lax and failing to fulfill their obligation. So here matters are explicit: the sages do not simply repeat what they know to be a revealed law, passed on through tradition. Rather, they intentionally refrain from indicating the correct parameters for proper practice, preferring, instead, to give their own reasoned opinion as to what the people should be told.

The form and concerns of this passage suggest that the rabbinic literature records discussions and opinions from the time of the rabbis themselves. This impression is supported by recent analyses of the content of the discussions found in the Mishnah as a whole. The consensus of this scholarship is that the ideals and principles that inform the Mishnah's rules are the creations of those same rabbis cited in that document. These rabbis, that is to say, report their own opinions and disputes on a variety of topics. They do not simply repeat, in their own names, laws that they inherited.

This point is illustrated by reference to the Mishnaic division of Agriculture, which contains the rabbinic treatment of Scripture's laws for tithing and maintenance of the holy land, e.g., observance of the prohibitions against planting mixed kinds and tilling the land during the Sabbatical Year. Observance of these restrictions would have been of central concern to the Israelite people from antiquity all the way through Second Temple times. Meticulous observance of the tithing laws also is generally considered one central characteristic of the Pharisaic movement. If the Mishnah preserves an ancient oral tradition at all, we should likely find substantial traces of it here.

This, however, is not the case. Like the rest of the Mishnah, the vast majority of the division of Agriculture is attributed to authorities who lived in the period after the destruction of the temple in 70 C.E., and, to an even greater extent, after the Bar Kokhba revolt of 133–35 C.E. (Avery-Peck 1985: 359–61). It is from this later period that most of the division's attributed laws and all of its anonymous materials appear to derive. Further, the smattering of facts and ideas attributed to authorities from the period before 70 does not present a coherent interpretation of the character or meaning of the agricultural law. Nor are these facts sufficient to allow practical implementation of Scripture's tithing restrictions. In all, then, it is clear that traditions of agricultural practice that might have existed in or prior to rabbinic times simply are not preserved in the rabbinic literature.

It is noteworthy, too, that the few extant details of agricultural practice attributed to authorities who lived during the Second Temple period do not provide the starting point for the later rabbinic deliberations. Within the division of Agriculture, that is, the rabbis followed their own interests. Their legal deliberations exhibit no significant dependence upon a knowledge of practices that might already have existed. These deliberations follow a path that is distinct even from the concerns introduced by the earliest cited rabbinic masters. The few extant details from this early period, that is, offer no clue to the character of the system of Mishnaic law as it develops in the later rabbinic academies. This suggests that both the topical interests of and the program of inquiry followed by the rabbis were their own, developed independently of any inherited body of law and interpretation.

This is not to suggest that traditions of agricultural and other practices were not known in the first centuries. From a variety of historical sources it is clear that from the time of Scripture itself, Jews did tithe and observe the other laws introduced in Scripture. Further, the Mishnah does assume a number of details not available in Scripture. These include the identification of the distinctive set of agricultural gifts discussed by the Mishnah's authorities. Accordingly, it is clear that at some point prior to the inception of the discussion later recorded in the Mishnah, unidentified individuals carefully read Scripture and delineated a set of agricultural tithes.

In light of this fact, the point must be clearly stated. It is not that traditions regarding ritual practice and the meaning of Scripture did not in all probability exist in late antiquity. The point, rather, is that so far as the literary evidence indicates, the rabbis did not take up and preserve any such traditions, using them as significant components of their own legislation. Rather than a compendium of prior oral traditions, the Mishnah and other rabbinic writings, as they have come down to us, are the independent intellectual and literary creations of rabbinic circles. These documents do not preserve an ancient tradition of law, but rather develop themes and ideas suggested by Scripture and worked out by the rabbis themselves.

This is not to deny that the sages did, at points, use facts, such as the definitions of the agricultural offerings, which antedate the discussions recorded in the Mishnah. But the historical provenance of these facts cannot be determined. Even in their case, therefore, it is impossible to speak with confidence about an ancient oral tradition, let alone about one going back to Sinai. Moreover, the way in which the rabbis took over such facts, incorporating them within their own systematic legal and theological discussions, means that the meaning and significance they might have had within a prior context cannot be recovered. In the division of Agriculture, like the rest of the Mishnah, accordingly, rabbinic authorities preserved little of any inherited corpus of laws and interpretations. The content and character of rabbinic law, rather, is worked out fully within the Mishnah itself, by the authorities cited there.

C. Past Perspectives on the Oral Tradition

The evidence of the Mishnah and other rabbinic literature does not disprove the existence within early Judaism of an oral tradition extending back into history. This evidence only shows that even if the rabbis knew such a tradition, they did not embody it within their own legal dicta and scriptural interpretations. As a result, what rabbinic Judaism calls Oral Torah in fact is the creation of the sages who flourished in the 1st through 6th centuries C.E.

An earlier generation of scholars of Judaism, however, failed to make this important distinction between the system of law and exegesis that the rabbis created and transmitted under the heading Oral Torah, on the one hand, and ancient traditions of practice and interpretation that theoretically existed, but for which we have no extant literary evidence, on the other. Instead these scholars largely accepted the rabbinic version of matters. They attempted, therefore, to conceive of how an oral tradition, beginning at or close to the time of Sinai, could have existed and developed so as ultimately to be codified and preserved in the rabbinic texts.

In light of this perspective, scholars argued that the very nature of the Written Torah necessitates the existence of an oral tradition. This view is described in detail by M. D. Herr (*EncJud* 12: cols. 1439–40):

> [I]t is clear that there can be no real existence for the Written Law without the Oral. The need for the positing of the existence of the Oral Law is inherent in the very character and nature of the Torah. The statutes of the Written Law could not have been fulfilled literally even in the generation in which they were given, since "that which is plain in the Torah is obscure, all the more that which is obscure" (Judah Halevi, *Kuzari,* 3, 35) . . .
>
> If, therefore, the statutes of the Torah could not be properly understood in the generation in which it was given, how much less could it be understood by later generations? In addition to this consideration, it was a fundamental doctrine of the rabbis that the Torah was given by God for all time, that it would never be exchanged for another Torah and certainly never rescinded, and that it provided for all possible circumstances which might arise at any time in the future . . . It can thus be regarded as a historical fact that the Oral Law existed not merely from the moment the Written Law was given (and in this sense it is correct to say that the Written and Oral Laws were given together to Moses at Sinai), but it may even be maintained that the Oral Law anticipated the Written Law, as the Written Law not only assumed the observance of the Oral Law in the future, but is in effect based on its previous existence. Since the written law relies—by allusion or by its silence—on statues, customs, and basic laws not explicitly mentioned in it (marriage, divorce, business . . .), these statutes are ipso facto converted into part of the Oral Law.

Herr continues by describing the continuous existence and development of the Oral Law throughout Jewish history, tracing it in the books of the Bible, the Jewish literature of the Second Temple period, the early Targums, and the rabbinic literature.

This approach, much like that of the rabbis themselves, sees the transmission of law and theology within Judaism as the result of a unitary and linear process, beginning with Scripture and continuing through all later developments within (Orthodox) Judaism. While Herr stops short of making claims concerning the divine origin of the oral tradition, his view still makes an important theological point. It argues that the corpus of law and interpretation embodied within rabbinic Judaism is authentic, having existed at least from the moment (if not before) the Written Law was given and having been accurately preserved and transmitted through the generations.

The problem, as we have seen, is not with the claim for the existence, throughout Jewish history, of traditions external to the Written Law. Certainly, in each period within Jewish history, cultural, legal, and ritual practice was determined not only by scriptural statements but, additionally, by interpretations of the meaning and import of those statements. The problem, rather, is how to conceive of and describe these traditions. Until recently, scholars understood them to comprise a monolithic corpus, rightly designated "the" oral tradition and correctly understood as being embodied in the rabbinic writings. This perspective failed to recognize the difference between any traditions that did in fact exist, on the one hand, and the intellectual and literary processes that gave way to the documents of rabbinic Judaism, on the other. As recent study of those documents has made clear, they are the products of the authorities cited in them and are not the end product of a long history of transmission of originally oral laws and interpretations.

In the minds of the rabbis, the oral tradition of Sinai took shape in the Mishnah and in the successive documents of rabbinic Judaism (Neusner 1986: viii). But this rabbinic notion of Oral Torah cannot be equated in any concrete sense with a corpus of laws and interpretations that actually existed throughout Israelite history. Clearly, Jews in different historical periods and places observed Scripture's dicta according to interpretations of the biblical text, some of which may have been transmitted from generation to generation. But there is no evidence that such traditions ever comprised a unitary tradition stretching back to Sinai. Even if such an oral tradition existed, the clear evidence of the rabbinic writings indicates that these texts do not embody it. They are, rather, the products of their authors, who pursued their own independent program in order to create a system of practice and belief that would take Judaism from their day to our own.

Bibliography

Avery-Peck, A. J. 1985. *Mishnah's Division of Agriculture: The History and Theology of Seder Zeraim.* Chico, CA.

Neusner, J. 1986. *The Oral Torah.* San Francisco.

Smith, M. 1956. Palestinian Judaism in the First Centuries. Pp. 75–76 in *Israel: Its Role in Civilization,* ed. M. Davis. New York.

ALAN J. AVERY-PECK

ORATORY. See RHETORIC AND RHETORICAL CRITICISM.

ORDAIN, ORDINATION. Appointment to formal functions in a religious community. Greeks and Romans knew a variety of modes of selection and installation to public office, and some of these influenced the later developments in the Church. Greek society commonly filled magistracies and priesthoods by election, by taking lots, or by a combination of the two methods. *Cheirotonia* was voting by a show of hands. Entrance into office involved the candidate undergoing a formal scrutiny of his qualifications, taking an oath, and bringing entrance sacrifices.

The Roman Republic chose magistrates by an election by the voting units of the assembly. Existing magistrates had great influence in determining the outcome and had the right to designate lesser magistrates. Colleges of Roman priests filled vacancies by co-optation. Offices were formally assumed by taking the auspices to determine divine favor and formally beginning to exercise the functions. The oath held a prominent place. Under the empire the imperial designation eclipsed other methods of selection.

The divine choice was determinative for positions of leadership in Israel. This may be seen in the hereditary principle governing the levitical priesthood (Numbers 3) and God's choice of kings, made known through prophets (1 Sam 9:16; 16:1; 1 Kgs 11:30–38). Out of the elaborate ceremony of consecration to the priesthood (Exodus 19; Leviticus 8), the anointing with olive oil was understood as the crucial element. The oil was sprinkled on all the priests, but it was poured on the head of the high priest (Lev 21:10), so that the term "anointed priest" referred to the high priest. Anointing with oil was likewise crucial in the appointment of kings (1 Sam 10:1; 16:13–14; 1 Kgs 19:16). Exodus 29 and Leviticus 8 use words from the root *ml*ʾ ("to fill") in reference to the installation of a priest. The full expression seems to have been "to fill the hand" (Judg 17:5, 12), but with what is not clear—portions of the sacrificial animal (Lev 8:27) or divining stones (Lev 8:8) are the most likely interpretations. In most OT passages the sense is "appoint" without reference to the original denotation. The OT accounts of consecration of priests did not influence early Christian practice of ordination.

Accounts of two special appointments became important in the later Jewish and Christian practices. In the account of the consecration of the Levites in Num 8:5–13 the people of Israel were instructed to "lay their hands upon the Levites" (v 10). This action perhaps expressed the idea that the Levites were a sacrificial offering or, more precisely, a substitute for the firstborn of the nation (vv 17–18). When Moses appointed Joshua to succeed to the leadership of Israel in Num 27:15–23, he laid his hands on him, so investing him with authority, and commissioned him. Although Num 27:18 says Joshua was chosen because the spirit was in him, Deut 34:9 seems to say that Joshua was full of the spirit of wisdom because "Moses had laid his hands on him." On the other hand, the text may be understood as saying that Moses' laying on of hands was evidence for and not the cause of the spirit of wisdom in Joshua.

By Herodian times, if not earlier, investiture with the garments of the high priesthood and not chrismation was constitutive in the making of the high priest (Josephus *Ant.* 20.6–14; *m. Hor.* 3:4; *b. Yoma* 12a–b).

Admission to the Sanhedrin was obtained by a formal seating in the chair of teaching and judging (*Assum. Mos.* 12.2; *Sipre* Num 27:18, 20). The Mishnah, therefore, may reflect pre-70 conditions in its description:

> The Sanhedrin was arranged like the half of a round threshing-floor so that they all might see one another. Before them stood the two scribes of the judges . . .
>
> Before them sat three rows of disciples of the Sages, and each knew his proper place. If they needed to appoint another as judge, they appointed him from the first row, and one from the second row came into the first row, and one from the third row came into the second; and they chose yet another from the congregation and set him in the third row. He did not sit in the place of the former, but he sat in the place that was proper for him . . .
>
> (*m. Sanh.* 4:3)

The same procedure apparently was employed for the lesser Sanhedrins of 23 in places away from Jerusalem (*b. Sanh.* 17b). A similar concern with being seated in one's proper place may be observed in the Qumran community (1QS 5.23–24; 6.8–13).

Ordination of individual rabbis is first attested for Johanan b. Zakkai after 70:

> Originally, every one [i.e. every teacher] ordained his own pupils, thus R. Johanan b. Zakkai ordained R. Eliezer and R. Joshua; R. Joshua ordained R. Akiba; R. Akiba ordained R. Meir and R. Simeon. They were anxious to honor this house [the house of the Nasi] and declared that if the Beth Din ordained without the approval of the Nasi the ordination was not valid, but if a Nasi ordained without the knowledge of the Beth Din the Semikah was valid; then again they made a regulation that ordination should be performed with the mutual approval of the Beth Din and the Nasi.
>
> (*j. Sanh.* 1, 19a, 43)

Private ordination of a student by his rabbi belongs to the troubled period between 70 and 135. The limitation to the Nasi presumably occurred after 135, and the requirement of mutual consent in the 3d century. Rabbinic ordination employed the imposition of hands, but not prayer, and developed its technical terminology from the Hebrew word *sāmak* ("to lean upon"). It granted an equal status and had a legal significance in that it conferred juridical functions.

Christian ordination did not derive directly from rabbinic ordination; rather, both practices were independent developments from the Jewish heritage.

The Qumran community was hierarchically organized with a priestly dominance. Nonetheless, the voice of the "many" was heard in the selection of leaders. The whole congregation appears to have made the choice of the ten judges (CD 10.4–6), and the phrase *yṣ*ʾ *hgwrl* ("the lot shall go out") was used figuratively for all decisions in which the whole assembly had a part, including the selection of leaders by the members (1QSa 1.13–17).

The divine initiative in the selection of leaders is manifested in Jesus' selection of the Twelve and in Paul's words about spirit-inspired ministers given to the Church. A selection of an inner circle of twelve disciples by Jesus is firmly embedded in the synoptic tradition (Matt 10:1–4; Mark 3:13–19; Luke 6:12–16). No special act accompanied their choice, although a later apocryphal tradition supplies an imposition of hands (*Acts Pet.* 10).

Paul often mentions gifts and functions bestowed on the Church by God (Rom 12:6–8; 1 Cor 12:28–30; cf. Eph 4:11); but these cannot be identified with offices in the Church, nor does Paul give any indication how these inspired functionaries might be recognized or set apart: presumably their charisma was self-evident and its own authorization. Paul does refer to churches' choosing messengers to carry their contribution to the Judean Christians (2 Cor 8:19), using the word *cheirotonein.* During Hellenistic times this word had come to mean "elect," in whatever way, or even "select" or "appoint." Philo and Josephus attest a religious usage of *cheirotonein* in Hellenistic Judaism in reference to the appointments of God, including his selection of leaders for his people (Philo *Quod Det* 39; Josephus *Ant.* 4 §34, 54, 66).

Acts and the Pastoral Epistles give evidence of more developed practices which later provided the precedents for the ceremony of Christian ordination.

The selection of Matthias to replace Judas (Acts 1:23–26, according to the best supported text) employed a procedure without parallel in the early history of the Church—the taking of lots, which preserved the idea of the Lord himself choosing his apostles. The prayer, particularly the designation of God as the "knower of hearts," found echoes in later ordination liturgies.

Acts 6:1–6, the most complete account of the selection and setting apart of Church functionaries in the NT, was one of the most influential texts. There are numerous verbal parallels with the Greek version of Num 27:15–23, as well as a common sequence: a command to select someone meeting definite qualifications to be appointed for a responsibility, who is then publicly presented to receive the laying on of hands. The roles, however, are in a measure reversed: the disciples take the place of God and Moses in making the selection (cf. Acts 15:22 for the whole Church choosing representatives), and the apostles take the place of Israel as witnesses before whom the appointees are formally presented to receive a public commissioning. Luke's linking of the first step in developing an organization for the Church with the first transmission of authority in Israel (an event which also served as the pattern for rabbinic ordination) was a bold claim that Christians were the true heirs of the biblical traditions.

Acts 13:1–3 refers to a choice by the Holy Spirit speaking through prophets, and based on this choice a human commissioning by fasting, prayer, and laying on of hands. The account has allusions to Numbers 8. The laying on of hands did not impart the Holy Spirit to Paul and Barnabas, but, as in Numbers 8, ratified the divine choice and set apart representatives who were offered to the Lord for his service. The significance of the event is made clear by Acts 14:26.

The linking of the laying on of hands with prayer points to the practice of bestowing a blessing in this manner (Gen 48:14, *šit*) as the primary origin of Christian usage. Jesus used this gesture in blessing (Mark 10:13–16); the varying usages of the act in early Christianity (healing, bestowing the Holy Spirit, reconciling penitents, exorcism) had in common the bestowal of a blessing; and the Church Fathers interpreted the act in terms of a benediction (Jerome *In Isa.* 16.58; John Chrysostom *hom. 14 in Ac.; Vita Polycarpi* 11).

The centrality of prayer emerges in the more summary account in Acts 14:23 of the appointment of elders in the churches. The chief problem of this text is the meaning of *cheirotonein.* Does it keep the Hellenistic meaning of "elect" or "select," so that Paul and Barnabas made the choice (cf. the meaning in *Did.* 15 and Ign., *Philad.* 10; *Smyrn.* 11; *Polyc.* 7 for congregational election)? Or is the word used in the sense of "appoint" or "install," and so looks in the direction of the later ecclesiastical meaning of "ordination" (for an appointment with the idea of commission, see Justin, *Dial.* 108)?

A set of passages which belong together—1 Tim 1:18; 4:14; and 2 Tim 1:6—provides a parallel to Acts 13:1–3. Prophecies pointed out Timothy, according to 1 Tim 1:18; in view of this verse, *dia prophēteias* in 4:14 should be taken as accusative and translated "on account of prophecies" (if "prophecy" is genitive, then the reference may be to prayer as the means of imparting the gift). Similarly, Acts 20:28 speaks of bishops made by the Holy Spirit, i.e. designated by spirit-inspired prophecies. The college of presbyters laid hands on Timothy (this was not laying on of hands to make him one of the presbyters, who are throughout distinct from Timothy). If the prepositions may be pressed, Timothy received the charisma "through" *(dia)* the laying on of Paul's hands (2 Tim 1:6) but "with" (*meta* as an accompanying circumstance) the laying on of the hands of the elders (1 Tim 4:14).

The *Apostolic Tradition* of Hippolytus from the beginning of the 3d century provides the first complete description of an ordination ceremony. Some of its features reflect widely representative practices: the congregation chose or approved the bishop; *cheirotonia* meant "ordination" (if the restoration of the text is correct); the right to confer ordination was limited to a bishop, although presbyters shared in the ceremony; the ordination was by the laying on of hands and a prayer for the bestowal of the Holy Spirit; the newly ordained bishop proceeded immediately to the celebration of the eucharist; and lesser clergy (appointed by the bishop) were named or received the symbol of their office.

Christian ordination put its emphasis on the divine choice of ministers for the Church, a choice mediated by prophetic utterance or by selection by the people. God bestowed with his call his blessing, mediated by prayer, which was reinforced by fasting and the laying on of hands. Although the central element of ordination was the benediction, there were the accompanying themes of commissioning or authorization and the ratification or creation of representatives for service to God.

Bibliography

Bârlea, O. 1969. *Die Weihe der Bischöfe, Presbyter, und Diakone in vornicänischer Zeit.* Munich.

Daube, D. 1956. *The New Testament and Rabbinic Judaism.* London.

Ehrhardt, A. 1954. Jewish and Christian Ordination. *JEH* 5: 125–38.

Ferguson, E. 1959. Ordination in the Ancient Church. Ph.D. diss. Harvard.

———. 1963. Jewish and Christian Ordination. *HTR* 56: 13–19.

———. 1974. Selection and Installation to Office in Roman, Greek, Jewish, and Christian Antiquity. *TZ* 30: 273–84.

———. 1975. Laying on of Hands: Its Significance in Ordination. *JTS* n.s. 26: 1–12.

Kilmartin, E. J. 1979. Ministry and Ordination in Early Christianity against a Jewish Background. *StLtg* 13: 42–69.

Kretschmar, G. 1975. Die Ordination im frühen Christentum. *FZPT* 22: 35–69.

Lohse, E. 1951. *Die Ordination im Spätjudentum und im Neuen Testament.* Göttingen.

Newman, J. 1950. *Semikhah.* Manchester.

Parratt, J. K. 1969. The Laying on of Hands in the New Testament:

A Re-examination in the Light of the Hebrew Terminology. *ExpTim* 80: 210–14.
Richter, K. 1974. Ansätze für die Entwicklung einer Weiheliturgie in apostolischer Zeit. *Archiv für Liturgiewissenschaft* 16: 32–52.
Siotis, M. A. 1949–50. Die Klassische und die Christliche Cheirotonie in ihrem Verhältnis. *Theologia* 20–22 (Greek).
Workentin, M. 1982. *Ordination: A Biblical-Historical View.* Grand Rapids.

EVERETT FERGUSON

ORDEAL. Like most of their contemporaries, the ancient Israelites were familiar with ordeal procedures. The conceptual basis for this judicial practice was the belief that God possessed a knowledge surpassing that of humans. A crime might have been committed without a soul in sight, but the Lord had been a witness. "The eyes of the Lord are in every place, keeping watch on the evil and the good," says Prov 15:3 (cf. Zech 4:10; 2 Chr 16:9). The Lord "tries the kidneys and the heart" of men (Jer 11:20; 17:10; 20:12; Ps 7:10—Eng v 9; 26:21, and from his investigation there is no escaping (Ps 139:1–12). In this respect, the Lord had assumed functions attributed elsewhere in the ANE to solar deities, like the Mesopotamian Shamash. Just as nothing remains hidden before the penetrating sunlight (Ps 19:7—Eng v 6), no sin remains hidden before the scrutinizing face of the Lord (Ps 19:13—Eng v 12). Should a judicial inquest prove inconclusive, an appeal to God for a verdict from on high was bound to clear things up.

The ordeal is not the only means by which humans could involve the supernatural in a legal case. It has close affinities with divination and oath, both of which could also be resorted to in cases where the court was unable to reach a verdict. In order to avoid confusion, one must try to distinguish between the three procedures. Generally speaking, divination is primarily used in the early stages of the legal process, as a preliminary procedure. It can be resorted to as a means of justifying bringing a charge against an individual. Ordeals, on the other hand, may be invoked to determine whether the accused is in fact guilty or not. Also, the ordeal involves the suspect in a far more direct manner than divination. In the ordeal, the accused is subjected to a physical test, the outcome of which decides his guilt or innocence. Such a test is also one of the elements in which the ordeal differs from the oath. In its simplest form, the oath consists of a solemn statement by which the juror refers his case to the heavenly court. It is fundamentally a transfer of jurisdiction. The divine agent invoked is expected to render a verdict by implementing the appropriate sanction. In the ordeal, verdict and punishment usually make up two separate phases. Once the deity has manifested his verdict in the ordeal, the human judges decide the measures to be taken in consequence.

In practice, however, these distinctions are often blurred, making it sometimes difficult to decide whether a given procedure is actually an oath, an ordeal, or a species of divination. A case in point is the treatment of the wife whom her husband suspects of adultery, dealt with in Num 5:1–31. Although the relevant passage probably belongs to the postexilic strata of the Pentateuch, it incorporates material that savors of great antiquity. In two originally separate literary strands, one and the same procedure is described. In summary, this is what the text says. Since legal proof is lacking, the suspected wife, possibly pregnant, is to be taken to the sanctuary where, among other things, her husband presents a "remembrance offering, a reminder of iniquity" (Num 5:15). The priest then sets the wife "before the LORD" and makes her take an oath. Thereupon she is given a powerful potion to drink, a mixture of "holy water" and dust from the temple floor, into which conditional curses, written in ink and erased in the liquid, have materially passed. In case of guilt, the water will turn out to be "bitter" and make the woman's body swell and her thigh fall away. Apparently, the sexual organs of the wife will be affected. If she is innocent, nothing will happen to the woman, who will then have no difficulty conceiving children.

In studies on Israelite jurisprudence, the case of the *sôṭâ*, "the errant woman" as the suspected wife is referred to in the Mishna, is often cited as a crown witness of trial by ordeal. In the strictest sense of the term, however, this can hardly be called an ordeal. Verdict and sanction coalesce, and the matter does not belong to the competence of the human judge. Perhaps we should speak here of a dramatized oath. As a rule, the oath is exacted from the accused on the assumption that God will curse the perjurer. In the case of Num 5:11–31 the penalty is specified beforehand. Through the consumption of the "bitter water that brings the curse" (Num 5:24), the sanction has been ritually anchored in the woman's body, ready to be activated when circumstances trigger it. Once the ceremony is over, the wife is left to her fate. No human jury intervenes to decide about the appropriate punitive measures. Also the delay in which the curse will go into effect is left vague; it may be a matter of hours, days, weeks, or months.

The procedure followed for the *sôṭâ* falls into the category of drinking trials. The latter have in common that the guilt of the suspect is established, and in some cases penalized, by his reaction to a special potion which he is made to drink. When one searches the OT for traces of this practice, one discovers that apart from Num 5:11–31, there are only indirect allusions. Yet these are clear enough to warrant at least a twofold distinction, based on the nature of the potion that is used. Sometimes the suspect is given water to drink; at other times it is wine. Setting aside Num 5:11–31, a drinking trial by means of water is alluded to twice. According to Exod 32:20, Moses made the Israelites drink water mixed with the powder of the ground "golden calf." Presumably, those guilty of idolatry would not prove impervious to this noxious mixture. The sober description is reminiscent of trial by ordeal and was interpreted as such in *b. ʿAbod. Zar.* 44a. Exod 15:22–26 can also be connected with the drinking trials, if the "bitter water" (Exod 15:23) of Marah was indeed used by the Lord to "try" his people.

The use of water in drinking trials was by no means restricted to the soil of Palestine. T. Frymer-Kensky (1977) found evidence for it in Susa texts, and could also point to a Hittite parallel. J. M. Sasson (1972) drew attention to a similar practice in Mari. There are also a few Neo-Assyrian texts which bear on the theme. They show that a promissory oath (as contrasted with the purgatory oath) could be accompanied by "drinking water from a *ṣarṣaru*-jar." In the same vein, the series *Šurpu* speaks of a "curse" *(māmītu)* incurred "by drinking water from a *ṣarṣaru*-jar" (III 62). Presumably, this water became harmful when the oaths were false. Thus, the taking of an oath was coupled with an act that linked it to threats of punishment in case of noncompliance. In other words, the perjurer was exposed to an imminent curse which would "enter his inwards like water," as Ps 109:18 puts it. There is no need to assume that some sort of poison was added to the water, since in the ANE the water itself was often rather unhealthy. Thus, a Babylonian extispicy text pictures the situation of an army overcome by thirst during a campaign. "They will drink bad water," goes the prediction, "and they will die." Similarly, the water around Jericho is purported to have caused death and miscarriages until the actions of Elisha made it wholesome (2 Kgs 2:19–22). Under such circumstances, water that had neither been filtered nor boiled could very well serve as a judgment drink.

Most of the OT allusions to drinking trials, however, seem to envisage the use of wine. The relevant texts are often referred to as the "cup of wrath" passages (Isa 51:17–23; Jer 25:15–29; 49:12; 51:7, 39; Ezek 23:31–34; Obadiah 16; Hab 2:15–16; Zech 12:2; Pss 60:5—Eng v 3; 75:9; Lam 4:21). They conjure up the image of an "anti-banquet" (W. McKane 1980), during which the Lord provides his guests with poisonous food and drink instead of wholesome dishes and wine that cheers the heart. A special emphasis falls on the "cup" *(kôs)* or "chalice" *(qubbaᶜat)* (Mayer *TWAT* 4: 107–11). It apparently contains wine (Jer 25:15; Ps 75:9), but this is "wine of poison" (Jer 25:15), according to the primary meaning of *ḥēmâ*, "venom, poison" (cf. Ug *ḥmt* and Akk *imtu*). Hab 2:15 indicates that poison could be purposefully added to the wine, partly at least in view of heightening the narcotic qualities of the beverage. The effect of the wine was expected to be twofold: it would bring about intoxication and drunkenness, making the drinkers totter and stagger, and would eventually lead to their destruction (Jer 25:27; 51:39). The ingestion of the potion resulted in the eliciting of a verdict, a proof of guilt, and the imposition of a penalty.

Although the imagery of the "cup of wrath" passages was inspired by ordeal procedures, the biblical authors detached it from its judicial context to serve as a literary motif in descriptions of God's judgment. The connection between the cup of judgment and the ordeal is still present, however, in some of the individual laments in the Psalter. In 1928, H. Schmidt published a monograph in which he argued that various psalms were purgatory prayers, spoken by suspects in the context of sacral jurisdiction (Psalms 3; 4; 5; 7; 17; 26; 27; 31:2–9—Eng vv 1–8; 57; 139; 142; cf. Pss 11; 13; 55:2–20—Eng vv 1–19; 56; 59; 94:16–23; 109; 140; Beyerlin 1970 added Pss 23; 63). Even though Schmidt has perhaps included too many psalms in his newly defined *Gattung*, the thrust of his argument appears to be valid. Several psalms do indeed hint at a nightly ordeal, to be followed by an acquittal in the morning (Ps 17:3, 15; cf. Pss 3:6—Eng v 5; 139:18). Because these prayers have come down to us without a description of the accompanying rituals, the nature of the ordeal must be pieced together from the oblique allusions occurring in the pertinent complaints. The recurrent reference to a "cup" *(kôs)* suggests that it was a drinking trial (Pss 11:6; 16:5; 23:5; cf. 116:13). The expected effect of this cup was dual: judgment upon the wicked, salvation for the righteous. Ps 11:6 says that the wicked will have "a scorching wind" *(rûaḥ zilᶜāpôt)* as "the portion of their cup" *(mĕnāt kôsām)*, whereas in Ps 23:5, the cup, said to be overflowing *(rĕwayâ;* Vg. *calix meus inebrians*), is drunk in a festive mood. Guilt or innocence determined one's attitude toward this cup: either fearful apprehension or joyful anticipation. Also the description of God's judgment in Ps 17:14 suggests that it materialized in the effects of a drinking trial.

The hypothesis of a drinking trial as the institutional background of the "Psalms of the Accused" makes sense when it is set in the broader context of the sacral repast. In the ANE, oath ceremonies were frequently connected with the celebration of a sacrificial meal. Pacts were concluded over a solemn banquet (Gen 31:53–54; Exod 24:11); according to a letter from the Mari archives, the partners "ate from the same platter, drank from the same goblet, and anointed themselves (or each other) with oil" (ARM VIII 13 rev. 11′–14′). The effect of the various actions—eating, drinking, being anointed—was twofold: it signified the mutual bond as well as the danger of disloyalty. In case the oath was taken in a callous way, the food would turn into a source of illness, and the water and the oil which had penetrated the body would prove to be the bearers of a curse (Ps 109:18). Traces of the belief that under certain conditions, normally harmless food could have detrimental effects are also contained in the Talmud. Significantly, the second cup drunk during a meal is called the "cup of retribution" *(kôs šel pûrᶜānût, b. Ber.* 51b), a designation used by the *Tg. Jon.*, Ezek 23:32 for the "cup of wrath." Paul's interpretation of the Lord's Supper seems to be indebted to similar conceptions. He says that "anyone who eats and drinks in an unworthy manner eats and drinks judgment upon himself," a judgment consisting of weakness, illness, and possibly death (1 Cor 11:27–30). The drinking trials alluded to in the Psalms and the various "cup of wrath" passages pertain to the same conceptual sphere. Through the consumption of a consecrated substance the faith of the juror was put to the test.

The instances of ordeal considered until now were all closely connected with the oath. A similar connection gleams through in Exod 22:7–10—Eng vv 8–11. When one Israelite has a grudge against another, suspecting him of the embezzlement of his property, "the case of those two shall come to the gods *(ᶜad-hāʾelōhîm);* the one whom the gods declare guilty shall restitute in double to his neighbor" (Exod 22:8—Eng v 9). Once the litigants had committed themselves by oath (Exod 22:10—Eng v 11), the deities—the term was later interpreted as "judges"—were to manifest their verdict. This is probably the clearest instance of an ordeal to be found in the OT, even though the actual procedure remains in the dark. The drinking trials discussed above implied a transfer of jurisdiction. In Exod 22:7–10, the sentence is determined by the human agents. The gods are asked to indicate the verdict, but the appropriate sanction is for the court to take.

A most unusual type of ordeal, bordering on divination, is to be found in Num 17:16–26—Eng vv 1–11. It is the story of Aaron's rod, miraculously transformed overnight. In its present form the passage looks like a piece of propaganda for the Levites. The episode relates how a dispute over sacrificial rights was settled by means of an ordeal. Twelve rods, each inscribed with the name of one of Israel's clans, were deposited in the "tent of meeting." On inspection the following morning only the rod of Aaron had sprouted, the sign agreed upon beforehand as indicating God's election. As far as we can see, this way of eliciting a divine verdict is unique and it hardly reflects actual custom. The etiological nature of the story is evident: the author may well have based his account on the presence in the sanctuary of a staff, a relic purportedly harking back to the time of Aaron (cf., perhaps, Jer 1:11). The described procedure, probably fictitious, stands between ordeal and divination.

Finally, the OT contains a literary reflection of ordeal by fire. The story of Daniel and his comrades in the fiery furnace (Daniel 3), legendary in nature, shows familiarity with the Persian trial by fire. The latter consisted of a passage through flames; it was introduced in Babylonia under the reign of the Achaemenids. Since the experiences of Daniel are set in a Babylonian milieu, the author probably used the Persian fire ordeal as a model. Rabbinical sources contain a similar account, also set in Babylonia, in which Abraham figures. This story of "Abraham in the Fiery Furnace," of which Pseudo-Philo offers an extended version (*L.A.B.* 6.15–18), is found in *Gen. Rab.* 38:13. In Israel itself, though, ordeal by fire was never practiced.

Judging by the biblical sources, the only type of ordeal to enjoy some popularity was the drinking trial. It should be kept in mind, however, that the latter was always preceded by an oath. The ordeal, taken in the broad sense of the term, served as an immediate test to verify the reliability of the oath-taker's witness. In many cases, the ordeal may not even have been necessary. Fear of God's curse was such that the prospect of the ordeal may have sufficed to scare feigned innocents into confessing.

Bibliography

Beyerlin, W. 1970. *Die Rettung der Bedrangten in den Feindpsalmen der Einrelnen auf institutionelle Zusammenhange untersucht.* FRLANT 99. Göttingen.

Frymer-Kensky, T. S. 1977. *The Judicial Ordeal in the Ancient Near East.* 2 vols. Ph.D. Diss. Yale.

———. 1981. Suprarational Procedures in Elam and Nuzi. *SCCNH,* pp. 115–31.

———. 1984. The Strange Case of the Suspected Sotah (Numbers v 11–31). *VT* 34: 11–26.

McKane, W. 1980. Poison, Trial by Ordeal and the Cup of Wrath. *VT* 30: 474–92.

Press, A. 1933. Das Ordal im alten Israel. *ZAW* 51: 121–40, 227–55.

Sasson, J. M. 1972. Numbers 5 and the "Waters of Judgment." *BZ* 16: 249–51.

Schmidt, H. 1928. *Das Gebet der Angeklagten im Alten Testament.* BZAW 49. Giessen.

Toorn, K. van der. 1985. *Sin and Sanction in Israel and Mesopotamia.* SSN. Assen.

———. fc. Ordeal Procedures in the Psalms and the Passover Meal. *VT.*

KAREL VAN DER TOORN

OREB AND ZEEB (PERSONS) [Heb *ʿōrēb ûzĕʾēb*]. The two "princes of Midian" who were captured and slain by the men of Ephraim when Gideon defeated the Midianites (Judg 7:25; 8:3; Ps 83:12—Eng 83:11). They were killed, respectively, at "the rock of Oreb" and "the winepress of Zeeb." The former location, at least, became legendary in later tradition (Isa 10:26), and it is uncertain whether these place names gave rise to etiological legends about "Midianite princes," or vice versa. Both names are authentic pre-Islamic Arabic personal names, common to the onomastics of the Arabian desert fringe area (but not Amorite, Ugaritic, or biblical Hebrew). The name Oreb can be compared with Safaitic and Old S Arabic *ġrb, ġurāb* ("raven"), *ġārib.* "Zeeb" can be compared with *d̲ʾb,* "wolf," found in Old S Arabic dialects, Thamudic, and very often in Safaitic and Nabatean (*dʾbw* and the diminutive *dʾybw, d̲uʾaib*); in Classical Arabic until recent times it was used as a personal and tribal name. Regardless of how the names got into the biblical tradition and Israelite toponymy, they must be associated with the pre-Islamic Arabic cultural and linguistic complex (Knauf 1988: 90).

Bibliography

Knauf, A. 1988. *Midian.* ADPV. Wiesbaden.

GEORGE E. MENDENHALL

OREN (PERSON) [Heb *ʾōren*]. Individual of the tribe of Judah, the third son of Jerahmeel who was firstborn of Hezron (1 Chr 2:25). His name is spelled the same as the mountain ash found in Isa 44:14.

DAVID CHANNING SMITH

ORIENTATION. See DIRECTION AND ORIENTATION.

ORIGEN (PERSON). An Alexandrian-born early Church Father (ca. 185–253); most of what we know about him comes from Eusebius' *Ecclesiastical History* (ca. 340).

A. Life
B. Works
  1. Treatises
  2. Homilies
  3. Letters
  4. Dialogues
C. Difficulties in Interpretation
D. Sources
E. Origen and the Church
F. Theology
G. Biblical Study
H. Piety
I. Origen's Legacy

A. Life

Not a biographer in the modern sense, Eusebius presents Origen as a model scholar and saint, combining in his person ideals admired by pagans and Christians alike (Cox 1983). We can also glean information from such sources as the *Panegyric* by a student of Origen traditionally identified as Gregory Thaumaturgus (ca. 213–ca. 270), occasional personal references in Origen's surviving works, and some of Jerome's (ca. 342–420) letters. Pierre Nautin (1977) provides the most persuasive account of Origen's life, based on a critical analysis of all sources, but has been challenged on many points (Barnes 1981: 81–93; Crouzel 1984).

Notwithstanding the difficulties involved in reconstructing the details of Origen's life and work, the following outline is reasonably certain. Origen was born, ca. 185, in Alexandria, where he was reared in a Christian family of some means. He received an education in Greek literature and the Christian Bible. During the reign of Septimius Severus (193–211), when Origen was in his teens, his father was martyred and his estate confiscated, leaving his family destitute. A wealthy Christian woman enabled Origen to complete his studies so as to become a teacher of Greek literature. During his youth Origen also became familiar with other intellectual traditions. His patron also supported a gnostic whose teaching Origen attended; he studied philosophy under the Platonist Ammonius Saccas (early 3d century), who later taught Plotinus (205–ca. 269); and he became familiar with Jewish exegetical traditions. He probably studied also with Clement of Alexandria (ca. 150–ca. 215), who dealt with many issues Origen was to develop more fully. During a second period of persecution under Severus, when Bishop Demetrius of Alexandria (d. ca. 231) and most of the Church's teachers hid or fled, Origen courageously provided Christian instruction. Shortly thereafter he underwent a conversion that led him to abandon pagan literature, to adopt a life of rigorous self-mortification (almost certainly including voluntary castration), and to restrict himself to Christian teaching.

Origen's learning commanded the respect of pagans and Christians alike. When he converted Ambrosius, a wealthy Alexandrian, from Gnosticism, he gained a lifelong friend and patron. Ambrosius encouraged Origen to write and provided Origen with stenographers and copyists so that he could compose treatises *ex tempore,* becoming one of the most prolific authors of antiquity. His fame soon spread far beyond Alexandria, reaching the highest circles of the empire. In 231 the dowager empress Julia Mammaea called him to audience at Antioch.

Although Bishop Demetrius gave after-the-fact approval to Origen's teaching, his efforts at establishing episcopal hegemony over the Church in Egypt provided little scope for a brilliant lay teacher. Journeys to Rome and to Greece, undertaken at various times, were probably attempts to find an intellectual center where the Church would be more congenial. After 233 Origen settled at Caesarea in Palestine, whose bishop, Theoctistus, had ordained him to the presbyterate during an earlier sojourn. This ordination infuriated Demetrius, who had come to view Origen as a heretic.

Most of Origen's surviving works were written at Caesarea, where he preached extensively. Although Heraclas (d. 247), Demetrius' successor as bishop of Alexandria, also considered Origen unorthodox, the bishops of Palestine and the nearby province of Arabia (modern Jordan) made use of his expertise at least twice in synods concerned with christological doctrine. After being imprisoned and tortured during the Decian persecution of 251, Origen died at Tyre, his health broken by his sufferings (ca. 253).

B. Works

The emperor Justinian (483–565) procured Origen's condemnation as a heretic in 553 and saw to the destruction of most his works. Even so, extensive writings have survived, some, including his treatise *On First Principles,* in Latin translations of regrettably questionable accuracy. Nautin (1977: 241–60) provides a comprehensive list of Origen's works and their editions. Origen wrote in four established genres: (1) learned treatises, (2) homilies, (3) letters, and (4) dialogues. Outside such classification is his massive *Hexapla,* an edition of the OT in which, most likely, six parallel columns enabled the reader to see the Hebrew text, its Greek transcription; and four translations into Greek, those of Aquila and Symmachus, the LXX, and that of Theodotion. To these Origen added two Greek translations of the Psalms that he had personally discovered.

1. Treatises. Most of Origen's treatises, including his earliest work, *On Psalms 1–25,* were biblical commentaries. He also wrote a commentary on Lamentations and began massive commentaries on Genesis and on John while still at Alexandria. Of these only the first two books of the *Commentary on John* (CJ), vital for understanding Origen's christology, survive in more than fragments. While there he also wrote treatises, now lost, *On the Resurrection,* against what he considered the crudely materialist views of simple Christians; *On Natures,* against Valentinian anthropology; and a work called *Stromata* (his use of this unusual title, evoking a variegated oriental carpet, is our best indication that he was familiar with Clement of Alexandria).

Origen's great treatise at Alexandria, *On First Principles* (OFP), often known by its Greek title, *Peri Archon,* was the first Christian attempt to provide a systematic and philosophically informed account of the principal doctrine of the faith. Recent scholarship has shown that the *Peri Archon* belongs to the genre of philosophical treatises on "physics" (the doctrine of God and God's relationship to the world). Such treatises are characterized by a two-part structure in which a general conspectus is followed by a treatment in more detail, but in the same order, of particular issues (Harl 1975; Dorival 1975). Origen's treatise actually has a fourfold structure. A preface briefly enumerates the "*archai,*" first principles in the philosophical sense employed by the pre-Socratics, but also, for him, elementary principles of the Christian faith as transmitted by the Church's tradition. The first major section of the work deals with God; rational creatures and their fall from God into various kinds of embodiment; and the world and its place in the process whereby God is bringing about the return of rational creatures to their original state. The second deals with particular issues such as the manner of the incarnation, the free will of rational creatures, and biblical interpretation. A short recapitulation sums up these doctrines and ties up loose ends.

Origen continued his never-completed commentaries on Genesis and John after removing to Caesarea. He also wrote commentaries on Proverbs, the Song of Songs, Isaiah, Ezekiel, the Minor Prophets, Luke, Matthew, and most of the Pauline Epistles, as well as a fuller commentary on the Psalms. Some books of the commentaries on John and Matthew survive in Greek, and more or less faithful translations of the commentaries on Romans, the Song of Songs, and much of the rest of the commentary on Matthew survive in Latin. The others survive, at best, only in fragments. In addition, Origen wrote *scholiae,* which appear to have been commentaries on selected passages of works or parts of works not covered by continuous commentaries (Nautin 1977: 372–75). We know of scholiae on the Pentateuch, the Psalms, Ecclesiastes, Isaiah, and John.

Three nonexegetical treatises written at Caesarea, his *Exhortation to Martyrdom, On Prayer,* and *Contra Celsum,* survive in Greek. A further work, a treatise (or homily) *On the Passover,* a spiritual interpretation of Exodus 12, has recently been discovered and edited (Nautin and Guéraud 1979). The *Exhortation to Martyrdom* exhibits the Maccabean veneration of martyrdom that suffused the Church of Origen's time. For him this signified a preference for intellectual over corporeal existence. *On Prayer* provides a concise introduction to Origen's piety; its justification of prayer for its own sake, as opposed to having petitions granted, places it at the head of a long succession of Christian mystical literature. The *Contra Celsum* (CC), in eight books, refutes Celsus' *True Logos.* Celsus, a 2d-century Platonist, attacked Christianity on philosophical grounds and provided a rationale for persecution by accusing Christians of disloyalty to the empire. Origen's reply is the most cogent apology for Christianity written in Greek.

2. Homilies. While in Palestine Origen preached homilies, recorded by stenographers, on Genesis, Exodus, Leviticus, Numbers, Deuteronomy, Joshua, Judges, 1 Samuel, Job, the Psalms, Proverbs, Ecclesiastes, the Song of Songs, Isaiah, Jeremiah, Ezekiel, Matthew, Luke, Acts, 1 Corinthians, 2 Corinthians, Galatians, 1 and 2 Thessalonians, Titus, and Hebrews. One hundred and fifty-six OT homilies, along with thirty-nine on Luke, survive in Latin translations by Jerome and Rufinus. Vittorio Peri (1980) has recently demonstrated that an additional seventy-five homilies in the Latin *Treatise or Homilies on the Psalms,* ascribed to Jerome, are in fact adaptations of homilies by Origen. Twenty homilies on Jeremiah (HJ) and one on 1 Samuel survive in Greek. These works do not display the oratory of the great 4th-century preachers, but employ the subtle diatribe style of philosophical teachers like Epictetus (ca. 55–ca. 135). Like the commentaries, they interpret the biblical text verse by verse, but they treat it in less detail and concentrate on moral exhortation.

3. Letters. Little is left of Origen's extensive correspondence, but those fragments that survive provide valuable insights into the man and his thought. We have one letter written to him along with his reply, his correspondence with Julius Africanus concerning the authenticity of the story of Susanna in the LXX version of Daniel.

4. Dialogues. Ancient sources mention among Origen's works a *Dialogue with Candidus* from his Alexandrian period; and part of his *Dialogues with Heracleides,* which almost certainly dates from his Caesarean period, has recently been discovered. Neither of these works were literary dialogues in the tradition of Plato, but were transcripts of debates in which Origen had engaged.

C. Difficulties in Interpretation

The loss of so many works makes interpreting Origen difficult. A comparison of Latin translations with Greek texts reveals, at the very least, a loss in nuance and subtlety. It is particularly regrettable that we lack the full Greek text of *On First Principles,* crucial for interpreting Origen's thought. That work was controversial in its own time. It became even more so as Christian doctrine became more fixed in the century and a half that elapsed between its composition and its translation. In his translator's preface Rufinus (ca. 345–410) justified correcting theological errors in the Greek text on the pretext that there had been heretical interpolations. However, if Rufinus understated putatively heterodox elements in Origen's works, others have overstated them. Antoine Guillaumont (1962) has shown that the views of Evagrius Ponticus, a 4th-century Origenist, have become confused with Origen's own, so that we cannot assume that Origen taught all the doctrines for which he was condemned in 553.

Origen's theological method also poses difficulties of interpretation. He presupposes a division between the vast majority of simple Christians, who accept the Church's teaching on faith and are motivated by fear, and a small minority of spiritual Christians, who rationally understand their faith and are motivated by love (Rius-Camps 1970; Hällström 1984). Valentinian gnostics made a distinction between psychics and pneumatics, but Origen differentiated his position from theirs by insisting that spiritual Christians differ from their simpler fellow believers not by nature, but because they have progressed further toward likeness to God. Origen taught that the Christian theologian should exercise a prudent reserve, extending even to deliberate deception (as, in his opinion, the biblical authors themselves did) in presenting profound doctrines that might shock or demoralize simple believers (CC 4.19 and HJ 20.3–7). We must, therefore, be attentive in studying Origen to determine to what extent doctrines simply hinted at or presented as mere speculations are in fact serious expressions of his thought. This difficulty has led to widely divergent estimates of Origen's thought.

D. Sources

Origen seldom cites authors outside the Bible, and those works that he did use he thoroughly transformed. When we speak of sources, therefore, we are not ordinarily speaking of borrowings but of constituent elements of a remarkably original intellectual synthesis. This is true of the Bible itself. Given Origen's intimate knowledge of and ardent devotion to the biblical text, it may seem paradoxical that the extent of this influence is a matter of controversy. Thus, for example, Eugène de Faye, author of a pioneering study of Origen, argued that the Bible was, in effect, an empty shell into which Origen poured his own thought (1923: 72–95). Henri de Lubac (1950), by contrast, presented Origen as a genuinely biblical thinker. Such widely divergent views are possible because Origen understood the Bible in terms of intellectual traditions of his time.

Origen received the Bible through the mediation of early Christianity. His statement of the fundamental principles of the faith conforms to earlier summaries by such authors as Irenaeus and Hippolytus and his ethical teaching reflects the asceticism and veneration of martyrdom which were current in the Church of his time. His christology depends on the Logos speculation which writers such as Justin Martyr (ca. 100–ca. 165) brought into the Christian tradition from Philo (ca. 29 B.C.–ca. A.D. 50). Although he mentions Ignatius of Antioch (ca. 35–ca. 107) and is said to have met Hippolytus of Rome (ca. 170–ca. 236), he does not mention either Irenaeus (ca. 130–ca. 200), whom he may have read, or, for that matter, Clement of Alexandria.

Gnosticism's influence on Origen is of a different character. Although one can speak of a limited positive influence of Gnosticism on Origen's exegesis (Daniélou 1955: 191–99), its principal influence is negative. Origen may justly be called the greatest of the anti-gnostic Fathers (le Boulluec 1985), and Hal Koch has shown that the refutation of gnostic understandings of God, the world, and the human condition is a mainspring of Origen's theology (1932). He never tired of refuting the schools of Valentinus, Basilides, and Marcion. He also denied any access to a secret, esoteric tradition such as many gnostics appealed to (Hanson 1956). Origen, by contrast with Irenaeus, sought not simply to refute the gnostics but to provide a reasoned response to the serious issues they raised. He regarded the refusal to identify the Creator and Lawgiver of the OT with the God and Father of Jesus Christ as the fundamental error of all gnostics (CC 5.4 and 5.61), and he felt obliged to demonstrate the fundamental consistency of the Christian tradition that identified them. In doing so, Origen was forced to go far beyond the Church's traditional rule of faith, which simply did not deal with such issues as why the world came into being or why some souls have a better lot than others. Ironically, this led him to develop an esoteric account of the origin and destiny of the cosmos that, as Hans Jonas (1934) has pointed out, is structurally much like a gnostic system.

Although Origen taught that Judaism was superseded by Christianity and engaged in anti-Jewish polemic occasioned by the intense competition between Christians and Jews in Caesarea, his relationship to Judaism is much more positive (de Lange 1976: Sgherri 1982). He regarded Philo more highly than any postbiblical Christian writer and he respected the learning of the rabbinic teachers of his time. Origen recognized the importance of the Hebrew text for the understanding of Scripture and he sought out and utilized, with or without attribution, Jewish Haggadah in his exegesis.

Origen's biblical interpretation constantly testifies to his training in Hellenistic literary theory, known as grammar, which determines his method of approaching a text and, for that matter, his literary, if unadorned, style (Neuschäfer 1987). He was also trained in the scientific and mathematical disciplines that made up encyclical education and could use the astronomical discovery of the precession of the equinoxes to refute astrology.

Origen studied under Ammonius Saccas and continued throughout his life to read and teach philosophy, which he saw as an indispensable preparation for biblical interpretation. He was a sophisticated philosopher of the school we call Middle Platonism, itself an eclectic blend of Platonic metaphysics, Aristotelian logic, and elements of Stoic ethics, along with Neo-Pythagorean mystical speculation (Berchman 1984). Philosophical terms continually occur in his writings, and philosophical concepts inform his theology. Origen, like Justin Martyr before him, considered Christianity the true philosophy and parted company with pagan philosophy when the Church's teaching compelled him to do so, most notably in his doctrine of the incarnation.

E. Origen and the Church

Origen described himself as a "man of the Church," remained throughout his life in communion with the Church, and vigorously defended its teachings against heretics, Jews, and pagans. Nonetheless, the Church has had difficulty assimilating his thought and, as his tensions with the Alexandrian episcopate indicate, he was already suspected of unorthodoxy during his lifetime. Origen, for that matter, frequently and unsparingly criticized bishops.

Origen's understanding of the Church and of his role as a theologian made tensions inevitable. Essential to both is the distinction between "spiritual" and "simple" Christians. Most Christians are simple, and, although this should not be the case, so are many who hold clerical office. Unspiritual clerics, however, have no right to arrogate for themselves disciplinary authority that can only be exercised by the spiritual. Furthermore, teaching, as a mediation of the word of God, is the highest ecclesiastical function and the source of genuine authority. The administration of the sacraments is distinctly subordinate to this function (Lies 1978). While Origen professed loyalty to the Church's rule of faith, he held that as a spiritual man, it was his duty to pass beyond the acceptance of such doctrines on faith, as is appropriate for the simple, and to acquire a rational understanding of them. Such an understanding would uncover the hidden system of thought that gave the Church's teaching its coherence (Kettler 1965). Not surprisingly, bishops considered such views subversive.

F. Theology

In *On First Principles* Origen discussed the doctrines which, in his opinion, the soul most needs in its journey toward God (OFP 4.2.7). Hal Koch (1932) has shown that Origen employed the Middle Platonic philosophy to construct a system in which the driving force is God's providence, which employs the material and spiritual worlds as *paideia* (a Gk word that means both "education" and "discipline") for rational beings while respecting their freedom of choice. Origen believed that such a system underlay and made sense of the Bible. In his doctrine of God (God the Father) Origen argued for the incorporeality of God and for God's utter unity and simplicity in contrast with the multiplicity of the created world. His understanding of God's purpose enabled him to provide a rational justification, over against the gnostics, for the Church's teaching that the Creator and Lawgiver in the OT is the Father of Jesus Christ in the NT.

For Origen the Son is God's Logos ("Word" or "Reason"), and Wisdom, a second divine hypostasis, or second God, subordinate to and eternally generated by the Father. Although consistent with Middle Platonic speculation about the divine hypostases, Origen's subordinationism was characteristic of Christian thought in his time; Arius' (ca. 250–ca. 336) retention of it comes not from Origenism, but from theological conservatism. By contrast, his concept of eternal generation was highly influential in the formation of the Christian doctrine of the trinity. The manifold aspects *(epinoiai)* of the Logos, the "express image of [God's] substance" (Heb 1:3), mediate between the absolute unity of God and the multiplicity of the Created World (Lyons 1982). Likewise, various aspects meet the needs of fallen rational spirits at every stage of their return to God (Harl 1958). The incarnation enables rational beings to know the Logos and, through the Logos, to know God. It involves the inseparable union between the Logos and a full human person. This is possible because of the Son's preincarnate union with his human soul, the one rational being who did not fall from its original adherence to God. The Holy Spirit, the third divine hypostasis, is eternally generated through the Son and shares in the Son's knowledge of and subordination to the Father. The Spirit's sphere is limited to sanctifying the saints, an activity which includes giving insight into those who wrote the Bible and to those who interpret it spiritually.

Rational beings were created in unity with God and all but the being who was united with the Logos fell from God through satiety. Some did not fall very far, and their return is relatively easy. These beings constitute the angels and the spirits that animate the heavenly bodies, whose task is to serve those below them. Other rational creatures fell more precipitously; these are called "souls" *(psychai)* because they have "cooled" *(psychesthai)* from their once ardent love of God. God created the material cosmos from nothing in order to arrest the fall of these beings and to facilitate their return. Origen thus affirmed, against the gnostics and with Plato and the Bible, the goodness of the cosmos.

Once in each world age these souls can become enfleshed in grossly material human bodies. Through God's providence, their situation in the world is a just recompense for their sin and their experience here provides a means for them to choose freely to return to God and, in so doing, to become intellectually and ethically more like God. Origen thus transforms Christian eschatology. Our experience in this life determines whether our future life will be a continual growth in the knowledge of God, including knowledge of the Bible and the created order, both of which reveal God, or will be the painful purgation symbolized by the fires of hell in which simple Christians do well to believe literally. Christian belief in the resurrection is a way of talking about the identity of the embodied person who dies in this world with the glorified person of the world to come. Similarly the advent (Parousia) of Christ that is significant for us is his advent in our souls.

Other rational beings, the adverse powers, have fallen too far for such embodiment to be useful. These beings continually attempt to frustrate the progress of human beings and, in the guise of pagan deities, to deceive them into worshipping them to the neglect of the one true God. Origen holds forth the hope that all creatures, however, shall eventually return to God. To deny even Satan, the prince of demons, the possibility of repentance would mean to deny the free choice of a rational being. To bring even the most obdurate beings to the point where their existence apart from God is unbearable, a very long cycle of world ages will be necessary.

G. Biblical Study

Origen is best known for his allegorical interpretation, but, in keeping with his training in Hellenistic literary study, he was a master of all aspects of biblical scholarship. This ranged from establishment of the text, through careful study of grammar and syntax, to the most speculative theological application. Origen's students reputedly dreamed about the Bible at night from having studied it so assiduously all day, and Origen found the erotic imagery of the Song of Songs entirely suitable to describe the soul's intercourse with the Logos in Scripture.

Origen never attained the ability to read Hebrew, even though keenly aware of its need. His *Hexapla* was an attempt to make up for this lack by enabling him to compare the Church's LXX text with all other Greek translations. Its use is apparent in his *Homilies on Jeremiah,* where he occasionally mentioned that he preferred another reading to that of the LXX. Origen used Hellenistic critical signs to mark places where the LXX evidently differed from the Hebrew. This immense work was probably never copied in its entirety and unfortunately perished with Origen's original manuscript.

Origen's works reveal him being careful of grammatical niceties and using historical or geographical information to illuminate the Bible's literal meaning, which he respected. Although he had a high doctrine of biblical inspiration and lacked a modern appreciation of history, Origen's approach to Scripture was neither naive nor insensitive. He was able, in his interpretation of Paul, for example, to grasp the overall thrust of a biblical author's argument and to recognize when that author was using categories of thought not identical to his own (Gorday 1983). He recognized serious inconsistencies in the Bible and explained them as a deliberate policy on the part of the inspired authors to hide deeper insights from the simple and to signal their presence to the more intelligent by interweaving falsehoods into the narrative. Intelligent readers of the Bible can recognize that a text is literally false when it is unworthy of God, contradicts another inspired text, or is manifestly improbable. A striking instance of interweaving is in the gospel of John, where Origen argues on the basis of inconsistencies among the gospel accounts and historical improbabilities that Jesus' entry into Jerusalem and cleansing of the temple did not literally happen at all (Grant 1961; Kettler 1973). Instead, the account symbolizes the Logos' entry into and purification of the soul (CJ 10.22–34).

Although he found historical investigation helpful in understanding the text, Origen rejected historical information as a goal of interpretation because he could see no way in which purely historical knowledge could lead the soul toward God. It is this attitude toward history that distinguishes Origen sharply from the approach exemplified by Theodore of Mopsuestia (ca. 350–428) and often referred to by the modern term "typology." While his allegory may initially strike the reader as arbitrary, it possesses remarkable internal consistency throughout his works. Origen believed in a natural symbolism, grounded in the sensible world's dependence on the intelligible world, which Charles Bigg (1913: 173) aptly referred to as a "sacramental mystery of nature."

The anti-gnostic thrust of Origen's theology, with its concern to vindicate the unity of the Creator and Lawgiver of the OT and the Father of Jesus Christ of the NT, implied exegetically the unity of the two testaments. God's command to consume the entire Passover lamb (Exod 12:10) symbolizes the need to interpret the whole Bible as a unity and is a standing rebuke to Jews and gnostics who only accept one testament (CJ 10.28.107). The Bible is treated as a consistent and harmonious whole, in which every part illuminates every other part; Origen frequently brings to bear a multitude of verses containing the same word or concept in order to elucidate a difficult passage. There is, however, a significant difference between the testaments: Christ, who is only announced in a shadowy way in the OT, is shone forth in the NT. Even so, the NT requires interpretation. An inspired interpreter must transform the sensible gospel shown forth in the NT into the eternal, or spiritual, gospel of Rev 14:6, which bears a relation to the NT similar to that which the NT bears to the OT (CJ 1.3.12–8.46).

H. Piety

Walther Völker's pioneering study (1931) demonstrated a rich affective piety in Origen and laid the groundwork for an appreciation of Origen's key role in the history of Christian spirituality. Origen depicted the Christian life as, ideally, a continual progress toward the knowledge of God, a progress by which we are transformed both ethically and intellectually so as to become more like God. Unlike the Cappadocians, whom he resembles in many ways, Origen, as Hans Urs von Balthasar noted (1936–37), locates the reason for our ignorance of God not in the absolute incomprehensibility of God, but in the silence of the Logos, who communicates to us what we need to know when we need to know it. For Origen, God, as Raoul Mortley puts it (1986: 84) "whilst incommunicable in language, is accessible to the mind and the object of knowledge."

There is no tension between Origen's piety and the intellectual rigor of his theology and exegesis (Crouzel 1961). Indeed, the latter is the highest expression of the former. It is precisely in the interpretation of Scripture, informed by the best insights of all aspects of learning, that the soul makes its progress. Spiritual interpretation was, in fact, the chief means by which the Logos conferred to souls at all levels of progress the saving knowledge of God. Origen's interpretation of Scripture is consistently oriented toward the transformation of the person who reads the Bible or hears it interpreted (Torjesen 1985). This process requires divine grace and a willingness to wait upon the Logos. Origen, in fact, believed that the Christian soul continues to study Scripture as it progresses toward God after death (CJ 32.3; OFP 2.11.3).

I. Origen's Legacy

Manlio Simonetti (1986) has pointed out that Origen presents an elitist way of living the Christian life which could only have arisen during a time when the Christian community permitted a relatively great freedom of thought and which was doomed by that community's organizational evolution. Nevertheless, while Origenism per se rapidly became a bypath in the history of Christianity, Origen's influence was immense. This is particularly true of monastic theology, where Origen's way of life to some extent survived. Athanasius and the Cappadocian Fathers freely adapted Origen to the needs of their own time and through them and others Origen became the father of scriptural study and systematic theology in the Christian tradition.

Bibliography

Balthasar, H. U. von. 1936–37. Le Mystérion d'Origène. *RSR* 26:513–62; 27:38–64.

Barnes, T. D. 1981. *Constantine and Eusebius.* Cambridge, MA.

Berchman, R. M. 1984. *From Philo to Origen.* BJS 69. Chico, CA.

Berner, U. 1981. *Origenes.* ErFor 147. Darmstadt.

Bigg, C. 1913. *The Christian Platonists of Alexandria.* Oxford.

Boulluec, A. le. 1985. *La notion d'hérésie dans la littérature grecque IIe-IIIe sciècles.* 2 vols. Paris.

Cox, P. 1983. *Biography in Late Antiquity: A Quest for the Holy Man.* Berkeley.

Crouzel, H. 1961. *Origène et la "connaissance mystique."* Bruges.

———. 1971. *Bibliographie critique d'Origène.* The Hague.

———. 1982. *Bibliographie critique d'Origène, Supplément 1.* The Hague.

———. 1984. *Origène.* Paris.

Daniélou, J. 1955. *Origen.* Trans. W. Mitchell. New York.

Dorival, G. 1975. Remarques sur la forme du *Peri Archon.* In *Origeniana,* ed. H. Crouzel; G. Lomiento; and J. Rius-Camps. Bari.

Faye, E. de. 1923–28. *Origène: Sa vie, son oeuvre, sa pensée.* 3 vols. Paris.

Gorday, P. 1983. *Principles of Patristic Exegesis: Romans 9–11 in Origen, John Chrysostom, and Augustine.* New York.

Grant, R. M. 1961. *The Earliest Lives of Jesus.* New York.

Guillaumont, A. 1962. *Les "Kephalaia Gnostika" d'Evagre le Pontique et l'histoire de l'origénisme chez les Grecs et chez les Syriens.* Paris.

Hällström, G. af. 1984. *Fides Simpliciorum according to Origen of Alexandria.* Helsinki.

Hanson, R. P. C. 1956. *Origen's Doctrine of Tradition.* London.

Harl, M. 1958. *Origène et la fonction révélatrice du Verbe incarné.* Paris.

———. 1975. Structure et cohérence du *Peri Archon.* In *Origeniana,* ed. H. Crouzel; G. Lomiento; and J. Rius-Camps. Bari.

Jonas, H. 1934. *Gnosis und spätantiker Geist.* 2 vols. Göttingen.

Kannengiesser, C., and Petersen, W. L., eds. 1988. *Origen of Alexandria.* Notre Dame, IN.

Kettler, F. H. 1965. *Der Ursprüngliche Sinn der Dogmatik des Origenes.* BZNW 31. Berlin.

———. 1973. Funktion und Tragweite der historischen Kritik des Origenes an den Evangelien. *Kairos* 15: 36–49.

Koch, H. 1932. *Pronoia und Paideusis: Studien über Origenes und sein Verhälnis zum Platonismus.* Berlin.

Lange, N. de. 1976. *Origen and the Jews.* Cambridge.

Lies, L. 1978. *Wort und Eucharistie bei Origenes.* Innsbruck.

Lubac, H. de. 1950. *Histoire et esprit: l'intelligence de l'Ecriture d'après Origène.* Paris.

Lyons, J. A. 1982. *The Cosmic Christ in Origen and Teilhard de Chardin.* Oxford.

Mortley, R. 1986. *From Word to Silence.* Vol. 2, *The Way of Negation Christian and Greek.* Bonn.

Nautin, P. 1977. *Origène: sa vie et son oeuvre.* Paris.

Nautin, P., and Guéraud, O., eds. 1979. *Origène sur la Pâque: Traité indédit d'après un papyrus de Toura.* Paris.

Neuschäfer, B. 1987. *Origenes als Philologe.* Basel.

Peri, V. 1980. *Omelie origeniane sui Salmi.* Vatican City.

Rius-Camps, J. 1970. *El dinamismo trinitario en la divinización de los seres racionales según Origenes.* OCA 188.

Sgherri, G. 1982. *Chiesa e Sinagoga nelle opere di Origen.* Milan.

Simonetti, M. 1986. La controversia origeniana. *Aug* 25: 7–31.

Torjesen, K. J. 1985. *Hermeneutical Procedure and Theological Method in Origen's Exegesis.* Berlin.
Trigg, J. W. 1983. *Origen: The Bible and Philosophy in the Third-Century Church.* Atlanta.
Völlker, W. 1931. *Das Vollkommenheitsideal des Origenes.* Tübingen.
JOSEPH W. TRIGG

ORIGEN'S HEXAPLA. See HEXAPLA OF ORIGEN.

ORIGIN OF THE WORLD (NHC II,5). See WORLD, ON THE ORIGIN OF (NHC II,5).

ORNAMENTS. See DRESS AND ORNAMENTATION.

ORNAN (PERSON) [Heb *ʾornān*]. An alternate form of ARAUNAH.

ORPAH (PERSON) [Heb *ʿorpâ*]. The wife of Chilion and sister-in-law of Ruth (Ruth 1:4; 4:10). See CHILION. Due to famine in Bethlehem, Elimelech and Naomi moved to Moab, where their sons, Mahlon and Chilion, married the Moabite women Ruth and Orpah (1:1–4). See RUTH, BOOK OF. With the deaths of Elimelech and his sons, Naomi and the Moabitesses were left without male progeny. Naomi decided to return to her homeland, but she urged her daughters-in-law to remain and marry Moabite husbands, where they could secure for themselves a future. Orpah elected to stay in Moab while Ruth insisted on accompanying Naomi (1:13–17).

Orpah's character in the story serves as a foil for Ruth. Since her decision to stay behind is not condemned by the story's narrator, Ruth's decision is recognized as an exceptional act of devotion to the family. By contrasting the women, the storyteller shows Ruth to be a woman of great value to Naomi and the family of Elimelech.

To highlight the difference in their characters, the story paints this word portrait of Orpah: "Orpah kissed her mother-in-law, but Ruth clung to her" (1:14). By subtle means, the story continues to compare Orpah with Ruth. Naomi says of Orpah, "See, your sister-in-law has gone back to her people and to her gods, return after your sister-in-law" (1:15). The reference to Orpah as "sister-in-law" *(yĕbimēk)* is the term occurring in Deut 25:5–10, which describes the responsibilities of the brother-in-law (or lever) to a widowed sister-in-law. See MARRIAGE (OLD TESTAMENT AND ANE); FAMILY. The irony of Naomi's statement is that it is Ruth who comes closer to playing that role than Orpah.

Also, the story contrasts Orpah with Ruth when Naomi remarks that Orpah has returned to her "people and her gods" (1:15). This is proleptic of Ruth's exclamation: "Your people shall be my people and your God my God" (1:16). The final gate scene provides another subtle comparison for the reader. A significant theme in the story is reward for faithfulness. When Boaz concludes his negotiations, he declares that he has purchased all that belonged "to Chilion and to Mahlon" (4:9). Whereas Ruth shall enjoy through Boaz both Chilion's and Mahlon's inheritance, Orpah is not present to benefit from the legacy of her deceased husband, Chilion.

The etymology of Orpah is usually related to *ʿōrep,* meaning "neck." Thus, Jewish midrash explains that Orpah turned her back on her mother-in-law. Jewish tradition also has Orpah and Ruth sisters, the daughters of the Moabite king Eglon. An alternative explanation for the name is *ʿarîp,* "cloud."

Bibliography

Beattie, D. R. G. 1977. *Jewish Exegesis of the Book of Ruth.* JSOTSup 2. Sheffield.
KENNETH A. MATHEWS

ORPHISM. A religious movement dating to the 6th century B.C.E. centering on the figure of Orpheus, producing a sizable literature with cosmogonic and theological themes, and inviting people to find salvation by living a particular lifestyle. Although the materials we may call "Orphic" first appear in the 6th centuries B.C.E. and much evidence comes from Neoplatonic authors living as late as the 6th century C.E., the movement was likely the strongest in the 6th and 5th century B.C.E. and lasted into the 3d century B.C.E. Three relatively discrete types of materials comprise Orphism: legends about Orpheus, an Orphic literature, and ritual practices and regulations for an Orphic way of life.

Orpheus was first and foremost a musician with shamanic powers. His voice and his lyre had the magical ability to charm animals and to change the course of rivers. He joined the expedition of the Argonauts, as Apollonios of Rhodes writes in the mid-3d century B.C.E., a somewhat effeminate man whose entertaining music prevented the sailors from quarreling and whose sacrifices won the blessing and aid of the gods. His journey to Hades to reclaim Eurydice remains ambiguous; Euripides (*Alc.* 357–59) indicates that Orpheus successfully retrieved his wife, but Plato (*Symp.* 179D) suggests that he left Hades without her because he lacked the courage to join her in death. Orpheus himself is portrayed on numerous vase paintings of the 5th century B.C.E. as dying at the hands of Thracian women and their spears, clubs, and stones, perhaps because he refused to initiate them into his mysteries or because his music enthralled their husbands. Somehow Orpheus managed to survive his death or at least to enjoy a pleasurable existence in Hades. A number of 4th- and 3d-century vases from S Italy show him playing his lyre in the underworld and his initiates holding a papyrus scroll, suggesting that victory over death was thought possible for those following an Orphic regimen, while the noninitiates would continue to suffer for their sin.

The Orphic literature of the 5th and 4th centuries exhibits a keen interest in the origin of the gods and the world. One of the richest creation accounts, the Derveni commentary of the 4th century, tells how Zeus, a monotheistic deity, produced the world through his power (Okeanos) and his thought (Moira). Although Zeus has no partner, he created the world by "aphroditing," or making love; his sexual energy functions as a metaphor rather than a mythical description of the world's beginning. A sharp distinction seems to identify Zeus as permanent and the world as temporal, perpetually undergoing change as its elements combine to form entities only to dissolve and recombine to make new entities. Even though deities and cosmos are distinct, continuity between them is assured because Zeus governs the world as its king. The author of the Derveni text developed his linguistic and allegorical theories to comment on Orpheus' creation account, for he tried to show that as sexual activity both unites and divides, so the linguistic act of naming objects and events indicates the unity of the world even as it shows its differences.

Other Orphic creation myths elaborate themes of the Derveni account and also introduce new topics. Most accounts show the world deriving from a primal unity, with strife or tension soon arising as the force which divides beings and objects. Descriptions of the bizarre Orphic deities demonstrate how Orphism differs from the orderly gods of the Olympian religion of the polis: bodies of dragons, multiple heads, angelic wings of gold, and voices of bulls. We also hear of incest and parental emasculation. Several accounts tell of a succession of rulers from Phanes to Ouranos and Gaia, thence to Kronos and Rhea, and finally to Zeus, the transitions anything but smooth yet all culminating in the reign of Zeus. Common to all myths is the recognition that the world cannot be sustained by its own power but instead needs the attention and effort of a ruler or a king who is beyond it. However, the monstrosity of the gods prior to Zeus' rule and the divine struggles before Zeus takes the throne are neither capricious nor fanciful, because they show the trials and experiments that preceded the rule of Zeus (and as one account has it, his son Dionysos). The rule of Zeus adds unity to the division and tension characterizing previous generations of rulers, and thus transforms deformity in to clarity and beauty; the birth of Dionysos makes salvation possible for humans caught in their hereditary sin.

Mention of Dionysos and soteriology prompts us to move from Orphic creation accounts to anthropological motifs in Orphic literature. Aristotle writes that the Orphic poems distinguish soul from body, holding, moreover, that the soul enters the body from the universe (*De An.* 1.5.410b). Plato adds that the body is a sort of prison for the soul, not one where the soul is punished but a garrison where it resides for safekeeping and with the gods as its guardians (*Cra.* 400C and *Phd* 62B). But why are souls in bodies? And how do they get there? The myth of the dismemberment of Dionysos by the Titans, considered by many scholars to be the cardinal Orphic myth, provides the clue to answers. According to the myth, when the Titans observed the child Dionysos at play, they disguised themselves and then dismembered Dionysos, boiled and roasted him, and finally ate him; Zeus, however, struck the Titans with his thunderbolt, reducing them to ashes. From the ashes, the human species arose—partly Titanic and partly Dionysiac. The myth is not the basis for a sacramental ritual of intimacy with the gods, but one which describes the divine deeds which led to the human plight.

Several times Plato refers to Orphic notions of a judgment and destiny of the human soul, as though to suggest that the duality of humans, i.e., their Titanic-Dionysiac nature, presents humans with choices and responsibilities. In the *Phaedo* and the *Gorgias,* Plato draws on the Orphics to develop his own views; to the Orphics he attributes the view that the human soul retains after the death of the body those traits and characteristics it had acquired when the two were together, and that the soul would be judged—naked, and thus without any ability to deceive the judges. Pure and just souls are to be rewarded, whereas impure and uninitiated souls are to suffer severe penalties in Hades.

Where a distinction between life before death and life after death is marked by a final judgment, a connection is also established by the belief that the soul's destiny after death is determined by its behavior in its body prior to death. An Orphic way of life provides both ritual and ethical foundations for happiness after death. Euripides (*Hipp.* 952–53), Aristophanes (*Batrachoi* 1032), and Plato (*Leg.* 6.782) refer to the Orphic initiatory rituals as well as their prohibition on eating meat and sacrificing animals. Plato (*Resp.* 364D–365A) also refers to a large number of Orphic books or liturgical texts used to persuade individuals as well as large groups that ritual participation can eliminate guilt and pardon injustices, and that proper sacrifices can save the dead as well as the living from punishment in the next world. Among the most interesting materials providing information about Orphic practices is a statement in the Derveni text about the wandering Orphic practitioners who journeyed from city to city to perform their rites and received payment for performing rituals to mollify fears about life after death. All these references to Orphic rituals and bans demonstrate that Orphism was more than merely a literary religion, and that it offered an alternative to the traditional Greek religion of warring deities and blood sacrifice.

At the center of the Orphic life was a ban on killing, be it for food or for sacrifice. This prohibition meant that those who followed an Orphic way of life put themselves in sharp and uncompromising opposition to the mainstream of Greek religion with its sacrifices, which served to distinguish eternal gods from mortal humans at the same time it linked the two by apportioning rights and duties among them. The Orphics renounced the general Greek way in favor of a life of purity, nonviolence, and vegetarianism. The negative model was the Titans who swallowed Dionysos to kill him; the positive model was Zeus who, according to one creation account, swallowed the entire universe in order to give it new life and peace and order. The Orphics could imitate Dionysos and thus transport themselves back to a pure time of the beginnings of the world, and thus procure salvation for their souls. Hence it was not the Titanic killing and eating of Dionysos that brought a sacramental intimacy with the gods but a rejection of killing based on Dionysiac hope that made salvation ritually and ethically possible for the Orphics. Here we have an encouragement to preserve life, for killing damaged the psyche in a body whereas avoidance of killing enhanced the psyche. And because the psyche continued to exist after the death of the body, it could anticipate a blessed life after death if it followed the Orphic way of life. Orphism became a religion of salvation—renouncing blood sacrifice, abandoning the Greek civil religion, and finding in liturgical and ethical practices a life of Dionysiac joy.

Orpheus does not appear as the historical or even legendary founder of Orphism. It is likely, however, that the people we have come to know as Orphics adopted Orpheus as their teacher and master because his nonviolence established a pattern they desired and his shamanic powers enabled them to look beyond society and nature to another world where their salvation was guaranteed.

Bibliography

Alderink, L. J. 1981. *Creation and Salvation in Ancient Orphism.* American Classical Studies 8.

Burkert, W. 1982. Craft versus Sect: The Problem of Orphics and Pythagoreans. Pp. 1–22 in *Jewish and Christian Self-Definition.* Vol. 3 of *Self-Definition in the Greco-Roman World,* ed. B. F. Meyer and E. P. Sanders. Philadelphia.

———. 1987. *Ancient Mystery Cults.* Cambridge, MA.

Detienne, M. 1979. *Dionysos Slain.* Trans. M. Muellner and L. Muellner. Baltimore.

Guthrie, W. K. C. 1952. *Orpheus and Greek Religion.* 2d rev. ed. London and New York.

Kern, O., ed. 1963. *Orphicorum Fragmenta.* 2d ed. Berlin.

Linforth, I. M. 1941. *The Arts of Orpheus.* Berkeley.

West, M. L. 1983. *The Orphic Poems.* Oxford.

LARRY J. ALDERINK

ORTHOSIA (PLACE) [Gk *Orthosias*]. A port city in Phoenicia to which Trypho, the usurper to the Syrian throne, fled in 138 B.C. when defeated in Palestine by Antiochus VII Sedetes (1 Macc 15:37). The site is attested in many ancient manuscripts and was later a bishopric. The name of the city indicates a great deal of Hellenistic influence. Its name is derived from an epithet attributed to Artemis, meaning "upright." This toponym was also used to name a city in the Maeander River drainage area of W Asia Minor. The port city of Orthosia is located by ancient geographers S of the Eleutherus River and N of Tripolis (Pliny *HN* 5.17; Ptolemy *Geog.* 5.14). It is located through the use of the Peutinger Tables to be in modern Lebanon in the vicinity of Ard Artuzi near the mouth of the Barid River (ca. 34°31′N; 35°57′E). Trypho's flight to Orthosia was a retreat toward his original base of support in Apamaea. He was not able to land at Tripolis since it was loyal to Antiochus. From Orthosia he was able to travel along the Barid River and through the Homs Gap in the Lebanon Mountains into the Orontes Valley.

ROBERT W. SMITH

OSNAPPAR (PERSON) [Heb *ʾosnappar*]. The king reported to have transported some of the people of Babylonia to Samaria (Ezra 4:10). The context clearly suggests an Assyrian king, and some Greek codices of Ezra read *salmanassarēs,* suggesting an identification with Shalmaneser. To the best of our knowledge, Samaria was besieged and captured by Shalmaneser V, while the various transfers of population groups were carried out by his successor Sargon II. See SARGON. There seems to be no way to reconcile the name "Sargon" with the biblical form Osnappar. Some scholars have suggested that the name is actually a corruption of the name of the last great Assyrian king Ashurbanipal, since he waged numerous campaigns against the Elamites and since Elamites and "men of Susa" are listed among those peoples deported to Samaria (Ezra 4:9).

A. KIRK GRAYSON

OSPREY. See ZOOLOGY.

OSTRACA, SEMITIC. The word "ostraca," plural of Gk *ostrakon,* "shell, sherd" (cf. Heb *ḥeres, ḥăsap*), is used in epigraphy for inscriptions written on sherds. Mostly written with ink but sometimes incised, these ostraca can be from various dimensions: from a few centimeters up to the size of a sheet of paper (ca. 21.5 × 28 cm; Lemaire and Vernus 1983). Written on one side (generally the convex one) or on both sides (recto and verso), they can contain texts ranging from one word (personal name) to several-dozen lines or columns of ciphers.

Sherd, as a material for writing, was not so practical as leather or papyrus but much cheaper: ostraca were mainly used for learning writing, for short and provisory administrative notes such as receipts, or for short letters, especially in war time, when it was difficult to get imported papyrus.

In Palestine, during biblical times, besides the Beth-shemesh and Izbet-Sartah ostraca from the late 2d millennium B.C. and a few Gk ostraca from the beginning of the Christian era, one may distinguish three groups of Semitic ostraca corresponding to three periods of writing.

(1) *Paleo-Hebrew ostraca* were mainly used in the royal administration from the 8th century B.C. to the fall of Jerusalem in 587. The main collections were found in Samaria, Lachish, and Arad (Lemaire 1977) but several other ones come from Jerusalem, Meṣad Hashavyahu, Kadesh-Barnea, and Ḥorvat ʿUza. From the same period, a few Ammonite, Moabite, Edomite, and Philistine (Naveh 1985b) ostraca were found in Transjordan, the Negev, and the Philistine plain. See EPIGRAPHY, TRANSJORDANIAN.

(2) *Aramaic ostraca* were used in administration during the Persian period. Two collections of these ostraca have been found in Arad and Beer-sheba while various exemplars were discovered at Samaria and several other places.

(3) *Square Hebrew ostraca* were used toward the turning of the Christian era at Qumrân, Massada, Murabbaʿât, and Herodium. They contain mostly abecedaries, names, and schoolboy's exercises. See also LACHISH LETTERS; ARAD OSTRACA; SAMARIA (PLACE) (OSTRACA).

Bibliography

Beit-Arieh, I. 1983. A First Temple Census Document. *PEQ* 115: 105–8.

———. 1986–87. The Ostracon of Aḥiqam from Horvat ʿUza. *TA* 13/14: 32–38.

Kaufman, I. T. 1982. The Samaria Ostraca. *BA* 45: 229–39.

Lemaire, A. 1977. *Inscriptions hébraïques.* Vol. 1, *Les ostraca.* LAPO 9. Paris.

———. 1978. Les ostraca paléo-hébreux des fouilles de l'Ophel. *Levant* 10: 156–61.

———. 1985. Vom Ostrakon zur Schriftrolle, Überlegungen zur Entstehung der Bibel. Pp. 110–23 in *XXII. Deutscher Orientalistentag, März 1983, Tübingen.* ZDMGSup 7. Stuttgart.
Lemaire, A., and Vernus, P. 1980. Les ostraca paléo-hébreux de Qadesh-Barnēa. *Or* 49: 341–45.
———. 1983. L'ostracon paléo-hébreu n° 6 de Tell Qudeirat (Qadesh-Barnēa). Pp. 302–6 in *Fontes atque Pontes,* ed. M. Görg. ÄAT 5. Wiesbaden.
Naveh, J. 1973. The Aramaic Ostraca. Pp. 79–82 in *Beer-Sheba I, Excavations at Tel Beer-Sheba 1969–1971 Seasons,* ed. Y. Aharoni. Tel Aviv.
———. 1979. The Aramaic Ostraca from Tel Beer-Sheba (Seasons 1971–1976). *TA* 6: 182–98.
———. 1985a. Published and Unpublished Aramaic Ostraca. *ʿAtiqot* 17: 114–21.
———. 1985b. Writing and Scripts in Seventh-century B.C.E. Philistia. *IEJ* 35: 8–21.
Pardee, A. D. 1982. *Handbook of Ancient Hebrew letters.* Chicago.
Puech, E. 1980. Abécédaire et liste alphabétique de noms hébreux du début du IIe s. A.D. *RB* 87: 118–26.
Smelik, K. A. D. 1987. *Historische Dokumente aus dem alten Israel.* Göttingen.

André Lemaire

OSTRICH. See ZOOLOGY.

OTHNI (PERSON) [Heb *ʿotnî*]. A Levitical gatekeeper in the Jerusalem temple, one of the sons of Shemaiah (1 Chr 26:7) who was the firstborn son of Obed-Edom (1 Chr 26:4). While no other mention is made of Othni, considerable discussion attaches to his grandfather, Obed-Edom: in this passage (1 Chr 26:4–8) he and his posterity are listed among the gatekeepers, while other passages include him among the Levitical musicians, of the clan of Asaph ("with harps and lyres," 1 Chr 16:5; "with lyres," 1 Chr 15:21). Perhaps the Obed-Edom clan members originally were temple musicians, but later were demoted to the rank of gatekeepers (1 Chr 15:24, which also designates them as gatekeepers, is often considered a later gloss; see Williamson *1 and 2 Chronicles* NCBC, 125–27, 169–71). If that shift actually happened, Othni may have been a temple musician who was later remembered as a gatekeeper when the reputation of his family was downgraded.

Bibliography

Williamson, H. G. M. 1979. The Origins of the Twenty-four Priestly Courses. A Study of 1 Chronicles xxiii–xxvii. Pp. 251–68 in *Studies in the Historical Books of the Old Testament,* ed. J. A. Emerton. VTSup 30. Leiden.

John C. Endres

OTHNIEL [Heb *ʾotnîʾēl*]. The first of the military leaders who "judged" Israel in the book of Judges (3:7–11). Only the Heb verb *šāpaṭ* "to judge," and never the noun *šōpēṭ* "judge," is used with reference to those leaders. In such usage, it appears, "to judge" is to organize successful counteroffensive against oppressive overlords.

Othniel's career description displays an outlook and employs framework rubrics that are variously observed in the stories of other "judges." It appears, therefore, that Othniel's story is offered as an example, presenting the relationship between Othniel and Israel as exemplary. It is told at the beginning of the book of Judges in such a way as to introduce the problems with which Israel and Yahweh would be confronted in Israel's remembering the rest of the era.

The narrative unit is compact. When Israelites forsook Yahweh and turned instead to Baal and Asherah, Yahweh sold them into the hand of Cushan-rishathaim, "king of *ʾărām nahărāyim*" (Judg 3:8; RSV: "Mesopotamia"). When the Israelites cried out to Yahweh, he raised up a savior who rescued them, Othniel the son of Kenaz, further identified as Caleb's younger brother (Judg 3:9; cf. Josh 15:17). Othniel's leadership was recognized as manifesting the spirit of Yahweh when he went forth to defeat Cushan-rishathaim and win forty years (a generation?) of "rest" for the land. Such, overall, will be the repeated pattern of the premonarchy period. Information about the protagonists here at the outset is minimal.

References to the spirit of Yahweh occur sporadically throughout Judges (6:34; 11:29; 13:25; 14:6, 19; 15:14), differently manifested in various individuals. Here it stands for an impersonal power or force which can be absorbed or can so envelope a person that he or she becomes capable of extraordinary deeds.

The meaning of Othniel's name is not clear, except for the final syllable, Heb *ʾēl,* "God." The first element is a root that appears elsewhere in OT only in the personal name Othni (1 Chr 26:7), who was a Levitical gatekeeper in the temple (note *TPNAH,* 96).

Othniel appears to be presented as Caleb's nephew, who won Caleb's daughter Achsah as his wife by capturing the town of Debir (Josh 15:15–19), a town apparently identical with Kiriath-sepher (Judg 1:11–15). The genealogy in 1 Chr 4:13 supports the statement in Judg 3:9 that Othniel was the son of Kenaz, Caleb's brother. On the other hand, Othniel is also a clan or tribal name in 1 Chr 27:15. Thus Othniel and Caleb are clans of the tribe of Judah. The eponymous hero Othniel is a southerner, from the area where Debir is also situated (probably Khirbet Rabud), not far from Hebron, which Joshua allotted to Caleb (Josh 15:13–14).

The name of the oppressor, "Cushan Doubly Wicked," is obviously a distortion, and "king of Mesopotamia" (Heb *melek ʾărām;* Judg 3:10) is problematical. (RSV's translation of *ʾărām* as "Mesopotamia" is unique here and dependent on the inferred meaning of Judg 3:8; elsewhere the name is translated "Aram" [e.g., Num 23:7] or "Syria" [e.g., Judg 10:6; 1 Kgs 10:29].) The oppressors of Israel in the premonarchy period never came from so far away as Mesopotamia. The suggestion that the oppressor's name may be related to one Irsu, a Syrian usurper in Egypt during the period of anarchy which concluded the 19th Dynasty (Malamat 1954), has not fared well. Recognizing the ease of misdivision in an unpointed consonantal Hebrew text, the oppressor might instead have been king of *ʾarmōn-hărîm,* "a hill country fortress" (Boling *Judges* AB, 81), located not far from Hebron and Debir. If so, and Othniel was a southern hill country liberator, then the story rings with a sound of more authenticity than is generally granted.

This tradition about the southerner Othniel as conqueror of Debir remains in tension with the tradition about the northerner, Joshua of Ephraim, who is elsewhere credited with the conquest of Debir (Josh 10:38–39). Or perhaps the place had changed hands again, in the interim.

Bibliography

Malamat, A. 1954. Cushan Rishathaim and the Decline of the Near East around 1200 B.C. *JNES* 13: 231–42.

ROBERT G. BOLING

OTHONIAH (PERSON) [Gk *Othonias*]. One of the sons of Zattu who returned with Ezra (1 Esdr 9:28). He was one of the Israelites who had married foreign wives and had to put them away with their children in accordance with Ezra's reform. The parallel list in Ezra calls him Mattaniah (Ezra 10:27).

JIN HEE HAN

OVENS, TOWER OF THE (PLACE) [Heb *migdal hattannûrîm*]. A tower in the outer wall of Jerusalem to the W of Ophel. Nehemiah refers to this tower in both the restoration (3:8–13) and the procession (12:38–39) texts and places the tower to the N of the Valley Gate and S of the Broad Wall and the Ephraim Gate. The Tower of the Ovens was probably an integral part of the bakers quarter NW of the City of David and near the royal residence where the "Bakers' Street" was found (Jer 37:21). Avi-Yonah (1954: 244) alludes to the prevailing breezes from the W that would provide the drafts and ventilation for such a complex of ovens. Those who have held to a maximalist view of Jerusalem during Nehemiah's reconstruction have associated the Tower of the Ovens with reinforcement of the Corner Gate by Uzziah (2 Chr 26:9; Sayce 1883: 218; Simons 1952: 234 and n. 2; and Vincent 1954: 243). Simons' suggestion that Nehemiah refers to the Corner Gate when he speaks of the Tower of the Ovens (3:11; 12:38) and Vincent's equation of the Tower of the Angle (2 Chr 26:9) with the Tower of the Ovens have obscured rather than clarified the location of the tower. The accumulative evidence appears to corroborate Avi-Yonah's proposal that the Tower of the Ovens should be placed near the NW limits of the City of David, N of the Valley Gate and S of where the Broad Wall intersects the W wall of the Temple mount (Avi-Yonah 1954: 244; Williamson 1984: 85).

Bibliography

Avi-Yonah, M. 1954. The Walls of Nehemiah—A Minimalist View. *IEJ* 4: 239–48.

Sayce, A. H. 1883. The Topography of Pre-exilic Jerusalem. *PEFQS,* 215–23.

Simons, J. 1952. *Jerusalem in the Old Testament.* Leiden.

Vincent, L.-H., and Steve, M.-A. 1954. *Jerusalem de l'Ancien Testament.* Paris.

Williamson, H. G. M. 1984. Nehemiah's Walls Revisited. *PEQ* 116/2: 81–88.

DALE C. LIID

OVERLAY. An English word that translates five different Hebrew terms signifying various technical applications of metal—gold, silver, and bronze—over a wooden or stone object or structural element. The most common term is from the verb *ṣph* and is used frequently in the tabernacle texts of Exodus to describe the covering of "pure gold" attached to various appurtenances such as the ark (Exod 25:11; 37:2) and its fittings. It also designates the brass and silver overlay for other tabernacle objects or structural features. Similarly, the holiest places and items of the First Temple are said to be overlaid with gold (e.g., 1 Kgs 6:20; 6:28; 2 Kgs 10:18) although the designation for gold in the Temple differs from that of the tabernacle texts. Similarly, the royal throne was overlaid with gold (2 Kgs 10:18; 2 Chr 9:17).

In several other passages, different Hebrew words are found for gold. They are probably not synonyms but rather indicate differences in technology. In 2 Chr 3:8, 9, *ḥph* is used with "fine gold" in Isa 40:19, *rkᶜ* is used to describe the covering of an image (made of metal?) with gold; and in Hab 2:19, gold and silver are said to overlay (from Heb *tpš*) stone idols.

The frequent use of the root *ṣph* apparently refers to the use of hammered-out sheets of metal. The other words may designate variations on the process that depend on the quality of the gold or the nature of the object to be overlaid. The technique for covering stone, for example, would have to be different than for that used to cover wood (acacia wood in the Tabernacle; cedar, olivewood, and cypress wood in the Temple).

CAROL MEYERS

OWL. See ZOOLOGY.

OX (ANIMAL). See ZOOLOGY.

OX (PERSON) [Gk *Ōx*]. A name given as part of the genealogy of Judith (Jdt 8:1). The name in its Greek form is non-Semitic. It appears in certain manuscripts as Oz (Gk *Ōz*; see Vaticanus, OLˢ, Syr), which is a translation of the Hebrew name Uzzi (Heb *ᶜuzzî*). If "Ox" is a corruption of "Oz," its Hebrew original, Uzzi, appears eleven times in the OT (Ezra 7:4, Neh 11:22, 1 Chr 5:31, etc.). However, none of these occurrences connect the name "Uzzi" with the tribe of Simeon, the tribe to which, according to the author, Judith belongs. Therefore, it is probable, given the genre of the book of Judith, that the name is part of what Noth *(HPT)* calls a "secondary genealogy," and thus completely fictitious. See further JUDITH, BOOK OF.

SIDNIE ANN WHITE

OXYRHYNCHUS SAYINGS. See SAYINGS OF JESUS, OXYRHYNCHUS.

OYSTERS. See ZOOLOGY.

OZEM (PERSON) [Heb *ʾōṣem*]. Two individuals of the tribe of Judah.

1. Sixth son of Jesse and the brother of David the King. The sons of Jesse are listed here as being seven whereas 1 Sam 16:10 indicates eight sons.

2. Fourth son of Jerahmeel (1 Chr 2:25).

David Channing Smith

OZIEL (PERSON) [Gk *Oziēl*]. A name given as part of the genealogy of Judith (Jdt 8:1). The Hebrew form of the name is Uzziel (Heb *ʿuzzîʾēl*), which occurs several times in the OT. The occurrence of which the author of the book of Judith was most likely thinking is 1 Chr 4:42, where a certain Uzziel appears as a member of the tribe of Simeon. Judith, according to the author, is also a Simeonite. The purpose of the genealogy is to prove the purity of Judith's Jewish descent, and to provide the story with verisimilitude. See JUDITH, BOOK OF.

Sidnie Ann White

OZNI (PERSON) [Heb *ʾoznî*]. Var. EZBON. OZNITE. One of the sons of Gad and founder of the clan of the Oznites, according to the genealogy of Num 26:16. He is preceded in the list by Shuni and followed by Eri. This second census in Numbers is closely related to the genealogy of Genesis 46. There (Gen 46:16) and also in *Jub.* 44:20, Ezbon is listed as the son of Gad between Shuni and Eri. There is no manuscript evidence which would support Ozni or Ezbon as the preferred reading in both places. Rather, there seem to be two renditions of the same name.

Christina de Groot van Houten

P

P. The abbreviation used in Pentateuchal source criticism to designate the Priestly Writer. See PRIESTLY ("P") SOURCE; TORAH (PENTATEUCH); SOURCE CRITICISM (OT).

PAARAI (PERSON) [Heb *paʿăray*]. One of "The Thirty," an elite group of the warriors of King David (2 Sam 23:35). He is called "the Arbite" (Heb *ʾarbî*), which is a reference to his home village, ARAB, in the hill country district of Hebron (Josh 15:52).

There is some textual confusion over both the name "Paarai," and the gentilic "Arbite." In the parallel list of David's champions in 1 Chr 11:26–47, the reading corresponding to "Paarai the Arbite" is "Naarai the son of Ezbai" (1 Chr 11:37; LXX supports this). Although certainty is impossible, scholars generally feel that Samuel has the superior reading, Naarai resulting from a confusion of the Hebrew letters *pe* and *nun,* and "son of Ezbai" being the result of corruption.

In the LXX of 2 Kgdms 23:35, Codex Vaticanus reads *Ouraioerchi* for the term "Arbite" in MT. This suggests the translator read Heb *ʾarḥi* instead of *ʾarbi,* "Archite" in place of "Arbite." This would then place the home town of Paarai in the hill country of Ephraim. Although some scholars have argued for the originality of this reading, it has a weak textual basis. It would also be incongruous with the geographical arrangement of the list, since Paarai's name is included with other warriors, all of whom came from the southern district of Judah (Elliger 1966: 101–2).

Bibliography

Elliger, K. 1966. Die dreissig Helden David. Pp. 72–118 in *Kleine Schriften zum Alten Testament,* ed. H. Gese and O. Kaiser. Munich.

STEPHEN G. DEMPSTER

PADDAN-ARAM (PLACE) [Heb *paddan-ʾărām*]. Var. PADDAN. A name for the area around Haran, the homeland of Abraham's family in upper Mesopotamia. This designation occurs only in Genesis and only in passages generally ascribed to the Priestly source. It appears particularly in reference to Jacob's sojourn with Laban at Haran in Genesis 28–31. It is to Paddan-aram that Isaac sends Jacob in Gen 28:1–7, and it is there that most of Jacob's sons are born (Gen 29:31–30:24; cf. Gen 35:26; 46:15). Scholars have generally seen it as an alternate name for ARAM-NAHARAIM, a substantial region of upper Mesopotamia located around the great bend of the Euphrates River (Skinner *Genesis* ICC, 358; de Vaux *EHI,* 195). On the other hand, some have argued that Paddan-aram was an Aramaic rendering of the city name HARAN (PLACE) (O'Callaghan 1948: 96).

These two distinct identifications depend upon the meaning of the word *paddān.* Those who argue that the name designates a large geographical area generally translate it as "field," thus making Paddan-aram mean "Field of Aram." This has been based largely on two arguments (already referred to in Rashi's commentary on Gen 25:20): (1) the noun *paddān* has a cognate in Arabic which means "field," and thus Aramaic may also have had a similar meaning for the word; and (2) Hosea 12:13 (—Eng 12:12) refers to this area as *śĕdēh ʾărām,* "Field of Aram," in a reference to Jacob's sojourn there, and this is deemed to be a Hebrew translation of *paddan-ʾărām* (de Vaux 1948: 323; Albright *FSAC,* 237; Skinner *Genesis* ICC, 358). However, neither of these arguments is conclusive. There appears to be no clear Aramaic or Syriac occurrence of *paddān* as "field." Its regular meanings in Aramaic and Syriac are "plough, yoke (of oxen)," and in Arabic the primary meaning is "yoke" as well. The derivative meaning, "field," may be an inner-Arabic development. As for the second argument, one must admit that the use of *śĕdēh ʾărām* in Hosea need not be understood as the translation of a place name at all.

The other proposal, that Paddan-aram is an Aramaic rendering of the city name Haran, relates *paddān* to the Akkadian *padānu/paddānu,* which means "road, highway." This is a synonym for Akkadian *ḫarrānu,* "road, highway, caravan," the probable source of the name, Har(r)an (O'Callaghan 1948: 96). But the argument depends on the Aramaic word also having the meaning "road" or "caravan," and there is no such evidence currently available. Thus the exact extent of the area designated by this name remains uncertain.

Bibliography

O'Callaghan, R. T. 1948. *Aram Naharaim.* AnOr 26. Rome.
Vaux, R. de. 1948. Les patriarches hébreux et les découvertes modernes. *RB* 55: 321–47.

WAYNE T. PITARD

PADON (PERSON) [Heb *pādôn*]. The head of a family of Nethinim (Temple servants) who returned from the Babylonian Exile (Ezra 2:44 and parallels in Neh 7:47 and 1 Esdr 5:29). The list in Ezra-Nehemiah implies that this return took place immediately in response to Cyrus's declaration in 538 B.C.E. But 1 Esdras places this return in its more probable date at the time of King Darius (ca. 522). As members of the guild of NETHINIM, the family of Padon would have had a special role in the temple cult, perhaps assisting the Levites (Levine 1963; Weinberg 1975). Although some scholars consider the Nethinim to be foreigners or of foreign origin (largely on the basis of later rabbinic sources), it is more likely that during the postexilic period the Nethinim, as cultic personnel, were neither considered foreigners nor slaves. Rather, like the Levites, they had been devoted to cultic service the precise nature of which can no longer be identified. The size of Padon's family, its origins, and specific role are no longer discernible. See Blenkinsopp *Ezra-Nehemiah* OTL; Williamson *Ezra, Nehemiah* WBC.

Bibliography

Levine, B. A. 1963. The Netinim. *JBL* 82: 207–12.

Weinberg, J. P. 1975. Nᵉtinim und "Söhne der Sklaven Salomos" im 6–4 Jh. v. u. Z. *ZAW* 87: 355–71.

TAMARA C. ESKENAZI

PAGANS. See NATIONS.

PAGIEL (PERSON) [Heb *pagʿîʾēl*]. The son of Ochran and the chief (*nāśîʾ*, Num 2:27) of the tribe of Asher during the wilderness sojourn after the Exodus. He is mentioned only five times in the OT in four different tribal lists. He helped Moses conduct a census of all able-bodied warriors among the Israelites (Num 1:13). He led the tribe of Asher to its proper place on the N side of the tabernacle in the Israelite camp (2:27) and to its position in the rear guard when the Israelites prepared to depart from Mt. Sinai (Num 10:26). He also presented the offerings of the tribe of Asher on the eleventh day of the twelve-day celebration of the dedication of the altar (Num 7:72, 77). While the meaning of the name "Pagiel" is uncertain, *HALAT* (861) suggests that it means "the one who intercedes with God"; Gray (*Numbers* ICC, 8) proposes the meaning: "the lot or fate given by God."

DALE F. LAUNDERVILLE

PAHAD. See NAMES OF GOD IN THE OT.

PAHATH-MOAB (PERSON) [Heb *paḥat-môʾāb*]. The name Pahath-Moab suggests a title, (military) governor of Moab, rather than a personal name. It is derived from the Hebrew word *peḥâ,* meaning military governor, and is related to the Akk *paḥâtu/piḥâtu* of the same meaning. The best explanation for the use of Pahath-Moab as a personal name is that a person of humble origins rose to a position as governor of Moab and assumed his title in place of his given name. One can only guess that this person was one of obscure background who achieved this position under David (1 Sam 22:1–2) and became the governor of the newly subjugated land of Moab (2 Sam 8:2). This person is never otherwise identified, however, and is known primarily as the ancestor of one of the large Judean clans which returned from the Babylonian exile with Zerubbabel (Ezra 2:6; 8:4; 10:30; Neh 3:11; 7:11; 1 Esdr 5:11; 8:31). Neh 10:15—Eng 10:14 names Pahath-Moab as one of the chiefs of the people who set his seal to Nehemiah's covenant.

D. G. SCHLEY

PAI (PLACE) [Heb *pāʿî*]. Var. PAU. Residence of the Edomite king Hadad (1 Chr 1:50). See also PAU (PLACE).

PALACE. Neither the Hebrew OT nor the Greek NT has a specific word for "palace," although various terms so translated suggest a structure that was an elite residence and at the same time served certain military, judicial, and even religious functions. For instance, *bêt hammelek* (2 Chr 9:11), "house of the king," denotes what we would call a palace. Similarly, in the NT, *aulē,* literally "hall" or "court," clearly implies in some passages a palace (cf. Matt 26:3; Luke 11:21).

Few actual palaces are known thus far from excavations in Palestine, and certainly none that compare to the famous palaces brought to light in ancient Egypt, Syria, and Mesopotamia. Ancient Palestine was a marginal region, relatively poor in material culture in comparison with Egypt, Syria, and Mesopotamia. It has thus yielded few remains of luxurious buildings such as palaces. This brief survey will note the principal structures that might be considered "palaces" in the pre-Classical sites and Classical periods (see articles on specific sites for further detail). We shall regard as a "palace" any unusually large and elaborate structure that is clearly not an ordinary private dwelling, especially those whose locations and/or contents and furnishings suggest both residential and administrative functions.

A. Bronze Age

1. The Early Bronze Age (ca. 3400–2000 B.C.). The only truly palatial structure known from the first urban era in the 3d millennium B.C. is the ʿAi *palais* of Mm. Marquet-Krause (1949), reinvestigated by J. A. Callaway. See Fig. PAL.01 and AIP.01. In its initial phase, it no doubt functioned as a temple, but by EB III (ca. 2600–2400 B.C.) it had become a citadel-palace, of monumental proportions and excellent stone masonry.

2. The Middle Bronze Age (ca. 2000–1500 B.C.). The phase of urban revival in the early 2d millennium B.C. produced a number of elaborate structures, possibly the residences and also administrative centers for local dynasts in Palestine's characteristic "city-state" system. "Palace 7200" adjacent to the city gate at Shechem (Dever 1974) is a large, two-story colonnaded structure, incorporating a tripartite temple and located on a public plaza. It resembles and even rivals the royal complex of stratum VII at Alalakh in Syria. Petrie's old "Palace II" at Tell el-ʿAjjûl (1931–34) is an impressive multiroomed structure, also near the city gate. The largest (and earliest) such structure is the Ras el-ʿAin/Aphek "Palace I" of MB I, with spacious, thickly plastered rooms and courtyards, and massive col-

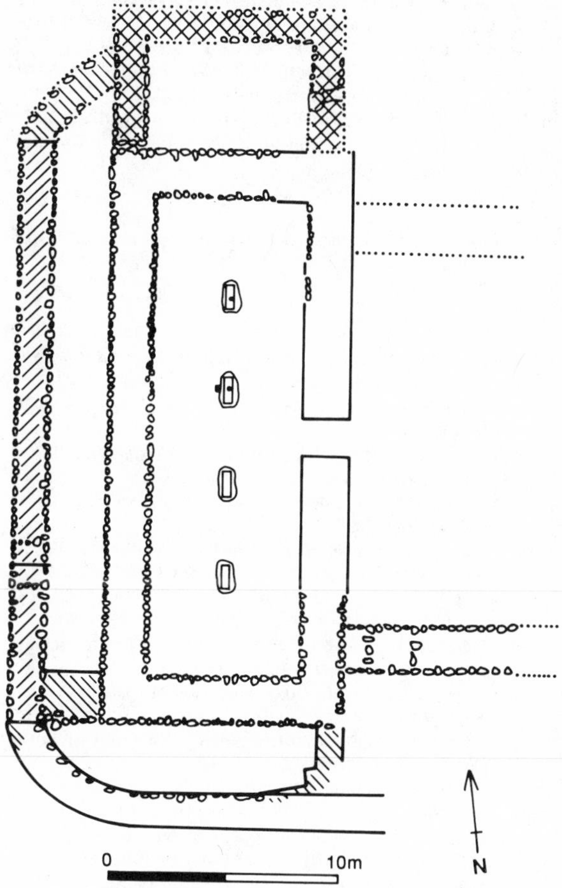

PAL.01. Plan of monumental citadel-palace at Ai—EB. *(Redrawn from Marquet-Krause 1949: pl. XCII)*

umn bases that rival or surpass any in contemporary Syria in size. A recently discovered palace at Kabri, in Lower Galilee, even boasts plastered floors with painted designs. It is likely that other Middle Bronze Age palaces existed in Palestine.

3. The Late Bronze Age (ca. 1500–1200 B.C.). When Palestine came under Egyptian New Kingdom domination in the Late Bronze Age—especially in the well-known "Amarna Age" of about the 14th century B.C.—a number of palatial structures appeared. Several were clearly palaces, since they were modeled along the lines of Egyptian-style "Governor's Residencies," as E. Oren has shown (1985). Among the latter are elaborate, multiroomed buildings such as those at Beth-shan, Aphek ("Palace 1"; Beck and Kochavi 1983; 1985), Tel Batash VII (Kelm and Mazar 1984), Tell esh-Shariya IX (Oren 1982), Tell el-ᶜAjjûl ("Palace III") (Petrie 1931–1934), Tel Masos, Tell Jemmeh, Tell el-Ḥesi, Tell el-Farᶜah (S), and Deir al-Bâlah in the Gaza strip. The Aphek palace is exceptional. It has two stories, the lower no doubt administrative and the upper residential. The lower story features an entrance court with a large water basin, several large work and service rooms, and a still larger area that is probably an audience chamber. The administrative function of the Aphek palace is indicated by its relative wealth of textual remains (for a Palestinian site), including cuneiform fragments, a lexical tablet in Akkadian, and a Hittite *bulla.* A monumental building unearthed at Gezer long ago by Macalister along the N "Inner Wall" may constitute another example, as does also the badly ruined "Palace 14120" of the modern excavations.

B. Iron Age

1. The Iron I Period (ca. 1200–900 B.C.). The periods of the Israelite settlement and early monarchy have yielded a few palacelike structures, such as Albright's "fortress of King Saul" at Tell el-Fûl/Gibeah (Albright 1924; Sinclair 1960; Lapp 1965). More certain are the Solomonic period *bit ḫilani*-style "Palace 6000" and Building 1723 (Ussishkin 1973) at Megiddo (both str. VA/IVB)—the latter possibly the residence of the district governor Baᶜana, who is known from the Hebrew Bible (1 Kgs 4:12). "Palace 10,000" at Gezer is connected with the city gate (Dever 1985), like "Palace 6000" at Megiddo, but it is less elaborate; both appear to be more administrative than residential, i.e., citadels. The most important Iron I palace in early Israel would have been, of course, the Royal Palace in Jerusalem. This is described in 1 Kgs 7:1–12 (cf. also 2 Sam 5:11–15 for David's palace), but no trace of this structure has been (or ever likely will be) discovered. Similar structures, however, which fit even the details of the biblical structure, have been found in 9th–8th century Syria at such sites as Zinjirli (ancient Samᶜal) and Tell Halaf. Here one finds, as with the Jerusalem temple, a location on the citadel near the main temple, ashlar (dressed) masonry construction, etc.

2. The Iron II Period (ca. 900–600 B.C.). Similar palaces at regional centers existed during the period of the divided monarchy. In Israel, was the Hazor VIII–V Citadel in the upper city, a massive residence-fortress. The Gezer "Palace 10,000" continued in use, but more as a residence. The most significant palace in the N kingdom of Israel was no doubt that of the Omride kings at the capitol of Samaria (Crowfoot, Kenyon, and Sukenik 1942), in the 9th–8th centuries B.C. The royal quarter on the acropolis was surrounded by a casemate (double) wall. The palace area included a splendid building constructed in the finest Phoenician ashlar masonry ever found in ancient Palestine. Dubbed the "ivory house" by the excavators, this building yielded more than 500 fragments of carved ivory inlays, no doubt from wooden furniture (see Ahab's "house of ivory" in 1 Kgs 23:39; cf. "beds of ivory" in Amos 6:40). These are the finest Phoenician-style ivories known from Palestine, and they hint at the luxury goods that once embellished the local palaces but which were almost always looted in antiquity. Just to the W of this building was found a group of 63 ostraca, mostly tax receipts, indicating the administrative functions of the palace.

In Judah, Ramat Raḥel (Aharoni 1962; 1964), on the outskirts of Jerusalem, may have been an auxiliary residence of the kings of Judah; it had splendid ashlar masonry, capitols, and balustrades of Phoenician style. Albright's "West Building" at Tell Beit Mirsim, a *ḥilani*-style structure built into a city gate, is probably another palace (Albright 1932; Albright and Kelso 1943). See Fig. PAL.02. The most monumental Iron II palace in Palestine is the strata V–II "Residency" at Lachish (Tufnell 1953; Aharoni 1975), an enormous masonry structure with several successive additions, still standing to an impressive height today. It continued in use until the Assyrian destructions, and was even rebuilt in the Persian period.

C. Later Palaces

There may have been Assyrian or Babylonian palaces in Palestine following the destruction of the N and S kingdoms, but no trace of these has survived, with one possible exception. A large building built in Assyrian-style vaulted mudbrick construction, containing Assyrian "palace ware," was found at Tell Jemmeh, possibly ancient Yurza, of the 8th–7th centuries B.C.

The Persian rebuild of the Lachish "Residency" has been mentioned above. The Hellenistic period in Palestine has yielded a number of monumental buildings, but none that can be positively identified as a palace.

In the Roman era, the most notable remains of palaces are those identified with the well-known building activities of Herod the Great (37–4 B.C.). His principal residence in Jerusalem is relatively well described by Josephus, and archaeological investigation has confirmed that it is to be identified in the earliest phases of the Citadel, now incorporated into the Jaffa Gate in the W wall of the Old City. Herod's "Winter Palace" on both banks of the Wadi Qelt, W of Jericho, has been investigated by both American and Israeli archaeologists (Pritchard 1958; Netzer 1982) and has produced splendid remains of residential areas, courtyards, and luxurious gardens. See Fig. JER.06. Another retreat of Herod's was the Herodium (Netzer 1981; Netzer and Arazi 1985), a fortress (and also Herod's tomb) 4 miles SE of Bethlehem, excavated in recent years. An even more grandiose Herodian palace and desert retreat was erected, along with other structures, at Masada, on the W shore of the Dead Sea. Masada was extensively cleared by Y. Yadin in 1965–67 (1966) and gives the visitor an unforgettable impression of Herod's ambition and his taste for the Roman lifestyle.

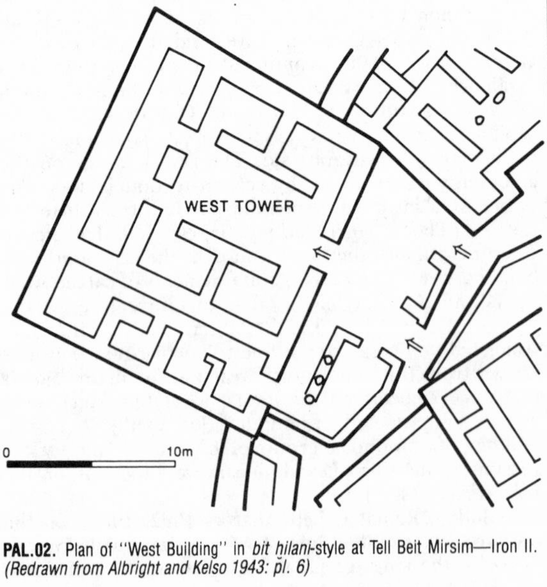

PAL.02. Plan of "West Building" in *bit ḫilani*-style at Tell Beit Mirsim—Iron II. *(Redrawn from Albright and Kelso 1943: pl. 6)*

Bibliography

Aharoni, Y. 1962. *Excavations at Ramat Rahel, Seasons 1959 and 1960.* Rome.
———. 1964. *Excavations at Ramat Rahel, Seasons 1961 and 1962.* Rome.
———. 1975. *Lachish V.* Tel Aviv.
Albright, W. F. 1924. *Excavations and Results at Tell el-Ful (Gibeah of Saul).* AASOR 4. New Haven.
———. 1932. *The Excavation of Tell Beit Mirsim in Palestine, I.* AASOR 12. New Haven.
Albright, W. F., and Kelso, J. L. 1943. *The Excavation of Tell Beit Mirsim, 3.* AASOR 21–22. New Haven.
Beck, P., and Kochavi, M. 1983. The Egyptian Governor's Palace at Aphek. *Qad* 16: 47–51 (in Hebrew).
———. 1985. A Dated Assemblage of the Late 13th Century B.C.E. from the Egyptian Residency at Aphek. *TA* 12: 29–42.
Crowfoot, J. W.; Kenyon, K. M.; and Sukenik, E. L. 1942. *The Buildings at Samaria.* London.
Dever, W. G. 1974. The MBIIC Stratification in the Northwest Gate Area at Shechem. *BASOR* 216: 31–52.
———. 1985. Solomonic and Assyrian Period "Palaces" at Gezer. *IEJ* 35: 217–30.
Kelm, G. L., and Mazar, A. 1984. Timnah: A Biblical City in the Sorek Valley. *Arch* 37: 58–59+.
Lapp, P. W. 1965. Tell el-Ful. *BA* 28: 2–10.
Marquet-Krause, J. 1949. *Les fouilles de ʿAy (et-Tell).* Paris.
Netzer, E. 1981. *Greater Herodium.* Qedem 10. Jerusalem.
———. 1982. Recent Discoveries in the Winter Palace of Second Temple Times at Jericho. *Qad* 15: 22–29 (in Hebrew).
Netzer, E., and Arazi, S. 1985. The Tunnels of Herodium. *Qad* 18: 33–38 (in Hebrew).
Oren, E. 1982. Ziklag: A Biblical City on the Edge of the Negev. *BA* 45: 155–66.
———. 1985. Governors' Residencies in Canaan Under the New Kingdom: A Case Study of Egyptian Administration. *Journal for the Society for the Study of Egyptian Antiquities* 14/2: 37–56.
Petrie, W. M. F. 1931–34. *Ancient Gaza I–IV.* London.
Pritchard, J. B. 1958. *Excavations at Herodian Jericho, 1951.* AASOR 32–33. New Haven.
Sinclair, L. A. 1960. *An Archaeological Study of Gibeah (Tell el-Ful).* AASOR 34–35: 1–52.
Tufnell, O. 1953. *Lachish 3.* London.
Ussishkin, D. 1973. King Solomon's Palaces. *BA* 36: 78–105.
Yadin, Y. 1966. *Masada.* London.

WILLIAM G. DEVER

PALAEOGRAPHY. Palaeography provides the student of the Bible with a tool for studying both the material culture of ancient civilizations and the religious, political, and intellectual culture of these societies. By providing a sound basis for establishing relative chronologies for manuscripts, inscriptions on monuments, potsherds, and coins, palaeography joins with other archaeological evidence in allowing the student to gain a better understanding of everyday life in the ancient world.

Palaeography is the study of ancient writing with reference to the way the letters are formed and how these letters change form over a period of time. There are several subcategories within palaeography which are defined in relation to the type of material the scribe wrote upon and the tools the scribe used. As a subcategory, *palaeography* refers to the study of writing drawn with a pen or a brush, upon any material which will hold the ink or paint, but particularly leather, parchment, papyrus, paper, and ostraca (Metzger, 1981: 1). *Epigraphy* refers to the study of writing carved into nonporous materials such as stone, metal, bone. *Numismatics* refers to the study of coins; coins often bear an inscription and other symbols or designs representative of the minting authority.

A. Functions and History

Once sufficient evidence is in hand, a palaeographer is able to establish a typological sequence of the changes which occur in the form and orientation of the characters written by the scribes. Not every newly discovered manuscript, inscription, or coin comes with an absolute date written upon it. But the palaeographer can date the newly discovered writing on the basis of the relative chronology that the typological sequence provides.

This makes palaeography an indispensable tool for detecting forgeries and authenticating genuine manuscripts, inscriptions, and coins. The science of palaeography was born out of an attempt to prove the authenticity of the credentials of several Benedictine monasteries through classifying Latin manuscripts by age using handwriting and other internal evidence. This led to the publication of *De Re Diplomatica* by Jean Mabillon (1632–1707) of St. Maur. Mabillon's methodology was soon adapted to the study of Greek manuscripts (Metzger 1981: 1).

With a sufficient base of evidence, one can even identify the work of individual scribes in a number of manuscripts or the hand of specific engravers in a number of different coin dies. An example of this is found in the palaeographic and numismatic study of the abundant Hasmonean coinage (ca. 103–37 B.C.) available for study. At least twelve different engravers made dies for the Hasmonean rulers (McLean 1982: 111).

B. Methodology and Techniques

The palaeographer tries to envision the ideal form which the scribe or engraver was trying to achieve. The scribe had in mind a basic form with a certain sequence and direction of strokes, and had some understanding of the proper proportions of the character to be produced, whatever the actual outcome might be. The feature of human nature that allows us to use typological analysis for scripts, pottery, and art forms is that the individual execution of the "ideal form" is different each time. No person signs his or her name exactly the same way each time. Yet the signature must be recognizable. Therefore the range of tolerated variation is limited in any given instance.

It is the innovations, whether accidental or deliberate, in the actual production of a form which result in reinterpretation of the form, its proportions, and even the sequence and direction of strokes. Subsequent students or apprentices have a new ideal form as their standard. It is this continual modification that allows us to determine typological sequences over the long term. The more frequent the use of a script or individual letter within the script, the greater is the possibility of innovations and reinterpretation. More frequent letters will have a faster rate of development than less frequently used forms.

However, one cannot study the change in any given letter in isolation from the rest of the letters of the script. Just as each of us learned that our printed and cursive letters have ideal proportions, spacing, and angular relationships with the other letters in a word or line, these same considerations must be taken into account. The palaeographer must create a horizontal script chart which displays examples of all the letters found in a given manuscript in alphabetical order. The proper proportions, spacing, and angular relationships must be recorded with reference to the ceiling or base line used in any given manuscript. The term "swing" is used for scripts hanging from a ceiling line; "stance" is used for scripts oriented to a base line.

Modern English and Hebrew alphabets are drawn in relationship to a base line. The early Semitic alphabets, including Aramaic, Hebrew, and Phoenician, were drawn hanging from a ceiling line. Often the ceiling or base line used by the original scribe is still visible on the manuscript. The Palaeo-Hebrew manuscript of Leviticus found in Cave 11 at Qumran (11QpaleoLev) provides a good example of the horizontal ceiling and vertical margin lines used by scribes (Freedman and Mathews 1985: pl. 9).

Inscriptions on coins and other media create special problems for determining the ideal swing or stance envisioned by the engraver. Stones and other natural objects have limitations of size, and possible flaws; miscalculation of available space by the engraver further modifies letter shape and stance or swing. The die cutter has limited space upon which to put the required inscription on the coin. Letters are often squeezed into odd corners at odd angles. A line of script will start at one angle and finish on another. A script chart for a Hasmonean coin might show extreme variations of swing or shape of letters owing to the engraver's attempt to use available space. The palaeographer must recognize that such variations have no bearing on the development of the script. Also, a common numismatic convention of writing the inscription around the circumference of the coin makes the establishment of an orientation line difficult.

Perhaps the most important development in palaeography is the continuing work of perfecting techniques in infrared and microphotography, computer enhancement, and digital recording of images. One of the scholars in the forefront of these developments is Prof. Bruce Zuckerman, director of the West Semitic Research Project of the University of Southern California. One of the major goals of the project is to make good-quality photographs of West Semitic inscriptions available to the whole scholarly community (Coughlin 1987). Standard photography has made reproductions of manuscripts, inscriptions, and coins available to the beginning and experienced palaeographer that would otherwise be unavailable because of the cost of travel and the restrictions of various institutions on access to their collections.

The use of photographic materials, however, is not without its dangers. Photographs of manuscripts do not pose too much of a problem. But a photograph of an inscription or a coin involves reducing a three-dimensional object to a two-dimensional reproduction. The position of the camera, the angle and type of lighting, the amount of relief in the original inscription or coin result in different images being recorded. The best palaeographic analysis remains dependent on access to as many of the original artifacts as is possible. The palaeographer can turn the objects to get different lighting effects and identify distortions caused by lighting that might be impossible to detect in a photograph.

The use of original coins or inscriptions does not completely solve the problem; the making of a script chart once again involves reducing a three-dimensional character to two dimensions. This reinforces the earlier observation that the palaeographer must be able to envision the ideal form behind the actual form which the scribe or engraver produced. Naturally, the palaeographer is limited by what she sees, or thinks she sees.

This interpretation and reproduction of what the palaeographer perceives means palaeography is both a science and an art. Therefore, the value of palaeographic analysis is dependent on the quantity of material available for comparison. The methodology, techniques, and abilities of the palaeographer are crucial. The information gleaned from palaeography is vital for creating, supplementing, or debunking relative chronologies or absolute datings not only for writings, but also for pottery and other archaeological artifacts. It is useful for determining the authenticity of manuscripts, inscriptions, and coins.

Bibliography

Avigad, N. 1958. The Palaeography of the Dead Sea Scrolls and Related Documents. *Aspects of the Dead Sea Scrolls.* ScrHier 4. Jerusalem.

Coughlin, E. K. 1987. Cameras, Computers Help to Decipher Ancient Texts. *Chronicle of Higher Education* 34/11: A6–A9.

Cross, F. M. 1968. The Phoenician Inscription from Brazil. A Nineteenth-Century Forgery. *Or* 37: 437–60.

Freedman, D. N., and Mathews, K. 1985. *The Paleo-Leviticus Scroll (11QpaleoLev).* Philadelphia.

Herr, L. G. 1978. *The Scripts of Ancient Northwest Semitic Seals.* HSM 18. Missoula, MT.

Lidzbarski, M. 1898. *Handbuch der Nordsemitischen Epigraphik.* 2 vols. Weimar.

McCarter, P. K., Jr. 1975. *The Antiquity of the Greek Alphabet and the Early Phoenician Scripts.* HSM 9. Missoula, MT.

McLean, M. 1982. The Use and Development of Palaeo-Hebrew in the Hellenistic and Roman Periods. Ph.D. Diss., Harvard.

Metzger, B. 1981. *Manuscripts of the Greek Bible: An Introduction to Palaeography.* New York.

Naveh, J. 1970. *The Development of the Aramaic Scripts.* Jerusalem.

Zuckerman, B. 1987. *Puzzling Out the Past: Making Sense of Ancient Inscriptions from Biblical Times.* Los Angeles.

MARK D. MCLEAN

PALAL (PERSON) [Heb *pālāl*]. One of those who worked on the wall of Jerusalem following the return from Babylonian exile (Neh 3:25). His name may be a shortened form of Pelaliah, which means "Yahweh has interposed/judged" (Brockington *Ezra, Nehemiah and Esther* Century Bible, 143). Palal was the son of Uzai.

MICHAEL L. RUFFIN

PALEO-HEBREW SCRIPT. See HEBREW SCRIPTS.

PALEOLITHIC. See PREHISTORY.

PALEOPATHOLOGY. The study of ancient health and disease in man and animals from the evidence of archaeological remains. While the term "paleopathology" itself is often thought to have been coined by Armand Ruffer early this century, it is clear that it was used in dictionaries as early as 1895 (Moodie 1921: 21), and as early as 1892 in articles dealing specifically with the subject (Zimmerman and Kelley 1982: 1). The terms "pathology" and "pathologies" are still often used incorrectly in the sense of "lesion(s)" or "disease process(es)," rather than correctly to mean the *study* of such conditions (see the Editorial 1985). The field of paleopathology is very broad and includes the study of disease processes in plants, lower and higher animals, and hominids from the earliest eras from which there is evidence to the recent historical past. One can find paleopathological studies on a variety of specimens—evidence of fungal parasitism in fossil plants, traumatic lesions in ancient crustaceans, fractures and arthritis in dinosaurs, osseous lesions in extinct cave bears and bison, dental attrition among Neanderthals, and a myriad of paleopathologic studies on recent man (Tasnadi-Kubacska 1962; Moodie 1921). The present discussion will necessarily focus on human paleopathology as it concerns the biblical world.

A. History and Development of Paleopathology
   1. Prior to ca. 1850
   2. From ca. 1850 to ca. 1930
   3. From ca. 1930 to ca. 1960
   4. From ca. 1960 to the Present
B. The Nature of the Evidence
   1. Decarnated Skeletal Remains, Including Teeth
   2. Preserved Soft Tissues and Hair
   3. Blood, Biological Pigments, and Stains of Biological Origin
   4. Coprolites, Soil from the Burial, and Ancient Cesspits
   5. Foreign Objects Associated with Grave Contents
   6. Fabricated Cultic, Artistic, and Other Fashioned Artifacts
C. Pseudopathological Changes in Human Remains
D. Animal Paleopathology
E. Are Archaeological Human Remains a Biohazard?
F. The Paleopathologist
G. Paleopathology and Reburial Laws
H. Paleopathology and Archaeology of the Biblical World

I. Observations on Health and Disease Applicable to the Biblical World
J. Conclusion

A. History and Development of Paleopathology

The science of paleopathology appears to have emerged nearly simultaneously in America and Europe near the turn of the century from out of its early beginnings in the late 18th century and early 19th century, with work based largely upon specimens indigenous to each hemisphere. It seems valid to speak of paleopathology in the narrower sense of the biblical world as its development is directly related to British and European advances in paleopathology which were early based almost entirely upon human and animal remains from Egypt. The history of paleopathology in the biblical world might be outlined as follows (for a worldwide perspective, see Pales 1930; Armelagos et al. 1971; Buikstra and Cook 1980; and Angel 1981).

1. Prior to ca. 1850. Before the mid-1800s, interest in human paleopathology ultimately emerged from curiosity and interest in the mummies which accompanied the flow of antiquities from Egypt into Europe and Great Britain. And indeed, human paleopathology is to a large extent the spawn of formative Egyptian archaeology. Already by 1662, German naturalist Andreas Gryphius (1616–1664) had published an anatomical treatise on two mummies which, however, stemmed from his preoccupation with mystery, ritual, and death (Neveux 1964). This early general curiosity surrounding Egyptian mummies soon developed into a more serious interest in their anatomy and health. In 1765, English physician John Hadley (1731–1764) published a scientific description of an Egyptian mummy belonging to the Royal Society (Dawson and Uphill 1972: 130). And in America as well, surgeon John C. Warren (1778–1856) of the Massachusetts General Hospital described a Ptolemaic period mummy in 1821 (Dawson and Uphill 1972: 298). A number of such accounts followed by physicians and others who had either acquired mummies locally or had purchased them as tourists in Egypt. Typical of the increasingly scientific and medical nature of early paleopathology, English physician A. B. Granville (1783–1872) published in 1825 an account of a Persian period mummy in which he observed a cystadenoma of the ovary. The report of the mummy and its unwrapping is still useful reading (Dawson and Uphill 1972: 77). Particularly important in this period is the work of surgeon Thomas J. Pettigrew (1791–1865), who studied a particularly large number of mummies and produced his *History of Egyptian Mummies* in 1834, recently reprinted (Pettigrew 1834). This work was an early landmark in paleopathology as well as being the first book written in England on the archaeology of Egypt (Dawson 1934). It contained, by the standards of the day, many important observations of mummification, anatomy, and other issues of interest to the paleopathologist. Serious accounts of mummies also began to appear early in the century from nonphysicians such as German anthropologist Johann F. Blumenbach, one of the early founders of the science of physical anthropology, and English historian William Osburn (Dawson and Uphill 1972: 31, 219).

Similarly, while studies of the human skeleton also dated back to the 1600s, detailed work did not appear until the 1800s, notably with the appearance in 1844 of such works as S. G. Morton's *Crania Egyptiaca* (Brothwell 1968: 1). Interest in skeletal remains would continue through the century, with the development of several models and theories concerning the various races of man as early understood and characterized from skeletal remains, especially the skull.

2. From ca. 1850 to ca. 1930. From the mid-1800s to roughly 1930, human paleopathology in the biblical world continued to center largely on mummified human and faunal remains from Egypt. Austrian physician Johann Czermak (1828–1873), who perfected the early laryngoscope, published the first microscopic anatomical and histological observations on mummified organs and tissues in 1852 (Dawson and Uphill 1972: 75). Among many other figures of importance in this period are physician D. M. Fouquet (1850–1914) (whose work on mummies was influential but contained many errors), and French naturalist Louis Charles Lortet (1836–1909), who continued work on mummified fauna of Egypt. Toward the turn of the century and later, human paleopathology in the biblical world was largely a British affair focused upon Egypt with landmark contributions by anthropologists G. Elliot Smith (1871–1937) and Frederic Wood-Jones (1879–1954) during the archaeological survey of Nubia, the first and largest systematic pathological survey of ancient human remains to date (Smith and Wood-Jones 1910).

Under the direction of Egyptologist Margaret Murray (1863–1963), the first serious interdisciplinary approach to the dissection and medical study of a mummy was made in 1907 before an audience at the Manchester Museum (Murray 1910). English pathologist Marc Armand Ruffer (1859–1917) made many important early contributions to descriptive paleopathology and the scientific study of mummified human tissues, and is commonly regarded as the "Father of Paleopathology," although others such as Pales have applied this epithet to the great Rudolph Virchow (ascribing to him "la paternité de la paleopathologie," and more accurately, it seems, calling Ruffer "le grand animateur" [Pales, 1930: 7, 13]). During the last part of the 19th century, Virchow reported on a broad group of paleopathological specimens ranging from early prehistoric mammals and hominids to the specifics of the hair of Egyptian mummies, quite aside from the fact that some of his conclusions were later shown to be incorrect. Ruffer's contributions were nevertheless a major landmark in paleopathological method also. While the first histological studies on mummified tissue dates to the work of Czermack in 1852, Ruffer left a lasting imprint on the field with pioneering work which employed relatively modern histological techniques on mummified tissues and also with the formulation of the so-called Ruffer's Solution. This histologic reagent is used in the rehydration of mummified human tissues, although the formula has been slightly modified in recent years (Sandison 1955, and others). A number of Ruffer's papers were collected and reprinted after his death (Sandison 1967; Moodie 1921).

Characteristics of this period is the descriptive paleopathology of human remains, centering largely on trauma, skeletal lesions, and early interest in infectious diseases, especially syphilis, which was then incorrectly diagnosed in human remains from early Egypt by Lortet, Zambaco

Pasha, and others (Lortet 1907; Zambaco Pacha 1897). Also, the period is marked by the first application in paleopathology of several scientific methods and technologies. Flinders Petrie, for instance, utilized X-ray studies on mummies just three years after its application in medicine (Petrie 1898).

3. From ca. 1930 to ca. 1960. It has been stated that the years of ca. 1930–1960 reflect a period of relative stagnation in paleopathology worldwide (Buikstra and Cook 1980). This was due in part to the criticism of several established racial osteometric models and theories and the subsequent shift of interest away from the study of bones to the study of living populations in anthropological circles (Brothwell 1968: 2). However, work did not cease entirely. Among the contributions of this period could be mentioned a number of papers by Douglas Derry on a variety of paleopathological subjects (see Armelagos et al. 1971) or the important work of British physician William C. Boyd, who surveyed a large number of mummies in the first large-scale effort to determine blood groups from associated ancient mummified tissues (Boyd and Boyd 1934; Boyd and Boyd, 1937). Also, in 1931 Moodie published X-ray studies of seventeen Egyptian mummies. However, aside from various individual studies, no attempts were made at assembling a major synthesis of paleopathologic knowledge on a scale such as those which had been produced earlier in the century by Moodie or Pales.

4. From ca. 1960 to the Present. Since about 1960 and more recently, and paralleling progress in technology and anthropological theory, there have been numerous advances in the field of paleopathology with an increase in the number of paleopathologic subspecialties as well. The increase in the number of published reports on human remains since about 1960 is notable (cf. Bass 1979). Several important syntheses and collections of paleopathologic knowledge have appeared, although none have dealt specifically with the biblical world (e.g., Brothwell and Sandison 1967; Brothwell 1968; Janssens 1970; Steinbock 1976; Cockburn and Cockburn 1980; Ortner and Putschar 1981; Cohen and Armelagos 1984; David 1986; Zimmerman and Angel 1986; others). Work on the histology of dessicated and mummified tissues has been advanced with the appearance of a paleohistological atlas and a number of detailed studies on the microstructure and staining characteristics of preserved soft tissues (Zimmerman and Kelley 1982). A radiographic survey of 133 mummies from museums in Europe and Britain was made by Gray in 1967 (Gray 1967), and an X-ray atlas and new pathological study of the royal mummies in the Cairo Museum has appeared (Harris and Wente 1980). Several specialized studies have provided vast improvements in the diagnostic criteria for the evidence of several diseases in skeletal remains, especially syphilis (Hackett 1976), and leprosy (Moller-Christensen 1961; 1978). Major advances have been made in the area of paleonutrition providing several new nonspecific skeletal indicators of metabolic stresses. Technological advances have provided medical diagnostic tools and techniques which have been of importance to paleopathology such as CAT (computed axial tomography) and scanning of human remains, and fiber optics, which allow the study of body cavities and the sampling of the internal tissues of mummified corpses without the unacceptable massive destruction of museum specimens previously associated with the gross dissection of autopsies. The facial reconstruction techniques of forensic medicine have been usefully applied to ancient human remains as well (David 1978). Indeed, the blossoming of paleopathology in recent years holds great promise for unprecedented discoveries and advances in our ability to extract knowledge from human remains. Achievements such as the successful cloning of ancient Egyptian mummy DNA in the modern laboratory demonstrates the potential for obtaining *direct* knowledge of the biological nature and makeup of the ancient inhabitants of the biblical world (Pääbo 1985).

Examples of what can be accomplished by interdisciplinary teams employing modern techniques can be seen from the efforts of Rosalie David, whose team conducted a thorough interdisciplinary mummy autopsy at the Manchester Museum, in the tradition established by Margaret Murray (David 1978; David and Tapp 1984). Important also is the more recent team study of the mummy of Ramesses II, which was flown to France for the application of a battery of modern diagnostic procedures, then sterilized by gamma radiation before being returned to Cairo (Balout and Roubet 1985).

However, with advances in techniques and technologies is associated the increasing cost of paleopathological research and the difficulty in applying some techniques to large numbers of specimens. From a practical standpoint, much that is potentially available for use in paleopathology is usually unavailable in the field to the archaeologist and paleopathologist. Advances in diagnostic technology which are relatively common in medicine are often applied only exceptionally to archaeologic period human remains. Unfortunately, paleopathology in the archaeological setting still relies largely on descriptive osteological studies with specialized study of smaller specimens or portions of specimens which can be studied at, or taken from, the site.

B. The Nature of the Evidence

The various specimens obtained from archaeological excavations from which paleopathologic data are obtained may be grouped as follows:

1. Decarnated Skeletal Remains, Including Teeth. Skeletal remains are the most frequently encountered human remains in biblical archaeology. A large variety of evidence can be obtained from the skeleton, such as information regarding the age, sex (still difficult or impossible with immature specimens), stature of the individual, identification of blood groups, relative health, and the existence of certain general disease processes, evidence of parturition (past childbirth), the presence of accidental and inflicted trauma, dietary information and nutritional status, several nonspecific markers for biological stress, and information about certain social customs (i.e., changes in bones owing to frequent kneeling). Often, evidence of specific diseases can be detected such as arthritis, leprosy, tuberculosis, treponemal infections, septic infection (pyogenic osteomyelitis), certain anemias and metabolic bone diseases, and malignancies and tumorlike processes (Steinbock 1976). A number of nonspecific indicators may be found singly or together in skeletal remains to suggest the presence of stress and disease, such as early age at death, Harris lines, dental crowding, dental hypoplasias, or thin long bone cortices. When large numbers of burials are found, populations may be profiled and defined by the application of osteometric analysis to the skeletons.

The information gained from skeletal material depends upon many factors, most important being the presence of a complete skeleton in good condition. However, much may still be learned from fragmentary skeletal remains as well. In fact, the probable sex, relative age, and an estimate of the stature of an ancient person may be determinable from a single recovered bone. An example of the wealth of data which can be extracted from an incomplete, poorly preserved, prehistoric skeleton in the hands of competent osteologists is seen in the recent and superb analysis of the paleolithic period skeleton from Wadi Kubbaniya, Egypt (Close 1986). The presence of a healthy skeleton does not eliminate the presence of disease since most acute illnesses and conditions resulting in death leave no imprint upon the bones. Teeth also may provide evidence of the age of the individual, the quality of the diet, and several nonspecific indicators of nutritional stress and growth disturbances (Price et al. 1985). Occasionally, evidence of certain social customs and occupations is present in teeth such as grooves in the teeth of weavers who pulled fibers from the mouth, etc.

2. Preserved Soft Tissues and Hair. With the survival of soft tissues is often preserved information regarding the specific health of that particular tissue, and thus certain implications may be drawn for the health of the individual. Important advances in the study of preserved tissues have been made in recent years (Zimmerman 1979; Zimmerman and Kelley 1982), and it is from Egypt that we have the greatest amount of knowledge in this regard. Zimmerman, for example, has shown the wealth of data extractable from preserved soft tissues in a recent study of a small group of mummies which demonstrated the presence of tuberculosis, anthracosis (the accumulation of carbon particles from inhaled smoke from cooking fires, etc.), severe atherosclerosis, a rare ancient occurrence of a benign dermatofibroma of the skin on the heel of one mummy, cases of spina bifida, and an infected but healed fracture (Zimmerman 1977). Work on the histology of mummified tissue has shown that many preserved tissues and lesions retain most of the characteristics comparable to freshly processed tissues of the same type. However, some inflammatory reactions (and associated neutrophils), areas of hemorrhage, malignancies of the colon, and evidence of acute myocardial infarction are poorly preserved in mummified tissues (Zimmerman 1979; Zimmerman and Kelley 1982).

Hair is important for the assessment of the nutritional status of the individual and for racial and population profiles (e.g., Hrdy 1978). The color of preserved hair must be interpreted cautiously especially when red-brown and near-blond colors are encountered in populations where dark and black hair is to be expected. Factors such as the oxidation of pigments, damage to the hair, the process of mummification, or fungal invasion of the hair shaft are all known to alter the color of hair.

3. Blood, Biological Pigments, and Stains of Biological Origin. Blood and other biological stains are encountered infrequently in archaeology and in the past were often ignored. However, when properly studied, such material can reveal extraordinary information. Dessicated ancient blood—indeed, the survival of even intact erythrocytes of several thousand years age has been demonstrated (Zimmerman 1973)—contains much potential information concerning the person to whom it belonged, at least the blood type (groups A, B, O, M, and N, usually excluding the Rh antigens, which are unstable over time) if not the manner in which the blood might have been shed. Wounds sustained before death may cause bloodstains on associated bone (Wood-Jones 1908a). Also, the discovery and proper analysis of the pink-colored bones from the cemeteries at Qumran revealed dietary practices among the monks at Qumran which are unattested by any of the published Dead Sea Scrolls or archaeological artifacts (Steckoll et al. 1971). The presence of bright yellow hematoidin on a femur from Tell esh-Shuqafiya, Egypt, is proof of the presence of an old wound and a subsequent nonacute or nonsudden death in the individual a few weeks after the wound was sustained (Jones 1988). However, quite unreliable are the conclusions drawn from the study of red-stained bedrock during the excavations at Bethel which attempt to link it with blood shed by sacrificial victims on a Canaanite altar (Kelso 1968).

4. Coprolites, Soil from the Burial, and Ancient Cesspits. Recent broadened interests in human paleopathology now require an examination of the soil of the burial, especially the soil in the pelvic and abdominal areas, for the presence of coprolites, or ancient fecal remains. Fecal remains may be found as part of the individual grave soil or in masses in ancient pit toilets. Archaeologic fecal remains may contain direct evidence of the diet of ancient man, data on the domestication of plants and the use of wild plant foods, the presence of hair and bone of animal and fish origin used as food, evidence of ancient technologies, the season of defecation of the specimen determined from seasonally specific food remains, as well as data on the microbiological and parasitic inhabitants of the human or animal alimentary tract. The soil from the pelvis and burial may also contain urinary parasites or various materials inserted into the rectum of the individual for medicinal or magical purposes prior to death. Unfortunately, much less may be learned concerning nutrition from fecal analysis owing simply to the fact that it is difficult or impossible to assess the nutritional value of foods assimilated by the body from the undigestible fibers and residues which are not assimilated. Many problems remain in the study of coprolites such as the difficulty in determining if a sample is of human versus animal origin, and various quantitative and qualitative assessments implied by the indigestible remains present in the coprolite. Attempts at culturing and recovering viable ancient human intestinal microorganisms from coprolites have failed repeatedly (see, Wilke and Hall 1975; Bryant 1974 and references).

With regard to the biblical world, paleofecal studies are very few. One analysis of coprolite specimens from caves near the Dead Sea dating to the late Second Temple period, suggest the presence, perhaps commonly, of *Entamoeba histolytica, Giardia lamblia,* and *Chilomastix mesnili.* All three are common intestinal protozoa in developing countries, the first two of which may cause diarrhea and abdominal complaints but also may be life-threatening, the latter being a harmless protozoan inhabitant on the colon (Witenberg 1961). Several studies of Egyptian coprolites have provided some data on food items and ancient parasites from various periods (Cockburn et al. 1975; Smith and Wood-Jones 1910: 181–220; Netolitzky 1911; 1912).

Occasionally, other biological artifacts are recovered with the burial soil such as tissue and arterial calcifications, urinary and gall stones, and echinococcal cysts, among others.

5. Foreign Objects Associated with Grave Contents. Burials may contain durable objects which provide considerable evidence for the paleopathologist. Among these may be weapons embedded within a portion of the skeleton such as arrowheads (Pahl 1983), the remains of rope nooses and garrotes (Wood-Jones 1908b), crucifixion nails (Zias and Sekeles 1985), the presence of splints or bandaging (Smith 1908b), and many other items.

6. Fabricated Cultic, Artistic, and Other Fashioned Artifacts. While this group of artifacts easily may fall within other spheres of study such as the history of medicine, sociology, cult, or myth, they often have relevance directly to paleopathology as well. Various objects found in association with human habitation and burials sometimes preserve replicas or images of certain human activities of medical importance or portrayals of pathological conditions. However, such artifacts must be interpreted with caution. For example, from Egypt, the painted limestone statue of the dwarf Khnumhotep (Egyptian Museum no. 160), the granite sarcophagus lid with the portrait of its dwarf occupant Djehor (Egyptian Museum no. 1294), or the statuette group of the dwarf Seneb with his wife (Egyptian Museum no. 6055) prove the existence of achondroplastic dwarfism in ancient Egypt, agreeing importantly with the literary and artistic evidence from ancient Egypt as attested by many examples (Ruffer 1911 = Moodie 1921: 35–48; Dawson 1938). However, the claim of Yoeli (1955 and 1968), that a single Canaanite figurine dated to the 14th century B.C. portrays the *facies leonis* of advanced leprosy at such an early date runs counter to current knowledge of that disease in antiquity. Also, several ancient portrayals of the Pharaoh Akhenaten have stimulated much discussion about several possible diseases he may have had although his mummy itself has not yet been found (Aldred and Sandison 1962).

Another area which holds some potential in anthropology, genetics, and paleopathology is the study of ancient fingerprints left on pottery by the potter, pressed into the insides of bivalve molded figurines, pottery, etc. Fingerprints on various objects uncovered by the archaeologist are a relatively common discovery, but little study has been made of these important sources of ancient dermatoglyphs.

More directly applicable to the biblical world is the unusual case of the famous woman Babata from the time of Bar Kokhba, whose artifacts were found in the so-called Cave of Letters in Nahal Hever. Her possessions included a basket (her "purse") which contained such traditional feminine objects as scraps of cloth, a mirror, household items, and various personal documents. Also recovered were two important and telling artifacts, her sandals. One sandal had a normal sole pattern, but the other was peculiarly shaped to conform to the outline of her pathologically malformed foot. Babata, it appears, was crippled and had a visibly deformed foot, the shape of which was reflected in her sandal, a disability she bore her entire life. She likely had the noticeable limp of a cripple, and certainly she could not run well. See LAME, LAMENESS. None of Babata's skeletal remains have yet been identified (Yadin 1963; 1971).

C. Pseudopathological Changes in Human Remains

An area of paleopathology of which we still know little is the study of false diseaselike lesions or changes in human remains which are due to factors in the burial environment and therefore occur *post mortem.* Relatively common are such changes as bending or warping of long bones due to grave soil pressure over time, tracks along bones made by roots or insects which mimic venous imprints in bone, or scratches and erosions due to carnivorous animals, all of which may appear pathologic in their origin (Wells 1967). Such alterations in skeletal remains may be particularly enigmatic—at times one may not be sure if certain lesions on ancient bone represent disease processes or are the result of innumerable environmental factors. One of the most important examples of pseudopathological changes in human bone being interpreted as truly pathological are the past attempts of several physicians to see the existence of syphilis anciently in skulls from Egypt dating many centuries earlier (even to the late Predynastic period of Egypt) than any previously known from any part of the world (Fouquet 1896; Zambaco Pacha 1897; Lortet 1907; others). These pseudo-syphilitic bony changes of the skull resembled true syphilitic changes so closely that the claims of ancient syphilis in Egypt remained unchallenged for more than a decade until it was shown that such changes were actually due to a combination of the effects of insects and sandy burials upon the skull (Smith 1908a).

A more recent example is the question of the true incidence of ochronosis in ancient Egypt. Several claims for its existence were called into question only because ochronosis in modern times is a rare autosomal recessive condition. X-ray films of the intervertebral discs of Egyptian mummies often present an impression indistinguishable from the densification of the intervertebral spaces characteristic of alkaptonuric ochronosis seen in modern examples, and thus several claims for the common existence of ochronosis in ancient Egypt have now been shown to be the result of artifacts owing to the processes of mummification (Sandison 1968; Vyhanek and Strouhal 1976).

D. Animal Paleopathology

Much of the present discussion may be relevant to the paleopathology of animal remains. Ancient animals also may be found to have had arthritis, broken bones, and other diseases, although the impact of such discoveries is often minor or insignificant in archaeological terms. However, other findings are clearly more applicable to the archaeological setting. Among the more important aspects of animal paleopathology are the evidences of man-inflicted wounds associated with hostilities, animal sacrifice, etc. (Holladay 1982).

E. Are Archaeological Human Remains a Biohazard?

The issue of biohazardous risk associated with archaeological period biological evidence has been raised occasionally, most recently with regard to the smallpox virus. Smallpox was eradicated worldwide by 1979, but some have cautioned that viable smallpox virus particles may be entombed in potential reservoirs such as the mummy of Rameses V, which is covered with smallpox pustules (Meers 1985). However, the infectious risks associated with archaeologic human remains appear to be extremely small, generally speaking. Smallpox virus particles have not been proven viable after more than a year in dormancy. It is often difficult or impossible to culture viable organisms from mummy viscera, or matter from ancient pit toilets which must have initially received a variety of contagious organisms. However, there are few studies of this question and presently there are no established guidelines regarding the biohazardous potential of archaeologic period human remains.

F. The Paleopathologist

During the early days of paleopathology, the paleopathologist (although many early researchers in ancient disease process never thought of themselves in such terms) was most often an anthropologist or physician, but sometimes an historian, antiquarian, or chemist. At the present day, and reflecting the diverse nature of diagnostic techniques and technologies, the paleopathologist, now more than ever, represents many fields and orientations—most often anthropologists and archaeologists specializing in osteology and paleopathology, and physicians who may represent such specialties as pathology and radiography. Also, one often finds paleopathological studies, especially in team efforts, which include the work of biochemists, microbiologists, demographers, forensic artists, and many others. Such diversity in paleopathologic science is its major strength and this interdisciplinary nature of paleopathology will only increase in the future. However, the paleopathologist must necessarily bridge several fields, no matter what one's initial training might be. The paleopathologist must understand human physiology and pathology, the concepts of diagnostic osteology (often not the same as that of modern surgical pathology), or such fields as paleoenvironment, biochemistry, and many others, while at the same time being aware of the requirements of solid archaeological technique and the elements and principles of accurate history. It is to be expected, therefore, that paleopathological studies may occasionally vary in quality.

G. Paleopathology and Reburial Laws

Without question, the greatest obstacle to the paleopathologist is the established laws and regulations in most modern countries of the biblical world which require reburial of excavated ancient human remains. The implications of such regulations are many, such as greatly restricting the length of time permitted for the study of human remains, restriction of the application of special techniques and technologies to the specimens, or elimination of the opportunity for future study of problems which were not touched upon initially in the field. For example, the reader will note that many of the references to studies of osteological material used in this article mention the frustration of time restrictions and reburial requirements attached to the study of human remains. Such laws also prevent the restudy of osteological samples years after an initial assessment. One possible effect of this is seen in a recent craniometric restudy of skulls from Lachish which determined that only 39 percent of the specimens had been assessed correctly in the initial study performed soon after their excavation. Had these skulls been reburied instead of deposited in the British Museum of Natural History, much of our data on the population at Lachish derived from these skulls would have remained forever incorrect (Keita 1988).

Local religious and cultural sensitivities often even prevent the excavation of human remains from their ancient burial sites. And so, for example, important sources of data for the anthropology and paleopathology of the ancient Jews, such as the Jericho necropolis containing many thousands of burials, or the cemeteries at Qumran containing approximately 1200 burials, still remain largely unstudied except for a few samplings (Hachlili et al. 1981; Steckoll 1967–69; Haas and Nathan 1967–69; Steckoll et al. 1971). One can appreciate and understand the many religious, social, and traditional motivations underlying the establishment of reburial laws, but clearly, the dead can only speak to us and tell us of their ancient lives when their remains are accessible for careful and reverent study by sympathetic modern scientists. Many ancient people still wait to speak. That skeletal remains may be housed in museums is only to their honor rather than the comparative anonymity of a cursory examination and haphazard reburial.

H. Paleopathology and Archaeology of the Biblical World

It is only in recent years that human and animal remains from archaeological excavations have begun to receive the attention they deserve. Today, it is apparent that paleopathology often touches upon issues which relate directly to biblical period history, problems, and personalities. Some random examples of this applicability might include the following out of many possible examples.

Without question, the best evidence for the paleopathologist is to be found in mummified human remains where the skeleton as well as some or all of the soft tissues are preserved. In this regard, we know that Merneptah, the probable Pharaoh of the Exodus, had severe periodontal disease and had lost all of his upper maxillary teeth in the molar-bicuspid regions, leaving only his frontal teeth with which to chew food. He also had extensive arteriosclerosis and was obese (Harris and Wente 1980: 330, 294). A restudy of male skulls from ancient Lachish has provided new confirmation of the multinational population suggested by data from the Bible and excavations at the site (Keita 1988).

Paleopathological studies of human skeletal remains from the ancient Middle East have yet to demonstrate the existence of leprosy and syphilis in the ancient biblical world before the 6th century A.D., although some biblical translations of and commentaries on Leviticus 13 and 15 have led many to believe that it existed at an earlier date. See LEPROSY; DISCHARGE. A skeleton from the Abba cave at Givʿat ha-Mivtar, thought to be that of one of the Maccabean heroes and which possessed evidence of wounds which generally agreed with that reported of his death, has been shown with reasonable probability by modern paleopathologists to be the remains of a woman who had sustained a sword wound to the face *post mortem* (Smith 1977). Important new contributions to our previously sketchy knowledge of the methods of crucifixion have also been reported (Zias and Sekeles 1985 and references).

Populations of several periods in ancient Israel have been osteometrically profiled (Arensburg 1973; Nathan 1961; Smith and Zias 1980; Arensburg and Rak 1985; others), and for example, the Jewish population during the Second Temple period has been described as generally of a robust short to medium stature, having brachycranic to mesocranic skulls, with short broad faces. Jewish families of this period were faced with a child mortality of 30 percent although this was lower than that experienced by non-Jewish neighbors of the same period (Smith and Zias 1980), and similar to that of Bedouin skeletal remains from Israel dating to the last century (Goldstein et al. 1976). Dental disease and arthritis were evident by middle age (Hachlili et al. 1981; Smith and Zias 1980). Specific diagnostic problems such as various forms of trauma in late ancient Israel have been described (Rak et al. 1976), as well as numerous observations on the health and diseases of Jewish inhabitants of Israel during the period of 100 B.C. to A.D. 600 (Arensburg, Goldstein, and Rak 1985).

Among the most important recent studies of human remains from Transjordan have been the series of reports dealing with EB Age human remains from shaft tombs at Bab edh-Dhra (Ortner 1979; Ortner 1981; Ortner 1982), and the skeletal remains from Tell el-Mazar which represent a significant number of Iron Age human remains known elsewhere in large numbers only from Kamid el-Loz and Lachish (Disi et al. 1983). Iron Age human remains are very much fewer from other sites in the biblical world such as Megiddo (Hrdlička 1938), Ain Shems (i.e., Beth-shemesh; Hooton 1939), Azur, or Gezer (Macalister 1912). All of these studies demonstrate that degenerative arthritic conditions, trauma, and dental attrition are the most obvious conditions reflected in these human remains. Trephaning is also evident in a significant number of crania from this period, however it is to be interpreted.

Less work has been done on the osteology and paleopathology of skeletal specimens from Mesopotamia. The region is most famous for the discovery of the prebiblical Neanderthal remains from the Shanidar Cave in N Iraq (Trinkaus 1983). Otherwise, a number of scattered and relatively recent reports have appeared which focus largely on isolated or small groups of human specimens, although "bin" ossuaries are known from several sites. Nevertheless, some of these studies present important and rare paleopathological cases such as the possible remains of conjoined ("Siamese") twins from early Tell Hassuna (Abdul Aziz and Slipka 1966). Clearly, the most important and only synthesis of paleopathological data from this area is the recent study of Rathbun which concentrates largely on specimens dated earlier than about 1000 B.C. (Rathbun 1984). In this region, he notes that "pathology has yet to be considered adequately," and further, although the majority of specimens date from the metal ages, superficial study and reporting in the past "again makes comprehensive comparisons tenuous" (Rathbun 1984: 138). However, several skeletal markers for inadequate or periodic nutritional stresses are present in remains from earlier periods, as is generalized dental attrition, especially in earlier specimens and in the Neanderthal remains. Bronze and Iron Age skulls from some sites show a very high incidence (40 percent) of advanced otitis media or inner ear infections and resultant sequelae with a presumably high incidence of associated deafness. Trauma, often violent in origin, was evident in four of six Shanidar Neanderthals and 15 percent of metal age specimens. Osteoarthritic changes were common in all specimens and the average age at death was low (Rathbun 1984).

From Egypt, there are of a host of studies, too many to be properly sampled here owing to space considerations. Egyptian specimens have given us the most comprehensive body of data on health and disease in the entire ancient world. Evidence of trauma of many types has long been known from this region. Several infectious diseases are known from ancient Egypt such as tuberculosis, poliomyelitis, smallpox, and degenerative vascular disease. Arthritis of several types was common. There is no evidence of vitamin D deficiency (rickets) or syphilis. Parasitism was widespread throughout the entire biblical world with a variety of probable sequelae such as anemia, reduced work output, poor health and longevity, and poor nutrition. Parasites such as schistosomiasis, for example, are well documented in ancient Egypt as early as 1000 B.C. beginning with the discovery of schistosome ova in the renal tubules of a mummy by Ruffer in his early landmark paper (Ruffer 1910). It was probably also present in much of ancient Mesopotamia as well since the habitat in this region was and is well suited for the spread of the disease and the shells of the snail intermediate host can be found in mudbricks used in the construction of ancient Babylonian *ziggurats*. Various other conditions are known, among them the presence of renal stones and gallstones, hernia, rectal disease, anthracosis, emphysema and pneumonia, acromegaly, achrondroplastic dwarfism, or vesicovaginal fistula associated with narrow pelvic architecture in childbirth (for further references, begin with Sandison 1985). The human remains also present us with some surprises. The high incidence of periosteal reactions in the tibias of ancient Egyptians is not convincingly accounted for, and sepsis seems only occasionally or rarely to have followed severe examples of broken bones which likely were compound fractures. Nearly all septic changes of the facial bones are due to advanced dental disease. Many other less threatening and less fatal conditions existed as well. Mummies from Egypt have shown that societies with high-population-density dwellings suffered from carbon deposits in the lungs owing to smoke inhalation from domestic fires (Zimmermann 1977).

I. Observations on Health and Disease Applicable to the Biblical World

While more specific information on health and disease in the biblical world can be had in another article in this dictionary, some results and inferences drawn from the efforts of paleopathologists may be summarized to provide here a broad general statement on the subject. Many things are clear from the study of ancient health and disease, that is, paleopathology, which are applicable to most or all of the biblical world. See SICKNESS AND DISEASE.

While there are always some long-lived individuals in every society, life expectancy in the ancient biblical world was short by modern standards, averaging in the range of 30 to 45 years depending upon the place and time. The advances of Greek society alone are credited by some with the extension of average longevity about five years to roughly 40–45 years of age, and it appears that at turn-of-the-era Jericho, one-fourth of the population survived beyond age 50. Women generally lived shorter lives than men by as much as ten years (Arensburg, Goldstein, and Rak 1985) in contrast to the life span of modern American women, which surpasses that of men by about ten years. Mortality associated with childbirth was greater, as was also infant and subadult mortality. Indeed, the figures obtained from some skeletal groups suggest that by age 18 as much as 30 percent of the population had already perished (Hachlili et al. 1981; Ortner 1979). More startling are the burials from the Meroitic cemetery at Aksha (N Sudan), where 45 percent of the burials were age 12 and less (Vila 1967).

In ancient times there was always the constant reality of uncertain nutrition, reflected by the presence of *cribra orbitalia,* a skeletal lesion which is apparently a reaction to sustained iron deficiency, found in the ocular orbits of the skull. This has been observed commonly, for example, in ancient Jewish skeletal remains, especially those of children, which date to the Second Temple period (Arensburg, Goldstein, and Rak 1985).

Trauma, accidental and inflicted, was one of the most common causes of injury and disability, and is one of the most frequent causes of pathological conditions apparent in ancient skeletal remains. Healed broken bones are often found in various states of union and disunion as evidence of accidents and inflicted wounds. Certain forms of arthritis and degenerative conditions were common. By the Coptic/Byzantine periods, dental caries became much more notable and increasingly so thereafter in association with refinements in diet and lifestyle, whereas before this time and in association with more unrefined diets, attrition (wear) was common and caries were rare (Arensburg, Goldstein, and Rak 1985; Brothwell 1959). Infectious diseases went largely unchecked except for natural immunity. A variety of states of disability must have existed anciently owing to many causes. It cannot be stressed too strongly that pain was a common fact of life for much of the ancient population.

Arterial disease was probably widespread anciently and is known to have existed in Egypt at least. Evidence of cancer from antiquity is very rare, but the reasons for this are not clear. A possible explanation may be the shorter life span of most people anciently, and thus the probability that malignancies were expressed in many fewer of the population. Another explanation may be that many malignancies often do not spread to the bone before death and are thus not apparent to the paleopathologist.

J. Conclusion

The importance of a serious study of human remains from archaeological excavations in view of the real and potential knowledge to be gained thereby has resulted in the frequent participation of a paleopathologist as part of the staff of archaeological expeditions, and reflects the increasing sophistication of the theory and method of the so-called "New Archaeology." See ARCHAEOLOGY, SYRO-PALESTINIAN. Clearly, as much may be learned about the inhabitants of an ancient tell from their skeletal remains as from associated artifacts.

Bibliography

Abdul Aziz, M. H., and Slipka, J. 1966. Twins from Tell Hassuna. *Sumer* 22: 45–50.

Aldred, C., and Sandison, A. T. 1962. The Pharoah Akhenaten: A Problem in Egyptology and Pathology. *Bulletin of the History of Medicine* 36: 293–316.

Angel, J. L. 1981. History and Development of Paleopathology. *American Journal of Physical Anthropology* 56: 509–15.

Arensburg, B. 1973. The People of the Land of Israel from Epipaleolithic to Present Times, Ph.D. diss., University of Tel Aviv, Tel Aviv.

Arensburg, B.; Goldstein, M. S.; and Rak, Y. 1985. Observations on the Pathology of the Jewish Population in Israel (100 B.C. to 600 B.C.). *Koroth* 9: 73–83.

Arensburg, B., and Rak, Y. 1985. Jewish Skeletal Remains from the Period of the Kings of Judaea. *PEQ* 117: 30–34.

Armelagos, G. J.; Mielke, J. H.; and Winter, J. 1971. *Bibliography of Human Paleopathology.* Amherst.

Balout, L., and Roubet, C., eds. 1985. *La Momie de Ramses II.* Paris.

Bass, W. M. 1979. Developments in the Identification of Human Skeletal Material (1968–1978). *American Journal of Physical Anthropology* 51: 555–62.

Boyd, W. C., and Boyd, L. G. 1934. An Attempt to Determine the Blood Group of Mummies. *Proceedings of the Society of Experimental Biology and Medicine* 31: 671–74.

———. 1937. Blood Group Testing on 300 Mummies with Notes on the Precipitin Test. *Journal of Immunology* 32: 307–19.

Brothwell, D. R. 1959. Teeth in Earlier Human Populations. *Proceedings of the Nutrition Society* 18: 59–65.

Brothwell, D. R., ed. 1968. *The Skeletal Biology of Earlier Human Populations.* Symposia of the Society for the Study of Human Biology 8. London.

Brothwell, D., and Sandison, A. T., eds. 1967. *Diseases in Antiquity.* Springfield.

Bryant, V. M., Jr. 1974. The Role of Coprolite Analysis in Archaeology. *Bulletin of the Texas Archaeological Society* 45: 1–28.

Buikstra, J. E., and Cook, D. C. 1980. Paleopathology: An American Account. *Annual Review of Anthropology* 9: 433–70.

Close, A. E., ed. 1986. *The Wadi Kubbaniya Skeleton: A Late Paleolithic Burial from Southern Egypt.* The Prehistory of Wadi Kubbaniya Vol. 1. Dallas.

Cockburn, A.; Barraco, R. A.; Reyman, T. A.; and Peck, W. H. 1975. Autopsy of an Egyptian Mummy. *Science* 187: 1155–60.

Cockburn, A., and Cockburn, E., eds. 1980. *Mummies, Disease, and Ancient Cultures.* London.

Cohen, M. N., and Armelagos, G. J. 1984. *Paleopathology at the Origins of Agriculture.* Orlando.

David, A. R., ed. 1978. *Manchester Museum Mummy Project: Multidisciplinary Research on Ancient Egyptian Mummified Remains.* Manchester.

———. 1986. *Science in Egyptology.* Manchester.

David, R., and Tapp, E., eds. 1984. *Evidence Embalmed: Modern Medicine and the Mummies of Ancient Egypt.* Manchester.

Dawson, W. R. 1934. Pettigrew's Demonstrations upon Mummies. A Chapter in the History of Egyptology. *JEA* 20: 169–82.

———. 1938. Pygmies and Dwarfs in Ancient Egypt. *JEA* 24: 185–89.

Dawson, W. R., and Uphill, E. P. 1972. *Who Was Who in Egyptology.* London.

Disi, A. M.; Henke, W.; and Wahl, J. 1983. Tell el-Mazar: Study of the Human Skeletal Remains. *ADAJ* 27: 515–48.

Editorial. "A Question of Style?" 1985. *Paleopathology Newsletter* 49: 5–6.

Egyptian Museum. 1986. *Egyptian Museum, Cairo. A Brief Description of the Principal Monuments.* Cairo.

Fouquet, [D. M.] 1896. Appendice. Note sur les squelettes d'El-'Amrah. Pp. 241–70 in *Recherches sur les Origines de l'Egypte,* ed. J. De Morgan. Paris.

Goldstein, M. S.; Arensburg, B.; and Nathan, H. 1976. Pathology of Bedouin Skeletal Remains from Two Sites in Israel. *American Journal of Physical Anthropology* 45: 621–40.

Gray, P. H. 1967. Radiography of Ancient Egyptian Mummies. *Med. Radiogr. Photogr.* 4: 34–44.

Haas, N., and Nathan, H. 1967–69. Anthropological Survey of the Human Skeletal Remains from Qumran. *RevQ* 6: 345–52.

Hachlili, R.; Arensburg, B.; Smith, P.; and Killebrew, A. 1981. The Jewish Necropolis at Jericho. *Current Anthropology* 22: 701–2.

Hackett, C. J. 1976. *Diagnostic Criteria of Syphilis, Yaws, and Treponarid (Treponematoses) and of Some Other Diseases in Dry Bones.* New York.

Harris, J. E., and Wente, E. F., eds. 1980. *An X-Ray Atlas of the Royal Mummies.* Chicago.

Holladay, J. S. 1982. *Cities of the Delta III: Tell el-Maskhuta.* Malibu.

Hooton, E. A. 1939. Report on the Skeletal Remains. Pp. 61–66 in *Ain Shems Excavations IV.* Haverford.

Horne, P. D., and Kawasaki, S. Q. 1984. The Prince of El Plomo: A Paleopathological Study. *Bulletin of the New York Academy of Medicine* 60: 925–31.

Hrdlička, A. 1938. Skeletal Remains. Pp. 192–208 in *Megiddo Tombs,* ed. P. L. O Guy and R. M. Engberg. OIP 33. Chicago.

Hrdy, D. B. 1978. Analysis of Hair Samples of Mummies from Semna South (Sudanese Nubia). *American Journal of Physical Anthropology* 49: 277–82.

Hughes, D. R. 1965. Human Remains. Pp. 664–85 in *Excavations at Jericho II.* London.

Janssens, P. A. 1970. *Paleopathology: Disease and Injuries of Prehistoric Man.* London.

Jones, R. N. 1988. Analysis of a Yellow-Stained Human Femur from Tell esh-Shuqafiya: Evidence of Ancient Trauma. *American Journal of Physical Anthropology* 77: 77–83.

Keita, S. O. Y. 1988. An Analysis of Crania from Tell-Duweir Using Multiple Discriminant Functions. *American Journal of Physical Anthropology* 75: 375–90.

Kelso, J. L. 1968. *The Excavation of Bethel (1934–60).* AASOR 39. Cambridge, MA.

Lortet, L. C. 1907. Crâne syphilitique et nécropoles préhistoriques de la Haute-Egypte. *Bulletin de la Société d'Anthropologie de Lyon* 26: 211.

Macalister, R. A. S. 1912. *The Excavations of Gezer (1902–1905, 1907–1909).* London.

Meers, P. D. 1985. Smallpox Still Entombed? *Lancet* 1: 1103.

Moller-Christensen, V. 1961. *Bone Changes in Leprosy.* Munksgaard.

———. 1978. *Leprosy Changes of the Skull.* Odense.

Moodie, R. L. 1931. *Roentgenologic Studies of Egyptian and Peruvian Mummies.* Chicago.

Moodie, R. L., ed. 1921. *Studies in the Paleopathology of Egypt by Sir Marc Armand Ruffer.* Chicago.

Murray, M. A. 1910. *The Tomb of Two Brothers.* Manchester.

Nathan, H. 1961. The Skeletal Material from Nahal Hever Cave No. 8—The "Cave of Horror." *ʿAtiqot* 3: 165–75.

Netolitzky, F. 1911. Nahrungs- und Heilmittel der Urägypter. *Die Umschau* 46: 953–56.

———. 1912. Hirse und Cyperus aus dem Prähistorischen Agypten. *Beihefte zum Botanischen Centralblatt* 29: 1–11.

Neveux, Jean B. 1964. Andreas Gryphius et les momies. *Études Germaniques* 19: 451–62.

Ortner, D. J. 1979. Disease and Mortality in the Early Bronze Age People of Bab edh-Dhra, Jordan. *American Journal of Physical Anthropology* 51: 589–97.

———. 1981. A Preliminary Report on the Human Remains from the Bab edh-Dhra Cemetery, 1977. Pp. 119–32 in *AASOR 46,* ed. W. E. Rast and R. T. Schaub. Cambridge, MA.

———. 1982. The Skeletal Biology of an Early Bronze IB Charnel House at Bab edh-Dhra, Jordan. Pp. 93–95 in *Studies in the History and Archaeology of Jordan I,* ed. A. Hadidi. Amman.

Ortner, D. J., and Putschar, W. G. J. 1981. *Identification of Pathological Conditions in Human Skeletal Remains.* Smithsonian Contributions to Anthropology 28. Washington.

Pääbo, S. 1985. Molecular Cloning of Ancient Egyptian Mummy DNA. *Nature* 314: 644–45.

Pahl, W. M. 1983. Medical and Archaeological Findings Concerning an Unusual Lethal Injury in an Ancient Egyptian. *Journal of Human Evolution* 12: 213–29.

Pales, L. 1930. *Paleopathologie et Pathologie Comparative.* Paris.

Petrie, W. M. F. 1898. *Deshasheh, 1897.* London.

Pettigrew, T. J. 1834. *A History of Egyptian Mummies. . . .* London. Repr. 1983.

Price, T. D.; Schoeninger, M. J.; and Armelagos, G. J. 1985. Bone Chemistry and Past Behavior. *Journal of Human Evolution* 14: 419–48.

Rak, Y.; Arensburg, B.; and Nathan, H. 1976. Evidence of Violence on Human Bones in Israel, First and Third Centuries C.E. *PEQ* 108: 55–64.

Ruffer, M. A. 1910. A Note on the Presence of *Bilharzia hematobia* in Egyptian Mummies of the Twentieth Dynasty (1250–1000 B.C.). *British Medical Journal* 1: 16.

———. 1911. On Dwarfs and Other Deformed Persons in Ancient Egypt. *Bulletin de la société archéologique d'Alexandrie* 13: 1–17.

Rathbun, T. A. 1984. Skeletal Pathology from the Paleolithic Through the Metal Ages in Iran and Iraq. Pp. 137–68 in *Paleopathology At the Origins of Agriculture.* ed. M. N. Cohen and G. J. Armelagos. Orlando.

Sandison, A. T. 1955. The Histological Examination of Mummified Material. *Stain Technology* 30: 277–83.

———. 1967. Sir Marc Armand Ruffer (1859–1917) Pioneer of Paleopathology. *Medical History* 11: 150–56.

———. 1968. Pathological Changes in the Skeletons of Earlier Populations Due to Acquired Disease, and Difficulties in Their Interpretation. Pp. 205–43 in *The Skeletal Biology of Earlier Human Populations,* ed. D. R. Brothwell. Oxford.

———. 1985. Diseases in Ancient Egypt. Pp. 29–44 in *Mummies, Disease, and Ancient Cultures.* ed. A. Cockburn and E. Cockburn. Cambridge.

Smith, G. E. 1908a. The Alleged Discovery of Syphilis in Prehistoric Egyptians. *Lancet* 2: 521–24.

———. 1908b. The Most Ancient Splints. *British Medical Journal* 1: 732–34.

Smith, G. E., and Wood-Jones, F. 1910. *The Archaeological Survey of Nubia: Report for 1907–1908. Vol. 2: Report on the Human Remains.* Cairo.
Smith, P. 1977. The Human Skeletal Remains from the Abba Cave. *IEJ* 27: 121–24.
Smith, P., and Zias, J. 1980. Skeletal Remains from the Late Hellenistic French Hill Tomb. *IEJ* 30: 109–15.
Steckoll, S. H. 1967–69. Preliminary Excavation Report in the Qumran Cemetery. *RevQ* 6: 323–36.
Steckoll, S. H. et al. 1971. Red-Stained Human Bones from Qumran. *Israel Journal of Medical Sciences* 7: 1219–23.
Steinbock, R. T. 1976. *Paleopathological Diagnosis and Interpretation: Bone Diseases in Ancient Human Populations.* Springfield.
Tasnadi-Kubacska, A. 1962. *Paläopathologie: Pathologie der Vorseithihen Tiere.* Jena.
Trinkaus, E. 1983. *The Shanidar Neanderthals.* New York.
Vila, A. 1967. *Aksha II. Le cemeterie meroitique d'Aksha.* Paris.
Vyhanek, L., and Strouhal, E. 1976. Radiography of Egyptian Mummies. *Zeitschrift für Ägyptische Studien und Altertumskund* 103: 118–28.
Wells, C. 1967. Pseudopathology. Pp. 5–19 in *Diseases in Antiquity,* ed. D. Brothwell and A. T. Sandison. Springfield.
Wilke, P. J., and Hall, H. J. 1975. *Analysis of Ancient Feces: A Discussion and Anotated Bibliography.* Berkeley.
Witenberg, G. 1961. Human Parasites in Archaeological Findings. *BIES* 25: 86.
Wood-Jones, F. 1908a. The Post-mortem Staining of Bone Produced by the Ante-mortem Shedding of Blood. *British Medical Journal* 1: 734–36.
———. 1908b. The Examination of the Bodies of 100 Men Executed in Nubia in Roman Times. *Lancet* 1: 736.
Yadin, Y. 1963. *The Finds from the Bar Kokhba Period in the Cave of Letters.* Jerusalem.
———. 1971. *Bar-Kokhba.* New York.
Yoeli, M. A. 1955. "Facies leontina" of Leprosy on an Ancient Canaanite Jar. *Journal of the History of Medicine and Allied Sciences* 10: 331–33.
———. 1968. Mot, the Canaanite God, as Symbol of the Leper. *Bulletin of the New York Academy of Medicine* 44: 1057–67.
Zambaco Pasha. 1897. L'antiquite de la Syphilis. *Paris Medicale* no. 52.
Zias, J., and Sekeles, E. 1985. The Crucified Man from Giv^{c} at ha-Mivtar: A Reappraisal. *IEJ* 35: 23–27.
Zimmerman, M. R. 1973. Blood Cells Preserved in a Mummy 2000 Years Old. *Science* 180: 303–4.
———. 1977. The Mummies of the Tomb of Nebwenenef: Paleopathology and Archaeology. *JARCE* 14: 33–36.
———. 1979. Paleopathologic Diagnosis Based on Experimental Mummification. *American Journal of Physical Anthropology* 51: 235–54.
Zimmerman, M. R., and Angel, J. L., eds. 1986. *Dating and Age Determination of Biological Materials.* London.
Zimmerman, M. R., and Kelley, M. A. 1982. *An Atlas of Human Paleopathology.* New York.

RICHARD N. JONES

PALESTINE, ADMINISTRATION OF. With the collapse first of Samaria (722 B.C.) and then of Jerusalem (586 B.C.), political control of the land of Canaan passed from Israelite/Judean hands into the hands of successive conquering empires. This entry surveys how those various imperial powers arranged to administer this territory. The entry consists of six sequential articles covering (1) Assyrian and Babylonian administration, (2) Persian administration, (3) local Judean officials during the Persian period, (4) Ptolemaic (Hellenistic Egyptian) administration, (5) Seleucid (Hellenistic Syrian) administration, and (6) Roman administration. For the Hellenistic Jewish administration of Palestine in the period between Seleucid and Roman rule, see HASMONEAN DYNASTY.

ASSYRIAN AND BABYLONIAN ADMINISTRATION

The administrative domination of Mesopotamia over Palestine, as manifested first in the Neo-Assyrian then in the Neo-Babylonian empire, spans the two centuries from the 730s to 539 B.C. "Palestine" here will be understood essentially as the territories comprising the biblical Israel and Judah. However, to follow the Mesopotamian impact on them, occasional notice must be taken of the contiguous regions of Transjordan, including Ammon, Moab, and Edom; of Philistia, including Ekron, Ashdod, Ashkelon, and Gaza; and of Phoenicia, especially Tyre and Sidon.

A. Neo-Assyrian Period
 1. First Contacts
 2. Neo-Assyrian Empire in Its Classical Period
B. Neo-Babylonian Period
 1. Preliminaries
 2. Samaria in the Neo-Babylonian Period
 3. Judah as Vassal
 4. Judah as Province

A. Neo-Assyrian Period

1. First Contacts (853–745 B.C.). Prior to the 730s, Mesopotamian (which at this time means Assyrian) contact with Palestine was intermittent and unimportant. Three moments are recorded in the sources available. Two of them come in the middle of the 9th century B.C., when the Assyrian king, Shalmaneser III, attempted to advance beyond the N Syrian region, attacked already by his predecessors, into S Syria: (1) 853, at the battle of Qarqar, near Hamath in Syria. Here Shalmaneser's advance was apparently stopped by a Syro-Palestinian coalition led by the Aramean Hadadezer of Damascus and Irhulena of Hamath, and among its other prominent members was Ahab of Israel (*ANET,* 278–79); (2) 841, in which Shalmaneser finally broke through the local coalition, overrunning S Syria and apparently Transjordan and Israel (Hos 10:14 may be an echo of this: cf. Astour 1971). In his mention of Syrian rulers who paid him tribute, Shalmaneser includes the apparent leader, Hazael, the recent usurper of the Aramean throne of Damascus who had been attacking Israel, and the ruler of Israel himself, who seems to be Jehu (*[I]Ia-ú-a/Ia-a-ú mār [I]Ḫu-um-ri-i*), the recent usurper of the dynasty of Ahab (*ANET,* 280–81; cf. P. K. McCarter's proposal that the king here is Jehoram, son of Ahab [McCarter 1974], and the responses by Weippert 1978 and Halpern 1987). Shalmaneser III's victory may have given Israel some relief from the Aramaeans, but it was only temporary. For with the withdrawal of Assyrian forces, Aramean pressure from Hazael returned, and another forty years remained before a "deliverer" appeared

(2 Kgs 13:5), in the person of Adad-nirari III. The latter king records in several inscriptions his defeat of Syria-Palestine, especially Damascus, and in one of them adds that he accepted tribute from "Joash, the Samarian" (Page 1968), i.e., Joash, grandson of Jehu, king of Israel. The date of submission is disputed between 803/802 (e.g., Schramm 1972) and 796 (e.g., Millard and Tadmor 1973), but two results can be discerned. First, the submission seems to have brought some Israelite captives to Assyria, as revealed by their inclusion in wine ration lists from Kalah a couple of decades later (Kinnier-Wilson 1972: 91–93). Second, the submission, with the defeat of Damascus, allowed Joash and his son, Jeroboam II, under the nominal protection of Assyria, to gain back territory in Transjordan previously lost to Damascus and then, eventually, when Assyria became too preoccupied elsewhere to interfere, to embark on an expansion of their own (2 Kgs 13:25; 14:25,28).

The three moments just noted represent no sustained concern for Palestine on the part of the Assyrians. Insofar as they had an interest in permanent control it extended, to the W, only so far as the Syrian states up to the W bend of the Euphrates, which were either annexed as provinces or, more often, kept as vassal states (e.g., Nasibina, Rasappa, Guzana, Harran, Bit Adini; cf. the Tell Fakhariyeh stela, probably of the middle 9th century B.C. [Abou-Assaf, Bordreuil, and Millard 1982]). Syria farther W and S was largely for periodic raids to gather booty and personnel and to keep lines of commerce open to the Mediterranean and beyond. Into this area N Israel—never Judah—was drawn, but Assyrian armies barely grazed its territory. The tribute and captives thus taken can be construed as a kind of imposition of vassalage upon the local Syro-Palestinian states, but it was a vassalage clearly not regularly enforced, all the more as Assyria in the century between 850 and 745 also faced serious challenges from other outsiders on other borders, especially Urartu to its N, and from rival elites within its midst.

2. Neo-Assyrian Empire in Its Classical Period (745–609 B.C.). a. Tiglath-pileser III and His Imperial Reforms. This pattern changed with the accession of Tiglath-pileser III as Assyrian king in 745. Apparently a usurper, who succeeded to the throne out of the struggle among rival elites, Tiglath-pileser undertook a vigorous program to rebuild the Assyrian state. On the one hand, he seems to have curtailed the independence of various high officials, who had become virtually kings in their own right. On the other, he initiated almost immediately upon his accession a wide-ranging series of military campaigns in all directions: first to the south to Babylonia (745); then to the E to the Zagros and W Iran (744); next to N and central Syria, detaching them from the Urartian sphere of influence (743–738); then to the N to Urartu and E to the Medes in W Iran (738–735); back to Damascus and Syria along with Palestine (734–732); and finally, to Babylonia once more (731–727), with which he was involved almost until his death in 727. The successes of these campaigns Tiglath-pileser sought to consolidate into an imperial system. While it rested on earlier Assyrian efforts, in extent and complexity it was really something new, and continued, with some modifications, as the basic political structure until the collapse of Assyria at the end of the 7th century.

This imperial system relied on a large-scale bureaucracy that radiated from the imperial cities in the Upper Tigris area outward, and more particularly on an increasingly professional army hardened by regular campaigning, a well-maintained road network, and an intelligence and propaganda apparatus to monitor potential trouble spots and spread the message of Assyrian invincibility. The areas conquered were arranged in two basic categories, both of which had been used by Assyrian rulers before Tiglath-pileser, though over a more limited territory. The first were the vassal states. Here the local state and ruler were kept intact—although if the ruler had been resistant, he could be replaced by someone else in his family or community who would be more pliant—in return for which the ruler had to agree to become a loyal subordinate of the Assyrian sovereign. The agreement seems to have been formalized in an oath-treaty to the Assyrian king directly, the *adê,* which stipulated loyalty to the king and his dynasty, coordination of foreign policy with that of the king, and approval from the king for any local change of ruler. The vassal was also obligated economically in the form of material goods and personnel. These were often taken in a large amount upon conquest by the Assyrian king, and after that the vassal sent them in smaller sums annually as tribute *(biltu, mandattu/maddattu)* as well as in occasional special taxes *(katru, tāmartu/nāmurtu).* It was also expected that the vassal would furnish men and supplies to Assyrian military campaigns and building enterprises conducted in his vicinity. What may not have been required was worship of the Assyrian gods (see further below). To ensure compliance with the obligations that were demanded, at least in the case of potentially uncertain vassals—it is not clear whether this applied to all vassals—the Assyrian central administration installed an official called a *qēpu* at or near the vassal's court, together with a small garrison, or sometimes it relied on a nearby governor *(šaknu)* for this task.

If the vassal rebelled or if the newly conquered state in other ways required it, the Assyrian king could annex it outright as a part of Assyrian territory (the formulas in the Assyrian royal inscriptions speak of "seizing it anew," which probably means "reorganize" [*ana eššūti ṣabātu*] or "reckoning the local population with my people/the Assyrian people" [*ana/itti nišê mātīya/māt Aššur manû*]). In this way, the state lost its independence and became an Assyrian province *(pīḫatu)* ruled directly by an Assyrian official labelled either *šaknu* (= Heb *sagan*) or *bēl pīḫati* (= Heb *peḥāh*). These two titles have been conventionally translated as "governor," but what difference, if any, existed between them has not yet been agreed on. The governor maintained his own palace complex in the capital city of the province. He also controlled various other locales of authority within the province: fortresses *(birtu, ḫalṣu),* royal roads, and stations for royal messengers and the army *(bīt mardīte).* Collecting taxes—in addition to the general terms for tribute, *biltu* and *mandattu/maddattu,* the particular categories used were the *ilku,* a tax in labor service, and the *šibšu,* a tax on agricultural produce—was one of the governor's main duties; part of these was sent on to the central imperial cities in the Assyrian heartland, while the other part remained in the province to maintain the local administration. The governor had to keep the imperial center regularly informed of all activities and to join the Assyrian army on campaign when ordered. He also, unlike the apparent situation in the vassal states, provided for Assyrian religious cults, though native gods and their worship were certainly not proscribed. And in the process of carrying out his duties, assisted by a variety of subordinates—the *rab ālāni,* in charge of a subdistrict (perhaps = *qannu*) of settlements with its own urban center, was the most important—the governor was normally able to gain profit of his own: at least of some of the taxes left over after the distribution to the central and provincial administrations could be used by him personally, and he was normally granted land by the king, often tax-free, outside his own province.

A province was created normally as a result of Assyrian military action, which resulted in the destruction of certain of the local cities and towns of the region and deportation of significant elements of the population, especially from the local elites and craftsworkers, to other parts of the empire, most prominently to the central imperial cities in the Upper Tigris triangle. Here the deportees entered the work force, as skilled craftsmen or as laborers, on state building projects, were mustered into the army, or became part of the governing bureaucracy. In turn, the lost population was replaced, at least partially, by deportees brought in from other provincial regions. While it is clear that Tiglath-pileser III created provinces and practiced deportation on a far larger scale than his predecessors, and that his policy was continued by his successors, the origins of this policy are no longer certain. Forrer (1920: 10–11) had argued that it began by his breaking up into smaller units the large provinces in existence from earlier decades in the area from the Tigris to the western bend of the Euphrates—provinces that had been controlled by powerful, rather independent governors. As noted above, it does appear that Tiglath-pileser curbed the power of these officials, but Garelli (Garelli and Nikiprowetzky 1974: 113–14, 232–34) has more recently cast strong doubts on the assumed breakup of territory as one of the means by which this was done.

This imperial system of vassal states and provinces exhibited several peculiarities or partial modifications. Babylonia, because of its ancient cultural associations, was the most troublesome part of the empire, and at various times was a vassal, province, and especially a state ruled by a member of the Assyrian royal family, whether a son, brother, or the reigning king himself. In the west, the Phoenician cities remained vassal states under special protection, so that their maritime commerce would flourish to Assyria's benefit. Vassals of another kind were the nomadic Arab tribes in the Syro-Arabian desert and the N Sinai—similar arrangements operated with other nomadic groups like the Medes—who were too elusive, resistant, and far away to be coerced into provinces. Rather, with their sheiks nominated as vassal rulers and pasture rights occasionally given on the margins of Assyrian imperial lands, the Arabs could be used to facilitate trade, the passage of Assyrian armies, and other kinds of communication through the deserts and other border areas over which they alone had mastery. This was particularly crucial in the Assyrian campaigns against Egypt, which had to go through the Sinai.

b. Israel in the Classical Neo-Assyrian Period. Within the imperial system just described, the fortunes of Israel and Judah can be followed. Israel, from the first campaigns of Tiglath-pileser III to the W in 743–738, passed rapidly from vassal to province. In 738, in the wake of Tiglath-pileser's defeat of a N Syrian coalition led by Azriyau of Yaudi (not = Azariah/Uzziah of Judah!), Menahem, king of Israel paid the Assyrian tribute (2 Kgs 15:18–20; *ANET,* 283a; Levine 1972: 18.II 5). The resulting vassal status, however, was shattered by 734, when a new Israelite king, Pekah, joined forces with the king of Damascus, Raẓyan II (= biblical Rezin), in an anti-Assyrian pact to enlarge their territory at the expense of Judah under Ahaz. This so-called Syro-Ephraimite war brought Tiglath-pileser back to the region, and in 732 he defeated the coalition and conquered the two states. Damascus became a set of provinces; Israel lost, it appears, its W and E territories to provinces (see below). The core of Israel, around the capital Samaria, was allowed to remain a vassal state under a new, seemingly pro-Assyrian ruler, Hoshea, whose accession had to be approved by Tiglath-pileser III (*ANET,* 284a; cf. Borger and Tadmor 1982: 244–249). But by 725 Hoshea was in open revolt against the successor of Tiglath-pileser, Shalmaneser V. And the response was equally decisive. Israel was attacked and Samaria was besieged. Hoshea seems to have been captured and deported at the beginning of this siege (2 Kgs 18:9–10 with 17:4–6), and after three years, during which time, leadership may have been assumed by city elders or generals, Samaria fell in 722, at the end of Shalmaneser's reign (2 Kgs 17:5–6; TCS 5: 73.I 28; cf. Tadmor 1958: 37). His successor, Sargon II, however unfairly claimed responsibility for this success (Tadmor 1958: 34), dating it to his accession year. But two years later, in 720, Sargon had a legitimate boast when Samaria revolted a second time, in conjunction with a widespread uprising of the W vassals and provinces supported by Egypt, and he put it down (*ANET,* 285, and victory stelae of Sargon from Samaria [Crowfoot, Crowfoot, and Kenyon 1957: 35 & Pl. IV 2] and Qāqūn [cf. *RLA* 5: 203b]. At this point, apparently, Samaria and its environs became definitively an Assyrian province, under the name *Sāmerīna,* the Assyrian equivalent of Hebrew *Šōmĕrōn* (= Samaria). And as in 722, population deportation took place.

After 720, therefore, no independent or vassal state existed in the territory of (N) Israel. The classic study of Forrer (1920: 60–61,63) had supposed that four provinces were established in what had been the Israelite state prior to 732. Three came in 732 after Tiglath-pileser III's campaign: Dor (= Assyrian *Du'ru*) on the Mediterranean coast from above Ashdod to the Mt. Carmel region; Megiddo (= Assyrian *Magiddû/Magaddû*) in the Jezreel Valley and Galilee; and Gilead (= Assyrian *Gal'a[d(d)a];* on the form see Weippert 1972: 154–55) in the N Transjordan. The fourth province was Samaria (= Assyrian *Sāmerīna*) in the hill country below the province of Megiddo, established in 722–20 under Sargon II. As Eph'al (*WHJP* 4/1: 284–86), however, has noted, no Assyrian or Biblical texts unequivocally mention Gilead as an Assyrian province; when the name occurs in Tiglath-pileser III's inscriptions, it designates only a city, and only by extrapolation from biblical texts that describe earlier periods and later Hellenistic Greek texts can one infer that Gilead in 8th–7th-century Assyrian history designated the capital city of a province. Similarly for Dor, the Assyrian references are only to a city, and one can only guess whether this was an isolated Assyrian center or the capital of an Assyrian province by the same name. Only for Megiddo and Samaria do the Assyrian records—and for Samaria, also the biblical (2 Kgs 17:24, 26)—testify clearly to their existence as provinces. And at least by Esarhaddon's time, the territory of Samaria appears to have included Aphek, close to the Mediterranean coast (Borger 1956: §76:16, as collated by Tadmor *apud* Cogan 1974: 100, n. 19).

As for the deportations, these proceeded over a number of decades, beginning with Tiglath-pileser III's campaign of 734–732. In 733–732, the king deported large numbers from the Transjordanian tribes of Reuben, Gad, and half-Manasseh, then within the N kingdom of Israel (1 Chr 5:6, 26) and from Upper Galilee (2 Kgs 15:29; Tiglath-pileser III annals, which give the number as 13,520 [Tadmor 1967: 66]). With the fall of Samaria in 722/720, the inscriptions of Sargon II number the deportees at 27,290 (*ANET,* 285a), but whether this figure represents the sum from the conquest in 722, by Shalmaneser V, and 720, by Sargon II, who also, it may be recalled, took credit for the 722 conquest, or just the sum from 720 is not clear. The Biblical record (2 Kgs 17:6; 18:11; 1 Chr 5:26) seems to record only the 722 deportation, which it indicates took the captives to the upper Euphrates, around the Habur River (Habor, river of Gozan), to the area apparently NE of Nineveh beyond the Tigris (Halah, cities of the Medes). Assyrian texts, in turn, indicate the presence of Israelites after 722/20 in Gozan (= Tell Halaf), Kalah (= Nimrud), and Nineveh as various kinds of officials and workers, military and otherwise. Of these, recent evidence from the reign of Sargon II suggests that the Assyrian especially prized Samarians for their expertise in chariot and equestrian warfare and deported them to serve both as contingents within and as experts to advise the army (Dalley 1985).

Doubtless not all the inhabitants of the former kingdom of Israel were exiled. But to replace those who were the Assyrians brought in deportees from other parts of the empire. 2 Kgs 17:24 (cf. 30–31) speaks of people brought from a variety of cities in Babylonia (Babylon, Kutha, perhaps Hamath and Sepharvaim), probably in Elam (Avva, though some have located this in Babylonia), and possibly in Syria (Hamath and Sepharvaim, if they are not in Babylonia). These are presented as coming in the wake of the 722/20 conquests (cf. also Sargon II annals, *ANET,* 284b; Tadmor 1958: 34), though it is likely that the 2 Kgs list is a composite of several deportations, both from 722/20 and later. Clearly later, either in 716 or in 715, Sargon records the transfer of parts of Arab tribes—the Tamudi, Ibadidi, Marsimani, and Hayyapa (*ANET,* 286a). And in Ezra 4:2, 9–10, there are notices of additional deportations to Samaria in the following 7th century by Esarhaddon and Ashurbanipal (= Heb Osnappar), the latter, according to vv 9–10, including people from Babylonia (Erech/Uruk and Babylon) and Elam (Susa) as well as other places.

The operation of Assyrian administration in these provinces of the former kingdom of Israel can be followed only in limited fashion. Sargon II's inscriptions speak of imposing on the newly created province of Samaria, after its conquest, tribute (Akk *biltu, mandattu/maddattu),* continuing "the *biltu* of their former king" (Winckler 1889: 1.100.24–25, *ANET,* 285a, which should refer to the tax system of Israel when it was an independent state). Three governors are known from Assyrian documents, all important enough to have achieved the status of eponym (references in *RLA* 5: 203): Itti-Adad-(a)ninu of Megiddo (679, reign of Esarhaddon); Nabu-kitta-uṣur of Samaria (690, reign of Sennacherib; in different documents he is described as *bēl pīḫati* [Grayson 1963: 96.120] and as *šaknu* [Postgate 1970: 148]); and Nabu-sar-ahhesu (646 or 645, reign of Ashurbanipal) also of Samaria. A *rab ālāni* is attested from an Assyrian document found in Samaria, in which he is to be given, apparently on order of the governor, a ration of animals (Reisner, Fisher, and Lyon 1924: 1.247; 2, pl. 56b). Samaria and Megiddo, apparently as capital cities of their respective provinces, are noted in several lists of Assyrian administrative centers, some of which indicate tribute submitted by these centers to the Assyrian crown. Dor is also listed in these texts, but note above Eph'al's caution about identifying it as the capital of a province. Several Assyrian texts, letters, and administrative lists, indicate contingents from Samaria in the Assyrian army, though it is not clear whether these represent forces sent by the province or deportees from the original Assyrian conquest in 722/720 (cf. Dalley 1985 and other references in *RLA* 5: 204). Akkadian texts reflecting Assyrian control have been found in three settlements: Samaria (Reisner, Fisher, and Lyon 1924: 1.247; 2, pl. 56a–b; Crowfoot, Crowfoot, and Kenyon 1957: 35, pls. II–III, XV: 18a), Gezer (republished by Becking 1981–82), and Tell Keisan near Acco (Sigrist 1982). The texts at issue include: for Samaria, a legal order, a bulla with the royal Assyrian seal that bears the name of a local resident, a cylinder seal of a Nabu-zabil with an inscription mentioning various Babylonian gods, and a fragment of an Assyrian royal stela, probably of Sargon II; for Gezer, two legal contracts, one dated to 651, recording the sale of an estate with houses and slaves, and the other dated to 649, describing the sale of a plot of land, in addition to several uninscribed cylinder and stamp seals and impressions (Reich and Brandl 1985: 45–48); for Tell Keisan, a list of bread rations perhaps for foreign soldiers or settlers. The texts, thus, are of standard Mesopotamian types, found elsewhere in the Assyrian empire, and reflect Mesopotamian/Assyrian administrative/legal procedures. The personnel involved, if one may judge from the names, are of mixed background—Assyrian, Babylonians, Egyptians, Aramaeans, Israelites—exactly what one would expect from Assyrian deportation policy and confirming, at least in broad outline, the range of population pictured for conquered Samaria in the biblical sources noted above (2 Kgs 17; Ezra 4).

The archaeological picture of the N kingdom after the Assyrian conquest correlates with the picture described in the written sources. Sites like Hazor (Level VA), Megiddo (Level IVA), Beth-shan (Level IV), and Gezer (Level VIA) show destruction in the latter 8th century that fits with the written evidence of Tiglath-pileser III's campaigning in their area in 733–32. In turn, the destruction of Samaria (Period V–VI)—not complete, but centered on the buildings of the Israelite royal quarter—and of other sites like Tell el-Farah of the N (Level VIIc–d) and Shechem (Level VII) can be attributed to the conquest of 722. Most of the destroyed sites—Beth-shan is one of the exceptions—were resettled, although not all immediately. Some like Tell el-Farah of the north (Level VII e) and Shechem (Level VI) were now poorer and less extensive than before. In the case of Samaria (Level VII), the earlier defensive walls seem to have been kept and restored, although the general rebuilding indicated by Sargon II in his annals (*ANET*, 284b) has not been found on the site.

Megiddo (level III), Hazor (Level IV), and Gezer (Level VB) evidence refortification that suggests their positions as Assyrian administrative centers: Megiddo as capital of the province of the same name; Hazor and Gezer as subprovincial centers perhaps for *rab ālāni,* Hazor within Megiddo and Gezer within Samaria or possibly Dor. At all three sites, the remains of fortified buildings were discovered that doubtless served administrative needs, and hence have been called palaces. The plan of the one at Gezer is unclear, but at Hazor (citadel) and Megiddo (buildings 1052 and 1369), the structures are of the "open court" type, in which a series of rooms is arranged along the four walls of the building with an open court in the middle. This type appears to derive from Babylonia, and was brought to Palestine, where it was previously unknown, by the Assyrians; Lachish (where, however, the structure, called by the excavators the Residency, is now to be dated to the Achaemenid Persian period), Tell Jemmeh, and Buseirah represent other (southern) sites in Palestine where the building is found. Note that at Hazor and Megiddo, these "open court" buildings were in central locations: at Hazor occupying the whole of the W bluff of the citadel; at Megiddo, both near the city gate. In addition, just NE of Hazor at Ayyelet Ha-Shahar a new settlement was established, more or less contemporaneous with the Assyrian occupation of Hazor III. The bulk of this is another palace, whose fragmentary plan seems directly to reflect the palaces of the Assyrian imperial capitals, with two, not one, open courtyards, slightly separated, around which rooms are arranged (Reich 1975). A recent suggestion by J. Bloom (1989) is that the Ayyelet Ha-Shahar palace represents the dwelling of the Hazor *rab ālāni,* while the open court building on the citadel of Hazor III is an Assyrian *ekal mašarti,* the armory and headquarters of the Assyrian garrison at Hazor. Indeed, that there appears to be no real settlement in Hazor III beyond this building suggests that the site served then exclusively military-administrative purposes.

Besides these architectural features, the Assyrian presence in Samaria and adjacent provinces can be traced in various artifacts. The small, but noticeable number of cuneiform texts and seals from Samaria, Gezer, and Tell Keisan has been described above. The other noticeable artifact is a distinctive pottery, hitherto unknown in Palestine, which has been labeled Assyrian palace ware because it is at home in the palaces of the Assyrian imperial capitals (Nimrud has furnished an especially large collection; see Oates 1959). This pottery is distinguished by its thin, fine ware, and its shapes include a bowl with a high flaring rim which reflects a metallic prototype. The pottery appears in Palestine primarily in the first years of Assyrian occupation both in imported and in local copy, and gives way rather soon to indigenous pottery styles.

What did the Assyrians expect from the population of natives and deportees settled in Samaria and the other provinces which they had created out of the former kingdom of Israel? Several inscriptions of Sargon II speak, as we have seen, of the tribute *(biltu, mandattu/maddattu)* imposed on the population, by which should probably be understood both the initial spoil and the subsequent regular payment of taxes. The inscriptions make a point that this was done "just as if they were Assyrian" *(ki ša Aššurî),* and add that "I also had them trained in proper behavior" *(inušunu ušāḫiz)* (Lie 1929: 6:7.17; Winckler 1889: 1.100–1.24; cf. *ANET,* 284–85). What is involved here is elaborated on in another inscription of Sargon, treating the resettlement of captives and others in his new capital of Dur-Sarrukin (Khorsabad): "I ordered citizens of Assyria, knowledgeable in all the proper behavior *(mūdûte ini kalama),* as overseers and supervisors to teach them correct conduct, the worship of god and king" *(ana šūḫuz ṣibitte pālaḫ ili u šarri)* (Lyon 1883: 12.74). These statements reflect, as Cogan (1974: 49–55) has pointed out, the effort to organize the new and mixed population of the provinces and to teach them proper obedience. Indeed, the possibility that such statements may have been broadcast to the local population, at least to the local elites, is suggested by the way they are echoed in a biblical text like 2 Kgs 17:27–28 (Paul 1969). What the obedience involved, certainly, was the orderly payment of taxes, service to the crown, and resistance to rebellion. Included as well was a degree of religious obeisance, which, as other Assyrian texts, not relating to Israel, suggest, could take such forms as taxes for support of the temples of the Assyrian gods in the imperial centers and the erection of images of deified weapons, particularly associated with the imperial god Ashur, in provincial cities, around which, one can assume, worship occurred. But obeisance to the Assyrian gods did not apparently displace the worship of other deities connected with the provincial populations. This is clearly indicated by the narrative in 2 Kings 17, which describes the various deportees in Samaria each worshipping their own gods along with Yahweh, whose cult is said to have been reactivated there with the approval of the Assyrian king, and eventually to have predominated among the population. While there is doubtless some special pleading in this narrative on the part of its Deuteronomistic editors, the religious tolerance it assumes from the Assyrian authorities is borne out by practice elsewhere in the empire (Cogan 1974: 55; 38 n. 101; 104–7).

The waning of Assyrian rule in Samaria and adjacent provinces seems to have begun, or at least becomes noticeable, in the late 640s, in the wake of Ashurbanipal's costly wars in the S and E parts of the empire, viz., against Babylonia (652–648) and Elam (647–646). Against the background of these wars, the West saw the opportunity to challenge Assyrian control, and the last attested Assyrian interventions in the S Levant were in the mid-latter 640s in response: a campaign against the nomads who were menacing the provinces from the middle Euphrates to the

Transjordan; and the conquest of mainland Tyre (Ushu) and Acco, which had rebelled. By the 620s and the death of Ashurbanipal (627), the situation of the empire as a whole became urgent, provoked and aggravated by strife within the ruling Assyrian elite joined to a resurgent independence in Babylonia and Iran. Not surprisingly, Egypt took advantage to extend its influence through Palestine, to which Assyria seems eventually to have agreed in return for support elsewhere; one by-product may have been the Assyrian cession of Megiddo to Egypt in this period (Malamat 1973; archaeologically this is Megiddo II). It is probably no accident as well that the 620s mark the full emergence of the political and religious reforms undertaken by Josiah of Judah, reforms that may have included a reclamation of territory in Judah previously removed by Sennacherib in his 701 campaign (2 Kgs 23:5, 8; 2 Chr 34:9, 32; letter from Meṣad Ḥashavyahu [*ANET,* 568) and an attempt to expand into Samaria and perhaps adjacent provinces (2 Kgs 23:15–20; 2 Chr 34:6–7, 9, 33; for the debate on this see D. Edelman 1991). Significantly, the extant sources on Josiah's reforms (2 Kgs 22–23; 2 Chr 34–35) do not report any concomitant defensive measures against Assyria nor, in turn, any Assyrian response.

c. Judah in the Classical Neo-Assyrian Period. Unlike Israel, Judah's involvement with Assyria, from the western campaigns of Tiglath-pileser III in the 730s B.C. until the collapse of the Assyrian empire in 614–609 B.C., shows a basic consistency: its status as vassal is never changed. That status first becomes clear in 734–732 B.C., when Judah was attacked by the "Syro-Ephraimite" coalition of Damascus and Israel as part of a general agitation against Assyrian authority in the region, and Tiglath-pileser III responded with a campaign of conquest through S Syria, Israel, Transjordan, and the Mediterranean coast from Phoenicia to "the city of the Brook of Egypt" in the Sinai (Wiseman 1951: 23.18). In this campaign, Ahaz of Judah affirmed his loyalty to the Assyrian, who secured his throne, and this affirmation is made clear in the biblical text (especially 2 Kgs 16:7–18) and in an Assyrian list of tribute providers either from 734 or 732 (*ANET,* 282a, where the name appears in Akkadian, as *ᴵIa-ú-ḫa-zi* = Jehoahaz). Sometime around his conquest of Samaria in 720, Sargon II noted in one inscription that he was "the subduer of the country Judah which is far away" (*ANET,* 287a), which would not seem to indicate that Judah had revolted at that time, but rather had paid tribute as a loyal vassal (so Tadmor 1958: 39 n. 146). And two other occasions of demonstrated loyalty are recorded in Assyrian texts for the long fifty-five-year reign of Manasseh of Judah: the first in the annals of Esarhaddon, where Manasseh is listed among twenty-two W vassal kings who were commanded, about 679 or 677, to bring to the imperial capital at Nineveh materials for the construction of the royal armory and storehouse *(ekal mašarti)* (*ANET,* 291); the second from the annals of Esarhaddon's successor, Ashurbanipal, in which many of the same rulers brought gifts to the king and troop contingents to join his first campaign against Egypt in 668/667 (*ANET,* 294).

This history of vassalship was disturbed on several occasions, but it is noteworthy that none of them resulted in a change of status for Judah. Thus, in the anti-Assyrian revolt of 713–712 led by Ashdod, Judah was at least tempted to join, if it did not actually do so (cf. Isa 20:1–6; Prism A of Sargon II in *ANET,* 287a). But the outcome for her was at the most a payment of tribute, as recorded in an Assyrian text that may date from the end of this revolt and lists tribute payments from various Palestinian and Transjordanian groups as well as Egypt (ND 2765; cf. Cogan 1974: 118). In the great rebellion against Sennacherib of 705–701, Hezekiah of Judah was one of the major western leaders, extending his influence perhaps to Samaria and the other N provinces (2 Chr 30:5, 10–11, 18; 31:1) as well as to Philistia (Sennacherib annals, *ANET,* 287b). In turn, Sennacherib's counterattack, in his third campaign of 701, resulted in a sizable conquest of Judean territory ("46 of his strong cities, walled forts and . . . countless small villages in their vicinity" [Sennacherib annals, *ANET,* 288a]), the transfer of this territory to loyal Philistine vassals (Mitinti of Ashdod, Padi of Ekron, and Ṣilli-bel of Gaza), large slaughter and deportations from the captured settlements (Sennacherib's annals number the deportees at 200,150 [*ANET,* 288a], and the slaughter and deportation from Lachish are the most graphically recorded in the excavations at the site and in reliefs from Nineveh [Ussishkin 1982]), and a very large payment of tribute from Judah as well as an increased annual tax. Yet the Assyrian siege of Jerusalem was suddenly withdrawn; and Judah, though now reduced essentially to Jerusalem and its environs, was allowed to retain its vassal status and even its rebel king, Hezekiah (Sennacherib annals, *ANET,* 287b–88; Naʾaman 1974; main Biblical sources are 2 Kgs 18–20 = Isa 36–39 and 2 Chr 32).

Judah's vassalship was again disturbed, though still not broken, in the reign of Hezekiah's successor, Manasseh. 2 Chr 33:11–13 reports that Manasseh was captured and brought before an unnamed Assyrian king in Babylon. If the incident is authentic, as seems likely, it cannot easily be equated with either the Esarhaddon or the Ashurbanipal mentions of Manasseh noted above. It may refer, rather, to the possible involvement of Judah, along with other W vassals, in the rebellion of the Egyptian Taharqa (biblical Tirhakah) in 671 against Esarhaddon (so Cogan 1974: 69 with earlier opinions). Or it may be connected with Judean (and other western) restiveness in reaction to the Babylonian war or Ashurbanipal in 652–648 (see in Cogan 1974: 68–69; as Cogan and others have also suggested, this same rebellion and war, respectively, may also be behind the deportations to Samaria in the reigns of Esarhaddon [Ezra 4:2] and Ashurbanipal [Ezra 4:9–10]). Whatever the case, the account in 2 Chronicles 33 makes clear that Manasseh was not removed from his throne, but with the help of Yahweh, restored to Jerusalem by the Assyrians, presumably after a sizable tribute payment (which is not, however, noted). Finally, we may recall the political and religious reforms of the last Judean king, Josiah, which went unchallenged by Assyria even though they appear to have become increasingly aggressive in the 620s. Indeed, the only external force Josiah had to deal with was Egypt, which moved, as noted above, to fill something of the Assyrian vacuum in Palestine. Whether Josiah actually became an Egyptian vassal is moot (cf. *HAIJ,* 388–90), but by 609, they were at odds. For in that year, Pharaoh Necho II slew Josiah at Megiddo, evidently when Josiah attempted to stop the Egyptians from marching to the aid of the beleaguered Assyrian army in Harran (2 Kgs 23:29–30; 2 Chr 35:22–24).

Within the historical framework just given, details about the Assyrian management of Judah as vassal are, as they were for Israel, sparse. The effectiveness of the Assyrian propaganda apparatus in communicating authority and demands is made clear by the many echoes of imperial rhetoric in the biblical texts of the period, none more than in (First) Isaiah (Cohen 1979; Machinist 1983). More concretely, as we have seen, the vassal's duty of regular tribute (*biltu, mandattu/maddattu* [= tribute] and *tāmartu/nāmurtu* [= supplementary gifts]) is documented for the reigns of Ahaz, Hezekiah, and Manasseh; the punitive tribute and spoil from rebellion for the reign of Hezekiah. Judeans in Assyrian army service are likewise known from Manasseh's reign, as mentioned, where they apparently were grouped into a separate unit, and the same is true for a regiment of Judeans from Lachish, deported in the wake of Sennacherib's campaign of 701, who served as palace guards in Nineveh (Barnett 1958; cf. Reade 1972: 106–7). The Assyrian practice of supervising a vassal state by placing one or more government commissioners *(qēpu)* in or near it, or of using a nearby governor *(šaknu),* is attested for several W states: e.g., the Arabs of Queen Samsi, under Tiglath-pileser III; Tyre and Ashdod, under Esarhaddon and Ashurbanipal and perhaps also, in the case of Ashdod, under Sargon II after the 713–712 rebellion (*WHJP* 4/1: 286–87; Elat 1975: 64–66; Tadmor 1966: 95). Whether such a commissioner was placed in Judah is moot. None is explicitly attested, but Elat (1975: 63–64) has argued on indirect grounds that one was appointed after the 701 campaign, and set up his headquarters in Lachish. This argument has been opposed by Ussishkin (1977: 53 and n. 14), who notes that there is nothing in the archaeological record of Lachish level II (the level of the post-701 period) that points to an Assyrian presence. Especially, Ussishkin (1977: 39) shows that the so-called Residency building, which was an "open court" structure and for Elat and Aharoni was used by the commissioner, belongs not to level II, but to level I of the Achaemenid Persian period. It represents, thus, a survival of the "open court" form beyond Assyrian times. Ussishkin's refutation notwithstanding, it makes sense to suppose that Assyrian garrisons and associated officials were at least within range of Judah to monitor affairs. Among the places they may be looked for are the sites of Tell esh-Sharia (probably Ziklag) and Tell Jemmeh (probably Arṣa) in the northwestern Negeb just inside or over the Judean border. Here excavations by Oren (1982: 159–61 for Level VI) and Van Beek (1983), respectively, have revealed in the 7th–century levels such features as Assyrian palace ware, iron spearheads, and massive fortresslike buildings. The Jemmeh building is of the "open court" form and has mud-brick barrel vaulting. Together such remains suggest that at that time both sites were Assyrian military posts.

Other archaeological traces of Assyrian activity may be found elsewhere in Judah. Thus, the devastation of Sennacherib's 701 campaign is attested at a number of sites, most dramatically at Lachish level III (on the dating see Ussishkin 1977), with such features as the massive siege ramp and counterramp against the city wall (Ussishkin 1983: 137–46; Eph'al 1984), tomb 120 with its mass burial of some 1500 persons, and numerous iron arrowheads; there is also, one will recall, the Assyrian record of all this in the extensive wall reliefs from Nineveh (Ussishkin 1982). Moreover, some pieces of Assyrian palace ware have turned up in Judah, though far less and generally later—in the latter half of the 7th century (e.g., Ramat Rahel Level VA)—than in Samaria and the other N provinces. In general, the archaeological indications, combined with other sources, suggest that Judah only slowly recovered from the devastation and truncation of its territory caused by the 701 campaign, and that the burden of heavy taxation never allowed a return to full economic health.

In the Assyrian management of its vassals, the matter of religious control has become a disputed question. Against an older opinion, Cogan (1974) and McKay (1973) have independently concluded that while religious obeisance in some form was expected of the provinces, it was not of the vassals. No Assyrian sources, they argue, indicate that vassals were required to support Assyrian sanctuaries or to maintain Assyrian religious symbols or cults within their own territory. On the other hand, vassals certainly had the option of making occasional gifts for Assyrian gods if they wanted to on their own volition. More recently, Spieckermann (1982) has returned to the older view; and while acknowledging that Assyrian texts rather infrequently mention demands for worship of the Assyrian gods, he believes that there are some instances (e.g., in Esarhaddon's treaty with the Median vassals, lines 393–96, 401–9 [*ANET,* 538a]) and that these are echoed by Assyrian practices such as deporting the statues of the gods of the people whom they conquer (e.g., for Samaria in 722/720: cf. Gadd 1954: 179, 4.32–33), presumably to be replaced (even if this is not explicitly stated) by the statues of Assyrian gods. The dispute between Cogan/McKay and Spieckermann is not easily resolved, but it appears to turn on the nature of the evidence each is seeking: Cogan/McKay looking for explicit concrete requirements and actual practices involving Assyrian cults; Spieckermann willing to infer such requirements from more generally phrased statements, such as in the Esarhaddon treaty, because of his conviction that the religiously grounded character of Assyrian imperial ideology—promoting the superiority of the god Ashur—makes religious impositions a logical part of imperial practice.

The relevance of this debate for Judah centers on the religious innovations associated with the kings Ahaz and Manasseh: the erection of a new altar in Jerusalem copied from one seen by Ahaz in Damascus during his meeting with Tiglath-pileser III; the passing of children through fire and the Molech cult; and astral cults, which included also horses (2 Kgs 16:3–4, 10–16; 21:5–6, 18, 26; 23:5, 10–12; 2 Chr 28:3; 33:5–6). For Cogan and McKay, these innovations reflect long-standing Syrian(Aramean)-Canaanite traditions, not Assyrian, except possibly for the cultic use of horses; and their promotion by Ahaz and Manasseh was a voluntary revival of these traditions in Judah, not an Assyrian imposition. The new altar, in any case, was adapted, as the biblical text makes clear (2 Kgs 16:12–16), for a specifically Israelite/Judean worship of Yahweh in Jerusalem, not for any Assyrian god. Spieckermann admits this latter point, but supposes that the new altar was part of a religious change enforced on Ahaz when he met and affirmed his loyalty to Tiglath-pileser in Damascus, and that the old altar became then, in Jerusalem, the vehicle for the worship of Assyrian deities. It is difficult, however, to infer such worship from the only source we have, 2 Kgs 16:14, 16.

d. Trade and the Neo-Assyrian Involvement in Israel and Judah. The Assyrian treatment of Israel and Judah in the latter 8th and 7th centuries B.C. does not make sense, finally, unless it is seen with Assyrian policy toward the S Levant as a whole. Clearly a crucial aspect of this policy was opening up and maintaining lines of trade into the Mediterranean, along the coast into Egypt, and through the Sinai and down the Jordan Valley into Arabia. From these channels came a great variety of natural resources such as wood, precious objects like glass and gold, animals like horses and camels, and human personnel, which the Assyrians increasingly desired for their capital cities and elsewhere in the empire. Menacing the flow of this trade, on the other hand, were the Egyptians, especially under the aggressive 24th and 25th Dynasties, and the nomads of the Syrian desert. These occasionally accepted peaceful relations with and even the domination of Assyria, but often as not resisted it, in the process encouraging the breakdown of authority among the Assyrian provinces and vassal states of the S Levant—the Egyptians focusing on those W of the Jordan, the nomads on those E.

The Assyrians, in turn, sought to deal with these challenges as inexpensively as possible. Accordingly, they preferred to maintain control through vassal states, which obviated the need for large commitments of Assyrian troops and bureaucrats. While continually restive vassals were converted to provinces, this was not done, as Otzen (1977–78: 103–6) has acutely observed, S of a line running roughly E-W above Jerusalem and the Dead Sea. Thus, Samaria, Megiddo, and perhaps Dor and Gilead became provinces; but S of them Judah, the four Philistian kingdoms (Ekron, Ashdod, Ashkelon, and Gaza), and Ammon, Moab, and Edom in the Transjordan—plus various Arab tribes in the Sinai—all remained vassals, despite the rebellions they occasionally offered. Their distance from the Assyrian imperial centers made it simply too costly to establish and supply them as full provinces—though Ashdod may have had a brief period as such shortly after 712. As vassals, then, these S states could serve as facilitators of trade with the Mediterranean, Egypt, and Arabia and as buffers against Egyptian and nomadic hostility when it appeared, their activities watched by isolated Assyrian administrative posts at sites like Tell esh-Sharia, Tell Jemmeh, Tell Abu Salima, and Tel Qatif/Tell Rukeish. (The latter two have each been identified with the commercial and administrative center [Akk *kāru*] set up by Sargon II in 716 to organize trade in the region; see Reich 1984 [who advocates Abu Salima] and Oren et al. 1986 [who prefers, probably correctly, Qatif/Rukeish]). One exception to this geographical division, it should be added, was the Phoenician cities, Sidon, Tyre, Aradus, and Byblos. Although in the latitude N of the Dead Sea and occasionally rebellious, these were nonetheless preserved mostly as vassals, presumably because the Assyrians felt that a heavy hand would interfere with their mercantile activities, and thus with the benefit the Assyrians sought to derive from them.

B. Neo-Babylonian Period

1. Preliminaries. When the Assyrian state collapsed in the years 614–609, its empire in Syria-Palestine fell largely under Egyptian control of the Pharaoh Necho II. This control did not last long. Babylonia, under the Neo-Babylonian or Chaldean dynasty, first challenged it, though unsuccessfully, in 607. Then in 605, at the battle of Carchemish, a Babylonian army led by the crown prince, Nebuchadnezzar II, decisively defeated the Egyptians and so opened Syria-Palestine up to Babylonian control. Nebuchadnezzar became king the next year, 604, and with his successors appears to have followed Assyrian imperial practices rather closely, preserving the division into provinces and vassal states and utilizing deportation.

Babylonian domination of Judah and the former territory of Israel was briefer than the Neo-Assyrian, and is more sparsely recorded. Nebuchadnezzar II appears to have taken control of the region if not immediately after his Carchemish victory, then within the next couple of years (on the question and a rather late date for the capitulation of Judah at the end of 603, see Malamat *WHJP* 4/1: 208–9 and references). Babylonian sovereignty remained until 539, when the whole of the empire passed into the hands of the Achaemenid Persian ruler, Cyrus II.

2. Samaria in the Neo-Babylonian Period. Within this chronological framework, hardly anything is known about the Babylonian treatment of Samaria and the other N provinces set up by the Assyrians. If these provinces came, partly or largely, under the control of Josiah of Judah in the 620s, it is possible that the Babylonians at first allowed them to remain as such. But by 599/98, Samaria, at least, seems to have been a separate entity, if we follow the LXX of 2 Chr 36:5, which reports that Nebuchadnezzar II included Samarians among the local contingents of troops that he sent to counter the rebellion of Jehoiakim of Judah in that period. (The parallel account in 2 Kgs 24:2, both in the MT and in the LXX, leaves out the Samarians.) This argument was advanced by Alt (1934/1953: 325 and n. 3; cf. also Malamat *WHJP* 4/1: 209 and n. 16). Much more debated, because more conjectural, is Alt's further contention (1934/1953: 328–29) that at a later point, perhaps after the deportation of 582, the Babylonians brought Judah under the jurisdiction of the province of Samaria, and that this arrangement prevailed through Achaemenid Persian rule until the arrival of Nehemiah. In any event, Samaria continued to be occupied in the period after 586, as Jer 41:5 makes clear (referring to inhabitants of Shechem, Shiloh, and Samaria), though this cannot be confirmed easily by the archaeology of the area, given the scanty and poorly defined materials uncovered.

3. Judah as Vassal. In regard to Judah, Babylonian control under Nebuchadnezzar II moved through two stages: vassal and then province. The first lasted for almost twenty years, from 605/603 to 586, and through three Judean vassal kings: Jehoiakim (605 [became king in 609]–598), his son, Jehoiachin (598–597), and his brother, Mattaniah/Zedekiah (597–586) (on the problem of the dates in this period, see Malamat 1968: 144–51; Cogan and Tadmor *II Kings* AB, 317 *ad* 2). But it was marked by several severe strains: rebellion against Babylonia (ca. 600–597) led by Jehoiakim and then Jehoiachin; a conspiracy of Judean and neighboring leaders from the Transjordan and Phoenicia, held in Jerusalem under the aegis of Zedekiah (apparently 595–594), and concerned to plan, through it did not fully implement, further anti-Babylonian resistance; and a major new rebellion against Babylonia (589–586) involving the same Zedekiah. These rebellions and conspiracy followed the earlier Assyrian pattern: they began while the Babylonians were occupied elsewhere and were inevitably opposed by other Judean groups which thought them counterproductive (the prophet Jeremiah was a prominent member of these). Yet they regularly involved not only Judah, but also some other Palestinian states, Phoenician and/or Transjordan, although the broad coalitions of rebel states of Assyrian times seem not to be found. In turn, encouragement to rebel was always supplied by Egypt, whether indirectly or directly by military confrontations with Babylonian forces, but Egypt never offered sufficient strengths or persistance to sustain the rebellions (cf. Egypt as "a broken reed" not to be relied on, a motif used both in the Babylonian [e.g., Ezek 29:6] and in the earlier Assyrian periods [e.g., 2 Kgs 18:21 = Isa 36:6]).

Nebuchadnezzar's response was in each instance a strong one, although sometimes it was delayed by the necessity to attend to troubles in other parts of the empire. Thus in 599–597, the king first sent local imperial garrisons and auxiliaries to harass the Judeans, followed up a year later by an invasion of Judah and capture of Jerusalem by the main Babylonian army, which resulted in a deportation of the local elites, including the rebel Judean king, Jehoiachin. The latter was replaced as vassal by his more pliant uncle, Mattaniah, renamed Zedekiah, who, in turn, was required, as in Assyrian practice, to pay a "heavy tribute" *(biltu kabittu)* (TCS 5: 102.11–13; 2 Kgs 24:1–17; cf. 2 Chr 36:5–10). Another Babylonian campaign to Syria-Palestine occurred in 594–593 (TCS 5: 102.25–26); and although not certain, this may have intersected with two events of the same year: the Jerusalem conspiracy, noted above, and the (enforced) visit of Zedekiah and/or one of his officials to Babylon (Jer 51:59). Finally, in 588 or 587—the date is disputed (cf. Malamat 1968: 150–51; Cogan and Tadmor *II Kings* AB, 317 *ad* 2)—Nebuchadnezzar invaded Judah once more, this time with much greater devastation of the countryside, and began a 1½–2-year siege of Jerusalem (2 Kgs 25:1–22; 2 Chr 36:11–21; Jeremiah 34; 37; 52:1–27). Briefly interrupted when an Egyptian force came to help the Judeans then withdrew, the siege was brought to a violent conclusion in the summer of 586. Deportation and heavy slaughter, including the sons of the vassal Zedekiah and the highest priestly echelon, destruction of the city, especially of the royal palace and the Temple, and wide plunder, including the Temple's sacred implements, all marked the Babylonian effort. Judah's vassalship was thereby ended and a new provincial status for it begun (see below), and what is significant is that this change had not been made earlier, as a result of the troubles of 600–597 or 594–593. Apparently, Nebuchadnezzar tried to hold on as long as he could to the Assyrian policy of not establishing provinces below the Jerusalem–Dead Sea line; only the tenaciousness of the rebellion in 589–586 made him decide that this policy was too mild and indulgent.

Within this twenty-year period of vassalship, several features of the Babylonian management of Judah are discernible. As in the Assyrian empire, the Judean vassal kings were called the "servants" of their sovereign (e.g., 2 Kgs 24:1 for Jehoiakim; cf. 2 Kgs 16:7 for Ahaz), and received their status from him through some kind of loyalty oath, akin to the Assyrian *adê*. To be sure, no Neo-Babylonian oath document actually survives, but of the three Judeans, Zedekiah is reported to have been brought to the imperial capital at Babylon to take such an oath in 597 (Ezek 17:12–21; Josephus, *Ant* 10.102).

Vassal activity must have been monitored, as in the Assyrian case, by various administrative centers and their associated garrisons. Riblah, near Hamath in Syria, appears to have been the main one for Syria-Palestine, taken over by the Babylonians from the Egyptians who preceded them (2 Kgs 23:33); it is here that Zedekiah and his entourage were brought before Nebuchadnezzar for judgment when caught trying to escape the siege of Jerusalem in 586 (2 Kgs 25:6, 20; Jer 39:5–7, 52:9–12, 26–27). Of Babylonian centers within or adjacent to Judah, there are no clear indications, but they must have existed, as in the Assyrian period, probably in the provinces of Samaria and the Transjordan. From these it may well be that the initial harassment of Judah in 599–98 was coordinated, using a mixture of Chaldean forces, with local troops from Moab, Ammon, Syria, and perhaps Samaria (2 Kgs 24:2; LXX to 2 Chr 36:5, as noted above).

Babylonian deportation policy, as revealed by the Judean deportations of 597 and 586, as well as a third carried out in 582, also reflected Assyrian practice, but with some variations. For both Babylonia and Assyria, deportation was aimed particularly at the leading elements of the local population—even more, it seems, under Babylonia than under Assyria—and served to punish and (it was hoped) weaken local resistance to imperial authority, as well as to furnish the empire with workers and soldiers. On the other hand, Babylonian deportation appears to have been less extensive than Assyrian; at least the numbers and frequency of deportations stand out less in texts about the Neo-Babylonian state than in texts about the Neo-Assyrian. Compare, for example, the numbers for the Assyrian deportations from Samaria and Judah—27,290 and 200,150, respectively—with those for the three Babylonian deportations from Judah—10,000, 8,000, 3,023 in 597, probably to be totaled at not more than 11,000; 832 from Jerusalem in 586; 745 in 582 (2 Kgs 24:14–16; Jer 52:28–30)—although it must be admitted that these numbers raise serious problems of interpretation (see, e.g., Ackroyd 1968: 22–23. n.24; Malamat *WHJP* 4/1:211; *HAIJ*, 419–20). Further, the Babylonians did not replace those taken from Judah with deportees from elsewhere in the empire, either while Judah was a vassal (when Assyrian did not do it either) or after 586, with its apparent conversion to a province (when Assyrian would have done it). The point is that Babylonian deportees seem to have been resettled virtually exclusively in Babylonia and not, as in Assyrian, all over the rest of the empire as well. And in resettling them, as the Judean deportees and other examples show (Jer 29:4–7; *ANET*, 308; cf. Eph'al 1978 and *WHJP* 5:17–27; 256–58, the Babylonians seem to have been more intent than the Assyrians on keeping exiled communities intact.

The deportation policy had another facet bearing on the management of Judah. This is the evidently deliberate tension created in 597, when the rebel Judean king, Jehoiachin, and his courtiers were exiled to Babylon and his uncle, Zedekiah, was appointed in his stead. As biblical (2 Kgs 25:27–30; Jer 52:31–34) and Babylonian sources (*ANET,* 308b) indicate, the exiled Jehoiachin was allowed to retain his community and treated reasonably well, if closely watched. He had the loyalty of many Judeans, both among the Babylonian exiles and back in Judah (Jer 28:4; note the dating by his reign even when in exile in Ezek 1:2). Since Babylonian records tell us of other exiled rulers who were similarly treated (*ANET,* 308a; *WHJP* 4/1: 213, 351 n. 26), the practice may have been, as Malamat notes (*WHJP* 4/1: 213), to keep the exiled ruler as a threatened replacement for the new vassal in case the latter failed or misbehaved. But if so, the situation had an unintended effect, since the tension it provoked with the new vassal helped, in Zedekiah's case, to weaken his authority and thus to reduce his chances for success as a Babylonian vassal.

4. Judah as Province. Nebuchadnezzar II was determined that after 586 Jerusalem should not remain the functioning capital of the area. This is clear from the biblical report about its massive destruction in that year, confirmed by the excavations in the ancient center of the city. See DAVID, CITY OF; OPHEL. Here the work of Kenyon (1974: 166–71) then of Shiloh (1984: 29 and *passim;* 1986; 1989) has laid bare the devastation of level X, with its revelations of collapsed city and house walls, scattered and crushed home furnishings, intermixed with arrowheads and other weapons and a hoard of inscribed bullae of Judean officials active on the eve of the destruction.

Babylonian destruction was not confined to Jerusalem. The biblical record only briefly alludes to this, in its note about the towns of Lachish and Azekah (Jer 34:7). One must go to the archaeological evidence, therefore, to get a sense of how much beyond Jerusalem destruction reached. The Babylonian goal seems to have been particularly the fortresses throughout Judah, and the evidence shows destruction, in levels regularly with groups of pottery similar to that found in the Jerusalem Ophel destruction, in the W hill country and Shephelah (Lachish II, Tell Beit Mirsim A_3, Gezer VA), in the central Judean hills (Beth-zur III, Khirbet Rabud [probably = Debir] IB, Ramat Rahel VA), in the Negeb (Arad VI, Tel Malhata, Tel Ira VI, Tel Masos, Aroer II, and Kadesh Barnea Upper Fort), and on the Western Dead Sea shores (Ein Gedi V). The letters written on ostraca from Arad VI and Lachish II add to this picture, by describing military activities at these two border fortresses just prior to or at an early stage of the rebellion, before matters became desperate (one exception may be Lachish letter 4, which may attest the fall of, or at least danger to, Azekah [*ANET,* 322]). Interestingly, the note about Lachish and Azekah in Jer 34:7 reports that while the Babylonians were besieging Jerusalem, only these two fortresses, of those outside the capital, remained in Judean hands. The indication is, then, that the Babylonians probably completed their devastation of the rest of Judah before they conquered Jerusalem, just as Sennacherib had undertaken to do in 701.

According to the biblical book of Chronicles (2 Chr 36:21), the Babylonian destruction and deportation were so thorough in 586 that the land "lay desolate" for seventy years thereafter, to "enjoy its sabbaths." But from other textual evidence and archaeological work, it becomes clear that this portrayal is inaccurate, the outgrowth of the particular ideological interests of the Chronicler. Some areas of settlement in fact survived. These included part of Jerusalem itself, notably the W quarter (note the rich burials from the Hinnom Valley [Barkay 1986]), but especially the territory of Benjamin N of Jerusalem. Whether because Benjamin had voluntarily surrendered to the Babylonians early in the 589–586 rebellion or because even earlier, perhaps in 598–597, the Babylonians had split it off from Judah (*WHJP* 4/1: 212; 217–18), Benjamin seems to have escaped extensive destruction. Although the stratigraphy is not always clear, it appears that Benjaminite sites like Bethel, Tell en Nasbeh (= Mizpah), Tell el-Ful (Gibeah), and Gibeon continued right though 586 without a break.

It was at an ancient political center of Benjamin, Mizpah (= Tell en Nasbeh), 12 km N of Jerusalem, that Nebuchadnezzar established a new Judean capital; and we should probably understand that the core of the new community was now in Benjaminite territory. The two deportations of 597 and 586 had depleted the land of many of its leading elements—most of the royal family, major officials, key military and religious figures, the upper class of landed wealth, and various skilled artisans (2 Kgs 24:12–16; 25:11–12; Jer 52:15–16; Jer 24:1; 27:20; 29:2, 21). Those who were left, according to the biblical sources, were "the poorest people of the land" (2 Kgs 24:14), "the poor people who owned nothing" (Jer 39;10)—that is, the peasantry and other lower classes who had owned little or no property before the destruction. In addition, there were still some of the ruling elite around, who had escaped harm by going into hiding or into the Transjordan or by professing loyalty to Babylonian rule (Jer 40:7–12; cf. *WHJP* 4/1: 220–21). From this elite, Nebuchadnezzar chose Gedaliah as the ruler of the surviving Judean community.

Gedaliah son of Ahikam came from a distinguished family of Judean royal officials (2 Kings 25:22; Jer 40:5), whose service reached back to the reign of Josiah. It makes sense that Gedaliah himself should also have had government experience, and that may be attested if we can connect him with the person named in a seal impression found at Lachish, apparently of the early 6th century (Tufnell 1953: 347–48 and pls. 44–45: No. 173). In that impression, which still bears traces of the papyrus fibers of the document to which it was fixed, the owner's name is written in the longer form, Gedalyahu, and is given the well-known title "the one over the house," which could designate a royal official. A similarly spelled Gedalyahu, together with his son, Hananiah, appears in another seal impression with papyrus fiber marks, which seems to date to about the same period (Avigad 1964: 193–94 + pl. 44C). Unfortunately, neither impression provides the name of Gedaliah's father, and since we know of other

Gedaliahs in the period (Jer 38:1), an identification with the new Judean ruler is not certain.

Once installed in Mizpah, Gedaliah was able to attract various Judeans who had earlier fled the Babylonian invasion (Jer 40:7–12). He also had the support, and supervision, of a Babylonian garrison at the site (Jer 41:3). The arrangement fits best with the supposition that Gedaliah functioned as Babylonian governor over a provincial Judah, and not, as Miller and Hayes have recently proposed (*HAIJ,* 423), as king. The indications that they find in the Biblical text for this are all highly indirect and can be interpreted otherwise. The fact remains that Gedaliah was not of royal blood, and it is hard to see what advantage the Babylonians would have gained by appointing him king and flouting so flagrantly and provocatively native Judean royal tradition. Indeed, though Gedaliah is not explicitly labelled a governor, the designation he is given, the one whom Nebuchadnezzar "appointed (*Hipʿil* < *pāqad*) over them (≠ the people left in the land)" (2 Kgs 25:22; Jer 40:7, 11; 41:2, 18), would suit an imperial official like a governor nicely (cf. Gen 41:34; Esth 2:3); it is, however, never used in the Bible for making a king (expected would be a *Hipʿil* verb from *mālak,* as in Nebuchadnezzar's making Mattaniah/Zedekiah vassal king [2 Kgs 24:17]).

In establishing Gedaliah's governorship, the Babylonians were determined not to allow the economy of the area to languish. The biblical texts report that Nebuzaradan, the leader of the Babylonian army against Jerusalem in 586, made the Judean poor who were left in the land "vinedressers and plowmen" (2 Kgs 25:12), "and gave them vineyards and fields" (Jer 39:10). In turn, Gedaliah advised his people to "dwell in the land, serve the king of Babylon" and "gather wine and summer fruits and oil, and store them in your vessels" (Jer 40:9, 10). Graham's recent study (1984) has made clear that behind these notices—and perhaps also various archaeological finds at Mozah, Gibeon, Tell en Nasbeh/Mizpah, and En Gedi, though the dating is not in all instances secure—is the establishment of a deliberate economic policy, in which the estates of the Judean wealthy who had been deported were transferred to the lower classes, to be worked by them for the benefit of the Babylonian state. Gedaliah was the local coordinator of this policy; and through taxes and trade, the products of the Judean economy, wine, balm, oil, and dyes, appear to have made their way beyond Judah to Babylonia itself.

What about religious practices in provincial Judah after 586? The Babylonians' deliberate destruction of the Jerusalem Temple, plunder of its sacred implements for removal to Babylon, and execution of its principal priests (2 Kgs 25:9, 13–21 = Jer 52:13, 17–27) indicate an effort to destroy the cult at least as it had been practiced in Judah. But there is evidence that the worship of Yahweh continued, albeit on a much more modest level, which the Babylonians presumably tolerated, although their attitude is not represented with any precision. The principal notice is Jer 41:4. It records a procession of pilgrims from Shechem, Shiloh, and Samaria, thus evidently from the Samarian province, coming in mourning garb to present *minḥāh* offerings and incense *(lebōnāh)* to the temple of Yahweh, all but ten of whom were waylaid and killed in Mizpah by Ishmael ben Nethaniah, who had assassinated Gedaliah the day before (vv 5–8). Mizpah has been suggested as the location of the temple in question (e.g., *HAIJ,* 426), but more likely it is the ruin of the Jerusalem Temple which was the goal, and the mourning garb was to lament its destruction. Whether within this ruin the altar survived as the point of worship is debated; those in favor point to the absence of any notice of the altar's destruction in the biblical descriptions of the Babylonian burning and sacking of the Temple. Likewise debated is the nature of the worship: whether animal sacrifices had ceased and only nonanimal sacrifices were continued, and whether sacrifices altogether were giving way to prayer. The passage of Jeremiah clearly indicates that sacrifices were still being made, but may suggest that these were only of the nonanimal kind, if *minḥāh* here means cereal offerings and is not used more ambiguously as a general term for sacrifice, animal and nonanimal. Who supervised the sacrifices is not specified. One would expect priests, but with the main Jerusalem leadership executed, it is possible that no priests were involved at the Temple ruin, or else other priestly orders, previously subordinate or peripheral, now took over. As for prayer, various biblical texts, for example 1 Kings 8 (especially vv 46–54), have been held to emphasize it over against sacrifice and to reflect the post-586 period in Judah (e.g., Jones 1963). But the interpretation and dating of these passages is far from clear, even though one should certainly not deny the existence of prayer in the worship of the period, ubiquitous as it was already in preexilic times when the Temple and other sanctuaries were functioning.

The tenure of Gedaliah, though not specified, seems to have been a short one. He had bitter enemies, opposed to his collaboration with Babylonia and perhaps to other things he stood for. The enemies centered on a group of royalists, led by Ishmael son of Nethaniah, of the royal family, who had initially professed support of him, but then conspired with the Ammonite king Baalis (= *baʿal-yišʿa,* in the seal impression referring possibly to this king: Herr 1985; Younker 1985) and assassinated Gedaliah, his entourage, and the Babylonian garrison at Mizpah (Jer 41:1–10). The aim of the plot may have been the restoration of an independent Judean kingdom, but the result was further disaster. Ishmael's forces were set upon by those Judeans supporting Gedaliah and Babylonian rule; the losing Ishmael and eight of his companions succeeded in escaping to their ally, Ammon. In turn, the bulk of the Gedaliah forces, fearing a severe Babylonian reaction, decided to flee Judah for Egypt, and took Jeremiah with them (Jer 41:11–43:7). The fear may have been warranted. Jer 52:30 mentions a third deportation from Judah in 582, after those of 597 and 586; and while the reason for this is not given, many scholars have connected it with the assassination of Gedaliah, thus yielding about four years for his rule. The matter is not resolved, because others have understood the laconic dating of the assassination to the "seventh month," without any elaboration (Jer 41:1–3), to imply a time within Gedaliah's first year of rule, i.e., 586–585 (cf. Holladay *Jeremiah 2* Hermeneia, 296). Be that as it may, the biblical authors provide no further notice about Judah under Babylonian rule. For them at least, the importance of Judah as a viable community had ceased for the moment, and all attention was turned to the exile in Babylonia.

Bibliography

Abou-Assaf, A.; Bordreuil, P; and Millard, A. R. 1982. *La statue de Tell Fekherye et son inscription bilingue assyro-arameenne.* Études assyriologiques. Paris.

Ackroyd, P. 1968. *Exile and Restoration.* OTL. Philadelphia.

Albright, W. F. 1958. The Assyrian Open-Court Building and the West Building of Tell Beit Mirsim. *BASOR* 149: 32.

Alt, A. 1934. Die Rolle Samarias bei der Entstehung des Judentums. Pp. 5–28 in *Festschrift Otto Procksch.* Leipzig. Repr. *KlSchr* 2: 316–45.

Amiran, R. B. K., and Dunayevsky, I. 1958. The Assyrian Open-Court Building and Its Palestinian Derivatives. *BASOR* 149: 25–32.

Astour, M. C. 1971. 841 B.C.: The First Assyrian Invasion of Israel. *JAOS* 91: 383–89.

Avigad, N. 1964. Seals and Sealings. *IEJ* 14: 190–94 + Pl. 44.

Barkay, G. 1986. *Ketef Hinnom: A Treasure Facing Jerusalem's Walls.* Jerusalem.

Barnett, R. D. 1958. The Siege of Lachish. *IEJ* 8: 161–64 + Pls. 30–32.

Becking, B. 1981–82. The Two Neo-Assyrian Documents from Gezer in Their Historical Context. *JEOL* 27: 76–89.

Bloom, J. 1988. *Material Remains of the Neo-Assyrian Presence in Palestine and Transjordan.* Ph.D. Diss. Bryn Mawr.

———. 1989. The Stratum III Citadel at Hazor: A Provincial Variant of the Neo-Assyrian *ekal mašarti*? [Abstract] Pp. 147–48: S141 in *Abstracts. American Academy of Religion/Society of Biblical Literature Annual Meeting 1989.* Atlanta.

Borger, R. 1956. *Die Inschriften Asarhaddons Königs von Assyrien. AfO* Beiheft 9. Graz.

Borger, R., and Tadmor, H. 1982. Zwei Beiträge zur alttestamentlichen Wissenschaft aufgrund der Inschriften Tigaltpilesers III. *ZAW* 94: 244–51.

Cogan, M. 1974. *Imperialism and Religion.* SBLMS 19. Missoula, MT.

Cohen, C. 1979. Neo-Assyrian Elements in the First Speech of the Biblical Rab-Šāqê. *IOS* 9: 32–48.

Crowfoot, J. W.; Crowfoot, G. M.; and Kenyon, K. M. 1957. *The Objects from Samaria. Samaria-Sebaste III.* London.

Dalley, S. 1985. Foreign Chariotry and Cavalry in the Armies of Tiglath-Pileser III and Sargon II. *Iraq* 47: 31–48.

Edelman, D. 1991. The Manassite Genealogy in 1 Chr 7:14–19: Form and Sources. *CBQ* 53: 179–201.

Elat, M. 1975. The Political Status of the Kingdom of Judah within the Assyrian Empire in the 7th Century B.C.E. Pp. 61–70 in *Investigations at Lachish. The Sanctuary and the Residency (Lachish V),* by Y. Aharoni. Tel Aviv.

———. 1978. The Economic Relations of the Neo-Assyrian Empire with Egypt. *JAOS* 98: 20–34.

———. 1982. The Impact of Tribute and Booty on Countries and People within the Assyrian Empire. Pp. 244–51 in *Vorträge gehalten auf der 28. Rencontre Assyriologique Internationale in Wien, 6.–10. Juli 1981. AfO* Beiheft 19. Horn.

Eph'al, I. 1978. The Western Minorities in Babylonia in the 6th–5th Centuries B.C.: Maintenance and Cohesion. *Or* n.s. 47: 74–90.

———. 1982. *The Ancient Arabs.* Jerusalem.

———. 1984. The Assyrian Siege Ramp at Lachish: Military and Linguistic Aspects. *TA* 11: 60–70.

Forrer, E. 1920. *Die Provinzeinteilung des assyrischen Reiches.* Leipzig.

Gadd, C. J. 1954. Inscribed Prisms of Sargon II from Nimrud. *Iraq* 16: 173–201 + pls. XLIV–LI.

Garelli, P., and Nikiprowetzky, V. 1974. *Le Proche-Orient asiatique: Les empires mésopotamiens. Israël.* Nouvelle Clio 2 *bis.* Paris.

Gonçalves, F. J. 1986. *L'Expédition de Sennacherib en Palestine dans la litterature hebraïque ancienne.* EBib n.s. 7. Paris.

Graham, J. N. 1984. "Vinedressers and Plowmen"; 2 Kings 25:12 and Jeremiah 52:16. *BA* 47: 55–58.

Grayson, A. K. 1963. The Walters Art Gallery Sennacherib Inscription. *AfO* 20: 83–96 + Tf. I–IV.

Hallo, W. W. 1964. From Qarqar to Carchemish: Assyrian and Israel in the Light of New Discoveries. *BAR* 2: 152–88.

Halpern, B. 1987. Yaua, Son of Omri Yet Again. *BASOR* 265: 81–85.

Henshaw, R. A. 1967. The Office of *Šaknu* in Neo-Assyrian Times I. *JAOS* 87: 517–25.

———. 1968. The Office of *Šaknu* in Neo-Assyrian Times II. *JAOS* 88: 461–83.

Herr, L. G. 1985. The Servant of Baalis. *BA* 48: 169–172.

Jones, D. 1963. The Cessation of Sacrifice After the Destruction of the Temple in 586 B.C. *JTS* n.s. 14: 12–31.

Kenyon, K. M. 1974. *Digging Up Jerusalem.* London.

———. 1979. *Archaeology in the Holy Land.* 4th ed. London.

———. 1987. *The Bible and Recent Archaeology.* Rev. P. R. S. Moorey. Atlanta.

Kinnier-Wilson, J. V. 1972. *The Nimrud Wine Lists.* Cuneiform Texts from Nimrud I. London.

Levine, L. D. 1972. *Two Neo-Assyrian Stelae from Iran.* Royal Ontario Museum Art and Archaeology Occasional Paper 23. Toronto.

Lie, A. G. 1929. *The Inscriptions of Sargon II, King of Assyria.* Pt 1, *The Annals.* Paris.

Lyon, D. G. 1883. *Keilschrifttexte Sargon's, Königs von Assyrien (722–705 v. Chr.).* Assyriologische Bibliothek 5. Leipzig.

Machinist, P. 1983. Assyrian and Its Image in the First Isaiah. *JAOS* 103: 719–37.

Malamat, A. 1968. The Last Kings of Judah and the Fall of Jerusalem. *IEJ* 18: 137–56.

———. 1973. Josiah's Bid for Armageddon. The Background of the Judean-Egyptian Encounter in 609 B.C. *JANES* 5: 267–79.

McCarter, P. K. 1974. "Yaw, Son of ʿOmri": A Philological Note on Israelite Chronology. *BASOR* 216: 5–7.

McKay, J. 1973. *Religion in Judah under the Assyrians.* SBT n.s. 26. London.

Millard, A. R., and Tadmor H. 1973. Adad-nirari III in Syria. *Iraq* 35: 57–64 + pl. XXIX.

Naʾaman, N. 1974. Sennacherib's "Letter to God" on His Campaign to Judah. *BASOR* 214: 25–39.

Naʾaman, N., and Zadok, R. 1988. Sargon II's Deportations to Israel and Philistia (716–708 B.C.). *JCS* 40: 36–46.

Oates, J. 1959. Late Assyrian Pottery from Fort Shalmaneser. *Iraq* 21: 130–46 + pls. XXXIV–XXXIX.

Oren, E. D. 1982. Ziklag: A Biblical City on the Edge of the Negev. *BA* 45: 155–66.

Oren, E. D. et al. 1986. A Phoenician Emporium on the Border of Egypt. *Qadmoniot* 19: 83–91 (in Hebrew).

Otzen, B. 1977–78. Israel under the Assyrians: Reflections on Imperial Policy in Palestine. *ASTI* 11: 96–110.

Page, S. 1968. A Stela of Adad-nirari III and Nergal-ereš from Tell al Rimah. *Iraq* 30: 139–53 + pls. XXXIX–XLI.
Paul, S. M. 1969. Sargon's Administrative Diction in II Kings 17: 27. *JBL* 88: 73–74.
Pečírková, J. 1977. The Administrative Organization of the Neo-Assyrian Empire. *ArOr* 45: 211–28.
———. 1987. The Administrative Methods of Assyrian Imperialism. *ArOr* 55: 162–75.
Postgate, J. N. 1970. More "Assyrian Deeds and Documents." *Iraq* 32: 129–64 + pls. XVIII–XXXI.
———. 1974. *Taxation and Conscription in the Assyrian Empire.* Studia Pohl, Series Maior 1. Rome.
———. 1979. The Economic Structure of the Assyrian Empire. Pp. 193–221 in *Power and Propaganda. A Symposium on Ancient Empires,* ed., M. T. Larsen. Mesopotamia 7. Copenhagen.
———. 1980. The Place of the *Šaknu* in Assyrian Government. *AnSt* 30: 67–76.
Reade, J. E. 1972. The Neo-Assyrian Court and Army: Evidence from the Sculptures. *Iraq* 34: 87–112 + pls. XXXIII–XL.
Reich, R. 1975. The Persian Building at Ayyelet ha-Shahar: The Assyrian Palace of Hazor? *IEJ* 25: 233–37.
———. 1984. The Identification of the "Sealed *kāru* of Egypt." *IEJ* 34: 32–38 + pl. 6A.
Reich, R., and Brandl, B. 1985. Gezer under Assyrian Rule. *PEQ* 117: 41–54.
Reisner, G. A.; Fisher, C. S.; and Lyon, D. G. 1924. *Harvard Excavations at Samaria 1908–1910.* Vols. 1–2. Cambridge, MA.
Schramm, W. 1972. War Semiramis assyrische Regentin? *Historia* 21: 513–21.
Shiloh, Y. 1984. *Excavations at the City of David I.* Qedem 19. Jerusalem.
——— 1986. A Group of Hebrew Bullae from the City of David. *IEJ* 36: 16–38 + pls. 4–7.
———. 1989. Judah and Jerusalem in the Eighth-sixth Centuries B.C.E. Pp. 97–105 in *Recent Excavations in Israel: Studies in Iron Age Archaeology,* ed. S. Gitin and W. G. Dever. AASOR 49. Winona Lake, IN.
Sigrist, R. M. 1982. Une tablette cunéiforme de Tell Keisan. *IEJ* 32: 32–35.
Smith, D. L. 1989. *The Religion of the Landless. The Social Context of the Babylonian Exile.* Bloomington.
Spieckermann, H. 1982. *Juda unter Assur in der Sargonidenzeit.* FRLANT 129. Göttingen.
Stern, E. 1975. Israel at the Close of the Period of the Monarchy: An Archaeological Survey. *BA* 38: 26–54.
Tadmor, H. 1958. The Campaigns of Sargon II of Assur. *JCS* 12: 22–40; 77–100.
———. 1966. Philistia Under Assyrian Rule. *BA* 29: 86–102.
———. 1967. The Conquest of Galilee by Tiglath-pileser III, King of Assyria. Pp. 62–67 in *All the Land of Naphtali* (in Hebrew). Jerusalem.
Tufnell, O. 1953. *Lachish III. The Iron Age.* 2 vols. London.
Ussishkin, D. 1977. The Destruction of Lachish by Sennacherib and the Dating of the Royal Judean Storage Jars. *TA* 4: 28–60.
———. 1982. *The Conquest of Lachish by Sennacherib.* Tel Aviv.
———. 1983. Excavations at Tel Lachish 1978–1983: Second Preliminary Report. *TA* 10: 97–175.
Van Beek, G. W. 1983. Digging Up Tell Jemmeh. *Arch* 36: 12–19.
Weippert, M. 1972. Review of *Neo-Assyrian Toponyms,* by Simo Parpola. *Göttingische Gelehrte Anzeigen* 224: 150–61.
———. 1978. Jau(a) Mār Ḫumri—Joram oder Jehu von Israël? *VT* 28: 113–18.
Winckler, H. 1889. *Die Keilschrifttexte Sargons.* 2 Vols. Leipzig.
Wiseman, D. J. 1951. Two Historical Inscriptions from Nimrud. *Iraq* 13: 21–26 + pls. XI–XII.
Younker, R. W. 1985. Israel, Judah, and Ammon and the Motifs on the Baalis Seal from Tell el-ʿUmeiri. *BA* 48: 173–80.

PETER MACHINIST

PERSIAN ADMINISTRATION

The period of Persian dominance in the ANE, ushered in by Cyrus in 539 B.C., is not easily documented by the available epigraphic and archaeological evidence. Persian rulers dealt with the region that came to be called Palestine, which was defined differently over time, by using political and administrative savvy to serve their own interests. Although Persian policies toward and administrative structures governing Palestine are difficult to reconstruct because of the meager evidence, an overview of administrative practice in the south, the north, Samaria, and Judah is possible.

A. Sources
B. The Region Called Palestine
C. Persian Administration
  1. In the South
  2. In the North
  3. Samaria
  4. Judah

A. Sources

The sources available for the study of the Persian administration of Palestine fall into two distinct groups, and the difficulty which confronts us in consequence is that of relating the one to the other. First, the literary and archaeological sources illuminate the history of Palestine (principally Judah) throughout this period. Alongside the relevant biblical texts, mention should also be made of the Aramaic texts from the Jewish community in Elephantine, Upper Egypt, of the Aramaic texts from Wâdī ed-Dâliyeh, of a number of seals and coins throughout the region, and of course, the general conclusions which may be drawn from a study of the material remains of the period. Of later textual sources, none is more important than Josephus, whose history of the period (*Antiquities* 11) probably includes a few items of authentic material not otherwise preserved. These sources are not comprehensive and so do not enable us to reconstruct a satisfyingly connected history even of Judah, let alone the remainder of Palestine (see Williamson 1990). However, this is less serious for our present purposes than might at first appear, in so far as our concern is with policy and administrative structures rather than with the course of events as such.

Second, we have a good deal of information regarding the affairs of the Achaemenid empire as a whole. Until the last century, this was confined to classical sources, such as Herodotus, Ctesias, Thucydides, and Xenophon. Now, however, it is possible to refine and sometimes modify this picture by firsthand texts from the center of the empire itself: monumental texts in Old Persian, such as Darius I's

Behistun inscription, have been joined by the Elamite and Aramaic texts from Persepolis, while information in local languages from Babylon, Egypt, Asia Minor, and elsewhere has helped to round out the picture (see Cook 1983; Frye 1984). Hardly any of these, however, make any mention whatsoever of Palestine; our problem, therefore, is to match what we know of Persian administrative practices in general with such specific texts as we have for the history of Palestine during this period.

B. The Region Called Palestine

"Palestine" was not a name or district officially recognized by the Persians. Furthermore, Herodotus is not fully consistent in his usage of the term. Generally in his writings, Palestine explicitly excludes Phoenicia (e.g., in his list of satrapies, 3.91: ". . . the whole of Phoenicia and that part of Syria which is called Palestine . . ."), but at 7.89, beyond the more restricted definition, he also goes on to say, "This part of Syria [i.e., including the land of the Phoenicians], together with the country which extends southward to Egypt, is all known as Palestine." In view of this ambiguity, it would seem best in the present context to concentrate attention primarily on the territories originally included within the preexilic kingdoms of Israel and Judah, but to include some comments on neighboring districts (where sources permit) for comparison and contrast.

At the macro level, the administrative status of this territory under the Persians is relatively straightforward. When Cyrus entered Babylon in 539 B.C., he inherited at a stroke the whole of the neo-Babylonian empire, which was made up of both Babylonia and former Assyria and thus stretched around the fertile crescent as far as Egypt. During the early years of Persian rule, this whole area ("Babylon and the land Beyond the River") was administered as a single unit under Gubaru, whom Cyrus appointed as governor.

Similarly, after Darius I crushed two rebellions in Babylon at the start of his reign, we find that a Persian named Ushtani is governor over the same extended area, but that in addition he has a subordinate with responsibility for "Beyond the River" (i.e., the western side of the fertile crescent) only, namely Tattannu Olmstead 1944), who is clearly to be identified with the Tattenai of Ezra 5:3, 6; 6:6, 13. Ushtani remained in office until at least 516 B.C. (Graf 1985: 87), and Tattenai until as late as 502 B.C. (Rainey 1969: 53, Oppenheim in Gershevitch 1985: 563). It is thus apparent, on the basis of firsthand sources, that we cannot follow without qualification the somewhat later account of Herodotus when he both implies that the major reform of the empire into twenty satrapies should be dated early in the reign of Darius I and that Babylon and Beyond the River were administered as separate satrapies (the ninth and fifth in his list respectively) from that time on. It is widely believed currently (though, cf. Dandamayev *CHJ* 1: 329) that whereas the major reorganization of the empire was achieved by Darius, the specific separation of Beyond the River to form a new satrapy was realized only in the early years of Xerxes' reign as part of his reforms following two Babylonian revolts (Rainey 1969: 57; Graf 1985: 89–93). Thereafter, Palestine will have remained as part of this new satrapy until the end of the Persian period.

There is little agreement as to where the capital of the new satrapy was located. Sidon, Tripolis, Damascus, Ashkelon, and Belesys all have some sort of claim (Cook 1983: 174), though the first-named seems most probable (Elayi 1980: 25–26). More interestingly, it appears from material remains that the Persian overlords limited their presence to a few specific garrison towns (notably Lachish, Hazor, Tel Poleg, Shiqmonah, Ramat Rahel, Ein Gedi, Tell es-Sadiyeh, Tell Mazar, Tell el-Hesi, Samaria. Tell el-Farah, and Gezer; see Kenyon 1987: 145–47), and were content thereafter to leave the administration in local hands. They will have relied upon their excellent road system and periodic inspections by high officials of the king, known as "the King's Eye" (who traveled the provinces with a military patrol drawn from the Persian army itself) to ensure stability and provide an independent check on the loyalty of both satraps and governors.

C. Persian Administration.

It is when we turn to the issue of provincial administration within this satrapy that we encounter great difficulties, and indeed the almost complete lack of connection between our two major blocks of sources (to say nothing of their spasmodic character) means that over many issues we cannot hope for more than reasonably informed conjecture. Nor should we assume that the Persians administered every province alike; a brief look at the situation in the extreme S and the extreme N of our area should underline this point before we move on to a more detailed discussion of Judah and Samaria.

1. In the South. The S border of the Persian province of Judah ran along a line to the N of Hebron and Lachish, so that these prominent centers, to say nothing of more southerly towns such as Arad and Beer-sheba, lay outside the Jewish province. This situation probably reflects a continuation of that which developed after the first Babylonian conquest (597 B.C.), when the territory of Judah was diminished and Edomite and other Arabian tribes expanded into the area.

Herodotus (3.4–9; 3.91; 3:97) tells us that in return for Arabian help during his Egyptian campaign, Cyrus' successor Cambyses did not subdue their territory but rather established "friendly relations" and that this was continued later in the sense that the Arabs were not obliged to pay revenue but that they did make annual contributions in the form of "gifts." From the Persian point of view, this may well have been regarded as a practical means of securing one of their borders with a minimum of effort, while Eph'al (1982: 206–10) has suggested that the "gifts" were in fact a fixed amount paid in return for the delegation to "the king of the Arabs" of the supervision of the spice trade from Arabia to the coast S of Gaza. A less generous attitude might be to observe that the arrangement was as much as the Persians could hope to achieve in the light of what we now know of the power and extent of this kingdom. Geshem the Arabian, who was an enemy of Nehemiah located to the S of Judah (cf. Neh 2: 19; 6:1–2, 6), is probably to be identified with the father of "Qainū son of Geshem, king of Qedar," whose name appears on a silver bowl found at Tell el-Maskhūṭa in lower Egypt, and perhaps with the Gashm ben Shahr referred to in a Liḥyanite inscription from Arabian Dedan (see the most recent defense of this identification by Graf fc., 10–11, *contra* Eph'al 1982: 213–14). This suggests that in the middle of the 5th century B.C., at any rate, the Qedarite confederation was an extensive and powerful force whose total subjugation the Persians may have considered too costly.

It has been reasonably argued, however, that following the Egyptian revolt at the very end of the 5th century, the relationship changed and the Persians established the province of Idumaea; a further reason for this may have been that the growth in population of S Palestine made this fiscally rewarding (de Geus 1979–80). This would then account for the presence of 4th-century Aramaic ostraca at Arad and Beersheba whose terminology is suggestive of Achaemenid administration, but whose late date cannot support Stern's conjecture (*CHJ* 1: 81) that the area was a regular Persian province throughout the period of Persian rule. The history of S Palestine thus makes clear that Persian administration proceeded on a pragmatic basis and was subject to development in the face of changing circumstances.

2. In the North. Administration of the Phoenician cities, located basically to the N of Palestine, but with influence on and hence implications for virtually the whole of the Palestinian coast, leads by a quite different route to a comparable conclusion (see especially Elayi 1980). In the early years of Persian rule it is clear that they shared many common objectives with the Persians in terms of control of the eastern Mediterranean seaboard. Not only, therefore, did they rapidly submit to Cyrus after he had entered Babylon (assuming that they are included among "the kings of the West land" mentioned in the Cyrus cylinder; see *ANET* 316), but they materially aided his successor Cambyses with naval assistance for his invasion of Egypt, as they did subsequent kings in the later Greco-Persian wars of the early 5th century.

In response to (if not indeed to secure) such loyalty, these Phoenician city-states seem to have been treated with a light hand by the Persians. They retained their hereditary monarchs, were able later to mint their own coinage (Betlyon 1982), and were given considerable freedom in their commercial enterprises. Thus although they were included within the fifth satrapy, it would be a mistake to think of them either individually or collectively as simply another province. Once again, Stern (1982: 239; *CHJ* 1: 80–81) rejects this conclusion, citing in particular the fact that the Eshmunazar inscription includes the description of a region which coincides with the boundaries of the Assyrian-Persian province of Dor. What he does not state, however, is (1) that this is south of the central area of the Phoenician city-states, (2) that the area was given to Sidon as a reward for loyalty by the Persian king (unidentified, but perhaps Xerxes I, following his wars with Greece), thus implying a change in what had formerly been the situation, and (3) that the area is geographically separated from Sidon by Tyre, so that it cannot be part of a single province. The political geography of this area is admittedly extremely complex (Elayi 1982) and we do not have sufficient sources to resolve all the issues satisfactorily. Furthermore, conditions did not remain static (Katzenstein 1979) and of course later on in the Persian period the area saw at least two major revolts against the central authorities, but none of this should detract from the fact that, once again, the Persians adopted a pragmatic approach to their administration in this area—granting considerable autonomy to a traditional way of government in order to secure the benefits of much-needed Phoenician maritime skills.

This brief survey of S and N Palestine has concluded that we cannot bring *a priori* considerations to bear on an analysis of the administrative structures of any given area within the satrapy of Beyond the River. Since we have to be alert to variety, we should not be afraid of concluding from a study of relevant evidence that one province may have been administered differently from another. Unfortunately, for parts of the coastal plain, as for Galilee and Transjordan, we do not have sufficient evidence to draw any firm conclusions whatever (for a survey of what is available, see Avi-Yonah 1966: 23–31; and Stern 1982: 237–53). But for the heartland of Judah and Samaria, the OT itself, together with epigraphic and other archaeological remains, enables us to be rather more positive.

3. Samaria. The first issue concerns whether these two districts were initially administered as a single province, or whether they were two separate provinces from the very start of Achaemenid rule. References to Sheshbazzar (Ezra 5:14) and Zerubbabel (Hag 1:1, 14) as "governors" of Judah, as well as to the territory of Judah as a "province" (Heb *hamědînâ,* Ezra 2:1), give initial support to the latter opinion (*IJH,* 510). This was challenged by Alt (*KlSchr* 2:316–37), however, who argued in an influential article that Judah became part of Samaria in Babylonian times and that this continued to be the case until Nehemiah's time, when Judah first gained its independence (hence the opposition which Nehemiah aroused). He further argued that *pḥh,* "governor," was a broad term that could equally well refer to a "special commissioner" (see more recently McEvenue 1981).

In a strongly worded riposte originally published in 1971, Smith (1987: 193–201) pointed to the hypothetical nature of Alt's case and to the fact that Neh 5:15 implies that there were governors of Judah before Nehemiah. In the second edition of his book (1987: 149–50), Smith was also probably right to draw attention to the appearance of "Elnathan the governor" on a bulla and seal published by Avigad (1976). Neither the precise significance of the title nor the date of this material is completely certain, although probability strongly favors Avigad's and Smith's position (Williamson 1988).

Finally, various historical considerations may be added to the foregoing proposals. For instance, it needs to be asked why, if Judah was not an independent province with Jerusalem as its capital, the various official enquiries in Ezra 4 and 5 were necessary. Presumably on Alt's view the governor of Samaria should have had authority to act within his own province (Ezra 4), while Tattenai in Ezra 5 should have approached him, and not the Jews, for an explanation of what was going on. On balance, therefore, we should conclude that Judah and Samaria were administered separately throughout the period of Persian rule.

What little further is known of Samaria may be conveniently summarized next. The precise boundaries of the province are uncertain, but Avi-Yonah (1966: 24–25) has argued convincingly that it did not include Galilee, the situation thus remaining as it had under the Assyrians.

The mixed population of the province (Stern 1982: 245) appears to be reflected in the names and titles of Ezra 4: 9–10, but textual difficulties preclude pressing this evidence further. By the middle of the 5th century B.C., however, when Nehemiah came to Jerusalem, Sanballat was acting as governor. The biblical text never ascribes this title to him, but it appears on a seal from Wâdī ed-Dāliyeh (Cross 1974: 18) as well as in the Elephantine papyri (*CAP* 30.29). Because he was succeeded by his descendants through a further four generations and appears himself to have been the first in his family to act as governor (for the evidence for both these assertions, see SANBALLAT), it is likely that his appointment reflects some administrative changes by the Persians following the revolt of the western satrapies under the leadership of Megabyzos in about 449 B.C., but unless Nehemiah's appointment a few years later is to be seen in the same context we do not know what further measures they took at this time.

4. Judah. a. Boundaries. Turning finally to Judah, we find our evidence to be more abundant than for any other of the provinces in Beyond the River. First, we can reconstruct not only the approximate boundaries of the province, but even its internal divisions. From the list of those who returned from Babylon (Ezra 2; Nehemiah 7) and that in Nehemiah 3, which details the participants in the reconstruction of the walls of Jerusalem, we learn that Gibeon, Mizpah, and Bethel were included, suggesting a northern border slightly more extensive than that of the kingdom of Judah after the division of the monarchy. To the east, the mention of Jericho points to the river Jordan continuing as the natural border. To the south, however, the border was pulled back to a line between Hebron and Lachish outside the province and Beth-zur and Keilah inside, as already noted, this probably continued the situation established by Nebuchadnezzar. The southwestern border, including Keilah and Zanoah, is not controversial, but in the northwest there is considerable dispute as to whether the trio of Lod, Hadid, and Ono (Ezra 2: 33) are to be included or not. For different reasons, Alt (*KlSchr* 2:338–45) and Avi-Yonah (1966), among others, have argued that this district lay outside the province of Judah, whereas to counter this Stern (1982: 245–49) has added archaeological considerations to the textual data, namely the place of discovery of a number of seal impressions which he believes belonged to the Judean administration and of coins bearing the legend *yh(w)d* (Judah). As regards the disputed area, he locates this within a district that he calls "north-west Shephelah," centered on Gezer, where such finds have been made. Unfortunately, however, this sort of evidence cannot at present finally settle the issue. The trio of towns are at quite some distance from Gezer, so that we cannot be sure exactly where the border lay. This leaves us with the literary evidence alone, which points unanimously to their inclusion. This may seem a little odd geographically, but it is possible to defend it on historical grounds (Williamson *Ezra, Nehemiah* WBC, 33–34, 254–55). It thus emerges that the province was probably no more than 40–50 km wide, less than half as large as the preexilic kingdom of Judah.

Again on the basis of Nehemiah 3, it is clear that the province was divided into at least five districts (themselves apparently further subdivided), with their "capitals" at Jerusalem, Keilah, Mizpah, Beth-haccherem, and Beth-zur. Some scholars accept that this reflects the actual situation (e.g., Aharoni *LBHG*, 364), while others believe that one or two districts may simply not be mentioned in the list. For instance, Avi-Yonah (1966: 22) adds Jericho, whereas Stern (1982: 248–49) adds Gezer and Jericho, but subsumes Beth-haccherem within Jerusalem. Such details, of course, are of less significance in the present context than the intensity of administrative structures which the data present as a whole.

b. Governor. As already noted, the Persians administered this province through a "governor" (Heb *peḥâ).* We may list the names of those known to us with the source which states their title, while recognizing that in the case of those known only from epigraphical sources, there can be little certainty as to absolute or relative chronology (Avigad 1976: 35; modified by Williamson 1988), as follows:

NAME	DATE	SOURCE
Sheshbazzar	538 B.C.	Ezra 5:14 (and 1:8?)
Zerubbabel	520 B.C.	Hag 1:1, 14
Elnathan	late 6th century B.C.	see Avigad 1976
Nehemiah	445–433 B.C.	Neh 5:14–15, 18; 12:26
Bagohi	408 B.C.	*CAP* 30:1
Yeḥezpîyâ	4th century B.C.	see Rahmani 1971; Mildenberg 1979; Betlyon 1986
Yehᶜezer	(uncertain)	Aharoni 1962: 28; Aharoni 1964: 19, 43
Ahzai	(uncertain)	Aharoni 1962: 28; Aharoni 1964: 19, 43

The dates refer to the year attested by the source, not the duration of the office, concerning which there is generally no information. The names "Yehᶜezer" and "Ahzai" appear on stamps from a refuse dump at Ramat Raḥel, but there is no means of telling whether they were governors before or after Nehemiah's time. It thus appears as if the administration was wholly in Jewish hands. The only possible doubt here concerns Bagohi, but since we know that, despite its Iranian etymology, this name could be used by Jewish families (Ezra 2: 2), it seems probable that this is also the case here. In any event, he should almost certainly not be associated with the famous general of Artaxerxes III (Williamson 1977).

c. Strategic Location. Moving beyond these rather severely factual matters, we should observe next that Judah probably benefited considerably under the Persian administration from its location near the border with Egypt. (The situation ought to have been the same in the case of such neighboring provinces as Ashdod, but we have no literary evidence by which to check.) Though Cyrus himself never invaded Egypt, there can be little doubt that he had it in mind, and his son Cambyses duly fulfilled his ambition. We have already noted how, in quite different ways, this turned out to the advantage both of the Arabs to the south and the Phoenician city-states to the north and west. The dealings of the early Achaemenids with Judah should be viewed in the same light. Although Cyrus is not so much regarded now as acting purely out of liberal humanitarian considerations (Kuhrt 1983), he was certainly not above making use of such when it could be seen to work to his advantage—and in the case of Judah, it surely was. The return of some of the exiles with their temple treasures from Babylon, together with permission to rebuild the temple itself, is not out of place in terms of Persian policy toward both the area of Babylon itself, as revealed in the Cyrus cylinder, or toward Beyond the River, as noted above.

Indeed, as it turns out, for most of the major turning points known to us in the history of the postexilic period which brought the Jews into close contact with the center of power in the empire, wider international considerations can always be postulated as motivation on the part of the king. In summary (and in addition to the factors already mentioned), we may link (1) the favor of Darius I (Ezra 5–6) with his desire to consolidate his rule after the spate of rebellions at its inception; (2) the mission of Ezra (on an early date) with the Egyptian revolt (though cf. Margalith 1986; (3) the harsh measures of Ezra 4: 8–23 soon after with the revolt of the satrap Megabyzos once he had successfully put down the Egyptian revolt; (4) the mission of Nehemiah with a postulated desire of Artaxerxes I to stabilize the position in the whole of the satrapy following Megabyzos' revolt (Williamson 1990); and (5) a late date of Ezra's mission (i.e., 398 B.C.) with a further Egyptian revolt (Cazelles 1954). Finally, the account of how one Bagoses "defiled the sanctuary, and imposed tribute on the Jews" because the high priest Joannes murdered his brother Jesus in the temple (Josephus, *Ant* 11.297–301) may be linked with the attempt by Artaxerxes III to recapture Egypt in 344–343 B.C. both because a Persian general named Bagoses played an important part in this campaign, and because it is possible that the Tennes revolt just before could well have divided Jerusalem into pro-Persian and pro-Egyptian parties; but this example is far less certain, and could equally well have been motivated by local issues alone.

Evidence is continuing to accumulate regarding the administrative procedures which undergirded this policy. Frei (1984) has collected examples from Egypt and Asia Minor as well as Judah to illustrate how frequently reforms in the spheres of law and the cult as they affected a particular province were initiated by the Persians in response to specific petitions by the local inhabitants under an indigenous leadership. Similarly, Blenkinsopp (1987) is only the latest in a long line of scholars who have compared the accounts of Ezra and Nehemiah with that of the Egyptian Udjahorresnet (for his inscription, see *AEL* 3: 36–41). He was a collaborator who, again explicitly by means of a petition, "used his new position to influence Cambyses to carry out a thorough restoration of the cult at the dynastic sanctuary of Sais" (*AEL* 3: 410), and who was almost certainly involved in the codification and enforcement of the ancient laws of Egypt, as recorded in the Demotic Chronicle (Spiegelberg 1914).

In the light of these and other examples that could be listed, a picture emerges with regard to Judah in which king and subject were each willing to make some concessions in return for what was regarded as an even greater good. As texts from various sources show, the Jews, for their part, were generally quite willing to act loyally toward the empire—including offering prayers and sacrifices on behalf of the king and his family (Ezra 6: 10; 7: 23)—in return for relative religious and legal freedom as well as tax concessions (elsewhere it has been argued that, ironically, it was this administrative convenience rather than any internal ideological development which was the primary catalyst for the exclusive stance of the Jewish reformers; see Williamson 1989). Conversely, it is likely that the Persians regarded this as a small price to pay for loyalty on their W border. But of course, as Ezra at least demonstrates, any suspicion of an abuse of this delicate arrangement was speedily treated in a harsh and peremptory manner.

Another important area in the Persian administration of Palestine is unfortunately one regarding which we have least information. As part of the satrapy of Beyond the River, Judah must have had to contribute its share toward the 350 talents of silver which, according to Herodotus 3.90–97, the satrapy as a whole was liable to pay as revenue each year, but how much and by what means the province made its contribution we have no way of knowing. On the one hand, Cyrus (Ezra 6: 4), Darius I (Ezra 6: 8–10), and Artaxerxes (Ezra 7: 20–24) all made grants for the support of the temple, and it has often been supposed that this was administered by deducting the amount expended from the amount of revenue owed by the province. In addition, there were specific tax concessions for the cultic personnel (Ezra 7: 24). On the other hand, it is clear from Neh 5: 4 that the burden of taxation fell heavily on many in the population and, from vv 14–19 of the same chapter, that several of Nehemiah's predecessors as governor exacted their dues from the people with a heavy hand. (It is possible, on the basis of evidence from the Persepolis tablets, that these dues in kind were accepted as part of the province's overall dues in revenue, but we cannot be sure.) In addition, steps were taken periodically (Nehemiah 10 and 13) to enforce the payment of tithes for the support of the temple.

Now, it has frequently been stated in the past that in the later part of the Persian period, at least, the situation already obtained which seems certain for the Hellenistic period, namely that civil as well as sacred authority lay in the hands of the high priest. If that were so, then several of the kinds of payment just listed would have been concentrated into one, and the whole system would be relatively clear. Unfortunately, however there is virtually no evidence for this hypothesis (nor have I been able to find any serious attempt to defend it; most scholars just assert it, though see Meyers 1985), and much that tells against it, such as the list of (secular) governors given above (see also Laperrousaz 1982). Thus, beyond the suggestion that the jar handles stamped with the official name of the province were once part of a system for collecting revenues in kind, we remain in the dark about this important topic.

Finally, we should observe that a number of coins stamped with the name of the province are now known from the 4th century B.C., again attesting both the administrative independence and favorable status which Judah enjoyed at that time. The occurrence of the name of a governor on some of these coins is thus not expected. More difficult to account for, however, is Barag's reading of one coin as *yḥn[n] hkhn* "Johanan the priest" (1985). Were there other evidence to support it, this might be taken as signifying that by the second half of the 4th century B.C. (i.e., just before the collapse of Persian rule) Judah was indeed governed as a hierocracy, but in fact both Barag and Betylon (1986) agree that this single coin more likely attests a time of revolt or subversive activity against Persian rule.

In sum, therefore, the Persian administration of Palestine can be best characterized as one of enlightened self-interest, exploiting with no little skill their varied ways of gaining favor with the local peoples for their own strategic and political ends.

Bibliography

Aharoni, Y. 1962–64. *Excavations at Ramat Rahel: Seasons 1959 and 1960* and *Seasons 1961 and 1962*. Rome.

Avigad, N. 1976. *Bullae and Seals from a Post-Exilic Judean Archive*. Qedem 4. Jerusalem.

Avi-Yonah, M. 1966. *The Holy Land From the Persian to the Arab Conquests (536 B.C. to A.D. 640): A Historical Geography*. Grand Rapids.

Barag, D. 1985. Some Notes on a Silver Coin of Johanan the High Priest. *BA* 48: 166–68.

Betlyon, W. 1982. *The Coinage and Mints of Phoenicia: The Pre-Alexandrine Period*. HSM 26. Chico, CA.

———. 1986. The Provincial Government of Persian Period Judea and the Yehud Coins. *JBL* 105: 633–42.

Blenkinsopp, J. 1987. The Mission of Udjahorresnet and those of Ezra and Nehemiah. *JBL* 106: 409–21.

Cazelles, H. 1954. La Mission d'Esdras. *VT* 4: 113–40.

Cook, J. M. 1983. *The Persian Empire*. London.

Cross, F. M. 1974. The Papyri and Their Historical Implications. Pp. 17–29 in *Discoveries in the Wâdī ed-Dâliyeh*, ed. P. W. Lapp and N. L. Lapp. AASOR 41. Cambridge, MA.

Elayi, J. 1980. The Phoenician Cities in the Persian Period. *JANES* 12: 13–28.

———. 1982. Studies in Phoenician Geography during the Persian Period. *JNES* 41: 83–110.

Eph'al, I. 1982. *The Ancient Arabs: Nomads on the Borders of the Fertile Crescent*. Leiden.

Frei, P. 1984. Zentralgewalt und Lokalautonomie im Achämenidenreich. Pp. 7–43 in *Reichsidee und Reichsorganisation im Perserreich*, ed. P. Frei and K. Koch. OBO 55. Freiburg and Göttingen.

Frye, R. N. 1984. *The History of Ancient Iran*. Munich.

Gershevitch, I., ed. 1985. *The Cambridge History of Iran*. Vol. 2, *The Median and Achaemenian Periods*. Cambridge.

Geus, C. H. J. de. 1979–80. Idumaea. *JEOL* 26: 53–74.

Graf, D. F. 1985. Greek Tyrants and Achaemenid Politics. Pp. 79–123 in *The Craft of the Ancient Historian*, ed. J. W. Eadie and J. Ober. Lanham, MD.

———. fc. Arabia during Achaemenid Times. *Papers Presented to the Sixth Achaemenid Workshop*.

Katzenstein, H. 1979. Tyre in the Early Persian Period (539–486 B.C.). *BA* 42: 23–34.

Kenyon, K. M. 1987. *The Bible and Recent Archaeology*. Rev. ed. Ed. P. R. S. Moorey. London.

Kuhrt, A. 1983. The Cyrus Cylinder and Achaemenid Imperial Policy. *JSOT* 25: 83–97.

Laperrousaz, E. M. 1982. Le régime théocratique juif a-t-il commencé à l'époque hellénistique? *Sem* 32: 93–96.

Margalith, O. 1986. The Political role of Ezra as Persian Governor. *ZAW* 98: 110–12.

McEvenue, S. E. 1981. The Political Structure in Judah from Cyrus to Nehemiah. *CBQ* 43: 353–64.

Mildenberg, L. 1979. Yehud: A Preliminary Study of the Provincial Coinage of Judaea. Pp. 183–96 in *Greek Numismatics and Archaeology*, ed. O. Mørkholm and N. M. Waggoner. Wetteren.

Meyers, E. M. 1985. The Shelomith Seal and the Judean Restoration: Some Additional Considerations. *EI* 18: 33*–38*.

Olmstead, A. T. 1944. Tattenai, Governor of "Across the River." *JNES* 3: 46.

Rahmani, L. Y. 1971. Silver Coins of the Fourth Century BC from Tel Gamma. *IEJ* 21: 158–60.

Rainey, A. F. 1969. The Satrapy "Beyond the River." *AJBA* 1: 51–78.

Smith, M. 1987. *Palestinian Parties and Politics that Shaped the Old Testament*. 2d ed. London.

Spiegelberg, W. 1914. *Die sogenannte Demotische Chronik*. Leipzig.

Stern, E. 1982. *The Material Culture of the Land of the Bible in the Persian Period 538–332 B.C.* Warminster and Jerusalem.

Williamson, H. G. M. 1977. The Historical Value of Josephus' *Jewish Antiquities* xi.297–301. *JTS* n.s. 28: 49–66.

———. 1988. The Governors of Judah under the Persians. *TynBul* 29: 59–82.

———. 1989. The Concept of Israel in Transition. Pp. 141–61 in *The World of Ancient Israel: Social, Political and Anthropological Perspectives*, ed. R. E. Clements. Cambridge.

———. 1990. Early Post-Exilic Judaean History. In *The Bible and the Ancient Near East*, ed. J. A. Hackett. Atlanta.

H. G. M. WILLIAMSON

POSTEXILIC JUDEAN OFFICIALS

A problem for exegesis of biblical references to officials lies in the fact that the official of preexilic towns called a *śar* seems to be accompanied by *sĕganîm* and *ḥōrîm*, instead of the earlier "elders," just as the previously rare *peḥâ* has now become a top-ranking "governor" or *tiršātā*ʾ. Such changes might be expected to have some relation with Persian administrative reforms, either under Darius I, or perhaps more likely in Xerxes' reorganization following the Babylonian and Egyptian revolts at his accession. But a lexical scrutiny of the terms involved, together with what little new light archaeology has shed, may point rather to developing outlooks held within the biblical period itself.

A. The Monarchic Period
  1. *śar*
  2. Other Officials
  3. *nāśî*
  4. *sāris*—"Eunuch"
  5. *sĕganîm*
  6. "Elders"
  7. Conclusion
B. The Postexilic Period
  1. Overview of Sources
  2. Ezra 9:1–2
  3. Nehemiah 2

4. Nehemiah 12
5. *rōʾš*

C. Ezra and Nehemiah as Officials

A. The Monarchic Period

1. *Śar*. In the Monarchic period, as reported in Kings and Chronicles, the typical upper-bracket official is *śar.* Though the term is taken from Akkadian *šarru,* "king," it rarely seems to mean so high a ruler. But it does have a wide variety of meanings. The term is applied to David in his condottiere days (1 Sam 22:2); to the top but rather collegial authorities of the Philistines (for *sarĕn* 5 times in 1 Samuel 29); and in Isa 49:7, the "Servant of Yahweh," though subject to *mōšlîm* (RSV "rulers"), will be honored by *mĕlākîm* and *śārîm* (RSV "princes"). The word *śar* is used for the highest officials of David (1 Chr 22:17); and Solomon (1 Kgs 4:2); for princes (Qoh 10:16; Hos 3:4); for magistrates, *per se* suggesting judicial powers (Isa 1:23); although in Deut 1:15 rather military, as distinct from *šōpēṭ* of 1:16; similarly Exod 2:14. But *śar* is also the "city-ruler" or mayor (Judg 9:30, of Shechem; "king" in Josh 12:9–24; 1 Kgs 22:26 = 2 Chr 18:25, Shomron?). In 2 Chr 34:8, Maaseiah is the *śar* of Jerusalem involved in the finding of "the [Deut-scroll] Law," but not in the parallel 2 Kgs 22:3, where 23:8 names Joshua as *śar* of Jerusalem. The *śārîm* of cities seem to have had an authority which was rather collegial (though not clearly in subordination to a single "ruler") and paired with "elders" (Judg 8:14, for Succoth; 2 Kgs 10:1, Shomron; 2 Chr 29:20, Jerusalem). The preexilic *śar* is quite insistently *ʿebed* of the king (Rüterswörden 1985: 4–19, 92–95), though in Zeph 1:8 he is distinct from the *bĕnê hammelek.* As synonym of *rōʾš, rab, pāqîd,* and *ʿal haṣṣebāʾ,* the *śar* is progressively militaristic, culminating in the "Archangel" Michael of Dan 12:1. Throughout Chronicles, as in Job 29:9–10, the plural *śārîm* is equated with *nĕgîdîm* (RSV "nobles"), though preexilically *nāgîd* occurs only in the singular for the king as Yahweh's choice (de Vaux *AncIsr*). The fact that *śar* is occasionally used for top authorities, even sovereigns, increases rather than diminishes its vagueness: like "leader," it is a term of honor even for the most supreme potentate, but is also fully applicable to a village mayor or razzia leader.

2. Other Officials. Flanking the preexilic *śar* are not only the *pāqîd* and *nāgîd* noticed above (really names for highest-level authority), but also his "counselors" (*yoʿaṣ, niṣṣāb* [de Boer 1955]), and "policemen" (*šōmēr;* also *šōṭēr* [van der Ploeg 1954]). Even *peḥâ* occurs as early as 1 Kgs 10:15 under Solomon, for a taxable official of "the land." It is not clear whether this is Israel or Judah, or perhaps the immediately preceding Arabia as in 2 Chr 9:14. In the relatively similar context of 1 Kgs 11:15, *śar* is plainly a military title, as indeed it is in a notable proportion of all its occurrences (BDB, 3ab), not unlike the military "dictator:" *qĕṣîn* (RSV "leader") of Isa 3:7 and Joshua-Judges. But no less than four times in 1 Kings 20 alone, *śar* seems to be the head of a *mĕdînâ:* no number of such *śārîm* is given, and they are curiously neither equated with, nor distinguished from, the exactly thirty-two "kinglets" *(mĕlākîm)* who were helping Ben-hadad and carousing with him (1 Kgs 20:16–17). The anomalous use of *mĕdînâ* here will reappear below in the controversy as to whether Judah ever became a separate province with its own top authority (? *peḥâ*/*tiršātāʾ*).

3. *nāśîʾ*. This term has a semantic and chronological range so similar to *śar* that it is striking not to find the two in parallel. Though it is used for Abraham by Hittites in Gen 23:6, for Solomon by Yahweh in 1 Kgs 11:34, and for top civil rulers in general in borrowed Israelite law (Exod 22:27), nevertheless already in Numbers and Ezekiel it is primarily used for lay posts in the religious organization. Mysteriously falling out of use in the postexilic period, it reappears shortly after as the rabbinic term for a high or highest religious office equated with *nāgîd.* Mantel (1961: 51) has only a fleeting allusion to the possible equating of *nāśîʾ* with *śar* (*m. ʾAbot* 1.2; Rost 1938: 65) or its Greek equivalents, or with *śārîm* as a group sometimes consulted by high priests. Schürer-Vermes's (*HJP*² 2: 203) discussion on *gerousia* is unrelated to *śar* or *nāśîʾ;* but the equivalence is examined by Horbury (1986) under the name "phylarch." The *nāśîʾ* of Ezra 1:8 for Sheshbazzar is declared "utterly unhistorical" by Donner (1986: 410).

4. *sāris*—"Eunuch." With two *sameks, sāris* only accidentally sounds to us like *śar;* its Akkadian origin is *ša rēšî,* "he who is chief," where *rôʾš* is made an adjective. In 1 Kgs 22:9 the *sāris* is exactly the kind of official for minor errands which concerns us here. But he is usually a much higher and *foreign* official; as in Genesis 37–38; Esth 1:10–11; and Rab-Saris in parallel with the famous Hebrew-speaking Rab-Šakeh of 2 Kgs 18:17. Though such an official was often called "eunuch" in the Orient, BDB is rather outdated in assigning this as its principal meaning and relating it to admittedly denominative verbs for "castrate" in Syriac, Aramaic, and Arabic. Hence it will hardly prove relevant to the long-standing debate as to whether Nehemiah (1:11) was really a eunuch, as in the corresponding Greek (*2 Esdras* 11:11: *euno-échos* is also explainable as inner-Greek variant for *oino-chóos* [as MT]; North "Chronicles/Ezra/Nehemia" *NJBC;* Yamauchi 1980). Even if Nehemiah was called "eunuch," this term, like our "chamberlain," may have really signified some administrative office. If so, it would seem to have been of a higher and more privileged rank than the local officials being discussed here.

5. *sĕgānîm*. It is not included among the dozen terms for postexilic officials studied by Rüterswörden. It does in fact occur some six times in the major prophets (Isa 25:41) for high officials of Assyria, Babylon (always parallel with *pāḥôt,* Ezek 23:6; 12:23; Jer 51:23,57), or Media (Jer 51:28). But it will be prominent in Nehemiah as an official of Judah distinct from, but equated, with *ḥōrîm.* This *ḥōr[îm]* virtually never occurs in preexilic sources. Isa 34:12 (LXX), concerning Edom, begins "And there shall be no *ḥōrîm* [which RSV connects with the preceding verse]; 'No kingdom there' they will call it." In the exilic horizon of Jer 27:20; 39:6 it occurs for "the (slain) nobles;" later still we have Qoh 10:17, "happy is your land when your king is a son of *ḥōrîm,* and your *śārîm* dine at the proper time."

6. "Elders." Apart from the "pre-state judges" (not really judges before 1 Sam 7:16, but rather charismatic "leaders"), great importance is attached in preexilic times to the "elders." The *zāqēn* is doubtless largely equated with *rōʾš,* presumably heads of families *(roʾšê ʾabôt),* and had great consultative influence but no real authority.

7. Conclusion. Really *all* the above biblical terms for civil authority are shifting and interchangeable. This was the (orally communicated) conclusion of Alonso-Schökel in preparing his Chronicles (1976), after an exhaustive effort to attach specific significances. This is also held by McEvenue (1981: 364), "the form of political authority in Judah from 597 to 445 B.C. remains obscure in our sources" (p. 359, "the head [*rōʾš*] of a district or [*ʾabôt*] family, *niṣṣāb* under Solomon [1 Kgs 4:5, 7], later *śar* [1 Kgs 20] and also *peḥâ* [1 Kgs 10:5 = 2 Chr 9:14] is a lower official whose chief responsibility is organizing the taxes").

B. The Postexilic Period

1. Overview of Sources. On the specifically postexilic administration our information comes wholly from Ezra, Nehemiah, and Chronicles. Their presumed authorship by the Chronicler, and also the likelihood of a post-Nehemiah date for Ezra, are now widely questioned but must still be regarded as fully open possibilities. In any case, terms for earlier history specific to Chronicles, some of which have been mentioned above, may reflect an Ezra-era usage. Furthermore, *śar* within Chronicles occurs frequently in combinations not attested earlier, and always plural: with *rěkûš*, "possessions" (1 Chr 27:31; cf. 28:1); *maḥlěqôt*, "departments" (1 Chr 28:1); *mělěʾket hammelek*, "royal works" (1 Chr 29:6); *šālîšāyn/milḥāmôt* (2 Chr 8:9; 32:6 "chief of the adjutants" [Rüterswörden 1985: 45]), comparing the only use of *śar* in the singular, "of determining the singers," Ezra 2:65). Also peculiar to the Chronicler is the equating of *śar* with *rōʾš;* Rüterswörden gives a number of examples, mostly of *śar* for *rōʾš*, but some of *rōʾš* for *śar*. His general conclusion is that the Chronicler differs from the Deuteronomist in two points (p. 145): (1) he marks no hiatus between kingdom and prekingdom practices (*šōṭēr* and *šōpēṭ* are used also for the Kings era) and he ignores the "King's *ʿăbādîm*" (2 Chr 8:9); and (2) he makes a distinction between secular and religious officials.

References in Haggai, Zechariah, Malachi, and such possibly contemporaneous works as Job, Joel, and Jonah are fleeting and vague. The Maccabees and the Wisdom Literature, while not ignored here, are not very instructive. De Vaux's *Ancient Israel* (1961: 98), though devoting a lengthy chapter to the Chr-Ezra priesthood, has only a half-page on the postexilic "state" (Ezra 5:9; 6:7, the *mišpāḥōt* and their *zāqēnîm*, families and elders).

2. Ezra 9:1–2. These verses provide the main source on administration. In v 1 a complaint against "mixed" marriages is lodged with Ezra by the *śārîm*. RSV and NJB render this "officials"; Fensham (*Ezra/Nehemiah* NICOT, 124) and NEB perhaps better use "leaders," whom they relate to the three groups immediately enumerated: "people" (laity), priests, and Levites—though the complaint will turn out to be precisely *against* these three groups. And the next verse comes to a climax with a claim that the worst offenders are the *śārîm* themselves and the *sěgānîm*. We might harmonizingly render "*some śarîm* protested against the widespread abuse in which (other) *śārîm* and even Seganim were involved." But it seems more objective to recognize that *śar* has become, or remains, a rather mild term for any kind of leadership, "important people," which would fit equally both verses. As for a distinction between *śārîm* and *sěgānîm*, Fensham admits it is very difficult to find any at all; he hesitantly suggests that the *sěgānîm*, of which we do not even know a singular form, are a kind of council for the *śar;* thus they would be a kind of *zāqēnîm* or *ḥōrîm*. And yet, with a casual reserve for the Nehemiah usages below, he audaciously equates the *sěgān* as Akkadian loanword *šaqnu* with *peḥâ/bēl peḥâtî* "governor." Henshaw (1968: 465–69) had found that *šaqnu* is never identical with *bēl peḥâtî*, but is also never clearly above or below him (see also Lipiński 1973).

3. Nehemiah 2. Neh 2:16 is a rich source of data on those *sěgānîm* and other officials who knew nothing of his night ride. The *sěgānîm* are mentioned first "because they were very important," says Fensham (*Ezra/Nehemiah* NICOT, 167); but he less guardedly adds (adapting Widengren 1977: 522) that they were "probably representatives who were chosen by the congregation"—like his "council" of Ezra 9:2, but not *zāqēnîm* as suggested above. Like *śārîm* in Ezra 9:1–2, *sěgānîm* seems to be used here in two different senses, first as a general term including also other officials about to be enumerated; then as a specific group among these officials, distinct from the four other groups.

One of these groups is suitably enough "the priests" as in Ezra 9:1 but surprisingly without "the Levites." A second group in Neh 2:16 is "the *ḥôrîm*", not noblemen in the real sense of the word, but persons with certain rights, "citizens" according to Fensham. Williamson (*Ezra/Nehemiah* WBC, 191) rejects Kellermann's attempt to take *ḥôrîm* as the local leadership distinct from *sěgānîm*, "Persian appointees." It is important to bear in mind that *ḥôr* nowhere in biblical Hebrew means "free" or "freedman" as it does in modern Hebrew, which follows Aramaic-Arabic (and perhaps Sabean-Amharic).

There remain in Neh 2:16 two anomalous groups. "The Judeans," even more than *sěgānîm* itself, is applicable to *all* the groups. The term is perhaps used in contradistinction to "the people of the land" (2 Kgs 25:22; see *NJBC* on Neh 4:1), those Judeans who had never gone into exile and thus had become administratively a part of the Babylonian-Persian Samarian province (Williamson *Ezra/Nehemiah* WBC)—and remained such to the bitter end, despite claims of a separate "Judah-province" to be noticed below. Nehemiah has a very prickly relationship with this "people of the land." Much of his polemic against "the [or specific] Samaritans" seems in fact directed against those full-blooded Judeans and Yahweh worshipers who had never been deemed worthy of the hardships of exile (inflicted on only the upper crust: 2 Kgs 24:14, 16). Nehemiah does not in fact elsewhere use "Judeans" as an appellative for "returnees only," "Judeans worth listening to," but we might find this implication here if our interpretation of "low-brow Samaritan-province people of the land (of Judah)" is correct.

The fifth and even more anomalous group of "officials left in ignorance" in Neh 2:10 are "the doers of the work" (RSV "the rest that were to do the work"), presumably the heads of the various guilds or locality groups immediately enumerated in Nehemiah 3, "but we cannot deduce this from the Hebrew," says Fensham (*Ezra/Nehemiah* NICOT, 167) overcautiously, citing Kaupel (1940). In that chapter indeed we have a *sixth* group to add to the five enumerated in Neh 2:16, namely the *śar* of *pelek* or half-*pelek*. The term is generally there taken as "chief of a district" (Neh 3:16, Bet-Zur; 3:15, Mizpah) or half-district (3:9, 12, Jerusalem; 3:17–18, Keilah; 3:16, Beth-zur, under a different Nehemiah). Rüterswörden (1985: 46) concludes that these uses of *śar* in the singular were formations invented by the Chronicler without foundation in actual usage, even in the postexilic period (except for *bîrâ* in Neh 7:2); more interestingly he claims that the *śar pelek* cannot be related to *rab pilkani,* because that Akkadian term relates to *building* supervision (Demsky 1983, "corvée"). But in this context of Nehemiah there is question precisely of building supervision; and even the more general commission of Nehemiah is primarily that of *building* contractor. In any case, mention of "the doers of the work" in Neh 2:16 may justifiably be focused as a very modern nuance: Nehemiah puts the labor union leaders on a par with the bureaucrats and hierarchs, even if only to bypass them all temporarily.

4. Nehemiah 12. Neh 12:40 is the third passage focusing on *sĕgānîm.* Here we have a procession, in which Nehemiah himself leads "half of the *sĕgānîm* with me," that is, the counterclockwise half of the parade. We may see in those *sĕgānîm* the *civil* authorities, or rather "Very Important Persons" including Nehemiah himself, since the clockwise half includes mostly priests. It also includes (obscurely in 33, but tardily as head of the procession in 36) "Ezra the scribe"; whereas Ezra "the priest, the scribe" is more directly paired with "Nehemiah the *peḥâ*" in Neh 12:26, but as a purely chronological colophon to a preceding list. Fensham discreetly finds it "of interest" that Nehemiah mentions only his own half of the leaders *(segānîm)* and not any other half under the leadership of Ezra. RSV flatly excises all three references to Ezra. We would say more cautiously that the common name "Ezra" may well belong to the obscure personage of Neh 12:33, and may have given rise to 36 assuming that *the* Ezra was meant, and he would thus of course go to the head of the parade. The chronological notice of Neh 12:26 does not imply that Nehemiah was *present* or even *contemporary* with Ezra any more than with Jeshua ben-Jozadak a century earlier (Ezra 5:2), but in noting this we must repeat that the question of whether Ezra was in fact at least briefly on the stage *with* Nehemiah, or only before or after him, is fully open, because the Albright-Rudolph emendation of 7th to 27th year of Artaxerxes in Ezra 7:7 is not one bit more audacious than to excise *all* the references to Ezra and Nehemiah functioning together.

In Neh 12:31 *both* groups of paraders are "marshaled" by Nehemiah as "master of ceremonies"—a very low place on the totem pole, whatever happens to be the actual rank of its incumbent; and the *śārîm* here used for the paraders doubtless means "the leaders of various degree along with their escorts." In verse 32 the clockwise half alone are called *śārîm,* which is thus a synonym of the *sĕgānîm* of the counterclockwise half in Neh 12:40.

5. *rōʾš*. This term has not shown up prominently in these key passages from Ezra-Nehemiah. It is used postexilically for special groups (Müller 1976; Bartlett 1969) and, as noted above, becomes interchanged with *śar.* Despite *adrazdāʾ* of Ezra 7:23 (Rundgren 1982), the Bible rarely gives a Persian title except through Akkadian, from which Aikhenwald (1985: 66) concludes that the Persian administration left no lasting trace.

All in all, our search for the above data on *minor* officials has revealed that these are at times varyingly equated with the highest local authority, sometimes having no other title, sometimes *peḥâ,* to which *sĕgan/šaqnu* is not probably equal, superior, or inferior.

C. Ezra and Nehemiah as Officials

In no case is there further evidence calling in doubt the published view that neither Nehemiah nor Ezra possessed any genuine permanent civil office within the Persian government (North 1972). The sporadically recurring claims that Nehemiah as governor stood in an unbroken line with Zerubbabel and the previous (or identical: so Lust 1987) Sheshbazzar; or that some or all of these were of Davidic lineage, thus putting this "governorship" on a far more solid and even messianic plane, have not been followed up.

But what is apparent is that more recent studies (Klein 1976), some even after respectful note of North (1972), continue to maintain in various ways that Nehemiah as *peḥâ* and *tiršātāʾ* was truly a governor, a cog in the Persian satrapy system, over Judah created into a *mĕdînâ* or province distinct from Samaria (Bengtson 1965; Frye 1984; Gershevitch 1985). These general histories of Persia draw their accounts of Judean administration mainly from the philology-based dictums of outdated exegetes, or from Herodotus, with no really new empirical data. This is despite interest in the questions raised by Cross (1975) in adding a new Sanballat to the dynasty of Nehemiah's opponents (Betlyon 1986).

The request made to the king by Nehemiah at his initial appointment (1:7–8) clearly excludes any civil authority. Nehemiah asks for a recommendation to the governors of the province and for help in his building project, and there is no evidence that the king's edict went beyond these modest requests. McEvenue (1981: 363; citing Nober 1961) demolishes Morton Smith's conclusions drawn from *peḥâ;* and he briefly dismisses *tiršātāʾ* as likewise ambivalent. Yet he goes on to maintain that Nehemiah had a genuine civil office in the Persian administration, proved not from his titles but from the way he is shown acting; and Alonso-Schökel agrees with this (oral communication). But as *Nehemiah* NJBC shows, what Nehemiah is actually shown doing is building a wall, incidentally surmounting "foreign intrusions" (Nehemiah 4), labor troubles (Nehemiah 5), and other national solidarity crises progressively taking on a religious tinge: mixed marriages, sabbath—his manhandling and threats in Neh 13:15, 21, 25 seem to imply he was exceeding whatever authority he may have had.

After surveying McEvenue's view that there was no independent province of Judah before Nehemiah, and equating it with Alt's, Williamson (1987: 40–50) goes on to prefer the position of M. Smith and Widengren: there was a Persian province of which Sheshbazzar was appointed governor, as Ezra 5:14 says. But in understandable diffidence about that verse, Donner (1986: 422) holds that Nehemiah's original Persian commission was simply to build the wall, and at a later stage he became the first real "governor" of the *newly constituted* province (*mĕdînâ;* Neh 11:3; 7:6 = Ezra 2:1; Esther often; but already also Neh

1:3) of Judah. No two events in the civil life of a region are less likely to pass unnoticed than its erection into a new degree of independence, or the inauguration of a ruler with the highest title thus far granted. It seems inconceivable that such a great day would have passed unnoticed either in Nehemiah's personal memoirs, or in the Ezra books otherwise so fond of describing in detail just such solemnities.

We know even less about Ezra (Donner 1986: 431), but what at any rate is certain is that between the two of them something momentous was accomplished in the creation of a new Israelite identity. For further discussion see Galling TGI, and *CHJ* 1: 130–61.

Bibliography

Aikhenwald, A. Y. 1985. Some Names of Officials in the Later Books of the Old Testament. *Vestnik Drevnej Istorii* 3: 58–65 (in Russian).

Alonso Schökel, L. 1976. *Crónicas, Esdras, Nehemias: introducciones y comentarios.* Madrid.

Alt, A. 1992. Das System der assyrischen Provinzen auf dem Boden des Reiches Israel. *ZDPV* 52: 220–42.

———. 1945. Neue assyrische Nachrichten über Palästina. *ZDPV* 67: 128–46.

Bartlett, J. R. 1969. The Use of the Word *rōʾš* as a Title in the Old Testament. *VT* 19: 1–10.

Bengtson, H. 1965. Syrien in der Perserzeit. Pp. 371–76 in *Fischers Weltgeschichte.* Vol. 5, *Griechen und Perser.* Frankfurt.

Betylon, J. W. 1986. The Provincial Government of Persian Period Judea and the Yehud Coind. *JBL* 105: 633–42.

Boer, P. A. H. 1955. The Counsellor. VTSup 3: 42–71.

Bogoliubov, M. N. 1974. Titre honorifique d'un chef militaire achéménide en Haute-Égypte. *Acta Iranica* 2: 109–14.

Cazelles, H. 1982. *Histoire politique d'Israël des origines à Alexandre le Grand.* Paris.

Cross, F. M. 1975. A Reconstruction of the Judean Restoration. *JBL* 94: 4–18.

Demsky, A. 1983. *Pelekh* in Nehemiah 3. *IEJ* 33: 242–44.

Donner, H. 1986. *Das persische Zeitalter.* Vol. 2 of *Geschichte des Volkes Israel und seiner Nachbarn in Grundzügen.* Göttingen.

Frye, R. N. 1984. *The History of Ancient Iran.* HAW 3/7. Munich.

Garbini, G. 1985. Aramaico *gemîr* (Esdra 7, 12). Pp. 227–29 in *Studi in onore di E. Bresciani,* ed. S. F. Bondì et al. Pisa.

Gerschevitch, I., ed. 1985. *The Cambridge History of Iran.* Vol 2.

Gordis, R. 1935. Sectional Rivalry in the Kingdom of Judah. *JQR* 25: 237–59.

Heichelheim, F. M. 1951. Ezra's Palestine and Periclean Athens. *ZRGG* 3: 251–53.

Henshaw, R. A. 1967–8. The Office of *šaqnu* in Neo-Assyrian Times. *JAOS* 87: 517–25; 88: 461–83.

Hinz, W. 1971. Achämenidische Hofverwaltung. *ZA* 61: 260–311.

Horbury, W. 1986. The Twelve and the Phylarchs. *NTS* 32: 503–27.

In der Smitten, W. T. 1971. Der Tirschātāʾ in Esra-Nehemia. *VT* 21: 618–20.

Japhet, S. 1983. Sheshbazzar and Zerubbabel against the Background of the Historical and Religious Tendencies of Ezra-Nehemiah. *ZAW* 95: 218–29.

Kaupel, H. 1940. Der Sinn von *ʿōśēh hammĕlāʾkâ* in Neh 2, 16. *Bib* 21: 40–44.

Klein, R. W. 1976. Ezra and Nehemiah in Recent Studies. Pp. 361–76 in *Magnalia Dei,* ed. F. M. Cross. New York.

Lipiński, E. 1973. *skn* et *sgn* dans le sémitique occidental du nord. *UF* 5: 191–207.

———. 1974. Nāgīd, der Kronprinz. *VT* 24: 497–99.

Lust, J. 1987. The Identification of Zerubbabel with Sheshbassar. *ETL* 63: 90–95.

McEvenue, S. E. 1981. The Political Structure in Judah from Cyrus to Nehemiah. *CBQ* 43: 353–64.

Macholz, G. C. 1975. Nagid, der Statthalter ("praefectus"). Pp. 59–72 *Festschrift R. Rendtorff,* ed. K. Rupprecht Diehlheim.

Mantel, H. 1961. *Studies in the History of the Sanhedrin.* HSS 17. Cambridge, MA.

Margalith, O. 1986. The Political Role of Ezra as Persian Governor. *ZAW* 98: 110–12.

Müller, H.-P. 1976. *Rôš,* Kopf. *THAT* 2: 701–15.

Nober, P. 1961. Notae philologicae. *VD* 39: 110–11.

North, R. 1972. Civil Authority in Ezra. Vol. 6, pp. 377–404 in *Studi in onore di E. Volterra.* Milan.

Ploeg, J. van der. 1950. Les chefs du peuple d'Israël et leurs noms. *RB* 57: 40–61.

———. 1954. Les *šoṭerîm* d'Israël. *OTS* 10: 185–96.

Reviv, H. 1983. *The Elders in Ancient Israel.* Jerusalem (in Hebrew).

Rost, L. 1938. *Die Vorstufen von Kirche und Synagoge im Alten Testament.* BWANT 76. Stuttgart.

Rundgren, F. 1982–83. Biblical Aramaic *adrazdā* (Ezra 7, 23) and *šam bal. Orientalia Suecana* 31–32: 143–46.

Rüterswörden, U. 1985. *Die Beamten der israelitischen Königszeit; eine Studie zu* śr *und vergleichbaren Begriffen.* BWANT 117. Stuttgart.

Sánchez Caro, J. M. 1985. Esdras, Nehemías y los orígenes del Judaismo. *Salman* 32: 5–35.

Smith, M. 1965. Das Judentum in Palästina während der Perserzeit. Vol. 5, pp. 356–70 in *Fischers Weltgeschichte,* ed. H. Bengtson. Frankfurt.

Soggin, J. 1985. *A History of Ancient Israel.* Philadelphia.

Vaux, R. de. 1939. Titres et fonctionnaires égyptiens à la cour de David et de Salomon. *RB* 48: 394–405.

Widengren, G. 1969. *Der Feudalismus im alten Iran.* Cologne.

———. 1977. The Persian Period. Pp. 489–538 in *IJH.*

Williamson, H. G. M. 1987. *Ezra and Nehemiah.* OT Guides. Sheffield.

Yamauchi, E. M. 1980. Was Nehemiah the Cupbearer a Eunuch? *ZAW* 92: 132–42.

ROBERT NORTH

PTOLEMAIC ADMINISTRATION

A. Chronology and Extent of Ptolemaic Control

After two brief periods of control (320–315 and 312 B.C.), Ptolemy I Soter gained permanent possession of Palestine in 301 B.C., when Antigonus the One-Eyed was defeated at the Battle of Ipsos. Ptolemy and his successors held "Phoenicia and Hollow Syria," as they called it, for a century until Antiochus III ("the Great") defeated the forces of Ptolemy V Epiphanes at Paneion in 200 B.C. During the intervening years, Ptolemaic and Seleucid forces fought several wars over control of Palestine, but with one exception we do not know of any significant and lasting gains by either side in these wars until the final Ptolemaic loss. Shortly before his death in 146 B.C., Ptolemy VI Philometor made an attempt to recover Palestine, but death cut short his early success (for the chronology and extent of Ptolemaic rule, see Bagnall 1976: 11–13).

The area under Ptolemaic control during the 3d century

was bounded on the S by Egypt, on the W by the Mediterranean, and on the N probably by the Eleutherus River (the modern Kebir), the northern boundary of modern Lebanon. It is clear that Arados and the territory to the N in general never came under lasting Ptolemaic control (Seyrig 1951: 206–20). Ptolemy III Euergetes did gain control of Seleucia-in-Pieria and of Laodiceia in the Third Syrian War (246–241 B.C.), but they were lost by his successor, Ptolemy IV Philopator, in 219 and not regained despite Philopator's victory at Raphia in 217 (for control of Laodicea, see Rey-Coquais 1978). The limits of Ptolemaic control to the E are less clear. Philadelphia (Rabbath-ammon, modern Amman) was certainly Ptolemaic, along with much of Transjordan, but we do not know how whether any of Moab was under Ptolemaic rule nor exactly how far N it extended E of the Jordan. Paneion (the site of the final loss in 200 B.C.) was probably part of the Ptolemaic domains; Damascus was in Ptolemaic hands at least from the 270s until the 250s, and perhaps throughout the period. It seems likely enough that Ptolemaic control extended to the E slopes of the Anti-lebanon Mountains throughout their extent.

B. Military Occupation and Settlement

The Ptolemies certainly kept garrisons in the principal cities of the region, made up of mercenaries recruited from all over the E Mediterranean (Bagnall 1976: 17; Rey-Coquais 1978). In peacetime their numbers were no doubt modest, but in time of war field forces were imported in much greater quantity. Most of the military commanders mentioned in the ancient sources appear in accounts of the Ptolemaic-Seleucid wars, and we know little about the regular garrisons and their commanders. There is not even any evidence until the last two decades of Ptolemaic rule of any military governor of the region as a whole. It seems likely, however, that as in many other regions of their empire (at varying dates), the Ptolemies appointed in Palestine a *stratēgos,* or provincial governor, who had both military and civil functions. But such an appointment may not have come until the second half of the 3d century (Bagnall 1976: 219). The first absolutely certain *strategos* of the area, indeed, is first found after Antiochus III's conquest; the title is mentioned in an inscription dealing with the property of Ptolemaius son of Thraseas, formerly a Ptolemaic general, who had gone over to the Selucid king at an unknown date and become a *stratēgos* and high-priest, evidently of Syria and Phoenicia (for this official and his landholdings, see Fischer 1979; Bertrand 1982).

The Ptolemies also settled troops on land in the region in much the same way they did in Egypt: a soldier was allocated land to support him and his family, but he held it on condition of continued military service, when needed, by him or his son. These soldiers evidently tried (as elsewhere) to take advantage of their superior economic positions to enslave natives, a practice firmly forbidden, with limited exceptions, by the Ptolemaic government (Liebesny 1936). Many of them married local women; and in the Ammanitis there was a group of them under the command of a local chieftain, Tobias (Edgar 1925: 1.59003). We have no idea of the numbers of these settlers, who provided substantial military reserves and helped ensure the loyalty to the Ptolemaic crown of the areas in which they were settled. Ptolemy II founded or refounded and renamed (as Greek cities) several towns (Ptolemais, from Acco; Philadelphia, from Rabbath-ammon; Philoteria, on the Sea of Galilee), and all of these presumably had Greek soldiers among the settlers and citizens.

C. Civil Administration in the Cities

The scarce inscriptions of the period give us almost no information at all about the administration of the cities of the inferior in this period, and only some limited facts about the coastal cities, which were no doubt the focus of Ptolemaic interest. Though the Phoenician monarchy was preserved for a time at least in Sidon (as some of the Cypriot monarchies had survived briefly under Ptolemaic rule), it probably did not outlast Philokles son of Apollodorus, who served as a Ptolemaic admiral (Merker 1970; Seibert 1970). Signs of Greek civic institutions soon appear: Sidon is called a *polis;* members of its upper class compete in Greek athletics at Delos, Delphi, and Nemea; and the city has an official in charge of athletic contests whose title *(agonothētes)* is Greek. The Greek civic title *archon* is attested for Sidon and Marissa. Even with all these signs of Hellenization, however, the substance of local government may not have changed very much. The Phoenician term *sufet,* president of the people, and its Greek rendering *dikastes,* appear in Tyre and Sidon.

In all probability the cities of the coast, and at least some of those in the interior, had some land attached to them and under their administration. But our evidence for this land under Ptolemaic rule is nonexistent. Nor do we have any real indication of the relationship of the civic officials to royal ones, either those at the level of the whole province or those with more local control. Ptolemaic administration elsewhere kept local governments in check with supervision by the garrison commander (or city commandant) and financial officials, and the same was probably true in Palestine.

D. Civil Administration in the Countryside

The countryside of the province of Phoenicia and Coele Syria was divided (at least by 261 B.C.) into administrative units called hyparchies *(hyparchiai),* of whose size and number we know nothing. At the head of the financial bureaucracy in each hyparchy, just as of each nome in Egypt, was an *oikonomos,* who was in charge of such things as supervising the underwriting of the collection of taxes to contractors, overseeing the actual tax collection, and registering ownership of slaves. (This information comes mostly from Lenger 1980: 21–22.) Administrative symmetry and Ptolemaic practice in Egypt suggest that the *oikonomos* operated collegially with at least one other official, who was probably called a *hyparchos.* So far, however, no evidence for these officials at the level of the entire region, to whom the *oikonomoi* probably reported at least in this aspect of their work, called "the manager of the revenues in Syria and Phoenicia." His one appearance in the papyrus uses a participle of the verb *dioikeo,* but he may well have held the title *dioiketes,* as did the finance minister in Egypt to whom he doubtless reported.

At the village level, the royal administration was represented by komarchs. They were responsible for seeing that the proper declarations of taxable or restricted property (such as livestock and slaves) were filed with the *oikonomos.* There were also royal judges, called *dikastai,* but we know virtually nothing about who they were, what areas they were responsible for, or what their jurisdictional competence was.

Despite this structure, which appears to be a Greek framework imposed on the country, the Ptolemies relied substantially on local institutions and magnates to rule the countryside for them, just as they did in the cities. The story of Joseph son of Tobias (see below) indicates that wealthy locals acted as tax farmers on a large scale, just as Tobias' role as the commander in charge of military settlers in his area shows an attempt to enlist the most powerful local figures in the military side of Ptolemaic rule.

E. Economic Management

Like any empire, the Ptolemaic was interested in exploiting its opportunities for income from the lands it controlled. Palestine was a useful backup source of wheat for Egypt when the Egyptian harvest was poor, but in ordinary times its agricultural interest was certainly more for the wide range of fruits, vegetables, oils, and wine that it produced than for wheat, which Egypt produced in abundance. The Phoenician ports had a long history as commercial centers, and these clearly offered numerous opportunities to Greeks in Ptolemaic service to make money. The Zenon papyri from the 250s show us some of the range of economic interests at stake (Harper 1928; Tcherikover 1937).

Royal interest in these activities, however, centered on taxing them. Export and import taxes at the ports, largely in the control of tax farmers, were undoubtedly important (as they were elsewhere in the Ptolemaic empire). The agricultural land of the province was also taxed. The career of Joseph son of Tobias, recounted in book 12 of Josephus' *Jewish Antiquities,* shows us a prominent local notable bidding for the tax contract for the entire province, outbidding the longtime holders of the contract and still making a fortune over more than two decades (the dates are disputed: see Bagnall 1976: 21 n. 42).

From the reign of Ptolemy II on, the coinage for the entire region was supplied by seven coastal mints (Tyre, Sidon, Ptolemais, Joppa, Gaza, Berytos, and Askalon). Like Ptolemaic coinage elsewhere, it was minted on a standard with a lower weight for the drachma than was common elsewhere. The Ptolemies systematically excluded coinage from elsewhere from Palestine (as they did from Egypt, Cyprus, and Cyrene), and hoard and excavation finds from the middle of the 3d century until its end show almost exclusively Ptolemaic coins. Many of them remained in circulation after the Seleucid conquest (Bagnall 1976: 180–83).

Bibliography

Bagnall, R. S. 1976. *The Administration of the Ptolemaic Possessions Outside Egypt.* Leiden.

Bertrand, J.-M. 1982. Sur l'inscription d'Hefzibah. *Zeitschrift für Papyrologie und Epigraphik* 46: 167–74.

Edgar, C. C. 1925. *Zenon Papyri.* Vol. 1. Cairo.

Fischer, T. 1979. Zur Seleukideninschrift von Hefzibah. *Zeitschrift für Papyrologie und Epigraphik* 33: 131–38.

Harper, G. M. 1928. A Study in the Commercial Relations between Egypt and Syria in the Third Century before Christ. *AJP* 49: 1–35.

Lenger, M. T. 1980. *Corpus des ordonnances des Ptolémées.* 2d ed. Brussels.

Liebesny, H. 1936. Ein Erlass des Königs Ptolemaios II: Philadelphia über die Deklaration von Vieh und Sklaven in Syrien und Phönikien (PER Inv. Nr. 24.552 gr.). *Aeg* 16: 257–91.

Merker, I. L. 1970. The Ptolemaic Officials and the League of the Islanders. *Historia* 19: 143–50.

Rey-Coquais, J.-P. 1978. Inscription grecque découverte à Ras Ibn Hani. *Syr* 55:314–25.

Seibert, J. 1970. Philokles, Sohn des Apollodoros, König der Sidonier. *Historia* 19: 337–51.

Seyrig, H. 1951. Antiquités Syriennes 49: Aradus et sa perée sous les rois Séleucides. *Syr* 28: 206–20.

Tcherikover, V. 1937. Palestine and the Ptolemies (A Contribution to the Study of the Zenon Papyri). *Mizraim* 4–5: 9–90.

ROGER S. BAGNALL

SELEUCID ADMINISTRATION

Only a few sources provide information about the Seleucid administration and staff in Palestine. The sources comprise a few inscriptions, the more or less extensive but tendentious accounts in 1–2 Maccabees, and the later works of Josephus. The works of Polybius and Poseidonius, who were the most important contemporary authors in the Greco-Roman ambit, as well as those of their immediate successors, are almost completely lost. The authors of the Roman Imperial period only imprecisely or summarily inform us about the management and bureaucracy of the Hellenistic period. In spite of the many problems and uncertainties concerning the historical and political development (in particular of Judea), the following survey will attempt to depict some basic features of the Seleucid administration of Palestine in the 2d century.

A. Seleucid Conquest and Maccabean Revolt
B. Rise of Hasmonean Rule
C. Remnants of Seleucid Sovereignty
D. Conclusion

A. Seleucid Conquest and Maccabean Revolt (200–157 B.C.)

During the Fifth Syrian War (202–ca. 195 B.C.) Ptolemy, the governor of the Ptolemaic border province of Syria and Phoenicia, sided with the Seleucid Antiochus III the Great and thus retained his position as provincial governor after Antiochus' victory. In 199 B.C. the Seleucid king perhaps regulated the legal and property relations of his newly won territory in a "decree;" in so doing, it is likely that he simply confirmed the existing Ptolemaic arrangements (see the inscription of Hefzibah, Fischer 1980: 1–3; see also Bengston 1964: 147–48; Fisher 1986: 66). Accordingly, Antiochus allowed the theocracy of Jerusalem and Judea to retain its conventional form, including the "high priest" *(archiereus),* the "council of elders" (*gerousia,* also in its traditional and unofficial sense called *hoi presbyteroi*), the "priests" *(hiereis),* and the "rest of the Judeans" *(hoi alloi Ioudaioi).* However, as far as we are aware he did this only indirectly in a formal message directed to his provincial governor, Ptolemy. In this letter, Antiochus allowed "the

Judean people" and their temple further "magnanimities" through the governor, although in a precarious and time-limited fashion (*Ant* 12.138–44; cf. *WHJP* 6: 81–86; Taylor 1979: 51–107, 169–70). A further "announcement" seeking to protect the domestic cult regulations in Jerusalem (*Ant* 12.145–46) may have been secured from the king by Jonathan, the father of Eupolemus. In the winter of 194/3 B.C. Antiochus married off his daughter Cleopatra to the Ptolemaic king; in so doing, he may have awarded her (rights to) half of the *phoroi* (tribute) of Phoenicia and Coele-Syria ("Syria," according to the earlier Ptolemaic nomenclature). However, this personal dowry was apparently understood by both Cleopatra and by the Egyptian (Ptolemaic) rulers as the Seleucid return, surrender, or renunciation of the (entire) province.

The hereditary Zadokite high priest in Jerusalem represented the now-subject "nation of the Judeans" to the king. His task included ensuring the deliveries of the *phoroi* to the king. He assumed the principal responsibility for the territorial administration, and with his own army, he assumed responsibility for the cultic, political, military, and administrative (juridical) interests of the Seleucid king on the regional level. Thus, for example, he communicated to the court the news of the "immeasurable wealth" of the temple in Jerusalem. He likewise presented to the sovereign an accusation emerging from the Judean council of elders against the high priest. He also presented to the sovereign "memoranda," that is, petitions, applications, or complaints. When appropriate, the Seleucid monarch informed him and/or assigned other functionaries to carry out his projects. In the sense of his royal "instruction," the governor apparently also issued executive "decisions" on behalf of the (pseudo-) autonomous congregations or cities of his region (2 Macc 6:8, according to Fischer 1985: 352, n. 10).

Unlike the *dynastēs,* the provincial governor—a Macedonian or Greek who was a foreigner and as such subject to transfer—could not normally bequeath his position to members of his own family. He probably dwelt in Acco-Ptolemais, which was officially called "Antioch-in-Ptolemais" from the time of Antiochus IV at the latest. Certainly this site was, in juridical terms, a *polis* which had its own more or less "free," "democratic," and/or Hellenized administration. The "people" plus their own "assembly," "council," and "magistrates" were the typical institutions of such communities. The Seleucids themselves, particularly Antiochus IV and his house, encouraged the urbanization and extension of such "Greek" *poleis* as Acco in order to support their rule, especially E of the Jordan. Moreover, in many cases such cities had originated in the foreign military settlements of the Macedonian kings.

According to *Ant* 12.154, 175, the province was originally divided into four(?) districts (*merides* in the official usage, perhaps *eparchiai* in the common usage): (1) Coele-Syria (in the strict sense); (2) Samaria (at least in the Maccabean period Judea seems to have belonged within its jurisdiction); (3) Idumea(?); and (4) Phoenicia (without the N parts, that is, the region N of the river Eleutherus). Each possessed its own district governors and troops. Similarly, at this district level "subcommanders" *(hyparchoi)* were empowered to act in the civil and particularly in the fiscal arena. They were served by the local leaders in the respective counties (Bengston 1964: 10–11, 21–29, 170; cf. *HJP*² 2: 186). According to the sources, there was, however, no satrap at the peak of the civil and financial administration of the province. It may be that the native and hereditary high priest of Jerusalem enjoyed the rank and/or function of "subcommander" *(hyparchus)* of Judea; the same possibly applied to the Samaritans. Galilee was perhaps a hyparchy within the district of Samaria. However, these details and functions remain quite unclear and problematical.

Stationed on the site itself, the "commanders of garrisons" (*phrourarchoi*; at larger places *akrophylakes* or *eparchoi*) exercised the supreme military authority. As representatives of the standing army they performed all the immediate and tangible functions of occupational, police, or general security forces. In this capacity they preserved the public order alongside the civilian functionary, the *hyparch* or high priest, and helped to ensure the regular payment of the tax monies to the crown. Occasionally such commanders were designated by the types of troops or weapons at their command (e.g., the "elephantarch," as well as the "Mysarch" and the "Kypriarch" who were, respectively, commanders of mercenary units from Mysias and Cyprus).

Local "mayors" *(kōmarchai)* are not attested in the entire province; however, it seems probable that the Hasmonean Mattathias (prior to the Maccabean Revolt) and (afterward) his son Jonathan exercised (as "judges") such an administrative function at Modein and Michmash, respectively (1 Macc 2:17; 9:73). Local traditions manifested themselves fairly strongly at the lower (local) level, whereas in the first half of the 2d century the Greco-Macedonian element predominated at the top of the administrative system.

It is not possible here to deal with the conflicts concerning the "immeasurable wealth" of the temple in Jerusalem, the rivalries about the position of high priest, or the events and prehistory of the Maccabean Revolt under Antiochus IV (175–164 B.C.), Antiochus V (164–162), and Demetrius I (162–150). See MACCABEAN REVOLT. Perhaps it would be best to emphasize the following points here in abbreviated terms. Jason had attempted to establish a sort of community or even a *polis* of the "Antiochenes-in-Hierosolyma" (Jerusalem). When he failed in the end to deliver "the immeasurable wealth" of the sanctuary (as Onias III had done before him), the Seleucid king appointed Menelaus, brother of the temple manager, to serve as the new Judean high priest. See MENELAUS. The appointment of Menelaus not only deposed the traditional Zadokite dynasty in this increasingly cosmopolitan town; it also shifted the focus of the office from the religious and cultic to the economic and political sphere. At first the league between Antiochus IV and his protégé Menelaus survived, but when Judas Maccabeus achieved preeminence among the people, the "failure" was liquidated by Antiochus V. The revolt itself began in 166; it extended steadily from the *phrourarch* of Jerusalem throughout the *meridarch* of Samaria up to the provincial governor *(stratēgos).* Finally, it escalated up to the central government, only to be put down by Demetrius I himself in 157 B.C. During the Revolt, the Hasmoneans had shown themselves to be capable military leaders and very able politicians, which recommended them to the king (note the personal meeting between

Antiochus V and Judas, when the latter received "forgiveness" but by no means renounced his "rebellious temper").

B. Rise of Hasmonean Rule (152–129 B.C.)

The Seleucid pretender and bastard, Alexander Balas (150–145 B.C.), considered the Hasmonean Jonathan his "brother and friend," and as early as 152 B.C. appointed him to the office of high priest in Jerusalem. After Alexander's subsequent victory over Demetrius I, the general conditions in Palestine changed drastically. In the course of the Seleucid succession struggle, which lasted until 138, the Hasmonean leaders brought increased autonomy to Judea. Henceforth, the local leader served (in the Seleucid staff) as a *dynastēs,* with his own military forces; he ascended swiftly and won advantages for his own country and for himself from his double function, that is, against the rivaling kings as well as against his own Judean compatriots. On the other hand, the royal power in Palestine diminished both quantitatively and qualitatively, as Rome now had no serious opponent in the E Mediterranean. In other words, an additional destabilizing factor had now entered the political arena. In addition to this, the native element of the population now began more strongly to assume leadership positions in competition with the Greek-born and with the immigrant "Macedonians," a phenomenon which allows comparison with simultaneous developments in Egypt.

The events which took place in these years may be summarized in the following manner. In 152/51 B.C. Demetrius I had ended the general occupation of the territory of Judea, with the exceptions of Beth-zur and the citadel of Jerusalem; he also granted to Jonathan the right to assemble his own troops and to fortify Zion. In 150/49 the victorious Alexander Balas appointed the Judean leader to be his provincial governor *(stratēgos)* and district governor *(meridarches)* (of Samaria, including Judea?); about 145 B.C. Jonathan received the court title of "relative of the king," plus the territory of Ekron as his personal, immediate, and privileged fief, on the rank order of a *dynastēs* within the Seleucid realm. The next ruler, Demetrius II (145–139, 129–125 B.C.), who maintained the garrisons in Jerusalem and Beth-zur, confirmed Jonathan's cultic, military, and political position; he laid claim to the military forces of his Judean vassal, and in fact received them. The same disposition was accepted by his rival, Balas' minor son Antiochus VI (145–142 B.C.), who additionally appointed Jonathan's brother Simon to be "*strategos* from the Ladder of Tyre to the border of Egypt" (1 Macc 11:57–59). In their victorious struggle as functionaries of the young Antiochus VI against Demetrius II, the two Hasmoneans attempted to extend their own rule, which is probably what finally cost Jonathan his life.

After this, Simon (142–134 B.C.) gathered the reins of power in Judea to himself and returned under the banner of Demetrius II. Presumably in the beginning of 141 B.C., the Demetrius II granted not only him (as "high priest and friend of the kings") but also the "elders *(presbyteroi)* and the people *(ethnos)* of the Judeans" both amnesty and deliverance from taxation, allowing them to enter the royal service (1 Macc 13:36–40).

As yet, there is no indication that the Judean dynast tangibly supported the Seleucid king; instead, we discover that "the people" dated their own (i.e., presumably the non-Greek, viz. Aramean) documents according to the reign (!) of "Simon, the great high priest, the commander-in-chief and leader of the Jews" (1 Macc 13:42; Josephus, however, differs, referring to the high priest [*archiereus*] Simon, as "the benefactor [*euergetēs*] of the Judeans and the ethnarch" [*Ant* 13.213–14; varia lectio: "eparch"]). The first year of this alleged freedom of Israel from the "yoke of the nations" corresponds to Seleucid Era 170 by the Babylonian (and therefore Judean) reckoning, that is, the year 142/141 B.C. (from spring to spring) by the Julian reckoning (1 Macc 13:41–42; 14:27; *Ant* 13.213–14). Henceforth, as of the beginning of the year 141 B.C., the Judeans considered themselves to be completely free and independent. However, the Seleucid king had neither agreed to nor pronounced the formal decree of independence. Thus the "honorary record of the great assembly of the priests, the people, the community authorities, and the elders of the country for Simon, the high priest *en asaramel* and his brothers" (1 Macc 14:25–49), which was composed in the late summer of 140, served as an additional, proper and quasi-"Israelite" legitimation of Hasmonean sovereignty (cf. *Ant* 13.215–17, which reveals a similarly plebiscitarian-"democratic" tendency). In 141/40 B.C. (= year 172 by the Macedonian Seleucid reckoning, i.e., from autumn to autumn) the considerable privilege of *asylia* was accorded by the king to the city of Tyre with its important sea harbor. In 138 the new king Antiochus VII Euergetes (139–129 B.C.), who later managed to retard the struggle for the Seleucid succession, directed some demands to Simon, the "high priest and people's leader of the Judeans." Simon only partially assented, and succeeded in repelling the retaliatory attack of the "high commander of the coastal district" (1 Macc 15:38), which was launched on Antiochus VII's personal order. However, in the beginning of 134 Simon fell prey to the plot of his son-in-law Ptolemy, the (royal?) chief, on the plain of Jericho. Once again (around 133 B.C.) Antiochus VII achieved the subjugation of Judea. In spite of several concessions, John Hyrcanus I (134–104 B.C.), the son of Simon, was confirmed as the legitimate dynast of the people and even received a limited right to issue his own coins. As vassal and military leader, he followed his lord Antiochus VII into the Parthian War of 131–129 B.C.

C. Remnants of Seleucid Sovereignty (129–63 B.C.)

Hyrcanus survived the death of Antiochus VII in the Parthian War. He was the first Hasmonean to hire foreign mercenaries (which apparently counted as a sign of royal power). According to Josephus (*Ant* 13.273), on his return he "fell away from the Macedonians (i.e., from the Seleucid kings) and did not concern himself with them as either subject or friend" (namely as functionary, vassal, or ally). Instead, he pursued his own successful policy of expansion everywhere in Palestine. Nevertheless, some vestige of Seleucid royal authority was officially retained, as evidenced by a document from 124/23 which reflects the usage of the Seleucid Era (2 Macc 1:9).

It was Alexander Jannaeus (104–78 B.C.), son and successor of Hyrcanus, who first assumed the most exalted title "king" (*melek* or *basileus*), who dated his documents (as the Ptolemies had already done) by the years of *his own* reign, and who formally declared himself free and independent. It is conceivable that the Seleucids never renounced their juridical claim to the possession of the Hasmonean territories.

In fact, it was the "Macedonian" kings who had exhausted themselves in passionate dynastic competitions in the years following the death of Antiochus VII in 129 B.C., while at the same time Ptolemaic (Egyptian) influence over Syria and Palestine had been steadily increasing. In 125, Tyre became completely free, and other coastal sites of the former province of Coele-Syria and Phoenicia followed suit shortly thereafter (Gaza between 112 and 103; Sidon in 111; Ascalon in 104/3; Acco probably in 103 or 102. In other places, particularly in the interior, local potentates (*tyrannoi, monarchoi*) established their own more or less independent governments—Zeno Cotylas had done so in Philadelphia already under Antiochus VII; somewhat later, his son Theodorus did so in Amathus on the Jordan; Zoilus would so do in Straton's Tower and Dora; Ptolemy, the son of Mennaeus, would do so in Chalcis in the Lebanon region, etc. Occasionally the fairly meager sources permit us to make out individual events clearly, as, for example, the controversy over Joppa and the territories which Antiochus VII had detached from Judea.

When Alexander Jannaeus laid siege to Acco at the beginning of his reign, neither of the two Seleucid pretenders—Gryphus (Antiochus VIII) or Cyzicenus (Antiochus IX)—was able to assist the town. By purest chance we happen to possess a dedicatory inscription from this city by a "first friend, minister for the land forces," who was also "local commander." The king honored in this document is possibly Antiochus IX (although this is debated). Actually, this Antiochus, who controlled S Syria and the coastal sites of Phoenicia and Palestine for a few years following 113/12, was able to assert himself in battle with his half-brother Antiochus VIII, who mainly ruled in the N. Shortly before the turn of the century, the Ptolemies and Hasmoneans ruled the field in swift succession. With only a few exceptions, especially on the coast, Judeans and Nabatean Arabs, under their own increasingly Hellenizing and pro-Greek princes, determined the development of the former province of (Coele-)Syria, Judea (to which Samaria had in the meantime become subject), Idumaea, and Phoenicia (*Ant* 13.395; cf. Justinus, *Epit.* 39, 5–4–6; 40, 2:4). Thus, in the course of a single century the juridical, political, military, and economic pace of events had considerably intensified and fundamentally changed through the disintegration of the sole determining central authority (Rome had not yet seized control of the region).

D. Conclusion

In the course of one century, the Seleucid administration continuously proved itself to be, in both its regular and its transient functions, neither rigid nor formalistic. Instead, it was capable of adaptation and thoroughly suited to build upon its Ptolemaic predecessor, organically and by varying degrees. For the moment it also proved to be able to compensate for the loss of its own Greco-Macedonian basis by the absorption of both new and domestic resources.

After the misconceived and unsuccessful policy of Antiochus IV in Judea, the Seleucid kings promulgated a policy which was at once indulgent yet determined; which ensured reciprocal advantages, took account of the actual situations, and allowed for contingencies. This was a policy of "good intention" of "faithfulness and obligation" in the form of "good deeds" with respect to the subject peoples. The Seleucids were thus able, with different intentions and in varying degrees of success, to attach the rebellious, aggressive, and ambitious clan of the Hasmoneans to their own "concerns." Moreover, they did so despite their losses of territory and power, despite the dynastic embroilments, despite Rome's continuously emergent influence, and above all despite the newly awakened senses of national and regional self-awareness which continually weakened their universal dominance, and which continually intensified the instability of the normally well-established power structures.

This process of gradual dissolution of central authority was accompanied by the continuous reevaluation and increased emancipation of the local and regional powers, that is, the dynasts, the *tyrannoi*, and the *monarchoi*, as well as of both the indigenous elite and the eminent individuals in the towns. These tendencies manifested themselves in an increase in privileges and in a refined and to some extent extremely complex "legal empowerment" of the ever more divergent and pluralistic instances.

With the death of Antiochus VII in 129 B.C. the final decline of Seleucid sovereignty began, at least in Palestine. Exalted titles replaced the *de facto* absent royal power and concealed the lack of real Seleucid authority. The political chaos was reflected by the dominance of the military, and by an unmistakable expansion in terms of industry, trade, and finance; in addition to this there was apparently a demographic increase. The dynasty of the Hasmoneans, with their success on the regional power level, did not end as Israelite "priests," genuine "judges," or true biblical "kings," as David and Solomon had done. Rather, they were very appropriate to their own time, "Hellenized," self-assertive, occasionally unscrupulous personalities who distinguished themselves as "leaders," "power holders," and finally as "kings" in the Greek sense, like the Seleucids and Ptolemies. This dynamic development of "decline and fall," like the once-great empire of Alexander, may have experienced a final, sometimes exaggerated and even exuberant flowering. However, unlike Poseidonius and the sectarians of Qumran, who deplored such a "denaturation" from very different points of view, the modern historian is in a considerably better position to study the transformation and the authentic achievements of the Seleucids as well as their fragmentation and "orientalization."

Bibliography

Avi-Yonah, M. 1966. *The Holy Land from the Persian to the Arab Conquests (536 B.C. to A.D. 640).* Grand Rapids.

———. 1974. Historical Geography of Palestine. Pp. 78–116 in *The Jewish People in the First Century,* ed. S. Safrai and M. Stern. CRINT 1/1. Philadelphia.

Bengtson, H. 1964. *Die Strategie in der hellenistischen Zeit.* Vol. 2. Rev. ed. Munich.

Bickerman, E. J. 1988. *The Jews in the Greek Age.* Cambridge, MA.

Bringmann, K. 1983. *Hellenistische Reform und Religionsverfolgung in Judaea.* Göttingen.

Cohen, G. M. 1978. *The Seleucid Colonies.* Wiesbaden.

Fischer, T. 1980. *Seleukiden und Makkabaeer.* Bochum.
———. 1981. Rom und die Hasmonaeer. *Gymnasium* 88: 139–50.
———. 1985. Review of Bringmann 1983. *Klio* 67: 350–55.
———. 1986. Zur Auswertung seleukidischer Muenzen. *Schweizerische Numismatische Rundschau* 65: 65–72.
———. fc. Hasmoneans and Seleucids. *Proceedings of the Conference "Greece and Rome in Eretz-Israel," Universities of Haifa and Tel Aviv (March 25–28, 1985).*
Gruen, E. S. 1984. *The Hellenistic World and the Coming of Rome.* 2 vols. Berkeley, CA.
Rajak, T. 1981. Roman Intervention in a Seleucid Siege of Jerusalem? *GRBS* 22: 65–81.
Taylor, J. E. 1979. Seleucid Rule in Palestine. Diss. Duke University.
Will, E. 1982. *Histoire politique du Monde hellénistique (323–30 av J.-C.).* Vol. 2, 2d rev. ed. Nancy.

THOMAS FISCHER
Trans. Frederick H. Cryer

ROMAN ADMINISTRATION

This article covers the period of Roman administration in Palestine from the time of Pompey's conquest in 63 B.C. until the crushing of the Bar Kokhba revolt in A.D. 135.

A. From Pompey's Conquest to the Parthian Invasion
B. Herod, King of the Jews
C. Herod's Legacy
  1. Sons of Herod
  2. Early Prefects of Judea
  3. Reign of Herod Agrippa
D. The Last Procurators of Judea
E. The War with Rome
F. Judea under Imperial Legates

A. From Pompey's Conquest to the Parthian Invasion

The establishment of Roman control over W Asia after Pompey's decisive overthrow of Mithridates VI of Pontus in 64 B.C. was bound to affect the state of Judea, which for nearly 80 years had enjoyed independence under the Hasmonean dynasty of priest-kings. But division within the Hasmonean camp at that time positively invited Roman intervention in Judea.

When Salome Alexandra, Hasmonean queen regnant, died in 67 B.C., rivalry broke out between her two sons—Hyrcanus II, who had occupied the high priesthood during her reign, and Aristobulus II, who had been her military commander-in-chief. Hyrcanus, the older son, was heir to the throne, but Aristobulus rebelled against him and defeated his forces. Hyrcanus relinquished his royal and high-priestly titles in his brother's favor. Hyrcanus was totally devoid of personal initiative or ambition, but he was manipulated by the ambitious Idumean Antipater. Antipater persuaded Hyrcanus that Aristobulus had designs on his life and that he should seek sanctuary with the Nabatean king Aretas III. Aretas invaded Judea on Hyrcanus's behalf and defeated Aristobulus.

Aristobulus and Hyrcanus both sent legations to Damascus, where Aemilius Scaurus, Pompey's lieutenant, had arrived in 65 B.C. Scaurus favored Aristobulus, and ordered Aretas to leave Judea. But when Pompey himself came to Damascus in 63 B.C., legations from the two brothers appeared before him in turn, and Pompey eventually gave his support to Hyrcanus. Jerusalem was surrendered to Pompey, but the followers of Aristobulus barricaded themselves in the well-fortified temple area and held out against Pompey's forces for three months. The temple area was stormed in July or August, 63 B.C.

Pompey confirmed Hyrcanus in power, but withheld the title of king from him, and released from his control the Greek cities of the Mediterranean seaboard and Transjordan which his predecessors had conquered, placing them under the direct authority of the Roman governor of Syria (Scaurus), who at the same time exercised general supervision over Judea.

In 57 B.C. Alexander, son of Aristobulus II, escaping from his Roman captivity, raised an army and occupied three fortresses in Judea. Aulus Gabinius, newly appointed proconsul of Syria, put down the rebellion and reorganized the province of Judea. Hyrcanus was left with the high priesthood and the custody of the temple; Judaea was divided into five districts, each administered by an aristocratic council.

In 54 B.C. Gabinius was succeeded as proconsul of Syria by Licinius Crassus, a member of the first triumvirate at Rome along with Pompey and Julius Caesar. Crassus plundered the temple treasury in Jerusalem to raise funds for his campaign against Parthia. In that campaign he was defeated and killed (53 B.C.). His quaestor Cassius (later to be one of Caesar's assassins) exercised supreme authority in Syria and Judea from 53 to 51 B.C.

The civil war which broke out in 49 B.C. between Pompey and Caesar ended the following year with Pompey's defeat at Pharsalus in Thessaly and his murder when he fled for asylum to Egypt. Hyrcanus, at the prompting of Antipater (who for several years had been quietly consolidating his power base in Judea), declared his support for Caesar. A material proof of this support was given in the spring of 47 B.C. when Caesar found himself outnumbered in Egypt: Antipater sent troops and other supplies to his aid, and Hyrcanus persuaded the large Jewish colony in Egypt to fight on his side. Caesar was grateful: when he came to Syria later that year he named Hyrcanus "ethnarch of the Jews" over and above his high priesthood, while he honored Antipater (the effective power behind Hyrcanus' throne) with Roman citizenship and freedom from taxation, and appointed him procurator of Judea. Gabinius' division of the province into five administrative districts was now canceled.

Antipater appointed his two sons, Phasael and Herod, military prefects in Judea and Galilee respectively. About the same time Herod, a young man of outstanding ability, was appointed military prefect of Coele-Syria by Sextus Caesar, governor of Syria.

Julius Caesar's assassination on March 15, 44 B.C., was a heavy blow to the Jews, both in Palestine and throughout the empire. Cassius, one of the leading assassins, came back to take control of Syria, and received from Hyrcanus and Antipater the support which they had given to Caesar. Antipater's policy, followed by his son Herod, was to support Rome, whoever might be the representative of Roman power in the east from time to time. Antipater was killed by a private enemy in 43 B.C.; his authority was taken over by his two sons. Next year they were nominated tetrarchs of Judea by Mark Antony, who became ruler of the Roman east when he and Octavian (Caesar's heir) defeated Cassius and Brutus at the battle of Philippi.

In 40 B.C. the whole of W Asia was overrun by the Parthians, from beyond the Euphrates. In Jerusalem they placed Antigonus, the last surviving son of Aristobulus II, on the throne as king and high priest. Phasael was captured and committed suicide; Herod escaped to Rome. There Antony and Octavian persuaded the Roman senate to recognize him as king of the Jews.

B. Herod, King of the Jews

It was now for Herod to give substance to his title by winning back his kingdom. The Romans lost no time in expelling the Parthians from the territories they had overrun, but left Antigonus on the throne in Jerusalem. Most of his subjects were well pleased to have an effective Hasmonean ruler again. It took long and hard fighting on Herod's part to reduce Judea. Jerusalem was taken in the summer of 37 B.C. after a siege of three months in which Herod's forces were augmented by Roman troops under the command of Sosius, governor of Syria.

For 33 years (37–4 B.C.) Herod reigned over Judea (including Samaria, Galilee and parts of Transjordan) as Rome's faithful ally. When civil war broke out between Antony and Octavian in 31 B.C. and Antony (with Cleopatra) was defeated at the battle of Actium (committing suicide at Alexandria the following year), Herod went to meet Octavian at Rhodes and undertook to be as loyal a friend to him as he had been to Antony. Octavian recognized Herod's worth to Rome and confirmed him in his status as king of the Jews.

Rome found it convenient to control several subject nations in the E part of the empire through client kings, who ranked officially as "friends and allies of the Roman people." These kings were completely dependent on Rome for their power, and were bound to retain the favor of Rome, but they enjoyed considerable freedom in the administration of their kingdoms. See CLIENT KINGS. If they kept the peace within their own boundaries and in adjoining territories, Rome was content: Rome reaped all the advantages from this arrangement, and the client kings incurred all the odium—and where Herod was concerned, there was no lack of odium. But when Herod subdued unruly tribes on his NE frontier, Augustus (the style which Octavian adopted from 27 B.C. on) knew that the best way to keep them pacified was to add them to Herod's kingdom. By the end of Herod's reign his dominions approached the dimensions of the empire of David and Solomon a thousand years before. But, whereas David and Solomon were overlords over weaker rulers, Herod could never forget that he was subject to the overlordship of Augustus, to whom indeed his subjects had to swear an oath of allegiance as well as to Herod himself (Joseph. *Ant.* 17.42).

C. Herod's Legacy

When Herod died in 4 B.C., his kingdom was at the disposal of Augustus. In his last will he had bequeathed his kingdom to three of his sons, but the will could not take effect until Augustus confirmed it. Judea and Samaria were bestowed on Herod's son Archelaus (cf. Matt 2:22), who received the title of ethnarch; Galilee and Peraea (S Transjordan) went to Archelaus' full brother Antipas ("Herod the tetrarch" of the gospel records), while their half-brother Philip received as his tetrarchy the territories which Herod had acquired E and NE of the Sea of Galilee in 23 and 20 B.C.—"the region of Ituraea and Trachonitis" (Luke 3:1).

1. Sons of Herod. Archelaus, who inherited his father's ruthlessness but not his statesmanship, proved so intolerable to his subjects in Judea and Samaria that after 9 years they threatened revolt if he were not removed. Augustus accordingly removed him in A.D. 6 and banished him to Gaul. His principality was transformed into a Roman province.

Philip governed his mainly gentile tetrarchy justly and peaceably. He built himself a capital at Banyas, near one of the sources of the Jordan, and named it Caesarea in honor of the emperor; it was known as Caesarea Philippi ("Philip's Caesarea") to distinguish it from other foundations of the same name. When he died in A.D. 34 his tetrarchy was added to the province of Syria.

Antipas was politically the ablest of Herod's sons. He governed Galilee and Peraea in the interests of Rome for over forty years. He vigilantly checked any movement which he suspected might lead to insurrection. His capital was Sepphoris, until he built a new one on the W shore of the Sea of Galilee and called it Tiberias in honor of the Emperor Tiberius. He fell from power in A.D. 39, when his nephew Agrippa I satisfied a grudge by poisoning the mind of Tiberius' successor Gaius (Caligula) against him. Gaius deposed and banished him, and gave his tetrarchy to Agrippa.

2. Early Prefects of Judea. When Archelaus was deposed in A.D. 6 his territory was placed under the general supervision of the imperial legate of Syria, with its own governor of equestrian rank. The first event of the new order was the census held by Quirinius, legate of Syria, to determine the amount of tribute which the province of Judea would henceforth have to pay to Rome. The idea that the people of God, living in the holy land, should pay tribute to a pagan ruler was offensive to many Jews, chiefly to Judas of Galilee and his followers, who led a rising against the Romans; this was inevitably put down (Acts 5:37). It is plain from the gospels that the propriety of paying tribute to Caesar remained a burning question in Judea and Jerusalem (Mark 12: 13–17; Luke 23:2).

The first provincial governor of Judea was Coponius. Between A.D. 6 and 41 he and his successors appear to have been called prefects. This is Pontius Pilate's designation in the Caesarea inscription which bears his name; if Tacitus, writing ca. 115–17, calls him a procurator (*Ann.* 15.44.4), that may be because the later governors of Judea (44–66) were called procurators.

The prefects had some cohorts of auxiliary troops under their command: garrisons were maintained at Caesarea (the Mediterranean port founded by Herod ca. 13 B.C., where the prefects set up their official residence), at Jerusalem (in the Antonia fortress NW of the temple area) and elsewhere in the province. If more force was required, the legate of Syria could supply it from the legionary troops at his disposal.

The internal affairs of the Jewish nation were administered by the Sanhedrin, their senate and supreme court. The prefect reserved the right of capital punishment; only for offenses against the temple was this right left in the hands of the Sanhedrin, by a special concession from the Romans. Jerusalem had the status of a holy city; when its sanctity was disregarded by an insensitive prefect, he was apt to incur the emperor's disapproval. Images were not to be introduced within the city limits (for their presence would infringe the second commandment); when Pilate nevertheless brought into the city military standards bearing busts of the emperor, the Jewish authorities protested and Pilate had to remove the busts (*Ant* 18.35; *JW* 2.169).

From A.D. 6 to 41 the prefects of Judea, or occasionally the legates of Syria, appointed and deposed Jewish high priests. Annas, for example, was appointed in A.D. 6 by Quirinius; his son-in-law Caiaphas was appointed in A.D. 15 by the prefect Valerius Gratus, and retained the office until 37, when he was removed by Vitellius, legate of Syria. In addition to his sacral duties, the high priest was president of the Sanhedrin. The prefects maintained further control of the high priests until 37 by keeping their holy vestments under armed guard in the Antonia fortress.

3. Reign of Herod Agrippa I. When Gaius (Caligula) succeeded Tiberius as emperor in 37, he made Agrippa, grandson of Herod the Great, ruler of Philip's former tetrarchy, with the title king. When, two years later, he deposed Antipas, he added Galilee and Peraea to Agrippa's kingdom. When Claudius became emperor in 41, he enlarged Agrippa's kingdom with the addition of Judea and Samaria, so that Agrippa ("Herod the king" of Acts 12:1) ruled a territory almost as extensive as his grandfather's.

Agrippa enjoyed considerable autonomy within his kingdom, but otherwise his authority was strictly limited. When, for example, he convened a conference of neighboring client kings at Tiberias, the legate of Syria ordered it to disband. His Jewish subjects were mostly pleased with his rule, but it lasted only three years: in 44 he died after a short and sudden illness (Acts 12:20–23; *Ant.* 19.343–50).

D. The Last Procurators of Judea

Agrippa's seventeen-year-old son, Agrippa the younger ("Agrippa the king" of Acts 25:13), was adjudged too immature to inherit his father's kingdom; Claudius gave him a tiny kingdom in South Lebanon. Judea (with Samaria, Galilee, and Perea) reverted to provincial status.

The governors of Judea from 44 to 66 were called procurators. Unlike the prefects from 6 to 41, they were not allowed to appoint high priests: this privilege was given to the late Agrippa's brother, Herod of Chalcis, and after him to the younger Agrippa.

Cuspius Fadus, first of the new procurators, tried to govern justly, but did not hold his office long. His successor, Tiberius Julius Alexander, an uncle of Philo, the Jewish philosopher of Alexandria, was unacceptable to most Jews because he was an apostate from his ancestral religion. He dealt sternly with insurgents, including two sons of Judas the Galilean, who were crucified by his orders. The next procurator, Ventidius Cumanus (48–52), experienced the difficulties inherent in governing both Jews and Samaritans. He intervened unsatisfactorily in a dispute between the two communities. Both sides appealed to the legate of Syria, who ordered their leaders, with Cumanus himself, to go to Rome and submit to Claudius' judgment. Claudius ruled in the Jews' favor, and Cumanus was deposed and exiled.

Cumanus' successor, Felix, was not a member of the equestrian order, like his predecessors, but a freedman who owed the appointment to the influence of his brother Pallas at the imperial court. Felix's procuratorship was disturbed by repeated outbreaks of insurgency, which his forces put down ruthlessly. A flattering description of his measures is given by Tertullus in his speech for the prosecution when Paul appeared on trial before Felix (Acts 24:2–3). His severity led to a stiffening of anti-Roman resistance in Judea. He was eventually recalled from office (A.D. 59) because of his inept handling of a feud between Jews and gentiles in Caesarea.

At his departure from Judea, Felix left Paul in custody for his successor, Porcius Festus (59–62) to deal with. It was at his appearance before Festus that Paul, exercising his right as a Roman citizen, appealed to have his case transferred from the subordinate provincial court to the supreme imperial tribunal in Rome (Acts 25:11–12).

Of Festus (exceptionally among the governors of Judaea), nothing discreditable is recorded, but he died suddenly after three years in office. Events in the three months' interregnum which followed his death showed how strictly Roman authority was maintained over a province even in the absence of a governor. The high priest Ananus took advantage of the interval which elapsed before the arrival of Festus' successor to assume the right of capital jurisdiction (one of his victims was James the brother of Jesus); this usurpation of an authority which was not his would have brought down Roman reprisals on the province if his action had not been disowned by his being deposed from the high priesthood.

Of the last two procurators of Judea, Albinus and Gessius Florus, nothing good is related. Their insensitivity and ineptitude were largely responsible for the Jewish revolt of 66, but Josephus depicts them as unworthy representatives of imperial Rome, which deserved better agents. Albinus accepted bribes impartially from the Jewish establishment and the insurgents, and on the eve of his departure, he released criminals from prison indiscriminately; Florus' misdeeds made Albinus appear a paragon of justice (*JW* 2.277; *Ant* 20.252). He flaunted his venality even more disgracefully than Albinus, and took savage reprisals when his vexatious treatment of the Jews became more than they could endure. Even Tacitus (*Hist.* 5.10) concedes that it was Florus' malevolence that made Jewish patience snap at last.

When the ensuing revolt quickly developed to a point where Florus could not cope with it, Cestius Gallus, legate of Syria, intervened with the twelfth legion and additional troops. On reaching Jerusalem, Gallus realized that the reduction of the strongly defended Temple area would require a greater force than he had brought, so he withdrew northward, and his troops were severely mauled by the insurgents on their way through the Pass of Bethhoron.

E. The War with Rome

A state of war now existed throughout all Palestine, and supreme authority was vested in Vespasian, the commander-in-chief sent by Nero with adequate forces (three legions and auxiliary troops) to put down the revolt. When, in the strife that followed Nero's death, Vespasian was proclaimed emperor by the eastern legions in July 69, he left for Rome with Jerusalem still unreduced, entrusting the prosecution of the war to his son Titus. When Titus in turn left for Rome, after bringing the siege of Jerusalem to a successful conclusion in September 70, his place as commander-in-chief was taken by Vettenius Cerialis.

F. Judea under Imperial Legates

After the war, Judea's status as a Roman province was raised: it was now governed by a legate of senatorial rank, no longer under the general supervision of the governor of Syria, like the earlier prefects and procurators, but directly responsible to the emperor, with legionary troops under his command. These troops belonged at first to one legion only, the tenth *(Fretensis)*; later, between 120 and 130, the sixth legion *(Ferrata)* was also stationed in Judea. The seat of government continued to be Caesarea, now a Roman colony.

The first three legates appear to have been Cerialis, commander of the fifth legion at the siege of Jerusalem; Lucilius Bassus, who stormed the fortresses of Herodium and Machaerus; and Flavius Silva, who reduced Masada. The extant list of legates is incomplete: Lusius Quietus, appointed by Trajan, had put down a Jewish rebellion in Mesopotamia in 115; Tineius Rufus, appointed by Hadrian, was legate when the Bar-Kokhba revolt broke out in 132. The governor under whom this revolt was crushed (135) was Julius Severus, who had earlier been governor of Britain. Thereafter the name of the province was Palestine (Syria Palaestina); Jerusalem was refounded as a Roman colony and renamed Aelia Capitolina.

Bibliography

Freyne, S. 1980. *Galilee from Alexander the Great to Hadrian.* Wilmington, DE and South Bend, IN.

Goodman, M. 1983. *State and Society in Roman Galilee.* Oxford Centre for Postgraduate Hebrew Studies. Totowa, NJ.

———. 1987. *The Ruling Class of Judea.* Cambridge.

Jones, A. H. M. 1967. *The Herods of Judaea.* 2d ed. Oxford.

Lémonon, J.-P. 1981. *Pilate et le Gouvernement de la Judée.* EBib. Paris.

Schalit, A. 1969. *König Herodes: Der Mann und sein Werk.* Trans. J. Amir. SJ 4. Berlin.

Smallwood, E. M. 1976. *The Jews under Roman Rule.* SJLA 20. Leiden.

F. F. Bruce

PALESTINE, ARCHAEOLOGY OF.

This entry consists of four articles surveying, respectively, the prehistoric periods, the Bronze and Iron Ages, the Persian period, and the New Testament period.

PREHISTORIC PERIODS

The study of prehistoric Palestine began with surface collections made during the 19th century by travelers who came to look for the country's biblical past. The first excavation was carried out by F. Turville-Petre (1925–1926) in Zuttiyeh and Emireh caves in Wadi Amud near Tiberias. He was followed by D. Garrod, who is known mostly for her excavations in the Carmel caves (1928–1934) and by R. Neuville in rock shelters in the Judean desert (1928–1935). He also dug in Qafzeh cave (near Nazareth) with M. Stekelis, the first Israeli prehistorian, who excavated Jisr Banat Yaʿaqub, a Lower Paleolithic site in the Jordan Valley. From the 1950s through the 1980s, a series of excavations have been conducted in various parts of Israel, and these, with the results of surveys and excavations in Sinai and Jordan, have provided a continuous cultural sequence for the Middle and Upper Paleolithic, Epi-Paleolithic, and Neolithic periods. Our knowledge of the earlier period is still fragmentary—the number of sites is small and they are poorly dated.

A. Paleolithic
B. Neolithic
  1. Pre-Pottery Neolithic (PPN)
  2. Pottery Neolithic (PN)
C. Chalcolithic

A. Paleolithic

The earliest occurrences of artifacts testifying of the presence of early hominids in the Near East were found during the excavations at UBEIDIYA, in the central Jordan Valley. The archaeological horizons of this site are embedded in a sequence of lacustrine and fluviatile deposits which is defined at the Ubeidiya Formation. This formation overlies the Erq el-Ahmar Formation, which contained Late Pliocene mollusks and is the earliest limnic formation within the Jordan Rift, which was formed by a series of tectonic movements younger than 3.2 million years. The excavations at Ubeidiya demonstrated the presence of numerous implementiferous layers but only 14 were extensively excavated. The lithic industries are characterized by the high frequencies of core choppers from which flakes were removed and used. Polyhedrons, spheroids, and a few hand axes form the rest of the assemblages. It is worth noting that most core choppers and polyhedrons were made of flint pebbles; spheroids were shaped from limestone, and hand axes were dominantly made of basalt and the rest from flint and limestone. Only the earliest levels at Ubeidiya do not contain bifaces. The assemblages resemble the Oldowan of Africa. However, as the rest of the assemblages includes bifaces, trihedral, or picks even in small numbers, the entire lithic sequence is cautiously attributed to the Early Acheulian.

Over 120 species of mammals, birds, and reptiles were identified. Among the most common mammals are the horse, deer, hippopotamus, elephant, several carnivores, and various rodents (which essentially characterize a forest-steppic environment). The paleoecological reconstruction of the immediate environment of the site encompasses a variety of habitats including an open fresh-water lake, pebbly beaches, thickets with reeds and tamarisk along laguna areas, open grassy meadows, partly forested western slopes of the Jordan Rift with some rocky exposures, a plateau covered with oak forest above the valley, and some dry wadis descending into the lake much as they do today.

The site of Ubeidiya is dated on the basis of faunal correlations. The presence of certain species including an elephant *(Mammuthus meridionalis tamanensis)*, rhinocerus *(Dicerorhinus etruscus)*, horses *(Equus tabeti, Equus caballus)*, deer *(Praemegaceros verticornis)*, warthog, and wild boar *(Kolpochoerus oldowayensis)* led to a long-distance correlation between the faunal biozones of W and E Europe and E Africa, and indicates the Ubeidiya should be dated to 1.4–1.0 million years ago. This is the best-dated Lower Paleolithic site in the entire Near East and represents one of the stations of *Homo erectus* as members of this genus moved from Africa into Asia and Europe.

Other Lower Paleolithic sites, all of which are classified as Middle or Upper Acheulian, are found in the Jordan Valley or the coastal plain, where considerable amounts of deposits are exposed. The hilly areas are often stripped of any Lower or Middle Pleistocene accumulations.

Evron-Quary is a small site including the remains of some Middle Pleistocene mammals. Its lithic assemblage contains a few large flint bifaces and a small flake industry indicating that part of the assemblages was transported into the site. See EVRON.

JISR BANAT YAᶜAQUB, on the banks of the Jordan River and currently under excavation, is known for its assemblages of lava flake cleavers which were made in the same technique so common in Africa. With the cleavers are lava bifaces and a collection of large mammalian fauna, which are best correlated with the European Cromerian fauna. They include elephants, rhinoceroses, hippopotamuses, wild boar, and deer. This site overlies a lava flow dated by Potassium/Argon (K/Ar) to 0.68 million years with a normal magnetic polarity. The age of the site is estimated to be around 0.5 million years old. According to the observations made by M. Stekelis in the 1930s, the upper layers of the site contained Acheulian industry in which the bifaces were mainly made of flint. Two fragments of human femora, without exact provenience, were collected from the dumps created by the deepening of the Jordan River channel, which considerably damaged the site.

Upper Acheulian materials, most of them collected from surface scatters, were located in the various regions of Palestine including the oases such as AZRAQ and Nahal Zin. However, it seems that hominids during the Lower and Middle Pleistocene were not able to cope with arid or semiarid conditions. Sites located in the deserts, therefore, signify pluvial times. Upper Acheulian assemblages were also excavated in cave sites such as Tabun cave and Umm Qatafa cave. See CARMEL CAVES. The animal bones are often those of large to medium mammals, probably indicating the scavenging activities of humans.

In several sites, the Upper Acheulian is overlain by a lithic industry which has several names. The current term "Mugharan Tradition" was suggested by A. Jelinek, on the basis of his excavations in Tabun cave. Others still use the term "Acheulo-Yabrudian." Both terms mean that this entity contains several facies of the same lithic industry. One "facies" contains thick scrapers of various shapes including canted and transverse forms, often demonstrating considerable resharpening ("Yabrudian"); the second together with the scrapers has varying frequencies of often small, oval or pointed bifaces; and the third "facies" is dominated by blades with a few bifaces and burins ("Amudian"). The first two facies are the most common.

The Acheulo-Yabrudian demonstrates a particular geographic distribution. This entity occupied the N Levant, and its S manifestations are just S of Mt. Carmel and into the Transjordanian plateau. U-series datings suggest that this entity lasted from about 180/150–120 thousand years ago.

Human relics in Acheulo-Yabrudian contexts include the fragmentary skull recovered in Zuttiyeh cave and a broken femur in Tabun cave. The Zuttiyeh skull is morphologically attributed to the late *Homo erectus* or the archaic *Homo sapiens.*

In stratified cave sites such as Yabrud (Anti-Lebanon mountains) or Tabun cave, the Acheulo-Yabrudian is overlain by the Mousterian complex. The long sequence of Tabun cave enabled the general description of three types of lithic industries, mostly made through the use of various methods of the Levallois technique. Each of these is named after the main layer in Tabun as identified by D. Garrod, although A. Jelinek was able to refine the subdivision and accurately relate the industries to their geological deposit.

In "Tabun B"–type industry, the blanks were removed by the unidirectional and convergent methods of Levallois. Short and broad points are common as well as side scrapers. A more "facies" with more blades and elongated points occurs at the lower levels of this entity in Tabun and Kebara caves. See KEBARA CAVE.

The "Tabun C"–type industry is often dominated by radial and bidirectional core reduction methods which were responsible for the production of large oval flakes. However, convergent flaking is present and resulted in the presence of a "facies" with Levallois points (such as in Tabun and Qafzeh caves).

The earliest industry is the "Tabun D" type, which contains numerous elongated points and blades, however, with side scrapers. Among the best examples are Tabun and Abu Sif caves. This type of industry seems to be more common in the Negeb and the S Transjordanian plateau than in the N part of Palestine. The lack of a sufficient number of well-founded dates precludes the establishment of the Mousterian sequence. Thermoluminescence (TL) and Electron Spin Resonance (ESR) dates from Qafzeh cave (averaging 90–100 thousand years for the hominid bearing layers) and Kebara cave (averaging 48–64 thousand years for the entire sequence in the site) support earlier contentions based on rodents' biozones. An estimated age for Tabun D–type industry will be in the order of 130/115–100/95 thousand years. However, the current use of these dating techniques and cross-checking by other radiometric methods makes any suggested conclusions premature.

The current surge of dates was motivated by the renewed discussion on the origins of anatomically modern humans. The number of Mousterian human remains discovered in Palestine is large when compared to other regions of the Old World. Several relics were uncovered by intentional burials such as in Tabun, Skhul, Kebara, Qafzeh, and Amud caves. The entire sample is considered to represent the West Asian Neanderthal (Tabun, Kebara, and Amud) or the archaic *Homo sapiens* (also referred to as "Proto-Cro-Magnon" at Qafzeh, Skhul). While one school views the entire collection as representing the same population, others see the Neanderthals as either emerging from local ancestors or as Europeans migrating into the Levant with the onset of glacial conditions (110 or 75 thousand years ago).

There is ample evidence to indicate that the Mousterian people gathered plant foods and hunted gazelles and fallow deer, although they did not refrain from opportunistic scavenging. The signs of utilization on their tools reflect hide and woodworking, and butchery. Levallois points bear impact marks as they have been employed as spear points. The use of red ocher is rare as is the collection of marine shells. Imported elements in sites include raw material for the production of artifacts and curated tools. Hearths were often rounded or oval, and amorphous ashy deposits are common in well-preserved situations in caves (e.g., Kebara).

The transition from the Middle Paleolithic to the Upper Paleolithic is reflected in the local evolution within the lithic industries. The best example is in Boker Tachtit, a site in Nahal Zin in the Negeb, excavated by A. Marks. The lithic sequence of this site demonstrates a transition in core reduction methods from a mixture of bidirectional Levallois cores and prismatic Upper Paleolithic cores for blade production to simple unidirectional Upper Paleolithic blade cores. The Transitional Industry includes Levallois points removed from blade cores with a bidirectional scar pattern. In Ksar Akil (Lebanon), the Transitional Industry represents an idea similar to that of the Upper Paleolithic. Tool types such as end scrapers are made on Levallois blanks. The specific tool type common in Lebanon, the chamferred blades and flakes, were not found in Palestine except for rare surface occurrences. The Early Upper Paleolithic sequence is therefore characterized by the dominance of tool types such as end scrapers and a few burins. The blanks are either mainly flakes (Emireh cave) or blades (Boker Tachtit).

It is the following industry which signifies the subsequent phases with the dominance of blades/bladelets (often removed from unipolar prismatic cores). This industry was called the Ahmarian Tradition and most of its sites are known from the Negeb and Sinai, but also include the early layers in some caves (e.g., Kebara). The dominant point forms are either the Ksar Akil type or the El-Wad type and retouched bladelets are often a steady component of these assemblages. The entire Ahmarian sequence is radio-carbon dated to 38,000–20/18,000 B.C. when it develops into the Kebaran Complex. Most of the sites indicate a greater mobility than in the Middle Paleolithic, accompanied by the hunting of gazelle, fallow deer, roe deer, and more ibex in the semiarid areas. Intensive use of red ocher is recorded and several grinding tools were also employed in the preparation of the color. Bone tools are quite rare and the manipulation of marine shells began around 20,000 B.C.

The Ahmarian sequence in the cave sites is interrupted by the distinct appearance of the first Aurignacian elements, such as carinated and nosed scrapers and later by the dominance of an industry essentially produced on flakes. It is this industry which is currently named Levantine Aurignacian.

With carinated and nosed scrapers, the Levantine Aurignacian assemblages contain El-Wad points which are also present in Ahmarian assemblages. However, rich bone and antler objects add to the distinction of this entity. Most of these objects were made by cutting and shaving with flint knives. Two split base points, a typical object in the European Aurignacian, were found in Kebara and El-Quseir caves. Two incised slabs, found in Hayonim cave, may represent artistic expressions.

The Levantine Aurignacian is only known from the N and central Levant and is not present in the Negeb or S Jordan. It is therefore considered as the archaeological expression of a social unit foreign to the Near East, which arrived in the region and lasted for some time between 32,000–28,000 B.C.

The following phase of the Upper Paleolithic is signified by an abundance of scrapers and burins (in several sites the latter is the dominant tool type) and it seems that in most assemblages, these tool types are made on flakes. In some sites the burins, especially those on truncation, dominate the assemblage. It is in this type of site (Nahal Ein Gev I, Jordan Valley) that a flexed burial of a woman, 30–35 years old, was uncovered.

The subsequent industries (ca. 25/24,000–20/18,000 B.C.) are characterized by the proliferation of blade/bladelet production, and microlithic tools become the dominant forms. This phase, which can be referred to as the Late Ahmarian, heralds the onset of what is known as the Kebaran cultural complex (ca. 18,000–12,500 B.C.), which encompasses a variety of assemblage types. The changes in the form of the microliths leads from nongeometric forms such as the obliquely truncated bladelets (Kebara points) to the elongated trapeze-rectangles, which characterize the ensuing cultural complex known as the Geometric Kebaran (ca. 12,500–10,800/10,500 B.C.).

The Kebaran sites are generally small and located in lower altitudes. Most are known from surface collections and limited excavations. The largest excavation is in Ein Gev I (on the E shores of Lake Tiberias), where a shallow basin dug into the sandy deposits which formed the foundations of a small hut (5–7 m in diameter) was exposed. Repeated occupations resulted in considerable accumulation of flints and animal bones (mainly deer and gazelle). A burial of a 30–35-year-old woman was found under one of the levels in the center of the hut. A mortar and several pestles were among the domestic utensils. Recent excavations in Urkan er-Rubb II, a site in the lower Jordan Valley, retrieved the only art object from this period—a flat pebble which bears several incised series of the "ladder" pattern.

The climatic conditions during the Kebaran Complex were cold and dry (the Late Glacial Maximum) and human occupations were limited to the belt of Mediterranean vegetation and margins of the steppic Irano-Turanian belt including some of the desert oases. The subsequent climatic amelioration which brought the increase in temperatures and precipitation enabled the Geometric Kebaran groups to inhabit many of the formerly arid areas. Moreover, the spatial expansion of vegetal and animal resources tempted groups from neighboring regions to move in. Such is the archaeological complex of the Mushabian, mainly known from Sinai; which is considered to be a penetration from NE Africa. Other groups moved into the inland basins on the Transjordanian plateau such as the Azraq.

The general increase in population within the entire

region and the different lithic knapping traditions imported into Palestine left a variety of assemblages which cannot easily be clustered under one or two taxons. However, the common denominators are the microliths, mostly the trapeze-rectangles, the triangles, and the lunates. In terms of lifeways, these were basically small groups of hunter-gatherers who left behind ample evidence for reconstructing small campsites with a hearth and a particular distribution of the dumps. The larger sites are either palimpsests of reoccupations where deflation and erosion obliterated many features or sites where rapid accumulation of sand and loam today enables the identification of discrete features such as hearths and activity areas. The consumption of seeds, grain, acorns, and nuts is best recorded in the use of pounding and some grinding tools such as mortars, pestles, and mullers. Marine shells were brought mainly from the closest shoreline—either the Mediterranean or the Red Sea. From the large Geometric Kebaran site of Neveh David (Mt. Carmel), two burials with fragmentary skeletons are known.

The settlement pattern reconstructed for the Epi-Paleolithic groups depends on the available resources and their seasonal distribution. On the whole, lowlands were better suited for winter exploitation while highlands were better suited for summer occupations. Water sources are abundant in the hills of Palestine (including the Transjordanian plateau) and the dry summer had no effects on the availability of this resource. Over one hundred species of plants can be exploited during the year and the stress period is often from November through late February. The common medium- to small-size mammal is the gazelle (mainly *Gazella gazella*), which is a stationary mammal with a very small home range territory (1–5 km^2). Such an availability, reliability, and accessibility of resources would encourage a semisedentary settlement pattern with some storage facilities.

A short and abrupt climatic crisis, probably around 10,000/10,500 B.C. was responsible for the disruption of the socioeconomic situation and caused some groups to resolve the seasonal shortages by settling down on the ecotone of the Mediterranean open forest and the steppic belt or on the boundary between the coastal plain and the hilly areas. This archaeological entity known as the Natufian culture has a distribution of sites which avoids the arid belt.

The Natufian large sites (or base camps) are up to 5,000 m^2 and contain rounded and oval houses (e.g., Ain Mallaha, Hayonim Cave and Terrace, Wadi Hammeh 26), burials, and rich lithic and bone industries. The houses are often dug into the ground and the walls of undressed stone are slanting inside. In one large house in Ain Mallaha a series of postholes were uncovered. There is no evidence for the use of mudbricks by the Natufian and it seems that the superstructures of the houses were built of organic substances.

Natufian burials display various styles in disposition of the dead. Collective burials are more common in the Early Natufian and positions are supine, semiflexed, and flexed. In rare cases, skulls of adults were intentionally removed. The late Natufian sites contain more single burials in flexed position. Grave goods possibly indicate social differentiation. They include body decorations made of bone and stone pendants, shell beads, often using the various species of *Dentalium* and rarely some mundane tools. The original places of the decorations were probably as headgear, garments, and belts. Of special importance is the burial of a woman with a young dog exposed in Ain Mallaha, indicating the domestication of this mammal.

The lithic industry of the Natufian culture often demonstrates a proliferation of geometric microliths, especially of lunates shaped by either Helwan or abrupt retouch. Sickle blades, burins, perforators, and a few delicate, elongated picks make for the rest of the assemblages. The production of small flakes and short bladelets as blanks for tools differentiate the Natufian from the former cultural complexes. The use of microburin technique to obtain oblique snaps possibly indicates the local tradition of certain groups which lasted through the two phases of the Natufian. However, Helwan retouch (a bifacial retouch on lunates) is more common in the Early Natufian. On the whole, the Early Natufian is better known from some large sites and small ephemeral occupations in the semiarid zone while the Late Natufian is poorly known from a few sites such as NAHAL OREN Terrace (Mt. Carmel), Salibiya I (Jordan Valley), Rosh Zin, and Rosh Horesha (Negeb).

Natufian art expressions are more numerous than in any of the preceding periods. They include the carving of heads of ungulates on sickle hafts, limestone figurines schematically representing humans and animals, zigzag and meander decorations incised or carved on domestic objects, and some incised slabs where the ladder pattern is dominant. The sudden increase in artistic activity in the Natufian is explained by the need to increase symbolic behavior to maintain social cohesion. Natufian sites also differ from each other by types of ornaments, especially the arrangements of *Dentalium* shells or common bone beads. It seems that body decorations were the salient means of group identification.

The Natufian economy was based on intensive collection of cereals (which left its marks as a special luster on the sickle blades) although some scholars have suggested that during this period emerged the earliest farmers. Unfortunately, plant remains in Natufian sites are scarce, mainly owing to bad preservation in Mediterranean soils. For pounding and grinding, they employed mortars and pestles which were made either of limestone or basalt. Hunting continued, and at some sites, the decrease in gazelle size is interpreted as overexploitation. Otherwise, the range of hunted game and collected reptiles or trapped water fowl is wider than in any previous Epi-Paleolithic entity. It seems that the Natufian subsistence strategy had responded to the increase of basic group size and sedentarism (which leads to increase of population). Even if Natufian groups were not permanently annually sedentary, the investments in building structures in the sites reflects a tight pattern of anticipated mobility.

The evidence for sedentarism is derived from the proliferation of commensals, such as house mice and house sparrows, in some Natufian sites. Recent chromosomal studies, as well as metrical analysis of living wild and domestic forms of house mice, confirm the identification of the Natufian mice populations as including both forms of this self-domesticated rodent.

The study of Natufian skeletal remains indicates that

they were generally healthy, with a stature of 153–160 cm (i.e., ca. 60–62.5 inches), a life expectancy of 32–35, and about 20–30 percent mortality of children 0–12 years old. Teeth attrition demonstrates (except for the Kebara sample) the eating of ground and pounded substances. Thus Natufian economy seems to have been a mixture of hunting and gathering of a large variety of foodstuffs which enabled the survival of larger groups. During the 11th millennium B.C. (based on uncalibrated C14 dates), the Near Eastern climate returned to cold and dry conditions. Natufian adaptations were slightly changed, but the most prominent example of efforts to retain the traditional lifeways are the archaeological remains of Late Natufian groups in the Negeb and N Sinai, who developed some special regional attributes and are therefore known as the Harifian culture.

The Harifian sites demonstrate a well-defined distribution. The small sites (sometimes less than 100 m^2) are dispersed in the lowlands (which in N Sinai and the W Negeb are covered with sand dunes). The larger sites were uncovered in the highlands of the Negeb, on the plateau of Har Harif and its vicinity which lies 1000 m above sea level. The sites contain semisubterranean buildings, often lined with stones. Mortars, pestles, grinding stones, and slabs with numerous cupholes are found either inside the huts or around them. The lithic industry is Natufian-like with numerous microliths dominated by lunates but with the inclusion of what seems to be a desertic projectile point—the Harif point. This is a microlithic point, with a rhomboid form, modified by abrupt retouch and microburin technique. Animal bones include mainly gazelle, ibex, and hare. No plant remains were recovered and charcoal samples indicate a similar vegetation, probably with a better cover of *Pistacia atlantica.* Radiocarbon dates indicate a distribution between 8700 and 8000 B.C. (uncalibrated). Taking into account the problems of "dead wood," typical to desertic sites, these dates could be interpreted as indicating the presence of humans during only one or two centuries.

B. Neolithic

The Natufian culture marks an important threshold in the cultural and social evolution in the Levant. The emergence of sedentary and semisedentary communities in which the social unit was larger than the smaller Paleolithic band demonstrates a change in human organization. Under the climatic circumstances prevailing in the Levant around 8000 B.C., with the increase of annual precipitation and an additional rise of temperatures, the adoption of systematic harvesting of natural stands of cereals led to the establishment of permanent farming communities. In these new and large villages, such as Jericho, Netiv Hagdud, and Gilgal (in the Jordan Valley), cultivation of barley was practiced. See GILGAL (PREHISTORIC SITES).

Archaeological observations dated to the Early Neolithic period (8300/8000–6000/5800 B.C.) provide ample evidence for the contemporary presence of farmer-hunters and hunter-gatherers in the S Levant. The sown land, which is a narrow "corridor" stretching from the Damascus basin through the W edges of the Transjordanian plateau into the Jordan Valley and the Edom Mountains (S Transjordan), was inhabited by the earliest cultivators. The coastal belt and the deserts were occupied by hunter-gatherers, who continued to survive while interacting with the villagers. While agriculture as a subsistence strategy expanded, the Lebanese mountains and the arid region remained the primary territories of hunter-gatherers, who continued their mutual exchange (food and commodities) with the farming communities.

Current researchers use a variety of archaeological terms to describe the material culture of the Neolithic period. Terms such as "Pre-Pottery Neolithic" or "Aceramic Neolithic" interchange with Archaic or Early Neolithic. The use of chronological terms such as Period 1, 2, 3, . . . etc., is based on C14 dates which are currently subject to calibration. In order to keep the basic terminology in line with those used in Palestinian archaeology, the terminology proposed by K. Kenyon during her excavations in Jericho will be used.

1. Pre-Pottery Neolithic (PPN). The number of sites excavated and studied from the Pre-Pottery Neolithic A (PPNA) (8300–7300/7200 B.C.) is small. Most of them were found in the Jordan Valley or the adjacent slopes of the Jordan Rift. On the basis of lithic studies, this period was subdivided into two phases—the Khiamian and the Sultanian. The Khiamian lithic assemblages contain moderate frequencies of microliths (mainly lunates and retouched bladelets), perforators, burins, some sickle blades, and arrowheads mostly of the El-Khiam type (a small projectile with bilateral notches near the often retouched base). The Sultanian contains the same components with the addition of axes-adzes and polished celts. Unfortunately the Khiamian is known from only one unicultural site (Salibiya IX) and from two sites where the Khiamian assemblages are partially mixed with the underlying Late Natufian industry (HATULA, El-Khiam Terrace). The Sultanian is well represented in Jericho, Netiv Hagdud, Gilgal, Gesher, and Hatula. It is possible that the Khiamian, as an archaeological phenomenon, represents the actual transition from the Natufian to the Early Neolithic, and the overlapping radiocarbon dates only indicate that this transition was a rather rapid change, which deserves the definition of the "Neolithic Revolution."

An additional aspect of this major cultural change is site size. PPNA sites vary in size from 2.5 hectares (Jericho), through 1.5–1.0 (Netiv Hagdud and Gilgal), to the smallest occupations of this period in the desert, which hardly cover 100 m^2. Minimal demographic estimates would suggest a population of 150 persons per hectare and thus a large village like Jericho probably had a population of about 450 people. If such minimal estimates are correct, then the largest villages held a sufficiently large social unit to maintain their biological vitality. Such a group size is a significant departure from the previous Paleolithic period.

The Sultanian architectural remains are best known from the excavations of JERICHO. The so-called "town wall," built of undressed stones 1.8 m thick and 3.5 m high, was exposed in the W trench. In front of the wall was a 3.5 m wide shallow ditch dug into the chalky bedrock. Behind the wall, inside the settlement, is the rounded tower, 8.5 m high, built of stone and covered with a thin layer of mud, with a small door and interior staircase with 22 steps. On the N side of the tower, a few large and deep rounded structures built of mudbricks were exposed. The "town wall" according to Kenyon's observations, was removed by erosion on the N end of the village and is only 1.6 m thick on the S end. The conventional interpretation is that the wall and the tower were part of a fortification system against human aggression. The ample evidence for the role of erosion evidenced in Jericho and neighboring sites in the lower Jordan Valley led to the alternative interpretation that the defense system was built in order to protect the settlement from flooding. Apparently, the PPNA period was wetter and slightly warmer than the preceding millennium. These conditions secured the success of the early farming communities, which otherwise under climatic conditions similar to today's, with frequent droughts, would have retreated to better-watered areas.

Domestic architecture is represented in Jericho, Netiv Hagdud, Gilgal, and Hatula in oval houses, the foundations of which were dug into earlier levels, which were lined with stones and a superstructure built of mudbricks. The shape of the roof is somewhat unclear, but some collapsed examples indicate that they had a flat roof with wooden beams and mats covered with mud. On the floors there is evidence for the use of mud and plaster. Mats covered the floors. Hearths were embedded into the floors, generally forming a sort of a shallow, well-paved basin. Some of the houses or structures were rounded with a smaller diameter of about 3 m. The walls were built of mudbricks which often have a planoconvex cross-section. Mud as a building material was brought from the vicinity of the site and thus "foreign elements" such as flints from earlier sites were incorporated in the site's deposits.

While burials are absent from some sites (such as Gilgal), they are otherwise found in various places, including situations which are often interpreted as under the floors. It is conceivable that some burials took place in open spaces which were later built up. Building required leveling and thus some burials, or storage installations, stratigraphically occur under the floors. Burials are generally single and only from adults were skulls removed while leaving the jaw in place. No grave goods were encountered in any of the sites.

The lithic industry of the PPNA is generally characterized by the production of blades, bladelets, and flakes. It differs from the Natufian by having much lower frequencies of microliths even in the desertic sites such as Abu Madi I in S Sinai. Among the retouched pieces, there are small projectiles such as El-Khiam point and a few others with a small tang or with a triangular shape. Perforators are common as are burins. Sickle blades are often plain and a few bear bifacial retouch and are known as Beit Ta'amir knives. The group of bifacial tools include axes-adzes (in which the transverse removal shaped the working edge; i.e., Tahunian axes), chisels (with narrow working edges), and picks. Polished celts made of basalt and limestone occur as well. In the desert sites, sickle blades and bifacial tools are missing. Instead higher frequencies of scrapers were noted. Retouched or used blades are common in most of PPNA assemblages.

Art objects are quite rare, but small figurines exist, which are made either of limestone or clay. A common type is the sitting female (most notably known from Netiv Hagdud), a female with a string skirt and birds (Gilgal), and schematic figurines of kneeling females (?) from Salibiya IX and Nahal Oren. It seems that the small number of excavations and the small areas dug in the sites are responsible for the poor sample of artistic representations.

The economic basis of the Sultanian villages was a mixture of cultivation of emmer (in the Damascus plain), barley, and legumes. Fruits and wild seeds, including nuts and acorns, were collected. Gazelle and foxes were the main game animals in the Jordan Valley with some fallow deer, bovids, and hare. Water fowl trapping was a major seasonal activity for the collectors in the village, and several species of ducks are evident. The health of the population (as inferred from the skeletal remains) was comparable to that of the earlier Natufian period. Similar frequencies of child burials are recorded. In some cases in Jericho skull deformation was practiced *in vivo.*

It is impossible to separate the cultural changes that took place in Palestine from those of the entire Levant. Although agriculture as a subsistence strategy was first established in the central and S Levant, it rapidly diffused northward and the ensuing technological changes in the N Levant began by the mid-8th millennium B.C. (uncalibrated).

The following period, the Pre-Pottery Neolithic B (PPNB; ca. 7300/7200–6000/5800 B.C. uncalibrated), is better known from Palestine and other parts of the Near East. It was recently suggested, on the basis of stratigraphic evidence from AIN GHAZAL (near Amman) to name the latest portion of this period as PPNC.

Climatic conditions during the PPNB were wetter than in the PPNA, at least until the second half of the 7th millennium B.C. (uncalibrated). Site size increased considerably, especially when the sizes of the largest sites of each period are compared. The surface size of Ain Ghazal is 12 hectares, Basta is 12 hectares, Beisamoun is 12, Yiftahel is 4, and Jericho is 2.5 hectares. The largest sites are about five times larger than the largest known PPNA sites. Even if the increase in size took only 500 years, it still reflects a population increase which is evident not only in the lusher areas of Palestine, but also in the desert region in the Negeb and Edom, where relatively large PPNB sites were discovered and several were excavated.

The change in domestic architecture, which among other archaeological criteria led K. Kenyon to propose her subdivision, is neatly expressed in the houses with a rectangular plan exposed in Jericho, Ain Ghazal, YIFTAHEL, Munhatta, Beisamoun, and Nahal Oren. The excavations in Beidha demonstrate that the appearance of rectangular houses was preceded, at least at this site, by polygonal buildings, where the roof was supported with wooden posts. The use of lime plaster for building floors and coating lower portions of the walls, as well as storage facilities, is recorded from various sites. This practice is not evenly distributed within the sites, and is therefore understood to indicate socioeconomic hierarchies. In Ain Ghazal, the preservation of postholes implies the use of timber, and in the later phases of the site's history, the diminishing of this resource is reflected in smaller spaces and fewer posts.

PPNB burials are found under floors and in open spaces. Skulls of adults were removed and in a few sites nests of skulls were found. Better known are the plastered skulls uncovered in Jericho, Beisamoun, and Ain Ghazal (as well as Tel Ramad in S Syria). An additional method of treating skulls was discovered in Nahal Hemar cave (Judean Desert), where the skulls were modeled in asphalt. There is a consensus that the special treatment of the skulls is a direct evidence for the "ancestors' cult." This is possibly supported by the important discovery of a cache of plaster statues of humans in Ain Ghazal. Similar, but fragmentary, remains were also found in Jericho and Nahal Hemar cave. The human statues, made of lime plaster and modeled on reed skeletons, represent males and females. The fashion in which they were constructed recalls the Mesopotamian legend of the creation of man, perhaps indicating the antiquity of this myth.

Additional insights on either domestic or cultic activities are gained from the numerous clay figurines which represent pregnant females, males, and animals, including oxen, sheep, goat, as well as some wild species. A cache of human figurines, stone masks, modeled skulls, and numerous domestic objects in a small, dark cave in Nahal Hemar in the S end of the Judean Desert indicates that ritual activities also encompassed special sites which perhaps marked territorial ownership.

The PPNB lithic industry differs from its predecessor by the heavy reliance on blade removal from bipolar cores, which in their more elaborate, elongated form, are known as "naviform" cores. The punched blades were shaped into arrowheads, perforators, burins, sickle blades, or simply used in their original shape. The typological changes in arrowhead types proved to be chronological indicators for the subdivision of the PPNB and for marking prehistoric provinces within the Levant. The earliest types are the Helwan point (with bilateral notches and a tang) and the Jericho point (with wings or clear-cut shoulders and a tang) and the later types are the Byblos point (leaf-shaped with a tang) and the Amuq point (leaf-shaped). The two latter types are often shaped by flat pressure flaking.

Sickle blades are either plain blades (which bear the luster resulting from the harvesting of cereals) or elongated, tanged blades, often finely serrated. A complete curved sickle made from a bent ibex horn, in which were three blades which had been attached with resin, was found in Nahal Hemar cave. Sickle blades are generally found only in sites within the sown land.

Burins are common in many, but not all, sites. In Transjordan there is a geographic province which stretches into the Syro-Arabian desert where burins are the most common tool type.

The group of bifacial tools including axe-adzes and celts see some changes through time. While in most early and middle PPNB sites, the Tahunian (tranchet) types dominate, there is a shift in the later PPNB to objects with rounded retouched or polished working edges. Triangular shapes increase in frequency. Desert sites contain none of these types, which seem to have been used in cutting and working wood and sometimes served as hoes.

Imported raw materials such as obsidian, which had first appeared in the Late Natufian, are more frequent in some PPNB sites although not necessarily at the large ones. The mechanism responsible for the distribution of this commodity is still poorly understood. Other exotic raw materials include greenstone (serpentine, malachite, rosasite), from which beads and pendants were made. Marine shells were collected on the shores of the Mediterranean and the Red Sea and distributed through the Levant. It seems that cowries *(Cyprea sp.)* and *Glycimerys sp.* are among the commonly used species. The preference for these forms marks a departure from the more *Dentalium*-shell-dominated assemblages of the Natufian and the PPNA.

The PPNB village economy was based on cultivation of domesticated species of cereals and legumes with the continuous collection of wild fruits and seeds. Hunting gazelles, along with a few roe deer, fallow deer, wild boar, and hare was supplemented in the villages (which were located within the core area of farming communities) by raising goats and sheep.

The domestication of goats and sheep is a controversial issue. While wild goats occur in the faunal collections of Epi-Paleolithic and PPNA sites (although in very small percentages), wild sheep were apparently absent from the original wild fauna of the Levant. Goats and sheep were most of the hunted game in the Zagros Mountains since Mousterian times. There is ample evidence to indicate that the domestication of these herd mammals took place during the Early Neolithic period in the Zagros region and perhaps in the E Taurus. The exchange networks which enabled the incorporation of domesticated cereals into the Zagros economy were probably responsible for the introduction of goats and sheep into the Levant. Thus, the shift in the faunal spectra is reflected in the PPNB sites, which in Palestine are located within the "corridor" which runs from the Damascus basin through the Jordan Valley. It is only in later times that both the W hilly slopes of Palestine and the desert fringes in Transjordan acquired the domesticated species.

In the late stages of the PPNB, new domestic objects were introduced. These products are known as the "White Ware," which is made of a mixture of ashes and plaster. The forms include bowls, open jars, and bowls on pedestals. Most of those are known from N Syria, and they rarely occur in Palestinian contexts.

The end of the PPNB period is not as clear as its beginning. Many sites were abandoned. The abandonment of villages either during the PPNA or the PPNB is an issue which has never received an adequate treatment. Suggested reasons which might cause a population to move out or not to return to their home base may include group aggression, salinization of fields, mortal epidemic, and temptation to move to an empty and a better environment. The "collapse" of the PPNB in the S Levant is known to have been a major break or an abrupt change of settlement pattern. In the site of Ain Ghazal, where this phase is named "PPNC," there is sufficient evidence to demonstrate the presence of two cultural changes. The first is signified by a change in the lithic industry and mortuary practices. The main core reduction strategy was based on the production of flakes and to a lesser extent of blades. The dominant tool types are burins, with low frequencies of other formal tool types including arrowheads. Burials were less organized and with no evidence for skull removal.

The second cultural change brought about the establishment of what is known as the Yarmukian culture, the assemblages of which contain ceremics. This introduction is part of the definition of the following period.

2. Pottery Neolithic (PN). The Pottery Neolithic is a

poorly known period, mainly because of a major change in settlement pattern. This change is archaeologically expressed in two ways: (1) in stratified sites the PN remains are found in numerous pits of various sizes which often penetrated and disturbed the wealth of PPNB rectangular buildings (Jericho, Munhatta, Beisamoun, etc.), and (2) many new settlements were established either in the Jordan Valley (Sha'ar Hagolan) or along the coastal plain. Most of these were abandoned after some time and their remains provide excellent examples of unicultural assemblages.

The invention of pottery and its introduction to domestic use took place first in the N Levant and later in Palestine. As mentioned above, the "White Ware" is made of lime plaster mixed with ashes. Clay pots outnumber in Palestine the White Ware products and the common forms are simple, including jars, cooking pots, and bowls. These were decorated first with chevron pattern and red paint and later by painting alone.

The economy of this period is based on the cultivation of cereals and legumes, herding goats and sheep, raising pigs in the more humid parts of the country, and some cattle. The activities of pastoral nomads, who partially subsisted on herding goats, are reflected in numerous desert sites. These groups continued to hunt and were possibly exchanging meat and other products for carbohydrates with the farming communities.

Evidence for burials is still rare, but indicates a shift from the earlier pattern. One burial under a small built-up cairn of rocks was exposed in Sha'ar Hagolan. Single flexed and semiflexed burials were found in other sites. Further indications concerning belief systems are reflected in clay and stone figurines. The Yarmukian culture, represented to date in Sha'ar Hagolan, Munhatta, Ain Ghazal, and Jericho, is famous for the female clay figurines which depict seated women, with tall headgear and a mask on the face, but exposed breasts. Schematic images of the same female were incised on river pebbles. The minimal representations kept the slanted eyes or the female organ. Additional patterns on the pebbles are the network and series of parallel lines.

Temples or shrines are as yet unknown from the more sedentary sites, but occur mainly in the desert sites. An open temple found in Biqat Uvda has an open courtyard and a small enclosure in one corner with miniature steles of undressed stones. Two small pebble-coated pits, which contained charcoal, were uncovered in the courtyard. Rock figures were found on the surface just outside the shrine. These were made by planting small stones which depict a series of panthers and one antelope. Panthers, more than lions, seem to have been part of the animal imagery of the Neolithic religious world.

The distribution of the PN sites in Palestine reflects a settlement pattern which was based on cultivation and herding with seasonal mobility. The investment in the more permanent sites seems to have been less than in the PPNB period and probably points toward a less anticipated pattern of mobility. It might reflect the unstable climatic conditions which by the mid-Holocene were changing from a stable pattern of precipitation to one which resembles much more today's unpredictable pattern.

C. Chalcolithic

The Chalcolithic period (5000–3500 B.C. calibrated) marks the establishment of a typical Mediterranean socioeconomic structure based on large and small communities, which practiced cultivation of cereals and legumes, herding goats and sheep, some cattle, raising pigs in suitable areas, and tending a variety of fruit trees. There are some regional subcultures, and in a few cases several scholars view them as chiefdoms. In the arid region, both pastoral nomads and seasonal herders from villages exploited the natural pastures maintaining constant interaction.

Several cultural attributes characterize the subregions and are archaeologically expressed in particular architectural remains and pottery types. It should be stressed that, contemporaneously, major urban centers were already established in Mesopotamia and the emergence of large human organizations—chiefdoms and states—was underway. By the end of the Chalcolithic period in Palestine, writing systems were employed in Mesopotamia and Egypt, and there is ample evidence of connections between the Sumerians and the Egyptians.

The Chalcolithic period suffers from the same taxonomical problems as almost every other archaeological period. Its earliest phase, which certain scholars still call "Late Pottery Neolithic" (spanning the last third of the 6th and first half of the 5th millennia B.C.) is sometimes known as the "Wadi Rabah culture," the sites of which were found only in N and central Palestine. Most of the sites of the second half of the 5th and first half of the 4th millennia contain the remains of the Ghassulian culture (named after Tuleilat el-Ghassul, a site in the lower Jordan Valley, across the river, and E of Jericho). However, in the Negeb, which is one of the most studied subregions, a sequence of local entities, beginning with the Qatifian (ca. 4500–4000 B.C.), followed by the Besor phase and then the Beersheba-Ghassulian culture (ca. 4000–3500/3300 B.C.) was suggested. See RABAH, WADI; GHASSUL, TULEILAT EL-; and BEER-SHEBA.

The climate of the Chalcolithic period was and is a subject for debate. The palynological evidence and the deposition of the loess in the N Negeb suggest a humid period with considerable precipitation in the S. The plant remains from the site of Shiqmim were interpreted as indicating a climate similar to today's. However, it is difficult to understand how the Negeb sites had flourished, while subsisting on farming and herding in an area with repeated droughts without economic support from a central political power. A low-level regional social organization (i.e., chiefdom) is inferred from the archaeological remains. Hence, favorable environmental conditions seem essential for the survival of semidesert Chalcolithic communities during the 4th millennium B.C.

The Wadi Rabah culture, considered here as Early Chalcolithic, is known from sites in the Upper Jordan Valley, the coastal plain, Mt. Carmel area, and the lower Galilee. It is characterized by the pottery known as Dark Face Burnished Ware. Some of the pots are angular, with red, brown, and black color and decorated with incisions, fingerprints, shell prints, and clay relief. Other types include the bow-rim jars. In some sites evidence for the influence of the Halafian culture (known from N Syria and S Turkey) is inferred from the ornamentation of the pots with geometric bicolor designs. The lithic artifacts are shaped in the forms which were common during the Chalcolithic period such as backed sickle blades, adzes with planoconvex longitudinal cross-section, robust perforators, cortical scrapers, and the lack of arrowheads.

The houses exposed in small excavations are either square or rectangular, built on stone foundations. Similar structures were uncovered in other sites which are not included in the Wadi Rabah entity, in other parts of the country. Additional common attributes are within the economic realm. All sites were those of farmers and herders. Because of the similarity of the material remains with the following millennium, the only reliable way to differentiate them is with C14 dates. It seems that communities of pastoral nomads continued to evolve in the Near Eastern desert, and still relied on herding goats and sheep. Most scholars view as autochtonic the development of Palestinian society from this phase into the Late Chalcolithic.

The Ghassulian culture is better known and is represented by a wide distribution of sites, mostly villages and hamlets of various sizes, often located on alluvial terraces. The basic house plan was the broad room type, with the entrance in one of the long walls of the house. Sometimes it is subdivided with one or two small rooms at the ends. Storage installations were built inside the houses or in the courtyards (which in Tuleilat el-Ghassul were encircled). In the Beer-sheba region subterranean rooms and tunnels, carved into the loess, were exposed by J. Perrot and other archaeologists. These unusual features ignited debate regarding their function. However, the objects found inside the underground rooms and tunnels indicate that they were intentionally closed, but the inhabitants never returned to retrieve their belongings.

Special buildings or compounds either (1) occupied a special topographic location, such as the temple of En Gedi, (2) were specifically decorated, such as the house with the frescos in Ghassul, or (3) contained special vessels and artifacts like the one in Gilat. The presence of temples or shrines is not a major change, as already noted above. This phenomenon began at least during the Neolithic when social cohesion among farming communities required a more permanent establishment. In this context the hoard found in a cave in Nahal Mishmar should be mentioned. The large collection of cult objects which include standards decorated with maceheads, animal figures, scepters, "crowns," decorated animal figures, doors (which resemble the ossuaries), standards, carved hippo tusks with numerous well-oriented holes, and numerous maceheads was related to the En Gedi temple. However, petrographic analysis of pottery derived from the two sites did not confirm this hypothesis. A similar analysis illuminated the important place of the temple exposed in Gilat, one of the Negeb village sites where two ceramic figurines were uncovered. One of these depicts a seated woman carrying a churn on her head while the other one is a ram with three cornets on its back. To the general description of cultic objects one should add the ivory male and female human figurines from Bir es-Safadi, near Beer-sheba, the schematic basalt face carvings known as the pillar statues from the Golan, and the numerous "fiddle" figurines, found in various sites, which sometimes were made of foreign metamorphic rocks and were brought into Palestine.

Mortuary practices are signified by the establishment of cemeteries which lie outside the habitation area. Such cemeteries with circular graves or tumuli were exposed in Adeimeh and near Shiqmim. Others were found in dugout caves in the kurkar (sandstone) ridges in the coastal plain. Clay ossuaries are an additional attribute of this culture. They have two basic forms, either circular like a jar with an opening at the top, or rectangular like a "house" with an opening in the narrow side. Both types were interpreted by M. Dunan as representing silos. The "house"-type ossuaries often have legs and a door in the upper part of the narrow side, a trait which resembles silos much more than the typical broad-room Chalcolithic house. Some of the ossuaries were decorated on the front pediment with attributes (e.g., horns) similar to those common on the Golan pillar statues or in the hoard of Nahal Mishmar, thus indicating a common belief system.

Craft specialization in the Chalcolithic is reflected in the lithic, pottery, and especially the metal assemblages. Among the lithics, the frequent tool types are adzes with the planoconvex cross sections, the scrapers on tabular flint (which seem to have been a trade item), backed sickle blades, some microlithic tools, and hammer stones. A special tool type is the starlike, perforated, bifacially retouched disk.

Ceramic technology was marked by the introduction of the slow wheel (tournette), the production of V-shaped bowls, the cornets (which are the hallmark of the Ghassulian), the churns (used for butter production), and a variety of pots including large pithoi, holemouth vessels, globular jars, basins, footed vessels, and vessels with multiple handles. Clay was used to construct large storage jars (i.e., pithoi) as tall as 2 m; these were decorated with rope designs. Pottery decorations, however, were minimal and the "hanging triangle," red painted stripes, and rope motifs in relief seem to have been the common ones.

Two other raw materials received careful attention by the artisans of this period—basalt and ivory. Basalt objects included, besides the traditional mortars, grinding bowls, pestles, handstones, fenestrated bowl stands, delicately shaped V-shaped bowls, and pillar statues. Ivory craftsmanship was well done and a workshop was discovered in Bir es-Safadi (Beer-sheba). Both elephant and hippopotamus tusks were exploited. Additional raw materials, which have been used, include mined malachite and turquoise which were quarried in Feinan, TIMNA (PLACE), and S Sinai. In addition to making beads and pendants, the Chalcolithic period is marked by the development of metallurgy.

The main evidence concerning the metallurgical achievements of this period come from the hoard of Nahal Mishmar cave (Judean Desert). The spectrographic analysis indicates that the mace heads and probably most of the elaborate forms were made by the lost wax-casting technique. Copper mines and smelting installations were uncovered in Timnaᶜ, but the full picture of the entire exploitation system (including investment in labor, food supplies for workers, exact sourcing, etc.) is not well documented.

The transition from the Chalcolithic to the Early Bronze

period is again not a simple subject for discussion. However, by the end of this social process, urban centers emerged in Palestine and thus marked another threshold in the history of the country.

Bibliography

Amiran, R.; Beck, P.; and Zevulun, U. 1970. *Ancient Pottery of the Holy Land.* New Jersey.

Arensburg, B., and Bar-Yosef, O. 1973a. Human Remains from Ein Gev I, Jordan Valley, Israel. *Paleorient* 1: 201–6.

———. eds. 1973b. *Eretz Israel* 13.

Arensburg, B., and Hershkovitz, I. 1988. Nahal Hemar Cave: Neolithic Human Remains. *ᶜAtiqot* 18: 50–58.

Aurenche, O.; Evin, J.; and Hours, F., eds. 1987. *Chronologies in the Near East.* BARIS 379. Oxford.

Bar-Yosef, O. 1980. Prehistory of the Levant. *Annual Review of Anthropology* 9: 101–33.

———. 1986. The Walls of Jericho: An Alternative Interpretation. *Current Anthropology* 27: 157–62.

———. 1987a. Late Pleistocene Adaptations in the Levant. Pp. 214–36 in *Old World Pleistocene: Regional Perspectives,* ed. O. Soffer. New York.

———. 1987b. Pleistocene Connexions between Africa and Southwest Asia: An Archaeological Perspective. *African Archaeological Review* 5: 29–38.

Bar-Yosef, O., and Alon, D. 1988. Nahal Hemir Cave: The Excavations. *ᶜAtiqot* 18: 1–30.

Bar-Yosef, O., and Belfer-Cohen, A. 1988. The Early Upper Palaeolithic in Levantine Caves. Pp. 23–41 in *Early Upper Paleolithic,* ed. J. H. Hoffeker and C. A. Wolf. BARIS 437. Oxford.

Bar-Yosef, O., and Tchernov, E. 1972. *On the Palaeoecological History of the Site of ᶜUbeidiya.* Publications of the Israel Academy of Sciences and Humanities. Jerusalem.

Bar-Yosef, O., and Vandermeersch, B., eds. 1989. *Investigations in South Levantine Prehistory/Préhistoire du Sud-Levant.* BARIS 497. Oxford.

Bennett, C.-M. 1980. Soundings at Dhea, Jordan. *Levant* 12: 30–39.

Bintliff, J. L., and van Zeist, W., eds. 1982. *Paleoclimates, Paleoenvironments and Human Communities in the Eastern Mediterranean Region in Later Prehistory.* BARIS 133. Oxford.

Cauvin, J. 1978. *Les premiers villages de Syrie-Palestine du IXème au VIIème millénaire avant J.C.* Lyon.

Cauvin, J., and Sanlaville, P., eds. 1981. *Prehistoire du Levant.* Centre national de la recherche scientifique 598. Paris.

Clark, J. D. 1975. A Comparison of the Late Achenian Industries of Africa and the Middle East. Pp. 605–60 in *After the Australopithecus,* ed. K. W. Butzer and G. L. Isaac. Hague.

———. 1982. The Transition from Lower to Middle Palaeolithic in the African Continent. Pp. 235–55 in Ronen, A., ed. 1982.

Clutton-Brock, J. 1981. *Domesticated Animals from Early Times.* Austin.

Epstein, C. 1977. The Chalcolithic Culture of the Golan. *BA* 40: 57–62.

Garfinkel, Y. 1987. Yiftahel: A Neolithic Village from the Seventh Millennium B.C. in Lower Galilee, Israel. *Journal of Field Archaeology* 14: 199–212.

Garrad, A. N., and Gebel, H. G., eds. 1986. *The Prehistory of Jordan, The State of Research in 1986,* Part i. BARIS 396. Oxford.

Garrod, D. A. E., and Bate, D. M. 1937. *Stone Age of Mount Carmel.* Vol. 1. Oxford.

Gilead, I. 1983. Upper Palaeolithic Occurrences in Sinai and the Transition to the Epi-Palaeolithic in the Southern Levant. *Paleorient* 9: 39–54.

———. 1988. The Chalcolithic Period in the Levant. *Journal of World Prehistory* 2/4: 397–443.

Gilead, I., and Grigson, C. 1984. Farah II: A Middle Palaeolithic Open Air Site in the Northern Negev, Israel. *Proceedings of the Prehistoric Society* 50: 71–97.

Goldberg, P. 1986. Late Quarternary Environmental History of the Southern Levant. *Geoarchaeology* 1: 225–44.

Goren-Inbar, N. 1985. The Lithic Assemblage of the Berekhat Ram Acheulian Site, Golan Heights. *Paleorient* 11: 7–28.

Goring-Morris, A. N. 1987. *At the Edge.* BARIS 361. Oxford.

Hennessy, J. B. 1982. Teleilat el Ghassul: Its Place in the Archaeology of Jordan. Pp. 55–58 in *Studies in the History and Archaeology of Jordan.* Vol. 1, ed. A. Hadidi. Amman.

Henry, D. O. 1983. Adaptive Evolution within the Epi-Palaeolithic of the Near East. Pp. 99–160 *Advances in World Archaeology,* vol. 2, ed. F. Wendorf and A. E. Close. New York.

———. 1985. The Natufian Example. Pp. 365–84 in *Prehistoric Hunter-Gatherers: The Emergence of Cultural Complexity,* ed. T. D. Price and J. Brown. New York.

———. 1989. *From Foraging to Agriculture.* Philadelphia.

Hershkovitz, I., ed. 1989. *People and Culture in Change.* BARIS 508. Oxford.

Horowitz, A. 1979. *The Quarternary of Israel.* New York.

Jelinek, A. J. 1982a. The Middle Palaeolithic in the Southern Levant with Comments of the Appearance of Modern *Homo Sapiens.* Pp. 57–104 in Ronen, A., ed. 1982.

———. 1982b. The Tabun Cave and Paeolithic Man in the Levant. *Science* 216: 1369–75.

Kenyon, K. M. 1957. *Digging Up Jericho.* London.

———. 1979. *Archaeology in the Holy Land.* 4th ed. London.

Kenyon, K. M., and Holland, T. A. 1981. *Excavations at Jericho.* Vol. 3. London.

———. 1982. *Excavations at Jericho.* Vol. 4. London.

———. 1983. *Excavations at Jericho.* Vol. 5. London.

Kirkbride, D. 1966. Five Seasons at the Pre-Pottery Neolithic Village of Beidha in Jordan. *PEQ* 88: 8–72.

Levy, T. E. 1983. Chalcolithic Settlement Pattern in the Northern Negev Desert. *Current Archaeology* 24: 105–7.

———. 1986. The Chalcolithic Period. *BA* 49/2: 83–108.

Marks, A. E. 1983b. The Middle to Upper Palaeolithic Transition in the Levant. *Advances in World Archaeology* 2: 51–98.

Marks, A. E., and Ferring, C. R. 1988. The Early Upper Paleolithic of the Levant. Pp. 43–72 in *Early Upper Paleolithic,* ed. F. Hoffeker and C. A. Wolf. BARIS 437. Oxford.

Moore, A. M. T., 1985. The Development of Neolithic Societies in the Near East. *Advances in World Archaeology* 4: 1–69.

Muheisin, M. 1985. L'Epipaleolithique dans le gisement de Khoraneh IV. *Paleorient* 11: 149–60.

Neuville, R. 1951. Le paleolithique et le Mesolithique du desert de Judee. *24e Memoire des Archives de L'Institut de Paleantologie Humaine.* Paris.

Noy, T.; Schuldenrien, J.; and Tchernov, E. 1980. Gilgal, A Pre-Pottery Neolithic A Site in the Lower Jordan Valley. *IEJ* 30: 63–82.

Ohel, M. 1986. *The Acheulian of the Yiron Plateau.* BARIS 307. Oxford.

Perrot, J. 1968. La Prehistoire Palestinienne. *DBSup* 8: 286–446.

Phillips, J. L. 1987. Sinai during the Palaeolithic: The Early Periods. Pp. 106–22 in *Prehistory of Arid North Africa,* ed. A. E. Close. Dallas.

Roe, D., ed. 1983. *Adlun in the Stone Age.* BARIS 159. Oxford.
Rollefson, G. O. 1985. The 1983 Season at the Early Neolithic Site of Ain Chazel. *National Geographic Research* 1: 44–62.
Ronen, A., ed. 1982. *Transition from Lower to Middle Palaeolithic and the Origin of Modern Man.* BARIS 151. Oxford.
———. 1984. *Sefunim Prehistoric Sites, Mount Carmel, Israel.* BARIS 230. Oxford.
Ronen, A., and Vandermeersch, B. 1972. The Upper Palaeolithic Sequence in the Cave of Qafza (Israel). *Quaternaria* 16: 189–262.
Ronen, A.; Ohel, M.; Lamdan, M.; and Assaf, A. 1980. Acheulian Artifacts from Two Trenches at Ma'ayan Baruch. *IEJ* 30: 17–33.
Rust, A. 1950. *Die Hohlenfunde von Jabrud (Syrien).* Neumunster.
Schwarcz, H.; Goldberg, P.; and Blackwell, B. 1980. Uranium Series Dating of Archaeological Sites in Israel. *Journal of Earth Sciences* 29: 157–65.
Sherrat, A. 1983. The Secondary Exploitation of Animals in the Old World. *World Archaeology* 15: 90–104.
Suzuki, H., and Takai, F. 1970. *Amud Man and his Cave Site.* Tokyo.
Tchernov, E. 1968. *Succession of Rodent Faunas during the Upper Pleistocene of Israel.* Hamburg.
———. 1984. Commensal Animals and Human Sedentism in the Middle East. Pp. 91–116 in *Animals and Archaeology,* vol. 3, ed. J. Clutton-Brock and C. Grigson. BARIS 202. Oxford.
———. 1987. The Age of the ʿUbeidiya Formation, an Early Pleistocene Hominid Site in the Jordan Valley, Israel. *Israel Journal of Earth Sciences* 36: 3–30.
Trinkaus, E. 1984. Western Asia. Pp. 251–93 in *Origins of Modern Humans: A World Survey of the Fossil Evidence,* ed. F. H. Smith and F. Spencer. New York.
Unger-Hamilton, R. 1989. Epi-Paleolithic Southern Levant and the Origins of Cultivation. *Current Archaeology* 30/1: 88–103.
Vandermeersch, B. 1981. *Les Hommes Fossiles de Qafzeh (Israel).* Centre national de la recherche scientifique. Paris.
———. 1982. The First *Homo Sapiens* in the Near East. Pp. 294–300 in Ronen, A., ed. 1982.
Wendorf, F., and Marks, E. A., eds. *Problems in Prehistory: North Africa and the Levant.* Dallas.
Wolpoff, M. H. 1980. *Palaeo-anthropology.* New York.
Young, C. T.; Smith, Ph. E. L.; and Mortensen, P., eds. 1983. *The Hilly Flanks and Beyond.* Chicago.
Zohay, D., and Hopff, M. 1988. *Domestication of Plants in the Old World.* Oxford.

OFER BAR-YOSEF

BRONZE AND IRON AGES

Ancient Palestine was geographically a small country, situated astride the narrow coastal "land bridge" between Egypt and Syro-Mesopotamia. Its vulnerable geopolitical position, in addition to its mountainous terrain and its semiarid agricultural conditions, made the country economically unstable, politically fragmented, and constantly subject to foreign domination. Palestine was thus a marginal area compared to its great neighboring empires; but its long history and contribution to universal culture were nevertheless uniquely important.

The archaeological history of Palestine has frequently been surveyed, and detailed data on individual sites and problems will be found in many publications (see also *EAEHL*; Aharoni 1979; Shanks and Mazar 1984; Mazar 1989; and, for Transjordan, especially Hadidi 1982–89). The present treatment, therefore, confines itself to an overview, concentrating on the Bronze and Iron Ages as is typical of the divisions usually made in Syro-Palestine archaeology. See also ARCHAEOLOGY. Major attention is given to discoveries and changed opinions since about 1970.

A. The Late Chalcolithic Age
B. The Early Bronze I–IV Age
C. The Middle Bronze Age
D. The Late Bronze Age
E. The Iron I Period
F. The Iron II Period

A. The Late Chalcolithic Age (ca. 3800–3400 B.C.)

The last "prehistoric" phase preceding the Bronze Age and its rapid urban development was the Chalcolithic (or "Copper-Stone" Age). Early Chalcolithic (sometimes called "Late Neolithic," ca. 4500–3800 B.C.) is not yet well defined, but it represents a transitional phase between the long Neolithic period (ca. 9th–6th millennium B.C.; see preceding article) and distinctive village cultures of "proto-urban" type. These later Chalcolithic sites (ca. 3800–3400 B.C.) consist mostly of small villages, grouped in several complexes and marked by strongly regional cultures. Some are in the N and inland, while others are along the coast and the river valleys, and especially in the lower Jordan Valley and the N Negeb. One of the first sites extensively investigated (in the 1920s), Tuleilat al-Ghassul, at the N end of the Dead Sea, produced a large, exceptionally well planned and laid out village. Grains and cereals were grown, possibly using primitive irrigation; olives and grapes were imported from the hill country; and copper was brought from mines farther S in the Jordan Valley. A sanctuary revealed frescoes with exotic cult scenes. The lithic and ceramic industries were technically and aesthetically very advanced, and both textiles and basketry were attested. More recent excavations at Nahal Ḥever along the W Dead Sea shore have yielded dozens of very elaborate arsenical copper implements, mostly cultic, produced by a lost-wax method of casting. Near Beer-sheba, a group of similar sites, most recently Shiqmim, has produced a series of ivory male and female figurines carved in the round, copper items, exotic painted pottery, rectangular houses, the first well-preserved tombs found (of *tholos*-type, at Shiqmim), and even some evidence for runoff irrigation agriculture (again at Shiqmim). The coastal sites near Tel Aviv are characterized by secondary burials in terra-cotta painted ossuaries, some in zoomorphic form, others representing domestic houses. The latest regional Late Chalcolithic family is in the far N, as exhibited for instance at Tel Teo near Shiqmonah, a well-planned village with exceptional stone-built rectilinear houses. On the Golan heights, Claire Epstein has investigated many pastoral nomadic camps and agricultural villages, the latter characterized by broadroom dwellings, rope-molded pottery, and curious basalt anthropomorphic and zoomorphic figurines.

The general picture of the Chalcolithic is that of a highly sophisticated society, based on intensive farming, and particularly concerned with religious expression. Although still regional, it represents a further development from "tribal" to a "chiefdom" level of social organization. Indeed, the last century or two is classed by some authorities (together with the early part of the following phase) as the "Proto-Urban" horizon. In Egypt and Mesopotamia, this is the Late Predynastic and Proto-Historic period, with monumental art and architecture, and even the beginnings of writing, already in evidence (see further Levy 1986).

B. The Early Bronze I–IV Age (ca. 3400–2000 B.C.)

Early Bronze Age studies have flourished since 1970, changing our views of every phase (see further Broshi and Gophna 1984; Richard 1987). Early Bronze I, ca. 3400–3100 B.C., appears more and more as a "Proto-Urban" (Kenyon's term), transitional phase between Late Chalcolithic and the true urban Early Bronze period. Among the key sites is 'En-Shadud in the Jezreel Valley, a well-developed agricultural village founded *de novo,* with typical broadroom dwellings. In the N Shephelah, Gezer continues the Chalcolithic occupation but remains, as most sites, an unwalled village. J. A. Callaway's reexcavation of ᶜAi, N of Jerusalem, greatly clarifies older work, revealing several well-defined "pre-urban" phases. The final publication of the Jericho volumes clarifies the occupational deposits that complement Kenyon's red-painted and red-burnished ceramic groups from tombs, upon the basis of which she (like Wright) had characterized this period. Kenyon's notion of three intrusive *ethnic* groups, however, finds little favor today. Bâb edh-Dhrâᶜ in S Transjordan exhibits a pre-town phase of occupation, with early disarticulated, secondary shaft-tomb burials supplanted by articulated primary burials toward the end of EB I (Wright's "EB IB"). Renewed workup of the unpublished Tel Gath materials will almost certainly clarify the Palestinian EB I–Egyptian Late Predynastic connection already attested. At Yiftaḥel, in lower Galilee, several long oval houses clearly dated to Early Bronze I apparently lay to rest the older notion of "apsidal" dwellings as characteristic of this period. All sites thus far excavated show that city walls were first built only in the succeeding phase (the former "EB IC," or transitional phase, now generally being abandoned).

Early Bronze II, ca. 3100–2650 B.C., is now richly documented as Palestine's first, and very impressive, urban period. By "urban," we mean a "complex society" that exhibits such features as densely nucleated population, in a hierarchically tiered settlement pattern with a few large sites; a stable subsistence system, in this case based on intensified agriculture, industry, and trade; social stratification; centralized political administration (not state-level formation in Palestine, but the typical "city-state"); and monumental art and architecture. In Egypt and Mesopotamia, this first urban era comprises the Archaic/Proto-Dynastic and Early Dynastic I–II periods, with writing well in evidence, but Palestine lags somewhat behind these developments.

The most important recent EB II site is Arad, E of Beersheba, where Ruth Amiran's exceedingly important excavations since the 1960s have revealed much of the 50-acre site's city plan. It includes a massive masonry wall with many round towers; an extensive and well-laid-out domestic quarter with broadroom dwellings; a "twin temple"; a "palace"; and an enormous catchment system and deep reservoir. Among the small finds are a potsherd with a signature of Narmer, the first pharaoh of Dynasty 1 in Egypt; imported Egyptian pottery; painted Abydos wares like those found in Dynasty 1–2 tombs; and materials linking Arad with a number of EB II "colonies" of Arad found by Israelis throughout the Sinai. ᶜAi is also important, with massive city walls, several gates, and a large colonnaded temple with Egyptian Dynasty 1–2 alabaster vessels. Egyptian trade is further illustrated at ᶜEn-Besor, a way station or trading emporium at the mouth of the Wadi Gaza, which has yielded more than 30 sealings for jars (or grain sacks) of Dynasty 1 date. Across the N Sinai, Israeli archaeologists have found small EB II camps along the caravan routes with both Palestinian and Egyptian materials, further evidence of a brisk trade. Current dates for EB II, ca. 3100–2650 B.C., emphasize the long-held correlation with the Archaic period in Egypt, Dynasties 1–2, and thus provide a relatively well-fixed chronology, although somewhat higher in accordance with the current tendency to raise the date of the beginning of Dynasty 1.

Early Bronze III, ca. 2650–2350 B.C., was a period of urban collapse in the N, still poorly illuminated. As previously, it was marked by lustrous "Khirbet Kerak" red and black pottery of Anatolian derivation. In the S, recent excavations have brought to light a renewed urban phase, with even larger fortifications. The main sites are Tel Y̩armut, near Beth-shemesh, with massive embankments, city walls, towers, and gate; Lahav, near modern Gath; and Petrie's old site of Tell el-Ḥesi, reexcavated by an American expedition. At the end of this period, however, these sites declined, like those of EB II, and there were only scattered unfortified settlements (e.g., Nahal Rephaim).

Several recent discoveries in Jordan testify to the fact that the Palestinian urban EB II–III cultures flourished to a hitherto unsuspected degree in Transjordan. W. Rast and T. Schaub have excavated the extensive town site of Bâb edh-Dhrâᶜ on the Lisan, which had large defenses, a temple area, and a vast cemetery that included unique charnel houses, nearly all abandoned by EB IV. To the S, Numeira is a one-period EB III walled site, destroyed (by earthquake?) at the end of EB III. A number of other EB II–III sites are now known in Jordan through surface surveys. In the N, German and Jordanian work at Mughayir, E of Irbid, has brought to light an urban center fully comparable to those in W Palestine. S. Helms' site of Jawa, far out in the NE desert near the modern Iraqi border, was founded at the beginning of EB I, but the date of the massive fortifications is not yet clear (i.e., they may belong to the Middle Bronze citadel). The Transjordanian sites, like those of W Palestine, generally ended as *urban* sites with EB II or EB III; but S. Richard's site of Khirbet Iskander, on the Wadi Wala, flourished precisely as a walled town in EB IV, thus far unique. Then it, too, like nearly all the other large EB sites in Jordan, was abandoned entirely throughout the MB and LB Ages.

The explanation for the end of the EB II–III urban period is sought today not in "Amorite invasions," as previously, but in a complex interrelationship of causes, among them possible climatic shifts, environmental degradation, overpopulation, bureaucratic mismanagement, and possibly the diminution of international trade with the beginning of Egypt's "First Intermediate period" (Dyn. 6–11).

Early Bronze IV, ca. 2400–2000 B.C. (Albright's "Middle Bronze I," Kenyon's "Intermediate EB–MB"), was the posturban phase. A former dark age, it is now illuminated by hundreds of newly discovered small settlements and seasonal camps in the marginal zones, especially the Jordan Valley and the Negeb-Sinai. Dozens of isolated cemeteries, represented by hundreds and hundreds of shaft tombs in S Palestine, have yielded secondary disarticulated burials. Thus the settlement at Be'er Resisim in the Negeb highlands, together with the vast cemetery at Jebel Qaᶜaqīr in the Hebron hills, excavated by W. G. Dever, seem to reflect the way of life of migratory pastoral groups. In central and N Palestine, however, as well as in the Jordan Valley, an increasing number of small, permanent agricultural villages are known; most are not on the older *tell* sites, most of which remain abandoned. The new evidence seems to confirm the notion of several distinct "families," or regional cultures. The Transjordanian family may have preserved some of the urban character of the preceding EB II–III period, for S. Richard has brought to light an EB IV fortification system and urban-style occupation at Kh. Iskander, on the Wadi Wala (see further Dever 1980; Richard 1987).

Palestine appears to have been a relatively isolated hinterland of Syria in EB IV, where pastoral nomadism and rural villages characterized the socioeconomic structure. This contrasts with Syria, where in EB IV, "Palace G" at Ebla produced evidence of a network of international relations and a large archive of texts. Some contacts between Palestine and Syria are attested, however, in a few items, probably brought by migrating pastoralists or by trade, such as Syrian "caliciform" pottery at several sites in the N, and a silver goblet of provincial Ur III style found in a shaft tomb at ᶜAin es-Sâmiyeh near Jerusalem. Contacts with Egypt, which was in its own "dark age" in the First Intermediate period (ca. 2315–1999 B.C.), were nonexistent.

C. The Middle Bronze Age (ca. 2000–1500 B.C.)

The MB has been well illuminated by recent archaeological work (see further Broshi and Gophna 1986; Dever 1987). The three phases designated by Albright as "Middle Bronze IIA–C" (using "Middle Bronze I" for the previous period) are increasingly termed Middle Bronze I–III, but not all authorities yet agree on the transitions, or on the absolute dates. Israeli archaeologists recognize only an "MB IIB" (i.e., combining the last two).

The first phase (ca. 2000–1800 B.C.), coinciding almost exactly with the renascent Egyptian Dynasty 12, witnessed a major shift in settlement patterns, back to the central agricultural zone (see further Gerstenblith 1983). This entailed the reoccupation of nearly all the older urban sites and the founding of numerous new, small unwalled settlements. Many of these sites would be fortified before the end of the period. Excavations of the Tel-Aviv University since 1973 at Tel Aphek are the most revealing, combined with extensive surface surveys throughout the Sharon Plain. Aphek exhibits an unfortified "pre-palace" phase, then a "palace" phase with city walls and a palatial administrative building. The rich ceramic repertoire is in the new fast wheelmade style, often beautifully burnished and sometimes painted, which seems to reflect Syrian influence. Recent publication of the earlier excavations at Dan, Akko, Beth-shan, Shechem, Gezer, and many isolated tombs reveal the same ceramic developments, along with the introduction of new cist tombs and the introduction of true tin-bronze metallurgy—often accompanied by early earthen ramparts and city walls. At Dan there was found an almost intact triple-entryway mudbrick and plastered city gate, still standing to its original three-story height (Biran 1984).

Middle Bronze II (ca. 1800–1650 B.C.), coeval with Egyptian Dynasty 13, saw the fuller development of highly urbanized city-states, nearly all of which were fortified (see further Kempinski 1983 on this and the following phase). Recent excavations at Dan, Hazor, Akko, Kabri, Shechem, Tel Zeror, Tel Poleg, Aphek, Jerusalem, Jericho, and elsewhere further document this trend. Some sites were first founded in this period, like Ashdod and its port, Tel Mor. Egyptian imports such as scrabs and alabasters increased, and Cypriot pottery was imported on a larger scale.

The final phase, Middle Bronze III (ca. 1650–1500 B.C.), marked the zenith of urban development in Palestine, and coincided exactly with the late "Second Intermediate" period and the Semitic "Hyksos" Dynasty 15 in Egypt. New sites like Gezer, previously unwalled, were heavily fortified; while existing defenses at other sites were augmented, often with several phases of construction in evidence. The typical system consisted of *terre pisée* embankments, a plastered *glaçis* (or ramp), at least one masonry and mudbrick city wall, often an outer revetment wall, and even dry moats or fosses. Both double- and triple-entryway gates were found, and both casemate and solid walls. Even tiny forts like Tel Mevorakh and Tel Mor on the coast near Tel Aviv, or small hill country sites like Shiloh, boasted massive fortifications.

Several small villages in the Jordan Valley, among the first such sites excavated, have brought to light MB III temples surprisingly like those formerly known at large urban sites such as Megiddo and Shechem. Among them are Kfar Ruppin and Tel Kittan near Beth-shan, and Tell el-Ḥayyat across the Jordan.

Two large urban sites demonstrate the main character of the period. Shechem had a massive embankment, revetted by an outer cyclopean Wall A (still standing 10 m high) and topped by casemate Wall B. Just inside the triple-entryway NW Gate was a two-story colonnaded palace, an attached tripartite private (?) temple, a barracks or citadel adjoining the gate, a large plastered plaza, and a *migdal* (or fortress) temple similar to the area D temple at Ebla. The entire complex is closely paralleled by stratum VII at Alalakh in Syria. Gezer exhibits an even larger wall and tower system, in places more than 15 m thick (the Inner Wall and Tower 5017), together with a large triple-entryway gate and a skillfully engineered, multilayered *glaçis*. To this period belongs the Gezer "High Place," an installation of 10 large steles in a N–S alignment with a stone basin and plastered pavement, probably a cult place of some sort.

The end of MB III saw virtually every site in Palestine violently destroyed, probably in connection with the expulsion of the Hyksos in Egypt under the renascent Dynasty 18 kings, ca. 1540–1480 B.C.. Nearly all the more recent sites noted above have produced clear evidence of these destructions, particularly Shechem and Gezer. The destruction of the Hyksos capitol of Avaris in the Delta, now positively identified by the excavations of M. Bietak at Tell ed-Dabʿa, must be related to these events. The site shows a Canaanite population and material culture, including tombs with Palestinian weapons and pottery, beginning as early as 1800 B.C. or even earlier (in Levels G–F).

Literacy seems to have begun in Palestine toward the end of the MB Age. A few more examples of the "Proto-Sinaitic" script have turned up (as at Gezer); and fragmentary cuneiform tablets are known from Hazor, Megiddo, Gezer, and Hebron.

D. The Late Bronze Age (ca. 1500–1200 B.C.)

The LB I, ca. 1500–1400 B.C., was a postdestruction horizon that is still not well illuminated (see further Gonen 1989; Leonard 1989). The LB IIA–B period, however (ca. 1400–1200 B.C.), is increasingly well known, especially the IIA phase of the "Amarna Age" in the 14th century B.C. The major sites recently investigated are Tell Abu Hawam, Tel Kittan, Tel Mevorakh, Aphek, Gezer, Jerusalem, Tel Batash in the Sorek Valley, Lachish, Ashdod, Tel es-Shariʿa in the N Negeb, and Deir al-Balaḥ in the Gaza area. Across the Jordan, important LB remains have come to light at Deir ʿAllā, Tell es-Sa'idiyeh, Pella, Irbid, Amman, and other sites.

Virtually all these sites, despite their strategic location and importance, remained unwalled, or simply made slight reuse of the old MB fortifications. The sole exception may be Gezer, where the "Outer Wall" system has been dated by the excavators to the LB IIA period.

Among the most important finds are new temples at Tel Kittan, Tel Mevorakh, and Lachish (the "Summit Temple"), and in Jordan at Deir ʿAllā and Amman. Large, multiroomed Egyptian "residencies" have been recognized now at major centers such as Gezer, Aphek, Ashdod, Tel es-Shariʿa, and Deir al-Balaḥ. Finally, rich LB II tombs have been partially published from Akko (the "Persian Garden"), Dan, Shechem, Gezer (Cave I.10A), Jerusalem, and elsewhere. The general picture of political conditions and socioeconomic structure in Palestine, as revealed in the well-known Amarna letters from Egypt, fits very well indeed with the most recent LB II archaeological discoveries. All indications point to Egypt's incorporation of Palestine into the New Kingdom empire.

There are now a number of confirmed destructions at the end of the LB and the beginning of the Iron Age, from ca. 1250–1150 B.C., but virtually none would any longer be attributed to an "Israelite conquest" under Joshua. Hazor appears to have been destroyed ca. 1250 B.C., Lachish ca. 1150 B.C., both by unknown agents. Tell Abu Hawam, Tel Mevorakh, Aphek, Ashdod, and other coastal sites were likely destroyed by the incoming Philistines and other "Sea Peoples." Many sites, such as Megiddo, Beth-shan, Shechem, and Gezer, show considerable continuity or were not destroyed at all. It is increasingly clear that Egyptian influence, despite declining Dynasty 20 power, continued even as late as Rameses VI.

E. The Iron I Period (ca. 1200–900 B.C.)

The early Iron Age ("Iron IA–B," 12th–11th centuries B.C.) saw the appearance of two new ethnic groups among the population of Canaanite Palestine, the Philistines and the Israelites. Both are well illustrated by recent archaeological finds, in what must be accounted among the most significant archaeological advances of our era (see further Dothan 1982; Callaway 1988; and especially Finkelstein *AIS*).

The main Philistine domestic sites are Ashdod, Gezer, and Tel Miqne (Ekron). The appearance of new architectural and ceramic styles is clearly evident, including both imported Late Mycenaean III:$C1_b$ monochrome pottery and its locally made bichrome derivatives—reminders of the Aegean origins of the "Sea Peoples." Tel Qasile, on the coast at the mouth of the Yarkon River, has revealed a sequence of several well-preserved temples with quantities of Philistine pottery and other Aegean elements. Deir al-Balaḥ, in the Gaza strip, has produced more than two dozen distinctive terra-cotta anthropoid coffins from the late 13th century B.C., similar to those long known from Beth-shan and elsewhere, but made in a local potter's workshop. These Egyptian-style coffins suggest that some of the earliest "Sea Peoples" appeared along the coast of Palestine as Egyptian mercenaries even before the time of Rameses III. Today many scholars believe, however, that the distinctive bichrome painted pottery of the Philistines came into vogue only in the second generation, ca. 1150 B.C., after these people were partly assimilated.

Early "Israelite" settlements (or better, "Proto-Israelite") have now been clearly recognized for the first time. Most were small, unwalled hilltop villages in central Palestine, Galilee, and possibly the N Negeb, established *de novo* and not on the ruins of Canaanite LB urban sites. Particularly important (although largely unpublished) are ʿAi, Raddanah, Shiloh, and Giloh, all near Jerusalem; ʿIzbet Ṣarṭeh, near Aphek (probably Biblical Ebenezer); and probably Tel Esdar, Tel Masos, and Beer-sheba, all in the N Negeb. These villages are characterized by early "four-room" courtyard houses, stone silos, rock-hewn cisterns, terrace farming, crude iron implements, transitional LB/Iron I pottery (including the well-known "collar-rim" store jars), and even a few Old Canaanite (or "Proto-Hebrew") ostraca (ʿIzbet Ṣarṭeh). Most sites were abandoned in the late 11th–early 10th century B.C. with the growth of urbanism under the United Monarchy of Israel. In addition, extensive Israeli surveys in ancient Ephraim and Manasseh, in Lower Galilee, and along the Sharon Plain have revealed several hundred small agricultural villages of the 12th–11th centuries, all probably "Israelite." These new discoveries clearly discredit the older "conquest" model of Albright. Instead, they support a modified version of the Alt-Noth "peaceful infiltration" model, or even the "peasants' revolt" model of Mendenhall, Gottwald, and others. *Any* model for the Israelite settlement must now take into account: (1) the *continuity* from LB Canaanite culture into early Iron I, especially in ceramics; and (2) the *indigenous* factors in the Iron I hill country settlement, i.e., changes in settlement patterns, demography, and socioeconomic structure, rather than supposed "invasions," from Transjordan or otherwise. See ISRAEL, HISTORY OF (ARCHAEOLOGY AND THE ISRAELITE "CONQUEST").

Two possible early Israelite cult sites are now known. The Mt. Ebal installation, a tower or large altarlike structure with pits containing many burnt animal bones, is dated clearly to the 12th century B.C., but its interpretation is disputed. The "Bull site" east of Dothan is of the same date, and its enclosed altar, standing stone *(māṣṣēbāh),* and a finely cast bronze bull strongly suggest an El (or Canaanite) sanctuary in the heartland of Israelite tribal territory.

The late Iron I period in the 10th century B.C. (Albright's "Iron IC," or Israeli "Iron IIA") is now best documented in a number of Davidic-Solomonic constructions at increasingly urbanized sites (see further Dever 1983). Nearly identical three-entryway city gates and casemate walls at Hazor, Megiddo, and Gezer provide a commentary on I Kgs 9:15; and both Megiddo and Gezer also have 10th-century "palaces" that were probably residences of royal governors. Of the Temple of Solomon in Jerusalem, nothing remains. The plan of the structure, however, and details of its decoration and furnishings, may now be confidently reconstructed from the increasing number of Bronze and Iron Age Canaanite-Phoenician temples and cultic artifacts brought to light. These include the MB tripartite "Temple 7300" at Shechem; similar temples at Mumbaqat and elsewhere in Syria; more "Proto-Aeolic" capitals; artistic motifs on ivories and seals; bronze stands; a life-sized horned altar from Beer-sheba; and other data. See TEMPLE, JERUSALEM.

The extension of Solomonic power is well illustrated by a string of forts recently investigated through the Negeb, extending to the earliest fortress at the oasis of Kadesh-barnea in the Sinai. Finally, Jerusalem itself has been extensively dug, where Y. Shiloh has uncovered several 10th century B.C. pillared houses on the E slope S of the Temple Mount, on a terraced and stepped stone podium that recalls the biblical *millo,* or "filling." On the coast, Tel Mevorakh provides rich evidence of imported Cypro-Phoenician pottery; and Tel Miqne and Ashdod illustrate the continuing culture of the Philistines along the coast, never fully assimilated. Increasing evidence points to the end of Iron I with the convergence of the death of Solomon, the raid of Shishak, and the breakup of the United Kingdom, ca. 920 B.C.

F. The Iron II Period (ca. 900–600 B.C.)

The Iron II period, representing the full development of the Israelite monarchy and the zenith of Israelite material culture, has been especially well documented by recent Israeli archaeology (see further Shiloh 1980; Horn 1988; Gitin and Dever 1989). Nevertheless, there are still serious chronological difficulties, and the 9th century B.C. in particular is still inadequately attested.

We can only mention the main sites, moving from N to S. Dan, excavated since 1966 by A. Biran, remains largely unpublished but has revealed a massive 9th-century "High Place" of ashlar masonry; an associated shrine with altars, anthropomorphic figurines, a horned altar, bronze implements and shovels, and burned animal bones; and both outer and inner triple-entryway city gates, with a connecting roadway. Yadin's last campaigns at Hazor (1969–70) brought to light a magnificent 9th-century water shaft hewn into the bedrock, with an underground gallery reaching the water table deep underground. Megiddo, reexcavated by Yadin in the 1960s, now makes clear that the well-known "stables" (perhaps storehouses) are 9th century B.C. (i.e., Ahab, rather than Solomon), as is its water system. Tell el-Farᶜah (N), dug in the 1950s–1960s by R. de Vaux, has finally published the Iron Age sequence, which has important domestic material and cultic remains. The 10th century B.C. elite quarter of the City of David in Jerusalem continued to develop, and it has yielded not only a good pottery sequence but also figurines, inscriptions, and a cache of late 7th century B.C. bullae featuring many Judean names known from the Hebrew Bible. Other Iron II Israelite sites include Yoqneam W of the Megiddo pass; Shechem, not yet published; and Gezer, with important domestic remains, reused and augmented city walls and gates, and destruction levels of the Neo-Assyrian period. Tell Keisan, near the bay of Haifa, gives evidence of Cypro-Phoenician cultural influence, as do Dor and Tel Mevorakh farther S on the coast.

In the S, both Arad and Beer-sheba, excavated by Y. Aharoni, yield nearly complete town plans of an Iron II Israelite fortress and district store-city, respectively, both with sanctuaries. At Arad, a collection of several dozen ostraca is especially noteworthy. Lachish, reexcavated since 1973 by D. Ussishkin, is perhaps the key site. The well-attested destruction of the gate area in stratum III can now be fixed to the raid of Sennacherib in 701 B.C. (not 598 B.C., as formerly). This raises the Iron II chronology of Judah by as much as 100 years and is of revolutionary import. Other important Judean sites recently dug are Khirbet Rabûd (now "Debir"), Lahav, and Tell el-Ḥesi. For the 7th–early 6th century B.C., both Tel Miqne (Ekron) and Tel Batash (Timna), in the Sorek Valley, provide a wealth of information, including evidence of industry and trade with the Philistine coast. The latter is also illustrated now by the upper levels at Ashdod.

In the Negeb-Sinai, some of the Iron I forts and the fortress at Kadesh-barnea continued into Iron II. The 8th century B.C. hilltop fort and shrine at Kuntillet ᶜAjrûd, in the E Sinai, are known only from preliminary publications. Kuntillet ᶜAjrûd has yielded dozens of graffiti and votives of a cultic nature, including a painted stone jar with two Bes figures, a half-nude enthroned female, and a Hebrew inscription mentioning in a blessing formula "Yahweh of Samaria and his Asherah." To the extreme S, Nelson Glueck's excavation of Tell el-Kheleifeh, on the Gulf of Eilat (Ezion-geber?), has finally been published as well as possible.

Among scattered finds are numerous Iron II chamber and bench tombs, yielding large collections of pottery, figurines, weights, and several inscriptions. Judean tomb inscriptions are now known from Khirbet Lei and Khirbet el-Qôm, in the Hebron hills, as well as from Silwan (Jerusalem). The 8th century B.C. el-Qôm inscription seems also to mention Yahweh and Asherah together.

Outside Israel, the contemporary Transjordanian states of Ammon, Moab, and Edom are increasingly well documented by a number of excavations. The main sites are Pella, Amman, Tel es-Sa'idiyeh, Amman, Heshbon, Dhibân, Buseira (Bosra), Tawilan (Tema?), and ᵓUmm el-Biyara (Sela?). The material culture is parallel to that of Israel, as are the closely related West Semitic dialects now reconstructed from a growing *corpus* of ostraca and seals (see further Dornemann 1983; Geraty and Herr 1986; Sauer 1986). The cult, however, differs substantially, to judge from the names of known deities and cult practices. The best evidence for the Edomite cult comes from a hoard of exotic 7th-century figurines found at Qitmit, S of Arad in SE Israel.

Both the Assyrian destructions in the N in 735–721 B.C., and those of the Babylonians in Judah in 587/586 B.C., are well attested in clear destruction levels at nearly all the sites mentioned above. Nevertheless, surveys have shown that many smaller sites escaped destruction, especially in Judah, where an "Iron III" phase may be detected extending well toward the end of the 6th century B.C.

Bibliography

Aharoni, Y. 1979. *The Archaeology of the Land of Israel.* Philadelphia.

Biran, A. 1984. The Triple-arched Gate of Laish at Tel Dan. *IEJ* 34: 1–19.

Broshi, M., and Gophna, R. 1984. The Settlement and Population of Palestine during the Early Bronze Age. *BASOR* 253: 41–53.

———. 1986. Middle Bronze II Palestine: Its Settlements and Population. *BASOR* 261: 73–90.

Callaway, J. A. 1988. The Settlement in Canaan. Pp. 53–84 in *Ancient Israel,* ed. H. Shanks. Washington.

Dever, W. G. 1980. New Vistas on the EB IV ("MB I") Horizon in Syria-Palestine. *BASOR* 237: 35–64.

———. 1983. Monumental Architecture in Ancient Israel in the Period of the United Monarchy. Pp. 269–306 in *Studies in the Period of David and Solomon and Other Essays,* ed. T. Ishida. Tokyo.

———. 1987. Palestine in the Middle Bronze Age: The Zenith of the Urban Canaanite Era. *BA* 50: 149–76.

Dornemann, R. H. 1983. *The Archaeology of the Transjordan in the Bronze and Iron Ages.* Milwaukee.

Dothan, T. 1982. *The Philistines and Their Material Culture.* New Haven.

Geraty, L. T., and Herr, L. G., eds. 1986. *The Archaeology of Jordan and Other Studies.* Berrien Springs, MI.

Gerstenblith, P. 1983. *The Levant at the Beginning of the Middle Bronze Age.* Winona Lake, IN.

Gitin, S., and Dever, W. G., eds. 1989. *Recent Excavations in Israel: Studies in Iron Age Archaeology.* AASOR 49. Winona Lake, IN.

Gonen, R. 1989. *Burial Practice and Cultural Diversity in Late Bronze Age Canaan.* Baltimore.

Hadidi, A., ed. 1982–89. *Studies in the History and Archaeology of Jordan,* vols. I–IV. Oxford/Amman.

Horn, S. 1988. The Divided Monarchy. Pp. 109–49 in *Ancient Israel,* ed. H. Shanks. Washington.

Kempinski, A. 1983. *Syrien und Palästina (Kanaan) in der Letzten Phase der Mittlebronze IIB-zeit (1650–1570 v. Chr.).* Wiesbaden.

Leonard, A. 1989. The Late Bronze Age. *BA* 52: 4–39.

Levy, T. E. 1986. The Chalcolithic Period. *BA* 49: 83–109.

Mazar, A. 1989. *The Archaeology of the Land of the Bible; 10,000–600 B.C.E.* Garden City, NY.

Richard, S. 1987. The Early Bronze Age: The Rise and Collapse of Urbanism. *BA* 50: 22–43.

Sauer, J. A. 1986. Transjordan in the Bronze and Iron Ages: A Critique of Glueck's Synthesis. *BASOR* 263: 1–26.

Shanks, H., and Mazar, B., eds. 1984. *Recent Archaeology in the Land of Israel.* Washington.

Shiloh, Y. 1980. The Population of Iron Age Palestine in the Light of a Sample Analysis of Urban Plans, Areas, and Population Density. *BASOR* 239: 25–35.

WILLIAM G. DEVER

PERSIAN PERIOD

Between 545 and 538 B.C.E., the whole of the Middle East—including Palestine—was conquered by the Achaemenid kings of Persia. During the reign of Darius I (522–486 B.C.E.), its borders were consolidated and its interior division was determined. Accordingly, some twenty satrapies were established, each of which was divided into subprovinces (compare the description in Esth 1:1).

Palestine constituted only a tiny part of one of these satrapies, named "Beyond the River" (Ezra 4:10–11), a term which was borrowed from the former Assyrian administration and perhaps from an even earlier period (see 1 Kgs 4:24). In addition to Palestine, the province included Syria, Phoenicia, and Cyprus. According to Herodotus (3.5), its N border was in Poseideion (now al-Mina at the mouth of the Orontes), and its S border was at Lake Sirbonis (Bardawil Lake).

The subdivision of Palestine appears to have been based on the older divisions of the Assyrian and Babylonian administration, probably related to the territorial boundaries of the various peoples living in the country during that period. The best known of these provinces were Megiddo, Dor, Samaria, Judea, Ashdod, and Gaza. At the head of each province was a Persian governor or a local representative who was responsible to the satrap of "Beyond the River" for its efficient administration, payment of taxes, etc. This arrangement lasted for some two hundred years, from 538 to 332 B.C.E., when the entire Middle East was conquered by Alexander the Great.

A. Archaeological Research

From the standpoint of archaeology, the history of the Persian period in Palestine is obscure, despite the fact that it is relatively recent. The information provided by the Bible, our major literary source for the Israelite period, gives anything but a clear picture, and even this does not go beyond the middle of the 5th century B.C.E. The same is true of the following period with regard to the information provided by Greek literature (Herodotus, Pseudo-Scylax) and the Apocrypha.

Some epigraphic sources have been added through recent discovery. Among them are the inscriptions of Darius I found at Persepolis, the inscriptions of the Phoenician kings discovered at Sidon, the archives of the Jewish military colony from Elephantine in Egypt, the inscriptions found at Tell el-Maskhuta in Egypt, where a similar Arab military base existed, and the archive of the satrap, ʾArsam.

Palestine, too, has yielded some outstanding discoveries. Of prime importance are the Samaritan papyri dating to 375–332 B.C.E. discovered in a cave at Wadi Daliyeh, and the hoard of bullae from a postexilic Judean archive found near Jerusalem. Also important are some Egyptian steles found at Gezer and Acco. But the main epigraphic materials in Palestine are the ostraca, discovered at many sites and written in Aramaic, Hebrew, and Phoenician. Most are lists of proper names (Hebrew, Phoenician, Arabic, Babylonian, Egyptian, etc.) or receipts for consignments of food, merchandise, etc. Although they give no indication of contemporary events, they are of considerable importance for our knowledge of the everyday life of the period.

They also shed light on the country's military and fiscal organization, and indirectly on the composition of the population. Short inscriptions, some with the titles of officeholders, have been discovered on seals, seal impressions, bullae, and coins.

However, the combined literary and epigraphic sources still provide little information of the history of Palestine during the Persian period, and the overall picture which emerges remains unclear. Unfortunately, our knowledge of the material culture of this period in Palestine has for many years been unorganized and has fallen short of that of the previous periods.

Significant advances in the study of the period have occurred relatively recently. Settlements of the Persian period have been discovered in Galilee and the coastal plain: Tel Dan, Tel Anafa, Hazor, Beth-Yerah, Taanach, Tel Qedesh, Tell Qiri, Tel Yokne'am, Akzib, Acco, Tell Keisan, Uṣa, Gil'am, Shiqmona, Tel Megadim, Tel Dor, Tel Mevorakh, Tel Zeror, Mikhmoret, Makmish, Jaffa, Tell Qasile, Tell Abu-Zeitun, Aphek, Tirat Yehudah, Ashdod, and Tel Sera', as well as the more recent excavations at Gezer, Lachish, Tell el-Ḥesi, and Tell Jemmeh. Excavations revealing Persian occupation have been conducted in the mountain region at Shechem, Gibeon, Tell el-Fûl, Jerusalem, Ramat Raḥel, and En-gedi; and in the Negeb, Persian-period remains were found at Beer-sheba, Arad, and Kadesh-barnea. Further evidence has come from excavations and surveys in Sinai. Of special importance were the excavations at Hazor, Shiqmona, Tel Megadim, Tel Dor, Tel Mevorakh, Tel Michal, and En-gedi, since at these the Persian strata were better preserved and could serve as a frame of reference to investigate the regional assemblages. These finds are now enriched by homogeneous assemblages from Shechem, Wadi Daliyeh, Qadum, the Sheikh Ibrahim cave near Jerusalem, the burial cave at ᶜAin ᶜArub, N of Hebron, as well as the recent finds from Tell el-Mazar E of the Jordan.

In some of these excavations the stratum of the Persian period contains two phases or more, while at other sites the finds belonged to only part of the Persian period. It is now possible to analyze the development of the Persian material culture in Palestine and to classify the finds into early and late.

Recent excavations have cast a new light on cult objects. Important collections of statuettes and figurines have been discovered at Tel 'Erani, Tel Ṣippor, and Tel Dor. Our knowledge of the various types of seal impressions has been expanded by the excavations at Ramat Raḥel and by the collection of bullae and seals from the Jerusalem area.

B. The Character of the Material Culture

1. Regional Diversity: Eastern and Western Influences. A study of the material culture of Palestine reveals that the country was divided into two distinct regions at the beginning of the period: one included the hill country of Judea and Transjordan (and to a lesser extent Samaria), while the other was Galilee and the coastal area. The border between these two cultural areas is at times very sharp—almost like a border dividing two countries. Without an understanding of this division of Palestine it is difficult to understand the material development of the culture of the period.

An analysis of the remains of these two regions demonstrates that the material culture of the hill country is basically "eastern" in character. It is made up of a local culture (which continues the Israelite tradition) and eastern influences (Assyrian, Babylonian, but also Egyptian). The coastal culture, on the other hand, is basically "western" in nature, containing eastern Greek, Cypriot, and Athenian elements. It is therefore probable that the Greek material culture considerably preceded the Macedonian conquest and that Greek materials had already been adapted to local traditions and customs. The main bearers of this new culture to Palestine were probably Phoenicians and only secondarily Greek soldiers and settlers.

It seems then that Albright's definition of "Iron III" for the culture of this period is justified if it is applied only to the mountain region of Judea and Benjamin; it seems much less appropriate, however, for other regions of the country. Moreover, it is now evident that the difference between the "coastal" culture and that of the "hill country" is not a chronological difference as proposed by Albright, but rather a question of concurrent influences from "western" and "eastern" cultures over these respective areas.

2. Achaemenid Influences. From all that has been said so far, the fact remains that in the case of the material culture in Palestine one cannot distinguish any influence of the *Persian* material culture (i.e., the culture of the rulers by whose name we identify the entire period). The scanty Persian influence is mainly expressed by isolated types of ceramics; by a small number of ornaments and Achaemenid style metal objects, which also appear to have been made by the Phoenicians; and by a few clothing accessories on some Phoenician figurines.

The main influence of the long period of Persian rule in Palestine is seen not in the material culture but only in those spheres immediately connected with political affairs, such as administration, military organization, finance, and taxation. In each of the few inscriptions from Wadi Daliyeh so far published, the dates given are according to the royal years of the Persian kings, and the officials named are local Persian administrators. Information about military organization is contained on an ostracon recently discovered at Arad, which mentions an individual who belongs to a certain "standard" (i.e., a Persian military unit also known from Elephantine in Egypt). The military strongholds and granaries discovered at nearly all the large sites in Palestine reflect the maintenance of the Persian military system. Many of the weapons and chariot accessories found in the tombs of the period are of the Scytho-Iranian type, just like those found in the guard rooms at Persepolis, confirming the earlier supposition that some of the tombs at Gezer were in fact the graves of Persian soldiers. Persian influence is most conspicuous, however, in matters of taxation and money. Whereas Persian rulers could be liberal and magnanimous toward the conquered people in matters of cult and administration, in matters pertaining to the economy and taxation they were rather severe. The taxes levied on the various provinces were determined according to their size and prosperity, and had to be paid in precious metals only. The seal impressions on the handles of vessels from Judea, which give evidence of the taxation system, use motifs taken from Achaemenid royal motifs. Their stratigraphic contexts (only from the end of the 6th to the end of the 5th century B.C.E.) prove that matters of administration and finance in Judea were only initially conducted by officials of the Achaemenid empire. Subsequently, these Achaemenid seals were replaced by seals written in Aramaic bearing the name of the province, *yhwd*. This implies a change in the administration of the province at the end of the 5th century B.C.E., perhaps at the time of Nehemiah or a little later. Alt surmised that Nehemiah freed Judea from its subjection to Samaria and turned it into an independent province.

C. Stratigraphic Evidence of Conflicts

A detailed study of the sites of this period in Palestine allows us to conclude with some measure of certainty that there were two waves of destruction during the Persian period. We learn about the first through the excavations in the territory of Benjamin. A large number of the towns which had been spared the destruction wrought by Nebuchadnezzar were destroyed about a hundred years later (ca. 480 B.C.E.). No historical explanation has been found for this destruction, though it may be assumed that it occurred in connection with some minor war, such as that which threatened Judea in the days of Nehemiah. The picture is different concerning the second wave of destruction, which affected only the coastal regions and the Negeb apparently around 380 B.C.E. This destruction is connected with the Egyptian struggle for independence (ca. 404–400 B.C.E.), which spread two decades later to the lowlands of Palestine. This assumption is strengthened by two important finds: an inscription of Nepherites I (399–393 B.C.E.) at Gezer, and steles of Achoris (393–380 B.C.E.) at Acco and Sidon.

The end of the Persian period in Palestine is marked by staggered destruction levels that testify not to a single "death blow" but to sporadic conflicts associated with the demise of Persian power. Such conflicts included the Sidonian revolt of 351 B.C.E., which brought about the destruction of the province of Dor; the wars associated with Alexander the Great in the territories of Tyre, Acco, and Gaza; and the Samaritan revolt against Alexander, which resulted in the destruction of many major cities in these regions (e.g.: Megiddo, Acco, Tell Abu Hawam, Samaria, and Gaza). Several cities (Shiqmonah, Tel Ṣippor) may have been destroyed even as late as the wars of the Diadochi, as is proved by the coins of Alexander the Great which were uncovered within the destruction levels of the Persian period.

Bibliography

Avigad, N. 1976. *Bullae and Seals from a Post-Exilic Judean Archive.* Qedem 4. Jerusalem.

Cross, F. M., Jr. 1963. The Discovery of the Samaritan Papyri. *BA* 26: 110–21.

———. 1971. Papyri of the Fourth Century B.C. from Daliyeh. Pp. 45–69 in *New Directions in Biblical Archaeology*, ed. D. N. Freedman and J. C. Greenfield. Garden City.

———. 1974. *Discoveries in the Wadi ed-Dâliyeh*, ed. P. W. Lapp and N. L. Lapp. AASOR 41: 17–29.

Davies, D., and Finkelstein, L., eds. 1984. *CHJ* 1.

Galling, K. 1929. Syrien in der Politik der Achämenider. *AfO* 28.

———. 1938. Die Syrische-Palästinische Küste nach der Beschreibung bei Pseudo-Skylax. *ZDPV* 61: 66–96.

Stern, E. 1987. *Material Culture of the Land of the Bible in the Persian Period 538–332 B.C.* Warminster.

Weinberg, S. S. 1969. Post Exilic Palestine. An Archaeological Report. *The Israel Academy of Sciences and Humanities Proceedings.* Vol. 4, no. 5. Jerusalem.

Widengren, G. 1977. The Persian Period. Pp. 489–538 in *IJH.*

EPHRAIM STERN

NEW TESTAMENT PERIOD

Scholars did not systematically pursue the archaeology of the NT period in Palestine, (ca. 50 B.C.–A.D. 150) until roughly the second half of the 20th century. This was because of the relative paucity of Roman monuments in Palestine at a time when archaeology was dominated by interest in major architecture. Roman Palestine seemed to furnish few Greek and Roman temples, aqueducts, theaters, circuses, hippodromes, etc. This was at the very time when the imaginations of the 19th and early 20th century pilgrims and scholars had been captured by the splendid monuments of Egypt, Asia Minor, and Mesopotamia, most of which related to the OT period. On the other hand, Greece, Italy, and W Turkey still appeared to provide more than enough attractive architecture to illustrate the NT narratives, while the seemingly paltry finds of a few potsherds and coins from Hellenistic and Roman Palestine hardly seemed worth the effort. Apart from the Temple Mount of Herod the Great in Jerusalem, most showpieces of Roman civilization came from other well-known Classical sites in the E Mediterranean. As late as 1960, W. F. Albright could cite relatively few discoveries of Roman Palestine in the revised edition of *The Archaeology of Palestine.* These included certain painted tombs of Tell Marissa, the mausoleum of the Tobiads at Araq el-Amir, the Hellenistic citadel at Beth-zur, the "fortress of Simon Maccabeus" at Gezer (now known to be misidentified), the town plan of Tell Marissa, ossuaries and tombs of the period, certain discoveries in Jerusalem (the walls, the Ecce Homo arch, the alleged Gabbatha pavement beneath the convent of the sisters of Zion), NT Jericho (excavated from 1950–51), the cities of Gerasa and Petra in Jordan, synagogues in Galilee (including Capernaum), and certain epigraphic discoveries, such as proper names, that echo those found in the NT. The Dead Sea Scrolls were not mentioned, but were discussed in detail by G. E. Wright in his 1962 work *Biblical Archaeology.* Thus interest in the archaeology of the NT period seemed to be dominated by the concerns of the classical archaeologist of the same period, including the hope of finding texts.

Researchers focused on sites mentioned in the NT. These included Capernaum, visited by Robinson in 1857, who identified the synagogue, but did not identify the site (Tell Hum) with Capernaum. The site was subsequently visited and probed by many until 1921, when it was systematically excavated by Dr. G. Orfali. In 1968, excavations resumed under Frs. Corbo and Lofredda. In Jerusalem, meanwhile, no less than 46 excavations were carried out before 1967 by a host of well-known archaeologists, including R. A. S. Macalister, E. L. Sukenik, J. W. Crowfoot, R. W. Hamilton, M. Avi-Yonah, K. Kenyon, and J. Hennessy. Among many questions pursued by excavators were the location of Golgotha and the tomb of Christ, the location and dates of the city walls of the Roman period, the search for Herod's palace, the discovery of the Ecce Homo arch, and the discovery and identification of the so-called Gabbatha pavement. Excavations at Caesarea, the political capital, were conducted from 1948 to 1963 by such luminaries as J. Ory, M. Avi-Yonah, A. Frova, A. Negev, and E. A. Link. Bethlehem and the Church of the Nativity fascinated generations of scholars, and publication of its remains by H. Vincent and F.-M. Abel began in 1914. Similarly Nazareth was excavated by M. Viaud from 1890–1909 and by B. Bagatti in 1954. Armchair archaeologists wrote about the archaeology of Antioch, Ephesus, Laodicea, and Athens.

A second focus of interest in archaeology of the period was on artifacts and items that illustrated the NT and other early Christian and postbiblical Jewish literature. Those who pursued this line described writing materials, the scroll and codex, the potter's craft, ancient tombs (so as to reconstruct on paper the tomb of Christ), inscriptions, ritual baths at Qumran as forerunners of Christian baptism, coins, and certain manuscripts discoveries (for example the Samaria Papyri, the Dead Sea Scrolls, the Bar Kokhba letters, the Bodmer papyri, and the Nag Hammadi finds), including papyri and codices containing alleged sayings of Jesus. This broad line of investigation promised less than the more narrowly defined study of inscriptions and papyri, which after all promised—and delivered—a host of evidence to solve various linguistic enigmas in the NT and other ancient literature. The study of the Roman period Egyptian papyri faced certain limits, namely, that one was extrapolating to Palestine from another Roman province with only similar, not the same, religious and political institutions.

On the other hand, the amount of archaeological knowledge about the NT period seems to have expanded exponentially since the 1960s. This is knowledge from systematic and large-scale excavations, thorough regional surveys, and pursuit of accidental discoveries. In this period the interests of the scholar have gradually shifted from those of Classical art and archaeology to include questions of the size and population of ancient cities and villages, reconstructions of rural and urban life, the nature and extent of Hellenism, the magnitude of Greek/Aramaic bilingualism, of the nature and extent of urbanism and of urban vs. village life, understanding of Jewish burial customs, evidence for the "God fearers" of the book of Acts, methods of identification of distinctively Jewish symbols, grasping more clearly early synagogue architecture, identification of house churches, understanding Herod the Great and his dynasty, developing the role of numismatics in historical reconstructions, realizing the dynamics of Roman-Jewish relations, and disclosing details of Roman rule. In addition, scholars have given attention to particulars of archaeological data of the period with a variety of goals in mind, such as determination of subsistence patterns, study of regional Roman architecture, investigation of water systems, and deduction of ancient methods of olive and wine production. Other scholars have attempted to understand early Christian symbols, or to specialize in Roman Jerusalem and its archaeological history, or to research other "holy places" such as the Tomb of Lazarus. Others debate the identification of the Emmaus of Luke or uncover campsites of the Sixth Legion "Ferrata" in Galilee or the Tenth Legion "Fretensis" in Jerusalem. These developments in archaeology show promise of linkage with NT scholarship in a more direct and fruitful way. On the other hand, the unfolding of allied specialties in the archaeology of the period has often proceeded without regard for connections with NT scholarship, research in Christian origins, or the study of Rabbinic Judaism. Such developments include stratigraphic excavation of Roman sites for purely scientific reasons, advances in numismatics, studies in ancient glass, neutron-activation analysis of ancient ceramics and other technological studies, or the formation of theory and models in archaeology. Probably the dominant trend in recent archaeology of the period is an attempt to place the archaeology of the NT period into the wider discipline of Roman archaeology in ancient Palestine and the E Mediterranean.

It is within this wider understanding of archaeology that we must place recent excavations in ancient Palestine. For example, excavations at Khirbet Shema, Meiron, Gush Halav, and Nabratein, all in Upper Galilee, have disclosed a vigorous Jewish village life from the 2d century B.C. to the 4th century A.D. and later. Similar conclusions must follow from excavations in a series of ancient villages and towns from the Negeb to the Galilee. Local and regional trade networks bore goods to the remotest parts of Upper Galilee. That is, town and village life was not isolated, but movement of goods, services, and ideas was extensive. Excavations of tombs and structures in Nazareth Ilit, to cite only one example, indicate that there was a tiny Roman agricultural village above Nazareth about a fifteen-minute walk away. In a similar vein, excavations at the Herodium near Bethlehem reveal an entire support village around the fortress, suggesting that similar support villages might be found elsewhere. The density of occupation in ancient Judea in the NT period appears to have been nearly the highest in the Roman Empire, if not the highest. On the other hand, excavations in a variety of cities and large towns indicate a degree of urbanization in ancient Palestine that goes beyond traditional understandings. For example, excavations at Magdala-Tarichaeae have disclosed a small portion of a Roman-style city complete with paved streets. The excavations at Tiberias have revealed a very large city and a detached city of Hammath to the S in the 1st century, confirming certain literary notices in Josephus and the Jerusalem Talmud. The same situation pertains at Hippos-Susita on the SE shores of the Sea of Galilee. Excavations at Sepphoris have unearthed remains of a robust Roman city of large Jewish population whose toparchy surely extended to Nazareth, suggesting a degree of urbanization of Lower Galilee heretofore only suspected. Similarly, recent excavations at Bethsaida (Roman Julias) have disclosed a rather small urban complex of the 1st century. Other excavations at Caesarea Philippi-Paneas have only begun to show the extent of the ancient city. A similar conclusion is supported by excavations at Caesarea, Jerusalem, Antipatris, Azotus (OT Ashdod), and others. Probably the most spectacular example of excavations in an urban center of this period are those at Beth Shean. In this case a truly striking Roman city of grand proportions has emerged since 1986. Although most of the finds postdate the NT period, there are sufficient remains to suggest the thoroughly Roman character of this city. For example, various inscriptions and temple architecture suggest that paganism in various forms flourished at Beth Shean, including the worship of Dionysus and Zeus-Akraios. An inscription and Roman temple correlate with the ancient local tradition that Dionysus founded the city and buried his nurse Nysa there. Also town and village planning is evident in their traces, suggesting a clear governing and planning structure. Excavations at Capernaum have combined to reveal a very large, well-planned town that thrived from the 2d century B.C. to the Arab period. The same degree of planning is visible at Chorazin, although the remains are largely Byzantine. Excavations at Horvat Amudim at the E end of the Beit Netopha valley reveal a large, thriving Roman town of unknown name in the 1st century that continued to the Byzantine period. The accidental find of a fishing boat in the mud of the Sea of Galilee has revealed the only 1st-century boat thus far found from ancient Palestine. The sophisticated level of shipbuilding revealed in the construction of the boat suggests that an infrastructure of shipbuilders and other artisans likely formed part of the population of the cities and villages of the lake. Interest in 1st-century synagogues, though the word is understood less as a dedicated cultic structure and more as a "gathering place" *(synagogēs)*, continues unabated. Probably the best known of these structures are at Masada, the Herodium (though it seems to be 2d-century), Gamala, and Magdala. In the last case, the Franciscans unearthed a likely synagogue of the 1st century situated at the corner of two paved streets. Also at Capernaum, their excavations beneath the 4th-century synagogue unearthed what is simplest to identify as a 1st-century synagogue. In the Golan Heights, just inside the city wall at Gamala, breached by the Romans in the First Revolt against Rome, was found a rectangular building with interior columnation and benches that is usually interpreted as a synagogue. It went out of use with the destruction of Gamala by the Romans in A.D. 67. Identification of house churches, besides the one at Dura-Europos, is an emerging controversy. Beneath the 5th-century octagonal church at Capernaum, one block away from the famous Byzantine synagogue, is an Early Roman house likely converted to a house church, the so-called "House of St. Peter." This was identified by its continuous history and use as a holy place right up to the 5th century. It is an interesting question how many house churches we may not be able to identify because such structures did not acquire a fixed architectural form nor contain a fixed iconography until later centuries.

Excavation of hundreds of tombs of the NT period mainly confirms the outline of Jewish burial custom known from rabbinic sources of the early centuries. Jewish tombs are usually of the loculus type and are very sparing in their finds. Artifacts found in tombs of the period are predominantly lamps and glass phials, perhaps lachrymortaria. Only a few clearly Jewish tombs have had coffins, as the rule was to bury first in a shroud directly in the loculus with subsequent reburial in an ossuary. Some tombs have burial inscriptions. These inscriptions were intended for the family and are almost always in Greek, though many names and epitaphs in Hebrew, Aramaic, and other languages are known. This is the most telling archaeological evidence for deducing bilingualism or trilingualism in ancient Palestine, since Greek is the norm within the tomb, that is, for the family. Since tombs are often equipped with a forecourt and other architectural features not required for inhumation itself, there was obviously a well-developed ritual of mourning, as the noncanonical Mishnaic tractate "Mourning" *(Ṣem.)* indicates.

The archaeological picture of the architectural culture to be associated with the dynasty of Herod the Great is coherent and striking. Herod and his sons (and grandsons) relied heavily upon developments in Roman engineering and architecture to produce buildings in grand style, as witness Ramat el-Khalil in Hebron, the city gates of Caesarea, Sebasté, and Tiberias, the stunning Temple Platform in Jerusalem, his palaces at Jerusalem, the Herodium, Masada, Jericho, and Machaerus in Jordan, his extensive waterworks traced from Bethlehem to Jerusalem, the building of Tiberias, Sepphoris, and Bethsaida-Julias by his sons, and by many other remains. Herod the Great relied upon delicate and expensive media in his decoration of the Temple Mount, but he relied upon painted and molded plaster in Masada and Herodium. Nevertheless the architecture of the Herods bespeaks the aesthetic and political ascendancy of Rome and the place of the Herods as client-kings or client-rulers for Rome.

The evidence from archaeology suggests that the overlay of Roman culture provided symbols, architecture, and conventions of its own that the underlying Jewish culture might accept or reject. The degree of participation in the overlay varied with the Roman institution and the century under discussion. For example, it is as yet a matter of controversy whether any Roman theaters in ancient Palestine so far excavated were built in the 1st century A.D. apart from the Herodian theaters at Caesarea and Jericho. Other theaters associated with the Roman cultural overlay have been surveyed or excavated at Abila, Philadelphia (Amman), Gerasa (Jerash), Botzra (Bosra), Gadara, Pella, Philipopolis, Hippos-Susitha, Hammath-Gader (el-Hammeh) and Petra E of the Jordan, and at Flavia Neapolis (Nablus), Eleutherapolis (Beth Guvrin), Sebasté (Samaria), Beth Shean-Scythopolis, Dora, Dionysias-Soada (Suweida), Legio, Maiumas near Caesarea, and Sepphoris W of the Jordan. The sheer number of theaters suggests that investigation of the social structures associated with Roman theaters in ancient Palestine may be a fruitful line of inquiry. Baths also were introduced with Greek culture, though the presence of Rome spurred construction of baths, since they were apparently somewhat less offensive to Jewish culture. The enormous bath complex at Hammath-Gader on the E shores of the River Yarmuk and S of the Sea of Galilee is almost totally Byzantine, but it raises the question of the degree of acceptance of a Roman cultural form such as public bathing in the period under discussion. In any case, it is clear that the architectural and aesthetic norms of Greek and Roman Hellenism, and certainly the Greek language, penetrated everywhere into ancient Palestine. What is not clear is the extent of penetration of other Hellenistic ideas such as rhetoric, Greco-Roman notions of the social position of women, or the relation of the human to the divine. Such abstractions are a greater challenge to assess archaeologically, though perhaps it is not impossible.

The future challenge to archaeologists of this period and to exegetes of the NT and other early Christian and Jewish literature is to combine insights from the two disciplines with the hope of achieving clear social-historical reconstructions of ancient Palestinian life. Since historical investigation at the moment is dominated by social history, and since exegesis of the NT and other ancient texts currently bears the same interpretative weight, it is possible to see a fruitful collaboration. For example, research into the social structures of Jewish society, of the imperial cult, and of the penetration of alternatives to the old Roman Religion, including Mithraism, into the cities of the provinces is in full swing among historians. Ever since G. Theissen and J. Gager, research into the social histories of early Christianity (the "Jesus movement") has expanded to include the social context of ancient Palestine, including aspects of temple and society or synagogue and society. It has already been suggested that one fruitful avenue of inquiry has been study of the structures of society relating to Roman theaters. This should be expanded to include study of other forms of Roman entertainment. Since 1931 archaeologists have excavated hippodromes at Bozra (Bosra), Kanath, Gadara, Gerasa, Caesarea, Jericho, and Beth Shean, with another possibly at Herodium. Josephus mentions one at Magdala-Tarichaeae (*Life* 132, 138) and at Jerusalem (*Ant* 17.193), though neither have been found. Another field of potential worthwhile inquiry is in the social norms of temple worship and cult in Judaism and the Roman world as revealed in texts and monuments, and there is no dearth of temple remains in Israel, Egypt, Syria, Lebanon, and Jordan. Recently considerable archaeological evidence has been adduced for reconstruction of the buildings and other remnants of Jewish cult on the S end of the Temple Mount, including ritual baths. Finally a potentially important area of study for the future is in theory and method in archaeology, especially the hermeneutics of monuments, and a comparative study of interpretation in archaeology and interpretation in textual studies. Some initial forays in this direction have been attempted.

Bibliography

Shanks, H., ed. 1984. *Recent Archaeology in the Land of Israel.* Washington.

———. 1988. *Ancient Israel.* Washington.

JAMES F. STRANGE

PALESTINE, CLIMATE OF. The climate of any particular region, by which is meant the general pattern of weather which recurs from year to year, is directly related to that region's position upon the surface of the globe. Thus, the climate of a region cannot be considered in isolation from the climates of other neighboring regions, but must be observed in relationship to them, since shifts in the distribution of high and low pressure systems, together with corresponding changes in global air-flow, have a profound impact upon regional climatic patterns.

Most of Palestine, except for the Jordan Valley and the area W of the Dead Sea (which is in a steppe climate zone), falls within the subtropical or Mediterranean climatic region, a region which is characterized by two distinct seasons per year—a dry one and a wet one (the terms "summer" and "winter" are sometimes used, but are not really descriptive of the seasons in Palestine). Being on the N margin of the subtropical zone, Palestine is situated between a subtropical arid zone to its S, the great deserts of Arabia and the Sahara, and a subtropical wet zone to its N. Even though Palestine itself is relatively small, this location results in some marked climatic differences between the N and S regions of the area. The climatic boundary position refers also to the W-E direction with the proximity of the Mediterranean on the W and the large Asian land mass on the E, with corresponding regional differences within the area from W to E.

A. Factors Influencing Climate
  1. Atmospheric Pressure and Winds
  2. Latitude and Insolation
  3. Relationship to Water and Land Masses
  4. Regional Topography
B. Seasonality in the Palestinian Climate
  1. The Rainy Season
    a. Limits and Development
    b. Variations in Rainfall
    c. Rain Days and Rainfall Intensity
  2. The Dry Season
    a. Limits
    b. Dew and Humidity
  3. The Transitional Periods
C. The Climate during Biblical Times and the Climate Today

A. Factors Influencing Climate

1. Atmospheric Pressure and Winds. One of the principal meteorological factors influencing the Palestinian climate is the shifting global system of high- and low-pressure areas. During the dry season, Palestine sits on the W edge of an extensive low pressure area which is centered over India (the cause of the Indian monsoons) and which extends over the Persian Gulf and Mesopotamia. There is also a secondary low centered over Cyprus. As the air circulates in a counterclockwise direction around the Indian low, and is in turn deflected by the Cyprus low, the resulting airflow over Palestine is from NW to SE, bringing what was known to the ancient Greeks as the "etesian winds."

The wet season commences when this entire system of low pressure areas is displaced southward by a shift in the path of the jet stream, which brings Palestine into the zone of the westerlies of the temperate zone, with its cyclonic storms, units of low barometric pressure with circular, counterclockwise airflow. These cyclonic storm systems move E toward Palestine following the path of a low-pressure trough in the Mediterranean, which is situated between one high pressure area in Central Asia and another in the Sahara. See Fig. PAL.03. As these cyclones (about twenty-five in an average year) travel across the Mediterranean (in four to six days), they are reinforced by the confluence of warm African air with cooler European air, producing unstable conditions in the atmosphere, commonly resulting in precipitation.

2. Latitude and Insolation. A second factor affecting

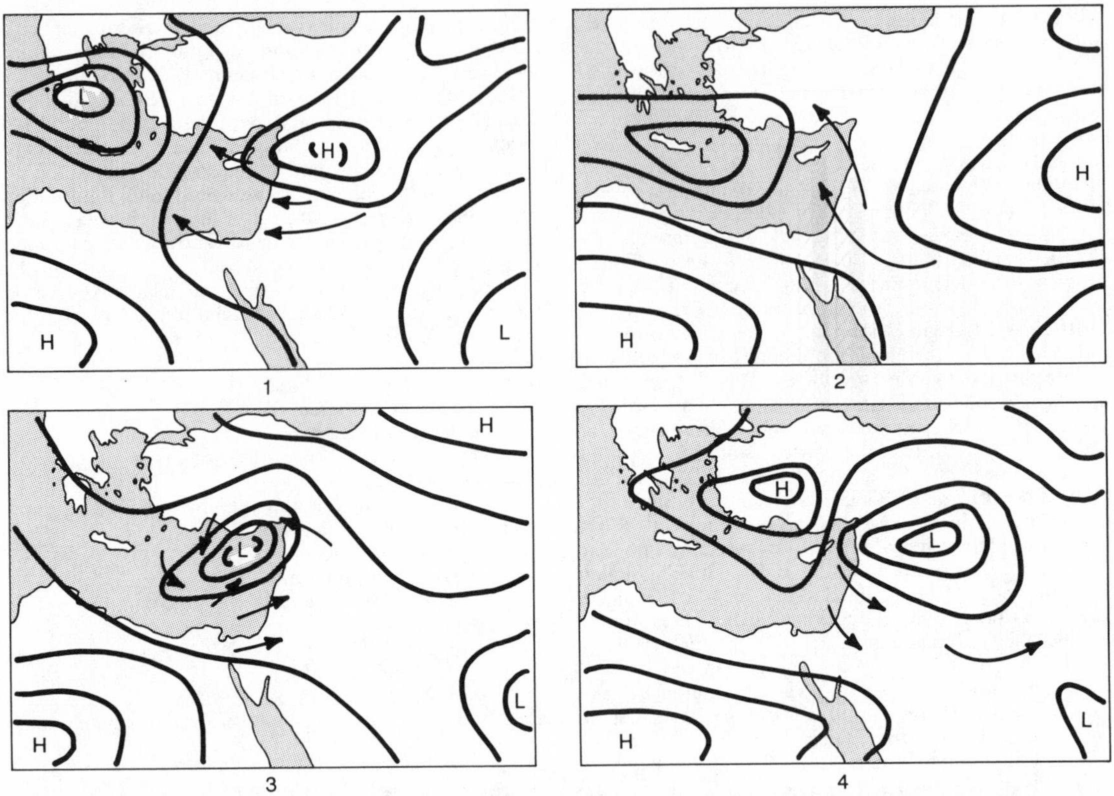

PAL.03. Weather maps showing (in four stages) the movement of a typical cyclonic storm system (L) along a low-pressure trough in the Mediterranean. The arrows indicate prevailing wind direction during this wet season in Palestine.

Palestinian climate, especially with respect to sunlight intensity (insolation) and temperature, is its distance from the equator, since this determines both the amount of heating from the sun and the moderate seasonal variations in the length of daylight hours. Palestine lies between 31°15′ and 33°15′ N latitude, which is approximately equivalent to S California.

With the stable conditions of the dry (summer) season, Palestine is typically sunny and warm, with insolation intensified by the extremely low degree of cloud cover. There are no completely overcast days in the summer, and only a fourth of summer days are partly cloudy, with fair-weather cumulus and stratocumulus clouds. In most of the area, cloud cover is less than 10% in July and August. Summer sunshine hours may approach close to 98% of the possible. Even in the winter season this figure remains at 50%, which is higher than either W Europe or E North America. The latitude also means that the sun strikes the ground at a high angle, as high as 80° during the dry season. This results in solar radiation at the rate of an annual mean of 5 million calories per square meter. On a summer day this figure rises to 7.5 million cal./m^2, while on a clear winter day it falls to 3 million cal./$m.^2$ Even on a cloudy winter day, however, this figure is still 1 million cal./m^2 (Ashbel *EncJud* 10: 184). Expressed in another way, this means that horizontal surfaces receive illumination of some 90 kilo-lux-hours at noon in summer, and an area perpendicular to the sun's rays receives over 130 klh, nearly the absolute maximum possible. These quantities of klh are reduced by only one-third in the wet season (Ashbel *EncJud* 10: 184–85).

Palestine's general temperature patterns are also a product of its latitude. While temperatures vary within the area from N to S and depend upon regional topography and distance from the sea as well, they are generally comparatively high owing to the high insolation. Highest temperatures normally occur in August and the lowest are in January in all four orographic regions of the area. See Fig. PAL.04. January averages are 53.5°F in the Coastal Plain, 46.5°–50°F in the W Highlands, 53.5°–55°F in the Jordan Valley, and 47°F in the Transjordanian Plateau. August figures are 75°–79°F in the Coastal Plain, 71.5°–79°F in the W Highlands, 82°–93°F in the Jordan Valley, and 78°F in the Transjordanian Plateau (Orni and Efrat 1973: 136).

3. Relationship to Water and Land Masses. Palestine's geographic position—at the SE corner of the Mediterranean, where the sea is in close proximity to the desert, and between the Sahara and Arabian deserts on the one hand and the Russo-Siberian plains on the other—greatly influences its climate.

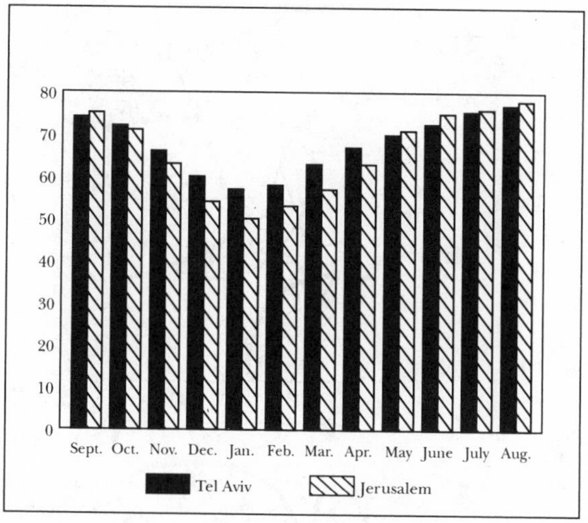

PAL.04. Comparative graph of monthly mean temperatures of coastal plain (Tel Aviv) and hill country (Jerusalem).

Local winds are generated by differences in temperature at the border of water and land masses. Land warms more quickly than the sea during the day and cools more rapidly at night. The land thus becomes cooler than the sea at night and develops higher atmospheric pressure over it, with the opposite occurring during the day. Therefore there are ordinarily offshore winds at night and onshore winds during the day. The onshore breeze is stronger and more persistent than the offshore breeze in the summer, owing to the low over the Persian Gulf. Rainfall tends to decrease and the temperature range tends to increase with distance from the sea.

The location of Palestine between the deserts and the Russo-Siberian plains also affects precipitation. Normally storms develop over the Mediterranean where the warm tropical air from N Africa clashes with cold air from Asia. Should, however, the high pressure systems in these two areas become linked at their margins instead of clashing, the resulting ridge of high pressure can block the progress of rain-bearing depressions, bringing drought to Palestine.

4. Regional Topography. While climatic contrasts between the S and N parts of the area are largely explained by Palestine's global position, other differences in weather within the area are due to the fact that there are four distinct orographic regions, whose lines of relief run in a N-S direction, at right angles to the movement of the cyclonic storms. Rainfall distribution is decisively influenced by landscape relief because air ascending a slope cools, while its relative humidity increases. Descending air warms and decreases in humidity. Not only do differences in elevation affect the flow of air, and thus the development of weather patterns, but also such things as the angle of slope and the direction the slope faces. While the general rule is that rainfall decreases with distance from the sea, an increase in elevation changes this. Higher elevations with seaward slopes show a true orographic increase in precipitation, while lee slopes of such elevations show a sharp orographic decrease in precipitation, in what is known as the rain-shadow effect. The angle of the slope is also relevant. The steeper the ascending slope, the smaller is the area where the amount of rain resulting from the cooling of the air can concentrate. While there is a general decrease in precipitation in the area from N to S and there are other variations within each region from N to S, the general climatic patterns of the four orographic regions can be described as follows:

The Coastal Plain, which includes the central section of the Esdraelon Plain, is naturally greatly influenced by the sea. Throughout the year, the relative humidity is high, averaging 65–70% (see Fig. PAL.05) and the diurnal temperature range

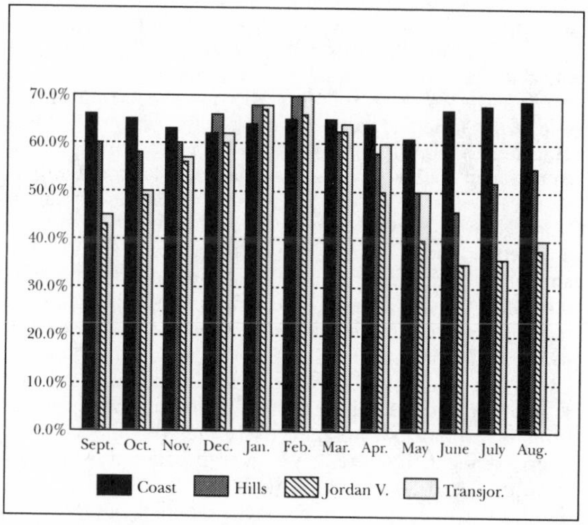

PAL.05. Comparative graph of average monthly relative humidity of coastal plain, hill country, Jordan Valley, and Transjordan.

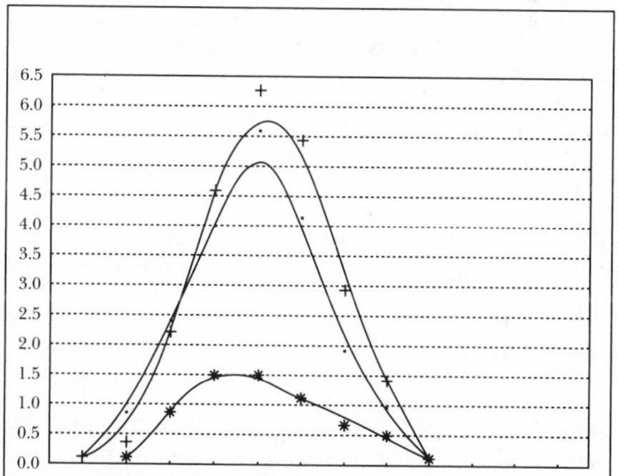

PAL.06. Comparative graph of average monthly precipitation of coastal plain (Lydda), hill country (Jerusalem), and Jordan Valley (Jericho).

(about 13°F) is considerably less than it is in the W Highlands. With a January average temperature of 55°F, both snow and frost are quite rare in this region (Orni and Efrat 1973: 151). The sirocco (see below) is less frequent here than in other parts of the country. Rainfall is both heavier and begins earlier than inland, with some 60% of the season's rain coming by the end of January. See Fig. PAL.06. Rainfall also increases from 10 inches annually in the S to 32 inches in the N (Orni and Efrat 1973: 152).

The Western Highlands, including Mount Carmel, have lower relative humidity than the coast, averaging 60%, and both the diurnal and annual temperature range is greater (Orni and Efrat 1973: 153). This area has the highest precipitation W of the Jordan, even though the onset of the rainy season is later than on the coast. Owing to considerable variations in topography, however, the rainfall map in the Highlands shows significant variability within the region. Both frost and snowfall are common in the higher elevations.

The Jordan Rift Valley is both in the rain shadow on the lee side of the Western Highlands and is below sea level in most of its length. This results in sharply decreased precipitation from that in the Highlands and in markedly warmer temperatures as well. The general rule of decrease in precipitation from N to S holds for this region, but there are other differences as well. In the N part of this region there is a large annual temperature range, with frost common in the winter, but long, hot summers. For example, Beth-shan has six months with average maximum temperatures above 86°F (*GB*, 59). To the S, around the Dead Sea, which is both the lowest spot on earth and is surrounded by mountains on the E and W, there are unique climatic conditions. The relative humidity is quite low, averaging 57%, but is modified to some degree owing to the extremely high evaporation rate of water from the Dead Sea, resulting from the high temperatures. The annual mean temperature at the S end of the Dead Sea is 78°F, and falls to only 62.5°F in January. The highest temperature ever recorded in Palestine, 124°F, was recorded here (Orni and Efrat 1973: 157). Precipitation amounts are the lowest in Palestine, less than 5 inches annually.

The Transjordanian Plateau has a climate which generally resembles that of the Western Highlands. There are, however, differences caused by its higher elevation and greater distance from the sea. The seaward slopes of these higher elevations see more rainfall than do the Western Highlands. The annual and diurnal temperature ranges are also greater. Frost and snow are even more common.

B. Seasonality in the Palestinian Climate

1. The Rainy Season. a. Limits and Development. The terms "summer" and "winter," which are used to describe the seasons in the temperate zone, are not as descriptive of the seasons in Palestine as are the terms "dry season" and "wet season," since, as an indicator of seasonality, temperature variation is not as marked as is the sharp bifurcation in the precipitation pattern. In the Bible this season (*ḥōrep*) is one of rainy, stormy weather (Lev 26:4; Deut 11:14; Isa 4:6; 25:4; Job 37:9; Ezra 10:9, 13; Cant 2:11; John 10:23; Acts 28:2). The word *sĕtāw*, another meteorological term in Hebrew, occurs only once in the Bible (Cant 2:11); but its Arabic cognate, *sitā*ʾ, is the common word for rain as well as winter in the dialect of

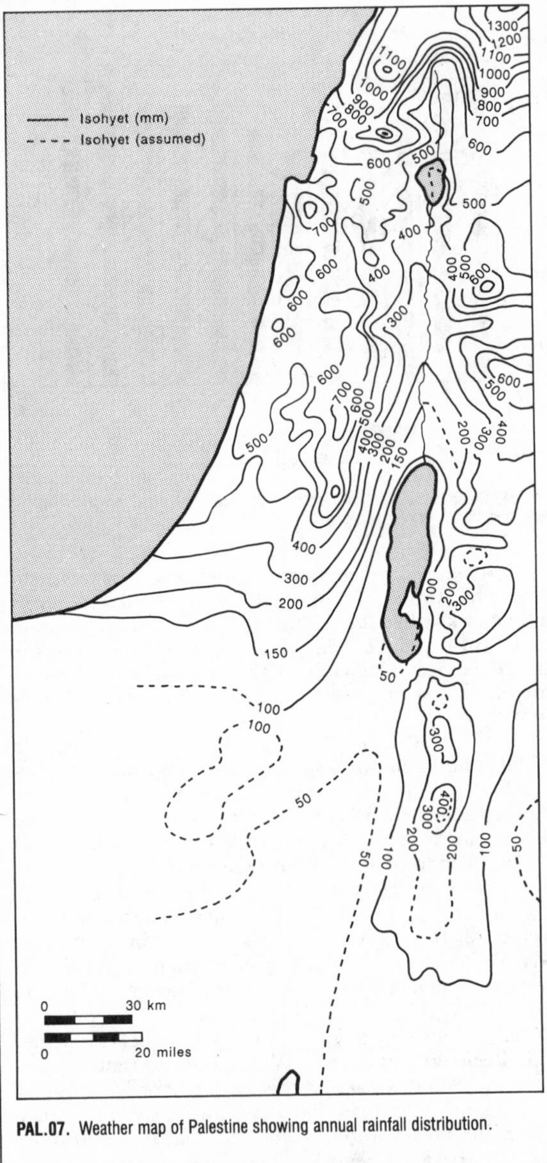

PAL.07. Weather map of Palestine showing annual rainfall distribution.

Jerusalem. The Greek term *cheimōn* in the NT means both "winter" and "storm" (Scott *IDB* 3: 623).

The wet season begins first in the N part of the area, usually in mid-October, and ends last there in the spring, usually in March. The rainy season starts as the cyclones of the temperate zone create steep pressure gradients which cause more rapid and steeper movement of air masses, cooling them and causing them to gain in relative humidity. When this moist air reaches its saturation point, its moisture precipitates in rain or snow.

About 70% of the rainfall in Palestine falls from November to February, with January being both the wettest and coldest month (Orni and Efrat 1973: 146). There are differences in rainfall patterns as well as amounts in the four orographic regions. The Coastal Plain receives 50% of its annual rainfall by early January, the Western Highlands attain that figure about the end of January, and the Transjordanian plateau only in February (Orni and Efrat 1973: 146). At the beginning and end of the rainy season come what the Bible speaks of as "the former and latter rains" (*malqôš* and *yôreh*). See RAIN.

b. Variations in Rainfall. The rainy season in Palestine is, however, highly unpredictable—both in its temporal distribution within a season and in successive seasons. Five types of seasonal distribution have been observed: (1) normal, with even distribution throughout the rainy season—occurs about one-third of the time in Jerusalem and 42% of the time in Haifa; (2) a wet early season with a dry second half—occurs about 20% of the time in Jerusalem and the Judean Mountains, only 6% of the time in the N; (3) a dry early season with a rainy second half—more common in the N than in the S; (4) heavy rains in the middle of the season with a relatively dry beginning and end—rare, occurring only 2–3% of the time; and (5) twin or multiple-peaked season with dry spells between the peaks—about 35% of the time in the Judean Mountains and 24% of the time in Haifa (Ashbel *EncJud* 10: 185). These variations in the temporal distribution of rainfall throughout the season have significant consequences for agriculture. Especially important for farming is the date of the initial rainfall that marks the end of the dry season and the date of the last rain, since the former is needed to prepare the soil for plowing and the latter influences the maturation of crops. Rain at the end of the season, if the timing is right and not too late, serves to bring cereal crops to successful maturation, especially wheat. But such rains, if too late, can easily devastate barley, which is particularly susceptible to rain during harvest. Such rain during the harvest season is a rare occurrence. In 1 Sam 12:17 Samuel says: "Is it not wheat harvest today? I will call to YHWH and he will give thunder and rain . . ." When the prophet successfully called for rain in a normally dry period, his prophetic credentials were confirmed.

In addition to such variations in the temporal distribution of rainfall in a season, there are significant variations from year to year. Two parameters come into play here: (1) the frequency of abnormal (+ or −) precipitation; and (2) the extent of deviation from the mean. In assessing these two variables, Jerusalem can be used as an example, since there exists for Jerusalem the longest series of recorded rainfall for the area, beginning in 1846/47. In the 42-year period 1920–1962, there were two series of years when there was an average deviation of 30% (±) or more from the mean annual rainfall, one dry cycle and one rainy cycle as follows (Amiran 1964: 104):

Dry Cycle (1920/21–1937/38)

	Total Amount of Deviation	Number of Years of Occurrence
Number of years		18
Positive deviations	26	4
Negative deviations	365	14
Positive deviations of 30% or more	0	0
Negative deviations of 30% or more	283	7
Negative deviations of 50% or more	106	2

Rainy Cycle (1944/45–1961/62)

	Total Amount of Deviation	Number of Years of Occurrence
Number of years		18
Positive deviations	85.4	4
Negative deviations	369	14
Positive deviations of 30% or more	79	2
Negative deviations of 30% or more	243	5
Negative deviations of 50% or more	117	2

What is most significant in these figures is the fact that even in the eighteen-year rainy cycle five of these years had negative deviations of 30% or more. Even more critical for agriculture, however, is the spacing of these years. A dry year in a series of more or less normal or wet years rarely has serious consequences for the farming economy. But while the farmer can weather a single dry year, a series of such years can be disastrous. Amiran (1964: 104) observes that three consecutive dry years, each with a negative deviation of 30% or more, are part of the experience of every farmer in Palestine. It is perhaps not coincidental that this same three-year figure is used to describe the disastrous drought in the time of Elijah (1 Kgs 18:1).

Jerusalem rainfall data for the years 1920/21–1949/50 are represented in Fig. PAL.08. The left side of the chart

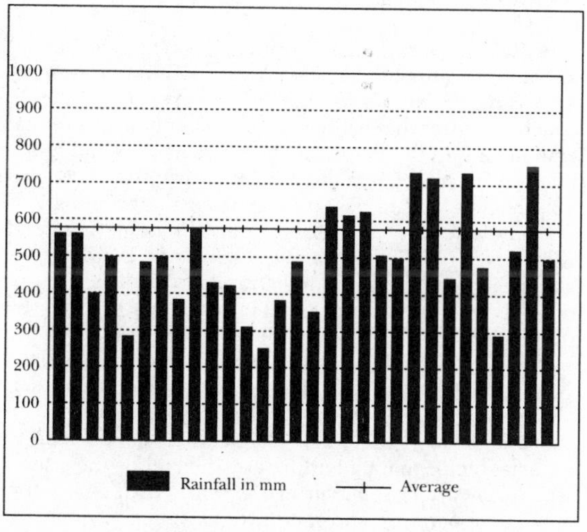

PAL.08. Graph of annual rainfall of Jerusalem—1920/21–1949/50.

represents 1920/21 and the right side 1949/50 (Rosenan 1955: 151). On the basis of this data, it can be observed that a cycle of three or more consecutive years with 30% or more negative deviation occurs twice within this relatively short span of years. Put in other terms, this means that three years out of ten will experience accumulation of rainfall about 16% less than the mean and that one or two of these years will experience more than 25% less.

Perhaps the most meaningful way of assessing the variability of rainfall and its impact on agriculture in Palestine is one developed by D. Sharon (1965: 172), who presents rainfall data by calculating the standard deviation (in percent) of the annual amount of rain, and then plotting standard deviation isopleths (1965: 172). On such a plotting, Jerusalem, together with much of the central hill country, falls within the 30%–40% range in the measure of standard deviation, with most of Galilee in the 20%–30% range. The 40% range encompasses Beer-sheba, the Negeb, and the Jordan Valley S of Beth Shean. Sharon then interprets such standard deviation figures of 20% and 40% by means of the following table (1965: 171):

	Probable Percentage of Years with Variation of		
Standard Deviation	≦ 20%	≦ 40%	≦ 60%
20%	68	96	99.7
40%	38	68	87

The conclusion to be drawn from this table is that wherever there is a standard deviation of 40%, variations of less than 20% from the average annual rainfall can be expected in only 38% of the years, whereas in 32% of the years, variations that exceed 40% will occur. Furthermore, in 13% of the years, deviations exceeding 60% can be encountered. Sharon concludes: "Thus, the data . . . supply valuable information on the variability of rainfall which might be expected at each specified level. The latter could also be interpreted in terms of the risk associated with the relative or absolute deviation of each size, at each station" (1965: 171).

c. Rain Days and Rainfall Intensity. While the annual amount of rainfall in farming areas in Palestine roughly approximates that of some agricultural areas in temperate zones, the difference between the two lies not in the annual amount of rain but in the number of rainy days and in the intensity of rainfall in a given hour or day (Ashbel *EncJud* 10: 185–86). A rain day, in international terminology, is one on which there is at least 0.1 mm of rainfall (Orni and Efrat 1973: 147). Thus, while Jerusalem and London have about the same average annual rainfall (22 inches), London has over 300 rain days while Jerusalem has only 50 (Orni and Efrat 1973: 147). The number of rain days per season (like the amount of annual rainfall) decreases from N to S and from W to E. Rain tends to be concentrated within a few hours of the day, with sunny intervals between showers (Karmon 1971: 28). The heaviest showers tend to occur at the beginning and toward the end of the season when there are clashing air masses which differ considerably in temperature and moisture (Orni and Efrat 1973: 146). The net result of these patterns is high-intensity rainfall, resulting in increased runoff and, consequently, frequent flooding.

2. The Dry Season. a. Limits. The dry season typically begins in May-June and lasts until September, with three to four completely rainless months. Even though the air moving into Palestine from the Mediterranean is moisture-laden during this season, rain cloud formation is inhibited by the presence of high pressure in the upper atmosphere, which causes air to subside and creates a thermic inversion over the E Mediterranean area. As air settles and is compressed, its temperature increases while its relative humidity declines, thus deferring rain (Hopkins 1985: 80).

b. Dew and Humidity. Although rainfall is not triggered during the dry season, the steady, moist W winds do bring dew, the formation and amount of which are dependent both on relative humidity and nighttime cooling as well as on the properties of the cooling surfaces of soil and vegetation upon which the dew falls. The distribution of the number of dew nights and the amount of dewfall, like that of rainfall, varies considerably from one area to another. But by comparison with dew amounts, the number of dew nights is relatively stable, just as the number of rainy days varies only slightly in comparison with variations in amounts of rainfall. There are three distinct dew regimes: (1) a coastal type with a summer maximum; (2) an interior type with a spring maximum; and (3) the hill type with an autumn maximum (Gilead and Rosenan 1954: 121). Dewfall is especially significant in the Coastal Plain (including the Jezreel Valley) and on the sea-facing slopes of the Western Highlands, where dew falls heavily and regularly during the dry season. See Fig. PAL.09. The Central Huleh Basin and the lower Beth-shan Valley also have considerable amounts of dew. Dew falls on nights when the soil becomes cooler than the air with which it comes into contact. The incidence of such nights increases as one travels S in the Coastal Plain, where the moisture-laden air from the sea is coupled with the cool nights

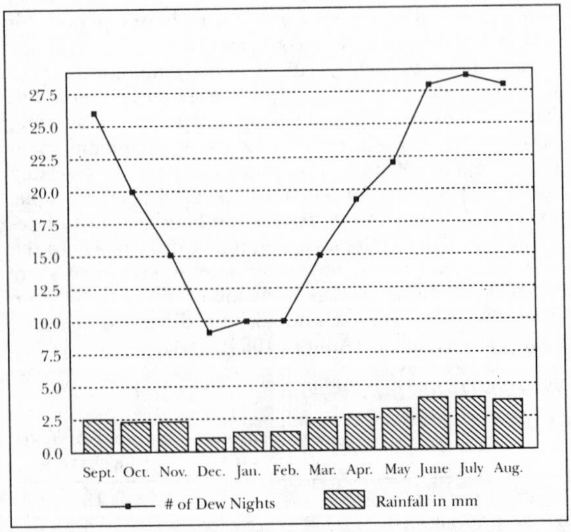

PAL.09. Graph of dew nights and amounts of coastal plain—1945–52.

caused by the nearby desert. Studies of dew show that the richest month for dew in the Coastal Plain is August. The number of dewfall nights in the Coastal Plain ranges from 138 in the N to 250 in the S, with an average of 200 (*GB*, 44). In the Western Highlands there are between 100 and 180 nights of dewfall per year (Orni and Efrat 1973: 155). See Fig. PAL.10.

Dewfall is important for agriculture, especially in the S Coastal Plain, where melons can be grown as a typical dry season crop. Its presence and value are frequently attested to in the Bible (Gen 27:28; Deut 33:28; Judg 6:38; 2 Sam 1:21; 1 Kgs 17:1; Isa 18:4; Hos 14:5; Mic 5:7; Zech 8:12; Hag 1:10; Job 29:19).

3. The Transitional Periods. Palestine does not have a spring and fall as they are known in the temperate zones, but rather two short, irregular transitional periods which fall between the dry and rainy seasons and which are characterized by particular weather patterns. These periods typically last about six weeks, with one occurring from early April to mid-June; the second from mid-September to the end of October. These transitional periods are clearly demarcated from the dry season and merge into the wet season, there being some overlap with the end of the rainy season in April-May and with its beginning in September-October.

Two important meteorological phenomena characterize these transitional periods: the sirocco and desert storms (Baly, *GB*, 52). The name "sirocco" is derived from the term *sharqiyyeh,* meaning an E wind, and is known in Egypt as *khamsin* and in modern Israel as *sharav,* although these terms do not refer to precisely the same conditions and thus are not strictly interchangeable (*GB*, 52). Israelis commonly use the term *sharav* as a general term for any kind of hot air that moves into the area from the E desert. Actually, however, there are three distinct situations which may give rise to *sharav* conditions of E and SE winds or a rise in barometric pressure: (1) the *khamsin* proper (which Baly [*GB*, 52] prefers to call the sirocco), in which a low over eastern North Africa causes warm, dry winds to blow over Palestine from the E; (2) the *sharav* proper, where a high over the area itself causes subsiding air to be compressed and heated; and (3) a situation in which a low moves into the area from the direction of the Red Sea, bringing with it unseasonably warm air (Orni and Efrat 1973: 141). Baly (*GB*, 52) suggests restricting the use of the term "sirocco," which is limited to the transitional periods, to the first of these conditions.

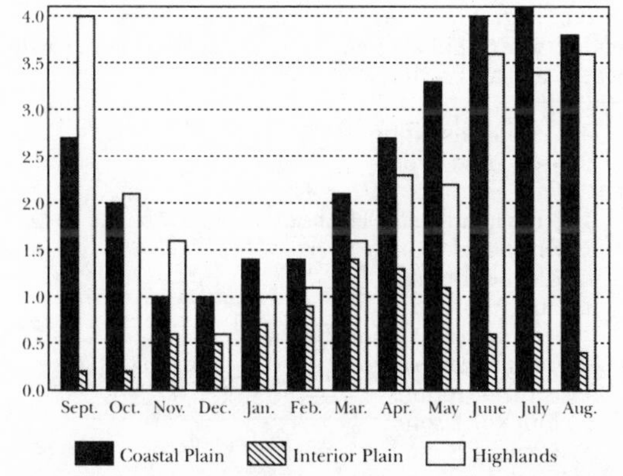

PAL.10. Mean monthly dew (in mm) of coastal plain, interior plain, and hill country—1943–52.

The sirocco proper (or true *khamsin,* which occurs sporadically during the transitional seasons) is characterized by a set of phenomena which includes strong thermal inversions which compress, heat, and desiccate trapped stagnant air, and strong dust-carrying E winds blowing across Palestine from the Arabian desert whence they are attracted by a low over Libya or Egypt (Karmon 1971: 24) [cf. Ezek 12:10; 19:12]. During a sirocco, which may last from two or three days to three weeks, temperatures may rise rapidly by as much as 16–22°F, with a corresponding lessening of the diurnal differential. Relative humidity can drop by as much as 40%, and the air becomes filled with very fine dust (*GB*, 52). Although the mean maximum daily temperature typically occurs in August, the record high temperatures for the area have been recorded in May and June during a sirocco. In such conditions, "People with a heart condition, nervous complaints, or sinus trouble are particularly affected, but even the mildest-tempered person is apt to become irritable and to snap at other people for no apparent reason" (*GB*, 52). Relief from the sirocco comes when the low-pressure area moves on eastward, bringing to the area a sudden shift to cooler, moister westerlies. The sirocco is characterized by variable intensity and duration in different regions of the area. Intensity increases as one goes from E to W, and becomes especially oppressive in the Jordan Rift Valley. Since it is a descending wind from the E, the Western Highlands have more days of sirocco than the lowlands to their W. Biblical references to the sirocco are frequent (Isa 27:8; 40:6–8; Ezek 17:10; Hos 12:1; 13:15; Ps 103:16; Job 37:16–17; Luke 12:55; Jas 1:11).

The second situation, the *sharav* proper, develops with rising barometric pressure under anticyclonic conditions, bringing an E wind which blows toward the area from a center of high pressure over Iraq, and sometimes also Turkey. This kind of storm is not restricted to the transitional periods, but may occur during the wet season (Ashbel *EncJud* 10: 189). Such a strong E wind in the wet season is referred to in the Bible as a *qādîm* (Exod 10:13; Ps 48:8; Jonah 4:8). Such a situation brings conditions which resemble those of a sirocco, but it is not only as hard to bear as a sirocco, but the high often becomes stationary and thus the *sharav* can last longer than the sirocco (Ashbel *EncJud* 10: 190).

C. The Climate during Biblical Times and the Climate Today

A theoretical comparison of the climate in Palestine in biblical times and today presents three possibilities: (1) that the climate during biblical times was more moderate; (2) that the climate was harsher than now; and (3) that the climate was similar to today's. Evidence for significant climatic variations in the ANE is diverse, multiform, of varying quality and applicability, and above all, widely open to competing interpretations. Among the various types of evidence that have been marshaled in support of significant climatic change are: (1) extrapolation from the reconstructions of climates of adjacent and climatically related areas (particularly NW Europe); (2) historical events (migrations, cultural breaks, etc.) purportedly tied to climatic variations; (3) hydrological evidence, especially regarding the level of the ground water table, the Dead Sea, and the fluctuation of the Mediterranean Sea coast; (4) dendroarchaeological and paleobotanical evidence; (5) palynological evidence; (6) fossil fauna (especially recovered from cave excavations); (7) pedological and sedimentary analysis; and (8) paleometeorological deductions (Hopkins 1985: 101). While individual pieces of such evidence may prove substantial, there have been no synthetic treatments of them with respect to their applicability in assessing climatic change.

Investigators have, however, established considerable support for the idea that in prehistoric times there were different climatic conditions in Palestine than exist there today. Animal bones characteristic of a hot and humid climate, for example, have been discovered in the Tabun F level in the Carmel Caves, which included small mammals that have become almost extinct today (Ben-Yoseph 1985: 226). It is thus concluded that archaeological data support the theory that, at least for some time at the end of the Pleistocene era, the Palestinian climate was similar to that of the tropics.

But have there been changes in the climate of Palestine during and since the biblical period? On the one hand, it seems clear that, in terms of what Butzer calls "third-order" changes profound enough to show up on the astronomical scale of climatic history (Butzer 1974: 730), the general pattern of the climate, with the alternation of dry and wet seasons, has not seriously changed since 6000 or 7000 B.C. in the Neolithic period. Below such third-order changes, paleoclimatologists speak of second-order variations, measured in hundreds of years, and first-order fluctuations which are observable within a lifetime (Butzer 1974: 730). With respect to such second-order variations and first-order fluctuations, Baly says, "That climate is not static but rather in a state of constant fluctuation is now beyond doubt, and it would be a great mistake to take any set of climatic figures as 'normal' " (*GB*, 65). But having said this, he also adds, "Any attempt to reconstruct theoretically the relationship between climatic fluctuations of western Europe [where there is more complete data than for Palestine] and those of Palestine is fraught with danger" (*GB*, 67). Ben-Yoseph concludes that the amounts of precipitation have not changed in Palestine, but their usefulness has decreased as a result of human land-use patterns. Erosion on hillsides, owing to poor land management, has led to an increase in the water lost to runoff after rain. Deforestation reduced the fog and the amounts of water that accumulated in the treetops. Thus the same amount of water falling on the land lost part of its effectiveness through an increase and expansion of human neglect of the land. The gradual decline of the land was not caused by a change in climate but rather by the people living there (Ben-Yoseph 1985: 237).

We can then conclude with Hopkins that the climate of Palestine in the biblical period has not changed appreciably from that of today, but only varied around a mean that closely resembles present conditions (Hopkins 1985: 107).

Bibliography

Amiran, D. H. K. 1964. Land Use in Israel. Pp. 101–12 in *Land Use in Semi-Arid Mediterranean Climates.* UNESCO International Geographic Union. Paris.

Ben-Yoseph, J. 1985. The Climate in Eretz Israel during Biblical Times. *HS* 26: 225–39.

Butzer, K. W. 1974. Climate Change. *EncBrit* 4: 730–41.

Gilead, M., and Rosenan, N. 1954. Ten Years of Dew Observation in Israel. *IEJ* 4: 120–23.

Hopkins, D. C. 1985. *The Highlands of Canaan: Agricultural Life in the Early Iron Age.* SWBA 3. Decatur, GA.

Karmon, Y. 1971. *Israel: A Regional Geography.* London.

Orni, E., and Efrat, E. 1973. *Geography of Israel,* 3d Rev. Ed. Philadelphia.

Rosenan, N. 1955. One Hundred Years of Rainfall in Jerusalem. *IEJ* 5: 137–53.

Sharon, D. 1965. Variability of Rainfall in Israel: A Map of the Relative Standard Deviation of the Annual Amounts. *IEJ* 15: 169–76.

FRANK S. FRICK

PALESTINE, GEOGRAPHY AND GEOLOGY OF.

See GEOGRAPHY AND THE BIBLE (GEOGRAPHY OF PALESTINE).

PALESTINIAN FUNERARY INSCRIPTIONS.

Palestine can be understood in a restricted sense as the "land of Philistia" but also in the sense intended by Greek and Latin authors to designate all the territory found between Syria-Phoenicia and Egypt, including the two banks of the Jordan. During the Byzantine period the word "Palestine" took on a still greater range, the area being divided into three provinces: *Palestina prima, secunda,* and *tertia* or *salutaris.* What will be presented here are the funerary inscriptions found in Palestine taken as "Cisjordan," from the most ancient times up until the Byzantine period, beginning with the reign of Constantine, and divided where possible chronologically by sites according to language and script.

A. Canaanite Inscriptions
B. Hebrew Inscriptions
  1. Jerusalem
  2. Jerusalem: Ketef Hinnom
  3. Khirbet el-Qōm
  4. Khirbet Beit Lei
  5. Conclusion
C. Phoenician Inscriptions: Achzib
D. "Idumean" Inscriptions: Marissa-Maresha
E. Jewish Inscriptions
  1. Tomb of Jason
  2. Tomb of Benê Hezîr
  3. Tomb Inscriptions
  4. Inscribed Sarcophagi
  5. Ossuaries

A. Canaanite Inscriptions

The short inscriptions from tombs at Lachish are not, strictly speaking, funerary inscriptions, but neither should they be set aside too quickly. The "Lachish Dagger" from tomb 1502, dated to the 17th century B.C., carries an engraving of a four-letter name, best understood as Turanza (Puech 1986–87). The cover of an incense burner from tomb 216, from the early 13th century, still shows traces in red ink of a date and the name of a person, "The month of Ziv for Baᶜal[x]." On the outside of a bowl from tomb 527 a date is painted in white, "The third of the month of [. . .]" and is to be dated in the 13th century (Puech 1986–87). Do these dates refer to the inhumation of the deceased? Whatever the case, as the oldest alphabetic inscriptions discovered in tombs, they merit being mentioned along with the anthropoidal clay sarcophagi with hieroglyphic inscriptions, slightly more recent, that mention proper names also.

B. Hebrew Inscriptions

1. Jerusalem. A necropolis from the monarchic period was discovered by the Frenchman Clermont-Ganneau in 1870 and 1881 on the slopes of the village of Siloam to the east of the old city of Jerusalem (Clermont-Ganneau 1871: 103; 1885: 217–18; 1899a: 305–16). He soon suspected its importance since, despite the poor state of preservation of the two inscribed panels on the walls of the rock-cut tomb that had served as a cell for Byzantine hermits and as a cistern during the Arab period, he suspected that this could be the tomb of Shebna, the steward of the palace (Heb *ʾăšer ᶜal habbāyit*) mentioned in Isa 22:15 (Clermont-Ganneau 1899a: 313). This pioneer of archaeology and Palestinian epigraphy succeeded in removing the two inscribed panels on behalf of the British Museum, where they are exhibited.

In 1946 a fourth inscription was discovered above the entrance to a tomb adjoining the one on the N (Reifenberg 1948). From the remains of three lines, one can read only two or three words: (1) "Tomb of . . . (2) who will o[pe]n (?) [. . .]," for the more usual "Tomb of PN[. . . Cursed be the person] who will o[pen . . .]." It was evidently the tomb of a person of high rank whose name still eludes a more secure interpretation (Ussishkin 1975).

It was not until 1953 that the longer inscription above the door of the "steward's" tomb was deciphered by Avigad with the help of photographs and a squeeze:

> (1) "This [is the tomb of x]yahu, steward of the palace. There is neither silver nor gold here, (2) only [his bones] and the bones of his maidservant with him. Cursed be the man who (3) would open this (tomb)!"

Only the theophoric name with a Yahwistic element is not restorable. Following Clermont-Ganneau, Avigad (Yadin) (1953) and Gibson (*TSSI* 1: 24) want to restore [Sheban]-yahu after Isa 22:15–16, but Katzenstein (1960) proposed [*Helqi*]yahu, father of Eliakim (2 Kgs 18:18). These two propositions seem hardly likely because of their length, which exceeds the space to be filled. From the Lachish ostraca and recently published bullae, other names of royal stewards from the end of the 7th century are known. It is therefore useless to speculate on the name of the owner of this tomb. Of the one-line inscription engraved in a rectangular panel to the right of the preceding one, only the first half is preserved: "(Sepulcral) chamber next to the (funerary) ch[amber . . .]" At most three words are missing; they could refer to the deceased or to the interdiction against opening the tomb (see Avigad 1955; Ussishkin 1969). These two inscriptions on panels on the W face of the same monolithic tomb probably refer to two separate sepulchral chambers, each probably furnished with a sarcophagus dug into the rock for different inhumations, probably for the same family. The short inscription designates the interior room on the S side that has no access to the exterior and so it describes the composite aspect of the tomb.

The monolithic tomb to the N known as that of the "wife of the pharaoh" also carries a one-line inscription in a rectangular panel above the entrance, but enlargement of the door in the Byzantine period almost completely destroyed it, with the exception of the last two letters (*dalet*/*reš* and *reš;* Clermont-Ganneau 1885: 217–18 and pl. IID). Although the inscription is incomplete, the remaining letters date the structure to the end of the monarchic period, contemporary with the two other monolithic tombs.

2. Jerusalem: Ketef Hinnom. Several tombs located on the SW side of Gehenna between the road toward Bethlehem and the Scottish Hospice, and dating from the end of the monarchic period to the Roman period were recently brought to light. In tomb 25 two small silver rolls were discovered, measuring respectively 2.75 cm long and 1.1 cm in diameter and 1.14 cm long and .55 cm in diameter. These rolls are amulets or charms finely engraved with more than twenty lines, for which we have presently only a summary publication (Barkay 1986). The clearest passage concerns the priestly benedictions of Num 6:24–26 in an abridged form: *ybrk yhwh wyšmrk yʾr yhwh pnyw ʾlyk wyśm lk šlm* "May Yahweh bless <you> and keep you. May Yahweh make his face to shine upon you and may he bring you peace!" Num 6:25b–26a adds "and may he be gracious to you. May Yahweh lift up his countenance upon you." The double mention of the tetragrammaton is paired with the benediction, the peace and the illumination of the face. The amulets worn by the living accompanied the dead in the tomb in order to continue in their favor their protective and apotropaic role. In this sense, these inscriptions also interest the world of the dead. They date paleographically to the end of the 7th century.

3. Khirbet el-Qōm. Clandestine excavations at Khirbet el-Qōm, located about 11 km E-SE of Lachish (and perhaps to be identified with MAKKEDAH [Dorsey 1980]), brought to light in 1967 two tombs of the Iron II period with a quantity of ceramic materials and inscriptions on the walls. See KOM, KHIRBET EL-. Tomb I to the E of the site is composed of a central room and three side rooms with benches, rooms 1 and 2 to the right and 3 facing the entrance. Inscription number 1 was engraved on the W wall of the central room, to the left of the entrance to room number 3. Inscription number 2 was painted on the lintel of this same entrance. Tomb II, to the S roughly halfway between the village and the wadi, contains a central room with two lateral rooms on either side of the entrance. Inscription number 3 was incised on the pillar-shaped wall between the two rooms on the right. The walls of Tombs I and II also bear a certain amount of graffiti.

a. Inscription 1. The deeply engraved inscription was cut out of the wall by its discoverers. The reading of the three lines is assured (Dever 1969–70: 151): "To Ophay, son of Natanyahu, (belongs) this room."

b. Inscription 2. The inscription painted on the lintel of the same room posed several problems with its reading (Dever 1969–70: 156–57), but the reading seems to be fairly certain: Ophay, rather than ʿUzah (Barag 1970), thus "To Ophay, son of Natanyahu." It thus concerns the same personage to whom belonged this burial chamber. The inscription incised to the left was meant to specify and fix through time the property already indicated by the dipinto. These two contemporary inscriptions date probably from the first half of the 7th century or even ca. 700.

c. Inscription 3. This inscription, less carefully incised above a very deeply engraved hand, has been the object of considerable research because of its importance, but its interpretation remains in dispute. The engraved right hand is hanging in the position of an amulet, as is well known, and it must have an apotropaic meaning (Schroer 1983). The maledictions and benedictions of the inscription should logically belong to the same literary genre, something that interpreters have generally not recognized. The inscription is an imprecation in favor of Uriyahu, as the first line says very clearly when correctly read and interpreted. The verb *hqšr* is of an assured reading (the letter *qop* is certain); the word should not be read *hqšb* "be careful" (*contra* Dever 1969–70), *hʿšr* "the rich," (Lemaire 1977; Miller 1980; Jaroš 1982; Zevit 1984; Hadley 1987), *ḥšr* "the singer" (Mittmann 1981; Spronk 1986: 307–10), *ḥśr* "the governor" (Naveh 1979a; Angerstorfer 1982), or *hʾšr* "the one who" (Shea 1990). However, *hqšr* does not mean "was added" (Garbini 1978; Catastini 1984) but in the *Hipʿil* "to conjure," "to bind by conjuration," as in Isa 8:12–13 (were one should read **tqšyrw*, which has been changed into *tqdyšw* by metathesis and the Yahwistic purism of a scribe). The entire inscription reads as follows (note that line 4 is written to the left of the engraved hand, and line 5 is written below the engraved hand).

1 *ʾrhyw . hqšr . ktbh*	"Uriyahu conjured his inscription.
2 *brk . ʾryhw . lyhwh*	Blessed be ʾUriyahu before Yahweh,
3 *wmṣryh . lʾšrth . hwšʿ lh*	and from his adversaries by his asherah he saved him/ save him!
4 *lʾnyhw*	From/by ʾOniyahu
5 *wlʾšrth*	and by his asherah."
6 [. . . . . . .] *ḥ*	[. . . .]

The third line is superimposed over another text; certain letters are repeated or displaced, and it is possible that the original phrase was a little different, perhaps "Blessed the Uriyahu (?) before asherah! Save him (from his enemies!)"; as a kind of doublet of line 2, this sentence was corrected to read "and from his adversaries by his asherah. . . ." The suffix pronoun *h* ("his") of *ʾšrth* ("his asherah," probably referring to the cultic pole rather than the deity) does not agree well with a parsing of *hwšʿ lh* as an imperative ("save him"), as might be expected in an imprecation. The *waw* of *wmṣryh* (at the beginning of line 3) could be consecutive: "*because* from his enemies by his Asherah He saved him." The engraving is the work of Oniyahu (line 4), and line 5, incomplete (but not a graffito), could repeat a precative formula, parallel to lines 2–3.

Whatever it may be, the sense of this inscription is clear: it is a conjuration-imprecation of an apotropaic character in which the benediction of the deceased Uriyahu before Yahweh and his asherah assures him of salvation, and serves at the same time as a malediction against encounter with his adversaries or enemies, perhaps violators of the tomb and dark forces of the netherworld. The hand in the shape of an amulet with magic powers reinforces this interpretation. This inscription would date from around 700 B.C.

d. Graffiti. Some letters were incised on the left wall, opposite room 2 of Tomb I: *ʾalep* (or *ʿayin* ?); *ʾalep, bet,* and *mem* (not *nun-lamed,* as read by Dever [1969–70: 157]). These letters could represent the initials of the zodiac signs "lion(-scorpion?)," "lion," "virgo," and "libra," the four consecutive and central signs (five through eight of the zodiac, and for this reason endowed with magic and apotropaic powers. The graffiti on the pillars and in rooms 3–4 of Tomb II do not make any sense, but the engraved hand belongs to the same context as inscription 3. The inscriptions on vases cannot be called funerary inscriptions: a proper name on a pitcher, *yḥml,* and on a bowl, *ʾl* "El." (The letters of "El" are the first and twelfth letters of the alphabet, that is to say the beginnings of the two halves, *ʾalep* [to *kap*] and *lamed* [to *taw*]. This alphabetic significance is more likely if the inscription had any link with the burial.)

4. Khirbet Beit Lei. On the E side of Khirbet Beit Lei 8 km E of Lachish, a tomb was discovered dug into the rock. It includes a principal room (2 × 3 m) with two burial chambers, one to the NW and the other to the SW, of the kind with three benches well known before the Exile. It held the remains of eight people, of which two are children, still *in situ* at the moment of discovery, and without ceramic vessels in the interior. The small amount of pottery found in the entrance well dates from the Persian period. The walls are covered with pictures and inscriptions.

a. The Pictures. The pictures incised on the walls represent three subjects: human figures, ships, and camps.

(1) The human figures are three in number:

(a) On the N wall of the central chamber is a crudely incised stocky man holding what is perhaps a lyre (Naveh 1963) or a bow and arrow (Bar-Adon 1975; Lemaire 1976: 567).

(b) On the lower part of the E wall of the entrance to the S burial chamber is a lightly engraved person with extended hands on both sides, as in a position of prayer or surrender. These two figures seem to have been executed by the same hand.

(c) On the W wall of the principal chamber to lower part and to the left of the entrance of the funerary chamber is another deeply engraved person with a well-drawn robe that reaches to the knees and a tall headdress, perhaps a crested helmet of the Assyrian kind, the hands at the height of the face.

(2) On the S wall of the central chamber are two crudely incised ships with sail and rudder that do not seem to have religious significance (Naveh 1963) but rather a military one (Lemaire 1976).

(3) On the N wall, facing the ships, two vaguely circular incisings represent an encampment: one is divided into four quarters like the camps of the Assyrian army on campaign according to friezes, and the other is divided into three parts, perhaps a tent.

b. The Inscriptions. At least seven texts are inscribed on the walls.

(1) Above and to the right of the "camp" can be read *ʾ(w)rr* "cursed" (Naveh 1963 pl. 11 E, F).

(2) Also on the N wall, facing the entrance to the S burial chamber, can be read (1) *ʾrr ḥ*(2)*rpk,* "cursed be the one that challenged you!" (Lemaire 1976); if the *kap* that precedes is joined to this inscription, its translation is "like a curse done, be the one that reproached you!" (Naveh 1963 pl. 11 D).

(3) On the W wall above and to the left of the person with the helmet and between the two "long" inscriptions, *ʾr* "cursed!"; to the right, more deeply incised, is the word *ʾtt* "signs" (Naveh 1963 pl. 13).

(4) On the S wall, between the ships and the entrance to the S chamber, (1) *ʾ ʾrr* (2) *yšr mḥr,* a text capable of being understood in several ways depending on whether one reads the two lines together. Naveh corrects the reading to suggest "Cursed be the one who pillages the tomb!" Bar-Adon (1975) and Lemaire (1976) transpose the first *ʾalep* and *yod* and correct the final *reš* to *he* to understand *ʾrr ʾšr ymḥh,* "Cursed be the one who erases!" This formula is found elsewhere in funerary inscriptions, but at the end of the text. One wonders what the reader is adjured not to erase, because nothing precedes this text and because there is no personal name! Without emending the text, one could suggest that it be understood "Cursed be the one who will sing (*šyr;* or 'govern' [*śrr*]/'behold' [*šwr*]) tomorrow!" (The word *mḥr* "tomorrow" is attested in epigraphic Hebrew at Arad.) The passage perhaps alludes to the national catastrophe.

(5) Above, to the left of the same entrance, is incised the inscription *hwšʿ yhwh,* "Yahweh, save!"

(6) On the W wall above (3) is a very lightly engraved inscription of two lines descending slightly to the left under the vein of the rock. The second line, perhaps the longer, is the most difficult to read (Naveh 1963 pl. 13). One possible reading is the following:

1 *ḥbrt(?) yhwh ʾlhyk . . . hʾrṣh*	"Blows of Yahweh, your God. It is he who favored
2 *lḥṣ yhdh wlʾ l<ʾ>ḥy yršlm*	the oppression of Juda, but not for the brethren (?) of Jerusalem."

Some have wanted to find biblical expressions in this passage, and therefore read it differently. One different reading is: (l) *kl hʾrṣ h*(2)*ry yhd(h) lʾlhy yršlm* (Naveh 1963; *TSSI* 1: 58; Lemaire 1976; Miller 1980); this reading disregards the dividers between words, traces of letters, and the lineation.

The fact of oppression inflicted by an enemy and the religious interpretation of oppression as permitted by the divine will are both well known in the Bible (Deut 26:7; 2 Kgs 13:4; Pss 42:10; 44:25), even with respect to Judah after the Assyrian and Babylonian campaigns. If God was favorable (*rṣh,* line 1) to or permitted this oppression (*lḥṣ,* line 2) of Judah (the reading *yhwd* is also possible in line 2), he did not allow it to touch the "living" (*ḥy,* or better, <ʾ>*ḥy* "the brethren") of Jerusalem, who were spared this time. A word perhaps preceded the beginning of the first line, to the left of the margin, but no clear trace can be made out.

(7) Below inscription (3), written with the same tool and above other crisscross patterns that were written earlier, another line in alignment with (6) seems to be the continuation of the preceding inscription. It reads: *(h?)bqd yhwh yḥnn . . . nqh yh yhwh,* to be understood either as "He (= Judah) was punished. Yahweh will be gracious; acquit Yah, Yahweh!" or (with asyndeton) "Yahweh has punished, he will show grace; . . ." The translations differ according to whether one reads a *he* at the beginning of the line; the verb *bqd* (in the orthography attested at Arad; biblical Heb *pqd*) is either a *Hopʿal* or (better) a *Qal,* but with a different subject. There is no question of Moriah (Naveh 1963; *TSSI* 1: 58), nor of "God the merciful" (Cross 1970; Lemaire 1976; Miller 1980), but of punishment, a request for grace, and acquittal.

In conclusion, these inscriptions and graffiti represent a coherent and lively description of a catastrophic situation. An encamped enemy received reinforcements from the sea, it oppressed Judah but spared Jerusalem, according to the will of God. May the one that defied you be cursed! One asks God to save, to absolve, and to show grace, and curses the one who will sing/govern (?) tomorrow. It is a moment for the survivors to mourn and to realize cause of the punishment (disobedience to the divine will?). The incised figure with extended hands could be a supplicant or someone giving up to the conqueror (Hezekiah capitulated in 2 Kgs 18:14); the one with the "lyre" might be a musician or an archer. The atmosphere is not that of a festival but of mourning (Isa 22:12–13).

Even if their literary genre is more varied than normal, in view of the particular circumstances these inscriptions of national lamentation are appropriate in a tomb in which were probably inhumed members of the resistance of the highest rank, victims of this oppression (the seige of Lachish) for which one lamented and called God to their aid. The texts are not of a prophetic or poetic nature (Miller 1980). The ships could be Philistine or Phoenician vessels allied to Sennacherib after the capture of Sidon and the enthronement of Ittobaal. Because Beit Lei is situated very close to Lachish, and because in the Bible the verb *ḥārap* occurs a number of times in the account of the campaign of Sennacherib (2 Kgs 19:4, 16, 22, 23; 2 Chr 32:17; Isa 37:4, 17, 23, 24), it is very probable that Sennacherib's campaign in Judea is alluded to here (so Lemaire 1976). Jerusalem was not taken (Isa 31:5) but the strongholds of Lachish and Shephelah fell and Juda was oppressed (2 Kgs

18:13–14). The paleographic dating would lend support to association of the inscription with the campaign of 701 B.C. and not 587 (Cross 1970; Naveh 1963). The circumstances of these burials doubtless explain the absence of pottery on the interior. Whatever the case, this new interpretation corresponds perfectly to the historical situation as it can be understood with the help of biblical and extrabiblical texts (discussed by Gonçalves 1986). Consequently these inscriptions, having come down to us because they were hidden in a tomb, are another extrabiblical testimony of contemporary events.

5. Conclusion. The funerary inscriptions from the four sites of the monarchic period are all in keeping with a certain concept of life after death. It is prohibited (in the Siloam inscription) to open the sarcophagus and thus to disturb the rest of the deceased; the conjuration of the Khirbet el-Qôm inscription invokes the blessing of Yahweh and his asherah or the magic hand to assure the salvation of the dead; amulets bear priestly benedictions of divine protection, illumination of the face, and peace upon persons living and dead (Ketef Hinnom); maledictions curse an enemy who sowed oppression and mourning, and the lamentation leads to an act of faith in the just punishment of God and a call for divine pardon so as to be saved (Beit Lei).

C. Phoenician Inscriptions: Achzib

In one of the cemeteries from the Phoenician site of Achzib on the Galilean coast, several funerary steles have been discovered. They bear the name of the deceased and sometimes his profession: "for Zakarmilk," "for ʿAmsakar," "for ʿAbdšamaš, son of 'Ušay," "for ʿAma, the founder," followed in this case by the *ʾankh* or sign of life in Egyptian hieroglyphics. What significance could this sign have on a funerary stele? In order to draw the most precise conclusions, one has to take into account all of the archaeological evidence of these necropolises and not only the epigraphic evidence. The writing and name forms are typically Phoenician, and date the steles to the 7th century.

D. "Idumean" Inscriptions: Marissa-Maresha

Some very beautiful tombs from the Idumean capital Marissa have revealed engraved and painted inscriptions in the frieze above the *loculi* or above the *loculi* themselves. The tomb of Appollophanes (no. 1) was decorated with a hunting scene with a series of domestic and wild animals, in color, designated by their names in Greek. Also painted were a Cerberus and an eagle or a phoenix. The long funerary inscription gives the age of the owner and underlines his good reputation during 33 years as the leader of the Sidonians. The other inscriptions give us the names of the dead, Phoenicians, Greeks, Idumeans for the most part. One reads twice or three times the phrase "do not open," but in one instance (no. 29) the malediction specifies damnation: "Let no one touch it, or else there will be no salvation for him!" Another Greek inscription of four lines is of uncertain interpretation; it could be a "monologue of a couple separated by death." The other inscriptions are of the more common sort: name of the deceased (patronymic, age). Several of them mention dates that probably relate to the reign of a Ptolemy. Thus the tombs would date from the 3d to the beginning of the 1st century B.C. Some of them were reused after the rejudaization of Idumea by the conquests of John Hyrcanus, but no Jewish inscription relative to this period has been found, read, or published. Only a short Nabatean inscription above a reinhumation niche (Oren and Rappaport 1984: 146) is to be read perhaps *šlm*(?) *qymw* "Salam (or Salmay), son of Qayamu."

These funerary inscriptions are important for the dating and the sociological milieu of Marissa and its region. As elsewhere, it is stressed that the repose of the dead should not be disturbed. Did the drawings of the Cerberus and the eagle/phoenix in the tomb perhaps have a religious signification respecting belief in life after death? The question must at least be asked.

E. Jewish Inscriptions

By the expression "Jewish inscriptions," one is to understand the inscriptions in Aramaic, Hebrew, and Greek from the Hellenistic and Roman periods, the two great periods of ancient Judaism, since the Persian period has not yet revealed any epigraphic funerary texts.

1. Tomb of Jason. Discovered in 1956 in the Rehavia quarter W of Jerusalem, this tomb contains two chambers, one with a *kokh* or *loculus* (place of inhumation) and an *ossilegium* chamber, and a porch which was also cut into the rock, with several connecting rooms (a forecourt, outer court, inner court, and the porch proper surmounted by a *nepeš*), in part dug into the rock, in part built (Rahmani 1967). Inscriptions, graffiti, and drawings are traced on the walls of the porch that gives access to the chambers.

a. Drawings. On the W wall are traced two warships, a troop transport ship, and drawings of palm trees. A recumbent deer is painted on the N wall above the entrance to the *ossilegium*. On the plaster of the E wall are engraved five *menorot* with seven branches, probably later than the preceding paintings. Other graffiti remain difficult to identify.

b. Aramaic Inscriptions. Five Aramaic inscriptions are more or less legible in the tomb.

(1) An inscription of four lines was written in charcoal on the left part of the N wall. Cursive writing and its poor preservation make the reading of it difficult (Avigad 1967; *MPAT* number 89; Puech 1983a; Beyer 1984). It reads:

1 *qw/ynʾ ʿlmʾ ʿwbd lyswn br pynḥs <ʾḥy> šlm dy(?) bnt(?) lk qbwr ṭ/sbʾ hwh šlm*
2 *byr[w]š[l]m*
3 *kdyn qw/ynʾ ʿlmʾ rḥmyʾ lmʿbdʾ lk zy hwyt šwʾ h(wh) šlm*
4 *ḥny br ywsh mḥy qw/ynʾ hyk ylyn šlm*

(1) This eternal abode was (re)built for Jason, son of Phinehas, <my brother.> Peace! Because I have reconstructed for you a tomb, o good (man) [or: elder] be in peace (2) in Jerusalem!

(3) This eternal abode the friends were obliged to build [or: built as a monument] for you who were worthy. Be (in) peace!

(4) Honi, son of Jose, restored this abode so that he could rest (there) (in) peace.

The Aramaic word *qwnʾ* or *qynʾ* (a medially weak noun) means "plot, abode," excluding "lamentation" (Avigad

1967; *MPAT*), but one can hesitate between *dy bnt lk* and *(ʾ)ry bnt lk* and between *ṭbʾ* and *sbʾ*. In line 3 for *kdyn* one can hesitate between "to be obliged to" (the normal sense) and "to do" (sometimes in Syriac). The phrase *lmʿbdʾ* could be nominal or infinitival.

(2) On the E wall are two lines of formal writing in black ink with a date; the numbers are written in figures, represented here As arabic numerals: (1) *b*27 *l*[false start!] (2) *b*24 *lʾlwl šnt* 22 (?) [. . .] "On the 24th (day of the month) Elul, year 22 [. . .]."

(3) On the E wall, one line in black ink that can be read: . . . *kwhntʾ w* . . . *ʾl ybzʾ śṭn yt b* . . . , ". . . (of) the priesthood and (of his anointed?). Let no adversary destroy the t[omb!]."

(4) On the E wall, an inscription of four lines in black ink. Two lines in closely written formal script probably carrying the mention of a "thousand" or a "ship" and sailors *(gbry ʾnywt)*, and of the littoral of Kanope. The two other texts in cursive script probably mention "Leah, daughter of Joseph, son of Menahem, son of Menahem."

(5) On the W wall, two lines of crude script in charcoal beneath a warship, illegible, reading partly, *bnth*. . . .

c. Greek Inscription. This text of two or three lines is written in charcoal under the Aramaic inscription (1) and is aligned to the right of it. The reading is certain (Puech 1983b).

1 *euphraineste (h)oi zōntes*
2 *adelphoi k(ai) pein (h)o(i) m(akarioi) a(nthrōpoi). O(udeis) athlan(atos)*

(1) Feast, you living (2) brothers, and drink, y(ou), h(appy) m(en). N(o one) is immor(tal)!

d. Significance. The inscriptions introduce the person for whom the tomb was built, Jason, son of Phinehas. This was very likely the grandson of Jason, the high priest of Jerusalem who was ousted by Menelaus, took refuge in Ammon, then in Egypt, and died in Lacedemonia; he was neither brought back nor mourned in Jerusalem (2 Macc 5:10). The name and the inscription (3) suggest that this is a family tomb of (high) priests (note the *menorahs*) that had to be restored after a *damnatio memoriae* (see (1) and the archaeological evidence that indicates a first use ca. 200). This Jason was a great personage, influential, probably the commander of Cleopatra's III's fleet (see (4) and the warships). Either he ended his days in Jerusalem, rehabilitated, or his remains were brought back to Jerusalem, where it was hoped he would rest in peace. The dated inscription (2) refers to the 22d year of a reign, probably of Alexander Jannaeus (103–75 B.C.), and thus 81 B.C. but the tomb was in use until 31 B.C. (when it was damaged by an earthquake) and, after being abandoned, again around A.D. 30–31. Although it is a property of the Sadducean party, the plans and furnishings of the tomb attest, it seems, to the general conception of life after death in the Judaism of the period. The epicurian tone of the Greek inscription reflects moreover the practice of the *marzeaḥ:* mourning and rejoicing with and because of the dead (see Tob 4:17). Inscription (3), although poorly preserved, carries a curse against anyone who would destroy the tomb (Puech 1983b).

2. Tomb of Benê Hezîr. On the W slope of the Mount of Olives in the Kidron Valley has been excavated a funerary monument (a tomb and its *nepeš*) for the Benê Hezîr family, the Hebrew inscription of which has been known for more than a century (de Vogüé 1864); but its exact reading was the work of Avigad (1954: 60). The inscription would date from the first half of the 1st century B.C., about two generations after the completion of the monument. It mentions the names of the deceased of the priestly family buried in the tomb: "This tomb and its *nepeš* (are) those of Eleazar, Oniah, Yoʿezer, Judah, Shimʿon, Yohanan sons of Joseph, son of ʿObed, of Joseph and Eleazar sons of Oniah, the sons of Hezîr."

3. Tomb Inscriptions. In the necropolis of Givʿat hamibtar, an Aramaic inscription engraved in (paleo-)Hebrew letters, was discovered above a *kokh* (the niche in which the bones of the deceased are deposited) in a panel divided into seven bands, bands two and five being painted in dark red (Beyer 1984: 347; *MPAT,* 68). The text reads: "I, Abba, son of the priest Eleazar, son of Aharon the Elder, it is I, Abba, the oppressed, the persecuted, who was born in Jerusalem, exiled in Babylonia, and who brought back Mattatia, son of Judah. And I have buried him in the grotto that I acquired by deed."

The author of the inscription, recalling his ancestry, relates his own story and the act of piety that he accomplished in bringing back to Jerusalem the bones of Mattatia, deposited in a tomb that he himself had acquired. The return to Jerusalem of the bones of Jews who died in foreign lands is now well known from the inscription of Jason (?) (Puech 1983a) and an Aramaic inscription on an ossuary from the Mount of Olives: "Joseph, son of Elasah, *ʾrtqʾ*, brought the bones of his mother (or our mother; Aram *ʾmk/nh*) Amma to Jerusalem" (Puech 1982a). The family may have come from N Mesopotamia. Another example of this phenomenon is the return of the family of Queen Helena of Adiabene (tomb of the Kings). Even the transfer of bones buried within Palestine to Jerusalem is also known. A slab for the closing of a loculus carries an engraving: "Here were brought the bones of Uzziah, king of Judah. Do not open" (Beyer 1984; 343; *MPAT,* 70). The king Uzziah (8th century B.C.) could not be buried with his fathers because of his leprosy, but the transfer was noted by this Aramaic inscription of the 1st century C.E. (its provenance is unknown).

An Aramaic dipinto in the Kidron Valley mentions another loculus (and its dimensions) for the gathering of ancestors' bones: "This loculus was made for the bones of our fathers, two cubits long. Do not open!" (Beyer 1984: 340; *MPAT,* 67; *CIJ* 1300; see also 1334).

4. Inscribed Sarcophagi. Despite the number of sarcophagi found at Jaffa, Azoth, Caesarea, Haifa, Apollonia, Gezer, and Jifna, few carry inscriptions of any interest. The best known is that of Queen Helena of Adiabene, discovered in the tomb of the kings N of Jerusalem (now in the Louvre in Paris; Beyer 1984: 343; *MPAT,* 132; *CIJ,* 1388). The name and title of the deceased are engraved in two scripts, Estranghelo and Palestinian Aramaic, "Saddan/Saran (or Saddah/Sarah), the queen"; this must be the Semitic name of Helena (Jos. *Ant* 20.92–96), and allows us to identify the funerary monument which is dated to ca. A.D. 50–60.

A sarcophagus cover has recently been discovered in a necropolis E of Jerusalem with a unique Aramaic inscription. In the absence of the name of the deceased, his last wishes are engraved on the tectiform cover. On one end of the sarcophagus and on one triangular side of the tectiform cover, above the depression that served as a handle, the word *skr* can be read; and on one of the two long sides of the cover, *skr ʾmr dy lʾ lhšnyh wlh ytqbr ʿmh bʾrnh dnh kwl ʾnš* "He (had it) closed. He said to not change it, and that no one should be buried with him in the sarcophagus" (Puech 1989). The dead man asked to remain alone for eternity and did not want to change his place of rest, for example by being placed elsewhere in an ossuary according to the practice of the period in order to reuse the sarcophagus. The cover should be considered as sealed by order *(skr)* and nobody else, not even a member of his family, should join him. Thus neither another inhumation nor a reinhumation was permitted, but only the first inhumation of the deceased, probably to avoid all impurity and/or the disturbing of the bones, in anticipation of general corporeal resurrection. These indications from the beginning of our era are based in the ancient practice "do not open" applied to tombs, sarcophagi, or *loculi.* The use of sarcophagi of wood or stone thus did not cease with the practice of reinhumation in ossuaries.

5. Ossuaries. Among the several thousand ossuaries brought to light in Palestine, a fairly large proportion carry signs and inscriptions more or less finely engraved on the coffin or the stone cover. Most of the inscribed ossuaries come from Jerusalem and its periphery (see *CIJ, MPAT,* Beyer 1984) and from Jericho (Hachlili 1978, 1979) but a few from Gezer (Macalister 1906; *CIJ* 1176–84), Lydda (*CIJ* 1173), Jaffa (*MPAT* 135), Ziph (Rahmani 1972), Nazareth (*MPAT* 109). The major period of their use extends from the end of the 1st century B.C. (ca. 40–30) up until around A.D. 70 as indicated by the pottery, the coins, and the paleography of some inscriptions. A Hebrew-Aramaic bilingual inscription mentions "Simon, the builder of the temple" (Naveh 1970) and another (Greek-Aramaic) "the bones of Nicanor of Alexandria who made the doors (of the temple)" (*CIJ* 1256; Clermont-Ganneau 1903; see *y. Yoma* 41a; Acts 3:2). An ossuary contained the remains of the granddaughter of the high priest Theophilus (to be dated after A.D. 37) (Barag and Flusser 1986), and another from Jericho mentions the queen Agrippina, spouse of the Emperor Claudius, Empress from 50 to 54 (Hachlili 1979). Certain inscriptions advert to the reinhumation of as many as three generations prior to A.D. 68–70; the *loculi* of these tombs remained in use. This was the case for the tombs of four families: Goliath at Jericho (Hachlili 1979), Dositheus (Sukenik 1928), Simeon the Elder (Savignac 1925), and Qallôn of Jerusalem (*MPAT* 90–95). These indications are important cautions against classing these ossuaries as Judeo-Christian without other evidence. The occasional mention of professions has the same import: priest (Puech 1983a; Milik 1958: 22; Naveh 1979b; Barag and Flusser 1986; *CIJ* 1317), rabbi (*CIJ* 1266, 1268–69), scribe (*CIJ* 1308; *MPAT* 99), artisan (Milik 1958: 12), potter (*MPAT* 86), Nazirite (*MPAT* 121–22), proselyte, and others are mentioned. The signs in the form of an X or a cross on the cover correspond normally to identical signs on the case, and have no religious significance; they indicate the proper position of the cover in order to close it correctly (Smith 1974; Puech 1982b). The rare injunction "do not open" (*MPAT* 95) still plays the role of metal seals (see Puech 1984), as also the *chi-rho* sign (Colella 1973); a divine threat is another protection, as in the (Aramaic) warning, "Whoever will use this ossuary to his own profit, a curse [= offering] of God on behalf of the one who is [enclosed] within" (Milik 1956–57). To these brief formulas can be added indications of consanguinity, "son," "daughter," "wife," "father," "mother," and sometimes the place of origin: Alexandria, Cyrenaica, Ptolemais (Avigad 1962), Beisan/Scythopolis (*CIJ* 1372–74), Bethel (*CIJ* 1283), Capua (*CIJ* 1284), Tyre, Sheba (Puech 1983b).

If these specifications indicate a desire for inhumation in Jerusalem, others, perhaps even families of priests originating in Jerusalem, had their tombs at Jericho (Hachlili 1978–79): "Ishmael, son of Simeon, son of Paltiya, of Jerusalem" (ossuary and inscribed bowl). At other times a surname may characterize a family (e.g., Goliath), or the age of the deceased may be indicated in Greek (Hachlili 1978; Avigad 1962). Finally, an inscribed ossuary found in the excavations of the street Midbar Sinai in Jerusalem carries the specification *šl by dwd* "belonging to the house of David" in Hebrew, but with the Aramaic form *by* for Heb *byt* (Flusser 1986). As evidence of the survival of several families claiming to be of the House of David, this discovery is not without importance for the NT and the Davidic origins of the Messiah Jesus.

The inscriptions on the ossuaries in particular show a surprising diversity of scripts: Aramaic and paleo-Hebrew (*CIJ* 1264), NE Aramaic (Puech 1982a), Palmyrene (Puech 1983b), and Greek (Estranghela on Helena's sarcophagus). Bilinguals are not rare, but trilinguals exist as well (*MPAT* 145). The Semitic, Greek, and even Latin names allow us to have a fairly good idea of the population, all the while aware that the owners of the rock-cut tombs, the sarcophagi, and ossuaries really represent only the elite and prosperous families of the country.

A beginning of the Greek alphabet, apparently followed by the Hebrew letters *aleph* (perhaps for *ʾ[rwr]* "cursed" and *qop* (perhaps for *q[dš]* "holy") in paleo-Hebrew, written in charcoal on the interior face of a cover found at the corner of the bench opposite the entrance of a tomb at Jericho (Hachlili 1979), must have a magic and apotropaic meaning, equivalent to the benedictions and maledictions and the engraved hand at Khirbet el-Qôm, the Hebrew alphabet from a tomb at Tell Eitun (unpublished; see E.6 below), and the amulets of Ketef Hinnom and Emmaus, discovered in a tomb (*CIJ* 1185, Beyer 383). It is not impossible that the inverted writing of several proper names also has such an apotropaic value. Names in Greek script include *naduol* (for *Ioudan* [*CIJ* 1232]), and in Hebrew script *mwlš* (for *šālôm* [*CIJ* 1258]) and *pswy* (for *Yôsēp* [Joseph; *CIJ* 1389]). Finally an ossuary cover brought to light in the tomb of Bethphage carries, inscribed in two columns, lists of names and sums paid. This reckoning is perhaps to be associated with work executed in the necropolis or in the workshop that made the ossuaries. By the paleography it would date to the last third of the 1st century B.C. (Milik 1971). The use of ossuaries may have continued sporadically up until A.D. 135, but epigraphic indications are lacking on this matter. This practice would have been that of the dominant party, the Pharisees, and the epigraphic evidence does not contradict it.

6. Necropolis of Beth Shearim. An important center for Jewish activity from the second half of the 2d century (centered around Rabbi Judah ha-Nasi) up until its destruction in 352, Beth Shearim became the Jewish capital, succeeding in some manner to Jerusalem. See JUDAH THE PRINCE, RABBI. Thus its necropolis attracted numerous rich Jews from abroad who desired to rest in Palestinian soil.

Most of the inscriptions come from numerous catacombs dug into the hills. They are engraved or written in charcoal or in red paint on the lintels, stones, and walls, or on the sarcophagi themselves. Among the several hundred inscriptions found in better and worse states of preservation and corresponding degrees of legibility, the great majority are in Greek; only about a fifth are Semitic, many of these in Hebrew, probably because of the influence of the rabbinical school. Palestinian Aramaic is scarcely found at all, but Palmyrene is well represented. Thanks to these documents, it is possible to have an idea of the sociocultural milieu of the inhabitants of the region and their places of origin, be it from abroad, Tyre, Sidon, Beirut, Byblos, Yaḥmur, Beqaᶜa, Phaene, Palmyra, Asia (Ezion Geber), Himyar, Meishan (Babylonia), Antioch, Pamphylia, or from Palestine itself, Gabara, Havara, Caesarea, Judea, Maᶜon. Also, it appears that the personal names, principally Semitic, come first of all from the biblical world; but there are also names identifiable as Palmyrene (e.g., Mokimos, Sassos, Zenobia, Barazabedia), Nabatean (e.g., Arthis), and Canaanite (e.g., Enebelos [Hannibal]). The most frequently found Greek names are based on Hebrew names (e.g., Theodotos) or phonetic approximations (e.g., Simon), but others are typically Greek, (e.g., Symmachos, Kyrilos, Korinthis, Seleukos), including even Greek and Egyptian theophorics (Diodorus, Dionysius, Eisas, Kalliope, Ourania), which is even more surprising in this Jewish milieu. A certain number of Latin names are attested (e.g., Sabinus, Severius, Germanicus). The use of a second name is not uncommon: Sarah or Maxima, Rael Ourania, etc. But even if one does not press the evidence too much, the names, with the language used, reveal a cultural and religious milieu and denote certain divisions, tolerances, and openness to other cultures. This is confirmed by the two epigrams and figurative representations found on the walls and sarcophagi (victories, the god Eros, amazonomachy). The period of codified interdictions seems largely over, at least for the Jews of the Diaspora. It is notable that in catacombs number 14 and 20, where rabbis were inhumed, the Hebrew inscriptions are more numerous, and that their names are in Hebrew and those of their wives in Greek or Latin. The Greek inscriptions sometimes give the profession (goldsmith, doctor, banker, dyer) and titles (head of synagogue, rabbi, priest [these last also in Hebrew], priestess).

Other than the new words to designate a tomb, *hapsis, krepis, osta, nepeš,* the Greek inscriptions in particular instruct us about postmortem beliefs. The interdiction against opening a sarcophagus in which a husband and wife repose is accompanied with a malediction concerning future life: "Whoever would dare to open what is above us, may he not have any part in eternal life" (no. 129). Another threatens divine judgment at the resurrection: "Whoever would move this one (fem.), he who has promised to resurrect the dead will judge him" (no. 162; cf. John 5:21). The only Aramaic inscriptions are in the same vein: "Whoever would open this sepulcher above the one it encloses, may he die an impious death" (Avigad 1976: 1–2). The Greek inscription (no. 134) stipulates: "No one has the right to open this, in accordance with divine and secular law." One cannot help but recall an imperial edict (exhumed in a village in Galilee and dating from the beginning of the current era) concerning the violation of sepulchers and the profanation or transfer of a corpse (Abel 1930). These unique formulas perfectly reflect Jewish beliefs of the period: a doctrine of the resurrection of the dead after the general judgment; the conviction that the wicked will not take part in the future life of the just; and the consequent opinion that the Jew who did not respect the eternal rest of the dead until the day of judgment as impious and merited the reward of the impious. A pious Jew hoped for the participation of the deceased in the resurrection of the just: *ᶜmydt[n ᶜm ḥṣdyqym]*, "[their] resurrection [with the just]" (Avigad 1976: 15). Certain inscriptions express the need for courage to face the journey toward eternal life, sometimes adding "and your soul will have immortal life" (no. 130). The use of the language "soul" and "immortality" translates the Jewish idea of eternal life that is not opposed to the resurrection of the body. But the Greek influence is perhaps felt more strongly in the Greek epigram of the mausoleum: ". . . I went to Hades . . . because the All-Powerful Destiny had decided it." If the Greek word "Hades" translates Heb Sheol in the LXX, the idea that the goddess *Moira* (fate) cuts the cord of life is not at all Jewish, and the formula seems surprising in this milieu. The second epigram (catacomb 18) expresses no Jewish ideas at all in designating the tomb as the riches in which a man rejoices after his death, a sentiment evidenced also by the Homeric inspiration of the poetic Greek phraseology.

On the arch of chambers II–VI in catacomb 1 are engraved the nine first letters of the Greek alphabet that must also have had a magic and apotropaic value (see B.2–3 and E.5 above) without having any direct or immediate relation to pagan influences. In catacomb number 35 an abecedary completely in Hebrew was discovered (unpublished). Graffiti represent the Menorah, boats, and animals.

7. The Coast. A series of tomb inscriptions dating from the first centuries of the current era have been discovered along the Palestinian littoral, in particular at Caesarea, Apollonia, Jaffa, Azotus, Ascalon, Gaza/Maioumas in particular. The contents of these inscriptions can be summarized in general as an indication of the name and patronymic of the deceased, sometimes the age, the profession, and the place of origin. Among this last are Babylonia (*CIJ* 902), Cappadocia (*CIJ* 910), Tarsus (*CIJ* 925, 931), Alexandria (*CIJ* 918, 928, 934), and Pentapolis (*CIJ* 950). Most often in Greek, they also can be written in Hebrew or Aramaic or be partially bilingual. The most important group was found at Jaffa. Several names of rabbis known in Jewish literature are found there (Klein 1931), but also a priest from Egypt (*CIJ* 930), and a centurion from a Jewish family (*CIJ* 920). Rarer, some inscriptions indicate

Roman soldiers from the 5th Macedonian legion at Emmaus, in Latin (Landau 1976; Negev 1971) or others in Greek, at Beit Nattif (Savignac 1903), at ᶜEitun (Tsaferis 1982a), and elsewhere.

8. Conclusion. These "Jewish" funerary inscriptions reveal a richness of sociocultural (languages, scripts, personal names, ethnography, history) and religious information (funerary customs of reinhumation, transfer of bones, beliefs, Sheol, immortality, resurrection, judgment, eternal life). The belief in resurrection seems already accepted, and is expressed to a certain extent in the practice of reinhumation in ossuaries, but not exclusively, because inhumation in sarcophagi or the gathering of bones in an *ossilegium* does not contradict that belief in any way. The attraction of Palestinian ground, and Jerusalem in particular, as a place of burial during the epoch of messianic effervescence is certainly linked. This attraction does not seem to have disappeared or diminished until the age of Constantine, according to the evidence that has been discovered.

Bibliography

Abel, F. M. 1913. Tombeaux et ossuaires juifs récemnent découverts. *RB* 22: 262–77.

———. 1925. Tombeaux recemment decouverts à Marisa. *RB* 34: 267–75.

———. 1930. Un rescrit impérial sur la violation de sépulture et le tombeau touvé vide. *RB* 39: 567–70.

Ameling, W. 1985. Phagōmen kai Piōmen. *ZPE* 60: 35–43.

Angerstorfer, A. 1982. Ašerah als "Consort of Jahve" oder Aširtah? *BN* 17: 9–10.

Avigad, N. 1953. The Epitaph of a Royal Steward from Siloam Village. *IEJ* 3: 137–52.

———. 1954. *Ancient monuments in the Kidron Valley.* Jerusalem.

———. 1955. The Second Tomb-Inscription of the Royal Steward. *IEJ* 5: 163–66.

———. 1962. A Depository of Inscribed Ossuaries in the Kidron Valley. *IEJ* 12: 1–12.

———. 1967. Aramaic Inscriptions in the Tomb of Jason. *IEJ* 17: 101–11 (= *ᶜAtiqôt* 4 [1964] 32–38 [in Hebrew]).

———. 1971. The Burial-Vault of a Nazirite Family on Mount Scopus. *IEJ* 12: 185–200.

———. 1976. *Beth Sheᶜarim: Report on the Excavations during 1953–1958.* Vol. 3, *Catacombs 12–23.* Jerusalem.

Bahat, D. 1982. Two Burial Caves at Sderot Ben Zvi. *Atiqôt* 8: 66–68.

Bar-Adon, P. 1975. An Early Hebrew Inscription in a Judean Desert Cave. *IEJ* 25: 231.

Barag, D. 1970. Note on an Inscription from Khirbet el-Qôm. *IEJ* 20: 216–18.

Barag, D., and Flusser, D. 1986. The Ossuary of Yehoḥanah Granddaughter of the High Priest Theophilus. *IEJ* 36: 39–44.

Barkay, G. 1986. *Ketef Hinnom: A Treasure Facing Jerusalem's Walls.* Jerusalem.

Ben Arieh, S. 1982a. A Burial Cave on Mount Scopus. *Atiqôt* 8: 59–60.

———. 1982b. A Tomb in Arnona. *Atiqôt* 8: 77–79.

Benoit, P. 1967. L'inscription grecque du tombeau de Jason. *IEJ* 17: 112–13.

Beyer, K. 1984. *Die aramäischen Texte vom Toten Meer.* Göttingen.

Catastini, A. 1984. Note di epigrafia ebraica I–II. *Hen* 6: 129–38.

Clermont-Ganneau, C. 1871. Notes on Certain New Discoveries at Jerusalem. *PEFQS* n.s. 1: 103–5.

———. 1885. Rapports sur une mission en Palestine et en Phénicie entreprise en 1881. Pp. 157–251 in *Archives des missions scientifiques et littéraires.* Paris.

———. 1899a. *Archaeological Researches in Palestine.* Vol. 1. London.

———. 1899b. Jewish Ossuaries and Sepulchres in the Neighbourhood of Jerusalem. Vol. 1. Pp. 381–454 in *Archaeological Researches in Palestine During the Years 1873–74.* London.

———. 1903. Archaeological and Epigraphic Notes on Palestine. *PEQ* 125–31 (= La "porte de Nicanor" du temple de Jérusalem. *RAO* 5: 334–40).

Colella, P. 1973. Les abreviations ţ et ☧ *(XP). RB* 80: 547–58.

Cross, F. M. 1970. The Cave Inscriptions from Khirbet Beit Lei. Pp. 299–306 in *Near Eastern Archaeology in the Twentieth Century,* ed. J. A. Sanders. Garden City, NY.

Dever, W. G. 1969–70. Iron Age Epigraphic Material from the Area of Khirbet el-Kôm *HUCA* 40–41: 139–204.

Diringer, D. 1934. Le iscrizioni di Silwân. Pp. 102–10 in *Le iscrizioni antico-ebraiche palestinesi.* Florence.

Dorsey, D. A. 1980. The Location of Biblical Makkedah. *TA* 7: 185–93.

Driver, G. R. 1953. Seals and Tombstones. *ADAJ* 2: 62–65.

Dussaud, R. 1912. *Les monuments palestiniens et judaïques.* Paris.

Flusser, D. 1966. "The House of David" on an Ossury. *Israel Museum Journal* 5: 37–40.

Garbini, G. 1978. Su un'iscrizione ebraica da Khirbet el-Kom. *AION* n.s. 38: 191–93.

Goncalves, F. J. 1986. *L'expédition de Sennachérib en Palestine dans la littérature hébraïque ancienne.* Etudes Bibliques 7. Paris and Louvain-la-Neuve.

Hachlili, R. 1978. A Jerusalem Family in Jericho. *BASOR* 230: 47–56.

———. 1979. The Goliath Family in Jericho: Funerary Inscriptions from a First Century A.D. Jewish Monumental Tomb. *BASOR* 235: 31–66.

Hachlili, R., and Killebrew, A. 1983. Jewish Funerary Customs during the Second Temple Period in the Light of the Excavations at Jericho Necropolis. *PEQ* 115: 109–30.

Hadley, J. M. 1987. The Khirbet el-Qom Inscription. *VT* 37: 50–62.

Hestrin, R., and Israeli, Y., eds. 1972. *Inscriptions Reveal.* Jerusalem.

Jacoby, R. 1987. *The Synagogues of Barᶜam: Jerusalem Ossuaries.* Jerusalem.

Jaroš, K. 1982. Zur Inschrift Nr. 3 von Hirbet el-Qōm. *BN* 19: 31–40.

Kane, J. P. 1978. The Ossuary Inscriptions of Jerusalem. *JSS* 23: 268–82.

Katzenstein, H. J. 1960. The Royal Steward. *IEJ* 10: 149–54.

Klein, S. 1920. *Jüdisch-palästinische Corpus Inscriptionum (Ossuar-, Grab-und Synagogeninschriften).* Vienna.

———. 1931. Inschriftliches aus Jaffa. *MGWJ* 75: 369–77.

Lagrange, M. J. 1893. Epigraphie sémitique. *RB* 2: 221–22.

Landau, J. H. 1976. Two inscribed Tombstones. *Atiqôt* 11: 89–91 (English Series).

Lemaire, A. 1976. Prières en temps de crise: les inscriptions de Khirbet Beit Lei. *RB* 83: 558–68.

———. 1977. Les Inscriptions de Khirbet el-Qôm et l'Ashérah de YHWH. *RB* 84: 595–608.

Lifshitz, B. 1963. Notes d'épigraphie grecque. *RB* 70: 259–65.

———. 1964. La nécropole juive de Césarée. *RB* 71: 384–87.

———. 1965. Inscriptions de Césarée en Palestine. *RB* 72: 98–107.

———. 1966. Notes d'épigraphie palestinienne, 1. L'exhortation à la jouissance de la vie dans une inscription tombale juive à Jérusalem. *RB* 73: 248–57.

Macalister, R. A. S. 1906. Three Ossuary Inscriptions from Gezer. *PEQ* 123–24.

Mazar, A. 1982. A Burial Cave on French Hill. *Atiqôt* 8: 41–45 (in Hebrew).

Mazar, B. 1973. *Beth She'arim: Report on the Excavations during 1936–1940.* Vol. 1, *Catacombs 1–4.* Jerusalem.

Meyers, E. M. 1971. *Jewish Ossuaries: Reburial and Rebirth.* BibOr 24. Rome.

Milik, J. T. 1956–57. Trois tombeaux juifs récemment découverts au sud-est de Jérusalem. *LASBF* 7: 232–67.

———. 1958. Le iscrizioni degli ossuari. Pp. 70–109 in *Gli scavi del "Dominus Flevit,"* ed. B. Bagatti and J. T. Milik. Studium Biblicum Franciscanum 13. Jerusalem.

———. 1971. Le couvercle de Bethphagé. Pp. 75–94 in *Hommages à André Dupont-Sommer.* Paris.

Miller, P. D. 1980. Psalms and Inscriptions. Pp. 311–32 in *Congress Volume.* VTSup 32. Leiden.

Mittmann, S. 1981. Die Grabinschrift des Sängers Uriahu. *ZDPV* 97: 139–52.

Naveh, J. 1963. Old Hebrew Inscriptions in a Burial Cave. *IEJ* 13: 74–92.

———. 1970. The Ossuary Inscriptions from Givᶜat ha-Mivtar. *IEJ* 20: 33–37.

———. 1973. An Aramaic Tomb Inscription Written in Paleo-Hebrew Script. *IEJ* 23: 82–91.

———. 1979a. Graffiti and Dedications. *BASOR* 235: 27–30.

———. 1979b. Varia Epigraphica Judaica. *IOS* 9: 17–31.

Negev, A. 1971. The Nabatean Necropolis of Mampsis. *IEJ* 21: 110–29.

Oren, E., and Rappaport, U. 1984. The Necropolis of Maresha-Beth Govrin. *IEJ* 34: 114–53.

Peters, J. P., and Thiersch, H. 1905. *Painted Tombs in the Necropolis of Marissa.* London.

Puech, E. 1982a. Ossuaires inscrits d'une tombe du Mont des Oliviers. *LASBF* 32: 355–72.

———. 1982b. Les nécropoles juives palestiniennes autour de notre ère. *Les Quatre Fleuves* 15–16: 35–55.

———. 1983a. Inscriptions funéraires palestiniennes: l. Tombeau de Jason. *RB* 90: 481–99.

———. 1983b. Inscriptions funéraires palestiniennes: 2. Ossuaires. *RB* 90: 499–533.

———. 1984. Un emploi méconnu de *WLʾ* en araméen et en hébreu. *RB* 91: 88–101.

———. 1986–87. The Canaanite Inscriptions of Lachish and Their Religious Background. *TA* 13–14: 13–25.

———. 1989. Une inscription araméenne sur un couvercle de sarcophage. *EI* 20: 161*–65*.

———. fc. Les deux derniers psaumes davidiques du rituel d'exorcisme 11QPsAp^{a} IV 4–V 14. In *Acts of a Symposium: Forty Years of Research in the Dead Sea Scrolls 20th–24th Mars 1988.* Jerusalem.

Rahmani, L. Y. 1961. Jewish Rock-cut Tombs in Jerusalem. *Atiqôt* 3: 93–120.

———. 1967. Jason's Tomb. *IEJ* 17: 61–100 (= *ᶜAtiqôt* 4 [1964] 1–32 [in Hebrew].

———. 1972. A Bilingual Ossuary-Inscription from Khirbet Zif. *IEJ* 22: 113–16; 235–36.

———. 1986. Some Remarks on R. Hachlili's and A. Killebrew's "Jewish Funerary Customs." *PEQ* 118: 96–100.

Reich, R., and Geva, H. 1982. Burial Caves on Mount Scopus. *Atiqôt* 8: 53–56.

Reifenberg, A. 1948. A Newly Discovered Hebrew Inscription of the Pre-exilic Period. *JPOS* 21: 134–37.

Rosenthal, E. S. 1973. The Givᶜat ha-Mivtar Inscription. *IEJ* 23: 72–81.

Savignac, R. 1903. Un tombeau romain à Beit Nettif. *RB* 12: 431–34.

———. 1904. Ossuaires juifs. *RB* 13: 262–63.

———. 1925. Nouveaux ossuaires juifs avec graffites. *RB* 34: 253–66.

———. 1929. Nouveaux ossuaires juifs avec inscriptions. *RB* 38: 229–36.

Schroer, S. 1983. Zur Deutung der Hand unter der Grabinschrift von Chirbet el Qôm. *UF* 15: 191–99.

Schwabe, M., and Lifshitz, B. 1974. *Beth She'arim.* Vol. 2, *The Greek Inscriptions.* Jerusalem.

Shea, W. H. 1990. The Khirbet el-Qom Tomb Inscription Again. *VT* 40: 110–16.

Smith, R. H. 1974. The Cross Marks on Jewish Ossuaries. *PEQ* 106: 53–66.

Spoer, H. H. 1907. Some Hebrew and Phoenician Inscriptions: 1. New Ossuaries from Jerusalem. *JAOS* 28: 355–59.

Spronk, K. 1986. *Beatific Afterlife in Ancient Israel and in the Ancient Near East.* AOAT 219. Neukirchen-Vluyn.

Sukenik, E. L. 1928. A Jewish Hypogeum near Jerusalem. *JPOS* 8: 113–21.

———. 1932. Two Jewish Hypogea. *JPOS* 12: 27–31.

———. 1937. A Jewish Tomb in the Kidron Valley. *PEFQS* 69: 126–30.

———. 1947. The Earliest Record of Christianity. *AJA* 51: 351–65.

Thomsen, P. 1921. Die Lateinischen und griechischen Inschriften der Stadt Jerusalem und ihrer nächsten Umgebung. *ZDPV* 44: 90–168.

Tsaferis, V. 1982a. A Monumental Roman Tomb on Tel ᶜEitun. *Atiqôt* 8: 23–25 (in Hebrew).

———. 1982b. Rock-cut Tombs on Mount Scopus. *Atiqôt* 8: 49–52 (in Hebrew).

———. 1982c. A Burial Cave in Meqor Ḥayim. *Atiqôt* 8: 70–73.

Ussishkin, D. 1969. On the Shorter Inscription from the "Tomb of the Royal Steward." *BASOR* 196: 16–22.

———. 1970. The Necropolis from the Time of the Kingdom of Judah at Silwan, Jerusalem. *BA* 33: 34–46.

———. 1975. A Recently Discovered Monolithic Tomb in Siloam. Pp. 63–65 in *Jerusalem Revealed.* Jerusalem.

Vincent, H. 1900. Hypogée judéo-grec découvert au Scopus. *RB* 9: 106–12.

———. 1902. Nouveaux ossuaires juifs. *RB* 11: 103–7; 276–77.

———. 1907. Ossuaires juifs. *RB* 16: 410–14.

———. 1913. Un hypogée juif à Djifneh. *RB* 22: 103–6.

———. 1931. Epitaphe prétendue de N.S. Jésus-Christ. *Rendiconti della Pontif. Accademia Romana di Archeologia* 7: 215–39.

Vitto, F. 1972. Chronique archéologique: Qiryat Tivᶜon. *RB* 79: 575–76.

Vogüé, M. de. 1864. *Le temple de Jérusalem.* Paris.

Weippert, M. 1964. Archäologischer Jahresbericht: *ḫirbet bet Lejj.* *ZDPV* 80: 161–64.

Zevit, Z. 1984. The Khirbet el-Qôm Inscription Mentioning a Goddess. *BASOR* 255: 39–47.

EMILE PUECH
Trans. Stephen Rosoff

PALESTINIAN JUDAISM. See JUDAISM (PALESTINIAN).

PALLU (PERSON) [Heb *pallûʾ*]. PALLUITE. The second of the four sons of Reuben (Gen 46:9; Exod 6:14; 1 Chr 5:3). Pallu was the grandson of Jacob and Leah. His name is included in the list of the seventy people who migrated to Egypt with Jacob and his family at the time of a great famine in Canaan (Gen 46:8–27). Pallu was the father of Eliab (Num 26:8). The redactor of Numbers provided some additional information about the descendants of Pallu through Eliab in order to show that Dathan and Abiram (Num 26:9) were the leaders of the group that was dissatisfied with Moses' leadership and who had opposed him in the wilderness (Num 16:1–30). It is possible that Pallu may be identified with Peleth, a son of Reuben mentioned in Num 16:1. According to the second census list of Israel mentioned in Numbers, Pallu became the eponymous ancestor of the Palluites, one of the Reubenite clans (Num 26:5).

CLAUDE F. MARIOTTINI

PALM TREES, CITY OF. See CITY OF PALM TREES.

PALMYRA (34°33′N; 38°17′E). An oasis in the Syrian desert halfway between the Phoenician coast and the Euphrates. It was an important caravan city in 1st–3d centuries A.D., then became a Byzantine frontier fortress. Occasional references from the 19th through 11th centuries B.C. (archives from Kaneš, Mari, Emar, and Assyrian annals) indicate limited importance of the site, whose native name, Tadmor, was already in use, going back to an Amorite dialect (possible meaning "guarding post"). Biblical references that Solomon founded Palmyra are late: 2 Chr 8:4 mentions "Tadmor in the wilderness," and apparently derives from 1 Kgs 9:18, where the *ketib* reads *tamar.* The context of 1 Kgs 9:18 suggests a location for Tamar S of the Dead Sea (cf. Gen 14:7; Ezek 47:18–19; 48:28). If the Chronicler understood *Tadmor,* and adapted the context accordingly, it proves only that the desert station had already some renown in the early Hellenistic period. Josephus (*Ant* 8.6.1) abounds in the same sense, as does modern Arab folklore. See TADMOR.

The Greek name *Palmyra* remains unexplained; it can hardly be related to the Latin *palma,* in spite of Hebrew *tamar* meaning "palm." Latin texts are extremely rare in Palmyra, but there are about two thousand inscriptions in local Aramaic, including the longest known NW Semitic inscription, the Tariff, which is a text of the law passed in 137 A.D. to harmonize and complete earlier rules concerning municipal custom duties and taxes. The language is practically the same as the contemporary Jewish Aramaic of the Dead Sea Scrolls, and is very close to the biblical Aramaic. The script is a monumental version of the Achaemenid chancery ductus, but there exists also a cursive script.

A. History of Palmyra

Disregarding some Paleolithic flint finds and a few Bronze Age sherds, the earliest remains discovered in Palmyra date to the 2d century B.C., and consist of burial deposits in the underground family tomb of Yediʿbel. The first safely dated inscription, commissioned by the priests of Bel in 44 B.C., is nearly contemporary with a failed attempt by troops of Mark Antony to loot the city, which had hastily been evacuated by the inhabitants (App., *BCiv* 5.9). A tiny chapel of the Arab goddess Allat was erected before ca. 50 B.C., but all other extant monuments were built around the B.C./A.D. transition or later.

The city was self-governed by an assembly composed of a number of tribes, four treasurers, and probably other elected officials, but it was at the same time a part of the Roman province of Syria. Statues of Tiberius and his kin were erected in the temple of Bel in 17 A.D. Under Nero, the Senate was created, and two archonts were placed at the head of the city, which was divided on territorial or religious criteria between four reformed tribes, in accordance with the Hellenistic institutions.

By the time of Nero, Palmyra had already risen to prominence as a major merchant power, with outposts in Babylon and Seleucia-on-Tigris, and later in Vologesias and Charax, river ports closer to the Persian Gulf. Its trade provided the Roman Empire with oriental luxuries and essentials such as frankincense, spices and scents, silk, cotton, and pearls, brought to the head of the Gulf from China and India. The Palmyrenes transported these goods by boat on the Euphrates and on camelback across the desert to the Mediterranean. To accomplish this, it was essential to maintain secure footholds on the river (such as the island of ʿAna) and especially to maintain security of the desert tracks, which they assured by promoting positive relations with the nomads. The heyday of their trade was between 130–160 A.D.

The emperor Hadrian visited Palmyra in 129 A.D. and made it a free city (i.e., autonomous in fiscal matters). Further privileges were granted when it was given the status of colony, awarded by Caracalla after 212 A.D. However, with the mounting danger of Sassanian expansion, trade came to a standstill and direct rule was introduced. Septimius Odainat, son of Hairan, is known to be the "Head of Tadmor" (Gk *exarch*) in 252, and then as Roman governor of the province Syria-Phoenicia in 258. After he defeated an attempted invasion by Sapor I in 260, he was proclaimed by Emperor Gallienus "corrector of the whole East" and took for himself the Persian title of "King of Kings." Such audacity was too much for the imperial government, and he was assassinated in 267/68, apparently the result of an official plot. His widow Zenobia, however, maintained power for her minor son Wahballat, and conquered Egypt and Asia Minor, forming a short-lived Oriental empire. The new "empire" was crushed in 272 by Aurelian who, after an uprising in Palmyra the following year, captured the city and devastated it.

Much reduced in size, Palmyra became then a legionary fortress of the *limes* of Diocletian (about 300 A.D.). It was restored in the 6th century by Justinian, but the caravan trade never revived. Taken by Moslems in 634, Palmyra continued as a town until the middle of the 8th century, and became a fortress again in the 12th century. After being an insignificant village for several centuries, Palmyra is now an expanding town of over thirty thousand.

B. Archaeological Remains

The present-day ruins correspond largely to the inner city of 2d–3d centuries A.D., as preserved within the reduced perimeter of the Diocletian's wall. The residential areas are practically untouched by research, but the street grid is clearly visible on the surface. The main thoroughfare was shaded, in a way typical of the Roman East, by two rows of columns. The road has been partly cleared, together with the neighboring complex of public buildings, which include a theater, a square agora, a caravan entrepôt, etc. A characteristic feature at Palmyra, which is found sparingly at other sites, is brackets fixed on columns at about two-thirds of their height; these held bronze statues of worthy citizens, but only the dedicatory inscriptions remain.

Immediately outside the city is the necropolis, which includes about 200 partly preserved tombs. The oldest type is the funerary tower, with multistoried loculi opening on each floor. There are also collective monuments sometimes called *nāpša* (i.e., "soul, person"), a term applied also to individual funerary stones. Other tombs are underground, which consist of long galleries with vertical niches, and in the 2d century the so-called funerary temples appeared, which are lavishly decorated mausolea of Classical inspiration.

The major monument of Palmyra is the sanctuary of Bel, erected on top of a mound which was the likely site of the early settlement and its temples. The present cella, dedicated in 32 A.D., but completed probably later, is outwardly Hellenistic, but contains at its short ends two deep, raised niches where cult images were exposed and sacred objects kept. The flat roof could accommodate some ceremonies, while other activities took place at the slaughtering altar, the lustration basin, and the banqueting hall, all set in the huge square courtyard surrounded by porticoes. The much smaller sanctuary of Baᶜal-šamīn consisted of an irregular temenos divided into several colonnaded courtyards. Founded at the beginning of the 1st century A.D., it received a Classical cella just before 131 A.D. to enshrine an older cult-relief in a richly adorned exedra. There was also the temple of Nebo, raised on a high podium in the middle of its courtyard, which apparently replaced an older building. The shrine to the goddess Allat was for a long time a small chapel, but later was preserved within a 2d-century cella. The temple of Arṣū is utterly destroyed, while those of Atargatis, ᶜAglibōl and Malakbel, and others, are not located yet.

The chief god of Palmyra was Bel, which reflects the Babylonian name of the archaic Bōl (apparently a dialectical rendering of common Semitic *baᶜal*), and was preserved only in composite names (e.g., the Moon-god, ᶜAglibōl; or the Sun-god, Yarḥibōl). These three, in company of Arṣu, ᶜAštart, and others, owned together the great temple and formed a group of planetary gods with Bel, as Jupiter, governing the Cosmos. They appear, however, in different combinations in other sanctuaries, preserving disparate tribal traditions; thus ᶜAglibōl was worshiped in the "Sacred Grove" together with Malakbel ("Angel of Bel"), a youthful vegetation god, but also a Sun-god distinct from Yarḥibōl, who presided over the source Efqa, the main water supply for the oasis. While these gods are unknown outside the sphere of Palmyra cults, others are more common: Arṣu is an Arab armed godhead equated with the Greek Ares and proceeding from the Safaitic Ruḍā; Herodotus (3.8) identified Orotal as the major god of the Arabs, and also identified Allat with Aphrodite. While Baᶜal-šamīn, "Lord of Heaven," is known in the 10th century B.C., he arrived in Palmyra as the supreme deity of a tribe, parallel to, but distinct from Bel. A crowd of lesser gods, often undistinguishable from each other, were imported by their nomadic worshipers from the desert. Characteristically, they are always armed, either in the bedouin way or wearing an armor as Roman soldiers did.

The forms of cult are known very imperfectly. In addition to the traditional holocausts, there were simple frankincense offerings on altars of which several hundreds survive. Ritual meals, organized by particulars or by associations (with that of the priests of Bel paramount), consisted in solemnly sharing food and wine in the presence of a god. Cult images were most often graven in relief and not sculpted in the round, so that some traditional offerings and trappings were obviously no longer appropriate, and a more spiritual understanding of divinity might be supposed. Such an understanding is certain in the case of the so-called anonymous god, which was apparently Baᶜal-šamīn, who was worshipped outside his sanctuary with ritual consisting of incense burning on votive altars. These altars bear formulas expressing the transcendent and ethical character of the god, whom they never call by name. However, in spite of some modern speculation, this cult was not monotheistic.

In the art of Palmyra the gods and their faithful are represented in relief, aligned in a strictly frontal view. This convention is also constant in funerary sculpture, which consists of plaques with half-figures of men and women in high relief; these are applied on grave slits, and larger plaques with family banquet scenes are placed on sarcophagi. Artists strove to express a vivid presence of the deceased and their contact with the beholder via a frontal posture and large open eyes. While they are keen on details of dress, jewelry, etc., a portrait likeness is seldom attempted. The relation to Byzantine art strikes the eye though direct links are missing, since the art of Palmyra became extinct in the late 3d century, shortly after those of Hatra and Dura, which had shared in the same artistic and religious outlook.

Bibliography

Browning, I. 1974. *Palmyra.* London.
Colledge, M. A. R. 1976. *The Art of Palmyra.* London.
Drijvers, H. J. W. 1976. *The Religion of Palmyra.* Leiden.
Starcky, J. 1957. Palmyre. *DBSup* 6: 1066–1103.
Starcky, J., and Gawlikowski, M. 1985. *Palmyre.* Paris.
Teixidor, J. 1974. *The Pantheon of Palmyra.* Leiden.

M. GAWLIKOWSKI

PALSY. See SICKNESS AND DISEASE.

PALTI (PERSON) [Heb *pālṭî*]. Var. PALTIEL. **1.** Son of Raphu, and a Benjaminite (Num 13:9). Palti's name appears sixth in a list of twelve men sent by Moses to spy out the land (Num 13:1–16). Each man represented a tribe, Palti representing the tribe of Benjamin.

2. Second husband of Michal, Saul's daughter; and the son of Laish from Gallim (1 Sam 25:44, 2 Sam 3:15). Palti's name appears in a note about David's wives (1 Sam 25:43–44) and in the narrative concerning David's negotiations with Abner (2 Samuel 12–21). (In the latter he is called Paltiel.) Saul gave Michal, David's wife, to Palti. No reason is stated for this action. After Saul's death, David stipulated the return of Michal as a condition of his talks with Abner, commander of Ishbosheth's army (2 Sam 3:14). Michal is taken from Palti, as David requested (v 15). Palti follows her, weeping, all the way to Bahurim. When Abner orders him to return, however, he obeys (v 16).

LINDA S. SCHEARING

PALTIEL (PERSON) [Heb *pālṭîʾēl*]. **1.** Son of Azzan; an Issacharite (Num 34:26). Paltiel's name appears eighth in a list of twelve tribal representatives designated by Moses to divide the land of Canaan (Num 34:19–29).

2. Second husband of Michal; son of Laish (2 Sam 3:15). See PALTI.

LINDA S. SCHEARING

PALTITE, THE [Heb *happalṭî*]. Occurs only in 2 Sam 23:26 as the gentilic designation of Helez, fifth in the main list of "the Thirty," David's corp of military elite *(haggibbōrim)*. See DAVID'S CHAMPIONS. It identifies him either as a Calebite through Pelet (1 Chr 2:47) or as a native of Beth-Pelet (M.R. 141079), a Judean town near Beer-sheba (Josh 15:27). The latter is more likely in view of the context, though the two may be associated. The LXX's *phelōthi* reflects the confusion found in the Chronicler's parallel and related lists (1 Chr 11:27; 27:10), where Helez is "the Pelonite" (MT *happĕlônî;* LXX *phelōni*).

Bibliography

Elliger, K. 1933. Die dreissig Helden Davids. *PJ* 31: 29–75.
Mazar, B. 1963. The Military Elite of King David. *VT* 13: 310–20.

DAVID L. THOMPSON

PAMPHYLIA (PLACE) [Gk *Pamphylia*]. A district in S Asia Minor bounded on the N by Pisidia and the Taurus Mountains, on the E by Cilicia Tracheia (later called Isauria), and on the W by Lycia. The district, which bordered the Mediterranean coast, covered a territory about eighty miles long and thirty miles wide. Several navigable rivers, including the Kestros and the Eurymedon, flowed through the region to the S coast of Asia Minor and emptied into the Pamphylian Sea. The major cities on the coast were Attalia, Side, and Coracesium and in the interior were Perga and Aspendus (Strabo 14.4.1–3; see also Bean 1968: 1053–81). The coastal towns were used as an operational base for pirates from Pamphylia and Cilicia (Strabo 12.7.2–3, 14.3.2). The climate along the coastal plain was uncomfortable and malaria was prevalent. The region produced abundant fruit crops and was renowned for its pharmaceutical products.

According to one tradition, Pamphylia was colonized by a mixed multitude of Greeks led by Amphilochus and Calchas after the fall of Troy (Herodotus 7.91; Strabo 14.4.3, 12.3.27, 14.5.23). Pamphylia literally means "many tribes, or nations," but the region had its own aberrant Greek dialect related to the Arcadian Greek (see Ramsay 1880 and Brixhe 1976; the city of Side had its own script and language which persisted until the 2d century B.C.E. and is still essentially undeciphered; cf. Acts 2:10). Pliny (the Elder) reports that the region was once called Mopsopia, after the celebrated soothsayer Mopsus (*HN* 5.26; Strabo 14.4.3; see Pausanius 7.3.2; compare with another earlier diviner by the same name in Pindar *Pyth.* 4.191; and Apollonius of Rhodes 1.1083, and 4.1502ff.). Mopsus shared an oracle-shrine with Amphilochus in Cilicia, where his name occurs in local place names and in 8th-century bilingual hieroglyph inscriptions from Karatepe.

Pamphylia was ruled by local kings before being absorbed into Croesus' Lydian empire. Pamphylia fell to the Persians and continued under Persian control until it submitted to Alexander the Great. Although Pamphylia was occupied by Ptolemy I and III, the district was generally controlled by the Seleucids. The region was surrendered to the Romans by Antiochus III in 189 B.C.E. The Attalids of Pergamum gained a small part of the W coastline, where they founded the city of Attalia.

Pamphylia was part of the province of Cilicia from 102 B.C.E. to 44 B.C.E. and then was included in the province of Asia. Antony granted Pamphylia to Amyntas in 36 B.C.E. and it was joined together with Galatia from 25 B.C.E. to 43 C.E. (see Smye 1934) when Claudius formed Lycia-Pamphylia. Pamphylia was reunited to Galatia by Galba, after the Lycians procurred a temporary independence, and was finally reunited again with Lycia by Vespasian. Luke's use of a common article bonding "Cilicia" and "Pamphylia" in Acts 27:5 was probably not to indicate a political entity (which did not exist) but rather a geographical unit, both sharing the S coastline of Asia Minor.

It appears that Pamphylia had a sizable Jewish population during the Maccabean period, considering that it was one of the countries notified by the Roman consul in 142 B.C.E. of a renewed alliance with the Hasmoneans of Judea (1 Macc 15:23). Side was specifically mentioned in the circular; however, inscriptions relating to Jews in this city date to a later period (*CLL* no. 781; Robert 1958: 36–47; Lifshitz 1967: nos. 36–37). Philo included it among countries having a significant Jewish population, and Pamphylian Jews were reported in Jerusalem at Pentecost (Philo *Gaium* 281–82; Acts 2:10). It is likely that there were Jews in the city of Perga during Paul's missionary activities there (Acts 13:13; 14:25).

Paul, Barnabas, and John Mark visited Pamphylia during their first missionary journey. They sailed from Paphos on Cyprus up the Kestros River to Perga (or an adjoining port town, Acts 13:13). There is no indication that Paul or his companions preached to the Pamphylians at this time. After an apparent difference of opinion, John Mark left his colleagues and returned to Jerusalem (Acts 13:13). Paul and Barnabas crossed the Taurus Mountains and preached in Pisidian Antioch (Acts 13:14). A possible explanation of the unusual course of events is that the three agreed to evangelize Pamphylia but for some reason there was a change of venue and John Mark refused to acquiesce. Some scholars have conjectured that Paul, who was probably enervated by the intense efforts at Paphos, may have contracted malaria in the moist Pamphylian climate (cf. Gal 4:13), forcing a change in itinerary. On their return, Paul and Barnabas preached in Perga and perhaps Attalia before sailing back to Antioch (Acts 14:24–26).

Bibliography

Bean, G. E. 1968. *Turkey's Southern Shore.* London.
Brixhe, C. 1976. *Le dialecte grec de Pamphylie.* Paris.
Lifshitz, B. 1967. *Donateurs et fondateurs dans les synagogues juives.* Paris.
Ramsay, W. M. 1880. On Some Pamphylian Inscriptions. *JHS* 1: 242–57.
Robert, L. 1958. Inscriptions grecques de Sidè en Pamphylie. *RP* 32 3d ser.: 15–53.
Smye, R. 1934. Galatia and Pamphylia under Augustus: The Governorships of Piso, Quirinius and Sivanus. *Klio* 27: 122–48.

Scott T. Carroll

PANEL [Heb *misgeret; sippûn*]. A word used to denote the sides of the lavers in Solomon's Temple and also the wooden (cedar) paneling of houses. The temple texts describe the elaborate stands for the lavers as having framed panels decorated with lions, oxen, and cherubim (see 1 Kgs 7:28, 29, 31, 32, 35, 36). See also LAVER. Otherwise, Jeremiah delivers an oracle against Shallum, who is berated (Jer 22:14) for building such a fancy dwelling, paneled with cedar. In Hag 1:4, the prophet urges the people to rebuild the desolate Temple since they already live in "paneled" *(sĕpûnîm)* houses. However, the Haggai passage may mean "finished" houses in contrast to God's ruined dwelling. An obscure Hebrew word *(śāḥîp)* is rendered "paneled" in Ezek 41:16.

Carol Meyers

PANTHEONS, MESOPOTAMIAN. In the polytheistic world of Sumer, Babylonia, and Assyria thousands of gods existed, and since the cuneiform scribes made and used all kinds of lists of signs, words, and numbers for various practical and theoretical needs, gods' names were also compiled in list form. In a restricted sense, the word "pantheon" can be used to describe these lists. The earliest such list is *ca.* 2600 from Ur (UET 2: 105), which consists of only twelve names, and its purpose is not clear. However, from Fara and Abu Ṣalābīkh *ca.* 2500 B.C. there are lists of between 600 and 400 names, as well as some shorter ones, which are clearly meant as comprehensive statements of the pantheon. The two longest, one each from Fara and Abu Ṣalābīkh, show set principles of arrangement. Both begin with the most senior members of the pantheon by rank, to express a theological statement, but later in the lists another principle of arrangement appears. For example, in the big Fara list there is a long section of names beginning with *Nin-*, put together only because they share the same first sign, something akin to our alphabetic arrangement, with no theological significance.

In the 2d millennium another type of list arose, which continued to be copied until the 1st millennium, namely gods' names written in signs which are not self-explanatory and so have the reading indicated in phonetic signs, thus being a philological tool. However, the 3d-millennium type continued to be compiled and used, at least for the first few centuries of the 2d millennium, and at least one of these survived into the 1st millennium. But before 1600 B.C. more systematic lists were being compiled, giving the major deities of the pantheon in order of rank, each with spouse, children, courtiers, and other related minor gods. Such single-column lists required considerable knowledge to use and understand, so a double-column format was introduced *ca.* 1500 B.C. The names were explained by being equated with another name, on the analogy of Sumero-Babylonian word lists, and explanatory notes followed or took the place of the equivalent name, e.g. "Asallukhi = Marduk, prime son of Enki." This kind of list is, of course, extremely informative for modern scholars, though in need of critical handling, and the longest list of this type is called *An = Anum* after its first line, and contains not far short of 2000 entries. It was compiled by expanding older lists in the second half of the 2d millennium. It continued to be copied until at least the period of the Persian empire.

A still more elaborate type of list also appeared in the second half of the 2d millennium, utilizing three subcolumns. As before, the name in the first subcolumn was explained by an equation with another name, and then a phrase indicated the special reference of this particular name of the god being dealt with, e.g., "An = Anum, of mankind." Instead of simple phrases, more elaborate epithets are used in some of these lists.

All but one of these lists are Sumerian or Babylonian, the exception being a single-column Assyrian list, known from 1st-millennium copies, but perhaps of 2d-millennium origin. For further discussion see *RLA* 3: 473–79.

Bibliography

Mander, P. 1986. *Il Pantheon di Abu-Ṣalābīkh.* Naples.

W. G. Lambert

PANTHER. See ZOOLOGY.

PAPHOS (PLACE) [Gk *Paphos*]. A city in the SW of the island of Cyprus (34°45′N; 32°25′E), seat of the island's administrative government during the NT period. The Paphos of Acts 13:6–13 is actually the newer of two neighboring cities bearing the same name, sometimes differentiated by the terms "New Paphos" (*paphos nea;* Pliny *HN,* 5.130) and "Old Paphos" (*palaipaphos;* Strabo 14.683).

The maiden missionary voyage of Saul and Barnabas took them to Cyprus at the very outset. They landed in Salamis and made their way to Paphos at the other end of the island. Here they encountered the Jewish magician Elymas and the proconsul Sergius Paulus, who was the first of many secular authorities to summon Paul to give an account of himself. Paul (as Saul is called for the first time in the course of this narrative) successfully curses one with blindness (the apostle's first recorded miracle) and converts the other. Given some of the external evidence, the references connecting this city to a Sergius Paulus, to proconsuls in general, and to a Jewish magician are not surprising. Cyprus had recently been made a senatorial province, and the capital, and therefore proconsular residence, was in Paphos. There seems to be evidence for the name "Sergius Paulus" in an inscription found in N Cyprus (*SEG* 20.302, lines 9–11), but the best conjectures at dating make it unlikely that it refers to the same man (cf. now Mitford *ANRW* 2/7/2: 1300, 1330). Josephus (*Ant* 20.142) mentions a Cypriot Jewish magician named Atomus, again unlikely to be identified with the man in Acts, unless perhaps one regards the Bezan text as preserving his name more accurately (*et*[.]*mas* for *elumas*). On all these matters see Hemer 1989: 108, 109, 166f.

Cyprus was annexed by Rome in 58 B.C. and, after a very short period as a province with a military governor, became a senatorial (proconsular) province in 22 B.C. Paphos was well known for its temple and cult of a goddess syncretistically identified as the Greek Aphrodite, who became known as the "Paphian goddess." She was allegedly born on the foam of the sea, and floated on a shell to the shore of Cyprus near Paphos. The city also had a history of earthquakes, and was virtually destroyed by one in the 4th century A.D. It was perhaps as a result of this that Paphos lost its title as the capital of the island to Constantia, which was the rebuilt city of Salamis. The modern name for Paphos is Baffo, and excavations have revealed parts of several public and private buildings from the Roman era, including the city walls, an amphitheater, and a luxurious villa which may have been the governor's palace.

Bibliography

Hemer, C. J. 1989. *Book of Acts in the Setting of Hellenistic History.* WUNT 49. Tübingen.

CONRAD GEMPF

PAPIAS (PERSON). The writings of Papias (traditionally, ca. A.D. 60–130) are known to the modern world only from fragments and would be neglected today if it were not for certain statements made by him about Mark and Matthew that have intrigued NT scholars. This interest has rescued Papias from obscurity but has also distorted his importance and skewed the significance of his role in the early church.

A. Papias the Man

According to Irenaeus, our earliest witness, Papias was "a hearer of John and a companion of Polycarp, a man of primitive times," who wrote a volume in "five books" (*haer.* 5.33.4; quoted by Eusebius *Hist. Eccl.* 3.39.1). Eusebius already doubted the reality of a connection between Papias and the apostle John on the grounds that Papias himself in the preface to his book distinguished the apostle John from John the presbyter and seems to have had significant contact only with John the presbyter and a certain Aristion (*Hist. Eccl.* 3.39.3–7). Eusebius' skepticism was no doubt prompted by his distaste—perhaps a recently acquired distaste (Grant 1974)—for Papias' chiliasm and his feeling that such a theology qualified Papias for the distinction of being "a man of exceedingly small intelligence" (*Hist. Eccl.* 3.39.13). Nevertheless Eusebius' analysis of the preface is probably correct; and his further point that Papias' chiliasm put him to the same camp as the Revelation of John is surely relevant. It is notable that Eusebius, in spite of his desire to discredit Papias, still places him as early as the reign of Trajan (A.D. 98–117); and although later dates (e.g., A.D. 130–140) have often been suggested by modern scholars, Bartlet's date for Papias' literary activity of about A.D. 110 has recently gained support (Schoedel 1967: 91–92; Körtner 1983: 89–94, 167–72, 225–26).

It is also Eusebius who informs us that Papias was "bishop of the community in Hierapolis" (*Hist. Eccl.* 3.36.2). A somewhat different impression is left by Irenaeus, who is interested in the connection between Papias and the "presbyters" of Asia Minor. In this context the term "presbyter" refers not to church officials but to followers of the disciples (notably John) who handed on the orthodox theological tradition. It seems unlikely, as Harnack thought, that Papias was Irenaeus' source for his knowledge of the presbyters (Körtner 1983: 36–43). For in the crucial passage, Papias is evidently treated by Irenaeus simply as one who reinforces the authority of the presbyters in handing on the saying of the Lord about the wonderful fruitfulness of the earth in the millennium (*haer.* 5.33.3–4). The likelihood is that the presbyters were charismatic leaders in Asia Minor who in some quarters were believed to have been followers of the apostles and sometimes of the Lord himself and who were responsible, among other things, for promoting an apocalyptic form of Christianity; and it seems probable that John the presbyter and Aristion were the most important of these figures for Papias (Körtner 1983: 114–32).

B. Papias' Exposition of the Lord's Logia

What has become for many the standard collection of fragments of Papias (in Bihlmeyer) contains some thirteen items, the most important of which are derived from Irenaeus (*haer.* 5.33.4–5) and Eusebius (*Hist. Eccl.* 3.39). Other collections have additional materials, including a number of minor references to Papias from the church fathers. Körtner, for example, numbers twenty-two items in his edition of the fragments. Efforts to enrich the collection from the traditions of the presbyters in Irenaeus (Loofs 1930: 325–38) or from Armenian sources (Siegert 1981; Kürzinger 1983) are problematic (Körtner 1983: 31–43).

Papias' book was entitled "Exposition of the Lord's Logia" (Eus. *Hist. Eccl.* 3.39.1). Papias uses the term *logia* also in his discussion of Mark where the words and deeds of Jesus are under discussion (*Hist. Eccl.* 3.39.15). To judge from the fragments, the term "exposition" *(exegesis)* refers primarily to the act of collecting and correlating the materials. We do not know to what extent (if any) the shape of the book was determined by the written sources used by Papias (Mark and Matthew). We do not know what the scope or structure of the book was. We do not know whether the five divisions of the work represent anything more than perhaps an imitation of the Pentateuch, the Psalms, or some other collection. We cannot specify the genre of the work with any confidence (though perhaps the relevant parallel is offered by the *apomnemoneumata*—

the memoirs—of antiquity). It is not known whether any polemical intent informs the writing of the work, although opposition especially in Gnosticism or to Paulinism or to the Gospel of John have often been named in this connection. We do know that the preface of Papias' book and his account of the gospels of Mark and Matthew reflect the horizons of Greco-Roman rhetorical theory and practice. But there is disagreement as to how deep the influence goes (for an extreme statement of the case, see Kürzinger). It is possible that Papias was exercising a kind of rhetorical criticism on the tradition primarily for historical purposes with a view to establishing the credentials of his own chiliastic theology and thus promoting his work as a resource for the Christianity dominant in his immediate environment or at most (if we are not dealing merely with rhetorical flourishes) as a response to vaguely defined tendencies that involved (as Papias saw it) an openness to "those who have much to say" and a receptivity to "alien commandments" (*Hist. Eccl.* 3.39.3). In any event, it is not to be taken for granted that the anti-Gnostic use soon to be made of such theology necessarily illuminates Papias' own purpose.

Somewhat similarly, Papias discloses his preference for oral tradition in good rhetorical style as a preference for "a living and abiding voice" (*Hist. Eccl.* 3.39.4), yet he clearly is also well disposed to his written sources. Thus he apparently was a man who within certain limits sought to soften rather than to sharpen polarities and apparent contradictions.

C. Papias' Sources

Papias mentions "the presbyters"—or more precisely, those "who had actually attended the presbyters"—as his oral source and in this connection names seven (presumably representative) disciples (Andrew, Peter, Philip, Thomas, James, John, and Matthew) and two others, "Aristion and the elder John," whom he also calls "disciples of the Lord" (*Hist. Eccl.* 3.39.3–4). These lines from Papias' preface can be read in a way that identifies the presbyters with the disciples. But it is more likely that Papias regarded the presbyters as followers of the disciples. If the latter is correct, Papias claims to have his information from the disciples at third hand (Schoedel 1967: 98). It is also possible to read the passage in a way that identifies the apostle John with the presbyter John. But this reading also seems very doubtful (Schoedel 1967: 98–99). Presumably, then, Aristion and the presbyter John were regarded as personal "disciples" of Jesus who were not among the twelve; and presumably John was called "the presbyter" (whereas Aristion was not) to distinguish him from the apostle, who had just been named (Munck 1959). In any event, Papias "often mentions them [Aristion and the presbyter John] by name and sets forth their traditions in his writings"; and the assertion of Eusebius that Papias was himself a hearer of Aristion and the presbyter John is probably based on nothing more definite than that (*Hist. Eccl.* 3.39.7).

D. Papias' Theology

It is presumably from (followers of) Aristion and the presbyter John, then, that Papias derived his chiliastic doctrine. This connects Papias with a distinctive theological tradition that involves especially the presbyters of Asia Minor, Montanism, and later enthusiasts for millennialism. Interest in this tradition may have been reinforced in the case of Papias by the use of the NT Apocalypse (Körtner 1983: 82), but that is not certain (Schoedel 1967: 113–14). Papias' own theology left its mark in Irenaeus and elsewhere (notably, it seems, in Victorinus of Pettau, who died ca. A.D. 304). The background of the famous saying of the Lord about the miraculous fruitfulness of the earth in the millennium has been found in Jewish apocalyptic literature (Gry 1944, 1946), and there is little in the fragments of Papias that could not be seen as inspired by an apocalyptically oriented form of Jewish Christianity. But there are occasional hints of other theological concerns such as Papias' account of "a woman reproached for many sins in the Lord's presence" (*Hist. Eccl.* 3.39.17). And the interest in literary and historical questions evidently has intellectual foundations independent of Jewish Christianity. Moreover, Papias' accounts of miracles—the resurrection of a dead body (a story "received from the daughters of Philip," presumably Philip the evangelist and not Philip the apostle as Eusebius asserts), and the drinking of poison by Justus without any harmful effects (*Hist. Eccl.* 3.39.8–10; cf. Mark 16:17–18), or the gruesome account of Judas' death (in a fragment stemming from Apollinaris of Laodicaea)—suggest the atmosphere of the legendary acts of the apostles. That such events functioned as eschatological signs for Papias is possible, but that is not at all obvious from the fragments themselves. That Papias was in such instances adapting to his purposes stories that had Gnostic dimensions (Beyschlag 1961) is even less likely (Schoedel 1967: 111–12, Körtner 1983: 137–44; 148).

E. Papias and the New Testament

What the fragments have to tell us about Mark and Matthew is information that Papias himself traces to "the presbyter" (Eus. *Hist. Eccl.* 3.39.15–16). Eusebius separates the statements about Mark and Matthew, but they may originally have followed one another and certainly seem closely related. Perhaps the simplest reading of the statement on Mark is that Mark served as Peter's interpreter (possibly in the role of *methurgaman*, or oral translator) and wrote down what he heard Peter say of the words and deeds of Jesus and that his writing is defective in "order," though not in accuracy or fullness of recollection, because Peter naturally referred to the Lord's *logia* in a random manner. Some have suspected that Papias did not have in mind the gospel of Mark that we know, but the arguments are tenuous. On another point, Kürzinger has attempted to show that Papias was speaking not of translation from the native language of Peter but of presentation of the reports of Peter (an interpretation which he applies also to Papias' statement about Matthew); but this seems to push a rhetorical approach to Papias' terminology too far (Schoedel 1967: 107; Körtner 1983: 203–4). On the other hand, an interpretation in rhetorical terms is somewhat more likely when it comes to the suggestion that Papias meant to say that Peter spoke "in *chria*-style" rather than "as needs *(chriai)* dictated." But the point that is debated more than any other is what Papias had in mind when he said that Mark did not write "in order." It is perhaps most likely that Papias was measuring Mark by Matthew (who is said by Papias to have made "an ordered arrangement" of the materials)—or perhaps more generally by Papias' own conception of what ought to be included in such an account—and that he had in mind completeness of information as well as "order" in the narrow sense of the term. In any event, Papias is defending Mark in spite of perceived deficiencies.

Perhaps the simplest reading of the much briefer statement of Papias on Matthew is that Matthew organized the Lord's *logia* in Hebrew (Aramaic?) and that people ("each one") translated them variously. Some have held that Papias had in mind something other than the gospel of Matthew as we know it (a collection of sayings like Q, for example, or a collection of *testimonia*), but such views enjoy little support today. Again Kürzinger thinks that Papias is speaking of materials written not in the Hebrew language but in a Semitic style and of the presentation of such Semitically colored materials in different ways by Mark and Matthew ("each one"); but this also seems to push the terminology unnaturally (Schoedel 1967: 110; Körtner 1983: 203–4). To be sure, it is unclear what Papias had in mind when he referred to the variety of translations of Matthew. Conceivably the Jewish model of the translation of Scripture orally by a *methurgaman* lies in the background, or it may be that Papias was trying to account for the existence of Jewish Christian gospels (like the *Gospel According to the Hebrews*) which rivaled the authority of our Matthew. In any event, it is likely that, in the case of both Mark and Matthew, Papias was offering an explanation of the fact that he possessed Greek versions of what he assumed must have had Semitic prototypes. In other words, the concern for the authenticity of the tradition is once again the main point. Clearly, then, Papias' purpose must be taken into account before his statements are scrutinized for clues to the origins of the gospels. For this and other reasons there is an understandable reluctance of scholars today to rely heavily on Papias in the unraveling of NT problems.

Some scholars have found hints in the fragments that Papias also knew the gospels of Luke and John (and was dissatisfied with them or, quite the opposite, used one or the other of them as the standard by which he measured the adequacy of Mark), but the evidence is fragile. In particular, the reference to Mark's lack of "order" has inevitably suggested a connection (positive or negative) with Luke's claim to have set his materials down "accurately in order" (1:3). And Papias' assertion that he will hand on only "commandments" given by the Lord and "coming from the Truth itself" has suggested dependence on the Gospel of John (14:6, 15). But it is hard to find much to support these points. Certainly the evidence of the so-called "anti-Marcionite prologue" that names Papias as the apostle John's amanuensis is not impressive (Schoedel 1967: 121–123). Also highly problematic, however, is the information contained in two interdependent fragments of Papias that links the (relatively early) martyrdom of James (Acts 12:2) with that of John and that has consequently often been used to question the apostolicity of the Gospel of John (Schoedel 1967: 117–21). At the same time, the distinction apparently made between the disciple John and the presbyter John in Papias' preface plays a legitimate role in assessing claims made for the authorship of the various writings attributed to John in the NT and in evaluating the tradition concerning the Ephesian ministry of John the apostle.

A complex relation obtains between Papias' story of "a woman reproached for many sins in the Lord's presence" (*Hist. Eccl.* 3.39.17), the *pericope adulterae* now located in John 7:53–8:11, and the *Gospel According to the Hebrews* that Eusebius names as containing the story (cf. Becker). Here it is worth noting only that it is Eusebius (and not necessarily Papias himself) who makes reference to the *Gospel According to the Hebrews*.

Finally, Eusebius says that Papias "made use of testimonies from the first letter of John and likewise from that of Peter" (*Hist. Eccl.* 3.39.17). If this is accurate, it seems unlikely that the theology of either of these two writings influenced Papias deeply. Conceivably an interest in the figure of Peter prompted by Papias' Jewish Christian orientation had something to do with his use of 1 Peter and his appeal to what the presbyter had to say about Peter's role in the formation of the gospel of Mark. But that is obviously tenuous, and it seems unlikely in any event that opposition between Peter and Paul would have been involved. Papias' Christianity was evidently non-Pauline, but it was not necessarily anti-Pauline.

Bibliography

Annand, R. 1956. Papias and the Four Gospels. *SJT* 9: 46–62.

Becker, U. 1963. *Jesus und die Ehebrecherin.* BZNW 28. Berlin.

Beyschlag, K. 1961. Herkunft und Eigenart der Papiasfragmente. Pp. 268–80 in *Studia Patristica IV.* TU 79. Berlin.

Bihlmeyer, K. 1956. *Die Apostolischen Väter, Neubearbeitung der Funkschen Ausgabe.* 2d ed. Ed. W. Schneemelcher. Tübingen.

Bligh, J. F. 1952. The Prologue of Papias. *TS* 13: 234–40.

Deeks, D. G. 1977. Papias Revisited. *ExpTim* 88: 296–301, 324–29.

Grant, R. M. 1943. Papias and the Gospels. *ATR* 25: 218–22.

———. 1974. Papias in Eusebius' Church History. Pp. 209–13 in *Mélanges d'histoire des religions offerts à Henri-Charles Puech.* Paris.

Gry, L. 1944. Le Papias des belles promesses messianiques. *Vivre et penser* 3: 112–24.

———. 1946. Hénoch X, 19 et les belles promesses de Papias. *RB* 53: 197–206.

Gryson, R. 1965. A propos du témoignages de Papias sur Mattieu, le sens du mot logion chez les pères du second siècle. *ETL* 41: 530–47.

Gutwenger, E. 1947. Papias, eine chronologische Studie. *ZKT* 69: 385–416.

Körtner, U. H. J. 1983. *Papias von Hierapolis.* FRLANT 133. Göttingen.

Kürzinger, J. 1983. *Papias von Hierapolis und die Evangelien des Neuen Testaments.* Eichstätter Materialien 4. Regensburg.

Loofs, F. 1930. *Theophilus von Antiochien Adversus Marcionem und die anderen theologischen Quellen bei Irenaeus.* TU 46. Leipzig.

Munck, J. 1959. Presbyters and Disciples of the Lord in Papias. *HTR* 223–43.

Schoedel, W. R. 1967. *Polycarp, Martyrdom of Polycarp, Fragments of Papias.* Vol. 5 in *The Apostolic Fathers,* ed. R. M. Grant. Camden, NJ.

Siegert, F. 1981. Unbeachtete Papiaszitate bei armenischen Schriftstellern. *NTS* 27: 605–14.

William R. Schoedel

PAPYRI, EARLY CHRISTIAN. "Papyri" is used as a generic term to refer to texts written on papyrus or similar writing materials (in particular parchment, ostraca, and wooden tablets) which have emerged through stray finds or excavation, mainly in Egypt. The word conveniently distinguishes these from the "manuscripts" (mostly on parchment) handed down through the medieval library tradition. The writing materials of Mediterranean antiquity—of which papyrus was the principal one (Lewis 1974)—in general failed to survive the passage of time. Arid and desolate conditions along the Nile valley, however, proved especially favorable to their preservation (the moister Delta region much less so), and papyri have turned up in large numbers from scrap heaps and other sites in Egypt since late in the 19th century (comprehensive surveys of papyrology, including treatment of Christian materials, are given by Montevecchi 1973; Turner 1980; and there are several standard bibliographies for the field; for explanations of sigla denoting papyrus editions see Oates et al. 1985). Outside Egypt, papyrus finds have been on a very much smaller scale and the attestation of early Christianity slight. A parchment fragment of Tatian's *Diatessaron* (P. Dura 10) was found at Dura-Europus, where Christianity was practiced alongside other worshipping traditions in this remote Roman outpost, destroyed by the Persians in A.D. 256/57.

In filling in some of the considerable gaps presented by the literary, epigraphic, and archaeological sources, papyri offer a type of documentation of great directness, and extend the range of evidence to times and places for which documentation is otherwise unavailable (the full range of source materials for Christianity in Egypt is considered in Pearson and Goehring 1986). Alexandria, pivotal in the history of Christianity as in cultural history more generally, has itself yielded no papyrus finds, a major gap in the documentation scarcely alleviated by the finding elsewhere of texts which emanate from or refer to Christianity there, and by the assumption that Alexandrian practice had a decisive influence on scribal and other aspects of Christian books in Egypt. Middle Egypt has yielded much, particularly the Fayum and Oxyrhynchus, as well as Hermopolis, Antinoopolis, and other places. Finds from Upper Egypt are fewer but highly significant; from there have come, or may have come, some of the best-preserved texts (notably the Bodmer and Chester Beatty biblical codices in Greek, and the Nag Hammadi Coptic Gnostic codices), with monastic milieux providing an important role in the transmission of theological literature. There is evidence of the spread of Christianity westward to the Great Oasis by the 3d century, a process stimulated by the flight or banishment of persecuted Christians to remote regions (on Christianity in the oases see Wagner 1987: 355–72). Traffic beyond the First Cataract is likely to have carried Christian influence into Nubia as early as the 4th century.

The chronology of the Christian texts presents a formidable problem, owing to the uncertainties of palaeographic dating (on handwriting and other aspects of scribal practices, see Metzger 1981, Turner 1987; Turner [1977] gives some important re-datings). Most datings are very approximate. None of the texts can be safely assigned to the 1st century. The 2d century provides the first sure glimpses of the penetration of Christian literature along the Nile. In the 3d century the number of biblical and theological texts increases substantially, and there are clear references to Christians in official documents. Official reaction to Christianity reached a turning point with the Diocletianic persecutions in the early years of the 4th century and then the toleration of Christianity under Constantine I, and these developments receive papyrus attestation. By the mid-4th century the Christianization of Egypt was considerably advanced, and ecclesiastical and monastic institutions were part of the social fabric (Bagnall 1982; 1987 uses the criterion of personal names to quantify the rate of the changes). Papyri reflect this consolidation in their number and range.

The papyri relating to Christianity add to the general store of textual data, and give firsthand evidence of the spread of Christian beliefs. They contribute to the question of defining "Christian," although owing to the limited evidence there is an inescapable circularity in the identifying of Christian elements in texts and the illumination of Christianity on the basis of the texts. The papyri bear out the view that there was a diversity of beliefs and practices, but the low proportion of specifically "unorthodox" material warns against overstating the diversity (Roberts 1979; Samuel 1985). Light is shed, albeit in a scattered and incomplete way, on some of the great developments, such as the introduction of Christianity into Egypt, the growth of Coptic Christianity, the rise of the monastic movement, the formulation of liturgy, and the transmission of the textual traditions of the OT (including pre-Hexaplaric and non-LXX material) and of the NT (including texts with "Western" affinities).

The bulk of the texts are in Greek (over 300 by the early 4th century; in the space available here only a representative sample of texts can be cited), a phenomenon reflecting the transplantation of Hellenic culture to Egypt through commerce and conquest and its continuance under the Roman administration (Lewis 1983, Bowman 1986 provide general perspectives on the period in the light of the evidence of papyri). Only a handful of texts are in Latin (Cavenaile 1987). Coptic scriptures (Metzger 1977: 99–152; T. Orlandi's survey of Coptic literature in Pearson and Goehring 1986: 51–81) begin to appear in the 3d century, as well as Coptic glosses to Greek texts (the glosses in a papyrus of Isaiah, P. Chester Beatty VII, being among the earliest specimens of Coptic). Some codices contain collections of both Greek and Coptic texts (as Hamburg Pap. bil. 1, with several OT books in Greek and Coptic along with the Acts of Paul in Greek), and there is evidence for Greek-Coptic glossaries (British Museum Pap. 10825 verso, for some or all of the Minor Prophets).

Papyri illuminate the cultural phenomenon of the form of Christian books, a feature which is of significance for questions of attribution and of the use to which texts were put, as well as for the cultural attainments of their copyists and readers. Typically (but not exclusively), Christian biblical papyri are written in informal styles of handwriting, are in codex form (varying in size from large to miniature, with one or two columns to the page), and have *nomina sacra* (distinctively Christian contractions of certain sacred names such as the word for God or Lord, e.g. $\overline{ks}$ = *kyrios*) (Turner 1977; Roberts 1979). This general picture of Christian books applies to both OT and NT texts. The possibility of a Jewish milieu, or at least the influence of Jewish scribal tradition, arises where an OT text is written calligraphically, is in roll form, uses the Tetragrammaton (the Hebrew *YHWH* = Lord, represented by paleo-Hebrew or square Hebrew characters), or carries a non-Septuagint Hebraizing version (as that of Aquila or Symmachus; on the various Greek translations and their attestation [Tov *ANRW* 2/20/1: 121–89]). A concurrence of several such features, suggesting Jewish attribution as unavoidable, occurs seldom. The Jewish presence in Egypt declined dramatically as a result of cycles of revolt and persecution, and Jewish papyri in this period are correspondingly few.

In the 2d and 3d centuries the Christian preference for the codex for biblical texts (the roll was not infrequent for Christian literary works) is in marked contrast with the still traditional use of the roll for works of classical literature, for which the codex did not become standard until the 4th century (Turner 1977; Roberts and Skeat 1983). In the same century parchment came into common use in Egypt; an increase in the proportion of parchment codices for biblical texts is part of this wider change. In addition to the codex form, Christian scribes used the roll form on exceptional occasions for biblical texts. Some biblical texts appear in the form of individual sheets, including instances (notably of Psalm texts) which are evidently for liturgical use, and texts used as amulets.

The consistency with which Christian scribes favored the codex is matched by the regularity with which they used *nomina sacra.* Like the codex, these are found in use in the earliest examples of Christian biblical papyri. The system shows some variety in its earlier stages, both in the choice of words abbreviated and in the methods of abbreviation. Abbreviations became normal for the following fifteen words, and could be employed whether in context the words had a "sacred" or "profane" sense: *theos, kyrios, Iēsous, christos, uios, pneuma, Daueid, stauros* (and *stauroō*), *mētēr, patēr, Israēl, sōtēr, anthropos, Ierousalēm* and *ouranos* (Paap 1959; Roberts 1979).

Biblical papyri (which are augmented by biblical quotations and reminiscences in apocryphal and literary papyri and in some of the letters) provide a core of evidence (biblical and literary papyri are catalogued in van Haelst 1976 [including a chronological list of early texts, pp. 409–13], with updates by Treu in his "Christliche Papyri" reports [Treu 1969–]; and Aland 1976 is confined to texts on papyrus specifically, as is the series of text volumes begun with Grunewald and Junack 1986). The biblical papyri are more abundant than texts in other categories, and provide a useful indicator of the geographical spread of Christianity along the Nile (Roberts 1979). They provide the earliest witnesses to many passages, and offer numerous variants. They shed light on scribal practices, on reading preferences, on the canon of scripture, and on text types current in Egypt. (Aland and Aland 1987 gives contents and textual evaluation of NT texts on papyrus and parchment. In these matters it needs to be remembered that statistical considerations are affected by the accidents of preservation and publication.)

Evidence for a complete Bible in a single codex is lacking. Most of the papyri survive as leaves or fragments of one book, and their original extent is unclear. Groupings of a small number of books frequently occur. There is evidence of varying clarity for collections of the usual subgroupings: the Pentateuch, the Psalms, the Wisdom books, the Minor Prophets, some of the Major Prophets, the Four Gospels, the Johannine books, the Pauline Epistles, the Catholic Epistles. From this list are absent as a group the historical books of the OT, which are weakly represented. The sequences of books within these groupings are frequently noteworthy (for example, the Pauline Epistles appear in descending order of length in P. Chester Beatty II). There are also some unanticipated groupings of biblical works (a striking instance is P. Oxy. VIII 1075 + 1079, from a papyrus roll with Exodus on the recto and Revelation on the verso), and combinations of biblical and other (such as patristic) material (where a theme may be discernible, as with the apparently Paschal contents of the Savery Coptic codex, which has Melito, *On the Pasch,* as well as 1 Peter, Jonah, and other texts).

Best represented of all are the Psalms (P. Bodmer XXIV being especially extensive), a reflection of their importance in worship and also in the schoolroom. Other examples of substantially preserved OT papyri include texts of Genesis (Berlin, Cod. Gr. fol. 66 I, II; P. Chester Beatty IV and V), Numbers and Deuteronomy (P. Chester Beatty VI), Proverbs, Wisdom and Ecclesiasticus (P. Ant. I 8 + II 210), the Minor Prophets (Washington MS. V), Isaiah (P. Chester Beatty VII + other fragments), Ezekiel, Daniel and Esther (P. Chester Beatty IX + X + other fragments). P. Chester Beatty I has the remains of the four Gospels and Acts. The Gospels of Matthew and John are particularly well represented. Strong attestation for the gospel of John (including the substantially preserved codices of John and Luke-John, P. Bodmer II and P. Bodmer XIV–XV), and the occurrence of noncanonical material with Johannine affinities, lead to the conclusion that Johannine thought had very considerable influence in early Egyptian Christianity. A work of similar popularity (to judge by the numbers) was the *Shepherd of Hermas,* which achieved some canonical status for a time; the papyri show it to have circulated in several of its component parts. P. Bodmer VII + VIII has 1 and 2 Peter and Jude complete. P. Chester Beatty III has a third of Revelation. Some casual biblical excerpts appear in the margins of documents (such as the beginning of the Lord's Prayer written beside accounts, P. Erl. 105–10).

With the canonical books must be considered the extracanonical or apocryphal texts, bearing in mind that the idea and content of the canon were in the process of clarification, and that authentic material, such as new sayings of Jesus, may be transmitted independent of the canon. The papyri attest several apocryphal gospels not otherwise known, among them one of the earliest Christian papyri, Greek fragments of an unidentified gospel or gospel harmony (P. Egerton 2 = P. Lond. Christ. 1, with another fragment recently identified in the Cologne collection, P. Köln VI 255). The identified NT apocrypha include the *Protevangelium of James* complete (P. Bodmer V), and Greek fragments of the gospel of Thomas (P. Oxy. I 1, IV 654, 655; now reedited in Layton 1989), recognized after the discovery of a Coptic translation of the work among the tractates of the Nag Hammadi codices.

Literary papyri include identified works of patristic authors, works which may be attributed to known authors on the grounds of content or style, and works of unknown authorship, among which homiletic literature and works of hagiography are prominent. The variety of writers attested goes beyond specifically Egyptian circles and, in fact, the Alexandrian theologians are weakly represented (some identifications for Origen, uncertain attribution for Clement; Alexandrian textual criticism is represented in P. Grenf. I 5, a papyrus of Ezekiel in which the Hexaplaric system of signs is used). Melito of Sardis is relatively well represented. Other writers found include Aristides, Irenaeus, Julius Africanus, Eusebius, and Pachomius. An epistle against the Manicheans (P. Ryl. III 469) may be a pastoral circular from an Alexandrian bishop. Two versions of the anonymous *Acts of Phileas* (P. Bodmer XX, P. Chester Beatty XV) illuminate the development of martyrological compositions based on the form of official reports of court proceedings.

Knowledge of Gnostic and related writings has been revolutionized by the finding of the Nag Hammadi codices, containing over 40 tractates in Coptic (most if not all translations of Greek originals, reaching back into the early period). There is a small number of distinctively gnostic papyri in Greek from our period, including portions of the *Gospel of Mary* (P. Oxy. L. 3525 as well as P. Ryl. III 463, the latter likewise from Oxyrhynchus), the *Sophia of Jesus Christ* (P. Oxy VIII 1081; also found among the Nag Hammadi tractates), and a work regarded as probably from the school of Valentinus (P. Oxy. I 4). Several Coptic Manichean codices were discovered in the Fayum in 1930 and the process of their preservation and publication continues to the present day.

The liturgical texts, prayers, and hymns which survive are for the most part unknown from other sources. As well as individual prayers from formal and private milieux (P. Oxy. III 407 is a well-preserved example), there are collections, one of them conspicuously syncretistic (B.K.T. VI 6 1, which includes a hymn from the *Poimandres,* with doxology added). P. Oxy. XV 1786, a hymn to the Trinity with musical notation, offers the earliest extant specimen of Christian hymnody.

There is a miscellaneous group of "subliterary" papyri, including biblical oracles, glossaries, onomastica and word lists, biblical passages used for school exercises, and glosses and other marginalia. Through the magical genre, preserved in Greek and Coptic, run crosscurrents of thought which typify the period, when biblical excerpts could be used as amulets or Christian ideas could be drafted into magical formulations. Some Christian symbols occur in texts of various genres, such as the staurogram worked into an abbreviated form of the word for "crucify" in biblical texts, or the number 99 (the numerical value of the letters of *amēn*) added to a private letter (P. Oxy. XXXI 2601).

The private letters, from ca. A.D. 200 onward, show persons expressing their beliefs, incidentally or more deliberately, in the course of everyday affairs (whether some letters assigned earlier actually refer to Christians is debated; this is part of a general problem of attribution, since monotheistic or other usages may be consistent with Christian belief without being distinctive of it [Naldini 1968; Wipszycka 1974; Tibiletti 1979]). The standard conventions of letter writing were adapted so that Christian phraseology appears in greetings, prayers, and salutations. The conveying of Christian sentiments in the body of a letter becomes frequent in the 4th century, and some biblical quotations and allusions occur. The correspondence of churches and monasteries—such as letters of recommendation—begins to appear in the latter half of the 3d century. Some light is thrown on Christianity in Alexandria; there is, for example, an apparent mention of the late-3d-century bishop of Alexandria Maximus (P. Amh. I 3 [c]), and a description of conflicts between adherents of Athanasius and supporters of the Meletian schism (P. Lond. VI 1914). P. Lond. VI 1913–1922 is a series of letters from around A.D. 330–40 from a Melitian monastic milieu (now further illuminated, though with a slightly later focus, by the archive of Nepheros in Trier and Heidelberg). The mutually supportive roles of church and military functionaries is documented by the archive (early 340s–early 350s) of Abinnaeus, a cavalry officer stationed in the Fayum (P. Abinn.). The papyrus letters give evidence of social and cultural levels, norms (such as the ascetic), and customs (such as the bestowal of Christian names). On the whole, in both the 3d and 4th centuries, the writers are from the higher levels of town or village society (Judge and Pickering 1977, with a list of letters and documents).

Some official and other documents refer to or originate with Christians, or are concerned with events of relevance to the history of Christianity. There is a tendency in the evidence of the documents toward depicting a transition from confrontation to integration in the community, a result of the types of circumstances which could lead to the appearance of persons in public records (such as the holding of property) or the public designation of persons as church-related (as when ecclesiastical titles became commonplace). Documents have the advantage that, in most instances, they contain specific dates or are susceptible of reasonably close dating (even here doubts over dating may arise, owing to questions of reading or interpretation). Firmly dated texts begin to emerge in the middle of the third century. Between A.D. 250 and A.D. 350 the focus of the documents changes from the investigation of Christians (in the latter half of the 3d century and the first few years of the 4th) to the role of church institutions in the social and economic order (particularly from the early 320s onwards). At the beginning of that period are certificates of sacrifice from the Decian persecution (the so-called Decian *libelli* [P. Oxy. XLI 2990 was the 44th to be published], not specifically referring to Christians), and soon after (at or near to the time of the persecution of Valerian) investigative documents in which the word "Christian" occurs (P. Oxy. XLII 3035, XLIII 3119); at the midpoint, the dismantling of churches under Diocletian is attested (P. Oxy. XXXIII 2673; cf. P. Harr. II 208); toward the end of the period, ecclesiastics and monks have become part of the daily scene (e.g. P. Col. VII 171), Sunday is referred to as "the Lord's Day" (P. Oxy. LIV 3579), an Egyptian monk is summoned by Constantine to the Synod of Caesarea (P. Lond. VI 1913, A.D. 334), and bishops are found as substantial landowners (P. Herm. Landlisten), a signal of the large role of the church in the politics and economy of Byzantine Egypt.

Bibliography

Aland, K., ed. 1976. *Repertorium der griechischen christlichen Papyri.* Vol. 1, *Biblische Papyri. Altes Testament, Neues Testament, Varia, Apokryphen.* Patristische Texte und Studien 18. Berlin and New York.

Aland, K., and Aland, B. 1987. *The Text of the New Testament.* Trans. A. F. Rhodes. Grand Rapids, MI and Leiden.

Bagnall, R. S. 1982. Religious Conversion and Onomastic Change in Early Byzantine Egypt. *BASP* 19: 105–24.

———. 1987. Conversion and Onomastics: A Reply. *Zeitschrift für Papyrologie und Epigraphik* 69: 243–50.

Bowman, A. K. 1986. *Egypt after the Pharaohs, 332 BC–AD 642, from Alexander the Great to the Arab Conquest.* London.

Cavenaile, R. 1987. Le latin dans les milieux chrétiens d'Égypte. Pp. 103–10 in *Miscellània papirològica Ramon Rocca-Puig en el seu vuitantè aniversari,* eds. S. Janeras. Barcelona.

Grunewald, M., and Junack, K., eds. 1986. *Das Neue Testament auf Papyrus.* Vol. 1, *Die Katholischen Briefe.* ANTF 6. Berlin and New York.

Judge, E. A., and Pickering, S. R. 1977. Papyrus Documentation of Church and Community in Egypt to the Mid-Fourth Century. *JAC* 20: 47–71.

Layton, B., ed. 1989. *Nag Hammadi Codex II,2–7 Together with XIII,2*, Brit. Lib. Or. (4926) 1, and P. Oxy. 1, 654, 655.* The Coptic Gnostic Library. NHS 20–21. Leiden.

Lewis, N. 1974. *Papyrus in Classical Antiquity.* Oxford.

———. 1983. *Life in Egypt under Roman Rule.* Oxford.

Metzger, B. M. 1977. *The Early Versions of the New Testament.* Oxford.

———. 1981. *Manuscripts of the Greek Bible.* New York and Oxford.

Montevecchi, O. 1973. *La Papirologia.* Turin.

Naldini, M. 1968. *Il Cristianesimo in Egitto. Lettere private nei papiri dei secoli II–IV.* Studi e testi di papirologia. Florence.

Oates, J. F.; Bagnall, R. S.; Willis, W. H.; and Worp, K. A. 1985. *Checklist of Editions of Greek Papyri and Ostraca,* 3d ed. BASPSup 4.

Paap, A. H. R. E. 1959. *Nomina Sacra in the Greek Papyri of the First Five Centuries A.D. The Sources and Some Deductions.* Papyrologica Lugduno-Batava. Leiden.

Pearson, B. A., and Goehring, J. E., eds. 1986. *The Roots of Egyptian Christianity.* Studies in Antiquity and Christianity. Philadelphia.

Roberts, C. H. 1979. *Manuscript, Society and Belief in Early Christian Egypt.* London.

Roberts, C. H., and Skeat, T. C. 1983. *The Birth of the Codex.* London.

Samuel, A. E. 1985. How Many Gnostics? *BASP* 22: 297–322.

Tibiletti, G. 1979. *Le lettere private nei papiri greci del III e IV secolo d.C. Tra paganesimo e cristianesimo.* Milan.

Treu, K. 1969–. "Christliche Papyri" [surveys in] *Archiv für Papyrusforschung* 19: 169–206 [and subsequent volumes].

Turner, E. G. 1977. *The Typology of the Early Codex.* Philadelphia.

———. 1980. *Greek Papyri: An Introduction.* Rev. ed. Oxford.

———. 1987. *Greek Manuscripts of the Ancient World.* 2d ed. rev. and enl., ed. P. J. Parsons. BICS Sup 46. London.

Van Haelst, J. 1976. *Catalogue des papyrus littéraires juifs et chrétiens.* Paris.

Wagner, G. 1987. *Les Oasis d'Égypte à l'époque grecque, romaine et byzantine, d'après les documents grecs (Recherches de papyrologie et d'épigraphie grecques).* Bibliothèque d'Étude, 100. Cairo.

Wipszycka, E. 1974. Remarques sur les lettres privées chrétiennes des IIᵉ–IVᵉ siècles (à propos d'un livre de M. Naldini). *Journal of Juristic Papyrology* 18: 203–21.

S. R. Pickering

PAPYRI, PAPYRUS. Articles on individual papyri can be found under the following titles: BODMER PAPYRI; CHESTER BEATTY PAPYRI; ELEPHANTINE PAPYRI; SAMARIA (PAPRYRI); and EGERTON PAPYRUS. On papyrus as a writing material, see FLORA; WRITING AND WRITING MATERIALS.

PARABLE. An extended metaphor or simile frequently becoming a brief narrative, generally used in biblical times for didactic purposes.

A. Parabolic Genre
B. Parabolic Corpus
   1. The Hebrew Scriptures
   2. The Jesus Tradition
C. Parabolic Interpretation

A. Parabolic Genre

The Greco-Roman literary tradition took the genre "parable" in a fairly restricted manner. In his *Rhetoric* (2.20) Aristotle distinguished two types of proof used in all types of rhetoric. First, there is the example *(paradeigma),* which is to be used inductively. This is divided into two classes, "one which consists in relating things that have happened before, and another in inventing them oneself." The former is history, the latter fiction. Those fictional examples are again divided into two subclasses: the fable *(logos)* and the comparison *(parabolē).* Fables are impossible or unrealistic fictions. Aristotle gives an instance from Aesop: The flea-ridden fox refuses the hedgehog's offer of help because his fleas are now sated. Parables are possible or realistic fictions. Aristotle gives an instance from Socrates: "If one were to say that magistrates should not be chosen by lot, for this would be the same as choosing as representative athletes not those component to contend, but those on whom the lot falls; or as choosing any of the sailors as the man who should take the helm, as if it were right that the choice should be decided by lot, not by a man's knowledge" (2.20.4). Second, there is the saying *(enthymēma),* which is to be used deductively. Here again there are two classes. One is the maxim *(gnōmē),* for instance: "There is no man who is really free." Another is the proverb *(paroimia),* for instance: "An Attic [i.e., troublesome] neighbor."

The Hebrew literary tradition gave the genre a much wider understanding. As we shall see in more detail below, the word *māšāl,* with its most usual Greek translation, *parabolē,* meant a similitude or comparison and the expression had a very wide range of application. In fact it is almost synonymous with metaphor.

Contemporary literary criticism agrees with the Greco-Roman tradition in emphasizing the narrative element in parable but with the Hebrew tradition in allowing both impossible and possible stories into the genre. Three elements are stressed in modern parabolic theory. Parables combine the qualities of narrative, metaphor, and brevity. A parable must tell, in as short a space as possible, a story with a double meaning. One meaning will usually be quite clear on the surface of the narration. Another, and presumably deeper meaning, or other, and possibly multiple meanings lie hidden within the complexities of the narrative, and these challenge or provoke the recipient to interpretation. Parables are lures for interpretation and also revelations of the very process of interpretation itself.

B. Parabolic Corpus

1. The Hebrew Scriptures. In the Hebrew scriptures the parabolic genre, as *māšāl* or *parabolē* is not limited to narratives but is concentrated around the idea of comparison, of one thing said and another intended. It therefore includes everything from proverb to allegory (Boucher 1977: 86–89). The full continuum of its usage can be seen even in a single book, for example, in Ezekiel.

The term can designate what we would call a proverb, and specific examples are italicized in the following cases. In Ezek 12:22–23 God says to the prophet, "Son of man, what is this proverb that you have about the land of Israel, saying, 'The days grow long and every vision comes to nought'? Tell them therefore, 'Thus says the Lord God: I will put an end to this proverb, and they shall no more use it as a proverb in Israel.' " In Ezek 16:43b–45b, God accuses Jerusalem, "Have you not committed lewdness in addition to all your abominations? Behold, every one who uses proverbs will use this proverb about you, 'Like mother, like daughter' . . . Your mother was a Hittite and your father an Amorite." Finally, in Ezek 18:2–3, in a text very similar to the first one in 12:22–23, God again refutes an Israelite proverb. "The word of the Lord came to me again, 'What do you mean by repeating this proverb concerning the land of Israel, "The fathers have eaten sour grapes, and the children's teeth are set on edge." As I live, says the Lord God, this proverb shall no more be used by you in Israel.' "

There is a special instance of parable-as-proverb in the case of proverbs of warning or bywords of caution. In Ezek 14:8 God is threatening idolators who seek prophetic guidance despite their infidelity: "I will set my face against that man, I will make him a sign and a byword and cut him off from the midst of my people; and you shall know that I am the Lord."

At the other end of the continuum are instances of what we would term allegory. Once again there are very good examples in Ezekiel. Here the parable designates a narrative comparison with the hidden meaning carried by both the narrative sequence and details of the story. In Ezek 17:2 God tells the prophet, "Son of man, propound a riddle, and speak an allegory to the house of Israel." There follows in 17:3–10 the parable-allegory of The Two Eagles, which is explained in detail in 17:11–21. The first or "great eagle" is Nebuchadrezzar of Babylon, the "young twig" is Jehoiachin, the "seed of the land" is Zedekiah. The "second eagle" is Pharaoh Psammeticus II of Egypt. The turning of the vine away from the first eagle which had planted it and toward the second eagle is Zedekiah's pro-Egyptian intrigues which will bring the wrath of Babylon down upon him. There is another parable-allegory in Ezek 20:45–49 where The Great Fire from the north will destroy the trees of the south, and Ezekiel protests, "Ah Lord God! they are saying of me, 'Is he not a maker of allegories?' " It should be noted that not every single element in the allegorical story has a specific referent in the allegorized history.

In those preceding instances the word *māšāl* or *parabolē* was explicitly used for those parabolic or allegorical stories. But even in Ezekiel there are allegories where the term does not appear. They are simply called prophetic lamentations. For example, The Young Lions in Ezek 19:1–9 has Judah as a lioness. Jehoahaz as the "young lion . . . brought with hooks to the land of Egypt," and Jehoiachin as "another of her welps . . . put . . . in a cage and . . . brought . . . to the king of Babylon." Similarly, The Vine's Branch in Ezek 19:10–14 has Judah as a vine, the "strongest stem" is Zedekiah, the "east wind" is Nebuchadrezzar, and the "transplantation in the wilderness" is the Babylonian Exile.

There are several instances elsewhere in the Hebrew scriptures where the specific term *māšāl* or *parabolē* is not used but which should also be considered as parables in the sense of allegories. Here the stories are taken not from natural events but from human actions. The most famous may well be The Ewe Lamb in 2 Sam 12:1–4. The "rich man" is David, the "poor man" is Uriah, the "ewe lamb" is Bathsheba, and Nathan traps David in his own indignation. Notice, once again, that even in such parabolic allegories, not every narrative element has an extranarratival referent. What, for example, in the story of David's adultery and murder corresponds to the narrative's "there came a traveler to the rich man"? Is it part of the allegorical challenge that the recipient must determine just how far such detailed references are to be passed? A similar allegorical trap is sprung on David by The Widow's Sons in 2 Sam 14:5–7. Here the first son is the murdered Amnon, and second son is the fugitive Absalom. One final example, which Aristotle would have termed a fable rather than a parable, is the case of the antimonarchic story in Judg 9:8–15. The trees sought a king but were turned down by olive, fig, and vine, and had to take in the end the useless and dangerous bramble. In that example there are no specific referents for olive, fig, and vine, but the bramble clearly applies to Abimelech.

Most of what will follow in this parabolic tradition is already set up by those preceding examples. Parable extends from nonnarrative proverb to narrative allegory, from fables with possible or impossible natural protagonists to stories with quite possible and plausible human protagonists, and with or without the specific title of parable being present.

2. The Jesus Tradition. The Christian tradition was consciously aware that Jesus spoke both in aphoristic parables and narrative parables. This is clear in two documents discovered at Nag Hammadi. The aphoristic parables are recalled by the comment in *Dial. Sav.* (NHC III.5) 139:8–11, "Mariam said, 'Thus about "The wickedness of each day," and "The laborer being worthy of his food," and "The disciple resembling his teacher." ' " Those three sayings are known to us also from elsewhere in the Jesus tradition. The Wickedness saying is in Matt 6:34b. The Laborer saying is in Matt 10:10b; Luke 10:7b; 1 Cor 9:14; 1 Tim 5:18b; *Did.* 13:1–2. The Disciple saying is in Matt 10:25a; Luke 6:40. The narrative parables are recalled by the comment in *Ap. Jas.* (NHC I,2) 8:1–10, "It was enough for some ⟨to listen⟩ to the teaching and understand 'The Shepherds' and 'The Seed' and 'The Building' and 'The Lamps of the Virgins' and 'The Wage of the Workmen' and 'The Didrachmae' and 'The Woman.' " Those seven parables are also known to us from elsewhere in the Jesus tradition. The Shepherds (despite the plural) is probably Matt 18:12–13; Luke 15:4–6. The Seed is Mark 4:3–8; Matt 13:3b–8; Luke 8:5–8a; *Gos. Thom.* 9. The Building is Matt 7:24–27; Luke 6:47–49. The Lamps is Matt 25:1–13. The Wage is Matt 20:1–15. The Didrachmae (despite the plural) is Luke 15:8–9. The Woman is either Matt 13:33 or *Gos. Thom.* 97.

Following from the Hebrew scriptural usage, we would expect the term "parable" to cover both the aphoristic and narrative metaphors of Jesus. Thus, when Jesus is accused of Satanic collusion, Mark 3:23 continues, "And he called them to him, and said to them in parables, 'How can Satan cast out Satan? If a kingdom is divided against itself, that kingdom cannot stand. And if a house is divided against itself, that house will not be able to stand.' " In this case of Kingdom and House the term "parables" refers to nonnarrative or aphoristic metaphors. Later in Mark 12:1, the story of The Evil Tenants is introduced with, "And he began to speak to them in parables," and in 12:12 it is concluded with, "And they tried to arrest him, but feared the multitude, for they perceived that he had told the parable against them; so they left him and went away."

This wide understanding of parable as including both aphoristic metaphor and narrative metaphor is present even within the same chapter in Mark 4. This opens in 4:2, "And he taught them many things in parables," and concludes in 4:33–34, "With many such parables he spoke the word to them, as they were able to hear it; he did not speak to them without a parable, but privately to his own disciples he explained everything." Yet inside those emphatic frames, the section includes both parables-as-narratives, for example, The Sower in 4:3–8, The Harvest Time in 4:26–29, The Mustard Seed in 4:30b–32, and parables-as-aphorisms, for example, Lamp and Bushel in 4:21, Measure for Measure in 4:24b. And both types of parable receive the warning, "He who has ears to hear, let him hear," in 4:9 and, "If any man has ears to hear, let him hear" in 4:23.

In general, therefore, the Jesus tradition follows the Hebrew scriptural precedent and places the emphasis on comparison or metaphor in applying the term "parable" to a unit. Whether the unit is aphoristic or a narrative metaphor is of no significance. The data of the Jesus tradition necessitates, however, the expansion of that double into a triple category: aphoristic parables, extended parables, and narrative parables.

a. Aphoristic Parables. There is a very high incidence of aphoristic metaphors in the Jesus tradition and these may be present with or without the explicit term "parable" being present. For example, Mark 2:21–22 says, "No one sews a piece of unshrunk cloth on an old garment; if he does, the patch tears away from it, the new from the old, and a worse tear is made. And no one puts new wine into old wineskins; if he does, the wine will burst the skins, and the wine is lost, and so are the skins; but new wine is for fresh skins." Matt 9:16–17 follows Mark in not calling this aphoristic metaphor about Patches and Wineskins a parable. And it also occurs without explicit parabolic characterization in *Gos. Thom.* 47d. But in Luke 5:36a the same unit is introduced by "He told them a parable also." Exactly the same phenomenon occurs in the case of The Blind Guide. Matt 15:14b reads, "And if a blind man leads a blind, both will fall into the pit." The aphoristic metaphor also appears in *Gos. Thom.* 34 and again without being explicitly called a parable. But Luke 6:39 reads, "He also told them a parable: 'Can a blind man lead a blind man? Will they not both fall into a pit?' "

It is already evident from some of the above examples that aphoristic parables often appear in doubled format. We just saw the doubled aphoristic metaphors of Patches and Wineskins. There are also several cases where an aphoristic metaphor appears as single in one text but as double in another. For example, the Dogs and Swine saying in Matt 7:6 reads, "Do not give dogs what is holy; and do not throw your pearls before swine, lest they trample them under foot and turn to attack you." *Gos. Thom.* 93 also has this saying as a doublet, "⟨Jesus said,⟩ "Do not give what is holy to dogs, lest they throw them on the dung leap. Do not throw the pearls to swine, lest they grind it [to bits]." Yet *Did.* 9:5 warns with a single aphoristic metaphor, "But let none eat or drink of your Eucharist except those who have been baptized in the Lord's Name. For concerning this also did the Lord say, 'Give not that which is holy to the dogs.' " Again, the sayings on Hating One's Family and Carrying One's Cross appear as a doublet in Matt 10:37–38; Luke 14:26–27; *Gos. Thom.* 55. But the latter saying appears alone in Mark 8:34; Matt 16:24; Luke 9:23; and the former appears alone in *Gos. Thom.* 101. Finally, the famous saying about the Prophet's Own Country appears as follows in *Gos. Thom.* 31 (P. Oxy 1.30–35), "Jesus said, 'No prophet is accepted in his own village; no physician heals those who know him.' " Instead of this double version, with prophet and physician present, there is a single version, with only prophet present, in Mark 6:4; Matt 13:57b; John 4:44.

In most of these cases it is almost impossible to decide whether a single saying has been doubled by analogous creation or an originally double saying has been contracted into single format. In that final instance, the second option seems more plausible. Prophet could be taken literally and the metaphorical physician could easily drop away. This is confirmed by Jesus' comment in Luke 4:23, "And he said to them, 'Doubtless you will quote to me this proverb, "Physician, heal yourself; what we have heard you did at Capernaum, do here also in your own country." ' " Luke, in other words, may have known the double aphorism but opted, unlike Mark and the rest, for the physician rather than the prophet.

There are even some cases where a single or double aphorism is moving on to become a triple version. We saw already the double saying on Kingdom and House in Mark 3:24–25 and Luke 11:17b. In this case Matt 12:25b almost triples it: "Every kingdom divided against itself is laid waste, and no city or house divided against itself will stand." One begins to glimpse a possible third saying about a divided city added to that on kingdom and house. Similarly the Serving Two Masters saying appears in single form in Matt 6:24, "No one can serve two masters; for either he will hate the one and love the other, or he will be devoted to one and despise the other." So also in Luke 16:13. But this is a triple version in *Gos. Thom.* 47, "Jesus said, 'It is impossible for a man to mount two horses or to stretch two bows. And it is impossible for a servant to serve two masters; otherwise he will honor the one and treat the other contemptuously.' "

Aphoristic parables, in other words, appear in single, double, triple, or even multiple units, and these may either expand or contract as the transmission progresses. And doublets, of course, could be formed either synonymously, with twin positives or twin negatives, or else antithetically, with a balanced positive and negative in whichever order. All the preceding doublets were in synonymous parallelism. Examples in antithetical parallelism appear in the next section.

b. Extended Parables. The distinction between extended and narrative parables may be clarified by an example. The narrative parable of The Treasure appears in Matt 13:44: "The kingdom of heaven is like treasure hidden in a field, which a man found and covered up; then in his joy he goes and sells all that he has and buys that field." On the one hand, this is much more than a simple aphoristic parable, as if it had said only, "the kingdom of heaven is like a treasure hidden in a field," and stopped right there. On the other, it is surely a minimal story, with beginning, middle, and end, with the three sequential elements of finding, reburying, and buying. Still, despite its brevity or maybe even because of it, one could certainly not guess from the opening sentence how the story would unfold. That is a narrative parable and the application depends on how one reads the entire story. There is, in other words, some at least minimal amount of surprise or unpredictability in narrative parables.

Extended parables, however, are but the predictable unfolding of what is implicit in aphoristic parables. Consider The Two Houses in Matt 7:24–27 or Luke 6:47–49, "Every one then who hears these words of mine and does them will be like a wise man who built his house upon rock; and the rain fell, and the floods came, and the winds blew and beat upon the house, but it did not fall, because it had been founded on the rock. And every one who hears these words of mine and does not do them will be like a foolish man who built his house upon the sand; and the rains fell, and the floods came, and the winds blew and beat against that house, and it fell; and great was the fall of it." That could be taken as a sequential narrative with beginning, middle, and end, with building, flooding, standing, or building, flooding, falling. It could be considered a narrative parable, just like The Treasure. But each half does no more than unpack the details already quite predictable in those opening aphoristic metaphors, "built on rock" or "built on sand." No doubt, the expanded metaphor is quite suitable as the climactic ending for Matthew's "Sermon on the Mount," but it is also a moot point in aesthetics whether expanded metaphors are not often ruined metaphors. It is sometimes best to leave the unpacking to the recipient's imagination.

In The Two Houses the extended parables were based on an aphoristic doublet but this doublet, unlike the synonymous ones seen earlier, was an antithetical formation. It balanced a positive with a negative rather than having a synonymous formation containing two of either. Several other extended parables contain antithetical parallelism. For example, notice the contrasted options in The Two Shepherds of John 10:11–13, The Two Positions of Luke 14:7–10, The Two Stewards of Matt 24:45–51; Luke 12:42–46; The Two Reactions of the master in Luke 17:7–9, The Two Refusals of the playing children in Matt 11:16–17; Luke 7:31–32; and The Two Sons of Matt 21:28–32. A graphic illustration of the difference between an extended parable and a narrative parable may be seen by comparing that last instance with the story of the two sons in The Prodigal Son of Luke 15:11–32.

Of course, not all extended parables have this antithetical format. Examples without it are the Fig Tree's Lesson in Mark 13:28 and Matt 24:32, but explicitly called a parable only in Luke 21:29–30; or Knowing the Danger in Matt 24:43; Luke 12:39; *Gos. Thom.* 21,103.

In the Jesus tradition, extended parables form the center of a parabolic continuum with clearly aphoristic parables at one end and clearly narrative parables at the other. There are, therefore, extended parables which are extremely close to aphoristic ones and others extremely close to narrative ones.

An example of the former instance is Before the Judgment. In Matt 5:25–26 and Luke 12:58–59 this reads: "Make friends quickly with your accuser, while you are going with him to court, lest your accuser hand you over to the judge, and the judge to the guard, and you be put in prison; truly, I say to you, you will never get out till you have paid the last penny." But the synoptically dependent version in *Did.* 1:5 is much shorter: "He . . . shall be tried . . . and being in prison he shall be examined as to his deeds, and he shall not come out thence until he pay the last farthing."

There are several examples of the latter instance, that is, of parables which stand on the exact borderline between an extended and a narrative parable. Examples are The Harvest Time in Mark 4:26–29; *Gos. Thom.* 21; The Mustard Seed in Mark 4:30–32; Matt 13:31–32; Luke 13:18–19; *Gos. Thom.* 20; The Leaven in Matt 13:33; Luke 13:20–21; *Gos. Thom.* 96; The Midnight Friend in Luke 11:5–8; The Tower Builder in Luke 14:28–30; The Warring King in Luke 14:31–32; The Unjust Judge in Luke 18:2–4; and all three parables from one of the Nag Hammadi texts, The Palm Shoot in *Ap. Jas.* 7:22–28; Grain of Wheat in *Ap. Jas.* 8:10–23; Ear of Grain in *Ap. Jas.* 12:20–27.

Finally, there is one very interesting parable, The Returning Master, which might be classified in any of the three categories. In Mark 13:34–36 and Luke 12:35–38, the combination of parabolic third-person and parenetic second-person discourse renders it hard to decide whether there might be a full narrative parable behind those units. But in any case, the synoptically independent version in *Did.* 16:1 is simply an aphoristic parable: "Watch over your life: let your lamps be not quenched and your loins be not ungirded, but be ready, for ye know not the hour in which our Lord cometh."

c. Narrative Parables. The most famous parables in the Jesus tradition are not the extended but the narrative parables. It is those, for example, that gave to our language the images of the prodigal son and the good Samaritan. It must be remembered, however, that Jesus was an oral teacher and that those stories may well be no more than plot summaries of stories which might have taken hours to tell.

In a famous article of 1909, Axel Olrik spoke of the epic

"laws" of folk narrative, and those traditions of oral storytelling are still obvious even in the necessarily summarized versions of Jesus' narrative parables. The "Law of Three" appears in the path, rocks, and thistles of The Sower in Mark 4:3–8; Matt 13:3–8; Luke 8:5–8a; *Gos. Thom.* 9; in the three servants of The Talents in Matt 25:14–30, in the "improved" version in *Gos. Naz.* 18, and even in Luke 19:15–26 despite the initial "ten servants" in 19:13; and in the Priest, Levite, and Samaritan of The Good Samaritan in Luke 10:30–35. But those last two cases also follow the "Law of Twins," that is, the first two servants in The Talents and the first two travelers in The Good Samaritan form a twinned situation as contrasted with the third one in each case. The Law of Contrast, of clearly polarized protagonists, appears in the farmer and his enemy in the Wheat and Weeds in Matt 13:24–30; *Gos. Thom.* 57; in the Rich Man and Lazarus in Luke 16:19–31; in the Pharisee and Publican in Luke 18:10–13; in the former and latter guests of The Feast in Matt 22:1–13; Luke 14:15–24; *Gos. Thom.* 64a; and in the wise and foolish bridesmaids of The Closed Door in Matt 25:1–12. The "Law of Concentration" on one leading character explains the emphasis on the master in The Vineyard Laborers in Matt 20:1–15. The "Law of the Single Strand," of unentangled plots, is clear in the three successive scenes of The Unmerciful Servant in Matt 18:23–35. The "Law of Opening," moving swiftly from rest to movement, is evident at the start of The Prodigal Son in Luke 15:11–32 or The Unjust Steward in Luke 16:1–7. But "The Law of Ending," returning terminally from movement to rest, is quite absent in those two parables. It is as if they are deliberately left hanging to force the hearer into judgment and commitment.

Another feature of Jesus' narrative parables, apart from their oral character, is their normalcy. The realities of Galilean life peer out from the everyday actions of peasant women, in The Lost Coin of Luke 15:8–9 and The Empty Jar of *Gos. Thom.* 97; and from the lethal actions of peasant rebels, in The Tenants of Mark 12:1–11; Matt 21:33–43; Luke 14:15–24; *Gos. Thom.* 65–66, and in The Assassin of *Gos. Thom.* 98. Parables speak of a fish, in The Fishnet of Matt 13:47–48; *Gos. Thom.* 8; of a flock, in The Lost Sheep of Matt 18:12–13; Luke 15:4–6; *Gos. Thom.* 107; and of a tree, in the Barren Fig Tree of Luke 13:6–9. One might move up in such a world, but it would take luck or even cunning, for example, in The Treasure of Matt 13:44; *Gos. Thom.* 109; or The Pearl in Matt 13:45–46; *Gos. Thom.* 76. To make a point about riches, a rich farmer is chosen, in The Rich Fool of Luke 12:16–20; *Gos. Thom.* 63.

C. Parabolic Interpretation

In the rabbinical tradition the interpretation of a parable is usually quite clear from the context. The classical sequence for rabbinical usage is: (1) the problem requiring a parable; (2) the introduction of the parable, often with a redundant emphasis, "They parable a parable. Unto what is the matter like? It is like . . ." but also with several abbreviated forms all the way down to the simple, "It is like"; (3) the parable itself; (4) the application, often introduced with some word like "thus"; (5) biblical quotation, often introduced with "as it is written" (Johnston 1978: 1.164–65, 2.526–38). In the Jesus tradition, however, the interpretation of the parables is much more problematic. This is probably because the parables were often told concerning the Kingdom of God and that explained a symbol by a metaphor. This meant that the first hearers and final writers were themselves forced both to transmit and to interpret the parables at the same time. The presumption is that Jesus intended this effect, namely, that the parables would be both provocative and unforgettable so that the recipient would be forced inevitably to interpret.

The narrative parables of Jesus can receive external and/or internal interpretation. The most obvious mode of external interpretation is by commentary. In this usage the parable is given a detail-by-detail interpretation, somewhat similar to what was seen already for The Two Eagles in Ezekiel 17. The classic example is The Sower in Mark 4:3–8; Matt 13:3–8; Luke 8:5–8a. This is interpreted by Jesus in Mark 4:13–20; Matt 13:18–23; Luke 8:11–15. The seed is the word of God and the earth is the hearers; the birds are Satan; the rocks are persecutions; the thistles are temptations. Similarly, the Wheat and Weeds in Matt 13:24–30 is interpreted by Jesus in 13:36–43, and The Fishnet in Matt 13:47–48 is interpreted by Jesus in 13:49–50. What is striking, however, is that all three of those parables are also known in *Gos. Thom.* 9, 57, 8, but they receive no interpretation at all in that gospel. It must therefore be considered quite possible that such commentaries derived not from Jesus but rather from the tradition itself. In doing so, the tradition may have placed more emphasis on the details of the parable than they will plausibly bear. Although one should not distinguish parable from allegory by saying that the former applies only one point from story to referent while the latter applies every detail, it is correct that the application of Jesus' stories seems to derive more from their general structure than from specific detail.

Another mode of external interpretation is from context. Luke 15:1–2 reads, "Now the tax collectors and sinners were all drawing near to him. And the Pharisees and the scribes murmured, saying, 'This man receives sinners and eats with them.' " Next comes The Last Sheep in 15:3–6, with the conclusion in 15:7, "Just so, I tell you, there will be more joy in heaven over one sinner who repents than over ninety-nine righteous persons who need no repentance." Then comes The Lost Coin in 15:8–9, with the conclusion in 15:10, "Just so, I tell you, there is joy before the angels of God over one sinner who repents." Finally, the chapter concludes with The Prodigal [Lost] Son in 15:11–32. It is clear that the opening sentence sets the context for the interpretation of all three parables which follow it. Yet, on the other hand, The Lost Sheep appears in Matt 18:12–13 and *Gos. Thom.* 107 without the same setting. Context, then, like commentary, is from transmissional process rather than original situation.

Three different interpretations by three different contexts are given to The Feast in Matt 22:1–13; Luke 14:15–24; *Gos. Thom.* 64. First, in the *Gospel of Thomas,* there are three parables in 63–64–65 linked together by their openings concerning "a man." They are also linked by content. *Gos. Thom.* 63 is The Rich Fool, also known from Luke 12:16–20. Then comes 64 about The Feast. Finally, there is 65, The Tenants, also known from Mark 12:1–11; Matt 21:33–43; Luke 20:9–18. All three parables, in other words, involve the dangers and temptations of wealth or greed. This is a first contextual interpretation for the meaning of the middle parable on The Feast. And in case there might still be doubt, that parable as found in the *Gospel of Thomas* concludes with this explanation from Jesus: "Businessmen and merchants will not enter the places of my Father."

Second, the Lukan version is located within Luke 14:1–24, which groups a series of Jesus' sayings concerning meal situations within an actual meal situation itself. There are four units involved and each one opens with a reminder of the symposium situation. Luke 14:1–6 has a healing "one sabbath when he went to dine at the house of a ruler who belonged to the Pharisees." Then in 14:7–10 he discusses The Two Positions "to those who were invited." Next in 14:12–14, "He said also to the man who had invited him, 'When you give a dinner or a banquet, do not invite your friends or your brothers or your kinsmen or rich neighbors, lest they also invite you in return, and you be repaid. But when you give a feast, invite the poor, the maimed, the lame, the blind, and you will be blessed, because they cannot repay you. You will be repaid at the resurrection of the just." Finally, in 14:15–24, the parable of The Feast is introduced with this dialogue: "When one of those who sat at table with him heard this, he said to him, 'Blessed is he who shall eat bread in the kingdom of God.' " All that preceding context serves to interpret the concluding parable. In it, those first invited are unable to come, and this reflects on the authorities among whom Jesus sits. Instead, their places are taken, in 14:21, by the outcasts of Israel, by the same four classes mentioned earlier in 14:13, the poor, maimed, blind, and lame.

Third, Matthew formed a parabolic diptych of two parables: The Tenants, concerning an owner and his tenants in 21:33–44, and The Feast, concerning a king and his guests in 22:1–14. He then placed as their interpretive hinge this statement in 21:45–46: "When the chief priests and the Pharisees heard his parables, they perceived that he was speaking about them. But when they tried to arrest him they feared the multitudes, because they held him to be a prophet." This means that Matthew intends each parable to throw contextual light on the other and for both to be understood against that dangerous situation noted in the middle.

Apart from those external interpretations from commentary and context, there are also manifold possibilities of internal interpretation by the very details imbedded in the story as it is told and retold. The same parable of The Feast may serve again as paradigmatic instance. First, in Luke 14:18–20, and despite the fact that in 14:16b the master had "invited many," only three guests have their refusals recorded. One had bought a field, another five yoke of oxen, and a third had got married. This same triad, reminiscent of Olrik's "Law of Three," reappears in Matt 22:5–6, although here it is almost totally swallowed up in the plurality of servants and refusals of that version: "But they made light of it and went off, one to his farm, another to his business, while the rest seized his servants, treated them shamefully, and killed them." But in *Gos. Thom.* 64 there are four guests and four refusals recorded and that is surprising within the "Law of Three." When you look closely at the four dialogues between servant and guests, the second one is doubly different from the other three. While they begin with "My master invites you" and conclude with "I ask to be excused (from the dinner)," that second one begins with, "My master has invited you" and concludes without any polite request to be excused. It seems most likely that *Gos. Thom.* is interpreting the parable internally by adding in that second instance to bring the total number up to four. This confirms what was seen already from external interpretation. The original three excuses involved claims against merchants, preparing a wedding for a friend, and buying a farm. That is, only two out of three involved business. But, since the concluding aphorism turned the parable against "businessmen and merchants," *Gos. Thom.* added in another commercial enterprise. Thus, he created his new second excuse, "I have just bought a farm" on the model of the old final one, "I have just bought a farm," and so had three out of four guests excused for the commercial activities which the ascetic Thomas considered an obstacle to heaven.

Second, we already saw that Luke had allowed the outcasts of Israel into The Feast instead of the authorities to whom Jesus was speaking. But that was not enough to fill the banquet. Therefore, besides those outcasts in 14:21, from "the streets and lanes of the city," the servant is commanded in 14:23 to "Go out to the highways and hedges, and compel people to come in, that my house may be filled." The new guests from near at hand are the outcasts of Israel but those from afar off are the gentiles. By these internal details Luke has interpreted the parable as an allegory of the history of salvation.

Third, after setting up The Feast in contextual parallelism with The Tenants, as seen above, Matthew also inserts internal details that draw attention to that interpretation. In The Tenants, instead of the single servants of Mark 12:2–5 and Luke 20:10–12, the owner in Matt 21:34 "sent his servants" and in 21:36 "again he sent other servants." Then, in parallelism with that plurality, and again in contrast with the single servants of The Feast in Luke 14:17–23 and *Gos. Thom.* 64, the king in Matt 22:3 "sent his servants" and in 22:4 "again he sent other servants." But by far the most striking interpretation through added internal detail is the incident of the wedding garment present in this parable only in Matt 22:11–14. This is best seen as Matthew's own creation and it interprets the parable as an allegory of Christian history, just as Luke had done, but now with a special terminal warning for Christians themselves. In Matthew's reading, God has invited his people to come to the marriage feast of Jesus. Their refusal has been punished by the destruction of "their city," presumably of Jerusalem by Titus in 70 C.E. Now the gentiles have taken their place at the feast. But, and this is characteristically Matthean, even among those actually at the feast, there are "both good and bad" (22:10). On the last day, at the final judgments, God will review the guests, and then it will not be enough to be at the feast, it will be necessary to be properly attired as well. Matthew, in other words, thinks certain members of the Church are destined for eternal condemnation. Possibly their attitude toward the Mosaic Law was one of which he disapproved. So also, in the preceding parable of The Tenants, the replacement tenants in 21:41 must make certain to "give him the fruits in their seasons." It is not enough just to have received the vineyard. And in the Wheat and Weeds, a parable recorded both in Matt 13:24–30 and *Gos. Thom.* 57 but interpreted only in Matt 13:36–43, Matthew knows that there are both wheat and weeds in the kingdom, but "at the close of the age," in the last judgment, "the Son of man will send his angels, and they will gather out of his kingdom all causes of sin and all evildoers, and throw them into the furnace of fire; there men will weep and gnash their teeth" (13:40–41).

All of those differing interpretations, with the difference most obvious in the case of The Feast, but actually present everywhere among the parables, should not be considered as the interpreter's failure but rather as the parable's success. It is a parable's destiny to be interpreted and those interpretations will necessarily be diverse. When the diversity ceases, the parable is dead and the parabler is silent.

Bibliography

Boucher, M. 1977. *The Mysterious Parable.* CBQMS 6. Washington, DC.

Crossan, J. D. 1973. *In Parables.* New York.

Funk, R. W. 1982. *Parables and Presence.* Philadelphia.

Jeremias, J. 1963. *The Parables of Jesus,* rev. ed. New York.

Johnson, R. M. 1978. *Parabolic Interpretations Attributed to Tannaim.* 2 vols. Ann Arbor.

Kissinger, W. S. 1979. *The Parables of Jesus.* American Theological Library Association Bibliography Series 4. Metuchen, NJ.

Olrik, A. 1965. Epic Laws of Folk Narrative, Pp. 129–41 in *The Study of Folklore,* ed. A. Dundes. Englewood Cliffs, NJ.

Perrin, N. 1976. *Jesus and the Language of the Kingdom.* Philadelphia.

TeSelle, S. McF. 1975. *Speaking in Parables: A Study in Metaphor and Theology.* Philadelphia.

Tolbert, M. A. 1979. *Perspectives on the Parables.* Philadelphia.

Via, D. O. Jr. 1967. *The Parables: Their Literary and Existential Dimension.* Philadelphia.

Wilder, A. N. 1971. *Early Christian Rhetoric,* rev. ed. Cambridge, MA.

J. DOMINIC CROSSAN

PARACLETE [Gk *paraklētos*]. Five distinct though related questions arise concerning the term *paraklētos,* which is found five times in the Johannine writings (John 14:16, 26; 15:26; 16:7; 1 John 2:1) and nowhere else in the NT. These are (1) the significance of the term in the Gospel (there is no problem about 1 John 2:1, where it is applied to Christ and means "advocate" or "intercessor"); (2) the meaning of the word itself; (3) the religious origins of the tradition concerning the Paraclete; (4) the functions assigned to him in the Gospel, (5) the relationship between the Paraclete logia and what is said about the Spirit in the body of the Gospel.

There is no single obvious meaning of *paraklētos* in the Gospel. As Lindars observes (1981: 63), the evangelist is aware that the title is not self-explanatory, since he accompanies each of its occurrences with an account of the Paraclete's function. If one of these occurrences could be shown to be the source of the others, this would prove a useful starting point. In 1907 Wellhausen argued that the farewell discourse comprises two variants placed one after the other. This view has subsequently become increasingly popular among scholars, though few would share Sasse's opinion (1925) that the second of these, chaps. 15–16, is actually the earlier and some would divide chaps. 15–16 into two or even three independent sections. In 1927 Windisch argued that the Paraclete sayings could be excised from the Gospel without loss of continuity and concluded that they had been inserted into the discourse by the evangelist from a source in which they were grouped together. If this were right, then it would be impossible to recover the source of the tradition by working directly from the Gospel text as it has been transmitted. Although the arguments are inconclusive, the most likely hypothesis is that chap. 14 was composed before chaps. 15–16 and consequently that the Paraclete was first seen as Jesus' representative after his death (14:16) and his successor in his teaching role (14:26). In that case, the other functions assigned to him, of witnessing (15:26) and of convincing or convicting the world (16:7) may derive from a source closely affiliated to the synoptic tradition, perhaps even from that tradition itself.

There are four reasons why it is difficult to recover the meaning of the Greek *paraklētos:* (1) Although the form of the word (a verbal adjective ending in *-tos*) points to a probable passive sense (hence Old Latin *ad-vocatus,* literally "called to the side of"), an active sense "Counselor," "Comforter") cannot altogether be excluded. (2) None of the possible meanings of *parakalein,* either active or passive, squares precisely with the various functions attributed to the Paraclete in the Gospel. (3) These functions cannot be reduced to or summed up in a single comprehensive term that could then be substituted for *paraklētos.* (4) The few earlier extant uses have been scrutinized by Grayston, who concludes (1981: 75) that "*paraklētos* was a word of general meaning which could appear in legal contexts, and when it did the *paraklētos* was a supporter or sponsor." This conclusion is too vague to be of very much use. Since all suggested The Feasts ("Advocate," "Counselor," "Comforter," etc.) are simply guesses, it is best to stick to the anglicized "Paraclete," which provides a distinct and recognizable *name* for the personage identified in the farewell discourse as "the spirit of truth" (14:17; 15:26; 16:13) or "the Holy Spirit" (14:26), thus performing for English-speaking readers the same service as *paraklētos* for readers of the original Greek and *Paracletus* for the readers of Jerome's Vulgate.

If the problem of the meaning of *paraklētos* cannot be solved linguistically, then can it be solved historically? Is it possible to find a figure in near-contemporary religious belief and practice who may plausibly be thought to have furnished a model for the Johannine Paraclete? Suggestions are wide-ranging and include the returning Elijah (Spitta); the Mandaean *Yawar* or helper (Bauer *Johannesevangelium* HNT; Bultmann); OT and Jewish intercessors, both angelic and prophetic, in particular the angel Michael or the mediator *(mēlīṣ)* in Job 33:23, translated in the Targum by the loanword *prqlyṭʾ* (Mowinckel, Johansson); the fusion of two figures from the Qumran documents, Michael and "the spirit of truth" (Betz), a fusion which, according to another scholar (Johnston), the Paraclete was designed to combat and displace, the second or successor figure in a tandem relationship: Joshua/Moses, Elisha/Elijah (Windisch), to which Bornkamm added John the Baptist/Jesus; late Jewish angelology and the figure of personified Wisdom (Brown 1966–67). Müller (1974) has supplemented these suggestions by arguing for a properly form-critical investigation into the testament or valedictory form. Another proposal comes from Franck (1985), who thinks that the Paraclete may have been modeled on the Methurgeman, who had to translate and (later) preach upon the Scripture readings in Aramaic-speaking synagogues. Lastly, one may mention Hermann Sasse's proposal (1925), revived by Culpepper (1975), that the Paraclete is simply to be identified with the Beloved Disciple. Of these suggestions two may be singled out as especially fruitful. The first is the comparison between the Paraclete's role as Jesus' representative and successor with that of Joshua, commissioned by Moses on the eve of his death to lead his people into the Promised Land. Here the *Testament of Moses,* itself largely a midrash of Deuteronomy 31–34, repays study along the lines proposed by Müller. The second is the evocation of the *angelus interpres* familiar from apocalyptic literature, a suggestion that may be reinforced by de la Potterie's study (1965) of the Greek verb *anangellein* (cf. John 16: 13–15), used by Theodotian to render Heb *pšr*ʾ in Daniel 2. It must be acknowledged, however, that arguments based on the methods of the history-of-religions school turn out to be almost as inconclusive as those based on lexicography. A good up-to-date summary of the various theories is to be found in the work of Burge (1987).

Fortunately the uncertainties concerning meaning and origin need not stand in the way of the actual exegesis of the farewell discourse, which is quite explicit about the roles assigned to the Paraclete. Most of these are straightforward, since they echo, as Brown (*John xii–xxi* AB, 1135–44) insists, the teaching and revealing activities of Jesus. Two of the terms employed by Windisch to describe the Paraclete's role are particularly suggestive: he is Jesus' *Doppelgänger* or *alter ego* (1927: 129), a term especially appropriate to the first logion (14:16); he is also Jesus' successor, his *Kalif auf Erden* (1933: 311), a term reminiscent of Tertullian's *vicarius Christi,* which well fits the second logion (14:26). The function of reminding (14:26) is probably to be associated with the passages earlier in the Gospel where the disciples are assured that they will remember Jesus' words (2:22) and actions (12:16), but only after he has been glorified. The function of witness (15:26) is in all likelihood derived from the Synoptic tradition (Matt 10:19–20 = Mark 13:11–12; Luke 21:16).

By far the most difficult saying is John 16:7–11, for it is impossible to give a single meaning to the verb *elenchein* "convince" (RSV), while at the same time taking the three words that follow, *hamartia,* "sin," *dikaiosynē,* "righteousness," and *krisis,* "judgment," in their natural sense, unless the phrase *elenchein ton kosmon peri,* "convince the world concerning . . . ," is taken to mean simply "to prove the world wrong in its ideas about," a usage which accords ill with the other instance of *elenchein peri* in 8:46. Windisch (1927: 120, n.2) suggested that the phrase concerning righteousness is a corruption. Worth mentioning, because it has been ignored by subsequent commentators, is Bammel's idea (1973) that the original logion spoke of the teaching functions of the Paraclete concerning themes which are the object of christological controversy elsewhere in the Gospel: the world's failure to respond to Jesus (= *hamartia,* 8:40); Jesus' justification by the Father (= *dikaiosynē*); the defeat of the prince of this world (= *krisis,* 12:30). Bammel admits, however, that this is not how the editor of the text, who added the three explanatory clauses, saw the matter.

Few commentators have attempted to link the Paraclete sayings with the other references to the Spirit. Exceptions are Porsch (1974) and Burge (1987). They can appeal to the fact that in many of its occurrences (e.g. 3:34; 6:63) the term *pneuma* is used in direct connection with the words of Jesus. Furthermore, even if the Paraclete passages came from an independent source, the evangelist felt able to identify him with the Holy Spirit (14:26), thus providing some justification for attempting an integral exegesis of all the allusions to the spirit in the Gospel. Additional support comes from the editorial comment interjected at 7:39: "for the Spirit did not yet exist *(oupō gar ēn pneuma)* because Jesus had not yet been glorified." Some allusions to the Spirit, however, e.g., 1:32–3; 3:5–8, are aligned with the Paraclete passages only with great difficulty and the editorial gloss in 7:39 cannot altogether disguise the conceptual differences.

Bibliography

Bammel, E. 1973. Jesus und der Paraklet in Johannes 16. Pp. 198–27 in *Christ and Spirit in the New Testament,* ed. B. Lindars and S. Smalley. Cambridge.

Betz, O. 1963. *Der Paraklet.* Leiden.

Bornkamm, G. 1949. Der Paraklet im Johannes-Evangelium. Pp. 12–35 in *Festschrift für Rudolf Bultmann.* Stuttgart.

Brown, R. E. 1966–67. The Paraclete in the Fourth Gospel. *NTS:* 113–32.

Bultmann, R. 1971. *The Gospel of John.* Trans. G. R. Beasley-Murray. Oxford.

Burge, G. M. 1987. *The Anointed Community.* Grand Rapids.

Culpepper, R. A. 1975. *The Johannine School.* SBLDS 26. Missoula, MT.

Franck, E. 1985. *Revelation Taught: The Paraclete in the Gospel of John.* ConBNT 14. Lund.

Grayston, K. 1981. The Meaning of PARAKLETOS. *JSNT* 13: 67–82.

Johansson, N. 1940. *Parakletoi: Vorstellungen von Fürsprechern für die Menschen vor Gott in der alttestamentlichen Religion, im Spätjudentum, und Urchristentum.* Lund.

Johnston, G. 1970. *The Spirit-Paraclete in the Gospel of John.* Cambridge.

Lindars, B. 1981. The Persecution of Christians in John 15:18–16:4a. Pp. 48–69 in *Suffering and Martyrdom in the NT.* ed. W. Horbury and B. McNeil. Cambridge.

Mowinckel, S. 1934. Die Vorstellung des Spätjudentums vom heiligen Geist als Fürsprecher und der johanneische Paraklet. *ZNW* 52: 97–130.

Müller, U. B. 1974. Die Parakletenvorstellung im Johannesevangelium. *ZTK* 71: 31–78.

Porsch, F. 1974. *Pneuma und Wort: Ein exegetischer Beitrag zur Pneumatologie des Johannesevangeliums.* Frankfurter Theologische Studien 16. Frankfurt.

la Potterie, I. de. 1965. Le Paraclet. Pp. 85–105 in *Le Vie selon l'Esprit, Condition du Chrétien.* ed. I. de La Potterie and S. Lyonnet. Unam Sanctam 55. Paris.

Sasse, H. 1925. Der Paraklet im Johannesevangelium. *ZNW* 24: 260–77.
Spitta, F. 1910. *Das Johannes-Evangelium als Quella der Geschichte Jesu.* Göttingen.
Wellhausen, J. 1907. *Erweiterungen und Änderungen im vierten Evangelium.* Berlin.
Windisch, H. 1927. Die fünf johanneische Parakletsprüche. Pp. 110–37 in *Festgabe für Adolf Jülicher.* Tübingen = *The Spirit-Paraclete in the Fourth Gospel.* Trans. J. W. Cox. Philadelphia, 1968.
———. 1933. Jesus und der Geist im Johannes-Evangelium. Pp. 303–18 in *Amicitiae Corolla,* ed. H. G. Wood. London.

JOHN ASHTON

PARADISE. A loanword from Old Persian *(pairi-daēza),* which means "enclosure," then "park" or "garden." It appears in Late Biblical Hebrew as *pardēs,* only with profane meaning (Neh 2:8 [RSV: "forest"]; Cant 4:13 [RSV: "orchard"]; Eccl 2:5 [RSV: "park"]). The profane meaning continues in Mishnaic Hebrew *pardēs* "park" (e.g., *t. Beṣa* 1.10) and in Jewish Aramaic *pardēs(āʾ)* "garden" (e.g., *B. Meṣ.* 103a).

The Old Persian etymon is also the source of the Greek loanword *paradeisos.* In the LXX *paradeisos* denotes God's garden (Gen 2:8–10, 16), and the shift from secular to religious meaning has been made. The religious meaning—God's garden or Paradise—entered Jewish thought and vocabulary after the Babylonian Exile, was combined with the hope of a blessed eschaton, and appears in the Apocrypha (2 Esdr 4:7; 6:2; 7:36, 123; 8:52) and frequently in other early Jewish writings (*Psalms of Solomon* 14; *Sib. Or.* frag. 3.46–48; *2 Enoch* 8–9; *3 Baruch* 4; *Joseph and Asenath* 18; *4 Baruch* 9). In the NT, the religious meaning "Paradise" alone is evident (Luke 23:43; 2 Cor 12:3; Rev 2:7).

The biblical Garden of Eden attracted non-Jewish conceptions of a paradisiac garden. The development of "Paradise" within Judaism was aided by the image of a special garden, Eden, free of any trouble or inconvenience, in which the human and divine were close and collegial, in which every tree was "pleasant to the sight and good for food" (Gen 2:8), and from which flowed four rivers (Gen 2:10–14). Mixed with these images were the following concepts: the Isaianic words that Zion will become like Eden and the garden of the Lord (Isa 51:3), that God's people will be as a watered garden (Isa 58:11), and his planting (of special trees in the desert [Isa 41:18–19]) for his glory (Isa 60:13); Jeremiah's vision that the righteous are those whom God will plant in the promised land in faithfulness (Jer 32:41). Related images are Ezekiel's images of the garden of God, the trees of Eden, and the trees by the waters (Ezek 31:8–9; cf. 36:35). Equally important for the understanding of the Jewish development of Paradise are the Psalmist's words, which were memorized by devout Jews: "Blessed is the man who . . . delights . . . in the Law of the Lord, . . . He is like a tree planted by streams of water, that yields its fruit in its season, and its leaf does not wither" (Ps 1:1–3).

This symbolic language, as well as other images and myths, combined in numerous ways to produce the Jewish concept of Paradise. One of the earliest passages is *1 Enoch* 32, according to which Enoch journeys to the east and "came to the garden of righteousness and saw beyond those trees . . . the tree of wisdom . . . from which (his) precursors, ate and . . . realized that they were naked and (so) . . . were expelled from the garden" (*1 En.* 32:3–6). Another early image is found in *Jubilees.* Abraham "perceived that from him there would be a righteous planting for eternal generations . . ." (*Jub.* 17:26). One of the most interesting early examples is found in the sectarian psalms from Qumran called the Hodayoth. According to column 8, the Righteous Teacher probably looks back on his life and allegorically forsees his community as the one that will produce the eternal planting from which shall issue the shoot for the glorious Eden (1QH 8, cf. 1QS 8.4–5; CD 1.7–8). The image of Paradise is fully developed in *2 Enoch* 8, according to which Enoch is taken "up to the third heaven, and . . . looked downward, and . . . saw Paradise. And that place is inconceivably pleasant. . . . And in the midst . . . the tree of life, at that place where the LORD takes a rest when he goes into paradise" (*2 En.* 8:1–3 [J]). According to the *Apocalypse of Moses,* Paradise is not only in the third heaven (40:2), it is also on the earth (38:5). Paradise is thus obviously situated in different places according to early Jewish documents. It is on the earth either far to the east (*1 En.* 32:2–3, *2 En.* 42:3–4), to the northeast perhaps (*1 En.* 61:1–13), between the northeast and the west (*1 En.* 70:3–4), to the north (*1 En.* 77:3–4), to the far west perhaps (Jos. *JW* 2.155–56), but never to the south (but see *1 En.* 77:1–2). It can be readily seen, from this brief list, that the books collected together as *1 Enoch* are a repository of many diverse Jewish ideas.

Paradise is sometimes perceived as the (post resurrection) intermediate abode of the righteous (*1 Enoch* 37–70), or as the hidden eschatological place of the righteous (*2 Enoch* 8). Other passages describe the righteous enjoying life in Paradise or Eden, but provide no indication of their duration there (*Apocalypse of Abraham* 21). It is also frequently portrayed as closed (*4 Ezra* 7), as one would expect from the Genesis account of the expulsion; note *2 En.* 42:3[J], "And I ascended into the east, into the Paradise of Eden, where rest is prepared for the righteous. And it is open as far as the third heaven; but it is closed from this world." This passage seems to result from an attempt to resolve the tension arising from placing Paradise on the earth and also in the third heaven. Jews did not think about diverse places, but only one and the same Paradise. In *4 Ezra,* Ezra is told, "for you . . . Paradise is opened, the tree of life is planted, the age to come is prepared, plenty is provided, a city is built, rest is appointed . . ." (8:52; cf. *Apocalypse of Abraham* 21). The Jewish apocalypses contain the conviction that the final (or second) age will be characterized by the blessed state at creation of the first age, but without the possibility of disobedience, disharmony, discomfort, and discontinuity. Only in this sense can it be said that the Paradise of the first age reappears in the second (final) age. The Jewish myth of Paradise is so developed by the end of the 1st century C.E. that the author of *Joseph and Aseneth* freely borrowed from it in describing the garden beneath Aseneth's tower.

Such creative ideas in early Jewish theology influenced Christians. According to Luke 23:43 Jesus tells the repentant thief that he will be with him that day in Paradise.

Paul reveals that he was taken up into the third heaven, and thus probably into Paradise (2 Cor 12:3). The author of the *Odes of Solomon* describes Paradise; as also in the *Psalms of Solomon* but in contrast to many other texts according to which the righteous eat the fruit of the trees (see *T. Levi* 18:11; Rev 2:7), the righteous are portrayed as "blooming and fruit-bearing trees." The poet proclaims, "Blessed, O Lord, are they who are planted in your Land, and who have a place in your Paradise" (*Odes Sol.* 11:18; cf. *Gos. Thom.* 19).

James H. Charlesworth

PARAH (PLACE) [Heb *pārâ*]. A settlement in the E half of Benjamin (Josh 18:23). The exact location of the site is unknown. Z. Kallai (*HGB,* 401) has recently argued that the settlement is likely to be situated near Bethel or Ophrah on grounds that the names in the list in which it appears are geographically grouped. Long-standing scholarly opinion has, however, identified the site with the modern Tell Fara some 6 mi (10 km) N of Jerusalem (M.R. 177137). It is possible that this latter site, being located both by a substantial spring (it still provides Old Jerusalem with water) and in close proximity to Anathoth, is also known by the name "Parath," the river to which Jeremiah went to hide his linen belt (Jeremiah 13).

Elmer H. Dyck

PARALEIPOMENA IEREMIOU. See BARUCH, BOOK OF 4.

PARALLELISM. Parallelism is the most prominent rhetorical figure in ancient Near Eastern poetry, and is also present, although less prominent, in biblical prose. It can be defined as the repetition of the same or related semantic content and/or grammatical structure in consecutive lines or verses. For example, in Ps 103:10 we find that both the sense and the structure of the first line are echoed, in different words, in the second:

> Not according to our sins did he deal with us;
> And not according to our transgressions did he requite us.

But, while the definition cited here works well for the most part, and the example of Ps 103:10 would be universally accepted as a parallelism, there is no consensus on precisely what parallelism is or how it works, and therefore no absolute criterion for identifying parallelisms. As we move farther away from identity or similarity between the two lines, more questions arise and there is more disagreement about the identification of a parallelism. For instance, some scholars would consider Ps 106:35 to be a parallelism while others would insist that it is not.

> They intermingled with the nations;
> They learned their ways.

What does seem certain, though, is that parallelism is a matter of relationships—between lines and/or parts of lines. The history of the study of biblical parallelism can be understood as a quest to determine the precise nature of the relationship between groups of words which give the strong impression of being related in at least one of a number of ways.

A. The Study of Parallelism, Past and Present
B. Types and Categories
  1. Synonymous, Antithetic, and Synthetic Parallelism
  2. Additional Types
    a. Chiastic Parallelism
    b. Staircase Parallelism
    c. Emblematic Parallelism
    d. Janus Parallelism
  3. Parallel Word Pairs
  4. Linguistic Models
    a. The Grammatical Aspect
    b. The Lexical Aspect
    c. The Semantic Aspect
    d. The Phonological Aspect

A. The Study of Parallelism, Past and Present

Biblical parallelism became the focus of scholarly attention as the result of Bishop Robert Lowth's discussion of it in his *De sacra poesi Hebraeorum (Lectures on the Sacred Poetry of the Hebrews)* in 1753 and his *Isaiah: A New Translation with a Preliminary Dissertation and Notes Critical, Philological, and Explanatory* in 1778. To be sure, Lowth was not the first to notice the phenomenon of parallelism (for the pre-Lowthian history of the study of parallelism see Kugel 1981: 96–286), but, due to the then-current trends in biblical studies and his own prominence in the field, it was his definition, articulated in the introduction to *Isaiah,* that became the classic definition of parallelism.

> The correspondence of one Verse, or Line, with another I call Parallelism. When a proposition is delivered, and a second is subjoined to it, or drawn under it, equivalent, or contrasted with it, in Sense; or similar to it in the form of Grammatical Construction; these I call Parallel Lines; and the words or phrases answering one to another in the corresponding Lines Parallel Terms.

Lowth spoke of the correspondence of parallel lines and terms. This was generally understood as sameness or identity by most of Lowth's successors; so the emphasis was put on the synonymity or redundancy in parallelism to the neglect of parallelism's other dimension: variation and continuity. Studies of parallelism from the late 18th century until the 1980s reiterated, with ever-increasing refinements, the basic sameness of parallel lines. Not until the work of J. Kugel and R. Alter was the balance rectified. Kugel rejected the notion of the synonymity of parallel lines, replacing it with the notion of continuity: "A, what's more, B." In a similar vein, Alter spoke of the "consequentiality" of parallel lines. The views of Kugel and Alter place the emphasis on the *difference* between parallel lines. Parallel lines could now be seen as adding new information, containing an intensification or a progression, rather than just going over old material in new words. This shift in perception can be illustrated in Ps 18:9—Eng 18:8 (= 2 Sam 22:9).

Smoke went up from his nostrils;
From his mouth came devouring fire;
Live coals blazed forth from him.

Most biblical scholars would view these lines as synonymous; Kugel and Alter would see in them an intensification and/or a progression. Actually, it is not a question of either sameness of difference, either synonymity or continuity; both dimensions are equally present in parallelism, and it is the creative tension between them that makes this such a pleasing figure.

Both Kugel and Alter came to the study of the Bible from literary criticism, and both brought their finely honed skills as readers to parallelistic texts. But literary criticism often eschews precise analysis in favor of more diffuse observations. So, while achieving a reorientation of the view of parallelism, Kugel and Alter achieve it only at a level of extreme generality. They offer only the vaguest definitions of parallelism and do not provide the criteria for deeper analysis of its workings.

There are at least two potentially more "scientific" models for the analysis of parallelism: the mathematical and the linguistic. A mathematical approach, stressing the symmetries between parallel lines, is espoused half-heartedly by W. G. E. Watson (1984: 114–119), but for the most part Watson relies either on grammatical models or those preceding them. Linguistic models have been proposed by S. A. Geller, E. Greenstein, and A. Berlin. All three draw on modern linguistics, especially transformational grammar and the views of R. Jakobson (see below).

While there are major differences between 18th and 19th century studies and the most recent studies of parallelism, they have some things in common. All attempt to analyze parallelistic texts with the most current literary and linguistic tools available; and all seek to define the relationships that pertain between parallel lines. In some sense, therefore, Lowth's definition remains classic, and his terms like "correspondence," "equivalent," and "contrasted," if interpreted in their broadest sense, remain relevant to the study of parallelism.

B. Types and Categories

The preceding section presented a simplified summary of the major approaches to the study of parallelism. But most scholars' energy was spent in the detailed analysis of specific types and subtypes of parallelism. Here, too, Lowth's work served as a guide to his own and later generations, for in his *Isaiah* he provided a framework for the classification of types.

1. Synonymous, Antithetic, and Synthetic Parallelism. Based on the semantic relationship of the parallel lines, Lowth reduced parallelism to three sorts: synonymous, antithetic, and synthetic. In synonymous parallelism the same sense is expressed in different but equivalent terms: "When a proposition is delivered; and is immediately repeated, in whole or in part, the expression being varied, but the sense entirely or nearly the same." An example is Ps 112:1:

Happy is the man who fears the Lord;
Who is greatly devoted to his commandments.

Notice that the meaning of both lines need not be identical, only "nearly the same," and that terms found in the first line may be lacking in the second (and vice versa). In fact, there is considerable latitude in all of Lowth's categories, which later biblicists sought to constrict.

In antithetic parallelism "two lines correspond with one another by an opposition of terms and sentiments." The antithesis may range from "exact contraposition of word to word" to "a general disparity." Prov 10:1 illustrates:

A wise son makes glad his father;
But a foolish son is the grief of his mother.

In synthetic parallelism (also called constructive or formal parallelism), according to Lowth,

> the parallelism consists only in the similar form of construction; in which word does not answer to word, and sentence to sentence, as equivalent or opposite; but there is a correspondence and equality between different propositions, in respect of the shape and turn of the whole sentence, and of the constructive parts . . .

Eccl 11:2 is an example:

Give a portion to seven, and also to eight;
For you do not know what evil shall be upon the earth.

This is the loosest of Lowth's categories, and the one that received the most criticism. Some viewed it as a catch-all of miscellaneous, difficult-to-categorize cases, and others did not think that it was a legitimate form of parallelism at all.

2. Additional Types. As parallelism was studied more closely, its many permutations became evident: word order might vary from line to line; some terms might be ellipsed and others added (i.e., the parallelism might be termed complete or incomplete; incomplete parallelism might or might not have compensation), and so forth. To some extent, Lowth had allowed for these permutations within his three types, but, given the scholarly penchant for categorizing and labeling, it was not long before the number of types grew. Many of the additional types are not of the same order as Lowth's; that is, in one sense they can be considered subtypes and in another sense they cut across the lines of the original three types. The most well-known of these additional types will be presented here.

a. Chiastic Parallelism. The order of the terms in the first line is reversed in the second line, yielding an AB//BA pattern, as in Jer 4:5a:

Proclaim in Judah;
And in Jerusalem announce.

More than two sets of terms may be involved: ABC//CBA, etc. Chiastic patterning is not limited to parallelism, but it is often found in parallel lines.

b. Staircase Parallelism. A steplike pattern in which some elements from the first line are repeated verbatim in the second and others are added to complete the thought. Judg 5:12 provides an illustration:

Awake, awake, Deborah;
Awake, awake, chant a song.

(Cf. Greenstein 1974 and 1977; Loewenstamm 1975; Watson 1984: 150–56).

c. Emblematic Parallelism. A parallelism in which a simile or metaphor forms one of the lines, as in Ps 42:2:

As a hind yearns for watercourses;
So my soul yearns for you, God.

d. Janus Parallelism. This type of parallelism hinges on the use of a single word with two different meanings, one of which forms a parallel with what precedes and the other with what follows. Thus, by virtue of a double entendre, the parallelism faces in both directions. An example is Gen 49:26:

The blessings of your father
Surpass the blessings of my ancestors/mountains [*hwry*]
To the utmost bounds of the eternal hills.

(Cf. Watson 1984: 159; Rendsburg 1980).

3. Parallel Word Pairs. Although 20th-century scholars continued to refine the distinctions involving the relationships between parallel lines as a whole, the major efforts were placed on the analysis of certain sets of parallel terms, or, as they came to be known, fixed word pairs. Lowth had mentioned parallel terms ("words or phrases answering one to another in corresponding lines"), but it was the discovery and decipherment of Ugaritic poetry, together with the ascendancy of the Parry-Lord theory of oral composition, that spurred the collection, from biblical and Ugaritic poetic texts, of sets of terms that recur frequently in parallelisms. The emphasis was on recurrence—those terms, like "day" and "night," "heaven" and "earth," which were found together frequently. It was thought that such pairs were the functional equivalents of the formulas in Greek and Yugoslavian poetry that enabled a poet to compose orally. Lists of these pairs grew long (they number over 1,000), as did the bibliography on word pairs (See primarily Dahood *Psalms* AB, 3.445–56; Dahood 1972, 1975, and 1981. See also Avishur 1977; Berlin 1983, 1985: 64–80; Boling 1960; Cassuto 1971; Craigie 1971, 1979a, 1979b; Culley 1967; Gevirtz 1963; Held 1953, 1962, 1965; Kugel 1981: 27–39; Melamed 1961, 1964; O'Connor 1980: 96–109; Watson 1984: 128–43; Watters 1976; Whallon 1963, 1969; Yoder 1970, 1971.) Attention was paid to frequency, to the order in which the members of a pair occurred, and to their grammatical form. Inevitably, there were attempts to categorize the semantic relationship between words in a pair: synonyms, antonyms, a whole and a part, abstract and concrete, common term and rare or archaic term, the breakup of stereotyped phrases. In the last, a conventional phrase is split, one part occurring in one line and the other in the next line (cf. Melamed 1961, 1964). For instance, the phrase "horses and chariots," a conventional combination (cf. Josh 11:4), is split in Zech 9:10:

I shall banish chariots from Ephraim;
And horses from Jerusalem.

Likewise in Ps 20:8—Eng 20:7:

These (call) on chariots;
And those on horses.

It was also noticed that numbers obey a formula, x // x + 1, when they appear in parallelism. Thus "three" parallels "four" (Amos 1:3); "six" parallels "seven" (Job 5:19). The principle may employ a factor of 10: "one thousand" parallels "ten thousand" (Ps 91:7).

Many scholars saw in word pairs the essence of parallelism, the *sine qua non* without which parallel lines could not exist. Furthermore, it was suggested, these pairs formed a kind of "poet's dictionary"—a poetic substratum on which poets might draw in order to compose parallelisms. These conclusions reflect the fact that the impetus for the study of word pairs was intimately bound up with theories of oral composition, unproved and unprovable at least for biblical poetry. But even when these theories came under criticism, the collecting of word pairs did not cease, for word pairs had taken on a life of their own in biblical studies. As such, this enterprise represents one of the most extensive lexical studies of ancient texts. The preoccupation with word pairs focused attention on the similarities between Hebrew and Ugaritic poetry, and on certain of their lexical aspects, but it did so to the neglect of the rest of the parallelism and the pairing of other terms in it which did not occur with any notable frequency. Moreover, it threatened to perpetuate certain misunderstandings about the nature of parallelism and the nature of word pairs. (Cf. Kugel 1981: 27–39; Berlin 1983, 1985: 64–80.)

4. Linguistic Models. By the 1970s the influence of modern linguistic research, especially structural linguistics and transformational grammar, began to be felt in biblical studies. Interest in the grammatical analysis of poetry grew, and with it, the grammatical analysis of parallelism. A number of scholars (Berlin, Collins, Geller, Greenstein, O'Connor, Pardee, Watson), working independently, offered grammatical treatments of parallelism. They varied somewhat in type and level of analysis (cf. Berlin 1985: 18–30), but they all signaled a return to the analysis of the line as a whole, rather than the concentration on word pairs; and they all showed that linguistics had something new and important to contribute to the study of parallelism.

No modern linguist has had more impact on the study of parallelism, both within and outside of the Bible, than Roman Jakobson. Jakobson's (1966: 423) most famous dictum on the subject was

> Pervasive parallelism inevitably activates all the levels of language—the distinctive features, inherent and prosodic, the morphological and syntactic categories and forms, the lexical units and their semantic classes in both their convergences and divergences acquire an autonomous poetic value.

This was taken by both Stephen Geller (1979) and Adele Berlin (1979, 1985) as a programmatic guide for the analysis of biblical parallelism. Geller limited his treatment to the grammatical aspect, as did Berlin 1979 (cf. also

Greenstein 1982), but Berlin's 1985 work offered a more comprehensive linguistic description, including areas and issues previously dealt with in word pair studies. Since this is the broadest and most recent study, a detailed summary of it will be presented here.

Parallel can be viewed as a linguistic phenomenon involving linguistic equivalences and/or contrasts that may occur on the level of the word, the line, or larger areas of text. (For the most part, biblical parallelism operates at the level of the line.) Equivalence does not mean only identity, but a word or construction that, linguistically speaking, belongs to the same category or paradigm, or to the same sequence or syntagm. One can discuss four linguistic aspects which may be activated in parallelism: the grammatical aspect, the lexical aspect, the semantic aspect, and the phonological aspect.

a. The Grammatical Aspect. In grammatical parallelism the syntax of the lines is equivalent; i.e., their deep structures (and perhaps their surface structures as well) are the same. For example, the surface structures are the same in both lines (in the Hebrew) of Ps 103:10:

> Not according to our sins did he deal with us;
> And not according to our transgressions did he requite us.

Many parallelisms, however, employ lines of different surface structure which can be related back, using the methodology of transformational grammar, to the same underlying deep structure. A nominal clause may be paired with a verbal clause, as in Mic 6:2b.

> For the Lord has a quarrel with his people;
> And with Israel will he dispute.

A positive clause may be paired with a negative clause, as in Prov 6:20:

> Guard, my son, the commandment of your father;
> And do not forsake the teaching of your mother.

The subject of one clause may become the object in the next clause, as in Gen 27:29:

> Be a lord over your brothers;
> Let the sons of your mother bow before you.

There may be contrast in grammatical mood: an indicative may parallel an interrogative, an imperative may parallel a jussive, etc. In Ps 6:6—Eng 6:5 a negative indicative is paired with an interrogative.

> For in Death there is no mention of you;
> In Sheol who can acclaim you?

The seeds of grammatical analysis are present in Lowth's definition ("similar to it in the form of Grammatical Construction"), but Lowth and his successors did not develop it because their understanding of grammar was quite different from that of modern linguists and they lacked the tools for this type of analysis.

Parts of lines are also subject to grammatical, or morphological, analysis. Parallel terms may be of different word classes: e.g., noun // pronoun; noun, adjective, or participle // verb, etc. The first is illustrated in Ps 33:2:

> Praise *the Lord* with a lyre;
> With the ten-stringed harp sing to *him.*

The second can be seen in Ps 145:18:

> The Lord is near to all his *callers;*
> To all who *call* him in truth.

This type of morphological pairing is possible because the forms paired can be substituted for each other in a sentence. That is, they belong to the same paradigm and are, therefore, linguistically equivalent.

When parallel terms are from the same word class (e.g., both nouns), there may be other morphological contrasts present: the tense or conjugation of verbs may be different; there may be contrast in the number, gender, or definiteness of nouns. In fact, to quote P. Kiparsky (1973: 235): "the linguistic sames which are potentially relevant in poetry are just those which are potentially relevant in grammar." One could easily substitute the word "parallelism" for "poetry" in this statement, for in parallelism any grammatically equivalent form ("linguistic same") can be paired with another. Some examples follow:

(a). The tenses contrast (*qtl* // *yqtl*) in Ps 26:4:

> I do not [Heb: did not] consort with scoundrels;
> And with hypocrites I do not [Heb: will not] associate.

(b) The conjugations contrast (*qal* // *nipḥʿal*) in Ps 24:7:

> Lift up, O gates, your heads;
> And be lifted up, O eternal doors.

(c) A singular parallels a plural in Prov 14:12 = 16:25:

> There is a right *path* before man;
> But its end is *paths* of death.

Note that the same word is used in both forms. Often different words, one in each number, are used, as in Deut 32:7 ("remember" [sing.] // "consider" [pl.]) and Lam 5:17 ("this" // "these").

(d) In Lam 3:47 the terms in the first line lack the definite article while those in the second line have it.

> Panic and pitfall were ours;
> The desolation and the destruction.

There are other types of grammatical equivalences and contrasts, and numerous examples of each. The benefit of such a grammatical approach to parallelism is that it can account for the many permutations which earlier approaches were at a loss to explain, and it can relate, under one rubric, in a holistic manner, many phenomena which were previously considered disparate.

b. The Lexical Aspect. Earlier approaches dealt with one facet of the lexical aspect of parallelism—fixed word pairs. But actually, there is no reason to limit the discussion only to fixed, or frequently recurring, pairs. All parallelisms involve the pairing of terms, and all lexical pairings can be better understood through recourse to linguistics.

The process whereby terms are paired in parallelism is similar to the process which generates associations in psycholinguistic word association games. That is, parallel word pairs are the product of normal linguistic association. Every word has a potential mate, and it does not require any special training or talent to produce one.

Linguists have discovered rules that account for the kinds of associations that are made. They have noted that in word association games a word may elicit itself; and so in parallelism, a word may be paired with the same word, or with a word from the same root (cf. 2 Sam 22:7; Job 6:15). They have also noted that a word may have a number of different associates, and that some are likely to be generated more often than others.

The rules for word association are categorized as paradigmatic or syntagmatic. In paradigmatic operations, a word is chosen from the same category and may substitute for the given word. The most common type of paradigmatic choice is one with minimal contrast, which produces an "opposite," as in *good-bad, man-woman.* A related type of operation invokes the "Feature Deletion and Addition Rule." The features of a word are listed hierarchically by linguists; for example, *father* = noun, singular, animate, human, parent, male. When a feature is deleted it is usually done from the end of the list, so that *father* will more likely generate *mother* (changing male to female) or *son* (changing parent to its reverse) rather than something involving a change higher on the list, like *ram.* The preferred change is the change of a sign (plus or minus), i.e., +/− male, +/− parent. This yields minimal contrast. If a feature is deleted, the result is a superordinate, as in *father-man.* An added feature produces a subordinate, as in *fruit-apple.* If another word is chosen with the same list of features, we have a coordinate, as in *cat-dog* (both are noun, singular, animate, mammal, domesticated, etc.). The higher on the list a feature is, the less likely that it will be changed. This accounts, first of all, for the tendency toward paradigmatic responses (i.e., associations involving the same class of words). It also explains why certain responses occur more frequently than others.

Syntagmatic responses involve the choice of an associate from the same sequence rather than the same class. Often this is realized in the completion of idioms. In English the word *cottage* will often evoke *cheese.* This is similar to the phenomenon described by Melamed (1961; 1964) as the breakup of stereotyped phrases. Conventional coordinates, like *sws-rkb* ("horse-chariot/driver"), *ḥsd-ʾmt* ("loyalty-truth"), may be paired in parallel lines. Another type of syntagmatic pairing in the Bible involves the splitting up of the components of a personal or geographic name: *Balak // king of Moab* (Num 23:7); *Ephrathah // Bethlehem* (Ruth 4:11). There are also other examples of syntagmatic pairings such as *chair // sit* (Isa 16:5; Lam 5:19) and *write // book* (Job 19:23).

While lexical parallelism, that is, the pairing of associated words, generally accompanies grammatical parallelism, it can occur in lines which are not grammatically parallel (at least paradigmatically). An example is Ps 111:6:

> The power of his deeds he told to his *people (ʿmw)*
> In giving to them the inheritance of *nations (qwym).*

The syntactic structure of the lines is not equivalent, but the pair *people-nation* is a known association. There are other cases in which the lexical pairing occurs in addition to semantic pairing; a creative tension between the two may be at play. Job 5:14 provides an illustration:

> By day they encounter darkness;
> And as in the night they grope at noon.

The semantic and grammatical pair is *day-noon,* but the common lexical associates *day-night* gives an added dimension to the parallelism.

c. The Semantic Aspect. The semantic aspect pertains to the relationship between the meaning of the parallel lines. It was this relationship that Lowth categorized as synonymous, synthetic, or synthetic; and which Kugel described as "A, what's more, B" (see above). From a linguistic perspective, the semantic relationships in parallel lines, like the lexical relationship between word pairs, can be viewed as either paradigmatic or syntagmatic.

It is not always so easy, however, to categorize particular examples as one or the other. Sometimes the relationship is ambiguous and would be interpreted differently by different readers. Take, for example, Hab 3:3:

> His glory covers heaven;
> And the earth is full of his praise

It is possible to analyze these lines as paradigmatic—each conveying a similar meaning; on the other hand, the second line may be perceived as a result of the first, in which case there would be a semantic sequence, or syntagm.

In many case both paradigmatic and syntagmatic elements are present, as in Isa 40:9:

> Ascend a high hill, herald (to) Zion;
> Lift your voice aloud, herald (to) Jerusalem.

The actions of the herald are sequential, but the vocatives ("herald to Zion/Jerusalem") are paradigmatic. It appears to be in the nature of parallelism to combine these two forces, so that the expression advances even as the lines are bound firmly together. In this way the second line of a parallelism often disambiguates, or clarifies, the first; or on a more abstract level, parallelism may serve as a metaphor.

> A thorn comes to the hand of a drunkard;
> And a proverb to the mouth of fools. (Prov 26:9)

d. The Phonological Aspect. Sound equivalences may be activated in parallelism just as grammatical and lexical equivalences are. Often this takes the form of sound pairs—the pairing of terms that are phonologically equivalent (i.e., they contain the same or linguistically related consonants). In some cases the sound pairs are also word pairs: *šlwm // šlwh,* "peace // tranquility" in Ps 122:7; *bwrk // bʾrk,* "your cistern // your well" in Prov 5:15; *šwṭ // šbt,* "whip

// rod" in Prov 26:3. More often, it seems, sound pairs are not lexical or semantic pairs; they may not even be from the same word class.

> He made the moon for *time-markers* [*mwᶜdym*]:
> The sun *knows its setting* [*ydᶜ mbwʾw*]. (Ps 104:19)
> I will cut off your horses *from your midst* [*mqrbk*];
> I will destroy *your chariots* [*mrkbtyk*]. (Mic 5:9)

(In this last verse the lexical pairs are *horses // chariots*.)

Several sound pairs may occur in a parallelism and they may be patterned in different ways: AABB, ABAB, ABBA. The effect of sound pairs is to reinforce the bond created by the other forms of equivalence between the parts of the parallelism. Sound pairs provide an added dimension, an additional type of linguistic equivalence. The more equivalences there are in a parallelism, the stronger is the sense of correspondence between one line and the next. This, in turn, promotes the perception of semantic unity. The various linguistic equivalences may act in concert, or they may produce an artistic tension, creating an interplay that adds to the interest of the parallelism.

Because there are infinite possibilities for activating linguistic equivalences, there are infinite possibilities for constructing parallelisms. No parallelism is "better" or "more complete" than any other. Each is constructed for its own purpose and context. The device of parallelism is extraordinarily flexible, and its expressive capabilities and appeal are enormous, as the poets of the ANE discovered long ago.

Bibliography

Alonso-Schökel, L. 1963. *Estudios de Poetica Hebrea.* Barcelona.

Alter, R. 1983a. The Dynamics of Parallelism. *Hebrew University Studies in Literature and the Arts* 11.1: 71–101.

———. 1983b. From Line to Story in Biblical Verse. *Poetics Today* 4: 615–37.

———. 1985. *The Art of Biblical Poetry.* New York.

Avishur, Y. 1972. Addenda to the Expanded Colon in Ugaritic and Biblical Verse. *UF* 4: 1–10.

———. 1974. Stylistic Common Elements Between Ugaritic Literature and Song of Songs. *Beth Mikra* 59: 508–25 (in Hebrew).

———. 1975. Word Pairs Common to Phoenician and Biblical Hebrew. *UF* 7: 13–47.

———. 1976. Studies of Stylistic Features Common to the Phoenician Inscriptions and the Bible. *UF* 8: 1–12.

———. 1977. *The Construct State of Synonyms in Biblical Rhetoric.* Jerusalem (in Hebrew).

Baker, A. 1973. Parallelism: England's Contribution to Biblical Studies. *CBQ* 35: 429–40.

Berlin, A. 1979. Grammatical Aspects of Biblical Parallelism. *HUCA* 50: 17–43.

———. 1983. Parallel Word Pairs: A Linguistic Explanation. *UF* 15: 7–16.

———. 1985. *The Dynamics of Biblical Parallelism.* Bloomington, IN.

Boling, R. 1960. "Synonymous" Parallelism in the Psalms. *JSS* 5: 221–55.

Bostrom, G. 1928. *Paronomasi i den aldre hebreiska Maschallitteraturen med sarskild hansyn till Proverbia.* Lund.

Bronznick, N. 1979. "Metathetic Parallelism"—An Unrecognized Subtype of Synonymous Parallelism. *HAR* 3: 25–39.

Cassuto, U. 1971. *The Goddess Anath.* Jerusalem.

———. 1973–75. *Biblical and Oriental Studies.* 2 vols. Jerusalem.

Ceresko, A. 1975. The A:B::B:A Word Pattern in Hebrew and Northwest Semitic with Special Reference to the Book of Job. *UF* 7: 73–88.

———. 1976. The Chiastic Word Pattern in Hebrew. *CBQ* 38: 303–11.

———. 1978. The Function of Chiasmus in Hebrew Poetry. *CBQ* 40: 1–10.

Clark, H. H. 1970. Word Associations and Linguistic Theory. Pp. 271–86 in *New Horizons in Linguistics,* ed. J. Lyons. Baltimore.

Collins, T. 1978. *Line-Forms in Hebrew Poetry.* Rome.

Craigie, P. C. 1971. A Note on "Fixed Pairs" in Ugaritic and Early Hebrew Poetry. *JTS* 22: 140–43.

———. 1979a. Parallel Word Pairs in Ugaritic and Early Hebrew Poetry. *JTS* 22: 140–43.

———. 1979b. The Problem of Parallel Word Pairs in Ugaritic and Hebrew Poetry. *Semitics* 5: 48–58.

Culley, R. C. 1967. *Oral Formulaic Language in the Biblical Psalms.* Toronto.

Dahood, M. 1972. Ugaritic-Hebrew Parallel Pairs. Pp. 71–382 in *Ras Shamra Parallels I,* ed. L. Fisher. AnOr 49. Rome.

———. 1975. Pp. 1–39 in *Ras Shamra Parallels II,* ed. L. Fisher. AnOr 50. Rome.

———. 1981. Pp. 1–206 in *Ras Shamra Parallels III,* ed. S. Rummel. AnOr 51. Rome.

Di Marco, A. 1976. Der Chiasmus in der Bibel. *LB* 36: 21–79; 37: 49–68.

Driver, G. R. 1953. Hebrew Poetic Diction. *VTSup* 1: 26–39.

Fox, J. 1977. Roman Jakobson and the Comparative Study of Parallelism. Pp. 59–60 in *Roman Jakobson: Echoes of His Scholarship,* ed. D. Armstrong and C. van Schooneveld. Lisse.

Freedman, D. N. 1980. *Pottery, Poetry, and Prophecy. Collected Essays on Hebrew Poetry.* Winona Lake, IN.

Geller, S. 1979. *Parallelism in Early Biblical Poetry.* Missoula, MT.

———. 1982a. The Dynamics of Parallel Verse. A Poetic Analysis of Deut 32:6–12. *HTR* 75: 35–56.

———. 1982b. Theory and Method in the Study of Biblical Poetry. *JQR* 73: 65–77.

Gevirtz, S. 1963. *Patterns in the Early Poetry of Israel.* Chicago.

———. 1973. On Canaanite Rhetoric: The Evidence of the Amarna Letters from Tyre. *Or* 42: 162–77.

Gluck, J. 1970. Paronomasia in Biblical Literature. *Semitics* 1: 50–78.

———. 1971. Assonance in Ancient Hebrew Poetry: Sound Patterns as a Literary Device. Pp. 69–84 in *De Fructu Oris Sui, Essays in Honor of Adrianus van Selms,* ed. I. H. Eybers, F. C. Fensham, and C. J. Labuschagne. Leiden.

Gordis, R. 1971. The Structure of Biblical Poetry. Pp. 61–94 in *Poets, Prophets, and Sages.* Bloomington, IN.

Gray, G. B. 1915. *The Forms of Hebrew Poetry.* New York. Repr. 1972.

Greenstein, E. 1974. Two Variations of Grammatical Parallelism in Canaanite Poetry and Their Psycholinguistic Background. *JANES* 6: 87–105.

———. 1977. One More Step on the Staircase. *UF* 9: 77–86.

———. 1982. How Does Parallelism Mean? A Sense of Text. *JQRSup* pp. 41–70.

Held, M. 1953. Additional Pairs of Words in Synonymous Parallelism in Biblical Hebrew and in Ugaritic. *Leš* 18: 144–60.

———. 1962. The YQTL-QTL (QTL-YQTL) Sequence of Identical Verbs in Biblical Hebrew and in Ugaritic. Pp. 281–90 in

Studies and Essays in Honor of Abraham A. Neuman, ed. M. Ben-Horin et al. Leiden.
———. 1965. The Action-Result (Factitive-Passive) Sequence of Identical Verbs in Biblical Hebrew and Ugaritic. *JANES* 6: 87–105.
Holenstein, E. 1976. *Roman Jakobson's Approach to Language: Phenomenological Structuralism.* Bloomington, IN.
Holladay, W. L. 1970. Form and Word-Play in David's Lament over Saul and Jonathan. *VT* 20: 153–89.
Jakobson, R. 1960. Linguistics and Poetics. Pp. 350–77 in *Style in Language,* ed. T. Sebeck. Cambridge, MA.
———. 1966. Grammatical Parallelism and its Russian Facet. *Language* 42: 399–429.
———. 1971. Two Aspects of Language and Two Types of Aphasic Disturbances. Pp. 239–59 in *Selected Writings.* Vol. 2. The Hague.
———. 1972. Verbal Communication. *Scientific American* 227.3: 73–80.
———. 1980a. On Poetic Intentions and Linguistic Devices in Poetry. A Discussion with Professors and Students at the University of Cologne. *Poetics Today* 2: 87–96.
———. 1980b. A Postscript to the Discussion on Grammar of Poetry. *Diacritics* 10.1: 22–35.
———. 1980c. Subliminal Verbal Patterning in Poetry. *Poetics Today* 2: 127–36.
Kaddari, M. Z. 1968. On Semantic Parallelism in Biblical Hebrew. *Leš* 32: 37–45 (in Hebrew).
———. 1973. A Semantic Approach to Biblical Parallelism. *JJS* 24: 167–75.
Kiparsky, P. 1973. The Role of Linguistics in a Theory of Poetry. *Daedalus* 102.3: 231–44.
Kselman, J. S. 1977. Semantic-Sonant Chiasmus in Biblical Poetry. *Bib* 58: 219–23.
Kugel, J. 1981. *The Idea of Biblical Poetry, Parallelism and Its History.* New Haven.
———. 1984. Some Thoughts on Future Research into Biblical Style: Addenda to the Idea of Biblical Poetry. *JSOT* 28: 107–17.
Landy, F. 1984. Poetics and Parallelism: Some Comments on James Kugel's *The Idea of Biblical Poetry. JSOT* 28: 61–87.
Levin, S. 1962. *Linguistic Structures in Poetry.* The Hague.
Loewenstamm, S. E. 1975. The Expanded Colon Reconstructed. *UF* 7: 261–64.
Lowth, R. 1753. *Lectures on the Sacred Poetry of the Hebrews.* London. Repr. 1835.
———. 1778. *Isaiah. A New Translation With a Preliminary Dissertation and Notes.* London. Repr. 1848.
Lundbom, J. R. 1975. *Jeremiah. A Study in Ancient Hebrew Rhetoric.* SBLDS 18. Missoula, MT.
McNeill, D. 1966. A Study in Word Association. *Journal of Verbal Learning and Verbal Behavior* 5: 548–57.
Malkiel, Y. 1968. Studies in Irreversible Binomials. Pp. 311–55 in *Essay on Linguistic Themes.* Berkeley.
Melamed, E. Z. 1961. Break-up of Stereotype Phrases. *ScrHier* 8: 115–53.
———. 1964. Break-up of Stereotype Phrases as an Artistic Device in Biblical Poetry. Pp. 188–219 in *Sefer Segal. Studies in the Bible Presented to Professor M. H. Segal,* ed. Y. Grintz. Jerusalem (in Hebrew).
Miller, P. J. 1980a. Studies in Hebrew Word Patterns. *HTR* 73: 79–89.
———. 1980b. Synonymous-Sequential Parallelism in the Psalms. *Bib* 61: 256–60.
———. 1984. Meter, Parallelism, and Tropes: The Search for Poetic Style. *JSOT* 28: 99–106.
Moor, J. C. de 1978a. The Art of Versification in Ugarit and Israel. Pp. 119–39 in *Studies in Bible and the Ancient Near East Presented to Samuel E. Loewenstamm,* ed. Y. Avishur and J. Blau. Jerusalem.
———. 1987b. The Art of Versification in Ugarit and Israel II: The Formal Structure. *UF* 10: 187–217.
———. 1980. The Art of Versification in Ugarit and Israel III: Further Illustrations of the Principle of Expansion. *UF* 12: 311–15.
Muilenburg, J. 1953. A Study in Hebrew Rhetoric: Repetition and Style. *VTSup* 1: 97–111.
Newman, L. 1918. *Studies in Old Testament Parallelism, I: Parallelism in Amos.* Berkeley.
O'Connor, M. 1980. *Hebrew Verse Structure.* Winona Lake, IN.
Pardee, D. 1980. Ugaritic and Hebrew Poetry: Parallelism. Paper read at the First International Symposium on the Antiquities of Palestine. Aleppo.
———. 1982. Types and Distributions of Parallelism in Ugaritic and Hebrew Poetry. Paper read at the Annual Meeting of the Society of Biblical Literature. New York.
———. 1984. The Semantic Parallelism of Psalm 89. Pp. 121–37 in *In the Shelter of Elyon,* ed. W. B. Barrick and J. R. Spenser. JSOTSup 31. Sheffield.
Parker, S. 1974. Parallelism and Prosody in Ugaritic Narrative Verse. *UF* 6: 283–94.
Popper, W. 1918–23. *Studies in Biblical Parallelism, Part II: Parallelism in Isaiah.* UCPNES. Berkeley.
Rendsburg, G. 1980. Janus Parallelism in Gen 49:26. *JBL* 99: 291–93.
Ridderbos, N. H. 1963. The Psalms: Style-Figures and Structure. *OTS* 13: 43–76.
Robinson, T. H. 1953. Hebrew Poetic Form: The English Tradition. *VTSup* 1: 128–49.
Sayce, R. A. 1971. The Style of Montaigne: Word-Pairs and Word-Groups. Pp. 383–405 in *Literary Style: A Symposium,* ed. S. Chatman. London.
Saydon, P. P. 1955. Assonance in Hebrew as a Means of Expressing Emphasis. *Bib* 36: 36–50, 287–304.
Schramm, G. M. 1976. Poetic Patterning in Biblical Hebrew. Pp. 167–91 in *Michigan Oriental Studies in Honor of George G. Cameron,* ed. L. Orlin. Ann Arbor.
Segert, S. 1960. Problems of Hebrew Prosody. *VTSup* 7: 283–91.
———. 1979. Ugaritic Poetry and Poetics: Some Preliminary Observations. *UF* 11: 729–38.
———. 1983a. Parallelism in Ugaritic Poetry. *JAOS* 103: 295–306.
———. 1983b. Prague Structuralism in American Biblical Scholarship: Performance and Potential. Pp. 697–708 in *WLSGF.*
Shapiro, M. 1976. *Asymmetry. An Inquiry into the Linguistic Structure of Poetry.* Amsterdam.
Steinitz, W. 1934. *Der Parallelismus in der finnisch-karelischen Volksdichtung.* Folklore Fellows Communication 115. Helsinki.
Watson, W. G. 1984. *Classical Hebrew Poetry: A Guide to its Techniques.* JSOTSup 26. Sheffield.
Watters, W. R. 1976. *Formula Criticism and the Poetry of the Old Testament.* Berlin.
Waugh, L. 1980. The Poetic Function and the Nature of Language. *Poetics Today* 2.1a: 57–82.
Werth, P. 1976. Roman Jakobson's Verbal Analysis of Poetry. *Journal of Linguistics* 12: 21–73.

Whallon, W. 1963. Formulaic Poetry in the Old Testament. *Comparative Literature* 15: 1–14.
———. 1969. *Formula, Character, and Context: Studies in Homeric, Old English and Old Testament Poetry.* Cambridge, MA.
Whitley, C. F. 1975. Some Aspects of Hebrew Poetic Diction. *UF* 7: 493–502.
Willis, J. T. 1979. The Juxtaposition of Synonymous and Chiastic Parallelism in Tricola in Old Testament Hebrew Psalm Poetry. *VT* 29: 465–80.
Yoder, P. 1970. *Fixed Word Pairs and the Composition of Hebrew Poetry.* Ph.D. Diss. University of Pennsylvania.
———. 1971. A-B pairs and Oral Composition in Hebrew Poetry. *VT* 21: 470–89.

ADELE BERLIN

PARALYSIS. See SICKNESS AND DISEASE.

PARAN (PLACE) [Heb *pā'rān*]. The name which designates the wilderness area S of Israel, W of Edom, and N of the wilderness of Sinai (*IDB* 3: 657). While this location is not given directly, it can be inferred from the several OT references to the wilderness of Paran. In particular, Num 13:3 and 26 report that the spies sent to scout out Canaan from the S were sent from and returned to Paran. Num 13:26 adds the specific note that the spies returned to Kadesh, apparently a town within the larger area designated by the "Wilderness of Paran." In Deut 1:22, the location is also given specifically as Kadesh-barnea. The site of Kadesh-barnea is located at Tell el-Qudeirat in N Sinai at the juncture of two ancient routes: the Way of Shur and a branch of the Via Maris (*EAEHL*, 697).

While Deuteronomy names the departure point of the S reconnaissance of Canaan as Kadesh-barnea at Deut 1:22, Deut 1:1 includes Paran in its list of locales which define the wilderness in which Israel encamped and locates this wilderness in the Arabah, which lies S of the Dead Sea and N of Sinai.

Additional information about the location of the Wilderness of Paran can be gleaned from the account of Abraham's victory over the coalition of kings in Genesis 14. Gen 14:6 states the limit of territory taken by the king Chedorlaomer to be "as far as El-paran on the border of the wilderness." N. Glueck (1935: 104) places the route of this action in the Arabah on the way to Sinai. From thence Chedorlaomer turned back to Kadesh (Gen 14:7), a note which strengthens the geographical tie between Paran and Kadesh.

Num 12:16 reinforces this general location for the Wilderness of Paran as it notes that the people of Israel travelled there from Hazeroth, which Numbers locates on the journey from the Wilderness of Sinai to the Wilderness of Paran. Gen 21:21 names the Wilderness of Paran as the place where Ishmael grew up, and the rest of the chapter allows us to infer that this must be placed beyond Beersheba (cf. Gen 21:15) on the way to Egypt (cf. Gen 21:21b); that is, in the general area S of Israel and N of Sinai. Such a general picture of the location of the Wilderness of Paran is confirmed in 1 Kgs 11:18, where Solomon's adversary Hadad the Edomite flees from Edom to Egypt by way of Midian and Paran (that is, W from Edom).

Num 33:36 has an additional geographical reference lacking in the MT which equates Paran and Kadesh, but this cannot be relied upon, as it could well be an attempt to harmonize the various references to Kadesh and Paran.

The other references to Paran are of a different sort. Deut 33:2 and Hab 3:3 bear great similarity to each other, as both describe in poetic terms the appearance of YHWH on the path of the Exodus (cf. Exod 15:15, Ps 68:7f, and Judg 5:4 for similar descriptions of the Exodus and the entry into Canaan as divine appearances).

1 Sam 25:1 should be read as "the Wilderness of Maon" with the LXX, since the continuation of this story about David, Abigail, and Nabal takes place in Maon (see McCarter *1 Samuel* AB, 388).

Bibliography

Glueck, N. 1935. *Explorations in Eastern Palestine II.* AASOR 15. New Haven.

JEFFRIES M. HAMILTON

PARAN, EL-. See EL-PARAN (PLACE).

PARAPET. See TEMPLE, JERUSALEM.

PARAPHRASE OF SHEM. See SHEM, PARAPHRASE OF (NHC VII,*1*).

PARBAR [Heb *parbār*]. An outer building or court mentioned by the Chronicler as one of the places where temple gatekeepers were stationed (1 Chr 26:18). The meaning of the Hebrew word is uncertain. It is often identified with *parwār* in 2 Kgs 23:11 referring to a structure attached to the side of the temple. Allegro (1960: 117), on the basis of usage in the Copper Scroll from Qumran, suggested that the word refers to a toilet or waste chamber for the high priest or king. *Parbār* in 1 Chr 26:18 would, thus, probably refer to a waste chamber connected with the temple. The word *parwār* is generally supposed to be a Persian loanword meaning "open pavilion." In an Aramaic-Lydian scroll from Sardis (Littman 1916: 26–27) *parwār* refers to the open anteroom of a tomb. In the Mishnah the word often means "suburb" or "adjunct."

Bibliography

Allegro, J. M. 1960. *Treasury of the Copper Scroll.* Garden City, NY.
Littmann, E. 1916. *Sardis.* Vol. 6, *Lydian Inscriptions,* Part 1. Leiden.

TOM WAYNE WILLETT

PARENESIS AND PROTREPTIC. Discourse whose aim is to exhort or persuade the reader or auditor to do good.

A. Background and Definitions
B. Literary Forms
C. Structure, Devices, and Techniques
D. Traditional and Commonplace Material
E. Parenesis in the Undisputed Pauline Letters

F. Parenesis in the Pastoral and Catholic Epistles
G. Parenesis and Apocalyptic Literature

A. Background and Definitions

Dibelius' comparison of the letters of James and Paul with the Mandates in the *Shepherd of Hermas,* the synoptic speeches of Jesus, and Greco–Roman parenetic works (*James* Hermeneia, 2–7) disclosed the common character of all of these as diverse collections of older sayings material arranged in no particular order and not focused on a particular situation or thought. In the Jewish milieu parenesis appears in the maxims in the didactic poetry of the Wisdom tradition and *Ps-Phocylides,* in the properly prose parenetic of Tob 4:5–19; 12:6–12, and the "Two Ways" teaching (*Didache* 1–6 and *Epistle of Barnabas* 19–20), in the sayings of Ps-Menander, and in the legendary and apocalyptic *Testaments of the Twelve Patriarchs.* In form, the didactic poetry of Hesiod, the prose tractates of Isocrates and Plutarch, the letters of Seneca, and the maxim collections of the *florilegia* parallel the Jewish and Christian parenesis. In content, too, the Christian authors, like the writers of Jewish Wisdom, incorporated into their generally applicable parenetic guidebooks or guidebook sections a vision of the correct way of life common to their Greco-Roman contemporaries.

Hartlich (1889: 328–29) distinguishes protreptic (*protropē, protreptikos logos,* an exhortation or persuasion to a commonly agreed upon good, associated with *paraklēsis* or exhortation) from parenesis (*parainesis,* proposal by precept of a debatable good, associated with *symboulē* or counsel, advice). Burgess (1902: 299) finds that the ancient theoreticians are not consistent in distinguishing the two terms, although many refer to a predominance of precept in parenesis. Vetschera (1911–12: 4–9), while agreeing that parenesis is distinguished by its use of precepts ("principles by which one should live"), also finds the parenetic work to be broader in content than the protreptic one. For him the protreptic piece, in popular philosophy as well as rhetoric, hopes to lead the addressee to obtain a certain knowledge and its *aretē* ("virtue"). The parenetic work, on the contrary, covers many areas of life, e.g., culture, friends, fortune, under the aspect of their usefulness for obtaining a happy and virtuous life. Thus, the distinction rests on both content and form. Given this mixed verdict from antiquity, Vetschera's definition of parenesis is a reasonable guide: "a literary work which by its structure and aim delineates a collection of precepts which relate unexceptionally to the practical conduct of life, indeed to promote it, as far as it can, and to lead to virtue." Protreptic is treated along with parenesis here since, though different, both apply to a range of hortatory devices to urge the audience to a virtuous and happy life.

A vital, though not yet fully clarified, role in the employment and development of the hortatory devices which serve parenesis in popular philosophy and education was played by the progymnatists (teachers of elementary rhetoric) and their handbooks of rhetorical theory and exercise. Clark (1957: 186–88) notes a protreptic-apotreptic (persuasion-dissuasion) end in the exercises (see Nicolaus and Aphthonius) on how to develop and apply a *chria* ("clever saying) and *gnomeē* ("epigram" or "proverb"). Coleman (1974: 280) finds this put to work in the moralist Seneca's letters. Epistle 104, for example, associates ideas, precepts, and rhetorical devices in a hortatory argument which parallels the school exercises.

B. Literary Forms

Burgess (1902: 186–87, 234–44) finds moralizing parenesis both in epideictic (displaying praise or blame) oratory, in the prose diatribe (conversational form of teaching), and in the half-dialogue or epistle, especially when adopted by rhetorically adept popular philosophers. Prior to the widespread use of the parenetic letter, Isocrates and his successors used parenetic discourses, like the *Ad Nicoclem, Ad Demonicum,* and *Nicocles,* to effect their parenetic ends. These "instruction booklets" for rulers and subjects are full not of new but of conventional prescriptive teachings, drawn from a variety of sources, arranged in a locally unstructured but nonetheless not haphazard order, and meant to be perennially valid. Though similar in content to poetic compendia of maxims and precepts, these discourses are couched in epistolary terms and carry a friendly tone proper to letters of exhortation.

The "Kingship Treatises" (*principis speculum*) of Plutarch and Dio Chrysostom make use of another typical parenetic feature, catalogs of virtues and vices, remarkably alike in content despite the different authors and contexts.

The parenetic aims in these "epistolary" discourses surface in the exhortation section of some actual official letter-memoranda prescribing the duties of newly appointed officials. More widespread, however, was the teaching letter, a development from the philosophical dialogue, for moral instruction. Indeed, Guillemin (1929: 32) notes that epistolary parenesis owes it success to the letter's friendly tone and that the parenesis is a concomitant of the teacher's friendly relations with the pupils. The letter's familiar and quietly persuasive conversational tone makes the friend present as he acquits himself of the friend's hortatory task. The correspondent in turn relies on the teacher–friend for guidance. The letter writer's self-presentation, which Ps-Demetrius *Eloc.* 223 considered the essence of a letter, serves as a surrogate for the actual presence and sharing of life circumstances. Seneca regarded this mutuality in the letter to be the most effective method of moral instruction. The letter may even be more effective than actual presence since it can propose an ideal model unequivocally expressive of the parenetic concepts. The practical situation of geographical distance and the theoretical superiority of the letter for parenesis led popular philosophers like Seneca and the Cynics to prefer the letter for their moral instruction and exhortation.

C. Structure, Devices, and Techniques

While parenetic works have been commonly thought to be random collections of hortatory material, structural principles do organize the parenetic texts. In addition to the characteristic commands, prohibitions, advice, warnings, maxims, and precepts, Cancik (1967: 23–24) finds a broad array of auxiliary hortatory devices like declarations, comparisons, examples, explanations, applications, and concluding calls to action. Others (Thyen 1955) add catalogs of virtues, vices, and sufferings, appeals to common knowledge and authority, together with rhetorical techniques like hyperbole, antithesis, paradox, and irony, which help make the exhortations strike home. Moreover, Cancik's (1967: 8–9, 25–26) study of Seneca's moral letters finds them to be carefully structured so as to build persuasive hortatory arguments either by themselves or mixed with theoretical observations. Before Seneca, Isocrates and his followers related example, a prime hortatory tool (*Evagoras* 73–81), to prescriptions by describing those characteristics in the positive and negative exemplars which correspond to the precepts. When the examples were only roughly sketched out (*Ad Demonicum* 11) the loosely organized prescriptive section which follows filled out their parameters. Similarly, when "Kingship Treatises" used catalogs of virtues and vices from popular philosophical moral teaching, they also delineated exemplary types to be imitated or avoided.

Malherbe sees the call to imitate the prescribed virtues embodied in exemplars and, presumably, in the teachers themselves, as typical. Catalogs of sufferings help establish the authoritative teacher–exemplar whose experiences and progress have shown that the task at hand is possible. The difficult task calls for persistent striving, often expressed in athletic images, and can occasion drastic interventions by the teacher-guides described with medical analogies. The teachers, though sometimes harsh, are really friends who by frankness rather than flattery seek not to harm but to improve their charges.

D. Traditional and Commonplace Material

To Verner (1983: 15–25) the parenetic material can be traditional in three ways: borrowed from other sources, arranged in typical structures, or inserted as self-contained units of generalized exhortation *(topoi)*. Its commonplace and general character argue against seeing therein reflections of the author's own outlook or a specific situation. He finds, however, that the more developed the structure of a parenetic section, the more likely does it reflect the author's perspective. Thus Romans 12–15 arguably contains not generalized *topoi* but concrete and personal applications of the gospel exposed theoretically earlier in the letter and even throughout Paul's letters. Similarly, 1 Cor 11:23–34 uses liturgical tradition and parenesis to meet the community's needs.

E. Parenesis in the Undisputed Pauline Letters

Paul, whose letters stand in for his personal presence in support of his parenesis, makes hortatory appeals which combine authoritative demands with diplomatic sensitivity and lead into parenetic sections (Rom 12:1–2; 15:30–32; 16:17; 1 Cor 1:10; 4:16; 16:15–16; 1 Thess 4:1, 10b; 5:12, 14). While these sections ordinarily appear after the body of the letter (Romans), they may precede it (1 Corinthians, actually framing the body) or even constitute the body (1 Thessalonians, prepared for by a long thanksgiving).

Paul's written parenesis echoes the traditional and comprehensive teaching on moral conduct which accompanied the missionary preaching. To Collins (1984: 327–32) this recalls the Jewish Hellenistic missionary sermon which grounds moral responsibilities in the convenantal relationship. The ethical life, a sign of the Holy Spirit, entails an ethic of response and growth. While urgent ("in the Lord Jesus") what Paul writes is not new but is a reminder of what his correspondents already know, so that they might continue along their chosen path. Beyond the specific questions and preparations for the parousia, building a life of virtue engaged Paul's efforts. Consequently, the motivation behind the parenesis is multiform, as in 1 Thessalonians which appeals to final judgment, the Christians' call to holiness, and their response to the gift of the Holy Spirit.

The parenetic character of a letter section explains the function of its diverse elements. Thus, for example, the hymn in Philippians 2 sets the positive example of self-sacrificing humility being urged; the vice and virtue lists in Galatians 5 provide a noncontrovertible reminder of Paul's original message about the Galatians' Spirit-filled existence; the opponents and exemplars (including Paul) in 1 Thessalonians alert the correspondents to well-known figures in and beyond the community whose way of life calls for emulation or avoidance. Paul goes beyond his contemporaries when he calls explicitly for imitation of himself as a prime example of the Christian life, resting this claim not on his own works (unlike some boastful Cynics) but on the gospel.

While some of Paul's material is Christian-specific, like motivation based on the presence of the Holy Spirit or on the eschatological implications of the resurrection, much, like the catalogs of virtues, vices, and sufferings, the images of father, nurse, pedagogue, and disease, the themes of money- or reputation-seeking teachers, the desire to be with the correspondents, the personal relationship and mutual concern among the correspondents, is common to Greco-Roman parenesis. The same is true for formal features like catalogs, prescriptions, contrasts, threats, reminders, affirmations of prior knowledge, model figures, the call the imitation, and expressions of frankness. In Paul, all of this complements his missionary preaching, setting out parameters of the Christian life-style which pleases God, however similar it is to that of their non-Christian neighbors.

F. Parenesis in the Pastoral and Catholic Epistles

The Pastoral Epistles, with their catalogs of virtues, vices, sufferings, and household duties; with the commonplace teachings on riches and women; and with their prescriptions of what to do and reject, whom to associate with and avoid, in an epistolary handbook for young officials from a teacher-friend-model, are unmistakably parenetic. Their apparently haphazard arrangement actually constitutes a developed hortatory argument, which ultimately rests on the logic of deduction and illustrative examples (Donelson 1986: 66–113). Their claim to Pauline authority and divine sanction for the sound teaching and ethical program finds support in a succession of teachers from Paul to Timothy and Titus to appointed officials in the context of the pseudepigraphical letters themselves. These all illustrate in action the letters' prescriptions and outlines of appropriate behavior, virtues, and qualifications for office, while the vice-laden and quarrelsome false teachers demonstrate the ill effects of heresy. The letters propose a typical, Greco–Roman, "bourgeois" morality, in a Christianized version (Schwarz 1983). Their insistence on propriety seems aimed at both innercommunity unanimity and stability (e.g., Titus 1:5–9) and extracommunity reputation of the increasingly well-established church members (e.g., 1 Tim 3:7).

The use of typical Greco–Roman *Haustafeln* (lists of household duties) in 1 Pet 2:11–3:12; 1 Tim 2:1–15; Titus 2:1–15 (and see Eph 5:21–6:9; Col 3:18–4:1) touches the larger question of the specifically Christian character of the parenesis in the letters. Balch (1981: 81–109) argues that the lists in 1 Peter are not an instance of de-eschatologized Christianity adopting the ethic of its environment, nor an attempt to suppress social unrest among slaves or women insisting on their baptismal equality (Gal 3:28), nor part of the Church's mission to convert by good example. Rather, by maintaining commonplace ethical standards, they seek to quiet the suspicions and ill will of masters and husbands toward their slaves and wives who have abandoned the traditional gods for the new Christian belief. The lists' traditional parenesis, which serves the apologetic purpose of giving assurance that traditional values are still being maintained, is furnished with properly Christian motivation of Christ's patient suffering, God's judgment, and Christ's guardianship.

G. Parenesis and Apocalyptic Literature

The imagery of current or impending crisis in apocalyptic literature, which works as motivation for their parenesis, has led to the search for likely persecution settings, like a Domitian reign of terror for the book of Revelation. Osiek (1986: 113–21), however, finds that the apocalyptic visionary myth in the *Shepherd of Hermas* is addressed not to the historical but to the social reality of the community, where the demands of religious visionaries either are losing their appeal or directly threaten the economically comfortable and upwardly mobile church members. The parenesis function to expand the horizons of the community and move them in the direction of a faith commitment explained and shaped by the apocalyptic myth.

Bibliography

Balch, D. L. 1981. *Let Wives Be Submissive: The Domestic Code in 1 Peter.* SBLMS 26. Chico, CA.

Burgess, T. C. 1902. *Epideictic Literature.* Studies in Classical Philology. Chicago.

Cancik, H. 1967. *Untersuchungen zu Senecas epistulae morales.* Spudasmata: Studien zur Klassischen Philologie und ihren Grenzgebieten 18. Hildesheim.

Clark, D. L. 1957. *Rhetoric in Greco-Roman Education.* New York.

Coleman, R. 1974. The Artful Moralist: A Study of Seneca's Epistolary Style. CQ n.s. 24: 276–89.

Collins, R. F. 1984. *Studies on the First Letter to the Thessalonians.* BETL 66. Louvain.

Donelson, L. W. 1986. *Pseudepigraphy and Ethical Argument in the Pastoral Epistles.* Hermeneutische Untersuchungen zur Theologie 22. Tübingen.

Fiore, B. 1986. *The Use of Personal Example in the Socratic and Pastoral Epistles.* AnBib 105. Rome.

Guillemin, A. M. 1929. *Pline et la vie littéraire de son temps.* Paris.

Hartlich, P. 1889. De exhortationum a Graecis Romanisque scriptarum historia et indole. *LSS* 11: 207–336.

Malherbe, A. J. 1983. Exhortation in First Thessalonians. *NovT* 3: 238–56.

Osiek, C. 1986. The Genre and Function of the *Shepherd of Hermas. Semeia* 36: 113–21.

Schwarz, R. 1983. *Bürgeliches Christentum im Neuen Testament?* ÖBS 4. Klosterneuburg.

Thyen, H. 1955. *Der Stil der jüdisch-hellenistischen Homilie.* FRLANT NF 47. Göttingen.

Verner, D. C. 1983. *The Household of God: The Social World of Pastoral Epistles.* SBLDS 71. Chico, CA.

Vetschera, R. 1911–12. *Zur griechischen Paränes.* Smichow and Prague.

BENJAMIN FIORE

PAREVE. See MEAL CUSTOMS (JEWISH DIETARY LAWS).

PARMASHTA (PERSON) [Heb *parmaštā*ʾ]. One of the ten sons of Haman (Esth 9:9). On problems surrounding this list of names see ADALIA (PERSON). Parmashta (LXX *marmasima*) may render the otherwise unattested Old Iranian name **Fra-mathista* "preeminent" (Scheftelowitz 1901) or **Parvaštā-* "standing before" (Hinz 1975: 183 s.v. **parvaštā-*).

Bibliography

Hinz, W. 1975. *Altiranisches Sprachgut der Nebenüberlieferungen.* Wiesbaden.

Scheftelowitz, I. 1901. *Arisches im Alten Testament.* Vol. 1. Berlin.

PETER BEDFORD

PARMENAS (PERSON) [Gk *Parmenas*]. One of seven gifted leaders, "of good repute, full of the Spirit and of wisdom" (Acts 6:3) who were chosen to look after the needs of the Hellenistic Jewish Christian widows who had been neglected in the "daily distribution" (Acts 6:1, 5). The name Parmenas may be a shortened form of Parmenides, which means "steadfast" or "trustworthy." It was a rather uncommon Greek name at the time (Foakes Jackson and Lake 1979: 66). Since all seven had Greek names and only one of them, Nicolaus, is explicitly called a Proselyte, it is probable that the other six, including Parmenas, were either Jews born in the Diaspora or Palestinian Jews with Greek names (as would be the case with Jesus' disciples Andrew and Philip). The work of two of them, Stephen (Acts 6:8–8:2) and Philip (Acts 8:5–40; 21:8) makes it clear that the Seven did not limit themselves to "serving tables" (Acts 6:2) but functioned for the Hellenists in the way that the Twelve did for the Hebrew Christians (See Simon 1958: 7). According to later tradition, Parmenas was one of the seventy appointed by Jesus (cf. Luke 10:1), became bishop of Soli on Cyprus (cf. Acts 11:19, 20) and was martyred at Philippi during the reign of Trajan (Schermann 1907: 302–3, 344).

Bibliography

Foakes Jackson, F. J., and Lake, K. 1979. *The Beginnings of Christianity.* Vol. 4. Grand Rapids.

Schermann, T. 1907. *Propheten-und Apostellegenden.* Leipzig.

Simon, M. 1958. *St. Stephen and the Hellenists in the Primitive Church.* London.

JON PAULIEN

PARNACH (PERSON) [Heb *parnak*]. The father of Elizapahan, leader of the tribe of Zebulun who was appointed to help distribute the land to the Israelites (Num 34:25). Parnach is taken to be a name derived from either Elamite or Persian. It means either "spendor" or "success." A similar name is found in a Neo-Babylonian text from the Achaemenid era. In the LXX, Parnach was rendered as *par(a)nax*.

RAPHAEL I. PANITZ

PAROSH (PERSON) [Heb *parʿōš*; Gk *phoros*]. Head of a family of Babylonian exiles who are listed as returnees under the leadership of Zerubbabel and others (Ezra 2:3 [= Neh 7:8 = 1 Esdr 5:9]) and later under Ezra (Ezra 8:3 [= 1 Esdr 8:30]). Some from this family married foreign wives and later agreed to divorce them in response to Ezra's reform (Ezra 10:25 [= 1 Esdr 9:26]). A member of this family assisted Nehemiah in rebuilding the walls of Jerusalem (Neh 3:25), and the leader of this clan affixed the family name to the covenant document of Nehemiah in Neh 10:15—Eng 10:14. For discussion of the list in Ezra 2, see AKKUB.

That the list of builders in Nehemiah 3 is a partial one is evident from the references to "second portions" in 3:11, 19, 20, 30 without previous notations of corresponding first portions (cf. 3:4, 21; 3:5, 27). There is widespread agreement that the list came from independent archives, perhaps in the temple, and was incorporated into the Nehemiah Memoirs by Nehemiah himself or by some other editor. (See Batten *Ezra and Nehemiah* ICC, 206–7; Clines *Ezra, Nehemiah, Esther* NCBC, 149; Williamson *Ezra, Nehemiah* WBC, 199–202.)

Many do not regard the list and covenant of Nehemiah 10 as belonging originally in this context. Williamson (325–30) surveys various views about the origins of this list. He concludes that it was compiled from other lists in Ezra and Nehemiah in order to be attached to the terms of an agreement drawn up by Nehemiah following his reforms of Nehemiah 13. This document was then kept in the temple archives until being inserted into its present position. (See also Clines, 199–200; Myers *Ezra, Nehemiah* AB, 174–75; Jepsen 1954: 87–106.)

Bibliography

Galling, K. 1951. The Gōlā-List According to Ezra 2 and Nehemiah 7. *JBL* 70: 149–58.
———. 1964. Die Liste der aus dem Exil Heimgekehrten. Pp. 89–108 in *Studien zur Geschichte Israels im persischen Zeitalter.* Tübingen.
Jepsen, A. 1954. Nehemia 10. *ZAW* 66: 87–106.

CHANEY R. BERGDALL

PAROUSIA. The Greek word *parousia* used in the NT to speak of the arrival (2 Cor 7:6f; Phil 1:26) or presence of someone (2 Cor 10:10). It is also used as a technical term to speak of the arrival or presence of Christ in glory at a particular point in the eschatological process (e.g., Matt 24:3). The belief in the Parousia or presence of Christ in glory is firmly rooted in all strands of the NT, though the expectation can be referred to apart from the word (Rev 19:11ff; 1 Cor 15:23ff; Mark 13:26; 14:62) or by use of other terms (e.g., *apokalypsis* in 1 Cor 1:7; 1 Pet 1:7). Even in those books where the person of Christ does not loom large (like the letter of James), the Parousia of the Lord (God or Christ?) is referred to (Jas 5:7).

A form of the Parousia hope does probably go back to the historical Jesus and represents part of that set of convictions most clearly represented in Matt 19:28 and par. in which Jesus uses eschatological imagery to speak of the future reign with his disciples in the kingdom of God (Kümmel 1966). There was probably no coherent Parousia doctrine in Second Temple Judaism, though the material in the *Similitudes of Enoch* (chaps. 37–71) comes very close to it. This material represents an interpretation of Daniel 7 in a direction parallel to what we find in the future Son of Man sayings in the Synoptic Gospels, though, with the exception of Matt 25:31 there is not much evidence to suggest that the NT was dependent on the *Similitudes* (or vice versa for that matter). There are hints that the expectation of an imminent return of the Messiah may have been deeply rooted in the earliest Aramaic-speaking church if 1 Cor 16:22 (cf. Acts 3:19ff) is anything to go by.

A. Revelation and the Jesus Apocalyptic Tradition
B. Pauline Letters
C. Synoptic Eschatological Discourses
D. Gospel of John
E. Delay of the Parousia
F. Conclusions

A. Revelation and the Jesus Apocalyptic Tradition

In the book of Revelation there is ample evidence of the belief in the imminent coming of Christ, especially in chaps. 1 and 22, and in Rev 19.11ff (Rissi 1972). This follows the Divine Warrior myth which is here applied to the future conquering messiah. There appears to be evidence here of the influence of the Jesus story: the Rider on the White Horse already bears the marks of his death (19:13). In addition, there are explicit links with the vision of the Son of Man in 1:14 which inaugurates John's vision of what is to come.

This section belongs to a much longer symbolic account of the manifestation of the divine righteousness within human history which culminates in the exaltation of the Lamb and its claiming the right to open the sealed scroll. This triumph immediately precedes the establishment of the messianic kingdom on earth, in which those who have been slain for the testimony to Jesus reign with the Messiah for a thousand years (v 4). Revelation 19–22 is not too far removed from the roughly contemporary eschatological accounts in *2 Bar.* 29–30 and *4 Ezra* 6:11ff and 7:32ff. A scheme of woes, messianic kingdom, resurrection, judgment and new age is clearly discerned in all three works. Revelation uses much more vivid imagery as compared to the prosaic prediction found in *4 Ezra* and *2 Baruch.* The role of the redeemer figure is much more obvious in Revelation than it is in the other two apocalypses where the Messiah's role is hardly touched on; indeed, there is little sign of the warrior role found in the *Psalms of Solomon.* A comparison between Revelation and these sections of *2 Baruch* and *4 Ezra* is necessary in order to note the way in which the Parousia passage in Rev 19:11f is part of a much larger complex of hopes for the dissolution of the present order, the overthrow of the hostile powers, and the establishment of a messianic kingdom on earth (Rowland 1982).

B. Pauline Letters

1 Thess 4:15–17 describes the moment of vindication of the elect (Jewett 1986). Paul indicates that it is a word of the Lord (v 15), and it has several points of contact with the account of the coming of the son of man in Matt 24:30–31. It is, of course, a fragmentary eschatology for a limited purpose (the encouragement of the community dealing with the death of some of their number before the coming of the Kingdom). It indicates how closely intertwined the fulfillment of the eschatological hope had become with the person of Christ, a significant development in emerging Christian eschatology.

A case can be made for supposing that Paul's eschatology in 1 Cor 15:22ff follows the general outline of that found in Revelation 19–21 and presupposes a messianic reign on earth, while Christ subjects the enemies of God to himself (cf. Rev 19:11ff), though this has been a matter of considerable debate (Davies 1965; Schweitzer 1931). Also similar to Revelation 19 is the account of the Parousia in 2 Thessalonians 2 (Jewett 1986). Once again this eschatological fragment is to be found in a context dealing with a particular pastoral problem. As such, like 1 Corinthians 15, it offers only a fragment of the eschatological drama, sufficient to deal with the particular issue confronting the writer: the threat of disturbance to the community because of an outburst of eschatological enthusiasm prompted by the belief that the day of the Lord has already arrived (2:2). To counteract such enthusiasm, readers are told that the rebellion must take place first along with the revelation of the man of lawlessness who opposes God and sits in the temple of God and makes himself God. It is clear that this sign of the coming of Christ has not yet taken place, because there is something restraining his appearance (2:5) at his proper time; (whatever that may be: Paul himself; the evangelizing of the gentiles; the Roman Empire, some divine/angelic restraint such as is found in, e.g., Rev 7:1). Meanwhile the mystery of lawlessness is already at work. In other words, the present is in some sense a time of eschatological fulfillment. In this sense it is similar to Revelation where the exaltation of the Lamb provokes the initiation of the whole eschatological drama, in which the seer and other prophetic voices have their part to play (chap. 10). Until the Restrainer is removed there cannot be the manifestation of the antichrist figure. The coming of the man of lawlessness will be accompanied by signs and wonders which will deceive those who are on the way to destruction, just as the activity of the beast and the false prophet deceive the nations of the earth in Rev 13:7 and 12ff. Finally the Lord Jesus will slay the man of lawlessness with the breath of his mouth.

C. Synoptic Eschatological Discourses

When viewed in the light of Rev 19:11f. the synoptic eschatological discourses (Matthew 24–25; Mark 13; Luke 21) show some remarkable omissions (Wenham 1984). It is true that they manifest the same kind of preoccupations with the messianic woes which are so characteristic of several eschatological passages from writings of this period of Judaism. While there may well be some kind of connection between the sort of focus of evil which is outlined so cryptically in Mark 13:14 and the hubris of lawlessness mentioned in 2 Thessalonians, nothing is said about the effects of the coming of the Son of Man on the forces of evil. Indeed, the description of the coming of the Son of Man in all three Synoptic Gospels is linked explicitly with the vindication of the elect, thus focusing on the final aspect of the messianic drama in the vision of the man from the sea in *4 Ezra* 13. The certainty of vindication is there but the lot of the elect when they have been gathered from the four corners of the earth is not touched on at all in Mark. The element of judgment at the Parousia of the Son of Man is not entirely absent, however, from the Synoptic discourses as the climax of the Matthean version is the account of the final assize with the Son of Man sitting on God's throne separating the sheep from the goats. But here as elsewhere in these discourses the focus of attention is on the present response of the elect. It is the recognition of the heavenly Son of Man in the brethren who are hungry, thirsty, strangers, naked, weak and imprisoned in the present age, who will inherit the kingdom prepared by God from the foundation of the world.

Similarly in Markan discourse, the preoccupation of the bulk of the material is not so much the satisfaction of curiosity about the details of the times and seasons so much as dire warnings of the threat of being led astray, of failing at the last and of the need to be ready and watchful to avoid the worst of the disasters which are to come. In the bleak moments of the last days in Jerusalem there is little attempt to dwell on the privileges of discipleship (though an eschatological promise is made to the disciples a little later in the Lukan version in Luke 22:29f. in the context of the supper discourse). It is not a future without hope but the thoughts of the hearers are made to dwell on responsibilities in the short medium term as the essential prerequisite of achieving millennial bliss. These are sentiments which are very much to the fore in *4 Ezra* where a convincing theodicy and the minutiae of eschatological destiny are relegated to the need to follow the precepts of the Most High in order to achieve eternal life. In comparison with the more extended accounts of the coming of the new age to be found in other material, both Christian and Jewish, the Synoptic Discourses concentrate on the period of strife and tribulation leading up to the coming of the Son of Man, what happens thereafter is not explored. In the Lukan account, however, there is the expectation that the arrival of the Son of Man is but the beginning of the process of liberation, for which the tribulations and destruction had been the prelude. This point is made very clearly in the climax of the discourse in Luke 21:26ff: "When these things come to pass, stand up right and hold your heads high, because your liberation draws near" (v 28). It is only when that which has been described in the series of predictions comes to pass that the kingdom of God begins to draw near. The implication is that the kingdom does not arrive with the coming of the Son of Man; that is only part of the eschatological drama whose climax is still to come, when there will be a reversal of Jerusalem's fortunes (v 24). Indeed, that is exactly what we would suppose if we followed the account in Revelation where the arrival of the Rider on the White Horse is the prelude to the struggle which must precede the establishment of the messianic kingdom.

D. Gospel of John

The Johannine Paraclete offered a compensation for the return of Jesus. Indeed, there are occasions in the farewell discourses (John 14–17) that the coming of Jesus and the coming of the Spirit/Paraclete are closely linked (Johnston 1970). What is not in doubt is that the Paraclete's function is to act as a replacement for the departed Jesus (John 14:15ff cf. John 16:9ff). This would become particularly appropriate at a time when the living exponent of the link with the past (such an important theme in the Johannine writings, e.g., John 1:14; 1 John 1:1 and John 21) had died. The Paraclete comes to the disciples; the world cannot receive him; and it is the Paraclete who enables the disciples to maintain their connection with the basic revelation of God, the Logos who makes the Father known (John 14:17ff; 15:26). The Paraclete thus points back to Jesus, the Word made flesh, and is in some sense at least a successor to Jesus, a compensation by his presence for Jesus' absence with the Father. See also PARACLETE.

The disciples are those to whom Jesus comes. The one who loves Jesus and keeps his commandments will be loved by him and Jesus will manifest himself to that disciple (John 14:21); indeed, to that disciple will both the father and the Son come and make their home (14:23). The dwellings which Jesus goes to prepare for the disciples with the father can be enjoyed by the one who loves Jesus and is devoted to his words (John 14:2; cf. 14:23). Likewise the manifestation of the divine glory is reserved not for the world but for the disciple (John 14:19). Whereas elsewhere in both OT and NT all flesh will see the salvation of our God (Isa. 52:3ff) and those who pierced the victorious Son of Man will look upon him in glory (Rev 1:9; cf. Mark 14:62), the world cannot see the returning Jesus. The goal of the new age in Revelation is that those who bear the name of God on their foreheads (Rev 22:3f) will see God face to face. In John this is part of the bliss reserved for the disciples in heaven. There they will be with him and see his glory (17:24).

Whatever hope there may be for the future (and there are signs that the Fourth Gospel has not moved entirely to a realized eschatology), the focus is on the first coming as the ultimate moment to which the witness of the community and the Spirit-Paraclete both point. Those who love Jesus and keep his commandments are those to whom the incarnate Son of Man comes and with whom the Father and the Son make their abode (John 14:21, 23). The presence of the eschatological glory among the disciples who love him has about it a "vertical" dimension in which the coming son of man is not primarily a figure who appears as a reproach to the nations. The lack of concern for the future of the world is not because the Johannine community is disappointed because of the nonfulfillment of the Promise but because of the concentration on those who are of the light rather than the children of darkness outside the elect group (Meeks 1972).

E. Delay of the Parousia

A question which always arises when the doctrine of Parousia is discussed is the issue of the problem caused for Christians of the nonfulfillment of the expectation. This theory is one which has been extraordinarily influential within biblical exegesis over the last century or so. The classic theory associated with Schweitzer (1931) and Werner (1957) which ascribes the emergence of orthodox Christian doctrine as part of the response to the problem caused by the delay has been subjected to critical scrutiny over the years (also Grässer 1957). There is little doubt that the explicit evidence for the delay of the Parousia being a problem within primitive Christianity is not as large as is often suggested; 2 Peter 3 is in fact a rather exceptional piece of evidence (Käsemann 1964). Other passages which are often mentioned in Matthew and Luke, for example, have to be set alongside other indications which point in the opposite direction. But while one would want to question the view that the delay of the Parousia must have been a problem, it would be wrong to dismiss some of the issues which this particular theory has highlighted. Early Christianity may have dealt with nonfulfillment of its grandiose hopes by intensifying those hopes such as we find, for example, in the vigorous expectation which is to be found in the pages of Matthew's gospel (Bornkamm 1963). The departure of apostolic figures may have caused a crisis of confidence within nascent Christianity. The apostle Paul's theology and self-understanding cannot be properly understood without reference to his expectation of the partial presence and imminent expectation of a new age. For example, the mission to the gentiles and probably also the collection for the saints in Jerusalem may have been linked with the framework of an eschatological drama in which Paul is a crucial actor. Thus it would be appropriate to consider the effect of Paul's departure on that doctrinal construction in which Paul's role was so important.

The issue can be illuminated by reference to Karl Mannheim's (1960) discussion of the utopian or, to use Mannheim's terms, "chiliastic mentality." One aspect of this type, he argues, is the way in which the present moment becomes the Kairos, the moment to take decisive action. The utopian then takes it upon himself:

> to "enable the absolute to interfere with the world and condition actual events" (p. 192) . . . the present becomes the breach through which what was previously inward bursts out suddenly, takes hold of the outer world and transforms it (p. 193) . . . the chiliast is always on his toes awaiting the propitious moment . . . he is not actually concerned with the millennium to come; what is important for him is that it has happened here and now . . . the chiliastic mentality has no sense for the process of becoming; it was sensitive only to the abrupt moment, the present pregnant with meaning (p. 195).

That sense of destiny which probably undergirded Paul's self-understanding and his activity actually enabled his thinking to cohere as an expression of the outlook of one who believed himself called to be an agent in the dawn of the new age, the means by which the gentiles became fellow heirs of the commonwealth of Israel. Once that sense of being part of the "propitious moment" disappears, however, the understanding of present activity as an integral part of that drama and its relationship with the future consummation of the divine purposes gradually disappears also. When that happens it does become more difficult to see that future consummation as anything other than an article of faith rather than a goal in which present activity forms an indispensable part in "interfering with the world and conditioning actual events."

Something similar may be found in the appendix to the gospel of John. One issue which is touched on in the closing verses of the chapter is the problem posed by the death of the Beloved Disciple. John 21:23 indicates that there was an expectation current among the members of the community that this disciple would not die before the return of Jesus. Now that he has, a question mark has been placed about the future coming of Jesus; the sense of being part of a "propitious moment," the "present pregnant with meaning" have been replaced by bewilderment in the face of the departure of a figure who had hitherto been the key to the ongoing story of the community. Indeed, the outlook of the community and its view of its future have been deprived of their eschatological significance. Accordingly, the basis for that view is questioned and the tradition on which it is based is subjected to scrutiny.

Early Christianity had ample resources for dealing with the nonfulfillment of their hopes, particularly from within precisely that vehicle of expression of that hope. The apocalypses are interested in the world above where God's reign is acknowledged by the heavenly host and where the apocalyptic seer can have access to the repository of those purposes of God for the future world (Rowland 1982 and 1985). Thus the apocalyptic seer can glimpse either in the heavenly books about the mysteries of eschatology or be offered a preview of what will happen in human history in the future. In most apocalypses that experience of a disclosure of the heavenly mysteries is reserved for the apocalyptic seer, but it was perfectly possible to extend that privilege to a wider group. It is that which we find in different forms in the *Hōdāyôth* (1QH) and the *Odes of Solomon* both of which offer the elect group a present participation in the lot of heaven and a foretaste of the glory which is to come. The identification of the ecclesia of the elect with Christ in the heavenly places is stressed in the letter to the Ephesians (1:21; cf. 3:5ff), so that the present life of the Church becomes a glimpse, a foretaste of the kingdom of God, just as the Spirit enables the believers to regard the present as a participation "in the powers of the age to come" (Heb 6:5) (Lincoln 1981).

The privilege granted to the apocalyptic seer of glimpsing the glory which is to come can be paralleled also in aspects of Paul's understanding of apostleship. See APOSTLE. The presence of the apostle whether in person, coworker, or through letter represented the presence of Christ confronting his congregations (Rom 15:14ff; 1 Cor 4:14ff; 1 Cor 5:3ff; Phil 2:12). When he finally reaches Rome he promises that his coming will bring blessing (Rom 15:29). Like the Risen Christ who stands in the midst of his churches, in Rev 1:13ff the apostle of Christ comes as a threat and a promise: a threat to those who have lost their first love or exclude the Messiah and his apostle; a promise of blessing at his coming for those who conquer. The direct commission from God not from other men to be an apostle of Jesus Christ (Gal 1:1) is central to Paul's role. That has set him apart like Jeremiah before him. He is no ordinary mortal sent by the God of Israel but one in whom the presence of the Messiah dwelt, as bearer of the marks of his death (Gal 6.17; 2 Cor 4.10; 2 Cor 10.10; Phil 3.10) (Funk 1967).

F. Conclusions

We saw in examining the Synoptic discourses that there is in fact very little attempt made to sketch the character of the liberation which draws near. The sketch of the ideal society or the ideal world is lacking, a mark of either a lack of any political realism or of a merely utopian fixation. But we should attempt to assess the significance of such an absence, for it would be wrong to suppose that the early Christian writings are devoid of any hope for a better world. Rather they prefer to hint at their conviction that one is coming without being too precise about what it will involve. It is the language of myth and metaphor which is to the fore rather than the offering of any detailed political manifesto. The point is made by the markers in the book of Revelation itself. The reader is reminded at the start of the vision of the Rider on the White Horse that discourse of a very different kind is being used here. The reference to the open heaven is a sign that we have to do with attempts to evoke rather than to describe exhaustively what is to come. It is about what is beyond in the sense that it is both future and different from the patterns of society currently offered. To speak of it, therefore, demands a language which is both less precise and yet more potent and suggestive, a language which after all is what is appropriate when one sets out to speak of that which is still to come.

The book of Revelation offers a timely reminder in its own form about supposing that its preoccupation with eschatological matters offers an opportunity to avoid the more challenging preoccupations of the present. Thus, the vision of hope inaugurated by the exaltation of the Lamb is set within the framework of the Letters of the Seven Churches. Even if we can discern a preponderance of "religious" issues in these letters (warnings against false teaching, suspicion of false prophecy, loss of an initial religious enthusiasm), we should probably regard the issues being touched on here as typical of a complacent second generation religious movement which is making too many accommodations with the surrounding culture and which needs to be brought back once again to its countercultural affirmation in the light of its witness to the new age. Thus the promise of a part in the New Jerusalem is linked with present behavior. The readers of the Apocalypse are not allowed to dream about millennial bliss without being brought face to face with the obstacles which stand in the way of its fulfillment and the costly part to be played by them in that process: they have to wash their robes and make them white in the blood of the Lamb, and avoid being marked with the mark of The Beast.

Similarly the eschatological discourse in the Synoptic Gospels must not be separated from th narrative of Jesus' proclamation and inauguration of the reign of God. It is that context which is necessary to prevent the discourse about the future becoming the goal of the narrative. Discipleship involves sharing the way of the cross of the Son of Man as he goes up to Jerusalem. What is offered to the disciple is the sharing of the cup of suffering of the Son of Man rather than the promise of sitting at his right hand and his left when he reigns on earth. It is not that this request is repudiated but, as the eschatological discourse makes plain, there can be no escape from the painful reality of the present witness with its need to endure the tribulations which precede the vindication. That is the challenge which faces those who wish to live out the messianic narrative in their own lives; no short cuts to the messianic reign are to be found here.

Within the NT the promise of his coming is found in different forms and functions in various ways. In 1 Thessalonians, that classic proof-text of the rapture of the saints, the concern is reassurance. However numerous may have been the words of the Lord known to Paul relating to this episode the piece chosen by him is intended to reassure the elect that even those who die before the coming of the Messiah will not forfeit the right to share in the privileges of that messianic period. We are told nothing of what will happen after the rapture; but in 1 Thessalonians that is not important, as the point of quoting the word of the Lord is to reassure rather than to provide information about what will happen hereafter. As such this passage, fragmentary as it is, conveys little of the threat to and struggle to be undergone by the disciples of Jesus which we find when we read the parallel passages in the wider contexts of Mark 13 and Matthew 24–25. Despite the similar promise to the elect in Mark 13:26 that they will be gathered by the returning Son of Man that deliverance is on the other side of the period of great tribulation from which they are not exempt and which promises real risks of apostasy (cf. Rom 8:19ff). Similarly in Rev 19:11ff the coming of the Messiah is a threat even to the elect. In Rev 1:13ff the Risen Christ may stand among his churches but frequently finds himself on the outside knocking at the door (Rev 3:21) and reproving those who have lost their first love (2:4f). All the inhabitants of the earth run the risk of falling for the illusion of greatness created by the Beast and its agents and finding that the same apocalyptic light which lights the way to the wedding feast of the elect shines with anger on the wicked (Jacob Boehme quoted by Bloch 1972: 182).

Bibliography

Bloch, E. 1972. *Atheism in Christianity.* London.

Bornkamm, G. 1963. *Tradition and Interpretation in Matthew's Gospel.* London.

Davies, W. D. 1965. *Paul and Rabbinic Judaism.* London.

Funk, R. et al. 1967. *Christian History and Interpretation.* Cambridge.

Gager, J. 1975. *Kingdom and Community.* Englewood Cliffs, NJ.

Glasson, T. F. 1963. *The Second Advent.* London.

Grässer, E. 1957. *Das Problem der Parusieverogerung in den Synoptischen Evangelien und in der Apostelgeschichte.* BZNW 22. Berlin.

Jewett, R. 1986. *The Thessalonian Correspondence.* Philadelphia.

Johnston, G. 1970. *The Spirit Paraclete in the Fourth Gospel.* Cambridge.

Käsemann, E. 1964. *Essays on New Testament Themes.* London.

Kümmel, W. G. 1966. *Introduction to the New Testament.* Trans. A. J. Mattill, Jr. Nashville.

Lincoln, A. 1981. *Paradise Now and Not Yet.* Cambridge.

Mannheim, K. 1960. *Ideology and Utopia.* London.

Meeks, W. 1972. The Man from Heaven in Johannine Sectarianism. *JBL* 91: 44–72.

Moore, A. L. 1966. *The Parousia in the New Testament.* Leiden.

Rissi, M. 1972. *The Future of the World.* London.

Rowland, C. 1982. *The Open Heaven.* London.

———. 1985. *Christian Origins.* London.

Schweitzer, A. 1931. *The Mysticism of Paul the Apostle.* London.

Wenham, D. 1984. *The Rediscovery of Jesus' Eschatological Discourse.* Sheffield.

Werner, M. 1957. *The Formation of Christian Dogma.* London.

CHRISTOPHER ROWLAND

PARSHANDATHA (PERSON) [Heb *paršandātāʾ*]. One of the ten sons of Haman (Esth 9:7). On problems surrounding this list of names ADALIA (PERSON). Parshandata (LXX *pharsannestain*) is the same name as Aramaic *pršndt* attested on a (late Achaemenid?) Mesopotamian seal. It perhaps renders Old Iranian **Pṛšanta-dāta-* "born to a multicolored person" (Zadok 1986: 108f).

Bibliography

Zadok, R. 1986. Notes on Esther. *ZAW* 98: 105–10.

PETER BEDFORD

PARTHIANS [Gk *Parthoi*]. An Iranian people who developed an empire (ca. 238 B.C.E.–224 C.E.) second only to Rome, a few of whom were present in Jerusalem at the feast of Pentecost (Acts 2:9). Most Parthians were polytheists but those visiting Jerusalem must have been some of the many Jews or Jewish proselytes who lived within the boundaries of the Parthian Empire (*Ant* 15.2.2 §14). According to Acts, the Parthians and people from many different nations heard their native languages being miraculously spoken by Christians who had just been filled with the Holy Spirit (2:1–13).

While Parthians are not explicitly mentioned anywhere else in the Bible, several of Revelation's apocalyptic scenes were almost certainly inspired by the dreaded Parthian cavalry. Caird suggests that the conquering bowman on the white horse in Rev 6:2 was not Christ, but rather an evil figure resembling a Parthian mounted archer (*Revelation* HNTC, 80). Three features of the terrible cavalry invasion described in 9:13–19 recalled the Parthians as well: (1) their origin near the Euphrates River, (2) the cavalry's bright plate armor (Beasley-Murray *Revelation* NCB, 165), and (3) the horses' ability to wound with their mouths and tails (9:19), suggesting the Parthian's tactics of shooting one volley of arrows as they charged and then shooting another volley over their horses' tails as they withdrew (Caird *Revelation* HNTC, 122). The threat of a Parthian invasion may also lie behind the invasion over the dried up Euphrates by the kings from the East (16:12).

The Parthians first rose to power in the mid-3d century B.C.E. when Arsaces led a successful revolt against the Seleucid Empire in what is now NE Iran. Two great kings, Mithradates I (ca. 171–138 B.C.E.) and Mithradates II (ca. 124–87 B.C.E.) expanded the Parthian Empire westward, not halting until they met Roman forces at the Euphrates River, which became the boundary between the two empires. The Parthians defeated Roman armies under Crassus at Carrhae (Haran) in 53 B.C.E., Mark Antony in 36 B.C.E., and Paetus in 62 C.E. Trajan finally defeated the Parthians and permanently ended their threat to Rome in 114–16 C.E. Their empire disintegrated in the 220's C.E.

The Parthians were influenced by Iranian, Greek, and Semitic cultures. The chief Zoroastrian god Ahura Mazda was widely honored as the most powerful of the deities, but Babylonian, Greek, and Hindu gods were also worshipped and the empire at its peak encompassed large numbers of Buddhists and Jews. See further *CHI* 3.

MARK J. OLSON

PARTITION/DIVIDING WALL. See TEMPLE, JERUSALEM.

PARTRIDGE. See ZOOLOGY.

PARUAH (PERSON) [Heb *pārûaḥ*]. The father of Jehoshaphat, who was in charge of one of the twelve administrative districts in Solomon's kingdom (1 Kgs 4:17). Jehoshaphat's territory was Issachar, one of the districts identified by its old tribal name. Other districts are designated according to cities or geographical regions. This may have been an attempt to incorporate Canaanite territory conquered by David (*AncIsr,* 135). Each district was responsible for providing food and supplies to Solomon's court one month of the year (1 Kgs 4:7, 27–28).

PHILLIP E. MCMILLION

PARVAIM (PLACE) [Heb *parwāyim*]. Presumably an area from which gold was secured for use in Solomon's construction of the Temple (2 Chr 3:6). This geographical interpretation is reflected in most early manuscripts and in the major English translations. The suggestion of the Syriac Peshitta (cf. the Vulgate) that the word is a descriptive category (i.e., "good," "fine") has not generally been accepted. It appears implausible since such descriptions immediately precede this reference (i.e., v 5 "pure"; v 6 "good").

Early rabbinic interpretation, however, was open to a descriptive use of the term when they sought an etymology for the word. It is associated with *parîm,* "young bulls," whose red blood suggested such a hue for the metal (*Midr. Cant.* 3:10; *Exod. Rab.* 35:1; cf. Milik 1959), and with trees bearing fruit *(pārâ)* of gold (*B. Yoma* 21b, 39b, 45a; *Num. Rab.* 11:3; see Del Medico 1963).

An early geographical understanding is evident in 1QapGen 2:23 where Parvain, a variant of Parvaim, is said to be the home of Enoch (Fitzmyer 1971: 52–53, 94). Here it seems to refer to some far-off, exotic land which might even be understood as mythical (Grelot 1961: 35). It is possibly associated with the apocryphal "Garden of Righteousness" (Enoch 60:23; 106:8; Grelot 1964). The actual location of the geographical source of the gold is not clear. Suggestions have been given linking it to Farwa in Yemen or el-Farwein in NE Arabia (Williamson *Chronicles* NCBC, 207).

Bibliography

Del Medico, H. E. 1963. *Zahab parwayim:* L'or fructifère dans la tradition Juive. *VT* 13: 158–86.

Fitzmyer, J. 1971. *The Genesis Apocryphon of Qumran Cave I: A Commentary.* 2d ed. BibOr 18a. Rome.

Grelot, P. 1961. Parwaim des Chroniques a l'Apocrypha de la Genèse. *VT* 11: 30–38.

———. 1964. Retour au Parwaim. *VT* 14: 155–63.

Milik, J. T. 1959. Notes d'épigraphie et de topographie palestinienne: traité des vases. *RB* 66: 568.

DAVID W. BAKER

PAS-DAMMIM (PLACE) [Heb *pas dammim*]. The scene of one of David's military victories over the Philistines (1 Chr 11:12–14). The name is a variant form of EPHES-DAMMIM.

PASACH (PERSON) [Heb *pāsak*]. A son of Japhlet listed in the genealogy of Asher in 1 Chr 7:33. While his grandfather Heber is mentioned in the parallel genealogies of Asher in Genesis 46 and Numbers 26, Pasach remains an obscure figure. He neither appears elsewhere in the Hebrew Bible nor is attributed with any descendants. While some scholars consider such unique names as fabrications of the Chronicler, Johnson and others suggest that this genealogy derives from military census lists, themselves arranged in genealogical form (Johnson 1969: 64–66).

Bibliography

Johnson, M. D. 1969. *The Purpose of The Biblical Genealogies.* Cambridge.

JULIA M. O'BRIEN

PASEAH (PERSON) [Heb *pāsēaḥ*]. **1.** The father of Joiada, one of those who repaired the wall of Jerusalem following the return from Babylonian exile (Neh 3:6). The LXX has *phasek.* The name means "lame" (Clines *Ezra, Nehemiah, Esther* NCBC, 57).

2. The forebear of the temple servants who came out of Babylon (Ezra 2:49). The LXX has *phasē;* the parallel listing in 1 Esdras 5:31 has *phinoe.* Clines (152) points out that Joiada could be a descendant of the temple servant Paseah. On the other hand, it is possible that we are dealing with two different persons named Paseah. Brockington (*Ezra, Nehemiah and Esther* Century Bible, 136) maintains that the Joiada of Neh 3:6 was probably not one of the temple servants because they are said to repair the wall at another place (Neh 3:26). In that case, the Paseah of Ezra 2:49 would be a different person than Joiada's father. It is not necessary to conclude, however, that all of the temple servants would have worked together.

3. A descendant of Judah (1 Chr 4:12). The LXX has *phissēe.*

MICHAEL L. RUFFIN

PASHHUR (PERSON) [Heb *pašḥûr*]. Name of five individuals in the Hebrew Bible and the Apocrypha. The name is derived from Egyptian and means probably either "Son of Horus" or "Portion of Horus" (Fowler *TPNAH,* 64–65).

1. Son of Malchiah (Jer 21:1; 38:2). In Jeremiah 21, Pashhur the son of Malchiah along with Zephaniah the priest—the latter subsequently executed by Nebuchadnezzar (Jer 52:24–27)—are sent by King Zedekiah to the prophet Jeremiah. The two are to inquire of the prophet if there is any hope that Yahweh will deliver Judea from the invading Babylonians (Jer 21:2). While this text does not indicate Pashhur's title or official position, he is presented as a person who has close connections with King Zedekiah. The focus of Jeremiah 21 is upon the message of Jeremiah that Judea must surrender to Babylon; the lives of those who surrender will be spared (Jer 21:9).

In Jeremiah 38, Pashhur, son of Malchiah, is among a group of officials who upon hearing the prophet Jeremiah's urging to surrender to Babylon (Jer 38:2; cf. Jer 21:9), appeal to King Zedekiah to be allowed to kill Jeremiah. Zedekiah turned Jeremiah over to these princes who lower the prophet into a cistern of the king's son, Malchiah. This account suggests that Pashhur would have been a royal prince, a grandson of Zedekiah. This would explain both the close connection to Zedekiah in Jeremiah, chaps. 21 and 38, as well as his association with those who regarded Jeremiah's plea to surrender to Babylon as treasonous.

In 1 Chr 9:12 and Neh 11:12, a Pashhur, son of Malchiah, is identified as the grandfather of Adaiah, one of the priests in Jerusalem after the exile. However, it is not clear if this is the same Pashhur found in Jeremiah, chaps. 21 and 38. In Jeremiah 21, only Zephaniah—not Pashhur—is designated as a priest. However, Chronicles and Nehemiah designate Pashhur as part of the priestly line.

2. Opponent of the prophet Jeremiah (Jer 20:1–6). Hearing Jeremiah's prophesy of doom against Jerusalem in Judea (Jer 19:14–15), the narrative indicates that Pashhur beat Jeremiah and placed him in stocks in the upper gate of the temple (Jer 20:2). When released, Jeremiah pronounces judgment upon Pashhur. This judgment includes a play upon Pashhur's name so he is no longer to be known as Pashhur but as *māgôr missābîb* ("Terror on Every Side"). The judgment also included a threat of death and exile to Pashhur and his family.

3. Father of Gedeliah, one of the supporters of Zedekiah and opponents of Jeremiah (Jer 38:1). It is not clear how, if at all, this Pashhur is related either to Pashhur, son of Immer, the priest in Jer 20:1–6, or Pashhur, son of Malchiah, of Jeremiah, chaps. 21 and 38.

4. One of the ancestors of the priests who return from the exile (Ezra 2:38; Neh 7:41; 1 Esdr 5:25). These descendants of Pashhur are among those who leave their foreign wives (Ezra 10:22; 1 Esdr 9:22).

5. One among those who participate in the sealing of the covenant with Nehemiah (Neh 10:3). It is not clear if there is a relationship between this priest and the "sons of Pashhur" whose return from exile is mentioned elsewhere in Nehemiah (see #4 above).

John M. Bracke

PASSION NARRATIVES. This term usually designates the sections of the canonical gospels that recount the suffering and death of Jesus of Nazareth: Matt 26–27; Mark 14–15; Luke 22:23; John 12–19.

Critical scrutiny of these sections as self-contained narratives originated from source-critical considerations. Schmidt (1919: 303–9), Dibelius (1935: 178–217), and Bultmann (1963: 262–84) saw in Mark 14–15 a continuity that their atomizing analyis did not find elsewhere in Mark, and they posited variously a pre-Markan passion narrative which had come to Mark in elaborated form. Subsequent form criticism focused on the tradition history of individual units (see esp. Linnemann 1970). The origin of narrative details was often ascribed to a process of primitive Christian scriptural exegesis.

The approach here will be literary and generic. The narratives have a literary shape and serve a function within the context of the gospels as wholes. Their literary shape originated in an identifiable genre of Jewish stories, and the narratives developed from pre-canonical sources into the texts of the four canonical gospels and the non-canonical *Gospel of Peter.*

A. Jewish Stories of Persecution and Vindication
B. Mark 11–15
C. Matthew 21–27
D. Luke 19–23
E. John 11–19
F. The *Gospel of Peter*
G. Pre-canonical Passion Narratives

A. Jewish Stories of Persecution and Vindication

The generic model for the passion narratives occurs in Jewish stories about the persecution and vindication of a wise or righteous protagonist: Genesis 37, 39–41; Esther (Mordecai); Daniel 3 and 6; Susanna; and, with modifications, 2 Maccabees 7; and Wisdom 2, 4 and 5 (Nickelsburg 1980). These stories originate as court tales (see also *Ahiqar*) about a wise man who, as the object of a conspiracy, is persecuted, consigned to death, rescued, vindicated, and exalted in the royal court. In Daniel 3 and 6 the courtier is a faithful Jew whose obedience to the Torah and trust in God lead to his condemnation. In Susanna the court setting is dropped and the protagonist is a god-fearing woman. In Wisdom 2, 4 and 5 the unnamed hero, a *type* of the wise and righteous spokesman of the Lord, is identified with the Servant of Second Isaiah and the story is recounted in language heavily influenced by Isa 52:13–53:12 (Nickelsburg 1980: 156, n. 15).

The plot of these stories is embodied in a series of common narrative elements that depict the actions and attitudes of the characters. The stories differ from one another in their specific settings and characters and the particular issues that give the stories their continuity (e.g., Joseph's ability to interpret dreams, Susanna's chastity, the righteous man's status as God's son). In 2 Maccabees 7 and Wisdom 2, 4, and 5 the vindication does not prevent death, but takes place in spite of it.

Three factors distinguish the gospel narratives from their Jewish prototypes. The protagonist is a historical figure of the recent past. Unique status is ascribed to him, as Messiah, Son of Man, Son of God. His divinity gives the narratives a special nuance: a genre that originally described the suffering of a righteous man now recounts the death of a divine being.

B. Mark 11–15

The literary genre of the Markan passion narrative is evident in the many narrative elements typical of the Jewish stories. These elements, of which there are more than in any single Jewish story of this genre, carry two major themes: Jesus' relationship to the temple and Jesus' messianic status.

The temple theme enters the gospel in chap. 11. In a provocation typical of the genre, Jesus "cleanses" the temple, explaining his actions by quoting two prophetic passages, one anticipated a new, eschatological temple (11:15–17). This action triggers a conspiracy by the temple authorities (11:18; cf. 11:22–33; 12:1–12). An oracle predicting the destruction of the temple is explicit in Jesus' private teaching in 13:1–2. The conspiracy reemerges in 14:1–2, usually designated as the beginning of the Markan passion narrative. Jesus' alleged claim that he would destroy the temple and build a new one appears in the accusation before the Sanhedrin (14:57–58). Although the charge is not substantiated, it is presumed at the crucifixion, where mocking bystanders challenge the validity of his alleged claim (15:29–30). The rending of the temple veil anticipates the vindication of Jesus' prediction (15:38).

The set of generic elements that bear the theme of Jesus' messiahship make use variously, and usually with irony, of the titles "Christ," "King of the Jews/Israel," "Son of God/the Blessed": Conspiracy (14:3–11, though the title does not appear, note the anointing); Accusation and Condemnation (14:61–64; 15:1–20); Acclamation (15:26); Ordeal (15:31–32); Vindication and Acclamation (15:39). Different from the temple theme, Jesus' identity as a divine being called "Son of God" and his status as Messiah are present from the beginning of the gospel. Both God and the evil denizens of the supernatural realm identify Jesus as God's Son and holy one (1:11, 24; 5:7; 9:7). His status as Messiah is suggested in the allusion to Psalm 2 in 1:11 and becomes focal in 8:29. In the latter context, however, Jesus interprets Messiah in terms of the "Son of Man" who must die (8:31–33). This crucial modification of any idea of a triumphant Messiah-King, is repeated three more times (9:9–13; 9:31; 10:32–45) in predictions that point the reader toward a denouement in which Jesus' status as Son and Messiah will be validated in his passion and death. Roman irony about "the King of the Jews," ridiculously condemned to die, shadows the truth of his messiahship. The crucifixion constitutes an ordeal; Jesus renounces the temptation that he prove his messiahship by miraculously saving himself (15:31–32), and, by losing his life, he affirms his vocation as Messiah (cf. 8:34–35). In the end, in another unwitting shadowing of the truth, the pagan centurion, seeing the proof of "this man's" mortality, becomes the only human being in the gospel to acclaim Jesus' divine identity as God's Son. Thus, in the context of the gospel, the passion narrative is the key that unlocks the significance of Jesus of Nazareth, revealing kingship in death and divinity in the determination to accept human mortality.

The passion narrative is inextricably connected to the story of the empty tomb. The Jewish stories saw vindication in a rescue from death. The pair, persecution/vindication, recurs in Mark's repeated passion predictions, in language beholden to the Deutero-Isaianic texts that inform Wisdom 2; 4–5. See SON OF MAN. The function of the Sanhedrin's "seeing" the enthroned Son of Man will be to vindicate Jesus' admission of messiahship and divine status, which was the immediate cause of his condemnation (Mark 14:62–64). Although the story climaxes christologically in the centurion's confession—however defective—the narrative pattern requires Jesus' resurrection and exaltation, though neither is described in narrative form.

While, from the point of view of genre, the pattern of persecution and vindication reflects the Jewish stories mentioned above, Mark's passion narrative also sounds this double motif through allusions to canonical psalms about the suffering and exaltation of the righteous one. Noteworthy are: 14:18 (Ps 41:9); 14:34 (Ps 42:5, 11; 43:5); 15:24, 29, 34 (Ps 22:18, 7, 1); 15:23, 36 (Ps 69:21). Although scripture is not cited in any of these cases (contrast, e.g., 14:27), the wording of the psalms is narrativized in a way that was typical of Jewish stories. Through this use of Israel's religious traditions, Mark and his source(s) cast the narrative of Jesus' suffering and death in a familiar mold that others had used to describe the suffering and vindication of the wise and righteous.

Mark's use of a traditional genre and pattern is governed and nuanced by his view of Jesus' unique status as the Messiah and God's Son. Jesus' unjust death served a unique divine purpose. Probably relying on ideas drawn from Isaiah 52–53, understood and nuanced in new ways, Mark's Jesus claims that his death initiates a covenant that will effect "a ransom for many." The idea is asserted in the climactic announcement that prepares for and interprets the passion narrative (10:45) and in the account of the Last Supper which was familiar to Mark's readers from the liturgical context in which they remembered and celebrated Jesus' death (14:22–25).

Although Jewish stories of persecution and vindication provide a model for most of the cast of characters, the plot, and many of the narrative elements of Mark's passion narrative, the prominence of Jesus' disciples and of episodes about them are worthy of special note, particularly because of their negative characterization. This Markan motif is introduced in chapter one and unfolded in the gospel's plot. The disciples' apostasy, recounted in the passion narrative, is an extension of the ignorance and misunderstanding described in chaps. 3–10. The historical setting and literary and theological function of this portrait of the disciples continues to be debated. Three facts are noteworthy. (1) In the pericopes about Gethsemane and the Sanhedrin trial, in episodes not typical of the genre, the disciples' apostasy is carefully contrasted with the faithfulness and obedience of Jesus, the righteous sufferer. (2) This faithless shrinking from appropriate and necessary suffering is linked to Mark's understanding of messiahship and to the disciples' calling to imitate Jesus' suffering service for others (cf. 8:31–38; 9:31–35; 10:32–45; 13:9–13). (3) Mark's allusions to his own time in chap. 13 suggest a polemic against false teachers who proclaim a Messiah much like the one wrongly expected by the Twelve. They also predict that the disciples must suffer like Jesus and they contain warnings against the kind of careless conduct attributed to the disciples in Gethsemane (cf. 13:32–37 with 14:32–42). Thus Mark's christology, which culminates in the narrative about Jesus' unique and saving death, does not exclude a paradigmatic aspect in the faithful and obedient suffering depicted in that narrative.

Mark's characterization of the antagonists is of special importance. In keeping with the temple motif, Jesus' enemies are the members of the Jerusalem establishment—the chief priests, scribes, and elders. Although the historical fact of the crucifixion presupposes condemnation by the Roman governor, Mark's narrative reflects a double tendency to exculpate Pilate and blame the Jewish authorities. In terms of the genre, Pilate plays the role of the friendly helper figure who attempts to deliver the protagonist, and the centurion's acclamation does not come from the lips of one who has been portrayed as Jesus' enemy. In contrast to these more or less well-disposed characters, the Jewish authorities pursue Jesus' destruction. These tendencies, which the other evangelists will underscore, are noteworthy because, with the exception of 1 Thess 2:14–16 and the book of Acts, they are otherwise absent in the NT. Their presence in the gospels and Acts reflects 1st century Jewish-Christian controversy and Christian apologetic vis-à-vis the Romans. Therefore, historical conclusions about Jewish participation in the arrest, trial, and death of Jesus must be drawn with much more caution and tentativeness than has been traditional.

With respect to their genre, contents, and necessary placement in the plot, the passion narratives of the other canonical gospels evidence many similarities to Mark's account. At the same time, in keeping with their purposes, the respective evangelists both emphasize and deemphasize aspects of Mark's account and add traditional and newly constructed material.

C. Matthew 21–27

From start to finish, Matthew repeatedly emphasizes that the Jews and their leaders have rejected their Messiah and that salvation now belongs predominantly to the gentiles. In keeping with this view, Matthew's major changes in the passion narrative expand on Mark's tendency to exculpate Pilate and blame the Jews. The malevolence of the Jewish leaders is evident in a number of Matthean editorial changes. The chief priests and the Sanhedrin seek *false* testimony against Jesus (26:59; cf. Mark 14:55). Different from Jesus' open claim to divine status in Mark 14:62, Matthew's Jesus responds ambiguously, "you say so" (26:64). Nonetheless, he is condemned for blasphemy. Matthew repeatedly contrasts the Jewish leaders' malevolence with the protests of Jesus' innocence expressed by other characters. The chief priests and elders pursue their death plot, cynically rejecting Judas' confession of sin and attestation of Jesus' innocence (27:3–10). In the trial before Pilate, the governor raises the issue of amnesty as a device to rescue Jesus (27:15–18; contrast the crowd's initiative in Mark 15:6–10). Following this and Pilate's wife's divinely prompted attestation of Jesus' innocence, the leaders incite the crowd to ask for Barabbas (27:19–20), and the curse is invoked in response to Pilate's public handwashing (27:24–25). The scene echoes the Judas story (vv 3–10). Contrast is again implied when only the centurion and the soldiers respond to the visible phenomena that vindicate Jesus' status as God's Son (27:51–54). The story of the guard at the tomb (27:62–66; 28:2–4, 11–15) emphasizes the Jewish leaders' hardheartedness. They attempt to prevent the disciples from stealing Jesus' body and claiming that he is risen. When the resurrection takes place, it is they who perpetrate a fraud.

Matthew moves significantly beyond Mark by ascribing responsibility for Jesus' death to the people as a whole, and he makes the consequences explicit. The elders are "the elders of the people" (26:3, 47; 27:1; cf. Mark 14:1, 43; 15:1). In 27:24–25, Mark's "crowd"—here identified as "all the people" (*laos,* the technical term for the nation)—invokes a curse on themselves and their descendants, which will be fulfilled in the destruction of Jerusalem, and the Jews' disenfranchisement as God's people. Matthew makes this point in 21:28–22:10, where he interpolates into his Markan source two parables that complement the parable of the vineyard (Mark 12:1–12) and identify Jesus' controversies in Jerusalem as confrontations inextricably related to the story of the passion and its consequences.

Matthew exploits the possibilities of the genre in order to underscore aspects of the christology implicit in Mark's narrative. He enhances the theme of Jesus' status as God's Son. This title is linked to that of "Christ" in the Sanhedrin trial (26:63; cf. Mark 14:61) and in Matthew's addition in 16:16 (cf. Mark 8:29). He keeps it in prominence in the crucifixion scene through a pair of additions to the narrative element of the ordeal (27:40, 43), which reflect the ordeal element in Wis 2:17–18 and its combination of "son of God" language with an allusion to Ps 22:8. Thus, as in Wis 5:5, the protagonist's vindication as God's Son (Matt 27:54) is a response to the cynical taunt that he prove his sonship by escaping death. Moreover, Matt 27:40 parallels Matt 4:6 and makes explicit that the taunt is a satanic temptation to obstruct God's purpose that Jesus must die (cf. Matt 16:21–23, par. Mark 8:31–33).

Matthew elaborates on Jesus' death as a saving event, retaining Mark 10:45 at 20:28 and Mark 14:24 at 26:28. In 26:28 he inserts the motif of "forgiveness of sins," deleted from his account of John's baptism (contrast Matt 3:1–2 with Mark 1:4). The eschatological aspects of soteriology appear in Matthew's crucifixion account. Cosmic signs, expected on the Day of the Lord, accompany Jesus' death, and the resurrection of the saints anticipates and is dependent on Jesus' resurrection (27:51–53).

Following Mark, and in keeping with his own interest in the fulfillment of scripture, Matthew ties the passion events to scripture and its traditional interpretation. At 26:24, 54 he follows or modifies Mark. At 27:9–10 he uses a typical citation formula. He retains the Markan allusions to the Psalms and adds the language of Psalm 22 and Wisdom of Solomon mentioned above.

D. Luke 19–23

Although the Lukan passion narrative retains the genre, the general order, and the contents of Mark's narrative, its omissions, additions, and transpositions have led some scholars to conclude that Luke used a traditional passion narrative in addition to Mark's (Taylor 1972). While Luke's narrative may well retain unique traditional material, most of the differences from Mark are understandable as expressions of Luke's literary and theological interests, and an independent passion narrative seems an unnecessary hypothesis.

Jesus' negative relationship to the temple is recast in Luke's narrative. The motif is present primarily in chaps. 19–21, where the temple is the setting for a major confrontation between Jesus and the Jewish authorities. Similar confrontations, also between Jesus' followers and the authorities, are a typical feature of Luke-Acts (Petersen 1978). In the passion narrative, however, the motif has disappeared from crucial elements of the genre. The conspiracy is tied to Jesus' teaching in general and not to his "cleansing" of the temple (19:47; cf. Mark 11:18). The accusation that he threatened to destroy the temple is deleted from the Sanhedrin trial (22:66–71) and the taunts at the crucifixion (23:35; cf. Mark 15:29–30). Only the rending of the veil remains, as one of several phenomena that *precede* his death. Most of the deleted material reappears in Acts in the confrontation stories about Stephen and Paul (see below).

Luke's view of Jewish responsibility for Jesus' death is ambivalent. The leaders' malevolence is emphasized. Their plot is a function of wholesale opposition to his teaching (19:47; cf. 4:25–30). The second mention of the conspiracy is juxtaposed to the statement that Judas acts at the prompting of Satan (22:1–3), whose "hour" and "authority" are present when the authorities and their soldiers arrive at Gethsemane (22:52–53). Although at the Sanhedrin trial Jesus twice avoids the Messianic claim explicit in Mark 14:61–62 (cf. 22:67–70), the authorities hear what they wish (v 71). Before Pilate they perpetrate a double lie: he claims to be Christ, a king; he forbids paying tax (23:2, anticipated in 20:20–26). The contrast between Pilate's estimation of Jesus and the leaders' accusations is also developed by Luke. Pilate becomes Jesus' advocate, and his threefold formal statement of Jesus' innocence is underscored by Herod's judgment (23:4, 14–15, 22). The condemnation is a capitulation "to their will" (23:25). By moving the soldiers' mockery to the crucifixion, Luke identifies as Jews rather than Romans the "they" who lead Jesus to Golgotha and crucify him (contrast 23:25ff with Mark 15:16ff).

Luke's ambivalence about Jewish responsibility appears in his statements about the "people" and the "crowd(s)." The "people" react in horror to the parable of the vineyard, while the leaders plot his demise (20:9–19). The death plot in 22:2 is a reaction to Jesus' popular support, not in spite of it (cf. Mark 14:2). On the way to Golgotha, Jesus is followed by a crowd of "the people" and lamenting women. At the cross, in contrast to the leaders, who mock Jesus, "the people" watch, and at the end these "crowds" beat their breasts in repentance (23:35, 48). Only in 23:4, 13 are "the crowds" and "the people" mentioned explicitly in a negative way. In Acts, Luke frequently reasserts the leaders' responsibility for Jesus' death and attributes Stephen's death to them, but he describes mass conversions of the people—though other "Jews" in Asia Minor and Europe persecute Paul.

The christology in Luke's passion narrative has its own nuances. Although for Luke, Jesus is God's Son, the title is lacking at 23:47, where the centurion sees in Jesus' death the evidence of his innocence or righteousness, not his divine status. More central—the leaders' lies notwithstanding—is Jesus' status as the Chosen One, the Christ, who must suffer to enter his glory (23:35, 42; 24:26, 46; cf. Acts 2:36).

Luke deemphasizes the idea of Jesus' death for others. At 18:34 he omits Mark 10:45 and replaces it at 19:10 with a logion that ties the Son of Man's saving work not to his death but to his reclaiming the likes of Zacchaeus. Other parts of Mark 10:35ff appear at the Last Supper, where the exemplary aspects of Jesus' death are stressed (22:24–30) in the context of the institution of the Eucharist—if the long reading is accepted. In spite of this interpretation of Jesus' death "for you", no statement of its vicarious function occurs in the "kerygmatic" formulae in Luke 24 and Acts, though his death is according to God's plan, and forgiveness and salvation are tied to his name. Central is the pattern of persecution and vindication/exaltation typical of the Jewish stories.

Luke's passion narrative portrays Jesus as a model of patient and selfless suffering. At the Last Supper he thinks of his disciples (22:15). In Gethsemane, he heals the high priest's servant (22:51). At the crucifixion the "cry of desperation" (Mark 15:34) is replaced with a prayer for forgiveness, comfort for a fellow sufferer (typically of Luke, an outcast to be saved), and the confident committal of his spirit to the Father (23:34, 42:43, 46). The paradigmatic quality of Jesus' passion is evident in Acts. In chaps. 6–7, Stephen's trial and death are cast in the genre of the passion narrative. The conspiracy results from his claim that Jesus threatened the temple (and Torah) (6:8–14). His vision of the glorified Son of Man (6:15; 7:54–56) parallels the Sanhedrin trial (22:69; Mark 14:62). His final words (7:59–60) parallel Jesus' words at Luke 23:46, 34. His death and the attack on the Christians is a persecution of Christ (9:4–5), and Saul's confession at 9:20 takes up the Markan centurion's acclamation dropped in Luke's passion narrative. Moreover, Saul will have to "suffer" for Jesus (9:16), and his journey to Jerusalem (20:22ff) parallels Jesus' journey in the gospels.

This relationship of the fate of master and disciples is enhanced by Luke's systematic expunging of most of the negative aspects of Mark's portrait of the disciples. They endure with him in his temptation (22:28). Their careless behavior in Gethsemane is minimized, and their sleep is attributed to grief (22:45). They do not apostasize (Mark 14:27–28, 50–52 are omitted), and they are present at the cross (23:49).

E. John 11–19

The Johannine passion narrative contains the major episodes common to the Synoptics: conspiracy (11:47–53); anointing (12:1–8); royal entrance (12:12–19); Last Supper and announcement of betrayal and denial (13:1–30, 36–38); Gethsemane (18:1–12); Jewish trial and Peter's denial (18:13–27); trial before Pilate (18:28–19:16); crucifixion with a final scene focusing on a Roman soldier's action which interprets Jesus' death (19:17–37); burial (19:38–42). The major formal difference from the Synoptics is the presence of the typical Johannine discourses, which function as testamentary instruction on the nature of Jesus' death and on the disciples' life afterwards (esp. chaps. 13–17).

Although John's passion narrative bears many resemblances to the Synoptic accounts, its episodes do not function as interrelated elements of a consistent and complete story of the genre described above. No single issue is the cause of a conspiracy, the substance of an accusation, the subject of an ordeal, and the object of a vindicative acclamation. The temple cleansing (John 2:13–22) has no plot as its consequence. In 11:45–53, the conspiracy, which results from the raising of Lazarus, alludes to the relationship between Jesus' death and the temple's destruction, but the issue is never again mentioned. Although Jesus' status as Christ and Son of God are at issue in the Roman trial (18:28–19:16), they have not been mentioned in the hearing before the high priest, and in the crucifixion account the messianic motif appears only in the superscription. Jesus' status as Son and Messiah is not vindicated at Golgotha.

These differences from the Synoptic Gospels are consonant with the context of the gospel. First, the charge that Jesus claims to be God's Son (19:7) reflects hints and open claims throughout the gospel (contrast Mark's secrecy motif) and follows through on two episodes in which these claims trigger charges of blasphemy and attempts to stone Jesus (8:31–58; 10:22–39). The climactic acclamation of Jesus' divinity occurs in Thomas' post-resurrection confession and the Evangelist's conclusion (John 20:28–31), which links messiahship and divine sonship (cf. also 11:27).

Secondly, different from the Synoptics, Jesus' death is integral and necessary to the plot of the whole gospel. John describes repeated attempts to capture or kill Jesus (5:16–18; 7:10–19, 25, 32; 8:37, 59; 10:22–39). These incidents reflect, in turn, the narrative pattern of John's christology. Jesus, the eternal Son of the heavenly Father, the Logos who became flesh to reveal God's will, is rejected by his own, and this rejection climaxes in the crucifixion. The passion narrative describes the death which is also the Son's departure to the realm from which he came, and the discourses in the narrative interpret this death as glorification and exaltation, employing a paradigm reminiscent of the Wisdom of Solomon. See RESURRECTION.

Through this structurally essential theme of rejection, John raises the anti-Jewish element to high relief. Different from the Synoptics (except Matt 21:45; 27:62), the Pharisees play a major role in the death plot (7:32, 45–52; 11:46–47, 57; 18:3). More important, John identifies "the Jews" as the antagonists who seek Jesus' death (passim). As in Matthew, responsibility for Jesus' death has been generalized from the leaders to the people. Moreover, these Jews are the historical agents of the primordial mythical darkness that opposes the heavenly light and salvation.

Although John's primary soteriological pattern depicts the descent of the Revealer who gives life to those who accept him, and although Jesus' death is the treacherous rejection of the Revealer, John sees positive value in Jesus' death. This paradox is presented at the introduction to the passion narrative, where unwittingly the high priest rightly interprets the death he is plotting (11:49–52). In passages that correspond to Mark 10:45; 14:24, Jesus describes himself as the Shepherd, or loving Friend, who lays down his life for the sheep, or friends (10:11–18; 15:12–15). The motif also occurs, though cryptically, in passages that allude to Jesus as the Passover lamb (19:14, 36; cf. 1:29).

Scholars debate the extent to which John understood Jesus to be a real human being. However one resolves the question, John's passion narrative lacks the features that stress Jesus' humanity and suffering in the other gospels (Käsemann 1968), although aspects of Luke's narrative approximate John's view. Especially noteworthy is John's Gethsemane story, where epiphany replaces agony (18:1–12; cf. 12:27–28, which takes up the synoptic Gethsemane logion and dismisses it). The crucifixion scene depicts a Jesus in control. It lacks the desolation suggested by the quotation of Ps 22:1, and it cites Ps 22:18 and Ps 69:21 not to attest the righteous one's suffering, but to prove how events took place to fulfill scripture and how Jesus orchestrated them to this end. It is in the citation of these Psalms and other scripture that John's passion narrative approximates the motif of vindication. What Jesus does and what happens to him define him as God's agent, but within a cosmic context. John describes not the vindication of the righteous one's conduct, but the fulfillment of a grand divine purpose.

The relationship between the Synoptics and John's gospel is debated. Recent discussion favors independence. This position must explain the following parallels with peculiarly Lukan details: John 13:2, Luke 22:3 (Satan and Judas); John 13:4–20, Luke 22:24–27 (servant motif at the supper); John 18:23, Luke 22:67–68 (double conditional sentence); John 18:38, 19:4, 6; Luke 23:4, 14, 22 (Pilate's triple response); John 19:12, Luke 23:2 (kingship and Caesar); John 19:25–26, Luke 23:40–43 (Jesus' concern for others); John 19:30, Luke 23:46 (he commits his spirit). Collectively, these similarities suggest John's dependence either on Luke or on a substantial parallel narrative.

F. The *Gospel of Peter*

This work exists in one fragmentary copy. It begins at the conclusion of the trial before Pilate and continues with the mockery, crucifixion, burial, and setting of the guard at the tomb. After a description of the resurrection and the discovery of the empty tomb, the story breaks off with Peter, Andrew, and Levi setting off for the Sea of Galilee (cf. John 21). The common opinion that the gospel contained an account of only the passion and resurrection can be neither proven nor disproven. Evidently it included an account of a trial before Jewish leaders, where the issues may have been a threat against the temple (see *Gos. Peter* 26), and Jesus' status as Son of God (see *Gos. Peter* 6–9, 45–46).

Most scholars believe that the gospel is dependent on the canonical gospels. Especially noteworthy are the parallels with material unique to Matthew, Luke, and John: the handwashing and the guard at the tomb (Matthew); the presence of Herod, the repentant thief, the lament about Jerusalem (found in a minor Lukan ms tradition), the people's repentance, the acclamation of Jesus as "righteous" (Luke); the breaking of the bones, and the fear of the Jews (John). Crossan (1988) ascribes many of these elements to a pre-Markan narrative that was supplemented by other material from the canonical texts. Although this analysis ascribes too much to primitive tradition, there seem to be some early elements in the *Gospel of Peter,* e.g., the story of the guard at the tomb.

Whatever its relationship to the other gospels, the *Gospel of Peter* attests the tendency to exculpate Pilate and blame the Jewish leaders. The author heaps up and reinforces anti-Jewish material spread through the other gospels and reshapes other pericopes to this end. Details in the Mathean handwashing scene appear twice (1, 46). The act of condemnation is attributed not to Pilate but to the Jewish king. Actions elsewhere ascribed to Roman soldiers are attributed to the Jews, the people, or their leaders. The request for Jesus' body and the necessity to bury him is mentioned three times in connection with a concern to obey the Law. The Jewish leaders are ready to commit the "great sin" of denying the resurrection, lest their admission of wrong lead to their execution by the people. The element of the miraculous, introduced through the signs at Jesus' death and the description of the resurrection, underscores the wickedness of the leaders, who refuse to repent with the people or to make a confession as Pilate does.

Although the document's fragmentary state obscures the author's christology, some tentative conclusions are possible. The name "Jesus" never occurs in the extant text. The author's titles for him, "the Lord" and "Son of God," emphasize Jesus' divinity, as does the description of the gigantic stature of the risen one. That such a gospel would have been a favorite among docetists (according to Serapion, ca. 200 C.E.) is not surprising, but it is not clear that only gnostics or other docetists could have written it.

G. Precanonical Passion Narratives

Many questions about the shape of pre-Markan passion traditions remain unresolved. The earliest textual evidence is in Paul. The eucharistic text in 1 Cor 11:23–26, which mentions the night, the betrayal, the words over the bread and cup, and an eschatological hope, may reflect a fuller account similar to the long text of Luke 22:17–22. The tradition in 1 Cor 15:1–5 may indicate knowledge of an account of the burial and, perhaps, the discovery of the empty tomb on the third day. Heb 5:7–10, a later nongospel text, knows either the Gethsemane story, or an account of the crucifixion. Form-critical analysis has shown that some of Mark's pericopes have developed from older traditions. The generic shape of Mark's narrative supports the earlier critical opinion about its unity. The presence of doubled narrative elements carrying two motifs may indicate that the material about the temple derives from an earlier running account (Nickelsburg 1980). The strange placement of the story of the resurrection of the holy ones in Matt 27:51–54 suggests that the pericope is traditional. Along with the *Gospel of Peter*'s post-Resurrection acclamation of Jesus, it may reflect an earlier narrative with a high christology tied to Jesus' miraculous vindication. The passion narratives in John and the *Gospel of Peter* deserve close scrutiny. The literary form in John resembles Mark's (even if the elements do not function as they do in its generic prototype), and its parallels to Luke are striking. If it is independent of these gospels, it attests an extensive early narrative of known generic shape. Even if the *Gospel of Peter* is not completely independent of the canonical gospels, it seems to contain pre-Markan material.

Bibliography

Bultmann, R. 1963. *The History of the Synoptic Tradition.* Trans. J. Marsh. Oxford.

Crossan, J. D. 1988. *The Cross that Spoke.* San Francisco.

Denker, J. 1975. *Die theologiegeschichtliche Stellung des Petrusevangeliums.* Europaischen Hochschulschriften 23/26. Bern and Frankfurt.

Dibelius, M. 1935. *From Tradition to Gospel.* Trans. B. L. Woolf. New York.

Dodd, C. H. 1963. *Historical Tradition in the Fourth Gospel.* Cambridge.

Käsemann, E. 1968. *The Testament of Jesus According to John 17.* Philadelphia.

Kelber, W. H., ed. 1976. *The Passion in Mark.* Philadelphia.

Linnemann, E. 1970. *Studien zur Passionsgeschichte.* FRLANT 102. Göttingen.

Maddox, R. 1982. *The Purpose of Luke Acts.* FRLANT 126. Göttingen.

Mara, M. G. 1973. *Évangile de Pierre.* SC 201. Paris.

Maurer, C. 1963. The Gospel of Peter. *NTApocr* 1: 179–87.

Mohr, T. A. 1982. *Markus- und Johannespassion.* ATANT 70. Zurich.

Nickelsburg, G. W. E. 1980. The Genre and Function of the Markan Passion Narrative. *HTR* 73: 154–84.

Petersen, N. R. 1978. *Literary Criticism for New Testament Critics.* Philadelphia.

Schmidt, K. L. 1919. *Der Rahmen der Geschichte Jesu.* Berlin.

Senior, D. P. 1975. *The Passion Narrative According to Matthew.* BETL 39. Leuven.

Taylor, V. 1972. *The Passion Narrative of St. Luke.* Ed. O. E. Evans. SNTSMS 19. Cambridge.

Vaganay, L. 1930. *L'Évangile de Pierre.* Paris.

GEORGE W. E. NICKELSBURG

PASSOVER MEAL. See UNLEAVENED BREAD AND PASSOVER, FEASTS OF.

PATARA (PLACE) [Gk *Patara*]. A prominent seaport city of Lycia, a region of SW Asia Minor (modern Turkey). Patara, which served as the port for the city of Xanthus (Xanthus = 36°22′N; 29°20′E), is located just 7 miles E of the mouth of the Xanthus River. The importance of Patara is indicated by its inclusion in the Lycian League of which it was the 6th largest member. The ruins of the city are situated near the modern village of Gelemish.

Paul sailed to this city from Rhodes on his last missionary journey (Acts 21:1–2). Most manuscripts record that once at the city he transferred to another ship which was sailing directly to Tyre. The prevailing winds of the area made the direct sailing route from Asia Minor to Phoenicia possible. The Codex Bezae and a few other manuscripts add "and Myra" to the phrase "to Patara" which indicates that Paul switched ships at the nearby Lycian city of Myra (Acts 27:5). The former reading, however, is thought by many scholars to be more reliable than the latter because of the preponderance of textual evidence and the preference for the Alexandrian over the Western text.

Patara was colonized at an early date by Dorians from Crete. It was highly regarded by the Greeks because Homer lists it as an ally during the Trojan War (*Il.* 2.876ff). The inhabitants of Patara, however, were not Greek, but spoke the Lycian language until Ptolemaic times. The name of the city is linked with Patarus the son of Apollo and like Delphi, the city was famous for its oracle of Apollo (Hdt. 1.182). The oracle was only active during the winter months because Apollo preferred to spend his winter months here instead of his normal home on the island of Delos.

The city issued its own coinage as early as the 4th century B.C. Alexander the Great captured the city during the winter of 334–333 B.C. The city was renamed briefly Asinoe after the wife of Ptolemy II after he appropriated the city in 275 B.C. Antiochus III seized the city in 197 B.C., but his control was short-lived because the region came under the control of Rhodes after the Peace of Apameia.

The Lycians were allowed by the Romans to form an autonomous league of cities in 167 B.C. This league developed a unique style of representative government called republican federalism. Twenty-three cities of the league had either one, two, or three seats in the assembly according to the size (Strabo *Geog.* 14.3.2–3); Patara controlled three seats. Pliny records that there were 32 member cities in his day (*HN* 5.101). Except for the brief control of Brutus in 42 B.C., the region enjoyed relative freedom until A.D. 43, during the reign of Claudius, when Lycia was joined with Pamphilia to form a new Roman province.

The legendary Saint Nicholas is thought to have been born at Patara, but he became the Bishop of nearby Myra where he is thought to be buried.

Patara was rediscovered in 1811 by the British survey team led by Francis Beaufort, but little archaeological work has been carried out at the site. The protected harbor of Patara which was well equipped with a lighthouse is now filled with alluvial deposits. Several travelers of the 19th century recorded the ruins visible to them. The remains are substantial including: portions of the city wall, a large theater dated to the reign of Tiberius and rebuilt in A.D. 147 during the administration of Antoninus Pius, and a granary erected by Hadrian.

Other information about the site has been gained through the discovery of numerous inscriptions. One inscription notes that Vespasian built a bath for the city. Other inscriptions record the gifts of renowned citizens of the city who had gained power and wealth through their involvement in Roman politics.

Bibliography

Jameson, S. 1966. Two Lycian Families. *AnSt* 16: 130–37.

Jones, A. H. M. 1971. *The Cities of the Eastern Roman Provinces.* 2d ed. Oxford.

Sams, G. K. 1975. Investigations at Patara in Lycia, 74. *Archaeology* 28: 202–4.

Yamauchi, E. 1983. Patara. Pp. 356–57 in *New International Dictionary of Biblical Archaeology,* ed. E. M. Blailock and R. K. Harrison. Grand Rapids.

JOHN D. WINELAND

PATHOLOGY. See PALEOPATHOLOGY.

PATHROS (PLACE) [Heb *patrôs*]. PATHRUSIM. According to the Table of Nations (Gen 10:14) and the parallel genealogy in 1 Chr 1:12, the Pathrusim were among the descendants of Mizraim (Egypt), the son of Ham, the son of Noah. The name of this population group only occurs here in the Bible, but the name of the geographical area Pathros also occurs in the prophets. In each occurrence, Pathros is linked to Egypt, just like it was in the genealogies. As part of the messianic kingdom, God will not only restore exiles found in Assyria and Elam, to the E of Israel, but also from the SW, from "Mizraim, Pathros and Cush (Ethiopia)" (Isa 11:11). In Jer 44:1, 15, God addresses people living in Egypt, including more specifically those living in Pathros, but they do not pay attention. Exiles from Egypt will be restored to Pathros (Ezek 29:14), and judgment upon Egypt and Noph will effect Pathros, among others (30:14). All of these references indicate that Pathros is a subsection of Egypt. The progression of the three Egyptian elements in Isa 11:11 could indicate a location of Mizraim (Egypt) in Lower (i.e., N) Egypt, Pathros in Upper (i.e., S) Egypt, and Cush (Ethiopia) furthest up the Nile. The same progression is exhibited in an Assyrian inscription of Esarhaddon (*ANET,* 290; *NBD,* 883), where Pathros is referred to as Petorisi. This location of Pathros between Memphis/Cairo and Aswan is supported by the Egyptian name for the area, *pꜣ-tꜣ-rs(y)* "the south land" (*NBD,* 883).

DAVID W. BAKER

Upper Egypt had often formed an administrative unit distinct from Memphis and the Delta in early periods of Egyptian history; but the final severance of any direct connection between Thebes and the royal house at the close of the New Kingdom (11th century B.C.) tended to increase the isolation of the valley. By the 7th century B.C., the term "House of Amun," i.e., the great estate of the Theban god who had been chief of the pantheon, was often used synonymously with "Upper Egypt." By the time of Esarhaddon's campaign against Egypt (671 B.C.), *Musru* ("Egypt," i.e., the Delta), *Paturisi* (= the Southland, Upper Egypt), and *Kusu* (Kush) together signified the totality of the Egyptian king Taharqa's holdings, from the Mediterranean to the Sudan.

The Saite kings of the 26th Dynasty (664–525 B.C.) separated off the Southland and treated it as an administrative unit once again. It was assigned a governor and a master of commercial shipping, mainly for purposes of taxation; while for purposes of cultic continuity, a princess of the royal line was installed at Thebes as "Divine Worshipper of Amun." A foreign garrison, including a paramilitary(?) unit from Judah, was installed at Elephantine on the S border. The Persians continued the Saite practice of assigning a single governor to the Southland and maintained the garrison, but did away with the role of the Divine Worshipper. "The Southland" survived in Coptic as *Mares,* the "Southern Country," the precursor of the modern Arabic *Sa'id,* "the South."

DONALD B. REDFORD

PATMOS (PLACE) [Gk *Patmos*]. One of the Sporades Islands in the Aegean Sea located off the coast of Asia

Minor, 37 miles SW of the city of Miletus and 28 miles SSW of the island of Samos (37°20′N, 26°34′E). The desolate volcanic island is 25 miles in circumference, about 10 miles long N to S and 6 miles wide at its broadest point (the N half). Mt. Elias, the highest point on the island, rises more than 800 feet. On the isthmus at the center of the island a Greek settlement has been excavated.

Patmos is mentioned by both Thucydides (3:33) and Strabo (10:5). However, the island is especially important for its relationship to the history of the early church. Patmos is the traditional location of John's visionary experiences recorded in the book of Revelation. John begins the Apocalypse by stating that he was banished to the island of Patmos (Rev 1:9). A cave on a hill in the S part of the island, below the monastery of St. John the Divine, is the traditional site of John's visions.

Roman prisoners and dissidents were often banished to islands, and three islands, in particular, in the Sporades were used for exiles (Pliny *HN* 4:69–70; Tacitus *Ann.* 4:30). John was exiled to Patmos, according to early church tradition, in the 14th year (95 C.E.) of the emperor Domitian (Eusebius *Hist. Eccl.* 3:18–20; see also Irenaeus *haer.* 5.30.3; Jerome *vir. ill.* 9). Legends about John's deeds on Patmos are preserved in the *Acts of John (by Prochorus)*, a 5th-century text pseudepigraphically attributed to the apostle's scribe. John was probably released during the reign of Nerva (Cassius Dio 68.1) and lived into the reign of Trajan (Irenaeus *haer.* 2.22.5), serving as pastor of the church at Ephesus.

The monastery of St. John the Divine was built over John's grotto in 1088 by St. Christodoulos. The monastery library, which still contains a large collection of biblical and patristic mss, is one of the major collections of Byzantine texts.

SCOTT T. CARROLL

PATRIARCHATE. The office of head of the Jewish community of Roman Palestine. The incumbent is called *patriarchēs* in Gk sources (occasionally *ethnarchēs*) and *nāśîʾ* in Heb ones. The office is fairly well documented in legal, literary, and epigraphic materials from the 2d century C.E. till its demise, for reasons not specified by the sources, between 415 and 429 (*Cod. Theod.* XVI, 8:22; 8:29). The incumbent of the patriarchal office, at its peak, wielded considerable power over the Jews of the eastern Roman Empire and was granted high honors by the Roman imperial authorities. Around 240 Origen noted that as a result of the great powers granted him by Caesar, the ethnarch differed in no way from a king. Origen illustrated these powers by reference to the ethnarch's *de facto* competence to try capital cases according to Jewish law (Or. *ep.* 1, 14). And laws preserved in the Theodosian Code show that the patriarchs of the late 4th and early 5th centuries were granted such honorifics as *clarissimus, illustris,* and *spectabilis,* titles used for the holders of the highest offices in the empire (*Cod. Theod.* XVI, 8:8; 8:11; 8:13; 8:15). It is not clear whether all the patriarchs enjoyed the same degree of power and recognition. Still, for most of its history the patriarchal office does approximate the position of a (client) king. The patriarch served as chief magistrate of the Jews, maintained a court and lived in splendor from the income on extensive landholdings and taxes paid by Jews, and the office was hereditary within one family. Let us examine each of these features in turn.

The patriarchs had the authority to appoint, supervise, and depose officials of the local Jewish communities—first in Roman Palestine and by the 4th century elsewhere in the empire as well. These communities enjoyed considerable autonomy in matters of personal status, civil litigation, and even minor criminal affairs. The patriarchs also judged cases themselves, heard appeals, and issued legal rulings. The editing and publishing of a compendium of traditional Jewish law, the Mishnah, by the patriarch Judah I early in the 3d century C.E. also relates to the role of the patriarch as chief magistrate. Since Jewish law did not distinguish between "religious" and "civil" matters, the patriarchs seem to exercise both types of authority. An example of a "religious" function is the authority of the patriarchs to regulate the Jewish calendar.

The patriarchs lived a style befitting a provincial magnate. In carrying out their judicial activities they were assisted by a *consilium* of advisors some of whom seem to have attended on the patriarch at all times. Fourth century sources mention *apostoloi,* delegates, who were sent abroad to carry out the patriarch's orders and supervise affairs in the local communities in his name (Epiph. *Adv. Haeres.* 30.4–12). They also collected a tax from the local communities for the maintenance of the patriarchate (*Cod. Theod.* XVI, 8:14; 8:29). Jewish sources describe the levees conducted by the patriarchs at which clients paid their respects daily in the manner of the Roman *salutatio* (y. Sabb. 12:3, 13c; *Taʿan.* 4:2, 68a; *Hor.* 3:9, 48c). They also refer to a police force, apparently composed of Gothic troops, which served the patriarchs (*y. Sanh.* 2:1, 19d; *Hor.* 3:1, 47a).

The patriarchate was hereditary within one family, the descendants of Gamaliel of Yavneh (Jamnia) who flourished around the end of the 1st century. Gamaliel appears to have been the scion of an aristocratic Jerusalemite family affiliated with the Pharisaic party and active in Judean politics. While the exact status of Gamaliel of Yavneh and of his son Simeon is debated, all agree on the preeminence of his grandson Judah I, referred to in Jewish sources simply as Judah the Patriarch (*yĕhûdâ hannāśîʾ*). It was in Judah's time that the family of Gamaliel began to claim descent from the ancient Judean royal house of David. The claim of Davidic descent provided a Jewish legitimation for the kingly prerogatives of the Gamalielan patriarchate.

Bibliography

The best survey of the patriarchate, broader in scope than its title suggests, is Levine 1979. He includes a bibliography of the important literature till 1977. Following are items published since then. See Linder 1987 for the Roman legal materials, Stern 1980 for the (possible) correspondence of Julian and Libanius with the patriarchs, Rubin 1982 on the account of the patriarchal court in Epiphanius, Dothan 1983 on an important epigraphic reference to the patriarch, and Goodblatt 1978 and 1983 on the origins of the patriarchal office and 1984 on the title *nāśîʾ*.

Alon, G. 1980. *The Jews in their land in the Talmudic age, 70–640 C.E.*, Vol. 1. Trans. G. Levi. Jerusalem.

Dothan, M. 1983. *Hammath Tiberias.* Jerusalem.

Goodblatt, D. 1978. The Origins of Roman Recognition of the Palestinian Patriarchate. *Studies in the History of the Jewish People and the Land of Israel* 4: 89–102.

———. 1983. The Jews in the Land of Israel, 70–132. Pp. 155–184 in *Judea and Rome—The Jewish Revolts,* ed. U. Rappaport. Jerusalem.

———. 1984. The Title *nāśî*ʾ and the Ideological Background of the Second Revolt. Pp. 113–32 in *The Bar-Kokhva Revolt—A New Approach,* ed. A. Oppenheimer and U. Rappaport. Jerusalem.

Levine, L. I. 1979. The Jewish Patriarch (Nasi) in Third Century Palestine. *ANRW* 19/2/2: 649–88.

Linder, A. 1987. *The Jews in Roman Imperial Legislation.* Detroit.

Rubin, Z. 1982. Joseph the Comes and the Attempts to Convert the Galilee to Christianity in the Fourth Century C.E. *Cathedra* 26: 105–16.

Stern, M. 1980. *Greek and Latin Authors on Jews and Judaism.* Vol. 2. Jerusalem.

David Goodblatt

PATRIARCHS, TESTAMENTS OF THE THREE.

Around the figures of the three first patriarchs of the Israelites—Abraham, Isaac, and Jacob—there grew a small body of apocryphal stories now called "testaments." This title, which was given to them at some time in the history of their transmission, is not very suitable, since drawing up wills and offering advice to future generations are not central. These stories, rather, emphasize the inexorableness of death, depict the fate of souls after death, and urge the keeping of basic moral laws.

All three works were preserved by Christians, and the *Testaments of Isaac* and *Jacob* may be originally Christian. Although the existing texts of the *Testament of Abraham* contain Christian elements, it was probably originally a Jewish work. The other two works are dependent on it, and the *Testament of Jacob* is also dependent on the *Testament of Isaac* (Stinespring, *OTP* 1: 903–4). Thus they were composed in the chronological order of the patriarchs themselves: Abraham, Isaac, and Jacob.

A. The Testament of Abraham

There are two principal recensions, a longer one (A), and a shorter (B). Both are preserved in Gk mss. The Gk recension A is supported on the whole by a Romanian version, while B is supported by another Romanian version, and also by Slavonic, Coptic, Arabic, and Ethiopic versions. There are wide variations at each stage; not only are there two different recensions, there are also fairly substantial differences from version to version and from manuscript to manuscript. The stories were very freely handled, and it is not possible to establish "the original text." Despite this, there is a good deal of common material, and there are even striking agreements between A and B in the Gk mss. There seems to have been a core story, best preserved in recension A, which was modified in various ways as it was copied and translated. B is probably an abbreviation of the longer story now found in A. *T. Ab.* B 9:8, for example, refers to "evenly balanced" deeds, but only A has a description of the weighing of deeds; B here has a reminiscence of the judgment scene of A (so Nickelsburg 1972; for the opposite view see Schmidt 1972).

The provenance, date, and original language of *Testament of Abraham* are uncertain. The Gk of recension B has a Semitic cast, which once led some to argue that it was earlier than A and that it was written in Hebrew. On examination, however, the Semitisms turn out to be biblical, and they are probably the result of imitation of the Bible in its Gk translation. Most scholars now think that the story was first composed in Greek (Turner 1955; Delcor 1973: 32–34; Janssen 1975: 198–99; discussion in Sanders, *OTP* 1: 873–74 and n. 14).

The basic story is earlier than the immediate ancestors of the surviving recensions. Although A has an earlier form of the story than B, it also contains more late words and shows clearer signs of Christian scribal work. As it now stands, the slightly Christianized version of A could be as late as the 6th century C.E. This only confirms, however, that scribes handled the text freely. The core story, which depicts a judgment in which Christ plays no role, was not composed by Christians. Yet it also lacks emphasis on aspects of the Jewish law which set Jews apart from Gentiles. The judgment falls on all equally, on the basis of the observance of extremely general moral laws, and there is no reference to specifically Jewish commandments (e.g., circumcision, sabbath, and food laws). This seems to require a time and place of relative peace between gentiles and Jews, when Jews were not being forced by pagan harassment to defend those parts of the law which distinguished them from gentiles.

The second clue to the date and provenance of the basic story is reference to the weighing of souls in *T. Ab.* A 12:13. Although the idea of weighing or balancing deeds is widespread, the weighing of souls is distinctive of Egyptian religion (Delcor 1973: 67–68, following James 1892). Thirdly, the closest parallels to recension A are found in *Testament of Job, 3 Baruch, 2 Enoch,* and *Apocalypse of Moses.* Of these, *Testament of Job* is probably, and *3 Baruch* and *2 Enoch* are possibly, from Egypt. It is thus not unreasonable to assign *T. Ab.* to Egypt, before the worst period of antagonism between Jews and Gentiles, that is, at the latest before 115 C.E. (there were troubles between Jews and others in Alexandria in 41, 66, 72, and 115–117 C.E.: see Smallwood 1981: 364–68; 393–96; 403–9; Tcherikover 1959: 356 and n. 65). It should, however, be borne in mind that ideas "floated" around the Mediterranean, and *T. Ab.* could have been written anywhere that Jewish, Greek, and Egyptian ideas came together.

Some scholars have attempted to attribute the work to one of the Jewish "sects" known from Josephus and the NT. What is truly distinctive about it, however, is not sectarian bias of some sort, but its completely commonplace view of God's mercy, the importance of avoiding heinous sins (such as murder and robbery), and the punishment of those who commit them (*OTP* 1: 877–78).

The setting of the narrative is the time just before Abraham's death. The story of recension A is this: The archangel Michael is sent by God to tell Abraham that his time has come and that he should prepare a will. (This is the "testamentary" element in the story.) He resists and refuses to go with the archangel. Michael then returns to God, who instructs him to show Abraham the inhabited world. Michael conducts him on a tour, during which the patriarch sees people engaged in various sins and calls down death upon them. God orders the tour stopped, since he, unlike Abraham, is merciful and wishes to give sinners time to repent. Michael then takes Abraham to the place of judgment, where he sees souls being tried. They are tried in three ways—by fire, by written record, and by the weighing of deeds. There are also three judgments—by Abel, by the twelve tribes of Israel, and finally by God himself. Abraham sees one soul that is judged to be neither righteous nor wicked, and he intercedes on its behalf. He then repents of his former harshness and pleads on behalf of the sinners whose death he had caused. God saves the soul whose fate was in doubt and restores the dead sinners to life. Michael then returns Abraham to his home. The patriarch, however, still refuses to die. God sends Death, who terrifies Abraham, so that he becomes faint. Death tricks Abraham into kissing his hand. The patriarch's soul cleaves to the hand of Death, and it is escorted to heaven by angels.

The shorter version, B, differs from A in two principal ways: (1) Abraham's view of the judgment of souls comes before his tour of the world rather than after; (2) the judgment itself is much less fully described.

The story is clearly Jewish: its hero is Abraham; the angel Michael is well known in Jewish literature; the first judgment is by Abel, who was one of the sons of Adam according to Genesis; the twelve tribes of Israel also figure in the judgment; the God of the story is clearly the God of Israel. Yet apart from these points, Jewishness plays no role. The sinners of Abraham's tour are robbers, murderers, adulterers, and thieves (*T. Ab.* A 10; B 12). The first judge, Abel, judges "the entire creation" on the same basis, since "every person has sprung from the first-formed," that is, Adam (A 13). The soteriology of the document is that one should avoid heinous sins, those regarded as such in all cultures, and repent in the case of disobedience. Being Jewish or not seems to be a matter of indifference.

The Christian elements in *T. Ab.* as it now stands are these: a concluding prayer refers to the Father and the Son and the Holy Spirit; this is obviously a scribal addition. At two points the wording of the NT has been influential: 11:2–10 reflects Matt 7:13–14 (the theme of two gates or ways is common and need not have been derived from Matthew, but there are a few striking verbatim agreements); 13:13 reflects 1 Cor 3:13–15 (testing by fire is also common enough, but again there are striking verbatim agreements). The work as a whole has not been revised by Christian hands. Its emphasis on common religious views—God's mercy, avoidance of wickedness, certainty of judgment, and efficacy of repentance—did not require Christianizing.

B. The Testaments of Isaac and Jacob

These are possibly Christian compositions (so Denis 1970: 34), written to commemorate Isaac and Jacob on the days set for honoring them in the calendar of the Coptic church. There are more reminiscences of the NT than there are in *T. Ab.* (e.g., the body is the temple of the Holy Spirit, *T. Isaac* 4:15, cf. 1 Cor 6:19; the unrighteous will not inherit the kingdom, nor will homosexuals, gluttons, or idolaters, *T. Jacob* 7:19f.; cf. 1 Cor 6:9–10). It is possible, however, that earlier Jewish stories have simply been taken over for use in the Coptic church (so Stinespring *OTP* 1: 904). These two Testaments exist only in Arabic, Coptic, and Ethiopic versions. They are usually dated to the 2d or 3d centuries C.E. although *T. Isaac* 7:12, which states that the Arabs have designated the three patriarchs as "the holy fathers," reflects the influence of Islam.

Whether these Testaments were originally Jewish or Christian, they add only a few themes to those of *T. Ab.* Neither contains elements which distinguish Jew from gentile. They have in common with *T. Ab.* emphasis on universally accepted standards of behavior, the need to repent before death, and God's mercy and forgiveness. The stories are built around the themes of *T. Ab.*: the time of death and a tour of heaven and hell. In addition, both condemn homosexuality (*T. Isaac* 5:27; *T. Jacob* 5:8). The *Testament of Isaac* champions asceticism—fasting, praying in the middle of the night, abstaining entirely from meat and wine, and not sleeping in the comfort of a bed (4:1–6)—as well as the virtue of charity towards the poor (6:11–13). Enmity towards one's neighbor is especially condemned (*T. Isaac* 5:17–20). The *Testament of Jacob* recommends prayer, fasting, reading the Torah of Moses, giving alms, and avoiding immorality. Generosity to strangers and charity to the poor are urged (*T. Jac.* 7:11, 21–25), especially clothing the poor (7:21; cf. Matt 25:36).

Bibliography

Delcor, M. 1973. *Le Testament d'Abraham.* SVTP 2. Leiden.

Denis, A. M. 1970. *Introduction aux pseudépigraphes grecs d'Ancien Testament.* SVTP 1. Leiden.

James, M. R. 1892. *The Testament of Abraham.* Cambridge.

Janssen, E. 1975. Testament Abrahams. Pp. 193–256 in *JSHRZ* 3.

Nickelsburg, G. W. E. 1972. Eschatology in the Testament of Abraham: A Study of the Judgment Scene in the Two Recensions. Pp. 23–64 in *Studies on the Testament of Abraham,* ed. G. W. E. Nickelsburg. SCS 6. Missoula, MT.

Schmidt, F. 1972. The Two Recensions of the Testament of Abraham: In Which Way did the Transformation Take Place? Pp. 65–83 in *Studies on the Testament of Abraham.*

Smallwood, E. M. 1981. *The Jews Under Roman Rule from Pompey to Diocletian.* SJLA 20. Leiden.

Tcherikover, V. 1959. *Hellenistic Civilization and the Jews.* Philadelphia.

Turner, N. 1955. The "Testament of Abraham": Problems in Biblical Greek. *NTS* 1: 219–23.

E. P. SANDERS

PATRIARCHS, TESTAMENTS OF THE TWELVE.

A book of the Pseudepigrapha that gives the parting words of each of the twelve sons of Jacob, spoken immediately before their deaths to their assembled sons (and grandsons or brothers). For text, see *OTP* 1: 775–828.

A. Content and Structure

In the *Testaments of the Twelve Patriarchs* (*T. 12 P.*) the emphasis is on exhortation: the sons should give heed to what their fathers command them and transmit their instructions to their descendants. Each testament deals with one or more virtues or vices, illustrated by the patriarch's own experiences or by references to the behavior of Joseph, the ideal son of Jacob (the exceptions here are *T. Levi,* which has very little exhortation, and *T. Asher* which has practically nothing about the patriarch's life). The illustrative material is taken from the chapters in Genesis which speak about the sons of Jacob (29:30–31:24; 34; 35:16–26; 37–50) and from related Jewish traditions. The sons should follow the good example of their father (and of Joseph) or avoid his sins. Taken together, the exhortatory passages in *T. 12 P.* give a colorful spectrum of virtues and vices within the framework of the general admonitions to obey the law of God and the commandments of the patriarch.

In all testaments the exhortatory section is connected with a prediction concerning the future of the tribe of the patriarch. It will forget the Lord's commandments and will be punished with exile, or it will rebel against Levi and Judah (the exception here is *T. Joseph*). The final note, however, is always one of peace and salvation. The sons and their descendants are warned beforehand and called to repentance. Only if they obey God's will as expressed by the patriarchs will there be a future for them. These passages about the future actually speak about events that have already taken place in the time of the author(s) as well as of events that are still unfolding.

The closing passages record the patriarch's wish to be buried in Hebron, and his death. The sons are said to have done what their father commanded them: they laid him in a coffin and brought him to Hebron.

The *T. 12 P.* are clearly pseudepigraphical. Their opening and closing passages are influenced by Gen 49:1–2, 29–33; 50:24–26, and their opening passages by that of 4QʿAmram (see below). This writing constitutes a fine example of the (in itself very variegated) genre "testament." Testaments of the form found in *T. 12 P.* are basically farewell discourses that receive special weight because they give the last words uttered by a great man of the past. The spiritual legacy of the fathers consists of closely connected exhortations and predictions, remaining authoritative to the end of times.

B. Textual Witnesses

Fourteen mss of *T. 12 P.* are known; one of these, and the marginal notes in one other, give only extracts, while a second gives only two fragments. The oldest Greek witness (Cambridge Univ. Libr., Ff I.24, ff. 203^{r}–261^{v}) dates from the late 10th century. The most important ancient version is the Armenian, over 50 mss of which are known; the oldest are from the 13th century. The date of the version is disputed, but it certainly existed in the 10th century. Of less importance are the Slavonic, Serbian, and New Greek versions. The Latin version known in many mss has served as a basis for a number of translations into European languages. It has no independent text-critical value since it was translated from the Cambridge ms.

The extant witnesses form two families, one consisting of only two mss: the Cambridge ms plus the "extracts-ms," the latter consisting of all the other witnesses. Here two subfamilies besides some independent witnesses can be distinguished. Reconstruction of the oldest attainable text is often rather difficult, due to the complexity of family II and, in a number of cases, the impossibility of making a clear choice between the readings of family I and family II.

In principle, the whole surviving ms tradition could derive from a single 9th- or 10th-century minuscule codex. In some instances, however, divergencies between family I and family II can be traced to different interpretations of uncial characters. This implies that the last common source was a manuscript in uncial script that was earlier than the 9th century, how much earlier we do not know. The few very short references to *T. 12 P.* in Origen (*Hom. in Joshua* 15.6) and in Jerome (*Tractatus de Psalmo 15*) prove that these authors knew the writing, but they do not enable us to determine the text these two authors had before them.

On the basis of this evidence we may conclude that *T. 12 P.* existed in the beginning of the 2d century A.D.; what happened between A.D. 200 and the archetype of the present manuscript tradition is unknown. How long before A.D. 200 the document was written, and whether it underwent any substantial changes before it reached Origen (or earlier Christian readers) will have to be determined otherwise (see below).

There is no reason to assume that *T. 12 P.* in their present form (or nearly their present form) were translated from Aramaic or Hebrew into Greek. Especially in the ethical passages, so many particularly Hellenistic words and phrases are found that it is practically impossible that they could have been written in any other language but Greek. It cannot be excluded, however, that parts of the material incorporated in *T. 12 P.* existed, at one time, in some Aramaic or Hebrew form.

C. Related Hebrew and Aramaic Material

Since the beginning of this century a number of fragments of an Aramaic Levi-text from the Cairo-Genizah have been known. They partly correspond with the second major addition found in one Greek ms (Athos, Koutloumous 39, ff. 198^{r}–229^{r}) of the 11th century, which is inserted after *T. Levi* 18:2. In 1955 a fragment consisting of part of one leaf, found in the fourth cave at Qumran, was published; it corresponds to the (fuller) Greek text found in the Greek ms, as an insertion in the middle of *T. Levi* 2:3. The Aramaic fragment belongs to a scroll now called 4*Q213* TestLevi[a]; additional (mostly very small) fragments of this scroll and of another document (4*Q214* TestLevi[b]) have been published or announced. Also in the first cave a number of fragments were found, most of them extremely small (1Q*21,* 1–60). There is also a small Syriac fragment.

A full and comprehensive survey of all the Genizah and Qumran material is urgently needed. Of course, the Greek additions to ms Koutl. 39 also have to be taken into account. Unfortunately, we do not know how this material reached the scribe of this ms (or the scribe of an earlier ms copied by him), nor do we know whether he had at his disposal more than he copied. Finally, it is completely uncertain at what time the Greek material was translated from Aramaic or Hebrew.

We are able to say, however, that the Greek additions and the Aramaic material of different provenance ultimately go back to a common ancestor. As far as we are able to reconstruct it, it must have contained a prayer and vision of Levi (cf. *T. Levi* 2–5), a report on the expedition against Shechem (cf. *T. Levi* 6, perhaps also 7), a vision like the one in *T. Levi* 8, the instructions of Isaac to Levi in a very extended form (*T. Levi* 9) and parallels to *T. Levi* 11–13. We know nothing about the end of the document; only a fragment of an invective against the Levitical priesthood corresponding to *T. Levi* 14:3–4 has been preserved. As far as we can make out it was not a testament like those found in *T. 12 P.* There are some links with 4QᶜAmram- and 4QQahat-fragments found at Qumran. Perhaps these three complete documents constituted a series of priestly (final) exhortations and visions of importance for the Qumran community.

T. Levi differs in many respects from the other eleven testaments, and this is clearly due to the fact that its author followed a "Vorlage" very similar to the hypothetical ancestor of the known Levi-material. Whether he consulted it in Aramaic (or Hebrew), or had it already before him in Greek, we do not know. Comparison in detail between the present *T. Levi* and Levi-material known to us makes it likely that the author of *T. 12 P.* abbreviated the text in many places (sometimes very drastically) and that he redacted it thoroughly.

A number of tiny fragments from the third and fourth cave at Qumran have been connected with *T. Judah* and *T. Joseph,* but this connection remains hypothetical. There is, however, a genealogy of Bilhah comparable to the one found in *T. Naph.* 1:6–12, of which 4QTestNapht. 1 II 4–5 (corresponding to *T. Naph.* 1:12) has been published. It has no connection with the medieval Heb *Testament of Naphtali.* However, this testament has two visions that are clearly related to those found in *T. Naph.* 5–7. Although the Hebrew text is much later, it helps us to get some idea of the fuller and more consistent account which must have formed the "Vorlage" of the present heavily redacted text of the visions in the present *T. Naphtali.*

Midr. Wayissaᶜu (found in later collections) gives an account of a war against the Amorites like that described in *T. Jud.* 3–7 (cf. also *Jub.* 34:1–9), followed by a description of the war against Esau and his sons, like that found in *T. Jud.* 9 (and *Jub.* 37:1–38:14). Again, this late midrash does not provide us with the document used by the author of the present *T. Judah,* but it shows that he could consult a more elaborate account of the wars, selecting and redacting material in order to illustrate Judah's heroic deeds.

The author of *T. 12 P.* had much more material at his disposal—e.g., traditions about Judah, his wife, his children, and Tamar in *T. Jud.* 8, 10–12 (etc.), showing points of contacts with *Jubilees,* and numerous haggadic details scattered all over the Testaments. We can also mention a list of seven spirits inserted in *T. Reu.* 2:3–3:1 (reflecting Stoic conceptions), and a list of parts of the human body and its functions in *T. Naph.* 2:8 (parallel to Heb *T. Naph.* 10:6).

There is a great diversity in the biographical material. The *T. 12 P.* are clearly a literary composition for which the author used traditions about the sons of Jacob from various sources. He incorporated whatever he could use, adapting the general pattern followed in each testament wherever this was necessary.

D. Jewish or Christian?

The *T. 12 P.* belong to the Jewish pseudepigrapha of the OT, and have found a place in all collections of OT pseudepigrapha published in the past hundred years. They contain a number of Christian passages, particularly in the sections dealing with the future, but these have usually been explained as the result of interpolation or of a more thoroughgoing Christian redaction. The remaining document is regarded by many scholars as Jewish. Even without the Christian passages it does not form a unity. Scholars differ, however, with regard to the earlier stages of redaction.

At the beginning of the 20th century, R. H. Charles distinguished between a 2d-century B.C. pro-Hasmonean original to which extensive anti-Hasmonean passages (advocating a Messiah from Judah) were added in the 1st century B.C. In 1970 J. Becker assumed a Hellenistic-Jewish "Grundschrift," stemming from Wisdom circles dated around 200–175 B.C. This formed the nucleus of the present writing that took shape in the subsequent centuries by the addition of Hellenistic-Jewish homilies, apocalyptic visions, midrashic expositions, etc. In 1977 A. Hultgård, in an analysis of the apocalyptic passages, found first an anti-Hasmonean stage with the expectation of an ideal Levi and an ideal Judah; later, in the beginning of the 1st century B.C., the emphasis was on intervention by God himself, on the expectation of a Davidic messiah and on the hope of the resurrection and the last judgment. In the 1st century A.D. there was a new redaction, introducing a central eschatological figure called the "priest-savior," the result of the merger of different traditions.

A different approach has also been advocated (de Jonge 1953). There is no doubt that *T. 12 P.* are Christian in their present form and must have received that form sometime in the second half of the 2d century A.D. One first has to establish the meaning of the present *T. 12 P.* (allowing, of course, for possible alterations in the period between their origin and the origin of the archetype of our manuscript tradition) for a Christian audience around A.D. 200. Because the Christian passages cannot be removed without damaging the fabric of large sections of the work, we must assume at least a thoroughgoing Christian redaction. It is very difficult, if not impossible, to establish the exact contents of this "original" (pre-Christian) Jewish document, let alone to detect different stages in the redaction of that document. It is, in fact, uncertain whether one should speak of a Christian redaction of an existing Jewish *T. 12 P.* or of a Christian composition.

It should be kept in mind that early Christians (with some exceptions) regarded the Jewish Bible as Holy Scripture and the great figures of the OT as their spiritual ancestors. They were interested in obtaining more information on those they read about in the OT, and took their exhortations and predictions seriously. Moreover, Hellenistic Judaism and early Christianity shared a great number of ethical notions derived from Hellenistic popular philosophy. Much of the exhortatory and biographical material contained in *T. 12 P.* could serve the purpose of Jews as well as of Christians; it is the overall context in which it functions that determines its present meaning.

E. Ethical Teaching

The exhortatory sections form the kernel of each testament. *T. Benj.* 10:4–5, at the end of *T. 12 P.*, characterizes the many ethical instructions in this and other testaments:

"For I teach you these things instead of any inheritance
And do you, also, therefore, give them to your children
for an everlasting possession;
for so did Abraham and Isaac and Jacob.
They gave us all these things for an inheritance, saying:
Keep the commandments of God,
until the Lord will reveal his salvation to all the
nations."

A description of all that will happen at God's final intervention follows, in agreement with the general pattern in *T. 12 P.;* in this case Israel's negative reaction to Jesus Christ is emphasized (vv 8–10). Yet the chapter ends in v 11 with the words:

"But you, if you walk in holiness before the face of the
Lord,
you will again dwell safely with me;
and all Israel will be gathered together unto the Lord."

The various testaments deal with a great number of vices and virtues. Of the vices we may mention the ignorance of youth and sexual impurity *(T. Reu.)*, envy *(T. Sim.)*, arrogance *(T. Levi)*, love of money and impurity *(T. Jud.)*, anger and lying *(T. Dan.)*, and hatred *(T. Jud.)*. Among the virtues are simplicity *(T. Iss.)*, compassion and mercy *(T. Zeb.)*, natural goodness *(T. Naph.)*, chastity and endurance *(T. Jos.)*, and a pure mind *(T. Benj.)*. *T. Asher* deals with the two faces of vice and virtue, and warns against "doubleness" (the opposite of simplicity). The warnings against vices are more prominent than the disquisitions on virtues. In many cases biographical examples are used by way of illustration. There is no regular pattern in the treatment of biography and exhortation; the author was not really interested in following a certain order as long as he made his exhortatory point, told the available stories about the patriarch, and linked the former with the latter.

The exhortations are also clearly connected with warnings against evil spirits. Beliar (Satan, the devil) and his evil spirits stand over against God and his angels. *T. 12 P.* have no systematic angelology and demonology; in general they think along dualistic lines; also in *T. Asher* where all sorts of "intermediate" cases are discussed, the emphasis is on a serving God with a single mind. Dualism and demonology serve to accentuate the ethical advices and warnings. Often (personified) vices and the spirits of those vices are mentioned together and are virtually interchangeable. The emphasis lies clearly on the struggle of individuals (in their own personal circumstances) with evil influences coming from outside but at work within their minds and bodies.

The exhortations are concerned with ethical matters. With regard to Jewish customs it is significant that *T. 12 P.* nowhere demand the observance of the sabbath, or of circumcision, or of the dietary laws. They assume that the patriarchs—before the revelation at Sinai—nevertheless observed a number of regulations in the Law of Moses; *T. Levi* 9:7–14, for instance, records instructions to Levi by Isaac concerning the priesthood, though in a very summary form (we happen to have here very detailed regulations in the passage in the Greek addition after *T. Levi* 18:2 in ms Koutl. 39). The situation is different with regard to the direct exhortations to the sons of the patriarchs. So marriage with gentile women is forbidden to Levi (*T. Levi* 9:10) and predicted among the sins of Levi's sons (14:6; cf. *T. Dan.* 5:5). Judah mentions his troubles when he married the Canaanite Bath-shua (*T. Jud.* 8:10–12), but in the exhortatory sections the warnings are against women in general, not against gentile women in particular. Joseph, the man who remains faithful to God in the midst of temptation and oppression, marries the daughter of his masters (*T. Jos.* 18:3); no specific conditions with regard to her are mentioned. The author of *T. 12 P.* obviously concentrates on what he regards as the essentials of the law. In *T. Levi* 16:3 Jesus is introduced as the "man who renews the law in the power of the Most High" (cf. *T. Levi* 14:4; *T. Dan.* 6:9). As the new priest predicted in *T. Levi* 18 he will spread the true knowledge of God over the entire world (see vv 3, 5, 9).

A very important virtue is *haplotēs,* i.e., simplicity, integrity, wholehearted obedience to God's commandments (against "doubleness" characterized and condemned in *T. Asher*). *Haplotēs* is the central virtue in *T. Issachar,* and there it is directly connected with the two great commandments, see 5:1–2:

"Keep, therefore, the law of God, my children
and acquire simplicity and walk in guilelessness,
not meddling with the commandments of the Lord
and the affairs of your neighbor.
But love the Lord and your neighbor,
show mercy to the poor and the weak."

These two commandments are also found together in *T. Iss.* 7:6–7; *T. Dan.* 5:2–3 (cf. *T. Gad.* 4:1–2; *T. Jos.* 11:1), and especially in *T. Benj.* 3:1–5. They also occur separately: for "to love (to fear) the Lord" see *T. Levi* 13:1; *T. Zeb.* 10:5; *T. Dan.* 6:1 (cf. *T. Gad.* 3:2; 5:2, 4–5; *T. Benj.* 10:10), and for "to love one's neighbor" see *T. Reu.* 6:9; *T. Sim.* 4:7; *T. Zeb.* 8:5; *T. Gad.* 6:1, 3; 7:7; *T. Jos.* 17:2.

An analysis of the ethics of *T. 12 P.* shows beyond doubt that this writing originated in a community wanting to make clear to anyone interested how one should obey the God of Israel and of the Gentiles. The author is well acquainted with distinctions and forms used in the Wisdom books of the LXX and with ideas propagated in Hellenistic popular philosophy. Occasionally there are notions that have only parallels in Christian sources. In general, the ethics of *T. 12 P.* may be characterized as Hellenistic-Jewish. If it were not for certain Christian elements, *T. 12 P.* could be regarded as a Hellenistic-Jewish document—and in fact many scholars have regarded them as such, removing Christian "additions." It should be remarked, however, that exhortatory passages in many writings of the early Church are in line with Hellenistic-Jewish and Hellenistic ethics; there is very little specifically Christian in them, either.

In this connection it is important to note that Justin Martyr in his *Dialogue with Trypho* distinguishes three periods in the history of humanity. First, before Moses, people were righteous and pleased God without obeying the specific commandments of the law—among these were Abel, Enoch, Noah, Abraham, Isaac, and Jacob (*Dial.* 19:3–4; 46:3). Then, at the time of Moses, the law was given and became a temporary legislation for the Jews. However now, after the coming of Jesus Christ, this law is no longer necessary: ". . . as an eternal and final law was Christ given to us" (*Dial.* 11:2). This law is not only eternal but also universal. Similar ideas are found in Irenaeus (*haer.* 4:13–16) and Tertullian (*Adv. Iud.* 2 and 3).

We may add that Justin, Irenaeus and Tertullian use the word "patriarchs" to denote the "saints" of the pre-Mosaic era, and that Justin includes the righteous Israelites in the final salvation: "The righteous Gentiles will be saved, with all the patriarchs, prophets, and the righteous men of Jacob" (*Dial.* 26:1; 45:2–4; 80:1–2; 130:2). *T. 12 P.* concentrate on the essential commandments and put them into the mouths of the twelve sons of Jacob belonging to the pre-Mosaic era. These commandments have to be obeyed by non-Jews *and* Jews alike in the period inaugurated by Jesus Christ, who is the savior of non-Jews *and* Jews alike. If the sons of Israel obey their patriarchs and give heed to their predictions, including those concerning Jesus Christ, they will share in God's final salvation together with the believing gentiles (cf. *T. Benj.* 10).

F. Expectations about the Future

Much attention has been devoted to the analysis of the eschatological passages in *T. 12 P.* It is here that the great majority of the explicitly Christian elements are found; many different attempts have been made to determine the extent of the Christian interpolations (or redactions) and to reconstruct the underlying Jewish passages. They have also been studied in view of the type(s) of eschatology reflected, and have been assigned to different redactions in different periods in Jewish history (see especially the studies of R. H. Charles and A. Hultgård).

In all testaments except *T. Reuben, T. Simeon,* and *T. Joseph* we find passages announcing the future sins of the sons of the patriarch, followed by exile, (repentance) and return. They represent an eschatological variant of the Deuteronomistic view of the history of Israel. It is eminently suited to describe the entire period from the patriarchs to the present time. It also brings out clearly the intrinsic connection between the exhortations and the predictions of the future. The Sin-Exile-Return pattern allows for repetition. In *T. Levi* 10; 14–15; 16, where the sins are those of Israel's priestly leaders against Jesus, the repetition serves to stress the hostility of Levi's sons. Yet there is salvation for them, too (16:5 "he will . . . in pity receive you through faith and water"). In 17:8–11 we find a description of a (final) seventh jubilee-period, according to a scheme of Sin-Exile-Return + (new) Sin, and in chap. 18 there follows a (Christian) description of a new priest as savior. In *T. Zeb.* 9:5–9 we find two Sin-Exile-Return passages with a short (Christian) savior passage in between. The second passage ends with a reference to the time of consummation, according to *T. Zeb.* 10 the time of the resurrection of the patriarch and (the faithful of) his tribe. Also, in *T. Naph.* 4 and *T. Asher* 7 history repeats itself. In the first instance Jesus Christ appears at the end (v 5); in the second at the end of the first sequence (v 3). We may add that *T. Jud.* 24, portraying a king as savior, follows after the Sin-Exile-Return sequence in *T. Jud.* (18:1); 23:1–5, and is, in turn, followed by a resurrection passage in chap. 25.

In the return element of the Sin-Exile-Return passage—as well as in the savior passages (to be supplemented with *T. Dan.* 5:10b–13 attached to the announcement of the salvation from Judah and Levi) and the resurrection passages (also in *T. Sim.* 6:7, and in *T. Benj.* 10:6–10 mentioned in the previous section)—there is no doubt that in the end the descendants of the patriarchs (i.e. Israel) will share in God's salvation for Jews and Gentiles. We should note that in *T. Sim.* 7:2; *T. Naph.* 4:5; *T. Jos.* 19:6 and *T. Benj.* 3:8b the gentiles are mentioned before Israel.

Levi-Judah passages are found in all testaments except *T. Zeb., T. Ash.* and *T. Benj.* In *T. Reu.* 6:5–7 and *T. Sim.* 5:4–6, (in testaments without Sin-Exile-Return passages) we find predictions of rebellion against these two tribes (cf. *T. Dan.* 5:4; *T. Gad.* 8:2). Here and elsewhere, we find injunctions to obey these two tribes, because Levi will be priest and Judah will be king; in *T. Jud.* 21:1–5 the sons of Judah are told that the priesthood (concerned with heavenly things) is superior to the kingship (an earthly matter). A few times Levi is said to act as a ruler and as a warrior (*T. Reu.* 6:7 (11); *T. Sim.* 5:5, cf. *T. Levi* 5–6).

This idea of a juxtaposition of priesthood and kingship, and the supremacy of the priesthood over the kingship, is a familiar one, and scholars have tried to establish links with similar ideas in the Qumran Scrolls. See MESSIAH. One should note, however, that in *T. Levi* 4:4; 5:2 (cf. *T. Reu.* 6:8) the period of priestly activity of Levi and his sons is limited. The new eschatological priest in chap. 18 is not said to be a Levite. And in the many Levi-Judah passages that announce that salvation or a savior will come out of these tribes (or out of Judah alone), clearly Jesus is meant (*T. Sim.* 7:1–2; *T. Naph.* 8:2; *T. Gad.* 8:1; *T. Jos.* 19:6; cf. *T. Levi* 2:11; *T. Jud.* 22:2; *T. Dan.* 5:10).

T. 12 P. are clearly concerned with the final destiny of Israel. The descendants of the sons of Jacob should realize that the savior of the world has come, they should realize "that the Lord will judge Israel first for the unrighteousness done to him, because they did not believe that God appeared in the flesh as deliverer" (*T. Benj.* 10:8). At the same time they may be convinced that, if it lives in holiness and believes in Jesus Christ, "all Israel will be gathered unto the Lord" (*T. Benj.* 10:11). The Christian group that was responsible for the present *T. 12 P.* was clearly concerned with the salvation of the Jews; in their thinking about and their contacts with their Jewish brethren they were certainly guided by the ideas expressed in this writing.

Bibliography

Becker, J. 1970. *Untersuchungen zur Entstehungsgeschichte der Testamente der Zwölf Patriarchen.* AGJU 8. Leiden.

———. 1974. *Die Testamente der Zwölf Patriarchen.* JSHRZ 3/1. Gütersloh.

Charles, R. H. 1908a. *The Greek Versions of the Testaments of the Twelve Patriarchs.* Oxford.

———. 1908b. *The Testaments of the Twelve Patriarchs Translated from the Editor's Greek Text.* London.

Hollander, H. W. 1981. *Joseph as an Ethical Model in the Testaments of the Twelve Patriarchs.* SVTP 6. Leiden.

Hollander, H. W., and de Jonge, M. 1985. *The Testaments of the Twelve Patriarchs. A Commentary.* SVTP 8. Leiden.

Hultgård, A. 1977. *L'eschatologie des Testaments des Douze Patriarches I. Interprétation des Textes.* Acta Universitatis Uppsaliensis, Hist. Rel. 6. Uppsala.

———. 1982. *L'eschatologie des Testaments des Douze Patriarches II. Composition de l'ouvrage, textes et traductions.* Acta Universitatis Uppsaliensis, Hist. Rel. 7. Uppsala.

Jonge, M. de. 1953. *The Testaments of the Twelve Patriarchs: A Study of their Text, Composition and Origin.* Assen.

———, ed. 1975. *Studies on the Testaments of the Twelve Patriarchs: Text and Interpretation.* SVTP 3. Leiden.

———, et al. 1978. *The Testaments of the Twelve Patriarchs: A Critical Edition of the Greek Text.* PVTG 1/2. Leiden.

———. 1984. The Testaments of the Twelve Patriarchs. Pp. 505–600 in *The Apocryphal Old Testament,* ed. H. F. D. Sparks. Oxford.

MARINUS DE JONGE

PATRIMONY. See FAMILY.

PATROBAS (PERSON) [Gk *Patrobas*]. A Roman Christian who received greetings from Paul in Rom 16:14. He was probably a gentile Christian. See NEREUS. A member of a Roman house-church (Lampe *StadtrChr,* 301) Asyncritus, Phlegon, Hermes, and Hermas were quoted by name, while the other participants were mentioned only generally as "the brethren who are with them." The five persons therefore may have played leading roles in the house-church. Patrobas' name is a short form of "Patrobios." According to the epigraphical and literary sources from the city of Rome, both names occur only very rarely ("Patrobios" eight times, "Patrobas" never except for one fictitious imperial freedman in Martial 2.32); Patrobas therefore may have been an immigrant in the capital (Lampe *StadtrChr,* 139–41, 148).

PETER LAMPE

PATROCLUS (PERSON([Gk *Patroklos*]. The father of Nicanor, who in 2 Macc 8:9 is appointed by Ptolemy to lead a large force of Seleucid troops "to wipe out the whole race of Judea." Nothing else is known of Patroclus except that he was named after the figure from Greek mythology. See NICANOR concerning whether his son is also the villain of the latter portion of 2 Maccabees (14:12ff.).

JOHN KAMPEN

PAU (PLACE) [Heb *pāʿû*]. Var. PAI. The residence of the Edomite king Hadar (= Hadad II?) who was married to Mehetabel daughter of Matred, daughter of Mezahab (Gen 36: 39; cf. 1 Chr 1:50). Hadad (II) is mentioned as the last of the Edomite kings in the Edomite king list (Gen 36:31–39), whose dating is very questionable, and in the parallel text 1 Chr 1:43–50. The place name could be traced back to the Arabic personal or clan name *faġw*. The LXX transmits it as *Phogō(r),* the Peshitta as *Peʿō* or *Paʿʿō,* the Samaritanus as *Fū* and the Vg as *Phau.* The site is localized in the Gebalene or in Edom by Eusebius, *Onomast.* 168.7; 170.13 *(Phogōr, Phogō)* and by Hieronymus, *Onomast.* 169.7; 171.10 *(Fogo).* It is not possible to locate it more precisely.

ULRICH HÜBNER

PAUL (PERSON) [Gk *Paulos*]. An early Christian apostle who was perhaps the most important and creative figure in the history of the early Church, whose formulations of Christian faith as expressed in his epistles to fledgling churches have become part of the foundation for orthodox Christian theology.

A. Sources
B. Life
  1. Name
  2. Ancestry
  3. Education
  4. Pre-Christian Career
  5. Conversion
  6. Apostolic Career
C. Paul's Image in Later Sources
D. Chronology
  1. Problems
  2. Datable Events
  3. Dating of the Letters
  4. Summary
E. Theology
  1. Methodological Problems
  2. Major Phases in the Development of Paul's Theology
  3. Summary

A. Sources

The primary sources for the study of the Apostle Paul are his authentic letters (1 Thessalonians, Galatians, Philippians, Philemon, 1 and 2 Corinthians, and Romans). Historical information can also be gleaned from the book of Acts (see D.1 below), the deutero-Pauline epistles (Colossians, Ephesians, 2 Thessalonians, 1 and 2 Timothy, and Titus), other NT writings (James, 2 Peter), and later apocryphal literature (apocryphal Acts [McDonald 1983], introductory information in NT manuscripts and canon lists, Pseudo-Clementine literature, Mani Biography [Betz 1986b]). These different groups of documents do not have clear-cut boundaries, though, since scholars still dispute whether or not some of the deutero-Pauline epistles are authentic, and whether the authentic letters contain later interpolations (see the articles on the various Pauline letters). Whether the apocryphal material provides reliable historical evidence independent of the NT presents a further problem, which must be decided on a case by case basis (*NTApocr* 2: 71–74; Schneemelcher 1987–1989; Betz 1986b: 215–34).

Secondary literature about Paul and his writings is vast; no exhaustive bibliography exists. For informative surveys see Schweitzer 1912; Bultmann 1929–36; Metzger 1960; Rigaux 1968; Merk 1988; *ANRW,* pt. 2, vol. 25/4: 2649–2840).

B. Life

1. Name. Paul is commonly known by his Greco–Roman *cognomen, Paulos,* but we know from Acts that he bore the Jewish name Saul as well (Acts 7:58; 8:1, 3; 9:1, 4, etc.). He himself never mentions his Jewish name in his letters, but always identifies himself as Paul (e.g., 1 Thess 1:1; 2:18; Rom 1:1; 1 Cor 1:1, 12–13; etc.).

2. Ancestry. While his Jewish name corresponds to his being a Benjaminite (Phil 3:5; Rom 11:1; cf. Acts 13:21), his Greco–Roman name may have been given to him in connection with his citizenship in Tarsus, a city in Cilicia where he was born and raised (Acts 9:11; 21:39; 22:3; cf. 9:30; 11:25). While there is some doubt with regard to his Roman citizenship, he certainly was not anti-Roman in his politics (Rom 13:1–7). His Roman citizenship plays an important role in Acts (16:37–38; 22:25–29; 23:27; 25:8–12, 21; 26:32; 27:24; 28:19), but there are questions prompted by the flogging (Acts 22:25; cf. 2 Cor 11:25; see Bauer 1988, *s.v. mastizō*) and the appeal to Caesar (Acts 25:8–12, 21; 26:32; 27:24; 28:19; see Conzelmann, *Acts* Hermeneia, 189–90, 203–4). If the author of Acts did have reliable information about Paul being a Roman citizen by birth (22:28), he certainly made the most of it in explaining how Paul got out of Jerusalem to Rome. At any rate, the family considered itself religiously "orthodox" (Phil 3:5; 2 Cor 11:22; Rom 11:1).

3. Education. What kind of education Paul may have received growing up in Tarsus (Acts 21:39; 22:3) is entirely a matter of speculation, although as Acts 22:3 presents it, he had an ideal Jewish education: "I am a Jew, born at Tarsus in Cilicia, brought up in this city [Jerusalem or Tarsus?], educated at the feet of Gamaliel, according to the strict manner of the law of our fathers." This claim suggests that Paul's family moved from Tarsus to Jerusalem, where he received his secondary education (26:4). But this claim must be weighed carefully because it corresponds with the tendencies in Acts to emphasize the apostle's regard for his Jewish heritage (13:14ff.; 14:1; 15:23–29; 16:1–3, 4, 13; etc.) and to link him with Jerusalem (7:58–8:1a; 8:1b–3; 9:1–2, 26–29; etc.). This latter tendency, together with Luke's attendant assumption of Paul's familiarity with Jerusalem, clashes with Paul's own testimony about his visits to the city (Gal 1:22). Luke's picture of Gamaliel is unclear as well (Acts 5:34; see *Acts* Hermeneia, 186). See also GAMALIEL. A further obstacle to reconstructing Paul's education arises from our ignorance of the specific content of Jewish education at that time, whether in Tarsus or in Jerusalem, whether elementary or secondary (see Safrai 1976; *HJP*² 2: 332–34, 415–22; Saldarini 1988: 137–39).

The fact that Paul acted as an international envoy, first on behalf of Jewish authorities (Acts 8:3; 9:1–2, 21; 22:4–5, 19; 26:10–11; Gal 1:13, 23; 1 Cor 15:9; Phil 3:6), then as a Christian missionary, means that he must have received a good Hellenistic education. He gave speeches, taught, wrote long letters, and was involved in highly specialized theological debates. His abilities as a founder of churches, working with many collaborators on an international level, make it impossible to conceive of him as an uneducated and culture-bound Jew from the East. Comparative figures of the time, especially Josephus and Philo show that being well-educated and Jewish did not exclude one other.

Objections to Paul's education as having been Hellenistic include recourse to his confession of being a layman in rhetoric (2 Cor 11:6; cf. 1 Cor 2:1–5) and his use of a secretary (Tertius, Rom 16:22). Such arguments, however, miss the fact that 2 Cor 11:6 is itself a rhetorical *topos* (see Betz 1972: 47–69; 1986a) and fail to explain how his letters became literary masterpieces. These letters—with their skillful rhetoric, careful composition, and elaborate theological argumentation—reflect an author who was in every way uniquely equipped to become the "apostle of the gentiles" (Rom 11:13; cf. Gal 2:8, 9; Rom 1:5). This much is clear also from a comparison with his sometime mentor and associate Barnabas, whose abilities fell short of what was needed. Similarly, Luke regards Paul as well-equipped to defend himself in court, while the Jewish priests must have a professional orator (Acts 24:1).

4. Pre-Christian Career. Before his conversion Paul actively preserved and protected the religious traditions of his forefathers. Considering himself an "orthodox" Jew, he was zealously committed to eradicating apostasy. Going further than his peers, he became a member of the Pharisaic sect (see Saldarini 1988: 134–43) and took it upon himself to persecute the Christian church (Gal 1:13, 23; Phil 3:6; 1 Cor 15:9). Exactly why he singled out the Christians for persecution is not clear, though a clue may be found in his particular dislike for the Christians in Damascus (Gal 1:17, 22–23; 2 Cor 11:32; Acts 9:2–25; 22:5–6, 10–11; 26:12, 20) and relative disinterest in those of Jerusalem and Judea (cf. Acts 8:3). The reason for persecuting the Christians of Damascus seems to have been that, though Jews, they had discontinued Torah observance, doing so as a matter of principle rather than casual neglect. But neither Paul nor Acts provides any detailed information.

5. Conversion. While Paul was approaching Damascus he suddenly experienced a vision of Christ. This experience had dramatic consequences, changing his entire life, self-understanding, theological views, and goals. Whether this vision occurred in his mind (Gal 1:12, 16) or externally (Acts 9:3–8; 22:6–11; 26:12–19) remains unclear, but it turned him from a persecutor to a propagator of Christianity. Christ himself commissioned him to proclaim the gospel among the gentiles (see also 1 Cor 9:1; 15:8, 9–11; Rom 1:5). Although we customarily label this experience Paul's "conversion," this can be done only in retrospect, for at that time Judaism and Christianity were not yet separate religions. In reality, then, Paul changed brands of Judaism, switching from Pharisaic to Christian Judaism.

6. Apostolic Career. a. The Autobiographical Résumé in Galatians. As Paul reports in Gal 1:17–24, the first part of his autobiographical résumé (see Betz, *Galatians* Hermeneia, 72–81; also GALATIANS, EPISTLE TO THE), after seeing Christ he left Damascus at once and went to Arabia, that is, the Kingdom of Nabataea, called *"Provincia Arabia."* See NABATEANS. This mission in Arabia, given the nature of Christ's commission to him, must have been among gentiles, not Jews. We may also infer that Paul did not initiate this mission but joined a venture already begun by the Damascus church, an inference confirmed by the fact that Paul afterward returned to Damascus. How successful his mission to Arabia was we do not know (see also Gal 4:25; Acts 2:11; *1 Clem.* 25:1, 3; cf. Rom 15:19).

Paul emphasizes that after Christ's appearance and commission he chose not to consult with the other apostles in Jerusalem. Why did he avoid this contact with the Christian authorities in Jerusalem? The reason seems to be connected with the Arabian mission. If Paul had persecuted the Damascus Christians because of their disregard for the Torah, and if those Christians had begun the mission in Arabia among the gentiles which Paul joined, then the Arabian converts in turn must not have submitted to Torah and circumcision. The Jerusalem church, however, must have looked at this enterprise with uncertainty or even disapproval, thus rendering plausible Paul's avoidance of Jerusalem.

Three years after his conversion Paul finally went to Jerusalem, a visit that he describes in Gal 1:18–24. Analysis of this trip to Jerusalem has been complicated since the writing of Acts, whose author assumed that Paul had come to Jerusalem, preached there, and moved freely in and out of the city (9:26–30). If we pay strict attention to Galatians, we realize that Paul had much less visibility during his stay there. What Paul tells us is that at that time he saw Peter for 15 days, an interview which presupposes Peter's sympathy with Paul's activity. The church as a whole, however, seems to have been divided, so that when Paul says, "I saw none of the other apostles, but only James the brother of the Lord" (Gal 1:19), he implies that he avoided them because they did not care for him. James, perhaps because he was not a (missionary) apostle, was agreeable to a visit. Did the churches of Jerusalem and Judea, when they praised God for Paul without ever having met him (Gal 1:22–24), know that he preached the Gospel without subjecting the converts to Torah and circumcision? At least we can say that no clear decision had been made and that tensions must have existed with regard to this question. We may conclude from this report that the tensions between Paul and the other apostles issued from their competing policies on foreign missions. Following his visit, Paul set out for another mission campaign in his home territory, Syria and Cilicia (Gal 1:21). It is not clear whether Peter and James approved of this campaign.

When Paul came to Jerusalem the second time "after fourteen years" (Gal 2:1), the mission to Syria and Cilicia had been carried out successfully. Paul names as his main collaborator Barnabas, a Jewish Christian like himself. According to Acts, Barnabas was Paul's Christian mentor (Acts 4:36–37; 9:27). The Jerusalem church had sent him to Antioch where he became the leading figure among the Jewish Christians from Phoenicia, Cyprus, and Syria/Cilicia. He went to Tarsus looking for Saul (Paul) to bring him to Antioch (Acts 11:25–26), where the mission to the Greeks was born (Acts 11:20) and where the name "Christian" *(Christianoi)* first came into use (11:26). From here Barnabas and Saul/Paul were sent out together on a missionary campaign (13:1–3) which first took them to Cyprus (13:4–12), then to Pamphylia and Pisidia (13:13–14:28). That this campaign is the same as the one mentioned in Gal 1:21 (Syria and Cilicia) is probable, but not provable.

The mission campaigns also brought to the fore a problem which could no longer be left undecided: Must the new gentile converts be circumcised or not? Is the church part of Judaism or a separate Christian religion? After considerable disagreements (Acts 15:1–2) and even a revelation (Gal 2:2), Paul and Barnabas went up to Jerusalem, taking along Titus, an uncircumcised gentile convert, as a test case. The Jerusalem conference (Gal 2:1–10; Acts 15:2–29; see Betz *Galatians*, 81–103) saw three parties, two of which had opposite answers to the main problem, while a third group stayed in the middle. After heated debates, Paul and his party (Barnabas and Titus) prevailed, gaining recognition of Titus as a Christian without circumcision; however, compromises had to be made. The Christian mission was divided into two thrusts, one to the Jews (under the apostolate of Peter), and the other under the leadership of Paul and Barnabas, without official titles (Gal 2:8–9). The acknowledged link between the two thrusts was the shared belief in the one God (2:8; Rom 3:30; 10:12). The agreement, which also included the pledge to collect money for the poor in Jerusalem (2:10), was approved by the three "pillars" (James, Cephas, and John), and the delegation from Antioch (Paul and Barnabas), but not by an intransigent third group, called by Paul "false brothers" (2:4). This conference had far-reaching consequences not only for the church, but in particular for Paul's future course of life.

One question which had been left undecided was whether the gentile *"Christianoi"* constituted a new religion, or whether Jewish and gentile Christians were together still part of Judaism. This indecision laid the seed for future conflict (see, e.g., the case of Timothy, Acts 16:1–4, and in general Cohen 1986; Bryan 1988), seed which came to fruition at Antioch (Gal 2:11–14). Confrontation arose there after Peter came to Antioch and dined with the gentile Christians, signifying their equal participation in salvation through Christ. This was subsequently contradicted by a delegation of "men from James" when they arrived from Jerusalem. After heated debates, Peter and the other Jewish Christians caved in to their visitors' censure and cut off table fellowship with the gentile Christians. Thus they reestablished the borders between clean and unclean foods *(koinophagia)*, leaving gentile Christianity outside. Paul, however, did not go along with his fellow Jewish Christians but remained with the gentile Christians. Confronting Peter in an open debate, he accused him of inconsistency ("hypocrisy") in theology and religious practice. The result was a complete break between Paul and the other Jewish–Christian missionaries, including his former mentor Barnabas (see also Acts 15:36–39). Henceforth Paul and the gentile churches founded by him were on their own, though plagued by contrary Jewish–Christian missionaries. To the end, however, Paul never lost hope that a reconciliation with the Jerusalem church might be accomplished, pinning this hope to the collection for the poor (1 Cor 16:1–4; 2 Corinthians 8 and 9; see Betz,

2 Corinthians 8–9 Hermeneia); and intercession by the church of Rome (Rom 15:30–32).

b. Further Data Concerning the Mission to Galatia. The biographical résumé in Gal 1:12–2:14 ends with the Antioch episode, but further data can be concluded from the letter. Although details are missing, the letter presupposes the founding of the Galatian churches. Later, anti-Pauline agitators appear, the result of which is the letter. If the founding visit can be correlated with Acts 16:6, it can also be coordinated with Gal 4:13, and Paul's second visit would be the one mentioned in Acts 18:23. It is, however, not clear whether Acts is at all informed about Galatian churches. Paul's itinerary in Acts appears to be based on good information only in some parts, while on the whole it is the creation of the author of Acts who attempted to fit pieces of tradition into what he envisioned to be a consistent narrative. There may have been journeys that Paul undertook but Acts did not include, just as there are reports about those that seem unlikely to us. The Galatian letter at any rate mentions a foundation visit (Gal 1:9; 4:13). A second visit that would match up with Acts 18:23 would depend on a special interpretation of *to proteron* (Gal 4:13). Following the founding of these churches, rival Jewish–Christian missionaries found a hearing among them, and in order to prevent their drifting away Paul wrote his letter. The founding of the Galatian churches must have preceded 1 Corinthians, since he mentions the Galatian churches and the collection for Jerusalem in 1 Cor 16:1–4.

c. The Mission to Macedonia and Greece. For information regarding the mission to Macedonia and Greece we must rely on Paul's letters to the Thessalonians and Corinthians, and on Acts. According to Acts 16:6–10, Paul went through Phrygia, Galatia, and, passing by Mysia, to Troas. From there he decided to go to Macedonia, responding to a vision of a Macedonian asking him to come. Timothy accompanied him on this trip (Acts 16:1–4), as did Silas (Acts 15:40; 16:19, 25, 29; 17:4, 10, 14, 15; 18:5; however, according to 15:33 he had already left for Jerusalem). Together, these three men (whose affiliation is verified by Paul's letters, 1 Thess 1:1 [2 Thess 1:1]; cf. also 1 Thess 3:2, 6; 2 Cor 1:19) sailed from Troas via Samothrace to Neapolis, the harbor of Philippi. They met their first success in Philippi, where they founded the first church in Macedonia (16:11–40). From Philippi they went to Thessalonica, establishing a church there as well (17:1–9). The next stations were Beroea (17:10–15), Athens (17:16–34; 1 Thess 3:1–2), and Corinth (18:1–17; 1 Cor 1:1–2, 14, 16; 3:5–15; 16:15, 17); in all these cities, churches were established. According to Acts, this concluded the second missionary journey. The third journey began with Paul sailing to Ephesus in the company of Priscilla and Aquila (18:18–21). Rather confusing is a strange trip Paul is said to have made from Ephesus "down" to Caesarea, then "down" to Antioch, and through Galatia and Phrygia back to Ephesus (18:22; 19:1).

d. The Journey to Jerusalem. Another revelation caused Paul to plan a second journey to Macedonia and Achaia, and then to Jerusalem and Rome (Acts 19:21–22). Sending Timothy and Erastus ahead, Paul followed after the riots in Ephesus stirred up by Demetrius had subsided (20:1). He went through Macedonia to Greece, that is Corinth (20:2). These scarce notes, which are based on some sources known to Luke, can be correlated only roughly with what we know from Paul's letters, esp. 1 Cor 16:1–11; 2 Cor 1:8–11, 15–18; 2:12–13; 7:5–7, 13–16; Rom 15:22–31. The main differences are (1) that the situation was much more complicated than Acts leads us to believe; (2) that Paul had to change his travel plans several times; and (3) that he almost lost his Corinthian church because of internal strife and opposition. See CORINTHIANS, SECOND EPISTLE TO THE.

Although Acts 20:1–6 also assumes that Paul changed his travel plans, these changes concern the final trip to Jerusalem, not the second visit in Corinth. While Rom 15:22–31 testifies that Paul was then in Corinth and would soon depart for Jerusalem, Acts 20:1–6 tells us that Jewish opponents prevented his going from Corinth to Syria directly. Instead he was forced to return to Macedonia and Troas. The delegation mentioned in 20:4 eventually assembled in Troas and left from Assos, sailing S along the coast to Mitylene, Chios, Samos, and Miletus, where Paul said farewell to the Ephesian elders who met him there (20:13–38). The voyage to Palestine is described in detail (21:1–7).

Upon arriving in Palestine, the party stayed in Caesarea and planned to continue to Jerusalem, although people warned Paul that calamity would be awaiting him there (21:8–15, cf. 20:22–24; Rom 15:30–31). At Jerusalem, Paul and his delegation were first greeted in a friendly manner (21:17), but when he visited James (21:18), he was informed about Jewish animosities. Paul's reports about the success of the mission among the gentiles (21:19–20a) were held against the fact that large numbers of Christian Jews in the Jewish heartland had remained faithful to the Torah and regarded Paul's mission among the gentiles as apostasy because he would not subject the new converts to the Torah of Moses, to circumcision and the Jewish way of life (21:20b–21). Yet, the elders of the church, including James, had a clever proposal ready for Paul, advising him to become one of four men who would take it upon themselves to complete a Nazirite vow, shave their heads, make the necessary offerings, and thus publicly demonstrate their adherence to the Jewish religion (21:22–26). The ploy almost worked, but failed at the last minute when Jews from Asia Minor recognized Paul in the Temple and incited the crowd to seize him (21:27–30). The Roman military intervened, rescuing him from being assassinated by the mob, but holding him under arrest (21:31–36).

e. The Trials in Jerusalem. As the narrative in Acts proceeds, the descriptions become increasingly dramatic and detailed with a good number of speeches and debates. To what extent these reports are based on reliable information is unknown. There appears to be some basic information worked in, but the total picture is certainly the result of Luke's imaginative history-telling techniques. From the data available to him, he tried to present a plausible picture of how Paul got himself arrested, extricated from the Jewish authorities and the lynch mobs, transferred to Roman protective custody, and eventually transported to Rome. The total result turns out to be a mixture of local politics, bizarre and fanatical maneuverings by dangerous mobs, and above all Paul's own strategies to escape certain death. Tragically, his final trump card, the appeal to Caesar, while saving him from death in

Jerusalem, made his transfer to Rome inevitable. Thus, in the end, Paul must go before Caesar because his own appeal to Roman law, and the will of God, require it (19:21; 21:14; 25:12; 26:31–32; 28:19).

The chain of events begins with Paul's defense (in Hebrew) to the Jewish crowds (21:40–22:21), which, however, led to renewed rioting, necessitating Paul's removal to the Roman barracks for protective custody (22:22–24a). Fearing that he would be flogged, he revealed that he was a Roman citizen, whereupon the Roman officer unfettered Paul and prohibited the soldiers from flogging him (22:24b–29). The next defense occurred before the Jewish high priests and the fully assembled Synhedrium/Sanhedrin, but this attempt also failed and the soldiers had to rescue Paul from another rioting mob (22:30–23:11). Next, Jewish fanatics conspired to murder Paul, but were foiled when his nephew told him of their plan and then informed the tribune as well (23:12–22). Almost 500 soldiers were needed to escort Paul safely from Jerusalem to Caesarea, where he was kept under guard in Herod's praetorium (23:23–35).

Paul's trial before the procurator Felix is narrated in dramatic detail (24:1–27). When the next procurator, Festus, wanted to move the trial to Jerusalem, Paul sensed the danger and appealed to Caesar (25:1–12). This appeal created a dilemma for the procurator because there were no charges against Paul that could stand up in a Roman court of law. When King Agrippa and Queen Berenice came to town, Festus brought Paul before them hoping that the king might help him dispose of the case (25:13–26:32). Indeed, Paul's defense before them is so convincing that Agrippa was ready to set him free, were it not for the appeal to Caesar which he could not overrule (26:32).

f. The Journey to Rome. Thus Paul, together with other prisoners, was dispatched to Rome. Under the protection of Julius, a friendly centurion of the Augustan Cohort, they sailed in a ship from Adramyttium via Sidon along the coast of Asia Minor to Myra in Lycia (27:1–5). From Myra they took a ship to Italy (27:6–8). This trip almost ended in disaster when they encountered a violent seastorm, suffer shipwreck, and barely made it ashore in Malta (27:9–44), not realizing where they were (28:1). Paul stayed for three months and was remembered in Malta for his extraordinary miracles (28:2–10). As the winter season drew to a close and the travel lanes reopened, Paul, still accompanied by the officer Julius, now his friend, took another ship to Syracuse in Sicily, continuing to Rhegium and Puteoli in Italy (28:11–14). Thus he arrived in Rome, where Roman Christians met him well outside the city (28:15–16). An attempt by Paul to explain himself before the Jewish leaders in Rome failed (28:17–28). The book of Acts then concludes by saying that Paul lived in Rome for two years at his own expense, "preaching the kingdom of God and teaching about the Lord Jesus Christ quite openly and unhindered" (28:30–31).

g. Death. Strangely, Acts has nothing to say about what happened when the two years were over. Coming to Rome fulfilled Paul's plan (and God's will) that he should go to Rome, although the way in which it came to pass differed from what he had imagined (19:21; 23:11; 27:24). Probably Luke, the author of Acts, knew that Paul was executed as a martyr in Rome (cf. 20:22–24; 21:11, 13). The reason Luke chose to end the book in this way (if this is the original end) is unknown, but there are various theories that try to explain it (see *Acts* Hermeneia, 227–28; Schneider 1980–82, 2:411–13).

Paul's letters confirm this foregoing narrative only in broad outlines. His plan to lead the delegation going to Jerusalem is affirmed by Rom 15:25–28, but Paul's earlier hesitation (1 Cor 16:3–4) is not known to Acts, nor does Acts seem to know why the delegation went to Jerusalem in the first place. The entire matter of the collection made by the Pauline churches seems to be unknown to Luke. Even when he found bits of information in his sources, he did not know what to do with them and therefore misplaced and misinterpreted the data (11:27–30; 21:24, 26; 24:17–18). Paul's self-understanding as the apostle of Christ, so preeminent in the letters, is alluded to only in Acts 14:4, 14. Paul's mission to Illyricum (Rom 15:19) and his plan to go to Spain (Rom 15:24, 28) were unknown to Luke as well (but cf. the Muratorian Canon, for which see *Acts* Hermeneia, xxxii). There can hardly be any doubt that Luke did not know Paul's letters. For him Paul was not a letter-writer but a powerful speaker, the opposite of what his opponents had concluded (cf. 2 Cor 10:10; 11:6). The accounts of Acts do not give any hint that Paul's major struggles were with opponents from Christian Judaism, not simply from Jews. Above all, there is a wide gap between what Acts reports about Paul's theology and what we learn at this point from Paul's own letters (see Vielhauer 1966).

C. Paul's Image in Later Sources

Paul's death as a martyr is also known to other NT authors, such as the followers of the apostles who wrote the epistles to the Colossians (see esp., 1:24), Ephesians (see esp., 3:13), and the Pastoral Epistles (see, esp., 2 Tim 4:6–8; and Wolter 1988). Still later testimonies are *1 Clem.* 5:5–7 and Ignatius of Antioch (Eph 12:2; Rom 4:3), and the apocryphal *Acts of Paul* (see esp., 11:1–7; and *NTApocr* 2: 73, 383–87). For further references see Schneider 1980–82, 2: 413; Lüdemann 1988. The historical information contained in these sources is extremely limited and does not significantly increase the data that can be obtained from the NT. Almost nothing is known about Paul's theology outside the Pauline and deutero-Pauline letters.

D. Chronology

1. Problems. Establishing a chronology for Paul's life and letters is beset by abundant difficulties. Four basic problems should be distinguished: (1) establishing the most probable sequence of Paul's letters and letter fragments, and the events to which they allude; (2) evaluating the sequence of events narrated in the book of Acts; (3) connecting the events reported in Acts with those mentioned in the letters; and (4) assigning actual dates to specific events. Two attendant circumstances further complicate matters. First, whereas Acts never refers to Paul's letters, some events reported in Acts can be correlated with events mentioned in the letters, although a further problem then arises since correlations can be made in several ways. Second, while scholars agree that priority of credibility should be given to Paul's own letters, without Acts no extended sequence of events can be determined. But all information yielded by Acts rests on the assumption that its author had access to historically reliable sources and that he used them in an historically responsible fashion, an assumption that is open to criticism. As a result, all attempts to determine a chronology for Paul's life and letters are hypothetical or even "experimental" (Jewett 1979: 95–104), even though several such hypotheses have been advanced in recent years.

Among these, notice should be given to the fact that Jewett (1979) and Lüdemann (1984; building on Knox 1950) have agreed that Paul made only three trips to Jerusalem after his conversion. The significance of this point lies in its deviation from the framework of Acts, which presents five such trips. Jewett and Lüdemann have therefore agreed to a major paradigmatic shift. Still, even this resembles other recent hypotheses in that all are based on older investigations and offer little in the way of new evidence (see *RGG* 1: 1693–94, and for surveys and bibliographies Rigaux 1968; Vielhauer 1975: 70–81; Suhl 1975; Dockx 1976; Jewett 1979; Lüdemann 1984).

2. Datable Events. The Gallio inscription enables us to date the reign of Iunius Gallio's proconsulship in Achaea to the years 51/52 or 52/53. These dates agree with Paul's 18-month visit in Corinth and the reference to Gallio in Acts 18:11–17. This visit would then have occurred in A.D. 51–53.

The conference of church leaders in Jerusalem, the so-called Apostolic Council described in Gal 2:1–10, presupposes that Peter was still in Jerusalem (his departure is reported in Acts 12:17), and that James and John, the sons of Zebedee, were still alive (their martyrdom is mentioned without dating in Mark 10:39). The John who attended the conference (Gal 2:9) was most likely one of the sons of Zebedee. If James, the brother of John in that text, was assassinated by Herod Agrippa I (Acts 12:2), and if this was also true of his brother John, then the Jerusalem conference must have occurred before that king's death in A.D. 44 (see *HJP*² 1: 442–54); the Jerusalem conference can thus be dated in ca. 43/44, a sequence roughly agreeing with Acts 11:27–12:1. If there is then the question about whether the events reported in Acts 12–17 are sufficient to fill the period from 43 to 51, it should not be assumed that Acts reports everything that happened. If the date of 43/44 for the Jerusalem conference is allowed to stand, Paul's conversion would have occurred ca. 15 years earlier (Gal 1:18; 2:1, counting 14 + 3 years, with the two beginning years included), that is, ca. 27–29. If so, Jesus would have been crucified some time earlier under Pilate's office as procurator (A.D. 26–36), that is, perhaps A.D. 27. Paul's conversion could then be dated in A.D. 28 (Vielhauer 1975: 78). These dates are all approximations.

Other synchronizations are even less certain. When Paul says he was driven out from Damascus three years after his conversion mission in Arabia and return to Damascus (Gal 1:17–18; 2 Cor 11:32–33), a precise dating within the reign of Aretas IV (ca. 9 B.C.–A.D. 40) seems impossible (see *HJP*² 1: 581–83; 2: 129–30; perhaps under Caligula [37–41]?). The edict of Claudius mentioned in Acts 18:1–2 is attested also by Suetonius, but the exact date cannot be ascertained. The date of A.D. 49 given by Orosius (5th century) would fit with the meeting of Aquila and Priscilla with Paul in Corinth (see *HJP*² 3: 77–78). Paul's two-year (Acts 24:27) imprisonment in Caesarea (Acts 23:23–26:32) occurred during the governorship of Felix, whose office lasted from ca. 52–60(?) (see *HJP*² 1: 460–66). The replacement of Felix by Festus (60–62 [?]), mentioned in Acts 24:27 (see *HJP*² 1: 467–68), may have taken place in the year 60, or two years earlier (see *HJP*² 1: 465). According to Acts, Paul was brought before Felix (Acts 23:33–24:26) and then Festus (Acts 25:6–26:32), events which may be dated so as to fall into the years 59/60 (*HJP*² 1: 467). If we knew precisely how long Paul stayed in Palestine and how long it took to travel from Ephesus to Palestine, his two and one-half years of residence in Ephesus (Acts 20:31) could be dated, but the time spans are a matter of guesswork. It may not be far off to put Paul's Ephesian residence sometime around A.D. 55. Also uncertain is the year of Paul's death. If he traveled to Rome in the year 60, stayed there for two years (Acts 28:30), and was martyred immediately afterwards, his death would fall into the years 63 or 64, a date coinciding with the persecution of Christians by Nero after the great fire (A.D. 64).

3. Dating of the Letters. The dating of Paul's authentic letters is a separate and related problem. While there is some agreement about the sequence of the letters, further complications arise if some of the letters (e.g., 2 Corinthians, Philippians) are actually collections of letter fragments. At a number of points, however, connections can be made between the letters and datable events in Acts.

Scholars agree that 1 Thessalonians is Paul's oldest extant letter. This letter appears to have been written not long after the founding of the church, which according to Acts 17:1–9 took place during the second missionary journey, perhaps in A.D. 49, when Paul came to Thessalonica from Philippi (1 Thess 2:2). Given that Silvanus and Timothy were with Paul (1 Thess 1:1; cf. Acts 18:5), the letter may have been sent from Corinth ca. 50/51 (Vielhauer 1975: 88–89).

The dating of Galatians is quite uncertain because Acts does not report the founding of any churches in Galatia; nevertheless, the itineraries recorded in Acts do leave open the possibility that Paul founded these churches during his second missionary journey (16:6–8) and visited them again during the third (18:23). It is unclear whether this return visit occurred before or after the Galatian crisis, which goes unnoticed in Acts. At any rate, the letter was written in response to the growing threat by anti-Pauline forces in these churches, perhaps during Paul's residence in Ephesus (Acts 20:31), ca. 52–54/55.

1 Corinthians may have been written at the same time that Galatians was, which would explain the reference to Galatia in 1 Cor 16:1. The Corinthian letters have a history in themselves, made up of a complex series of letters. If the Corinthian church was founded during the second missionary journey (Acts 18:1–18), ca. 50/51, the possible dates for the letters cover the period between Paul's first departure from Corinth and his final return to that city. 1 Corinthians was written from Ephesus (1 Cor 16:8) near the end of his residence there (ca. 54/55). See CORINTHIANS, FIRST EPISTLE TO THE.

The letter fragments in 2 Corinthians were written after 1 Corinthians and before Paul's third and final visit to Corinth, perhaps written from Ephesus and various places in Asia and Macedonia, ca. 55–56. See CORINTHIANS, SECOND EPISTLE TO THE.

The Philippian correspondence seems to have been sent some time after the foundation of that church (Acts 16:12–40), after Jewish Christian opponents had appeared and threatened Paul's work (Phil 3:2, 17–19), and at a time when Paul was in prison (in Ephesus? [see Vielhauer 1975: 170]). Whether Philemon, also a prison letter (Phlm 9), comes from the same time and place cannot be determined. The Epistle to the Romans was sent from Corinth shortly before Paul's departure for Palestine, probably A.D. 56.

4. Summary. Although efforts to pin precise dates on events in Paul's life usually fail to convince, the same cannot be said in regard to the general parameters of Paul's ministry. Here we find general agreement in assigning the apostolic conference to the 40s and the extant letters to the early and mid-50s. All of these rest within the period of Paul's Christian ministry, which at most extends from about A.D. 28 to A.D. 64.

E. Theology

As NT scholars have refined their methods, describing Paul's theology has become more exacting and complex. The following can provide no more than a sketch.

1. Methodological Problems. a. Sources. By common agreement, the primary source for Paul's theology should be his recognized authentic letters; the deutero-Pauline and, to a lesser degree, the Pastoral Epistles may receive limited consideration, inasmuch as they reflect Pauline tradition after his death. However, the speeches attributed to him in the book of Acts express the theology of the author of Luke-Acts, not Paul, and should not be used (see Vielhauer 1966).

Having identified the sources, one must decide *how* to use Paul's letters to arrive at his theology. Clearly, gathering a mosaic of quotations from the letters and putting them together under doctrinal headings will not add up to a theology of Paul, for it fails to account for the origin of Paul's ideas and the dialogical nature of his statements through successive letters. On the whole, Paul sets forth his theology not in doxographical abstractions but in contextual letters reflecting ongoing debates.

Paul's letters provide access to his theology on two levels: that of doctrinal presuppositions and that of applications to specific problems within his churches. These occur in the course of extended arguments in which Paul moves from his theological premises to the resolution of specific issues, both practical and theoretical. In arguments where Paul actually cites his presuppositions, they often have the form of abbreviated principles or formulae, sometimes lifted from another context (e.g., hymns or creeds). Such references occur as they are needed from case to case, so that in one sense none of the letters provides a complete description of his theological "system" (if he ever had a "system"); in another sense, every argument is itself a complete theological statement.

Not only does Paul's theology lie embedded within extended arguments, but his arguments lie within an epistolary context. This first requires that due consideration be given to the argument of an epistle as a whole. Second, this requires that attention be given to the place of the letter within the entire discussion of which it is a part, for Paul's arguments take place within an ongoing dialogue. Whatever Paul argues for and against in any given letter represents no more than one "picture" in an entire sequence, which includes a previous history, other discussion partners who often hold differing viewpoints, envoys and couriers who provide further commentary, and a subsequent history of exchanges, until the point when the dialogue breaks off. As in any exchange of letters or dialogue, the same or similar issues may be brought up repeatedly, and Paul may respond differently in each case. Depending on the circumstances, Paul can change his argumentation, present a revised version of it, or even change his position.

b. Character of His Thought. Although differing circumstances effected change and revision within Paul's thinking, some balance should be maintained in analyzing these variations. It would be as wrong to overlook the differences between Paul's letters as it would be to treat these differences as substantive self-contradictions, as opportunistic accommodations to what is deemed desirable, or as evidence of emotional instability. Räisänen (1987) certainly advanced criticism when he pointed out contradictions between Paul's letters; unfortunately, he largely ignored the structure and epistolary nature of Paul's arguments. Such oversight allows surface-level contradictions to obscure consistency of thought at a deeper, presuppositional level (see Boers 1988; Beker 1988). Admittedly, though, if Paul did pursue a consistent theological position throughout his letters, despite the differences between them, this consistency remains to be demonstrated.

This situation raises further questions with regard to Paul's thought. Did he work with a fixed theological "system" in the back of his mind? Or did he develop his arguments *ad hoc,* based only on a limited set of assumptions? Did Paul have a consistent theology throughout his apostolic career, or did his theology gradually evolve in the context of mission and controversy in which he was constantly involved? If he worked from a fixed theological system, was that system pre-Christian (Pharisaic, rabbinic, or apocalyptic) with his Christian convictions simply overlaid or appended? Or was his theology something altogether new that grew out of his vision of Christ and his commission to take the gospel to the gentiles? In short, how creative and dynamic a theologian was the apostle Paul? Such questions form the substance of the present debate in NT scholarship.

c. Understanding His Thought. Paul's theology is as difficult to grasp as that of any creative thinker. It is more than the sum of his extant letters and letter fragments, and more than a string of surface-level quotations. Rather, it involves analysis of Paul's arguments as part of an ongoing debate, so as to reveal the methods Paul uses to move from certain principles to the positions he adopts. This approach places us more in step with the apostle himself, because, while he no doubt does hold some non-negotiable assumptions, his theology is primarily the result of *processes of thought.*

Paul's thinking also contains development. As a result, positions taken in his last letter, Romans, are considerably more advanced that those in his first (extant) letter, 1 Thessalonians. This does not mean, however, that he would repudiate his earlier letters, for each letter is designed to respond to particular readers and a specific set of theological problems. Each letter must therefore be judged sufficient in itself theologically, though insufficient to the extent that it calls for future follow-up.

Paul's theology as a whole can be conceived of in different ways. If conceived of as the totality of all his thinking, involving all the letters he ever wrote and all the speeches and activities he ever undertook, this theology is inaccessible to us. As readers of his letters, however, we have access to his theology in another way: these letters allow us to enter into the apostle's thought processes. By analyzing Paul's arguments concerning specific issues and the positions he took throughout an ongoing debate, we as readers can learn to think like Paul and in this way gain entrance into the world of Paul's theological thinking. If this theology always remains incomplete, credit it to the fact that Paul's thinking was always open-ended. Even Paul's final and theologically most complete letter, Romans, points beyond itself. Such open-endedness encourages the reader to take Paul's theology beyond Paul, which is precisely what happens in the deutero-Pauline letters (2 Thessalonians, Colossians, Ephesians, the Pastorals).

2. Major Phases in the Development of Paul's Theology. If analyzed according to their chronological sequence, Paul's letters evidence major phases of his theological development. Such developments and their implications for the understanding of the apostle's thought are the subject of current scholarly discussions (see *ANRW,* pt. 2, vol. 25/4; 2653–54). Traces of development include direct references by Paul himself to views held in the past but now overcome, citations of pre-Pauline traditions taken over by him, or shifts in his thinking observable by critical investigation.

a. Pre-Christian Pharisaism. Although reliable sources here are extremely scarce, some conclusions can be drawn from Paul's own references to his pre-Christian past and the theology he affirmed at that time (see Gal 1:13–14; 1 Cor 15:9; 2 Cor 11:22; Phil 3:5–6; perhaps also Gal 5:11; see also *ANRW,* pt. 2, vol. 25/4: 2658–67; Saldarini 1988: 134–43, with bibliography). According to his own witness, Paul was an Israelite from the tribe of Benjamin, a "Hebrew from Hebrews" circumcised on the eighth day of his life (2 Cor 11:22; Phil 3:5). He was a member of the Pharisaic sect (Phil 3:5; Acts 23:6; 26:5) and devoted to upholding "the traditions of the forefathers" (Gal 1:14).

If this is assumed, he must have been a well-versed member of the Pharisaic party. This much can be said, although a paucity of sources leaves us unable to say anything specific about the education of diaspora Pharisees in Asia Minor (see Saldarini 1988: 137–41). The affirmation that he was "a son of Pharisees" (Acts 23:6) at the least assures us that his Pharisaism was genuine. That he was authorized to persecute Christians means that his aims received official recognition. Although our sources regarding early Pharisaism are scarce, there is reason to assume that these Pharisees had educational standards and theological consciousness, even if their criteria may have been quite different than later rabbinic orthodoxy. One should not assume that Pharisaic theological education of a serious nature could be obtained only at Jerusalem (against Oepke 1933: 444; see *ANRW,* pt. 2, vol. 25/4: 2660).

The information given in Acts that Paul came from Tarsus to Jerusalem to study with Rabbi Gamaliel I (22:3; cf. 26:4; see GAMALIEL) flatly contradicts Gal 1:22, a discrepancy which raises questions about the historical reliability of Acts 22:3. Those who nevertheless trust Acts (Oepke 1933: 440–46; van Unnik 1973: 259–320) draw further conclusions from it, mostly by consulting later rabbinic sources. If Paul, as Oepke suggested (1933: 412), was an ordained rabbi and educated in Jerusalem, serious problems arise. Is it conceivable that a pupil of Gamaliel displays no evident knowledge of Hebrew scripture, instead always citing the LXX? Jeremias (1969) even postulated that Paul was a Hillelite because he shared doctrines and exegetical methods attributed to Rabbi Hillel. Haacker (1972) advanced the opposite hypothesis, labeling Paul a Shammaite. But the historical evidence concerning the teachings of Hillel and Shammai is as shaky as the alleged connections between their teachings and Paul's theology (see Davies 1955: 1–16). One should, in fact, ask why it is almost impossible to establish any connections between Paul and the rabbinic sources. Whatever the answer may be, the accuracy of the information about Gamaliel (Acts 5:34; 22:3) is dubious. Furthermore, one cannot ignore how perfectly Acts' information about Gamaliel fits Luke's ideas (Strecker 1976: 482 n. 10). Still, if what Acts says is accurate, Gamaliel's theology was remarkably Hellenistic-Jewish and very different from the later rabbinic standards, a possibility not to be dismissed offhand.

At any rate, Paul's testimony leaves no doubt that his primary concern as a Pharisee was Torah and righteousness. A conscientious Jew, with respect to the Torah Paul stood "blameless" (Phil 3:6; cf. Gal 1:13, 14; Acts 22:4; 26:5). Paul describes in Gal 5:3 what he thought about the law, not without polemic poignancy: "I testify again to every man who has become circumcised, that he is obliged to do the whole Law." The concept of "the whole Law" is presupposed also in Gal 3:10 (LXX Deut 27:26), where "everything that is written in the book of the Law" defines quantitatively what is meant by "the whole Law"; anything less amounts to being "under the curse." This view does have an affinity to the rabbinic concept of the Torah as consisting of 613 prescriptions and prohibitions, as well as to the rigoristic position attributed to Shammai (*b. Sabb.* 31a; see Betz *Galatians,* 260; *ANRW,* pt. 2, vol. 25/4: 2665).

If Paul claims to have been "blameless" in terms of the Torah, he went further in his zeal by persecuting the Jewish Christians of Damascus, whom he, in agreement with the authorities at Jerusalem, regarded as "apostates" (Gal 1:13; 1 Cor 15:9; Phil 3:6; Acts 8:3; 9:1–2, 21; 22:4, 19; 26:10–11). The main reason for this persecution seems to have been that these Jewish Christians did not subject gentile proselytes to Torah and circumcision, discontinuing "the traditions of the forefathers" which Paul so zealously enforced (cf. perhaps Gal 5:11). At any rate, it seems to be clear that already the pre-Christian Paul had focused his theological concerns on the Torah, circumcision, and other ancestral traditions. He was, of course, not alone in this, as demonstrated by his later opponents in Jerusalem, Galatia, and elsewhere, who (even as Christian Jews) continued to hold the same views Paul once held and then rejected. See GALATIANS, EPISTLE TO THE.

It is not inconceivable that some of Paul's earlier concerns emerge in a later Christian context. Paul's sharp critique of Jewish claims in Rom 2:1–29 includes a discussion of Jewish prerogatives: the possession of the Jewish Torah (2:12–16), the honorific name "Jew" (2:17–24), and the ritual of circumcision (2:25–29). Essentially, the passage involves painful Jewish self-criticism, no doubt informed by Paul's intimate knowledge of Jewish theology. Does his critique of false Torah observance (2:12), pretentiousness (2:18–20), hypocrisy (2:21–22), and mere external ritual (2:25–29) reflect concerns he had felt already as a Pharisee? (This critique has close parallels in the Sermon on the Mount.) See SERMON ON THE MOUNT/PLAIN. Romans 9–11, a discussion of Judaism's eschatological destiny, may also draw on material coming from an earlier period of Paul's life. These possibilities, however, raise two fundamental questions which non-existent sources keep us from answering: Did Paul really believe that his personal "blamelessness" assured his salvation (cf. Sanders 1977: 442–43)? Or did he harbor some doubts, like the would-be disciple of Jesus in Mark 10:20 who, having done all of the Torah from his youth on, was still unsure of the way to eternal life? And did Paul share the view that his individual salvation was all he had to be concerned about, or the other view that his individual salvation was conditional upon the salvation of "all Israel" (Rom 11:25–26)? If these questions could be answered positively, we would begin to understand why he was impressed, first negatively, then positively, by the Christian gospel.

b. Conversion to Jesus Christ. According to his own testimony (Gal 1:1, 11–12, 15–16; 1 Cor 9:1; 15:8; Phil 3:5–6), the greatest change in Paul's thinking was brought about as a consequence of his vision of Christ on the road to Damascus. Appearing to him in this vision, Christ commissioned him to "preach the gospel to the gentiles." Paul at once dedicated himself to this task. At this point, the accounts in Acts (9:1–19a; 22:1–16; 26:9–18) differ in that Ananias mediated Paul's commission to him (9:15–16; 22:10, 14–15; cf. 26:16–18). What were the consequences of this event for Paul's theology? Four things immediately present themselves.

(1) Paul's commitment to Pharisaism came to an abrupt end, as he switched from Pharisaic to Christian Judaism.

(2) Paul's assignment to preach the Gospel to gentiles first meant that he joined the missionary enterprises of the Damascus church, from which he must also have received his first instruction in Christian theology. Unfortunately, our knowledge of this old church is extremely limited, so that we do not precisely know what kind of instruction and tradition Paul received at that time (see also Betz *Galatians,* 64–66). What did the Christians of Damascus have in mind when they converted non-Jews? How did they, as Jews, justify it? Clearly, the reason for Paul's persecuting them was that they failed to subject the new converts to circumcision and Torah. What was their theological reason for making converts outside of the Torah covenant? Was it in fact done outside of the Torah covenant? At any rate, they must have had theological reasons, but we do not know what they were. Nor do we know what the Jewish-Christian church in Jerusalem thought about this: Did they approve or disapprove? Or were they already divided over the question, as they obviously were later on?

(3) The next immediate question to be raised is whether and in what way the new converts from paganism were to become partakers of the (Sinai?) covenant. See COVENANT. If they were not circumcised and did not observe the Mosaic Torah, how could these converts hope to be partakers of salvation? Perhaps some conclusions can be drawn from Acts, provided of course it reflects the actual practices of the Damascus church. Since after his conversion Paul was baptized (Acts 9:18; 22:16), the ritual of baptism must have served as an initiation to the Christian faith. In connection with the gift of the spirit (9:17), the effect of baptism was purification and remission of sins (Acts 22:16: "Rise and be baptized, and wash away your sins, calling on his name."). To be sure, this theology agrees with Luke/Acts (see also Acts 1:5; 2:38; 5:31; 7:60; 10:43; 13:38; 26:18), but it may also reflect views held much earlier in the Damascus church. If this ritual of baptism was indeed administered to gentile converts in Damascus as well, taking the place of circumcision, then the new gentile Christians would have thereby joined the community of the sanctified. Christological and soteriological beliefs would have justified this status (cf. 1 Cor 1:13–17; 6:11; 10:2; 12:13), just as Christian ethics amounted to a preservation of sanctity until the Last Judgment (1 Thess 5:23; 1 Cor 1:8; 2 Cor 11:2). If, broadly speaking, this theology was affirmed by the Damascus church, it came close to Paul's theology in 1 Thessalonians [see below, E.2.c.(1)]. In fact, some of the pre-Pauline formulae cited in Paul's letters may go back to traditions taught in Damascus.

(4) One must keep in mind that when Paul spells out the changes in his life and thought, he does so retrospectively, yet this does not necessarily mean that these recollections were completely beside the point. As he affirms, the changes brought about by his conversion involved his entire life and thinking, not only certain aspects. Four of the most important changes are highlighted by Paul himself.

(a) The most immediate change was Paul's recognition and confession of Jesus Christ as "lord," *kyrios,* and "son of God," *hyios tou theou* (Gal 1:16; 1 Cor 9:1; Phil 3:8; cf. Acts 9:5, 10; 22:8, 10; 26:15). In contrast, the title "messiah," *christos,* does not seem to play an important role in Paul's conversion (cf. 1 Cor 15:3; see Bauer 1988: 1768–69). To be sure, it is remembered in his christology, but it was not the fulcrum of his conversion (differently Acts 9:22; 17:3; 18:5, 28; see Bauer 1988; *s.v. Christos*). This role was played by *kyrios.* This revelation of Jesus as *kyrios,* "lord," certainly received reinforcement by the confessions made in the first Christian worship service Paul attended (cf. e.g., Rom 10:9–10; Phil 2:11; 1 Cor 8:6; 12:3; 2 Cor 4:5). From this point, adopting already-existing christological and soteriological formulae and hymns was a small step, although when Paul cites such material in his letters it may not come only from Damascus (see especially, Gal 1:4; 4:4–6; Phil 2:6–11; 3:7–11; Rom 1:3–4; 1 Cor 15:3–5; Phil 3:7–9).

(b) An immediate consequence of Paul's invocation of Christ was the reevaluation of the fundamental concept of "righteousness," *dikaiosynē* (see *BTNT* 1: 270–85; Conzelmann 1969: 214–20; *Galatians,* 116–119; *2 Corinthians* 8–

9, 114–116; *ANRW,* pt. 2, vol. 25/4: 2694–2709, 2721–29; with further bibliography). In retrospect, Paul described the changes in two texts. The first was Gal 2:15–16: "We who are Jews by birth and not sinners know from [the] gentiles that a person is not justified by works of [the] Law but [only] through faith in Christ Jesus. So we also have come to believe in Christ Jesus, in order that we might be justified by faith in Christ and not by works of the Law, since it is not by works of [the] Law that all flesh will be justified." Paul's new Christian view is that Jesus Christ, by virtue of his death and resurrection, has acquired righteousness and that those who believe in him "in obedience of faith" (Rom 1:5; 6:12, 16, 17; etc.) are already now and will be at the Last Judgment beneficiaries of that righteousness (Gal 5:5–6; see *BTNT* 1: 274–79). The opposite, as it now appears to his Christian understanding, is a "righteousness based on the works of the Torah" (Gal 2:16; see Betz *Galatians,* 116, n. 35).

The second text in which Paul described his reevaluation of the concept of righteousness was Phil 3:7–9: "But whatever gain I had, I counted as loss because of the surpassing worth of knowing Christ Jesus my Lord. For his sake I have suffered the loss of all things, and count them as refuse, in order that I may gain Christ and be found in him, not having a righteousness of my own, based on [the] Law, but that which is through faith in Christ, the righteousness from God that depends on faith . . ." (RSV). This newly found "righteousness" is "in Christ" (Gal 1:22; 2:4, 16, 17; etc. See Conzelmann 1969: 208–12; Betz *Galatians,* 119, n. 60); indeed, Christ is that righteousness (1 Cor 1:30), which is "the righteousness of God" (Rom 1:17), a gift of grace to those who believe in Christ (Gal 5:5–6; 2 Cor 5:17; Rom 1:16–17; 3:21–22; etc.). The opposite is described as "my own righteousness" (Phil 3:9), i.e., basing one's hope for eternal salvation entirely on the individual's sufficient Torah observance. Paul claims that his reevaluation of the notion of righteousness is more than a second track to accommodate the admission of gentile Christians into the church and in salvation. Gal 2:16 states that Paul belongs to those Jews who have become Christians because they have come to recognize the insufficiency of their pre-Christian notions concerning eschatological righteousness. Up to this point there seems to have been broad agreement in Jewish Christianity. Disagreement arose, however, about the consequences.

(c) The most difficult question to solve was, What impact does the Christian Gospel have on the concept and observance of the Law (Torah)? This question is still disputed today. The basic problem is that Paul seems to be vacillating between two concepts of law, a Jewish concept and his own Christian concept. How are the two related to one other? (For discussion and bibliography, see *BTNT* 1: 259–69; Conzelmann 1969: 220–28; Räisänen 1987; Sanders 1977; 1983; Wilckens 1982; Hübner 1984; *ANRW,* pt. 2, vol. 25/4: 2668–94; *TRE* 13: 64–72; Westerholm 1986: 229–37; 1988.) For Paul, reevaluating his position on the Torah meant the rejection of his former Pharisaic concept, which he described in Gal 5:3: "I testify again to every man who has become circumcised, that he is obliged to do the whole law." As he now sees it, this Torah has come to an end with the coming of Christ (Gal 3:22–25; Rom 10:4). His judgment is therefore rather negative: "What then is the Law?—Because of the transgressions it was given in addition, till the offspring should come to whom the promise had been made, ordained through angels, through a mediator" (Gal 3:19). All Paul is willing to concede at this point is the inferior role the Torah has played in the history of salvation (3:23): "Before the faith came we were kept in custody under [the] Law, confined until the coming faith was to be revealed." This Torah did not have the capacity to "make alive" and generate "righteousness" (3:21).

This does not mean, however, that Paul was an antinomian who rejected the law in any form, or even the Torah. There could be no question that the demands of the Torah had to be fulfilled, if righteousness as the prerequisite for entering into the kingdom of God was to be obtained. Furthermore, there were not two different Torahs, an older one to be rejected and a new one to be approved. Rather, there were competing definitions of what the Torah was.

According to Paul, the Pharisaic Torah was deficient because it summarized the Torah in the wrong way. In this Pharisaic view, God revealed his will in the form of many laws, all of which must be obeyed. For the Pharisees, then, fulfilling "the whole law" meant keeping the quantitative sum total of all laws (Gal 5:3). This notion is, however, not the only possible one.

Paul called his new concept "the law of Christ" (6:2; cf. 1 Cor 7:19; 9:21). This law summarized the many prescriptions and prohibitions of Scripture in another way by regarding the love command Lev 19:18 as the common denominator *(kelal):* "For the whole Law is fulfilled in one word: 'you shall love your neighbor as yourself' " (Gal 5:14; cf. Rom 13:8–10). This concept of Torah as a single principle was apparently taken over from Jewish Christianity (see Matt 5:43; 19:19; 22:39; Mark 12:31, 33; Luke 10:27; Jas 2:8), coming probably from the historical Jesus himself, although it was also attributed to R. Hillel (see Betz *Galatians,* 274–76). The important difference is that this concept of the Torah does not require the specifically Jewish Torah observance, but it can in principle be fulfilled by every human being. If the love command is "fulfilled," the "whole Torah" is fulfilled, and thus righteousness is assured. This concept, therefore, permits gentiles to access salvation without their having to pass through the religion of Judaism. How Christians, whether Jews or gentiles, might then fulfill this Torah is the next question.

(d) Since gentiles by definition do not partake of the Mosaic covenant, extending salvation to them required a special act of God in order to extricate them "from the present evil aeon" (Gal 1:4). Even before Paul, early Christianity interpreted Jesus' death on the cross as his voluntary self-sacrifice "for our sins" (Gal 1:4; 1 Cor 15:3; cf. 1 Thess 5:10). His death was in accordance with God's will, so that it was a manifestation not only of Christ's love (Gal 2:20) but also of God's (Rom 8:3–4, 32, 39). As a righteous man "without sin" (2 Cor 5:21), Christ took the curse (Gal 3:13) and the accumulated burden of human sinfulness on himself (2 Cor 5:21). His absolute obedience to his Father, manifest in his willingness to be crucified, though innocent, was meritorious enough (Phil 2:6–11; Rom 1:3–4; 5:19) to provide a ransom from eternal condemnation for those who believe in him (1 Thess 1:10; Gal 3:13; 4:5;

1 Cor 6:20; 7:23). Thus achieving "reconciliation" with God on behalf of sinful humanity (2 Cor 5:18–21; Rom 5:10–11), Christ cleared the way (Rom 5:1) for gentile Christians to become partakers, not of the Mosaic covenant, but of the prior promise God had made to Abraham. As believers in Christ they have become "sons of Abraham" (Gal 3:6–18, 29; cf. Rom 4:1–25).

Several christological and soteriological formulae, most probably going back to pre-Pauline Jewish Christianity and still somewhat controversial as to their exact meaning, describe the two acts initiated by God, through Christ, to integrate gentile Christians into the salvation process. (1) The formulae interpret Christ's death as a voluntary self-sacrifice and atonement (Gal 1:4; 2:20; 3:13; 4:4–6; Phil 2:6–11; 1 Cor 1:23, 24, 30; 15:3–8; 2 Cor 5:17–21; Rom 3:24–26; 4:25; 5:6–11; 8:3, 32). Its meritoriousness means the remission of the sins that have accumulated beforehand (Rom 3:25; 4:25). (2) In formulaic language Paul also wrote about the work of the divine spirit which enables the believer to "fulfill the demands of the Law" (Rom 8:4). The formula in Gal 4:4–6 contains a summary of these doctrines: "When, however, the fullness of time had come, God sent his son, born by [a] woman, put under [the] Law, in order that he might redeem those who are under [the] Law, in order that we might receive the adoption as sons. And, since you are sons, God sent the spirit of his son into our hearts, crying out 'Abba! Father!' " (for interpretation, Betz *Galatians,* 205–11).

c. Earlier Phases of Paul's Theology. (1) The letter of 1 Thessalonians reflects Paul's theology during his early mission to the Greeks, a phase prior to the great confrontations with his Jewish-Christian opponents. In this epistle, Paul looks back at the turbulence surrounding that church's foundation (1:5–6; 2:1–2; cf. Acts 17:1–9), turbulence which for the time being (cf. 3:2–5) appears to have subsided, giving way to "peace" (cf. 1:1; 5:3, 13, 23). Paul recalls how the Thessalonians accepted the "gospel" (1:5–6; 2:2, 4, 8, 9; 3:2) and cites a summary of it as a reminder (1:9–10; cf. 4:5). This summary reflects the mission *kerygma* (i.e., preaching), which includes the turning away from idols to the worship of the living and true God, and the awaiting of the *parousia* of Christ (cf. 2:19; 3:13; 4:15; 5:23). The *kerygma* is based on the christology of the death and resurrection of Jesus Christ (1:10; 2:15; 4:14), the "son of God" (1:10) and "Lord" (1:1, 3, 6, 8; 2:15, 19; 3:8, 11, 12, 13; 4:1, 2, 6, 15, 16, 17; 5:2, 9, 12, 23).

The church (1:1; 2:14) consists of those who have been called to the kingdom of God (2:12; 4:7; 5:24). They have been given the holy spirit (1:5, 6; 4:8; 5:19), and have thus been purified (2:3; 4:7). As believers in the gospel (1:7; 2:10, 13; 4:14) they have thereby obtained the status of "holiness" (3:13; 4:3–7; 5:23) without recourse to the Torah. They are addressed as "the holy ones" (3:13; 5:27) and as "the sons of [the] light and the sons of [the] day" (5:5). Preserving this state of holiness "unblemished" until the *parousia* (3:13; 5:23), when they will greet the coming Christ in mid-air (4:13–18), is the purpose of Christian ethics. Paul described the desired ethics only in general terms as "how you must conduct your lives and please God" (4:1; cf. 2:12, 15; 4:12, 5:12–22), and cited the temptations of the devil as the primary cause for concern (3:5; cf. 4:3–8). However, the faith of the Thessalonians was still young and insecure; deficiencies exist (3:10) and strengthening was needed. For this reason Paul sent the letter, and in keeping with this purpose he included comfort for the unsettling death of some members (4:13–18; 1:10).

(2) While 1 Thessalonians barely mentions "sin" and "righteousness" (2:10, 16), the conspicuous role in Galatians of justification by faith in Jesus Christ and related concepts indicates that Paul wrote this letter in a very different situation. Basically, however, Paul's theology in this letter is the same as in 1 Thessalonians, and the Galatian letter lends confirmation to it, rather than changing it. See also GALATIANS, EPISTLE TO THE.

Accordingly, Christian salvation is based on the death and resurrection of Jesus Christ (1:1, 4; 2:19–20; 3:1, 13; 4:4–6; 5:11, 24; 6:12–14), the gift of the spirit (3:2–5, 14; 4:6; 5:5, 16, 17, 18, 22, 25; 6:1, 8), the "putting on" of Christ in baptism (3:26-28), and living the new, Christian life as "new creation" (6:15), filled with "the fruit of the spirit" (5:22–23a; cf. 5:16–18, 25). The Christian is "in Christ," i.e., a member of the "church of God" (1:2, 13, 22; 2:4, 17; 3:26–28; 6:15–16). This church moves forward under the guidance of the spirit and awaits the eschaton (5:5, 10, 21; 6:7–9).

This basic conception has been radically challenged by the Jewish–Christian opponents of Paul who invaded the Galatian churches. See GALATIANS, EPISTLE TO THE.

As Paul presents the matter, these opponents have almost persuaded the Galatians to circumcise themselves and to accept the Jewish Torah (1:6–7; 5:1–12, 13, 15–16). This could only mean the abandonment of the Pauline Gospel and its substitution by another version of the Gospel that included observance of the Torah (1:6–9; cf. 1:11; 2:2, 5, 7, 14). Such a move would reverse Paul's own "conversion" from Pharisaic Torah observance to the Christian Gospel without the Torah. Speculation about the reasons for the Galatians' impending switch is difficult, but they must have had serious reasons. The problem they seemed to have had to face was the occurrence of serious moral failure (6:1). With only Gospel and spirit, they probably felt they lacked adequate protection against the temptations by the "flesh" (3:3; 4:13, 14, 23, 29; 5:13–24; 6:1, 8, 12–13). Under the tutelage of the Mosaic Torah, they would be given clear directives about what to do and from what to abstain.

Against his adversaries' doctrines the apostle spells out his doctrine of justification by faith in Jesus Christ (2:15–21; 3:2–5, 6–18, 19–25, 26–28, 29; 5:5–6; 6:7–10, 14–16). This doctrine originated in Jewish Christianity itself and had in fact legitimated the early mission to the non-Jews (2:1–10, 15–16; see Betz *Galatians,* 115–19). But Paul presses the revolutionary contrast between justification by faith in Jesus Christ and by "works of the Law" (2:16–21; 3:2–5, 10–13, 18, 19–25; 5:4; 6:13) only when his Jewish-Christian competition threatened his entire mission. In his Galatian letter we see how for the first time this doctrine became the main subject of a theological argument.

The doctrine of justification by faith basically affirms the sufficiency of salvation through Christ, without the Torah, for gentile Christians. In fact, Paul's strongest counterargument against his opponents contrasts the sufficiency of Christ with the insufficiency of the Jewish Torah. This insufficiency became manifest in Christ's death (2:21; 4:4–5), in the Jewish-Christians' belief in Christ (2:15–16), and in the previous history of the church. As a result of these unmistakable factors the Galatian churches had been founded without subjection to the Torah (1:16–2:14; 3:1–5; 5:1–4, 18), nor need it ever be, for, as Paul points out, the Torah was no longer the agent of salvation (2:19; 3:11–13, 19–25; 4:4–6; 5:18). Once this was recognized, those who had been born Jews were free to continue their Jewish life. It is, however, a completely different matter for Gentiles like the Galatians to feel they must accept circumcision and Torah, because they thereby concede that faith in Christ alone is not sufficient for salvation. Such a concession, to be sure, means cutting themselves off from the benefits of Christ (1:6–7, 8–9; 2:21; 3:1–5; 5:2, 4, 6; 6:12–16). Ceasing to be partakers in Christ's salvation, they would in effect become converts to Judaism.

Therefore, when Paul reaffirms his original message to them (1:8–9; 6:14–16), he advises the Galatians to rely on the spirit, as they have done before (3:1–5; 5:5, 16–18, 25; 6:1, 7–9). Such reliance on the spirit is sufficient as a weapon to deal with the temptations of the "flesh." On the other hand, abandoning the preciously won "freedom in Christ" (2:4–5; 3:26–28; 4:21–31; 5:1, 13) and taking up the yoke of the Torah (5:2) can only mean voluntarily entering into the confinement and slavery under law, sin, and flesh (2:4–5; 3:22–24; 4:4–5, 21–31; 5:1–12), that is, the "elements of this world" (4:3–11). Therefore, Paul's letter ends by affirming a "rule": "Neither circumcision nor uncircumcision is [worth] anything but [a] new creation [is worth everything]" (6:15; cf. 5:6; 1 Cor 7:19). This reflects the sufficiency of the spirit which he summarizes earlier in the letter: "If the spirit is the source of our life, let the spirit also direct our course" (5:25).

(3) Although written after Galatians, Paul's Philippian correspondence contains a theology in many ways similar to that of Galatians. One feature unique to Philippians—Paul's rumination on his possible, impending death—comes as little surprise given that he writes this letter while imprisoned, most probably in Ephesus (Phil 1:7, 12–26; cf. 1 Cor 15:32; 2 Cor 1:8–11; Acts 19:32–40). In the short run this reflection on the proper attitude to take when confronted with the threat of one's own death would prove premature (2 Cor 1:8–11; 11:23); nevertheless, in the long run it was quite realistic (cf. Rom 15:30–32). Although not entirely new (cf. 1 Thess 1:6; 2:14; Gal 6:14, 17), another prominent theme in the Philippian letter fragments (see Koester 1961; 1982, 2: 132–34) is Paul's participation in Christ's suffering, death, and resurrection. This partnership provides the logic for the conspicuous role in Philippians that Christ's and Paul's examples play in the apostle's exhortation. Paul bases such imitation chiefly on the Christ hymn cited in 2:6–11 (see Betz 1967). This hymn also anchors Paul's main parenetical concern in Philippians, the unity of the church (esp. 1:5–11, 27–30; 2:1–4, 17–18; 4:1, 2, 7). A completely different tone appears in the fragment 3:2–4:3, where Paul sharply attacks his Jewish–Christian adversaries. On the whole, though, Paul's theology in Philippians again includes the doctrine of justification by faith in Jesus Christ (Phil 1:11; 3:5–11) and reliance on the spirit (1:19, 27; 2:1; 3:3).

The letter to Philemon may also have been written during the Ephesian imprisonment. Regardless, its basic theology again resembles the previous letters, although the major subject matter is of course different.

d. The Crisis at Corinth. The great crisis in the church of Corinth (for details, see CORINTHIANS, FIRST EPISTLE TO THE and CORINTHIANS, SECOND EPISTLE TO THE) confronted Paul with new, rapidly changing situations and challenges. Although the causes that gave rise to the crisis are to some extent confusing, it appears that, as far as theology is concerned, the problem stemmed neither from disagreement with what Paul taught, nor, in the first stages, from outside interference. Apparently, some of the Corinthians themselves had developed Paul's own theology in directions unpalatable to the apostle. As a result, charismatic experiences and ecstatic prophecy, though not unfamiliar to Paul (see 1 Thess 1:5; 5:20; Gal 3:5; Phil 3:10; 1 Cor 14:18), played too large a role in this church: the overwhelming abundance of and superior status attributed to their enthusiastic displays went beyond anything Paul had seen. Based on these experiences, members of the church apparently created their own theologies and modes of behavior without taking into account that this new Corinthian diversity posed a threat to the very existence of the church. Feeding into the crisis were other factors of social and religious origin, complicated by outside interference (Apollos? Cephas? [see 1 Cor 1:12; 3:4–6, 22; 4:6; 9:5; 16:12; Acts 18:24–19:1]). Interacting with each other, these factors gave the crisis a life of its own that at times drove Paul to the brink of his own demise.

The theological issues Paul confronted are stated succinctly in the prooemium of 1 Corinthians, the thanksgiving prayer (1:4–9). Since much of the language in the passage appears to conform to the Corinthians' self-understanding, Paul expected the Corinthians to agree when he saw "God's grace *(charis)* given in Christ Jesus" being manifest among them: "in everything you have been made rich through him [sc. Christ], in every form of speech and in every form of knowledge" (1:5; see Betz 1986a). The Corinthian church experienced this spiritual wealth in its abundance of spiritual gifts, *charismata,* which had become a source of pride (1:7; 7:7; 12:4–31). Being Greeks, they especially cherished, "eloquence and knowledge" (1:5; cf. 2 Cor 8:7). These cherished gifts were all derived from the divine spirit which revealed them through prophecy (see, esp. 1 Cor 12:8; 14:1–40). These experiences also satisfied the Greek cultural expectation that they possess "wisdom" (*sophia* [1:22]). But Paul considered the Corinthians' pride to be compromised severely by the fact that they seemed unable to cope with cosmopolitan diversity and sophistication in the church and that their pride created strife and factionalism (see 1:10–17; 3:3–4; 11:18–19; 12:25). These deteriorating developments created an intolerable discrepancy between claim and reality. As Paul put it, the Corinthians' wealth of *charismata* was still deficient: they lacked mature love among each other and consequently congregational harmony (1:7–9, 10, 13a; 3:1–2; 8:1; 13:1–13; 16:14). This discrepancy not only disrupted their congregational life in a threatening way, but also raised the question whether this church would be able to appear at the Last Judgment, as it would be required to do, "blameless" (1:8; cf. 15:58).

Paul's theology in 1 and 2 Corinthians differs markedly from his earlier letters because the crisis in Corinth solicited a new response with a new, special kind of theology. Since the Corinthians' ideas were not simply imported from the outside but were mostly based on assumptions in Paul's own theology, he could not simply repudiate their ideas, but had to take them up and develop them in a different direction. Thus, Paul agreed with the Corinthians that a wealth of eloquence and knowledge is certainly a laudable blessing; he added, however, that it ought to add up to "wisdom of God" and not "wisdom of this world" (1 Cor 1:18–3:23). This new theology of wisdom is designed to affirm the Corinthian claims on the one hand, but correct them on the other by bringing them in line with Paul's own theology of the cross.

In order to meet the challenge, Paul proceeded from his established positions on theology and christology (see, esp. 1:1–3, 4–9, 18–24; 8:6; 12:3; 15:3–5). Dealing not with Jewish but Greek claims (1:22), he applied the principles of his theology of justification by faith in Jesus Christ not to "works of the law" (as in Galatians), but to the claim to possess wisdom (1:18–31). The common denominator was the principle of proper and improper "boasting" (1:29–31; 3:21; 4:8; 5:6; 9:15–16; 15:31). In the first part of 1 Corinthians (1:18–3:23) Paul demonstrated what in his eyes really constituted Christian wisdom by critically analyzing the concept. In the second part he brought these clarifications to bear on his own role as church leader (chap. 4) and on the concrete problems which disturbed the church (chaps. 5–15). Since 1 Corinthians evidently did not achieve its goals, the fragments assembled in 2 Corinthians provide further insights into Paul's monumental struggle to get the church to understand and accept his theological viewpoint. Thus, the entire Corinthians correspondence, at least to the extent we possess it, amounts to an education in the apostle's theological thinking. Within the parameters of the struggle, he worked out positions on a broad range of issues, from legal and ethical issues to those of religion and worship, including even self-evaluation of his own role and conduct. See CORINTHIANS, FIRST EPISTLE TO THE; CORINTHIANS, SECOND EPISTLE TO THE.

On the whole, the Corinthian crisis subjected Paul's theology to the test of fire (1 Cor 3:13–15). Apparently, he had no time for critical reevaluation of his theological premises, in particular his doctrines of the spirit, sin, and the law. It is, however not surprising that after the struggle was over, Paul took the time to revise his thinking in rather substantial ways, resulting in his *magnum opus,* Romans.

e. The Later Paul. When Paul wrote his letter to the Romans, he took the occasion to summarize his theology in a more systematic fashion than in his previous letters. This letter does not, however, present a complete and final statement, but rather a résumé of a more mature stage in his theological development. Paul felt the need for this summary for a number of reasons. First, since he did not found the Roman church yet intended to visit it, the letter served as an appropriate way to introduce himself. Second, the apostle also realized that he had to counteract the hostile rumors circulated by his opponents and the caricatured versions of his teaching with which they slandered him (Rom 3:5–8; 6:1). Third, because he knew that dangers awaited him in Jerusalem (15:30–32), Paul sent this letter to Rome, and possibly a copy to Ephesus, as something like a theological "testament" (see Bornkamm 1971a: 88–96; 1971b).

Although presented as a defense argument, the main thesis of which is stated in 1:16–17, Paul's letter contains more than merely an apology for views he has always held. In comparison with his earlier letters, Paul in Romans writes with much greater circumspection and complexity. This letter includes elaborate discussions of theological topics previously argued, or at least mentioned, topics that are entirely new, and, most importantly, revisions of earlier positions on significant theological doctrines. It is incorrect to think, therefore, that in Romans Paul merely presents a fuller version of what he more briefly sets forth in other letters.

The point of Paul's argument as a whole is to explain the reasons why he still refuses to be ashamed of the gospel as he has been preaching it, and why his gospel is indeed God's power achieving salvation for every believer, Jew or Greek (1:16–17). If he can successfully demonstrate this, he can hope the Romans will not be embarrassed by his visit and will support his plans for a mission in Spain (15:22–24).

As the opening thesis (1:16–17) indicates, Paul bases his entire argument on the doctrine of justification by faith in Jesus Christ. This doctrine had, of course, been argued before in Galatians and Philemon, and with special application in the Corinthian letters, but its full development in terms of a history of salvation reaching from Adam (5:12) to the *parousia* (2:5, 16; 8:31–39; 13:11–14) occurs only in Romans. The application of this pivotal doctrine to history has abbreviated parallels in 1 Cor 15:21–22, 45–49 and Gal 3:6–29, but the thoroughness and comprehensiveness of the approach in Romans is a new achievement.

As Paul begins citing his proofs, he first offers a radical critique of paganism (1:18–32) and Judaism (2:1–3:8); this approach is new as well, although elements have occurred in earlier letters (cf. Gal 3:19–25; 4:8–10; Phil 3:2–9; 1 Cor 8–10; 2 Cor 10:1–13:10). While all ancient religions are, according to the apostle, corrupt to the core, divine restitution began with Abraham and reaches all the way to Christ (Rom 4:1–25; cf. Gal 3:6–25). Abraham and Christ, therefore, are the two main pillars on whom the doctrine of justification by faith rests (3:9–31). Unlike Galatians, in Romans Paul does not repudiate the Torah (see 7:12, 16, 21–23; 8:2–8), but instead argues in favor of being a "genuine" Jew and against being a Jew by pretense (2:1–29). The prototype of the genuine Jew is Abraham, who was declared righteous by God even though neither Torah nor circumcision existed at that time. His righteousness was his unconditional faith in God, on account of which he received God's promise. This promise finds fulfilment in Jesus Christ, and is subsequently applied to all who believe in him (4:1–25); therefore, Christ, not Abraham, provides access to God's grace for all believers (5:1–12). Jesus Christ, and Jesus Christ alone, the new and second Adam, has overcome the human corruption endemic in the race since Adam and now makes possible for humanity a means of deliverance from the domination by sin and death that resulted from Adam's fall (5:12–21; cf. 1 Cor 15:21–22, 45–49).

Chapters 6–8 set forth the benefits of Christ's salvation. Initially Paul refers to the doctrine of baptism into the death and resurrection of Christ (6:1–11), writing that through baptism the Christian is sacramentally initiated into and made a partaker of Christ's death and resurrection as a salvation event (see *BTNT* 1: 292–314; Conzelmann 1969: 199–212; Wedderburn 1987). Though Paul has mentioned the basic components of this teaching in Gal 3:26–28 (cf. 1 Cor 1:13–17), the comprehensiveness of what he says here goes beyond anything he previously wrote about baptism. He has spelled it out here because baptism links the Christian to Christ's salvation and thereby provides the basis for the Christian's participation in the benefits of Christ's salvation about to be discussed. The first of Christ's benefits which Paul presents is liberation from the enslaving power of sin (6:12–23), a doctrine which seems to be older and already presupposed in the earlier letters (1 Thessalonians, however, does not mention it). The second benefit, liberation from the law (7:1–25a), expands what Paul had previously said only when referring to his own paradigmatic experience (Gal 2:19–20; Phil 3:7–8). The third benefit is liberation from death (Rom 8:1–30), an idea with antecedents in 1 Thess 4:13–17 and Gal 2:19–20 (also Phil 1:12–26; 1 Cor 15:50–57; 2 Cor 1:3–11; 2:14–17; 4:7–5:15; 13:3–4), but not before stated as a part of an overarching salvation doctrine. These benefits reach their climax with the fourth, viz. the eschatological union with God (Rom 8:31–39; cf. 1 Cor 15:20–28).

The final section on the history of salvation concerns the relationship between Jews and Christians in future history (Romans 9–11), a dimension which Paul had never before addressed. Recognition of this as an issue presupposes Paul's concession that the *parousia* will not be imminent (cf. 13:11–14) and that there will be two religions, Judaism and Christianity, existing side by side for some time to come. Paul still argues on the premises of his doctrine of justification by faith in Jesus Christ that Jews and Christians will have to coexist, stimulating and checking one another by peaceful competition (11:13–24). The final "mystery" will be disclosed when "the fullness of the gentiles enter into" the kingdom of God, and "all Israel will be saved" (11:25–26).

This entire history of salvation is regarded as a succession of God's merciful deeds (12:1), beginning with Abraham and ending when no accuser remains for the Last Judgment (8:31–39; 11:33–36). This grandiose historical and eschatological panoply is yet another new development in Paul's theology.

A further significant shift in Paul's thinking takes place in his ethics, for which the apostle finds a new foundation (Betz 1988). Instead of grounding Christian ethics simply in the spirit, as he does in his earlier letters, Paul develops a new concept in Rom 12:1–15:13. Paul now conceives of ethics as the human response to God's merciful deeds in the history of salvation (chaps. 4–11). This response is a matter of obligation and involves the self-dedication, and, indeed, the self-sacrifice of the whole human person, body and mind (12:1).

Paul has also integrated the notion of spirit into the benefits of Christ (5:5; 7:6; 8:2–27). Thereby Paul has prevented the (Corinthian) misunderstanding of spirit in terms of individualistic spirit possession. The spirit cannot be divorced from the body because self-sacrifice includes the whole person. This person also belongs to the corporate body of the church (12:3–8; see also 1 Cor 12:12–27; Gal 3:26–28) and does not exist in isolation. Moreover, Christian existence is inconceivable without the norms set by the notion of love (*agapē* [12:9–21]). Concretely, Christian ethics is a matter of obligations toward society at large: the state (Rom 13:1–7), the law (13:8–14), and the weaker members of the Church (14:1–15:18).

3. Summary. The extant letters and letter fragments show an author constantly involved in debates and conflicts, trying to explain, defend, and recommend what he sees to be the implications of Christian life and thought. The urgency to engage in this dialogue grew out of Paul's awareness that he and his assistants were taking part in momentous historical developments. This urgency pressed even harder when doom threatened Paul's gentile mission, requiring that he provide theological warrant for it. Thus, through the course of his ministry Paul increasingly found that his task was not only to bring the Gospel to the gentiles, but to bring theological clarification to the Gospel.

As Paul attempted to make sense of Christian theology, the Damascus event provided an unexpected answer to an old Jewish question: "Is God the God of Jews only? Is he not the God of gentiles also?" Because Christ ordered Paul to preach the gospel to the gentiles, Paul could now answer boldly: "Yes, of Gentiles also" (Rom 3:29). Thus the universality of the gospel commission confirmed the unity of God. The Damascus event also demonstrated that the Damascus Christians were correct, righteousness was available apart from Torah. Combining this realization with the unity of God, Paul concluded that the Gospel must provide a single, inclusive means of justification: "Since God is one, he will justify the circumcised on the ground of their faith and the uncircumcised through their faith" (Rom 3:30). Thus, the doctrine of justification by faith was implicit in the Gospel message itself as Paul experienced it: coming to grips with it and making it explicit in ever greater clarity and detail is the thread that runs through Paul's life and letters.

To raise a basic question yet again, does any continuity and consistency of thought underlie the shifts and changes, the theological reformulations and revisions evident in Paul's letters? From the foregoing, we can say that despite changes of position, such as his realization that the *parousia* would be delayed and that the historical coexistence of Christian and non-Christian Judaism would persist for some time, Paul steadily held on to justification by faith. Moreover, if there was anything that established the theological identity and legitimacy of Christianity as a new religion, it was Paul's discovery and exposition of the God who "in Christ" justifies a sinful and godless humanity.

Bibliography

Barrett, C. K. 1982. *Essays on Paul.* Philadelphia.

Bauer, W. 1988. *Griechisch-deutsches Wörterbuch zu den Schriften des Neuen Testaments und der frühchristlichen Literatur.* 6th ed., ed. by K. and B. Aland. Berlin.

Baumgarten, J. 1975. *Paulus und die Apokalyptik.* WMANT 44. Neukirchen-Vluyn.

Baur, F. C. 1845. *Paulus, der Apostel Jesu Christi.* Stuttgart.

Beker, J. 1980. *Paul the Apostle: The Triumph of God in Life and Thought.* Philadelphia.
———. 1988. Paul's Theology: Consistent or Inconsistent? *NTS* 34: 364–77.
Betz, H. D. 1967. *Nachfolge und Nachahmung Jesu Christi im Neuen Testament.* BHT 37. Tübingen.
———. 1972. *Der Apostel Paulus und die sokratische Tradition.* BHT 45. Tübingen.
———. 1986a. The Problem of Rhetoric and Theology according to the Apostle Paul. Pp. 16–48 of *L'Apôtre Paul: Personnalité, style et conception du ministère,* ed. A. Vanhoye. BETL 73. Leuven.
———. 1986b. Paul in the Mani Biography (Codex Manichaicus Coloniensis). Pp. 215–34 in *Codex Manichaicus Coloniensis,* ed. L. Cirillo. Cosenza.
———. 1988. Das Problem der Grundlagen der paulinischen Ethik (Röm 12, 1–2). *ZTK* 85: 199–218.
Boers, H. W. 1988. The Foundation of Paul's Thought: A Methodological Investigation: The Problem of a Coherent Center of Paul's Thought. *StTh* 42: 55–68.
Bornkamm, G. 1971a. *Paul.* Trans. D. M. G. Stalker. New York and Evanston.
———. 1971b. Der Römerbrief als Testament des Paulus. Vol. 4, pp. 120–39 of his *Gesammelte Aufsätze.* Munich.
Braun, H. 1967. *Gesammelte Studien zum Neuen Testament und seiner Umwelt.* 2d ed. Tübingen.
Bryan, C. 1988. A Further Look at Acts 16:1–3. *JBL* 107: 292–94.
Bultmann, R. 1929–36. Zur Geschichte der Paulusforschung. *TRu* N.F. 1: 26–59; 6: 229–46; 8: 1–22.
———. 1967. *Exegetica: Aufsätze zur Erforschung des Neuen Testaments,* ed. E. Dinkler. Tübingen.
———. 1984. *Theologie des Neuen Testaments.* 9th ed., ed. O. Merk. Tübingen.
Cohen, S. D. 1986. Was Timothy Jewish (Acts 16:1–3)? Patristic Exegesis, Rabbinic Law, and Matrilineal Descent. *JBL* 105: 251–68.
Conzelmann, H. 1969. *An Outline of the Theology of the New Testament.* Trans. J. Bowden. London.
———. 1974. *Theologie als Schriftauslegung: Aufsätze zum Neuen Testament.* BEvT 65. Munich.
Cullmann, O. 1959. *The Christology of the New Testament.* Trans. S. C. Guthrie and C. H. Hall. London.
Dahl, N. A. 1977. *Studies in Paul.* Minneapolis.
Davies, W. D. 1955. *Paul and Rabbinic Judaism.* 2d ed. London.
———. 1984. *Jewish and Pauline Studies.* Philadelphia.
Dietzfelbinger, C. 1985. *Die Berufung des Paulus als Ursprung seiner Theologie.* WMANT 58. Neukirchen-Vluyn.
Dinkler, E. 1967. *Signum Crucis: Aufsätze zum Neuen Testament und zur christlichen Archäologie.* Tübingen.
Dockx, S. I. 1976. *Chronologies néotestamentaires et vie de l'église primitive.* Gembloux.
Dodd, C. H. 1953. *New Testament Studies.* Manchester.
———. 1968. *More New Testament Studies.* Manchester.
Furnish, V. P. 1968. *Theology and Ethics in Paul.* Nashville.
———. 1986. Development in Paul's Thought. *JAAR* 48: 289–303.
Georgi, D. 1986. *The Opponents of Paul in Second Corinthians.* Rev. ed. and trans. Philadelphia.
Güttgemanns, E. 1966. *Der leidende Apostel und sein Herr.* FRLANT 90. Göttingen.
Haacker, K. 1972. War Paulus Hillelit? Pp. 106–20 of *Das Institutum Judaicum der Universität Tübingen in den Jahren 1971–72.* Tübingen.
Hahn, F. 1969. *The Titles of Jesus in Christology.* Trans. H. Knight and G. Ogg. New York.
Hanson, A. T. 1974. *Studies in Paul's Technique and Theology.* Grand Rapids.
Hoffmann, P. 1978. *Die Toten in Christus.* 3d ed. NTA 3. Münster.
Hübner, H. 1984. *Law in Paul's Thought.* Edinburgh.
Jeremias, J. 1969. Paulus als Hillelit. Pp. 88–94 in *Neotestamentica et Semitica* (M. Blackfestschrift). Ed. E. E. Ellis and M. Wilcox. Edinburgh.
Jewett, R. 1979. *A Chronology of Paul's Life.* Philadelphia.
Jüngel, E. 1962. *Paulus und Jesus.* HUTh 2. Tübingen.
Käsemann, E. 1964. *Essays on New Testament Themes.* Trans. W. J. Montague. London.
———. 1969. *New Testament Questions of Today.* Trans. W. J. Montague. Philadelphia.
———. 1971. *Perspectives on Paul.* Trans. M. Kohl. London.
Klein, G. 1988. Ein Sturmzentrum der Paulusforschung. *VF* 33: 40–56.
Knox, J. 1950. *Chapters in a Life of Paul.* Nashville. Rev. ed. Macon, GA, 1987.
Koch, D.-A. 1986. *Die Schrift als Zeuge des Evangeliums.* BHT 69. Tübingen.
Koester, H. 1961. The Purpose of the Polemic of a Pauline Fragment (Phil III). *NTS* 8: 317–32.
———. 1982. *Introduction to the New Testament.* 2 vols. Berlin.
Kümmel, W. G. 1975. *Introduction to the New Testament.* Trans. H. C. Kee. Nashville.
Lindemann, A. 1979. *Paulus im ältesten Christentum.* BHT 58. Tübingen.
———. 1986. Die biblischen Toragebote und die paulinische Ethik. Pp. 242–65 of *Studien zum Text und zur Ethik des Neuen Testaments.* Berlin.
Lüdemann, G. 1980–83. *Paulus, der Heidenapostel.* 2 vols. FRLANT 123, 130. Göttingen.
———. 1983. *Paulus und das Judentum.* Munich.
———. 1984. *Paul, Apostle to the Gentiles: Studies in Chronology.* Trans. F. S. Jones. Philadelphia.
———. 1988. *Early Christianity According to the Traditions in Acts.* Trans. F. S. Jones. Philadelphia.
McDonald, D. R. 1983. *The Legend and the Apostle.* Philadelphia.
Meeks, W. A. 1983. *The First Urban Christians.* New Haven.
Meeks, W. A., ed. 1972. *The Writings of St. Paul.* New York.
Merk, O. 1988. Paulus-Forschung 1936–1985. *TRu* 53: 1–81.
Metzger, B. 1960. *Index to Periodical Literature on the Apostle Paul.* NTTS 1. Leiden.
Nock, A. D. 1938. *St. Paul.* London.
Oepke, A. 1933. Probleme der vorchristlichen Zeit des Paulus. *TSK* 105: 387–424.
Ollrog, W. H. 1979. *Paulus und seine Mitarbeiter.* WMANT 50. Neukirchen-Vluyn.
Pedersen, S., ed. 1980. *Die Paulinische Literatur und Theologie.* Århus.
Räisänen, H. 1987. *Paul and the Law.* 2d ed. WUNT 29. Tübingen.
Rengstorf, K. H., ed. 1964. *Das Paulusbild in der neueren deutschen Forschung.* Darmstadt.
Rigaux, B. 1968. *The Letters of St. Paul: Modern Studies.* Chicago.
Safrai, S. 1976. Education and the Study of the Torah. Pp. 945–70 of *The Jewish People in the First Century.* CRINT 1/2. Philadelphia.
Saldarini, A. J. 1988. *Pharisees, Scribes and Sadducees in Palestinian Society.* Wilmington, DE.
Sanders, E. P. 1977. *Paul and Palestinian Judaism.* Philadelphia.
———. 1983. *Paul, the Law and the Jewish People.* Philadelphia.

Schmeller, T. 1987. *Paulus und die "Diatribe."* NTAbh N.F. 19. Münster.
Schneemelcher, W. 1987–89. *Neutestamentliche Apokryphen.* 2 vols. 5th ed. Tübingen.
Schneider, G. 1980–82. *Die Apostelgeschichte.* 2 vols. HTKNT 5. Freiburg, Basel, Vienna.
Schoeps, H. J. 1961. *Paul: The Theology of the Apostle in the Light of Jewish Religious History.* Trans. H. Knight. Philadelphia.
Schweitzer, A. 1912. *Paul and His Interpreters: A Critical History.* Trans. W. Montgomery. London.
Stendahl, K. 1976. *Paul among the Jews and Gentiles and Other Essays.* Philadelphia.
Strecker, G. 1976. Befreiung und Rechtfertigung. Zur Stellung der Rechtfertigungslehre in der Theologie des Paulus. Pp. 479–508 of *Rechtfertigung. FS für E. Käsemann,* ed. J. Friedrich et al. Göttingen.
Suhl, A. 1975. *Paulus und seine Briefe.* SNT 11. Gütersloh.
Thüsing, W. 1986. *Per Christum in Deum. Studien zum Verhältnis von Christozentrik und Theozentrik in den paulinischen Hauptbriefen.* 2 vols. 3d ed. NTAbh 1. Münster.
Vanhoye, A., ed. 1986. *L'Apôtre Paul: Personnalité, style et conception du ministère.* BETL 73. Leuven.
Van Unnik, W. C. 1973. Tarsus or Jerusalem: The City of Paul's Youth. Vol. 1, pp. 259–320, 321–27 of his *Sparsa Collecta.* Leiden.
Vielhauer, P. 1966. On the "Paulinism" of Acts. Pp. 33–50 of *Studies in Luke-Acts,* ed. L. E. Keck and J. L. Martyn. Nashville.
———. 1975. *Geschichte der urchristlichen Literatur.* Berlin.
Wedderburn, A. J. M. 1987. *Baptism and Resurrection.* WUNT 44. Tübingen.
Westerholm, S. 1986–87. On Fulfilling the Whole Law (Gal. 5:14). *SEÅ* 51–52: 229–37.
———. 1988. *Israel's Law and the Church's Faith.* Grand Rapids.
Wilckens, U. 1982. Zur Entwicklung des paulinischen Gesetzesverständnisses. *NTS* 28: 154–90.
Wolter, M. 1988. *Die Pastoralbriefe als Paulustradition.* FRLANT 146. Göttingen.

HANS DIETER BETZ

PAUL AND SENECA, EPISTLES OF. A series of 14 Latin letters that comprise an apocryphal correspondence between Paul and the Roman philosopher Seneca. They were most likely written in the 3d or 4th century to commend Seneca to Christians or to recommend Paul's letters to members of Roman society. The correspondence is attested in numerous corrupt manuscripts, most of which date from the 13th, 14th, and 15th centuries, although a few are as early as the 9th. The letters were known to Jerome and Augustine, but scholars disagree over whether they regarded them as authentic. Some scholars suggest that the letters we now possess are not the ones known to Jerome and Augustine (Lightfoot 1953: 330–31). The correspondence remained popular throughout the Middle Ages. It is noted by Peter of Cluny in *Tractatus adversus Petrobrusianos* (*PL* 189.737C); by Peter Abelard in *Introductio ad Theologiam* 1.24 and in *Expositio in epistolam Pauli ad Romanos* 1.1; and in the *editio princeps* of Erasmus (Kurfess *NTApocr* 2:135). English translations are provided by James and Kurfess.

The correspondence alternates, with letters 1, 3, 5, 7, 9, 11, 12, and 13 purportedly written by Seneca, and letters 2, 4, 6, 8, 10, and 14 supposedly written by Paul. In letter six Paul greets Lucilius along with Seneca; letter seven is addressed to Paul and Theophilus. The letters contain an exchange of compliments between the two writers.

Seneca begins the series by praising the "wonderful exhortations for the moral life" contained in Paul's letters (Kurfess *NTApocr* 2:135). Paul responds, in letter two, by thanking Seneca for his high praise. Letter three tells of Seneca's desire to read some scrolls to the emperor. Letter four expresses Paul's desire to meet with Seneca. In letter five Seneca is distressed that Paul has not come to see him, and wonders if it is because he is afraid that the empress is displeased over his giving up the beliefs of Judaism. Seneca says that a visit might enable Paul to explain why he has given up these beliefs and practices. The sixth letter provides an opportunity for Paul to encourage Seneca and Lucilius to treat all people with respect.

In letter seven Seneca reports that he agrees with what Paul says in his letters to the Galatians, Corinthians, and Achaians (= 2 Corinthians; see 2 Cor 1:1), and that Paul's thoughts have made a positive impression on the emperor. Paul uses the eighth letter to tell Seneca that, while showing love and respect for him, he must take care not to offend the empress. In letter nine Seneca expresses his new understanding of Paul's concerns and his desire that they begin to work afresh. Letter ten concerns Paul's acknowledgement that his name should have been placed last on a letter he previously sent to Seneca. Seneca sends the eleventh letter to indicate his distress and grief over the persecution experienced by Paul and other Christians. Letter twelve is Seneca's response to the issue, raised in letter ten, of the placement of Paul's name. He indicates that he is not at all offended by the placement and suggests that they are equals. In letter fourteen, Seneca encourages Paul to write with refinement. Finally, in letter 14 Paul pushes Seneca to write in such a manner as to "make yourself a new herald of Jesus Christ" (Kurfess *NTApocr* 2:141).

Bibliography

James, M. R. 1924. *The Apocryphal new Testament.* Oxford.
Kurfess, A. 1952. "Zu dem apokryphen Briefwechsel zwichen dem Philosophen Seneca und dem Apostel Paulus" *Aevum* 26: 42–48.
Liénard, E. 1932. Sur La Correspondance Apocryphe De Sénèque et de Saint Paul. *Revue belge de philologie et d'historie* 11: 5–23.
Lightfoot, J. B. 1953. "The Letters of Paul and Seneca." Pp. 329–31 in *St. Paul's Epistle to the Philippians.* Repr. Grand Rapids.
Sevenster, J. N. 1961. *Paul and Seneca.* Leiden.

DANA ANDREW THOMASON

PAUL'S NEPHEW. The report about an unnamed nephew in Acts 23:16–22 is the only reference we have to Paul's family connections. Naturally, there is the temptation to view the incident as a Lukan creation. However, since Paul as a Roman citizen would in any case have been brought to Caesarea as the first stage in any judgment process, Luke would have had no motive for creating the incident (Williams *Acts* BHNTC, 251). The account must go back to an eyewitness (Hengel 1983: 175); at least, Paul's sister and nephew appear to be historical (Lüdemann 1987: 254–55). Moreover, Paul's sister's family or the nephew himself must have had connections in Jewish circles for him to have heard of the ambush. This story may belong to a tradition about Paul's family moving from Tarsus to Jerusalem and about his education there under Gamaliel (cf. Acts 22:3).

Not unreasonably, scholars infer from Phil 3:8, "For his (Christ's) sake I have suffered the loss of all things," that Paul was disinherited for his acceptance and proclamation of Jesus. Such a situation would explain how his sister's family might still have Jewish connections (Bruce *Acts* NICNT, 457–58). Also, visits to persons in prison were possible (e.g., Luke 7:18; Matt 11:2; 25:36; Acts 24:23; 28:30; Phil 2:25–30). Nonetheless, because there is a minimum of verifiable evidence, much that is said is conjectural.

The text reports that Paul's nephew learned of the ambush planned against him and told him about it. Paul then appears almost to order the centurion to lead his nephew to the tribune since he has something to tell him. The centurion does this. The tribune takes Paul's nephew aside and inquires what he has to say. Paul's nephew tells him about the Jewish ambush, that they will ask him to bring Paul down to the Sanhedrin the next day, and that more than 40 individuals have bound themselves by oath to kill Paul at that time. Paul's nephew urges the tribune not to agree to their request. The tribune tells him to tell no one that he has informed him of the plot, and then dismisses him.

In the story, Paul does the reasonable thing, and the centurion does his duty. Both Paul's nephew and the tribune demonstrate moral character. The nephew cares enough about Paul to risk informing the Romans, and the tribune is well disposed and attentive, yet cautious. The story of Paul's nephew belongs to Luke's theme that the Roman officials are well disposed toward the Christians (O'Toole 1984: 160–66).

Bibliography

Hengel, M. 1983. Der Historiker Lukas und die Geographie Palästinas in der Apostelgeschichte. *ZDPV* 99: 147–183.

Lüdemann, G. 1987. *Das frühe Christentum nach den Traditionen der Apostelgeschichte: Ein Kommentar*. Göttingen.

O'Toole, R. F. 1984. *The Unity of Luke's Theology: An Analysis of Luke-Acts*. GNS 9. Wilmington, DE.

ROBERT F. O'TOOLE

PAUL, ACTS OF. A 2d-century Christian writing recounting the missionary career and death of the apostle Paul and classed among the NT Apocrypha. In this work Paul is pictured traveling from city to city, converting gentiles and proclaiming the need for a life of sexual abstinence and other encratite practices. Though ancient evidence suggests that the *Acts of Paul* was a relatively lengthy work (3600 lines according to the *Stichometry* of Nicephorus), only about two-thirds of that amount still survives. Individual sections were transmitted separately by the medieval manuscript tradition (Lipsius 1891), most importantly the *Acts of Paul and Thekla* and the *Martyrdom of Paul*, both extant in the original Greek and several ancient translations. Manuscript discoveries in the last century have added considerable additional material. The most important of these include a Greek papyrus of the late 3d century, now at Hamburg (10 pages), a Coptic papyrus of the 4th or 5th century, now at Heidelberg (about 80 pages), and a Greek papyrus of correspondence between Paul and the Corinthians (*3 Corinthians* = Testuz 1959), now at Geneva. These finds have confirmed that the Thekla cycle and story of Paul's martyrdom were originally part of the larger *Acts of Paul* (details in Bovon 1981 or *NTApocr.*). See also PAUL, MARTYRDOM OF; THEKLA, ACTS OF.

The papyrus discoveries have suggested that the story of the *Acts of Paul* was organized according to an itinerary of missionary visits to the leading cities of the Roman East (Schmidt 1905), including at least Antioch of Syria, Iconium, Antioch of Pisidia, Seleucia, Myra, Sidon, Tyre, Ephesus, Philippi, Corinth, then on to Italy, and finally martyrdom at Rome. In each city Paul encounters believers, sometimes already known to him; whether he has sent fellow workers ahead or is now visiting previously established communities is not always clear. A constant theme is the opposition engendered by Paul's preaching of conversion to a Christianity marked especially by renunciation of ordinary life and values. Because the work is incomplete and its original sequence of events not entirely recoverable, however, arguments from silence about its contents or interests must remain more than usually tentative (Schmidt 1905 and 1936; Schneemelcher *NTApocr.*, and 1974; Bovon 1981).

There are many coincidences of names and places with the account in the NT Acts of the Apostles, but very little actual agreement in detail for any particular event or place. There is some diversity in the manner of Paul's preaching from city to city, but consistency in his message: the need for conversion to a life of celibacy in Christ. In Iconium, for example, we see Paul pronouncing beatitudes that stress the value of a life of renunciation: "Blessed are those who have kept the flesh pure . . . Blessed are the continent . . . Blessed are those who have renounced this world . . . Blessed are those who have wives as though not having them. . . . Blessed are the bodies of the virgins . . ." (*Acts of Paul and Thekla* 5–6). This stress on encratism, that is, a life of ascetic renunciation and physical denial, represents an important current within earliest Christianity (Tisserot in Bovon 1981; Brown 1988).

In several places, following a theme familiar in the Apocryphal Acts in general, social and legal conflict arises because of Paul's success in summoning pagans (especially women) to the celibate or virginal life. The best-known surviving section was transmitted separately in late antiquity and the Middle Ages as the *Acts of Paul and Thekla* due to St. Thekla's importance as a figure of cult in Christian Asia Minor (for the extensive hagiographical tradition see Dagron 1978). This story portrays a young woman, about to be married to a leading city figure, who upon hearing Paul instead adopts the celibate Christian life and attempts to journey with the apostle and then herself become a missionary. Paul is not very encouraging until Thekla proves her mettle (and her vocation?). Thekla's stubborn celibacy twice provokes anger, first in her native Iconium from her rejected fiancé, whereupon she is arresed, condemned to death in a public beast-fight, but ultimately rescued by divine intervention. In the second case, in Seleucia, Thekla is condemned to the beasts by another rejected man, and then baptizes herself when in imminent danger; after her second miraculous rescue, she adopts an apostolic life and finally receives Paul's blessing and approval for her work.

The motifs of travel, frustrated love, and other entertaining elements are reminiscent of many aspects of the ancient popular genre of romance novels (Söder 1932; Pervo 1987), with the important difference that in these ascetic acts the tone is less erotic than anti-erotic. There is very little theological argument or speculation, but instead the narrative describes the dangers and successes of those steadfast in their renunciatory behavior. The early Christian communities are portrayed as joyfully united in prayer and simple communion, looking for the soon and sudden end of the world, portrayed in the traditional apocalyptic imagery.

The themes, locales, and external evidence all point to a composition date sometime in the mid-2d century, somewhere in Asia Minor. Tertullian claimed to know that the work was the product of an Asian presbyter who however was quickly exposed as a fraud (*De baptismo* 17). Tertullian's objection to the work is the leading role, self-baptism, and attitude assigned to Thekla, and his response is a good indication of both the appeal and the threat embodied in the work. Some modern scholars suggest that the authors of at least the Thekla cycle, perhaps in an earlier oral form, were women seeking affirmation of their celibate way of life and leadership role in Asian Christianity (see esp. Davies 1980 and Burrus 1987). Certainly the stories in the *Acts of Paul* reflect the more radically renunciatory side of 1st and 2d century Pauline Christianity and uphold the tradition of sexual equality over the subordination of women (cf. e.g., 1 Corinthians 7 vs. 1 Timothy 2), but specific claims about the gender of the writer(s) go beyond the evidence available (see MacDonald 1983 and 1986).

The nature of the relationship between the *Acts of Paul* and the NT Acts is disputed, though traditionally, as with most "apocryphal" literature, scholars suggest that these stories are intended to supplement the canon (Söder 1932; Schneemelcher 1964 and 1974). But some have argued more recently that while the author(s) of the *Acts of Paul* may well have known the NT Acts, that work was not in any way decisive for his (or her!—see above) own understanding of Paul's story (esp. Pervo 1987). For example, the dominant motif of Jewish hostility to Paul's mission in the NT Acts, along with at least passive acceptance from Roman authorities, is entirely missing. In the *Acts of Paul* the Jews and their synagogues are offstage; the apostle preaches to the gentiles and encounters opposition from the social and governmental elite and indeed finishes by being executed at Rome at Nero's command. Only in this last episode it is not Paul's preaching of celibacy that puts him in danger—instead Nero perceives a social, political, and perhaps even a military threat from "Christ's army" as led by Paul. If the NT Acts are known, in sum, they are not used as a source either of reliable information or of authoritative interpretation about Paul's life and theological orientation.

Bibliography

Bovon, F., ed. 1981. *Les Actes apocryphes des Apôtres: christianisme et monde païen.* Publications de la Faculté de Théologie de l'Université de Genève 4. Geneva.

Brown, P. 1988. *The Body and Society.* New York.

Burrus, V. 1987. *Chastity as Autonomy: Women in the Stories of the Apocryphal Acts.* Studies in Women and Religion 23. Lewiston.

Dagron, G. 1978. *Vie et miracles de sainte Thècle.* Sudsidia Hagiographica 62. Brussels.

Davies, S. L. 1980. *The Revolt of the Widows: The Social World of the Apocryphal Acts.* Carbondale, IL.

James, M. R. 1924. *The Apocryphal New Testament.* Oxford.

Lipsius, R. A., and Bonnet, M., eds. 1891. *Acta Apostolorum Apocrypha.* Leipzig. Repr. Hildesheim, 1959.

MacDonald, D. R. 1983. *The Legend and the Apostle.* Philadelphia.

———, ed. 1986. *The Apocryphal Acts of the Apostles.* Semeia 38. Atlanta.

Pervo, R. I. 1987. *Profit with Delight: The Literary Genre of the Acts of the Apostles.* Philadelphia.

Schmidt, C. 1905. *Acta Pauli.* 2d ed. Leipzig. Repr. 1965.

Schmidt, C., and Schubart, W. 1936. *Praxeis Paulou: Acta Pauli nach dem Papyrus der Hamburger Staats und Universitäts-Bibliothek.* Glückstadt.

Schneemelcher, W. 1964. Die Apostelgeschichte des Lukas und die Acta Pauli. Pp. 236–50 in *Apophoreta: Festschrift für Earnst Haenchen.* BZNW 30. Berlin.

———. 1974. *Gesammelte Schriften.* Thessaloniki.

Söder, R. 1932. *Die apokryphen Apostelgeschichten und die romanhafte Literature der Antike.* Würzburger Studien zür Altertumswissenschaft 3. Stuttgart.

Testuz, M., ed. 1959. *Papyrus Bodmer X–XII.* Geneva.

Vouaux, L. 1913. *Les Actes de Paul et ses lettres apocryphes.* Les Apocryphes du Nouveau Testament. Paris.

PHILIP SELLEW

PAUL, APOCALYPSE OF. The name of two different apocryphal works, both inspired by the tradition of Paul's "rapture" into the heavens (2 Cor 12:2–4). One, an extensive tour of paradise and hell, composed sometime in the 4th or 5th century C.E. is preserved in a long Latin version; a Greek abridgment, and in Armenian, Old Russian, Syriac, and Coptic versions. It also appears to have been an important source for later Christian works which described the geography of the fiery punishments in hell (see A below). The other, a Christian gnostic work from the 2d or 3d century C.E. (NHC V,*2*), emphasizes Paul's ascent with the twelve apostles through the eight heavens of Jewish and Christian traditions into the "tenth," the resting place of the elect (see B below). It survives in a single reasonably well-preserved Coptic version found among the gnostic writings at Nag Hammadi. There are some parallels between its vision of the souls being punished in the fourth and fifth heavens and the punishments reported in the *Testament of Abraham* 10. Epiphanius alludes to an *Ascension of Paul* used in some gnostic groups (*Pan.* 38.2). Since that work had only three heavens, it may indicate that yet a third apocalypse of the heavenly journey type circulated in early Christian circles.

A. Latin Version

Although *Apoc. Paul* was originally composed in Greek, the long Latin version represents the best text for this early Christian work. It is first clearly attested in Augustine (*In Joh. Tract.* 98.8; *Enchir.* 112–13). An ancient introduction to the work claims that is was composed in the late 4th century C.E. Many modern scholars think that the body of the apocalypse may have been written in the early 3d century, since Origen refers to an *Apoc. Paul* as accepted by the church and also gives a description of the fate of the soul similar to that beginning in chap. 13 *(Hom. in Pss. 5).* The author praises asceticism (chaps. 9, 24, 26, 39–40) and condemns persons who only appear to renounce the world by wearing the garb of the ascetic (chap. 40). But unlike later texts it does not refer to the extensive development of monastic asceticism.

The so-called "Tarsus introduction" (chaps. 1–2) claims that the manuscript was found in 388 C.E. by a person living in a house once owned by Paul. Following instructions given by an angel in a dress, the finder discovered in the foundations a marble box containing the revelation. Chaps. 3–10 detail creations complaint against the sinfulness of humanity. God's forebearance is demonstrated in the delay of judgment. Nevertheless all the deeds of humans are reported by angels every morning and evening. Paul's journey to the third heaven enables him to see how the wicked and righteous souls depart from the body at death (chaps. 11–18). Journeys in the heavenly regions allow Paul to see Enoch and Elijah in paradise, the land where the righteous dwell during the millennium and the city of Christ. The righteous ones of the Hebrew Bible and the altar where David sings are found in that city (chaps. 19–30). Then Paul is taken to see the extensive punishments suffered by sinners. At the end of the journey he and the archangel Michael plead for mercy for sinners. Christ responds by rebuking the sinners but granting them rest from punishment on Sunday (chaps. 31–44). The journey ends in paradise where Paul is met by the righteous including the Virgin Mary, the patriarchs, Moses and Adam (chaps. 45–51). Adam blesses Paul for the many persons he has brought to faith. On the Latin version, see James 1893; Duesning 1965; Himmelfarb 1983.

B. Coptic (Gnostic) Version

The first of four gnostic apocalypses, in the Achmimic dialect, from Codex V at Nag Hammadi, this work bears the title *Apocalypse of Paul* at the beginning and end of the writing (NHC V,2). It is not related to the *Apoc. Paul* preserved in the Latin, though Paul does witness the judgment of various souls in his ascent through the fourth and fifth heavens. Reincarnation is presented as the punishment extracted by the demonic guardians of the heavens from those souls which have not obtained true knowledge (21, 18–22).

The book opens with Paul meeting a small child, his guiding angel, also identified with the Holy Spirit on "the mountain in Jericho." The divine figure will lead the apostle in his ascent to Jerusalem. Gnostic revelations frequently picture the risen Christ as a polymorphic figure who appears like a child. Thus the opening appears to recall Paul's resurrection vision and his going up to Jerusalem to visit the apostles (Gal 1:11–17; 2:1–2). Here he is taken into the heavenly Jerusalem where he will meet his "fellow apostles," the Twelve. As they begin the ascent, Paul is shown his body and those of the Twelve on the earth below. In the shining light of the sixth heaven, Paul must utter a formula, "open to me and the [Holy] Spirit, who is before me," in order to pass by the toll collector (22, 21–23). Passing into the seventh heaven, he encounters an old man on a throne who acknowledges Paul's election in terms drawn from Gal 1:15. An extended dialogue in which Paul speaks the gnostic formulas about returning to the "place from which he came" and leading others from the captivity of the lower world shows that the old man is the Jewish creator god. Paul goes beyond that god's heaven and authority when he gives the "sign" that makes it possible for him to enter the next heaven, the Ogdoad. There the Twelve greet Paul, and they continue in the company of the elect to the tenth heaven.

This *Apoc. Paul* has clearly used the genre of heavenly journey to embody the gnostic formulas for the post mortem ascent of the soul. This theme along with the formulaic dialogues necessary for the soul to gain its freedom appears in a number of gnostic writings (*Gos. Mary, 1 Apoc. Jas., Gos. Thom.* Log. 50). On the Coptic version, see Murdock and MacRae 1979; Fallon 1979; Kasser 1965; Krause 1983; Orbe 1983.

Bibliography

Duesening, H. 1965. Apocalypse of Paul. *NTApoc* 2: 755–98.

Fallon, F. 1979. The Gnostic Apocalypse. *Semeia* 14: 123–58.

Himmelfarb, M. 1983. *Tours of Hell.* Philadelphia.

James, M. R. 1893. *Apocrypha Anecdota.* TextsS 2 3. Cambridge.

Kasser, R. 1965. Textes gnostiques: Remarques à propos des éditions récentes du Livre secret de Jean et des Apocalypses de Paul, Jacques et Adam. *Mus* 78: 71–98.

Krause, M. 1983. Die literarischen Gattungen der Apokalypsen von Nag Hammadi. Pp. 621–37 in *Apocalypticism in the Mediterranean World and the Near East,* ed. D. Hellholm. Tübingen.

Murdock, W. R., and MacRae, G. W. 1979. Apocalypse of Paul. *Nag Hammadi Codices V, 2–5 and VI,* ed. D. M. Parrott. NHS 11. Leiden.

Orbe, A. 1983. Gli Apocrifi cristiani a Nag Hammadi. *Aug* 23: 83–109.

PHEME PERKINS

PAUL, MARTYRDOM OF. A document describing Paul's encounter with the emperor Nero in Rome and his subsequent trial, execution, and miraculous appearance after death. Originally the *Martyrdom of Paul* was the concluding section of the 2d century apocryphon the *Acts of Paul,* but it was separated very early and transmitted independently in medieval Christianity in connection with the cult of the holy apostle and martyr. The story tells how Paul runs afoul of Nero by resurrecting and converting Patroclus, the imperial cupbearer. A search leads to Paul's arrest and that of many other Christians, all of whom are condemned to death when Nero hears Paul's threats of apocalyptic judgment with fire. Paul predicts that the emperor will see him after his death; after his execution by beheading, when milk miraculously spurts from his neck rather than blood, the apostle does appear, causing Nero to free the remaining Christians. While in jail awaiting execution, Paul had begun to convert the Roman centurion Cestus and the prefect Longus, who at his instructions visit his tomb at dawn and receive baptism from Titus and Luke. The historical value of the story is minimal, as is suggested by its borrowing of many motifs from similar accounts of the deaths of holy people, and its literary merits are few; but the *Martyrdom of Paul* nonetheless achieved great popularity. See also PAUL, ACTS OF.

PHILIP SELLEW

PAUL, PASSION OF. See PETER AND PAUL, PASSION OF; PAUL, MARTYRDOM OF.

PAUL, PRAYER OF THE APOSTLE (NHC I,*1*). Inscribed in the front flyleaf of Codex I of the Nag Hammadi collection is a brief (2 page) work followed by a title and colophon. Apart from a few lines missing at the top of the first page, the work is well preserved. Although it survives in Sahidic Coptic, the *Prayer of the Apostle Paul* (NHC I,*1*), like most of the other works in the Nag Hammadi collection, was probably composed in Greek, the language of the colophon and title. The date of composition is uncertain, although it was clearly written before the final copying of the collection in the mid-4th century, and probably after the mid-2d century, when the Valentinian Gnosticism evidenced in the text emerged.

In form, the text resembles prayers and hymns in other gnostic, Hermetic, and magical sources. The extant portion begins with a series of invocations of the redeemer, "Jesus Christ, the Lord of Lords." He is asked to bestow on the supplicant his blessings, including bodily healing and eternal salvation.

The major motifs of the prayer are gnostic commonplaces. Thus, the invocations identify the redeemer as the "source," "mind," "fullness," and "repose" of the supplicant, who asks for the redemption of "my eternal light-soul and my spirit." Yet the text also owes some of its motifs to the Psalms and to the Pauline epistles. A clear example of dependence on Paul, and at the same time another indication of gnostic orientation, is the request to be granted "what no angel-eye has seen and no archon-ear has heard and what has not entered into the human heart" (cf. 1 Cor 2:9). The Gnosticism involved is probably Valentinianism, which is represented in several other works contained in the codex, including the *Gospel of Truth* (NHC I,*3*), *The Treatise on Resurrection* (NHC I,*4*), and *The Tripartite Tractate* (NHC I,*5*). The invocations of the redeemer would be at home in Valentinianism, as are the designations of the redeemer as "First-born" and "First begotten." The disparaging reference to the creation of the human heart "after the image of the psychic God" evokes the common gnostic reading of Genesis and the Valentinian tripartite schema which consigns the creator God of the OT and all his works to the "psychic" realm.

Bibliography

MacRae, G. W. 1987. Prayer and Knowledge of Self in Gnosticism. Pp. 218–36 in *Studies in the New Testament and Gnosticism,* ed. D. J. Harrington and S. B. Marrow. Wilmington, DE.

Mueller, D. 1985. The Prayer of the Apostle Paul. Pp. 5–11 in *Nag Hammadi Codex I (The Jung Codex),* ed. H. W. Attridge. NHS 22. Leiden.

HAROLD W. ATTRIDGE

PAULUS, SERGIUS (PERSON) [Gk *Sergios Paulos*]. The proconsul of Cyprus converted by Paul when he and Barnabas visited that island on their first missionary journey (Acts 13:7).

The Roman cognomen "Paulus" is found in two inscriptions which have been thought to identify the proconsul mentioned in Acts 13 (*IGRR* III.930 and *CIL* VI.31545). The "Paulus" mentioned in the first inscription is too late be connected with Paul. The second inscription mentions an L. Sergius Paulus who was curator of the Tiber, but does not connect him with Cyprus. He could be the Paulus mentioned in Acts if it is assumed that he was later appointed to Cyprus in the right time frame. A third inscription (*IGRR* III.935) has been restored to read "Q. Sergius Paulus." The identification of this person with the proconsul of Acts is more probable than the other two inscriptions but conclusive proof is lacking (Van Elderen 1970: 155f). If a definite inscriptional identification of Sergius Paulus could be made it would be important for establishing the chronology of the Pauline missionary journeys in Acts.

Because Luke fails to mention the baptism of the proconsul some have thought that he was not actually converted. The Lukan emphasis on repentance and baptism as a sign of conversion found in the early chapters of Acts is less prominent in the Pauline sections of Acts. But Luke's use of *pistis* (faith) and *pisteuō* (believe) in connection with Paul is an effort to mimic Pauline language and connotes conversion. In Luke's eyes, Sergius Paulus is a convert. Ramsay (1920: 150–72) attempted to use inscriptional evidence mentioning other members of the family to substantiate Luke's claim as historically accurate. His results are intriguing but inconclusive.

The portrayal of Sergius Paulus as a convert may be important to the theology of Acts in two ways. First, it has been thought to reflect a pro-Roman apologetic. Luke is said to be seeking Roman acceptance of Christianity by stating that a Roman of the Senatorial Order had found it acceptable. But since there are other aspects of Acts which make a Roman apologetic problematic a second explanation may be suggested. From a sociological perspective the story about Sergius Paulus functions to provide social legitimacy for the Christians who were reading Acts. Rather than indicating that Luke's community actually had such upper-class members, this story of an aristocratic Roman convert would help Christians from marginalized groups or others experiencing status inconsistency to see themselves as on a par with other religions groups in the Greco-Roman world. See ELYMAS.

Bibliography

Ramsay, W. M. 1920. *The Bearing of Recent Discovery on the Trustworthiness of the New Testament.* London.

Van Elderen, B. 1970. Some Archaeological Observations on Paul's First Missionary Journey. Pp. 151–61 in *Apostolic History and the Gospel.* Ed. W. W. Gasque and R. P. Martin. Grand Rapids.

THOMAS W. MARTIN

PAVILION. See ART AND ARCHITECTURE.

PEACE. This entry consists of two articles. The first one deals with peace in the OT, and the second one covers peace in the NT.

OLD TESTAMENT

The principal word used to express the idea of peace in the Hebrew Bible is *šālôm.* The root of the word is found in many Semitic languages. The Akkadian *salāmū* comes closest to the core meaning of the root, "to be hale, whole, complete." In one form or another the notions of wholeness, health, and completeness inform all the variants of the word. Peace is not, then, simply a negative, the absence of war. Peace is a positive notion, a notion with its own content.

Šālôm is the daily greeting in Israel; *šālôm ʿălêkem* "peace upon you (pl.)" is a common expression we could translate as "good day." But it really is closer to "may you be well." To be well is, of course, to be "whole, to be complete," to have physical and spiritual resources sufficient to one's needs.

Wholeness or completeness can be ascribed to things as well. Thus Solomon in 1 Kgs 9:25 offers peace offerings *(šelāmîm)* in the temple he completed *(šillam).* A debt is made good *(šallēm)* through payment of money. Vows are completed *(šallēm)* through sacrificial offerings.

Peace is contrasted with war. Qoheleth notes that "there is a time for peace and a time for war" (Qoh 3:8). In numerous passages peace is negotiated to end or preclude hostilities (Deut 20:10–12; Jos 9:15; 10:1; 10:4; 11:29). R. de Vaux (*AncIsr,* 254) notes that "peace in a political sense is not only the absence of war in a purely negative sense, but it includes the idea of friendly relations between two peoples" (see Judg 4:17; Isa 7:14; 1 Kgs 5:4, 26; 22:45). Peace is also synonymous with victory (Judg 8:9; 2 Sam 19:25, 31; 1 Kgs 22:27–28; Jer 43:12). Peace and prosperity are paired (Mic 3:5; Zech 8:12; Mal 2:5). In this pairing it would seem that peace is seen as a sort of economic freedom.

Then there is the idea of dying peaceably. "You shall go to your fathers in peace" (Gen 15:15) is a promise to Abraham; this peace is contrasted to disquiet. The peace of the blessed rest overcomes the natural anxiety about death and the afterlife. These usages of *šālôm* are "secular" or "profane," in contrast to the theological understanding of *šālôm.*

G. von Rad (*ROTT,* 1:130) observed that "the relationship guaranteed by a covenant is commonly designated by the word *šlm*" (see Gen 26:30ff; 1 Kgs 5:26; Isa 44:10; Job 5:23). The Hebrew Bible speaks of the *bĕrît šālôm* "covenant of peace" (Num 25:12; Ezek 34:25; 37:26). This notion of a covenant of peace is particularly useful in developing our understanding of *šālôm.* The covenant initiates a relationship which is based in some sense on mutually assured obligations. Though God cannot be said literally to be "obliged," there is an implicit contract that attaches transcendent values to ordinary or customary human actions.

It is this association of *šālôm* with *bĕrît* "covenant" and also with *mišpat* "judgment, justice" that ties together the nuance of wholeness with the notion of peace as an action. In Ps 34:14 the psalmist charges hearers, "Do good, seek peace, pursue it." Here peace is not something that simply happens; it is a content-laden thing that one can lay hold of. And, further, peace is not seen as a mere product but as an end in itself.

In Zech 8:16–19 the notion of peace is joined with *mišpat;* where the root *šlm* again is used in its meaning of true or complete justice. And *šālôm* is joined with *ʾemet* "truth." Peace, truth, and justice are parallel terms. Their association in this passage implies that peace has a content like justice and truth. Peace encompasses a relationship that is ordered, a relationship of equity. So in Ps 85:10 "righteousness and peace shall kiss"; the two join together as partners in the blessed life. And in Isa 32:17 the prophet avers that "peace is the effect of righteousness," which in the Vulgate becomes *"opus justitiae pax"* or "peace is the work of justice." In this we see a profound theological sense to peace which is far beyond the simple idea of the cessation of war or the absence of conflict. Indeed, peace is not seen as tranquility and order, but rather as the deep commitment to the work of justice.

Peace also points to the future, because it reconnects an ideal of justice that is remembered and expected. That the figure of the herald of glad tidings (Nah 1:15), whose task it is to announce a victory, did so to inaugurate peace is very important. The herald contrasts with the false prophet who announces "peace, peace, but there is no peace" (Jer 6:6; 8:11; 8:15). Jeremiah's contrast is, like that in Isaiah, between justice and injustice, righteousness and unrighteousness. Peace is clearly associated with justice and often synonymous with justice.

The figure, then, of the *śar šālôm* "Prince of Peace" (Isa 9:5—Eng 9:6) is to be seen as the bringer of justice, as the vindicator. He is "in purpose wonderful, in battle God-like, Father of all time, Prince of peace" and his kingdom shall be established and sustained with justice and righteousness. The same confluence of the peace-bringer with the renewal of justice and righteousness is found in Isaiah 40.

Isa 9:5 should be seen also in the light of Isa 11:1–5, where the figure is described who shall inaugurate the peaceable kingdom in which lion and lamb shall dwell together, while "they shall not hunt or destroy in all my holy mountain" (Isa 11:9). This image of peace as an eschatological event manifests the sense of completion inherent in the idea of peace. Von Rad writes that the anointed one in Isaiah will establish a "paradisal peace . . . to bring order over into the world of nature and to resolve its conflicts" (*ROTT,* 2:170). Peace is, in fact, the order of creation (ibid., 147).

The theological implications are clear enough. Creation is depicted as an act of divine completion. "On the sixth day God completed all the work he had been doing" (Gen 2:2). "And God saw all that he had made and it was very good" (Gen 1:31). The order of the cosmos created harmony and peace. Justice, righteousness, and peace are all present in this "original state." The parable of Adam and Eve is one in which sin is unknown and even "good and evil" are unknown. The depiction of the dissolution of paradise in J's narrative leads from the serpent's wiles to the murder of Abel, the Flood, and the division of the peoples of the earth. In brief, creation, once completed, is now fractured and scattered, disunited and without peace.

The apocalyptic eschatology of the late kingdoms and early exile envisioned the restoration of the created order. Deutero- and Trito-Isaiah refer repeatedly to this glorious new creation. "I will make your government peace, and righteousness rule over you" (Isa 60:17). "I will send peace flowing over her like a river" (Isa 66:12). This peace is the mark of the new heavens and the new earth which the Lord will make (Isa 66:22). So peace, *šālôm,* embraces the notion of the restoration of creation to justice, truth, and righteousness. Peace is a blessing and a sign of the blessed life of the new creation just as it was the hallmark of the first creation. Peace is "from the Lord" (1 Kgs 2:23) and is "the Lord's own work" (Isa 52:7). Peace is both a restoration of the divine plan of creation and the harbinger of the completion of life to come. And to the ears of a weary planet it brings the good news that strife shall cease and that the peoples of the earth "shall beat their swords into plowshares and their spears into pruning hooks."

Bibliography

Blank, S. 1967. *Prophetic Faith in Isaiah.* Detroit.
Childs, B. 1986. *Old Testament Theology in a Canonical Context.* Philadelphia.

JOSEPH P. HEALEY

NEW TESTAMENT

The word *eirene* (peace) appears in almost every writing of the NT. It describes an international calm and a relationship of goodwill between God and humans. Most frequently it describes a social reality, a state of reconciliation and wholeness among a group of people.

A. Classical Words
B. Judaism and Peace
C. Early Christian Views of Peace
  1. Jesus
  2. Paul
  3. Other Early Christian Writings

A. Classical Words

In classical Greek three words can be translated "peace": (i) *galēnē:* the calm of nature, specifically at sea; of the mind or spirit and even of the conscience (Arist.*Ep.*5); (ii) *homonoia:* concord, or the quality of community life which emerges when people think alike or agree; and (iii) *eirēnē;* the most frequently used and the most inclusive of the terms. Plato speaks of the "profound peace" which comes to older persons when they no longer need to be concerned about their passions (*Resp.*329c).

The Greek view of peace has often been portrayed as consisting primarily in the absence of war: the normal human state (Fuchs 1965). More precisely, two contrasting ideals exist alongside each other: the Homeric, or heroic ideal, which presupposes that war will be the arena in which the truly human virtues can be displayed. The other, the unheroic ideal, presupposes that human beings achieve their true potential in work which produces peace and justice (Hesiod). The dominant note in the iambic poets is not exaltation of heroes but using all the resources of art to hold up to ridicule the faults and weaknesses of human nature. Competition in the arts is encouraged (Klassen 1984).

The Homeric ideal is praised in classical literature (tragedy, historical writing, political propaganda) and even dominates the political agenda of the polis. Peace is seen as a positive value, even as the highest value, and war is seen as a necessary stage and the means by which peace is attained. *Si vis pacem, para bellum* ("if you wish peace, prepare for war") went the ancient, widely quoted slogan (Haase 1977).

One exception is comedy, especially the comedy of Aristophanes whose anti-war position merits further exploration. The power of Euripides' protest against war in his plays, *The Women of Troy* and *Medea* is felt even to this day.

Prior to Socrates, the adage, "Do good to your friends and harm your enemies" seems to have held the day. With his fundamental dictum that "it is never right to repay anyone evil for evil" (Apol. 30D) a new approach to the resolution of conflict emerged (Dihle 1962). Both Cynics and Stoics built upon Socrates' insight but forged different concepts of peace. The Cynics praised world citizenship and used illustrations from animal life to deprecate human wars (Malherbe 1977). The Stoics opted for a concept of peace as internal control or inner tranquility *(ataraxia)* which ran the risk of becoming insensitive to one's own feelings as well as to the attacks of others. The Stoics however have deeply influenced the later prevailing view of peace through Varro (ca. 40 B.C.E.) whom Augustine copied, and Epictetus (1st century C.E.), whose manual was for centuries the handbook of the soldier (Klassen 1977).

The Latin words *concordia* and *pax* correspond to the Greek *homonoia* and *eirēnē* respectively. A significant shift has taken place, however, in that *pax* commonly refers to an enforced pacification program.

B. Judaism and Peace

The Jewish concept of *šālôm* undergirds the Christian view of peace. For the early Hebrews Yahweh could be designated *Shalom* (Judg 6:24) and the word designates the state of being well. Whereas the Greeks were clearly comfortable applying peace to the inner nature of humans, the Hebrews tended to use the term primarily for interpersonal or social relations where it comes very close to meaning "justice." When justice is done it is seen as God's gift to the people, and the prosperity *(šālôm)* comes to the people when they live faithfully under God's covenant (Ravitsky 1987).

The concept of peace undergoes many changes in the Jewish literature preceding and contemporaneous to the early Christian period. Already in the LXX we perceive the tendency to interiorize peace as the term *eirēnē* begins to be used in connection with the "soul" (Lam 3:17). Most illuminating for our time period, however, may be an intriguing shift in the tradition as reflected in the Talmud about the altar made of unhewn stones. As J. Neusner

(1970) has observed, the Ishmaelite version, commenting on Deut 27:6 that no iron tools are to be used on the stones of the altar led R. Simon Eleazer to say that the altar was meant to prolong life, iron however shortens it. "It is not right for that which shortens life to be lifted up against that which prolongs life."

R. Yohanan b. Zakkai (16–80 C.E.) spells it out specifically for peace: "The whole stones are to establish peace, although they do not see, hear nor speak, yet they serve to establish peace between Israel and their Father in heaven . . . How much the more then should the child of peace who establishes peace between people, between husband and wife, between city and city, between nation and nation, between family and family, between government and government, be protected from harm."

One generation later, Rabbi Aqiba commenting on the same text left out all references to peace. The "children of peace" became the children of Torah. For the Aqiban party during the war of Bar Kokhba, which they endorsed, the exegesis of Yohanan ben Zakkai was rejected (so Neusner). For Yohanan the atoning function of the altar and the life-enhancing role of the altar was displaced by human beings: children of peace. In this respect Yohanan stood very close to his fellow rabbi, Jesus of Nazareth.

C. Early Christian Views of Peace

The NT uses *galene* once to refer to the calmness of the Sea of Galilee (Mark 4:39 and parallels). The second, *homonoia,* meaning concord or harmony among people, is never used in the canonical NT although it is frequent among the Apostolic Fathers. By far the largest number of occurrences are of the word *eirēnē,* which appears in every NT author except 1 John and in its various forms about 100 times in total.

In Christian ethical thought, *eirēnē* is deeply influenced by the function *šālôm* had in Jewish literature. Thus it is used most often as a greeting of encounter (John 20:19, 21, 26) or as a departing salutation (Mark 5:34). In the NT epistles it has clearly become formulaic; joined with the word "grace" (Rom 1:7; 1 Cor 1:3; 2 Cor 1:2; Phil 1:2; Col 1:2; 1 Thess 1:1; 2 Thess 1:2; Titus 1:4; Phlm 3; 1 Pet 1:2; 2 Pet 1:2; Rev 1:4); and with the word "mercy" as well (1 Tim 1:2; 2 Tim 1:2; 2 John 3; Jude 2) at the beginning of the letters, sometimes at the end (3 John 15; 1 Pet 5:14), and occasionally at both (Eph 1:2; 6:23; Gal 1:3; 6:16).

1. Jesus. Behind the emphasis placed by NT writers on peace lies the teaching and practice of Jesus. With the words: "Go in peace" he dismissed both the woman healed of her hemorrhaging (Mark 5:34; Luke 8:48) and the sinful woman who came to see him while he was at a meal (Luke 7:50). In the Fourth Gospel in particular peace appears both as a parting gift (14:27) and as a greeting by the risen Christ to his disciples (20:19, 21, 26).

According to Mark the gift of peace is not only to be granted to people as they leave but is also an action which can be commanded. He transmits a word that urges the early disciples to share the salt of friendship, i.e., to eat together and by doing so to keep the fellowship or community intact: Mark 9:50c: "Have salt among yourselves and keep peace with each other" (Lattke 1984). Although we cannot be certain Jesus spoke these words, there are no inherent grounds to deny their genuineness. It is reasonable to assume that Jesus wanted the relationships among his disciples to have integrity. What is noteworthy is the imperative verb which is repeated in later Christian texts. If peace can be commanded it clearly takes effort and not just receptivity to divine gifts.

There is of course the disclaimer: "Do not think that I have come to cast peace upon the earth, I have not come to cast peace but a sword" (Matt 10:34 = Luke 12:51). To take this to mean that Jesus literally promoted the sword or violence contradicts all the other evidence found in the Gospels. When a disciple used a sword, Jesus firmly rebuked him and the damage was undone (Luke 22:51). The saying signifies, rather that Jesus will bring division into the lives of people by his claim to their loyalty and allegiance. The most sacred of all obligations, that of the family, will be attenuated by his call. Jesus declares that not all that the world terms peace is truly that. Jesus has not come to bring a false peace in which outer quietness rules while storms rage within but rather to cut clean as a sword the division between truth and falsehood, between idolatry and true service of God.

Closer to the central element in Jesus' work and that of his disciples is the term of self-designation he suggests for his disciples: "child of peace" (Luke 10:6). The Jewish custom of the time was to designate persons in accordance with their behavior (sons of light, sons of darkness, sons of Beliar, sons of righteousness). Given the central place peace holds in Judaism one would expect 1st-century Jews to designate peace-loving people as "children of peace." One group which could have been called that was the "peace party" during the war of 66–74 C.E. But Jesus is the only 1st-century Jew to whom this phrase is attributed; Hillel, his contemporary, preferred to invite: "Be of the disciples of Aaron, loving peace and pursuing peace" (*Pirke Aboth* 1:12). Little is said about Aaron and his peacemaking in Jewish sources. One can only conclude that when the figure of Aaron is cited Stoic virtues were invoked and that sons of Aaron are those who quietly stand by (Rabinowitz 1967; Klassen 1981).

The phrase "child of peace" which appears only here, is most likely a genuine coinage of Jesus. After him, only Luke and Tertullian used it. It did not emerge as a term for post-Easter Christians, perhaps because of the presence of the "peace party" in the revolt against Rome in 66–70 C.E. The more assertive term: "Peacemaker" (Matt 5:9: noun; Col 1:20 as an aorist participle and Jas 3:18 [noun] combined with the verb "to make") upstaged it.

The formula "to make peace" is found in the OT (Isa 27:5); generally God is the subject of the verb. It appears in such a context in the LXX (Josh 9:15) but it also is used of military leaders, as those who pacify the countryside. 1 Maccabees prefers its usage for a state of real peace without battle (11:51; 13:37; 14:11) but also once uses it for a military action (6:49). In a later Jewish text the term is used for the male organ that makes peace between husband and wife (*Midr. R. Lev.* 18:1).

In the NT, the term goes back first of all to Jesus and the beatitude which promises the high calling of being a child of God to those who are peacemakers (Matt 5:9). The promise of being called a child of God is well known in Jewish circles (Sir 4:10) and is generally associated with keeping the covenant (*Pss. Sol.* 13:8; 17:30; *Deut. Rab.* 7:9), observing the law and, in general, remaining faithful to God.

Among the beatitudes of Jesus the term "peacemaker" is the most assertive. All the rest designate a state or an attitude while this one describes a concrete act (Windisch 1925). Some of the other occurrences enforce this point: Jesus is described as "having made peace" (Eph 2:15) through the blood of his cross (Col 1:20). By interposing himself between the warring parties, Jesus atoned for their sin and made peace by reconciliation.

More problematic is the usage in Jas 3:18. Various diverse renderings of this sentence have been proposed. One acceptable translation is: "For the (fruit or) harvest of justice has been sown in peace by those who make peace." A reading of Isaiah 32–33 in the LXX makes it clear that a connection exists between justice and peace and even the image of sowing is introduced here (Isa 32:20).

James utilizes the theme of sowing and reaping and those two terms describe very well the relationship between peace and justice. It is an organic relationship—that of seed and fruit but it is also clear that their sequence can be reversed. In order to receive the gift of God's peace one can do justice, when Yahweh is heeded then peace will flow down like a river (Isa 48:18; 66:12). If one makes peace then justice will grow like a flower (Isa 32:16–19). Paul too sees peace and justice as integrally bound to each other (Rom 14:17).

In Mark both the verb "be at peace" (9:50) and the noun (5:34) appear only once. In Luke's gospel the noun appears 13 times and in the Acts another seven times. Luke speaks explicitly of peace more often than Mark, Matthew, and John combined. He obviously has a particular interest in the topic of peace (Swartley 1983; Donahue 1982). He reads the Christ event through the eyes of his contemporaries who have heard much of the peace of Augustus. They have identified the Jews as those who disrupted that peace in the war of 66–74 and with whom the Christians could be all too easily identified.

The forerunner of the Messiah in Luke signals that "in the tender compassion of our God . . . the morning sun will rise upon us to shine on those who live in darkness, under the cloud of death, and to guide our feet into the path of peace" (Luke 1:79). The allusions are to Isa 59:9–10 and its vivid description of how hard it is to find one's way when there is neither justice nor peace.

In the infancy narratives "peace is virtually identified with that salvation which will characterize the new age" (Donahue). Luke also has the angelic hymn promising peace on earth to those responding to that event (2:14). The inverted doublet appears in 19:38 where Luke follows Job 25:2 in affirming that God has established "peace" in heaven; both have "glory to God in highest heaven." Job's assumption is that peace must be brought to heaven before it can be brought to earth, although the LXX translators cannot bring themselves to affirm that *eirēnē* is needed in heaven. They change the meaning to "he made the universe" (Gk *sympasam*), from "he established order or peace in the heavens."

Luke, however, can also use the term, *eirēnē,* to describe the more secular or mundane security involved in peace: from theft (11:21), averting war (14:32; Acts 12:20), release from persecution (Acts 9:31), reconciliation after an altercation between two people (Acts 7:26), or the end of a disagreement within the Church (Acts 15:33).

An early lament over Jerusalem (Luke 13:34) bemoans Jerusalem's treatment of the prophets. Luke, and only he, depicts most poignantly Jesus' last lament over Jerusalem: "Seeing the city he wept over her saying: 'If only you had known on this day that which brings peace; but now it is hidden from your eyes' " (Luke 19:42). In no other place is it so movingly stated that Israel's national tragedy is a result of her refusal to live according to the covenant with God. Even the desire to make Jesus a good Stoic who would not weep yields here to the historical reality. Similar statements are found in Josephus twenty years after the event.

Finally, the formula: "he gave the good news of peace through Jesus Christ, who is Lord of All," (Acts 10:36) indicates that the author of Luke-Acts saw the word "peace" as a capsule for that which the good news about Christ contains. It is incorrect to restrict the meaning to peace between God and humans (Haenchen *Apostelgeschichte* MeyerK, 304; Zahn *Apostelgeschichte* HKNT, 355–56). Especially in this context of the gentile mission—where the universality of God's love and acceptance is being proclaimed—it is not irrelevant that one of the greatest human divisions of ancient society, that between Jew and gentile, is described as overcome. The similarities between this and Ephesians are worthy of note.

The Fourth Gospel affirms that peace is intimately related to Jesus himself. It is a gift related to the commission to forgive sins (20:19, 21, 26) and go forth in the power of the Holy Spirit, but also before his death he promises them: "Peace I leave to you, my peace I give to you, the kind of peace the world cannot give" (14:27). The difference between the world's peace and that of Jesus is not explained, but it has to do with John's notion of the world *(kosmos).* "In the world you will have trouble. But courage! The victory is mine; I have conquered the world" (16:33). In Christ peace is available to them. The difference must not be drawn along Stoic lines, as if the peace of Christ "has nothing to do with the absence of warfare nor . . . with an end to psychological tension, nor with a sentimental feeling of well-being" (Brown *John xiii–xxi* AB, 653). Caesar's peace enforced by violence is not the same as the peace of Christ which derives from his victory over evil through the absorption of suffering. The two are dramatically different ways of bringing peace. In general, the Johannine community has little interest in the topic of peace. The word appears only six times in the Fourth Gospel and is christologically determined.

2. Paul. The matter stands very differently with Paul. His roots in Judaism are firmly established and yet he lives in the Roman Empire as a Roman citizen. From many angles he would clearly appreciate the *pax Romana.* At the same time he is captivated by the *pax Christi.* Paul begins with God and not with Christ.

We find here the surprising fact that the formula, "the God of Peace" if not a Pauline construct, was so attractive to him that he avails himself of it more frequently than any other ancient writer. It is known to appear in only one other ancient writer prior to Paul.

The *T. Dan* boldly pronounces: "Speak the truth each one to their neighbor and you will not fall into anger and confusion, but will remain in peace and have the God of peace and no war will conquer you" (5:2). The author promises that if Israel repents they will find mercy and be given peace, even as the Lord wages war against Beliar. Those who call upon the Lord will have "eternal peace" (5:9–10). The author is convinced that if Israel repents the kingdom of Beliar will come to an end and the "angel of Peace himself will strengthen Israel, so that it will not fall into deepest evil" (6:5).

The "angel of peace" appears also in the *T. Asher* where the soul at peace going forth with joy will learn to know the angel of peace who will lead him into eternal life (*T. Asher* 6:6). The *T. Benj.* even says that "if you have a good attitude, then even evil people with be at peace with you" (5:1). Here the role of the angel of peace is to lead the soul of the good man (*T. Benj.* 6:1), "who loves those who wrong him as he loves his own life" (4:3). He believed firmly that good will conquer evil and that the pious man when attacked will through his mercy bring the wanton man to repent because he showed mercy and maintains silence. And a righteous man because he prays, even though for a brief time he may be humbled, later he will appear far more illustrious, . . . for the angel of peace guides his life" (5:4–6:1).

The angel of peace appears also in Ethiopic Enoch as a guide to follow and interpreter. These writers instead of speaking of the God of Peace envision an angel of peace as an intermediary.

Paul used the formula, "the God of Peace" a total of six times. The earliest reference is 1 Thess 5:23 and the latest is Phil 4:9. Most often (five times) it appears as a benediction or prayer but also to enforce an ethical admonition: "God is not of chaos but of peace" (1 Cor 14:33). Once it is combined with the "God of Love" (2 Cor 13:11) and once changed to "the Lord of Peace," (2 Thess 3:16). Here he prays that peace will be given to his readers always and in every way. In another text the God of peace will "sanctify" them completely (1 Thess 5:23).

In a strikingly unique reference Paul predicts that "the God of Peace will soon crush Satan under your feet" (Rom 16:20). In this sole reference to Satan in Romans, Paul used traditional apocalyptic language for the defeat of evil (Malherbe 1983) and only here is it perhaps possible to describe "peace as essentially an eschatological concept and not a social-political one" (Furnish 1984), a set of alternatives ordinarily foreign to his thinking. Obviously Paul while eschewing the term, "the God of War" (Exod 15:3) does not leave behind conflict terminology when he develops a new term to describe the God he has learned to know through Jesus Christ (Delling 1975). The morality he has described in Romans (esp. 16:17–19) will be the instrument by which Satan is crushed under *your* feet (Malherbe 1983).

Paul speaks, moreover, not only of the God of Peace but also of the peace of God (Phil 4:7); and of the peace of Christ (Col 3:15). In the first instance he stresses that the peace of God transcends human reason and comprehension. Nevertheless, it is his prayer that it may protect his readers' hearts and minds from wrongful intrusion. Although it may transcend human comprehension, its major domain of operation is still the human mind as well as the heart.

Similarly, the author of Colossians prays that the peace of Christ may serve as an arbitrator or referee in the hearts of those who hear him read (3:15). The author sees peace as the purpose of their calling, just as in 1 Cor 7:15 Paul states that being called to a relationship of peace is more important than maintaining a marriage between a believer and unbeliever.

In rabbinic sources it was affirmed that God had lied to retain peace between Sarah and Abraham and that peace was more important than truth (*Yebam.* 65b, *Midr. Rab. Gen.* 48, *Der. Er. Zuṭ.* 9). Paul affirms a similar position: Peace between husband and wife is a major objective, it is their calling (1 Cor 7:15). Peace stands third in the fruit of the spirit (Gal 5:22) and in Rom 14:17 the kingdom of God is defined as consisting of justice, joy, and peace in the Holy Spirit. Paul also prays that the God of Hope will fill the Romans with all joy and peace, so that they, while they believe, may abound in hope in the power of the Holy Spirit (15:13).

The imperative "be at peace among yourselves" occurs three times in the Pauline letters: once in Romans urging his readers to make peace with all people (12:18) and twice urging unanimity among the believers (1 Thess 5:13; 2 Cor 13:11). These imperatives, without parallel in Greek and Roman literature, have the same impact as the imperatives to "pursue the things that pertain to peace" (Rom 14:19); "send him (Timothy) on ahead in peace" (1 Cor 16:11) and "Take heed to keep the unity of the spirit in the bond of peace" (Eph 4:3). The impact is strengthened when the verb "pursue" is used as in 2 Tim 2:22; Rom 14:19; Heb 12:14 (with all people) and 1 Pet 3:11: "Seek peace and pursue it"; (quoting from Ps. 34:14). In total there are eleven imperatives "to seek" or "pursue peace" and several specify to live at peace with all people. The cumulative impression of these texts is that for the early Christian community peace had a very high priority. Could this stress on the value of harmonious life within community and beyond have come from Jesus himself?

The richest source for understanding peace in the NT is found in the letter to the Ephesians. In part this is true because of the affirmation: "Christ is himself our peace" (2:14). Further the term "proclaim good news" of peace is used twice, once in a noun phrase ("the gospel of peace" 6:15), and once in a verbal phrase (2:17). This author is working in a situation where he is not only eager to show that Jew and Greek are no longer separated by cultural or religious differences but he seems also to be dealing with a Caesar-cult which elevates the contribution Caesar has made to peace.

Against the credit bestowed on Caesar for peace, this author credits Jesus for having broken down the wall of partition, with "having made peace." He seeks to strengthen the Ephesians' devotion to Jesus, who is described not only as peacemaker but as peace himself. Later Christianity could have avoided individualism, anti-semitism, and blind obedience to Caesar if it would have taken this view of peace more seriously. For the focus is on communities, reconciled in one person.

Paul's contemporaries excelled in attempts to glorify and even deify peace or the emperor who had been effective in restoring order to the empire. In an allusion to the coinage of the empire, Paul warned about the people who promised "peace and security" (1 Thess 5:3). Important as these may be, if they are obtained only through repression they have to be discarded as alien to the manner of peacemaking associated with Jesus (Wengst 1987). In a highly militant passage, the author of Ephesians, borrowing freely from other precedents (Isaiah 59; Wis 11:20ff) prescribes as part of the armor: "let the boots you wear be the gospel of Peace" (6:15). The trampling boot of the soldier has been transformed into good news that peace has arrived. It is not an accident that in Cynic circles as well one of the profoundest statements in the 1st century about war and peace is found in a letter attributed to Heraclitus, directed at Ephesus (Malherbe 1977). In any case that letter was a brilliant rejection of war rather than a statement on how peace could be achieved.

There is only one reference in Paul to peace between God and humans (Rom 5:1). It forms part of his argument in the first part of Romans that a profound alienation has crept into God's relationship with humankind, an alienation from which no one is exempt and from which no one can be humanly extricated. Only God's act of sheer mercy makes peace with God a possibility. Once that peace is achieved then a new relationship with life is available. It is a new life, "those who live on the level of the spirit have a spiritual outlook and that is life and peace" (Rom 8:6).

3. Other Early Christian Writings. The letter to the Hebrews also, used the designation "God of peace" in the finest prayer found in the NT (13:20). Melchizedek is called "a king of peace" and a parallel is drawn between him and Jesus, both of whom were kings of justice and peace (7:2). In the hortatory section (12:7–15) sonship, peace, justice, and holiness, are joined.

There is finally one reference in the NT to peace in which eschatology plays a major role. The author of 2 Peter foresees the time when the world will go up in flames and, as if it is inevitable, urges "since the whole universe will break up in this way, think about what sort of people you ought to be, what devout and sanctified lives you should live!" (3:11–12). Christians look forward to a new heaven and a new earth, "the home of justice."

The final advice remains: "With this to look forward to, do your utmost to be found in a good relationship *(eirēnē)* with him, unblemished and above reproach in his sight" (14–15). This, like Romans 5, stresses "peace" as a relationship with God, without however ignoring the human dimension. It shares with other texts concern with justice (v 13) and holiness (v 11). It could emerge from a community influenced by Stoicism which had resigned itself to the inevitable. Convinced that the course of history cannot be changed the Stoics stress a holy life which is tied to peace with God. The issue of justice is not muted and the combination: "Pursue peace with all and holiness without which no one will see the Lord" (Heb 12:14) is clearly also evident here.

Ever since the days of Augustine, when he dipped into pre-Christian Stoic thought (Varro) for his definition of Christian peace (Fuchs 1965), peace as an inner feeling has had a pervasive influence. This text, however, while it takes eschatology seriously, brings no support for escape from the present world. The next world can be brought not by quietism but by repentance (3:9). The prophet's conviction that repentance influences history overrides the apocalyptic tendency to determinism.

The sharpest challenge to the Christian concept of peace came with the ascendance of the Caesar cult and the attendant persecution. The response was an immersion in the apocalypse, not as a diversion from history but rather as a use of the imagination which allows one to take the enemy seriously and to project the battle against a mightier screen. Much of the ancient apocalyptic literature was subversive, and apocalyptic imagery could be used for communication among the persecuted minority without unduly endangering the group. So books like the *T. Moses* affirm that Divine sovereignty will be maintained, but they also affirm that the role of the faithful is to endure suffering without retaliation. For the Christian community represented by the Revelation, one secure anchor is the assurance that the blood of the martyrs will be vindicated. God will rule in history because history's greatest show of power came in the Lamb that was slain. History is the unfolding of the rule of the Lamb. It will end when the throne of the Lamb becomes also the throne of God (21:22; 22:2, 3).

Thus the plot of the book is the realization in history of that which is perceived as proleptically accomplished in chaps. 4 and 5. The main purpose of the book is to encourage those who follow the Lamb to remain faithful to his manner of dealing with evil and with power; especially they must endure suffering patiently and remain true to the Lamb (Lampe 1981). By concentrating on the glory and power of the Lamb and ascribing all honor and power and glory to him, their loyalty to the emperor is of course lessened and they resist the temptation of worshipping the beast. At the same time the Lamb overcomes his enemies through the Word that proceeds out of his mouth, and although that is described as a "sword," what comes out of the mouth can heal as well as hurt (19:15). The difference between the two is decided by the receiver.

The apocalyptic persuasion, sometimes seen as hostile to peace in history, "for you shall hear of wars and rumours of wars, do not be alarmed" (Mark 13:7 = Matt 24:6 = Luke 21:9), makes no claims about the inevitability or necessity of war. It simply affirms that as long as there are people who grasp for power and promote violence, war is predictable. Clearly the Lamb does not initiate war, for the beast and the dragon (those committed to war with the Lamb) use that method (17:14). The Lamb will overcome, and in that terminology the Apocalypse of John uses conflict terminology in a highly symbolic way. Accordingly peace does not become internalized, and the struggle is public, but it also safeguards early Christianity from joining in the revolution against Rome from 66–74 C.E. and in subsequent revolts. At least for the first 200 years the early Christian movement followed the understanding of the relation of peace to war left them by their Teacher. This was true even when the basic usage of words for peace changed (in *1 Clement*, Beyschlag 1972; van Unnik 1970) and when they adopted Roman ways of thinking about peace.

Early Christian views on peace were anchored in theology and Christology, what members believed about God and what they believed about Jesus. This had profound implications for their self-understanding as a community and for their convictions about how people could live together. Within the community, openness or freedom of speech was practiced. It was believed, following the proverb that "a frank rebuke leads to peace" (Prov 10:10). It was also united with joy (Rom 14:17), just as the Proverb already predicts that those who seek peace will find joy (Prov 12:20). So peace had inner dimensions, but was not confined to inner attitudes, just as it had theological roots but profound implications for community living. Beyond the inner-personal and the interpersonal community aspects, the NT views on peace also included a concern for the outsider. They followed Judaism in prescribing the pursuit of peace with all people and in every way as one of the highest priorities of Christian conduct (1 Pet 3:11; Heb 12:14; Rom 12:18; 14:19).

Bibliography

Batto, B. F. 1987. The Covenant of Peace: A Neglected Ancient Near Eastern Motif. *CBQ* 49: 187–211.

Beyschlag, K. 1972. Zur EIRENE BATHEIA (I Clem. 2:2) *VC* 26: 18–23.

Bonk, J. 1988. *The World at War, The Church at Peace.* Winnipeg.

Brandenburger, E. 1971. Grundlinien des Friedenverständnisses in NT. *WD* 11:21–72.

———. 1973. *Frieden im Neuen Testament.* Gütersloh.

Comblin, J. 1963. *Theologie de la Paix.* Paris.

Delling, G. 1975. Die Bezeichnung 'Gott des Friedens' und ähnliche Wendungen in den Paulusbriefen. Pp. 76–84 in *Jesus und Paulus,* ed. E. E. Ellis and E. Grässer. Göttingen.

Dihle, A. 1962. *Die goldene Regel.* Göttingen.

Dinkler, E. 1973. *Eirene, der urchristliche Friedensgedanke.* Heidelberg.

Donahue, J. R. 1982. The Good News of Peace. *The Way* 88–99.

Fuchs, H. 1965. *Augustin und der antike Friedensgedanke.* Berlin.

Furnish, V. 1984. War and Peace in the NT. *Int* 38: 363–73.

Gnilka, J. 1970. Christus unser Friede—ein Friedens-Erlöserlied in Eph. 2,14–17. Erwägungen einer neutestamentlichen Friedenstheologie. Pp. 190–207 in *Die Zeit Jesus, Festschrift für H. Schlier,* ed. G. Bornkamm und K. Rahner.

Haase, W. 1977. *"Si vis pacem, para bellum"*: Zur Beurteilung militärischer Stärke in der römischen Kaiserzeit. Pp. 721–55 in *Akten des XI. Internationalen Limeskongresses.* Budapest.

Hanson, P. 1984. War and Peace in the Hebrew Bible. *Int* 38: 341–62.

Hastings, J. 1922. *The Christian Doctrine of Peace.* Edinburgh.

Hopwood, K. 1986. Peace in the Ancient World. Vol. 2, pp. 197–208 in *World Encyclopedia of Peace,* ed. E. Laszlo and Jong Youl Yoo. New York.

Klassen, W. 1977. "Humanitas" as seen by Epictetus and Musonius Rufus. *Studi Storico Religiosi* 1: 63–82.

———. 1981. A "Child of Peace" (Luke 10:4) in First Century Context. *NTS* 27: 484–506.

———. 1984. *Love of Enemies: The Way to Peace.* Philadelphia.

———. 1986. Peace. Pp. 767-69 in *Illustrated Dictionary and Concordance of the Bible,* ed. G. Wigoder. New York.

Klemm, M. 1977. *Eirene im neutestamentlichen Sprachsystem.* Bonn.

Lampe, P. 1981. Die Apokalyptiker—Ihre Situation und ihr Handeln. Pp. 61–114 in *Eschatologie und Friedenshandeln,* ed. U. Luz. Stuttgart.

Lattke, M. 1984. Salz der Freundschaft in Mk. 9:50c. *ZNW* 75: 44–59.

Leipoldt, J. 1965. Herrscherkult und Friedensidee. Pp. 127–42 in *Umwelt des Urchristentums.* Berlin.

Levick, B. 1978. Concordia at Rome. Pp. 217–33 in *Scripta Nummaria Romana. Essays presented to Humphrey Sutherland.* London.

Luz, U. et al. 1981. *Eschatologie und Friedenshandeln Exegetische Beiträge zur Frage christlicher Friedensverantwortung.* Stuttgart.

Malherbe, A. J. 1977. *The Cynic Epistles: A Study Edition.* Missoula, MT.

———. 1980. *The Cynic Epistles.* Missoula, MT.

———. 1983. Antisthenes and Odysseus and Paul at War. *HTR* 76: 143–73.

McSorley, R. 1984. *New Testament Basis of Peacemaking.* Scottsdale, PA.

Meurer, S. 1971. *Das Recht im Dienst der Versönhnung und des Friedens.* Zürich.

Nestle, W. 1938. *Der Friedensqedanke in der antiken Welt.* Leipzig.

Neusner, J. 1970. The Babylonian Talmud as a Historical Document. *Conservative Judaism* 24: 48–57.

North, R. 1985. Violence and the Bible: The Girard Connection. *CBQ* 47: 1–27.

Rabinowitz, L. I. 1967. The Study of a Midrash. *JQR* 58: 143–61.

Ravitsky, A. 1987. Peace. Pp. 685–702 in *Contemporary Jewish Religious Thought,* ed. A. A. Cohen and P. Mendes-Flohr. New York.

Schmidt, H. 1969. *Frieden.* Stuttgart.

Schrey, H. 1981. Fünfzig Jahre Besinnung über Krieg und Frieden. *TRu* 46: 58–96; 149–80.

Sisson, J. P. 1986. Jeremiah and the Jerusalem Conception of Peace. *JBL* 105: 429–42.

Stier, H. E. 1975. Augustusfriede und römische Klassik. *ANRW* 2/2: 4–54.

Stuhlmacher, P. 1970. Der Begriff des Friedens im Neuen Testament und seine Konsequenzen. Vol. 4, pp. 21–69 in *Studien zur Friedensforschung.*

Swartley, W. 1983. Politics and Peace in Luke's Gospel. Pp. 18–37 in *Political Issues in Luke-Acts,* ed. R. J. Cassidy and P. J. Scharper. Maryknoll, NY.

Unnik, W. C. van. 1970. "Tiefer Friede" (I Klemens 2,2). *VC* 24: 261–79.

Vögtle, A. 1983. *Was ist Frieden? Orientierungshilfen aus dem Neuen Testament.* Freiburg.

Wald, M. 1944. *Shalom: Jewish Teaching on Peace.* New York.

Weigel, R. D., and Matthew, M. 1981. *Peace in the Ancient World.* Jefferson, NC.

Wengst, K. 1987. *Pax Romana and the Peace of Jesus Christ.* Trans. J. Bowden. Philadelphia.

Windisch, H. 1925. Friedensbringer—Gottessöhne. *ZNW* 24: 240–60.

Yoder, P. B. 1986. *SHALOM: The Bible's Word for Salvation, Justice, and Peace.* Newton, KS.

Zampaglione, G. 1973. *The Idea of Peace in Antiquity.* Notre Dame.

WILLIAM KLASSEN

PEACEMAKING, PEACEMAKERS. Making peace *(eirēnopoieō)* and peacemakers *(eirēnopoios)* occur each once in the NT (Col 1:20; Matt 5:9). Until now there has been no consensus among scholars as to who is the subject of "peacemaking" in Col 1:20. For some it is God or the "fullness" of v 19, for others it is Christ. Most recent commentators and authors of monographs distinguish two layers in Col 1:15–20: an early Christian (or even pre-Christian) hymn and a comment on it. Burger (1975: 3–79) distinguishes three layers. The oldest was an original

(Christian) hymn that spoke of Christ as "beginning, firstborn from the dead, in whom all the fullness dwelt . . . whether on earth or in heaven" (vv 18b–20). A subsequent editor made God the subject of the whole strophe vv 18b–20 (i.e., of the work of atonement and peace among the heavenly and the earthly beings through Christ by virtue of his resurrection). The final author of Colossians then reinterpreted this work of God by reference to the redeeming death of Christ. The double "through him" in v 20c still shows the insertion. On this level, the "peacemaking" refers probably to the reconciliation of heaven and earth with God. (For the word, cf. Prov 10:10; for the idea Rom 5:1, 10; 2 Cor 5:20.)

There is an echo of Col 1:20 in Eph 2:15, where "making peace" *(poiōn eirēnēn)* is said of Christ. The author of Ephesians seems to have used, in addition to Colossians 1, a hymnic fragment apparent in Eph 2:14–17. This fragment speaks in cosmic language of Christ as unifying two divided areas (heaven and earth). It ends with a reference to Isa 57:19 combined with 52:7: the announcement of peace to those distant and near (v 17). Whereas the hymn speaks of the reconciliation of heaven and earth and their atonement with God, the author of Ephesians seems to have understood the "atonement" mainly as reconciliation between Jews and gentiles. He took the concept of "peace" from the quotation of Isaiah, made it the main theme of the whole strophe (v 14), and referred the peace in v 14b–15 to the unity of Jews and gentiles, and in vv 16–17 to their common atonement with God (cf. Burger 1975: 117–39.)

To those who "make peace" (same expression), Jas 3:18 announces a "fruit of righteousness sown in peace" (dat. *commodi* rather than *auctoris: BDF* 188, 1; it is sown probably by God in the sense of a passivum divinum). "Making peace" refers here to a peaceful attitude in the community as a sign of divine wisdom, as the preceding vv 13–17 show.

The beatitude of the "peacemakers" in Matt 5:9 is one of a group of passages common to Matthew and Luke (Matt 5:34; 6:11–12 par.) going back either to a pre-Matthean expansion of Q, to tradition, or to the redactional activity of Matthew. The opinion of McEleney that it goes back to tradition, together with vv 7 and 8, is well founded. In the present context "peacemaking" may refer to both one's own enemies or to those of the community (vv 10–12, 21–26, 38–47: cf. Schnackenburg).

Bibliography

Burger, C. 1975. *Schöpfung und Versöhnung.* WMANT 46. Neukirchen.

McEleney, N. 1981. The Beatitudes of the Sermon on the Mount/Plain. *CBQ* 43: 1–13.

Schnackenburg, R. 1982. Die Seligpreisung der Friedensstifter (Mt 5,9) im mattäischen Kontext. *BZ* 26: 161–78.

JOHANNES BEUTLER

PEARL, HYMN OF THE. See HYMN OF THE PEARL.

PEARLS. See DRESS AND ORNAMENTATION.

PEDAHEL (PERSON) [Heb *pĕdahʾēl*]. The son of Ammihud, the leader of the tribe of Naphtali who was appointed to help distribute the land to the Israelites (Num 34:28). Pedahel is a theophoric name, consisting of the element *pdh,* "ransom," "redeem" and the common term for the divine, *ʾel.* Thus, Pedahel may be translated as either "the divine has ransomed" or "the divine has redeemed." The name has been found, outside of Scripture, in a Phoenician seal from Damascus dated to the 8th century B.C.E., and an Assyrian cognate, Padu-ilu, occurs in a text from Nineveh (*APNM,* 256; *IPN,* 180).

RAPHAEL I. PANITZ

PEDAHZUR (PERSON) [Heb *pĕdāhṣûr*]. The father of the chief (*nāśîʾ*, Num 2:20) Gamaliel of the tribe of Manasseh. Each of the five times that Pedahzur is mentioned in the OT occurs in a tribal list where his mark of distinction is his status as the father of Gamaliel. Under the leadership of Pedahzur's son Gamaliel, the tribe of Manasseh participated in the census of Israelite fighting men carried out by Moses (Num 1:10, 34–35), presented its offerings on the eighth day of the twelve-day celebration of the dedication of the altar (Num 7:54, 59), took its proper place on the west side of the tabernacle in the Israelite camp (Num 2:20), and assumed its position in the order of march at the Israelites' departure from Mt. Sinai (Num 10:23). The name Pedahzur means "the Rock has rescued," where "the Rock" is an appellative rather than a proper name and serves as a metaphor for the Lord (cf. Ps 18:3). Noth (*IPN,* 181) speculates that a child would be named Pedahzur because the mother was delivered from danger at the time of childbirth.

DALE F. LAUNDERVILLE

PEDAIAH (PERSON) [Heb *pĕdāyāh*]. The name Pedaiah was held by seven people in the Hebrew Bible. The name is attested more frequently in the postexilic period and may have been more popular then. The meaning is "Yahweh has ransomed" with the shortned forms "Yah" or "Yahu."

1. The maternal grandfather of king Jehoiakim of Judah (608–598 B.C.E.). His daughter's name is given in the MT as either Zebiddah (Kethib) or Zebuddah (Qere) (2 Kgs 23:36). The latter might mean approximately "gifted." Pedaiah came from the town of Rumah which was in the N near Rimmon. The name occurs in extrabiblical sources in the Ophal seal (6th century B.C.E.) and in the Elephantine papyri, AP, 43 (Myers *1 Chronicles* AB, 21).

2. The third son of Jeconiah/Jehoiakin and, contrary to most other traditions, the father of Zerubbabel (1 Chr 3:16–24). Compare Ezra 3:2, 8; 5:2; Neh 12:1; Hag 1:1, 12, 14; 2:2, 23; and in the New Testament Matt 1:12 and Luke 3:27. Williamson has suggested that since the genealogical list in 1 Chronicles is later than the other materials and puts Zerubbabel in a less exalted position it is likely to rest on an accurate tradition (Williamson *Chronicles* NCBC, 57). But it is just as possible that this list reflects Zerubbabel's mysterious loss of importance in the postexilic community after the completion of the temple. Note that the LXX substitutes the name Shealtiel in our text for Pedaiah.

3. The father of Joel from the half tribe of Manasseh W of the Jordan River (1 Chr 27:20). The list in 1 Chr 27:16–22 purports to give the rulers of each tribe under David. The list is, in the opinion of some scholars, integral to vv 23–24 which follow and have as their main purpose to exonerate David from blame for the census. The list may then give the names of the tribal rulers who were responsible in this matter (Williamson *Chronicles* NCBC, 175–176).

4. The son of Parosh in Neh 3:25 (LXX 2 Esdr 13:25). He helped to rebuild the walls of Jerusalem under Nehemiah.

5. The man who stood on the left of Ezra when he read the Book of the Law to the people in Jerusalem. This was probably a place of honor, but we do not know anything more about him or his position (Neh 8:4 = 1 Esdr 9:44).

6. The father of Joed and the son of Kolaiah of the tribe of Benjamin (Neh 11:7 = 2 Esdr 21:7). They are listed in chap. 11 along with the other leaders of the people dwelling in Jerusalem and in the provinces during the time of Nehemiah.

7. The Levite who was appointed by Nehemiah to supervise the distribution of the portions of the Levites from the temple storehouses (Neh 13:13). The appointment of officers to oversee the distribution of the portions was the last action in a series which Nehemiah took apparently following the reading of the "Book of Moses" which is mentioned in v 1. The room which he caused to be cleansed and used for this purpose was the same one that Tobias the Ammonite had been given the use of by the high priest. In reinstituting the distribution of the levitical portions Nehemiah not only solved the problem of supporting the Levites, the skilled help of the Second Temple, but also got rid of an antagonist who, being an Ammonite, was supposed to be barred from the Temple anyway.

RUSSELL FULLER

PEDESTAL [Heb *kēn*]. The Hebrew word is probably a variant of *mĕkōnā* (cf. 1 Kgs 7:27; Exod 30:18), and is a technical designation for part of the base of each of the bronze stands of the temple courtyard (1 Kgs 7:31).

CAROL MEYERS

PEDIMENT [Heb *marṣepet*]. A word found in conjunction with the way in which King Ahaz partly dismantled the bronze Sea of the temple courtyard (2 Kgs 16:17). He removed the bronze oxen that held the Sea, which he then set upon a stone "pediment." Since this word is related to a more common word meaning "pavement," the elevated connotations of "pediment" may make that word a less appropriate translation.

CAROL MEYERS

PEGAI. See FEJJA.

PEKAH (PERSON) [Heb *peqaḥ*]. A king of N Israel ca. 735–732 B.C., Pekah was the son of Remaliah. He succeeded to the throne after his assassination of King Pekahiah who had united Israel for two years (2 Kgs 15:23).

The name Pekah is closely related to Pekahiah, the name of the king whom the Bible reports Pekah succeeded. Pekahiah in Hebrew means "Yahweh opened [the eyes]" (*TPNAH*, 94) or "Yahweh is open-eyed or alert" (*IPN*, 186). Pekah is a shortened form of the name derived from the same Hebrew verbal root *pqḥ*. This verbal root occurs in the Hebrew Bible in a name only in connection with the names of these two kings. The similarity of the two names and the distinctiveness of the verbal root have raised the possibility that the two kings were actually one and the same person. However, this is unlikely. The two kings have two different fathers: Remaliah is the father of Pekah (2 Kgs 15:27), Menahem of Pekahiah (2 Kgs 15:23). It is quite possible that Pekah originally had another name. When he murdered King Pekahiah and usurped the throne, he may have taken the closely related name Pekah for himself as a means of identifying himself as a legitimate successor. Isaiah 7 provides some evidence that the name Pekah may have been perceived as a usurped and illegitimate name for the new king. The prophet Isaiah mentions the name of Rezin king of Syria, but the prophet simply refers to the king of Israel as "the son of Remaliah" with no mention of his name (Isa 7:4–5, 9; 8:6). Isaiah may thereby signal a refusal to acknowledge the legitimacy of Pekah's reign by avoiding the name stolen from the previous king Pekahiah. In any case, it seems clear that Pekah and Pekahiah are two distinct royal figures.

The second and most troublesome issue connected with Pekah is the question of the precise number of years which he reigned as king of Israel. 2 Kgs 15:27 reports that Pekah "reigned twenty years." The difficulty is that contemporary Assyrian records contradict such a lengthy reign. The extrabiblical evidence indicates that Menahem reigned as king of Israel at least until 738 B.C. and probably a year or two thereafter. Menahem is reported to have paid tribute to the Assyrian conqueror Tiglath-pileser in 738 B.C. Pekahiah was Menahem's son and reigned after him for two years (2 Kgs 15:23) which places his reign somewhere in the years 737–736 B.C. Thus, Pekah's rule did not probably begin until 735 B.C.

Moreover, Assyrian records indicate that in 732 B.C. Tiglath-pileser conquered N Israel and soon replaced Pekah with another king, Hoshea. This puts the end of Pekah's reign during either 732 or 731 B.C. Therefore, Pekah could not have ruled N Israel for more than five years and more probably for only four years (735–732 B.C.). But what then is the origin of the tradition of a twenty-year reign for Pekah?

Three major solutions have been proposed. Thiele (1951: 113–14) has argued that Pekah was already a member of the inner court during the reigns of King Menahem and his son King Pekahiah. In support of this assumption, Thiele pointed to 2 Kgs 15:25, where Pekah is called a "captain" (Heb *šālîš*), which Thiele understood to be a very high officer in the royal court. Thus, when Pekah actually took over the kingship from Pekahiah, Pekah figured the years of his reign to include the years he had served in the court under Menahem and Pekahiah as well as the years he actually held the kingship in N Israel.

A second solution has been proposed by H. J. Cook

(1964: 126–27), who argued that the term "captain" (*šālîš*) does not necessarily imply a high rank but may at times designate a class of warriors of lesser rank. Thus, Pekah may not have been a part of the inner court of Menahem and Pekahiah. Rather, Cook argued that the kingdom of N Israel in this period was torn apart into two rival kingdoms. Menahem and Pekahiah ruled only a portion of the N kingdom of Israel, the district of Samaria. Gilead and some of the N parts of Israel were ruled by the "captain" Pekah, who moved these areas toward independence from Samaria during the reign of Menahem (cf. the reference to Gileadites in 2 Kgs 15:25). Thus, Pekah ruled over a part of N Israel, according to Cook, for twelve years and over all of the N kingdom for eight more years, which calculates to a total of 20 years. Cook's assignment of eight full years for Pekah's rule over all Israel may be questioned in light of the Assyrian records mentioned above which place Menahem as still ruling in 738 B.C. Cook's attempt to dissociate Pekah's function as "captain" from a role within Pekahiah's inner court strains the biblical text, which explicitly calls Pekah "his [i.e., Pekahiah's] captain" and thus suggests an internal court revolt.

A third proposal advanced by Naʾaman (1986: 74–82) maintains that Pekah's only tenure as king was his rule over N Israel for five years (736–731 B.C.). Pekah perceived himself as the only legitimate ruler since the dynasty of Jehu which had continued until its interruption by Menahem and Pekahiah. These latter two kings had been pro-Assyrian and had thus forfeited the consistently anti-Assyrian tradition of the preceding Jehu dynasty. Pekah may have seen himself as resuming this anti-Assyrian tradition. Thus, Pekah rejected the legitimacy of the reigns of Menahem and Pekahiah and counted their years of kingship as his own. An early Israelite historian recorded Pekah's reign as twenty years long, including in the total Pekah's actual reign and the reigns of Menahem and Pekahiah. This tradition was written into the royal records and was part of the tradition which was later faithfully recorded but not fully understood by the writer of Kings.

Another issue associated with Pekah is N Israel's relationship with the empire of Assyria in this period. The previous kings, Menahem and Pekahiah, had been pro-Assyrian and paid tribute to them; this was apparently supported in the district of Samaria. The Gilead faction in the N led by Pekah apparently did not support such overtures to Assyria and desired independence. When Pekah became king of all N Israel, he joined King Rezin of Syria in an anti-Assyrian coalition. Pekah and Rezin joined together in a military expedition to Jerusalem to force Ahaz, the S king of Judah, to collaborate with them against Assyria. Ahaz quickly summoned the aid of Assyria whose army under Tiglath-pileser came and conquered the rebellious forces of Pekah and Rezin. The Assyrians took the Syrian capital of Damascus and killed the Syrian king Rezin (2 Kgs 15:37; 16:1–9; cf. Isaiah 6–12).

Finally, two traditions differ about the details of Pekah's eventual demise as king of N Israel. In Assyrian records, Tiglath-pileser himself takes credit for setting up Hoshea as successor after the overthrow of Pekah: "they (the Ephraimites) overthrew their king Pekah and I placed Hoshea as king over them" (*ANET,* 284). In contrast, the biblical tradition indicates that Hoshea overthrew Pekah and set himself up as king, with no mention of Tiglath-pileser's support. 2 Kgs 15:30 reports that Hoshea organized a conspiracy against Pekah and killed him and usurped his throne. The two versions of the same event, one Assyrian and one biblical, simply represent two different perspectives. Hoshea was probably designated by the Assyrians as their choice to succeed the rebellious Pekan. But it was Hoshea who had to obtain the support and means by which to overthrow Pekah, thus providing the basis for the biblical tradition (Hayes and Hooker 1988: 64–65).

Bibliography

Cook, H. J. 1964. Pekah. *VT* 14: 121–35.

Hayes, J. H., and Hooker, P. K. 1988. *A New Chronology for the Kings of Israel and Judah.* Atlanta.

Naʾaman, N. 1986. Historical and Chronological Notes on the Kingdoms of Israel and Judah in the Eighth Century B.C. *VT* 36: 71–92.

Thiele, E. R. 1951. *The Mysterious Numbers of the Hebrew Kings.* Chicago.

Wiseman, D. J. 1956. A Fragmentary Inscription of Tiglath-pileser III from Nimrud. *Iraq* 18: 117–29.

DENNIS T. OLSON

PEKAHIAH (PERSON) [Heb *pĕqaḥyāh*]. A king of N Israel ca. 737–736 B.C. Pekahiah was the son of Menahem, who had reigned over N Israel for ten years before his son. The name "Pekahiah" in Hebrew means "Yahweh opened [the eyes]" or "Yahweh is open-eyed or alert." See PEKAH (PERSON). The biblical account of Pekahiah's reign is brief and couched in the Deuteronomistic introductory and closing formulas regularly used for the kings of Israel (2 Kgs 15:23–26). The report of the conspiracy concerning the overthrow of Pekahiah introduces the most important dimension of Pekahiah's reign.

Pekahiah's kingship was overthrown by a man named Pekah who was a son of Remaliah; Pekah may have usurped not only Pekahiah's throne but also his name (2 Kgs 15:25). In this verse, Pekah is called "his [i.e., Pekahiah's] captain" (Heb *šālîš*), which suggests that Pekahiah was the victim of an internal court revolt led by one of the king's own officers. However, the biblical account also notes that the rebel Pekah was abided by "fifty men of the Gileadites." It seems likely that Pekah was indeed a court officer who also had his origins and an independent base of support in the province of Gilead, whence he drew the core of his fighting force. Thus, Pekahiah's downfall was the product both of internal court intrigue as well as resistance from at least certain areas within the N kingdom of Israel.

What were the reasons for this resistance and revolt? Pekahiah and his father Menahem stand out among the kings of N Israel as allies of the Assyrian empire (2 Kgs 15:19–20). A long line of Israelite kings before them since King Jehu had been vigorously anti-Assyrian, struggling to maintain the independence of Israel. Many Israelites likely perceived the capitulation to Assyria by Menahem and Pekahiah as a threat to Israel's integrity. While Menahem seems to have been an able ruler with a relatively lengthy tenure of ten years, Pekahiah's reign was short-lived, indicating some weakness as a ruler.

Another possible reason for Pekahiah's fall may have been a popular resistance in the N kingdom of Israel to any notion of a hereditary dynasty. The S kingdom of Judah had a political tradition and a theological foundation for the hereditary succession of kingship from father to son in the promise to David of an eternal dynasty in 2 Samuel 7. The N kingdom of Israel did not have such a tradition or theological rationale, and the practice of hereditary succession of kingship seemed to be resisted among at least some groups within Israel. This resistance may account for the fact that Menahem's kingship was not overturned, even though it may not have been popular among all segments of the population. However, when Pekahiah became king and aroused hostility for both his pro-Assyrian stance and his role as part of an hereditary dynasty, popular outcry may have provided the base of support necessary for his assassination and the usurpation of his throne by Pekah.

One final issue relates to the translation of 2 Kgs 15:25. The RSV notes the place where Pekahiah was killed as "in the citadel of the king's house." The Hebrew of the MT adds the phrase, "Argob and Arieh," which is problematic in meaning. Some scholars have suggested emending the Hebrew to render the translation, "and his four hundred warriors," indicating the small army who had supported Pekah's revolt. Another scholar has suggested translating the Hebrew terms as meaning "near the eagle and near the lion," suggesting that Pekahiah was murdered between two palace statues of an eagle and a lion which were intended ironically to represent the guardians of the palace (Geller 1976: 374–77). Perhaps the most likely suggestion is that "Argob and Arieh" were displaced by a scribal error from the list of place names conquered by Tiglath-pileser in 2 Kgs 15:29. Both verses contain a reference to Gilead so that a scribe's eye may have jumped from one to the other as the text was copied. See also ARGOB AND ARIEH (PERSONS).

Bibliography

Geller, M. J. 1976. A New Translation for 2 Kings XV 25. *VT* 26: 374–77.

DENNIS T. OLSON

PEKOD (PLACE) [Heb *peqōd*]. An E Aramean tribe resident in the territory E of the Tigris, centered between the Sealand in the S and the Diyala River to the N (Jer 50:21; Ezek 23:23). In the migration of the Arameans in the Fertile Crescent during the 2d millennium B.C. the Puqudu appear to have arrived in their settlement several centuries before the reign of Tiglath-pileser III, King of Assyria (744–727) and King of Babylon (728–727 synchronously). During the Assyrian and Neo-Babylonian empires the Puqudu were generally subject to the regnant powers, but repeatedly expressed their rebellious spirit, as the Assyrian royal correspondence indicates (cf. Waterman 1936 s.v.) even in the days of Tiglath-pileser and his successors. A similar pattern of refractoriness continued into the Babylonian regime, though it appears that they were politically subservient to this dominant power (Cooke *Ezekiel* ICC, 253). The Puqudu were a formidable Aramean tribe, capable of military might, and enjoyed considerable prosperity as an agrarian society.

The Peqod (Puqudu) are referred to twice in the OT. First, in an extensive taunt song (Jeremiah 50:1–51:58), its composer mingles imprecations presaging the demise of the great Babylonian power, yet here and there are mingled promises of hope for the depressed people of Judah. The date for the composition may be generally set ca. 545 B.C. For this intermingling of woe to the foe but redemption for Judah one may witness such in the passionate enunciation of woes, incisive mockeries, and vehement taunts hurled upon Babylon in vv 2–3, 9–10, 11–16, 21–33; and, on the other hand, passages of promise for the enslaved Judeans in 50:4–5, 6–7, 17–21.

Now in the midst of this martial excitation the poet bids the rising military avenger to invade the land of Merathaim and move against the inhabitants of Peqod, to slay, destroy utterly, and perform all the command of Yahweh (v 21). That the poet should single out the far flung SE border states of the empire indicates the depth of the enemies' penetration and suggests the total fragmentation of the glory that once was Babylon.

The two tribal areas of MERATHAIM and Pekod are in parallelism and have been considered paronomasia. Merathaim is cognate with the Hebrew *m-r, m-r-r,* "bitter, to be bitter" and/or the derivative *m-r-h,* "to rebel." On the other hand, it would appear that the name Merathaim was derived when the Aramaic tribe settled on the banks of the lagoon of the S Tigris, the *mar marratu* or "bitter river." That this possesses greater verisimilitude than the notion of rebellion is more easily argued from the unlikelihood than any nation would call itself "Rebellion," but the term Merathaim is dual so it has been interpreted to mean "Double Rebellion." But this is the paronomasia that the poet uses to indicate the massive breakup of the Aramean settlements.

The term in parallelism to Merathaim is Pekod which has as it root meaning "visit," "visitation," or "to visit." The term is basically a neutral word: visits may be benign (Gen 50:24) or punitive (Exod 32:34; cf. *HALAT* s.v. *pāqad*). No tribe would call itself "punishment," but the poet seizes upon this derivative nuance and selects Pekod as a pun, suggesting that the incursion will be a punishment to the Aramean tribe of Pekod. That the Hebrew writers often used paronomasia in regard to geographical terms may be gathered from Mic 1:10–16. Accordingly, two remote areas of the Babylonian Empire will spell out in the day of the coming invasion "Double Rebellion" and "Punishment" for the power of Babylon.

The second occurrence of Pekod appears in Ezek 23:23, a verse in a lengthy censorious allegory depicting the sheer wickedness of Judah under the guise of a loose and sensuous maiden. The vivid portrayal of the Judean aristocracy as steeped in religious and moral harlotry climaxes with the thundering woes that the Lord Yahweh will make Judah abhorrent in the eyes of her erstwhile friends (lit. "lovers"), the great Babylonian Empire, and will gather together such a military force of Babylonian power even summoning tribal regiments from the extremities of her borders: the Chaldeans, Pekod, Shoa, Koa, and the defecting(?) Assyrians; and with these Judah will feel the judgment of God for her multiplied infidelities. This prophecy may be dated shortly before the fall of Jerusalem to the Babylonians.

Bibliography

Streck, M. 1918. *Assurbanipal und die letzten assyrischen Könige bis zum Untergang Ninivehs.* VAT 7/3. Leipzig. Repr. 1973.

Waterman, L. 1936. *Royal Correspondence of the Assyrian Empire.* Ann Arbor. Repr. 1972.

EDWARD R. DALGLISH

PELAIAH (PERSON) [Heb *pĕlā(ʿ)yāh*]. The name Pelaiah occurs three times in the Hebrew Bible, all three times referring to persons in the postexilic Judean community. The name may mean "Yahweh is wonderful" or "Yahweh has done a wonder."

1. Pelaiah is listed as the third son of Elioenai in the genealogy of postexilic Davidic descendants in 1 Chr 3:16–24. Not much is known of these individuals. The Chronicler may have intended to end on a positive note by listing the seven sons of Elioenai.

2. In Neh 8:7; 10:10 (cf. 1 Esdr 9:44) Pelaiah is given as the name of one of the Levites who attended the reading of the Law by Ezra and helped the people to understand (Heb *mebînîm ʾet hāʿām*). In addition in Neh 10:10 he is listed as one of the Levites who affixed his seal (Heb *ḥātûm*) to the covenant which the community made. The passage in Nehemiah 8 shows the Levites acting in a teaching capacity which became one of their functions in the postexilic period.

RUSSELL FULLER

PELALIAH (PERSON) [Heb *pĕlalyāh*]. A person listed in the genealogy of Adaiah, one of the priests who settled in Jerusalem upon returning to Judah during the days of Ezra (Neh 11:12). Pelaliah was the grandfather of Adaiah, the third member of a linear genealogy extending seven deep (Adaiah < Jeroham < Pelaliah < Amzi < Zechariah < Pashhur < Malchiah). A parallel genealogy for Adaiah is presented in 1 Chr 9:12, with the difference that its depth is reduced from seven to four members. As a result, the middle three members of the longer genealogy, including Pelaliah, have dropped out, and 1 Chronicles gives the genealogy as Adaiah < Jeroham < Pashhur < Malchiah. The LXX reading of Neh 11:12 also abridges the genealogy to four members, but effects the reduction by deleting not the three central members but rather the first three members (i.e., Adaiah, Jeroham, Pelaliah), thereby beginning with Amzi. Such genealogical variability is not surprising given the nature and function of genealogies. Because the social function of linear genealogies is to legitimate the status of present institutions by linking them to primary ancestors, it is commonly the middle members of such genealogies which would cease to function and therefore be dropped. This principle accounts for the shorter form of the genealogy presented in 1 Chr 9:12. However, it cannot explain the reading of the LXX, beginning as it does with Amzi rather than Adaiah.

The function of this genealogy relates to the postexilic need to link the priestly family of Adaiah with the eponymous figure Malchiah to whom, according to 1 Chr 24:9, David granted the fifth priestly course. That Pelaliah drops out in the version presented in 1 Chr 9:12 simply illustrates the primary social function of such genealogies.

Bibliography

Wilson, R. R. 1975. The Old Testament Genealogies in Recent Research. *JBL* 94: 169–89.

ROD R. HUTTON

PELATIAH (PERSON) [Heb *pelāṭyāh*]. The name Pelatiah is held by four persons in the Hebrew Bible. With one exception the name, which may mean "Yahweh delivers," is attested only during the Persian period. Pelatiah also occurs in the Elephantine papyri (Myers *1 Chronicles* AB, 21).

1. The first son of Hananiah in the list of David's postexilic descendants in 1 Chr 3:16–24 (1 Chr 3:21). This would make Pelatiah the grandson of Zerubbabel although some see no connection between this list and the descendants of Zerubbabel due to textual problems in v 21.

2. One of the sons of Ishi of the tribe of Simeon. In 1 Chr 4:42 Pelatiah is one of the captains of a group of five hundred Simeonites who destroyed a settlement of Amalekites on Mt. Seir during the reign of Hezekiah king of Judah (727–698 B.C.E.). This fragment of tribal history seems to preserve the justification for the Simeonites presence on Mt. Seir.

3. The son of a certain Benaiah (Ezek 11:1, 13). He was one of two Judean princes mentioned by the prophet in his judgment oracle against the leaders of Jerusalem, they are termed officers of the people (Heb *śarê hāʿām*) an expression which occurs elsewhere only in postexilic materials (Zimmerli *Ezekiel* Hermeneia, 257). At the end of Ezekiel's vision Pelatiah falls dead. This may represent the fulfillment of the prophet's word in the context of the judgment oracle.

4. One of the chiefs of the people (Heb *roʾšê hāʿām*) who affix their seals to the covenant which the postexilic community entered into under Nehemiah.

RUSSELL FULLER

PELEG (PERSON) [Heb *peleg*]. Son of Eber when he was 34, brother of Joktan, and at 30 the father of Reu, in the line from Noah to Abraham (Gen 10:25; 11:16–19). Peleg lived 239 years. During his life "the earth was divided" (10:25); the meaning of this expression and the meaning of Peleg's name are two disputed issues.

As to the name, there are three related sources. First, Peleg is composed of the Hebrew root, *plg,* "to divide; division," which appears only in the *Piʿel* and *Nipʿal.* Here it may function as an appellative (Malamat 1968: 166). Second, the Akkadian *palgu,* "canal," appears as early as the Old Akkadian period (Gelb 1957: 214) and throughout the later periods. The only known personal name related to this root is found in a 7th century B.C. Akkadian text from Ur, *pal-gu.* Whether it is to be understood as Akkadian or as Aramaic is uncertain (Zadok 1977: 334). Third, the origin of Peleg has been associated with a geographic name, known in Hellenistic times as Phalga, which may lie where the Upper Euphrates and the Balikh divide (Thompson 1974: 306; *HALAT,* 878). In fact, the only clear example of the geographic name *phalga,* is quoted in a Byzantine source as located in Seleucia and Mesopotamia (PW 19: 1668). In addition, Old Babylonian *pulukkum* (Hallo 1964: 69; Groneberg 1980: 186), New Babylonian *pallukkatu* (Zadok 1985: 245–46), and proposed Arabian place names (Thompson 1974: 306) appear as possible locations for Peleg, but these are no closer phonologically and farther removed from N Mesopotamia, which appears to be the origin of a number of the place names associated with figures mentioned in Genesis 11. See also NAHOR (PERSON); HARAN (PERSON).

As to the meaning of the "division of the earth" during the life of Peleg, this may be related to any of the proposed explanations of the name. If Peleg is meant to reflect the W Semitic root, "to divide," then the division may simply refer to that between the descendants of Peleg and those of his brother Joktan. See JOKTAN. If Peleg is suggestive of the Akkadian word for "canal," the division may refer to that between civilized canal builders and nomadic peoples. If Peleg is a geographic name in N Mesopotamia, then the division may suggest the events of Gen 11:1–9.

Bibliography

Gelb, I. J. 1957. *Glossary of Old Akkadian.* Chicago.

Groneberg, B. 1980. *Répertoire Géographie des Textes Cunéiformes.* Vol. 3, *Die Orts- und Gewässernamen der altbabylonischen Zeit.* BTAVO B7. Wiesbaden.

Hallo, W. W. 1964. The Road to Emar. *JCS* 18: 57–88.

Malamat, A. 1966. King Lists of the Old Babylonian Period and Biblical Genealogies. *JAOS* 88: 163–73.

Thompson, T. L. 1974. *The Historicity of the Patriarchal Narratives.* BZAW 133. Berlin.

Zadok, R. 1977. *On West Semites in Babylonian during the Chaldean and Achaemenian Periods. An Onomastic Study.* Jerusalem.

———. 1985. *Répertoire Géographie des Textes Cunéiformes.* Vol. 8, *Geographical Names According to New- and Late-Babylonian Texts.* BTAVO B7. Wiesbaden.

RICHARD S. HESS

PELET (PERSON) [Heb *pelet*]. **1.** A Calebite, one of the sons of Jahdai (1 Chr 2:47). The genealogy of the descendants of Caleb in 2:42–55 balances the earlier list in 2:18–24. 1 Chr 2:46–47 report Caleb's descendants through his concubine Ephah.

2. One of the ambidextrous warriors from the tribe of Benjamin who joined David during the period of his fleeing from Saul (1 Chr 12:3). He was a brother of Jeziel and son of Azmaveth; Azmaveth should perhaps be identified with David's warrior in 11:33. The Chronicler has doubled the list of warriors who supported David (1 Chr 11:41b–12:40) beyond what was contained in the parallel narrative (2 Sam 23:8–39 = 1 Chr 11:10–41a). The source for these additional lists can only be a matter of conjecture, though Williamson has provided a convincing argument for the structure of 1 Chronicles 11–12. The long list reflects the Chronicler's concern to show "all Israel" united in support for David, a characteristic theme of his history. Within the immediate context (1 Chr 12:1–8—Eng 12:1–7) the Chronicler is concerned to show the support David enjoyed among Saul's kinsmen before Saul's death; the twenty-three Benjaminite warriors named here joined David while he was at Ziklag, the Philistine city given to David by Achish, King of Gath (1 Chr 12:1; 1 Sam 27:6). Ambidexterity or left-handedness among Benjaminites is also noted in Judg 3:15; 20:16.

Bibliography

Williamson, H. G. M. 1979. Sources and Redaction in the Chronicler's Genealogy of Judah. *JBL* 98: 351–59.

———. 1981. We Are Yours, O David. *OTS* 21: 164–76.

RAYMOND B. DILLARD

PELETH (PERSON) [Heb *pelet*]. **1.** The father of On, one of the conspirators who, alongside Korah, Dathan, and Abiram, challenged the authority of Moses and Aaron in the wilderness (Num 16:1). The MT reading, ". . . and On the son of Peleth, sons of Reuben (i.e., Reubenites)," is difficult for at least three reasons. First, unlike Korah, Dathan, and Abiram, On has no further role in the narrative, and the name here seems out of place. Second, the use of Heb *benê reʾûbēn* to mean "generic Reubenites" is unusual, given the use of *benê ʾelîʾāb* in the preceding phrase to refer to children of a specific person. Third, the text does not correspond to the given genealogies of the descendants of Reuben. Such confusion has led to different emendations. Some would delete the entire reference to "On the son of Peleth" (Budd *Numbers* WBC, 179). Others reconstruct the genealogy based upon the information given in Gen 46:9 and Num 26:5, 8. There the genealogy is given as follows: Reuben > Pallu > Eliab > Nemuel/Dathan/Abiram. Accordingly, Peleth is equated with the Pallu ben Reuben mentioned in those texts. By deleting "On" (or emending to read "and he" as in *BHS*) and by changing Peleth to Pallu, the text is commonly emended to read ". . . and he [i.e., Eliab] was the son of Pallu the son of Reuben" (so *BHS*).

2. One of the descendants of Jerahmeel and Judah (1 Chr 2:33). The genealogies of 1 Chronicles 1–9 function at a general level to establish the continuity of "all Israel" through the disruptive period of exile. By beginning with the genealogy of Judah, however, there is also a claim being made for the priority of this specific tribe, resulting from the importance of David in the Chronicler's perspective (Braun *1 Chronicles* WBC, 3). The first genealogy to be developed, therefore, is that of Ram, leading as it does to David (2:9–17), even though Jerahmeel has genealogical priority. Peleth appears alongside Zaza as the final member of the genealogy of Jerahmeel. To this base genealogy has been added a longer linear genealogy of Sheshan (vv 34–41), which likely functioned to establish the authority of the family of Elishama in the postexilic community. Peleth, therefore, represents the end point of a truncated early base genealogy which was later reworked for new purposes in the postexilic period.

Bibliography

Johnson, M. D. 1969. *The Purpose of the Biblical Genealogies.* New York.

ROD R. HUTTON

PELETHITES [Heb *pĕlētî*]. A group of mercenaries in David's employ, always mentioned in conjunction with the Cherethites; as a military force distinct from the regular army, they were under the command of Benaiah (2 Sam 8:18; 20:23; 1 Chr 18:17). Their allegiance to David was evidenced by their support of him at the time of his flight from Absalom (2 Sam 15:18), by their pursuit of Sheba during his revolt against David (2 Sam 20:7), and by their actions in support of the coronation of Solomon as David's successor in which they were following the political policy of their leader Benaiah (1 Kgs 1:38, 44). Although the Cherethites appear in clear ethnic contexts (1 Sam 30:14; Ezek 25:16; Zeph 2:5) from which their settlement in S Philistia and their Aegean origin can be deduced (see CHERETHITES), similar claims cannot be made with any certainty for the Pelethites. The most common assumption regarding the identity of the Pelethites is that they were Philistines. According to this view, the Heb *pĕlētî* "Pelethite" is derived from *pĕlištî* "Philistine" (Montgomery *Kings* ICC, 86). Evidence for the otherwise unattested assimilation of *šin* and *taw* is sought in the Gk *pheleththei,* with its doubled *theta* reflecting the supposed original form of the name. The change from *pĕlištî* to *pĕlētî* would have been occasioned by analogy from *kĕrētî.* Thus in this view the Heb *hakkĕrētî wĕhappĕlētî* should be translated as "Cretans and Philistines." On the basis of an alleged parallel with the Gk *peltē* "light shield," Albright (*CAH*[3] 2/2: 512) surmised that the biblical expression is a hendiadys referring to "light-armed Cretan" mercenaries. Delcor (1978: 421) hinted at a possible connection between the Pelethites and Peleth son of Jonathan from the Jerahmeelite genealogy (1 Chr 2:33). A possible parallel to the biblical Pelethite has been identified in a Punic inscription, in which a certain Hannibal son of Baalhanun is referred to as *hplty,* which term presumably indicated his place of origin (Schult 1965: 74–79). Be that as it may, the evidence is insufficient to allow us to determine with any measure of certainty a clear identification of the Pelethites.

Bibliography

Delcor, M. 1978. Les Kéréthim et les Crétois. *VT* 28: 409–22.

Schult, H. 1965. Ein inschriflicher Beleg für "Plethi"?. *ZDPV* 81: 74–79.

Carl S. Ehrlich

PELLA (M.R. 207206) An ancient city situated in the foothills of the Transjordanian plateau, a little less than 5 km E of the Jordan river and 32 km S of the Sea of Galilee.

A. The Site.

The central occupational area of Pella is today a flattened ovoid mound some 300 m long that rises 30 m above a small valley immediately to the S known as the Wadi Jirm. Mild winters and abundant water from a spring which flows into the Wadi Jirm from the base of the mound made Pella one of the most habitable locations in the Jordan valley. Although summer temperatures often exceed 100° F, the vicinity has considerably less summer heat than localities in the S part of the Jordan valley. Unlike some sites in the N Jordan valley, Pella remains free of frost in the winter. In most years, winter rains are sufficient to permit abundant spring crops. The rolling hills that surround the site were once forested, but ancient lumbering and continued grazing by sheep and goats have left the hillsides largely denuded of trees except where reforestation has been carried out in recent years.

Immediately W of the mound is a narrow tableland (Ar *ṭabaqah,* which appears in the present name of the site, Ṭabaqat Faḥl), extending about 800 m toward the Jordan valley. N of the mound, across a small valley, is a low outcropping of the marly limestone which underlies the entire site. On the E rises a large hill known as Jebel Abu el Khas. S of the mound, across the Wadi Jirm, lies a dome-shaped natural hill called Tell el Ḥuṣn. All of these locations show evidence of occupation at various times.

Pella is mentioned briefly in more than one hundred ancient texts. *Faḥl* is a corruption of an earlier Arabic place name *Fiḥl,* the phonetic equivalent of the Semitic name *Piḥil(um)* by which the city was known at least as early as the 19th century B.C. The language that was spoken was a dialect of NW Semitic related to Ammonite and Moabite. The Hellenization of the name to Pella honored the Macedonian birthplace of Alexander the Great, who conquered of the region in 332 B.C.

B. Excavations

Major archaeological research at the site was begun in the spring of 1967, the results of which have been published in the first volume of the excavation report series (Smith 1973). Field operations at the site were disrupted by the 1967 war, but were resumed in 1979. Preliminary reports on the individual seasons have been published in the *ADAJ* and the *BASOR,* commencing in 1980. An interim report on the 1979–81 seasons was published in 1982 (McNicoll, Smith, and Hennessy 1982). In 1989, a second volume of the final excavation reports was published (Smith and Day), and other volumes were in preparation.

C. History

Excavations and surface surveys have revealed a very long occupation at Pella and in its vicinity. A broad slope half a mile NE of the mound is littered with Paleolithic chert implements, some of which date from one-half to one million years ago. A short distance beyond are Kebaran and Natufian sites dating from 20,000–8,000 B.C. Pre-Pottery Neolithic and Pottery Neolithic artifacts of the 8th–5th millennia B.C. have been found on the mound itself and at a number of places near Pella.

Chalcolithic occupation in the 4th millennium B.C. is attested on the mound, and a small site of the same period was excavated on a slope to the SE of Tell el Ḥuṣn. The EB city has not yet been found, but potsherds excavated on the mound attest to a flourishing occupation in EB I, and occasional sherds of EB II–III suggest that a settlement continued to exist through much of the 3d millennium B.C. Toward the end of the EB Age occupation may have dwindled.

During the 2d millennium B.C., when the name of the city appears in Egyptian lists of foreign conquests, Pella stood firmly within the Canaanite cultural milieu. The MB period, ca. 1950–1550 B.C., was a time of prosperity. Numerous tombs found on Tell el Ḥuṣn reveal the urbanity of the inhabitants in the latter part of this period. During much of the LB Age there seems to have been a decrease in the city's prosperity, but a revival is attested around 1200 B.C.

Several centuries during the Iron I and early Iron II periods (ca. 1200–600 B.C.) are not well attested at Pella. It is possible that around 1100–800 B.C. the city underwent a decline in population. The relative lack of archaeological evidence for these centuries may explain, in part, why Pella is not mentioned in the OT; there may, however, have been other factors that figured in this silence, since Pella remained outside the sphere of Hebrew cultural influence, clinging to old Canaanite ways.

Thick deposits of debris dating from the end of the Iron II period show that Pella enjoyed a resurgence around the 7th century B.C. The occupational area of the town may, however, have extended across only the E portion of the mound. Although pottery from this time is abundant, there is little to suggest that the city was highly prosperous or trade-oriented; the culture appears to have been largely local, with relatively little trade between Pella and other regions.

Archaeological evidence for Pella during the Persian period, from the mid-6th century until the late 4th century B.C., is slight. Persian suzerainty may not have been conducive to Pella's prosperity, but the specific occasion for the near-abandonment of the site in the 6th century may have been the Neo-Babylonian conquest of the region early in the 6th century.

In 332 B.C. Alexander the Great marched near Pella in his conquest of the East, and was later credited by some ancient writers with the refounding of the city. There is at present, however, little evidence of the Early Hellenistic period at Pella. Whether or not it was ever actually refounded, the city began a gradual revival by the end of the 3d century B.C. It greatly increased in vigor in the 2d century, when its population grew rapidly and the city expanded from the central mound to adjoining areas, including the Wadi Jirm and Tell el Ḥuṣn. Participating in international trade, the inhabitants grew sufficiently prosperous that they could eat on dishes manufactured in Asia Minor, drink wine bottled in Syria or Rhodes, use fish sauce prepared in Egypt, and decorate their homes with figurines that may have been manufactured on the coast of the Levant. Greek came into increasing use as the language of both trade and culture.

This comfortable existence was abruptly terminated in the year 83/82 B.C., when Alexander Jannaeus, the Hasmonean ruler of Israel, ordered his troops to cross the Jordan and destroy Pella because the inhabitants refused to practice circumcision and other Jewish customs. Excavation has brought to light a thick stratum reflecting that destruction, but unfortunately most of the remains were churned up during the rebuilding of the city in the Roman Period.

When the Roman general Pompey marched through Syria and Palestine in 64/63 B.C. and claimed the entire region for Rome, Pella lay in ruins. Pompey freed a number of cities in N Transjordan from Hasmonean domination, thereby gaining a measure of gratitude from the citizens. At this time, if not before, Pella became part of the DECAPOLIS, a loose federation of ten commerce-oriented cities in N Transjordan. Its location also placed the city on the N border of Peraea, E of the Jordan river.

Pompey's actions did not have an immediate impact on Pella, but the city began to revive toward the end of the 1st century B.C. or early in the following century. Under the aegis of Rome, new patterns of trade were established. As Pella regained prosperity, new streets were laid out on the mound and more dwellings and commercial buildings began to be constructed. By the time that civic leaders decided to embellish the city with some public buildings in Roman style, the mound had apparently become well-filled with houses and shops; consequently the builders were obliged to construct the larger structures in a new civic area located at the SE base of the mound. It is likely that these public buildings were clustered around a forum that was constructed in the Wadi Jirm. Most of this burst of construction probably took place in the later 1st century or the 2d century A.D. The civic pride of the Pellaeans is reflected in the fact that in A.D. 82, the city issued its first coinage, consisting of four different bronze types. Among the civic buildings constructed during the Early Roman Period were a large temple (shown on a coin of Pella, but not yet found at the site), an odeum (excavated in 1979–81), and public baths (partly excavated in 1981–83). Little of these buildings survived into the 20th century; earthquakes, to which the Jordan valley is prone, may have damaged some of them, but in any case their building stones were extensively robbed for use in later structures.

Pella is not mentioned by name in the NT, but Jesus certainly would have known of the city, and could have visited it on his travels in the region of the Decapolis and Peraea (Mk 5:1–20; 7:31–37; 10:1–16 and par.). A few decades later Pella played a distinctive part in the history of the nascent church. Around A.D. 67, when the Roman army began to threaten Jewish insurgents in Jerusalem during the First Jewish Revolt, the Christians of that city are reported to have fled to Pella in obedience to an oracle delivered by a prophet active in the church. It is possible that the apocalyptic passage in Mark 13:3–37 and parallels, which includes Jesus' instruction that when Jerusalem is desecrated his followers in Judea should "flee to the hills" (v 14), is related to the oracle which prompted Jerusalem Christians to seek refuge at Pella. That Pella would have been considered an appropriate refuge is plausible if one considers that the Christians who fled to Pella may have been primarily Hellenists, of which there were many in the Jerusalem church from the earliest days (cf. Acts 6:1). Precisely because Pella was known as a non-Jewish city, it could be presumed to be safe from Roman aggression during the Jewish Revolt.

The length of time that these early Christians stayed at Pella is not recorded. Perhaps some of the refugees chose never to return to Jerusalem; in any case, Christianity had gained a foothold in the city. It would hardly be surprising if no evidences of earliest Christianity were found at Pella, since Christians during the first two centuries used no religious symbols, built no churches, and otherwise left no material remains that would readily distinguish them from others in the population; nevertheless, a late 1st- or early 2d-century sarcophagus found beneath the floor of the West Church in 1967 may possibly be a relic of the Jerusalem Christian community at Pella (Smith 1973: 143–49).

By the mid-2d century, Christianity was firmly enough established at Pella that the city was home to the early Christian apologist Aristo.

The Late Roman period and earliest phase of the Byzantine period, from the middle of the 2d century through the end of the 4th century, is not adequately known at Pella. It appears to have been a time in which the population again declined. Family tombs which had been cut in the Early Roman period continued to be utilized, however, a fact which suggests that there was continuity of population and local practices. There was little or no new public construction, unless the widely-known baths of the city (which are mentioned in a 4th-century text) were possibly remodeled and enlarged.

During the Byzantine period, paganism rapidly disappeared at Pella, as it did elsewhere in the empire, although it continued to survive in indirect ways as pre-Christian elements found their way into the local Christianity. Excavated artifacts show that a former mother goddess was assimilated to the Virgin Mary, and pagan elements were incorporated into amulets that were intended to protect the wearer from evil. Although possibly attracted by some E heresies, the Christians of the city continued to affirm orthodox beliefs. The city's major architecture during this period consisted of ecclesiastical structures such as the West Church, the East Church and the Civic Complex Church (which was probably the Cathedral), all of which have been partly or entirely excavated.

The 6th century saw Pella's population and prosperity reach their maximal extent. Many new houses, ranging from villas to hovels, were built, often with the lower parts of walls constructed of hewn stones and the upper parts of mudbricks. Space was at such a premium that houses were built on some of Tell el Ḥuṣn's steep slopes. The city's merchants carried on extensive trade with Syria, Egypt, the coast of Palestine, and other places in the Byzantine world, and the households of the city were well stocked with imported goods. But the secure roads and far-flung markets of the empire were already beginning to deteriorate, and the 7th century must have been as grim for the inhabitants of the city as the 6th century had been pleasant. The climate may have turned slightly drier, bringing drought to many parts of Transjordan. Large cisterns constructed during this century indicate that the water supply from the spring had dwindled until it no longer sufficed for a large population.

Capitulation to Islamic forces in A.D. 635 brought further changes in the city's pattern of life. Byzantine social and economic institutions weakened or disappeared entirely, while caravan trade with regions to the E, made newly accessible because of Muslim conquests, brought fresh commercial contacts to the city. These developments were not sufficient, however, to prevent further decline of the city's fortunes during the next hundred years. Severely damaged by an earthquake in the year 717, Pella virtually ceased to exist in 747, when a massive earthquake destroyed most of its surviving buildings. Excavations have provided vivid pictures of the devastation which brought the city's existence to an end.

Bibliography

McNicoll, A.; Smith, R. H.; and Hennessy, B. 1982. *Pella in Jordan, 1*. Canberra.

Smith, R. H. 1973. *Pella of the Decapolis, Volume 1*. Wooster, OH.

———. 1981. Pella of the Decapolis. *Archaeology* 34/5: 46–53.

———. 1985. Excavations at Pella of the Decapolis, 1979–1985. *National Geographic Research* 1: 470–89.

Smith, R. H., and Day, L. P. 1989. *Pella of the Decapolis, Volume 2*. Wooster, OH.

ROBERT HOUSTON SMITH

PELONITE [Heb *pĕlōnî*]. A descriptive adjective of Helez, one of David's champions, a select class of warriors directly attached to the king for special assignments, named in the list of 1 Chr 11:10–47 (v 47), a list which, up to v 41a, parallels that of 2 Sam 23:8–39. No such place as "Pelon" or group of people as "Pelonites," have been identified. In the parallel text (2 Sam 23:26) Helez is called a Paltite, a designation which has been identified as either a member of the clan of Calebites who descended from Pelet (1 Chr 2:47) or an inhabitant of Beth-pelet, a town in S Judah (Josh 15:27) which might have been associated with the Calebite clan (McCarter *2 Samuel* AB, 497). Therefore, it has been suggested that "Pelonite" is a corruption of the original "Paltite" (Rudolph *Chronikbücher* HAT, 102). However, the same Helez appears to be mentioned in a list of commanders found in 1 Chr 27:1–15 (v 10). Here Helez the Pelonite is also said to be "of the sons of Ephraim," a designation which would conflict with the interpretation that Helez of 2 Sam 23:26 is from Beth-pelet in Judah.

"Pelonite" also occurs as a descriptive adjective for Ahijah (1 Chr 11:36); however, this construction, "Ahijah the Pelonite," seems to have arisen through a corruption of the text. The parallel text (2 Sam 23:34b) reads, "Eliam, son of Ahithophel of Gilo" (*ʾlyʿm bn-ʾḥytpl hglny*), who is also encountered at 2 Sam 15:12 and 31. It is possible that in one or more stages of translation the eyes of the transmitter skipped from the first to the second *ʾalep,* omitting "Eliam, son of," then jumped from the first to the second *l,* resulting in *ʾḥytplny,* and finally "corrected" the *t* to *h,* to read in accord with v 27b, *ʾḥy(h) hplny,* "Ahijah the Pelonite" (Rudolph *Chronikbücher* HAT 102).

RODNEY K. DUKE

PELUSIUM (PLACE) [Heb *sin*]. A city in the 14th Lower Egyptian nome, 30–40 km E of the Suez Canal, just S of the coast and E of the Pelusiac mouth and Lake Manzala (31°02′N; 32°32′E), mentioned in Ezekiel's oracle against Egypt (30:15–16). For general information and additional references, see Thissen 1982. In both commerce and warfare it has been a point of entry into Egypt at the NE frontier; it served as a "customs-house" for trade in the Hellenistic period (Kees 1961: 210), and it is mentioned in the Roman *Itinerarium Antonini* as the starting point of roads across the Egyptian Delta (Kees 1961: 183). Herodotus (2.141) ascribes the Assyrian retreat from Pelusium under Sennacherib to an onslaught of mice (Gardiner 1961: 345); he also notes a garrison at "Daphnae of Pelusium" (2.30) in the Saite period (Gardiner 1961: 357). Pelusium was taken by the Persians to usher in both the "first" and "second" Persian dominations of Egypt, in 525 and 343 B.C.E. respectively (Gardiner 1961: 364, 343); was ordered by the Persian satrap to open its gates to Alexander in 332 B.C.E. (Bevan 1927: 2f.); was taken by Octavian in 30 B.C.E. (Bevan 1927: 380); and fell to the Arabs after a month of fighting in 640 C.E. (Lane-Poole 1925: 2).

The name Pelusium is first used by Herodotus, and the corresponding Demotic form is first attested in Ptolemaic times (Cheshire 1985: 20, 23 n. 21). According to Classical authors, the town was founded by the eponymous Peleus, father of Achilles (Amm. Marc. 22.16.3) or by Isis in memory of her foster-son Pelusios (Plutarch *De Is. et Os.* 17), or is named for the region's characteristic mud (*pēlós*—Strabo 17.1.21). This last statement has led most Egyptologists to identify it with the toponym *Swn,* attested since the Old Kingdom, which resembles the word *s'in* "mud," a position supported by the rendering of *Swn* as *Ṣinu* in cuneiform, *sîn* in the Hebrew Bible (Ezek 30:15), *Sain* in *LXX,* and *Pelusium* in the Vulgate (Cheshire 1985: 20; Kitchen 1973: 393 n. 877). Doubt is cast on this identification by a demotic onomasticon, P. Cairo 31169, which contains a geographical list giving *P3-ʾi-ʾir-ʾImn* followed immediately by *T3-ʿmy* "The mud," and, much later in the text, *Swn* (Cheshire 1985).

Amun was the preeminent deity of Pelusium (as reflected in the demotic form of the name), Isis and Harpokrates were venerated there, and a temple of Zeus Kasios was founded under Hadrian. The veneration (or, sometimes, abomination) of the onion is ridiculed by Classical and patristic writers as *Religio Pelusiaca* (thus Jerome, Commentary on Isaiah, 13, 46; cf. Juvenal 15, 9; Thissen 1982; Griffiths 1984). In the mid-19th century, Lepsius suggested that Per-Rameses (biblical "Raamses") was located in the vicinity of Pelusium, a view first upheld and then abandoned by Gardiner (Rowley 1950: 27–28). Per-Rameses is now agreed to be located in the Khatana-Qantir region (Van Seters 1966: 127–51; Bietak 1979). Pelusium was renowned as a source of fine wine (Kees 1961: 81–82). There was another town named Pelusium in the Fayum (Cheshire 1985: 22 n. 6).

Bibliography

Bevan, E. 1927. *The House of Ptolemy.* Chicago. Repr. 1968.
Bietak, M. 1979. Avaris and Piramesse. *Proceedings of the British Academy* 65: 225–90.
Cheshire, W. 1985. Remarks on the Names of Pelusium. *Göttinger Miszellen* 84: 19–24.
Gardiner, A. H. 1961. *Egypt of the Pharaohs.* Oxford.
Griffiths, J. G. 1984. Religione Pelusiaca. *LÄ* 5: 229–30.
Kees, H. 1961. *Ancient Egypt.* London.
Kitchen, K. A. 1973. *The Third Intermediate Period in Egypt.* Warminster.
Lane-Poole, S. 1925. *A History of Egypt in the Middle Ages.* 4th ed. London.
Rowley, H. H. 1950. *From Joseph to Joshua.* London.
Thissen, H. J. 1982. Pelusium. *LÄ* 4: 925–26.
Van Seters, J. 1966. *The Hyksos.* New Haven.

EDMUND S. MELTZER

PENDANTS. See JEWELRY, ANCIENT ISRAELITE.

PENINNAH (PERSON) [Heb *pĕninnâ*]. The second wife (1 Sam 1:2, 4) of Elkanah, the father of Samuel. Elkanah may have married her because his first wife, Hannah, was barren. The mother of several children, Peninnah became Hannah's rival and taunted her at every opportunity (1:6–7). In time the Lord honored the prayers of the pious Hannah, who herself eventually became the mother of four sons and two daughters (1:21; 2:21). In her song of thanksgiving and praise, Hannah apparently made several references to her tormentor Peninnah, though not by name (2:1, 3, 5–8).

Unique to 1 Samuel 1, the name Peninnah is sometimes compared to Ar *faynānā,* "woman with luxuriant hair," or *fanan,* "tree branch" (in reference to her fecundity). It is perhaps better, however, to assume that *pĕninnâ* is the feminine singular form of the plural *pĕnînîm,* the meaning of which is uncertain ("coral," "pearls," and "rubies" all have their advocates) but which denotes a reddish substance (Lam 4:7).

With the possible exception of Prov 20:15, all the other attestations of *pĕnînîm* in the OT (Job 28:18; Prov 3:15; 8:11; 31:10; Lam 4:7) and Apocrypha (Sir 7:19; 30:15) describe someone, or something, as being better than *pĕnînîm.* Especially instructive is Sir 7:19:

> Do not divorce a prudent wife,
> for her charm/grace (*ḥn*) is worth more than rubies (*pnynym*).

Perhaps Ben Sira was alluding to 1 Sam 1:4–5, where it is implied that Hannah (*ḥnh,* "Grace")—at least in Elkanah's eyes—was better than Peninnah (*pnnh,* "Ruby").

RONALD YOUNGBLOOD

PENTATEUCH. See TORAH; also SAMARITAN PENTATEUCH.

PENTECOST [Gk *pentēkostē*]. The Greek name for the Jewish Feast of Weeks, deriving from its occurrence 50 days after Passover (Acts 20:16; 1 Cor 16:8). Because the early Christians received the baptism of the Holy Spirit on this day, the term is now more commonly used to refer to that event recounted in Acts 2:1–13.

The Feast of Weeks was the second of the three great Jewish feasts. Its name signified that it concluded the period of seven weeks which began with the presentation of the first sheaf of the barley harvest during the Passover celebration (Lev 23:15–16; Deut 16:9). Thus it was originally an agricultural feast marking the end of the grain harvest and was celebrated during the month of Sivan (May/June). Both Josephus (*Ant* 3.10.6 §252; *JW* 1.13.3 §253) and Jewish intertestamental writings (Tob 2:1; 2 Macc 12:31–32) refer to the feast as Pentecost.

According to Acts, the apostles remained in Jerusalem after the Resurrection appearances. On the day of Pentecost they were gathered in one house when the Holy Spirit came upon them, sounding like a mighty wind and appearing like tongues of fire upon each of them. Then the apostles began miraculously to speak in foreign languages, attracting the attention of foreign Jews who were amazed to hear their native languages spoken by Galileans. This set the stage for Peter's sermon which resulted in the conversion and baptism of about 3000 people (Acts 2:1–47).

Scholarly reaction to Luke's account has ranged from Marshall's defense of the basic historicity of the entire narrative (1977: 347–69) to Haenchen's conclusion that it is essentially Luke's theological attempt to explain the coming of the Spirit, not an historical account of actual events (1971: 172–75). Objections to the Pentecost narrative center on the miraculous elements as well as John's very different retelling of the giving of the Spirit (20:19–23). Dunn defends the miraculous elements, noting that the believers expected nothing similar to what occurred (1975: 148). He also defends Luke's dating of the gift of the Spirit at Pentecost against John's placing it at Jesus' first Resurrection appearance to the disciples (1975: 139–41).

Various passages in OT and Jewish writings have been suggested as providing the background against which the Pentecost events might be best understood: Philo *Dec* 33, God created a sound on Sinai and changed it into fire; Exod 19:18, the Lord descended in fire; and Gen 11:1–9, the confusion of languages at Babel. More important from Luke's perspective are the prophecies by Joel (2:28–32, cited in Peter's speech in Acts 2:17–21), John the Baptist (Luke 3:16) and Jesus (Acts 1:5) regarding the pouring out or baptism of the Spirit. Luke also closely associates the baptism of the Spirit at Pentecost with the mission and expansion of the church to people of every nation.

Bibliography

Dunn, J. D. G. 1975. *Jesus and the Spirit.* London.
Haenchen, E. 1971. *The Acts of the Apostles: A Commentary.* Trans. B. Noble et al. Philadelphia.
Kremer, J. 1973. *Pfingstbericht und Pfingstgeschehen.* Stuttgarter Bibelstudien 63–64. Stuttgart.
Marshall, I. H. 1977. The Significance of Pentecost. *SJT* 30: 347–69.

MARK J. OLSON

PENUEL (PERSON) [Heb *pĕnû'ēl*]. Two individuals mentioned in the OT bear this name.

1. The son of Hur and grandson of Judah, and listed as the father of Gedor (1 Chr 4:4). If Gedor is identified with Jedur, a town in the hill country near Jerusalem, then Penuel was a co-founder with Jered (1 Chr 4:18).

2. The son of Shashak of the tribe of Benjamin (1 Chr 8:25). The RSV renders the name according to the *Qere*; however the *Ketib* is *pny'l,* perhaps reflecting a variation similar to Gen 32:31–32 (Eng 32:30–31) where both spellings Penuel and Peniel are used for the same location. See PENUEL (PLACE); *GKC* § 90 k.

DAVID CHANNING SMITH

PENUEL (PLACE) [Heb *pĕnû'ēl*]. A city in E Palestine on the Jabbok river where Jacob wrestled with the angel (Gen 32:32). The place is located E of the Jordan river and E of Succoth. According to the Genesis story (Gen 32:24–32), as Jacob was returning home from Paddan-aram, he spent the night at the ford of the Jabbok. That night he wrestled with a man (Hos 12:4 calls this "man" an angel) who ultimately blessed him and renamed him Israel, "Prince of God." So moved by this experience, Jacob names the place Penuel, "the face of God."

Jacob's name for the ford eventually became the name for a town built on that site, for the name is mentioned again in the period of the Judges. When Gideon was pursuing the Midianite kings, Zebah and Zalmunna, he asked for provisions for his army from the towns of Succoth and Penuel. Fearing reprisals from the Midianites, the two towns refused Gideon's request and insulted him. After Gideon had defeated the Midianites, he returned to Penuel and destroyed the tower of the city and every man in it (Judg 8:8–9, 17). Later Jeroboam rebuilt the town fortifying the site to ward off attacks on the E frontier (1 Kgs 12:25).

The site of Penuel is identified with Tell edh-Dhahab esh-Sherqiyeh, "the Hill of Gold" (M.R. 215177), on the brook Jabbok, Nahr ez-Zerqa. Some suggest that Pernoual, number 53 in Pharaoh Shishak's list of conquered cities, is the same as Penuel. Later Assyrian documents call the city Panili.

Bibliography

Glueck, N. 1968. *The River Jordan.* New York.
Gross, H. 1963. Penuel. *LTK* 8: 266.
McKenzie, J. L. 1963. Jacob at Penuel: Gn 32,24–32. *CBQ* 25: 71–76.
Merrill, S. 1881. *East of Jordan.* New York.
Schmidt, N. 1926. The Numen Penuel. *JBL* 45: 260–79.

JOEL C. SLAYTON

PEOPLE OF THE EAST. See EAST, PEOPLE OF THE.

PEOPLE OF THE LAND. See AM HA'AREZ.

PEOR (PLACE) [Heb *pe'ôr*]. **1.** A mountain in Moab to which Balak took Balaam in hopes of securing a curse against Israel (Num 23:28). After his two previous attempts resulted in blessings rather than curses (Num 23:7–10, 18–24), Balak led Balaam to the top of Peor for a third and final pronouncement. Once again, a blessing followed. According to Num 24:2, the view from Peor enabled Balaam to see the Israelite camp in the plains of Moab below. As such, it must have been located somewhere in the vicinity of Mt. Nebo. See NEBO, MOUNT. Although Eusebius situated the mountain just over 6 miles W of Heshbon, a precise identification has not been made.

In addition to the incident involving Balak and Balaam, Peor appears in connection with Israelite apostasy. Associated with the site are intermarriages with foreigners as well as the idolatrous worship of BAAL-PEOR, the god of this particular mountain (Num 25:3, 5, 18; 31:16; Deut 4:3; Ps 106:28). Such apostasy later served as a comparison to the apparently disloyal act of the Reubenites, Gadites, and the half tribe of Manasseh, who built an altar E of the Jordan (Josh 22:17).

2. A town in the hill country of Judah, referred to only in an expanded list appearing in the LXX (Josh 15:59).

Peor has been identified with Kh. Faghur (M.R. 164119), located some 5 miles SW of Bethlehem.

TERRY L. BRENSINGER

PERAZIM, MOUNT [Heb *pĕrāṣîm*]. See BAAL-PERAZIM (PLACE).

PEREA (PLACE) [Gk *Peraia*]. A territory E of the Jordan river, described by Josephus as extending "in length from Machaerus to Pella, in breadth from Philadelphia to the Jordan" (*JW* 3.3.3 §44).

A. Identity

The name Perea is found in variant readings of Luke 6:17 (Codex Sinaiticus, Freer Gospel; Sinaitic Syriac). Elsewhere the Gospels refer to the region as "beyond the Jordan" (Matt 4:15; 4:25 [= Mark 3:8] ; 19:1 [= Mark 10:1]; John 1:28; 3:26; 10:40). Alternate readings of Mark 10:1 indicate some confusion over the identity of the district. The difficulty involves a description of the region as an extension of Judea. The Alexandrian text reads, (he) "went to Judea and beyond the Jordan," while the Western, Caesarean, and Antiochian texts have, (he) "went to Judea beyond the Jordan." There is great diversity of support for the Alexandrian text, but this may reflect an attempt to harmonize Mark 10:1 with the parallel in Matt 19:1 (Metzger 1971: 103). A third variant, mainly attested in later witnesses, reads in translation, "he came into the territories of Judea via Transjordan." This rendering appears to be an attempt at clarification by copyists who were troubled by the geographical difficulties involved in the two readings.

B. Boundaries

The W boundary of Perea was fixed by the Jordan river and the Dead Sea. In the S the region was bounded by the land of Moab (*JW* 3.3.3 §47). N. Glueck's survey of the Transjordan put the S frontier running E from the Dead Sea on a line with the fortress of Machaerus (el-Mukawer M.R. 209108) to the "top of the western edge of the Moabite plateau" (1939: 140). Avi-Yonah extended the border S to the Arnon and its confluent Aidonas (Sel Heidān), so as to include the land around Machaerus (1966: 170–80). To the E Perea was bounded by Philadelphia, Gerasa, Arabia, and Heshbonitis (*JW* 3.3.3 §47). Glueck's survey marked the E boundary of Perea by a N–S line to the W of Gerasa, Philadelphia, Heshbonitis, and Medeba. Gerasa (Jerash M.R. 234187) was a city of the Decapolis and therefore probably not part of Perea. A bloody boundary dispute between the Pereans and the inhabitants of the village of Zia (Kh. Zey M.R. 217166), fifteen Roman miles W of Philadelphia (*Ant* 20.1.1 §1–3), would seem to confirm the frontier was W of Philadelphia (Rabbath-ammon M.R. 238151). Josephus included Heshbonitis (Heshbon, Esbus, Hesban M.R. 226134), twelve miles E of the N end of the Dead Sea, among the cities of Moab in *Ant* 13.15.4 §497, while in *Ant* 15.8.5 §294 he placed Heshbon in Perea. It may be that Heshbon, which was part of Jewish territory during the reigns of Alexander Jannaeus and Herod the Great, fell into the hands of the Arabians after the death of Herod. At the beginning of the Jewish War 66–70 C.E., Heshbonitis was not part of Jewish hegemony (*JW* 2.18.1 §458). Eusebius claimed that Perea bordered on Heshbon (*Onomast.* 136, 7, 13; 18, 3). Medeba (Madeba M.R. 225124) was not considered Perean territory. In the N, according to Josephus, the frontier reached to Pella (*JW* 3.3.3 §47). According to Eusebius, the N border was actually located six miles from Jabesh (Tell el-Maqlub M.R. 214201) on the road leading to Gerasa (*Onomast.* 32, 5–7; 33, 5–7). Gersa was to the S of the Wadi Jabis and Pella (M.R. 207206) was N. At the outbreak of the Jewish War, Jews attacked Pella, an unlikely strike if the city were within Jewish territory since the Jewish attacks were directed against Syrian villages and the non-Perea cities of Philadelphia, Heshbon, Gerasa, Sythopolis, Gadara, Hippos, and Gaulanitis (*JW* 2.18.1 §458–59). It is probable that the N boundary ran along the Wadi Jabis including the city of Amathus (Tell Amtah M.R. 208182) 18 to 20 miles S of Pella and NE of the Jabbok (Avi-Yonah 1969: 179–80).

C. History

In the OT, the Transjordan territory from the Jabbok to the Arnon was known as Gilead (Josh 12:2). Moses gave this land to the tribes of Reuben and Gad and the half tribe of Manesseh (Josh 12:6; 22:9). During the monarchies of Saul and David, the land was occupied by the Israelites and the prophetic literature refers to the balsam (Jer 8:22) and pasturage for which the district was known. The Syrians controlled the land from 900 to 780 B.C.E. when Jeroboam II retook the territory. He held it only briefly. In 733 B.C.E., the Assyrians conquered the area. They carried out a deportation of the local population (2 Kgs 15:29). There is no further mention of a Jewish presence in the Transjordan until the Maccabean era.

During the conquests of Alexander the Great, Greeks immigrated into Perea. By the time of the Maccabees the area was inhabited mainly by gentiles (Hoehner 1972: 54–55) who threatened the Jewish minority (1 Macc 5:1; 45–54). Schürer suggested that the opposition of the local population to the Jews living beyond the Jordan indicates a decline in Jewish inhabitants and the existence of a dispersion among the gentiles (*HJP*[1] 1/1: 192). John Hyrcanus (135–104 B.C.E.) and his successors concentrated on Judaizing the region. Early in the years of his reign the Hasmonean monarch Alexander Jannaeus (104–78 B.C.E.) besieged Gadara and Amathus, the most important fortresses beyond the Jordan (*JW* 1.4.2 §86). Jannaeus succeeded in subduing the greater part of Perea reaching from the vicinity of the N city of Pella S to the fortress of Machaerus on the E shore of the Dead Sea (*JW* 7.6.2 §171). Despite the conquest of Perea ca. 88 B.C.E., Jannaeus was apparently unable to secure the territory. Around 57 B.C.E., Gabinius, a former legate of Pompey, made Amathus (Tell Amtah M.R. 208182) one of five administrative districts in Palestine. Each of these regions was governed by a sanhedrin under his general direction. The duration of the administrative districts was probably limited to the rule of Gabinius, although the sanhedrin continued to function after his time (Smallwood 1976: 31).

During the Roman period, Perea was considered a Jewish territory. Its capital was Gadara (Gedor, Tell Jedur,

Gedora M.R. 220160) eighteen miles N–NW of the N tip of the Dead Sea near es-Salt. This Gadara should not be confused with Gadara (Umm Qeis M.R. 214229) in the Decapolis. Herod the Great (37–4 B.C.E.) built additional fortresses in the Transjordan and established military colonies there (*Ant* 15.8.5 §294). Near the end of his life, Herod unsuccessfully sought relief in the baths of Callirrhoe (Zereth-shahar, ez-Zarat M.R. 203111) on the E shore of the Dead Sea (*Ant* 17.5.1 §171–72). In 20 B.C.E. with the permission of Augustus, Herod appointed his brother Pheroras to the post of tetrarch of Perea with control of its revenues (*Ant* 15.10.3 §362). After Herod's death, Perea was assigned with Galilee to Herod Antipas' tetrarchy. In Perea, Antipas (4 B.C.E.–39 C.E.) fortified a city which he named Julias (Livias, Betharamphtha, Tell er-Rame M.R. 211137) in honor of the empress Julia. It may be, as Schürer (*HJP*[1] 2: 214–15) and others have suggested, that the city was originally named Livias in honor of Livia, Augustus' wife, and later (14 C.E.) renamed Julias when Livia was adopted into the *gens Julia*. The name reverted to Livias after the 1st century. The boundary dispute between the Jews of Perea and the Philadelphians over the frontier of Zia climaxed ca. 44 C.E. Fadus the procurator arrived in Judea and discovered that the Pereans had taken arms without the consent of their rulers. He arrested three of the revolt leaders, condemning one to death and two to exile (*Ant* 20.1.1 §2–4).

From this period on, Galilee and Perea were included in the provincial designation of Judea, together with districts formerly identified as Judea, Samaria, and Idumea (Smallwood 1976: 1). In 54 C.E., when Nero acceded to the throne he granted Agrippa II (28–100 C.E.) two-thirds of Perea, specifically the toparchies of Abila (Abel, Tell Abil M.R. 231231) and Julias. Agrippa's ambition was to reign over a territory equal to that of his father and grandfather, but his dream was brought to an end by the outbreak of the Jewish War in 66 C.E. During Vespasians's campaign in Perea in 68 C.E., many Jews fled to Jericho. The Roman general captured Gadara, described as a "city of some strength" (*JW* 4.7.3 §413), and subsequently subdued the whole of Perea as far as Machaerus, which he did not take. After Agrippa's death in 100 C.E., Perea became part of the Roman province of Syria.

D. NT and Rabbinic Sources

In the NT, Perea is the land "beyond the Jordan" (Mark 3:8). Galilean Jews making the trip to Jerusalem traveled via Perea in order to avoid contact with the Samaritans. Those making the journey by crossing the Jordan thought they never left Jewish territory, reinforcement for the Jewish character of the population in the 1st century (Hoehner 1972: 56). John the Baptist was active in the district. According to the gospel of John, the Baptist responded to priests and Levites who had come from Jerusalem questioning his baptisms (John 1:28). Later John's disciples asked him about Jesus "who was with you beyond the Jordan" (John 3:26)—an indication that John's main activity was in the Transjordan. Around the time of the Battle of Actium, Antipas imprisoned and executed John in the fortress of Machaerus (*Ant* 18.5.2 §116–19). Josephus does not record the details of John's arrest as described in the Gospels (Matt 14:6–12 [= Mark 6:22–28]; Luke 9:9), but attributes the execution to Antipas' fear that John might incite a revolt. Jesus also ministered in Perea. He answered the Pharisees concerning divorce (Matt 19:1–9), blessed children (Matt 19:13–15), taught the disciples concerning marriage (Matt 19:10–12), withdrew from the Jews (John 10:40) and attracted crowds who had heard of his reputation as a healer (Mark 3:8 = Matt 4:25).

Jewish literature assumes that Perea was a land inhabited by Jews (*Seb.* 9.2; *Ketub.* 13.10; *B. Bat.* 3.2; *Menah.* 8.3). In the Talmudic period, Perea did not have as favorable a reputation as Judea and Galilee. According to the Aboth of Rabbi Nathan, Judea represented the grain, Galilee the straw and "ha-Yarden" (Perea) the chaff (Neubauer 1868: 241–51).

Bibliography

Avi-Yonah, M. 1966. *The Holy Land from the Persian to the Arab Conquests.* Grand Rapids.

Glueck, N. 1939. *Explorations in Eastern Palestine III.* AASOR 18–19. New Haven.

Haefeli, L. 1913. Samaria and Peräa bei Flavius Josephus. *BS* 18: 66–120.

Hoehner, H. W. 1972. *Herod Antipas.* Cambridge.

Metzger, B. M. 1971. *A Textual Commentary on the Greek New Testament.* London.

Neubauer, A. 1967. *La Géographie du Talmud.* Hildesheim.

Smallwood, E. M. 1976. *The Jews Under Roman Rule from Pompey to Diocletian.* Leiden.

DIANE I. TREACY-COLE

PERESH (PERSON) [Heb *pereš*]. The Manassite son of Machir and his wife Maacah (1 Chr 7:16). According to the genealogy of Manasseh in 1 Chr 7:14–19, his brothers included Sheresh and Gilead, and perhaps Huppim and Shuppim, too. Peresh is omitted, however, from other Manassite genealogies and biblical texts.

There are several difficulties in 1 Chr 7:14–19 that have bearing on the identity of Peresh. First, Maacah, the mother of Peresh, is called the wife of Machir (v 16), as well as his sister (v 15). In addition, Gilead appears to be the brother of Peresh (v 14), but in v 17, he is included among the "sons of Gilead." There have been several attempts to resolve these difficulties, but none is completely satisfying. Curtis and Madsen (*Chronicles* ICC, 151–52) emended "Machir" in v 16 to "Gilead." Therefore, Maacah was Machir's sister but Gilead's wife (as well as his aunt), and Gilead, rather than Machir, was the father of Peresh. In addition, the names of Shuppim and Huppim (v 15) should be deleted, since they are glosses from v 12 (the genealogy of Naphtali) and so cannot have been the brothers of Peresh. Rudolf (*Chronikbücher* HAT, 68–71), however, reconstructs 1 Chr 7:14–19 extensively on the basis of Num 26:29–34. In his arrangement, Maacah becomes the daughter of Gilead and the mother of Peresh, but the name of her husband is missing from the text.

M. PATRICK GRAHAM

PEREZ (PERSON) [Heb *pereṣ*]. Var. PHARES. PEREZITES. The son of Judah and Judah's daughter-in-law

Tamar (Gen 38:28; 1 Chr 2:4; 4:1). He was the brother of Zerah (Gen 38:29) and the father of Hezron and Hamul (Gen 46:12; Num 26:21; 1 Chr 2:5).

The story of his birth provides a popular etymology for his name. When the time came for Tamar to give birth there were twins in her womb. One of them stretched out his hand and the midwife placed a scarlet thread on it to indicate that he was the first born. After the hand was withdrawn, the other brother came bursting forth. At this the midwife exclaimed: "What a breach you have made for yourself." For this reason he was named Perez, a name which means "breach" (Gen 38:27–29). The story of Perez's birth is an attempt to explain the preeminence of the younger clan Perez over the older clans of Judah. In the second census list of the tribes of Israel mentioned in the book of Numbers, Perez is listed as the eponymous ancestor of the Perezites (Num 26:20). In addition, two other Judean clans come from Perez, the Hezronites and the Hamulites (Num 26:21). The superiority of Perez and his clan is due to the fact that David descended from Perez through Boaz and Ruth (Ruth 4:18–22).

The reference to Perez in the blessing which the leaders of Bethlehem bestowed upon Boaz, "May your house be like the house of Perez, whom Tamar bore to Judah," (Ruth 4:12) reflects the belief that Perez enjoyed numerous progeny. Because of Perez's prominence among the clans of Judah, the Perezites occupied important positions in Judean society. One of his descendants was the commander of the first division of David's army (1 Chr 27:2–3). Some of the Perezites lived in Jerusalem after the return of the exiles from Babylon (1 Chr 9:4), among them there were 468 who were "valiant men" (Neh 11:4–6). Zerubbabel, the son of Shealtiel, who returned to Jerusalem from Babylon, and who was exhorted by Haggai and Zechariah to rebuild the temple, was from the clan of Perez (RSV and Gk *Phares*; 1 Esdr 5:5). In the NT, the ancestral line of Jesus is traced through Perez (Matt 1:13; Luke 3:33).

Bibliography

Emerton, J. A. 1975. Some Problems in Genesis xxxviii. *VT* 25: 338–61.

Zimmermann, F. 1945. The Births of Perez and Zerah. *JBL* 64: 377–78.

CLAUDE F. MARIOTTINI

PEREZ-UZZAH (PLACE) [Heb *pereṣ* ʿ*uzzâ*/ʿ*uzzāʾ*]. Appears twice in the Bible (2 Sam 6:8 = 1 Chr 13:11). A place of uncertain location between Jerusalem and Baalah-Judah (Kiriath-jearim; cf. Josh 15:10), 14 miles to the NW. Here, as the ark of God was being brought from Baalah to the City of David, Uzzah, son of Abinadab, took hold of the ark to steady it and died. The name reflects that tragedy. The text explains that "Yahweh broke forth against Uzzah" (*pāraṣ yhwh pereṣ bĕ*ʿ*uzzâ*), translating *pĕrōṣ b-* as in Exod 19:22, 24 and 1 Chr 15:13. If the place name carries that understanding, as the LXX, Vg, Tg and most modern English versions hold, it means "the breaking forth upon Uzzah" (e.g., Hertzberg *1 and 2 Samuel* OTL, 276). McCarter takes *pereṣ* to mean "an interruption in . . . family line," as in Judg 21:15. He translates the etiology "Yahweh made a breach in Uzza," and the place name "Uzza's Breach." The name may originally have referred to a breach in the wall of Jerusalem where the incident occurred, with later theological reflection prompted by the various meanings of *pereṣ* (McCarter *2 Samuel* AB, 161, 170).

DAVID L. THOMPSON

PERFUMES AND SPICES. A variety of perfumes and spices are named in the Bible. Perfumes and spices were important items of trade in the ancient world.

A. Perfumes

Although the human sense of smell has atrophied over the millennia as hunting and being hunted became less of a pastime, our delight over pleasing smells—especially those which function as an aphrodisiac—has grown. Like many products desired and manufactured by early cultures, individual perfumes were identified by chance or experimentation. Most are derivatives of plants, although a few are extracted from animals. Some probably were discovered as medicinal potions were concocted, but in many cases their origin is found in the natural smells of the forest and desert, which attracted humans just as the scent of flowers drew insects.

1. Biblical Terms. Specific Hebrew terms for perfume or those associated with the perfume industry in the Bible are *rôqēaḥ* (Exod 30:25, 35; 37:29; Eccl 10:1), *raqqāḥ* (1 Sam 8:13; Neh 3:8), *mirqaḥaṯ* (2 Chr 16:14), *riqqûaḥ* (Isa 57:9), *rîaḥ* (Exod 30:38), *nûp̱* (Prov 7:17), *qeṭōreṯ* (Prov 27:9), *mequṭṭereṯ* (Cant 3:6), *bātê hannep̱eš* (Isa 3:20), *bōśem* (Isa 3:24).

2. Sources. Since most of the substances (with the exception of stacte and gum) used as perfumes in the Bible are not native to Canaan, they had to be acquired through trade. Caravans carried these precious commodities from the Arabian desert or from ports along the Red Sea and the Mediterranean coast where Egyptian, Phoenician, and later Roman ships (Miller 1969: 120) had deposited them. The places of origin for the plant-based perfumes mentioned in the biblical narrative include Arabia (bdellium, frankincense, myrrh—Isa 60:6; Jer 6:20), India (aloes, calamus, saffron), Nepal (nard), Sri Lanka (cassia, cinnamon), Iran (galbanum), Somaliland (frankincense, myrrh). The one perfume derived from animals, Onycha, was extracted from the muscle of a Red Sea mollusk.

The trade in perfumes and spices created an elaborate network of land and sea routes from the sources to the markets (Van Beek 1960: 106). One such route used by the Ishmaelite traders, who were carrying "gum, balm, and myrrh" from Gilead to Egypt, brought them in contact with Joseph's brothers as they pastured their flocks near Dothan (Gen 37:25). The biblical narrative describes how in the monarchical period, Solomon participated in a joint venture with the Phoenicians. According to this account a fleet of "Tarshish" ships was constructed which plied the waters of the Red Sea and the Arabian and East African coasts for three years at a time (1 Kgs 10:22–26; 2 Chr 9:21). The cargoes included luxury items such as "gold, silver, ivory, apes, and peacocks" as well as myrrh and spices (Stieglitz 1984: 141).

In order to gain a fuller understanding of the extent of

trade in the ancient world, two accounts are instructive: Ezekiel's "lamentation over Tyre" (chap. 27) and the "lamentation over Babylon (= Rome)" in Revelation 18. A vast array of products are listed from metals to jewels to slaves. Among the perfumes and spices listed are balm from Judah (Ezek 27:17), cassia and calamus from Uzal (27:19), and "the best of all kinds of spices" (27:22) from Sheba and Ra'amah (all in SW Arabia). The Roman merchants are said to have trafficked, among other things, in "cinnamon, spice, incense, myrrh, and frankincense" (Rev 18:13). Eastern trade routes stretched along the coast of Africa down Somaliland and Madagascar, across the Indian Ocean to Indonesia, and all along the Persian Gulf and the W coast of India (Miller 1969: 145–47; Van Beek 1960: 109).

3. Manufacture. Raw materials for the manufacture of perfumes in ancient times can be divided into two categories. The first consists of plant materials, including "essential oils" (which are obtained through distillation or expression), flower oils, and gums, resins, and exudations. The second category is made up of a variety of animal secretions (Balsam 1972: 600).

Collection of these materials depended upon the form that they took in nature. In some cases, bark was stripped from trees (cinnamon), roots dug from the ground (mandrake, nard) or gathered from flowers (saffron). Another method consisted of tapping trees (frankincense and myrrh) and collecting the "tears" of resin once they had had time to dry (Van Beek 1960: 101; *IDB* 3: 731). Packaging for storage could be as simple as a cloth bag or as elaborate as a finely shaped alabaster jar (Matt 26:7) or perfume box (Isa 3:20). A large number of these perfume jars have been uncovered in excavations throughout the Near East, some still containing minute amounts of their contents.

Some fragrances, like frankincense and myrrh, did not require refining. They were simply transported to buyers and then burnt as incense (Exod 30:34; Cant 3:16). However, myrrh at least was also pulverized into a fine powder and placed in a sachet worn between a woman's breasts (Cant 1:13). Recipes also exist for the blending of fragrances to create sweet smelling incense and perfume. For instance, Exod 30:23–25 contains a list of ingredients (myrrh, cinnamon, aromatic cane, cassia, olive oil) and their proportions for use in the creation of "anointing oil" to be used in the tabernacle. The profession of perfumer is first ascribed to Bezalel in Exod 37:29. The industry was restricted in part to the priestly community (Exod 30:37–38; 1 Chr 9:30), but there was obviously a large secular market. For instance Samuel mentions that women will be drafted to work for the palace as perfumers (1 Sam 8:13).

The utensils and methods for blending, however, are missing in these texts. Clues to that process can be found in Middle Assyrian texts dating to the 13th century B.C.E. (Ebeling 1948: 132–43). They, along with Egyptian tomb paintings from the time of Tuthmosis IV (1397–1384), contain evidence of an elaborate series of steps which included steeping and boiling the ingredients while oil and other items were added until they were properly mixed (Shelmerdine 1985: 16). Recent excavations at Ein Gedi have also revealed the tools and furnaces used for the commercial production of balm in ancient Judah (Zohary 1982: 198).

4. Uses. Some of the substances mentioned above have few uses in antiquity. Frankincense, for example, was primarily burnt as incense in religious ceremonies (Exod 30:34; Lev 2:2), although it occasionally is mentioned as a perfume or fumigant (Cant 3:6). Myrrh, however, was used in many ways—for example, as incense (Exod 30:23), as a perfume to freshen garments (Ps 45:9), and as a cosmetic treatment (Esth 2:13). In Mark 15:23 myrrh mixed with wine was offered as a painkiller to Jesus on the cross, and in John 19:39, a hundredweight of myrrh and aloes was used to embalm Jesus' corpse and line his linen shroud.

Of course, perfumes functioned as a cosmetic, providing pleasing fragrance as well as needed protection for the skin in the hot and dry climate of the ANE (Cant 1:3, 5:5). The more costly fragrances made them the rivals of gold (Matt 2:11) for the attention of the wealthy and a remarkable gift. The reaction of the disciples over the use of an alabaster jar of nard to anoint Jesus' feet (Mark 14:3–5) is thus quite understandable. It was made even more expensive (300 denarii = worker's pay for half a year) by its costly container and the distance from which it had come (Nepal).

B. Spices

In biblical usage, spices [Heb *bōśem*] are associated with aromatic oils, perfumes, incense, and embalming substances. There are no references to their use with food except in a cultic context—the placing of frankincense on the Bread of the Sanctuary (Lev 24:7), which was later consumed by Aaron and his sons (Van Beek 1960: 113). However, cuneiform texts from Mesopotamia contain recipes which include lists of spices used to flavor food (Bottero 1985: 38), and there is mention of spiced wine in Cant 8:2.

Spices, generally in pulverized form and mixed in combination with each other and oil had many uses. These included anointing oil (Exod 30:23–25—for use on the tent of meeting and the ark; Cant 1:3, 12 and Esth 2:12—as a fragrance or cosmetic), sweet smelling incense for the exclusive use of the priests (Exod 30:34–38; 2 Chr 2:4), and a freshener, providing an enticing fragrance to a home (Cant 7:13) or a lover's bed (Prov 7:17–18). They were also widely used in connection with funerals. In the latter case spices could be applied to the corpse (Luke 23:56; 24:1; John 12:3–7) or used to mask the odors of a funeral pyre (2 Chr 16:14).

Since most spices had to be obtained from merchants who had traveled great distances, they were prized and displayed as part of a king's treasury (2 Kgs 20:13). Only the kings and the very wealthy could afford to use them lavishly (Solomon's perfumed litter in Cant 3:6–7; the king's robes "fragrant with myrrh and aloes and cassia" in Ps 45:7–8) or expect them to be burnt at their funerals (Jer 34:5). They also served as appropriate presents when trying to make a good impression or a peace offering, as Jacob does in his gift to Pharaoh in Gen 43:11.

While the medicinal qualities of spices are rarely mentioned in the biblical text because Yahweh was considered the source of healing (Zohary 1982: 183; 2 Chr 16:12–13), some were undoubtedly cultivated or obtained for their pharmaceutical value. For instance, mandrake is mentioned twice in connection with its aphrodisiac qualities (Gen 30:14–15; Cant 7:13). In Jer 8:22, the "balm of Gilead" (Heb *ṣŏrî*) is described in medicinal terms. It is obtained by "wounding" the storax-gum tree and does contain a significant amount of balsamic acid (Zohary 1982: 192).

Bibliography

Balsam, M. S. 1972. Fragrance. Pp. 599–634 in *Cosmetics Science and Technology*, ed. M. S. Balsam and E. Sagarin. New York.
Bottero, J. 1985. The Cuisine of Ancient Mesopotamia. *BA* 48/1: 36–47.
Ebeling, E. 1948. Mittelassyrische Rezepte zur Herstellung von wohlriechenden Salben. *Or* 17: 129–45.
Miller, J. I. 1969. *The Spice Trade of the Roman Empire 29 B.C. to A.D. 641.* Oxford.
Shelmerdine, C. W. 1985. *The Perfume Industry of Mycenaean Pylos.* Göteborg.
Stieglitz, R. R. 1984. Long Distance Seafaring in the Ancient Near East. *BA* 47/3: 134–42.
Van Beek, G. W. 1960. Frankincense and Myrrh. *BAR* 2: 99–126.
Zohary, M. 1982. *Plants of the Bible.* Cambridge.

VICTOR H. MATTHEWS

PERGA (PLACE) [Gk *Pergē*]. An important Greek city in Pamphylia, visited by Paul at the beginning and end of his first missionary excursion into the interior of Asia Minor ca. A.D. 47–48 (Acts 13:13; 14:25).

According to the book of Acts, Paul and his associates, Barnabas and John (Mark), sailed for the mainland following their evangelistic excursion across Cyprus (13:13). They arrived in Perga, a river port on the S coast of Asia Minor (36°59′N; 30°46′E), some 7 miles up the river Cestrus (modern Aksu). Strabo (*Geog.* 14.42) says that it could be reached directly from the sea, as suggested by the narrative of Acts; but this would have demanded a scala on the river at the nearest point approaching the city (Bean 1979: 25). John Mark left the company of Paul and Barnabas here and returned to Jerusalem. We are not told by the narrator why he left, though many commentators have offered their creative speculations to remedy our historical ignorance (e.g., hesitancy with the way Paul was moving in regard to Jewish-Gentile relations; afraid of the rugged journey across the mountains and into Galatia; homesick for his mother and friends in Jerusalem, etc.). We are told, however, that his departure was not regarded in a favorable light by Paul and was the source of the break of the cooperative missionary venture of Paul and Barnabas (Acts 15:36–40).

Perga was founded by a mixed multitude of Greek immigrants after the Trojan War. Recent excavations have turned up a number of statue bases of "founders" of the city—some of them the legendary leaders of the original migration (such as Calchas and Mopsus), but others who are known to have been prominent historical personages (such as M. Plancius Varus and his son, C. Plancius Varus, fl. second half of 1st century A.D., who were originally Italians) who were designated "founders" as a result of their personal philanthropy on behalf of the community (Bean 1979: 31–32).

The Plancius family had great wealth and influence in various parts of Asia Minor and were the leading family in Perga during the first two centuries A.D. M. Plancius Varus had a political career in Rome under Nero and managed to survive the intrigues of A.D. 69 to become proconsul of Bithynia under Vespasian. He had served as a Roman senator, and his son was later to achieve the double distinction of being a successful athlete and also consul during the reign of Hadrian (A.D. 117–38). A descendant of the family was to become a celebrated philosopher (Varus). But it was his daughter, Plancia Magna, who exercised the greatest influence in her day. Dozens of texts have been found with her name on them, more than in the case of any other civic personage. She was responsible for the erection of a magnificent array of statues of the Roman imperial family just inside the S gate, many of which are now in the fine museum in Antalya. Plancia herself was priestess of Artemis and held the highest civic office of state (*demiurgus*). Several striking statues of her have also been uncovered.

The city of Perga was a very wealthy and beautifully decorated city from Hellenistic times. Its remains today are second only to Ephesus among the cities associated with the apostle Paul. At least three aqueducts supplied water to the city. The towers of the 3d century B.C. gate are still standing and are among the most impressive of any city of the period. One of the best preserved stadiums in Asia Minor is found just outside the wall of Perga, as is a moderately well preserved Greek theater that was later converted to the Roman style and which would have been operative when Paul visited the city in ca. A.D. 47–48. Perga's theater could accommodate up to 14,000 spectators (Bean 1979: 29). There were numerous elaborate Roman baths in the city and also a very large gymnasium with a *palaestra* (lit. wrestling place) adorned with statues and dedicated to the emperor Claudius (A.D. 41–54). At the foot of the acropolis was a handsome *nymphaeum* (fountain) adorned with a reclining statue of Kestros [Cestrus] (god personifying the local river). Although there was a famous temple to Artemis in Perga that appears on the coinage of the city from the 2d century onward and served as an "inviolable" sanctuary of refuge from the time of Domitian (A.D. 81–96), its location has not yet been determined. In spite of its Asiatic setting, the culture of Perga was almost entirely Greek and, to a lesser extent, Roman. Only about one or two percent of the names represented at Perga are Anatolian; a third of them are Roman. There was presumably a synagogue, where Paul may have preached on his return visit from Galatia (Acts 14:25), but there is no tradition of any early church having been established here.

Bibliography

Bean, G. E. 1979. *Turkey's Southern Shore.* London.

W. WARD GASQUE

PERGAMUM (PLACE) [Gk *Pergamos*]. One of the seven cities whose Christian community was addressed in the book of Revelation (1:11; 2:12). Also known by the form "Pergamon," this city had a long history. Pergamon (modern Bergama; 39°07′N; 27°11′E) emerged as the center of the most important kingdom in W Asia Minor during the early 3d century B.C. and remained one of the cultural and political centers of the region into the 4th century A.D.

The oldest portion of the city is the acropolis, which rises steeply to a height of nearly 1,300 feet above the plain of the Caicus river. This acropolis, powerfully fortified by the rulers of the Attalid dynasty in the 3d and 2d centuries B.C., was the base from which these dynasts could extend their power throughout the region and the fortress to which they could retire when overmatched in the field. The portion of the city lying around the base of the acropolis (much of it built over by modern Bergama) seems to have developed under the protection of the kings and to have expanded in the years of peace after Roman control was firmly established in Asia Minor in the 2d and 1st centuries B.C.

The earliest record of settlement at Pergamon comes in the course of Xenophon's description of the Spartan campaigns of 399 (*Hell.* 3.1.6). He says that the city was one of several which had been given to the descendants of the Spartan king Demaratus, who had been driven from his throne in 490 and became a close adviser to the Persian king Xerxes. The city itself does not appear to have been a very important place at this point, and it is possible that the Persians discouraged extensive development on a site of such great natural strength. It was not until after Alexander the Great's conquest of Asia (334–323 B.C.) that Pergamon began to emerge, first as a major military center, and then as a major political center. By the time of the battle of Courepedium, fought between Lysimachus and Seleucus in 281, the last of the *diadochoi* or "successors" of Alexander, the acropolis had become one of the most important fortresses in western Asia Minor. It was here that Lysimachus had deposited a significant portion of his treasury under the care of the eunuch Philetaerus. In the confusion which had preceded Lysimachus' defeat at Courepedium, Philetaerus had begun to assert his independence from the king (283) (Allen 1983: 11). The years after the battle were even more confused, because of the chaos in the Seleucid court after the murder of Seleucus I shortly after his victory, and because of the Celtic invasion of Asia Minor in 278/277. Philetaerus took advantage of these troubles to begin building up his own kingdom around Pergamon (283–263).

Philetaerus was succeeded by his brother, Eumenes I (263–241), who continued the work of expanding Pergamene power. Eumenes I met with considerable success in the face of the continued Celtic threat to the Greek states off the coast and the endemic military and political crises of the Seleucids (Will 1979–82, 1: 135–52; 234–301). Eumenes' son, Attalus I (241–197), made even more important contributions in this regard. It was Attalus who first claimed the title of *basileus* or "king" (as opposed to *dynastes* or "ruler") for the family after his crushing defeat of the Celts early in his reign and it was Attalus who initiated the alliance between Pergamon and Rome in 212. It seems that he made it to protect himself from the Seleucids, who had reduced his realm on one occasion to little more than the acropolis, and from the aggression of King Philip V of Macedon as well. The result of this alliance was perhaps more spectacular than anything that Attalus could ever have anticipated: the destruction of Seleucid power in Asia Minor. In 193 Rome went to war with the Seleucid king, Antiochus III. In 189 a Roman army, with Pergamene assistance, defeated Antiochus at the battle of Magnesia so decisively that in the treaty of Apamea (187) he had to surrender his family's claim to rule any territory north of the Taurus. The Romans rewarded the Pergamenes, who were then ruled by Attalus' son Eumenes II (214–153), with massive grants of the territory taken from Antiochus throughout Anatolia and in Thrace. Although Rome's relations with Eumenes were strained during the last decade of his life, the kingdom of Pergamon remained Rome's most important ally in the E Mediterranean for the remainder of his reign and throughout the reigns of his brother, Attalus II (153–138), and son, Attalus III (138–133) (Hansen 1971: 70–163; Allen 1983: 76–135; Will 1979–82, 2: 210–38, 285–93, 379–85, 416–25). This situation came to an end in 133 when Attalus III died without issue and left the royal lands to Rome. Rome accepted the bequest in the face of an effort to seize the throne made by a man named Andronicus, who claimed to be the bastard son of Attalus II (for discussion of the circumstances and earlier bibliography, see Potter 1988). The Romans suppressed the revolt of Andronicus and created the province of Asia out of the old Attalid kingdom.

The status of the city of Pergamon remained somewhat ambiguous in the years of Attalid rule. On the one hand it functioned as the royal residence; on the other, it continued to be administered as a normal Greek city, and royal institutions never replaced civic magistracies in the administration of its daily affairs. While the kings ruled their lands and provinces through their appointed officials, Pergamon itself was governed by a council (*boulē*) and board of ten *stratēgoi* (generals). An official known as the *prytanis* appears to have been the chief executive officer of the *boulē,* though his duties appear to have been mostly ceremonial, while the *stratēgoi* looked after most matters of importance. Other important officials were the *nomophylakes* and *astynomoi* (both groups concerned with maintaining public order), the *tamiai* (treasurers) and, after the great expansion of the Attalid kingdom in 188, a royal officer, "the overseer of the city" or "overseer of the sacred revenues," who looked after the interests of the kings (Allen 1983: 159–77). After the establishment of Roman rule, the "overseer" disappeared and was not replaced, but the civic constitution remained essentially unchanged. Aside from these officials, the most important positions were the various superintendencies of the major civic festivals, the priesthoods of the city's gods, of the royal cult, and in the years after Augustus (31 B.C.–A.D. 14) the priesthoods of the cult of the Roman emperors. These offices, as was the case in all classical cities, would have entailed substantial expenditures by the holders.

In the 2d century B.C. Pergamon emerged as one of the great artistic and intellectual centers of the Greek world. This was reflected by the construction program of Eumenes II on the acropolis (for a thorough summary, see Hansen 1971: 234–433). When he took the throne there were a few sacred buildings, including a temple of Demeter, a temple of Athena, a temple to the Magna Mater and a temple to Aphrodite, some royal palaces, a theater and two monuments which Attalus I had erected to commemorate his victories over the Celts and the Seleucids. Eumenes II made the acropolis an architectural marvel. He enclosed it with a magnificent new circuit wall and built imposing monuments: among them a new theater, a new palace, the great altar, the upper agora and the new precinct of Athena. Eumenes' temple of Athena stood on the W side of a square above the theater. The N, E, and S sides of this square were enclosed by new stoae, and behind the N stoa he constructed a new library which became one of the great centers of learning in the ancient world. The patronage of the kings also provided opportunities for the practice of the plastic arts, and the works of sculpture which adorned their monuments remain some of the most magnificent examples of Hellenistic art.

The institution of direct Roman rule in Asia Minor did, however, result in problems for Pergamon. Although certain of her citizens such as the Mithridates (not to be confused with the homonymous Pontic king) who gave Julius Caesar invaluable assistance in the 40s were clearly men of great importance, her position declined in relation to other cities in the Roman province, and Ephesus replaced her as the leading city in the region. This may have been due, in part, to Ephesus' location at the mouth of the Cayster river and her superb harbor, but it also may have resulted from the damage that Pergamon suffered in the wake of the first war between Rome and Mithridates of Pontus in 89–84 B.C. Mithridates swept over the Roman province, ordered the massacre of all Romans in the area and established Pergamon as one of his capital cities. The Roman general Cornelius Sulla exacted a heavy price from Pergamon after his defeat of Mithridates, and a period of relative decline seems to have lasted until the end of the century. It was only in the reign of Augustus that Pergamon began to recover, and this recovery seems to have owed a great deal to the efforts of one of her citizens, Julius Quadratus. This man greatly enhanced the sanctuary of Asclepius (Asclepeium) just outside the city (Bowersock 1969: 19; Habicht 1969: 1–4), and it soon became a major intellectual center. This development may be connected with the growth of its medical staff, which appears to have been deeply concerned with both medical and rhetorical studies.

In the early years of the 2d century, Pergamon was once again one of the great cities of the region. The vigorous intellectual life of the city is eloquently reflected by inscriptions; remarks in Philostratus' *Lives of the Philosophers*; in the works of Galen, the greatest doctor of antiquity, who was born in Pergamon in 129 and practiced there in his early years; and in the remarkable spiritual autobiography, *The Sacred Tales*, of the professional rhetorician or *sophist*, Aelius Aristides, who lived in the Asclepium for many years (for the intellectual life of this period, see Bowersock 1969; for Galen, see Bowersock 1969: 59–75; for the Asclepeium, see Habicht 1969: 6–18). Even though the city seems to have suffered in the course of the 3d century—as did the other cities of Asia Minor—the writings of the 4th-century historian and biographer Eunapius of Sardis provide further glimpses of life in the city which suggest that it retained its importance as an intellectual center into his own time. His evidence also suggests that, despite the presence of a Christian community in the city since the 1st century (Habicht 1969: 19), the city as a whole was very slow to adopt the new faith. One reason for this may have been the importance to the city of the cult of Asclepius, who was himself a god of healing, and the feeling among many pagans that the healing miracles which Asclepius was believed to have performed proved that he was a true protector of his people. It is therefore not surprising that it was at Pergamon that the future emperor Julian first encountered important teachers of the Neoplatonic school. This was a decisive point in the intellectual odyssey which ended in his apostasy from the Christian faith and his effort to restore the worship of the pagan gods during his brief reign (361–363). The continuing importance of the cult of Asclepius may also be illustrated by the fact that one of Julian's closest advisers was the doctor Oribasius, who was a native of the city (Bowersock 1978: 28–29).

Pergamon appears to have declined in the centuries after Julian's visit, and it was never able to recover from the damage that it sustained during the Arab invasions of 663 and 716. The story that, in the course of the siege of 716, the defenders of the city cut a pregnant woman to pieces, and dipped their gauntlets in the pot where they had boiled the remains of mother and child (Theoph. 390), suggests that the sophistication of the inhabitants at this point was somewhat less than it had been in the 4th century. These inhabitants had, by this time, largely withdrawn to the acropolis where their humble dwellings were nestled among the monuments of the Attalid monarchy, which were torn apart to supply building materials. When the future emperor Theodore Lascaris visited the site in the 12th century he wrote with sadness that the poor modern buildings that he saw among the remains of the classical city revealed what he felt was the poverty of his own age in comparison with that of the ancients (*Ep.* 80; Foss 1977: 479–81).

Bibliography

Allen, R. E. 1983. *The Attalid Kingdom. A Constitutional History.* Oxford.

Bowersock, G. W. 1969. *Greek Sophists in the Roman Empire.* Oxford.

———. 1978. *Julian the Apostate.* Cambridge.

Foss, C. 1977. Archaeology and the "Twenty Cities" of Byzantine Asia. *AJA* 81: 469–86.

Habicht, C. 1969. *Alterümer von Pergamon VIII.3. Inschriften des Asklepeions.* Berlin.

Hansen, E. V. 1971. *The Attalids of Pergamon.* 2d ed. Ithaca.

Potter, D. S. 1988. Where did Aristonicus' Revolt Begin? *Zeitschrift für Papyrologie und Epigraphik* 74.

Will, E. 1979–82. *Histoire politique du monde hellenistique.* 2 vols. 2d ed. Nancy, France.

D. S. POTTER

PERIDA (PERSON) [Heb *pĕrîdāʾ*]. See PERUDA (PERSON).

PERIPHRASIS. See BIBLE, EUPHEMISM AND DYSPHEMISM IN THE.

PERIZZITE [Heb *pĕrizzî*]. Group of pre-Israelite inhabitants of Canaan. The term is always used with the definite article as a collective name for Perizzites. The term Perizzite is found in 21 of the 27 lists of pre-Israelite nations. It occurs in ten-name lists (Gen 15:20), seven-name lists (Josh 3:10), six-name lists (Josh 7:1), five-name lists (1 Kgs 9:20), and two-name lists (Gen 34:20). In the most common six-name lists the Perizzites always occur in the fourth position in the latter half of the lists among other little known nations including the Jebusites and the Hivites (Exod 3:8; 33:2).

The fact that Canaanites and Perizzites occur together four times in two-name lists suggests that each of these groups stands for a larger combination of peoples (Gen 13:7; 34:30; Judg 1:4–5). Some have suggested that Perizzites is etymologically linked to *pĕrazî* "rural country" and that " 'Canaanites' and 'Perizzites' here stand for 'those living in fortified cities,' and 'those living in unwalled towns or hamlets' " (Ishida 1979: 479). Ishida argues, however, for an ethnic distinction between the terms and suggests that "Canaanites" refer to Semitic people and "Perizzites" refer to non-Semitic people (1979: 480).

According to Josh 11:3 the Perizzites are located in the hill country of Canaan. On the basis of Gen 15:19–21 and Josh 17:15 Ishida suggests that the Perizzites and Rephites can be "positioned in the forest country between Judah and Ephraim" (1979: 483; see also *GTTOT,* 71–72).

While the land of the Perizzites was promised to Abraham and his descendants (Gen 15:20) the Israelites found it difficult to totally defeat these people. In spite of reports that they were defeated (Josh 12:8) intermarriage took place between them and the Israelites (Judg 3:5) and the Israelites did not totally separate from them (Ezra 9:1). The descendants of the pre-Israelite nations who still lived in the land were reportedly reduced to slavery by Solomon (1 Kgs 9:20–21). The Perizzites continued to find their place in the traditional lists of pre-Israelite inhabitants of Canaan (Neh 9:8; Jdt 5:16; 1 Esdr 8:69).

There is no scholarly consensus about the ethnical or etymological background of the term Perizzites. Boling and Wright suggest that "The term may be ethnic (Hurrian) or appellative (cf. *pĕrāzôt,* 'unwalled villages,' Esth 9:19; Ezek 38:11; Zech 2:8)" (*Joshua* AB, 166). Speiser suggests that the term Perizzites is probably non-Semitic and since its suffix *-izzi* is also independently attested in Hurrian that it might be a local group of Hurrians (*IDB* 3: 242).

Bibliography

Ishida, T. 1979. The Structure and Historical Implications of the Lists of Pre-Israelite Nations. *Biblica* 60: 461–90.

STEPHEN A. REED

PERSECUTION OF THE EARLY CHURCH. There were many reasons for the persecution of the Christian church in the four centuries preceding the conversion of Constantine. Different reasons predominated at different times; no single reason or simple set of explanations can explain persecution in any given period. As a result, the most promising approach to the subject as a whole is an examination of the institutions involved: the imperial government, the local civic authorities and the church itself. This makes it possible to review the different concerns of each and the changes that occurred. Scholars have had difficulty arriving at a consensus with regard to persecution because the sources are diffuse and often tendentious. Some account of these sources is therefore necessary before exploring the causes, effects and changing nature of the persecutions in more detail.

A. The Sources
B. The Imperial Government
C. Persecution and Local Government
D. Persecution and the Church

A. The Sources

The sources for the persecution fall into three categories: statements by the imperial authorities and pagan writers; Christian apologetic works and other theoretical discussion of persecution; and the extant Christian martyr acts.

The first of these three categories is the least well represented. All that survives is the correspondence between Pliny and Trajan on the subject of the Christians when Pliny was governor of the province of Bithynia-Pontus (in N Turkey) in 111 or 112; a rescript (a response to a written inquiry which had the force of law) from the emperor Hadrian to a governor of the province of Asia (W Turkey) in 122/123; *libelli* (certificates of sacrifice) preserved on papyri from Egypt from the time of Decius' edict on sacrifices in 249/250; the text of Valerian's edict of 258 summarized in a letter of Cyprian and a number of documents connected with the great persecutions of 303–313 that are either quoted in Christian writers or can be reconstructed from their accounts. Finally, there are the fragments of authors such as Celsus (whose *On True Doctrine* is quoted extensively by Origen in his response, *Against Celsus*) and some passing remarks in Suetonius' biographies and Tacitus' *Annals.* As a whole, these texts reveal the attitude of the state towards the church and the steps that the imperial authorities thought would be effective against the church.

The Christian apologetic and historiographic tradition, which begins with the Gospels, is extremely complicated. The authors of these works seem to give straightforward explanations for persecution, such as the jealousy of the Jews or Nero's edict of A.D. 64 (Nero reigned from A.D. 54–68), but these explanations often fall apart on close examination. The standard explanation from the 2d century onwards was that the "Christian name," the *nomen Christianum* (membership in the Church) was persecuted as a result of Nero's edict; persecution was an *institutum Neronianum,* a Neronian practice, that was only permitted by emperors who all agreed were evil. This explanation is unsatisfactory and was influenced by a tendency of Christian writers to interpret Roman history in the same terms as Jewish history had been presented in the OT, that "good kings" honored Yahweh and "bad" did not. The other explanation that they offer, that persecution was the result of ignorance of Christian doctrine on the part of ill-educated pagans, is similarly too simplistic. Nonetheless, these works often shed valuable light on relations between the church and the imperial authorities and the most important of them, Eusebius' *Ecclesiastical History,* written in the early years of the 4th century, preserves a number of documents which are crucial for an understanding of the persecutions. Other works such as Tertullian's *To the Martyrs* and *Concerning Flight in Persecution* or Cyprian's *Concerning the Lapsed* reveal that persecution caused serious doctrinal problems. The question that they sought to answer was "Is persecution the work of the Devil or of God?" A person's behavior in time of persecution would be conditioned by his answer to this problem.

The martyr acts, accounts of the execution of individual martyrs or groups of martyrs, are the most difficult source, but when handled with sufficient care, also the most important. Care in their interpretation is essential as these acts vary greatly in their content. Some are rhetorical fictions which provide, once the gory details of a martyr's death are stripped away, no more than the fact of the martyrdom and its date—and even these might not be authentic. Others, such as *The Passion of Pionius and his Companions* contain vivid eyewitness accounts and even documents composed by martyrs as they lay in prison awaiting execution. The details which they present are of great value for reconstructing the attitudes of both the persecutors and the persecuted, and the doctrinal statements which many of them contain shed important light upon the tensions to which persecution gave rise within the church.

B. The Imperial Government

The Gospels and *Acts* show that the Jewish communities in Palestine and other cities of the Greek East drew Romans into the persecution of the church. Suetonius' obscure allusion to problems at Rome in the reign of Claudius (A.D. 41–54) between Jews and the "followers of Chrestus" suggests the same thing, although it is debated whether there "followers of Chrestus" were Christians (Suet. *Claud.* 25). The executions of Peter and Paul at Rome, before Nero issued his edict against the Christians in 64, may have been the result of complaints about their activity from the Jewish community. But these actions can only have had a tangential relationship to that edict. When a great fire ravaged Rome in 64, Nero attempted to shift the blame for the fire from himself onto another party and ordered the mass arrest and execution of Christians in Rome. This was the event which led later Christian writers to claim that persecution was a "Neronian institution." In fact, it is not likely that Nero's edict extended to Christians who lived outside of the city and it may have been no more than an extreme version of earlier edicts, of both Republican and imperial date, which banned or restricted the practice of certain cults within Rome or Italy. As was the case with these earlier edicts, Nero's edict probably ceased to be enforced after the immediate crisis ended. It is certainly true that Pliny does not seem to be aware of the edict when he investigates Christianity in 111/112.

The opening lines of Pliny's letter to the Emperor Trajan (98–117) reveal that he was not sure of either the specific reasons for the persecution of the church, or of the proper procedure for deciding the cases before him. He wrote (*Ep.* 10.96): "I have never been present at investigations of Christians; so I do not know how or to what extent they are to be punished or sought out. I have thought about these questions a great deal: should some distinction be shown on grounds of age, or should there be no difference in the treatment of children and adults; should mercy be given to the repentant, or should nothing be forgiven to a person who was once a Christian, should the fact of being a Christian (the *nomen Christianum*) be punished, even if there was no other crime, or should only the crimes connected with the name be punished?" Thus Pliny knew that people had been tried for being Christians, and since we know that he spent most of his adult life in Rome and Italy, we may surmise that he means Christians had been tried at Rome during his mature years. He knew the charge against these people was that they were members of a religious sect that indulged in criminal activity. This is an important point. He knew that members of the sect were punished because of crimes that they were believed to be committing in his own time, not because of anything that had happened in the reign of Nero. The explanation for this may have been that the Emperor Domitian (81–96) had taken some action against the cult—though the evidence for this is open to dispute—or it may have been that Pliny and all other Roman magistrates were charged with protecting the areas under their administration from "evil men." Whatever the case, it was membership in the cult that was at issue, and whether by being a member of that cult a person had broken the law. We know from other sources that the crimes associated with Christianity were attacks on pagan temples or images of the gods, cannibalism and incest. It is also clear from this letter that Pliny attempted to discover whether or not the Christians in his area were actively engaged in these crimes. He discovered that they were not. In the meantime he executed any Christians who were not Roman citizens if they refused his order to sacrifice to "our gods," the grounds being insolence in the face of his authority; and he sent Roman citizens who were guilty of the same offense to be tried at Rome. While he awaited Trajan's response he treated the church as an illegal private association (see de Ste Croix 1969).

Pliny's question was whether he should treat Christians as guilty because of their beliefs or simply because the church was one of a number of the private associations (*collegia*) that Trajan had banned. Trajan's response made it clear that the practice of Christianity was defined as a religious offense and that, as a cult, it was illegal. A person charged with Christianity could be forgiven past membership in the cult if he recanted and offered sacrifice to the gods. Trajan added the further provision that Pliny, whose other duties were onerous enough, should not spend his time seeking out Christians and that he should not investigate charges against people which he found in anonymous denunciations (Pliny, *Ep.* 10.97). The implication is that if someone came to Pliny in person and denounced another, that person could be charged. This decision was restated by Hadrian (117–138) in a letter that he sent to Minicius Fundanus in 122/123.

The practice of the Christian faith was therefore illegal because the Roman authorities thought that it involved the commission of crimes, but it was up to individual governors and other magistrates to act against Christians as they saw fit. They had a great deal to do: they had to maintain the tranquillity of their provinces, prevent riot and insurrection in the cities under their control, keep the highways free of brigands, and ensure that cities were able to pay their taxes. Most if not all governors probably felt that they had more important tasks than dealing with the Christians and, with the passing of time, some may even have come to feel that there was nothing wrong with the religion so long as its practitioners did not disturb the peace. In one case, a provincial governor even rescued a Christian congregation from brigands after its bishop had led it out into the desert to greet Christ at his second coming. Tertullian tells of another governor who let an unrepentant Christian go free after only "moderate torture" and of yet another who refused to act when he was confronted by a Christian community asking to be put to death. He suggested that they jump off cliffs or hang themselves instead (Ter. *ad Scap.* 4.3; 5.1). It is a universal literary device of the martyr acts that the magistrate presiding at the investigation of Christians always asks the prospective martyrs to recant. The authorities seem always to have been more interested in convincing Christians to apostatize than in executing them. To this end the punishments inflicted were more often flogging, imprisonment, and exile, rather than death.

This state of affairs continued until the middle of the 3d century. In 249, the Emperor Decius (249–251) ordered all inhabitants of the empire to sacrifice to the ancestral gods and to obtain a certificate (*libellus*) proving that they had done so. Failure to sacrifice could result in exile, the confiscation of property, prison, or death. The edict was not aimed at eradicating Christianity, but rather at ensuring the goodwill of the ancestral gods in a time of crisis. Nonetheless, it had a significant impact on some Christian communities. In North Africa, Cyprian, the bishop of Carthage, took a very strong line against members of his congregation who either sacrificed (*sacrificati*) or fraudulently obtained *libelli* (*libellatici*). There seems to have been a great number of people who took one or the other of these options, perhaps believing that under the circumstances such a sacrifice was not a serious sin. We know of bishops who retained their sees after sacrificing, and obedience to the edict seems to have been so widespread in the east that the issue never arose as to the terms under which those who had sacrificed should be re-admitted to communion.

The edicts of Valerian (253–260) in 257 and 258 were very different matters. They represent the first empire-wide efforts to destroy the church. The first edict seems to have included the following provisions: Christians should honor the traditional gods of the empire (this did not mean that they had to cease to honor their own god, but only that they had to show respect for the others as well), clergy who would not obey the edict should be arrested and of church property confiscated. The second edict, which may have been motivated by the recalcitrance of members of the clergy who had been arrested, seems to have been concerned entirely with the treatment of unrepentant Christians. According to its terms all members of the clergy who persisted in the faith would be executed, male Christians who were members of the highest orders of society (the equestrian and senatorial) would suffer confiscation of their property and death if they persisted, and Christian women (presumably women of the same social classes) would suffer the confiscation of their property and exile. Members of the imperial household who had been or were Christians would be condemned to work in chains on the imperial estates. The reasoning behind these edicts is obscure. It is clear that they represented a radical departure from Valerian's earlier policy towards the church and it may be, as the bishop of Dionysius of Alexandria suggested (Eus. *Hist. Eccl.* 7.10), that court politics had something to do with the decision to attack the church. In any event, the edicts did not remain in force for long. Valerian was captured by the Persians in the summer of 260 and his son Gallienus (253–268) issued an edict of toleration in the same year. This edict legalized the practice of Christianity and ordered the restoration of church property that had been confiscated under the earlier edicts.

In 260, therefore, Christianity was recognized as a legal cult in the empire and persecution came to an end for a generation. We even hear of Christian bishops asking the emperor Aurelian (270–275) to intervene in a dispute over the see of Antioch and to expel the bishop, Paul of Samosata. This state of affairs continued until the very last years of the reign of Diocletian (284–305).

Diocletian's decision to issue an edict of persecution is difficult to understand. Up to this point in his reign he had been openly tolerant of the church. Christians held high positions in his court and a Christian, Lactantius, held the prestigious chair in Latin rhetoric in his capital Nicomedia (in NW Turkey). The reason may, in fact, lie in the politics of his reign, for Diocletian's edict seems to have come at the end of an elaborate campaign within the court to promote hostility to the church. This campaign appears to have been the work of the *Caesar* Galerius (an important feature of Diocletian's reign was the creation of a college of four emperors, the two senior emperors, or *Augusti,* were Diocletian and Maximian Herculius, the two junior emperors, or *Caesares,* were Galerius and Constantius, father of the future emperor Constantine). In the later years of Diocletian's reign Galerius appears to have exerted a tremendous amount of influence over the senior emperor, and he appears to have been a fervent anti-Christian (Barnes 1981: 21–27). This also appears to have caused a split in the imperial college, for the persecution edicts—as was also the case with other measures taken in these years—were not enforced as vigorously by Maximian Herculius and Constantius as they were by Diocletian and Galerius.

The first edict was promulgated on February 23, 303. Its terms were as follows: Christian churches and houses where Christian scripture was discovered were to be destroyed, copies of scripture were to be burned, church property was to be confiscated, and meetings for Christian worship were forbidden; Christians who persisted in the faith would lose the capacity to bring actions in court; Christians whose status exempted them from physical coercion in courts (*honestiores*) would lose the protection of their status; Christian members of the imperial household would be enslaved. A few months later—in the spring or summer of 303—a second edict was issued, ordering the arrest of Christian clergy. This led to a crisis for the state as the prisons filled up, and in the autumn of 303 yet another edict was handed down, stating that Christian prisoners who sacrificed would be released. Finally, in January or February, 304, an edict was posted ordering all the inhabitants of the empire to sacrifice. None of this succeeded, in great measure because such measures depended upon the willingness of imperial officers to execute them and there were not many who went beyond token obedience. In fact, Constantius seems to have refused to act on them in anything more than the most cursory way and Maximian did not enforce any edict except the first.

Diocletian and Maximian abdicated in favor of Galerius and Constantius on May 1, 305, and this in effect ended what persecution there had been in the W since Constantius assumed supreme power there. When Constantine succeeded his father on July 25, 306, he issued a general edict of toleration in the part of the empire that he controlled (at first only Britain and Gaul). In the E, Galerius continued to enforce the edicts until 311, when he too issued a general edict of toleration a few months before his death. There were only two further outbreaks after that. Maximin Daia (*Caesar* under Galerius after 305 and *Augustus* in his own right after 311), influenced by a powerful anti-Christian lobby at court, engaged in a brief persecution between 311 and 312/313 when he issued an edict of toleration before going to war with Galerius' successor, Licinius. In July of 313, Licinius, who had defeated Maximin, issued a general edict restoring Christian property throughout the E (this edict, issued at Nicomedia, is often referred to as the "edict of Milan" because it was believed that it was the result of a meeting between Constantine and Licinius in that city during 312). Although Licinius restricted Christian worship before his final defeat by Constantine in 324, this edict effectively marked the end of imperial efforts to act against the Christian church. It was in the time of Constantine that the power of the imperial government came to be directed instead against Christian heretical sects in defense of what Constantine defined as orthodoxy, as well as, by gradual stages, traditional cult.

C. Persecution and Local Government

In the first three centuries A.D. most outbreaks of persecution did not begin with the imperial authorities. They began as local pogroms inspired by a feeling on the part of the inhabitants of individual cities that the Christians in their midst were atheists whose presence upset the traditional gods. It was a reaction that is summed up best by Tertullian's observation (*Apol.* 40.1) that, "if the Tiber rises to the walls, if the Nile does not rise to the fields; if the sky stands still, if the earth moves, if there is famine, if there is pestilence, the cry goes up, 'Christians to the lion.' "

It was the dislike of the provincials for the Christians in their midst that led Pliny to investigate the sect, and this often seems to have been the case elsewhere. Thus in 177 there was a serious outburst at Lyons which resulted in the death of a number of Christians. The incident began when a mob seized a group of Christians and dragged them to the town forum where the civic authorities asked them about their beliefs. When they confessed their faith, they were imprisoned to await the governor (who would be coming to the city in the course of his annual tour of the province). Thereafter, the governor sentenced unrepentant Christians before large and enthusiastic crowds (Eus. *Hist. Eccl.* 5.1.7–10). The members of these crowds seem genuinely to have believed that the Christians were dangerous "atheists," and also to have believed the charges that were extracted from the slaves of some of the members of the congregation: that the Christians regularly committed incest (a misunderstanding of the Christian use of the terms "brother/sister") and that their rites involved cannibalism (a misunderstanding of the Eucharist). The charge of atheism could move crowds to a great frenzy. It was leveled against Polycarp when he was sentenced to death at Smyrna in the 150s, crowds cried, "away with the atheists" during his trial and during an earlier execution (*Mart. Pol.* 3.2; 9.2). Mobs at Alexandria tried to force Christians whom they seized to sacrifice to the gods, and Alexander, priest of an oracular cult of Glycon, is said to have had Christians cursed as atheists at celebrations of the mysteries of his god.

As the church became more familiar to people in general and Christians were more frequently people of high social status, such charges became less common, and the local authorities at times appear reluctant to engage in full-scale persecution. It is clear from the *Acts of Pionius*, that Pionius' refusal to recant and the prospect of his death at the hands of the governor deeply upset the local magistrates. It is also clear that the officials charged with enforcing Valerian's edicts in North Africa made a real effort to convince Christians to apostatize and appear to have been extremely uncomfortable when they were faced with the prospect of executing Christians who were members of the highest levels of society. A local magistrate at Cirta, in North Africa, who was charged with enforcing Diocletian's first edict, appears to have been on familiar terms with the local Christians and averse to the use of violence in carrying out his orders. The local Christians were equally averse to forcing him to do so (von Soden 1913: 28). It seems to be a general rule that in the later part of the 3d century and early 4th century, as the state became more directly involved in the persecution of the faith, local authorities became less willing to join in and there were fewer anti-Christian riots.

The exception to this general rule appears in cases where entire communities were Christian. In such cases, however, it would appear that the local jealousies characteristic of the cities and towns of the empire were more important than issues of religion. From the time of Constantine onwards we hear much about towns such as Orcistus in Phrygia, which suffered at the hands of their neighbors during the persecution of Galerius and Maximin Daia and were rewarded for their faith under the new dispensation. In the 4th century, local pride came to be intertwined with issues of religion and a new chapter opened in the tale of intercity violence in the Roman Empire, as Christians destroyed temples and pagans fought back.

The total number of Christians who suffered death or imprisonment for their faith is difficult to estimate. Pliny's letter to Trajan suggests that he killed a number of people in the course of a routine investigation and the records of local pogroms suggest that from time to time individual Christian communities suffered heavy losses. Even though enforcement was erratic, the edicts of Decius, Valerian,

Diocletian and his successors caused substantial casualties in some areas. But, the numbers were probably not enormous in absolute terms: most Christian communities were not large and no community is known to have been destroyed by a persecution. A figure of around 30,000–50,000 victims in the centuries before Constantine, which would allow for an average of between 75 and 125 victims a year throughout the empire, may be roughly correct.

D. Persecution and the Church

As the attitude of the state and local authorities changed towards the church, so too did the attitude of the church towards persecution. From the earliest period, Christians who were willing to endure death, torture, and imprisonment for the faith were greatly honored. The cult of martyrs quickly came to play an important role in the church, and some movements, such as Montanism, placed a premium upon martyrdom. For any Christian, persecution was seen as a time to prove ultimate devotion, and in facing the authorities a Christian might feel that he was reenacting the Passion. The emotion is summed up most eloquently by martyrs imprisoned at Carthage in the late summer of 250: "what . . . could, through God's favor, befall any man which might bring him greater glory or bliss than this: in the very midst of his executioners, undaunted, to confess the Lord God . . . to become, by confessing the name of Christ, a partner of Christ in his passion; to have become, by God's favor, a judge of his own judge (Cyp. *Ep.* 31, 2, 3)." A number of Christians even went so far as deliberately to attract the attention of the authorities so that they might suffer for the faith. But this also led to problems within the Church.

One difficulty persecution caused the church (above and beyond the physical suffering of some of its members and the intellectual problems it raised about the nature of evil) was the challenge that martyrs posed to the established hierarchy of the church. Montanists certainly taught that martyrs were closer to God than the authorities of the church, and that attitude was also common in more conventional circles. Cyprian treated the question at length in his *Concerning the Lapsed* (*de Lapsis*, 15–21) and argued that the absolution granted by martyrs to those who had sacrificed or obtained *libelli* during the reign of Decius had no effect—that penance had to be imposed by the duly constituted officers of the church. But this did not solve the issue, even in Cyprian's own province. At the time of the great persecution there is a great deal of evidence for efforts by the church to restrict the title of martyr and regulate the celebration of the cult. The early 4th century council at Elvira in Spain ruled that "voluntary martyrs," people who were killed while insulting traditional cult, could not be regarded as true martyrs. Mensurius of Carthage refused the title of martyr to people who did not try to evade the authorities. It would even appear that he forbade members of his congregation to bring food to such people when they were in prison (cf. Jonkers 1954: 18 n. 60; von Soden 1913: n. 4, 6). But his ruling did not go unchallenged; even a Christian, such as Lactantius, who subscribed to the doctrine that people should not offer themselves to the authorities, could not restrain his admiration for a man who was executed after tearing down a copy of Diocletian's first persecution edict (Lactant. *de Mort. Pers.* 13.2–3). The problem did not end for the orthodox church until the end of the persecutions.

The second major problem was that persecution gave rise to schism. People responded differently to persecution, and while all might agree that "authentic martyrs" should be treated with the highest regard, not all could agree as to what constituted proper behavior on the part of their weaker brethren. Debate over this question became particularly vehement at the time of the Decian edict on sacrifices and even more so in the time of the Great Persecution. The great Donatist and Melitian disputes arose directly out of this issue: both sects challenged the orthodox church's more moderate treatment of those who were weak in the face of persecution. Such disputes were not easily quelled and were carried on with great vehemence, as may be seen in the statement of the schismatic bishop Majorian of Carthage at the time of his consecration in 311. He said, "I am the real vine and my father is the gardener. Every barren branch of mine he cuts away; and every fruiting branch he cleans (John 15:1–2). Thus I cast off the barren branches which have been cut, thus the incense burners, the *traditores,* who are hateful to god, may not remain in the church of god, unless, confessing their grief they are reconciled through penance. Hence it is not fitting to have communication with Caecilian, a heretic, ordained by *traditores*" (von Soden 1913: 6).

It was through the promotion of schism that persecution by the imperial authorities caused the most difficulty to the Church. The quarrels which arose in the wake of the Great Persecution did not end with the victory of Constantine. In fact, they led to the opening of a new chapter in the relationship between the Church and the empire. This was the violent persecution of heretical sects by the imperial government in defense of the orthodox faith.

Bibliography

Barnes, T. D. 1968. Legislation Against the Christians. *JRS* 58: 32–50.

———. 1981. *Constantine and Eusebius.* Cambridge, MA.

Clarke, G. W. 1984. *The Letters of St. Cyprian.* ACW 43, 44, 46. New York.

Delehaye, H. 1921. *Les Passions des martyrs et les genres littèraires.* Brussels.

Frend, W. H. C. 1965. *Martyrdom and Persecution in the Early Church.* Oxford.

Gregoire, H. 1964. *Les persécutions dans l'empire romain.* Académie royale de Belge. Classe des lettres et des sciences morales et politiques. Mémoires 56.3. Brussels.

Jonkers, E. J. 1954. *Acta et symbola conciliorum quae saeculo quarto habita sunt.* Textus minores 19. Leiden.

Knipfing, J. 1923. The *libelli* of the Decian Persecution. *HTR* 16: 345–90.

Lane Fox, R. J. 1986. *Pagans and Christians.* New York.

Musurillo, H. 1972. *The Acts of the Christian Martyrs.* Oxford.

Soden, H. von. 1913. *Urkunden zur Enstehungsgeschichte des Donatismus.* KlT 122. Bonn.

Ste. Croix, G. E. M. de. 1954. Aspects of the Great Persecution. *HTR* 47: 73–113.

———. 1963. Why were the Early Christians Persecuted. *Past and Present* 26: 1–38.

———. 1969. Christianity's Encounter with the Roman Imperial Government. Pp. 345–46 in *The Crucible of Christianity,* ed. A. J. Toynbee. London.

D. S. Potter

PERSEPOLIS (PLACE) [Gk *Persepolis*]. One of the ancient capitals of the Achaemenid kings of Iran (the others were Susa, Ecbatana, and Babylon). Now called Takht-i Jamshid (the Throne of Jamshid), it is located in SW Iran (29°57′N; 52°52′E) in the province of Fars (the homeland of the Achaemenids), approximately 32 miles NE of the modern city of Shiraz. The Old Persian name for the site was *Parsa.* It is mentioned in 2 Macc 9:2 as a city which rebelled against and defeated Antiochus.

The site is situated on a large platform, partially artificial and partially carved from the native rock at the W foot of the Kuh-i Rahmat (Mountain of Mercy). The platform, the cistern, an elaborate system of drains, the central part of the Apadana or large audience hall, and several sections of the Treasury building were founded and, in the main, brought to completion by Darius I (522–486 B.C.). Construction probably began shortly after 520 B.C. Late in the reign of Darius, and in the early years of Xerxes, the platform was expanded to the W and Darius' private palace, a second phase of the Treasury, part of the fortifications, the main stair and the Gate of All Nations were built. Xerxes himself built a new, larger private palace, the central building (Tripylon), and the Harem. He also reorganized and enlarged the Treasury, and laid the foundations for, and perhaps completed, a large new audience hall, the Hall of a Hundred Columns. All remaining construction can be dated to the reigns of either Artaxerxes I or his successors, but any further construction is nothing more than the completion, or the enlargement, of the building plans laid down by Darius and modified by Xerxes.

The Persepolis platform and the buildings on it are a remarkable artistic and architectural statement. It is probable, however, that what has been exposed is only the "fortification," or the citadel, of a far more extensive complex. There are several palaces on the plain to both sides of the platform, and no doubt more await excavation. It is, therefore, reasonable to suppose that a much larger "City of the Persians" stretched across the plain at the front and to the sides of the platform.

The characteristic architectural feature of the Persepolis building complex is the columned hall. Other individual elements, such as the Mesopotamian-inspired winged bulls which guard Xerxes' Gate of All Nations, are clearly borrowed from other cultures, but the columned hall is rooted in the experiences of the Iranians on the Iranian plateau. The prototypes of the great halls, such as the Apadana and Hall of a Hundred Columns, can be found in the columned structures of Hasanlu V and IV (1400–800 B.C.) and in the columned halls of the Median sites of Nush-i Jan and Godin II (8th–7th centuries B.C.).

Another major feature of the site is the relief sculpture which adorns almost every building. Characteristic of these reliefs is that they are entirely unhistorical; they tell no developing story, as did many reliefs of the Assyrians and the Egyptians. Instead they give a static picture of something that is already done, that already exists, that is accomplished (tribute brought, monsters slain, fire honored, dignitaries received). More important, the king is everywhere and is the focus, in one way or another, of almost all the reliefs. Yet this king is not an individual; there are no portraits of Darius, Xerxes, or Artaxerxes. Instead they project a dynastic image of the glory and concept of kingship, rather than a realistic depiction of a particular king. Thus the whole of even a complex composition such as the great reliefs on the stairways of the Apadana present a planned, spiritual, abstract, and almost cosmic composition of static totality.

It can be suggested that the ultimate goal of both the architecture and the decoration of Persepolis was to present to the world the concept of a *Pax Persica*—a harmonious, peaceful empire ruled by a king who contained within his person and his office the welfare of the empire.

T. CUYLER YOUNG, JR.

PERSEUS (PERSON) [Gk *Perseus*]. Illegitimate son of Philip V and the last king of Macedonia, whose defeat is mentioned in a list praising Roman accomplishments (1 Macc 8:5). In the 180s B.C.E., Perseus helped his father prepare Macedonia for war against Rome, while his legitimate half brother, Demetrius, defended Philip in the Senate against accusations of illegally seizing Thrace. Jealous of Demetrius' success in Rome, Perseus engineered his death in 181 with a forged letter implicating him in treason. Later Philip learned the truth, but he died too suddenly to prevent Perseus' accession to the throne in 179.

Perseus continued to arm Macedonia and make alliances with Rome's enemies. Seleucus IV married his daughter Laodice to Perseus in 177 to join the Macedonian cause. After Seleucus' assassination in 175, the pro-Roman King Eumenes of Pergamum put Antiochus IV on the Seleucid throne to block a Seleucid alliance with Perseus. Though Antiochus IV negotiated with Perseus, he did so secretly so as not to anger Rome.

The accusations against Perseus and the fears about his military buildup led Rome to invade Macedonia in 171. In the Third Macedonian War, Perseus would neither capitalize on his victories by destroying the Romans nor could he get them to surrender. On June 22, 168, the Roman general Aemilius Paulus finally defeated Perseus at Pydma and took him captive to Rome. Perseus lived in a dungeon in Alba until Aemilius convinced the Senate to give him better quarters. However, after two years, Perseus so antagonized his guards that they kept him awake constantly until he died from sleeplessness.

Rome's involvement in the Third Macedonian War permitted Antiochus IV to invade Egypt in 171 and to control it until 168, when Rome forced him to leave Egypt.

Bibliography

Bevan, E. R. 1966. *The House of Seleucus.* Vol. 2. New York.

MITCHELL C. PACWA

PERSIAN ART. See ART AND ARCHITECTURE (PERSIAN ART).

PERSIAN EMPIRE. In the third quarter of the 6th century B.C., the political geography of the Middle East underwent a profound change. Divided around 550 between powerful contemporary kingdoms (Babylonia, Egypt, Media, Lydia), it would be, in the decades that followed, unified by the conquests of the Persians, a small group practically absent from historical documentation until the time when, under Cyrus the Great (560/59–530), they began their indomitable expansion. Under the reigns of the first three representatives of the new "Achaemenid" dynasty, the territory controlled by the Persian armies continued to extend in all directions at a very rapid pace.

A. The Creation of an Empire
  1. The Persian Kingdom Before 550 B.C.
  2. The Conquests of Cyrus
  3. Cambyses and the Conquest of Egypt
  4. Uprising, Revolts, and New Conquests
  5. The Organization of the Empire under Darius
B. The Empire in the 5th Century
  1. The First Retreats on the Mediterranean Front
  2. Imperial Strength and Royal Power
C. From Artaxerxes II to Alexander
  1. Dynastic Crisis and Royal Power
  2. The Retaking of Asia Minor
  3. Egyptian Danger and Satrapic Revolts
D. Alexander and the End of the Persian Empire

A. The Creation of an Empire

1. The Persian Kingdom Before 550 B.C. We know very little about the Persians before the appearance of Cyrus. They were an Iranian people who, coming directly from Central Asia or via the Caucasus and the Zagros around 1000 B.C., settled in the region that would become Persia (Fārs), i.e., the heart of the Persian Empire. The way of life of these Persians is poorly understood. Herodotus makes reference to tribes of nomads and tribes of farmers, but this text remains too schematic. The Persians settled in a region that had traditionally been held by the masters of Susa, the Elamite kings. It is therefore hardly surprising that the first title held by the Persian kings was that of "king of Anshan," a direct reference to the Fārs region near Maliyan, traditionally under Susa. The expansion of the first Persian kingdom was done at the expense of Susa and the Neo-Elamite kings. But the Perso-Elamite contacts did not take place solely during periods of war. The Fārs was then inhabited by Elamite populations with whom the Persians had established fruitful contacts. The "Acropolis Tablets," whose dating is still contested (second half of the 7th century or the first half of the 6th century), attest to the presence of a Persian population in Susa during this period. All of this explains why Elamite influence was so powerful in the institutions of the Persian State: for example, the Persepolis tablets that date from the reigns of Darius and Xerxes are written in the Elamite language (sprinkled with Persian terms).

In the absence of indisputable written documents, we cannot reconstruct with certainty the different stages of the history of the Persian kingdom before Cyrus the Great. In his genealogy, Darius I affirms that eight kings reigned before him. But Darius' pretentions are highly debatable (see below). On the other hand, an inscription by Ashurbanipal (669–630 B.C.) refers to a certain Kurash, "king of Parsumash," who rendered homage to the Assyrian king and sent him his son as hostage ca. 640 B.C. It is now doubtful that this was actually Cyrus I: a recent study (de Miroschedji 1985) places his reign ca. 610–589 (Cambyses I [585–559] and Cyrus II [the Great] succeeded him). The only evidence pertaining to Cyrus I remains a seal from Persepolis referring to "Kurash of Anshan, son of Teispes." We are forced to admit that the current state of the evidence does not allow us to create a picture of Persian politics and society at the time when Cyrus II began his assault on the kingdoms of the Middle East.

2. The Conquests of Cyrus (550–530 B.C.). Cyrus' first target was the Median kingdom of Astyage and its capital Ecbatana (Hamadan). The relationship between the Medes and the Persians was ancient: they were both peoples of Iranian culture. The different versions of the "legend of the founder" transmitted by classical sources (as well as from a passage of the Sippar Cylinder) attest to the Persian kingdom's status as vassal to Ecbatana. It is probable that Cyrus was able to benefit from a certain weakening of Astyage before a group of nobles. Whatever the reason, the Median army was defeated and Cyrus seized Ecbatana and imposed himself as successor to the Median kings. Most likely the peoples of Central Asia (Hyrcanians, Parthians, Sakai, and Bactrians) who had been linked to Ecbatana came to renew their (more or less lax) state of dependence: Cyrus could certainly demand contingents of them to reinforce his army, which was already swollen with Median troops. The conquest of Ecbatana also allowed Cyrus to obtain the treasure of Astyage and to remove it to Persia.

His first conquest resulted in his territorial expansion up to the border of the Lydian kingdom of Croesus, that extended to the Halys River. Croesus, who had an alliance with the Babylonian king Nabonidus, himself took the offensive. He was defeated in pitched battle at Pteria, and the following winter (546?) Cyrus laid seige to Sardis. Most of the Greek cities, subjects of Croesus, underestimated Cyrus' power and refused to surrender. Only Miletus, a city traditionally "Medizing," abandoned Croesus' camp. After the fall of Sardis, Cyrus was called back to the E front, while his generals, under the high command of the Mede Harpage, continued to assault the recalcitrant Greek cities, which soon had to submit after hard combat. Only Miletus was able to strike an advantageous agreement with its new masters.

The reasons for Cyrus' rapid departure are thus presented by Herodotus: "Babylon in effect created difficulties for him, the Bactrian people, the Sakai, and the Egyptians; it is against these adversaries that he proposed to march in person" (1.153). After a little-known expedition on the Iranian plateau, Cyrus decided to march against the principal power opposing him, the Neo-Babylonian kingdom and its king Nabonidus. The conditions and the circumstances of the capture of Babylon in 539 are presented by classical sources (Herodotus, Xenophon) and by contemporary Babylonian texts. Cyrus' Cylinder (*ANET,* 315–316), drawn up after the Persian victory, affirms that Cyrus' victory was facilitated by the Babylonians themselves, who were eager to get rid of Nabonidus, whom they considered impious. In reality, the conquest of Babylonia was not so simple. Nabonidus and the Babylonian army tried to resist the invaders, but after a Babylonian defeat at Opis (October 539) the road to Babylon was open. One of Cyrus' generals, Gobryas, was able to enter the next day, and shortly after, Cyrus himself made his solemn entrance. The Persian propagandists knew how to present Cyrus as a good king coming to restore order and security and to reconstruct the sacred temples.

The conquest of Babylonia allowed Cyrus the opportunity to seize the territories of the Outer-Euphrates. Several kings and cities from this region soon submitted to him. There was no doubt that Cyrus intended to march on these regions, but it was not necessary to launch any military expedition during his reign. However, it was decided to allow the Judeans who had been in exile in Babylon to return to Jerusalem. The text of the edict is cited twice in the Hebrew Bible (2 Chr 36:23; Ezra 1:2–4; cf. 1 Esdr 2:3–7). The Judeans could resettle in Judea and reconstruct the temple of Jerusalem, taking with them the objects of the cult that had been taken as booty by the Babylonians. The biblical texts present the act of Cyrus as being directly inspired by Yahweh (cf. also Isa 45:1–7). In reality, contrary to what has often been said, Cyrus had no special sympathy for Yahwism. He acted with respect to the Yahwist cult as he had acted with respect to the Babylonian temples. Placed in the historical context of the ANE, the royal decision takes on its true character: while it was a decisive episode for the Judeans themselves, at the same time it was a common and banal event for the Persian political establishment. It is probable that, in doing this, Cyrus had political objectives in mind, probably already anticipating an expedition against Egypt, which was located on the other side of Judea.

3. Cambyses and the Conquest of Egypt (530–522 B.C.). Cyrus himself was not able to lead the conquest into Egypt for reasons that are not exactly known. It is known that the king disappeared during combat in Central Asia against the Massagetai. The task of leading the Persian armies against the pharaoh fell to his son Cambyses, who had a sizeable fleet at his disposal, thanks to the support of the Ionians and the Phoenicians. The new pharaoh, Psamtik III, soon suffered a decisive defeat, and in the spring of 525 Cambyses was able to enter Saïs, the capital of the dynasty. He had less success with his expedition against Ethiopia, which ended in a military disaster. Thus, the empire had practically attained the dimensions that would stand until the arrival of Alexander, reaching from Central Asia to the Mediterranean. Certainly the next king Darius led important expeditions, but one can say that the work of conquering these lands was accomplished essentially by the first two kings. By 525 B.C., the Persians had no more neighbors in the Middle East: the ancient kingdoms of Media, Lydia, Babylonia, and Egypt had been transformed into satrapies administrated by the Persians.

Contrary to what the Greek tradition (especially Herodotus) claims, the conduct of Cambyses with respect to the Egyptian temples was not fundamentally different than that of Cyrus in Babylon. Certainly there were depredations, to which the Judeans of Elephantine would allude a century later. But the Egyptian documents attest to the respect that the king paid to the sacred bull Apis, and the autobiography of Ujahorresne, a newly-conquered Egyptian noble, indicates that Cambyses protected everything, especially the temple of the goddess Neith in Saïs. It was, moreover, necessary for the new conqueror to mold himself in Egyptian traditions: thus he also adopted the pharaonic title, and there is little doubt that he was seen as a pharaoh by the vast majority of the Egyptian population. In fact, Cambyses "pharaonized" himself in Egypt, just as Cyrus had "Babylonized" himself in Babylon. The attitude taken by the first two kings constituted the basis of a flexible policy that the Achaemenids constantly implemented within the diverse populations of their empire.

4. Uprising, Revolts, and New Conquests (522–500 B.C.). Called back to Persia by an uprising, Cambyses died on the return road (522). The consequent dynastic struggle is known to us not only from Herodotus but also from Darius, who had the facts engraved on the rock of Behistun after his victory. But Darius' account is hardly adequate for the historian. According to Darius, the uprising was the work of a magi, Gaumata, who posed as Cambyses' younger brother, Bardiya (called "Smerdis" by Herodotus). Darius presents himself as the legitimate successor to the eight previous kings, the hero who took control of a conspiracy of nobles, killed the usurper, and immediately ascended the throne (the end of September 522). But this version of events is questioned by many historians who think that Gaumata was indeed Cambyses' brother. In that case, Darius himself would have been the usurper. This dynastic competition was accompanied by a series of revolts against the Persian power. Although Darius cites Egypt among the rebels, it seems that the most important rebellions took place in the heartland (Persia, Elam, Babylonia, Media) and to the E on the Iranian Plateau.

With the help of a necessarily reduced army, Darius launched numerous counter-offensives led by generals who remained loyal to him. The different royal armies had to fight on several fronts at the same time: in December 522, for example, one notes two victories by Darius in Babylonia, the quelling of a rebellion in Elam, a victory in Arachosia, and another in Assyria. Fortunately for Darius, two satraps on the Iranian Plateau (in Bactria and in Arachosia) joined him in the fight against the rebels, as did Darius' real father, Hystaspes, in Parthia-Hyrcania. Darius' consolidation of power was, however, long and difficult: Elam abandoned the struggle definitively only in 520. It is even later still, in 518, that Darius reestablished order in Egypt.

These revolts show a marked dynastic character. The rebels borrowed the name of a king, thereby attaching themselves to a dynasty deposed by the Persians: one of the Babylonian rebels presented himself as the son of Nabonidus, while a Median chief posed as a member of the Cyaxares family. The symbolism is clear—they were trying to terminate the short period of Persian domination and to link themselves to the history of different preexisting kingdoms (Babylonia, Media, Elam, etc.). All the rebel chiefs succeeded in mobilizing large armies against the Persians, as attested by the high number of losses recorded in the Akkadian and Aramaic versions of the Behistun inscription. The danger was greater in Asia Minor, where the satrap Oroites tried to profit from the troubles by declaring independence from the central power. Elsewhere, the problems confronting the central power instilled hope in people who did not directly take part in the revolts. There exists an echo of this in certain prophetic texts (Haggai, Zechariah) documenting Judean hopes for a restoration of the Israelite monarchy. Furthermore, the Persian people were themselves divided when Darius confronted a native Persian competitor in the person of Vahyazdata, who took for himself the name of Bardiya, thus indicating clearly that he considered himself to be Cyrus' legitimate successor. This dynastic crisis thus added to the imperial crisis.

Inversely, the victories won by Darius attest to the stability and sturdiness of the empire established by Cyrus and Cambyses. Many satraps remained loyal, and Darius found devoted aides among the nobles who had actively participated in the elimination of Gaumata-Bardiya. It is with the support of the aristocratic Persians that he was able to put an end to the secession of Oroites in Asia Minor without a military campaign. He was even able to take strong measures against the noble intaphernes who had defied his authority; no aristocrat would take Intaphernes' side. One thus understands why Darius proudly celebrated his victories on the rock of Behistun: under his feet lay Gaumata, and before him were drawn the "lying kings" he had recently vanquished. According to his own declarations, it was the victory of the Truth (*arta*) over the Lie (*drauga*), in other words, the triumph of loyalty over the rebellion. The strength of the king and the empire would soon be magnified by the construction of a new capital, Persepolis. Shortly after his victories he led a major expedition into Central Asia and India, whereby the Indus valley was annexed to the empire. In 513 the expedition into Scythia was less successful, but it still allowed the Persians to settle in Thrace and to reduce the Macedonian kingdom to vassalage. The empire had thus reached its largest extension.

5. The Organization of the Empire under Darius. According to Herodotus, Darius' victory in 520 was followed by a reorganization of the empire: "He established in the Persian Empire twenty governments (*archai*) called satrapies; the various governors were appointed, and each nation assessed for tributes (*phoroi*) that should revert to him" (3.89). In reality, satraps and tribute already existed during the reigns of Cyrus, Cambyses, and Bardiya, but Darius was the first to unify and systematize the administrative practices. The people (*ethnē*) were reunited from within the large governmental provinces (the satraps) and made to pay a tribute each year, probably calculated in pro-rate of cultivatable lands. Only some people (Arabs, Ethiopians, Colchidians) maintained their status as donors. The Persian territory itself was exempted from tribute. Several Achaemenid documents (royal lists, "Gift Carriers" of Persepolis, "Throne Carriers," a statue of Darius, Egyptian steles) refer to lists that have often been considered lists of satraps. They were actually selective lists of countries (*dahyu- ava*), upon which one should not base conclusions about an administrative structure. It is also necessary to underscore the fact that both the number and the specific responsibilities of the satraps evolved over time.

Each satrapy was given to a high Persian aristocrat, aided by administrators. The satrap could call upon garrison and occupation troops. The satrapy had to pay its tribute every year to the Persian king, who deposited the sum in the stores and treasuries of the empire. The size of the stocks of precious metals later found by Alexander the Great is an indication of the viability of the system. In order to control the satraps more effectively, large numbers of native Persians were installed and were given sizeable plots of land along with the obligation of leading their cavalry troops as requisitioned by the satrap. In Babylonia, the land was awarded to the *hatru,* collectivities of diverse ethnic origin that in return were supposed to provide soldiers and diverse taxes. The satraps were required to be diligent in implementing the royal orders that they regularly received from royal couriers.

Within the satrapy the local peoples, dynasties, and other recognized communities continued to enjoy a certain degree of autonomy (e.g., the dynasties of Cilicia and of Caria remained in place). It was up to the local chiefs to conduct their contingent of the royal army. By the same token, the internal organization of the conquered Greek cities was essentially unchanged; in fact the first Persian kings happily relied on the local tyrants. Darius essentially continued his predecessors' policies with respect to conquered populations. In Egypt, he continued to present himself as pharaoh, as attested by the title engraved on his statue found at Susa. In the same way, he confirmed to the Judeans the privileges that Cyrus had granted them (Ezra 6). In a general manner, the king also recognized the earlier practices of the temples, as is so eloquently attested by the letter he sent to Gadatas, who was accused of having violated the privileges of the temple of Apollo near Magnesia of Meander (in Asia Minor). This policy has been erroneously labeled "religious tolerance"; actually it was an attempt to reconcile the central power with the local subjects, and the fundamental objective remained maintenance and reinforcement of the Persian Empire. The royal policy with respect to Babylonian temples clearly shows this orientation, since one can find abundant evidence attesting to the intervention of the Persian administration in the management of the wealth of these temples, while at the same time the cults and local temples were not threatened.

The entire imperial system was dominated by the king. While not regarded as a god himself, the Persian king was viewed as the earthly lieutenant of the great deities of the empire, the first among them being the god Ahura-Mazda. The king was consecrated at Pasargadae during the course of a religious ceremony (which is described by Plutarch). But the new king did not take his power only from the gods: he also held it from filiation. Custom required that the eldest son succeed his father, and that he, in turn, designate his heir. This frequently-attested custom did not stop the drama of succession, since certain younger brothers did not easily accept being bypassed (e.g., Bardiya's struggle against his elder brother Cambyses, and also the case of the succession after the assassination of Xerxes, when Artaxerxes II came to power after eliminating his older brother Darius in a bloody struggle).

The monumental structures built in the large capitals symbolized the new power attained by Darius' empire. During his reign the first improvements were made at the site of Susa, improvements attested both archaeologically and from numerous inscriptions of Darius and Xerxes. Darius also had a large palace built in Babylon, and work was continued at Parsagadae, the capital founded by Cyrus. It is probably during the period of Cambyses that Persepolis was first chosen as a site, but it was up to Darius to design the plan and to him and his successors to construct it. The style and grandeur of the buildings are amply documented by archaeological evidence and by a group of Elamite tablets, the Treasury Tablets, published by G. C. Cameron in 1948. Another group of contemporaneous tablets, an important part of which were published by R. T. Hallock in 1969, attest to productive activities in Persis under Darius. They are also interesting because they shed light on persons such as Artaphernes, Mardonios, and Datis, who are mentioned in classical sources. The land was worked by laborers from all parts of the empire, who are often identified in the tablets as *kurtash,* a generic term which applied to a wide variety of persons (prisoners of war, dependent peasants, "free" salaried workers). A similar ethnic diversity is found among the groups of workers employed at the building sites at Persepolis. All the buildings and inscriptions there function to exalt the vastness and the richness of the territory ruled by the Great King. If Susa had become (according to the Greek testimony) the most frequented capital of the court, Pesepolis was always clothed with an essentially ideological function. During the course of the year, the Great King and the court moved from capital to capital: Persepolis, Susa, Babylon, Ecbatana.

A system of royal roads completed the unification of the empire. Herodotus (5. 52–53) gives a precise description of the route and the organization of the Royal Road that during Darius' reign went from Sardis to Susa. But there existed many other royal roads linking the capitals of the empire to the satraps' capitals. A group of tablets from Persepolis gives precise descriptions of the roads and the rights enjoyed by officially-authorized travelers, including the right to travel on the roads and to receive rations at wayside inns. Among other functions, these well-maintained and protected roads allowed troop convoys to deploy to various places where they had been ordered; thus the military played an essential role in the survival of the road system.

The Persian king had numerous troops at his disposal in order to control the territories and populations of the empire. In order to regulate local problems, the satraps could summon the troops of their government. Sometimes a satrap could be given command of the troops of several satraps: he would thus receive the title of *karanos.* If the king decided to mount a large campaign, he convened the royal army, composed of contingents from all the countries of the empire. Darius assembled them to lead his expeditions of conquest. The best known example is the army raised by Darius and then by Xerxes to march against the Greeks. The royal army is described in detail by Herodotus (7. 60–99). Each ethnic contingent kept its own weapons. Each of the large divisions of the army was commanded by a Persian, often a relative of the king; similarly the naval contingents were given to Persian commanders. The diversity of the contingents and the disordered character of this army (often emphasized by Greek authors) should not be misleading. Within this array, several contingents constituted the army of the elite, the real fighting army—the Persians, the Medes, the Bactrians, and the Sakai. The components of the royal army thus corresponded in effect to the political and ideological motives: it visually symbolized the grandeur and the diversity of the empire.

B. The Empire in the 5th Century

1. The First Retreats on the Mediterranean Front (500–448 B.C.). The first setbacks took place on the W front at the very beginning of the 5th century B.C. For reasons still not completely clear, the tyrant Aristagoras of Miletus led a revolt against the Persians. At the head of these forces, he ravaged Sardis (499), initiating the Ionian revolt. But the land and naval superiority of the Persians would soon become obvious, despite the fact that the cities of the straits (Bosporus) and the Cypriot kingdoms joined the rebellion. After 497 or 496, the Persians retook Cyprus and then obtained the submission of the cities to the N. After a Greek naval defeat at Lade, Miletus was taken in 494. The Persians destroyed the city and deported part of the population. Then the satrap Artaphernes relinquished the office of tyrant and accepted the democratic regimes, fixing norms for levying tributes on the territories of the cities. The Persians profited from their victory by sending an army into Thrace in 492 under the command of Mardonios, son-in-law of the king.

An expedition against Greece was launched in 490; it is referred to as the First Persian War. The objective was less the annexation of Greece than domination over the Cyclades. The Persian defeat at Marathon revealed the Persian vulnerability in the Aegean. Almost immediately Darius began a new expedition, this time directed against the Greek cities themselves. His death in 486 and the subsequent revolts in Babylonia and Egypt slowed down his son and successor Xerxes, and it was only in 480 that the immense land and sea force finally set off (the contingents are counted and described by Herodotus). Faced with this threat, Athens and Sparta concluded an alliance of common action, and Themistocles decided to abandon Attica to concentrate his effort on the sea. Although Athens was thus taken by the Persians, the Persians then suffered a major naval defeat at Salamis, which forced Xerxes to return to his kingdom. The elite-army left in Greece under the command of Mardonios suffered a disaster the following year at Plataea (479). This defeat caused renewed hope in the Asian cities, so much so that the same year the Greek fleet won yet another victory at Mykale. Soon, under the aegis of Athens, a league was formed to which a number of Asian cities adhered. The objective was to lead reprisal expeditions against the Achaemenid territories and to protect the cities against Persian counterattacks.

In three years the strategic situation had thus been upset. The Persians had lost Thrace (where only a few garrisons still resisted) and no longer enjoyed hegemony on their Mediterranean front. Furthermore, Athens emerged from the war strong. The city had access to important resources, a first rate navy, and its leaders had decided to launch a large offensive against the Achaemenids' possessions. Around 466, Cimon achieved a double victory over Persian forces in Pamphylia. Several years later, the Athenians came to the aid of the Inaros dynasty in Egypt, which had revolted against the Persians (460). The arrival of a Persian army under the command of Megabyze (Xerxes' son-in-law) resulted in a complete disaster for the Athenians—Egypt came once again under Achaemenid domination. Several years later, after an Athenian success in Cypriot waters (450), negotiations were opened that would lead to the Peace of Callias (448), about which there has been much dispute. The two adversaries, Athens and Persia, wanted to put an end to the hostilities. Even if the Persian king continued to affirm his dominion over these cities, he still had to concede the Athenian presence, a notable setback to the Achaemenid power on the Mediterranean front. Peace was renewed later by Darius II shortly after his accession.

2. Imperial Strength and Royal Power. It is often assumed that Xerxes' setbacks inaugurated a long period of decline in Achaemenid history that would culminate with the conquest of Alexander. This is a very tendentious assumption that has no documentary foundation. The relative importance of Darius' reign and that of Xerxes is a misleading result of the unequal division of narrative Greek sources. Herodotus' work ends with the Persian defeats of 479 in Greece and Ionia. No author of his stature undertook a record of Persian affairs. Today's historian must go to Diodorus of Sicily and to Ctesius. The latter devoted several books of his *Persika* to the actions of the kings after Cyrus up until the year 398 B.C., the 7th year of king Artaxerxes II. For the most part, his story refers to dynastic problems, to the intrigues of the court, and to the difficulties encountered by the royal power. See CTESIAS. However, his vision of Persian history at the least must be nuanced because it is at the same time very biased. The paragraphs that he devotes to the reigns of Xerxes (486–465) and Artaxerxes I (464–424) are less centered on royal politics than on the picturesque and novel-like story of the noble Megabyze. As for the reign of Darius II (425–405/4), he summarizes the difficulties of the accession of the king and the revolts that he had to put down. The idea of a Persian decline beginning with Xerxes is found in other Greek authors of the 4th century (Plato and Xenophon in particular), but their interpretations arise more from their Greek ideological biases than from a reasoned analysis of the course of Persian history.

On the Persian side, the documentation is unfortunately very scanty. However, everything leads one to believe that neither the royal power nor the imperial domination were ever seriously or profoundly jeopardized by the setbacks on the Mediterranean front. The tablets from the Treasury of Persepolis recount that the construction work was more active than ever during the reign of Xerxes and the first years of Artaxerxes I (486–461). The activities of these kings are confirmed by royal inscriptions. The importance of an inscription by Xerxes must also be considered. In it, the king recalls first of all that he restored order in the provinces that had rebelled. He also affirms the preeminence of the god Ahura-Mazda. This has been seen as a modification of the religious policies of the Achaemenids—Xerxes attempting to impose the cult of the supreme Persian god by forbidding the cult of local gods. However, this is not the case. The document makes no reference to any specific measures taken in Babylonia or anywhere else. Above all, it attests to the strength of the monarchic ideology, still reinforced and codified in a rigorous manner during Xerxes' reign and fully maintained by his successors.

The strength of the monarchic ideology did not prevent dynastic difficulties, which were numerous and serious during the 5th century. If, as designated heir, Xerxes succeeded his father without difficulty, his own succession was much more tumultuous. He was assassinated by rebels, as was his eldest son Darius. The younger son, Artaxerxes, came to power only after difficult combat. In 424, the death of Artaxerxes I was soon followed by the assassination of his son Xerxes II, who reigned only a few weeks. Fierce competition then ensued between two of his illegitimate sons, Sogdianos and Ochos. The latter was finally recognized as king under the name of Darius (II) at the end of an intense civil war, recounted by Ctesias and echoed in Babylonian tablets. At the end of his life, Darius II followed the Achaemenid custom of designating his eldest son Artaxerxes as his successor. But, his accession in 405/404 precipitated a war of succession instigated by his younger brother Cyrus and supported by their mother Parysatis, a war (401) of which Xenophon (*Anabasis*) and Ctesias have left accounts. However, one cannot talk about a deterioration of the dynasty since such dynastic struggles occurred from the beginning of Achaemenid history. They never threatened the hegemony of the Achaemenids with respect to the great aristocratic Persian families.

On the other hand, existing documentation does not allow for a continuous reconstruction of imperial affairs in the 5th century. Babylonia and Egypt are the best known governments, thanks to Babylonian tablets on the one hand, and Aramaic documents on the other. The archives of the house of Murashû give important information concerning economic and social life in Babylonia between 455 and 403. They allow us to have a precise idea as to the condition of the land and people, in particular the operation of the *hatru*-system and the military and fiscal obligations that were levied on the plots of land of the communities located in this region. Other archives also attest to the new place held by the Babylonians in the administration. One example is Belshunu who, after having been "governor of Babylon" between 421 and 404, was named satrap of Syria (i.e., Trans-euphrates) between 407 and 401; he is the Belesys of Xenephon.

In Egypt, the Aramaic documents furnish information about the satrapic government of Arshama and about the management of the large Persian domains in the Nile river valley during the last quarter of the 5th century. A group of letters (*DOTT, 260–69; ANET,* 492) refers to the hostilities that the Judean garrison of Syene-Elephantine encountered ca. 410 B.C. from the Egyptians and the Persian governor Widranga. After the destruction of the local temple of Yahweh, the dispute was taken before the king and the satrap, who judged in favor of the Judeans, who were then permitted to reconstruct their temple. The Aramaic documents and the Greek sources also point out the difficulties encountered by the Persians in Egypt from the revolt suppressed by Xerxes at the beginning of his reign (485) to the Inaros revolt crushed by Megabyze at the end of Xerxes' reign (456). The defeat of another dynasty, Amyrtaios, had not meant the end of this principality in the Delta. In 445/44, Psamtik still seemed to be a powerful pharaoh. In 404, another Amyrtaios succeeded in implanting himself firmly in Upper Egypt then, several years later (398), in Lower Egypt. That would mark the end of the Persian domination of Egypt until 343 (see C.3 below).

The Athenian defeat in Sicily in 412 and its repercussion in Ionia put Asia Minor in full light in the accounts of

Thucydides (*The Peloponnesian War*, Book 8) and Xenophon (*Hellenics*). This front had practically disappeared in the documentation since the middle of the 5th century, except for Ctesias' reference to a satrapic revolt. In 412, the two principal satraps of Asia Minor—Pharnabazus (Hellespontine Phrygia) and Tissaphernes (Sardis)—tried to ally themselves with Sparta. Both had received from Darius II the order to force the Greek cities once again to pay the royal tribute. But the Greek sources for the most part treat the struggles between Athens and Sparta, disregarding Achaemenid affairs. The nomination of Cyrus in 407 as commander in chief of the Persian troops allowed the reestablishment of Achaemenid positions, but these were soon jeopardized by Cyrus' subsequent revolt against his brother Artaxerxes (404–401), the designated successor to the throne.

C. From Artaxerxes II to Alexander (404–334 B.C.).

1. Dynastic Crisis and Royal Power. Menaced on the western front, the empire once again experienced serious dynastic problems during the course of the 4th century. The succession of Artaxerxes was difficult. His eldest son and designated heir, Darius, was put to death for treason. His younger son, Ochos, was recognized under the name of Artaxerxes III (359–358). The succession of the latter took place in the middle of a bloodbath. He was assassinated by the chiliarch Bagoas who had Oarses, youngest son of Artaxerxes III, recognized as king, before making him disappear and pushing Darius (III) onto the throne. According to Diodorus, the reason for this was that the "Royal House was extinguished and there was no longer anyone to whom birth permitted them to inherit the power" (17.5.5)—an excessive judgment, given the fact that Darius was an Achaemenid. His selection is explained by the Achaemenid custom of endogamy that had always enabled power to be conserved in the "royal line"; Darius III was in effect married to his own sister Stateira—they were both born to one of Darius II sons. Thus, dynastic continuity was maintained.

The prestige and power of the last Persian kings remained strong, as attested by their inscriptions and by their continuation of the work at Persepolis. The desire of the kings to restore and to strengthen their ties with the different Persian communities located in the different regions of the empire also attest to it. Ever since the first kings, the Persian communities of the *diaspora* constituted the "backbone" of Persian power in the empire's territories. They were under obligation to continue to live according to the Persian way of life, to promote a cult to the Persian gods, and to obey in every way the satrap, lieutenant of the king in the satrapy. An inscription found at Sardis shows that a temple and a statue dedicated to Ahura-Mazda existed there (named Zeus Baradates: "Legislator"): the text indicates that a high administrator of Sardis prohibited the followers of the cult of Ahura-Mazda from participating in the Anatolian mystery cults. One should probably link this decision to the order given by Artaxerxes II to the Persians of the large capitals of the empire reinforcing their devotion to Anahita, one of the three great deities of the Persian Empire (along with Ahura-Mazda and Mithra). This complemented similar measures aimed at identical objectives: regrouping the Persian *diaspora* around traditional Persian ideas, and thus around the royal person.

2. The Retaking of Asia Minor. On the Asia Minor front, the reign of Artaxerxes II—once the danger of Cyrus had been eliminated—showed a clear consolidation of power. The years following the defeat of Athens in 404 saw a series of expeditions by Sparta, presented as campaigns to liberate the Greek cities from Achaemenid rule. But even the most ambitious of the Spartan chiefs, Agesilaus, never threatened Persian domination. Soon the Persians supported the Athenian Konon against Sparta. The Persian king quickly became the arbiter for quarrels between Greek cities, to such a point that in 386 Artaxerxes II imposed his will on all the Greek cities by unilaterally enacting a treaty called "the Peace of Antalkidas" (from the name of the principal Spartan negotiator). The royal edict was brought to the attention of the Greek ambassadors in the following terms: "The King Artaxerxes considers the cities of Asia as belonging to him, as well as the islands Clazomenes and Cyprus; on the other hand, the other cities, large or small, remain autonomous, except for Lemnos, Imbros, and Skyros, which, as in the past, will belong to the Athenians." In other words, the Greek cities of Asia Minor reverted to direct domination of the Achaemenids. The royal decision was, in addition, accompanied by an unambiguous threat: "Those who do not consent to these conditions of peace, I will personally make war upon them with the help of all those who accept them, on land, on sea, with my fleet, and with my treasure" (Xen. *Hell.* 5.1.31). The Persians were wise enough to permit some internal autonomy for the subjugated cities. An inscription shortly after the Peace of Antalkidas indicates that, after a territorial conflict between Miletus and Myous, the satrap Strouses submitted the decision to a tribunal of Ionians, the king and the satrap confirming the judgment of the tribunal. This document attests to great continuity in Persian policy with respect to the Greek cities dating back to the measures taken by Artaphernes a century earlier.

3. Egyptian Danger and Satrapic Revolts. On the Aegean front—the only region the Greek sources talk about—the Persians won no victories. For several decades the central government tried to retake Egypt, which had been independent since 404 B.C. Numerous armies were mobilized in Syro-Palestine; all failed. Furthermore, under the reigns of Hakoris (392–380) and his successors, Egypt led a political offensive in the E Mediterranean. The successive Persian defeats in 385–382, 373, and again in 360–359 represented serious military failures and cruel losses of prestige for the Great King. The need to amass troops against Egypt was one of the reasons that pushed Artaxerxes to the Peace of Antalkidas in 386. In fact, the Persian defeats incited other revolts. Thus a two-year long war (382–381) was required to suppress the rebellion of Evagoras of Salamis, who could rely on the aid of Hakoris.

The Persian position was even more precarious because the central power had to face several satrapic rebellions in Asia Minor during the course of the 4th century. The most important was the one traditionally called the Great Revolt of the Satraps (360 B.C.) that itself led to individual revolts, of which the best known is that of Datames in Cappadocia. According to Diodorus, the revolt, directed by Orontes, covered the entire Aegean front from Asia

Minor to Cyprus; however, it probably did not have the global character that the Greek historian has given it. However, it is clear that it represented an evident danger for the Persian power. Paradoxically, the revolt dissipated after the initial successes of the royal armies. Orontes, soon followed by other chiefs, submitted to the Persian king by betraying his comrades. This alone attests to the solidarity of loyalist sentiment among the Persian chiefs of the provinces.

One of the first measures taken by Artaxerxes III upon coming to the throne was to order the satraps to dismiss their Greek mercenary troops. The massive enrollment of mercenaries had become commonplace from Cyrus' expedition on. The Persians and also the Egyptian pharaohs used them with increasing frequency. For the Greek authors of the 4th century, this growing demand for mercenary Greeks attested to the military deterioration of the Achaemenid Empire. Such a polemical view cannot be accepted without reservation. The Persian armies of the 4th century were certainly not composed only of mercenaries, and (contrary to an interpretation currently defended) the Babylonian tablets do not bring indisputable proof of the decline of the *hatru* system during the 4th century. But faced with enemies that fought like the Greeks, the satraps of Asia Minor very naturally used troops for which they themselves did not have the equivalent and that they could quickly enroll and mobilize. The existence of an increasingly abundant market in Europe and a growing demand in Asia is sufficient explanation of the phenomenon. Artaxerxes III himself did not hesitate to enroll numerous mercenaries in the army that he would lead to reconquer Egypt, but at the same time he had understood that it was extremely dangerous to leave the recruitment up to the satraps.

A new defeat at the hands of Egypt in 351–350 B.C. had disastrous consequences. The Phoenician cities revolted the following year. Artaxerxes III prepared an immense army and fleet. The campaign was initiated by the satraps Belesys and Mazaios in 345. Sidon had to surrender and suffered terrible reprisals. In 343, the Persian army (containing a large contingent of Greek mercenaries) won a victory in Egypt. Thus, around 340, the Persian Empire recovered the territorial boundaries of 480. Despite the revolts, the central power had succeeded in maintaining Persian domination. Even in Asia Minor the regions formerly left in the hands of more or less submissive dynasties had been transformed into satrapies in their own right: this was the case with Cilicia and with Caria (where the satraps were from the family of Hekatomnids, at least until 340 when a Persian acquired the satrapy). The regions that chronically proved difficult to control were thus included in the satrapies. This was the case of Lycia, now reunited with the satrapy of Caria, as the inscription of Xanthos shows. The Persian Empire was thus far from experiencing the profound decadence to which the Greek polemic authors of the 4th century constantly referred.

D. Alexander and the End of the Persian Empire (334–330 B.C.)

Reassured on the interior front, without worrying unduly about the Greeks, the Persian kings realized too late the growing power of the kingdom of Macedonia during the period of Philip II (359–336). Within several years he had extended the Macedonian territory to the Straits, had given his kingdom an army without compare, and had defeated the Greek cities at Chaeronea (338). This victory was followed by the founding of the Corinthian League, whose proclaimed objective was the liberation of the Greek cities of Asia Minor. However, from this date on, a strong Macedonian force operated within Asia Minor. The victories won by Memnon in 337 and a certain lack of lucidity no doubt explain why the central Persian power did not consider it advantageous to mobilize the royal army in 334 to oppose the young Alexander, who had succeeded his father Philip in 336. The task of pushing the Macedonian forces back to the sea was thus given to the satraps of Asia Minor. The defeat of Graneikos (May 334) would be of great importance. Alexander would soon capture Sardis, which would give him the Persian Mithrenes as well as the logistic means that he lacked. In several months (spring–winter 334), the Persian king lost Asia Minor. During the following spring (333), the death of Memnon ended an enormous naval counterattack by the Persians that might prove capable of pushing Alexander back into Europe.

Facing this danger, Darius III decided to mobilize the royal army. Almost all of the contingents of the empire, except the contingents to the E of Iran, were assembled in Babylon and marched to Cilicia to stop the Macedonians. The battle of Issos (November 333)—represented on the famous mosaics of Neapels—was a severe defeat for Darius, who had to flee the battleground and to leave royal women and children to fall into the hands of the enemy. The negotiations initiated by the Great King proved uneventful. Incapable of defending the Syro-Phoenician coast and Egypt and abandoned by the Persian forces, Darius decided to raise a new army in which he could this time enroll the contingents from E Iran. The troops were assembled and trained in Babylonia, then dispersed in the upper valley of the Tigris, to the W of Arbela, a famous stop on the Royal Road. In the beginning of the month of October 331 Darius was again defeated. He fled toward Ecbatana, leaving open the road toward the great capitals. Babylon and then Susa without resistance fell into the hands of the conqueror, who seized the immense royal Treasuries. Alexander would soon (end of 331) come to Persepolis, which would be surrendered by the Persian governor before being pillaged in the spring of 330.

During this time, Darius tried to mobilize a new army in Media. But the rebellions within his entourage and the speed of the advancing Macedonians prevented him from even engaging in battle. The Great King was soon assassinated by a plot conceived by Bessos, satrap of Bactria (July 330). Bessos took the royal title under the name of Artaxerxes, hoping to stop Alexander at Bactria; however, he was soon handed over to the conqueror and put to death. Despite some resistance led by the small princes of Sogdia and Bactria, Alexander succeeded in imposing his dominion over E Iran (329–327), before taking the Indus River valley (327–325). Two years after his return to Babylonia, he died, at last conquered by malaria (June 323).

If one considers rightly that the death of Darius III in July of 330 marks the end of the Achaemenid Empire founded by Cyrus and his successors, one must also emphasize the imperial structures that remained intact during Alexander's lifetime. The conqueror left unchanged the satrapies and the tributary system. On the other hand, one of his concerns had been to call Persian and Iranian nobles into his service. In 334 he admitted the Persian Mithrenes into his entourage, but in 330 he made a decision of great importance by giving satrapic governments to Mithrenes himself and to Mazaios, command posts he had up until then reserved for Macedonians and Greeks. Without compromise he pursued this policy of Macedono-Iranian collaboration. Numerous Iranians were named satraps in the countries of the Iranian plateau, and Iranian contingents served in the army side by side with Greeks and Macedonians. In 327, Alexander married an Iranian princess, Roxane who, after the death of the young conqueror, gave birth to his son, Alexander IV. In Persia itself, he was careful to name as satrap his companion Peukestas, who demonstrated his goodwill by adopting the Persian way of life. As for the conqueror himself, he put to his own profit the customs of the Achaemenid court, despite opposition from within part of his entourage. His ultimate objective was to allow the Persians and the Iranians to evolve in a flexible and gradual manner into the ruling class of the new empire, that the defeat of Darius III had allowed him to create on the ruins and on the model of that of Cyrus and his successors.

Bibliography

Briant, P. 1982. *Rois, tributs et paysans.* Paris.

———. 1987. *Alexandre le Grand.* Paris.

Cook, J. M. 1983. *The Persian Empire.* London.

Dandamaev, M. D. 1976. *Persien unter der ersten Achämeniden.* Wiesbaden.

Frye, R. N. 1984. *The History of Ancient Iran.* Munich.

Miroschedji, P. de. 1985. La fin du royaume d'Anshan et de Suse et la naissance de l'Empire perse. *ZA* 75: 265–306.

Olmstead, A. T. 1959. *The History of the Persian History.* Repr. Chicago.

Sancisi-Weerdenburg, H., and Kuhrt, A., eds. 1987–1988. *Achaemenid History,* I–III. Leiden.

Walser, G. 1984. *Hellas und Iran.* Darmstadt.

PIERRE BRIANT
Trans. Stephen Rosoff

PERSIAN LANGUAGE.

See LANGUAGES (LANGUAGES OF ANCIENT IRAN).

PERSIS

(PERSON) [Gk *Persis*]. A Roman Christian who received greetings from Paul in Rom 16:12 as "the beloved Persis." Having been close to Paul in the E of the Roman Empire, she had immigrated to Rome. This latter fact is confirmed by the epigraphical and literary sources from the city of Rome which show the name "Persis" only six times; the Romans very rarely used the name (Lampe *StadtrChr,* 138–41). Persis had "worked hard in the Lord" (for discussion of this phrase, see TRYPHAENA AND TRYPHOSA). As with all names recalling a geographical area, "Persis" ("Persian") was a typical slave name; two out of three set "inscriptions" in the city of Rome attribute the name to (freed) slaves (Lampe *StadtrChr,* 145–46, 153). Persis was probably a gentile Christian. See NEREUS.

PETER LAMPE

PERSONALITY, CORPORATE.

See CORPORATE PERSONALITY.

PERUDA

(PERSON) [Heb *pĕrûdāʾ*]. Var PERIDA. Head of a family belonging to Solomon's servants who had returned from the Babylonian Exile (Peruda in Ezra 2:55; Perida in the parallels in Neh 7:57 and 1 Esdr 5:33). The list in Ezra-Nehemiah implies that this return took place immediately in response to Cyrus' declaration in 538 B.C.E. But 1 Esdras places this return in its more probable date at the time of King Darius (ca. 522).

Some have used 1 Kgs 9:20 to conclude that Solomon's servants were originally enslaved foreigners. Levine (1963), however, suggests that the term denotes Israelite officials supervising foreigners. In the postexilic era, when the family of Peruda appears, the term "servant" typically refers to officials. Like the temple servants (Nethinim), Solomon's servants are temple functionaries. They are members of the congregation of Israel and separated thereby from ordinary slaves (Ezra 2:65). The name Peruda could mean "the solitary one." The number, origin, and specific tasks of the Peruda family are no longer discernible. See Blenkinsopp *Ezra-Nehemiah* OTL; Williamson *Ezra, Nehemiah* WBC.

Bibliography

Levine, B. A. 1963. The Netinim. *JBL* 82: 207–212.

Weinberg, J. P. 1975. Nᵉtinim und 'Söhne der Sklaven Salomos' im 6–4 Jh. v. u. Z. *ZAW* 87: 355–371.

TAMARA C. ESKENAZI

PESACH.

The Hebrew name for the festival known as Passover. See UNLEAVENED BREAD AND PASSOVER, FEASTS OF.

PESHARIM, QUMRAN.

The discovery of the Qumran library has brought to light a hitherto unknown type of biblical commentary, employed by the Qumran community, which has come to be known as "pesher" (pl. pesharim). This name derives from the frequent use of the term "pesher" (Heb *pšr*—in the OT it occurs only once at Qoh 8:1; Akk *pišru,* Aram *psrʾ*) to introduce an interpretation of a biblical text. The word is used in the sense of "interpretation, realization" (Rabinowitz 1973: 226 suggests: "a presaged reality"), akin to the Heb *ptr.*

The term "pesher" is currently used in four different senses: (a) a Qumranic biblical commentary written in pesher-like form; (b) the formal term used to introduce the expositionary section of this kind of commentary; (c) the literary genre of these commentaries; and (d) the particular exegetical method of these Qumranic commentaries.

A. Form and Content of the Extant Pesharim
1. Continuous Pesharim
2. Thematic Pesharim
3. Isolated Pesharim
4. Other Forms of Pesharim
B. Nature and Structure of the Pesharim
C. Literary Genre of the Pesharim
D. Exegetical Method Used by the Pesharim

A. Form and Content of the Extant Pesharim

The importance of the Scriptures in the life and ideology of the Qumran community is expressly stated in the writings of the Qumranites (CD 6:3–11; 1QS 6:6–8; 8:2, 15–16; 1QpHab 2:8–10; 7:7–8), from which we learn that exposition and interpretation of the Torah and the Prophets constituted an important part of the community's special teaching. This is corroborated by the numerous biblical texts and biblical commentaries found among the Qumran scrolls. Significantly, most of the surviving commentaries offer expositions of divine discourses, mainly from the Prophets, but also from the Torah, as well as from the Psalms and the book of Daniel (4QPs37 on Ps. 37; 11QMelch ii.9–12 on Pss. 82:1–2 and 7:8–9; 4QFlor 1–2.i.14 on Ps. 1:1 and elsewhere; 4QFlor 1 + 3 ii.3 on Dan 12:10; 11QMelch ii.8 on Dan 9:25), since both David and Daniel were considered prophets (11QPs^{a} 27:11; 4QFlor 1 + 3 ii.3). The commentaries are identified as belonging to the Qumran community by virtue of their terminology, subject matter, and ideology. These commentaries are the only Qumran texts so far published that refer to historical persons and events, and they constitute the main evidence for dating the Qumran community and understanding its history. Some scholars have concluded, based on the fact that the extant pesharim are all single Herodian mss with no copies or overlapping sections, that the pesharim were autographs and produced within the community at a later stage in its history (Milik 1959: 41; Cross 1980: 114–15). However, some pesharim betray a copyist's hand (e.g., 4QpIsa 5:5a–5, which has an interlinear addition that appears to be a correction; Horgan 1979: 3–4) and therefore may not be autographs. Moreover, the exegetical method of the pesharim is to be found already in much older Qumranic works such as 1QS, CD, and 1QM. It is possible therefore, that some of these pesharim, or their sources, may be attributed to an early stage in the community's history, or even to the founder of the community himself.

The extant pesharim appear in several forms: (a) *continuous pesharim*—running commentaries (section by section) on single biblical books, mainly the Prophets; (b) *thematic pesharim*—exposition of verses from various biblical books, organized around a common theme, such as 4QFlorilegium and 11QMelchizedek; (c) *isolated pesharim*—exposition of one or two biblical verses, within a work of a nonpesher genre (e.g., Isa 40:3 in 1QS 8:13–16; Isa 24:17 in CD 4:13–15; and Num 21:18 in CD 6:3–10). These first three forms share a common lemmatic structure: a biblical citation followed by an exposition, usually introduced by the term "pesher." There are also (d) *other forms of pesharim*.

1. Continuous Pesharim. Most of the extant pesharim are of this type. Fragments of 15 mss were discovered in Qumran Caves 1 and 4 (editions: Allegro 1968, to be used with Strugnell 1969–71; cf. also Horgan 1979). These include:

4QpIsa^{a} (= 4Q*161*, on Isa 10:22–27, 33–34; 11:1–5),
4QpIsa^{b} (= 4Q*162*, on Isa 5:5–30),
4QpIsa^{c} (= 4Q*163*, on Isa 8:7–8; 9:11–20; 10:24; 14:8, 26–30; 29:10–23 [with a quotation from Zech 11:11]; 30:1–21; 31:1),
4QpIsa^{d} (= 4Q*164*, on Isa 54:11–12),
4QpIsa^{e} (= 4Q*165*, on Isa 40:11–12; 14:19; 15:4–5; 21:10–15; 32:5–7; 11:11–12),
4QpHos^{a} (= 4Q*166*, on Hos 2:8–14),
4QpHos^{b} (= 4Q*167*, on Hos 5:13–15; 6:4–11; 8:6–14),
1QpZeph (= 1Q*15*, on Zeph 1:18–2:2),
4QpZeph (= 4Q*170*, on Zeph 1:12–13),
1QpMic (= 4Q*14*, on Mic 1:2–9; 6:15–16),
4QpNah (= 4Q*169*, on Nah 1:3–6; 2:12–14; 3:1–14),
1QpHab (the Habakkuk pesher, the longest and best preserved ms, containing a pesher on Hab 1:1–2:20),
1QpPs (= 1Q*16*, on Ps. 68:13, 30),
4QpPs^{a} (= 4Q*171*, on Pss. 37:2–39; 45:1–2; 60:8–9), and
4QpPs^{b} (= 4Q*173*, on Ps. 129:7–8).

Most of the continuous pesharim have a common structure, exegetical method, and subject matter. They all refer in a similar way to a certain community, its leaders and opponents, and its history. Similar references appear also in other Qumran documents. It is generally assumed that the pesharim, as well as writings such as 1QS and CD, refer to a community of Essenes, one of the three Jewish sects that, according to Josephus, flourished in Judaea during the Second Temple era. See also ESSENES.

a. The Pesher on Habakkuk (1QpHab). This pesher, the first to be published, has received the most attention. The ms is written in an early Herodian hand (Trever and Cross 1972); thirteen columns have been preserved but, owing to extensive decay, without their lower edge (Cross 1972: 4). The author expounds the first two chapters of Habakkuk verse by verse, reading contemporary events into the prophecy.

The exposition refers repeatedly to three main persons, designated by special sobriquets, and to events connected with them. The first figure, the Teacher of Righteousness (based on Hos 10:12; Joel 2:23), is the leader of a group whose members are described as "The Men of Truth" and "The Doers of the Torah" (7:1, 10–14; 8:1–3). This leader is an inspired teacher of the Torah (5:11–12) and the Prophets. Being divinely inspired, he is able to decipher the hidden historical and eschatological meaning of the prophetic words (2:7–10; 7:4–5). The Teacher of Righteousness is involved in a bitter controversy with a second person, an ideological opponent, a person referred to as "The Man of Lies" or "The Spouter of Lies" (based on Mic 2:11), who was at one time the Teacher's follower but broke away, together with his adherents, to form his own group (2:1–3; 5:9–14; 10:9–13). The third person, yet another adversary of the Teacher, is a political leader, a ruler of Israel, who is accorded the sobriquet "The Wicked Priest" (1:12–15; 11:4–8). This Wicked Priest is described as one "who was called by the true name at the beginning of his course" (8:8–9), but who, corrupted by wealth and power, defiled the Temple (12:2–10) and amassed wealth by violent and sinful means (8:8–13; 9:8–12; 11:12–16; 12:10). He pursued the Teacher of Righteousness to "his place of exile," and disturbed his rest on the Day of Atonement (11:5–7, which seems to indicate that "The Wicked Priest" used a different calendar from that of the Teacher and his followers; Talmon 1965: 166–167; for polemic in matters concerning the calendar and festivals, cf. also CD 3:12–16; 4QpPs[a] 1–10 ii 10–11; 4QpHos[a] ii 16–17).

The external and internal conflicts of the Teacher and his followers were seen by the pesher as signs of the approaching eschatological era and the End of Days (7:7–14). The Qumranites believed that the day of final judgment was imminent, and hoped to see their wicked opponents punished and their own faithfulness to the true way of the Torah rewarded (8:2; 10:3; 12:14; 13:3). One of the contemporary events which made a deep impression on the author of the pesher was the approach and attack of a terrible people, the Kittim, whom he identified with the Chaldeans in Habakkuk. The Kittim are depicted as swift, cruel, mighty, merciless, and invincible (2:10–4:16; 6:1–2). Their attack is interpreted by many of the pesharim as a divine punishment of their wicked adversaries.

There is no reason to believe that all these details are invented. It is generally assumed that they refer to real persons and events. At present, the most plausible identification is that the Kittim are the Romans (note 1QpHab 6:1–12, which appears to refer to the Roman military standards. The identification of the Kittim as Romans is corroborated by 4QpNah 3–4 i 3; Milik 1959: 64–65; Cross 1980: 123). Similarly plausible is the identification of the Wicked Priest as one of the early Hasmonean rulers, generally assumed to be either Jonathan (161–142 B.C.E.; Milik 1959: 65–71; Vermes 1981: 151; Murphy-O'Connor 1974: 229–33; Delcor, *DBSup* fasc. 51: 907) or Simon (142–134 B.C.E.; Cross 1980: 142–52; Nickelsburg 1976). Both more or less fit the description in 1QpHab 9:1–2 and 11:15. Others identify the Wicked Priest as Alexander Janneus (103–76 B.C.E.; Delcor 1951; Nitzan 1986: 132–33) or Hyrcanus II (Dupont-Sommer 1980: 274). The identity of the Teacher of Righteousness remains, however, an enigma. Initially, it was argued that he was a descendant of the high priests of the Zadokite lineage who was ousted from office by the Hasmonean Jonathan (Stegemann 1971: 250–51), but this explanation is too conjectural. See also TEACHER OF RIGHTEOUSNESS. As for the Man of Lies, he was sometimes identified as the leader of the Pharisees. This is based on 4QpNah 3–4 ii 2, 4 (cf. also 4QpIsa[c] 23 ii 10), in which the community's opponents are referred to as "the Seekers of Smooth Things," an expression interpreted as a cryptogram for the Pharisees (Amoussine 1963; Flusser 1970). Others see him as identical with the Wicked Priest (Vermes 1981: 143), but the different characteristics of the two men make this identification unacceptable.

b. The Pesher on the Psalms (4QpPs[a]). Substantial fragments of four columns of this Herodian ms have been preserved (Stegemann 1963–64; 1967–69). The author reads the dichotomy of the Righteous and the Wicked, as described in the Psalms, as referring to the Teacher of Righteousness and his followers on the one hand and their opponents on the other. The Teacher is referred to here as "the Priest" (1–10 iii 15). He is persecuted both by the Wicked Priest (1–10 iv 8) and the "Wicked ones of Ephraim . . . who will seek to lay their hands on the Priest and his partisans" (1–10 ii 18). This is seen by the author as part of the events taking place "at the time of testing that is coming upon them" (1–10 ii 19–20). The community believed that its own salvation by God was imminent, as was the punishment of their enemies. The Man of Lies also figures here. He is the one "who led many astray" with false teaching (1–10 i 26–27).

The sharp contrast between the Teacher (and his followers) and their opponents is also reflected by the various epithets applied to each party. The Teacher and his adherents are variously called "those who practice the Torah" (1–10 ii 15, 23), "the Congregation of the Meek" (1–10 ii 10; iii 10), "the congregation of his chosen ones" (1–10 ii 5), and "those who returned from the wilderness" (1–10 iii 1; cf. 1QM 1:2–3; 4QpIsa[a] 2–6 ii 18). Their adversaries are referred to as "the Ruthless Opponents of the Covenant" (1–10 ii 14; iv 1–2), "the Wicked of Ephraim and Manasseh" (1–10 ii 18), and "the Wicked Princes" (1–2 iii 7). The contrast between the community and its opponents is seen as part of the cosmic battle between the forces of Good and the forces of Evil (1–10 ii 7–11).

c. The Pesher on Nahum (4QpNah). Substantial fragments of five columns of this late Hasmonean or early Herodian ms have survived (Strugnell 1969–71: 205). Published after 1QpHab, this pesher was the first of the Qumran writings to mention historical names. It mentions "[Deme]trius King of Greece" (4QpNah 3–4 i 2), probably referring to the Seleucid ruler Demetrius III Eukerus (95–88 B.C.E.; Cross 1980: 124–25; Milik 1959: 72). It also mentions "the kings of Greece from Antiochus until the rise of the rulers of the Kittim" (4QpNah 3–4 i 3). While it is difficult to ascertain which specific king this refers to, it is at least clear that the kings of Greece (= *yawan,* as in Dan 8:21; 10:20; 11:2; also referred to in CD 8:11–12), namely the Seleucids, are distinct from "the rulers of the Kittim" (mentioned also in 1QpHab 3:5), who must then be the Roman governors. These references, therefore, place the events and persons alluded to in the pesharim on a firm historical footing, dating them in the 2d century B.C.E.

The Nahum pesher seems to refer to events dating from Alexander Janneus to the fall of the Hasmonean kingdom following the conquest of Palestine by Pompey (63 B.C.E.; cf. 4QpNah 3–4 iv). Perhaps the clearest indication is the allusion to Alexander Jannaeus, referred to here as "the Lion of Wrath." This Lion is one "who would hang men up alive" (4QpNah 3–4 i 7), apparently alluding to Alexander Jannaeus' crucifixion of the Pharisees who had transferred their allegiance to Demetrius III (cf. Josephus *Ant* 13.14.2 §§379–83; *JW* 1.4.6 §§96–98). The pesher, though it may appear to be condemning Jannaeus' act, may in fact be approving it as an appropriate punishment for the Pharisees' treachery (thus Yadin 1971, relying on the ruling of 11QTemple 64:6–13 to hang traitors alive [cf. Deut 21:22–23]; also Yadin 1983, 1: 378).

"The Seekers of Smooth Things" (4QpNah 3–4 i 7, based on Isa 30:10; cf. Ps. 21:3; Dan 11:32), namely the Pharisees, appear both as the foes of the Lion of Wrath and as the adversaries of the Qumranites. Most of the pesher's polemic is directed against them. They are referred to as "those who lead Ephraim astray; with their false teaching, their lying tongue, and deceitful lip they lead many astray" (4QpNah 3–4 ii 8; cf. 4QpPs^a 1–10 ii 18–19). A similar charge is leveled by 1QpHab against the Spouter of Lies and his followers. 4QpNah refers to three distinct groups within Israel, by means of three biblical symbols: Ephraim, Manasseh, and Judea. Ephraim stands for the Seekers of Smooth Things, namely the Pharisees (4QpNah 3–4 ii 2, 8). A second group, represented by Manasseh, is also condemned by the author (4QpNah 3–4 iii 9–11, iv 1–7). The third group appears to refer to the Qumran community itself, and is represented by Judea and Israel (4QpNah 3–4 iii 4–5).

It had been concluded from other Qumran writings (1QS and CD) that the Qumran community must be identical with some branch of the Essenes. If the pesher's tripartite symbolism is equated with the three Jewish sects referred to by Josephus—Pharisees, Sadducees, and Essenes (*Ant* 13.5.9 §§171–73; 18.1.2–5 §§11–22; *JW* 2.8.2–14 §§119–166)—the second group, Manasseh, must be identified with the Sadducees (Amoussine 1963; Flusser 1970; the same tripartite symbolism underlies 4QpPs^a 1–10 ii 18–19 and other pesharim). However, new evidence shows that the members of the Qumran community adhered to a Sadducean halakhah (Qimron and Strugnell 1985, citing the yet unpublished work 4QMMT; see also MIQSAT MAᶜASE HATORAH), so that the identification of the triple symbolism of the pesharim with the three sects of Josephus must be modified.

d. The Pesher on Isaiah (4QpIsa^d). A fragment of this pesher offers an interesting insight into the self-image of the Qumran community. The pesher interprets the description of the eschatological Jerusalem in Isaiah 54 as symbolic of the eschatological community and its leadership: "the council of the community was established [among the] priests and the p[eople] [in the midst of] the congregation of his chosen ones, like a stone of lapis lazuli in the midst of the stones" (1 2–3). Underlying the equation of the eschatological Jerusalem with the community is also the equation of Jerusalem with the Temple and, consequently, the equation of the community with the Temple (also in 1QS 5:5–6; 8:5–6; 4QFlor 1–2 i 6–7; cf. Dimant 1986: 184–89). The pesher appears also to connect the twelve community leaders (cf. the twelve apostles of the early Christian community) with the twelve precious stones on the breastpiece of the High Priest (Exod 28:4, 15 etc.). A similar theme and approach are to be found in the description of New Jerusalem in Revelation 21. The concept of community as temple is applied also to the early Christian community by several NT writers (e.g., Matt 16:17–18; Eph 2:19–20; Rev 3:12; cf. Baumgarten 1977; Flusser 1965).

2. Thematic Pesharim. Unlike continuous pesharim, the thematic pesharim do not provide a running commentary on a single biblical text; they are a collection of pesharim of various biblical verses on a single, or several themes. The theme thus dominates the structure and development of the pesher, and dictates the choice of biblical texts to be interpreted. These pesharim use a structure similar to the continuous pesharim, but modify it in some ways.

a. 4QFlorilegium (4Q*174*). Several fragments of this ms together preserve most of one column, and parts of another two columns (editions: Allegro 1968: 53–57; Strugnell 1969–71: 220–25; Brooke 1985: 86–91). The ms dates from the end of the 1st century B.C.E. or the beginning of the 1st century C.E. (Brooke 1985: 83–84). Organized around citations from 2 Sam 7:10–14 (1 Chr 17:9–13); Exod 15:17–18; Amos 9:11; Ps. 1:1; Isa 8:11; Ezek 37:23; and Ps. 2:1; the work expounds various eschatological themes.

The best preserved column contains a pesher on 2 Samuel 7. It interprets the prophecy of Nathan concerning the House of David as alluding to three temples (Schwartz 1979; Dimant 1986): the future eschatological temple (Heb *mqdš ʾdny*) to be built by God (1–2 i 1–5; also mentioned in 11QTemple 29:10); the Temple of Israel (Heb *mqdš yśrʾl*), which was the temple built by Israel and later desecrated (probably to be equated with the contemporary temple; 1–2 i 5–6); and the Temple of Men (Heb *mqdš ʾdm*), that is, the temple created and fashioned by the life and deeds of the Qumran community itself. The pesher accordingly states (1–2 i 6–7) that the sacrifices in this third temple are not of animals but of "deeds of Torah" (Heb *mᶜśy twrh;* cf. 4QMMT *mᶜśy mṣwh;* Qimron and Strugnell 1985: 406). The author goes on to interpret 2 Sam 7:11–14 as referring to the Shoot of David, the eschatological leader of the community (mentioned also in 4QPatrBless 3; cf. 4QpIsa^a 7–10 ii 22; CD 7:16), who will appear together with another leader of the community, the Interpreter of the Torah (mentioned also in CD 6:7; 7:18).

This first section (4QFlor 1–2 i 1–13) does not use the term "pesher" at all, whereas the second section (4QFlor 1–2 i 14–19) does. Moreover, this second section opens with the formula "Midrash of 'happy is the man . . .' " (Ps. 1:1) (Heb *mdrš mʾšry hʾyš*). These distinctions were taken to indicate that this second section (4QFlor 1–2 i 14–1–3 ii 1–6) is a real pesher in the form of a midrash, whereas 4QFlor 1–2 i 1–13 is not (Brooke 1985: 140–41, 154–55). This view is, however, questionable, since both sections employ the same exegetical procedures and syntactic patterns as other pesharim. The differences of style and terminology between the two sections may indicate that 4QFlor was originally a collection of various eschatological pesharim.

b. 11QMelchizedek (11QMelch). Parts of three columns of this early Herodian ms have survived (de Jonge and van der Woude 1965–66; fresh edition Puech 1987: 488–89). The fragments describe the events as taking place during the tenth eschatological jubilee, so that originally they must have formed part of a larger pesher on ten jubilees. But differences of style and subject matter make it doubtful whether the fragments 4Q*180–181* are to be considered as part of this pesher (as Milik 1972 has suggested; cf. Dimant's criticism 1979: 89–90).

In 11QMelchizedek the author strings together pesher-type expositions of various biblical texts (Lev 25:9–10, 12:13; Deut 15:2; Isa 49:8; 52:7; 61:1–3; Pss. 7:8–9; 82:1–2; Dan 9:25). He interprets the freedom accorded in the biblical jubilee as the eschatological liberation of the Sons of Light imprisoned by the evil Belial (ii 1–6). This liberation will take place at "the End of Days" (ii 4), at the end of the tenth jubilee (ii 7), which implies a division of historical time into ten jubilees (cf. *1 En.* 93:1–10; 90:12–17; Kobelski 1981: 49–51). The chief actor in these events is Melchizedek, the eschatological judge who figures as a priest in Gen 14:18 and Ps. 110:4. In this capacity he acts as liberator and expiator of sins for the Sons of Light while wreaking vengeance upon Belial and his hosts (ii 13–14). By applying Ps. 82:1 to Melchizedek (ii 13), the author of the pesher treats him as a supernatural figure.

3. Isolated Pesharim. Most of the isolated pesharim come from the first part (the admonition) of the *Cairo Damascus Document:* 3:20–44 (on Ezek 44:15); 4:13–19 (on Isa 24:17); 6:3–11 (on Num 21:18 + Isa 54:16); 7(B):10–21 (on Isa 7:17 + Amos 9:11 + Num 24:7); 8(A):8–15 (on Deut 32:33); and 19(B):7–13 (on Zech 11:11 + Ezek 9:4). Only one isolated pesher is to be found outside this document (the *Community Rule* interprets Isa 40:3; note also 9:20). Significantly, all the isolated pesharim occur in paraenetic sections, where the pesharim serve as prooftexts both for events in the history of the community and for its ideological tenets. The texts commented upon in this way are mostly prophetic, but a few are taken from ancient songs found in the Torah (Num 21:18; 24:7; Deut 32:33). This means that these songs were considered prophetic and were interpreted as such.

4. Other Forms of Pesharim. Another type of biblical interpretation is the use of various sobriquets in the pesharim to refer to historical persons. Most of these sobriquets serve as cryptograms for pesher-type interpretations of biblical passages (cf. above and the examples discussed by Nitzan 1986: 43–46). Thus, for instance, the epithet "The Seekers of Smooth Things" for the community's opponents clearly refers to Isa 30:10, but implies a pesher of the entire context of Isa 30:8–14. The epithet "The Teacher of Righteousness" is based on Hos 10:12 and Joel 2:23, but has its source in a pesher of the larger context of the two verses (note esp. Joel 2:18–27). Although these sobriquets cannot formally be considered "pesharim," they are derived by the same exegetical principles.

Another form of pesher is interpretation of biblical verses by allusion, that is, without explicit quotation (cf. 1QpHab 11:12–14 on Hab 2:16, alluding to Deut 10:16; Jer 4:4; see other examples cited by Nitzan 1986: 61–78). These interpretations of alluded vv are also derived by the pesher's exegetical method. The fact that pesher-like characteristics appear in various other literary forms indicates that continuous or thematic pesharim were not the only literary forms that employed the pesher-type exegesis.

B. Nature and Structure of the Pesharim

Besides the pesharim, the members of the Qumran community employed several other modes of biblical interpretation (Gabrion, *ANRW* 2/19/1: 779–848; Fishbane 1988). However, it is the pesharim which are most typical of the community. Their distinctive historical-eschatological subject matter and typical lemma-and-exposition form reflect in a unique way the doctrines and attitudes of the Qumran community.

The *Pesher on Habakkuk* claims that the pesharim are of divine origin. It states that "God divulged all the mysteries of the words of His servants the Prophets" to the Teacher of Righteousness (1QpHab 7:4–5), and these mysteries relate to the historical events leading to the eschatological era (1QpHab 2:8–10). Biblical prophecies are, therefore, interpreted as enigmatic predictions relating to events of the Last Day, revealed to the Prophets who perhaps did not understand them (being too far removed in time from the events about which they prophesied). These enigmatic mysteries (Heb *rzym;* e.g. 1QpHab 7:8; 1QS 3:23; 1QH 2:13; 1QM 3:9; CD 3:18; cf. Dan 2:29 et al) could therefore only be unraveled by an inspired person living close to the time of the actual events. The Teacher of Righteousness, according to 1QpHab, not only possessed such great visionary powers, but was also inspired and guided by God (Elliger 1953: 154–55; Nitzan 1986: 25–26). We should not conclude from this that all the extant pesharim were necessarily composed by the Teacher of Righteousness himself, but the pesher-method, as developed within the Qumran community, may ultimately derive from him. The numerous exegetical techniques the pesharim share with other contemporary literary corpora seem to indicate that the Teacher of Righteousness, like other contemporary Jewish writers, also drew on traditional exegetical modes and traditions (Fishbane 1988: 340–41; Dimant 1988: 379–84).

The character and form of the pesharim are best understood by observing the relationship between their formal structure and their content. The lemmatic pattern makes for a structural and stylistic distinction between the biblical citation and its exposition, thus differentiating between the word of God and man's interpretation of it. The *Pesher of Habakkuk* provides the most comprehensive illustration of pesher patterns. The work consists of small pesher units. Because the main text expounded is known, each unit opens with a biblical citation without any introductory term. The interpretation which follows is, however, always introduced by the term "pesher." Such pesher-interpretation identifies parts of the biblical citation with contemporary personages or activities (Rabinowitz 1973: 226), with further explanations (Brooke 1979–80: 498).

When applied to *persons* the identification is introduced by the formula *pšrw ʿl* ("its interpretation concerns") + a noun + the relative *ʾšr* ("who"/"which") + verb/s describing the activities of the persons mentioned. An alternative formula uses *pšr hdbr ʿl* ("the interpretation of it concerns"; cf. 1QpHab 10:9; 12:2, 12–13). A good illustration is 1QpHab 6:8–10:

> THEREFORE HE DRAWS HIS SWORD CONTINUALLY TO SLAUGHTER NATIONS AND HE HAS NO COMPASSION [Hab 1:17]. Its interpretation concerns the Kittim, who destroy many with the sword . . .

When applied to *activities* the identification is introduced by the formula *pšrw ʾšr* ("its interpretation is that") or *pšr hdbr ʾšr* ("the interpretation of it is that") + verb. A good illustration of this form is found in 1QpHab 7:7–7:

> FOR THERE IS YET A VISION CONCERNING THE APPOINTED TIME. IT TESTIFIES TO THE END, AND IT WILL NOT DECEIVE [Hab 2:3]. Its interpretation is that the last end will be prolonged . . ."

The pesher unit may be elaborated by repeating a portion of the citation and giving it a fresh interpretation. The subordinate character of such elaborations is indicated by special introductory terms: the quotation is always introduced by the formula *wʾšr ʾmr* ("and as for what he said"; cf. 1QpHab 6:2; 7:3; 9:3; 10:1–2) or *hwʾ ʾšr ʾmr* ("this is what he said"; cf. 1QpHab 3:2, 14). Such repeated quotations are followed by additional identifications, again introduced by the term "pesher" (e.g., 1QpHab 5:6–7; 7:3–4). These identifications are in the form of nominal sentences which repeat some terms from the quotation itself, and equate them with other, nonbiblical, terms. For example, 1QpHab 12:3–4 (on Hab 2:17) reads: "for 'Lebanon' *is* the council of the community, and the 'beasts' *are* the simple ones of Judah."

The above formal patterns are employed, with slight modifications, by all continuous pesharim (Brooke 1979–80: 498–500; Horgan 1979: 239–44), with a single exception: 4QpIsa^c, which omits comment on some passages of its main Isaiah text, contains quotations from Jeremiah and Zechariah (Horgan 1979: 237–38).

The thematic pesharim also employ the basic patterns of the continuous pesharim, with appropriate modifications. But unlike the continuous pesharim, they employ a combination of main text with subordinate ones. Thus, for example, 4QFlorilegium, like the continuous pesharim, quotes the main text of 2 Samuel 7 without any introductory formula (1–2 i 10–11) because the main text had been cited explicitly in the initial section of the pesher (which has not been preserved). As with the continuous pesharim, the interpretation which follows the quotation is identifactory, but takes the form of nominal equations (4QFlor 1–2 i 2, 11) instead of a "pesher." This is followed by fresh quotations from other biblical books, considered by the author to refer to the same exegetical subject. Since these quotations come from biblical books other than that of the main text, their source is explicitly mentioned. These quotations are introduced by the term *kʾšr ktwb* ("as it is written"; cf. 4QFlor 1–2 i 2, 12), a typical introductory formula for scriptural prooftexts (also used in explicit nonpesher quotations, chiefly in legal sections of Qumran works; cf. CD 5:1–2; 11:10; 1QS 5:15). These quotations are in turn interpreted as subordinate units (which repeat a quotation and introduce it with "and as for what he said" [4QFlor 1–2 i 7], or introduce nominal equation [4QFlor 1–2 i 12–13]). 11QMelch is too fragmentary to permit a full reconstruction of the structural patterns. The surviving quotations are all introduced by formulas used to mark subordinate elaborations ("and as for what he said"; "this/as it is written"). The main quotation appears, therefore, to be missing.

C. Literary Genre of the Pesharim

The fact that the term "pesher" is not always used in the pesharim indicates that the use of this term is not constitutive to the genre (Brooke 1979–80: 492). Rather, the structure, terminology, and exegetical purpose of the work are of greater importance. The exegetical procedure underlying each pesher-unit may be reconstructed as follows (similarly Brooke 1979–80: 497).

The first step consists in locating within the biblical citation the subject of the exposition and identifying it with a contemporary figure or situation. The subject may be located in a noun, a verb, or a pronoun of the biblical text. These identifications may appear to the modern reader to be very arbitrary, but they are often based on an already existing exegetical tradition. Thus, for instance, the equation of the Chaldeans with the Kittim goes back to a well-established exegesis (cf. Num 24:24 together with Isa 23:12–13 and Dan 11:30; Brooke 1985: 328–29). Similarly, the identification of the term "Lebanon" in Hab 2:17 with the community (1QpHab 4:12) rests on the traditional equation of Lebanon with the Temple (in the Targums tradition; cf. Brownlee 1956; Vermes 1961: 28). It is this initial step of applying the ancient prophecy to a contemporary situation that is the most difficult. This is often done through symbolic or allegorical equations: the lion of Habakkuk stands for a human king (4QpNah 3–4 i 1–6), the eschatological Jerusalem stands for the Qumran community (4QpIsa^d), a reference to "a town" stands for "the town of vanity," namely, for a group of opponents led by the Spouter of Lies (1QpNah 10:9–10).

Having established the identification, the author sets out to relate the various details in the citation to the identified subject (the second step). In order to bridge the gap between the literal meaning of the biblical prophecy and the sense attributed to it in the pesher, the author will indicate the presence of analogy, similarity, or identity between various elements of the two texts.

Finally, the above aims are achieved by the application of various exegetical techniques (the third step; see D below).

The exegetical steps described above, as well as their eschatological subject matter, though not always explicitly formulated, are essential components of (and underlie all forms of) pesharim. They are the distinctive features of the pesher-commentary. The presence or absence of these constituents is, therefore, sufficient to decide if a work is to be defined as a pesher or not. The occurrence of the term "pesher" is important, but not indispensable, for such a definition. We may find pesher-type works which do not employ the term "pesher," but employ other terminological equivalents to perform the same task (cf. 4QFlor 1–2 i 1–13). Conversely, the pesher exegetical method may be employed in a different literary form and with different structural patterns (compare isolated pesharim and the sobriquets; cf. also 1 Macc 7:16–17 commenting on Ps 79:2–3; cf. Dimant 1988: 390–91).

It should be noted, however, that two Qumranic texts make a different use of the term "pesher": the text known as 4QOrdinances (= 4Q*159*) 5:1, 5 uses the term to introduce a pesher on a legal passage from the Pentateuch (Lev 16:1?). In another text, 4Q*180,* the term "pesher" introduces abstract themes later to be interpreted by means of pertinent quotations. This indicates that the use of the term "pesher" may have been wider than what can be gathered from the evidence of the continuous and thematic pesharim (Brownlee 1979: 28; Dimant 1979: 96).

What is the genre of the pesharim? A heated debate on this question was conducted in the years following their publication. It was argued that the pesher, serving as it does to disclose contemporary events presaged in ancient biblical prophecies, should not be termed "interpretation" or "exposition" of scripture, for it does not aim at explaining or clarifying biblical verses, but rather at disclosing coming events (thus Rabinowitz 1973). Nevertheless, the lemmatic structure and the exegetical techniques used by the pesharim link them firmly with other types of lemmatic commentaries, such as the rabbinic midrashim and the commentaries of Philo. Some scholars have, in fact, classified the pesher as a sort of Qumranic midrash (Brownlee 1979; Brooke 1985). Other scholars have discovered an affinity between the pesharim and the interpretation of dreams as practiced in the ANE and as evidenced in the biblical stories of Joseph (Gen 40–41) and Daniel (chaps. 2–6). The pesharim, like the interpretation of dreams, aim at revealing future events alluded to in visions, and do so by similar exegetical means (Rabinowitz 1973: 230–32; Finkel 1963–64).

But although the pesher has some affinity with all these literary forms, and especially with the prophetic dreams and apocalyptic visions, it has a distinct form, distinct aims, and a distinct background. The distinctiveness of the Qumranic pesharim lies in their peculiar structure and terminology, and in their systematic application of the biblical text to the historical circumstances of the community itself. The immediate purpose of the pesharim is to vindicate the Teacher of Righteousness and his followers in their struggle against their opponents, to strengthen the adherents' faith and their powers of endurance, and to inspire them with hope for the future (Brownlee 1979: 35–36). The Qumranic pesher should, therefore, be considered as a commentary of a special kind.

D. Exegetical Method Used by the Pesharim

The pesher's strict formal distinction between the biblical lemma and its interpretation indicates the interpreter's main task: to extract the desired sense from the biblical citation by indicating the analogy and similarity between the text and the community's situation. To accomplish this a number of exegetical techniques were used (Elliger 1953: 130–48; Brownlee 1951; Bruce 1960: 11–18; Horgan 1979: 244–49; Brooke 1985: 279–352; Nitzan 1986: 39–79):

(1) modeling the interpretation on the syntactic and lexical patterns of the citation (cf. 4QFlor 1–2 i 1–13; Dimant 1986: 174);

(2) using, in the pesher, lexical synonyms of words occurring in the biblical citation;

(3) punning on words of the citation (paranomasia);

(4) atomizing;

(5) vocalizing or grouping the consonants of words in the citation in a different way; and

(6) adducing other biblical quotations which share one or more terms with the main citation.

These procedures have close parallels in the rabbinic midrashim, in early biblical versions, and in early apocalyptic literature. It is, therefore, often asserted that they are identical with the techniques used in the rabbinic midrashim (Silberman 1961–62; Slomovic 1969–71; Brooke 1985: 154–55, 283–92). These procedures, though similar, are nevertheless not identical; they are used in widely different texts, different in character, period, and social background. Identity cannot, therefore, be established until further research is carried out. However, the affinity between the exegetical methods used in all these corpora seems to indicate that the Qumranic pesher is not a unique phenomenon, but it must be placed within the wider framework of Jewish exegesis of the Second Temple era.

Bibliography

Allegro, J. M. 1968. *Qumran Cave 4 I (4Q158–4Q186).* DJD 5. Oxford.

Amoussine, J. D. 1963. Ephraim et Manasse dans le Pesher de Nahum (4Qp Nahum). *RQ* 4: 389–96.

Baumgarten, J. M. 1977. The Duodecimal Courts of Qumran, Revelation and the Sanhendrin. Pp. 145–71 in *Studies in Qumran Law.* Leiden.

Brooke, G. J. 1979–80. Qumran Pesher: Towards the Redefinition of a Genre. *RQ* 10: 483–503.

———. 1985. *Exegesis at Qumran.* Sheffield.

Brownlee, W. H. 1951. Biblical Interpretation Among the Sectaries of the Dead Sea Scrolls. *BA* 14: 54–76.

———. 1956. The Habakkuk Midrash and the Targum of Jonathan. *JJS* 7: 169–86.

———. 1979. *The Midrash Pesher of Habakkuk.* Missoula.

Bruce, F. F. 1960. *Biblical Exegesis in the Qumran Texts.* London.

Cross, F. M. 1972. Introduction. Pp. 1–5 in Trever and Cross 1972.

———. 1980. *The Ancient Library of Qumran.* Grand Rapids.

Delcor, M. 1951. Le Midrash d'Habacuc. *RB* 58: 521–48.

Dimant, D. 1979. The 'Pesher on the Periods' (4Q180) and 4Q181. *IOS* 9: 77–99.

———. 1986. *4QFlorilegium* and the Idea of the Community as Temple. Pp. 165–89 in *Hellenica et Judaica: Hommage A Valentin Nikiprowetzky,* ed. A. Caquot et al. Paris.

———. 1988. Use and Interpretation of Mikra in the Apocrypha and Pseudepigrapha. Pp. 379–419 in *Mikra,* ed. M. J. Moulder. CRINT 3/1. Assen.

Dupont-Sommer, A. 1980. *Les Écrit Esséniens.* Paris.

Elliger, K. 1953. *Studien zum Habakuk-Kommentar vom Toten Meer.* Tübingen.

Finkel, A. 1963–64. The Pesher of Dreams and Scriptures. *RQ* 4: 357–40.

Fishbane, M. 1988. Use, Authority and Interpretation of Mikra at Qumran. Pp. 339–77 in *Mikra,* ed. M. J. Moulder. CRINT 2/1. Assen.

Flusser, D. 1965. Qumran und die Zwolf. Pp. 134–46 in *Initiation,* ed. C. J. Bleeker. Supp Numen 10. Leiden.

———. 1970. Pharisees, Sadducees and Essenes in Pesher Nahum. Pp. 133–68 in *Essays in Jewish History and Philology in Memory of Gedaliahu Alon,* ed. M. Dorman et al. Tel Aviv (in Hebrew).

Horgan, M. P. 1979. *Pesharim: Qumran Interpretations of Biblical Books.* CBQMS 8. Washington.

Jonge, M. de, and van der Woude, A. S. 1965–66. 11QMelchizedek and the New Testament. *NTS* 12: 301–26.

Kobelski, P. J. 1981. *Melchizedek and Melchireša*ᶜ. CBQMS 10. Washington.

Milik, J. T. 1959. *Ten Years of Discovery in the Wilderness of Judaea.* Trans. J. Strugnell. London.

———. 1972. *Milkî-ṣedeq* et *Milkî-reša*ᶜ dans les anciens ecrits juifs et chrétiens. *JJS* 23: 95–144.

Murphy-O'Connor, J. 1974. The Essenes and their History. *RB* 81: 215–44.

Nickelsburg, G. W. E. 1976. Simon—A Priest with a Reputation for Faithfulness. *BASOR* 223: 67–68.

Nitzan, B. 1986. *Pesher Habakkuk.* Jerusalem (in Hebrew).

Puech, E. 1987. Notes sur le manuscrit de *11QMelkîsédeq*. *RQ* 12: 483–513.

Qimron, E., and Strugnell, J. 1985. An Unpublished Halakhic Letter from Qumran. Pp. 400–7 in *Biblical Archaeology Today*. Jerusalem.

Rabinowitz, I. 1973. Pesher/Pittaron. *RQ* 8: 219–32.

Schwartz, D. R. 1979. The Three Temples of 4QFlorilegium. *RQ* 10: 83–91.

Silberman, L. H. 1961–62. Unriddling the Riddle: A Study in the Structure and Language of the Habakkuk Pesher (1QpHab). *RQ* 3: 323–64.

Slomovic, E. 1969–71. Towards an Understanding of the Exegesis in the Dead Sea Scrolls. *RQ* 7: 3–15.

Stegemann, H. 1963–64. Der Pešer Psalm 37 aus Höhle 4 von Qumran (4QpPs37). *RQ* 4: 235–70.

———. 1967–69. Weitere Stücke von 4 QpPsalms 37, von 4 Q Patriarchal Blessing und Hinweis auf eine unedierete Handschrift aus Höhle 4 Q mit Exzerpten aus dem Deuteronomium. *RQ* 6: 193–227.

———. 1971. *Die Entstehung der Qumrangemeinde* (privately published).

Strugnell, J. 1969–71. Notes en marge du volume V des 'Discoveries in the Judaean Desert of Jordan.' *RQ* 7: 163–276.

Talmon, S. 1965. The Calendar Reckoning of the Sect from the Judaean Desert. *ScrHier* 4: 162–99.

Trever, J. C., and Cross, F. M. 1972. *Scrolls from Qumran Cave I*. Jerusalem.

Vermes, G. 1961. Lebanon. Pp. 26–39 in *Scripture and Tradition in Judaism*. SPB 4. Leiden.

———. 1981. *The Dead Sea Scrolls: Qumran in Perspective*. Philadelphia.

Yadin, Y. 1971. Pesher Nahum (4QpNahum) Reconsidered. *IEJ* 21: 1–12.

———. 1983. *The Temple Scroll*. 3 vols. Jerusalem.

DEVORAH DIMANT

PESHITTA. See VERSIONS, ANCIENT (SYRIAC); CHRISTIANITY (SYRIA).

PESTILENCE. See SICKNESS AND DISEASE; PALESTINE, CLIMATE OF.

PETER (PERSON) [Gk *Petros*]. Var. SIMON PETER; SIMON; CEPHAS. The most prominent of the 12 disciples of Jesus.

A. Pauline Letters
B. Book of Acts
C. Gospel of Mark
D. Gospel of Matthew
E. Gospel of Luke
F. Gospel of John
G. The Petrine Epistles
H. The Apocryphal Writings

A. Pauline Letters

There are undisputed references to Peter in 1 Corinthians and Galatians; some would hold that there are also veiled references to Peter in 2 Corinthians. Not only do the Pauline letters represent the earliest extant literature in the canonical NT but they also contain references to Peter which predate considerably the time of their writing. However, when Paul relates such meetings with Peter, he does so in a context which is intended to reinforce his apostleship and his understanding of the gospel.

According to the evidence in Galatians and 1 Corinthians, Paul sees Peter serving at least four important functions: (1) Peter is the first-named witness to whom the risen Christ appeared according to the list in 1 Cor 15:5; (2) Peter was a source of tradition about Jesus if one accepts *historēsai* in Gal 1:18 as meaning that Paul went up to Jerusalem "to get information [about Jesus] from Cephas;" (3) Peter served as a leader in Jerusalem during the time of the Christian Paul's first visit (Gal 1:18) and continued to have a position of importance during Paul's second visit (Gal 2:1–10); (4) Peter participated in the apostolate to the circumcised as Paul did in the apostolate to the uncircumcised (Gal 2:8).

1. Galatians. In order to understand Paul's assertions about Cephas (Paul uses the name "Cephas" in Gal 1:18; 2:9, 11, 14 and in 1 Cor 1:12; 3:22; 9:5; 15:5, but the name "Peter" only in Gal 2:7–8) it is necessary to understand what factors in the Galatian controversy prompted Paul to include references to him. Since it is unlikely that Paul believed Peter himself was causing the difficulty in Galatia by preaching "a different gospel" (1:6) the solution must lie elsewhere. According to one explanation Paul's primary opponents were Judaizers who were incorrectly invoking the name of Peter in support of their position. That the Galatians understood Peter as an authority figure, either because of his personal apostolate or because of the significance of Jerusalem, is suggested by Gal 1:18. However one may wish to define the specific profile of these Judaizers this much is clear: that their "different gospel" included such Jewish practices as circumcision (5:1–6) and the celebration of feasts according to the Jewish calendar (4:10). Thus, on the one hand, Paul refers to Cephas in terms of past history: at Jerusalem (Gal 2:1–10) and at Antioch (Gal 2:11–14) Peter had been involved in two of Paul's prior confrontations with Judaizers, and in each of them he refused to capitulate to those demands which would have imposed Jewish practices on gentile converts. On the other hand, this review of the past serves to refute the attempt of the Galatian Judaizers in associating their position with that of Peter and those "who were men of repute" (2:2) at Jerusalem. Thus, for example, the fact that "those who were of repute" extended to Paul and Barnabas "the right hand of fellowship" (2:9) would certainly weaken the claim of the Galatians. Paul, then, rejects the legalistic mentality common to the groups in Jerusalem, Antioch, and Galatia.

In order to determine Paul's perception of Peter, three encounters between the two must be taken into consideration: (1) Gal 1:18, Paul's initial visit to Jerusalem and meeting with Peter; (2) Gal 2:1–10, Paul's second visit to Jerusalem concerning the circumcision issue; and, (3) Gal 2:11ff., Paul's rebuke of Peter at Antioch.

With regard to the first of these meetings, one meaning of the verb *historēsai* is "to gather information from someone" and it is possible that Paul received information about Jesus during this visit, perhaps including the Risen Christ's appearance to Cephas (1 Cor 15:5). Concerning the second visit to Jerusalem, Paul went privately to "those who were of repute [. . .] lest somehow I should be running or had run in vain" (2:2). Critical is how one is to understand this latter phrase. Paul may have regarded himself inferior to these Jerusalem authorities, including Peter, and was concerned that if Jerusalem did not approve of his policy in not circumcising gentile converts he might be doctrinally "running in vain." Or Paul may not have been concerned about winning the doctrinal approval of the authorities in Jerusalem but rather much more concerned in bringing clarity to the political intrigues which had been launched against his policies. The degree of authority which Paul attached to Peter is conditioned by the interpretation of this phrase. At the very least, one may say that Paul took these leaders seriously even if he did not understand them to be his ecclesiastical superiors. With regard to the final encounter at Antioch it is probable that Paul is not challenging the person of Peter but rather the fact that Peter acted without principle with regard to the "truth of the gospel." The main issue is that Peter was not drawing consistent consequence from the one and only gospel (1:7; 2:14).

This incident at Antioch raises another set of interesting questions concerning possible changes in the relationship between Peter and Paul and between Peter, James, and John. With regard to the former, does the phrase "I opposed him to his face" mean that Paul opposed "*even* Peter," in the sense of implying Peter's superiority? Or does Paul's challenge of Peter face to face suggest an increasing self-assurance on Paul's part? Read in this way, one could understand 1:18 as suggesting Paul as inferior to Peter; 2:7–8 indicating that both are equal; and 2:11–21 implying Paul's superiority as a result of his ability to confront Peter. If such a tentative interpretation is followed, one could argue for a shift in power. With regard to the latter point (Peter's relation to James and John), it is also possible, more convincingly, to suggest a change in this relationship. In 1:18–19, Cephas is named before James; in 2:9 James is mentioned before Peter and John. Thus, at least by the time Paul writes Galatians, *James,* and not Peter as was the case during Paul's first visit, is recognized as the major figure in Jerusalem.

2. 1 Corinthians. Cephas is referred to in 1:12, 3:22, 9:5, and 15:5. The first two references involve the tendency toward division in Corinth (those belonging to Paul, to Apollos, and to Cephas) and they raise the question whether Peter had ever been in Corinth. That he engaged in missionary activity is made clear by Gal 2:7–8, 11 but also by Acts 1–12 where Peter is active in Samaria, Lydda, Joppa, and Caesarea. That he was in Corinth is possible; in that case the existence of a Peter-party in Corinth included those who were converted by him during the time that he preached there. However, other cogent explanations have been put forth, viz., that the Corinthians, in an attempt to end the in-fighting decided to appeal to a higher earthly authority, Cephas. The reference to Christ would then be understood similarly. Or, the Cephas-party might have included those baptized by him in Palestine and who subsequently migrated to Corinth. Paul's reference to Peter in 1 Cor 15:5, "Do we not have the right to be accompanied by a wife, as the other apostles and the brothers of the Lord and Cephas?", unfortunately does not help decide this issue since this verse can be used on both sides of the argument. However this matter may be decided there is a likely consensus that the Cephas-party in Corinth does not necessarily reflect the views of Peter any more than the Paul-party accurately reflected the views of Paul.

In 1 Cor 15:5 a different set of problems is encountered. Verse 5 is set in a very carefully structured context which continues through 15:8: "And that he appeared: [1] to Cephas, [2] then to the Twelve; [3] and then he appeared to more than 500 brethren at one time, and then he appared: [4] to James, [5] then to all the apostles; [6] last of all, as to one irregularly born, he appeared also to me."

Most would agree that these verses contain an early tradition that the first appearance of the resurrected Christ was to Cephas, a tradition that is consonant with that in Luke 24:34; by Paul's own admission the appearance to him was the "last of all." Other than these chronological references, few would assert that the entire list as we have it before us follows any chronological order. The problem is twofold: (1) Where does the pre-Pauline tradition end and where does Pauline redaction begin; (2) how do the two groupings of three relate to one another?

Concerning the first issue the question arises whether the fact that Jesus *appeared* originally belonged to a pre-Pauline formula or derives from Paul himself. Also, were the names of Cephas and the Twelve already in the pre-Pauline formula or did Paul add these names? Even if the latter should be the case he was dependent on earlier tradition for information about those to whom the Risen Jesus appeared. Concerning the second problem, several solutions have been offered—none without difficulty, however. Some suggest that the first three appearances (Cephas, the Twelve, more than 500 brethren) represent those who had been Jesus' followers during his lifetime; the second three appearances (James, all the apostles, Paul) were directed to more recent followers of Jesus. Another suggestion understands the first group as a "church-founding" appearance and the second as a "mission-inaugurating" one. Another explanation wishes to see rival lists reflected in these groupings, a suggestion that coheres with the thesis of a shift in power as reviewed in the discussion of Galatians. Still others would explain these lists as duplicate reports of the same appearances with James substituted for Cephas and "all the apostles" substituted for the Twelve. Finally, if Paul is dependent on tradition it may be that these lists have no functional significance as he uses them in 1 Cor 15:5–8. If a functional significance is to be found one should look to 1 Cor 15:11: "Whether then it was I or they, so we preach and so you believed." Whatever differences may have existed between Paul and the others, whether Christ appeared to them first or last, is irrelevant since they all preach the same gospel. By underscoring this harmony in the apostolic preaching Paul wishes to show the absurdity of the party rivalries and tendency toward division present in the Corinthian church.

3. 2 Corinthians. Although there are no specific references to Peter in 2 Corinthians, there are, nevertheless, some scholars who detect indirect references in this probably composite letter. In 10:7 Paul argues: "If someone is confident that he is Christ's, let him remind himself that we are Christ's as much as he is." Again in 11:4–5: "If someone comes who proclaims another Jesus, not the Jesus whom we proclaim [. . .] you submit to it readily enough. But I think that I am not least inferior to these superlative apostles." According to the interpretation under consideration, this "someone" is Peter and it is he who is causing the difficulties in Corinth. Thus it is necessary for Paul to refute him in sharp and polemical language. This view is usually rejected because it is based on a speculative identification of vague references in 2 Corinthians and because it runs counter to the neutral, if not favorable, interpretion of Peter in 1 Corinthians.

B. Book of Acts

This review of Peter in the NT attempts to follow a chronological sequence with the exception of the books of Acts. There are two primary reasons for departing from chronological order: first, the book of Acts describes activities of Peter roughly contemporaneous with those mentioned by Paul; and second, even though Acts is "volume two" of Luke's portrait of primitive Christianity, to have discussed Acts after Luke's gospel would effectively break the sequence of reviewing the portrait of Peter in all four gospels. However, this treatment of Acts after the Pauline letters does not suggest that Acts is a consistently reliable historical source of the events Luke describes. Luke is a theologian who shapes early traditions for his literary purposes. One of the chief problems in the study of Acts is the discrimination between Lukan redaction and Lukan sources. Even more difficult is to move behind both source and redaction to the historical level. Despite these problems an attempt will be made to describe both Luke's understanding of Peter and, where possible, that of the sources used by Luke.

The following functions of Peter (Luke prefers the name "Peter," using "Simon" in Acts only in 10:5, 18, 32, and "Cephas" not at all) are brought to prominence in Acts: (1) Peter is first mentioned in the post-resurrectional list of the Eleven in Acts 1:13; (2) Peter guides the process leading to the election of Matthias to fill the place left vacant by Judas (Acts 1:15–26); (3) Peter is a preacher both within the Jerusalem church and as a missionary to those outside (Acts 2:14–36; 3:12–26; 4:8–12; 5:29–32; 10:34–43); (4) Peter is a miracle worker and, as in the case of Paul, some of these miracles resemble those of Jesus as presented in the gospels (Acts 3:1–10; 5:1–11, 15; 9:32–42); (5) Peter is the object of miraculous divine care and receives visionary or heavenly guidance (Acts 5:17–21; 10:9–48; 12:6–11); and (6) Peter is a spokesman for the Jerusalem community (Acts 8:14–25; 11:1–18 [where Paul has to defend the actions described in the previous text to the entire community]; 15:7–11).

Three significant matters in Acts need to examined more closely. The first of these is Acts 10:1–11:18 which discusses the issue of Peter and the conversion of the gentiles. The problem in this text is twofold: (1) How much of this account is historical and how much is the result of Luke's theological program? (2) What is the relationship of Peter's apparent precedence in, if indeed not his inauguration of, the gentile mission to Paul's statement in Gal 2:7–8 that he, Paul, had been entrusted with the gospel to the uncircumcised?

With regard to the first difficulty, two explanations are possible. First, that Peter's conversion of the Roman centurion Cornelius at Caesarea Maritima is a historical fact incorporated by Luke into a theological context and that this incident was then recalled at the Jerusalem conference where the issue of Paul's large-scale conversion of gentiles was the subject of discussion. A second explanation is that the entire scene is a creation of Lukan theology, viz., that the mission to the gentiles had to have the approval of the Twelve and that Peter's action serves as the legitimation of the decision recounted in Acts 15 that the gentiles did not need to be circumcised. Common to both views is that the editorial hand of Luke is evident in this text and that God intended salvation to be extended to the gentiles (10:18) through Peter's conversion of Cornelius. Not unimportant is that Paul's first missionary journey only takes place after this event.

The second difficulty with this text is its relationship to Gal 2:7–8. How does Peter's conversion of Cornelius and his statement in Acts 15:7, "God made choice among you that by my mouth the gentiles should hear the word of the gospel and believe," relate to the conclusion found in Gal 2:7 that "Peter had been entrusted with the gospel to the circumcised." One resolution is to acknowledge a contradiction. Another would be to note that Gal 2:9 does not contrast Peter and Paul on a one-to-one basis, but rather each is part of a larger mission team; this suggests a more complicated missionary pattern. One also needs to take into account the fact that Luke prefaces and modifies the Petrine inauguration of the gentile mission by describing that there were missionaries to the gentiles before either Paul or Peter and that Luke records in Acts 8 the missionary activity of Philip among the Samaritans and Philip's baptism of an Ethiopian eunuch, as well as the fact that in Acts 10:2 it is emphasized that Cornelius was "a devout man who feared God." Thus, as a "God-fearer" he was already positively inclined toward Judaism and an observant of some Jewish practices. This last view would suggest that Peter's missionary relationship to gentiles might be different from that of Paul insofar as it does not involve the conversion of large numbers of gentiles who had no previous attachment to Judaism.

The second significant matter which needs to be examined is the relationship of Peter to the Jerusalem church. In Acts 8:14, 9:32, and 15:6–7, 22–23, Peter and the Jerusalem apostles are mentioned at significant points in the development of the Christian missionary strategy. Who is supervising this development? Peter? The Jerusalem church? If the latter, who is in charge? A review of the evidence in Acts would suggest the following possible models of church leadership involving Jerusalem:

(1) Peter and the other members of the Twelve were involved with a Christian missionary strategy far more extensive than just Jerusalem. Peter was not a local church leader, and once the Jerusalem church grew to the point of requiring consistent administrative leadership this role was assumed by James, the brother of the Lord. He continued in Jerusalem even after Peter and the others were no longer present either because of missionary journeys or death. The authority of James extended only to the Jerusalem church; however, he was more widely known because of his relationship to Jesus. Paul's regard for James would

have been for him as a local church leader and his primary loyalty would have been to the Jerusalem church as a whole because of its historical priority as the "mother church."

(2) Although Peter was widely known because of his relationship with the ministry of Jesus, he was essentially a local church leader in Jerusalem. At some latter point James took Peter's place as the leader of the Jerusalem church. Neither had a role as leader in the churches beyond Jerusalem.

(3) Peter was a leader in the universal church centered in Jerusalem. This position of universal leadership, with the exception of his apostleship, was transferred at some latter point to James.

Whichever hypothesis one finds most convincing, each seems to support the thesis that Galatians 2 suggests a shift in leadership (however narrowly or widely one may wish to define this) from Peter to James. As one turns to Acts 15 this understanding of Galatians 2 also gains support: there one observes that Peter speaks first (15:7–11) and that the final persuasive words are spoken by James (15:12–31).

The third and last significant area that needs to be reviewed is the important chapter dealing with Peter and the gathering in Jerusalem, Acts 15. The problems as well as the proposed solutions are myriad. The issue which calls forth the gathering of the apostles and elders is the assertion by certain persons from Judea who insisted that "Unless you are circumcised according to the custom of Moses, you cannot be saved" (15:1). In partial agreement with the position outline in Gal 2:7–9, Peter, James, the apostles and the elders take a stand for freedom, not requiring that gentile Christians be subject to circumcision and the whole law, "It has seemed good to the Holy Spirit and to us to lay upon you no greater burden than these necessary things" (15:28). Even though Luke stresses the theme of "accord" *(homthymadon)* in 15:25, there are differences in the position of Peter and James. While Peter recommended to the "council" no circumcision or law based on the precedent of his conversion of Cornelius, James urges a few regulations to be observed by the gentiles. Not only did James concede less than Peter did on this issue, the apostles and elders followed James in their decision to enforce these regulations in a letter to those "who are of the gentiles in Antioch and Syria and Cilicia" (15:23). Thus in Luke's presentation all play a decisive role: Peter through his witness; James in his judgment; and, the apostles and elders in their letter of enforcement.

One of the difficulties in using chap. 15 as a straightforward historical account of the events is one we have encountered earlier: the difficulty in determining what belongs to Luke's sources and what results from his redaction of earlier materials. A few illustrations will suggest the complexity of the issue. If one accepts the dominant scholarly view that Acts 15 corresponds to the events described by Paul in Gal 2:1–10, how should one understand the four regulations of Acts 15:20–29 (abstention from the pollution of idols, from unchastity, from what is strangled, and from blood) which are not mentioned by Paul. Further, how could Paul dispute with Peter at Antioch (Gal 2:11–14) if these regulations had been sent to the church at Antioch with Paul and Barnabas? Such inconsistencies between the two accounts lead many scholars to question the historical reliability of the Lukan portrait and even whether such a letter was ever sent by the Jerusalem gathering. It is likely that Luke had at his disposal a tradition that the Jerusalem leaders together with Paul had reached an agreement and a tradition that from an early period gentiles in mixed Christian communities had to observe certain Jewish regulations concerning impurity so that fellowship might exist with the Jewish Christians.

Although what has just been outlined represents a position frequently found in the literature, there are many alternatives. One such alternative, by way of example, would take seriously the redactional creativity of Luke while asserting the essentially reliability of the underlaying historical data. It suggests that Acts 15 conflates two Jerusalem meetings: the one is represented by Peter's address in Acts 15:6–11 and that this coheres with Paul's description in Gal 2:1–10; the other meeting took place later and was provoked by controversies about meals jointly shared by gentile and Jewish Christians. An example of such an argument can be found in Gal 2:11–14. As a result of such unrest, James and the Jerusalem church issued the four regulations described in Acts 15:20 and 29. Paul was not present at this second meeting and he may, therefore, not have known of these regulations or, perhaps, they were addressed only to that area for which the Jerusalem church had jurisdiction. By placing the confrontation between Paul and Peter prior to this second meeting, a number of the tensions between Acts 15 and Galatians 2 are resolved.

The fact that there are no further references to Peter in the book of Acts, which for the historian is regrettable, is due to Luke's primary interest in portraying the missionary advance of the early church. Luke's literary plan moves from Jerusalem and from Peter (Acts 1–15) to the gentile churches of Asia Minor/Greece/Rome and to Paul (Acts 16–28). This author is also concerned to show the links between the late 1st-century churches and the early period. Thus Acts begins in Jerusalem with the twelve apostles (Acts 2:37), with particular emphasis on Peter and John, continues on with "the apostles and the elders" (Acts 15:6, 22; 16:4) and finally to "James and all the elders" (Acts 21:18). For the purposes of his theological perspective, it is Paul who is the key figure in this latter period, and it is he who is the missionary successor to Peter—the one who had played such a dominant role in the foundational period of the early church in Jerusalem.

C. Gospel of Mark

Most contemporary NT scholars assert that Mark was the first gospel written and that Matthew and Luke used it as a source. Further, it is almost universally held that the Gospels are multidimensional, viz., they contain various levels of tradition: (1) materials and redaction stemming from the gospel writer; (2) written or oral pre-gospel sources and traditions; and, (3) material that is derived from the historical Jesus. Although it is not always possible to distinguish these levels with great certainty, the attempt is necessary and is bound to affect not only one's understanding of Mark's intention and theology but also Mark's interpretation of the role of Peter. For example, is Mark pro-Petrine, and anti-Petrine, both, or neither? In accepting these presuppositions of the historical-critical method, contemporary scholarship places little value on Papias' statement that Mark was "Peter's interpreter" and that he was dependent on Peter's testimony.

In Mark 3:16 the evangelist refers to "Simon whom he surnamed Peter." Thereafter Peter is the dominant name (eighteen times) for this disciple with only one reference to "Simon" thereafter (14:37; prior to 3:16 also in 1:16, 29, 30, 36).

The following general picture of Peter emerges in Mark's gospel: Simon and his brother Andrew were fishermen on the Sea of Galilee where Jesus called them as his first disciples to follow him and become fishers of men (1:16–18). At the house of Simon and Andrew in Capernaum, Jesus healed Simon's mother-in-law (1:29–31). Following additional healings in Capernaum, Simon, together with others, report to Jesus that people were seeking him (1:35–38). Of the Twelve appointed by Jesus the first of these in the list of their names is Simon "whom he surnamed Peter" (3:14–16). When Jesus revived the ruler's daughter he permitted only Peter, James, and John to follow him. This is the first of three traditional scenes (cf. 9:2–13 and 13:3–8) involving an "inner group" of three disciples (but in 13:3–8 Andrew is also included in this group) among the Twelve (5:37). Peter's confession on the way to Caesarea Philippi that Jesus is the "Messiah" and Jesus' subsequent rebuke of Peter referring to him as "Satan" (8:27–33). The transfiguration of Jesus before Peter, James, and John. Peter "did not know what to say" and offered to make 3 booths for Jesus, Moses, and Elijah (9:2–13). Peter, somewhat perplexed, responds to Jesus, "Lo, we have left everything and followed you," to which Jesus responds with a word of promise concerning this life and the age to come (10:28–30). As Peter and the others pass by the fig tree which Jesus had cursed on the previous day (11:12–14) he remarks, "Master, look! The fig tree which you cursed has withered" (11:21). Peter, James, John, and Andrew ask Jesus privately when the temple buildings would be destroyed, a question which gives occasion to Jesus' apocalyptic discourse (13:3–8). Despite Peter's assertions to the contrary, Jesus predicted that Peter would deny him three times that very night (14:27–31). At Gethsemane, Jesus took Peter, James, and John and shared with them his great distress. Asking them to remain and watch, he went further to pray. Upon his return he found them sleeping and said to Peter, "Simon, are you asleep? Could you not watch one hour?" Twice again Jesus leaves only to return to a similar situation (14:32–42). Following Jesus' arrest, Peter followed him at a distance into the courtyard of the high priest. Having denied Jesus three times prior to the cock crowing a second time, Peter remembered Jesus' prediction and broke down and wept (14:54–72). A young man dressed in a white robe sitting on the right side of the tomb where Jesus had been laid, announces to the women who had come to anoint him, "But go, tell his disciples and Peter that he is going before you to Galilee; there you will see him, as he told you" (16:7).

1. Peter's Confession of Jesus as Messiah (8:27–33). The question of the historicity of this pericope is a difficult one and the opinions of scholars vary. Unfortunately, since Matthew and Luke are dependent on Mark, these gospels do not assist in evaluating this question. Some have noted a general sequential parallel between this Markan account and John 6:66–71 and have suggested that Mark may have altered and adopted a pre-Markan tradition, especially at 8:27b.

If Peter did in fact make a confession that Jesus was Messiah he probably understood that term in a way consonant with that of intertestamental Judaism, viz., as the anointed king of the House of David who would come and deliver Israel from its enemies and establish a world empire characterized by peace and justice. That some understood Jesus' role in such a regal way is confirmed by his crucifixion as a would-be Messiah king.

Jesus' charge to his disciples not to tell anyone about him (8:30) and the prediction that the Son of Man must suffer, be killed, and be raised after three days (8:31) is generally thought to stem from Markan redaction although, especially with regard to the latter, it is quite possible that Mark was drawing upon an earlier tradition concerning the passion of Jesus. Further, there is much agreement that Peter's refusal to accept the suffering of the Son of Man, Jesus' rebuke of Peter (8:32–33), and the unfavorable reaction of Peter to Jesus, all in their present wording and location stem from the hand of the evangelist. However, Jesus' rebuke of Peter in 8:33, "Get behind me, Satan! For you are not on the side of God, but of men," may well be a traditional saying which contains a historical reminiscence. In such an understanding, Peter's misguided confession and Jesus' rebuke suggest a picture of Peter marked by bungling enthusiasm.

This pericope and the general portrait of Peter outlined above raise the question of Mark's intention. Is his picture of Peter essentially a negative or a positive one? At several points Peter serves as a spokesman for others, and there are three scenes where he appears with James and John as constituting an "inner group." And yet, there are other scenes in which Peter is portrayed as the embodiment of the disciples failure, as for example in 14:50 where all the disciples forsake Jesus and flee but only Peter's denial is singled out and underscored. Is Mark hostile to Peter and does he seek to highlight his failings? Or, is Mark emphasizing the prominence of Peter in order to rehabilitate his memory and counter attacks made by a larger anti-Petrine movement? One popular view suggests that Mark's gospel is an effort to counteract a *theios aner* christology in Mark's community. In this effort the disciples are portrayed as holding the view that Jesus was predominantly a miracle-worker. Mark has Jesus correct this view by insisting on a theology of suffering. According to this understanding of Mark's theology, Peter is presented by the evangelist as the spokesman of an erroneous christology. This later view of Mark's theological intention would see Mark 8:27–33 as a classic example of Peter's role as a spokesman for an erroneous christology which must be rejected. However, there are other scholars who would understand Mark's insertion of 8:31 not as a rejection of Peter's confession but as a corrective through the addition of the theme of suffering. Peter's confession is inadequate and must be corrected in this way. Thus, Jesus does not rebuke Peter for his confession of him as Messiah but for tempting Jesus with an understanding of messiahship that does not recognize the suffering and death of Jesus.

2. A Post-Resurrectional Message to Peter (16:7). A young man sitting in the tomb speaks to the women: "But go, tell his disciples and Peter that he is going before you to Galilee; there you will see him, as he told you." This verse is paralleled in both Matthew and Luke, although only Mark explicitly refers to Peter. Such a reference to Peter can be interpreted either positively or negatively depending on one's understanding of Mark's overall intention. If, as many scholars agree, 16:7 is a redactional insert (note the tension between verses 7 and 8: in v 7 the women are told to go to the disciples and Peter with a message and according to v 8 they said nothing to anyone), it is possible that this verse allows for a post-resurrectional appearance and even the fact that Mark was aware of a tradition that the risen Jesus had appeared first to Peter (according to this interpretation Mark means, "Tell the disciples, *especially* Peter"). Obviously such an interpretation would present Peter in a most positive light: he was one of the most important witnesses of the risen Jesus. However, there are those scholars who insist that 16:7 refers not to a post-resurrectional appearance but to the parousia. Since such appearances are linked with a *theios aner* christology Mark wishes to counteract such traditions with an emphasis on the parousia in Galilee when his disciples will Jesus return as the Son of Man. Such a perspective would interpret this specific reference to Peter negatively: Mark is attempting to discredit the tradition that Jesus had appeared to Peter by emphasizing that they all will see Jesus when the parousia occurs—"Go tell the disciples, *even* Peter . . ." Once again it is evident that one's understanding of Markan theology as a whole influences one's interpretation of specific pericopes.

D. Gospel of Matthew

Matthew's unique contribution to the image of Peter in the NT can be found particularly in three passages: Peter walking on the water, sinking, and being rescued by Jesus (14:28–31); Peter's confession of Jesus as Messiah and the Son of the living God and Jesus' response in the form of a blessing and promise concerning the church (16:16b–19); and Peter's question about paying the temple tax (17:24–27).

Since Matthew is dependent on Mark, most of the Petrine scenes and pericopes found there also appear in Matthew, sometimes with insignificant variations. For example, where Mark in 1:35–38, 5:37, 11:12–14, 13:3ff., and 16:7 includes a specific reference to Peter, it is omitted in Matthew. This apparent "lessening" of Peter's importance is balanced by Matthew's insertion of "first" *(prōtos)* before Matthew's name in the list of the Twelve (10:2) and the introduction of Peter in Matt 15:15 and 18:21–22, for which there are, respectively, Markan and Lukan parallels, and thus to be attributed to Matthean redaction.

Before analyzing in greater detail the three passages where Matthew makes his most important contribution, one should note that all three of these pericopes are found in the context of Matthew's fourth book (13:53–18:35), a section which reveals particularly Matthew's ecclesiastical concerns. It is in this book, for example, where the only two occurrences (Matt 16:18; 18:17) of the word *ekklēsia* (church) appear in the four gospels, and thus it is likely that we shall gain insight into Matthew's perspective about the role of Peter in the 1st-century church from these texts.

1. Jesus Rescues Peter (14:28–31). Matthew modifies Mark 6:45–52 (for example, the omission of Jesus' intention of passing by the disciples) and adds the material now found in Matt 14:28–31. As a result, there is a more positive picture of the disciples. The Markan scene ends with words of amazement: "for they did not understand about the loaves, but their hearts were hardened." Following Jesus' rescue of Peter, both get into the boat and those in the boat worship Jesus saying, "Truly, you are [the] Son of God." Since there are no parallels for the Matthean material the question of source and historical value are difficult to evaluate. Certain similarities can be noted with the scene in John 21:7–8 where Peter rushes from the boat to Jesus who stands on the shore of the Sea of Tiberias. There one finds the same basic pattern of leaving the boat in a context of hesitation concerning the identity of Jesus and the confession of Jesus as "Lord." The suggestion that we may have here a post-resurrectional appearance (modified and retrojected by Matthew back to a point in the life of the historical Jesus) is a plausible one: the theme of Peter as a man of little faith who sinks and has to be saved by Jesus coheres well with an appearance of the risen Jesus to Peter following his denial.

In this scene Peter is portrayed as a disciple who has genuine love for Jesus as he desires to go to him but also as one who has an insufficient faith during Jesus' earthly ministry. When this tension is not held together, widely differing interpretations as to Matthew's view of Peter can be given. If only the latter is stressed, then one might be inclined to stress Peter as a man "of little faith," as one possessed by a presumptuous and misguided enthusiasm. If only the first element is stressed, it results in interpretations which view this pericope as illustrating the primacy of Peter. Perhaps more nuanced would be the view that Peter is indeed given a prominence among the disciples; certainly he had an insufficient faith, but at least there was the first glimmering of faith. Although Peter is weak, he begins to see with the help of Jesus, and although Peter sinks, Jesus rescues him. While there is an element of typical discipleship portrayed in this scene, there is also a singular emphasis on Peter; since Peter will soon be declared the rock on which the church is to be built, it becomes important for Matthew's congregation to know that Jesus saves Peter even when he begins to sink. Before leaving this pericope, one should also note that, contrary to Mark, the *disciples* confess Jesus as "Son of God." In the structure of Matthew's gospel this confession anticipates virtually the same confession that Peter will make in Matt 16:16b and for which Jesus praises him.

2. Peter's Confession and Jesus' Promise (16:16b–19). Matthew has preserved all the key elements of the Markan account and has expanded it at two points: first, in addition to confessing Jesus as Messiah, Peter also confesses him to be "the Son of the living God" (Matt 16:16b); and second, following this confession Matthew has inserted three verses (16:17–19) in which Jesus calls Simon blessed and calls him Peter, promises that his church which will be built on this rock (Peter?; see below) and that the powers of death shall not prevail against it, and the promise is made that the keys of the kingdom shall be given to Peter. Also, Matthew expands the rebuke of Peter in Mark, "Get behind me, Satan!", by adding: "You are a stumbling block for me" (16:23). Because of the complexity of this entire pericope, it is best to analyze it in several parts.

a. *Peter's confession of Jesus as "the Son of the living God"* (16:16b). In Matthew, as opposed to Mark, there is no suggestion that Peter misunderstands the title Messiah, for Jesus himself praises it (16:17) as a result of divine revelation. As we noted, this confession is expanded to include one of the most exalted titles for Jesus in the NT, "Son of God." It is frequently coupled with the title Messiah in the NT as, for example, in John 20:31: "That you may believe that Jesus is the Messiah, the Son of God." The Johannine context is certainly post-resurrectional and belongs to an appearance of the Risen Jesus to Peter. It could be argued that in Matthew 16 we have a combination of two different Petrine confessions: one located in the earthly ministry of Jesus and one located in the post-resurrectional context. This view gains some support from our previous analysis of the confession of Jesus as "Son of God" in Matt 14:33, a scene which, together with Jesus' promise to Peter that he would be the rock on which the church would be built (Matt 16:18) and the giving of the power of binding and loosing (Matt 16:19) may also be post-resurrectional in origin. Thus, while Matthew does not say that Peter was the first among the Twelve to see the risen Jesus (as some interpret Mark 16:7), much of Matthew's special material about Peter appears to have had as its original context a post-resurrectional setting.

The combination of these two confessions into one scene result in the alteration of Peter's role over against the Markan portrayal. Not only is he the spokesman for the disciples but he is the recipient of a revelation that is not shared with the other disciples. For Matthew, Peter's confession is no longer the turning point in the gospel: His messianic origins have been the subject of reflection from the very beginning of this gospel (1:1, cf. 9:27; 12:23 and 15:22) and all the disciples confessed him as Son of God in 14:33. Although Peter's confession no longer has a chronological priority in Matthew, it will be given an ecclesiastic priority in the words that follow.

b. *"And Jesus answered him, 'Blessed are you, Simon Bar-Jonah! For flesh and blood has not revealed (this) to you, but my Father who is in heaven'"* (16:17). This verse adds strength to the suggestion that we may be dealing with an originally post-resurrectional context. The clause, "*flesh and blood* has not revealed [*apokalyptein*] this to you" is remarkably similar to Paul's description of his experience with the resurrected Jesus in Gal 1:16: when God "was pleased to reveal [*apokalyptein*] his Son to me [. . .] I did not confer with *flesh and blood*." Both Matthew and Galatians contrast a revelation from God with mere human information ("flesh and blood"). In all likelihood neither is dependent on the other; more probably, both have taken up a traditional way of describing post-resurrectional appearances.

Although Matthew received such a post-resurrectional tradition there are some signs of Matthean redactional elements. "Father who is in heaven" is found in Matthew's version of the Lord's Prayer (Matt 6:9) whereas Luke has the almost certainly more original "Father" (Luke 11:2). The macarism "Blessed are you" is not used by Mark and is found in Matthew's gospel 13 times. However, the fact that it is used in Luke, which may suggest that this represents a "Q" pattern, and that it is part of a post-resurrectional scene in John 20:29 might suggest that it comes from Jesus himself.

c. *"And I tell you, you are Peter; and on this rock I will build my church, and the gates of Hades shall not prevail against it"* (16:18). The argument for a pre-Matthean origin for the basic material contained in this verse is strengthened by the recognition of an Aramaic substratum lying behind Matthew's Greek. In Aramaic the Greek play on the word "Peter" is marked by an identity: "You are *Kepha* and upon this *kepha* I will build my church." Further, the Semitisms, "gates of Hades" (interpreted by the RSV as the "powers of death") as well as "flesh and blood" and "bind and loose," all suggest that 16:17–19 originated in an Aramaic-speaking environment.

The setting of this verse is in all probability post-resurrectional. While one should not exclude the possibility that Jesus might have thought of building *a church* in the sense of organizing a people in preparation for the imminent end, the reference to the "gates of Hades" not prevailing over the church does seem to suggest a permanence which would go beyond the supposed intentions of the earthly Jesus. The intentions expressed here cohere more closely with those post-resurrectional appearances described previously as "church-founding."

The identity of "the rock" is an important exegetical question. In view of the Aramaic identity of *Kepha/kepha* there can be no doubt that the rock on which the church is to be built is Peter. Even though there is a slight difference between *Petros/petra* in the Greek text of Matthew, most scholars today would hold that this same identity between the rock and Peter is also the intention of Matthew. However, other views are possible. One such view found in the Church Fathers (e.g., Origen, Ambrose, Chrysostom) and advocated by some today is that *petra* is not Peter himself but Peter when he confessed and "thinks the things of God" (16:23).

If indeed Peter is to be the rock on which the church is to be founded, how does this relate to the image of Peter as the "stumbling block" *(skandaion)* (16:23) for Jesus, an image which represents a sharpening of the Markan form of Jesus' rebuke. Although the issues are complex, one commonly held view would suggest that in response to Peter's confession "You are the Messiah" (16:16) he is given a name which will signify his *future* role as the rock on which the church will be built, a role which according to Matthew's presentation Peter would assume after the resurrection. Further, in response to misunderstanding the necessity of Jesus' suffering, Peter is referred to as a stumbling block for Jesus, as one advocating human rather than divine values. It is the same kind of weakness which Peter will display in his final denial of Jesus, a denial from which Jesus will have to save him so that he can play the role of the foundation rock.

d. *The passage that relates Peter to the "power of the keys"* (16:19) *reads as follows:*

(a) "I will give you the keys to the kingdom of heaven.
(b) Whatever you bind on earth shall be bound in heaven;
(c) whatever you loose on earth shall be loosed in heaven."

This division of v 19 not only demonstrates the parallelism between parts (b) and (c), but also raises the question about the relationship of parts (a) to (b) and (c). In other words is "the power of the keys" defined by that which follows so that they are identical or is the reference to the "keys" a reference to a more general authority of which only a part is further specified in (b) and (c)? A further difficulty is the relationship of these verses in Matthew 61 to those found in Matt 18:18. Is the power of binding and loosing given to Peter the same in *all* its aspects to that which is given to the disciples in general in Matt 18:18? If the power is the same, then it would follow that all the disciples, not just Peter, received an identical power of the keys.

Much of the uncertainty involved in answering these questions would be removed if one could with certainty define the significance of the reference to the "power of the keys." Some have suggested that the background is that of Isa 2:15–25 where Eliakim is installed as the new prime minister of King Hezekiah and on whose shoulder God places "the key of David; he shall open [. . .] and he shall shut." The prime minister is given the power to allow or refuse entrance to the palace, that is, access to the king. Matthew, then, would be portraying Peter in a similar way and also giving to him a broad power of the keys, viz., allowing or refusing entrance into the kingdom. One part of this broader power would be the specification of binding and loosing, but others might include baptismal and post-baptismal discipline, excommunication, legislative powers, and the power of governing. Other interpretations are possible and one of these would assert that the power of the keys originally referred to the authority to forgive sins through baptism and that this authority was then at a later time reinterpreted in terms of the rabbinic pattern of binding and loosing.

What exactly is meant by the power to bind and loose? These two verbs in combination are found in at least two different contexts in rabbinic literature. Most often they are used in the sense of imposing or removing an obligation by an authoritative decision. These verbs are also used in the sense of imposing or lifting a ban of excommunication. Which meaning is intended in Matt 16:19 and 18:18? Are the meanings identical or are they being used in different ways? A key issue is to what extent 16:19 gives Peter a responsibility that is distinguished from that given to the other disciples. Some have understood Matt 16:19 as representing the first usage; Peter seen as a chief rabbi issuing binding rules in contrast to "the teaching of the Pharisees and Sadducees" (16:12), and Matt 18:18 as representing the second usage. Such a view presupposes Matthew's congregation as one which had recently emerged from within Judaism and is now in tension with it. Since other understandings of Matthew's situation are possible, other solutions to the above questions can be offered. And yet when all of these options are reviewed one can conclude that, while for Matthew Peter does function as a model of discipleship in general, Matthew does give him a prominence that the others do not receive. See also KEYS OF THE KINGDOM; BINDING AND LOOSING.

3. The Temple Tax (17:24–27). Matthew interrupts the Markan sequence he is using and inserts this unique Petrine scene. The collectors of the half-shekel tax (the didrachma) ask Peter, "Does your [in the plural; Peter representing the disciples?] teacher not pay the tax?" Peter answers in the affirmative and then in the house Jesus, addressing him as Simon, asks from whom earthly kings collect their toll and tribute. Following Peter's response "From others," Jesus concludes that the sons, therefore, are free of such tolls. In order not to give offense "to them" Peter is to go fishing and give "to them" the shekel which he will find in the mouth of the fish.

The central issue in this pericope is whether the Temple tax is to be paid. Which tax is meant? That by which every male Jew above 19 years of age had to pay, a half-shekel yearly for the maintenance of the temple prior to its destruction in A.D. 70? Or, the *fiscus iudaicus,* a poll tax imposed on the Jews after A.D. 70 for the support of the temple of Jupiter Capitolinus? Even if 17:25b–26 goes back to the historical Jesus (note, for example, the reference to "Simon" as in 16:17), which is possible, no clear answer can be given for Matthew's redaction of this traditional saying, although it is likely that he may have been addressing this later development *(fiscus iudaicus).* At both levels, viz., during the ministry of Jesus and Matthew's redactional level, Peter is able to give the correct answer because Jesus showed him the way. Even if the pre-Matthean elements of this passage can no longer be described with complete accuracy, it is certain that for Matthew's community Peter exercises a teaching authority in the name of Jesus, an authority already ascribed to him in Matt 16:18–19. Not only in terms of this pericope but for Matthew's presentation of Peter as a whole, it can be said that he extends Peter's preeminence from the ministry of Jesus into the church situation which Matthew addresses. As in 15:15 (Jewish food regulations) and 18:21–22 (forgiveness), so here it is Peter who poses a problem facing the Christian community.

E. Gospel of Luke

As in the case of Matthew, this gospel was written toward the end of the 1st century and used Mark, Q, and some other special material as sources. That this author wrote not only the gospel but Acts as well must be kept in mind as one considers the Lukan portrait of Peter in the gospel.

One has in Luke's gospel a portrait of Peter written about the same time as Matthew's, but directed to a Christian community in a different location and context. In general it is possible to make this generalization: Luke is interested in presenting a positive picture of Peter and he effects several changes in his sources to achieve this purpose. Some examples of this intent would include Luke's omission in 9:18–21 of any reference that Peter refuses to accept Jesus' prediction about the suffering of the Son of Man and to Jesus' rebuke of Peter (Mark 8:31–33). In Mark 13:3, Peter, James, John and Andrew ask a question which could be understood as a misunderstanding on their part, viz., when will the Temple be destroyed. In Luke 21:7 this question is asked by an anonymous "they." This Lukan tendency to omit or reduce all that is blameworthy in the life of Peter is also evident in the passion narrative. The prediction of Peter's denials (Mark 14:29–31) is prefaced in Luke's account by Jesus' prayer that Simon's faith will not fail and that he will turn again and strengthen his brethren (Luke 22:31–32). Also Peter is not referred to by name in the Gethsemane scene and therefore does not receive any special blame from Jesus for sleeping as is the case in Mark 14:32–42. The denials of Jesus in Mark (14:66–72) are softened by the Lukan Peter. Not only is the intensity of these denials reduced, it is only in the Lukan account that one reads, "The Lord turned and looked at Peter," an *implicit* reproach that causes Peter to weep bitterly (Luke 22:62).

This positive Lukan view of Peter both prepares the way for his second volume, the Acts of the Apostles, and allows the image of Peter to be enhanced even further in Acts. In Mark 14:12–17 and Matt 26:17–20, it is the "disciples" who prepare the Passover meal; in Luke 22:8 it is "Peter and John" who are asked to prepare this meal for Jesus and his disciples. Not only does Luke give Peter a prominent and praiseworthy role in Acts, often, in the early chapters of Acts, this is carried out in association with John (Acts 3:1–11; 4:13–22; 8:14).

Even though they are too numerous to describe in detail, one should be cognizant of numerous other, relatively minor, changes which Luke makes in his description of Peter when contrasted with Mark and Matthew. A few examples must suffice. Unlike Matthew, Luke 4:42–43 reproduces the scene found in Mark 1:35–38 (Simon searching for Jesus) but replacing the reference to Simon with "the people," probably because he had not yet been called to follow Jesus. In Luke the message of the young man to the women to the empty tomb (Mark 16:7, "Go, tell his disciples and Peter") is omitted and replaced with a tradition that the risen Jesus had appeared to Simon (24:34). In Luke 8:45 it is Peter who responds to the question, "Who was it that touched me?" in the healing account of Jairus' daughter, information not found in Mark or Matthew. Where in Matt 18:21 Matthew inserts the name Peter to identify the questioner, it is not found in Luke 17:4. On the contrary, in Luke 14:41, Luke inserts the name of Peter in identifying the questioner, whereas in Matt 24:44–45 no name is specified.

Three Petrine scenes found in Luke's gospel must be discussed in detail and it will be necessary to ask whether the striking consistency of the use of the name "Simon" in these scenes would suggest that they have come to Luke from pre-Lukan sources. These pericopes include the miraculous catch of fish, a scene which serves as the context for the call of Simon (5:1–11); Jesus' prayer at the Last Supper that Simon's faith will not fall but that he will turn and strengthen his brethren (22:31–32); and the tradition that the risen Lord appeared to Simon (22:34).

1. The Call of Simon (5:1–11). The call of the first disciples in Mark (1:16–20) and Matthew (4:18–22) is straightforward and to the point: "Follow me and I will make you become fishers of men;" they respond by leaving their nets and following him. The story before us in Luke 5 is considerably more detailed. What is Luke's source for this information? Does he have a source independent of Mark and Matthew or has he added to the call of the disciples another narrative about Peter and a miraculous catch of fish? There are a number of awkward elements in the account of Luke 5:1–11—the transitions between Peter's response, the belated identification of James and John, Jesus' subsequent address only to Simon, as well as the fact that the response "Depart from me" would be more appropriate on land—which suggest that it originally belonged to a setting other than that of the call of the first disciples.

There are some striking similarities between this Lukan scene and the account of Simon Peter's catch of fish in John 21:1–13. Among these many similarities, one should not overlook the identical use of the name "Simon Peter" in both accounts. Although this combination of names is used more frequently by John than any other NT writer, it is found only here in Luke. These similarities have led many scholars to conclude that both Luke and John are using a common source independently of one another and that this source recounted the story as a post-resurrectional appearance as is the case in John 21. If the suggestion of a post-resurrectional context is valid, one finds Luke employing a literary technique similar to the one used by Matthew in 16:16b–19: the retrojection of post-resurrectional material into the ministry of Jesus.

Only in Luke 5:10 do we find these words of promise by Jesus to Simon: "Do not be afraid; henceforth you will be catching men." This redactional intention of Luke is preparing for the prominent role that Simon will have among the disciples in Acts. Thus, it is evident that Peter's missionary endeavors related in Acts are rooted in the pre-Easter intention of Jesus where these endeavors are always grounded in the power of Jesus which alone allows the sinful Simon to become a fisher of men.

2. Jesus' Prayer for Simon's Faith (22:31–32). Not only are these words absent from Mark and Matthew, the entire context leading up to Peter's denial (Luke 22:54ff.) is different in Luke's account. The Lukan tendency to deemphasize the weakness of the disciples is evident in these verses in which their falling away is only obliquely hinted.

In order to deal with the question of the origin of these words, we need to look at them more closely: "(31) Simon, Simon, behold, Satan demanded you [pl.] to sift like wheat. (32) But I have prayed for you [sing.] that your [sing.] faith may not fail. And you [sing.], when you [sing.] have turned again, strengthen your [sing.] brothers."

That part of this text addressed to Simon in the second person singular ("Simon, Simon [. . .] I have prayed for you that your faith may not fail") is likely to be pre-Lukan. This proposal is strengthened by the double use of "Simon" which contrasts with the prediction of *Peter's* denials which follow. As the use of "to strengthen" suggests, this pre-Lukan source was modified by Luke and then incorporated into the present context where Luke may be following a source independent of Matthew and Luke. This would help one make sense of the awkward plural-to-singular shift which occurs here.

At the level of Lukan redaction Simon is part of the larger apostolic group (the pl. "you") whom Satan demanded so that he might sift them like wheat. For Luke the disciples are also subject to temptation, and that includes Simon. Although there is no Lukan equivalent to Mark 8:33 ("He rebuked Peter and said, 'Get behind me Satan' "), there is the implication of some kind of failure in the words "turning again" and in the denials themselves. Since the phrase "turning again" precedes the period of Peter's denial of Jesus, it is likely that Luke intends that through Jesus' prayer the lack of faith implicit in the denials would not become a permanent failure and that his faith would be revived following the resurrection.

Jesus also prays that when Simon had turned again that he would strengthen his brothers. Since Luke has never referred to a failure of such magnitude that their faith needed to be restored, it is not probable that this is the intended reference. To be preferred is that interpretation which understands "brothers" in the broader sense of strengthening the *larger Christian community* through his missionary preaching. Such activity is described in Acts and Acts 15:32 may serve as an example: "Judas and Silas, who were themselves prophets, exhorted the *brothers* . . . and *strengthened* them." Thus in Luke 22:31–32 the author is preparing for Peter's missionary career and role as the leading spokesman for the faith of the Jerusalem Church as portrayed in the first fifteen chapters of Acts. By calling special attention to Simon by the use of singular "you" one again observes (as was the case in Luke 5:1–11) how Luke wishes to prepare for Peter's post-resurrectional prominence as described in Acts.

3. The Lord's Appearance to Simon (24:34). When the two disciples to whom the Risen Jesus had appeared on the road to Emmaus (24:13–32) returned to Jerusalem, they immediately told the Eleven gathered there, "The Lord has been raised indeed and appeared to Simon" (24:34). There are several problems involved in Luke's presentation of all the appearances of the risen Lord on one day and it is therefore best to understand that this announcement to the Eleven originally belonged to a kerygmatic formula that Luke has placed awkwardly into the present context. This suggestion is supported by the use of the term "Simon" in 24:34, as opposed to the previous reference in 24:12 to Peter, and the fact that this formula in 24:34 from early Christian proclamation is remarkably similar to the one found in 1 Cor 15:4–5: "He was raised [. . .] and appeared to Cephas." Luke probably knew nothing more about the original setting of this announcement than the fact that it was the first appearance of the risen Jesus to a member of the Twelve. By inserting this piece of kerygmatic tradition, Luke is the only gospel writer to make explicit reference to a special appearance of the risen Jesus to Peter. Perhaps this was one more way in which Luke wished to prepare for Peter's post-resurrectional role. Thus, it is not by accident that Peter is the last of the Twelve to be referred to by name in the gospel and the first of the Twelve to be mentioned by name in Acts. If for Luke the Twelve are the link between the historical Jesus and the church, Peter is the most prominent example of such a link.

F. Gospel of John

The Fourth Gospel was written about the same time as the gospels of Matthew and Luke or perhaps slightly later. It was addressed to a community different from the communities addressed by the Synoptic Gospels and one familiar with a different gospel tradition. Characteristic of this divergent tradition is its emphasis on a certain unknown "disciple whom Jesus loved" (John 19:35; 21:24). Given the current state of the scholarly discussion, it is impossible to establish with any certainty that John's gospel was dependent on the synoptic tradition. It is possible, however, that this writer may have drawn upon sources independent of even the pre-synoptic sources. As a result there are a number of important scenes involving Peter that are unique to the gospel of John, such as the footwashing scene (13:6–11) and Simon's cutting off the ear of the servant of the high priest at the time of Jesus' arrest (18:10–11). While not frequent, there are several references to Peter in the Fourth Gospel which parallel those found in the synoptics: Simon Peter is called a disciple; his name is changed from Simon to Cephas (1:42); he confesses Jesus, serving as a type of spokesman for the Twelve (6:67–69); Jesus predicts his denial (13:36–38); and he denies Jesus three times (18:17–18, 25–27).

The material dealing with Peter in the gospel of John may be placed under the following headings: those passages where he appears without the Beloved Disciple; those where he appears with the Beloved Disciple; and the role of Simon Peter in John 21.

1. Peter Apart From the Beloved Disciple (John 1–20). There are six references to Simon Peter without mention of the Beloved Disciple. These include: (1) 1:40–42, Jesus meets Simon and indicates that he will be called Cephas; (2) 6:67–69, Simon Peter confesses Jesus as the Holy One of God; (3) 13:6–11, Jesus washes Simon Peter's feet; (4) 13:36–38, Jesus predicts Simon Peter's denials; (5) 18:10–11, Simon Peter cuts off the servant's ear in the garden; (6) 18:17–18, 25–27, Simon Peter denies Jesus three times.

The first two of these passages have certain parallels in the Synoptics. In the first of these (1:40–42) Jesus gives to Simon the name Peter. However, in the Johannine account it is Andrew who announces "We have found the Messiah," and it is he who leads his brother Simon to Jesus. Although Jesus' response, "So you are Simon, son of John? You shall be called Cephas (which means Peter)," has certain similarities with Matt 16:17–18—especially that the name change follows the confession of Jesus as the Messiah—here it is Andrew, not Peter, who has made the acknowledgment. In the second of these passages (6:67–69), it is Peter who was the one who spoke for the Twelve in confessing Jesus at a critical time. Important as this confession is in the Fourth Gospel, it does not play the decisive role it did in Mark's gospel, or in a different way in Matthew's gospel, primarily because Simon is portrayed as already having participated in a similar confession in 1:40–42. In John's gospel, Simon Peter is neither rebuked as in Mark and Matthew or praised as in Matthew. While cast in the role of spokesman for the Twelve, he is given no special prominence because of his confession of Jesus.

In John 13:6–11, the third Johannine passage to refer to Peter, he does not understand the significance of Jesus washing his feet and thus insists, "You shall never wash my feet." However, when Jesus points its necessity, Peter overreacts: "Lord, not my feet only, but also my hands and my head." While having no exact parallel in the Synoptic Gospels, this scene is consistent with the image of Peter as a somewhat impulsive figure who at times misunderstood the intention of Jesus.

This same impulsive tendency is found in the fifth scene, John 18:10–11. Only in John is Simon Peter identified as the swordsman who cut off the ear of the high priest's servant. Jesus' response to Peter, "Put your sword into its sheath; shall I not drink the cup which the Father has given me?" does appear to echo Peter's misunderstanding of Jesus as the suffering Son of Man following his confession at Caesarea Philippi and Jesus' subsequent reprimand (Mark 8:31–33; Matt 16:21–23).

The fourth and the sixth scenes both refer to Peter's denials of Jesus. In 13:36–38 the reference is the prediction of the denials and in 18:17–18, 25–27 to the three denials themselves. These references are substantially the same as those found in the synoptics. In John 13:36 there is indeed a word of Jesus to Simon Peter not found elsewhere: "Where I am going, you cannot follow me now, but you shall follow afterward." That the reference in John 21:18–19 to Peter's death has some connection to John 13:36 is evident. Either the writer of 13:36 had already known of Peter's death and made subtle reference to it or the connection may have been made by the redactor who wrote 21:18–19.

2. Peter and the Beloved Disciple (John 13–20). Unique to John's gospel is the relationship between the Beloved Disciple and Peter. Although there are many unanswered questions concerning the identity of the Beloved Disciple, it is reasonable to suggest that for this congregation he was a real person who had been a companion of Jesus and whose career was dramatized so that he could serve as a model for all believers. There are three pericopes which associate Simon Peter and the Beloved Disciple that deserve our special attention in John 13–20: (1) 13:23–26 at the Last Supper; (2) 18:15–16 in the courtyard of the high priest; (3) 20:2–10 at the empty tomb of Jesus.

The "disciple whom Jesus loved" appears for the first time in the setting of the Last Supper (13:23–26). In 13:23 he is "reclining on Jesus' bosom" (13:23), a reference, no doubt, to Jesus' affection for him. Simon Peter, at some distance from Jesus, must ask the Beloved Disciple what Jesus meant with regard to his statement that one of those eating at table with him would betray him. It is then in response to the Beloved Disciple's question that Jesus answers by identifying the traitor. That Simon Peter has at least a secondary part in this story indicates that he too was an important figure in the community's memory of the career of the earthly Jesus. The texts which follow will confirm the importance of both these disciples while always giving the indication that it was the Beloved Disciple who was closest to Jesus.

In 18:15–16 there is reference to "another disciple" and to "the other disciple." That this refers to the Beloved Disciple is suggested by John 19:25–27 where he is the only male disciple who stands at the foot of the cross together with Jesus' mother. It is to him and not Simon Peter that the mother of Jesus is entrusted. Thus, the Beloved Disciple, in contrast to Peter, is held up as the faithful one, as the one who neither denied Jesus nor fled during the passion.

In John 20:2–10, Simon Peter and "the other disciple, the one whom Jesus loved," run to the tomb together. Although the Beloved Disciple arrives first, he waits for Peter to enter before him. When the Beloved Disciple finally enters after Peter, it is reported in 20:8 that he "saw and believed," a possible indication that for the Johannine community it was the Beloved Disciple who first came to resurrection faith, a thesis that is strengthened when John 21:7 is examined.

That the Beloved Disciple was a basic source of tradition for this community is obvious (19:35). Thus he had to be depicted as one close to the events surrounding Jesus. Yet at the same time this community also knew that it was impossible to tell the Jesus story without reference to Peter. While the Beloved Disciple was of enormous internal importance to the Johannine church, Peter was essential to an accurate transmission of the Jesus tradition.

3. Peter and the Beloved Disciple in John 21. Although John 21 is usually considered to be an addition by a later hand to the materials collected in John 1–20, that ought not to suggest that it might not contain traditions older than that found in the preceding chapters. Since the entire chapter is constructed around the twin figures of the Beloved Disciple and Simon Peter, it will be well to subdivide this chapter into three small units: (1) the appearance of the risen Jesus and the miraculous catch of fish (21:1–14); (2) the risen Jesus instructing Simon to feed his sheep (21:15–17); and (3) Jesus referring to the destinies of Simon Peter and the Beloved Disciple (21:18–23).

Where the story about the miraculous catch of fish in John 21:1–14 is most markedly different from the similar account in Luke 5 is in the contrast between the Beloved Disciple and Peter. Although both see a stranger on the shore, it is the Beloved Disciple who recognizes that it is the Lord and who then relays this information to Peter. As in 20:8 and elsewhere in John's gospel, Peter is important to the story, but it is the Beloved Disciple who is most closely attuned to Jesus and the events surrounding him. Also consistent with 18:10–11 where Peter rushes to defend Jesus with a sword is Peter's impetuosity in jumping from the boat to rush to Jesus.

Other changes between this Johannine account and the one reviewed previously in Luke 5 would include the fact that Simon is no longer portrayed as being alone in importance next to Jesus, but now he is in the midst of six other disciples. Nevertheless, Peter still is portrayed as having a prominent role: he takes the initiative to go out fishing; he jumps into the sea to go and meet Jesus; and he brings the nets from the boat to the shore. One would be able to say more about the symbolism involved if one could be sure that for John, as for Luke, this scene was also referring to future missionary work.

In 21:15–17 the Beloved Disciple is absent and full attention is given to Peter. The threefold question, "Simon, son of John, do you love me?" is often described as a rehabilitation of Peter following his threefold denial. Since the Beloved Disciple never denied Jesus he need not be rehabilitated.

Although some elements in 21:15–17 gain clarity from an examination of the shepherd imagery in John 10, a more immediate background to the threefold giving of pastoral authority to Simon may be an OT text such as Ezekiel 34 where the king is described as a shepherd and where the shepherd, in turn, is given enormous pastoral authority. Similarly, in John 21, Simon is given a pastoral authority rooted in love in which he is instructed to feed *Jesus'* sheep.

This scene may simply attest to Peter's rehabilitation or it may also reflect the fact that Simon Peter is increasingly being perceived by some circles in primitive Christianity as a symbol of pastoral authority. If the latter is indeed the case, then there are some partial parallels to Matt 16:18–19, although John 21 is more concerned to stress the theme of Peter's love and obligation to the sheep in contrast to Matthew's stronger emphasis on authority and legal imagery. Perhaps closest to 21:15–17 is a text which has yet to be discussed, 1 Peter 5:1–4. There, Peter addressing his fellow presbyters, urges: "Tend the flock of God that is in your charge, exercising oversight not by constraint but willingly [. . .] not as domineering over those in your charge but being examples to the flock. And when the Chief Shepherd is manifested, you will obtain the unfading crown of glory." Here the good shepherd language of John 10 is incorporated with the themes of an authority grounded in love and an obligation to the flock.

In John 10 it is stated that the good shepherd protects his sheep even if it means laying down his life for the sheep (10:11–18). The connection between John 10 and John 21 is strengthened by the fact that the command to feed the sheep is followed by the prediction that Peter will die by laying down his life for the sheep. The language used in 21:18–23 is reminiscent of martyrdom and the invitation of Jesus in 21:19, "Follow me," may well be an invitation to martyrdom.

In this scene (21:18–23) one notes both similarities and dissimilarities between Simon Peter and the Beloved Disciple. Both are witnesses but in quite different ways. It is only Simon Peter who receives the commission to be a shepherd, a commission that involves a willingness to die. Since Jesus willed the Beloved Disciple's witness, it is not inferior, but of a different type. He "remained" as Jesus desired, viz., he lived out a long life in the love of Jesus. The Johannine community realized that, as they could not narrate the details about Jesus of Nazareth without reference to Simon Peter, so too they could not recount the story of the Christian church without mention of Peter's important missionary and pastoral role. And yet the community made sure to place their model of discipleship, the Beloved Disciple, alongside Simon Peter and emphasized his primacy in love. For them such a manifestation of discipleship was just as authentic as that of the other traditional apostles.

G. The Petrine Epistles

1. The First Epistle of Peter. In order to discuss the role and function of Peter in this document, two items must be discussed: the origin and nature of the epistle; and the description of Peter as shepherd in 5:1–4.

Both the question of authorship and the destination of this epistle are significant for understanding the perspective of Peter presented in 1 Peter. Most NT scholars argue that 1 Peter is pseudonymous and written by someone invoking Peter's name, authority and memory; a likely dating would be late in the 1st century. Pseudonymity does not lessen the importance of this writing as a witness to Peter. If anything, it enhances its importance since it implies that some 20 or 30 years after his death Peter's name could still be thought to carry weight and be invoked to instruct Christian churches, especially if the area of Asia Minor (Pontus, Galatia, Cappadocia, Asia, and Bithynia) addressed is not Petrine territory. With regard to this latter point, it is impossible to judge with certitude whether Peter or his co-workers had missionized in this area, some of which had been evangelized by Paul. If this is not the case then 1 Peter would testify to the fact that Peter's authority extended to areas where other apostle's had worked and that one would hope to guide such churches by invoking Peter's name.

Another not unimportant issue is raised by the greetings in 5:13 from "the woman who dwells in Babylon" to these churches addressed in Asia Minor. Since "Babylon" is commonly understood to be a symbolic name for Rome it raises the question of Peter's relationship with Rome. Does this epistle attempt to exercise not only Petrine but also Roman influence over churches that may originally have been outside the orbit of Peter's influence? Not unimportant in evaluating this question is the evidence of *1 Clement*, a document of the 1st century, in which the Roman church writes to the church at Corinth, a church which had been founded by Paul.

In the description of Peter as shepherd in 5:1–4, Peter assumes the title of "fellow presbyter" and addresses the presbyters of the communities of Asia Minor. His authority is greater than simply being a "fellow presbyter" for in 1:1 his authority is defined as apostolic and in 5:1 he is identified as a "witness *(martys)* of the sufferings of Christ," a reference that may reflect knowledge that he died as a martyr *(martys)*.

The relationship between 1 Peter 5 and John 21 has already been touched on and it is quite possible that they are dependent on a common tradition related to the Province of Asia (for many the gospel of John is composed in Ephesus). This would explain the relationship between Peter's instruction to his fellow presbyters to "tend the flock of God" *(poimainein)* in 1 Peter and the fact that he had himself been charged to tend *(poimainein)* the sheep of Jesus. A similar reference to feeding *(poimainein)* is made in Acts 20:28 where Paul instructs the presbyters of Ephesus. Not only had the term "shepherd" taken on specific meaning for those who were presbyters in the churches of that area, but also for Peter who is being portrayed as the principal presbyter-shepherd.

2. The Second Epistle of Peter. The strong consensus among scholars is that 2 Peter is also pseudonymous and may well be the last NT book to be composed, perhaps in first decades of the 2d century. Peter is presented as an eyewitness authenticator of tradition about the historical Jesus (1:16–18) and as an authority who can correct misunderstandings of Paul (3:14–16). On the basis of the author's statement in 3:1 that this is "the second letter that I have written to you" one can assume that the same audience is intended although such a specific reference is absent.

The threat being addressed by this document is that of false teaching and moral confusion, a situation not dissimilar to that addressed in Acts 20:28–30. Peter is being presented as the guardian of the orthodox faith and serves to counteract the teachings of the false prophets (2:1). To their assertion that there will be no future coming of Jesus in glory (3:1–10), Peter is portrayed as an eyewitness, presumably of the Transfiguration, when Jesus received honor and glory from God the Father (1:17). Peter is in a strong position to refute their false assertions not only as one who saw the first coming of Jesus in glory, but also because he was one of those for whom the prophetic word was made more sure (1:19) and who had been given the authority to interpret prophecy and Scripture (1:20–21). Peter's apostolic authority does not stop here: he can even correct the false interpretations attributed to other apostles and particularly those ignorant and unstable persons who are twisting the letters of Paul (3:15–16) "to their own destruction." In offering such interpretations, 1 Peter has presented us with a Petrine teaching office not dissimilar to the one outlined in Matthew 16 and one to which there could be authoritative recourse in refuting the appeal of his opponents, probably some sort of gnostics, to the letters of Paul.

H. The Apocryphal Writings

This subject is one of several important areas which go beyond the scope of this essay. Others would include the role of Peter in the Apostolic Fathers and the archaeological evidence for the presence of Peter in Rome. With regard to the latter, while it is likely that Peter did get to Rome late in his career and was martyred and buried there, the exact results of recent excavations under St. Peter's Basilica in Rome continue to be debated. Nevertheless, a brief indication of the use of the Peter tradition in some of these apocryphal writings will be useful in understanding the variety of ways in which Peter was interpreted in gnostic circles and also as a background to the kind of problems being addressed in 2 Peter and elsewhere in the NT.

Several of the church fathers (Irenaeus, Hippolytus, Tertullian, and Origen) refer to strong anti-Petrine tendencies in the literature of various gnostic groups. In some cases (e.g., Carpocratians) this is the result of a denigration of the wider body of the apostles; in other cases it is due either to their elevation of Paul into a central position (e.g., Valentinians) or to their elevation of some lesser apostle (James, Thomas, Mary Magdalene) because he or she received a special revelation. Many of these anti-Peter tendencies reflect the gnostic-orthodox controversies of the period. In the *Gospel of Thomas* 51:18–25, for example, Peter appears to represent the orthodox objections against the role of women in the gnostic groups: "Let Mary leave us, for women are not worthy of life." Peter also represents these orthodox objections to the gnostic claim that certain of their model apostles had experienced a separate and unique vision of the Lord. Thus, groups that venerate Mary, James, and Thomas precisely because of such visionary experiences would tend to elevate the importance of their model over Peter or to polemicize against Peter. In the *Apocryphon of James,* James, not Peter, is consistently regarded as the apostolic leader in the early church. In fact, in the *Apocryphon of James* many of the items attributed to Peter in the NT are reformulated and now attributed to Peter. Thus in 13:39–14:1, Jesus' response to a question asked by Peter is given to James, "I have revealed myself to you, James." Similar tendencies can be found in the *Gospel of Thomas* and in the *Acts of Thomas.*

As a result of the discovery of the Nag Hammadi texts, it is now possible to point to at least three gnostic writings which are pro-Petrine: the *Acts of Peter and the Twelve Apostles,* the *Epistle of Peter to Philip,* and the *Apocalypse of Peter.* Whereas some of the gnostic writings radically alter Matt 16:16b–19 in a derogatory way, the *Acts of Peter* accepts and amplifies this high Matthean view of Peter and understands Peter as the unquestioned apostolic leader. In the *Epistle of Peter to Philip,* heavily dependent on Luke-Acts, the reinterpreted Peter speeches are understood to be models of gnostic teaching. Peter is the apostle who has true gnostic insight. The *Apocalypse of Peter* provides several visions experienced by Peter in which Jesus explains to him the true, gnostic teachings, especially with regard to the nature of Jesus. It is a docetic view of Jesus in which a literal crucifixion, preceded by Jesus' suffering, is denied. Here, too, Peter serves as the transmitter and guarantor of the authentic gnostic teaching and here, also, Matt 16:16b–19 is reinterpreted in a gnostic manner: "But you yourself, Peter, become perfect in accordance with your name with myself, the one who chose you, because from you I have established a base for the remnant whom I have summoned to knowledge" (*Apoc. Pet.* 71:15–21). These three Nag Hammadi documents confirm Basilides' description of a secret, gnostic, Petrine apostolic tradition in which Peter is viewed most positively. But since both the gnostic anti- and pro-Petrine tendencies present a view of Peter reconstructed through gnostic eyes, both tendencies would be rejected by such NT writings as 2 Peter.

Bibliography

Brown, R. E.; Donfried, K. P.; and Reumann, J., eds. 1973. *Peter in the New Testament.* Minneapolis.

Pesch, R. 1980. *Simon-Petrus.* Päpste und Papsttum 15. Stuttgart.

Smith, T. V. 1985. *Petrine Controversies in Early Christianity.* WUNT 2/15. Tübingen.

KARL P. DONFRIED

PETER AND PAUL, ACTS OF. The *Acts of Peter and Paul* is a 6th or 7th century Greek expansion of the Pseudo-Marcellus *Passion of Peter and Paul.* It survives in an Armenian translation as well. Elaborations of Paul's travels and martyrdom give Paul a role more nearly equal to that of Peter. The Jews in Rome convince Nero to order Paul's execution, but believers in Rome express their wish to have "the two great lights" united in their city. Dioscuros, the shipmaster who brought Paul from Gaudomelite to Syracuse, converts and accompanies him to Italy. Paul ordains a bishop when he stops in Messana. In Puteoli, Dioscurus is mistaken for Paul, since both are bald. He is seized and beheaded. The town later sinks into the sea. Paul, informed by a dream, corrects the behavior of the Roman bishop Juvenalias, who had been ordained by Peter. From the point of Paul's arrival in Rome, the story follows the longer version of the *Passion of Peter and Paul.* The discussion of circumcision does not appear. The story of Perpetua is inserted into Paul's martyrdom (cf. Plautilla in the Pseudo-Linus *Passion of Paul*). Perpetua, who is blind in one eye, gives her handkerchief to Paul as he is led out to execution. Immediately after the apostle's death, the cloth is returned to Perpetua and her eye is healed. These events led to the conversion of the soldiers who beheaded Paul. Perpetua and the soldiers are eventually martyred for their faith. See also PETER AND PAUL, PASSION OF.

Bibliography

Amann, E. 1928. Les Actes de Pierre. *DBSup* 1: 499.

Charlesworth, J. H. 1987. Greek Acts of Peter and Paul. Pp. 287–89 in *New Testament Apocrypha and Pseudepigrapha*. Metuchen, NJ.

Leloir, L. 1986. *Ecrits apocryphes sur les apotres*. CChr Series Apocryphorum 3. Turnhout.

Lipsius, R. A. 1891. Pp. 178–222 in *Acta apostolorum apocrypha*. Vol. 1/1. Leipzig. Repr. Darmstadt 1959.

Walker, A. 1951. Acts of the Holy Apostles Peter and Paul. *ANF* 8: 477–86.

ROBERT F. STOOPS, JR.

PETER AND PAUL, PASSION OF. The *Passion of Peter and Paul,* an account of the martyrdoms of the two apostles which circulated under the name of Peter's follower Marcellus, survives in two forms. The longer version is extant in Greek, Latin, and Slavonic. Composed perhaps in the 6th century, it is based loosely on the *Acts of Peter,* but shows knowledge of the Pseudo-Clementine Romances and the *Acts of Paul* as well. One early manuscript incorporates material from Pseudo-Hegesippus, *De excidio Hierosolymae* 3.2 (Migne, *PL* 15.2169–71). The longer version was used in the *Acts of Peter and Paul.* The briefer version of the *Passion of Peter and Paul* is a 6th or 7th century compilation of Latin sources. It deletes most of the speeches and the letter of Pilate, but adds narrative details. In both versions Paul's role is minor compared to Peter's.

The longer text of the *Passion of Peter and Paul* begins with Paul's return to Rome from Spain. Jews who have opposed Peter's gentile mission seek Paul's help but find that the two apostles agree in their teaching. Simon Magus, who claims to be the Christ, takes advantage of the disturbance to appeal to Nero against the apostles. Simon has demonstrated his divinity by appearing alive three days after an illusory decapitation (cf. *Martyrdom of Paul* 4). When Peter and Paul come before Nero to dispute with Simon, they produce the *Letter of Pilate to Claudius.* Peter demonstrates his ability to read minds by secretly blessing bread. When Simon sends a large dog against him (cf. *Acts Pet.* 7), Peter displays the bread causing the dog to disappear. Simon is silenced in a debate concerning circumcision. To prove his divinity, Simon promises to fly from a tower (cf. *Acts Pet.* 32). At the prayers of Peter and Paul, the demons supporting Simon drop him to his death.

The apostles are condemned by Nero for having caused Simon's death. The prefect Agrippa (Clement in some mss) suggests appropriate modes of execution. Paul is beheaded on the road to Ostia. Peter is hung upside down from a cross. From that position he reports the *Quo vadis* story. Strange men appear from Jerusalem to help Marcellus bury Peter's body on the Vatican hill. Nero is forced to flee the city and dies in the desert. Finally, men from the E attempt to steal the bodies of the apostles. The relics are given temporary burial on the road to Ostia. Thus, the *Passion of Peter and Paul* authenticates the various cult sites for the apostles which had been used in Rome from the mid-3d century.

In the shorter version of the *Passion of Peter and Paul,* the two apostles arrive in Rome together. They lodge there with relatives of Pilate, believers who first bring the apostles to the attention of Nero. Other additions, drawn from the *Acts of Peter* by way of Pseudo-Hegesippus, include the resurrection of a young man, Nero's anger over Simon's death, the *Quo vadis* scene in its proper place, and the placing of Simon's death in Aricia. The apostles are sentenced by Clement rather than Agrippa. The deaths of the apostles are not described, so neither Peter's speeches at the cross nor the disposition of the relics is reported.

Bibliography

Amann, E. 1928. Les Actes de Pierre. *DBSup* 1: 499.

Charlesworth, J. 1987. Peter, Passions of Peter and Paul. Pp. 329–30 in *New Testament Apocrypha and Pseudepigrapha.* Metuchen, NJ.

Cullmann, O. 1962. *Peter: Disciple, Apostle, Martyr.* Philadelphia.

Lipsius, R. A. 1883–90. Pp. 207–17, 284–366 in *Apokryphe Apostelgeschichten und Apostellegenden.* Brauschweig. Vol. 2/1. Repr. Amsterdam 1976.

———. 1891. Pp. 118–77, 223–34 in *Acta apostolorum apocrypha.* Vol. 1/1. Leipzig.

Vouaux, L. 1922. *Les actes de Pierre, introduction, textes, traduction et commentaire.* Paris.

Walker, A. 1951. Acts of the Holy Apostles Peter and Paul. *ANF* 8: 478–865.

ROBERT F. STOOPS, JR.

PETER AND THE TWELVE APOSTLES, THE ACTS OF (NHC VI,*1*). This tractate is the first in the miscellaneous collection of Sahidic Coptic tractates comprising Nag Hammadi Codex VI. For all its brevity (12 pages) it is a remarkably complex document. The first half consists mainly of an account, with heavy allegorical overtones, about a pearl merchant who attracts the poor but is shunned by the rich, and who turns out not to have the pearl he is hawking; it is available only to those willing to journey to his city. The pearl merchant's name is Lithargoel, which means, according to the text, a lightweight, glistening stone (5.16–18) (Wilson and Parrott 215 n.). The account takes place in an island city identified simply as "Habitation" (the Coptic for which may be a translation of the Greek word meaning "inhabited world").

The observer of all this is Peter, who, with the other disciples, was brought to the city by an apparently chance wind (1.26–28) shortly after setting sail to begin what seems to be the post-resurrection apostolic ministry (relevant details at the beginning of the tractate are missing due to lacunae).

The transition between the first and second half of the tractate is briefly interrupted by Peter's vision of the waves and high walls that surround the city. An old man (angelic interpreter?) interprets it in such a way that the city is seen as a symbol of the community of the faithful who have to endure in this world in order to enter the kingdom of heaven (6.27–7.19).

The remainder of the tractate recounts the dangerous journey of Peter and the other disciples to Lithargoel's city and their meeting with a physician, who subsequently reveals himself as Christ (9.8–15), and still later makes it clear indirectly that he is also Lithargoel (10.8–13). The disciples are instructed about undertaking a ministry of healing in the city from which they had just come. Christ ends with a warning against the wealthy in the church.

Evidence of editorial activity abounds (Krause 1972; Wilson and Parrott 1979) and leads to the conclusion that *Acts Pet. 12 Apost.* is a composite, the earliest level of which was probably the allegory of the pearl merchant Lithargoel. It may be that the story was originally about a god who bore that name (Krause 1972: 51), but in the absence of evidence of a Lithargoel cult in antiquity, it seems better to assume that the name was originally created as a cover name for Christ within the context of the allegory.

Although it has been identified as gnostic (Perkins 1980: 127), there is in fact nothing within the tractate that compels that conclusion, and, furthermore, it stands within a codex that has a number of tractates that are clearly not gnostic. It seems likely, however, that the tractate could have been used by gnostics. The allegory may well have had a Jewish Christian origin. That is suggested by the name Lithargoel, which has the form of Jewish angel names, the attraction of the poor (alone) to the pearl merchant (the Jewish Christians called themselves Ebionites, or the Poor), and the similarity of the allegory to some found in the Jewish-Christian *Herm. Sim.* The discourse of Christ and the disciples, which assumes a ministry within a church made up of both rich and poor (10.1–7; 12.8–13), may well have been added by an orthodox editor, who felt the church was becoming too worldly. The material in which Christ is identified as a physician may reflect the effort of Christians to counter the widespread attraction of the cult of Asclepius.

The earliest portion of the tractate—the allegory—probably should be dated no later than the middle of the 2d century, because of the affinity with *Herm. Sim.*, which is dated in the mid-century or before. The tractate as a whole, then, may have been put together in its present form toward the end of the 2d century, or early in the 3d.

It has been suggested that *Acts Pet. 12 Apost.* might have been part of the lost first third of the apocryphal *Acts of Peter* and perhaps even its introductory section (Krause 1972). Both share encratite characteristics and there are some connections to be made with *Act of Peter* in Papyrus Berolinensis 8502 (BG). On the other hand, the encratism of *Acts Pet. 12 Apost.* lacks the sexual element found in *Acts of Peter,* and the connections with *Act of Peter* do not clearly lead to the conclusion of a prior literary relationship; moreover, there are significant reasons for thinking they were not connected (e.g., *Act of Peter* is set in Jerusalem, which was also the setting of the first part of *Acts of Peter; Acts of Pet. 12 Apost.* is not). It seems best to think of *Acts Pet. 12 Apost.* as one of the independent narratives about the apostles that began to appear in the 2d century.

Bibliography

Haas, Y. 1981. L'exigence du renoncement au monde dans *les Actes de Pierre et des Douze Apôtres, les Apophtegmes des Pères du Désert, et la Pistis Sophia.* Pp. 296–303 in *Colloque international sur les textes de Nag Hammadi,* ed. B. Barc. Québec.

Krause, M. 1972. Die Petrusakten in Codex VI von Nag Hammadi. Pp. 36–58 in *Essays on the Nag Hammadi Texts in Honour of Alexander Böhlig,* ed. M. Krause. Leiden.

Krause, M., and Labib, P. 1971. *Gnostische und hermetische Schriften aus Codex II und Codex VI.* Gluckstadt.

Perkins, P. 1980. *The Gnostic Dialogue: The Early Church and the Crisis of Gnosticism.* New York.

Schenke, H-M. 1973. Die Taten des Petrus und der zwölf Apostel. *TLZ* 98: 13–19.

Wilson, R. McL., and Parrott, D. M. 1979. Pp. 197–229 in *Nag Hammadi Codices V.2–5 and VI with Papyrus Berolinensis 8502.1 and 4.* ed. D. M. Parrott. Leiden.

Douglas M. Parrott

PETER TO PHILIP, LETTER OF (NHC VIII,*2*).

The *Letter of Peter to Philip* is the second and concluding tractate within Codex VIII of the Nag Hammadi library. Situated immediately after the long tractate *Zostrianos* (NHC VIII,*1*), *Ep. Pet. Phil.* fills most of the last nine pages of Codex VIII (132,10–140,27). The tractate opens with a superscribed title ("The letter of Peter which he sent to Philip," 132,10–11) that places the text within the tradition of letters ascribed to Peter (e.g., 1–2 Peter, and the *Epistula Petri* at the opening of the Pseudo-Clementines). *Ep. Pet. Phil.*, however, is not to be identified with any of the previously known letters attributed to Peter, and represents a newly discovered work in the Petrine corpus.

The body of *Ep. Pet. Phil.* may be divided into 2 major sections: the letter itself (132,12–133,8), and the account of the meetings of the apostles (133,8–140,27). The letter of Peter describes the separation of Philip and the need for a meeting of all the apostles. At 133,8 the letter concludes, and after the reference to the willing response of Philip to Peter, Philip disappears from the scene, and is only implicitly present as an anonymous member of the apostolic group assembled around Peter.

The balance of *Ep. Pet. Phil.* (133,8–140,27) provides an account of the apostolic gatherings, frequently in the form of a "dialogue" between the resurrected Christ and the apostles. Peter and the apostles come together for the first meeting on the Mount of Olives and offer prayers to the Father and the Son. The risen Christ appears as a light and voice, and the apostles raise several questions for Christ to answer. The voice from the light responds by discoursing on the deficiency of the aeons and the fullness (*plērōma*), and the detainment and struggle of the apostles. At the conclusion of this meeting the apostles return to Jerusalem, and on the way the discussion about the problem of suffering prompts a response by Peter as well as by the revelatory voice. After the apostles reach Jerusalem, they teach and heal, and Peter delivers an exemplary sermon. The apostles are filled with holy spirit and part in order to preach the gospel. Finally, Jesus appears again to commission the apostles, and the tractate closes with the apostles departing "into four words" (140,25; possibly the four gospels to be sent to the four directions).

As the contents of the tractate indicate, *Ep. Pet. Phil.* bases itself upon a variety of early Christian and gnostic traditions, and interprets these traditions in a Christian gnostic fashion. Thus, numerous parallels may be noted between the tractate and portions of the first (Petrine) section of the NT Acts of the Apostles (chaps. 1–12), including scenes, themes, and terms. The revelatory discourse on fullness (136,16–137,4) also resembles the hymn to the Logos in John 1:1–18, and the little "Pentecost" of *Ep. Pet. Phil.* (140,1[?]–13) recalls not only Acts 2 but also the Johannine "Pentecost" account (John 20:19–23). Further, the depiction of the resurrected Christ as a light and voice throughout the text represents a primitive means of describing glorious appearances of Christ in the NT and other early Christian literature (e.g., Mark 9:2–8 par.; 2 Pet 1:16–19; Acts 9:1–9; 22:4–11; 26:9–18; 1 Corinthians 15; Rev 1:12–16). Conversely, the discourse on the deficiency of the aeons (135,8–136,15) addresses specifically gnostic issues by providing an abbreviated myth of the mother (cf. Eve/Sophia) which shows no overtly Christian features whatsoever. This discourse, adopted as a revelatory discourse of the risen Christ, reflects a simple version of the myth, and is similar to the Sophia myth of the *Apocryphon of John* (NHC II,*1;* III,*1;* IV,*1;* Berlin Gnostic Codex 8502,*2*) and the Barbelognostics of Irenaeus (*Adv. haer.* 1.29.1–4).

On the basis of such traditions as these, *Ep. Pet. Phil.* proclaims its Christian gnostic message. The tractate legitimates its message by deriving it from Peter and the apostles and, ultimately, from Jesus. Now, the tractate maintains, the risen Christ must speak again as a light and voice in order to provide a renewed revelation of the Christian gnostic message. The tractate thus shows its concern that the apostles, and the Christian gnostic believers themselves, be empowered to act as "illuminators in the midst of mortal people" (137,8–9). They are to gather for worship and go forth to preach, "in the power of Jesus, in peace" (140,27).

The evidence of the tractate suggests that *Ep. Pet. Phil.* very likely was composed in Greek around the end of the 2d century C.E. or into the 3d, and was translated into Coptic some time thereafter. The Coptic dialect of the tractate resembles Sahidic to a considerable extent, although dialectical peculiarities, including forms traditionally called Subachmimic and Bohairic, are also to be found. See LANGUAGES (COPTIC). In addition to the Coptic text of *Ep. Pet. Phil.* from the Nag Hammadi library, another copy of the Coptic text is reported to have been found in a papyrus codex which is not yet published or available for study.

Bibliography

Bethge, H.-G. 1978. Der sogenannte "Brief des Petrus an Philippus". *TLZ* 103: 161–70.

———. 1984. "Der Brief des Petrus an Philippus": Ein neutestamentliches Apokryphon aus dem Fund von Nag Hammadi (NHC VIII,2). Diss. Humboldt-Universität, Berlin.

Koschorke, K. 1977. Eine gnostische Pfingstpredigt. *ZTK* 74: 323–43.

———. 1979. Eine gnostische Paraphrase des johanneischen Prologs: Zur Interpretation von "Epistula Petri ad Philippum" (NHC VIII,2) 136,16–137,4. *VC* 33: 383–92.

Luttikhuizen, G. P. 1978. The Letter of Peter to Philip and the New Testament. Pp. 96–102 in *Nag Hammadi and Gnosis*, ed. R. McL. Wilson. NHS 14. Leiden.

Ménard, J.-E. 1977. *La Lettre de Pierre à Philippe*. BCNHT 1. Quebec.

Meyer, M. W. 1981. *The Letter of Peter to Philip: Text, Translation, and Commentary*. SBLDS 53. Chico, CA.

Parrott, D. M. 1986. Gnostic and Orthodox Disciples in the Second and Third Centuries. Pp. 193–219 in *Nag Hammadi, Gnosticism, and Early Christianity*, ed. C. W. Hedrick and R. Hodgson. Peabody, MA.

Tröger, K. W. 1977. Doketistische Christologie in Nag-Hammadi-Texten. *Kairos* 19: 45–52.

Wisse, F., and Meyer, M. W. fc. The Letter of Peter to Philip. In *Nag Hammadi Codex VIII*. NHS, Coptic Gnostic Library. Leiden.

———. fc. The Letter of Peter to Philip. In *The Nag Hammadi Library in English*, ed. J. M. Robinson. 2d ed. San Francisco.

MARVIN W. MEYER

PETER, ACT OF. The apocryphal *Act of Peter* recounts the story of Peter's paralyzed virgin daughter for purposes of encratite edification. While elements of the story were previously known through secondary sources, the sole primary text came to light in 1896 with the purchase in Cairo of a Coptic papyrus codex (*P. Berol.* 8502). *Act Pet.* is the last of four tractates preserved in the codex, the other three of which are decidedly gnostic in character (*Gos. Mary, Ap. John,* and *Soph. Jes. Chr.*). *Act Pet.* itself contains no clearly gnostic theologumena (Parrott 1979: 475–76). The text, written in the Sahidic dialect with a few non-Sahidic forms, is generally well preserved (Parrott 1979: 473).

Act Pet. reports how, while Peter was healing the sick on the Sabbath, an individual asked him why he did not heal his own beautiful virgin daughter who lay paralyzed in a corner. Peter, to reveal the power of God, restores her body whole, and the crowd rejoices. He then commands her to return to the corner where her paralysis reafflicts her. The crowd weeps.

Peter explains why this is necessary. The girl, when young, was very beautiful. Her beauty tempted a certain Ptolemy, who saw her bathing with her mother. He abducted the girl when his offer of marriage was rejected. But before he could seal the relationship through intercourse, the girl was paralyzed in answer to Peter's prayers. Ptolemy returned the child with her virginity intact. Smitten with grief, he became blind and through a vision learned that God's vessels were not given for corruption and pollution.

When he narrated these events to Peter, Ptolemy's sight was restored. He died shortly thereafter, leaving a parcel of land to Peter's daughter for her support. Peter reports that he sold it and gave the proceeds to the poor, since God cares for his own. The story finished, Peter distributes bread to the crowd and then returns to his own home.

Act Pet. represents a single act in the genre of the Acts of the Apostles. It belongs to the beginning of the longer *Acts of Peter,* though the story is missing in the surviving witnesses (especially the Latin *Actus Vercellenses*) of the longer work (Schmidt 1903: 21–25; 1924: 321–48; Vouaux 1922: 35–38; Schneemelcher *NTApocr,* 269–70; Parrott 1979: 474–75; contra Ficker 1904: 402–3; 1924: 227–28). The content is encratite and serves to warn the reader of the dangers associated with sexuality. The fact that marriage and sexual relations are not explicitly denounced and that Peter remains married to his wife may suggest a less-pronounced encratism (Parrott 1979: 475). However, the idea that beauty entices sin and that paralysis serves as an appropriate defense of virginity underscores the author's view of human sexuality as corrupting and polluting of the body.

Act Pet. was in existence by the end of the 2d century when it appeared in the longer *Acts of Peter* (*NTApocr,* 275; Parrott 1979: 476). It is an important witness to a strong encratite or ascetic presence in early Christianity in general and within the Petrine tradition in particular.

Bibliography

Ficker, G. 1904. Petrusakten. Pp. 400–4 in *Handbuch zu den neutestamentlichen Apokryphen,* ed. E. Hennecke. Tübingen.

———. 1924. Actus Vercellenses. Pp. 226–30 in *Neutestamentliche Apokryphen.* Ed. E. Hennecke. 2d ed. Tübingen.

Krause, M. 1972. Die Petrusakten in Codex VI von Nag Hammadi. Pp. 36–58 in *Essays on the Nag Hammadi Texts in Honour of Alexander Böhlig,* ed. M. Krause. NHS 3. Leiden.

Parrott, D. M., and Brashler, J. B. 1977. The Act of Peter (BG 8502, 4). *NHL:* Pp. 475–77.

———. 1979. The Act of Peter. BG, 4: 128,1–141,7. Pp. 473–93 in *Nag Hammadi Codices 5. 2–5 and 6 with Papyrus Berolinensis 8502, 1 and 4.* NHS 11, ed. D. M. Parrott. Leiden.

Schmidt, C. 1903. *Die alten Petrusakten im zusammenhang der apokrypen Apostelliteratur nebst einem neuentdeckten Fragment.* Leipzig.

———. 1924. Studien zu den alten Petrusakten. *ZKG* 43: 321–48.

Till, W., and Schenke, H.-M. 1972. Die Praxis des Petrus. Pp. 8, 296–321, 333–34 in *Die gnostischen Schriften des koptischen Papyrus Berolinensis 8502 herausgegeben, übersetzt und bearbeitet von Walter C. Till,* ed. H.-M. Schenke. 2d. enl. ed. *TU* 60/2. Berlin.

Vouaux, L. 1922. *Les Actes de Pierre.* Paris.

JAMES E. GOEHRING

PETER, ACTS OF. One of the earliest of the apocryphal acts of the apostles, the *Acts of Peter* reports a miracle contest between Simon Magus and the apostle Peter in Rome. It concludes with Peter's martyrdom. The *Acts of Peter* was originally composed in Greek during the second half of the 2d century, probably in Asia Minor. The majority of the text has survived only in the Latin translation of the Vercelli manuscript. The concluding chapters are preserved separately as the *Martyrdom of Peter* in three Greek manuscripts and in Coptic (fragmentary), Syriac, Ethiopic, Arabic, Armenian and Slavonic versions. See PETER, MARTYRDOM OF.

The stichometry of Nicephoros indicates that roughly one-third of the original *Acts of Peter* has disappeared. Schmidt (1903) suggested that the missing portions recounted Peter's activities in Jerusalem, including Simon Magus's first confrontation with Peter and Paul (cf. *Acts of Peter* 23). The story of Eubula, now found in *Acts of Peter* 17, may have originally appeared in this section. Similarly, two episodes mentioned by Augustine (*Contra Adimantum* 17) probably belonged to this lost section: the story of Peter's daughter (partially preserved in the Berlin Coptic Codex), and the story of the gardener's daughter (summarized in the Pseudo-Titus Epistle). Krause's suggestion that the *Acts of Peter and the Twelve Apostles* from Nag Hammadi represents lost portions of the *Acts of Peter* has not won acceptance.

The surviving sections of the *Acts of Peter* describe the end of Paul's ministry in Rome and his departure for Spain. Soon thereafter, Simon Magus arrives in Rome, where he uses both wonders and arguments to seduce all but a handful of those who believe in Christ. To counter the works of Simon, Christ sends Peter from Jerusalem to Rome. Peter converts the ship's captain during the voyage. Once in Rome, Peter restores many to faith by preaching. Peter confronts Simon, using as intermediaries a dog and an infant, both of whom gain the powers of prophetic speech for the purpose. Marcellus, a senator who had been the patron of believers before he was misled by Simon, is restored to faith. He miraculously repairs a statue of the emperor which had been shattered during an exorcism (cf. Philost. *VA* 24).

Further visions, public miracles, and teaching from Peter lead up to a public contest with Simon. A brief debate about the identity of God and Christ precedes the contest of miracles during which Peter raises three men from the dead and exposes Simon's deceptions. When Chryse, a wealthy woman of the worst reputation, donates money to Peter in response to a vision, he takes it as a demonstration of Christ's ability to care for believers in material as well as spiritual matters. Simon tries to regain his influence by flying above the city of Rome, but he is brought down by Peter's prayer. Simon withdraws to Aricia, where he dies from the injuries suffered in his fall.

Peter's martyrdom follows. Agrippa, the prefect, is angered when his concubines decline his advances after hearing Peter preach on chastity. Xanthippe, wife of Albinus, is converted and withdraws from her husband's bed. The two men conspire to kill Peter. Peter is warned and persuaded to leave the city. At the city gate he encounters Christ entering Rome "to be crucified again." Peter recognizes his own destiny in these words and returns to be arrested. Peter asks to be crucified upside-down and explains the soteriological significance of that position in a lengthy speech from the cross. After his death, Peter appears to Marcellus to rebuke him for attending to the apostolic corpse. Meanwhile, Nero, angered at having missed the chance to torture Peter, begins to persecute the other believers. Nero is stopped by a vision, and peace comes to the faithful in Rome.

The *Acts of Peter* interweaves stories, mostly miracles, and teachings of diverse origins. It is less closely related to romance literature than are other early apocryphal acts of apostles. Travel plays a small role, because Peter is not portrayed as a wandering missionary but as the reestablisher of the Roman church. The theme of chastity is present but not dominant. Physical persecution is not important except in the martyrdom section; rather Simon is called a "persecutor" for uprooting Christians from their faith. The main concern of the *Acts of Peter* is the restoration and maintenance of faith in the face of competition from other cults. Simon is a composite figure representing a number of challenges to the faith of believers rather than a particular heresy. Each side competes for loyalty by claiming to offer superior benefits. The *Acts of Peter* shows great concern for the newly converted and the possibility of returning to the church after apostasy. Peter's falterings during the lifetime of Christ are repeatedly mentioned, as is Paul's initial role as a persecutor.

Lipsius's identification of the *Acts of Peter* as gnostic has been rejected. The theological stance represented in Peter's speeches and the stories is eclectic. The *Acts of Peter* affirms God's role as creator and the reality of Christ's sufferings. It stresses the polymorphism of Christ, a motif often associated with docetism, but used here to show that Christ takes on whatever form is necessary to aid those in need (Cartlidge). The *Acts of Peter* reflects the piety of popular Christianity rather than the thoughts of the theologians.

Research on the questions of sources, redaction, and genre continues (Poupon). Studies of the social world of the apocryphal acts have included the *Acts of Peter.* The stories concerned with chastity have been analyzed as reflections of the roles and concerns of Christian women (Davies 1980, and Burrus 1987). It has been suggested that patron/client relationships provided a model for both Christology and propaganda in the *Acts of Peter* (Stoops 1986).

The *Acts of Peter* mentions a written gospel and may have been intended to supplement the canonical Acts of the Apostles, although it does not agree with it in detail. The *Acts of Peter* is more clearly related to the *Acts of Paul,* although which text has priority is debated. The solution depends in part on whether the first three chapters dealing with Paul and the final chapter reporting the Neronian persecution belong to the original of the *Acts of Peter.* General similarities with the *Acts of John* have been noted, but literary dependence cannot be demonstrated.

The *Acts of Peter* was not widely circulated (Eus. *Hist. Eccl.* 3.3.2), perhaps because of its association with Manichaeism (cf. Augustine and *Manichean Psalm-book*). However, the *Acts of Peter* did serve as an important source for much of the later Petrine literature. The Pseudo-Clementine Romances show a general familiarity with the *Acts of Peter* and may be designed to fit into the period between Peter's activity in Jerusalem and his journey to Rome. The *Acts of Peter* follows the Clementine *Recognitions* in the Vercelli manuscript. The Martyrdom section was expanded in the Pseudo-Linus *Passion of Peter.* The *Acts of Peter* also lies behind alternative accounts of Peter's death in Pseudo-Hegesippus and in the Pseudo-Marcellus texts, the *Passion of Peter and Paul,* and *Acts of Peter and Paul.* The later currency of these secondary texts is shown by the *Apostolic History* of Pseudo-Abdias, which drew on them all in the late 6th or early 7th century.

Stories and speeches from the *Acts of Peter* were also incorporated into other works. Elements appear in the 3d century *Carmen apologeticum* of Commodian and perhaps in the *Didascalia.* In the 4th and 5th centuries, the *Life of Abercius* and *Acts of Philip* used the *Acts of Peter.* It was used again in the *Acts of Xanthippe and Polyxena,* the *Acts of Saints Nereus and Achilleus,* and in the Syriac *Teaching of Simon Cephas in Rome* and the *History of Simon Cephas in Rome.*

Bibliography

Amann, E. 1928. Les Actes de Pierre. *DBSup* 1: 496–501.

Burrus, V. 1987. *Chastity as Autonomy: Women in the Stories of the Apocryphal Acts of the Apostles.* Lewiston.

Cartlidge, D. 1986. Transfigurations of Metamorphosis Traditions in the Acts of John, Thomas, and Peter. *Semeia* 38: 53–66.

Charlesworth, J. 1987. Peter, Acts of; and Peter Cycle. Pp. 309–14 in *New Testament Apocrypha and Pseudepigrapha.* Metuchen, NJ.

Davies, S. 1980. *The Revolt of the Widows: The Social World of the Apocryphal Acts.* New York.

Ficker, G. 1903. *Die Petrusakten: Beiträge zu ihrem Verständnis.* Leipzig.

Flamion, J. 1909–11. Les actes apocryphes de Pierre. *RHE* 9: 233–54, 465–90; 10: 5–29, 215–77; 11: 5–28, 223–56, 447–70, 675–92; 12: 209–30, 437–50.

Grenfell, B., and Hunt, A. 1908. *Oxyrhyncus Papyri.* Egypt Exploration Fund 6: 6–12. London.

Krause, M. 1972. Die Petrusakten in Codex VI von nag Hammadi. Pp. 36–58 in *Essays on the nag Hammadi Texts in Honour of Alexander Bohlig,* ed. M. Krause. NHS 3. Leiden.

Lipsius, R. A. 1883–90. *Apokryphe Apostelgeschichten und Apostellegenden.* Brauschweig. Repr. Amsterdam 1976.

———. 1891. Pp. 45–103 in *Acta apostolorum apocrypha.* Vol. 1/1. Leipzig.

Plümacher, E. 1978. Apokryphe Apostelakten. *PWSup* 15: 19–24.

Poupon, G. 1988. Les 'Actes de Pierre' et leur remaniement. *ANRW* 25 6; 4363–82.

Schmidt, C. 1903. *Die alten Petrusakten im Zusammenhang der apokryphen Apostelliteratur, nebst einem neuentdeckten Fragment, untersucht.* TU 24/1. Darmstadt.

———. 1924–27. Studien zu den alten Petrusakten. *ZNW* 43: 321–48; 45: 481–513.

Stoops, R. 1986. Patronage in the *Acts of Peter. Semeia* 38: 91–100.

Turner, C. 1931. The Latin Acts of Peter. *JTS* 32: 119–33.

Vouaux, L. 1922. *Les acts de Pierre.* 1–214. Paris.

———. 1922. *Les actes de Pierre, introduction, textes, traduction et commentaire.* Paris.

ROBERT F. STOOPS, JR.

PETER, APOCALYPSE OF (NHC VII,*3*). This Gnostic tractate bears no relationship to two other apocryphal writings of the same name, the one partially preserved in Greek and fully in Ethiopic translation, the other extant only in Arabic. A complete copy of the Gnostic *Apoc. Pet.* in Sahidic Coptic is present in the Nag Hammadi Codex VII, pp. 70:13–84:14. There can be little doubt that the original was written in Greek. The title found at the beginning and end of the tractate preserves the Greek case endings and the many serious grammatical and syntactical problems suggest an incompetent translator (as in the case of NHC VI,*5; Plato Rep. 588b–589b*) rather than an inept Coptic author or major corruptions in the ms transmission. These philological problems seriously hinder the interpretation of the text.

Apoc. Pet. was appropriately named, for it confirms well to the literary genre of the apocalypse. The introductory section (70:14–72:17) places the two main characters, the Savior and Peter, in the temple, apparently shortly before the crucifixion, where they are threatened by the priests and the people. This leads to a vision (72:17–73:10) which, similar to the experience of Elisha's servant in 2 Kgdms 6:17, opens Peter's eyes to the truth about the opponents. This vision becomes the occasion for a lengthy discourse (73:10–81:3) in which the Savior reveals to Peter that there will be many who do appear to accept "our teaching" but who in reality oppose the truth. In 81:3–82:16 Peter receives another vision, or perhaps two, during which his eyes are opened for the true reality of the crucifixion. The vision is again followed by an explanatory revelation (82:17–83:15). The tractate closes by specifying those who are worthy to receive the revelation (83:15–84:13).

The generally gnostic character of *Apoc. Pet.* is evident from a radical dualism which distinguishes between two levels of reality which closely resemble each other but are opposites. The one is material, mortal and counterfeit; the other is spiritual, immortal and true. The teaching of *Apoc. Pet.* focuses on the implication of this dualistic worldview for ecclesiology and Christology. Thus in the Church there are those who have only mortal souls and who form an imitation sisterhood which stands over against the true brotherhood of the immortal ones. These false teachers, who follow the "Father of their error," are blind and deaf in that they are only able to recognize material reality. They are unaware that the one who died on the cross was only the physical Jesus and not the spiritual, living Christ. These blind Christians praise Christ in a *apokatastasis* (74:9) which probably refers to their belief in the restoration of the physical body of Jesus. There is a similar polemic against carnal resurrection in *The Testimony of Truth* (NHC IX,*3*, pp. 34:26–37:5). Another Nag Hammadi tractate, *The Second Treatise of the Great Seth* (NHC VII,*3*) joins *Apoc. Pet.* in its denial that the heavenly Christ was crucified and in portraying Christian opponents as an imitation church.

The polemic of the tractate is directed against several groups of Christians. The references, however, are so general or enigmatic that it is impossible to identify them with positions known from Patristic sources. The main opponents appear to be the bishops and deacons of the orthodox church (79:5f.). In spite of his heretical Christology, the author does not appear to speak from a sectarian viewpoint. He acts more as a champion of the "little ones" who are temporarily dominated by the counterfeit leaders, but who will eventually reject their rule (80:8–29).

As in the case of most other gnostic writings, it has not been possible to assign *Apoc. Pet.* to any of the sects described by the heresiologists. Most likely we are dealing with an idiosyncratic text and not with sectarian teaching. It is quite unnecessary to see *Apoc. Pet.* as a representative of a pro-Petrine form of Gnosticism. The figure of Peter was simply taken from the canonical literature which the author knew and accepted. On the basis of the late 4th century date of Codex VII and the nature of the polemic in *Apoc. Pet.*, one would guess that the Greek original was written not earlier than the 3d century and possibly as late the early 4th. Nothing in the tractate betrays the identity and provenance of the author.

Bibliography

Brashler, J., and Bullard, R. A. 1988. Apocalypse of Peter (VII,3). *NHL*, pp. 372–78.

Koschorke, K. 1978. *Die Polemik der Gnostiker gegen das kirchliche Christentum unter besonderer Berücksichtigung der Nag-Hammadi-Traktate "Apokalypse des Petrus" (NHC VII,3) und "Testimonium Veritatis" (NHC IX,3).* NHS 12. Leiden.

Krause, M. 1973. Die Petrusapokalypse. Vol. 2, pp. 152–79 in *Christentum am Roten Meer*, ed. G. Altheim and R. Stiehl. Berlin.

Schenke, H.-M. 1975. Bemerkungen zur Apokalypse des Petrus. Pp. 277–85 in *Essays on the Nag Hammadi Texts in Honour of Pahor Labib*, ed. M. Krause. NHS 6. Leiden.

Smith, T. V. 1985. *Petrine Controversies in Early Christianity. Attitudes Towards Peter in Christian Writings of the First Two Centuries.* WUNT 2. Reihe 15. Tübingen.

FREDERIK WISSE

PETER, FIRST EPISTLE OF.

PETER, FIRST EPISTLE OF. One of the so-called Catholic Epistles in the NT; written by, or in the name of, Peter the apostle to Christians of Pontus, Galatia, Cappadocia, Asia, and Bithynia.

A. Introduction
B. Ancient Reception and Modern Reassessment
C. Literary Genre and Integrity
D. Literary Relations and Traditional Sources
  1. NT Literary Affinities
  2. The Influence and Use of Common Tradition
E. Style, Vocabulary, and Composition
  1. Style
  2. Vocabulary
  3. Compositional Devices
F. The Transmitted Greek Text
G. Structure
H. The Addressees and Their Situation
  1. Geographical Location
  2. Social and Ethnic Composition
  3. Societal Status and Situation
I. Strategy
  1. Dignity and Status Conferred by God
  2. Demarcation from Non-Christian Outsiders
  3. Distinctive Holy Behavior
  4. Solidarity in Suffering
  5. Christian Community as the Household/Family of God
J. Date, Authorship, and Place of Composition
  1. Date
  2. Authorship and Provenance: A Petrine Group in Rome

A. Introduction

1 Peter is a letter of encouragement and exhortation written in the name of the apostle Peter during the latter third of the 1st century C.E. to Christian communities scattered throughout Asia Minor suffering as an oppressed minority in an alien society. Its eloquent articulation of the meaning of Christ's death and resurrection for Christian life in society, its rich use of common Christian tradition, its lofty expression of the divinely conferred dignity and responsibility of the elect and holy people of God, its courageous summons to brotherly solidarity and hope in the face of social hostility, and its moving pastoral tone gained for the letter rapid recognition in the early Church and an undisputed place in the biblical canon. Though figuring prominently in subsequent centuries of Christian theology and worship, questions raised by modern scholars regarding virtually all features of its composition, setting, and aim have made it a continuing "storm-centre of New Testament studies" (Neill 1964: 343).

B. Ancient Reception and Modern Reassessment

External attestation of 1 Peter was early and widespread. 2 Pet 3:1 may be among the earliest witnesses to its existence, though the precise letter implied is by no means certain. Numerous certain echoes of the letter, however, are contained in *1 Clement* (Lohse, in Talbert 1986: 53–55), Polycarp's letter to the Philippians (Bigg *Epistles of St. Peter and St. Jude*[2] ICC) and Justin Martyr (Bigg *Peter and Jude* ICC, 10). Irenaeus (*Haer.* 4.9.2; 16.5; 5.7.2) was the first to cite 1 Peter by name, followed by Tertullian (*Scorp.* 12), and Clement of Alexandria (*Str., Paed., Hypotyp.*). Known in Rome by the end of the first century (*1 Clement*) and recognized in both East and West in succeeding centuries, the letter was ranked by Eusebius in the fourth century among those canonical writings about which there was universal agreement (*Hist. Eccl.* 3.25.2). "There is no book in the New Testament which has earlier, better, or stronger attestation" (Bigg *Peter and Jude*[2] ICC, 7).

Centuries later in the Reformation era, it was 1 Peter along with the gospel of John and Paul's letter to the Romans, which Luther singled out as "the true kernel and marrow" of all the NT books. "For in them you . . . find depicted in masterly fashion how faith in Christ overcomes sin, death, and hell, and gives life, righteousness, and salvation" (*Prefaces to the New Testament,* 1522).

Such earlier enthusiasm has waned considerably since the advent of modern biblical criticism. Preoccupation with the Gospels and the historical Jesus, Paul, and supposed Petrine-Pauline polarities in the early Church has tended to reduce 1 Peter and other neglected NT writings to the status of exegetical step-children. Often arbitrarily assigned to the Pauline orbit of early Christianity, 1 Peter has been assessed as an inferior product of a "Paulinist," a dim and deficient reflection of the Pauline legacy. Within recent decades, however, the tide has begun to change. Studies of its source and redaction, specific passages with long histories of theological importance (2:4–10: Elliott 1966 and 1976: 250; 2:21–25: Osborne 1983; Elliott 1985; 3:18–4:6: Reicke 1946; Dalton 1989; Vogels 1976), and distinctive social ethic, have led to a renewed appreciation of this letter's witness to the struggle of the early Christian movement to maintain its mission and cohesion in the face of vigorous social opposition. Goppelt (*Der erste Petrusbrief* MeyerK, 179) is not alone in the judgment that "the First Epistle of Peter was the NT document that most vigorously united the witness of the word with the witness of Christian presence in society." (For research trends and literature since Reicke's 1964 AB commentary, see Beare 1970: 212–27; Schelkle *Petrusbriefe/Judasbrief* HKNT 13: 249–55; Elliott 1976, 1981; Goppelt *Petrusbrief* MeyerK; Brox 1978; Cothenet 1980; Sylva 1986. For an earlier survey, see Martin 1962.)

C. Literary Genre and Integrity

1 Peter bears all the essential characteristics of a conventional Greek letter. It opens with an epistolary salutation including the name of the chief sender, the apostle Peter (on Peter in the early Church see Cullmann 1958; O'Connor 1969; Brown et al. 1973), a description of the "elect" addressees and their location, and a greeting (1:1–2). Following the communication proper (1:3–5:11), it concludes with a commendation of its probable bearer, Silvanus, and the personal greetings of the co-senders, including Mark and an unnamed sister in the faith (5:12–14). The mention of specific names with only minimal introductory detail ("Peter, apostle of Jesus Christ," 1:1, cf. 5:1; "Silvanus, faithful brother," "Mark, my son," 5:12, 13) implies that the senders were known to the addressees and that the former counted on this personal familiarity to underscore the common bonds of experience and faith of which they wrote.

In contrast to the letters of Paul, 1 Peter was addressed to a much wider audience which was located not in a single city but throughout several Roman provinces of Asia Minor (1:1; cf. Jas 1:1). For this reason it is included among the "general" or "catholic" epistles of the NT (James, 1–2 Peter, 1–3 John, Jude) although it nevertheless remains a particular message for a particular audience facing a particular set of circumstances. Included in the address were two large provinces (Bithynia-Pontus and Cappodocia) with no record of Pauline activity. Thus 1 Peter was not directed to an exclusively "Pauline" mission area. The interior of the territory circumscribed in 1:1, moreover, was agricultural and grazing land, a predominantly rural and less urbanized area quite distinct from the urban centers which attracted Paul (Puig Tarrech 1980; Elliott 1981: 59–65). The size of the total area addressed, moreover, presupposes a substantial advance of the Christian mission beyond the limits reached by Paul. This strongly suggests that 1 Peter was written decades after the Pauline mission to communities some of which had little if any contact with Paul.

Although the *final* and present form of 1 Peter is that of a letter, its *original* components have been the subject of sustained debate (surveyed by Martin 1962; Dalton 1989: 62–71; Elliott 1966: 11–13; Kelly *Peter and Jude* HNTC, 15–20; Goppelt *Petrusbrief* MeyerK, 37–40). Beginning with the influential study of the German scholar Richard Perdelwitz in 1911, some commentators have suspected hints of the letter's composite character. Claiming a break in thought between 4:11 (doxology) and 4:12 (new address) and a shift in situation from potential (1:3–4:11) to actual (4:12–5:11) suffering, as well as a distinction between the "hortatory" nature of the former section with its focus on baptism and the "epistolary" character of the latter, these scholars have hypothesized that 1:3–4:11 originally constituted a "baptismal homily or discourse" addressed to newly baptized converts. This sermon was subsequently incorporated into a letter (1:1–2, 4:12–5:14) intended as a message of consolation for these converts when the suffering anticipated in the sermon had become a reality (Reicke *James, Peter, and Jude* AB; Beare 1970; and the scholars listed in Kümmel 1975: 419–20). Further elaborations of the composite theory and the assumed cultic setting of 1 Peter propose that the document consisted mainly of a baptismal liturgy (Windisch and Preisker *Katholischen Briefe* HNT, 156–61) or even the celebrant's part of a baptismal eucharist occurring on the Paschal vigil of Easter eve (Cross 1954).

On the whole, such theories based on the purported composite character of 1 Peter must be judged more imaginative than cogent. Externally, there is no manuscript evidence of 1 Peter in any other than in its present form; internally, the consistency and coherence of the letter demonstrate its epistolary integrity. In ch. 4, vv 11 and 12 mark not a sudden break but rather a transition in the line of thought, similar to the transition at 2:10/11. The actual suffering of the readers is presumed throughout the letter (1:6; 2:18–20; 3:9, 13–4:6, 12–19; 5:7–10). The frequent use of the verb *paschein* ("suffer," 12x) appears prompted not by liturgical recollection during the paschal (*pascha*) vigil but by the social experience of the readers. Mention of baptism (3:21) and its related imagery (rebirth, 1:3, 23; 2:2; sanctification, 1:2, 15–16, 22; 2:5, 9; 3:5, 15; Exodus and redemption, 1:13, 18–19) and exhortation (1:14–16, 22–23; 2:1–3; 4:1) indicates the use of common Christian liturgical, catechetical and hortatory material, but provides no clear evidence that the document itself or any segment thereof was a baptismal homily or liturgy. Moreover, comparable contemporary examples of Christian homilies or liturgies embodied in letters are completely lacking. Accordingly, the theory that 1 Peter is the result of the combination of independently composed parts is both improbable and unnecessary. The consistency and coherence of its language, style, arrangement and line of argumentation indicate that 1 Peter was, in its origin, an integral letter (Selwyn 1947; van Unnik *IDB* 3: 758–66; Dalton 1989; Kelly *Peter/Jude* HNTC; Goppelt *Petrusbrief;* Elliott *James, 1–2 Peter, Jude* ACNT; Shimada 1985; Brox *Erste Petrusbrief* EKKNT[2]).

D. Literary Relations and Traditional Sources

Relative to its length, 1 Peter has more affinities to more NT writings than any other NT document. Its apocalyptic perspective on the Christian social situation and the imminence of final divine judgment, its christological focus on suffering and its vindication, its stress on the distinctive corporate identity and responsibility conferred by baptismal conversion, its image of the Christian community as household of God, and the content of its moral exhortation link 1 Peter with a majority of the NT writings.

1. NT Literary Affinities. Particularly noteworthy are 1 Peter's affinities with Romans, Ephesians, the Pastorals, James, Hebrews, the Synoptic Gospels, and Acts (Forster's full listing [1913] is more useful than his analysis). In regard to the *Pauline and Deutero-Pauline writings,* compare 1 Pet 1:14–16 (Rom 12:2); 1:21 (Rom 4:24); 1:22, 3:8–9 (Rom 12:9–19); 2:4–10 (Rom 9:25, 32–33); 2:5 (Rom 12:1); 2:13–17 (Rom 13:1–7); 2:21 (Rom 4:12); 3:22 (Rom 8:34); 4:1 (Rom 6:7); 4:7–11, 14–16 (Rom 12:3–8, 13:8–10); 4:12–13, 5:1 (Rom 8:17); 1 Pet 1:3–12 (Eph 1:3–14, 3:2–6; cf. 2 Cor 1:3–11); 1:14–18, 4:2–3 (Eph 4:17–18, 5:8); 1:20 (Eph 1:4); 2:1 (Eph 4:25, 31); 2:4–6 (Eph 2:20–21); 3:1 (Eph 5:22); 3:22 (Eph 1:20–21); 5:8–9 (Eph 6:11–13); 1 Pet 1:3–5 (Titus 3:4–7); 2:1 (Titus 3:3); 2:9 (Titus 2:14); 2:13–3:7, 5:1–5 (1 Tim 2:8–15, 6:1–2; Titus 2:1–10, 3:1–2; cf. Eph 5:22–6:9, Col 3:18–4:1).

Beyond the Paulines, similarities with *James* include 1 Pet 1:1 (Jas 1:1); 1:6–7 (Jas 1:2–3. cf. Wis 3:5–6); 1:23–2:2 (Jas 1:18–22); 1 Pet 5:5 (Jas 4:6); 1 Pet 5:8–9 (Jas 4:7) and the common OT citations of Isa 40:6–8 (1 Pet 1:24–25; Jas 1:10–11), Prov 10:12 (1 Pet 4:8; Jas 5:20), and Prov 3:34 (1 Pet 5:5; Jas 4:6). Affinities with *Hebrews* include 1 Pet 1:1, 2:11 (Heb 11:13); 1:2 (Heb 12:24); 1:23 (4:12); 2:24 (Heb 10:10); 2:25, 5:4 (Heb 13:20); 3:9 (Heb 12:17); 3:18 (Heb 9:28); 4:14 (13:13) and the themes of social alienation and solidarity with the suffering of Jesus Christ.

Links with *Mark and the Synoptic tradition* include 1 Pet 2:4–8 (Mark 12:1–12 par.); 2:18–3:7, 5:2–5 (Mark 10:2–45 par. and domestic instruction for the household of God [cf. 1 Pet 2:5, 4:17 and Mark 3:20–35, 13:33–37 par.]); 1 Pet 1:19–21, 2:21–25, 3:18 (Mark 14–16 par.); 1 Pet 4:13 (Mark 13:9–13 par.); and 1 Pet 5:2–5 (Mark 10:35–45 par.). Affinities with specific *dominical sayings* include 1 Pet 1:10–12 (Matt 13:17; Luke 24:26); 1:13 (Luke 12:35); 1:17 (Matt 6:9; Luke 11:2); 2:12 (Matt 5:16); 2:19–20 (Luke 6:27–36); 3:9, 14; 4:5 (Matt 12:36); 4:13–14 (Matt 5:10–11, 39; Luke 6:22–23, 28); 5:6 (Luke 14:11); 5:7 (Matt 6:25–27).

From such similarities, earlier scholars concluded that 1 Peter manifested direct literary dependence upon much of the NT or at least upon the writings of Paul (e.g. the representative positions of Forster [1913] and Beare [1970]). More recent form-critical and traditional-critical analysis of the NT and 1 Peter in particular, however, have made it evident that similarities between 1 Peter and other Christian writings were the result not of literary dependency but of the common use of a wide stream of oral and written tradition (Selwyn 1947: 363–466; Lohse 1954; Kelly *Peter and Jude* HNTC; Best *1 Peter* NCBC; Elliott 1976; Goppelt *Petrusbrief* MeyerK; Brox 1978; *Petrusbrief* EKKNT[2]; Cothenet 1980). 1 Peter has been aptly labeled an "Epitre de la Tradition" (Spicq *Les épîtres de Saint Pierre* SB, 15).

2. The Influence and Use of Common Tradition. The themes, images, and formulations of the letter reflect the influence of a broad range of Jewish, Judaeo-Christian and Hellenistic tradition. From the Greek OT (LXX) use was made of no less than twenty-four texts or combinations of texts. Linking the eschatological community with the history of God's covenant people, this material served to stress the social estrangement and oppression of God's people as resident aliens in diaspora (1:1, 17–18; 2:11; 3:6 [Gen 23:4, cf. Gen 12:1–20, 20:1–18; Isa 52:3, 5]; 3:10–12 [Ps 33(34)]; 4:14 [Isa 11:2]; 5:8–9, 13 [Jeremiah 50:51]); their election and holiness (1:15–16 [Lev 19:2]; 2:5, 9 [Exod 19:6; Isa 43:20; Hos 1:6, 9; 2:1, 3, 25]); the rejection, suffering, and exaltation of the Messiah-Servant (2:4–8 [Isa 8:14, 28:16; Ps 117(118):22]; 2:22–24 [Isa 53:4, 6, 9]); divine redemption of the righteous and oppressed (1:13 [Exod 12:11]; 1:17–19, cf. 1:2 [Exod 12–15; Isa 52:3, 5]; examples of Sarah, 3:5–6, and Noah, 3:20); fear of God rather than man (2:17 [Prov 24:21]; 3:6 [Prov 3:25]; 3:14–15 [Isa 8:12–13]); moral conduct (3:10–12 [Ps 33(34):13–17]; 4:8 [Prov 10:12]); the imminence of divine judgment (2:12 [Isa 10:3]; 4:17 [Ezek 9:6]; 4:18 [Prov 11:31 LXX]); and God's nurture (2:3 [Ps 33(34):9]) and exaltation of the humble (5:5 [Prov 3:34 LXX]; 5:7 [Ps 54(55):23]).

Though supplying no direct sources for 1 Peter, *1 Enoch* (6–16, 65–67, 106–8) illuminates the worldview behind 3:18–22 (Dalton 1989: 163–76); the Qumran writings reveal similarities in thought but differences in strategy (Goppelt *Petrusbrief* MeyerK *passim*); and works of Philo show similar expositions of the Exod 19:6 tradition (Elliott 1966: 96–101; 1981: 170–74) and similar appropriation of the Hellenistic household management tradition (Elliott 1981: 208–20).

The Christian tradition underlying 1 Peter, discernible from its contacts with other early Christian literature, is both parenetic and kerygmatic in character and Palestinian and Hellenistic in coloration (Lohse 1954). The *parenetic material,* comprising wisdom sayings on conduct (Psalms and Proverbs), Jewish-Hellenistic traditions (the domestic code in 2:13–3:7, 5:1–5; "virtues" in 3:8, 4:8–9, 5:5; "vices" in 2:1, 4:3, 15), and isolated sayings of the Lord (1:10–11, 13, 17; 2:12, 19–20; 3:9, 14; 4:13–14) was employed for the purpose of moral instruction and exhortation. The *kerygmatic material,* embodied in creedal or hymnic-like formulae (1:18–21, 2:21–25, 3:18–22; cf. 4:1), provided a christological basis for this exhortation (cf. also 1:3, 11; 2:4–10; 4:13; 5:4). Further traces of liturgical custom may be seen in the kiss of love (shared in the worship assembly, 5:14) and in the blessing (1:3) and doxology (5:10–11; cf. 4:11) with which the letter commences and concludes.

The liberal use of such a broad range of traditions served several significant ends. The socially estranged yet divinely elected company of believers was portrayed as the eschatological fulfillment of the covenant people of God. Suffering Christians were provided a rationale for endurance, hope, and God-pleasing conduct through their solidarity with the rejected yet divinely vindicated Lord. And communities dispersed throughout Asia Minor were assured by distant fellow believers at "Babylon" of the breadth of the tradition which united the universal Christian brotherhood.

E. Style, Vocabulary, and Composition

1. Style. In 1 Peter this abundance of diverse tradition has been skillfully integrated in a composition consistent in style and coherent in theme. The letter was written in a polished Greek revealing numerous traces of literary refinement. The near-classical employment of the article and exact use of tenses is coupled with a more semitic appreciation of rhythm and parallelism (2:14, 22–23; 3:18; 4:6, 11; 5:2–3); the adept use of prepositions (1:2, 3–5, 21; 2:4; 3:18); and the effective rhetorical use of repetition, allied terms and contrasts (1:3–5, 7–8, 12, 14, 18–19, 23, 2:1, 4–10, 3:3–4, 13–17; 4:12–19; 5:2, 6–7). Evidence of the letter's predominantly hortatory tone includes some fifty-one imperatival constructions (including participles used as imperatives, 1:14; 2:18; 3:1, 7–9; 4:7–10), frequent use of the second person plural "you" (51 times), the parenetic "therefore" (2:1, 7; 4:1, 7; 5:1, 6; cf. 1:13), and the persistent thematic stress on behavior consistent with the will of God. The sequence of imperatives followed by supporting indicatives (2:18–20, 21–25; 3:3–4, 5; 3:13–17, 18–22; 4:12–16, 17–19; 5:7a, 7b; 8–9, 10) differs markedly from Paul who normally follows the reverse procedure.

2. Vocabulary. The Greek text of 1 Peter contains a total of 1,675 words and a vocabulary of 547 terms, sixty-one of which occur nowhere else in the NT. Several of these so-called *hapax legomena* express fundamental emphases of the letter: the Christian community as a "brotherhood" (*adelphotēs,* 2:17, 5:9; cf. 3:8 and 5:12) and covenant people of God (*hierateuma,* "body of priests" from the covenant formula of Exod 19:6 cited in 2:4, 9); "being (doing) good" (*agathopoios,* 2:14; *agathopoiia,* 4:19) over against "being (doing) evil" (*kakopoios,* 2:12, 14; 4:15) as characteristic of Christian conduct and holiness (Elliott 1966: 179–82). Further distinctive features include the frequent and refined use of the comparative particle "like/as" (*hōs,* 27x); the highest occurrence (12x) of *paschein* ("to suffer") in the NT; identification of the believer as "Christian" (*Christianos* [4:12], elsewhere only in Acts 11:26, 26:28), but no use of the terms *ekklēsia* ("church") or "body of Christ" as so frequently in Paul; and stress upon the believers as "elect/chosen" (1:1, 2:4–10, 5:13) "resident aliens and strangers" (1:1, 17; 2:11; cf. "Babylon," 5:13) which runs like a golden thread through the epistle.

3. Compositional Devices. Several types of compositional devices were employed to give the letter its structural and thematic coherence (Dalton 1989: 72–86; Combrink 1975; Talbert 1986: 141–51). (1) Many terms or images are repeated throughout the several sections of the letter ("elect/chosen," "call," "holy," "grace," "peace," "mercy," "believe," "hope," "(brotherly) love," "gospel/proclaim good news," "test/trial," "suffer," "rejoice," "exhort," "do(be) good versus evil"; and contrasts between righteous believers and unrighteous non-believers, "will of God" and "be subordinate," and images of Christian community such as "flock of God" or "household-family-brotherhood of God." (2) Parallel patterns of arrangement (main statement/negative/positive/conclusion) are evident in 1:13–16, 2:13–17, 3:8–9, 4:1–6; 2:18–21, 3:1–6, 13–17, 4:12–19; and 1:17–21, 22–25, 5:1–4. (3) Link-words are used to unite ideas or sources and effect continuity: "salvation" in 1:9/10 linking 1:6–9 with vv 10–12; "living stones[s] linking 2:4 and 5 and its different traditions (Elliott 1966); "evil (do evil, harm)" in 3:12/13 linking 3:10–12 and 13–17; "(be) humble" in 5:5/6 joining 5:1–5 and 6–11. (4) Chiastic arrangements have been observed (Combrink 1975 with varying degrees of cogency) in both smaller (1:10–12; 2:7, 17, 19–20; 3:19–22; 4:1–3, 16) and larger (1:3–12, 13–21[25]; 3:1–7; 4:1–6; 4:12–19; 5:12–14. (5) Some terms serve to mark the beginning ("exhort, beseech" in 2:11, 4:12, 5:12) or conclusion ("good news" in 1:12, 25; 4:6, 17) of sub-sections. (6) The device of inclusion (repetition of terms or motifs to signal the beginning and end of sections) was employed to integrate not only smaller units (1:13–21 ["hope"]; 1:3–2:10 ["mercy"] but also to unify and frame the letter as a whole. At both the outset and close of the letter the paradoxical relation of suffering and glory is stressed (1:6–8, 12; 5:10), peace is enjoined (1:1, 5:14), the grace of God (1:2) in which the believers are to stand fast (5:12) is given as a theme encompassing the entire letter (cf. 1:10, 13; 3:7; 4:10; 5:5), and the common social condition (diaspora, 1:1; Babylon, 5:13), familial unity (1:1, 5:12–14), and divine election (1:1, 5:13) of both senders and recipients of the letter are emphasized.

F. The Transmitted Greek Text

The Greek text of 1 Peter is relatively well preserved. The complete text is contained in Bodmer Papyrus 72 (3d century), nine chief uncials, and more than 500 minuscules. The history of its textual transmission involves no major problems, and only variants of minor significance (Beare 1970: 1–14; Schelkle *Petrusbrief,* 16–17; Goppelt *Petrusbrief,* 72–74).

G. Structure

The foregoing evidence of its genre, thematic emphases and compositional elements indicates the structure of the letter and its general line of argument. Framed by an epistolary salutation (1:1–2) and conclusion (5:12–14), the body of the letter combines an affirmation of the distinctive communal identity and divinely conferred dignity of Christian believers (1:3–2:10) with exhortation concerning their appropriate collective behavior within a hostile society (2:11–5:11). Underlying this union of affirmation and exhortation was the basic tension between the social condition of the suffering Christians and their divine vocation, their contrast to nonbelievers and their communion in Christ, their "homelessness" in society and their new home in the family of God.

H. The Addressees and Their Situation

Information concerning the addressees, their geographical location, social and religious features, and their problematic standing in society provides important indications of both the situation which prompted this letter and the strategy which shaped its response (Elliott 1981: 59–100).

1. Geographical Location. The geographical location of the addressees is indicated in 1:1: ". . . to the elect visiting strangers [and "resident aliens," 2:11] of the dispersion in Pontus, Galatia, Cappadocia, Asia, and Bithynia." These Roman provinces of Asia Minor (modern Turkey) were formerly independent territories which since 133 B.C.E. had gradually come under Roman control through bequest or annexation. Their total population of ca. 8.5 million included an estimated 1 million Jews and 80,000 Christians by the end of the 1st century C.E. Apart from Syria-Palestine, it was here in Asia Minor that the Christian movement made its earliest and most extensive advance. The sequence of provinces in 1:1 and the unusual separation of Bithynia and Pontus (a single unified province since 62 B.C.E.) are probable indications of the intended route of this circular letter, commencing in Pontus and concluding in Bithynia. Such a route would be compatible with a Western (Roman) origin of the letter and its emissary, arriving and departing by ship at the northern shores of Bithynia-Pontus.

2. Social and Ethnic Composition. In regard to the social composition of the audience, the letter specifically refers to free men (2:16), household slaves (2:18–20), wives with nonbelieving husbands (3:1–6), husbands with Christian wives (3:7), community leaders ("elders," 5:1–4) and recent converts ("younger persons" [in the faith], 5:5). Culturally and religiously, the audience belonged to a worldwide brotherhood (5:9) originating in a Jewish messianic sect which believed that the life, death and resurrection of Jesus as the Christ had ushered in the final age and the culmination of the history of God's chosen people (1:3–2:10). Forming a distinctive minority whose members were identified as "Christians" (4:16), this movement was engaged in a universal mission (2:12, 3:1–2) among the "gentiles" (nonbelievers including both Jews and pagans).

The audience comprised an ethnic mix of converts from both Judaism and paganism. Indicative of the former is the frequent use of the Jewish scriptures (see 3. below), reference to messianic tradition (2:4–8) and venerated Hebrew figures (prophets and their search for the Christ, 1:10–12; Sarah and Abraham, 3:5–6; Noah, 3:20), comparative allusion to key events in Jewish history (Abraham as resident alien, 2:11 [Gen 23:4]; Passover and Exodus of Israelite aliens, 1:13, 18–19; alien existence in the dispersion, 1:1, and Babylon, 5:13), and stress on the distinctive features of Israel's identity (holy, 1:14–16; 3:5; elect, 1:1; 2:4–10; 5:13) which now characterizes the believers in Christ. On the other hand, reference to an earlier ignorance of and alienation from God (1:14, 2:10) and the behavior and idolatry typical of gentiles (1:14, 18; 2:11; 4:2–4) which was to be renounced also points to many pagan converts among the readers.

3. Societal Status and Situation. The vulnerable social standing of the addressees and the conflict in which they were engaged was due to a combination of factors: their social status as "strangers and resident aliens" and the exclusive form of their religious allegiance. This, in turn, set the stage for the hostility they encountered and the suffering this brought.

a. "Visiting Strangers and Resident Aliens." One of the most notable features of 1 Peter is the identification of its addressees by a pair of Greek terms best rendered as "visiting strangers" (*parepidēmoi,* 1:1, 2:11) and "resident aliens" (*paroikoi,* 2:11; cf. *paroikia,* 1:17). Translations such as "exiles," "pilgrims," or "sojourners" (e.g., KJV, RSV, JB, NAB), along with the unwarranted addition (e.g., NEB, TEV) of "on earth" in 1:17 (absent in the original Greek), distort the social and political connotations of these terms. They likewise have led to the equally unwarranted assumption that 1 Peter advocates a spiritual "pilgrimage on earth" for believers whose ultimate goal is a "heavenly home." Such a theme underlies the cosmic theology of the letter to the Hebrews but hardly the perspective of 1 Peter with its focus on societal conflict and social rather than cosmic contrasts.

In the Greco-Roman world of 1 Peter, as in the Greek OT, *paroikoi* and *parepidēmoi* were regarded and treated as permanent or temporary "strangers in a strange land" (Elliott 1981: 24–37). Literally, *paroikoi* were foreigners who lived "alongside" *(par-)* the "home" *(oikos)* of others. This condition of geographical and social displacement (*paroikia* and related terms) was the constant and typical lot of God's ancient people. As Abraham was a resident alien in Egypt (Gen 12:10) and Canaan (Gen 23:4, 26:3; Heb 11:8–9), so Moses in the land of Midian (Exod 2:22; Acts 7:29), Israel in Egypt (Gen 15:13; Acts 7:6) living in a foreign "house of bondage" (Exod 20:2; Deut 5:6), Judah in Babylon (1 Esdr 5:7), and later the Jewish settlement in Ptolemaic Egypt (*3 Macc.* 7:19). Inscriptional evidence from Greek secular sources indicates that resident aliens formed a specific social stratum of local populaces (ranked below full citizens and above complete foreigners [*xenoi*]) and slaves. Their cooperation or noncooperation with the native population could result in their moving up or down the social ladder. Legally, such aliens were restricted in regard to whom they could marry, the holding of land and succession of property, voting, and participation in certain associations and were subjected to higher taxes and severer forms of civil punishment. Set apart from their host society by their lack of local roots, their ethnic origin, language, culture, and political or religious loyalties, such strangers were commonly viewed as threats to established order and native well-being. Constant exposure to local fear and suspicion, ignorant slander, discrimination and manipulation was the regular lot of these social outsiders.

In Asia Minor, resident aliens were found among both the urban and rural populations, working as artisans, traders and dispossessed farmers (Magie 1950: 639–40, 1503). Because of their marginal status as outsiders, they frequently joined clubs or cults which offered the promise of social acceptance, mutual support, or even salvation. As the Christian movement expanded beyond Palestine and throughout the Jewish diaspora, it moved along the trade routes of the empire. Spread by itinerant artisans and traders, it enlisted no small number of converts who were strangers and resident aliens in their local communities. As the movement grew, it experienced increased resistance from local populations of Jews and gentiles alike. By the time of 1 Peter, the precarious social condition of the movement as a whole had begun to mirror that of many of its individual adherents. Strangers who had embraced the Christian faith for the communion, hope, and salvation it promised were discovering that membership in this sect provided no escape from the prejudices and animosities of the larger society. To the contrary, membership in this strange and exclusive movement from the East resulted only in an increase in social friction and suspicion of strangers now banded together in a missionizing movement. As Israel's history indicated, social alienation and oppression had been the regular experience of God's chosen and estranged people. From this history 1 Peter drew on models and memories of dispersion and gathering, suffering and deliverance, societal rejection and divine acceptance so that continuity with the past, along with faith in the present, might serve as an effective basis for hope in the future.

b. Local Hostility, Not Official Roman Persecution. An attempt to link 1 Peter and the Christian suffering it describes to a general persecution of Christianity initiated by Rome (Beare 1970: 28–38; Windisch-Preisker *Katholischen Briefe* HNT, 76–77) has justifiably been rejected by the majority of scholars. 1 Peter speaks of Christians suffering "throughout the world" (5:9) but the first general imperial persecution of Christianity did not occur until 251 C.E. under Decius. Earlier anti-Christian actions under Nero in 64–65 (Tac. *Annals* 15:44; Suet. *Ner.* 16:2), possibly Domitian in 93–96 (Suet. *Dom.* 10–17), and Trajan (Pliny *Ep.* 10:96–97) were limited in scope to Rome or Pontus and *were* the product of sporadic local incidents rather than of universal legal proscription. Nor is a state persecution envisioned where respect for the emperor and civil law is enjoined (2:13–17) and a positive outcome of good behavior is anticipated (2:11–12; 3:13–17). The nature of the hostility encountered—verbal abuse and reproach (2:12, 3:16, 4:14), curiosity concerning Christian hope (3:15), anger at the severance of former social ties (4:4)—likewise makes the theory of a state-sponsored persecution both improbable and unnecessary. Details of the situation point rather to social polarization and conflict which was local, disorganized and unofficial in character (Selwyn 1947; van Unnik *IDB* 3: 758–66; Reicke *James, Peter, Jude* AB; Kelly *Peter* HNTC; Best *1 Peter* NCBC; Goppelt *Petrusbrief* MeyerK; Elliott 1981; Brox *Petrusbrief*² EKKNT). As strangers and aliens belonging to a novel cult and exclusive minority actively seeking adherents, these Christians were the victims of the harassment and discrimination regularly experienced by those suspected of posing a disruptive threat to local peace and prosperity.

Branded by pagans with the opprobrious label "Christians" (literally "Christ-lackeys"), and reproached for their allegiance to Christ (4:14, 16) they were called to account for their curious hope (3:15), reviled (3:9) and unjustly slandered as immoral or criminal wrongdoers by the ignorant (2:12, 14–15; 3:13–17; 4:15). Subjected to unjust treatment (2:18–20) and fear (3:6, 14), they were also abused as a result of their termination of previous social associations and modes of behavior (4:3–4). Faced with grief, sorrow, and suffering (1:6; 2:19–20; 3:14, 17; 4:1, 12–19; 5:9–10), the addressees were in danger of doubting the benefits of their conversion, abandoning hope in God's mercy, and abdicating their proper responsibilities toward both the brotherhood and the society at large.

I. Strategy

The expressed aim of 1 Peter was to encourage its suffering readers to stand fast in the grace of God (5:12). Its literary, theological, and social strategy was to set the issue of Christian suffering within the context of the tension between the readers' social estrangement and their divine vocation, their "homelessness" in society and their "at-homeness" in the family of God. To counteract the divisive and erosive effect of innocent suffering upon the confidence, cohesion, and commitment of the brotherhood and its mission, the letter reassures its readers of their distinctive communal identity as God's favored family, encourages winsome conduct among the gentiles along with love within the brotherhood, and urges continued trust in God who vindicates the faithful who share the suffering and glory of their exalted Lord.

1. Dignity and Status Conferred by God. At the outset of the letter (1:1–2:10), a rich array of terms, images, and contrasts serve to underscore the dignity and distinctiveness of the community to which the readers belonged. Elected by God (1:1), sanctified by the Spirit (1:2; cf. 1:22), redeemed by Christ's blood (1:18–19), believers in Jesus Christ, God's elect agent of salvation, belong to the elect and holy covenant people of God, the household in which the Spirit resides (2:4–10; Elliott 1966). In contrast to Jews (1:4, 10–12), pagans (1:18), and all who reject Jesus as the Christ (2:4–8), those believing the enduring good news (1:23–25) have a permanent inheritance, a sure salvation, and a firm basis for hope (1:3–5, 13, 21). Reborn by God the Father (1:3, 23; 2:2), believers as his obedient children are not to conform to the passion of their former ignorance but to the holiness of the Wholly Other in the time of their alien residence (1:14–17). Through sincere love of brothers and sisters in the faith and avoidance of divisive behavior, they are to maintain the solidarity of the brotherhood (1:22; 2:1; 3:8; 4:8).

2. Demarcation from Non-Christian Outsiders. As conversion confers new dignity and status before God, so it also demarcates believers from unbelievers and the old way of life from the new. In addition to the distinctive union that Christians are said to have with God and Jesus Christ, this point is further accentuated by the numerous contrasts drawn throughout the letter between past and present (1:14–15, 18; 2:10, 25; 4:2–3), impermanence and permanence (1:4–5, 23–25; 5:4), nonbelievers and the faithful (2:7–10), sinners and the righteous (2:24; 3:12, 18; 4:18), human desires and the will of God (2:11, 15; 4:1–3), abuse and innocent suffering (2:11–12, 18–25; 3:13–17; 4:4, 12–19; 5:8–9), devouring devil and brotherhood united with God (5:8–9). As children of God's family, Christians were indeed different and should remain so. Within a society governed by the self-interests of human passion, futile traditions, hopelessness, and fear, Christians formed a distinctive community enlivened by mercy, faith, hope, and love.

3. Distinctive Holy Behavior. This difference, however, did not imply a Christian disdain of all societal norms and values. Although 1 Peter was hardly written to warn against Christian involvement in anti-imperial subversive activity (as argued by Reicke *James, Peter, and Jude* AB, xv–xxix and refuted by Sleeper 1968), it did stress the importance which Christians, like gentiles, attached to good conduct in both civic and domestic spheres (2:12, 14, 15, 20; 3:6, 10–12, 13–17; 4:15, 19). The ultimate norm of Christian behavior, however, was fear of God alone (1:17; 2:17, 18; 3:2, 15) and obedience to his will as exemplified by Jesus Christ (1:2, 14–17; 2:15, 18–25; 3:17; 4:2, 19). Where no conflict existed between conformity to God's will and submission to human authorities established by God (2:13), subordination was appropriate (2:13–3:7, 5:1–5) "because of the Lord" (2:13, 21–25; 3:18–22; 5:4). Respect for public law and domestic harmony was as typical of Christians as it was of gentiles. In the face of ignorant popular suspicion to the contrary, believers were urged to set the record straight.

On the other hand, the readers were reminded that they were ultimately servants of God (2:16), co-servants with the Christ (2:21–25), whose holy conduct was aimed also at gentile conversion and the glorification of God (2:11–12, 3:1–2, 4:11, 5:10). The letter's promotion of good conduct and domestic order is insufficient reason for concluding that its intention was to advocate Christian acculturation to Roman values (Elliott 1981; 1986 against Balch 1981; Stambaugh and Balch 1986). Where Christian adherence to gentile values, customs, and moral standards would obscure or contradict the distinctive features of Christian community and allegiance, there believers were to desist (1:14–19; 2:1, 11; 4:1–4), resist (5:8–9) and stand firm in God's grace (5:12). Respect was due the emperor, as to all men; but fear (awe and reverence) was to be reserved for God alone, and love, to members of the brotherhood (2:17). Retaliation sanctioned in society would be inconsistent with the solidarity believers have with their non-retaliating Lord (2:18–25; 3:9, 15–16). Exploitation of role and rank would put the lie to the humility, love, and mutual service owed one another by all believers (1:22; 2:17; 3:8; 4:8–9; 5:2–5) as "good household stewards of God's varied grace" (4:10–11). Continued association with nonbelievers and their selfish desires and futile ways (1:18; 2:11; 4:1–4) would deny the reality of their conversion, their holy union with God and Jesus Christ, and their incorporation into a new brotherhood of faith and hope (1:3–2:10). Thus the behavior encouraged in 1 Peter, while superficially consistent with some conventional standards, is ultimately and distinctively grounded in God's will for his holy children and their solidarity with Jesus Christ, God's suffering servant.

4. Solidarity in Suffering. Stress on the readers' special union with God and Jesus Christ likewise figures prominantly in the letter's discussion of their suffering. This innocent suffering is seen as a key symptom of their paradoxical situation: their estrangement in society and their union with God. In startling contrast to societal attitudes, suffering is described not as a bane but as a blessing, evidence of divine favor and sign of Christian solidarity. In continuity with earlier Jewish and Christian tradition emphasizing "joy in suffering" (Selwyn 1947: 439–58), 1 Peter regards the suffering of God's people as a sign of the end time, the day of judgment and salvation (1:6–9; 4:5–7, 17–19). Suffering, moreover, is an occasion for the divine "testing" of the purity and constancy of faith (1:6–7; 4:12). Suffering for doing good in obedience to God's will has as its reward "praise, glory, and honor" (1:7; 2:7; 5:10). Through such suffering, believers are united with their suffering Lord; his suffering serves as the model and means for theirs; and his glorification, as the basis for their endurance and hope (2:18–25; 3:13–4:6; 4:12–19; 5:1; Osborne 1983; Elliott 1985; Richard 1986). Righteous suffering is therefore a "blessing" and an opportunity to "keep the Christ (as) Lord holy in your hearts" (3:14–15). It is a sure sign of the presence of the "glory and the Spirit of God" (4:13–14) and the occasion in which those who bear Christ's name "give glory to God" (4:16). Through innocent suffering believers are united not only with God and the Christ but also with the worldwide Christian brotherhood (5:9). Therefore the suffering which the readers endure is not a reason for grief or despair but for "inexpressible and exalted joy" (1:8; cf. 4:13).

5. Christian Community as the Household/Family of God. The strategy of 1 Peter was to mobilize the resources of faith and concerted action which would enable the Christian addressees to stand firm and persevere as the community of God in a society from which they are estranged. Basic to this strategy, as the stress upon solidarity in suffering illustrates, was an emphasis upon the distinctive collective identity and responsibility of the believers. Although the term "church" *(ekklēsia)* is never employed, in the broader theological sense 1 Peter is one of the most church-oriented compositions in the NT. Through faith, believers are one "in Christ" (3:16; 5:10, 14). Their innocent suffering unites them with the suffering Christ and suffering Christians everywhere (2:18–25; 3:13–4:6; 4:12–16; 5:1, 8–9). Christians together constitute the "flock of God" (5:2). Once scattered, this flock is now being saved and gathered by its "chief shepherd" and guardian, Jesus Christ (5:4; 2:25). Within this one flock, Christian leaders ("elders"), as "under-shepherds," are to set the proper example for the people to follow (5:2–3). In 2:9–10, the culmination of a grand description of the people of God (1:3–2:10), a series of traditional communal epithets is used to depict the eschatological community of faith. This community is an "elect race, a royal residence [of God the King], a holy body of priests, God's own special people." Once the addressees were, like Hosea's illegitimate offspring, "Not-my-people" and "Without-mercy." Through God's mercy (1:3), however, they, like Hosea's contemporaries, have become the "People-of-God" and the "Ones-Shown-Mercy" (2:10; cf. Hosea 1:6; 2:1, 23). Those once alienated from God are now the very children of God (1:14).

Among these various images of community, it is the identification and exhortation of Christians as members of the *household* or *family of God* which dominates the letter from beginning to end. In two key passages of the letter, 2:4–10 and 4:12–19, the community is explicitly called the "household *(oikos)* of the Spirit" (2:5) or the "household *(oikos)* of God" (4:17). In the former passage, this phrase interprets the covenantal epithet *basileion* (Exod 19:6) cited in 2:9, and describes the eschatological community as the "house(hold) in which God's Spirit dwells" (Elliott 1981: 167–69). In the latter passage, "house(hold) of God" likewise identifies the community united with Christ and upon which God's Spirit rests. Consistent with this household metaphor are further instances of *oikos*-related terminology. The readers also are assured that they are being "built up" (*oikodomeisthe,* 2:5) by God and at the letter's conclusion this metaphor of construction and confirmation is repeated (5:10). In the household instruction of 2:18–3:7, the servant-slaves are addressed not with the conventional term for slaves (*douloi,* Eph 6:5; Col 3:22; Titus 2:9) but with the word for "household servants" (*oiketai,* 2:18). In its only NT occurrence, *synoikein* is used to exhort Christian husbands to "live together" with their wives in the knowledge that both spouses are co-heirs of the grace of life (3:7). Similarly, all the addressees are encouraged to practice hospitality, love, and mutual service as "household stewards *(oikonomoi)* of God's varied grace" (4:7–11).

In conjunction with this image of household/family, the process of salvation and conversion is pictured as a "rebirth" (1:3, 23; 2:2) initiated by God, the father of a new human family (1:2, 3, 17). Those who have been reborn have become his "children" (1:14; 2:2) subject to his will and protected by his power and care (1:14–17; 4:19; 5:6–7, 10). This process of "infamilialization" transforms believers into brothers and sisters. The senders (5:12, 13) and recipients of the letter belong to a "brotherhood" (2:17; 5:9)—the only NT occurrence of this term—whose cohesion is maintained through the practice of "brotherly love" (1:22; 3:8; 4:8) and expressed through the familial "kiss of love" (5:14). The roles, relations, and mutual responsibilities within this community are therefore appropriately defined according to the pattern of household instruction (2:13–3:9; 5:1–5). And the service owed by Christians to one other is compared to that of humble household servants (*diakonein,* 4:10, 11) and stewards (*oikonomoi,* 4:10).

The depiction of the universal believing community as the household or family of God functions as a comprehensive metaphor for coordinating the distinctive features of communal Christian identity and affirming the relation between identity and ethos. In addition to its literary utility, the image of the household constitutes a symbol of Christian community closely related to the history of the Christian mission. Most importantly, the psychological, social, and religious connotations of "house and home" make this image of community a compelling response to the problem of social estrangement.

It was the conversion of households which served as the focus and springboard of the nascent Christian mission (Luke 19:9; John 4:46–53; Acts 10–11; 16:15, 31–34; 18:8; 1 Cor 1:14, 16; 16:15). Households provided the base of Christian operations, the places of worship and centers for support and mutual aid (Acts 2:26; 5:42; 9:10–19; 12:12; Rom 16:1–23; 1 Cor 16:15; Col 4:15; Phlm 2). Household hospitality (1 Pet 4:9) facilitated the mobility of missionaries and thus the rapid expansion of the movement. The unity of this movement of household networks was expressed in several instances of greetings from "our house to yours" (Rom 16:5; 1 Cor 16:19; Col 4:15; Phlm 2; 1 Pet 5:12–14). It was a logical extension of this social reality when the Christian community as a whole was then described as the "household of God" (Gal 6:10; Eph 2:19–21; 1 Tim 3:5, 15; Heb 3:1–6, 10:21; 1 Peter).

Throughout ancient society the household or family was considered the fundamental form and model of social, political, and religious organization. For Judaism and Christianity, the house of Abraham, of Jacob, of Israel, of David, and of the new household of Jesus (Mark 3:21—35 par.) reckoned prominently in the history of salvation. With its diverse connotations, the reality and symbol of "household-family-brotherhood" provided a pregnant and powerful metaphor for describing a community created and sustained by God as Father, King, and Provider.

Finally, with this symbolization of Christian community, the letter addresses most directly the situation of its recipients, their social condition and their divine vocation. In society Christians are indeed strangers and strangers they should remain, as signs of holiness and beacons of hope. Endurance of suffering and steadfastness in faith is possible because of their incorporation in the household of God. In the family of the faithful the homeless of society *(paroikoi)* have a home *(oikos)* with God. The church, according to 1 Peter, is a home for the homeless.

J. Date, Authorship, Place of Composition

1. Date. The ambiguous nature of the letter's internal evidence concerning its date, authorship, and place of composition requires a consideration of several interrelated literary, historical, and social factors. Both a time frame for the letter's composition and a place of origin is suggested by its close links (Forster 1913: 398–411, 424–42) to two letters of Roman provenance, Romans (ca. 57 C.E.) and *1 Clement* (ca. 96). The nature of the numerous thematic affinities among all three documents, while not indicating direct literary dependency, points to the existence and use of a body of tradition common to the Christian community at Rome (Lohse, in Talbert 1986: 53–55; Best *1 Peter* NCBC, 32–36, 64–65; Goppelt *Petrusbrief,* 345–55). As Romans contributed to the tradition of the Roman church upon which 1 Peter drew, so 1 Peter subsequently added traditions and themes which recur in *1 Clement.* Accordingly, 1 Peter was written sometime between the years 57 and 96.

Other features of the letter are consistent with this general time frame and help to reduce its limits. Since the suffering described in 1 Peter was not the result of imperial persecution, scholars convinced of its Petrine authorship assign the letter to the years preceding the great fire in Rome (64 C.E.) and Nero's subsequent anti-Christian campaign (Bigg *St. Peter and St. Jude*[2] ICC, 87; Selwyn 1947: 56–63; van Unnik *IDB* 3: 765; Reicke *James, Peter, and Jude* AB 71; Spicq *Épîtres Pierre* SB, 26; Kelly *Peter and Jude* HNTC, 30). Further factors, however, including indications of the letter's pseudonymity, indicate the likelihood of a later date of composition in the middle years of the Flavian period, ca. 73–92 (Elliott 1981: 84–87; Best *1 Peter* NCBC, 63–64; Goppelt, 64–65; Brox, 38–47).

The vast scope of the letter's address (four provinces comprising ca. 129,000 sq. mi. and two provinces not reached by Paul [Bithynia-Pontus and Cappadocia]) requires the allowance of sufficient time for the spread of Christianity in this area subsequent to the mission of Paul. Moreover, the sequence of provinces given in 1:1 may reflect not only the intended route of the letter but also the alteration of these provincial boundaries undertaken by Vespasian in 72 C.E. (Elliott 1981: 60). Distance from the Pauline period and the early 60s is also indicated by the growth and coalescence of diverse traditions reflected in 1 Peter and the shift from an internal Jewish debate over the Mosaic law to a struggle of believers now labeled as "Christians" with an alien and hostile society. An accompanying shift in political perspective from the positive view of Roman government expressed in Rom 13 to the neutral stance of 1 Peter (2:13–17) would be a consequence of Nero's pogrom against the Christians of Rome, including Peter (65–67 C.E.), as viewed from the distance of a decade or more. Though no longer under imperial attack, Christians had learned a sobering lesson about esteeming Roman officials as "ministers of God" (Rom 13:6).

The figurative use of the term "Babylon" to signify the letter's place of origin (5:13) likewise indicates its post-70 date and composition at Rome. The lack of any trace of Petrine activity in the Mesopotamian city of Babylon, or in the Roman military outpost in Egypt also known as Babylon, makes it virtually certain that, in accord with later Jewish and Christian usage, "Babylon" referred figuratively to Rome, the city attested by the unanimous witness of the early church as the location of Peter's final ministry and martyrdom. Rome, like Babylon of old (Isa 13; 43:14; Jer 50–51; Dan 1–7), was seen as the seat of a godless empire which also had destroyed Jerusalem and its temple and now marked an important site of God's dispersed people. This designation of Rome as "Babylon," occurring only in literature composed after the fall of Jerusalem in 70 C.E. (*Sib. Or.* 5:143, 159; *2 Bar.* 11:1, 67:7, *4 Ezra* 3:1, 28, 31; Rev. 14:8, 16:19, 17:5, 18:2, 10, 21), constitutes further cogent evidence for the post-70 composition of 1 Peter.

On the other hand, a date of composition no later than the early 90s is also likely. By the time of Revelation (ca. 95) the situation of Christianity in Asia, one of the provinces also addressed in 1 Peter, had worsened. In contrast to the conditions and political perspective reflected in 1 Peter, many believers had suffered martyrs' deaths (Rev 2:13; 6:9–10; 16:6; 18:24; 19:2) and the attitude toward Rome had changed to a thoroughly negative one (chaps. 12–18). Likewise, in Pontus, another province addressed in 1 Peter, Christian defections had begun by the mid 90s (Pliny, *Ep.* 10.96) and in Rome Domitian's "reign of terror" (93–96) was underway. 1 Peter reflects none of these later developments; its situation rather presupposes an earlier Flavian period marked by a relative tranquility which encompassed imperial-Christian relations as well (Magie 1950: 566–92).

These various factors taken together make it likely that 1 Peter was written from Rome sometime during the years 73 to 92 C.E. Consistent with this period of the Church's situation and theological development are further features of the letter such as the rudimentary mode of organization (4:10–11) and presbyteral leadership (5:1–5); the emergence of the household as ecclesial model (Mark, Luke-Acts, Colossians, Ephesians, Hebrews); a "servant" christology (Mark, Luke-Acts) which was later abandoned; a christological motivation of moral conduct (contrast later appeals to apostolic authority in Jude, 2 Peter and Pastorals); absence of contention over gnosis and heresy; and a still lively apocalyptic eschatological orientation.

2. Authorship and Provenance: A Petrine Group in Rome. This date of composition rules out authorship by the apostle Peter who, according to the most reliable evidence (Cullmann 1958: 70–152; O'Connor 1969), suffered martyrdom in Rome ca. 65–67. The letter's refined literary style, rich, often rare, vocabulary not occurring elsewhere in the NT; and consistent citation of the Greek OT are also difficult to reconcile with the NT picture of Simon Peter as an unschooled (Acts 4:13) and Aramaic-speaking Galilean fisherman (Schrage *Katholischen Briefe* NTD, 62–64; Brox *Petrusbrief*[2] EKKNT 43–47). The hypothesis that 5:12 identifies Silvanus as Peter's secretary and co-author (Selwyn 1947: 9–17, 241; Reicke *James, Peter, Jude* AB, 69–71) lacks convincing proof (Beare 1970: 212–16). Even less is known of Silvanus and his literary ability than of Peter and the commendation of Silvanus as "a faithful brother" would then appear a deceptive form of self-praise. The Greek expression employed in 5:12 *(dia Silouanou . . . egrapsa)* conventionally identifies the *emissary* through whom a letter is delivered (cf. *Ign. Rom.* 10:1; *Ign. Phild.* 11:2; *Ign. Smyrn.* 12:1; cf. Polyc. *Ep.* 7:3) and occurs also in Acts 15:23 to identify Silas/Silvanus and Judas Barsabbas as emissaries of the letter of the Jerusalem council to the believers at Antioch (15:22–34).

Additional information from Acts records not only the personal association of Peter and Silvanus/Silas in Jerusalem and their important role in the promotion of the Gentile mission (Acts 15 and Silvanus's subsequent activity with Paul, 15:40–18:22). It also indicates Jerusalem (Acts 12:12, 13:13) as the place where both Peter and Silvanus also had contact with Mark, probably the same person identified in 1 Pet 5:13 as "my [Peter's] son." The absence of further introductory information concerning Silvanus and Mark in 1 Peter suggests that they, like Peter, were known to the addressees by reputation, if not through personal contact. In all likelihood, therefore, the Silvanus and Mark of 1 Peter were the same persons associated with Peter in Jerusalem, later co-workers with Paul (Acts 13:4–13; Col 4:10; Phlm 24; 2 Tim 4:11; 2 Cor 1:19; 1 Thess 1:1; 2 Thess 1:1), and eventually reunited with Peter in Rome.

All three of the persons expressly named in 1 Peter would thus constitute important figures through whom the Palestinian tradition of Jesus' words and the kerygma of his death and resurrection was transmitted from East to West. The explicit mention of these three names indicates that 1 Peter is the communication not so much of an individual as of a *group,* a circle once gathered around the apostle Peter and now writing in his name. Less important than the question of who actually wrote the letter is the fact that 1 Peter represents the witness of the apostle Peter, the personal networks of a brotherhood reaching from Jerusalem to Rome, and the rich tradition of the Roman Christian community (Lohse, in Talbert 1986: 53–55; Best, 32–36, 64–65; Goppelt, 37, 65–70, 347–49; Elliott 1981: 267–95). The letter was ascribed most naturally to this group's apostolic leader, Peter, one who in his own life and death bore witness to Christ's suffering (5:1) and who was later attested as Mark's associate in Rome (Papias, Irenaeus, Origen, in Eus. *Hist. Eccl.* 3.39; 5.8.3; 6.25.3–6) and a major figure of the Roman community (*1 Clem.* 5:4; *Ign. Rom.* 4:3). Speaking in the name of their martyred leader, this Petrine branch of the family of God in "Babylon" assured fellow members of the household dispersed throughout Asia Minor of the bonds of suffering, faith, and hope which united the worldwide Christian brotherhood. In 1 Peter, accordingly, the ecumenical roots and vision of Christianity at Rome received their first significant articulation. (See also Michaels *1 Peter* WBC; Olsson *Forsta Petrusbrevet* Kommentar till Nya Testament; Schrage and Balz *Katholischen Briefe* NTD.)

Bibliography

Adinolfi, M. 1988. *La prima lettera di Pietro del mondo greco-romano.* Bibliotheca Pontificii Athenaei Antoniani 26. Rome.

Balch, D. L. 1981. *Let Wives Be Submissive.* SBLMS 26. Chico, CA.

Beare, F. W. 1970. *The First Epistle of Peter.* 3d rev. ed. Oxford.

Brown, R. E.; Donfried, K. P.; and Reumann, J. 1973. *Peter in the New Testament.* Minneapolis.

Brox, N. 1977. Situation und Sprache der Minderheit im ersten Petrusbrief. *Kairos* 19: 1–13.

———. 1978. Der erste Petrusbrief in der literarischen Tradition des Urchristentums. *Kairos* 20: 182–92.

Calloud, J., and Genuyt, F. 1982. *La première épître de Pierre: Analyse sémiotique.* LD 109. Paris.

Combrink, H. J. B. 1975. The Structure of 1 Peter. *Neotestamentica* 9: 34–63.

Cothenet, E. 1980. Les orientations actuelles de l'exégèse de la première lettre de Pierre. Pp. 13–42 in *Études sur la première lettre de Pierre,* ed. C. Perrot et al. Paris.

Cross, F. L. 1954. *1 Peter: A Paschal Liturgy.* London.

Cullmann, O. 1958. *Peter: Disciple, Apostle, Martyr.* Trans. F. V. Filson. New York.

Dalton, W. J. 1989. *Christ's Proclamation to the Spirits.* AnBib 23. 2d rev. ed. Rome.

Elliott, J. H. 1966. *The Elect and the Holy. An Exegetical Examination of 1 Peter and the Phrase basileion hierateuma.* NovTSup 12.

———. 1976. The Rehabilitation of an Exegetical Step-child: 1 Peter in Recent Research. *JBL* 95: 243–54. Repr. pp. 3–16 in Talbert 1986.

———. 1981. *A Home for the Homeless: A Sociological Exegesis of 1 Peter, Its Situation and Strategy.* Philadelphia.

———. 1985. Backward and Forward "In His Steps": Following Jesus from Rome to Raymond and Beyond: The Tradition, Redaction, and Reception of 1 Peter 2:18–25. Pp. 184–209 in *Discipleship in the New Testament,* ed. F. F. Segovia. Philadelphia.

———. 1986. 1 Peter, Its Situation and Strategy: A Discussion with David Balch. Pp. 61–78 in Talbert 1986.

Forster, O. D. 1913. *The Literary Relations of "The First Epistle of Peter" with Their Bearing on Date and Place of Authorship.* vol. 17, pp. 363–538 of the Transactions of the Connecticut Academy of Arts and Sciences. New Haven.

Goppelt, L. 1982. The Responsibility of Christians in Society according to the First Epistle of Peter. Vol. 2, pp. 161–78 in *Theology of the New Testament.* 2 vols. Trans. J. E. Alsup. Grand Rapids, MI.

Guthrie, D. 1970. *New Testament Introduction.* 3d rev. ed. Downers Grove, Il.

Kümmel, W. G. 1975. *Introduction to the New Testament.* Rev. ed. New York and Nashville.

Lohse, E. 1954. Paraenese und Kerygma im 1. Petrusbrief. *ZNW* 45: 68–89; Repr. pp. 37–60 in Talbert 1986.

Magie, D. 1950. *Roman Rule in Asia Minor.* 2 vols. Princeton.

Martin, R. P. 1962. The Composition of 1 Peter in Recent Study. *VE* 1: 29–42.

Munro, W. 1983. *Authority in Paul and Peter.* SNTSMS 45. Cambridge.

Neill, S. 1964. *The Interpretation of the New Testament 1861–1961.* London.

O'Connor, D. W. 1969. *Peter in Rome: The Literary, Liturgical, and Archaeological Evidence.* New York.

Osborne, T. P. 1983. Guide Lines for Christian Suffering: A Source-Critical and Theological Study of 1 Peter 2:21–25. *Bib* 64: 381–408.

Perrot, C. et al. 1979. *Études sur la première lettre de Pierre.* LD 102. Paris.

Puig Tarrech, A. 1980. Le milieu de la première épître de Pierre. *RCT* 5: 95–129, 331–402.

Reicke, B. 1946. *The Disobedient Spirits and Christian Baptism.* ASNU 13. Copenhagen.

Richard, E. 1986. The Functional Christology of First Peter. Pp. 121–39 in Talbert 1986.

Selwyn, E. G. 1947. *The First Epistle of St. Peter.* 2d ed. London.

Shimada, K. 1985. Is I Peter a Composite Writing? *AJBI* 11: 95–114.

Sleeper, C. F. 1968. Political Responsibility According to 1 Peter. *NovT* 10: 270–86.

Stambaugh, J. E., and Balch, D. L. 1986. *The New Testament in Its Social Environment.* Philadelphia.

Sylva, D. 1980. A 1 Peter Bibliography. *JETS* 25: 75–89. Repr. pp. 17–36 in Talbert 1986.

Talbert, C. H., ed. 1986. *Perspectives on First Peter.* National Association of the Baptist Professors of Religion Special Study Series 9. Macon, GA.

Unnik, W. C. van. 1980. *Sparsa Collecta.* Vol. 2. NovTSup 30. Leiden.

Vogels, H. J. 1976. *Christi Abstieg ins Totenreich und das Laeuterungsgericht an den Toten.* FTS 102. Freiburg.

JOHN H. ELLIOTT

PETER, GOSPEL OF. The *Gospel of Peter* (= *Gos. Pet.*) was a narrative gospel of the synoptic type which circulated in the mid-1st century under the authority of the name Peter. An earlier form of the gospel probably served as one of the major sources for the canonical gospels. Neither quoted nor extensively described by patristic authors, *Gos. Pet.* is preserved today only in two very fragmentary manuscripts. The partially preserved story begins abruptly with the trial scene where Pilate washes his hands, includes a unique and unusual account of the resurrection, and concludes in mid-sentence with, apparently, the beginning of a resurrection appearance scene at the Sea of Galilee.

A. Patristic Sources and Manuscripts
   1. Eusebius and Origen
   2. Akhmim Papyrus
   3. Oxyrhynchus Papyrus Fragments
   4. Identifying the Text

A. Patristic Sources and Manuscripts

1. Eusebius and Origen. The church historian Eusebius (ca. 303 C.E.) passes on a tradition about bishop Serapion of Antioch (ca. 200 C.E.) in W Syria who had received a report about a certain Gospel of Peter which was in use at the church in nearby Rhossus (*Hist. Eccl.* 6.12.2–6). Bishop Serapion had no serious objections to the use of the text but determined that it could be understood by some to promote a docetic Christology. An even more obscure reference is made by Origen (ca. 250 C.E.) in his commentary on Matt 10:17 (*PG* 13, 876C–877A). The patristic authors transmit no quotes from the gospel so that its contents and nature remained a mystery until the end of the last century.

2. Akhmim Papyrus. The French archaeological mission in Cairo discovered a Greek manuscript containing part of *Gos. Pet.* in the winter season of 1886–87 while excavating in the ancient Christian cemetery of the modern Egyptian town of Akhmim (ancient Panopolis), sixty miles N of Nag Hammadi (Bouriant 1892–93). While the monk's grave in which the manuscript was found dates from the 8th to 12th century (Bouriant 1892–93: 93–94; Swete 1893: xlv–xlvii), the scribal hand of the *Gos. Pet.* text dates from the 7th to 9th century (van Haelst 1976: no. 598) giving us a tentative date in perhaps the latter half of the 8th century for the copying of the *Gos. Pet.* text (750–800 C.E.). The text has been available for the past century in a photographic facsimile edition (Lods 1892–93: pls. I–XXXIV, esp. II–VI) accompanied by a critical text edition (Lods 1892–93: 219–24). Today the manuscript is conserved in the papyrus collection of the Cairo Museum.

The Akhmim manuscript is in the form of a codex (book) which was rather crudely constructed out of pages from other manuscripts. Following the facsimile edition of Lods (1892–93: pls. I-XXIV), the codex measures six inches high by four-and-a-half inches wide and has 33 unpaginated leaves (= 66 pages). The codex contains four separate texts: (1) part of *Gos. Pet.*, (2) part of the *Apocalypse of Peter*, (3) part of *1 Enoch* (1:1–32:6), and (4) part of the martyrdom of a certain Julian. The texts are copied by two or three different scribes, the two Petrine texts copied by the same scribe. Van Haelst dates the hand of the *1 Enoch* text from the 4th to 6th centuries and thus as the earliest hand in the codex (1976: no. 595).

For our purposes, it is noteworthy that the Akhmim text of *Gos. Pet.* is surrounded by typical though crude scribal decorations both at the beginning of the texts (where the scene of Pilate washing his hands abruptly begins) and also at the conclusion of the text (where the text suddenly ends in the middle of a sentence). This means that the earlier manuscript containing *Gos. Pet.* from which the Akhmim scribe copied was already a broken fragment. There was certainly enough room on the bottom part of the last page containing the *Gos. Pet.* text (= codex page 10) for the scribe to have copied more of that Petrine text onto his page, verifying that the scribe copied all of the *Gos. Pet.* text that was available to him from an earlier and fragmentary manuscript. As a result, we know nothing of the contents and nature of *Gos. Pet.* in the portions that originally preceded the scene of Pilate's handwashing and originally followed the beginning of the resurrection appearance scene of the Sea of Galilee.

3. Oxyrhynchus Papyrus Fragments. Cambridge University Press published in 1972 an edition of two small and fragmentary Greek papyri which probably belong to *Gos. Pet.* (Coles 1972: 15–16 and pl. II). The fragments are part of the larger sensational find known as the Oxyrhynchus Papyri, first discovered in 1897 in the rubbish heaps of the ancient town of Oxyrhynchus (modern el Bahnasa, north of Akhmim halfway to the delta). The editor of the text, R. A. Coles, observes (1) that the two fragments are from the same manuscript, (2) that the manuscript was a scroll rather than a codex, (3) that the extant, though brief, text has significant affinities with the text of *Gos. Pet.* from the Akhmim manuscript, (4) that the text of the Oxyrhynchus manuscripts can be identified with *Gos. Pet.* 2:3–5a from the Akhmim manuscript, (5) that the text of *Gos. Pet.* in the Oxyrhynchus fragments represents a different recension of the text from what we find in the Akhmim manuscript (cf. Crossan 1988: 6–9), and (6) that the informal type of scribal hand can be dated to the early 3d or possibly late 2d century (Coles 1972: 15–16).

Thus, the Oxyrhynchus fragments give us a papyrological witness to the *Gos. Pet.* which predates both to the patristic allusions to the text and also predates the Akhmim manuscript by about 500 to 600 years. Further, it is clear that the early papyrological evidence for *Gos. Pet.* is now as strong as that for the gospels of Matthew and Luke (Lührmann 1981: 225) and probably *better* than that for Mark, *Gos. Thom.*, and *Gos. Mary.* The 2 Oxyrhynchus fragments are generally considered a single manuscript and so are given the single inventory number P. Oxy. 2949. The papyri are now conserved in the Ashmolean Museum, Oxford.

4. Identifying the Text. Following such analyses as those of Lührmann (1981: 216–26) and Crossan (1988: 3–9), most scholars today identify the texts on the Oxyrhynchus and Akhmim manuscripts with the *Gos. Pet.* mentioned by Eusebius. Since none of the surviving fragments contains the title of gospel, and since none of the patristic authors preserved quotes from the *Gos. Pet.*, the gospel text on the Oxyrhynchus and Akhmim manuscripts is technically from an unknown gospel. The strongest evidence which equates the gospel text of the papyri with the *Gos. Pet.* mentioned by Eusebius and used by western Syrian Christians in the late 2d century, is that the voice of the text's narrator-author is identified in the first-person singular as "Simon Peter" ("But I, Simon Peter . . ." 14:60; cf. 7:26; note the closely related third-person singulars in 7:27 and 14:59). Another, though weaker, indicator is that the gospel text of the papyri can be read, without too much trouble, as the same text which Serapion obliquely describes (Crossan 1988: 12).

B. Debate over Literary Relations

1. Overview of the History of Research. Debate continues over the relationship of *Gos. Pet.* to the canonical gospels. In line with the generally more conservative, and perhaps less critical approach of an earlier generation, *Gos. Pet.* was first understood to be a literary pastiche of texts borrowed from the canonical gospels and then embellished by fanciful oral traditions (esp. Robinson 1892: 11–36, 82–88, and Vaganay 1930: 18–27; cf. also Swete 1893 and Zahn 1893). Adolf von Harnack proposed, as early as his lectures of November 3 and 10, 1892, that *Gos. Pet.* might preserve some independent traditions, but his discussion is too vague to be anything more than suggestive (1893: 32–37, 47). Clearer arguments for independent traditions in *Gos. Pet.* were later made by Gardner-Smith (1925–26a, b), Denker (1975), and most notably by Helmut Koester (1980: 126-30; 1982: 2.162–63). The most useful and fully documented analysis is the recent work of Crossan (1988: 16–30 and passim), who laments the early years of scholarly analysis with appropriately incisive statements: "one cannot help wondering if scholarship would have been better served by everyone taking a little more time instead of rushing to judgement. . . . scholarship is at an impasse on the *Gospel of Peter* . . . it has accepted that impasse much too readily" (1988: 13–14).

2. Crossan's Hypothesis. A new direction in the study of the *Gos. Pet.* was initiated by the publication of Crossan's study in 1988. Rather than rephrase Crossan's statement, the present author presents here Crossan's own concise description of his hypothesis on the textual history of *Gos. Pet.*:

> I find three major stages in the compositional history of the present *Gospel of Peter*. . . . I call the first and earliest stage the *Cross Gospel*, a document presently imbedded in the *Gospel of Peter*, just as Q is in Matthew and Luke. . . . The second stage is the use of the preceding document by all four of the intracanonical Gospels. I hold it to be the only passion and resurrection narrative used by Mark and, along with him, by Matthew and Luke, and, along with them, by John. . . . all the intracanonical passion and resurrection narratives are dependent on the *Cross Gospel*. . . . The third and latest stage occurs when this *Cross Gospel*, like John before it, comes under pressure to adapt itself to the intracanonical endings with their stories of honorable burial, discovery of the empty tomb, and apparition for missionary mandate to the apostles. This expanded composition is attributed pseudonymously to Peter, but it is already far too late to save it for intracanonical inclusion (Crossan 1988: xii–xiv).

Crossan's interpretation clearly falls into the camp of those, like Koester before him, who argue for independent traditions in *Gos. Pet.* Crossan's distinct contribution is twofold: (1) the identification of redactional strata within the present text, and (2) the construction of a theory of the development of those strata in relation to the development of the gospel tradition in general, especially the canonical gospels, Q, *Gos. Thom.*, and numerous related texts.

The implications for the Koester-Crossan line of reasoning are clear. The sources now incorporated into the extant text of *Gos. Pet.* go back to the preformative stages of the development of the passion narrative and the empty tomb story, thus dating them to the mid-1st century. Koester argued for a text which was older than and "independent of the canonical gospels" (1982: 2.163) while Crossan has gone the distance in isolating those sources and demonstrating their place within the development of the tradition. One can expect that all future research on *Gos. Pet.* will need to begin with a serious consideration of Crossan's work.

C. Contents and Story Line

The standard text in English translation is divided into 14 short chapters and 60 continuously numbered verses (yet it is standard practice to list both the chapter and verse numbers). The following resume of the story line follows the larger text from the Akhmim fragment (*NTApocr*, 183–87): *1:1–2* the conclusion of the trial scene with the presence of Jesus, Pilate (who alone washes his hands), Herod (who proclaims judgment) and his judges, and the people; *2:3–5a* (also in P. Oxy. 2949) Joseph the friend of Pilate asks to bury the body of Jesus before the Sabbath so as to keep the law; *2:5b–3:9* Jesus is delivered to the people who mock and beat him; *4:10–14* he is crucified with two malefactors who suggest he is innocent, only to enrage those who cast lots for his garments and thus refuse to break his legs so that his suffering might be extended; *5:15–20* the sky darkens at noon, the people are thus afraid that the Sabbath has begun with the body still on the cross, he cries out his last words and is taken up, then the veil of the Temple is rent in two; *6:21–24* the Jews bring Jesus down from the cross, at the ninth hour the sun shines again and the Jews rejoice, Joseph prepares the body for burial and puts it in his own sepulchre; *7:25–27* the Jews begin to lament as Peter and his fellows hide with mourning and weeping; *8:28–9:34* some Jews entreat Pilate to seal the tomb and set guards to prevent a theft of the body and consequent supposition of a resurrection; a large crowd gathers; *9:35–11:49* the tomb opens with a voice from heaven, two men (angels) enter the tomb, three men (the two angels and the resurrected Jesus) come out of the tomb with a walking-talking cross following them, the soldiers report the event to Pilate and confess "in truth he was the Son of God"; then Pilate commands the soldiers to be silent about what they had heard and seen; *12:50–13:57* Mary Magdalene and some unidentified women friends go to the tomb to prepare the body (?), find the tomb opened, and speak with a young man who tells them Jesus "is risen and gone thither whence he was sent"; the women flee the scene in fear; *14:58–59* after the feast the people return to their homes; the twelve (!) disciples are still weeping and mourning and also return to their homes; *14:60* "But I, Simon Peter, and my brother Andrew took our nets and went to the sea. And there was Levi, the son of Alphaeus, whom the Lord . . ." [note: sudden conclusion of extant text in mid-sentence].

D. Supposed Gnostic and Docetic Features

The history of research on *Gos. Pet.* shows a definitive preoccupation with the issue of the supposed gnostic or at least docetic character of the gospel's christology. The supposed gnostic and docetic features of the text are found in 4:10, where it is said that at the crucifixion Jesus "held his peace as if he felt no pain"; at 5:19, where it is said that at his death he was "taken up"; and at 10:39–42 where the cross walks out of the tomb behind the resurrected Jesus with the two angels, and it then replies "yes" to the voice from heaven. Such features are hardly representative of any gnostic or docetic theology, and have been given ample consideration by Crossan (1988: 10–12) and Maurer (*NTApocr,* 100–81).

Crossan (1988: 10–12) extends the theological analysis into the Serapion tradition transmitted by Eusebius and notes that Serapion's concern was not with any gnostic or docetic features in the text, nor did he consider *Gos. Pet.* to be an unacceptable text, but rather that some persons (a certain Marcianus) were able to read *Gos. Pet.* in a docetic manner. Serapion then proceeds to list what he considers docetic additions to the text, but at that point Eusebius moves on to another issue. We have no reason to suppose that the docetic additions to the text which Serapion identified were found anywhere in the brief remains of the story as we have them in the extant text from the Akhmim fragment; they could have been found in scenes preceding or following the extant story.

Bibliography

Bouriant, U. 1892–93. Fragments du texte grec du livre d'Enoch et de quelques écrits attribués a saint Pierre. Pp. 91–147 in *Mémoires publiés par les membres de la Mission archéologique française au Caire* 9/1, ed. U. Bouriant. Paris.

Coles, R. A. 1972. Oxy P 2949 = Gospel of Peter 2. Vol. 41, pp. 15–16, pl. II in *The Oxyrhynchus Papyri,* ed. G. M. Browne et al. Cambridge.

Crossan, J. D. 1988. *The Cross that Spoke.* San Francisco.

Denker, J. 1975. *Die theologiegeschichtliche Stellung des Petrusevangeliums.* Europäische Hochschulschriften 23/36. Frankfurt am Main.

Gardner-Smith, P. 1925–26a. The Gospel of Peter. *JTS* 27: 255–71.

———. 1925–26b. The Date of the Gospel of Peter. *JTS* 27: 401–7.

Haelst, J. van. 1976. *Catalogue des Papyrus Littéraires Juifs et Chrétiens.* Série Papyrologie 1. Paris.

Harnack, A. von. 1893. *Bruchstücke des Evangeliums und der Apokalypse des Petrus.* Leipzig.

Koester, H. 1980. Apocryphal and Canonical Gospels. *HTR* 73: 105–30.

———. 1982. *Introduction to the New Testament.* 2 vols. Philadelphia.

Lods, A. 1892–93. Reproduction in héliogravure du manuscript d'Enoch et des écrits attribués a Saint Pierre. Pp. 217–35, pls. I–XXXIV in *Mémoires publiés par les membres de la Mission archéologique française au Caire,* ed. U. Bouriant. Paris.

Lührmann, D. 1981. POx 2949: EvPt 3–5 in einer Handschrift des 2./3. Jahrhunderts. *ZNW* 72: 216–26.

Robinson, J. A. 1892. The Gospel According to Peter. Pp. 11–36 [lecture] and 82–88 [Greek text] in *The Gospel According to Peter, and the Revelation of Peter,* ed. J. A. Robinson and M. R. James. London.

Swete, H. B. 1893. *Evangellion Kata Petron: The Akhmim Fragment of the Apocryphal Gospel of St. Peter.* London.

Vaganay, L. 1930. *L'Evangile de Pierre.* 2d ed. EBib. Paris.

Zahn, T. 1893. *Das Evangelium des Petrus.* Erlangen.

PAUL ALLAN MIRECKI

PETER, MARTYRDOM OF. The final chapters of the 2d century *Acts of Peter* circulated independently as the *Martyrdom of Peter.* See PETER, ACTS OF. The *Martyrdom* survives in three Greek manuscripts and in the Latin translation of the Vercelli *Acts of Peter.* Versions of varying completeness also survive in Arabic, Armenian, Coptic, Ethiopic, Slavic, and Syriac. The text is often found in association with the *Martyrdom of Paul.*

One Greek manuscript from Mt. Athos begins with the story of Chryse in *Acts Pet.* 30 and so contains the story of Simon Magus's final flight. The other versions begin with Peter's preaching of continence and conclude with the end of Nero's persecution of believers in Rome (cf. *Acts Pet.* 33–41). Attributing persecution to the concupiscence of prominent men is a common motif in early Christian literature. The prominence of Peter's preaching on chastity in the *Martyrdom* may have led to an overestimation of its importance in the *Acts Pet.* as a whole.

Interest in Peter's status as a martyr appears by the beginning of the 2d century in both Asia Minor and Rome. All traditions which locate Peter's martyrdom place it in Rome, often connecting it to Paul's martyrdom. By the end of the 2d century, the location of Peter's martyrdom was more precisely fixed at the Vatican hill, and soon took on significance in church politics. The failure of the *Martyrdom of Peter* to locate the place of Peter's execution or burial was corrected in later developments of the tradition, such as the *Passion of Peter* and the *Passion of Peter and Paul.* See PETER, PASSION OF; PETER AND PAUL, PASSION OF.

Bibliography

Burrus, V. 1987. *Chastity as Autonomy: Women in the Stories of the Apocryphal Acts of the Apostles.* Lewiston.

Cullmann, O. 1962. *Peter: Disciple, Apostle, Martyr: A Historical and Theological Study.* Philadelphia.

Kaestli, J.-D. 1986. Response. *Semeia* 38: 119–31.

Leloir, L. 1986. *Ecrits apocryphes sur les apotres: Traduction de l'edition Armenienne de Venise.* CChr Series Apocryphorum 3. Turnhout.

Lipsius, R. A. 1891. *Acta apostolorum apocrypha.* 1.1: 45–103. Leipzig.

Smith, J. Z. 1969. Birth Upside Down or Right Side Up? *HR* 9: 281–303.

Vouaux, L. 1922. *Les acts de Pierre.* 1–214.

———. 1922. *Les actes de Pierre, introduction, textes, traduction et commentaire.* Paris.

ROBERT F. STOOPS, JR.

PETER, PASSION OF. The *Passion of Peter* is a 4th or 5th century Latin elaboration of the *Martyrdom of Peter* from the *Acts of Peter.* It is based on the Greek original rather than the Vercelli Acts. Although presented as a report to the Eastern churches from Linus, Peter's successor as bishop of Rome, it is attested only in Latin. The *Passion of Peter* specifies the date and place of Peter's death and seems to have been prepared for use in the June 29 commemoration of the apostles Peter and Paul. In the ancient manuscripts, it is frequently followed directly by the Pseudo-Linus *Passion of Paul.* The *Passion of Peter* begins with Peter's conflict with Simon who is identified as the anti-Christ. It moves to Peter's preaching of chastity (cf. *Acts Pet.* 33). Because the four concubines of the perfect Agrippa follow his teaching, Peter is arrested. After Xanthippe, the wife of Albinus, visits Peter in prison, she also takes up the life of chastity. The jailors, Processus and Martinian have been converted and baptized by Peter in a miraculous spring. They add their urgings to the pleas of Marcellus and other believers to convince Peter to leave the city. The *Quo vadis* scene follows. Peter asks to be crucified head downward because he is not worthy of dying in the same manner as the Lord. The location of Peter's execution is specified as the Naumachia, near the obelisk of Nero on the hill, i.e. the Vatican. Peter's speech at the cross is retained and slightly expanded. God opens the eyes of the witnesses so that they are able to see angels crowned with flowers standing near the cross. They also see Peter standing at the top of the cross where he reads the words of his speech from a book handed to him by Christ (cf. *Acts John* 97–101).

Bibliography

Amann, E. 1982. Les Actes de Pierre. *DBSup* 1: 496–501.

Charlesworth, J. H. 1987. Peter, Martyrdom of. Pp. 328–29 in *New Testament Apocrypha and Pseudepigrapha: A Guide to Publications with Excurses on Apocalypses.* Metuchen, NJ.

Lipsius, R. A. 1883–90. *Apokryphe Apostelgeschichten und Apostellegenden.* Brauschweig. Repr. Amsterdam 1976.

———. 1891. Pp. 45–103 in *Acta apostolorum apocrypha.* Vol. 1/1. Leipzig.

Vouaux, L. 1922. *Les actes de Pierre, introduction, textes, traduction et commentaire.* Paris.

ROBERT F. STOOPS, JR.

PETER, PREACHING OF. The customary translation of the title of the *Kerygma Petrou,* which is an example of apocryphal missionary literature attributed to Peter by various early Christian writers. Not an "Acts of Peter," but rather a document that was probably made up of a series of sermons, the primary source for the "Preaching of Peter" is Clement of Alexandria, who gives a sequence of quotations from the *Kerygma Petrou* in his *Stromateis* (1.29.182; 2.15.68; 6.5.39–41; 6.5.43, 6.6.48; 6.7.58; 6.15.128, see also *ecl.* 58). Although it is clear that Clement of Alexandria considered this work to be genuine, Origen no longer accepted it as part of legitimate Christian tradition, possibly because of its use by the gnostic Heracleon (*Jo.* 13.17). The apologist Aristides as well as Theophilus of Antioch may also have known this work, although neither of them quote the *Kerygma Petrou* by name. Eusebius, however, clearly lists it under the heading of non-canonical writings (*Hist. Eccl.* 3.3.2). From the attestation and surmised use of the *Kerygma Petrou* by early Christian writers, it is thought to have been composed sometime in the early part of 2d century C.E., possibly in Egypt.

Due to the fragmentary nature of the evidence for the *Kerygma Petrou* little can be said concerning the nature of the work as a whole or concerning the order of its composition. What does remain indicates that the *Kerygma Petrou* contained supposedly Petrine discourses, the contents of which are reminiscent of later 2d century apologetic literature. Peter, a likely choice as the authoritative missionary leader of early Christianity, is depicted as preaching on such topics as monotheism, the dangers of paganism, as well as the falsity of Jewish religion and worship. The *Kerygma Petrou* may also have included christological sections which utilized OT passages in its Christian interpretation of Jesus death and resurrection. Whether the christological passages are meant to be discourses of the resurrected Christ or further sermons attributed to Peter is not clear. The emphases on monotheism and paganism, as well as the negative assessment of Judaism found in the *Kerygma Petrou* connect it to the literature of the early Christian apologists. However, the *Kerygma Petrou* also manifests tendencies of early Christian missionary preaching found in the Acts of the Apostles, and is therefore seen as a possible intermediary tradition between Christian Greek apologetic literature and early Christian missionary proclamation. Although the *Kerygma Petrou* contains discussions concerning the attributes of God and comparisons of pagan, Jewish, and Christian worship, it is not therefore surmised that the author of the document was necessarily a Jewish Christian, as such topics were common in Christian literature of the 2d century.

Other less explicit references in early Christian literature have been suggested as further fragmentary evidence for the *Kerygma Petrou,* such as a "Doctrine of Peter" mentioned by Origen (*princ* praef. 8) or a "Teaching of Peter" quoted by Gregory of Nazianzus (*ep.* 20; *or.* 17.5). However, the identification of such documents with the *Kerygma Petrou* is seen to be questionable.

Bibliography

Mees, M. 1975. Das Petersbild nach ausserkanonischen Zeugnissen. *ZRGG* 27: 193–205.

Nautin, P. 1974. Citations de la Predication de Pierre dans Clement d' Alexandrie, Strom. vi.v.39–41. *JTS* 25: 98–105.

Quispel, G. and Grant, R. M. 1952. Note on the Petrine Apocrypha. *VC* 6:31–32.

KATHLEEN E. CORLEY

PETER, SECOND EPISTLE OF. A composition of the post-apostolic period that claims to be the testament of the apostle Peter dispatched as a letter. It is included in the canonical NT.

A. Introduction
B. Reception and Importance
C. Literary Genre and Pseudonymity
D. Sources
E. Style and Structure
F. Situation
G. Strategy
H. Origin, Destination, and Date

A. Introduction

The Epistle's words of encouragement, warning, and reminder, supposedly composed shortly before the apostle's death (1:12–15), were actually intended for Christians of a later generation beset by internal division and doubt concerning the Lord's final coming.

Because its addressees are unnamed (1:1), the letter has been included among the 7 "Catholic Epistles" (James, 1–2 Peter, 1–3 John, Jude) whose destinations are less specific than the letters of Paul. Nevertheless, it provides a specific response to an urgent crisis. Gentile converts had begun to introduce novel doubts about theological assumptions long taken for granted along with forms of behavior deviating seriously from ancient norms. The letter's double aim was to refute these "false teachers" (2:1), their theory and praxis, and to reinforce stability and commitment among the faithful through reminder of their divine gifts and calling.

Its rather unique blend of apocalyptic message and Hellenistic expression gives it a culturally catholic character. Old and new are combined as in a new arrangement of an old song: a jazz improvisation on "Rock of Ages" or, more appropriately, "Give Me That Old Time Religion." To contend effectively in the present and to prepare for the future, it is argued, requires a recalling of the past. Thus 2 Peter outlines an interim ethic for the present (1:5–11, 19; 3:11–18) which is framed and guided by lessons from the past (prophecy: 1:19–21; 3:2; world history: 2:4–10a, 15–16; 3:5–6; apostolic witness: 1:12–18; 3:1–4) and by the prospect of judgment and cosmic renewal in the future (3:7, 8–10). Basic to this ethic is the assurance of God's continual and consistent action in human affairs in past (1:3–4; 2:2–8; 3:5–6), present (1:20–21; 2:3, 9–10a; 3:8–9) and future (3:7, 10–12).

B. Reception and Importance

Together with 1 Peter and a large body of non-canonical Petrine literature (including the *Apocalypse of Peter, Gospel of Peter, Preaching of Peter, Acts of Peter,* and the pseudo-Petrine gnostic writings), 2 Peter illustrates the prominence attributed to the apostle Peter in orthodox and heterodox circles. Despite its Petrine pedigree, however, no NT writing was so poorly attested among the Church Fathers or received into the canon with greater hesitation than was 2 Peter. It left no certain early traces among the churches of Antioch, Asia Minor, Africa, or Rome. In Egypt, however, the *Apoc. Pet.* (ca. 135) made use of it while Origen (died ca. 253) is the first extant author to mention it by name (*Commentary on John* 5:3). Here too it was translated into Sahidic and Bohairic versions and also included in P^{72} (ca. 350). Nevertheless doubts concerning its canonicity (Eus., *Hist. Eccl.* 3.3, 3.25) or at least its authenticity (Jer., *Epist.* 120.11; Erasmus, Luther, Calvin, and most modern scholars) have persisted down to modern times. For some contemporary commentators, particularly German Protestant exegetes (represented by the influential study of E. Kaesemann [1964]), it is the content of 2 Peter which raises serious theological problems. An identification of gospel with tradition and faith with doctrinal assent, it is claimed, and an ethic based on final retribution rather than on the christological kerygma must be seen as a loss of the authentic evangelical spirit of Paul as the Church embarked on the regrettable path of "early catholic" institutionalization.

Such a negative assessment, however, has not gone unchallenged (Green 1960; Bauckham *Jude, 2 Peter* WBC, 151–54) and more recent studies (Fornberg 1977; Neyrey 1980a, 1980b; Bauckham *Jude, 2 Peter* WBC; Elliott and Martin *James, 1–2 Peter/Jude* ACNT) have sought to provide a more comprehensive basis for appreciating the letter's situation and strategy. 2 Peter remains an important NT document for both historical and theological reasons. It records the effort of Christianity in a transitional post-apostolic period to communicate effectively in a pluralistic cultural environment while at the same time remaining faithful to its apostolic heritage and underlying worldview.

C. Literary Genre and Pseudonymity

The epistolary salutation (1:1–2) and reference to its being a "second letter" (3:1) show that 2 Peter was dispatched as a letter. However, its formal character is determined primarily by 1:12–15 and the recurrent theme of prediction and reminder (2:1–3; 3:1–4, 17). Accordingly, this letter contains the "testament" or farewell address of the apostle Peter intended to forewarn and remind Christians living after his death.

2 Peter thus resembles other parting addresses or testaments contained in the NT (of Jesus: Mark 13 par.; John 13–17; of Paul: Acts 20:17–35; 2 Timothy), the OT (of Jacob: Gen 47:29–49:32; Deuteronomy 1–3; 28–31; of Joshua: Joshua 23–24; of Samuel: 1 Samuel 12), and especially in the OT Pseudepigrapha (*Testament of Abraham, Testament of Moses, Testament of Job,* and *the Testaments of the Twelve Patriarchs*). Such testaments typically included notice of the speaker's impending death, the prediction of "future" events, and exhortation regarding the appropriate behavior of the righteous. Generally pseudepigraphical, the testament was a literary form employed to address current issues as the anticipation or forecast of some venerable figure of the past and thereby secure for its teaching the authority antiquity confers.

This appears to have been the chief motive behind the "Petrine testament" of 2 Peter. The use of this literary convention here (1:1, 3–11, 12–15; 2:1–3a; 3:1–4, 11–14, 17), along with arguments based on language and style, sources used, problems addressed, and theological content, points to pseudonymous authorship and a date long after Peter's death (Guthrie 1970: 820–48; Bauckham *2 Peter* WBC, 131–35, 158–62 for arguments for and against Petrine authorship; Metzger 1972 on the issues concerning canonical pseudepigrapha). Moreover, in the shift from future to present tense verbs (2:1–10a/10b–22; 3:2–4/5–18) "Peter's" prediction is abandoned altogether and the real author speaks to his present situation.

Aside from his familiarity with Hellenistic rhetoric, Jewish and Christian apocalyptic traditions, the Letter of Jude and unidentified letters of Paul, little can be said of 2 Peter's actual author. Considering his own identity less weighty than that of an apostle, he wrapped himself fully in Peter's mantle. Through the fiction of a Petrine testament and appeal to the apostle's eyewitness of Jesus' transfiguration (1:16–18; cf. Mark 9:2–8 par.), he attempted to combat powerful opponents and novel ideas with the authority conferred by apostolicity and earlier historical experience.

D. Sources

2 Peter is replete with anomalies (Elliott ACNT, 120–26). Two of them concern its main source and the Hellenistic stylization of its Jewish-Christian apocalyptic message.

In many respects the letter is an eccentric NT writing, outside the mainstream of early Christian kerygmatic and catechetical tradition. The author knows of a collection of Pauline letters (3:15–16) but is concerned less with their evangelical content than with their distortions by the "ignorant." Affinities with the Gospels are also few and vague, deriving from oral rather than from literary sources (compare 1:14 and John 21:18; 1:16–18 and Mark 9:1[2]–8 par.; 2:20 and Matt 12:45 = Luke 11:26; 3:4 and Mark 9:1, 13:19; 3:10 and Matt 24:43–44 = Luke 12:39–40). Not once is the OT cited explicitly though the letter abounds with OT allusions (compare 1:19 and Num 24:17; 2:4–5 and Genesis 6–8; 2:6–8 and Genesis 19; 2:15–16 and Num 22:21–35; 2:22 and Prov 26:22, Isa 66:3 [dog and sow]; 3:3 and Isa 3:4 LXX, cf. 66:4; 3:5–6 and Gen 1:6–8; 3:7, 10 and Isa 66:15–16; 3:8 and Ps 90[89]:4; 3:9, 12–14 and Hab 2:3; 3:10–13 and Isa 66:15–16, 22). Among the OT Pseudepigrapha, 2 Peter shows several striking similarities with the Syriac apocalypse of *2 Baruch* (text in *OTP* 1: 615–52) in both form (cf. the letter in chaps. 76–86) and content (delay of God's coming, divine forbearance, judgment of corruption). This late NT writing thus shows close ties with Jewish apocalyptic tradition in particular, affinities shared also by *1* and *2 Clement* and Hermas (Bauckham *2 Peter* WBC, 140).

The statement in 2 Pet 3:1 "This is now the second letter that I have written to you," along with other similarities, would seem to suggest 1 Peter as a source (Boobyer 1959). The affinities, however, are minor and superficial and derive from common convention and tradition rather than from literary dependency. The letters are thoroughly different in form, language and style, sources used, social situation and issues addressed, and theological message (Mayor 1907:lxviii–cv; Bauckham *2 Peter* WBC, 285–87).

The continuation of 3:1 in vv 2–3, however, is virtually identical with vv 17–18 of the Epistle of Jude. Moreover, of the 25 vv of Jude no less than 19, in whole or in part, have parallels in 2 Peter. Of Jude's 460 word vocabulary almost one quarter (111) are found in 2 Peter. This extraordinary correspondence of vocabulary, phrasing, ideas, and sequence argues against the use of common oral tradition (as suggested by Reicke *The Epistles James, Peter, and Jude* AB, 190) and for direct literary dependence. Earlier commentators (Bigg *Epistles of St. Peter and St. Jude* ICC^2, 216–24; Luther, Spitta, Zahn) considered Jude an excerpt of 2 Peter. However, the broad current consensus is that the longer letter is clearly a later revision and expansion of the shorter one (Mayor 1907:i–lxvii, 1–15; Grundmann *Judas and der Zweite Brief des Petrus* THKNT, 102–07; Fornberg 1977:33–59 for detailed comparisons). 2 Pet 2:1–18 reproduces Jude 4–16 in the same general sequence; 3:2–3 echoes Jude 17–18; 3:13–14, 18 reflect and modify Jude 24–25, 1:5 and 12; and other parallels occur in 1:1–2 = Jude 1–2; 1:5 = Jude 3; 1:12 = Jude 5; 3:13–14, 18 = Jude 24–25. Jude thus constituted the main source employed in 2 Peter and supplied the latter with both the material for the polemic of chap. 2 and the important theme of apostolic prediction and reminder.

2 Peter revised and expanded upon this material and set it within a larger framework of thought provided by chaps. 1 and 3. The OT examples from Jude 5–7 were arranged chronologically and references to Noah and Lot were added to balance the themes of destruction and deliverance (2 Pet 2:4–10a). Jude's references to the apocryphal traditions regarding Michael and Enoch (vv 9, 14–15) were omitted. The "way" of truth (2:2) and righteousness (2:21; cf. 2:15) was stressed as a Christian moral norm. The disruptive Christians were identified as "false teachers" (2:1) and apostates (2:20–22). The substance of their deviant teaching was identified and refuted (1:16–21; 2:19; 3:4–7, 15–16). The theme of appropriate response to God's benefactions and coming was developed (1:3–11, 3:8–18). And the whole of this expanded revision of Jude was presented as the testament and predictive warning of the apostle Peter (1:1, 12–15; 3:1–2).

E. Style and Structure

The letter's vocabulary and style also distinguish it from other NT documents. Fifty-eight of its 402 word vocabulary (1,105 total words) are unique in the NT—the highest proportion in the NT (14.4 percent). This taste for obscure and grandiose language is matched by a style marked by excess rather than economy of expression. Many passages in the Greek original contain verbal repetitions and recurrent sounds (1:3–4, 5–7, 12–15, 17–18, 19–21; 2:1–3, 7–8, 13; 3:6, 9, 16), pairs of synonym (1:7, 10; 2:13; 3:14), and graceful rhythmic formulations (1:16, 17, 19–21; 2:4–9; 3:13). The opening section of the letter (1:3–11), as Danker (1978; 1982: 453–67) has shown, mimics the stereotyped diction and style of the omnipresent public inscriptions celebrating the virtues and deeds of benefactors and saviors.

Much of the content also has a pronounced Hellenistic hue: the conventional Greek virtues encouraged in 1:5–7; the notion of death as a "putting off of the bodily tent" (1:13–14); identification of the realm of the dead or "hell" (RSV, NEB) as "tartarus" (2:4); dispute about myths (1:16–18), prophecy (1:20–21), and involvement of the gods in human history and final judgment (3:3–7); interest in knowledge as a means of access to God (1:2, 3, 6, 8, 12; 2:20, 21; 3:3, 17, 18); salvation conceived as godliness (1:3), escape from corruption (1:4, 2:20), and participation in divine being (1:4); and the conception of God and/or Jesus Christ as Benefactor and Savior (1:1, 11; 2:20; 3:2, 18). The author is quite conversant with popular philosophies, the mystery religions, and especially with the beliefs and behavior of, as well as arguments directed against, rationalists and sceptics who disputed divine providence, life after death, and post-mortem retribution.

All these features indicate an author and audience at home in a pluralistic Hellenistic society (Fornberg 1977: 111–48). At the same time, the Jewish-Christian scripture and apocalyptic traditions employed in the letter's argument reveal that this environment embraced Jewish-Christian as well as Greco-Roman cultures. In such environments the merging as well as clash of cultures was inevitable. 2 Peter was designed to communicate effectively across these cultures while at the same time contending for the ancient truth in the face of its novel distortion. With a diction that was exceptionally Hellenistic in its makeup, the letter formulates a message that was remarkably "primitive" and Jewish in its moral and apocalyptic orientation.

The Greek text and syntax of the letter is uncertain at several places and its meaning often obscure. The many textual variants reflect early attempts to make sense of these obscurities (1:4, 10, 15; 2:1, 4, 6, 12–18, 21–22; 3:5, 7–12). Bauckham's (*2 Peter* WBC) discussion is comprehensive and is based on the most recent edition of the Greek text (NovTG^{26}).

A coherent development of themes and line of argumentation and a consistency of terminology and style mark the integrity of the document as a whole. It is structured in three major sections. Following the address and salutation (1:1–2), a preamble establishes at the outset how the addressees are to respond to the divine gifts and promises to which they owe their Christian existence and future hope (1:3–11). Then, 1:12–3:13 comprises a double apostolic and prophetic reminder serving as the basis for the denunciation and refutation of sceptical false teachers. A concluding exhortation (3:14–18), paralleling 1:3–11, reaffirms the gifts and responsibilities of the faithful.

Within these major sections, the units 1:12–15; 16–21; 2:1–22; 3:1–7; 8–13 are marked off by internal content and/or inclusions (1:12–15 "remind"/"recall;" 2:1–22 ("way of truth, righteousness") and by the introductory address, "beloved" (3:1, 8, 14). Linkwords ("knowledge," 1:2, 3, 8; "borne," 1:17, 18, 21; "prophecy," 1:19–22, cf. 2:1; "ignore," 3:5, 8; "forbearance," 3:9, 15; "wait," 3:13, 14), as well as frequent demonstratives ("these things," 1:8, 9, 10, 12; 2:20; 3:11, 14) are used to relate and join smaller units of thought. A major inclusion is evident in the combination of "grace and knowledge of our God (Lord) and Savior Jesus Christ" in 1:2 and 3:18 (cf. also "stabilized" and "stability" in 1:12 and 3:17) which thereby frames the letter as a whole.

F. Situation

2 Peter was directed to a Christian community in which converts from paganism (2:20), assuming the mantle of teachers (2:1), had begun to challenge traditional Christian beliefs and norms of behavior. Their divisive factional views ("heresies," RSV) had strong appeal apparently for members who had grown impatient with the delay of the Lord's coming *(parousia)* and had begun to lose faith in its promise (3:4). In his *Anchor Bible* commentary on this letter, Reicke (pp. 160–61) imagined a different situation more political in character. He proposed that the troublemakers were greedy Christian leaders who had accepted bribes from Roman aristocrats intent on gathering support for a revolt against the Roman emperor Domitian (81–96). There is no trace of these particulars in the text, however. Here the issue is described as an internal Christian problem. Covert introduction of alluring alien ideas was endangering the community's cohesion and stability (2:1–3, 14, 18; cf. 1:10 and 3:17).

This situation is further clarified by other explicit and implicit indicators of the dissenters' program. They "deny the Master who bought them" and "despise authority" (2:1, 10a). They deny the final "coming" *(parousia)* of God in judgment and cosmic renewal, and consider its promise empty (3:4, refuted in 3:5–10). On the other hand, they themselves promise "freedom" (2:19a, refuted in 2:19b–22), a deviant brand of freedom for self-indulgence probably gained through an idiosyncratic interpretation of Paul's writings (3:15–16). As Neyrey (1980a; 1980b; followed by Bauckham *2 Peter* WBC) has shown, the formula "not . . . but" employed in 1:16a/16b–18, 1:20/21 and 2:3b/4–10a also identifies teaching refuted by the author. This included rejection of the Lord's previous coming *(parousia)* in power as a "myth," individualistic and idiosyncratic interpretation of scripture ("prophecy"), and again denial of divine destruction and deliverance. In sum, these sceptics denied God's past, present, and future involvement in the world and human affairs, divine communication through and control over prophecy, and divine judgment of either sinners or the righteous.

Consonant with this theoretical position, they flaunted a supposed freedom from judgment as a release from the commandment of the Lord (2:21, 3:2) and a license for self-indulgence (2:2, 10a, 13, 18), "pleasure" (2:13), and personal gain (2:3, 15–16). Over against the common good and the binding norms of the community they advocated pursuit of individual interests and rejections of social constraints.

The repeated stress in 2 Peter upon an authentic "knowledge" (1:2, 3, 5,6, 8; 2:20; 3:17) as well as upon a correct understanding of the apostolic and prophetic tradition (1:16–21; 3:1–4, 15–16) has led many scholars to identify the opponents as Christian Gnostics (from the Greek *gnosis* meaning "knowledge"). However, interest in knowledge and wisdom as a means to perfection of salvation was by no means restricted to these heretical Christian groups of the 2d and later centuries. It was rather typical of the Hellenistic age in general, in secular as well as Jewish and Christian milieux.

Since the spread of Greek culture with the advance of Alexander's armies (333 B.C.E.), numerous philosophical and religious movements had competed with one another over the nature and source of knowledge and the means it provided for discovering the nature and goal of life, the essence of human happiness, and the way to attain it. Beside the schools of Plato, Aristotle, the Cynics and Stoics, the school of Epicurus (341–270 B.C.E.) propounded views and practices with which the false teachers of 2 Peter seem to have much in common.

Among its basic tenets, this rationalistic and quasi-religious philosophy held that: knowledge derives from sense perception of the physical world, the "nature of things" (the title of a widely influential didactic poem by Lucretius, 94–55 B.C.E.); this perception teaches that all matter is composed of atoms and eventually disintegrates; hence everything is mortal and there is no "life after death;" the gods are distant from and uninvolved in the affairs of this world; hence the notion of post-mortem retribution or divine punishment is absurd and the "myths" concerning the gods held by the general populace are ridiculous; mortals should not be motivated by fear of the gods, death, or divine judgment but by pursuit of "pleasure" (*hēdonē* in Greek, whence "hedonist"), i.e., the absence of pain and disturbance; such knowledge frees one from fear, guilt, superstition, and involvement in the affairs of social and political life.

The founder of this philosophy was generally honored for his wisdom and personal morality and was celebrated as a "savior." Later adherents, however, came under severe censure for their "atheism" (rejection of the gods as popularly worshipped), their exclusiveness and especially for their alleged immoral conduct, whence the pejorative connotation of the related labels, "Epicurean" and "hedonist." They were, in fact, compared to pigs wallowing in their self-serving passions. This practical philosophy flourished for half a millennium in the ancient world and attracted adherents from all social strata and walks of life (DeWitt 1954).

To the outsider as well as to many a Christian convert, Epicureanism and Christianity appeared to have much in common, including their repudiation of popular religion, their sectarian exclusiveness, and their disengagement from political life. In the popular mind the two groups were closely associated and commonly subjected to the same condemnation. The description of those labeled "false teachers" in 2 Peter includes numerous traits typically associated with Epicureans. In addition to the substance of their teaching, the reference to their pursuit of "pleasure" (2:13) and their comparison with dogs and swine (2:22) is particularly striking. Most significantly, as Neyrey has shown (1980a; 1980b), the critique of the opponents' teaching closely resembles the polemic regularly leveled by Jews and Gentiles alike against Epicureans and those thought tainted by Epicureanism such as the Sadducees. In all likelihood, the Christians censured in 2 Peter were perceived as persons under the influence of Epicurean thought seeking to attract other members of the community to their new amalgamation of Christian freedom and rationalistic scepticism.

G. Strategy

This serious erosion of the confidence and cohesion of the community as well as of its public reputation (2:1–3) called for a persuasive response. To combat this situation the author combined a rebuke and refutation of the sceptics with a reaffirmation of the faithful. The letter of Jude, conventional anti-Epicurean polemic, language and motifs of benefactor commemoration, apocalyptic tradition, and apostolic-prophetic testimony provided the models and substance of the argument.

To isolate and discredit the sceptics, a comprehensive contrast is drawn between their behavior and that of the faithful, their new and alien false teaching and the ancient prophetic and apostolic testimony verified by God. Those who scoff at the Lord's coming are "false teachers" who exploit and entice with "false words" like the "false prophets" of old (2:1–3, 14–16). By contrast, you the faithful know the "truth" and its reliable source (1:12–21, 3:1–2; cf. 1:2–3, 5–8; 3:17–18). They are "ignorant" (3:16) like "irrational animals" (2:12, 22); they "forget" (1:9) and "ignore" (3:8) what they once knew (2:20–22). You should "not ignore" (3:8) but "remember" the testimonies (1:12–15, 3:1–2) and advance in all the gifts you have received from God (1:3–11, 3:14–18). They have followed Balaam's "way" of error (2:15), whereas you adhere to the "way of truth and righteousness" (2:2, 21). They are "unstable" apostates who mislead others (2:2, 15, 20–22; 3:16); you must resist their efforts and remain "stable" (3:17; 1:10, 12). They distrust God's "promise" (3:3–4; but their own "promise" of freedom is vacuous (2:17–19). However, the "promises" you have are reliable for they come from God (1:4; 3:9, 13). They are "ungodly," "lawless men" (3:17; cf. 2:6, 8) seeking their own self-serving passions and interests (1:20, 2:2–3, 10–11, 13–14, 18); they are unholy "slaves of corruption" (2:19–20). But you have "escaped corruption" and "passion" and share in God's holy nature (1:3–4; 3:11, 14). They, like the sinners of old, will be "condemned," though they doubt God's judgment (2:3, 4–10a; 3:4–7). but you can trust God's coming. If, like righteous Noah and Lot of old, you remain faithful, you will be rescued (1:10–11, 3:11–18).

Accompanying this strategy of demarcation was an argument based on historical precedence and antiquity. To allay doubt in God's present and future involvement in human judgment and cosmic renewal, the author recalled scriptural evidence and apostolic eyewitness testimony from the past. God's creative and destructive action in the world is recorded in history (2:4–8; 3:5–6). This history establishes the certainty of his present and future involvement in human judgment and cosmic renewal (2:9–10a, 12; 3:7, 8–13). As God spoke at creation (3:5), so he also spoke through the prophets and to his Son (1:16–21). This word and coming of God in the past is attested by the personal experience of the earliest of the apostles, Symeon Peter. This "coming in power," already experienced in human history, is a model for, and basis for confidence in, the parousia to come at the end of time (3:1–11).

Over against the novel and alien vagaries of the false teachers, 2 Peter thus posed the older, venerable, and more probative testimony of prophetic and apostolic tradition. Over against their aberrant and divisive sense of freedom, he emphasized the unifying way of truth and righteousness and the holy commandment received from Jesus Christ. Over against scepticism concerning the future, he urged recollection of what the believers had already received and knew. "Entrance into the eternal kingdom of our Lord Jesus Christ" would be theirs if they awaited the day of the Lord in patient confidence and grew in the gifts already granted.

2 Peter has been faulted for its lack of reference to the heart of the kerygma, the death and resurrection of Jesus Christ, and its implications for Christian faith and conduct. The nature of the error confronted, however, concerned theological assumptions underlying that kerygma rather than the kerygma itself: the ancient Jewish and primitive Christian belief concerning divine providence and the exercise of divine justice. It was this previously unquestioned belief which converts from paganism had begun to challenge. Their scepticism focused not the person and role of Jesus but rather on the presence and participation of God in human history. In response, the author marshaled arguments and sources useful for the reaffirmation of this belief and the refutation of those who challenged it. Jude and anti-Epicurean polemic supplied the model and substance for the critique of the false teachers. Apocalyptic tradition likewise was used to reassert the universal scope of God's reign and to stress the link between present, past and future, protology and eschatology. The fiction of a Petrine testament supplied the letter with apostolic credentials which were older and therefore superior to those of Paul and Jude, the author of 2 Peter's chief source. Furthermore, Peter's eyewitness of Jesus' transfiguration, the foreshadowing of the future parousia in past time and space, countered the sceptics' charge that the parousia of God (or the gods) was merely a fanciful "myth." Finally, the testament form itself provided a means for depicting events of the present as already anticipated and addressed in an authoritative legacy from the past.

Linked to its theological eschatology of the endtime, 2

Peter proposed an "interim ethics" for Christians awaiting the dawning of the final day of the Lord. Between Christian conversion and cosmic consummation believers were to grow in the gifts and their stability and salvation by resisting the seduction of Christian subversives who deviate from the prophetic and apostolic norms of truth; avoid the corruption of the world by leading holy, godly and peaceful lives in accord with the way of righteousness; and with patient confidence await the promised day of the Lord.

Despite its marginal status within the course of Christian theology, the concerns of this letter retain perennial significance. For when sceptics of any age question the rule of God in human history, the certainty of afterlife, Christ's coming in power and judgment, and the implications of this for Christian morality, then this recollection of the ancient apostolic tradition assumes fresh urgency and vitality.

H. Origin, Destination, and Date

2 Peter contains only implicit information concerning its origin, destination, and date of composition. The letter's salutation (1:1–2) does not specify the geographical location of its intended audience. The situation, style, and content of the letter indicate that both author and audience resided in culturally pluralistic Hellenistic environments. Both addressees and false teachers are said to have "escaped from the world's corruption" (1:4, 2:20), a characterization which is more appropriate to gentile rather than Jewish converts. On the other hand, the frequent allusions to the Jewish scriptures, the occasional use of Semitic turns of phrase (2:1, 2, 12–14; 3:3), and the strong reliance on Jewish apocalyptic materials, suggest that the audience on the whole was familiar with and could be persuaded by tradition drawn from the Jewish-Christian heritage. The addressees were also assumed to have known of Paul and at least some of his letters (3:15–16), of a previous Petrine letter, and possibly of the letter of Jude (3:1–3).

The location of the audience could have been in any of the cosmopolitan centers of the Mediterranean world penetrated by Christianity such as Antioch in Syria, Alexandria in Egypt, Ephesus in Asia Minor, or Rome. However, the cumulative evidence argues most strongly for Asia Minor. Here pagan, Jewish, and Christian cultures coexisted and clashed, Epicureans had a firm foothold, Pauline letters were gathered, and another epistle of Peter was known. Egypt as a possible, though less likely, place of destination is suggested by the early use of 2 Peter in the Egyptian *Apocalypse of Peter* (ca. 135 C.E.) and its first explicit citation by Origen of Alexandria (217–ca. 251).

Although the letter's place of origin is also unspecified, several indications point to Rome. This was the site of Peter's death and the location of the Petrine circle from which 1 Peter issued. The numerous affinities between 2 Peter and the clearly Roman documents of *1* and *2 Clement* and the *Shepherd of Hermas* suggest dependence on a common Roman Christian tradition (Bauckham *2 Peter* WBC, 145–51, 158–62). These documents, along with 1 Peter, also attest the pastoral concern of the Christian groups in Rome for the churches abroad.

The lower and upper limits of the letter's date of composition are established by its use of Jude (ca. 70–90) and its probable use by the author of the *Apocalypse of Peter* (ca. 135). This time frame also accords with its concerns, content, and retrospective perspective. The advanced Hellenistic spirit of the letter, the Christian divisions it describes, the delay of the parousia it must explain and the doubts it must dispel, its retrospective appeal to the legacy of an apostle no longer alive, the misuse of prophetic and Pauline writings it must correct, along with its relatively late attestation are all features which indicate that 2 Peter is, with great likelihood, the latest composition of the NT, written sometime in the first quarter of the 2d century. Composed in the name of Peter who had long since died (ca. 65–67 C.E.), it nevertheless claims to preserve a testament which provides a formal link with the past and a guideline for present and future. (See also Chase *HDB* 3: 779–96; Fuchs and Reymond *La deuxième épître de Saint Pierre. La épître de Saint Jude* CNT 2/13b; Kelly *The Epistles of Peter and of Jude* HNTC; Schelkle *Die Petrusbriefe, Der Judasbrief* HTKNT; Schrage and Balz *Die "Katholischen" Briefe* NTD 10; Spicq *Les Epitres de Saint Pierre* SB.)

Bibliography

Boobyer, G. H. 1959. The Indebtedness of 2 Peter to 1 Peter. Pp. 34–53 in *New Testament Essays,* ed. A. J. B. Higgins. Manchester.

Danker, F. W. 1978. 2 Peter 1: A Solemn Decree. *CBQ* 40: 64–82.

———. 1982. *Benefactor: Epigraphic Study of a Graeco-Roman and New Testament Semantic Field.* St. Louis.

DeWitt, N. W. 1954. *Epicurus and His Philosophy.* Minneapolis.

Fornberg, T. 1977. *An Early Church in a Pluralistic Society. A Study of 2 Peter.* ConBNT 9. Lund.

Green, E. M. B. 1960. *2 Peter Reconsidered.* Tyndale New Testament Lecture. London.

Guthrie, D. 1970. *New Testament Introduction.* 3d rev. ed. Downers Grove. IL.

Kaesemann, E. 1964. An Apologia for Primitive Christian Eschatology. Pp. 169–95 in *Essays on New Testament Themes.* London.

Mayor, J. B. 1907. *The Epistle of St. Jude and the Second Epistle of St. Peter.* London. Repr. Grand Rapids, MI.

Metzger, B. M. 1972. Literary Forgeries and Canonical Pseudepigrapha. *JBL* 91: 3–24.

Neyrey, J. H. 1980a. The Apologetic Use of the Transfiguration in 2 Peter 1:16–21. *CBQ* 42: 504–19.

———. 1980b. The Form and Background of the Polemic in 2 Peter. *JBL* 99: 407–31.

Smith, T. V. 1985. *Petrine Controversies in Early Christianity: Attitudes towards Peter in Christian Writings of the First Two Centuries.* WUNT 2/15. Tubingen.

JOHN H. ELLIOTT

PETHAHIAH (PERSON) [Heb *pĕtaḥyāh*]. **1.** A priest who appears in an organizational list associated with David (1 Chr 24:16). According to the genealogical information in 1 Chronicles 24, Pethahiah was a descendant of Aaron through the family of either Eleazar or Ithamar. When lots were cast in order to organize the various officers of the temple, he was assigned to the nineteenth of twenty-four divisions. In light of the postexilic perspective of Chronicles, Pethahiah is further seen as an ancestor of a later priestly family (Braun *1 Chronicles* WBC, 228).

2. A Levite (Neh 9:5) who participated in the ceremonies preceding the "sealing" of the new covenant (Neh 9:38). These ceremonies included both communal confession and worship. According to Neh 9:5, Pethahiah and other selected Levites called the assembly to join in a liturgical blessing of Yahweh prior to Ezra's prayer. In addition, this is most likely the same Pethahiah who, along with other Levites, priests, and laymen, listened to Ezra and agreed to renounce their foreign wives and children (Ezra 10:23; 1 Esdr 9:23).

3. The son of Meshazabel and a descendant of Judah, he appears in a catalog of officials who served the postexilic community in and around Jerusalem (Neh 11:24). Specifically, Pethahiah "was at the king's hand in all matters concerning the people." While some have suggested that such a description indicates a Jewish representative residing in Persia and functioning in a capacity quite similar to the one held earlier by Ezra (Ezra 7:12; Brockington *Ezra, Nehemiah, and Esther* NCBC, 195; Fensham *Ezra-Nehemiah* NICOT, 248), the phrase "at the king's hand" can just as well be understood in a figurative sense. Given the general setting of Jerusalem and the surrounding towns in this passage, Pethahiah was likely a local advisor who reported to the king through regional officials (Blenkinsopp *Ezra-Nehemiah* OTL, 327).

TERRY L. BRENSINGER

PETHOR (PLACE) [Heb *pĕtôr*]. The home of Balaam, the Mesopotamian seer who was summoned by Balak to curse the Israelites (Num 22:4–6; Deut 23:4). According to Num 22:5, Pethor was located near the Euphrates River in the land of AMAW. Mentioned in occasional extrabiblical inscriptions, Amaw lay to the W of the Euphrates. Additional information concerning Pethor is provided in both the book of Numbers as well as the inscription of Shalmaneser III. In Balaam's first oracle, he mentions that he had been brought from Aram and the eastern mountains (Num 23:7). While such descriptions are noticeably vague, they suggest the general region that included central Syria and extended to the Euphrates (Budd *Numbers* WBC, 267; Noth *Numbers* ET, OTL, 183). Shalmaneser III's inscriptions, however, are a bit more precise. In this case, Pitru (the Hittite name for Pethor and the equivalent of the Assyrian *Ana-Aššurutîr-aṣbat,* meaning "I founded [it] again for Aššur") is positioned "on the other side of the Euphrates, on the river Sagur" (*ANET,* 278). Insofar as the Sagur joins the Euphrates some 60 miles NE of Aleppo, Pethor was situated on the W bank of the Euphrates in Upper Mesopotamia near the point where the two rivers meet. While a specific site defies certain identification, Tell Aḥmar (36°40′N; 38°08′E), located 18 miles S of Carchemish, has been suggested (Snaith *Leviticus and Numbers* NCBC, 287).

TERRY L. BRENSINGER

PETHUEL (PERSON) [Heb *pĕtûʾēl*]. According to Joel 1:1, the name of the father of the prophet Joel. The name may mean "youth of El" or "a youth belonging to El" (*TPNAH,* 116, 123).

RICHARD D. WEIS

PETRA (PLACE). See NABATEANS.

PEULLETHAI (PERSON) [Heb *pĕʿullĕtay*]. Among the gatekeepers at the temple in Jerusalem, Peullethai (whose name means "recompense" or "reward") is named in 1 Chr 26:5 as the last of the eight sons of Obed-Edom cited. The list in which his name occurs (1 Chr 26:4–8) appears to be the contribution of a reviser of the Chronicler's organization of the gatekeepers (Williamson Chronicles NCBC, 160–70; Rudolph *Chronikbücher* HAT, 173).

J. S. ROGERS

PHALTIEL (PERSON) [Lat *Phalthihel*]. A "chief of the people" who came to visit Ezra between Ezra's first and second vision, according to 2 Esdr 5:16. Phaltiel comes to Ezra's residence on the day after the first vision, and urges him to revive himself and lead the people. The Codex Complutensis renders the name as *Salatiel,* which is equivalent to the Heb name Shealtiel (Myers *1 and 2 Esdras* AB, 168). Shealtiel is the father of Zerubbabel in Ezra-Nehemiah (see SHEALTIEL), and so an identification of Phaltiel with Shealtiel is both possible and intriguing.

PHANUEL (PERSON) [Gk *Phanouēl*]. Phanuel, whose name means "the face of God" (cf. Gen 32:32 LXX), is the father of Anna the prophetess and a member of the tribe of Asher (Luke 2:36). Asher was one of the lost northern tribes and the reference here indicates that after the exile some of the lost tribes returned to full membership in the Jewish nation.

JOANN FORD WATSON

PHARAKIM (PERSON) [Gk *Pharakim*]. Forefather of a family included under the heading the "temple servants," which returned with Zerubbabel (1 Esdr 5:31). See also NETHINIM. However, this family is not included in the parallel lists in Ezra 2 and Nehemiah 7.

Bibliography

Haran, M. 1961. The Gibeonites, the Nethinim and the sons of Solomon's Servants. *VT* 11: 159–69.

CRAIG D. BOWMAN

PHARAOH. Egyptian *Pr-ʿ3* (pronounced something like *pārĕō), literally (the) "Great House;" a later designation of the king of Egypt.

The monarch who sat on the throne of Egypt was traditionally accorded a number of names and titles encompassing his divine and terrestrial roles in the scheme of things: "Horus" (the falcon-god incarnate), "Golden Horus," "Favorite of the Two Ladies" (i.e., the cobra and vulture, tutelary goddesses of Upper and Lower Egypt), "He-of-the-Sut-plant-and-the-bee" (i.e., King of Upper and Lower Egypt), "son of Re" (the sun-god) etc. The word "Pharaoh," however, was not initially part of his titulary. Attested from the early 3d millennium B.C. as a designation of part of the large palace complex at Memphis wherein the king and the officers of his administration lived, the term by extension came to signify the authority of the central government. During the 18th Dynasty (ca. 1560–1320 B.C.), and certainly before the reign of Thutmose III (1504–1451 B.C.), "Great House" was occasionally applied to the person of the king himself by metonymy, much as "the Porte" stood for the Turkish sultan, or the "White House" betokens the President of the U.S.A. While initially this semantic development took place within the realm of the vernacular, before the close of the New Kingdom (ca. 1070 B.C.) "Pharaoh" had become a polite circumlocution for the reigning king in official jargon, and as such from the reign of Sheshonk I (last quarter of the 10th century B.C.) is sometimes included within the king's titulary in formal inscriptions. By the 8th century B.C. it was an integral part of the royal cartouche itself (i.e., the oval within which the king's name was written in hieroglyphs); and from the 7th century on was nothing but a synonym of the generic "king," the older word which it rapidly replaced. Its occurrence in the Bible in Genesis, Exodus, and 2 Kings as synonymous with "king of Egypt" conforms to the final stage of its native evolution.

The word did not escape oblivion itself. Although Ptolemaic temples (ca. 300–30 B.C.) display "Pharaoh" frequently and consistently in the context of inscriptions where it means only "king," the termination of the monarchy by the Roman emperor Augustus rendered it obsolete. Coptic Christianity (beginning in the late 3d century A.D.) wholly misinterpreted "Pharaoh" (as definite article *p-* followed by *-rero,* "king"—no such word exists); while classical and Islamic tradition transmogrified it into a personal name for a few individual kings (see also *LÄ* 4: 1021).

Bibliography

Gardiner, A. H. 1953. *Egyptian Grammar.* 3d ed. Oxford.
Posener, G. 1960. *De la divinité de la Pharaon.* Paris.
Vergote, J. 1959. *Joseph en Égypte.* Louvain.

DONALD B. REDFORD

PHARATHON (PLACE) [Gk *Pharathōn*]. Variant spelling of PIRATHON.

PHARES (PERSON) [Gk *Phares*]. See PEREZ.

PHARISEES [Gk *Pharisaios*]. Recent research on the Pharisees has paradoxically made them and their role in Palestinian society more obscure and difficult to describe. The three ancient sources—Josephus, the NT, and rabbinic literature—have very limited information which is difficult to interpret. Scholars have pictured the Pharisees as a sect within Judaism, a powerful religious leadership group, a political leadership group, a learned scholarly group, a lay movement in competition with the priesthood, a group of middle class urban artisans, or some combination of these. In most historical reconstructions of Jewish society the categories used to describe these groups, such as sect, school, upper class, lay leadership, etc. are ill defined or misused and not integrated into an understanding of the overall structure and functioning of society. Bits of evidence are often taken out of context, harmonized with each other, and used as building blocks for very improbable structures. Because Josephus names the three leading Jewish "schools of thought" as the Pharisees, Sadducees, and Essenes, and because the Pharisees, scribes, and Sadducees appear in the NT as opponents of Jesus, the importance and roles of these groups in Jewish society is vastly overemphasized. The proliferation of hypotheses about the Pharisees shows how poorly they are understood. After a review of previous scholarship, the evidence from Josephus, the NT, rabbinic literature, and Qumran will be reviewed and the historically reliable conclusions synthesized.

A. Previous Scholarship and Theories
B. Josephus
  1. Hasmonean Period
  2. Herodian Period
  3. War against Rome
  4. Political Role
  5. Descriptions
  6. Organization
C. New Testament
  1. Paul
  2. Mark
  3. Matthew
  4. Luke-Acts
  5. John
D. Rabbinic Literature
  1. 1st Century Sages
  2. 1st-Century Laws
  3. Pharisee Texts
E. Qumran Literature
F. Synthesis

A. Previous Scholarship and Theories

Studies of the Pharisees in the last century have been beset with a number of political and methodological problems. Jewish interpretations of the programs of the Pharisees and Sadducees have often been covertly influenced by modern conflicts between traditional and progressive Jews. Many Christian accounts of the Pharisees have been vitiated by either uncritical acceptance of the anti-Jewish polemics of the NT or modern anti-Semitism. Apologetic defenses of the Pharisees by both Jewish and Christian scholars have distorted or romanticized the Pharisees and separated them from their historical context. Many traditional and historical studies of the Pharisees have been marred by an uncritical acceptance of some or all of the sources (Josephus, NT, rabbinic literature) without sophisticated interpretation of the purpose, date, and natures of each. The fragmentary nature of the texts referring to the Pharisees has prompted scholars to harmonize the sources with one another, to fill in gaps with very speculative hypotheses, and to create historically unproven accounts of their origin, nature, history, teaching, and goals. Lack of evidence about the Pharisees and great discord over related issues such as the nature of Second Temple Judaism, its thought, laws, practices, and social structure, have joined to produce a welter of unproven theories concerning every aspect of the Pharisees' thought and history.

Only the most influential writers and theories will be reviewed here.

A. Geiger's work on the Pharisees set the terms for the debate in the 19th and 20th centuries. He interpreted the Hillelites as more liberal and adaptable to evolving circumstances than the more conservative and literalistic Sadducees and Pharisaic Shammaites. The contrast between the rigidity of the old halakha (condemned in the NT according to Geiger) and the new halakha of the Pharisees (whom Geiger admired) roughly parallels the conflict in 19th century Germany between traditional Judaism and the Reform. Geiger's approach was popularized by the historians H. Graetz and I. H. Weiss and has continued with many modifications and variations to govern most accounts of the Pharisees until the present.

Christian accounts of the Pharisees have been greatly influenced by Wellhausen, Schürer (*HJP*), Bousset, and Meyer, all of whom interpreted "late" Judaism as a legalistic degeneration of Judaism in comparison with prophetic ethics. Wellhausen and other 19th century writers were influenced by Hegelian and evolutionary ideas in their construction of historical schema and conveniently saw the Pharisees as symptomatic of a legalistic and materialistic Judaism, both deteriorating and about to be replaced by Christianity. This type of view, popularized by the influential histories of Schürer, Bousset, and Meyer has dominated much of Christian scholarship on the Pharisees and Judaism in general.

At the turn of the century a number of Jewish scholars had begun to argue against the prevailing Christian interpretation of the Pharisees (see the review of fourteen items by Box 1908–9). In the early part of this century, British and American scholarship was greatly influenced by the interpretations of the Pharisees by J. Lauterbach, L. Ginzberg, L. Finkelstein, L. Baeck, and H. Loewe. Lauterbach continued Geiger's tradition of reformed scholarship in a series of essays (1913–29) which relate the history of the Pharisees to the development of midrash and Mishnah in Jewish history. He interpreted the Pharisees as progressive lay leaders opposed to the conservative Sadducean priestly aristocracy. Ginzberg criticized Geiger's contention that the Pharisees changed and adapted the law and affirmed its antiquity. He related differences in the law to social and historical factors, especially the relationship of the Sadducees and Shammaite Pharisees to the aristocracy, and the Hillelite Pharisees to the common people. The laws of these groups focused on different concerns and produced different legal interpretations. Ultimately, Ginzberg's characterization of the Pharisees resembles that of Geiger. Finkelstein in early articles and studies and finally in his book, *The Pharisees,* took the sociological study of the Pharisees in a different direction, attributing differences in law and custom, not to liberalism and conservatism but to social class and geographical location, with the Pharisees representing the urban plebians and the Sadducees the rural patricians. He also attributed to some rabbinic laws and customs an origin in the monarchic period. Baeck, defending Judaism against the onslaughts of German anti-Semitism in the 1930's, understood the Pharisees as a movement which sought the dominance of religion over all of Jewish life and stressed a holiness which did not compromise with a hostile culture. The Pharisees were close to the people and led Judaism in changing social circumstances. H. Loewe, following Lauterbach and others, gave a comprehensive and sympathetic account of the Pharisees in a famous series of lectures presented to a Jewish and Christian audience in Britain.

All these scholars accepted at face value the sources which speak of the Pharisees, criticizing them only when they contradicted one another or seemed very improbable. The continuity of the Pharisaic and rabbinic movements and the pertinence of rabbinic literature for describing Pharisaic history and thought was assumed. Most understood the Pharisees as a lay movement or sect with scribal connections which was based on certain interpretations of the law. In general the rabbinic view of the Pharisees as a powerful governing force, in competition with and eventually dominating the priesthood and other aristocratic leaders, was accepted. Their synthesis of the Pharisees and the rest of early Judaism, derived mainly from rabbinic literature's later understanding of its origins, was accepted by a new generation of Christian scholars.

R. T. Herford published a number of books which sought to counteract Christian polemics and anti-Semitism. In his study of the Pharisees he followed Lauterbach and presented a sympathetic portrait of the Pharisees as teachers of the oral law. He based his account of their teachings almost wholly on rabbinic literature and turned Wellhausen's theory on its head by arguing that the Pharisees continued the ethical tradition of the prophets. Herford, and Moore after him, encouraged an appreciation of the deep religious significance in the Pharisaic/rabbinic way of life and recognition of the vitality of Pharisaism which was the foundation of rabbinic Judaism and contributed so much to early Christianity. Herford's approach, based on the work of the Jewish apologists, influenced the presentation of Judaism in Gressmann's third edition of Bousset.

G. F. Moore's masterful and judicious synthesis of Jewish thought in the first two centuries has dominated the English-speaking world. Moore, who mastered both the primary and secondary sources, made use of rabbinic and other literature with attention to the problems of dating and continuity. His famous synthesis of "normative Judaism" which he argued formed the inner core of Judaism in all its manifestations has been decisively refuted by recent finds and research, but his study still retains value as a thoughtful summary of major themes in Jewish thought. In his account of the Pharisees and their place in Jewish history Moore followed the main lines sketched out by Geiger, Ginzberg, and others, with special emphasis on theological disagreement between the Pharisees and Sadducees, including a rough analogy between the Pharisees and Puritans.

S. Zeitlin, in numerous articles and his history of the Second Commonwealth, distinguished various meanings of the term "Pharisee" in rabbinic literature so that the historical group opposed to the Sadducees could be distinguished from other groups of "separatists" who were not Pharisees. The Pharisees according to Zeitlin had their origin in the 5th century and were not a sect, but emerged from a lay scribal movement which was focused on the oral law. Zeitlin makes critical use of the sources, but his methods for solving many problems and his exegeses of numerous texts are idiosyncratic; thus his work should be used with care.

Ellis Rivkin has taken up Zeitlin's work on the Pharisees with numerous modifications. The Pharisees are not a sect or movement, but a scholarly class dedicated to the teaching of the twofold law and interalizing Judaism through belief in life after death. They revolutionized Judaism by creating new institutions such as the synagogue, the *bêt dîn* (court), the dominance of the scholarly class, the master-disciple relationship, and the formulation of Mishnaic type law. The Pharisees originated in the Hasmonean period and were socially powerful leaders (Rivkin takes Matt 23:2 as historically accurate on this point). Rivkin more consistently distinguishes the varied uses of Pharisee in rabbinic literature, but in doing so he uncritically combines texts from very diverse documents and periods as if they formed one homogenous corpus. He too readily accepts rabbinic texts referring to the Pharisees, as well as the NT and Josephus, as reliable historical sources without taking into account the authors' purposes and historical distance from the Pharisees. In addition, he identifies Pharisaic teachings with much of rabbinic literature and Pharisees with scribes and sages. With these qualifications Rivkin's reconstruction of the Pharisees is the most detailed and critical since World War II, with the exception of that of Jacob Neusner.

Jacob Neusner has pioneered the use of rigorous historical-critical analysis of the full range of rabbinic sources. The stories of the Second Temple sages, which are usually used as the building blocks for reconstruction of the Pharisees, are found to be generally unreliable. The teachings of these sages can be accepted as 1st or 2d century only if the substance of the teaching is attested (that is, referred to or assumed) by a sage of the same or the next generation. The whole Mishnah also has been subjected to a formal and logical analysis to unravel its earlier and later layers. While no certain results can be achieved by these methods, some probable conclusions concerning the teachings of the Pharisees have been reached and correlated with the evidence in Josephus and the NT.

When the Mishnah and Tosefta are analyzed using Neusner's criteria (the logic of Mishnah's argument and the attested attributions), by far the largest body of law which can be somewhat reliably assigned to the early- and mid-1st-century concerns: ritual purity, tithes and other food laws, and Sabbath and festival observance. These laws set out an agenda of holiness for the land and people which was a fitting response for a powerless people dominated by the Romans because these laws pertain to the parts of domestic life—food, sex, and marriage—which can be controlled by people out of power in their own society. Food and reproduction within the household, rather than the public cult at the Temple and the governance of society, are within the grasp of a subject people. Neusner argues that the legal agenda of the Pharisees, centered around food laws and festivals, bespeaks a sectarian table fellowship which was not part of the political struggle or 1st-century Palestine. Neusner theorizes that the Pharisees were an active political party under the Hasmoneans (cf. Josephus), but were driven from the political arena by Herod's repression. He has further suggested that the absence of a coherent body of laws concerned with civil law and sacrifice in the Temple, though an argument from silence, indicates that the Pharisees were not in control of the Temple cult or the dominant force in society. Talmudic stories which depict the Pharisees as rulers of society are later retrojections of 3d to 6th century rabbinic power onto the Pharisees of the 1st century. It is more likely that the Pharisees had been under the Hasmoneans, and remained under the Romans, one of a large number of political-interest groups which combined a social-religious reform program with a search for power and influence over Jewish society and government. Though the Pharisees were less successful in the 1st century than in the Hasmonean period, they were still oriented toward power and continued to work for it after the destruction of the Temple. On the whole Neusner's theory is much more critical and adequate than those of his predecessors.

Two other overviews of the Pharisees by J. Bowker and H. Mantel are deserving of mention. Bowker thinks that Pharisees was the pejorative name for a movement of scholars called *ḥăkāmîm* (sages) who sought to make the laws fit daily life and extend priestly holiness to the people. They became a sect only when they were expelled from the Sanhedrin by John Hyrcanus and finally dominated Judaism after the destruction of the Temple. The *hakamic* movement embraced scribes and associates, *ḥăbērîm,* of *Tractate Demai* as part of their larger movement. In order to create the overarching *hakamic* movement, Bowker must uncritically meld a number of texts into an artificial whole. H. Mantel, who has written extensively on the Sanhedrin, oral law, and origins of rabbinic Judaism, locates the original disputes which separated the Pharisees and Sadducees in the time of Ezra, and envisions a scholarly social movement focused on the study of Torah spanning the centuries from the exile to the destruction of the Second Temple. His focus is on the origin and development of rabbinic halakha which he sets in the Second Temple period. Mantel accepts the rabbinic sources as historically accurate and critically assesses the sources only when they contradict each other or are incoherent. His account of the Pharisees is derived from the interpretation of rabbinic literature found in the German Jewish scholars of the 19th century.

Truly critical interpretation of the rabbinic sources and assessment of their contributions to the history of the Pharisees and their Second Temple context has only recently begun. The redactional tendencies of individual documents must be taken into account, the literary forms analyzed, and the antiquity of traditions established by comparison among many sources and with datable texts and events. As such research progresses (cf. the work of J. Neusner), hypotheses concerning the Pharisees' organization, social type, program, and purposes may be generated and tested. For the present, despite the contribution and theories of past research, much is not known concerning the inner workings of the Pharisees and their social roles in society.

B. Josephus

In his many volumes Josephus mentions the Pharisees less than twenty times, a reflection of their minor role in society. In the *Jewish War* the Pharisees are mentioned four times. Their great influence on Queen Alexandra and consequent political power in the early 1st century, B.C.E. is recounted disapprovingly. Later in that century, Herod accused his brother Pheroras' wife of subsidizing the Pharisees against him. After the long, laudatory description of the Essenes, the Pharisees are described briefly with the Sadducees as one of the three traditional Jewish philosophies. Finally, at the beginning of the Great War the most notable Pharisees along with other Jewish leaders tried to prevent the revolt and the cessation of the sacrifices offered for Rome.

Pharisees as a group or as individuals are mentioned nine times in the *Jewish Antiquities,* three of which are parallel to passages in the *Jewish War.* Josephus gives a brief description of the Pharisees in Book 13, as he treats the Hasmonean period, and a longer one at the beginning of Book 18 (which covers the beginning of the 1st century, C.E.), parallel to the description in the *JW.* He recounts their conflict with John Hyrcanus which led to loss of influence, their political power under Alexandra, and their loss of it again at her death. During the Herodian period, Samaias and Pollion, who are Pharisees, appear in several incidents, including the defense of Herod (in a manner of speaking) at his trial before the Sanhedrin. Herod showed favor to Samaias and Pollion when he took Jerusalem and later exempted them from taking an oath of loyalty to him. Near the end of Herod's life the Pharisees formed an alliance with Pheroras' wife and her faction against Herod, an association which led to the execution of a number of Pharisees.

In the *Life,* Josephus says that he tried the Pharisaic way of life along with the Essenes, Sadducees, and an ascetic named Bannus; finally he chose the Pharisees. On the eve of the revolt, the leading Pharisees, along with the chief priests and Josephus, appear as a leadership group. Simon ben Gamaliel, a Pharisee, is the prime mover in Jerusalem to have Josephus removed from command in Galilee, and the delegation finally sent to remove Josephus from command has a priest Pharisee and two lay Pharisees along with a young chief priest.

1. Hasmonean Period. The nature of the Pharisees can be inferred from their activities during the Second Temple period. During the reign of John Hyrcanus (134–104 B.C.E.) the Pharisees were initially very influential on Hyrcanus, who was guided by their views of Jewish law and life (*Ant* 13 §288–98). Hyrcanus gave a banquet for his valued supporters, and when he asked them for any criticisms they might have, the Pharisees, like tactful clients, praised their patron. The Pharisees seem to have been allies and aids to Hyrcanus, probably as lower officials and functionaries in the newly organized Hasmonean rule. One Pharisee, Eliezer, did criticize Hyrcanus (a serious political attack is implicit) and was rejected by his fellow Pharisees. Nevertheless, a Sadducean friend of Hyrcanus, Jonathan, fanned the flames of the dispute, succeeded in outmaneuvering the Pharisees, and broke their influence on Hyrcanus. This tale of court intrigue and social conflict reflects the struggle for control of Jewish society which endured throughout the Second Temple period. In this complex political, social, and religious competition the Pharisees had at different times both major and minor roles.

The conflict between Hyrcanus and the Pharisees continued through the reign of his son, Alexander Jannaeus (103–76). Though Alexander expanded Jewish territory, Josephus criticizes him for his untactful policies and oppressive cruelty which aroused the people to disturbance and revolt and filled his reign with conflict (*JW* 1 §67–69; *Ant* 14 §85–106). On his death bed Alexander bequeathed his kingdom to his queen, Alexandra, and quieted her fears about the hostility of the people with the advice that she win the Pharisees over to her side so that they would control the people (*Ant* 13 §399–417). Alexander stresses to his wife the ability of the Pharisees to harm or help people by influencing public opinion, despite the fact that they sometimes act out of envy. He also reveals the Pharisees' political agenda, that is, their desire for power over the laws governing domestic Jewish life. Alexandra is to render them benevolent by conceding to them a certain amount of power. Alexandra followed this advice and also let the Pharisees have control over Alexander's corpse and burial, as he advised. The Pharisees, in turn, forgot their anger and gave speeches praising Alexander as a great and just king, which moved the people to give him a splendid burial. Josephus neither praises nor blames the Pharisees for their actions. He sees them as one of the political interest groups competing for power and influence. They are useful for the governing class because of their status and influence among the people. He seems to approve of Alexander's advice to his wife to win over the people and end the civil disorder which marked the end of his reign. The Pharisees are seen here as a force for order and thus win Josephus' approval. Josephus shows no interest in the details of the Pharisaic program, nor in their motives. He takes for granted their self-interested quest for power and cynical posthumous praise of Alexander. Subsequently, however, he criticizes them for causing disorder by trying to take vengeance on their enemies among Alexander's supporters and officials, and he criticizes Alexandra for weakness in letting the Pharisees rule. Under Alexandra the Pharisees had substantial direct bureaucratic power in domestic affairs, recalled exiles, and freed prisoners; but they did not have unlimited power, because they could not punish on their own authority Alexander's old advisors and allies who had crucified eight hundred opponents of Alexander (*Ant* 13 §379–83).

In the confusion which followed the death of Alexandra the Pharisees are not mentioned. It is likely that they had lost influence and popularity with the people because of the way they had exercised power over them and thus lost political power to rival interest groups, coalitions, and factions. Though both of Alexandra's sons, Aristobolus and Hyrcanus, had supporters within Jewish society, neither is said to have turned to the Pharisees for support. The rise and fall of the Pharisees fits the pattern found in many other societies. In times of turmoil many groups and individuals emerge as partially independent power centers and compete for control and frequent changes of leadership are normal.

2. Herodian Period. Herod (37–4 B.C.E.) kept a tight hold on power, so all other groups receded before him and his network of spies. Two Pharisaic leaders, Samaias and his teacher Pollion, protested against the weak leadership of the Sanhedrin by giving Herod backhanded support (*Ant* 14 §163–84; 15 §1–4). Herod responded by treating them as favored clients. Twenty years later he exempted the Pharisees from an oath of loyalty because of his respect for Pollion (*Ant* 15 §368–72).

That the Pharisees remained a social and political force can be seen at the end of Herod's reign when the Pharisees participated in a factional intrigue over the succession to Herod with catastrophic results. Herod's brother Pheroras, the tetrarch of Perea, along with Pheroras' wife, mother, and sister, and Antipater's mother, conspired to have Antipater, Herod's son, succeed him (*JW* 1 §567–71; *Ant* 17 §32–60). Josephus recounts disapprovingly the Pharisees' long relationship with Pheroras's wife and their role in the plots. "There was also a group of Jews priding itself on its adherence to ancestral custom and claiming to observe the laws of which the Deity approves, and by these men, called Pharisees, the women (of the court) were ruled" (*Ant* 17 §41). The Pharisees are here pictured as influencing prominent women just as they had Alexandra in the previous generation. For Josephus, they are just one more group of court retainers surrounding Herod and scheming for power. "These men were able to help the king greatly because of their foresight [prediction], yet they were obviously intent upon combating and injuring him" (*Ant* 17 §41). If the number of Pharisees, six thousand, is accurate, it suggests that they were an organized group or movement with clear enough boundaries to be identified and with enough influence to be recruited by one faction of the royal family.

3. War against Rome. The Pharisees are next active during the revolt against Rome in 66 C.E. the chief priests, leading citizens, and notables (well-known leaders) of the Pharisees tried to persuade the people not to revolt but failed (*JW* 2 §409–17). Josephus makes a clear distinction between these legitimate leaders and the revolutionaries. The Pharisees, or at least their leaders, were part of the established leadership of Jerusalem during its last days. Josephus reaffirms their position when he recounts that he "consorted with the chief priests and the leading Pharisees" (*Life* 20–23) on the eve of the revolt. During the revolt while Josephus was general in Galilee his opponent, John of Gischala, recruited as an ally Simon ben Gamaliel, a high-born leader and member of the Pharisees (*Life* 189–98). Finally, when a delegation of four leaders was sent to remove Josephus from power in Galilee (*Life* 196–98), it consisted of a young chief priest, a Pharisaic priest, and two Pharisees from the common people. Clearly the Pharisees were enmeshed in the fabric of Jewish society and governance, but not in control.

4. Political Role. The minor role played by the Pharisees in Josephus is explained by his concentration on the governing class and its political and military fortunes which were so crucial for Jewish society as a whole. Neither the priesthood, the aristocrats, nor the peasants are treated except when they have an impact on the fortunes of the nation as a whole. The Pharisees are mentioned at times of change, crisis, or transition in government because when power shifted they and many other social and political forces in Jewish society became active in the competition for power and influence. When John Hyrcanus shifted his allegiance from the Pharisees to Sadducees, when Alexandra struggled to maintain control after her husband's death, at the beginning and end of Herod's reign, at the transition from Herodian rule to Roman procurators, and in the complex events at the beginning of the war against Rome, the Pharisees and Sadducees are treated by Josephus as part of the political and social competition for power and influence.

The Pharisees functioned as a political interest group which had its own goals for society and constantly engaged in political activity to achieve them, even though they did not always succeed. They were not themselves the leaders of the Jewish community, though prominent leaders of the Pharisees—either by their station in the Pharisaic group or because of family status—were part of the governing class. The Pharisees as a group did not have direct power (except to a limited degree under their loyal patron, Alexandra) and were not as a whole members of the governing class. They were a literate, organized group which constantly sought influence with the governing class.

The Pharisees' precise goals for society and the laws by which they wished society to live are not described by Josephus, but the traditions which they promoted were popular with the people, especially in the Hasmonean period, according to Josephus. Both their activities in the Hasmonean period and the description of them at the end of Archelaus' reign imply that they were allied with traditional, nonrevolutionary Judaism. Whatever influence they achieved, they usually achieved with the help of a powerful patron, and they entered into coalitions with other groups among the upper classes in order to gain influence and move those who had power.

5. Descriptions. Josephus' descriptions of the Pharisees (along with the Sadducees, Essenes, and "Fourth Philosophy") are generally consistent with his accounts of them in action (*JW* 2 §119–66; *Ant* 18 §11–25; 13 §171–73, 297–98). However, the descriptions are far from complete and do not present a coherent picture of the groups' thought and organization. The Pharisees were noted for their practice of the law and their ability to interpret the law in their own way. This implies that they had particular views about how to live Jewish life and probably followed communal customs within an organizational structure. However, Josephus does not give us any information about the inner workings of the Pharisees or their presumably learned leadership. The Pharisees' acceptance of life after death and resurrection as well as reward and punishment is contrasted with the Sadducees' rejection of these teachings. Likewise, their positions on fate (meaning divine providence) and on free will and human responsibility are contrasted. The Pharisees' positions on life after death and divine providence are consistent with one another and probably derive from their eschatology and apocalyptic expectations: they picture God and humans as in a close relationship both in this life and the next. The Pharisees are said, both in the *Jewish War* and in the *Antiquities,* to be the leading and most influential school of thought, but their social class and status is not specified, except that most of them were of a lower social station than the Sadducees. The description of social relations among the Pharisees and with outsiders is consistent with their place in society. Since the Pharisees lacked direct political power, they cultivated harmonious relations with all and sought support for their mode of life through respect for tradition and their elders. (The Sadducees, like many who exercise power, were perceived as competitive, argumentative, and hard to get along with.) The Pharisees, most of whom did not have hereditary ties to positions of power, struggled to influence society as a group by winning influence. Consequently, they stressed social relations to build up their own group and win it favor and influence with others. That their struggle for power and influence was a group struggle is shown by the absence of names of Pharisaic leaders in most cases. Only Eleazar who attacked John Hyrcanus, Samaias and Pollion who struck up a peculiar and ambivilent relationship with Herod, Simon ben Gamaliel, and the three Pharisees who were part of the delegation sent to Josephus in Galilee (Jonathan, Ananias, and Jozar) are named.

6. Organization. Josephus says nothing about the Pharisees' internal organization. The beliefs which they espoused concerning afterlife, divine activity in history, and human freedom were most probably different enough from the traditional Jewish teachings and attitudes to require some positive commitment and explicit organization. However, their leadership structure, educational system, and criteria for membership are not described. Josephus calls them a *hairēsis,* a term often translated as "sect" or "school" (of thought). A *hairēsis* was a coherent and principled choice of a way of life, that is, of a particular school of thought (Simon 1979: 110, 104). In the view of the ancients and most importantly Josephus, once a few basic principles of a tradition were accepted one could then expect some diversity, that is, some choice of particular ways of life and thought. Greek philosophical schools were usually ways of life based on a certain understanding of the universe and of moral law. Thus, Josephus uses *hairēsis* to describe the great currents of thought and practice in Judaism—espoused by the Pharisees, Sadducees, Essenes, and "Fourth Philosophy" revolutionaries—in such a way as to bring respectability to Judaism and attest to the antiquity and value of its traditions. The translation "sect" may be used if it does not imply withdrawal from political and social action. (Sect in classical sociological usage refers to a religious group which is in reaction to the main religious tradition and which sees itself as the true religion and an exclusive replacement for the dominant tradition.) With their distinctive interpretation of Jewish life and desire for political influence and power the Pharisees may be understood as a reformist sect. *School of thought* as a translation of *hairēsis* may be closer to what Josephus meant, though not necessarily to what the Pharisees were. Josephus is certainly comparing the Pharisees, Sadducees, and Essenes to the Greek schools of philosophy in order to show that Jews are a respectable, civilized people with its own wisdom. The comparison is at least partially appropriate because Greek schools of philosophy did not just engage in the academic study of a group of doctrines, but urged on their members and students a way of life. That the Pharisees actually were similar to a philosophical school is likely because the formation of voluntary associations and social groups was a characteristic of Hellenistic society.

C. New Testament

The Pharisees appear in the gospels and Acts, mostly as opponents of Jesus and his followers. Different roles and characteristics are assigned to the Pharisees in each source. In addition, Paul refers to himself as a Pharisee once in his letters.

1. Paul. Paul is the only person beside Josephus whose personal claim to be a Pharisee is preserved (Phil 3:5) and he is the only diaspora Jew identified as a Pharisee. Paul argues in Philippians against those who propose that Christians be circumcised that, though he has every reason to have confidence in his Jewish birth and heritage (3:4–6), he counts all that as loss in comparison with Jesus (3:7–11). In recounting his Jewish past Paul refers to his circumcision, his membership in Israel and the tribe of Benjamin, and his way of life in Judaism: "in relation to law, a Pharisee; in relation to zeal, a persecutor of the church; in relation to righteousness in law, being blameless." Paul's single allusion to his having been a Pharisee is related to living Jewish life according to the Pharisaic interpretation of Torah. The two characteristics of his Jewish way of life which follow his claim to be a Pharisee seem to derive from his Pharisaism. First, his adherence to the Pharisaic mode of interpreting the law led him zealously to attack the followers of Jesus, a group which had mounted a major challenge to the Pharisaic way of life. Second, he kept the law as one was supposed to and achieved the righteousness from law which was proper to it. Paul is not referring to a highly complex doctrine of work righteousness vs. grace righteousness, but simply saying that he live a good life according to Pharisaic standards. Paul's casual reference to Pharisaism in Philippians implies that it is well known and accepted as a legitimate and strict mode of living Jewish life.

Paul's very brief description of his Jewish way of life as a Pharisee partly fits the view of the Pharisees found in Josephus. Both Josephus and Paul say that the Pharisees had an interpretation of the law, though neither says what it is, and both refer to the Pharisees as a well-known group which does not need detailed identification. Like Josephus, Paul does not tell us of the inner organization of the Pharisees. Both Paul and Josephus say that they were once Pharisees, but never again refer to Pharisaism as part of their Jewish identities. Perhaps both habitually thought of themselves as Jews against the larger horizon of the Greco-Roman world where inner Jewish distinctions, such as membership in the Pharisees, were important.

Paul never says where he made contact with Pharisaism (Tarsus, Syria, or Jerusalem?). Since he never refers to Pharisees as his opponents nor as leaders in the Jewish community in any of the letters addressed to communities in Asia Minor and Greece, it is very probable that Pharisees were not found in those communities. Since Paul lived and worked in greater Syria as a Pharisee, it is possible that Pharisaism had some influence there and that some Pharisees lived outside Jerusalem and Judea.

Paul does not say how he came to know about Pharisaism, why he was attracted to it, and what the Pharisaic life entailed. Pharisaism, as depicted as Josephus, the New Testament and rabbinic writings, concerned itself with Palestinian Jewish political and social issues and with a certain style of Jewish life which included tithing and ritual preparation of foods. It was especially suited to life in Jewish villages and towns. Since Paul used purity language metaphorically to describe and maintain the new boundaries of the Christian community, he was familiar with

Jewish and perhaps Pharisaic purity rules. Paul consciously created a new community with a new understanding of purity, just as the Pharisees had for Judaism.

In the diaspora it is unclear what the Pharisaic life might have meant. Both Josephus and Paul claimed to be Pharisees while living in the larger world of the Roman Empire. Perhaps they found the Pharisaic view of how to live Judaism as a viable response to the intellectual and spiritual challenge of Hellenism. Pharisaism probably brought Jewish practices into daily life and created a conscious way of life which answered the questions and crises felt by some Jews when confronted with the Greco-Roman culture.

Paul's social class and status as a Pharisee is imperfectly transmitted. Though Paul's letters present him as an artisan (1 Thes 2:9; 1 Cor 9:6) and so a member of the lower classes, some facts about Paul's life suggest that he had connections with the upper classes and was more than an uneducated and powerless artisan. That he was a city dweller does not mean that he was educated or influential, though the city offered opportunities usually lacking in rural areas. His letters, written in good but not highly literate Greek, testify that Paul received basic education in grammar. His familiarity with and interpretations of the Bible show that he had received a solid Jewish education (Luke's claim [Acts 22:3] that he studied with Gamaliel is not verified by his letters). It is likely that he spoke and read Hebrew and Aramaic. Paul travelled, like many artisans in antiquity, and as an artisan he could find employment in urban centers. In the account of his life in Galatians, he says he persecuted the church of God. Acts locates this activity in Jerusalem, Judea, Palestine, and S Syria, but Paul's own letters leave this vague. Nor do the letters say why Paul had left his home in the first place or what his relationship to Jewish authorities in Jerusalem and elsewhere was before he followed Jesus.

2. Mark. The gospels and Acts do not easily provide information for the historical understanding of the Pharisees because they date from the last third of the 1st century and thus do not give firsthand witness to the period before the destruction of the Temple in 70 C.E. they project onto the life of Jesus later controversies between the Christian and Jewish communities and reflect later authors' misunderstandings of tradition and of Palestinian society. In all cases the gospel authors have woven Jesus' opponents as characters into a dramatic narrative which is controlled by their purposes in writing the story rather than by a desire or ability to reproduce faithfully the historical events of Jesus' life. Thus the Pharisees undergo mutation for dramatic and theological purposes and are often attacked as Jesus' opponents.

Mark places the Pharisees in Galilee on all occasions except one (2:16, 18, 24; 3:2, 6; 7:1, 5; 8:11; 10:2; in a Galilean setting in 7:3; 8:15). The Pharisees meet Jesus at Capernaum and other rural towns (3:2, 6; 7:1, 5) and in many often indeterminate places (2:18, 24; 8:11; 10:2). In contrast with Josephus, who shows the Pharisees closely linked with the leadership in Jerusalem. Mark sees them as active only in Galilee. They do not lack alliances, for they plot with the allies of Herod Antipas, the ruler of Galilee (3:6), join the scribes in conflict with Jesus, and have some scribes in their midst (2:16). They appear in Jerusalem only once, but this is probably due to the literary arrangement of Mark. In chap. 12, just before his arrest, Jesus meets a series of opponents: the Pharisees and Herodians (12:13), the Sadducees (12:18), and a friendly scribe (12:28). It is likely that Mark brings the Pharisees into this Jerusalem context as a dramatic device to create a complete roster of Jesus' opponents just before the arrest and crucifixion.

The Pharisees dispute with Jesus over fasting (2:18), sabbath observance (2:24; 3:2), and divorce (10:2). The scribes and Pharisees dispute with Jesus over purification of hands (7:1), and the scribes of the Pharisees question his eating with sinners (2:16). This agenda resembles the pre-70 C.E. legal agenda isolated from the Mishnah by J. Neusner. The Pharisees also question Jesus authority by demanding a sign (8:11). In concert with the Herodians, the Pharisees try to trap Jesus in a political matter—the question of Roman taxes (12:13)—and they enter into a plot with the Herodians against Jesus.

Because the Pharisees in Mark have relationships with other groups in society, enter into a political alliance with the Herodians against Jesus (3:6), and put Jesus to the test with the Herodians at the instigation of the Jerusalem leaders (12:13), they appear to be a well-connected political interest group, of which the "scribes of the Pharisees" (2:16) may be the Jerusalem representatives. Since their religious views are integral to the way Jews live in Palestine, they sought to control or influence the political, legal, and social factors which might determine the social practices and views of the community. The Pharisees were the defenders of a certain kind of community and Jesus challenged the Pharisees' vision of community by attacking their purity regulations concerning washing and food, as well as Sabbath practice. The effect of Jesus' teaching was to widen the community boundaries and loosen the norms for membership in his community. Jesus thus created a new community outside the Pharisees' control and quite naturally provoked their protest and hostility.

Mark differs from Josephus in placing the Pharisees and their allies, the scribes, in Galilee as potent political and religious forces. Since Mark writes just before or after the war against Rome, he is not anachronistically reading the later rabbis back into Jesus' life as Pharisees. His traditions reflect the mid-1st century experience of the early Christian community if not the experience of Jesus himself. Galilee was ruled by Herod Antipas during Jesus' life and was not under the direct control of the Temple authorities. It was divided into upper and lower Galilee by topography and tradition and had several major towns (such as Sepphoris and Tiberias) which served as regional centers for tax collection and security. In view of the complex social and political structure of Galilee, Jesus and his opponents in Galilee, the Pharisees, scribes, and Herodians, must be seen as minor actors in the larger political struggle for control during the 1st century. The Pharisees, one of many political and religious interest groups seeking power and influence over Jewish society, exercise influence on the people and compete with Jesus for social and political control. They enter into political alliances with the Herodians and are associated with the scribes, who have some political control and a presence in Jerusalem. Though we cannot be certain that Mark and his sources give us a completely accurate picture of the Pharisees as a strong community force in Galilee in the early and mid-1st century, such a role in Galilean society for the Pharisees is intrinsically probable.

3. Matthew. Matthew tends to insert the Pharisees into more narrative situations than Mark, but less than Luke. He also pairs them differently from Mark. The Pharisees and Sadducees appear together in two contexts (3:7; 16:1–12). The formulaic pair scribes and Pharisees, not found in precisely that form in Mark, appears in a large number of places (5:20; 12:38; 23:2, 13, [14], 15, 23, 25, 27, 29; in 15:1 the order is reversed to conform to Mark). In several passages Matthew eliminates Mark's scribes when they are opponents of Jesus and replaces them with Pharisees (9:11, 34; 12:24; 21:45) whom he considers to be Jesus' opponents par excellance.

The scribes and Pharisees are presented as the pious and zealous official representatives of Judaism whose practice and interpretation of the Bible are contrasted with Jesus' interpretation of biblical law and with Matthew's interpretation of how Christians and especially Christian leaders should function in the second generation of Christianity. In the background of Matthew's polemic against the scribes and Pharisees are the Jewish and Christian communities in Matthew's day. The Pharisees and Jesus' followers are competing groups, each with their own teachings, practice, and identity, a situation similar to that of the Matthean and Jewish communities a generation later. The polemic against the "scribes and Pharisees, hypocrites" (23:13, 15, 16, 23, 25, 27, 29) is noteworthy. The scribes and Pharisees are attacked for their failure to practice Judaism sincerely, guide others to live Judaism correctly, interpret the Bible correctly, and attend to the major principles of the law and Jewish way of life. They are used as negative examples for how a community leader should act (23:4–7) and are contrasted with Christian leaders, who should not use titles and should be characterized by lowliness (23:8–12). Matthew pairs the Pharisees and scribes without regard for any differences in their interests and functions (chap. 23), in contrast to Luke who carefully separates the woes against the Pharisees and lawyers so that they are condemned for failings appropriate to their respective activities in society (11:37–52). Matthew has provided a traditional list of improper attitudes and activities of which he accuses both the opponents of Jesus and the adversaries of his own community, both internal and external. The list is so polemical and the Pharisees and scribes so identified with one another that little reliable historical information can be gleaned from it.

Matthew, in comparison with Mark, expands the role of the Pharisees as opponents of Jesus. The Pharisees comprise the most constant opposition to Jesus in Galilee and are concerned with the same agenda as Mark's Pharisees: Sabbath observance, food rules, and purity (9:6–13, 14–17; 12:1–14). The Pharisees in Matthew have a wider role and are less distinct from the scribes than in Mark. They challenge Jesus' authority as a religious and social leader by assaulting its divine source (9:32–34; 12:22–30) and argue with him concerning divorce (19:3–9 in Judea). After Jesus attacks the Pharisees with a series of parables which they perceive as directed against them (21:45–46), they plot against Jesus (22:15). Thus they are active in Judea and Jerusalem, in contrast to Mark's Pharisees. The hostility of the Pharisees brackets the crucifixion in which they take no direct part. A lawyer of the Pharisees asks the last hostile question (22:34–35), and the Pharisees join the chief priests in requesting a guard for Jesus' tomb (27:62–65). The Pharisees are not only part of the local leadership whose influence over the people and power over social norms are being challenged and diminished by Jesus, but they are also in direct contact with the more powerful forces of the Jerusalem leadership.

These peculiar Matthean characteristics, which are generally but not exclusively attributed to his redaction of Mark and other traditional materials, prompt questions concerning Matthew's purposes in writing. Recent work on the role of the Jewish leaders in Matthew has been dominated by a redactional perspective which has emphasized the dramatic and theological use to which Matthew has put these leaders and doubted that either Matthew or the traditions he passes on provide any accurate, recoverable knowledge of these groups (Tilborg typifies this view). Some see Matthew's characterization of the Jewish leaders as a literary and theological device for identifying the Christian community in contrast to Judaism and explaining the rejection of Jesus by Judaism. In Matthew's narrative the leaders form a united front against Jesus and need not be precisely distinguished from one another in themselves or by specific function in the community. But, though the lines which distinguished the scribes and Pharisees from other groups and from each other have become somewhat blurred, the groups are not simply identified with one another. Some argue that Matthew's view of Jewish leaders, especially the prominence given to the Pharisees, reflects the polemical confrontation between the Matthean community and the post-70 C.E. Jewish community which was dominated by the Pharisees-become-rabbis (Davies 1963). This position has been overstated as the social positions and functions assigned to the scribes and Pharisees fit 1st-century Jewish society as we know it from Josephus, other NT books, and later rabbinic sources.

4. Luke-Acts. Luke is notable for adding references to the Pharisees a number of times (alone 7:36; 13:31; 14:1; 16:14; 17:20; 18:10–14; with scribes 11:53; with lawyers or teachers of the law 5:17; 7:30; 14:3). Many have claimed that the author has a less-hostile attitude toward the Pharisees both in the gospel and especially in Acts (Ziesler). The situation is not simple, however, for in the gospel Luke inserts hostile Pharisees into several situations but removes them from some places where Mark and Matthew portray them as hostile (Sanders 1985: 149–54). It is clear that Luke is not unreservedly friendly toward the Pharisees and has his own specific and limited complaints about them.

Some aspects of the Pharisees in Luke-Acts are unique. Three times Jesus dines with Pharisees (17:36; 11:37; 14:1). The Pharisees are community leaders (14:1) involved with wealth (16:14) and are politically active and informed (13:31). Though Luke follows Mark in locating the Pharisees in Galilee and not in Jerusalem, they are more ubiquitous and powerful than in Mark or Matthew. Along with the scribes they are a leadership group with power and wealth in the Galilean villages (5:17–26, 30–32; 6:7–11; 11:37–53; 14:1–3; 15:2). Finally, the Pharisees seem sympathetic to Jesus and Christians on several occasions (Luke 13:31; Acts 5:34–39; 23:6–9). Acts especially treats the Pharisees well because the Pharisees accept resurrection. Also in Acts, Jesus' followers are seen (along with Judaism) as a small part of the larger and more diverse Greco-Roman world. Finally, the positive view of some Pharisees toward Christianity and one reference to Christian Pharisees (Acts 15:5) fit Luke's theme of continuity between Judaism and the church.

Luke's presentation of the Pharisees and other Jewish leaders is part of a theologically motivated literary inversion of ordinary society. The leaders of the Jews, the rich, the other established citizens, and sometimes Israel itself are pictured as rejecting Jesus and thus rejecting God and ultimately any hope of salvation. By contrast, the poor, the sinners, the non-Jews, and the outcasts like tax collectors accept Jesus and salvation from God and "become" Israel. This new community is gradually outlined and formed in the narrative and the Pharisees, scribes, and other leaders serve this overarching narrative theme. Luke objects that the Pharisees and other leaders do not care for the poor who depend on them and have a claim on their generosity (14:1–24; 17:14; 18:9–14). Luke also complains that the Pharisees' use of purity regulations to maintain social order leads to unjust relationships in which the poor are deprived of justice because they are judged to be unclean and outside of the social order (14:15–24). In response Luke defines true uncleanness as a moral, not ritual, deficiency and thus opens Christianity's group boundaries to the outcasts, Gentiles, and sinners.

New aspects of the Pharisees, scribes, and Sadducees appear in Acts. Pharisees appear as members of the Sanhedrin twice. Gamaliel, a Pharisee and a member of the Sanhedrin, had enough wisdom, respect, and influence to be able to overcome the Sanhedrin's rage and to counsel prudent caution in dealing with the apostles (5:33–40). Luke's attitude toward Gamaliel was positive because Gamaliel helped the apostles and because he was open to the possibility that their teaching might come from God. Luke has Paul cite his study with Gamaliel as a warrant for his respectability as a Jew (Acts 22:3) and thus testify to Gamaliel's importance and honored place in both Judaism and Christianity. Whether the presentation of Gamaliel in Acts is historical can be questioned because as a literary figure he serves Luke's purpose of showing Christianity's continuity with Judaism. When Paul appeared before the Sanhedrin, he declared that he was a Pharisee and the son of a Pharisee, and thus garnered the support of the Pharisees in the Sanhedrin (Acts 23).

Some Jerusalem Christians are identified as Pharisees by Luke. At the meeting of the Jerusalem community with Paul "some believers of those from the school *(hairēsis)* of the Pharisees" claimed that gentile believers had to be circumcised and instructed to keep the law of Moses (15:5). This zeal for the law of Moses fits Luke's idea of the Pharisees in both the gospel and Acts, and it is consistent with his picture of Paul when Paul later claims that he lived Judaism according to the strictest school *(hairēsis),* the Pharisees (26:5). The author of Acts uses the same word as Josephus to describe the Pharisaic group and identifies them by the strict way of life they lead according to their interpretation of the biblical law. In a way similar to Josephus, Luke presents Pharisaism as a political force noted for its renewal of Jewish life. Acts also agrees with Paul's own characterization of Pharisaism where he implies that the Pharisaic way of life is a recognized, demanding, and accepted way of living Jewish life (Phil. 3:5).

A word must be said about the historicity of Luke's account of the Pharisees. That some were members of the Sanhedrin and competed for power in Jerusalem is likely on the basis of Josephus' account. However, Luke's idea that Paul could be a Pharisee and a Christian and that there were Christians who remained Pharisees is very unlikely, especially granted all the conflicts with Jewish authorities recounted in Acts and alluded to in Paul's letters. Since the Pharisees were a political interest group with a program for living Judaism and a sect-like organization, any interpretation of Christianity, no matter how Jewish, would have found itself in conflict with them. In trying to establish the continuity between Christianity and Judaism, Luke maximizes their agreements and common interests. He associates the Jews who were strict in observance of the law (Pharisees) with the Jewish Christians who wished to remain faithful to the Mosaic law. Luke correctly perceives many things about the Pharisees, but he probably overemphasizes their positive relations with the early followers of Jesus.

5. John. The Pharisees in John function both as government officials and as the learned doctors of the law who are interested in Jesus' teaching and dispute its truth. (Scribes do not appear in John, except in 8:3 [the woman caught in adultery], a non-Johannine pericope.) The presentation of the Pharisees in John differs greatly from that in the Synoptic Gospels though a few common features remain. In both Galilee and Jerusalem the Pharisees are an ominous presence, ever-watchful and suspicious adversaries of Jesus who keep the people under surveillance and influence it with their propaganda. They compete with Jesus for influence with the people and attempt to undermine his teaching. All through the gospel the Pharisees are allied with the chief priests in taking official action against Jesus, especially on his trips to Jerusalem. In addition, the Pharisees, either alone or with other officials, control the synagogue and the judicial processes for removing those whom they oppose. This picture of the Pharisees as an officially powerful group has significant features in common with Josephus' presentation of them during the Hasmonean period. According to both accounts they attained real political power even though it was derived from the governing class which they served. That they are not the highest authorities is clear in the account of Jesus' condemnation to death, during which the Pharisees drop from view. Thus, John follows the Synoptic Gospels in the passion account in assigning the highest leadership and contact with the Romans to the chief priests.

The Pharisees are first mentioned in connection with a delegation sent from Jerusalem to the Jordan to investigate John the Baptist (1:19–28). The Pharisees in the incident are located in Jerusalem, engage in official inquiry of John, and are interested in his precise teaching and the authority for it. Here and elsewhere John locates the Pharisees in Jerusalem, contrary to the synoptic tradition but in agreement with Josephus. The supervisory role of the Pharisees in society is further attested when Jesus' trip to Galilee from Judea (4:1) is said to be motivated by his hearing that the Pharisees know that he is making more disciples than John the Baptist. The implication is that the Pharisees will disapprove of Jesus and be a threat to him in some tangible way. The characterization of Nicodemus as a Pharisee and a "ruler" *(archōn)* of the Jews confirm this picture (3:1). He has an official capacity in Jerusalem, knows about Jesus, has a learned and positive interest in his teaching, and feels the threat of disapproval from his fellow Pharisees (7:52).

The Pharisees are threatened by Jesus' teaching and reject him because none of the authorities *(archontes)* or Pharisees have believed in him, and the people who have do not know the law (7:48–49). Only once do the Pharisees directly debate with Jesus (8:13–20); usually they maintain a superior position based on social recognition of their learning, their influence with the people, and their political power in conjunction with the chief priests—and so refuse to treat Jesus as an equal.

The story of the healing of the man born blind (9:1–39) and the controversy following it reveal much about John's view of the Pharisees' place in the community. When the man born blind had been cured and returned to his neighborhood in Jerusalem, those who knew him sought an explanation for his cure and took him to the guardians of community order and custom, the Pharisees, for an evaluation of the situation. The Pharisees questioned the man and upon discovering that Jesus had mixed clay on the Sabbath dismissed him as a sinner who broke the Sabbath rest (9:13–17). In this narrative the Pharisees are leaders concerned with teaching, order, and the exercise of power in the community. They use their socially accepted role as accurate interpreters of the tradition to condemn Jesus according to the laws and customs which give the community its identity and shape. What is especially noteworthy is that the people turn to them as the local officials concerned with public order and community norms. Similarly, when Lazarus had been raised from the dead, some went and reported to the Pharisees what Jesus had done. They then met in council with the chief priests to decide how to prevent disruption of the social order and loss of power (11:46–47; also 12:19). The Pharisees are presented as having either direct power or decisive influence in determining who is recognized as a Jew in good standing. This function is made clear in the summary which ends the first half of the gospel (12:36–50). Many believed, including leaders *(archontes)*, but did not admit it because of fear of the Pharisees who might put them out of the synagogue (12:42–43).

As presented by John, the Pharisees were a learned group who had influence with the people because they were accepted by them as guides in Jewish behavior and belief. As such they were community leaders, perhaps with some direct power in both the synagogue and government council in Jerusalem, and certainly with great influence in conjunction with the chief priests and other community leaders ("the Jews"). Like Josephus, John emphasizes those Pharisees (probably only a small leadership core) who were in Jerusalem and participated in the direct leadership of the nation. In contrast with the Synoptic Gospels, John emphasizes the Pharisees' leadership role in the community. They kept watch over Jesus and how people reacted to Jesus. They were the ones the people consulted or reported to when they were disturbed or confused by Jesus. They discussed Jesus' teachings and authority to teach, but except in one case, they did not directly challenge Jesus. Rather, they acted as established leaders should; they kept their distance from the newcomer and schemed to blunt his influence and preserve their own. When they took official action it was with the cooperation of the chief priests and other officials. They were not the main political leaders, for the chief priests took over as the main opponents of Jesus in the passion narrative just as in the Synoptic Gospels. John has undoubtedly merged many forces which opposed Jesus into one figure: the Pharisees. However, John, who partly reflects mid-1st century traditions, agrees in some particulars with Josephus in his presentation of the Pharisees and may be critically appropriated into a synthetic presentation of the Pharisees.

D. Rabbinic Literature

Most studies and textbook treatments of the Pharisees cite the rabbinic sources extensively because they provide much more information than Josephus and the NT and are assumed to be less biased. But such reconstructions of Pharisaism have been based on an uncritical reading of a diverse body of later Jewish sources, including the Mishnah (ca. 200 C.E.), Talmuds (5th-6th centuries), and early medieval midrashic collections. These texts have usually been culled for the few passages which spoke of Pharisees; for the more numerous laws, sayings, and stories attributed to the sages who dated from before the destruction of the Temple; and for anonymous passages which seem to refer to pre-destruction society. Such materials, taken out of context, have been treated as historically accurate 1st century traditions and patched together into a narrative. Rabbinic literature must be read with the same kind of critical methodology used on Josephus and the NT, because each of the rabbinic sources tells stories of earlier times and records laws to accomplish its own religious purposes. With these cautions in mind, three bodies of evidence will be evaluated: (1) sayings and stories about 1st-century C.E. sages; (2) 1st-century C.E. laws; and (3) texts which mention the Pharisees by name.

1. 1st-Century Sages. Stories and sayings attributed to sages of the 2d and 1st centuries, B.C.E. are very few in number and almost impossible to evaluate historically. Of all the pre-70 sages, only Hillel has a large body of sayings and stories attributed to him (33 traditions in 89 pericopae according to Neusner 1971, 2: 185–302; 3:255–72). Because the talmudic rabbis conceived of Hillel as their founder and major teacher, they consistently depicted him as an appealing, wise, and patient person and surrounded his legal teachings with an array of wise sayings, stories of his origin and status, and accounts of his disciples. Hillel is even made the ancestor of Gamaliel and Simon ben Gamaliel and thus a founder of the patriarchal house, though there is no evidence for this in either *m. ʾAbot* or the Babylonian Talmud. The search for legitimacy through descent reaches it speak in the later claim of the patriarchal house that Hillel was a descendent of David (*j. Taʿan.* 4:2). The stories about Hillel in the later rabbinic sources serve to legitimize the patriarchal house of the 2d to 5th centuries. Hillel's rise to power, wisdom, moral teaching, and dominance on matters of law make him (and implicitly his successors) a leader of great influence and power in all areas of life.

The Hillel of these rabbinic sources is not simply historical any more than the Jesus of the gospels is. The rabbinic sources show with relative certainty only that he was a dominant Pharisaic teacher at the turn of the era whose influence was felt after his death. When he was adopted as the originator of the Pharisaic and later rabbinic patriarchate, he was turned into a larger-than-life figure and even compared to Moses (*Sipre* Deut 357). Most of the stories about Hillel come from the mid-2d century and later and attest to the rabbis' self-understanding rather than to the history of Hillel.

Shammai, Hillel's opponent, appears almost exclusively within the Hillel materials. The rabbis claimed Hillel as their own and did not independently preserve Shammaite material nor did they present a fair picture of him and his teachings. The Mishnah and Tosefta show Shammai accepting the dominance of Hillelite positions and thus coopt him for one of their purposes, convincing all Jews to accept the mishnaic interpretation of Jewish life. The Palestinian Talmud and midrashim are less hostile to Shammai than the Babylonian Talmud, which totally stereotypes him.

The materials attributed to the Houses of Hillel and Shammai outnumber all materials attributed to pre-70 sages, even those of Hillel. The houses' materials are highly stylized and reflect a large measure of redaction during the 2d century. Since the attributions of materials to particular rabbis cannot be presumed to be accurate, rules and disputes can only be reliably dated if they are assumed or referred to in materials attributed to sages in a later generation (Neusner 1971, 3: 180–83). For example, if the Jamnian (70–130) or Ushan (140–170) sages know of a teaching or dispute, then it existed at that time and probably came from the previous generation. The rules attributed to the houses mostly concern tithes, purity, and Sabbath observance and not other wider concerns characteristic of the late 2d century. Thus, the 2d century sages seem to have had a group of disputes which came from the 1st century and which they preserved as part of their teaching. However, the houses' disputes do not give a full or first hand view of the 1st century Pharisees. The formulation of the legal materials attributed to the Houses of Hillel and Shammai is so stereotyped and pithy that they are surely literary constructions and neither the record of lively debate from the middle of the 1st century nor the verbally exact repetition of teachings from that period.

Little more is known about the 1st century sages following Hillel. A number of named authorities are mentioned, but not many traditions are assigned to them. The major figures of the 1st century are Gamaliel I (the elder); Simon his son; and, after the destruction of the Temple, Gamaliel II. The materials which mention these leaders are mostly stories, rather than the standard legal rulings assigned to later sages. The agenda of Gamaliel the Elder is broader than that of earlier sages and its scope is consistent with the station and duties of a member of the Sanhedrin (Acts 5:34–41). Simon is known from Josephus where he was active in the Jerusalem leadership during the war (*Life* 189–98). After the destruction of the Temple, Simon's son, Gamaliel II, gained power over the fledgling rabbinic movement which owed much to Second Temple Pharisaism. Little more can be reliably known about their teachings and activities.

The Second Temple sages and the Houses of Hillel and Shammai have usually been understood as scholarly rabbinic groups. But this view, fostered by the Talmuds, is a retrojection of later rabbinic schools onto the 1st century. Given the interpenetration of religion with politics and the rest of society, it is doubtful that the picture of the Houses of Hillel and Shammai as sectarian debating societies is accurate. Since the two groups identify themselves by the name of a leader or founder, they can best be understood as factions, that is temporary associations of disparate people grouped around a leader. Later after the deaths of the leaders, these factions became institutionalized into formal, corporate groups as part of 1st century society. Factions thrive when society's central authority is weak, disorganized, or unaccepted by much of the population, exactly the sociological conditions in 1st century Palestine. Judea was subordinate to Rome, and many popular movements, both violent and nonviolent, arose in response to this situation, as Josephus attests. The priests and leading families strove to keep the populace quiet, but ultimately they failed, with catastrophic results for the Jewish nation. Amid this maelstrom of activity many groups carved out their own ways of living Judaism to preserve their identities as Jews. Generally speaking, factions which persist for a long time and outlive their leaders become a formal group with an organized, self-perpetuating leadership and defined social identity. The late 1st century and early 2d century accounts of the Houses suggest that they were this type of group, and as such, two of many organizations of zealous Jews which provided a program for defending and reforming Judaism in the face of Roman and Hellenistic pressure. Hillel, Shammai, Judas the founder of the Fourth Philosophy, Jesus the preacher of the kingdom of God, Simon bar Giora the messianic pretender, and others were very common in 1st century Judaism and easily gathered modest groups of enthusiastic followers who strove to convince other Jews to join them in seeking influence and power over social policy.

2. 1st-Century Laws. When the Mishnah and Tosefta are analyzed using Neusner's method (the logic of Mishnah's argument and the attested attributions), by far the largest body of law which can be somewhat reliably assigned to the early and mid-1st century concerns ritual purity, tithes, food laws, and Sabbath and festival observance (1981: 45–75). These laws set out an agenda of holiness for the land and people. We do not know for certain who developed these laws dating from before the destruction, but the usual hypothesis, that it was the Pharisees who bequeathed these laws to the first generation of rabbis after the destruction of the Temple, is most probable. The gospel evidence of Pharisaic interest in purity and food and Josephus' claim that the Pharisees had their own interpretation of some Jewish laws converge with Neusner's analysis of early mishnaic law.

The stress on strict tithing, on observance of ritual purity by non-priests, and on strict observance of Sabbath and other festivals probably reflects the Pharisees' internal rules and program for a renewed Judaism. The articulation of the group's program and the recounting of disputes among various factions is common in the literature of political and religious social groups. Rules concerning food, purity, and group practices are typical boundary-building mechanisms. Ethnic groups in the Roman empire needed to maintain strong boundaries in order to keep the larger Hellenistic-Roman society and culture from absorbing them. Internal rules, such as food rules, kept the intimates of Jewish groups united to one another and distinct from gentiles and even from other Jews with whom they constantly had to interact and with whom they competed. While the precise mode of living Judaism is distinctive in these laws, the Pharisees drew on an old tradition of using priestly laws concerning purity, food, and marriage in order to separate, protect, and identify Judaism. The development of the priestly tradition in the Exile and the regulations for Judaism championed by Ezra and Nehemiah in the restoration period were forerunners of the type of regulations adopted by the Pharisees in the Greco-Roman period.

Associations or fellowships, mentioned a number of places in rabbinic literature, have often been identified with or compared to the Pharisees. The associates in *Tractate Demai* who were devoted to maintaining the rules of ritual purity and tithing are the best known. Other associations in Jerusalem seem to have been devoted to good works of various types, especially burial rites (*t. Meg.* 4:15). What is unclear in all these cases is what exactly is meant by the term "associate," how the texts differ from one another in their use of the term, and whether it is even a technical term at all. The Hebrew words *ḥăbûrâ* (association, fellowship) and *ḥăbērîm* (associates) are common words which simply refer to one's fellows, that is, one's townsfolk or social familiars, with no technical meaning or special organization implied. Thus, the tendency of scholars to gather together all the citations of *ḥābēr* and *ḥăbûrâ* and create a single historical group is misguided. The Pharisees have often been identified with the associates who appear in *m. Dem.* 2:2–3 because both groups are associated with tithing and ritual purity. The associates promised one another to tithe their food and to observe certain kinds of ritual purity. This means that the associates could confidently buy and sell to one another and also eat together without fear of breaking any of the laws they wished to keep. By contrast, they had to take great care in their dealings with the "people of the land," the *ʿam hāʾareṣ*, because the "people of the land" did not keep the special priestly laws of purity and did not tithe properly and fully. Their food was not properly sanctified and could not be eaten by associates. It had to be tithed if it was acquired by an associate. The Tosefta (2:2–3:9) sets out rules for accepting a person as an associate and stages of initiation (which are unclear and have provoked numerous disputes among scholars). It also discusses doubtful cases of reliability within the family and marginal cases in relations with the *ʿam haʾareṣ*. Though the associates have been linkled to numerous historical periods and groups, no certain identification can be made.

3. Pharisee Texts. The designation Pharisee is relatively infrequent in rabbinic literature and the texts using that term, which derive from several centuries of rabbinic literature, use it in different and sometimes pejorative senses. The etymology of the term "Pharisees" is disputed. The name seems to come from the Hebrew and Aramaic root *prš* which means "separate, interpret." The most common etymological understanding of Pharisees is "separate ones," though separate from whom or what is disputed. In a good sense it would mean people who separated themselves from normal Jewish society or from gentile society in order to observe Jewish law (purity, tithing?) more rigorously. In a negative sense it would mean sectarians or heretics, that is, people who separated themselves illegitimately from society at large because of beliefs and practices judged illegitimate. Rabbinic literature uses the term in both senses. Another possible meaning of their name is "interpreters"; this meaning would fit with the observations in Josephus and the New Testament that the Pharisees had their own interpretation of Jewish law and were considered accurate interpreters of the law. The two senses of the root could imply that the Pharisees separated themselves from the priestly or dominant interpretation of Jewish law. No decisive evidence or arguments have solved this issue.

No Jewish group refers to itself as Pharisees. The authors of rabbinic literature referred to themselves and their forbearers as "sages" *(ḥăkāmîm)* and after the destruction of the Temple, used the title "rabbi" for sages. They had no name for their movement, but called themselves Israel because they considered themselves to be simply proper Jews. The name Pharisees is a name used by outsiders, such as Josephus (taking the stance of a Hellenistic historian) and the New Testament. The sages do not customarily identify themselves or their predecessors as Pharisees, except when they implicitly ally themselves with the Pharisees in disputes with the Sadducees.

The Babylonian Talmud quotes the well-known list of seven types of Pharisees as a comment on *m. Soṭa* 3:4 (*b. Soṭa* 22b): "There are seven types of Pharisee, the *sykmy* Pharisee, the *nyqpy* Pharisee, the *qwzʾy* Pharisee, the *mdwkyʾ* Pharisee, the Pharisee (who says) Let me know my duty and I will do it, the Pharisee from love, the Pharisee from fear." The transliterated words are all obscure, but all are meant pejoratively. The Babylonian Talmud explains all five etymologically, but the Palestinian Talmud, which cites the list in two places (*j. Soṭa* 5:7 [20c]; *j. Ber.* 9:5 [13b]), gives different explanations. In *Soṭa* both Talmuds are discussing motives for studying Torah and avoiding hypocrisy. Several of the names are made to refer to hypocritical behavior or obedience to the law from imperfect motives. The Babylonian Talmud even rejects the last two—those who have motives of love and fear—in favor of the study of Torah for its own sake. It ends this section with a saying of King Yannai (Alexander Jannaeus) who warns his wife against those "painted ones" who pretend to be Pharisees.

Since these lists are found for the first time in Talmudic sources, they probably do not give accurate information about 1st century Pharisaism. By the 5th and 6th centuries Christianity had attained a position of power in the empire and since both the New Testament and early Christian writings contained attacks on the Pharisees as hypocrites, these lists may be a response to Christian polemics in which the talmudic authors defuse Christian criticism by agreeing with their attack on hypocritical Pharisees and by separating some Pharisees and themselves from those being attacked.

Some texts refer to Pharisees in a positive way, with the assumption that they keep ritually pure (*t. Šabb* 1:15; *m. Ṭohar.* 4:15; *m. Ḥag.* 2:7). A number of Mishnah and Tosefta passages polemically contrast the Pharisees and Sadducees (e.g., *Yad.* 4:6–7; *m. Nid.* 4:2; *m. Para* 3:7; *t. Ḥag.* 3:35). Most of the disputes between the Sadducees and Pharisees (and others) concern interpretations of the laws of ritual purity. If the Pharisees based much of their program for Jewish life on a revised understanding of the purity laws and an application of them to all Israel, as has been argued above, then the conflict between the Sadducees and Pharisees on this issue is comprehensible and probably historical in its general content. The application of purity laws to the people at large was a new mode of understanding Jewish life, law, and Scripture and it is reasonable and even inevitable that the Sadducees or someone else should oppose them. Other texts contrasting Pharisees or sages with the Sadducees or Boethusians can be found in the Talmuds and midrashic collections. Despite the claims of Rivkin (1969–70) that many of the Pharisees-Sadducees texts in the Talmud and other later sources are historically reliable, most of these passages reveal the assumptions of their rabbinic authors rather than the nature of the Second Temple Pharisees.

E. Qumran Literature

Many commentators have claimed that certain polemical Qumran texts which mention the "seekers after smooth things" refer to the Pharisees. Qumran literature is filled with polemics and invective which bear witness to the social, political, and religious strife among Jewish groups during the Hasmonean period. The wicked priest, the man of lies, the man of scorn, the spouter of lies, the lion of wrath, and the seekers after smooth things are only some of the adversaries condemned for a variety of crimes by the Qumran literature. Though the allusions to the Qumran community's opponents, which are contained in the pesharim to Habakkuk, Nahum, Psalm 37, and other documents, are very difficult to correlate with history, they testify to the political and religious strife at the inception of the Qumran community in the 2d century B.C.E. (probably under Jonathan or Simon) and also under Alexander Jannaeus. Pesher Nahum certainly refers to events in the reign of Alexander Jannaeus. It names two Greek kings, Antiochus and Demetrius, who have been convincingly identified with Antiochus IV Epiphanes (175–164 B.C.E.) and Demetrius III Eukairos (95–88 B.C.E.). The lion of wrath who opposed these kings and crucified his opponents is almost certainly Alexander Jannaeus (*Ant* 13 §379–83).

The identity of the "seekers after smooth things" remains a problem. The crucified opponents of Alexander and the seekers after smooth things are usually said to be the Pharisees because when they attained power under Alexandra (after Alexander's death), they sought to take vengeance on Alexander's allies who had supported the crucifixions (*Ant* 13 §410–15; *JW* 1 §96–98). However, Joseph does not identify Jannaeus' opponents as Pharisees. He says that Alexander's Jewish opposition came from many of the people and their leaders, not from one, limited group, such as the Pharisees (*Ant* 13 §372–76; *JW* 1 §90–92). After six years of civil disturbances in which 6,000 were killed by Alexander, this broadly based anti-Jannaeus movement asked Demetrius to intervene. After Demetrius had Alexander Jannaeus on the run, some people switched sides to give Alexander the victory. He then defeated and besieged his opponents and crucified the 800 survivors. Nowhere does Josephus identify this broad coalition with the Pharisees, though it is likely that they were partners in it.

According to Pesher Nahum, the seekers after smooth things called on Demetrius to intervene (4QpNah 3–4.1.2) and then were crucified by Alexander Jannaeus, an act which the Qumran community probably approved (4QpNah 3–4.1.7). If the identification of events is correct, the seekers after smooth things would be the coalition opposing Alexander Jannaeus. The metaphoric characterization of Alexander's and the community's opponents as "seekers after smooth things" *(dôršê ḥălāqôt)*, found a number of times in Qumran literature (4QpNah 3–4.1.2, 7; 2.2, 4; 3.3, 6–7; 4QpIsa[c] 23.2.10; 1QH 2:15, 32; CD 1:18) is derived from the Bible. The word *ḥălāqôt* means "smooth things, flattery, and falsehood." Isa. 30:10 contrasts true prophecy with the smooth things *(ḥălāqôt)* and delusions desired by rebelious Israelites who will not listen to the Torah of the Lord. Daniel 11:32 says that Antiochus Epiphanes will seduce by flatteries *(ḥălāqôt)* those who act wickedly against the covenant. Thus the term "seekers after smooth things" suggests that the Qumran community found their opponents too accommodating to changes in Jewish society, either because they twisted the meaning of the law (Isa 30:10) or allied themselves too closely with non-Jewish authorities and practices. The use of various epithets connected to "lie" and "falsehood" suggests that the community disagreed with its opponents on many points of interpretation and practice. Since the Qumran group had left Jerusalem, the seekers after smooth things were probably still there and active in Palestinian political struggles in a way the Qumran community did not approve. The Qumran polemics against their opponents testify to the diversity and conflicts in Jewish society. Thus their opponents, the seekers after smooth things, were probably a broad coalition of groups which included the Pharisees.

F. Synthesis

The Pharisees in Josephus' narrative function as a political interest group which had its own goals for society and constantly engaged in political activity to achieve them, even though it did not always succeed. They generally did not have direct power as a group and were not as a whole members of the governing class. They were members of a literate, corporate, voluntary association which constantly sought influence with the governing class. As such they were above the peasants and other lower classes but dependent on the governing class and ruler for their place in society. They were found in Jerusalem, and they probably fulfilled administrative or bureaucratic functions in society at certain times. They appear in each era of Jewish history from the Hasmonean period until the destruction of the Temple struggling to gain access to power and to influence society.

The Pharisaic association probably functioned as a social movement organization seeking to change society. The social, political, and economic situation of Palestinian Jews underwent a number of upheavals in the Greco-Roman period which demanded adaptation of Jewish customs and a reinterpretation of the Jewish identity fashioned by the biblical tradition. The Hasmoneans and the governing class changed Israel into a small, militarily active Hellenistic kingdom and took control of political and economic resources in order to control society. The Pharisees probably sought a new, communal commitment to a strict Jewish way of life based on adherence to the covenant. If they did so, they sought to capitalize on popular sentiment for rededication to or reform of Judaism. Such popular sentiment can produce a social movement which seeks reform, but a long-lasting, complex campaign for reform or renewal requires the formation of a social movement organization which aims at promoting or resisting change in society at large.

If the Pharisees are called a sect, they are of the reformist type which seeks gradual, divinely revealed alterations in the world (Wilson 1973: 23–26; 38–49). This type of sect engages in political and social activities similar to those of the Pharisees. Wilson characterizes reformist sects as "objectivist" because they seek change in the world, not just in individuals or in a person's relations with the world. A reformist sect differs from the three other objectivist types of sect: the revolutionist, which awaits destruction of the social order by divine forces (apocalyptic groups); the introversionist, which withdraws from the world into a purified community (the Qumran community); and the utopian, which seeks to reconstruct the world according to divine principles without revolution. However, these types are not hermetically sealed off from one another. A group may have more than one response to the world at the same time, that is, it may overlap two or three of these categories. It may also change over time and even cease to be a sect if social conditions change. Consequently, if the Pharisees are understood as a sect, they may have had introversionist tendencies, manifested in their purity regulations, without losing their involvement or desire for involvement in political society.

The Pharisees may also be compared to Hellenistic philosophical schools or schools of thought if the analogy is cautiously and loosely applied. They had a program of reform for Jewish life, a particular interpretation of Jewish tradition and a definable and sometimes controversial outlook on fundamental matters crucial to Judaism. Since the Pharisees as depicted by Josephus acted as a political interest group, they went beyond the activities of many Greek schools. The designation school (of thought) is appropriate as long as this expression is not understood to refer to an exclusively academic and theoretical association.

A major question unanswered by the sources concerns the daily activities of the Pharisees and the source of their livelihood. The older theory that they were urban artisans is very unlikely because artisans were poor, uneducated, and uninfluential. The more common theory that the Pharisees were a lay scribal movement, that is, a group of religious scholars and intellectuals who displaced the traditional leaders and gained great authority over the community (most recently, Rivkin 1978: 211–51), is likewise very unlikely. Though some Pharisees were part of the governing class, most Pharisees were subordinate officials, bureaucrats, judges, and educators. They are best understood as retainers, that is, literate servants of the governing class, who had a program for Jewish society and influence with both the people and their patrons. When the opportunity arose, they sought power over society. This means that their organizations cannot be viewed as a monastic-like community or withdrawn sect which demands primary and total commitment from every member. It is most likely that Pharisees were active in a number of occupations and roles in society and were bound together by certain beliefs and practices and by endeavors to influence social change.

Concretely, a person was not primarily a Pharisee. A member of the Pharisees retained his family and territorial allegiances, his roles in society and occupation, his friends and network of associates. In some way not revealed in reliable first-century sources he committed himself to be a Pharisee, and this commitment with its particular understanding of the Jewish covenant and Jewish life guided many of his endeavors and claimed a part of his time, energy, and resources. The Pharisaic movement has some characteristics in common with Greek schools of thought and must have educated its members to some degree. This view of the Pharisees, admittedly hypothetical due to lack of evidence, is consistent with what the sources tell us of the Pharisees, including the information given by Saul the Pharisee.

The accounts of the Pharisees' beliefs in Josephus and the gleanings available in rabbinic literature and the NT provide incomplete information which is difficult to interpret. According to Josephus, who sought to relate the Jewish schools of thought to Greek philosophy, they affirmed the influence of divine activity on human life, the joint effect of human freedom and fate, and reward and punishment in the afterlife. Josephus' contrast of the positions of the three schools of thought probably derives from their eschatology and apocalyptic expectations. The Pharisees probably held positions on eschatology, divine providence, and human responsibility which were different enough from traditional Jewish teachings and attitudes to require some positive commitment and explicit defense. In this the Pharisees were not unusual, as the great diversity of outlook in Second Temple apocryphal and pseudepigraphical literature shows.

The rabbinic laws and stories which can be somewhat reliably dated to the 1st century show that the Pharisees had a strong interest in tithing, ritual purity, and Sabbath observance and not much of an interest in civil laws and regulations for the Temple worship. The New Testament also shows that the Pharisees had unique interpretations of these matters and sought to promote their observance and defend their validity against challenge by other establishment and reform groups, including the priests, Qumran community, and Jesus and his early followers. Serious differences in the understanding of Jewish covenant and commitment to God, people, and land separated these groups and factions within Judaism. Implicit in these programs for living Judaism were profound judgments concerning the meaning of Judaism and its place in the larger world where it was politically subordinate.

The purity rules, which seem so arcane to modern westerners, regularized life and separated that which was normal and life-giving from that which was abnormal or ambiguous, and so was a threat to normal life. Such a set of categories and rules excluded that which is foreign or strange; their usefulness against the attraction and influence of the Romans and Hellenistic culture is obvious. Purity and tithing rules separated the Pharisees, Sadducees, and Essenes, all of whom affirmed the biblical rules and had a distinctive interpretation of them in daily life, from one another and from the followers of Jesus as well as from numerous other messianic, apocalyptic, political, and reformist groups.

Bibliography

Baeck, L. 1927. Die Pharisäer. *Jahresbericht der Hochschule.* Berlin = The Pharisees. Pp. 3–50 in *The Pharisees and Other Essays.* New York. 1947.

Baumgarten, A. I. 1983. The Name of the Pharisees. *JBL* 102: 411–28.

Bousset, W. 1903. *Die Religion des Judentums im neutestamentlichen Zeitalter.* Berlin.

Bowker, J. 1973. *Jesus and the Pharisees.* Cambridge.

Box, G. H. 1908–9. Survey of Recent Literature on the Pharisees and Sadducees. *Review of Theology and Philosophy* 4: 129–51.

Carroll, J. T. 1988. Luke's Portrayal of the Pharisees. *CBQ* 50: 603–21.

Cohen, S. J. D. 1979. *Josephus in Galilee and Rome: His Vita and Development as a Historian.* Leiden.

———. 1986. Parallel Historical Traditions in Josephus and Rabbinic Literature. Vol. 1, pp. 7–15 in *Proceedings of the Ninth World Congress of Jewish Studies* B. Jerusalem.

Davies, W. D. 1963. *The Setting of the Sermon on the Mount.* Cambridge.

Finkelstein, L. 1938. *The Pharisees.* 2 vols. Philadelphia.

Geiger, A. 1857. *Urschrift und Übersetzung der Bibel.* Breslau.

———. 1863. Sadducäer und Pharisäer. *Jüdische Zeitschrift für Wissenschaft und Leben* 2: 11–54.

———. 1910. *Kebuzat Ma'amarim.* 2d ed. Warsaw.

Ginzberg, L. 1928. The Religion of the Pharisees. Pp. 88–108 in *Students, Scholars and Saints.* Philadelphia.

———. 1955. The Significance of the Halachah for Jewish History. Pp. 77–124 in *On Jewish Law and Lore.* Philadelphia.

Graetz, H. 1891–98. *History of the Jews.* Philadelphia.

Herford, R. T. 1924. *The Pharisees.* New York.

Klijn, A. F. J. 1959. Scribes, Pharisees, Highpriests and Elders in the New Testament. *NovT* 3: 259–67.

Lauterbach, J. Z. 1951. *Rabbinic Essays.* Cincinnati.

Loewe, H. 1937. Pharisaism. Vol. 1, pp. 105–90, and The Ideas of Pharisaism. Vol. 2, pp. 3–58 in *Judaism and Christianity,* ed. W. O. E. Oesterley and H. Loewe. London.

Mantel, H. 1977. The Sadducees and the Pharisees. Vol. 8, pp. 99–123 in *WHJP.*

Marcus, R. 1952. The Pharisees in the Light of Modern Scholarship. *JR* 32: 153–64.

Meyer, E. 1921–23. *Ursprung und Anfänge des Christentums.* 3 vols. Stuttgart.

Moore, G. F. 1927–30. *Judaism in the First Centuries of the Christian Era.* 3 vols. Cambridge, MA.

Neusner, J. 1971. *The Rabbinic Traditions about the Pharisees Before 70.* 3 Vols. Leiden.

———. 1973. *From Politics to Piety.* Englewood Cliffs.

———. 1981. *Judaism: The Evidence of the Mishnah.* Chicago.

———. 1983. *Formative Judaism.* 3d Series. *Torah, Pharisees, and Rabbis.* BJS 46. Chico, CA.

———. 1986. *Formative Judaism.* 5th Series. *Revisioning the Written Records of a Nascent Religion.* BJS 91. Chico, CA.

Rivkin, E. 1969–70. Defining the Pharisees: The Tannaitic Sources. *HUCA* 40–41: 205–49.

———. 1978. *The Hidden Revolution: The Pharisees' Search for the Kingdom Within.* Nashville.

Saldarini, A. J. 1988. *Pharisees, Scribes and Sadducees in Palestinian Society.* Wilmington, DE.

Sanders, J. T. 1985. The Pharisees in Luke-Acts. Pp. 141–88 in *The Living Text: Essays in Honor of Ernest W. Saunders,* eds. D. Groh and R. Jewett. New York.

Schwartz, D. R. 1983. Josephus and Nicolaus on the Pharisees. *JSJ* 14: 157–71.

Simon, M. 1979. From Greek Hairesis to Christian Heresy. Pp. 101–16 in *Early Christian Literature and the Classical Intellectual Tradition,* eds. W. R. Schoedel and R. L. Wilken. ThH 53. Paris.

Smith, M. 1956. Palestinian Judaism in the First Century. Pp. 67–81 in *Israel: Its Role in Civilization,* ed. M. Davis. New York.

Stowers, S. 1984. Social Status, Public Speaking and Private Teaching: The Circumstances of Paul's Preaching Activity. *NovT* 26: 59–82.

Tilborg, S. van. 1972. *The Jewish Leaders in Matthew.* Leiden.

Weiss, H. 1871. *Dor Dor Ve-Dorshav.* Vienna.

Wellhausen, J. 1874. *Die Pharisäer und sadducäer.* Greifswald.

Wilson, B. 1973. *Magic and the Millennium.* London.

Zeitlin, S. 1962–67. *The Rise and Fall of the Judean State.* 2 vols. Philadelphia.

———. 1974. *Solomon Zeitlin's Studies in the Early History of Judaism.* New York.

Ziesler, J. A. 1978–79. Luke and the Pharisees. *NTS* 25: 146–57.

Anthony J. Saldarini

PHARISON (PERSON) [Gk *Pharisōn*]. 1 Maccabees 9:66 relates that Jewish forces under Jonathan the Hasmonean killed the sons of Pharison along with Odomera and his brothers near Bethbasi S of Jerusalem (ca. 160 B.C.E.). On the sons of Pharison see ODOMERA.

Michael E. Hardwick

PHARPAR (PLACE) [Heb *parpar*]. A river in Syria near Damascus. 2 Kgs 5:1 records that Naaman, the commander of the Syrian army, had leprosy. An Israelite captive girl informed him that a prophet in Samaria could cure him. So he went to Elisha (v 9) who did not bother to come out of the house to see him but simply told him to go wash in the Jordan. Naaman became angry and argued: "Are not Abana and Pharpar, the rivers of Damascus, better than all the waters of Israel?" (v 12). The Abana is the modern Nahr el-Barada which flows through the middle of Damascus, dividing the city in half.

The Pharpar is probably the 40-mi-long Nahr el-Awaj, "the crooked river." It is formed by two small brooks at Sasa on Mt. Hermon where the waters form in a valley below a sheer wall of 6,000 feet. It runs NE ca. 6 mi. and then E in a deep tortuous channel to Kiswe. In this first section, it is called the Sabirany. Several canals which irrigate southern parts of the Damascus oasis tap into either side of Kiswe. The Awaj passes between Jebel Maani and Jebel Aswad and then turns SE. In the rainy season, surplus water empties into Lake Hijaneh (Bahrat el-Hijaneh), a salt lake or swamp ca. 10 mi. S of Lake Ateibeh. The river runs ca. 10 mi. S of Damascus. As such, it is not a river of Damascus, the city, but of a river of the larger oasis of Damascus, the Ghouta. The oasis, at an altitude of 2,650 feet, slopes slightly eastward. It owes its fertility to the Barada/Abana, Awaj, Wadi Mnin, and other small streams with sources in Hermon and Jebel Kalamun. The Awaj roughly separates the limestone region of the Damascus oasis from the basalt formation of the Hauran (Syria 1943: 23, 32, 50). The amount of water varies greatly. In the spring, when snows are melting, there is a good supply. During the summer, there is much less. The productivity of the S part of the Damascus oasis depends on the Awaj/Pharpar. Its cool, fresh waters, particularly in the early spring, could provide a favorable contrast to waters of the lower Jordan (Bowling 1975: 752). A tributary of the Awaj is called the Wadi Barbar which would preserve the biblical name. The Arabic for Pharpar is *farfara,* "move," "shake." Gehman (1970: 742) notes that local tradition, traced back to the 16th century, identifies the Pharpar as the Nahr Taura, one of seven canals drawn off from the Barada as it nears Damascus.

Bibliography

Bowling, A. 1975. Pharpar. Pp. 752 in Vol. 4 of *Zondervan Pictorial Encyclopedia of the Bible,* ed. M. C. Tenney and S. Barabas. Grand Rapids.

Gehman, H. S. 1970. *New Westminster Dictionary of the Bible.* Philadelphia.

Syria. 1943. Geographical Handbook Series. Naval Intelligence Division.

HENRY O. THOMPSON

PHASELIS (PLACE) [Gk *Phasēlis*]. A city on the S coast of Asia Minor (modern Turkey) in the region of Lycia near the region of Pamphylia. Located on a headland, Phaselis controlled three harbors and thereby became an important point linking E and W trade.

Phaselis is mentioned in a list of cities receiving a letter circulated by the Roman consul Lucius (1 Macc 15:23). This letter, which was to circulate to several rulers and municipalities instructed those who received it to treat the Jews in their region with favor. This request was prompted by the gift of a shield made from 1,000 minas (1 mina equals about 1.25 pounds) of gold which the Jewish ambassadors brought to the Roman ruler.

The city may have been first settled by Dorian colonist and soon became an important center for trade. The geographical setting of the city isolated it from the surrounding region and this may have contributed to its independent nature. Settlers from Rhodes established the city as a trade center in the 7th century. Soon other colonists from Naucratus, the Greek outpost in Egypt, established trade routes between the two cities.

The city struck its own coins while under the control of the Persian Empire in the 6th and early 5th centuries. Phaselis joined the Athenian League in 466 B.C. and soon established important trade contacts linking Greek cities with the Phoenician coast (Thuc. *Peloponnesian Wars* 2.69). Phaselis as indicated by the minting of its own coinage, was relatively independent during the 4th and 3d centuries B.C.

The city first came under the control of the Ptolemies in 276 B.C., who were replaced by the Seleucids from 204–190 B.C. When Phaselis regained independence in 190 B.C., it began to mint coins once again. The city may have joined the Lycian League by 168 B.C., because it began minting coins that were typical of that confederation.

The inclusion of Phaselis separately on the city list of the Roman consul Lucius (1 Macc 15:23) dated to ca. 139 B.C., may indicate that the city had separated from the league at that time. The Roman consul Servilius Isauricus seized the city in 77 B.C. because it had become the base of the leader of the Cilician pirates, Zenicetes. The city declined in importance in later times, however it was the home of a Byzantine bishopric.

The site of the ruins of the city is near the modern village of Tekrova. The remains of the city include a stadium, a Roman aqueduct, and two temples, one constructed during the reign of Trajan and the other dating from the Greek era.

JOHN D. WINELAND

PHICOL (PERSON) [Heb *pîkōl*]. An army commander who accompanied the king Abimelech when covenants were made with Abraham (Gen 21:22, 32) and Isaac (Gen 26:26). It is not likely that Phicol and Abimelech were involved with both covenants since a period of some 70 to 80 years lies between the two events. In this light, scholars have generally taken one of two positions. One the one hand, some assert that there never were two separate covenants. According to Speiser (*Genesis* AB, 203), for example, behind the accounts is "a single incident which was differently reported in two independent sources." Noth (*HPT,* 102) asserts as a general rule that elements of tradition which appear in duplicate belong originally to Isaac rather than to Abraham, a position with which de Vaux (*EHI,* 167) concurs. On the other hand, some scholars feel that "Abimelech" and "Phicol" were titles or family names (Kidner *Genesis* TOTC, 154). In this view, both patriarchs could have made a covenant with an "Abimelech" and a "Phicol." See also AHUZZATH.

DAVID SALTER WILLIAMS

PHILADELPHIA (PLACE) [Gk *Philadelpheia*]. A city of the Roman province of Asia addressed by the risen Jesus in the book of Revelation (3:7–13).

Located in ancient Lydia, in the W of what is today Asiatic Turkey, Philadelphia was founded by Eumenes II, King of Pergamum (197–159 B.C.) or possibly his brother, Attalus II (159–138 B.C.), whose loyalty had earned for him the epithet "Philadelphus," hence the city's name. It is located near the upper end of the very fertile plateau in the Cogamus River (today Koca Çay) valley, a tributary of the Hermus River, E of Sardis and on the route into the interior from Smyrna on the coast (38°22′N; 28°32′E). It is in the midst of a very prosperous agricultural region, though it was (and is) notoriously subject to frequent earthquakes. A severe one in A.D. 17 destroyed the city, and this was followed by a series of intermittent shocks which led the people to continue living outside the city for some years because of the structural instability of many of the city buildings and walls (Strabo, *Geog.* 12.8.18; 13.4.10; cf. Hemer 1986: 156–57). This disaster made an indelible impact on the contemporary world as the greatest in human history (Pliny *HN* 2.86.200). The nearby city of Sardis was equally badly hurt (Tacitus *Ann.* 2.47.3–4), but Philadelphia was among the cities whose tribute was remitted for five years to allow the people to have the resources to rebuild. Hemer (1986: 157) finds an historical allusion to this situation in the promise of Rev 3:12a: "He who conquers, I will make him a pillar in the temple of my God; never shall he go out of it. . . ." The citizens of Philadelphia subsequently expressed warm gratitude on inscriptions and coins to the emperor Tiberius for his assistance in the process of rebuilding their city, and they later took the name "Neocaesarea." Still later, under Vespasian, it took another imperial name, Flavia (*BMC,* 60 and 60 of Vespasian; 62 of Domitian). Hemer suggests that this adoption of the name of the divine emperor is referenced and contrasted with the offer of a better and more lasting name in Rev 3:12b: "And I will write on him the name of my God, and the name of the city of my God, the new Jerusalem which comes down from my God out of heaven."

Another negative event that burned itself upon the collective memory of the people of Philadelphia was an edict from the emperor Domitian in A.D. 92 (practically contemporary with the probable date of the Apocalypse). In the interest of protecting the vine growers of Italy (or perhaps to encourage the production of grain at the expense of grapes), Domitian required at least half the vineyards in the provinces to be cut down and no new ones planted (Suet. *Dom.* 7,2; 14.2; Philostr. *VA* 6.42; *VS* 1.21). As can be imagined, this edict was bitterly unpopular in Asia and the source of severe hardship in a city like Philadelphia, which was so dependent on viticulture (cf. Rev 6:6) and where Dionysius was the chief deity. Thus the contrast between the character of Christ, who will never betray his people who have continued to confess his name even when they are weak and rejected (Rev 3:8, 10, 11), and that of the imperial god who had disappointed them so severely.

Ignatius, the bishop of Antioch on the Orontes, visited the city on his way to his martyrdom in Rome (A.D. 107) and also sent a letter from Troas to the church at Philadelphia. Some of the members of the church of this city were martyred ca. A.D. 155 along with Polycarp (*Mart. Polyc.* 1). Philadelphia was a center of prophecy in the post-apostolic age, a place where Christians tended to be fearless and aggressive in their witness for the faith, and possibly the birthplace of Montanism (Calder 1923: 309–54; cf. Hemer 1986: 170–74). Today, the Hellenistic and Roman remains are located underneath the modern Turkish town of Alaşehir. There is an ancient acropolis with a few minor excavations, an ancient church (with traces of 11th century frescoes), and a rather extensive portion of the city wall from Byzantine times. Finds from Philadelphia are located in the Manisa museum, some distance away.

Bibliography

Calder, W. M. 1923. Philadelphia and Montanism. *BJRL* 7: 309–54.

Finegan, J. 1981. *The Archaeology of the New Testament.* Boulder, CO.

Hemer, C. J. 1986. *The Letters to the Seven Churches of Asia in Their Local Setting.* JSNTSup 11. Sheffield.

Yamauchi, E. 1987. *New Testament Cities in Western Asia Minor.* Grand Rapids.

W. WARD GASQUE

PHILEMON, EPISTLE TO.

One of the epistles of St. Paul that now stands as the 18th book of the NT (between Titus and Hebrews).

A. Orientation to the Letter and Its Interpretation
B. Authorship and Rhetoric
C. Legal Context and Obligations
D. The Letter's Story

A. Orientation to the Letter and Its Interpretation.

While under arrest for his activities as a Christian, Paul of Tarsus with his "brother" Timothy wrote a personal but not private letter to his "beloved fellow worker" Philemon, to Apphia and Archippus (family members?), and to the congregation meeting in Philemon's house. The letter has a single theme: the future of the relationships among at least three persons: Paul, who identified himself as "a prisoner for Christ Jesus" and a "brother"; Philemon, a slave owner, who had become a Christian directly or indirectly in response to Paul's work sometime before he received this letter; and Onesimus, a male slave owned by Philemon, who was with Paul at the time of the writing and who had become a Christian directly under Paul's influence since leaving Philemon's household without permission. Paul seems to have intended also to put in question Philemon's future relationship to the Christians who met in his house (note the plural "you" in vv 22b, 25) and to "all God's people" (vv 5, 7).

The letter is correspondingly brief: 335 words encompassing an occasionally specialized vocabulary of 143 words. As such, it is the shortest extant Pauline letter in the NT canon. In its form, Paul followed more closely than in any of his other writings the pattern of Hellenistic letters known to us, particularly letters of intercession (see Stowers 1986). See also LETTERS (GREEK AND LATIN). In the context of Greek rhetoric (see below), the book of Philemon (hereafter Plmn) divides readily into five paragraphs:

Vv 1–3	Opening Greetings
4–7	Thanksgiving, Intercession, and Praise for Philemon (the exordium)
8–16	Appeal on behalf of Onesimus (the body or proof)
17–22	Reiteration and expansion of the appeal (the peroration)
23–25	Concluding Greetings

This brief document has attracted a large amount of scholarly attention during the past forty years (Schenk 1987), much of which has continued earlier efforts to explain the perplexing legal context and the extraordinary rhetorical aspects of this succinct, winsome, yet apparently slight document. Of particular importance is Petersen's attempt (1985) to embrace and move beyond these concerns in order to clarify the larger story (including the "social structures" and the "symbolic universe") within which Plmn first made sense. This story is grounded in profound theological convictions, even though Paul did not treat in the letter itself any of the obvious doctrinal or ecclesiastical issues that characterize all his other letters.

To be sure, even without focusing on the larger story as such, every scholar of Plmn has felt obliged in some way to propose as the context for exegesis a reconstruction of at least some of the circumstances which provoked the writing and preserving of this letter. Chief among the questions energizing these reconstructions and explanations have been:

Why did Onesimus decide to leave Philemon's household, and by doing so did he make himself a fugitive slave? Did Onesimus then come into contact with Paul because he searched for him and found him under arrest, or rather as an unintended result of being arrested himself as a lawbreaker? Or had his owner sent him to help Paul (see Winter 1987)?

Did the prohibition of Deut 23:16–17 (—Eng 23:15–16: "You shall not give up to his master a slave who has escaped from his master to you. He shall dwell with you . . .") play a role in Paul's keeping Onesimus with him during the period in which he became a Christian? And did it influence his choice of words in vv 13–14?

To what extent was Paul constrained by Roman law in his relationships with Philemon (not a Roman citizen) and Onesimus? In any case, was Paul's eventual urging of Onesimus to return to Philemon (with Plmn as a "cover letter") motivated primarily by his respect for Roman or local laws applying to the harboring and returning of fugitive slaves, or by his respect for Philemon's rights and feelings (see Getty 1987), or by his theology which required him to encourage reconciliation among estranged Christians (see 1 Cor 6:7)?

Exactly which actions was Paul urging Philemon to take with respect to Onesimus (vv 14, 16–18, 20–21)? For example, would Philemon have concluded from v 16 that Paul wanted him to change Onesimus's legal and social status from that of his slave to being his freedman (see SLAVERY) because of Onesimus' new status as a Christian "brother" (see Daube 1986: 41)? Did Paul hope that his new "father/child" relationship with Onesimus (with implications of ownership—vv 10, 12) would strike Philemon as a prevailing counterweight to his own claims on his slave, leading to new perceptions of who was whose patron (v 11, 13, 15–17)? In any case, was Paul appealing to Philemon's honor (see vv 4–7) with the implication (vv 13–14, 21) that Philemon's "goodness" should lead him not only to restrain himself from punishing Onesimus and to reconcile with him but also to send him back to help Paul in prison or in the Christian mission (see Ollrog 1979: 101–6)?

Where and when was Paul imprisoned when he wrote (vv 1, 9–10, 13, 23)? Rome? Ephesus? Caesarea? And what should be concluded about the relation of Plmn to the Letter to the Colossians which includes references to both an Onesimus (4:9), and Archippus (4:17), and an Epaphras (4:12—see Plmn 23) whose home is Colossae? For example, could Plmn be the letter to nearby Laodicea mentioned in Col 4:16?

Was Archippus, rather than Philemon, the real addressee of Paul's appeals (see S. Winter 1986, following J. Knox)?

What role should Paul's direct advice to Christians in slavery in 1 Cor 7:21 play in interpreting Paul's letter to Philemon?

What circumstances in the subsequent lives of Paul and Onesimus contributed to the preservation of Plmn in the NT canon?

B. Authorship and Rhetoric

Although a few scholars seriously questioned Pauline authorship of Plmn in the 4th and 5th centuries (because the content seemed too slight) and again in the 19th century (because the situation presupposed by Plmn appeared too novelistic), the language, style, and structure of argumentation found in Plmn are unmistakably Paul's (Schenk 1987: 3142–3145). Many exegetes have concluded that Paul did not dictate these words but wrote the entire letter in his own hand (see Stuhlmacher 1975: 50).

Some of the many distinctively Pauline features are his self-designations in combination with "Christ Jesus" in vv 1 and 9, his use in vv 1 and 24 of the term *synergos* ("co-worker"), the phrase *en kyrio* ("in the Lord") without the definite article in Gk (vv 16, 20), participles as transitions to new clauses (vv 4, 5, 21), and the intensifying phrase *hina mē lego* ("to say nothing of") in v 19b, which suggests that he could indeed overlook a matter that by mentioning he especially emphasizes (see 2 Cor 9:4). Even the sentence that has provoked the greatest disagreements among translators (v 6) contains characteristic Pauline features (see Riesenfeld 1982).

Paul's artistry in crafting such a carefully woven argument and appeal has been widely recognized. Only recently, however, have scholars shown the strong influence of Greek rhetorical conventions on Paul's masterful argumentation in Plmn, in particular the genre of deliberative rhetoric (Church 1978; see White 1971; Schenk 1987). By use of skillful appeals to the reason, the emotions, and the character of their hearers, rhetoricians sought to establish two motives for action: maintaining honor and gaining advantage (Quint. *Inst.* 3.8.1–15, 6.2.9–14). According to Aristotle, Cicero, and Quintilian, such a deliberative statement was divided into three parts: (1) the exordium: for setting up the fitting mood and winning the favor of the hearer through praise and then linking that praise to the subject at hand; (2) the main body or proof: for making the aforementioned appeals to honor and advantage; and (3) the peroration: for restating the request, appealing again to the hearer's goodwill, expanding the argument, and placing the reader in an emotional frame of mind (Arist. *Rh.* 3.14–19).

Whether by training or observation, Paul used deliberative rhetoric when he appealed to Philemon, adapting this genre to his particular style and structure for letter writing. Following his characteristic salutatory format in vv 1–3, vv 4–7 function as Paul's exordium. With tact and succinctness, he first sought favor by praising Philemon for his love and faith (vv 4–5), then he focused the praise on those practical qualities especially pertinent to Philemon's positive response to the appeal (v 6), and then he referred to particulars (Philemon's loving care for God's people resulting in Paul's own joy and comfort) that he later developed in the body and underscored in the peroration (Church 1978: 20–24).

The body or proof is expressed in vv 8–16, opening with a perfectly balanced appeal to Philemon's character and feelings (vv 8–10a). Paul first applied the rhetorical convention of openly abandoning an apparently strong line of argument by referring to himself as an "ambassador" and a "prisoner" for Christ, and then for love's sake waiving that authority in order to make his first appeal to the free expression of Philemon's honor and love. In a further rhetorical move focused on Philemon's feelings, Paul duplicated the expression of his appeal (vv 9–10a) before finally mentioning its object—Onesimus—and punning effectively on the name's meaning: "profitable/useful." By doing so, Paul appealed to the second motive for action: Philemon's gaining advantage.

In vv 12–14 Paul returned to the first motive: maintaining honor. Not only has Onesimus become far more profitable to Philemon by becoming a Christian, but also Philemon has been presented with a further opportunity to express his true character, his "goodness." Paul emphasized the decisive character of this opportunity by stressing how important Onesimus was to him. While with Paul, Onesimus not only became his "son," but his "very heart," his own self (v 12). Thus Paul would regard Philemon's manner of dealing with Onesimus as treatment of himself (see v 17). Furthermore, by urging Onesimus to return home and depriving himself of his "son's" comfort and service, Paul set an example of selfless love for Philemon and established the basis for true reciprocity among the three men. By these means Paul was able to force a point of honor while ostensibly restraining himself from pressuring Philemon, who thus retained the freedom to respond honorably on his own.

Paul concluded his proof with reasoning that went beyond conventional rhetoric: it may have been necessary, i.e., providential, for Philemon to lose Onesimus as a slave in order to gain him as a "beloved brother" (vv 15–16).

Paul's words in vv 17–22 fulfilled all four requirements of a peroration with a fitting invoking of feelings: (1) Verse 17 restated his request. (2) Verses 18–19 expanded the argument with two strong rhetorical devices: anticipating a potential objection (by promising to compensate Philemon for any loss Onesimus had caused him), and emphasizing a point by claiming that it does not have to be made (Philemon owed Paul his life). (3) Verse 20 attempted to put Philemon in an emotional state of mind. (4) Verses 21–22 further sought Philemon's favor (Church 1978: 28–30). Paul poignantly concluded this rhetorical section with requests for hospitality (thus announcing his intention to follow the letter with a personal visit) and prayers for his release from imprisonment.

Rhetorical analysis of Paul's use of deliberative rhetoric in Plmn highlights its contrast to Pliny's Letter to Sabinianus (*Ep.* 9.21) about an errant freedman, to which Plmn is often compared. Pliny used a contrasting rhetorical model, the plea for pardon, stressing the freedman's youth and "genuine repentance" as well as the harm Sabinianus was causing himself with his understandable anger.

C. Legal Context and Obligations

Recent investigations have shown that a number of legal assumptions essential to the generally accepted reading of Plmn must be questioned: that Onesimus was a fugitive slave, that Paul in relation to Philemon was obligated to obey Roman laws regarding slavery, and that Onesimus would probably not ever have been made a freedman if Paul had not intervened on his behalf (if indeed that was included in Paul's request).

Until quite recently, leading exegetes of Plmn (e.g., Stuhlmacher 1975: 17–23; Suhl 1981: 21–23; O'Brien, *Colossians, Philemon* WBC, 266–67) have generally presupposed that according to Roman or Greek law Onesimus became a fugitive slave (Lat: *fugitivus*) when he left Philemon's household (Winter 1987 and Schenk 1987 argue that Philemon *sent* Onesimus to help Paul in prison). They have assumed that Onesimus belonged to the category of those slaves who ran away from their owners in order to find a life of freedom—by going underground in a large city, or in a faraway country, or in an outlaw band. Also noted is the possibility, respected particularly in the eastern Roman provinces, for such fugitives to seek asylum in a temple, such as the one dedicated to Artemis in Ephesus, or at a statue of the emperor, in order to beg the priests or attendants to broker their sale to a more humane owner.

Against this background, scholars have noted their varying degrees of surprise that the fugitive Onesimus chose none of these options but rather seems to have sought out the assistance of a person respected by his owner. Or they have suggested that Onesimus did not seek out Paul but rather unintentionally met up with him in prison after having been caught as a fugitive in a large city such as Rome or Ephesus, thus assuming (or concluding) that Onesimus only decided to return to Philemon because of Paul's urging. With Onesimus' putative fugitive status in mind, exegetes have discussed the range of punishments such a captured *fugitivus* could anticipate—beatings, chains, branding, in some cases even crucifixion—and concluded that part of Paul's intent in writing to Philemon was to persuade him to restrain himself from castigating Onesimus for running away.

In contrast to these longstanding assumptions, the Roman legal evidence presents as a common case a triangular situation in which a slave who got into some difficulty with his or her owner sought out a third party for the purpose of persuading that person to become the slave's advocate before the angry owner. The slave's goal was not to run away successfully but rather to return to the owner's household under improved conditions. According to Proculus, the foremost Roman jurist in the early 1st century C.E., such a slave emphatically did not become a *fugitivus* (*Dig.* 21.1.17.4). This opinion was echoed by such jurists as Vivianus during Trajan's reign, who mentioned the slave's mother as a natural advocate (*Dig.* 21.1.17.5), and by Paulus at the end of the 2d century, who specifically mentioned a slave who sought refuge and assistance from a friend of his owner (*Dig.* 21.1.43.1).

Among Roman models, this unexceptional triangular

scenario provides the most adequate context for explaining the relationship among Onesimus, Paul, and Philemon in juristic terms (Lampe 1985: 135–37). Onesimus, then, was not a fugitive slave, nor had Paul been harboring a fugitive slave. If Onesimus had indeed intended to run away, there were surely much more promising and less risky places in which to "disappear" than at the side of a friend of his owner. But in this scenario, after causing his owner some serious loss (v 18), Onesimus sought out a respected friend of Philemon precisely in order to appeal for help in smoothing things out at home. This means that Onesimus' wrongdoing was neither running away nor stealing from household funds in order to finance his travel. Rather, something that he had done wrong led Onesimus to decide to seek out Paul as his advocate.

Lampe (1985: 137) acutely observes that this decision created a delicate situation: Onesimus, who was not yet a Christian, hoped to gain advantage by persuading one honored Christian teacher to put pressure on another Christian. Onesimus' initial trust in his owner's friend and "partner" (v 17) clearly bore surprising fruit: Paul led him to become a Christian (v 10), a "usefulness" (v 11) that Philemon had been unable to achieve in his own household. And Paul himself offered to make good whatever loss Onesimus had caused Philemon (vv 18–19). With these results in view, Paul appealed to Philemon to receive Onesimus back into the household as he would Paul himself, without mentioning directly the anger that had to be put aside and the forgiveness that was needed. Did Paul also anticipate that Philemon would make the new Christian Onesimus his freedman?

Innumerable former slaves throughout the Empire were living proof that neither Greek nor Roman slavery was usually a permanent state. Most commonly, an owner granted manumission to a *servus fidelis* as the due reward for faithful work and loyalty; this was frequently done by the owner's will at death. On the other hand, owners could punish disloyal slaves by including in their wills a clause prohibiting the heirs from ever manumitting them (Wiedemann 1985: 165). Yet there is also much evidence that owners while living had a variety of reasons for choosing to manumit some of their slaves (Bartchy 1973: 88–91), many of whom had reason to anticipate being set free about the age of thirty (see Alföldy 1972, opposed by Wiedemann 1985). (This is the appropriate context for resolving the famous disagreement about Paul's advice in 1 Cor 7:21 to Christians in slavery.) See SLAVERY (NEW TESTAMENT).

In this social-legal context the question regarding manumitting Onesimus was most likely *when,* not if, Philemon planned to set Onesimus free. Paul's climactic appeal in v 16 (receive him "no longer as a slave but . . . as a beloved brother") seems best understood as Paul's request that Onesimus' manumission not be delayed because of any wrongdoing (see v 18) and that Philemon forgive his slave and manumit him very soon. By this appeal Paul confronted Philemon with the choice either of continuing to regard himself as Onesimus' owner or of becoming his "brother" and "partner" (v 17) in a new social reality. Paul may well have hoped that Onesimus would then be sent back to help him, in the status of Philemon's freedman (v 13).

What role, then, did Roman law as such play in this triangular relationship? There is no evidence that Philemon, a Phrygian, was a Roman citizen; therefore Paul was not obligated to extend to him the protections of Roman private law (see Derrett 1988: 73). And in any case, scholars must beware of accounting for any of Paul's actions solely in terms of Roman or Greek or even Jewish laws; at the least, matters depended on the respective civic statuses of the persons with whom he was involved. Nevertheless, general Roman principles regarding treatment of slaves, especially those who had left their owners for any reason, seem to have been broadly respected in the empire. Among the options known from Greek and Jewish law, this Roman model does seem to account best for the story in Plmn.

D. The Letter's Story

Every letter is a part of a story, arising out of some form of previous relationship between the writer and the reader, then itself creating a new dimension in the relationship, and finally implying at least one future event: the response of the reader(s). The writers, readers, and persons mentioned in letters are related to each other as superiors, equals, and inferiors, and the fact that Paul, Philemon, and Onesimus play multiple roles has made interpreting Plmn particularly difficult (see Petersen 1985: 63–64).

Thus every interpretation of Plmn has been based on some explicit or implied reconstruction of the personal stories of which it is a part. The most adequate interpretation of Plmn will integrate those stories into the letter's own story, a brief version of which follows.

Such a story begins, to be sure, prior to the writing of Plmn—with Paul's activities as a Christian evangelist in Asia Minor and his attempts in various cities to gather household-based communities of Christians characterized by their exclusive faith in the God of Israel, their merciful love for each other, and their hope in the future mercy of Jesus Christ (see 1 Thess 1:2–10). Paul's God was seeking to create a new social reality and solidarity among people long separated by religious, ethnic, and class barriers. Before having to consider the relations among Philemon, Onesimus, and himself, Paul had become well practiced in stimulating reconciliation and developing social cohesiveness among his surprisingly heterogeneous groups. And his other letters suggest that he sensed well how to use patron-client relationships to further his goals (see Elliott 1987).

Plmn's story becomes more focused with Paul's encountering Philemon somewhere along the way (Ephesus seems quite likely) and persuading him to become a Christian. This established Paul as Philemon's patron, as v 19 especially emphasizes: "you owe me even your own self." Probably the next step was Philemon's own evangelistic work, most likely in Colossae, resulting at the least in the community of Christians who met in his house, including Apphia and Archippus (v 2). In any case, Philemon had opened his household (see Elliott 1984) to this group of Christians and gained a glowing reputation as their patron (vv 5–7).

During this period Paul was taken prisoner either in Ephesus (ca. 54–56) or Rome (ca. 60–62). (In view of Acts 24:26–27, Caesarea has been proposed for more than a century, but this seems unlikely.) Ephesus was the closest large city to Onesimus' home, less than 100 miles distant, and many scholars have suggested that one of the imprisonments mentioned by Paul in 2 Cor 11:23 (see also his "affliction in Asia," 2 Cor 1:8) was there. In addition, Paul's request for hospitality (Plmn 22) has seemed to many to fit most easily with an arrest in Ephesus. This part of the story has been complicated by the traditional association of Plmn with the Letter to the Colossians and a Roman imprisonment, in which Onesimus is mentioned with Tychicus (4:9) as the bearer of the letter. In any case, because of his public activities as a Christian, Paul was under arrest in a kind of imprisonment that permitted him sufficient freedom to have personal contact with Onesimus and to write to Philemon.

At this point the scenario described above (in C) enters the story. A slave of Philemon named Onesimus, who had not become a Christian, caused his owner some serious loss (v 18). He then decided to leave his troubles behind and to seek out a respected friend of his owner in order to appeal for help in assuaging Philemon (v 15), probably hoping to use the Christian bond between these two men to his own advantage. Onesimus found Paul under arrest (v 13), and while visiting and assisting him was himself persuaded to become a Christian (v 10). He thereby won Paul as his own patron and "father" and successfully persuaded him to become his advocate before his wronged owner.

At some point along the way Paul had heard about Philemon's great faith and love (vv 4–7), perhaps from Onesimus himself. Paul then built on that knowledge, on his friendship (v 17) and on his patron-client relationship with Philemon (vv 19–21), on Onesimus' personal service to him (v 13), and on the fact that Onesimus had become a Christian "brother" (v 16) and his own very dear "son" (v 10) by "pulling out all the stops" in a rhetorically crafted letter to Philemon on Onesimus' behalf. He even offered to pay from his own account for any damages done or debts Onesimus owed to Philemon, an amount Philemon may well have been able to cover from Onesimus' personal funds. See SLAVERY (NEW TESTAMENT).

Onesimus then returned to Philemon with Paul's strong, written appeal. If Philemon was moved by Paul's appeals to his advantage and his honor and then did all that Paul requested, he put aside his anger, forgave Onesimus, began to treat him with honor as a "brother," and smoothed out any remaining difficulties within the household (as he would have done for Paul, if needed). By these deeds he would have maintained his honor as a generous patron within his Christian community and before his own patron, Paul.

Moreover, the most direct way for Philemon to have stopped treating Onesimus as a slave (v 16) would have been to manumit him, probably well ahead of previous plans for doing so, especially in view of his wrongdoing. By making Onesimus his freedman he would have created a far more credible basis for functioning as his "brother" and "partner" (v 17) in the new kinship group they shared, their Christian community.

If Philemon, Apphia, Archippus, Onesimus, and the other Christians in their house-church accepted Paul's request that they pray for his anticipated stay with them (v 22), Philemon may well have waited for this visit to decide if he would encourage Onesimus to join Paul's group of "fellow workers" in the gospel. In any case, the return of Onesimus as a Christian, with Paul's strong support, presented Philemon with a major and pressing decision: would he deny his Christian identity by acting first of all with the prerogatives of an angry slave owner, or would he strengthen it by doing all in his power as Onesimus' patron to make him his "beloved brother" (see Petersen, *HBC*, 1245–48)? His house-church was watching, and Paul hoped to be there soon to see for himself.

Bibliography

(For additional bibliography, see SLAVERY (NEW TESTAMENT).

Alföldy, G. 1972. Die Freilassung von Sklaven und die Struktur der Sklaverei in der römischen Kaiserzeit. *Rivista Storica dell'Antichita* 2: 97–129.

Bartchy, S. S. 1973. *MALLON CHRESAI: First Century Slavery and the Interpretation of 1 Cor. 7:21*. SBLDS 11. Missoula, MT. (Repr. 1985).

Church, F. F. 1978. Rhetorical Structure and Design in Paul's Letter to Philemon. *HTR* 71: 17–33.

Daube, D. 1986. Onesimos. *HTR* 79: 40–43.

Derrett, J. D. M. 1988. The Functions of the Epistle to Philemon. *ZNW* 79: 63–91.

Elliott, J. H. 1984. Philemon and House Churches. *BToday* 22: 145–50.

———. 1987. Patronage and Clientism in Early Christian Society. *Forum* 3/4: 39–48.

Feeley-Harnik, G. 1982. Is Historical Anthropology Possible? The Case of the Runaway Slave. Pp. 95–126 in *Humanizing American's Iconic Book,* SBL Centennial Addresses 1980, eds. G. M. Tucker and D. A. Knight. Chico, CA.

Getty, M. A. 1987. The Theology of Philemon. Pp. 503–8 in *SBLSP,* ed. K. H. Richards. Atlanta.

Gnilka, J. 1982. *Der Philemonbrief.* HTK 10/4. Freiburg.

Hahn, F. 1977. Paulus und der Sklave Onesimus. *EvT* 37: 179–85 (review of Stuhlmacher 1975).

Lampe, P. 1985. Keine "Sklavenflucht" des Onesimus. *ZNW* 76: 135–37.

Ollrog, W.-H. 1979. *Paulus und seine Mitarbeiter.* WMANT 50. Neukirchen-Vluyn.

Petersen, N. R. 1985. *Rediscovering Paul: Philemon and the Sociology of Paul's Narrative World.* Philadelphia.

Riesenfeld, H. 1982. Faith and Love Promoting Hope: A Interpretation of Philemon v. 6. Pp. 251–57 in *Paul and Paulinism: Essays in Honour of C. K. Barrett,* ed. M. D. Hooker and S. G. Wilson. London.

Schenk, W. 1987. Der Brief des Paulus an Philemon in der neueren Forschung (1945–87) *ANRW* 2/25/4: 3135–55.

Stowers, S. K. 1986. *Letter-Writing in Greco-Roman Antiquity.* Philadelphia.

Stuhlmacher, P. 1975. *Der Brief an Philemon.* EKKNT 18. Neukirchen-Vluyn.

Suhl, A. 1973. Der Philemonbrief als Beispiel paulinischer Paraenese. *Kairos* 15: 267–79.

———. 1981. *Der Brief an Philemon.* ZB. Zurich.

White, J. 1971. The Structural Analysis of Philemon. A Point of Departure in the Formal Analysis of the Pauline Letter. Pp. 1–47 in *SBLSP.* Missoula, MT.

Wiedemann, T. 1981. *Greek and Roman Slavery.* Baltimore.
———. 1985. The Regularity of Manumission at Rome. *Classical Quarterly* 35: 162–75.
Winter, S. C. 1987. Paul's Letter to Philemon. *NTS* 33: 1–15.

S. SCOTT BARTCHY

PHILETUS (PERSON) [Gk *Philētos*]. A Christian who, along with Hymenaeus, had "swerved from the truth by holding that the resurrection is past already" (2 Tim 2:18). Because Hymenaeus can be linked with Ephesus (1 Tim 1:3), it can be assumed that that area was also the sphere of Philetus' activity. For further discussion on Philetus and related issues, see HYMENAEUS.

FLORENCE MORGAN GILLMAN

PHILIP (PERSON) [Gk *Philippos*]. **1.** Philip II, King of Macedonia (359–336 B.C.) and father of Alexander the Great (1 Macc 1:1, 6:2). Philip began his political career as the regent for the infant son of his dead brother Perdiccas III, but he soon displaced his nephew and became king instead. Five other contenders for the throne opposed him, but Philip captured coastal towns and the Chalcidian league, securing control over Macedon in the process. He founded new cities, beautified the Macedonian capital of Pella, and poured heavy resources into armaments. Then he turned his attention W toward Greece itself, conquering its city states and leagues in turn, ending with the defeat of Thebes and Athens in 338 and the formation of a league with all the cities except Sparta in 337. Philip next opened war on the Persian Empire, but was murdered by a Macedonian noble in 336 at the wedding of his daughter.

2. Philip V, ruler of Macedonia 221–179 B.C. mentioned (1 Macc 8:5) along with his son Perseus, the last Macedonian king, as a foe defeated by the Romans. As a young king he joined with Hannibal and waged the First Macedonian War (215–205) against Rome. Rome won, but at great cost. Hence, Philip V began attacking neighbors in the Agaean, while Antiochus III (Seleucid ruler 223–187) asserted Seleucid ambitions in Palestine and Asia Minor, causing Rome to attack Philip. After Antiochus took Palestine from the Egyptians at the outset of the reign of the child-king Ptolemy V (198), Philip V was able to secure land in Thrace and Asia Minor formerly held by Egypt. Rome, however, defeated Philip at the Battle of Cynoscephalae in 197. Philip was stripped of much of his territory and weapons, but left in power in Macedonia as a buffer against the ambitions of Antiochus III.

3. Phrygian governor of Jerusalem appointed by Antiochus IV Epiphanes (2 Macc 5:22) in 169 B.C. to complete the punishment of Jerusalem begun by Antiochus. Antiochus had attacked the city because he had been thwarted in his second campaign against Egypt in 169, causing a rumor to spread in Judea that he was dead and a battle to break out. Antiochus thought that Jerusalem had revolted and came to the city to take vengeance, ultimately robbing the Temple. He then appointed Philip to finish the task while he returned to Antioch. Philip proved more ruthless even than Antiochus, killing pious Jews who had assembled in caves to worship secretly (2 Macc 6:11). This Philip is mentioned once more (8:8), when he wrote to Ptolemy for help against the rising power of Judas Maccabeus. (According to 1 Macc 3:38, which is likely more accurate, Lysias was in charge, not Ptolemy, and dispatched Ptolemy, Dorymenes, and Gorgias to meet Judas.)

4. Foster brother of Antiochus Epiphanes (1 Macc 6:14). Upon his deathbed in Persia, Antiochus IV named Philip regent over his kingdom (6:14) and guardian of his son Antiochus V Eupator (6:55), roles he had previously entrusted to Lysius. See LYSIAS. Philip apparently carried the body of Antiochus back to Antioch (2 Macc 9:29), but the assertion that Philip fled to Egypt out of fear of Antiochus seems wrong. For one thing Antiochus was but a child, so Philip would have feared Lysias, if anyone. Second, 1 Macc 6:63 says that Lysias returned to Antioch, found Philip in control of the city, and defeated him, apparently contradicting 2 Macc 9:29. Goldstein (*2 Maccabees* AB, 372–73) argues that 1 Maccabees is incorrect and that 2 Macc 9:29 is correct that Philip fled to Egypt, not, however, at the death of Antiochus in November or December, 164 B.C., but after April of 163. In the absence of better data, one should approach Goldstein's reconstruction with caution. If Philip did indeed flee to Egypt, perhaps he was retreating before the advance of Lysias on Antioch.

Bibliography

Sealey, R. 1976. *A History of the Greek City States ca. 700–338 B.C.* Berkeley.
Starr, C. G. 1974. *A History of the Ancient World.* New York.

PAUL L. REDDITT

5. The son of Herod the Great and Cleopatra of Jerusalem. Josephus reports that he spent part of his youth in Rome, during which time Antipater made accusations against him to Herod: Antipater alleged that Philip had denounced Herod as the murderer of Aristobulus and Alexander and had said that he, Philip, would be Herod's next victim (*Ant* 17.80). These allegations caused Herod to hate Philip (*Ant* 17.146). But, discovering that Antipater's allegations were false, Herod was reconciled to Philip and made him a beneficiary under his last will, allotting to him Gaulonitis, Trachonitis, Batanaea, and Panias, with the title of tetrarch (*Ant* 17.189).

Philip played a part in the disputes which followed Herod's death. When Archelaus visited Rome to press his own case with Augustus, Philip remained in Judaea as his viceroy (*Ant* 17.219). But Varus, the Roman governor of Syria, soon persuaded Philip that he, too, should travel to Rome in order to support Archelaus there and to ensure that he would also receive a share if Augustus decided to partition Herod's kingdom (*Ant* 17.303). Under Augustus' final settlement, Philip received Batanaea, Trachonitis, Auranitis, Gaulonitis, and portions of the "domain of Zenodorus" in the vicinity of Panias. Our sources are imprecise as to the full extent of his territories: the Panias region is presumably the Ituraea of Luke 3:1 (cf. *HJP*^{2} 1: 336). Philip ruled these territories as tetrarch, and received from them an annual income of 100 talents (*Ant* 17.319; *JW* 2.95).

Philip is known primarily as a builder. He re-founded the city of Panias and named it Caesarea—the Caesarea Philippi (literally, "Philip's Caesarea") of the New Testament (Matt 16:13; Mark 5:27). He also refounded the town of Bethsaida: he supplemented its population, strengthened its fortifications, and named it Julias after Julia, Augustus' daughter. The refoundation will therefore have taken place early, presumably before Julia's exile in 2 B.C. (*Ant* 18.27–8). The foundation and refoundation of cities named after the emperor and his family was characteristic of client rulers under the Principate (Suet. *Aug.* 60 with Braund 1984: 107–11). Such cities tended to be centers of imperial cult: Herod the Great had already built a splendid temple near Panias for Augustus (*Ant* 15.363–64; *JW* 1.404–6). Philip's subjects were predominantly non-Jewish. Thus Philip's coinage bears images, most notably the heads of Augustus and Tiberius respectively. They also depict a temple, probably the temple which Herod had built near Panias. These coins indicate that Philip called himself simply "Philip, tetrarch" (*HJP*² 1: 340 n. 9).

Philip reigned as tetrarch from 4 B.C. until his death in A.D. 33/4. According to Josephus, he was a good ruler. His reign was mild and he avoided external entanglements. He traveled about his territories with only a small, select entourage, which would not be a burden upon his subjects. He dispensed justice promptly and fairly from a throne which he took with him in his travels around his tetrarchy. He died at Julias, where, after a costly funeral, his body was consigned to a tomb which he had built in preparation for his death (*Ant* 18.106–8).

Philip had married Salome, daughter of Antipas and Herodias, whose dancing had cost the head of John the Baptist (Mark 6:22) and who survived Philip to marry again (*Ant* 18.137). But Philip had no children: Tiberius annexed his territories upon his death (*Ant* 18.108). Philip the tetrarch is probably to be distinguished from another son of Herod named Philip (Mark 6:17 has the best mss authority; cf. also Matt 14:3; Luke 3:19; Josephus *Ant.* 18.5.1 §109). It is possible, however, that this second Philip is the product of confusion in our sources. See HEROD PHILIP.

Bibliography

Braund, D. 1984. *Rome and the Friendly King.* New York.

DAVID C. BRAUND

6. One of the twelve disciples of Jesus. In the Synoptic Gospels, he is only mentioned in the list of the disciples (Matt 10:3 = Mark 3:18 = Luke 6:14). More is known of him from the gospel of John where Jesus called Philip to be one of the Twelve (1:43–44). Philip may have been a disciple of John the Baptist because his call took place near Bethany beyond the Jordan where John was baptizing (1:28). Philip is central in bringing Nathanael to Christ as one of the Twelve (1:45–46). Jesus tested Philip regarding how to feed the 5,000 in the wilderness, and Philip looks only to the expense of the matter (6:5–7). He acts as intermediary between Christ and Greeks who had come to worship at the Passover. They wanted to be introduced to Jesus and they sought out Philip to help them (12:20–26). He may have been chosen because he spoke Greek, had a Greek name, and came from Bethsaida, a predominantly Greek area (12:21). Within the confines of the Farewell Discourse, Philip asks Jesus for a vision of the Father, only to be told by Jesus that he already had seen the Father in him (14:8–9). Philip was present among the disciples in the Upper Room who were waiting for the coming of Holy Spirit (Acts 1:13). According to one tradition, Philip is the disciple who asked to go bury his father before following Jesus (Matt 8:21; Luke 9:56; Clem. *Str.* 3.4.25; 4.9.73).

7. One of the Seven chosen by the Jerusalem Church chosen to be an almoner to serve at table, administrate, and care for the poor and widows. The Seven were appointed as a response to the growing tension between the Hellenistic Jewish Christians and the Hebrew Christians of the Jerusalem Church. They served to relieve the disciples of such duties and permit them full time evangelism (Acts 6:1–7).

After the martyrdom of Stephen, Philip was forced to leave Jerusalem. As part of Luke's account of the spread of the Gospel to all the nations as a response to the Great Commission, an account of Philip relays his missionary work as an evangelist (Acts 8). He is noted for the conversion of non-Jewish believers. He made many converts, cast out demons, and healed the lame in the city of Samaria, even thwarting the influence and eventually converting the magician Simon Magus. Upon hearing of Philip's work, the apostles at Jerusalem sent Peter and John to Samaria to sanction officially the work and baptize the new converts in the Holy Spirit (vv 4–25).

In an episode on the road between Jerusalem and Gaza, Philip met a eunuch, the treasurer to the Candace, Queen of Ethiopia. Philip interpreted the Servant Song of Isa 53:7–8, identifying Jesus as the Servant. The eunuch was subsequently converted and baptized (vv 26–39). Philip then evangelized Azotus, the old Philistine city of Ashdod, about 20 miles N of Gaza, and proceeded to preach to cities along the coastal road until settling in Caesarea. Paul later stayed there with Philip and his four prophesying daughters (see below) on his last journey to Jerusalem (Acts 21:8–9).

Later tradition confuses Philip the Apostle and Philip the Evangelist. Confusion may have occurred as early as Papias (60–130 C.E.), for he refers to Philip the Apostle as living in Hierapolis with his daughters (Eus. *Hist. Eccl.* 3.39.8–10), but it was Philip the Evangelist who had notable daughters (see below). Also, Polycrates identified Philip the Apostle as buried at Hierapolis with his two aged virgin daughters and having another daughter buried at Ephesus (Eus. *Hist. Eccl.* 3.31.3). Eusebius does not catch Polycrates's mistake for he then quotes the *Dialogue* of Gaius to claim that Philip and his four prophetess daughters were buried at Hierapolis and goes on to quote Acts 21:8–9 (Eus. *Hist. Eccl.* 3.31.2–5).

The four virgin daughters of Philip the Evangelist are mentioned in Acts 21:8–9. Philip's daughters were Jewish-Christians who lived with their father in his home in Caesarea in Judea. They possessed the gift of prophecy and are literally called "virgin *(parthenos)* prophesying daughters." They are evidence that the gift of prophecy was the privilege of women in the early Church (cf. 1 Cor 11:5; Rev 2:20) and that the practice of prophecy among women evident in the OT was again manifested (e.g. 2 Kgs 22:14; Neh 6:14). Within Acts, these four prophetesses demonstrate the fulfillment of Joel's prophecy that in the latter days the spirit of God would be poured out on the daughters of Israel (Joel 2:28–29; Acts 2:14–21; cf. Eus. *Hist. Eccl.* 5.17.2–3).

Luke may have received information about persons and events of the early years of Christianity in Judea from the daughters of Philip. Papias received information about Joseph Barsabbas (Acts 1:23) from the daughters of Philip (he confuses him with Philip the Apostle) (Eus. *Hist. Eccl.* 3.39.9–10). Polycrates, bishop of Ephesus, mentions that Philip, one of the twelve apostles, and two virgin daughters who grew quite old were buried in a tomb at Hierapolis (Eus. *Hist. Eccl.* 3.31.2–3). Eusebius understands this reference to be to Philip the Evangelist, for he goes on to quote Proclus from the *Dialogue* of Gaius that the four daughters of Philip were prophetesses who worked and were buried in Hierapolis along with their father Philip. In support, Eusebius cites Acts 21:8 as the biblical reference to the family (Eus. *Hist. Eccl.* 3.31.4–5).

Bibliography

Strobel, A. 1972. Armenpfleger "um des Friedens willen" (Zum Verständnis von Act 6,1–6). *ZNW* 63: 271–76.
Swindler, L. 1979. *Biblical Affirmations of Women.* Philadelphia.

JoAnn Ford Watson

PHILIP, ACTS OF. A text which chronicles the adventures and martrydom of Philip at Hierapolis. About 50 Greek manuscripts, menologia for the most part, transmit the *Martyrdom of Philip.* This tale, which circulated in three divergent forms, was extracted from a larger work, the *Peregrinations* or *Acts of Philip the Apostle.* The remainder of the work—long lost—has been progressively recovered. This is especially so in the following manuscripts: Vatican, gr. 824 for *Acts Phil.* I–IX; Athos, Xenophontos 32 for the overall work in its long form less the essential of *Acts Phil.* II and VIII; the totality of *Acts Phil.* IX–X and the beginning of XI, folios having been mislaid or torn away; Athens, B.N. gr. 346 which gives a long form of the beginning of *Acts Phil.* VIII; and, if it really is the original end, Oxford, Bod. Baroccianus 180, which relates the translation of the apostle's relics from Ophiorymos to Hierapolis. The work was either dismantled for liturgical reasons (extraction of the *Martyrdom* as the reading for the Feast of St. Philip, 14 November) or else expurgated for doctrinal reasons (especially encratism).

The overall work was not, moreover, a single aggregate. *Acts Phil.* VIII and what follows until the end constitute a homogenous work and relate the journey of Philip the Apostle, accompanied by his sister Marian and his friend Bartholomew, to the city of Ophiorymos where he preached an encratic message, converted Nikanora the governor's wife, and Stachys the Blind, before being martyred by order of Tyrannognophos the governor. If Baroccianus 180 is followed, the tale finishes by the translation of the apostle's relics from Ophiorymos to Hierapolis where the tomb of Philip was venerated since the 2d century (Eus., *Hist. Eccl.* 3.31.1–4). On the other hand, *Acts Phil.* I–VII is a composite: *Acts Phil.* II, an independent episode (the confrontation at Athens between Philip, some Greek philosophers, and the High Priest of Jerusalem, inspired by Acts 17), *Acts Phil.* III–IV, a whole (the divine confirmation of Philip in his ministry and the healing of a young girl); *Acts Phil.* V–VII (the controversy with a Jew, a successful miracle, and the construction of a church). Certain of these episodes, as the proper names Azotus and Candankians suggest (*Acts Phil.* 33), must have originally been about Philip the Deacon (Acts 8) and not about the apostle. Different indices (2d century sources which were used as well as the mention of the *Acts Phil.* in the Decree of Ps-Gelatus 5.2.5, line 268, 5th–6th century) suggest that these different documents were grouped together into a single work by a 4th century author. This author or the editors of the sources relied on information relative to Philip which began circulating from the 2d century (the sepulcher at Hierapolis, the resurrection of a dead man; cf. Eus., *Hist. Eccl.* 3.31.1–4 and 39.9, as well as on a few legends [cf. the Manichean Psalm, "There were ten virgins," Allberry 1938: 192]). These also adapted passages from the other apocryphal Acts transferring them to Philip (cf. *Acts Phil.* VI, the joust between Peter and Simon, *Acts Pet.* 23–28), as well as different prayers of uncertain origin. The presence of this archaic material confers an importance on the *Acts Phil.* unsuspected until now.

In order to define the author's religious conceptions, one has to rely on the least normalized form of the *Acts Phil.*, i.e., Xenophontos 32. The work is encratic, hostile to marriage, favorable to sexual continence and abstention from meat, as is evident in such passages as "Purity *(hagenia)* communicates with God" (*Acts Phil.* V, 46). Mariamne is saved and fulfills a ministry, but only insofar as she is dressed as a man and inwardly has adopted a masculine dispostion. God and Christ generously offer salvation and confer on the believer a power capable of exorcism and healing. In addition, the apostles received from Christ a special dress (*Acts Phil.* I, 6) and a small coffer or case (*Acts Phil.* XIII). Coming in Christ's wake, they are healers of the soul; they settle in an abandoned dispensary.

The *Acts of Philip* is not hostile to the OT which is quoted in the dispute between Philip and Aristarchus (*Acts Phil.* VI, 77–79). Moreover the work transmits previously unpublished sentences of Jesus of a synoptic type, doubtlessly coming from a document of the same type as the source of the Logia (Q; *Acts Phil-Mart. Phil.* 135).

Bibliography

Allberry, C. R. C. 1938. A Manichean Psalm Book, Part 2. Stuttgart.
Bovon, F. fc. Les Actes de Philippe. *ANRW* 2/25/4.
Lipsius, R. A. 1884–1890. *Die apocryphen Apostelgeschichten und Aspostellegenden,* 2. Braunschweig repr. 1976.

François Bovon

PHILIP, GOSPEL OF (NHC II,*3*). A Valentinian Christian document included among the Nag Hammadi Coptic codices discovered in Egypt in 1945. The text is extant only in this ms (Codex II,*3;* pp. 51-29-86:19), very likely a translation of an original Greek work. A Syrian provenance for the Greek text is suggested in part by the interest shown in the meaning of Syriac words (63:21–23; 56:7–9). Our Coptic copy is dated ca. A.D. 350.

A. Title

The text is anonymous and may bear Philip's name merely because he is the only apostle referred to by name

(73:9–14). Among gnostics, however, Philip was considered a privileged recipient and caretaker of the Lord's revelation (*Pistis Sophia* 1:42). The apocryphal *Acts of Philip* portrays its protagonist as an ascetic who taught chastity and continence in marriage and who overcame heavenly demons by sacramental means.

B. Composition

Gos. Phil. is not like one of the NT Gospels. It is a compilation of statements in a variety of literary types: parable, paraenesis, narrative dialogue, dominical saying, aphorism, and analogy, along with samples of biblical exegesis, dogma, and polemics. These statements, however, are not placed into a narrative framework but are arranged in a sequence that is neither strictly topical nor predictable. Efforts to analyze the scheme of arrangement are hampered by inconvenient lacunae in the ms.

Some continuity of thought can be observed in the linkage of similar materials (e.g., 51:29–52:35, series of contrasts) or in the use of catchwords (e.g., 77:15–78:24, "love"). Abrupt changes of thought are frequent. Certain themes recur at unequal intervals (e.g., the need to rise before one dies, 56:15–20; 56:26–57:22; 66:16–23; 73:1–8), but with no obvious intervening development. There is a possibility that the compiler has broken coherent paragraphs into pieces (e.g., read in this order 70:5–9; 76:22–77:1; 66:7–29; or 75:13–14 followed by 61:36–62:5; or 63:5–11 prefixing 70:22–29).

C. Content

Gos. Phil. contains eight brief, enigmatic "new" sayings of Jesus (55:37–56:3; 58:10–14; 59:25–27; 63:29–30; 64:2–9; 64:10–12; 67:30–35; and 74:25–27). In addition it quotes five sayings of Jesus from Matthew (3:15; 6:6; 15:13; 16:17; and 27:46 [= Mark 15:34]) and three from John (6:53; 8:32, 34). The only other NT passages cited are Matt 3:10; 1 Cor 8:1; 15:50; and 1 Pet 4:8. There are many allusions to NT contexts and expressions, and the early chapters of Genesis receive an ongoing exegesis. There is no disparagement of the OT in *Gos. Phil.*, and the citation of Matt 3:10 is said to be as "the word says" (83:11).

Gos. Phil. tells several extracanonical stories about Jesus. He changed his appearance to suit the nature of those to whom he was revealing himself (57:28–58:10). His three female companions were each named Mary (59:6–11), though Mary Magdalene alone received many kisses from him (63:32–64:2). The result of mixing 72 colors together was a vat of white (63:25–30).

Gos. Phil. is very short on speculation about Sophia, the nature of the Pleroma, or the myth of creation. The tripartite division of humanity—fleshly, psychic, pneumatic—is not emphasized. *Gos. Phil.* speaks rather of being "a Hebrew," or "a Christian," or "a Christ."

The primary interest of *Gos. Phil.* is the restoration of Adam's original androgynous nature. Christ came expressly "to repair the separation" (70:12–17), which has brought death (68:22–26). The reunion is also spoken of as "the resurrection" (67:9–18) and must be attained before one dies, as pioneered by "the lord" (56:15–19). The reunion can be effected in the sacramental bridal chamber (70:17–22), where "the mysteries of truth" are revealed in type and image (84:20–21; 85:14–19).

Only "free men and virgins" may enter the bridal chamber; "animals, slaves, and defiled women" are excluded (69:1–4). A "virgin" is one never defiled by sexual intercourse (55:27–28), a "free man" does not sin (77:15–18); together they are called "Christians" (74:13–16), who possess "the resurrection, the light, the cross, the Holy Spirit" (74:18–21). Since "Christian" in the gnostic glossary normally designates the psychic rather than the pneumatic, *Gos. Phil.* is offering the psychic the chance to rise to the pneumatic level—by sacramental means (64:22–31; 74:12–15; 67:26–31). Even "a slave" can advance to a higher level (79:13–18).

Gos. Phil. summarizes: "The lord did everything in a mystery, a baptism and a chrism and a eucharist and a redemption and a bridal chamber" (67:27–30). This is probably the complete initiation sequence for a gnostic Christian. Initiation in the Church at the time of *Gos. Phil.* normally included baptism in water, chrism, and eucharist, set against a nuptial background. "Bridal chamber" in *Gos. Phil.* may be a covering term for the whole initiation, since a benefit of a particular sacrament (cf. 67:5–6; 69:12–14; 57:27–28) may also be associated with "bridal chamber" (86:4–11; cf. 70:5–9; 74:12–24). The converse is also the case (58:10–14; 69:4–14; 73:1–19; 75:14–24).

What the mystery of "redemption" accomplished is not explained. It is associated with both baptism and bridal chamber (69:25–27). Both Irenaeus (*Haer.* 1.21.2) and Hippolytus (*Haer.* 6.41) say that a second baptism called "redemption" was in use among Valentinians. The ritual action in the sacramental bridal chamber has been variously estimated: an act of sexual intercourse by married couples (cf. 65:1–26), or a holy kiss shared by celibates (69:1–4; 59:2–6; 63:32–64:9; 82:4–7).

Bibliography

Buckley, J. J. 1980. A Cult-Mystery in *The Gospel of Philip*. *JBL* 99: 569–81.

Grant, R. M. 1961. The Mystery of Marriage in the Gospel of Philip. *VC* 15: 129–40.

Isenberg, W. W. 1988. The Gospel of Philip. Pp. 131–51 in *NHL*.

Isenberg, W. W., and Layton, B. fc. The Gospel of Philip: Introduction, Translation, Coptic Text, and Notes. In *Nag Hammadi Codex II,2–7*, ed. B. Layton. NHS. Leiden.

Segelberg, E. 1960. The Coptic-Gnostic Gospel According to Philip and its Sacramental System. *Numen* 7: 189–200.

Wilson, R. M. 1962. *The Gospel of Philip*. London.

WESLEY W. ISENBERG

PHILIPPI (PLACE) [Gk *Philippoi*]. Situated in N Greece at the border of E Macedonia and Thrace, ancient Philippi was the site of Paul's earliest extensive missionary activity in Europe (Acts 16:11–40; Philippians). The city (41°00′N; 24°16′E) stood about 16 km NNW of the port city Neapolis (modern Kavalla) and originally bore the name Krenides (from the Greek for "spring") in recognition of the abundance of streams in the area.

A. Historical Overview
B. Krenides, Philippi, and the Thracians
C. Hellenistic Philippi
D. Early Roman Philippi

E. Later Roman Philippi
F. Sanctuaries and Rock Reliefs
G. Early Christian Philippi

A. Historical Overview

Greek colonists from the nearby island of Thasos founded Krenides in 360–59 B.C.E. under the leadership of the exiled Athenian politician Kallistratos. In 356, King Philip II of Macedon brought the city under Macedonian dominion and renamed it after himself. It is likely that the financial resources which propelled Philip's hegemonic policies in Greece derived in large part from the precious metals mined at Mt. Pangaion overlooking the plain of Datos in which Philippi was located.

Rome's successful campaigns against Macedonian dynasts and dynastic pretenders in the 2d century B.C.E. led to the establishment of a Roman province of Macedonia. Over the course of the next century (mid-2d to mid-1st B.C.E.), Philippi served as a provincial outpost on the Via Egnatia, the main overland artery linking Rome to the East. Two battles fought near the city in 42 B.C.E. resulted in the defeat of the "liberators" Cassius and Brutus who had been instrumental in the assassination of Julius Caesar. The victors at Philippi, Octavian (later titled Augustus) and Antony, emerged as the dominant powers of the Roman Mediterranean basin. Following the battles, Philippi became a Roman colony and discharged veterans receiving land allotments settled permanently in the area. Within a few years after Augustus' defeat of Antony at the battle of Actium (30 B.C.E.), as many as 500 more Roman soldiers—mostly veterans of Antony's praetorian guard who had lost their claims to land in Italy—received allotments and accompanying privileges in Philippi. Renamed Colonia Julia Augusta Philippensis, in honor of Augustus' daughter, the colony of Philippi embraced an area of more than 700 square miles extending from the Pangaion mountain range in the north to the colony's seaport of Neapolis in the S and from the Nestos river in the E to the Strymon in the W. The city of Philippi was the urban political center of the colony and with its proximity to the Via Egnatia also dominated the colony's commercial life.

Epigraphic evidence from Philippi indicates that the Egnatia in E Macedonia and Thrace was in a state of disrepair in the early Roman Imperial period. During the reigns of Augustus' immediate successors (Tiberius, Gaius, and Claudius) the colony may have been dependent largely on its access to the sea via Neapolis for commerce and communication. It was by the sea route—Alexandria Troas in Asia Minor to Neapolis and overland to Philippi—that the apostle Paul traveled to the city in 49 C.E. during the reign of the Emperor Claudius (41–54 C.E.). Trajan's (97–117 C.E.) and Hadrian's (117–138 C.E.) activities in the East occasioned the repair and upkeep of the Egnatia, and it is from this period and the time of their successors, Antoninus Pius (138–61 C.E.) and Marcus Aurelius (161–80 C.E.), that most of the Roman buildings now visible at the site originated.

Excavations at Philippi have revealed further building activity in the 3d and 4th centuries C.E. including the construction of one of the earliest known Christian churches in Greece. At least six more churches were built at or near the city during the 5th–7th centuries C.E. attesting to Philippi's dramatic ascendancy as an episcopal and ecclesiastical center and perhaps also as an important object of Christian pilgrimage. Taking their toll in this period was a series of extremely destructive earthquakes which disrupted construction and repair activity at some of the ecclesiastical sites and may have resulted in the city's general depopulation. In medieval times, there is evidence of a castle fortification at Philippi (mid-10th century C.E.) and of Christian burials (10th and 11th centuries C.E.), but by the 16th century only a small and scattered settlement occupied the site.

(Reports of the Greek Archaeological Service excavations at Philippi are included in the "Chronika" of *Archaiologikon Deltion* [in Greek]. Excavations of the Archaeological Society of Athens were reported in *Ergon,* 1958–69 [in Greek], and in *Pratika Archaiologikes Hetaireias,* 1958–67 [in Greek].)

B. Krenides, Philippi, and the Thracians

Of the Thasian settlement of Krenides little is known. Herodotus reports (7.112) that Thracian tribes were active in the Pangaion area at the time of Xerxes' invasion of Greece and that they held gold and silver mines in the region. According to Diodorus Siculus (16.3.7; 16.8.6–7), Philip II's takeover of Krenides came after the original Thasian settlers requested assistance in curbing Thracian hostilities. The impact of the native Thracians was durable throughout Philippi's early history, especially in local military, political, and religious matters. Thracian military contingents guided both Antony's and Octavian's forces as well as those of Cassius and Brutus before the first battle of Philippi—this, apparently, to insure that Thracian interests would be served whatever the battle's outcome. Inscriptions provide evidence of high civic honors bestowed by the Roman colony on Thracian dynasts who served as Roman client-rulers in the early Imperial period. Thracian royalty occupied the highest civic priesthoods even in the Roman province's capital, Thessalonica. Particularly acute was Thracian influence in Philippi's local religions. Herodotus reports a Thracian oracle of Dionysos at nearby Mt. Pangaion (7.111). The Thracian Bacchus, Bendis (associated with Artemis and Diana), and the rider hero are prominent features of Philippi's religious environment and their influence may explain certain peculiarities in the city's religious history.

C. Hellenistic Philippi

Few archaeological remains of the Hellenistic city have survived. A dedicatory inscription from the late 4th century B.C.E. provides some evidence for a temple of Apollo Komaios and Artemis. Foundations of fortification walls enclosing the acropolis and habitable area below date probably from Philip II's reign. Below the acropolis on the E within the city walls was an early theater of the Hellenistic period which was transformed on at least two occasions in Roman times.

At the SW base of the acropolis was a small Ionic prostyle structure (3d or 2d century B.C.E.) which may have served as a hero's shrine. Philippi's largest Christian basilica was to be built immediately adjacent to the sanctuary, and the church's outermost structures expanded to incorporate it into the ecclesiastical complex. Another heroön dating from the 2d century B.C.E. has been excavated in the Hellenistic city's center. A monumental temple-like structure was built above an earlier Macedonian tomb containing the remains of a young man thought to be associated with one of the city's or region's cults (as inferred from a religious relief on a pendant worn by the deceased). An inscription identifies the youth as Euephenes son of Exekestos, a name known from lists of initiates into the Samothracian cult of the "Great Gods." The earliest known Christian church at Philippi abutted the heroön which was later built over by an ecclesiastical establishment.

D. Early Roman Philippi

In the early 1st century C.E., a marble arch (no longer extant) was located two kilometers W of the city and marked the limit of Philippi's *pomerium*—an area which, according to Roman convention, was left uninhabited and uncultivated. Dating also from the early Roman colonial settlement are the foundations of a sanctuary of the Egyptian gods, a cult which enjoyed considerable popularity in Roman Macedonia. Judging from the use of expensive imported marble in the sanctuary's construction, Philippi's Egyptian cult establishment appears to have enjoyed the support of at least some wealthy adherents. The sanctuary commanded a prominent location on a central ledge at the base of the acropolis overlooking the Hellenistic Ionic prostyle heroön.

About 400 meters S of the Egnatia, a small structure was identified beneath a later Roman bath complex. Five inscriptions recovered in the bath's excavation suggest that the building was an early Roman Imperial period sanctuary of Bacchus and other gods and goddesses associated with him at Philippi. Three of the inscriptions are dedicated to Liber, Libera, and Hercules, and the other two to Liber Pater, the Roman religious analogue of the Greek Dionysos. A predominance of female dedicants in the inscriptions is striking. Dedicating a water system at the sanctuary to Liber, Libera, and Hercules was a thiasus of maenads, a cultic association of women distinctive to Dionysos religion. Three of the other inscriptions record devotional activity by individual women: one involved an offering to Liber Pater of a sestertia (1,000 denarii); another apparently the dedication of a statue directed to Liber, Libera, and Hercules. The fifth inscription was dedicated by a husband and wife to the divine triad. In addition to attesting to the financial well-being and independence of the female dedicants, the inscriptions reflect the participation of women in cultic activity involving Hercules. Such participation was unusual in Greek and Roman environments. At Thasos and Rome, for example, women could not take part in sacrificial activity for Hercules. Since Dionysos and Hercules were patron deities of Thasos, the origin of the site's original settlers, it is possible that the cult of Liber, Libera, and Hercules at Philippi stems from early Thasian devotions. In view of the cult's peculiarities (involvement of women and the additional attention to Libera), the influence of Thracian attachment to Bacchus, Bendis, and the rider hero also may have had an impact on the cult of Liber (in association with Libera and Hercules) at Philippi.

At the time of Paul's visit, the population of the colony would have included a relatively privileged core of Roman veterans and their descendants; Greeks descended from the inhabitants of the earlier Hellenistic cities (Krenides and Philippi) and from other Greek settlements in the area (e.g., Amphipolis, Maroneia, and Neapolis); Greeks involved in commerce who had migrated from Asia Minor (exemplified by the figure of Lydia of Thyatira mentioned in Acts 16:14); and native Thracians. Most of the colony's inhabitants probably lived in agrarian rural settlements, including those Roman veterans who established agricultural estates with slave work forces in the countryside. Although there is little archaeological evidence of such estates from the colony of Philippi, an excellent example of such villas from the later Roman period has been excavated at the site of Tsoukalario on nearby Thasos. The presence of villages in the colony is attested by burial sites, inscriptions from which designate the deceased person as "villager" *(vicanus)*. Epigraphic data indicate that Romans dominated the city's and colony's administration which was typically Roman (duumviri, aediles, and quaestors are in evidence). While Latin predominates in the inscriptions from the period, traces of the continued use of Greek and Thracian are apparent especially in cultic contexts. Half of the inscriptions pertaining to the Egyptian cult, for example, are in Greek—a number out of all proportion to the preponderance of Latin inscriptions in Philippi's epigraphic record. The Greek-speaking Paul was understood sufficiently well to have undertaken an extended stay at the city.

E. Later Roman Philippi

With the repair of the Egnatia during Trajan's reign (97–117 C.E.) and the increasingly eastward-oriented policies of his successors, Hadrian (117–138 C.E.) and Antoninus Pius (138–61 C.E.), Philippi enjoyed a period of extensive building activity. In the south-central part of the city, excavations have revealed a palaestra dating from the Antonine period. It included an exercise field, a compact amphitheater, a cavernous underground latrine complex, and various rooms for users of the facility. About 200 meters S of the palaestra were ornate public baths with richly decorated mosaic floors (no longer extant). Dating from the 2d century C.E., the baths were built over the earlier structure associated with dedications to Liber, Libera, and Hercules.

The palaestra's northern entrance issued onto a large street running parallel to the Via Egnatia which intersected the city as the decumanus maximus some forty meters to the N. Lying just off the large street immediately east of the palaestra was a market complex with a facade of Corinthian columns. A row of shops lined the other (N) side of the street across from the palaestra and market. Abutting the rear of the shops was the S wall of the forum.

Most of the remains of the forum presently visible date to the period of Marcus Aurelius' reign (161–80 C.E.). The forum is a clearly defined rectangle which encloses a marble-paved court measuring 100 meters from E to W and 50 meters N to S. Its N side is parallel and immediately adjacent to the Via Egnatia and features an imposing speaker's rostrum in the center, flanked by two shrine-like structures and two large fountains on either side.

Located along the forum's N axis in its E and W corners are two small temples very similar in size and ground plan.

The two buildings frame the N forum complex and are aligned with stoas to the S which run along the forum's E and W sides. The structure in the W corner consisted of a pronaos *in antis* and a rectangular room within which a bench lined the side and back walls. A dedicatory architrave inscription suggests that the building may have been the scene of banquets held in honor of the divine Antoninus Pius ([. . . *ex*] *voluntate sua a divo* [*A*]*ntonino ex epulis . . .*). The corresponding temple on the E side of the forum had a pronaos with two Corinthian columns *in antis* with a naos characteristic of a temple cella and not furnished with benches. Although there is an architrave inscription which appears to be quite similar to that of the W building, the central block presumably bearing the honored deity's name has not been recovered. An inscription on a small statue base recovered inside the cella refers in dedicatory style to Faustina Augusta, probably Marcus Aurelius' wife Faustina the Younger whose tenure as "Augusta" spanned the years 147 to 175 C.E. The presence of the statue of an emperor's wife suggests that the temple was the site of honors for the Roman imperial house as was its twin temple on the forum's E side. That the emperor's wife received divine honors at the colony is affirmed by inscriptions mentioning a priesthood of the divine Augusta recovered at Philippi and Neapolis.

Behind the stoa defining the forum's E side are a row of rooms some of which were occupied by the city's library. 2 Timothy 4:13 reflects the importance of popular literary culture in the period: Paul is portrayed as requesting the return of a cloak together with his books and parchments. Government buildings appear to have dominated the W side of the stoa in the center of which stood the curia chamber. Along the forum's S side was a large double-aisled stoa probably for the general use of the city's inhabitants and visitors.

F. Sanctuaries and Rock Reliefs

North of the Via Egnatia along the base of the acropolis were a number of sanctuaries situated in a quarry which had been used in the Hellenistic period. A well-executed inscription in Latin records devotees of Silvanus, a Roman god of woods and forests. The quarried-out rock face on which the inscription was carved served apparently as the back wall of a sanctuary otherwise constructed of semipermanent materials. Shrines dedicated to Magna Mater and Diana also are in evidence and if enclosed at all, would have been made of wood and other less durable materials. Though extremely difficult to date, the sanctuaries probably originated in the 1st or 2d centuries C.E.

The acropolis at Philippi bears 187 rock-cut reliefs. While a variety of deities are associated with the carvings (the Thracian rider, Magna Mater, Jupiter, Minerva, Isis), the vast majority of them represent a hunting goddess Diana, related to the Greek Artemis and Thracian Bendis. Some of the reliefs depicting Diana are in proximity to carvings of what appear to be human women accompanied, in some instances, with typically domestic paraphernalia. Interpreters of the reliefs have suggested that the women may have been worshippers of the goddess, as clearly was the case in certain ex votos with female dedicants and representations of a deity. It also is possible that human women depicted in the carvings were understood as being associated through funerary iconography with the protective powers of the goddess. Although the cemetery conventionally was located outside the city, the reliefs may have been religious memorials celebrating the deceased's assumption of immortal status. An analogous phenomenon occurs in mortuary iconography depicting deceased males as the Thracian rider hero.

Another set of reliefs depicting women and/or goddesses in a fairly remote area above the theater reflects perhaps the devotions and memorial activity of a group of women cult officials (priestesses of the Augustae) or associated adherents of Libera or Bacchus. However one understands the reliefs on the Philippian acropolis, it is unwise to attribute them to a single underlying religious motivation. They appear to be monuments to a rich variety of religious and honorific perspectives which were expressed in very different styles over a period of two or three centuries.

G. Early Christian Philippi

The earliest Christian building identified at Philippi is a small rectangular structure in the area just E of the Roman forum. Dedicated to Paul, the church was built in the second quarter of the 4th century C.E. (a floor inscription records donations by a bishop at Philippi who from independent testimony is known to have attended the Council of Serdica in 342 C.E.). While the church was immediately adjacent to the heroön built over the Macedonian tomb, there is no indication of a cultic relationship between the two establishments. It is noteworthy, however, that the earliest large basilica at Philippi (5th century C.E.) was constructed in immediate proximity to the heroön just above the Egnatia. This church complex, known as Basilica A, spread over an area almost as large as the Roman forum. The two-storied basilica with its apse oriented typically to the E, featured elegant frescoes in its various chambers, a long, broad nave, and an expansive narthex and exonarthex to the W. Excavations have revealed another basilica N of the Egnatia, to the W of and below Basilica A, which was carefully built and richly appointed with fine marble materials.

An even more grandiose church building (the so-called "Direkler Basilica" or Basilica B) was begun S of the forum adjacent to the palaestra. It was to have been crowned by an enormous free-standing dome which collapsed prior to completion of the church. A church of more modest dimensions later was built at the site.

East of the forum and incorporating the earlier church dedicated to Paul was an ecclesiastical complex designated by excavators as an "episkopeion" (installations associated with a bishop's residence). A monumental entryway to the complex consisted of a double-colonnaded stoa leading S from the Egnatia. Through the stoa, one gained access to a large octagonal chapel with a stepped apse to the E. Before reaching the octagon, one would have passed a number of rooms off the stoa's E edge: a pyramidal-shaped fountain (Phiale), a room of uncertain identity just above the heroön, a Diakonikon with a table or bench on its E wall, and a Prothesis which communicates with the chapel. Suggestions that an early Christian saint's cult involving water rituals continued the earlier cult at the heroön cannot be confirmed. Over 1,500 coins have been recovered in the area above the heroön, but these date only from the 4th to 6th centuries C.E. and not before. There are no architectural or other archaeological grounds for presuming cultic continuity between the two establishments.

North of the Phiale is an ensemble of elegantly executed rooms clustered around a baptistery which probably was covered with a dome, decorated on its walls and ceilings with mosaics. Hot water for the baptistery came from an adjacent thermae (bath) complex complete with caldarium, tepidarium, frigidarium, swimming pool, toilets, and perhaps a shower. The intimate proximity of such an extensive bath complex communicating with the ecclesiastical installation is a distinctive feature of the episcopal establishment at Philippi. Extensive storage areas which served the complex have been excavated as has a small burial site for infants located N and E of the octagon's apse.

Outside the city walls in the modern village of Krenides is another basilica from the early Christian period (the "Extra-muros Basilica"). Originally constructed in the 5th century C.E. in an area containing tombs, the "Extra-muros Basilica" was the site of later Christian burials some of whose epitaphs may include sectarian distinctions applied to the deceased. A series of earthquakes in the 6th and 7th centuries C.E. damaged the church, apparently beyond repair since a small Byzantine chapel was built on the site using remains from the earlier basilica. In the 10th and 11th centuries C.E., the area around the chapel served as a Christian cemetery.

In the immediate vicinity of the "Extra-muros Basilica" excavations have uncovered the apse of a much larger basilica dating from the 4th century C.E. At the site, a large funerary mosaic of the 6th century C.E. has come to light which indicates the titles of the deceased and the names of the bishops who had served during his lifetime. The mosaic is an important source in the reconstruction of Philippi's officialdom in the early Byzantine period. A possible explanation for the large number of imposing churches at Philippi is that in addition to its episcopal importance, the city enjoyed a special status as the site of early Christian pilgrimages focusing on Paul or other unknown saints. To establish whether or not this evolved out of regional attraction to Philippi's hero and/or healing cults of an earlier period will require further investigation.

Recovered near the "Neapolis Gate" SE of the theater were fragments of an inscription containing a version of the apocryphal correspondence between Abgar of Edessa and Jesus. The inscription has been dated from the mid-4th to mid-5th centuries and probably served as a device intended to protect the city.

Bibliography

Abrahamsen, V. 1986. *The Rock Reliefs and the Cult of Diana at Philippi.* Th.D. Thesis, Harvard.

———. 1987. Women at Philippi: The Pagan and Christian Evidence. *JFSR* 3: 17–30.

Collart, P. 1929. Le sanctuaire des dieux égyptiens à Philippes. *BCH* 53: 70–100.

———. 1933. Inscriptions de Philippes. *BCH* 57: 313–79.

———. 1935. Une réfection de la "Via Egnatia" sous Trajan. *BCH* 59: 395–415.

———. 1937. *Philippes. Ville de Macédoine depuis ses origines jusqu' à la fin de la l'époque romaine.* Paris.

———. 1938. Inscriptions de Philippes. *BCH* 72: 409–32.

Collart, P., and Ducrey, P. 1975. *Philippes I. Les reliefs rupestres.* BCHSup 2. Paris.

Daux, G. 1962. Excavation Report 1961. *BCH* 86: 826.

———. 1965. Excavation Report 1964. *BCH* 89: 832.

Elliger, W. 1978. *Paulus in Griechenland: Philippi, Thessaloniki, Athen, Korinth.* SBS 91/92. Stuttgart.

Heuzey, L., and Daumet, H. 1876. *Mission archéologique de Macédoine.* Paris.

Hoddinott, R. 1963. *Early Byzantine Churches in Macedonia and Southern Serbia.* New York.

———. 1981. *The Thracians.* New York.

Jones, A. H. M. 1971. *The Cities of the Eastern Roman Provinces.* Oxford.

Kanatsoulis, D. 1964. *History of Macedonia.* Thessaloniki (in Greek).

Lazarides, D. 1976. Philippi (Krenides). Pp. 704–5 in *Princeton Encyclopedia of Classical Sites,* ed. R. Stillwell. Princeton, NJ.

Lemerle, P. 1935. Inscriptions latines et greques de Philippes. *BCH* 59: 126–64.

———. 1937. Nouvelles inscriptions latines de Philippes. *BCH* 61: 410–20.

———. 1945. *Philippes et la Macédoine orientale à l'époque Chretienne et Byzantine.* Paris.

Pandermalis, D., and Papazoglou, F. 1983. Macedonia under the Romans. Pp. 192–221 in *Macedonia: 4,000 Years of Greek History and Civilization,* ed. M. Sakellariou. Athens.

Papazoglou, F. 1979. Quelques aspects de l'Histoire de la province de Macédoine. *ANRW* 2/7/1: 302–69.

———. 1982. Le territoire de la colonie de Philippes. *BCH* 106: 89–106.

Pelekanidis, S. 1955. The *extra muros* early Christian Basilica of Philippi [in Greek]. *Archaiologike Ephemeris* (1961): 114–79.

———. 1967. Excavations in Philippi. *Balkan Studies* 8: 123–26.

———. 1978. Kultprobleme in Apostel-Paulus-Oktogon von Philippi im Zusammenhang mit einem aelteren Heroenkult. Pp. 393–97 in *Studi di antichità cristiana* 32. *Atti del IX Congresso Internazionale di Archeologia Cristiana.* Vol. 2. Vatican City.

Perdrizet, P. 1898. Voyage dans la Macédoine première (1). Un tombeau du type "macédonien" au N.O. du Pangée. *BCH* 22: 335–53.

———. 1900. Inscriptions de Philippes. *BCH* 24: 299–323.

Picard, C. 1922. Les dieux de la colonie de Philippes vers le Ier siècle de notre ère, d'après les ex-voto rupestres. *RHR* 117–201.

Portefaix, L. 1988. *Sisters Rejoice: Paul's Letter to the Philippians and Luke-Acts as Seen by First-century Philippian Women.* ConBNT 20. Stockholm.

Salac, A. 1923. Inscriptions du Pangée, de la région Drama-Cavalla et de Philippes. *BCH* 47: 49–96.

Witt, R. 1977. The Egyptian Cults in Ancient Macedonia. Pp. 324–33 in *Ancient Macedonia II.* Thessaloniki.

HOLLAND L. HENDRIX

PHILIPPIAN JAILOR. Not named in Acts 16, although two late minisucle manuscripts, 2147 of the 11th century and 614 of the 13th, call him Stephanas (Metzger 1980: 41). Acts 16:23, 27, 36 are the only places in which *desmophylax,* "jailor," appears in the NT. According to Haenchen *Acts* (MeyerK, 501), Acts 16:25–34 contain so many improbabilities that these verses cannot be historical. However, vv 25–29 very likely contain a historical kernel, because according to 1 Thess 2:2, Paul had suffered and been shamefully treated in Philippi. This narrative would have also contained miraculous elements (Giesekke 1989: 348–51): the earthquake, opened doors, being freed from the stocks, and Paul's seeing through walls. In parallel fashion, Luke writes of the apostles (5:17–26) and Peter (12:3–17) being freed from prison (Lüdemann 1987: 187–91).

The jailor was instructed to guard Paul and Silas carefully, and he did. They were put in the inner prison and their feet were placed in stocks. Later, after the earthquake had opened the doors of the prison and the prisoners appeared to be gone, the jailor wanted to kill himself. But Paul prevented him and assured him that all the prisoners were still there. The jailor demanded a light and rushed and fell at Paul's and Silas' feet. He then led them outside and asked the question, "Men, what must I do to be saved?" Their answer was that he should believe in the Lord Jesus and he and his household would be saved, and then they spoke the word of the Lord to them. The jailor washed their wounds and was at once baptized with all of his family. He brought Paul and Silas into his household and set food before them and rejoiced with all his household that he had believed in God. The next day, the jailor delivered to Paul and Silas the magistrates' instruction that they were to be freed, and let them go in peace.

To show an appropriate equality, Luke draws parallels between men and women. Both Lydia (vv 13–15) and the jailor convert, and with their households believe and are baptized. Both show Paul hospitality. In addition, God protects the Christians. The security measures taken by the jailor are to no avail. Actually, Paul's calm confidence is contrasted with the agitated state of the jailor, who later humbly recognizes the importance of Paul and Silas. Consequently, through the Philippian jailor, Luke develops his themes of salvation, belief with one's whole household in the Lord Jesus, recognition of Jesus as "Lord," the word of the Lord, baptism, sexual equality, hospitality, and rejoicing in these things (O'Toole 1984: 33–61, 86–92, 125, 206–10, 225–47).

Bibliography

Giesekke, F. 1989. Zur Glaubwürdigkeit von Apg. 16, 25–34. *TSK* 71: 348–51.

Lüdemann, G. 1987. *Das frühe Christentum nach den Traditionen der Apostelgeschichte: Ein Kommentar.* Göttingen.

Metzger, B. M. 1980. *New Testament Studies: Philological, Versional, and Patristic.* NTTS 10. Leiden.

O'Toole, R. F. 1984. *The Unity of Luke's Theology: An Analysis of Luke-Acts.* GNS 9. Wilmington, DE.

ROBERT F. O'TOOLE

PHILIPPIAN SLAVE GIRL. See SLAVE GIRL AT PHILIPPI.

PHILIPPIANS, EPISTLE TO THE. Written by the apostle Paul to the church in the NE Macedonian city of Philippi, the letter to the Philippians is the eleventh book of the NT canon. It is traditionally referred to as one of Paul's four "Prison" or "Captivity" Epistles, because in this letter as well as in Ephesians, Colossians, and Philemon the author indicates that he is incarcerated at the time of writing. The contents of Philippians may be briefly summarized as follows: After a salutation (Phil 1:1–2) and thanksgiving (1:3–11), Paul discusses his imprisonment and its effects on the progress of the gospel (1:12–26). Next, he gives exhortations to the church (1:27–2:18), citing a famous hymn from the early Christian liturgy (2:6–11). After indicating his plans to send Timothy and Epaphroditus to Philippi (2:19–30), Paul warns the Philippians about false teachers who would thwart their spiritual progress (3:1–21). Finally, he concludes the letter with various exhortations (4:1–9), an expression of gratitude for a gift sent to him by the Philippians (4:10–20), greetings (4:21–22), and a benediction (4:23).

A. Establishment of the Church
B. Paul's Continuing Contact with Philippi
C. Analysis of the Letter to Philippi
   1. Authenticity
   2. Character and Contents
   3. Integrity and Purpose
   4. Place and Date of Composition
D. Opponents
E. The Christ Hymn
F. Text and Early Versions

A. Establishment of the Church

According to Acts 16, Paul established the church in Philippi on his so-called second missionary journey. He was accompanied by Silas, Timothy, and possibly a third, anonymous individual whose presence may be implied by the use of "we" in the narrative of Acts (16:10–17; cf. also 20:5–15; 21:1–18; 27:1–28:16). With the founding of the church in Philippi, Christianity made its first appearance in Europe, a development that Luke attributed to divine intervention (Acts 16:6–10). Paul also attached special significance to his activity in and from this Macedonian city and referred to it as constituting "the beginning of the gospel" (Phil 4:15). It is appropriate that the first convert is identified in Acts as a woman, Lydia of Thyatira, for women played an important role not only in Macedonian social life but also in the church at Philippi (Phil 4:2–3; cf. Thomas 1972; Portefaix 1988). Paul's work in the city was marked by conflict and persecution (Phil 1:29–30). According to his own testimony, he was shamelessly mistreated there (1 Thess 2:2), and suffered abuse of the sort instanced by the account in Acts, in which he is seized, dragged into the marketplace, accused of crimes, publicly beaten with rods, and incarcerated, with his feet fastened in stocks (16:19–40). After a stay of uncertain length in Philippi (Acts 16:12, 18) and the conversion of a jailer (Acts 16:27–34) along with an unspecified number of others (Acts 16:40), Paul departed and went to Thessalonica (1 Thess 2:1–2; Acts 16:40–17:1). The preceding depiction, which incorporates the evidence of Acts, suggests a date of approximately 49 or 50 C.E. for Paul's ministry in Philippi (cf. Bruce 1977: 475; Schenke and Fischer 1978: 124; Lohse 1981: 80; Koester 1982: 103). For a different reconstruction, based on Phil 4:15 and the rejection of

Acts as a reliable source for the dating and description of Paul's Macedonian ministry, see Luedemann (1984: 262), who places Paul at Philippi in either 36 or 39 C.E.

B. Paul's Continuing Contact with Philippi

Paul's departure from Philippi did not end his contact with the church there. The narrative of Acts may suggest that he left behind one of his associates (compare Acts 17:14–15), viz., the anonymous eyewitness of the "we" sections who is traditionally identified as Luke. Similarly, the resumption of first person plural language in Acts 20:5–6 in connection with another visit of Paul to Philippi may imply that this anonymous associate either remained in the city until that time or returned there to rejoin Paul. These suggestions, however, cannot be confirmed by Paul, who never mentions Luke in connection with the Philippians, and the use of "we" may be simply a stylistic device by the author of Acts (Robbins 1978). By his own account, Paul had a unique relationship with the church in Philippi. Departing from his usual practice of refusing compensation from his converts (1 Corinthians 9), Paul accepted financial support from the Philippian church while he was in Thessalonica, and he did so on more than one occasion (Phil 4:15–16). Funds were also supplied to him later when he was in Corinth (2 Cor 11:7–9), and Paul's receipt of still another monetary gift occasioned at least part of his correspondence with the Philippians (Phil 4:10–20). Since the Philippians shared in the Macedonians' abject poverty (2 Cor 8:2), such largess was not a sign of their affluence, but of their genuine affection for the apostle and of their support of his labors (Phil 1:5; 4:10; cf. also Rom 15:26). These gifts served to solidify the bond between Paul and the Philippians and to nurture their special relationship. But communication was maintained not simply by the Philippians sending their envoys (such as Epaphroditus [Phil 2:25]) with gifts and probably letters to Paul (so Zahn 1909: 1.526; Moffatt 1923: 168). Paul, for his part, sent his co-workers to Macedonia and Achaia with messages for churches in those provinces (Acts 19:22). Timothy, who had played a part in the founding of the church at Philippi, probably traveled through that city on his way to Corinth (1 Cor 4:17; 16:10). In writing to the Philippians, Paul not only mentioned Timothy in the prescript (1:1) but also announced his intention once again to send him to Philippi (2:19, 23). Silas may also have been sent back to Philippi (cf. Milligan 1908: xxx; Lake 1919: 74). Paul was not content, however, to send his companions with oral or written messages; he had a long-standing desire to return to Macedonia in person (1 Cor 16:5; 2 Cor 1:15). This hope was finally realized after he paid a painful visit to Corinth and wrote a severe letter to the church there (2 Cor 2:13; 7:5; Acts 20:1–2). According to Acts, he paid a third and final visit to the city on his way to Troas (Acts 20:5–6; cf., however, 1 Tim 1:3). How these visits are to be related to the expectations and plans expressed in Philippians (1:19, 26; 2:24) depends on the date and place of the letter's composition (see below).

C. Analysis of the Letter to Philippi

Four matters especially germane to the interpretation of Philippians are its authenticity, character and contents, integrity and purpose, and place and date.

1. Authenticity. Four basic positions have been taken by NT scholars during the last two centuries in regard to the authenticity of the letter to the Philippians. First, a number of scholars in the 19th century denied the authenticity of the letter. The most important to do so was Ferdinand Christian Baur (1875: 2.45–79), who regarded Romans, 1 and 2 Corinthians, and Galatians as the only genuine Pauline letters. Baur argued that the letter used Gnostic ideas in 2:6–11, was dependent on the Corinthian correspondence (esp. 2 Corinthians), contained monotonous repetitions, and lacked anything distinctly Pauline, including a concrete historical occasion and purpose (cf. Mengel 1982: 119–27). He viewed Philippians as a 2d century document that was intended to glorify Paul's success in Rome and to lessen the conflict between the Jewish Christian and the gentile Christian parties in the church. His rejection of Philippians was shared by most scholars of the early Tübingen School (e.g., Schwegler 1846: 1.168–69, 298; 2.133–35) as well as the later radical skeptics, who regarded all letters in the Pauline corpus as inauthentic (e.g., van Manen [*Philippians EncBib*, 3703–13]). Although the strongest arguments for the inauthenticity of Philippians were marshalled by Carl Holsten (1875; 1876), not many scholars found his interpretation of the evidence persuasive. Consequently, this extreme position had few advocates by the end of the century and has little support today (cf., however, Morton and McLeman 1966).

The second position, a compromise adopted by some scholars, is that Philippians contains both authentic and inauthentic material. A few interpreters (e.g., Völter 1892; 1905: 286–323) have discerned large blocks of non-Pauline material in the letter, whereas several others (e.g., Barnikol 1932) have limited the inauthentic parts to glosses added by a later redactor. Critics frequently have viewed the reference to "bishops and deacons" (1:1), for instance, as an ecclesiastical anachronism and dismissed it as an ancient gloss (so, e.g., Riddle and Hutson 1946: 123; Schmithals 1971: 89–90 n. 14; Schenke and Fischer 1978: 126; Schenk 1984: 78–82, 334). Many older scholars who rejected Philippians as completely inauthentic naturally used this same reference as part of their case against Pauline authorship. (For discussions of the first two positions and bibliography, cf. esp. Lipsius *Philippen* HKNT, 211–15; Vincent *Philippians* ICC, xxvi–xxx; and Mengel 1982: 317–24).

The third position, the traditional view that Paul wrote all the material contained in Philippians, was maintained by the majority of 19th- and early-20th-century scholars and still has numerous adherents. Current advocates include those who believe that Paul is the composer of the hymn found in 2:6–11; they view the hymn as either written by Paul at the time of the letter or, as is more likely, composed on a prior occasion and incorporated in the letter as part of his exhortation (so, e.g., Scott *IDB* 1: 46–47; Furness 1959: 240–43; Kim 1981: 147–49; Wright 1986: 352; cf. also the discussion by Martin 1983: 55–61).

The fourth position on the authenticity of Philippians, a variation of the traditional view, is held by the majority of contemporary interpreters. Paul's authorship of Philippians is affirmed, but his use of traditional Christian material is also recognized (cf. Schenk 1984: 336–38). Some, for example, see in Phil 3:20–21 either Paul's creative use of traditional motifs (so Siber 1971: 122–34; Collange 1979: 139; Martin *Philippians* NCBC, 146–51) or his citation of a non-Pauline hymn (so Strecker 1964: 75–78; Güttgemanns 1966: 240–47; Becker 1971; 1976: 106–16; Reumann 1984; for a different view, cf. Kim 1981: 150–56). Again, the hymn in 2:6–11 is viewed as pre-Pauline by a wide spectrum of scholars, who usually affirm that Paul has redacted the hymn by adding one or more glosses, such as "even death on a cross" (2:8; cf., e.g., Lohmeyer 1928; 1964: 91, 96; Bonnard *Philippians* CNT, 42, 47–49; Jeremias 1953: 152–54; Gnilka *Philipperbrief,* HTKNT, 131–47; Ernst 1974: 65–79; Barth *Philipper* ZB, 40–48; Martin 1983: xviii, 42–54, 297–305; Egger 1985: 59–60; compare Hofius 1976: 1–17). It is this fourth position that is adopted in this article.

2. Character and Contents. Paul's letter to the Philippians is essentially a letter of friendship. Addressed to a church which had supported him financially and with which he had a deeply personal relationship, the letter is replete with language and concerns drawn from the ancient topic of friendship. These include the idea that friends are of "one soul" (Phil 1:27; 2:2) and "one mind" (2:3) and thus think the same (2:2; 4:2). Friendship is a fellowship (2:1) or partnership (Gk *koinonia:* 1:5) that necessitates mutuality and reciprocity, the sharing of feelings (2:17–18) and hardships (4:14) as well as giving and receiving (4:15). Certain attitudes and actions are conducive to friendship (4:8), while others are inimical to it (1:15, 17; 2:3; 3:2). Because friendship often involves finances and patronage, the issue of its relationship to other ideals, such as self-sufficiency [Gk *autarkeia*], frequently needs to be addressed (4:10–20). The meaning of friendship is often clarified by a discussion of its antithesis, viz., enmity; the use of invective (3:2) and ridicule (3:2, 19) to castigate one's enemies (3:18) is as natural as it is conventional in Greco-Roman society (cf. Marshall 1987: 1–129, esp. 35–69).

Letters play an important role in the maintenance of friendship and serve during a time of absence (2:12) as effective substitutes for personal presence. In friendly letters such as Philippians, it is natural for writers to employ the vocabulary of gratitude (1:3–5) and affection (4:1), to recall past and current experiences (1:30; 2:22; 4:15–16), to express both yearning for the friends from whom they are separated (1:7–8) and an anticipation of seeing them in the future (2:24), to provide information about their own situation (1:12–26), to offer the advice and exhortation that is appropriate to their relationship (1:27–2:18; 4:2–7), to commend friends (2:19–30) and ideals (4:8–9) shared in common, and to give warnings about enemies whose values are alien to the basis of their friendship (3:1–21). Philippians is written at a time when Paul is in prison and thus involuntarily separated from the church at Philippi. He is fairly sanguine that he will be released from prison and see his friends again, though he must reckon with the possibility that his imprisonment will be followed by his execution rather than his acquittal and release (1:19–26). The correspondence with the Philippians is ultimately occasioned by the arrival of a gift from them, which Paul accepts as an expression of their friendship and support. Using traditional literary devices such as lists of virtues (4:8) and *peristasis* catalogues (4:11–12; cf. Fitzgerald 1988: 45, 205), he thanks them for their gift (4:10–20) and encourages them to be a community that is characterized by friendship (1:27–2:11; 4:2–9) and is active in the proclamation of the gospel (2:12–18), neither stampeded by opposition (1:27–30) nor deluded into believing that their spiritual goals already have been attained (3:12–16).

3. Integrity and Purpose. Serious doubts about the unity of Philippians began to be expressed during the 19th century (Clemen 1894: 133–41) and have increased greatly in the last 30 years. At the current time, three basic positions are held concerning the question of the letter's literary integrity. Given the importance of this subject in recent scholarly literature, each of these three positions will be presented in some detail, with a judgment on this question deferred until the end of the discussion.

First, the traditional view that canonical Philippians is a unity is defended by a number of scholars (Mackay 1961; Furnish 1963; Pollard 1966; Jewett 1970a; Ernst 1974: 27–31; Kümmel 1975: 332–35; Dalton 1979; Lindemann 1979: 23–25; Garland 1985). According to this *One-Letter Hypothesis,* the epistle was prompted by a gift from Philippi brought to Paul by Epaphroditus, who at some point fell seriously ill and nearly died. It is debated whether Epaphroditus fell ill on his way to Paul or after his arrival. A possible reconstruction of events based on the former of these options is as follows (cf. Bruce *Philippians* GNC, xxv, 71):

1. The Philippians learn of Paul's imprisonment;
2. they send Epaphroditus with a gift to deliver to Paul;
3. Epaphroditus falls seriously ill on his way to Paul and nearly dies;
4. the Philippians learn of Epaphroditus' illness and become concerned;
5. Epaphroditus recovers, completes his journey to Paul, and delivers the gift;
6. Epaphroditus learns of the Philippians' anxiety for him and becomes distressed;
7. Paul sends Epaphroditus back to Philippi with a letter in which he commends Epaphroditus, thanks the Philippians for their gift, warns them about false teachers, and informs them about his own circumstances and plans.

Next, numerous contemporary scholars are convinced that canonical Philippians is a composite work. In support of this possibility in general, appeal is made to the following four considerations: (a) Paul wrote letters that either have not been preserved (1 Cor 5:9; cf. also Col 4:16) or have been partially preserved in other letters (possibly 2 Cor 10–13); (b) Phil 3:1a suggests previous correspondence with the Philippians (cf. NEB: "To repeat what I have written to you before is no trouble to me"); (c) one of the Apostolic Fathers of the 2d century C.E., Polycarp of Smyrna (*Phil.* 3:2), uses the plural *(epistolas)* to refer to Paul's correspondence with Philippi; and (d) Polycarp's own *Letter to the Philippians* seems to preserve two originally independent letters to the church at Philippi (so Harrison 1936).

Critics who posit redactional activity in regard to Philippians differ, however, as to the number of letters or fragments of letters contained in the document and the content that originally belonged to each piece of correspondence. Some scholars adopt a second basic position and divide the canonical letter into two separate letters, whereas others hold a third distinct position and divide it into three originally independent pieces. The basis of the division into two letters is primarily fourfold: (a) Paul's use of "finally" (i.e., "in conclusion") in 3:1a seems to suggest he is about to close the letter (cf. 2 Cor 13:11); (b) a sharp change in tone and content occurs after 3:1a; the invective that follows is out of harmony with the overall tone of the letter and interrupts the exhortation to rejoice (3:1a; 4:4); (c) the discussion of travel plans (2:23–24, 28–29) normally occurs toward the end of Paul's letters; and (d) different dangers face the church in chaps. 1 and 3; in 1:27–30 the church is threatened from without, whereas in chap. three the threat comes at least in part from those within the church. A *two-letter hypothesis* is seen by many scholars (e.g., Keck 1971: 846; Friedrich *Philipper* NTD, 126–28) as the best explanation of these peculiarities.

An early supporter of this hypothesis was Goodspeed (1937: 90–96), who argued that 3:1b–4:20 was originally part of the letter that Paul wrote upon receipt of the gift brought by Epaphroditus. The latter fell sick only after this first letter was sent. Upon his recovery he was sent back to Philippi with the letter that is preserved in 1:1–3:1a; 4:21–23. These two letters were later combined by an editor who placed the earlier letter at the end.

A more recent advocate of the two-letter hypothesis is Gnilka (6–18), who divides the material into Letter A: 1:1–3:1a; 4:2–7, 10–23 and Letter B: 3:1b–4:1, 8–9. Letter A is sent following the receipt of the Philippians' gift and Epaphroditus' recovery. While Paul expresses thanks for the gift, his primary purpose is to discuss the impact of his imprisonment and possible execution on the progress of the gospel. The letter is pastoral rather than polemical; false teachers have not yet appeared in Philippi, and the church's chief internal problem is lack of love. Letter B is writter later, after Paul has been released from prison and after false teachers have invaded Philippi. Hence, Paul is no longer concerned with the fettering of the gospel, but with its endangerment. The purpose of this passionate, polemical piece is to protect his beloved community from the pernicious propaganda of his opponents.

The *three-letter hypothesis* is usually distinguished from the two-letter hypothesis by the isolation of 4:10–20 as an independent letter of thanks for the Philippians' gift. This letter's existence is predicated on four considerations: (a) it is likely that Paul acknowledged the receipt of the Philippians' gift soon after it arrived, and the statement in 4:10–20 appears to be his first expression of thanks for it; that is, it is improbable that he waited so long to do so as the one-letter or two-letter hypotheses usually require (contrast Michael *Philippians* MNTC, xxi–xxii, 208–27; (b) in 4:18, Epaphroditus seems to have just arrived, whereas in 2:25–30 he has clearly been with Paul for some time; (c) the introduction of a new subject in 4:10 following the use of "finally" and a benediction in 4:8–9 is abrupt; and (d) the discussion of the gift is a self-contained unit that concludes with a doxology. Particular reconstructions of the three proposed letters differ widely in regard to details, but 4:10–20 is usually assigned to Letter A, 1:1–3:1a to Letter B, and 3:2–4:1 to Letter C. Advocates of this hypothesis include Müller-Bardorff (1958), Beare (*Philippians* HNTC 1–5), Rathjen (1960), Bornkamm (1962), Koester (1962; *IDBSup*, 666; 1982: 132–34), Fuller (1965: 34–37), Fitzmyer (*JBC*, 248), Marxsen (1970: 61–62, 66–68), Schmithals (1972: 65–122), Vielhauer (1975: 159–66), Collange (1979: 3–15), Barth (*Philipper* ZB, 10–11) and Lohse (1981: 81–82). Of the various sequences of events reconstructed by defenders of this position, that offered by Schenke and Fischer (1978: 125–29) is one of the most detailed and suggestive:

1. Epaphroditus is sent by the Philippians with a twofold mission: to deliver the church's monetary gift to Paul and to serve Paul for a certain period of time; the purpose in both cases is to provide support for Paul, who has not yet been arrested;
2. Paul accepts this gift from the Philippians, just as he had previously at Thessalonica and Corinth; in gratitude he writes Letter A (4:10–20);
3. soon thereafter Paul is arrested and placed in prison;
4. while Paul is in prison, Epaphroditus falls ill and nearly dies;
5. when Epaphroditus finally recovers, Paul sends him back to Philippi with Letter B (1:1–3:1; 4:4–7, 21–23), which is ultimately a letter of recommendation and certificate of good conduct for Epaphroditus;
6. in keeping with his expectations (1:19), Paul is soon thereafter released from prison;
7. Paul sends Timothy to Philippi (2:23; Acts 19:22) and Corinth (1 Cor 4:17; 16:10–11);
8. Timothy returns to Paul (1 Cor 16:11);
9. instead of going himself, Paul once again sends Timothy back to Philippi and somewhat later sends Titus to Corinth;
10. Paul learns that his opponents have invaded Philippi and sends Letter C (3:2–4:3; 4:8–9) to the Philippians and Timothy, who not only is to defend the church against these false teachers but also, as the "true yokefellow" of Phil 4:3, is to help solve the dispute between Euodia and Syntyche.

Each of the three positions presented here has its strengths and weaknesses, but the presumption of the letter's literary integrity is probably correct. Defenders of the unity of Philippians correctly point to thematic elements that link the sections of the letter and structural considerations that favor the one-letter hypothesis. The extensive use of friendship language throughout the letter points toward the same conclusion. When viewed from the perspective of ancient discussions of friendship and enmity, the sharp change of tone at 3:2 and the strong use of invective in 3:2–19 are not even surprising; the ridiculing of one's enemies is but the natural antithesis to the praising of one's friends. Furthermore, Paul's strong desire to have both Timothy and Epaphroditus in Philippi (2:19–30) is related to the danger of the "dogs" of chap. 3. Indeed, the discussion of the opponents and of the strife between Euodia and Syntyche (3:1–4:3) is framed by the commendation of Timothy and Epaphroditus (2:19–

30) and Paul's other co-workers (4:3), and it is followed by the apostle's parenesis (4:4–8) and presentation of himself—along with the others (3:17)—as a proper model for the church's imitation (4:9). Such framing of a discussion is rhetorically proper, as is the combination of parenesis and the presentation of both positive and negative models of conduct.

Finally, many of the peculiarities of Philippians listed above can be adequately if not convincingly explained without recourse to a partition theory. The postponement of the discussion of the gift until the end of the letter, for example, may well be part of a strategy that reserves until the end of a communication the treatment of the most important matters. In that case, 4:10–20 will be no postscript, but the climax to Paul's whole discussion of his partnership with the Philippians in the gospel. The primary purpose of 4:10–20 is certainly not to thank the Philippians for their gift. The gift provides the ultimate occasion for the letter, but not its immediate purpose. Paul here uses the gift as the occasion for commenting on their long-standing partnership in the gospel. Their recent gift is proof of their continuing friendship, and Paul discusses it so as to strengthen his special bond with them. Similarly, the emphasis on "thinking the same" in 2:2 is probably foundational for his appeal to Euodia and Syntyche in 4:2–3; their harmony is likely to be the key for the harmony of the church as a whole (cf. also Garland 1985: 171–73). This makes it unlikely that 4:4 was originally the resumption of 3:1, as many partition theories suggest. Such theories would have much greater probability if some traces of editorial activity were evident in the textual tradition (cf. Gamble 1975: 418), but this is not so in the case of Philippians. For these and other reasons, the one-letter hypothesis seems preferable, but Philippians' literary integrity will doubtless remain a greatly disputed issue for the foreseeable future.

4. Place and Date of Composition. Another highly contested issue involves the place and date of the letter's composition. The dating of the correspondence is determined by the decision made in regard to both the letter's integrity and the place of Paul's imprisonment. If Philippians is indeed a composite of 2 or 3 Pauline letters, the possibility of more than one place and date of origin must be considered. The choices as to Paul's place of imprisonment are essentially three: Rome, Caesarea, and Ephesus. Other locations, such as Corinth (Dockx 1973), have been proposed but are not likely.

In favor of Rome are the following considerations: (a) Paul was both imprisoned and executed there, facts which are consonant with the references to Paul's bonds (Phil 1:7, 13–14, 17) and his contemplation of martyrdom (1:19–26; 2:17) (see also SUICIDE); (b) the references in Philippians to the praetorium (1:13) and Caesar's household (4:22), though applicable to other cities, are most appropriate for Rome; (c) of the imprisonments described by Acts, the one in Rome (Acts 28:14–31) most closely matches the circumstances described by Paul in his letter; and (d) the early Church was virtually unanimous in assigning Philippians to Rome. The major argument against Rome is its great distance from Philippi (ca. 800 miles) and the consequent length of time necessary for the occurrence of the number of communications presupposed and three more are contemplated prior to Paul's anticipated visit. Supporters of Rome (e.g., Dodd 1953: 85–108; Cullmann 1953: 104–6; Buchanan 1964; Reicke 1970: 282–86) usually stress the relative speed of travel in this period and seek to reduce the number of communications between Paul and the Philippians as well as the length of time required for these to take place. If all or part of Philippians emanates from Rome, it would come from ca. 58–60 or 60–62 C.E., either early in Paul's imprisonment (so Lightfoot 1891: 30–46) or, as is far more likely, toward its end (so J. Weiss 1959: 1.389). In that case, it would be the last of his authentic letters (so Moffatt 1923: 166, 168, 170).

Advocates of Caesarea (Johnson 1957; Lohmeyer 1964: 3–4; Hawthorne *Philippians* WBC, xxxvi–xliv) typically assert that Paul's description of his situation corresponds more closely to Acts' account of the imprisonment there (23:33–26:32) than it does to the one in Rome. Paul is kept under guard in the praetorium of Herod (23:35; cf. Phil 1:13), but his friends are permitted access to him to attend to his needs (24:23; cf. Phil 2:25, 30). His incarceration is of sufficient duration (24:27) to accommodate the number of communications with Philippi, and during this period Paul is called upon several times to offer an *apologia* (24:10; 25:8, 16; 26:1–2, 24; cf. Phil 1:7, 16) for his activities. If the opponents of chap. 3 are non-Christian Jews (see below), a connection can be posited between Paul's philippic against the "mutilators" (3:2) and the Jewish opponents of Acts 21–26, who were responsible for his incarceration (compare 1 Thess 2:14–16). Finally, Paul could also anticipate, if released at Caesarea, a trip to Philippi on his way through Rome to Spain; no change in his travel plans of Rom 15:28 would have to be assumed. Support for this theory must rely entirely on Acts, for the Pauline corpus is silent as to an imprisonment in Caesarea. Yet Acts' depiction of Paul's Caesarean imprisonment does not suggest that death was an imminent possibility in that locale. Freedom could always be purchased (24:26), or an appeal made to Caesar (25:10–12). Furthermore, Paul is depicted, even prior to his arrival in Caesarea, as knowing by divine revelation that his final place of witness will be Rome (23:11); execution in Caesarea is simply not an option entertained by Acts. Finally, in view of the great distance from Philippi to Caesarea, travel considerations also militate against this option. But if Caesarea is nevertheless accepted as the place of origin, correspondence would derive from ca. 56/57–58/59 C.E.

Suggested as an option only at the turn of the 20th century, Ephesus has been adopted by an increasing number of scholars and now rivals or even surpasses Rome as the imprisonment site favored by most (cf. Feine 1916; Deissmann 1923; Duncan 1929; Michaelis 1933; *An die Philipper* THKNT, 2–6; 1961: 204–10). The great argument in its favor is its close proximity to Philippi, a location that would have facilitated numerous communications with that city. In addition, the parallels in subject matter, vocabulary, and tone with 2 Corinthians 10–12 and Galatians suggest to many that all three were written about the same time, that is, during the three-year period that Paul was in Ephesus. This would be ca. 52/53–55/56 C.E., and such a dating allows the identification of the proposed visits of Timothy and Paul (Phil 1:26; 2:19, 23–24) with the ones recorded by the apostle (1 Cor 16:10; 2 Cor 2:13; 7:5) and Acts (19:22; 20:1–6). Finally, nowhere in Philippians does Paul indicate that he has returned to the city since he founded the church there (Phil 1:26, 30; 2:12, 22; 4:15; contrast 2 Cor 2:1; 13:1); if that is the case (and he has not simply failed to mention the trips of Acts 20:1–6), both Caesarea and Rome are excluded as possibilities. The major difficulty of this option is that neither Paul nor Acts mentions an imprisonment in Ephesus. One can only be inferred on the basis of such passages as 2 Cor 1:8–10; 6:5; and 11:23 (but not 1 Cor 15:32, which refers instead to the Heraclean contest with hedonistic opponents; cf. Malherbe 1968). Yet only on the basis of this hypothesis can Philippians (or at least 1:1–3:1) be assigned to Ephesus. On the other hand, Phil 3:1b–4:9 does not mention imprisonment. Those who regard this passage as part of another letter can assign it to Ephesus without necessarily postulating an imprisonment there. Thus one could, for example, assign Phil 1:1–3:1a to Rome and 3:1b–4:9 to Ephesus (compare Bruce, xxviii). But, in that case, 3:1b–4:9 might just as easily be assigned to Corinth (so, e.g., Gnilka, 25).

In view of the uncertainty involved, all reconstructions of the historical setting of Philippians necessarily remain highly tentative. Those that presuppose an imprisonment in either Ephesus or Rome are the most persuasive, and a decision between them is difficult. In the final analysis, however, Meeks (1983: 63) is probably correct when he says that "Rome still seems the most likely" place of composition for the letter.

D. Opponents

Two key issues have dominated the discussion of the opponents mentioned by Paul in the letter. The first has to do with the number of groups presupposed. As many as five are possible: the partisan proclaimers of Christ (1:15–18), the adversaries destined for destruction (1:28), the dogs and evil workers (3:2–4), the "perfectionists" (3:12–16), and the enemies of the cross of Christ (3:18–19). The partisan proclaimers of Christ, whose relationship to the group spoken of in 2:21 is disputed, were active in the city of Paul's imprisonment, not in Philippi, though the claim is sometimes made that they were itinerant Christian missionaries whose presence in Philippi was not desired by Paul (so Jewett 1970b: 363–71). The adversaries of 1:28 were located in Philippi, but it is debated whether the opponents of chap. 3 were already active in the city and thus posed an actual threat for the Philippians or were active elsewhere (perhaps in the city of Paul's imprisonment) and were only potentially dangerous. Whether present or imminent, however, the urgency of Paul's warning (3:2) suggests the danger was real. The opponents in 1:28 and 3:2–19 occasionally are identified as four separate groups (so, e.g., Michael, 69, 133, 160, 172); often three groups are detected (so, e.g., Hock *HBD*, 1223–24); frequently only two groups are identified, with those in chap. 1 distinguished from those denounced in chap. 3 (so, e.g., Barth, 37, 67); and sometimes a single group is inferred (so, e.g., Mearns 1987).

The second issue concerns the identification of these opponents, and the decision as to the number of groups involved obviously determines the material used to describe them. Moreover, to the extent that they are equated with opponents mentioned in Galatians, 2 Corinthians, and Romans, material from those letters is employed to elaborate their portrait. As a consequence of all these factors, a plethora of portraits has been offered, but no broad consensus has yet emerged. Indeed, no fewer than 18 different descriptions of the opponents of chap. 3 have been offered (Gunther 1973: 2).

Even when only one group in Philippi is presupposed, assessments as to their identity differ widely. For example, Schmithals (1972: 58–122) sees them as Jewish Christian Gnostics with libertine tendencies, Collange (1979: 10–14, 75) as Jewish Christian itinerants with a "divine-man" Christology and self-understanding similar to that espoused by the opponents whom Paul confronts in 2 Corinthians, and Hawthorne (xliv–xlvii, 58, 125, 163) as non-Christian Jewish missionaries who were punctilious in their observance of the law (cf. also Klijn 1965). Many interpreters agree that the adversaries of 1:28 are non-Christian opponents (so, e.g., Vielhauer 1975: 160, 163) but view them as Gentile persecutors rather than Jewish agitators (cf. Martin *Philippians* NCBC, 22, 83; Friedrich, 147; compare 1 Thess 2:14). The opponents of 3:2, on the other hand, are clearly Jewish, though the conjecture is occasionally made that they are proselytes (so, e.g., Jülicher and Fascher 1931: 119), in which case Paul's emphasis on being "a Hebrew born of Hebrews" who was "circumcised on the eighth day" (3:5) would have special point. The debate historically has centered on the question of whether these people are Jewish propagandists (so, e.g., Benoit 1969: 31; Caird 1976: 133; Houlden 1977: 95–105) or Jewish Christian Judaizers (so, e.g., Vincent, 92; Jewett 1970b: 382–89; Bruce, 79, 81).

Sharply debated also is the question of whether Paul discusses one or two (or even three) groups in 3:2–19. Dibelius (*An die Philipper* HNT, 93), for instance, identifies two groups (Jewish agitators in 3:2–4 and immoral Christians in 3:18–19), whereas Koester (1962) discerns a single group of Jewish Christian missionaries with gnostic tendencies. Crucial to the decision is often the interpretation of Paul's damning indictment of his opponents in 3:19: "their god is the belly, and they glory in their shame." Some interpret "belly" and "shame" in terms of Judaizers' values. Thus Fitzmyer (252) sees in them a reference to the Judaizers' dietary observances and their advocacy of circumcision, and Mearns (1987: 198) sees both terms as "euphemisms for the circumcised male organ." Paul's words could easily suggest, however, a devotion to sensual and sexual pleasures, so that other scholars view them as libertines (so, e.g., Delling *RGG*^{3} 5: 334; Beare, 136). It was common in rhetorical circles to accuse one's enemies of immorality (cf. Marshall 1987: 62–63), and Paul may be doing that here. Indeed, the group he has in mind could be the hedonistic opponents ("wild beasts") against whom he struggled at Ephesus (1 Cor 15:32; cf. Malherbe 1968: 79). Whoever they were, however, they seem to have been Christians whose perfectionist tendencies had a basis in a radically realized eschatology (cf. Holladay 1969).

E. The Christ Hymn

As was indicated previously, most modern interpreters regard the hymn in Phil 2:6–11 as pre-Pauline (see above).

The discussion has therefore centered on questions concerning the hymn's original literary form, authorship, background, setting, and meaning, as well as its use and redaction by Paul. Of the various proposals in regard to the hymn's structure, those of Lohmeyer (1928: 5–6) and Jeremias (1953: 152–54) deserve mention. The former divides the hymn into six strophes (A-F) of three lines each (A: v 6; B: v 7a–c; C: vv 7d–8b; D: v 9; E: v 10; F: v 11), with v 8c treated as a Pauline gloss. The latter divides it into three strophes (A-C) of four lines each (A: vv 6–7b; B: vv 7c–8b; C: vv 9–11), with vv 8c, 10c, and 11c viewed as Pauline additions. Proposed sources for the hymn include the gnostic scheme of the Primal Man myth (Käsemann 1968); the Genesis story of Adam as well as later Jewish speculation about two Adams (Héring 1936; 1959); the Deutero-Isaianic figure of the Suffering Servant (Cerfaux 1954; 1959: 374–401); and the figure of divine Wisdom in Hellenistic Judaism (Georgi 1964). Sometimes only one source is recognized in the hymn, but more often the confluence of motifs from several sources, both Hellenistic and Jewish, is detected (Sanders 1971: 58–74). The author of the hymn has been sought in Jewish gnostic circles (Bonnard, 49), the early Palestinian church (Lohmeyer 1928: 9, 66), and the Hellenistic Jewish mission represented by Stephen (Martin 1983: 304–5, 318–19; cf. also Fuller 1965: 204–6). Early Christians used the hymn in a cultic setting, either at the Eucharist or during baptism. Whatever its original function may have been, Paul uses the hymn here in service of his parenesis. It is usually assumed that the beginning of the hymn (2:6–8) refers to Christ prior to the Incarnation, so that his preexistence is presupposed (so, e.g., Bornkamm 1969: 113). Recently, however, this interpretation has been attacked by a number of scholars who insist that the hymn speaks only of the human Christ (Talbert 1967; Robinson 1973: 162–66; Bartsch 1974: 24–27; Murphy-O'Connor 1976; Howard 1978; Dunn 1980: 114–28). This controversy (Hurst 1986; Wanamaker 1987) and the continuing debate about the meaning of the term *harpagmos* (RSV: "a thing to be grasped") in 2:6 (Hoover 1971; Glasson 1974: 133–37; Moule 1970; Wright 1986) indicate that the hymn will continue to attract scholarly attention (cf. Rissi *ANRW* 2/25/4: 3314–26; Schenk *ANRW* 2/25/4: 3299–303). An excellent orientation to all the central questions involved in the study of the hymn is provided by Martin (1983; cf. also *Philippians* NCBC, 90–102, 109–16), whose survey is foundational for an understanding of current analyses of the hymn (cf. also Deichgräber 1967: 118–33; Sanders 1971: 9–12, 58–74).

F. Text and Early Versions

The text of Philippians is preserved in three fragmentary papyri, 18 parchment uncials (of which nine contain the entire text, three are fragmentary, and six are accompanied by commentary), and more than 625 minuscules (cf. Gnilka, 25–27). The earliest is P^{46}, one of the three Chester Beatty papyri of the NT. It dates from about C.E. 200 and contains 1:1, 5–15, 17–28, 30–2:12, 14–27, 29–3:8, 10–21; 4:2–12, 14–23. A second early papyrus is P^{16}, which dates from the 3d or 4th century and contains 3:10–17 and 4:2–8. The three earliest parchment uncials that contain the entire text of Philippians are Codex Sinaiticus (01), Codex Vaticanus (03), and Codex Alexandrinus (02). These five mss, plus three minuscules containing Philippians (33, 1739, and 2427), belong to the text critical "Category I," which indicates that they are "of a very special quality" and "should always be considered in establishing the original text" (Aland and Aland 1987: 105). There are ten additional manuscripts of Philippians that are of generally high quality and belong to the next class, "Category II" (Schenk 1984: 331). They include three 5th-century fragmentary uncials (04, 016, 048), the bilingual Codex Claromontanus (06, 6th century), P^{61} (ca. C.E. 700) and 5 minuscules (81, 1175, 1881, 2127, and 2464). On the basis of these and other witnesses, a fairly reliable text of Philippians which involves no major textual problems can be reconstructed.

Philippians, along with the other letters in the Pauline corpus, was translated into a number of ancient languages. It was almost certainly translated into Old Syriac, though no copy of any of Paul's letters is extant in this early version. It is, however, preserved in the later Syriac versions, esp. the Peshitta. Other extant eastern versions that contain Philippians include Coptic, Armenian, Georgian, and Ethiopic. Of the Western versions, it is extant in Old Latin (Frede 1971), the Vulgate, Gothic, and Slavonic (cf., in general, Metzger 1977).

Bibliography

Aland, K., and Aland, B. 1987. *The Text of the New Testament.* Trans. E. F. Rhodes. Grand Rapids and Leiden.

Barnikol, E. 1932. *Philipper 2: Der marcionitische Ursprung des Mythos-Satzes Phil. 2,6–7.* Forschungen zur Entstehung des Urchristentums des Neuen Testaments und der Kirche 7. Kiel.

Bartsch, H.-W. 1974. *Die konkrete Wahrheit und die Lüge der Spekulation.* Theologie und Wirklichkeit 1. Frankfurt.

Baur, F. C. 1875. *Paul the Apostle of Jesus Christ.* 2 vols. Trans. A. Menzies. London.

Becker, J. 1971. Erwägungen zu Phil. 3,20–21. *TZ* 27: 16–29.

———. 1976. *Auferstehung der Toten im Urchristentum.* SBS 82. Stuttgart.

Benoit, P. 1969. *Les Épîtres de saint Paul aux Philippiens, à Philémon, aux Colossiens, aux Éphésiens. SBJ.* 4th ed. Paris.

Bornkamm, G. 1962. Der Philipperbrief als paulinische Briefsammlung. Pages 192–202 in *Neotestamentica et Patristica.* NovTSup 6. Leiden.

———. 1969. On Understanding the Christ-Hymn: Philippians 2.6–11. Pages 112–22 in *Early Christian Experience.* Trans. P. L. Hammer. New York.

Bruce, F. F. 1977. *Paul: Apostle of the Heart Set Free.* Grand Rapids.

Buchanan, C. O. 1964. Epaphroditus' Sickness and the Letter to the Philippians. *EvQ* 36: 157–66.

Caird, G. B. 1976. *Paul's Letters from Prison.* New Clarendon Bible. Oxford.

Cerfaux, L. 1954. L'hymne au Christ—Serviteur de Dieu (*Phil.*, II,6–11 = *Is.*, LII,13–LIII,12). Vol. 2, pp. 425–37 in *Recueil Lucien Cerfaux.* BETL 6–7. Gembloux.

———. 1959. *Christ in the Theology of St. Paul.* Trans. G. Webb and A. Walker. New York.

Clemen, C. 1894. *Die Einheitlichkeit der paulinischen Briefe.* Göttingen.

Collange, J.-F. 1979. *The Epistle of Saint Paul to the Philippians.* Trans. A. W. Heathcote. London.

Cullmann, O. 1953. *Peter: Disciple, Apostle, Martyr.* Trans. F. V. Filson. London.
Dalton, W. J. 1979. The Integrity of Philippians. *Bib* 60: 97–102.
Deichgräber, R. 1967. *Gotteshymnus und Christushymnus in der frühen Christenheit.* SUNT 5. Göttingen.
Deissmann, A. 1923. Zur ephesinischen Gefangenschaft des Apostels Paulus. Pp. 121–27 in *Anatolian Studies Presented to Sir William Ramsay,* ed. W. H. Buckler and W. M. Calder. Manchester.
Dockx, S. I. 1973. Lieu et date de l'épître aux Philippiens. *RB* 80: 230–46.
Dodd, C. H. 1953. *New Testament Studies.* Manchester.
Duncan, G. S. 1929. *St. Paul's Ephesian Ministry.* London.
Dunn, J. D. G. 1980. *Christology in the Making.* Philadelphia.
Egger, W. 1985. *Galaterbrief, Philipperbrief, Philemonbrief.* NEBib NT 9, 11, 15. Würzburg.
Ernst, J. 1974. *Die Briefe an die Philipper, an Philemon, an die Kolosser, an die Epheser.* RNT. Regensburg.
Feine, P. 1916. *Die Abfassung des Philipperbriefes in Ephesus.* BFCT 4. Gütersloh.
Fitzgerald, J. 1988. *Cracks in an Earthen Vessel.* SBLDS 99. Atlanta.
Frede, H. J. 1971. *Epistulae ad Philippenses et ad Colossenses.* Vetus Latina: Die Reste der altlateinische Bible 24/2. Freiburg.
Fuller, R. H. 1965. *The Foundations of New Testament Christology.* New York.
Furness, J. M. 1959. The Authorship of Philippians 2.6–11. *ExpTim* 70: 240–43.
Furnish, V. P. 1963. The Place and Purpose of Phil. III. *NTS* 10: 80–88.
Gamble, H. Y. 1975. The Redaction of the Pauline Letters and the Formation of the Pauline Corpus. *JBL* 75: 403–18.
———. 1985. *The New Testament Canon.* GBS. Philadelphia.
Garland, D. E. 1985. The Composition and Unity of Philippians. *NovT* 27: 141–73.
Georgi, D. 1964. Der vorpaulinische Hymnus Phil. 2,6–11. Pp. 263–93 in *Zeit und Geschichte,* ed. E. Dinkler. Tübingen.
Glasson, T. F. 1974. Two Notes on the Philippians Hymn (II. 6–11). *NTS* 21: 133–39.
Goodspeed, E. J. 1937. *An Introduction to the New Testament.* Chicago.
Güttgemanns, E. 1966. *Der leidende Apostel und sein Herr.* FRLANT 90. Göttingen.
Gunther, J. J. 1973. *St. Paul's Opponents and Their Background.* NovTSup 35. Leiden.
Harrison, P. N. 1936. *Polycarp's Two Epistles to the Philippians.* Cambridge.
Héring, J. 1936. Kyrios Anthropos (Phil 2,6–11). *RHPR* 16: 196–209.
———. 1959. *Le Royaume de Dieu et sa venue.* 2d ed. Neuchâtel.
Hofius, O. 1976. *Der Christushymnus Philipper 2,6–11.* WUNT 17. Tübingen.
Holladay, C. R. 1969. Paul's Opponents in Philippians 3. *ResQ* 12: 77–90.
Holsten, C. 1875. Der Brief an die Philipper: Eine exegetisch-kritische Studie I. *Jahrbücher für protestantische Theologie* 1: 425–95.
———. 1876. Der Brief an die Philipper. Eine exegetisch-kritische Studie II. III–VI. *Jahrbücher für protestantische Theologie* 2: 58–165, 282–372.
Hoover, R. W. 1971. The Harpagmos Enigma: A Philological Solution. *HTR* 64: 95–119.
Houlden, J. 1977. *Paul's Letters from Prison.* Philadelphia.
Howard, G. 1978. Phil 2:6–11 and the Human Christ. *CBQ* 40: 368–87.
Hurst, L. D. 1986. Re-Enter the Pre-Existent Christ in Philippians 2.5–11? *NTS* 32: 449–57.
Jeremias, J. 1953. Zur Gedankenführung in den paulinischen Briefen. Pp. 146–54 in *Studia Paulina in honorem J. de Zwaan septuagenarii,* ed. J. N. Sevenster and W. C. van Unnik. Haarlem.
Jewett, R. 1970a. The Epistolary Thanksgiving and the Integrity of Philippians. *NovT* 12: 40–53.
———. 1970b. Conflicting Movements in the Early Church. *NovT* 12: 362–90.
Johnson, L. 1957. The Pauline Letters from Caesarea. *ExpTim* 68: 24–26.
Jülicher, A., and Fascher, E. 1931. *Einleitung in das Neue Testament.* 7th ed. Tübingen.
Käsemann, E. 1968. A Critical Analysis of Philippians 2:5–11. Pp. 45–88 in *God and Christ: Existence and Province,* ed. R. W. Funk. JTC 5. Trans. A. F. Carse. Tübingen and New York.
Keck, L. E. 1971. The Letter of Paul to the Philippians. Pp. 845–55 in *The Interpreter's One-Volume Commentary on the Bible,* ed. C. M. Laymon. Nashville.
Kim, S. 1981. *The Origin of Paul's Gospel.* WUNT 2/4. Tübingen.
Klijn, A. F. J. 1965. Paul's Opponents in Philippians iii. *NovT* 7: 278–84.
Koester, H. 1962. The Purpose of the Polemic of a Pauline Fragment (Philippians III). *NTS* 8: 317–32.
———. 1982. *History and Literature of Early Christianity.* Vol. 2 of *Introduction to the New Testament.* Hermeneia. Philadelphia and Berlin.
Kümmel, W. G. 1975. *Introduction to the New Testament.* Rev. ed. Trans. H. C. Kee. Nashville.
Lake, K. 1919. *The Earlier Epistles of St. Paul.* 2d ed. London.
Lightfoot, J. B. 1891. *Saint Paul's Epistle to the Philippians.* London.
Lindemann, A. 1979. *Paulus im ältesten Christentum.* BHT 58. Tübingen.
Lohmeyer, E. 1928. *Kyrios Jesus: Eine Untersuchung zu Phil. 2,5–11.* SHAW Phil.-hist. Kl. Heidelberg.
———. 1964. *Die Briefe an die Philipper, an die Kolosser und an Philemon.* MeyerK 9. 13th ed. Göttingen.
Lohse, E. 1981. *The Formation of the New Testament.* Trans. M. E. Boring. Nashville.
Luedemann, G. 1984. *Paul: Apostle to the Gentiles.* Trans. F. S. Jones. Philadelphia.
Mackay, B. S. 1961. Further Thoughts on Philippians. *NTS* 7: 161–70.
Malherbe, A. J. 1968. The Beasts at Ephesus. *JBL* 87: 71–80.
Marshall, P. 1987. *Enmity in Corinth.* WUNT 2/23. Tübingen.
Martin, R. P. 1983. *Carmen Christi: Philippians 2:5–11 in Recent Interpretation and in the Setting of Early Christian Worship.* 2d ed. Grand Rapids.
Marxsen, W. 1970. *Introduction to the New Testament.* Trans. G. Buswell. Philadelphia.
Mearns, C. 1987. The Identity of Paul's Opponents at Philippi. *NTS* 33: 194–204.
Meeks, W. A. 1983. *The First Urban Christians.* New Haven.
Mengel, B. 1982. *Studien zum Philipperbrief.* WUNT, 2d Ser., 8. Tübingen.
Metzger, B. M. 1977. *The Early Versions of the New Testament.* Oxford.
Michaelis, W. 1933. *Die Datierung des Philipperbriefes.* NTF 8. Gütersloh.
———. 1961. *Einleitung in das Neue Testament.* 3d ed. Bern.

Miligan, G. 1908. *St. Paul's Epistles to the Thessalonians*. London.
Moffatt, J. 1923. *An Introduction to the Literature of the New Testament*. International Theological Library. 3d ed. New York.
Morton, A. Q., and McLeman, J. 1966. *Paul, the Man and the Myth*. New York.
Moule, C. F. D. 1970. Further Reflections on Philippians 2:5–11. Pp. 264–76 in *Apostolic History and the Gospel*, ed. W. W. Gasque and R. P. Martin. Grand Rapids.
Müller-Bardorff, J. 1958. Zur Frage der literarischen Einheit des Phil. *Wissenschaftliche Zeitschrift der Friedrich v. Schiller Universität Jena* 7: 591–604.
Murphy-O'Connor, J. 1976. Christological Anthropology in Phil., II, 6–11. *RB* 83: 25–50.
Pollard, T. E. 1966. The Integrity of Philippians. *NTS* 13: 57–66.
Portefaix, L. 1988. *Sisters Rejoice: Paul's Letter to the Philippians and Luke-Acts as Received by First-Century Philippian Women*. ConBNT 20. Uppsala.
Rathjen, B. D. 1960. The Three Letters of Paul to the Philippians. *NTS* 6: 167–73.
Reicke, B. 1970. Caesarea, Rome, and the Captivity Epistles. Pp. 277–86 in *Apostolic History and the Gospel*, ed. W. W. Gasque and R. P. Martin. Grand Rapids.
Reumann, J. 1984. Philippians 3.20–21—A Hymnic Fragment? *NTS* 30: 593–609.
Riddle, D. W., and Hutson, H. H. 1946. *New Testament Life and Literature*. Chicago.
Robbins, V. K. 1978. By Land and By Sea: The We-Passages and Ancient Sea Voyages. Pp. 215–42 in *Perspective on Luke-Acts*, ed. C. H. Talbert. Edinburgh.
Robinson, J. A. T. 1973. *The Human Face of God*. Philadelphia.
Sampley, J. P. 1980. *Pauline Partnership in Christ*. Philadelphia.
Sanders, J. T. 1971. *The New Testament Christological Hymns*. SNTSMS 15. Cambridge.
Schenk, W. 1984. *Die Philipperbriefe des Paulus*. Stuttgart.
Schenke, H.-M., and Fischer, K. M. 1978. *Einleitung in die Schriften des Neuen Testaments*. Vol. 1. Gütersloh.
Schmithals, W. 1971. *Gnosticism in Corinth*. Trans. J. E. Steely. 1965. Nashville.
———. 1972. *Paul and the Gnostics*. Trans. J. E. Steely. Nashville.
Schwegler, A. 1846. *Das nachapostolische Zeitalter in den Hauptmomenten seiner Entwicklung*. 2 vols. Tübingen.
Siber, P. 1971. *Mit Christus leben: Eine Studie zur paulinischen Auferstehungshoffnung*. ATANT 61. Zürich.
Strecker, G. 1964. Redaktion und Tradition im Christushymnus Phil 2,6–11. *ZNW* 55: 63–78.
Talbert, C. H. 1967. The Problem of Pre-Existence in Philippians 2:6–11. *JBL* 86: 141–53.
Thomas, W. D. 1972. The Place of Women in the Church at Philippi. *ExpTim* 83: 117–20.
Vielhauer, P. 1975. *Geschichte der urchristlichen Literatur*. Berlin and New York.
Völter, D. 1892. Zwei Briefe an die Philipper. *TT* 26: 10–44, 117–46.
———. 1905. *Paulus und seine Briefe*. Strassburg.
Wanamaker, C. A. 1987. Philippians 2.6–11: Son of God or Adamic Christology? *NTS* 33: 179–93.
Weiss, J. 1959. *Earliest Christianity*. 2 vols. Trans. F. C. Grant. New York.
Wright, N. T. 1986. *Harpagmos* and the Meaning of Philippians 2:5–11. *JTS* n.s. 37: 321–52.
Zahn, T. 1909. *Introduction to the New Testament*. 3 vols. Trans. M. W. Jacobus et al. New York.

JOHN T. FITZGERALD

PHILISTINES. This entry consists of two articles. The first surveys the history of the Philistines as it is presented in various historical sources. The second focuses particularly on Philistine material culture as it has been revealed through archaeological work.

HISTORY

The Philistines (Eg *P-r-š-t-w;* Heb *pĕlištîm*), whose country of origin is still unknown, must have come to Canaan through the Aegean basin, destroying the Mycenaean and Minoan civilizations. They came partly overland via Anatolia, destroying the Hittite empire, Ugarit, and Amurru, and partly by ship via Crete (Caphtor of the Bible, cf. Amos 9:7 and Jer 47:4; Keftiu of the Egyptians) and Cyprus ("Ships come from the quarter of Kittim," i.e. Cyprus [Num 24:24] probably alludes to the first waves of the Sea Peoples). They were allied with other Sea Peoples, and their ultimate goal was to settle in Egypt. In about 1190, Rameses III clashed with them and defeated them. Rameses settled the conquered Philistines, mostly as Egyptian mercenaries, in the coastal towns, Gaza, Ashkelon, and Ashdod (cf. Deut 2:23, where "Caphtorim" refers to the Philistines). The connection between Egypt and Caphtorim is reflected in Gen 10:13–14 (cf. Speiser, *Genesis* AB). The term "the Negeb of the Cherethites" (1 Sam 30:14) may reflect Philistine occupation of that part of the Negeb (for the identification of Cherethites as Philistines, cf. Ezek 25:16).

The references to the Philistines in Gen 21:32–34; 26:1, 8, 14–15; and in Exod 13:17; 15:14; 23:31) are all anachronisms, although the expression "the Sea of the Philistines" may reflect Philistine naval supremacy in the 12th and 11th centuries.

The signs of destruction in Ashdod, Ashkelon, and Gaza suggest that sometime after the reign of Rameses VI (ca. 1150 B.C.E.), the Philistines drove out their Egyptian overlords by force. The Philistine Pentapolis was formed, a confederation of Gaza, Ashkelon, and Ashdod, together with two towns in the Shephelah which had already been settled by Philistines: Ekron and Gath. Each of these towns was a city-state, consisting of a "royal city" ruling a number of "country towns" (1 Sam 27:5, cf. 1 Sam 6:18). The rulers of these city-states were called *sĕrānîm* (singular, **seren*), a title whose etymology has not yet been satisfactorily explained; it may be from the Hittite word for "judge." For the next 150 years, until about 1000 B.C.E., the Philistine confederation was the most powerful entity in this corner of the world, occupying the land strip from Raphia in the S to Joppa, spreading gradually N (they founded Tell Qasile) and E through the Jezreel Valley to Beth-shan, and even establishing their hegemony over the Israelite tribes in the hill country (cf. 1 Sam 10:5; 13:23–14:16, and also 2 Sam 23:13–17). The source of Philistine power was apparently in the jealously defended monopoly of iron wares and the art of forging iron (1 Sam 13:19–21).

Very early the Philistines accepted the local Canaanite deities, dedicating temples to Dagon in Gaza (Judg 16:21–23), Ashdod (1 Sam 5:2–3), and Beth-shan (1 Chr 10:10–12), and to Astarte (1 Sam 31:10).

The clashes between the Philistines and the Israelites are

vividly reflected in the book of Judges. Despite the heroic exploits of Samson (Judges 13–16) and Shamgar son of Anath (Judg 3:31), the pressure of the Philistines was relentless, as seen in the tales of the migration of part of the tribe of Dan, who traveled N in their search for a safe refuge.

Further evidence of the advance of the Philistines can be found in the defeat of the Israelites at Ebenezer (the Philistines had already reached Aphek), resulting in the loss of the ark of the covenant and the destruction of the holy precinct Shiloh (1 Sam 4; cf. Jer 7:12, 14).

Samuel's victory over the Philistines (1 Sam 7:5–14), even if it is historical, did not appreciably reduce the pressure of the Philistines. The people demanded a king to lead them in war. The king chosen was Saul, whose wars with the Philistines can be traced from the beginning of his reign (1 Sam 13) until its tragic end on Mount Gilboa (1 Samuel 31). The eventual victor, however, was David, whose triumphs over the Philistines (1 Samuel 17; 18:6–9, 25–27, 30; 19:8) had gained him such renown as to arouse the jealousy and hatred of Saul. David was forced to flee, and eventually to become a vassal to his former foes the Philistines (1 Samuel 27, 29).

After the death of Saul, David was crowned king of Judah in Hebron (2 Sam 2:1–4), apparently with the consent of the Philistines. When David was chosen king over all Israel, however, and moved his capital to Jerusalem, the Philistines realized their danger and attacked. David's victories over the Philistines made Israel the leading power in the land of Canaan. We may assume that Gath became a vassal state to Israel. This change is suggested by David's mercenaries from Gath, who were under the command of Ittai the Gittite (cf. 2 Sam 15:18–22), and by his bodyguard, the Cherethites and the Pelethites (2 Sam 8:18; 15:18; 20:7, 23; 1 Kgs 1:38, 44; 1 Chr 18:17). The crushing defeat inflicted by David appears to have put an end to the Philistine Pentapolis; henceforward each city-state acted independently in its own selfish interest. It seems likely that the Philistines made a defensive alliance with Pharaoh to protect them against David; otherwise it is difficult to explain how Pharaoh was able to capture Gezer and give it as a dowry to his daughter, the wife of Solomon (1 Kgs 9:16). Forty years later apparently the same geopolitical situation enabled Shishak to invade Judah and Israel (1 Kgs 14:25), because no Philistine city, except Gaza, his starting point, is mentioned in his list of conquered towns. After the death of Shishak, Egypt was no longer a power in Asia. In the constant struggles between the Philistines and Israel (cf. 1 Kgs 15:27; 16:15) and the Philistines and Judah, in which the Philistines turned to the Edomites and the Arabs as allies (cf. Amos 1:6–8; 2 Chr 21:16–17), Judah sometimes prevailed (2 Chr 17:11; 26:6), and sometimes the Philistines (2 Chr 21:16–17; 28:18, until a new factor appeared on the scene, Assyria.

Philistia (Akk *Pa-la-aś-tu*) appears in Assyrian records for the first time in the inscriptions of Adad-nirari III (810–783 B.C.E.; *ANET,* 281b, 282a), but Assyrian domination of Philistia started only after the conquest of Syria by Tiglath-pileser III, when the Assyrian empire reached the Mediterranean, and the Assyrians began to try to dominate the maritime trade of the coastal towns of Phoenicia and Philistia. In 734 B.C.E., the first Assyrian campaign against Philistia began; its main object was the conquest of Gaza (the sequence of events is very fully expressed in Zech 9:5–6). The king of Gaza, Hanno, fled to Egypt, but later returned and was reinstated as a vassal of Assyria. The Assyrians were not interested in incorporating the Philistine territories into the Assyrian empire. They preferred to leave the towns as more or less autonomous tribute-bearing states. In the long list of kings bearing tribute are Mitinti of Ashkelon, Hanno of Gaza, and *Mu-še-ḫu-(. . .)* of Ashdod or Ekron. It appears that Mitinti of Ashkelon was allied with Rezon of Damascus, because when the latter was defeated by Tiglath-pileser, Mitinti "disappeared," and his son Rukibtu became king in his place. Because of the heavy hand of Tiglath-pileser, all these petty states breathed a sigh of relief when he died in 727 B.C.E., but their rejoicing was premature (cf. Isa 14:29, 31).

About five years later, when Sargon ascended the throne of Assyria, Hanno joined the Syro-Palestinian rebellion headed by the king of Hamath, which was also supported by Egypt. In 720, Sargon, having crushed the rebels near Qarqar, attacked Philistia. Hanno called on the Egyptian army for help. The Assyrians met the Egyptians near Raphiah, defeated them, captured Hanno and took him captive to Assyria. Gaza subsequently remained a loyal vassal until the end of the Assyrian empire.

In 713 or the beginning of 712 B.C.E., Ashdod rebelled against Assyria, and in 712 Sargon sent an army to crush the rebellion (cf. Isa 20:1). This campaign is well documented in the annals, and two reliefs from Khorsabad, which depict the sieges of Gibbethon and Ekron. Sargon's victory is also attested on a stela, pieces of which have been found in the excavations in Ashdod. Ashdod was made a province, but the political arrangement is problematic since we also hear of kings in Ashdod, Mitinti in 701 and Ahimilki in 677 and 667.

The death of Sargon in battle in 705 set off a wave of rebellions in nearly all the vassal states in W Asia, who were apparently supported by Egypt. The loyal king of Ashkelon was replaced by his brother. In Ekron the local nobility deposed their king Padi and sent him to Jerusalem for safekeeping. Probably it is to this time that we must ascribe the notice in 2 Kgs 18:8 that Hezekiah "overran Philistia as far as Gaza and its border areas." In 701, after having suppressed the revolt in Babylon, Sennacherib appeared in the W. Near Tyre he received tribute from the vassal kings of Amurru, but of the Philistine kings, only Mitinti of Ashdod is mentioned. The king of Gaza does not appear on the list, perhaps because he had not rebelled. The rebel king of Ashkelon, Sidqia, was deported to Assyria and replaced with a new king with a typically Assyrian name, Sharruludari. When Ekron was besieged, the Egyptian army came to the support of the rebels but was defeated at Eltekeh. Ekron was conquered and its loyal king, Padi, restored to kingship as part of Hezekiah's submission. The loyal Philistine kings (Mitinti of Ashdod, Padi of Ekron, and Sillibel of Gaza) were rewarded with towns that had formerly belonged to the kingdom of Judah (cf. Isa 1:7). Philistia was thus both enriched and more firmly established as a buffer region between Assyria and Egypt.

The more belligerent policy toward Egypt which Sennacherib's successor, Esarhaddon, pursued involved a firm grip on Philistia, too. In his first campaign (679) Esarhaddon plundered Arzâ, apparently a town on the Egyptian border, and took its king captive. Four Philistine kings, Sillibel of Gaza, Mitinti of Ashkelon, Ikausu (a Philistine name!) of Ekron, and Ahimilki of Ashdod, appear among "the kings of the country Hatti" who were required to do corvée work for Esarhaddon in Nineveh, apparently in 677/76. Esarhaddon conducted three campaigns against Egypt, and we may assume that in all these campaigns the Philistine towns served as depots and secured the long line of communication, although they are never mentioned, except for indications that in the second campaign Ashkelon supported Egypt, which was defeated.

All the vassal kings in W Asia, among them the four Philistine kings, Sillibel, Mitinti, Ikausu, and Ahimilki, were called upon to be auxiliary troops when Esarhaddon's successor, Assurbanipal, resumed the campaign against Egypt, which this time proved successful. About ten years later, however, Psammetichus I (656–610), prince of Saïs and founder of the 26th Dyn., was able to establish his independence.

As the Assyrian empire declined, Egypt seized dominion over the Philistine city-states. Herodotus (2.157) records that Psammetichus besieged Ashdod for twenty-nine years before he could conquer it. Psammetichus' invasion may be reflected in Zephaniah's prophecy against Philistia (Zeph 2:4), which describes events from the S (Egypt) to the N, Gaza, Ashkelon, Ashdod, and Ekron. Jeremiah's phrase "what is left of Ashdod" (Jer 25:20) may also reflect the conquests of Psammetichus I. A witness to Egypt's dominion over Philistia is the statuette of Padese "the king's envoy to The Canaan (Gaza?) and Philistia." The fact that the Philistine cities were vassals of Psammetichus I and his son Neco II enabled these kings to come to the aid of a failing Assyria against the rising power of Babylonia. Nebuchadnezzar's great victory over Neco at Carchemish in 605 (cf. Jer 46:22–26) changed the whole situation, and in the following years the Babylonian armies swept through Philistia. The Aramaic letter found in Saqqara, in which a Philistine king asks urgent help from Pharaoh against the Babylonian king, probably belongs to this time. Only Ashkelon made any opposition, and it was turned into a heap of ruins for its temerity (cf. Jer 47). Some years later (592/1), the sons of Aga king of Ashkelon became hostages and they along with other exiles from Ashkelon are mentioned in a provisions list of the Babylonian court.

In 601/600 Neco II defeated Nebuchadnezzar decisively at Migdol, and occupied Gaza (Hdt. 2.159; cf. Jer 47:1). Three years later, Nebuchadnezzar returned and conquered Jerusalem (cf. Jer 52:28; 2 Kgs 24:12). It is probable that Gaza profited by Jerusalem's revolt in 598, sharing with Edom, the Negeb that had been lost by Judah (cf. Jer 13:19 and also Ezek 25:15–17).

When Pharaoh Hophra (Apries) succeeded to the throne of Egypt in 589 B.C.E., he persuaded Zedekiah to revolt and even came to the aid of Zedekiah against Nebuchadnezzar, but the Egyptian army retreated as soon as the main Babylonian forces left Jerusalem to fight them (cf. Jer 37:7). It is likely that the Philistine cities joined in the revolt, and it was probably at this time that Nebuchadnezzar deported people from the Philistine towns and settled them in the vicinity of Nippur, although our evidence comes from later times. The kings of Gaza and Ashdod appear (together with several other kings from W Asia) at the end of a list of high court officials from ca. 570 B.C.E. During the reign of Nabonidus, there existed a place named Gaza (*Ḫa-za-tu*), which must have been founded by exiles from Gaza although the people mentioned all had Babylonian names. The archives of the Murasu family from Nippur (455–403 B.C.E.), also mention settlements near Nippur named "Ashkelon," "Bît Arsa," and "Gaza."

By the time the Persians became masters of Philistia (in 539 B.C.E.), the Philistine element in the language and culture had disappeared. ("Ashdodite" [Neh 13:24] was probably an Aramaic dialect). The towns became Persian towns, some belonging to Sidon or Tyre, some autonomous. Gaza became the base for Persian military operations against Egypt.

After the conquest by Alexander the Great in 332 B.C.E., Ashdod, Ashkelon, and Gaza became Greek *poleis* in every respect. The only trace of the Philistines that remained was the name Palestine, which was first used in Greek by Herodotus (1.105; 2.104) and in Latin by Pliny (*HN* 5.12), and which Hadrian made the name of the region for nearly two thousand years.

Bibliography

Albright, W. F. 1975. Syria, the Philistines, and Phoenicia. *CAH*³ 2/2: 507–16.

Barnett, R. D. 1975. The Sea Peoples. *CAH*³ 2/2: 371–78.

Ephᶜal, I. 1978. The Western Minorities in Babylonia in the 6th–5th Centuries B.C. *Or* 47: 80–83.

Kitchen, K. A. 1973. The Philistines. Pp. 53–78 in *POTT.*

Macalister, R. A. S. 1965. *Philistines, Their History and Civilization.* Chicago. Repr.

Mitchell, T. C. 1967. Philistia. Pp. 404–27 in *Archaeology and Old Testament Study,* ed. D. W. Thomas. Oxford.

Sandars, N. K. 1985. *The Sea Peoples.* Rev. ed. London.

Strange, J. 1980. *Caphtor/Keftiu.* Leiden.

Tadmor, H. 1966. Philistia under Assyrian Rule. *BA* 29: 86–102.

Wainwright, G. A. 1959. Some Early Philistine History. *VT* 9: 73–84.

Weidner, E. F. 1939. Jojachin, König von Juda. Vol. 2, pp. 928 in *Melanges Syriens offerts à M. René Dussand.* Paris.

H. J. KATZENSTEIN

ARCHAEOLOGY

The Philistines were among the Sea Peoples, probably of Aegean origin, who first appeared in the E Mediterranean at the end of the 13th century B.C. These peoples were displaced from their original homelands as part of the extensive population movements characteristic of the end of the LB Age. During this period, the Egyptians and the Hittites ruled in the Levant, but both powers were in a general state of decline. The Sea Peoples exploited this power vacuum by invading areas previously subject to Egyptian and Hittite control, launching land and sea attacks on Syria, Palestine, and Egypt, to which various Egyptian sources attest.

The various translations of the name *Philistine* in the different versions of the Bible reveal that even in early times translators and exegetes were unsure of their identity. In the LXX, for example, the name is usually translated as *allopsyloi* ("strangers"), but it occurs also as *phylistieim* in the Pentateuch and Joshua. In the Hebrew Bible, the Philistines are called *pĕlištîm,* a term defining them as the inhabitants of *pĕlešet,* i.e., the coastal plain of S Palestine. Assyrian sources call them both *Pilisti* and *Palastu.* The Philistines appear as *prst* in Egyptian sources.

Encountering the descendants of the Philistines on the coast of S Palestine, the historian Herodotus, along with sailors and travelers from the Persian period onward called them *palastinoi* and their country *palastium.* The use of these names in the works of Josephus, where they are common translations for *Philistines* and *Philistia* and, in some cases, for the entire land of Palestine, indicates the extent to which the names had gained acceptance by Roman times. The emperor Hadrian officially designated the province of Judaea *Provincia Palaestine,* and by the 4th century C.E., the shortened name *Palaestina* had become the general term for the whole of Palestine.

The biblical references to Philistine origins are few and enigmatic. The first appears in the "Table of Nations" in Gen 10:14. The probable meaning of this verse, insofar as it relates to the Philistines, is ". . . and the Caphtorim, out of whom came the Philistines." The homeland of the Philistines, Caphtor (cf. Amos 9:7, Jer 47:4, Deut 2:23), is generally recognized by scholars as Crete, although some believe Caphtor to be located in Cilicia in Asia Minor. In other biblical references, the Philistines are synonymous with the Cherethites, that is Cretans (cf. Zeph 2:5, Ezek 25:16). Various biblical traditions, then, suggest that the Caphtorim are to be identified with the Cherethites, thus linking the Philistines with a Cretan homeland. The evidence supplied by the architectural remains, material culture and pottery from archaeological sites in Israel, strongly suggests that the Philistines originated in the Aegean.

Several key references to the Sea Peoples have been identified in Egyptian sources. According to inscriptions of Pharaoh Merneptah (ca. 1236–1223 B.C.), the Sea Peoples attempted to invade Egypt from the direction of Libya. The attack was led by Libyans joined by "foreigners from the Sea"—the Sherden, Sheklesh, Lukka, Tursha (Teresh), and Akawasha. This list of Sea Peoples does not, however, include references to the Philistines and Tjekker, who are first mentioned as invaders during the reign of Rameses III (ca. 1198–1166 B.C.). The reliefs and inscriptions at his mortuary temple at Medinet Habu in Thebes describe fierce naval and land battles with the Sea Peoples. An inscription under the land battle scene indicates that the Egyptian army fought the Sea Peoples in the "land of Djahi," i.e., the Phoenician coast and hinterland down to Palestine.

This information is supplemented by the Harris Papyrus I, in which Rameses' decisive defeat of the Sea Peoples, including the Philistines, is described. Subsequently, Rameses gave the Philistines permission to settle on the S coastal plain of Palestine. There they vied with the disunited Canaanite city-states and the newly arrived Israelites for cultural and political domination of the country.

The Onomasticon of Amenope, which dates from the end of the 12th or beginning of the 11th century, mentions the areas settled by the Sea Peoples in Palestine, as part of the sphere of Egyptian influence. It records a number of peoples, lands, and cities. Three ethnic groups, the Sherden *(srhn),* the Tjekker *(tkr),* and the Philistines *(prst)* are listed, together with Ashkelon, Ashdod, and Gaza, cities situated in the territory controlled by the Philistines.

Philistia, "The land of the Philistines," consisted of five major cities—Gaza, Ashkelon, Ashdod, Gath, and Ekron—which were united in a confederation. In addition to the Pentapolis, several smaller Philistine cities, called *ḥăṣērîm* ("villages") or *banôt* ("daughters"), are mentioned in the Bible. These include Ziklag, Timna, and Jabneh. The role of these smaller cities was as secondary, nearly autonomous centers under the control of the capitals of the city-states.

The territory of the Philistines as defined in Josh 13:2–3 designates the Brook of Egypt (Wadi el-Arish) and the Sihor as the S border, the N boundary as defined by the region N of Ekron, Judah as the E border, and the Mediterranean Sea as the W boundary. This region, as corroborated by archaeological evidence, was occupied by the Philistines for several generations after their arrival in Palestine and before their expansion in the 11th century. Major excavations have established a clear stratigraphic sequence by which the initial appearance, then the flourishing, and subsequently the assimilation of the Philistines can be traced, a process spanning most of the Iron I period (c. 1200–1000 B.C.E.). The discovery of archaeological remains of unmistakably Philistine character at sites quite distant from this area has raised the question of how Philistine culture spread beyond the confines of Philistia—through military conquest, through the establishment of military outposts, or through peaceful trade and commerce.

Four of the cities of the Philistine Pentapolis have been positively identified—Gaza, Ashkelon, Ashdod, and Ekron. The location of the fifth, Gath, remains an open question. At Gaza, the ancient tel lies beneath the modern city and as a result, large-scale excavations have not been undertaken. Excavations at Ashkelon have revealed that the last Canaanite stratum was destroyed, followed by a Philistine settlement. The most extensive evidence of Philistine settlement and expansion is provided by excavations at Ashdod, Ekron, and Tell Qasile on the N border of Philistia. These sites provide complementary data on the nature of Philistine urban settlement, facets of their material culture, and cultic structures and practices.

Philistine occupation at Ashdod began in the early 12th century B.C.E. The first indication of the arrival of a new population was the partial destruction of the Egyptian-Canaanite fortress over which was built an open-air cultic installation. Adjacent to this installation was a potter's workshop in which was found a rich assemblage of locally made Mycenaean IIIC:1b pottery, Aegean in style and a precursor of the earliest Philistine bichrome pottery. In the following occupational phases, Ashdod was a well-planned, fortified city. Two building complexes were uncovered, one of which included an apsidal structure with adjacent rooms and a courtyard. The last phase of Philistine settlement (ca. 1050 B.C.E.) at Ashdod was the largest and most prosperous. At that time, the lower city outside the acropolis area was occupied for the first time and massive mudbrick walls and a gate were built to protect the enlarged city. While the Philistine population had grown and flourished, the pottery and material culture reflect assimilation of local tradition and new Phoenician influences.

A clear understanding of the ceramic repertoire within the stratigraphic sequence is one of the keys to defining the settlement pattern of the Philistines, both within the borders of Philistia and beyond. The initial phase of Philistine settlement has been recognized at Ashdod and Ekron by virtue of the appearance of locally made Mycenaean IIIC:1b pottery (see Fig. PHI.01), while the second phase of Philistine settlement and expansion is associated with the Philistine bichrome wares. The shapes and decorative motifs of Philistine pottery were a blend of four distinct ceramic styles: Mycenaean, Cypriot, Egyptian, and local Canaanite. The dominant traits in shape and almost all the decorative elements were derived from the Mycenaean repertoire and point to the Aegean background of Philistine pottery. Philistine shapes of Mycenaean origin include bell-shaped bowls, large kraters with elaborate decoration, stirrup jars for oils and unquents, and strainer-spout "beer jugs." A few of many decorative motifs are stylized birds, spiral loops, concentric half-circles, and scale patterns. Although Philistine vessels were richly decorated with motifs taken from the Mycenaean repertoire, these motifs were rearranged and integrated with other influences to create the distinctive "signature" known as Philistine.

PHI.01. Philistine pottery with stylized bird motif from Gezer—Mycenaean IIIC:1b. *(Redrawn from J. G. Duncan,* Corpus of Dated Palestinian Pottery, *Publications of the British School of Archaeology in Egypt 49 [London: British School of Archaeology in Egypt, 1930], pl 64.G, fig. 339)*

Excavations at Ekron (Tel Miqne) have revealed a LB Canaanite city-state which was transformed by the Philistines in the 12th century B.C.E. into a large, well-planned, fortified city which included industrial and elite quarters. A monumental building, possibly a palace with shrines, was discovered at the heart of the city in the elite quarter. See Fig. PHI.02. This building, probably part of a larger complex, included rooms which contained mudbrick altars and a number of bronze and iron artifacts of cultic significance. These rooms opened onto a hall in which was constructed a circular hearth flanked by two pillar bases. Hearths are an important feature in the Aegean and Cyprus where they are the central architectural element in the plan of the megaron. Mudbrick altars, a continuation of local Canaanite tradition, are also well-known in Cyprus and the Aegean at such sites as Enkomi, Kition, Phylakopi, and Mycenae.

The city at Tell Qasile was founded by the Philistines in the first half of the 12th century B.C.E. on the N bank of the Yarkon River. The site was obviously chosen because it was a perfect inland port site. Established on virgin soil, Tell Qasile was undoubtedly part of the Philistine expansion which followed their initial phase of settlement. In addition to industrial and residential structures found in other quarters of the city, three superimposed temples dating from the end of the 12th to the beginning of the 10th century B.C.E. were uncovered in the sacred precinct. These structures in their various phases included raised mudbrick platforms, mudbrick benches, pillars, and small chambers at the back of the temples interpreted variously as holy-of-holies or treasuries. A related building adjacent to the earliest temple (12th century B.C.E.) contained a hearth and two pillars, similar in plan and conception to the hearth and pillars found at Ekron.

There is both agreement and discrepancy between the Bible and the archaeological record with respect to Philistine religious organization and beliefs. The Aegean background of Philistine religion, which is not disclosed in the Bible, is evident through cultic architectural features such as the hearth mentioned above, as well as through small finds such as the "Ashdoda," a ceramic figurine found at Ashdod. See Fig. PHI.03. The Ashdoda is most likely a schematic representation of a female deity and throne, and is evidently a variant of the Mycenaean female figure seated on a throne, sometimes holding a child. These figurines are usually associated with the worship of the "Great Mother" or "Great Goddess." Several figurine fragments of the "Ashdoda" type have also been discovered at Ekron and Tell Qasile. At Ekron, head fragments with spreading headdress and birdlike features resemble the Ashdoda, while at Qasile the torso of a flat figurine of the Ashdoda type was found.

Archaeological evidence has revealed that in the Aegean, female, not male deities were primarily worshipped. Apparently by the 11th century this predominantly female pantheon was replaced by a male Canaanite pantheon reflecting the Philistines' more recent cultural milieu. The head of the Philistine pantheon appears to have been the

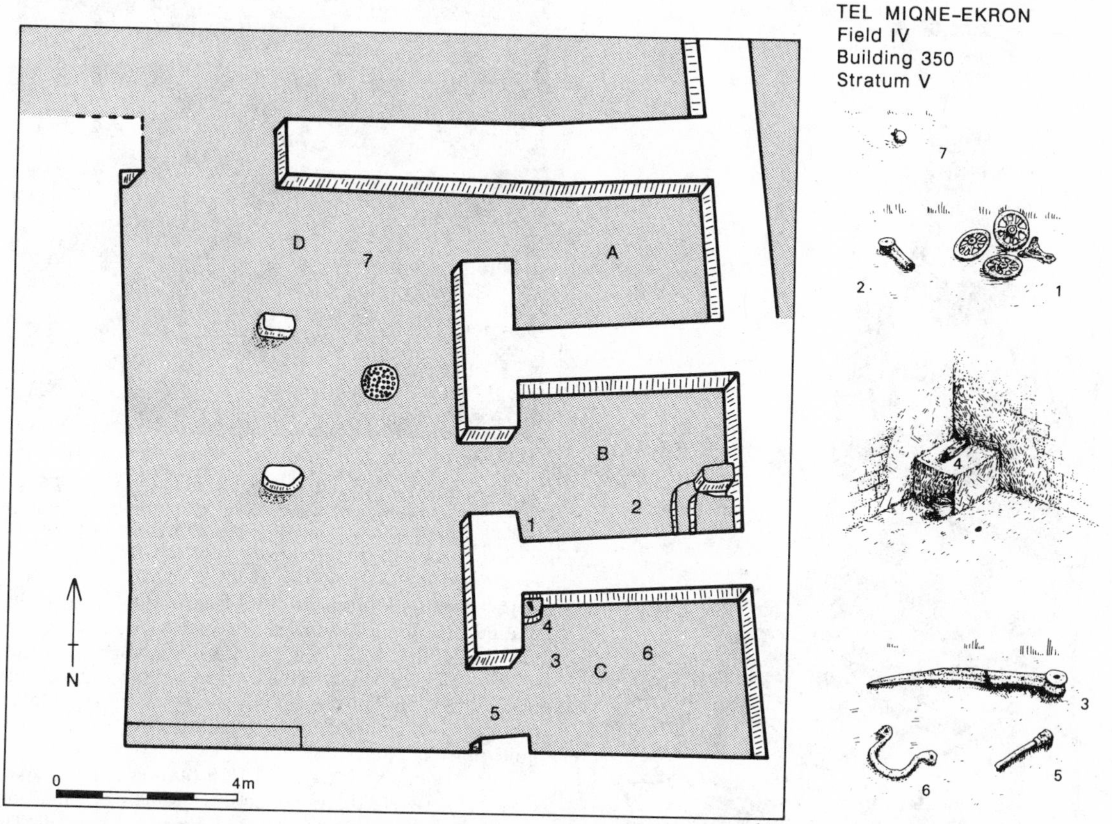

PHI.02. Schematic reconstruction of the monumental building (with find spots) at Tel Miqne-Ekron—Stratum V: (1) Bronze wheels and a bronze corner of a stand; (2) ivory handle of an iron knife; (3) iron knife with ivory handle; (4) an iron object; (5) bronze peg with two faces; (6) bronze horizontal handle; (7) bronze plug in the shape of a pomegranate. *(Drawing, by permission, Tel Miqne-Ekron Project)*

Canaanite god, Dagon (1 Chr 10:10), to whom the temples of Gaza and Ashdod, and possibly also at Beth-shan, were dedicated. Another god, Baal-zebub (Baal-zebul), has his oracular temple in Ekron. The goddess Ashtoreth apparently also had a temple at Beth-shan (1 Sam 31:8–13). Philistine priests appear only once in the Bible, when the Ark was captured and taken to Ashdod (1 Samuel 5). The Bible also refers to the Philistine custom of carrying idols into battle (2 Sam 5:21) and to "Houses of Images," apparently a reference to temples in which images of the gods were kept. Among the few specifically Philistine religious beliefs that appear in the Bible are the golden images of mice and boils that were sent as a guilt *(ʾašam)* offering to God (1 Sam 6:4–16).

Philistine cult vessels also provide insights into Philistine rituals and beliefs. The *kernos,* reflecting Aegean influences, is a hollow ceramic ring on which objects such as birds, bulls' or rams' heads, or pomegranates are set. See Fig. PHI.04. It was apparently used for the pouring of libations in some religious ritual. Examples of *kernoi* decorated in Philistine style are known from Ashdod, Ekron, Gezer, and Megiddo.

A distinctive Philistine cult vessel is the one-handled lion-headed rhyton, a ritual or drinking cup. Similar rhyta have been found at Tell Jerishe, Tell Zeror, Megiddo, Tell es-Safi, Tell Qasile, and Ekron. The Philistine rhyton is a ceramic adaptation of animal-headed rhyta in metal and stone of Mycenaean-Minoan tradition.

Three high cylindrical cult stands from Tell Qasile were found in the Philistine temple. Each had a bowl topped with a bird's head. Another cult stand found at Ashdod features five musicians around its base. Each of the five figures plays a musical instrument: cymbals, double pipe, frame drum, and stringed instrument that is probably a lyre. These musicians represented on the stand were probably part of a Philistine cult, their role similar to that of the "Levites who were singers" in the temple of Jerusalem (2 Chr 5:12–13).

Other facets of Philistine life, such as mourning customs and burial practices, may be understood through several interesting types of finds. For example, terra-cotta female mourning figurines from Philistine burials at Tell 'Aitun and Azor show women with both hands on their heads, or with one hand on their heads and one on their breasts.

PHI.03. Philistine "Ashdoda" figurine from Ashdod—Stratum XII, 12th Century B.C.E. *(Redrawn from* BA *50/4 [1987]: 203)*

Similar mourning figures are closely associated with the burial customs and the cult of the dead found in the Aegean world at the end of the Mycenaean period.

Burial customs are generally a sensitive indicator of cultural affinities, and Philistine burial customs reflect the same fusion of Aegean background with Egyptian and local Canaanite elements that distinguishes every other aspect of their culture. The use of anthropoid clay coffins (an Egyptian custom) and interment in rock-cut chamber tombs (of Mycenaean affinities) are two such indicators.

Anthropoid coffins are built roughly in the outline of a body. The lids are ineptly modeled with faces in what has been termed the "grotesque" style, with only a schematic outlining of facial features and arms. Five such coffins dating from the 12th–11th centuries B.C.E. were discovered at Beth-shan. The distinctive feature of the Beth-

PHI.04. *Kernos,* cultic libation vessel with Philistine style decorations from Megiddo—Iron I. Various hollow forms are attached to the hollow *kernos* ring. The gazelle's head was flanked by two jars (one of which has broken off), and these in turn are flanked by two pomegranates. Opposite the gazelle's head is a cup flanked by two doves. *(Courtesy of the Oriental Institute of the University of Chicago)*

shan "grotesque" lids is the applique headdress. However, one lid portrays a headdress crowned by vertical fluting, identical to the "feathered" cap worn by the Peleset (Philistines), Tjekker, and Denyen on the Medinet Habu reliefs of Rameses III. This headgear provides decisive evidence that the bodies buried in these coffins were Sea Peoples, quite possibly Philistines.

Several stamp seals found in 12th-century strata at Ashdod may provide the only extant examples of Philistine language and writing. Used to imprint a lump of clay affixed to a letter, the text is apparently related to the Linear A and B scripts and the Cypro-Minoan syllabary utilized in the Aegean during the LB Age. Philistine words and personal names as they are preserved in the Bible are another possible key to the enigma of the origins of the Philistines and their language. The word *seren,* the head of each Philistine city-state, seems to be linguistically related to the Greek *tyrannos* ("tyrant"), likely a proto-Greek Illyrian or Lydian word that later entered the Greek language. The name Achish, *Agchous* in the LXX and Homer, which closely resembles the name Ikusu, king of Ekron in the Essarhadon annals, is sometimes compared with *Agchisēs* (Homer, *Il.* 2.189). *Agchisēs,* in Greek tradition, was related to the Dardanians, one of the Illyrian tribes that later migrated to Asia Minor and Greece. Scholarly opinion is divided on Goliath, which is sometimes compared to the Lydian *Alyattēs.*

Archaeological finds illuminating Philistine material culture are not limited to the ceramic medium. Though it is the latter that appears in greater quantities at excavations, no less significant is the Philistine contribution in the area of metallurgy. A key biblical reference in 1 Sam 13:19 reads: "Now there was no smith found throughout all the land of Israel; for the Philistines said, 'Lest the Hebrews make them swords and spears.' " Here it is clear that a worker in metal, without specifying whether the material was bronze or iron or both, is intended. Material evidence for bronze-working has been found at numerous sites associated with the Philistines, including Ekron, Tel Mor (harbor of Ashdod), and Tell Qasile. Significant small finds in bronze from the city of Ekron include wheels of a cultic stand similar to the type found at Cypriot sites of the same period, and a double-headed peg with suspension hole which may have parallels in Crete.

The discovery of various iron artifacts, including several bimetallic knives from 12th century strata at Philistine sites, raises the question of the role of the Philistines in the introduction of iron-working technology to Israel. Though it cannot be demonstrated with certainty that it was they who introduced this new technology, it is very likely that these new settlers brought with them a knowledge of iron-working which acted as a stimulus to local industry.

A superior knowledge of metal-working, whether in bronze or iron, may have given the Philistines a military advantage in their early conflicts with the Israelites. The well-known biblical account in 1 Samuel 17 of the duel between David and Goliath provides a detailed description of Philistine armaments. Unlike the Philistines in the Medinet Habu reliefs, which depict an earlier period, Goliath of Gath wears a bronze helmet rather than a "feathered" headdress. Nevertheless, Goliath's spear, helmet, coat of mail, and bronze greaves, as well as the duel itself, are all features of Aegean arms and warfare. The Bible compares Goliath's spear to a "weaver's beam" because this type of weapon was new to Canaan and had no Hebrew name. Mycenaean warriors are depicted very similarly equipped on the 12th century Warriors' Vase from Mycenae.

Philistine material culture is a syncretistic blend of Aegean, Egyptian, and Canaanite elements. The dominant element is Aegean, as demonstrated by decorative motifs on pottery, cult practices, burial customs and funerary rites, and architectural styles. The same period which witnessed the collapse of empires in the Levant with the resulting cessation or reduction of trade (13th century B.C.E.), also produced migrations of populations, among them the Sea Peoples. When they settled, as they did on the coastal plain of Israel, these peoples introduced by means of material culture, cultic practices, and architecture a new ethnic element which reflected their origins in the Aegean. This period, from the beginning of the 12th century to the end of the 11th century B.C.E. was the Philistines' most flourishing era, both historically and culturally. From the early 10th century on, the Philistines gradually lost their cultural distinctiveness and assimilated into the Canaanite population, steadily declining in importance until they played no more than a minor role in the history of Palestine.

Bibliography

Dothan, M. 1972. The Relation Between Cyprus and the Philistine Coast in the Late Bronze Age (Tel Mor, Ashdod). *Praktika* 1: 51–56.

Dothan, M., and Freedman, D. N. 1967. *Ashdod 1.* ᶜAtiqot. Jerusalem.

Dothan, M., et al. 1971. *Ashdod II–III.* ᶜAtiqot 9–10. Jerusalem.

Dothan, M., and Porath, Y. 1982. *Ashdod IV.* ᶜAtiqot 15. Jerusalem.

Dothan, T. 1973. Philistine Material Culture and its Mycenaean Affinities. Pp. 187–88 and 376 in *Acts of the International Archaeological Symposium: The Mycenaeans in the Eastern Mediterranean.* Nicosia.

———. 1982. *The Philistines and Their Material Culture.* Jerusalem.

———. 1983. Some Aspects of the Appearance of the Sea Peoples and Philistines in Canaan. Pp. 99–120 in *Griechenland, die Ägäis, und die Levante während der "Dark Ages,"* ed. S. Deger-Jalkotzy. Vienna.

———. 1989. The Arrival of the Sea Peoples: Cultural Diversity in Early Iron Age Canaan. Pp. 1–14 in *Recent Excavations in Israel,* ed. S. Gitin and W. G. Dever. AASOR 49. Winona Lake, IN.

———. 1990. Part I: Where They Came From, How They Settled Down and the Place They Worshiped In. *BARev* 16/1: 26–36.

Dothan, T., and Gitin, S. 1990. Ekron of the Philistines. *BARev* 16/1: 20–25.

Gitin, S. 1990. Part II: Olive-Oil Suppliers to the World. *BARev* 16/2: 33–42, 59.

Gunneweg, J.; Perlman, I.; Dothan, T.; and Gitin, S. 1986. On the Origin of Pottery from Tel Miqne-Ekron. *BASOR* 264: 17–27.

Mazar, A. 1980. *Excavations at Tell Qasile,* 1. Qedem 12. Jerusalem.

———. 1985a. *Excavations at Tell Qasile,* 2. Qedem 20. Jerusalem.

———. 1985b. The Emergence of the Philistine Material Culture. *IEJ* 35: 95–107.

Sandars, N. K. 1978. *The Sea Peoples.* London.

TRUDE DOTHAN

PHILO OF ALEXANDRIA.

A Hellenistic Jewish philosopher of 1st-century Alexandria.

A. The Man and His Family
B. Philo's Writings
  1. Exposition of the Laws of Moses
  2. Exegetical Commentaries
  3. Remaining Writings
C. Philo and the Jewish Community in Alexandria
D. Philo as Biblical Exegete
E. Central Ideas and Perspectives
F. The Significance of Philo

A. The Man and His Family

Philo was a prominent member of the Jewish community of Alexandria, the largest Jewish settlement outside Palestine. The only certain date known from his life comes from his account of the great pogrom in Alexandria which started in A.D. 38 under the prefect Flaccus, during the reign of the Roman emperor Gaius Caligula. Philo was then chosen to head a delegation (*Gaium* 370) sent in A.D. 39/40 by the Jewish community to Gaius Caligula in Rome.

A few other datable events are found in his writings. In *Alexander,* or *Whether the Animals Have Reason* (*Anim*) 27, Philo speaks of the celebrations in various places given by Germanicus Iulius Caesar, probably in A.D. 12, when he entered on his first term of consulship. The horse race account in *Anim* 58 is found also in Pliny *HN* 8:160–61, where the event is said to have occurred during the games of Claudius Caesar in A.D. 47. Philo was aged already at the time of the embassy. On the basis of these observations, the time of Philo's death should probably be set around A.D. 50, and his birth to around 20–15 B.C.

Philo belonged to one of the wealthiest Jewish families in Alexandria. His brother, Alexander, was probably chief of customs (alabarch) of the Eastern border of Egypt and guardian of the Emperor Tiberius' mother's properties in Egypt. Alexander was rich enough to lend money to the Jewish king Agrippa I, and to plate the gates of the Temple of Jerusalem in gold and silver. Alexander's apostate son, Tiberius Iulius Alexander, born ca. A.D. 15, had a public career which took him to the highest post of a Roman official in Egypt, that of prefect (A.D. 66–70). He had then already served as procurator of Judaea (A.D. 46–48) and served as chief of staff under Titus during the siege of Jerusalem A.D. 70.

On the basis of information from Philo and Josephus, A. Terian has set up the following tables (*ANRW* 2/21/1: 282–83):

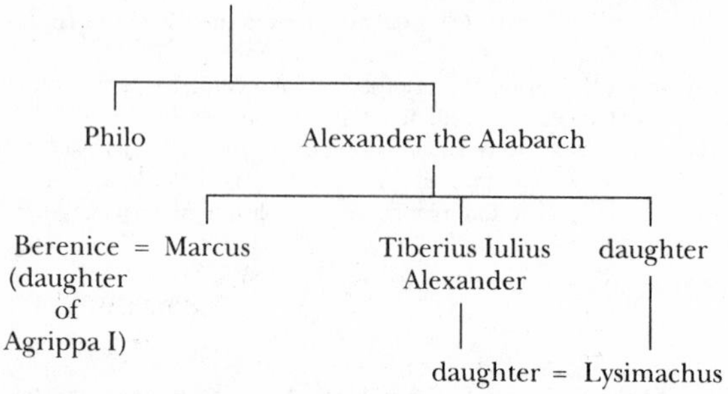

PHI.05. Genealogical chart of Philo.

Although direct and datable information about Philo is scanty, it is possible to give a picture of him. His role as political leader is mentioned above. He was the head of the Jewish delegation sent to Gaius Caligula in Rome. A competing legation was sent by the Greek citizens of Alexandria, headed by Apion. Philo's mission turned into failure. The Jews thought they should meet a judge and get their rights, but discovered that Gaius Caligula was their foe. Gaius Caligula died in A.D. 41, and his successor, Claudius, issued an edict to normalize conditions in Alexandria. Claudius confirmed the particular religious and judicial rights of the Jews, but denied them equal rights with the Greek citizens.

Also apart from this legation to Gaius Caligula, Philo had political responsibilities. He tells in *Spec Leg* III:1–5 that circumstances forced him to leave philosophy and contemplation because envy had plunged him into the ocean of civil cares. By envy, Philo seems to allude to the tensions which existed between the Jews and other ethnic groups in Alexandria.

Philo was a learned person. In his youth he received the Greek general education of the encyclia. This general education consisted of literature, rhetoric, mathematics, music, and logic. Philo's writings show that he had a broad education also beyond the encyclia. He not only had excellent command of Greek language and literary style, but was well acquainted both with Greek authors and philosophers.

Although Philo was clearly conscious of being a Jew, he took an active part in the social life of Alexandria. He attended banquets, frequented the theatre, watched boxing matches, and attended horse races. Nevertheless, he was a religious person, loyal to Judaism and its institutions. His engagement in philosophy had its setting in the activities of the synagogues, which according to Philo were schools of philosophy. His writings prove that his philosophical interest largely was expressed in exegesis of the laws of Moses. At times (*Spec Leg* III:1ff; *Cher* 27) Philo indicates that he had mystical experiences in connection with his exegetical activity. At least once in his life he made a pilgrimage to the Temple of Jerusalem to offer up prayers and sacrifices. He was so strict in his emphasis on loyalty to the Jewish ethnic community and its cause, that he advocated immediate execution of apostates without any formal trial (*Spec Leg* I:54–56; 315–18).

B. Philo's Writings

There has long been general agreement among scholars on the classification of Philo's expository writing. These fall into two main groups:

1. Exposition of the Laws of Moses *(Op; Abr; Jos; Dec; Spec Leg All; Virt; Praem)*. These writings are but parts of one comprehensive rewriting of the law of Moses. On the basis of Philo's own terminology and outline, the "Exposition" can be divided in three parts: the story of creation, the historical part, and the legislative part. The *Life of Moses* was formerly classed in a group of miscellaneous writings, but Goodenough has shown that this and the "Exposition" were companion works. In these exegetical works, Philo paraphrases and expands the biblical text and so gives his own views. A similar method may be found in the book of *Jubilees*, the *Genesis Apocryphon*, and the *Biblical Antiquities of Pseudo-Philo.*

2. Exegetical Commentaries. These fall into two subordinate series:

(a) Questions and Answers on Genesis and Exodus, which is a brief commentary in the form of questions and answers on parts of the first two books of the Pentateuch. Most of the Greek original has been lost; modern editions depend mainly on the ancient Armenian version. The original work may have included other books of the Pentateuch, but Eusebius knew only the section on Genesis and Exodus. Greek fragments preserved by Byzantine writers deal only with Genesis or Exodus with two doubtful exceptions. Therefore we probably have the whole of the work.

(b) Allegorical Interpretations of Genesis, which consists of *Leg All* I–III; *Cher; Sacr; Quod Det; Post; Gig; Quod Deus; Agr; Plant; Ebr; Sobr; Conf; Migr; Heres; Congr; Fuga; Mut; Somn; Deo.* This series covers the main parts of Genesis 2–41. They have the form of a verse-by-verse commentary on the biblical texts. These commentaries vary in length and are more complex in form than Questions and Answers, though the question-and-answer form is also used. In this respect they are closer to the Midrashim than to the commentaries found at Qumran. Originally the title of all these commentaries seems to have been *Legum Allegoriae*. This name is now given only to the first work, on Gen 2:1–3:19. The others have different titles.

The commentary is mostly on two levels: the literal and the allegorical. The relationship between Questions and Answers and the Allegorical Interpretation of Genesis 2–3 is much discussed. Both works have the form of a commentary on verses or passages from the Pentateuch. Some scholars have suggested that "Questions" is catechetical, while "Allegorical Interpretation" is more scholarly. Against this is the fact that in general, where *Quaes* overlaps with sections of questions and answers in the "Allegorical Interpretation," there is no substantial difference. Moreover, the question-and-answer form also occurs in the "Exposition of the Laws of Moses," where it does not serve a catechetical aim. Scholars have observed that the question-and-answer form is also found in Greek commentaries on Homer. But it equally occurs in Palestinian exegetical tradition, and Philo may therefore share this influence from Greek exegetical forms with Jewish tradition.

3. Remaining Writings. There has been more uncertainty in the classification of the remaining writings. In general they have been divided into purely philosophical writings (*Aet; Provid; Anim; Quod Omn*) and historical and apologetic treatises (*Flacc;* 118 *Gaium; Vita Cont; Apol Jud; Vita Mos*). E. R. Goodenough (1933: 109–25) has rightly challenged the placement of *De vita Mosis* among the historical and apologetic writings. He has shown that this treatise and the Exposition of the Laws of Moses were companion pieces.

Apart from the questions related to *Vita Mos,* the classification of other writings as historical and apologetic is also rather unsatisfactory. The main weakness of this heading is that it fails to integrate these treatises with the other works of Philo. It therefore also seems pertinent here to start from the fact that Philo was an exegete. Against this background, the classification of these writings should be given the heading: Pentateuchal principles applied to contemporary issues and events.

These writings fall into three groups: (1) Writings in which Pentateuchal material, considered as literal narrative or as an adumbration of deeper principles, is applied to socioreligious factors in the Jewish community. *Apol Jud* and *Vita Cont* fall into this category. (2) Writings in which Pentateuchal principles are applied to, or are developed in dialogue with contemporary philosophical issues and religious phenomena: *Quod Omn, Aet, Provid,* and *Anim.* (3) Writings in which Pentateuchal principles are applied to specific historical events and persons: *Flacc* and *Gaium.*

The preserved fragments of *Apol Jud* deal with events and laws which cover parts of the Pentateuch from Jacob (Genesis 25) to the conquest of Palestine in the books of Joshua and Judges. The emphasis in *Apol Jud* is placed on a characterization of Judaism in Philo's own time, and it can therefore be listed among Philo's writings on contemporary issues.

In *Vita Cont,* Philo tells about the religious community of the Therapeutae to illustrate the aspect of heavenly ascent (*Vita Cont* 11). They are citizens of Heaven even in this life in the world (*Vita Cont* 90). They are in this way model Jews, since to be a true Jew is to be a citizen of Heaven; a proselyte receives a place in Heaven when he becomes a Jew (see for instance *Praem* 152).

The second group of treatises deals with philosophical issues. In these writings Philo uses his interpretation of the laws of Moses in evaluating and developing philosophical notions (see especially *Quod Omn* 42ff.; 53–57; 75–91; *Aet* 13–19; *Provid* I:22; 35; 84).

Even the view expressed by Philo in the treatise *Anim* seems to be selected on the basis of his Jewish attitude, and can be combined with ideas which he puts forward in other writings: the animals know nothing of God, cosmos, law, ancestral customs, state and political life. These attributes are exclusive to man. Some of these Stoic ideas are part of Philo's Exposition of the Laws of Moses. Thus, in saying that the animals know nothing about man's conscious and purposeful art, Philo in *Congr* 141 gives the full Stoic definition of art in the course of his exposition of Gen 16:5. Notwithstanding the Stoic influence, the Mosaic treatment of animals must be considered as the determining factor in moulding his thought. And the philosophical ideas of God, cosmos, ancestral customs, state and political life are points which in several places are central to Philo's interpretation of the Pentateuch. The conclusion is that Philo's views stated in *Anim,* as elsewhere, are influenced by his attitudes and views as a Jew in the sense in which he himself defines Jewish ideas in his other writings.

When Philo draws on Pentateuchal passages and principles in his philosophical writings, he presupposes the kind of exegesis which he has developed in his various expository works. They therefore presuppose Philo's work as an exegete, and do not belong to a period of his life before he had settled down to interpret the laws of Moses.

The hypothesis that Philo's philosophical writings were written prior to his expository works is built on the doubtful assumption that Philo had less interest in philosophy after he began to interpret the Pentateuch. But his expositions show that he was continually drawing on Greek philosophy and philosophical works. Some of the philosophical writings point rather to a later period than to youth: *Alexander,* or *Whether the Animals have Reason,* for example, must have been written some time after the year A.D. 12, and in it there is also probably a reference to the Jewish Alexandrian embassy to Rome in A.D. 39/40 of which Philo himself was the head. And if, as it seems, his own nephew Alexander was old enough to be his dialogue partner, Philo was most probably of advanced age.

It is, therefore, doubtful whether Philo's life should be divided into his philosophical period as a young man and his exegetical period as a mature and old man. He lived all his life in the double context of the Jewish community and the Alexandrian Greek community. Philosophy was Philo's life interest. The dialogues seem to be apologetic writings and thus to fall in line with the rest of his works.

The third group, the writings on contemporary matters, deals with the historical events connected with the pogrom in Alexandria in A.D. 38. The situation is portrayed as a conflict between the Jewish belief that they were the elected people of the one God, the Creator, and the usurpatory claim of power and of divine prerogatives of the Greek *polis* and the Roman emperor.

The connection between the historical writings *Flacc* and *Gaium* and Philo's expository writings can be quite closely drawn. In his exegetical works also Philo at times applies Pentateuchal principles to historical events and persons. Thus as an example of persons who (as seen in Gen 37:9–11) exalt themselves above men and the world of nature, he lists Xerxes, who was punished with insanity. Another example was a governor over Egypt who attempted to disturb the ancestral customs of the Jews (*Somn* II:123ff.).

In *Flacc* and *Gaium* the same approach is followed, in such a way that the Pentateuchal principles—as understood by Philo—are used as an interpretative key, and the actual biblical passages are presupposed as background.

Of particular interest is *Gaium* 3–7, where Philo gives a summary of the main points of his interpretations of the laws of Moses and thus of the Jewish religion. He places emphasis here as elsewhere on God's creative, kingly, and providential powers, and on such of the other powers which serve both beneficial and punitive purposes (*Quod Deus* 77–78; *Plant* 50). This nation, whose God is the Creator, is according to Philo the race of suppliants (§3) in the sense that they serve as link between God and man. God's care for all men is in a sense the outcome of His care for the Jews (cf. *Praem* 44). Philo then tells how Flaccus and Gaius Caligula proved to be enemies of the Jews (*Flacc* 24 *Gaium* 373), but were in reality enemies of God himself: Flaccus was puffed up with arrogance (*Flacc* 124; 152), and Gaius even overstepped the bounds of human nature and claimed to be god (*Gaium* 75; 367f.).

Philo here narrates theologically interpreted history. In this respect these treatises show a similarity to history writing in the Old Testament, in Judaism, and in the New Testament. In the New Testament especially, the Passion narrative in the Gospels and the persecutions of the early church according to the Acts of the Apostles describe historical events and interpret them on the basis of the Old Testament. As for Philo's specific point about rulers being punished for their blasphemous arrogance, the brief story in Acts 12:20–23 applies this principle to the same King Herod who aided the Alexandrian Jews: "And the people shouted, 'The voice of a god, and not of a man!' Immediately an angel of the Lord smote him, because he did not give God the glory; and he was eaten by worms and died."

Philo's works are based on the interpretation of the Pentateuch, although also other LXX books are used. The predominance of his use of the Pentateuch probably reflects the reading practice in the Alexandrian synagogues. In this case, Pentateuchal pericopes were read in the synagogal gatherings, and other writings would have been drawn upon only in expositions or in other parts of the services. It should also be added here that the Pentateuchal books would be of special interest to the Jewish community in Egypt, since Egypt and the Exodus are central geographical and theological elements in these books.

Since Philo builds his exegesis on the Greek text of the LXX, he develops a theological understanding of this translation: the LXX is an exact and inspired translation of the Hebrew original. Moreover, it has a central role, since it serves as a revelation of the sacred writings to the Greek-speaking part of mankind. In spite of this fact, many details of the textual affinities of Philo's LXX text are uncertain, particularly because he sometimes departs from the LXX readings. The reason is that in the paraphrasing expositions Philo deals with the text as an active exegete; moreover, he works exegetical traditions into his paraphrase. Thus, it is impossible to reconstruct an original LXX text on the basis of his exegesis.

The question whether Philo knew Hebrew has been much discussed, but no consensus has been reached. The question is not of decisive importance, however. He undertakes etymological interpretations based on Hebrew, and he employs some traditions which were common to Greek-speaking and Hebrew-speaking Jews. He may have relied on written documents or on oral traditions in the Synagogues. Philo's broad knowledge and his role and place in the Jewish community suggest that he used both kinds of sources.

C. Philo and the Jewish Community in Alexandria

The situation of the strong Jewish community in Alexandria from the Roman takeover in 30 B.C. to the settlement of the increasing unrest by the Emperor Claudius in A.D. 41 has been subject to thorough examination.

The general conclusion can be summed up in this way: the Romans made a distinction between, on the one hand, the citizens of the Greek cities and the Hellenes of the provincial towns and villages, and on the other, the native Egyptian population. The first group was either exempted from the poll tax, in the case of the Greek citizens, or paid a lower rate, as did the Hellenes, while the native Egyptians paid the tax in full. For the Jews in Alexandria, therefore, the question of their legal status was a burning issue, and they pressed for equal status with the Greek citizens of the city. The Greek citizens, on the other hand, tried to deprive the Jews of the privileges granted them by the Emperor Augustus and wished the Jews to be classified together with the native Egyptians.

After Gaius Caligula became emperor in A.D. 37, this state of cultural, judicial, and religious strife led to anti-Jewish riots which grew into a pogrom. A military uprising by the Jews against the Greeks followed in A.D. 41 on the death of Gaius Caligula and the accession of Claudius to the throne. Jews from Palestine and Egypt took part in the armed revolt, as can be seen from the fact that Claudius forbade the Alexandrian Jews to permit Jews from Syria and Egypt to enter the city. The emperor, furthermore, would not permit Jews to participate in the various activities connected with the gymnasium.

From these observations the following hypothesis can be formulated: It is probable that some Jews in Alexandria were content with the status quo under which they were permitted to live according to their own laws and customs as a separate *politeuma* of its own. Furthermore, it is certain that others coveted Greek citizenship for the sake of higher social and political prestige and greater economic advantages.

Strong forces among the Alexandrian Jews, however, seem to have entertained the (eschatological) expectations that other nations would acknowledge the law of Moses, and the people of God, the Jews, as the center of the world. Among these Jews there seem to have been two different perspectives as to methods which should be used. Some were in favor of using force, even arms, if necessary. The armed revolt by the Jews in Alexandria in 41 seems to have been inspired by such convictions, since the rebels were able to motivate even Jews from Syria and Egypt to come and join them. Others among the Alexandrian Jews advocated that the Jews were to conquer their surroundings by peaceful means; i.e., by their religion, based on the laws given by the Creator, and by their growing prosperity. Philo was of this opinion. In *Vita Mos* II:44, he expresses the conviction that increased prosperity and progress among the Jews will lead other nations to accept the laws of Moses; and Philo's writings serve the general aim of interpreting these laws to the surrounding world and preparing the Jews for their universal task.

Accordingly, in *Somn* II:83, Philo advises his fellow Jews to be cautious and not to use revolutionary provocations in their dealings with the non-Jewish political authorities: ". . . Surely then they are all lunatics and madmen who take pains to display untimely frankness, and sometimes dare to oppose kings and tyrants in words and deeds. They do not perceive that not only are their necks under the yoke like cattle, but that the harness also extends to their whole bodies and souls, their wives and children and parents, and the wide circle of friends and kinsfolk. . . ." The conclusion drawn from this evidence is that Philo supported the policy that Jews should participate actively in the social life of Alexandria. He therefore belonged himself to those who infiltrated the Greek milieu centered around the gymnasium. At the same time, however, he attacked and passionately criticized pagan worships and pagan life-standards.

Among the burning issues are mentioned the paying of fees and participation in the life of the clubs. Reluctantly, Philo says: ". . . when the object is the share in the best of possessions, prudence, such payments are praiseworthy and profitable; but when they are paid to obtain that supreme evil, folly, the practice is unprofitable" (*Ebr* 20ff.), and it can lead to Egyptian animal worship (*Ebr* 95). Another issue is participation in the triennial festivals of athletic contests, which were organized by the cities. To Philo, these festivals are examples of contests in rivalry, lust, anger, and licentiousness. A Jew should try to avoid participation in these, but if compelled to take part, he should not hesitate to be defeated (*Agr* 110–21). In *b. Giṭṭin* 47a we find an example of this attitude. According to this text, Simeon S. Lakish at one period of his life was a professional gladiator. He justified this on the ground of grim necessity.

The treatise *De Josepho* reflects problems related to sexual ethics and to table fellowship. In *Jos* 42ff. and in 56–57 the difference is pointed out between the Hebrew nation and other nations in sexual ethics and marriage laws. The Hebrews have strict customs and strict laws on marital matters, while licentiousness has destroyed the youth of the Greek race and the barbarians. In Egypt it is easy for Jewish youth to leave the ancestral way of life and change to alien ways, because the Egyptians deify things created and mortal and are blind to the true God (*Jos* 254).

Another area of tension was that of table fellowship. Joseph gave a feast both for his own family and for Egyptians. Joseph feasted each party according to its ancestral practice, but Philo adds that the Egyptians followed the same seating order as the Hebrews. The Egyptians indicated that in other times the style of life in their country was less civilized, until Joseph introduced good order (*Jos* 202–6).

Philo speaks of Jewish institutions in Alexandria. He refers to the Jewish council of elders. There were many synagogues in each section of the town, and one synagogue was very large and notable. He often describes how the synagogues function, stressing the reading and explanation of the Bible: "And will you sit in your conventicles and assemble your regular company and read in security your holy books, expounding any obscure point and in leisurely comfort discussing at length your ancestral philosophy." Unfortunately, he does not provide any definite information about Jewish education or his own part in it. With regard to the LXX Philo refers to an old custom "to hold every year a feast and general assembly in the island of Pharos, whither not only Jews but multitudes of others cross the water, to do honour to the place in which the light of that version shone out."

Philo's writings show that he had a wide Greek education. He has an excellent command of Greek, a good literary style, and knows many Greek philosophers and writers. Some conclusion about Philo's knowledge of Greek philosophy may be drawn from explicit quotations, and the philosophical ideas he uses. Stoicism, Pythagoreanism, and Platonic traditions predominate. Philo's view that general education prepares for philosophy and his definition of philosophy as "the practice or study of wisdom, which is the knowledge of things divine and human in their causes." (*Congr* 79) are Stoic, as is also his division of philosophy into logic, ethics, and physics. From the Platonic tradition he takes over the distinction between the "forms" or ideas and the visible world, and between soul and body. From the Pythagoreans come speculations on numbers. Philo also shows familiarity with other philosophical schools and with Greek literature in general.

Non-Jewish sources have been incorporated in such a way that on the whole little identification of authors seems possible, but in some cases names of philosophers and authors are given.

D. Philo as Biblical Exegete

With regard to Philo's exegetical aims and methods, some scholars see him as the main representative of Hellenistic Diaspora Judaism, in contrast to Palestinian Judaism as represented in the rabbinic sources. This distinction does not do justice to Philo's own view of the situation. While he is involved in debates with fellow Jews in Alexandria, their views may, from this perspective, reflect debates in Judaism in general, Palestine included. Philo is primarily an exegete. Sometimes he agrees with other exegetes, sometimes he supplements them, and often he repudiates them; but he does not reveal the identity, whereabouts, or social status of his partners in debate. Indeed, more research is needed to examine whether his interlocutors represent specific schools. Tentatively, the following observations can be made.

Philo seems to refer to two different varieties of exegetes who championed literal exegesis. One was faithful to Judaism, while the other used literal exegesis to attack and ridicule the Pentateuch and Judaism. Some of the views of the "faithful literalists" are: in Deut 34:4 God humiliates Moses by not permitting him to enter the promised land; in Gen 11:7–8 the confusion of tongues refers to the origin of the Greek and barbarian languages; Gen 26:19–32 tells about actual digging of wells; in Exod 22:26–27 material return of garment is meant; the consistency of the rules about leprosy in Lev 14:34–36 is a matter of discussion. In arguing with the other group, Philo reflects disputes between non-Jews or Jewish apostates and Jews. The treatise *On the Change of Names* serves as defense against the literalism of a jester whom Philo himself had heard, and who committed suicide as a punishment from God (*Mut* 60–

62). The change of one letter in Abram/Abraham and Sarai/Sarah is ridiculed by this group, as is the story of Jacob and Esau and their food; some of them maintain that the Bible contains myths (such as the story about the tower of Babel) similar to those which Jews themselves ridicule when recited by others. *On the Confusion of Tongues* serves also as defense against such mockery.

Philo also tells of Jews who used allegory to such an extent that valid Jewish custom was undermined. The central passage is *Migr* 89–93:

> There are some who, regarding laws in their literal sense in the light of symbols of matters belonging to the intellect, are overpunctilious about the latter, while treating the former with easygoing neglect. Such men I for my part should blame for handling the matter in too easy and off-hand a manner: they ought to have given careful attention to both aims, to a more full and exact investigation of what is not seen and what is seen, to be stewards without reproach. As it is as though they were living alone by themselves in a wilderness, or as though they had become disembodied souls, and knew neither city nor village nor household nor any company of human beings at all, overlooking all that the mass of men regard, they explore reality in its naked absoluteness. These men are taught by the sacred word to have thought for good repute, and to let go nothing that is part of the customs fixed by divinely empowered men greater than those of our time. It is quite true that the Seventh Day to meant to teach the power of the Unoriginate and the non-action of created beings. But let us not for this reason abrogate the laws laid down for its observance, and light fires or till the ground or carry loads or institute proceedings in court or act as jurors or demand the restoration of deposits or recover loans, or do all else that we are permitted to do as well on days that are not festival seasons. It is true also that the Feast is a symbol of gladness of soul and of thankfulness to God, but we should not for this reason turn our backs on the general gatherings of the year's seasons. It is true that receiving circumcision does indeed portray the excision of pleasure and all passions, and the putting away of the impious conceit, under which the mind supposed that it was capable of begetting by its own power: but let us not on this account repeal the law laid down for circumcising. Why, we shall be ignoring the sanctity of the Temple and a thousand other things, if we are going to pay heed to nothing except what is shown us by the inner meaning of things. Nay we should look on all these outward observances as resembling the body, and their inner meanings as resembling the soul. It follows that, exactly as we have to take thought for the body because it is the abode of the soul, so we must pay heed to the letter of the laws. If we keep and observe these, we shall gain a clearer conception of those things of which these are symbols; and besides that we shall not incur the censure of the many and the charges they are sure to bring against us (Loeb ed.).

In this passage, Philo summarizes his attitude as an exegete. The allegorical, though higher and more important, practically never invalidates the literal. (Only exceptionally does Philo discard the literal meaning altogether or allow it only a limited role.) Philo combines literal and allegorical methods of exegesis, stressing allegorical exposition against literalists and the literal sense against overspiritualization.

Philo discusses other views which do not readily sort into the classes of literal and allegorical exegesis, although they may be combined with such an approach. As an example, we quote the following: "There are some whose definition of reverence is that it consists in saying that all things were made by God, both beautiful things and their opposites. We would say to these, one part of your opinion is praiseworthy, the other part on the contrary is faulty . . ."

The sources of Philo's allegorical method have been much discussed. Did he draw on Greek allegorical methods (especially as employed by the Stoics on Homer) or on Jewish traditions? He undoubtedly followed the Stoics, who read natural phenomena and ethical norms into Homer, though Philo emphasized the ethical, which he based on his concept of God. But other parallels are found in the Haggadah, especially as regards the idealization of the patriarchs and other biblical persons, often by means of etymologies.

It may be maintained that Philo attempts to make the allegorical method serve his aims as a Jewish exegete. In this respect, his allegorical interpretation shows affinities with the hermeneutical concept of prophecy and fulfillment. He spells out abstract principles which he sees in the biblical text, and these in turn can be applied to individuals and the Jewish community, serving to interpret specific events. Philo also adapts allegorical interpretation to the Jewish notion of election, which he uses to claim for the Jews and their sacred writings elements from Greek philosophy, education, ethics, and religion. Conversely, to Philo, allegorical interpretation is a way in which the wisdom of the laws of Moses and Jewish religious institutions can be disclosed to the world.

Philo often indicates that he uses other Jewish sources as well as the Bible. He refers to these sources in *On the Life of Moses:* "But I will . . . tell the story of Moses as I have learned it, both from the sacred books . . . and from some of the elders of the nation; for I always interwove what I was told with what I read." The question arises here whether Philo depended only on local Jewish tradition, or also on wider ones, including Palestinian Haggadah and Halakah. Philo's own visit to Jerusalem, his knowledge of conditions and events in Palestine, the frequent contacts between Alexandrian and Palestinian Jews, and the fact that both groups recognized the Temple of Jerusalem as their center, at least strongly indicate that Philo knew and followed Palestinian traditions. This conclusion is confirmed by a comparison of Philo with the rabbinic writings.

Philo practiced the common Halakah with regards to worship in the Temple of Jerusalem, the Temple tax, and pictures and statues in Temple and synagogues. His visit to the Temple may indicate that he recognized its rules about calendar and sacrifices. Philo knew of the conflicts between Pilate and the Jewish authorities in Palestine arising from the Halakah. In some cases where Philo's views are in conflict with the rabbinic Halakah, it can be proved that they represent an earlier stage of common practice (Alon 1977). Examples of haggadic views in Philo which have parallels in the rabbinic writings are: the rivalry among the stars as to precedence, the angel who appeared to Moses in the burning bush being the image of God; Moses growing extraordinarily fast; why Adam was last to be created; the manna and the well not conforming to the regular sequence of rain from heaven and bread from earth.

E. Central Ideas and Perspectives

At times Philo maintains that God is unknowable, transcending virtue and the good and the beautiful. He is "that which exists" *(tò on),* or "he who exists" *(ho ōn).* But, although God himself is unknowable, his activities, which are called his powers *(dynameis)* can be known. Central powers are: God's activity in creating the world, represented by the name "God" *(Theos),* and his continued activity in governing the world, indicated by the name "Lord" *(Kyrios).* The universe consists of the intelligible and the sensible world, both created and governed by God. God's powers are in the intelligible sphere, but reach into this world and are knowable by man.

Philo's technical use of the term *Logos* connotes God's mental activity during the act of creating. The parable of the architect in *Op* 15–25 illustrates this point: Philo tells about an architect who made a model of the various parts of the city he was to build. Similarly, *Pirqe R. El.* 3, portrays a king who wanted to build a palace, and first modeled on the ground its foundations, entrances, and exits. According to Philo, the architect thought out in his mind how he should build. Similarly, in an anonymous midrash, it is stressed that the man first sat and calculated how he wanted the building (Urbach 1975: 1.200–1). Philo applies this picture to the creation of the world; and he identifies the intellectual planning of the architect with Logos, meaning God's mental activity during the act of creating. Similarly, the parable of the architect in the anonymous midrash is supported by Ps 33:6: "By the word of the Lord the heavens were made." In his use of the parable of the architect, Philo thus to a large degree stays within the context of Jewish exegesis of the creation story. Nevertheless, Philo develops a philosophical exegesis on this basis. He focuses the attention on the intellectual activity of the architect, and in this way the model is not an "empirical" sketch or model, but the image of the city in the mind of the architect. Thus, the parable expresses the idea that the model of the world is the intelligible world (of ideas) conceived by God before he created the world perceived by the senses. Here Jewish exegetical tradition about God as architect and Stoic and Platonic terminology and thought categories are brought together in a synthesis. The Logos, as one of the powers of the intelligible world, reaches into our world, mainly through the mediators Moses and Aaron, both called Logos. The plural *logoi* can indicate the heavenly principles which are embodied in the laws and precepts given to the Jews through Moses.

In another sense, the Logos and the logoi may be conceived as heavenly figures such as angels and archangels. The Logos is also called a "second god," or God's firstborn. This Logos has many names: "the beginning," "the name of God," "the man after his image," and "he that sees" (Israel). The meaning of Philo's Logos is therefore complex: it embraces the scriptural "word," biblical figures, heavenly beings, the laws of Moses and Platonic and Stoic elements. In some places Philo uses the related concept of wisdom, *Sophia.* When Sarah is a cosmic and heavenly figure she can be named Sophia, following Jewish Wisdom tradition.

Philo sometimes uses sexual imagery to describe the relationship between God and the world. The contrast between male and female means the contrast between the spiritual and the irrational or between the eternal and the transitory. Matter is female, while form and logos is male. The highest Logos and God himself are essentially asexual.

In Philo's anthropology, humans consist of soul and body, but Philo utilizes a variety of concepts such as soul, mind, and spirit. He distinguishes between the lower mind and soul, which operate within the context of sense perception and are mortal, and the higher mind and soul, which are indestructible and immortal. In Philo the higher soul does not have primarily an individualistic sense. In *On Drunkenness* 36–37 Philo writes: "He (Moses) in his wisdom was recalling the whole *people of the soul* to piety and to honouring God and was teaching them commandments and holy laws." Thus "the soul" is associated with piety, the honoring of God, the commandments and holy laws, the very characteristics of the Jewish people, in contrast with "a city of commonwealth peopled by a promiscuous horde, who swing to and fro as their idle opinions carry them."

Philo's dualism must also be connected with the distinction made between the chosen people, the Jews, and other nations. Philo combines an ethical dualism between heaven and earth and between soul and body with the dualism between Judaism and the pagan world. For example, the Jews who make education, wealth, and office serve the heavenly values, as manifested in the laws of Moses, bring heaven to rule over earth. If, on the other hand, the Jews have luxurious living, political careers, and licentiousness as their objectives, they join with the earthly, pagan disorder. Accordingly, when Philo interprets references to Egypt and Egyptians allegorically to mean the body, passions, moral values, etc., he combines these two aspects of his dualism: Egypt and Egyptian represent the pagans in contrast to the Jewish nation, and at the same time they represent evil body over against the Jewish nation which has the heavenly quality of the soul. When Jews yield to the somatic passions and other evils, they then join with the Egyptians in their vices.

Looking for a dominant feature in Philo's thought, some scholars have pointed to the tendency to bridge the gap between the transcendent God and man by intermediaries, such as Logos, the powers, etc. This is not enough. To Philo, it is specifically the Jewish people which intermediates between God and man. The notion of the cosmic and universal significance of Israel dominates in this thought.

The center of Jewish existence is Jerusalem and its Temple. All Jews see Jerusalem as mother city, their metropolis. Its earthly buildings are not its totality, but essentially represent God's cosmos. Surprisingly, the Logos is equally characterized as a "metropolis," and Philo regards Jerusalem as a manifestation of the divine Logos spoken by God when he created the world. Indeed the chief, surest, and best mother city—which is more than just a city—is the Divine Logos, and to take refuge in it is supremely advantageous. Furthermore, Philo seems to expect that all Jews of the Diaspora would be brought back to Jerusalem and the Holy Land in the eschatological age.

Equally, the Temple in Jerusalem is an earthly counterpart of the cosmic heavenly Temple:

> The highest and in the truest sense the holy, temple of God is, as we must believe, the whole cosmos, having for its sanctuary the most sacred part of all existence, even heven, for its votive ornaments the stars, for its priests the angels who are servitors to His powers . . . There is also the temple made by hands; for it was right that no check should be given to the forwardness of those who pay their tribute to piety and desire by means of sacrifices either to give thanks for the blessings that befall them or to ask for pardon and forgiveness for their sins. But he provided that there should not be temples built either in many places or many in the same place, for he judged that since God is one there should be also only one temple (Loeb ed.).

Of the Levitic priests, Philo says that their perfection of body and soul makes them the image of God. This requisite perfection of body is a token of the perfection of the immortal soul, fashioned after the image of God, i.e. of the Logos through whom the whole universe was created. So, the high priest in the Jerusalem Temple is the true portrait of man.

Again, the biblical picture of Aaron as a mediator and as Moses' interpreter is developed into the high priest as the sacred Logos who separates and walls off holy thoughts from the unholy. Aaron was Logos in utterance, and the perfect interpreter. Along the lines of Jewish tradition, Philo attributes cosmic significance to the high priest. His vestments symbolize the whole cosmos, he is consecrated to the Father of the world, and thus is invested with universal meaning for the service of the Creator. The worship of the One God is seen in contrast to the erroneous polytheism of other nations. Therefore, it is worship on behalf of all mankind: through the Levites, the Jewish nation is the priesthood of all nations.

Philo's explanation of the feasts, of which only the Sabbath can be mentioned here, is illuminating. Jews, he says, regard the Sabbath with great reverence and will not yield to political authorities who want to abolish it. Already in the Pentateuch, the celebration of the Sabbath is founded on creation (Gen 2:2–3), and Philo is fertile in his interpretation of the Sabbath and its cosmic role. For instance, he elaborates in Pythagorean fashion on the number seven. One example out of many may be given: Moses recognized in the seventh day the birth of the world, celebrated in heaven and on earth, as all things rejoice in the full harmony of the sacred number seven. Hence, the Hebrew people, who follow the laws of nature, must celebrate this festival too. Basically, feasts and joy belong to God alone, for God alone is entirely blessed, exempt from all evil. But from this joy of God the joy of man flows, as a mixed stream.

The above illustrates how Philo gives a cosmic and universal relevance to Jerusalem, the Temple and the Sabbath, as also to the laws of the Jewish nation and the role of Moses. By introducing his laws into the story of creation, Moses implies that the universe is in harmony with the Law and the Law with the world. Thus the man who observes the Law is constituted a loyal citizen of the world. Primarily, this is Moses, a true cosmopolitan, in accordance with the development of that idea. In the second place, the people of Israel is meant.

Like Aaron the high priest, Moses is a messenger and mediator between God and man. As such, he is identified with an archangel, or with the Logos and in this capacity says: "and I stood between the Lord and you" (Deut 5:5), that is neither uncreated as God, nor created as you, but midway between the two extremes, a surety to both sides, . . . For I am the harbinger of peace to creation from that God whose will is to bring wars to an end, who is ever the guardian of peace. Similarly, Moses was one among the many angels when he mediated at Sinai and spoke on God's behalf to the people. He served as one of the logoi. Philo can even say that God sent Moses as a loan to the earthly sphere.

In *Vita Mos* 1:158 Philo interprets Moses' ascent of Mount Sinai to mean that he ascended into the realm of God. In rabbinic writings the same interpretation is found, and both Philo and the rabbis see Moses as god and king (cf. Exod 7:1). This explains Moses' authority: Though a figure of the past, he still is to determine the lives of Jews in the time after him. In his ascent and vision of the divine world they are to imitate him. They are Moses' disciples.

It was Moses who communicated the basic self-revelation of God as "I am He that is." This means that "God alone has veritable being," and that God's nature is to be, not to be spoken. Yet, so that the human race should not lack a title to give to the supreme goodness, he allows them to use the title of "Lord God."

In his references to examples and persons outside Judaism, Philo can use various lines of argumentation. In his discussion of the free men (in: *Quod Omn*) he says that the various levels of freedom of the worthy man receives their full dimension and true expression in Moses and in those who follow him in worshipping the Self-existent only. At several places Philo maintains that the Greek philosophers drew their thought from Moses and his Laws, *Heres* 214, *Leg All* I:108, *Spec Leg* IV:61, *Post* 133, *Quaes Gen* IV:152, *Quod Omn* 53–57, *Congr* 176. In agreement with this, Philo pictures Moses as the embodiment of all knowledge and wisdom. Although Moses had Egyptian and Greek teachers, he was independent in his apprehension so that he seemed a case rather of recollection than of learning.

Abraham, the ancestor of the Jewish race, is at the same time the prototype of proselytes, since he left his native country and its polytheism to discover the One God. In doing so he gained all the other virtues. Philo distinguishes three types of men: the earth-born, the heaven-born, and the true men of God. Abraham began as a man born of heaven, searching into the nature of the ethereal region. Later, he became a man of God, and the God of the Universe was his God in a special sense and by a special grace. The sons of earth are those who follow the pleasures of the body. By combining these notions, we see that the sons of earth are in fact pagans or apostates. The men of heaven are pagans who, like young Abraham, seek heaven and the Creator. The men of God then are the Jews, who like the older Abraham are wholly owned by God.

Philo's concept of revelation can now be better understood. According to some scholars, he distinguishes in a general way between the lesser mystery of knowing God through creation and the greater mystery in which man experiences the vision of God himself. This distinction should be understood more specifically on the basis of the difference between Jews and other men: the chosen people received the revelation of God. Although other men share in a certain knowledge of God through creation and reason, it is only through the revelation received by the Jews that man is truly known by God.

F. The Significance of Philo

Scholars have interpreted Philo in a variety of ways. He has been seen as a great (Pharisaic) system builder and philosopher (Wolfson); as a representative of anti-normative Hellenistic Judaism, a Jewish mystery religion (Goodenough); as a representative of gnosticism (Jonas, Klein, Käsemann, etc.); or as a representative of Middle Platonism (Theiler, Früchtel, Dillon, Pearson). Since Philo combines motifs of Platonic/Pythagorean and Stoic nature, he shows obvious kinship with Middle Platonism. These Greek elements of Middle Platonic background are woven together with biblical and Jewish notions. His writings reflect the fact that different streams and traditions were present in Alexandrian Judaism. Philo's own emphasis on heavenly ascent and the complementary roles of ruler (Moses) and law-abiding person suggests that he draws on traditions from early Jewish mysticism. Furthermore, Philo and mystical Judaism share the idea of a heavenly being or angel, Israel, understood by means of a pseudo-etymology to mean "the one who sees God."

Was Philo then fundamentally Greek or Jewish? His loyalty to the Jewish institutions, the laws of Moses, the role of Israel as the priesthood of the world, and his harshness against renegades (even to the point of advocating lynching) shows that he was fundamentally a Jew. When Philo draws on Greek philosophy and various notions from pagan religions, his intention was not to compromise Jewish convictions and aims. He was such an extreme Jew that he referred all ideas and phenomena of value, also including those outside Judaism, to Moses as their origin and/or authentic formulation. Whatever good there was had its source in Scripture and thus belonged to the Jewish nation and its heritage. Consequently, being so extreme in his claims, he was on the verge of ending at the other extreme, that of being overcome by the ideas he wished to conquer. In this way, Philo's extreme form of particularism risked ending up in a universalism where Jewish distinctiveness was in danger of being lost.

Philo may have belonged to an elite group, small in number within the Jewish community of Alexandria. Nevertheless, his place is clearly within the community in such a way that he took part in debates and conflicts among different Jewish streams, and understood himself to represent traditions and interpretations of the synagogues, the Jewish schools of philosophy.

Philo reflects more firsthand knowledge of Hellenistic culture in general and Greek philosophy in particular than earlier Alexandrian Jewish writers, though direct historical lines can be drawn from Aristobulus' allegorical and philosophical exegesis and the philosophical language of the Wisdom of Solomon to Philo. Philo was literally the culmination of a literary tradition within Alexandrian Judaism: apparently, no significant works were produced after him by Alexandrian Jews.

Philo remained almost unknown in Jewish tradition until the 16th century. It was the Christian Church which preserved and adopted Philo; Byzantine anthologies even cite excerpts of Philo under the heading "of Philo the Bishop." Clement of Alexandria, Origen, and Ambrose were influenced by Philo in their allegorical exegesis and their use of such concepts as wisdom, Logos, and faith.

In modern historical research, Philo is studied as a source for Greek philosophy, as a representative of Second Temple Judaism and as a forerunner of early Christian thought. As for the latter, Philo has especially been studied to throw light on the concept of Logos in the Gospel of John, on Platonisms in the Epistle to the Hebrews, and on exegetical techniques and forms used in the New Testament. Philo's writings reflect a variety of movements within Judaism in the time of the beginnings of Christianity, and this observation has thrown light on some of its conflicts and debates, particularly in relation to Judaism and the Hellenistic world.

Bibliography

Texts and Translations

Machine-readable Greek Text of Philo's Works. (The Cohn-Wendland Text and the Greek Fragments). Ed. P. Borgen and R. Skarsten. Trondheim and Bergen, 1972. Magnetic Tape.

Les Oeuvres de Philon d'Alexandrie. Ed. R. Arnaldez; L. Pouilloux; and C. Mondésert. 35 Vols. Paris, 1961–79.

Philo, with an English Translation. Ed. F. H. Colson; G. H. Whittaker; and R. Marcus. 10 Vols and 2 Supplementary Vols. LCL. Cambridge, MA, and London. 1929–62.

Philonis Alexandrini de Animalibus. The Armenian Text with an Introduction, Translation and Commentary by A. Terian. Chico, CA. 1981.

Philonis Alexandrini opera quae supersunt. Ed. L. Cohn and P. Wendland. 7 Vols in 8. Berlin, 1896–1930. Repr. Berlin, 1962. Editio Maior.

Die Werke Philos von Alexandria in deutscher Übersetzung. Ed. L. Cohn; I. Heinemann; M. Adler; H. Lewy; J. Cohn; and W. Theiler. 7 vols. Breslau and Berlin, 1909–1964.

Bibliographies. Surveys of Research. Concordances

Borgen, P. 1984. Philo of Alexandria. A Critical and Synthetical Survey of Research since World War II. *ANRW* 2/21/1: 97–154.

Borgen, P., and Skarsten, R. 1973. *Complete KWIC-Concordance of Philo's Writings.* Trondheim/Bergen. Magnetic Tape.

Feldman, L. H. 1963. *Scholarship on Philo and Josephus (1937–1962).* New York.

Goodhart, H. L., and Goodenough, E. R. 1938. A General Bibliography of Philo. Pp. 125–348 in Goodenough 1938.

Hilgert, E. 1984. Bibliographia Philoniana 1935–1981. *ANRW* 2/21/1: 27–97.

Marcus, R. 1935. Recent Literature on Philo (1924–1934). Pp. 463–91 in *Jewish Studies in Memory of George A. Kohut,* ed. S. W. Baron and A. Marx. New York.

Mayer, G. 1974. *Index Philoneus.* Berlin.

Nazzaro, A. V. 1973. *Recenti Studi Philoniani (1963–1970).* Naples.

Radice, R. 1983. *Filone di Alessandria: Bibliografia Generale 1937–1982*. Naples.
Radice, R., and Runia, D. T. 1988. *Philo of Alexandria: An Annotated Bibliography 1937–1986*. Leiden.
Thyen, H. 1955. Die Probleme der neueren Philo-Forschung. *TRev* n.s. 23: 230–46.
Völker, W. 1938. *Fortschritt und Vollendung bei Philo von Alexandrien*. TU 49. Leipzig.

Other Works

Alon, G. 1977. On Philo's Halakha. Pp. 89–137 in *Jews, Judaism and the Classical World,* ed. G. Alon. Jerusalem.
Amir, Y. 1983. *Die hellenistische Gestalt des Judentums bei Philon von Alexandrien*. Neukirchen-Vluyn.
Belkin, S. 1984. *Philo and the Oral Law*. Cambridge, MA.
Borgen, P. 1965. *Bread from Heaven*. Leiden. Repr. 1981.
———. 1984. Philo of Alexandria. Vol. 2/2, pp. 233–82 in *Jewish Writings of the Second Temple Period,* ed. M. Stone. CRINT 2 Philadelphia.
———. 1986. *Philo, John, Paul*. Brown Judaica Series. Atlanta.
Borgen, P., and Skarsten, R. 1976–77. Quaestiones et solutiones: Some Observations on the Form of Philo's Exegesis. *StPhilon* 4: 1–15.
Bréhier, E. 1908. *Les Idees Philosophiques et Religieuses de Philon d'Alexandrie*. Paris.
Chadwick, H. 1966. St. Paul and Philo of Alexandria. *BJRL* 48: 286–307.
Christiansen, I. 1969. *Die Technik der allegorischen Auslegungswissenschaft bei Philon von Alexandrien*. Tübingen.
Cohn, L. 1899. Einteilung und Chronologie der Schriften Philos. *Philologus* Sup 7: 385–435.
Daniélou, J. 1958. *Philon d'Alexandrie*. Paris.
Dillon, J. 1977. *The Middle Platonists*. London.
Früchtel, U. 1968. *Die kosmologischen Vorstellungen bei Philo von Alexandrien*. Leiden.
Goodenough, E. 1929. *The Jurisprudence of the Jewish Courts in Egypt*. New Haven. Repr. Amsterdam, 1968.
———. 1933. Philo's Exposition of the Law and his De Vita Mosis. *HTR* 26: 109–25.
———. 1935. *By Light, Light*. New Haven.
———. 1938. *The Politics of Philo Judaeus*. New Haven. Repr. Hildesheim, 1967.
———. 1940. *An Introduction to Philo Judaeus*. New Haven.
Heinemann, I. 1932. *Philons griechische und jüdische Bildung*. Breslau. Repr. Hildesheim, 1962.
Käsemann, E. 1939. *Das wandernde Gottesvolk*. Göttingen.
Klein, F. -N. 1962. *Die Lichtterminologie bei Philon von Alexandrien und in den Hermetischen Schriften*. Leiden.
Meeks, W. 1967. *The Prophet-King*. Leiden.
Mendelsohn, A. 1982. *Secular Education in Philo of Alexandria*. Cincinnati.
Nikiprowetzky, V. 1977. *Le commentaire de l'Ecriture chez Philon d'Alexandrie*. Leiden.
Otte, I. 1968. *Das Sprachverständnis bei Philo von Alexandrien*. Tübingen.
Pearson, B. 1984. Philo and Gnosticism. *ANRW* 2/21/1: 295–342.
Runia, D. 1986. *Philo of Alexandria and the Timaeus of Philo*. Vols. 1–2. Leiden.
Sandmel, S. 1979. *Philo of Alexandria: An Introduction*. New York.
Smallwood, E. M. 1976. *The Jews under Roman Rule*. Leiden.
Tcherikover, V. A. 1963. The Decline of the Jewish Diaspora in the Roman Period. *JJS* 14: 1–32.
Urbach, E. 1975. *The Sages: Their Concepts and Beliefs*. 2 vols. Jerusalem.
Williamson, R. 1970. *Philo and the Epistle to the Hebrews*. Leiden.
Wilson, R. McL. 1972. Philo of Alexandria and Gnosticism. *Kairos* 14: 213–19.
Winston, D., and Dillon, J. 1983. *Two Treatises of Philo of Alexandria*. BJS 25. Chico, CA.
Wolfson, H. A. 1947. *Philo*. Vols. 1–2. Cambridge, MA.

Peder Borgen

PHILO OF BYBLOS. One of a number of learned scholars of Near Eastern origin active in the Roman empire. He was born ca. A.D. 70 and died in 160; we have no information where he lived, although Byblos and Rome are the obvious possibilities. His circle of friends centered around the ex-consul Herennius Severus, and included men such as Hermippos of Beirut, an exceedingly learned slave, who wrote *Concerning Dreams*. Philo himself was the author of several works. Worthy of particular notice is his encyclopedic compilation *Concerning Cities and the Illustrious Men Each of Them Produced*. This book was eventually abridged, and while it has not survived either whole or in abridgement, numerous citations from it can be found in the writings of Stephanus of Byzantium (who lived in the 7th century A.D.).

Philo is, however, best known for his *Phoenician History (PH)*. The *PH* has not been preserved intact, and we know it only through the mediation of Eusebius of Caesarea (ca. 260–340), who quoted extensively from it in his *Praeparatio Evangelica*. The *PH* suited Eusebius's apologetic and polemical interests almost perfectly. The principal pagan competitors of Christianity in his day were mystery cults, often based on allegorizing or physiologizing interpretations of myths. Philo opposed mystery cults as humbuggery, and strongly rejected allegorizing and physiologizing interpretations. Philo argued for a Euhemeristic interpretation of mythology, maintaining that the gods of myth were either immortal forces of nature or humans deified for their contribution to culture by a grateful posterity. As such, Philo provided Eusebius with a pagan witness whom he could employ to attack pagan opponents.

The excerpts preserved by Eusebius do not read as a smooth whole. Transitions are abrupt, and there are rarely more than two sentences devoted to any topic; hence Philo's comments are often difficult to understand. This obscurity may explain part of the fascination Philo has held for scholars over the centuries. More substantial reasons for scholarly interest in Philo are the obvious importance of the Phoenicians for understanding the background of the biblical world, and the desire to evaluate the material preserved by Philo in the light of our growing knowledge of the ANE. Indeed, for the past century, work on Philo has usually been undertaken under the influence of the latest discoveries from the Near East: there was a new impetus to read Philo at the time of the discovery of ancient Babylonian literature, and a similar wave in the aftermath of the publication of Ugaritic and Hittite myths. The latest scholarly tendency, however, has been to emphasize that Philo was an author in the Hellenistic-Roman world, and to balance interpretations of his work in ANE terms against those that employ the culture Philo himself knew as a frame of reference.

Philo's work has a strong polemical quality. It is Euhemeristic to the core, and it agrees on a relatively large number of small points with the little we know of the writings of other Euhemeristic historians. In this sense, the *PH* conforms to the canons of Euhemeristic historiography. As noted above, Philo opposed mystery cults which were growing popular in his day (cf. Lucian of Samosata) and violently attacked allegorizers and physiologizers (Plutarch may be a convenient example of the sort of opponent Philo had in mind). The antipathy between allegorizers and physiologizers on the one hand, and Euhemerists on the other, was mutual: thus Plutarch presented a "critical" attack against Euhemerus, while Philo argued at length against the interpretations of myths proposed by allegorizers and physiologizers.

Philo was also a strong Phoenician nationalist. He writes as if everything important happened first in Phoenicia, or was discovered by a Phoenician. He displayed a deep dislike of Greeks typical of learned Near Easterners of his day. For all these reasons, we should not expect objectivity of the *PH*. Philo was not a dispassionate historian, but an author determined to make a case with important contemporary implications, concerning which he felt intensely. All of this, as noted above, made Philo especially useful to Eusebius, but should be a constant source of caution in reading and evaluating the fragments of the *PH*.

The surviving extracts of the *PH* fall into a number of distinct sections. Eusebius has preserved part of Philo's introduction in which he discussed the purpose of the work and described Sanchuniathon, his supposed source, whom he claimed to be translating from Phoenician to Greek. Sanchuniathon was also known to Porphyry (232/3–ca. 305), and Eusebius cited a passage from the latter's polemic against the Christians in which Sanchuniathon was described and praised. According to both Porphyry and Philo, Sanchuniathon was a learned man of great stature and antiquity, antedating Hesiod, and either prior to or contemporary with the Trojan War.

Eusebius then presented passages from Philo's supposed translation of Sanchuniathon, beginning with a verse cosmogony, and continuing with a section on discoverers of essentials of civilized life. The latter are regularly gods, who have been turned into mortals by Philo (in accordance with his Euhemeristic beliefs) and whose area of divine function has become a discovery or invention. Philo continued with a long section on Kronos and his wars, describing the division of the world by the victorious party at the end of the battles. One of the major events of the conflict between Kronos and Ouranos is the castration of the latter by the former. Philo concluded this discussion with harsh criticism of the Greeks, foremost of whom was Hesiod, who misappropriated this Phoenician material and fashioned theogonies, gigantomachies, and castration stories of their own. Philo commented that we have become so accustomed to these distortions of the truth that it has become difficult to give up the incorrect versions and to recognize the authentic story—as he has presented it from Sanchuniathon—for its true worth.

Eusebius cited two additional sections from Philo's work, one explaining the origins of child sacrifice, and another on the nature of snakes. Snakes played an important role in some mystery cults (such as the rites created by Alexander of Abonuteichos, described by Lucian). Philo is therefore anxious to explain the true nature of snakes lest we be misled and accept the interpretation of them offered in the mysteries he hated.

Philo's work raises a number of questions around which scholarly interest has focused. What sources did Philo use in composing the *PH*? Did he have any very ancient document(s) from which he worked directly? What is the true relationship between Philo and Hesiod? Finally, was Sanchuniathon a historical personality, a legendary hero, a religious authority, or a fiction created by Philo or some prior forger?

As noted above, there have been several cycles in the answers proposed to these questions. Philo's claims are now, however, regarded with considerable skepticism. His cosmogony was written in the verse technique typical of Ugaritic, Phoenician and biblical poetry, but the contents stress a scientific explanation of meteorological phenomena difficult to conceive before the rise of rationalism in 6th-century Greece. In the Wars of Kronos, Philo tells a Byblian version of the common Mediterranean myth of "Kingship in Heaven," also known in Babylonian, Hittite, and Greek forms, but Philo knows these Byblian myths in their classical or Hellenistic versions; they have been touched up to look more like Hesiod. Moreover, Philo has exploited the similarities with Hesiod for his polemical purposes: to attack the Greeks as being inferior to the great ancient cultures of the Near East.

Philo does present Phoenician traditions—this is indisputable—but he has not discovered and somehow preserved unaltered texts from hoary antiquity. Rather he has retold contemporary versions of Phoenician myths, modified them to suit his pet theories, and presented the results as the true ancient versions. We therefore do not read relatively unaltered Bronze Age or early Iron Age sources in Philo.

As for Sanchuniathon, his name is a good Phoenician one, attested in inscriptions. He may have been a venerable figure of Phoenician religion, and Philo's sources must have been connected in some way with this outstanding authority. Unfortunately, the Sanchuniathon strata in Philo's work are beyond recovery. That material was part of a living tradition and was further modified by Philo as part of his reworking the stories to fit his personal hypotheses. What little we are told of Sanchuniathon is of dubious value: he supposedly dedicated his book to Abibalos, king of Beirut; but book dedication did not become widespread until the Hellenistic period. The early date claimed for him is typical of the desire of barbarian historians to make their authorities equal in age with or older than Homer. Sanchuniathon therefore remains a shadowy figure of antiquity.

The *PH* and the Bible illuminate each other on a large number of points. For example, the verse cosmogony has the seeming anomaly of having the first stages of animal life preceding the blazing forth of the sun and moon. This seems so contrary to the logic of our expectations that one scholar proposed reorganizing the text of the *PH* so that animal life would commence after the sun and moon shone forth. Such drastic measures are, however, unnecessary, particularly in the light of Genesis 1, where the heavenly luminaries are created after the plants—another sequence jarring to the modern mind.

Philo's entire section on discoverers is reminiscent of Gen 4:19–22, where the Bible mentions several people who were the first to invent crafts or skills. Philo tells of mortal giants who gave their names to mountains which they conquered: to the Kassios, Lebanon, Anti-lebanon and Brathys(?). Their descendants were called after their mothers, because the women of the time had sexual relations with anyone upon whom they chanced. Philo is clearly writing about the Baals of these mountains, of whom the Baals of Kassios, Lebanon, and Anti-lebanon are known from other sources. The enigmatic Brathys may be an error for Itaburion, the usual name for Mt. Tabor in Greek. If this suggestion is correct, it would fit well with biblical evidence for the worship of Baal Tabor (Hos 5:1, Deut 33:18–19).

The entire section on these giants and their mountains is connected with the enigmatic passage in Gen 6:1–4. The Bible tells a fragment of myth about the union of divine beings or minor gods with human women. This story is further expanded in Jewish legend. Two hundred angels, under the leadership of Shemhazai, were attracted by the lewd practices, beauty, and sensual charm of human women. They descended on Mt. Hermon (= Anti-lebanon) and swore to cooperate in choosing wives. Giants resulted from these unions and the fallen angels then taught mankind all sorts of evil practices, from weapons and cosmetics to exorcism, magic, and divination. The version in Jewish legend is a relic of Canaanite myth: Danel (the hero of Ugaritic epic) appears among the fallen angels, and one of the skills humans learn is that of dyeing cloth—a reference to the chief industry of Phoenicia. Both the similarities and differences between Philo's story and the Jewish legend are clear. The original story, if there ever was one common source behind Philo and Jewish legend, would have spoken of gods or heroes. Philo has turned these into mortals, while Jewish legend would have transformed them into angels.

Deuteronomy 32:8 contains an account of the division of the world by *ᶜelyôn,* the "Most High" one. As the text now stands, this *ᶜelyôn* is the God of the Bible, who as the senior deity assigning shares could have taken any nation for his own, but chose to take Israel. In earlier versions of the text things might not have been so clear, as is suggested by fragments of Deuteronomy found at Qumran, in which the God of the Bible might have had a subsidiary role, with the main part assigned to El. On this understanding, Philo's account of the division of the world by the victorious El-Kronos is especially important.

In summary, there was extensive contact between the world of the Bible and the Phoenicians. Philo's sources go back to good Phoenician tradition, even if that material has changed with time and been modified by Philo to suit his polemical purposes. It is therefore appropriate that a number of points of contact between the *PH* and the Bible remain visible.

Bibliography

Baumgarten, A. I. 1981. *The Phoenician History of Philo of Byblos: A Commentary.* EPRO 89. Leiden.

Ebach, J. H. 1979. *Weltentstehung und Kulturentwicklung bei Philon von Byblos.* BWANT 6/8. Stuttgart.

Oden, R. A., and Attridge, H. W. 1981. *Philo of Byblos: the Phoenician History: Introduction.* CBQMS 9. Washington, DC.

Albert I. Baumgarten

PHILO, PSEUDO-.

Pseudo-Philo's retelling of the biblical story from Adam to David is known by its Latin title *Liber Antiquitatum Biblicarum (L.A.B.)* and its English equivalent *Biblical Antiquities.* But the title is late, and the text itself makes no claim to have been written by Philo of Alexandria. The Latin title appeared first in the 1552 printing of the work, though one 14th-century manuscript bore the heading *Liber Antiquitatum.* The term "Antiquities" suggests that some analogy was perceived with Josephus' *Antiquities,* and thus the work was attributed to Philo of Alexandria as the other great Jewish writer of antiquity known to Christian scribes. Manuscripts of *Biblical Antiquities* were transmitted along with the Latin translations of Philo's writings. Nevertheless, the nonallegorical approach to the biblical text, the likelihood that it was composed in Hebrew in Palestine, and the conflicts with Philo's genuine works indicate that the ascription to Philo has no historical foundation.

Biblical Antiquities exists in 18 complete and three fragmentary Latin manuscripts (Harrington and Cazeaux 1976: 15–57), all of German or Austrian origin, from between the 11th and 15th centuries. All break off abruptly in the midst of Saul's speech in chap. 65 and have gaps in content between 36:4 and 37:2 and between 37:5 and 38:1. The most important Latin manuscripts are Fulda-Cassel Theol. 4°, 3 (11th cent.) and Phillipps 461 (12th cent.). The Hebrew sections of *L.A.B.* in the medieval *Chronicles of Jerahmeel* appear to have been translated from Latin (Harrington 1974).

Pseudo-Philo retold the biblical story from Adam to David by selecting material from Genesis (1:1–8:14), Exodus (9:1–13:2), Leviticus (13:3–10), Numbers (14:1–18:14), Deuteronomy (19:1–15), Joshua (20:1–24:6), Judges (25:1–48:5), and 1 and 2 Samuel (49:1–65:5). Some biblical material was greatly expanded (especially the Kenaz story in chaps. 25–28 [see Judg 3:9, 11]), and other sections were severely abbreviated or bypassed almost completely (e.g., Genesis 1–3, Leviticus). Particular attention is given to the leaders of ancient Israel: Abraham, Moses, Joshua, Kenaz, Zebul, Deborah, Ehud, Gideon, Abimelech, Jair, Jephthah, Abdon and Elon, Samson Micah, Phinehas, Samuel, Saul, and David (Nickelsburg 1980: 49–65).

While incorporating various literary forms (genealogies dream visions, apocalypses, prayers, speeches, poems etc.), *L.A.B.* is best described as an example of the "rewritten Bible" (Vermes 1961) comparable to *Jubilees, Genesis Apocryphon,* and Josephus' *Antiquities.* It treats the biblical texts more freely than the Targums and is not as directly concerned with the exposition of the biblical texts as the midrashim. It may reflect popular biblical interpretation as practiced in the ancient Palestinian synagogues.

Even though Latin is the language of the most important extant manuscripts, several passages are best explained by assuming a Greek stage in the transmission of the wor and by supposing mistranslation from Hebrew to Greek (Harrington 1970). Therefore it seems likely that *L.A.B.* was composed in Hebrew, translated into Greek, translated into Latin, and partly retroverted into Hebrew *(Chronicles of Jerahmeel)*.

A Palestinian origin is indicated by its original composition in Hebrew, use of a Palestinian biblical text, knowledge of Palestinian geography, literary parallels to *4 Ezra* and *2 Baruch,* and theological interests. A date at the turn of the era is suggested by the silence about the destruction of the Second Temple, the assumption that worship continued at the Jerusalem Temple, and the use of a Hebrew biblical text-type that was suppressed around 100 C.E. (Perrot and Bogaert 1976: 22–74). Those who argue for a late 1st- or early 2d-century C.E. dating (James 1917) appeal to the parallels with *4 Ezra* and *2 Baruch* (both post-70 C.E.), the great interest in Jewish leaders, and the possible allusion to the fall of the Second Temple in 19:7.

Attempts at relating *L.A.B.* to specific Jewish groups (e.g., Essenes, Pharisees, Samaritans, anti-Samaritans) are not convincing. Rather the work appears to reflect the general spirit of the Palestinian synagogues. It illustrates how Jews read the Bible, tells us about the popular theology of the day, and contains some legends and motifs not found elsewhere in ancient Jewish literature. It may have been intended as a complement to the canonical books of Chronicles, though its theological interests were different.

Biblical Antiquities is the earliest witness to some popular Jewish motifs (Ginzberg 1909–38; Feldman 1971): Abraham's escape from Ur (6), Israel's being spared from the Flood (7:4), Job as Dinah's husband (8:8), Moses' being born circumcised (9:13), etc. It also contains some unique motifs and material: e.g., the connection between the tower of Babel and casting Abraham into the fire (6:3–18), the long section on Kenaz (25–28), and the idols of Micah (44:5). The focus of Pseudo-Philo's eschatological teaching was what happens after death (33:2–5; 44:10) and what will happen during and after God's eschatological intervention. He looked on idolatry and intermarriage of Jews with gentiles as especially reprehensible offenses against God's covenant with Israel. Other special interests included prophecy, the "holy spirit," good and bad leaders, angels, and the Deuteronomic interpretation of history (sin, punishment, salvation).

L.A.B. provides important evidence about the text and interpretation of the Hebrew Bible from Genesis to 1 and 2 Samuel around the turn of the era. It also contains references to Psalms, Isaiah, and Jeremiah. It shares many apocalyptic motifs with *4 Ezra* and *2 Baruch,* though it lacks their four-empire scheme of history and any interest in the messiah. In addition to some verbal parallels with the NT, its stories about the birth of Moses (9:9–16) and Samson (42:1–10) share features with the Matthean and Lukan infancy narratives. Its treatment of Abraham's sacrifice of Isaac according to Genesis 22 (see 18:5; 32:2–4; 40:2) may have influenced early Christian ideas about Jesus' sacrificial death.

Medieval Christian writers (Rhabanus Maurus, Rupert of Deutz, Peter Comestor) referred to the work. The earliest explicit Jewish reference was by Azariah dei Rossi in the 16th century. Leopold Cohn's 1898 article revived modern scholarly interest in the document, but its omission from important modern collections of Jewish writings has prevented it from being taken as seriously as it deserves. The Latin text was edited by Kisch (1949) and Harrington (1976). It has been translated into English by James (1917) and Harrington (*OTP* 2: 297–377), German by Riessler (1966) and Dietzfelbinger (1975), Modern Hebrew by Hartom (1967), French by Cazeaux (1976), and Spanish by de la Fuente Adánez (1984).

Bibliography

Cohn, L. 1898. A Apocryphal Work Ascribed to Philo of Alexandria. *JQR* 10: 277–332.

Dietzfelbinger, C. 1975. Pseudo-Philo: Antiquitates Biblicae (Liber Antiquitatum Biblicarum). *JSHRZ* 2: 91–271.

Feldman, L. 1971. *Prolegomenon to M. R. James's The Biblical Antiquities of Philo.* New York.

Fuente Adánez, A. de la. 1984. Antigüedades Biblicas (Pseudo-Filon). Vol. 2 pp. 195–316 in *Apocrifos del Antiguo Testamento,* ed. A. Díez Macho et al. Madrid.

Ginzberg, L. 1909–38. *The Legends of the Jews.* Vols. 1–7. Repr. 1946. Philadelphia.

Harrington, D. J. 1970. The Original Language of Pseudo-Philo's *Liber Antiquitatum Biblicarum. HTR* 63: 503–14.

———. 1971. The Biblical Text of Pseudo-Philo's *Liber Antiquitatum Biblicarum. CBQ* 33: 1–17.

———. 1974. *The Hebrew Fragments of Pseudo-Philo's* Liber Antiquitatum Biblicarum *Preserved in the* Chronicles of Jerahmeel. SBLTT 3. Cambridge, MA.

Harrington, D. J., and Cazeaux, J. 1976. *Pseudo-Philon: Les Antiquités Bibliques.* Vol. 1. SC 229. Paris.

Hartom, A. S. 1967. *Sēper Qadmônîot Hammiqrâ.* Tel-Aviv.

James, M. R. 1917. *The Biblical Antiquities of Philo.* Translations of Early Documents 1: Palestinian Jewish Texts. London and New York. Repr. 1971.

Kisch, G. 1949. Pseudo-Philo's *Liber Antiquitatum Biblicarum.* Publications in Mediaeval Studies 10. Notre Dame.

Nickelsburg, G. W. E. 1980. Good and Bad Leaders in Pseudo-Philo's *Liber Antiquitatum Biblicarum.* Pp. 49–65 in *Ideal Figures in Ancient Judaism. Profiles and Paradigms,* ed. J. J. Collins and G. W. E. Nickelsburg. Chico, CA.

Perrot, C., and Bogaert, P.-M. 1976. *Pseudo-Philon: Les Antiquités Bibliques.* Vol. 2. SC 230. Paris.

Riessler, P. 1966. Philo: Das Buch der Biblischen Altertümer. Pp. 735–861 in *Altjüdisches Schrifttum ausserhalb der Bibel.* Darmstadt.

Vermes, G. 1961. *Scripture and Tradition in Judaism: Haggadic Studies.* SPB 4. Leiden.

DANIEL J. HARRINGTON

PHILOLOGUS (PERSON) [Gk *Philologos*]. A Roman Christian who received greetings from Paul in Rom 16:15. He was probably a gentile Christian. See NEREUS. That Philologus was the husband (or brother) of Julia, being coupled with her in v 15, is only a possibility. According to the literary sources and to more than 37,000 Roman inscriptions, the name "Philologus" occurs only twenty-three times (whereas "Julia" appears more than 1,400 times; Lampe *StadtrChr,* 139–41). Since the name was not very common in the city, it probably indicates that Philologus had immigrated there.

PETER LAMPE

PHILOMETOR (PERSON) [Gk *Philomētoros*]. The coronation of Philometor as king of Egypt and his antipathy for the Seleucid king Antiochus IV are mentioned in 2 Macc 4:21. Philometor was Ptolemy VI Philometor, son of Ptolemy V Epiphanes and Cleopatra, daughter of Antiochus III. Philometor was born ca. 184 B.C.E. and ruled from ca. 180–145. Philometor ruled under the regency of his mother until her death in 176 B.C.E. during which time relations between Ptolemaic Egypt and Seleucid Syria were cordial. Upon Cleopatra's death in 176 B.C.E., the regency was assumed by Eulaios and Lenaios, who were opposed to Seleucid control of Coele-Syria. The deterioration of relations between Egypt and Syria, due to the regents, and not Philometor's personal opposition, led to Antiochus' hostile actions in Coele-Syria described in 2 Macc 4:21–22. The reference in 2 Macc 4:21 to Philometor's "coronation" (RSV; Gk *prōtoklēsia*) may be erroneous. *Prōtoklēsia* is found in Codex Alexandrinus but *prōtoklisia,* "first reclining" from the Gk roots for "first" (*prōt-*) and "recline" (*klin-*), appears in numerous other authorities. As *ēta (ē)* and *ipsilon (i)* were pronounced alike by the time of Codex Alexandrinus (Goldstein *II Maccabees* AB, 234), scribal error is possible. This "first reclining" or taking the place of honor at a banquet would possibly indicate a coming of age ceremony for Ptolemy VI Philometor rather than a coronation (Otto 1934: 16 and Robert 1969: 13). Polybius (xxvii 12.8–13.4) mentions Ptolemy Philometor's *anaklētēria* which is described as a coming of age ceremony. However, although the practice was known in Hellenistic Egypt, no such royal ceremony is known from the Ptolemaic period.

Bibliography

Otto, W. 1934. *Zur Geschichte der Zeit des 6. Ptolemäers.* ABAW phil.-hist. Kl. n.s. 11. Berlin.

Robert, L. 1969. Inscriptions d'Athènes et de la Grèce Centrale. *Archaiologikē ephēmeris,* 1–58.

MICHAEL E. HARDWICK

PHILOSOPHY [Gk *philosophia*]. Referring most obviously to the classical Greek schools of thought and their investigation of nature and truth, "philosophy" could denote the study and scientific treatment of, or speculation about, diverse subjects. Besides the intellectual disciplines, it could signify prescribed training or, even more broadly, a way of life. Thus, Diodorus of Sicily (1st century B.C.E.) calls the priestly discipline and the study of astrology and divination undertaken by the Chaldeans of Babylon "philosophy" (2.29.1–4). (See *TDNT* 9: 172–88.)

In the LXX, "philosophy" occurs only in *4 Maccabees,* where it has a broad meaning. Countering the charge that the religion *(thrēskeia)* of the Jews is foolish philosophy (5:7–11), the author defends obedience to the Law as sound philosophy because it enables one to achieve the cardinal Greek philosophical virtues (5:22–24). Philo, too, characterizes Judaism as a philosophy. In a discussion of Sabbath, he notes that the day of rest prescribed by Jewish law allows for the pursuit of wisdom and the study of the ancestral philosophy (*Mos.* 2.39. §211, 216). Josephus uses the term more narrowly, applying it to each of the religious parties in pre-70 C.E. Jewish Palestine; the Pharisees, Sadducees, and Essenes constitute the philosophies of the Jews (*Ant* 18.1.2. §11; cf. *JW* 2.8.2 §119).

"Philosophy" appears only once in the NT (Col 2:8). In that context, the writer combats a threat to the Christian community at Colossae, disparaging the threat there as empty deceit and philosophy, specifically, a philosophy according to human tradition and the elements of the world, and not according to Christ. The label "philosophy," by itself, says nothing certain about what the letter writer opposes. The term's lack of any pejorative connotation may indicate that "philosophy" is the self-designation of a group at Colossae, but the semantic breadth of the word precludes any further deductions. (See Lohse *Colossians* Hermeneia, 127–31.)

Since contemporary Jewish writers describe Judaism as a philosophy, and both dietary regulations and Sabbath observances belong to the practices of the Colossian philosophers (2:16), the Colossian philosophy may have been a form of Judaism. On the other hand, philosophical schools of the period, particularly Middle Platonism and Neo-Pythagoreanism, exhibited a markedly religious hue. The letter writer may have applied the term "philosophy" to a brand of pagan philosophy in Colossae that had adopted certain Jewish practices.

Bibliography

Brehier, E. 1965. *The Hellenistic and Roman Age.* Vol. 2 of *The History of Philosophy.* Chicago.

RICHARD E. DEMARIS

PHINEHAS (PERSON) [Heb *pînĕḥās*]. Var. PHINEAS. The name most likely derives from Eg *nḥsj* which meant "southerner" (the preformative *pꜣ* adds the definite article "the"). "The southerner" was a term which referred to those people from south of ancient Egypt, such as the Nubians, and hence it implied those of "dark skin." The association of Phinehas #2 with Hophni, another name of Egyptian origin, supports the contention of the Egyptian origin of Phinehas.

1. Phinehas was the son of Eleazar and Putiel, the grandson of Aaron and a descendant of Levi (Exod 6:25; Num 25:7; Judg 20:28; 1 Chr 5:30—Eng 6:4; 1 Chr 6:35—Eng 6:50; Ezra 7:5; *4 Ezra* 1:2b; *Ps-Philo* 28:1, 3). He was a priest (Num 25:7) and, as demonstrated by several passages, he was known for his strong and sometimes violent defense of the Israelite worship of Yahweh.

When the Israelites began to worship Baal-peor instead of Yahweh, Phinehas stood against them (Num 25:1–13; see also Ps 106:28–31; Sir 45:23–24; 1 Macc 2:26, 54; *4 Macc.* 18:12; *Hel. Syn. Pr.* 8:4–5, where Phinehas' actions are seen as exemplary). In particular, when an Israelite brought a Midianite woman into his family, Phinehas slew the man and woman with a spear (Num 25:6–8). Phinehas action brought forth four reactions by Yahweh: (1) Yahweh's anger toward the people was tempered and, as a result, only 24,000 people died by a plague (Num 25:8–9); (2) Yahweh praised Phinehas for his action in abating the wrath of God against the people (Num 25:11); (3) Yahweh rewarded Phinehas with a "covenant of peace" *(bĕrît šālôm)* (Num 25:12); and (4) Yahweh conferred on Phinehas and his descendants the "covenant of priesthood forever" (*bĕrît kĕhunnat ʿôlām*) (Num 25:13; 1 Macc 2:54). This last point refers to the fact that this passage is one in which the Israelite priesthood is established. Another such text is Exod 32:25–29, where the Levites "ordain" themselves to the service Yahweh as a result of their violent killing of the unfaithful; it is another account where militaristic actions lead to priesthood. A third passage is Exod 28:1, where Aaron and his descendants become priests; however in this instance it is not as a consequence of any violent action on their part (see also Num 1:47–54; 8:5–26; Deut 33:8–11).

A second incident where Phinehas was involved with the defense of the worship of Yahweh was in the holy war against Midian (Num 31:1–54). Phinehas, as priest, accompanied 12,000 people into battle at Peor (Num 31:6). The battle concluded with the slaying of all males and females, except the young women who were virgins (Num 31:17–18), and a long instruction, in part by Phinehas' father, Eleazar, on the proper handling of the spoils of war (Num 31:21–54).

In Joshua 22, when the Reubenites, Gadites, and the half-tribe of Manasseh returned to the Transjordanian region, they built an altar near the Jordan River (Josh 22:10). The priest Phinehas and 10 leaders of Israel took offense at this construction, claiming it indicated a turning away from Yahweh (Josh 22:11–20). The situation was resolved only when the Reubenites, Gadites, and half-tribe of Manasseh asserted that the altar was an "altar of witness" (Josh 22:26–27) to remind their children of their relationship with the 10 tribes of Israel, not an altar of sacrifice (Josh 22:28). This story not only reflects the defense of the worship of Yahweh, but it also introduces and defends the concept of a single central sanctuary, as is advocated in Deuteronomy 12.

A fourth episode which indicates Phinehas' defense of Yahweh is found in Judges 20. Here, the tribes of Israel are seeking revenge upon the Benjaminites in retaliation for their atrocities against the concubine of a Levite (Joshua 19). Just before the battle at Gibeah, Phinehas stood (*ʿmd*) before the ark of the covenant, consulting Yahweh and seeking his blessing prior to commencing the battle. Phinehas' role is again to defend the mainline Israelite tradition against those who would violate or turn away from that tradition.

Finally, Phinehas appears in the midst of a genealogy in 1 Chronicles 9. In this late genealogy, various priests, Levites, and temple servants are mentioned, and in the list of Levites who were gatekeepers at the temple, Phinehas, the son of Eleazar, is named as the one who rules over these gatekeepers (1 Chr 9:20). This relationship indicates the tension and rivalry between the Aaronite priesthood represented by Phinehas and the Levitical priesthood represented by the gatekeepers. Furthermore, these gatekeepers act as guards for the temple and temple treasury (1 Chr 9:26–27) which again reflects the military nature of the priesthood.

Three factors of significance can be derived from examining the activities of this Phinehas. Yahweh bestows the priesthood on Phinehas and his descendants, and all priestly factions (Aaronites, Levites, and Zadokites) must somehow be related to Phinehas. Secondly, Phinehas is a priest of Yahweh whose zealous defense of Yahweh becomes a model for subsequent generations. Finally, Phinehas' defense of Yahweh, like that of other priests and priestly groups, clearly takes on militaristic characteristics.

The descendants of Phinehas are prominently mentioned among those who returned from Exile at the time of Zerubbabel and Ezra (Ezra 8:2; 1 Esdr 5:5). In 1 Esdr 8:29, the RSV form is Phineas (Gk *Phinees*), though the same Greek spelling appears throughout the LXX for Phinehas, including the parallel passage in Ezra 8:2.

2. Phinehas was the brother of Hophni, the son of Eli the priest (1 Samuel 1). These priestly brothers began as good priests, but they quickly turned into bad priests who abused their sacred trust (1 Sam 2:12–17). This deterioration is in sharp contrast to Samuel who was portrayed as a model priest. These incidents in 1 Samuel 1–4 thus provide reason for the later elimination of the Elide priesthood (see 1 Kgs 2:27). The story also asserts that ritual cleanliness was essential for participation in holy war. See HOPHNI for a more detailed discussion of the brothers Hophni and Phinehas.

At the end of 1 Samuel 4, Phinehas' wife had a child (1 Sam 4:19). She named the child Ichabod ("no glory") since Eli, Hophni, and her husband Phinehas were dead and the ark of the covenant was in the hands of the Philistines (1 Sam 4:21–22). She died almost immediately after naming her son (1 Sam 4:20).

According to 1 Sam 14:3, Phinehas had a brother, Ahitub, whose son was Ahijah the priest. Abiathar, the priest Solomon banished when he assumed the throne, is apparently the son of Ahimelech, who was the brother of Ahijah (1 Sam 22:20). Thus, the genealogical connection between Phinehas and Abiathar is established, the guilt of Phinehas and Hophni was visited upon Abiathar, and the line of Eli was at an end (1 Kgs 2:27).

3. Phinehas was the father of Eleazar (Ezra 8:33; 1 Esdr 8:63). Eleazar was one of the people, along with Meremoth the priest and Jozabad and Noadiah the Levites, who received the temple vessels and gold when they were returned from their captivity in Babylon. See ELEAZAR #5.

JOHN R. SPENCER

PHLEGON (PERSON) [Gk *Phlegōn*]. A Roman Christian who received greetings from Paul in Rom 16:14. See PATROBAS. He was probably a gentile Christian. See NEREUS. According to the epigraphical and literary sources from Rome, the name "Phlegon" occurs only nine times (Lampe *StadtrChr,* 139–41). Because the name was not common there, it probably indicates the Phlegon had immigrated to Rome. It has been proposed that he was a (freed) slave, but the inscriptions do not support the argument that the name was one commonly held by slaves (see Lampe *StadtrChr,* 150, 152–53; three out of seven inscriptions show slaves or freedman).

PETER LAMPE

PHOCYLIDES, PSEUDO-. A gnomic poet who lived in Milete in the 6th century B.C.E. Only a very few lines of his poetry are still extant, but ancient testimonies make abundantly clear that throughout antiquity he was regarded as a great authority in matters of ethics and correct behavior in daily life (van der Horst 1978a: 59–63). Under his mask a Jewish Wisdom poet, who probably lived in the second half of the 1st century B.C.E., or in the first half of the 1st century C.E., wrote a gnomic poem of 230 hexameters in the old Ionic dialect. It is a skillful forgery that remained unrecognized as such until the end of the 16th century. Up to that time this poem enjoyed an enormous popularity as a schoolbook; hence it is extant in over 150 mss (Derron 1980). From the early 17th to the middle of the 19th centuries it was often regarded as a Christian forgery because of its biblical resonances, until Jacob Bernays demonstrated its undeniably Jewish origin (Bernays 1856). In recent times there have been new critical editions (Young 1971; Derron 1986), translations and commentaries (van der Horst 1978a; Walter 1983), and several important studies on the poem (e.g., Küchler 1979 and Niebuhr 1987; further details in van der Horst 1988).

One of the striking characteristics of the poem is that on the one hand it draws heavily upon the Pentateuch (esp. Leviticus 18–20 and the Decalogue) and on the other hand it consistently avoids references to specifically Jewish precepts like sabbath observance, circumcision, and dietary rules. All cultic precepts are passed over in silence, only "moral" precepts for conduct in daily life are presented, with a very heavy emphasis on sexual matters and on avarice, an emphasis to be found in other Jewish writings as well. Much of his material is also found in the "summaries of the Law" as presented in Philo's *Hypothetica* (in Eus. *P.E.* 8: 7, 1–9) and in Jos. *AgAp* 2 §190–219. They draw upon a common source in which the essentials of the Torah are summarized in the form of a short catechism. These catechism-like summaries (more examples in Neibuhr 1987) do not give any or only a minimum of cultic rules, but all of them emphasize strict sexual ethics, the viciousness of greed, the duty to care for the poor and the needy, honesty, modesty, and moderation. Mixed with these biblical and early Jewish rules one finds, both in *Ps.-Phoc.* and in Philo and Josephus, precepts of originally pagan Greek provenance, which are also presented as God's Law. Although not deriving from the Torah, this material is presented as God's commandments since it can be derived from the Torah and is in essential accordance with its intentions. Hence there are a great many lines in *Ps.-Phoc.* that have only pagan parallels (van der Horst 1978a: 105–262; Derron 1986: 35–54).

A much debated question is that of the author's purpose. Why did a Jew write a summary of the Torah, mixed with non-biblical ethical rules, under a heathen pseudonym? It has often been thought that he had a pagan audience in mind and wanted (*not* to make converts to Judaism but) to bring pagans to a kind of "ethical monotheism" (Crouch 1972: 89, 97); one scholar even asserted that this author cannot have been a Jew but must have been a "sympathizer" or "God-fearer" who wished to win over others to his way of life on the fringes of the synagogue (Rossbroich 1910). But there is a growing consensus now that the author's intended audience was Jewish and that what he hoped to achieve was to make clear to Hellenized Jews who were fascinated by the dominant Greek culture and were in danger of dropping Jewish values: (1) that biblical and Greek ethics are not incompatible; (2) that even the famous pagan Wisdom poet Phocylides promulgated biblical ethics; and (3) that their attachment to Judaism should be reinforced instead of slackened because it is perfectly possible to reconcile the Jewish religion with the surrounding Greco-Roman culture (Goodman *HJP*[2] 3: 687–92; van der Horst 1988).

The poem shares the characteristics of both Greek gnomologies and Jewish Wisdom literature and is as such a typical example of cross-cultural didactic poetry. In spite of its use of the old Ionic dialect, its origin in the late Hellenistic or early Imperial period is betrayed by its vocabulary, meter, and syntax (van der Horst 1978a: 55–58; Derron 1986: LXVI–LXXXII). Its place of origin is unknown but Alexandria is a good possibility since v 102 prohibits dissection of the deceased which was practiced in Alexandrian medical circles; but other possibilities cannot be excluded. The poem is an important source for our knowledge of popular morality in diaspora Judaism and as such it sheds light on several parenetic passages in the NT (van der Horst 1978b). See also *OTP* 2: 565–82.

Bibliography

Bernays, J. 1856. *Über das phokylideische Gedicht.* Berlin.

Crouch, J. E. 1972. *The Origin and Intention of the Colossian Haustafel.* Göttingen.

Derron, P. 1980. Inventaire des manuscrits du Pseudo-Phocylide. *Revue d'histoire des textes* 10: 237–47.

———. 1986. *Pseudo-Phocylide.* Paris.

Horst, P. W. van der. 1978a. *The Sentences of Pseudo-Phocylides.* SVTP 4. Leiden.

———. 1978b. Pseudo-Phocylides and the New Testament. *ZNW* 69: 187–202.

———. 1988. Pseudo-Phocylides Revisited. *JSP* 3: 3–30.

Küchler, M. 1979. *Frühjüdische Weisheitstraditionen.* Freiburg.

Niebuhr, K.-W. 1987. *Gesetz und Paränese: Katechismusartige Weisungsreihen in der frühjüdischen Literatur.* Tübingen.

Rossbroich, M. 1910. *De Pseudo-Phocylideis.* Münster.

Young, D. 1971. *Theognis, Pseudo-Pythagoras, Pseudo-Phocylides, Chares, Anonymi Aulodia, Fragmentum Teleiambicum.* Leipzig.

Walter, N. 1983. Pseudo-Phokylides. *JSHRZ* 4/3: 182–216.

PIETER W. VAN DER HORST

PHOEBE (PERSON) [Gk *Phoibē*]. A woman from Cen-chreae (near Corinth) commended by Paul in Rom 16:1–[illegible] to the recipients of that letter, evidently because she wa[s] delivering it to them. Paul's reference to Phoebe uses thre[e] titles to describe her: *adelphē,* "sister"; *diakonos,* "deacon"[;] and *prostatis,* "patroness." The first term indicates that sh[e] was a Christian; the second and third denote various role[s] she had as a believer and each has inspired much discus-sion.

While some translations such as the RSV render *diakon[os]* as "deaconess," this is not an appropriate translation [of] the Greek. From the term Paul uses, Phoebe must be calle[d] a "deacon." For, to say Phoebe was a deaconess implie[s] that Paul used the term *diakonissa,* which in fact is n[ot] known to have been used in 1st century C.E. Greek. Fu[r]thermore, it also suggests, in view of later deaconess mov[e]ments, that Phoebe's role was subordinate to male deaco[ns] or that it primarily involved ministry to other women. B

Paul's description of her implies no such restrictions. In his eyes she was a deacon in the same sense as he applied the term to himself (e.g., 1 Cor 3:5; 2 Cor 3:6; 6:4; 11:23) and to various co-workers (e.g., Apollos in 1 Cor 3:5; Timothy in 1 Thess 3:2). Since in these texts Paul portrayed himself and his co-workers as missionaries who preached and ministered within churches, the same role must be attributed to Phoebe. Apparently she was a ministerial leader in the church at Cenchreae. The possessive expression "deacon of the church" (16:1) makes it probable that, unlike Paul and some others, hers was a local function rather than an itinerant one.

In describing Phoebe as *prostatis* to himself and to many others (16:2), Paul uses the feminine form of a term not found in either the feminine or masculine elsewhere in the NT. While in wider Greek usage the masculine *prostatēs* definitely has the technical sense of a legal patron, it has been argued by Käsemann, for example, that in Phoebe's case the term "cannot in the context have the juridical sense of the masculine form, i.e., the leader or representative of fellowship," since women could not take on legal functions (1980: 411). Rather, in this scholar's view, "the idea is that of the personal care which Paul and others have received" at Phoebe's hands (1980: 411). Schüssler Fiorenza has assessed this interpretation as "an androcentric model of historical reconstruction [which] cannot imagine or conceptualize that women such as Phoebe could have had leadership equal to and sometimes even superior to men in early Christian beginnings" (1986: 425). Also, Jewett has argued that recently published data indicates that women actually did function in many instances in a legal role as a *prostatis* (1988: 149).

Paul's statement that Phoebe was a *prostatis,* i.e., patroness, to many as well as to himself suggests she was prosperous and thus assumably had a high social standing. Probably Phoebe's house was large enough to accommodate the Cenchreaen Christian gatherings. She would have been not only hostess but also a leader in her role as deacon. In Jewett's judgment, with respect to Phoebe as such a key member of the church of Cenchreae, specifically as benefactress, Paul would have had a "relatively subordinate social position as her client" (1988: 150).

Paul's commendation of Phoebe asks the Romans to "receive her in the Lord as befits the saints, and help her in whatever she may require from you" (16:2). This has invited some speculation concerning the purpose of Phoebe's trip to Rome (or Ephesus, according to those who defend that city as the destination of Romans 16). Several commentators have thought that perhaps business or family matters occasioned her travel, and thus she could also conveniently deliver Paul's letter. Recently Jewett has advanced the provocative theory that Phoebe actually went to Rome to persuade the church there to support Paul's planned evangelization of Spain (cf. Rom 15:24, 28). In his judgment Phoebe "had agreed to cooperate with Paul as the patroness [*prostatis*] of the Spanish mission" (1988: 151). A problem with the theory, however, is that when Paul refers to his Spanish plans and his desired support from the Roman church in Rom 15:24, he does not immediately mention Phoebe as one would expect were she such an integral link in his plans.

Bibliography

Gibson, M. 1911–12. "Phoebe," *ExpTim* 23: 281.

Gillman, F. M. 1989. *Women Who Knew Paul.* Wilmington.

Jewett, R. 1988. Paul, Phoebe and the Spanish Mission. Pp. 142–61 in *The Social World of Formative Christianity and Judaism: Essays in Tribute to Howard Clark Kee,* ed. J. Neusner et al. Philadelphia.

Käsemann, E. 1980. *Commentary on Romans.* Trans. and ed. G. W. Bromiley. Grand Rapids.

Lohfink, G. 1980. Weibliche Diakone im Neuen Testament. *Diakonia* 11: 385–400.

Schüssler Fiorenza, E. 1986. Missionaries, Apostles, Coworkers: Romans 16 and the Reconstruction of Women's Early Christian History. *WW* 6: 420–33.

FLORENCE MORGAN GILLMAN

PHOENICIA, HISTORY OF.

Phoenicia was the Greek name for the Syrian littoral north of Palestine. The name meant "dark red" and was applied first to the people and region renowned for dyes of this color, and then to some of the natural products that became associated with them in international trade. Phoenicia was neither a country nor a nation but a conglomerate of city-states that was distinguished from adjacent areas by its habitual outreach into the Mediterranean world and by its preferred dealings with Indo-Europeans and Greeks. Its history consists in the contribution of these individual cities and their dominions to the civilization and gradual maturation of the Mediterranean world.

A. Sources
  1. Judean
  2. Phoenician
  3. Egyptian
  4. Greek
  5. Assyrian and Babylonian
B. Chronology

A. Sources

The Phoenician cities are known from their own records and from Egyptian, Greek, Assyrian, Babylonian, and Judean sources. Their own records are inscriptions and artifacts that attest their influence on art and culture, religion, politics, international trade, and commerce in the 1st millennium B.C. The main Egyptian sources are the Amarna letters and the mid-11th-century story of Wen-Amon. The Greek sources include references in Mycenaean texts but begin coherently with Homer and continue through Herodotus and later historians and in scattered epigraphic materials. The Assyrian and Babylonian sources are the intermittent records of subjugation and conquest in the annals and chronicles of the kings. The Judean sources include some 7th-century geographical references, a few inscriptions, a 6th-century encomium of Phoenician economic and cultural superiority, and some contemporary allusions to the grandeur of the past and to the gradual deterioration of Israelite-Phoenician relations.

1. Judean. The earliest biblical reference to the Phoenicians includes them in the world of the Greeks. In the 7th-century geography composed by P the Kittim (Gen 10:4) are listed as descendants of Japheth, children of Ionia, and brothers of Cyprus, Tarshish, and Rhodes (Westermann *Genesis* BKAT, 673–81). But they were, in fact, the Phoenician inhabitants of Kition in Cyprus, a city founded in Mycenaean times, resettled by the Phoenicians early in the 1st millennium and continuing as the center of Phoenician expansion in the Mediterranean until the 4th century B.C. (Karageorghis 1976). Jeremiah, later in the 7th century, still thought of the Kittim as inhabitants of the far W islands (Jer 2:10; 31:10). In early 6th-century letters from Arad (AI) they are mentioned as recipients of rations and seem to have been agents or mercenaries stationed in S Judah. Later in the 6th century Ezekiel included them in the Tyrian fleet (Ezek 27:6), the Dtr historian thought of them as pirates (Num 24:24), and 2 Isaiah described them as inhabitants of an island, trading partners with Sidon, and adventurers on the high seas (Isa 23:1, 12). Still they retained their mysterious character, and as late as Daniel and Maccabees the Kittim symbolized the power that lurked on the far shores of the Mediterranean (Dan 11:30; 1 Macc 1:1; 8:5).

The earliest biblical reference to particular Phoenician cities is in Ezekiel's lamentation for Tyre (Ezekiel 26–28; Zimmerli *Ezechiel* BKAT, 600–96). He describes an imagined capture and destruction of the city (Ezekiel 26), its effect on Mediterranean trade (Ezekiel 27), and its consequences for the Phoenician way of life (Ezekiel 28). The Phoenician cities are mentioned by name but are included indiscriminately with Greece, Cilicia, and Anatolia in a catalogue of the nations of the world.

Tyre is described as a fortified island city with mainland dominions and an interest in the overland trade routes (Ezek 26:1–6). The supposed destruction of the city by Nebuchadnezzar (Ezek 26:7–14) is portrayed in detail: the invasion, the capture of its mainland possessions, construction of siege mounds and redoubts, attacks with battering rams on the walls and towers, the taking of the city, execution of its inhabitants, demolition of its pillars, plunder and total destruction—leaving Tyre a bare rock in the water, a place for drying nets. Tyre had been settled by seafarers (Ezek 26:17 *nôšebet miyyammîm*) and the repercussions of its sudden collapse were felt throughout the Mediterranean by the people and princes who enjoyed its renown and relied on its naval power (Ezek 26:15–18). But its destruction was by divine decree and Tyre had descended into the netherworld never to rise again (Ezek 26:19–21).

The effect of Tyre's symbolic demise on Mediterranean trade and economic stability is the topic of a lament (Ezekiel 27) that compares Tyre to a ship and describes how it was built and why it foundered (Ezek 27:1–7, 31–36), where its crew was hired and how they were stunned by its loss (Ezek 27:8–11, 25–30), where it loaded cargo and where it traded (Ezek 27:12–16, 20–24), and where it got the provisions it carried on its long voyages (Ezek 27:17–19). Provisions were gathered from its overland trade with Judah, Israel, and Damascus. Its cargo came from Ionia and Rhodes, Cilicia, Anatolia, and the Arameans of N Syria, and was traded to Arabia and N Mesopotamia. But its crew was Phoenician from Sidon, Arvad, Tyre, and Byblos; its troops were mercenaries from Persia, Lydia and Libya; its garrison was recruited from Arvad and her dependencies in the North. Tyre, in this portrayal, is a great cosmopolitan city, unrestricted in its foreign relations, the convener of the Mediterranean world.

The contrast that Ezekiel draws is between Tyre, lamented by the whole world, and Jerusalem whose destruction did not matter to anyone else. For Tyre, in particular, the fall of Jerusalem was an opportunity to trade with Judah's neighbors to the E ("So Jerusalem is broken, the gate to the nations has swung open to me, I will get my fill from her destruction" [Ezek 26:2]). Ezekiel eulogized Tyre's worldliness but castigated its insouciance and its sense that life goes on by depicting Tyre as a royal city that thinks it will live forever like a god (Ezek 28:1–5) but will die, he protests, and will not return from the dead (Ezek 28:6–10; cp. 26:19–21; 32:17–32; 37:1–14).

The Dtr historian, writing in the mid-6th century, was familiar with Tyre's preeminence in the Mediterranean world but was also interested in Phoenician geography and ethnography. The Phoenicians are Canaanites who live in the E and in the W, along the coast and in the Jordan valley (Gen 10:19; Num 13:29; Deut 1:8; 11:30; Josh 11:3; Judg 18:7, 28). They are called Sidonians (Gen 10:15; Judg 3:3; 10:11–12; 18:7; 1 Kgs 5:20; 11:1, 5, 33; 16:31; 2 Kgs 23:13). Their land is N of Philistia and S of Amurru, and includes both the littoral and the possessions of Byblos in Mt. Lebanon as far as Lebo Hamat in the interior (Deut 3:9; Josh 13:2–6). Some of their towns, such as ʿAkko and ʿAkzib, belonged theoretically to Asher (Judg 1:31), other towns such as ʿArqa, Siyannu, Arvad, and Ṣumur were N of Canaan in Amurru (Gen 10:17–18; Westermann *Genesis* BKAT, 694–99) but Phoenicia was not part of the land of Canaan that had been allotted to the tribes of Israel (Gen 10:15–19; 49:13; Josh 11:8; 19:28; 2 Sam 24:6–7).

Tyre is mentioned in the Dtr history only in connection with David and Solomon and the building of the temple. This history ascribes to Solomon the wealth, wisdom, and world renown that Ezekiel admired in the king of Tyre (1 Kgs 3:1–15; 5:1–14; Ezek 28:1–5). Solomon, like Ezekiel's king of Tyre, achieved world dominion (1 Kgs 5:1; 10:23–24; Ezek 26:17–18; 27:1–36) and acquired his wealth from international trade (1 Kgs 10:14–15; Ezek 28:1–5). They both had ships of Tarshish (1 Kgs 10:22; Ezek 27:12, 25), traded with Sheba (1 Kgs 10:1–13; Ezek 27:22) and all the countries from Cilicia and Anatolia to Egypt (1 Kgs 10:26–29; Ezek 27:7, 12–16), and sent their fleets on joint expeditions to Ophir (1 Kgs 9:26–28; 10:11, 22). For both, their grandeur and the richness of their foreign relations was ultimately their downfall (1 Kgs 11:1–3; Ezek 28:1–10).

The Dtr historian portrayed Solomon as a Phoenician king, made him the contemporary and friend of Hiram of Tyre, and gave them joint responsibility for building the temple. Israel exchanged ambassadors with Tyre and made a treaty (2 Sam 5:11–12; 1 Kgs 5:15–20, 26). The Tyrians, following the pattern described by Ezekiel, bartered their materials and expertise for wheat and oil (1 Kgs 5:21–25; Ezek 27:17), summoned the Byblians to help them with the timber and masonry (1 Kgs 5:27–32; Ezek 27:9), imported all the wood and gold and precious stones needed for the construction of the temple (1 Kgs 9:26–28; 10:11–22; Ezek 27:22; Lemaire 1977: 253–55), supplied the bronze for the temple vessels and for the two pillars that stood before it (1 Kgs 7:13–47; Ezek 26:11; 27:13

and acquired the right to settle by the coast in return for their wares (1 Kgs 9:10–14; Ezek 27:3). The magnificence of the temple matched the splendor of its founder. Together they represented the wonder of new beginnings and the innocence of primordial times. The temple was the replica of the created order, a place like sky and earth where Yahweh might dwell (1 Kgs 8:12–13, 27–30), with pillars to sustain the heavens (1 Kgs 7:15–22; cp. Ps 75:4) and a bronze sea to contain the mighty waters (1 Kgs 7:23–26). The king, like God and Adam, had the knowledge of good and evil (1 Kgs 3:9; Gen 3:22) and, like Adam, was led astray by his wives to worship other gods (1 Kgs 11:1–3; Gen 3:8–13). He was like the king of Tyre in the book of Ezekiel who was created in the garden of Eden but sinned and defiled his temples and was removed from the mountain of God (Ezek 28:11–19).

This Tyrian interlude in the Dtr history makes the beginning of the Davidic dynasty coincide with the origin of right worship in the distant and idyllic past. But it differs from the usual Dtr interpretation of Israel's dealings with the Phoenicians and Sidonians. The Dtr historian included them among the nations left in the land to test Israel (Josh 13:2–6; Judg 3:3). They were mentioned with the Philistines in a list of Israel's oppressors (Judg 10:11–12). Their women lured Solomon into the worship of Astarte (1 Kgs 11:1, 5; 2 Kgs 23:13). The worship of Baʿal was introduced into Israel in the early 9th century when Ahab married Jezebel the daughter of ʾIttôbaʿal the "king of the Sidonians" (*mlk ṣdnm,* 1 Kgs 16:31; Katzenstein 1973: 129–192). This critical attitude toward the Sidonians and Phoenicians was governed by the Dtr interpretation of Israel's distinctiveness that required its separation from all the nations of the world. But Tyre's exemption from criticism was based on the Dtr reconstruction of history that reflected 2 distinct phases in Phoenician expansion. The inveterate conflict with the Phoenicians or Sidonians corresponds to the era of Sidonian expansion that began, as the Dtr writer affirmed, at the time of Israel's struggle for independence and that lasted, as the Dtr author suggested, almost until the fall of the Northern Kingdom. The following era of Tyrian supremacy that continued to the fall of Judah and beyond inspired Ezekiel's eulogy and lament and was the paradigm of prosperity and good relations that the Dtr historian used to describe the time of Solomon.

The works of Ezekiel and the Dtr historian were known to all the later biblical authors who wrote about Tyre or Sidon. The revision of the book of Amos, for instance, includes an oracle against Tyre (Amos 1:9–10) that is copied from its context (Amos 1:6–8) but also refers to the treaty between Hiram and Solomon recorded by the Dtr historian (Amos 1:9; 1 Kgs 5:26), and to the Tyrian slave trade and commerce with Judah's neighbors to the E that were exposed and condemned by Ezekiel (Amos 1:9; Ezek 26:2; 27:13). Joel considered the same topics, criticizing Tyre and Sidon for their slave trade with the Greeks and for dedicating in their temples the silver and gold they took from trade with Judah (Joel 4:4–8). Joel was also familiar with the Dtr geography, which associated Philistia with the Phoenician cities (Joel 4:4) and put Sheba at the ends of the earth (Joel 4:8; 1 Kgs 10; cf. Gen 10:7; Ezek 27:22). Ezekiel had connected Sidon with Arvad and the principalities of the N (Ezek 27:8; 32:30) but the revision of his book made Sidon an accomplice of Tyre in the economic repression of Judah (Ezek 28:20–26). The psalms reminisce about Tyre's grandeur and great wealth (Ps 45:13) and perpetuate the idea that Tyre belonged with Philistia among Israel's enemies on the seacoast (Ps 83:8; 87:4). Second Isaiah reviewed Ezekiel's lamentation on Tyre but included Sidon as an equal partner and predicted that the wealth of the two cities eventually would belong to the people of Yahweh (Isaiah 23). The book of Jeremiah mentioned Tyre and Sidon among the traditional enemies of Judah (Jer 25:22), observed in passing that Jerusalem was a negotiant in their trade with Judah's neighbors to the E (Jer 27:3), and condemned Philistia in the S as an accessory after the fact (Jer 47:4; cp. Zeph 2:5). Zechariah was familiar with the geography of the coast, condemned Philistia for its alignment with Tyre and Sidon, and rebuked Ionia for its participation in the slave trade (Zechariah 9). But at the end of the 6th century the Chronicler interpreted Solomon's dealings with Hiram of Tyre as trade relations with both Tyre and Sidon (1 Chr 22:4; cp. 1 Kgs 5:15–26), and these relations evidently had withstood the test of time and theological tradition and persisted through the era of the restoration to the building of the second Temple (Ezra 3:7; Neh 13:16).

The Tyrians and Sidonians were famous and successful merchants living in coastal Canaan (cf. Obad 20) and the geographical designation, consequently, acquired a commercial connotation. Hosea criticized Ephraim for its deceitfulness and dealings with the powerful nations of the world (Hos 12:1–3) and then illustrated his point by comparing Ephraim to a wealthy and arrogant Canaanite merchant with no sense of allegiance (Hos 12:8–9). In the mid-6th century the book of Zephaniah blamed the leading people of Jerusalem for the downfall of the city and included among them the merchants (*ʿam kĕnaʿan*) who made their money at the Fish Gate and in the marketplace (Zeph 1:11). But at the end of the century the book of Proverbs compared a good wife to a shrewd dealer in purple garments trading with the Phoenicians (*kĕnaʿănî,* Prov 31:24). The attitude of biblical writers to the Phoenicians of Tyre and Sidon reflected diverse historical situations but was dictated by theological theory and often conflicted with an implicit admiration for the relentless adventurers who had discovered the Mediterranean world and given the East a new role in the history of civilization.

2. Phoenician. The Phoenician discovery of the Mediterranean world proceeded initially from the mainland via Cyprus to N Syria, Cilicia, Anatolia, through the Aegean to Greece and W to Italy, North Africa, and Spain (Coldstream, *PhönWes,* 261–75; Riis, *PhönWes,* 237–60). It was primarily a Sidonian venture with some collaboration or competition from Byblos. A later series of expeditions was conducted mainly by Tyre and led through Philistia and Egypt, along the Libyan coast past Malta and North Africa to the Atlantic (Breglia 1955). Both directions of discovery are marked by inscriptions and artifacts that delineate the features of Phoenician culture and civilization and confirm the evidence of the biblical sources.

The northward expansion of the Phoenician cities was a reflex of the invasion of the Philistines and the other Sea Peoples. The earliest distinctive Phoenician pottery was a derivative of Cypro-Aegean fashions of the 11th century B.C. (Culican, *PhönWes,* 45–82). The earliest E Phoenician inscriptions are from Crete and Cyprus from the end of the 11th century and later (Cross 1979a: 105; 1980: 15–17). Inscriptions of the 9th and 8th centuries from Zinjirli and Karatepe attest the continuing coexistence of Phoenicians with the Danunian Sea People *(dnnym, KAI* 24.7; 26 A I 2, 3, 4 [etc.]). A 9th-century inscription from Nora in Sardinia shows that the Phoenicians knew the Sherden Sea People *(šrdn)* and had learned from them the navigation of the W seas (Cross 1972).

From the time of their earliest voyages the Phoenicians were in immediate contact with the Greek cities and emerging Greek civilization. The Greeks borrowed the alphabet from them and finally developed their own in the 9th century, but they knew the Phoenician scripts and scribal traditions of the 11th century and later (Cross 1979a: 105–11). Ninth-century ivories in the N Syrian style still betray an early Mycenaean influence (Winter 1976: 9–10). The Phoenicians had settled in Spain by the early 8th century B.C. (Aubet Semmler 1985) but their products were Greek and their business was the transport of Greek goods (Shefton 1982). One of the first Phoenician inscriptions from Carthage is on a gold pendant from the early 7th century and it is dedicated to Phoenician Astarte and her Greek associate Pygmalion (*KAI* 73).

Byblos was the most ancient and renowned of the Phoenician cities and maintained the strictest ties with its traditions. The earliest mainland inscriptions are from the 11th century, one a commercial agreement (McCarter and Coote 1973), two others with personal names illustrating familial (*ʾḥʾš,* "My brother has given") and cosmological (*ʿbdḥmn,* "Servant of [Baʿal] Ḥamōn") aspects of the local Phoenician religion (Cross and McCarter 1973). Royal inscriptions from the 10th century and again from the 5th manifest a similar concern, in the same language and style, for the long life and welfare of the king, and attest the constant devotion of the city to Baʿal the king *(bʿl, mlk)* and to the "Mistress of Byblos" (*bʿlt gbl KAI* 1–10; Bordreuil 1977). Two other royal inscriptions from the early 5th century (Cross 1979b; *KAI* 9) have lexical and ideological connections with contemporary texts from Sidon and suggest a change in Byblian foreign policy during the Persian wars (cp. Dunand 1969), but Byblian adherence to tradition is evident in a 1st-century offering to Baʿal that continues to petition for the long life and welfare of its donor (*KAI* 12).

Byblos and its dominions were distinguished from the other Phoenician cities by their language (Lane 1969), script (Peckham 1968: 42–63), politics, and belief, but they shared some religious traditions with Israel. The kings of Byblos expected long life *(ʾrk ymm)* and blessing *(brk)* from their gods, things that the Dtr historian promised to Israel (e.g., Deut 6:2–3; 22:7) and, exceptionally, to Solomon (Deut 17:20; 1 Kgs 3:10–14). They and their subjects looked to the gods for life *(ḥwh)* and based this hope on their justice and observance of the laws *(ṣdq, mšpṭ, yšr),* in substantial agreement with the correlations established by the Dtr historian between life, justice, and obedience to Yahweh (e.g., Deut 6:24–25; 8:1; 9:4–6; 30:15–20). From the 5th century onward, at Byblos, at Lapethos in Cyprus and at Pyrgi in Italy, kings were concerned with their physical appearance in the tomb, people were eager to make living likenesses of themselves before they died, and kings and commoners alike celebrated the annual death and resurrection of the gods. Hosea, Ezekiel, the Dtr history and 2 Isaiah were familiar with the rituals of death and resurrection (Hos 6:1–4; Ezek 28:1–10; 37:1–14; 1 Sam 28:3–19; 1 Kgs 18:20–29; Isa 14:12–21), but the principles of physical representation that they entailed were excluded by the biblical tradition (e.g., Deut 4:15–24).

Sidon was most active in international trade and established colonies all around the Mediterranean. Its earliest permanent settlement was at Kition in Cyprus in the wake of Mycenaean and Achaean colonists (Karageorghis 1976). From this seaport its power radiated NW across the island: the earliest Phoenician inscription from Cyprus, the Honeyman tomb text, is probably from one of its domains in the interior (Masson and Sznycer 1972: 13–20); another inscription just like it from the early 7th century was found at Chytroi to the NW (Masson and Sznycer 1972: 104–7); in the 5th century Kition extended its boundaries to include Idalion, and in the 4th century it took control of the kingdom of Tamassos (Peckham 1968: 18–20). But the settlers lived among Cypriots and Greeks, maintained their own traditions in symbiosis with the native population, and had little influence on the cultural or political history of the island (Moscati 1968: 103–10). Typically, the Sidonians in Cyprus were merchants and seafarers who exported Cypriot products rather than their own goods to the rest of the Mediterranean world (Coldstream 1979).

Sidon's Anatolian interests are represented by its settlement in the region of Zinjirli. It began at least in the early 9th century with the installation of a local Phoenician dynasty (*TSSI* 3: 30–41). At the end of the century it could still produce a literary Phoenician inscription (Fales 1979), but its king Kilamuwa had an Anatolian name. In the 8th century the whole region was Aramean, and the dynasty became a Phoenician-Aramean hybrid (*TSSI* 2: 60–93). The inscriptions record the difficulty the kings encountered in maintaining their authority and the Kilamuwa inscription in particular mentions internal conflicts between the natives and the Phoenician settlers and external pressures from the surrounding Danunians (*KAI* 24.5–8). The king makes no territorial claims, but describes the benefits that trade has brought to the region—the wealth, fine clothing, and good food. His description anticipates the fuller catalogue in Ezekiel's lamentation over Tyre by mentioning an excess of silver and gold (cf. Ezek 28:4) and the fine linen *(bṣ)* that Ezekiel says was imported from the Arameans (Ezek 27:16). It also makes the king the benefactor of the people, much as Yahweh was to Israel (cf Deut 8:3–4; 10:18) and attributes to him the sort o fatherly role that the Dtr historian assigned to Yahwel (Deut 8:5; cf. Hos 11:1–4; Jer 3:4).

In the neighboring kingdom of Karatepe in Cilicia th inscription of Azitawada evinces a similar settlement pat tern in the 8th century (*KAI* 26; *TSSI* 3: 41–64). Azita wada, as his father before him, was the ruler of Adana i the Cilician plains, the territory that had belonged to th Greek house of Mopsos and that he held as an ally c Urikki of Que, king of the Danunians. In his inscriptio he is accommodating to both indigeneous populatio groups, explaining how he enlarged the borders of the Danunians, and how he subdued the brigands that the house of Mopsos could not control. He was a foreigner, in an area traditionally aligned with Sidon, whose scribes wrote elegant and contrived Phoenician, but he had assimilated to the region, his name was Luwian, his subjects were natives, and his inscription was translated into Hieroglyphic Luwian. He was a merchant prince who claims to have secured the trade routes and rid the country of bandits. His region's exports were horses, weapons, and mercenaries; Ezekiel and the Dtr historian mention such exports from this area (Ezek 27:10–11, 13–14; 1 Kgs 10:26–29). He was a king in the Sidonian tradition, attributing to himself qualities that the Dtr historian ascribed to Yahweh and the people or, exceptionally, to Solomon: he was wise and just (*ḥkm, ṣdq;* cf. Deut 4:6–8; 1 Kgs 5:9–14; Ezek 28:1–5), a father to kings (*ʾb;* cf. 2 Sam 7:14), the benefactor of his people (*śbʿ;* cf. Deut 8:1–20; 10:18; 11:15), the enlarger of their land (*rḥb;* cf. Exod 34:24; Deut 12:20), the source of rest and tranquillity (*nwḥ,* cf. Deut 12:9), the inaugurator of the annual and seasonal festivals (*zbḥ ymm, bʿt ḥrš, bʿt qṣr;* cf. Exod 23:14–17; 34:18–22; Deut 16:1–17, 1 Kgs 9:25). He is representative of the Sidonian spirit of cooperation that brought cohesion, stability, and prosperity to the Mediterranean world.

The Phoenicians who traveled the Aegean to Greece and the West were mostly from Sidon, from Kition and its colonies in Cyprus, or from Arvad and other Sidonian satellites in N Syria (*KAI* 53–60; Röllig 1972). They traveled with foreign wares and adapted thoroughly to the culture of strange places, but they brought with them settlers and skilled artisans trained in the artistic traditions of their own cities (Moscati 1968: 42–81, 145–74). They arrived in Sardinia by the end of the 9th century (Cross 1972), in Italy and in Spain by the early 8th century (Buchner, *PhönWes,* 277–306; Niemeyer, *PhönWes,* 185–206; Schubart, *PhönWes,* 207–34). They maintained relations with their home cities and preserved the religious traditions of the mainland that are known from other Phoenician and from Hebrew sources. An 8th-century inscription from Spain was dedicated to the Astarte worshipped in Sidon (Cross 1971). A 7th-century text from Kition preserves a ritual in her honor that resembles the ritual of the nazirite vow (Num 6:1–20; Dupont-Sommer 1972). An early 5th-century inscription from the same place has details of a celebration in her honor that is also mentioned in contemporary biblical texts (*TSSI* 3: 123–31; Jer 7:16–34; 44:15–30). Fifth-century inscriptions from Sidon confirm her veneration as queen of heaven and tutelary goddess of the city and substantiate the Dtr contention that Astarte was the goddess of the Sidonians (*TSSI* 3: 101–18; 1 Kgs 11:5; 2 Kgs 23:13).

The Phoenicians of Tyre were influential in the S countries and voyaged later than the Sidonians to the western Mediterranean (Bunnens, *StudPhoen* I–II: 7–21). They had separate jurisdiction in Cyprus and founded a new city, Carthage, at Limassol on the SE coast (Lipiński, *StudPhoen* I–II: 209–34). In the latter part of the 8th century Cypriot Carthage was still governed by a viceroy and was under the protection of Baʿal Lebanon, the god of Carmel (*KAI* 31; 1 Kgs 18:20–40); in the 5th century it was an independent city with its own royal house (Masson and Sznycer 1972: 91–94). They founded another Carthage in North Africa from this base in Cyprus and an early 7th-century dedication to Astarte and Pygmalion still attests the Cyprian origin of the colony (Ferron 1958–59). There are ivories in the S Phoenician style from 8th and 7th-century sites in Cyprus, Palestine, North Africa, Etruria, and Spain, and exceptionally from Khorsabad and Arslan Tash (Winter 1976). In the 7th and 6th centuries Phoenicians from Tyre settled at Sarepta and ʿAkzib (Prausnitz, *PhönWes,* 34–44; Pritchard, *PhönWes,* 83–92; Peckham 1968: 130), with Judeans at ʾAzor and ʿArad (Peckham 1968: 125–27; Cross 1979c), in Egypt at Daphne and Abu-Simbel (*KAI* 48–52; Peckham 1968: 127–29), and in Malta (*KAI* 61–62; Ciasca, *PhönWes,* 133–54). In the 5th and 4th centuries they could still be located on the coast of Palestine at Shiqmona, Nebi Yunus and Bat Yam, with Edomites at Elath, and with Judeans in the colony at Elephantine (Peckham 1966; Cross 1968; Delavault and Lemaire 1976).

The Tyrians were more cosmopolitan than the Sidonians and in religious matters remarkably eclectic. Their artistic inspiration was Egyptian (Gubel, *StudPhoen* I–II: 23–52) and at Tyre until the end of the 1st millennium they worshipped Egyptian gods (Dunand and Duru 1962: 181–96). At Arslan Tash, if the texts are genuine (Teixidor 1983), they invoked indigeneous gods like ʿAtaʾ, a provincial antecedent of Atargatis (Pope 1970), and the genius Sasam, whom they identified as the son of a local god, or they worshipped their own chthonic gods like Baal the lord of the earth and Horon the lord of death, or they appealed to the great god Asshur of Assyria and included him in their pantheon with all the sons of El and the assembly of the holy gods (Cross and Saley 1970; Cross 1974). At Carthage they venerated Astarte's Greek consort Pygmalion, at Daphne they worshipped both Baʿal Saphon and the local pantheon (*wkl ʾl tḥpnḥs; KAI* 50.3), and elsewhere in Egypt they paid reverence to Harpocrates (*KAI* 52; Röllig 1969). On the mainland they had particular devotion to derivative gods like *Mlkʿštrt* and Tanit (Yadin 1970; *CMHE* 28–35) but persisted as well in the worship of ancient gods like El and Baalshamem. Tyrians in Malta in the 2d-century thought of Melqart or Heracles as their tutelary god (*bʿl ṣr; KAI* 47.1), and the god is mentioned in contemporary texts from Tyre (Bordreuil 1986a), their own names reveal them to be worshippers of the Egyptian Osiris.

3. Egyptian. The Egyptian sources mark the transition from Canaanite to Phoenician times in the coastal cities. The Amarna letters (EA) depict relations between Canaan and Egypt in the early 14th century and indicate the various political alignments of Tyre, Sidon, and Byblos. The Report of Wen-Amon from the early 11th century (Albright 1975; Goedicke 1975) portrays the new regimes that prevailed in these cities after the Philistines had settled along the coast. Together they suggest continuity rather than great change (Sasson 1966) and anticipate the characteristic features of the principal Phoenician cities in the 1st millennium.

In the Amarna letters Sidon is mentioned mainly in complaints to the Pharaoh from the kings of Tyre and Byblos. The king of Sidon in one of his own letters agreed to give the Pharaoh all the information that he received about Amurru, but the contemporary king of Byblos regularly complained that Sidon was allied with Amurru and Arvad. In his other letter he mentioned problems with the local insurgents, but at the same time the king of Tyre protested that Sidon was interfering in his territory and restricting his essential supplies from the mainland. Tyre considered itself a great city (Akk *ālu rabītu*) and was effusive in its declarations of loyalty to Egypt. It sent ships to transport Egyptian troops and informed on Sidon and its allies in the N: it reported that the king of the Danunians had died but had been succeeded by his brother, that Ugarit had been partly destroyed by fire, that Amurru was encouraging rebellion, that Sidon and Arvad had gathered ships and chariots against Tyre. A cosmopolitan city, Tyre demonstrated its eclectic taste in religion by adopting the new Egyptian devotion to Aton and assimilating it to the local cult of Baalshamem. Byblos was equally loyal to Egypt and, as a buffer against Amurru, more dependent on her military aid. It was isolated from the other cities, under attack by Sidon, and rebuffed by Tyre when it offered assistance against the local insurgents. Byblian territory along the coast and dependent cities in the mountains and in the interior were gradually lost to the incessant attacks of Amurru. Byblos was bound by a tradition of good relations with Egypt. It was tenacious in its fidelity to religious tradition, acceding to the divine pretensions of the Pharaoh, but simultaneously invoking in all its correspondence with Egypt the protection of the Mistress of Byblos (*bʿlt gbl*).

The Report of Wen-Amon gives the impressions of an emissary from Egypt, confirms the relative autonomy of Tyre, Sidon and Byblos, and alludes to their separate dealings with the Sea Peoples. Tyre was in alliance with the Tjekker of Dor. Sidon was conspicuous for its large fleet and had formed a syndicate with the Sea Peoples from Cilicia and Anatolia. Byblos was a small independent port that maintained friendly relations with Egypt but could not compete either with Sidon or with Dor and the Tyrians. Coastal Canaan was no longer an Egyptian province but a conglomerate of maritime powers on the verge of discovering a new world.

4. Greek. The Greek writings confirm or elaborate what is known from other sources and are often derivative. In Linear B texts the word "Phoenician" *(po-ni-ki-yo)* may mean purple or crimson. Homer sometimes mentions Phoenicians, but means the Sidonian merchants and craftsmen who had traveled N and W through the Aegean and were still renowned in his own time (Muhly 1970). Herodotus in his history of the Babylonian and Persian periods was more familiar with Tyre and almost ignored Sidon, although he knew the geography of Phoenicia and was aware that Phoenicians had sailed in search of Europe (3.44, 49; 5.58) before they settled in Egypt and along the Libyan coast (2.32, 112).

Josephus elaborated on the biblical text with information from other historians of the Hellenistic era and naturally ascribed to Tyre preeminence among the Phoenician cities (Katzenstein 1973). He embellished the biblical account of the building of the temple with a parallel account of the reign of Hiram and a chronology of Tyrian kings up to the founding of Carthage (*AgAp* 1.112–27; *Ant* 8.141–47). He retold the story of Ahab and Jezebel (*Ant* 8.316–24; 9.132–39) but used the Tyrian king-list to correct the Dtr historian (1 Kgs 16:31) and called Jezebel's father ʾIttôbaʿal king of the Tyrians, or king of the Tyrians and Sidonians, rather than simply king of the Sidonians. He recounted the fall of Samaria and related it to Shalmaneser V's invasion of Phoenicia in the reign of Elulaios (*Ant* 9.283–87). He elaborated on the destruction of the temple with an account of Nebuchadnezzar's contemporary siege of Tyre and another excerpt from the Tyrian king-list (*AgAp* 1.156–60). He followed the biblical precedent that situated Israel in world history by magnifying the significance of its association with Tyre, but he neglected the other cities and was a partial witness to the history of Phoenicia.

Although Josephus duplicates the biblical narrative, his synchronisms and system of parallel accounts preserve items of interest for the history of Tyre. His Tyrian king-list is fairly accurate and has been corrected and completed by Phoenician and Assyrian sources (Cross 1972: 17; Katzenstein 1973: 349). His story of Hiram's religious reforms includes an oblique reference to the famous pillars of Tyre (*AgAp* 1.118) that are mentioned by Ezekiel (26:11) and Herodotus (2.44) and depicted on Assyrian reliefs (Barnett 1969). The invasion of Phoenicia in the time of Elulaios (ʾIluʾili) is also recorded in the Assyrian annals but is assigned by them to the reign of Sennacherib rather than Shalmaneser V (Pritchard *ANET* 287–88) and is described as an attack on Sidon rather than Tyre (Katzenstein 1973: 220–58). The Babylonian siege of Tyre lasted thirteen years (*Ant* 10.228), and the city's resistance, combined with the earlier Assyrian conquest of Sidon, seems to have inspired Ezekiel's eulogy of the island fastness and lamentation for the Mediterranean world (Ezekiel 27).

Herodotus had heard of early contacts between the Phoenicians and Greece. He knew of Phoenicians particularly as sailors and mercenaries in the service of Egypt and Persia. He recalled that Phoenicians in the time of Cadmus had brought the alphabet to Boeotia and Attica, where it was learned and adapted by Ionian residents (2.57–59). He recorded that Phoenicians in the service of Pharaoh Necho (610–595 B.C.) sailed around Africa from the Red Sea to the Mediterranean, anticipating and partly duplicating Hanno's circumnavigation of the continent in the opposite direction (Harden 1962: 170–77). Among the exploits of Pharaoh Apries (589–570 B.C.) he included an expedition against Tyre and Sidon (2.161) that was meant to deter them from cooperating with the Babylonians in the siege of Jerusalem (Freedy and Redford 1970: 481–84). He knew that the Phoenician fleet gave the Persians naval supremacy (1.143) and he noted that they refused to obey Cambyses' orders to attack their own colony in North African Carthage (3.19; Elayi 1981). He observed that the Phoenician ships, and especially those of Sidon, were the best in the Persian navy and that their kings sailed with the fleet, notably Tetramnestos the son of Anysos of Sidon, Mattan the son of Hiram of Tyre, and Maharbaal the son of ʾAbîbaal of Arvad (7.96–98).

In the Persian and Hellenistic periods, the coastal cities were drawn progressively further into the Greek world and their political history is known almost exclusively from Greek literary and epigraphic sources (Bengston 1962; Peckham 1968; Katzenstein 1973; Elayi 1980; 1982; 1987). But in the 5th century, under Persian administration, the also acquired territory in Palestine and showed some interest in Judean affairs (Ezra 3:7; Neh 13:16; Barag 1966; Peckham 1968: 78–87; Müller 1971; Stern 1982a; 1982b). Sidon, in particular, seems to have profited from the exchange and its inscriptions from the middle of the century demonstrate familiarity with Hebrew literature and religious practice (Greenfield 1971: 258–65). A similar but more developed familiarity with biblical traditions is evident in the later work of Philo of Byblos (Attridge and Oden 1981) who synthesized the religious practice of the coastal cities in an eclectic system derived from Greek theogony and oriental, specifically biblical, cosmology. The speculation of the *Phoenician History* is in striking contrast to Lucian's descriptive account of practices in Tyre, Sidon, Byblos, and Hierapolis (Oden 1977) but shares with it, despite his use of Phoenician sources, a disparagement of native Semitic elements and a naive exaltation of their Greek equivalents.

5. Assyrian and Babylonian. Assyrian intervention on the Phoenician coast followed the era of Sidonian expansion to the N and W and coincided with the beginning of Tyrian predominance in the S states. This period of greatness lasted as long as Tyre could rely on Egyptian support but dwindled after the Babylonian siege of the city and ended with the Persian conquest of Egypt (525 B.C.).

Sidonian expansion N did not go unnoticed by the world powers. In the years just before the voyage of Wen-Amon, Tiglath-pileser I (1114–1076 B.C.) went to Mount Lebanon where he erected a stele and received tribute from Sidon and Byblos, then marched against Amurru where he received tribute from Arvad and sailed in an Arvadian ship (*ANET,* 275; Katzenstein 1973: 175). In the 9th century, Asshurnasirpal II (883–859 B.C.) made a similar expedition to Mount Lebanon and the seacoast, but he also listed the merchandise that he received as tribute and was the first to include Tyre among the tributary cities (*ANET,* 276). Shalmaneser III (858–824 B.C.) also mentioned Tyre among the coastal cities that brought him tribute, but his campaigns were directed mainly against the Arameans and the N coalition on whom Sidon depended for trade (Pritchard *ANET* 276–81; Katzenstein 1973: 173–82). Hayanu (*ḥyʾ* [*KAI* 24.1]), the father of Kilamuwa, was among the rulers of northern Syria, Cilicia, and Anatolia defeated in his first campaign; at the battle of Qarqar (853 B.C.) his opponents included Arvad, ʿArqa, and Siyannu, the Phoenician cities in Amurru mentioned by the Dtr historian (Gen 10:17–18), as well as Damascus, Arabia, and the other regions that Ezekiel included in his catalogue of Phoenician trade centers (Ezekiel 27).

From the early 8th century Palestine was included among the regions subject to Assyria (*ANET,* 281; Katzenstein 1973: 200) and in the second half of the century the Assyrian kings began their policy of total conquest. Tiglath-pileser III (744–727 B.C.) conquered ʿArqa, Siyannu, and the northern coastal towns and incorporated them, and a few years later Arvad, into the Assyrian province of Ṣimirra (= Ṣumur [Gen 10:18]; Kessler 1975–76). This ended the era of Sidonian supremacy and allowed Tiglath-pileser to concentrate on Tyre and its Philistine allies. He received tribute from ʾIttôbaʿal of Tyre before 738 B.C. (Levine 1972; Cogan 1973) and defeated Hiram of Tyre a few years later (734–732 B.C.). Although Philistia was defeated at the same time and eventually became the province of Dor, Tyre retained its independence and continued to pay tribute (Oded 1974). This contravened Assyrian policy in the West (Weippert 1982) and, with Sidon's isolation from its northern resources, it assured Tyre's supremacy in the E Mediterranean (Oded 1974). Tyre became the leading city of Phoenicia, and its kings, earlier entitled "King of the Tyrians" (*mlk ṣrm;* Bordreuil 1986b: 298–305) assumed the title "King of the Sidonians" (*mlk ṣdnm* [*KAI* 31.1]).

At the end of the 8th century ʾIluʾili (Gk *Elulaios* Akk *Luli*) of Sidon attempted to restore the city's control of Kition in Cyprus and regain its former stature in Mediterranean affairs, but he was defeated by Sennacherib and (704–681 B.C.) escaped to Cyprus, where he was assassinated (Elayi 1985). He was succeeded by ʾIttôbaʿal (Katzenstein 1973: 220–58). In the reign of Esarhaddon (680–669 B.C.) ʿAbdimilkut of Sidon made another attempt to escape Assyrian domination but he and his Cilician allies were defeated, the kings of Cyprus submitted to Assyria, and Sidon was destroyed (*ANET,* 290–91). Tyre remained the only naval power in the East, and the treaty with Esarhaddon that gave it access to harbors in Philistia and Phoenicia invoked all the gods of the coast including the seafaring Baals of Tyre, Eshmun of Sidon, and Melqart. The treaty gave Esarhaddon control of Mediterranean trade and restricted Tyre's local autonomy. Tyre rebelled, was besieged, captured, and put under Assyrian administration; Egypt, on which it had relied for support, was invaded and conquered (671 B.C.; Spalinger 1974). In its expansion southward Tyre cooperated with Phoenician kings in the coastal cities of Philistia, but all of these cities paid tribute to Ashurbanipal (668–633 B.C.) and were forced to accompany him on his first campaign against Egypt (*ANET,* 294). Tyre revolted again but was reconquered and incorporated into the Assyrian provincial system (Katzenstein 1973: 288–94). It may have prospered in the lull before the Babylonian invasions, but Tyre was besieged again by Nebuchadnezzar (605–562 B.C.) and its king, with the kings of Gaza and Ashdod, of Sidon and Arvad, was taken captive to Babylon (Katzenstein 1973: 319). When the Phoenician cities were restored and regained their power in the Persian period, the Mediterranean world they helped create had fallen to the emerging world powers.

B. Chronology

The king-lists of the principal Phoenician cities are reconstructed from Hebrew (*), Greek (+), Assyrian (-), Egyptian (=) and Phoenician sources (Albright 1947; Cross 1972: 17; Katzenstein 1973: 349; Mullen 1974). The dates are approximate and often conjectural.

BYBLOS

=Zakarbaʿal	1050
ʾAḥîrām	1000
ʾIttôbaʿal	975
Yaḥîmilk	950
ʾAbîbaʿal	930
ʾElîbaʿal	920
-Šipṭîbaʿal I	740

-ʾUrîmilk I	701
-Milkʾasap	670
Šipṭîbaʿal II	500
ʾUrîmilk II	480
Yîḥarbaʿal	460
Yaḥawmilk	440
ʾElpaʿal	420
ʿOzîbaʿal	400
Zakarbaʿal II	380
ʾAddīrmilk	360
ʿAyyinʾel	340

TYRE

+ʾAbîbaʿal	1000
*+Ḥîrām I	980
+Baʿalʿazor I	950
+ʿAbdʿaštart	930
+ʿAštart	920
+Dalayʿaštart	900
+ʿAštartrām	890
+Pilles	880
+ʾIttôbaʿal I	880
-+Baʿalʿazor II	850
+Mattan I	840
+Pygmalion	830
-ʾIttôbaʿal II	760
-Ḥîrām II	738
-Mattan II	734
-Baʿal I	680
+ʾIttôbaʿal III	590
+Baʿal II	575
+Yakînbaʿal	565
+Kalbay	564
+ʾAbîbaʿal	563
+Mattan III	562
+Baʿalʿazor III	555
+Maharbaʿal	554
+Ḥîrām III	551
+Ḥîrām IV	500
+Mattan IV	480
+ʿOzîmilk	350

SIDON

*ʾIttôbaʿal I	880
-ʾIluʾili	720
-ʾIttôbaʿal II	700
-ʿAbdimilkut	680
+Anysos	520
+Tetramnestos	500
ʾEšmunʿazor I	480
Tabnît	470
ʾEšmunʿazor II	465
Yatonmilk	450
Bodʿaštart	440
Baʿalšillem I	430
ʿAbdʾešmun	420
Baʿnaʾ	400
Baʿalšillem II	380
+Straton I	375
+Mazaeus	360
+Tannit	357
+Evagoras	345
+Straton II	343

Bibliography

Albright, W. F. 1947. The Phoenician Inscriptions of the Tenth Century B.C. *JAOS* 67: 153–60.

———. 1975. Syria, the Philistines and Phoenicia. Pp. 507–36 in *CAH*³ 2/2.

Attridge, H. W., and Oden, R. A., Jr. 1981. *Philo of Byblos: The Phoenician History.* Washington.

Aubet Semmler, M. E. 1985. Los fenicios en España: estado de la cuestión y perspectivas. *AulaOr* 3: 9–38.

Barag, D. 1966. The Effects of the Tennes Rebellion on Palestine. *BASOR* 183: 6–12.

Barnett, R. D. 1969. Ezekiel and Tyre. *EI* 9: 6–13.

Bengston, H. 1962. *Die Staatsverträge des Altertums.* Vol. 2, *Die Verträge der griechisch-römischer Welt von* 700 bis 338 v. Chr. Munich.

Bordreuil, P. 1977. Une inscription phénicienne champlevée des environs de Byblos. *Sem* 27: 23–27.

———. 1986a. Attestations inédites de Melqart, Baal Ḥamon et Baal Ṣaphon à Tyr. StudPhoen IV, 77–86.

———. 1986b. Charges et fonctions en Syrie-Palestine d'après quelques sceaux ouest-sémitiques du second et du premier millénaire. *CRAIBL* 290–308.

Borger, R. 1956. *Die Inschriften Asarhaddons Königs von Assyrien.* Graz.

Breglia, L. 1955. Le antiche rotte del Mediterraneo documentate da monete e pesi. *AANLR* 30: 211–326.

Cogan, M. 1973. Tyre and Tiglath-Pileser III. *JCS* 25: 96–99.

Coldstream, J. N. 1979. Some Cypriote Traits in Cretan Pottery ca. 950–700 B.C. Pp. 257–263 in *Acts of the International Archaeological Symposium 'The Relations between Cyprus and Crete, ca. 2000–500 B.C.'.* Nicosia.

Cross, F. M. 1967. The Origin and Early Evolution of the Alphabet. *EI* 8: 8*–24*.

———. 1968. Jar Inscriptions from Shiqmona. *IEJ* 18: 226–33.

———. 1971. The Old Phoenician Inscription from Spain Dedicated to Hurrian Astarte. *HTR* 64: 189–95.

———. 1972. An Interpretation of the Nora Stone. *BASOR* 208: 13–19.

———. 1974. A Second Phoenician Incantation Text from Arslan Tash. *CBQ* 36: 486–90.

———. 1979a. Early Alphabetic Scripts. Pp. 97–123 in *Symposia Celebrating the Seventy-Fifth Anniversary of the Founding of the American Schools of Oriental Research (1900–75),* ed. F. M. Cross. Cambridge.

———. 1979b. A Recently Published Phoenician Inscription of the Persian Period from Byblos. *IEJ* 29: 40–44.

———. 1979c. Two Offering Dishes with Phoenician Inscriptions from the Sanctuary of ʿArad. *BASOR* 235: 75–78.

———. 1980. Newly Found Inscriptions in Old Canaanite and Early Phoenician Scripts. *BASOR* 238: 1–20.

Cross, F. M., and McCarter, P. K., Jr. 1973. Two Archaic Inscriptions on Clay Objects from Byblus. *RSF* 1: 3–8.

Cross, F. M., and Saley, R. J. 1970. Phoenician Incantations on a Plaque of the Seventh Century B.C. from Arslan Tash in Upper Syria. *BASOR* 197: 42–49.

Delavault, B., and Lemaire, A. 1976. Une stèle 'molk' de Palestine dédiée à Eshmoun? RES 367 reconsidéré, *RB* 83: 569–83.
Donner, H., and Röllig, W. 1968. *Kanaanäische und aramäische Inschriften.* 3 vols., Wiesbaden.
Dunand, M. 1969. Byblos, Sidon, Jerusalem: Monuments apparentés des temps achémenides. *VTSup* 17: 64–70.
Dunand, M., and Duru, R. 1962. *Oumm el-ᶜamed: Une ville de l'époque hellénistique aux échelles de Tyr.* 2 vols. Etudes et documents d'archéologie 4. Paris.
Dupont-Sommer, A. 1972. Une inscription phénicienne archaïque récemment trouvée à Kition (Chypre). *Mémoires de l'Institut National de France, Académie des Inscriptions et Belles-Lettres* 44/2: 273–94.
Elayi, J. 1980. The Phoenician Cities in the Persian Period. *JANES* 12: 13–28.
———. 1981. The Relations between Tyre and Carthage during the Persian Period. *JANES* 13: 15–29.
———. 1982. Studies in Phoenician Geography during the Persian Period. *JNES* 41: 83–110.
———. 1985. Les relations entre les cités phéniciennes et l'empire assyrien sous le règne de Sennachérib. *Sem* 35: 19–26.
———. 1987. *Recherches sur les cités phéniciennes à l'époque perse.* Naples.
Fales, F. M. 1979. Kilamuwa and the Foreign Kings: Propaganda vs. Power. *WO* 10: 6–22.
Ferron, J. 1958–59. Le médaillon de Carthage. *CaByr* 8: 45–59.
Freedy, K. S., and Redford, D. B. 1970. The Dates in Ezekiel in Relation to Biblical, Babylonian and Egyptian Sources. *JAOS* 90: 462–85.
Goedicke, H. 1975. *The Report of Wenamun.* Baltimore.
Greenfield, J. C. 1971. Scripture and Inscription: The Literary and Rhetorical Element in Some Early Phoenician Inscriptions. Pp. 253–68 in *Near Eastern Studies in Honor of W. F. Albright,* ed. H. Goedicke. Baltimore.
Harden, D. 1962. *The Phoenicians.* New York.
Karageorghis, V. 1976. *Kition: Mycenaean and Phoenician Discoveries in Cyprus.* London.
Katzenstein, H. J. 1973. *The History of Tyre.* Jerusalem.
Kessler, K. 1975–76. Die Anzahl der assyrischen Provinzen des Jahres 738 v. Chr. in Nordsyrien. *WO* 8: 49–63.
Lane, W. R. 1969. The Phoenician Dialect of Larnax tes Lapethou. *BASOR* 194: 39–45.
Lemaire, A. 1977. *Inscriptions Hébraïques.* Vol. 1, *Les Ostraca.* Paris.
Levine, L. 1972. Menahem and Tiglath-Pileser: A New Synchronism. *BASOR* 206: 40–42.
McCarter, P. K., Jr., and Coote, R. B. 1973. The Spatula Inscription from Byblos. *BASOR* 212: 16–22.
Masson, O., and Sznycer, M. 1972. *Recherches sur les Phéniciens à Chypre.* Paris.
Moscati, S. 1968. *The World of the Phoenicians.* Trans. A. Hamilton. London.
Muhly, J. D. 1970. Homer and the Phoenicians: The Relations between Greece and the Near East in the Late Bronze and Early Iron Ages. *Berytus* 19: 19–64.
Mullen, E. T., Jr. 1974. A New Royal Sidon Inscription. *BASOR* 216: 25–30.
Müller, H. P. 1971. Phönizien und Juda in exilisch-nachexilischer Zeit. *WO* 6: 189–204.
Oded, B. 1974. The Phoenician Cities and the Assyrian Empire in the Time of Tiglath-Pileser III. *ZDPV* 90: 38–49.
Oden, R. A., Jr. 1977. *Studies in Lucian's De Syria Dea.* HSM 15. Missoula, MT.
Peckham, B. 1966. An Inscribed Jar from Bat-Yam. *IEJ* 16: 11–17.
———. 1968. *The Development of the Late Phoenician Scripts.* Cambridge.
Pope, M. H. 1970. The Saltier of Atargatis Reconsidered. Pp. 179–95 in *Near Eastern Archaeology in the Twentieth Century: Essays in Honor of Nelson Glueck,* ed. J. A. Sanders. Garden City.
Röllig, W. 1969. Eine neue Harpokrates-Statuette mit phönizischer Inschrift. *WO* 5: 118–20.
———. 1972. Alte und neue phönizische Inschriften aus dem ägäischen Raum. Vol. 1, pp. 1–8 in *Neue Ephemeris für Semitische Epigraphik,* eds. R. Degen, W. W. Müller, and W. Röllig. Wiesbaden.
Sasson, J. M. 1966. Canaanite Maritime Involvement in the Second Millennium B.C. *JAOS* 86: 126–38.
Shefton, B. B. 1982. Greeks and Greek Imports in the South of the Iberian Peninsula: The Archaeological Evidence. Pp. 337–70 in *PhönWest.*
Spalinger, A. 1974. Esarhaddon and Egypt: An Analysis of the First Invasion of Egypt. *Or* 43: 295–326.
Stern, E. 1982a. *Material Culture of the Land of the Bible in the Persian Period 538–332 B.C.* Warminster.
———. 1982b. A Favissa of a Phoenician Sanctuary from Tel Dor. *JJS* 33: 35–54.
Teixidor, J. 1983. Les tablettes d'Arslan Tash au Musée d'Alep. *AulaOr* 1: 105–9.
Weippert, M. 1982. Zur Syrienpolitik Tiglathpilesers III. Pp. 395–408 in *Mesopotamien und seine Nachbarn. 25th Renconere Assyriologique Internationale.* Berlin.
Winter, I. J. 1976. Phoenician and North Syrian Ivory Carving in Historical Context: Questions of Style and Distribution. *Iraq* 38: 1–22.
———. 1981. Is There a South Syrian Style of Ivory Carving in the Early First Millennium B.C.? *Iraq* 43: 101–30.
Yadin, Y. 1970. Symbols of Deities at Zinjirli, Carthage and Nazor. Pp. 199–231 in *Near Eastern Archaeology in the Twentieth Century. Essays in Honor of Nelson Glueck,* ed. J. A. Sanders. Garden City.

BRIAN PECKHAM

PHOENICIAN LANGUAGE. See LANGUAGES (PHOENICIAN).

PHOENICIAN RELIGION. The eastern littoral of the Mediterranean sea S of the Amanus mountains and N of Mt. Carmel was occupied in historic times by people whose language and culture were sufficiently uniform in antiquity to be recognized as distinct. The land was called CANAAN by its inhabitants, *fnḫw* by Egyptians (see Vandersleyen 1987), *phoinikē* by Greeks. The name "Phoenicia" is properly applied to this area, and "Phoenician" to its inhabitants, from about 1200 B.C.E. onward. See PHOENICIA, HISTORY OF. The beliefs and activities of the ancient Phoenicians that can be designated "religion" in modern usage are of interest to readers of the Bible principally with respect to the religion of ancient Israel and Judah as depicted in the Hebrew canon. Less readily perceived is the contribution of Phoenician mythology to Jewish thought as set down in the Apocrypha of the Greek canon and in the writings known as Pseudepigrapha (on Phoenician traditions of secret writings, see Ribichini 1987b). Even more obscure is the degree to which elements of early Christian theology incorporated motifs associated with Phoenician religion (for an example, see HERAKLES).

A. Sources
 1. Textual
 2. Artifactual
 3. Condition and Utility of Sources
B. Scope
 1. Geographical
 2. Historical
C. Cult
 1. Sacrifice
 2. Gifts
 3. Prayer
 4. Purity
D. Cult Sites
 1. Natural
 2. Constructed
E. Cult Personnel
 1. Priesthoods
 2. Other Functionaries
F. Festivals
 1. Seasonal Celebrations
 2. Sports
G. Revelatory Institutions
 1. Prophecy
 2. Other Mantic Activities
H. Divinities
 1. Phoenician Polytheism
 2. Dynamics of Pantheons
I. The Dead

A. Sources

1. Textual. Literary and epigraphic texts are the written sources of information about Phoenician religion. Literary texts include the Hebrew Bible; portions of the Apocrypha and Pseudepigrapha; Greek texts by classical, Hellenistic, and Christian writers; and Latin works. Epigraphic texts include cuneiform texts in the Akkadian language and inscriptions in the Phoenician language; the form of Phoenician used at Carthage and elsewhere in the W Mediterranean is called Punic (Lat *Poenus,* "Phoenician"), and the form used after the fall of Carthage is known as Neo-Punic. See LANGUAGES (PHOENICIAN).

Evidence derived from the biblical traditions will be discussed separately. Among Greek writers, Homer provides no substantive information about Phoenician religion, though the Phoenicians figure in the verse epics attributed to him. Herodotus, whose history explores relations between Greek and Phoenician societies, nonetheless provides no sustained discussion of religious beliefs and practices among the latter. Works of the Greek historians Ephorus and Timaeus survive only in the fragments cited by other Greek writers. Details of the military and political history of Carthage, founded as a Phoenician colony in N Africa, were preserved with these fragments, chiefly in the *Library of History* compiled by Diodorus Siculus (Pearson 1984); but Phoenician and Punic religion is represented only episodically, and with tendentious hostility (Simonetti 1983).

The text of a treaty concluded in 215 B.C.E. between Hannibal of Carthage and Philip V of Macedon is preserved in the history written by Polybius (7.9). See HISTORIOGRAPHY (GRECO-ROMAN). It has been plausibly argued (most recently and thoroughly in Barré 1983) that the divine witnesses listed in the text of the treaty, in spite of their Greek names, are to be understood as their Phoenician or Punic "equivalents," and that the list represents the pantheon of Carthage at the time of Hannibal. (For a different perspective, see Huss 1986.) The historian Pausanias and the geographer Strabo preserve details of Phoenician religion as observed by Greeks.

A narrative description of religious practices of Phoenician derivation is found in the Greek work *Concerning the Syrian Goddess* attributed to Lucian of Samosata, a satirist who wrote in the 2d century C.E. (Oden 1977). The 4th-century Christian historiographer Eusebius presented Phoenician mythology as an example of the sort of nonsense from which his own church had liberated the theological intellect. Eusebius cited generous portions of a work entitled *Phoenician History,* said to be translated by PHILO OF BYBLOS from an older work in the Phoenician language compiled by Sanchuniaton (*Hist. Eccl.* 1.10.23–1.10.53; see Attridge and Oden 1981; Baumgarten 1981; Schiffmann 1986).

Among texts in the Latin language, the epitome or summary compiled by Justin from the (now lost) world history of Pompeius Trogus includes a section on the history of Carthage (chaps. 18 and 19 of Justin; the standard edition of the text is by Seel [1972]). The accurate historical details of Trogus' compilation can be traced to Timaeus; of Phoenician religion there is nothing of substance.

The principal epigraphic sources are those in cuneiform and others in the linear Phoenician alphabet. A vassal treaty imposed by the Neo-Assyrian ruler Esarhaddon on Baal, king of Tyre about 675 B.C.E. (*ANET,* 533–34) lists among its divine witnesses deities that must be Tyrian (on the list, Barré 1983: 45–50). See also BETHEL. Other documents in cuneiform provide incidental details pertinent to a reconstruction of Phoenician religion.

A small corpus of inscriptions in the Phoenician language has survived (CIS I 1–121; *KAI* 1–60; additional texts published in a variety of journals remain uncollected); a larger corpus of Punic and Neo-Punic inscriptions (CIS I 122–6068; *KAI* 61–173, 277) is comprised almost entirely of votive texts which repeat stereotyped formulas. Less than half a percent of the surviving corpus is non-dedicatory, and again these offer only glimpses of Phoenician religious thought and practice.

2. Artifactual. Architecture, sculpture, glyptics (including coins), and other craft products constitute a fragmentary record of the social manifestations of Phoenician religion. See LEBANON; PALESTINE, ARCHAEOLOGY OF.

3. Condition and Utility of Sources. With the exception of Phoenician inscriptions, all sources of information about the religion of Phoenicia are secondary. Any information derived from them must become part of a modern narrative whose major components are deduction, inference, and speculation. The quality of the resulting reconstruction is inherently dependent on the organizing scheme according to which fragments of fact have been related to one another. Any reconstruction of Phoenician religion must necessarily be tentative.

B. Scope

1. Geographical. "Phoenicia" was spatially dispersed. A series of coastal cities and villages from Myriandos in Cilicia (modern Turkey) to Gaza were Phoenician in language and religion. Cyprus supported a Phoenician population in its E and S portion. Phoenician was written in W Cilicia, and Phoenicians settled on the Aegean islands, on the Italian peninsula, on Sardinia, in N Africa, in W Sicily, on other islands of the W Mediterranean, and extensively in Spain. See PHOENICIA, HISTORY OF.

2. Historical. While it has been argued (Garbini 1980) that the term "Phoenician" is appropriate to the Bronze Age culture of the E Mediterranean littoral, most scholars accept the chronological constraints for which Moscati (1968: xxii) has made a case, and reserve the word "Phoenician" for the Iron Age, i.e., the period following the invasions of "Sea Peoples," and later.

C. Cult

1. Sacrifice. The Phoenician words for sacrifice and related activity derive in large part from the common Semitic lexical stock (Fronzaroli 1965: 252–56) traceable to a very early period. From this and other evidence it can be deduced that sacrifice is a practice of great antiquity among Semitic-speaking societies. The procedures and perceived significance of particular sacrificial types, however, undoubtedly changed and varied over time.

Both faunal and floral sacrifices were made by Phoenicians. Mammalian victims were oxen, bulls, sheep, goats, and varieties of deer. Among birds, columbine species (doves and pigeons) seem to have been preferred as victims. Pools of sacred fish are mentioned by classical writers, but there is no evidence of piscatory sacrifice.

Faunal sacrifices necessitated the death and (in cases involving larger animals) partial consumption of the victim. Nothing is known about the method of dispatching the victim, although it is reasonable to suppose that a variety of procedures were employed. In certain categories of sacrifices all or part of the victim was incinerated on an altar. Other sacrifices may have involved suspending the victim from a sacred tree or post.

Floral sacrifices included offerings of cereal grains and plant derivatives such as oil. There is no evidence that floral offerings were consumed.

The most detailed documentary evidence concerning sacrifice of Phoenician derivation is late (after 350 B.C.E.) and Western. The Carthage tariffs (among which is included the Marseilles Tariff [*KAI* 69]) were temple documents regulating payments due priests for a variety of sacrifices and (in cases of faunal sacrifices) specifying the distribution of portions of the victim not destroyed in the sacrificial procedure. A limited continuity can be traced in the names of sacrifices found in Ugaritic ritual texts (see UGARIT), biblical legislation (see SACRIFICE), and the Carthage tariffs (Guzzo Amadasi 1967: 169–82).

The most vivid biblical narrative concerning a sacrifice performed by Phoenicians is legendary and highly polemical (1 Kgs 18:20–40). It concerns a sacrificial contest staged by the Israelite prophet Elijah at Mt. Carmel, a site that, according to one writer, was "sacred above all mountains" to the Phoenicians and of restricted access (Iamb. *Vit. Pyth.* 3:15). The sacrifice is performed by "prophets of Baal" convened for the purpose by Elijah (1 Kgs 18:25); the victim is a bull, which is killed, butchered, and arranged in pieces on wood placed on an altar. Fire to consume the sacrifice is sought (unsuccessfully) from "Baal" in shouted invocations while the sacrificers dance around the altar and lacerate themselves (1 Kgs 18:26–28).

One of the goals of this story is to make Phoenician sacrifice appear ridiculous, and it is possible that in such a distorting context the details of sacrificial procedure are not accurately representative. But the implicit assumption of the narrative that identical sacrificial procedures are appropriate for both "Baal" and Yahweh may be an indication of a perceived common derivation of Israelite and Phoenician sacrifice.

The narrative of Jehu's bloody suppression of a Phoenician cult in Samaria (2 Kgs 10:18–27) indicates that the "great sacrifice" which Jehu convened consisted in part of holocausts (vv 24–25; Heb *ʿōlôt*). Jehu himself, as king, may have performed the sacrifices (the pronominal reference of these sentences is ambiguous).

As a social institution, sacrifice in Phoenicia probably shared structural features with Israelite sacrifice. Presumably it operated in a system of male bonding and genealogical legitimation (Jay 1988) in which women were marginal participants (Winter 1983: 1–69). Phoenician and Punic texts commemorating sacrifices generally include a genealogy of the offerer which lists male ancestors; this is true in the case of women as well as men (Amadasi Guzzo 1988).

The Phoenician inscription from Karatepe in Anatolia (*ANET,* 653–55; *TSSI* 3: 41–64) claims for its author Azatiwata. Significant military and diplomatic achievements which culminate in the refoundation of the city bear his name. The climax of Azatiwata's narrative is the establishment of the cult of the god *bʿl krntryš* (the second half of the name is not Phoenician) with seasonal sacrifices of oxen and sheep (*KAI* 26 A ii 19–A iii 2). It is apparent from the benedictions which follow the narrative that not only Azatiwata himself but the entire city anticipated life, health, political prowess, reliable food supplies, and reproductive success to follow from their assiduous maintenance of the sacrificial cult.

Insofar as the sacrificial cult in Phoenician cities operated within a centralized palatine economy exploiting outlying villages for agricultural produce and redistributing goods and services within a stratified urban social structure, expectations such as those expressed in the Karatepe inscription may have been more than wishful thinking (Liverani 1974). In the Persian period the construction of cultic installations remains among the chief accomplishments of kings (*ANET,* 656 [Yehawmilk of Byblos]; *ANET,* 662 [Eshmunazar of Sidon]).

The inscribed base of a statue erected by Yatonbaal, a local official in the Ptolemaic administration of Cyprus (see Parmentier 1987), records the building of altars and the institution of daily sacrifices on behalf of the dedicator's immediate family in conjunction with monthly sacrifices for the reigning Ptolemy and dependents (*TSSI* 3: 133–41).

2. Gifts. In common with the practices of other Semitic cultures, Phoenician religion included offerings of objects specially dedicated to a deity. Agricultural and industrial products were equally presentable gifts. Carved work (such as the ivory casket dedicated to Astarte by a Phoenician woman [*TSSI* 3: 71–74]); metal objects (of which an elegant silver bowl found in 1876 at Praeneste, Italy, is a fine example [*TSSI* 3: 71]), sculpture, ceramics, and terracottas were all offered in dedication. Spoils of war were frequently dedicated, and the presentation of gifts in temples was an important element of interstate relations linking colonies (or former colonies) to their mother cities (Diod. 13.108.4; 17.41.8) and vassals to their suzerains.

Dedications were commonly made in fulfillment of a vow (Phoen *ndr*). Phoenician and Punic inscriptions on steles set up to record the fulfillment of a vow *(ndr)* by means of a gift (Phoen *mtt,* Pun *mtnt*) comprise more than 95 percent of the textual remains of these languages. The relative abundance of votive texts witnesses to the importance of vows and their fulfillment in Phoenician religion.

Certain categories of vows may have been fulfilled by the immolation of neonatal or prepubescent children of either sex. Evidence for human sacrifice as an institution of Phoenician religion is, however, limited and ambiguous. A few passages from the Hebrew Bible have been understood as referring to the sacrifice of children in connection with the cult of a divinity called Molech (a god whose very existence has been doubted; see Heider 1985). Archaeological evidence of human sacrifice among Levantine Phoenicians is lacking (a point stressed by Ribichini 1987a; 1988). Sites of Phoenician origin in the W Mediterranean have provided considerably more artifactual and osteological evidence, but the interpretation of these remains is controversial. Excavations of the topheth at Carthage have led certain archaeologists and historians to conclude that an institution of ritual infanticide was maintained for at least five centuries (ca. 700–200 B.C.E.) among the Carthaginians (Stager 1980; 1982; Stager and Wolff 1984; Lipiński 1982; 1988; Heider 1985; S. Brown 1987). Moscati (1987) has denied the existence of such an institution. Other scholars have remained agnostic on the subject (Benichou-Safar 1988). But an analysis of the osteological remains from the *tophet* of Tharros in Sardinia, where controlled excavation and interpretation have been possible, indicates that neonatal and prepubescent humans probably were sacrificial victims (Fedele and Foster 1988).

Certain passages from Greek and Latin writers purport to describe the sacrifice of children as carried out at Carthage and other Punic sites. These are all highly polemical, histrionic, and perhaps interdependent. They thus invite proper scepticism in their interpretation (as Simonetti 1983 as shown).

3. Prayer. Prayer is intimately related to the taking and fulfillment of vows. Numerous Phoenician and Punic inscriptions make the association explicit. Most votive texts end with a formulaic statement that the divinity or divinities to whom the dedication has been made "heard the sound" of the voice of the dedicator. Presumably vows were most often made in the context of prayer, and the necessity of their fulfillment was communicated through revelation to the vower (biblical parallels have been drawn out by O'Brien 1987).

Phoenician and Punic inscriptions provide examples of prayerful dedication. Here can be seen truly touching examples of marital devotion (*KAI* 48) and filial piety (*KAI* 34). The benedictory section of the Karatepe inscription (*KAI* 26 A iii 2–11) has the characteristics of prayer in spite of its rhetorical origins and propagandistic purpose.

A Punic prayer is incorporated in a soliloquy spoken in Punic by the character Hanno at the beginning of the fifth act of the *Poenulus,* a play in Latin by the playwright Plautus (d. 184 B.C.E.). The Punic text is genuine but corrupt. The opening line can be translated "I invoke the gods and goddesses . . . of this city" (1. 930), but the remainder of the text is replete with difficulty (see Sznycer 1967; Krahmalkov 1970; 1988: 55–62). Also, the Carthaginian general Hannibal prayed for his troops before battle (Polyb. 3.44.13).

Maledictions are amply attested in Phoenician sources (Gevirtz 1961; *IDB* 1: 749–50). Blasphemy was attached to a famous Carthaginian commander: Himilco, returning in shame from defeat in Sicily, is said by Trogus to have accused his gods of perfidy before finally committing suicide (Justin 19.3.3 [Seel 1972: 166]).

4. Purity. Systems of sacrifice and ritual express conceptual analyses of the world in related taxonomies of purity and impurity, benefit, and danger (Douglas 1966). The conceptualization of purity in Phoenician religion and the rules according to which Phoenicians maintained ritual purity have been largely lost. Surviving details do not imply any particular system.

Classical writers mention Phoenician abstention from pork (Herodian 5.6.9; Porph. *Abst.* 1.14); archaeological confirmation has been inferred from the absence of pig bones from the earliest levels of Phoenician settlements in the W Mediterranean, even at sites where pig bones are found in pre-Phoenician levels (Whittaker 1974: 71).

Endogamy also knew exceptions among the Phoenicians. The notorious Jezebel was a daughter of the Phoenician Ethbaal, "king of the Sidonians" (1 Kgs 16:31), given in marriage to Ahab, king of Israel. Psalm 45 envisions such a royal wedding between an Israelite king and a Phoenician princess. Sallust (*Iug.* 78.4) says that Tyrians intermarried with Libyans at Lepcis Magna in N Africa. Intermarriage of Phoenicians with Judeans took place near Larnaca, Cyprus (ancient Kition) early in the Persian period, to judge from Judean names in the genealogies on Phoenician gravestones there (Hadjisavvas, Dupont-Sommer, and Lozachmeur 1984; Hadjisavvas 1986). Hamilcar, a 5th-century Carthaginian general (d. 480 B.C.E.), was the son of a Carthaginian father and a Syracusan Greek mother (Herod. 7.167).

A late and fragmentary Punic inscription (*KAI* 76) appears to be a calendar of purificatory rituals. The word *qdš* "holy" occurs three times, and there is mention of fruit, bread, incense, and (perhaps) naphtha. The text gives directions for the cultic manipulation of these items on specified days. Also associated with Carthage is a legend that a sacred oil-spring in a Carthaginian sanctuary would not flow except for persons who were ceremonially pure (Pseud. Arist. *Mir. Ausc.* 113).

The violation of a deity's prerogatives with respect to

purity or custom might result in death, illness, or madness. A case of sacrilege is the subject of a recently discovered Akkadian letter from the king of Sidon to the king of Ugarit (Arnaud 1986–87: 189–90; the date appears to be ca. 1225 B.C.E.). Plague resulting from sacrilege is a motif seized upon by Greek historians recounting Carthaginian military losses (e.g., Diod. 13.85–86). It is in the context of sacrilege, plague, and military defeat that narratives of human sacrifice are to be found (Diod. 13.86.3; 20.13.5–6).

D. Cult Sites

1. Natural. Any distinctive feature of the topography might be a sacred site among the Phoenicians, as among Mediterranean peoples generally. Caves, peaks, stone outcroppings, springs, rivers, and lakes were sacred, and frequently the sites of cults. Natural and cultivated groves of trees were centers of worship. The sacred grove and pool of Afqa at the source of the river Adonis (modern Nahr Ibrahim in Lebanon) was the most celebrated holy place in Phoenicia (Euseb. *Vita Const.* 3.55; Ribichini 1981: 159–65).

2. Constructed. Altars, chapels, images, and temples were constructed at sacred sites. See HIGH PLACE. The foundation or refurbishing of cultic installations is a recurring subject of Phoenician and Punic inscriptions (e.g., *KAI* 19; 277). Maintenance of temples was an obligation of kings in the E Phoenician cities; among colonies of Phoenicians in the W, such obligations might fall to private individuals (as did *leiturgia* among the Greeks). Private expenditures on cultic service could be lavishly rewarded (*KAI* 60).

The temple of Yahweh in Jerusalem, which was built for Solomon by Tyrian architects and laborers (1 Kings 5–6), was an elegant example of Phoenician temple design. See TEMPLE, JERUSALEM. A Phoenician temple of Astarte in Kition, Cyprus, datable to the 8th century B.C.E., provides a parallel.

E. Cult Personnel

1. Priesthoods. Two priesthoods, *khn* and *kmr,* existed among the Phoenicians. The former is the only class of priesthood recognized as legitimate in the Hebrew Bible, where it is restricted to men and, at least in the divided monarchy, not a royal prerogative. The Phoenicians, in contrast, admitted male *khnm* and female *khnt,* who might also be king and queen, or queen mother (*DISO,* 116). As in Israelite religion, Phoenician *khn* priests were organized in colleges presided over by a *rb khnm* "high priest."

The *kmr* priesthood is little known either in the Hebrew Bible (BDB, 485) or in Phoenicia (*DISO,* 122). Both in the Bible (2 Kgs 23:5) and at Carthage (*KAI* 76.6 [restored]), *kmr* priests are associated with the offering of incense in rituals of Tyrian origin. (Aramaic inscriptions mention *kmrt* "*kmr*-priestesses.")

2. Other Functionaries. The names of extra-priestly cultic offices are known, but little can be said about the specifics of these. The *ʿzr* (CIS I 6000bis.3) was probably a temple administrator; the *zbḥ* presided over bloody sacrifices. Specific to the cult of Melqart were the offices *mqm ʾlm* "waker of the god" and (probably) *mtrḥ ʿštrny,* variously interpreted (see Lipiński 1970). The record of expenditures of a Phoenician temple in Kition (*TSSI,* 123–31) lists payments to builders, assistants, bakers, and barbers. Another term listed there—*klbm* "dogs"—has been interpreted as a variety of male sex worker (*TWAT* 4: 163; Margalith 1983; Brunet 1985).

Among biblical scholars it has unfortunately become a truism that male and female sex workers were cultic functionaries in the religions of Canaan, and that considerable polemic was exerted against this practice by the classical prophets. The marriage of Hosea, for example, is regularly interpreted against the background of a fertility cult in which unrestricted sex is the religious obligation (or privilege) of certain women (Wolff *Hosea* Hermeneia; Andersen and Freedman *Hosea* AB). Partial illumination of the modern fascination with sacred prostitution is to be had from the sociology of biblical studies as a discipline (Schüssler Fiorenza 1988). Cross-cultural studies of the prostitution calumny itself and of the economics of ancient religions have raised new questions.

All of the classical accounts of ritual sex among Semites appear to derive from Herodotus (Oden 1987: 140–47). The words in all Semitic languages alleged to be designations of ritual sex workers are euphemistic and polyvalent. And the very existence of a "fertility cult" has never been convincingly demonstrated, although fertility, both human and agricultural, was certainly a concern of all ancient societies. Incidents of female prostitution in ancient Israel and elsewhere are perhaps better accounted for in terms of economic marginalization (see PROSTITUTION, CULTIC; van der Toorn 1989).

F. Festivals

1. Seasonal Celebrations. It is reasonable to assume that religious festivals marked the New Year, the vernal equinox, the summer solstice, and the autumnal equinox in Phoenicia, but evidence of festivals tied to the solar cycle is tenuous. Such evidence as is available suggests that seasonal festivals combined elements of agricultural and mythopoeic origin. A Tyrian celebration of the resurrection of the god Melqart may have coincided with the vernal equinox (Lipiński 1970). The festival of Adonis in Byblos, known from Greek sources, probably was held in early summer (Ribichini 1981: 150–51). Other festivals are known only as names. The *ym qbr ʾlm* lit. "day of the god's burial" is mentioned in the Phoenician inscription from Pyrgi in Italy (lines 8–9; see *TSSI* 3: 151–59). The phrase *zbḥ šmš* "sun sacrifices" designated a month, perhaps the month of the winter solstice (*TSSI* 3:156; cf. *KAI* 43.4).

2. Sports. Athletic contests and paramilitary maneuvers were part of the ritual activities of Phoenicians. The former has been linked to the origins of the Olympic games (Boutros 1981).

G. Revelatory Institutions

1. Prophecy. The Elijah narrative refers to "the four hundred and fifty prophets of Baal and the four hundred and fifty prophets of Asherah who eat at Jezebel's table" (1 Kgs 18:20). In this biblical narrative, the prophets of Baal perform the priestly function of animal sacrifice. Priests and prophets were bearers of religious tradition according to one source of Phoenician origin. The *Phoenician History* of Philo of Byblos relates that the first Phoenician hierophant, a certain Thabion, transmitted his allegorical interpretations of myths and of natural and cosmic phenomena "to the priests and to the prophets who led the rites" (Euseb. *Praep. Evang.* 1.10.39 [Attridge and Oden 1981: 61]).

Traces of prophetic activities remain in the epigraphic record, as well. An Etruscan ruler declares in the Phoenician-Etruscan bilingual text he commissioned at Pyrgi in Italy that he built a sanctuary for Astarte because she requested it of him (*TSSI* 3: 157). Presumably the request was made through prophets or oracles. Responsibility for the erection of an Astarte shrine at Hammon, S of Tyre, is attributed jointly to the *mlʾk* (traditionally "angel") of the god Milk-Astarot (*KAI* 19.2) and the citizens of the city. It can be inferred from the rhetoric of the inscription that prophetic agency may have been involved in the decision to undertake the project.

2. Other Mantic Activities. In recounting the Carthaginian siege of Akragas in Sicily, Diodorus (13.86.2) alleges that soothsayers (Gk *manteis*) warned the Carthaginian general against dismantling Greek tombs for the siegeworks. The *Periplus* attributed to Hanno the Navigator, probably a Greek translation of a 5th-century Punic document, describes a fearful night passed by a shore crew on an island in a lake near the W African coast. Soothsayers (Gk *manteis*) commanded them to leave the dreadful place (line 77; Oikonomides 1977: 29).

H. Divinities

1. Phoenician Polytheism. The very concept of divinity in NW Semitic religion is fuzzy. Divinities achieve definition relatively: in relation to one another and in relation to human beings. The mutual relations of divinities are expressed in the schematic associations called pantheons. The organizing principles of pantheons are analogical. Human structures organizing power, generative and coercive, provide the lines of analogy. Thus divinities may associate in triadic nuclear families (father/mother/son); or as conjugal pairs; or as kin groups spanning several generations. Alternatively they rank in power strata like the population of a city-state. Minor groupings of deities are iconic and thereby mutable.

The pantheons of Phoenician city-states have been described as incorporating a divine triad consisting of a god and goddess with a divine male child begotten by them (Teixidor 1977: 35–39; van den Branden [1981: 36] extends the triad beyond the nuclear family of parents and child). But the triad is imagistic rather than structural (a point missed by van den Branden 1981, argued in essence by Xella 1981: 14–15). The iconography of Astarte, for example, includes erotic groupings of three female deities (Delcor 1986: 1080 and pl. 20). The motif of a dying-rising god, traditionally linked with the triadic arrangement of divine families, need not be coupled with triadism.

Paired deities are a more enduring element of Phoenician religion (Servais-Soyez 1986). The pair Elyon and Baalat have been associated with Byblos on the basis of combined epigraphic and literary evidence (Moscati 1968: 31–32). At Tyre, Astarte is coupled with Melqart (Herakles) in texts (Moscati 1968: 34–35) and iconography (Delcor 1986: 1081). At Carthage the god Baal Hammon is paired with the goddess Tinnit from the early 5th century onward (CIS I 5510 is probably the earliest textual evidence).

The phylogeny of divine beings was expressed in theogonic myths. Apart from Ugaritic texts with theogonic interests (see CANAAN, RELIGION OF), the only extant Phoenician theogony is from the *Phoenician History* of PHILO OF BYBLOS (the detailed investigation of this text by Movers [1848] still repays close reading; the most extensive recent analysis is by Schiffmann 1986).

2. Dynamics of Pantheons. It is a commonplace that the ranking and grouping of divinities in pantheons mirrors the social and political relations of human society. The occupational specializations of urban society are likewise represented in the restricted ambit of any single deity. The pantheons of Phoenician cities were dynamic: new deities were assimilated or invested; old deities waxed or waned in prominence; some became senescent.

The dynamism of Phoenician polytheism accounts for the considerable discontinuity between Bronze Age and Iron Age pantheons of the same regions (noted by Xella 1981: 12–13). The historical development of Phoenician religion involved innovation, openness to elements of non-Phoenician origin, and periodic divestment of innovative elements (Garbini 1981). First-millennium Phoenician pantheons, for example, show the emergence of guardian deities, such as Shadrapa, Horon, Sid, and Bes, to a new prominence (Garbini 1981: 33–36). Two-element divine names are widely diffused in the 1st millennium: Milk-Astarot (see Pardee 1988 on this name), Tinnit-Astarot, and Baal Hammon are examples; "double-gods," e.g., Eshmun-Milqart, also show a renewed prominence in the late Iron Age.

I. The Dead

On Phoenician cults of the dead, see DEAD, CULT OF THE.

Bibliography

Amadasi Guzzo, M. G. 1988. Dédicaces de femmes à Carthage. *StudPhoen* VI: 143–49.

Amiet, P. 1983. Observations sur les "Tablettes magiques" d'Arslan Tash. *AulaOr* 1: 109.

Arnaud, D. 1986–87. Religion Assyro-Babylonienne. *AEPHE* V 95: 187–91.

Attridge, H. W., and Oden, R., eds. 1981. *Philo of Byblos: The Phoenician History.* CBQMS 9. Washington, D.C.

Barré, M. L. 1983. *The God-list in the Treaty between Hannibal and Philip V of Macedonia.* Baltimore.

Baumgarten, A. I. 1981. *The Phoenician History of Philo of Byblos.* EPRO 129. Leiden.

Benichou-Safar, H. 1981. A propos des ossements humains du tophet de Carthage. *RSF* 9: 5–9.

———. 1988. Sur l'incineration des enfants aux tophets de Carthage et de Sousse. *RHR* 125: 57–68.

Boutros, L. 1981. *Phoenician Sport: Its Influence on the Origin of the Olympic Games.* Amsterdam.

Branden, A. van den. 1981. La triade phénicienne. *BeO* 23: 35–64.

Brown, S. S. 1987. Late Carthaginian Child Sacrifice and Sacrificial Monuments in Their Mediterranean Context. Ph.D. diss., Indiana.

Brunet, G. 1985. L'Hebreu *keleb. VT* 35: 458–88.

Delcor, M. 1986. Astarte. *Lexicon Iconographicum Mythologiae Classicae* 3/1 (addendum): 1077–85.
Douglas, M. 1966. *Purity and Danger.* London.
Elayi, J. 1987. *Recherches sur les cités phéniciennes a l'époque perse.* AIONSup 51. Naples.
Fedele, F., and Foster, G. V. 1988. Tharros: ovicaprini sacrificali e rituale del *tofet. RSF* 16: 29–46.
Fronzaroli, P. 1965. Studi sul lessico comune semitico iv.: La religione. *AANLR* 20/5–6: 253–55.
Garbini, G. 1980. *I fenici, storia e religione.* Series minor—Istituto universitario orientale, seminario di studi asiatici 11. Naples.
———. 1981. Continuita e innovazioni nella religione fenicia. Pp. 29–42 in *La religione fenicia.* SS 53. Rome.
Gevirtz, S. 1961. West-Semitic Curses and the Problem of the Origins of Hebrew Law. *VT* 11: 137–58.
Guzzo Amadasi, M. G. 1967. *Le iscrizione fenicie e puniche delle colonie in occidente.* SS 28. Rome.
Hadjisavvas, S. 1986. Greek and Phoenician Influences on Cyprus as Evidenced in the Necropolis of Kition. Pp. 361–68 in *Acts of the International Archaeological Symposium "Cyprus between the Orient and the Occident"*, ed. V. Karageorghis. Nicosia.
Hadjisavvas, S.; Dupont-Sommer, A.; and Lozachmeur, H. 1984. Cinq stèles funéraires découverts sur le site d'Ayios Georghios, à Larnaca-Kition, en 1979. *RDAC* pp. 101–16.
Heider, G. C. 1985. *The Cult of Molek: A Reassessment.* JSOTSup 43. Sheffield.
Huss, W. 1986. Hannibal und die Religion. *StudPhoen* IV: 223–38.
Jay, N. 1988. Sacrifice, descent and the Patriarchs. *VT* 38: 52–70.
Krahmalkov, C. R. 1970. The Punic speech of Hanno. *Or* 39: 52–74.
———. 1988. Observations on the Punic Monologues of Hanno in the *Poenulus. Or* 57: 55–66.
Lipiński, E. 1970. La fête d'ensevelissement et de la resurrection de Melqart. Pp. 30–58 in *Actes de la XVIIe Rencontre Assyriologique Internationale,* ed. A. Finet. Ham-sur-Heure.
———. 1982. Syro-Fenicische wortels van de Karthaagse religie. *Phoenix* 28: 51–84.
———. 1988. Sacrifices d'enfants à Carthage et dans le monde sémitique oriental. *StudPhoen* VI: 151–62.
Liverani, M. 1974. La royaute syrienne de l'age du bronze recent. Pp. 329–56 in *Le Palais et la royaute,* ed. P. Garelli. Paris.
Margalith, O. 1983. *Keleb:* Homonym or Metaphor? *VT* 33: 491–95.
Moscati, S. 1968. *The World of the Phoenicians.* Trans. A. Hamilton. New York.
———. 1987. *Il sacrificio punico dei fanciulli: Realta o invenzione?* Problemi attuali di scienza e di cultura, Quaderno 261. Rome.
Movers, F. C. 1848. Phoenizien, Phoenizier. Vol. 24, pp. 319–443 in *Allgemeine Encyklopädie der Wissenschaften und Künste,* ed. J. S. Ersch and J. G. Gruber. Leipzig.
O'Brien, J. 1987. Because God Heard My Voice: The Individual Thanksgiving Psalm and Vow-fulfillment. Pp. 281–98 in *The Listening Heart,* ed. K. G. Hoglund, et al. JSOTSup 58. Sheffield.
Oden, R. 1977. *Studies in Lucian's De Syria Dea.* HSM 15. Missoula, MT.
———. 1987. *The Bible Without Theology.* New Voices in Biblical Studies. San Francisco.
Oikonomides, A. N. 1977. *Hanno the Carthaginian: Periplus.* Chicago.
Pardee, D. 1988. A New Datum for the Meaning of the Divine Name Milkashtart. Pp. 55–67 in *Ascribe to the Lord,* ed. L. Eslinger and J. G. Taylor. JSOTSup 67. Sheffield.
Parmentier, A. 1987. Phoenicians in the administration of Ptolemaic Cyprus. *StudPhoen* V: 403–12.
Pearson, L. 1984. Ephorus and Timaeus in Diodorus: Laquer's Thesis Rejected. *Historia* 33: 1–20.
Ribichini, S. 1981. *Adonis: Aspetti "orientali" di un mito greco.* SS 55. Rome.
———. 1987a. *Il tofet e il sacrificio del fanciulli.* Sardò 2. Sassari.
———. 1987b. Traditions phéniciennes chez Philon de Byblos: une vie éternelle pur des dieux mortels. Pp. 101–16 in *Apocalypses et voyages dans l'au delà,* ed. C. Kappler. Paris.
———. 1988. Review of Heider 1985. *RSF* 16: 122–25.
Schepens, G. 1987. The Phoenicians in Ephorus' Universal History. *StudPhoen* V: 315–30.
Schiffmann, I. 1986. *Phönizisch-Punische Mythologie und geschichtliche Überlieferung in der Widerspiegelung der antiken Geschichtsschreibung.* Collezione di studi fenici 17. Rome.
Schüssler Fiorenza, E. 1988. The Ethics of Interpretation: De-Centering Biblical Scholarship. *JBL* 107: 3–17.
Seel, O., ed. 1972. *M. Iuniani Iustini Epitoma Historiarum Philippicarum Pompei Trogi.* 2d ed. Stuttgart.
Servais-Soyez, B. 1986. La "triade" phénicienne aux époques hellénistique et romaine. *StudPhoen* IV: 347–60.
Simonetti, A. 1983. Sacrifici umani e uccisioni rituali nel mondo fenicio-punico. *RSF* 11: 91–111.
Stager, L. E. 1980. The Rite of Child Sacrifice at Carthage. Pp. 1–11 in *New Light on Ancient Carthage,* ed. by J. G. Pedley. Ann Arbor.
———. 1982. Carthage: A View from the Tophet. *PhönWest* pp. 155–62.
Stager, L. E., and S. R. Wolff. 1984. Child sacrifice at Carthage—Religious Rite or Population Control? *BARev* 10: 30–51.
Sznycer, M. 1967. *Les passages puniques en transcription latine dans le "Poenulus" de Plaute.* Etudes et commentaires 65. Paris.
Teixidor, J. 1977. *The Pagan God.* Princeton.
Toorn, K. van der. 1989. Female Prostitution in Payment of Vows in Ancient Israel. *JBL* 108: 193–205.
Vandersleyen, C. 1987. L'étymologie de Phoïnix, "Phénicien." *StudPhoen* V: 19–22.
Whittaker, C. R. 1974. The Western Phoenicians. *Proceedings of the Cambridge Philological Society* 200: 58–79.
Winter, U. 1983. *Frau und Göttin.* OBO 53. Freiburg and Göttingen.
Xella, P. 1981. Aspetti e problemi dell'indagine storico-religiosa. Pp. 7–25 in *La religione fenicia.* SS 53. Rome.
———. 1986. Le polythéism phénicien. *StudPhoen* IV: 29–40.

PHILIP C. SCHMITZ

PHOENIX (BIRD AND POEM). In the ancient world, the phoenix was a bird whose symbolic power proved international and durable. Although its long history, including occurrences in Egypt, Greece, and Rome, exhibits significant and interesting variety, several constant factors define the boundaries and establish the identity of the phoenix: bird of the sun, an immensely long life, the capacity for self-renewal or self-regeneration after its death, and a sign of the human soul and its destiny.

In Egypt, the phoenix is early (2500 B.C.E.) attested in the Heliopolitan mythology of Atum/Re. The creation account portrays the emergence of land and life from the primeval waters, with Atum a self-generating deity whose shape became definite as a mound or hill in the waters and whose spirit was a light sending the rays of the sun into the world from the temple in Heliopolis. In the very beginning, the Phoenix perched on the Benben stone, located in the temple of Atum, marking the origin of the inhabited world and the reign of Atum:

> O Atum! When you came into being you rose up as a High Hill.
> You shone as the Benben Stone in the temple of the phoenix in Heliopolis
> (*Pyramid Text* 600, in Rundle-Clark 37)

The self-emergent Atum and the self-emergent phoenix received the adoration befitting their status:

> Hail to you, O Atum!
> Hail to you, O Becoming One who came into being of himself!
> You rose up in this your name of High Hill,
> You came into being in this your name of "Becoming One."
> (*Pyramid Text* 587, in Rundle-Clark 38)

Creating the world was not the only time when the phoenix was active, for the daily and monthly ritual were performed in the temple of the Benben stone, suggesting that important moments in social life were assimilated to the activity of Atum and the bird and noted in the liturgical calendar. The *Book of the Dead* 17 extends the influence of the phoenix to the journey of the soul from the underworld to the sun. As the bird was a manifestation of Atum at the beginning, so it aids the dead who return to Atum at the end. The pervasive character of the phoenix is underscored in the words of Atum:

> The Word came into being.
> All things were mine when I was alone.
> I was Re in his manifestations:
> I was the great one who came into being of himself . . .
> I was that great Phoenix who is in Heliopolis,
> who looks after the decision of all that is
> (Rundle-Clark 79)

Yet another feature of the phoenix is seen in the ancient Egyptian view of time as cyclical and composed of segments of the day, the week of ten days, the year, and longer periods of 400 and 1,460 years. Since the bird was present when the world emerged from the waters, it initiated the cycles as well as the world; it also began each new period in the flux and flow of the world. The recurring appearance of the phoenix is a corollary of the meaning the bird occupied in ancient Egypt: the presence of Atum/Re and his word which became the destiny of the world and humans.

When we move from the Egyptian to the Greco-Roman world, we meet new developments in the symbol of the phoenix. The earliest reference is found in a fragment of Hesiod (ca. 700 B.C.E.), preserved in Plutarch (*De def. or.* 415), from which we learn that Hesiod thought that time is divided into periods or cycles which are the lives of nine ravens. Even in ancient times, Hesiod's statement was enigmatic, but van den Broek (76–97) has demonstrated that the life of the bird was 540 years and that it appeared at the end of one and the beginning of another historical cycle. Herodotus, in the 5th century B.C.E., gives an extensive description and interpretation based on pictures and Egyptian myths:

> Another bird also is sacred; it is called the phoenix. I myself have never seen it, but only pictures of it; for the bird comes but seldom into Egypt, once in five hundred years, as the people of Heliopolis says. It is said that the phoenix comes when his father dies. If the picture truly shows his size and appearance, his plumage is partly golden but mostly red. He is most like an eagle in shape and bigness. The Egyptians tell a tale of this bird's devices which I do not believe. He comes, they say, from Arabia bringing his father to the Sun's temple enclosed in myrrh, and there buries him. His manner of bringing is this: first he moulds an egg of myrrh as heavy as he can carry, and when he has proved its weight by lifting it he then hollows out the egg and puts his father in it, covering over with more myrrh the hollow in which the body lies; so the egg being with his father in it of the same weight as before, the phoenix, after enclosing him, carries him to the temple of the Sun in Egypt. Such is the tale of what is done by this bird.
> (Histories 2.73, trans. Godley 359–61)

Here we have considerable information which was to become standard for much Greek and Roman thought about the bird: its origin in Arabia and appearances in Heliopolis and its burial of its dead father in the temple of the Sun in Egypt. A fragment of the 4th century B.C.E. poet Antiphanes, preserved in Athenaeus (*Deipnosophists* 14.655) also connects the Greek phoenix with Egypt. Another fragment, from the 2d-century-B.C.E. Hellenistic Jewish writer Ezekiel the Dramatist and preserved in Eusebius (*P.E.* 9.29.16), says that this bird, king of all birds, sang beautifully. And from a fragment of Aenesidemus, preserved by Diogenes Laerteius (9.79) we learn that the phoenix reproduces asexually, a theme that Christians will develop into a symbol for life after death. But the most complete account of the phoenix comes from a Roman senator, Manilius, who indicates that a new bird is reborn from the decaying remains of its own body, with each death-birth occurring every 540 years to mark political, social, and religious renewals (Pliny 10.4–5), with which Ovid (*Met.* 1.108–10 and 15.392–407) and Seneca (*Ep.* 42.1) agree. Tacitus provides an account with several characteristic themes belonging to the symbolism of the phoenix:

> . . . the bird known as the phoenix visited Egypt . . . I propose to state the points on which they [the tales] coincide, together with the larger number that are dubious. . . . That the creature is sacred to the sun and distinguished from other birds by its head and the variegation of its plumage, is agreed by those who have depicted its form: as to its terms of years, the tradition varies. The generally received number is five hundred . . . phoenixes flew to . . . Heliopolis. . . . When its sum of years is complete and death is drawing on, it builds a

nest in its own country and sheds on it a procreative influence, from which springs a young one, whose first care on reaching maturity is to bury his sire . . . he lifts up his father's corpse, conveys him to the Altar of the Sun, and consigns him to the flames.

(*Ann.* 6.28, trans. Jackson 201–3)

Several Christian texts contain copious references to the phoenix. Two invite discussion, for they demonstrate how Christians adopted and utilized a pagan symbol as a vehicle for expressing new religious content. The first is the 3d-century C.E. poem of Lactantius, *De ave phoenices.* Here we are told that the bird dwells in a far-off land from which the Sun sends its spring rays, a place higher than any known mountaintop and where vegetation is always green, water from a fresh spring ever sweet, and life is eternal. Indeed, the bird dwells in Paradise where the sun shines with eternal brightness as the place to which the soul ascends and where it is nourished by food reminiscent of the sacraments. Lactantius exhibits continuity between Christian and pagan culture, and thus shows that his conversion to Christianity did not prevent him from using a Greco-Roman symbol as a means to express Christian ideals and beliefs. The phoenix became a symbol of life after death, of "gaining eternal life by the boon of death" (trans. in Duff and Duff 665).

A Coptic Christian text dating to the first half of the 6th century C.E., the *Sermon on Maria,* is among the symbolically richest descriptions of the phoenix (van den Broek 33–47 for translation and discussion). According to this sermon, the bird appeared at crucial junctures in the divine efforts to redeem humans—at Abel's sacrifice, when God delivered the Israelites from Egypt, and for the tenth and last time, when the Virgin sacrificed in the temple at the birth of Jesus. In addition to mentioning the death and rebirth of the phoenix, the preacher alludes to the resurrection of Jesus and explicitly refers to the bird as a symbol of the general resurrection and of life after death.

The phoenix was an unusually powerful symbol in the ancient world. Because the myth moved across cultures, it could gain or lose a particular meaning. Whereas in Egypt it served as a manifestation of deity, in the Greco-Roman world it came to express a view of history as periodical and, in Christianity as well, as a symbol for existence in a paradisal state presaged by living as a Christian.

Bibliography

Athenaeus. *Deipnosophists.* 7 vols. Trans. C. B. Gulick. LCL. Cambridge, MA, 1961.

Broek, R. van den. 1972. *The Myth of the Phoenix according to Classical and Early Christian Traditions.* Leiden.

Herodotus. *Histories.* 2 vols. Trans. A. D. Godley. LCL. Cambridge, MA, 1946.

Lactantius. *Phoenix.* Trans. J. W. Duff and A. M. Duff in *Minor Latin Poets.* LCL. Cambridge, MA, 1961.

Morenz, S. 1960. *Egyptian Religion.* Trans. A. E. Keep. London.

Plutarch. *De defectu oraculorum.* Trans. F. C. Babbitt. Vol. 5 in *Plutarch's Moralia.* LCL. Cambridge, MA, 1957.

Rundle-Clark, R. T. 1959. *Myth and Symbol in Ancient Egypt.* London.

LARRY J. ALDERINK

PHOENIX (PLACE) [Gk *Phoinix*]. A harbor of Crete near the W end of its S shore (Acts 27:12). The Greek designates both the date palm (from which the harbor name probably arose) and the mythical bird of Egypt (see van den Broek [1972: 51–66] for the common origin of these). The harbor and nearby town were W of Fair Havens (Strabo 10.4.3; Ptolemy *Geog.* 3.17.3.) and offered a secure winter haven for the grain ship from Alexandria on which Paul was traveling to Rome (Acts 27). The deep harbor of modern Loutro E of Cape Mouros would fit the classical references but the description in Acts that the harbor faced SW and NW *(bleponta kata liba kai kata chōron)* has caused some debate since the Loutro harbor faces E. Three main theories exist: (1) Since Luke had not visited Phoenix and his knowledge of the discussion in vv 9–12 was secondhand, he mistakenly identified the orientation of the harbor; (2) the Gk phrase may mean "looking down the SW and NW wind" (Smith 1880: 87–89; 251–53) so that the harbor actually "looked NE and SE" as in the RSV; (3) a shallow open bay just to the W of Cape Mouros called locally Phineka was the harbor of Acts 27:12 not Loutro harbor. Ogilvie (1958: 308–14) argues that the classical references actually favor the E facing harbor of Cape Mouros which was deeper and well protected in Paul's day. He suggests earthquakes in the 6th century A.D. raised the ocean floor, closed an inlet facing NW, and caused the remaining SW inlet and W facing bay to be abandoned in favor of the E bay of Loutro.

Bibliography

Broek, R. van den. 1972. *The Myth of the Phoenix.* Leiden.

Ogilvie, R. M. 1958. Phoenix. *JTS* 9: 308–14.

Smith, J. 1880. *The Voyage and Shipwreck of St. Paul.* 4th ed. London.

DANIEL L. HOFFMAN

PHRYGIA (PLACE) [Gk *Phrygia*]. The land of the Phrygians, a territory of W central Asia Minor, between the N Aegean and the river Halys (modern Kizil Irmak).

A. History of Phrygia
B. Phrygia in the Bible
C. Phrygia and Early Christianity

A. History of Phrygia

1. The Early Period. The Phrygians migrated to Asia Minor in the 12th century B.C. Herodotus (6.45; 7.73) refers to an ethnic group in Thrace and Macedonia called *Brygoi* or *Briges* (Macedonian *b* replaces common Gk *ph,* as in Berenice/Pherenice). What is known of the Phrygian and Thracian languages indicates that they belong to the same Indo-European group, called Thraco-Phrygian. A legend recorded by Herodotus (2.2) makes the Phrygians the most ancient of all nations—a claim with no substance to it.

In Homer (*Il.* 2.862, etc.) the Phrygians are closely associated with the Trojans. They displaced the Hittites as the dominant power in central Asia Minor. Their kings bore the alternate dynastic names Midas and Gordios, the latter being linked with the name of the capital of Phrygia, Gordion (about 50 miles WSW of Ankara). The situation of Gordion, commanding the trade routes between the

Hellespont and the Cilician gates, was symbolized in the Gordian knot: whoever untied it would control all Asia Minor.

The Phrygian kings were proverbial for their wealth, derived perhaps from gold mines and commemorated in the legend of Midas and the golden touch. Midas' name appears (in the form "Mita") in Assyrian records of 710 B.C. The power of Phrygia was broken by the Cimmerian invaders from the Russian steppes; during their invasion Midas, the last Phrygian king, committed suicide (693 B.C.).

When the Cimmerian invasion receded, Lydia, with its capital at Sardis, emerged as the leading Anatolian power, extending its dominion over Phrygia as far east as the Halys. From then on Phrygia was subject to one imperial power after another—to the Persians after Cyrus' overthrow of the Lydian Croesus in 546 B.C. and to the Macedonians after Alexander's conquest of Asia Minor in 333 B.C.

Under the Persian Empire Phrygia was divided into two satrapies, Greater Phrygia and Lesser or Hellespontine Phrygia, which were separated from each other by the Mysians, Bithynians, and other immigrants from Europe. With Hellespontine Phrygia may be associated the traditional Phrygian thalassocracy from 905 to 880 B.C. (Diod. Sic. 7.11; cf. Hom. *Il.* 24.545).

On his westward march against Greece in 480 B.C. (Hdt. 7.27) Xerxes traversed Phrygia, after crossing the Halys, until he reached the city of Celaenae (the later Apamea, modern Dinar in the Maeander valley). A Phrygian contingent marched in his army (Hdt. 7.73). Other Phrygian cities through which the army passed were Anaua and Colossae in the Lycus valley. On the Phrygian-Lydian border it came to Cydrara (Hdt. 7.30), later known as Hierapolis.

When Cyrus the younger led his army of Greeks east from Sardis in his bid to seize the Persian throne from his brother Artaxerxes II (401 B.C.), they crossed the Maeander from Lydia into Phrygia; then one day's march of 24 miles took them through Phrygia to Colossae, "a large and prosperous city." From there a three days' march of 60 miles took them to Celaenae, where Cyrus was joined by reinforcements from other parts of the Greek world. From there they advanced to Peltae (a two days' march of 30 miles) and then on to Potters' Market (a two days' march of 36 miles) and then again to Caÿster plain (a three days' march of 60 miles). Two days' march from there (30 miles) took them to Thymbrion, where there was a fountain named after Midas. Another two days' march of 30 miles took them to Tyriaion, from which a three days' march of 60 miles took them to "Iconium, the last city of Phrygia." On leaving Iconium they crossed from Phrygia into Lycaonia (Xen. *An.* 1.2.6–19).

2. After Alexander. Alexander the Great also passed through Phrygia on his way from the Granicus (which flows into the Sea of Marmara) to Issus in SW Cilicia (334–333 B.C.); it was at Gordion, the former Phrygian capital, that he is said to have ensured his mastery of Asia by "cutting the Gordian knot."

After Alexander's death (323 B.C.), Antigonus, his governor of Phrygia, was proclaimed king by his army; but Ptolemy and Seleucus, with Lysimachus of Thrace and Cassander of Macedonia, combined against him and killed him at the battle of Ipsus in central Phrygia (301 B.C.). Lysimachus then gained control of Asia Minor, but soon lost most of it, including Phrygia, to Seleucus.

Seleucus I is said to have granted citizenship to Jewish settlers in cities which he founded in "Asia and Lower Syria" (*Ant* 12.119); among these Antioch-near-Pisidia is probably to be included.

In 278/277 B.C. three tribes of migrant Celts or Galatians crossed the Hellespont into Asia Minor at the instance of the king of Bithynia, who hoped to use them as mercenaries against his enemies. For a generation and more the Galatians menaced their neighbors in Asia Minor, until a series of defeats at the hands of Attalus I, king of Pergamum, confined them within strict limits, in territory which had formerly been NE Phrygia (232 B.C.). This territory became the kingdom of Galatia, which expanded until by the reign of its last king, Amyntas, it bordered on Cappadocia to the E, Pamphylia to the S, and the Roman province of Asia (formerly the kingdom of Pergamum) to the W. When Amyntas fell in battle in 25 B.C., his expanded kingdom became the Roman province of Galatia.

When Antiochus III succeeded to the Seleucid throne in 221 B.C., he had to win back Lydia and Phrygia from his rebellious kinsman Achaeus, who seized those regions and had himself crowned king at Laodicea (220 B.C.). When Antiochus recovered those regions, he settled two thousand Jewish families from Babylonia in them to ensure their continued allegiance (*Ant* 12.149). The Jewish population flourished in the Lycus valley and other parts of Phrygia: in 62 B.C., for example, the annual half-shekel tax for the maintenance of the Jerusalem temple amounted to nearly 100 gold *librae* ("pounds") at Apamea and just over 20 at Laodicea, which points to a population of well over 50,000 male Jews between 20 and 60 years of age in the areas of which these cities were the centers (Cic. *Flac.* 68). An often-quoted Talmudic saying to the effect that "the baths and wines of Prugitha separated the ten tribes from their brethren" (*b. Šab.* 147b) has been thought to refer to the assimilationist tendencies of Phrygian Jews; but Prugitha may not be Phrygia.

In 204 B.C., during the Hannibalian war, the Romans sent a deputation to Pessinus in Phrygia to acquire, by the good offices of Attalus I of Pergamum, the black stone in which the ancient Anatolian mother goddess *(Mater Deum Magna Idaea)* was believed to reside (Livy 29.10); her cult—so unlike any traditional Roman cult—was from then on established in Rome. Other Phrygian divinities whose worship persisted into Roman times were the moon god Mēn, who had important cult centers at Pisidian Antioch (Mēn Askainos) and near Laodicea (Mēn Karou), and the nature god Sebazios (identified with Dionysus).

Later in the reign of Antiochus III the Romans compelled him to hand over southwestern Phrygia to their ally the king of Pergamum. (Attalus I of Pergamum had already annexed part of northwestern Phrygia, called thenceforth Phrygia Epiktētos, "Acquired Phrygia.") When in 133 B.C. the last king of Pergamum bequeathed his kingdom to the senate and people of Rome, it was reconstituted as the Roman province of Asia, which included a good part of Phrygian territory. Over a century later, when the Romans reconstituted the kingdom of

Galatia in turn as an imperial province, the remainder of Phrygia came under their direct control.

Phrygia was thus divided between the provinces of Asia and Galatia, its western part being known as Asian Phrygia (Gal. *De aliment. facultat.* 1.13.10), and its E part probably as Galatic Phrygia (cf. Calder 1956). The territory between Emir Dağ and Sultan Dağ was called Phrygia Paroreios, "Phrygia near the mountain(s)"; the extreme SE part of Phrygia was called Phrygia-near-Pisidia (Strab. 12.8.13), having Pisidian Antioch as its chief city (cf. Acts 13:14).

In A.D. 295 the provincial system in central Asia Minor was reorganized: a new, enlarged province of Pisidia was created with Pisidian Antioch as its capital—a situation reflected in the later texts of Acts 13:14, which change "Pisidian Antioch," i.e., Antioch-near-Pisidia (Strab. 12.3.31, etc.), to "Antioch of Pisidia" (cf. KJV). At the same time Phrygia became a provincial title for the first time under the Roman Empire: two new provinces were called Phrygia Prima (Phrygia Pacatiana), to the W, with its capital at Laodicea (cf. the appended note to 1 Timothy, KJV), and Phrygia Secunda (Phrygia Salutaris), to the E, with its capital at Synnada.

The Phrygians were apparently an unwarlike people, subject for centuries to other races; hence perhaps the disparaging use of "Phrygian" (Gk *Phryx*) as a slave name (e.g., Ar. *Vesp.* 433); cf. the proverb "as timid as a Phrygian hare" quoted by Strabo (1.2.30).

In ancient Greek music the Phrygian scale (Pl. *Resp.* 3.399A; Arist. *Pol.* 4.3.4; 8.7.89; cf. Eur. *Or.* 1426; *Tro.* 545), commonly associated with the flute, was a mode of two tetrachords with a semitone in the middle of each and a whole tone between the two.

B. Phrygia in the Bible

1. In the Greek OT. There is no reference to Phrygia in the Hebrew Bible, although the Moschi (Assyrian *Muški*), who occupied part of the Phrygian territory, appear as "Meshech" in Gen 10:2 = 1 Chr 1:5; Ezek 27:13; 32:26; 38:2, 3; 39:1. In the Greek OT the only relevant instance is the mention of "Philip, by birth a Phrygian (Gk *Phryx*)," whom Antiochus IV appointed governor of Jerusalem in 168 B.C. (2 Macc 5:22).

2. In the NT. According to Acts 2:10, a contingent of Phrygian Jews was present in Jerusalem at the first Christian Pentecost; they are possibly mentioned because the evangelization of Phrygia is to be related later in the book.

Pisidian Antioch and Iconium, cities of Phrygia, were evangelized by Paul and Barnabas during their missionary tour of central Asia Minor (Acts 13:14–14:4). Pisidian Antioch lay in "Phrygia near Pisidia." While Iconium is referred to as a city of Lycaonia by Cicero (*Fam.* 15.4.2) and the elder Pliny (*HN* 5.25), Phrygian was spoken there from Xenophon's time to the end of the 2d century A.D., as inscriptions show (Calder 1911: 188–94). In A.D. 165 Hierax, an associate of Justin Martyr, when put on trial with him at Rome, tells the examining magistrate that he was "dragged away from Iconium in Phrygia" (*M. Just.* 4). Indeed, as late as 232 a Church council is described as being held at "Iconium, a place in Phrygia" (Cyprian *Ep.* 75.7). That Iconium was reckoned to be in Phrygia and not in Lycaonia is implied in Acts 14:6, where Paul and Barnabas are said to have fled from Iconium "to Lystra and Derbe, cities of Lycaonia."

In Acts 16:6 (RSV) Paul, with Silas and Timothy, is said to have gone "through the region of Phrygia and Galatia" on a westward journey through Asia Minor. The phrase is best translated "through the Phrygian and Galatic region" (Gk *dia tēs Phrygias kai Galatikēs chōras*). For the high probability that the genitive *Phrygias* is an adjective here and not a noun see Hemer (1976; 1977). The region traversed was that which was both Phrygian and Galatic, i.e., that conveniently called Phrygia Galatica (the part of Phrygia included in the province of Galatia).

When in Acts 18:23 Paul is described as going "from place to place through the region of Galatia and Phrygia" (Gk *tēn Galatikēn chōran kai Phrygian*), the wording is different and may denote the Galatic region of Lycaonia (in which Lystra and Derbe lay) together with Phrygia, both Galatic and Asian (Ramsay 1896).

The churches of Colossae, Laodicea, and Hierapolis, in the Lycus valley in the SW part of Asian Phrygia, were planted evidently by Epaphras during Paul's Ephesian ministry, A.D. 52–55 (Col 1:7; 4:12–13). The church of Laodicea is the only Phrygian one included in the seven churches of Asia addressed in Rev 1:11; 3:14–22.

C. Phrygia and Early Christianity

Phrygia was one of the most important centers of Christian life and activity in the generations following the apostolic age. This may have been partly due, but was by no means entirely due, to the immigration of outstanding Palestinian Christians in the later part of the 1st century, such as "John the disciple of the Lord" and Philip of Caesarea and his family. From Phrygia comes a greater concentration of Christian inscriptions in the 2d and 3d centuries than from any other place except Rome. Three main lines of Christian penetration have been traced: (1) up the Lycus and Maeander valleys and radiating out to Eumeneia and Akmonia, (2) southeastern Phrygia and Lycaonia, (3) NW Phrygia, especially the Tembris valley (Ramsay 1897: 511, 715).

Among outstanding Phrygian bishops were Papias and Claudius Apollinaris of Hierapolis and (toward the end of the 2d century) Abercius (Avircius) Marcellus of Hierapolis in Phrygia Salutaris. In Phrygia the Montanist movement arose in the middle of the 2d century; it was sometimes referred to as the Cataphrygian heresy. The 60 canons traditionally promulgated by the Council of Laodicea (ca. 363) were treated by later Church councils as a basis of canon law.

Phrygian Christianity suffered severely during the last imperial persecution. One Phrygian city, said to have been entirely Christian (possibly Eumeneia), was destroyed by fire with its inhabitants (Eus. *Hist. Eccl.* 8.11.1).

Bibliography

Anderson, J. G. C. 1897–98. A Summer in Phrygia. *JHS* 17: 396–424; 18: 81–128.

Calder, W. M. 1911. Corpus Inscriptionum Neophrygiarum. *JHS* 31: 159–215.

———. 1956. The Boundary of Galatic Phrygia. Pp. ix–xvi in *Monumenta Asiae Minoris Antiqua* 7, ed. W. M. Calder. Manchester.

Friedrich, J. 1932. *Kleinasiatische Sprachdenkmäler.* Kleine Texte 163. Berlin.
Gabriel, A., and Haspels, C. H. E. 1941–65. *Phrygia,* 4 Vols. Paris.
Haas, O. 1966. *Die phrygischen Sprachdenkmäler.* Linguistique Balkanique 10. Sofia.
Hemer, C. J. 1976. The Adjective "Phrygia." *JTS* n.s. 27: 122–26.
———. 1977. Phrygia: A Further Note. *JTS* n.s. 28: 99–101.
Jones, A. H. M. 1971. *The Cities of the Eastern Roman Provinces.* 2d ed. Oxford.
Ramsay, W. M. 1890. *The Historical Geography of Asia Minor.* London.
———. 1895–97. *The Cities and Bishoprics of Phrygia.* Part 1, Vols. 1 and 2. Oxford.
———. 1896. The "Galatia" of St. Paul and the "Galatic Territory" of Acts. Pp. 15–57 in *Studia Biblica et Ecclesiastica* 4. Oxford.
Young, R. S. 1958. The Gordion Campaign of 1957. *AJA* 62: 147–54.

F. F. BRUCE

PHRYGIAN LANGUAGE. See LANGUAGES (INTRODUCTORY SURVEY).

PHYGELUS (PERSON) [Gk *Phygelos*]. Phygelus, along with Hermogenes, is named in 2 Tim 1:15 as being one of those from Asia who had "turned away" from Paul during his imprisonment in Rome. Unlike Hermogenes, who appears also in the apocryphal *Acts of Paul,* Phygelus is not known apart from his mention in 2 Timothy. On the basis of what can be pieced together about Hermogenes, it is reasonable to conjecture that he and Phygelus were at odds with Paul due to their understanding of the resurrection. See the fuller discussion and bibliography under HERMOGENES.

FLORENCE MORGAN GILLMAN

PHYLACTERIES [Gk *phylaktērion*]. This term appears once in the NT in Matt 25:3, where Jesus is said to accuse the scribes and Pharisees of ostentatiousness for "they do all their deeds to be seen by men; for they make their phylacteries broad and their fringes long." The Greek word passed to the Vulgate and entered English Bibles through the Geneva Bible, 1557. It is universally accepted that by "phylactery" Matthew meant the Aramaic word *tĕpillîn,* the name given in rabbinic sources to two black leather boxes containing scriptural passages which are worn by Jews on the forehead and left arm.

The Mishnah, *Šebu.* 3.8, 11, requires Jewish males thirteen years and older to wear *tĕpillîn* each day. Women are explicitly exempt from this religious obligation (*m. Ber.* 3.3). The basis for wearing phylacteries was derived by the rabbis from four biblical verses: Exod 13:9, 16; Deut 6:8; 11:18. These four verses require the Jew to put "these words" as "a sign upon your hand and a frontlet (Heb *ṭôṭāpōt*) between your eyes" (Exod 13:9 has *zikkārôn,* "memorial," instead of "frontlets"). Thus both the head and hand phylacteries contain four passages from Scripture which include these verses: Exod 13:1–10, 11–16; Deut 6:4–9; 11:13–21. The head phylactery worn on the head consists of four compartments, each containing one section of Scripture, while the hand phylactery has one compartment containing all four passages on one parchment. The boxes of the phylacteries must be exactly square, and both the boxes and the straps which hold them firm must be painted black. The head phylactery is imprinted twice with the Hebrew letter *šin:* once on the side which is to the left of the wearer, and once on the opposite side. The *šin* on the right has four rather than the usual three prongs, as a reminder of the four scriptural passages contained in the phylacteries (*b. Menaḥ.* 35a). Each box is sewn to a base of thick leather with twelve stitches, one for each of the twelve tribes of Israel (*b. Šabb.* 8b). The phylacteries are not worn at night, nor on festivals or the Sabbath (*b. Menaḥ.* 36a–b). The hand phylactery is donned first: the box is placed on the inner side of the upper arm (facing the heart) and the strap is wound seven times around the arm. The head phylactery is placed in the middle of the forehead, with the two ends of the strap hanging over the shoulders. The placing of each phylactery is accompanied by certain blessings and by the recitation of Hos 3:21–22. They are worn during the morning prayer and removed in the reverse order in which they were placed on the body.

While the classical Jewish commentators on the Bible take the verses in Exodus and Deuteronomy as literally commanding the wearing of the phylacteries (see, however, Samuel ben Meir on Exod 13:19), the rabbis of the Talmud were aware that the Bible gives absolutely no description of the phylacteries or the laws concerning them. These laws were understood as the classic example of a biblical precept whose details are elaborated only in the oral law (*m. Sanh.* 11:3), and almost all of the details of their construction are attributed to those oral laws which God purportedly taught Moses at Sinai (*b. Menaḥ.* 34b–37a). Given the tenuous relationship between the laws of phylacteries described in the Talmud and the alleged scriptural basis for them, it is far from apparent at exactly what point in the history of the Israelite religion phylacteries were introduced.

The first question is thus whether the "signs" and "frontlets" of Exodus and Deuteronomy were intended to describe objects in some way similar to phylacteries, or if they were figurative terms. Some interpreters have taken the Exodus passage literally, based on the facts that the word for "memorial" almost always has a literal reference and that Exodus 13 consists primarily of ritual injunctions which were obviously intended to be performed as commanded (*IDB* 3: 809). However, the referent of Exod 13:9, "it shall be for a sign unto you on your hand and for a memorial between your eyes," is the Feast of Unleavened Bread, and the "it" of Exod 13:16 which was to serve as a "sign" and "frontlet" is the dedication of the firstborn. Neither of these two ceremonies can be understood to be literally bound upon the body of the Israelite; rather, they are to serve as perpetual reminders of how God redeemed Israel from the hands of the Egyptians. The passage in Deuteronomy also must be read figuratively, because "these words" (Deut 6:6 and 11:8) must refer at least to Deuteronomy chaps. 5–11, if not to the entire book (Kennedy *HDB* 3: 871). Thus it would seem likely that originally the expressions "sign," "frontlet," and "memorial" were intended figuratively, as were other expressions in these same passages ("The Law of the Lord shall be in your mouth," Exod 13:9; "You shall place My words in your heart and in your soul," Deut 11:18).

One reason for supposing the literal intention of the passages in question is alleged evidence for a widespread custom among ANE religions of tattooing or branding various parts of the body with the name of a deity, particularly the forehead and hands, as a prophylactic measure. Hints of such a practice can be found in the Bible, such as the sign (*ʾôt*) on Cain's forehead (Gen 4:15) which placed him under divine protection (see also Ezekiel's cross, Ezek 9:4, 6; cf. Rev 7:3; 14:1). Thus while arguing that the intention of the scriptural passages in question is figurative, it is important to note that the language chosen is borrowed from actual customs familiar to the author of these passages (*HDB* 3: 871).

At what date, then, did Jews begin to wear phylacteries and to interpret the passages from Scripture literally? Hirsch (*JEnc* 10: 26) claimed that phylacteries were used as early as the 4th century B.C.E., but there is no support for this view. Josephus (*Ant* 4.213) regards the phylacteries as dating from the time of Moses, though he makes this claim of all of the daily customs that he mentions which revolve around prayer, many of which are known to be later innovations. The LXX translates the word *ṭôṭāpōt* as *asaleuton,* "that which is fixed, immovable." This implies that in Egypt in the middle of the 3d century B.C.E. the institution of phylacteries was not yet known. Rather, the four scriptural passages were interpreted as meaning that the laws and rituals of Exodus 13 and Deuteronomy 6 and 11 should remain the unchanging subjects of one's thoughts. The earliest explicit reference to phylacteries in a literary work is the *Letter of Aristeas,* sec. 159, where only the phylactery of the hand is mentioned. Scholars differ as to the dating of this text. Most place it in the 2d century B.C.E. (Shutt *OTP* 2: 9–10), though some claim that parts of it, including secs. 128–71, date from the 1st century C.E. (Andrews *APOT* 2: 87). See also ARISTEAS, LETTER OF. It therefore seems prudent to attribute the introduction of the phylacteries to the period between 250 and 100 B.C.E.

Yet the literary evidence can only suggest the existence of some object worn on the head and the arm: it cannot tell us to what extent these objects were similar to the *tĕpillîn* as they are described in rabbinic sources. All statements as to the nature of phylacteries in pre-Mishnaic times were mere conjecture until the discovery forty years ago of the remains of phylacteries at the caves of Murabbaʿat, which were occupied by refugees at the time of the Bar Kokhba revolt (135 C.E.), and at the caves at Qumran. While the exact dating of the material from Qumran remains uncertain, all agree that it reflects the late Second Temple period, and thus provides us with evidence on the nature of phylacteries which predates the earliest material in the Mishnah by one if not two centuries (see *DJD* 2: 80–85).

Prior to 1967, the only fragments discovered came from the hand phylacteries, and while some of the boxes which housed the biblical passages were found, all the parchments were without their original containers. Then, on January 31, 1968, Y. Yadin acquired the only known capsule of head phylacteries, together with four parchments. Scientific examination revealed that three of the four scriptural passages were still in their original compartments (Yadin 1969: 9), thus providing new evidence for the manner in which the passages had been folded and tied. The form of the phylacteries, the material used for the parchment and the tying, all conform to the regulations given in the Talmud. Most surprisingly, the difference of opinion between two 12th-century Talmudists as to the proper order of arranging the four scriptural passages in the head compartments is reflected in the Qumran fragments. Thus we know that the dispute did not originate during the medieval period, as some scholars had previously thought, but rather reflected divergent traditions which go back at least to the 1st century.

Another stage in the development of phylacteries was revealed when it was discovered that the Qumran phylacteries contained the Decalog. According to *m. Tamid* 5:1, the Decalog was recited daily in the temple along with Deut 6:4–9 and 11:13–21. A statement in *y. Ber.* 3c implies that these same texts were also recited outside the temple. The custom of reciting the Decalog along with Deut 6:4–9 is reflected in the Nash Papyrus, a 2d-century-B.C.E. papyrus allegedly from the Fayyum region of Egypt. Therefore it appears that the Decalog was at one time part of the daily liturgy in both Palestine and Egypt (Vermes 1959: 69). According to both Palestinian and Babylonian traditions, the practice of daily recital of the Decalog was suspended because the sectarians claimed "these alone were given to Moses at Sinai" (*y Ber.* 3c; *b. Ber.* 12a).

As early as 1927, Mann (291) claimed that pre-rabbinic *tĕpillîn* contained the Decalog. This would explain the comments of Jerome on Ezek 24:16 that the Babylonian magistrates who observe the law surround their heads with the Decalog written on leather. Mann also points out that *m. Sanh.* 11.3 expressly forbids the use of five rather than four passages in the phylacteries. Since *Sipre* to Deuteronomy, secs. 34–35, uses two exegetical interpretations to justify the exclusion of the Decalog from phylacteries, it seemed logical to Mann that the fifth forbidden passage is the Decalog. Mann's hypothesis was confirmed by the evidence at Qumran. Since those phylacteries found at Qumran contain the Decalog while those at Murabbaʿat do not, it is clear that the Mishnaic reform mentioned above had taken effect by 135 C.E. Thus we see that while the physical elements of the phylacteries, i.e., the case, the parchment, the ties, etc., were already fixed by the 1st century, the final uniformity of the text was not established until the 2d century, and even then, two traditions remained as to the ordering of the four passages.

While the laws concerning phylacteries were fixed by the middle of the 2d century, it is not clear how widespread the custom of wearing phylacteries was in the first two centuries of the Common Era. The majority of those who wore phylacteries did not wear them all day; to do so was seen as a special act of piety (*b. Sukk.* 28a; *b. Taʿan.* 20b). According to *b. Ber.* 47b and *b. Soṭa* 22a, the wearing of phylacteries was seen as one of the criteria distinguishing a *ḥābēr* (member of the rabbinic "society") from an *ʿam hāʾāreṣ* (one not observing rabbinic customs). Possibly the requirement of ritual purity while wearing phylacteries (*y. Ber.* 4c) prevented many from wearing them. A tannaitic statement found in the Babylonian Talmud suggests another reason why the masses did not embrace this custom.

During the Hadrianic persecutions the wearing of phylacteries was banned on pain of death (*y. Ber.* 4c; *m. ᶜErub.* 10.1; *m. Meg.* 4.8). According to *b. Šabb.* 130b, because the people were not willing to martyr themselves for the wearing of phylacteries, this precept remained "weak in their hands" even after the persecution.

Most scholars assume that the origin of the custom of wearing phylacteries was connected with their use as amulets or charms. The Greek word *phylactērion* means "safeguard," "that which protects"; hence, an amulet. However since the term "phylactery" is never attested in Jewish sources even as a foreign word, this etymology (underlying the word's use in Matt 25:3) at best reflects the view of the Christian community in 70 to 90 C.E., and sheds no light on the origin of the institution. As mentioned above, the biblical verses undoubtedly adopted the language of contemporaneous magical and apotropaic charms.

The meaning of the MT's Heb *ṭôṭāpōt* is unclear. It probably should be vocalized as a singular noun, *ṭôṭepet.* Some scholars derive it from the root *ṭpp,* meaning "to tap or strike," "make an incision," with implicit reference to an actual sign or mark made in the flesh. Others prefer the root *ṭûp,* from Akk *ṭaṭâpu,* meaning "to encircle," "surround," thus "headband" for *ṭôṭepet* (BDB, 377). However, this does not fit the descriptive expression "between your eyes." Most scholars prefer to connect the word with *neṭipōt* (Judg 8:26; Isa 3:19) meaning "round jewel." This opinion is supported by *m. Šabb.* 6:1, where *ṭôṭāpōt* is used to describe a jewel worn by a woman on her forehead. Thus the word *ṭôṭāpōt* does not necessarily indicate a sign with magical properties. (See also the discussion in *TDOT* 5: 320, with additional bibliography.)

The derivation of the nonbiblical Hebrew word *tĕpillîn* is likewise unclear (see *TWAT* 6: 608–9). The singular *tĕpillâ* is identical with the Hebrew word for "prayer," but it may be a homonym, deriving not from *pll,* "to intercede," but from *plh,* "to separate, distinguish," indicating that which distinguishes the Jew from the non-Jew. The word *tĕpillîn* appears a number of times in lists with *qāmêaᶜ*, "an amulet" (*m. Miqw.* 10.2; *m. Kelim* 23.1; *m. Šabb.* 6.2), but no connection is suggested between them. While there is no evidence in rabbinic literature that phylacteries were ever regarded as amulets, it is possible that at the time they were first adopted, the masses regarded them as possessing magical properties similar to those of the *qāmêaᶜ*, which were also written on parchment by a professional scribe or exorcist and worn on one's body. Indeed, the very custom of wearing phylacteries might have emerged as a popular superstition, one which was then made normative by the leaders of the Jewish community, who stripped the symbol of its original magical overtones and infused it with a more "legitimate" religious significance. The choice of the term *tĕpillîn,* seen as the plural of "prayer," would thus be part of the rabbinic polemic to replace the original prophylactic nature of phylacteries with the liturgical nature of *tĕpillîn.*

Bibliography

Goren, S. 1962. The Phylacteries of the Judean Desert in Light of the Halacha. *Mahanayim* 62: 5–15.

Kuhn, K. G. 1957. *Phylakterien aus Höhle 4 von Qumran.* AHAW Phil.-hist. Kl. 1. Heidelberg.

Mann, J. 1927. Changes in the Divine Service of the Synagogue due to Religious Persecution. *HUCA* 4: 288–99.

Vermes, G. 1959. Pre-Mishnaic Jewish Worship and the Phylacteries from the Dead Sea. *VT* 9: 65–72.

Yadin, Y. 1969. *Tefillin from Qumran.* Jerusalem.

RUTH SATINOVER FAGEN

PI-BESETH (PLACE) [Heb *pî-beset*]. One of the Egyptian cities mentioned in Ezekiel's oracle of doom against Egypt (Ezek 30:17). The Hebrew represents Egyptian *Pr-b3stt,* "house of Baste," which was rendered "Bubastis" in Greek. The city is associated with extensive ruins of Tel Basta on the SE limits of modern Zagazig in the E Delta, 39 miles NNE of Cairo. The ancient city lay on the right bank of the easternmost of the three major Nile branches, in the Delta. Undoubtedly of prehistoric foundation, Bubastis was originally a metropolis of the thirteenth township of Lower Egypt and came to prominence during the Old Kingdom due to its strategic location at the junction between the river route to the NE frontier and the land route through the Wâdī Tumilat into Sinai. Old Kingdom pharaohs built extensively at the site, and blocks have been found of Khufu and Khafre (Dyn. 4) (Naville 1891: pl. 32); both Tety (Dyn. 5) and Pepy I (Dyn. 6) built chapels there (Bietak 1975: 99 n. 365; Habachi 1957: 11–43). The Middle Kingdom kings lavished building projects on the site, refurbishing older buildings and adding new ones, including palaces (Gomaà 1987: 2–8, 215).

While the fate of the site under the Hyksos is unknown (although blocks of Khiyan and Apophis have been found there; Naville 1981: pl. 35), the 18th Dynasty renewed its interest in Bubastis, and the temples were rebuilt under Thutmose III and Amenhotep II (Urk. IV: 1443; Naville 1891: pl. 35). Thutmose IV left an important historical inscription at the site (ibid.), and Amenhotep III built a new temple (Habachi 1957: 102–7). After the vandalism attendant upon the Amarna heresy, Sety I restored inscriptions (cf. Naville 1891: pl. 35), and his son Rameses II contributed extensively to rebuilding an expansion of all structures and temples.

Bubastis enjoyed its greatest prosperity from about 900–711 B.C., when it was closely associated with the Libyan 22d and 23d dynasties, the latter in fact using it as a residence (Gomaà 1974: 126–37). It is from this period (ca. 850 B.C.) that the great festival hall of Osarkon II dates (Naville 1892). Bubastis, which under the Libyans had been the chief principality of the district Ranofer (stretching from the Nile to the NE frontier), was, at the end of the 23d Dynasty, made into the metropolis of a new nome, the Eighteenth of Lower Egypt (Helck 1974: 196). Though deprived of its political primacy, the city remained prosperous and favored, and one of the prominent cities of the kingdom (cf. Ezek 30:17). Herodotus describes its breathtaking temples in glowing terms (ii. 137–38), and claims that in his day the local festival was the largest in Egypt (ii. 67–69). Bubastis was the site of a decisive battle in the attempt of Artaxerxes III to recapture Egypt (343 B.C.; Diod. xvi. 49–51), but retained its prominence throughout Ptolemaic times (Strabo xvii, 1. 27; Sauneron 1957), and its cults continued to operate in the 3d century A.D. (Aelian xii. 29).

The principal deity at the site was the lioness goddess Bast, later associated with the cat (*KG,* 373 n. 3; te Velde 1982), a feline type of deity associated variously with Sekhmet, the Eye of Re (Habachi 1957: 118), Hathor, Isis, and others (*RÄR* 80–82). Bast's son was Miusis, the "fierce-eyed lion," and she herself was identified by the Greeks with Artemis.

Bibliography

Bietak, M. 1975. *Tell el-Dab^ca.* Vol. 2. Vienna.

Gomaà, F. 1974. *Die libyschen Fürstentümer des Deltas.* Wiesbaden.

———. 1987. *Die Besiedlung Ägyptens während des Mittleren Reiches.* Wiesbaden.

Habachi, L. 1957. *Tell Basta.* Cairo.

Helck, W. 1974. *Die altägyptischen Gaue.* Wiesbaden.

Kees, H. 1958. Bubastis. *OLZ* 53: 309ff.

Naville, E. 1891. *Bubastis.* London.

———. 1892. *The Festival Hall of Osorkon II in the Great Temple of Bubastis.* London.

Sauneron, S. 1957. Un cinquieme exemplaire du decret de Canope: la stele de Boubastis. *BIFAO* 56: 67ff.

Velde, H. te. 1982. The Cat as Sacred Animal of the Goddess Mut. Pp. 127–37 in *Studies in Egyptian Religion.* Leiden.

DONALD B. REDFORD

PI-HAHIROTH (PLACE) [Heb *pî haḥîrōt*]. A stopping place on the itinerary of the Israelites from Goshen to the wilderness (Exod 14:2, 9; Num 33:7–8). In Exod 14:2 the place is reached after "turning back" from Ethan, and in v 9 and Num 33:7 it is said to be "in front of" or E of Baal-zephon. Neither of these passages, however, is of much assistance in locating the place, and they seem to betray a flawed knowledge of delta geography. As transcribed the word resembles a Hebraized form of Akkadian origin, *Pi-hiriti,* "the mouth of the canal," which would be an appropriate toponym for the E edge of the heavily canalized E delta.

No Egyptian toponym of this form has yet been found, the closest approximation being *Pa-Kherta,* a town dedicated to the goddess Tefnut, somewhere on the E edge of the delta (El Arish naos, rev., 6: 5th–4th centuries B.C.), or (the variant of the letter) "the Pond of *Ta-Kherta*" (P. Dem. Cairo 31169 iii, no. 18: Ptolemaic). It is conceivable that these could be garblings of the earlier Akkadian geographical terms postulated above. Other candidates, such as Per-Hathor ("House [of the Goddess] Hathor"), between Tanis and Bubastis ("Hyksos" to post-Saite attestations), or Pa-Hiret (Ramesside), near Qantir, are disqualified for both linguistic and geographical reasons.

Bibliography

Redford, D. B. 1987. An Egyptian Perspective on the Exodus Narrative. In *Egypt, Israel, Sinai,* ed. A. F. Rainey. Tel Aviv.

DONALD B. REDFORD

PIG. See ZOOLOGY.

PIGEON. See ZOOLOGY.

PILATE, ACTS OF. An ancient and extended account of the trial, crucifixion, and resurrection of Jesus. The initial episode of the narrative, which is dependent in part upon the canonical Gospels, centers around the activities of Pontius Pilate during the trial. It is this episode that provides the inspiration for the title of the work.

In many medieval manuscripts a text that is known as "Christ's Descent into Hell" has been appended to the Acts. The two writings often were circulated together in this form under the title of the "Gospel of Nicodemus." The Descent itself is a report upon the activities and the ministry of Christ while in hell, after the crucifixion and before the resurrection. It embodies a purportedly first-hand account of Christ's activities, as they are told by the aged Symeon and his two sons.

A firm date for the original composition of the Acts cannot be established with certainty. The canonical Gospels already reveal a concern among the authors of late-1st-century Christianity for the participation of Pilate in the judgment and execution of Jesus. This general concern for Pilate's role was not resolved by the gospel accounts, however, as is evident from the reappearance of the Pilate theme in the 2d-century *Gospel of Peter.* See PETER, GOSPEL OF.

The first possible reference to the Acts comes through Justin Martyr, who twice makes a specific appeal to a writing that he calls the "Acts of Pontius Pilate" (*Apol.* 1.35, 48). He cites this document as evidence for his own interpretation of the passion episode, but, unfortunately, he does not quote directly from the text. This silence concerning the specific wording of the Acts may suggest either that Justin lacked any intimate familiarity with the writing or perhaps that he only presumed that such a text existed (*NTApocr.* 1: 444).

Though probably a separate document and therefore not a reference to our Acts, Tertullian (*Apol.* 5 and 21) knows of a tradition in which Pilate was believed to have sent letters to Tiberius that contained detailed accounts of the wonderful deeds which were performed by Jesus. Tertullian is convinced by the tone of this correspondence that Pilate himself could be regarded as a Christian based upon the strength of his personal conviction. Additional support for the tradition that is attested by Tertullian is offered by Eusebius (*Hist. Eccl.* 2.2.1–2). But Eusebius also records that a "forgery" of the Acts text itself was circulated during the reign of Daia Maximinus (ca. 311–12) with the intent of engendering animosity against the Christians (*Hist. Eccl.* 1.9.3; 9.5.1). Despite the attestation of Eusebius, it is impossible to know with certainty whether any extant copies of the Acts actually reflect a text that predated the late 3d century. While it is possible that the forgery to which Eusebius refers was in fact a perversion of some earlier form of the Acts, the prevailing scholarly view is that the "Christian Acts" were written only subsequently to any such forgery and that they were considered in order to diffuse the effect of its damage.

Two basic editions of the Acts have been identified among the many copies of the text that are available. The older edition (Recension A), which is attested in Greek, Latin, Coptic, Syriac, Armenian, and Arabic translations, also appears as the basis of a 12th-century Greek manuscript which stands as the oldest copy of the Acts that is known to modern scholars. A second edition of the Acts (Recension B), which has been preserved only in Greek, reveals numerous alterations from the first edition. These obvious additions and expansions indicate that this edition is a secondary construction of the Acts. Included among the changes in Recension B are the introduction of additional biblical materials and the insertion of lamentations over Jesus by his mother, Mary Magdalene, and Joseph of Arimathaea. A pronounced concern for the mother of Jesus as *theotokos* suggests that the earliest form of this second and more recent edition probably should not be dated prior to the Council of Ephesus.

Many versions of the Acts contain a prologue that is attributed to a certain Ananias (Coptic: Aeneas; Latin: Emaus), who claims to have received the text in Hebrew and to have copied it into Greek during the 5th century (425). This prologue specifies that the passion of Christ occurred on the eighth day before the calends of April. Epiphanius (*Haer.* 50.1.5) observes that the heretical Quartodecimans claimed a knowledge of this date which was based upon information that could be found in the Acts. It therefore is probable that the Quartodecimans already had some form of the Acts, with this prologue attached, by the time of Epiphanius in the late 4th century.

The narrative of the Acts is ordered according to the passion sequence of Jesus as it is preserved within the canonical gospel record. The author, however, has added substantial detail to the accounts in order to complete the panorama of events. At the insistence of the Jewish authorities, Pilate summons Jesus for examination, but upon the entrance of Jesus, the Roman standards bow to the amazement of all those who are present (chap. 1). After testimony is offered by twelve men that he was not "born of fornication" (chap. 2), Jesus is examined and released to the will of the Jews, who assume the responsibility for his death (chaps. 3–4). Further testimony on behalf of Jesus then is offered by Nicodemus, by numerous persons whom Jesus healed (including the woman with the "issue of blood," who here is named Bernice [Latin text: Veronica]; Mark 5:25–34), and by another unspecified group of persons who witnessed the teachings and miracles that were performed during his ministry (chaps. 5–8). After the crucifixion and the burial by Joseph of Arimathaea (chaps. 9–11), a series of miracles and proofs of the resurrection are provided as evidence that the deeds of the Jewish authorities were undertaken in error (chaps. 12–16).

Bibliography

Cameron, R. 1982. *The Other Gospels.* Philadelphia.
Finegan, J. 1969. *Hidden Records of the Life of Jesus.* Philadelphia.
James, M. R. 1924. *The Apocryphal New Testament.* Oxford.
Tischendorf, C. 1876. *Evangelia Apocrypha.* Leipzig.

CLAYTON N. JEFFORD

PILATE, PONTIUS. See PONTIUS PILATE.

PILDASH (PERSON) [Heb *pildāš*]. The sixth son borne by Milcah to her husband Nahor, Abraham's brother (Gen 22:22). The name Pildash seems to be used here as a personal one. If it is also a tribal name, the location is unknown but is perhaps to be sought in N Arabia with other Nahorites. Some surmise that all the Aramaean tribes descended from Nahor and his twelve sons (vv 20–24). The Israelites knew that they were related to this other people, and links uniting the ancestors of Israel to other groups of people were always expressed genealogically (*EHI,* 212, 240). The etymology and meaning of the name are uncertain. The first of two leading candidates would have it originate from an animal term, *piddāš* (Ar *fuds,* "spider"). The second main view proposes a relationship to Ar *fandaš,* "to conquer," and a comparison with the Nabataean personal name *pndšw.* Moritz (1926: 93) supplies evidence for the permissible interchange of the letters *l* and *n*—viz., in Nabataean *tntnw* parallels *tntlw.* A couple of other equally valid speculations could be, similar to the first, a connection with Ar *faddâš,* "shatterer" (from the base *fadaš*), and, similar to the second, one with *fandas,* "to run."

Bibliography

Moritz, B. 1926. Edomitische Genealogien. I. *ZAW* 44: 81–93.

EDWIN C. HOSTETTER

PILHA (PERSON) [Heb *pilḥāʾ*]. A leader of the people and a signatory to the covenant established by Ezra (Neh 10:24). The name means "millstone," but nothing else is known about Pilha, who is mentioned only here.

FREDERICK W. SCHMIDT

PILLAR OF FIRE AND CLOUD. The theophany of cloud and glory that guided Israel during the wilderness journey. The phrase "pillar of fire and cloud" only occurs once (Exod 14:24), but there are a number of instances when the separate phrases "pillar of fire" (Exod 13:21, 22; Num 14:14; Neh 9:12, 19) and "pillar of cloud" (Exod 13:21, 22; 14:19; Num 14:14; Neh 9:12, 19; Ps 99:7) occur. Each phrase describes the same manifestation of divine presence.

The Exodus text does not introduce the theophany by description. The title itself became the description. When Israel left the bonds of Pharaoh, departing from Succoth (Tell el-Mashkutah), and reached the edge of the wilderness, the divine presence went before them as a pillar of cloud by day and a pillar of fire by night (Exod 13:21). God's presence not only guided them, but protected them; for the cloud moved to the rear of the Israelite host when the Egyptians approached. The pillar of cloud also represented divine presence when Moses entered the tent of the Lord and conversed with God (Exod 33:7–9), again when the authority and leadership of Moses was confirmed after Aaron and Miriam murmured against him (Numbers 12:5 ff.), and a third time when Joshua was appointed successor to Moses (Deut 31:15).

God is often represented in the OT by fire and cloud. The symbol of the cloud both reveals and conceals the divine presence (Mendenhall 1973: 32–66). The cloud would indeed reveal truth but, at the same time, would limit that revelation. On the other hand, fire symbolized the power of the one leading them.

Any natural explanation of these phenomena seems to be strained. Some have suggested that a large fire on a pole was placed at the head of the host. Though this practice was common in festivals (1 Kgs 7:15) and military campaigns, it does not appear the case here. Others have proposed the cloud and fire to be the embers of an active volcano in the area. This theory is difficult to prove geologically.

The pillar of fire and cloud according to OT tradition represented God's miraculous provision and protection for the Hebrews during a time marked by many supernatural phenomena.

Bibliography

Davies, G. H. 1962. Pillar of Fire and Cloud. *IB* 3: 817.

Mann, T. W. 1971. The Pillar of Cloud in the Reed Sea Narrative. *JBL* 90: 15–30.

Mendenhall, G. 1973. *The Tenth Generation.* Baltimore.

JOEL C. SLAYTON

PILLARS, HALL OF (PLACE) [Heb *ʾûlām hāʿammûdîm*]. See JUDGMENT, HALL OF.

PILTAI (PERSON) [Heb *pilṭāy*]. The head of the priestly family of Moadiah in the time of the high priest Joiakim (Neh 12:17). The name is an abbreviated form (KB; cf. Pelatiah, Heb *pĕlaṭyāhû,* "Yahweh has saved").

NORA A. WILLIAMS

PIN. See DRESS AND ORNAMENTATION.

PINE TREE. See FLORA.

PINNACLE. See TEMPLE, JERUSALEM.

PINON (PERSON) [Heb *pînōn*]. One of the persons mentioned among the eleven names in the list of Edomite "tribal chiefs" *(ʾallūpîm)* in Gen 36:40–43, an addition probably originating from the Priestly Source. The name also recurs in 1 Chr 1:51b–54, an addition which represents a shortened version of Gen 36:40–43. Although some of the names cannot be classified with any certainty, "Pinon" and "Mibzar" are likely place names. The original (?) place name was obviously understood as a tribal or a district name. The name Pinon/Punon (Num 33:42–43)—Greek *Phinan, Phinō, Phainō*—is identical with Arabic *Fênān* and probably with Egyptian *pwnw,* the mining colony Kh. Fênān (M.R. 197004) in the Wâdī ʿAraba. See also FEINAN, WADI.

ULRICH HÜBNER

PIPE. See MUSIC AND MUSICAL INSTRUMENTS.

PIRAM (PERSON) [Heb *pirʾām*]. The Amorite king of Jarmuth at the time of Joshua, according to biblical tradition (Josh 10:3). His name, which occurs only once, appears to be a form of the Hebrew term *pereʾ,* "wild ass," with the ending *-ām.* A similar construction may be attested in the name Balaam (Heb *bilʿām* = *belaʿ* ["confusion," "slander"] + *-ām*). Piram joined with Adoni-zedek of Jerusalem, Hoham of Hebron, Debir of Eglon, and Japhni of Lachish to oppose Joshua and the Gibeonites. This coalition was defeated by Joshua and its five kings fled to the cave of Makkedah, from which Joshua took them and hanged them on five trees nearby.

D. G. SCHLEY

PIRATHON (PLACE) [Heb *pirʿātôn*]. Var. PHARATHON. PIRATHONITE. A town in the central hill country of Ephraim that was controlled by Amalekites prior to Israelite domination (Judg 12:15). It was the home of Abdon, the judge who led Israel for eight years (Judg 12:13–14), and of Benaiah, one of David's thirty mighty men (2 Sam 23:30; 1 Chr 11:31; 27:14). A location bearing the same name along with other sites in Judea was later reportedly fortified by the Seleucid general Bacchides ca. 160 B.C. as a means of controlling the rebellious forces of Jonathan and Simon Maccabeus (Josephus *Ant* 13.1.3 (§14–16); 1 Macc 9:50). The Pharathon (RSV var. of "Pirathon") reported by the author of Maccabees may not be the same as that attested earlier in the OT. Goldstein (*1 Maccabees* AB) contends that the author of Maccabees purposely attempted to compare the exploits of the Maccabees with the venerated heroes of the conquest under Joshua. The reference to Pharathon could then be a case where the name was used as an allusion to places that had been captured by the Jews in antiquity. Textual difficulties in the account of 1 Maccabees have caused some to believe that "Pharathon" was the second half of a compound name, Timnath-pharathon, rather than the name of separate fortified towns. Some doubt concerning the equation of the town in Ephraim mentioned in Judges and Samuel with that fortified by Bacchides has arisen because 1 Macc 9:50 and Josephus *Ant* 13.1.3 (§14–16) locate the town in Judea as opposed to Ephraim. Clearly the author of Maccabees understood Judea as Jewish-occupied territories, including land N of Jerusalem in the ancient tribal allotment of Ephraim. The sites of Bethel and Beth-horon which were listed along with Pharathon as being fortified by Bacchides were also located in the traditional territory of Ephraim.

The location of Pirathon is widely accepted as modern Farata (M.R. 165177), which is six miles SW of Shechem. Attempts to locate the site in the territory of Benjamin are based upon the mistaken identification of the judge Abdon with other Abdons, one who was a Benjaminite tribal chief (1 Chr 8:23) and another who was an ancestor of King Saul (1 Chr 8:30; 9:36).

ROBERT W. SMITH

PISGAH (PLACE) [Heb *pisgâ*]. A mountain in the Abarim range of NW Moab, close to Mt. Nebo. The "mountains" in this region are actually narrow extensions of the Transjordanian tableland that has been deeply eroded by scarp streams, mostly running E-W. These plateau remnants tower above the floor of the Jordan Rift valley, but they are no higher than the tableland to which the mountains are attached on the W.

Both Mt. Nebo and Mt. Pisgah are in this region (cf. Deut 34:1). Whereas Nebo is mentioned only twice in the Bible, Pisgah is named eight times, always with the definite article and always in combination with one of two terms that highlight features of the mountain. In four passages, "the top of Pisgah" occurs: (1) Num 21:20, where it is mentioned as a station on the Hebrew migration through Moab and as a peak "which looks down upon the desert"; (2) Num 23:14, where it is named as one of the peaks on which Balak made sacrifices in an effort to induce Balaam's curse on Israel; (3) Deut 3:27, where it is identified as a peak from which Moses viewed the promised land; and (4) Deut 34:1, where it is named as the point from which Moses again saw the territory which the Hebrews would occupy and on which Moses died.

In four OT passages, "the slopes of Pisgah" are named: (1) Deut 3:17, in which they are referred to as being E of the Salt Sea, one of the boundaries of Reuben and Gad; (2) Deut 4:49, in which they are named again as towering above the Sea of the Arabah, a boundary of Israel's conquests; (3) Josh 12:3, in which they are identified as a border of Sihon's kingdom; and (4) Josh 13:20, in which they are mentioned again as one of the borders of Sihon's realm and of the tribe of Reuben. Contrary to these RSV uses of the phrase "slopes of Pisgah," the KJV has "springs of Pisgah" in Deut 4:49 and "Ashdoth-pisgah" in Deut 3:17; Josh 12:3; 13:20.

Eusebius located Phasgo (Pisgah) along the way from Livias in the Arabah to Esbus on the tableland, in the same vicinity as Mt. Peor. Most interesting is Jerome's translation of "Fasge" (Pisgah) by the Lat *abscisum,* meaning "steep" or "broken off." This corresponds to the LXX's translation of Heb *pisgâ* with Gk *laxeuō.* Thus, LaSor (*ISBE* 3: 873) notes that the name Pisgah, which derives from Heb *pāsag* ("split," "cut off"), means "cleft." It is suggested that Pisgah's projection from the plateau had this appearance when viewed from the E.

Most scholars identify Mt. Nebo and Mt. Pisgah as the two peaks on Jebel Shayhan, with Pisgah (M.R. 218130) located ca. 1.5 miles W-NW of Nebo, beyond a small saddle. Jebel en-Nebu (2,739 feet above sea level) is located ca. 4 miles NW of Medeba, and Ras es-Siyagha (2,329 feet above sea level) is located ca. 5.5 miles NW of Medeba. Though this widely accepted location of Pisgah is slightly lower than Jebel en-Nebu, Siyagha's projection from the tableland affords magnificent views of the Rift valley and points beyond.

GERALD L. MATTINGLY

PISHON (PLACE) [Heb *pîšôn*]. The first of the four rivers into which the stream that springs from the Garden of Eden is divided (Gen 2:11). The Pishon surrounds the land of Havilah, where there is gold. Several proposals have been made to identify this country and its river. If, however, Havilah is to be equated with the large and old tribal federation of Ḫaulān in SW Arabia, the Pishon likewise is to be localized in that region. See HAVILAH (PLACE). A second biblical reference is found in Sir 24:25, where a parallel is drawn between wisdom, of which the divine law is full, and the plenteous waters of the Pishon river.

A. Sprenger (1875: 49) was the first one who compared the biblical *pîšôn* with the Wâdī Baiš in the SW of the Arabian peninsula. Al-Hamdānī (1884: 73) nevertheless writes that the Wâdī Baiš is fed from tributaries from the N of the land of Ḫaulān before it flows into the Red Sea. As was probable already in antiquity, in the 10th century the Wâdī Baiš, abounding in water, formed the N boundary of the densely populated and terraced mountainous region of Ḫaulān (and until 1934 it was the border between the kingdom of Yemen and Saudi Arabia). Moreover, it is quite possible that the names of the rivers Baiš and Bīša are contained in the name "Pishon," since both rise not far from each other in the mountains of ʿAsīr. However, while the Wâdī Baiš flows SW toward the coastal plain, the Wâdī Bīša flows N into the Wâdī Dawāsir, which discharges itself into the central Arabian desert. For another southern tributary of the Wâdī Dawāsir, al-Hamdānī (1884: 141) furthermore records the name Faišān. Since the Wâdī Baiš offers the best access to the upper course of the Wâdī Bīša, the two valleys were possibly regarded to be one single river, ignoring the real geographic facts. Ptolemaios, too, fell into the same error when he designated not only the small Wâdī Baiḍ to the N of Wâdī Baiš but also the Wâdī Bīša as *Baitios potamos* (*Geog.* 6.7.5).

However, one must admit that neither the name Baiš, Bīša, nor Faišān corresponds correctly to the Heb *pîšôn;* one would rather expect a form **Fīšān.* Sprenger (1875: 49) wanted to see in the ending *-ôn* the rendering of the Arabic nunation *-un* suffixed to the name *Baiš.* Hommel (1926: 564ff.) believed that the first element of the name was the Hebrew word *pī,* "mouth (of a river)." M. Görg (1977) derived the name from the Egyptian because the initial *pī-* corresponds to the Egyptian masculine article; according to him, *pîšôn* designates simply "the river," i.e., the Nile. The name Pishon has also been repeatedly combined with the Heb root *pûš,* "to jump, skip," and it is quite possible that the vocalization of the form *pîšôn* resulted from an assimilation to the name of the river mentioned in the following verse (Gen 2:13): Gihon.

Bibliography

Al-Hamdānī. 1884. *Ṣifat Ǧazīrat al-ʿArab,* ed. D. H. Müller. Leiden.

Görg, M. 1977. Wo lage das Paradies? *BN* 2: 23–32.

Hommel, F. 1926. *Ethnologie und Geographie des Alten Orients.* HAW 3/1/1. Munich.

Sprenger, A. 1875. *Die alte Geographie Arabiens.* Bern.

Wissmann, H. von. 1975. *Über die frühe Geschichte Arabiens und des Entstehen des Sabäerreichs.* SÖAW 301/5. Vienna.

W. W. MÜLLER

PISIDIA (PLACE) [Gk *Pisidia*]. A mountainous area in the southernmost part of the Roman province of Galatia, bordered by Phrygia to the N, Lycaonia to the E, Pamphylia to the S, and Lycia to the W. Pisidia is mentioned twice in the Acts of the Apostles (13:14 and 14:24), where Pau passes through the area on his way to and from his mission in S Galatia.

Although the majority textual reading in Acts 13:14 is "Antioch of Pisidia" (Gk *Antiocheian tēs Pisidias,* genitive case), "Pisidian Antioch" (Gk *Antiocheian tēn Pisidian,* accusative case; supported by numerous manuscripts) is probably the best reading (Metzger *TCGNT,* 404–5; Hemer 1989: 228). In the first instance, the reading would suggest that Antioch was in Pisidia; in the second, "Pisidia" functions as an adjective, meaning "Antioch [of Phrygia] toward [sc. facing or near] Pisidia" (Strabo has the more complete phrase, 12.6.4; cf. Bruce *Galatians* NIGTC, 6, n. 17). At the time of Paul and earlier, only the latter would be correct. Thus the majority mss tradition reflects the situation following the reorganization of the E provinces under Diocletian when this Antioch was assigned to the extended province of Pisidia and made its capital (A.D. 295). This descriptive title served to distinguish it from the many other cities of the same name founded by the Seleucids throughout Asia Minor.

There were three possible routes for Paul as he journeyed from Perga, in Pamphylia near the coast, through Pisidia to Pisidian Antioch (Finegan 1981: 90). There was a Roman road that traversed the W side of the region. Another route would have been to go straight N up the Kestros river and past Lake Limnae (modern Egridir), following the SE shore to the Anthios valley and on to Pisidian Antioch (Broughton 1937: 131–33). It is possible that Paul would have chosen this second route, but it is more likely that he would have followed the Roman road to Side and from there traveled N along the E shore of Lake Beysehir. It would have involved a steep climb over very rugged mountains to the inner plateau of some 3,000 feet or more and a distance of at least 80 miles. The time required would have been about 6 days. It would have taken much longer if Ramsay is correct in his speculative suggestion (1920: 94–97; followed, apparently, by Finegan 1981: 90), on the basis of Gal 4:13, that Paul moved from the hot, mosquito-infested coastal region to recover from malaria.

It was not merely the rugged terrain of Pisidia that was treacherous, but its native people also had a fierce reputation. Alexander the Great had great difficulty in subduing Pisidia, and throughout the Hellenistic and Roman periods the area is described as the home of marauding bandits. It has been frequently observed that the words of 2 Cor 11:26 ("on frequent journeys, in danger from rivers, in danger from robbers") would have been especially appropriate to his trip across Pisidia. To secure the region, Augustus had established a series of military colonies, including the garrisons of Lystra (Acts 14:8–21) and Pisidian Antioch (Acts 13:14–50; 14:21) visited by Paul. The latter was the chief colony and the center of the military administration of the region. An inscription indicates that P. Sulpicius Quirinius, mentioned in Luke 2:2 as governor of Syria in the year of Christ's birth, was an honorary magistrate of Antioch during the time of his campaign (ca. 8 B.C.) against the Homonades (Frend *ISBE* 3: 874).

Pisidia continued to be a part of the province of Galatia until A.D. 74, when the S part was assigned to the newly created province of Lycia-Pamphylia. The N part continued to be a part of Galatia until the end of the 3d century, when the province of Pisidia was formed and Antioch named the capital. The whole of the S part of the province of Galatia, including the region of the four cities visited by Paul (Pisidian Antioch, Iconium, Lystra, and Derbe [Acts 13 and 14], probably home of the churches addressed in Paul's letter to the Galatians), was co-opted into the new province. From this time onward it became technically correct to speak of "Antioch of Pisidia," though because of the close link of the city with the region, the designation may have been in use at an earlier period.

Like the N part of the province of Galatia, the interior of Pisidia was little affected by either Hellenic or Roman culture. The Roman presence was primarily military, and the countryside was largely rural. There are few evidences that Christianity made very deep inroads into Pisidia until it was legally recognized under Constantine. There is also little evidence for the presence of Jews, except at Antioch, which, as has been noted, was not strictly in Pisidia.

Bibliography

Broughton, T. R. S. 1937. Three Notes on St. Paul's Journeys in Asia Minor. Pp. 131–38 in *Quantulacumque: Studies Presented to Kirsopp Lake,* ed. R. P. Casey and A. K. Lake. London.

Finegan, J. 1981. *The Archaeology of the New Testament.* Boulder, CO.

Hemer, C. J. 1989. *The Book of Acts in the Setting of Hellenistic History,* ed. C. Gempf. WUNT 49. Tübingen.

Ramsay, W. M. 1920. *St. Paul the Traveller and the Roman Citizen.* London.

W. WARD GASQUE

PISPA (PERSON) [Heb *pispâ*]. A descendant of Asher, listed in 1 Chr 7:38. Pispa is recorded as the son of Jether, who perhaps is to be identified with Ithran (7:37). If this identification is correct, then Pispa stands within the last listed generation of Asher. Nothing is known of this figure: he is not mentioned elsewhere in the Hebrew Bible, and none of his descendants are given. According to Johnson (1969: 64–66) and others, the Chronicler's unique genealogies may draw from military census lists, themselves arranged in genealogical form.

Bibliography

Johnson, M. D. 1969. *The Purpose of the Biblical Genealogies.* Cambridge.

JULIA M. O'BRIEN

PISTACHIO. See FLORA.

PISTIS SOPHIA (CODEX ASKEWIANUS). Coptic (Sahidic) parchment codex of 178 leaves inscribed in double columns on both sides. This codex contains gnostic treatises known by the title given in a later hand in the manuscript, *Pistis Sophia.* The original title, which appears at the end of books 2 and 3, appears to have been *Books of the Savior.* The provenance of this codex is unknown. It was acquired by a London doctor, named Askew, around 1772 and purchased by the British Museum in 1785. The first editions of the complete text and translations did not appear until the mid–19th century. The standard edition was published by C. Schmidt for the *Griechischen christlichen Schriftsteller* series in 1905 with a second edition in 1925; that edition was revised by W. Till in 1954 and 1959 (see this publication history in Schmidt 1981, the 4th edition edited by H. M. Schenke). It forms the basis for the text, notes, and English translation by V. MacDermot in the *Nag Hammadi Studies* series (Schmidt and MacDermot 1978). Modern editors have divided the codex into a continuous series of chapters.

In its present form, *Pistis Sophia* is divided into four books. Books 2 and 3 conclude with a title in the original hand. A later scribe separated books 1 and 2 by introducing a title, "The Second Book of the Pistis Sophia." Book 4 is clearly a different work from the earlier books. It contains a new setting, on Easter rather than after eleven years of instruction by the risen Jesus as in Book 1. The disciples are shown the zodiac as they stand in the "Midst." They receive revelations about the punishment of the evil archons, who are bound by the zodiac in the regions of fate and the various punishments there. They are promised forgiveness and access to the divine mysteries by which they can escape judgment. These mysteries include magical words recited by Jesus and rituals of offering wine, water, and loaves while sacred words are pronounced (chap. 142).

Book 1 and Book 2 through chap. 82 are primarily concerned with the repentance of the fallen Sophia, Pistis Sophia. She is the mother of the gnostic seed. Chaps. 30–58 detail her wanderings in darkness and her lamentation. Jesus, acting in the power of light, serves as Savior to bring her out of chaos, and she sings hymns of gratitude to the "First Mystery" (chaps. 58–62). These hymns are then interpreted by the disciples with reference to the Sophia story (chaps. 63–82). The rest of Book 2 (chaps. 83–101) details the mysteries of various ranks and types of souls, including the origins of the passions which destroy the soul. It concludes with the promise that the person who discovers the truth of these mysteries will be equal to the "First One" (God), having gained knowledge (gnosis) of the Ineffable.

Book 3 elaborates on the standard conclusion of gnostic revelation dialogues, the command to the disciples to preach gnosis either to the world (as here) or to the elect. Humanity is to be summoned to renounce sin, to be saved from the various regions of punishment and become worthy of the mysteries (chap. 102). Dialogue between Jesus and the disciples concerning the mysteries of repentance and the punishments of those who do not receive them includes application of Matthew 10 to the gnostic missionary (chap. 107).

Pistis Sophia is a late compendium of gnostic lore complied from earlier writings. It contains Coptic versions of five *Odes of Solomon* and refers by name to the two *Books of Jeu* found in the Bruce Codex. Elaborate exposition of the Psalms, the hymns of Pistis Sophia, magical formulas, variants of the Sophia story, and various allusions to sacred formulas and ritual suggest that the work has drawn on extensive gnostic lore. Therefore most would suggest that it was composed sometime in the late 3d or early 4th century. For *Pistis Sophia,* gnosis is clearly an extensive body of esoteric Christian wisdom, not a dynamic system of speculation.

Bibliography

Amélineau, E. 1895. *La Pistis Sophia: ouvrage gnostique de Valentin.* Paris.

Carmignac, J. 1964. Le genre littéraire du péshère dans la Pistis Sophia. *RQ* 4: 497–552.

Kragerud, A. 1967. *Die Hymnen der Pistis Sophia.* Oslo.

Ludin, J. H. 1960. Gnostic Interpretation in Pistis Sophia. Pp. 106–11 in *Proceedings of the IXth International Congress for the History of Religions.* Tokyo.

———. 1967. Er Sofia-teksten en mysterieliturgi? *NorTT* 68: 92–93.

Schmidt, C. 1981. *Die Pistis Sophia.* Vol. 1 of *Koptisch-gnostische Schriften.* 4th ed., ed. H. M. Schenke. Berlin.

Schmidt, C., and MacDermot, V. 1978. *Pistis Sophia.* NHS 9. Leiden.

Trautmann, C. 1979. La citation du Psaume 85 (84), 11–12 et ses commentaires dans la Pistis Sophia. *RHPR* 59: 551–57.

Unnik, W. C. van. 1963. Die "Zahl der vollkommenen Seelen" in der Pistis Sophia. Pp. 467–77 in *Festschrift für Otto Michel,* ed. O. Betz; M. Hengel; and P. Schmidt. AGSU 5. Leiden.

Widengren, G. 1969. Die Hymnen der Pistis Sophia und die gnostische Schriftauslegung. Pp. 269–81 in *Liber Amicorum.* SHR 18. Leiden.

Worrell, W. H. 1912. The Odes of Solomon and the Pistis Sophia. *JTS* 13: 29–46.

PHEME PERKINS

PIT. See DEAD, ABODE OF THE.

PITHOM (PLACE) [Heb *pītōm*]. One of the two storage cities built by the Hebrews while in Egypt (Exod 1:11) laboring under an oppressive pharaoh. The city also served as a fortress to help guard Egypt from invasion from the east.

The Hebrew *pītōm* has been shown to be a transcription of the Egyptian phrase *pr ʾitm* (see Redford 1963: 403). The Egyptian expression means "house of Atum." The word *pr* means "abode," "temple," or "house," while *ʾitm* is the name of the god Atum, personifying the sun. From Egyptian texts such as the Abu Simbel stele (*AEL* 2: 57–78), Papyrus Harris, and Wadjhoresne's inscription, it is evident that *pr ʾitm* was also used in reference to temple estates. From the end of the Saite period (that is, after 525 B.C.E.), the phrase appears to name a city.

The city is only once directly mentioned as "Pithom" in the Bible (Exod 1:11). However, some scholars suggest that Gen 46:28 may also refer to the same place. Although the MT reads "Goshen," the LXX reads *hērōōn polin,* which has been linked to Pithom through the equivalency of Atum to the god Ero. Moreover, the Bohairic Coptic Version reads "Pithom" in place of *hērōōn polin.*

The question which continues to linger concerning Pithom is: where is the location of the city? One may ascertain certain clues from the biblical account in Exod 1:11, such as (1) Pithom is probably located close to the city of Rameses, a city which is located in the Wâdī Tumilat historically renowned as a route between Egypt and the East, and (2) Egyptian architecture should remain from the time of the Exodus in the LB Age. The evidence from archaeology is consequently of utmost significance in the identification of this site.

Excavations in Egypt have resulted in three major assessments of the archaeological evidence for the location of Pithom. The first location was proposed by Edouard Naville in 1888. After excavating Tell el-Maskhuta in the E delta, he concluded that the site was biblical Pithom. Alan Gardiner, later challenging Naville's theory in 1918, proposed another site at Tell el-Ratabah. Finally, in 1968 E. P. Uphill suggested a third location at the site of the ancient capital city Heliopolis (Egyptian Innu) just one mile north of Matariyeh.

Édouard Naville's proposal has received the most attention by subsequent scholars. See MASKHUTA, TELL EL-. After his archaeological expedition began in 1883, he reported his findings which led him to conclude that Tell el-Maskhuta ("mound of idols/images") was Pithom. First, he found the toponym *pr ʾitm* used of this site, along with *ṯkw(t)* (identified also with Succoth). He argued that *pr ʾitm* was the religious name given to the site, while *ṯkw(t)* was the civil name. Second, Naville concludes that the remains of the tell evidence a construction which was both a fortress and a storage building. Third, a Latin inscription found at the site mentions Ero (or Gk Hero), commonly associated with *hērōōn polis.* Hero is the Greek equivalent for Atum (see Gardiner 1918: 267–69), hence making *hērōōn polis* connected with *pr ʾitm.* Finally, a parallel is drawn between bricks found at Tell el-Maskhuta without straw and the bricks of Exod 5:6–10, which were made by the Hebrews without straw.

Alan Gardiner disagreed with Naville's finds and conclusions. In particular, he translated one of the Latin markers differently, concluding that the message identified the present site (Tell el-Maskhuta) as nine miles away from Ero. Consequently, Tell el-Maskhuta could not be Pithom. A site identified as Tell el-Ratabah was his choice for the city of Pithom.

The third option appeared as E. Uphill, disagreeing with Naville, proposed the site of Heliopolis as Pithom. Uphill's approach posed the question of how the Egyptians would have understood *pr ʾitm.* His assumption was that the Egyptians' understanding of *pr ʾitm* would also be the Hebrew writer's understanding. He observed that contemporaries would view the phrase as designating the national shrine located at Heliopolis. In support of his view, Uphill observed that Sir Flinders Petrie discovered a temple, possibly for the god Atum, at Heliopolis. Gardiner objects to this proposal, as no definite proof exists that the temple was so dedicated (the temple has been typically viewed as dedicated to the diety *Rēʿ-Harakhti*). However, Uphill points out that Innu was closely related to Atum. Hence the possibility of the temple for Atum cannot be ruled out absolutely.

An important addition to the three ideas proposed is the evidence given by John S. Holladay in 1983. Speaking on the ongoing excavations concerning the Wâdī Tumilat, he remarks that many statues of Rameses II have been discovered since Naville (1883) at Maskhuta, but the pottery and the habitation found are not pre–7th century.

With three different assessments of the archaeological evidence available, scholars find no unanimity in identifying the location of Pithom. While some scholars view Pithom as probably Tell el-Maskhuta, others view the tell as Succoth (*ṯkw(t)*). While some see Tell el-Ratabah as probably Pithom, others claim that Tell el-Ratabah was the city Rameses. About the only existing consensus among scholars is that more archaeological evidence is needed to make a definite conclusion.

Bibliography

Bleiberg, E. L. 1983. The Location of Pithom and Succoth. *AW* 6: 21–27.

Gardiner, A. H. 1918. The Delta Residence of the Ramessides. *JEA* 5: 267–69.

Helck, W. 1965. *Ṯkw und die Ramses-stadt. VT* 15: 35–48.

Naville, E. 1903. *The Store City of Pithom and the Route of the Exodus.* 3d ed. Egypt Exploration Fund, Memoir No. 1. London.

Peet, E. T. 1924. *Egypt and the Old Testament.* Liverpool.

Redford, D. B. 1963. Exodus 1, 11. *VT* 13: 401–18.

Uphill, E. P. 1968. Pithom and Raamses: Their Location and Significance I. *JNES* 27: 291–316.

———. 1969. Pithom and Raamses: Their Location and Significance II. *JNES* 28: 15–39.

Tom F. Wei

PITHON (PERSON) [Heb *pîtôn*]. A Benjaminite, son of Micah, great-great-grandson of King Saul (1 Chr 8:35; 9:41). The etymology of the name is unclear, but it might be related to Hebrew *peten,* "an adder" (Noth *IPN,* 254). The section that lists Micah's children is segmented, listing four children; it is unclear why this segmented section appears in what is a generally linear genealogy. Pithon's line is not the main line, which derives instead from his brother Ahaz. The name appears in the two nearly identical genealogies of Saul's family in 1 Chr 8:33–40 and 1 Chr 9:39–44. This list is from the end of the First Temple period (Demsky 1971: 20), and was preserved by Benjaminite families that survived the Babylonian Exile (Williamson 1979: 356). The existence and preservation of the Saulide genealogy probably reflects the continued prominence of Saul's family, and perhaps even their hope that they would return to power (Ackroyd *Chronicles, Ezra, Nehemiah* TBC, 42; Flanagan 1982: 25). See MELECH.

On the repetition of the genealogy in 1 Chronicles 8 and 9, and its structure within the genealogies in Chronicles, see AHAZ.

Bibliography

Demsky, A. 1971. The Genealogy of Gibeon (1 Chronicles 9:35–44): Biblical and Epigraphic Considerations. *BASOR* 202: 16–23.

Flanagan, J. 1982. Genealogy and Dynasty in the Early Monarchy of Israel and Judah. *PWCJS* 8: 23–28.

Williamson, H. G. M. 1979. Sources and Redaction in the Chronicler's Genealogy of Judah. *JBL* 98: 351–59.

Marc Z. Brettler

PLAGUES. See SICKNESS AND DISEASE; EGYPT, PLAGUES IN.

PLANE TREE. See FLORA.

PLANK [Heb *lûaḥ*]. A construction term designating the planking of a Tyrian ship (Ezek 27:2; cf. Acts 27:44). This Hebrew term is sometimes rendered "board," as in the tabernacle text of Exodus in reference to wooden (acacia) "boards" used for the altar (Exod 27:8; 38:7; cf. Cant 8:9). The Heb *ṣĕdērôt* is translated "planks" in the temple texts in 1 Kings, where it designates, together with "beams," the components of the cedar ceiling of the Jerusalem temple (1 Kgs 7:9). These words are part of a nuanced terminology for building materials with the distinctions among the various terms being difficult to ascertain.

CAROL MEYERS

PLANTS. See FLORA.

PLATO: REPUBLIC 588B–589B (NHC VI,*5*). This brief fragment is a very poor translation of a section from Plato's *Republic* (588B–589B) on the theme of justice. The poor quality of the translation reveals that the Coptic author had no knowledge of classical Greek nor of Plato's writings. The Coptic dialect of the fragment is Sahidic with Subachmimic influence. See LANGUAGES (COPTIC). The Greek original was most likely circulated in a school handbook of similar quotations because the fragment is either alluded to or cited by a number of ancient authors. In the context of the Nag Hammadi Library, the fragment is included in a codex containing several hermetic writings: *The Discourse on the Eighth and the Ninth* (NHC VI,*6*); *The Prayer of Thanksgiving* (NHC VI,7); *Asclepius 21–29* (NHC VI,*8*). The belief among hermeticists that Hermes was the teacher of Plato best explains its inclusion among these particular texts. However, the fragment was not identified as a quotation from Plato for some twenty years after its discovery because of the distorted nature of the translation. Some scholars argue that the fragment is not gnostic in any special sense, but that it was included in the Nag Hammadi Library because of its strong ethical appeal. Others argue, however, that the Coptic text has been consciously reworked by its author and is thus a true redaction and not simply a paraphrase or bad translation. A final point of view opts for a middle position, viz. the author is a bad translator who has interpreted the text in a gnostic direction but is not a true redactor. To date, there is no scholarly consensus on these various opinions.

In general, the text deals with the problem of justice in relation to three "images" within the individual: a many-headed beast, a lion, and an inner human. The just person tramples the beast and lion, the unjust or weak person does not. In a Platonic context, the three images relate to the tripartite nature of the soul: appetitive, spirited, rational. In a gnostic context, however, the three images would allude to the three races of humankind: hylics, psychics, pneumatics. Additional gnostic themes would be a probable allusion to the archontic creation of the world (49,4–50,19) as well as an implied reference to the eschatological choice the psychic race must make between a just life and one of archontic or "beastly" domination (50,4–51,23). Jackson (1985: 204–13) now cites logion 7 of *The Gospel of Thomas* (NHC II,2) as another example of gnostic usage of this Platonic parable and, in doing so, explores in detail numerous examples of leonine imagery in a variety of gnostic sources. In gnostic circles, the lion becomes a powerful symbol of sexual passion or the "beastly" dimension of human existence that the ascetic gnostic strives to subdue and control. If *Plato Rep.* has been consciously shaped with these various gnostic concerns in mind, then the Coptic author can be viewed as a probable Christian gnostic in touch with Sethian cosmogonic notions and Valentinian ideas of salvation. Otherwise, the gnostic affinities of the author, if any, cannot be determined.

The date of the Coptic translation is toward the middle of the 4th century C.E., or the approximate date of the copying of Codex VI. The Greek original can be dated in either the 2d or 3d century C.E. The locale cannot be determined, but Alexandria is a reasonable hypothesis because the author is clearly an Egyptian living in an eclectic milieu with only superficial Greek contacts (Poirer and Painchaud 1983: 122–23).

Bibliography

Brashler, J. 1979. Plato, Republic 588B–589B: VI,*5*:48,16–51,23. Pp. 325–39 in *Nag Hammadi Codices V,2–5 and VI with Papyrus Berolinensis, 1 and 4*. NHS 11. Leiden.

Jackson, H. M. 1985. *The Lion Becomes Man: The Gnostic Leontomorphic Creator and the Platonic Tradition*. SBLDS 81. Atlanta.

Krause, M., and Labib, P. 1971. *Gnostische und Hermetische Schriften aus Codex II und Codex VI*. Glückstadt.

Matsagouras, E. G. 1976. *Plato Copticus, Republic 588b–589b*. M.A. diss., Dalhousie University.

———. 1977. Plato Copticus. *Platon* 29: 191–99.

Orlandi, T. 1977. La traduzione copta di Platone, Resp. IX, 588B–589B: problemi critici ed esegetici. *AANLR* 32 fasc. 1–2: 45–62.

Poirer, P.-H., and Painchaud, L. 1983. *Les Sentences de Sextus (NH XII,1)/Fragments (NH XII,3) et Fragment de la République de Platon (NH VI,5)*. BCNHT 11. Quebec.

Schenke, H. M. 1974. Zur Faksimile-Ausgabe der Nag-Hammadi-Schriften: Nag-Hammadi-Codex VI. *OLZ* 69: 235–42.

RUTH MAJERCIK

PLATONISM. Platonism, as understood here, is to be distinguished from the philosophizing of Plato himself, although it is very largely a formalization of his teachings. Ever since the beginning of the last century (Schleiermacher), it has been customary to distinguish the philosophy of Plato's dialogues from the later Platonic tradition, and that procedure is a sound one. Platonism marks its rise from Plato, certainly, but it was a lively philosophic tradition in its own right, which developed in various ways over the 800 years or so which are the subject of this survey. Historically, Platonism may be regarded as progressing through four chief periods in ancient times: the Old Academy (347–267 B.C.E.), the "New" (Skeptical) Academy (267–ca. 80 B.C.E.), Middle Platonism (ca. 80 B.C.E.–250 C.E.), and Neoplatonism (ca. 250 B.C.E.).

A. The Old Academy

After Plato's death in 347 B.C.E., the school was taken over by his nephew Speusippus (ca. 407–339), an idiosyncratic thinker but not one who had much influence on later Platonism. Platonism as a formalized philosophical movement is best seen as beginning with his successor, Xenocrates (396–314). He put out a comprehensive series of works covering all areas of philosophy (the three branches of which, physics, ethics, and logic, he is credited with being the first to distinguish formally). He is also probably responsible for the "official" edition of Plato's works. Xenocrates' successor, Polemon (ca. 350–267), was chiefly concerned with ethics (indeed, with practical morality), and seems to have been prepared to accept the ethical theories of Aristotle and Theophrastus back into the school, thus completing what later came to be seen as the Old Academic synthesis of Plato's doctrines.

The chief features of this are the following: (1) a strong distinction between two levels of reality, the intelligible world (God, and the Ideas—transcendent models, mathematical in form, of which the things of this world are images and constitute the contents of the Divine Mind), and the sense-perceptible world. In the former, all is eternal, unchanging, perfect. Its first principles are the Monad (which for Xenocrates is God, and an Intellect), and the Dyad, a principle of plurality, on which the Monad acts to produce first the Ideas and the World-Soul, and then the physical world; (2) a belief in the immortality of the soul (or at least of the rational part; what became of the irrational is less than clear), and in reincarnation (possibly into animals as well as other human bodies, though that is never quite settled in the tradition); (3) a moderately ascetic ethics, which had the aim of separating the soul as far as possible from the influences of the body (though Aristotelian ethics was generally accepted by the end of the period, as has been said); (4) in epistemology, a prejudice against the evidence of the senses, in favor of the processes of pure reason *(epistēmē, noēsis)*; (5) in logic, an acceptance of the substance of Aristotle's great discoveries (though some traces of a more primitive "Old Academic" system of *diaeresis* ["division"], based more closely on Plato, can still be discerned). It is this system that constitutes the basis of the philosophical *koinē* with which Christianity was later confronted.

B. The New Academy

Before that, however, much was to happen. After Polemon, the headship of the school passed to Arcesilaus, who inaugurated a period of Skepticism, the so-called New Academy, where the academy, in opposition to the new dogmatism of the Stoics, returned to what Arcesilaus saw as its "Socratic" roots, the position of challenging all assumptions without necessarily asserting anything positive. Arcesilaus denied that there was any sure criterion of knowledge, and exercised himself largely in demolishing the claims of the Stoics in this area. About a century after his time, the school found another distinguished leader in Carneades (head ca. 160–128 B.C.E.), who appears to have entertained slightly more positive views in that he distinguished levels of "probability" in our perceptions, his highest level being in the nature of a Skeptical "answer" to the Stoic doctrine of certainty. Under a successor of his, Philo of Larissa, (fl. ca. 110–80 B.C.E.), the Skeptical position was undermined still further, leading to a return to dogmatism under Antiochus of Ascalon.

C. Middle Platonism

Antiochus, who established a Platonic school in Athens in the 70s B.C.E., was actually too much influenced by Stoic materialism to be the true founder of the later "Middle Platonic" synthesis of doctrine, but he turned the Platonic movement back from Skepticism to a belief in the possibility of certain knowledge, paving the way for further developments. He also gave the movement a view of its own history, which proved influential (though controversial), taking Aristotle and his followers back into the fold and designating the Stoics as the true heirs of the Old Academy, thus rejecting the New Academy as an aberration. Only with Eudorus of Alexandria (fl. ca. 25 B.C.E.), however, do we find a clear reinstatement of belief in a transcendent first principle, and the beginnings of a hierarchy of levels of being, together with an interest in Pythagoreanism and number theory, which are characteristic of the renewed Platonist movement.

In the generation after Eudorus, we find the same type of Middle Platonism represented by the Jewish philosopher Philo of Alexandria (ca. 30 B.C.E.–45 C.E.). For Philo, the (previously Stoic) concept of the Logos as the active, immanent aspect of God in the world, the unifying principle and transmitter of the Forms (seen as *logoi*), comes to be of central importance, as does a creative adaptation of the Pythagorean-Platonic dyad to the late Jewish concept of God's Wisdom (Sophia).

Both these developments, together with a pronounced dualism (belief in a disorderly, "evil" World Soul) are characteristic of Plutarch in the next century (ca. 45–120 C.E.). Plutarch, though not a great philosopher, is well known as an essayist and biographer. More obscure Platonists of the age are Albinus (fl. 150), author of a handbook of Platonism, the *Didaskalikos,* on the "Peripatetic" wing of the movement, and Atticus (fl. 175), who was hostile to Aristotle, maintaining a "purified" Platonism and agreeing with Plutarch on the creation of the world. A distinct movement within Middle Platonism is constituted by the Neo-Pythagoreans, notably Moderatus of Gades (fl. ca. 100), Nichomachus of Gerasa (fl. ca. 145), and Numenius, who even more than Plutarch is a strong dualist. He had considerable influence on Neoplatonism, through Plotinus and Porphyry, but they modified his dualism.

A number of basic themes of Middle Platonism should be given special mention, as they are of concern to Christianity.

1. A basic tenet of ethical theory was the so-called "end of goods," the *telos* or *summum bonum,* at which all rational activity should aim. Antiochus of Ascalon seems to be the first Platonist to formulate this as such. He was under Stoic influence and adopted the Stoic *telos* of "Life in agreement with Nature," though he attributed this back to the Old Academy and specifically to Polemon. When we turn to Alexandrian Platonism in the next generation, however, with Eudorus, we find the ideal of "Likeness to God" (taken from Plato's *Theaetetus,* 176a) propounded as the *telos,* and so it remained for the rest of antiquity. This ideal was taken in a "strong" sense—in Plotinus' striking phrase, "Our concern is not to be free of sin, but to be god (*Enn.* 1.2.6)." A certain degree of asceticism, though not necessarily of a world-negating type, is inseparable from Plato-

nist ethics, ranging from Plutarch's genial Peripateticism to the dualistic pessimism of Numenius.

2. A subject of major concern in later Platonism, arising out of the challenge posed by Stoic determinism and thus not a concern for Plato himself (in its starker form, at least), is that of free will and necessity, and thus of God's providence. If one accepted, as Platonists generally did, the Stoic argument that nothing takes place without an antecedent cause, and indeed as the culmination of a chain of causes running back to the beginning of the world, it became difficult to maintain another tenet which Platonists held dear (and felt they had a text for in the myth of Plato's *Resp.* 10), the autonomy of the rational soul. It was also difficult to see how God's knowledge of the totality of causes was reconcilable with the concept of our free will, and thus of an element of contingency. These problems were wrestled with by Platonists (Albinus *Didask,* 26; Ps.-Plutarch *On Fate*; Plotinus *Enneads* 3.2–3 "On Providence") without any very satisfactory solutions and bequeathed by them to contemporary Christianity.

3. A further issue of concern to Christianity, on which there were differing views among the Platonists of the first two Christian centuries, was that of the creation of the world. The Greek philosophical tradition in general rejected the concept of creation from nothing, but creation of an ordered world *(kosmos)* from preexistent chaotic matter was a recognized possibility. Here, for Platonists, the interpretation of Plato's *Timaeus* (a dialogue of great significance throughout our period) becomes crucial. On the whole, from Speusippus and Xenocrates on, the tendency was to deny that the account of creation presented there (and therefore the Creator God, or Demiurge, who figures in it) was to be taken literally. The creation is an eternal process and the Demiurge is the incessantly active cosmic Mind. In later times, an elaborate list of senses in which the world could be said to be "created" was drawn up (the most favored being "dependent upon a cause outside itself"), but two influential Platonists of the 2d century C.E., Plutarch and Atticus, maintained the literal interpretation of the *Timaeus,* and held that the world was created from precosmic disorderly matter. Plutarch, at least, saw this matter animated by a disorderly, "evil" soul (which he saw described by Plato in *Laws* X), and thus introduced a strongly dualist element into Platonism, also shared by the Neo-Pythagorean Numenius, but decisively rejected by mainstream Platonism after Plotinus.

4. Of concern to Christians also, since it bears on the vexed question of the relation of the Father to the Son, and later, the mutual relations of all three persons of the Trinity, is the gradual development of a hierarchy of being, arising out of the ambiguity of the relationship between the Good of Plato's *Republic* and the Demiurge of the *Timaeus.* Eudorus postulated a supreme One above a pair of Monad and Dyad; Plutarch seems to envisage a supreme God, a Logos, and an essentially irrational World Soul; Albinus, a supreme God, and a Mind and Soul of the World. On the Pythagorean wing, Moderatus postulated a sequence of three "Ones," derived from a metaphysical interpretation of the *Parmenides* and of a passage in the *Second Letter,* (312 E), while Numenius recognized a sequence of God the Father (the Good), Demiurge, and World Soul. Gradually a triadic sequence emerged, which became formalized (and further elaborated) in the philosophy of Plotinus and his successors.

D. Neoplatonism

This is a term coined in modern times to denote the type of Platonism inaugurated by Plotinus (204–70 C.E.) and continued by his successors Porphyry (ca. 232–305) and Iamblichus (ca. 245–320), and later by the Athenian and Alexandrian schools of the 5th and 6th centuries. The term has sometimes even been used to characterize the whole Platonist movement after Plato. Plotinus would have indignantly repudiated any such name. He saw himself (*Enn.* V I) as, if anything, restoring the true teachings of Plato after centuries of distortion. But, in fact, a number of new elements enter at this stage. Most notable is the demoting of Intellect *(nous)* from the position of first principle: Plotinus argued that the concept of Intellect involves a certain duality—of thinking element and object of thought—which the first principle should not include. His principle, the One, is therefore prior to Intellect, though Plotinus allows it a certain self-awareness. It produces by "overflowing," and thus all subsequent entities, Intellect, Soul, Nature, World, even Matter, are generated by a constant dynamic tension of procession and return (this latter process producing consciousness and self-definition in the entities concerned). Matter and Evil are simply negativities, the dark at the edges of the light radiated by the One. All other Neoplatonic elaborations (and, beginning with Iamblichus and continuing with Syrianus [d. 437 C.E.], Proclus [412–485], and Damascius [fl. 520], these became increasingly complex) stem from Plotinus' new vision of reality, though his successors' views were very different from his.

E. Christian Platonism

A word should be said of the phenomenon, which can be divided broadly into two phrases, that dependent on Philo and Middle Platonism, and that dependent on Neoplatonism. All Christian theology is dependent, to an extent at least, on contemporary Greek philosophy, primarily Platonism, but some Christian thinkers fall particularly strongly under Platonic influence, and properly merit the title of Christian Platonists.

Earlier Christian Platonism is represented, in a rudimentary way, by Justin Martyr (fl. ca. 150 C.E.), but in a developed form by the Alexandrians Clement (ca. 150–215) and Origen (ca. 176–254). Clement is overtly hospitable to Platonism, Origen covertly, though he is the more deeply influenced of the two. Doctrines that especially got him into trouble were his view of the Son as a Logos or Demiurge figure, his belief in a sequence of incarnations and worlds, and his denial of eternal punishment, all profoundly non-Christian ideas, arising from a creative interpretation of both Stoicism and Platonism.

In the next century, the Cappadocian Fathers, Basil of Caesarea (ca. 330–379 C.E.), Gregory of Nazianzus (329–ca. 390), and Gregory of Nyssa (d. 394), are influenced despite their overt hostility, by the Platonism of Plotinus and Porphyry (though also, even more, by Origen) and later again, in the 6th century, the mysterious figure of "Dionysius the Areopagite" is deeply influenced by Proclus and Damascius. In the Latin West, Marius Victorinus (fl.

350 C.E.) is a thoroughgoing Platonist, deeply influenced by Porphyry, and of course Augustine is profoundly, though not slavishly, under the spell of Platonism. Later again, Boethius (490–525) shows he is knowledgeable about contemporary Platonism.

Platonism is thus the single greatest outside intellectual influence on Christianity in its formative stages. This influence continues through the Middle Ages (the School of Chartres) and the Renaissance (the Florentine Academy) to the Cambridge Platonists of the 17th century (chiefly More and Cudworth) and modern times, but that is beyond the scope of the present article. Unlike Aristotelianism, Platonism was fated always, despite its influence, to be in opposition to Christianity, since Platonism was always something more than a philosophical system; it was, like Christianity, a religion, and religions tend to brook no rivals.

Bibliography

Armstrong, A. H. 1979. *Plotinian and Christian Studies.* London.
Armstrong, A. H., ed. 1967. *The Cambridge History of the Late Classical and Early Mediaeval Philosophy.* Cambridge.
Betz, H. D., ed. 1975. *Plutarch's Theological Writings and Early Christian Literature.* Leiden.
Blumenthal, H. J., and Marcus, R. A., ed. 1981. *Neoplatonism and Early Christian Thought: Essays in Honour of A. H. Armstrong.* London.
Cherniss, H. 1945. *The Riddle of the Early Academy.* Berkeley.
Dillon, J. 1977. *The Middle Platonists,* Ithaca, NY.
Dörrie, H. 1976. *Platonica Minora.* Munich.
———. 1987–. *Der Platonismus in der Antike.* Stuttgart and Bad Cannstatt.
Festugière, A.-J. 1950–54. *La Révélation d'Hermès Trismégiste.* 4 vols. Paris.
Glucker, J. 1978. *Antiochus and the Late Academy.* Göttingen.
Lilla, S. 1971. *Clement of Alexandria: A Study in Christian Platonism and Gnosticism.* Oxford.
O'Meara, D., ed. 1964. *Neoplatonism and Christian Thought.* Albany.
Rist, J. M. 1964. *Eros and Psyche: Studies in Plato, Plotinus and Origen.* Toronto.
———. 1985. *Platonism and Its Christian Heritage.* London.
Theiler, W. 1930. *Die Vorbereitung des Neuplatonismus.* Berlin.
Whittaker, J. 1984. *Studies in Platonism and Patristic Thought.* London.
Zeller, E. 1923. *Die Philosophie der Griechen.* Vol. 3/2. 7th ed. Leipzig.

JOHN M. DILLON

PLEDGE. See DEBTS.

PLINY THE YOUNGER. Born Publius Caecilius Secundus in A.D. 61 or 62, Pliny the Younger belonged to a prosperous landowning family of northern Italy. In Rome, he attended the lectures of the illustrious Quintilian, who had been appointed professor of Latin rhetoric by Vespasian. The most influential member of the family was his mother's brother, Gaius Plinius Secundus (Pliny the Elder), whose monumental *Naturalis Historia,* a type of ancient encyclopedia surviving in 37 books, was dedicated to Titus; he had served in the army with Titus and had been appointed by Vespasian to various senior equestrian posts, including the command of the fleet at Misenum, from where he sailed to observe and inspect the eruption of Mt. Vesuvius and perished in the fumes (August 29, 79). Under the terms of his will, his nephew inherited his property, was posthumously adopted, and thereby acquired the name Gaius Plinius Caecilius Secundus.

In Titus' reign, Pliny the Younger (as he now was) began a legal career, specializing in inheritance cases. He prospered under Domitian, holding a number of official posts, including the praetorship (93) and the prefecture of the military treasury (ca. 94–96). Later, however, he asserted that his life had been in danger at the time: "I stood amidst the flames of thunderbolts dropping all round me and there were certain clear indications that a like end was awaiting me" (*Ep.* 3.11.3). This was untrue, and, despite his friendship with members of the "Stoic Opposition," his political and legal career proceeded unhindered. With the accession of Nerva and Trajan (96 and 98), he continued to flourish, being appointed to a second treasury post (the prefecture of the treasury of Saturn) and then to a consulship (100). He maintained his legal work and was best known, early in Trajan's reign, for his defense of Julius Bassus and Varenus Rufus, two governors of Pontus-Bithynia. In 104, he accepted a senior position in Rome involving flood and drainage control and, in this period, was invited to join Trajan's cabinet on a number of occasions as a judicial adviser. Finally, ca. 110, he was appointed special commissioner to settle the financial and political problems of Pontus-Bithynia, when he died prematurely, about 51 years old.

Thanks to his letters and to four inscriptions, Pliny's is one of the best documented careers of the early empire. It was remarkable in many ways. The legal minimum age for the consulship was 42 and very few were appointed at that age; yet, with imperial favor, Pliny gained the honor at 39, while his consular colleague was almost 60 on his appointment. Again, it was almost unparalleled for an ex-consul to govern a province when he had not had similar experience at a lower level. Equally unusual was his appointment to a second treasury post. Thus he emerges as a highly competent administrator and lawyer, trusted by every regime. He was also extremely wealthy, investing most of his funds in property (*Ep.* 3.29.8), with a house in Rome on the Esquiline, another near Ostia, at least three on the shores of Lake Como, and a villa on his estates at Tifernum.

His fame, however, is based on his letters. Unlike those of Cicero, written a century and a half previously, Pliny's were intended for publication, carefully composed and subsequently edited. The first nine books, consisting of 247 personal letters, were published at intervals between ca. 100 and 109, while the tenth appeared posthumously and contained 121 official letters written during his term in Pontus-Bithynia. The former are polished essays, providing an elegant portrait of contemporary upper-class activities and attitudes both in the capital and elsewhere, particularly in northern Italy. The topics are varied: domestic and social issues (treatment of slaves, public entertainment), events in politics and the law courts, descriptions of a villa, scenery, interpretation of a dream, eulogies of famous writers (Silius Italicus and Martial), a murder, ghost stories, and letters of recommendation or advice.

Some are addressed to literary friends such as Suetonius and Tacitus (perhaps the most famous is 6.16, written to Tacitus and describing the death of Pliny the Elder following the eruption of Vesuvius), others to young men undertaking a political career, others to people from the area of Lake Como, his birthplace, others to eminent senators (Arrius Antoninus, Vestricius Spurinna), generals (Sosius Senecio, Licinius Sura), and equestrians (Septicius Clarus, later Hadrian's Praetorian Prefect).

The tenth book is different. Written in a simpler and less mannered style, it is a unique record of a Roman province's administrative problems and the solutions proposed or implemented. Pliny is revealed as a thorough, painstaking administrator with an apparent tendency to refer to the emperor even the most mundane of problems. But Pliny's was not an ordinary province. Pontus-Bithynia faced a political and financial crisis, and it is impossible to assess the extent to which strict imperial guidelines limited Pliny's freedom of action. Trajan's replies are briefer and more concise, revealing his concern for consistency and equity. Of particular interest is Pliny's request to Trajan for guidance on the treatment of Christians (*Ep.* 10.96) and Trajan's reply (*Ep.* 10.97). Pliny had, so he told the emperor, executed those who had admitted that they were Christians but had freed any who denied the charge and who were prepared to sacrifice to the gods (and to an image of the emperor). Pliny's problem, however, was twofold: anonymous accusations and lapsed Christians. Trajan indignantly rejected the former as being "out of keeping with the spirit of the age" and, perhaps inconsistently, pardoned the latter "however suspect their past conduct (might have been)." What the letters do not make clear is precisely why those who confessed to being Christians were executed, a point still debated by scholars. However, they do provide crucial evidence on the problem of Christianity's legal status at the end of the 1st century and until the time of Decius' persecution (ca. 250). For further discussion see *ANRW* 2/2.

Bibliography

Sherwin-White, A. N. 1966. *The Letters of Pliny.* Oxford.
Syme, R. 1958. *Tacitus.* Oxford.

Brian W. Jones

PLOW, PLOUGH. See ZOOLOGY.

PLUTARCH.

Greek biographer, essayist, Platonist, priest of Apollo, and Roman citizen (ca. A.D. 50–120). He was born into a well-to-do family of the Boeotian town of Chaeronea, located approximately eighty miles NW of Athens, during the reign of the Roman emperor Claudius. At the time of Nero's visit to Greece in 66/67, Plutarch was in Athens studying philosophy under Ammonius, then head of the Platonic Academy. After completing his studies he returned to Chaeronea, where he continued to live until his death in the time of Hadrian, taking a leading part in the public life of his city and directing a philosophical academy of his own.

What we know of Plutarch and his family is derived principally from his own writings, a very personal example of which is the *Consolatio ad uxorem* ("Consolation to my wife"), the letter he wrote to his wife, Timoxena, after the death of their two-year-old daughter. Timoxena also bore Plutarch four sons, only two of whom survived into manhood. Both she and her husband were at some time initiated into the Dionysiac mysteries. The experiences of Plutarch's own happy marriage are perhaps reflected in the *Conjugalia praecepta* ("Advice about marriage"), which he sent to a bride and groom, and in the respect for the moral and intellectual qualities of women he evinces in the *Mulierum virtutes* ("Courage of women"), the *Amatorius* ("Conversation about Eros"), and elsewhere.

Plutarch himself, his teacher Ammonius, his friends, and members of his family regularly appear as speakers in his dialogues, among which the nine books of *Quaestiones convivales* ("Table talk") constitute a mine of incidental information about the concerns and habits of Plutarch and his circle. As a man of wealth and political influence and of literary and philosophical prominence, Plutarch enjoyed the society of a large number of important individuals throughout the Greek world and in Rome, those in the latter category including the consulars L. Mestrius Florus, whose gens name, Mestrius, he bore as a Roman citizen and who was probably responsible for his receiving the citizenship, and Q. Sosius Senecio, to whom Plutarch dedicated the *Parallel Lives,* the *Quaestiones convivales* ("Table talk"), and an anti-Stoic essay on making progress in virtue. It may be, though the evidence is disputable, that Plutarch attained equestrian rank, was awarded consular dignities by Trajan, and was appointed procurator of Greece by Hadrian.

Plutarch's social and intellectual life as well as his diplomatic and religious duties took him abroad frequently. He was often in Athens, where he was honored with Athenian citizenship, and at Delphi, the oracular center near Chaeronea where he served for many years as priest of Apollo and the scene of his four theological dialogues. In addition, Plutarch traveled throughout the Greek mainland, to Alexandria in Egypt (his treatise on Isis and Osiris is an important source for our knowledge of Egyptian religion), probably to Asia Minor—and at least twice to Italy, where in Rome he was sought out as a teacher and delivered lectures, presumably in Greek.

Plutarch was a polymath and undoubtedly one of the most learned men of his day. His general education would have included the standard training in rhetoric, and mathematics was a significant component in his philosophical studies. He was, moreover, steeped in the literature of his Hellenic past, its poets as well as its prose writers, and his reading included virtually every genre. He also kept *hypomnēmata,* notebooks of a sort in which he recorded material suitable for incorporation into his own writings. Beyond this, there is every indication that he worked quickly and composed with ease. All of these factors are reflected in the large and varied corpus of his surviving works, fifty biographies and over seventy miscellaneous pieces traditionally grouped under the heading *Moralia,* and even in the mere titles of the many additional works listed in the so-called Lamprias Catalogue, an ancient compilation of 227 works attributed to Plutarch. Many of Plutarch's writings, including the *Lives,* appear to belong to a later part of his life, but their order of composition is generall impossible to determine. Plutarch's Greek is a literary Attic, his style learned yet relaxed, and his vocabulary, developed from the entire sweep of a literature extending seven centuries into the past, immense.

The *Moralia,* traditionally cited by Latin translations of their Greek titles, with rare exception take the form of essays, dialogues, and collections, although many of the essays were originally delivered as lectures; the dialogues frequently have the tone and purpose of essays, and their historicity appears to be generally limited to a reflection of the interests and conduct of Plutarch and his society. In total substance, the *Moralia* offer a survey of virtually every topic that was subjected to inquiry and discussion in classical antiquity. Extant treatises concern, among other subjects, ethics (*De cupiditate divitiarum* ["On love of wealth"]), psychology (*De tranquillitate animi* ["On peace of mind"]), medicine (*De tuenda sanitate praecepta* ["Advice about keeping well"]), politics (*Praecepta gerendae reipublicae* ["Advice about public life"]), religion (*De genio Socratis* ["On the sign of Socrates"], *De sera numinis vindicta* ["On the slowness of divine punishment"]), animal psychology (*De sollertia animalium* ["On the intelligence of animals"]), natural science (*De facie quae in orbe lunae apparet* ["On the face that appears in the orb of the moon"]), and literary criticism (*De Herodoti malignitate* ["On the malice of Herodotus"]). Rhetorical features permeate the *Moralia,* as does the influence of Aristotle and the Peripatetics the ethical and psychological treatises, which are usually popular and practical in purpose and approach. Nevertheless, Plutarch was fundamentally a Platonist, as is evident both in numerous treatises and from two technical works, the *Platonicae quaestiones* ("Platonic questions") and the commentary on a section of Plato's *Timaeus* entitled *De animae procreatione in Timaeo* ("On the creation of the soul in the *Timaeus*"); he was also firm in his opposition to the Epicureans (in *Adversus Colotem* ["Against Colotes"]) and the Stoics (in *De Stoicorum repugnantiis* ["On the contradictions of the Stoics"]), though he sometimes treated the latter as *adversaires privilégiés.* (The titles of all the surviving *Moralia* are listed in both Latin and Greek at the beginning of each of the 15 *Moralia* volumes in the Loeb Classical Library.)

The extant *Lives* are of political and military personages and, with four exceptions, are "parallel" in that they are arranged in pairs consisting of a Greek and a Roman biography; the pairing is based on similarities of character and career, and all but four of the pairs are followed by a *syncrisis,* a short comparison, primarily ethical, in which Plutarch tends to emphasize the differences between the two individuals. Several of the *Lives* take us in varying degrees into the realm of myth and legend (most notably, those of the pairs Theseus and Romulus and Lycurgus and Numa, and that of Coriolanus, who is paired with the historical Alcibiades), but the large majority are of men who were fully historical (Pericles and Fabius Maximus, Nicias and Crassus, Alexander and Caesar). Plutarch is not, however, oblivious to a distinction between myth and history (*Theseus* 1), although he makes abundant use of anecdote and does not hesitate to include material he judges possibly apocryphal, especially when it is useful for illustrating character (*Solon* 27.1). While Plutarchan biography is grounded in Peripatetic ethics, it is, nevertheless, without precise literary antecedents. The evidence, moreover, is substantial that Plutarch himself, not some hypothetical intermediary, is mainly responsible for the collection and synthesis of the biographical and historical information on which each *Life* is based; nor did Plutarch's imperfect knowledge of Latin (*Demosthenes* 2) prevent him from making an ample use of Latin sources in the Roman *Lives.*

Plutarch insists that he is writing "lives," not "histories" (*Alexander* 1), and that he is doing so for the moral edification of himself as well as others (*Aemilius Paulus* 1). He has, therefore, chosen as his subjects personages whose life and character merit and inspire emulation, and whose moral failures are entirely attributable to humanity's incapacity for absolute virtue (*Cimon* 2); the only clear exception is the pair Demetrius and Antony, who serve expressly as negative examples and a foil to the subjects of the other *Lives* (*Demetrius* 1). But Plutarch the moralist and biographer is also Plutarch the storyteller, and the *Lives* contain many narrative passages which go beyond what is required merely for the illustration of character. The *Demosthenes-Cicero* gives full and exact expression to Plutarch's biographical concepts and purposes.

Plutarch's grand literary achievement is that the *Lives* and *Moralia* together constitute a synthesis and interpretation of the thought and events of all antecedent classical antiquity. In the Greek East, he continued to be read throughout later antiquity and the Middle Ages; and when Greek literature was restored to the West with the Renaissance, Plutarch came to occupy a central place in Western letters, particularly in France and England, which he held until the 19th century, when changing literary, historical, and educational values began their steady erosion of his influence and popularity. The last prominent literary figure to be significantly influenced by Plutarch was Emerson, but he was preceded by a host of major and minor authors that included Erasmus, Rabelais, Montaigne, Corneille, Rousseau, Shakespeare, Bacon, Dryden, and Schiller. Impetus was given to Plutarch's growing literary and educational influence by Jacques Amyot, who translated both the *Lives* (1559) and *Moralia* (1572) into French, and by Sir Thomas North, who rendered Amyot's version of the *Lives* into English (1579). It was principally through the agency of Amyot's translations that Plutarch had such a profound effect on Montaigne, and it was North's version of the *Lives* that Shakespeare used as the source for his Roman plays. Since World War II, there has been a resurgence of scholarly interest in Plutarch, which led to the establishment of the International Plutarch Society in 1983.

Bibliography

General Works:

Babut, D. 1969. *Plutarque et le Stoïcisme.* Paris.

Barrow, R. H. 1967. *Plutarch and His Times.* Bloomington, IN.

Dihle, A. 1956. *Studien zur griechischen Biographie.* Göttingen.

Dillon, J. 1977. Plutarch of Chaeroneia and the Origins of Second-Century Platonism. Pp. 184–230 in *The Middle Platonists.* Ithaca, NY.

Jones, C. P. 1971. *Plutarch and Rome.* Oxford.

Russell, D. A. 1973. *Plutarch.* New York.

Theander, C. 1950–51. *Plutarch und die Geschichte.* Bulletin de la Société Royale des Lettres de Lund. Lund.

Texts and Translations:

Moralia

Babbitt, F. C., et al., eds. and trans. 1927–76. *Plutarch's Moralia.* 15 vols. LCL. Cambridge, MA.

Betz, H. D., ed. 1975. *Plutarch's Theological Writings and Early Christian Literature.* SCHNT 3. Leiden.

———., ed. 1978. *Plutarch's Ethical Writings and Early Christian Literature.* SCHNT 4. Leiden.

Flacelière, R., et al., eds. and trans. 1972–. *Plutarque: Oeuvres morales.* Paris.

Hubert, C., et al., eds. 1925–. *Plutarchus: Moralia.* Leipzig.

Warner, R., trans. 1971. *Plutarch: Moral Essays.* Baltimore.

Lives

Flacelière, R., et al., eds. and trans. 1957–79. *Plutarque. Vies.* 15 vols. Paris.

Perrin, B., ed. and trans. 1914–26. *Plutarch's Lives.* 11 vols. LCL. Cambridge, MA.

Scott-Kilvert, I., trans. 1960. *The Rise and Fall of Athens.* New York.

———. 1965. *Makers of Rome.* New York.

———. 1973. *The Age of Alexander.* New York.

Warner, R., trans. 1958. *The Fall of the Roman Republic.* New York.

Ziegler, K., ed. 1957–73. *Plutarchus. Vitae Parallelae.* 3 vols. Leipzig.

HUBERT M. MARTIN, JR.

POCHERETH-HAZZEBAIM

POCHERETH-HAZZEBAIM (PERSON) [Heb *pōkeret haṣṣĕbāyîm*]. Head of a family belonging to Solomon's servants who had returned from the Babylonian Exile (Ezra 2:57 [= Neh 7:59; 1 Esdr 5:34]). The list in Ezra-Nehemiah implies that this return took place immediately in response to Cyrus' declaration in 538 B.C.E. But 1 Esdras places this return in its more probable date at the time of King Darius (ca. 522).

Some have used 1 Kgs 9:20 to conclude that Solomon's servants were originally enslaved foreigners. Levine, however, suggests that the term denotes Israelite officials supervising foreigners (1963). In the postexilic era, when the family of Pochereth-hazzebaim appears, the term "servant" typically refers to officials. Like the temple servants (Nethinim), Solomon's servants are temple functionaries. They are members of the congregation of Israel and separated thereby from slaves (Ezra 2).

The feminine form of the name Pochereth-hazzebaim has been taken to refer to an occupation (cf. Qohelet, the so-called "Preacher" of Ecclesiastes). The name has been translated as "gazelle hunter" (e.g., Blenkinsopp *Ezra-Nehemiah* OTL, 91) or "gazelle binder," since the word *ṣĕbāyim* can mean "gazelles." It is plausible, however, that the word here means "beauty" or "decorations," a usage frequently found in the singular in Ezekiel (20:6) and Daniel (11:45). Hence, the name could suggest a guild of temple functionaries, which Solomon's servants clearly were, whose specific task centered on beautification or decoration. The feminine form may also suggest that either the founder of the guild or its members were females. The designation of a clan by the name of its mother is attested in Ezra 2:61 (and the parallels in Nehemiah 7 and 1 Esdras) where the Barzillai family is specifically named after the wife because the man has taken her name. Possibly a similar process has shaped this professional guild or family of Solomon's servants. See Williamson *Ezra, Nehemiah* OTL.

Bibliography

Levine, B. A. 1963. The Netinim. *JBL* 82: 207–12.

Weinberg, J. P. 1975. Nᶜtinim und 'Sōhne der Sklaven Salomos' im 6–4 Jh. v. u. Z. *ZAW* 87: 355–71.

TAMARA C. ESKENAZI

POETRY, HEBREW. See PSALMS, BOOK OF; PARALLELISM; BUDDE HYPOTHESIS.

POLIS. See CITIES (GRECO-ROMAN).

POLITARCHS

POLITARCHS. The politarchate was a senior, annual magistracy attested predominantly in cities of Macedonia after Roman intervention in the 2d century B.C. The geographical spread of attestations of the word "politarch" includes Egypt, Bithynia, the Bosporan Kingdom, Thrace, Illyria, and (in a dialectically distinct form) Thessaly, as well as Macedonia. Chronological witness to the office stretches from the late 3d century B.C. to the last quarter of the 3d century A.D. While they are best known from the reference to them at Thessalonike in Acts (17:6–8), most of our information about politarchs comes from documentary texts.

Much of the writing on this subject from the late 19th and early 20th centuries is now superseded. Dimitsas' edition of Macedonian inscriptions (1896) is still of some use, and is now accessible again as a reprint; but a considerable number of his texts either have been improved or are in need of reediting. Burton's article was a particular landmark for NT studies, and is still often referred to in modern discussion; but his research was published in 1898, and our knowledge of the subject has advanced considerably since then. The score of texts he examines as evidence for politarchs has more than tripled. Nevertheless, his article continues to provide the most accessible, complete (if not most reliable) version of some of the inscriptions. Ferguson's dissertation has only a couple of pages on politarchs (1913: 65–66), and hence contributes little. Greek scholars have continued to show an interest in this subject: reference should be made particularly to Pelekides (1934) and Kanatzoulis (1956). In fact, it is Schuler's 1960 article, which, although focusing upon the Macedonian evidence alone, has provided the benchmark for subsequent research because of his valuable tabulation of known inscriptions from there (note, however, that his no. 16 must now be deleted because it does not refer to a politarch; the latest version of this text is published as *IG* 10/2: 1.181). Schuler's list of politarchs is now superseded by Hatzopoulos (1984: 147–49), whose tabulation includes 50 items from Macedonia (49 inscriptions and the reference in the book of Acts). The tally in the present article is somewhat higher, reflecting both new discoveries and the decision to incorporate evidence from a broader geographical area. Since 1970, the number of significant contributions which focus on the office of politarch has increased markedly: Gschnitzer (PWSup 13: 483–500); Hell

(1977); Koukouli-Chrysanthaki (1981); Hatzopoulos (1984); and Papazoglou (1986). Edson's publication of the *IG* volume (10/2) covering Thessalonike has made many of the texts far more accessible, although the *IG* volumes covering Beroia and certain other Macedonian cities are yet to appear.

By 1988 there were possibly as many as 64 known nonliterary references to the politarchate, all but one occurring in inscriptions. Over three quarters of them are from Macedonia, and nearly half of all the attestations are from Thessalonike alone. Literary attestation is rarer: apart from the two occurrences in Acts 17, Chrysostom mentions politarchs five times in allusions to the Acts incident (*PG* 60.263.26, 34; 60.677.41; 62.394.26; 62.395.35). The epitome to the 5th-century *Acts of Philip* mentions a politarch named Irōn (Lipsius and Bonnet 1903: 2.1. 46–50). The word occurs once in one of the works attributed to Macarius, the late 4th-century ascetic from Egypt. Finally, a politarch is referred to in the 7th-century *vita Cyri et Joannis* by Sophronios (*PG* 87.3401D). The only other mention in literary texts is much earlier: the 4th-century-B.C. writer Aeneas Tacticus uses the form *politarchos* (26.12).

The known documentary references to politarchs are listed in Table 1. Each item includes the provenance, date, details of the most accessible/reliable complete text, and, where appropriate, brief remarks. Not included in this list are texts with wording like *prōtos archōn,* although such terminology has been suggested as indicating politarchs in Macedonian inscriptions (Hatzopoulos 1984: 139). Very little information is known about no. 64.

Until the 1970s, the dominant view of the politarchate—most clearly formulated by Schuler (1960)—was that it was introduced into Macedonia by the Romans, either after 167 B.C., when democratic institutions were imposed by L. Aemilius Paullus after the Third Macedonian War (171–168 B.C.), or after 146 B.C., when Macedonia was accorded provincial status. Certainly, the great bulk of attestations of politarchs from Macedonia belong to the 2d century B.C.–2d century A.D. Yet Schuler did not exclude absolutely the possibility of pre-Roman politarchs in Macedonia. Pointing to an inscription of 243/42 B.C., the last year of the reign of Antigonos II Gonatas, in which *archontes* are mentioned (*SEG* 12.373, line 32), he raises the possibility (1960: 93) that politarchs may have been among the magistrates alluded to in this more general term. Hatzopoulos, too, has suggested (1984: 139) that the politarchate is reflected in phraseology such as *prōtos archōn, prōtarchōn,* and *arxas tēn prōtēn archēn,* occurring in inscriptions from Thracian Philippopolis. Such terminology is indubitably attested once of a politarch at Thessalonike (see Table 1, no. 50). Acceptance of this argument leads to the consequential one (Hatzopoulos 1984: 144, n. 39) that the politarchate is attested in a larger number of Thracian cities than merely Philippopolis, where alone the actual word occurs (Table 1, nos. 57–58).

Contrary to Schuler, Gschnitzer (PWSup 13: 493) and Hatzopoulos (1984: 139) have more recently advanced different strands of the same argument which now place beyond doubt the pre-Roman institution of the politarchate. Studying the presence of the magistracy in separate regions (Table 1, no. 9 in Macedonia, nos. 57–58 in Thrace, respectively), they have demonstrated that the politarchate existed in the Roman period in areas which had been under the Antigonids but which were still not subsumed by the Romans before mid–2d century B.C. Papazoglou has clinched this with her argument (1986: 448) concerning the sole instance from Illyria (Table 1, no. 1), that the institution of the politarchate in this lone polis among the Illyrian cities can be accounted for only by an alliance or dependent state relationship having been established between Olympe and Macedonia under Philip V before the Second Macedonian War (200–197 B.C.). This most recently published of the attestations is thus also the earliest (3d century B.C. fin.). Another attestation (no. 3) originally was held to be pre-Roman, being dated to 179–171 B.C., during the reign of Perseus (Koukouli-Chrysanthaki 1981), but doubt has been raised subsequently whether that stone may actually carry two separately inscribed texts of different date (Papazoglou 1986: 442–43, n. 19).

The fact that the politarchate can now be shown to predate 167 B.C. does not resolve the issue whether this office underwent changes of function over time. It would not be surprising if there were alterations; and some of these may well have been introduced by the Romans. Combining the evidence from the inscriptions, certain of the functions of the Macedonian politarchate in the Roman period emerge clearly. It was an annual magistracy (*ton kata etos geinomenon poleitarchēn,* Table 1, no. 9) which could be held more than once (no. 35). That politarchs had an administrative/executive function is attested by no. 16, where they are responsible for introducing motions to the *boulē,* and for effecting its decisions (nos. 9, 10). That politarchs possessed judicial authority is clearest from the incident at Thessalonike (Acts 17): they were responsible for maintaining the peace in their city (Gschnitzer, PWSup 13: 491). Although the magistrates at Beroia are not mentioned in the following section of Acts (17:10–14), the analogous situation there to what occurred at Thessalonike, together with the firm attestation of the politarchate at Beroia (Table 1, nos. 6–8), suggests that it may have been these officials who had to quell the disturbances in that city as well (*NDIEC* 2: 35).

There are only two certain instances of a community having a single politarch per year (Table 1, nos. 9, 59). Where the evidence is clear elsewhere, a collegial arrangement was used. Sometimes one of the politarchs in such a group is specified (or at least implied) as the eponymous magistrate by the phrase *politarchōn tōn peri* NN, *vel sim.* (nos. 10, 12, 19, 53; cf. *archittoliarchentos* in no. 56). He may be inferred to have functioned as president of the council and of the citizen assembly. The number forming a college varied both from city to city and from time to time. Two Thessalonikan inscriptions of similar date (nos. 24 and 25) attest five and two politarchs respectively. The regular number of politarchs in the late 1st century B.C. was five (nos. 26–29). In the mid–2d century A.D. the size of the college appears to vary from three to perhaps seven (nos. 35–38). By the early 3d century A.D. their number had reached nine (no. 44). The three Amphipolitan inscriptions attest five, two, and perhaps three politarchs respectively (nos. 2–4). No convincing reason for such fluctuation can be suggested on the basis of the present evidence. To

Table 1
Documentary References to Politarchs

NO. PROVENANCE	DATE	MOST ACCESSIBLE/ RELIABLE TEXT	REMARKS
ILLYRIA			
1. Olympe	III B.C. fin.	*Historia* 35 (1986): 438	Politarch and 4 others called *hoi synarchontes*
MACEDONIA			
2. Amphipolis	167 B.C.	Schuler 1960: 94–95	5 politarchs
3. Amphipolis	Roman period?	*SEG* 31.614	2 politarchs
4. Amphipolis	Roman period	*SEG* 27.248	3(?) politarchs
5. Apollonia in Mygdonia	I A.D.	unpublished	cf. Hatzopoulos 1984: 147, no. 4
6. Beroia	mid–II B.C.	*SEG* 28.261	140–120 B.C. (Helly 1977: 544, n. 32)
7. Beroia	40–50 A.D.	*SEG* 27.263	5 politarchs, if stem of participle is correctly restored
8. Beroia	I A.D.	Kanatzoulis 1955: 20, n. 6	5 politarchs
9. Community of the Battynaioi	143/44 A.D.	*JHS* 33 (1913): 337–46, no. 17; re-ed. of lines 1–42 in *SEG* 30.568	1 politarch chosen annually
10. Derriopos	95 A.D.	Burton 1898: 615–18, no. 9	1 eponymous politarch and colleagues implied by *tōn peri NN politarchōn*
11. Drymos	69–79 A.D.	*SEG* 29.579	2(?) politarchs(?)—verb stem almost entirely restored
12. Edessa	129/30 or 245/46 A.D.	Burton 1898: 614–18, no. 8	1 eponymous politarch and colleagues implied by *politarchountōn tōn peri NN;* Hatzopoulos 1984: 149, no. 44, for reference to improvement to part of text
13. Gortynna(?)	after 180 A.D.	*Spomenik* 98 (1941–48): no. 101	*non vidi;* cf. Schuler 1960: 97, no. 25
14. Herakleia Lynkestis	II A.D.	Burton 1898: 618–19, no. 11	Schuler 1960: 98, no. 30
15. Herakleia Lynkestis	II A.D.	G. Tomašević, *Herakleia,* vol. II (Bitola, 1965): 15–23	*non vidi;* cf. Hatzopoulos 1984: 149, no. 48
16. Lete	118 B.C.	*Syll.*[3] 700	politarchs responsible for introducing motion to *boulē* and for effecting its decisions
17. Lete	121/22 A.D.	*SEG* 1.276	*apo politarchias* used to refer to former politarch
18. Lyke	II A.D.	*SEG* 24.489	
19. Parthicopolis(?)	158 A.D.	*IGBulg.* 4: 2263	3(?) politarchs; 1 eponymous and colleagues implied by *p. tōn peri* NN
20. Pella	I B.C. or I A.D.	*Pella,* vol. I (Athens, 1971): 144	*non vidi;* Hatzopoulos 1984: 149, no. 39
21. Pella	44/45 A.D.	Burton 1898: 611, no. 6	2 politarchs
22. Serrai	n.d.	*SEG* 30.616	[*hoi p*]*ol*[*it*]*ạrchoi* or [*ton p*]*ol*[*it*]*ạrchon*

Table 1 (continued)
Documentary References to Politarchs

NO. PROVENANCE	DATE	MOST ACCESSIBLE/ RELIABLE TEXT	REMARKS
23. Styberra	imperial period	Burton 1898: 618, no. 10	
24. Thessalonike	before end II B.C.	*IG* 10/2 1.27	5 politarchs
25. Thessalonike	II or I B.C.	*IG* 10/2 1.28	2 politarchs
26. Thessalonike	39/38 B.C.?	*IG* 10/2 1.30	5 politarchs
27. Thessalonike	39/38 B.C.?	*IG* 10/2 1.50	same 5 politarchs as in no. 26
28. Thessalonike	39/38 B.C.?	*IG* 10/2 1.109	same 5 politarchs as in no. 26
29. Thessalonike	27 B.C.–14 A.D.	*IG* 10/2 1.31	5 politarchs
30. Thessalonike	I B.C. or I A.D.	*IG* 10/2 1.86	verb stem largely restored
31. Thessalonike	I B.C. or I A.D.	*IG* 10/2 1.129	5(?) politarchs(?)—verb entirely restored
32. Thessalonike	ca. I A.D.	*IG* 10/2 1.848	funerary epigram; *ptoliarchos;* I–II A.D.—Helly 1977: 537
33. Thessalonike	before end I A.D.	*IG* 10/2 1.32	verb stem entirely restored
34. Thessalonike	I–III A.D.	*IG* 10/2 1.128	
35. Thessalonike	137–61 A.D.	*Makedonika* 9 (1969): 143–44, no. 45	3 politarchs; *non vidi;* cf. *BE* (1970): 367
36. Thessalonike	March 16, 141 A.D.	*IG* 10/2 1.137	4(?) politarchs
37. Thessalonike	after 153/54 A.D.	*IG* 10/2 1.133	5 politarchs; first third of I A.D.—*RPh* 48 (1974): 210–15
38. Thessalonike	mid–II A.D.	*IG* 10/2 1.126	6 or 7 politarchs; 1–late II A.D.—*RPh* 48 (1974): 208–10
39. Thessalonike	II A.D.	*IG* 10/2 1.226	5(?) politarchs
40. Thessalonike	end II A.D.	*IG* 10/2 1.252	adjectival stem mostly restored
41. Thessalonike	II or III A.D.	*IG* 10/2 1.37	
42. Thessalonike	II or III A.D.	*IG* 10/2 1.228	adjectival stem mostly restored
43. Thessalonike	200–40 A.D.	*IG* 10/2 1.201	politarch referred to as *arxanta dis tēn prōtēn archēn*
44. Thessalonike	shortly before 212 A.D.	*IG* 10/2 1.127	9 politarchs; verb entirely restored
45. Thessalonike	240/41 A.D. or slightly later	*IG* 10/2 1.214	politarchate accorded as honorific title
46. Thessalonike	246/47 A.D.	*IG* 10/2 1.162	
47. Thessalonike	after 246/47 A.D.	*IG* 10/2 1.197	
48. Thessalonike	248/49 A.D.	*IG* 10/2 1.163	politarchate possibly accorded as honorific title
49. Thessalonike	ca. mid–III A.D.	*IG* 10/2 1.199	
50. Thessalonike	III A.D.	*IG* 10/2 1.181	politarch described as *prōtarchēsanta*
51. Thessalonike	undatable	*IG* 10/2 1.962	
52. Thessalonike	undatable	*CIG* 2.1967	7 politarchs; not in *IG* 10/2 1
53. unknown provenance within Macedonia	136/37 or 137/38 A.D.	unpublished	letter of Hadrian to Macedonian *koinon*. One eponymous politarch and colleagues implied by *politarchountōn tōn peri NN*

Table 1 (continued)
Documentary References to Politarchs

NO. PROVENANCE	DATE	MOST ACCESSIBLE/ RELIABLE TEXT	REMARKS
THESSALY			
54. Krannon	III² B.C.	*SEG* 23.437	4 *ttoliarchoi;* cf. BE (1965) 216
55. Krannon	III² B.C.	*REA* 66 (1964): 314, n. 4	5 *ttoliarchoi;* most of verb stem restored by analogy with *SEG* 23.437; re-ed. of *IG* 9/2. 459
56. Phalanna	III B.C.	*IG* 9/2. 1233	5 *ttoliarchoi* one of whom is chief politarch *(archittoli-archentos)*
THRACE			
57. Philippopolis	Flavian	*IG Bulg.* 3: 1.913	
58. Philippopolis	Flavian	*IG Bulg.* 3: 1.1023	most of noun stem restored
BOSPORAN KINGDOM			
59. Pantikapaion	276–79 A.D.	*CIRB* 36	1 politarch
60. Phanagoreia	179 A.D.	*CIRB* 1000	
BITHYNIA			
61. Kios	109 A.D.	*Ath. Mitt.* 24 (1899): 415–21, no. 14	
EGYPT			
62. Leontopolis	I A.D.	*CPJ* III, App. I, inscr. 1530A	metrical epitaph
63. Oxyrhynchos	ca. 1 A.D.	*P. Oxy.* 4.745	private letter
GREEK ISLANDS			
64. Paros	?	——	cf. Burton 1898: 625–26

the extent that we can infer the size of the college in Illyria (no. 1), Thessaly (nos. 55–56), and Macedonian Beroia (nos. 7, 8), five is again the regular number.

This range of information leads to the legitimate inference that the politarchs were the chief magistrates in their cities. Yet it is possible that by about the mid-3d century the title was becoming merely honorific (nos. 45 and 48, though these two texts do not indicate such a change as certainly as has sometimes been supposed; cf. Schuler 1960: 99, n. 14; Gschnitzer, PWSup 13 489). Another reasonable conclusion to draw from the evidence is that the politarchs came from the wealthier families (Schuler 1960: 90, cf. 98, n. 9), who will also have comprised the social elite of their city.

Two caveats should be mentioned. First, it is not only within urban centers that politarchs exercise their position. Hammond and Griffith note (1972 1: 87) that in Table 1, no. 10, Derriopos is not a city but a district inhabited by the Derripes, and the politarchs of Derriopus are officials of the tribal state *hē polis tōn Derriopōn.* In this inscription the politarchs convene the *boulē* which decides to honor a Roman citizen. Again, in no. 9 we see the politarch convening the *ekklēsia* not of a city but of a tribal community in the SW Macedonian canton of Orestis (Hammond and Griffith 1972 1: 114–15). The resolution concerning a land dispute is passed by the politarch and citizens together.

The second qualification to be made is that most of our evidence relates to Macedonia; whether the functions of politarchs elsewhere were identical is unclear. There is a natural presumption in favor of a similar role in those regions which came under Macedonian influence (Table 1 nos. 1, 57–58). In the sole papyrological example (no. 63), however, it is quite uncertain what duties the politarch Theophilos performs, from the passing comment included in this private letter. In fact, this is our only instance from Egypt where the term may be used in a technical sense. The usage in the metrical epitaph for Abramos from Leontopolis (no. 62) is clearly more fluid, probably to indicate his leadership of two Jewish communities *(dissō gar te topōn politarchōn autos eteimō).* The sole text from Bithynia which mentions a politarch (no. 61) similarly does not clarify the function for that city. Accordingly, the politarch at Kios has been seen as both a minor official (Schuler 1960: 99, n. 21; Hatzopoulos 1984: 143, n. 20) and also as one holding a post similar to that of *censor/timētēs* (Vidman 1960: 70; Ameling 1984: 27–28, and n. 70).

This possibility of the term being employed for officials exercising different responsibilities in different locations leads to the question whether the Macedonian politarchs and the Thessalian politarchs are in fact to be identified. Generally, they have been differentiated (Schuler 1960: 92; Gschnitzer, PWSup 11: esp. 1112; PWSup 13:483–500); but Helly (1977) has shown that these and related terms are essentially the same. The difference is one of dialect. No. 32 in Table 1 may help to reinforce this conclusion: it is a metrical text from Thessalonike, but with the spelling *ptoliarchos,* one of the forms which occurs in the Thessalian inscriptions (for three Classical and Hellenistic literary verse occurrences of *poliarchos*—all non-technical uses—see Gschnitzer, PWSup 11: 1112).

Bibliography

Ameling, W. 1984. Das Archontat in Bithynien und die *lex provinciae* des Pompeius. *Epigraphica Anatolica* 3: 19–31.

Burton, E. D. 1898. The Politarchs. *AJT* 2: 598–632.

Dimitsas, M. G. 1896. *Hē Makedonia en lithois phtheggomenois kai mnēmeiois sōzomenois.* Athens. Repr. as *Sylloge inscriptionum Graecarum et Latinarum Macedoniae.* 2 vols; Chicago, 1980.

Edson, C. 1972. *Inscriptiones Graecae.* Vol. 10/2/1. Berlin.

Ferguson, W. D. 1913. The Legal and Governmental Terms Common to the Macedonian Greek Inscriptions and the New Testament. Diss., Chicago.

Hammond, N. G. L., and Griffith, G. T. 1972, 1979. *A History of Macedonia.* 2 vols. Oxford.

Hatzopoulos, M. 1984. Les politarques de Philippopolis: Un élément méconnu pour la datation d'une magistrature macédonienne. Pp. 137–49 in *Dritter internationaler Thrakologischer Kongress zu Ehren W. Tomascheks, 2.-6. Juni 1980.* Sofia.

Helly, B. 1977. Politarques, Poliarques, et Politophylaques. Vol. 2, pp. 531–44 in *Ancient Macedonia.* Thessaloniki.

Kanatzoulis, D. 1955. *Makedonika Meletēmata.* Thessaloniki.

———. 1956. Peri tōn politarchōn tōn Makedonikōn poleōn. *Epistēmonikē epeteris Philosophikēs scholēs (Thessaloniki)* 7: 157–79.

Koukouli-Chrysanthaki, C. 1981. Politarchs in a New Inscription from Amphipolis. Pp. 229–41 in *Ancient Macedonian Studies in Honor of Charles F. Edson,* ed. H. Dell. Thessaloniki.

Lipsius, R. A., and Bonnet, M. 1903. *Acta Apostolorum Apocrypha.* Vol. 2/2. Leipzig.

Oliver, J. H. 1963. Civic Constitutions for Macedonian Communities. *CP* 58: 164–65.

Papazoglou, F. 1986. Politarques en Illyrie. *Historia* 35: 438–48.

Pelekides, S. 1934. *Apo tēn politeia kai tēn koinōnia tēs archaias Thessalonikēs.* Thessaloniki.

Schuler, C. 1960. The Macedonian Politarchs. *CP* 55: 90–100.

Touratsoglou, J. P. 1977. Apo tēn politeia kai tēn koinōnia tēs archaias Beroias: epigraphikēs semeiōseis. Vol. 2, pp. 481–93 in *Ancient Macedonia.* Thessaloniki (in Greek).

Vidman, L. 1960. *Etude sur la correspondence de Pliny le Jeune avec Trajan.* Prague.

G. H. R. Horsley

POLITICAL IDENTITY. See NATIONALITY AND POLITICAL IDENTITY.

POLYCARP (PERSON). Bishop of Smyrna in Asia Minor, born ca. 70 C.E. and martyred in Smyrna ca. 156 C.E. Our sources for the life of Polycarp include Ignatius' letter to Polycarp, Irenaeus' *Adversus Haereses,* Eusebius' *Historia Ecclesiastica,* and most importantly, the anonymous *Martyrdom of Polycarp.* Irenaeus, quoted by Eusebius (*Hist. Eccl.* 5:20:6), states that Polycarp was a disciple of John the Apostle. Some scholars doubt the accuracy of this assertion, especially considering Eusebius' preoccupation with demonstrating apostolic succession. Neither Ignatius nor Polycarp himself mentions any connection with John. According to a scribal addition to the *Martyrdom of Polycarp* (22:2), Irenaeus was a disciple of Polycarp.

Polycarp was the author of one extant writing, a letter to the Philippians. Harrison (1936) has argued persuasively that Polycarp's *Philippians* is actually two letters (1–12 and 13–14). Chief evidence for this theory is the presupposition in 1–12 that Ignatius of Antioch has already died (9:1), whereas in 13–14 Ignatius clearly is still living (13:2). Since Ignatius was martyred ca. 108–15, the two letters were probably written shortly after and shortly before this time.

Moral exhortation dominates Polycarp's *Philippians.* He exhorts the Philippians to the highest standards of personal morality in forgiveness (2:2–3), righteousness (3:1–2), avoidance of love of money (4:1, 3; 11:1–2), chastity (4:2), compassion (6:1), and endurance under persecution (8:2–9:2). The predominant theological emphasis of the letter is anti-Docetism (7:1; 8:1). Polycarp's writing is thoroughly infused with brief quotations and allusions to lst-century Christian writings, indicating his familiarity with Matthew, Acts, Romans, 1 and 2 Corinthians, Galatians, Ephesians, Philippians, 1 and 2 Timothy, 1 Peter, 1 John, and 1 Clement. The thought and literary style of Polycarp's *Philippians* so closely resembles that of the Pastoral Epistles in the NT that von Campenhausen (1963) has even proposed Polycarp as the author of the Pastorals, although this hypothesis has not gained widespread scholarly acceptance.

The *Martyrdom of Polycarp* was written not long after the time of the event (ca. 156) and was known to Irenaeus around 180. It describes the events of Polycarp's martyrdom as follows. During a persecution at Smyrna he was found, arrested, and brought to the stadium by a police chief named Herod (6:1–2). When asked by the proconsul to "swear by the Genius of Caesar" (9:2), Polycarp replied, "For eighty-six years I have served [Christ], and he has done me no wrong. How can I blaspheme my king who saved me?" (9:3). He was soon afterward executed by burning, but when the flames would not consume his body, the executioner plunged a dagger into him. A mass of blood spurted forth from the wound, quenching the fire and amazing the crowd (16:1).

The *Martyrdom of Polycarp* holds a special place in Christian literature as the first example of the literary genre, acts of Christian martyrs. Scores of such acts of martyrs would be written in subsequent centuries. Although some of the miraculous elements in the *Martyrdom of Polycarp* appear to be legendary (15:2; 16:1), the work claims to have been written by an eyewitness (15:1). See also POLYCARP, EPISTLE OF; POLYCARP, MARTYRDOM OF.

Bibliography

Bihlmeyer, K. 1956. *Die Apostolischen Väter.* Sammlung Ausgewählter Kirchen und Dogmengeschichtliche Quellenschriften. Tübingen.

Campenhausen, H. F. von. 1963. *Aus der Frühzeit des Christentums.* Tübingen.

Harrison, P. N. 1936. *Polycarp's Two Epistles to the Philippians.* Cambridge.

Köster, H. 1957. *Synoptische überlieferung bei den Apostolischen Vätern.* TU 65. Berlin.

Lake, K. 1912. *The Apostolic Fathers.* LCL. Cambridge. Repr. 1965.

Lightfoot, J. B. 1890. *The Apostolic Fathers,* Pt. 2, vols. 2–3. Grand Rapids. Repr. 1981.

Schoedel, W. R. 1967. *The Apostolic Fathers: A New Translation and Commentary.* Vol. 5, *Polycarp, Martyrdom of Polycarp, Fragments of Papias.* Camden, NJ.

J. Christian Wilson

POLYCARP, EPISTLE OF. The primary source of our knowledge of Polycarp of Smyrna (traditionally ca. A.D. 69–155) is a letter which he wrote to the Church at Philippi early in the 2d century. See also POLYCARP, MARTYRDOM OF. The letter is not a distinguished document from a literary or theological point of view, but it reveals a man who could be relied on for a sane and cautious approach to religious and administrative problems. The importance of the letter is enhanced by the fact that Polycarp's career intersected that of others who left a deeper impression on the early Church than Polycarp himself.

A. Polycarp and Ignatius

Of first importance in this regard is Ignatius of Antioch, who was allowed by his guards to meet with the Christians of Smyrna while en route to Rome and who subsequently dispatched two letters to the Smyrnaeans and their leader, Polycarp, from Troas (Eus. *Hist. Eccl.* 3.36). Polycarp was evidently stirred by the intense spirituality of his visitor from Antioch and proved to be his most enthusiastic advocate. In the end, he agreed to help organize the flow of representatives and congratulatory notes to Antioch requested by Ignatius (Ign. *Phld* 10; *Smyrn* 11; *Pol.* 7–8; Pol. *Phil.* 13.1). He also indicates that he had made a collection of Ignatius' letters at the request of the Philippians (*Phil.* 13.2), perhaps on the model of a corpus of Pauline letters.

Ignatius is mentioned again along with two other Christian martyrs in *Phil.* 9. These same "patterns of true love" are alluded to at the beginning of the letter in a statement that seems to presuppose their presence in Philippi not long before (*Phil.* 1.1). Polycarp's references to Ignatius do not, however, harmonize easily: in *Phil.* 9 our author seems to speak of Ignatius' martyrdom, presumably in Rome, as a past event, whereas in *Phil.* 13 he asks to be informed if the Philippians have learned "anything more certain" about Ignatius and those with him. This apparent contradiction led P. N. Harrison (1936) to suggest that *Phil.* 13–14 (or 13 alone) was written as a covering letter for the Ignatian corpus soon after Ignatius had passed through Philippi, whereas *Phil.* 1–12 (or 1–12 + 14) was composed later (ca. 135 A.D.) to meet other problems. Among these, according to Harrison, was the desire to combat the Marcionite heresy implied by the polemics of *Phil.* 7 and by the identification there of the docetic opponent of the truth as "the firstborn of Satan" (*Phil.* 7.2). For according to Irenaeus, precisely this phrase was applied to Marcion by Polycarp during a famous encounter between them (*Adv. haer.* 3.3.4; Eus. *Hist. Eccl.* 4.14.7). It remains very doubtful, however, that *Phil.* 7 has Marcion's teaching in view (Schoedel 1967: 23–26); and it is surely possible that Polycarp used the expression "firstborn of Satan" on more than one occasion or that the story reported by Irenaeus grew up around Polycarp's bon mot later. In any event, the allusion to the martyrs in *Phil.* 1, suggesting as it does a fresh memory of the martyrs, indicates that the divergence between *Phil.* 13–14 and *Phil.* 1–12 cannot be pressed. Either the two letters were close to one another in time, or there was in fact but one letter. To be sure, those who regard the references to Ignatius in Polycarp as interpolations point to a grammatical inconsistency in *Phil.* 1 that they take as evidence of the inauthenticity of the reference to the martyrs in that passage. There are indications, however, that the peculiarities of the text arise from an unusual manipulation of a standard transitional device (a "joy expression") often found at the beginning of the body of ancient letters (Schoedel 1987).

It should be noted that those who regard Polycarp's references to Ignatius as interpolations are primarily concerned to deny the authenticity of the letters of Ignatius (i.e., the "middle recension" generally considered authentic since the research of Zahn [1873] and Lightfoot [1885]). A form of the argument presented by Joly (1979: 17–37) has it that the interpolator built on an authentic reference to an otherwise unknown Ignatius in *Phil.* 9, added *Phil.* 13 to turn the communication into a covering letter for the Ignatian corpus, and inserted the allusion to the martyrs in *Phil.* 1 to set the stage for the new picture of Ignatius that was being created. Here, however, too much depends on the prior conviction that the middle recension of Ignatius is inauthentic; and again too much is probably made of the grammatical inconsistency in *Phil.* 1.

B. Polycarp and Apostolic Tradition

Our assessment of the place of Polycarp in the early church is further complicated by the fact that he was soon appealed to by Irenaeus (and Eusebius after him) as an important link in a line of orthodox tradition stretching back to the apostles, especially John. In one passage Irenaeus claims to have known Polycarp personally "in my early youth" (*Adv. haer.* 3.3.4; Eus. *Hist. Eccl.* 4.14); and he goes on to make the following points about him: Polycarp visited Rome in the time of Anicetus, whose accession to the episcopal office took place perhaps no earlier than A.D. 155, and Polycarp opposed heresy there; Polycarp related a story about John, the disciple of the Lord, who "going to bathe at Ephesus and seeing Cerinthus within, rushed out of the bathhouse without bathing, saying, 'Let us flee lest the bathhouse fall down because Cerinthus the enemy of the truth is within' "; and when Polycarp encountered

Marcion, he identified him as "the firstborn of Satan." In this connection, Irenaeus also refers to Polycarp's "very able" letter to the Philippians. But when he speaks elsewhere of Polycarp's letters in the plural (Eus. *Hist. Eccl.* 5.20.8), he was probably going on much less. In yet another passage, Irenaeus links Polycarp and Papias, calling the latter "the hearer of John, and a companion of Polycarp" (*Adv. haer.* 5.33.4). The importance of Polycarp to Irenaeus also emerges from a fragment of his letter to Florinus: "When I was still a boy," says Irenaeus, "I saw you [Florinus] in lower Asia in the company of Polycarp, faring brilliantly in the imperial court and endeavoring to secure his favor." Irenaeus also claims to have remembered what Polycarp did and said and "how he would tell of his intercourse with John and with the others who had seen the Lord" (Eus. *Hist. Eccl.* 5.20.4–8). Finally, a letter of Polycrates of Ephesus (ca. A.D. 190) to Victor, bishop of Rome (A.D. 189–98), on the paschal controversy names Polycarp, among others, as preserving Quartodeciman practice from the time of the apostle John (Eus. *Hist. Eccl.* 5.24.2–7). Irenaeus also wrote to the Roman bishop on this matter, reminding him that when Polycarp visited Anicetus in Rome, there was mutual respect in spite of disagreement on the date of the celebration of Easter (Eus. *Hist. Eccl.* 5.24.14–17).

In spite of all this, a link between Polycarp and John is not assured. Irenaeus was young when he heard Polycarp and may well have taken references to John the elder (Eus. *Hist. Eccl.* 3.39.3–7) as references to John the apostle. Polycarp himself certainly makes no appeal to having known any of the disciples of the Lord, and he does not claim to have been appointed by one of them over the Church in Smyrna. He does not even lay claim to the title of bishop. And although it was no doubt appropriate for Ignatius to refer to Polycarp as bishop in Smyrna (Ign. *Magn* 15; *Pol.* 6.1), it is also evident that the title meant more to Ignatius than to his host. Yet even Ignatius makes no use of the idea of apostolic succession in this connection. And when he writes against Docetism on Polycarp's behalf (Ign. *Smyrn.* 1–9), he never appeals to the special authority of John. A link between Polycarp and John, then, seems just about as unlikely as a link between Papias and John. In any event, Irenaeus evidently remembered very little of what Polycarp may have said concerning his mentor John. For it is significant that he presents the story of the encounter between the apostle and Cerinthus—a high point of his account of the bishop of Smyrna—as derived from others.

C. Polycarp and the Philippians

The authority that Polycarp exercised beyond the Smyrnaean Christian community can be judged by the task that he was asked to assume by the Philippians. They requested that he give his opinion on what should be done about the elder Valens and his wife in the Philippian congregation, who had misused funds of the Church. Polycarp's advice was to "bring them back as weak and erring members" (Pol. *Phil.* 11.4). The incident serves to illustrate the informal authority enjoyed by prestigious outsiders who could be trusted to give an unbiased judgment. The situation is comparable to that presupposed in *1 Clement,* which was written by a leader of the Roman Church in response to an appeal from Corinth to help deal with internal difficulties there.

Polycarp's references to the martyrs (*Phil.* 1; 9; 13), to Docetism (*Phil.* 7), and to Valens' love of money (*Phil.* 11) are embedded in a theology that emphasizes the preservation of the blessings of salvation (especially the resurrection) through a faith that bears fruit in sober living and a forgiving attitude (*Phil.* 1–2; 8; 10; 12) and that recognizes responsibilities articulated in tables of duties for wives, children, widows, deacons, young men, virgins, and elders (*Phil.* 4–6). Again, there is no mention of a bishop or bishops. Special attention to the Pauline theme of "righteousness" (*Phil.* 3) suggests that Polycarp was reacting to an exegesis of Romans and Galatians by gnosticizing enthusiasts for the apostle. Polycarp himself emphasizes the settled spiritual and ethical attitudes that the term implies. Similarly, he works with a moralized version of the eschatological outlook of the early Christian movement (Bovon-Thurneyson 1973). Indeed, the theology of the letter is so close to that of the Pastorals that von Campenhausen (1951) argued for Polycarp's authorship of them as well. The theory is not fully persuasive, but the affinities are striking.

Although the letter to the Philippians to all appearance consists of a collection of disconnected points, it is likely that Polycarp saw a relation between them (Meinhold PW 21/2: 1662–93; Schoedel 1967; Steinmetz 1972). Thus it may be said that Polycarp opposes Docetism and the misinterpretation of righteousness by appealing to the witness that martyrdom gives to a life of endurance and love and to the reality of the cross of Christ. And it seems that he deals with Valens' love of money as a symptom of hidden impulses at work in the congregation as a whole and that he deepens its significance for the Philippians by treating greed as the moral corollary of heresy.

D. Polycarp and the New Testament

An extraordinary feature of the letter is the extent to which Polycarp pieces together words, phrases, and sentences from the Christian literature of the 1st century to say what he does. There are strong echoes of Matthew along with hints of Luke. And there may also be dependence on Acts in one passage (*Phil.* 1.2). As regards Paul, language reminiscent especially of Romans, 1–2 Corinthians, Galatians, Philippians, and Ephesians is found. Similarities with the Pastorals may depend on the use of traditional themes in pagan and Christian moralists. At the same time, there is the possibility that 1 Tim 6:7, 10 was before Polycarp in *Phil.* 4.1 and 2 Tim 4:10 in *Phil.* 9.2. There seem to be numerous clear reflections of 1 Peter in the letter. But the fact that Polycarp and the First Letter of John have anti-Docetic themes in common (*Phil.* 7) does not necessarily point to a literary relation between them. In view of the presumed connection between Polycarp and "John," it is striking that echoes of neither the gospel of John nor of the Apocalypse are to be found. On the other hand, Polycarp appears to have known *1 Clement* fairly well. And the allusions to Synoptic materials seem clearly to presuppose the use of written documents—perhaps atypically for the Apostolic Fathers (Koester 1957)—with the exception of a collection of items in *Phil.* 2.3 that apparently depends on *1 Clem.* 13.2 or on traditional materials somehow related to *1 Clem.* 13.2 (Hagner 1973: 279). None of the material discussed above seems to have been regarded as Scripture by Polycarp, though there is a problematic passage in *Phil.* 12.1. Yet Polycarp makes relatively little use of the OT and professes inferiority to the Philippians in the knowledge of Scripture (*Phil.* 12.1). Nevertheless, traces of language derived directly or indirectly from the Psalms, Proverbs, Isaiah, Jeremiah, Ezekiel, Tobit, and other biblical books are found.

Bibliography

Bovon-Thurneyson, A. 1973. Ethik und Eschatologie im Philipperbrief des Polycarps von Smyrna. *TZ* 29: 241–56.

Campenhausen, H. F. von. 1951. *Polykarp von Smyrna und die Pastoralbriefe.* SHAW Phil.-hist. Kl. 36/2. Heidelberg.

Damme, D. van. 1985. Polycarpe de Smyrne. *Dictionnaire de spiritualité* 12: 1902–8.

Hagner, D. A. 1973. *The Use of the Old and New Testaments in Clement of Rome.* NovTSup 34. Leiden.

Harrison, P. N. 1936. *Polycarp's Two Epistles to the Philippians.* Cambridge.

Joly, R. 1979. *Le dossier d'Ignace d'Antioche.* Université libre de Bruxelles, faculté de philosophie et lettres 69. Brussels.

Koester, H. 1957. *Synoptische Überlieferung bei den Apostolischen Vätern.* TU 65. Berlin.

Lightfoot, J. B. 1885. *S. Ignatius, S. Polycarp.* Vol. 2 of *The Apostolic Fathers.* London. Repr. Grand Rapids, 1981.

Paulsen, H. 1985. *Die Briefe des Ignatius von Antiochia und der Brief des Polykarp von Smyrna.* 2d rev. ed. HNT 18. Die Apostolischen Väter 2. Tübingen.

Schoedel, W. R. 1967. *Polycarp, Martyrdom of Polycarp, Fragments of Papias.* Vol. 5 of *Apostolic Fathers,* ed. Robert M. Grant. Camden, NJ.

———. 1987. Polycarp's Witness to Ignatius of Antioch. *Vig Christ* 41: 1–10.

Steinmetz, P. 1972. Polykarp von Smyrna und die Gerechtigkeit. *Hermes* 100: 63–75.

Zahn, T. 1873. *Ignatius von Antiochien.* Gotha.

William R. Schoedel

POLYCARP, MARTYRDOM OF. The account of the martyrdom of Polycarp (*MPol*) is contained in a letter written by the Church in Smyrna to the Church in Philomelium (a small but reasonably important city in Phrygia) and beyond that "to all the communities of the holy and catholic church sojourning in every place." The conclusion indicates that a certain Marcion was responsible for the composition of the letter (*MPol* 20.1) and that a person named Evarestus served as scribe (*MPol* 20.2), although the text may also be taken to mean that Marcion was "the authoritative witness" and Evaristus the author (Dehandschutter 1979: 280). The connection between the epistolary framework and the account of the martyrdom is purely ad hoc, however, and does not justify the identification of a separate category for Christian martyria in epistolary form (Dehandschutter 1979: 157–89). Thus *MPol* is the first of the narrative martyria from the early Church.

The contents of the document may be outlined as follows: an introduction concerning "martyrdom in accord with the gospel" (*MPol* 1); an account of the martyrdom of those who preceded Polycarp (2–4), including especially the description of the courage of "the most noble Germanicus" in *MPol* 3 and the rueful reflections on Quintus the Phrygian in *MPol* 4 (who at first forced himself and some others to come forward and then lost his nerve); a lengthy recital of the martyrdom of Polycarp himself (5–18); and a conclusion (19–20). There follows a number of appendixes: a chronological note that may or may not be part of the original letter (*MPol* 21); a conclusion that echoes vocabulary and themes from the beginning of the letter and that also may or may not be part of the original letter (22.1); a note on the transmission of the manuscript of *MPol,* quite possibly reformulated by the same copyist who identifies himself in the last section (22.2); and the last section, a note by Pionius—probably a 4th-century writer masquerading as the 3d-century martyr Pionius—who explains the circumstances under which he copied *MPol* and who suggests that *MPol* was to be part of a collection of materials devoted to Polycarp (22.3). Also note that the Moscow ms of *MPol* breaks off before the doxology at the end of *MPol* 21 and adds at that point its own elaborate version of *MPol* 22.2–3. The recital of Polycarp's martyrdom is the heart of the document and includes the following elements: Polycarp's preliminary withdrawal to safety (*MPol* 5); his arrest (6–8); his summary trial before the proconsul in the stadium (9–11); the martyrdom itself (12–18). The martyrdom itself recounts the reactions of the crowd (12–13), Polycarp's prayer of thanksgiving, modeled to a certain extent on early eucharistic materials (14), the burning of Polycarp (15–16), and the treatment of his remains (17–18).

The authenticity of the letter was proved to the satisfaction of most by Lightfoot. Skepticism on this point has not been entirely banished (Schwartz 1972), but far more significant has been the challenge of Grégoire and Orgels (1951) to the long-accepted dating of *MPol* and the questions raised by von Campenhausen (1957) about the integrity of the document. To understand the debate it is necessary to recall that *MPol* is known to us not only in an independent form from Greek mss and early versions but also from Eusebius' discussion of it (*Hist. Eccl.* 4.15). The historian represents *MPol* by quoting the address, paraphrasing *MPol* 1–6, and then returning to the text itself of *MPol* 7–19. To be more precise, he breaks off shortly after the beginning of *MPol* 19 (at the words "so that he is spoken of in every place even by the heathen"); and thus Eusebius either did not know the chronological note in *MPol* 21 or did not see fit to deal with it. Eusebius' paraphrase of *MPol* 1–6 is noteworthy for the absence of the theme of the imitation of Christ prominent in the mss of *MPol.* And his form of the text of *MPol* 7–19 stands out for its omission of the reference to the dove in *MPol* 16.1 which was said to fly from the wound inflicted on the martyr by the executioner.

The older scholarship is dominated by the date of A.D February 23, 155, or A.D. February 22, 156, for the martyrdom of Polycarp. These suggestions rest on complex arguments brought to bear on the chronological note in *MPol* 21. The surprisingly late date of A.D. 177 for the martyrdom of Polycarp proposed by Grégoire and Orgel (1951) depends on regarding the chronological note in *MPol* 21 as a late addition to the text, offering a fresh analysis of the data provided by Eusebius, both in his Church history and his chronicle, and treating the discussion of Quintus in *MPol* 4 as a response to Montanism. The arguments against this interpretation of the evidence are strong, however, and it is likely that an earlier date should be preferred. Some have defended A.D. 167 (the date that Eusebius actually gives in his chronicle) or thereabouts (Marrou 1953; Brind'Amour 1980). Others have been willing to give greater credit to the chronological note in *MPol* 21 (partially supported by the reference to the Asiarch Philip in *MPol* 12.2) and to suggest a date of ca. A.D. 155–60 (Schoedel 1967: 58, 68, 78–79; Barnes 1967; 1968; Dehandschutter 1979: 191–219). This approach to the data supplied by the chronological note involves setting aside the mention of "a great Sabbath" (the day on which Polycarp was martyred) as helpful in being any more precise. The uncertainty about the meaning of this much-discussed expression is well illustrated by the effort of Rordorf (1980) to take it as a reference to a celebration of the pagan Terminalia that happened to coincide with a Sabbath. Rordorf notes that *MPol* pictures pagans and Jews as equally free to attend the festivities. Any earlier date for the martyrdom of Polycarp than those suggested above is ruled out by the fact that Polycarp is said by Irenaeus (Eus. *Hist. Eccl.* 5.24.16) to have visited Anicetus in Rome; for it is generally thought that Anicetus became bishop of Rome about A.D. 155 (perhaps A.D. 155 at the earliest).

Another approach to the problems presented by *MPol* has led to theories of interpolation. This line of argument was pursued most persuasively by von Campenhausen (1957). He called into question not only elements absent from Eusebius' paraphrase of *MPol* 1–6 (notably the theme of the imitation of Christ), but also certain materials already present in the text known to Eusebius. Among the latter are the discussion about Quintus in *MPol* 4, elements of the miraculous in the account, and the points in *MPol* 17–18 that seem to reflect a veneration of martyrs and a theological assessment of such veneration too highly developed for the 2d century. The chronological note in *MPol* 21 is regarded as a later addition, and the conclusion in *MPol* 22.1 is seen as the work of the same redactor who developed the theme of "martyrdom in accord with the gospel" (*MPol* 1.1) and who presumably drew out the parallels between the death of the martyrs and the passion of Jesus.

Von Campenhausen's view of the matter has been developed and refined by Conzelmann (1978), significantly modified by Schoedel (1967: 47–82), and now more or less abandoned by Barnard (1970), Dehandschutter (1979: 131–55), and Saxer (1982). A fundamental error of von Campenhausen was his failure to examine more carefully how Eusebius dealt with his sources. Moreover, most of the parallels drawn in *MPol* between the death of the martyrs and the passion of Jesus are, as Barnard observed, also found in Eusebius' report. And von Campenhausen's reasons for judging certain items as anachronistic were not always clear. But it is perhaps not yet certain that he was mistaken on every point, including especially the highly developed martyrological themes in *MPol* 17–18. In any event, one general result of recent criticism of *MPol* is the virtual elimination from scholarship of the notion that originally the letter would naturally have contained a more or less factual account devoid of elements of the miraculous and of explicit theological reflection. Indeed, we now have a theory of the textual transmission of *MPol* that calls into question any tendency to favor the evidence of Eusebius and that also sees no reason to follow him in eliminating the reference to the dove which is said to fly from the wound inflicted on Polycarp by the executioner in *MPol* 16.1 (Dehandschutter 1979: 27–129).

It has not proved easy to describe with clarity the idea of martyrdom that comes to expression in the letter. *MPol* naturally shares with postbiblical Judaism and early Christianity an emphasis on the importance of affirming a way of life in obedience to the will of God and of being committed to it, if need be, to the point of death. *MPol* also naturally shares with Judaism and early Christianity the confidence that God will reward those who endure to the end with a "crown of incorruption" (*MPol* 17.1). In the early Church, however, new horizons were opened up by the fact that the requirement of loyalty to the law was replaced by the experience of communion with Jesus Christ. In working out the implications of this difference, it is still useful to view the martyr as the antecedent of the saint in the later technical sense of the term. Thus in *MPol*, martyrs show themselves, by their endurance in suffering, to be people who are no longer human but already "angelic" (2.3), and the martyrdom of Polycarp is marked by a display of miracles (5.2; 9.1; 15.2; 16.1). Moreover, the faithful, who had treated Polycarp when alive with such reverence that they constantly sought to "touch his flesh" (13.2), also attempt to recover his body "to have fellowship with his holy flesh" (17.1). When that is denied them, they gather up his bones, set them in a "suitable" place (18.2), and plan to celebrate "the birthday of his martyrdom" on the anniversary of his death (18.3). Such acts seem to presuppose an established cultic pattern (Rordorf 1972); and though the careful distinction here between the "worship" due Christ and the "love" due martyrs (17.3) evidently reflects a developing debate concerning the veneration of martyrs, the author is prepared to come to terms with popular attitudes on this point (Saxer 1982: 992–99). Some scholars, however, deal with such elements in *MPol* merely as naive anticipations of later developments and stress the extent to which the annual celebration was intended, as *MPol* 18.3 itself says, "in memory of those who have already contested and for the training and preparation of those whose lot it will be." Dehandschutter (1982), for example, presents *MPol* as focused on obedience to the will of God (2.1; 7.1) and concerned about the salvation of "all the brethren" rather than of "oneself alone" (1.2). From this point of view, the rule to withdraw and not to thrust oneself forward for martyrdom (1.2; 4) not only reflects an awareness of the dangers of enthusiasm for institutional stability and social respectability, it also suggests that the theological center of *MPol* is to be found less in an emphasis on individual salvation and the achievement of a special sanctity than in a call to obey God and to attend to the Church's mission.

The problem of the theological outlook of *MPol* comes to a head in the interpretation of the theme of the "imitation of Christ" (1.1; 17.3; 19.1) and the assessment of the role of the parallels drawn between the martyr's lot and the passion of Christ. These features of *MPol* have been regarded as too highly developed for the 2d century by those who see them as setting the martyr apart from other Christians and establishing him as an independent focus for piety alongside of Christ (von Campenhausen 1957). More particularly, a distinction has been drawn between *Nachfolge* in the NT (a following after Christ in terms of obedience and faith) and *Nachahmung* in *MPol* (an imitation of Christ that implies an emphasis on the martyr's special sanctity). The imitation theme in *MPol,* however, is not carried through with great consistency and, in the opinion of many, is compatible with the treatment of Stephen in Acts 7 (Irenaeus, *Adv. haer.* 3.12.10–13) or with James in Hegesippus (Eus. *Hist. Eccl.* 2.23.4–18). Thus it may be correct to say that *MPol* does not intend so much to imitate the passion as to show that Polycarp's behavior was in harmony with the will of God and in conformity with the gospel (Schoedel 1967: 51–82; Dehandschutter 1982).

The effort of Kretschmar (1972) to read *MPol* from a quite different angle against the background of a popular Christian Passover tradition and to see martyrdom as a quasi-Eucharistic event (*MPol* 14) is both highly suggestive and highly problematic.

The theology of *MPol* is clearly directed against a misunderstanding of martyrdom. A number of scholars have thought that Montanism, with its home in Phrygia and its special enthusiasm for martyrdom, is represented by Quintus (*MPol* 4). This interpretation is connected with the problems of dating and the possibility of interpolations outlined above. Another suggestion is that *MPol* represents a response to Gnosticism which in some forms opposed martyrdom and in other forms (notably in the *Apocryphon of James*) encouraged self-willed martyrdom (Dehandschutter 1982: 665–67). It seems more likely, however, that *MPol* is confronting difficulties that could arise in any Christian community from inordinate caution or excessive zeal in meeting hostile challenges from the social environment of the churches. Thus *MPol* provides a balanced outlook that would presumably have helped to preserve the stability of the group and to have made measured responses to outside pressure possible. At the same time, it seems likely that *MPol* was also taking into account an incipient tendency within the churches to honor the martyr too highly. For if the distinction between the worship of Christ and the love of martyrs in *MPol* 17.3 does not serve as evidence of interpolation, the author of the document is surely reacting against what he regarded as an exaggerated veneration of these figures.

The foundation for such an exaggerated veneration was likely to have been laid in the popular culture of the Greco-Roman world with the piety that surrounded heroes and their relics. Even Klauser (1974), who had contested such influence, withdrew his arguments for the purely Jewish roots of the Christian idea of martyrdom in a note appended to the reprinting of his much-cited essay on the subject. In this connection, it may be relevant to note that the cult of martyrs and the common cult of the dead are not sharply distinguished from each other (Saxer 1982: 995), and that consequently the normal treatment of the dead may have paved the way in some communities for more highly developed practices. Influences from Hellenism are also to be found, however, at another level in *MPol.* It may be recalled that Jewish ideas of martyrdom had an impact on Christianity in the 2d century and beyond, primarily through 2 Maccabees (6–7) and *4 Maccabees,* and that *4 Maccabees* in particular presents the Jewish martyrs as spiritual "athletes" who embody the traditional Greek virtues. Echoes of this literature are frequent in *MPol* (Baumeister 1980: 295–99), and this background partly accounts for the emphasis here on the spiritual qualities of those who contend for Christ in the arena. New dimensions are added to the conception of such qualities in the Christian context where there is the possibility of "becoming a partaker of Christ" (*MPol* 6.2; cf. Phil 3:10) and of being "no longer people but already angels" (*MPol* 2.3; cf. John 17). Such a heightening of the virtues of the martyr seems likely to be linked with a growing enthusiasm for miracles inspired by popular conceptions of the preternaturally endowed "divine man" (Baumeister 1980: 302–6). *MPol,* however, still stands at the beginning of this transformation of the martyr into a saint. The theology and spirituality of the document belong fundamentally to the world of postbiblical Judaism and NT Christianity.

Bibliography

Barnard, L. W. 1970. In Defense of Pseudo-Pionius' Account of Saint Polycarp's Martyrdom. Vol. 1, pp. 192–204, in *Kyriakon.* 2 vols. Münster.

Barnes, T. D. 1967. A Note on Polycarp. *JTS* 18: 433–37.

———. 1968. Pre-Decian *Acta Martyrum. JTS* 19: 509–31.

Baumeister, T. 1980. *Die Anfänge der Theologie des Martyriums.* Münsterische Beiträge zur Theologie 45. Münster.

Brind'Amour, P. 1980. La date du martyr de saint Polycarpe (le 23 février 167). *AnBoll* 98: 456–62.

Campenhausen, H. F. von. 1957. *Bearbeitungen und Interpolationen des Polykarpmartyriums.* SHAW Phil.-hist. Kl. 3. Heidelberg.

Conzelmann, H. 1978. *Bemerkungen zum Martyrium Polykarps.* NAWG Phil.-hist. Kl. 2. Göttingen.

Damme, D. van. 1985. Polycarpe de Smyrne. *Dictionnaire de spiritualité* 12: 1902–8.

Dehandschutter, B. 1979. *Martyrium Polycarpi: Een literair-kritische studie.* BETL 52. Louvain.

———. 1982. Le martyre de Polycarpe et le développement de la conception du martyre au deuxième siècle. Vol. 2, pp. 659–68, in *Studia Patristica, Vol. XVII,* ed. E. A. Livingstone. New York.

Grégoire, H., and Orgels, P. 1951. La véritable date du martyre de Polycarpe (23 février 177) et le "Corpus Polycarpianum" *AnBoll* 69: 1–38.

Klauser, T. 1974. Christlicher Märtyrerkult, heidnischer Heroenkult und spätjüdische Heiligenverehrung: Neue Einsichten und neue Probleme. Pp. 221–29 in *Gesammelte Arbeiten zur Liturgiegeschichte, Kirchengeschichte und christlichen Archäologie,* ed. E. Dassmann. JACSup 3. Münster.

Kretschmar, G. 1972. Christliches Passa im 2. Jahrhundert und die Ausbildung der christlichen Theologie. *RSR* 60: 287–323.

Lightfoot, J. B. 1885. *S. Ignatius, S. Polycarp.* Vol. 2 of *The Apostolic Fathers.* London. Repr. Grand Rapids, MI 1981.

Marrou, H.-I. 1953. La date du martyre de S. Polycarpe. *AnBoll* 71: 5–20.

Rordorf, W. 1972. Aux origines du culte des martyres. *Irenikon* 45: 315–31.

———. 1980. Zum Problem des "grossen Sabbats" im Polkarp-und Pioniusmartyrium. Pp. 245–49 in *Pietas.* JACSup 8. Münster.

Saxer, V. 1982. L'authenticité du "Martyre de Polycarpe": Bilan de 25 ans de critique. *Mélanges de l'école francaise de Rome, Antiquité* 94: 979–1001.

Schoedel, W. R. 1967. *Polycarp, Martyrdom of Polycarp, Fragments of Papias.* Vol. 5 of *The Apostolic Fathers,* ed. R. M. Grant. Camden, NJ.

Schwartz, J. 1972. Note sur le martyre de Polycarpe de Smyrne. *RHPR* 52: 331–35.

William R. Schoedel

POMEGRANATE. See FLORA.

POMPEY (PERSON). Gnaeus Pompeius, later surnamed Magnus, or "Pompey the Great," is mentioned mainly in Plutarch's *Life of Pompey,* though he is frequently mentioned in other ancient sources, especially the contemporary speeches and letters of Cicero, and the relevant books of Appian's *Civil Wars* and Cassius Dio's *History of Rome.* Born in 106 B.C., Pompey developed his early career through abnormal military commands, first in the service of the dictator Sulla from 83–80, and subsequently as the senate's commander against Lepidus in Italy in 78 and the rebel Sertorius in Spain from 76–71. In 71 he assisted in mopping up the slave insurrection led by Spartacus, and in 70 pressured the senate into allowing him to become consul (with Crassus as his colleague), even though he was too young and had held none of the necessary prior magistracies. Then followed extensive commands to clear the Mediterranean of pirates in 67 and to complete the campaign against Mithridates in the east from 66–62.

Toward the end of this campaign (63), Pompey intervened in a civil war in Judea between Hyrcanus and Aristobulus; his brief campaign against the latter culminated in a three-month siege of the temple in Jerusalem and its capture. Though he entered the holy of holies, Pompey did not take any temple treasure; he installed Hyrcanus as high priest and made Judea tributary to Rome, but did not annex the country, placing it instead under the supervision of the Roman governor of Syria. He returned to Rome soon after, taking Aristobulus and his children with him as hostages.

On returning to Italy, Pompey found that his opponents in the senate were able to refuse grants of land to reward his veterans and to block ratification of the massive reorganization which he had carried out in the east. This unexpected opposition led Pompey to form a private political alliance with Crassus and Caesar, known as the "First Triumvirate," to push through the legislation which each desired. To cement the alliance Pompey married Caesar's daughter Julia (all of Pompey's five marriages were made for political purposes).

In the following years, with Caesar away campaigning in Gaul, Pompey appeared to be losing political ground gradually: the senators were suspicious of him, and the people deserted their military hero for others. As Caesar's reputation increased with his victories, Pompey grew more jealous. The breach was widened by the death of Julia in childbirth in 54, and increased by the death of Crassus, fighting against the Parthians in 53. To regain his standing, Pompey aligned himself with the conservatives in the senate, who were happy to use him to quell the increasing political chaos and against the rising power of Caesar (whom they feared more). This alignment culminated in Pompey being made sole consul in 52, which made him now the acknowledged leader of the conservative senators.

Civil war now appeared inevitable. When Caesar invaded in 49, Pompey sacrificed the advantages he had in Italy by leaving for Greece. Though he outmaneuvered Caesar on a number of occasions in the subsequent campaign and had a numerical superiority, he lost the final battle at Pharsalus in August 48. Pompey fled to Egypt, but was murdered on landing by the local ruling dynasty. Pompey's sons and supporters carried on the republican cause, but they were eventually overcome by Caesar.

Pompey does not appear to have been cultured or affable; he had spent most of his life on military campaigns. These had given him enormous wealth, which was the basis of his great popularity and later political influence. His success as a general resulted more from his ability to organize and to ensure numerical superiority. He had a tendency to take over command of campaigns when the hard work had already been done by others, to abandon those who had previously helped him, and to change sides frequently to suit his own political purposes. He also tended not to make his wishes clear, leading to the view that he was not politically astute, but it may have been a deliberate policy to foment uncertainty, which he could then be called upon to sort out. Despite his abnormal and extensive military powers and commissions, Pompey was essentially a constitutionalist and never used them to take over the state.

Bibliography

Greenhalgh, P. A. L. 1980. *Pompey, the Roman Alexander.* London.

———. 1981. *Pompey, the Republican Prince.* London.

Bruce A. Marshall

PONTIUS PILATE (PERSON) [Gk *Pontios Pilatos*]. The fifth Roman governor of Judea, during whose tenure Jesus of Nazareth was executed. Pilate is known primarily from Josephus and the Gospels. Philo reports in some detail an incident during Pilate's service in Judea, Tacitus mentions him in passing in connection with Christian origins, some of Pilate's coins have survived, and an inscription discovered in Caesarea Maritima in 1961 completes the primary evidence. This dossier is larger and more detailed than that of any other Roman governor of Judea, a circumstance which is probably to be explained by the special Christian interest in him. Such an interest explains not only the data in the Gospels and Tacitus' reference, but also the availability to Josephus, in Rome, of so much information about this governor. Nevertheless, we are totally in the dark about Pilate's life before and after his Judean governorship, and much remains unclear about that period as well.

A. Chronology
B. Title and Responsibilities
C. Pilate and Rome
D. Pilate and the Jews

E. The Events of Pilate's Governorship
F. Aftermath and Afterlife

A. Chronology

The year of Pilate's appointment to office is commonly given as 26 or 27 C.E. This results without difficulty from Josephus' statements that Pilate's predecessor, Valerius Gratus, was appointed after the death of Augustus (August of 14 C.E.) and served eleven years before being replaced by Pilate (*Ant* 18.2.2 §§33, 35). One should probably suppose that a few months passed, perhaps until the spring of 15 C.E., before Gratus was dispatched to Judea. Similarly, an appointment of Pilate in 26 or 27 C.E. is corroborated by Josephus' notice (*Ant* 18.4.2 §89) that Pilate served for ten years before being suspended from office shortly before the death of Tiberius, which came in March of 37 C.E.

Over against this usual dating of Pilate's term, to ca. 26–37 C.E., there has been some major argumentation about its beginning and some minor uncertainties about its end. The difficulties associated with the end of his term result from the data Josephus supplies in *Ant* 18.4.2–3 §§89–90, on the one hand, and in 18.5.3 §§122–24, on the other. According to §§89–90, after L. Vitellius, the Roman governor of Syria, suspended Pilate from office the latter hurried to Rome but arrived only after Tiberius died; Vitellius, in the meantime, went on to visit Jerusalem during a Passover festival. Given Tiberius' death in mid-March of 37 C.E. and Passover in April, these data clearly indicate that Pilate was suspended from office ca. March of 37 C.E. However, in §§122–24 we read of a visit by Vitellius to Jerusalem during a Jewish festival, at which time news reached him of Tiberius' death. It seems most likely that this news would have reached Judea within a month, and that this account is therefore referring to Passover of 37 C.E. However, such a conclusion would seem to push the visit mentioned in §90 back to Passover of 36 C.E., but it seems most unlikely that Pilate, if suspended prior to April of 36 C.E. would not have reached Rome (to which he is said to have hurried; §89) until March of 37 C.E.

To resolve this conundrum, some would move the first visit (§90) to Tabernacles in the fall of 36 C.E. (Holzmeister 1932: 228–32) or even ignore Josephus' reference to a festival and place it between December of 36 C.E. and January of 37 C.E. (Smallwood 1954: 12–21). Others (Blinzler 1959: 180, n. 8) would move the second visit (§§122–24) back to Pentecost (ca. May–June) of 37 C.E., leaving the first one, as Josephus says, on Passover. It seems preferable, however, to assume with Otto (1913: 192–94, n. *) that both accounts in Josephus in fact refer to one and the same visit, during Passover of 37 C.E. The fact that each account focuses on different events reflects the fact that they are based on sources which were interested, respectively, in the high priesthood and in Herodian affairs (Schwartz 1981–82: 383–98). Thus, we may maintain the plain implication of §§89–90, namely that Pilate was suspended and sent to Rome ca. March of 37.

The issue concerning the beginning of his term is much more complicated. As we have noted, Josephus clearly states (*Ant* 18.2.2 §§33–35) that Pilate's predecessor (Gratus) was appointed after Augustus' death (14 C.E.) and served eleven years. It is odd, however, that these two, Gratus and Pilate, are the only governors of Judea for whom Josephus states the duration of their tenure (eleven and ten years, respectively). This oddity may become suspicious in light of a number of indications that Gratus' term was in fact much shorter, and Pilate's correspondingly longer. The following are the main indications that this was the case.

Josephus reports the end of Gratus' term and Pilate's appointment in his stead (*Ant* 19.2.2 §35) just before the founding of the city of Tiberias in ca. 19–21 C.E. (18.2.3 §§36–38), and the latter is followed by a long account of eastern events culminating (18.2.5 §§53–54) in Germanicus' mission to the East and his death there in 19 C.E. Only thereafter does Josephus begin his account of Pilate's term (18.3.1 §35). The implication is that the latter began ca. 19 C.E.

Similarly, Josephus interrupts his account of Pilate's term in Judea with an account of scandals concerned with Jews and Isis worshipers in Rome, which occurred, he says, "about the same time" (18.3.4–5 §§65–84); thereafter, he reverts to Pilate and Judea. The events in Rome are also recounted by Tacitus, who clearly dates them to 19 C.E. (*Ann.* 2.85). Here too, then, as in the preceding paragraph, the implication is that Pilate's term had begun by ca. 19 C.E.

All that Josephus recounts of Gratus' term as governor of Judea (18.2.2 §§33–35) is the removal and appointment of high priests. Gratus is said to have deposed one and appointed another, "not long thereafter" appointed a third, and "after a year" a fourth, who also served "for not more than a year" before he was replaced by a fifth, Joseph Caiaphas. At this point Josephus concludes his account of Gratus by saying that "having done these things Gratus returned to Rome." While Josephus goes on to say that Gratus had spent eleven years in Judea, the impression given by his narrative is of a term lasting more like four or five years.

According to Eusebius (*Hist. Eccl.* 1.9), anti-Christian *Acta Pilati* circulated in the early 4th century were obviously false since they were dated to 21 C.E., several years before Pilate was appointed, according to Josephus' chronological data. As Eisler (1931: 13–20) has argued, however, it is unlikely that falsifiers would have been so stupid as to have misdated Pilate, and it could well be that their copies of Josephus did not contain the data regarding his and Gratus' lengths of service.

It seems that coins were minted in Judea for 15, 16, 17, and 18 C.E., but thereafter only in 24 C.E. (Meshorer 1982: 177). An obvious explanation is that there was some administrative change in ca. 19 C.E., and such might well have been accompanied by a change of governors.

Moreover, while it is often argued, in this connection, that Josephus' account is in chronological disorder (and that little weight, therefore, may be ascribed to arguments from context and order), such a generalization should be applied with caution in any particular case. Furthermore, it seems that Josephus in fact ordered his material quite well. One need only realize that he generally brings events of marginal importance to his story (such as affairs in Parthia and in Rome) *after* the narration of events in Judea during the same period. This procedure at times results in Josephus placing such "marginal" events—which actually occurred *earlier* than the "main" events of a given period (e.g., term of a governor of Judea)—after his narration of the "main events," which actually occurred *later* (for a detailed analysis of *Ant* 18–20 which demonstrates Josephus' practice, see Schwartz 1982–83). In our case, Josephus' narrative seems to indicate the following: the fact that the account of the "main events" in *Ant* 18.2.2 (Judean governors and their administration of the province) is followed by accounts of "marginal events" in Galilee ca. 19–21 C.E. and in Parthia and Commagene ca. 2 B.C.E.–19 C.E. (i.e., before the beginning of Pilate's affairs) indicates that Josephus viewed the period before Pilate as one covering the years up to ca. 19 C.E. Similarly, the fact that Josephus narrates events in Rome in 19 C.E. after his central narrative on Pilate's affairs in Judea (18.3.4–5 §65–84), before returning to relate Pilate's final adventure, which led to his suspension from office (18.4.1–2 §§85–89), again indicates that Josephus viewed Pilate's term as one which began ca. 19 C.E.

That Pilate was appointed in that year is all the more likely in view of the fact that the years 17–19 C.E. saw Germanicus' mission to the East, a mission inspired, in part, by complaints from Syria and Judea over the tax burden (Tac. *Ann.* 2.42.5). It is not difficult to imagine Germanicus' efforts to appease the overburdened population including the replacement of Gratus with Pilate. In this connection we may note, finally, that Gratus' frequent firing and appointment of high priests contrasts sharply with Pilate's retention of Joseph Caiaphas, Gratus' last appointee, throughout his entire term. It may well be that Germanicus, as part of an attempt to assuage irate Judeans whose religious sensitivities had surely been wounded by Gratus' high-handed approach to their highest religious authority, denied Pilate the power to exercise further such control of the high priesthood.

B. Title and Responsibilities

While Josephus and Philo call Pilate *epitropos* (*JW* 2.9.2 §169; *Gaium* 299) and Tacitus uses its Latin equivalent, *procurator* (*Ann.* 15.44), various scholars early on suggested, on the basis of various comparable data from elsewhere in the empire, that pre-Claudian provincial governors were in fact known as "prefects," the later term "procurator" thus being anachronistic with regard to Pilate (Hirschfeld 1905: 382–85; Jones 1960: 115–25). Indeed, alongside *epitropos* Josephus uses *eparchos,* the Greek equivalent of "prefect," for several of Pilate's predecessors and successors (Lémonon 1981: 46–47), thus indicating that his usage of the latter for Pilate is probably not to be pressed. And the building inscription discovered in Caesarea in 1961 (Lémonon 1981: 23–32), which refers to him as "Pontius Pilatus Praefectus Iudaeae," would seem to settle the question. See Fig. PON.01. The NT uses only the nontechnical term *hēgemōn* (ruler) for him as for others, a usage paralleled in Josephus both with regard to Pilate (*Ant* 18.3.1 §55) and others (Lémonon 1981: 43–44). A similar popular insouciance concerning the fine points of titulary lies behind Luke's willingness (Acts 4:26–27) to identify Pilate as an "archon" referred to in Ps 2:2 (LXX).

However, while "prefect" is a term with connotations more military than those of the administrative "procurator," it does not seem that this should guide our characterization of Pilate's responsibilities. While there certainly were troops at Pilate's disposal—auxiliary units of infantry and cavalry (*Ant* 18.4.2 §87)—they functioned more as police than as military forces. For more serious military endeavors responsibility rested with the legate of Syria, who had four legions at his disposal. In 37 C.E. we find one of those legates assisting Herod Antipas, and in 39–41 C.E. another was charged with enforcing Gaius' order to erect a statue in the temple of Jerusalem. But we hear of no involvement of the legate of Syria in Palestine during Pilate's tenure, a fact which might indicate that the period was generally quiet.

PON.01. Building inscription of Pontius Pilate at Caesarea. *(Courtesy of Israel Department of Antiquities and Museums)*

As governor of Judea, Pilate was responsible for all aspects of the Roman administration of the province. First of all, this meant he was at the head of its judicial system: note that when Josephus uses a shorthand phrase to indicate the governor's authority, that phrase is "with power even to execute" (*JW* 2.8.1 §117; in the parallel *Ant* 18.1.11 §2, he says simply "with full power"). The only details regarding Pilate as judge come from the NT with regard to the trial of Jesus. Pilate's other main responsibilities were fiscal: he was responsible for the collection of tributes and taxes, for the proper disbursement of funds for provincial needs, and for the forwarding to Rome of revenues and reports. However, we have no evidence regarding Pilate's activities in these fields, apart from his construction of an aqueduct—for which he is said to have used Jewish sacred monies (*Ant* 18.3.2 §2). Similarly, among the hundreds of Roman milestones testifying to Roman road building in Palestine, none so far indicates any such activity by Pilate. At best, one might note his coins (Meshorer 1982: 177–80) as evidence of care for the proper functioning of the marketplace.

C. Pilate and Rome

We have no information about any special background for Pilate's appointment to office. The governorship of Judea was not a very prestigious post and all of Pilate's predecessors in the position, as most of his successors as well, are otherwise unknown. While it has been speculated that Pilate may have had close ties to L. Aelius Seianus, the praetorian prefect who came to be the real ruler of Rome until his execution in 31 C.E. due to Tiberius' retirement to Capir, this hypothesis seems to lack any reasonable basis. Its main prop, Philo's claim that Seianus plotted against the Jews (*Gaium* 159–60), is unsupported and so difficult to square with the other known data that is better attributed to Philonian rhetoric, namely the need to have a dark backdrop against which Tiberius' benevolence to the Jews—which Philo presents before Gaius as an example—can shine out clearly (Hennig 1975: 160–79). On the other hand, John 19:12 need not mean that Pilate had specifically been awarded the title *philos tou kaisaros* ("friend of Caesar"). John's use of the title might only reflect his knowledge, or that of the Jews he "quotes," that such a title existed, a fact which they could have learned, for example, from the titulary of Agrippa I and II.

Pilate seems to have been given a free hand in governing his province. It is true, however, that on two occasions Pilate's Jewish subjects exerted pressure upon him by threatening to complain to Rome about him, and in one instance, we are told, they actually did so. But neither case appears to be historical. Namely, John 19:12 is part of that gospel's attempt (similar to that of other gospels) to portray a Pilate desirous of freeing Jesus; the Jewish threat to appeal to Caesar is therefore introduced in order to explain why the governor yielded to Jewish pressure. And Philo's claim (*Gaium* 301–5) that the Jews threatened to send an embassy to Tiberius, and in fact sent a letter which brought Tiberius' wrath down upon Pilate, is all only a part of this apologetic historian's attempt to portray Tiberius as beneficent to the Jews and therefore a proper model for Gaius. Only at the end of Pilate's governorship do we see imperial intervention, and it is interesting to note that this was in response to complaints not of Jews but rather of Samaritans (although some witnesses incongruously read "Jews" instead of "Samaritans" in *Ant* 18.4.2 §89). After Pilate had used violence to stop an armed demonstration by Samaritans near Mt. Gerizim, and had executed a number of their leaders, a Samaritan delegation complained to Vitellius, the legate of Syria. As we have already seen in our discussion of Pilate's chronology, Vitellius responded by suspending Pilate from office and sending him off to the emperor Tiberius (who died before Pilate arrived). This is a good example of the ambiguous relationship between the Roman governors of Judea and the legates of Syria: while the former were responsible to Rome and not to Antioch (for which reason Vitellius could neither remove Pilate from office nor appoint his successor), it was nevertheless clear that when a nearby representative of Rome was needed, Rome's senior official in the East and governor of the large province adjacent to Judea, headquartered at Antioch, was the natural address for both the governor of Judea and its population (Lémonon 1981: 59–71).

D. Pilate and the Jews

Apart from the Samaritan episode mentioned in the preceding paragraph, wherein everything but the unfortunate bloody end is unclear, all of the known episodes of Pilate's term of office concern his clashes with his Jewish subjects. The result is an impression of a very turbulent period characterized by hostility and violence between the governor and his subjects. Josephus created this impression by using *thorybos,* "tumult," as the leitmotiv of his pages on Pilate (*Ant* 18 §§58, 62, 65, 85, 88; Norden 1913: 638–44). Similarly, Philo generally describes Pilate's administration as one characterized by "his venality, his violence, his thefts, his assaults, his abusive behavior, his frequent executions of untried prisoners, and his endless savage ferocity" (*Gaium* 302, trans. Smallwood 1954).

However, both of these Jewish historians should be taken here with more than a grain of salt. Philo's characterization of Pilate is part of his exaltation of Tiberius, and we may now add that it is so reminiscent of his general characterization of corrupt governors (*Flac* 105), even to the point of several cases of verbal identity, that it cannot be taken as being particularly applicable to Pilate (Schwartz 1987: 213–14). Josephus' implication that the word *ethorybei,* "outrage" (*Ant* 18.3.5 §65) properly characterizes the execution of Jesus and the scandal in Rome (18.3.5 §§81–84) is misleading. Neither event in fact seems to have been associated with a "tumult," although there has been much speculation about the original text of the *Testimonium Flavianum.* Moreover, the Roman affair had nothing to do with Pilate. Josephus' narrative thus leaves us with only two clashes between Pilate and the Jews: the issues of the military ensigns (18.3.1 §§55–59) and the aqueduct (18.3.2 §§60–62). Of these, only the latter (perhaps to be identified with the enigmatic episode mentioned in Luke 13:1) ended with bloodshed. This is not a bad record for a term as long as Pilate's; later governors, who served for much shorter periods, would do much worse. Similarly, we may recall here the fact that Pilate, as opposed to his predecessor, left the same high priest in office throughout his term, something which probably contributed to maintaining Jewish acceptance of Roman rule. And while it is true that some of Pilate's coins included Roman cultic symbols, we hear of no opposition on this ground. Indeed, only a few years after Pilate's suspension Agrippa I, a Jewish king, was minting coins showing human figures and cultic scenes potentially more abrasive to Jewish religious sensitivities than Pilate's (Burnett 1987: 35–37). Apparently most Jews, being practical with regard to Roman and Herodian rule, were willing to let Caesarea be Caesarea as long as Jerusalem—where Agrippa minted only aniconic coins (Burnett 1987: 25; Meshorer 1982: 57–60)—could remain Jerusalem. Just as Pilate learned this lesson through the episode of the military ensigns, he may well have applied it with regard to his coins as well.

Thus, the impression that Pilate's tenure was stormy is

probably misleading. This impression, cultivated by Josephus, should be viewed as part of his general apologetic attempt to portray Roman governors as incompetent and cruel, thereby helping to explain the eventual rebellion against Rome. Pilate's tenure was probably one of continued underlying friction between governor and governed, now and then breaking out in brief incidents (note "the riot" of Mark 15:7), but not so much as to stop him from becoming, apparently, the longest-serving Roman governor of Judea. While Rome would be happy to seek a form of government for Judea which, after Pilate, would insert a Jewish, not Roman, middleman between Rome and the Jews, we need not assume that the grounds for the friction were to be found in the particular characteristics of Pilate's personality, policies, or administration. Rather, the friction was inherent in the very phenomenon of Roman rule in the land many Jews considered to be God's.

E. The Events of Pilate's Governorship

We read of several discrete incidents during Pilate's term of office, but in a few cases it is difficult to decide whether different references allude to the same events. Such is especially the case for two of the events mentioned in the NT: "the Galileans whose blood Pilate had mixed with their sacrifices" (Luke 13:1) and the "riot" (Mark 15:7; Luke 23:19). It may well be that these two references refer to the same event, and it may be that one or both of them allude to the event reported in *Ant* 18.3.2 §§60–62, but there still appears to be no way of proving or eliminating any of these possibilities.

This type of question can be considered, however, with regard to an incident described by Josephus (*JW* 2.9.2 §§169–74 and *Ant* 18.3.1 §§55–59) and one reported by Philo (*Gaium* 299–305). The incidents reported are strikingly similar: both report that Pilate introduced into Jerusalem items in honor of Tiberius which aroused Jewish protests on religious grounds; eventually, Pilate removed the offending items to Caesarea. So great is the similarity of the two accounts that it was formerly common to assume that both refer to the same event. Since the 19th century, however, it has become much more common to emphasize the differences between the two accounts. These are, especially, the fact that Philo refers to aniconic shields while Josephus refers to busts of Tiberius, and the fact that Josephus portrays Pilate backing down in the face of the Jews' obdurate willingness to suffer martyrdom rather than tolerate the iconic ensigns while Philo describes how the Jews brought Tiberius into the picture, and it is only at his orders that Pilate removes the offending shields from Jerusalem.

It seems that the earlier view (that the two authors describe the same event) is to be preferred (Schwartz 1983). Both of the above-mentioned differences in Philo's account must be seen as part of his attempt to portray Tiberius as a role model for Gaius. Namely, such a motive explains not only the introduction of Tiberius into the story, but also the transformation of the offending object into something aniconic. This allows for a striking *argumentum a minori ad maius,* which Philo makes quite explicit (§306): if Tiberius was upset over the attempt to bring something aniconic into Jerusalem, how much the more so should Gaius refrain from bringing in a statue. And, similarly, if Tiberius defended the sanctity of Jerusalem, how much more should Gaius respect the sanctity of the very Holy of Holies of the temple. In any case, it is quite difficult to understand why the Jews protested Pilate's act if, as Philo claims, the shields were aniconic; for other cases of Philonic denials which patently contradict the rest of his story, see *Gaium* 261, *Flac* 27–28 (Schwartz 1987: 86–87, n. 37). As for the discrepancy between Philo's shields and Josephus' standards, note that in *Ant* 18.3.1 §§55–56 (as in 18.5.3 §121) Josephus refers to the offending objects as images *attached to* the military standards and not as the standards themselves. There is ample evidence for such attached images being embossed upon shields (Schwartz 1983: 33). It is thus easier to assume that the two historians are referring to the same event.

After reporting the incident associated with the military standards, Josephus, in both of his works, goes on to report that Pilate used Jewish sacred funds to construct an aqueduct and that he encountered Jewish opposition which his troops put down bloodily. While it may be that the Jewish protestors were upset by the use of sacred funds for secular purposes (Feldman, *Josephus IX* LCL, 46–47 N.B.), insufficient attention has been paid to Josephus' statement that the Jews' complaint had to do with "what was done regarding *the water*" (not "the money," *Ant* 18.3.2 §60). This being the case, and given the fact that one of the aqueducts which brought water to Jerusalem in the Roman period ran through a cemetery (a fact which aroused the opposition of some if not all Jews; Patrich 1982: 25–39), it may be that the issue was not so much the use of sacred funds as a lack of concern for the water's ritual purity. As for the precise identification of Pilate's aqueduct, the matter is complicated by the conflict between Josephus' works regarding its length: 400 furlongs according to *Jewish War,* but only 200 according to *Antiquities* (corresponding to approximately 46 and 23 miles, respectively; for the remnants of aqueducts to the S of Jerusalem and their possible attribution to Pilate, see Lémonon 1981: 168–70).

Apart from the clash with the Samaritans, about which little may be said with certainty except that it led directly to Pilate's suspension from office (*Ant* 18.4.1–2 §§85–89), the only other notable event was the trial and execution of Jesus of Nazareth. See TRIAL OF JESUS. Here we are concerned only with Pilate's role. Tacitus simply states that Pilate had Jesus executed (*Ann.* 15.44), and Josephus, in the *Testimonium Flavianum* as we have it (*Ant* 18.3.3 §§63–64), adds only that Pilate did so upon Jesus' being accused by prominent Jews. See also JOSEPHUS (PERSON). Neither historian tells us what charge(s), if any, was brought against Jesus. Nevertheless, the Gospels make it abundantly clear that the charge was one of rebellion, one which was eminently in the domain of the Roman prefect. As for the Gospels' claim that Pilate was in fact unconvinced of Jesus' guilt and was forced by the Jewish mob to execute Jesus against his own better judgment, this appears to be part of the apologetics of the early Church. The Gospels' portrayal of a Jesus who posed no threat to Roman order is to be classed along with Josephus' many portrayals of 1st-century charismatics who were, it would seem, uninvolved in anything political but nevertheless executed by the Romans. They all reflect the situation of apologists for religious groups which had learned how to get along in the Roman Empire: by worshipping deities whose kingship was not of this world, and therefore did not compete with the emperor's kingship. Indeed, we may well believe Luke's report (23:12) that after Jesus' trial Pilate and Herod Antipas became friends, since only recently Herod too had executed someone very similar to Jesus, John the Baptist, whose teachings had won him popularity. We may assume that the reasoning Josephus gives for Antipas' move—"it would be much better to strike first and be rid of him before his (John's) work led to an uprising, than to wait for an upheaval, get involved in a difficult situation and see his mistake" (*Ant* 18.5.2 §118, trans. Feldman)—was good enough for Pilate vis-à-vis Jesus; for a similar "nipping in the bud," see *JW* 2.13.4 §260. As for the "prior enmity" between Pilate and Antipas which Luke mentions, one may only speculate (Otto 1913: 182–83; Hoehner 1972: 175–83).

F. Aftermath and Afterlife

After Vitellius suspended Pilate from his post in the spring of 37, we hear of no governors in Judea until the appointment of Cuspius Fadus in ca. 44 C.E., after the death of Agrippa I (*Ant* 19.9.2 §363). Fadus was appointed, according to Josephus, in order to avoid the attachment of Judea to the province of Syria, whose governor at the time had been hostile to Agrippa. The obvious implication of this explanation is that the province of Judea had been abolished, so that the end of the Jewish monarchy would lead to the land being part of Syria. This makes sense only if Judea had been attached to Syria during the years 37–41, that is, between Pilate's suspension from office and Agrippa's enthronement as king of Judea; indeed, the same is implied not only by Philo's designation of Petronius, the Syrian legate in 39/40 C.E., as "the governor of *all* Syria" (*Gaium* 207), but also by other considerations as well (Schwartz 1987: 72–77). In other words, after Pilate was suspended Caligula seems to have annexed Judea temporarily to Syria, just as Tiberius had done a few years previously with regard to Philip's territories (*Ant* 18.4.6 §108). And just as the latter were passed on to Agrippa in 37 C.E. (*Ant* 18.6.10 §237), so too was he to be given Judea as well. The move probably reflects, apart from Caligula's friendship with Agrippa, a basic underlying dissatisfaction with the system of direct rule, which all too frequently resulted in friction between the governor and the governed. Thus, Pilate's term of service played an important role in paving the way for the establishment of the last attempt at Jewish rule of Judea under Roman auspices.

Virtually nothing is known about Pilate's personal later life. Claiming a basis in ancient historical sources, Eusebius reports that Pilate came to be afflicted with such calamities that he committed suicide in 39 C.E. (*Chron.*, Helm, 178; *Hist. Eccl.* 2.7.1). The reliability of this notice has been doubted (Lémonon 1981: 268), due to its lateness and due to a certain vacillation in the way in which Eusebius refers to his sources. Nevertheless, the insistence that the notice was transmitted by ancient historians should not be lightly dismissed. Moreover, Eusebius' claim represents such a pointed deviation from the thrust of prior Church tradition that it is reasonable to assume that he wrote of Pilate's suicide precisely because he had uncovered material to that effect. Of course, we have no reason to assume that Pilate's troubles were due to his execution of Jesus or to remorse over that act; the complaints which brought about his suspension from office could well have resulted in proceedings in Rome which became unbearable (Brunt 1961).

The general thrust of Church tradition about Pilate consisted of a continuation of the Gospels' tendency to exonerate Pilate and put all the onus for the death of Jesus upon the Jews. In various *Acta Pilati* and related early Christian literature we find the repeated emphasis that Pilate had recognized Jesus' innocence and that Jesus was in fact executed by the Jews; and from portraying Pilate as recognizing Jesus' innocence it was a short step to present Pilate actually recognizing Jesus' divinity as well. See PILATE, ACTS OF. Thus, already Tertullian (ca. 200) could state that Pilate was a believer in the truth of Christianity. This was a very necessary and functional procedure, given the threatened status of the missionary religion in the empire: its spokesmen had to be able to argue that the empire's representative who had actually had the closest contact with Jesus, far from considering him a criminal worthy of condemnation, in fact thought him innocent or even more. Thus, what Paul could not do to Agrippa (Acts 26:28), the Church in fact did do to Pilate (Lémonon 1981: 249–71). As Winter points out (1974: 88–89), it was only the Christianization of the empire which removed the need for such apologetics: "Constantine eventually became converted—and Pilate missed canonization." But not totally—in the Ethiopic and Coptic churches he is indeed counted among the saints (Volkoff 1969–70).

Bibliography

Bammel, E., ed. 1970. *The Trial of Jesus.* SBT 2/13. Naperville, IL.

Blinzler, J. 1959. *The Trial of Jesus.* Trans. I. and F. McHugh. Westminster, MD.

Brunt, P. A. 1961. Charges of Provincial Maladministration under the Early Principate. *Historia* 10: 189–227.

Burnett, A. 1987. The Coinage of King Agrippa I of Judaea and a New Coin of King Herod of Chalcis. Pp. 25–38 in *Mélanges de numismatique offerts á Pierre Bastien á l'occasion de son 75ᵉ anniversaire,* ed. H. Huvelin; M. Christon; and G. Gautier. Wetteren, Belgium.

Davies, P. S. 1986. The Meaning of Philo's Text about the Gilded Shields. *JTS* n.s. 37: 109–14.

Eisler, R. 1931. *The Messiah Jesus and John the Baptist according to Flavius Josephus' Recently Rediscovered "Capture of Jerusalem" and the Other Jewish and Christian Sources.* Trans. and ed. A. H. Krappe. New York.

Hennig, D. 1975. *L. Aelius Seianus: Untersuchungen zur Reqierung des Tiberius.* Vestigia 21. Munich.

Hirschfeld, O. 1905. *Die kaiserlichen Verwaltungsbeamten bis auf Diocletian.* 2d ed. Berlin.

Hoehner, H. W. 1972. *Herod Antipas.* SNTSMS 17. London.

Holzmeister, U. 1932. Wann war Pilatus prokurator von Judaea? *Bib* 13: 228–32.

Jones, A. H. M. 1960. Procurators and Prefects in the Early Principate. Pp. 115–25 in *Studies in Roman Government and Law.* Oxford.

Laet, S. J. de. 1939. Le successeur de Ponce-Pilate. *L'Antiquité classique* 8: 413–19.

Lémonon, J.-P. 1981. *Pilate et le gouvernement de la Judée: Textes et monuments.* Paris.

Meier, P. L. 1971. The Fate of Pontius Pilate. *Hermes* 99: 362–71.
Meshorer, Y. 1982. *Ancient Jewish Coinage, II: Herod the Great through Bar Cochba.* Dix Hills, NY.
Müller, G. A. 1888. *Pontius Pilatus, der fünfte Prokurator von Judaäa und Richter Jesu von Nazareth.* Stuttgart.
Norden, E. 1913. Josephus und Tacitus über Jesus Christus und eine messianische Prophetie. *Neue Jahrbuecher für das klassische Altertum, Geschichte und deutsche Literatur* 31: 637–66.
Otto, W. 1913. *Herodes: Beiträge zur Geschichte des letzen jüdischen Königshauses.* Stuttgart.
Patrich, J. 1982. A Sadducean Halakha and the Jerusalem Acqueduct. *The Jerusalem Cathedra* 2: 25–39.
Scheidweiler, F. 1963. The Gospel of Nicodemus, Acts of Pilate and Christ's Descent into Hell. *NTApocr* 1: 444–84.
Schwartz, D. R. 1981–82. Pontius Pilate's Suspension from Office: Chronology and Sources. *Tarbiz* 51: 383–98 (in Hebrew).
———. 1982–83. Pontius Pilate's Appointment to Office and the Chronology of Josephus' *Jewish Antiquitites,* Books 18–20. *Zion* 48: 325–345 (in Hebrew).
———. 1983. Josephus and Philo on Pontius Pilate. *The Jerusalem Cathedra.* 3: 26–45.
———. 1987. *Agrippa I: The Last King of Judaea.* Monographs in Jewish History. Jerusalem (in Hebrew).
Smallwood, E. M. 1954. The Date of the Dismissal of Pontius Pilate from Judaea. *JJS* 5: 12–21.
Volkoff, O. V. 1969–70. Un Saint oublié: Ponce Pilate. *Bulletin de la Société d'archéologie copte* 20: 167–75.
Winter, P. 1974. *On the Trial of Jesus.* 2d ed. Studia Judaica 1. Berlin and New York.

DANIEL R. SCHWARTZ

PONTUS (PLACE) [Gk *Pontos*]. The name of a kingdom which occupied much of the S seaboard of the Black Sea (Gk *Pontus*), after which it was named. Residents of this region are referred to in several NT passages (Acts 2:9; 18:2; 1 Pet 1:1). The S part of this region contained a series of mountain ranges running E–W which collectively constituted the Paryadres range. Two large river systems (Halys and Iris) ran N through the mountains and provided both water and routes for communication. The kingdom's large Iranian population constructed relatively few cities, in this resembling its S neighbor, Cappadocia. Settlement remained mainly rural throughout antiquity, the principal pursuit being the growing of widely varying crops, including grains, fruits, and nuts. Rich pasturelands and an ample supply of timber, metals, and salt added to the considerable wealth of Pontus.

Pontus displayed the typical Iranian pattern of a powerful nobility with rich estates, controlling society under the suzerainty of a monarch who normally descended from a single royal family. The Hellenistic practice of intermarriage with other dynasties also prevailed in Pontus; Seleucids, Cappadocians, and Ptolemies appeared prominently in various marriages. The ruling house of Pontus prided itself on descent from the Achaemenid Persian Darius the Great.

The dominant figure in Pontic history of the late 2d and early 1st centuries before Christ was Mithradates VI, known to the Greeks as Mithradates Eupator. Soon after his accession in 120 B.C., he revealed his ambitions by murdering his mother, Queen Laodice (a Seleucid), and then his brother. Early on he determined to expand his ancestral kingdom into an empire, gradually extending his power over the Black Sea coast, Colchis, and northward into the Crimea. Then he turned S and conquered Paphlagonia, Phrygia Major, Armenia Minor, and subsequently Cappadocia.

This led him toward conflict with Rome, which regarded Cappadocia as an essential constituent of its own nascent empire in Asia Minor. To prepare himself for the inevitable struggle, Mithradates sought alliance with Parthia and with Armenia, marrying his daughter to Tigranes the Great of Armenia.

The hereditary claims of Mithradates to portions of his new holdings did not offset in Roman eyes their treaties, especially with Paphlagonia and Cappadocia. Nicomedes III of Bithynia at first cooperated with Mithradates, but soon perceived his danger. After marrying Laodice, the daughter of Mithradates who had entered the Cappadocian royal line, Nicomedes III boldly invaded Cappadocia himself. This failed, but Mithradates had to abandon plans to control Cappadocia through his sister, instead installing there his son as King Ariarathes IX.

The Cappadocians preferred to avoid rule by Pontus, however disguised, and appealed to Rome. The famous election of a new dynasty under Ariobarzanes I merely shifted the strategy of Mithradates to a series of invasions, expelling the new king five or six times in the following 30 years. This policy led Mithradates into three wars with Rome, precipitated in 89/88 B.C. by his slaughter of thousands of Romans then resident in Asia Minor and adjacent islands.

The dynastic policy of holding territory through the installation of relatives as rulers helped Mithradates during this long period of warfare. In this way, he held a considerable block of territory. His armies ranged throughout Asia Minor and parts of the Balkan peninsula, penetrating as far S as Athens. Control of these forces usually lay in the hands of close relatives of Mithradates.

Though regarded initially as a savior, Mithradates gradually lost favor among the Greeks. His measures seldom accorded with the aspirations of free cities; his Persian satrapal system entailed, rather, a governor for most cities, directly responsible to himself, and the Greek cities came to resent this. For example, Ephesus openly turned from support for him to an alliance with Rome.

As the years of warfare wore on, his commanders increasingly defected. The rise of a Pontic empire to take its place alongside those of Armenia, Parthia, and Rome began to lose momentum by 69 B.C., when Lucullus won a great victory for Rome at Tigranocerta. Tigranes retired to his own kingdom of Armenia, and Mithradates spent six largely fruitless years trying to hold his own empire together. At the end of his life, in 63 B.C., he succumbed to the treachery of a faithless son.

This man, Pharnaces II, now succeeded, but found it necessary to submit to Pompey. In return for recognition as king of Bosporus, he watched while Rome began to subdue Pontus and convert it into a province.

The mixture of royal precincts, temple estates, Greek states on the coast, and a rural hinterland made it difficult for Romans to organize. In any case, a large part of the former kingdom of Pontus lay outside the new province; these regions were held by neighboring kings.

About a dozen years after the death of Mithradates, Pharnaces II felt strong enough to begin recovering portions of the ancestral kingdom. The civil war between Pompey and Caesar seemed to him an opportunity to accelerate this movement, and he regained much of Pontus. The arrival of Caesar in 47, who "came, saw, and conquered" Pharnaces, ended this phase.

A branch of the family now took up rule in the Bosporus, and from it descended a long line of rulers there.

A son of Pharnaces II named Darius reigned in Pontus from 39 to 37 B.C., but this ended rule by the ancient royal line. In his arrangements for the East, Antony put forward several new kings, loyal to himself, including Archelaus of Cappadocia. He found as well a new king for Pontus.

Polemo I, the son of an aristocrat from the Greek city of Laodiceia on the Lycus in Asia Minor, proceeded to the rule of Pontus in 37. He bore no relation to any royal family in Asia Minor, so far as presently known. If that was his situation, Antony chose him to ensure that his loyalty would remain undivided.

Polemo served vigorously, soon gaining full control of Pontus and then assisting Antony against Parthia. He extended his control into Colchis and later into Armenia Minor.

At Actium, Polemo was represented by an army, but did not attend in person. At least by 26 B.C., he received the recognition of Augustus, and became a "friend and ally" of the Roman people. Polemo moved to reestablish the claims of Pontus to Bosporus, where he married its queen Dynamis, granddaughter of Mithradates Eupator.

The marriage may not have lasted: she is later recorded ruling apparently alone, and he eventually had another wife, Queen Pythodoris, probably a granddaughter of Marc Antony by an eastern woman (*ANRW* 2/7: 913–30). She, like Polemo, came from W Asia Minor, in her case the town of Tralles near the Maeander river, lying some 60 miles W of his ancestral town, Laodiceia.

From this marriage, Polemo had three children, one of whom later served as queen of Thrace and one as king of Armenia. His five grandchildren included another queen of Thrace and a king of Thrace, a king of Armenia Minor, a queen of Bosporus, and King Polemo II of Pontus.

Polemo met his death fighting in the Bosporus, perhaps about 8 B.C. Queen Pythodoris succeeded to the throne of Pontus, where her coins mount to "Year 60." Estimates of her regal span run as high as A.D. 35. She survived a second husband, King Archelaus of Cappadocia; he died in Rome in A.D. 17.

The last king of Pontus, Polemo II, the grandson of Pythodoris and Polemo I, came to the throne in A.D. 38, recognized by Caligula, with whom he had been "raised together." Polemo ruled during the demanding times when the Julio-Claudians sought to solve "the Armenian question" by force; under Nero, he occupied a portion of Armenia. He also ruled part of Cilicia.

Polemo attended an important meeting of allied kings held by Agrippa I, grandson of Herod the Great, in A.D. 44. Josephus (*Ant* 19 §338–42) records this assembly of six kings and notes that it alarmed the Roman governor of Syria.

Polemo's marriage to Julia Bernice of Judea, a great-granddaughter of Herod the Great, failed early. However, he apparently married a princess from Emesa who became Queen Julia Mamaea; a joint coinage with her calls him "Great King," possibly referring to his brief rule in a part of Armenia.

The Parthians took over Armenia in A.D. 66, but by then Polemo had lost Pontus. He was said to have abdicated voluntarily, about A.D. 63 (Suetonius, *Nero* 18). He apparently retained his responsibilities in Cilicia and issued coins there for several years more. One type can be dated to the reign of Galba in A.D. 68 (Sullivan 1979: 6–20).

Pontus earned its prominence in NT times. Two dynasties, the ancient house to which Mithradates Eupator belonged and the "Zenonid" house from which both Polemos arose, conferred stability on Pontus during the 1st century B.C. and most of the 1st century after. After 63, the land entered the Roman system of provinces. For centuries longer, ecclesiastical lists and the general Church councils continued to note some of its cities under the descriptive rubric, "Pontus Polemoniacus" (Jones 1971: Appendix IV, Table xxiii).

Bibliography

Gutschmid, A. von. 1892. *Untersuchungen über die Geschichte des pontischen Reichs.* Leipzig.

Hoben, W. 1969. *Untersuchungen zur Stellung kleinasiatischer Dynasten in den Machtkämpfen der ausgehenden Römischen Republik.* Mainz.

Jones, A. H. M. 1971. *Cities of the Eastern Roman Provinces.* 2d ed. Oxford.

Reinach, T. 1890. *Mithridate Eupator, Roi de Pont.* Paris.

Sullivan, R. D. 1979. King Marcus Antonius Polemo. *Numismatic Chronicle* (ser. 7) 19: 6–20.

———. 1989. *Near Eastern Royalty and Rome, 100–30 B.C.* Toronto.

RICHARD D. SULLIVAN

POOL OF SHELAH. See SHELAH, POOL OF.

POOL OF SILOAM. See SILOAM, POOL OF.

POOR, POVERTY. This entry consists of two articles, one surveying how the subjects of poverty and poor people are treated in the Hebrew Bible, and the other surveying how these subjects are handled in the New Testament.

OLD TESTAMENT

Poverty in the Hebrew Bible denotes (1) a lack of economic resources and material goods; and (2) political and legal powerlessness and oppression. Neither a social class nor a political party in ancient Israel, the poor constituted a diverse body of social actors: small farmers, day laborers, construction workers, beggars, debt slaves, village dwellers.

Various strands of the biblical text discuss the plight of the poor, offering diverging analyses of their situation. *Legal texts* regulate the treatment of the poor; in particular, the legal codes seek to ensure the social well-being of the poor through the redistribution of goods and food, and through the establishment of restrictions regarding slave ownership (i.e., the system of debt servitude) and the treatment of wage laborers. *Prophetic texts* concern themselves with the poor who are economically exploited by the large landowners and ruling members of ancient Israelite society. The *wisdom tradition* divides over the question of poverty: Proverbs, in a somewhat condescending and possibly censorious tone, promotes the traditional wisdom view that poverty is the undesirable consequence of laziness, whereas Job, and to a lesser extent Ecclesiastes, understand poverty to be the result of political and economic exploitation. The *Psalms* display a rich language for poverty and many texts discuss God's concern for the poor at least in general terms. However, though much scholarly work has been devoted to characterizing the ideas of poverty found in the Psalter, it is difficult to determine to what extent the language has moved away from concrete cases of poverty to a more spiritualized level of worship discourse. Outside of these blocks of literature, the topic of poverty is treated only occasionally. The *narrative literature* of the Pentateuch is unconcerned with the issue; likewise, the Deuteronomistic History does not take up the topic. Ruth (3:10), Esther (9:22), and Daniel (4:24—Eng 27) only touch on poverty in an ancillary way. More significantly, the question of poverty emerges as an issue in the reforms of Nehemiah (5:1–13).

When investigating the meaning of these words, it is important to keep in mind that context and usage, *not* etymology, are decisive in determining the meaning of a word. While this observation may seem obvious, too many of the studies of the Hebrew terms for "poor," particularly of the vocabulary in the Psalms (e.g., Rahlfs 1892; Birkeland 1932), have mistakenly become enmeshed in a discussion of Hebrew verbal roots or the Semitic cognate background of the term, rather than on a word's actual usage. It is far more important to explicate the semantic field of these words as they actually appear in the biblical text (cf. Wittenberg 1986).

It is also important to note the distribution of the vocabulary throughout the Hebrew Bible: no one biblical writer or text uses all the Hebrew terms for "poor"/"poverty." In fact, the distribution reveals a selectivity on the part of the biblical authors: *rāš,* for example, is a wisdom word and not a prophetic word. This selectivity should also alert us to the fact that even when the various blocks of the biblical text make use of the same Hebrew term, the writers may not mean the same thing by that term: in Proverbs, for example, the *dal* is a lazy person; whereas for the prophets, the *dal* is an object of exploitation. By way of a contemporary illustration, we would say that a future historian investigating religious and political movements of the late 20th century would need to be aware that groups using the word "liberty" and groups using the word "liberation" diverge from one another in terms of their social analysis and often in terms of their sociological background. This is the case, even though the terms "liberty" and "liberation" share a common etymology. The same considerations apply where these political movements make use of the same term, such as "poor," since they mean radically different things by this word.

There are a number of Hebrew words for "poor"/"poverty": *ʾebyôn, dal, dallâ, maḥsôr, miskēn, miskĕnût, ʿānî, ʿănāwîm,* and *rāš.* (The reader may wish to note that these words are treated in Hebrew alphabetical order, with the exception of *raš,* which has been moved forward to highlight its connection with other wisdom words for "poor.")

A. The Beggarly Poor: *ʾebyôn*
B. The Poor Peasant Farmer: *dal*
C. The Lazy Poor: *maḥsôr*
D. Poverty Is Better: *miskēn*
E. Political and Economic Inferiority: *rāš*
F. The Injustice of Oppression: *ʿānî*
G. A Political Movement of the Pious Poor?: *ʿănāwîm*
H. Conclusion

A. The Beggarly Poor: *ʾebyôn*

The term *ʾebyôn* ("economically or legally distressed; destitute; beggar") occurs 61 times in the Hebrew Bible.

1. In the Prophetic Corpus. The word appears 17 times in the prophetic literature, where it can connote (1) general physical insecurity and homelessness (Isa 14:30; 25:4; Amos 8:4); (2) hunger and thirst (Isa 32:6–7; 41:7; Ezek 16:49); (3) mistreatment by the rulers of society and other evildoers (Isa 29:19; Jer 2:34; 20:13; Ezek 18:12; 22:29; Amos 4:1); (4) unfair handling of legal cases (Isa 32:7; Jer 5:28; 22:16; Amos 5:12); and (5) economic exploitation (Amos 2:6; 8:6). Humbert characterizes the occurrences of this term in the prophetic literature as "sporadic" (1952: 3). However, it seems more correct to suggest that *ʾebyôn* appears in a particular strain of the prophetic material, and, when used in tandem with *ʿānî* and *dal,* represents a stylized mode of expression for speaking of poverty (cf. van Leeuwen 1955: 16; see further under F.1 below). It is noteworthy that Micah chose not to use *ʾebyôn* or any of the other terms for "poor," even though his oracles addressed the subject of poverty in stark detail. (The divergence in word choice may lend additional support to Wolff's thesis that Micah stems from a rural background; 1978; 1981: 17–25).

2. In the Psalms. The word *ʾebyôn* appears 23 times in the Psalms, most often in Psalms of Lament. The situation of the *ʾebyôn* is described rather vaguely by such terms as "robbed" (Ps 35:10; Heb *gzl*) or "suffering" (107:41; Heb *ʿônî*). They are the victims of the "wicked" (Heb *rāšāʿ*), an otherwise undefined group (109:16). Only two psalms give more specific data. In one (Ps 37:14), the poor are depicted as the victims of the swords and bows of the wicked; perhaps the writer intends us to understand this concretely, though it is also possible that it is metaphorical for any kind of suffering. From the other text (Ps 132:15)—with its statement that God gives food to the *ʾebyôn*—we can infer that the poor are those who lack nourishment, a concrete understanding of the term that is consistent with the word's usage in the prophetic (see above) and legal materials (described below). The notion that God assists the poor *(ʾebyôn)* is expressed in a number of psalms: some portray God as the one who rescues the poor (Pss 35:10; 40:18—Eng 17; 69:34—Eng 33; 70:6—Eng 5; 72:12, 13; 109:31; 113:7; 140:13—Eng 12), while others are prayers calling on God to help the *ʾebyôn* (Pss 72:4; 82:4; 86:1; 109: 22).

Humbert maintains that since the Psalms were cultic texts, they were infused with royal ideology and governed by foreign influence (1952: 3). However, the high proportion of instances of *ʾebyôn* in the Psalter contrasts markedly with the rarity of the term in Proverbs and the complete absence of *ʾebyôn* in the narrative literature of the Pentateuch and Deuteronomistic History (DH)—texts that certainly reflect royal literary traditions. The Psalms' diverse vocabulary for poverty requires an explanation other than Humbert's view that they are imbued with royal ideology. The diverging vocabulary distribution between the Psalter and the narrative literature would seem to favor the view that the Psalms embody a variety of cultural influences, not simply royal tradition, and reflect a diverse set of ideas regarding matters of social justice, though with a less sharply defined agenda than the prophets.

3. In Wisdom Texts. The term *ʾebyôn* occurs in the wisdom texts of Proverbs (4 times) and Job (6 times). In Proverbs, the word only occurs once in all of the sentential literature of Proverbs 10–29, and there it is linked with the word *dal*; the text states that helping the *ʾebyôn* is one way to honor God (Prov 14:31). (When discussing poverty, Proverbs 10–29 typically uses *dal, maḥsôr,* and *rāš*; see below.) The other three occurrences of the term are found in chaps. 30–31 of Proverbs, and there it is always paired with *ʿānî*. In the words of Agur (Prov 30:1–33), it is said that there are some who devour the poor (Prov 30:14), though the precise meaning of this statement is not specified. In the sayings of Lemuel's mother, the hearer is enjoined to assist the poor (Prov 31:20) and speak out for them in their legal cases (Prov 31:9). The rarity of the term *ʾebyôn* in Proverbs is significant: it was definitely a prophetic (see above) and legal term (see below) and not the preferred word for Israel's "wise" to describe poverty (for wisdom terms, see *dal, maḥsôr, miskēn,* and *rāš* below).

In Job, the *ʾebyôn* are victims, whether of economic injustice (Job 24:4) or murder (Job 24:14). The book explores Job's relation to the poor, tracing Job's efforts to assist and defend them: he assisted them as a father would (Job 29:16); he grieved for them in their misfortune (Job 30:25); and he clothed them (Job 31:19). The book emphasizes these concrete deeds as the basis of Job's innocence before his friends (and to God). Job's actions match those of the God who saves the poor *(ʾebyôn)* from the strong (Heb *ḥāzāq*), a theme set out early in the book (5:15) and to which the book inexorably works as it seeks a solution to the problem of the suffering of the innocent.

The term *ʾebyôn* occurs more times in Job than it does in Proverbs, and while it is difficult to know precisely what significance to accord such a small sampling, this slightly larger number of instances in Job does seem to fit a curious distribution pattern for the words for "poor" in the Hebrew Bible: the terms for "poor" in Job *(ʾebyôn, dal, ʿānî)* are those also found in the prophetic writings, while the most distinctive wisdom words for "poor" *(maḥsôr, miskēn, rāš)* are conspicuously absent from Job. This gives the book of Job its "prophetic" character. Likewise, the book's defense of the poor and its concrete understanding of their situation mirrors the prophetic analysis of poverty (see Pleins 1987).

4. In Historical Narratives. It is striking that the term *ʾebyôn* is missing from the narrative materials of the DH and of the Pentateuch. Indeed, the overall scarcity of any of the terms for "poor" in these extensive bodies of narrative material is noteworthy, suggesting that ancient Israel's historians were reluctant to take up the topic of poverty (see further E.3 below). For the DH, this means a rejection (or at least an avoidance) of the prophetic contention that both Israel and Judah were destroyed in part because they mistreated the poor. This historian instead attributed the collapse of the kingdoms to the failure of kingship and to cultic abuses.

In the course of the DH, the word *ʾebyôn* occurs only in the Song of Hannah (1 Sam 2:8), a poetic text inserted into the larger block of narrative materials. This solitary appearance casts in sharp relief the historian's preference to avoid the topic of poverty. Clearly, the radical sentiments regarding poverty expressed in the Song of Hannah have little to do with the overall agenda of the Deuteronomistic Historian, who has selected the poetic text mainly because it enhanced the writer's support of the establishment of the rule of David through the agency of Samuel.

The only other occurrence of *ʾebyôn* in historical narratives is in the later text of Esther (9:22), where the term appears to refer to those to whom alms are given, that is, to beggars (cf. *BLe,* 500; Humbert 1952: 6). This reference lends support to the view that *ʾebyôn* refers to the beggarly poor.

5. In the Legal Materials. When *ʾebyôn* does appear in the Pentateuch, it occurs (9 times) only in restricted sections of the legal materials in Exodus and Deuteronomy (Exodus 23; Deuteronomy 15; 24). In Exodus, one is enjoined not to subvert the legal judgments made on behalf of the *ʾebyôn* (Exod 23:6); elsewhere they are permitted to eat the food that grows on land that has been left fallow (23:11). Humbert's observation that the legal material envisions the *ʾebyônîm* (plural) as those who are deprived of a proper diet (1952: 4–5; cf. Exod 23:11) is consistent with other instances of *ʾebyôn* in the Hebrew Bible (Isa 32:6–7, 41:7; Ezek 16:49; Ps 132:15). Deuteronomy 15 picks up on this latter Exodus text and expands on the topic of the fallow year by taking up the knotty issue of lending to the poor as the Sabbatical Year approaches, which is repeatedly encouraged throughout the passage (vv 4, 7, 9, 11). The term occurs only one other time in Deuteronomy, where it is legislated that poor laborers, whether natives or foreigners, must receive their wages (Deut 24:14). From these legal texts we obtain the picture that the *ʾebyôn* are landless wage laborers living on the edge of existence. Certainly this is consistent with the notion that this level of poverty includes begging as a way of life.

6. Meaning, History, and Etymology. There seems to be no evidence for the view that the term *ʾebyôn* has a religious connotation of patient, pious endurance amid misery as some have maintained (Kuschke 1939: 53; *GesB,* 4; van Leeuwen 1955: 16). The term simply points out severe economic deprivation. This condition may evoke the concern of God and the community, but the poverty of the *ʾebyôn* in and of itself is not considered a virtue or a way of life to be pursued for religious reasons.

On the basis of the use of *ʾebyôn* in Exodus 23 and in Amos, Humbert argues that the word came into play during the royal period; he further maintains that it did so under foreign influence, as evidenced by its appearance in such literature as the Psalms and the wisdom writings—texts which have "royal" connections (Humbert 1952: 3–

4). However, it is terribly difficult to date the psalmic and wisdom materials; furthermore, the Covenant Code of Exodus 23 doubtless reflects premonarchic (not royal) legal traditions. Likewise, it is very difficult to agree with Humbert that the word *ᵓebyôn* held a more important place in the time of the monarchy but fell into disuse in later periods (Humbert 1952: 3). The term is found throughout the Psalms—texts that are difficult to date, but which surely stem from both preexilic and postexilic times. Finally, it is hard to know how to assess the possible effects of foreign influence on Israel's literature as mediated through monarchic institutions.

As an adjective, the word *ᵓebyôn* has been commonly linked with and derived from the verb *ᵓābâ,* "be willing, consent" (*BDB,* 2) and its Semitic counterparts (cf. Birkeland 1932: 21; *TDOT* 1: 27–41; *THAT* 1: 20–25; Kuschke 1939: 53; van Leeuwen 1955: 15; von Soden 1969). One problem with the linkage between *ᵓebyôn* and *ᵓābâ* is that many of the analyses tend to confuse English "want" in the popular and active sense of "to be willing" with "want" in the older and passive sense of "to be lacking something"; *ᵓābâ* appears only to mean "to be willing; to desire" and not "to be in need" (von Soden 1969: 324). This interpretation finds support in the Old Aramaic Barrakab inscription from Zinjirli (THAT 1: 20; Barrakab line 14; KAI no. 216; cf. *TSSI* 2: 90), which reads: "And my brothers, the kings, desired [*htnᵓbw*] all the richness of my house." Yet, this would argue in favor of linking *ᵓebyôn* with the verb *yᵓb*/*tᵓb,* "long for," attested only in Psalm 119 and possibly representing Aramaic influence (Ps 119:40, 131, 174; cf. *THAT* 1: 21; Honeyman 1944: 81). This suggestion finds some support from *Leviticus Rabbah,* which states, "He is called *'ebyon'* because he longs [*mtᵓb*] for everything" (*Lev. Rab.* 34:6, Soncino edition). On the whole, however, the precise relation between *ᵓebyôn* and *ᵓābâ* remains difficult to specify, and in any event does not clarify the meaning of *ᵓebyôn.* The problems associated with the search for a Semitic background for *ᵓebyôn* have led some to postulate an Egyptian origin for the term in the Coptic *EBIHN* "a poor, wretched person" (Crum 1939: 53; cf. *TDOT* 1: 28–29; Lambdin 1953: 146). However, since counterparts to *ᵓebyôn* crop up in Ugaritic (*ᵓabynt*; Aqhat I:17) and Amorite (von Soden 1969), there seems to be no need to seek a Coptic derivation for the term. Ward, in fact, suggests that the Coptic was borrowed from a Semitic original (1960: 32).

B. The Poor Peasant Farmer: *dal*

The term *dal* ("poor; weak, inferior; lacking") is used 48 times in the Hebrew Bible, and half of these occur in prophetic and proverbial texts. In many cases it seems to allude to the plight of the beleaguered peasant farmer.

1. In the Prophetic Corpus. The term *dal* appears 12 times in the prophetic literature, less frequently than the words *ᵓebyôn* or *ᶜānî.* It can connote (1) unfair treatment in legal cases (Isa 10:2; 11:4); (2) unfair grain taxes paid to the large landowners (Amos 5:11); (3) abuses in the debt-slavery system (Amos 8:6); and (4) a lack of grazing land (Isa 14:30). Elsewhere, the term is used of those who suffer exploitation and oppression of an undefined character (Isa 26:6; Amos 2:7; 4:1). On two occasions God is depicted as the protector of the *dal* (Isa 25:4; Zeph 3:12). For Isaiah, God's liberation of the poor will lead to their trampling those who are in power (Isa 26:5–6). For Jeremiah, the *dal* stand in contrast to society's political and religious authorities (Jer 5:4–5; Heb *gĕdōlîm*). One text in Jeremiah explicitly defines *dal* as one "who has nothing" (Jer 39:10), meaning people who lack vineyards and fields. In the prophetic texts, therefore, the term *dal* depicts the politically and economically marginalized elements of society. The mention of severe grain taxes (Amos 5:11) and lack of sufficient grazing and farmland (Isa 14:30; Jer 39:10) suggests an agricultural background for this word—a background that is confirmed by uses of the word *dal* elsewhere in the Hebrew Bible (see below).

2. In Narrative and Legal Texts. The term *dal* appears only 5 times in the Pentateuch. It is found twice in legal contexts where the exhortation is made not to show favoritism toward persons, whether rich or poor, when making legal decisions (Exod 23:3; Lev 19:15). The word appears twice in ritual contexts, once where the *dal* is enjoined to pay the same census tax as the "rich" (Heb *ᶜāšîr*), and once where the poor are permitted to bring less costly offerings because of their status as people of lesser means (Exod 30:15; Lev 14:21). It is difficult to know why in the one case the rich and poor are not distinguished, whereas in the other, the poor are treated according to their financial circumstances (cf. Lev 5:11; 12:8). It may be that the principle of not showing favoritism to the poor had its limits, or it may be that the *dal* was not the poorest of the poor, that is, a person entirely without property, but was someone of modest means who stood somewhat above the *ᵓebyôn* on the social ladder (cf. *TDOT* 3: 219; Kennedy 1898: 84–86). Because of the agricultural nature of the passages (*TDOT* 3: 219), the texts may have in mind the "small farmer" (cf. the discussion on *dallâ* below). The only other occurrence of *dal* in the Pentateuch is in a narrative context where the subject is not poverty but a description of the emaciated condition of the cows in Pharaoh's dreams (Gen 41:19). This most vividly captures something of the image that must have come to mind when an Israelite thought of the condition of the *dal.* Note that the distribution of the word *dal* follows the same pattern as other words for "poor" in the Pentateuch: it occurs almost exclusively in legal texts and is only rarely found in the narrative materials, and when found in the narrative materials, the terms are rarely used to discuss poverty per se.

The term appears incidentally three times in the DH, not surprisingly in contexts focusing on issues other than poverty. Twice the word is used to indicate the political weakness of one group in relation to another (Judg 6:15; 2 Sam 3:1), and once it is used to speak of Amnon's dejected and haggard appearance—the result of his frustrated sexual desires for Tamar (2 Sam 13:4). Thus, though rare in the DH, the use of the word in this narrative material gives us two layers of meaning that illuminate the notion of *dal* elsewhere in the Hebrew Bible: (1) political weakness; (2) physically worn out. However, none of the occurrences of the term *dal* in the DH carries with it the notion of "poverty," which does set its usage apart from usage elsewhere in the Hebrew Bible. Finally, we may note that in the course of the DH, the word *dal* also turns up in a poetic context (1 Sam 2:8), the Song of Hannah (see A.4).

Elsewhere in the narrative texts, *dal* appears only in Ruth (3:10), where it stands opposite *ʿāšîr*, "rich," and means simply "poor": Boaz praises Ruth for not turning to younger men, whether poor or rich. Considering the agricultural context of the book of Ruth, it is perhaps no coincidence that the narrator chose to use a word for "poor" that applies to poor peasant farmers.

3. In the Psalms. Notably, the word *dal* is quite rare in the Psalter, occurring only 5 times in 4 psalms. Most of the occurrences concern God's care of the poor (Pss 72:13; 82:3, 4; 113:7), though the situations are largely left undefined. One text alludes to injustices in matters of law, for God calls on the divine assembly to judge the poor justly (Ps 82:3). While most of the texts concern God's attitude toward the *dal,* only one text deals with a person's relation to the poor, where a blessing is pronounced on those who are considerate toward them (Ps 41:2). The Psalms are thus even more vague about the *dal* than they are about the *ʾebyôn,* making it difficult to know how explicit these texts intend to be about physical poverty.

4. In Wisdom Texts. In contrast with these rather sporadic occurrences throughout the biblical corpus, the frequent use of *dal* in Proverbs (15 times) and in Job (6 times) suggests at least in part that this was a wisdom term. This is particularly the case for Proverbs: when one considers the statistics for those words for "poor"/"poverty" that Proverbs shares with other blocks of biblical material—namely *ʾebyôn, dal,* and *ʿānî*—the word *dal* is definitely the preferred proverbial word for expressing the wisdom tradition's understanding of poverty. The statistical difference between the frequent use of *dal* in Proverbs and its rare occurrence in the Psalms is thus primarily a synchronic matter of conscious word choice (reflecting diverging ideological perspectives) rather than a diachronic matter of the Psalms being later than Proverbs (when *dal* supposedly fell into disuse in the postexilic period, as Fabry [*TDOT* 3: 215] suggests; cf. Donald 1964: 29). The fact that *dal* appears 11 times in Sirach confirms the notion that *dal* is a favorite word of wisdom writers, even in very late periods.

In Proverbs, the term *dal,* like *maḥsôr* and *rāš* (see C. and E. below), is used only in chaps. 10–29, i.e. the sentential literature (contrast *ʾebyôn* above). This type of poverty is contrasted with wealth: it shatters the poor (10:15); it is a friendless circumstance (19:4); however, it may produce insight that the rich can fail to grasp (28:11). Charity toward the poor is elevated as a virtue of the wise person, though the motivation for such benevolence is to reap the rewards that come from having a reputation for magnanimity (19:17; 22:9; 29:9). Although the life of poverty is certainly no virtue to the proverbial writers, the pursuit of wealth should not involve mistreating the poor. Frequently wisdom warns of the dangers inherent in attempting to profit off the *dal* (14:31; 21:13; 22:16; 28:3, 8, 15).

In Job, the word *dal,* like *ʾebyôn,* becomes the measure of Job's innocence. However, unlike *ʾebyôn,* which is nearly always on the lips of Job, the word *dal* is almost always used by one of Job's accusers. This is appropriate if we consider that Job's friends are caricatures of wisdom teachers—the word *dal* is supposed to be on their lips. In the first instance (5:16), Eliphaz uses the term *dal* (along with *ʾebyôn*) to frame the book's challenge against Job concerning his treatment of the poor—a theme that is pursued in greater detail after chap. 20. Zophar speaks of the *dal,* and in true proverbial fashion he notes that the wicked who profit off the poor will lose their wealth (Job 20:10, 19). Zophar's use of the word *dal* is the first use of a term for "poor" since Eliphaz's challenge in chap. 5; we should see in this a conscious effort on the writer's part to reassert the accusation against Job regarding his treatment of the poor. In so doing, the writer uses this word to mark a significant turning point in the discussion: from this chapter on, the treatment of the poor becomes a major motif in the book and for Job's friends it is a central issue in assessing Job's integrity. Twice Elihu mentions the *dal* and speaks of God's attitude toward the poor. On the one hand, God is impartial toward both poor and nobles (Heb *śārîm;* 34:19); on the other hand, God is said to strike down the wicked, and thus the cry of the poor comes to God (34:28; the statements of Elihu have notable counterparts in the Pentateuch, see above; cf. the later Sir 35:12–14, also in the wisdom tradition). All of these uses of *dal* in accusatory contexts render Job's own use of *dal* most poignant: he claims to have met the needs of the poor (31:16). In each occurrence, it is clear that the writer has in mind the very concrete suffering of the poor—suffering that is not experienced by the well-to-do. Unfortunately, the text does not seek to further specify the nature of the deprivation experienced by the *dal.*

5. A Ugaritic Text. The ancient and widespread concern for the *dal* is strikingly confirmed in the Keret Epic (14th century B.C.E.). In one passage, King Keret is denounced by his son Yassib, who accuses his father of failing to execute the duties of the royal office, blaming this failure on his father's weakness and illness. In the course of his diatribe, Yassib sustains his critique of the king by pointing out how the poor, specifically the *dl,* have been treated: "You do not banish the extortioners of the poor [*dl*]" (Gibson 1977: 102). Interestingly, this passage groups together the mistreatment of the *dl* with the failure to feed the orphan *(ytm)* and the widow *(ʾalmnt)*—a word grouping that directly parallels the biblical vocabulary concerning the disenfranchised (cf. Isa 10:2; Ps 82:3–4; Job 31:16–17).

6. *dallâ,* pl. *dallôt.* A related term, *dallâ,* occurs twice in 2 Kings and three times in Jeremiah. In all these passages, the term refers to a social grouping or class at the time of the Exile, a group generally thought to represent the lowest orders of society (2 Kgs 24:14; 25:12; Jer 40:7; 52:15, 16). The *dallat ʿam hāʾāreṣ,* "poor of the people of the land," *dallat/dallôt hāʾāreṣ,* "poor of the land," and the *dallôt hāʿām,* "poor of the people," are those who remained in Judah after the Babylonian invasion of 587 B.C.E. They are explicitly depicted as people who were forced to work for the Babylonian conquerors as agricultural laborers, suggesting that this phrase may refer to "poor farm laborers" (cf. CAD 3: 173). Curiously, the narrative in Jeremiah (39:10) diverges significantly from its counterpart in 2 Kings (25:12). Whereas in 2 Kings the Babylonian commander is said to force the *dallâ* to be vineyard workers and field laborers for the conqueror, the reading in Jeremiah is altered to produce a radically different picture: there the *dal* are not forced laborers, but simply people to whom vineyards and fields are given. It would seem that the writer of Jeremiah has toned down the depiction of the Babylonians to cast the conqueror in the best possible light—a view that is consistent with other sections of Jeremiah (e.g., chaps. 27 and 29). In any case, these passages link the terms *dallâ* and *dal* to agricultural vocations, and their usage in 2 Kings and Jeremiah lends support to the view developed in this section that these terms refer to poor peasant farmers.

C. The Lazy Poor: *maḥsôr*

The word *maḥsôr* ("lack of, or need for, material goods") occurs 13 times in the Hebrew Bible, mainly in Proverbs. Its rarity throughout the rest of the Hebrew Bible would seem to mark off *maḥsôr* as a wisdom term.

1. In Wisdom Texts. Of the 8 occurrences in Proverbs, only one (6:11) is outside chaps. 10–29. Similarly, *dal* and *rāš* only occur in Proverbs 10–29. This vocabulary distribution serves to bind together chaps. 10–29 and isolate them from chaps. 1–9 and 30–31. Proverbs 1–9 is instruction that is largely unconcerned with the topic of poverty; chaps. 30–31 use a different terminology, namely the combination *ʿānî* and *ʾebyôn* (see A.3). In Proverbs, *maḥsôr* connotes (1) poverty that results from laziness (6:11; 14:23; 21:5; 24:34), and (2) poverty that results from excessive living (21:17). Since the ethic of Proverbs is the ethic of the bureaucratic elite (cf. Pleins 1987), the text tends to stress hard work and moderation. As a result, the wise are terribly concerned about the dangers of laziness. And yet, the wisdom teachers do not completely denigrate those who are poor: generosity toward the poor is a virtue in the wisdom tradition, and the wise warn that a lack of generosity can lead one into poverty (11:24; 22:16; 24:34).

Significantly, the word does not appear at all in Job or Ecclesiastes. The absence of this term and several others from Job is one line of argument for separating the social agenda of Job from that of Proverbs.

2. In Legal Texts. The term appears only once in the Pentateuch in the legal materials of Deuteronomy, where the community is enjoined to lend to the poor what they lack in material goods *(maḥsôr)* as the Sabbatical Year approaches (Deut 15:8). The context implies concrete items, though they are not specified. The rarity of the term in the Pentateuch is one indication that the *maḥsôr* had particular importance in the wisdom sphere.

3. In the Psalms. The word *maḥsôr* appears only once in the Psalter, in a supposed Thanksgiving Hymn (Psalm 34). However, the particular verse in question (v 10) is part of a section that looks more like a Wisdom Psalm (viz. 34:9–15). The text states that those who fear God lack *(maḥsôr)* nothing, and by implication appears to mean they do not lack food (cf. 34:11), though this may be metaphorical.

4. In Historical Narrative. Elsewhere, the word is found only in Judges (3 times). One occurrence is in the story of the Danite spies (Judg 18:1–31), who investigate the town of Laish and find it a prosperous place like Sidon (cf. Judg 18:7), a town where nothing is lacking (*maḥsôr;* Judg 18:10). Clearly, material goods are meant here. Twice the term *maḥsôr* occurs in the story of the Levite's concubine (Judg 19:1–30). The Levite and his concubine report that they do not lack *(maḥsôr)* any necessary supplies, listing in their possession such items as animal fodder, bread, and wine (Judg 19:19). And in reply the Ephraimite man tells them that "all you need [*maḥsôr*] I will take care of" (Judg 19:20). In both cases, *maḥsôr* denotes a lack of material goods.

D. Poverty Is Better: *miskēn*

The word *miskēn,* "poor," is a late Hebrew term for "poor," appearing only in the wisdom text of Ecclesiastes (4 times).

One text in Ecclesiastes (4:13) advises that it is better to be a poor *(miskēn)* youth than an old, foolish king who fails to heed warnings. The youth can rise out of the prison of poverty (Heb *bēt hāsûrîm*), but the king is in danger of collapsing into poverty *(rāš).* Another text (9:14–16), elevates the wisdom of a poor but wise man, who could have saved the town in time of siege if only the people would have heeded the poor man's advice. Such comparative statements about wisdom amid poverty are also found in Proverbs (19:1, 22; 28:6). While Ecclesiastes reflects the typical wisdom teaching on this point, the writer also acknowledges the systemic nature of poverty (see E.1 below).

A related term denoting scarcity of material goods, *miskĕnût,* appears once in Deuteronomy (8:9).

E. Political and Economic Inferiority: *rāš*

The word *rāš* ("economically poor, of modest means; beggar, bum") occurs 22 times in the Hebrew Bible, mainly in wisdom texts, and should be viewed as a wisdom term (it does not appear at all in the Pentateuch or the prophetic writings); the word *rāš* refers to someone who is politically and economically inferior, frequently referring to someone who is lazy.

1. In Wisdom Texts. The majority of occurrences are in Proverbs (15 times), all restricted to the sentential literature of chaps. 10–29 (cf. the usage of *dal* and *maḥsôr* in this regard). In Proverbs, this term connotes (1) poverty that results from laziness (10:4); and (2) want that arises from disordered living (13:23). This type of poverty is seen to be a friendless condition (14:20; 19:7; 28:3). The wisdom analysis of the origins of poverty in personal laziness diverges radically from other streams of biblical tradition, such as the prophetic and legal, which see the problem of poverty in terms of social structures and power arrangements. The wisdom analysis is to be explained by the fact that sociologically it finds its home in the educational circles of the social elite of ancient Israel (see Pleins 1987). Thus the term *rāš* often stands in contrast to "rich" (Heb *ʿāšîr* in 13:8; 14:20; 18:23; 22:7; 28:6; verb *ʿāšār* in 10:4). In one of these texts (18:23), the word *rāš* would seem to be best translated as "beggar" or "bum," for the text depicts this person imploring the rich for assistance. Consistent with the proverbial philosophy, this type of poor person is not to be mocked because God creates all people (17:5; 22:2; 28:27; 29:13). The term *rāš* is used on several occasions to teach that there are worse things than poverty, namely perverse speech and stupidity (19:1), lying (19:22), and evil deeds (28:6). Obviously, the use of this teaching device does not mean that the wise cultivated poverty as a virtue; rather, they drew on these proverbs to help their students grasp how one acts if one embodies wisdom. Wisdom is more than knowing how to respect wealth and poverty.

The word *rāš* is used twice in Ecclesiastes. One text (4:14) concerns the contrast between the poor but wise youth and an old, foolish king who does not heed warnings and collapses into poverty (see D. above). In another passage, the word *rāš* is used in the context of structural economic exploitation, a usage that is unusual for *rāš*. The writer says that one must not be surprised by the "exploitation of the poor [*rāš*]" in a province, for society is structured in such a way that those above exploit those who are below them on the social ladder (Eccl 5:7). Though the writer's sentiment is rather cynical about the situation of the poor, the author turns the meaning of the word *rāš* on its head by suggesting that *rāš* is *not* a poverty that results from laziness as the writers of Proverbs maintained; this inversion of categories moves Ecclesiastes in the direction of Job and the prophets, who also emphasize the structural origins of poverty.

The word *rāš* does not appear at all in Job; this lack is yet another factor that sets Job apart from Proverbs, even though both are generally regarded as wisdom texts (see C.1 above). That the book of Job avoids the term *rāš* strengthens the view we have argued for above that the book of Job is more akin to the prophetic materials in terms of language and social analysis than it is to the wisdom tradition, at least insofar as Proverbs is a typical representative of this tradition (a comparison with Egyptian wisdom materials shows Proverbs to be quite typical of the international wisdom tradition with regard to its understanding of poverty; see Pleins 1987).

2. In the Psalms. The word *rāš* appears only once in the Psalter, in a so-called prophetic oracle, where God calls on the divine assembly to bring about just legal decisions for the poor (Ps 82:3). This passage is rich in its use of terms for the "poor" (*dal, ʿānî, rāš, ʾebyôn,* and *yātôm* ["fatherless"] all occur in 82:3–4). All are victims of the ill-defined *rĕšāʿîm,* "wicked, guilty" (cf. Baudissin 1912: 216–17; Munch 1936: 19).

3. In Historical Narrative. Like the word *dal,* the word *rāš* is unusual among the words for "poor" in that it crops up at least a few times (4 times) in the course of the DH. The first instance concerns the rising figure of David in the court of Saul; David sees himself as an insignificant individual when compared to the importance of the ruling king, Saul (1 Sam 18:23). This use of *rāš* is comparable to DH's use of the term *dal:* the word is not used to bring up the topic of poverty; rather, it specifies political inferiority. The other uses of *rāš* in 2 Samuel all occur in the context of Nathan's parable addressed against the adulterous affair and murder perpetrated by King David. In the immediate context of the parable, the *rāš* is depicted as one who owns only one small sheep in contrast to the rich person who owns many flocks and herds (2 Sam 12:1–4). Clearly the term has a strong economic flavor to it, and the text tacitly recognizes the cruelty of the rich when they steal what little the poor possess. However, the purpose of the text is not to critique economic relations in the manner of the prophetic texts or the book of Job (the term *rāš* is not prophetic and is the wrong word to put in the mouth of a prophet); rather, the text seeks to make explicit the political miscalculations of King David. In this way, the Deuteronomistic writers are actually quite consistent in their use of *rāš* and *dal:* these words are used to stress political weakness and are not drawn on to analyze or critique the situation of the poor in their society. The topic of poverty is not on the agenda of DH.

F. The Injustice of Oppression: *ʿānî*

The term *ʿānî* ("economically poor; oppressed, exploited; suffering") is the most common term in the Hebrew Bible for "poverty," occurring 80 times in the biblical corpus.

1. In the Prophetic Literature. The word *ʿānî* is the most prominent of the terms for "poor" in the prophetic literature, where it appears 25 times and connotes (1) economic oppression (Isa 3:15; Ezek 18:12; cf. Deut 24:12; Ezek 22:29; Amos 8:4); (2) unjust treatment in legal decisions (Isa 10:2); and (3) victimization through deception (Isa 32:7). Concretely, the society's leaders are said to have robbed the poor of their possessions (Isa 3:14; cf. Second Isaiah below). In another case, Ezekiel actually transforms the story of the destruction of Sodom by applying an economic interpretation: Sodom was destroyed because it withheld food from the poor (Ezek 16:49; cf. Gen 18:16–19:29). For First Isaiah and Jeremiah, the liberator of the poor is the king (Isa 14:32; Jer 22:16). In other prophetic texts, Yahweh alone is portrayed as the champion of the oppressed (Hab 3:14; Zeph 3:12; cf. Second Isaiah below).

The term *ʿānî* is used in two characteristic ways in the prophetic literature. First, it is frequently paired with *ʾebyôn* (Isa 14:30–32; 32:7; 41:17; Jer 22:16; Ezek 18:12; 22:29; Amos 8:4), a grouping found frequently in the Psalms (15 times), and to a lesser extent in Proverbs 30–31 (3 times), Job (3 times), and Deuteronomy (2 times). The pair represents a somewhat stylized rhetorical device for speaking of poverty, and is the product of either prophetic or cultic influence, though which is difficult to determine. If the pair represents prophetic influence, this would lend further weight to the thesis that Job is adapting prophetic rhetoric. Secondly, on several occasions in the prophetic literature, the term *ʿānî* is linked with the word "people" (Heb *ʿam;* Isa 3:15; 10:2; 14:32; Zeph 3:12). Curiously, the only other uses of *ʿānî* with "people" occur in Exodus (22:24) and in two psalms (18; 72). The Exodus text represents premonarchic legal traditions and is probably the precursor to the other uses of *ʿānî* plus "people." This may put into context Micah's appeals on behalf of the "my people" (Mic 3:3, et al.), indicating that the prophet is in touch with ancient, possibly village, legal traditions. However, the Psalms use the combination of *ʿānî* and "people" in royal contexts (18:28; 72:12), which indicates a shift from a village to an urban context. It seems, therefore, appropriate that Isaiah, whose teachings are preoccupied with a royal ideology, should use this combination as well.

Perhaps the most significant use of *ʿānî* in the prophets occurs in Isaiah 40–66. The writer(s) of these chapters makes exclusive use of *ʿānî* in all but one passage, and even there *ʿānî* is combined with *ʾebyôn* (41:17). This nearly exclusive emphasis on *ʿānî* represents a deliberate word choice as the writer reshapes the prophetic notion of the "oppressed poor" to apply it to the sufferings of the exiles in Babylon. According to the earlier prophets, Israel and Judah were judged for their exploitation of others, i.e., for making others *ʿānî.* With Second Isaiah, the entire nation has endured divine judgment, and through its captivity in Babylon, Israel as a whole has become *ʿānî.* The prophet seeks to explain the implications of this new phase in the community's historical experience. To this end, the prophet develops two main themes around the term *ʿānî.* The first theme is that the wrath of God against Jerusalem is temporary (51:21; 54:11; cf. 48:9–10). The community will not remain in captivity forever as if abandoned by God. Judgment will give way to a new exodus and liberation (cf., e.g., 43:16–20; 63:9–13). The prophet's second theme is that the people should, therefore, continue to hope amid the debilitating circumstances of exile, standing firm in the face of the oppressor, namely Babylon (49:17; cf. 51:12–14, 22–23). Second Isaiah's view is that God takes note of and will assist the nation that has suffered political and economic oppression at the hands of one of the major political powers of the day. God is particularly concerned about this kind of suffering (66:2); and it would seem that the traditional translation of this text, that God looks to the "humble," seriously weakens the creative force of Second Isaiah's understanding of Israel as *ʿānî,* "politically oppressed."

This prophet's notion of *ʿānî,* while somewhat more abstract than previous prophetic usage, continues to contain concrete aspects. The *ʿānî* are those who search for water, but have none (41:17), though this may be a somewhat metaphorical statement concerning the general yearnings of the exiles for liberation. The *ʿānî* are also depicted as homeless (58:7), though this passage is more in the spirit of the earlier prophets since it seems to apply to a portion of the people and not the people as a whole. Admittedly, the prophet has expanded the concrete character of the term in most instances; nevertheless, the general and terribly concrete situation of political and economic oppression indelibly stamps Second Isaiah's concept of poverty. This is not a theology of humility in the more detached or spiritualized sense.

2. In the Psalms. The word *ʿānî* occurs 31 times in the Psalter (30 Kethib; 1 Qere) and represents the preferred term for "poor" among the cultic writers. The term appears most often in Psalms of Lament. As with the Major Prophets and Amos, the Psalms frequently pair up *ʾebyôn* and *ʿānî* (15 times; see A.1 and F.1 above). The poets utilize the term *ʿānî* when characterizing God's relation to the poor: they call on God not to ignore or forget the *ʿānî* (9:13—Eng 12; 9:19; 10:12 [= 9:33]; 70:6—Eng 5; 74:19). In many cases, this is a self-reference to the one who sings the Psalms (25:16; 40:18—Eng 17; 69:30; 86:1; 88:16; 102:1; 109:22). It is God who rescues or provides for the *ʿānî* (12:6—Eng 5; 18:28; 22:25; 34:7; 35:10; 68:11; 82:3; 140:13—Eng 12).

Rarely do the Psalms give specific details about the sufferings of the *ʿānî.* The poor are depicted generally as being hounded and seized by the wicked and strong (10:2, 9; 14:6; 35:10; 37:14; 106:16) or being plundered (12:6—Eng 5). Most concretely, the *ʿānî* are homeless (25:16; Heb *yaḥîd*); murdered with bows and swords (37:14; unless this is metaphorical); and in physical pain (69:30).

Only one royal psalm expressly depicts the king to be the champion of the poor (Psalm 72). The poet calls on God to give the king the ability to judge justly (72:2), which translates into upholding the legal claims of the poor (72:4, 12). The rarity of the connection between the king and the poor in the Psalms would seem to indicate that the Psalms do not intend to work out a theology detailing the state's responsibilities toward the poor or one that challenges the rulers for their failure to face societal injustices; this contrasts sharply with the social burden of the prophets.

3. In Wisdom Texts. The word *ʿānî* finds frequent usage (16 times) throughout the wisdom literature, appearing 8 times in Proverbs, 7 times in Job, and once in Ecclesiastes.

In Proverbs, the word is scattered through the major blocks of the text. The term appears once in the instructional texts of Proverbs 1–9. This is unusual since none of the other words for poverty except *maḥsôr* (6:11) occur in this part of the book. The passage (3:34) relates the attitude of God who scorns the scoffer but favors the righteous and the *ʿānî.* In the sentential literature of Proverbs 10–22, the term *ʿānî* occurs four times. Three of these occurrences reflect themes that are developed in greater detail through the use of other words for "poor" in Proverbs: (1) showing favor to the *ʿānî* brings fortune to the giver (14:21); (2) the lot of the *ʿānî* is terrible (15:15); and (3) it is better to be among the poor than to share the plunder of the arrogant (16:19). The most unique use of *ʿānî* in the sentential literature occurs in a section that is known as the "Sayings of the Wise" (Prov 22:17–24:34), a text which has clear connections to the Egyptian instruction of Amenemope (Bryce 1979: chaps. 1–3). The writer exhorts the student not to rob the *dal* or "crush the afflicted [*ʿānî*] at the gate" (22:22). While it is true that the wise often oppose the abuse of the poor, this is the only text that speaks of the gate, i.e., the mistreatment of the poor in legal cases. The atypical nature of the text must be taken as a sign that there is legal or prophetic influence at work here, strongly suggesting that the wise exerted little direct influence on the direction of the legal system in ancient Israel. The only other points where the wisdom, prophetic, and legal traditions really meet concern false weights and measures (Prov 11:1; 16:11; 20:10, 23) and property lines (Prov 23:10–11). In any case, the Proverbial tradition lacks the comprehensive and rather concrete social justice vision for the *ʿānî* that we find in the legal and prophetic materials (contra Malchow 1982).

Chaps. 30–31 of Proverbs make use of the pair *ʾebyôn* and *ʿānî* (see A.1 and F.1 above)—one fact among several considerations that sets these chapters off from the rest of the text of Proverbs. All three occurrences in these chapters reveal an awareness of the concrete suffering of the *ʿānî* that is unique in Proverbs. The *ʿānî* are devoured by the power-holders of society (30:14). In chapter 31, King Lemuel is exhorted to defend the legal case of the *ʿānî* (31:9). The wise and capable wife shows her compassion by opening her hand to assist the *ʿānî* (31:20). The meaning of *ʿānî* that we gain from these texts is one of concrete suffering and exploitation, though it must be observed that the specific situations of the *ʿānî* are not detailed by the sages.

A comparison of the various terms for "poor" in the

Psalms and Proverbs makes it clear that while both use the term *ʿānî,* the difference in the distribution of the terms reflects the differing social visions of the writers. On the one hand, for the psalmists, the term is of distinctive importance in the context of worship and liturgy. By contrast, the divergent social agenda of Proverbs is underscored by the fact that Proverbs proportionately uses the cultic/prophetic term *ʿānî* less and the wisdom-nuanced term *dal* more than the Psalter. To put this another way, the cultic social agenda, however ill-defined it may seem, did not exert great influence on wisdom views about poverty; likewise, whatever wisdom influence there may be in the Psalms (especially the so-called "wisdom" Psalms), that influence did not extend to the shaping of the Psalter's understanding of the poor.

The book of Job again yields a vocabulary that diverges from Proverbs, a rhetorical feature that also serves to distance Job from the ideology of traditional wisdom thought. In the discussions between Job and his friends, it is only Job that uses the term *ʿānî.* The sufferings of the *ʿānî* are very concrete: they are forced into hiding (24:4); their children are seized as a pledge (24:9; cf. 2 Kgs 4:1–7); and they are murdered (24:14). Once again, the substance of Job's language is prophetic in character: he speaks quite concretely about the suffering of the *ʿānî.* Job's wise friends scrupulously avoid the term, as one would expect from the distribution in Proverbs. Job finds the solution to the question of suffering in his posture toward the poor: he rescued those who cried out (29:12). Curiously, the other uses of *ʿānî* in Job are on the lips of Elihu (who twice uses the term *dal*). This is rather anomalous and may lend support to the view that the Elihu chapters are a later addition to the text. In many ways, Elihu speaks like a psalmist, for he stresses God's action in coming to the aid of the *ʿānî* (34:28; 36:6, 15). Perhaps then we should see Elihu not as a "wisdom character" but as a representative of the cultic community.

For the writer of Ecclesiastes, the *ʿānî* find no benefit in this world, even when they may acquire the ability to manage their own affairs. Pondering the fact that God gives wealth only to deny its enjoyment (Eccl 6:1–7), the writer asks, "What advantage then has the wise man over the fool, what advantage has the pauper [*ʿānî*] who knows how to get on in life" (Eccl 6:8, *JPS*). The writer focuses on the negative side of the ancient wisdom view that the gods or fate bring both prosperity and misfortune (cf. Ptahhotep #10; Amenemope VII:1–6, XXI:15–16; Ankhsheshonq 12:3; 22:25; 26:8; 26:14; P. Insinger 7:18; 17:2; 28:4; 30:15).

4. In Legal Texts. The term *ʿānî* finds its way only into restricted sections of the Pentateuch 7 times: 5 times in the legal materials (Exodus 22; Deuteronomy 15; 24) and twice in the priestly writings of Leviticus. The legal texts are keyed to the Covenant Code's (Exodus 21–23) concern for lending to "my people," i.e., the *ʿānî* among the people. One cannot exact interest when lending to the poor. Statements concerning the *ʿānî* in Deuteronomy 15 and 24 simply represent a later commentary on the text in Exodus. Both chapters elaborate on lending to the poor. In one passage, provision is made to ensure that the poor continue to receive loans even as the time of loan suspension, the Sabbatical Year, approaches (15:11). In the other passage, lending is likewise the topic, but here the concern is to forbid the lender from keeping and sleeping in the garment a poor person has given in pledge (24:12). The use of the term *ʿānî* in this passage causes the editor to mention another law related to the *ʿānî,* in this case the poor laborer. Such laborers, whether foreigners or nationals, are not to be mistreated; they should receive their wages the same day (24:14–15). The priestly material on the *ʿānî* is likewise very concrete: these poor are reduced to gleaning the edges of harvest fields and vineyards for food (19:9–10; 23:22). The *ʿānî* is someone who has no real estate (cf. Rahlfs 1892: 74–75) and little to eat. All the legal and priestly texts clearly focus on the economic deprivation of the *ʿānî,* as do the prophetic texts. Yet, unlike the prophetic texts, the pentateuchal materials try to spell out the specifics of society's obligations toward those who are economically deprived.

5. In Historical Narrative. As with other terms for poverty, the word *ʿānî* does not appear in the narrative portions of the Pentateuch or the DH. In fact, the only appearance of the term in the DH is in the poetic text of 2 Samuel 22, which actually represents the transferral of a liturgical text (roughly parallel to Psalm 18) into the narrative material. The contrast between the overwhelming number of occurrences of this word throughout large tracts of the Hebrew Bible and its striking absence from the Pentateuchal narrative and DH shows us how relatively unimportant the issue of poverty was for Israel's early "historians." This has direct implications for our understanding of the contrast between the philosophies of history held by the prophets and by the "historians" (see further E.3 and H).

6. Semitic Cognates. Discussion of the word *ʿānî* cannot be entirely separated from a discussion of the related verbal form *ʿānâ,* often defined as "be bowed down, afflicted" (BDB, 776). The *Piʿel* or transitive form of the verb, which constitutes the bulk of the verb's occurrences (57 out of 80), has a very concrete sense, namely "to oppress, abuse, rape." In a major study of the terms for oppression in the Hebrew Bible, Pons (1981: 103) concluded that *ʿānâ* "never has as its object something inanimate, but always persons, and, in particular, the body" (cf. *THAT* 6: 247–70; *TDNT* 6: 885–915; contrast Delekat 1964). A vivid cognate example appears in the famous Moabite stele: "Omri, the king of Israel, oppressed [*wyʿnw*] Moab for a long time because Chemosh was angry with his land. Then his [Omri's] son [Ahab] succeeded him and he also said, 'I will oppress [*ʾʿnw*] Moab' " (lines 4–6; cf. *TSSI* 1: 74; *KAI* no. 181). As in biblical Hebrew, the Moabite text confirms that the verb denotes political oppression. A possibly related example occurs in the Baal Cycle (14th century B.C.E.). Tsumura (1982) suggests that the text reads: "Give up Baal, and I will *humble* [*ʿnn*] him/ Dagan's son, that I may dispossess his gold" (*KTU* 1.2:I:35; cf. *OTA* 1983: 246–47). This interpretation of the passage, while not certain, is possible, and the pairing of *ʿnn* with the rather concrete phrase "dispossess his gold" suggests that "to humble" must also be understood as some sort of concrete suffering or deprivation, not simply as personal humiliation.

The experience of poverty is brought out in a related Aramaic example from the text of Ahiqar (line 105): "I have tasted even the bitter medlar and have eaten *endives* but there is nothing more bitter than poverty [*ʿnwh*]" (Lindenberger 1983: 89). Another cognate occurs in biblical Aramaic, where Daniel (Belteshazzar) calls on Nebuchadnezzar to "do away with your sins through righteousness and [get rid of] your offenses by showing kindness to the poor [*ʿnyn*]" (Dan 4:24—Eng 27).

Some treat *ʿānî* and *ʿānāw* as products of the same root with no differentiation in meaning (Hupfeld 1867; van den Berghe 1962; Aartun 1971). Rahlfs derives them both from the same root meaning, "the lower position that a servant takes toward a master," but he suggests that *ʿānî* denotes the condition of suffering, whereas *ʿānāw* bears a more religious sense, that of humbling oneself before God (1892: 70, 73–80). Rahlfs' view has tended to dominate the discussion. Some argue that the two terms have separate origins, but not necessarily distinct meanings: Birkeland (1932: 19–20) held that *ʿānāw* may not have existed in early biblical Hebrew but entered at a later point under the influence of Aramaic, a position advocated by George (*DBSup* 7: 387). Birkeland denied the view that *ʿānāw* is more religious or that *ʿānî* is more secular in tone (1932: 15), though by this he meant that *ʿānî* at times may mean "humble" (Birkeland 1932: 16)—a view that is difficult to sustain in light of its usage throughout the biblical corpus.

G. A Political Movement of the Pious Poor?: *ʿănāwîm*

The term *ʿănāwîm* ("poor; pious, humble[?]") is a plural form for a supposed singular *ʿānāw* and occurs 24 times in the Hebrew Bible. The word appears in the prophetic literature, in the Psalms, and in wisdom texts. Although this is not the most common word for "poor" in the Hebrew Bible, it is one of the most frequently discussed among scholars because many see in *ʿănāwîm* a merger between poverty and piety, possibly marking a political movement among the pious poor (see Lohfink 1986). A problematic singular form that appears in Num 12:3 is discussed below.

1. In the Psalms. The word *ʿănāwîm* appears 13 times in the Psalms, where it appears mainly in Psalms of Lament. As with the term *ʿānî*, the poets draw on *ʿănāwîm* to characterize God's relation to the poor. In the psalmists' vision, God actively relates to the *ʿănāwîm* by rescuing and guiding them, though precisely what this entails is difficult to determine from the texts (25:9; 34:3—Eng v 2; 69:33—Eng v 32; 76:10—Eng v 9; 147:6; 149:4). The poets observe that God does not forget the poor (9:13, 19—Eng vv 12, 18), and they call on God not to ignore the poor (10:12; 10:17—Eng v 16). As with the term *ʿānî*, few passages allude to the concrete circumstances of the *ʿănāwîm*, but what we do find is quite revealing. They lack food (22:27—Eng v 26); they are landless (37:11); and they are in pain (69:33—Eng v 32; cf. 69:30—Eng v 29). One text makes it clear that the opponents of the *ʿănāwîm* are the wicked (Heb *rĕšāʿîm;* 147:6), though again, as with so many of the Psalms texts, the precise sociological setting presupposed by "wicked" is difficult to determine. When we consider the usage of the term *ʿănāwîm* throughout the Psalms, it is striking to notice that this word matches *ʿānî* in its range of meaning and usage. This is one important piece of evidence for the theory pursued below that the term *ʿănāwîm*, is simply a plural form for *ʿānî*, and that the two actually should be treated together.

2. In the Prophetic Corpus. The word *ʿănāwîm* occurs in a few scattered places in the prophetic literature (7 times). The poor are victims of social injustice (Isa 32:7; Amos 2:7; 8:4). Several texts in Isaiah lay emphasis on hope for the poor: they will find a just judge in a future king (11:4); they will rejoice before God when God topples the tyrants (29:19); and they are the exiles to whom the announcement of release is presented (61:1; on Second Isaiah see F.1 above). These texts all have a concrete socioeconomic or political flavor to them. This is less clear for Zephaniah, where the text treats the *ʿănāwîm* as those who follow God's laws and who seek *ʿănāwâ*, a word that in this context appears to mean "humility" (Zeph 2:3). This is the only passage in the entire Hebrew Bible where the term *ʿănāwîm* seems to have the less concrete meaning of "humble," although even here this is not altogether certain (see below).

3. In Wisdom Texts. The term *ʿănāwîm* occurs only 3 times in Proverbs and once in Job. The occurrences in Proverbs all represent the spoken form (Qere) for the written (Kethib) plural of *ʿānî* (3:34; 14:21; 16:19); as such, these are all discussed above under F.3. The only occurrence in Job is a Kethib form for the Qere plural for *ʿānî* and is likewise treated above.

4. Semantic Meaning. The word *ʿănāwîm* falls into the same general semantic field as other words for poverty, although there has been tremendous debate over the links between "poverty" and "humility" (another possible meaning of the term *ʿănāwîm*).

For Baudissin, the key issue is how the psalmists' more positive view of poverty (expressed in the *ʿănāwîm* passages) arose given the negative depiction of poverty in the rest of the Hebrew Bible, where poverty is an evil that has no inherent spiritual value and must be uprooted from the community of God (1912: 202, 209). Baudissin suggests that Israel's experience of the Exile brought about a reevaluation of the nature and value of poverty, and he credits Second Isaiah as the first to characterize Judah as God's "poor people" in a positive sense: through repeated invasions by the Babylonians, deportation, and plundered cities, Judah, as a nation, joined the ranks of the poor and came to understand the Exile as an act of humbling by God (1912: 211–12). Poverty and humility eventually dovetail as theological concepts: they are the precondition for experiencing the compassion of God, a more positive assessment of humble poverty that comes to fruition in the Psalms (Baudissin 1912: 213–14, 216).

Baudissin's view is open to several lines of criticism. His hypothesis rests in part on the probably faulty linguistic analysis that the word *ʿănāwîm*, "humble," came to color the meaning of *ʿānî*, which originally characterized the socioeconomic plight of one who is poor (Baudissin 1912: 195). Moreover, it is not clear that *ʿănāwîm* means "humble." Baudissin is correct in suspecting that Second Isaiah shifts prophetic thinking about poverty, but this development occurs along different lines than Baudissin outlines and involves the term *ʿānî* (see F.1 above).

Another issue in the interpretation of *ʿănāwîm* concerns the possible sociological background of the people who are characterized as *ʿănāwîm*. Loeb (1892) and Rahlfs

(1892) held that especially in the Psalms they represented a party of the pious in ancient Israel. Munch (1936: 21), under the influence of Lurje's class analysis (1927), modified the notion of party from a spiritual movement to that of "the class of the oppressed," although Munch's analysis is, in part, dependent on a reassessment of the socioeconomic dimension of the term *ʿānî* and not on a reading of *ʿănāwîm* itself (Munch 1936: 26). Kittel (1914), Causse (1922; 1937), and Birkeland (1932) denied the party thesis, preferring instead to characterize the *ʿănāwîm* as a religious movement or tendency within the population (cf. van der Ploeg 1950: 237–40), though Birkeland was forced to revise his ideas in light of a reevaluation of the socioeconomic dimension behind the term *ʿānî* (1933: 317–20). A variant of this position goes back to Renan (1891: 37–50), who saw in the *ʿănāwîm* a religious movement of the preexilic period.

Bruppacher (1924) and van der Ploeg (1950) have sharply criticized the attempted link between "poverty" and "piety." In the first place, Bruppacher contends that there is no ideal of poverty in the Bible, nor is it the case that poverty is exalted (1924: xi). Secondly, he maintains that the evidence for a religious or political movement built around the pious poor is weak. In particular, he criticizes Loeb's view (1892: 147) that the poor of the Psalms are the pious Israelites of the postexilic period who had come together as "the party of the poor" (1924: xii, 89). Bruppacher denies the party thesis, contending that the biblical text provides no clear sociological picture for an organized movement of poor people in ancient Israel; like the "wicked" of the Psalms, it is not certain who the "poor" of the Psalms actually are (1924: 90–91).

Van der Ploeg's critique (1950) seeks to separate the term *ʿănāwîm,* "religious humility," from the terms *ʿānî, ʾebyôn,* and *dal,* which mean "socioeconomic poverty." Working from the prophets, van der Ploeg maintains that the descriptions of the poor are so concrete that the poverty the prophets were concerned about was not some spiritual phenomenon; rather, it was social and economic oppression (1950: 244, 250). In the prophets and elsewhere in the Hebrew Bible, there is no positive evaluation of poverty; the poor are "just" only insofar as they are the innocent victims of injustice, and poverty does not translate automatically into piety, even if God displays a special concern for the situation of the poor (1950: 245–46). Nowhere does the Hebrew Bible romanticize poverty; it is not a voluntary condition but the product of oppressive practices in society. Having disconnected poverty from a religious ideal such as humility, van der Ploeg then suggests that the term *ʿănāwîm* must refer to plain humility (a character trait) and must not be confused with the poverty of the *ʿānî* (a socioeconomic condition). Van der Ploeg understands *ʿănāwîm* as the general attitude of submission before God on the part of believers no matter what their social status or economic condition may be, and poverty does not necessarily predispose one to this virtue (1950: 263–65).

5. *ʿānāw* and *ʿānî*. Since the analyses of van der Ploeg and Baudissin hinge in part on a particular understanding of the relationship between *ʿānî* and *ʿānāw,* it is necessary to sort out the issues behind this linguistic debate.

The word *ʿānāw* occurs in its plural form *(ʿănāwîm)* in all but one (problematic) case (Num 12:3); consequently, there is some question whether or not the word is simply a variant plural form for *ʿānî.* It is difficult to know how to settle this debate: on the one hand, the LXX renders *ʿănāwîm* as *praûs* (Gk "mild, soft, gentle, meek") in 9 of its 24 occurrences, whereas it renders *ʿānî* as *praûs* in only 4 instances, preferring instead to render it in numerous instances by *ptōchós* (Gk "one who crouches or cringes; a beggar"; cf. Hands 1968: 62–76; Martin-Achard 1965: 355; van den Berghe 1962: 275). On the basis of this evidence, it would seem reasonable to suggest that some sort of differentiation in meaning between *ʿānî* and *ʿănāwîm* is warranted, and hence to maintain that these are indeed two different words (Rahlfs 1892: 56–60; contrast Birkeland 1932: 20).

However, in no case does the plural form *ʿănāwîm* occur side by side with the plural of *ʿānî* in such a way that would lead us to think that specific authors used these as two different words (cf. Delekat 1964: 45). The only exceptions are in the Psalms (9–10; 22; 25; 34; 37; 69), where *ʿăniyyîm* and *ʿănāwîm* are mixed, though because these texts do represent the exceptions, we must remain open to the possibility of scribal error in these instances (Birkeland 1932: 14–15; cf. Gillingham 1988–89: 17). Furthermore, many of the plurals represent Kethib (written) and Qere (spoken) variations in the scribal editorial tradition of the Hebrew text (on 5 occasions the term *ʿănāwîm* is used as the Qere for a Kethib *ʿăniyyîm:* Pss 9:13; 10:12; Prov 3:34; 14:21; 16:19; while *ʿăniyyîm* on 4 occasions is the Qere for a Kethib *ʿănāwîm:* Isa 32:7; Amos 8:4; Ps 9:19; Job 24:4; cf. Orlinsky and Weinberg 1983).

Those who argue that *ʿănāwîm* and *ʿānî* are different words would have to see in this state of affairs scribal confusion over the two words. However, it is much more likely (from our knowledge of ancient scribal practices) that the variation simply reflects the differences between historic spellings and spoken dialect. It is preferable to see in *ʿānî* (whether singular or plural) and *ʿānāw* (almost exclusively plural) linguistic variants of the same word. It may be the case that by the time of the LXX, the translators thought that *ʿănāwîm* and *ʿăniyyîm* carried different meanings (a distinction maintained in postbiblical Hebrew), but a comparison of their usage in the Hebrew Bible shows this is not the case. We may finally note that since the plural forms *ʿăniyyîm* and *ʿănāwîm* go back to at least the 8th-century prophets (Isaiah uses *ʿăniyyîm;* Amos uses *ʿănāwîm*), this Hebrew dialectical and spelling variant is quite old and should not be explained as a product of Aramaic influence, as Birkeland seeks to do (1932: 15–16 19–20).

A problematic singular form *ʿānāw* occurs in Num 12:3 The word is commonly translated "humble," pointing to Moses as the most humble person in the world. Rash sustains this interpretation in his commentary on Number when he says that *ʿānāw* means "humble" *(šāpāl)* and "patient" *(sabĕlān).* If this is true, this would be one case wher *ʿānî* and *ʿānāw* clearly diverge from one another as separate words. However, while the Kethib is *ʿānāw,* the Qere the unusual *anyw.* Gray explains the *yōd* in the Qere as " *mater lectionis* to indicate that the last syllable is to b pronounced as in *dĕbārāw*" (*Numbers* ICC, 124; cf. Rahlfs 1892: 95–100). If this is the case, the Qere is comparable to that for *stw* (Cant 2:11), which has a *yōd* inserted before the *waw* in the Qere to indicate that the word is to be read *sĕtāw* (cf. Rahlfs 1892: 98–99). This reading for *ʿānāw* is known from Qumran and later rabbinic writings, although curiously it does not appear at all in the Mishnah, which knows only *ʿānî* and *ʿăniyyîm* (Kandler 1957). While this analysis is possible, there are other equally plausible interpretations for this scribal notation (cf. Birkeland 1932: 18–20). The consonantal form of the Qere appears to combine both *ʿānî* and *ʿānāw*, perhaps to indicate scribal uncertainty over this word, or to note dialectical variation, or to indicate that *ʿānāw* is to be read as *ʿānî*. This latter suggestion is supported by the Samaritan Pentateuch, which may read *ʿānî* in Num 12:3 and not *ʿānāw* (cf. *THAT* 6: 259). In light of the ambiguity of this situation, it is quite possible that the *ʿānāw* in Num 12:3 should be treated as *ʿānî* and translated: "Moses had suffered more/was more oppressed than any other person in the world."

If *ʿănāwîm*, then, is nothing more than a plural form of *ʿānî*, the meaning of *ʿănāwîm* must be sought in conjunction with all the *ʿānî* texts. Three things will follow from this. (1) The term *ʿănāwîm* will be understood to denote concrete socioeconomic forms of poverty: it cannot be viewed as a condition that occurs by chance or by not being upright; rather, it is the product of oppression (Kuschke 1939: 48–51). (2) The religious connotation of "humbleness" will be rejected, although it will not be necessary to lay aside the biblical idea that God is concerned for the oppressed, and we can still see that the poor are depicted as those who do call on God in their oppression (cf. *THAT* 2: 345); in other words, the relation between God and the poor is a matter of justice, not based on piety (*THAT* 2: 352–55). (3) The statistics for word distribution will be combined, making *ʿānî*/*ʿănāwîm* the predominant word for poverty in the Hebrew Bible.

For another noteworthy discussion of the semantic meaning of *ʿănāwîm*, see Kraus 1986: 150–54. Other important discussions on poverty in the Psalms include Bolkestein 1939: 23–32; and Stamm 1955: 55–60.

H. Conclusion

This survey of the various terms for "poor" in the Hebrew Bible vindicates the context-oriented method outlined at the beginning of this article. Close attention to the precise usage and statistical distribution of these terms makes us aware of the diverging notions about poverty that infuse the biblical text. The classic discussions of the etymologies of the terms, while certainly important exercises, are generally unhelpful as guides to the meaning of these terms. Furthermore, the etymological approach fails to grapple with the diverging ideologies that exist in the text, and that are brought to the surface in a contextual analysis of the terms for "poor."

Some streams of the biblical tradition are clearly concerned about poverty, although their theologies and analyses of poverty differ radically. Nevertheless, the legal, prophetic, wisdom, and liturgical traditions all see poverty as a matter of grave significance to the community. The philosophies that drive these streams of tradition, in part, derive and explain their social visions in light of their confrontation with the realities of poverty in ancient Israelite society. Poverty is a decisive issue in the prophetic and legal traditions. It is in these traditions that we are brought face-to-face with the harsh living conditions of the poor: hunger and thirst, homelessness, economic exploitation, legal injustices, lack of sufficient farmland. All these form the web of poverty in ancient Israel. The prophets protest what they see to be the oppression of the poor at the hands of the society's rulers, while the legal tradents offer some limited provisions to ease the burdens of those who suffer in this situation. The liturgical tradition, as represented in the Psalms, presents a God who assists the poor in their distress, and the psalmists offer many prayers on their behalf. However, as we have seen, the Psalter's use of terms for the poor tends to be rather vague with regard to their specific circumstances, causing us to wonder if the text is more metaphorical in its use of the terms and therefore more spiritualized in its approach to the topic. The wisdom tradition offers divergent positions. Proverbs, in part by drawing on a different vocabulary for poverty, develops a markedly different view of poverty: to the wise, poverty is either the result of laziness or represents the judgment of God. By contrast, the book of Job moves in the direction of the language and analysis of the prophets. In this book, the poor are victims of economic and legal injustices. Furthermore, poverty becomes one of the book's major issues: Job has to defend himself against the charge that he has exploited the poor. One of the arguments for his innocence is built around the fact that he has defended the cause of the poor.

One unexpected conclusion we have arrived at through this study is that the plight of the poor was not a vital issue for ancient Israel's "historians," material that in this article has been termed the "narrative literature." A notable lack of poverty language distances the pentateuchal and Deuteronomistic historical writers from the issues of socioeconomic injustice; one must press the text to have these chroniclers address the topic of oppression. It is true that the narratives about Solomon's use of forced labor (1 Kgs 5:27–32; 9:15–22; 12:1–17), the text of Samuel's critique of kingship (1 Samuel 8), and the story of Ahab's taking of Naboth's vineyard (1 Kings 21) are potentially useful for developing sociological perspectives on the treatment of the poor in ancient Israelite society; likewise, one may choose to read the Exodus events as God's intervention on behalf of the poor (cf. Gutiérrez 1973: 155, 157). But in each case, the language of poverty is not present, and it would seem that this is deliberately the case, for in the few cases these "historians" do make use of the words for "poor," these terms either take on different nuances or are used to discuss matters that have nothing to do with the situation of the poor. It would seem, then, that the writers of the pentateuchal and Deuteronomistic narratives are not concerned with a critique of poverty and injustice, even in the case of the Exodus text. An alternative analysis of these texts would argue that the writers of Exodus and Samuel–Kings are concerned with developing a critique of kingship and foreign domination, but not with an analysis of the structures of poverty in their society. This latter conclusion, though somewhat negative, reveals an important insight into the diverse character of social thought in the Hebrew Bible.

Bibliography

Aartun, K. 1971. Hebräisch ʿānî und ʿānāw. *BiOr* 28: 125–26.
Baudissin, W. 1912. Die alttestamentliche Religion und die Armen. *Preussische Jahrbücher* 149: 193–231.
Berghe, P. van den. 1962. ʿĀnî et ʿānāw dans les Psaumes. Pp. 273–95 in *Le Psautier* (Orientalia et Biblica Lovaneinsia IV), ed. R. De Langhe. Louvain.
Birkeland, H. 1932. *ʿĀnî und ʿānāw in den Psalmen. SNVAO* 4. Oslo.
———. 1933. *Die Feinde des Individuums in der Israelitischen Psalmenliteratur.* Oslo.
Bolkestein, H. 1939. *Wohltätigkeit und Armenpflege im Vorchristlichen Altertum.* Utrecht.
Bruppacher, H. 1924. *Die Beurteilung der Armut im Alten Testament.* Zurich.
Bryce, G. 1979. *A Legacy of Wisdom.* Lewisburg, PA.
Causse, A. 1922. *Les "Pauvres" d'Israël.* Paris.
———. 1937. *Du Groupe Ethnique à la Communauté Religieuse.* Paris.
Crum, W. 1939. *A Coptic Dictionary.* Oxford.
Delekat, L. 1964. Zum Hebräischen Wörterbuch. *VT* 14: 7–66.
Donald, T. 1964. The Semantic Field of Rich and Poor in the Wisdom Literature of Hebrew and Accadian. *OrAnt* 2: 27–41.
Gibson, J. 1977. *Canaanite Myths and Legends.* Edinburgh.
Gillingham, S. 1988–89. The Poor in the Psalms. *ExpTim* 100: 15–19.
Gutiérrez, G. 1973. *A Theology of Liberation.* Maryknoll.
Hands, A. 1968. *Charities and Social Aid in Greece and Rome.* Ithaca, NY.
Honeyman, A. 1944. Some Developments of the Semitic Root *ʾby. JAOS* 64: 81–82.
Humbert, P. 1952. Le mot biblique *èbyon. RHPR* 32: 1–6.
Hupfeld, H. 1867–71. *Die Psalmen: Übersetzt und Ausgelegt,* 2d ed. 4 vols. Gotha.
Kandler, H.-J. 1957. Die Bedeutung der Armut im Schrifttum von Chirbet Qumran. *Judaica* 13: 193–209.
Kennedy, J. 1898. *Studies in Hebrew Synonyms.* London.
Kittel, R. 1914. Exkurs: Die Armen und Elenden im Psalter. Pp. 314–18 in *Die Psalmen.* Leipzig.
Kraus, H.-J. 1986. *Theology of the Psalms.* Trans. K. Crim. Minneapolis.
Kuschke, A. 1939. Arm und Reich im Alten Testament mit besonderer Berücksichtigung der nachexilischen Zeit. *ZAW* 57: 31–57.
Lambdin, T. 1953. Egyptian Loan Words in the OT. *JAOS* 73: 145–55.
Leeuwen, C. van. 1955. *Le Développement du Sens Social en Israël avant l'ère Chrétienne.* Studia Semitica Neerlandica, 1. Assen.
Lindenberger, J. 1983. *The Aramaic Proverbs of Ahiqar.* Baltimore.
Loeb, I. 1892. *La Littérature des Pauvres dans la Bible.* Paris.
Lohfink, N. 1986. Von der "Anawim-Partei" zur "Kirche der Armen." *Biblica* 67: 153–76.
Lurje, M. 1927. *Studien zur Geschichte der Wirtschaftlichen und Sozialen Verhältnisse im Israelitisch-Jüdischen Reiche.* BZAW 45. Giessen.
Malchow, B. 1982. Social Justice in the Wisdom Literature. *BTB* 12: 120–24.
Martin-Achard, R. 1965. Yahwé et les ʿănāwîm. *TZ* 21: 349–57.
Munch, P. 1936. Einige Bemerkungen zu den ʿănāwîm und den *rĕšaʿîm* in den Psalmen. *Le Monde Oriental* 30: 13–26.
Orlinsky, H. M., and Weinberg, M. 1983. The Masorah on ʿănāwîm in Amos 2.1. Pp. 25–36 in *Estudios Masoreticos* (V Congreso de la IOMS), ed. E. Tejero. Madrid.
Pleins, J. D. 1987. Poverty in the Social World of the Wise. *JSOT* 37: 61–78.
Ploeg, J. van der. 1950. Les Pauvres d'Israël et Leur Piété. *OTS* 7: 236–70.
Pons, J. 1981. *L'Oppression dans l'ancien Testament.* Paris.
Rahlfs, A. 1892. *ʿĀnî und ʿānāw in den Psalmen.* Göttingen.
Renan, E. 1887–93. *Histoire du Peuple d'Israël.* 5 volumes. Paris.
Soden, W. von. 1969. Zur Herkunft von hebr. *ʾebjôn* "arm." *MIO* 15: 322–26.
Stamm, J. 1955. Ein Vierteljahrhundert Psalmenforschung. *TRu* 23: 1–68.
Tsumura, D. 1982. *Sandhi* in the Ugaritic Language. *Bungei-Gengo Kenyu* 7: 111–26.
Ward, W. 1960. Comparative Studies in Egyptian and Ugaritic. *JNES* 19: 31–40.
Wittenberg, G. 1986. The Lexical Context of the Terminology for "Poor" in the book of Proverbs. *Scriptura: Tydskrif vir bybelkunde* (Stellenbosch) 2: 40–85.
Wolff, H. 1978. Micah the Moreshite—The Prophet and His Background. Pages 77–85 in *Israelite Wisdom: Theological and Literary Essays in Honor of Samuel Terrien,* eds. J. G. Gammie, et al. Missoula, MT.
———. 1981. *Micah the Prophet.* Trans. R. D. Gehrke. Philadelphia.

J. David Pleins

NEW TESTAMENT

A. Methodology
B. Terminology
C. Epistle of James
D. Gospel Source "Q"
E. Mark
F. Matthew
G. Luke–Acts
H. The Pauline Letters
I. Deutero-Pauline Letters
J. The Pastoral Letters
K. 1–2 Peter, Jude
L. Revelation
M. Gospel and Letters of John
N. Hebrews
O. Conclusion

A. Methodology

Despite much excellent work on countless individual texts (and even authors such as James and Luke), and innumerable general studies following the classical word-study methodology, we still lack a solid, thorough overview of NT teaching on the poor/poverty. The utter inadequacy of word-study approaches may be seen in the common omission of such theologically fundamental texts as Matt 25:31–46, where poverty is concretely described ("I was hungry . . . thirsty . . . naked") but without a general word for poor/poverty. Sweeping theological conclusions drawn from highly selective word studies have tended to be misleading. While much of homiletical value can be found in existing works, the common tendency to systematize (with forced ideological harmonization) makes clear the need for further interdisciplinary and integrative study. Continual disagreement about socioeconomic background, date and authorship of many NT documents makes any effort at comprehensive overview tentative, but growing sensitivity to NT diversity, ideological pitfalls, and new anthropological perspectives are making possible considerable advances on previous studies in an area that undoubtedly will involve much debate for years to come. In the Gospels, in addition to texts that refer explicitly to the poor, debate continues regarding the socioeconomic level of Jesus, his disciples, the author of each gospel, and the ecclesiastical situation addressed. Anthropological and feminist studies often broaden definitions and concerns to include groups socially weak, marginated, and despised: women, the sick and handicapped, tax collectors, sexual minorities, etc.

B. Terminology

Classic word-study approaches (*TDNT* 6: 885–915; *NIDNTT* 2: 820–28) focused especially on *ptōchós* ("poor, oppressed," lit. "beggar"), by far the most common term for the utterly destitute in the NT (34 times). However, in ancient Greece the most common term was *pénēs*, describing one who has little and must live frugally (used only in 2 Cor 8:9 in the NT). Other terms include *penichrós* ("poor," Luke 21:2; cf. *hystérēmatos*, v 4, "want") and *endeḗs* ("needy," Acts 4:34). Terms for need and want tend to be neglected in vocabulary surveys (see *chreia* 49 times in the NT; Acts 2:45; 4:35; Phil 4:16, 19; Titus 3:14; 1 John 3:17). The words for "poor" cannot be "defined" exhaustively and statically, but generally designate persons and groups lacking (totally or in some degree) the necessitites of life: food, drink, clothing, shelter, health, land/employment, freedom, dignity and honor, etc. (cf. Job 24:1–12). While poverty may be concretely indicated by specific manifestations (hungry, thirsty, naked, homeless, unemployed, despised), the presence of specific manifestations cannot simply be equated with a socioeconomic condition of poverty (Peter became hungry, Acts 10:10). In addition, various texts speak of poor/poverty metaphorically (Rev 3:17), though in certain cases exegetes continue to debate whether the usage is literal or metaphorical (2 Cor 8:9; Stegemann 1984: 14–15).

Malina (1986: 156) has argued from anthropology that in biblical cultures (as in modern Latin America) economics, politics, and religion commonly are embedded in kinship institutions, with the result that "wealthy 'sonless' women whose husbands have died are referred to as 'poor widows.'" Poverty in such contexts refers to "the inadequacy of life without honor, with consequent social and personal inability to participate in the activities of the community, the inability to maintain self-respect as defined by community social standards." While this inclusion of dimensions of kinship and honor is helpful, the NT often is quite specific about the economic condition of "poor widows" (Luke 21:4–5) and those in need of healing (Hanks 1983: 111). The socioeconomic dimension of Pauline teaching on justification (as "good news to the poor") is best understood against the kind of background described by Malina (Rom 5:1–11; Hanks 1986a: 14–16), and the Pauline preoccupation with empowering the weak (2 Cor 12:9–10) is closely related to the Synoptic concern for healing the sick, empowering the poor, and accepting the marginated and "unclean" (Countryman 1988).

C. Epistle of James

James is the NT writing that stands closest to the OT prophets in its perspective on poverty and oppression (Hanks 1983: 45–50), not surprising if it be the earliest NT writing (45–50 A.D.?) and written by Jesus' brother (Davids, *James* NIGTC, 21–22; Maynard-Reid 1987: 8). The Jewish-Christian recipients are not for the most part destitute beggars (2:2), but neither are they wealthy (2:6; 5:1–6). As a minority group ("Diaspora," 1:1) they appear to consist mainly of small farmers and artisans—those who have little and must live frugally (Stegemann 1984: 40–41).

In addition to the term for the beggarly poor (4 times *ptōchós*, 2:2–5), related terms James employs include the "humble" (*tapeinós*, 1:9; cf. 4:6, 10); "orphans and widows" (1:27); "workers and harvesters . . . the just" (5:4, 6). The beggarly poor are characterized by shabby clothing (2:2); being naked or lacking in daily food (2:15–16); the weak, needy, and marginated also include women (2:15), sexual minorities (widows; the prostitute Rahab, 2:25), and the sick (5:14–15).

In continuity with the OT (Exodus paradigm; prophets) James never blames the victims (for sloth, vice, genetic inferiority, etc.); rather he focuses on oppression as the basic cause of poverty (cf. Luke 4:18–19; Hanks 1983: 38–39). The "affliction" *(thlipsis)* suffered by orphans and widows may refer explicitly to oppression (Hanks 1983: 47; Tamez 1989: 17).

The oppression of the poor and weak appears to function basically in three ways in James (Davids *James* NIGTC; Maynard-Reid 1987; Tamez 1989): (1) financial-legal mechanisms, especially against poor debtors (2:1–12); (2) greedy and boastful merchants (4:13–17; cf. "covet"); (3) wealthy landowners withholding wages, a common mechanism of oppression (5:4). The rich "oppress" (*katadynasteúo*, 2:6) James' recipients, dragging them to court. Such "injustice/oppression" *(adikía)* is basically what characterizes the entire worldly system (2:6; Pons 1971: 166; cf. 4:4; "trials," 1:2, 12).

James, like Jesus, seems not to know Paul's doctrine of the fall; rather he espouses a more typical Jewish doctrine of creation (3:9) and individual sin (1:13–15; everyone is "Adam"; *2 Bar.* 54:19). He appears to place little stress on evangelism as popularly defined. However, such limited categories may fail to recognize that the prophetic denunciation of oppression is an essential part of evangelism, conceived as the proclamation of good news—preferentially—to the poor (Luke 3:10–14; 4:18–19; 6:20–26; Hanks 1983: 109–19). James envisions a community of disciples whose new lifestyle (stressing above all a loving response to the destitute, weak, and marginated) embodies the "word" proclaimed in a "world" characterized by greed, domination, and oppression of the poor and weak (1:18, 21; 4:6; 5:19–20; Tamez 1989: 56–69).

James is concerned especially with the kinds of sins of the tongue that create a false sense of importance and security for the affluent, but which deny dignity, honor, and justice to the poor and weak (2:6–7). His understanding of justification (cf. "condemnation," 2:12–13; 3:8–9; 4:11–12; 5:6) dignifies the poor (Hanks 1986a: 14–16), focusing on the paired examples of Abraham, an immigrant (like James' recipients), and Rahab, the woman who showed hospitality to Israel's migrant ancestors. As elsewhere in the NT, becoming "doers of the word," the performance of "good works," involves above all responding in practical ways to the material needs of destitute brothers, sisters, and neighbors (1:22–25; 4:17; cf. "forgiveness" in 5:14–16). Failure to be a doer of the word in helping the poor, oppressed, and marginated is to become guilty of murdering the poor (5:6) and committing "adultery" with the world (4:4–6; cf. 1 John 3:17).

Although James commends the peaceful nonresistance of oppressed harvesters, he is not passive in the face of such injustice and oppression. Rather, he vigorously denounces the cruel oppression and violence that impoverish and kill (2:11; 3:8; 5:5–6). For his recipients he commends a wise response (cf. Q and wisdom; Adamson 1989: 363–90) of "militant patience" (Tamez 1989: 52–56; James 1:3–4, 19; 5:7–11), nonresistance (5:6), peace (4:17–18), and prayer (1:5–7; 5:13–17; Tamez 1989: 69–72). The Parousia hope continues to function vigorously as the focus of an expectation of direct divine intervention (5:7–9), which consummates the promise of a kingdom characterized by liberation, justice, peace, and love (1:12, "life"; 2:5, "kingdom"; Tamez 1989: 33–50).

Although closest to the OT, James already is at a distance from the earliest NT traditions about poverty (see D below): the Jewish Christians addressed are in exile (1:1), but are not itinerant prophets. They live in a settled community of "brothers" and "sisters" (2:6–7, 15; cf. 1:27; 2:25–26), but one which is racked with (class?) conflict (4:1–3). While James is one of the three NT authors explicitly said to be married (1 Cor 9:5; cf. Peter and Jude), his exaltation of a single woman and prostitute, and his neglect of specific family virtues and responsibilities, are closer to Q's ideal (see below) than to the teaching of some later NT writings (1 Peter, Deutero-Pauline letters and pastorals). See also HAUSTAFELN; HOUSEHOLD CODES. James prophetically denounces oppression and abuse of wealth, but does not advocate total abandonment of home, family, possessions, and trade.

D. Gospel Source "Q"

Scholarly studies suggest that the very earliest NT traditions, which are reflected in the Q source (non-Markan material common to Luke and Matthew), also provide us with the most radical presentation of NT teaching on the poor and poverty (Lührmann 1989: 70). Q materials reflect the teaching of charismatic itinerant prophets who still took the instruction of Jesus' mission discourse literally: homelessness (Luke 9:57–58 = Matt 8:19–20), and a radical separation from family (Luke 9:59–60 = Matt 8:21–22) and from property, possessions, and trade (Luke 10:2–12 = Matt 9:37–38; 10:7–16; Luke 12:33–34 = Matt 6:20–21; Luke 11:2–4 = Matt 6:9–14). This *Wanderradikalismus,* attributed by Gerd Thiessen to the Jesus movement in general, is now more commonly understood to reflect the teaching of Jesus as preserved by the Q group. For the Q group, Jesus is viewed primarily as the prophet, and his homeless followers are also prophets (Lührmann 1989: 64, 71). The final redaction of Q is commonly dated around 60 A.D., while Mark, writing around 69 A.D., speaks not of homelessness as an inalterable condition of discipleship, but of settled communities of Christians who are incorporated into social structures (Mark 10:29–30; cf. Stegemann in Schottroff and Stegemann 1984: 158). In Q the priority attention given to the poor and evangelism of the poor is evident from the first beatitude (Luke 6:20 = Matt 5:3; cf. Luke 7:22 = Matt 11:55; Luke 4:18–19).

In the history of NT studies the apostle Paul repeatedly has been portrayed as a kind of "conservative" who betrayed Jesus' more radical teaching (on slavery, women, the poor, social outcasts, etc.). Surprisingly, however, Paul is "the only person really known to us from early Christianity who might be called a 'wandering radical' or a 'radical wanderer' " (Lührmann 1989: 70). Paul was a homeless prophet who wandered through the world without wife or family ties (1 Cor 9:5). Contrary to Jesus' mission instruction, Paul often earned his livelihood as a tentmaker (1 Cor 9:14–15). This need not be viewed, however, as "relativizing" Jesus' more radical teaching (pace Lührmann 1989: 70–71) but as an alternative expression of radical Christian freedom not so dependent upon the hospitality and donations—and ideological control—of established communities (1 Cor 9:1). For in fact, the homeless prophets portrayed in Q could only exist in dependence upon communities already existing or established by them. Paul, with his synagogue contacts and church planting, only applied to the gentile world the dialectic between homeless prophets and hospitable Palestinian Jewish communities implicit in Q's portrayal of the prophet Jesus and his homeless followers.

E. Mark

Mark employs *ptōchós* only five times in three contexts (10:21, the rich man; 12:42–43, the widow's mite; 14:5, 7, the anointing in Bethany), but a careful reading reveals abundant indirect references to poverty: the lifestyle of John the Baptist (1:6; 6:17, 27) and of Jesus (6:3; 11:12; 14:65; 15:15, 19; Pallares 1986: 176); the voluntary deprivations of the disciples (1:18, 20; 2:23–25; 6:8–9, 36–37; 9:41; 10:28–31); the socioeconomic level of the "crowds" (Myers 1988: 120) and their environment as reflected in Jesus' teaching (2:21, the use of old, mended clothes; 5:2–3, 5; 7:11–13; 8:1–2; 12:1–2).

Such evidence leads Stegemann (1984: 23) to conclude: "The movement within Judaism in Palestine associated with the name of Jesus was a movement *of the poor for the poor.*" Jesus' identification as a "carpenter" (Mark 6:3) in an insignificant Galilean hamlet suggests the situation of a wage-earning day laborer: "Probably neither Jesus nor his first disciples were professed beggars, yet they shared the desperate situation of many of their fellow country folk—particularly in Galilee—barely avoiding utter poverty" (Stegemann 1984: 24; see Waetjen 1989: 10–11). Mark's gospel may be directed to a similarly poor church in Roman-occupied Syria (Waetjen 1989: 4, 15) at a time of persecution (A.D. 67–70) and before significant number of more affluent members were added. The paucity of explicit references to the beggarly poor *(ptōchós)* in Mark (5 times; cf. 10 times in Luke) is quite compatible with the indications of pervasive poverty (in the broader sense of the classical term *pénēs*). Numerous comments about water need not be expected from the fish that swim therein (pace Bammel in *TDNT* 6: 903).

If tradition is correct in ascribing the gospel to th

unmarried young rebel (from a well-to-do Jerusalem family) who agreed to share the deprivations and rigors of Paul's itinerant missionary lifestyle (Acts 12:13–14; 13:5, 13; 15:37–40; 2 Tim 4:11; 1 Pet 5:13), we can understand the proximity of his gospel to the Q source.

F. Matthew

Paradoxically, Matthew begins his account of Jesus' teaching with an apparent "spiritualizing" reference to the poor (5:3 = Luke 6:20); however, his version of Jesus' final discourse closes with what may be the most radical text on poverty in the NT (certainly, along with Luke 4:18–19 it has served as one of two pillar texts for liberation theology (Gutiérrez 1973: 254–65; Pikaza 1984). Probably, then, we should not understand Matt 5:3 as a species of Neoplatonic "spiritualizing" long dominant in church tradition, but as a call to high-risk solidarity with poorer disciples at a time of persecution (Hanks 1986b; Pantelis 1989).

Despite the length of his gospel and his inclusion of five lengthy discourses of Jesus' teaching, Matthew contains no more explicit references to the poor *(ptōchós)* than Mark (5 times each). Three of Matthew's references (19:21; 26:9, 11) are taken from Mark (10:21; 14:5, 7); the other two (5:3; 11:5) are from Q (= Luke 6:20; 7:22). However, Matthew's option for the poor is also evident in the importance he attaches to almsgiving (6:1–4) and in his fierce denunciation of oppression (23:1–36; cf. Luke 6:24–26). In 25:31–46, writing in a conflictive situation, Matthew sets forth this option (good works) for the poor, weak, and oppressed as the *only* criterion for the final judgment—a truly radical conclusion (Miranda 1974: 118; *NIDNTT* 2: 826; Hanks 1986a: 18).

If "Matthew" was in fact the unmarried tax collector of tradition, his inclusion of sexual minorities in his genealogy is consistent with his praxis (9:9–11; cf. 19:11–12), the option he advocates not only for those poor economically, but also for despised, marginated classes (poor in terms of honor). His predominantly Jewish readership and the context of severe persecution may largely explain the necessity of his more subversive strategy (7:6).

G. Luke–Acts

Uncritical readings and word-study approaches easily established Luke's special concern for the beggarly poor (*ptōchós* 10 times plus *penichrós,* 21:2; cf. *ptōchós* 5 times each in Mark and Matthew); however, the total absence of these words in Acts has raised questions. Of the six uses of *ptōchós* in Luke which are not dependent on Mark or Q, five occur in the travel narrative of 9:51–19:27: 14:13, 21; 16:20, 22; 19:8. Also unique to Luke is 4:18, which stands as a programmatic introduction to Jesus' ministry (Ringe 1985; Hanks 1983: 97–119; cf. 6:20 = Matt 5:3).

Within Acts another problem posed is the relative concentration on the needs of the poor in the first half of the book: having all things in common (2:42–47; 4:32–37), with the poor described as those having "need" (*chreia,* 2:45; 4:35); the appointment of seven deacons to correct injustice in the church's ministry to Hellenistic widows; the exemplary ministries of Dorcas (9:36–43) and Cornelius (10:2, 4, 31) in providing alms, etc. (Moxnes 1988: 159–62). Such explicit concern for the poor, however, is almost totally lacking in the narrative of Paul's missionary travels in Acts 13–28. Paul is characterized as exemplary in his freedom from love of money (20:33–34), but his strategic gift to the poor saints in Jerusalem (which looms so important in his epistles) receives the barest mention in Acts (24:17). What recent studies have tended to overlook is the anthropological perspective, according to which the gentiles in Acts 13–28—although traditionally Israel's oppressors—were excluded and marginated from Jewish life and worship because of their uncleanness (Countryman 1988). Acts 13–28 may be criticized for concentrating too much on the quantitative aspect of church growth, but the kind and quality of community life had already been amply established in Luke and Acts 1–12, and the purpose in Acts 13–28 involves concentration on the miraculous incorporation of gentiles who are "cleansed by faith" without submission to circumcision and the law.

While older studies tended to view Luke as the "social radical" among the gospel writers, recent studies tend to view the Q source and/or Mark as reflecting more radical perspectives on the poor. Little attention has been paid to Luke's concern for the "immoral minorities" commonly marginated from society: tax collectors, prostitutes, etc. (7:2, 34, 37, 39; Hanks 1986a: 12; Countryman 1988: 66–74). Luke's heavy concentration on the economic dimension of the gospel (only partly reflected in word-study data; cf. 1:51–53; 3:10–14; 6:34–36; 9:58; 11:41; 12:33; 14:12–14, 33) is now commonly understood to respond to a situation of a relatively poor church (Caesaria/Antioch?) ca. A.D. 70–85 faced with an unprecedented influx of more affluent members and in danger of succumbing to the "love of money" characteristic of certain Pharisees (16:14; Moxnes 1988: 1–21). Luke addresses such an economically upwardly-mobile Christian community, drawing on an extensive store of Jesus' teaching appropriate to the crisis. W. Pilgrim (1981) analyzed Luke's teaching on wealth and poverty as involving three basic categories: (1) total renunciation of wealth; (2) warnings against the dangers of wealth; and (3) right use of wealth. Zaccheus' example ("I give half of my possessions to the poor," 19:8; cf. 3:10–14) is now commonly viewed as Luke's preferred paradigm for the influx of recently converted "wealthy disciples" (a contradiction in terms for Q and Mark). Johnson (1977) argues that money in Luke often has a symbolic function linked to the acceptance or rejection of Jesus.

If the author of Luke–Acts is the traditional unmarried "beloved physician" and sometime companion of Paul in his apostolic deprivations, Luke's missionary praxis, culminating in his literary effort, undoubtedly has been correctly understood as an impressive testimony to solidarity with the poor, weak, and marginated—but perhaps a more moderate response than that epitomized by Jesus and his disciples according to Q and Mark.

H. The Pauline Letters

The seven unquestioned letters of Paul constitute documents that largely predate Q and the four Gospels. Paul's proximity to Jesus' praxis and teaching on poverty is best perceived by attention to the apostolic praxis as reflected in the "catalogs of affliction/oppression" in 1 Cor 4:10–13a; 2 Cor 4:8–10; 6:4b–10; 11:23b–29; 12:10; Rom 8:35; Phil 4:12 (Hodgson 1983).

Linguistically, all seven uses of the more explicit vocabulary for poor/poverty occur in the unquestioned Paulines. In Gal 2:10 "continuing to remember the destitute" *(ptōchós)* is viewed as a nonnegotiable element in Christian praxis common to both Petrine and Pauline circles; cf. the weak elements *(stoicheia),* also metaphorically described as "beggarly" *(ptōchós)* in Gal 4:9. In 2 Cor 6:10 the apostle concludes the catalog of affliction, describing his own lifestyle as "poor [*ptōchós*] but enriching many; *having nothing,* and yet possessing all things." These seven "catalogs of affliction" might just as well be described as "catalogs of oppression" (Hanks 1983: 48–49). Concrete expressions of injustices suffered, with poverty and deprivation often consequent, dominate the lists.

The remaining four uses are to be found in Rom 15:26 *(ptōchós)* and 2 Corinthians 8–9, where Paul deals with the offering for the destitute among the saints in Jerusalem (Nickle 1966). The only NT use of *pénēs* (the more common word for "poor" in classical Greek) comes in 2 Cor 9:9 in the LXX-based citation of Ps 112:9 ("He scatters abroad, he gives to the poor; his justice endures forever"). Still greatly disputed is the interpretation of Paul's reference to the incarnational paradigm for the offering: "For you know the grace of our Lord Jesus Christ, that though he was rich, yet for your sake he *became poor* (verb *ptōchéo,* only here in NT), so that you through his *poverty (ptōcheia)* might become rich." Commentaries commonly have suggested Neoplatonic and metaphorical interpretations, but cf. Stegemann (1984: 15) and many liberation theologians; also the reference to the "poverty" *(ptōcheia)* of the Macedonian churches (2 Cor 8:2).

Much recent study has focused on the socioeconomic level of the Pauline churches (Theissen 1982; Meeks 1983). Stegemann (1984: 31–38) speaks of a new consensus according to which most of the early Christian communities were made up predominantly of "the little people" *(pénēs),* including neither the destitute *(ptōchós)* nor the wealthy. However, the interpretation of texts such as 1 Cor 1:26–29 (stressing lack of honor) continue to be disputed (Stegemann 1984: 35–36). Since more spacious houses and leadership for house churches tended to come from the more affluent and educated sectors, situations arose (1 Cor 11:17–32) in which a kind of conflict could flare up between some who became drunk (11:21) and others who "hungered" and "had nothing" (11:22)—even in the Lord's Supper. Theological elements so basic as the Eucharist ("*For* I received . . . , 1 Cor 11:23–33; cf. 11:17–22), variations in spiritual gifts (1 Corinthians 12; 14) and the urgency of agape love (chap. 13) are best understood in the context of the socioeconomic conflict or "class struggle" between more affluent and poorer members.

However, despite such conflicts and Paul's deprivations, a degree of accumulated wealth (capital) was to be expected in the house churches he founded: more affluent churches are expected to save up and share with poorer ones, and parents are expected to save for their children (2 Cor 12:14). Such provisions provide continuity with the teaching in the Deutero-Pauline letters.

I. Deutero-Pauline Letters

Since 2 Thessalonians, Colossians, and Ephesians generally occupy a place between the seven unquestioned Pauline letters and the Pastorals (both stylistically and theologically), we may ask whether specifically this is true regarding their perspective on poverty.

Despite questions about authorship and date, 2 Thessalonians has much in common with 1 Thessalonians in perspectives on poverty. Both stress the Church's experience of oppression in the form of persecution, which inevitably impoverished the artisan class and manual laborers addressed (Hanks 1983: 49; Meeks 1983: 64–65). In 2 Thessalonians particularly, distorted eschatological speculation, resulting in idleness, only augmented the problem (2:1–12; 3:3–12; cf. 1 Thess 4:13–5:11; 4:11–12 ("need," *chreia*). Paul's apocalyptic gospel, however, created viable community (Meeks 1983: 174) and instilled a more sober hope. Elitist Greek prejudices against manual labor were aggressively corrected by strong exhortation to work and by Church discipline (2 Thess 4:10, 14–15).

In Colossians no explicit language for poverty occurs. However, as in the unquestioned Paulines, oppression . . . and persecution directed against Paul and certain churches may be viewed as the basic cause of suffering, imprisonment, and poverty (*thlîpsis,* 1:24; cf. 4:10, 18; Hanks 1983: 47–50; *adikia,* 3:25, Hanks 1983: 128).

In the *Haustafeln* (Col 3:18–4:1), the inclusion of husbands, fathers, and lords (3:19, 21; 4:1) may indicate an upward penetration of the gospel in the social structure (cf. 1 Peter), but the priority given to women (3:15) and children (3:20), plus the more detailed treatment of slaves (3:22–25) suggests that the weaker and poorer classes continue to dominate in the Church membership. Noteworthy is the explicit stress on "justice" for slaves, in the explicit sense of equality *(isótēs),* demanded of converted lords (4:1)—especially radical if lords and slaves together are regarded as "brothers" with equal rights (4:7, 9), and if the lords were formerly characterized by covetousness rationalized by idolatrous religion (3:5) and particularly oppressive practices (1:21; 3:8; 3:25 *adikéō,* 2 times).

Colossians places special emphasis on a false philosophical teaching (proto-Gnosticism?) that "robs" the church, and on the true "riches" and "treasures" (2:2–3) of Christ's wisdom (undoubtedly metaphorical language), which may reflect certain literal economic effects of the authentic good news to the poor, contrasted with rapacious itinerant philosophers (2:8). Proper teaching on the positive goodness of creation (1:15–17) would counteract oppressive ideological tendencies in proto-Gnosticism.

In addition to authentic wisdom (2:2–3), which may reflect traditional Hebrew concerns for universal literacy, immediate solutions for poverty may be indicated in the kind of evangelization that implants a hope for radical social change (1:5, 12–13), in agape-love solidarity with the saints of all social classes (1:4; 2:2, 13; 3:12–14), forgiveness that probably includes debts (3:13), and good works to meet the needs of the more destitute members (1:6, 10; 4:10; cf. 1:7, 25; 4:2).

Analysis of Ephesians reveals a perspective that is similar to Colossians, but not identical. Direct reference to poorer classes may be seen in the former unemployed "thieves" and the one having "need" (*chreia,* 4:28) who is to be aided by "sharing" *(metadidōmi).* "Good works" directed to the needy are seen (as in Titus) as the immediate goal of "salvation" (2:8–10). Paul suffers imprisonment (3:1; 4:1; 6:20), a result of oppression-persecution (*thlîpsis,* 3:13), producing deprivation. Slaves (6:5–8) precede lords (6:9) in the *Haustafeln,* but husbands (5:25–33a) now receive more attention than wives (5:22–24, 33b). The concern in the *Haustafeln* to strengthen the family structure (which included household servants) may reflect not only a shift in evangelistic strategy (husbands, lords) but an adaptation to bureaucratic realities in the churches' ministry to the poor (cf. 1 Timothy 5). Evangelism is now directed aggressively toward the oppressive ruling classes ("boldness . . . ambassador") and not just to the little people (6:19–20). Hence prophetic denunciation of oppression and injustice ("darkness," 5:11), fervent intercession, and the practice of liberating justice (6:14; cf. Job 29:11–17; Isa 59:17) are advocated in the face of demonic structures of evil (6:1–18). Many perspectives similar to Colossians are repeated (love, inheritance, covetousness, God's universal Fatherhood, deacon ministry, forgiveness).

J. The Pastoral Letters

The focus of the Pastorals on the poor must take into account the socioeconomic status of the purported author (Paul), the recipients (Timothy and Titus) and the churches in Ephesus (1 Tim 1:3) and Crete (Tit 1:5) where they minister, as well as their explicit teaching about wealth and poverty.

Basically we find "Paul" in the same conflictive, oppressed, impoverished status of the apostle in the "tribulation lists" of 1–2 Corinthians and Romans. He who once persecuted the infant Church, even supporting violence (1 Tim 1:13) is now the victim of continual persecution and oppression (2 Tim 1:12; 4:14–15), unjust imprisonment (2 Tim 1:15–18; 2:9–13; 3:10–12), deserted by friends and colleagues (2 Tim 4:9–12, 16), facing the death penalty (though innocent of all wrongdoing; 2 Tim 4:6–8, 17–18), fearful of entering into a cold winter without his cloak (2 Tim 4:13, 21). Both Timothy and Titus are expected to continue the conflictive, impoverished apostolic lifestyle (1 Tim 1:18; 6:12; 2 Tim 1:6–8; 2:3–6; 3:10–14; 4:5) as originally exemplified by Jesus in the gospel (Tit 2:11–14; 1 Tim 1:11–12; 2:5–6; 2 Tim 1:10–12; 3:8–10, 13), who similarly suffered oppression and violence (2:5–6; 3:11–12), yet loved even his oppressors and persecutors (1 Tim 1:13–14, 16; 3:16–17), and was vindicated by his resurrection (3:16–17).

Analysis of the Pastorals' controverted teaching ("bourgeois"? see below) to the churches in Ephesus and Crete should not be carried out in isolation from the above-mentioned elements of continuity with the Jesus of the Gospels and the Paul of the seven unquestioned Pauline letters. Significant elements of discontinuity are discernible, but many studies oversimplify or exaggerate them.

The lowly socioeconomic status of the churches in Ephesus is reflected in 1 Timothy, especially in the detailed instructions given to counteract ecclesiastical bureaucratic paternalism in the care for "real" (impoverished) widows (5:3–16) and the maintenance of social responsibility in the extended family; in the qualifications for deacons (and deaconesses? 3:8–13) who minister primarily to the poor; and in the instructions to slaves (household servants, 6:1–2; cf. Tit 2:9–10; note the omission of parallel instructions for slave owners; cf. Philemon).

Women of means are frequent converts, but exhorted to minimize socioeconomic differences by their simple dress style (1 Tim 2:9; cf. 1 Pet 3:3). The good works, so central in Titus (1:6; 2:7, 14; 3:1, 13–14; cf. 1 Tim 2:10; 5:25; 2 Tim 2:21), represent the chief aim of redemption (Tit 2:14) and the second great purpose of inspired Scripture (2 Tim 3:14–17; Hanks 1986a: 19). These are works particularly defined as undertaken on behalf of those who lack the essentials of life (Tit 3:14; cf. Matt 25:31–46; Miranda 1974: 18).

Often cited without reference to the above contexts and teaching are two texts in 1 Timothy commonly said to represent a bourgeois adjustment—or contradiction—of Jesus' radical teaching in Luke. The first, 6:6–10, counsels those like Timothy, who have only the bare necessities of existence, to be content and avoid the love of money ("a root of all kinds of evil," 6:10). The second, 6:17–19, instructs Timothy how to reform the lives of the rich. Whereas Jesus in Luke often called for total renunciation of wealth, the "Paul" of the Pastorals would have his emissary in Ephesus simply advocate generosity and good works. Undoubtedly a certain diversity of historical contexts and teaching is found here. However, the generosity and good works that would be demanded of the rich in an impoverished church undoubtedly would involve something far more stringent than in a modern affluent neighborhood—especially when backed up by the radical examples of Jesus and Paul (cf. Zaccheus under Luke). The "generosity" to be demanded (*"koinōnikós,"* 6:18) may involve a kind of solidarity or pooling of resources and sharing that really has no limits (cf. Acts 2; 4). Another factor is that the Jesus of Luke's gospel often confronts the unconverted rich directly (6:20–23), while in the Pastorals, "Paul" speaks to wealthy converts—and then only indirectly through his emissary ("command them . . . ," 6:18).

Factors that produce poverty indicated in the Pastorals include especially persecution, oppression, and injustice (2 Tim 2:19; 1 Tim 1:19); idolatry and the false teaching of the pseudoprophets (2 Tim 2:16); and coveting (2 Tim 2:22; 3:6; 4:3; 1 Tim 3:3–8; 6:9; Tit 1:7–11; 2:12). As in the early Paulines, the consummation of God's kingdom in the Parousia stands as the ultimate solution, but is no longer expected to occur within Paul's lifetime (cf. 1 Tim 6:14; 2 Tim 4:8; Tit 2:13).

The evangelization of the world with the gospel remains (at least implicitly) as good news that gives special hope to the poor, as evidenced by the ready response of widows and slaves. Salvation is never limited to a Platonic heavenly sphere (2 Tim 4:18), but includes material relief in this life (2 Tim 4:18).

The church is the "pillar and ground of truth," particularly because it represents the new alternative community where God's just and loving purpose for all humanity begins to be realized. Prophetic denunciation of persecution and oppression may be seen in the remarks on Alexander the coppersmith (2 Tim 4:14; cf. 1 Tim 6:13), but the false teachers condemned held numerous tenets that would be detrimental especially to the poorer members (see food prohibitions, 1 Tim 4:3). Thus, even proper church government (so central a concern in 1 Timothy and Titus) becomes a means for ensuring that the churches, like their apostle, "remember the poor" (Gal 2:10). It might even be argued that historically, these most "conservative" epistles have contributed most to economic development and the liberation of oppressed classes in those countries which early extended the Calvinistic interpretation of their teaching on church government to the national political level (López Michelson 1947).

K. 1–2 Peter, Jude

1 Peter, probably a baptismal homily/tract proceeding from the Petrine circle (1:1; 5:12–13) in Rome (ca. 80 A.D.?), addresses churches in five provinces of Asia Minor (1:1; modern Turkey). Although the general technical terms for poor/poverty are absent, the relatively impoverished situation of the churches is clearly represented in various ways.

First, the Jewish and gentile believers are described as homeless, either "visiting strangers" (1:1), "resident aliens" (1:17), or both (2:11), sharing the Diaspora exile experience of non-Christian Jews in Asia Minor (1:1). Whether these terms be limited to a literal sense (Elliott 1981), or begin to include the (neo)Platonic cosmology explicit in the book of Hebrews, a large measure of socioeconomic content is increasingly recognized.

Second, the paradigmatic and major subgroup within the churches addressed is that of "household servants" (2:18–25) working in mainly non-Christian manors. The second major subgroup is that of the wives of unbelieving husbands in households whose economic means (2:2) obviously exceed those of the house servants. Recent converts include especially younger men of uncertain economic means (5:7).

Analysis of the causes for poverty may begin by studying the socioeconomic situation of the five provinces, of Diaspora Jews in the area (Elliott), and of gentile converts (largely former God-fearing proselytes) in the new sect. Particularly, the Diaspora experience of homeless aliens and separation from official Judaism resulted in frequent oppression and persecution (1:6; 2:12, 18–21; 3:14–17; 4:1, 12–19; 5:8–10).

The suffering and deprivations of uprooted "homeless" is countered in 1 Peter by incorporation into the new community of the church as the "household of God" (2:5; 4:17). In this new home (cf. "heaven" in the book of Hebrews), God is the gracious Father (1:2–3). The few affluent male converts (3:7; 2:13–17) are encouraged not to withdraw from public life, but to set examples as public benefactors (2:14; cf. Rom 13:3), a function which often included political and structural economic measures in times of scarcity and famine (Winter 1988a; 1988b). The proclamation of the gospel as "good news to the homeless" (1:12, 25; 2:9–10) thus imparted to uprooted recipients a sense of dignity and status (1:5, 9; 2:9–10). Tendencies toward unhealthy paternalism (see 1 Timothy 5) were thus vigorously counteracted.

The identification of imperial Rome with the name "Babylon" (5:13) suggests not only the resort to pseudonymity common in times of persecution (cf. book of Daniel), but also the kind of prophetic denunciation against oppressors elaborated in Revelation and James. 1 Peter is realistic in recognizing that such oppression may continue to occur even within the household of God (5:2–3), where all such behavior is subjected to divine judgment (4:17).

The newly baptized converts were born again to a living hope (1:3, 21) that included life in the new people of God, which was to be consummated at the Parousia (2:12; 4:13), seen as the ultimate solution to all persecution, homelessness, oppression, poverty, and suffering.

Although Jude purports to be the brother of James (1), his undisguised fury against false teachers (4–19) seems far removed from James' indignation against the rich who oppress the poor. Conceivably Jude attacks the kind of ideology that evolves to rationalize injustice, oppression, and indifference to the material needs of the poor, whose needs should be ministered to in the "love feasts" (12, "feed themselves"; cf. "coveting" in 16, 18). The "impiety" (*asébeia* 6 times 4, 15, 18), which appears to be the keynote of the epistle (Bauckham, *Jude, 2 Peter* WBC, 37) commonly translates the Heb *ḥamas* ("violence") in the LXX (Pons 1971: 166), and may be understood as reflecting the kind of violence the poor suffer at the hands of the wealthy and powerful. Even the sexual excesses Jude so vigorously condemns (*asélgeia,* 4; cf. 8, 10) may also involve oppression and force against the weaker elements in society.

While Jude made no reference to the common cause of poverty signified by *adikia* (injustice, oppression), 2 Peter makes this concept basic to the epistle (2:9, 13, 15) and juxtaposes the injustice-oppression of the world (1:4; 2:20) with the justice of the kingdom of God and the promised new heavens and earth (1:1, 11, 13; 2:5, 7–8, 21; 3:13). As in Jer 22:16, "knowing God" involves doing justice (1:2, 8; 2:20–21; 3:18; Miranda 1974: 44–53). The use of *asébeia* strengthens the case for a reference to the violence commonly suffered by the poorer and weaker sectors of society (2:5; cf. *ḥamas* in Gen 6:11, 13). Traditional elitist Greek virtues (1:5b–6) are placed in a radical Christian framework, beginning with faith (1:5a) and culminating in the brotherly friendship and agape love that characteristically maintained the solidarity of the socioeconomically diverse Christian communities (1:7; cf. 18; 3:1, 8, 14–15, 17; cf. 2:13).

L. Revelation

Word-study approaches on poverty gave rather meager results for the book of Revelation. The poverty *(ptocheia)* of the church in Smyrna is attributed to the oppression-persecution proceeding from certain "Jews" (2:9; Hanks 1983: 48). The reference (3:17) to the "poor" *(ptochós)* Laodicean church, although metaphorical, has been found particularly helpful in delineating the literal sense: having "need" *(chreia)* = wretched, pitiable . . . blind and naked . . . shame. Rich and "poor" alike succumb to the idolatrous economic demands of the second beast in 13:16 (*ptochós,* parallel to small and great . . . free and slaves; cf. the denunciation of the slave traffic in the "bodies and souls of men," 18:13; "slaves and small," 19:18). Such skimpy linguistic data, coupled with the current popular escapist eschatological "interpretations," ill prepare us to understand why F. Engels in 1883 should select Revelation as the subject of his only article on a biblical book (Engels 1974).

However, recent Latin American studies (Stamm 1978; Foulkes 1989) and sociological approaches (Schüssler Fiorenza 1985b) make clear the truly radical character of apocalyptic and utopian genres, which commonly proceed from poor, oppressed, and persecuted groups (see the exiled author's description of his situation, 1:9). Stamm called attention to the severe denunciation of imperial oppression and obscene luxury, rationalized by idolatrous religious claims (1978, chaps. 13, 17–18). Schüssler Fiorenza writes: "To those who are poor, harassed, and persecuted, the promises to the 'victor' pledge the essentials of life for the eschatological future: food, clothing, house, citizenship, security, honor . . ." (1985b: 196; cf. 124–25).

The perspective on sexual minorities in Revelation is paradoxical. Prostitutes undoubtedly would have felt much more comfortable sitting at Jesus' feet by the Sea of Galilee than in the seven churches in Asia Minor, listening to John's description of imperial idolatry with all the lurid references to the "Great Harlot" (chaps. 17–18). On the other hand, the seer's declaration that sexual relations with woman are "defiling" (14:4) brought unspeakable joy for centuries of medieval monks, who delighted to see themselves as the "virgins" espoused to the Lamb (Boswell 1980: 216–18). Post-Reformation heterosexist Protestant exegesis commonly confesses the text to be one of the most "difficult" in the NT (Schüssler Fiorenza 1985b: 181–92; Countryman 1988: 137–38).

M. Gospel and Letters of John

The gospel and letters of John may appear singularly deficient in specific ethical content. Jesus reveals only that he is the Revealer and in another apparent tautology commands a love, which keeps his commandment, which is to "love one another." The four references to the ever-present beggarly poor (*ptōchós,* John 12:5–6, 8; 13:29) hardly are such as to inspire great concern (*TDNT* 6: 907). Hence First World Johannine scholarship has focused on other areas, largely ignoring significant questions raised by Miranda (1977; see below) and a few other liberation theologians (Herzog 1972) and Third World exegetes. However, a growing minority of theologians interpret the Johannine writings as representing a unique, radical perspective. Just as they have opposed traditional "feudalizing" of the kingdom in the Synoptics, so they reject the "Platonizing" of (eternal) life in the Johannine writings.

John's prologue speaks of the Word become "flesh," which if not explicitly designating an option for a humanity that is "intrinsically poor" (Pixley and Boff 1986: 69), at least points to characteristic weakness (6:63), of which human poverty was a dominant expression. The homelessness and margination of the incarnate Word (1:11, 46; cf. 14:2–3) is another Johannine motif that expresses a painful dimension of poverty (Pixley and Boff 1986: 72–74; Fraijo 1985: 62). Mainline scholarship stresses persecution and excommunication as dominant formative experiences in the history of the Johannine communities, but has not commonly recognized the deadly economic deprivation and violence involved. As in the Synoptics, Jesus' healing miracles are usually directed toward the poor (e.g., John 9:8, "beggar") and the weak (5:1–13; 4:43–54), and the same is true for the provision miracles (2:1–11; 6:1–15). The forward placement of the temple cleansing (2:13–22, following the provision of wine for an obviously poor family) gives prominence to John's critique of the oppressive Jewish oligarchy, for "it is precisely in the limits of the Temple where Jesus opts for the marginated: the sick, poor, publicans, women, children, foreigners" (Zorrilla 1988: 71).

Above all, the Johannine substitution of (eternal) life for the Synoptic stress on the kingdom must be understood dialectically (Barrett 1972) and polemically in the context of excommunication, persecution, and violence. Traditional Platonizing interpretations of John radically distort the original meaning and seek to elude the painful "bite" of the polemic. The "abundant life" John offers (10:10) avoids extremes of nondialectical Pentecostal-charismatic "prosperity theology," but is not limited to a Platonically spiritualized (nonmaterial) realm (3 John 2). Miranda (1977) may have erred by succumbing to Bultmann's elimination of futuristic eschatology, but not in delineating the radical character of the Johannine perspective on the poor, justice, injustice/oppression (*adikia,* 1 John 1:9; 5:17), sacrificial love, and life.

In synthesis the gospel of John may be viewed as outlining the causes of poverty in the persecution, oppression, and violence suffered by the community; 1 John points explicitly to the poverty commonly resulting (1 John 2:17, "need"; cf. 3 John 5–8), and the appropriate response of agape love in the context of Christian communities characterized by *koinōnia* sharing. "John's love is love of the deprived, the poor, the needy" (Miranda 1977: 95). Despised and marginated sexual minorities are treated with concern and given special honor (4:1–42; cf. 8:1–11).

N. Hebrews

Paradoxically, Hebrews makes unprecedented use of the OT (particularly in the radical Exodus-Wilderness-Conquest traditions), yet also is commonly believed to represent an extreme in the NT writings in the degree of (neo)-Platonizing evident in its language and theology. In its perception of poverty and its causes, Hebrews is basically continuous with the Exodus paradigm. The question still debated is whether the solution is conceived of in (neo)Platonic terms: an Exodus-type escape, but to a spiritualized, nonmaterial heaven; or whether the eschatology of Hebrews is basically consistent with the apocalyptic-utopian perspective common to the rest of the NT. The author obviously represents an educational elite and addresses well-educated readers who seem more impoverished from persecution than originally poor (ca. 67–70 A.D.?). The two leading candidates, Apollos and Barnabas, each shared Paul's itinerant lifestyle (cf. 13:2–3 on hospitality and imprisonment).

The key passages are few but eloquent and significant for the NT teaching on the poor. The most explicit text climaxes the great faith chapter, countering the militarism and political triumphalism of 11:32–34a with reference to "others . . . of whom the world was not worthy," whose poverty (v 37, *hystereōmenoi*) is exemplified in their lack of adequate clothing (37a), and accompanied by brutal violence (35, 37a), ridicule and torture (36a), and unjust imprisonment (36b). Such impoverished, brutalized souls, like the elect in James (2:5), are particularly rich in faith (Heb 11:39–40). Related but less explicit references to impoverished saints may be observed in the mention of new converts whose possessions were plundered (10:32–34), and of the poor Israelite slaves in Egypt (11:24–26; cf. Exodus). Women and sexual minorities receive special attention (Rahab 11:31; Melchizedek 7:3 with Isa 56:3–5), but family integrity is defended against some who despised marriage (13:4).

Since Hebrews begins by stressing that God spoke through the prophets (1:1), it is not surprising that the prophetic emphasis on oppression and persecution as the fundamental cause of poverty dominates (10:33; 11:25, 37; Hanks 1983: 38–39). Such oppression impoverishes not only the original targets of persecution and discrimination but those who demonstrate solidarity with them as well (10:33, *koinōnia;* 11:25; cf. Matt 5:3; 25:31–46).

Hebrews shares with the rest of the NT an emphasis on the Church's ministry as a provisional and partial solution to the suffering of the poor. The "meeting together" is for providing for material needs as well as for spiritual edification (10:24–25). The Church's present ministry may be viewed theologically as the internalization of God's just law in the new covenant (8:8–12, note *adikia,* "oppression," v. 12; cf. 6:10; 10:17; Jer 22:16) or externally in the good works to the needy, agape solidarity, and ministry *(diakonéō)* to the saints (6:10). Brotherly love *(philadelphia)* is to be manifest in hospitality to homeless visitors (13:2, itinerant prophets and evangelists like Apollos?); ministry to those unjustly suffering imprisonment (13:3, 23), physical solidarity with the "excommunicated" (13:12–13), good works and sacrificial sharing *(koinōnia;* 13:15–16, 21). A life free from "the love of money" is prerequisite to such sacrificial external measures (13:5).

More "structural" approaches to the elimination of oppression and poverty may be seen in the new covenant provision (which internalizes Torah as a whole, not just its reformist and merciful elements; cf. the Exodus-Wilderness-Conquest traditions in 3:1–4:11) and in the military-political triumphalism of 11:32–35 (all of which are past, not contemporary realities). While not so explicit as Luke in presenting the gospel as good news to the poor, Hebrews does stress evangelism involving an integral salvation-liberation.

A more (neo)Platonist reading of the book would lead us to perceive a conflict between the utopian apocalyptic of other NT writings (Revelation 20–22; 2 Pet 3:13). However, despite some tendentious English translations, it is possible to read even the apparently (neo)Platonic texts in ways more consistent with materialist Hebrew thought and other NT books. Above all, "Mount Zion, the Heavenly Jerusalem" (12:22–24; cf. 11:10, 16) need not be interpreted as a nonmaterial realm eternally removed from the earthly scene, but as "coming" in space as well as time (13:14), like the new Jerusalem of Revelation, which finally descends to earth to consummate the kingdom of God (Heb 12:26–28 "receive"; Matt 6:10). Whichever reading is correct (neo-Platonic or materialist Hebrew), the consummation of the kingdom of God is viewed as elsewhere in the NT as the final glorious solution to the sufferings of the poor and oppressed. Certainly the book's teaching on creation (1:1–14) and resurrection (11:35; 13:20) is more consistent with a materialist reading. Even if an intermediate state and heavenly sphere receive more development and emphasis here than in other NT books, this reading need not contradict an ultimate apocalyptic, earthly-material resolution. The portrayal of Moses' decisive option for the poor and oppressed (11:24–26) is the most vivid and explicit NT paradigm of this element so basic to contemporary liberation theologies (strangely ignored by Boff and Pixley 1989, the Eng trans. of Pixley and Boff 1986). Hebrews' educated, eloquent author undoubtedly identifies with that picture.

O. Conclusion

Just as the OT presents considerable diversity of perspectives regarding the poor/poverty (see the 8th-century prophets and Proverbs), so considerable diversity must be recognized in the NT. Attempts to synthesize and harmonize biblical teaching and to draw general theological conclusions tend not to pay sufficient attention to this diversity. Heavily ideological and propagandistic works exalting the "Christian virtues of capitalism"—or socialism/communism—abound, usually highly selective in their use of "control texts" and often lacking in careful exegesis.

Liberation theology, with its emphasis on the Exodus paradigm of oppression and liberation, has planted fundamental challenges to traditional neo-Platonic interpretation of the NT. Certain liberation theologians and exegetes have made extreme statements regarding the poor/poverty in the NT. However, their perception that some kind of "option for the poor" is represented in most if not all the NT literature (far transcending occasional references to the "beggar poor") marks a major advance in NT interpretation, as is now widely recognized (*ISBE* 3: 609–11, 905–8, 921–26; Sugden 1988; cf. Adie 1984). Socio-economic and anthropological studies of the NT continue to debate and refine theological perceptions of the various documents regarding the poor.

However, Third World liberation theologians have only begun to take into account feminist perspectives, and feminist theology itself often has been somewhat elitist in its concerns. The socioeconomic polarization of women in the NT (poor widows or wealthy converts) has received little attention in studies on poverty and wealth. And liberation theologians have scarcely even raised any questions about NT perspectives on despised sexual minorities and uncleanness (Countryman 1988). Medieval monks assumed the NT to represent the perspective of continent bachelors; Protestantism has tended to assume that everyone except Paul must have had a wife and children. The failure to challenge sexual and family ideological assumptions has been a glaring weakness in theological efforts to delineate NT perspectives on oppression and poverty (Greenberg 1988).

Basic continuity between OT and NT perspectives on poverty and oppression is evident. However, for analysis of the factors in oppression, evaluation of the experience of poverty, and understanding of authentic liberation and integral salvation, the NT makes contributions of fundamental importance to biblical theology. Contemporary theological use of these perceptions, of course, must involve careful recourse to hermeneutics. The fact that poverty basically was caused by oppression at the time of the Exodus or in the NT does not prove that such is the case today, nor that biblical paradigms of liberation for the poor can now be slavishly imitated.

Bibliography

Adamson, J. B. 1989. *James: The Man and His Message.* Grand Rapids.

Adie, D. K. 1984. Christian View of Wealth. Pp. 1159–63 in *Evangelical Dictionary of Theology,* ed. W. A. Elwell. Grand Rapids.

Barrett, C. K. 1972. The Dialectical Theology of St. John. Pp. 49–69 in *New Testament Essays.* London.

Beals, A.; with Libby, L. 1985. *Beyond Hunger: A Biblical Mandate for Social Responsibility.* Portland, OR.

Belo, F. 1981. *A Materialist Reading of the Gospel of Mark.* Trans. M. J. O'Connell. Maryknoll, NY.

Berguist, J. A. 1986. "Good News to the Poor"—Why Does This Lucan Motif Appear to Run Dry in the Book of Acts? *BTF* 18/1: 1–16.

Boff, C., and Pixley, G. V. 1989. *The Bible, the Church and the Poor.* Maryknoll, NY.

Boswell, J. 1980. *Christianity, Social Tolerance, and Homosexuality.* Chicago.

Brummel, L; Valle, C. A.; and Rios, R. E., eds. 1978. *Los Pobres: Encuentro y compromiso.* Buenos Aires.

Burge, G. M. 1984. Alms, Almsgiving. Pp. 34–35 in *Evangelical Dictionary of Theology,* ed. W. A. Elwell. Grand Rapids.

Cassidy, R. J. 1978. *Jesus, Politics and Society.* Maryknoll, NY.

———. 1987. *Society and Politics in the Acts of the Apostles.* Maryknoll, NY.

Cassidy, R. J., and Scharper, J. P., eds. 1983. *Political Issues in Luke–Acts.* Maryknoll, NY.

Countryman, L. W. 1988. *Dirt, Greed, and Sex: Sexual Ethics in the NT and Their Implications for Today.* Philadelphia.

Elliot, J. H. 1981. *A Home for the Homeless: A Sociological Exegesis of I Peter, Its Situation and Strategy.* Philadelphia.

Ellul, J. 1977. *Apocalypse: The Book of Revelation.* Trans. G. Schreiner. New York.

———. 1988. *Jesus and Marx: From Gospel to Ideology.* Trans. J. M. Hanks. Grand Rapids.

Engels, F. 1974. El Libro del Apocalipsis. Pp. 323–28 in *Sobre la Religion,* eds. H. Assmann and R. Mate. Salamanca.

Foulkes, R. 1989. *El Apocalipsis de San Juan.* Buenos Aires.

Fraijo, M. 1985. *Jesus y los Marinados: Utopia y esperanza cristiana.* Madrid.

Greenberg, D. F. 1988. *The Construction of Homosexuality.* Chicago.

Gutiérrez, G. 1973. *A Theology of Liberation.* Maryknoll, NY.

Hanks, T. D. 1983. *God So Loved the Third World.* Trans. J. C. Dekker. Maryknoll, NY.

———. 1986a. The Evangelical Witness to the Poor and Oppressed. *TSF Bulletin* (Sept.–Oct.): 11–20.

———. 1986b. La Navidad segun San Mateo. *Mision* 18: 94–101.

Herzog, F. 1972. *Liberation Theology: Liberation in the Light of the Fourth Gospel.* New York.

Hodgson, R. 1983. Paul the Apostle and First Century Tribulation Lists. *ZNW* 74: 59–80.

Johnson, L. T. 1977. *The Literary Function of Possessions in Luke–Acts.* SBLDS 39. Missoula, MT.

Koenig, J. 1985. *New Testament Hospitality.* Philadelphia.

Lee, P. 1986. *Poor Man, Rich Man: The Priorities of Jesus and the Agenda of the Church.* London.

López Michelson, A. 1947. *La estirpe calvinista de nuestras instituciones.* Bogota.

Lührmann, D. 1989. The Gospel of Mark and the Sayings Collection Q. *JBL* 108: 51–71.

Malina, B. J. 1986. Interpreting the Bible with Anthropology: The Case of the Poor and the Rich. *Listening: Journal of Religion and Culture* 21: 148–59.

Maynard-Reid, P. U. 1987. *Poverty and Wealth in James.* Maryknoll, NY.

Meeks, W. A. 1983. *The First Urban Christians: The Social Word of the Apostle Paul.* Binghamton, NY.

Miranda, J. 1974. *Marx and the Bible.* Trans. J. Eagleson. Maryknoll, NY.

———. 1977. *Being and the Messiah: The Message of St. John.* Trans. J. Eagleson. Maryknoll, NY.

Moxnes, H. 1988. *The Economy of the Kingdom: Social Conflict and Economic Relations in Luke's Gospel.* Philadelphia.

Mullin, R. 1983. *The Wealth of Christians.* Exeter, UK.

Myers, C. 1988. *Binding the Strong Man: A Political Reading of Mark's Story of Jesus.* Maryknoll, NY.

Neyrey, J. H. 1988. *An Ideology of Revolt: John's Christology in Social Science Perspective.* Philadelphia.

Nickle, K. 1966. *The Collection: A Study in Paul's Strategy.* SBT 48. London.

Pallares, J. C. 1986. *A Poor Man Called Jesus: Reflections on the Gospel of Mark.* Trans. R. Barr. Maryknoll, NY.

Pantelis, J. 1989. Los Pobres en Espiritu Bienaventurados en el Reino de Dios. *RevistB* 1: 1–9.

Peterson, N. R. 1985. *Rediscovering Paul.* Philadelphia.

Pikaza, X. 1984. *Hermanos de Jesus y Servidores de los mas Pequenos (Mt 25, 31–46).* Salamanca.

Pilgrim, W. 1981. *Good News to the Poor: Wealth and Poverty in Luke–Acts.* Minneapolis.

Pixley, J., and Boff, C. 1986. *Opcion por los pobres.* Buenos Aires.

Pons, J. 1971. *L'Oppression dans l'Ancien Testament.* Paris.

Ringe, S. H. 1985. *Jesus, Liberation, and the Biblical Jubilee.* Philadelphia.

Schmidt, T. E. 1987. *Hostility to Wealth in the Synoptic Gospels.* Sheffield.

Schottroff, L.; and Stegemann, W. 1986. *Jesus and the Hope of the Poor.* Maryknoll, NY.

Schottroff, W.; and Stegemann, W., eds. 1984. *God of the Lowly: Socio-Historical Interpretations of the Bible.* Maryknoll, NY.

Schüssler Fiorenza, E. 1985a. *In Memory of Her.* New York.

———. 1985b. *The Book of Revelation.* Philadelphia.

Stamm, J. B. 1978. El Apocalipsis y el imperialismo. Pp. 359–94 in *Capitalismo, Violencia y Antivida* vol. 1, eds. E. Tamex and S. Trinidad. San José, Costa Rica.

Stegemann, W. 1984. *The Gospel and the Poor.* Trans. D. Elliot. Philadelphia.

Sugden, C. M. N. 1988. Poverty and Wealth. Pp. 523–34 in *New Dictionary of Theology,* ed. S. Ferguson, et al. Downers Grove, IL.

Tamez, E. 1989. *Faith without Works Is Dead: The Scandalous Message of James.* Bloomington, IN.

Theissen, G. 1978. *Sociology of Early Palestinian Christianity.* Trans. J. Bowden. Philadelphia.

———. 1982. *The Social Setting of Pauline Christianity.* Trans. J. H. Schütz. Philadelphia.

Via, D. O., Jr. 1985. *The Ethics of Mark's Gospel in the Middle of Time.* Philadelphia.

Waetjen, H. C. 1989. *A Reordering of Power: A Socio-Political Reading of Mark's Gospel.* Minneapolis.

Winter, B. 1988a. "Seek the Welfare of the City": Social Ethics According to 1 Peter. *Themelios* 13/3: 91–94.

———. 1988b. The Public Honouring of Christian Benefactors. *JSNT* 34: 87–103.
Zorrilla, C. H. 1980. *La Fiesta de Liberacion de los Oprimidos: Relectura de Jn. 7.1–10.21.* San José, Costa Rica.
———. 1988. *La Fiestas de yave.* Buenos Aires.

THOMAS D. HANKS

POPLAR. See FLORA.

PORATHA (PERSON) [Heb *pôrātāʾ*]. One of the ten sons of Haman (Esth 9:8). On problems surrounding this list of names, see ADALIA (PERSON). Poratha (LXX *pharadatha;* A *gagaphardatha*) perhaps renders the otherwise unattested Old Iranian name *Paru-raθa, "having many chariots" (Zadok 1986: 109) or *Paurāta-, a short form of a name such as *Paurubāta (Hinz 1975: 191).

Bibliography

Hinz, W. 1975. *Altiranisches Sprachgut der Nebenüberlieferungen.* Wiesbaden.
Zadok, R. 1986. Notes on Esther. *ZAW* 98: 105–10.

PETER BEDFORD

PORCH. One of several words used to designate architectural spaces that are transitional between the closed interior of a building and the courtyards that are clearly external. Some of these spaces are roofed; others are open to the sky. RSV "porch" denotes the space in front of the Hall of Pillars of Solomon's palace (1 Kgs 7:6). The Hebrew *ʾûlām* is elsewhere rendered "nave" or "vestibule," in reference to the forecourt of the temple. In the RSV, that feature is denoted by "porch" only in Ezek 8:16 (cf. Matt 26:71, where *pulōn* may mean the entrance to a courtyard). The term *ʾûlām* is discussed in TEMPLE, JERUSALEM.

CAROL MEYERS

PORCIUS FESTUS (PERSON). See FESTUS, PORCIUS.

PORCUPINE. See ZOOLOGY.

PORTICO, SOLOMON'S. See SOLOMON'S PORTICO.

POSIDONIUS (PERSON) [Gk *Posidōnios*]. One of three members of a delegation sent by Nicanor, according to 2 Macc 14:19, to work out the terms of a peace with Judas Maccabeus and his followers. This envoy, bearing a familiar Greek appellation, was named after Poseidon, the Greek god primarily of earthquake and water who in cult was viewed as the sea god. For the other members of the delegation, see THEODOTUS and MATTATHIAS.

JOHN KAMPEN

POSTSTRUCTURAL ANALYSIS. Structuralist studies, which have influenced literary criticism during the last twenty years, represent a rejection of two earlier, time-honored philosophical proposals about how it is that texts communicate their meanings to readers. They reject the view that texts are meaningful because they refer in a straightforward and simple way to the world we all inhabit. Language, it used to be supposed, is, or at least should be, a clear window on the world. Such a view of most language was always recognized as problematic, and a distinction was made between an "ideal" language which would exactly picture the world and other forms, like those of poetry and fiction, which were considered to be merely "emotive." But even in plain discourse, this picture theory of language is unhelpful. If I write that "I am sitting at a desk," the reader may have a picture of a desk, but not because "desk" has come to have a meaning for the reader from his or her observation of desks, but because "desk" is distinguished in the English language from "table," and other furniture, and the reader has learned how to make that distinction. We can easily imagine a language in which the distinction does not exist. Structuralism insists that words have a relational, rather than an essential, meaning. Each word fits into a complex pattern of binary oppositions, contraries, and contradictories, and it is this structure which gives it meaning.

Similarly, in literature, longer units of text are related to one another through binary oppositions like parallelism and inversion. Structuralism has therefore tended to treat languages and literatures as autonomous and has examined their internal structures. It has highlighted the distance between language about the world and the world itself, and has seen languages and literatures as cultural rather than natural phenomena.

Structuralism also rejects a second account of how texts become meaningful for readers. In our Western tradition, it is often assumed that texts convey meanings because the author intends a meaning and readers are able to look through the text into the mind of the author, who is conceived as a transcendent, disembodied, thinking self behind the text. Writing is thus understood as a kind of second-order speech, in which one person directly communicates his or her intention to another. In one-to-one conversation, however, the intention of the speaker is perceived by the recipient not only through the spoken utterance but also through the context. If I say "Please close the door," the listener is likely to understand my command in a context in which the door to the room is open, but to be puzzled if the only door visible is already closed. He or she may also understand my command to suggest that I am intending to go on and say something private, if, for example, I have just broken off my previous remarks. But if I have just shivered, he or she will think my intention is to exclude the draft. Again, if there is a noise in the corridor which makes communication difficult, the listener will suppose I am intending to muffle the noise. Moreover, if the recipient fails to understand, clarification can be requested. Even so, in present one-to-one conversation, misunderstanding is not always avoided. Communication depends on speaker and hearer sharing the same competence, and this cannot invariably be guaranteed. Nor are ambiguities in language and context always sufficiently recognized to ensure against misunderstanding. How much more problematic is the conception of meaning in terms of an author's intention when it is applied to texts, written, published, and read in quite different contexts, with the reader unable to cross-question the author to discover whether the supposed interpretation is the right one? Even when a writer and author share a common culture and language, and live at the same time, the reader can discover different plausible interpretations of the same text, and difficulties are increased when author and reader are separated by time and language. Structuralism therefore abandons the search for the intentions of the author and acknowledges a text's multiplicity of possible meanings.

The work of the French philosopher Jacques Derrida (b. 1930) has focused and intensified structuralism's questioning of common-sense attitudes to meaning. His books and essays examine philosophical literature in the Western tradition, from Plato to the present day; his method has sometimes occasioned superficial misunderstandings, so it will be useful to begin by clearing these out of the way. Derrida's writings encapsulate a very careful reading of philosophical texts, drawing attention not only to the main lines of argument which they contain, but also to the metaphors in which the argument is expressed, and which, as it transpires, undermine the argument itself. This endeavor has sometimes been characterized as the triumph of literary criticism over philosophy, and has been taken to warrant a completely free interpretive game with texts, irrespective of subject matter, genre, or any rational constraints. That such an understanding is superficial will become clear by examining an example of Derrida's work.

Plato's *Phaedrus* contains a discussion by Socrates about the dangers of writing and the superiority of direct speech (LCL, 275b–78). Commentators on the *Phaedrus* have usually bypassed this section because they have found it peripheral to their main interest. Derrida not only insists on treating the text seriously in the sense of refusing to omit sections from consideration, but also draws out its implications for Plato's philosophy and for the Western philosophical tradition which has been influenced by it. Socrates is depicted as favoring speech over writing because in speech the speaker is present and able to authorize where, how, by whom, and to whom his philosophy is taught. Once philosophy is written down, the text seems to open its wisdom to anyone who has access to a copy at any time. It allows people to repeat what is written without understanding it. The preference for speech, in which the speaker is present, over writing, in which the speaker is absent, is what Derrida calls *logocentrism.* But in reading the *Phaedrus,* Derrida draws attention to two important contradictions (Derrida 1981). The first and most obvious is that Plato has written this account of Socrates' castigation of writing. The second is that when Socrates tries to indicate the superiority of speech, metaphors from writing are used to describe speech. For example, speech is the word written in the mind of the speaker (LCL, 276a) or is writing inscribed on the soul (278b). The binary opposition of speech/writing, which the *Phaedrus* explores, is undermined by this interplay between the two. *Deconstruction* is the name given to this detailed elucidation of a text, which takes account both of explicit oppositions and of the ways in which they dissolve into an exchange which can give precision or preference to neither.

Moreover, the supposed "presence" of the speaker in his or her speech is just as illusory as the writer's "presence" in writing. Speech is no more a spiritual reality than writing is. Speech is not innocent, not an unmediated expression of the self. As soon as sensations are transformed into utterances about human experiences, they become entangled in the web of differential terms and relations. Both speaking and writing are attempts to make the inchoate coherent, but their achievements are only partial, open-ended approximations, which are suggestive rather than definitive.

The same *logocentrism* is present in biblical texts. God's creative and self-authorizing word brings creation into being and inspires the law and the prophets. In Christianity there is a similar mistrust of writing ("the letter kills but the spirit makes alive" [2 Cor 3:6]; cf. 2 John 12) but the same contradiction: the Bible indicates the priority of speech over writing in a written text. And when speech's superiority is described, use is made of a metaphor from writing: "I will put my law within them, and I will write it upon their hearts" (Jer 31:31).

It is just this privileging of speech and presence as somehow more original, a view which is fundamental to Western perceptions, that Derrida calls into question. The relation cannot simply be inverted to make writing privileged, but the interplay of the two must acknowledge the absence of an authoritarian presence prescribing meaning. To capture this sense of the opaqueness of language, Derrida invents a new French word, *différance,* which both expresses the insights of structuralism, that meaning is relational rather than essential, and conveys the further insight that meaning is indefinitely deferred, never completely captured and defined by an utterance.

Not only Derrida, but many modern philosophers have argued that language does not give us a clear picture of the world. Language is rather an expression of cultural and institutional ways of life. Pragmatists have been content to accept that language is useful in affording communication within social systems, without searching for a metalanguage which would allow escape from this relativist prison. Such a stance involves a conservative attitude toward the institutions which give language its sense and significance. In biblical studies, too, we cannot always be unaware of cultural and institutional influences on religious language, even when presented in the form of commentaries on the Bible. Commentaries from the Middle Ages seem alien in their interests and concepts to people living in the 20th century, but even commentaries written by contemporaries in English betray their sectarian bias. Derrida offers no solution to this relativist dilemma, but he is neither content to ignore it, nor accept it.

We may not be able to escape from the limitations that language imposes on thought, but we can at least become aware of the limits and of the ways in which those limits are undermined by the very language which expresses them. *Deconstruction* questions not only the definitive meanings of texts, but the societies and institutions which validate their use.

One feature of Derrida's writings which has given rise to interpretations that take no account of the text's form or genre is the practice of setting one text alongside another so that each is illuminated (for example, texts by Plato and Mallarmé in "The Double Session," Derrida 1981). It is common for interpreters to confine their discussions of literature to a single book, or to the books of a single author, or to books within the same genre. But Derrida's concern encompasses a whole cultural tradition and its intertextual influences. While recognizing that some insights can be gained by restricting the range of examples, Derrida also explores the interrelatedness of texts from quite different genres to gain new insights. Specialization in universities and colleges often serves to obscure links between different areas of discourse. Biblical studies could be enriched by examining some of the connections.

For example, scholarly English commentaries on the NT resurrection narratives could usefully be read alongside John Locke's *Essay Concerning Human Understanding* (1689), chap. 27, to discern their mutual influences and blind spots. A commentary which marginalizes the accounts of the empty tomb by calling them late legends or secondary traditions allows an interpretation of resurrection in terms of the binary opposition of soul and body in John Locke's anthropology. On the other hand, Locke's dualism and individualism owes something to the problematic presentation of the gospels' stories. Moreover, "soul," which is privileged in Locke's account, is distinguished from "body" by regarding it as a kind of body: "one person in two distinct bodies" is like "one man in two distinct clothings." Locke's essay uses metaphors in spite of empiricism's suspicion of metaphorical language.

In one respect at least, biblical texts encourage their own deconstruction. As Schneidau has argued, "the biblical insistence on our understanding ourselves in relation to an historical past, rather than in terms of a static cosmic system, breaks with the tendencies of logocentrism and allows us to align Derrida and the Bible" (1982: 5). He quotes Derrida on the relation of history to writing and Judaism: "The painful folding of itself which permits history to reflect itself as it ciphers itself. This reflection is its beginning. The only thing that begins by reflecting itself is history. And this fold, this furrow, is the Jew. The Jew who elects writing which elects the Jew" (Schneidau 1982: 9). Derrida does not encourage us to ignore history in our readings of texts, but, on the contrary, to take our readings and our history all the more seriously by noticing that we have not arrived at a final meaning.

Since Derrida insists that meaning is always deferred, never finally closed, it is interesting that one of his essays should include readings of the Revelation of John, which concludes the NT. Derrida's essay "Of an Apocalyptic Tone Recently Adopted in Philosophy" (1982) takes its title from Kant's "Of an Overlordly Tone Recently Adopted in Philosophy" to explore both old and new apocalyptic predictions of the imminence of the end of philosophy, of Western culture, and of the world. Kant offered a truce to his opponents, to the mystagogues who predicted the imminent demise of philosophy because they thought they perceived the truth for which it was searching. Derrida seeks to comprehend this apocalyptic tone. He observes that the revelation is precisely a revelation of truth; the tone of apocalyptic is self-assured, both in its conviction that the end is imminent and in its confidence in its own ability to reveal the truth about the end (Derrida 1982: 84–85).

But the Revelation is not an unmediated perception of the present and the future, nor is its delivery to the seven churches straightforward. There is rather a whole series of speakings, hearings, writings, and readings, as the opening verses of the book (Rev 1:1–3) show. Jesus indeed commands that John "write what you see, what is, and what is to take place hereafter" (1:19), and goes on to dictate letters to the angels of the seven churches. But this form soon gives way to descriptions of heavenly visions of a scroll written on both sides and sealed with seven seals (Rev 5:1); in the shift of images, seeing and hearing merge with reading. There are more confessions, more messages, more envoys to be dispatched, and a scroll to be eaten. The concluding words of Jesus in the book verify the dispatch of a messenger: "I, Jesus, have sent my angel to you with this testimony for the churches" (22:16); warnings are given against altering the words of the prophecy of the book (22:18–19). Derrida observes (1982: 87) that the imagistic structure of the Revelation—"dispatches [that] always refer to other dispatches without decidable destination"—is an image of writing itself.

Kant's essay lampooned mystagogues whose writings failed the criteria of rational philosophy. Derrida discovers that the opposition between philosopher and mystagogue, between rational philosophy and mystification, begins to dissolve on examination (1982: 88–89).

The Revelation has one other important lesson to teach those who suppose that the author owns the book's message or determines its meaning with any finality:

> It is said at the very end (22:10): Do not seal this: "Do not seal the words of the inspiration of this book. . . ." "Do not seal," that is to say, do not close, but also do not sign (Derrida 1982: 95).

Bibliography

Derrida, J. 1978. *Writing and Difference.* Trans. A. Bass. London.

———. 1981. *Dissemination.* Trans. B. Johnson. London.

———. 1982. Of an Apocalyptic Tone Recently Adopted in Philosophy [trans. J. P. Leavey, Jr.]. *Semeia* 23: 63–97.

Detweiler, R. 1978. *Story, Sign, and Self.* Missoula, MT, and Philadelphia.

Norris, C. 1982. *Deconstruction: Theory and Practice.* New York.

Schneidau, H. N. 1982. The Word against the Word: Derrida on Textuality. *Semeia* 23: 5–28.

MARGARET DAVIES

POTIPHAR (PERSON) [Heb *pôṭîpar*]. The name of the first master of Joseph (Gen 37:36; 39:1). The name belongs to a common Egyptian type attested from the 10th century B.C. through Roman times (although sporadic examples may be found in the 11th century B.C.), and means "He-whom-(the sun god)-Re-gives." Several examples of this very name occur, ranging from the 7th through the 3d centuries B.C. The similar name of Joseph's father-in-law, Potiphera, is closer to the Egyptian original. The Potiphar of Joseph's first employment in Egypt is described as "a eunuch of Pharaoh and the captain of the butchers (guard)" (Gen 39:1). The former designation is derived from an Assyrian title and only occurs in Egypt during the Persian domination (in the 5th century B.C.); the latter has no obvious Egyptian original.

Bibliography

Kadish, G. E. 1969. Eunuchs in Ancient Egypt. Pp. 55–62 in *Studies in Honor of John A. Wilson.* Chicago.

Redford, D. B. 1970. *A Study of the Biblical Joseph Story.* Leiden.

Schulman, A. R. 1975. On the Egyptian Name of Joseph: A New Approach. *SAK* 2: 235–43.

Vergote, J. 1959. *Joseph en Egypt.* Louvain.

———. 1985. Joseph en Egypt: 25 ans après. Pp. 289–306 in *Pharaonic Egypt, the Bible, and Christianity,* ed. S. Groll. Jerusalem.

DONALD B. REDFORD

POTIPHERA (PERSON) [Heb *pôṭî peraᶜ*]. The father-in-law of Joseph. His daughter Asenath was given by Pharaoh as a wife to Joseph (Gen 41:45). Out of their marriage two children were born: Manasseh, the firstborn, and Ephraim (Gen 41:50–52; 46:20).

"Potiphera" is a longer version of the name Potiphar, borne by the captain of the guard who bought Joseph as a slave from the Midianites (or according to the Yahwist, from the Ishmaelites, cf. Gen 37:25–28). The name in Egyptian is *pꜣ- dỉ-pꜣRᶜ*, and it means "He whom Re [the sun god] has given." The LXX treats the two names as identical and transliterates both names as *Petephres.* Potiphera was a priest of On, a city NW of modern Cairo. The city was later renamed Heliopolis by the Greeks. On was the center of sun worship in ancient Egypt, and the temple of Re had become the most important place in the city as early as the 5th Dynasty. When the worship of the sun god came into greater prominence in early Egyptian history, the priests who ministered at the temple gained more power and prestige in Egyptian society (Wilson 1951: 88). The high priest of On was a very influential and important figure in Egyptian religious life. There is no way of knowing if Potiphera was the high priest or only one of the many priests who ministered at On. However, because the narrative presents Joseph as a prominent officer of Pharaoh, answerable only to him, it is highly probable that Potiphera was to be regarded in the story as the high priest of On (Ward 1957: 51). The name does not appear in Egyptian inscriptions until the middle of the 10th century B.C., during the 22d Dynasty. This may provide some indication of the time when the Joseph narratives were written.

Bibliography

Ward, W. 1957. Egyptian Titles in Genesis 39–50. *BSac* 114: 40–59.

Wilson, J. A. 1951. *The Burden of Egypt.* Chicago.

CLAUDE F. MARIOTTINI

POTSHERD GATE (PLACE) [Heb *šaᶜar haḥarsît*]. A gate of Jerusalem at the S tip of the City of David (Jer 19:2), adjoining the juncture of the Hinnom and Tyropoeon or Central valleys, which is considered by most (Avi-Yonah 1954: 245) to be identical to the Dung Gate of Neh 2:13; 3:13, 14; and 12:31. An alternate translation is Gate of Earthenware (*BDB,* 360) or Gate of Potters (Simons 1952: 230, n. 1), which is erroneously translated in the AV as the East Gate. The Potsherd Gate should be identified with the wall and gate found by Bliss and Dickie (1894–1897) in the Tyropoeon or Central valley (Bliss and Dickie 1898: 116–26). Jeremiah's illustrated sermon at this gate, where broken pottery was discarded, was situated adjacent to the Hinnom valley where Israelites were participating in pagan liturgies (Jer 19:4–5). The Dung Gate may also be translated "Gate of the Refuse Pile" (*BDB,* 1046), a great deal of which would have been broken and discarded pottery, particularly if (as suggested by Simons 1952: 230) the gate adjoined an installation for the manufacturing of pottery. It has been suggested that this may be related to the name Topheth (another name used for the Hinnom valley, Jer 19:6).

Nehemiah's inspection tour took him S from the Valley Gate past the Jackal's Well to the Dung Gate or the Potsherd Gate (of Jeremiah's time) just before he rounded the S tip of the City of David. This gate was repaired by Malchijah son of Rechab, the ruler of the district of Beth-haccherem, and is the first landmark noted in the dedicatory procession (Neh 12:31) that went S and counterclockwise from the Valley Gate.

Bibliography

Avi-Yonah, M. 1954. The Walls of Nehemiah—A Minimalist View. *IEJ* 4: 245.

Bliss, F. J., and Dickie, A. C. 1898. *Excavation at Jerusalem, 1894–1897.* London.

Simons, J. 1952. *Jerusalem in the Old Testament.* Leiden.

DALE C. LIID

POTTER'S WHEEL. Pottery was made and used throughout the ancient world. Special wheels for fashioning pottery came into use at an early period, and were used throughout Palestine and neighboring areas. The Hebrew word designating a potter's wheel, *ᵓobnāyim,* occurs only once in the OT (Jer 18:3). The word's literal meaning, "pair of stones," is indicative of the configuration of the device itself.

From the MB I period (ca. 2000 B.C.) onward, pottery in Palestine was generally "thrown" on a fast wheel; i.e., it was made on a wheel spinning fast enough so that the centrifugal force formed the vessel, with the potter merely guiding the clay with his hands to attain the desired shape. Prior to the MB I period, pottery vessels were formed on a simple tournette. The Hebrew name for the potter's wheel may derive from the fact that the earliest potter's wheel, the tournette, was no doubt comprised of a pair of stone disks.

Stone bearings from "fast" potters' wheels have been found in abundance in excavations in Palestine. Usually made of basalt, but occasionally of limestone, they consist of one or both of two components: a lower whorl with a cavity, or socket, in the center, and an upper whorl with a projection, or tenon, in the center. See Fig. POT.01. The two whorls fit together, with the tenon mating the socket. From the wear marks on such whorls, it is evident that the upper whorl (sometimes called a pivot) rotated on the

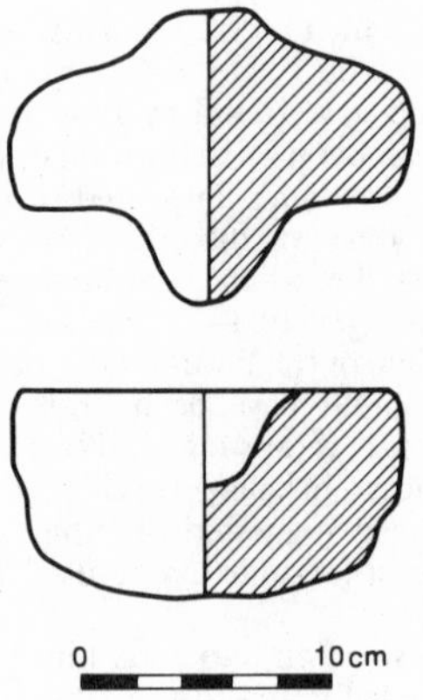

POT.01. Upper and lower thrust bearings for a potter's wheel from Jericho—MB. *(Drawing by B. G. Wood from Garstang 1934: pl. 19.2)*

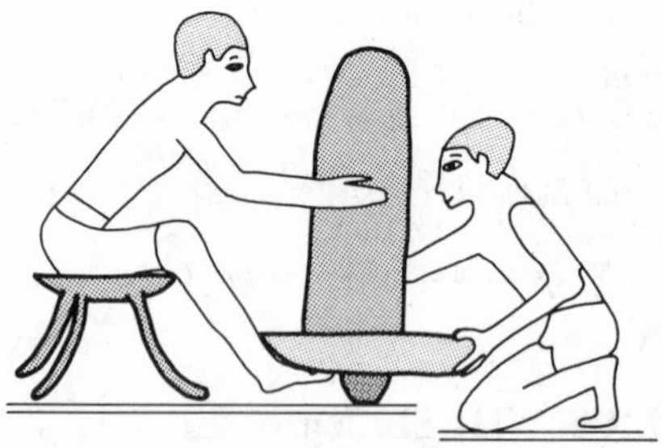

POT.02. Representation of potter's wheel from tomb of Kenamun at Thebes—18th Dynasty. Potter fashions a vessel from a conical lump of clay on a single potter's wheel, while an assistant turns the wheel. *(Drawing by B. G. Wood from Davies 1930: pl. 59)*

lower whorl. In reality, these stone whorls are thrust bearings from a more elaborate apparatus made of wood. From archaeological evidence and ethnographic analogy it is possible to reconstruct the "fast" potter's wheel of ancient Palestine. Two types were in use, the single wheel and the double wheel.

In the single or simple wheel (also called a hand wheel), the lower bearing is secured in the ground or on a platform or bench. A wooden disk (called a flywheel, wheel head, table, or platform) is attached to the upper bearing and the assembly is placed on the lower bearing with the tenon inserted in the socket. The wooden disk is then rotated by hand by an assistant while the potter fashions his vessels. The tenon in the upper bearing acts to keep the wooden disk centered and running true. An 18th-Dynasty Egyptian potter is seen using such a single wheel. See Fig. POT.02. The lower portion of the potter's wheel (shown in Fig. POT.02 without the shaft or upper wheel) is, in effect, a single potter's wheel. In a LB IIA (14th century B.C.) potter's workshop at Hazor a platform or workbench made of fieldstones was found (Yadin et al. 1960: 101–3). On top of the platform was a complete thrust-bearing assembly. The bearing assembly undoubtedly belonged to a single-wheel type of potter's wheel since a double wheel would not have been placed on such a bench.

The second type of fast wheel is the double or compound wheel (also called a combined wheel, foot wheel or kick wheel). In this type a wooden disk (the flywheel) is attached to the upper bearing as with the simple wheel, but now a vertical shaft is attached to the center of the wooden disk. See Fig. POT.03. At the end of the shaft is a second, smaller, wooden disk (the wheel head, working platform or table) where the vessel is fashioned. The shaft is steadied by a horizontal wooden bar with a hole in it, through which the shaft passes. Since the potter can now rotate the wheel by kicking the lower disk with his foot, an assistant is no longer needed (Foster 1959: 104; Childe 1965: 201; Nicklin 1971: 35–38; Holthoer 1977: 31). In an early Iron I (12th century B.C.) potters' cave at Lachish, two shallow pits (Pits C and D; Tufnell et al. 1958: 91, 292, pl. 92) appear to be emplacements for double potters' wheels. Similarly, Pit H in Cave 37 at Megiddo (Iron II period, 9th–7th centuries B.C.), with a worn stone socket found *in situ* (Guy 1938: 80, fig. 84), was most likely an installation for a double potter's wheel.

Bibliography

Childe, V. G. 1965. Rotary Motion, Vol. 1, pp. 187–215 in *A History of Technology,* ed. C. Singer, E. J. Holmyard, and A. R. Hall. Repr. London.

Davies, N. G. 1930. *The Tomb of Ken-amun at Thebes.* The Metropolitan Museum of Art Expedition, Vol. 11. New York.

Foster, G. M. 1959. The Potter's Wheel: An Analysis of Idea and Artifact in Invention. *Southwestern Journal of Anthropology* 15: 99–117.

Garstang, J. 1934. Jericho: City and Necropolis, Fourth Report. *Annals of Archaeology and Anthropology* 21: 99–136.

Guy, P. L. O. 1938. *Megiddo Tombs.* OIP 33. Chicago.

Holthoer, R. 1977. *New Kingdom Pharaonic Sites: The Pottery.* The Scandinavian Joint Expedition to Sudanese Nubia, Vol. 5/1. Stockholm.

Nicklin, K. 1971. Stability and Innovation in Pottery Manufacture. *WoAr* 3: 13–48.

Tufnell, O., et al. 1958. *Lachish 4: The Bronze Age.* London.

Yadin, Y., et al. 1960. *Hazor 2: An Account of the Second Season of Excavations, 1956.* Jerusalem.

BRYANT G. WOOD

POTTERY. Pottery can be defined as utensils or other artifacts made of clay and hardened by fire. Ever since the 6th millennium B.C. pottery has played an important role in the material culture of the ANE. Palestine was not a country particularly rich in artistic forms of expression or literary accomplishments. Material remains from biblical times are generally common and ordinary during most periods, and even poor and fragmentary at times. But pottery is always found. This entry consists of two articles pertinent to ancient Palestinian pottery. The first surveys the technology of producing pottery in ancient Palestine. The second surveys the role that pottery artifacts play in

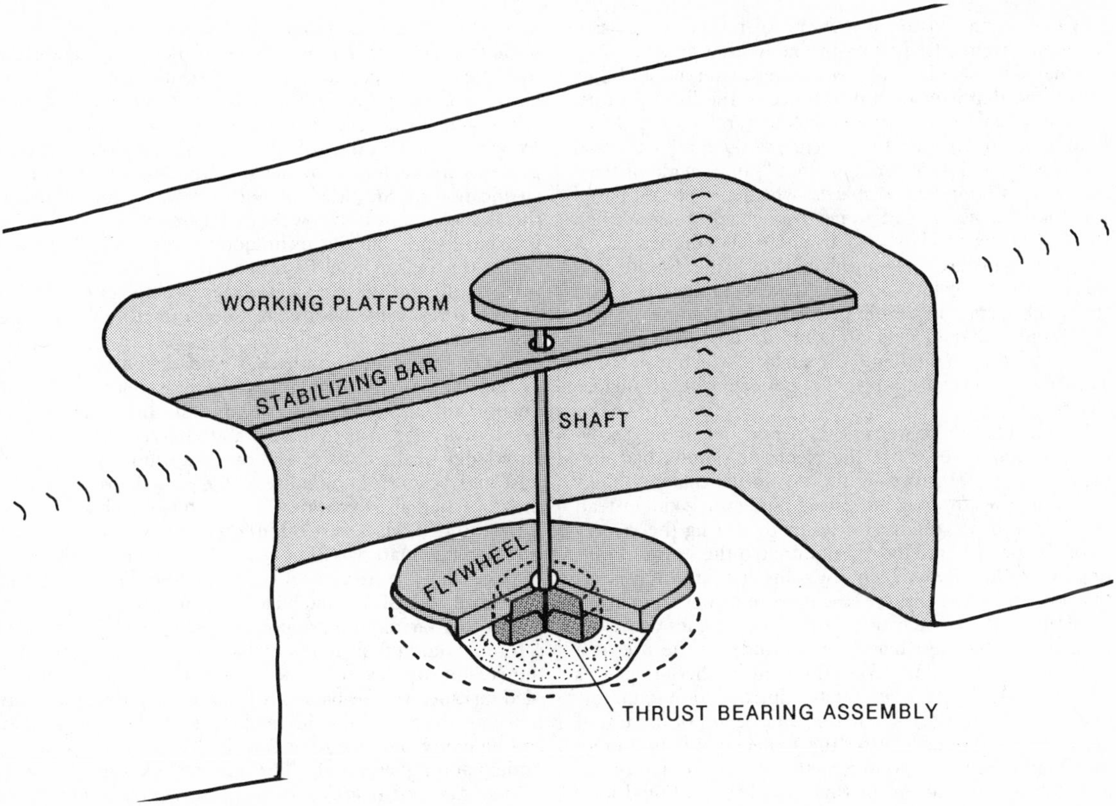

POT.03. Reconstruction of a double potter's wheel. *(Drawing by B. G. Wood)*

helping the archaeologist establish a chronological date for strata and other excavated artifacts.

POTTERY TECHNOLOGY IN ANCIENT PALESTINE

The study of pottery technology of antiquity seeks to find an explanation for the observable features of excavated pottery. It is normal practice in archaeology to describe the shapes and other features of excavated pottery on the basis of visual examination. The aim of technological studies is to add another dimension to these studies. For instance, one can identify Neolithic pottery from the visual descriptions, but how this pottery was invented cannot be deduced; only a technological study can help in solving this problem. But there are also other questions which cannot be solved without the aid of technological research, as will be shown in this article.

One can only speak about the invention of pottery making from the moment the process of manufacture was repeated with success and became a regular feature of Neolithic culture. The fact that pottery making had become a routine demonstrates that the makers understood what was happening, and that the invention was not a chance discovery. The first potters had acquired certain kinds of knowledge before they achieved regular production. They could distinguish between clays and other soils, and they knew how to make clay mixtures which could be shaped into a bowl by exercising pressure on the inside of a clay ball, and counterpressure from the outside. They knew that the shape had to dry, and that during the drying process the bowl shape would shrink and crack unless special care was taken to prevent it. They also knew that during firing the temperature had to be high enough to create a dark red glow in the clay, and that this temperature had to be maintained for some time. They knew how to do this because the technology for lime burning had already been invented. There were even experiments with making "pottery" from lime. In the case of the Neolithic pottery from ancient Jericho, it has been demonstrated that the potters used kilns and not open fires for pot making.

Thus it can be shown that people in Neolithic times experimented with different earths because they were seeking a substitute for the stone bowls which took a great deal of effort to make. However, once they had succeeded in producing fired clay vessels and could repeat this process, they continued with the experiments, some of which are mentioned here. Since the beginning of the Neolithic period people had known that to make sun-dried bricks, one had to mix the clay with chopped straw or similar dry materials. This gave cohesion to the brick and prevented it from flaking during the drying period. Similarly one finds very fine organic matter in pottery, or rather, the holes it left after firing. The potters probably used animal dung, but they also experimented with other materials, and they discovered that it made a difference to the fired product whether one used quartz sand or lime sand, coarse or fine sand. They discovered that calcite would render a vessel more heat-shock resistant, and that "sand" made of fired clay such as pounded potsherds, which can be compared with our chamotte, had some distinct advantages when shaping pottery. They also invented the decoration of vessels with different clays which, after firing, would show up in different colors. Such clays were applied as a thin slip to the surface in certain patterns, and as some of these slips would tend to peel off after drying or firing, the potters would rub them into the surface, which resulted in so-called burnished pottery or pottery with a surface sheen.

It seems that there was not very much left to be discovered in later times, since the Neolithic potters had also experimented with turning the pot in the making. They even knew the advantages of firing pottery in a kiln instead of in open fires. The discoveries made during the Pottery Neolithic period have indeed dominated the world of potting in the Near East, except for some comparatively short periods, until this century. New inventions were, in chronological order: (1) the production of what comes very close to stoneware in the Chalcolithic period; (2) the use of a "kick wheel" in the MB Age (followed by the loss of this device during the LB Age); (3) its reintroduction sometime during the Iron Age; (4) the slow perfection of the use of the wheel in the period after the Exile, culminating in an unrivaled mastery of potting techniques in Roman times; and (5) the introduction of what had been invented long before, but had never been taken into regular production: the application of glazes to pottery, and the many ways of manipulating the effects of glazes and metal oxides to obtain the magnificent effects of Islamic glazed wares. What could not have been invented was porcelain. Kaolin, which is the basic ingredient in the production of porcelain, is not found in any quantity anywhere in the entire area.

It is necessary to consider an aspect of pot making which is not generally understood. One common impression is that potters can make any shape when asked to do so. This is by no means true. The shapes potters can make depend largely on two aspects: the type of clay which the potter is accustomed to using, and the traditional knowledge accumulating over generations of potters who knew how to work that clay. Clays resemble wood in that different kinds must be used for different purposes. The traditional knowledge is often so attached to the special properties of the clay which the potter knows and uses, that he cannot imagine other shapes being made from it. The Neolithic potters have been depicted here as people who were very busy inventing and experimenting, as one does in a laboratory. The other side of the picture is, however, that traditional potters belong to that group of very conservative people who will not readily accept innovations and rationalizations in their crafts. And as far as they can, they work according to the traditional rules or "laws" passed down through the generations. After the Neolithic Age there were long periods in which little seemed to change in the potters' production. In Chalcolithic times there were some technical developments; one of them may have been that the very large storage jars were no longer fired in kilns but in open fires in which they became buried in hot ashes, preserving the heat for long hours and keeping oxygen out. The effect of this was that the iron and lime present in the local clay acted as fluxes, which caused vitrification or the development of a glassy phase in the clay at a comparatively low temperature. This produced a very hard ware, but this technique was abandoned in later times; the reason may have been that it took too much fuel. By the end of the Chalcolithic period, much of the natural forest had already been consumed by the village cultures.

Although the technical background remained the same during the first few millennia of potting, both in its production and in its means of decoration, different regions developed their own traditions and characteristics. While knowledge of the craft spread over the whole of the Near East and beyond, knowledge of the varied properties of the clays used also expanded, and potters who had to work with "difficult" clays were often forced to experiment anew with the raw materials. The rewards of their struggle can be seen in their results. Bronze Age potters in Cyprus produced beautifully shaped and decorated pottery which points to a far more advanced knowledge of potting than is found among their fellow craftsmen in Palestine. Clearly the reason for this difference is not that potters E of the Mediterranean were backward people, but that they did not have the right soils for making really fine ware, and consequently did not have the chance to develop better understanding and skill. The history of potting in the Bronze Age and Iron Age confirms this explanation.

Near the beginning of the Bronze Age the first walled settlements appeared, and with them probably pottery markets. The villages of the previous age may also have had such markets, but the tradition that families made their own pottery must already have existed. One might speculate that the inhabitants of the first towns were supplied with pottery partly by professional potters and partly by villagers. This is inferred, for instance, from study of the pottery excavated at EB Jericho. Small jugs and bowls were often made by hand, exactly as in the Neolithic. Embellishment often consisted of a dark red slip applied over the entire body, which was sometimes polished. Similarly one finds the use of a slow wheel which was turned by hand, besides the use of little woven mats on which a pot was built up and which could also be turned by hand. There were apparently professional potters working in the neighborhood, since the production of such classes as storage jars of the hole-mouth type required efficient mass production. One striking aspect of the pottery found at such sites is the care which was taken to make pleasant shapes, and to give them a strong and shiny color. Another striking feature is the occurrence of jars which had a whitewash applied to the surface, which was then decorated with red painted bands. This could only be done as long as firing temperatures were kept well below 825° C, the temperature at which lime turns into quicklime. Much of this pottery was fired in kilns with maximum temperatures of between 700° and 900° C. The firing method probably being practiced in this period was to fire quickly and briefly at probably over 900°C, so that the temperature in the lower levels of the kiln would be sufficient to produce fairly hard pottery, whereas in the upper part of the kiln the temperature would be enough to fire the pots but not enough to make them really hard. Another aspect of kiln firing was that the relation between the influx of oxygen and the escape of hot gases from the kiln was not well balanced. The oxygen flow was often hampered, and as a result the colors of the pottery are often dull or—in technical terms—either neutral or reduced. It was only after the Exile that this aspect of kiln firing was mastered. Pottery in use in small villages was still produced by the families.

In the EB IV, the pottery acquired more uniformity of shape and technique. Much of the pottery had flat bases that were made on flat stone slabs that could be turned, and molds were used to make the walls of jars from two parts that were later fitted together. Due to this device walls could be made very thin. In the E parts of the country these potters did not use a wheel, and even the regularly shaped, flaring rims of storage jars were handmade.

In the MB Age pottery was made on a heavy and rapidly turning wheel. This brought with it other new developments. The fast wheel was in use in Mesopotamia from the 3d millennium B.C. When a fast wheel is used, pottery can be made with elegant profiles, but rather plastic clays must be used which may contain only very fine sand. The wheel creates centrifugal force in the clay on the wheel head by turning at 50 r.p.m. or more. It is rather difficult to attach other parts such as handles to the pots. Finished shapes must dry evenly and slowly to prevent cracking, and firing the pots requires much skill. This complex of new technology was almost certainly introduced from the N. It had some revolutionary results. The use of a fast wheel could speed up production tenfold or more, and slow methods of pot making soon disappeared. A uniformity in shapes developed, and geometrically painted decoration disappeared simultaneously because the production was linked to speed. Light or dark red firing slips were used to cover the entire surface of bowls and dippers, and it is only late in the period that potters again turned to painting decoration on their wares. This new technique of painting (with a red or "black" firing paint made of iron oxides mixed with fine clay slips) was successful because great care was taken that the body of the vessel was well covered with a clay slip that would be nearly white after firing, regardless of the atmosphere in the kiln, which through lack of oxygen could turn a red firing body into a dark gray. The thick slip would also reduce the chance of scum forming on the red paint. In potting in the Near East, scum has always spoiled the potters' attempts to use contrasting surface colors as decoration. Scum forms during kiln firing when there is excessive salt in the clay; it turns the surface color pale greenish yellow, which also affects the painted parts.

An additional problem in the production of painted pottery was that clays containing a large amount of lime (as do most clays in Palestine) will cause iron oxide paints to become volatile at temperatures above 925° C. White firing slips that did not contain iron or lime were ideal as a basis for decoration, but sources for such were probably rare. Some potters applied a white slip first, as a basis for a red slip, in order to create a good surface for a painted decoration.

During the LB there was a slow but distinct decline in every respect. At first production continued with many decorated pieces, but in LB II the problems seem to have begun. Less slip was used to cover the pot surface, which gave scum more chance to influence the decoration. Then the sand used as a filler, which sometimes consisted entirely of lime rock, was no longer sieved, so that coarse particles were introduced in the clay. This tended to break up the surface of the pot after it had been fired. The presence of coarse lime sand indicates that potters returned to the use of slow wheels and less plastic clays. Perhaps the return to simpler production methods was provoked by two aspects of daily life. The mass-produced thin-walled thrown pottery of the MB was fragile, and it became expensive, so it was replaced by pottery with much thicker walls which lasted longer. Since the production process no longer had to be carefully watched, the potters seem to have become careless. In LB IIb a low point was reached. The pots were very heavy and most had cracks in the bases, which the potters had to mend with lime or bitumen before the pots could be used. Decorations fell victim to the same lack of understanding of basic principles in potting, and practically disappeared by the end of the period. By the end of the 13th century the potters had begun to experiment again and find solutions to their problems.

The transition from the 13th to the 12th century B.C., or from the LB Age to the Iron Age, has attracted much attention, because the question is thought to be related to the appearance of the Israelites in Canaan. When seen in this light, the question is: can pottery be used to indicate the presence of the Israelites? Unrealistically high expectations have been raised by earlier pottery studies. The question of what is exclusively Israelite pottery in the 12th and 11th centuries B.C. cannot be answered satisfactorily. Amiran thought that the Israelites took over the craft of potting from the Canaanites, and very soon developed the craft in their own way. If this were so, then pottery could indicate an Israelite presence. However, the end of the 13th century B.C. marks the absolute nadir of the craft, and there was not much to be learned from it; moreover, why should Israelites not have known how to make pottery? To take the problem out of the realm of pure speculation, we need more evidence about the technical development of the craft, and it is hard to obtain such evidence. What is clear, however, is that early in the 12th century B.C. potting was tackled in a fresh spirit of determination to overcome the problems of production, and this process was crowned with success. Since we know about the problems of decoration we do not expect developments in painted pottery, yet the potters invented a strong red slip which was applied to small items and burnished. Potters made better use of the raw materials, and coarse lime sand was no longer used. Potters from Jerusalem preferred to use fine quartz sand, even though it had to be brought from a considerable distance. Late in the 8th century B.C., after the Assyrians had taken Samaria and many people took refuge in or near Jerusalem, pottery production had to be greatly expanded. Lime sand replaced quartz sand; it was available in abundance locally, but it did not improve the quality of the product. The improvements consisted of the production of pottery that was lightweight in relation to its size; potters again made thin-walled pottery which was nevertheless not so fragile as that of the MB (less elegant but more shock resistant). Problems such as inferior bases to the pots no longer occurred.

What happened in the course of the Iron Age can be characterized as the rationalization of production. It was not a matter of mechanization, but a thoughtful development of means and methods of production, resulting in a useful and fairly cheap product, adapted to changing demands. Potters used a slow wheel which was probably hand operated. Small items such as drinking bowls, lamps, small plates, and small jugs were shaped from a cone of clay, which allowed the potter to make a number of pots one after the other. The upper part of the wall was made to the required thickness, but the lower part and the base were made rather thick because, as long as the clay was wet, a thin lower section could collapse under the weight of the upper part. When the rough shape was finished, the potter cut it loose from the clay cone with a string and put it aside to dry for a while. When the upper part (the thin part) was stiff enough, the unfinished shape was put back on the wheel upside down, and the potter scraped clay from the still-wet area to make the lower part and the base as thin as possible. At the same time he would give the base its required shape, such as a ring to stand on. To make larger pots such as storage kraters and water jars, the potter started by making a base and a small part of the wall. This then had to dry because from then on the potter added clay coils to build up the wall to the required height, while at the same time widening the shape. To prevent the wet shape from collapsing under its own weight, he tied string around the belly of the pot, which was removed when the shape had dried but left impressions in the clay wall. The potter scraped away as much surplus clay as possible from the inside near the base. The potters were aware of the need to give walls and base equal thickness. To make a rim shock-resistant it had to be thicker than the wall. The local clays were not sufficiently plastic to fold the top of the neck of a jar down, either to the inside or the outside, as can be done with plastic clays. Instead it had to be pressed down to the outside while the pot was rotated several times, as too much pressure would spoil the pot.

A fair degree of uniformity was largely due to the customers' behavior. Taking the cooking pot as an example, one can notice that in the beginning every potter had his own way of finishing the rim, making it somewhat longer or more flaring, or bending it down or up, and so forth. The customers noticed that rims with a certain profile resisted being struck by accident much better than rims with other profiles. Thus they became conscious of differences in quality, and when buying pots they began to look for the better-constructed ones. Slowly the potters followed this trend, and all began to give the same sturdy rim to their pots. On the other hand, cooking pots were not in daily use. They were probably only used on the occasion of religious festivals and at large family gatherings.

This can be demonstrated in the following way. A technological study of the pottery from Jerusalem in the 9th–6th centuries B.C. resulted in a fairly clear definition of the various classes of pottery, and a distinction could be made between some of the potters producing them. When production of the various classes was worked out statistically, it was found that cooking pots formed only a small part of total production during the 7th century B.C., roughly 5–8 percent. These were produced to replace broken ones—cooking pots had a short life. They were not only more vulnerable than most other shapes, but the base burnt through after some use. Masses of broken bases are always excavated together with fragments of other parts of the pottery, but bases of cooking pots are rare. They crumble away when burnt. If a cooking pot had been used every day, it would have lasted between four and six months. According to the percentages of broken pottery from the different classes, it appears that over the same period in which three cooking pots were broken in a family's daily life, nine rather strong deep storage bowls, twenty-seven small bowls used for drinking and eating, four storage jars, four plates, one lamp, four cylindrical storage jars, and one small jug were broken. This is far too much, and a more realistic estimate would start with the assumption that one cooking pot would last three years, in which case the average family would replace one deep storage bowl, three small bowls, one water jar, one plate, and one cylindrical jar in a year, but the lamp and the small jug would last for nine years. The cooking pot, the lamp and the (perfume?) jug were not for daily use but for festivals. When the sun went down people sat in the dark or enjoyed the moonlight, and they did not normally cook a meal. They baked their daily bread in a small bread oven, and if they had two meals a day, they ate their bread with thick milk probably prepared in several different ways, with cheese, olives, various fresh or dried herbs, dried fruits, and some honey if they could afford it. People ate and drank from small bowls, which represented more than 50 percent of the pottery in daily use through the Iron Age. Meat could be roasted in the bread oven, but it was certainly not part of the daily diet for the average family. The diet of the Israelite family must have changed during the Iron Age, since in the early days there were no real cooking pots, but only very wide and rather shallow frying pans without handles. When people in the 7th century used pots for cooking during festivals, they were probably boiling lentils or preparing special meals.

After the Exile, pottery production did not change until the country revived economically, and then we find a rationalized production. In Hellenistic and Roman times pottery was turned out in large quantities as a result of the throwing technique. The traditional clays were no longer used, being unsuitable for this technique. Pottery firms used fine plastic clays and mixed clays in order to adapt the properties to the shaping techniques. Mass production had become the only way to survive. Jars were thrown in two halves which were luted together, and the lower half was made upside down on the wheel, as were deep bowls and cooking pots. The percentages of cooking pots are not known for this period, but from finds at the Amman Citadel it can be concluded that people used them every day. The pottery became much lighter than it had been in the Iron Age; it had very thin walls and was seldom decorated. People who could afford to buy a good dinner service used terra sigillata or pottery of comparable quality, which was imported from overseas. There was no large-scale trade in fine pottery, such as that produced in Petra in New Testament times, but the potters at Qumran were very fine craftsmen who made high-quality utility wares, as did other potters in the country. This was the time in which, technically speaking, potters had reached the limits of what could be done with the local clays. Petra clays are of a totally different nature to those found in the mountainous areas of Palestine, and this is clearly shown in the products of the potters' workshop.

H. J. Franken

POTTERY CHRONOLOGY OF PALESTINE

Because pottery is almost always found in excavations from biblical sites in Palestine, and because pottery shapes and forms tended to change and develop over time, the historian, and particularly the archaeologist, turns to pottery remains for cultural and chronological information.

A. Importance of Pottery
B. As Chronological Indicators
C. In Survey Work
D. Other Clay Artifacts
E. As Cultural Artifacts
F. In Excavation, Study, and Publication
G. Biblical References
H. Characteristics by Period
  1. Neolithic
  2. Chalcolithic
  3. Early Bronze
  4. Middle Bronze
  5. Late Bronze
  6. Iron Age I
  7. Iron Age II
  8. Exilic and Persian
  9. Hellenistic
  10. Roman
  11. Byzantine

A. Importance of Pottery

Pottery's importance as an artifact of antiquity is due in part to its durability. Once a clay object is fired at a high degree it will harden and although it will break, it will not decay or disappear. Except for those of stone, other ancient artifacts of wood, cloth, reed, or vegetable matter, or even metal, have a limited life span and disintegrate on exposure to air and humidity. Pottery does not disintegrate, but it breaks rather easily on impact and has to be replaced. Once the art of pottery making was mastered, clay vessels were cheap and easy to replace. Clay beds are plentiful in the Near East, and artisans learned to seek out the superior sources of clay. Pottery vessels became the main type of containers in most Near Eastern cultures. Yet the vessels were fragile and their life spans were probably a few years at the most. The broken pieces of pottery, i.e., potsherds, would be discarded, but since they do not disappear they remain as evidence of the ancient peoples who first made them.

A complementary factor has made pottery important as an interpreter of history. Pottery types—their variety in form and texture, style and decoration—developed differently in different places and cultures and changed over time. Standard types were developed according to the needs of a particular people, and there was general conformity in form and design, but over a period of time the needs and styles would change as vessels had to be replaced. Although styles were conservative by today's standards, materials, decorations, and particularly forms changed. For example, Cypriot bilbils and Attic black-figured wares are associated with particular times and places. Wherever they are found they imply manufacture, trade, and cultural exchange during a specific time in history. Neolithic pottery of the Jordan valley indicates contacts with Anatolia, Syria, Egypt, and Mesopotamia. Even the common household wares have become known for their typical forms during a particular period and their changes of style over time. The symmetry and construction techniques of pottery manufacture make it possible to determine the whole form of vessels from "diagnostic" fragments—i.e., parts of vessels that are characteristic of a form such as typical rims, handles, bases, or decorated sherds. The occasional unbroken pot, the restorable vessels, and abundant potsherds found on Palestinian sites are thus invaluable when collected and studied in accordance with advanced archaeological techniques.

B. As Chronological Indicators

Pottery has had a particular historical importance in Palestine because of the lack of written material and rich architectural finds. Thus far the archival collections of tablets and texts known from Mesopotamia, Antolia, and Syria have yet to be found in Palestine and Transjordan. Monumental palaces, pyramids, and tombs have not been uncovered. Many times it has been the lowly potsherd that has revealed a story. The chronological factor reaches beyond dating the pottery for its own sake. Pottery has become the chronological indicator for other artifacts, architecture, and cultural features. This is possible through two principles which go hand in hand: stratigraphy and typology.

The first to realize the potential of pottery dating in Palestine was Sir Flinders Petrie in his excavations at Tell el-Hesi in 1890. As he isolated individual layers of occupation he noted the distinctive pottery types, their disappearance after a time, and the appearance of new forms. He developed what became known as sequence dating, assigning numbers to types, noting the levels in which they first appeared (lower levels) and then disappeared or became infrequent (at a higher level). His division of pottery into groups, such as bowls, jars, jugs, and cooking pots, was the beginning of pottery typology in Palestine. By relating his typology to the stratigraphy he was able to develop a relative chronology. When he found pottery types he recognized from similar finds in Egyptian tombs which were datable by scarabs and inscriptions, he was able to introduce some absolute dates. Pottery was on the way to becoming Palestine's main chronological indicator.

The latest pottery dates the particular layer of earth or debris in which the pottery was found. Pottery can then be used to date the other finds found with it, artifacts which did not change in style as rapidly or for which typologies are not yet known. It becomes possible to date buildings, fortifications, and other cultural remains.

Petrie used the knowledge he gained at Tell el-Hesi in the following years as he excavated other sites, and his ideas were adopted by other Palestinian explorers. As archaeological methods developed, with emphasis on trained staff, detailed records, plans, photographs, and an understanding of the complex nature of the tell (the Reisner-Fisher method of the early 20th century), pottery took on corresponding significance. Ceramic chronology took a major step forward with the publication of W. F. Albright's excavations at Tell Beit Mirsim (1926–32) and his pottery studies from the EB through the Iron Age. By emphasizing the sorting and dating of the pottery which was found in a room, on a floor, or beside a wall, he distinguished building periods as comparative ceramic groups were assigned a particular stratum. In other words, the evidence of contemporary pottery types determined the stratum. It was the Wheeler-Kenyon method, developed principally in Palestine at Jericho (1952–58), that put emphasis on observable layers of debris and the use of vertical sections to examine, correlate, and record the layers of soil, particularly in relation to walls. Structures and artifacts, including pottery, are recorded in relation to the observed debris. Applications of these methods, along with modifications such as larger horizontal areas of excavation, more elaborate systems for saving and recording pottery, and wider ecological and environmental studies, are now generally used.

Because of comparative studies between sites excavated stratigraphically, it is now possible to date pottery within 50 to 100 years for many periods of Palestinian history. Although pottery dating is still the most helpful method for the Palestinian archaeologist, he must use it in coordination with more recently developed scientific methods. Radiocarbon, thermoluminescence, tree rings, magnetic measurements, must all be used, but as yet none of these are as refined and available as the ordinary potsherd. But the ceramic specialist is always open to new advancements in methods and scientific discovery.

C. In Survey Work

Pottery plays a significant role in archaeological surveys. When one desires to learn the history of a particular area, one unexplored or when more thorough or detailed information is desired about a previously explored area, an archaeological survey may be undertaken. Although methods may differ, the collection of artifacts found on the surface is the primary activity. From these finds, suggestions can be made as to the occupational history of a site or area. The most likely artifacts to be on the surface are stone tools or flints for pre-Chalcolithic sites, and pottery for sites occupied thereafter. Although there is always the possibility that the evidence may be lacking, in most cases sherds from every period of occupation have worked their way to the surface. The ability to date groups of diagnostic sherds means tentative conclusions can be reached concerning historical problems and the desirability of excavation and further study.

The ability to date sherds found on the surface has played a part in site identification ever since Petrie's work at the end of the 19th century. As knowledge and methods have improved, older identifications have been many times revised. With new surveys, theories such as those of Nelson Glueck after his explorations in Transjordan and the Negeb have had to be reexamined.

D. Other Clay Artifacts

Although the principal efforts of the potter went toward manufacture of vessels, other clay artifacts are also found in excavations. Loom weights, sometimes of unbaked clay, and spindle whorls are common at some sites which seem to be dyeing and weaving centers. Clay figurines are unbaked in the EB. In the LB, they are made in molds. In the Iron Age they are partly formed by hand and partly in the mold. Ceramic animal figures and small pots, which may be toys, also appear.

Even broken pots were often reused in other ways. They were formed into lids or stoppers, or used as scrapers. Occasionally bowls were mended, as holes along broken edges testify. At Bethel a sherd was found with a piece of a drill through it, apparently broken off in attempting to mend the vessel.

Pottery occasionally provides written material. Sometimes vessels were impressed with seals or scratched with letters that marked ownership or destination. *LMLK* ("belonging to the king")-stamped handles are frequently found on Judean sites in Iron II. Rhodian jars were stamped for export. Records and messages were written on potsherds. These are known as ostraca and important historical evidence has been provided by such collections found at Samaria, Lachish, and Arad.

E. As Cultural Artifacts

Pottery's importance as a cultural artifact may first depend upon its date, that is the particular place and people with which it was associated. But along with its chronological value, pottery needs to be studied as a cultural artifact in its own right. Its style and decoration, its technique and care in making, its form and the possible use to which it was put—all can reveal something about its maker and the culture of those who used it. Its distribution over space and sources of manufacture tell something about the trade and economy of the ancient world. Complex economic, political, and social factors contribute to the movements of peoples, and the distribution of pottery is part of the evidence.

Renewed effort has been directed toward technical studies of pottery. See also the preceding article, POTTERY (TECHNOLOGY IN ANCIENT PALESTINE); POTTER'S WHEEL. Research concerning manufacturing methods and the kinds, sources, and qualities of clays indicate levels of skills, knowledge of environment, trade, and intergroup relations. Application of scientific techniques have served to determine clay composition and its sources. X-ray fluorescence spectrometry, neutron activation, and examination of thin sections under a petrologic microscope have helped to understand pottery manufacture and the raw materials.

Observations of modern potters disclose knowledge of clays and tempers, use of the wheel, and firing techniques that can be applied to the understanding of ancient cultures. Ethnological studies reveal information about the social setting of the makers and users. Pots and potters of a society are important vehicles for the understanding of that society.

F. In Excavation, Study, and Publication

It is obvious that the method of handling pottery on an excavation is very important. Every sherd must be collected, and the debris and locus from which it has come must be recorded. The usual method is to place each sherd in a bucket or container that is identified by locus. It is important that those that come from the same floor, room, or fill be kept in relation to each other so that the possibility of reconstructing vessels may be facilitated. As the sherds are brought in from the field they need to be carefully washed or dipped so that wash, paint, or ink is not removed. As soon as possible the ceramic specialist on the excavation will examine the pottery with the field supervisor of the area excavated so that tentative conclusions can be made as to date and the kind of debris being excavated. Incongruous results may send them back to the field to reexamine their work. A decision must be reached as to what sherds will be saved. If there are possibilities of reconstructing vessels everything is kept. Particularly important loci may demand that all pottery be saved. Some recent excavations have attempted to save every sherd, but on a large excavation sheer volume may make it impossible to handle all the material and storage itself may be impossible. In any case diagnostic sherds (rims, handles, bases, and decorated ware) will be labeled in indelible ink so that any individual piece may be identified. The sherds may be bagged or boxed at this point, but hopefully not long after the conclusion of the fieldwork the field supervisor and ceramist who is responsible for the publication of the material will examine it again. The pottery then serves at least two important purposes. The sherds themselves will be used to date or corroborate the debris, constructions, and other finds from which the material came. This may take much comparative study, depending upon the familiarity of the material. Further, this pottery will also have a contribution to make to further ceramic studies and excavation, as it becomes a part of the total corpus of datable excavated pottery.

The publication of the pottery may include groups published by loci in order to show how particular areas and constructions are dated; it may include publication by type, as the dated pottery makes its contributions to archaeological data. Pottery may be published by photograph, but data is generally best presented visually by drawings in section and in profile. This takes a person skilled in drawing, and consistent methods must be followed in showing form and decoration. Plate layout must be meaningful and attractive. Ware descriptions should accompany each published sherd. The use of the Munsell Soil Color Charts is the usual standard to describe the hue, lightness value, and chroma of the ware. If further technical studies have been undertaken (see above), they will also be fully published.

G. Biblical References

The material remains of the Iron Age demonstrate the importance of pottery and the potter in Israelite society. However, specific biblical references are rather few. In the elaborate descriptions of the temple vessels and offerings, it is evident that the most luxurious and valuable vessels were of metals—bronze, gold, and silver (Exod 27:3; 37:24). However, clay pots were also used (Lev 14:5, 50; Num 5:17), perhaps so they could be destroyed if they became ritually unclean (Lev 6:28). In contrast, the Lord ordered Jeremiah to preserve his land deed in a clay jar (*kĕlî-ḥāreś;* Jer 32:14) a practice well known from Qumran and the caves of the Dead Sea. A piece of pottery, a potsherd (*ḥereś*), was used by Job to scrape his sores (Job 2:8).

Metaphoric use of clay vessels and their makers is the most usual reference to pottery in the Hebrew Bible. An ordinary household item and a necessary and flourishing industry was a natural way to express deeper truths for the biblical writers. The potter (*yôṣēr*) as maker of the pot (*ḥōmer*) is a metaphor for God, the creator of man (Isa 45:9; 64:7 [—Eng 64:8]; Job 10:9). Jeremiah used the figure of the potter (*yôṣēr*) reforming his imperfect objects of clay (*ḥōmer*) into other forms as what the Lord might do to Israel (Jer 18:1–6), and Jeremiah's breaking a clay jar symbolized the breaking up of the kingdom (Jeremiah 19). In Daniel's vision, the wild beast (Dan 2:31–45) had feet which were part iron and part clay (Aramaic *ḥesap*), symbolizing the empire as partly strong and partly weak.

Figurative and vivid uses of clay as a simile appear in the Psalms: "You will shatter them in pieces like a clay pot" (*kĕlî yôsēr,* Ps 2:9); "My throat is as dry as clay" (*ḥereś,* Ps 22:16—Eng 22:15). In the poetry of Isaiah, "He tramples over rulers as if they were mud, like a potter (*yôsēr*) tramples clay (*ṭîṭ*)" (Isa 41:25), and in Proverbs (26:23) your fine talk covers what you really are like, "the fine glaze on a cheap clay pot (*hereś*)."

In the NT, Paul compares God's control to the potter's (*kerameus*) over the clay (*pelos;* Rom 9:20–21), and our treasure as being in "earthen vessels" (*ostrakinos skeuos*), i.e., power is of God, not our own (2 Cor 4:7).

The metaphoric use of clay in the Bible is perhaps the best commentary on the properties of clay and its use in antiquity: its form is at the mercy of the potter, in its hardened form it breaks easily, and the household pot is simple and ordinary.

H. Characteristics by Period

1. Neolithic (ca. 5500–4300 B.C.) Pottery is first known in Palestine toward the end of the Neolithic period. At Jericho, it was preceded by plastered floors and walls, vats and basins, clay figurines and plastered decorated skulls. Although the intermediate steps are not known, these activities could have led directly to the first use of fired pottery. Immediately new levels of civilization were possible: food could be cooked and preserved as never before. This was a major step toward a food-production economy.

The first pottery probably appeared about 5500 B.C. Handmade methods included forming "pinch pots" from a lump of clay held in one's hand, molding in or around a basket or stone vessel, slabs joined by slip (a more liquid clay), or building up by coils. Technical developments were rapid, as pottery from the Jordan valley shows evidence of firing in kilns to 800° C or higher. Various tempers were used before the end of the Neolithic period, including fine-ground pottery (grog). Decoration includes fine slips, and experiments were made with various methods of turning pottery. The usual forms include cuplike bowls, medium and large bowls with sloping or curved sides, and globular jars with flat bases. Rims are very simple, and handles may be simple loop handles, small pierced lugs, or incipient ledges. There are both fine and coarse wares. The coarse is very crude; it had considerable temper and was fired at a low temperature, making it soft and crumbly. The fine wares are of cleaner clay and considerably better fired. The finish is especially attractive; in cream and red-burnished slips a reserved portion is left in various patterns of zigzags, chevrons, or triangles. There are also decorations with incisions, and sometimes a combination of incisions and slip or paint.

At Jericho the Pottery Neolithic B people improved on the Pottery Neolithic A pottery: it is much better fired, the ware is thinner and contains less straw as temper. The forms include jar rims which are concave on the interior, and the loop handle is common. The red-on-cream slips of the earlier fine wares is succeeded by a deep red slip, sometimes burnished. Characteristic is a band of herringbone incisions, sometimes covered by a cream slip.

2. Chalcolithic (ca. 4300–3200 B.C.). The transition from Neolithic to Chalcolithic is not sudden but gradual, and it is not yet clear whether some cultures are transitional, contemporary, or continuous. The Yarmukian and Jericho Pottery Neolithic B are transitional and may fit best into the early part of the Chalcolithic period. In any case, the Ghassulian–Beer-sheba cultures are widespread by Late Chalcolithic times. Wares are more advanced—harder, thinner, and better fired. Pots are still handmade, but there is some evidence of a slow wheel or tournette. New varied forms include V-shaped bowls, goblets and chalices, churns, and cornets. Ear handles are common, sometimes in such excess that they must be merely decorative. Other forms of decoration include impressing, plastic, and paint. Large coil-made pithoi had elaborate rope-like clay bands, most likely in imitation of the rope which was necessary to hold them together as the pots were made. Holemouth jars (POT.04:a), which became so popular in the EB, began to appear. In addition to the household vessels the typical clay ossuaries of the Chalcolithic period should be mentioned; most were shaped like houses or animals, but jars were adapted also for this purpose.

3. Early Bronze (ca. 3200–2200 B.C.). The transition and degree of interruption between the Chalcolithic and EB ages has yet to be settled. Kenyon has called the early period of EB I the Proto-Urban period, beginning EB I with what others call EB IC. It was with the EB that the first correlations with Egypt were made, and the absolute chronology of the Bronze Age depends on correlation with predynastic and dynastic material of Egypt. Canaanite pottery found in Egyptian tombs and Egyptian artifacts found at EB sites in Palestine, along with local stratified Palestinian pottery, serve as the basis for EB chronology.

The periods of the EB Age are best delimited by the introduction of new pottery forms. Typical throughout the age is the ledge handle (POT.04:h). It apparently originated in Canaan, and from there spread N as far as Upper Galilee, and Canaanite jars with ledge handles have been found in Egyptian tombs. The plain (or duckbill) handle and indented ledge handles were probably the first. Typical of the N are red- and gray-burnished wares, including various kinds of teapots, small bowls with conical omphali, bowls with molded decorations or projecting knobs below the rim (POT.04:b), high loop-handled juglets, amphoriskoi, large jars, and wide-mouthed jars. In the S the typical decoration late in EB I is a painted ware called "line group," usually straight or wavy lines in groups crossed by diagonal lines. Plain bowls often have a row of impressed dots or slashes below the rim. Juglets, amphoriskoi, and bowls are common, but most of the N shapes are present and there was undoubtedly intermingling between the two regions. To these forms, which are best known from tombs, platters and hole-mouth cooking pots found at stratified sites should be added.

Most of these forms of EB I continue to appear in EB II. Platters become plentiful, and amphoriskoi, particularly with the "line group" decoration, are less common. Combing as a finishing makes its appearance. Most typical of EB II are the Abydos wares, called such because they were found in the Egyptian tombs at Abydos and this was the first Palestinian type pegged to Egyptian chronology. The most typical characteristic is a symmetrical oval-shaped jug with a loop handle, red-slipped and hard-baked to a metallic quality. Sometimes they have one or two degenerate loop handles on the side in addition to the regular loop handle, and a form with a stump base develops. There are also jugs with a brown- or red-painted decoration—rows of triangles filled with incisions and separated by bands. The jug forms and types also appear as juglets.

In EB III many of the EB II forms continue. Platters and bowls, some of them deep, continue with more elaborate rims developing. Wavy ledge handles on jars are common (POT.04:i). Pattern combing is characteristic on jars and bowls. The unique feature of EB III, however, is the introduction of KHIRBET KERAK WARE. Known first from Khirbet Kerak in Galilee, it seems to be introduced into Palestine from the N. The ware itself is brittle and poor and the pots are entirely handmade, showing no knowledge of the wheel. However, the vessel is covered with a heavy slip which is polished or burnished to a high gloss. The method of firing produces vessels partly black and partly red, witnessing to a sophisticated knowledge of smoke blackening. The usual Palestinian pot sits on a base as wide or almost as wide as its mouth and gently curves up to its rim. Khirbet Kerak vessels have small bases, sometimes appearing top-heavy, and the profile often curves up in an S-form. Most common are bowl forms, but there are also jugs, stands, and lids. New rim and handle types are introduced, and decoration includes incisions and reliefs, unlike any previously known Palestinian pottery.

Unique vessels sometimes found at EB sites are incense stands and kernoi (three or more small bowls or cups on a ring, probably also cultic in use). EB lamps are hardly more than shallow bowls with a slight pinch blackened by a burnt wick.

The next period sometimes is considered the final period of the EB and is known as EB IV (Dever). Others prefer an "Intermediate EB–MB" designation (Kenyon, Kochavi), emphasizing possible relations with the following period as well as the EB. It was formerly known as MB I

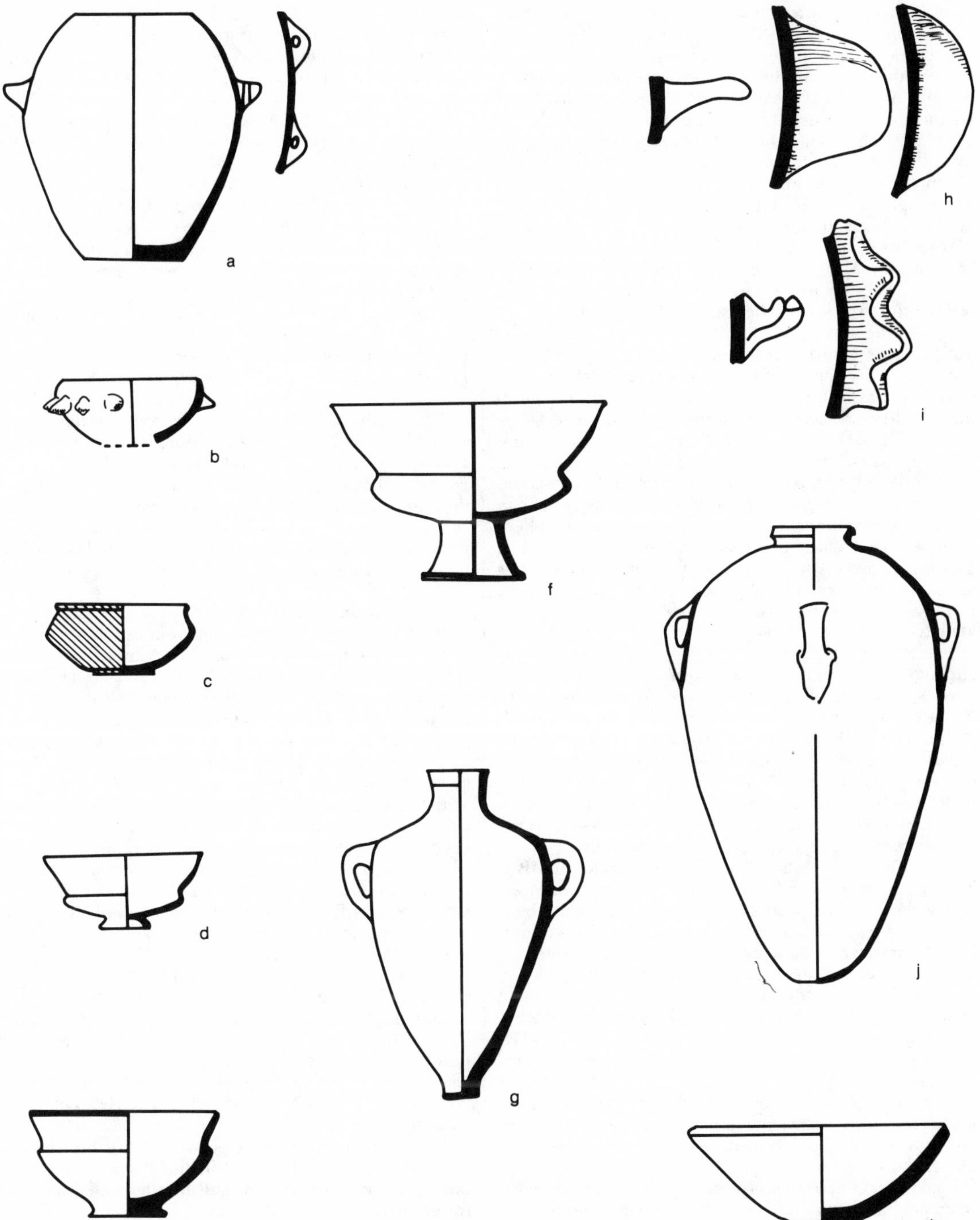

POT.04. Pottery of Palestine—Chalcolithic and Bronze Age: (a) holemouth jar from Ghassul—level IVA, Late Chalcolithic; (b) bowl from el-ʿAffula—EB I; (c) carinated bowl from Megiddo—level XIV, MB I; (d) carinated bowl from Megiddo—level XII, MB II; (e) carinated bowl from Megiddo—level VIII, LB II; (f) chalice from Megiddo—level XI, MB II–III; (g) Canaanite jar from Abu Hawam—level V, LB; (h) ledge handles from Deir Saʾaneh Mahladeih/Ras Abu Lofeh—EB I; (i) wavy ledge handle from Tell es-Saidiyeh; (j) storage jar from Tell Beit Mirsim—level E, MB II; (k) bowl from Megiddo—level VIII, LB II.

(Albright), and this is still preferred by some (Amiran). The urban life of EB II–III as known from large sites in Palestine and Transjordan largely disappears, and in some respects the pottery of the final EB phase is similar to that of EB I. As a rule, types of pottery are very localized and attempts have been made to find many migrations or influences coming into the country and to set up chronological frameworks. It is likely, however, that changes are as much due to the breakup of the city-state system as to new peoples coming into the land, and many of the varied groups may be contemporary.

Wide bases and gently curving sides in jars, jugs, and bowls continue. A profiled rim is typical of many large bowls. Teapots are particularly common. Lamps are open bowls with four wide-pinched spouts (POT.06:a).

Toward the end of the period or in MB I, "caliciform" ware appears. Probably introduced from Syria, the typical decorations are incised wavy lines between straight lines below the rim of the vessel. The jars usually have handmade bodies with necks and rims finished on a wheel.

4. Middle Bronze (1900–1550 B.C.). In the MB, technical advancements from the widespread use of the potters' wheel resulted in improvements in form and decoration. A heavy and fast-turning wheel required a fine temper in the clays and additional care in drying and firing. There were new possibilities in delicate rim and base forms and pleasing shapes. The pottery and other material finds indicate a prosperous society with time for luxury items. Improvements in technology probably helped bring this about.

The MB is easily distinguished from the earlier periods, although the beginning of the technical improvements were already emerging. Similar types occur throughout the MB, but some distinctions can be made between MB I, II, and III. A deep red burnished slip is common in MB I, and there are also cream-slip burnished vessels. Painted decoration is found. In MB II, burnishing continues but many vessels are plain, and painted decoration is less often found. However, Tell el-Yahudiyeh ware, dark-burnished with white-filled punctured holes, is characteristic.

Open, rounded bowls had gently curved sides in MB I. The bases were flat or low disk, and a shallow ring base was beginning to appear (POT.04:c). In MB II the bowl walls are less rounded and sometimes almost straight. Platters or large shallow bowls with a plain, slightly inverted rim are common. Bases are higher, often with a ring, but a concave disk base is also characteristic. The carinated bowls (POT.04:d) are small and closed in MB I with both sharp and rounded carinations. In MB II–III, they are much more varied; they are often flared and vary the place and angle of the carination. The base is better formed and the trumpet base and chalice (POT.04:f) have made their appearance. White or pale-colored thin wares are popular. Occasionally attractive bowls with three handles as bases appear.

Cooking pots are of two types. The flat-based, straight-sided pot has a molded band with thumb impressions and a row of punctures or holes below the rim. In MB II–III, the predominant type is round-based with carinated sides, usually handleless, with the rim rolled or folded outward.

Jugs and juglets take many forms and MB II–III types are generally a continuation of the MB I. Dipper, pyriform, and cylindrical jugs and juglets begin in MB I and branch out into many variations. The double and triple handles are common. Narrow necks with small mouths and outturned rims are typical of both pyriform and cylindrical juglets. The button base on pyriform juglets appears in MB II. Variations with flat, concave, or pointed bases may be MB III variations of the typical form. Tell el-Yahudiyeh juglets with their dark clay and slip, and punctured design filled with white chalk, follow the development of the common pyriform juglets. Cylindrical juglets appear as early as MB I in the coastal region and Jezreel plain, but they appear infrequently in more central regions until late in MB II and then largely replace the pyriform juglet in MB III.

The classic MB II jar is ovoid in shape, tapering to a small flat base (POT.04:j). Two handles are smoothly attached on opposite sides at its widest girth, hardly interfering with the contour of the vessel. The neck is relatively short. Rims may be plain or profiled externally, internally, or both, with rounded, flattened, or tapered edges. Elaborate profiles seem to be more popular as the MB progresses. Bases may be slightly convex and also rounded. Four handles are found as well as two. Combed incised decoration and brownish-red-painted alternating wavy and straight lines over a white slip are also found.

Cypriot imports, so typical of the next period, began to be imported into Palestine in the MB. White-painted and white-slipped wares are found.

5. Late Bronze (ca. 1550–1200 B.C.). The LB is largely contemporary with the New Kingdom of Egypt, and during most of this period Canaan was dominated by Egypt. It is generally divided into LB I, II A, and II B. Most pottery forms are a direct development or degeneration of MB forms. There are many Mediterranean imports and local painted wares, but especially toward the end of the period the local ware becomes cruder and heavier. Analysis at Deir Alla in Jordan has shown that there was a return to the slow wheel and coil-made pottery. The area of this decline and its duration needs to be further tested.

Carinated bowls continued to be made, but by LB II the carination had become not much more than a ridge (POT.04:e). Concave disk bases are more usual than the ring base. By LB II the more usual open bowl has rounded or straight sides (POT.04:k). Chalices and decorated goblets are characteristic throughout LB.

Kraters are also characteristic LB forms. There are two handles, either vertical or horizontal. In LB II they are usually painted, and the metope style is the most popular. The rounded-body cooking pot continues the MB tradition, and the everted rounded rim continues into LB I. A triangular rim also develops and became the most common type in LB II. Late in the period (LB II B) an elongated triangle is typical.

A distinction can be made between the "Canaanite" jars (POT.04:g), used for export in the flourishing international exchange of the LB, and the decorated store jars for domestic consumption. The jar for export was heavier, with thicker walls, slanting from a pronounced shoulder, and a botton or stub base. The domestic jars were usually decorated (a custom begun in the MB) and had thinner walls, an oviod body and a round base (POT.05:a). Large pithoi are also known from N Canaan.

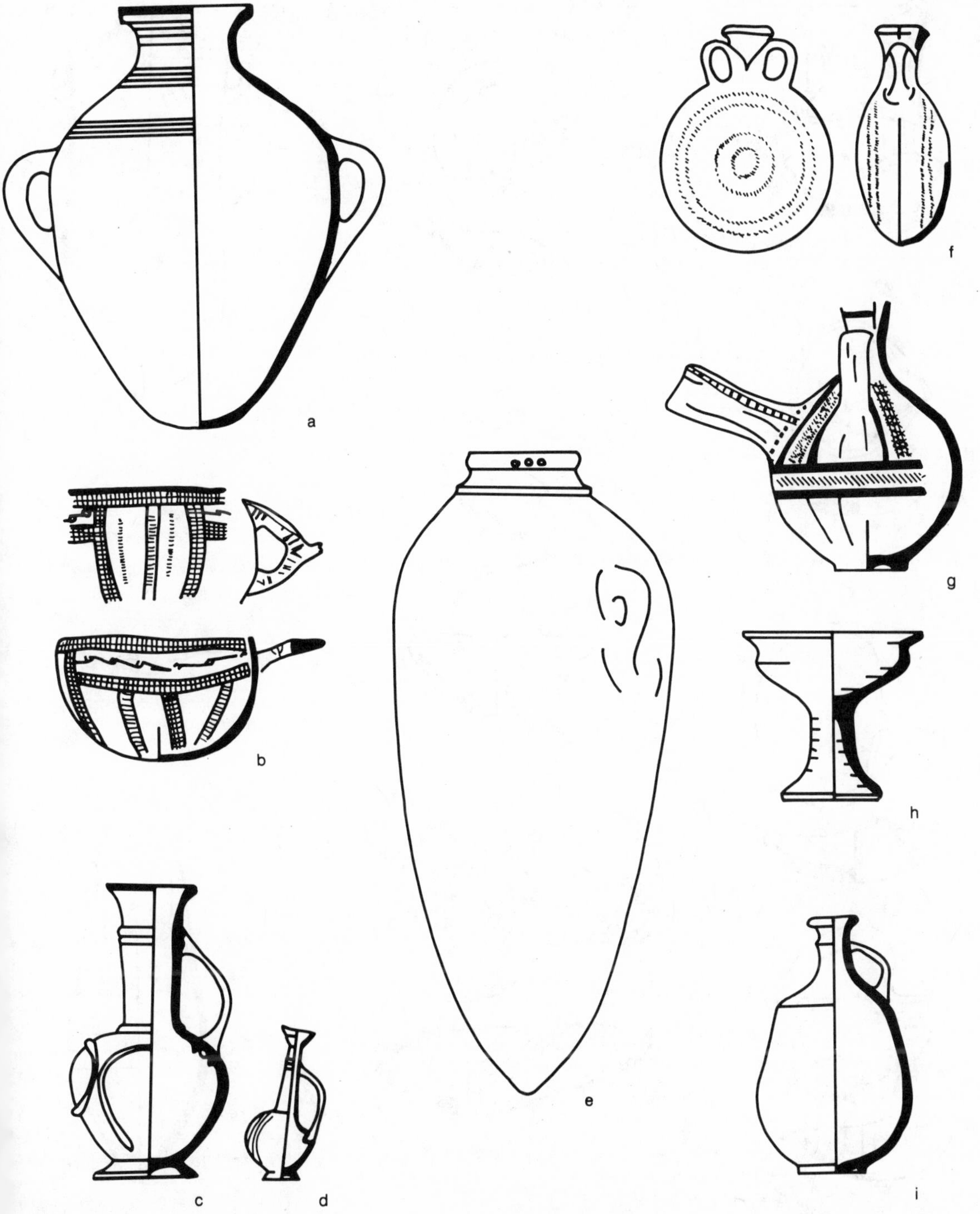

POT.05. Pottery of Palestine—LB and Iron Age. (a) domestic jar from Megiddo—level VIII, LB; (b) Cypriot milkbowl from Lachish—LB; (c) base ring II bilbil from Jerusalem—LB; (d) base ring I bilbil from Jerusalem—LB; (e) collar rim storage jar from Shiloh—Iron I; (f) pilgrim flask from Hazor—level 1B, LB; (g) beer jug from Megiddo—level VIA, Iron I; (h) chalice from Beth-shemesh—level III, Iron I; (i) decanter from Lachish—level II, Iron II.

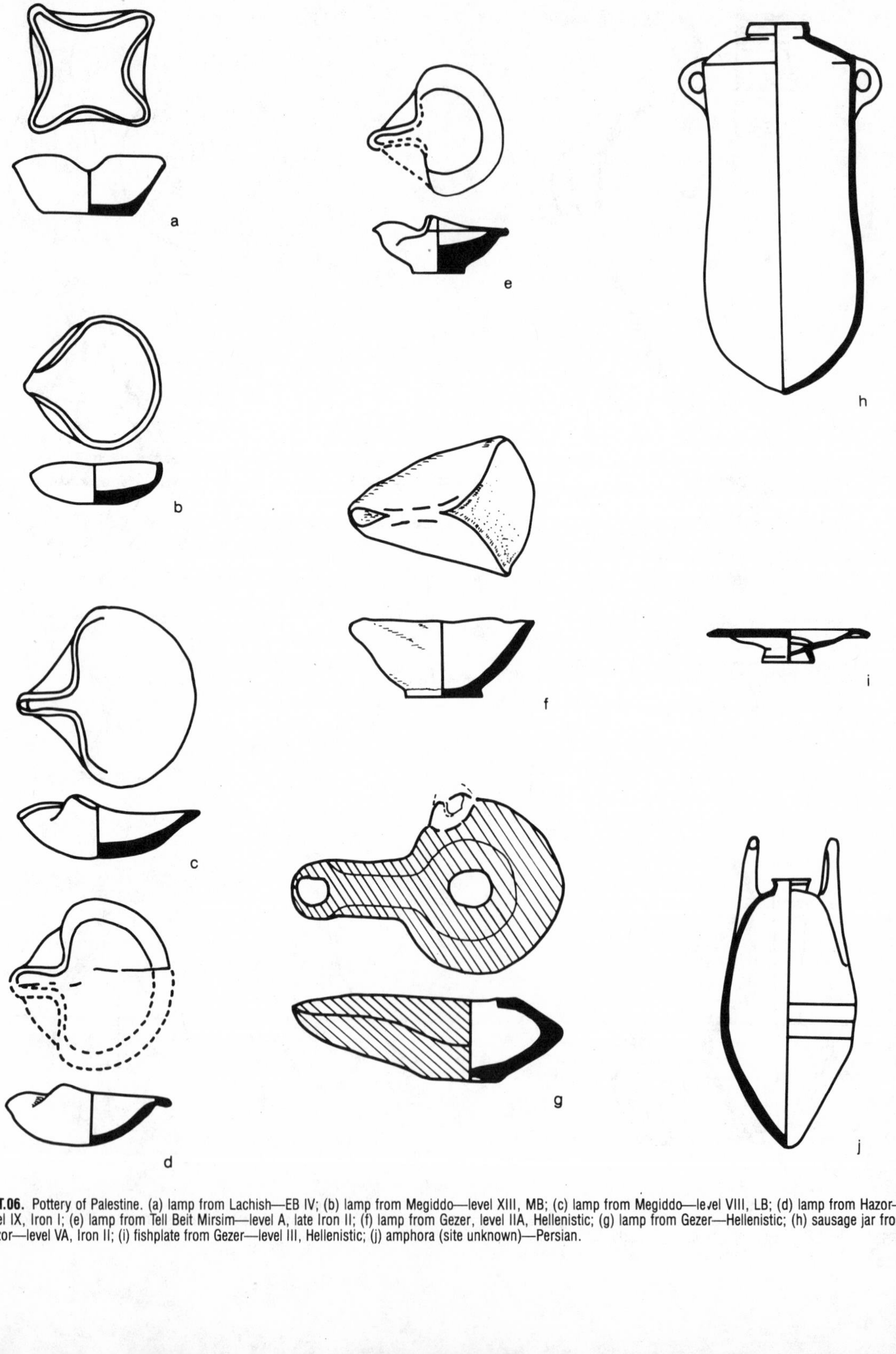

POT.06. Pottery of Palestine. (a) lamp from Lachish—EB IV; (b) lamp from Megiddo—level XIII, MB; (c) lamp from Megiddo—level VIII, LB; (d) lamp from Hazor—level IX, Iron I; (e) lamp from Tell Beit Mirsim—level A, late Iron II; (f) lamp from Gezer, level IIA, Hellenistic; (g) lamp from Gezer—Hellenistic; (h) sausage jar from Hazor—level VA, Iron II; (i) fishplate from Gezer—level III, Hellenistic; (j) amphora (site unknown)—Persian.

Jugs and juglets continue the ceramic tradition of the MB. Zones of painted metopes are common decorations. Biconical jugs, where the upper part of the vessel is about equal in height to the lower, have a shoulder handle and the metope design on the upper part. Biconical craters are similar but have two shoulder handles. Juglets tend to lose their shoulders and their necks become shorter and wider. Dipper juglets are not as elongated as MB forms.

A new form in the LB is the pilgrim flask (POT.05:f). It differs from other closed vessels in that its lentoid form cannot be thrown on the wheel all at once, but must be thrown as two plates and molded together. Development is seen in the handle attachments, and by the Iron Age they are smaller.

At the beginning of the LB, lamps are not too different from those of the MB, which had slight single spouts (POT.06:b). In LB II they become larger with a pinch that almost meets, and a rim develops (POT.06:c). As sometimes in the MB, and later in the Iron Age, full-body female figurines, known commonly as "Astarte" plaques, are found with varying frequency at LB Palestinian sites. Their varied arm postures, hairstyles, and decoration show some affinities with curvaceous female representations of deities on Egyptian wall reliefs.

An important and characteristic part of the LB repertoire is the amount of painted and imported ware, found more often at this time than in any other period of antiquity in Palestine. Perhaps this accounts for the crudeness of much of the ordinary household pottery. Luxury items were made by specialists or imported.

The bichrome ware seems to be the result of a school of artisans working in the coastal area of Canaan. The wheel-made pottery is of high quality, of fine light-colored clay and well burnished before painting. The decoration is on the shoulder zone of the vessel in a frieze divided into patterned metopes enclosing ibex, birds, and fish. Vessel forms are those of the plain ware as well as some unique bichrome types. The "chocolate on white" ware is distinctive particularly because of its finish—a creamy-white-burnished slip on which the thick chocolate or reddish brown paint has been applied. The patterns are largely geometric. Both these wares appear at the end of MB III and flourish during LB I. In addition to these two wares, the palm tree and ibex motifs in a frieze, typically in metopes between triglyphs, occur on all kinds of closed vessels throughout the LB. Sometimes it appears to have disintegrated in LB II B specimens.

The typical imported wares, present in almost any LB Palestinian site or tomb, include Cypriot, Mycenaean, and some Egyptian wares. Well known of the Cypriot wares are the white-slipped "milk bowls" with "wishbone" handles and brown or reddish-brown ladder-painted designs (POT.05:b). The delicate patterns become more schematic in LB II. The other common Cypriot imports are jugs and juglets in Base Ring ware, known as "bilbils" (POT.05:c, d). They are of a well-fired clay, with a dark burnished slip, and are thin, hard metallic ware in appearance and resonance. Handmade, they may appear skewed in stance. Base Ring I is characterized by plastic decoration around its neck. Base Ring II is usually white-painted, and often more squat and considerably larger than Base Ring I. These vessels were imitated locally, and the local vessels can be easily recognized because they were wheel-made of poorer ware.

Mycenaean vessels of excellent workmanship are imported all over the E Mediterranean. They are wheel-made, and the glossy black paint of the design was also largely done by wheel. Typical forms are the pyxis, stirrup jar, and kylix. These were imported throughout the LB; they were also imitated locally, but lesser skill in craftsmanship is evident.

6. Iron Age I (ca. 1200–918 B.C.). This is the time when the Israelites came into the land of Palestine and formed an independent kingdom under Saul, David, and Solomon. Iron Age II begins with the division into the N and S kingdoms and lasts until the fall of Jerusalem in 587 B.C. However, the assumed distinctions between Canaanite and Israelite pottery beginning around 1200 B.C. can no longer be made with the assurance once assumed, since the Israelites slowly took over the land and pockets of Canaanite culture remained.

Another element, the Philistines and Sea Peoples, also settled in the land during Iron I. Their pottery is more distinctive, and where it is found gives some indication of their settlement, influence, or trade. But again, conclusions must be drawn carefully.

Albright made his first division of Iron I on the appearance of this "Philistine" ware at Tell Beit Mirsim in the second period, about 1150 B.C., but pottery of the Sea Peoples is now known earlier at other sites. Although the pottery was made locally, connections with the Aegean are obvious in the decorated Philistine ware. The black and red paint appears usually over a white slip, covering the upper and central zone of the vessel. The central zone is divided into metopes containing geometric patterns such as spirals or circles with crosses, or more characteristically, large-feathered birds. Some of the forms are also Mycenaean: kraters with tilted handles, stirrup jars, and pyxides. However, local forms are also introduced, most typically the "beer jug" (POT.05:g), as well as various jugs, juglets, and pilgrim flasks.

Local painted wares continued to some extent into Iron I, but often in a debased LB style. A bichrome style is introduced which may be of local Phoenician-Palestinian origin. The decoration is typically red and black with concentric circles on the sides of jugs or inside bowls.

No sharp division occurs between the pottery forms of the Iron and LB ages. Carinated bowls, decorated rounded bowls, and small bar handles develop from LB forms. In addition, irregular hand burnishing has its beginning in this period. The chalice (POT.05:h) reaches the height of its popularity in Iron I, whereas a low-footed vase or goblet is dying out. The krater continues earlier traditions in form and painted decoration. There are sometimes four or more handles, as well as the horizontal handles known from the earlier period. A typical Iron Age thickened rim develops.

The cooking pot continues the LB shape: relatively shallow and carinated body with rounded base, usually without handles. The triangular rim is elongated in various forms.

The first pithoi are largely transitional from the LB, but the body becomes more elliptical and the neck narrower and shorter. A ridge develops at the base of the neck, and

Albright was first to recognize the "collar rim" store jar (POT.05:e). He identified this jar with the early Israelite settlers, but the history is probably much more complicated. Other Iron I store jars have ovoid bodies, and a painted jar with a spout appears. Amphoriskoi continue their Canaanite form. Typical jugs have globular bodies and trefoil mouths. Painted jugs and jugs with strainer spouts also appear. The popular juglet types are those with an ovoid body, trefoil mouth, and a slightly pointed base, and the small black-burnished juglet, more graceful and with a longer neck than in Iron II. In Iron I the upper handle attachment is below the rim. A "Cypro-Phoenician" imported juglet appears in the 11th century in black-on-red wares.

The lamps are relatively small with a flat base or larger with a rounded base (POT.06:d). Distinctive cultic vessels are frequently found in Iron I contexts, particularly incense burners and kernoi. Figurines and spouted animal bases also appear.

7. Iron Age II (ca. 918–587 B.C.). Iron II begins with the division into the N and S kingdoms and lasts until the fall of Jerusalem in 587 B.C. The pottery at present can generally be divided into an early and late phase. Tell Beit Mirsim A should now be recognized as belonging mainly to the early phase along with Lachish III, Beer-sheba II, Samaria, and other N sites. To the later period ending in the fall of the kingdom belong Lachish II, Ramet Rahel V, most of the Tell el-Ful and Beth-zur Iron II occupations, and En-gedi V. Also important during Iron II are the regional differences between the N and S, more apparent than earlier in the Iron Age. This probably reflects the political situation, the division of Solomon's kingdom into N (Israel) and S (Judah) entities.

The technical advances should also be recognized. Most pottery is wheel-made, and it is well fired. Many different forms and types are found, but large quantities of similar forms, often in varied sizes, indicate mass production. Every clan and family unit must have had their ceramic wares. Imported and painted pottery is not so common. Much of the local ware is slipped, often in red but in other colors also, and then burnished. This finish seems to be preferred over, or perhaps easier produced than, painted wares.

Improved workmanship is easily recognized in the bowls. Many are red-burnished. Irregular hand burnishing came in at the end of Iron I. By the latter part of Iron II the typical bowl has a thickened rim, is slightly carinated, and has a wheel-burnished reddish-brown slip on the interior and rim. It is made in a variety of sizes. There are also rounded, slightly flaring, and shallow platelike bowls, some plain-rimmed and some with different patterns of burnishing, but similar features are repeated over and over. A type of bowl found at many N sites with a high-quality red slip and burnish has been called Samaria ware.

The shallow Iron I cooking pot continues into Iron II, usually with a lower carination and a shorter triangular section in the rim. Later in Iron II the pot becomes more squat and rounded and has two handles, and the rim becomes ridged and appears in many variations. In the S a deep type appears with a rather high, narrow neck, often rilled, and two handles from the rim to the shoulder.

Storage jars with pronounced shoulders are typical. Ovoid jars with ridged necks and "sausage jars" (POT.06:h) are popular in the N. The ovoid jar with a wide rounded shoulder, tapering neck, and four handles is the type on which the *lmlk* ("belonging to the king") seal impressions have been found in the S. See STAMPS, ROYAL JAR HANDLE. Jar handles with personal stamps, a few with names found in the Bible, are found fairly frequently. A popular S form was the hole-mouth jar of two types: a rather small cylindrical and a large heavy, sometimes more rounded or barrel-shaped with sloping shoulders. Jars with three handles and a spout are found in both the N and the S. Amphoriskoi appear in both large and smaller variants, and a particular type with painted bands has been found in Jordan and suggests Assyrian influence.

Wide-mouthed jugs often with pinched lips continue Iron I types. Variants of jugs with strainer spouts also continue. The characteristic new form of Iron II is the well-made and often beautiful decanter (POT.05:i). There are some variations between the N and S forms. The dipper juglet is typically cylindrical with a plain rim and appears in a range of sizes. Likewise the black-burnished juglet is found, some very tiny in size, others up to ten cm or more in height. Its handle is now attached to the rim. The pilgrim flask continues to appear to the end of the Iron Age. The pyxis has almost completely disappeared. Imported Cypro-Phoenician ware is found in small quantities to the end of Iron II. Lamps have rounded or flat bases, sometimes with a wider lip and pronounced rim. Late in the Iron Age in the S a high-based lamp appears and continues into the next period (POT.06:e). Figurines with molded heads and handmade bodies are frequently found on Judean sites.

8. Exilic and Persian (ca. 587–332 B.C.). Iron II ends with the fall of Jerusalem in 587 B.C. and is followed by what is usually called the Persian period. Before the Persian occupation, though, there is the period of the Babylonian Exile, ca. 587–532 B.C., and at some sites, particularly in Judah, pottery types have been distinguished that belong to this period. Apparently small colonies of Israelites continued to live in towns outside Jerusalem.

Typical of this exilic period are heavy high-based lamps, rather deep round cooking pots with ridged rims which first appeared late in Iron II and are a development of Iron II shallow pots, elongated juglets, wide-mouthed jugs, and large bowls, still sometimes irregularly burnished but more often not. An impressed chevron design sometimes appears on the shoulders of high straight-rim kraters.

During the Persian period, 532–331 B.C., some differences have been distinguished between the pottery in the highlands and that of the coastal plain and Galilee. The coastal regions were more influenced by the E Mediterranean—Cyprus, the Aegean, Anatolia, and Egypt. However, most of the influences also reached inland as seen in the rich imported wares which have been found at Shechem, Samaria, and Jerusalem.

It is the imported Greek wares which were the first and the most easily recognized and often the determining chronological factor for this period. Though often fragmentary, imported black-figured ware of the late 6th century and early 5th, red-figured ware of the 5th, lecythoi of the 4th, and the black-glazed wares of the 4th have assisted in giving absolute dates to strata and in developing typologies for local wares.

Local wares are sometimes developments of Iron Age types and other times are influenced from the W. The shallow mortaria with wide thickened rims, sometimes with ribbed sides, and with flat, ring, or high-footed bases are characteristic. Typical particularly of coastal areas, as it was used for international trade in the Mediterranean world, is the flat-shouldered jar with cylindrical body tapering to a pointed base. Sometimes the handle is twisted and ugly or the rim and handles have thick black-painted lines. An amphora with "basket handles" (two loop handles attached horizontally and extending high above the rim) is characteristic in both Cyprus and Palestine (POT.06:j).

Rounded and elongated juglets have characteristic forms. Cooking pots tend to be deep with necks developing, predecessors of Hellenistic deep cooking pots. Lamps take a very characteristic form, with a wide rim and more flattened profile than in any other period. Molded and glazed imported lamps are also found and will soon be copied locally.

9. Hellenistic (ca. 332–63 B.C.). During the Hellenistic period, 332–63 B.C., influence from the E Mediterranean and the Greek world continues, but in many cases local attempts at imitation take the place of actual imports. Increased trade and contact point to similar pottery forms throughout the Hellenistic world. In Palestine Attic bowls are copied in form, and a poor paint or wash imitate the glazed wares. In time even the paint is omitted and round bowls with incurved rims and flat straight-sided bowls, descendants of "fish plates," are characteristic. The Attic fish plate (POT.06:i) had a depression in the center, sometimes stamped with a fish impression, and the oil could run down in the bottom of the dish. The pottery as a whole is hard-fired, but sometimes quite carelessly, and disfigured forms result.

Storage jars are elongated to bag-shaped with sloppily attached handles. Rims with undercuts develop into typical rounded rims, then are more flattened until an elongated flattened rim is typically late Hellenistic. Imported Rhodian jar fragments are easily recognized by their finely levigated orange or buff ware, high necks with rounded rims, stump bases, and angular handles with stamps. The inscriptions have been thoroughly studied and can be accurately dated. On one handle the name of the potter will be given and on the other, the priest in whose tenure of office the vessel was manufactured.

Wide-mouthed globular jugs with smoothly concave bases are characteristic. Flasks are varied and develop longer necks and become smaller as the Hellenistic period progresses. Cooking pots are deep with rather long necks and two strap handles from the rim to the shoulders. The ware is often quite thin. Late in the Hellenistic period there is also a shallow type with a ridge to accept a lid.

Except for a small folded lamp whose sides are folded over to meet (POT.06:f), lamps are now made in molds (POT.06:g). They are imitations of Greek forms, but the local ones are generally rather plain with a ridge or incised circle around the small oil hole and sometimes a small knob or vestigial handle. Ray, floral, and other motifs become common in the 1st century B.C.

A unique and characteristic Hellenistic form is the unguentarium. The early ones, sometimes known as "spindle bottles," are elongated at both ends and rather long and heavy. They become lighter and more delicate in the 1st century B.C. Later a pyriform juglet replaces them and this lives on into the Roman period.

Nabatean pottery first appears in the Hellenistic period and its typical forms and ware continue well into the Roman period. It is mainly found in S Transjordan, with its center at Petra, but there are also Nabatean sites in the Negeb and evidence of trade as far N as Damascus. This is the finest and most attractive pottery in the history of Palestine and Transjordan. It is red- or orange-colored, thin, hard-fired, and often beautifully decorated. The finest of clays and excellent firing techniques were used. Most forms are small compared with other Palestinian pottery: small bowls and plates, small jugs and cooking pots, juglets and unguentaria. Fine bowls and painted decorations developed sometime after 100 B.C. and for the next two centuries the painted ware is common. Initially the decoration is of a flowing, naturalistic style, executed in bright orange or light red paint with a delicate brush technique. Late in the 1st century B.C. another style appears—heavier and more formal, in a solid purplish-red pigment. This type seems to span the 1st century A.D. Other vessels are impressed, usually with rouletted designs. Jugs, juglets, and cooking pots are sometimes ribbed.

10. Roman (63 B.C.–324 A.D.). Terra sigillata, a red-glazed ware, is one of the best recognized wares of the Early Roman period. Besides the red glaze, rouletting on the interior or rim is common. Roman red wares of various kinds are imported from the W Mediterranean throughout the Roman period. Large amphorae with stamps in Greek and Latin continue to be found in Palestine as the containers for imports.

Local Early Roman forms are direct developments from Hellenistic wares. Rims on storage jars become long collars with a characteristic ridge below. A cylinder-type jar is known from Qumran. The concave base on Hellenistic jugs becomes sharper. Narrow-necked jugs are common. Pyriform juglets replace the fusiform unguentaria. Asymmetrical pot-bellied flasks develop exaggerated, twisted handles. Cooking pots have shorter necks and flat, ribbonlike handles. Ribbing becomes more common and extensive ribbing is typical of the following Byzantine period. Small incurved rim bowls continue for some time. In Jerusalem thin-walled bowls with red, brown, or black stylized floral patterns have been found in recent excavations. At first they were called "Pseudo-Nabatean," but they are different in motif and ware.

The "Herodian" lamp is typified by its bow spout and plain body, made in a mold as all lamps are by this time. Many elaborately designed lamps are imported from Italy and other places to the W by the 2d century A.D. Besides floral designs, some have mythological scenes.

11. Byzantine (A.D. 324–630). The Byzantine period is beyond the scope of biblical times, but archaeology of this period, as well as of later Islamic and Crusader times, is receiving more attention in Palestine and Transjordan in relation to early Christianity as well as the history and culture of the land.

Pottery characteristics include pronounced ribbing on jugs, juglets, jars, and cooking pots. Decoration includes straight and wavy incised lines on jugs and bowls. "Frying pans" are shallow cooking pots sometimes with hollow handles. There are slipper and channel nozzle lamps, and "candlestick" lamps with six, seven, or eight branches around the spout and occasionally a cross or Greek inscription.

Bibliography

Albright, W. F. 1932. *The Excavation of Tell Beit Mirsim in Palestine, I.* AASOR 12. New Haven.

———. 1933. *The Excavation of Tell Beit Mirsim, IA.* Pp. 55–127 in AASOR 13. New Haven.

———. 1938. *The Excavation of Tell Beit Mirsim, II.* AASOR 17. New Haven.

———. 1943. *The Excavation of Tell Beit Mirsim, III.* AASOR 21–22. New Haven.

———. 1960. *The Archaeology of Palestine.* Baltimore.

Amiran, R. 1969. *Ancient Pottery of the Holy Land.* Jerusalem.

Avigad, N. 1983. *Discovering Jerusalem.* Nashville.

Cole, D. P. 1984. *Shechem I.* Winona Lake, IN.

Homès-Fredericq, D., and Franken, H. J., eds. 1986. *Pottery and Potters—Past and Present.* Tübingen.

Kenyon, K. 1960. *Excavations at Jericho, I.* London.

———. 1965. *Excavations at Jericho, II.* London.

———. 1970. *Archaeology in the Holy Land.* 3d ed. New York.

———. 1981. *Excavations at Jericho, III.* London.

Kenyon, K., and Holland, T. A. 1982. *Excavations at Jericho, IV.* London.

———. 1983. *Excavations at Jericho, V.* London.

Lapp, N. L., ed. 1981. *The Third Campaign at Tell el-Ful.* AASOR 45. Cambridge, MA.

Lapp, P. W. 1961. *Palestinian Ceramic Chronology, 200 B.C.–A.D. 70.* New Haven.

———. 1970. The Pottery of Palestine in the Persian Period. Pp. 179–97 in *Archäologie und Altes Testament,* ed. A. Kuschke and E. Kutsch. Tübingen.

———. 1975. *The Tale of the Tell,* ed. N. L. Lapp. Pittsburgh.

Matson, F. R., ed. 1965. *Ceramics and Man.* Chicago.

Moorey, R. 1981. *Excavation in Palestine.* Grand Rapids, MI.

Sauer, J. A. 1973. *Hesbon Pottery 1971.* Berrien Springs, MI.

Stern, E. 1982. *Material Culture of the Land of the Bible in the Persian Period 538–322 B.C.* Warminster.

Wright, G. E. 1937. *The Pottery of Palestine from the Earliest Times to the End of the Early Bronze Age.* New Haven.

———. 1965. The Archaeology of Palestine. Pp. 85–139 in *BANE.*

NANCY L. LAPP

POUND. See WEIGHTS AND MEASURES.

POVERTY. See POOR, POVERTY.

POWER, NT CONCEPT OF. The message of salvation in the NT is a message of power: God raised Jesus from the dead. The cross-resurrection event not only demonstrated God's power over death, but also marked the defeat of the opposing sphere of power and its forces (Satan and his demons). Just as God delivered his people from bondage in Egypt "by his mighty right hand," the NT proclaims that he has now delivered his people from the bondage of death, the dominion of Satan, and the compelling influences of "sin" and "the flesh."

The most common word for power in the NT is *dynamis* (and its cognates), occurring some 375 times and used by every NT writer. Less common are the terms *ischus* and *kratos,* which are probably not to be distinguished sharply in meaning from *dynamis.* All three terms denote the inherent or derived ability to accomplish a given end. The plural form of *dynamis* is used frequently in the NT to describe powerful supernatural acts such as healings or exorcisms, and is normally translated "miracle." The effectual exercise of power is indicated by the term *energeia* and its forms. It is only used of supernatural beings in the NT and is often used to describe God's manifestation of power in raising Christ from the dead. The term *exousia,* usually translated "authority," has primary reference to one's right to exercise power but implies an ability to exercise that right. The concept of power is also conveyed in many other terms and units of thought (grace, light, fullness, glory, word, spirit).

In the Judaism of the NT era, the OT idea of a powerful personal God involved in history was prominent. A future direct intervention of God in history to exercise judgment, overthrow evil, and bring salvation was integral to the Jewish hope. Just as God powerfully wrought deliverance in the past, the Qumran community envisioned a future triumph over "the children of darkness" (1QM 1:14; 6:6; 11:4, 9; 13:13–14). This victory would take place not only on the physical battlefield but, more importantly, in the heavens against the supernatural forces of evil. Throughout the Qumran documents, the manifestation of divine power is conceived of primarily in a salvation-historical sense (1QH 1:34; 4:28–29; 13:9; 14:13). Future deliverance was also expected to come through a divinely empowered Messiah as seen most clearly in the *Psalms of Solomon* (17:21–44): "Undergird him with strength to destroy the unrighteous rulers . . . and he will not weaken in his days, relying upon his God, for God made him powerful in the Holy Spirit" (vv 22, 37). God's saving events of the past, particularly the deliverance from Egypt, also become the basis for an expectation for military victory in the Maccabean wars (1 Macc 4:9–11; *3 Macc* 2:6). Josephus' use of power terminology is almost exclusively tied to military activity. For Josephus, the Greek term *dynamis* has become a technical term for an "army" (e.g. *JW* 7 §252, 275).

In the 2 centuries leading up to the time of Christ, Judaism shows an increasing interest in supernatural power, especially the invisible realm of the angelic and demonic (see, for example, *Jubilees, 1–2 Enoch,* and *Testament of Solomon*). This appears to correspond to the heightened interest in divine power in the Greco-Roman religions. In Hellenistic religion, the gods were seen less as personalities and more as powerful beings needing propitiation or capable of manipulation. People sought divine power through invoking a deity (or a series of gods), by participating in the bloodbaths of a god (e.g. the *Taurabolium* of Cybele and Mithras), through being initiated into the mystery of a god, or by employing magical arts, which were well known to the masses of the Roman world. Asklepios could be praised because "every place has been penetrated by the saving power of the god" (*POxy.* 1381.215), especially for physical healing and rescue from dangers at sea. The moon god Mên received adulation for his power: "There is one great god in heaven, the heavenly Men, the great power *(dynamis)* of the invisible god" (see Moulton and Milligan 1930: 172). The magical texts of this period are filled with recipes for the attainment of supernatural power. *PGM* 4.1024–25 is representative of the request for power: "You who break apart rocks and change the names of gods, enter in, appear to me, lord, you who have in fire your power and strength." William Ramsay observed that "power" *(dynamis)* was one of the most common and characteristic terms in the language of pagan devotion (Moulton and Milligan 1930: 172).

In the Jewish writings of the Hellenistic era, the primary Greek term for power *(dynamis)* came to be used as a technical expression for angelic and demonic forces—perhaps due to the LXX expression "Lord of Hosts." These beings are seen as having widespread control over human existence and over all aspects of nature (*Jub.* 2:2). Philo comments: "The air He allotted to winged visible beings, and to other forces *(dynameis)* which cannot be perceived at all; these are the host of incorporeal spirits ordered according to differences in rank . . . We are told that some enter into mortal bodies . . . while others, endowed with a diviner constitution, have no regard for any earthly quarter, but exist on high next to the ethereal region itself" (*Plant.* 14). The Jewish literature of this period frequently depicts human existence as the battlefield between angels and demons, between God and Satan (*TDNT* 2: 296).

When we approach the NT, the person of Christ surfaces as decisive in understanding the NT concept of power. According to the Synoptic Gospels, Jesus conducted his ministry on the basis of the divine power imparted to him through the Holy Spirit (Luke 4:14). After resisting the temptations of the devil (Luke 4:1–13), Jesus waged a powerful confrontation with the realm of Satan. The exorcism in the synagogue at Capernaum led many to recognize the authority of Jesus over the dominion of Satan (Mark 1:21–28; Luke 4:31–36). It was necessary for Jesus to wage a powerful assault on the dominion of the "strong man" (Satan) in order for salvation to be procured (Mark 3:27; Luke 11:21–22). In the incident with the Gerasene demoniac, Mark indicates that no one had been strong enough to bind the man (Mark 5:4), yet Jesus displayed his power by driving out the entire legion of demons. Jesus' manifestation of divine power in exorcisms signifies that the salvation of God has finally come in the person of Jesus (Luke 11:20; Matt 12:28).

The miracles of Jesus, or his "works of power" *(dynameis)*, are seen by the evangelists as an indication that God himself was at work (Acts 2:22). Mark, for instance, records that the healing of the paralytic demonstrates that Jesus is the Son of Man and, as such, has authority to forgive sins (Mark 2:1–12). These works of power should produce repentance and incite faith (Matt 11:20–23; 13:54, 58; Luke 10:13; Mark 6:2, 5).

The power of God was manifest in the life of the historical Jesus in the context of the weakness and limitation of his human flesh. As such, the example of his dependence upon the power of God through the spirit becomes paradigmatic for the Church. For Jesus, his access to divine power did not circumvent his need to suffer and die. The evangelists agree that Jesus was aware of his need to experience the passion in order for God's plan of salvation to be consummated. Jesus indicates that his followers could also expect to suffer, particularly as a result of their witness for him (Mark 13:9). At the same time, Jesus bestowed his power and authority on his followers (first on the Twelve: Mark 3:15; 6:7; Luke 9:1; Matt 10:1; then on the seventy-[two]: Luke 10:17–20, esp. v 19, probably prefiguring the mission of the Church in this context). This access to the power of God would assist Jesus' followers in their mission and in gaining victory over the influence of the realm of evil. Jesus realized that his earthly ministry was not the time for a glorious display of divine omnipotence, but he did anticipate exaltation (Luke 22:69) and a glorious and powerful return (Matt 24:30; 26:64; Mark 13:26; 14:62; Luke 21:27).

In comparison to the Synoptics, John emphasizes the world as under the authority of Satan, who is described as "the prince *(archon)* of this world" (John 12:31; 14:30; 16:11). Unbelievers belong to his realm; the devil is their "father" (8:42–47). Jesus, however, drives out the devil and condemns him (12:31; 16:11). The strongly dualistic flavor of John's gospel (above versus below; light versus darkness) highlights the human isolation from God's realm and thus an inability to enter the kingdom of God (8:21–24; cf. also 7:34, 36; 14:17); the Father, however, extends the power and authority for one to come to Christ (6:44, 65). Those who would enter the kingdom must exercise faith (1:12; 8:24). The Nicodemus account illustrates the powerful divine work enabling a person to enter the kingdom, a process summarized by the metaphor of rebirth (3:1–16; note the usage of the six occurrences of *dynamai*). In John's gospel, it is the Father who comes into prominence as the immediate source of Jesus' power (5:19, 27; 10:18; 17:2).

In the programmatic statement of the book of Acts, divine power through the agency of the spirit is promised to the disciples to enable them to give effective witness throughout the world about Christ (Acts 1:8). Luke summarizes the early manner of the apostles' preaching by stating, "With great power the apostles gave their testimony to the resurrection of the Lord Jesus" (Acts 4:33). He then further illustrates the fulfillment of this promise by giving an account of the establishment of the church throughout Palestine and the Mediterranean region. Throughout the book of Acts, Luke clearly interprets the rise of the church as a powerful work of the Holy Spirit (note the usage of the 70 occurrences of "spirit" in Acts).

For Paul, the apostle to the gentiles, the message of the gospel was the power of God (Rom 1:16; 1 Cor 1:18). The gospel encapsulated the message of the crucified Christ who was raised from the dead by the power of God (1 Cor 6:14; 15:43). This was a message of deliverance and salvation. God had acted through Christ to destroy the influence of the realm of Satan (Col 2:15) and the bondage of death, sin, flesh, and the law (Rom 5:12–8:39).

Paul conducted his ministry by the enabling power of God (Eph 3:7; Col 1:29). In spite of the fact that he was painfully aware of his inherent weaknesses by virtue of his humanity, his preaching was a demonstration of the power of the spirit (1 Cor 2:3–5; 1 Thess 1:5). Paul thus endeavored to insure that the faith of his converts was based on the power of God rather than on human wisdom and rhetorical prowess. Paul believed that the limitations of human flesh provided an opportunity to display the enabling power of God (2 Cor 4:7). To the Corinthians, who entertained inflated notions about their access to the power of God, Paul stressed his own weakness and suffering in the carrying out of his ministry. In fact, he claimed that the Lord allowed a messenger of Satan to harass him in order that he might be even more cognizant of his weakness (2 Cor 12:7). Paul concludes, "I am content with weaknesses . . . for when I am weak, then I am strong" (2 Cor 12:10; 13:4). Nevertheless, Paul believed that by virtue of his union with the resurrected and exalted Lord, he was capable of doing great things (Phil 4:13). In doxological praise, he exclaims, "Now to him who by the power at work within us is able to do far more than all that we ask or think, to him be the glory . . ." (Eph 3:20).

Paul sought to gain an increasingly deeper awareness of the power of God (Phil 3:10). He also prayed earnestly that his converts might grow in their knowledge of God's power (Eph 1:15–23) and that they would be divinely strengthened in their innermost beings (Eph 3:14–19) for the purpose of resisting the "powers" of the devil (see PRINCIPALITIES AND POWERS) and for manifesting love in the life of the early Christian communities. Paul highlights the role of God's power as the ethical enablement for the Christian. Life by the spirit enables the Christian to eradicate vices and appropriate virtues, the foremost of which is love (Gal 5:13–26; Rom 8:13). Furthermore, Paul also stresses the need for dependence on the power of God for the fulfillment of the mission of the Church in the spread of the gospel (Rom 15:19; Eph 6:15–20).

Faith is the necessary human response to God in order for his power to be manifest. The writer of Hebrews, for example, stresses the pattern of the saints of the past who appropriated the power of God in difficult circumstances by exercising faith (Heb 11:11, 34; Rom 4:18–25). Faith is commonly expressed by God's people in the context of prayer. Paul models this to his congregations (Eph 3:14–19; cf. Eph 6:18–20).

The Apocalypse anticipates the coming of one like a son of man endued with power (Rev 1:16). Through him, God Almighty *(pantokrator)* will vanquish evil and reign by his power (Rev. 11:15–17; 12:10). This end-time triumph will entail the ultimate defeat of the dragon, Satan, and his powers (Rev 12:7–9). Both God and "the lamb" will receive eternal praise, with continual ascriptions of power and glory to their names (Rev 1:5–6; 4:11; 5:12–13; 7:12; 19:1).

Bibliography

Arnold, C. E. 1989. *Ephesians: Power and Magic. The Concept of Power in Ephesians in the Light of Its Historical Setting.* SNTSMS 63. Cambridge.

Grundman, W. 1932. *Der Begriff der Kraft in der Neutestamentilichen Gedankenwelt.* Stuttgart.

Moulton, J. H., and Milligan, G. 1930. *The Vocabulary of the Greek Testament.* Grand Rapids.

Nielsen, H. 1980. Paulus' Verwendung des Begriffes *Dunamis.* Pp. 137–58 in *Die Paulinische Literatur und Theologie,* ed. S. Pederson. Århus.

Nock, A. D. 1925. Studies in the Graeco-Roman Beliefs of the Empire. *JHS* 48: 84–101. Repr. 1972. Vol. 1, pp. 176–94 in *Arthur Darby Nock: Essays on Religion and the Ancient World.* Oxford.

Schmitz, O. 1927. Der Begriff *Dunamis* bei Paulus. Pp. 136–67 in *Festgabe für Adolf Deissmann.* Tübingen.

CLINTON E. ARNOLD

PRAETOR. See CITY AUTHORITIES.

PRAETORIAN GUARD. This is the name regularly applied to the substantial bodyguard maintained at Rome by the emperors. Under the Roman Republic a magistrate on campaign often formed a *cohors praetoria* ("headquarters" or "household" cohort) which was his combined staff and bodyguard. During the civil wars which brought the Republic to a close, various generals each formed more than a single cohort as the threats to their security became more severe. After the defeat of Antony and Cleopatra (31 B.C.), Octavian (soon to be the emperor Augustus) retained his own cohorts as a peacetime bodyguard. This was a force of nine cohorts, each probably 480 men strong. At first they had no single camp at Rome, but were billeted in private homes in small groups; some cohorts were outstationed in nearby towns. It is evident that Augustus wished to avoid flaunting republican tradition, which frowned on the presence of troops in the capital. No separate commander or commanders were appointed until 2 B.C. when Augustus chose two prefects of equestrian status, with the title *praefectus praetorio* ("prefects for the headquarters").

The influence of the Praetorian Cohorts (or Praetorian Guard as they are generally known in English) grew under Tiberius, when their number was increased to 12, and they were concentrated in a newly built fortress on the eastern outskirts of Rome, named the *castra Praetoria.* Both developments can be ascribed to the initiative of L. Aelius Sejanus, sole prefect from 14 to 31 A.D. Sejanus' influence became even more preeminent after Tiberius went into virtual retirement on the island of Capri from A.D. 26 onward; the prefect controlled the flow of information to the emperor and access to him. The influence of some later prefects also (Afranius Burrus [A.D. 51–62] and Ofonius Tigellinus [A.D. 62–68]) was considerable.

During the civil wars of the Late Republic praetorian cohorts were recruited from among serving legionaries; they were thus a corps of elite, experienced troops. But Augustus and subsequent emperors drew recruits directly from the civil population. They served 16 years, in contrast to the 25 years expected of legionaries. Their splendid uniforms, much higher pay, and pampered lifestyle made them the envy of the legions, and while the latter came to be recruited increasingly from provincials, the Praetorians remained predominantly Italians. The guard thus provided an outlet for the military aspirations of Italians unwilling to contemplate long service far from home. Each cohort was commanded by a tribune, normally an ex–chief centurion of a legion; the cohort was divided into six centuries led by a centurion who was normally promoted from the ranks. The guard contained numerous specialists in artillery, surveying, and engineering who could be seconded to the armies on the frontiers.

During the Julio-Claudian age the Praetorians saw little active service, though several cohorts are likely to have accompanied Claudius to Britain in A.D. 43. Their chief duties were ceremonial: a guard for the emperor at his palace in Rome, and on state occasions. The Praetorians retained for ceremonial wear the military equipment of the Late Republic (e.g., the oval shield), which was no longer used by the legions.

In A.D. 69 Vitellius, briefly victorious in a period of civil war, added many of his own legionaries to the guard by way of reward, boosting its numbers to 16 cohorts of 1,000 men. But his successor, Vespasian, who made his son Titus prefect of the Guard to keep it under tight control, reduced the total of cohorts to nine. Some time later Domitian increased the strength to 10 cohorts, which became the standard total. The guard thus constituted a military force of some 10,000 men in Rome, a sort of "household division" equivalent in size to two legions. From the Flavian period of the later 1st century the cohorts frequently went on campaign with the emperor, as the latter was compelled actively to defend the empire's frontiers.

In the 2d century the guard had a lower profile in the face of strong political leadership. Often the prefect functioned as a senior military adviser to the emperors; at other times, by virtue of the prefect's increasingly important judicial role in the hearing of court cases, prominent lawyers were appointed.

In A.D. 193 the guard was bribed by the senator Didius Julianus, in a notorious auction for power, to support his brief tenure of the purple. Soon after, Septimius Severus disbanded the existing guard, which he replaced with legionaries from his own victorious armies. The guard continued thereafter to be recruited chiefly from serving legionaries so that it became again a *corps d'elite* to which ordinary soldiers could aspire. In October 312, after the battle of the Milvian Bridge, in which the Praetorians had fought for the emperor Mexentius, the guard was abolished by the victor, Constantine.

In about A.D. 65, when the apostle Paul, having appealed directly to Caesar, was brought to Rome, he was placed under house arrest, with a soldier to watch him (Acts 28:16). Often the Praetorians were entrusted with the guarding of such prisoners and the prefect might sit in judgment on them. Paul wrote to the Philippians, apparently from Rome, that he had made the gospel known not only in the praetorium but to the population at large (Phil 1:13). "Praetorium" was the term used at Rome to describe the emperor's military headquarters, to which the Praetorians were attached.

Bibliography

Durry, M. 1938. *Les cohortes prétoriennes.* BEFAR 146. Paris.

Passerini, A. 1939. *Le coorti pretorie.* Istituto italiano per la storia antica, fasc. 1. Rome.

LAWRENCE KEPPIE

PRAETORIUM [Gk *praitōrion*]. The name given to the headquarters of the *praefectus praetorii,* a Roman official who resided as the supreme administrator and judge of a region. The praetorium was usually, but not necessarily, also the living quarters (Gk *oikia*) of the prefect or governor.

Several praetoriums are mentioned in the NT. Acts 23:25 refers to a praetorium in Caesarea Maritima, built by Herod the Great (37–4 B.C.), in which Paul was kept prisoner. No remains of this building have yet been discovered. If one dates Paul's letter to the Philippians to the time of this imprisonment, then this praetorium is also referred to in Phil 1:13. The Gospels refer to a praetorium in Jerusalem where Jesus was tried by Pontius Pilate (Matt 27:27; Mark 15:16; John 18:28, 33; 19:9). In Mark 15:16 it is also called a "palace" (Gk *aule*), suggesting an identification with an Herodian royal residence. Opinions about the location of this praetorium/royal residence differ, and several possible candidates have been considered.

One possible candidate has been the fortress Antonia, which stood on a rock escarpment in the NW corner of the Temple Mount. For a long time this was the most popular candidate for the Jerusalem praetorium (Vincent 1954; Finegan 1969: 156–62; van Elderen *ISBE* 3: 929; Mare 1987: 189) The current Via Dolorosa (the route along which Jesus is supposed to have carried the cross to Golgotha) begins at this site. Some earlier scholars (Vincent and Stéve 1954: 193–221; de Sion 1956) believed that the Antonia was a large fortress including in its inner court the pavement (thought to be the *Lithostroton* of John 19:13) found in the Ecce Homo Convent of Notre Dame de Sion. However, this position is no longer tenable (Benoit 1971): the pavement in question was evidently built over the Strouthion Pool, which had been kept open until the destruction of Jerusalem in A.D. 70 (*JW* 5 §467). After the 1985–86 excavations even the Sisters of Zion (proprietors of the site) abandoned the identification of this pavement with the *Lithostroton* of John's gospel. Furthermore, the historical sources, especially Josephus (*Ant* 15 §292), prove decisively that the Antonia was never used as a royal residence either by Herod or by his successors. Indeed, the traditions of the Antonia as Pilate's praetorium started only with the Crusaders late in the 12th century (see below; Baldi 1982: 588ff).

Another possible candidate is Herod's Upper Palace. In the year 23 B.C., around the middle of his reign, Herod the Great built a luxurious palace in the area of today's Citadel (near the Jaffa Gate) and the area to the S of it (Armenian Garden). He resided there with his many wives and children (*JW* 5 §§161–83; *Ant* 15 §318). Most modern scholars have so far held this site to be the most probable candidate for Pilate's praetorium (Mommert 1903; Dalman 1924: 355–63; Benoit 1952; Blinzler 1959: 173–76; Maier 1968: 215–40; Vanel *DBSup* 8: 513–54; Murphy-O'Connor 1986: 23). The main argument which speaks against this possibility is the complete lack of any Christian tradition regarding such a location (Bagatti 1973).

Earliest Christian tradition held that the praetorium of the Gospels stood somewhere on the W slope of the Tyropoeon valley, just opposite the SW corner of the temple enclosure (Pixner 1979: 57–72). The oldest pilgrim report, the Anonymous of Bordeaux in A.D. 333 (Baldi 1982: 583), described the remaining walls of the praetorium as situated somewhere toward the valley (i.e., facing the Tyropoeon). The ruins of the judgment house of Pilate were known to Bishop Cyrill of Jerusalem in A.D. 348 (Baldi 1982: 583), and in the first part of the 5th century it was (according to the old Armenian Lectionary) used as a station during the Good Friday procession (Renoux 1969–71).

Around A.D. 450 a church was built on the site (Wilkinson 1977: 58), which later was called Hagia Sophia, i.e., "Holy Wisdom," because Jesus as God's Wisdom stood there before a human judge (Baldi 1982: 585). This church is always mentioned in close proximity to the Nea (New) Church, the large Marian shrine built by Emperor Justinian (A.D. 483–565). Recent archaeology has identified the remains of this magnificent church in the S section of today's Jewish Quarter (Avigad 1983: 229–46). Following the itinerary described by an anonymous pilgrim of Piacenza in A.D. 580 (Baldi 1982: 584f) and the representation of the contemporary Mosaic Map of Madaba (Avi-Yonah 1954: 55; Donner and Cüppers 1977: 112f.) showing another church NE of the Nea, the approximate location of the Sophia Church can be established. This is the region where today stand both the ruins of the Crusader Church St. Mary of the Teutonic Knights and the Jewish Yeshiva Porat Joseph, next to the steps leading from the "Wailing Wall" to the Jewish Quarter. Indeed the ruins of an important Byzantine church were discovered beneath this modern yeshiva (Vincent 1914: 429–36). All the vestiges of this church, however, were destroyed, but there is now a general agreement that the Byzantine praetorium must have been in this vicinity (Otto 1980: 152f.; Benoit 1984).

If early Christian tradition had remembered the correct site of Pilate's praetorium, the only palace that could have stood in this vicinity was the ancient royal palace built by the Hasmoneans. According to Josephus, the Hasmonean Palace was located "at the very edge of the Upper City" (*JW* 2 §344) and gave one a rooftop view of the sacrificial altar in the temple compound (*Ant* 20 §189ff.). This seems generally to fit the area where ancient Christian tradition located Pilate's praetorium (Pixner 1979: 78–85). Some scholars (Jaroś 1980; Riesner 1986; Pixner 1987; Kroll 1988: 335–49) believe that the magnificent ruins called "the Herodian Palatial Mansion," with its splendid mosaics similar to those in Masada (Avigad 1983: 95–120), could very well have been a part of the Hasmonean Palace that was rebuilt by Herod and renovated by Agrippa II (cf. *Ant* 20 §222). Unfortunately, its E wing (with the Sophia Church) and N section have completely disappeared.

From 37 to 23 B.C. Herod the Great used the Hasmonean Palace for administrative and judicial purposes (*JW* 1 §443; *Ant* 15 §229, 247f., 286). It probably continued to serve the same purpose after he moved (for safety reasons) to the new Upper Palace (see above), which was fortified by three mighty towers. In A.D. 6, when his son Archelaus was banished by imperial decree, the Roman prefects took over all the Herodian palaces and the Antonia fortress (cf. *JW* 2 §111; *Ant* 17 §344). After the untimely death of Agrippa I in A.D. 44, the Hasmonean Palace was not handed back to the subsequent Roman governors (*Ant* 20 §189f) but remained in the hands of the Hasmonean-Herodian family (Herod of Chalcis; Agrippa II), who from then on were put in charge of temple affairs (*Ant* 20 §16).

Closely related to the question of Pilate's praetorium is the itinerary of the Way of the Cross, whose end point has always remained the Golgotha rock (inside today's Church of the Holy Sepulchre). However, the starting point (the praetorium) has undergone curious alterations throughout the centuries. This can be seen from the different routes followed by the Good Friday processions of the Jerusalem Church recorded in the ancient liturgical lectionaries (Pixner 1979–80). From earliest times, this procession visited the different sites of the passion of Jesus, beginning at the Mount of Olives, passing through Gethsemane, and crossing the Kidron valley to the "House of the High Priest" (i.e., Caiaphas) on the E slope of Mt. Zion. It then continued by passing through a city gate to the "Palace of the Judge" (Praetorium of Pilate, later Church of Sophia), finally winding its way to Golgotha (Church of the Holy Sepulchre). On this last leg of the route (the original Via Dolorosa), Luke's gospel account of the carrying of the cross (23:26ff.) was read.

The Sophia Church and the neighboring Nea Church were destroyed during the Persian invasion in A.D. 614. After the subsequent Muslim conquest, permission to rebuild these churches was withheld; consequently a surrogate station for the Good Friday procession had to be found. A small church with its pavement just N of Mt. Zion's Hagia Sion Basilica temporarily served as a *Lithostroton* (Baldi 1982: 586f.). For some reason even the station of Caiaphas' house moved to this locale in the 9th century, according to Epiphanius Hagiopolita (Baldi 1982: 586). The Crusaders inherited this tradition, but since they felt uncomfortable with so many stations of the passion being situated on such an unlikely spot, they relocated Pilate's judgment house to the ruins of the Antonia (Baldi 1982: 588ff). Thus began the tradition of equating Pilate's praetorium with the Antonia Fortress, an idea that was adopted by the Franciscan friars and developed over the following centuries into the modern Via Dolorosa with its traditional fourteen stations.

Bibliography

Avigad, N. 1983. *Discovering Jerusalem.* Nashville.

Avi-Yonah, M. 1954. *The Madaba Mosaic Map.* Jerusalem.

Bagatti, B. 1973. La tradizione della chiesa di Gersaleme sul Pretorio. *RBI* 21: 429–32.

Baldi, D. 1982. *Enchiridion locorum sanctorum.* 3d ed. Jerusalem.

Benoit, P. 1952. Prétoire, Lithostroton et Gabbatha. *RB* 52: 531–50. Repr. vol. 1, pp. 316–39 in *Exégése et théologie.* Paris.

———. 1971. L'Antonia d'Hérode le Grand et le Forum Oriental d'Aelia Capitolina. *HTR* 54: 135–67. Rev. repr. vol. 4, pp. 311–46 in *Exégése et théologie.* Paris.

———. 1984. Le Prétoire de Pilate á l'ère byzantine. *RB* 91: 161–77.

Blinzler, J. 1959. *The Trial of Jesus.* Westminster, MD.

Dalman, G. 1924. *Orte und Wege Jesu.* 3d ed. BFCT 2/1. Gütersloh.

Donner, H., and Cüppers, H. 1977. *Die Mosaikkarte von Madeba.* Vol. 1. Wiesbaden.

Finegan, J. 1969. *Archaeology of the New Testament.* Princeton.

Jaroś, K. 1980. Ein neuer Lokalisierungsversuch des Prätoriums. *BLit* 53: 13–22.

Kroll, G. 1988. *Auf den Spuren Jesu.* 10th ed. Leipzig.

Maier, P. L. 1968. *Pontius Pilate.* New York.

Mare, W. H. 1987. *The Archaeology of the Jerusalem Area.* Grand Rapids.

Mommert, C. 1903. *Das Prätorium des Pilatus oder der Ort der Verurteilung Jesu.* Leipzig.
Murphy-O'Connor, J. 1986. *The Holy Land: An Archaeological Guide.* Rev. ed. Oxford.
Otto, E. 1980. *Jerusalem—die Geschichte der Heiligen Stadt.* Urban-Taschenbücher 308. Stuttgart.
Pixner, B. 1979. Noch einmal das Prätorium: Versuch einer Lösung. *ZDPV* 95: 65–86.
———. 1979–80. Where Was the Original Via Dolorosa? *Christian News from Israel* 27: 7–10; 51–53.
———. 1987. Was the Trial of Jesus in the Hasmonean Palace? Pp. 66–80 in *Jerusalem: City of Ages,* ed. A. L. Eckardt. Lanham, MD.
Renoux, A. 1969–71. *Le codes arménien Jérusalem 121.* 2 vols. PO 35/1 and 36/6. Turnhout.
Reisner, R. 1986. Das Prätorium des Pilatus. *BK* 41: 34–37.
Sion, M. A. de. 1956. *La forteresse Antonia à Jérusalem et la question du Prétoire.* Jerusalem.
Vincent, L. H. 1914. Vestiges antiques dans ḥâret el-Moghârbeh. *RB* 11: 429–36.
———. 1954. L'Antonia, palais primitive d'Hérode. *RB* 61: 87–107.
Vincent, L. H., and Stéve, M. A. 1954. *Jérusalem de l'Ancien Testament.* Vol. 1. Paris.
Wilkinson, J. 1977. *Jerusalem Pilgrims before the Crusades.* Jerusalem.

BARGIL (VIRGIL) PIXNER

PRAYER IN EARLY JUDAISM. The great hymnbook of the Second Temple was the Davidic Psalter, although it was not closed and defined before 70 C.E. Prior to that, the Psalter often contained additions, growing in some circles to 151 psalms, 153 psalms, and even 155 psalms, and with psalms later categorized as apocryphal within it (see 11QPsAp). It was not so much rivaled as complemented by other psalmbooks, like the Hodayoth (the Qumran Thanksgiving Hymns) in the late 2d century B.C.E. and the *Psalms of Solomon* in the late 1st century B.C.E., and by the hundreds of psalms and prayers used to illustrate the narratives in early Jewish literatures—the apocalypses, testaments, and expansions of the Hebrew Bible or Old Testament—and especially by the earliest statutory prayers used in the places of worship, notably the synagogue (Heinemann 1977).

The beginning and end of the day were celebrated by special prayers (see in addition to the old rabbinic liturgies the Qumran Daily Prayers = 4Q503). The end of the week was heralded by Sabbath services in the home, synagogue, temple, and other religious gatherings (e.g., the Qumran Angelic Liturgy). The year began, at Rosh Hashanah and Yom Kippur (see the rabbinic prayers and the Qumran Prayer for the Day of the Atonement Fragment = 1Q35b), with special prayers and psalms, and was divided by the great festivals—notably Passover *(Pesaḥ),* the Feast of Weeks (Pentecost), and the Feast of Booths (Sukkoth)—and their liturgies (which were often transferred from the temple to the synagogue [Safrai]). Jewish time was hence liturgical time; it is easy to understand such specific clarifications as "at the hour of prayer" (Acts 3:1). Foundational for Jewish prayer were the daily prayers in the home (esp. grace after meals) and the frequent spontaneous prayers of the individual.

During the Second Temple period the Hebrew Bible or OT evolved through a refined script—and an authoritative order, content, and form for each book—to a closed canon of books. See CANON. At the same time an equally important development was taking place: the basic themes in Jewish liturgy were being normalized (Hoffman 1979). While spontaneous prayers were preferred by some rabbis, set prayers with varying wording appeared in Judaism before the destruction of 70 C.E. (Heinemann 1977; Talmon 1978; Reif 1982).

Jewish prayers were not, like in many of the cultures contiguous with Palestine, pleas for material possessions or rewards, or magical manipulations of a deity who could be controlled by special deeds or words. The author of Daniel has Shadrach, Meshach, and Abednego confess that even if God would not deliver them, he was their God (Dan 3:16–18). As is well known, Palestinian Jews resisted the Romans, notably Pilate, and offered their lives in the refusal to compromise their law and liturgical customs (see Jos. *JW*). Even in the apocalypses, which tend to describe God's abode as far removed from the earth, the accent falls heavily on the claim that the angels, who link humans with God, receive the prayers of the faithful ones:

> And there was a great sound like thunder, and I said, "Lord, what is this sound?" And he said to me, "The Commander-in-Chief Michael is descending to receive the prayers of humans."
> (*3 Bar.* 11:3–4; all translations are those of the author)

Jews lived out the conviction, expressed throughout early Jewish literature, that God does hear and answer prayers (*4 Ezra* 8:40). Note the 15th Blessing in the *Amidah* or *Tefilah (18 Benedictions)* according to the Palestinian (Cairo Geniza) Version:

> Hear, O Lord our God, the voice of our prayers,
> And have compassion upon us,
> For you are a gracious and compassionate God.
> Blessed are you, O Lord, who hears prayer.

The author of *1 Enoch* 83–90, long before the destruction, prays to God, asking him "to sustain" the righteous and upright. This book of *Enoch* concludes with a dream in which the prayer is answered and fulfilled: "All the sheep were invited to that house (= the temple) but it could not contain all of them . . . I noticed that the house was large, wide, and exceedingly full" (*1 En.* 90:34–36). Paradigmatic for this constant theme is the Psalter itself, especially Psalm 116:

> I love the Lord
> for he hears my voice, my pleas;
> for he inclines his ear to me whenever I call.
> (Ps 116:1)

Today the sources for the study of Jewish prayers before the cessation of sacrifices in the temple are abundant. Many of the Dead Sea Scrolls are hymns and prayers. The Apocrypha and pseudepigrapha are replete with prayers, both as collections, individual works, and poetic compositions to illustrate apocalypes, testaments, and narrative expansions of biblical stories (see MANASSEH, PRAYER OF, also *Pr. Jac.*, *Pr. Jos.*, *Pr. Mos.*). The present state of research is preoccupied with textual and analytical studies; it is not possible yet to attempt a synthesis of the hundreds of early Jewish prayers. When that time comes sensitivity must be given to the variations among groups within early Judaism (ca. 250 B.C.E. to 200 C.E.). It can be said, however, that no other period in the history of Jewish liturgy is so important as the first two centuries C.E. See also FORGIVENESS (EARLY JUDAISM).

Bibliography

Charlesworth, J. H., ed. 1982. A Prolegomenon to a New Study of the Jewish Background of the Hymns and Prayers in the New Testament. *JJS* 33: 265–285.

———. 1986. Hymns, Odes and Prayers (ca. 167 B.C.E.—135 C.E.). Pp. 411–36 in *Early Judaism and Its Modern Interpreters*, ed. R. A. Kraft and G. W. E. Nickelsburg. Philadelphia and Atlanta.

Elbogen, I. 1931. *Der jüdische Gottesdienst in seiner geschichtlichen Entwicklung.* 3d ed. Frankfurt.

Flusser, D. 1984. Psalms, Hymns and Prayers. Pp. 551–77 in *Jewish Writings of the Second Temple Period*, ed. M. E. Stone. CRINT 2/2. Philadelphia.

Gaster, T. H. 1952. *Festivals of the Jewish Year.* New York. Repr. 1978.

Grant, F. C. 1953. Modern Study of the Jewish Liturgy. *ZAW* 65: 59–77.

Heinemann, J. 1977. *Prayer in the Talmud.* Trans. R. S. Sarason. Studia Judaica 9. New York.

Heinemann, J., and Petuchowski, J. J., eds. 1975. *Literature of the Synagogue.* New York.

Henrix, H., ed. 1979. *Jüdische Liturgie.* QD 86. Freiburg.

Hoffman, L. A. 1979. *The Canonization of the Synagogue Service.* Notre Dame.

Jeremias, J. 1966. *Abba: Studien zur neutestamentlichen Theologie und Zeitgeschichte.* Göttingen.

———. 1967. *The Prayers of Jesus.* Trans. J. Bowden; Burchard; and J. Reumann. SBT n.s. 6. London. Repr. Philadelphia, 1979.

Neusner, J. 1979. *From Politics to Piety: The Emergence of Pharisaic Judaism.* 2d ed. New York.

Petuchowski, J. J., and Brocke, M., eds. 1978. *The Lord's Prayer and Jewish Liturgy.* New York.

Reif, S. C. 1982. Some Liturgical Issues in the Talmudic Sources. *Studia Liturgica* 15: 188–206.

Safrai, S. 1987. The Temple and the Synagogue. Pp. 31–51 in *Synagogues in Antiquity*, ed. A. Kasher et al. Jerusalem. (In Hebrew).

Talmon, S. 1978. The Emergence of Institutionalized Prayer in Israel in the Light of the Qumran Literature. Pp. 265–84 in *Qumrân: Sa piété, sa théologie et son milieu*, ed. M. Delcor. BETL 46. Paris and Louvain.

JAMES H. CHARLESWORTH

PRAYER OF AZARIAH. See DANIEL, ADDITIONS TO.

PRAYER, LORD'S. See LORD'S PRAYER.

PRAYERS, HELLENISTIC SYNAGOGAL. The title "Hellenistic Synagogal Prayers" *(Hel. Syn. Pr.)* summarizes what scholars such as K. Kohler, W. Bousset, and E. R. Goodenough have concluded regarding certain prayers in the Greek language scattered throughout the Christian Apostolic Constitutions *(Apos. Con.)*. Historians had for a long while known that the eight volumes of the *Apos. Con.* were a 4th-century compilation from a multitude of sources, including the 3d-century *Didascalia* (*Apos. Con.* volumes 1–6), the 2d-century *Didache* (*Apos. Con.* 7.1–32), the 3d-century *Apostolic Tradition* (dispersed throughout vol. 8), and the Clementine Liturgy of uncertain date (*Apos. Con.* 8.5–15). Kohler (1924), Bousset (1915), and Goodenough (1935) suggested that a prayer collection from the Greek synagogues of the Diaspora was a fifth source and stood behind the following prayers in the *Apos. Con.*:

Kohler's List	Bousset's List	Goodenough's List
7.26.3		7.26.1–3
7.33	7.33	7.33
7.34	7.34	7.34
7.35	7.35	7.35
7.36	7.36	7.36
7.37	7.37	7.37
7.38	7.38	7.38
	7.39.2–4	7.39.2–4
	8.5.1–4	8.5.1–4
	8.6.5	8.6.5–8
	8.9.8f	8.9.8f
	8.12.6–27	8.12.6–27
	8.15.7–9	8.15.7–9
		8.16.3
	8.37.1–4	8.37.1–4
	8.37.5–7	8.37.5–7
	8.38.4f	8.38.4f
	8.39.3f	8.39.3f
		8.40.2–4
	8.41.4f	8.41.2–5

A host of liturgical scholars, Church historians, and specialists in Talmudic-era Judaism have accepted this conclusion with only a few raising voices of dissent.

Such a conclusion yielded important results when applied to the study of Judaism and Christian origins. If the prayers are a good example of the liturgy of the Diaspora synagogues, then writers such as Philo are not isolated phenomena in Judaism and do not express an aberrational theology. Rather, Philo is a true representative of the theology and piety of non-Palestinian Jews generally, for the religious concepts of the prayers are virtually identical with Philo. The prayers then, it was believed, give us a glimpse into the typical Greek synagogue. Goodenough (1935) went so far as to divide all Judaism into normative and mystic (i.e. Hellenistic) segments and to claim that the Jewish prayers embedded in the *Apos. Con.* were the "mystic liturgy."

A more probable view of the prayers, however, is that only some of them originate from a Jewish substratum and that even those bear the theological imprint of the 4th-century compiler/redactor of the *Apos. Con.* This compiler—who may or may not have been the semi-Arian Pseudo-Ignatius who interpolated the writings of Ignatius—was certainly profoundly influenced by "Alexandrian theology." A redactional analysis based on a comparison of the *Apos. Con* with the existing sources reveals certain linguistic traits and theological tendencies with unmistakable similarities to Philo and Origen. Such traits and tendencies abound in the prayers of books 7–8.

The redactional analysis of the prayers leads to the conclusion that the methodology of many of the scholars working on these "Jewish" prayers was flawed. They based their identification of the prayers as Jewish on Jewish-sounding phrases or concepts found in the prayers. But many of these expressions appear to be redactional. One must then reject not only the theological analysis of the prayers since the analysis does not take note of redactional elements, but also the argument that the prayers are Jewish at all.

Only the argument of Kohler (1924) with respect to *Apos. Con.* 7.33–38 is valid. Kohler discovered that these six prayers correspond exactly to the first six of the Hebrew Seven Benedictions for Sabbaths and holidays. The prayers (minus the redactional elements) have many of the same themes as the Seven Benedictions and even some of the same wording. What is even more important is that the prayers are in the same order as the Seven Benedictions.

The first prayer (7.33) praises the God of the patriarchs, as does the first benediction. The second prayer (7.34) extols God's power and ends with a reference to God as the "reviver of the dead," as does the second benediction. The third prayer (7.35) concerns the hallowing of the name and the fourth (7.36) the hallowing of the Sabbath day, both of which correspond to the third and fourth benedictions. The fifth prayer (7.37) corresponds to the fifth benediction on temple service and the sixth prayer (7.38) is quite similar to the thanksgiving prayer of the sixth benediction. In addition, some of the prayers contain other portions of the Hebrew prayer book such as the *Kedûšâ* (7.35) and the *Nišmat* (7.38). Nothing in *Apos. Con.* 7.33–38 or following is reminiscent of the seventh benediction, the priests' blessing. Perhaps this omission is because the prayer was supposed to be recited only in the Hebrew language (*M. Soṭa* 7.2), and the prayers in the *Apos. Con.* are in Greek.

The Jewish prayers of *Apos. Con.* 7.33–38 are evidently the product of the Syrian synagogues. The *Apos. Con.* itself was compiled in Syria and most of its other sources originated in Syria. Also, Syrian Christianity always maintained close contacts with Judaism, which would facilitate the inclusion of a Jewish prayer collection into the *Apos. Con.*

The date of the form of the Seven Benedictions as found in the *Apos. Con.* 7.33–38 is probably between 150 C.E. and 300 C.E. The earliest possible date is when the form of the *Kedûšâ* as found in Apos. Con. 7.35 (a combination of Isa 6:30 and Ezek 3:12) first appeared. The latest date is a few years before the compilation of the *Apos. Con.*

No particular Jewish milieu is evident for the prayers except perhaps post-Jamnia Pharisaism. The prayers certainly betray no origin in mysticism, Samaritanism, or Essenism, contrary to what has been suggested. The prayers in the *Apos. Con.* without the redactional elements are very similar theologically to the Hebrew benedictions. For text see *OTP* 2:671–97.

Bibliography

Baumstark, A., and Botte, B. 1958. *Comparative Liturgy.* Trans. F. L. Cross. Westminster, MD.

Bousset, W. 1915. Eine jüdische Gebetssamlung im siebenten Buch der apostolischen Konstitutionen. Pp. 438–85 in *Nachrichten von der Königlichen Gesellschaft der Wissenschaften zu Göttingen* Phil.-hist. Kl. Göttingen.

Bouyer, L. 1966. *Eucharistie.* Tournai, Belgium.

Brightman, F. E. 1896. *Liturgies, Eastern and Western.* Oxford.

Fiensy, D. A. 1985. *Prayers Alleged to be Jewish.* Chico, CA.

Funk, F. X. 1905. *Didascalia et Constitutiones Apostolorum.* Paderborn, Germany.

Gavin, F. 1969. *The Jewish Antecedents of the Christian Sacraments.* New York.

Goodenough, E. R. 1935. *By Light, Light.* New Haven.

Heinemann, J. 1977. *Prayer in the Talmud.* Trans. R. S. Sarason. Berlin.

Kohler, K. 1924. The Essene Version of the Seven Benedictions as Preserved in the vii Book of the Apostolic Constitutions. *HUCA* 1: 410–25.

Lietzman, H. 1953. *Mass and the Lord's Supper.* Trans. D. H. G. Reeve. Leiden.

Simon, M. 1948. *Verus Israel.* Paris.

DAVID A. FIENSY

PREEXISTENCE OF SOULS.

See SOULS, PREEXISTENCE OF.

PREACHER, THE.

See ECCLESIASTES, BOOK OF.

PREACHING.

To preach is to proclaim, to announce, to declare a word from God, to present publicly the good news, to deliver a religious discourse related directly or indirectly to a text of Scripture. Apart from a specific context, preaching is difficult to define. Even though preaching has long been significantly linked to the life and activity of both Jewish and Christian communities, it is so varied in content, mode, audience, and purpose that it resists the constraints of a dictionary, even a Bible dictionary.

A. Preaching as Mode
  1. Terminology in Hebrew Scriptures
  2. Terminology in the NT
B. Preaching as Content
  1. John the Baptist
  2. Jesus
  3. The Early Church
C. Preaching as Distinguished from Teaching

A. Preaching as Mode

In the histories of both synagogue and church, preaching as a mode of communication has ranged from an informal discussion called homily (from *homilein*, translated in the RSV as "talking," Luke 24:14, 15, and as "conversing," Acts 20:11) to a carefully constructed speech following the instructions of ancient rhetoric. The words which can be translated "preaching" in the biblical texts, however, do not yield much clear information on the mode or modes of communication.

1. Terminology in Hebrew Scriptures. The Hebrew Scriptures contain few clear references to that which we term "preaching." However, two activities seem clearly to fall in this category: prophetic proclamation and the teaching of Torah. The word *bašēr,* containing "joy" in its stem, refers to bringing or announcing good news or a message of joy, as in 2 Sam 4:10; Ps 40:9; Isa 40:9; 61:1. The other term meaning "to proclaim or to call," *qĕrā*ʾ (Jer 11:6; Mic 3:5; Jonah 1:2; 3:2), can also be translated "to read aloud," as in the public reading of the Torah in Neh 8:8–9. In the Greek translation of the Hebrew Bible these two words were rendered most often by *euangelizō* and *kērussō,* the two most common terms for preaching in the NT. See below. And finally, the NT refers to certain persons in the Hebrew Scriptures as preachers: Jonah (Luke 11:32), Noah (2 Pet 2:5), and Enoch (Jude 14, 15).

2. Terminology in the NT. In the NT, terms which refer to preaching are basically of two types.

a. Terms Which by Definition Refer to Preaching. These are primarily *kērussō,* meaning, first of all, "to announce or to proclaim publicly," a word used approximately sixty times (Mark 1:14; 1 Cor 1:23; Acts 10:42), and *euangelizō,* meaning "to announce good news" (Acts 5:42). The stem word *angellō,* from which we get "angel" or "messenger," appears in the NT with a variety of prefixes and in the RSV is variously translated: "to proclaim" (Acts 17:23); "to declare" (1 Pet 2:9); "to command" (Acts 17:30); "to preach" (Acts 5:42).

b. Terms Which by Context Refer to Preaching. These are words which do not intrinsically specify such activity but which by reason of context clearly indicate a public telling of the Christian message. There are many such terms. The more common among them are: "to cry out" (Acts 23:6; Rom 9:7); "to speak" (Rom 15:19; 2 Cor 2:12); "to talk" (Mark 2:2); "to make known" (Eph 6:19); "to prophesy" (1 Cor 14:1–4; 1 Pet 1:10); "to speak boldly" (Acts 13:46; 18:26); "to exhort" (Acts 2:40; 15:32); "to bear witness, to testify" (Acts 2:40; 20:24; John 1:15).

B. Preaching as Content

The NT employs a number of nouns to designate that which is preached. The most commonly used are *kērygma* (that which is proclaimed), Matt 12:41; Rom 16:25; 1 Cor 1:21; Titus 1:3; *euangelion* (the good news, the gospel), Matt 4:23; Mark 14:9; Acts 15:7; Rom 15:19; *logos* (the word), Acts 6:2; 1 Tim 5:17; *akoē* (report; that which is heard), John 12:38; Gal 3:2, 5; Rom 10:16. In each case, specificity as to content must be supplied by context.

1. John the Baptist. According to the Synoptics, John preached "a baptism of repentance for the forgiveness of sins" (Mark 1:4; Luke 3:3). He called upon his listeners to prepare for the advent of one stronger than he who would come baptizing with the Holy Spirit (Mark 1:8) and with fire (Matt 3:11; Luke 3:16). Luke says John gave specific ethical instructions to those who came (3:10–14). None of the Synoptics indicate that John publicly pointed specifically to Jesus as the one who was to come. In John, however, that Jesus was the Son of God was divinely revealed to the Baptist (1:33–34), and therefore, his entire message was one of bearing witness to Jesus as the Christ (1:7, 15, 19, 30, 34).

2. Jesus. That which Jesus preached is variously called the gospel of God (Mark 1:14), the gospel of the kingdom (Matt 4:23) and the gospel of the kingdom of God (Luke 4:43). Mark summarizes Jesus' preaching as threefold: "The time is fulfilled, and the kingdom of God is at hand; repent, and believe in the gospel" (1:15). Luke's summary draws on Isa 61:1–2: good news to the poor, release to the captives, sight to the blind, liberty to the oppressed, and for all the year of God's favor (4:18–19). Although the continuities between the preaching of John and of Jesus are evident, it is also clear that in the person, work, and words of Jesus a new era begins. The reign of God has broken in and continues to do so. Scholars continue to debate Jesus' own expectations concerning the kingdom's coming: how soon, how completely, how radically. The debate is sustained by the fact that in the records of Jesus' preaching the kingdom of God is both present and future.

3. The Early Church. The tradition of preaching from the prophets, John the Baptist, and Jesus continued with the apostles (Acts 5:42). In addition, other persons shared in gospel proclamation (Acts 21:8; Eph 4:11); in fact, the whole Church at times became involved in forms of preaching (Acts 8:4). In its preaching the Church understood itself as continuing the message of Jesus, but there was one major difference: Jesus the messenger of the kingdom was now the central feature of the message itself. From the beginning, preaching seems to have been varied in both mode and content. The Epistle to the Hebrews, for example, is a sermon (13:22), representing a style of preaching (citing, interpreting, and applying a text) which later became popular and widespread. But it does not stand alone in the NT. Most investigators of early Christian preaching look to Acts and the epistles of Paul.

Acts contains a number of sermons and portions of sermons (2:14–36; 3:12–26; 13:16–41; 17:22–31), most of them delivered by Peter and Paul. One should keep in mind that all the preaching reported in Acts comes to us from Luke, whose own fingerprints are on the reports. In fact, Luke had earlier stated the content of the proclamation as "repentance and forgiveness of sins" (Luke 24:47), and the sermons in Acts convey those two themes regularly. While it may remain an open question as to how broadly representative of the whole Church Luke's sermon reports are, it has long been the practice of historians to draw upon Acts to provide summary sketches of early Christian preaching. The most influential of these digests is that of C. H. Dodd (1937), whose reading of Acts (and Paul, but sermons are fragmentary in the letters) rendered the following: prophecies are fulfilled and the new age is launched by the coming of Christ; Christ was born of the seed of David, died according to the Scriptures to deliver us from this present evil age, was buried, and rose on the third day according to the Scriptures; Christ is exalted at the right hand of God as Son of God and Lord of all; Christ will come again as Judge and Savior. In short, God has in Jesus Christ done the promised work of salvation and all persons are now invited to turn from their former ways and believe the good news. In the above summary, the expression "according to the Scriptures" should alert the reader of Acts to the clear differences in the preaching of the Church to those who knew and believed the Hebrew Scriptures (2:16–36; 3:12–26; 13:16–41) and the messages to audiences totally unfamiliar with the Scriptures (14:8–17; 17:22–31). The points of contact with the listeners are quite different. Before moving to preaching as reflected in Paul's letters, it should be remembered that quite a number of NT scholars believe that the four Gospels are our primary sources for getting at the content of early Christian preaching. That these narratives represent Christian preaching is not a position in direct conflict with the preaching reflected in Acts. There is a difference in form, to be sure, but it is hardly reasonable to suppose that the Church's preaching would be silent about "all that Jesus began to do and teach until the day when he was taken up" (Acts 1:1–2).

That Paul understood his mission to be that of a preacher is quite clear from Paul himself: "For Christ did not send me to baptize but to preach the gospel" (1 Cor 1:17); "Woe to me if I do not preach the gospel!" (1 Cor 9:16). However, his letters, usually occupied with issues within the young congregations, do not offer the reader samples of his preaching. Instead there are reminders to the churches of what he preached when he was present with them. "Now I would remind you, brethren, in what terms I preached to you the gospel" (1 Cor 15:1). This statement is followed by a summary: Jesus died for our sins according to the Scriptures, was buried, was raised on the third day according to the Scriptures, and has appeared to his followers, including Paul (1 Cor 15: 3–8). Sometimes Paul was more brief: he preached Christ crucified (Gal 3:1). What is of special importance, however, is that Paul says his message was what he received, the tradition which had been given to him and which he passed along to the churches (1 Cor 15:3; 11:23). This says not only that Paul had predecessors but that there was strong continuity between his preaching and that done by others. Whatever the distances he experienced, and at other times helped create between himself and other apostles, Paul did not preach a new or different gospel. So strongly did Paul feel about his message that he called it a revelation of Jesus Christ (Gal 1:12) and pronounced anathema upon anyone offering a different gospel (Gal 1:8–9).

Much has been made of the scarcity of stories about and sayings of Jesus (such as we have in the Gospels) in the letters of Paul. Did he not know them? Did he not regard them as ingredient to the *kērygma*? Or is it simply the case that his letters, in form, purpose, and focus, did not provide the vehicle for such recitals? Whatever one's conclusion, the evidence is clear that the governing center of Paul's preaching was the death and resurrection of Christ. This was the basic paradigm both for his message and his lifestyle (Gal 6:14–17; 2 Cor 4:10–11). The Roman letter, Paul's most complete statement of his preaching, focuses not on Jesus' life or preaching but on his death and resurrection as the demonstration of God's righteous grace.

In those Christian communities in which Paul is the canon for preaching, there has been a tendency to treat the Gospel stories of Jesus as background to the passion, as prolegomena to the gospel, functioning homiletically as illustrative material for elaborating on the meaning of the death and resurrection. In the Roman Catholic Church and associated traditions, the gospel readings have provided the center for interpreting all other texts in the proclamation of the gospel. As one can see readily, this treatment of Paul's letters and the Gospels as distinctly different raises not only the question of content (what is the *kērygma*?) but also the question of the mode of preaching. This is to say, is preaching most properly narrative or direct address, recital or confrontation? The canon of the NT affirms both.

C. Preaching as Distinguished from Teaching

Given the difficulties in arriving at a specific and complete definition of preaching, both as mode and as content, some have sought clarity by distinguishing between preaching and teaching. C. H. Dodd (1937) again has been most influential in separating *kērygma* and *didache* (teaching). He argued his case from the NT, and there is to be found there textual support for his thesis. Matthew describes Jesus' ministry as threefold: teaching, preaching, and healing (9:35). Paul lists separately the gifts of prophecy and teaching (Rom 12:6–7; Eph 4:11). And in Acts 2, following the preaching which resulted in a large ingathering of converts, Luke says the new Christians attended to the apostles' teaching (2:42). There is a clear good sense to the arrangement that those who respond to the proclamation of the gospel be taught what it means to be a disciple among other disciples and in the world. Much of the NT consists of such instruction.

However, such a sharp distinction cannot be maintained on the basis of either biblical texts or careful thought. For example, the Sermon on the Mount (Matthew 5–7) is a body of teaching (5:2; 7:29) about life and relationships in the kingdom, and yet the audience consisted not only of Jesus' disciples but also "the crowds" (5:1; 7:28). Documents describing synagogue activity of the period refer to preaching and teaching interchangeably. Israel gathered on occasions to be renewed and reconstituted by the recital of the Exodus, the narrative which created the community. It seems unreasonable to suppose that the early Christian Church, created by the proclamation of the gospel, did not gather again and again to be renewed and reconstituted by the preaching which first called it into being. In fact, many of the words cited above which in some contexts clearly refer to preaching are the same words ("speak," "say," "exhort," "state boldly," etc.) which elsewhere indicate instruction to Christians. Modes of communication do not always distinguish preaching and teaching, and neither does audience. As to content, preaching without instruction lacks substance; teaching without *kērygma* lacks identity.

Bibliography

Baird, W. 1957. What Is the Kerygma? *JBL* 76: 184–87.

Dodd, C. H. 1937. *The Apostolic Preaching and Its Development.* Chicago.

Filson, F. V. 1963. *Three Crucial Decades.* Richmond.

Keck, L. E. 1979. *Paul and His Letters.* Philadelphia.

Patte, D. 1984. *Preaching Paul.* Philadelphia.

Smith, D. 1980. *Interpreting the Gospels for Preaching.* Philadelphia.

Wilder, A. N. 1964. The Word as Address and the Word as Meaning. Pp. 198–218 in *The New Hermeneutic.* Vol. 2 of *New Frontiers in Theology,* ed. J. M. Robinson and J. B. Cobb. New York.

Worley, R. C. 1967. *Preaching and Teaching in the Earliest Church.* Philadelphia.

FRED B. CRADDOCK

PRECINCT. See PARBAR.

PREFECT. See PALESTINE, ADMINISTRATION OF (ROMAN); PRAETORIUM; PROCURATOR.

PREHISTORY. Articles concerning the prehistory of selected regions and nations of the ANE will be found under the name of the region or nation. See especially ANATOLIA; ARABIA; EGYPT; IRAN; MESOPOTAMIA; PALESTINE, ARCHAEOLOGY OF; and SYRIA.

PRESENCE, BREAD OF THE. See BREAD OF THE PRESENCE.

PRIDE. See VIRTUE/VICE LISTS.

PRIESTLY ("P") SOURCE. The composite material of two schools of redactors, which reformulates the message of the Pentateuch according to a theology of monotheistic holiness and the importance of the cult. The Priestly Source, or "P," is distinguished by its use of particular terms and its theological perspective(s), both of which reflect a preexilic provenience.

A. The Text
B. P and H: Distinctions in Terminology and Style
C. The Priestly Theology
  1. Polemic against Paganism and the Evisceration of the Demonic
  2. A Gradual "Revolution"
  3. Holiness Contagion
  4. A Symbolic System: Life versus Death
  5. The Universal Blood Prohibition
  6. Theological Distinctions between P and H
  7. The Theology of Sacrifice
  8. The Ethical Basis of the Priestly Theology
D. Preexilic Provenience of the Priestly Source: Terminological Testimony
  1. The Evidence
  2. Refutation of Archaizing
  3. Summary
E. Relative Proveniences of P and H
  1. P and the Sanctuary at Shilo
  2. The Shilo Tradition Reworked

A. The Text

Scholarly consensus holds that the Priestly Source prevails throughout the Pentateuch and Joshua (see Driver 1913). The modifications which have subsequently been proposed have proven slight (see below). A greater challenge has been generated by the proposition that the P narrative (in Genesis, Exodus, and Numbers) is not an independent source but a redaction (e.g., Cross *CMHE* 293–325). The recognition that the purity texts are the products of two distinct schools, designated by the sigla P and H, helps to resolve this problem.

B. P and H: Distinctions in Terminology and Style

The vocabulary of the priestly writings is so markedly different from the other pentateuchal sources (JED) that introductions to the Bible or Pentateuch take pains to supply lists of their distinctive words and idioms (e.g., Driver 1913: 131–35). The problem with these lists is that they do not distinguish between P and H. The best way to gauge the differences between P and H is to identify words or idioms in one source that are consistently altered or synonymized in the other. This is precisely what I. Knohl has done in his study of the priestly texts. He enumerates 44 priestly terms, nine of which are worded differently in P and H (Knohl 1988: 97–99). This list can be supplemented by employing another criterion: terms carrying a precise meaning in P lose their precision in H. The study of the priestly style has also been immeasurably advanced by the finely honed investigation of M. Paran (1983), though—like his predecessor and probable pioneer (McEvenue 1971)—he unfortunately fails to distinguish between P and H. Paran singles out the following priestly literary devices: circular inclusions, poetic elements, refrains, and closing deviations (1983: 28–173). All these, however, are commonly shared by P and H. There exists another literary artifice that holds better promise of yielding a distinction between P and H—structure, in particular, the chiastic form, alternately called introversion (Kikawada 1974) or palistrophe (McEvenue 1971: 29, n. 18).

C. The Priestly Theology

1. Polemic against Paganism and the Evisceration of the Demonic. When it comes to theology, P and H mostly form a single continuum; H articulates and develops what is incipient and even latent in P.

The basic premises of pagan religion are (1) that its deities are themselves dependent on and influenced by a metadivine realm, (2) that this realm spawns a multitude of malevolent and benevolent entities, and (3) that if humans can tap into this realm they can acquire the magical power to coerce the gods to do their will (Kaufmann 1937–47 1: 297–350; 1960: 21–59). The priestly theology negates these premises. It posits the existence of one supreme God who contends neither with a higher realm nor with competing peers. The world of demons is abolished; there is no struggle with autonomous foes because there are none. With the demise of the demons, only one creature remains with "demonic" power—the human being. Endowed with free will, his power is greater than any attributed to him by pagan society. Not only can he defy God but, in priestly imagery, he can drive God out of his sanctuary. In this respect, humans have replaced the demons.

a. Sanctuary Pollution and Purification. The pagans secured the perpetual aid of a benevolent deity by building a temple residence in which the god was housed, fed, and worshiped in exchange for his protective care. Above all, his temple had to be inoculated by apotropaic rites—utilizing magic drawn from the metadivine realm—against incursions by malevolent forces from the supernal and infernal world. The priestly theologians make use of the same imagery, except that the demons are replaced by humans. Humans can drive God out of the sanctuary by polluting it with their moral and ritual sins. All that the priests can do is periodically purge the sanctuary of its impurities and influence the people to atone for their wrongs.

b. Nondemonic Conception of Impurity. This thoroughgoing evisceration of the demonic also transformed the concept of impurity. In Israel, impurity is harmless, retaining potency only with regard to sanctums. Laypersons—but not priests—may contract impurity with impunity; they must not, however, delay their purificatory rites lest their impurity affect the sanctuary. The retention of impurity's dynamic (but not demonic) power in regard to sanctums serves a theological function. The sanctuary symbolizes the presence of God; impurity represents the wrongdoing of persons. If persons unremittingly pollute the sanctuary, they force God out of his sanctuary and out of their lives.

The priestly texts on scale disease (Leviticus 13–14) and chronic genital flows (Leviticus 15) give ample witness to the priestly polemic against the idea that physical impurity arises from the activity of demons who must be either exorcised or appeased. Purification is neither healing nor theurgy. The afflicted person undergoes purification only after being cured. Ablutions are wordless rites; they are unaccompanied by incantation or gesticulation—the quintessential ingredients in pagan healing rites. The Heb adjective used in Leviticus 13–15 (*tāhēr*) means "purified" not "cured," whereas the verb *rāpāʾ*, "cure," never appears in the ritual. A moldy garment or a fungous house (Lev 13:47–58; 14:33–53) does not reflect on the character of its owner, for he brings no sacrifice and performs no rite that might indicate his culpability. Even though the scale-diseased person does bring sacrifices for possible wrongdoing, the only determinable "wrong" is that his impurity has polluted the sanctuary. Especially noteworthy is the bird rite at the beginning of his purification process (Lev 14:4–7) which, in spite of its clear exorcistic origins, carries only a symbolic function in Israel. Above all, it seems likely that most, if not all, of the varieties of scale disease described in Leviticus 13 are not even contagious, supporting the conclusion that scale disease is only a part of a larger symbolic system (explained below).

Another example of how the priestly legists excised the demonic from impurity is the case of the person afflicted with chronic genital flux (Lev 15:1–15, 25–30). It is the discharge that contaminates, not the person. Hence, objects that are underneath him: bed, seat, saddle—but no other—are considered impure. In Mesopotamia, however, his table and cup transmit impurity. The difference is that in Israel the afflicted person does not contaminate by touch as long as he washes his hands. Consequently, he was not banished or isolated but allowed to remain at home. The same concessions were extended to the menstruant, who was otherwise universally ostracized. She, too, defiled only that which was beneath her. Touching such objects, however, incurred greater impurity than touching her directly (Lev 15:19b, 21–22). As illogical as it seems, it makes perfect sense when viewed from the larger perspective of the primary priestly objective to root out the prevalent notion that the menstruant is possessed by demonic powers.

c. The Cult. The parade example of the evisceration of the demonic from Israel's cult is provided by Azazel (Lev 16:10). Though Azazel seems to have been the name of a demon, the goat sent to him is not a sacrifice requiring slaughter and blood manipulation; nor does it have the effect of a sacrifice in providing purification, expiation, etc. The goat is simply the symbolic vehicle for dispatching Israel's sins to the wilderness (Lev 16:21–22). The analogous elimination rites in the pagan world stand in sharp contrast. The purification of the corpse-contaminated person with the lustral ashes of the red cow (Numbers 19) can also claim pride of place among Israel's victories over pagan beliefs. The hitherto demonic impurity of the corpse has been devitalized, first by denying its autonomous power to pollute the sanctuary and then by denying that the corpse-contaminated person must be banished from his community during his purificatory period (Milgrom 1976).

2. A Gradual "Revolution." Israel's battle against demonic beliefs was not won in one stroke. Scripture indicates that it was a gradual process. The cultic sphere attests a progressive reduction of contagious impurity in all three primary human sources: scale disease, pathological flux, and corpse contamination. The earliest priestly tradition calls for their banishment (Num 5:2–4) because the presence of God is coextensive with the entire camp, but later strata show that banishment is prescribed only for scale disease (Lev 13:46). The fact that genital flux and corpse contamination permit their bearers to remain at home indicates that the divine presence is now viewed as confined to the sanctuary. Henceforth in P, the only fear evoked by impurity is its potential impact on the sanctuary. The driving force behind this impurity reduction is Israel's monotheism. The baneful still inheres in things but it spreads only under special conditions, for example, carrion when consumed and genital discharges when contacted. But note that impurity springs to life resuming its virulent character only in regard to the sphere of the sacred, and that these impurities are not to be confused with evils.

3. Holiness Contagion. A similar gradation in the contagion of holiness is also exhibited in Scripture, but for different reasons. In the earliest traditions of the Bible, the sanctums communicate holiness to persons, the sanctuary's inner sanctums more powerfully so—directly by sight (if uncovered) and indirectly by touch (if covered), even when the contact is accidental. According to the early narratives this power can be deadly; note the stories about the ark (1 Sam 6:19; 2 Sam 6:6–7), Mt. Sinai (Exod 19:12–13), and the divine fire (Lev 10:1–2). In P a major change has occurred. This fatal power is restricted to the rare moment when the tabernacle is dismantled (Num 4:15, 20), but otherwise the sanctums can no longer infect persons, even by touch (Milgrom 1981). Clearly, this drastic reduction in the contagious power of the sanctums was not accepted by all priestly schools. Ezekiel holds out for the older view that sanctums (in his example, the priestly clothing, 44:19; 46:20) are contagious to persons (contrary to P).

The texts are silent concerning the motivation behind this priestly reform. Undoubtedly, the priests were disturbed by the superstitious fears of the fatal power of the sanctums that might keep the masses from the sanctuary (cf. Num 17:27–28). To the contrary, they taught the people that God's holiness stood for the forces of life, and only when approached in an unauthorized way (e.g., Lev 10:1–2) would it bring death. Contact with the sanctums would be fatal to the nonpriest who dared officiate with the sanctums (e.g., Num 16:35; 18:3) but not to the Israelites who worshipped God in their midst. There is also a more realistic, historically grounded reason that would have moved the priests in this direction—the anarchic institution of altar asylum. Precisely because the altar sanctified those who touched it, it thereby automatically gave them asylum regardless of whether they were murderers, bandits, or other assorted criminals. By taking the radical step of declaring that the sanctums, in particular the altar, were no longer contagious to persons, the priests ended, once and for all, the institution of altar asylum. In this matter they were undoubtedly abetted by the king and his bureaucracy, who earnestly wanted to terminate the veto power of the sanctuary over their jurisdiction (details in Milgrom 1981).

4. A Symbolic System: Life versus Death. Obviously, the ritual complexes of Leviticus 1–16 make sense only as aspects of a symbolic system. As noted, only a few types of scale disease (many clearly noncontagious) were declared impure. Yet, to judge by the plethora of Mesopotamian texts dealing with the diagnosis and treatment of virulent diseases, it is fair to assume that Israel knew them as well (see *Leviticus 1–16* AB, Introduction) but did not classify them as impure. The same situation obtains with genital discharges. Why are secretions from other orifices of the body not impure: mucus, perspiration, and, above all, urine and feces? This leads to a larger question: why are there only these three sources of impurity—corpse/carcass, scale disease, and genital discharges? There must be a comprehensive theory that can explain all of the cases. Moreover, since the phenomena declared impure are the precipitates of a filtering process initiated by the priests, the "filter" must be their invention. In other words, the impurity laws form a system governed by a priestly rationale.

This rationale comes to light once it is perceived that there is a common denominator to the three above-mentioned sources of impurity—death. Genital discharge from the male is semen; from the female, blood. They represent the life force and their loss represents death. The case of scale disease also becomes comprehensible with the realization that the priestly legists have not focused on disease per se but only upon the *appearance* of disease. Moldy fabrics and fungous houses (Lev 13:47–58; 14:35–53) are singled out not because they are struck with scale disease but because they give that appearance. So too the few varieties of scale disease afflicting the human body: their appearance is that of approaching death. When Miriam is stricken with scale disease, Moses prays: "Let her not be like a corpse" (Num 12:12; cf. also Job 16:13). The wasting of the body, the common characteristic of the highly visible, biblically impure scale disease, symbolizes the death process as much as the loss of blood and semen.

It is of no small significance that the dietary laws (Leviticus 11), which are contiguous to and form a continuum with the bodily impurities (chaps. 12–15), are also governed by criteria, such as cud chewing and split hooves, which are equally arbitrary and meaningless in themselves, but serve a larger, extrinsic purpose. This purpose can be deduced both from the explicit rationale of holiness (Lev 11:43–45) and the implicit assumption of relevant texts (Gen 9:4; Lev 17:3–5, 10–14), to wit: animal life is inviolable except for a few edible animals provided they are slaughtered properly (i.e., painlessly) and their blood (i.e., their life) is drained and thereby returned to God (Milgrom 1963). To be sure, the rationale of holiness and the equation of blood and life are first fully articulated in H (Lev 11:43–45; 17:10–14), but they are already adumbrated in P (e.g., Gen 9:4).

Since impurity and holiness are antonyms, the identification of impurity with death must then mean that holiness stands for life. No wonder that reddish substances, the surrogates of blood, are among the ingredients of the purificatory rites for scale-diseased and corpse-contaminated persons (Lev 14:4; Num 19:6). They symbolize the victory of the forces of life over death. A further example: the blood of the purification offering symbolically purges the sanctuary by symbolically absorbing its impurities (see below)—another victory of life over death. Moreover, the priest is commanded to eat the flesh of the purification offering (Lev 6:19, 22; 10:17; Milgrom 1976), and the high priest dispatches the sanctuary's impurities together with the people's sins (Lev 16:21). In neither case is the priest affected. Again, holiness-life has triumphed over impurity-death. Impurity does not pollute the priest *as long as he serves God in His sanctuary*. Israel, too, as long as it serves God by obeying His commandments can overcome the forces of impurity-death.

Since the quintessential source of holiness resides with God, Israel is enjoined to control the occurrence of impurity lest it impinge on His realm (see below). The forces pitted against each other in a cosmic struggle are no longer the benevolent and the demonic deities who populate the mythologies of Israel's neighbors but the forces of life and death set loose by man himself through his obedience to or defiance of God's commandments. Despite all the changes that are manifested in the evolution of Israel's impurity laws, the objective remains the same: to sever impurity from the demonic and to reinterpret it as a symbolic system reminding Israel of the divine imperative to reject death and choose life.

5. The Universal Blood Prohibition. It would be well to point out that the blood prohibition is an index of P's concern for the welfare of humanity. In Leviticus, to be sure, all of P is directed to Israel. But one need only turn to the P stratum in Genesis to realize that it has not neglected the rest of humankind. P's blood prohibition in Genesis appears in the bipartite Noachian law which states that human society is viable only if it desists from the shedding of human blood and the ingestion of animal blood (Gen 9:4–6). Thus it declares its fundamental premise that human beings can curb their violent nature through ritual means, specifically, a dietary discipline that will necessarily drive home the point that all life (Heb *nepeš*), including animals, is inviolable, except—in the case of meat—when conceded by God (Milgrom 1963).

The P strand in Genesis also indicts the human race for its Heb *ḥāmās* ("violence," Gen 6:11). Since the Noachian law of Genesis 9 is the legal remedy for *ḥāmās* (Frymer-Kensky 1977), it probably denotes murder (as in Ezek 7:23), though in subsequent usage, especially under prophetic influence, it takes on a wide range of ethical violations (Haag *TDOT* 4: 478–86). Thus, the blood prohibition proves that P is of the opinion that a universal God imposed a basic ritual code upon humanity. Israel, on the other hand, bound by its covenantal relationship with the deity, is enjoined to follow a stricter code of conduct.

6. Theological Distinctions between P and H. One would expect a sharp cleavage separating the theology of P from the nonpriestly strands of the Pentateuch. However, it may come as a shock to realize that even the two priestly sources, P and H, sharply diverge on many theological fundamentals. The most important ideological distinction between P and H rests in their contrasting concepts of holiness. For P, spatial holiness is limited to the sanctuary; for H, it is coextensive with the promised land. Holiness of persons is restricted in P to priests and Nazirites (Num 6:5–8); H extends it to all Israel. This expansion follows logically from H's doctrine of spatial holiness: since the land is holy, all who reside in it are to keep it that way. Every adult Israelite is enjoined to attain holiness by observing the Lord's commandments, and even the Heb *gēr*, "resident alien," must heed the prohibitive commandments, for their violation pollutes the land (e.g., Lev 18:26).

P's doctrine of holiness is static; H's is dynamic. On the one hand, P constricts holiness to the sanctuary and its priests. P assiduously avoids the Heb term *qādôš*, "holy," even in describing the Levites (compare their induction rites, Num 8:5–22, with the priestly consecration, Leviticus 8). On the other hand, though H concedes that only priests are innately holy (Lev 21:7), it repeatedly calls upon Israel to strive for holiness. The dynamic quality of H's concept is highlighted by its resort to the same participial construction Heb *mĕqaddēš*, "sanctifying," in describing the holiness of both the laity and the priesthood. Sanctification is an ongoing process for priests (Lev 21:8, 15, 23; 22:9, 16) as well as for all Israelites (Lev 21:8; 22:32). No different from the Israelites, the priests bear a holiness that expands or contracts in proportion to their adherence to God's commandments.

The converse doctrine of pollution also varies sharply: P holds that the sanctuary is polluted by Israel's moral and ritual violations (Lev 4:2) committed anywhere in the camp (but not outside), and that this pollution can and must be effaced by the violator's purification offering and, if committed deliberately, by the high priest's sacrifice and confession (Lev 16:3–22). H, however, concentrates on the polluting force of Israel's violation of the covenant (Lev 26:15), for example, incest (Lev 18; 20:11–24), idolatry (Lev 2:1–6), or depriving the land of its sabbatical rest (Lev 26:34–35). Pollution for H is nonritualistic, as shown by the metaphoric use of Heb *ṭāmēʾ* (e.g., Lev 18:21, 24; 19:31) and by the fact that the polluted land cannot be expiated by ritual, and, hence, the expulsion of its inhabitants is inexorable (Lev 18:24–29; 20:2).

7. The Theology of Sacrifice. The sacrificial system is intimately connected with the impurity system. Nonetheless, it possesses a distinctive theology (rather, theologies) of its own. No single theory embraces the entire complex of sacrifices (Milgrom 1976). All that can be said by way of generalization is that the sacrifices cover the gamut of the psychological, emotional, and religious needs of the people. We therefore seek the specific rationale that underlies *each* kind of sacrifice. Even with this limited aim in mind, the texts are not always helpful. However, hints gleaned from the terminology and the descriptions of the rites themselves will occasionally illumine our path. The comprehensive rationales for two sacrifices, the burnt and cereal offerings, remain unclear, whereas the three remaining sacrifices, the well-being, purification, and reparation offerings, can be satisfactorily explained.

a. The Well-Being Offering. The well-being offering is associated with the blood prohibition, although this connection was not present from the beginning. In the P stratum, the well-being offering is brought solely out of joyous motivations: thanksgiving, vow fulfillment, or spontaneous free will (Lev 7:11–17). The meat of the offering is shared by the offerer with his family and invited guests (1 Sam 1:4; 9:21–24). The development of H brought another dimension to this sacrifice. H's ban on nonsacrificial slaughter meant that all meat for the table had initially to be sanctified on the altar as a well-being offering (Lev 17:3–7). To be sure, the prohibition to ingest blood had existed before (Gen 9:4; cf. 1 Sam 14:32–35), implying that though man was conceded meat, its blood, which belongs to God, had to be drained. Now that the blood had to be dashed on the altar (Lev 3:2, 8, 13) it served an additional function—to ransom the life of the offerer for taking the life of the animal (17:11; Milgrom 1971). Thus the principle of the inviolability of life was sharpened by this new provision: killing an animal was equivalent to murder (Lev 17:3–4) unless expiated by the well-being offering.

b. The Purification Offering. The rationale for the purification offering has been alluded to above. The violation of a prohibitive commandment generates impurity and, if severe enough, pollutes the sanctuary from afar. This imagery portrays the priestly theodicy. It declares that while sin may not scar the face of the sinner it does scar the face of the sanctuary (Milgrom 1976). This image graphically illustrates the priestly version of the old doctrine of collective responsibility: when the evildoers are punished they bring down the righteous with them. However, those who perish with the wicked are not entirely blameless. They are inadvertent sinners, who by having allowed the wicked to flourish have also contributed to the pollution of the sanctuary. In particular, the high priest and the tribal chieftain, the leaders of the people, bring special sacrifices (Lev 4:9, 23) since their errors cause harm to their people. Thus, in the priestly scheme, the sanctuary is polluted (read: society is corrupted) by brazen sins (read: the rapacity of the leaders) and also by inadvertent sins (read: the acquiescence of the "silent majority"), with the result that God is driven out of his sanctuary (read: the nation is destroyed). In the theology of the purification offering, Israel is close to the beliefs of its neighbors and yet so far from them. Both hold that the sanctuary stands in need of constant purification lest it be abandoned by its resident god. But whereas the pagans hold that the source of impurity is demonic, Israel, having expunged the demonic, attributes impurity to the rebellious and inadvertent sins of man instead (details in Milgrom 1976).

c. The Reparation Offering. The reparation offering (Lev 5:14–26) seems at first glance to be restricted to offenses against the property of God, either his sanctums or name. It reflects, however, wider theological implications. The Heb noun *ʾāšām,* "reparation, reparation offering," is related to the Heb verb *ʾāšam,* "feel guilt," which predominates in this offering (Lev 5:17, 23, 28) and in the purification offering as well (Lev 4:13, 22, 27; 5:4, 5). This fact bears ethical consequences. Expiation by sacrifice depends on two factors: the remorse of the worshipper (verb *ʾāšam*) and the reparation (noun *ʾāšām*) he brings to both man and God to rectify his wrong. This sacrifice strikes even deeper ethical roots. If someone falsely denies under oath having defrauded his fellow, subsequently feels guilt and restores the embezzled property and pays a twenty percent fine, he is then eligible to request of his deity that his reparation offering serve to expiate his false oath (Lev 5:20–26). Here we see the priestly legists in action, bending the sacrificial rules in order to foster the growth of individual conscience. They permit sacrificial expiation for a deliberate crime against God (knowingly taking a false oath) provided the person repents before he is apprehended. Thus, they ordain that repentance converts an intentional sin into an unintentional one, thereby making it eligible for sacrificial expiation (details in Milgrom 1976).

8. The Ethical Basis of the Priestly Theology. It should already be clear that the priestly polemic against pagan practice was also informed by ethical postulates. The impurity system pits the forces of life against the forces of death, reaching an ethical summit in the blood prohibition. Not only is blood identified with life but it is also declared inviolable. If the unauthorized taking of animal life is equated to murder, how much more so is the illegal taking of human life. And if the long list of prohibited animals has as its aim the restriction of meat to three domestic quadrupeds, whose blood (according to H) must be offered up on the altar of the central sanctuary, what else could the compliant Israelite derive from this arduous discipline except that all life must be treated with reverence?

The reduction of sanctum contagion may have been motivated by the desire to wean Israel from the universally attested morbid fear of approaching the sanctums. But as indicated above, there coexisted the more practical goal of breaking the equally current belief that the sanctuary gave asylum even to the criminal. As noted above, the ethical current ran strong also in the rationale for the sacrifices. The purification offering taught the ecology of morality, that the sins of the individual adversely affect his society, even when committed inadvertently, and the reparation offering became the vehicle for an incipient doctrine of repentance. The ethical thrust of these two expiatory sacrifices can be shown to be evident in other respects as well. The priestly legists did not prescribe the purification offering just for cultic violations but extended the meaning of the term *miṣwâ* (Lev 4:2) to embrace the broader area of ethical violations. And the texts on the reparation offering make it absolutely clear that in matters of expiation man takes precedence over God; only after rectification has been made with man can it be sought with God (Lev 5:24b–25).

A leitmotiv of the sacrificial texts is their concern for the poor: everyone, regardless of means, should be able to bring an acceptable offering to the Lord. Thus, birds were added to the roster of burnt offerings (Lev 1:14–17), and the pericope on the cereal offering (Leviticus 2) was deliberately inserted after the burnt offering, implying that if a person could not afford birds he could bring a cereal offering. Indeed, this compassion for the poor is responsible for the prescribed sequence of the graduated purification offering: flock animal, bird, cereal (Lev 5:6–13). This concession of a cereal offering, however, was not allowed for severe impurity cases (Lev 12:8; 14:21–32; 15:14) because of the need for sacrificial blood to purge the contaminated altar.

The ethical impulse attains its zenith in the great Day of Purgation, Yom Kippur. What originally was only a rite to purge the sanctuary has been expanded to include a rite to purge the people. As mentioned above, the pagan notion of demonic impurity was eviscerated by insisting that the accumulated pollution of the sanctuary was caused by human sin. Moreover, another dimension was introduced that represented a more radical alteration. The scapegoat which initially eliminated the sanctuary's impurities now became the vehicle of purging their source—the human heart. Provided that the people purged themselves through rites of penitence (Lev 16:29; 23:27, 29; Num 29:7), the high priest would confess their released sins upon the head of the scapegoat and then dispatch it and its load of sins into the wilderness. Thus, an initial widely attested purgation rite of the temple was broadened and transformed into an annual day for the collective catharsis of Israel. God would continue to reside with Israel because his temple and people were once again pure.

D. Preexilic Provenience of the Priestly Source: Terminological Testimony

1. The Evidence. This priestly work can be dated. There is ample evidence that its terminology is preexilic. Thus far the chief investigator of priestly terminology has been A. Hurvitz (1981; 1982; 1988). Using the book of Ezekiel as a standard against which to measure the life span of priestly terms, Hurvitz finds ten such terms that are absent from Ezekiel in contexts where one should expect to find them. Moreover, he and Paran (1983) adduce 22 P terms that are replaced by synonyms in Ezekiel and in postexilic books. Hurvitz's examples can be supplemented by the key terms of Israel's sociopolitical structure. This area is more decisive because these terms describe living institutions (details in Milgrom 1978; 1989). The terminology for the doctrine of repentance also exhibits this diachronic transformation. P clearly posits repentance not by the prophetic (and postbiblical) root *šwb* but by its unique verb *ʾāšam* (Milgrom 1976: 3–12).

2. Refutation of Archaizing. Only one argument carries

some weight: P is guilty of archaizing. So writes Wellhausen, "It (P) tries hard to imitate the costume of the Mosaic period . . . to disguise its own" (*WPHI,* 9). In our day F. M. Cross echoes a similar view (*CMHE,* 322–23; cf. also Hoffman 1986). Hurvitz counters this argument by maintaining that archaizing is discernible only if "one can furnish positive evidence proving the existence of *late* linguistic elements in the same work" (1982: 163). That is, an author, particularly one represented by such an extensive corpus as the priestly writings, would surely betray himself by some anachronistic slip. Nonetheless, the possibility must be granted that the priestly redaction may have succeeded in concealing its true (late) period. Another control, however, is at hand that can vitiate the charge of anachronism. What if a term undergoes a change of meaning and there are ample attestations of this term in the early and late biblical literature so that the change can be accurately charted? Moreover, what if the new meaning is incompatible with, and even contradictory to, its predecessor so that it is inconceivable that both meanings could have existed simultaneously? The term *mišmeret* exemplifies the first case and *ʿăbōdâ* the second.

a. The Evidence from *mišmeret*. The Heb term *mišmeret* occurs 76 times in Scripture, chiefly in P. In connection with the tabernacle it means "guard duty" *and nothing else,* as observed by the medieval Jewish exegete Abrabanel (ca. 1437–1508) in his commentary on Num 3:5. When *mišmeret* is in construct with Yahweh, the context involves proscriptions and taboos so that "guarding" against the violation of the Lord's commandments is always meant (details in Milgrom 1970: 8–12). The evolution of *mišmeret* from "guard duty" to postbiblical "service unit" is barely detectable in Scripture. This later meaning is found only in Nehemiah (Neh 12:9, 24; 13:30; correcting Milgrom 1970: 12, n. 41) and Chronicles (1 Chr 25:8; Paran 1983: 205, n. 42). But it is not even adumbrated in any of P's 43 attestations (details in Milgrom 1970: 12–16).

b. The Evidence from *ʿăbōdâ*. The second Heb term, *ʿăbōdâ,* is of weightier import. In P it occurs some 70 times and it always denotes "physical labor" (Milgrom 1970: 60–82). However, in postexilic cultic texts (even when they cite pentateuchal passages) it means "cultic service" (Milgrom 1970: 82–87). These two meanings clearly contradict each other and therefore cannot coexist. Levites, on pain of death, are forbidden to officiate in the cult (Num 18:3b), and hence their *ʿăbōdâ* is confined to the job of physically removing the tabernacle. But in postexilic texts the contrary is true. Priests alone may perform *ʿăbōdâ* because this term now means "cultic service."

3. Summary. In sum, the terminological study of Ezekiel 44, supplemented by the studies of Hurvitz and Paran of the 22 Ezekielian passages adduced above, demonstrates that Ezekiel is the chronological watershed of Israel's cultic terminology. His book confirms the conclusions derived from P's central vocabulary in the area of cult (*mišmeret; ʿăbōdâ*), theology (absence of *šwb*), and sociopolitical institutions (Heb *ʿēdâ; maṭṭeh; ʾelep; nāśîʾ*) that P is a product of the preexilic age (cf. also Grintz 1974–75; Polzin 1976; Guenther 1977; Rendsburg 1980). Furthermore, not a single priestly term has been shown to be of postexilic coinage. Finally, the allegation that P is archaizing has proven baseless. No postexilic writer could have used *ʿăbōdâ* in its earlier sense of "physical labor" when it flatly contradicted the meaning it had in his own time. His readers would have been confused, nay, shocked, to learn that "cultic service," exclusively the prerogative of priests and fatal to nonpriests, had been assigned to the Levites.

E. Relative Proveniences of P and H

H probably arose out of the socioeconomic crisis at the end of the 8th century (Knohl 1988: 179–93). Following a suggestion of M. Haran (*EncMiqr* 5: 1098; 1981) that H's interdiction of the Molech and the *ʾōb* and *yiddĕʿōnî* corresponds with the proliferation of these cults into the royal court during the second half of the 8th century, Knohl postulates that H must be a product of that period (1988: 178, 263, n. 19, 264, n. 22). Here Knohl has been anticipated by Eerdmans (1912: 101), who added to the Molech factor the occurrence of *ʾĕlîlim* both in H (Lev 19:4; 26:1) and profusely in First Isaiah (9 out of a total of 16 times: 2:8, 18, 21; 10:10, 11; 19:11; 31:7; see also Elliott-Binns 1955: 38; Feucht 1964: 166–67). Knohl differs from all of them in that he alone postulates the priority of P, whereas the others hold with the consensus that H is earlier than and is absorbed by P. According to Knohl, the new issues that concern H are idolatry, social injustice, the gap between ethics and the cult, and the *gēr* (1988: 176–77, 188–89). "HS's (the Holiness School) writings become clear against the background of the socio-economic polarization and the religious crisis that developed in that period. The crisis that led to the attacks by classical prophecy on the ritual and Temple institutions . . . HS expresses the attempt by priestly circles in Jerusalem to contend with the prophet's criticism. In reaction . . . HS created the broader concept of holiness that integrates morality and cult and drew up a comprehensive program for social rehabilitation formulated in social terms" (1988: x; cf. 178–87). The priestly answer to this crisis eventuated in the composition of the Holiness Code (1988: 173–76).

Since H also includes the redaction of P, this can only mean that P—not just its teachings but its very texts—was composed not later than the middle of the 8th century (ca. 750 B.C.E.). As for determining the provenience, the veritable Sitz im Leben of P, it is likely that P presumes the existence and the legitimacy of common slaughter. More accurately, P espouses a modified form of common slaughter, one evidenced in Saul's battle against the Philistines (1 Sam 14:31–35; details in *Leviticus 1–16* AB, Introduction).

Thus H is not the innovator of centralization; it has inherited P's explicit demand that all sacrifice take place at the tabernacle. H is after something else—the banning of common slaughter. It claims that "all suet is the Lord's" and therefore demands that all animal flesh should first be offered as a well-being offering. If H is to be associated with Hezekiah's reform (see above) which was operative solely in the land of Judah, then the edict of Leviticus 17, though idealistic, is still feasible. D's centralization, however, takes place under different historical circumstances. The expanded borders of Josiah's kingdom had made common slaughter an absolute necessity (Deut 12:15–16, 21–25). Even at the risk of chthonic worship, D ordains that "[the blood] shall be spilled on the ground like water" (Deut 12:16, 23). This prescription may reflect D's fear that the example of Saul's stone ultimately turning into an altar (1 Sam 14:35) might subvert D's centralization imperative by leading to the consecration of other slaughtering stones as altars.

1. P and the Sanctuary at Shilo. It is clear that P as well as H speaks of the tent of meeting as the only legitimate sanctuary. H clearly has the Jerusalem temple in mind, but for P, there are only two possibilities. Being anterior to H, P's reference could be the pre-Hezekian temple (Knohl 1988: 189–91). Or P may advert to an anterior institution—the sanctuary at Shiloh (Haran 1962; 1978: 175–204).

The intensive excavations at the site of Shiloh and the survey explorations thoroughout the central hill country have yielded valuable information concerning Shiloh's regional role during Iron Age I of the premonarchic period (Finkelstein 1985: 164–74; 1988). The pertinent results can be summarized as follows: At the beginning of Iron Age I (end of 12th century B.C.E.) there was a dramatic increase in the number of permanent settlements in the central hill country. In the tribal territories of Ephraim and Manasseh, 27 sites during the Late Bronze Age grew to 211 sites, nearly an eightfold increase. Most of the growth was registered in Ephraim (23 times, to 4.4 times in Manasseh), especially around Shiloh (22 sites within a 5 or 6 km radius). The Shiloh temple located in the heart of this population must have served as the regional center for the entire area before it was destroyed in the middle of the 11th century. Expansion southward took place later, after the destruction of Shiloh. This meant that Shiloh probably was the first and only interregional, transtribal religious center before the Jerusalem temple. Other important sanctuaries, such as Benjaminite Bethel and Gilgal (of Samuel and Saul) could not have borne regional significance while the Shiloh sanctuary existed.

2. The Shiloh Tradition Reworked. The basic presuppositions of P fit the archaeological data of Shiloh to perfection. P prescribes a central sanctuary containing the tabernacle with its ark and other cultic paraphernalia. It also presupposes common slaughter at home (see above), so that households would journey to Shiloh only for the annual pilgrimage (1 Sam 1:3; 2:19) or festival (Judg 21:19). On the other hand, P does not claim that the tabernacle is the only legitimate sanctuary. There is neither admonition nor ban against worshiping at other altars—unlike H (Leviticus 19) and D (Deuteronomy 12). Though biblical scholarship registers other opinions regarding the provenience of P's tabernacle, the absence of any prohibition against multiple sanctuaries limits P's tabernacle to either the temple of Shiloh or that of Jerusalem before Hezekiah's edict of centralization (2 Kgs 18:4).

Both locations are possible. The sacrificial procedures attested in P probably had their origin at Shiloh. Some texts, like the thanksgiving offering pericope, were reworked by the Jerusalem priesthood so thoroughly that even where the seams are visible it is no longer possible to recover the original text. Others, like the cereal and well-being offerings, received interpolations or supplementary verses which when removed reveal the original text (details in *Leviticus 1–16* AB, Introduction). These additions are the work of subsequent generations of Jerusalem priests, but still from the time prior to Hezekiah. In substance these additions are not significant; they probably reflect the "in-house" adjustments of the priests regarding their sacrificial income as the one-family sanctuary gave way to the multifamily temple. It would take the momentous events at the end of the 8th century, which led to an infusion of refugees from north Israel and the prophetic rebuke concerning the social and economic injustices gripping the land, to provoke a major priestly response resulting in the creation of the radically new vistas and ideology of H (see Knohl 1988: 146–93).

Bibliography

Aharoni, Y. 1973. The Solomonic Temple, the Tabernacle and the Arad Sanctuary. *Beer-Sheva* 1: 79–86 (in Hebrew).

Albright, W. F. 1942. *Archaeology and the Religion of Israel.* Baltimore.

Aloni, J. 1983–84. The Place of Worship and the Place of Slaughter according to Leviticus 17:3–9. *Shnaton* 7–8: 21–50 (in Hebrew).

Barkay, G. 1986. *Ketef Hinnom: A Treasure Facing Jerusalem's Walls.* Jerusalem.

Brichto, H. C. 1976. On Slaughter and Sacrifice, Blood and Atonement. *HUCA* 47: 19–55.

Cohen, C. 1969. Was the P Document Secret? *JANES* 1/2: 39–44.

Cross, F. M. 1947. The Priestly Tabernacle. *BA* 10: 45–68. Repr. in *BAR* 1: 201–28. Repr. 1978.

Driver, S. R. 1913. *Introduction to the Literature of the Old Testament.* Edinburgh.

Duke, R. K. 1988. Punishment or Restoration? Another Look at the Levites of Ezekiel 44: 6–16. *JSOT* 40: 61–81.

Eerdmans, B. D. 1912. *Das Buch Leviticus.* Giessen.

Elliot-Binns, L. E. 1955. Some Problems of the Holiness Code. *ZAW* 76: 26–40.

Feucht, C. 1964. *Untersuchungen zum Heiligkeitsgesetz.* Berlin.

Finkelstein, I. 1985. Excavations at Shilo 1981–1984. Summary and Conclusions: History of Shilo from Middle Bronze Age II to Iron Age II. *TA* 12: 159–77.

———. 1988. *The Archaeology of the Israelite Settlement.* Jerusalem.

Friedman, R. E. 1980. The Tabernacle in the Temple. *BA* 43: 241–48.

Frymer-Kensky, T. 1977. The Atrahasis Epic and Its Significance for Our Understanding of Genesis 1–9. *BA* 40: 147–55.

Gertner, M. 1960. The Masorah and the Levites. Appendix on Hosea XII. *VT* 10: 241–84.

Gray, G. B. 1925. *Sacrifice in the Old Testament.* Oxford.

Grintz, Y. M. 1966. Do Not Eat on the Blood. *Tsiyon* 31: 1–17 (in Hebrew). Eng. trans. *ASTI* 8 (1970–71): 78–105.

———. 1974–75. Archaic Terms in the Priestly Code. *Leš* 39: 5–30, 163–81; 40: 5–32 (in Hebrew).

Guenther, A. R. 1977. *A Diachronic Study of Biblical Hebrew Prose Syntax: An Analysis of the Verbal Clause in Jeremiah 37–45 and Esther 1–10.* Ph.D. diss., University of Toronto.

Gurney, O. R. 1952. *The Hittites.* London.

Haran, M. 1962. Shilo and Jerusalem: The Origin of the Priestly Tradition in the Pentateuch. *JBL* 81: 14–24.

———. 1978. *Temples and Temple Service in Ancient Israel.* Oxford.

———. 1981. Behind the Scenes of History: Determining the Date of the Priestly Source. *JBL* 100: 321–33.

Hoffman, Y. 1986. Concerning the Language of P and the Date of Its Composition. *Teʿudah* 4: 13–22 (in Hebrew).

Hurvitz, A. 1981. The Language of the Priestly Source and Its Historical Setting—the Case for an Early Date. *PWCJS* 8: 83–94.

———. 1982. *A Linguistic Study of the Relationship between the Priestly Source and the Book of Ezekiel.* CahRB 20. Rome.
———. 1988. Dating the Priestly Source in Light of the Historical Study of Biblical Hebrew a Century after Wellhausen. *BZAW* 100: 88–99.
Ibn Ezra, Abraham. 1988. *Commentary on the Pentateuch.* Vol. 1, *Genesis.* Trans. H. N. Strickman and A. M. Silver. New York.
Kaufmann, Y. 1937–47. *The Religion of Israel.* Vols. 1–3. Tel Aviv (in Hebrew).
———. 1960. *The Religion of Israel.* Trans. M. Greenberg. Chicago.
Kikawada, I. M. 1974. The Shape of Genesis 11:1–9. Pp. 18–32 in *Rhetorical Criticism,* ed. J. J. Jackson and M. Kessler. Pittsburgh.
Knohl, I. 1983–84. The Priestly Torah versus the Holiness School: Sabbath and the Festivals. *Shnaton* 7–8: 109–46. Eng. trans. *HUCA* 58 (1987): 65–117.
———. 1988. *The Conception of God and Cult in the Priestly Torah and in the Holiness School.* Ph.D. diss., Hebrew University.
Kuenen, A. 1886. *An Historico-Critical Inquiry into the Origin and Composition of the Hexateuch.* Trans. P. H. Wicksteed. London.
Lambert, W. G. 1959. Morals in Ancient Mesopotamia. *JEOL* 16: 184–96.
Levine, B. A. 1983. Late Language in the Priestly Source: Some Literary and Historical Observations. *PWCJS* 8: 69–82.
Loewenstamm, S. E. 1972–73. The Relation of the Settlement of Gad and Reuben in Num 32:1–38. *TA* 42: 12–26 (in Hebrew).
Malamat, A. 1979. *Ummatum* in Old Babylonian Texts and Its Ugaritic and Biblical Counterparts. *UF* 11: 527–36.
McEvenue, S. E. 1969. A Source-Critical Problem in Num 14, 26–38. *Bib* 50: 453–65.
———. 1971. *The Narrative Style of the Priestly Writer.* AnBib 50. Rome.
Milgrom, J. 1963. The Biblical Diet Laws as an Ethical System. *Int* 17: 288–301.
———. 1970. *Studies in Levitical Terminology.* Berkeley.
———. 1971. A Prolegomenon to Leviticus 17:11. *JBL* 90: 149–56.
———. 1976. Profane Slaughter and a Formulaic Key to the Composition of Deuteronomy. *HUCA* 47: 1–17.
———. 1978. Priestly Terminology and the Political and Social Structure of Pre-Monarchic Israel. *JQR* 69: 65–81.
———. 1981. Sancta Contagion and Altar/City Asylum. *VTSup* 32: 278–310.
———. 1983. Magic, Monotheism, and the Sin of Moses. Pp. 251–61 in *The Quest for the Kingdom of God,* ed. H. H. Hoffman; F. A. Spina; and A. R. W. Green. Winona Lake, IN.
———. 1989. *The Book of Numbers.* Philadelphia.
Nilsson, M. P. 1940. *Greek Folk Religion.* New York.
Paran, M. 1983. Literary Features of the Priestly Code: Stylistic Patterns, Idioms and Structures. Ph.D. diss., Hebrew University (in Hebrew).
Paton, L. B. 1897. The Original Form of Leviticus XVII–XIX. *JBL* 16: 31–77.
Polzin, R. 1976. *Late Biblical Hebrew.* Missoula, MT.
Reiner, E. 1956. *Lipshur* Litanies. *JNES* 15: 129–49.
———. 1958. *Šurpu. AfO* 11. Graz.
Rendsburg, G. 1980. Late Biblical Hebrew and the Date of "P." *JANES* 12: 65–80.
Renger, J. 1967. Untersuchungen zum Priestentum in der altbabylonischen Zeit. *ZA* 24: 110–88; 26 (1969): 104–230.
Sauneron, S. 1960. *The Priests of Ancient Egypt.* New York.
Schley, D. 1989. *Shiloh.* JSOTSup 66. Sheffield.
Scott, J. A. 1965. *The Pattern of the Tabernacle.* Ph.D. diss., University of Pennsylvania.
Toeg, A. 1974. Num 15:22–31. A Halakhic Midrash. *TA* 43:20 (in Hebrew).
Zevit, Z. 1982. Converging Lines of Evidence Bearing on the Date of P. *ZAW* 94: 481–511.

JACOB MILGROM

PRIESTS. See LEVITES AND PRIESTS.

PRIMEVAL HISTORY. A modern label that scholars have applied to Genesis 1–11 and to a particular type of narrative pattern reflected not only in Genesis 1–11 but in other ANE literary sources.

A. Definitions
B. Patterns of Primeval History
 1. Narrative Pattern
 2. Genealogical Pattern
C. Purpose
D. Genesis 1–11
 1. Narrative Pattern
 2. Genealogical Pattern
E. Other "Primeval History" Patterns in the Bible
 1. Exodus 1–2
 2. Matthew 1–3
 3. Other Biblical Books
F. Indo-European Literature
 1. Iranian Tradition
 2. Indian Tradition
 3. Classical Tradition

A. Definitions

When a child asks, "Mommy, where did I come from?" the awareness of historical thought begins. When society asks us, "Who are you, anyway?" we begin to formulate history. We start to form a list of credentials, of memorable and significant events, including the definite point at which our historical accounting begins. One could start one's own history at this point, but ANE society seems to have demanded that history, whether personal or national, should begin rather with the very beginning of the world.

The problem with this requirement is that there were no human observers at the beginning of the world. But the people of the ANE knew that there must have been a more distant past lying behind the knowable past. To account for this, ancient historians had to posit the beginning of history, speculative both factually and philosophically. From that point on, going forward in time, they speculated about how the world in its fullness, including their untenable past and unknowable ancestors, came to be.

This speculative, often mythological history between the creation of the world up to the point when one's historical memory begins became well patterned and traditional in the ANE. This patterned portion of history is here termed "primeval history."

The primeval history is a long and well-established literary convention (Kikawada 1974) in the ancient world, first detected in the Sumerian literature of the 21st century B.C. and continuing through the Semitic literature in Akkadian and Hebrew down to classical and later Indo-European literature. One may consider it as an indication of the ANE people's awareness of what the modern geologist calls "deep time."

Accordingly, Genesis 1–11 is the primeval history of the Bible on the cosmological and world-historical levels. There are also many passages on the level of biography in the Bible, such as Exodus 1–2 and Matthew 1–3, that must be included in the literary category of primeval history (Kikawada and Quinn 1985).

B. Patterns of Primeval History

Since the "patterns of primeval history" are common to biblical and other literature, for convenience and clarity the two distinct patterns are described in terms of the Mesopotamian cuneiform literature. The first pattern is the *narrative pattern* of primeval history and it is derived from the Akkadian Epic of Atrahasis, the so-called Babylonian Flood Story (Lambert and Millard 1969). The second is the *genealogical pattern,* derived from the Sumerian genealogical material known as the Sumerian King List (Jacobsen 1939) and other Mesopotamian genealogical material. The common characteristic of the two is the great Flood standing at the end of the mythological or quasi-mythological epoch and ushering in the new, and more or less "factual," epoch. The great Flood is the epoch divider, signaling the end of the primeval history and anticipating the beginning of a new age.

1. Narrative Pattern. The Atrahasis Epic furnishes us with the basic narrative pattern of the primeval history (Laessøe 1956) in a five-story outline. The epic starts with the beginning of the world, when only the gods existed. The story tells us the reason why and the process by which the gods created human beings. The next three stories are concerned with the very successful procreation and multiplication of the human population and the gods' attempt to exterminate the ever-increasing population in three stages. But the human beings are saved from extinction at each of the three attempts. The second stage has two steps; somehow the gods had to intensify the extermination effort, for the plan was not working well. In the third stage we find the great Flood story. The last story relates the postflood compromise among the gods concerning population control (Kilmer 1972). Thus, the topical outline of the primeval history narrative may be articulated as follows:

A. Creation: Gods' Work and Creation of Mankind
B. First Threat to Mankind: Overpopulation and Control by Plague
C. Second Threat: Overpopulation and Control by Drought
C′. Threat Intensified—Severer Means
D. Third Threat: Overpopulation and Control by Flood
E. Resolution: Population Control

The historical time covered is from before the creation of mankind through the great Flood, to the post-Flood resolution regarding the increasing population. Note that there are only three narrative generations of expansion and diminution of the population, although these generations are of 1,200 years each. The predominant theme is how to deal with the ever-increasing population which even the great Flood could not resolve. The Atrahasis Epic resolves the problem by instituting "birth control" by means of the gods creating barrenness among women, demons to cause crib death, and three types of nuns to put some women out of procreation. The greatest variation among the specimens of primeval history discussed in this article is in the means of resolution to the problem of overpopulation.

The Sumerian forerunner to the Atrahasis pattern of primeval history may be obtained from the Sumerian Deluge story, but extreme caution must be applied since only 20 percent of the story is preserved. There is also a view that the Enki and Ninmah story plus the Sumerian Deluge may give us a more nearly complete pattern (Kilmer 1976). The Akkadian story of the Worm and Toothache intriguingly gives us the genealogical narrative of a worm that claims as its ancestry none other than the retired chief of the Mesopotamian pantheon, Anu himself, but this story lacks the great Flood. This may indicate either that the entire story is in the primeval historical context, or that it is from a separate tradition.

2. Genealogical Pattern. The Sumerian King List furnishes the basic genealogical pattern with seven to ten generations from the beginning to the great Flood, depending on how one counts them. The main characteristic of these antediluvian kings is their extreme longevity, such as King Alulim reigning for 280,000 years. This makes the antediluvian period, though consisting only of seven or ten generations, much longer than the postdiluvian period, comprised of many generations. The postdiluvian King Zambia, for instance, reigned only three years. The great Flood (Sum *AMARU,* Akk *abūbu*) thus bisects ancient world history, establishing a historiographic time axis with such expressions as "before the Flood" (Akk *lām abūbi,* cf. *lammabbûl,* Ps 29:10) and "after the Flood" (Akk *arki abūbi,* cf. Gen 9:28; 10:1, 32; 11:10), analogous to our convention of B.C. and A.D. divisions in world history and "antebellum" and "postbellum" in American history.

Although the Sumerian King List establishes the basic genealogical pattern of primeval history, perhaps more relevant to biblical studies is the Akkadian synchronic "List of Sages" (van Dijk 1962). The kings and sages (Akk *apkallu* for antediluvian and Akk *ummannu* for postdiluvian "sage") are listed side by side in this genealogy before the Flood as "[in the] time of Aialu the king, U'an was the sage *(apkallu)*" and after the Flood as "[during the reign of Gilgam]sh, Sinligunninni was the sage *(ummannu).*" In this list, the antediluvian period is accounted for in two genealogical lines, one line of kings and the other of sages. Also note that the kings are associated with cities according to the Sumerian King List, whereas the sages are linked to clever cultural inventions such as music, metallurgy, and the religious cult, and to "walking with god," especially in the light of the "List of Sages" and another list of sages known as "The Etiological Myth of the 'Seven Sages' " (Reiner 1961).

C. Purpose

The main purpose of the primeval history, be it in the form of narrative or genealogy, appears to be establishing one's first section of credentials, tracing back to the very beginning of the world. The primeval history, in a small neat package, is a formal introduction to a history or to a biography, adding to it the notion of "deep time." Once the primeval history became concisely patterned in both the narrative and genealogical tradition, it became a literary convention easily prefixed to any memory-based history, whether national or personal.

The great Flood became the primeval historical device to separate the two major epochs; it is the ANE epoch divider par excellence, lying between speculative history and memory-based history. Conversely, it may be considered as a bridge to fill in the gap between the two epochs. The great Flood is a very convenient literary device for the ancient historians; they need not claim any factual knowledge of earlier things, since symbolically the flood washed away all records. Thus, the great Flood signaled to the ancient reader that anything that had happened before it was speculative and mythological rather than factual and concrete.

D. Genesis 1–11

In the first eleven chapters of Genesis we have an example of a full primeval history, where the five-point-outline narrative and the double-line genealogical traditions (Wilson *GHBW*) are fused together into a single literary unit. The primeval history in turn constitutes the first and introductory cycle of the five cycles of the book of Genesis. Then, on a still larger scale, the book of Genesis constitutes the literary unit that introduces a five-book Torah (for a brief discussion, see below). Observe also that all three of the succeedingly larger units—the primeval history, the book of Genesis, and the Pentateuch—conclude with exactly the same motifs, among them the references to Abraham, to someone (Terah, Joseph, Moses) dying, and to the promised land still unreached.

1. Narrative Pattern. There are five major stories told in Genesis 1–11:

A. Creation, God's Work and Rest (1:1–2:3)
B. Adam and Eve, First Threat to Mankind (2:5–3:24)
C. Cain and Abel, Second Threat to Mankind (4:1–16)
C′. Threat Intensified—Lamech's Taunt (4:23–24)
D. The Great Flood, Third Threat, and Noah's Ark (6:1–9:29)
E. Tower of Babel, Population Control by Dispersion (11:1–9)

The narrative structure of Genesis 1–11 conforms to the five-point outline of the primeval history narrative of the Atrahasis Epic (cf. Millard 1967). The creation story is the cosmic introduction, majestically telling the story of divine work and rest in the uniquely Hebrew seven-day week. Then, three stories of the near extinction of newly created mankind follow. Adam is almost killed, but is allowed to live on and even to have children. Fifty percent of the following generation is eliminated when Abel is killed, but Cain lives on. Virtually everyone of Noah's generation is wiped off the earth, but the remaining ones repopulate the earth. Note that the sevenfold revenge instituted for Cain is echoed in Lamech's taunt but is intensified seventy times (C and C′). The story of dispersion as a resolution to the population problem concludes the primeval history.

While the form and themes of the Genesis 1–11 narrative parallel those of the Mesopotamian forerunners, the resolution of the population problem is diametrically opposed. The book of Genesis insists that the multiplication of people is a divine blessing and tries to accommodate it by dispersion of the population upon the face of the whole earth, whereas in the Babylonian epic, birth control measures are divinely instituted. This theological opposition may be accounted for by assuming two sociologically different communities; the Babylonian society was urban, confined to a limited space, and menaced by overpopulation, while the Hebrew society was more rural, welcoming population expansion. For the Hebrews, there was the whole earth to expand into, while the Babylonians locked themselves in the limited space of the walled city.

Certainly the themes of the biblical narrative are more complex than just the compounding stages of population expansion and diminution, although they are highlighted as the predominant theme of the primeval historical narrative. The biblical author, for instance, overlaid the narrative with the ethical structure that makes it a complementary part of the larger scheme of the whole Torah. In the first story ethical perfection is declared: all things God created were "very good." From the following story on, people degenerate ethically, but God repeatedly tries to set them right by forgiving them. Despite repeated disobedience and rebellion in the three narrative generations (namely Adam, Cain, and Noah), mankind is allowed to exist and continues to propagate, as commanded in the blessing of the creation story, "Be fruitful and multiply and fill the earth" (Gen 1:28). As though to implement this blessing, the fifth and last story (Gen 11:1–9) accommodates the expanding population in a distinctively Hebrew way. Note that this dispersion produces Abram in the genealogy that follows, and that Abram is the key link between the antediluvian primeval history and the postdiluvian patriarchal narrative (contra von Rad, *Genesis* OTL). Thus, the primeval history of the Bible concludes with the introduction of the first hero of the next epoch, Abram.

2. Genealogical Pattern. The genealogy (*tôlĕdôt*) links the five stories of Genesis 1–11 together and binds them to the rest of the book (contra Westermann, *Genesis* BKAT). Thus, there is a genealogy line corresponding to the story line described in the previous section. See Fig. PRI.01. The genealogy from Adam to Noah is either seven or ten generations deep (Wilson *GHBW*), but the narrative represents only three generations. Significantly, Genesis 4–5 preserves the antediluvian genealogy in double lines,

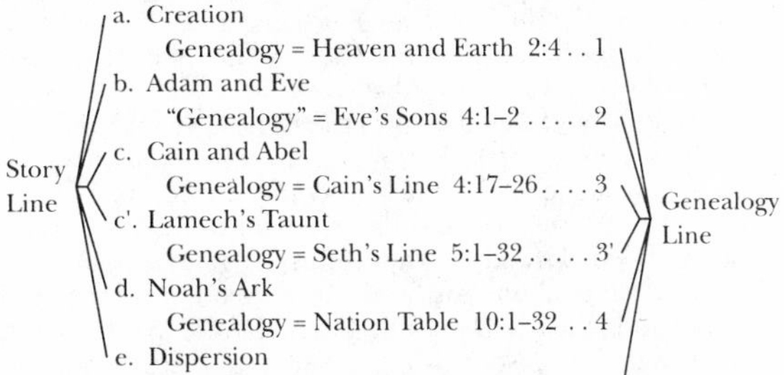

PRI.01. Pattern of story line and genealogy line in Genesis 1–11.

briefly interrupted by Lamech's taunt. Note that Cain is associated with a city as in the Mesopotamian genealogy of kings, while Jabal, Jubal, Tubal-cain, and Enoch are attributed with cultural inventions and "walking with God," just as are the Mesopotamian sages. The preservation of both the king-type figure and the sage-type figure in Genesis 4–5 may reflect the ancient Mesopotamian synchronic list of sages and kings, and this may perhaps help explain the existence of two genealogies linking Adam to Noah (cf. Indian double genealogies of Manu).

Also note that the historiographic expression "after the Flood" is preserved in Gen 9:28; 10:1, 32; 11:10, indicating that the Flood is the epoch divider in the biblical tradition as it is in the Mesopotamian. In this context, *lammabbûl* of Psalm 29:10 may be seen contextually as an equivalent to "before the Flood," since this expression is paralleled to the cosmic time expression, "forever."

E. Other "Primeval History" Patterns in the Bible

Although there are many manifestations of the patterns of the primeval history in both the OT and NT, either directly conforming to them or obliquely alluding to them, the intent and purpose of these passages must be evaluated according to the position of each passage in its larger literary context. First, let us look at other biblical examples of the primeval history that preface the biography of Moses (Exodus 1–2) and Jesus (Matthew 1–3). Second, let us examine a few sample passages that make oblique reference to the primeval history.

1. Exodus 1–2. A type of primeval history is prefaced to the biography of Moses. The narrative outline of Exodus 1–3 is identical to Genesis 1–11:

A. Creation by Procreation—Genealogy Linking to Genesis
B. First Threat to Hebrew Population—Affliction with Heavy Burdens
C. Second Threat—Tale of Two Midwives
C′. Threat Intensified—Drowning of Children
D. Third Threat—"the Flood" and Moses' Ark
E. Resolution—"Exodus" into Midian

The predominant theme of population expansion and diminution is clearly present and the solution to the population problem here is identical to the nomadic solution of Genesis 11, that is, "dispersion" or a little "exodus," wherein Moses goes away from the center of activity into the wilderness of Midian, just as Abram leaves an urban center. Moses' murder of an Egyptian and relocation of himself to the wilderness may be analogous to the motif sequence of the Cain and Abel story.

Note some verbal allusions to the Genesis narrative, such as Moses' mother making for him the "ark" (Heb *tēbâ*) of bulrushes pitched with pitch and mortar (Exod 2:3; cf. Gen 6:14); Moses' mother "saw that he was good" (Exod 2:2; cf. Gen 1:4, etc.); the children of Israel became "fruitful" and abundant, and "multiplied" and became strong, and "the earth was filled with them" (Exod 1:7, 12, 20; cf. Gen 1:28). Note also the rhetorical features such as those seen in the speech of Pharaoh, "Come, let us deal wisely with them, lest they multiply . . ." (Exod 1:10), echoing the speech of YHWH in Gen 11:7 ("Come, let us go down . . . , lest they may not . . ."); and the way in which the two midwives are named, "the name of the one is Shiphrah and the name of the other is Puah" (Exod 1:15), echoes the way Lamech's wives are named in Gen 4:19.

While Exodus 1–2 parallels the Genesis 1–11 narrative, perhaps more striking parallels are found between it and the Atrahasis Epic, especially in regard to the two opposing divine forces working to destroy and to save the Hebrew population in Egypt. The primeval historical section of Moses' biography, however, upholds the blessing of Genesis 1:28, symbolically removing Moses from the urban center to the wilderness, anticipating the forthcoming event of the massive Exodus from Egypt. This, as well as the dispersion story of Gen 11:1–9, may be considered an example of anti-Babylonian, antiurban rhetoric from the extraurban point of view.

The genealogical element of the primeval history is concentrated in the beginning of the narrative and constitutes a story unit (A. Creation by Procreation). "Joseph was already in Egypt" (Exod 1:5) links this story unit to the book of Genesis; genealogically, Moses becomes linked to Adam. This genealogical line then is punctuated by Moses' own miniature Flood (D. Third Threat—"the Flood"). Thus, complete history from the beginning on is told on a biographical scale; one may state this as "biography recapitulates historiography."

2. Matthew 1–3. The same phenomenon is observable in Matthew's primeval history. "The book of 'Genesis' [Gk *Genesis*] of Jesus Christ" is how Matthew begins his gospel (1:1) and as such one may expect allusion to the book of Genesis. Matthew 1–3 certainly parallels not only Genesis 1–11 but also Exodus 1–2; thus, it is also a primeval historical biography. The following is the basic five-point outline:

A. "Creation" by Genealogy—Abraham to Jesus
B. Birth of Jesus
C. Three Wise Men
C′. Slaughter of the Innocents
D. Flight to Egypt and Return—a Little "Exodus"
E. Baptism and Dove—a Little "Flood"

The story of three wise men is consigned here as a foil story to the slaughter-of-the-innocents story, yielding C and C′ in the outline, primarily because (1) the principal character of the birth, slaughter, and flight stories is the divine agent who commands Joseph, whereas in the wise men story Herod is the one who commands and whose command was not heeded by the wise men, and (2) there are almost verbatim threefold repetitions of the introduction to the angelic speeches in the birth, slaughter, and flight stories, while the angel does not speak in the wise men story but compromises Herod's plan.

The birth story here fills B, and the story of the extermination of the undesirable population is now concentrated in C′. The "flood" and "exodus" now switch places; the flight into Egypt and return to Israel occupy D, while the miniature "flood" (reminiscent of Exodus 2) occupies E in the form of the baptism, the salvation out of water with the presence of a dove. Nonetheless, at the end of Matthew 3 Jesus is placed in the wilderness just as was Moses in Exodus 2.

The structure of the narrative as a whole thus places Jesus formally in the antediluvian primeval history like Noah and Moses, while the genealogy of A links Jesus to the first Hebrew of the postdiluvian history. Thereby, Matthew has recast the time span from creation to Jesus in the primeval historical form of narrative.

3. Other Biblical Books. Both the OT and NT are full of allusions to and reflections of the primeval historical outline and motifs. The following are some examples, and one might be reminded that this is still a fruitful field of future study. Aside from the basic organization of the Torah and of Genesis, which is similar to that of Genesis 1–11, the court history of David and Solomon is considered to parallel the narrative progression of the primeval history of Genesis as originally suggested by Walter Brueggemann (1968). The five-point outline of the parallel accounts is shown in Table 1.

Genesis 1–11	*2 Samuel–1 Kings*
A. Creation—God saw everything very good: *ṭôb mĕʾōd*	David saw Bathsheba very good: *ṭôb mĕʾōd*
B. Adam and Eve—death threat and curse	David and Bathsheba—death threat and curse
C. Cain and Abel—anger, murder, exile	Amnon and Absalom—hate, murder, exile
D. Noah and the Flood—new beginning for Noah	Rebellion of Absalom—new beginning for David
E. Dispersion—Tower of Babel, name, city building, scattered people	Solomon—Dispersion, name, city building, scattered realm

Hesse and Kikawada (1984) have shown that the book of Jonah reverses the topical progression of Genesis 1–11. That is, the book of Jonah ironically reverses the primeval history, ending up with the creation motif in order to interpret the Mosaic covenant in a new light. It begins with the "dispersion" story of Jonah, who is unwilling to go to Nineveh and so journeys away from Mesopotamia. The miniature "flood" story follows with many verbal echoes of the Noah story, then comes the "Cain and Abel" story of angry dialogue between YHWH and Jonah in which YHWH asks, "Does it do any good (*hêṭēb,* 4:4; cf. Gen 4:6–7) to be angry?" Also, the name Abel (*hablê šāwʾ*) is hidden in the conclusion of the hymn of thanksgiving (Jonah 2:8). A little "Adam and Eve" story is told next in the episode of the worm and the gourd tree under which a life-and-death conversation takes place. The sixth day of the "creation" story in which man and cattle were created is again alluded to at the very end of the Jonah book in the phrase "and much cattle." Note that the entire Jonah book is set in seven narrative days; three days in the fish's stomach, three days to go across the great city, and the seventh day just to sit and talk with God. In fact, the allusions to creation are abundant, not only in that Jonah "fears YHWH, the God of Heaven, who created the sea and the dry land," but all through the book when God creates, destroys, and manipulates natural phenomena at will as the creator.

F. Indo-European Literature

A trace of the ANE convention of the primeval history can be felt in the Old Iranian and Indian literature to the east and in the classical material to the west.

1. Iranian Tradition. The second book of the Vendidad (*Vidēvdāt*) includes a Zoroastrian version of the great Flood story, featuring Yima as the hero in a five-point outline with the predominant theme of overpopulation:

A. Introduction and Institution of First King Yima
B. Overpopulation and the First Expansion of Earth
C. Overpopulation and the Second Expansion of Earth
D. Overpopulation and the Third Expansion of Earth
E. Overpopulation and the Preparation for the Flood

Note that while retaining the basic five-point outline of the primeval history, this account makes the Flood story occupy the last position. However, Yima, the first man and the first king (Christensen 1943), lives through all the generations of overpopulation, interceding for his people as did Atrahasis. In the end, to save mankind and preserve the best of the creatures from the impending flood, Yima is instructed to build an elaborate structure for salvation. But it is not clear whether the Flood is something that happened in the past or that is going to happen in an eschatological future (cf. Gunkel 1895).

2. Indian Tradition. From India we can recover both the narrative and genealogical traditions that featured Manu Vaivasvata as the Flood hero. He is the seventh Manu according to the *Viṣṇu Purāna* genealogy (Thapar 1976) and the Flood hero according to the 9th-century-B.C. story of Manu and a Fish (O'Flaherty 1975). In the story of Manu and a Fish we have a one-man or one-fish "overpopulation" and Flood story. One day Manu saves a fish that rapidly grows big. He tries to accommodate it in succeedingly larger containers but finally he has to release it in the ocean. Some time later, the fish reappears to Manu, instructing him to tie a boat onto the horn growing on its head so that Manu can be towed to the highest mountain to save himself from the impending Flood.

The Indian genealogical material is more pertinent to the OT tradition than to Mesopotamian, for it preserves a compound pattern similar to the OT genealogy rather than to the simple linear genealogies of Mesopotamia. The genealogical material of the Purāna as summarized by Thapar and compared to a summary of the OT genealogy is depicted in Fig. PRI.02.

Observe the tripartite genealogical scheme: *A* is the primeval historical section in double lines of sages/kings; *B* is the branched genealogy section; and *C* returns to the linear genealogy. In both the Indian and the OT genealogies, *A* and *B* are demarcated by the great Flood and *B* and *C* are separated by the war—i.e., the Mahabharata War for the former and the war between YHWH and Pharaoh (cf. Exod 15:1–22) for the latter.

3. Classical Tradition. Beside Berossus' account of Babylonian history, we have the story of Deucalion and the flood, from which we can recover many elements of primeval history. The Latin tradition also preserves it in the story told by Ovid. The most striking example, however, is a brief scholiastic commentary on "the will of Zeus" (*Iliad*

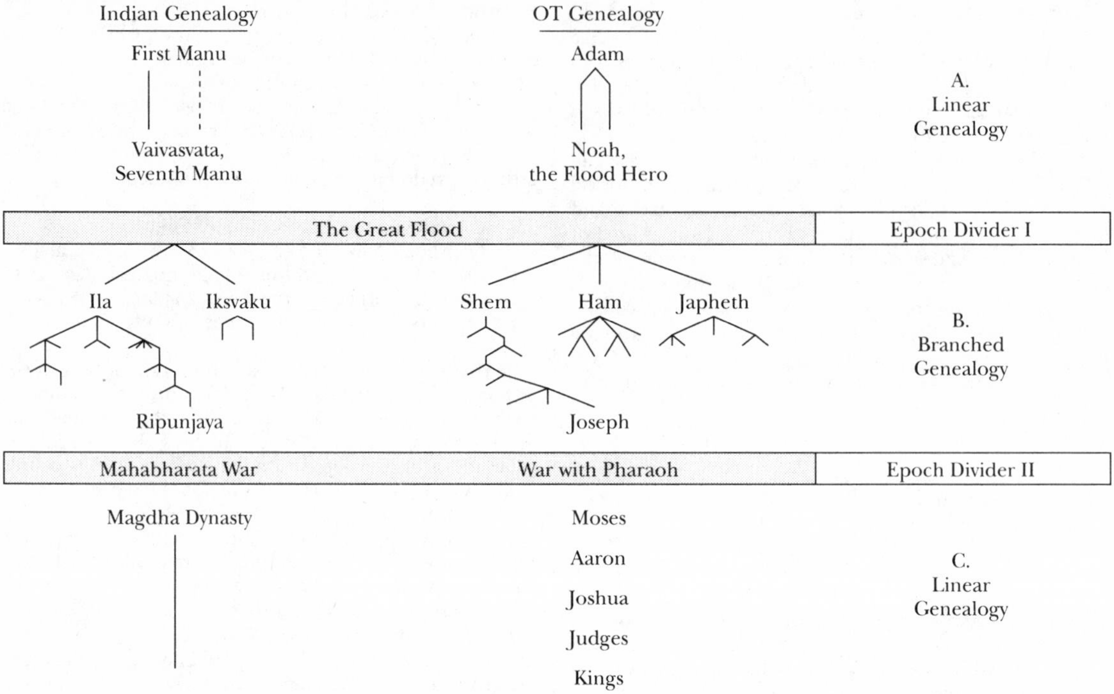

PRI.02. Comparative chart of Indian and OT genealogical patterns.

1.5). In it we find a summary of a long-lost story whose outline is as follows:

A. Problem—burdened earth, overpopulation
B. First Threat—Zeus sends Theban War, many destroyed
C. Second Threat—Zeus plans to destroy people by thunderbolts or flood. Momos dissuades Zeus from this plan
D. Third Threat—Momos suggests that Thetis marry a mortal to create Achilles and that Zeus seduce Leda to create Helen of Troy. This results in the Trojan War
E. Resolution—many destroyed: earth's burden lightened

Although we may never know where and when the concept of the primeval history was conceived and developed, we find it earliest in Mesopotamian cuneiform literature, and traces of it in the OT and in the literature of India as well as Europe. Many other examples of this literary tradition may be hidden in other unexpected places.

Bibliography

Ball, I. J. 1972. *A Rhetorical Study of Zephaniah.* Diss., Graduate Theological Union.

Brueggemann, W. 1968. David and His Theologian. *CBQ* 30: 150–81.

Christensen, A. 1943. *Les Types du Premier Home et du Premier Roi.* Archives d'Etudes Orientales 14/2. Leiden.

Dijk, J. van. 1962. Die Inschriftenfunde. *Vorlaeufinger Berich über die von der Notgemeinschaft der Dautchen Wissenshaft* 18: 45.

Gunkel, H. 1895. *Schöpfung und Chaos im Urzeit und Endzeit.* Göttingen.

Hesse, E. W., and Kikawada, I. M. 1984. Jonah and Genesis 1–11. *AJBI* 10: 3–19.

Jacobsen, T. 1939. *Sumerian King List.* AS 11. Chicago.

Kikawada, I. 1974. Literary Conventions for Primeval History. *AJBI* 1: 3–21.

Kikawada, I., and Quinn, A. 1985. *Before Abraham Was.* Nashville.

Kilmer, A. 1972. The Mesopotamian Concept of Overpopulation and Its Solution as Reflected in the Mythology. *Or* 41: 160–77.

———. 1976. Speculations on Umul, the First Baby. *AOAT* 25: 265–70.

Kramer, S. 1968. The "Babel of Tongues": A Sumerian Version. *JAOS* 88: 108–11.

Laessøe, J. 1956. The Atrahasis Epic: A Babylonian History of Mankind. *BiOr* 13: 90–102.

Lambert, W. G., and Millard, A. R. 1969. *Atra-Hasis: The Babylonian Story of the Flood.* Oxford.

Millard, A. R. 1967. A New Babylonian "Genesis" Story. *TynBul* 18: 1–18.

O'Flaherty, W. 1975. *Hindu Myths.* Harmondsworth.

Reiner, E. 1961. The Etiological Myth of the Seven Sages. *Or* 30: 1–11.

Thapar, R. 1976. Genealogy as a Source of Social History. *The Indian Historical Review* 4: 126.

Isaac M. Kikawada

PRINCE. See PALESTINE, ADMINISTRATION OF (POSTEXILIC JUDEAN OFFICIALS).

PRINCIPALITIES AND POWERS. A common translation of the NT terms *archai* and *dynameis,* which are used primarily by Paul to designate angelic beings, both good and evil, but most commonly in reference to the realm of Satan. Several other terms are used in conjunction with these to denote supernatural beings: *exousiai* ("authorities"), *archōntes* ("rulers"), *thronoi* ("thrones"), *kyriotētes* ("lordships"), *kosmokratores* ("world rulers"), and *stoicheia* ("elemental spirits").

This collection of terms was not coined by the early Christians, but was probably taken from the reservoir of terminology in 1st-century-C.E. Jewish and pagan belief in reference to the angelic realm. The terms appear in the OT pseudepigrapha, particularly the apocalyptic writings (e.g., *2 En.* 20:1; *1 En.* 41:9; 61:10; cf. also *Testament of Levi* 3:8; *Testament of Solomon* 8:2; 18:2; 20:15). Many of the terms are also used in the syncretistic Greek Magical Papyri (PGM) to denote various supernatural beings (e.g., PGM I. 215; III. 35; IV. 1193, 1275, 1599, 2198–99; XXIIb. 2, 4, 7 [= the *Prayer of Jacob*]).

In Ephesians, where there are more references to the principalities and powers than any other epistle, they are regarded as evil and under the authority of the devil (Eph 6:12; 2:2). Consequently, believers are called to resist their influence by appropriating the power of God. The compelling influence of these evil powers has been broken by the Christ event. Christ has been exalted to the right hand of God, a position of authority far above every conceivable evil angelic being (Eph 1:20; cf. also 1 Pet 3:22). By virtue of their union with him, believers share in the authority of Christ over the powers (cf. Eph 2:6) and may thereby break the power of their control and influence (see Arnold 1989: chap. 3).

The powers are seen by Paul as a fundamental factor in the heretical teaching threatening the health of the Colossian church. Paul therefore stresses a cosmic christology (Col 1:15–20) affirming the superior position of Christ in relation to the powers. Christ is also asserted as the ruling "head" over the principalities and powers (Col 2:10). The cross is seen as the point of decisive defeat: "on that cross he discarded [or, disarmed] the cosmic powers and authorities like a garment; he made a public spectacle of them and led them as captives in his triumphal procession" (Col 2:15; NEB). The Colossian believers should therefore not submit themselves to the tenets of the heretical teaching, which were ultimately inspired by the "elemental spirits" (Col 2:8). In their solidarity with Christ's death, they should consider themselves immune to the influences of these evil spirits (Col 2:20).

Deeply aware of the influence of "the god of this age" (1 Cor 4:4), Paul sees demonic rulers (*archontes*) as ultimately responsible for the death of Christ (1 Cor 2:8; see Eph 2:2 for a similar use of *archon* as an evil spirit being). These powers did not understand the wisdom of God, who would use Christ's death for the actual defeat of the realm of evil and thereby procure salvation for his people. Divine deliverance was necessary since humanity was in bondage to the realm of Satan and his minions (Eph 2:2; Gal 4:3, 8). The resultant emergence of the Church, the body of Christ, testifies to the evil powers of the vast wisdom of God (1 Cor 2:6–7; Eph 3:10). Although defeated by the cross-resurrection event, the powers are still active (Eph 6:12; Gal 4:9). They are in the process of being abolished (1 Cor 2:6) and will finally be destroyed at the consummation (1 Cor 15:24). Because of the work of Christ and his superior power, Paul can comfort the Church by assuring its members that no evil angelic power can separate them from the love of God in Christ Jesus the Lord (Rom 8:38).

Bibliography

Arnold, C. E. 1989. *Ephesians: Power and Magic.* SNTSMS 63. Cambridge.
Berkhof, H. 1977. *Christ and the Powers.* Scottdale, PA.
Caird, G. B. 1956. *Principalities and Powers.* Oxford.
Carr, W. 1983. *Angels and Principalities.* SNTSMS. Cambridge.
Dibelius, M. 1909. *Die Geisterwelt im Glauben des Paulus.* Göttingen.
Everling, O. 1888. *Die paulinische Angelologie und Dämonologie.* Göttingen.
Morrison, C. 1960. *The Powers That Be.* SBT 29. London.
Schlier, H. 1961. *Principalities and Powers in the New Testament.* Freiburg.
Wink, W. 1984. *Naming the Powers.* Philadelphia.
———. 1986. *Unmasking the Powers.* Philadelphia.

CLINTON E. ARNOLD

PRISCA (PERSON) [Gk *Priska*]. Var. PRISCILLA. An important Christian missionary in the mid-1st century C.E., mentioned in 1 Cor 16:19, Rom 16:3–5, and 2 Tim 4:19. She is called by the diminutive "Priscilla" in Acts 18:2–3 (historically reliable traditions; Lüdemann 1987: 206, 209–10); and 18:18, 26.

Prisca was probably freeborn; epigraphical material indicates that ordinarily her name was not a slave name (Lampe *StadtrChr,* 151–52). She married Aquila, a tentmaker of Jewish origin. The couple were among the first Christians in Rome who also belonged to the synagogues of the city. Together with her husband and others, Prisca spoke of Christianity in at least one of the Roman synagogues. This Christian proclamation led to tumultuous controversies among the Roman Jews, so that the administration of the emperor Claudius in 49 C.E. expelled from Rome the main quarrelers, including Prisca and Aquila.

The couple moved on to Corinth, where Paul first met and lodged with them and worked in Aquila's workshop (Acts 18:2–3). After more than a year and a half (Acts 18:11, 2; cf. Lüdemann 1987: 207; Lampe *StadtrChr,* 7–8), they moved to Ephesus, where they again were active as missionary co-workers of Paul and formed a church in their home (1 Cor 16:19; cf. 2 Tim 4:19; Acts 18:18). The couple "risked their necks" for Paul's life (Rom 16:4), probably during this stay in Ephesus, where Paul was exposed to serious dangers (1 Cor 15:32; 2 Cor 1:8–9). The historicity of the Ephesian episode about Apollos told in Acts 18:26 is very doubtful (Lüdemann 1987: 215–16); *parrēsiazesthai* is a Lukan word; and there is a tension between v 25 and v 26: Apollos already taught "accurately" about Jesus (v 25) *before* he was instructed "more accurately" by Prisca and Aquila (v 26). Luke, the advocate of the apostle Paul, suggests in v 26 that Prisca and Aquila turned Apollos into a staunch supporter of Pauline Christianity. Pre-Lukan tradition (cf. vv 24–25), however, knew only that Apollos once worked in Ephesus at the same time as Paul, Prisca, and Aquila (cf. also 1 Cor 16:12, 19) and that Apollos was a Christian pneumatic (cf. also the Apollos party in Corinth, 1 Cor 1:12, in the context of the Corinthian pneumatics and enthusiasts, e.g., 1 Corinthians 12–14). As such, Apollos was more likely a competitor of Paul (1 Cor 1:12; cf. 3:10b, 12–15) on whom the apostle could not at all impose his plans while he stayed in Ephesus (1 Cor 16:12). We do not know whether Prisca and Aquila at least housed Apollos in Ephesus (Acts 18:26; Weiser 1985: 508).

The couple has often been depicted as wealthy, with Prisca of even higher social status than Aquila since her name in most cases is placed before his (Rom 16:3; 2 Tim 4:19; Acts 18:18, 26; e.g., McNicol *HBD,* 823–24). But evidence points against the couple's wealth. For a discussion, see AQUILA. References to Prisca before Aquila more likely indicate that she was even more active in church life than her craftsman husband. The context, Rom 16:21–23, shows that socially respected persons were not necessarily named first (Gaius with his spacious dwelling and Erastus, the city treasurer, appear last). Paul esteemed a person's work for the church (Rom 16:3b, 4, 5a, 21), not the person's status in the pagan society (cf. Gal 3:28). Luke, on the other hand, mentioning Prisca first in Acts 18:18, 26, would probably have liked to report her elevated social status if he had known about it; he frequently pointed out the participation of distinguished women in Christianity (e.g., Luke 8:3; Acts 17:4, 12; cf. 17:34; 16:14).

Around 55 or 56 C.E. (after Claudius' death in 54 C.E. and between the writing of 1 Corinthians and Romans), the couple returned to Rome (Rom 16:3–5). This last move may have been strategically motivated: Prisca and Aquila were possibly sent as Paul's vanguard to Rome, where he wanted to establish a firm footing for his gospel before continuing to Spain. In Rome Prisca and Aquila again hosted a house-church. They were the first to receive greetings from Paul in Romans 16, where Paul praised them. Their prominence as Paul's co-workers was remembered by the later church; 2 Timothy used their names for its fictitious historical frame, at the beginning of a list of greetings (4:19). Church tradition of the 6th century claimed that the house-church of Prisca and Aquila was the basis of the later Roman "title"-church, "Prisca," on the Aventine. There is no proof for this connection or for any relation to the Roman catacomb "Priscilla" (Lampe *StadtrChr,* 11, 24–25).

Bibliography

Lüdemann, G. 1987. *Das frühe Christentum nach den Traditionen der Apostelgeschichte.* Göttingen.

Schüssler Fiorenza, E. 1983. *In Memory of Her.* New York.

Weiser, A. 1985. *Die Apostelgeschichte II.* ÖTK. Gütersloh.

PETER LAMPE

PRISON. In ancient Israel, mere imprisonment was not recognized as a formal punishment. When a convict was sentenced to prison (Ezra 7:26), he was to make good his offense by carrying out dull and heavy labor. The modern idea of a prison as a penitentiary, where criminals are to be reformed into decent citizens, was foreign to ANE conceptions. For various other reasons, however, prisons played an important role in the penal system of the ancients.

Pending his case, a suspect could be held in temporary confinement. Thus, the Israelite woman's son guilty of blasphemy was put in custody (Heb *mišmār*), until a divine verdict was reached (Lev 24:10–12). A similar treatment was given to a violator of the Sabbath, until his death sentence was pronounced (Num 15:32–36). It should be noted that, in these two instances, final judication was reached through the consultation of the Lord. In this respect, the custody pending trial can be compared to the Mesopotamian practice of detaining convicts in a temple prison prior to the river ordeal, attested in the so-called Nungal Hymn. Not all cases of temporary detention were concluded by a divine verdict. Micaiah, the son of Imlah, was put in prison (*bêt hakkeleʾ*) to allow the authorities to verify his prophecy (1 Kgs 22:27; 2 Chr 18:26); and Joseph's objective in putting his brothers in custody (*mišmār*) was to pressure them to comply with his demand (Gen 42:17). In Old Babylonian letters from Mari, reference is sometimes made to a period of detention during which the king can make up his mind what to do with the wrongdoer (e.g., ARM VI 42: 8–10). Examples of temporary detention pending clarification of a case are also found in the NT (Acts 5:17–25; 16:23–24).

The need for cheap labor forces often led the authorities to create compounds where prisoners of war and political adversaries were put to work. These places are sometimes designated as "prisons," though the Latin term *ergastula* (i.e., places of enforced labor) might be more correct. The practice is exemplified in the treatment Samson received at the hands of the Philistines: they gouged out his eyes, bound him with bronze fetters (Heb *nĕḥuštayim*), and forced him to grind (*wayĕhî ṭōḥēn*) in "the house of the prisoners" (*bêt hāʾăsîrîm,* Judg 16:21). Jer 52:11 offers a parallel in the description of Zedekiah's fate: Nebuchadnezzar punished his rebellious vassal by blinding him, binding him with bronze fetters, and putting him into "the house of the mill" (LXX). The more fragmentary indications concerning the measures taken against Hoshea (2 Kgs 17:4), Manasseh (2 Chr 33:11), and Jehoiachin (2 Kgs 25:27; cf. Jer 52:31) do not exclude the possibility that they were submitted to analogous humiliations (cf. 2 Kgs 25:7 and Jer 39:7 with Jer 52:11; for the blinding of enslaved prisoners—a preventive against attempts to escape—see also 1 Sam 11:2; Isa 42:7; and Hdt. 4.2). The designation "house of the mill," preserved by the LXX in Jer 52:11, reflects the Akkadian term *bīt ararri,* "house of the miller, mill," mentioned in a number of cuneiform texts as a place of detention for either distrainees or persons under arrest pending their case. In fact, many of the Akkadian terms rendered somewhat indifferently as "prison," such as *ṣibittum* and *nupārum,* refer to "workshops" where forced labor was performed. According to Ps 107:10–16 the deported Israelites ended up in such a place; they had "hard labor" (*ʿāmāl*) imposed on them, while they were bound with iron and locked behind doors of bronze with metal bars (see also Isa 42:7; Ps 105:17–18; Lam 5:13).

In some cases imprisonment was resorted to less for economic than for political reasons. The Aramaic Sefire inscriptions suggest that a high-ranking political rival was more likely to be imprisoned (*ʾsr*) than to be killed (*KAI* 224.18). The treatment of several Israelite and Judean kings referred to above corroborates this impression (see also 1 Macc 14:2–3 for similar measures taken by Arsaces against Demetrius). Such a solution was not adopted on humanitarian grounds but because of fear of an outburst of popular indignation. That is why Herod preferred to send John the Baptist to jail instead of executing him (Matt 14:3–5). Similar considerations may have underlain the decision to incarcerate Jeremiah (Jer 37:15–16) and the seer Hanani (2 Chr 16:10). Conditions in the prison were such, however, that many a prisoner died of disease or malnutrition, as Mesopotamian ration lists show. Since food rations were meager (1 Kgs 22:27) and the treatment harsh, a prisoner (*ʾāsîr*) might appropriately be counted among "those doomed to die" (Pss 79:11; 102:21). Considering these circumstances, imprisonment could be a convenient way of disposing of opponents; without incurring apparent bloodguilt, one simply made one's adversary "disappear" (cf. Gen 37:22–24; Jer 38:6–9).

Defaulting debtors were a specific category of prisoners, constrained to forced labor until their debt had been paid (Matt 18:28–30; Luke 12:58–59). The tasks imposed on them were similar to those performed by prisoners of war; judging from the cuneiform records, grinding and weaving were their main activities. Oftentimes it was not the debtor himself, but his wife or children, who were taken by the creditor (2 Kgs 4:1; Isa 50:1; Neh 5:5). Isa 40:2 refers to this practice, using it as a metaphor for the situation of the deported Israelites: the Exile has been their involuntary service by which they had to pay off (*rṣh*) their guilt (*ʿāwôn*). Study of the Mesopotamian evidence makes it likely that the debtors and/or their families were not simply toiling in the home of their creditor, but in constructions that are called "prisons" (Akk *bīt kīli*) or "houses of servitude" (Akk *bīt kiššātim;* cf. Heb *bêt ʿăbādim*). Reduced to (temporary) slavery, they probably found themselves in the company of prisoners of war, together with whom they formed the group of people referred to as *ʾăsîrîm,* "detained persons" (cf. Akk *asīrū*).

Closely related to imprisonment because of guilt was the practice of forcing a debtor to pay by taking a distrainee. B. Porten and J. C. Greenfield see this custom reflected in pleas such as Isa 38:14, which they translate, "Oh Lord, I am being distrained; be Thou my guarantor" (cf. Ps 119:122). The distrainee served in fact as a hostage. Such a hostage could be kept in a "house of custody" (*bêt mišmār*) for other reasons as well (Gen 42:18–20).

In its simplest form the prison was a cave (Josh 10:16–18) or—more frequently—a "pit" (*bôr*), a usage reminiscent of a nomadic lifestyle (Gen 37:22–24; Jer 38:6–13; Zech 9:11; cf. ARM III 36:17–20, where an evildoer risks being thrown into a "pit" [*ḫirītum*]). This ancient form of imprisonment has survived in the Hebrew term *bêt habbôr* (or simply *bôr,* Gen 40:15; 41:14), designating various types of prisons (Exod 12:29; Jer 37:16). In Gen 40:15 the term *bôr* refers to the *bêt hassōhar,* "house of the enclosure" (LXX *ochyrōma,* "fortress") in which the *ʾăsîrîm* (Ketib: *ʾăsûrim*) of the pharaoh were kept. The biblical description corresponds to Egyptian practice as we know it from the hieroglyphic records: those who were condemned to detention and forced labor were relegated to a fortified building (often called *pr šnʿ*), supervised by one of pharaoh's officials. How general a term *bêt habbôr* came to be is apparent from Jer 37:15–16, where the four terms *bêt hāʾēsûr,* "house of the fetters," *bêt hakkeleʾ,* "house of detention," *bêt habbôr,* and *haḥănuyôt,* "the storerooms," are applied to one and the same place, viz., an ordinary dwelling house which had been turned into a prison.

The multiplicity of nonspecific terms suggests that in ancient Israel no special constructions were designed in which prisoners could be lodged. This situation compares well with the data furnished by Mesopotamian texts, according to which persons under arrest were occasionally confined for work in rather harmless places like the *nakkamtum,* "granary," or the *kalakkum,* "silo" (cf. the reference in Isa 42:22 to *ḥûrîm,* LXX *tamieia,* "storerooms," as a Babylonian place of detention). People could be detained in a palace "court of the guard" (*ḥăṣar hammaṭṭārâ,* Jer 32:2) equipped with a dungeon (*bôr,* Jer 38:6), in an annex of the temple (Jer 20:2) or in a private house. Other Hebrew terms, such as *masgēr* (cf. Aram *msgrt* in *KAI* 215.4, 8), "place of imprisonment," (*bêt*) *mišmār,* "(house of) custody," *bêt happĕquddōt* (Jer 52:11), *bêt hammahpeket,* "house of the stocks" (2 Chr 16:10), *kĕlûʾ,* and *kĕlîʾ,* remain too general for identification with specific buildings. More is known of the prisons mentioned in the NT (called *phylakē* or *desmōtērion*). They sometimes consisted of several cells (called *oikēmata,* Acts 12:7), the central one of which was considered the most secure and unpleasant (Acts 16:24).

Bibliography

Frymer, T. S. 1974. The Nungal-Hymn and the Ekur-Prison. *JESHO* 20: 78–89.

Gelb, I. J. 1973. Prisoners of War in Early Mesopotamia. *JNES* 32: 70–98.

Porten, B., and Greenfield, J. C. 1969. The Guarantor at Elephantine-Syene. *JAOS* 89: 153–57.

Toorn, K. van der. 1986. Judges XVI 21 in the Light of the Akkadian Sources. *VT* 36: 248–53.

Vergote, J. 1959. *Joseph en Egypte.* Louvain.

Karel van der Toorn

PRISON, SPIRITS IN. See SPIRITS IN PRISON.

PROCESSIONS. Ancient cultures throughout the world performed processions for any number of reasons: to avert disaster, to ensure the fertility of crops, to enthrone a king, to welcome a conquering ruler, to accompany a wedding or funeral, or to honor a deity. Religious processions, for the most part, fell into one of three categories: (1) the magic procession, a ritual meant to ensure a beneficial or prevent a harmful effect, (2) the offering procession, a presentation of gifts to the gods, and (3) the epiphany procession, which featured the manifestation of a particular deity through the symbols or the image of that god, and which sometimes also included ritually reenacted myths of the deity.

Processions, a significant part of the cultus of ancient Israel, are depicted throughout the OT. The NT also has a few accounts of processions. In addition, the NT includes some passages where processional language is used figuratively. The processions portrayed in the Bible grew out of the ritual practices of the ANE culture and the Hellenized culture of the E Roman Empire. The present study will investigate the processions of the above-mentioned cultures insofar as they provide a context for understanding the processions in the Bible. (See Nussbaum *RAC,* 9: 908–1049; Bömer PW, 21: 1878–1974; Cross *CMHE.*)

A. Processions in the ANE and Greco-Roman World
  1. Processions in the ANE
  2. Greek and Hellenistic Processions
  3. The Roman Triumphal Procession
  4. The Procession as a Literary Motif
B. Processions in the Bible
  1. OT
  2. NT

A. Processions in the ANE and Greco-Roman World

1. Processions in the ANE. The majority of the processions in the ANE were epiphany processions which symbolically repeated and so reactualized the mythic actions of the gods. These epiphany processions usually occurred in the context of a religious festival. In fact, they represented the high point of the religious festivals in the ANE. One such procession, often compared to the Feast of Tabernacles procession and other rituals in the Hebrew Bible, was the procession which took place at the climax of the Babylonian *akîtu* festival. See AKITU; NEBO (DEITY).

The *akîtu* festival was a New Year Festival which reenacted the myth of creation. As such, it ritually reestablished the order of nature and society. The procession took place at the climax of the festival, featuring the king leading the statue of the god Marduk and the other major deities of the empire through Babylon to the *bit akîti* ("the temple of the *akîtu* festival"), which lay outside the city. The procession symbolized the victorious army of the gods who, together with Marduk, destroyed the forces of chaos prior to creation.

2. Greek and Hellenistic Processions. While epiphany processions dominated ANE cultic practices, offering processions were prominent in the classical Greek world. In Greece, as in the ANE, processions usually occurred in a larger ritual context as demonstrated by the fact that all of the great Greek processions were connected with festivals and, conversely, nearly every important festival contained a procession as part of its celebration. The close ties between the festivals and processions can be seen by the frequent use of the suffix *-phoria* in the festival names (e.g., Thesmophoria, Arrephoria, Oschophoria, Daphnephoria). This suffix is derived from the verb *pherein* ("to carry") signifying the bearing of specific offerings or cult objects in procession.

One of the most important processions in Athens was connected with the great Panathenaea, a festival held every four years. During this festival, a *peplos,* or robe, was paraded through the streets of Athens which the people of Athens presented, along with many other offerings, to Athena, the city's patroness. The Parthenon frieze, now in the British Museum, depicts this procession.

In the later Hellenistic culture and the Hellenized culture of the E portion of the Roman Empire, there was an increasing flexibility in the structure of religious processions. Although most of these processions were modeled after the processions of the classical Greek polis, there were, nevertheless, significant changes which resulted from various factors, such as the cultural influence of the East, the prosperity of the age, and the separation of the procession from the specific ritual function it had in the Greek city. Among the more important changes were: (1) processions coming into the hands of private cults or individuals who used them primarily for propagandistic purposes, (2) epiphany processions becoming the dominant type of procession, and (3) processions often becoming more extravagant at the expense of their underlying religious meaning.

3. The Roman Triumphal Procession. Probably the most famous procession in Roman times was the Roman triumphal procession celebrated at Rome on the occasion of a victory over enemies of state. The Roman procession, the offspring of an ancient Etruscan ritual, was originally an epiphany procession, with the triumphant general appearing as the living image of Jupiter Optimus Maximus. By the time of the empire, however, the triumph was celebrated as an offering procession held to honor the gods in thanksgiving for the victory. The procession consisted of the entrance into the city of the Roman magistrates, the Senate, people carrying booty from the campaign, sacrificial bulls, and enemy captives (who were executed at the end of the ceremony), followed by the victorious general on a chariot leading his army.

4. The Procession as a Literary Motif. Given the importance of religious processions in Greco-Roman times, it is not surprising that the procession came to be used as a common literary motif. For example, the popular philosophers of the time condemned the procession for its extravagance and frivolity, and as a result, it became the metaphorical equivalent of the ostentatious ceremony devoid of content. Likewise, the triumphal procession was used figuratively in Latin literature and poetry. Seneca compares his dependence on his benefactor to the humiliating experience of being "led in triumph" (*Ben.* 2.11.1), whereas Ovid writes of love having vanquished and led him in a triumphal procession (*Am.* 1.2.27–30). On the other hand, religious writers, both Christian and non-Christian, used the image of the epiphany procession as a metaphor to compare the fact that the human person bears the image of God in the same way that the epiphany procession carries around the deity (Ign. *Eph.* 9.2; Clem. Al. *Protr.* 4.59.2; *Midr. Ps* 17:8).

B. Processions in the Bible

1. OT. a. Elements of OT Processions. The elements of the ancient Israelite procession can be culled from various places in the OT. 2 Samuel 6 and 1 Kings 8 give specific accounts of cultic processions. The Psalms also contain numerous allusions to processions (Psalms 68; 47; 118). In addition to these passages, several etiological accounts of cultic processions from early OT times appear in Joshua 3–6. These passages demonstrate some of the most important elements of Israelite processions.

The focus of the Israelite procession was the ark. This is clearly evident in 2 Samuel 6, the most detailed processional account in the OT. Music also figured prominently in these processions. 2 Samuel 6 depicts musicians playing lyres (*knrwt*), harps (*nblym*), tambourines (*tpym*), systrums (*mnᶜnᶜym*), and cymbals (*ṣlṣlym*); whereas the procession in Ps 68:25–27 is accompanied by singers (*šrym*), musicians (*ngnym*), and young women playing tambourines (*twppwt*). 2 Sam 6:15 and Ps 47:6 also mention a "cry of homage" (*trwᶜh*) performed by the people and the sounding of the ram's horn (*šwpr*).

Processions in Jerusalem entered the temple court through the Eastern gate, possibly on a highway (*mslwt,* Ps 84:6) built especially for these events. At the gate of the courtyard, prior to the entrance of the procession, an entrance liturgy was intoned. The liturgy consisted of a litany of questions and answers performed by those inside the courtyard and those in the procession (Psalms 15; 24; cf. Ps 118:19–20; Isa 26:1; 33:14–16).

As the above survey shows, certain details about processions in ancient Israel can be extracted from the biblical texts. Nevertheless, the origin, frequency, and significance of Israelite processions are disputed, primarily because of the uncertainty of the origin and significance of Israelite cultic practices. Two schools of thought, the Myth and Ritual school and the History of Redemption school, dominate the discussion.

The Myth and Ritual school traces its origin to Sigmund Mowinckel (1884–1965). From his analysis of the Psalms, Mowinckel speculated that the rituals of Israel dramatically reenacted a common ANE cosmogonic myth. Subsequent studies by students of the Myth and Ritual school have further developed Mowinckel's theory, filling out details by investigating similar festivals from surrounding cultures. They have emphasized the central role played by the Israelite king, positing him as Yahweh's representative who performed in the ritual and in history what Yahweh accomplished in the mythical and cosmic realm. The History of Redemption school based its theory on form-critical investigation of early historical and covenant traditions. This school has interpreted the ritual practices of Israel as dramatically reenacting the significant events of Israel's history: the Exodus and Conquest.

Cross has attempted to synthesize these two viewpoints. In his studies on the background and function of Israelite ritual, Cross (1966; *CMHE,* 79–111) argues that "the apparently opposed views of the history of Israel's cultus prove to be complementary" (1966: 27). He contends that the cosmogonic elements in the cultus were from the earliest strata of Israelite history and experienced a revival in the cultus of the Monarchy, whereas the historical elements in the cultus originated at the time of the Israelite league.

b. 2 Samuel 6. Scholars have generally regarded the procession described in 2 Samuel 6 as part of the yearly celebration of the Feast of Tabernacles in ancient Israel despite the fact that they have disputed whether that festival was a celebration of cosmogonic events, of Israelite history, or of a combination of the two. Mowinckel (1962: 106–92) has claimed that the ancient autumn Feast of Tabernacles was originally a New Year Festival, a finding which would suggest that the Feast of Tabernacles shared many characteristics with the Canaanite and Babylonian New Year Festivals. Mowinckel further postulated that, as a New Year Festival, the Feast of Tabernacles featured as its primary event the enthronement of Yahweh. As in the Babylonian *akîtu* festival, one of the central elements of the autumnal Feast of Tabernacles was the procession. The Israelite procession featured the carrying of the ark, the symbol of Yahweh, to the temple, where Yahweh, having previously defeated the forces of chaos, was proclaimed king. Although Mowinckel saw this annual festal procession reflected in the description of the consecration festival of 2 Samuel 6, he also suggested that Psalm 132 is the "text" of this ritual procession (1962: 174).

Kraus (1965: 183–88) has agreed that an important Israelite ritual, culminating in a procession to the temple, occurred during the Feast of Tabernacles. Kraus has also connected this procession with that described in 2 Samuel 6 and, like Mowinckel, understood Psalm 132 to be "a selection of the ritual" (1965: 185). However, Kraus maintains that the procession to the temple was strictly a reenactment of historical events, specifically the arrival of the ark in the city chosen by Yahweh and the covenant with the Davidic dynasty.

Porter's work (1954) provides a compromise to these seemingly contrary positions. Porter suggests that the description of the procession and festival found in 2 Samuel 6 is the account of the festival which was celebrated at the enthronement of David in Jerusalem, while Psalm 132 reflects the cultic commemoration of that event in Israelite worship. According to Porter, the procession and festival depicted in 2 Samuel 6 were part of a Canaanite coronation rite introduced by David on the occasion of his accession to the throne in Jerusalem. As such, 2 Samuel 6 depicts the earthly exaltation of David which, in turn, reflects the cosmic exaltation of Yahweh. This coronation rite was later celebrated in the cultus, and it is the later celebration which is reflected in Psalm 132. The psalm recalls the historical hope of the perpetuation of the Davidic dynasty promised by Yahweh.

Miller and Roberts (1977) have challenged the assumption that 2 Samuel 6 is connected to the annual Feast of Tabernacles. Instead they have described 2 Samuel 6 as the account of a singular event, a procession celebrating the return of an exiled god to his city. They have cited as evidence parallels from Babylonian annals which describe Marduk's return, in procession, to the city of Babylon after an exile of eleven years.

More recently, McCarter (*2 Samuel* AB, 180–82) has suggested that 2 Samuel 6 is neither the account of a procession of the Feast of Tabernacles nor a depiction of the return of an exiled deity. Instead, he has proposed that this passage reflects a ceremony introducing a god into a new royal city.

c. Processions of the Gilgal Sanctuary. The acts of worship at the sanctuary of Gilgal, one of the most important sanctuaries in early OT times, apparently included several processions of the ark. The cultic legend of the crossing of the Jordan and of the entry into Canaan preserved in Joshua 3–4 bears all the marks of a ritual procession reenacting a significant event from Israelite history. In this account the ark led the procession (Josh 3:3) while the Israelite people followed at a specified distance (Josh 3:4). Kraus (1965: 159) has suggested that Psalm 114 is a hymn based on the cultic tradition of this passage.

Joshua 6 contains a report of the circumambulation of the ark with priests and trumpets (*šprwt*) around the city of Jericho. Since this passage reads more like an account of a cultic procession than a record of a military maneuver, it seems to be an etiological justification for the ritual practices of a later time, most likely a procession which ritually repeated Israel's conquest of the Canaanites.

d. Processions in the Apocrypha. There are several places in the Apocrypha which mention Hasmonean processions (1 Macc 13:5; 2 Macc 10:7). Additionally, 2 Macc 6:7 describes a Dionysus procession in which Antiochus Epiphanes forced the Jews to participate.

1 Macc 13:51 reports the triumphal entry of Simeon and the Jewish people into Jerusalem after enemy troops had been expelled from the Akra, the fortified citadel within the city. This procession featured musicians playing harps (*kinyrai*), cymbals (*kymbala*), and stringed instruments (*nablai*), while the people carried palm branches and sang hymns. 2 Macc 10:7 portrays a procession celebrating the purification of the temple. The latter procession is particularly interesting because it reflects both Jewish and Greek cultic practice, clearly demonstrating the flexibility of processions in the Hellenistic period. In this procession, the Jews carried branches, palm fronds, and *thyrsoi* or ivy-wreathed staffs. On the one hand, the Mishna reports that branches were carried in the Feast of Tabernacles procession (*Sukk.* 4:5). On the other hand, *thyrsoi* were well-known implements from the cult of Dionysus, ivy being sacred to that deity.

2. NT. a. The Entry of Jesus into Jerusalem. The most significant of the few processions depicted in the NT are the accounts of Jesus' entry into Jerusalem (Matt 21:1–9; Mark 11:1–10; Luke 19:28–40; John 12:12–19). The Synoptic accounts portray an impromptu procession of Jesus and his followers entering the holy city, while John describes a large crowd of people from the city who have come out to meet Jesus and escort him into Jerusalem. All four evangelists portray Jesus as a royal figure. The mention of David in Matt 21:9 and Mark 11:10, Luke's insertion of *ho basileus* ("the king") into the quotation of Psalm 118, and John's addition of *ho basileus tou Israel* ("the king of Israel") to the quotation of the same psalm demonstrate that the procession represents the victorious entry of a king into his city. The leafy branches (*stibades*) in the Markan account and the palm branches (*ta baia ton phoinikon*) in the Johannine report are reminiscent of the foliage carried in the procession of the Feast of Tabernacles and the palm branches carried in the procession of Simeon into Jerusalem after Israel's enemies had been expelled from the Akra (1 Macc 13:51). See also HOSANNA. In the latter account, the Jews enter Jerusalem in procession in order to reclaim their city. Likewise, the evangelists portray Jesus as the messianic king who enters Jerusalem in the manner of a royal figure come to claim his city. The spreading of garments before Jesus in the Synoptic accounts calls to mind a similar incident reported in the OT at the acclamation of Jehu as king (2 Kgs 9:13). John's depiction of people coming out of Jerusalem to meet Jesus corresponds to Hellenistic convention. Rulers claiming sovereignty over a city were sometimes met outside the gates of that city by its citizens and escorted inside in procession.

b. The Procession as a Literary Motif in the Pauline Literature. While there are not many actual processions portrayed in the NT, there are several passages where the procession is employed figuratively. One passage, Col 2:15, uses the verb *thriambeuein*, a term associated with the Roman triumphal procession, to portray Christ leading the "principalities" (*archai*) and "powers" (*exousiai*) in procession. The verse shows Christ in the position of the triumphant general parading his defeated prisoners.

Language from Greco-Roman processions also appears in 2 Cor 2:14–6:13; 7:2–4 (Duff 1988). Throughout this section, Paul uses the motif of the procession to describe his apostolic ministry. The section begins in 2:14: "Thanks be to God, who in Christ always leads us in triumph (*thriambeuein*)." 2 Cor 2:14, like Col 2:15, allludes to the triumphal procession, as the use of *thriambeuein* clearly shows. However, Paul's meaning in 2 Cor 2:14 is disputed. Paul obviously describes himself as a participant in God's triumphal procession, but what exactly is his role? Some scholars would interpret 2 Cor 2:14 in the manner of Colossians. In this case Paul would be describing himself as a prisoner of war, defeated by God. Other scholars insist that this image is too harsh, and they would read the passage as comparing Paul to the soldiers in the victorious general's triumphant army. In 2 Cor 2:14b–16 Paul further describes himself as the "aroma" (*osme*) and "incense" (*euodia*) of Christ. This description recalls the fragrant substances that frequently accompanied epiphany processions in the ancient world. Paul depicts his apostolic role in 2 Cor 4:10 with the verb *peripherein* ("to carry around"), a term often used to depict the bearing of cult objects or offering gifts in procession. He describes himself as "always carrying around (*peripherein*) the dying of Jesus" in his body. The self-description figuratively portrays Paul's missionary journeys as a cultic procession. Paul recognizes that his attempts to spread the gospel were not unlike the proselytizing efforts of the epiphany processions of the time. His self-characterization as "carrying around the dying of Jesus" calls to mind the display of cult objects or even the portrayal of scenes from the life of a deity in the epiphany processions of the Greco-Roman world. At the close of the section, in 2 Cor 6:13 and 7:2, Paul addresses the Corinthians directly: "Be wide open for us. . . . Make room for us" (*platunthete kai hymeis. . . . choresate hemas*). This language is reminiscent of the cry of the herald, the cultic official responsible for leading the procession. Apuleius, in his account of the Isis procession, illustrates the role of this official (Apul. *Met.* 273.13–14): "And there were many whose job it was to cry out, 'make the road clear for the sacred objects' " (*et plerique qui facilem sacris viam dari praedicarent*).

Bibliography

Cross, F. M. 1966. The Divine Warrior in Israel's Early Cult. Pp. 11–30 in *Biblical Motifs,* ed. A. Altmann. Cambridge, MA.
Duff, P. 1988. Honor or Shame: The Language of Processions and

Perception in 2 Cor 2:14–6:13; 7:2–4. Ph.D. Diss., University of Chicago.

Kraus, H.-J. 1965. *Worship in Israel.* Trans. G. Buswell. Richmond, VA.

Miller, P. D., Jr., and Roberts, J. J. M. 1977. *The Hand of the Lord.* Baltimore.

Mowinckel, S. 1962. *The Psalms in Israel's Worship.* 2 vols. Trans. D. R. Ap-Thomas. Oxford.

Nilsson, M. P. 1916. Die Prozessionstypen im griechischen Kult. *JDAI* 31: 309–39.

Pallis, S. A. 1926. *The Babylonian Akîtu Festival.* Det. Kgl. Danske Videnskabernes Selskab. Historisk-filologiske Meddelelser 12/1. Copenhagen.

Porter, J. R. 1954. The Interpretation of 2 Samuel VI and Psalm CXXXII. *JTS* 5: 161–73.

Versnel, H. S. 1970. *Triumphus.* Leiden.

PAUL BROOKS DUFF

PROCHORUS (PERSON) [Gk *Prochoros*]. The name Prochorus, a rather uncommon Greek name at the time (Foakes Jackson and Lake 1933: 4, 66), occurs only in Acts 6:5, where Prochorus is one of seven gifted leaders "of good repute, full of the spirit and of wisdom" (Acts 6:3) who were chosen to look after the needs of the Hellenistic Jewish Christian widows who had been neglected in the "daily distribution" (Acts 6:1). Since all seven had Greek names and only one of them, Nicolaus, is explicitly called a proselyte, it is probable that the other six, including Parmenas, were either Jews born in the Diaspora or Palestinian Jews with Greek names (as would be the case with Jesus' disciples Andrew and Philip). The work of two of them, Stephen (Acts 6:8–8:2) and Philip (Acts 8:5–40; 21:8), makes it clear that the seven did not limit themselves to "serving tables" (Acts 6:2) but functioned for the Hellenists in the way that the Twelve did for the Hebrew Christians (see Simon 1958: 7).

While Prochorus is otherwise unknown in the Bible, tradition suggests that he was one of the Seventy (Luke 10:1; cf. Schermann 1907: 302–3), was the scribe to whom the Apostle John dictated the Fourth Gospel, became bishop of Nicomedia, and died a martyr at Antioch. A 5th-century work, the *Acts of John* (an orthodox work not to be confused with the earlier work of the same name by the gnostic Lucius) was written in his name (see Bruce *Acts* NICNT, 121). See JOHN, ACTS OF (BY PROCHORUS).

Bibliography

Foakes Jackson, F. J., and Lake, K. 1933. *The Beginnings of Christianity.* 5 vols. London.

Schermann, T. 1907. *Propheten- und Apostellegenden.* Leipzig.

Simon, M. 1958. *St. Stephen and the Hellenists in the Primitive Church.* London.

JON PAULIEN

PROCONSUL. See PALESTINE, ADMINISTRATION OF (ROMAN).

PROCURATOR. The title of a governor of equestrian rank for one of the lesser provinces of the Roman Empire, such as Judea, or a personal agent of the emperor. The Latin word *procurator* derives from the preposition *pro,* "on behalf of," and the verb *curo,* "to care for." A procurator is, then, one who acts to care for something on behalf of someone else. The only usage of the word in the 500-year period of the Roman Republic was as a technical juridical term signifying the legally authorized agent of an individual charged with the conduct of business or the supervision of property on behalf of that individual. The term continued to have the same meaning throughout the imperial era and was generally so used. When applied to personal agents of the emperor, however, *procurator* could either indicate anyone acting on the emperor's business or signify a specific government officer whose service for the emperor warranted the official title of procurator (Jones 1960: 117–18).

Under the empire minor Roman provinces such as Judea, Thrace, Rhaetia, Noricum, and Mauretania were governed by officials designated procurators. These governors had risen through the military and civil service career ladder habituated by ambitious equestrians and, if successful in their procuratorial post, could anticipate advancement to one of the several prefectures which comprised the ultimate office for men of equestrian rank. The establishment of equestrian procuratorships has traditionally been linked to the inception of the principate with Augustus' division of the empire for administrative purposes into imperial and senatorial provinces (Pflaum 1950: 1–56, passim; Salmon 1968: 74–94). In light of recently discovered epigraphic evidence, that view is no longer tenable. A variety of inscriptions indicate that during the reigns of Augustus and Tiberius, the later procuratorial provinces were in fact administered by equestrians with the title of *praefectus.* Jones (1960: 117–25) not only calls attention to this information, but rightly notes the inconsistency of believing two emperors so meticulous in their observation of constitutional formalities to have bestowed on government officials titles which grew out of private administrative or household functions. Accordingly, prefect must be assumed to have been the proper title of equestrian provincial governors, at least until the reign of Claudius, when inscriptional evidence attests the usage in this context of the title procurator.

This is particularly significant in respect to Pontius Pilate and the governorship of Judea. Pilate has frequently been identified as procurator because of Tacitus' (*Ann.* 15.44) anachronistic use of the term when writing a century later, and because Josephus (*JW* 2.8.1; 9.2 §§117, 169) describes him as *epitropos,* the normal Greek rendering of the Latin *procurator.* Of course, Josephus is prone to identify the governors of Judea in a rather careless and imprecise fashion, sometimes designating the same individual by several different titles (Jones 1960: 119). Greater attention should be devoted to the more contemporary record of Philo (*Gaium*), who properly identifies Pilate as *praefectus Iudaeae,* and to the telling evidence of a recently unearthed inscription (*AE* 1963 no. 104) which demonstrates Pilate's official title to have been *praefectus Iudaeae.*

In addition to procuratorial governors possessing within their provinces full civil and criminal jurisdictional powers, there were other imperial officials as well as private agents of the emperor who bore the designation of procurator.

In large and important provinces of the emperor, governed in his stead by imperial legates (*legati Augusti pro praetore*), procurators were assigned as the chief financial officer of the province, paralleling the role of quaestors in senatorial provinces and having similar authority to collect taxes and tribute and to pay troops (Dio Cass. 53.15.3; Strab. 3.167). Procurators sometimes were also found in provinces administered by the Senate, but their role in such instances was without public authority and served only to administer and oversee imperial properties in the capacity of personal agents of the emperor. Finally, the term *procurator* was applied to other personal representatives of the emperor, who were often commoners or even freedmen, with responsibility for directing business enterprises or managing an emperor's personal holdings in Italy or the provinces (Millar 1964: 180–87). The activities of specific individuals in any level imperial procuratorial post are the subject of a detailed three-volume study by H. G. Pflaum (1960). See also PRAETORIUM.

Bibliography

Jones, A. H. M. 1960. *Studies in Roman Government and Law.* New York.

Millar, F. 1964. Some Evidence of the Meaning of Tacitus *Annals* XII.60. *Historia* 13: 180–87.

Pflaum, H. G. 1950. *Les procurateurs equestres sous le haut-empire romain.* Paris.

———. 1960. *Les carrières procuratoriennes equestres.* 3 vols. Paris.

Salmon, E. T. 1968. *A History of the Roman World 36 BC to AD 138.* 6th ed. London.

John F. Hall

PROLOGUES, GOSPEL (ANTI-MARCION).

See ANTI-MARCION (GOSPEL) PROLOGUES.

PRONOUNCEMENT STORY.

See APOPHTHEGM.

PROPAGANDA. Propaganda, i.e., the deliberate (albeit mostly dissimulated) spreading of ideas, information, rumors, etc. in order to support one's own political (or religious) cause, to acquire more proselytes, and in the last analysis to gain more power, has become a common practice in the modern world as a consequence of the availability of mass media (press, radio, television). It is being studied therefore especially with reference to the modern world (Katz 1954; Lasswell and Leites 1965; Gordon 1971; Domenach 1973) and in the frame of contemporary political language (Dovring 1959; Faye 1972; Klaus 1971; Robin 1973). Even though the common meaning as "forgery," "falsehood," or the like is certainly inaccurate, it is true that propaganda is more interested in effectiveness than in correctness, and its informations are biased as a result of unfair selection, cunning deformation, and subtle connotation. The "rate of truth" necessary for an effective propaganda (a patently false statement would be almost useless) is a function of the free circulation of ideas and information in the society. The most coarse propaganda is produced by totalitarian governments (and is mostly studied in the Nazi, Fascist, Communist cases); in capitalist societies, commercial propaganda (advertising) is most widespread (also in "hidden" forms).

A. Propaganda in the Ancient World
B. Propaganda in the ANE
C. Propaganda in the OT

A. Propaganda in the Ancient World

Propaganda is not limited to the contemporary world, however (Ellul 1976; Thomson 1977; Lasswell, Lerner, and Speier 1979). Since the constitution of complex political entities (based on a differentiation of socio-economic roles and rewards), the ruling elites have always pursued political consent and social cohesion by adding the instruments of persuasion to those of repression: in general, in order to confirm the actual rule, or in particular, in order to help the acceptance of new (possibly unpopular) legal or administrative measures or of irregular personal positions. Later on, since religions of universalistic extent have come into being (endowed with spreading power beyond their original communities), also a religious propaganda has become common practice (proselytism). Ancient propaganda is best studied with reference to the Roman world (Sordi 1974, 1975, 1976).

B. Propaganda in the ANE

The "despotic" states of the ANE (especially Egypt and Assyria) are a fertile field for political propaganda (Posener 1956; Williams 1964; Liverani 1973a; Finkelstein 1979; Oppenheim 1979). Sometimes propaganda is addressed to foreign states: cf. the explicit case of a letter sent by a middle-Assyrian king to the vassals of the Hittites after a victory over the Hittite king (Lackenbacher 1982); or the largely biased reconstruction of past relationships in the historical introduction to the Hittite treaties (Liverani 1973b); or the clear apologetic tone in the war declarations; or the pro-Babylonian reconstruction of events in the "Chronicle P" as contrasted to the pro-Assyrian one in the "Synchronistic History" (TCS 5: 50–59); or finally the elaborate piece of political propaganda that is the "Tukulti-Ninurta Epic" (Ebeling 1938; Machinist 1976, 1978).

More often the propaganda is directed to the inner subjects of the state. Usurpers are obviously in need of propagating apologetic texts in which they underscore their heroic behavior, or their justice, or their divine support—so counterbalancing the negative effect of an illegitimate seizure of power (Telipinu: Liverani 1977; Idrimi: Liverani 1974; Ḫattusilis: Archi 1971; Hoffner 1975; Assyrian kings: Tadmor 1983). But, more in general, the royal inscriptions can be viewed as pieces of propaganda and are in fact effective in spreading the political ideologies of the respective kingdoms, a task which becomes more necessary with kingdoms engaged in "imperialistic" expansion, like Egypt in the New Kingdom (Bleiberg 1985–86; Grimal 1986) and especially Assyria (Liverani 1979; Fales 1981; Garelli 1982). In their celebrative effort, the royal inscriptions reveal all the biased deformations typical of propaganda in all times: only the successes are reported, and never the losses or the defeats; "our" reasons are always good, while those of the enemies are wicked; the king who is author of the text constitutes the apex (in glory, bravery, power, justice, and the gods' favor) in the course of history for his own country and for the entire world. In Egypt the literary genre of the *Königsnovelle* becomes the stereotyped form of the royal self-celebration (Herrmann 1938; lastly Spalinger 1982; and see Herrmann 1953–54; Whybray 1968: 96–105 on its influence in the OT). The royal inscriptions displayed on the monumental buildings are not the only ones to convey messages of propaganda: royal hymns have the same purpose yet a different audience; prayers to the gods can contain pieces of political propaganda; and quite a number of "literary" or "historiographic" texts have the purpose of celebrating and propagating the ruling ideology.

Of course the written documents as such can be read only by a small minority in the populace—even though this is the minority engaged in public activities (scribes, administration and cult officials, members of the court). The texts keep in any case the most detailed formulations of the political ideology. More generic, but more widespread pieces of propaganda are also available: the royal titulary is a privileged carrier for propagandistic values; the periodic amnesties or debt remissions have the clear intent of captivating the popular favor; the public parades of troops or of foreign booty have a celebrative effect (cf. Aldred 1970); and the same holds true for the public reading of "letters to the god" reporting the king's victories (Oppenheim 1960). Even the names given to newly established settlements have generally a celebrative flavor; and the royal genealogies have in some cases been forged to attribute legitimacy and nobility to kings of doubtful origin. Besides the written, oral, and ceremonial propaganda, art and architecture can also convey similar effects. The monumental buildings (temple and royal palaces) in the capital city celebrate the king's power and his good relations with the divine sphere; in some cases the sculptured (or painted) decoration is such to underscore the power of the sovereign or to discourage the enemies' resistance (Egypt: Tefnin 1981; Assyria: Reade 1979; Winter 1981; Persia: Root 1979); even the different building materials, coming from distant regions, celebrate the worldwide spread of the king's fame.

C. Propaganda in the OT

If compared to the propagandistic apparatus of the Near Eastern empires, ancient Israel is noteworthy for the lack of an explicit propaganda. This is obvious for the nonmonarchic periods, especially when the society was ordered according to a "tribal" pattern and the political consent was based on a network of kinship relations. But this seems true also for the kingdoms of Israel and Judah (and especially for the most glorious reigns of David and Solomon): no royal inscriptions are extant from those kingdoms (in contrast to the contemporary Aramaic, Phoenician, and Neo-Hittite states in the same area; cf., e.g., Fales 1979); no iconic representations of the Israelite kingship are known (and the iconic representation is generally a depressed topic in ancient Israel); even the public buildings so far excavated are not conspicuous for their monumental features. It has been recently suggested that the lack of royal inscriptions (the most obvious channel for propaganda) is a result of their intentional destruction, connected with a (periodical?) rewriting of former history by the ruling political circles (Garbini 1986). This seems practically impossible. A more acceptable explanation should take into account the following elements: (1) no royal palaces have been archaeologically recovered so far (in Jerusalem or elsewhere); (2) Israel and Judah were relatively small (in wealth and power) in comparison to other Near Eastern kingdoms; (3) a peculiar "tribal" legacy survived all along their history; (4) an especially strong relation of dependence on the national god was established in the course of time.

Whereas no pieces of propaganda are extant from the archaeological record of ancient Israel, it cannot be denied that the OT as a whole can be considered as a huge propagandistic work and that many texts or passages constitutive of the OT (or embedded in it) display a more or less clear propagandistic purpose, both in the political and the religious field. The study of OT passages as "pieces of propaganda" has generally won a scarce success, however. This is understandable, since a negative connotation is always applied to the term, and we are as prompt to find out the elements of forgery or distortion in the others' propaganda as we are unable to recognize similar features in the formulation of our own ideology. Even more, the appreciation of the OT as "divine word" (necessarily built up of "true" statements) has discouraged a similar approach, both in the Jewish and Christian circles and in the scientific world largely belonging to such religious environments. Yet the kind of literary and ideological analysis elaborated for the study of propaganda (and of political language in general) could also be applied to the study of some literary forms or specific passages in the OT, in order to point out the procedures employed in expressing the political and religious ideologies of the time (see esp. Whitelam 1984, with further bibliography).

The most obvious field of application is the prophetic corpus. An old proposal (Winckler 1903) to consider the prophets as political activists was generally criticized and discarded (e.g., Elliger 1935). In more recent times, even though the term "propaganda" is seldom used in its explicit form, some studies on the political aspects of the prophetic books do in fact contain pertinent observations (e.g., Kraus 1952; Gottwald 1964; Dietrich 1976). In particular the oracles "against the Nations" (and in general the "weal" and "woe" oracles) are obvious pieces of political propaganda, certainly composed in the frame of a multidirectional network of charges and countercharges, apologies, and celebrations, in the Syro-Palestinian world threatened by the Assyrian, Babylonian, and Egyptian empires but still engaged in internal struggles. The same holds true for the inner political debate in Israel and in Judah, especially facing the problem of the political strategy to be chosen toward Assyria and Babylon: the prophecies are clearly the form of the local political debate of the time. On the other side the famous case of the *rab-šāqēh* (2 Kgs 18:17–37) shows how the Assyrian propaganda was received by the Israelites (Cohen 1979; Machinist 1983; cf. more in general Cogan 1974; Childs 1967).

The royal propaganda toward the inner population may have left some trace in the "royal" Psalms: these have been mostly studied in their obvious religious relevance (as expression of "divine kingship"), yet an appreciation of them as political messages cannot simply be discarded.

This focus applies even better to the prophecies intended to legitimize the king, like the Nathan prophecy (2 Samuel 7). Also some remains of "royal inscriptions" (or more properly of "royal apologies") are to be found in the historical books: the story of the rise and enthronization of David (1 Samuel 16–2 Samuel 4) contains obvious apologetic features (as expected in the case of a usurper) that can go back to materials propagated by the king himself or by his circle in order to support his legitimacy (Weiser 1966; McCarter 1980; Whitelam 1984). This is true also of the "Succession Narrative" (2 Samuel 9–20; 1 Kings 1–2) since Solomon's legitimacy was in need of some justification too (Whybray 1968: 50–55; Würthwein 1979). Another case has been studied from this point of view: the story of Joash (2 Kings 11–12) clearly goes back to an autobiographical inscription of the kind well known from the Idrimi statue and from related Hittite texts (Liverani 1974). Finally, a clear case of propagandistic forgery is to be seen in the episode of the old manuscript of the "Law" discovered in the temple in Josiah's times (2 Kgs 22:3–23:3): a stratagem commonly used in order to bestow the authoritativeness of time on a newly composed normative text. More cases could be singled out; and the large units in the historical texts can also be studied from the point of view of the propagandistic procedures employed in order to support the respective political or religious ideologies (a vein best represented by Smith 1971).

Bibliography

Aldred, C. 1970. The Foreign Gifts Offered to Pharaoh. *JEA* 56: 105–16.

Archi, A. 1971. The Propaganda of Hattušiliš III. *Studi Micenei ed Egeo-Anatolici* 14: 185–215.

Bleiberg, E. 1985–86. Historical Texts As Political Propaganda during the New Kingdom. *Bulletin of the Egyptological Seminar* 7: 5–13.

Childs, B. S. 1967. *Isaiah and the Assyrian Crisis.* SBT, n.s., 3. London.

Cogan, M. 1974. *Imperialism and Religion.* SBLMS 19. Missoula, MT.

Cohen, C. 1979. Neo-Assyrian Elements in the First Speech of the Biblical Rab-šāqē. *IOS* 9: 32–48.

Dietrich, W. 1976. *Jesaja und die Politik.* BEvT 74. Munich.

Domenach, J.-M. 1973. *La propagande politique.* Paris.

Dovring, K. 1959. *Road of Propaganda: The Semantics of Biased Communication.* New York.

Ebeling, E. 1938. *Bruchstücke eines politischen Propagandagedichtes aus einer assyrischen Kanzlei.* MAOG 12/2. Leipzig.

Elliger, K. 1935. Prophet und Politik. *ZAW* 53: 3–22.

Ellul, J. 1976. *Histoire de la propagande.* Paris.

Fales, F. M. 1979. Kilamuwa and the Foreign Kings: Propaganda vs. Power. *WO* 10: 6–22.

———, ed. 1981. *Assyrian Royal Inscriptions: New Horizons.* Orientis Antiqui Collectio 17. Rome.

Faye, J. P. 1972. *Théorie du recit: Introduction aux "langages totalitaires."* Paris.

Finkelstein, J. 1979. Early Mesopotamia, 2500–1000 B.C. Pp. 50–110 in Lasswell, Lerner, and Speier 1979.

Garbini, G. 1986. *Storia e ideologia nell'Israele antico.* Brescia.

Garelli, P. 1982. La propagande royale assyrienne. *Akkadica* 27: 16–29.

Gordon, G. N. 1971. *Persuasion: The Theory and Practice of Manipulative Communication.* New York.

Gottwald, N. K. 1964. *All the Kingdoms of the Earth.* New York.

Grimal, N.-C. 1986. *Les termes de la propagande royale égyptienne de la XIX dynastie à la conquete d'Alexandre.* Mémoires de l'Académie des Inscriptions et Belles-Lettres 6. Paris.

Herrmann, A. 1938. *Die ägyptische Königsnovelle.* Leipziger Ägyptologische Studien 10. Glückstadt.

Herrmann, S. 1953–54. Die Königsnovelle in Ägypten und in Israel. Pp. 51–62 in *Festschrift Albrecht Alt.* Leipzig.

Hoffner, H. A. 1975. Propaganda and Political Justification in Hittite Historiography. Pp. 49–62 in *Unity and Diversity,* ed. H. Goedicke and J. Roberts. Baltimore.

Katz, D., ed. 1954. *Public Opinion and Propaganda.* New York.

Klaus, G. 1971. *Sprache der Politik.* Berlin.

Kraus, H.-J. 1952. *Prophetie und Politik.* ThEH 36. Munich.

Lackenbacher, S. 1982. Une lettre royale. *RA* 76: 141–49.

Lasswell, H. D., and Leites, N. 1965. *Language of Politics.* Cambridge, MA.

Lasswell, H. D.; Lerner, D.; and Speier, H., eds. 1979. *Propaganda and Communication in World History.* Vol. 1, *The Symbolic Instrument in Early Times.* Honolulu.

Liverani, M. 1973a. Memorandum on the Approach to Historiographic Texts. *Or* 42: 178–94.

———. 1973b. Storiografia politica hittita. I. Šunaššura ovvero della reciprocità. *OrAnt* 12: 267–97.

———. 1974. L'histoire de Joas. *VT* 24: 438–53.

———. 1977. Storiografia politica hittita. II. Telipinu ovvero della solidarietà. *OrAnt* 16: 105–31.

———. 1979. The Ideology of the Assyrian Empire. Pp. 297–317 in *Power and Propaganda,* ed. M. T. Larsen. Copenhagen.

Machinist, P. 1976. Literature As Politics: the Tukulti-Ninurta Epic and the Bible. *CBQ* 38: 455–82.

———. 1978. The Epic of Tukulti-Ninurta I. A Study in Middle Assyrian Literature. Ph.D. diss., Yale University.

———. 1983. Assyria and Its Image in the First Isaiah. *JAOS* 103: 719–35.

McCarter, P. K. 1980. The Apology of King David. *JBL* 99: 489–93.

Oppenheim, A. L. 1960. The City of Assur in 714 B.C. *JNES* 19: 133–47.

———. 1979. The Neo-Assyrian and Neo-Babylonian Empires. Pp. 111–44 in Lasswell, Lerner, and Speier 1979.

Posener, G. 1956. *Littérature et politique dans l'Égypte de la XII dynastie.* Paris.

Reade, J. 1979. Ideology and Propaganda in Assyrian Art. Pp. 329–43 in *Power and Propaganda,* ed. M. T. Larsen. Copenhagen.

Robin, R. 1973. *Histoire et linguistique.* Paris.

Root, M. C. 1979. *The King and Kingship in Achaemenid Art.* Acta Iranica 19. Leiden.

Smith, M. 1971. *Palestinian Parties and Politics That Shaped the Old Testament.* New York.

Sordi, M., ed. 1974. *Propaganda e persuasione occulta nell'antichità.* Milan.

———. 1975. *Storiografia e propaganda.* Milan.

———. 1976. *I canali della propaganda nel mondo antico.* Milan.

Spalinger, A. J. 1982. *Aspects of the Military Documents of the Ancient Egyptians.* YNER 9. New Haven.

Tadmor, H. 1983. Autobiographical Apology in the Royal Assyrian Literature. Pp. 36–57 in *History, Historiography and Interpretation,* ed. H. Tadmor and M. Weinfeld. Jerusalem.

Tefnin, R. 1981. Image, écriture, recit. A propos des representations de la bataille de Qadesh. *Göttinger Miszellen* 47: 55–76.

Thomson, O. 1977. *Mass Persuasion in History*. Edinburgh.

Weiser, A. 1966. Die Legitimation des Königs David: zur Eigenart und Entstehung der sogen: Geschichte von Davids Aufstieg. *VT* 16: 325–54.

Williams, R. J. 1964. Literature As a Medium of Political Propaganda in Ancient Egypt. Pp. 14–30 in *The Seed of Wisdom*, ed. W. S. McCullogh. Toronto.

Winckler, H. 1903. Pp. 170–75 in *Die Keilinschriften und das Alte Testament*, ed. E. Schrader. Berlin.

Whitelam, K. W. 1984. The Defence of David. *JSOT* 29: 61–87.

Whybray, R. N. 1968. *The Succession Narrative*. SBT 2/9. London.

Winter, I. 1981. Royal Rhetoric and the Development of Historical Narrative in Neo-Assyrian Reliefs. *Studies in Visual Communication* 7: 1–31.

Würthwein, E. 1979. *Die Erzahlung von der Thronnachfolge Davids—theologische oder politische Geschichtsschreibung?* TSK 115. Zürich.

MARIO LIVERANI

PROPHECY. This article consists of four entries. The first is a discussion of prophecy and related phenomena in the ANE, with particular attention to the "prophetic" letters from the Mesopotamian site of Mari. The second is a survey of prophecy in Israel before the Exile. The third examines postexilic prophecy, and the fourth entry treats prophecy in the NT and early Christianity.

ANCIENT NEAR EASTERN PROPHECY

The label "prophetic" has been applied to various texts and roles known from the ANE. The texts so described involve predictions, or apparent predictions, eschatology or apocalyptic, social or religious criticism, and commissioned messages from deities. The roles include those of ordinary priests (Egypt), technical diviners (Western Asia), and those who speak directly under orders from a deity. The comparative discussion of prophecy is guided by whichever particular definition of prophecy is used. For some, the prophet is the critic of society; for others, the prophet is the announcer of the future; for yet others, the prophet is the charismatically authorized messenger. Although necessarily referring to materials reflecting this wider range of definitions, this entry focuses on prophecy understood as inspired speech at the initiative of a divine power, speech which is clear in itself and commonly directed to a third party.

A. Syria-Palestine
  1. North Syria: Ebla and Emar
  2. Ugarit
  3. Phoenicia
  4. Aram
  5. Ammon
B. Anatolia
C. Mesopotamia
  1. Uruk (Southern Babylonia)
  2. Mari (Middle Euphrates)
  3. Ishchali (East Tigris)
  4. Assyria
D. Egypt

A. Syria-Palestine

1. North Syria: Ebla and Emar. The Ebla texts, dating to the middle of the 3d millennium B.C., have been cited as evidence of prophecy, but those claims have yet to be substantiated. From Emar (Meskene), on the Middle Euphrates, texts from ca. 1300 B.C. indicate an office with the Akkadian designations *anabbiʾātu* and *munabbiʾātu* associated with the goddess Išhara. The editor (Arnaud 1986: 118, 360, 375, 377, 403; cf. 386) translates this title of office "prophetesses," but nothing is indicated of the role; cf. Akk *munambû*, "wailer."

2. Ugarit. Among the Ugaritic texts there are announcements of future blessing that have been labeled "prophetic" (van Selms 1971) as well as references to technical divination that have been referred to as "prophecy," but there is no evidence as yet for a divinely commissioned messenger.

3. Phoenicia. The Bible has many references to prophets of the Phoenician god Baal (and even of Asherah), using for them the same Hebrew term, *nābîʾ*, used for Israelite prophets. The Baal prophets share ecstatic behavior with the Israelite prophets, but they are not identified as giving oracles. However, the Egyptian report of Wen-Amun (*ANET*, 25–29; *AEL* 2: 224–30) states that while Wen-Amun was in Byblos (ca. 1090 B.C.), one of the Phoenician prince's young attendants became ecstatic and delivered an oracle authenticating Wen-Amun's mission from the god Amun (*ANET* 26; *AEL* 2: 225). Primarily because of these references it was at one time argued that biblical prophecy derived from Canaanite (Phoenician) prophecy.

4. Aram. Noteworthy among the small corpus of Old Aramaic inscriptions is that of Zakkur, king of Hamath and Luash (ca. 800 B.C.). While besieged in one of his cities, Zakkur records that "I lifted up my hands to Baal-Sha[may]n and Baal-Shamay[n] answered me [and spoke] to me by means of visionaries *(ḥzyn)* and . . . *(ʿddn)*. Baal-Shamayn [said] to me, 'Fear not, for I have made [you kin]g [and I will st]ay with you and rescue you'." The text does not indicate how the speakers received their message. Presumably this classic salvation oracle in response to the king's petition derived from prophetic inspiration; note the title *ḥzyn*, as with the Balaam text (below), parallel with *ḥôzeh*, "visionary," frequently used of biblical prophets.

5. Ammon. The plaster inscription from ca. 700 B.C., found at Tell Deir ʿAlla in 1967 refers to Balaam, son of Beor, a "visionary of the gods" *(ḥāzēh ʾilāhīn)* who saw a vision during the night and obtained a somewhat enigmatic revelation from a group of numinous beings *(šdyn)*. This is reinforced by Num 24:4–5, in which Balaam, son of Beor, "hears the words of God, sees a vision of the Almighty *(maḥăzê šadday)*."

B. Anatolia

In 14th-century B.C. texts of King Mursilis II and of his uncle (?) Kantuzilis, who seek relief from plagues or more personal sufferings, there are inventories of means of divine communication. It is in these inventories—cf. 1 Sam 28:6 (dreams, lots, and prophets)—that references to inspired speakers occur. In addition to direct communication to the petitioner through a dream, the deity might use indirect communication through incubation, liver divination, an "inquirer-sibyl" (ENSI), or a so-called "Old

Woman" (šu.gi); or—in the case of Mursilis II—a "man of god" (*šiuniyanza*) might "(come and) declare" the cause of suffering (Lebrun 1980: 113, 160, 209; Kammenhuber 1976: 16–17, 19–23). Although there is no further significant information about this "man of god," the Hittite texts are important as an attestation of the dispersion of such phenomena and as evidence for such activity in the latter part of the mid-2d millennium B.C.

C. Mesopotamia

A rich variety of texts comes from Mesopotamia, including Babylonia, Assyria, and the domain of the Mari texts, even though the Mari texts relate to an area reaching into NW Syria. Among the texts, a number have been published under the label "(Akkadian) prophecies" (Grayson 1975: 13–37; Hunger and Kaufman 1975), one of them being the "Uruk prophecy." These texts, though not of a uniform nature, essentially contain prophecies *ex eventu,* i.e., cast as predictions (e.g., "a king will arise . . ."), and are allied with the omen literature. The prophecies may even take the form of first person speeches of a deity (Marduk) or a divinized king (Shulgi). In some texts the wide-reaching time perspective is more reminiscent of apocalyptic (Hallo 1966; Kaufman 1977). Revelatory intermediaries are not involved.

1. Uruk (Southern Babylonia). A text from ca. 1850 B.C., distinct from the "Uruk prophecy" (above), reports a visit to an unnamed person by a deity who speaks directly to him concerning the future of Uruk and its ruler, whom the deity will appoint. The person responds to the deity and reports to the king "the words which Ishtar spoke to me" (*ANET,* 604). The text is not well enough preserved to indicate whether or not it is an example of inspired speaking.

2. Mari (Middle Euphrates). From the several thousand texts now published from Mari and dating to the first half of the 18th century B.C., there are many references to prophetic activity, using a variety of titles (*ANET,* 623–32; Huffmon 1970). Over a dozen deities are involved; and some eighteen prophets are named, apart from many others who are unnamed. Both male and female prophets are cited. For those with cultic titles, about four-fifths are male. Those without such titles are about evenly divided between men and women.

The small size of the corpus does not allow differentiation among the various titles in terms of specific roles, although there are some suggestive contrasts between those prophets with titles and those without them. This prophetic activity, regarded as marginal from the viewpoint of Mari court circles, doubtless to some extent reflects the Amorite cultural substratum. In keeping with that, the geographical range of references extends from Mari and nearby Terqa along the Euphrates (note Emar, above) to Aleppo in the west. The reference to Shamash of Sippar suggests activity even in Babylonia, although the reference may be to the cult of Shamash of Sippar within the Mari region. With the 1988 publication of the first two parts of *Archives Royales de Mari, XXVI,* the corpus of Mari Letters expanded by almost 500 new letters, and the number of "prophetic" letters increased by more than 20 (to a total of about 50, depending on the criteria for selection). Additionally, almost all of the previously published "prophetic" texts were reedited, frequently with important new readings. (One of the reports was formerly interpreted as a metallurgical text!) With the greatly enlarged corpus of letters, not to mention possible integration with data from the thousands of economic and administrative texts, the picture of prophecy in the Mari archives is in the process of considerable adjustment. The editor's introductory discussion offers an important new beginning (Durand 1988: 377–412, 455–63).

a. Prophets with Titles. These persons are associated with particular deities, though at times they communicate requests from other deities as well. The frequent bestowal on them of garments and other items from the royal stores—and at times their requests for such items—point to their regularized, significant status, analogous to that of typical letter couriers.

(1) *Āpilu/āpiltu,* "answerer." An ordinary Akkadian form, this title for both men and women seems restricted to the Mari texts and lexical compilations. The title implies that the person provides an answer to an explicit or implicit inquiry, although the texts do not exemplify the process. The "answerer" is normally associated with a specific deity, though a unique letter from the *āpilu* of Shamash of Sippar conveys requests for Shamash, Addu of Aleppo, and Nergal of Hubshalum, while mentioning also Dagan of Terqa (Charpin and Durand 1985: 332–33). Two texts mention the receipt of royal rations, suggesting that the "answerer" had an official standing. One of the most important letters, sent from Aleppo, concerns the "answerer" of Addu, lord of Kallassu, who "reclaims the territory of Alahtum as property" (Lafont 1984; the passage was previously translated "is standing guard over the tent-shrine of Alahtum to [be] an estate" [Malamat 1980], illustrating the problems of translation). This same letter refers to "what the 'answerers' (pl.) have said." The writer adds that when he had been in Mari itself, he had sent on to the king "whatever word the 'answerer' (male) or the 'answerer' (female) would say." The "answerer" is thus someone who "came and spoke" or "got up (in the temple) and spoke," addressing a court official with a message for the king.

The new texts include even an *āpilu* of Marduk, in Babylon—presumably a Mari designation for a different Babylonian title or a Mari functionary acting for the god of Babylon—and such initiatives as demanding a skillful scribe to write down the news which the deity had sent for the king. (That letter itself is now published in full [Durand 1988: 417–19].) The "answerer" can travel about in the king's realm and apparently can provoke oracles.

(2) *Assinnu,* "cult functionary." Although in later texts this title refers to a member of the cultic staff of Ishtar, connected especially with singing—perhaps even a eunuch—the Mari occurrences are much earlier and their meaning is uncertain. The two *assinnu* attested are affiliated with Annunitum, a form of Ishtar. One of them speaks in a state of ecstasy. Another *assinnu* apparently resides in an abandoned and partly ruined sanctuary.

(3) *Muhhû/muhhūtu,* "ecstatic." Deriving from the Akkadian root meaning "to become ecstatic," this is the most common prophetic title at Mari. The range of behavior may involve self-wounding, as suggested by a text from Ugarit ("my brothers bathe with their own blood, like *maḫḫû* [pl.]"). "Ecstatics" are associated with the deities Nergal, Itur-Mer, Ninhursaga, Annunitum, and especially Dagan. One Mari text detailing the cult of Ishtar mentions that a *muḫḫû* "is not [. . .] to become ecstatic" and hints at a connection of the *muḫḫû* with watered-down beer. Otherwise the Mari texts do not explicitly point to ecstatic behavior. Rather, the "ecstatic" "gets up/comes and speaks," sometimes in association with sacrifice. Also, it is an "ecstatic" who says "I will continue to answer *(atanappal),*" using a verb related to the title *āpilu.* Like the "answerer," the "ecstatic" occasionally receives garments from the royal stores (in five texts). One Mari "ecstatic," Irra-gamil, associated with Nergal, may even be the same person as Irra-gamil, servant of Nergal, known from a contemporary cylinder seal (Anbar 1976: 63). From Larsa in S Babylonia there are references to the female slave of the *maḫḫû.*

One report (partly restored) involves a person who becomes ecstatic, a person whose name is identified elsewhere as that of an "ecstatic" (Durand 1988: 398, 451–52). Such behavior for an "ecstatic" is otherwise specified only in the Ishtar Ritual Text from Mari. Also, a strikingly assertive "ecstatic" requests a lamb from the king, which he proceeds to eat raw—possibly reflecting an oath ceremony. He then assembles the elders at a city gate to hear his message and ends by requesting a garment, which he is provided (Durand 1988: 434–35).

(4) *Nabû,* "diviner (?)." This appears for the first time as a "prophetic" title in the Mari texts (Durand 1988: 444–45). A Mari functionary advises the king that he went to meet with a Hanaean leader. He then assembled the *nabû* (pl.) of the Hanaeans and had an omen taken on the king's behalf, putting a binary question to them and obtaining, apparently, a favorable answer. The new Mari title parallels the Hebrew *nābî,* but little is known of the function. It may be a question of conventional divination.

(5) *Qam(m)ātum,* unclear title. The reading *qabbātu(?),* "speaker (fem.)," an attractive interpretation confidently accepted by the major dictionaries in correction of the original editor's reading, *qamātum,* is no longer tenable. The reading *qam(m)ātum* is confirmed by collation and a further example—possibly two. Durand (1988: 396) suggests that the term refers to a prophetess with a characteristic hairstyle.

b. Prophets without Titles. Those without titles include a slight majority of women, one of whom was a high official at Mari. Also, a majority of the revelations derive from dreams—a means not yet attested for those prophets with titles; one revelation involves ecstasy. The locus of revelation is commonly a temple.

Also associated with untitled persons are some letters concerning divine revelations of unclear derivation (*ANET,* 629–30, 631). A divine word is sought through "a man and a woman," or Dagan speaks in some unspecified fashion. These texts may conceal prophetic activity, or forms of technical divination may be involved.

Dreams predominate among untitled prophets. In a well-known text the dreamer heard an administrative priest *(šangû)* speaking; in one of the new texts the dreamer reports the speech of two "ecstatics," apparently deceased. But generally the private persons report more directly.

c. The Context of the Oracles. A number of the texts provide information about the context of the message. The typical locus of revelation is a temple, either in reality or by dream visit. In some texts, the revelation by an "answerer" or an "ecstatic" seems to be a response to a sacrifice, whether favorable or unfavorable, but there is no clear example of a revelation in response to a petition of despair. One correspondent advises the king that "(when) I offered a sacrifice to Dagan for the life of my lord, the 'answerer' [masc.] of Dagan of Tuttul got up and spoke as follows, saying, 'O Babylon, . . . (here follows an oracle against Babylon).' " Another correspondent advises that the king's sacrifice has arrived and has been presented, apparently successfully, yet "the 'ecstatic' [masc.] got up before Dagan and spoke as follows: 'I (Dagan) am not given pure water to drink. Write to your lord so that he may give me pure water to drink.' " Most such oracles, however, do not specify cultic prompting.

Another text, referring to a female "ecstatic," suggests a sequence of messages: "O Zimri-Lim, do not go on a campaign. Stay in Mari and I will continue to answer."

The message is usually communicated to a royal official, but in two cases a temple administrator *(šangû),* who is not a cultic priest, serves as intermediary with the royal official. The *šangû* presumably had some jurisdiction over such temple activity. One letter even reports that a *šangû* himself had a revelatory dream.

A number of the oracles are public, even in the presence of the assembly of the elders. The connection of the oracles with times of political and personal (royal) crisis is even clearer with the publication of the additional texts. Also, the initiatives that the prophets can take—especially the "official" speakers—are striking.

d. The Content of the Oracles. Because of the nature of the Mari archives, the oracles deal almost exclusively with the king's affairs. Commonly the prophet communicates a message from a deity speaking in the first person, often referring to being "sent" by the deity. The message may begin with a formula such as "thus says [the deity X]." The content is generally an assurance to the king or a warning to the king of dangers (and an assurance of divine assistance); but a number of messages deviate from this pattern.

A unique letter from an *āpilu* contains cultic requests from several deities and promises support for the king. In other cases the king is chided for not meeting the cultic expectations of the deity—failing to provide "pure water" or neglecting the funerary offering for a predecessor or ancestor. More serious charges come from Addu of Aleppo and Addu of Kallassu: the king, who owes his throne to the deity, has been inattentive in offerings and in recognition of the deity's claims—what Addu has given, Addu can take away. Moreover, the deity does not speak in terms of self-interest, for the king has a fundamental obligation to deal justly in his realm with all who appeal to him. An obedient king will be richly rewarded (Lafont 1984).

At least one oracle is directed to a different audience. The citizens of Terqa are warned through a young man's dream revelation from Dagan that they should not (re)build a certain house (temple?).

There is some sense of community among the "prophets." The proverb "Under the straw, water flows" is now attested in two messages by a *qam(m)ātum* and one by an "ecstatic." The oracles center on the king's person and his political affairs, but include some rather personal elements, such as the notice to the king that his newly born(?) daughter has died, just as predicted by an "ecstatic" while in a trance state. Cultic requests are prominent. A deity advises the king, through a woman (as summarized; title perhaps lost), that "I have been safeguarding you since your youth; and I have continually led you in good ways," so send me what I ask for.

e. The Status of the Oracles. The marginal character of these prophetic revelations is underscored by the frequency with which the king's correspondents either report on means of confirmation which they employed, including technical divination, or encourage the king to examine the matter by means of technical divination. Several letters specify that a portion of the prophet's hair and a piece from the fringe of the prophet's garment are being sent on to the king. These items surely were intended for use in a confirmation process involving technical divination, as confirmed by a contemporary text from Karana (Dalley, Walker, and Hawkins 1976: 64–65, pl. 19).

The new texts show the prophets as rather assertive at times; together with administrative texts, new texts indicate a significant personal status for the titled prophets. Yet the prophets continue to be one channel of divine communication among others, and their messages continue to be sent on either with supportive statements or with the recommendation to seek a means for confirmation.

3. Ishchali (East Tigris). A number of OB texts from Babylonia proper evidence the title *muḫḫûm/muḫḫūtum*, at times associated with specific deities, although there is no explicit indication of oracular activity. Recently published texts from Ishchali, however, may indicate prophetic practice. Two letters are addressed directly to the king by the goddess Kititum, a manifestation of Ishtar. The best-preserved letter contains a message with similarities to some of the Mari prophecies (Ellis 1987). Unfortunately, the means of transmission are not indicated. The text may report a message from an individual intermediary, as at Mari, or a message obtained in response to a technical divination process.

4. Assyria. Especially characteristic of the reigns of Esarhaddon (680–669 B.C.) and Ashurbanipal (668–627 B.C.) is their special interest in a wide variety of modes of communication with the divine powers, including prophetic-type speakers. Esarhaddon adjures vassals not to conceal anything they hear that is derogatory to the crown prince, including any word from "a proclaimer" *(raggimu)*, "an ecstatic" *(maḫḫû)*, or "a dream interpreter." The existence of prophetic revelations in particular may reflect the influence of Aramean culture (Tadmor 1982: 458), though none of the titles is Aramean in origin. Unlike the Mari texts, the NA texts do not point to a marginal status for the prophetic speakers. Again, the focus of activity is the royal court. Many of the prophets, at least, seem to be attached to the court.

Many of the texts, some of which have been known for almost a century, present special linguistic problems and have been inadequately published. Careful study must await new publication of these important texts.

a. Prophets with Titles. (1) *Maḫḫû/maḫḫūtu*, "ecstatic." This title, in this spelling, is known from the OAkk period on, and as a variant of Mari *muḫḫû/muḫḫūtu* (above) provides the only continuity with the older titles. Esarhaddon and Ashurbanipal make frequent reference to messages from "ecstatics." Though these messages are at times associated with dreams sent by Ishtar, no verbatim messages are reported. The "ecstatic," predominantly male in the NA period, has a role in some rituals. The character of the oracular activity of "ecstatics" remains basically unknown.

(2) *Raggimu/raggimtu*, "proclaimer." This title, which also occurs as a divine epithet, is first attested in a MA text—without specification of function. In the 7th century B.C. the "proclaimer" delivers prophetic messages—one text contains two series of three oracles each addressed to Esarhaddon, one series from Asshur, and one from Ishtar; another contains an oracle from Ninlil/Mullissu for Ashurbanipal (Strong 1894). Also, the "proclaimer" plays a role, whether by agreement or by presumption, in connection with the substitute king ritual. Another reference suggests that "proclaimers" might be active as a group. Presumably the "proclaimer" had status within the cult, though there is no specific information concerning this.

(3) *Šabrû*, "revealer." One lexical text identifies this title with that of the "proclaimer." To be separated from the homonym referring to an administrative officer, this title derives from Akk *barû*, "to see." The "revealer" has a message dream—apparently through incubation—from Ishtar and reports it to Ashurbanipal. The LÚ.KAL, who has a message dream from Sin intended for Ashurbanipal, closely parallels the "revealer" (*ANET,* 606; Oppenheim 1956: 249–50).

(4) *Šēlūtu*, "(female) votary." Literally "someone sent up (for a deity)," this title identifies one of the speakers in a long collection of individual oracles for Esarhaddon (*ANET,* 605), a woman presumably devoted by the king to the deity. The title is known from contemporary contracts recording dedications to Ninlil/Mullissu. As a "votary" given by the queen, one contract notes, no creditor or legal adversary can seize her, though she is married.

b. Prophets without Titles. Two major collections of individual oracles for Esarhaddon are identified as being from the mouth of so-and-so, from such and such a city—apart from the one oracle from a "votary." One speaker even appears in both collections (and, for that matter, uses some identical terminology, otherwise unknown). The absence of a title for all speakers but one in these two collections suggests the lack of an official position in the cult. These speakers, male and female in roughly equal proportion, are especially—but not exclusively—associated with Ishtar of Arbela.

c. The Context of the Oracles. Virtually all of the oracles can fit within the pattern indicated in the fullest record of the context of an oracle. A crisis situation—minor or major—prompts a complaint to or an inquiry of a deity, who responds with a message of reassurance. Communication of the oracle to the king (or queen mother) may be oral or written down, deposited in the temple, and presented to the king in connection with ritual acts. The fullest report says, "Now these rebels have incited against you, they have made you come out, they have surrounded you. You (Esarhaddon) opened your mouth. Now I, Ashur, have heard your distress cry. From the gate of heaven I soar down(?). . . . I will surely have fire consume them. . . . I slaughtered your enemies. I filled the river with their blood. Let them see, let them praise me, for I am Ashur, lord of the gods. This is the greeting which is (placed?) before the (divine) statue. This is the sworn tablet of Ashur. It comes in before the king upon a . . . They sprinkle special oil, they make sacrifices, the incense burns, (and) they read out (the tablet) before the king" (Strong 1894: 637–39). At times the oracle is clearly received in a temple, sometimes specifically associated with sacrifices. On another occasion the setting is a political assembly.

One of the oracles seems to concern the occasion of a treaty ceremony: "Should you (pl.) go to your cities and your districts, eat food and forget these oaths, (then) when you drink from this water you will remember me (Ishtar) and keep this sworn agreement which I made concerning (your obligations to) Esarhaddon" (Strong 1894: 639–41).

Some of the oracles seem to be unsolicited, but there are many indications of a response to an inquiry. Those oracles by "proclaimers" (female) in connection with the substitute king ritual may reflect divine initiative. There is no reference to the speaker's being "sent" with the message, but a commissioning is at times implied.

d. The Content of the Oracles. The oracles are typically oracles of assurance for the political and succession concerns of the king, communicated directly, as it were, from the deity. "Fear not" is a common phrase, as in other ANE oracles of assurance. The oracles also emphasize the deity's power and reliability. The speakers rarely admonish the king; and if so, they use a mild form, such as saying that former utterances by the deity have been ignored.

The principal association of the prophets is with Ishtar or Arbela (and allied deities), though a number of other deities provide oracles.

e. The Status of the Oracles. The oracles are reported individually to the king, noted in the official annals, and collected into cumulative records. Sometimes the oracles are grouped by the deity involved. One collection appears to be oracles—perhaps even from two different deities—from a particular "proclaimer," but the concluding section is poorly preserved. There is also some evidence for the copying and transmission of oracle collections.

The (occasional) formality of the process of presentation and the attention to preservation point to the normalization of prophetic communication in the circles of Esarhaddon and Ashurbanipal.

D. Egypt

The problem of definition is especially well illustrated by the Egyptian materials. "The Admonitions of Ipu-wer," a critique of the sociopolitical order, is labeled by some as prophetic in a biblical sense. Texts such as "The Prophecy of Neferti" are cast as foretelling a future deliverance for a country in a time of trouble, though written *ex eventu.* This sequence has been taken as a forerunner to the biblical prophets and their sense of a time of crisis that will give way to a messianic age. But these texts illustrate more a relationship with wisdom, drawing on the past to anticipate the future; Neferti is a lector priest and a "wise man of the East," not a charismatic prophet. A major order of priests, the *ḥmw nṯr* (literally, "servants of god"), were described by Hellenistic Greek commentators with the term *prophētēs* because of their role in reporting oracles. Accordingly, the scholarly literature abounds with references to these priests under the rendering prophets—even in the hierarchy of the "first prophet" (high priest) through "fourth prophet" of Amun in Karnak. In actuality there is very little known from Egypt that illustrates the prophet as an inspired speaker of divine oracles. Plutarch reports that Pamyle—foster parent of Osiris—heard a voice from the temple of Zeus (Amun) instructing Pamyle to announce that Osiris had been born (Ray 1981: 174). Generally, however, Egyptian oracles result from a form of manipulate divination, such as movements of a deity during a public procession.

Bibliography

Anbar, M. 1976. Trois documents de la collection Leo Perutz. *IOS* 6: 59–63.

Arnaud, D. 1986. *Recherches au pays d'Aštata. Emar VI.3. Textes sumériens et accadiens. Texte.* Paris.

Charpin, D., and Durand, J.-M. 1985. La prise du pouvoir par Zimri-Lim. *MARI* 4: 293–343.

Charpin, D.; Joannes, F.; Lackenbacher, S.; and Lafont, B. 1988. *Archives epistolaires de Mari I/2.* ARM 26. Paris.

Dalley, S.; Walker, C. B. F.; and Hawkins, J. D. 1976. *The Old Babylonian Tablets from Tell al Rimah.* London.

Durand, J.-M. 1988. *Archives epistolaires de Mari I/1.* ARM 26. Paris.

Ellis, M. de J. 1987. The Goddess Kititum Speaks to King Ibalpiel: Oracle Texts from Ishchali. *MARI* 5: 235–66.

Grayson, A. K. 1975. *Babylonian Historical-Literary Texts.* Toronto.

Gurney, O. R. 1981. The Babylonians and Hittites. Pp. 142–73 in *Oracles and Divination.* ed. M. Loewe and C. Blacker. Boulder, CO.

Hallo, W. W. 1966. Akkadian Apocalypses. *IEJ* 16: 231–42.

Herrmann, S. 1963. Prophetie in Israel and Ägypten: Recht und Grenze eines Vergleichs. Pp. 47–65 in *Congress Volume, Bonn, 1962.* VTS 9. Leiden.

Huffmon, H. B. 1970. Prophecy in the Mari Letters. *BAR* 3: 199–224.

Hunger, H., and Kaufman, S. A. 1975. A New Akkadian Prophecy Text. *JAOS* 95: 71–75.

Kammenhuber, A. 1976. *Orakelpraxis, Träume und Vorzeichenschau bei den Hethitern.* Heidelberg.

Kaufman, S. A. 1977. Prediction, Prophecy, and Apocalypse in the Light of New Akkadian Texts. *PWCJS* 6/1: 221–28.

Lafont, B. 1984. La roi de Mari et les prophètes du dieu Adad. *RA* 78: 7–18.

Lebrun, R. 1980. *Hymnes et prières hittites.* Louvain-la-Neuve.

Malamat, A. 1980. A Mari Prophecy and Nathan's Dynastic Oracle. Pp. 68–82 in *Prophecy: Essays Presented to Georg Fohrer,* ed. J. A. Emerton. BZAW 150. Berlin.

———. 1987. A Forerunner of Biblical Prophecy: The Mari Documents. *AIR,* 33–52.

Noort, E. 1977. *Untersuchungen zum Gottesbescheid in Mari.* AOAT 202. Kevelaer.

Oppenheim, A. L. 1956. *The Interpretation of Dreams in the Ancient Near East. TAPhS* 46/3. Philadelphia.

Ray, J. D. 1981. Ancient Egypt. Pp. 174–90 in *Oracles and Divination,* ed. M. Loewe and C. Blacker. Boulder, CO.

Sasson, J. 1983. Mari Dreams. *JAOS* 103: 283–93.
Schmitt, A. 1982. *Prophetischer Gottesbescheid in Mari und Israel.* BWANT 114. Stuttgart.
Selms, A. van. 1971. CTA 32: A Prophetic Liturgy. *UF* 3: 235–48.
Strong, S. A. 1894. On Some Oracles to Esarhaddon and Ašurbanipal. *Beiträge zur Assyriologie* 2: 627–45.
Tadmor, H. 1982. The Aramaization of Assyria: Aspects of Western Impact. Vol. 2., pp. 449–70 in *Mesopotamien und Seine Nachbarn,* ed. H.-J. Nissen and J. Renger. Berlin.
Weippert, H.; Seybold, K.; and Weippert, M. 1985. *Beiträge zur prophetischen Bildsprache in Israel und Assyrien.* OBO 64. Freiburg and Göttingen.
Weippert, M. 1981. Assyrische Prophetien der Zeit Asarhaddons und Assurbanipals. Pp. 71–113 in *Assyrian Royal Inscriptions: New Horizons,* ed. F. M. Fales, Rome.

H. B. HUFFMON

PREEXILIC HEBREW PROPHECY

A. Vocabulary for Prophets
B. General Ideas and Description of Prophets
C. Prophets in the Biblical Books
  1. Narrative Books: Torah
  2. Narrative Books: Former Prophets
  3. Prophetic Anthologies: Latter Prophets
D. Language of the Prophets
E. Psychological Considerations
F. Themes of the Preexilic Prophets
  1. God
  2. Israel
  3. The Relation between God and Israel
  4. The Future
G. The Prophets' Relation to the Institutions of Israel
  1. Monarchy
  2. Cultus
  3. Wisdom
H. Reception of the Prophets
I. The Study of the Prophets

A. Vocabulary for Prophets

The word "prophet" most frequently translates the Heb word *nābîʾ*. This word is probably not of Hebrew origin; the Akk *nabītu* seems the closest cognate, although the title *nabû,* "diviner" (?), is now attested at Mari. This probable loanword in Hebrew suggests that prophecy in Israel was not a phenomenon unrelated to ideas and practices outside Israel. Israelite prophecy can rather be understood as a concept and an activity that Israel shared with other cultures and peoples among whom the Israelites lived and experienced God.

Other words are also used by the biblical tradition to describe persons who acted in the way that Israel saw its prophets behave. One passage claims that in former times the prophet *(nābîʾ)* was known as a seer *(rōʾeh)* (1 Sam 9:9). Two other terms also are occasionally used for the role: man of God *(ʾîš [hā]ʾĕlōhîm)* and visionary *(ḥōzeh).*

B. General Ideas and Description of Prophets

There seems to have been no standard prerequisite for a person to become a prophet in Israel. Divine inspiration was what made a person a prophet, and what caused the prophet to speak out, and what made others listen to the prophet as a legitimate spokesperson for the divine. For the early period, a favored conception is that "the spirit of the Lord" speaks through the individual (e.g., 1 Sam 10:10; 1 Kgs 22:24). Later terminology preferred "the word of the Lord came to" the person (e.g., Jer 1:2, 4; Ezek 1:3). The general idea remains: the prophet is the one who can speak in the name of God.

Prophets came from all walks of life. Indeed, some seem to have had a wide variety of experience and a deep acquaintance with various aspects of life and work in Israel. They claim or are given backgrounds as varied as sheepherder, priest, agriculturalist, scribe. They spoke where and when they thought they would be effective. They spoke frequently, no doubt, in places where people most readily gathered—the marketplace, the temple, the city gates (cf. Jer 7:2). They may have spoken less formally in other places as well.

A distinction has sometimes been made that, for some interpreters, marks a dramatic development in the history of Israelite prophecy. Many of the early prophets speak only to individuals, especially kings or other officials, while other, later prophets address large groups of people—rhetorically, the whole nation or an entire city. No doubt this variation depends on who the prophet thinks is the appropriate recipient of a particular utterance, whether that message is a threat or something else.

C. Prophets in the Biblical Books

1. Narrative Books: Torah. Some biblical personages of the early periods are called prophets long before prophecy in the usual biblical sense appears in ancient Israel. Thus, Torah contains no prophets in the technical sense of the term, even though the term is given to some individuals anachronistically.

The first four books of the Bible do not offer the reader any figure that resembles a prophet such as Isaiah. Although Abraham is identified as a prophet by the source usually called E, Abraham does not function as the other prophets do. He does not address people in the name of God. In Exodus, Aaron, the brother of Moses, will act as a "prophet" in relation to Moses (Exod 7:1). But he never actually says "Thus says the Lord." Miriam, the sister of Moses, gets the title "prophetess," but she performs actions that exhibit a character that is more cultic than prophetic (Exod 15:20; Num 12:1–15). A passage deals with competition among those who would claim exclusive right to prophetic activity (Num 11:26–30), and Num 12:6 mentions the possibility of a prophet in Israel whose vision of and insight into the divine would be less than Moses'.

Deuteronomy (a purported address of Moses within the narrative) presupposes the existence of prophets in an institutional setting. Grounds are given for withholding belief in a given prophet, i.e., if the prophet tries to lead people away from Yahweh (Deut 13:2–6—Eng 13: 1–5) and if what the prophet says does not come true (Deut 18:20–22). The text must have originated in a time when people wanted to hear the word of God but were troubled by the existence of numerous prophets, some of whom were in reality not sent from God. Moreover, it is Deuteronomy that identifies Moses as the great prophet sent from God, the model of one who is to come (Deut 18:15–19; 34:10).

Torah, then, gives the terms "prophet" and "prophetess" to individuals in the first four books by retrojection. The second section of the Hebrew canon, "Prophets," is divided into the Former Prophets and the Latter Prophets. The Former Prophets are the narrative books (Joshua through Kings) that follow the outlook of Deuteronomy (together called by modern scholars the Deuteronomistic History). The Latter Prophets comprise four books: Isaiah, Jeremiah, Ezekiel, and the book of the Twelve.

2. Narrative Books: Former Prophets. The first book of the Former Prophets (Joshua) does not use the term *nābîʾ*, but the second book (Judges) uses the feminine form, *nĕbîʾâ*. Deborah is called "prophetess" once in Judg 4:4. Just how the writer means the word in that setting is somewhat unclear. In that scene her work is described as that of a judge or ruler. In chap. 5, however, she is implored to "utter a song" (Judg 5:12).

Some scholars stress that Samuel is the beginning of the prophetic development in ancient Israel (Albright). The figure of Samuel certainly does present a prophetic facet of his being. He speaks in the name of God to oppose the idea of monarchy (1 Sam 8:7, 10) and then to proclaim Saul the divinely chosen king (1 Sam 10:24). But that figure also has several other facets as well. He is judge, priest, and leader of the group called "the sons of the prophets."

Nathan was a court prophet of David. He appears in the narrative only after David takes the city of Jerusalem (2 Sam 5:9). He may have been a native of this city, and hence have some non-Israelite prophetic heritage. Through him David is promised an eternal dynasty (2 Sam 7:13).

The prophetic groups, "the sons of the prophets," led lives of asceticism and probably partial seclusion. They function somewhat as intermediaries with the divine, and seem to use physical means, as the slashing of oneself and the chanting of songs, to produce an ecstatic trance (1 Kgs 20:35). They were sought out by individuals in special need.

Also connected with the sons of the prophets are the memorable figures of Elijah and Elisha. Elijah is called, on the one hand, to challenge the infidelity of the people and, on the other hand, to foment revolution both within and outside Israel (1 Kgs 19:15–16). Elisha, his successor, functions as a dramatic miracle worker (2 Kings 4–7).

The depictions of prophets within the Deuteronomistic History naturally are constructed according to the designs and purposes of the writers and for their purposes. Prophets in the narrative function in specific roles. They give legitimacy to a new dynasty (e.g., Nathan, 2 Sam 7:12; Elijah, 1 Kgs 19:16; and Ahijah, 1 Kgs 11:31). Moreover, they are sent successively by God to warn the people. Although for the Deuteronomists the kings are, in a special way, responsible for the infidelity of the people, nevertheless, the people themselves should heed the call of the prophets to repent. The disaster is announced, and the call is made, but there is no heeding. The prophets preach repentance in vain, and the two kingdoms fall.

This idea that the prophet's basic role is to preach repentance is a conception that often influences the interpretation of prophecy in general. Just how much this understanding of prophecy as the preaching of repentance should apply to the classical prophets has been a topic of debate.

Important too for the Deuteronomistic History is the efficacy of the predictions that prophets make in the name of God. Explicit emphasis on prediction of specific events and the fulfillment of those predictions recurs frequently in these books. On the general point of the future, the anthologies of prophetic sayings agree with these narrative books.

3. Prophetic Anthologies: Latter Prophets. The Hebrew canon places the anthologies of the prophets immediately after this extended narrative about the monarchy in Israel. The Latter Prophets are called "latter" simply because they are placed after the Former Prophets (the Deuteronomistic History). Other terms used for these books (and the prophets after whom they are named) are the "classical" or "canonical" prophets, and even, inappropriately, the "writing" prophets. The term "writing" is inappropriate because the preexilic prophets themselves did not write down the words they spoke. Prophets are speakers. (Perhaps Second Isaiah, in the Exile, is the prophet who began to use the written word as a prophetic medium.)

Because the preexilic prophets did not commit to writing what they had to say, the books of these prophets come to the reader today from many hands. It could have been that the first written collection of a prophet's words was made during the prophet's lifetime, but that is not the emphasis or the claim of the books themselves. Perhaps the death of the prophet was the stimulus for the first collections to be made (with the exception of Jer 36:2, 32). Then the process of editing, clarification, explanation, and expansion began. The process of the formation of the prophetic books was a long and complicated one. Much of that process remains unclear, even after much analysis.

In the most frequent terminology, the sequence of classical prophets begins with Amos, followed soon by Hosea, both of whom spoke in the northern kingdom in the 8th century. They are succeeded (with some overlap) by Micah and Isaiah, who both preached in Judah in the same century. The late 7th century claims Zephaniah, Jeremiah, Nahum, Habakkuk, and Ezekiel.

D. Language of the Prophets

The language of the prophets is probably what most strikes a reader today. They spoke in poetry, and some of the poetry that the prophets created is virtually unmatched in world literature. On the other hand, some of the sayings are cryptic, or crabbed, or too tied to a particular setting for them to offer a clear meaning today. But sometimes even these passages contain striking images that can haunt the reader.

The prophets understand themselves to be inspired by God and to speak the word of God. The most common evidence of this conviction is the ever recurring "Thus says the Lord." This kind of messenger formula is found elsewhere in the ancient Near East on the lips of an emissary from one monarch to the court of another. This form and formula are examples in which the language that the prophets use often contained oral forms or speech patterns from daily or routine life.

There are abundant examples of other borrowings from

varied kinds of activities with specific speech patterns. The judge's court is one area which offered many such forms that prophets used to convey their own message: the summons of the judge, the charge of the prosecutor, the claim of the defendant, or the lament of those who were denied justice. Songs and parables were also imitated by various prophets. Even the funeral service seems to have contributed a frequent form used by the prophets, the "Woe" oracle. It is sometimes claimed that no area of Israelite life was untouched by this borrowing of forms that appear in the prophetic books.

The preexilic prophets who preach a coming catastrophe sometimes can be found using a form, or parts of it, that has become standard in many analyses of prophetic speech, the "reproach and threat." The ideal form is "Because you have done this evil, therefore, thus says the Lord, disaster will come upon you." One finds many other terms to describe the two parts of the form: "invective," "reason," "accusation" for the "reproach," and "judgment," "sentence," "verdict" for the "threat." The analysis of this form shows that, regardless of the way in which the prophet receives the word of God, the prophet does contribute personal reflections and reasoning, which the prophet speaks before giving the divine decision of judgment.

E. Psychological Considerations

The actual state of a prophet when receiving the divine word has been the subject of much investigation and debate. Many scholars have found helpful comparisons with somewhat comparable phenomena from various other societies. Indeed, the choice of the society and the kind of comparison one makes will influence the outcome. Comparisons with the mystics of various traditions (Lindblom 1962), with the visionaries among the Native Americans (Overholt 1989), with intermediaries, ecstatic or possessed, of various cultures (Wilson 1980), and with many others have been made and have also been critiqued. All of these studies shed some light on the prophetic experience, but the reader is left to decide which are most appropriate and satisfying.

One remarkable thing is clear regarding the language and psychology of the prophets. The prophets share in the long literary tradition of Canaan, for the poetry that the prophets speak borrows much from the literary tradition found also in the Ugaritic poetry of half a millennium before the biblical prophets and only a few hundred miles to the north.

Not only did the Israelite prophets speak their words in the form of poetic parallelism, but they also used the same kind of word pairs that their Ugaritic predecessors had used. It is not clear how much a prophet would simply have "picked up" this tradition or how much the prophet actively set out to acquire it. The reality of the participation in the tradition is clear. A fairly recent proposal suggests that the poetry in the prophetic books is primary and the religious interpretation of it secondary (Auld 1980).

F. Themes of the Preexilic Prophets

1. God. The God whom the preexilic prophets experience is a God who demands certain actions from human beings. The 8th-century prophets appear with a disturbing message: Israel has not lived up to its calling. The prophets see basic moral laws broken or ignored. The prophets proclaim that the God who stands behind those laws will come to uphold those demands.

The first demand of the prophets was that the people worship only Yahweh. Although the preexilic prophets did not make theoretical statements about the existence or (non)existence of other gods, they did require the Israelites to worship only the God of Israel. The reality of God demands that Israel worship Yahweh. Moreover, the right worship of God requires of a person the right treatment of one's fellow human beings. The prophets do not tolerate worship of God that is not linked to proper behavior toward one's neighbor.

Rarely do the prophets identify the basis of God's claim of sole worship and just treatment of one's neighbor. Whether it was the election and protection of Israel or, as some say, a universal law within God's creation that the prophets relied on for their evaluations, God does demand proper actions. The universality of the moral claim is almost surprising. God judges Israel severely, but the prophets also view God as judging other nations as well (Amos 1–2). The moral sovereignty of God parallels the sovereign majesty of God. All humanity stands judged before God.

God has, however, revealed a special way of life to Israel. And that revelation must not be ignored. It is clear that God's position cannot be compromised. Although the prophets make no explicit claim that God was revealed to Israel, a moral revelation is the implicit presupposition in much of what the prophets said (Amos 3:7). The prophets do claim that God reveals the divine plans to the prophets. And the prophets invoke the traditions that were understood to have been revealed in the past about how humans are to behave.

In addition to the demands that God puts on human beings, the prophets also point to the love that God has for humanity and for Israel in particular. God's love extends to humans even in the face of unfaithfulness and of backsliding. The images that the prophets use for the love of God are themselves revealing. Parent, teacher, healer, counselor—these are some of the roles that the prophets give to God, roles that reveal the concern and passion God has for people.

A facile contrast is sometimes made between God's love and divine justice (often erroneously restricting the former to the NT and the latter to the OT). One might better say that God's justice is responsive, that is, that God's justice is an act of love rather than of vengeance. When things begin to get out of hand, when people's negligence goes so far that there is no expectation that things will improve, then God must step in to take action. God's delay in bringing the results of infidelity on the people cannot be extended indefinitely. The preexilic prophets are distinctive in speaking about a coming disaster for Israel, but there are also statements of God's regret about this future. For the prophets God could no longer delay the end.

One can ask whether the prophets took their own images for God in a literal sense. When they spoke of God as an unmoved judge, as a raging parent, as a plotting monarch, did the prophets think that God was completely and adequately represented by these images? We cannot know. But the Bible reader of today must realize the danger of taking literally these descriptions of the indescribable. The prophets used whatever images they thought appropriate for their society. Their statements remain part of the theology of 8th- and 7th-century Israel.

2. Israel. The unfaithfulness of the people is what struck and disturbed the classical prophets. The time of infidelity in which the prophets lived seems to some readers to be an expected development in Israel's history. The rise and history of prophecy in Israel virtually coincide with the history of the monarchy. It was the monarchy that allowed, perhaps encouraged, the so-called Canaanization of Israelite culture, both socially and religiously. The development of social and economic ranks or classes in Israel led to the oppression of the poor and the needy. The rich grew more wealthy, profiting from the labors and losses of the lower classes. The prophets decry this deterioration of Israel's soul.

The prophets feel the urge and conviction to speak out against this situation. When the prophets charge their audience with this infidelity, their speech is quite varied. They addressed various people on different occasions, so one expects variety in their collected sayings. The classical prophets usually addressed their words to people at large. It is noteworthy that they sometimes address or speak of the people in various linguistic forms. Sometimes they speak of the people in the grammatical form one would most expect, masculine plural. But Israel is also addressed as masculine singular. (Israel was the alternate name of the ancestor Jacob; and the name retained its masculine gender, not just because Jacob was male, but also because the names of people are masculine in biblical Hebrew.) Recent studies claim that the addressee or subject in the feminine singular is not Israel as such, but rather a city. When the people are addressed in the imagery proper to cities, images occur such as mother, wife, virgin, widow, sister, and harlot. When Israel as a people is addressed, those feminine images do not occur.

The message of the prophets varied also according to the time and the place of the speech, and the people involved. Preexilic prophecy can generally be depicted as prophecy of judgment. The prophets are the conscience of Israel, alerting it to the injustice and infidelity that each of the prophets sees.

On both accounts, the rights of God and the rights of their fellow human beings, Israel has to be judged as having failed in the eyes of God. Israel is seen by the preexilic prophets as unfaithful to the God who called them.

3. The Relation between God and Israel. As already stated, the preexilic prophets for the most part saw a deterioration in the relation between God and Israel. Israel no longer keeps the original faith they had in their God. (Alternatively, Ezekiel believes that Israel was wrong-headed from the start.) The relationship is coming to an end. The very end was in sight for some of the prophets. No more can God put up with the careless and faithless behavior of the people.

There is variation in the images that the prophets use for the end of this relationship. Amos speaks quite directly: "the end has come upon my people Israel" (Amos 8:2). Other images for the relation are used. God is called the parent of Israel (Hos 11:1), the shepherd (Ezek 34:1), the king (Isa 6:5). When the prophets speak of the relation between God and Jerusalem (and Samaria), the image is marital, and the act of separation is divorce (Jer 3:2; Ezek 16:8; Hos 2:4—Eng 2:2).

One image for the relation between God and Israel that has caused continued controversy regarding its age is the metaphor of covenant. This image, taken from the political realm, has been claimed by some scholars as the major and defining image for the God-human relation in ancient Israel. Other scholars point out that the 8th-century prophets do not employ it. They claim that it is an image that gained popularity in later times. One must admit that covenant is sometimes lost in the vast sweep of images that the prophets use.

Whatever the image used, the preexilic prophets say that there is something gone wrong with the relationship. Israel has become a wayward son, a sinful people, a man who needs to flee, a society that is corrupted. Some later prophetic writers speak of the broken covenant, the field of dry bones, the relationship that cannot endure.

Along with all the images of punishment and finality, there are some statements of God's enduring love and of the chance that God might not carry out the threat. There are even images of hope and restoration. The son will be taken back, the sins will be forgiven, the man can stop running, the society will be cleansed. Are these too from the same prophets? This question, of course, deals with the formation of the prophetic books.

4. The Future. Critical scholars ask the question whether to understand the promises that the books of the preexilic prophets contain as actually coming from those prophets or from later speakers and writers. The question that is inevitable for some critical thinkers is whether promises of restoration actually belong side by side with threats. Can the same person see total disaster coming and see beyond it a bright future?

Amos says that the end has come for Israel, the capital is virtually fallen. Jeremiah is just as definitive about the end of his city and the hopelessness of the situation. Can these men turn around and predict a time of fulfillment for their audience?

Often scholars point out that the prophetic word differs from day to day and from time to time. Indeed, times do change the message. For example, Isaiah may have held the idea of Zion's inviolability; but Jeremiah, about a century later, flatly contradicts the concept. For some scholars, the promises and hopes were given in the time of the prophet for a different generation, and these sayings were preserved for them and understood only later.

Around the turn of the 20th century, there was a proposal that the alternation of woe and weal, of threat and promise, was part of the standard way of prophetic speech (Gressmann 1905). Certain scholars, especially those who stressed the oral transmission of the prophetic sayings, repeated this solution to the phenomenon of seeming contradictions.

For many scholars, newness is the salient reality of the prophetic vision. The prophets see that Israel has reached a new stage in its relation to God. A turning point, a critical one, is near at hand. The way that Israel had lived to the time of the prophet has led to a particular crisis. For the most part, the preexilic prophets focus more on the immediate problems and the immediate future that Israel's infidelity would bring on. The hope that lay beyond that crisis has to be argued very carefully and forcefully to be persuasive.

G. The Prophets' Relation to the Institutions of Israel

1. Monarchy. Prophecy throughout the ANE was often connected with the kings and rulers. In Israel, the classical period of prophecy coincides with the time of the monarchy. There are court prophets in Israel at the very beginning of the monarchy, that is, with Saul and David. And after the secession of the North, one finds prophets of the kings of the independent kingdoms (1 Kgs 22:8; cf. 2 Kgs 20:1). Although prophecy continues after the demise of the active monarchy, nevertheless, the last large book of one prophet, namely Ezekiel, is named from a prophet who had lived under kings in Jerusalem.

The view of the monarchy that individual prophets took was, no doubt, influenced by a wide variety of things, many of which we cannot know. In general, however, Amos, Hosea, and Micah all take a dim view of the monarchy. Hosea even says that kingship was not something from God (Hos 8:4). Isaiah, the only 8th-century prophet who was a native of Jerusalem, does not speak against the kings. Indeed, it may be Isaiah, in his book, who depicts a bright future under a majestic monarch (Isa 9:5–6—Eng 9:6–7; 11:1–9). The editors of the book of Amos speak of the restored tent of David (Amos 9:11).

In both Isaiah and Jeremiah, there are passages that suggest that these prophets were advisers to the kings in their times (Isa 7:1–17; Jer 21:10; 37:16–21). To see such passages as actual records of historical facts is, to the critical reader, not the most obvious way to read these passages. Actually in both cases these prophets oppose the king or his plans. By and large the prophets who worked for the kings of Israel and Judah were not the prophets whose words survive in our prophetic books.

Nevertheless, the prophetic tradition one finds in the edited books of the Bible continues to use the imagery of the book of Isaiah. The future king is part of the developing hope for the future. The Heb word *mašiaḥ* (Eng "Messiah") is never used for the future king. (The word is used for the reigning king and others who are actually anointed.) Nevertheless, the monarchy clearly furnishes ideas that messianic expectation in later times expanded and developed.

2. Cultus. There are passages in the preexilic prophets which suggest to some readers that the prophets advocated a religion that did away with the traditional religious practice, specifically Israel's festivals, sacrifices, and offerings. The prophets speak about the seeking of God in purity of heart. The prophets clearly have God say that none of what the people offer is pleasing or required (Amos 5:21–23; Isa 1:12–15). Indeed, 19th-century scholarship understood these statements as a total rejection of the sacrificial system and of any material things involved in worship.

The immediate response to this view would have to be that in the ancient world and in Israel in particular, no person could conceive of worship without external expression, that is, without the rituals and actions that traditionally accompany the worship of a community or that of an individual. No one, especially before the Exile, could say that God did not require the worship in the temple as that worship had been offered from Solomon on.

Many of the charges that the prophets in their times raise against the cultus denounce worship that has been influenced by Canaanite practice and belief. The Canaanite "high places" were things that the reforming kings found virtually indestructible. The remnants of foreign worship survive even the Exile. These popular forms of infidelity, both in worship and in unjust social practices, were the object of the prophets' indignation.

The prophets, when they have a moment of hope, look forward to a purified cultus, one which truly manifests a commitment and a continued faithfulness to the God who called Israel. The prophets condemn the worship offered by certain individuals and groups only because it is the worship of other gods and the worship of the Lord without relation to one's treatment of one's fellow human beings.

Occasional words of the prophets are directed against the priests (e.g., Hos 4:4–10). They charge the priests with negligence and insincerity (Ezek 22:26). The prophets suggest that the priests are leading the people astray, away from God, rather than toward God (Mic 3:11). This criticism of the cultic personnel may be a different route to critiquing the cultus itself. But here again the words of the prophets are directed toward those priests who did stray from the path of priestly devotion and purity of life.

Moreover, these attacks on the priests are often accompanied by critiques of "the prophets." The prophets describe a society they see as corrupt, and they speak out against all forms of injustice and infidelity. The classical prophets often speak of priests and prophets in the same breath. The famous passage in Jer 18:18 speaks of the priest, the wise, and the prophet. All had their own roles to play in the society; all had their burdens to bear if the society failed.

3. Wisdom. In the past few decades, a most interesting development in the study of the prophets has been a focus on the relation of the prophets to the realm of wisdom. Israel's search for wisdom and the writing of its Wisdom Literature may have begun as early as the time of Solomon. If this is the case, prophecy and wisdom are parallel phenomena for the monarchic period. It would be unlikely if these parallel phenomena would not have some interrelation and interaction.

Isa 5:19–24 lashes out against those who have a pretended wisdom. Later, Isa 30:1–5 attacks those who plan things without consulting the wisdom of God. Isaiah seems to be attacking those whose profession is to treat and apply the traditional political wisdom.

There are indeed other passages in the prophets which manifest a more positive relationship. One finds some sayings that suggest a real wisdom background or origin (Isa 14:24–27; Jer 19:7–15). Although the prophets sometimes do seem to speak against the professional class of the wise, nevertheless, they share in their excellent use of language, an ability that normally requires training and practice. Often the same vocabulary is shared by the two groups.

Some scholars have proposed that the basis for the prophets' judgment against unjust practices was the teaching of the wise men, formulated and passed on from earlier generations. On the other hand, there is a proposal that there was no class of "the wise" in Israel. The people referred to by that term were simply the educated, the intellectually alert individuals. If this claim is true, the prophet's training would have been from and with such a group of educated people.

The difference between the wise man and the prophet remains, of course: the prophets speak the word of God, and wise men pass on the word they have received from their predecessors. The difference between the prophet and the wise man enriched life in the society of ancient Israel and our reading of the biblical books.

H. Reception of the Prophets

None of the canonical prophets seems comfortable with being called a *nābîʾ* (cf. Amos 7:14). None of the canonical prophets seems to have been a popular success in the sense of having a large following. All the preexilic prophets have rather harsh things to say, and it is not surprising that they did not immediately win the hearts of all.

That they do not call themselves *nābîʾ* or let others apply this term to them suggests that the term had connotations with which each of the prophets did not want to identify. Much scholarship claims that the word *nābîʾ* implies induced ecstacy, manic bizarreness, and irrational activity in general. Other studies have suggested that the professional aspect of prophecy is what Amos rejects in Amos 7:14. Yet another proposal is that the difference in terminology is mainly regional, Amos being from the South.

It is in the narratives about the prophets that a prophet is called *nābîʾ* without any hesitation. A recent scholarly tendency has been to say that the narratives come from a time after the historical prophet. In this view, the narratives are better understood as legends about the person for the purpose of enhancing or clarifying the figure rather than as manifestations of the personality of the prophet. Many scholars today are far more reluctant than those of a generation or two ago to write a biography or even a personality assessment of a given prophet.

There are indeed passages in which a prophet seems to express poetically the difficulty he has in speaking to the people and being heard by them. Isaiah is one example (Isa 8:16–18). But Jeremiah has a whole sequence of "laments" which have been interpreted as his inner soul emerging (Jer 12:1–6; 15:10–21; 17:14–18; 18:18–23; 20:7–13, 14–18). Yet even here, some scholarship attempts to read these as liturgical pieces or as evidence of inner-community strife. These interpretations suppose that the prophet wanted to reveal the divine word rather than individual feeling, and that the prophet's tradition continued to grow after the life of the prophet.

A claim that appears in the NT, which seems perhaps odd to the reader of the OT, is that Jerusalem killed the prophets sent to it (Luke 13:34). The Deuteronomistic History does emphasize the stream of prophets who were sent to warn the people of Israel, and in response the people and their kings would not listen. But there is no biblical scene to which the author of Luke could be referring.

A report of the killing of prophets appears only once in the OT. In 1 Kgs 18:4, 13, Queen Jezebel, who had been acquired by King Ahab from outside Israel, kills the prophets of Yahweh. Although in the next chapter, Elijah attributes the slaughter to "the people of Israel" (1 Kgs 19:10, 14), the killing neither occurs in nor is done by Jerusalem. The killing of the prophets is a postbiblical tradition that develops for different reasons both within Judaism and within Christianity (Amaru 1983).

I. The Study of the Prophets

Although over the centuries certain readers of the Bible had noticed that particular sayings within the books of the prophets did not seem to come from the people to whom they were ascribed, it was mainly in the 19th century that certain scholars vigorously attempted to sort out the authentic from the inauthentic sayings within the books of the prophets. The position, popularized especially by Julius Wellhausen, regarding the relation of the prophets to the Pentateuch encouraged this particular kind of study of the prophets. The insight that the law came after the prophets allowed certain scholars to set out in new directions in the study of the prophets. This newfound approach analyzes the prophetic books on their own rather than as precursors of a new revelation or as the commentaries and expansions on the Pentateuch.

Since the study of the Pentateuch had shown that many hands had contributed to those books, similar methods could be applied to the prophets. The approach that tries to determine whether all the words attributed to a prophet actually come from that prophet utilizes the many different clues within the text itself and raises other considerations from outside as well. It could be pointed out that the question of authenticity of the sayings is not asked in order to "challenge" the Bible or the believer, but simply to determine the real theology, the real thinking, of a given prophet. To seek to establish that original prophetic content is not to deny or to reject the Bible as normative.

The effort to determine what were the authentic words of the prophet has engaged a great number of scholars. Various methods are used to decide whether a particular saying can rank as authentic. Whether it be on the bases of the language and vocabulary used, of the ideas expressed, or of the historical events alluded to, the critic pares away certain words, verses, and passages to arrive at the substance of the prophet's preaching or writing. German scholarship has excelled in seeking to identify the authentic words of the prophets. Mainly as a result of this kind of analysis of the prophetic books, one concludes that the preexilic prophets were truly prophets of doom. Careful analysis of the books allows one to see and appreciate the original thoughts and words of the prophets.

A reaction to this approach of dissecting the texts to find the original meaning inevitably arises. Such a critique underlines the difficulty in deciding objectively what are the words and sections that have to be judged as additions. One's own presuppositions can intrude and influence the judgment. A modern conception of how books come into being can impede one's understanding of the development of the biblical text. Moreover, one might better stress the oral origins of prophecy and the oral transmission of the prophet's words to show the reliability of the text. Certain scholars pointed out that our current prophetic books differ in their origin and contents. Two kinds of prophetic material exist: the *diwan,* a collection of diverse sayings of a single prophet, passed on without much variation, and the *liturgy,* a unified piece which originated in the cultic performance of a prophet. The liturgy is the more unified of the two, weaving a pattern of themes and developing, in its own style, a complex work. This approach was fostered among Scandinavian scholars (Engnell 1969). It has stressed the impossibility of really sorting out the authentic sayings from the additions.

A different approach to the prophets is to take the prophetic book basically as the tradition has given it to us. Only those passages which are obviously not from the prophet need be cut away from the authentic words. The critic's task is to see how the words of the prophet reflect the situation in which the prophet existed. Archaeological research can be very helpful in understanding the message and even the style of the prophets in their own time and setting. This approach to the prophetic books, by and large, is pursued especially in the United States (King 1988).

More specific and distinctive approaches to the study of the prophets have arisen. The question of a prophet's relation to previous tradition returns in various ways. Gerhard von Rad's response is to show that each of the prophets speaks within one of the three election traditions of ancient Israel: those of Exodus, Zion, or David. The prophets see that Israel is entering a new stage of its history. Israel is encountering God on a new level. Yet that level always relates to the past. The prophet reinterprets the old election tradition and applies it (or them) to the new situation. The prophet's formulation of both judgment and promise depends on the specific tradition that prophet knows. Naturally the prophet's place of origin influences the election tradition out of which he speaks. Isaiah, e.g., was from Jerusalem and operated with the Zion and David traditions; Hosea, from the North, used the Exodus tradition.

Another approach which utilizes the places from which the prophet came and the particular ways of thought proper to that locality is the study of Wilson (1980). The Ephraimite prophetic tradition of the North differs from the Judean tradition of the South in matters of the vocabulary used for the prophet and his pronouncement, the manner of viewing the prophet, and the process of intermediation. Isaiah and Micah are the classical preexilic prophets in the Judean tradition (although Isaiah gets a Deuteronomic/Ephraimite depiction in the Deuteronomistic History); Hosea, of course, is Ephraimite. This sociological study underscores the importance of each prophet's support group, the specific segment of the society which encourages and sustains the prophet.

Sociology also offers David L. Petersen (1981) a particular approach to the prophets. Prophets come to a society that has certain kinds of expectations regarding the manner in which prophets should act and behave. Prophets can vary in the degree of involvement with which they play these roles. Their acceptance by the various segments of the society is indeed crucial. Some prophets operate with the support of the political or religious authorities and thus become central prophets, while other prophets receive the support only of the less powerful and outcast in the society, thus becoming peripheral prophets. The social dimension of Israelite prophecy continues to be one of the most lively areas of contemporary study on the prophets.

With regard to the prophetic writings, great emphasis has been given to the formation of the books of the prophets. Because the prophets themselves did not write, one must understand the words of the prophet as having been selected, edited, probably reinterpreted, and then expanded. The editorial remarks and expansions, once ignored by some scholars as inauthentic, are now analyzed to order to see the history of the book's growth. This growth of the prophetic books offers insights into the history of biblical religion from a new and different perspective.

Along with this interest in the formation of the books goes the attempt to analyze larger sections of the books as units rather than the smaller passages and individual sayings that had been passed on orally at some early stage. The editors of the books are increasingly given credit for intelligence, understanding, and organization in their work. The growth of the books is generally not seen as haphazard or unthinking.

The emphasis on the books as canonical sacred writings to be interpreted with the entire canon of the Bible has received a fresh proposal (Childs 1979). The only reasons these books have been preserved by the generations are the meanings that the whole books offer within the canon of the Bible. Critics of this approach suggest that this kind of analysis ignores all the advances of the historical-critical study of the prophetic books. The proponents of this method insist, however, that the approach does not deny any of those advances but simply puts them in the proper perspective. The debate on this approach has not yet concluded.

Bibliography

Albright, W. F. 1961. *Samuel and the Beginnings of the Prophetic Movement.* Cincinnati. Repr. in *Interpreting the Prophetic Tradition,* ed. Harry Orlinsky. Cincinnati, 1969.

Amaru, B. H. 1983. The Killing of the Prophets: Unraveling a Midrash. *HUCA* 54: 153–80.

Auld, A. G. 1980. Poetry, Prophecy, Hermeneutic: Recent Studies in Isaiah. *SJT* 33: 567–81.

Blenkinsopp, J. 1983. *A History of Prophecy in Israel.* Philadelphia.

Carrol, R. P. 1981. *From Chaos to Covenant: Prophecy in the Book of Jeremiah.* New York.

Childs, B. S. 1979. *Introduction to the Old Testament As Scripture.* Philadelphia.

Coggins, R.; Phillips, A.; and Knibb, M., eds. 1982. *Israel's Prophetic Tradition.* Cambridge.

Engnell, I. 1969. *A Rigid Scrutiny.* Trans. and ed. J. T. Willis. Nashville.

Fohrer, G. 1975–76. Neue Literatur zur alttestamentliche Prophetie (1961–70). *TRu* N.F. 40: 193–209, 337–77; 41: 1–12.

Gressmann, H. 1905. *Der Ursprung der israelitisch-judischen Echatologie.* Göttingen.

Heschel, A. 1962. *The Prophets: An Introduction.* 2 vols. New York.

King, P. J. 1988. *Amos, Hosea, Micah: An Archaeological Commentary.* Philadelphia.

Koch, K. 1983–84. *The Prophets.* 2 vols. Philadelphia.

Kselman, J. S. 1985. The Social World of the Israelite Prophets *RelSRev* 11: 120–29.

Lindblom, J. 1962. *Prophecy in Ancient Israel.* Oxford.

Overholt, T. W. 1989. *Channels of Prophecy: The Social Dynamics of Prophetic Activity.* Minneapolis.
Petersen, D. L. 1981. *The Roles of Israel's Prophets.* JSOTSup 17. Sheffield.
Schmitt, J. J. 1983. The Gender of Ancient Israel. *JSOT* 26: 115–25.
———. 1989. The Wife of God in Hosea 2. *BR* 24: 5–18.
Westermann, C. 1967. *Basic Forms of Prophetic Speech.* Philadelphia.
Wilson, R. R. 1980. *Prophecy and Society in Ancient Israel.* Philadelphia.

JOHN J. SCHMITT

POSTEXILIC HEBREW PROPHECY

The Babylonian Exile of the 6th century B.C.E. caused a sharp break in many of the traditions and institutions of ancient Israel. Its effect on the character of prophecy, however, was less marked than its social and political consequences; and there is a clear line of continuity linking Amos and Isaiah of Jerusalem with Ezekiel, Deutero-Isaiah, and Zechariah. Nevertheless, in time prophecy did gradually evolve into something very different from what had been known in preexilic Israel; and by the NT period the designation "prophet" applied to people in whom few of the characteristic features of the preexilic prophets are discernible. This change in turn had an effect on the way people in the Greco-Roman period perceived the preexilic prophets. At some point in the postexilic age, the idea began to develop that prophecy in the strict sense of the word had ceased from Israel, though certain groups, notably the Qumran community and the early Christians, held that it had recently revived. The interpretation of postexilic prophecy has many disputed areas, and in general it has not received as much scholarly attention as its preexilic counterpart. We shall examine five questions: the message of the postexilic prophets, their role and status in the community, the nature of prophetic experience after the Exile, the forms of prophetic literature, and the editing of prophetic books.

A. The Message of the Postexilic Prophets
  1. From Doom to Hope
  2. Calls to Repentance
  3. The Prophets and the Cult
  4. Oracles about Foreign Nations
  5. Eschatology
B. The Role of Prophecy in the Postexilic Age
C. Prophetic Experience
D. The Forms of Prophetic Literature
E. The Editing of Prophetic Books

A. The Message of the Postexilic Prophets

1. From Doom to Hope. The most obvious shift in the message of the prophets which begins with the Exile is the gradual loss of the sense that God was about to bring disaster on Israel and Judah. Scholars continue to disagree about the extent to which the preexilic prophets had seen hope beyond judgment, or had even thought that the judgment they predicted could be averted; but whether or not the preexilic message of judgment was total, there can be no doubt that it was an important part of the prophets' teaching. Amos had said "The end has come upon my people Israel" (Amos 8:2); Hosea, "Compassion is hid from my eyes" (Hos 13:14); Isaiah, "His anger is not turned away, and his hand is stretched out still" (Isa 9:12, 17, 21). In Jeremiah, and in the early oracles of Ezekiel, we hear the same message of impending doom, foretelling the disaster of the Exile. But once the Babylonian invasion had happened and all false hopes of averting it had come to nothing, prophets began to look beyond disaster to more favorable divine purposes for Israel, "plans for welfare and not for evil, to give you a future and a hope" (Jer 29:11). This is already clear in some of the oracles collected in Jeremiah 30–33 (although many scholars believe these to be additions to the words of Jeremiah, they cannot be much later than the work of the prophet himself), in Ezekiel 36–39 and the early postexilic appendix to Ezekiel (Ezekiel 40–48), and above all in the oracles of Deutero-Isaiah (Isaiah 40–55).

But exilic and postexilic prophecy of blessing is continuous with the preexilic judgment prophecy that it gradually displaced; it does not represent the triumph of the facile, optimistic prophets condemned by Jeremiah, who said "Peace, peace" when there was no peace (Jer 6:14). The stories of Jeremiah's activities during the early years of the exile of Jehoiachin make it clear that Yahweh has not in any sense changed his mind about the fate of Judah; no speedy return of the exiles or simple restoration of the preexilic kingdom is to be looked for. In Jeremiah 28 we read how Jeremiah disputed with a prophet, Hananiah, who had said "Within two years I will bring back to this place all the vessels of the Lord's house" (28:3). Jeremiah rejected such optimism as a failure to see that the Babylonian conquest was not a temporary setback, but part of a consistent divine plan, and that far worse was to come before there could be any thought of a change in Judah's fortunes. As late as Deutero-Isaiah, who prophesied just before the return of the first people back to the land of Israel, there is no suggestion that the disaster of Exile had been against the will of Yahweh, or that the better times which were now coming marked a change of heart by Yahweh or invalidated the judgment prophecy that had gone before. On the contrary, the Exile was a vindication of the prophets who had predicted doom: "Your first fathers sinned, and your mediators transgressed against me; therefore I profaned the princes of the sanctuary, I delivered Jacob to utter destruction and Israel to reviling" (Isa 43:27–28). The possibility of a better future results from the fact that Yahweh has now exacted the punishment which earlier prophets had correctly maintained that he would insist on. There is thus, in postexilic prophecy, a strong sense of identity with the teaching of previous prophets.

Nevertheless, the belief that Yahweh's judgment had now been fully exacted and so had come to an end did gradually change the prophetic message into something substantially different from what it had been before. Already in Deutero-Isaiah we find the idea that the punishment imposed on Judah was measured and could in principle be paid in full, so that a time would come (and had now come, according to the prophet) when the nation would owe Yahweh no more suffering by way of payment: "her time of service is ended . . . for she has received from the Lord's hand double for all her sins" (Isa 40:2). This could easily lead to a belief that the Babylonians, Yahweh's instruments of punishment, had afflicted the Israelites *more* than they deserved and so stood under imminent judgment themselves. Such seems to be the perception both of Deutero-Isaiah (Isaiah 46–47) and of the early postexilic prophet Zechariah (see Zech 1:15: "while I was angry but a little they furthered the disaster").

Soon the notion took root that Yahweh had vented his full anger on his people in the past, in the Exile which was now over, and that there was no danger that he would ever have cause to do so again. After the Exile, oracles predicting judgment on Israel still appear fitfully, in Haggai's warnings that sin leads to drought and famine (Hag 1:6–11), in Malachi's insistence that blemished offerings lead to divine displeasure (Mal 1:6–2:9), or in Trito-Isaiah's condemnation of social injustices and pagan practices which lead God to blight social relations and bring national calamity (Isaiah 59). But increasingly divine judgment was thought to fall selectively on those elements in Israel which continued to deserve it, and the overwhelming sense of impending *national* calamity which had been so marked a feature in the preexilic prophets was lost. Eventually even the theme of selective judgment died away, and the role of the prophets came to be understood as one of comfort and consolation for Israel, and of judgment only on her enemies.

2. Calls to Repentance. The question of whether the preexilic prophets preached "repentance" (i.e., a change in social and political attitudes and actions) is a vexed one, and the answer to it affects our assessment of how far the postexilic prophetic message is novel. There is no doubt that Jeremiah urged his contemporaries to "repent," that is, to alter their attitude toward the Babylonian threat by capitulating rather than resisting, and that he urged them to reform the religious customs of the day—to move away from the syncretistic practices that had replaced a purer Yahwism. It is clear, however, that he did not expect such repentance to lead to a simple change in Yahweh's plans for Israel. There was no question of averting the disaster of the Exile, whatever the people did; and the course of action he most urgently wished the leaders of Judah to adopt was to come to terms with this reality, not to resist it. Their "repentance" would thus consist more in recognizing the justice and inevitability of the Babylonian invasion and victory, and in adjusting to the new state of affairs this would imply, than in reforming the national life so as to persuade Yahweh to alter the course of international events—the time when that might have been possible was already past. Similarly, after the major deportations of 597 and 586 his advice to the exiles (according to the account in Jeremiah 29) is to settle down and come to terms with the reality of life in the land of Exile and not to act as if it were merely a temporary aberration in Yahweh's designs for his people.

Jeremiah's calls to repent are thus in practice calls to embrace realism and to abandon false hopes. Much the same may be said of the early oracles of Ezekiel, whose aim seems to have been chiefly to dissuade his contemporaries in Exile from believing that there would be a speedy restoration, and to accept that they were responsible for the fate that had befallen them and for the disasters which were still in store for the city of Jerusalem (Ezekiel 18). In this early exilic period attention shifts from the earlier prophetic concern with social justice and religious purity to the question of how the community will react to the conditions of life under Babylonian domination. Calls to reform the national life, even if these had once been typical of prophets, cease to be appropriate, in view of the total lack of self-determination possible for a nation in Exile or living in the ruins of its land.

In the period of postexilic reconstruction, however, prophets appear much more as teachers whose role is to induce a change of heart and of conduct in the community now striving to repair its national and social life. Haggai in particular quite clearly sees his task as being to persuade the people to make an effort to rebuild the temple (1:4, 9), while Zechariah seems to combine a similar concern for restoring the nation's cultic life with an interest in questions of social justice that reminds us of Amos or Isaiah (see, for example, Zech 8:16–17). It is possible, of course, that passages of moral exhortation in the postexilic prophets owe something to the work of editors, but these passages are in keeping with the much more positive and constructive role of these later prophets as compared with the doom-laden words of their preexilic predecessors.

By NT times it was widely held that all the prophets had been essentially moral teachers, whose function had been to exhort rather than to foretell disaster. This idea seems to owe much to the early years after the Exile, when prophets such as Haggai and Zechariah had directed their efforts to improving the moral condition of the nation, at a time when it was no longer believed that national disaster was impending. Whereas preexilic prophets had been concerned to discern God's hand in contemporary international affairs, and to show Israel the signs of the times, postexilic prophets became directly involved in social and political questions, as respected, official teachers of morality. The tenor of the preexilic prophets' message (continued by Jeremiah and Ezekiel) is that the people should accept the justice of Yahweh's impending punishment for their sins; that of the postexilic prophets is that Yahweh seeks moral reformation and renewal, and will reward them with his favor.

3. The Prophets and the Cult. Anyone who comes to the postexilic prophets after reading their preexilic predecessors is immediately struck by how differently they react to the place of the cult in Israel's national life. Amos had condemned the religion of the sanctuaries (4:4–5; 5:4–5), and Jeremiah had dismissed the temple as a false focus of security for the nation (7:1–4). But Haggai and Zechariah regard rebuilding the temple as crucial to national reconstruction (Hag 1:4; Zech 4:8–10); the appendix to Ezekiel places cultic institutions at the center of national life (Ezekiel 40–44); Malachi rebukes the priests for neglecting the detail of ritual ordinances (Mal 1:6–10); and in the work of the Chronicler prophets are consistently represented as concerned with the cultic life of the nation (cf. 2 Chr 13:8–11; 15:1–7). The reason for this may be that there had been a change in the prophetic message—perhaps a necessary change in view of the different conditions of life for the postexilic Jewish community, deprived of its political institutions and obliged to embrace distinctive ritual and cultic ordinances as an alternative focus for national life. Alternatively, it may simply mean that the postexilic prophets who are represented in the OT happen to be those who came from a cultic milieu, though in this respect they were not necessarily typical of postexilic prophecy in general. (This point will be discussed again below in relation to the question of the role of the prophet in postexilic society.) Only in Trito-Isaiah (Isa 66:1) do we find hints that not all postexilic prophets were enthusiastic supporters of the renewed temple cult.

Connections between prophets and cult may be reflected not only in the content of the prophetic message but also in the form of prophetic books, for it is after the Exile that these begin to show influence from literary forms whose natural home is public worship. Deutero-Isaiah makes extensive use of hymns, royal oracles probably taken from coronation or enthronement rituals, and cultic exhortations; indeed, it has sometimes been suggested that the whole collection is liturgical in origin, or at least that the prophet was a temple singer or poet by profession. If we follow the division of prophetic collections into *diwan* (collected oracles) and liturgy types (as proposed by Engnell 1969), it is noteworthy that the postexilic period contributes by far the most examples of the liturgy type to the prophetic corpus of the OT. Postexilic prophecy almost wholly lacks the antipathy to national cultic life which is so marked a feature of the teaching of Amos, Hosea, and Isaiah. Perhaps this is because the cult had ceased to be a cause for complacent self-satisfaction, preventing the people from hearing the prophetic warning that sacrifices would not save a nation steeped in social injustice. Instead it had become the essential rallying point for renewal and reconstruction.

4. Oracles about Foreign Nations. Israelite prophets had probably uttered oracles about foreign nations from the earliest times, since prophets seem to have been retained by kings to foretell the downfall of their enemies—and perhaps to help bring it about, through what we might call magic. Amos (in chaps. 1–2) seems to presuppose that his audience was familiar with the custom of uttering oracles predicting the fall of Israel's enemies. However, one of the most radical changes effected by the preexilic classical prophets was to replace such prophecies, which foretold disaster for the nation's enemies, with condemnation of Israel itself. Thus by the time of Jeremiah, there was a strong tradition among the prophets of seeing Israel itself as the enemy whom Yahweh had cursed. But in either case, down to the early exilic period prophets evince little interest in the fate of foreign nations except as this bears on the fate of Israel. Other nations may be doomed because they are Israel's enemies, or they may be Yahweh's instruments to punish his sinful people. Sometimes both themes may appear: Isaiah 10 contains a number of oracles in which the eventual downfall of the Assyrians is prophesied after they have carried out their commission to punish Israel.

From Jeremiah onward, however, the interest of Israel's prophets widens to include the fate of foreign nations as a theme in its own right. In Ezekiel, Deutero-Isaiah, Haggai, and Zechariah the downfall of Babylon is the prelude to the eventual restoration of Israel to its land; and the old tradition of cursing the enemies of Israel reemerges in the form of oracles against Babylon: Isaiah 46–47 is the most extended example. The Babylonians are denounced for their arrogance (cf. Isaiah 10 on the Assyrians), and their speedy collapse is promised by Yahweh. Probably from the same period are the oracles in Jeremiah 50–51 against Babylon. The logical implication of this is that Yahweh has appointed the Persian king, Cyrus, as his agent of judgment on Babylon and hence of salvation for the Jews, and this results in one of the earliest examples of an oracle's promising divine blessing to a foreign king (Isa 45:1–7). Here Cyrus is actually described as Yahweh's "anointed one"—a title previously used only for the Davidic king. The generally favorable view of the Persians continues to be characteristic of postexilic prophecy, which contains no explicitly anti-Persian oracles.

But alongside the specific oracles of doom on Babylon and of blessing on Persia, the prophetic tradition from Deutero-Isaiah onward comes to contain vaguer oracles about "the nations," in which virulently xenophobic sentiments alternate with an attitude which seems incipiently universalistic. Most of the prophetic books now contain a cycle of "oracles against the nations," in which (sometimes named, sometimes anonymous) nations are threatened with Yahweh's wrath. These oracles are notoriously difficult to date, but must in most cases derive from the Persian or Hellenistic age. At the same time, many prophetic books include oracles foretelling the "gathering in" of the nations to Jerusalem, and seem to envisage a future in which the barriers between Jew and gentile will break down and all mankind will come to acknowledge Yahweh as the one God. There is dispute about whether this is how we should understand passages in Ezekiel and Deutero-Isaiah which say that Yahweh will become known to the nations. They may rather be a promise that the nations (who have derided fallen Israel) will come to acknowledge the reality of Yahweh's power when he punishes them and restores his own people. But in Zechariah and Trito-Isaiah there can be little doubt that foreigners are regarded positively (cf. Zech 8:20–23; Isa 56:3–8), while Malachi seems to contrast the worship offered by gentiles favorably with the blemished offerings of Israelite priests (Mal 1:11–14). The book of Jonah—a legend about a prophet rather than a collection of prophetic oracles—seems designed to teach a similar message, perhaps in reaction against the exclusivism of some Judaism of the Second Temple period. Isaiah 19 concludes with five oracles of a strikingly universalistic tone, including the remarkable prophecy, "In that day Israel will be the third with Egypt and Assyria, a blessing in the midst of the earth, whom the Lord of hosts has blessed, saying, 'Blessed be Egypt my people, and Assyria the work of my hands, and Israel my heritage' " (Isa 19:24–25).

5. Eschatology. It is sometimes said that postexilic prophecy became more "eschatological" than prophecy had been in the preexilic period. This may mean one of several things.

First, sometimes this is a convenient way of expressing the idea that the time scale of prophetic predictions became longer after the Exile. Instead of foretelling the immediate consequences of national sin, prophets now came to be interested in a longer sweep of history; and, in particular, they started to think that God has a detailed plan for the history of all the nations which he was working out in a more or less predetermined manner. The preexilic prophets give the impression that Yahweh reacts sharply and immediately to human conduct, but not that he has a grand design coming to fruition in preplanned stages. But already in Ezekiel and Deutero-Isaiah, and to an increasing extent in the thought of Trito-Isaiah, Zechariah, and the forerunners of apocalyptic—such as the authors of Isaiah 24–27 or Zechariah 9–14—history seems to form an orderly progression, with human volition playing a role clearly subordinate to the divine plan. When the prophets after the Exile are said to have "an eschatology," this is the aspect of their message that is often being referred to. Of course they also had an interest in what the immediate future held for Israel, but (as noted in the preceding section) the scope of their concern was perceptibly wider. It should be noted, however, that it is not until a few of the apocalyptic works of the NT period that the events foretold can be called "eschatological" in the full technical sense the term has in traditional Christian theology, where it implies an end to the whole world order and also refers to the fate of the individual after death.

Second, "eschatology" may also be used (as it frequently is by NT scholars) to point not so much to the long-term plan found in the thinking of postexilic prophecy as to the transcendent character of the divine action in history. This is another aspect of the tendency to determinism just noted: the prophets stress that what happens in human history is *divine* action, the coming to fruition of a divine purpose, accomplished through more than human means. God breaks into the progression of human history and takes control of it in a direct and uncompromising way, leaving little to human agents. This is certainly the impression created, for example, by Zechariah 14, where God stands in person on the Mount of Olives and causes it to be split in two, or in Isaiah 34, where he himself wields the sword that first destroys the heavenly hosts and then descends in judgment on Edom. The expectation of God's personal, decisive intervention in human history seems to be a feature of prophecy as it develops toward what we call apocalyptic. There are few parallels to this way of thinking in the preexilic prophets, for whom divine involvement in human affairs is more often expressed through the mediation of human agency.

Third, some scholars hold that the failure of prophetic predictions to materialize led to their being projected into the remote ("eschatological") future as a way of retaining their authority, when a simpler reaction would have been simply to conclude that they had been proved wrong. On this view, the postexilic prophets themselves did not hold any longer-term view of history than their predecessors; it was their disciples who, faced with the apparent failure of the prophets' predictions, reworked their oracles so as to make them refer to the very remote future. Thus they made it impossible that the prophecies would ever be falsified by events. On this interpretation, "eschatology" is thus not a development within the prophetic tradition, but an interpretative category applied to prophetic oracles by those who edited and reused them in later generations.

B. The Role of Prophecy in the Postexilic Age

We noted above that alongside collections of oracles, the postexilic prophetic books also contain many works which are closer to the "liturgy" type. This observation, combined with the evidence of the books of Chronicles, where "prophets" often appear in a liturgical role, may suggest that there was a significant shift after the Exile toward a closer alignment of the prophetic tradition with the institutions of the cult. Haggai and Zechariah might already be examples of this, with their concern for the reestablishment of temple worship among the returned exiles. Even Ezekiel, during the exilic period itself, shows many more points of contact with priestly circles than is the case with the preexilic prophets: the sins listed in chap. 18, for example, include a number of "cultic" offenses such as we do not find in Amos or Isaiah. Even if Ezekiel 40–48 is a postexilic addition, the perception of Ezekiel as a prophet deeply concerned with the ordering of worship may well be the reason why it was to his oracles that this appendix was added.

Late 19th-century scholarship was inclined to regard almost all postexilic prophecy as the product of cultic circles. This was thought to mark a decline in the institution of prophecy, from the high ethical concerns of the 8th and 7th centuries into an incipient "legalism" and obsession with ritual matters. On this view, prophecy in the sense the term has when applied to Amos, Hosea, or Isaiah more or less ceased to exist after the Exile; the term "prophet" *(nābîʾ)* came to be used as the title of one among the many different types of temple officials. Other terms certainly underwent similar shifts—"Levite," for example, ceased to mean any sort of priest and became the name for a temple singer.

In recent years, however, a more nuanced interpretation of these postexilic developments has been proposed by Hanson (1975), building on the work of Plöger (1968). Hanson argues that there are two distinct strands within postexilic prophetic writings. The first is indeed a drift toward the institutionalization of prophets as temple officials, whose function was to produce liturgical texts. Their "oracles" consisted only of exhortations to keep the Torah and be regular in worship, or of promises that God would bless the cultic community around the temple. Hanson sees this trend as beginning with Ezekiel, continuing in Haggai and Zechariah, and passing on into the Chronicler's understanding of prophets.

But in tension with this shift toward the cult, there was also a second, minority tradition which kept alive "authentic" prophecy, the inheritance of Amos and Isaiah. This prophetic movement had as its task to protest against the increasingly static and complacent institutions of Second Temple Judaism. Its best representative is Trito-Isaiah (Isaiah 56–66). Trito-Isaiah's opposition to rebuilding the temple (66:1) stands in continuity with the preexilic prophetic protest against the centrality of the temple, expressed most clearly by Jeremiah (see, for example, Jer 7:4, "Do not trust in these deceptive words: This is the temple of the Lord, the temple of the Lord, the temple of the Lord"). According to Hanson, prophets such as Trito-Isaiah were not officials appointed by the Second Temple state but outsiders, just as the great preexilic prophets had been, denouncing the society of their day and attacking its cultic life as an empty show. This Isaiah 58 attacks solemn fasts in terms very similar to those used by the preexilic prophets to condemn feasts. The message here is that Yahweh hates fasting unaccompanied by social justice, and (by implication) will punish those who use such pentitential practices as a cover for an unreformed life. It contrasts with Zechariah's cheerful optimism that fasts will cease merely because (in the newly restored and forgiven Jerusalem, which is to enjoy God's blessing) they will no longer be appropriate (Zech 8:18–19). Trito-Isaiah is full of sharp condemnations of the corruption of cultic life (56:9–12; 57:1–13; 59:1–8; 65:1–12). It is hard to see him (or them, if the work is a collection of oracles by many hands) as any kind of temple official paid to maintain the institutional stability of the restored nation.

Hanson suggests that it is in this prophetic protest movement that the roots of apocalyptic are to be found, and that Trito-Isaiah represents "the dawn of apocalyptic." The insights of this movement continue in the works commonly called "proto-apocalyptic"—Isaiah 24–27, Joel, and Zechariah 9-14. Thus the "liturgy" type of prophecy by no means succeeded in completely displacing the old independent prophetic spirit, which continued to exist and to resist the tendency toward "establishment" attitudes in the Second Temple period. These independent prophets believed that Yahweh's hands were not tied by the institutional structures that had been established. Yahweh was still free to intervene dramatically in human affairs and, if he saw the need, to punish Israel as of old. To use the terms proposed by Plöger (1968), the postexilic *theocracy* succeeded in taming most prophets and reducing them to mere state officials—not unlike the "institutional prophets" whom Elijah, Micah, and Jeremiah had opposed; but there remained a loyal band of prophets who insisted that Yahweh's word to Israel included an *eschatology*—a message of doom on a disobedient people.

Hanson's theories have been widely accepted in OT scholarship, with the result that the picture of prophecy in postexilic times has become more subtle than it was at the end of the last century. There is no single model that will account for the role and function of "prophets" in the Second Temple period, as though all prophets were the same. Rather, we seem to have at least two radically different types. Some have asked whether there is really such a sharp distinction to be drawn between, for example, Trito-Isaiah and Zechariah; for Zechariah seems also to envisage the need for moral (not merely cultic) reform—Zech 7:17 criticizes fasting in much the same terms as Isaiah 58. Conversely, Isaiah 56–66 contain some oracles that seem perfectly well-disposed toward the restoration of Jerusalem and its cultus (the whole of Isaiah 60–62 belongs to this tradition). It has also been noted that the apocalyptic movement is by no means homogeneous and that not all apocalypses can be regarded as anti-"theocratic"; some indeed are entirely noneschatological. However, Hanson's work has been important in establishing that something akin to the preexilic tradition of noninstitutional, independent prophets did continue after the Exile. We should not be misled by the fact that many of those responsible for our finished OT tried to erase the traces of this movement by preserving rather few of its works, and by hijacking the term "prophet" for use as a technical term in describing the personnel of the temple. Enough remains in the OT to show that there were prophets who had no official role even after the Exile, and that these persisted in denouncing the hierarchy of temple and nation when they saw fit.

C. Prophetic Experience

The question of prophetic experience is an obscure one in every period of OT history. In the postexilic age the most noticeable development is a greater emphasis on the *spirit* of God as the motive force behind prophetic utterance. Ezekiel speaks of the spirit of Yahweh transporting him from place to place, and this seems intended to imply an "out-of-the-body" experience or perhaps even literal levitation (at one point he is picked up by a lock of his hair: see 3:12; 8:3; 11:1, 24). Trito-Isaiah contains a famous reference to the spirit of Yahweh as the inspiration behind his prophecy (Isa 61:1); and throughout Haggai and Zechariah there are repeated references to the spirit (Hag 1:14; 2:5; Zech 4:6; 7:12), though some scholars think that these are additions by the editors of the books, for whom it was important to stress the activity of the spirit in the restored community. Joel 3:1–2—Eng 2:28–29 explicitly refers to the gift of prophecy as resulting from the pouring out of God's spirit, predicting that a time will come when this gift will be extended to all humankind.

As is well known, references to the spirit are very rare in the preexilic prophets, so that we have clear evidence here of a shift in understanding of the prophetic experience. It is not clear, however, whether this reflects any change in the experiences prophets actually had—whether, for example, the postexilic experience was more dramatic, or "ecstatic," or was in some sense a return to the uncontrolled, frenzied activity of the preclassical prophets whom we meet in the books of Samuel and Kings and upon whom the spirit of Yahweh "came mightily" (cf. 1 Sam 10:10), driving them to act in uncontrollable, dervishlike frenzy. While this is possible, it may be simply that the post-exilic community spoke more of the spirit as the motive force behind prophecy as a way of emphasizing its divine origin, without meaning to imply that the psychological experience involved had changed significantly from preexilic times. It may be better to ask why the great classical preexilic prophets seem to *avoid* reference to the spirit of Yahweh, when both their predecessors and their successors seem to take it for granted that this is the best language to use in explanation of prophetic gifts.

A more significant shift may lie behind the greatly increased interest in visions and dreams in postexilic prophetic books. The passage from Joel just cited glosses the extension of prophetic gifts to all by saying, "Your sons and your daughters shall prophesy, your old men shall *dream dreams,* and your young men shall *see visions.*" If it is right to see significance in the insistence by preexilic prophets on hearing the word of Yahweh rather than on seeing visions or dreams, this change may well indicate an important new departure. Jeremiah once explicitly distinguishes true prophecy from seeing visions: "Let the prophet who has a dream tell the dream, but let him who has my word speak my word faithfully. What has straw in common with wheat? says the Lord" (Jer 23:28). This appears to imply that true revelations from Yahweh do not come in visions or dreams, though it is not clear what experience is concretely implied by "him who has my word." Does this refer to "audition," a supernatural but literal hearing of voices, or to some more subtle inner conviction that Yahweh has spoken in the heart? In any case, preexilic prophets are not uniformly opposed to visions: both Amos (7:1, 4, 7; 8:1; 9:1) and Isaiah (6:1) report visions which enshrine the word Yahweh is speaking to his people, and they show no embarrassment about this mode of revelation—unless these reports are the work of postexilic redactors.

At all events postexilic prophets and the collectors of the oracles seem to have regarded visions as the normal method by which God communicates with his messengers; and sometimes the visions in question are detailed and full of symbolism, a kind of pageant played out in front of the prophet's eyes, each incident within which has allegorical significance (see, for example, the vision reports in Zechariah 1–6). Amos' visions already contain a symbolic component. In that a commonplace object (a basket of summer fruit, a plumb line) is given a deeper meaning, often through wordplay (cf. also Jer 1:11–12). But in the postexilic period the visions become lengthier, and sometimes a whole drama is acted out in symbolic form, requiring interpretation (often by an angel) before its significance can be grasped by the prophet and communicated to his hearers. The earliest example of this is Ezekiel's vision of the coming fall of Jerusalem, recorded in Ezekiel 9. In later apocalyptic works such visions become deliberately obscure and riddling, so that it is quite impossible to understand them without the appended explanation. Such is the case, for instance, with the visions of Daniel, or (outside the Bible) of Enoch in the various books attributed to him.

A question which this often raises in the minds of students of apocalyptic, but one which is equally useful in studying the prophets, is whether in some cases the vision is not a "genuine" vision at all, but a literary convention deliberately and consciously adopted by the prophet. If so, then the "prophet" or apocalyptist is to be seen more as a writer than as a speaker. This question arises already with Ezekiel and Zechariah, for their allegorical visions seem to lack the immediacy and directness of the brief vision reports in Amos or Isaiah. There is no reason to rule out the possibility that some postexilic prophecy may have been communicated in writing, by the production of fly sheets which could be passed around among a literate religious group, rather than by the kind of public declamation that we associate with prophets like Isaiah or Jeremiah. In the case of apocalyptic works, it is virtually certain that this is how the works were appropriated by their intended audience. Of course the suggestion that some prophecy may have been literary from the beginning does not in itself detract from its inspiration; but it does imply that the prophet was a learned writer rather than a simple and perhaps illiterate spokesman for Yahweh. Since Hebrew culture seems to have lacked any conventional ways of describing literary inspiration, it may have seemed natural to account for such prophecies by attributing them to an origin in dreams and visions which had afterward to be written down—by contrast with the directness of the "word" of Yahweh which passed immediately through the prophet's mouth as he spoke to the people.

D. The Forms of Prophetic Literature

The postexilic period witnessed a breaking down of some of the distinctive forms of prophetic utterance. Oracles beginning "Thus says the Lord" or ending "oracle of Yahweh" continue to appear, but are less characteristic than they were in the books of the preexilic prophets. Sometimes these formulas seem to be scattered almost at random as a guarantee of prophetic authenticity, and have lost their original character of marking the beginnings and ends of distinct oracles. This is particularly marked in Haggai and Zechariah, where the phrase "says the Lord of hosts" appears more or less as a refrain (e.g., Hag 2:4–9; Zech 1:2–6, 14–17). Furthermore, what is introduced by such formulas is often not what we would recognize as an "oracle" in earlier prophetic writings. In Deutero- and Trito-Isaiah many of the oracles use liturgical forms, and this is part of a general drift toward the use of cultic forms by the prophets (as discussed above).

On the other hand, the postexilic prophets do not seem to follow their preexilic predecessors in using forms borrowed from other spheres of Israel's life with deliberately ironic or sarcastic effect. There is nothing like Amos' parodying of priestly *tôrôt* (e.g., 4:4–5) or his use of lament forms to suggest that Israel is already spiritually dead (e.g., 5:2). One has the impression that the forms of prophetic oracles are not taken directly from this or that everyday use, but are imitated from what is by now perceived to be "normal" prophetic style, without any awareness that originally each prophetic oracle had a distinct origin. It is as though postexilic prophets are producing imitations or pastiches of the existing prophetic collections, and whereas these are often jumbled because of the vagaries of transmission and editing, the imitations are jumbled because postexilic writers felt that this is how a prophetic book should look.

At the same time, some forms that scarcely occur at all in the preexilic prophets now come into prominence, notably the allegory, and the extended vision report (with its interpretation by an interpreting angel), which eventually becomes the form known as the apocalypse. There is also a profusion of oracles beginning "in that day" or "in the end of the days," which perhaps reflect the increasingly eschatological interest of these prophets. In general the developments are all consistent with the suggestion made in the preceding section, that prophecy gradually turned from a spoken into a written phenomenon, so that the forms used came increasingly to reflect leisurely literary composition rather than the needs of oral delivery, memorability, and immediate impact.

E. The Editing of Prophetic Books

This leads naturally into the next question: the editing of the prophetic books. A marked feature of the postexilic age is the growth of official or semiofficial versions of older writings, which gradually moved in the direction of becoming "Holy Scripture." Just as the Persian period saw the codification of the pentateuchal books to form the Torah, so at about the same time collections of prophetic oracles began to take on the character of sacred writings. At first perhaps these were revered by particular groups, but in due course they became part of the shared heritage of all Jews.

It is usually thought that the Exile itself provided the initial impetus toward the collection and codification of prophetic writings. For one thing, the event itself had vindicated the predictions of the preexilic prophets and so turned them from objects of scorn into venerable figures whom God himself had shown to be in the right; for another, the separation of so many Jews from their homeland made the preservation of the national literature imperative if Jewish culture and religion were to survive.

The process by which the prophetic books were compiled was almost infinitely complex, but it involved at least three separate elements. First, the authentic utterances of the prophets were arranged in order, sometimes chronologically (so far as the editors could guess at what this might be), sometimes thematically or on a catchword principle. Secondly, narratives about the prophet, which might or might not be of any historical value, were added. In the case of some prophets, such as Amos, very little such material was available, but with others, notably Jeremiah, it was very extensive. And thirdly, further oracles which had no original connection with the prophet in question were appended or worked into the earlier collection, until the ordinary reader could no longer discern the difference. With a book such as Isaiah this third stage probably contributed the greater part of the book. Indeed, from chap. 40 onward we have at least two collections which had probably existed in a semifinished form under who knows what name before they were added to Isaiah 1–39. Whether the editors intended to assert that the prophet named in the book's superscription had in fact delivered all these oracles himself remains wholly uncertain. Later generations certainly took this to be implied. Some of the additional oracles may very well be genuinely prophetic, in the sense that they were originally delivered by people who would have claimed for themselves the same kind of inspiration as those in whose names the present books appear. But others may have always been essentially the work of scribes, composing what they took to be plausible "prophetic" utterances in an endeavor to update or revise existing oracles. And it seems clear that the same sort of process operated with all the prophetic books; the words of late postexilic prophets, once uttered and remembered, became subject to just the same procedures of redaction, addition, and embellishment that had by then already produced something like the present form of older books, such as Amos or Hosea. Only the beginnings of a distinct "canon" of Scripture eventually set limits to this kind of editorial work, and ensured that from then on comment and interpretation would have to take the form of acknowledged commentary rather than changes to the text of the prophetic books themselves.

How far the work of editors should itself be regarded as "prophetic" is largely a matter of our definitions. No doubt there were some for whom the work of interpretation entailed in the work of editing constituted a sharing in the inspiration of the prophet himself. Some people may have believed that Isaiah or Jeremiah himself continued to speak through the disciples who revised and collected his oracles—much as in later times the disciples of rabbis would give their own teaching but claim (and believe) that it was given "in the name" of their teacher, and of his teacher, and of the whole line of teachers in whose succession they stood.

Matters are complicated further when one remembers that, by the NT period, it was widely believed that the gift of authentic prophecy had died out in Israel—though its restoration, promised (it was felt) in Joel 3—Eng chap. 2, was eagerly hoped for. This belief could make claims to have received a *direct* divine revelation automatically suspect. The strange prediction in Zech 13:2–6, which regards "prophets," like idols and "unclean spirits," as a blight which Yahweh will remove from the land, may belong to a movement of thought in which any claim to be a prophet branded the claimant as an impostor. In such circumstances anyone who believed that God had spoken to him was obliged to dress his message up as the utterance of some ancient prophets, speaking in the time before "the spirit departed from Israel," as the Talmud expresses it. This is undoubtedly part of the reason for the pseudonymity of apocalyptic works; and it no doubt also explains some of the more improbable additions to the prophetic books, such as those which imply that Isaiah addressed the problems of the Babylonian or Persian periods, or that Zechariah was interested in the Greeks. There is, however, little evidence that prophecy did in fact die out, if by "prophecy" we mean the phenomenon of inspiration such as existed in the 8th century. Indeed, theories such as those of Hanson (discussed above) have made it seem probable that the postexilic age saw just as active a prophetic movement as the preexilic. But the forms of expression did change significantly, and postexilic prophets often expressed their oracles as additions to existing collections, or even as whole new works falsely attributed to figures from the past, rather than speaking in their own persons as earlier prophets had done.

Bibliography

Ackroyd, P. R. 1968. *Exile and Restoration.* London.

Barton, J. 1986. *Oracles of God: Perceptions of Ancient Prophecy in Israel after the Exile.* London.

Blenkinsopp, J. 1983. *A History of Prophecy in Israel.* Philadelphia.

Carroll, R. P. 1979. *When Prophecy Failed: Reactions and Responses to Failure in the Old Testament Prophetic Tradition.* London.

Coggins, R.; Philips, A.; and Knibb, M., eds. 1982. *Israel's Prophetic Tradition.* Cambridge.

Engnell, I. 1969. Prophets and Prophetism in the Old Testament. Pp. 123–79 in *A Rigid Scrutiny.* Trans. and ed. J. T. Willis. Nashville.

Fishbane, M. 1985. *Biblical Interpretation in Ancient Israel.* Oxford.

Hanson, P. D. 1975. *The Dawn of Apocalyptic.* Philadelphia.

Koch, K. 1982. *The Prophets.* 2 vols. Philadelphia.

Levenson, J. D. 1976. *Theology of the Program of Restoration in Ezekiel 40–48.* Missoula, MT.

Mason, R. A. 1977. *The Books of Haggai, Zechariah, Malachi.* Cambridge.

Petersen, D. 1977. *Late Israelite Prophecy.* Missoula, MT.

Plöger, O. 1968. *Theocracy and Eschatology.* Oxford.

Whybray, R. N. 1975. *Isaiah 40–66.* NCBC. London.

Wilson, R. R. 1980. *Prophecy and Society in Ancient Israel.* Philadelphia.

Zimmerli, W. 1979–83. *Ezekiel.* 2 vols. Hermeneia. Philadelphia.

JOHN BARTON

EARLY CHRISTIAN PROPHECY

The phenomenon in early Christianity of inspired speech in the name of God, the risen Jesus, or the Spirit.

Prophecy and its effects are evident in the books of the NT and in other early Christian writings.

A. Terminology and Definitions

A glance at the entry on "prophecy" in the standard dictionary of ancient Greek (Liddell and Scott) will reveal that in the world into which Christianity was born the terms *prophet, prophecy, prophesy,* and *prophetic* did not function univocally, but were used with reference to a variety of figures and functions (cf. Fascher 1927). *Prophētēs* in Greek was a synonym for *hypophētēs.* Originally, both meant simply "spokesperson" or "announcer," but both were used in derivative and metaphorical senses. "Prophet" was used not only to mean "one who speaks for a god and interprets his will" to human beings, but also for the cultic official keepers of the oracle (at Branchidae), for members of the highest order of the priesthood (in Egypt), for herbalists and quack doctors, for the interpreters of the oracles of the *mantis* (Plato, *Ti.* 72a), and hence derivatively for poets as such (cf. Titus 1:12, of Epimenides), and then metaphorically for proclaimers in general, including the announcer at the games. On the other hand, "prophet" and related words represented only one set of terms used for the claim to communicate messages from the gods, with other designations such as "seer," *mantis,* and "sibyl" being used in related and overlapping ways.

In the light of this state of affairs, the 1973 Seminar on Early Christian Prophecy of the Society of Biblical Literature adopted a definition based on the common features of the use of the "prophet" word group in a number of early Christian sources. This definition has been widely received. The following adaptation of it expresses the understanding of prophecy assumed in this article: "The early Christian prophet was an immediately-inspired spokesperson for God, the risen Jesus, or the Spirit who received intelligible oracles that he or she felt impelled to deliver to the Christian community or, representing the community, to the general public." Since the term "inspiration" is used in a variety of senses, "immediately-inspired" is used here to express the prophetic claim that what he or she says represents the present, immediate voice of the deity. This does not exclude the use of sources, traditions, or the prophet's own reflections, all of which may be involved in the delivery of what the prophet perceives as directly revealed from the deity. This article investigates the phenomenon of prophecy so defined, whether or not it is labeled as prophecy. Conversely, other uses of the "prophet" word group are not explored.

B. Prophecy in the Hellenistic World

1. Gentile. The Judeo-Christian tradition did not introduce prophecy into the Hellenistic world. The inspired spokesperson for the gods, the oracle giver, the ecstatic mouthpiece for the deity, frequently called "prophet," was a familiar figure to the Greco-Roman populace. Many gods could speak through their prophets, of whom Apollo was only one of the more active. There were many shrines where he could be consulted by means of the oracle, of which Delphi was only the most famous.

Prophecy was located within the broad spectrum of devices by which information from the world of the gods was transmitted. There was a tradition at least as old as Plato of distinguishing *artificiosa divinatio* and *naturalis divinatio.* The former refers to divination by technical means such as the interpretation of dreams and reading the will of the gods from the flight of the birds and the livers of sacrificed animals, while the latter refers to communication of a message from the gods by inspired speech received in trance, ecstasy, or vision (Aune 1983: 24, 349 n 9). Greek prophecy was not always ecstatic. The spectrum of prophetic experiences ranged from raging loss of consciousness to sober declaration of the message from the god. Plutarch describes (*De def. or.* 431d–438e) the Pythia at Delphi as inhaling the vapors from a fissure in the earth, becoming "inspired," and delivering unintelligible utterances that were then translated by the "prophets." In other descriptions, the Pythia became inspired by drinking from the sacred spring, and delivered oracles that were quite intelligible. Probably different practices occurred at different times and places, even in the history of one oracle center such as Delphi. Plato's description (*Ti.* 71–72) of the mantic behavior of the agents of revelation, and the translation of their utterances into intelligible speech by the prophets, has perhaps been too influential in the scholarly assessment of Greek prophecy. Generalizations about prophecy in the Greco-Roman world should be avoided, but in a context where early Christian prophecy is being explored, some features that were usually characteristic of Hellenistic prophecy should be noted: (1) Hellenistic prophecy could be the result of the spontaneous inspiration by the deity, but it was normally a response to inquiries in which human beings took the initiative and was subject to manipulation. (2) Prophecy was not a function of a particular religious group and was not directed to a group of insiders, but was a part of the general public cultural scene, available to any interested person. (3) Prophecy was generally directed to the needs and inquiries of individuals, revealing the will of the deity or future information concerning the personal lives of individuals. (4) Oracles were generally ambiguous. Heraclitus' remark with reference to the Delphic oracle is characteristic: *oute legei, oute kruptei, alla sēmainei* ("she neither reveals nor conceals, but signifies"). (5) Oracles were generally brief and expressed in metrical form. (6) Collections of oracles were made, and later generations interpreted them with reference to their own situation. While Christian prophecy resembled pagan prophecy on points #5 and #6, prophecy in the Church was in contrast to its pagan counterpart on points #1–#4.

2. Jewish. Some streams of rabbinic Jewish tradition held the view that prophecy had ceased in the time of Ezra and would not return until the eschatological age (e.g., *Song of Songs Rab.* 8.9–10; *Num. Rab.* 15.10; *b. Yoma* 9b, 21b; *t. Sota* 13.2; *ʾAbot* 1). This view was reinforced by the widespread influence of the later Protestant canon of Scripture, in which there was presumed to be a gap of 400 years from Malachi to John the Baptist. Hence the popular tradition of the "four-hundred silent years." Except for the case of John the Baptist, who was incorporated into the Christian stream of history, the NT presents only minimal and indirect evidence for contemporary Jewish prophecy (cf. John 11:51; Acts 13:6). There is massive evidence for 1st-century Jewish prophecy, however, from the Jewish sources themselves.

a. Philo. If Philo was aware of the tradition of the cessation of prophecy, he ignored it. Prophecy had been available to every good Israelite and was still available to "every worthy man" (*Heres* 259). Like other Hellenistic Jews (e.g., Wis Sol 7:27), Philo understood all the religious leaders in Israel's history in prophetic terms, and understood prophecy in Hellenistic terms, using the complete range of the vocabulary of Greek ecstatic experience to portray biblical prophets. Moses and Abraham were prophets, and the Pentateuch was a collection of oracles. Like Josephus, Philo never explicitly calls himself a prophet, but his extraordinarily frequent discussions and detailed descriptions of the prophetic experience strongly suggest that he was describing a contemporary phenomenon he had observed in the synagogue, indeed that he himself experienced a kind of inspiration akin to the prophetic (cf. e.g., *De mig. Abr.* 35; *De Cher.* 27; esp. *Heres* 259–60).

b. Rabbis. The rabbis, too, testify to the fact that the prophetic spirit was alive and well in the Judaism from which Christianity was born. The heavenly voice *(Bath Qol)* was heard even by those rabbis who believed that it could not take precedence over traditional Halakah. Though by no means a major element in rabbinic religious experience, a significant number of prophetic phenomena may be documented even among those rabbis where the dogma of the end of prophecy might be expected to have been most influential. We should not, therefore, be surprised to find an abundance of evidence for prophets and prophecy in those circles where the rabbinic dogma was less influential, namely among the Zealots, Essenes, and other apocalyptically oriented groups (though conspicuously absent among the Sadducees).

c. Josephus. Josephus claimed that during the 66–70 war he presented himself to the conquering Vespasian as a messenger sent from God to announce that Vespasian would be the new Roman emperor (*JW* 3.400–402). Without using the word, he thus claimed to be a prophet himself. The term "prophet" is used in several senses by Josephus, who used it to describe Zealot prophets and Essene seers, as well as folk prophets among the people, especially during the critical period of the war and siege of Jerusalem (66–70 C.E.). The result is that it is not always clear that he refers to persons characterized by the claim to be inspired spokespersons for God, as in the definition used here. It is equally clear, however, that he does describe such people, though for his own political purposes he often describes them as "false prophets." That the prophetic phenomenon was alive in 1st-century Judaism is illustrated in Josephus' account of Joshua (Jesus) ben Ananiah, an unlettered peasant who began in 62 constantly to repeat an oracle of doom against the city, and continued despite insults and torture to repeat his oracle until the last days of Jerusalem in 70, when he was killed by a Roman projectile (*JW* 6.300–309).

d. Qumran. Qumran illustrates the presence of prophecy in one Jewish fringe group, which believed that it lived in the last days, within which the gift of prophecy had been renewed. The Teacher of Righteousness did not use the word "prophet" of himself, but functioned as a prophet, speaking from the mouth of God (1QpHab 2:2–3), taught by God himself, who has poured out his spirit upon him (7:4–7). As in early Christianity, prophecy was related to the interpretation of Scripture and to the eschatological theology of the community.

e. John the Baptist. The first prophet described in the New Testament is John the Baptist, whose career was contemporary with, and in some respects like, that of Jesus: he was a popular charismatic figure who created eschatological excitement, was alienated from conventional culture, was critical of the established authorities and suffered death at their hands, and had a community of disciples that continued to revere him after his death, Matt 3:1–12 (= Mark 1:4–8; Luke 3:2–18); 11:2–19 (= Luke 7:18–35); 14:5 (= Mark 6:17–29; Luke 3:19–20); 17:10–13 (= Mark 9:11–13); John 1:19–36; Luke 1:5–80; Acts 19:1–7. As a result, the Christian tradition, which could not ignore him, was at pains to fit him into a Christian understanding of the founding events and to show his subordination to Jesus. This means that the portrait of the historical John cannot be read off the surface of the NT text, but must be disentangled from the later layers of Christian interpretation. One way some, but not all, early Christians came to terms with John was by interpreting him as Elijah, understood as the forerunner of the Messiah (Matt 17:9–13; but contrast John 1:21). It is thus difficult to determine, for example, if John's strange dress is historical reminiscence or the later effort to describe him as Elijah (compare Mark 1:6 and 2 Kgs 1:8). Luke in particular is intent on describing John as belonging to the prophets of Israel described in the Hebrew Bible (3:10–14, peculiar to Luke). Still, it is clear that John was a prophet conscious of a direct call by God, who called for repentance on the basis of the eschatological judgment in the near future (Matt 3:7–12 = Luke 3:7–9). John's baptism could well be understood in the category of the symbolic actions of the prophets. He expected an eschatological "mighty one" who would execute the fiery baptism of God's judgment on those who had not received his baptism with water as the sign and seal of their repentance. John is thus pictured in the NT as belonging to the prophetic line of biblical prophets, but as "more than a prophet," i.e., the eschatological prophet who serves as the immediate forerunner and herald of the final act of God's saving history (Matt 11:9 = Luke 7:26).

f. Jesus. All four Gospels picture Jesus as a prophet. He is regarded as a prophet not only in the eyes of the people (Matt 16:14; 21:11; cf. 26:68; Mark 6:15; 8:28; 14:65; Luke 7:16; 9:8, 19; John 4:19; 9:17), but in one of the few sayings preserved in all four Gospels, he applies the proverb of the prophet rejected in his native land to himself (Matt 13:57; Mark 6:4; Luke 4:24; cf. 13:33; John 4:44). Moreover, Jesus is pictured as receiving a vision at the beginning of his ministry corresponding to a prophet's call (Matt 3:13–17; cf. Isa 6:1–10, and the role that 6:9–10 plays in the Gospels' accounts of Jesus' ministry; Mark 4:10–12 [= Matt 13:10–11 = Luke 8:10]). The spirit that he received in baptism would be understood in a Jewish context as the spirit that made one a prophet. Jesus is described as having apocalyptic visions of the fall of Satan (Luke 10:18) and even of delivering prolonged apocalyptic discourses, Mark 13:4–37 (= Matt 24:3–36 = Luke 21:7–36); Luke 17:21–37. For Luke especially, "prophet" is not a mistaken, preliminary, or minor category, but is one of his major categories of christological thought: Jesus is indeed the eschatological prophet promised in Scripture (Luke 24:19; Acts 3:22–23; 7:37; cf. Deut 18:15–18), who specifically identifies the Spirit that empowers him as the prophetic Spirit of Isa 61:1–2 (Luke 4:16–21). Jesus' authority is not the derived authority of the scribe, but the immediate authority of the inspired prophet (Matt 7:29).

Yet, if in the case of John the Baptist the historical figure of the prophet John is covered with layers of Christian interpretation, this is all the more true in the case of Jesus. Was the historical Jesus a prophet; or does "prophet," i.e., "eschatological prophet," the final messenger from God before the end, belong to the early layers of Christian interpretation of the significance of Jesus? Christian scholars of the most varied theological positions have generally agreed that the NT's picture of Jesus as prophet is historical bedrock. Conservative and evangelical Christians, while affirming the "higher" christological titles as more important, have, nonetheless, concurred in asserting that Jesus was also a prophet (Jeremias 1971). Liberal theologians, while considering other titles such as "Son of God" to be later church interpretation, have celebrated Jesus as the prophet of social justice (Rauschenbusch 1917; Enslin 1968). Rudolf Bultmann's agnosticism about the historical Jesus did not extend to his doubting that Jesus was a prophet, and his students who returned to the ("new") quest of the historical Jesus found "prophet" to be the key category (Bultmann 1958; Bornkamm 1960; Conzelmann 1969). Some recent American study of Mark (Mack 1988) and Q (Robinson 1987; Kloppenborg 1987) has argued that the prophetic picture of Jesus was a church construction, and that Jesus was more like a Cynic sage than a Jewish prophet, but the majority of scholarship would see two prophetic figures, John and Jesus, at the beginnings of the Christian movement.

C. Prophecy Reflected in the Literature of Early Christianity

The following survey presents the documentation for the phenomenon of Christian prophecy from its origins to the middle of the 2d century, i.e., prior to the advent of the "New Prophecy" with Montanus.

1. Paul. The first reflection of Christian prophecy in Christian literature is 1 Thess 5:19–20, in which Paul appears as the advocate of the prophetic gift over against its detractors. Prophecy has appeared in the Thessalonian congregation, had created some sort of problem that caused some of the Thessalonians to reject it, and Paul promotes their acceptance of the phenomenon as a gift of the Spirit, but not without critical evaluation. The most extensive discussion of Christian prophecy in the NT is found in 1 Corinthians 12–14. As in 1 Thessalonians, the discussion has a polemical tone, again revealing Paul as an advocate of prophecy, this time over against an inappropriately high valuation of glossolalia. These prophecies were more than normal pastoral preaching; it was a matter of direct revelation (cf. 1 Cor 14:29–32). It is impossible to gain any idea of the content of the revelations of the Corinthian prophets, except that in contrast to glossolalia they were expressed in intelligible language, and in Paul's view were directed to the edification of the whole church rather than responses to the private inquiries of individuals. The brief reference to prophecy in Rom 12:3–8 is valuable in that it is not polemical. Rather, a fundamental assumption of Paul's comes to expression here, namely, that wherever there is a church the Holy Spirit is at work, and wherever the Spirit is to be found there is a principal manifestation of the Spirit, the gift of prophecy. Prophecy, in fact, is the only constant in Paul's "lists" of charismata (1 Cor 12:8–11, 28–30; 13:1–2; Rom 12:6–8). When Paul "ranks" spiritual gifts, prophecy appears second only to the apostolic office or, from another perspective, love.

Since Paul insists so adamantly on his apostleship and thus does not refer explicitly to himself as a prophet, it has often been overlooked that, when defined functionally as above, Paul is a prophet who does in fact implicitly claim to exercise the prophetic gift (1 Cor 13:2; 14:6, 37). Though reluctant to parade it, he has "visions and revelations of the Lord" (2 Cor 12:1–10). The many points of contact between Paul's own biographical statements and the prophets of the Hebrew Scripture document Paul's awareness of standing within the prophetic succession (cf., e.g., Gal 1:15–16; Jer 1:5; Isa 49:1). Scholars have identified numerous passages in Paul's epistles where he is incorporating his own prophetic revelations or the oracles of some other Christian prophet. Three that are commonly so identified are 1 Thess 4:15–17; Rom 11:25–26; and 1 Cor 15:51–52, while a larger number are identified more tentatively. Paul's epistles also contain a large number of prophetic forms and formulas, which he seems to use habitually and unconsciously even when he is not citing a prophetic oracle (Müller 1975).

Paul's prophetism was once understood as of a piece with Hellenistic prophecy generally (Reitzenstein 1927; Leisegang 1919). More recent study has indicated that Paul's understanding of prophecy was not simply a reflection of the prophetic phenomena experienced in his churches but stands in tension with them (cf. 1 Thess

5:19–20 and especially 1 Corinthians 12–14). While the line between "Greek" and "Jewish" understanding of prophecy should not be drawn too neatly, it is, nevertheless, the case that Paul's understanding of prophecy is shaped by his Scripture and Jewish tradition, as well as by the understanding of prophetism in early Jewish Christianity.

2. Deutero-Paul. It is striking that there is no reference at all to prophecy in Colossians, and that "spirit" occurs only twice, each time with reference to the human spirit. "Spiritual" in 1:9 and 3:16 does suggest insight and songs given by the spirit (not just "lively tunes"), but Colossians seems very reserved with reference to the Pauline enthusiasm for prophecy, and may already express a reaction.

Ephesians, on the other hand, looks back upon the first generation and considers prophets, along with apostles, to be a constituent element in the foundation of the Church (2:20; 3:5; 4:11). The great spiritual insight of the inclusiveness of the Church was given through the post-Easter Christian prophets (not the historical Jesus!). While it is clear that the author of Ephesians admires prophets, it is equally clear that they are no longer a living reality in his church.

Likewise in the Pastorals, prophecy is primarily a remembered phenomenon from the Pauline past, rather than a vital part of the Pastor's own church, in which not charisma but "regular" ordination at the hands of authorized officials designates people for leadership in the Church. There may still be some stirrings of the prophetic spirit manifest in the references in 1 Tim 1:18; 4:14 and 2 Tim 1:14, but if they refer to the time of the author, then the gift of prophecy is regarded with more than a bit of suspicion. The point seems to be that claims to charismatic endowment should lead to regular ordination, and in fact operates properly only with the legitimately ordained channels and in connection with the deposit of tradition (*hē parathēkē*). More likely these texts, like 1 Tim 4:1–5, belong to the fictive world of "Paul" in the first generation. As in Ephesians, prophecy seems to be admired from a safe distance.

3. Q. Our earliest source for Palestinian Christianity is the hypothetical document Q, which is often considered a witness to the prophetic nature of earliest Christianity. "Prophets" are mentioned in six pericopes of Q. Of these, four refer to the prophets of Hebrew Scripture (the convention of designating Q passages by their Lukan location is here followed): 6:23; 10:24; 11:47; 16:16. ("Prophesy" in the Q passage Matt 7:22 is a Matthean addition; "prophets" in the Q text Luke 13:28 is a Lukan addition.) The way in which these texts are used indicates that for the Q community the prophets were considered the key leaders of ancient Israel. Two references point to prophets of the Q community's own time. In 7:26 John is called "more than a prophet," a designation that would include both John and Jesus as the twin messengers of transcendent Wisdom (cf. 7:33–35). In 11:49 the prophets of the Q community are included in this same line. The result is that for the Q community there was an unbroken succession of prophets from the times of Israel through John and Jesus to the Christian prophets of their own community. Rejection and persecution were the common lot of all (11:47–51). The Q document is replete with prophetic forms such as [*amēn*] *legō de hymin* ("[Amen] I say to you"). Whether some sayings of Christian prophets may be contained in Q as sayings of Jesus is discussed below.

4. Mark. Though he quotes their writings often, Mark specifically refers to OT prophets only twice (1:2; 7:6, both times to Isaiah), and makes two incidental references in connection with the understanding of Jesus as a prophet (6:16; 8:28). He never refers to John the Baptist or Jesus as a prophet (except for the implied self-identification by Jesus in 6:4). His only reference to prophets in the post-Easter time of the Church is 13:22, where they are considered false prophets, and are the Church's only opponents specifically named. Mark seems to be opposed to the prophetic phenomenon, which may indicate that Christian prophets who announced new sayings of the Lord were a problem in his church.

5. Matthew. The gospel of Matthew, on the other hand, seems to represent a church where prophecy is present and critically affirmed by the author, much as was the case with Paul and the Pauline churches. Unlike Paul, the author himself is not a prophet, but more of a scribal type (he seems to be describing himself in 13:52). His church may have been "founded" by the Q messengers (Luz 1985); he seems to stand in a later phase of the Christian prophecy manifest in the Q community. Matthew rephrases his Q source to read "the prophets *who were before you*" in 5:12, joining his own community to the prophetic community of Israel and Q. A saying peculiar to Matthew, 10:41, concludes his version of the "Missionary Discourse," indicating that Christian prophets were among the missionaries sent out by Matthew's church. In 7:15–23, general exhortations to the Christian community, in which neither the word nor idea of prophecy appears, have been altered to deal specifically with the problem posed by prophecy in the Matthean church. The passage makes clear that for Matthew the gift of prophecy did not guarantee that one was a true disciple; "doing the will of God" was the ultimate criterion.

6. Luke-Acts. Acts is the only NT document that purports to describe prophets in the earliest Church. Agabus stands out most clearly (11:27–30; 21:1–14) as one who is not only called "prophet" by Luke but fits the functional definition given here as well. Judas and Silas are prophets (15:32). Philip has four daughters who prophesy (21:9). Anonymous prophets proclaim their message by the Spirit, a term used interchangeably in such contexts with "Holy Spirit," "Spirit of the Lord," and "Spirit of Jesus," showing that it is the exalted Christ who is thought of as active in the prophetic event (16:6–7; 20:23; 21:4). A group of prophets and teachers at Antioch includes Barnabas and Paul (13:1–2). That Luke intends to include Barnabas among the prophets seems to be clear both from the grammar of this text and from 4:36; whether or not Paul is called a prophet in 13:1–2 is not absolutely clear. At the least, Paul is associated very closely with church prophets and is described by Luke as functioning as a prophet (9:3–6; 13:9–12; 16:6–9; 18:9–10; 22:6–21; 26:9–20; 27:23–24). In addition to this portrayal of particular individuals who manifest the prophetic gift, Luke understands that the Spirit has been poured out on the whole church, and this Spirit is preeminently the Spirit of Prophecy (2:17–18, 38; 4:31; 6:10; 16:6–7). This means that, though Luke does recognize certain persons in the Church who function consistently as prophets (whom he so designates), he does not draw a sharp line between prophets and non-prophets. For Luke, whoever in the church acts in the power of the Spirit is something of a prophet.

Luke is obviously interested in portraying the Church as the continuation of the OT people of God, which leads him to portray Christian prophets (as well as John the Baptist and Jesus) as similar to the prophets of his Bible. Agabus' binding himself with Paul's belt, for example, is reminiscent of the symbolic acts performed by Isaiah, Ezekiel, and Jeremiah (Acts 21:10–14; cf. Isa 20:2–6; Ezekiel 4–5; Jer 13:1–11). This and other Lukan *tendenzen* make it difficult to extract the historical reality that lay behind Luke's theological portrayal. Prophets may have been much more active in the leadership of the earliest Church, for example, than Luke's account indicates, for it emphasizes his own interests in ordered apostolic leadership. In this, Luke-Acts belongs with the Deutero-Pauline tradition discussed above. This means that in the gospel of Luke, where Jesus is portrayed in the garb of a biblical prophet, it is difficult to distinguish history from Luke's own theologizing. An exception may be provided by the outburst of prophetic phenomena in the Lukan Birth story (cf. Luke 1:35, 41–45, 67–79; 2:29–35), which may preserve memories and materials from early Christian prophets.

7. John and the Johannine Tradition. Only Jesus is called "prophet" in the gospel of John (4:19, 44; 9:17), and only Caiaphas is said to "prophesy" (11:51). Yet the function of Christian prophecy seems to be clearly evidenced in the Johannine church. Whether or not the author of Revelation is regarded as a member of the Johannine "school," the numerous points of contact between the gospel and the Apocalypse indicate interaction between the evangelist and Christian prophecy, since the Apocalypse obviously was written by a prophet. The letters, too, come from a circle that was familiar with the prophetic phenomenon and was beginning to experience some manifestations of it as problematic, without denying its validity per se (1 John 2:20, 27; 4:1–3). And since the "we" of 1 John cannot be separated from the "we" of the Fourth Gospel, we would expect a priori that the gospel would also originate from a circle in which the prophetic ministry was alive. The internal evidence of the gospel bears out this expectation. The Johannine portrayal of both the Paraclete and Jesus seems to be influenced by the author's perception of the ministry of Christian prophets in the Johannine church (cf. Boring 1978). On the night before Jesus' death, the disciples are promised that the Spirit will come in Jesus' name and speak with Jesus' authority, the Paraclete who will both keep alive the memory of Jesus and reveal new truth after Jesus' death (14:15–17, 25–26; 15:26–27; 16:8–11, 12–15). The functions of Christian prophets are here described.

8. Revelation. The Apocalypse is our most obvious, and most extensive, example of Christian prophecy among our earliest documents, being rivaled only by the later Hermas. Like Paul, the author does not specifically use *prophētēs* of himself, but nonetheless claims to write *prophēteia* (1:3; 19:20; 22:7, 10, 18–19) and to belong to a group of *prophētai* (22:9). the "book" (i.e., letter) is throughout the address of the risen Lord to his church through his immediately inspired spokesman. It is not only chapters 2–3 that are presented as the word of the exalted Lord, but the document as a whole. The subjective genitive of 1:1 embraces the whole document (cf. the series of quotations in 21:9, 15; 22:1, 6, 8, 9, 10, 12). Although the apocalyptic form of sealed scroll and interpreting angel is retained, it is subordinated to the understanding of revelation as Christian prophecy in which the risen Lord speaks through his prophet. Though saturated with apocalyptic content as well as apocalyptic forms, Revelation is thus, nonetheless, a thoroughly prophetic document. "Prophetic" and "apocalyptic" are not alternatives. Unlike the apocalyptists, John speaks in his own name the revelations he receives from the exalted Lord. That he uses traditional materials and stereotyped forms is no objection to the reality of his visionary experiences, for prophets customarily made use of traditional forms and materials to convey their messages received in various degrees of "ecstatic" experience.

9. Didache. The Manual of Church Order (*Didache* 6–15) comes from a Christian community that both honors prophecy and has come to experience it as a problem. This is the reason for the intense interest of the author(s) in prophecy, an interest that causes the instructions on prophets to be elaborated far beyond what is said about "apostles" and "teachers." These instructions do not seem to be all of a piece, indicating that they came into being from different hands over an extended period. For example, the prophet is considered to be above question when he speaks "in the Spirit," so that to challenge him is the unforgivable sin (11:7); and yet some things that he says are not to be tolerated, even if said "in the Spirit" (11:12). The criterion of true prophecy is whether he teaches according to the truth (11:1); but even that prophet who teaches according to the truth is a false prophet "if he does not practice what he teaches" (11:10). The *Didache* has been most influential in supporting the one-sided theory that early Christian prophets were itinerant "wanderers" rather than "settled" (Harnack 1910), but a close reading of the *Didache* indicates that its support for this purported characteristic of early Christian prophetism has been overemphasized.

10. Ignatius. The one instance in the Bishop of Antioch's letters that may refer to Christian prophets is not clear; it may refer to biblical prophets (*Phld.* 5:2). In any case, the reference is only incidental and provides no information. On the other hand, Ignatius speaks of himself as having "cried out" with a "great voice," the "voice of God," in which "the Spirit was speaking" (*Phld.* 7:1–2), in a context which suggests he thought of himself as speaking prophetically. The content of his oracle is an admonition to "give heed to the bishop, the presbyter, and the deacons," so Ignatius is somewhat like the Pastorals in that charisma serves primarily to reinforce church order through the developing regular channels.

11. Odes of Solomon. The prophetic spirit was thought to inspire not only oracles but hymns (cf. 1 Cor 14:15; Col 3:16; Eph 5:19; cf. the *Hodayot* from the prophetic Teacher of Qumran). The collection of forty-two hymns, all composed by the same author, seems to express the claim to prophetic inspiration. In some of them Christ speaks in the first person, as in Revelation. Particularly well-known is the concluding hymn, which expresses the prophetic self-consciousness in the words (42:6).

> Then I arose and am with them,
> and will speak by their mouths.

12. Hermas. The *Shepherd of Hermas* likewise emanates from within a structured ecclesiastical context, the Roman church in the first half of the 2d century, and is written by an author who never refers to himself as a prophet. Unless the "prophecy" of the author is only a literary device, the author is, nonetheless, a prophet by our definition, for the document repeatedly presents itself as the revelation of the Holy Spirit or Son of God to his church in the latter days (e.g., *Vis.* IV. 1.3; *Sim.* IX 1.1). The prophetic phenomenon seems still to be present in the author's church, where both "true" and "false" prophets can be observed and must be tested (*Man.* XI). There still seem to be some marks of genuine prophetic self-consciousness, e.g., the revelation of a second chance of repentance in view of the impending persecution and the imminent return of the Lord (*Vis.* III. 1.9). But even if the author does have some personal prophetic experiences, for the most part his writing is a tedious, labored, uninspired, and uninspiring work, formally in the prophetic category but written by one for whom prophecy is already a traditional phenomenon that may be stereotyped. In him, we hear the last faint echoes of the "old" prophecy. After him, references to prophecy in the Church are oriented to the "New Prophecy" of Montanism, either in affirmation or in repudiation.

D. General Characteristics and Themes of Early Christian Prophecy

1. Extent, Uniformity, and Variety. The survey above indicates that prophecy was not rare, episodic, or isolated, but was a widespread phenomenon in early Christianity that has left its traces in a variety of early Christian literature. Christian theology's emphasis on "the Prophets" (of the Hebrew Scripture) as those who predicted the days of Jesus and the Church has contributed to the fact that "prophecy" is frequently neglected as a major category for comprehending early Christianity and its own self-understanding. In fact, prophets and prophecy form a primary common denominator and line of continuity between the Hebrew Bible and the Christian Scripture. We have seen that there is considerable variety in the manifestations of prophecy in early Christianity. There are, nonetheless, enough common features to permit some general impressions, to which there are always exceptions.

2. Prophets as Church Figures. The context of prophecy is the worshipping congregation, to which prophets belong as constituent members. Although prophets, like others, on occasion travel from place to place, it is overdrawn to impose a doubtful interpretation of prophecy in the *Didache* on all our other sources, and picture itinerary as of the essence of Christian prophetism.

3. Prophets as Religious Figures. While Early Christianity generally believed that the Spirit was given to the body of believers as a whole, and not only to gifted individuals within it, prophecy was not an amorphous potentiality diffused throughout the Christian community. There was usually an identifiable group that functioned as prophets, who were recognized as such by the Church. Since the Spirit was given to the Church at large, however, the prophetic gift did not separate prophets from the Christian community. The Church as a whole, which also possessed the Spirit, was charged with critically evaluating the utterances of the prophets (Rev 2:2, 6, 14, 15, 20; 1 Corinthians 14). The prophets spoke with authority as they announced the unqualified word of the Lord, but it is also clear that they should expect a deliberate, engaged response from the community. The prophets functioned in the gathered worship of the community, not in private séances or consultations. The burden of their message was the edification of the community, not the satisfaction of private curiosity.

4. Prophets and Tradition. Tradition and revelation are not alternatives. The reality of the revelatory experiences of the prophets did not mean that they were divorced from tradition. Their oracles could be expressed using words from Scripture or other Christian tradition as the vehicle of their message.

5. Prophets and the Continuing Voice of Jesus. Prophets could express their revelations in words of the historical Jesus, which they sometimes took up and re-presented in a modified form more relevant to the new situation. Many scholars believe that new sayings of Jesus were spoken by church prophets. These sayings were blended into the Church's tradition of Jesus' words and appear in the narrative framework of the Gospels as sayings of the earthly Jesus. Since to early Christianity the earthly Jesus and the heavenly Lord were one and the same person, prior to the fixation of the tradition in the writing of the Gospels no consistent distinction was made between sayings of the pre-Easter Jesus and post-Easter revelations through church prophets. Although the presence of such prophetic sayings in the gospels is generally acknowledged, whether particular sayings that originated as Christian prophecy can be identified with any degree of confidence is a disputed point among scholars (pro: Boring 1982; con: Aune 1983; Hill 1979).

Bibliography

Aune, D. E. 1983. *Prophecy in Early Christianity and the Ancient Mediterranean World.* Grand Rapids.

Boring, M. E. 1978. The Influence of Christian Prophecy on the Johannine Portrayal of the Paraclete and Jesus. *NTS* 25: 113–23.

———. 1982. *Sayings of the Risen Jesus.* Cambridge.

———. 1989. *Revelation: A Commentary for Teaching and Preaching.* Louisville.

Bornkamm, G. 1960. *Jesus of Nazareth.* New York.

Bultmann, R. 1958. *Jesus and the Word.* New York.

Conzelmann, H. 1969. *An Outline of the Theology of the New Testament.* London.

Crone, T. 1973. *Early Christian Prophecy.* Baltimore.

Dautzenberg, G. 1975. *Urchristliche Prophetie.* Stuttgart.

Ellis, E. E. 1978. *Prophecy and Hermeneutic in Early Christianity.* Grand Rapids.

Enslin, M. S. 1968. *The Prophet from Nazareth.* New York.

Fascher, E. 1927. *PROPHETES: Eine sprach-und religionsgeschichtliche Untersuchung.* Giessen.

Harnack, A. von. 1910. *The Constitution and Law of the Church in the First Two Centuries.* New York.

Hill, D. 1979. *New Testament Prophecy*. Richmond, VA.
Horsley, R. A. 1986. Popular Prophetic Movements at the Time of Jesus: Their Principal Features and Social Origins. *JSNT* 26: 3–27.
Jeremias, J. 1971. *The Proclamation of Jesus*. Vol. 1 in *New Testament Theology*. New York.
Kloppenborg, J. S. 1987. *The Formation of Q*. Philadelphia.
Leisegang, H. 1919. *Die vorchristlichen Anschauungen und Lehren vom pneuma und der mystisch-intuitiven Erkenntnis*. Vol. 1 in *Der Heilige Geist*. Leipzig.
Lindblom, J. 1968. *Gesichte und Offenbarungen*. Lund.
Luz, U. 1985. *Das Evangelium nach Matthäus (Mt 1–7)*. Neukirchen-Vluyn.
Mack, B. 1988. *A Myth of Innocence*. Philadelphia.
Müller, U. 1975. *Prophetie und Predigt im Neuen Testament*. Gütersloh.
Panagopoulos, J. 1877. *Prophetic Vocation in the New Testament and Today*. Leiden.
Rauschenbusch, W. 1917. *A Theology for the Social Gospel*. New York.
Reitzenstein, R. 1927. *Die hellenistischen Mysterienreligionen: Nach ihren Grundgedanken und Wirkungen*. Leipzig (ET 1978).
Robinson, J. M. 1987. The Jesus Movement in Galilee: Reconstructing Q. *Bulletin of the Institute for Antiquity and Christianity*. 14/3: 4–5.
Sato, M. 1988. *Q und Prophetie*. WUNT 2/29. Tübingen.
Schmeller, T. 1989. *Brechungen: Urchristliche Wandercharismatiker im Prisma soziologisch orientierter Exegese*. SBS 136. Stuttgart.

M. EUGENE BORING

PROPHETS, LIVES OF THE. A short Jewish writing, deriving probably from the 1st century C.E. Its opening words describe the work's content: "The names of the prophets, and where they are from, and where they died and how, and where they lie."

Although Syriac, Ethiopic, Latin, and Armenian versions are extant, these all appear to derive from Greek originals. The numerous Greek witnesses are generally sorted into four major recensions: long and short recensions attributed to Epiphanius, another ascribed to Dorotheus, and an anonymous recension. Of these the last appears to be the earliest and to preserve the best text. It is best represented by Codex Marchalianus (Cod. Vaticanus Gk. 2125, 6th century, Vatican Library), known by the siglum Q. The Greek manuscripts differ considerably in the order in which the canonical prophets are presented and in their choice of nonliterary prophets to be treated.

Because of provenance and subject matter it is often assumed that the document was written originally in a Semitic language: Syriac, Hebrew, or Aramaic. Torrey (1946) believed it possible to demonstrate that certain problems in the Greek text are due to the mistranslation of an underlying Hebrew writing. Klein, on the other hand, maintained that an Aramaic original was as possible as a Hebrew one (1937). Schermann (1907a), whose work on the document remains fundamental, postulated a Hebrew source, but insisted that the earliest Greek text was not simply a translation. It thus remains possible that, despite an origin in the folklore of Jewish Palestine, the work may have first assumed its present shape in Greek.

Some of the Greek mss are clearly Christian products, incorporating sections concerning John the Baptist, his father Zechariah, and other early figures referred to in the NT. Fortunately, the Q ms contains none of these obvious interpolations, but more subtle Christian alterations are suspected at a few points. A date after the emergence of Christianity is probable if 2:13 ("And this will be for you a sign of [the Lord's] coming, when all the gentiles worship a piece of wood") is taken as a Jewish expression of disgust at Christian superstition, but the words may just as well represent a Christian interpolation anticipating Jesus' Parousia, when the full number of gentiles have been converted. (References and quotations follow the translation of Hare *OTP* 2: 379–99.) Perhaps significant is the fact that there is no clear mention of the destruction of Jerusalem in 70 C.E. (a possible allusion may be found in the ambiguous language of 12:11); such an omission would be surprising in the opening passage concerning Isaiah's grave, which seems to assume that the readers can make a pilgrimage to the site. Moreover, it has been proposed that this same passage presupposes that the pool of Siloam is situated outside the walls of Jerusalem. This was no longer the case after Herod Agrippa added a new southern wall to the city's fortifications in 41–44 C.E. An early date is also suggested by the author's allusion to Elijah as "a Thesbite, from the land of Arabs" (21:1), since Nabatean control of this area ended in 106 C.E. Of still greater importance for the dating of the document is the fact that its interest in the graves of the prophets is paralleled by the erection of an impressive monument at David's tomb by Herod the Great (Jos. *Ant* 16.7.1 §182). We may suppose that this interest in venerating David's resting place spread to include other ancient worthies, as witnessed in the saying attributed to Jesus by Matt 23:29 ("Woe to you . . . for you build the tombs of the prophets and adorn the monuments of the righteous"; cf. Luke 11:47–48). Since there is no mention of newly constructed monuments in the *Lives,* it is even possible that its publication early in the 1st century was one of the factors encouraging the activity to which Jesus' saying alludes.

The author appears to have precise knowledge of Jerusalem. This inclined Torrey (1946) to the opinion that the author was a Jerusalemite Jew. Since both the Hebrew and Greek textual traditions of Scripture are reflected in the document, we can postulate that its author was a bilingual Jew living in Judea.

In Codex Q, twenty-three prophets are treated, in the following order: Isaiah, Jeremiah, Ezekiel, Daniel, Hosea, Micah, Amos, Joel, Obadiah, Jonah, Nahum, Habakkuk, Zephaniah, Haggai, Zechariah, Malachi, Nathan, Ahijah, Joad (the unnamed "man of God" of 1 Kings 13), Azariah, Elijah, Elisha, and Zechariah, son of Jehoiada. It is to be noted that the position of Daniel conforms with the sequence of the LXX, not with that of the MT, and that the order in which the Twelve are presented is likewise closer to that of the LXX.

The amount of space devoted to the various prophets varies greatly. Joel receives the least attention: "Joel was from the territory of Reuben, in the countryside of Bethomoron. He died in peace and was buried there." The major prophets and Daniel, however, are treated at considerable length through the incorporation of legendary traditions, many of which are known to us from other Jewish sources.

The sections devoted to Elijah and Elisha are also extended, but in these two cases the material is primarily a summary of "signs" attributed to the two prophets in the canon (1–2 Kings). This material is omitted by the Dorotheus recension, and is replaced by shorter additions in the two recensions attributed to Epiphanius. Torrey is therefore justified in regarding these passages of Codex Q as later additions (1946).

Of special interest is the fact that in all four recensions the sections dealing with Elijah and Elisha contain brief birth narratives. Respecting Elijah, for example, it is reported: "When he was to be born, his father Sobacha saw that men of shining white appearance were greeting him and wrapping him in fire, and they gave him flames of fire to eat. And he went and reported (this) in Jerusalem, and the oracle told him, 'Do not be afraid, for his dwelling will be light and his word judgment, and he will judge Israel.' " This is one of the earliest witnesses to the belief that Elijah has been assigned a judging role in the eschatological drama.

The document is not profoundly theological. It is a good example of "folk religion," replete as it is with legend and superstition. Interest in Jeremiah's grave, for example, is motivated by its effectiveness in healing snake bites: "And those who are God's faithful pray at the place to this very day, and taking the dust of the place they heal asps' bites" (2:4). In terms of the history of religion, the document provides evidence of the emerging practice of venerating the saints, which later became such a prominent feature of popular Christianity.

Bibliography

Jeremias, J. 1958. *Heiligengräber in Jesu Umwelt.* Göttingen.

Klein, S. 1937. *'al-ha-seper* Vitae Prophetarum. Pp. 189–208 in *Sefer Klozner,* ed. H. Torczyner. Tel Aviv (in Hebrew).

Schermann, T. 1907a. *Prophetarum vitae fabulosae Indices apostolorum, discipulorumque Domini: Dorotheo Epiphanio Hippolyto aliisque vindicate.* Leipzig.

———. 1907b. *Propheten- und Apostellegenden nebst Jüngerkatalogen des Dorotheus und verwandter Texte.* TU 31/3. Leipzig.

Torrey, C. C. 1946. *The Lives of the Prophets.* SBLMS 1. Philadelphia.

Douglas R. A. Hare

PROSELYTE [Gk *proselytos*]. In antiquity the term "proselyte" was used only in the context of Judaism. In the LXX it translates Heb *gēr,* a word designating a resident alien or sojourner in the land. Later it became a technical term for a convert to Judaism, thus representing one aspect of the more general phenomenon of conversion in antiquity (the basic work on this subject remains Nock 1933). The term is used in Matt 23:15 and Acts 2:11 (—Eng 2:10); 6:5 and 13:43. The difficulties in determining this word's meaning include the relative paucity and frequent obscurity of the extant occurrences, and the lack of a thorough critical analysis. Not only do scholars today differ widely in their interpretation of the evidence, even the Jews of antiquity seem to have held a wide range of opinions regarding the proselyte (Cohen 1989: 14). To establish the background for the NT meaning of the term, here the most important Jewish (OT, Apocrypha and Pseudepigrapha, Philo, Josephus, rabbinic literature, and epigraphic evidence) and Greco-Roman sources concerning conversion to Judaism are presented.

In the Hebrew Bible the *gēr* was an alien who resided in the land, thereby lacking the protection and privileges associated with blood relationship and native birth. The term occurs most frequently in the Pentateuch. The Book of the Covenant portrays the *gēr* as standing in a special relationship to Yahweh (see Exod 20:10; 22:21; 23:9, 12). Even so, the *gēr*'s status was not religious, but reflected the fact that the *gēr,* as an alien, was under the influence of the God, to whom the land belonged. While Deuteronomy includes the *gēr* in the observance of some religious rites and festivals (5:14; 16:11, 14; 29:11), when 31:12 explicitly states that the *gēr* must be present for the solemn reading of the law, the intent was to expose the *gēr* to the demands of the law, not to imply that he was a full-fledged member of the cultic community (*TDOT* 2: 455). In P nearly the same religious rights and duties apply to the *gēr* as to the full citizen (Num 15:14–16). This inclusion of the *gēr* in the religious life of the nation arose from the people's sense of their own separateness, which demanded full differentiation from all foreigners. Since the people could not avoid contact with the *gērîm,* they had to provide a place for them in the religious community (*TDNT* 6: 730). In the late strata of P, the *gēr* was fully integrated into the life of the community by circumcision and mode of life (*TDOT* 2: 447). In the prophetic literature the *gēr* is routinely associated with defenseless widows and orphans as those who are unjustly oppressed (Jer 7:6; 22:3; Ezek 22:7, 29; Zech 7:10; Mal 3:5) and is said to have a share with the tribes of Israel in the promised inheritance (Ezek 47:22–23).

The LXX translated Heb *gēr* with Gk *prosēlytos* 77 times, but only in those cases where the context suggested a religious meaning, employing the terms *xenos* and *paroikos* elsewhere. This narrowing of the definition was a result of the Jews' altered circumstances in the Diaspora. The translators of the LXX appropriated the OT concern for resident aliens on behalf of the gentiles who adopted the religion and customs of Judaism, thereby providing a biblical basis for a practical reality.

Proselytes play a minor role in the Apocrypha and Pseudepigrapha. Achior the Ammonite believed firmly in God, was circumcised, and joined the house of Israel (Jdt 14:10). In *Joseph and Aseneth* the Egyptian Aseneth converted to Judaism in order to marry the patriarch Joseph.

While Philo did use the term proselyte for converts to Judaism (*Somn* II 273; *Spec Leg* I.51, 308), he seems to have preferred the more familiar term "alien" *(epēlus, epēlutes, epēlytos).* Philo asserted that converts had equal status with those who were Jews by birth. Moreover, because of their conversion they deserved special attention, having left country, family, friends, customs, tributes, and honors for the sake of the truth (*Spec Leg* I.51–53; 4.178; *Virt* 102–4, 219). He contrasted the virtues of the converts with the vices of those Jews by birth who had forsaken the faith (*Virt* 182; see *Praem* 152; *Spec Leg* I.51).

Josephus avoided using the term "proselyte." The closest he came was to call Fulvia, a Roman woman of high rank, a "convert to Judaism *[proselēlythuian tois Ioudaikois]*" (*Ant* 18.82). Normally he employed such phrases as those who "adopt our laws *[nomous eiselthein]*" (*Ag Ap* 2.123); those "aliens *[allophylous]*" who "elect to share" Jewish customs and who "desire to come and live under the same laws with us" (2.209–10); or those who "became converts to Judaism *[eis ta Ioudaiōn ethē ton bion metebalon]*" (20.17; see also 20.139). Even so, Josephus remains the foremost source for accounts of conversion to Judaism in the biblical period. The most extensive surviving account of a convert is that of Izates, king of Adiabene, who was instructed in the Jewish faith by a merchant named Ananias (*Ant* 20.17–95). Izates' mother, Helena, while sympathetic, warned that his subjects "would not tolerate the rule of a Jew over them." Ananias agreed with her, contending that Izates could "worship God without being circumcised." Another Jew, Eleazar, a Galilean with a reputation for strict adherence to the ancestral laws, told Izates that he "ought not merely to read the law but also, and even more, to do what is commanded in it." Izates took this advice and was circumcised. Later his brother, Monobazus, seeing that the king's pious worship of God "won the admiration of all men," likewise wished to convert to Judaism. Some members of the royal family subsequently supported the Jewish revolt against Rome (*JW* 2.520; 5.474).

In addition to accounts of conversion, Josephus also related that Jewish customs held some attraction for gentiles: "There is not one city, Greek or barbarian, nor a single nation, to which our custom of abstaining from work on the seventh day has not spread." Some also observed fasting, the lighting of lamps, and many of the dietary regulations. Moreover, the gentiles imitated "our unanimity, our liberal charities, our devoted labor in the crafts, our endurance under persecution on behalf of our laws" (2.281–83; see 2.179–80). The wealth of the Jewish temple was attributable to contributions from Jews and "those who worshipped God *[Ioudaiôn kai sebomenôn ton theon]*" (*Ant* 14.110). Nero's wife Poppaea, was "a worshipper of God *[theosebês]*" and pleaded on behalf of the Jews (*Ant* 20.195). The Jews in Antioch attracted "multitudes of Greeks" to their religious ceremonies (*JW* 7.45).

Because we lack a critical analysis of the rabbinic literature on the topic, it is difficult to state with any certainty the importance of this evidence for understanding conversion to Judaism in the biblical period. Schiffman presents a brief summary of the evidence drawn from the Tannaitic literature (1985: 19–39). There conversion to Judaism entailed acceptance of the Torah, including an identification with the historic experience of the Jewish people. For males, circumcision was required as the ultimate sign of Jewish identity; the convert must be purified in a ritual bath; and the convert was to bring a sacrifice to the temple. The requirements of baptism and sacrifice are not attested before the end of the 1st century C.E. (Collins 1985: 171).

Kuhn has identified ten inscriptions referring to Jewish proselytes, including two from Jerusalem and eight (out of a total of 554 inscriptions referring to Jews) from Italy, a number he considers "surprisingly small" (*TDNT* 6: 732–34). The Roman inscriptions come from the catacombs, where the proselytes were buried with the Jews, an indication that they were accepted as full members of the community.

Greco-Roman sources include scattered references to conversion to Judaism, many of which are openly hostile. Horace (65–8 B.C.E.) is often cited as the earliest attestator of Jewish proselytizing zeal, when he stated: "We [poets], like the Jews, will compel you to make one of our throng" (*Sat.* 1.4, 138–43). Nolland, however, attributes this statement to the realm of politics and personal advantage and not to that of the propagation of religious ideals (1979: 353). Epictetus (ca. 55–ca. 135 C.E.) contrasted those who observed some Jewish customs with those who were true converts: "Whenever we see a man halting between two faiths, we are in the habit of saying, 'He is not a Jew, he is only acting the part.' But when he adopts the attitude of mind of the man who has been baptized and has made his choice, then he both is a Jew in fact and is also called one" (cited in Arr., *Epict. Diss.* 2:19–20).

Tacitus (b. ca. 55 C.E.) considered those who were attracted to Judaism "the worst rascals," for they renounced their ancestral religions and sent contributions to Jerusalem. The Jews, he said, were extremely loyal toward one another, but toward everyone else they exhibited only hatred and enmity. They adopted circumcision to distinguish themselves from other peoples. Moreover, those who converted to their ways followed the same practices, so that the earliest lesson they received was "to despise the gods, to disown their country, and to regard their parents, children, and brothers as of little account" (*Hist.* 5.5). Juvenal (b. 67 C.E.), in a satire on the bad influence of parental vices, described a progressive attraction to Judaism from one generation to the next. The father, he said, observed the Sabbath. His offspring worshipped nothing but the clouds and the divinity of the heavens, and would no sooner eat swine's flesh than human. In time they were circumcised. Then they would give directions only to those who worshipped as they did, and would conduct none but the circumcised to the desired fountain. "For all which the father was to blame, who gave up every seventh day to idleness" (*Saturnae* 14.96–106). Cassius Dio (ca. 160–230 C.E.) observed that the title "Jews" applied both to those who are from Judea and "to all the rest of mankind, although of alien race, who affect their customs," a class which had increased "to a very great extent" (*Roman history* 37.17.1). Tiberius banished the Jews from Rome because they "were converting many of the natives to their ways" (57.18.5a). Those who "drifted into Jewish ways" were subject to the charge of atheism, which was punishable by death or at least by the confiscation of their property (67.14.2).

These references in Greco-Roman literature to conversion to Judaism are consistent with the unsympathetic attitude these sources display toward Judaism in general. Their hostility is confirmed by Philo's and Josephus' references to the difficulties converts encountered. Given this context, Millar states, the ability of the Jewish apologists to present Judaism as appealing depended on three factors. These authors focused on issues for which they could expect a sympathetic hearing, such as their conception of God, and they emphasized the role of Judaism in training for the conduct of life. Moreover, the Hellenistic world was receptive to new cult forms, especially those, like Judaism, which included a monotheistic element, emphasized the expiation of sins, and expected a happy afterlife (*HJP*² 3/1: 153–58).

To a certain extent the Jewish apologetic was clearly successful. Both Jewish and pagan sources attest that at least some Jewish practices gained wide acceptance in the Greco-Roman world. Cohen has identified a diversity of favorable responses to Judaism, ranging from admiration for some aspects of Judaism to conversion (1989: 15–30). Those gentiles who displayed some sympathy for Jewish religion without actually converting to Judaism are sometimes called "God-fearers." See DEVOUT. Determining the number of gentiles who converted remains problematic. Millar suggests that at one point (probably in the last centuries B.C.E.) their numbers may have been considerable, based on the "immense expansion of Judaism" that seems to have taken place during that time. During the Roman period, he says, actual conversions to Judaism seem to have been less frequent than other less formal associations (*HJP*² 3/1: 171).

This evidence indicates that in the NT the term "proselyte" refers to gentiles who had converted to Judaism. Proselytes from Rome were present at Pentecost (Acts 2:11). Nicolaus, a proselyte of Antioch, was one of the seven deacons (6:5). "Devout proselytes *[tôn sebomenôn prosêlytôn]*" and Jews followed Paul and Barnabas out of the synagogue at Antioch in Pisidia (13:43). The reference in Matt 23:15 to the scribes and Pharisees who "traverse sea and land to make a single proselyte" has frequently been taken to refer to the missionary zeal of the Jews in general and the Pharisees in particular. Little other evidence suggests that the Pharisees (or their descendants) were concerned with the conversion of the gentiles, except as a theoretical question. Alternately, if this saying originated with the evangelist writing after 70 C.E., rather than with Jesus speaking before 70, it would serve as an example of the Christian polemic against the nascent "normative" Judaism of the rabbis (see Wild 1985: 123). This passage is akin to the references to the "circumcision party" in Acts 11:2 and the Pauline Epistles (parallel also to Eleazar's approach to Izates of Adiabene): once a gentile became a Christian, some Jews and Jewish Christians would attempt to bring the convert into full conformity with the requirements of the law.

Bibliography

Cohen, S. J. D. 1989. Crossing the Boundary and Becoming a Jew. *HTR* 82: 13–33.

Collins, J. J. 1985. A Symbol of Otherness: Circumcision and Salvation in the First Century. Pp. 163–86 in *To See Ourselves as Others See Us,* ed. J. Neusner and E. S. Frerichs. Scholars Press Studies in the Humanities. Chico, CA.

Nock, A. D. 1933. *Conversion.* Oxford.

Nolland, J. 1979. Proselytism or Politics in Horace Satires 1, 4, 138–143? *VC* 33: 347–55.

Schiffman, L. H. 1985. *Who Was a Jew?* Hoboken, NJ.

Stern, M. 1974. *Greek and Latin Authors on Jews and Judaism.* 3 vols. Jerusalem.

Wild, R. A. 1985. The Encounter between Pharisaic and Christian Judaism. *NovT* 27: 105–24.

Williams, M. H. 1988. *Theosebes gar en:* The Jewish Tendencies of Poppaea Sabina. *JTS* 39: 97–111.

PAUL F. STUEHRENBERG

PROSTITUTION [Heb *zĕnût, zĕnûnîm, taznût*]. The practice of indiscriminate sexual relations in exchange for payment is attested throughout antiquity, as well as in the Bible. This entry consists of two articles that survey this practice. The first provides an overview to the phenomenon of prostitution as it is attested in the OT, as well as the metaphorical references to prostitution contained in the biblical text. The second focuses particularly on the question of whether and how extensively cultic (or sacred) prostitution was practiced in the ancient and biblical world.

OLD TESTAMENT

Although the Hebrew root *znh* underlies all the major OT words for "prostitute" and "prostitution," derivations from the root also refer to premarital sex and to adultery (extramarital sex). The prostitute is called a *zônâ* or *ʾiššâ zônâ* but perhaps also a *qĕdēšâ*. Evidence for male prostitution is lacking (but see B below).

A. The Prostitute in the OT
B. Cultic Prostitution in the OT
C. Prostitution as a Metaphor

A. The Prostitute in the OT

The label *zônâ* is used for the professional prostitute who accepts payment for her services, but perhaps can also be applied simply to a woman who had sex before marriage (Lev 21:7, 14 and the opinion of R. Elazar in *b. Yebam.* 61b). Israelite society's attitude toward prostitution was decidedly negative; yet despite legislation intended to outlaw this institution (Lev 19:29; for Deut 23:18, see B below), the prostitute seems to have been tolerated. While priests were not allowed to marry prostitutes and their daughters were burned for plying this trade (Lev 21:7, 9, 14), these strict standards did not apply to the lay Israelite. Prostitutes had access to the king for judgment (1 Kgs 3:16), and scholars find it worthy of mention that the Bible passes no moral judgment against Tamar, who posed as a prostitute (Genesis 38); Rahab (Joshua 2, 6); or Samson, who frequented a prostitute (Judg 16:1). Rahab in particular is cited as evidence of the Bible's ambivalent view of prostitutes, because it is she who shows exemplary wisdom and faith—so much so that in later tradition she is the progenitrix of great men (*b. Meg.* 14b; Matt 1:5).

On the other hand, this toleration is accompanied by a great degree of contempt. Bird (1974: 67) writes that the stories of Rahab and Tamar

> . . . also presuppose their low repute. In both accounts the harlot heroines are made to demonstrate in their words and actions faith, courage and love that would scarcely be expected of the average upright citizen and thus is all the more astonishing and compelling as the response of a harlot—that member of society from whom one would least expect religious and moral sensitivity.

Treating a girl as a prostitute was seen as a grave offense to family honor, one that justified, in the eyes of Simeon and Levi at least, death (Gen 34:31). The prostitution of one's wife was considered a horrible event on par with the death of one's children and the loss of one's patrimony (Amos 7:17). In 1 Kgs 22:38, the mention of harlots washing in the pool of Samaria where Ahab's bloody chariot was flushed out is no doubt intended as an insult to his dignity, similar to his blood being lapped by dogs. Having relations with prostitutes carried a stigma (Gen 38:23). While Lev 21:7, 14 presuppose that an Israelite would marry a former prostitute, Jer 3:3 suggests that prostitutes were a stubborn, unrepentant lot.

In Mesopotamia, prostitutes were also a tolerated, yet deprecated class of women (see the entry *ḫarīmtu,* "prostitute," CAD 6:101–2; having seven daughters become prostitutes is on par with having seven sons immolated "before Adad" [*AfO,* Beiheft 1 73 No. 8:7, NA]). The goddess Ishtar is compared to a "loving *ḫarīmtu,*" yet this is probably more of a negative reflection on Ishtar than an allusion to the exalted status of the prostitute (*Sumerisch-babylonisch Hymnen,* 106: 51). Their rights and restrictions are mentioned in law codes (Lipit Ishtar #27, *ANET,* 160; Middle Assyrian Law (henceforth MAL) #40, #49, #52, *ANET,* 183–85). This legal recognition stands in contrast with the *de jure* prohibition of prostitution in Israel, whatever the case *de facto.* Thus, Lev 19:29 prohibits the Israelite from selling his daughter into prostitution "lest the land be filled with depravity." This probably reflects the practice of selling one's children into debt slavery hinted at in Exod 21:7; 2 Kgs 4:1; and Code of Hammurabi (henceforth CH) #117 (*ANET,* 170). Deuteronomy's prohibition is more absolute: "No Israelite woman shall be a prostitute" (23:18; see B below).

Israel's greater intolerance of prostitution was probably influenced by several factors. First, paternity would be largely unknown with regard to the children of a prostitute (Jephthah in Judg 11:1 is an exception; for another, see the case in Lipit Ishtar #27, *ANET,* 160). MAL #49 (*ANET,* 184) probably reflects the normal situation in that the paternity of the harlot's children is unknown; and so they inherit from their mother: "If a prostitute dies, her children will receive a share like a brother together with the brothers of their mother." In both Israel and Mesopotamia, property and status were normally inherited patrilineally. Adoption, the transfer of the legal paternity of a child, was practiced in Mesopotamia, as evidenced by legal texts and wills (CH #185–87, *ANET,* 174; MAL #28, *ANET,* 182; for Nuzi, see Paradise 1972: 269–80). This did not seem to be the case in Israel, where we find almost no mention of the transfer of legal paternity outside of the family (Tigay, *EncJud* 2: 298–300; Moule, *IDB* 1, 48). Adoption is not mentioned in biblical law. A society which valued the patrilineal bloodline so highly would logically have a real abhorrence of children with no known paternity and of the mother who bred them. These offspring would have no proper inheritance and no patronym. Also, unknown paternity could lead to unwitting incest, another practice abhorred by YHWH (Leviticus 18, 20).

Second, Israel was to aspire to be a "holy nation," and this included a strict code of sexual morality. A comparison of the sexual ethics in biblical law with those reflected in Mesopotamian law codes reveals the absolute nature of the former. For example, Hittite law #200 (*ANET,* 197) absolves a man who had sexual relations with a horse or mule but not with a pig or bovine (#187, #199, *ANET,* 196), while Lev 18:23, 20:16 prohibit the Israelite from having carnal relations "with any beast." MAL #14 (*ANET,* 181) decrees punishment for an adulterer only if he was informed of the married status of the woman, while the OT makes no such exception (Exod 20:14; Lev 18:20; 20:10; Deut 22:22). CH #154 (*ANET,* 172) imposes banishment for the man who has intercourse with his daughter, and death by fire for he who lies with his mother (#157). In Israel, the punishment for incest seems to be more uniformly severe. In Leviticus 20, execution (probably stoning), death by fire, *kārēt* (the imminent end of the family line according to traditional Jewish exegesis and Wold 1978), dying childless, and "bearing one's iniquity" (probably a reference to *kārēt*) are the sentences imposed upon those who commit incest. It is difficult to decide which is more severe, death by stoning or the end of one's line through divine intervention. Israel's God was highly intolerant of sexual relations outside of narrowly prescribed circumstances. The activities of a prostitute certainly fell outside of these limitations.

Third, the metaphor of apostasy as *zĕnût,* "harlotry," linked the breaking of the exclusive bond with YHWH, the Sinaitic covenant, with the rupture of the most exclusive bond known in Israelite society, marriage (Jer 2:20, 25; 3:1–13; Ezekiel 16; 23; Hosea 1–3). Apostasy, therefore, seemed all the more unacceptable because of its association with adultery and promiscuity. The process, however, may have been bidirectional in that sexual promiscuity may have seemed all the more heinous because of its kinship with religious infidelity. The title of the prostitute, *zônâ,* and her activities, *zĕnût* or *zĕnûnîm,* carried the cargo not only of sexual, but also of religious infidelity because of the currency of the expression *zānâ ʾaḥărêy ʾĕlōhîm ʾăḥērîm* (Exod 34:15–16; Deut 31:16; Judg 2:17; 8:33; 1 Chr 5:25). The use of this metaphor therefore may have served not only to make apostasy more repulsive but also prostitution, which came to symbolize infidelity and lack of discrimination in the religious sphere as well.

Possible allusions to the prostitute's distinctive garments or ornaments have been found in several OT texts. Gen 38:15 reports concerning Tamar that, "When Judah saw her, he took her for a harlot; for she had covered her face." While some see the veil alluded to here as the customary garb of a harlot, an alternative explanation is preferable: her situation suggested her vocation because a crossroads (v 14) is a traditional place for a harlot to sit (Jer 3:2; Ezek 16:25), and because Tamar's face was covered, Judah could not identify her as his daughter-in-law (so suggests Rashi and LXX's surplus at the end of the verse, "and he didn't recognize her"). MAL #40 (*ANET,* 183) prohibits the common harlot from wearing a veil. Jeremiah's allusion (3:3) to a prostitute's distinctive "forehead" (Heb *mēṣaḥ*) could suggest some peculiar ornament (Holladay *Jeremiah* Hermeneia, 115), yet it is more likely that an internal trait is intended. The forehead is the seat of obstinacy (Ezek 3:7; Isa 48:4), and *Tg. Neb.* translates here *ḥûṣpā,* "impudence." Prov 7:10 may allude to the distinctive dress of a prostitute (for the unusual term *šît,* see also Ps 73:6). In Hos 2:4, the prophet implores his straying wife to "put away her harlotry from her face and her adultery from between her breasts." While this could be a dramatic and graphic way of telling her to refrain from her promiscuity, a more literal meaning is also possible (Andersen and Freedman, *Hosea* AB, 224–25). Perhaps she wore some badge or adornment which suggested that she was a harlot. In v 5, the enraged husband threatens to strip his wife if she does not voluntarily remove these items, while v 15 mentions a nose ring and pendants. Alternatively, these adornments need not be the badges of prostitution, but rather the items that women customarily used to make themselves more attractive—cosmetics (2 Kgs 9:30; Jer 4:30) and jewelry (Isa 3:16–23).

The prostitute's fee was called *ʾetnan* (Deut 23:19; Isa 23:17–18; Ezek 16:31, 34, 41; Hos 9:1; Mic 1:7) and perhaps *ʾetnâ* (Hos 2:14; see Andersen and Freedman, 254). Ezek 16:33 uses the terms *nēdeh* and *nādān* for the gifts given to a prostitute. The use of these wages for sacrificial purposes was prohibited (Deut 23:19). Mic 1:7 may suggest that the *ʾetnan* was not an insignificant source of income for a temple (van der Toorn 1989: 193–201). Prov 6:26 seems to compare the meager price of a prostitute's serves (a loaf of bread) with the heavy cost of adultery—one's precious life. Prov 29:3, on the other hand, suggests that keeping company with prostitutes leads to poverty. Prostitutes were commonly encountered in public places such as highways (Gen 38:14; Jer 3:2; Ezek 16:25; Prov 7:11–12) or pilgrimage sites (Hos 4:14), yet Jer 5:7 condemns those Jerusalemites who go "trooping to a harlot's house." Isa 23:15–16 suggests that prostitutes commonly sang and played the harp.

The "foreign woman" (*ʾiššâ zārâ* or *nōkriyyâ)* of Proverbs 2; 5–7 is probably not a harlot but rather an adulteress (2:16–17, 6:29–35; 7:19). Prov 6:26 seems to contrast the prostitute and the adulteress, who is also called an "alien" (*nōkriyyâ,* v 24). In Proverbs 7, the seductress appears in a harlot's garb (if that is the intent of *šît zônâ,* v 10) yet she does not receive wages as a harlot, but rather rewards her paramour with a feast (v 14). Only Prov 23:27 identifies the *nōkriyyâ* as a *zônâ,* but the LXX reads here *zārâ,* not *zônâ.*

B. Cultic Prostitution in the OT

It has long been assumed that the terms *qādēš/qĕdēšâ* allude to the practice of cultic prostitution in Israel, yet recent studies seriously question this widespread assumption. See also PROSTITUTION (CULTIC). The supposed role of the Mesopotamian *qadištu* as a cult prostitute has been thought to provide proof that her Hebrew counterpart, the *qĕdēšâ,* likewise had a sexual function in the cult. Yet the research of Gruber (1986: 133–48), Hooks (1985: 15–17), and Gwaltney (1964) gainsays this assumption. The *qadištu* assumed various cultic roles, yet none of these were sexual. Among other classes of female cultic functionaries, only the *kezertu* and perhaps the *ḫarīmtu* may have combined both cultic and sexual functions (Gallery 1980: 333–38; entry *ḫarīmtu,* CAD 6: 101–2). Further, the term *qdšm* at Ugarit signifies a class of male cult personnel, who are generally mentioned after the *khnm,* "priests." Any insinuation of sexual activity is lacking (Kinet 1977: 80; von Soden 1970: 329–30; Gruber 1983: 170–71). Extrabiblical sources, therefore, cannot be used as evidence for the sexual/cultic role of the *qādēš/qĕdēšâ,* nor does the LXX provide proof for the translation "cultic prostitute" (Dion 1981: 41–48).

In the OT, the assumption of sexual/cultic functions for these groups may result from the mistaken conflation of the discrete roles of these two groups, *qādēš* and *qĕdēšâ.* On the basis of Ugaritic texts and various passages in the books of Kings which refer to the *qādēš* (1 Kgs 14:24; 15:12; 22:47; 2 Kgs 23:7), it can be concluded that *qādēš/qĕdēšîm* refer to a priestly class rejected by orthodox Yahwists. The nature of their activities is not specified. In contrast, the feminine *qĕdēšâ* always appears as a synonym of *zônâ,* the common Hebrew word for prostitute (Genesis 38; Deut 23:18–19; Hos 4:14). This suggests a bifurcation of these two closely related words, *qādēš* and *qĕdēšâ,* masculine and feminine, as they seem to refer to two very different phenomena. This proposed distinction stands in opposition to the consensus of commentators that the collective noun *qādēš* refers to both the male and female members of the same class, *qĕdēšîm* and *qĕdēšôt* (e.g., Gray, *Kings* OTL, 311).

That these two homonymous nouns should refer to professions so different may be inferred from two biblical passages. 2 Kgs 23:7 could suggest that *qĕdēšîm* refers only to males since it reports that the women *(nāšîm)* present in the *bāttêy haqqĕdēšîm* were involved in weaving and nothing else. The second passage is Deut 23:18: "No Israelite woman shall be a *qĕdēšâ* nor shall any Israelite man be a *qādēš.*" If the collective noun *qādēš* referred to both male and female cult prostitutes, then only one clause would be needed—*Lōʾ yihyeh qādēš mibbĕnê yisrāʾēl,* "No Israelite shall be a *qādēš*"; this would be sufficient to prohibit all Israelites, male and female, from the act of sacred prostitution. The bipartite nature of the verse, with each half referring to gender, may suggest that the feminine and masculine nouns should be distinguished and could refer to two distinct classes of people, pagan or non-Yahwistic priests and common harlots. The Deuteronomist treated both of these classes in the same verse because both of these professions were seen as abhorrent to the pious writer and, more obviously, because of the similarity of the two words, *qādēš* and *qĕdēšâ.* Deut 23:18, accordingly, serves as a blanket prohibition against Israelite women becoming sexual mercenaries *in general,* and not specifically cult prostitutes.

When this verse is considered with its complement, v 19, the matter becomes more complicated because of *keleb,* "dog." While it can be suggested that there is no necessary connection between the two verses and that v 19 should not be used to explicate v 18 (or vice versa), the appearance of *qĕdēšâ* and *zônâ,* which are used together in Hos 4:14 and Genesis 38, makes this disjunction unlikely. Most commentators read v 18 and v 19 together as an attempt to limit prostitution, especially of the cultic sort, in Israel; and they understand *keleb,* "dog," as a reference to a male cultic prostitute so that *qādēš* is thereby provided with a synonym (e.g., Driver *Deuteronomy* ICC, 265; Mayes, *Deuteronomy* NCB, 320). This cultic interpretation of *keleb* is also based on an extra-Israelite inscription from the 4th century B.C.E. found at Kition. This inscription lists the expenses of a temple and its various personnel who receive stipends (*KAI* 2: 54–55; Cooke 1903: 65–70). While *klb* here could refer to a canine, a human referent is plausible because of the widespread use of *klb* in the ANE as a term equivalent to "faithful servant" (see *kalbu,* CAD 8:72; the Lachish Ostraca, *ANET,* 322; and personal names in Akkadian, Ugaritic, and Hebrew). A *keleb* would therefore be a servant at the sanctuary whose activities are unclear. The terms *klb*/*klbm* are also found at Ugarit; while the singular clearly refers to a canine (*UT* 125: 2, 15; Krt: 123, 226), the referents of the plural are unclear (*UT* 305: 4; 329: 18). Some scholars have suggested that the "dogs" listed among those not allowed into messianic Jerusalem in Rev 22:15 are male cult prostitutes, but this interpretation is based on Deut 23:19 and the Kition inscription. The use of "dogs" elsewhere in the NT offers no support (Matt 7:6; 15:26; Phil 3:2). In any event, no extrabiblical proof speaks for the identification of *keleb* in Deut 23:19 as "male cult prostitute."

Other interpretations of Deut 23:19 are possible. First, the verse may actually refer to a canine. The Mishna adopts this interpretation: "What is the 'price of a dog' (*mĕḥîr keleb*)? When one says to his fellow: 'Take this lamb in exchange for this dog' " (*m. Tem.* 6:3). The lamb, which would otherwise be suitable for the altar, is prohibited in this case because it was acquired in exchange for a dog. This association is not surprising since dogs were used for herding in Israel's pastoral economy (Job 30:1; Isa 56:10–11). The exchange of a lamb for a "sheepdog" in the Mishna's example may therefore reflect everyday practice.

Deuteronomy's prohibition of the "price of a dog" should then be viewed against the background of the OT's attitude of disgust and contempt toward these animals: a dog returns to its own vomit (Prov 26:11) and eats the unclean (Exod 22:30), including human flesh (1 Kgs 14:11; 16:4; 21:23–24; 2 Kgs 9:10, 36; Jer 15:3). A "dead dog" is synonymous with a despised and worthless object (2 Sam 9:8; 16:9), and Job 30:1 may be an adaptation of a popular expression of contempt (Pope, *Job* AB, 193). It is therefore understandable why the "price of a dog" would have been prohibited from donation to the temple. The word *mĕḥîr* also suggests that a canine may be the intention of the verse since it refers to the price in exchange for an object rather than a "wage" (2 Sam 24:24; 1 Kgs 10:28; 21:2; Jer 15:13; Prov 27:26; Lam 5:4; in Isa 45:13; and Mic 3:11, it appears as a synonym of *šōḥad*, "bribe," yet this too would be inappropriate for a professional prostitute's fee). Canines and prostitutes are also linked in 1 Kgs 22:38, and here both serve to symbolize Ahab's final disgrace.

According to this approach, Deut 23:18 and v 19 are juxtaposed because they both mention prostitutes, the *qĕdēšâ* and *zônâ*. The *qādēš* in v 18 refers to pagan priests, and the *keleb* in v 19 refers literally to canines (although the association of these two in parallel may be intended to mock and disparage these non-Yahwistic cultic officials).

A second possible interpretation of Deut 23:19 is offered by Gruber (1983: 167–76; 1986: 133 n. 1). On the basis of the books of Kings and Ugaritic texts, he concludes that the *qādēš* had no connection with cultic sex, but rather, as suggested above, was an official in a pagan cult. Further, in the inscription from Kition, the "dogs" seem to be some sort of temple servants. Gruber thus concludes that *both* verses, 18 and 19, contain references to common prostitution and to a kind of pagan cultic official; thus, as in many other places in the Bible, a cultic prohibition and an ethical prohibition have been placed side by side. An A-B-A′-B′ pattern (*qĕdēšâ-qādēš-zônâ-keleb*) becomes apparent, with A/A′ containing synonymous terms for the common prostitute and B/B′ containing labels for unorthodox cultic officials.

These two interpretations of *keleb* offered above (literal canine and cultic servant) are important to the better understanding of Deut 23:18–19 because either allows us to see the traditional translation of *qādēš*, "cultic prostitute," as only one, and perhaps not the best, understanding of the text.

How then are we to explain the use of the title *qĕdēšâ*, which suggests a relationship to holiness, for the common prostitute? From the premodern exegetes, Naḥmanides explains the term as the result of the phenomenon in Hebrew that one word can have a certain meaning along with its opposite (commentary on Deut 23:18). Thus, she who separates herself from holiness, just as she who guards herself from defilement, can be labeled with the root *qdš*. Further, two passages in the Bible employ the root *qdš* in the sense "to separate," "set apart" (Josh 20:7; Jer 12:3); and perhaps the title *qĕdēšâ* is derived from this—the prostitute by virtue of her unmarried status and ill-repute is alienated from the community and so "set apart." According to Snijders, the promiscuous woman in Proverbs is labeled *ʾiššâ zārâ*, a "foreign woman," for the same reason (1954: 96).

Gruber cites a linguistic analogue to the label "holy one" for a prostitute. He writes that the use of the same root for "prostitute" (*qĕdēšâ*) and "cultic functionary" (*qādēš*) is not surprising, since from *ḥrm*, a root synonymous with *qdš*, we have in Hebrew the noun *ḥerem*, "the ban," and the verb *lĕhaḥărîm*, "to ban, devote, consecrate" (Lev 27:28), but in Akkadian the term *ḫarīmtu* "prostitute." This can be explained by the fact that the root meaning of the term is "she who is set apart," whether for exaltation or degradation (Gruber 1986: 148).

Two passages other than Deut 23:18 mention the *qĕdēšâ*, and neither necessarily justifies the translation "cult prostitute." In Genesis 38, Judah encounters Tamar at a crossroads, not a temple or shrine, and takes her for a *zônâ*, common harlot (v 15). It is Judah's Canaanite friend, Hirah, who introduces the word *qĕdēšâ* in his query to the people of Timnah, and they reply with the same term (vv 21–22). The variation, therefore, may be based on their different ethnic backgrounds, since Hirah inquires of the harlot's whereabouts with a term that suggests her identity as he and the townsmen would know it, but with a term different from that used by Judah. On the other hand, if *zônâ* and *qĕdēšâ* are synonymous, the retort, "there has been no *qĕdēšâ* here" (v 22), makes little sense because Tamar did indeed pose as a harlot and the townsmen would have been aware of it. It can be argued, however, that Tamar offered herself not to any and every man but only to Judah, and that she stationed herself at a public place just long enough to catch his eye. That the men of Timnah did not take note of her is then understandable (Hooks 1985: 169). The Israelite audience would have been familiar with the equivalence of these two words and perhaps amused by the Canaanite's ascription of holiness to a sexual mercenary who sits at crossroads.

Hos 4:13–14 offers a cultic setting for the activities of the *qĕdēšâ*, with the mention of mountaintops, shade trees, incense, and sacrifice. Debatable, however, is the relationship of her activities to the cultic event, since the presence of prostitutes at a religious festival could be just one of the excesses such merrymaking would precipitate (van der Toorn 1989: 202). Ginsberg comments that "inviting prostitutes to the sacrificial banquets was a feature of the festivity rather than of the ritual" and that "the prophet's fulminations are aimed at the depravity of this dalliance not at its alleged rituality. . . ." (*EncJud* 8: 1019; also Gruber 1986: 134, n. 5). This interpretation of the verse sees the presence of a harlot at a high place for a feast as natural as her modern counterpart's appearance at a Mardi Gras or saint's day. Further, Hos 4:13–14 can be compared to Deut 23:19, which bars the donation of a whore's wages to the temple: if a whore's wages are prohibited, how much more the whore herself!

C. Prostitution as a Metaphor

Prostitution is widely used in the OT as a metaphor for Israel's defection from its covenant god. In fact, "prostitution" (Heb *znh*) is the dominant term when apostasy is characterized as illicit sex. This is surprising, since "adultery" (Heb *nʾp*) is, strictly speaking, more suitable for the characterization of Israel's relations outside of its "marriage bond" (the covenant) than is *znh*, the legal term which applies also to premarital sex.

Several factors may account for this: (1) *znh* implies that the illicit activity is habitual or iterative since the participle *zônâ* describes the professional whore; (2) the motive, personal gain, is supplied; and this is exploited by the prophets who point to Israel's folly in her pursuit of material goods from "no-gods" (Hosea 2); (3) *znh* implies a multiplicity of partners, and this all the more ridicules Israel's indiscriminate choice of fetishes for worship (Jer 2:20, 28); (4) the participle *zônâ* suggests a treacherous and hardened woman (Jer 3:3), and the concrete image of the whore is well suited for the personification of Israel as a woman; and (5) the root *znh* refers to illicit sex only by females, and because Israel in the covenant relationship adopts the feminine role, it is more fitting that a verb used strictly for females play a central role (*nʾp*, on the other hand, refers to illicit sexual activity by both sexes—a *nōʾēp* is a man, whether single or married, who engages in sex with a married woman [Lev 20:10]). The root *znh*, while strictly speaking less appropriate for symbolizing Israel's covenant breaking, was therefore a more effective rhetorical tool.

Prostitution is used as a metaphor for subjects other than Israel's apostasy, and even foreign cities in the OT are labeled *zônôt*. In Isa 23:15–18, Tyre, the great commercial emporium, is likened to a whore and her profits called *ʾetnan*, "a harlot's hire." Because the issue here is not fidelity to any covenant, a probable motive is the prophet's negative view of commerce. Israel was chiefly an agricultural nation with only sporadic experience with far-flung trade (Reviv, *EncJud* 15: 1294). In Isa 23:8; Hos 12:8; Zech 14:21; Prov 31:24; and Job 40:30, traders are called "Canaanites" and the international trade mentioned in 1 Kgs 9:26–28; 22:49 seems to be the exception. This disapproving attitude toward international trade no doubt facilitated its comparison to prostitution, a decidedly negative pursuit. Further, prostitution, by itself a commercial act, is akin to commerce because of the indiscriminate attitude which the seller has toward his/her customers. Other forms of commerce as well as prostitution can therefore be labeled "promiscuous." These factors, in addition to the OT's poetic convention of treating cities as women, explain the prophet's use of a prostitute in the personification of Tyre.

In Nah 3:4–7, Nineveh, the capital of Assyria, is depicted as a whore who charms nations and leads them to their downfall. "Harlotries and enchantments," (v 4) i.e., seduction and love spells, are the devious means by which a woman could exercise power over men and, in the eyes of the wisdom teacher, lead them to destruction (Prov 2:16–19; 5:7–14; 6:24–36; 7:6–27). Nineveh's means of allurement could be a reference to its physical splendor (*tôbat ḥēn* in v 4) or military might.

According to Isa 1:21, Jerusalem, "the faithful city that was filled with justice," has become a harlot. The prophet's charge isn't based on the worship of other gods, but rather on immorality and injustice. The root *ʾmn* (v 21), which represents concepts such as faithfulness, trust, and stability, finds its antithesis in *znh*.

Prostitution is also used to represent political alliances with foreign nations. In several OT passages, political and military allies are called "lovers," and the image suggested is that of Judah as a woman married to YHWH but pursued by (and pursuing) lovers who ultimately disappoint her (Lam 1:2, 19; Jer 4:30–31; 22:20–23). While the reliance of Israel and Judah upon other nations was condemned by the prophets as an affront to YHWH (Isaiah 30–31; Jer 2:18, 36–37; Hos 5:13; 7:11–12; 12:2; 14:4), only Ezekiel specifically labeled this activity *zěnût*, "harlotry" (16:26–29; chap. 23). In Ezekiel 23, however, the boundaries between political and religious apostasy are blurred since the prophet also focuses upon cultic transgressions, with the mention of idolatry (vv 7, 30), the sisters' "whoring" during the sojourn in Egypt (v 3; certainly not a reference to political alliances; cf. Ezek 20:7–8), and the repeated use of the verb *ṭmʾ*, "to defile," (vv 7, 13, 17), which is more suggestive of idolatry than political dealings. The prophet seems to suggest that Israel's foreign alliances brought about the worship of foreign gods. While strategic alliances, strictly speaking, may not have encouraged heterodoxy, royal marriages with foreign princesses for diplomatic purposes seem to have inspired apostasy on even a popular level (1 Kgs 16:31–32; 18:21–22; in the case of Solomon, only the king himself seems to have gone astray; 1 Kgs 11:1–10). Further, the cosmopolitan atmosphere in Jerusalem during the age of Assyrian hegemony seems to have inspired the worship of new gods (Cogan 1974: 91–96). These two factors, therefore, may supply the background of Ezekiel's association of political alliances and religious apostasy.

Bibliography

Bird, P. 1974. Images of Women in the OT. Pp. 41–88 in *Religion and Sexism*, ed. R. Ruether. New York.

Cogan, M. 1974. *Imperialism and Religion*. SBLMS. Missoula, MT.

Cooke, G. A. 1903. *A Textbook of North-Semitic Inscriptions*. Oxford.

Dion, P. E. 1981. Did Cultic Prostitution Fall into Oblivion during the Postexilic Era? Some Evidence from Chronicles and the Septuagint. *CBQ* 43: 41–48.

Fisher, E. 1976. Cultic Prostitution in the Ancient Near East? A Reassessment. *BTB* 6: 229–36.

Gallery, M. 1980. Service Obligations of the *Kezertu*-Women. *Or* 49: 333–38.
Gruber, M. 1983. The *qādēš* in the Book of Kings and in Other Sources, *Tarbiz* 52: 167–76 (in Hebrew).
———. 1986. Hebrew *qĕdēšâh* and Her Canaanite and Akkadian Cognates. *UF* 18: 133–48.
Gwaltney, W. 1964. The *Qadištum* and *Ištaritum* in Mesopotamian Society. Ph.D. diss., Hebrew Union College.
Hooks, S. M. 1985. Sacred Prostitution in the Bible and the Ancient Near East. Ph.D. diss., Hebrew Union College.
Kinet, D. 1977. *Baal und Yahweh.* Frankfort.
Lerner, G. 1986. The Origin of Prostitution in Mesopotamia. *Signs* 11: 236–54.
Paradise, J. S. 1972. Nuzi Inheritance Practices. Ph.D. diss., University of Pennsylvania.
Snijders, L. A. 1954. The Meaning of *Zār* in the Old Testament. *OTS* 10: 1–154.
Soden, W. von. 1970. Zur Stellung des "Geweihten" *(qdš)* in Ugarit. *UF* 2: 329–30.
Toorn, K. van der. 1989. Female Prostitution in Payment of Vows in Ancient Israel. *JBL* 108: 193–205.
Wold, D. 1978. The Meaning of the Biblical Penalty *Kārēth.* Ph.D. diss., University of California, Berkeley.

ELAINE ADLER GOODFRIEND

CULTIC PROSTITUTION

In OT commentaries and textbooks the existence of "cultic" or "sacred" prostitution in ancient Israel is frequently presented as a historical fact. On the basis of such texts as 1 Sam 2:22; 2 Kgs 23:7, 14; 2 Chr 15:16; Ezek 8:14; Hos 4:13; and others, it is assumed that in paganized Israelite cults, worshippers engaged in sexual intercourse with devotees of the various shrines, as a way to promote fecundity and fertility. Under the influence of Canaanite mythology, so the argument runs, many Israelites had come to see the processes of nature as the result of the relations between gods and goddesses. Divine intercourse would lead to abundant harvests and an increase of cattle. Cultic prostitution, performed by humans, was a form of imitative magic by which the gods could be moved to engage in similar activities, with all the ensuing beneficial results. Corollary to this view is the interpretation of the terms *qādēš* and *qĕdēšâ* as male and female "cult prostitute." Orthodox Yahwism combated these evils. Priests, prophets, and wise men alike denounced cultic prostitution as idolatry and utter foolishness. The fierceness of their reproval is all the more understandable when the heathen background of the sexual rites is taken into account.

In recent years, however, the widely accepted hypothesis of cultic prostitution has been seriously challenged. Various scholars have argued that the current view rests on unwarranted assumptions, doubtful anthropological premises, and very little evidence. At the same time the Ugaritic and Mesopotamian material, often referred to as evidence of cultic prostitution in neighboring civilizations, has been critically reevaluated and shown to be less unambiguous than it has often been assumed. These reasons call for a fresh look at the biblical material, to see to what extent prostitution in Israel may have been "cultic" or "sacred."

In order to dispel the possibility of terminological confusion, let us first define the content of the notion "cultic prostitution." When speaking of cultic prostitution, scholars normally refer to religiously legitimated intercourse with strangers in or in the vicinity of the sanctuary. It had a ritual character and was organized or at least condoned by the priesthood, as a means to increase fecundity and fertility. There is, however, another, more restricted way in which one can speak of cultic prostitution. We may use the term to call attention to the fact that the money or the goods which the prostitutes received went to the temple funds. A careful scrutiny of the evidence will show that the term "cultic prostitution" can be maintained only when used in the latter, limited sense. For the sake of clarity, however, it might be better to abandon the term altogether and to stick to circumscriptions such as "prostitution that was profitable to, and at times organized by, the temple and its administration."

An important argument of those who claim the existence of cultic prostitution in ancient Israel rests upon the various texts which picture debauchery as a corollary of communal rites. The OT contains indeed ample evidence of religious feasts that led to sexual excesses. The description of the cult of the golden calf, projected back into the misty times prior to the settlement in Canaan, can be considered as an archetype of the events (Exodus 32). During the celebrations "the people sat down to eat and drink, and rose up to play" (Exod 32:6). The latter verb, *ṣaḥēq,* is an unmistakable euphemism for sexual activities, similar to the Akk *ṣiāḫu,* "to laugh," "to make merry." In all likelihood, the story reflects the preexilic practices in the N kingdom, where the Lord was worshipped in tauromorph form (1 Kgs 12:26–33). Despite the presence of the image of a young bull, however, nothing indicates that the participants in these Bacchanalia were consciously playing their part in a fertility cult. We must bear in mind that the Israelite festivals were among the rare occasions where one could eat to satiety and drink one's fill, with song and dance contributing to the festive mood. Under such circumstances one could easily lose one's sense of propriety and momentarily indulge in a type of behavior that would otherwise be deemed inadmissible. The same holds true of the cult of Baal-Peor (Numbers 25; 31:13–20; Ps 106:28–31) and the cultic parties denounced by Hosea (Hos 4:13ff.; 9:10). The ban on transvestism, laid down in Deut 22:5, is also probably directed against such religious orgies, during which the customary distribution of roles was, by way of exception, suspended. One can imagine the licentious behavior to which this could lead.

It deserves to be emphasized that nothing warrants us to speak of cultically organized prostitution in connection with these instances of debauchery. Sexual libertinage was simply a frequent ingredient of the ANE festivals. A paragraph in the Middle Assyrian Law (tablet A, §55) deals with the case of a young woman who has been seized and violated "within the city or in the open country or at night in the street or in a storehouse or at a festival of the city." One is reminded of Judg 21:19–23, where the yearly feast of the Lord at Shiloh becomes an occasion for the Benjamites to take a wife by force. In both cases the relationship was perhaps established in a less brutal way than the texts affirm. According to the Babylonian Talmud, on Ab the 15th and on Yom Kippur, the Israelite girls dressed in white, danced in the vineyards, and invited the boys to make their choice (*b. Ta*ʿ*an.* 26b, cf. 31a). This tradition suggests that the affairs developed with the accord of both partners, the regulation of the Middle Assyrian Laws being merely a juridical construct to settle the ensuing situation of the girl. In all this, ANE man does not considerably differ from us. Sexual excesses were part of the expected ritualized behavior at festivals and belonged as such to the popular culture of the time. The same could be said of fraternity parties, New Year's parties, and the like in our own secular religion.

Besides the attestations to incidental sexual promiscuity at the occasion of festivals, however, the OT also mentions a specific category of people who are generally considered to have been the "professionals" of "cultic" prostitution in ancient Israel. These are the *qĕdēšîm,* a term frequently rendered as "cult prostitutes." Although the traditional understanding of this term has been challenged on the basis of the evidence concerning the Ugaritic *qdšm,* the parallelism between *qĕdēšâ* and *zônâ* in Genesis 38 and Deut 23:18–19 (—Eng 17–18) favors the idea that the *qĕdēšîm* engaged primarily in sexual activities. The Ugaritic *qdšm* seem to have consisted of all the nonpriestly temple personnel, who had been dedicated to a deity. They were free to marry and have children and could be released from their service by a royal decree. The situation of the Israelite *qĕdēšîm* may, to some extent, have been similar. Their functions need not be narrowed down to those of prostitutes; they may have performed a variety of menial tasks in the sanctuary as well. It cannot be denied, though, that during some periods they also functioned as prostitutes in the service of the temple. According to 2 Kgs 23:7, they had special rooms in the Jerusalem temple, a state of affairs intolerable to the zealous reformers, yet apparently accepted by the clergy in earlier times. Prostitutes operating as it were in the shadow of the temple, then, existed in ancient Israel. However, any links between the latter and a hypothetical fertility cult, it need hardly be said, belong to the domain of speculation. Prostitution as a source of profits for the temple?—yes; prostitution as an integrating part of fertility rituals?—no.

In a number of texts, the fulfillment of a vow appears to have been one of the motives for occasional prostitution. In ancient Israel the vow enjoyed great popularity, especially among women. A discreet indication of this popularity is found in the regulations concerning the Nazirite vow. The pertinent text, Numbers 6, specifies that members of both sexes are free to take this vow ("man or woman," Num 6:2). In a context which usually speaks only of men, this detail is striking indeed. Ordinary vows, too, were frequently resorted to by women. Childless wives were sometimes led to take a pledge by their desire for offspring, as 1 Sam 2:11 and Prov 31:2 show. At the time of fulfillment, however, difficulties could arise. Since women were financially dependent upon their husbands, the latter had to supply the means of payment. When a husband was unaware of his wife's religious pledge or did not agree with it, she found herself in a delicate situation. What was she to do when he refused to take responsibility for her actions? Was the vow to remain unfulfilled? Under such circumstances prostitution might seem to a woman the only solution left.

An illustration of such recourse to prostitution as a means to pay vows is given by Proverbs 7, where we find a portrait of the *nōkriyyâ,* the "strange" woman. She is described as a danger for the adolescent, whom she tries to persuade into accepting her erotic proposals: "Come, let us be satiated with love play till morning, let us delight ourselves with love" (Prov 7:18). In order to make the young man accept her offer, she refers to the predicament she is in: "I must provide a sacrificial meal, today I am to fulfill my vows" (Prov 7:14). Nothing obliges us to say that the vows of the woman were vows of fertility. Apparently, the term of her engagement has expired and the promised offerings are due today. What can she do? Her husband, she explains, has gone on a long journey; he took the bag of money with him, and will not be home until the full moon (vv 19–20). These words are indeed meant to seduce her victim. Yet they are not mere reassurances, designed to allay the youngster's fear of an untimely intrusion by the husband. Nor is the detail of the "bag of money" simply an indication of the duration of the business trip. No, the woman implies that she does not have access to the money she needs in order to discharge her religious obligations. The only way out she can think of is prostitution. Of course, she is no common whore! Under normal circumstances she would not dream of doing such things. But necessity knows no law. This woman from outside is using her (fictitious?) situation as an excuse for her desire of sensual enjoyment. Yet her arguments presumably impress her potential companion. Of course, adultery is wrong, but do not the ends justify the means in this case? He would not be merely buying a pleasure, but contributing to a good cause.

There are various reasons to assume that situations such as the one hinted at in Proverbs 7 arose rather frequently in ancient Israel. One of the texts on which this assumption is based is Num 30:1–16. The issue raised in this chapter concerns the vows taken by women. Only the widow and the divorced woman are regarded as independent and must at all times abide by their vows. Unmarried daughters, betrothed girls, and married women, on the contrary, are all subject to the authority of a man, be it their father or their husband. In case they should take a vow, father or husband has a right to cancel it, though only within a period of twenty-four hours on their hearing of the woman's engagement. Apparently, specific circumstances called for these rules. It has been suggested that the female vows referred to implied the abstinence from marital intercourse; thus, the husband would be directly affected by the consequences of his wife's piety. The text, however, does not say this. Ordinarily, vows were paid in movable goods, and there is no reason to assume that this was different in the case of women. In her case, though, it was her father or husband who had to furnish the promised goods. Since the latter had a stake in the matter, he was entitled to a say as to the validity of the vow. A woman could have her reasons, however, to hide her vow from her husband. When the time of payment came, she had to find means of her own to discharge herself of her pledge. Unless she resorted to prostitution as a way to acquire the necessary means, she had to retract her promise, which was considered a very serious offense (Deut 23:22—Eng 21; Eccl 5:3). In certain sections of the population, prostitution under these circumstances may have seemed preferable, so long as the revenues were set apart for the temple treasury.

Other biblical texts, too, allude to the practice of paying vows with money acquired by prostitution. The clearest instance is found in Deut 23:18–19 (—Eng 17–18).

> There shall be no *qĕdēšâ* among the daughters of Israel,
> nor shall there be a *qādēš* among the sons of Israel.
> You shall not bring the hire of a harlot or the wages of
>   a dog
> into the house of the Lord your God in payment for
>   any vow:
> for both of these are an abomination to the Lord your
>   God.

The verses show that, also among Israelites, the custom of paying vows by means of prostitution was a known phenomenon. Two distinct, yet connected practices are put in parallelism. The service of "consecrated persons" *(qĕdēšîm)* from Israelite extraction and the annex custom of paying vows with money acquired by prostitution are prohibited in the same breath. What the two have in common, it seems, is the recourse to prostitution as a way to make profits for the temple. The "harlot" *(zônâ)* parallels the *qĕdēšâ,* while the "dog" (*keleb,* a euphemism for the catamite) parallels the *qādēš.* Because of the destination of their income, their activities can be presented under the cloak of religion. The temple used the money it thus acquired, among other things, to pay for the production of divine images. Therefore Mic 1:7 can speak of Samaria's idols that have been gathered "from the hire of a harlot" (cf. also Isa 23:17–18). See also PROSTITUTION (OLD TESTAMENT).

The concept of prostitution as a means to pay vows was so well-known, that the Greek translators of Prov 19:13b had recourse to it in elucidating a passage that otherwise remained obscure to them. Whereas the Hebrew text speaks of a wife's quarreling that is likened to "a continual dripping of rain," the LXX talks about the unholy "votive gifts (*euchai,* the current translation of Heb *nĕdārîm*) from the hire of a hetaera." From a text-critical point of view the Masoretic Text is to be preferred, but the Greek rendering reveals the notoriety of the custom that interests us here. On the basis of these texts, we may conclude that the phenomenon of women—and, occasionally, men—prostituting themselves in order to obtain the money to fulfill their vows was known and to some extent accepted in broad layers of the Israelite society. Until the Deuteronomic reform it seems to have been tolerated by the official religion, which preferred the resulting votive gifts over an ethical rigorism.

Considering the available evidence, then, there is no need to postulate the existence of sacred prostitution in the service of a fertility cult. The witness of the OT certainly does not compel us to posit that the Israelites had recourse to such forms of sympathetic magic. The comparative material that is adduced to demonstrate a common ANE pattern of ritually staged copulation as a magical means to promote fertility is not as conclusive as is sometimes said. Prostitution whereby the income fell to the temple was definitely known, but its alleged magical connotation remains unproved.

Without going into a discussion of all the available ANE evidence, it will be useful to conclude this survey with a succinct analysis of the Mesopotamian data. Both the Sumerian and the Akkadian lexicon contain a number of words meaning "female prostitute." Generally, the attention of OT scholars has been monopolized by the *qadištu,* clearly cognate with Heb *qĕdēšâ.* The connection between the two terms is frequently said to go beyond the level of etymology; both would have been designations of the "cult prostitute." A survey of the texts in which *qadištu* occurs, however, shows that the term is frequently used, especially in the 1st millennium B.C.E., for a wet nurse or a midwife. One should therefore avoid narrowing down her activities to those of a prostitute. Nevertheless, the term does at times refer to a prostitute. Together with the *ḫarīmtu* and the *ištarītu,* the *qadištu* operated under the patronage of Ishtar, the goddess of love. There is no evidence, however, that such prostitution was ritual in the sense that it was part of a fertility cult. In Akkadian texts, the brothel can be called "the house of Ishtar," even though the entertainment offered there involved nothing particularly religious. Prostitution was a profane profession, unattractive perhaps, but on the whole not dishonorable. Also, the frequent connection of prostitutes with temples should not be interpreted as proof of the sacred character of their profession. Neo-Babylonian records from the Ishtar temple of Uruk show that the temple hired out certain members of its lower female personnel as concubines to private citizens. The relations between the hierodule and the man were conducted at the home of the latter, and nothing indicates that he had any higher designs than to have a pleasurable time. To the temple, prostitutes could be a source of income, but they were not cultic functionaries.

In a famous passage of the *Histories,* Herodotus tells us that every Babylonian woman had to prostitute herself, once in her life, to a stranger within the precincts of the Ishtar temple (1.199). Assyriologists disagree about the accuracy of this information. Supposing Herodotus was right, one cannot make him say that the women did so as part of a fertility rite. The only thing the "Father of History" tells us is that the piece of silver the woman received in payment belonged to the deity. This is precisely what we have found in the OT. We may even wonder whether Herodotus might not have mistaken the prostitution in payment of a vow for a general, once-in-a-lifetime duty. However that be may, the cuneiform evidence does not warrant the conclusion that the Mesopotamians practiced cultic prostitution in order to enhance the fertility of the soil or the flocks. The only instance one could quote to support the idea of a connection between sexual intercourse and fertility in nature is the so-called "sacred marriage." Evidence for this custom, however, is scarce and stems mainly from the late 3d millennium B.C.E. Also the term "prostitution" could hardly be applied to this.

In short, both the evidence from the OT and the Akkadian and Ugaritic data do not support the hypothesis of "cultic prostitution." Ancient Near Eastern civilizations were familiar with prostitutes working in the service of the temple, as they were with the phenomenon of prostitution as a means to pay vows. In neither case, however, does there seem to have been a conscious connection with fertility rites.

Bibliography

Arnaud, D. 1973. La prostitution sacrée en Mésopotamie, un mythe historiographique? *RHR* 183: 111–15.
Diakonoff, I. M. 1986. Women in Old Babylonia Not under Patriarchal Authority. *JESHO* 29: 225–38.
Gruber, M. I. 1983. The *qādēš* in the Book of Kings and in Other Sources. *Tarbiz* 52: 167–76 (in Hebrew).
———. 1986. Hebrew *qĕdēšâh* and Her Canaanite and Akkadian Cognates. *UF* 18: 133–48.
Hooks, S. M. 1985. Sacred Prostitution in the Bible and the Ancient Near East. Ph.D. diss., Hebrew Union College.
Soden, W. von. 1970. Zur Stellung des "Geweihten" *(qdš)* in Ugarit. *UF* 2: 329–30.
Toorn, K. van der. 1989. Female Prostitution in Payment of Vows in Ancient Israel. *JBL* 108: 193–205.
Yamauchi, E. M. 1973. Cultic Prostitution: A Case Study in Cultural Diffusion. Pp. 213–22 in *Orient and Occident: Essays Presented to Cyrus H. Gordon on the Occasion of His Sixty-fifth Birthday,* ed. H. A. Hoffner, Jr. AOAT 22. Neukirchen-Vluyn.

Karel van der Toorn

PROTO-LUKE. See LUKE-ACTS, BOOK OF.

PROTREPTIC. See PARENESIS AND PROTREPTIC.

PROVERBS, BOOK OF. The twentieth book of the OT in most English versions. The book is an anthology of admonitions and isolated sayings concerning wisdom and wise conduct.

A. Title of the Book
B. Authorship
C. Date
D. Content
E. Function
F. Affinities with Other Biblical Literature
G. Canonization

A. Title of the Book

The Hebrew title for the book of Proverbs, *mišlê šĕlōmōh,* derives from the superscription in 10:1 (cf. also the longer form in 1:1 and 25:1). Variants to this title are *sēper ḥokmāh* and *mišlôt* (the latter derives from Eusebius and uses a plural form of *māšāl* otherwise unknown, the usual plural being *mĕšālîm*). The Septuagint (LXX) title is *paroimiae;* and the Vulgate has *proverbia,* from which comes the English title "Proverbs." In the Hebrew Bible *māšāl* designates a wide range of literary types—taunt, allegory, lament, simile, and so on—but its etymology implies likeness and, in the view of some interpreters, authoritative word (from *mšl,* "to rule"). The fundamental feature of the sayings within the book therefore seems to be "comparison." Brief proverbial sayings set one image over against another, making an explicit or implicit comparison. Not every isolated saying compares two things, however, and some sayings extend considerably beyond a single distich, in the process multiplying the number of likenesses under consideration.

B. Authorship

Although certain features of the book associate the name "Solomon" with discrete units, other names also occur in connection with specific sections of the book. Some textual units lack any name whatever. Furthermore, the superscriptions may derive from a time later than the actual composition of the sayings within a given collection. The book therefore takes the shape of an anthology, its individual components coming from various periods of Israel's history. At least two, and probably three, short sections (Nos. 3, 6, and 7 below) stem from non-Israelite sources, making the anthology truly international.

Superscriptions set off seven distinct collections from their present context.

1. 1:1–9:18 The Proverbs of Solomon, David's son, king of Israel.
2. 10:1–22:16 The Proverbs of Solomon.
3. 22:17–24:22 The Words of the Wise.
4. 24:23–34 These also belong to the Wise.
5. 25:1–29:27 These also are Proverbs of Solomon that the men of Hezekiah, king of Judah, transcribed.
6. 30:1–14 The Words of Agur, son of Jakeh, the Massaite.
7. 31:1–9 The Words of Lemuel, king of Massa, with which his mother instructed him.

The last two brief collections have attracted miscellaneous sayings in the first instance and an alphabetic poem in the second.

8. 30:15–33 Numerical Sayings (except vv 20, 32–33).
9. 31:10–31 An Acrostic poem on a virtuous Woman.

Various signs of disunity within collections one and five, particularly arguments of style, content, and grammar, suggest that even further discrete units once existed (10:1–14:35; 15:1–22:16 and 25:1–27; 28:1–29:27).

In LXX the different location of material and additional sayings indicates conscious acknowledgment of foreign material and a desire to promote specific concepts. The Greek text gathers together the collections of foreign extraction, yielding the following sequence: 22:17–24:22; 30:1–14; 24:23–34; 30:15–33; 31:1–9; 25:1–29:27; 31:10–31. Much additional material in LXX appears toward the end of various collections (for example, 9:12, 18; 15:27, 29, 33; 16:1–9; 24:22; 27:24–27).

The occurrence of the same proverb in more than one larger entity gives further indication of multiple collections. For example, the same conclusion reinforces instruction about industry akin to the ant's and an object lesson concerning the effects of neglect on a vineyard (6:6–11; 24:30–34). Brief sayings occur more than once in identical form and in slightly altered language, and specific expressions appear in more than one literary context.

A satisfactory explanation has not surfaced for the prominence of Solomon's name in the book of Proverbs or for the implicit attribution of Ecclesiastes to him and explicit mention of him as author in Song of Songs and Wisdom of Solomon. Ordinary citizens venerated kings of the ancient Near East as patrons of wisdom if not actual possessors of extraordinary insight. The praise of Solomon for wisdom surpassing that of all other kings acknowledges this fact and is perhaps a product of his subjects' strong wish to be ruled by an astute monarch.

The tradition in 1 Kgs 5:8–14 (—Eng 4:29–34) that Solomon composed three thousand proverbs and one thousand and five songs actually summarizes their subject matter. One searches almost in vain within the book of Proverbs for sayings and songs about trees, beasts, birds, reptiles, and fish. Such encyclopedic lists have survived in Egypt and Mesopotamia, but biblical onomasticons have vanished if they ever existed. Given the tradition that Solomon's wisdom excelled that of everyone else in the Near East, it seems reasonable to assume that Israelite sages would have vigilantly preserved his noun lists.

Even those interpreters who think the tradition about Solomon's wisdom stems from his patronage of sages rather than from his actual authorship have difficulty explaining the divergence between the descriptions in 1 Kings 5 and the book of Proverbs. Some critics understand the reference in Kings as legend designed to legitimate a harsh regime that operated on the principle of might rather than justice. The apologia certainly depicts the young king as recipient of divine wisdom, which he promptly exemplifies in the judgment concerning the actual mother of a surviving infant, a story found in numerous cultures, and in his riddle contest with the Queen of Sheba. Whether such stories succeeded in counteracting the baneful effects of living memory remains unanswered, for this oppressive side of Solomon's reign was not totally suppressed in the biblical record. In this ancient apologia the climactic place of the references to Solomon's vast wealth may be instructive, for the belief that wise persons prospered became axiomatic at one time. As the wealthiest king in Israel's memory, Solomon must naturally have invited thoughts associating him with extraordinary wisdom. In all likelihood, the allusion to Hezekiah's men represents accurate recollection of a powerful and prosperous king of Judah whose patronage of sages allowed them to collect and transcribe earlier proverbial sayings. The ambiguous expression, men of Hezekiah, recalls the Masoretic Text of 1 Kgs 10:8, in which the Queen of Sheba expresses admiration for Solomon: "Happy are your men, happy these your servants who stand before you continually, hearing your wisdom."

The initial collection is preceded by an introductory paragraph similar to the one in the Instruction of Amenemopet. The biblical preface (1:2–6) concludes with a thematic statement (1:7); together they serve as an introduction to the first collection and possibly to the whole book. Technical vocabulary of the wise abounds here: wisdom, discipline, discerning words; perceptive discipline, i.e., correct, fair, and upright; prudence, knowledge, and perspicacity; teaching and steering; simile, enigma, words of the wise, and riddles. In addition, verbs emphasize the learning and teaching process: to know, to perceive, to receive, to give; to hear, to add, to obtain; to understand. Distinct groups of people are also mentioned: the simple, youth, the wise (singular and plural). The thematic statement, "The fear of the Lord is the beginning *(rēʾšît)* of knowledge; fools despise wisdom and instruction," grounds intellectual pursuits in religion. The word *rēʾšît* may extend beyond the temporal to the substantive, making piety the fundamental ingredient of all knowledge. The use of the Tetragrammaton, rare in Wisdom Literature such as Job and Ecclesiastes, is very much at home in Proverbs 1–9.

C. Date

Biblical wisdom is notoriously difficult to date, largely because of the timeless quality of its teachings. Sages endeavored to communicate insights that transcend space and time. Their teachings aimed at universal assent by any intelligent individual, Israelite or non-Israelite. Accordingly, the wise remained silent about the specifics of national history, choosing rather to dwell on things accessible to every human being. With Ben Sira a decisive shift took place, and Israel's sacred traditions entered the repertoire of professional teachers. In contrast to earlier Wisdom Literature, Sirach (Ecclesiasticus) can be dated with confidence to the decade between 190 and 180 B.C.E. See WISDOM OF BEN-SIRA.

Assigning relative chronology to the various collections in the book of Proverbs must therefore be done with considerable reservation. The previous tendency to date segments of the book on the basis of a form-critical judgment that brief sayings in distich or tristich form (sentences) antedate longer imperatives accompanied by warnings or exhortations (instructions) has collapsed because of Egyptian evidence. The discovery of Papyrus Insinger and the Demotic writings of Onkhsheshonqy demonstrated the existence in very late times of sentences, whereas instructions from the 3d millennium have survived. It appears that genre was more a matter of social setting than chronological period; in general, rural folk had a natural affinity for sentences, and members of the court preferred instructions.

Although the form-critical argument for the lateness of Proverbs 1–9 does not require an early date for this collection, other features do come into play, especially the role of *ḥokmāh,* whether merely an elaborate metaphor or an actual personification, and the heightened emphasis on piety, possibly even influenced by the Torah in its Deuteronomic form. In addition, the earlier literal use of *bĕnî,* "my son," and *ʾābîkā,* "your father," appears to have given way to technical nuances for student and teacher, just as *ḥākām,* "intelligent one," has taken on the sense of "professional sage." It follows that the present order of collections in the book of Proverbs does not reflect the chronology of the separate entities, and the clue from LXX that other factors shaped the sequence seems valid for the Hebrew as well. Although conjectural at best, a plausible reconstruction of the various stages of development reads as follows. An ancient collection of family teaching (10:1–22:16) was enlarged by a body of knowledge with conceivably broader application (25:1–29:27), then supplemented by professional instruction, first in a collection that duplicates several instructions preserved elsewhere in an earlier Egyptian text (22:17–24:22) and later by a body of instructions in which Egyptian imagery is completely integrated (1:1–9:18). The miscellaneous collections in 24:23–34 and

30:15–33 may very well have preceded the last mentioned unit, possibly even antedating 22:17–24:22. The sayings of Agur (30:1–14) and instruction of Lemuel's mother (31:1–9) probably followed the larger collections temporally, despite stylistic features in Agur's remarks that echo Canaanite literature. Actually, numerical sayings were widespread in the ancient world; and Agur seems to cite Job and certainly quotes from Psalms and Deuteronomy. His sentiments resemble the words of Qoheleth (Ecclesiastes), who probably was active about the middle of the 3d century. The latest section in the book of Proverbs, 31:10–31, appears to draw its power from the personification of Wisdom but extols wives of flesh and blood.

An interesting case has been made for the present arrangement of the book as a creative reinterpretation of old wisdom for theological purposes. The essence of the argument is this. Chapters 1–24 have a framing device and cyclic composition, whereas 25–31 use an additive technique. Chapters 1–9 combine two elemental or core blocks (2–4, the personal acquisition of wisdom, and 5–7, ethical advice, mostly about sex). A speech in first person (1:20–33 and 8:1–36) and a framing ring (the prologue, 1:2–7, and the final contrasting "allegory" about wisdom and folly, 9:1–18) enclose the two kernel blocks. Chapter 10 serves as an entranceway into the following collection, and chap. 15 functions as a second theological focus. Verses 4–5 in chap. 10 offer the kernel saying on poverty and riches, and verses 1–8 constitute a minicomposition around older wisdom, infusing new meaning into earlier teaching. Within chaps. 10–15 only 14:7 uses the style of instruction, but in 16:1–22:16 it occurs frequently (16:3; 18:22; 19:18, 20, 27; 20:16; 22:6, 10). Instruction style therefore wraps itself around the central unit of proverbial wisdom, providing an effective transition to 22:17–24:22, where imperatives increase noticeably. Chapters 25–27 appear to be more empirical and general, whereas 28–29 contain a pronounced theological bent. A plait pattern is discernible in chap. 29, a linking of a verse with the one after its immediate sequel (1 and 3; 2 and 4; 7 and 9; 12 and 14; 15 and 17; 19 and 21; 20 and 22).

D. Content

1:1–9:18. This section purports to give parental advice to children. The chief literary device is that of a father (the "I") speaking to a son (the "you"), for the most part warning against rival discourse and thus reinforcing an ideology, the ethos of the family. Readers assume the role of sons who must choose between those values that preserve society and alternative actions that undercut family stability. Various dangers threaten young men, but two stand out here: the encouragement from young companions to unite in an endeavor to get rich quickly through criminal activity and the seductive invitation to sensual pleasure from illicit sources. In both instances the father manipulates the rival discourse, underscoring the dangers accompanying such misconduct. He even reinforces his own authority by appealing metaphorically to a higher level, the transcendental, on which God disciplines wayward children. Furthermore, the father confesses that he was once a child, in this way drawing adults into the discourse and uniting the generations. Occasionally, the father appeals to the authority of torah, a body of teaching that protects those who walk in its paths.

A mother's voice, although never audible, gives additional weight to the warnings against dangerous conduct. Because the principal threat to young men involves a specific kind of woman, the father's discourse receives an ally in feminine form. The voice of Wisdom comes to the assistance of the father, openly inviting young boys to share her feast and, like a prophet, sternly warning those who resist her advances. Together, the two encourage youth to direct their erotic impulses toward their own wives and to pursue knowledge with the same passion. In this context, metaphorical language functions to explore the mystery of eros, which has a dark side in addition to its luminous one. Woman represents access to ecstasy and agony; hence she offers pleasures that seem to justify any risk. That situation enables females whose ways are foreign to wreak havoc as harlots; and adulterous women disseminate their poison, prepared in attractive vials. The discourse acknowledges the power inherent in seductive speech, for it corresponds to secret desire in the hearts of those being addressed. Nevertheless, clear warnings accompany the verbal allure: follow her and die; she speaks folly, behaving unacceptably all the time.

The son's silence contrasts markedly with vocal appeals from various quarters. He faces a choice of allegiance, whether to contribute to consensus or to join the ranks of society's dissidents. He can resist his father's voice, learning how to do so from the very one who urges him to obey parental instruction. An Egyptian instruction, Anii, has a rare instance in which a son actually responds to his dad's teachings, insisting that the vigorous moral demands are beyond his capability although appropriate for the father, who counters such claims with weighty arguments. The son's silence in the book of Proverbs may have contributed to the climate in which the books of Job and Ecclesiastes give voice to rival discourse of a different kind. The call for all readers to adopt the position of a son subject to an authoritative father yields to outright challenge of traditional authority. On his part, the father adheres to belief that allegiance precedes knowledge, so that habitual conduct eventually creates its own ethos in which such behavior becomes natural, like breathing.

Modern interpreters have divided 1:1–9:18 into ten speeches, but they differ on the precise delineation of each unit and the criteria for identifying distinct sections. Introductory formulas consisting of direct address ("my son") and of an appeal to hear or receive instruction suggest the following divisions: (1) 1:8–19; (2) 2:1–22; (3) 3:1–12; (4) 3:21–35; (5) 4:1–9; (6) 4:10–19; (7) 4:20–27; (8) 5:1–23; (9) 6:20–35; (10) 7:1–27. These units assert the personal authority of the teacher and understand wisdom as ordinary human capacity, in contrast to the two places in this larger collection where a personified Wisdom claims to possess godlike power to bestow life and riches.

10:1–22:16. The second collection in the book of Proverbs consists of brief observations about life that make their point in distich form. These two halves of a line balance one another synonymously, antithetically, or synthetically.

1. Condemnation is ready for scoffers,
   and floggings for the backs of fools (19:29).

2. The poor use entreaties,
   but the rich answer roughly (18:23).
3. The eyes of the Lord are in every place,
   keeping watch on the evil and the good (15:3).

Some observations begin with a particle of existence that functions merely to introduce an anomaly.

There is a way which seems right to a man,
but its end is the way to death (14:12).

Others judge one thing to be preferable to another.

Better is a dry morsel with quiet
than a house full of feasting with strife (17:1).

Still other observations make simple comparisons.

Like vinegar to the teeth, and smoke to the eyes,
so is the sluggard to those who send him (11:26).

Occasionally, a question expresses utter astonishment at incongruities.

Why should a fool have a price in his hand to buy wisdom,
when he has no mind? (17:16).

Because these sayings are complete in a single stich, the relationship to the larger context is uncertain. A few modern critics have posited thematic units, particularly in chaps. 10–15. For example, 11:3–8 introduces a topic (the just and the wicked), 11:9–14 [17] specifies the effects of conduct on neighbors and society in general, and 11:18–20 repeats the two themes. In verses 9–12, 14 the Hebrew letter *bet* occupies the initial position, although this phenomenon may be accidental. Similar repetition occurs in 15:13–14 (*lēb*, "heart") and in 16:27–29 (*ʾîš*, "person"). If the principle linking the individual sayings expresses intentional design, no one has discovered a clue to the structure, which gives the appearance of randomness.

The sayings in this collection lack the distinctive features of the instructions in 1:1–9:18, specifically imperatives and the direct address, "my son" (but see 19:27). The "sentences" capture a single facet of reality, stating the truth in a "matter-of-fact" way. Readers are expected to give their assent, for the observations derive from collective experience. Hence the sayings dispense with reinforcements of any kind; they thus resemble traditional sayings embedded within biblical narrative and oracular literature, e.g., "The fathers have eaten sour grapes, and the children's teeth are set on edge" (Jer 31:29; Ezek 18:2).

The observations constitute astute insights about human behavior, both the good and the bad; and they probe the inner spirit as well: the significance of a wink (16:30), the effectiveness of a bribe (17:8), the unpredictable manner in which generous persons acquire more wealth and stingy ones become poorer (11:24), the posturing of a buyer before and after a purchase (20:14), the necessity of looking beneath the surface of things (13:7), the power of speech to beget good or ill (15:1), the allure of gossip (18:8), the loneliness of the heart in its moments of grief or joy (14:10), the underlying sadness that laughter obscures (14:13). A few proverbial sayings explore the limits imposed by the deity on human beings (16:9, 33; 19:21), even on kings (21:1). For the most part these sayings exude optimism (12:21; 13:9; 15:3), a confidence that the Lord holds the reins of the universe securely in hand.

22:17–24:22. The unusual feature of these instructions is their affinity with the earlier Egyptian Instruction of Amenemopet. That relationship has been shown as follows:

PROVERBS	AMENEMOPET	SUBJECT
22:17–18	3:9–11, 16	Appeal to hear
22:19	1:7	Purpose of instruction
22:20	27:7–8	Thirty sayings
22:21	1:5–6	Learning a worthy response
22:22	4:4–5	Do not rob a wretch
22:24	11:13–14	Avoid friendship with violent people
22:25	13:8–9	Lest a trap ruin you
22:28	7:12–13	Do not remove landmarks
22:29	27:16–17	Skillful scribes will be courtiers
23:1–3	23:13–18	Eat cautiously before an official
23:4–5	9:14–10:5	Wealth flies away like an eagle/geese
23:6–7	14:5–10	Do not eat a stingy person's food
23:8	14:17–18	Vomiting results
23:9	22:11–12	Do not speak before just anyone
23:10–11	7:12–15; 8:9–10	Do not remove landmarks of widows
24:11	11:6–7	Rescue the condemned

The principle of polygenesis may explain some similarities, for identical proverbial sayings occasionally emerge in cultures where no direct contact with one another has taken place. Nevertheless, the astonishing affinities in this instance indicate that the biblical author drew upon the earlier literary tradition or both authors used a common source. The reference to thirty (sayings) becomes understandable in light of the thirty chapters in Amenemopet.

The long rhetorical unit about the dangers associated with excessive drinking (23:29–35) also has a close parallel in Egypt, but nothing here seems to require a theory of dependence. The idea of the deity weighing the heart (24:12) has its closest analogue in Egyptian symbolism about a final judgment of human deeds. Furthermore, the frequent mention of kings and service at the court stands out in this larger unit, 22:17–24:22. Presumably, such notions corresponded to reality in Israel only briefly, although literary conventions persist long after the social conditions giving birth to them have vanished.

24:23–34. A miscellaneous collection overlapping with 6:6–11, this brief section witnesses to the value of justice in society, offers helpful advice on priorities when embarking on a major undertaking like building a house, and encourages nonretaliation for offenses. The overlap with 6:6–11 has a different introductory scenario, but both discuss the folly of laziness.

25:1–29:27. The essential meaning of *māšāl* as similitude comes to expression in this early collection, for an impressive number of sayings begin with the preposition of comparison, "like," whereas others achieve the same thing by juxtaposing competing images. The social setting of this collection has generated considerable speculation, one scholar proposing two distinct settings, the court for 25–27 and rural society for 28–29. Evidence hardly supports the thesis that the former unit served as a mirror for princes and the latter unit as advice to peasants. The opening section, 25:2–10, does reflect on the different functions of God and king, pausing to offer sound counsel about the means of securing royal authority and of finding one's appropriate niche in the councils of power. The remaining sayings apply broadly to Israelite society, without dwelling on peculiar concerns of the royal court. To be sure, eloquence and accuracy in reporting facts apply to persons in the king's service, and courtiers profit from keeping a civil tongue. So do other people, who must learn self-discipline, the right time to act, the advantages of breaking free from the rule of lex talionis (an eye for an eye), the necessity of speaking at crucial times and the folly of doing so in some circumstances, the dangers of initiating violence, the advantage of intellectual discussion, and so on. The concluding section in 27:23–27 reverts to royal imagery, specifically wealth and a crown, but makes a sharp transition to the concerns of everyday sustenance.

The contrast between poor and rich surfaces again and again in chaps. 28–29, and the responsibility of a ruler to assure justice constitutes a society's deepest hope and harbors its greatest fear at the same time. Experience finds expression in the concession that a king's favor can be bought, so that pure justice rests with Yahweh alone. Nevertheless, the divine empowerment of poor people and their oppressors (29:13) has not escaped this astute observer of human experience.

30:1–14. Extraordinary disagreement characterizes scholars over the scope of this unit and its essential character, whether skeptical or pious. Some interpreters follow LXX's lead in viewing the teaching as humble piety, while others think Agur takes conventional wisdom to task. A strong argument can be made for understanding verses 1–14 as a coherent unit, either as a dialogue between two people or as a teacher citing popular views in order to refute them. More probably, a skeptic challenges traditional wisdom, questioning God's existence and feigning ignorance, although insisting that those who profess orthodox views should demonstrate their knowledge of the Creator. An interlocutor rebukes Agur for heterodoxy, quoting Scripture, and is in turn warned against adding to the teacher's words. A sublime prayer follows, one that by distinguishing social status may mount further attack on the privileged teacher who has forgotten God while basking in the lap of luxury. The concluding section has a transitional statement about servants and masters, one that functions with reference both to humans and to God, together with four incisive observations about types of people who are worse than honest skeptics like Agur: children who dishonor their parents, hypocrites, proud persons, and rapacious cutthroats.

This section demonstrates remarkable skill at rhetoric, utilizing double meanings and clanging symbols, the dashing of expectations. Promising prophetic revelation, it offers human words that are either Delphic gibberish or astonishing confession of practical, at least, atheism. Theophanic language evokes derision in a citation from God's speech in Job ("Surely you know"). The request to be spared poverty and riches demonstrates unusual perception about the role of sociological status in shaping one's religious views. This negative attitude toward wealth accords ill with the prevailing understanding of virtue and its rewards, but Israel's teachers seem to have had difficulty adopting a consistent attitude toward the poor.

30:15–33. Graded numerical sayings alternate with three observations that allude to the four types of persons in 30:11–14. Those who show disrespect for parents will suffer hideously (30:17); adulteresses eat and wipe their mouths without any awareness of offense, consequently remaining pure in their own eyes (30:20); proud individuals ought to refrain from boasting (30:32); and violent people should control their tempers (30:33). The numerical sayings isolate for scrutiny various categories that resemble one another: things that are never satisfied (Sheol, the barren womb, a thirsty ground, fire), movement that leaves no trace (an eagle in the sky, a serpent on a rock, a ship at sea, a young man and a maiden), intolerable circumstances (a king who once was a slave, a fool with a full stomach, a previously spurned woman who weds, a maid who succeeds her mistress), four small creatures able to adapt to circumstances (ants, badgers, locusts, and lizards), and four "prancing" (self-important?) creatures (a lion, a cock, a billy goat, and a king).

31:1–9. This instruction consists of a superscription (31:1), a queen mother's direct appeal to her son (31:2), and four "words" of advice. These admonitions concern relationships with women and excessive drinking. Lemuel's mother tells her royal son to provide strong drink for oppressed victims of society who need something to forget their misery. She also urges him to pay special attention to the matter of justice, becoming a powerful advocate for vulnerable members of society whose voice would otherwise go unheeded. The entire instruction makes effective use of rhetoric, combining terms of endearment, repetition, inclusion, suspension of subject matter, and double entendre.

31:10–31. The personification of Wisdom as a woman served to correct many sayings that emphasize women as temptresses and disrupters of harmony within households. Nevertheless, personified Folly neutralized this embodiment of discernment. Therefore another means of salvaging women's reputation was needed; the final poem endeavors to do just that. Its effectiveness suffers because of its orientation toward the good wife's contribution to her husband and children. Her worth seems to depend on how successfully she enhances his standing in the community. The description of their entrepreneurship suggests that Israelite women took an active role in business. The religious criterion for evaluating women (31:30) comes as something of an afterthought.

E. Function

During the earliest phases of Israelite society, power rested in elders, who perpetuated their singular authority through legal statute and traditional saying. Apodictic law compelled assent insofar as it voiced the will of respected figures whose wide experience, fairness, and good judgment set them apart from ordinary citizens as custodians of valuable lore. Similarly, proverbial sayings carried the weight of cumulative experience, hence embodied a way of life that was binding on everyone but persons who questioned the fundamental basis of society. These two, law and traditional saying, constitute ancient Israel's attempt to establish and maintain order in complex human relationships.

Although the locus of both law and aphorism reached beyond the privacy of a family's tent to the centers of daily deliberation, particularly the gates where important judicial decisions were rendered, the lofty position of parents in the early system of clans reinforced the authority of these literary forms. This domestic setting left its mark on proverbial teaching, which strengthened its own appeal to hearers by adopting the emotion-laden language of father to son. Older proverbial collections in the book of Proverbs dispensed with such specific designations of speaker and addressee, but ancient Near Eastern parallels from Egypt and Mesopotamia demonstrate the antiquity of this language, which eventually took on the technical sense of teacher (*ʾāb,* "father") and student (*bĕnî,* "my son") so prevalent in Proverbs 1–9.

These parental teachings emerged from persistent efforts to penetrate reality so as to order life for maximum success in achieving honor, wealth, health, and offspring. The notion of steering lay at the heart of such instruction, and an appreciable amount of self-discipline too. Optimism prevailed about the extent to which individuals controlled their own destiny. Virtue received its reward and vice, its punishment, with rare exceptions, which emphasized divine freedom. In due time, skepticism made its presence felt, particularly with regard to the impenetrability of the universe. In Egypt a noticeable increase in piety accompanied such pessimism, and the same may actually have occurred in Israel as well. Although an attitude of confident reverence pervades much of the proverbial literature, growing insecurity seems to have evoked opposite responses, skepticism and dogmatic assertions.

The introduction of monarchy in Israel brought about a definite shift in the power base, the center of authority moving from the heads of families to a chief of state. This change came slowly and after much resistance on the part of those who watched their status in the community dwindle year by year. Concentration of power in Jerusalem and international commerce hastened the emergence of a professional class of courtiers equipped to handle the complex affairs of state on behalf of royalty. Such learned figures graced the courts of Egypt and Mesopotamia from early times. Precisely when they first appeared in Israel remains a mystery; but they were firmly planted in the 8th century B.C.E., producing a tradition associating them with the court of King Hezekiah. Even David enjoyed the benefits of two counselors, Ahithopel and Hushai, whether in fact or as a piece of literary fiction.

One can easily imagine the responsibilities of such courtiers, despite the silence about their duties in Wisdom Literature. International diplomacy must have stood high on their agenda, and thus the mastery of various foreign languages. The educating of young princes may also have fallen to these courtiers, and perhaps, too, the entertaining of nobility with feats of eloquence like those in 1 Esdr 3:1–4:41. The courtiers probably kept records, both political and economic, and prepared propaganda for aspiring and fading regimes. Considerable attention would have gone to the training of young potential courtiers, hence to perpetuating their profession. In all likelihood instructional literature in the book of Proverbs belongs to such "in-house" pedagogy. This scholarship for internal consumption may have encouraged the kinds of philosophical reflection that eventuated in the books of Job and Ecclesiastes.

The disappearance of monarchy in 587 B.C.E. and the drastic alteration of lifestyle, whether in Exile or in the Judean countryside, brought about a radically different job description for professional sages. The accompanying loss in perceived status further fueled fires of discontent, already exacerbated by historical circumstances involving the populace at large. Adversity propelled these learned teachers into strange alliances with the ruling priestly class, or alternatively with persons located on the fringes of society, at least in their conviction that justice had departed once and for all. This retreat in opposite directions suggests that wisdom may always have possessed distinct perspectives corresponding roughly to the differences in literary genre that have complicated all attempts to comprehend the phenomenon. However, the two different orientations, the experiential aphorism and the reflective probing, functioned in a complementary way, possibly to the very end. Their union in Sirach merely continues a trend set in motion by the authors of Job and Ecclesiastes.

The preceding account of professional sages in ancient Israel suggests that they possessed remarkable adaptability, a willingness to change with the times. A Hellenistic text, Wisdom of Solomon, shows how far the sages proceeded in their accommodation to new modes of thought. See SOLOMON, WISDOM OF. Such radical departures inevitably threatened to introduce a new entity altogether, making it difficult to determine the actual successors of the wise in later Judaism. Furthermore, this partial rendering of the development of the sapiential enterprise, like the biblical literature itself, maintains silence about onomasticons. One wonders why Israel's teachers did not compile comprehensive taxonomies of flora and fauna, among other things. Perhaps they did, and this particular feature of their intellectual achievement has vanished.

Changes in the meaning of *ḥokmāh* over the years suggest yet another means of tracing the development of the sapiential enterprise. Just as the adjective *ḥakam* and its plural assumed a technical sense in some instances (the sage or the wise), the noun *ḥokmāh* also acquired a rich nuance of astonishing magnitude. Foreign influence definitely played a part in this fascinating speculation about a personified figure who embodied the highest and noblest aspirations of the sages, but Israelite ideas laid the foundation itself. As a matter of fact, prophetic language dominates the initial appearance of *ḥokmōt* (Prov 1:20–33), specifically the image of pouring out the spirit, the description of stubborn refusal to hear, and the references to undesirable consequences of such action. The people refused to listen to the proclamation; they spurned the outstretched hand; Wisdom will mock them in their distress; when they call, she will not answer; unable to find her, they will eat the fruit of their way and gorge themselves on their own misconduct. This threatening posture approximates that of a prophet who speaks in God's name, the prophetic ego merging with the divine. These foolish individuals have not just ignored a human teacher; they have also treated God with contempt.

The plural *ḥokmōt* has caused considerable speculation, none of which satisfactorily explains the form: a plural of abstraction, an ancient Canaanite goddess, an orthographic mistake. Curiously, the next section to introduce this figure, Prov 8:1–36, uses two expressions in parallelism (*ḥokmāh* and *tĕbûnāh,* although referring to a single individual (cf. 7:4). Several links with the earlier text stand out—the place of instruction, the objects of the teaching, the allusions to "seeking and finding" and to fruit, both positive here. New ideas also surface: the extraordinary worth of Wisdom, surpassing the value of jewels; Wisdom's role in the manifest rule of the earth; the integral relationship between Wisdom and morality; and her presence with God at creation.

The latter complex of ideas concerning creation, echoing sentiments from Egypt, particularly the emphasis on her presence before the various creative deeds and the picture of Wisdom as a source of God's pleasure, describes a transcendent figure loftier by far than the earlier prophetic one. The result of God's first creative deed, she therefore preceded earth itself. Either as artisan or darling child, she witnessed the firmament taking shape and rejoiced constantly as Yahweh established order despite chaotic forces of the deep. A merging of egos occurs here too, as Wisdom assures those who find her that they will discover Yahweh's favor and therefore life itself.

The third passage about an extraordinary figure known as *ḥokmāh,* Prov 9:1–6, describes a building project on a smaller scale. She constructs a house, fashions its seven columns, and prepares a lavish banquet, enlisting the aid of servants to issue an invitation to townspeople. Just as Yahweh had to contend with the waters of the deep, Wisdom must reckon with a rival force who promises sensual pleasure. Given the powerful role of erotic imagination, sweet water and pleasant bread transform a simple meal into a sumptuous feast (Prov 9:13–18).

F. Affinities with Other Biblical Literature

Proverbial sayings occur in various contexts other than the book of Proverbs. Besides traditional sayings preserved in narratives and prophetic literature, one finds similes and aphorisms in Psalms that closely resemble those in Proverbs. For example, Ps 37:16 expresses the judgment that the meager possessions of virtuous people are better than the abundance of many wicked persons. Similarly, 37:21 states that a wicked individual borrows and cannot repay, but the righteous is generous and gives away. Verse 23 insists that God directs a person's steps, establishing the one who finds divine approval. Ps 94:8–11 uses rhetorical questions in composing a didactic essay on divine sovereignty that hears, sees, and chastens. The motto in Prov 1:7a occurs in Ps 111:10a ("The fear of the Lord is the beginning of wisdom"); and the comparison of parental teaching with a lamp and light appears in Ps 119:105, here with reference to God's word. The sons of youth are likened to arrows in the hands of a warrior in Ps 127:4.

The use of *miṣwāh* and *tôrāh* in Proverbs raises the possibility that the Mosaic law lies behind the vocabulary about parental instruction. The use of these words with reference to paternal and maternal teaching in 6:20 suggests that they have the same referent in 6:23 ("For the commandment is a lamp and the teaching is a light, instruction and discipline are the way of life"). Nevertheless, an association with Deut 6:4–9; 11:18–20 seems likely, if unconscious. The Mosaic law may rest behind the language of Prov 28:4, 7, 9; and 29:18, particularly if this last verse also refers to prophecy, but all of these references may have in mind laws of the state.

Although Job and Ecclesiastes represent different genres within Wisdom Literature, they contain many proverbial sayings like those in the book of Proverbs. Perhaps Prov 30:4 alludes to God's mocking remark in Job 38:5 ("surely you know"). Sirach also has numerous proverbial sayings and didactic essays on individual themes, in both instances following in the footsteps of the unknown authors who composed the book of Proverbs. The popularity of such aphorisms is evidenced by their being embedded within devotional narratives such as Tobit (12:7–10).

G. Canonization

The sacred character of Proverbs seems never to have been in doubt, although remarks about its vivid description of a harlot in the act of seduction and about direct contradiction in 26:4–5 have survived in Jewish sources. Christian acceptance of the book seems not to have been contested, and its secular character did not pose any obstacle to considering the book canonical. In some circles, modern scholars have declared its contents pagan, but the criterion they use (proclamation of saving history) leaves much to be desired.

The Greek text has about 130 stichs more than the Hebrew, many of them highly Hellenized. Some haggadic tendencies intermingle with apparent mistakes. Other renderings may harmonize related texts in several different books, especially Psalms, Sirach, and Wisdom of Solomon.

Bibliography

Aletti, J. N. 1977. Seduction et parole en Proverbs 1–9. *VT* 27: 129–44.

Alonso Schökel, L., and Vilchez, J. 1984. *Proverbios.* Nueva Biblia Espanola. Madrid.

Barucq, A. 1964. *Le Livre des Proverbes.* SB. Paris.

Bryce, G. 1979. *A Legacy of Wisdom.* Lewisburg, PA.

Bühlmann, W. 1976. *Von Rechten Reden und Schweigen.* OBO 12. Freiburg and Göttingen.

Camp, C. V. 1985. *Wisdom and the Feminine in the Book of Proverbs.* Bible and Literature Series 11. Sheffield.

Crenshaw, J. L. 1988. A Mother's Instruction to Her Son (Prov. 31: 1–9). Pp. 9–22 in *Perspectives on the Hebrew Bible,* ed. J. L. Crenshaw. Macon, GA.

———. 1989a. Clanging Symbols. In *Justice and the Holy,* ed. D. A. Knight and P. Paris. Philadelphia.

———. 1989b. The Sage in Proverbs. In *The Sage in the Ancient Near East,* ed. L. G. Perdue and J. Gammie. Winona Lake, IN.
———. 1989c. Proverbs. In *The Books of the Bible,* ed. B. W. Anderson. New York.
Crossan, J. D., ed. 1980. *Gnomic Wisdom.* Semeia 17. Chico, CA.
Fontaine, C. R. 1982. *Traditional Sayings in the Old Testament.* Bible and Literature Series 5. Sheffield.
Gese, H. 1984. Wisdom Literature in the Persian Period. *CHJ* 1: 189–218.
Hermisson, H.-J. 1968. *Studien zur israelitischen Spruchweisheit.* WMANT 28. Neukirchen.
Kayatz, C. 1966. *Studien zu Proverbien 1–9.* WMANT 22. Neukirchen.
Lang, B. 1972. *Die weisheitlichen Lehrrede.* SBS 54. Stuttgart.
———. 1986. *Wisdom and the Book of Proverbs.* New York.
Lemaire, A. 1981. *Les écoles et la formation de la Bible dans l'ancien Israel.* OBO 39. Göttingen.
Lindenberger, J. M. 1983. *The Aramaic Proverbs of Ahiqar.* Baltimore.
Naré, L. 1986. *Proverbes salomoniens et proverbes Mossi.* Frankfurt.
Nel, P. J. 1982. *The Structure and Ethos of the Wisdom Admonitions in Proverbs.* BZAW 158. Berlin.
Shupak, N. 1987. The "Sitz im Leben" of the Book of Proverbs in the Light of a Comparison of Biblical and Egyptian Wisdom Literature. *RB* 94: 98–119.
Skehan, P. 1971. *Studies in Ancient Israelite Poetry and Wisdom.* CBQMS 1. Washington.
Skadny, U. 1962. *Die ältesten Spruchsammlungen in Israel.* Göttingen.
Trible, P. 1975. Wisdom Builds a 1975 Poem: The Architecture of Proverbs 1:20–33. *JBL* 94: 509–18.
Van Leeuwen, R. C. 1988. *Context and Meaning in Proverbs 25–27.* SBLDS 96. Atlanta.
Vawter, B. 1980. Prov. 8:22: Wisdom and Creation. *JBL* 99: 205–16.
Whybray, R. N. 1965. *The Intellectual Tradition in the Old Testament.* BZAW 135. Berlin.
———. 1972. *Wisdom in Proverbs.* SBT, n.s., 45. London.
Williams, J. G. 1981. *Those Who Ponder Proverbs.* Sheffield.

JAMES L. CRENSHAW

PROVIDENCE. The word "providence" derives from the Latin *providentia,* the noun from the verb *providere* "take thought for," "look ahead." The Greek equivalent is *pronoia,* from the verb *pronoeisthai,* having more or less the same meaning.

As a philosophical or religious concept, Providence denotes the care of God for his creatures, "God" standing for a personal, sentient first principle. The requirement that providence stem from a personal agent might seem absolute, but in fact, among the Greeks, the Stoic philosophers adopted the concept of *pronoia* to describe the rational ordering of the universe emanating from a first principle which they designated as *theos,* "God" but which they conceived of simply as the immanent active principle of the universe.

In early Greek thought, Zeus and the other gods are portrayed as exercising care for individual mortals, and in Zeus' case even in a general way for the world as a whole, but there was no overarching idea of divine providence as embracing all human activity, nor was the word *pronoia* used in this context, apart from one remarkable passage in Aeschylus' *Agamemnon* (684–85), where the chorus, speculating on the name of Helen of Troy, speak of "someone whom we do not see, guiding his tongue fortunately *(en tychâi)* to the mark with foresight of destiny *(pronoaisi tou peprômenou).*" Even here, though, *pronoia* is used for someone discerning the course of destiny rather than steering it.

In general, it might be said to be characteristic of early Greek thought, and of writers like Pindar and Herodotus in particular, to regard the gods as being just as likely to be envious of human success, and offended by human self-assertion, as to be benevolent. There is even an undercurrent of thought (represented, for instance, in the Prometheus myth and in the post-Homeric *Cypria*) that Zeus had plans to destroy humankind and start again with a less flawed race of creatures.

The first thinker to assert a systematic doctrine of divine providence is Plato, particularly in the *Timaeus* and in Book X of the *Laws.* In the *Timaeus* (29E), he makes an assertion which was to have great impact on later philosophy, and even on Christian theology, when he states that the Demiurge, the creator god presented in that dialogue, "was good, and in the good there subsists no envy ever about anything; being free of this, then, he wished that everything be so far as possible like unto himself." *Pronoia* is not mentioned here (though the concept is clearly implied, as the opposite of "envy"), but the word is used a little later (at 30C and 44C), referring this latter time to the forethought of the planetary gods, the Demiurge's assistants.

Later, in *Laws* X, by way of proving the existence of the gods, Plato presents us (896Eff.) with a World Soul which guides the whole universe benevolently (though hampered to some extent in its operations by another soul of opposite tendency—possibly just the negative force of Matter, though many later Platonists, such as Plutarch, took this to be an Evil World Soul in the *Timaeus,* but it was portrayed in the *Laws* as a creation soul). In the *Timaeus,* soul is an instrument of the Demiurge; but in the *Laws,* soul has the executive function of the Demiurge himself and is described as a god, with each of the heavenly bodies being a god as well (899B).

Plato then proceeds to argue against what was later the Epicurean doctrine that the gods exist but exercise no care over human affairs (899D–905D), and in the process he produces all the arguments that would later be used to support the doctrine of divine providence. This is therefore a text of fundamental importance. Plato asserts that the divinity cares for things both small and great (901B) and that we are all the possessions of the gods (902B), in which they therefore have a proprietorial interest, but that we cannot expect our personal convenience always to be served by divine providence since we are only parts of a larger whole and Providence looks to the whole (903Bff.).

The Stoic philosophers inherited this view of divine providence, but adapted it to their own materialist philosophy, God becoming now the immanent mind or soul of the universe. The Stoic doctrine of Providence thus becomes confused with their doctrine of Fate, and disputes in fact arose in the school as to the proper relation between the two concepts. We have record of a dispute between Cleanthes and Chrysippus as to whether everything fated is also providential. Chrysippus held that it is; Cleanthes that it is not (*SVF* 2.933). It is not quite clear what Cleanthes had in mind, but his view may have been that divine providence does not concern itself with a certain level of details (side effects of chains of causation), which are, nonetheless, fated.

Such an argument has some importance for later Platonist and Aristotelian doctrine. Albinus (*Didaskalikos,* chap. 26) though talking here of Fate, rather than Providence, makes the distinction that all things are comprehended by Fate, but not all things are *fated,* which may well be the distinction that Cleanthes was trying to make. Pseudo-Plutarch, in his treatise *On Fate,* presents an elaborate scholastic system (572Fff.), according to which there are three levels of Providence, the highest of which—the "intellection" or "will" of the Supreme God—transcends the sphere of Fate and "encloses" it, while lower levels of providence are coordinate with, or even subordinate to, Fate. Both Albinus and Pseudo-Plutarch, however, seek to preserve within this overarching framework of providence and fate a place for free will.

On the other hand, the Aristotelian tradition (represented most conspicuously in the later period by Alexander of Aphrodisias in his treatise *On Fate*) tended to restrict the sphere of God's Providence to the supralunary realm, leaving our world to Fate and Chance, and thus acquired the reputation of abolishing Providence, which is not quite fair, though it is admittedly not a concept that Aristotle had much use for. The Aristotelian God thinks himself (as in *Metaph.* 12), and the universe relates to him rather than the other way around.

The greatest statement of the theory of Providence in the Hellenic tradition is the treatise of Plotinus *On Providence* (*Enn.* 3.2–3), composed in the latter half of the 3d century C.E. While basically accepting the Stoic theory of Fate and Providence, Plotinus seeks to justify the rationality and goodness of God in the face of the multifarious evil observable in the world. Like the Stoics, he regards free will as a subjective phenomenon and holds that true freedom consists in understanding the way of the world and assenting to it. His treatise is the finest attempt that we have at a comprehensive Hellenic theodicy.

Two other treatises on Providence, however, should not be neglected, though they do not rise to the heights of Plotinus. One is the two-part treatise of the Platonizing Jewish philosopher Philo of Alexandria (fl. ca. 25 C.E.). This work presents the Platonic, and especially Stoic, arguments for Providence, of which it constitutes a most useful exposition, but also comes closer to Christian thought in that Philo believes in a personal God, which is not the case with the Greeks. The second book of the treatise takes the form of a dialogue with Philo's nephew Alexander, who presents Peripatetic and Skeptical arguments against Providence for refutation.

The essay of the Roman Stoic philosopher Seneca (4 B.C.E.–65 C.E.), commonly entitled *On Providence,* is really devoted to the more restricted question, "Why, if there is Providence, do some misfortunes befall good men?" and is a rhetorical elaboration of the theme that no evil can befall a good man. It does, however, touch briefly on most aspects of the topic of Providence in general, showing how closely enmeshed that concept is, for the Stoics, with Fate.

Pronoia is also an important concept in gnostic thought. The Father, in the *Tripartite Tractate* from the Nag Hammadi Corpus, is described as "the providence *[pronoia]* of those for whom He providentially cares" (66). Pronoia figures largely also in the *Apocryphon of John* (4–7), where it is identified with Barbelo, and in the treatise *On the Origin of the World* (108–11), where Pronoia is interestingly personified, and a lower Pronoia is envisaged, left by the Light-Adam in the heavens when he reascends to the Pleroma. In each, Pronoia is to be contrasted with Fate *(Heimarmene),* which is proper to the Demiurge and his realm.

Bibliography

Koch, H. 1932. *Pronoia und Paideusis.* Leipzig.

Parma, C. 1971. *Pronoia und Providentia: Der Vorsehungsbegriff Plotins und Augustins.* Leiden.

Rist, J. M. 1969. *Stoic Philosophy.* Cambridge.

JOHN M. DILLON

PROVINCE. See PALESTINE, ADMINISTRATION OF (ROMAN).

PRUSA (40°12′N; 29°04′E). The site of the city of Prusa is now occupied by the town of Bursa in NW Turkey. Prusa and its successor occupy a fine plateau site on the N slopes of Ulu Dag (in ancient times the Mysian Mt. Olympus), overlooking the coastal plain of the Sea of Marmarra. There are medicinal hot springs at Çekirge, near the town, which have been in use since classical times. No references to Prusa occur in the Bible.

The first systematic description of Prusa-Bursa was provided by Philippson in 1913. Earlier contributions had been made by von Moltke (1836), von Hammer, and Hommaire de Hell (1846). No systematic excavations have been carried out. However, Bursa was chosen as the site for one of Turkey's first museums, which was catalogued by Mendel (1909).

The ancient geographers (Strabo 12.504; Pliny *HN* 5.148) associate the foundation of Prusa with either Hannibal or a legendary King Prusias of the 6th century B.C. In fact Hannibal spent the last few years of his life in exile at the court of King Prusias I (ca. 235–183 B.C.) of Bithynia, who is commemorated on the city's coins as founder. Dörner (PW 23.1: 1071–86) considers that Prusias I probably founded the city with the advice and assistance of Hannibal, a view supported by the evidence of the fragments of Arrian, a Roman senator and historian from Nicomedia. A fragmentary inscription from Bursa contains a city decree of, apparently, 188 or 187 B.C.; this text mentions an *epistates,* or royal governor, indicating that Prusa was firmly under royal control at the start of its existence (Robert 1937: 229). During the wars between Mithridates of Pontus and Rome, which preceded the final annexation of Bithynia by Rome in 72 B.C., Prusa was occupied by Mithridates and besieged by the Romans.

The growing prosperity of the Roman Empire is reflected at Prusa by the resumption of local coinage under Nero (54–68). Under Trajan (98–117) Prusa became one of the assize towns of the province of Bithynia, where the

Roman governor conducted judicial business during his tours through the province. Assize towns benefited from the regular influx of litigants, traders, and entertainers attracted by the presence of the governor; a vivid, if satirical picture of the animated scene is drawn by the orator Dio Chrysostom, "golden mouthed," who was a native of Prusa (*Or.* 35.15–17). Of interest to biblical scholars is the 5th-century bishop Synesius' report that Dio referred to the Essenes of Palestine in favorable terms. It would be unwise to assume any great significance in this reference for the history of Judaism or Christianity in Asia Minor. The traditions of popular Hellenistic philosophy on which Dio drew included a certain superficial taste for "barbarian" (i.e., non-Greek) wisdom. So we find Dio in his surviving speeches referring favorably to Scythian morals, to the Brahmans and the Magi, and telling a philosophical myth with a Persian setting (*Or.* 35.22; 36.39–60; 49.7; 69.6).

A brilliant light is shed on the political life of Prusa during the time of Trajan by the political speeches of Dio of Prusa (ca. 40–after 110) and by some of the correspondence of Pliny and Trajan, when the former was governor of Bithynia (109–11; *Ep.* 10.17A, 17B, 23–24, 58, 70–71 deal with the affairs of Prusa). Like most Greek cities, Prusa enjoyed a measure of local autonomy under the supervision of the Roman authorities. Local government was largely in the hands of the wealthy civic aristocracy, who were expected to contribute liberally from their personal resources to public life. The evidence of inscriptions and of Dio and Pliny shows that Prusa's constitution followed the pattern set for Bithynia by the *lex Pompeia:* there was a city council, with (probably) a property qualification for membership, and a college of magistrates presided over by a chief magistrate (*protos archon;* Dörner PW 23.1: 1071–86; Sherwin-White 1966: 720; Ameling 1984). The speeches of Dio and the letters of Pliny illustrate the danger of civic ambitions leading to rash expenditure on prestige public projects. The evidence is presented and discussed by Jones (1978) and Sheppard (1984).

The hot springs were noted for the fact that the water required no cooling before being used for bathing. There was a cult of Asclepius, Hygieia ("Health"), and the Nymphs at the springs (Robert 1946: 93–102). Prusa was the home of two noted doctors of the Roman world: Asclepiades (1st century B.C.), who specialized in water and wine cures, and C. Calpurnius Asclepiades, active in the time of Trajan.

The prosperity of Roman Prusa was founded on the combination of the rich arable land and olive groves of the coastal plain with the timber resources of Ulu Dag. Peace and prosperity were, however, rudely shattered when Prusa was plundered by the Goths in 256. There is little evidence for the later history of Greco-Roman Prusa. A bishop is attested from 325 (until 1712). During the 5th century a number of Huns were settled in the area. In 1236 the city fell to Orhan Gazi, the second Sultan of the Ottoman dynasty, who made it his capital. Today the tombs and mosques of the early Ottoman sultans are the principal monuments of the town of Bursa.

Bibliography

Ameling, W. 1984. Das Archontat in Bithynien. *Epigraphica Anatolica* 3: 19–31.

Jones, C. P. 1978. *The Roman World of Dio Chrysostom.* Cambridge, MA.

Robert, L. 1937. *Etudes anatoliennes.* Paris.

———. 1946. *Hellenica II.* Paris.

Sheppard, A. R. R. 1984. Dio Chrysostom: the Bithynian Years. *L'Antiquité Classique* 53: 57–73.

Sherwin-White, A. N. 1966. *The Letters of Pliny: A Historical and Social Commentary.* Oxford.

ANTHONY SHEPPARD

PSALMS, BOOK OF. The book of Psalms is unique in the Bible because it is a collection of literature of prayer, praise, and meditation. If the Bible's narrative materials relate what God has done and the prophetic literature reports what God has said, the Psalms present the response of the people to the acts and words of God. As a book of the people, the book of Psalms has been especially valued for both public worship and private devotion among Jews and Christians alike. It has also been the focal point of much scholarly research. For useful summaries of the major trends and positions in this research (and related bibliography), see Clements 1976: 76–98; and Hayes 1979: 139–43, 285–317.

A. The Name
B. The Text
  1. The Dead Sea Psalms Scroll
  2. The Hebrew *Tehillim*
  3. The Greek Psalter
C. The Origin and Function of the Psalms
  1. The Psalms as Response
  2. The Psalter as Worship Book
  3. The Psalter as Scripture
D. The Book and the Books
  1. The Beginning and Ending
  2. The Five Books
  3. The Titles
E. The Poetry of the Psalms
  1. Balance or Parallelism
  2. Other Relationships between A and B
  3. Repetition
  4. Alphabetic Acrostics
  5. Metaphors and Similes for God
  6. Metaphors and Similes for People
F. Types of Psalms
  1. Laments or Prayers
  2. Hymns or Songs of Praise
  3. Songs of Thanksgiving
  4. Royal Psalms
  5. Songs of Zion
  6. Liturgies
  7. Wisdom and Torah Psalms
G. Theological Themes
  1. "The Teaching of the Lord Is His Delight"
  2. "O Lord, My Rock and My Redeemer"
  3. "What God is Great Like Our God?"
  4. "Human Beings Are Like the Beasts That Perish"
  5. "I Have Set My King on Zion"

A. The Name

The English title "Psalms" is derived from the Greek *psalmoi,* "songs of praise," by way of the Latin *Liber Psalmorum,* "book of psalms." Among ancient Greek manuscripts of the OT, *psalmoi* appears in Codex Vaticanus as a title for the book. Codex Sinaiticus has no title, though "psalms of David" appears at the end. Codex Alexandrinus has as the title for the book *psalterion,* the name of a stringed instrument and the basis for the English "psalter"; *psalmoi* appears at the conclusion. The noun *psalmos* is found often in titles to the psalms, as in "psalm of David." The noun comes from the Greek verb *psallo* meaning "sing (to the accompaniment of a harp)" (BAGD, 899), as in the references to David in 1 Sam 16:16, 17, 23 or to the minstrel in 2 Kgs 3:15.

The NT refers to the three-part division of the Hebrew Bible, speaking of "the law of Moses and the prophets and psalms" (Luke 24:44), with "psalms" representing the as-yet incomplete third division; note also reference to the "Book of Psalms" in Luke 20:42.

The oldest Hebrew manuscripts do not have a title for the collection as a whole. The note at the end of Book II, Ps 72:20, says, "The prayers *[tĕpillôt]* of David, the son of Jesse, are ended," thus designating the foregoing psalms as "prayers." In rabbinic and later literature, the book is called *Sefer Tehillim,* "book of praises," or simply *Tillim.* The noun *tĕhillîm,* "praises," is derived from the Hebrew root *hll,* "praise." That root also appears in "hallelujah" ("praise Yah," or "Yahweh"), found only in the Psalter, always at the beginning or ending of psalms (104:35; 106:1, 48; 113:1, 9; 146–50, beginning and end of each; etc.).

The noun "praise" occurs often in the psalms: "He put a new song in my mouth, a song of praise *(tĕhillâ)* to our God" (40:3; also 22:25; 33:1; 34:1; 48:10, etc.). Psalm 145 is the only psalm to be designated a *tĕhillâ* in the title, translated "Song of Praise."

Of the 206 occurrences of *hll,* "praise," in the OT (146 verbal, 60 nominal), about two-thirds are in the psalms or in phrases taken from the psalms (*THAT,* 493). Because the collection of psalms contains so many expressions of praise to God, it became known as "praises" or "Tehillim."

The two names preserved in the Hebrew tradition, "prayers" *(tĕpillôt)* and "songs of praise" *(tĕhillîm),* may be taken as representing two fundamental types of psalms: prayers in time of need, or laments, and songs of praise, or hymns.

B. The Text

1. The Dead Sea Psalms Scroll. Some 30 texts containing portions of the Psalter have been found at Qumran near the Dead Sea since the discovery of the scrolls there in 1947 (in Caves 1, 2, 3, 4, 5, 6, 8, and 11). Three psalm texts have been found at other sites (parts of Psalms 15 and 16 found S of En Gedi in 1960; parts of Psalms 81 through 85 and Psalm 150 at Masada between 1963 and 1965; Sanders 1967: 145–46). In addition, the caves have yielded four commentary texts containing portions of psalms.

The most dramatic find is the Psalms Scroll from Cave 11. Discovered in 1956, it was unrolled by James Sanders in 1961 and published by him in 1965 and 1967. Sanders dates the scroll to around A.D. 50. It is made of five sheets of leather sewn to a length of almost 13 feet and is presently 6 to 7 inches wide; originally its width was 9 or 10 inches, making it about the same width as the Isaiah Scroll from Cave 1. The scroll contains all or parts of 41 canonical psalms from Books IV and V of the Psalter, beginning with Psalm 101; as well as 2 Sam 23:1–7; four noncanonical psalms (151A, B; 154; 155; and Sir 51:13ff.); and four other nonbiblical works (Plea for Deliverance, Apostrophe to Zion, Hymn to the Creator, and David's Compositions; these are interspersed in the book at a variety of places).

The psalms appear to have been popular at Qumran. "There were undoubtedly more copies of psalms in the Qumran library than of any other biblical writing. . . ." (Sanders 1967: 9). The text of the psalms recovered thus far, says Sanders, is in close agreement with the standard Ben Asher manuscripts (Leningradensis and the Aleppo Codex), with most of the variations matters of orthography. An exception is Psalm 145, in which every verse has a refrain, "Blessed be the Lord and blessed be his name for ever and ever." The superscription to 145 reads *tĕpillâ,* "prayer," instead of *tĕhillâ,* "song of praise" (RSV); the psalm also has a subscript reading "This is for a memorial. . . ." (Sanders 1967: 64–67). The ordering of the psalms in this scroll differs from that of the MT (Sanders 1967: 10, 16).

2. The Hebrew *Tehillim* (Songs of Praise). The critical edition of the Hebrew text of Psalms found in *BHS* is based upon the MT as represented by Codex Leningradensis (B19A or L), dated in 1008 C.E. and identified in the colophon as a production of the Ben Asher family (Würthwein 1979: 168).

The basis for a new critical edition of the Hebrew Bible being prepared at the Hebrew University in Jerusalem is the Aleppo Codex, so named because though it was originally in Jerusalem, it was moved to Cairo and then to Aleppo in Syria. Again a Ben Asher manuscript, it is dated from the first half of the 10th century. The manuscript lacks Pss 15:1–25:2. For progress reports, see *Textus: Annual of the Hebrew University Bible Project;* the publication of Psalms has not yet appeared.

3. The Greek Psalter. The Greek OT or Septuagint (LXX) was produced by the Jewish community in Alexandria, Egypt, during the first half of the 3d century B.C. Intended for Hellenistic Jews, this translation was immediately accessible to Greek-speaking gentiles as well and eventually became the OT for the Christian movement. Because of the popularity of the psalms, there are many more Greek manuscripts of that book available than of any other Old Testament book (Rahlfs 1967: 61). As the LXX became more and more the Bible for Christians, it lost popularity in the Jewish community.

The convenient edition of Alfred Rahlfs, *Septuaginta,* is based mainly on the three oldest major Greek manuscripts, all of which include both OT and NT. Codex Vaticanus (B) is a 4th-century manuscript; Pss 105:27–137:6 were lacking but were added in the 15th century. Codex Sinaiticus (S) is another 4th-century manuscript, containing the entire Psalter. Codex Alexandrinus (A) is a 5th-century manuscript, lacking Pss 49:20–79:11.

Each of these three includes Psalm 151, in which David

celebrates victory over Goliath. While this psalm is not in the Hebrew Bible, it is among those noncanonical pieces included in the Dead Sea Psalms Scroll. All three manuscripts have a superscription identifying the psalm as an addition to the 150 canonical psalms: "This psalm is ascribed to David and is outside the number. . . ." Codex S has a subscript reading "the 151 psalms of David." The subscript to A reads "the 150 psalms and one ascribed." B has no subscript.

The numbering of the psalms in the Greek OT differs from the Hebrew. The following table indicates the differences:

MT (also RSV)	*LXX*
Psalms 1–8	Psalms 1–8
9–10	9
11–113	10–112
114–15	113
116:1–9	114
116:10–19	115
117–46	116–45
147:1–11	146
147:12–20	147
148–50	148–50
———	151

As Christians transmitted the text of the Greek OT, a number of interpolations began to appear in the text. One example: in Rom 3:10–18, Paul uses parts of Ps 14:1–3 as well as Pss 5:9; 140:3; 10:7; and 36:1 to support his argument that all are sinners. In LXX Psalm 13 (Heb 14), manuscripts B and S insert precisely these quotations from other psalms in v 3. Thus, Christians enriched their Greek OT by adding this chain of quotations (see Rahlfs 1967: 30–32, for further examples).

C. The Origin and Function of the Psalms

The psalms originated in the midst of Israel's life and have continued to function in the lives of both Jews and Christians as a hymnbook for worship and a prayer book for devotion.

1. The Psalms as Response. Psalms 1 and 2 provide an introduction to the Psalter (see D below). The psalms that follow offer clues to the way in which the psalms originated.

These psalms are addressed to God, as is clear from reading the opening lines of Psalms 3–10: "O Lord . . ." (Psalm 3), "Answer me when I call, O God" (Psalm 4), "Give ear to my words, O Lord" (Psalm 5), etc. They address God in response to a crisis, such as being ill (Psalm 6) or being surrounded by enemies who may make false accusations (Psalms 3; 4; 5; 7; 9/10). The same crises brought on by illness (31; 32; 38; 39; 41; 51; 88; 102), enemies (17; 23; 26; 27; 57; 63), or the distress of sin (40; 51; 130) appear through the psalter. Such prayers in times of crisis are commonly called "laments," since one of the constant elements in these psalms is a complaint or lament, against God in "thou" form ("But thou, O Lord—how long?" 6:3), concerning oneself in "I" form (". . . for I am languishing," 6:2), or concerning others in "they" form ("for there is no truth in their mouth . . . ," 5:9). These first laments in the Psalter voice an individual's complaint and cry for help. The superscription to Psalm 102 describes the situation that gave rise to such prayers of the individual in times of crisis: "A prayer of one afflicted, when he is faint and pours out his complaint before the Lord" (see F.1 below).

The entire community may cry out for help: "Do thou, O Lord, protect us. . . ." (Ps 12:7). The Community Laments (see F.1 below) provide clues to the situation giving rise to these prayers. The people may have experienced a defeat (44:9–16), or the temple and the city of Jerusalem have been devastated (74:4–8; 79:1), or they may be suffering at the hands of enemies (80:6; 12–13) or in exile in Babylon (137).

Psalms also arise out of good times, the psalmist responding to a situation of experiencing blessing. Psalm 8 celebrates God's work as Creator, addressing God with general words of praise, "O Lord, our Lord, how majestic is thy name in all the earth!" Such psalms are designated as "hymns." Psalm 30 expresses praise and thanks to God for a specific act, in this case for healing in answer to prayer (vv 1–3). Psalms of this type may be called Thanksgiving Psalms (see F.3 below).

Other psalms arose out of particular occasions. The Royal Psalms were composed for use in connection with events in the life of a king (see F.4 below). Several psalms were produced to suit liturgical needs, providing the script for a procession around the city (Psalm 48) or for the offering of sacrifices (Psalm 66; see F.6 below). More than two dozen "Wisdom Psalms" (see F.7 below) offer short observations growing out of life's experiences (Psalms 127, 128) or longer reflections on the great problems of life (37, 73); or they may commend Torah (instruction) and its study (1; 19; 119). The alphabetical acrostic psalms were built on the pattern of the Hebrew alphabet, probably both to facilitate memorization and also for the sheer delight of producing such a work (see E.4 below).

In sum, the psalms arose out of the midst of Israel's life in the presence of God, responding to good times and bad, providing words for the celebrations of the community, and offering guidance and reflection on the opportunities and problems of life.

2. The Psalter as Worship Book. Since the Psalter is not a manual providing directions for those leading worship but a collection of hymns, prayers, and poems for the people, the settings for these psalms in worship and other occasions must be inferred from the psalms themselves.

The hymns (see F.2 below) suggest congregational worship utilizing vocal and instrumental music and marked by exuberance and creativity (the "new song"; Ps 33:1–3). They often begin with a call to praise in the imperative plural, "Praise the Lord" (Heb "Hallelujah"; 33:1; 111:1; 113:1; 146–50), thus assuming the presence of a community. Ps 111:1 makes the congregational context for praise explicit: "Praise the Lord. I will give thanks to the Lord with my whole heart, in the company of the upright, in the congregation" (cf. 149:1; 150:1). The praise that takes place in connection with these psalms was lively, involving singing and shouting (33:3), dancing (149:3; 150:4), and the use of string, wind, and percussion instruments (33:1–3; 149:3; 150). The forms of worship change, with the community called to update its materials in a manner appropriate for new times (33:1; 96:1; 98:1; 149:1). Those engaged in praise may be standing in the temple (135:1–2), even for a service of worship at night (134). Praise came from different groups within the assembled congregation (135:19–20). The repeated refrain of Psalm 136 suggests a worship leading calling out or chanting the first part of each line and the congregation responding with "for his steadfast love endures forever." The rubric, "let Israel now say" (124:1; 129:1), again calls the gathered people to respond.

Some psalms were used as liturgies (see F.6 below), with actions accompanying the words of the psalm. Psalm 66 functioned in connection with the making of an offering (66:13–15). Psalms 48 and probably 132 were associated with processions; the latter would fit a reenactment of David's bringing the ark into the city (2 Samuel 6). Pss 24:7, 9 and 118:19–20 suggest a procession passing through the temple gates, with participants carrying branches (118:27). Ceremonial washings are suggested by 26:6 and perhaps 51:7 (cf. Num 19:18). Psalms 15 and 24 apparently functioned as entrance liturgies, the worshipper about to enter the temple area asking a question and a priest or temple official responding with the answer (15:1–5; 24:3–6; cf. Mic 6:6–8). Various attempts have been made to reconstruct liturgies and entire festivals on the basis of the psalms, but such reconstructions remain notoriously hypothetical.

The "Songs of Ascents" or "Pilgrimage Psalms" (120–34) seem to have been used as a collection especially designed for those "going up" (122:4; the root is the same as "ascents" in the titles) to Jerusalem for one of the regularly occurring festivals (Deut 16:16–17). They fit a broad pattern of anticipating the journey (122:1), setting out (121), joyful arrival (133), and concluding evening worship (134).

At one time the Community Laments (see F.1 below) functioned as part of community services of prayer and fasting, called the "fast" (*ṣôm;* Joel 1:14). These were gatherings convened at times of national emergency such as a military crisis (2 Chronicles 20) or natural disasters such as drought and famine or plague (Joel 1; cf. the listing in 1 Kgs 8:33–40). A picture of these services can be pieced together: the entire community was assembled, including the children and the newly married (Joel 1:14; 2:15–16; 2 Chr 20:13). The extremity of the emergency was demonstrated by the destruction of beauty: clothing was torn or removed (Joel 2:12; Isa 32:11), the hair was cut off, the people wept and mourned (Isa 15:2–3; 22:12), even gashed themselves (Hos 7:14), rolling in dust (Mic 1:10), putting on sackcloth, and rolling in ashes (Jer 6:26). While these Community Lament psalms grew out of times of specific national need, their continued use indicates that they were appropriated and adapted for other sorts of situations.

The Individual Laments (see F.1 below) arose out of a variety of personal crises and must have continued to function in a great variety of life situations. Childless Hannah poured out her heart in the sanctuary at Shiloh; her prayers probably used the language of the individual laments. The priest says to Hannah, "Go in peace, and the God of Israel grant your petition. . . ." which may account for the abrupt change of mood in many of the laments (1 Samuel 1; cf. the change from Ps 13:5 to Ps 13:6). Hezekiah's prayer from his sickbed suggests another obvious setting for these prayers (Isaiah 38; cf. the psalms associated with illness as listed above).

The book of *4 Maccabees,* written sometime between A.D. 20 and 54, concludes with a scene suggesting how the psalms were used in the setting of the family. In the last words of the mother who had lost her seven sons in persecution (2 Maccabees 7), she recalls her late husband, saying to her remaining children, "A happy man was he, who lived out his life with good children . . . while he was still with you, he taught you the law and prophets. . . . He sang to you psalms of the psalmist David, who said, 'Many are the afflictions of the righteous' " (*4 Macc.* 18:9–10, 15).

Gerstenberger (1988) has suggested that there were a variety of occasions when family and friends came together and utilized the psalms. These would include not only the events of birth, marriage, and death, but also special gatherings at times of illness and sorrow and joy and thanksgiving. The laments, he suggests, were used at times of crisis in the circle of family and caring friends, under the direction of a ritual expert. Gerstenberger has compared these groups to contemporary group therapy movements under the direction of an expert in such processes. His work is a reminder that people's lives are lived not only as individuals or in congregations, but also in the world of the small group of family and friends.

Again, these occasional services cannot be reconstructed with certainty. But there is enough evidence in the OT to suggest that the prayers and songs of praise found in the Psalter were not confined to the sanctuary. The psalms came out of a variety of situations from the midst of the life of the people; it is reasonable to assume that they also functioned in a variety of life situations.

3. The Psalter as Scripture. The psalms are now in the form of a book, called the "Psalter" since the time of the Greek translations. Recent studies have demonstrated that this book has been carefully shaped and edited (see D below). That editing placed Psalm 1 at the beginning in order to suggest another way in which this collection is intended to function.

The first picture that appears in the Psalter is that of a tree, planted by a river, flourishing, yielding fruit (1:3). Used as a comparison, this is an image of a human life that is deeply rooted and marked by productivity, prosperity, and beauty. The reader asks: How could one attain to such a life? The answer is explicit: by meditating, both day and night, on the Torah of the Lord. The verb *hāgāh,* translated "meditate" (v 2), is also used for the growling of a lion as he enjoys his prey (Isa 31:4); the sense here is of the sound made as one studies the Lord's instruction in Scripture. This psalm thus suggests that the way to the kind of life symbolized by the tree involves delighting in and meditating upon Torah, here referring to the Lord's instruction that follows in the Psalter.

A second psalm with a concern for Torah—Psalm 19 (cf. v 7, translated "law")—also refers to meditation, asking that such reflecting and speaking be acceptable in the Lord's sight (19:14).

Finally, Psalm 119 offers a lengthy treatise which speaks of the Lord's Torah as a delight (v 92), of loving Torah (vv 97, 113, 163, 165), and of mediating (Heb *śîaḥ,* synonymous with *hāgāh* in 77:13—RSV 12) upon it all day (v 97). The psalm commends reflection upon God's precepts (v 15), statutes (vv 23, 48), works (v 27), and promises (v 148). It seems likely that the two Torah psalms, 1 and 119, once framed an early version of the Psalter (see D.2 below; see also Westermann 1981: 253). In any case, both suggest a particular use of the psalms of which they are a part. These ancient psalms of Israel are not only hymns and prayers to be sung and prayed at a place of public worship; they are also Scripture, designed to nurture the piety of the people in devotion and meditation.

D. The Book and the Books

The Psalter in its present form consists of 150 psalms divided into five books. Editorial work included the collecting and arranging of the individual psalms, the division into books, and the supplying of superscriptions or titles for 116 of the psalms.

1. The Beginning and Ending. The editors of the psalter placed Psalms 1 and 2 at the beginning as an introduction to the collection as a whole. These two psalms may be considered together: neither has a title; they are framed by the "blessed" formulas in 1:1 and 2:11 (the formula in 2:11 may be a contribution of the editor); and they are linked by the catchword *hāgāh,* translated "meditate" in 1:2 and "plot" in 2:1. In Acts 13:33, the 6th-century Greek Codex D as well as a number of other witnesses introduce Paul's citation of Ps 2:7 with "as also it is written in the first psalm," thus indicating either that Psalms 1 and 2 were considered as one psalm, or that there was a Psalter in existence in which the present Psalm 2 was the first psalm.

As noted above (C. 3), Psalm 1 functions as an invitation to meditate upon the psalms which follow. While Psalm 1 has its focus on the individual ("Blessed is the man. . . ."), the focus of Psalm 2 is international because it speaks of the nations, their kings, and the Lord's anointed king on Mt. Zion in Jerusalem. Since a psalm like 137 assumes the Exile in Babylon, the final editing of the Psalter had to have taken place sometime after 587 B.C. With the time of the Monarchy past, Royal Psalms (see F.4 below) such as Psalm 2 were no longer applicable to an actual king; nevertheless, they were collected and continued to be used, providing the seedbed out of which grew the hope for a new anointed one (2:2), or in Hebrew, a "messiah."

These two introductory psalms thus suggest a reading of the Psalter for individual edification and also within an international context which included hope for a future king to take up rule from Mt. Zion.

After this introduction the Psalter begins with a series of five psalms of lament of the individual (3–7); the bulk of Book I (Psalms 1–41) consists of further Individual Laments. Moving toward the end of Book IV (Psalms 90–106), the sound of praise dominates with the Kingship of the Lord Psalms (93; 95–99) and in a series of hymns (103–6). With the beginning of Book V (Psalms 107–50) praise continues, up to Psalm 119 (109 is an exception); and the Psalter concludes with five psalms of praise, each framed with "Praise the Lord" ("Hallelujah"). Thus one can speak of a broad movement in the Psalter as a whole from lament to praise.

2. The Five Books. The Psalter is divided into five "Books" (Psalms 1–41; 42–72; 73–89; 90–106; 107–50). According to the Talmud, this is to correspond with the five part division of the Pentateuch: "Moses gave Israel the five books, and David gave Israel the five books of the Psalms" (*Midrash Tehillim* on Psalm 1). Each Book ends with a doxology, probably not an original part of the final psalm in each book, but an insertion made in the final editing (Pss 41:13; 72:20; 89:52; 106:48). Psalm 150 provides a concluding doxology for Book V and for the Psalter as a whole.

Book I is made up almost entirely of Psalms associated with David in the titles. Psalms 1 and 2 are introductory. Psalm 10 has no title because it is linked with Psalm 9 by a broken alphabetic acrostic pattern (see E.4 below). This leaves only Psalm 33, which, though not having a Davidic superscription, has clear links with Psalm 32: *BHS* indicates that some Heb mss join the two psalms; 32:11 and 33:1 are linked by "righteous" and "upright," and Psalm 33 may be regarded as carrying out the exhortation of 32:11 (Wilson 1985: 174–76). The majority of these are psalms of the individual; exceptions include 19 and 29, which are hymns; 24, which is a liturgy; and 12, which is a lament giving voice to the hurts of the community (v 7).

Within Book II Psalms 42–49 are identified with the "Sons of Korah," members of a musical guild (2 Chr 20:19; cf. also the Korah psalms 84–85; 87–88). Psalms 42–83 (extending into Book III) are called the "Elohistic Psalter" because of a preference for the divine name "Elohim" (RSV, "God") in contrast to "Yahweh." A comparison with psalms that have near duplicates elsewhere in the Psalter is instructive. Psalm 53 is almost identical with Psalm 14, but note the replacement of "Yahweh" in 14:2, 4, 7 by "Elohim" in 53:2, 4, 6. Psalm 40 (13–17) is almost the same as Psalm 70; the situation in comparing these two is more complicated. "Yahweh" of 40:13a, 16 is replaced by "Elohim" in 70:1a, 4; but "Yahweh" of 40:13b remains as "Yahweh" in 70:1b, while "Elohim" of 40:17b is replaced by "Yahweh" in 70:5b. In general, however, Psalms 42–83 exhibit a marked preference for "Elohim," in comparison with the remainder of the Psalter. (In the 41 psalms of Book I, Yahweh appears about 275 times, Elohim 50 times. In the 42 psalms of the Elohistic Psalter, Yahweh occurs 43 times and Elohim just under 240 times. In Psalms 84–150, Yahweh again predominates.) The production of this "Elohistic Psalter" suggests an editor preparing a collection of psalms for use in the temple at a time when the name Yahweh was being used less frequently and was being replaced by the more general "Elohim." Book II ends with a collection of Davidic psalms (51–65; 68–70; 71 is untitled; as was the case with 33, *BHS* indicates that many Heb mss link it with the preceding psalm and that the LXX associates it with David). The note at the end of Psalm 72, "The prayers of David, the son of Jesse, are ended," indicates that a Davidic collection once ended at this point. This seems to be an editorial comment, since the title of Psalm 72 associates it with Solomon and since 72 comes to a definite ending in vv 18–19. The fact that Book II includes duplicates of psalms in Book I (cf. 53 and 14, 70 and 40:13–17) might suggest that these two books once had a separate existence. However, it is possible that 72:20 once referred to the contents of both Books I and II, where the majority of Davidic psalms (55 out of the 73 so titled) are concentrated.

Book III (73–89) contains only 17 psalms. Most of the Community Laments (see F.1 below) are gathered here; these include 74, 79, 80, 83, 85 (the others are Psalms 44 and probably 12). The majority of these psalms are associated with Asaph in the titles (73–83; 50 is the only other Asaph psalm), referring to a musician from the tribe of Levi who was appointed by David to provide music when the ark was brought to Jerusalem (1 Chr 6:39; 15:17–19; 16:4–6) and who was present at the dedication of Solomon's temple (2 Chr 5:12). Asaph's family was still active in music at the time of Josiah in the 7th century B.C. (2 Chr 35:15) and also at the time of Nehemiah and Ezra in the 5th century, furnishing trumpet players when the wall was rebuilt (Neh 12:35) and instrumental music when the foundation of the Second Temple was complete (Ezra 3:10).

Book IV (90–106) also consists of 17 psalms. Here are gathered 6 of the 7 psalms that declare Yahweh's kingship (93; 95–99). Other devices link psalms together: 103 and 104 both have "Bless the Lord, O my soul" at beginning and end; 105 and 106 both recite God's mighty acts in Israel's history, though with different emphases; and both begin with "O give thanks to the Lord" and end with "Praise the Lord." Principles of arrangement here are thus thematic grouping and similarity of beginnings and endings. Book IV ends with a series of hymns (103–6), the last one framed by "Praise the Lord" ("Hallelujah").

Book V (107–50) is the largest of the five books, with 44 psalms. Davidic psalms are grouped at the beginning (108–10) and toward the end (138–45). The unique Psalm 119, an acrostic with eight lines for each letter of the Hebrew alphabet, is included here. Linked to Psalm 1 with the Torah theme, it may have concluded an early form of the Psalter. Psalms 120–34 are a collection of "Songs of Ascent" (see C.2 above). Psalms 140–43 constitute a final series of Individual Laments. Book V concludes the Psalter with a series of five "Praise the Lord" or "Hallelujah" psalms, which may be viewed as carrying out the resolution of 146:21 (Wilson 1985: 193–94).

In conclusion, the locations of two types of psalms may be noted. Royal Psalms are scattered throughout the Psalter, especially at the beginning and ending of books. Psalm 2 introduces the whole Psalter and Book 1; Psalm 72 ends Book II; Book III ends with Psalm 89. At the time of the final composition of the Psalter, the monarchy had long been an institution of the past. These Royal Psalms, distributed throughout the Psalter, serve to keep alive the picture of the ideal king, or "anointed" (messiah; cf. 2:2; 45:7; see G.5 below).

Psalms framed with "Hallelujah" appear at strategic places. They may close a book (106) and the Psalter itself (146–50) or come at the conclusion of a collection of psalms (Psalm 100, after the Kingship of the Lord Psalms, 93 and 95–99; and Psalm 135, after 120–34). In several instances a psalm framed by "Praise the Lord" is followed by a psalm beginning "O give thanks" (106 and 107; 117 and 118; 135 and 136).

3. The Titles. One hundred and sixteen of the 150 psalms have superscriptions or titles in the Hebrew text, ranging from one word (98) to a lengthy comment (18). The 34 psalms that do not have titles are distributed as follows:

Book I: Psalms 1, 2, 10, and 33.
Book II: Psalms 43 and 71.
Book III: all have titles.
Book IV: Psalms 91, 93, 94, 95, 96, 97, 99, 104, 105, and 106.
Book V: Psalms 107, 111–19, 135–137, and 146–50.

Psalms 10 and 43 do not have titles because they are linked to the preceding psalms either by an alphabetical acrostic pattern (10) or by a refrain (43). Psalms 33 and 71 may lack titles because they are thematically linked to the psalms preceding them. The first two psalms themselves function as something of a "superscription" to the entire Psalter. Psalms 111–13, 117, 135, 146–50 all begin with the imperative "Praise the Lord," which also may serve as a title. In sum almost all of the psalms in Books I–III are titled; the great majority of untitled psalms are found in Books IV (10 psalms) and V (18 psalms).

Much of the information in these titles consists of specialized musical terms which are no longer understood (for discussion, see Kraus 1988: 21–32). However, other types of information are also communicated.

The title for Psalm 6 may be taken as an example, indicating these various types of information.

(a) "To the choirmaster: with stringed instruments; according to The Sheminith." Here are *directions for musical performance, addressed to the musical director.* The phrase "to the choirmaster" (JPS, "for the leader") occurs in initial position in more than a third of the psalms. Associated with the notion of overseeing ("oversight," Ezra 3:8, 9), it is understood to refer to the director of the choir. Reference may be made to the instruments to be used: "with stringed instruments" (4, 6, 54, 55, 61, 67, 76; cf. 1 Sam 16:16, 23, where the related verb refers to playing with the hand). Other instruments are sometimes referred to: the RSV translates "for the flutes" in Psalm 5, but the Hebrew is not certain; and the expression, "according to The Sheminith" (Psalms 6, 12) means literally, "according to/on the eighth," possibly referring either to the eighth musical pattern or to an eight-string instrument.

Though the matter is debated, some of these musical directions may refer to melodies, such as "according to The Gittith" (8, 81, 84), "according to The Hind of the Dawn" (22), "according to Lillies" (45, 69, 80), "according to The Dove on Far-Off Terebinths" (56), "according to Mahalath" (53, 88), "according to Do Not Destroy" (57–59, 75). "According to Muth-labben" (9), "according to Alamoth" (46), and "according to Mahalath Leannoth" (88) are unexplained. Often the Greek translators did not understand these terms and simply transliterated them; this same approach is taken in many instances by the JPS translators.

Two technical terms appearing not in the titles but in the course of the psalms are also unexplained. The meaning of *higgaion* in 9:16 is unknown; it occurs in 19:14 with the sense "meditation" and in 92:3, translated "melody." Finally, the meaning of "selah," which occurs 71 times in 39 psalms (also in Hab 3:3, 9, 13) remains unexplained. The Greek, where it occurs 92 times, translates it as *diapsalma,* which means an instrumental interlude (see Kraus 1988: 27–29).

(b) "A psalm" indicates the *type of composition.* The Hebrew *mizmôr* was translated in the Greek Bible as *psalmos* and has thus given the name to the book. *Mizmôr* occurs a total of 57 times and only in psalm titles. In 36 instances it refers to a "psalm of David." Only in Psalm 98 does it stand alone.

Other types of compositions indicated in the psalm titles include the following: "Song" *(šîr)* occurs in 30 titles, 13 times with *mizmôr* (30, 48, etc.); the term may also be used of secular songs (Isa 23:16). In the title of Psalm 45 *šîr yĕdîdōt* means "love song." "A Song of Ascents" (lit. "for goings up") is the title for each of Psalms 120–34, most likely referring to the "going up" to Jerusalem for festivals (cf. 122:4), and thus suggesting a translation such as "Pilgrimage Psalm." "Song of Praise" translating *tĕhillâ* occurs in Psalm 145; the plural form provides the Hebrew title for the Psalter. It occurs only here as a title but within psalms at 22:25; 33:1; 34:1; etc. "Prayer" translating *tĕpillâ* is found in the titles of Psalms 17, 86, 90, 102, 142 (and Habakkuk 3); also in the plural form in 72:20.

Several terms are not understood and are thus left untranslated. *Miktām* occurs 6 times, always "of David" (16; 56–60). *Maskîl* occurs 13 times, always associated with a proper name and probably meaning "skilled or artistic piece" (cf. 2 Chr 30:22)—Psalms 32, 42, 44, 45, 52–55, 74, 78, 88, 89, 142; it occurs once within a psalm, translated "psalm" (47:7). *Shiggaion* occurs in Psalm 7 and (in the plural) in the heading for Habakkuk 3.

(c) The title may also *associate the psalm with an individual or group,* in the case of Psalm 6, "of David." In these cases the Hebrew preposition *lĕ-* appears with the name; since that preposition can mean "to," "for," "of," or "belonging to," the sense of the title is not always clear. The preposition *lĕ* occurs in the expressions "to the choirmaster" (RSV) or "for the leader" (JPS) in 55 psalms, and in these cases it does not indicate authorship.

In the Hebrew text, 73 psalms include in the title, "*lĕ*David." In 13 instances (3, 7, 18, 34, 51, 52, 54, 56, 57, 59, 60, 63, 142) the title associates the psalm with an event in David's life. In Psalm 18, the extended note identifies David as the author, "A Psalm of David, the servant of the Lord, who addressed the words of this song to the Lord . . ." Since all of these events are recorded in 1–2 Samuel, these notes appear to have been provided by someone searching for an appropriate setting for the psalm in the life of David as known from the biblical account, thereby attributing authorship to him.

The biblical tradition depicts David as a composer of psalms (2 Sam 1:17), as a musician (1 Sam 16:16–23; cf. Ps 151:2, "My hands made a harp, my fingers fashioned a lyre"), and as the "sweet singer of Israel" (2 Sam 23:1); since the 13 psalms associated biographically with David point to David as an author, it would seem that authorship is the intent of the expression in many cases. But because the meaning of the preposition is ambiguous, it is not possible to identify specific psalms with David as author. As the psalm tradition develops, the tendency is to ascribe more and more psalms to David; thus the LXX associates (Hebrew/RSV numbers) Psalms 33, 43, 71, 91, 93–99, 104, and 137 with David (though omitting mention of David in the titles of 122 and 124), for a total of 85 Davidic psalms. The Talmud thinks of him as the author of the psalms, just as Moses was author of the Pentateuch (*Midrash Tĕhillîm* on Ps 1:2). An insert near the end of the Dead Sea Psalms Scroll says:

> And David, the son of Jesse, was wise, and a light like the light of the sun, and literate, and discerning and perfect in all his ways before God and men. And the Lord gave him a discerning and enlightened spirit. And he wrote 3600 psalms; and songs to sing before the altar over the whole-burnt perpetual offering every day, for all the days of the year, 364; and for the offering of the Sabbaths, 52 songs; and for the offering of the New Moons and for all the Solemn Assemblies and for the Day of Atonement, 30 songs. And all the songs that he composed were 446, and songs for making music over the stricken, 4. And the total was 4050. All these he composed through prophecy which was given him from before the Most High (column xxvii, 2–11; Sanders 1967: 137)

Further individuals associated with psalms are Solomon (72 and 127), Heman (88), Ethan (89), Moses (90), and Jeduthun, one of David's musicians (39, 62, and 77; 1 Chr 25:1–2; 2 Chr 5:12).

(d) Other psalm titles include *suggestions for the use of the psalm.* In surveying these examples, it becomes apparent that the titles are part of the history of the interpretation and use of the psalms. The *content* of Psalm 30, for example, identifies it as suited for an individual giving thanks after experiencing healing; the *title,* however, suggests its use as "A Song at the dedication of the Temple." Psalms 38 and 70 are designated "for the memorial offering," Psalm 92 as "A Song for the Sabbath" (in the Gk translation, Psalm 24 is designated for Sunday, 94 for Wednesday, and 93 for Friday) and Psalm 100 "for the thank offering." The title to Psalm 60 includes the comment, "to be taught" (JPS; RSV, "for instruction"); cf. Deut 31:19; and 2 Sam 1:18).

In sum, while the psalm titles were not parts of the original psalms, they provide important clues to the history of the interpretation of the psalms and to their use in the lives of the people both individually and in the community.

E. The Poetry of the Psalms

The chief characteristic of Hebrew poetry in the Bible is balance or symmetry, commonly called parallelism. Biblical poetry is also marked by the use of repetition, a fondness for alphabetical acrostics, and the employment of metaphor and simile.

1. Balance or Parallelism. A line of Hebrew poetry is made up of two parts or cola (singular colon) which may be designated A and B. For example:

(A) When Israel went forth from Egypt,
(B) the house of Jacob from a people of strange language, (114:1)

In this example, "Israel" is balanced by "house of Jacob" and "Egypt" by "a people of strange language." Since the balancing words and phrases are synonymous and since the two cola parallel one another in meaning, this is called "synonymous parallelism." The book of Psalms, and indeed the entire Hebrew Bible, is full of this kind of synonymous parallelism (e.g., Pss 4:2–6; 8:4; 19:1–2; 24:1–3; etc.). See also PARALLELISM.

Parallelism or balancing may extend to more than two cola, with whole lines balancing one another:

(A + B) The precepts of the Lord are right, rejoicing the heart;
(A′ + B′) the commandment of the Lord is pure, enlightening the eyes (19:8; cf. vv 7, 9).

In the examples given, the ordering of the words in the balancing cola is the same. In Ps 114:1 "Israel . . . Egypt" is balanced by "house of Jacob . . . people of strange language." This order may be represented as A + B balanced by A′ + B′. The order may also fall into a chiastic pattern, where A + B is balanced by B′ + A′ (cf. "When the going gets tough, the tough get going"). For example:

(A + B) His mischief returns upon his own head,
(B′ + A′) and on his own pate his violence descends (7:16).

(A + B) Praise the Lord with the lyre,
(B′ + A′) with the ten-stringed harp make melody to him (my trans., 33:2; cf. also 137:5–6).

It is also possible that B may stand over against A, stating its opposite or standing in contrast to it. This is called antithetic parallelism:

(A) The wicked borrows, and cannot pay back,
(B) but the righteous is generous and gives;
(A) for those blessed by the Lord shall possess the land,
(B) but those cursed by him shall be cut off (37:21–22; cf. 1:6; 20:8; 32:10, etc.).

Antithetic parallelism is especially characteristic of proverbial literature (e.g., Prov 10:1–12; Eccl 8:4; 10:2, 12).

Kugel has suggested that the most general way to describe the relationship between A and B in examples such as these is the formula, "A is so, and what's more, B." He proposes a metaphor drawn from parliamentary procedure to understand the relationship between B and A; A is stated, and B then has an emphatic "seconding" character (1981: 51).

2. Other Relationships between A and B. The cola A and B may relate to one another in a number of other ways:

A makes a statement, B provides a reason:

(A) Blessed be the Lord!
(B) for he has heard the voice of my supplications (28:6).

A makes a statement; B balances with a question:

(A) For in death there is no remembrance of thee;
(B) in Sheol who can give thee praise? (6:5).

A asks a question; B gives an answer:

(A) How can a young man keep his way pure?
(B) By guarding it according to thy word (119:9).

A makes a statement; B balances with a quotation:

(A) I had said in my alarm,
(B) "I am driven far from thy sight" (31:22).

A sets forth something "better than" B:

(A) Better is a little that the righteous has
(B) than the abundance of many wicked (37:16; cf. 118–8–9; 119:72; also Proverbs).

A varies; B repeats:

(A) O give thanks to the Lord, for he is good,
(B) for his steadfast love endures forever.
(A) O give thanks to the God of gods,
(B) for his steadfast love endures forever (136:1–2 and throughout).

A makes a statement with an abstract noun; B sharpens the focus with a concrete noun:

(A) Therefore the Lord has recompensed me according to my righteousness,
(B) according to the cleanness of my hands in his sight (18:24).

A states the whole; B balances with a part which stands for the whole (synecdoche):

(A) For thou dost deliver a humble people;
(B) but the haughty eyes thou dost bring down (18:27).

A and B name two terms which mark boundaries in order to designate a totality (merismus):

(A) The sun shall not smite you by day,
(B) nor the moon by night (121:6).

A may provide a simile, B balancing with the reality:

(A) As a father pities his children,
(B) so the Lord pities those who fear him (103:13; cf. 103:11–12; 42:1).

3. Repetition. The psalms utilize a variety of forms of repetition. A psalm may begin with a repetition, for the sake of emphasis:

My God, my God, why has thou forsaken me? (22:1).

A repetition may conclude a psalm for the same reason:

Wait for the Lord;
be strong, and let your heart take courage;
yea, wait for the Lord! (27:14).

The same word may stand at the beginning of a succession of cola, again for the sake of emphasis:

> Surely every man stands as a mere breath!
> Surely man goes about as a shadow!
> Surely for nought are they in turmoil. . . . (39:5–6).

An entire colon may be emphasized through repetition:

> My soul waits for the Lord
> more than watchmen for the morning,
> more than watchmen for the morning (130:6).

This emphasis may take the form of a refrain (42:5, 11; 43:5; 46:7, 11; 49:12, 20; 56:4, 11; 57:5, 11; 59:6, 14; 59:9, 17; 67:3, 5; 99:5, 9; 107:8, 15, 21, 31).

A thematically central expression may recur throughout a psalm, such as the sevenfold occurrence of "the voice of the Lord" in Psalm 29.

The same statement may begin and end the psalm, tying the whole together (the *inclusio,* or inclusion), as in Pss 8:1, 9; 118:1, 29; note also "Praise the Lord" in Psalms 106, 113, 117, 146–150; and how the "blessed" formula in 1:1 and 2:11 links these two psalms together as an introduction to the Psalter.

In Ps 118:2–4 (cf. also 135–19–20), an initial colon A grows longer with each repetition, while coupled with a B colon that remains constant:

> (A) Let Israel say,
> (B) "His steadfast love endures for ever."
> (A) Let the house of Aaron say,
> (B) "His steadfast love endures for ever."
> (A) Let those who fear the Lord say,
> (B) "His steadfast love endures for ever."

In Ps 118:10–12, three A cola play upon the word "surround" and grow successively longer while the B colon again remains the same:

> (A) All nations surrounded me;
> (B) in the name of the Lord I cut them off!
> (A) They surrounded me, surrounded me on every side;
> (B) in the name of the Lord I cut them off!
> (A) They surrounded me like bees, they blazed like a fire of thorns;
> (B) in the name of the Lord I cut them off!

Note also the threefold repetition with variation of "the right hand of the Lord does valiantly/is exalted" (118:15–16).

Repetition may serve a liturgical purpose. The opening words of a psalm are sounded, followed by a call for the congregation to join in; and the initial words are stated again:

> If it had not been the Lord who was on our side,
> let Israel now say—
> if it had not been the Lord who was on our side (124:1–2; cf. 129:1–2).

4. Alphabetic Acrostics. A number of psalms are constructed on an acrostic pattern, the initial letters of each line following the order of the Hebrew alphabet. The clearest examples are Psalms 25, 34, 111, 112, and 145. Psalms 9 and 10 together constitute a broken acrostic with some of the letters of the alphabet missing. Psalm 119 is unique, an acrostic with eight lines built on each of the 22 letters of the Hebrew alphabet, for a total of 176 lines. The acrostic form was probably chosen as an aid for memorization (cf. Prov 31:10–31, an alphabetical acrostic in praise of a good wife; in later Jewish tradition, recited by a husband to a wife), though it may also have been used out of pleasure at the challenge of preparing such a composition. See also ACROSTIC.

5. Metaphors and Similes for God. A *metaphor* lets one reality stand for another, as in "the Lord is my shepherd" (23:1). A *simile* is a comparison using "like" or "as," for example, "my heart is like wax" (22:14).

The Psalter is rich in metaphors for God. Most frequent are those that portray God as a place of refuge, shelter, or protection. "Rock" as metaphor for God appears 21 times, translating Heb *ṣûr* and *selaʿ*. These are most often in expressions of trust in God. The word *miśgāb,* which has the root sense of "being high" or "inaccessible," occurs thirteen times, translated as "stronghold," "refuge," "defense," or "fortress." The word "fortress" also translates *mĕṣudâ,* always occurring with other metaphors (18:2; 31:2, 3; 71:3; 91:2; 114:2). "Refuge," *maḥseh,* which has the sense of shelter from storm and rain (Isa 4:6) or from the sun (Judg 9:15), is used as a metaphor for God eleven times in the Psalms. The Heb *māʿôz* is also translated as "refuge," "stronghold" (27:1; 31:2, 4; 37:39; 43:2; 52:7); the sense of "protection" is clear from the expression "*māʿôz* of my head" or "helmet" in Ps 60:7. God is named "hiding place," "cover," "shelter" (Heb *sēter*) in Pss 27:5; 31:20; 32:7; 61:4; 91:1; 119:114. The Lord is called a "dwelling place" (90:1), "habitation" (91:9), and "rock of refuge" (71:3), all translating *māʿôn.* The sense of *mānôs,* "refuge" (59:16; 142:4), is a place of escape. Related to these examples that portray the Lord as protection is the picture of the Lord as "shield" (3:3; 7:10; 18:2; 18:30, 35; 28:7; 33:20; 59:11; 84:11; 115:9, 10, 11; 119:114; 144:2), always in expressions of trust. The extraordinary number of such examples indicates that those praying these psalms were a people hurting, looking to their God for help.

God is portrayed as "king" in many psalms. The expressions "God reigns" and "the Lord reigns" occur as part of the Kingship of the Lord Psalms in 47:8; 93:1; 96:10; 97:1; 99:1; cf. 146:10. If one adds references to the Lord's throne (9:4, 7; 47:8; 89:14; 93:2; 103:19), it is apparent that "king" is a central metaphor for God in the psalms. God as "judge" also occurs many times.

A number of metaphors and similes appear less frequently. The Lord is "shepherd" for the individual (23:1; 119:176) or for the people as a whole (28:9; 80:1). The people may be portrayed as a "flock," implying the picture of shepherd for the Lord (74:1; 77:20; 78:52; 79:13; 95:7; 100:3). The Lord is a farmer caring for a vineyard (80:8–12) or feeding livestock (145:15–16). The Lord may be called "my portion," the sense being that the Lord is like a share or portion of land that one inherits (16:5; 73:26; 119:57; 142:5); closely related is the picture of the Lord as "my cup," i.e., my share (16:5). The Lord is a "sun" (84:11). The Lord as "father" occurs in 68:5; 89:26; and in the simile of 103:13. The Lord is a warrior (68:1–2, 11, 17, 21–23; 89:10) using nations as needed (60:7–8). The Lord may even be compared to a person awaking from a hangover (78:65).

The Songs of Ascent (120–34) are rich in imagery. The Lord is keeper and provider of shade (Psalm 121), builder and watchman (127:1), master and mistress (123:2), like a nursing mother (131:2), or like the mountains providing protection around Jerusalem (125:2).

In some instances the metaphor is implied by the action of the subject. The Lord is an archer (7:12–13; 18:14; 21:12; 38:2) firing lightning bolts as arrows (77:17; 144:6). The Lord is a bird whose wings provide protection (17:8; 36:7; 57:1; 61:4; 63:7; 91:4), a builder (102:25; 104:5), a host (23:5), a knitter (139:13), even a moth (39:11).

6. Metaphors and Similes for People. Much of the imagery for people comes from agricultural life. The person who delights in meditating on Scripture is like a tree, firmly rooted and productive (1:3). The righteous are like the palm or cedar, flourishing and productive even in old age (92:12–14). A family is blessed with a wife who is like a fruitful vine and children sprouting up like olive shoots around the table (128:3; in 127:4–5 children are called arrows in a quiver, affording protection to their parents). The psalmist trusting in God's love is "like a green olive tree" (52:8). Psalm 144 asks for God's blessing, including the wish that children "in their youth be like plants full grown" (144:12). The picture of God's people as a vine is developed in 80:8–13 (cf. 44:2).

The relationship of the individual to God may be described in terms of a sheep and a shepherd (23:1–4; 119:176); more frequently the whole people is described as a flock of sheep (28:9; 74:1; 77:20; 78:52; 79:13; 80:1; 95:7; 100:3) or even as sheep ready for slaughter (44:11, 22).

The fellowship of believers is as pleasant as an abundance of expensive perfume or the cooling morning dew (133).

The complaint section of the laments is rich in figurative language. The one suffering may use comparisons from animal life, calling himself a worm (22:6) or comparing his situation to a vulture of the wilderness, an owl of the waste places, or a lonely bird on the housetop (102:6–7). His longing for the Lord's deliverance is more than the longing of a night watchman for the morning (130:6); it is like the thirst of a person about to faint (63:1), of a deer yearning for flowing streams (42:1), or of a parched land needing water (143:6). The present situation of the people is like that of a dry creek in the Negeb (126:4). The psalmist describes his personal distress as being poured out like water, having a heart like wax, with his strength dried up like a potsherd (22:14–15). He is shriveled up like a dried out wineskin (119:83), broken like a pot (31:12), lonely as a person who is deaf and dumb (38:13–14). His life is passing away like a shadow that disappears at sundown, or it will vanish as quickly as a grasshopper that is shaken away (109:23). He may portray himself as drowning (69:1–2, 14–15; 88:7, 17). In several instances the psalmists lament the brevity of life, comparing people to grass or a flower (90:5–6; 102:11; 103:15–16, in a Thanksgiving Psalm); human life is a mere breath or a shadow (39:5–6; 102:11; 144:4), or a puff of smoke (102:3). The length of life is a mere handbreadth (39:5); a statement comparing the brevity of human life to that of the beasts becomes a repeated element in a Wisdom Psalm (49:12; 20). The Lord punishing the people made their days vanish like a breath (78:33), but their very impermanence was a ground for the Lord's mercy (78:39). The psalmist declares that he is not a permanent resident but a guest, a sojourner (39:12; 119:19).

Finally, we note the metaphors and similes that the psalmists use for the wicked person or the enemy. The wicked sprout up like grass (92:7; in contrast to the righteous who are like palm or cedar trees, 92:12–13). But they are in reality as impermanent as grass (37:2, 20), like chaff, dust, or the mire of the streets (1:4; 18:42). They are as transitory as a dream (73:20). They are like trappers, setting snares for the righteous (141:9; 142:3). They wear curses like clothing (109:18). Especially frequent is the comparison of the wicked to the lion (7:2; 10:9; 17:12; 22:13, 21; 35:17; 57:4). They may also be compared to bulls (22:12), dogs (22:16, 20; 59:6–7, 14–15), the wild ox (22:21), wild beasts (74:19), a boar (80:13), a serpent (58:4; 140:3), even bees or a blazing fire (118:12). Their tongue is like a razor (52:2) or a sword (64:3); their words are like arrows (64:3). One day they shall be shattered like a smashed rock (141:7).

The language in curses against the enemy is especially colorful: "May these lions have their teeth broken and be defanged" (58:6). "May they disappear, like water running away, like grass trodden down, like a snail disappearing into the slime, or a birth that is aborted" (58:6–8). "May they be as impermanent as smoke or wax before a fire" (68:2), or "as grass on a roof" (129:6). "May they be blown away like whirling dust and chaff" (83:13). "Let them be like a forest consumed by a fire" (83:14–15), "like dung ground into the earth" (83:10). "May their name be blotted out of the book of the living" (69:28). "May dishonor and shame be their clothing" (109:29).

The variety and vividness of the imagery in the Psalter are evidence of the lively imagination that animates this poetry.

F. Types of Psalms

The psalms originated as Israel's response to the acts and words of God and, in fact, to what the psalmists saw as God's inaction and silence. As such, they reflect the polar experiences of human life: joy and sorrow. Joy brought before God is praise; sorrow is taken to the Lord in the form of the lament. With this, the fundamental themes running through the Psalter—praise and lament—are identified (Westermann 1981).

As literature that arose out of the varied situations of human life, the psalms are as varied as human experience itself and cannot all be neatly categorized. Nevertheless, those coming from similar situations have similar features and can be profitably considered as a group. Lines of classification cannot always be firmly drawn, for example, between a "lament" and a "psalm of trust." (In the categories below, a psalm number in parentheses indicates that the psalm only partially fits in that category.)

1. Laments or Prayers (Heb *tĕpillâ*). The Community

Laments arose from times of national crisis. These include Psalms (12), 44, 60, 74, 79, 80, 83, 85, 90, 94, (108), 123, (129), and 137; five of these are gathered in Book III (73–89). The typical elements in the community lament include:

(*a*) the *address* (simply "O God" in 44:1; 80:1–2);
(*b*) the *complaint* in three forms, where the subject of the verb is "we" (44:22, 25), "they" (i.e., the enemy; 80:12b–13, 16a) or "thou" (i.e., God; 44:9–14; 80:4–6a; 12a);
(*c*) the *request for help* addressed to God (44:23, 26; 80:1a, 2b, 3, 7, 14–15, 17, 19);
(*d*) the *affirmation of trust* in God, which may take the form of recalling the Lord's previous saving acts (44:1–7; 80:8–11);
(*e*) a *vow to praise God* when the crisis has passed (44:8; 80:18).

Specific psalms can be considered against the background of this pattern of typical elements: Psalm 79 develops the *request* at length (vv 6–12), while Psalm 74 extends the *they-complaint* (vv 4–8). The *affirmation of trust* is developed in 74:12–17; it can so dominate a psalm that the entire psalm can be considered a Community Psalm of Trust: 125, (126). Psalm 60 adds a divine oracle to the typical elements (vv 6–8).

The Individual Laments arise from a variety of situations of individual crisis. Included in this category are:

Book I:	3–7; 9–10; 13; (14); 17; 22; 25; 26; 28; 31; 35; (36); 38; (39); 40:11–17; 41;
Book II:	42–43; 51; (52); (53); 54–59; 61; 64; 69; 70; 71;
Book III:	77; 86; 88;
Book IV:	102;
Book V:	109; 120; 130; 140–43.

Like the Communal Laments, the typical elements in the Individual Lament are:

(*a*) the *address* (13:1, "O Lord"; 22:1, "My God, my God");
(*b*) the *complaint* in three forms, with the subject "I" (13:2a; 22:2, 6, 14–15, 17a), "thou" (13:1; 22:1), or "they" (13:2c; 22:7–8, 12–13, 16, 17b–18);
(*c*) the *request for help* (13:3–4; 22:11, 19–21);
(*d*) the *affirmation of trust* (13:5; 22:3–5, 9–10);
(*e*) the *vow to praise God* when the crisis is past (13:6; 22:22–31).

When the *affirmation of trust* dominates, the psalm may be called an Individual Psalm of Trust: 11; 16; 23; 27; 62; 63; 131.

2. Hymns or Songs of Praise (Heb *tĕhillâ*). Included here are Psalms 8; 19:1–6; 29; 33; 47; 65; 66:1–12; 78; 93; 95–100; 103–6; 111; 113; 114; 117; 134; 135; 136; 145–50.

Many of these hymns begin with a *call to praise* in the imperative plural, summoning the assembled community to praise the Lord (33:1–3; 66:1–4; 100:1–3a; 105:1–6; 111:1; 113:1–3; 117:1; 135:1–3; 136:1a; 146–50). This imperative makes clear the congregational setting for these psalms. Following the call to praise (113:1–3; 117:1) are *reasons* for the praise (113:4–6; 117:2), which may include God's might and majesty (113:4–5) as well as God's mercy in caring for individual persons (113:6–9).

The theme of God's might as a reason for praise is developed in those psalms which place particular emphasis on the work of God the Creator (8; 19A; 104; 148; cf. 139) or on God's acts in history (78, 105, 106). A number of psalms celebrate God's work in both nature and history (33; 65; 66; 114; 135; 136; 146; 147).

Some psalms are dominated by the imperative call to praise. Psalms 146–50 are each framed with the plural imperative, "Praise the Lord!" The imperative to praise completely controls Psalms 148 and, especially, 150.

The hymns extolling the Kingship of the Lord ("Enthronement Psalms") describe the Lord as King (47; 93; 95–99); a number of these include the declaration, "The Lord reigns" (93:1; 96:10; 97:1; 99:1).

3. Songs of Thanksgiving (Heb *tôdâ*). Included here are Psalms 18; 30; 32; (34); 40:1–10; 66:13–20; 92; 116; 118; and 138. These psalms originated as a grateful response to God for a specific act of deliverance, such as healing from illness (30; 32; 116), which may be a physical manifestation of unforgiven sin (32), or deliverance from enemies (18; 92; 118; 138), or simply rescue from trouble (66:14). The title to Psalm 18 indicates how the origin of that particular psalm was understood at the time of the Psalter's editing: "A Psalm of David the servant of the Lord, who addressed the words of this song to the Lord on the day when the Lord delivered him from the hand of all his enemies, and from the hand of Saul."

These psalms assume the presence of the congregation, which is gathered either for worship (30:4–5; 34:5, 8, 9; 118:1–4, 24, 29) or for instruction (32:8–11; 34:11–14) and who hear the story of the deliverance (40:9–10; 66:16–19). There are hints indicating how these psalms were used in worship: 118:19–29 assumes a procession, while 66:13–15 and 116:12–19 point to a thank offering accompanying the psalm. In Psalm 138 the worshipper is in the outer court of the temple (v 2).

At the heart of these psalms is the *story of the deliverance*, summarized briefly, "O Lord my God, I cried to thee for help, and thou hast healed me" (30:2; cf. 18:3; 34:4, 6; 40:1–2; 66:19; 92:4; 116:1–2; 118:5; 138:3) and often expanded (18:4–19, 31–45; 30:6–11; 32:3–5; 66:16–19; 92:10–11; 116:3–4, 6–9, 16; 118:10–18).

A psalm of this type has been called a *tôdâ*, Hebrew for "thanksgiving" (116:17). The related verb, *yādāh*, occurs frequently in these psalms and is variously translated: 18:49 (RSV "extol"); 30:4 (RSV "give thanks"); 30:9 and 138:4 (RSV "praise"); 32:5 (RSV "confess"); 30:12; 92:1; 118:1, 19, 21, 28, 29; 138:1, 2, (all RSV "give thanks" or "thank," but JPS "praise"). Westermann has argued that the verb *yādāh* should be translated "praise" (cf. JPS) rather than "thank," and on that basis prefers to classify these psalms as "narrative praise of the individual" (1981: 25–30; 1989).

A number of psalms express the praise and thanks of the community or groups within the community for God's blessings or for specific acts of deliverance. These may be described as Community Thanksgiving Psalms (Crüsemann argues against such a category; 1969: 155–209). Psalm 67 expresses thanks for the blessing of a good harvest (vv 6–7). Psalm 75 gives thanks for "wondrous deeds" (v 1). Psalm 107 tells four stories of deliverance which are the basis for a refrain calling for thanksgiving (vv 4–9, 10–16, 17–22, 23–32). Psalm 124 again tells a story of deliverance, summarized in the doubled "we have escaped" of v 7. Psalm 136 begins with the triple imperative "O give thanks. . . ." (vv 1–3) and continues by reciting God's mighty acts in creation (vv 4–9) and in history (vv 10–25) as a basis for the refrain of every verse, "for his steadfast love endures forever."

4. Royal Psalms. These are psalms composed for an event connected with the life of the king. Included are Psalms 2; 18; 20; 21; 45; 72; 89; 101; 110; 132; and 144:1–11. Psalm 45 was written for a royal wedding. Psalm 2 was intended for a king's coronation, a time when the vassal nations would be considering rebellion (vv 1–3). Psalm 18 is a royal thanksgiving, in which the king expresses gratitude for a victory in battle (vv 6–19, 31–45). Psalm 20 is a prayer for the king's victory before battle; Psalm 21 gives thanks for answered prayers (vv 1–7) and promises future victories (vv 8–12). Psalm 72 is a prayer for the king, probably at the time of his coronation or at its anniversary. Psalm 89 is a lament, a prayer for deliverance from enemies. In Psalm 101 the king promises to rule with loyalty and justice. Psalm 110 again fits a coronation setting. Psalm 132 recalls the divine choice of the Davidic line (vv 11–12, 17–18) and of Zion (vv 13–16). In Ps 114:1–11 the king prays for victory.

These psalms originated during the period of the Monarchy and functioned during that period. After the fall of Jerusalem in 587 B.C., they took on another significance, projecting into the future a description of an ideal king to come (see G.5 below).

5. Songs of Zion. A number of psalms celebrate the Lord's choice of Mt. Zion in Jerusalem as the earthly center of the Lord's presence. These Songs of Zion (for this title, see 137:3) include 46, 48, 76, 84, 87, and 122 (cf. also 132:13). These psalms declare the Lord's presence in Jerusalem (46:7, 11), which is the city of God (46:4–5; 48:8; 76:2; 87:1–3), where beautiful Mt. Zion is located (48:1–3). Ps 48:12–14 suggest a procession around the city walls. Psalm 84 expresses the thoughts of one longing to visit the temple, where even the sparrows find refuge (vv 1–4; cf. v 10); Psalm 122 expresses the joy of a pilgrimage to the city and prays for the peace of Jerusalem.

6. Liturgies. Psalms designed for antiphonal dialogue or which associate liturgical action with the words of the psalm are called Liturgies. Here may be included Psalms 15, 24, 50, (68), 81, (82), 95, 115, 132. Psalm 15 appears to have functioned as a liturgy for entrance into the temple area, with the worshipper asking the question in v 1, "O Lord, who shall sojourn in thy tent?" and the priest responding with the answer in vv 2–5, "He who walks blamelessly, and does what is right. . . ." Psalm 24 is similar, with the worshipper's question in v 3, "Who shall ascend the hill of the Lord?" and the answer in vv 4–6, "He who has clean hands and a pure heart. . . ." Like Psalm 48, this psalm appears to be associated with a procession, probably including the ark. Those outside the temple area make the request, "Lift up your heads, O gates . . . that the King of glory may come in." Those inside respond with the question, "Who is this King of glory?" and the first group replies, "The Lord, strong and mighty. . . ." (vv 7–8). The same exchange is then repeated in vv 9–10.

Three psalms include extensive words from the Lord delivered in liturgical settings. Psalm 50 assumes a ceremony renewing the covenant (vv 5, 16). After a description announcing God's presence, including a word from God delivered by a cultic official gathering the covenant people (v 5), there are further words from God calling for genuine prayer and thanksgiving, instead of a mechanical offering of sacrifices (vv 7–15, 16b–23). The ceremony must have included a recitation of the covenant requirements (as v 16 suggests). Ps 81:1–3 is suited to a worship setting on a "feast day." The main part of the psalm consists of words from the Lord delivered by the proper official, here reminding Israel what the Lord has done (vv 6–7, 10a), recalling their past disobedience (vv 11–12), and calling for new loyalty and obedience (vv 9, 13). Psalm 95 appears to be connected with a procession (vv 1–2) which culminates in bowing before the Lord (v 6). Once again, a divine word spoken by a cultic official calls for obedience (7b–11).

Psalm 68 refers to "solemn processions," described in vv 24–27, while Psalm 82 depicts a legal process where God pronounces judgment on the gods making up the "divine council."

Psalm 115 assumes a variety of voices. One voice (or group) asks the question in vv 1–2, and another answers with vv 3–8; three groups are exhorted and then respond in vv 9–11; the psalm concludes with a word of blessing (14–15) and praise (16–18).

Psalm 118 appears to have been connected with a ceremony entering into the temple area (vv 19–20, 26–27). Psalm 132 may have been used in connection with a procession reenacting David's bringing of the ark (v 8) to Jerusalem and thus celebrating the Lord's choice of David (v 11; cf. the Royal Psalms) and of Zion (v 13; cf. the Songs of Zion).

As one of the "Pilgrimage Psalms," Psalm 121 appears to have been used as a liturgy for travelers, with those going on a journey reciting vv 1–2 and those remaining at home speaking the words of encouragement and blessing in vv 3–8.

7. Wisdom and Torah Psalms. Included here are Psalms 37, 49, 73, 112, 127, 128, 133, and Psalms 1, 19, and 119. One does not hear the tones of either lament or praise in the Wisdom Psalms; for the most part, they are not even addressed to God. Rather, they offer reflections on the possibilities and the problems of life before God and advice on how best to live that life. In so doing, they are linked with the biblical Wisdom Literature (Proverbs, Job, Ecclesiastes). Wisdom Literature in the Bible is represented by two basic kinds of materials: the short saying (as found in Proverbs and Ecclesiasticus) and the longer, reflective essay or drama (Ecclesiastes, Job). Both types are represented in the psalms.

Psalms 127, 128, and 133 are each made up of short sayings, reflecting on such everyday themes as piety and daily work (127:1; 128:1–2), the balance between work and rest (127:2), and the blessings of life together as a family (127:3–5; 128) and as a community of believers (133).

Psalm 37 (an acrostic) presents the thoughts of an older person (v 25) to one who is discouraged because of the apparent triumphs of the wrongdoers. Psalm 73 deals with the same theme, now in the words of one who had almost lost faith because of the prosperity of the wicked (vv 2–13); this psalm concludes with words of trust and praise addressed to God (vv 21–28). Psalm 49 offers a meditation (v 3) on wealth and wisdom. Psalm 112 is again acrostic, reflecting on the blessings of those who fear the Lord and the emptiness of the lives of the wicked.

Closely related are the Torah Psalms, which focus on the importance of instruction or *tôrâ* (Psalms 1; 19; 119) in the life of piety. Psalm 1 introduces the entire Psalter by commending meditation on the teaching of the Lord as the way to the blessed life, here imaged by a tree, deeply rooted and prospering. Psalm 19 is likewise identified as a meditation (v 14). The first part is a hymnlike affirmation of God the Creator, and the second part revels in the desirability of the Lord's instruction (*tôrâ,* testimony, precepts, etc.), described as "sweeter than honey." The acrostic Psalm 119 is unique in the literature of the Bible. After the introduction (vv 1–3) it addresses the Lord, praying for insight into the wonders of the Lord's teaching (v 18). Again, it commends meditation and reflection on the Lord's works (v 27), statutes (v 48), promises (v 148), and instruction (*tôrâ,* vv 97–105). Such meditation is a joy (vv 97, 103) and furnishes direction for the walk of the believer, pictured as a sojourner on this earth (vv 1, 19, 35, 105), even as a sheep who has lost its way (v 176).

G. Theological Themes

What do these psalms say about God, God and people, and God and the universe?

1. "The Teaching of the Lord is His Delight." Psalms 1 and 2 provide an introduction to the Psalter as a whole. Psalm 1 speaks of meditating on the "torah of the Lord." The Hebrew *hāgāh,* translated "meditate," denotes the contented growing of a lion anticipating a feast after prey has been captured (Isa 31:4), the cooing of a dove (Isa 38:14), or the rumbling of thunder (Job 37:2). The notion in Psalm 1 is the sound one of reading, studying, and pondering the instruction of the Lord as written down in Scripture; since the book of Psalms is being introduced, the reference is to reading and reflecting on the psalms. This sort of meditation takes place "day and night" (cf. 63:6). The modern equivalent would be to speak of "theological reflection" upon Scripture.

This reading and reflecting is described as a delight (Ps 1:2), using the same vocabulary as that employed to describe the delight of a lover with a beloved (Gen 34:19) or the preciousness of jewels (Isa 54:12). Other Torah Psalms also refer to the joy of the study of Scripture. Psalm 19 speaks of Torah, the Lord's written instruction, as "sweeter also than honey, and drippings of the honeycomb" (vv 7, 10). Psalm 119 says, "O, how I love thy Torah! It is my meditation all the day" (v 97). Luther catches the spirit of this delight in the study of Scripture in his comments on Psalm 1:

> It is the mode and nature of all who love, to chatter, sing, think, compose, and frolic freely about what they love and to enjoy hearing about it. Therefore this lover, this blessed man, has his love, the Law of God, always in his mouth, always in his heart and, if possible, always in his ear (*Luther's Works* 14: 297–98).

The person who takes such delight in the study of Scripture—here the Psalms—is compared to a sturdy and productive tree, planted by a river (1:3).

The images evoked by Psalm 2 are in sharp contrast. The first psalm suggests individual meditation on the teachings of the Lord; the second uses the same verb, *hāgāh,* in reference to the plotting and conspiring of nations against the Lord and the Lord's chosen king. This second psalm makes an abrupt move from the world of private individual meditation into that of public international intrigue. Psalm 2 suggests that the devout and delightful study described in Psalm 1 takes place in a world where "the nations so furiously rage together," where their armies dash one another to pieces like weapons of iron smashing clay pots (v 9). But this is also a world where the Lord is ruling through the Lord's anointed or messiah (v 2), and where the oppressed may find refuge with the Lord (2:12).

Taken together, these psalms set the tone and suggest the direction for reflection on the psalms that follow. Those who engage in such meditation will find joy in so doing, and will be well nourished and productive, like trees planted by the riverside. But this theological reflection is not done in isolation. It takes place in the context of a world where nations plot and engage in war, a world, nevertheless, ruled by the Lord and where those who are hurting can find refuge in God.

Consideration of these two introductory psalms suggests a procedure for organizing theological reflection on the psalms that follow. First, what theological themes are introduced in other psalms that speak of meditation on the Lord and the Lord's teaching (such as Psalms 19, 77 and 49)? What do the psalms say about God and the individual (Psalm 1)? Then, what do they say about God and God's people in the context of the nations of the world (Psalm 2)? What do the psalms say about the problems of those who are seeking refuge and who are suffering (2:12)? And finally, what about the Lord's anointed or messiah (Psalm 2)?

2. "O Lord, My Rock and My Redeemer." Psalm 19 offers the results of meditation (v 14) upon the work of God in creation (vv 1–6) and upon the revelation of God in torah or Scripture (vv 7–13). The one who has been considering these things concludes with a prayer naming the Lord, "my rock and my redeemer" (v 14). These two metaphors suggest two assertions about God that run throughout the Psalter, especially the psalms of lament, trust, and thanksgiving: God protects and provides security for the individual, and God delivers those who are hurting from situations of crisis.

The final line of Ps 2:12, "Blessed are all who take refuge in him," links with 1:1 but also points ahead to the psalms which follow. Those needing refuge are those who are experiencing crisis. The Psalter begins with a gathering of prayers of individuals in such times of crisis, so that the bulk of Book I consists of Individual Laments. Individual Laments continue through the Psalter so that they make up about one-third of the psalms, forming the backbone of the Psalter.

What do these laments (and the closely related Psalms of Trust) assert or assume about God? A good number of them portray God with pictures that denote security for a person in a situation of distress. The largest single group of metaphors and similes describing God are in this category (see E.5 above). The psalmist asserts that God is a rock, a place of safety and security (18:2, 31, 46; 19:14); or he may pray that God be such a place of security (31:2). In a number of instances, several similar figures are clustered together, describing God as rock, fortress, shield, horn of salvation, stronghold (18:2) or as refuge, rock of refuge, fortress, and rock (71:1–3). To be "set . . . high upon a rock" means to be in a place of security and hiding; it is God who provides such a place (27:5). Common to these variations on the theme of God as rock is the trustworthiness of God; in 91:2 God is addressed as refuge and fortress and then the statement is made, "my God in whom I trust." There are more metaphors and similes in this broad category than in any other, primarily because the Psalter contains such a large collection of prayers coming from individuals who are in a situation of crisis and who need a person to help and a place where they can find security.

The Psalms of Trust (see F.1 above) speak of the Lord with a variety of imagery. The Lord is the place where the hurting take refuge (11:1; 16:1; cf. 2:12). The Lord is a shepherd who guides and comforts his sheep or a gracious host who provides a banquet in the midst of danger (Psalm 23). The Lord is a rock, refuge, and fortress (62:2, 6–7), or like a mother providing peace and safety for a nursing child (Psalm 131). The Lord is even compared to a bird, under whose wings the faithful can find both security and joy (63:7).

These psalms assert that the Lord provides security, but they also describe the Lord as one who rescues from distress; in metaphorical language, the Lord is rock but also redeemer (19:14). The laments describe a variety of situations of distress: those praying may be ill (Psalms 61; 32; 102) or lonely (102:7), harassed by enemies making false accusations (3; 4; 5; 7) or plagued by sin (40; 51; 130; see C.1 above). The "request for help" sections of the individual laments pray for deliverance out of such situations. When deliverance comes, the psalms of praise and thanksgiving tell the congregation the story of what God has done (30:2; 34:4) and invite them to discover God's goodness (34:8) and to join in singing God's praises (30:4–5; see F.3 above for further references).

3. "What God Is Great Like Our God?" Psalm 77 also makes reference to meditating upon the deeds of the Lord or, in modern terms, to "theological reflection." In this instance the reflection is done during a time of great personal difficulty, so that the psalmist can even ask, "Has God forgotten to be gracious?" (v 9). In thinking about what God has done, this psalmist makes a number of assertions which are central to the theology of the Psalter. First, the God of Israel is incomparable: "What god is great like our God?" he asks (v 13). Second, this God has rescued the people of Israel from bondage in Egypt, leading them through the sea and through the wilderness (vv 15, 19–20). Finally, this God also has control over nature, turning back the sea, sending rain, thunder, lightning, and earthquake (vv 16–18). In other words, the psalmist speaks of God as unique, as acting in the history of nations, and also as active in the events of nature. These themes are played upon throughout the Psalter, especially in the hymns (see F.2 above).

The most explicit OT statements declaring the Lord to be the only God are found in Isaiah 40–44 (44:6–8; 45:5–7; etc.). A number of statements in the Kingship of the Lord Psalms, however, point in the same direction, declaring that the Lord is king over the whole earth (47:2, 7, 8; 95:3–5; 97:1–5; 99:2) and over heaven and earth (103:19–22), that other gods are mere idols (96:4–5), and the Lord will judge the whole earth (96:13; 98:9).

These hymns celebrate what the Lord has done in Israel's history, telling "to the coming generation the glorious deeds of the Lord, and his might" (78:4). They center on the events of the Exodus and leading through the wilderness (78; 105; 106; cf. also Psalms 75; 107; and 124, which give thanks for specific acts of deliverance). The Kingship of the Lord Psalms cited above assert that the Lord rules over all the nations and is active in their histories as well; note also other references to the Lord judging the nations, such as 7:8; 9:8, 19; 58:11; 82:8. Some of the hymns celebrate the Lord's mighty acts in both history and in nature, including God's work in creation (33; 65; 66; 114; 135; 136; 146; 147).

God's work in creation is the theme of another group of hymns. The psalmists are astonished at the universe, "the work of thy fingers" (8:3), calling the attention of the witness of the created order to the Creator (19:1–6), reveling in the wonders of this earth (104), marveling at the forming of an individual person (139:13–18), and calling upon everything that breathes to join in praise to God (148; 150). These hymns praise God not only for creating the world and the universe, but also for maintaining and blessing that world (e.g., Psalm 104; cf. also Psalms 65 and 67, giving thanks for a good harvest and for blessings).

4. "Human Beings Are Like the Beasts That Perish." Psalm 49 is another psalm explicitly offering the results of "theological reflection," this time identified as "the meditation of my heart" (v 3). This and other Wisdom Psalms deal with the great mysteries of life and death. These reflections are here offered to rich and poor alike (v 2). The writer of this psalm is being persecuted by certain persons who are wealthy (vv 5–6). Consideration of this situation leads to two conclusions. First, the wealthy cannot buy eternal life (vv 7–9) nor will they take their wealth with them after death (v 17); they will die, like all human beings, even those who are wise (vv 10, 18–19). Second comes a more comprehensive conclusion, repeated as a refrain: human beings cannot survive their splendor but are like the beasts that perish (vv 12, 20). There is, however, a word of hope: if humans cannot ransom themselves from death's power, God can and will do so (v 15).

Other wisdom psalms also reflect on life's mysteries. Psalm 37 is addressed from the perspective of age and experience (v 25) to those disturbed by the prosperity of the wicked (v 1). Such prosperity is only temporary (vv 10, 12–13, 17, 35–36), and the wicked will soon come to an end (vv 2, 9, 20, 38). In the meantime, those bothered by the inequalities of life should not worry but be patient (vv 1, 7, 8, 34) and find their security with the Lord (vv 39–40). Psalm 73 also deals with the problem of the success of the wicked, telling in an autobiographical fashion of one who had almost slipped away from the community of the faithful because of that problem (vv 1–14; note vv 2, 13). The psalmist kept the problem to himself, though it wore away at him (vv 15–16). In his ordinary attendance at community worship (v 17), he gained perspective and understanding, even the assurance that he was still with God and would always be so (vv 23–26). Finally, the psalmist claims God as his refuge and promises to continue to tell of what God has done (v 28). Wisdom Psalms also comment on the blessings of life in the midst of the community of worshippers (Psalm 133) and of family (127; 128).

5. "I Have Set My King on Zion." The theme of the Lord's anointed or messiah is introduced early in the Psalter, with Ps 2:2. Forming a double-psalm introduction to the Psalter, Psalm 2 is closely linked to Psalm 1, which speaks about theological reflection or meditation.

Psalm 2 is the first of the Royal Psalms, scattered throughout the Psalter. During the time of the Monarchy, these psalms functioned in connection with events in the life of the king. They articulate some extravagant hopes for the monarch. He is described as the Lord's son (2:7) and firstborn (89:27), from the line of David (89:20–37; 132:11–12; 144:9–10). He will be victorious in battle (21:7–12; 132:18; 144:10–11) and rule the nations of the earth (2:7–9; 72:8–11). Psalm 72 prays that the king might rule with justice and righteousness (vv 1–4, 7), which means special concern for the poor (vv 12–14); that he might bring prosperity and peace (vv 3 and 7, both translating Heb *šālôm*); and that he might rule forever (v 5; cf. 45:6). Ps 110:1 describes the king ("my lord") as seated at the right hand of Yahweh, victorious over all enemies, also identifying him as a priest (v 4). Many of these psalms speak of the king as being "anointed" (45:7; 89:20) or as the "anointed" (2:2; 18:50; 20:6; 89:38, 51; 132:10, 17).

After 587 B.C., there were no more kings in Jerusalem; nevertheless, the extravagant hopes articulated in these psalms remained and were projected into the future, describing an ideal anointed one, a messiah, who would finally bring about righteousness, justice, and *šālôm*. In this way these Royal Psalms became the seedbed out of which grew Israel's messianic hope. The prophets picked up these messianic themes and developed them (Isa 9:1–7; 11:1–10; Jer 23:1–8; Micah 5:2–6; Zech 9:9–10); and the NT declares that these promises find their fulfillment in Jesus of Nazareth, naming him the anointed one or (from the Greek *Christos*) the Christ (Matt 16:13–20; Mark 8:27–30; Luke 9:18–22; etc.).

Thus, the book of Psalms sounds the major theological themes that run throughout the OT and carry over into the NT. Luther perhaps understood this when he wrote the following as the introduction to his translation of the Psalms in his German Bible:

> [The Psalter] might well be called a little Bible. In it is comprehended most beautifully and briefly everything that is in the entire Bible. It is really a fine enchiridion or handbook. In fact, I have a notion that the Holy Spirit wanted to take the trouble himself to compile a short Bible and book of examples of all Christendom or all saints, so that anyone who could not read the whole Bible would here have anyway almost an entire summary of it, comprised in one little book (*Luther's Works* 35:254).

Bibliography

Clements, R. E. 1976. *One Hundred Years of OT Interpretation.* Philadelphia.

Crüsemann, F. 1969. *Studien zur Formgeschichte von Hymnus und Danklied in Israel.* Neukirchen-Vluyn.

Gerstenberger, E. S. 1988. *Psalms: Part I with an Introduction to Cultic Poetry.* Grand Rapids.

Hayes, J. H. 1979. *An Introduction to OT Study.* Nashville.

Kraus, H.-J. 1986. *Theology of the Psalms.* Trans. K. Crim. Minneapolis.

———. 1988. *Psalms 1–59.* Trans. H. C. Oswald. Minneapolis.

———. 1989. *Psalms 60–150.* Trans. H. C. Oswald. Minneapolis.

Kugel, J. 1981. *The Idea of Biblical Poetry.* New Haven.

Miller, P. D., Jr. 1986. *Interpreting the Psalms.* Philadelphia.

Rahlfs, A. 1967. *Psalmi cum Odis.* Göttingen.

Sanders, J. A. 1967. *The Dead Sea Psalms Scroll.* Ithaca, NY.

Seybold, K. 1978. *Die Wallfahrtspsalmen.* Neukirchen-Vluyn.

———. 1986. *Die Psalmen: Eine Einführung.* Stuttgart.

Westermann, C. 1980. *The Psalms: Structure, Content, and Message.* Trans. R. D. Gehrke. Minneapolis.

———. 1981. *Praise and Lament in the Psalms.* Trans. K. Crim and R. Soulen. Atlanta.

———. 1989. *The Living Psalms.* Trans. J. R. Porter. Grand Rapids.

Wilson, G. H. 1985. *The Editing of the Hebrew Psalter.* Chico, CA.

Würthwein, E. 1979. *The Text of the Old Testament.* Trans. E. F. Rhodes. Grand Rapids.

JAMES LIMBURG

PSALMS, SYRIAC (APOCRYPHAL).

The Syriac Apocryphal Psalms are found numbered consecutively from 151 to 155—subsequent to the canonical psalms—in a 12th-century Nestorian manuscript of the Psalter in Syriac. In all later Syriac mss where all five psalms appear together, these psalms are found in an order different from that of the oldest extant manuscript: 151 (also designated as Psalm I), 154 (II), 155 (III), 152 (IV), and 153 (V). These psalms are also found as filler material between parts one and two of *The Book of Discipline*, a theological treatise by Bishop Elijah, a Syrian church father who lived during the first half of the 10th century C.E. Three of these psalms (151, 154, and 155) are also found in the Psalms Scroll from Qumran Cave 11 (11QPs^a). Additionally, Psalm 151 is found in Greek, Latin, Coptic, Arabic, Armenian, and Ethiopic versions.

Psalm 151 is found in Hebrew (11QPs^a) as two separate psalms known as 151A and 151B. The Psalms Scroll is badly damaged where 151B is found, so that all that is left is the heading, half of verse 1, and a few letters of verse 2. The Greek and Syriac verses 6 and 7 seem to correspond in theme to the heading of 151B; however, Psalm 151B was probably much longer than these two Syriac and Greek verses indicate. Psalm 151 in the later versions is dependent on the Greek. The Greek is an obvious conflation and condensation of the Hebrew 151A and 151B, so that it portrays a drastic change in the text of the Hebrew. This change probably occurred in the Hebrew version.

Psalm 151A has undergone considerable controversy as to its translation and theology. Two verses of Hebrew 151A are absent from the Syriac and the Greek versions. Some scholars posit that these lines were intentionally edited from the original work because of Orphic influences. From this perspective the translation proclaims that the hills and the mountains do not witness to God, a nonbiblical statement. Other scholars view the psalm as being very biblical in style and theology. In this view, the psalm forms a chiasmus in structure and theme, which provides a key to its translation and interpretation. The disputed verses are thus read: "Do not the mountains bear witness to me," or "O, that the mountains would bear witness to me." It is an autobiographical psalm relating the praise of David after his election as king over Israel. The Greek and Syriac versions are not completely coherent. This psalm could be dated to the 6th century B.C.E., or earlier, on stylistic grounds; but it contains certain phrases which suggest a later date.

Psalm 152, an individual lament, and Psalm 153, a thanksgiving hymn, are both chiasmus, and relate the cries and thanks, respectively, of the psalmist upon the crisis of and deliverance from the threat of death. The psalms imitate the autobiographical style of Psalm 151A and deal heavily with the themes of death and rendering thanks. The psalms may have had Hebrew originals, but most likely, they were originally composed in Syriac imitating the Hebrew style. Therefore, they can be dated much later than Psalm 151A.

Psalm 154 could have been originally two independent psalms (a call to worship and a thanksgiving hymn) which were combined together by a redactor. If this is the case, a remarkable cohesiveness existed between the two psalms, enabling them to form a final psalm with a significant degree of internal integrity. Some scholars argue for the unity of the composition of Psalm 154. If this is the case, the author took great care to compose a psalm which easily could have been two individual psalms of integrity. It is possible that an editor composed a second psalm around or within a preexisting psalm. This alternative allows for the integrity of an individual smaller composition without relegating the unifying elements to chance. In this psalm, "Wisdom" is personified, and the faithful praise of God is exhorted. Although the psalm contains no elements unique to Qumran, several phrases and themes are congruent with Qumranic ideas. The psalm may be Proto-Essenian in origin. This psalm probably arose in the second quarter of the 2d century B.C.E.

Some scholars argue that Psalm 155 is the combination of two smaller psalms. Within the psalm is found an alphabetic acrostic from *he* to *pe*. According to this view, the original acrostic portion from *ʾalep* to *he* was mutilated and then inserted into another psalm. Other scholars provide a convincing argument for a unified psalm and argue that the acrostic can be seen from *ʾalep* to *he* with minor reconstructions of the text, if one views the first stanza as containing shorter metrical units. The psalm contains three stanzas, which move from staccato cries for deliverance in the first stanza to the repentant desire of the psalmist to be taught God's ways in the second stanza. The third stanza is a thanksgiving praise to God for the deliverance sought in section one, and experienced in section two. The psalm is biblical in style and theology and is difficult to date. This psalm probably arose during the 2d century B.C.E.

These psalms and their presence within the Psalms Scroll (11QPs[a]) have been significant for the discussion of the formation of the Psalter canon. Some scholars view the Qumran Psalms Scroll as evidence of the slow formation and canonization of the last third of the Psalter. Others see the scroll as an example of an early hymnbook or liturgical Psalter which existed apart from the history of the Psalter formation. The psalms are also significant for determining characteristics of late Jewish psalmody. During this period the breakdown in conventional psalm forms can be seen, and the use of borrowed biblical materials is evident. Traditional structuring devices were still in use, such as the alphabetic acrostic and chiasmus.

Bibliography

Baars, W. 1972. "Apocryphal Psalms." In *The Old Testament in Syriac according to the Peshitta Version.* Pt. IV, fas. 6. The Peshitta Institute. Leiden.

Pigué, S. 1988. The Syriac Apocryphal Psalms: Text, Texture, and Commentary. Ph.D. diss., Southern Baptist Theological Seminary.

Sanders, J. A. 1965. *The Psalms Scroll of Qumran Cave 11.* DJD 4. Oxford.

———. 1967. *The Dead Sea Psalms Scroll.* Ithaca, NY.

STANLEY C. PIGUÉ

PSALTER. See PSALMS, BOOK OF.

PSEUDEPIGRAPHA, OT. A modern collection of ancient writings that are essential reading for an understanding of early Judaism (ca. 250 B.C.E. to 200 C.E.) and of Christian origins. Many of these documents were compiled or composed by Jews, while others were written by Jews but eventually were expanded or rewritten by Christians. A few seem to have been composed by Christians who depended with varying degrees on pre-70 Jewish documents or oral traditions. Almost always the Pseudepigrapha are influenced by the so-called OT: many supply revelations reputed to have been received by persons prominent in the OT; others are rewritten versions or expansions of biblical narratives; some are psalms that are occasionally modeled on the Davidic Psalter; and a few are compositions shaped by Jewish Wisdom Literature. Although these writings were composed long after Abraham, Moses, David, Solomon, Jeremiah, Isaiah, Ezra, and other famous men, they were often intentionally but incorrectly (pseudepigraphically) attributed to one of them.

Copies of *Jubilees, 1 Enoch,* and the *Testaments of the Twelve Patriarchs* were found among the Dead Sea Scrolls. These fragments enable us for the first time to date these and related documents with some assurance. *Jubilees* and *1 Enoch* clearly predate 70 C.E. The *Testaments of the Twelve Patriarchs* in its Greek and Armenian recensions is clearly Christian, but early Semitic fragments of some testaments show that at least portions of this document are Jewish.

Many Jewish documents in the Pseudepigrapha are linked in various ways with these writings or with the Dead Sea Scrolls. They now can be reliably dated to the period before the Roman destruction of the temple in 70 C.E.

Since 1970 there has been a renaissance of interest in and appreciation of the Pseudepigrapha. Since then collections and translations of the Pseudepigrapha have appeared in Danish, Japanese, Greek, modern Hebrew, Spanish, French, Italian, German, and English. The documents in the Pseudepigrapha which are Jewish and early are probably our main source for understanding and reconstructing the lives of Jews in Palestine and the Diaspora, especially before the destruction of 70.

It is not possible to define "Old Testament Pseudepigrapha." The modern collections represent a lack of consensus regarding the contents of this collection. Most scholars throughout the world are not concerned about this failure to define Pseudepigrapha. They do agree that some writings within the Pseudepigrapha are not pseudepigraphical, i.e., "falsely attributed" to another person. However, scholars agree that some writings in the OT and NT are pseudepigraphical, for example the Davidic Psalms, the Proverbs of Solomon, and the letters incorrectly attributed to Paul, especially Hebrews, Colossians, and the Pastoral Epistles.

The Pseudepigrapha can be described if we think about the canonical OT, which was not closed when the pre-70 Jewish documents in it were composed. Many of the writings in the Pseudepigrapha were considered by Jews to be as inspired as the OT documents. Since many of them were full of prophecies, they were attributed to ancient biblical heroes such as Adam, Enoch, Noah, Abraham, Moses, David, Solomon, Ezra, and others who lived before prophecy was considered by many Jews to have ended.

The oldest Jewish documents in the Pseudepigrapha date from about the 3d century B.C.E. Others date to the period from 70 to 200 C.E., the dates assigned to the destruction of Jerusalem and the compilation of the Mishna. The latest ones date from sometime after the 4th or 5th centuries.

It is not easy today to decide whether a document is originally Jewish or Christian. Many early Christians were Jews, and they interpreted scriptures and related documents in terms of their conversion, especially their beliefs in Jesus. Sometimes they even edited Jewish documents to specify how they were to be understood. The alterations are usually christological additions. Hence, it is unwise to exclude from the Pseudepigrapha a document that is Christian in its final form since it may be an edited form of an early Jewish work. The Christian documents, or sections of them, in the Pseudepigrapha usually date from approximately 100 to about 400 C.E., although Christians frequently continued to alter the texts whenever they copied them.

The most comprehensive edition of the Pseudepigrapha, *OTP*, contains 65 documents. The names of the documents in this collection (all of which have separate *ABD* entries) and their broadly conceived genres are as follows:

Apocalyptic Literature and Related Works

1 Enoch
2 Enoch
3 Enoch
Sibylline Oracles
Treatise of Shem
Apocryphon of Ezekiel
Apocalypse of Zephaniah
The Fourth Book of Ezra
Greek Apocalypse of Ezra
Vision of Ezra
Questions of Ezra
Revelation of Ezra
Apocalypse of Sedrach
2 Baruch
3 Baruch
Apocalypse of Abraham
Apocalypse of Adam
Apocalypse of Elijah
Apocalypse of Daniel

Testaments (Often with Apocalyptic Sections)

Testaments of the Twelve Patriarchs
Testament of Job
Testaments of the Three Patriarchs (Abraham, Isaac, and Jacob)
Testament of Moses
Testament of Solomon
Testament of Adam

Expansions of the OT and Legends

Letter of Aristeas
Jubilees
Martyrdom and Ascension of Isaiah
Joseph and Aseneth
Life of Adam and Eve
Pseudo-Philo
Lives of the Prophets
Ladder of Jacob
4 Baruch
Jannes and Jambres
History of the Rechabites
Eldad and Modad
History of Joseph

Wisdom and Philosophical Literature

Ahiqar
3 Maccabees
4 Maccabees
Pseudo-Phocylides
Syriac-Menander

Prayers, Psalms, and Odes

More Psalms of David
Prayer of Manasseh
Psalms of Solomon
Hellenistic Synagogal Prayers
Prayer of Joseph
Prayer of Jacob
Odes of Solomon

Fragments of Judeo-Hellenistic Works

Philo the Epic Poet
Orphica
Fragments of Pseudo-Greek Poets
Demetrius the Chronographer
Eupolemus
Cleodemus Malchus
Pseudo-Hecataeus
Theodotus
Ezekiel the Tragedian
Aristobulus
Aristeas the Exegete
Pseudo-Eupolemus
Artapanus

The documents in the Pseudepigrapha that are Jewish and antedate the destruction of the temple in 70 C.E. are indispensable sources for perceiving the life and thought of early Jews in Palestine and elsewhere, especially in Alexandria. They show us not a monolithic, closed, and orthodox Judaism but a variegated, open, and cosmopolitan Judaism which was vibrantly alive and impregnated by the thoughts in all the contiguous cultures, notably Egypt, Persia, Syria, Greece, and Italy. In these writings, as in the Dead Sea Scrolls, we are introduced to the ideas, symbols, perceptions, fears, and dreams of pre-70 Jews. Since none of them can with assurance be assigned to Pharisees, Sadducees, Zealots, or Essenes, it is wise not to describe early Judaism in terms of four such sects; rather we must now think of many groups and numerous subgroups.

A good example of the influence of Wisdom thought on the apocalypses is found in the apocalypse attributed to Enoch:

> Then Wisdom went out to dwell with the children of
> the people,
> but she found no dwelling place.
> (So) Wisdom returned to her place
> and she settled permanently among the angels.
> Then Iniquity went out of her rooms,
> and found whom she did not expect.
> And she dwelt with them,
> like rain in a desert,
> like dew on a thirsty land (*1 Enoch* 42: 2–3; *OTP*).

This excerpt from the Pseudepigrapha discloses the pessimism about the present condition of the earth. The people reject Wisdom and willingly accept Iniquity, which are not concepts but hypostatic beings (hence the capitalization).

Another representative excerpt from the Pseudepigrapha is an account attributed to Enoch, who claims to have experienced a journey to the heavens:

> And those men took me from there, and they brought me up to the third heaven, and set me down there. Then I looked downward, and I saw paradise. And that place is inconceivably pleasant (*2 Enoch* 8:1; *OTP*).

An interest in esoterica pervades pseudepigraphic writing. Places, like paradise and the abode of the Rechabites, and persons, like Adam, Eve, and Melchizedek—all of which are mentioned in the OT with tantalizing brevity—are often described in the Pseudepigrapha. These accounts often reflect the power of folklore in early Judaism.

Like most early Jewish writings, the Jewish Pseudepigrapha rarely mention "the Messiah." Some passages, however, are highly significant for an assessment of this Jewish belief. One of the classic passages is found in the Pseudepigrapha:

> See, Lord, and raise up for them their king,
> the son of David, to rule over your servant Israel
> in the time known to you, O God.
> Undergird him with the strength to destroy the
> unrighteous rulers,
> to purge Jerusalem from gentiles
> who trample her to destruction. . . .
> And he will purge Jerusalem
> (and make it) holy as it was even from the beginning.
> . . .
> There will be no unrighteousness among them in his
> days,
> for all shall be holy,
> and their king shall be the Lord Messiah (*Ps. Sol.*
> 17:21–32; *OTP*).

The Messiah shall not be a militant hero in the normal sense, for "he will not rely on horse and rider and bow. . . ." The gentiles who are hated are those "who trample" down Jerusalem. The *Psalms of Solomon* were written in Jerusalem sometime in the second half of the 1st century B.C.E. They contain valuable insights into the social and economic problems facing many devout Jews.

The study of Christian origins has also been revolutionized thanks to the study and appreciation of the Pseudepigrapha and of the Dead Sea Scrolls. Not only synagogal, or rabbinic, Judaism, but also earliest Christianity (from 30 to at least 70 C.E.) was part of and eventually developed out of the complex "Judaisms" which made up early Judaism. What was seen as only the "background" of Christianity is now acknowledged to be part of the "foreground" of Christianity. In particular, many of Jesus' symbols and terms, like "Kingdom of God," "Son of Man," and "living water" are not to be attributed to the post-70 Church, as many distinguished specialists claimed; they are now found in pre-70 Jewish works in the Pseudepigrapha.

The Pseudepigrapha poses a perplexing problem for many readers: Why did the authors of these writings attribute them falsely to other persons? These authors did not attempt to deceive the reader. They, like the authors of the Psalms of David, the Proverbs of Solomon, the Wisdom of Solomon, and the additions to Isaiah, attempted to write authoritatively in the name of an influential biblical person. Many religious Jews attributed their works to some biblical saint who lived before the cessation of prophecy and who had inspired them. Also, the principle of solidarity united early Jews with their predecessors who, in their eyes, had assuredly been guided by God himself. To place one's own name on a work was exceptional and ran against the tradition in the synagogue and temple: wisdom was the result of God's guidance and was often made possible through the devotion of a gifted teacher or rabbi. It is also conceivable that some of the apocalyptic writers had dreams or visions in which they experienced revelations given to Enoch, Abraham, Elijah, Ezra, Baruch, and others.

One Jewish apocalypse, Daniel is found in the OT; and one Christian apocalypse, Revelation, is in the NT. All the other early Jewish apocalypses are now placed in the Pseudepigrapha. OT specialists now observe scattered elements of apocalyptic thought in OT theology. The oldest apocalypse, however, is not Daniel, which is dated around 165 B.C.E., but *1 Enoch,* the earliest sections of which date from the 3d century B.C.E.

Jesus was influenced in some ways by apocalypticism. In particular his concept of the Kingdom of God, his contention that his own day was the end of time, and his belief that God was rapidly moving to act dynamically in the present were all shaped in some ways by Jewish apocalyptic thought. Many specialists on Paul now emphasize that he was profoundly shaped by Jewish apocalypticism. Christianity was shaped early by the visions and dreams of apocalypticism. Hence, we can grasp the significance of the Pseudepigrapha for NT research.

Finally, it is essential to state that the Pseudepigrapha is a *modern* collection. It is neither closed nor a canon. Many of the writings in it were, of course, as influential in Jewish circles (especially before the end of the Bar Kokhba revolt in 135 C.E.) and in Christian circles (especially before the Council at Nicea in 325 C.E.) as the writings later canonized. Many early Jews and many of the earliest Christians considered these documents infallible and full of divine revelation. For further information see *APOT,* JSHRZ, and *HJP*² 3/1 and 3/2.

Bibliography

Caquot, A., ed. 1985. *La littérature interestamentaire.* Paris.

Charlesworth, J. H. 1981. *The Pseudepigrapha and Modern Research with a Supplement.* SBLSCS 7S. Chico, CA.

———, ed. 1985. *The OT Pseudepigrapha and the NT.* SNTSMS 54. Cambridge. Repr. 1987.

Denis, A.-M. 1970. *Introduction aux pseudépigraphes grecs d'Ancien Testament.* SVTP 1. Leiden.

Diez Macho, A., ed. 1982–89. *Apocrifos del Antiguo Testamento.* 5 vols. Madrid.

Dupont-Sommer, A., and Philonenko, M., eds. 1987. *La Bible: Écrits intertestamentaires.* Paris.

Jonge, M. de, ed. 1985. *Outside the OT.* Cambridge.

Leaney, A. R. C. 1984. *The Jewish and Christian World: 200 B.C. to A.D. 200.* Cambridge.

Nickelsburg, G. W. E. 1981. *Jewish Literature between the Bible and the Mishnah.* Philadelphia.

Russell, D. S. 1987. *The OT Pseudepigrapha.* Philadelphia.

Sacchi, P., ed. 1981–89. *Apocrifi dell'Antico Testamento.* 2 vols. Turin.

Sparks, H. F. D., ed. 1984. *The Apocryphal OT.* Oxford.

Stone, M. E. 1980. *Scriptures, Sects and Visions.* Philadelphia.

———. 1984. *Jewish Writings of the Second Temple Period.* CRINT 2/2. Assen and Philadelphia.

JAMES H. CHARLESWORTH

PSEUDO-. Falsely attributed names may be found under the second element of the name; for example: EUPOLEMUS, PSEUDO-; HEGESIPPUS, PSEUDO-; PHILO, PSEUDO-.

PSEUDONYMITY AND PSEUDEPIGRAPHY. Scholars employ the term "pseudonymity" to specify a fictitious name placed on a document, either originally by the author or during transmission by a copyist. The term derives from the Gk *pseudōnymous,* which means "under a false name." Similarly "pseudepigraphy" denotes the incorrect (i.e., false) attribution of authorship to famous persons. This term derives from two Greek words: *pseud,* "false," and *epigraphos,* "superscription." Emphasis must be placed on the fact that scholars judge only the titles to be "false"; the writings themselves can be invaluable.

In the 2d century C.E. Serapion employed *ta pseudepigrapha* (cf. Eusebius, *Hist. Eccl.* 6.12) to denote documents he considered falsely attributed to a NT author. Occasionally specialists use the same term to denote writings incorrectly attributed to nonbiblical authors such as Socrates, Pythagoras, and Philo of Alexandria; but more frequently they employ it to describe a large number of noncanonical texts that were improperly attributed, either originally or subsequently, to a person mentioned in the Bible or to an author of one of the biblical books. However, it is the case that some books in the OT are pseudepigraphical in the strict sense even though the term is not employed to describe them; for example, the Psalms were not composed by David, Proverbs was not created by Solomon, and Isaiah 40–66 was not written by the 8th-century prophet Isaiah. Many NT documents are also technically pseudepigraphical, including the gospels attributed to the apostles Matthew and John. For example, John 7:53–8:11 and chap. 21 are certainly not by the author of the rest of the gospel. Likewise several epistles traditionally ascribed to Paul, including Ephesians, 1 and 2 Timothy, Titus, and possibly 2 Thessalonians, are pseudepigraphical.

A large number of writings of early Judaism (ca. 250 B.C.E.–200 C.E.) are also pseudepigraphical, including most of the OT Pseudepigrapha and numerous Qumran Scrolls (cf. the *Prayer of Nabonidus* and the *Apocryphal Psalms* [11QPsᵃ]). During this formative period, for example, more than five significant collections of writings, many of them composite, were attributed to the antediluvian sage Enoch. In early Christianity, an abundance of writings were ascribed to OT figures like Solomon; the *Odes of Solomon* are a collection of hymns composed probably by a convert from Judaism to Christianity, perhaps in the early 2d century C.E., but attributed to the famous son of David. Other early Christian compositions were associated pseudepigraphically with Mary, Paul, Peter, and most of the leading characters in the NT, including Jesus. These works are collected into the NT Apocrypha and Pseudepigrapha.

Thus "pseudepigraphy" covers a wide range of writings, extending from texts included in the canon, to those that may be closely tied to the Bible, to those that were generated by other ideological (usually social) concerns. Many of the latter texts postdate the establishment of Christianity as the religion of the Roman Empire and the closing of the canon of biblical books.

To clarify the use of "pseudepigraphy" as applied to books related to the Bible and antedating 325 C.E. and the Council of Nicea, it is helpful to observe seven interrelated literary categories: (1) works not by an author but probably containing some of his own phrases or thoughts (the oldest psalms in the Psalter that may be in some ways Davidic, 2 Thessalonians, Ephesians, and perhaps Colossians); (2) documents by an author, perhaps a pupil, who was genuinely inspired by the person to whom the work is attributed (1 Peter, and perhaps James); (3) compositions influenced by earlier works by an author to whom they are connected (Deutero- and Trito-Isaiah) or assigned (1 Timothy, 2 Timothy, Titus); (4) writings attributed to a person but deriving from later circles of schools of learned individuals (Lamentations, Proverbs, Wisdom of Solomon, *Psalms of Solomon, 1 Enoch, 2 Enoch, 3 Enoch,* all the works in the Ezra cycle [viz., *4 Ezra*], Matthew, John, and virtually all the apocryphal gospels); (5) Christian writings attributed by their authors to an OT personality (*Testament of Adam, Odes of Solomon, Apocalypse of Elijah, Ascension of Isaiah*); (6) once anonymous works now incorrectly attributed to someone (Hebrews is sometimes falsely attributed to Paul); and (7) compositions that intentionally try to persuade the reader to think the author is someone famous (Psalms 151; 2 Peter [in a deceptive manner]). Such varieties of pseudepigraphy must be perceived. For many early Jews and Christians it was considered proper to attribute a thought or a document to someone who had inspired them; they employed no footnotes to hide the fact that almost all thoughts are derivative, especially when the source for a composition is God's words recorded in Scripture.

By at least 250 B.C.E. pseudepigraphy was the norm for writing in biblically inspired groups. While some of the intracanonical works are anonymous (the Pentateuch and the complex writings woven together in these books, Acts, Hebrews), many others are pseudonymous or incorrectly attributed to someone. Many of the Jewish works related to the Bible and placed within the Qumran Scrolls, the Apocrypha, and the Pseudepigrapha of the OT are attributed falsely to others for several reasons; for example, the reverence for biblical heroes and the creative thoughts their lives and traditions evoked in Jewish culture and within the individual author, the legendary accretion to biblical lore and the human need to fill in missing details in a cherished story (as in the *Genesis Apocryphon* and *Pseudo-Philo*), and especially the pervasive contention that prophecy had ceased (but cf. the *Pesher of Habakkuk* 7).

In a later period many works are attributed to outstanding people in the NT because of the reverence for them and the contention that the new revelation was only authoritative when linked with the first generation of Jesus' followers. Extracanonically, for example, numerous works were incorrectly attributed to Paul or claimed to contain authentic data about him, including *3 Corinthians,* the *Epistle to the Alexandrians,* the *Epistle to the Laodiceans,* the *Epistles of Paul and Seneca,* the *Apocalypse of Paul,* the *Vision of Paul,* the *Acts of Paul,* the *Martyrdom of Paul,* and the *Martyrdom of Peter and Paul.* Documents were also falsely attributed to Peter, namely, the *Apocalypse of Peter,* the *Gospel of Peter,* the *Preaching of Peter,* the *Acts of Peter,* the *Acts of Andrew and Peter,* and the *Martyrdom of Peter.* For the first time, however, perhaps beginning around the mid-2d century C.E., interest in Jesus' mother gave rise to many pseudepigrapha of Mary, notably the *Birth of Mary,* the *Gospel of the Birth of Mary,* the *Passing of Mary,* the *Questions of Mary,* the *Apocalypse of the Virgin,* the *Assumption of the Virgin,* and the *Coptic Lives of the Virgin.*

Early biblical exegesis in Christian circles frequently took the form of pseudepigraphy. Dogma, curiosity, apologetics, and especially the need to fill in gaps in the history of the drama of salvation gave rise to legends, storytelling, and pseudepigraphy; all of these forces need to be distinguished. Some of the pseudepigraphical works were produced by learned and gifted scholars; all of them are essential reading for a balanced view of the biblical world from 250 B.C.E., the probable time when the first works were composed in the name of Enoch, to 325 C.E., when the first Christian Council convened at Nicea.

Bibliography

Aland, L. 1965. The Problem of Anonymity and Pseudonymity in Christian Literature of the First Two Centuries. Pp. 10–13 in *The Authorship and Integrity of the New Testament.* Theological Collections 4. London.

Brox, N. 1975. *Falsche Verfasserangaben: Zur Erklärung der frühchristlichen Pseudepigraphie.* SBS 79. Stuttgart.

———, ed. 1977. *Pseudepigraphie in der Heindnischen und Jüdisch-Christlichen Antike.* Wege der Forschung 484. Darmstadt.

Charlesworth, J. H. 1985. *The Old Testament Pseudepigrapha and the New Testament.* SNTSMS 54. Cambridge.

———, ed. 1983–85. *The Old Testament Pseudepigrapha.* 2 vols. Garden City.

Charlesworth, J. H., and Mueller, J. R. 1987. *The New Testament Apocrypha and Pseudepigrapha.* ALTA Bibliography Series 17. Metuchen, NJ.

Donelson, L. R. 1986. *Pseudepigraphy and Ethical Argument in the Pastoral Epistles.* Hermeneutische Untersuchungen zur Theologie 22. Tübingen.

Goodspeed, E. J. 1937. Pseudonymity and Pseudepigraphy in Early Christian Literature. Pp. 169–88 in *New Chapters in New Testament Study.* New York.

Meade, D. O. 1986. *Pseudonymity and Canon.* WUNT 39. Tübingen.

Metzger, B. M. 1972. Literary Forgeries and Canonical Pseudepigrapha. *JBL* 91: 3–14.

JAMES H. CHARLESWORTH

PTOLEMAIS (PLACE) [Gk *Ptolemaeis*]. See ACCO (PLACE).

PTOLEMY (PERSON) [Gk *Ptolemaios*]. A name of Macedonian origin (Gk *ptolemaios* "warlike") borne by the founder and, as a dynastic name, by all subsequent rulers of the line of Greek-speaking kings who ruled Egypt after the death of Alexander the Great (323 B.C.) until the country's annexation by Rome (30 B.C.). Hence the line is known as the Ptolemaic dynasty; the period of its rule is often referred to as the Ptolemaic period; and the kings are usually referred to as the Ptolemies. They are of biblical interest because the struggles of the earlier Ptolemies with the Seleucid kings of Syria for control of Palestine led them into close contact with the Jews, toward whom they were generally well-disposed. Moreover, their promotion of Alexandria as a center of literature and scholarship was to have a profound effect upon the development of scholarship and learning in the early Christian church because the Church Fathers in essence adopted the scholarly methods of the classical tradition while rejecting its pagan content.

Fifteen kings and many persons outside the Ptolemaic royal house bore this popular name. Only those most relevant to the study of the Bible are treated here.

1. *Ptolemy I Soter* ("savior") (323 [king from 305 B.C.]–282 B.C.). Born ca. 367/366 B.C., son of the Macedonian general Lagus (hence the alternative name Lagidae for members of the dynasty) and Arsinoe, perhaps a concubine of Philip II of Macedon. After a distinguished career as one of the generals of Alexander the Great, he became satrap of Egypt in 323 B.C. and consolidated his position by hijacking Alexander's body, en route to burial in Macedonia, and taking it to Egypt. In 319 B.C. he seized Jerusalem on the Sabbath (*Ant* 12.1.1 §§3–4) in a first unsuccessful attempt to annex Palestine and Coele-Syria. The Jews taken as prisoners of war on this occasion formed the nucleus of what was to become a large and important Jewish community in Alexandria, with its own citizen rights and quarter of the city (*JW* 2.18.7 §§487–88). See ALEXANDRIA. They were followed later in Ptolemy's reign by many others who came as free settlers or mercenaries (*AgAp* 1.22 §186; *Ant* 12.1.1 §§7–9; *Let. Aris.* 12–14).

Subsequent struggles for power among the Diadochi

(successors to Alexander) found Ptolemy giving refuge to Seleucus when he fled Babylon in 315 B.C. (Dan 11:5 refers to Seleucus as "one of his princes") and allied with Ptolemy against Antigonus, whose forces he defeated at Gaza in 312 B.C. However, the tables were turned in 306 B.C., when the Egyptian fleet was routed by Antigonus off Salamis in Cyprus and Ptolemy's attempts to establish a presence outside Egypt were temporarily halted.

He declared himself king in 305/304 B.C. (the title Soter was acquired from his defense of the Rhodians in 306 B.C.). After Antigonus had been defeated and killed at Ipsus (301 B.C.), Ptolemy (although he had not been present) at last contrived to occupy Palestine and Coele-Syria (the cause of the five Syrian Wars between the Ptolemies and the Seleucids over the course of the 3d century B.C.). Later he got control also of Cyprus, the Aegean islands, and the S part of Asia Minor. In March/April 285 B.C. he took Ptolemy II, his son by his third wife Berenice, into co-regency with him (his eldest son Ptolemy Ceraunus, by his second wife Eurydice, having been excluded at the time of Ptolemy's remarriage). He died in the first half of 282 B.C.

Tenacious in pursuit of his political objectives, Ptolemy was also a skilled organizer (laying down the main features of the Ptolemaic government of Egypt) and a person of learning in his own right. The (now lost) account he wrote late in life of the campaigns of Alexander the Great, although not widely read later, was admired by Arrian, who used it as a source. It was he, too, who was responsible for founding the famous museum and library in Alexandria, after he moved the capital there from Memphis (ca. 313 B.C.), and for establishing there the worship of Serapis, a Greek interpretation of Osiris, the patron god of Memphis in his incarnation as the Apis bull.

2. *Ptolemy II Philadelphus* ("sister-loving," 282–246 B.C.). Born in 308 B.C., son of Ptolemy I, with whom he was coregent from 285 B.C., and Berenice. Married to Arsinoe I, daughter of Lysimachus (ca. 289/288 B.C.), he later divorced her and married (ca. 279–274 B.C.) his full sister Arsinoe II, whom he associated with him as co-ruler. Hence his title Philadelphus ("brother/sister-loving"), originally a cult title of Arsinoe but applied later also to Ptolemy himself.

Overseas, his initial conflict with Antiochus I of Syria, who was challenging for control of Asia Minor (280/279 B.C.), was followed by the First Syrian War (274–271 B.C.) over Palestine and Coele-Syria. Details are unclear except that Ptolemy retained control of these areas. The result was that the way was now open for the gradual exposure of the Jews to Greek ideas and institutions; Ptolemy was responsible for the foundation there of Philoteria on the Lake of Galilee, the Hellenization of Philadelphia on the site of Rabbath-Ammon (modern Amman) (Jerome, *Commentary on Ezek 25:1–7),* and the renaming of Acre in Phoenicia as Ptolemais. His generous treatment of the Jews is also reflected in the tradition (generally and rightly rejected) in the fictitious *Letter of Aristeas* that it was he who initiated the translation of the Hebrew Bible into Greek (the LXX), seventy (Gk *septuaginta,* "seventy") scholars being dispatched from Jerusalem, for the purpose at Ptolemy's request. See also ARISTEAS, LETTER OF.

Ptolemy had less military success later in his reign; interference in the Chremonidean War (267–261 B.C.) between the Macedonians and Athens and Sparta may have led to an Egyptian naval defeat by the Macedonians (261 B.C.), while a challenge to Antiochus II soon after the latter's accession only resulted in Ptolemy's losing territory in Asia Minor (Second Syrian War, 260–253[?] B.C.).

Within Egypt, Ptolemy promoted the spread of Hellenization and increased the country's prosperity by establishing Greek settlements (cleruchies) and bringing new areas under cultivation, particularly in the Fayum; and it was he who established the Ptolemaic ruler cult (both he and Arsinoe were proclaimed gods in 272/271 B.C.). He is chiefly remembered, however, for his generous patronage of science and the arts. The most notable results were a renaissance in Greek literature, with the work of the poets Apollonius of Rhodes, Callimachus, and Theocritus and the establishment of Alexandria as the new cultural capital of the Greek world. Yet along with his generosity toward the arts and sciences (in which he appears to have had a genuine interest), Ptolemy combined a vulgar and sensual extravagance. He is just as noted for the many mistresses he kept, his love of ostentatious display, and the magnificence of the court he established (an expense which the evidence suggests was beginning to impoverish Egypt in the last years of his reign).

3. *Ptolemy III Euergetes I* ("benefactor") (246–222 B.C.). Born ca. 284 B.C., oldest son of Ptolemy II and his first wife Arsinoe I. His marriage to Berenice II, daughter of Magas of Cyrene, resulted in the unification of Cyrenaica and Egypt. His reign began with an invasion of Syria and its territories in reprisal for the murder of his sister Berenice, wife of Antiochus II (Third Syrian [or Laodicean] War, 246–241 B.C., alluded to in Dan 11:7–9). Although he is said to have advanced as far as Bactria, his success was to be shortlived when Seleucus II combined with his brother Antiochus Hierax to force him to come to terms. Ptolemy did, however, gain some territory in Asia Minor and Thrace. On his return to Egypt, he is said to have offered sacrifice in Jerusalem (*AgAp* 2.5 §48).

Ptolemy's return had been prompted by a native Egyptian uprising, the result of Ptolemy II's extravagance having been compounded by the economic strain of the Syrian War and a series of poor Nile floods. Over the next decade Ptolemy's policy of reconciliation, shown in concessions to the Egyptian priesthoods and a generous program of temple building and restoration (the Horus temple at Edfu, begun in 237 B.C., was his foundation), did much to restore the country's prosperity. In the 220s B.C. Ptolemy began to look overseas again, assisting Athens after her liberation from Macedon (228 B.C.) and financially supporting Cleomenes III of Sparta for a period against Aratus of Sicyon (ca. 225–222 B.C.). He died probably late in 222 B.C.

4. *Ptolemy IV Philopator* ("father-loving") (222–204 B.C.). Born after 240 B.C., oldest son of Ptolemy III and Berenice II. On his accession he was challenged by Antiochus the Great, (Fourth Syrian War, 221–217 B.C.) who by the winter of 218/217 B.C. had taken control of the Ptolemaic possessions in Asia and had reached Ptolemais in Phoenicia. Assisted by 20,000 native Egyptian troops, Ptolemy defeated him decisively at Raphia in Gaza on 22 June 217

B.C. (Polyb. 5.51–87, and alluded to in Dan 11:11–12) and so regained control of Coele-Syria.

A highly colored story in *3 Maccabees* 1–2 tells how after the battle Ptolemy was thrown to the ground in a fit when he attempted to enter the high temple in Jerusalem; another (*3 Maccabees* 3–7, even more lurid in its details) recounts how on his return he vented his rage on the Jews of Alexandria, only to be thwarted again by divine intervention. Although this appears to be the etiology for a local Jewish festival, it may be that some of the Jews' rights and privileges were curtailed under this king.

While Ptolemy failed to capitalize upon his victory at Raphia, the role which the Egyptians had played in the battle did much to reawaken their sense of national identity. A period of serious internal unrest followed, with Upper Egypt seceding and being ruled by Nubian kings from 207 B.C. to 187 B.C. There is no doubt that the situation was aggravated by Philopator's weak and self-indulgent nature, and his reign is rightly identified as marking the beginning of the dynasty's decline. Yet his character is perhaps blackened to excess by Polybius (5.34) and Plutarch (Cleom. 33).

5. *Ptolemy V Epiphanes* ("manifest" [as a god]) (204–180 B.C.). Born 210 B.C., only son of Ptolemy IV and his sister-wife Arsinoe III. He was only a child when he became king under the regency of his ministers Sosibius and Agathocles. Antiochus the Great seized the opportunity to attack Egypt and in the Fifth Syrian War (202–200[?] B.C.) managed to extend Seleucid domination to the Sinai. The Egyptians rallied temporarily, but they were finally defeated at Panium (200 B.C.) and lost control of Palestine as well as most of their possessions in Asia Minor and the Aegean. Under the peace settlement Ptolemy married (194 B.C.) Antiochus' daughter Cleopatra I, ostensibly with the revenues of Coele-Syria and Palestine as her dowry. In fact the Ptolemies were never again to regain permanent possession of these areas. The events of this period are alluded to in Dan 11:13–18.

Within Egypt itself, however, control of Upper Egypt was regained in 187/186 B.C.; and the last native revolt in the delta was put down in 184/183 B.C.

6. *Ptolemy VI Philometor* ("mother-loving") (180–145 B.C.). Born 186 B.C., elder son of Ptolemy V and Cleopatra I. As a child, he ruled under the regency of his mother until her death in 176 B.C. In 175/174 B.C. he married his sister Cleopatra II. When Egypt was invaded by Antiochus Epiphanes (170 B.C.; referred to in 1 Macc 1:17–19), both she and his younger brother Ptolemy VIII Physcon were associated with him as co-regents (170–164 B.C.).

After Antiochus was compelled by the Roman Senate to withdraw from Egypt in 168 B.C., a struggle for power broke out between the brothers. Philometor was expelled by Physcon late in 164 B.C. but on appeal to Rome was reinstated in 163 B.C., Physcon being granted Cyrene.

In the 160s B.C. Ptolemy attempted to regain a foothold in Asia by supporting the pro-Ptolemaic group in Jerusalem under the high priest Onias III against the Seleucid faction there; and when Onias IV fled to Egypt (162 B.C.), Ptolemy and Cleopatra granted him permission to build a replica of the high temple in Jerusalem at Leontopolis (*Ant* 13.3.1–3 §§62–73). Later, with the Syrians weakened by squabbles over the Seleucid succession, Ptolemy became more open in his attempts to reestablish Egyptian power in Asia. From 150 B.C. he supported the rival claimants Alexander Balas and Demetrius II in turn, marrying his daughter Cleopatra Thea first to one (*Ant* 13.4.1 §§80–82; 1 Macc 10:51–56), then the other (*Ant* 13.4.7 §§109–10). Invading Syria, he was hailed in Antioch as king of Asia as well as Egypt but (under the eye of Rome) wisely declined the latter title (*Ant* 13.4.7 §§111–15; a more hostile account is in 1 Macc 11:1–19). He died (145 B.C.) of wounds received fighting in support of Demetrius against the forces of Alexander Balas in the plain of Antioch.

The Jewish philosopher Aristobulus from Alexandria dedicated his work on the Pentateuch (now extant only in fragments) to this Ptolemy.

7. *Ptolemy VII Neos Philopator* ("new, father-loving") (145 B.C.). Born ca. 162/161 B.C., second son of Ptolemy VI and Cleopatra II. Briefly associated in the kingship with his father in 145 B.C., he was disposed of by his uncle Ptolemy VIII Physcon after the latter's return and marriage to Cleopatra II; he was "murdered in the arms of his mother at her wedding-feast" according to Justin (38.8.4).

8. *Ptolemy VIII Euergetes II Physcon* (145–116 B.C.). Born after 182 B.C., younger son of Ptolemy V and Cleopatra I, he was nicknamed Physcon ("pot-bellied") from his gross appearance. He was co-ruler with his brother Ptolemy VI and sister Cleopatra II in 170–164 B.C., sole ruler in 164/163 B.C. after expelling his brother, and king of Cyrene (163–145 B.C.) after Ptolemy VI's restoration. Returning to Egypt on the latter's death (145 B.C.), he married Cleopatra II and, having disposed of her son Ptolemy VII, had himself crowned sole ruler (144 B.C., although he continued to count his regnal years from 170 B.C.).

His marriage (142 B.C.) to his niece Cleopatra III, without divorcing Cleopatra II, led to a rift between them and eventually to a civil war (132/131 B.C.). First Ptolemy and then Cleopatra II were forced to flee Egypt; and although Ptolemy regained Alexandria early in 130 B.C., hostilities continued. To block Cleopatra's plan to make her son-in-law (the Seleucid Demetrius II) king of Egypt, Ptolemy supported the pretender Alexander Zabinas but in 126/125 B.C. switched his alliance to Antiochus VIII Grypus, to whom he married his daughter by Cleopatra III.

A reconciliation between Ptolemy and Cleopatra II was effected in 124 B.C.; and thereafter the three of them shared uneasily together in the rule, with Ptolemy bequeathing the kingdom to Cleopatra III and whichever of her two sons, Ptolemy IX and Ptolemy X, she should choose.

Physcon is said to have been hostile to the Jews, and Josephus (*AgAp* 2.5 §§50–55) tells against him the same lurid story of persecution which *3 Maccabees* 3–7 attaches to Ptolemy IV. If he was (which is by no means certain; indeed the Greek translations of Sirach (Ecclesiasticus) and Esther were both made in Egypt during his reign [Sir, prologue; Add Esth 11:1]), then it was on account of their political support for Cleopatra II, not on any religious grounds.

9. *Ptolemy IX Soter II Lathyrus* (116–107 B.C. and 88–81 B.C.). Born 143/142 B.C., elder son of Ptolemy VIII and Cleopatra III, he was nicknamed Lathyrus ("chickpea") by the Alexandrians, who made him co-ruler with his mother (116 B.C.) against her wishes. He was twice temporarily replaced as king in favor of his brother Ptolemy X (late 110–early 109 B.C. and March–May 108 B.C.), and then he was expelled more permanently in 107 B.C. Fleeing to Cyprus, he was king there from 107 B.C. to 88 B.C.

An early attempt to retake Egypt (103 B.C.), during which he defeated the Jewish army under Alexander Jannaeus besieging Ptolemais (*Ant* 13.12.2–5 §§324–44), failed when Cleopatra's army advanced into Palestine against him. After his brother's expulsion and death (88 B.C.), the Alexandrians accepted him back as sole ruler, but the native Egyptians in Upper Egypt revolted against him (88–86 B.C.). Tragically, the revolt ended with the destruction of the ancient Egyptian capital of Thebes by Ptolemy's army.

10. *Ptolemy X Alexander I* (107–88 B.C.). Younger son of Ptolemy VIII and Cleopatra III. Governor (114/113–110 B.C.) and then king of Cyprus (110–107 B.C.) during the first period of his brother's rule, he was twice recalled to reign jointly with Cleopatra III for short periods (see Ptolemy IX above) before Ptolemy IX's final expulsion in 107 B.C. He ruled jointly with Cleopatra III until her death or murder in 101 B.C. Shortly afterward he married his niece Cleopatra Berenice, daughter of Ptolemy IX, and associated her with him in the kingship. Expelled by the Alexandrians (88 B.C.), he died in a naval battle off Cyprus while attempting to recover Egypt.

11. *Ptolemy XI Alexander II* (80 B.C.). Born ca. 105 B.C., the son of Ptolemy X and an unknown first wife, he was sent to Cos for safety (103 B.C.) by his grandmother Cleopatra III. Captured by Mithridates (88 B.C.), he escaped to Sulla (84 B.C.) and lived under his protection in Rome until the death of Ptolemy X. Married to his stepmother Cleopatra Berenice and made joint ruler with her (80 B.C.) by Sulla, he murdered her nineteen days later and was killed in turn by the enraged Alexandrians. He was the last legitimate male successor of the Ptolemaic line.

12. *Ptolemy XII Auletes* (80–58 B.C. and 55–51 B.C.). Born 111–108 (?) B.C., the illegitimate son of Ptolemy IX by a concubine. Nicknamed Auletes ("the piper") by the Alexandrians for his devotion to the cult of Dionysus, he was raised to the throne by them after their murder of Ptolemy XI (80 B.C.). He was permitted by Rome to remain king, sending troops to help Pompey in the east (63 B.C.), but was driven out by the Alexandrians (58 B.C.) after having been forced to cede Cyprus to the Romans. On appeal to Rome and the promise of 6000 talents, he was restored by Gabinius in 55 B.C. He was father of Ptolemy XIII, Ptolemy XIV, and Cleopatra VII, last of the Ptolemaic line.

13. *Ptolemy XIII* (51–47 B.C.). Born ca. 61 B.C., elder son of Ptolemy XII. Co-regent with his sister-wife Cleopatra VII until he attempted to expel her, he was defeated fighting against Cleopatra and Julius Caesar in the Alexandrine War and drowned in the Nile.

14. *Ptolemy XIV* (47–44 B.C.). Born ca. 59 B.C., younger son of Ptolemy XII. Made king of Cyprus by Julius Caesar (58 B.C.), after Ptolemy XIII's death he was married to Cleopatra and made co-ruler with her by Caesar but was murdered by her, probably in August 44 B.C.

15. *Ptolemy XV Caesarion* (44–30 August 30 B.C.). Born 47 B.C., son of Cleopatra VII by Julius Caesar (it is claimed). Hence his nickname Caesarion ("little Caesar"). Cleopatra made him co-ruler with her (44 B.C.), and in 34 B.C. he was declared "King of Kings." After the battle of Actium, he was put to death on Octavian's orders in 30 B.C.

16. The son of Dorymenes, one of the generals whom Antiochus Epiphanes dispatched to exterminate the Jews in 165 B.C. (1 Macc 3:38; 2 Macc 4:45; 6:8). Also known as (Ptolemy) MACRON, he took the lead in eventual peace-seeking efforts with the Jews; but these efforts were undermined; and he had to commit suicide (2 Macc 10:10–13).

17. Son-in-law of Simon Maccabeus, whom he murdered with two of Simon's sons, Mattathias and Judas, in February 135 or 134 B.C. (1 Macc 16:11–17; *Ant* 13.7.4 §§228).

18. The father of Lysimachus (the Jerusalem resident who translated Esther into Greek).

19. The son of the Levitical priest Dositheus. This Ptolemy, along with his father, brought Lysimachus' translation of Esther from Jerusalem to Egypt, most probably in 114 B.C. (Add Esth 11:1).

20. Ptolemy Mennaeus, king of the Ituraeans ca. 85–ca. 40 B.C. (*Ant* 13.5.2 §§392; and 14.13.3 §330; *JW* 1.13.1 §248).

21. Ptolemy, brother of the historian Nicholas of Damascus, and like him a trusted counselor of Herod the Great (*Ant* 17.9.4 §225; *JW* 2.2.3 §21).

22. Ptolemy, finance minister of Herod charged with his signet ring and will (*Ant* 17.8.2 §195 = *JW* 1.23.8 §667).

23. Ptolemy, perhaps of Ascalon, author of a lost biography of Herod (*HJP* 1: 27–28).

Bibliography

Bevan, E. R. 1927. *A History of Egypt under the Ptolemaic Dynasty.* London.

Bouché-Leclerq, A. 1903–1907. *Histoire des Lagides.* 4 vols. Paris.

Otto, W., and Bengtson, E. 1938. *Zur Geschichte des Niederganges des Ptolemäerreiches.* ABAW, n.s., 17. Munich.

Préaux, C. 1978. *Le monde hellénistique.* 2 vols. Nouvelle Clio 6. Paris.

Samuel, A. E. 1962. *Ptolemaic Chronology.* Münchener Beiträge zur Papyrusforschung 43. Munich.

Will, E. 1979, 1982. *Histoire politique du monde hellénistique (323–30 avant J.-C.).* 2 vols. 2d ed. Nancy.

JOHN WHITEHORNE

PTOLEMY MACRON (PERSON). See MACRON (PERSON).

PUAH (PERSON) [Heb *pûʿâ, pûʾâ*]. Var. PUVAH. **1.** One of two named midwives of the Hebrews in Egypt (Exod 1:15). The midwives were ordered by the king of Egypt to kill all the male infants of the Hebrews at birth. An engaging question has to do with the ethnicity of the midwives. The ambiguous text of v 15 can be translated either "Hebrew midwives," or "midwives of the Hebrews"—a rendering which leaves unanswered whether they were Hebrew or Egyptian. Childs (*Exodus* OTL, 16) has enumerated some arguments on both sides. On the one hand, the names of the women are Hebrew or at least Semitic; and it is perhaps unlikely that Egyptians would have been accepted in this delicate task (but since they were slaves, the Israelites may have had no choice). On the other hand, Pharaoh probably could not have expected Hebrew women to betray in secret their own people in this way (yet Ackerman [1974–82: 86] submits that the king was depending on their demoralized position as slaves). The force of "the midwives feared God" may be somewhat reduced if they were Israelite (though certainly far from all Hebrews feared God, and such an attitude was hardly restricted to the Hebrews).

Various explanations have been suggested for the reason why only two midwives are mentioned. Either these were the only two, the only two who disobeyed, or the only two whose names were remembered. The two may have been the head officials of the guild. However, perhaps this detail is attributable merely to the literary style of the narrative. Durham (*Exodus* WBC, 13) considers any speculation about the number of midwives and pregnant women as irrelevant. The point is the midwives' faith and its effects both for Israel and for themselves.

The name "Puah" (Heb *pûʿâ*) is probably cognate to Ug *pǵt*, signifying "(young) girl," which occurs also as the name of the daughter of *dnʾil*, *ʾaqht*'s father. Albright (1954: 233) found "Puah" to be a good northwest-Semitic feminine name from the first half of the 2d millennium B.C.

Bibliography

Ackerman, J. S. 1974–82. The Literary Context of the Moses Birth Story (Exodus 1–2). Vol. 1, pp. 74–119 in *Literary Interpretations of Biblical Narratives,* 2 vols., ed. K. R. R. Gros Louis, J. S. Ackerman, and T. S. Warshaw. Nashville.

Albright, W. F. 1954. Northwest-Semitic Names in a List of Egyptian Slaves from the Eighteenth Century B.C. *JAOS* 74: 222–33.

EDWIN C. HOSTETTER

2. The second son of Issachar according to the genealogical list of Issachar's clans preserved by the Chronicler (1 Chr 7:1). In the parallel genealogies of Issachar in Gen 46:13 and Num 26:23 his name is listed as Puvah.

3. A man of the tribe of Issachar. He is mentioned in Judg 10:1 as the "son of Dodo" and the father of Tola, a man from Issachar and one of the minor judges of Israel. The relationship between Puah (Heb *pûʾâ*) and Tola is not very clear (McKenzie 1967: 119). In the genealogies of Issachar (Gen 46:13; Num 26:23) Tola is the son of Issachar and one of the leading clans of that tribe. He is also presented as the brother of Puah (1 Chr 7:1), also known as Puvah. The LXX renders the expression "son of Dodo" (Heb *ben dôdô*) as "the son of his uncle" and says that Tola was the son of Puah, "the son of his father's brother," that is, the son of Abimelech. It is possible that the relationship between Puah and Tola is one of political affiliation rather than a father-son relationship.

Bibliography

McKenzie, D. A. 1967. The Judge of Israel. *VT* 17: 118–21.

CLAUDE F. MARIOTTINI

PUBLIUS (PERSON) [Gk *Poplios*]. A fairly common Roman praenomen (first or personal name), the Latin equivalent of the Gk *Poplios.* In Acts 28:7, 8 Publius is the chief man *(prōtos)* on the island of Malta. Because it would have been unusual to call a governor by his praenomen, Ramsay (1905: 343) speculates that *Poplios* is actually the Greek form of the Latin surname *Popilius.* Foakes Jackson and Lake (1933, 4: 342), however, reject this view. Since Polybius (2d century B.C.E.) habitually called the great general Scipio *Poplios,* his Roman first name being Publius, the usage in Acts 28:7, 8 should not be considered unusual (cf. Polybius books 10–15 passim). The use of the first name therefore may reflect, according to Zahn (1921, 2: 846), the friendly relationship that had arisen among Publius, Paul, and Luke during their time together on Malta. Or it may reflect the common usage among the peasants around Publius' estate.

Zahn (2: 843) documents the fact that two inscriptions found on the island, one in Greek and one in Latin, demonstrate that the term "chief man" *(prōtos)* in Acts 28:7 is an official title. Thus Publius was either the highest Roman official on the island or its chief native officer, serving under the governor of Sicily. As is the case with the "city authorities" *(politarchas)* of Thessalonica (Acts 17:6, 8), the author of Acts uses a governmental term that is appropriate to the location in question.

According to Acts 28, the ship on which Paul, his guards, and his fellow prisoners were traveling to Rome wrecked on the coast of the island of Malta near the estates *(chōria)* belonging to Publius. As the leading official of Malta, Publius would automatically be responsible for any Roman soldiers or prisoners who might arrive on the island. Acts 28:7, however, indicates that he went beyond the minimum when he "entertained us hospitably" *(philophronōs)* for three days (no doubt more permanent arrangements were made thereafter). If the "us" includes all 276 passengers on the ship (Acts 27:37), Publius must have had extensive possessions. Quite possibly, however, the "us" may be limited to selected passengers (such as Paul, Luke, the ship's captain, and the centurion) in whom Publius took a personal interest. According to Acts 28:8, Paul rewarded his kindness by healing his father of fever and dysentery. Harnack (1908: 176–77) and Haenchen (1971: 714) disagree as to whether the exactness of the medical terms used in Acts 28:7–10 indicates that the author of Acts was a physician.

According to the church father Jerome, a man named Publius was the predecessor of Quadratus as the bishop of Athens and suffered martyrdom (*De vir. ill.* chap. 19). Although the martyrdom may have occurred during the lifetime of Publius, we cannot be certain that the two men were the same.

Bibliography

Foakes Jackson, F. J., and Lake, K. 1933. *The Beginnings of Christianity.* 5 vols. London.

Haenchen, E. 1971. *The Acts of the Apostles.* Trans. B. Noble et al. Philadelphia.

Harnack, A. 1908. *Luke the Physician.* Trans. J. R. Wilkinson. Ed. W. D. Morrison. New York.

Ramsay, W. M. 1905. *St. Paul the Traveller.* London.

Zahn, T. 1921. *Die Apostelgeschichte des Lucas.* 2 vols. Kommentar zum Neuen Testament 5. Leipzig.

JON PAULIEN

PUDENS (PERSON) [Gk *Poudēs*]. A Christian mentioned before Linus and Claudia in 2 Tim 4:21, who along with them sent greetings to Timothy. Pudens apparently knew Timothy personally. Based on the assumption that the Pastorals were written in Rome (cf. 1:17), or are reflective of traditions from the Roman church, it has been supposed that Pudens lived in that city. It has also been theorized that he was the husband of Claudia, with Linus perhaps being their son, although this creates the problem of explaining why Pudens and Claudia are not mentioned together before Linus.

Some have thought that Pudens was Aulus Pudens, the soldier and husband of a British woman, Claudia Rufina, and friend of the Latin poet Martial referred to in Martial's *Epigrams* 4.13. This identification has been taken a step further, probably inspired by the hope of finding a link between Pauline Christianity and the British church—by those who equate Pudens with the person of the same name suggested by a fragmentary inscription at Chichester. That text has been interpreted as indicating that a certain Roman soldier, Pudens, donated the site for a temple to Neptune to the British king, Tiberius Claudius Cogidubnus, whose daughter, Claudia Rufina, he had married in Rome (*CIL* VII.17). While marriage to this British woman, Claudia Rufina, makes it quite likely that the Pudens of Martial and the Pudens of the Chichester inscription are the same person, the commonality of the names Pudens and Claudia argues strongly against extending the identification to the Pudens and Claudia of 2 Timothy. The same objection must also be advanced to any proposed link with Titus Claudius Pudens, husband of Claudia Quintilla. This couple lost an infant son who was memorialized on an inscription found on the road between Rome and Ostia (*CIL* VI.15,066). Finally, there is a theory which reasons that since some of the persons named Pudens were soldiers, then the Pudens of 2 Timothy must have held a similar occupation and was probably a prison guard in charge of Paul. But this is conjecture.

As for the ancient traditions surrounding Pudens mentioned in the *Acta Sanctorum,* e.g., that he was the son of Priscilla and that he was a Roman senator who extended hospitality to Peter, one is unable to determine where fact has been enveloped in legend.

Bibliography

Redlich, E. G. 1913. *S. Paul and His Companions.* London.

FLORENCE MORGAN GILLMAN

PUL (PERSON) [Heb *pûl*]. The king of Assyria who campaigned against Samaria during the reign of Menahem (ca. 745–738 B.C.; 2 Kgs 15:19; 1 Chr 5:26). From Assyrian texts we know that *pulu* was a nickname of the Assyrian king TIGLATH-PILESER III, who reigned from 744–727 B.C.

A. KIRK GRAYSON

PUNIC LANGUAGE. See LANGUAGES (PHOENICIAN).

PUNISHMENTS AND CRIMES (OT AND ANE). Analysis of ANE concepts of criminal offenses and their punishment as reflected in the cuneiform and biblical traditions of jurisprudence.

A. Background and Sources
   1. Date
   2. Ideology
   3. Context
B. Theoretical Basis
C. Public Offenses
   1. Apostasy
   2. Blasphemy
   3. Misappropriation of *ḥrm*
   4. Sorcery
   5. Violation of the Sabbath
   6. Incest
   7. Bestiality
   8. Homosexuality
D. Private Offenses
   1. Homicide
   2. Personal Injury
   3. Rape
   4. Adultery
   5. Theft
   6. Treason
   7. Against Parents
   8. False Accusation
E. Offenses Against the Legal System
   1. Abuse of Legal Authority
   2. Contempt of Court
F. Methods of Punishment
G. Summary and Conclusions

A. Background and Sources

The societies of the ANE, with the possible exception of Egypt, shared a common legal tradition, which is nowhere more clearly marked than in the sphere of criminal law. In historical times this tradition finds expression in the legal sources written in cuneiform script, which may itself have been the vehicle for the spread of legal ideas.

The best known of these sources are the cuneiform law codes: Code of Ur-Nammu (CU)—Sumerian (21st century); Code of Lipit-ishtar (CL)—Sumerian (19th century); Code of Eshnunna (CE)—Akkadian (18th century); Code of Hammurabi (CH)—Akkadian (18th century); the Middle Assyrian Laws (MAL)—Akkadian (12th century); the Hittite Laws (HL)—Hittite (13th century).

Those law codes were not legislation in the modern sense. Although they may have had diverse secondary uses (such as political propaganda), initially they were scientific treatises, which described the law rather than prescribed it. The cuneiform scribal schools were the universities of the ANE; within their walls not only was the art of cuneiform writing taught, but scholarly research was pursued in areas such as medicine, mathematics, omens, and law.

The "scientific" method used to examine the law was as follows. A judgment in a legal case was taken, stripped of all extraneous detail so that only the bare precedent remained, and then cast into a hypothetical form, usually expressed by a casuistic style, e.g., "If a man rapes a woman who is betrothed but not yet married . . . ," followed by the judgment applicable in that case. The case was then elaborated by considering various alternatives—if the woman was married, if she was willing, if she was unwilling but unable to call for help—so that a multifaceted legal problem was constructed through which the principles of the law could be taught, albeit not explicitly. Eventually there came into being a canon of classic scholarly legal problems which could be drawn upon in order to draft a written law code. The law code itself would contain no more than a small proportion of the oral canon, generally recording only one or two aspects of selected classic legal problems (together with excerpts from unworked judgments and other legal sources such as royal edicts).

As cuneiform scribal schools spread through the ANE from Mesopotamia, the Mesopotamian scientific tradition in its oral as well as its written aspects was adopted in the local academies. Law codes were composed on the Mesopotamian model, in the same casuistic style, and drawing in part upon the canon of scholarly legal problems, in part on local judgments elaborated in the same way. In the sphere of criminal law, a particularly high proportion of the material comes from the common canon of scholarly problems, although it is not always evident at first because different aspects of the same multifaceted problems are incorporated in different codes. By combining the similar and not-so-similar provisions of the various codes, however, the original scholarly problem that lay behind them may sometimes be reconstructed. When this process is complete, the result is not always a monolithic, cuneiform law. Differences between the legal systems can be seen in the rulings on particular aspects of the same problem.

Although biblical Israel lay outside the sphere of cuneiform writing, its law was pervaded by the same tradition. Two law codes in the Pentateuch, the Covenant Code (Exod 21:1–22:19) and the Deuteronomic Code (principally Deut 21:15–22:29) draw from the same canon of scholarly problems as the cuneiform codes. A third source, the Priestly Code (the legal provisions scattered through Leviticus and Numbers) shares the same intellectual background but draws mainly on a tradition that is poorly preserved in the cuneiform sources. There appears to have been a scholarly literature on specifically priestly regulations which find some reflection in the biblical provisions on the same subject (e.g., Geller 1980); but the only extant example is *Šurpu* (Reiner 1958), a recitation of sins to be atoned for with the help of the priest. Some parallels have also been shown with Hittite instructions to temple officials (Milgrom 1976).

The Ten Commandments, which contain no sanctions, are a collection of moral principles rather than a law code. Nonetheless, the negative commandments refer to crimes for which punishments were imposed in the biblical legal system.

The position of biblical law within the cuneiform tradition provides the Pentateuch's sparse and obscure provisions with the necessary background for their elucidation and enables us to view the whole system which they represent. There are, however, significant differences between the biblical and cuneiform sources.

1. Date. The biblical codes are from the 1st millennium; the cuneiform codes from the 2d and 3d millennia. The legal tradition was very conservative, with the same rules recurring millennia apart; but there are signs that from the 8th century on an intellectual revolution began in the Eastern Mediterranean that was eventually to herald the world of classical antiquity and a complete change in the conception of law, especially criminal law. While the earliest of the biblical codes, the Covenant Code, which perhaps dates back as far as the turn of the millennium, is squarely in the old cuneiform tradition, the Deuteronomic Code from the 7th century and the Priestly Codes from either the same period or up to several centuries later show signs that new conceptions were beginning to affect that tradition.

2. Ideology. The cuneiform codes derive from royal jurisprudence and represent the voice of the establishment. The Deuteronomic and Priestly Codes are from circles not necessarily sympathetic to the king. Although based on the existing law, they are polemical tracts which advocate reforms. While it may be that the cuneiform codes show some tendency to idealize the law, as one might expect in an academic work, in the two biblical codes this tendency is blatant, with outright utopian measures such as the Sabbatical and jubilee years, which could never have been part of the law in practice. Criminal law in the societies of the ANE was essentially customary law which had existed from time immemorial. Innovations occurred through precedent where new circumstances arose or occasionally through administrative orders issued by the ruler. The latter, however, were of marginal importance, effecting no fundamental change in the principles of the law. The Deuteronomic and Priestly codes, on the other hand, contain the first glimmerings of a new idea of criminal law that was eventually to become the norm in Talmudic jurisprudence.

3. Context. The biblical codes are not independent documents like the cuneiform codes but have undergone a process of editing and are inserted in a secondary context, a religious historiography. As a result, they are more heterogeneous and draw upon a variety of sources. To find the same context in the cuneiform material, it is necessary to consult diverse sources, the sum of which does not, however, add up to the same as the integrated biblical text. Furthermore, editing of the biblical text may have distorted the original meaning of the provisions (through devices such as *inclusio* and selectivity) in order to harmonize them with a particular religious perspective. On the other hand, the fact that, in contrast to the cuneiform codes, God, rather than a mortal king, is the purported author of the biblical codes should not overshadow his *function* as lawgiver. The biblical God is a divine king, whose legal role is the same as that of a mortal king except that he is the ideal king of justice, establishing equity and protecting the poor and oppressed—which is exactly how the kings of the cuneiform codes represented themselves.

The cuneiform codes provide us with a fragmentary view of the substantive law, partly because of restrictions in their length and partly because their casuistic style resulted in isolated examples. Documentary evidence of the criminal law in practice is scarce, being confined to reports of trials, which usually are concerned with the facts and the decision rather than with the legal rules at issue, and occasional references in letters.

Israelite literary tradition has yielded almost no documents of practice, but the nonlegal parts of the Bible contain numerous examples of the criminal law in practice. Of the narratives especially noteworthy are etiological stories establishing precedents such as the case of the wood gatherer on the Sabbath (Num 15:32–36) and the blasphemer (Lev 24:10–23) and juridical fables such as the woman of Tekoah (2 Sam 14:1–20) and the poor man's ewe lamb (2 Sam 12:1–14). While both types of account are fictional, they rely for their credibility on the contemporary audience's familiarity with the applicable law.

Prophetic and Wisdom Literature use familiar examples from everyday law to reinforce arguments on religious or moral issues; e.g., the punishment for adultery in the simile of marriage between God and his wayward people (Hos 2:5; Ezek 16:37–39) and in the admonitions of the book of Proverbs (e.g., 6:32–35).

The pentateuchal law codes do not always seem to be in accord with the law in practice as evidenced in other parts of the Bible. For example, the incest laws of Leviticus are stricter than those that the biblical account records elsewhere, in terms of forbidden degrees of relationship. Whether this reflects actual changes in the law or whether such changes are merely being advocated by the Priestly source is difficult to say. Caution must be exercised in comparing the two types of sources. The biblical codes, like their cuneiform counterparts, were not legislation in the modern sense. Their text was not interpreted by the courts as authoritative (except perhaps at the very end of the biblical period); and far from being comprehensive, it presented only a small fraction of the law and assumed knowledge of the rest. Where the text of a law code is silent, therefore, it cannot be taken as rejection of a rule found in a different source without further evidence.

B. Theoretical Basis

In dealing with wrongful conduct leading to harm (other than by breach of an agreement), modern legal systems distinguish between *torts* and *crimes*. Torts are generally wrongs with a lower level of moral culpability, such as negligence, but the same act may be both a tort and a crime. A tort is conceived of purely as a personal wrong against the victim. The initiative for proceeding against the tort-feasor (guilty party) is solely in the hands of the victim, and the purpose of the court's intervention is to *compensate* the victim for any harm caused him. A crime, by contrast, is conceived of as a wrong to society, in which the harm to the particular victim is incidental—indeed, there may be no specific victim at all. The initiative is in the hands of the state, which may proceed irrespective of the victim's wishes; and the purpose is to *punish* the offender.

The ANE legal systems dealt with wrongs in a different manner. Three main categories can be discerned:

First, acts causing damage where the level of moral culpability is low, e.g., a wound inflicted in a fight where the victim is equally to blame, or negligence causing damage to a neighbor's crops by fire or flood. The initiative was in the hands of the victim, and the purpose of the court's intervention was to award compensation. This category is comparable to the modern law of torts.

Second, acts which carried a high level of moral culpability, such as incest or blasphemy, which were conceived of as bringing down divine wrath on the whole society in a form such as drought, plague, or military defeat. The link between the act and its retribution was understood as an intangible pollution by the offender of his environment. It was society through its official organs that took the initiative to protect itself by removing the pollution, usually by killing or exiling the offender, thereby appeasing divine anger. Any resemblance to modern criminal law is superficial; the analogy is rather to a contagious disease, since innocent persons who had been polluted by contact with the offender might be dealt with in the same way as the offender.

Third, acts which would constitute the principal examples of crimes in modern systems, such as homicide, rape, wounding, and theft (but also adultery). Such offenses gave rise in principle to a dual right for the victim or his family: to take revenge on the offender or his family, or to accept ransom in lieu of revenge. The initiative was therefore with the victim; and the role of the court was seen as setting a limit on the level of revenge, or in some cases, of ransom, in accordance with the seriousness of the case. Where physical punishments appear in the law codes for such offenses, they are in fact limits on revenge, and the hidden assumption is that ransom may be demanded in lieu of them. Where these payments are fixed, they are neither fines nor compensation but limits on the ransom that may be exacted, and the hidden assumption is that the right to revenge will revive if they are not paid. It must be emphasized, however, that the right to revenge was a *judicial* remedy exercisable through the courts, not a simple expression of blood feud. Uncontrolled revenge was considered the antithesis of legal order, as in the boast of Lamech (Gen 4:23–24), which typified the wicked, lawless society before the Flood.

The above three categories overlap considerably. For less serious cases in the third category, revenge may be limited to loss of freedom, which would also be the fate of a tort-feasor unable to pay the compensation demanded, while the most serious cases might also create some degree of pollution and thus involve society as a whole. For convenience, the second and third categories, which together cover the area regarded as criminal law today, will be discussed separately under the headings "Public Offenses" and "Private Offenses," although they have no real equivalent in modern systems. A further minor category of wrongs has been brought together under the heading "Offenses Against the Legal System."

C. Public Offenses

1. Apostasy. Although apostasy was not considered by its polytheistic neighbors, Israel was forbidden to have gods other than Yahweh or to worship images of them (Exod 20:2–5). One who sacrifices to another god is made *ḥrm* (Exod 22:19; see below), which entails the death penalty (Deut 17:2–7). If an entire city is implicated, its inhabitants are killed and the city with all its contents burned and reduced to rubble (Deut 13:13–18). Incitement to apostasy is also punishable by death (Deut 13:2–12). Giving one's offspring to Molech (if a god) creates pollution and carries the death penalty (Lev 20:2–3). Prosecution of apostasy is by the public authorities (Deut 13:15–16, cf. Lev 20:2) based on evidence from informants (Deut 13:9).

Its theoretical basis is illustrated by the story of the people's apostasy to the Moabite gods (Num 25:1–9). Yahweh's anger is incurred; and the result is a plague—a typical consequence of pollution. The remedy is for Moses to have the leaders impaled, while the plague is actually stopped by the exemplary act of a zealot, Phinehas, in killing an apostate (cf. Ps 106:30).

2. Blasphemy. In MAL Tablet A 2 a woman who speaks blasphemy "shall bear her punishment; they shall not touch her husband, children, or daughters." The exact punishment is not stated, but King Assurbanipal (Weidner 1932: 184, 28) tells of two enemies "who spoke gross blasphemy against Assur, my god who created me: I ripped out their tongues and skinned them alive." The Akkadian term in both sources is *šillatu,* the cognate of which is found in Dan 3:29, where Nebuchadnezzar decrees that anyone who speaks *šlh* against the god of the Jews will be dismembered and his house destroyed (Paul 1983).

In the biblical laws, two associated terms are used: "curse" *(qll)* and "slander the name" *(nqb ʾt/b–šm).* Cursing of God is prohibited (Exod 22:27—Eng 22:28). Lev 24:15–16 states that one who curses God shall bear his punishment—i.e., his family shall not be touched, as in the Assyrian Laws—and that one who slanders the name is to be stoned.

The Levitical rule is purportedly based on an actual case where the offender slandered the name and cursed, and was accordingly executed (24:10–14, 23). The two actions, therefore, if not synonymous, have the same consequences in law (cf. 1 Kgs 21:13).

3. Misappropriation of *ḥrm*. In Mesopotamia, property that was reserved for a god or king might be placed under a taboo and was then known as *asakku.* To misappropriate it was to violate the taboo and incur a penalty, which apparently varied, but could be death if the circumstances warranted (Malamat 1966). A priestess who repeatedly steals the *asakku* is burned (Anbar 1974: 173), and a man who takes booty previously declared *asakku* is "not to be spared," but possibly has his death sentence commuted (ARM 5.72).

In the Bible the same institution is called *ḥrm,* but the term is used only of taboo property reserved for God. Reservation is achieved by total destruction, as in the case of the apostate city (Deut 13:13–16), and the same applies where the enemy is declared *ḥrm.* Consequently, taking enemy property as booty instead of destroying it amounts to misappropriation of *ḥrm,* a crime that will incur divine anger (1 Sam 15:1–33).

When Achan takes booty from Jericho, in spite of the city's having been declared *ḥrm* (Josh 6:17), divine anger manifests itself in military defeat for Israel (Josh 7:1–12). In punishment, Achan is to be stoned and burned, along with his family, livestock, and possessions, including specifically the *ḥrm* property taken by him and also the tent in which it had been concealed (Josh 7:22–25).

4. Sorcery. Sorcery was considered a public danger, and special procedures applied to its prosecution. According to the Edict of the Hittite king Telipinus (Hoffmann 1984: 54 §50), persons were expected to denounce members of their own family. Denunciation is to the king (Hoffmann, §50), who also interrogates the witnesses (MAL A 47). Sorcery is, therefore, the "judgment of the king" (HL 44).

Little is known of the practices that were forbidden. HL 170 mentions the killing of a snake while pronouncing a man's name. HL 44B declares the dumping on a man's land of residue from a purification ceremony to be sorcery, i.e., connected with the concept of pollution.

In the Bible, Exod 22:17—Eng 22:18 states: "You shall not suffer a sorceress to live." The addressees are presumably a public body. The only type of forbidden sorcery explicitly mentioned is that of mediums calling up a spirit of the dead (*ʾwb* or *ydʿny:* Lev 20:27). If Molech sacrifice is to the spirits of the dead, then its prohibition would belong in this category.

The role of the king is illustrated by the notice that Saul attempted to extirpate the mediums from the land (1 Sam 28:9). The practice incurs divine anger: one who consults a medium—typically a secret, collusive act not amenable to human justice (cf. 1 Sam 28:8–10)—is threatened with divine punishment (Lev 20:6).

5. Violation of the Sabbath. The biblical prohibition of work on the Sabbath (Exod 20:10; Deut 5:14) is not found elsewhere in the ANE. The penalty for infringement is death (Exod 31:14–15; 35:2). An etiological story defines gathering wood as forbidden work (Num 15:32–36). Jeremiah's appeal to the kings and inhabitants of Jerusalem to cease work on the Sabbath (Jer 17:19–27) suggests that the prohibition was not then enforced through the public authorities. Nehemiah does enforce it (Neh 13:15–22) but by administrative measures rather than direct sanctions.

6. Incest. HL 189–195A list a series of incestuous relationships classified as *hurkel.* No punishment is prescribed; but from another Hittite source, the Instructions to the Border Guard Commander (*ANET,* 211), we learn that *hurkel* was punished by death or banishment, according to local custom. Where the offender was banished, the town had to purify itself afterward. CH prescribes the same two alternatives according to type of incest: with a daughter—banishment (154); with a daughter-in-law—death (155); between mother and son after the father's death—death for both (157).

Lev 18:6–19 likewise contain a list of incestuous relationships, which it forbids and labels "abominations" *(twʿbwt).* The offender is said to pollute himself (v 24), and failure to curb such pollution may lead to defeat and exile (v 28). Lev 20:11–21 include a further list with specific punishments, human and divine; see below.

The lists of prohibited relationships vary, even within the two levitical sources (cf. Deut 23:1; 27:20, 22–23); and none of them is comprehensive. Undoubtedly, relations with a daughter were prohibited, although this prohibition is missing from the biblical lists. All sources prohibit relations not only with blood relatives but also with certain relatives by marriage. In the latter case, the relation would already be adulterous, so that the incest prohibition perhaps refers either to widowhood (cf. CH 157) or to collusion with the husband; the point being that in spite of his acquiescence it is still an offense because it pollutes (see below). In three cases the biblical code prohibits relations that are licit elsewhere in the Bible: (1) marriage with a paternal half-sister (Lev 18:9; Deut 27:22; cf. Gen 20:12; 2 Sam 13:13); (2) marriage with two sisters (Lev 18:18; cf.

Jabob's marriage to Leah and Rebekah); and (3) levirate marriage (Lev 18:16; 20:21, if not confined to the brother's lifetime), although it is enjoined as a duty by Deut 25:5. (Cf. HL 193, which specifically exempts the levirate as opposed to relations during the brother's lifetime [195A].)

7. Bestiality. HL 187–188 and 199 classify sexual relations between a man and a cow, sheep, pig, or dog as *hurkel.* They explicitly call for the death penalty but with a right in the king to grant pardon. Curiously, 200A exempts relations with a horse or mule, although in this case and where the offender is pardoned, he remains ritually impure. Lev 18:23 includes in the list of "abominations" intercourse by a man or woman with any animal, and Lev 20:15–16 prescribes the death penalty for both the offender and the animal.

8. Homosexuality. To "lie with a male the lying of a woman" is regarded as another "abomination" by Lev 18:22 and is punished with the death of both parties in Lev 20:13. In MAL 20, the same offense is punished with the offender himself being sodomized and castrated. It has been suggested (Daube 1986) that this curious punishment is based on a distinction between active and passive sodomy, the latter being the lot of the lower orders of society. Such a distinction finds no echo in the biblical law.

D. Private Offenses

1. Homicide. The basic principle was that the victim's family had a right to revenge through the death penalty or to ransom, at their choice. As the Edict of Telipinus, a Hittite king, puts it (Hoffmann 1984: 52 §49):

> A matter of blood is as follows. Whoever does blood, whatever the owner of the blood says:—If he says "Let him die!" he shall die. If he says "Let him pay ransom!" he shall pay ransom. . . .

The "owner of the blood" is the closest male relative of the victim. He is known by the same name in Neo-Assyrian sources, and as the "owner of the life" in MAL B 2. The biblical equivalent is "redeemer of the blood" *(gwʾl hdm),* i.e., one who brings it back within the family, like redeemed family land; and it is slaying of the killer that achieves restoration. As a letter from the Babylonian king to the pharaoh (EA 8) puts it: ". . . the men who killed my subjects—kill them! Return their blood!" If not restored, the victim's blood may "cry out" from the ground (Gen 4:10).

By the same token, if the homicide is justified for some reason and therefore does not give a right to revenge, the blood can remain where it is. In Leviticus 20, it is said of the offender who commits a polluting act, and may therefore be killed without revenge as a measure of public safety, "his blood is on his head." Exod 22:1—Eng 22:2 expresses the same idea even more strongly: the burglar killed while breaking in at night "has no blood."

a. Aggravating Factors in Cuneiform Sources. Telipinus' Edict presents the theoretical principle, which in practice was confined to aggravated homicide. In the cuneiform sources, three aggravating factors can be discerned:

(1) Premeditation. In the case referred to by the Babylonian king, where three men conspired to murder a fourth, a Mesopotamian court rules: "As men who have killed a man, they are not live men" (Jacobsen 1970). Where circumstances suggest lack of premeditation, CH 207 allows the killer to swear an oath to this effect and receive a much lighter penalty.

(2) Gross Negligence or Recklessness. CH 229 prescribes death for the negligent builder whose construction collapses on the house owner, killing him, as does CE 58 for the owner of a dangerous wall that collapses with fatal results, if the owner failed to repair it in spite of due warning. The family's right to revenge is against the offender himself, or as HL 43 puts it: "they shall receive that very man," in the case of one whose reckless behavior at a river crossing causes another to drown.

(3) Threshold Offense. Where the offender *unlawfully* distrains a member of the debtor's family (i.e., takes him into debt slavery) and causes his death through maltreatment, it is the distrainer himself who suffers death (CE 24). In normal circumstances the penalty for such an offense would be vicarious revenge, i.e., revenge against the equivalent member of the offender's family.

b. Mitigating Factors in Cuneiform Sources. Vicarious revenge was regarded as a mitigated punishment (cf. 2 Sam 12:13–14) of the offender. When there was a mitigating factor in homicide, the courts intervened to restrict revenge either by this means or by setting a limit on the ransom that might be demanded in lieu of it. Mitigating factors are:

(1) Lack of Premeditation. A classic scholarly problem concerns a fight, in which blame must be apportioned between both parties. If the death of one party ensues, HL 1 imposes a limited ransom, as does CH 207, but with the added proviso that the other party is to swear as to his lack of premeditation. Lack of premeditation (or of foreseeability of death) may lie behind HL 44A's allowing only vicarious revenge where death is the result of the victim's being pushed into a fire.

(2) Negligence. In the guarding of a goring ox or vicious dog, even when the owner has been warned of its propensity, negligence does not in the eyes of the cuneiform codes amount to aggravated homicide where the animal subsequently kills. Limited ransom is allowed, probably as an alternative vicarious revenge (CE 54, 56; CH 251).

(3) Status of the Victim. If it is the house owner's son who dies as a result of the builder's negligence (CH 230) or the debtor's son who is distrained and dies at the hands of a creditor (CH 116), then it is the offender's son upon whom revenge is exacted. If the offense is lesser, as in the case of the goring ox, and the victim is a son, limited ransom is allowed in lieu of vicarious revenge (CH 251).

The blow to a pregnant woman which causes a miscarriage is a classic scholarly problem. If it also causes her death and she is a daughter, the penalty will be vicarious revenge on the offender's daughter (CH 210), or limited ransom if the victim is from the poorer classes (CH 212—*muškēnum*). A fragmentary Sumerian code (Civil 1965: 4–5, lines iii 7′–8′) takes a more serious view, prescribing death for the offender himself.

The death of a slave invariably results in a low payment to the master. It is doubtful whether this is in lieu of revenge; it may be simple compensation, as with loss of property.

Causing the miscarriage of a fetus results in a small payment (CH 209; HL 17), which may be simple compensation. The fragmentary Sumerian code (Civil 1965: 4–5, lines iii 6′–7′) demands a much higher sum, which suggests that it is in lieu of revenge.

c. Aggravating Factors in the Bible. The same system of revenge and ransom, limited according to the circumstances, lies behind the biblical provisions but with important variations. Aggravating factors are:

(1) Premeditation. The killer who lay in wait for his victim is handed over to the redeemer of blood for revenge (Exod 21:14; Num 35:20–21; Deut 19:11–12). The victim's clan might demand that the killer be delivered up for this purpose (2 Sam 14:7). The victim's relatives would be entitled to ransom but in a case of deliberate murder might well insist on revenge. Thus the Gibeonites, whose people Saul had murdered (by waging war in breach of treaty), specifically forego their claim to ransom and demand Saul's sons, Saul being deceased (2 Sam 21:1–9).

In the case of Cain, the punishment imposed is exile, not death; but this turns out to be equally harsh, since Cain may then be killed by anyone without fear of retribution (Gen 4:11–14). Accordingly, God grants him protection and agrees to become his surrogate avenger (v 15). King David performs the same function in restraining revenge against the Tekoan woman's son (2 Sam 14:11) and acts as a surrogate avenger for Ish-bosheth (2 Sam 4:11).

(2) Gross Negligence. The scholarly problem of the goring ox is presented in Exod 21:28–32 in the same terms as in the cuneiform codes, but as aggravated rather than mitigated homicide. If the owner has previously been warned, revenge is against him in person, with no limit on ransom (v 30). Even if the victim is a subordinate member of the family, no vicarious revenge is allowed (v 31). Furthermore, the ox itself is to be stoned and not eaten (vv 28, 32), which may have been regarded as punishment of the animal.

d. Mitigating Factors in the Bible. (1) Status of Victim. If the victim of the goring ox is a slave, the negligent owner's liability is a low payment, as in the cuneiform provisions (Exod 21:32).

Where a member of the debtor's family dies as a direct result of abuse while in debt slavery, vicarious revenge is appropriate, as in CH 116. This is the import of *nqm ynqm* ("he shall surely be avenged") in Exod 21:20. Later sources polemicized against vicarious revenge (Lev 19:18; Deut 24:16), but it is not clear that it was actually abolished. Where the causal nexus between abuse and death cannot be conclusively established (Exod 21:21, "But if he survives a day or two . . ."), then only ransom is allowed, being limited to the amount of the debt (and thereby canceling it): ". . . he shall not be vicariously revenged, but it (the revenge) is his silver (the debt) (*lʾ yqm ky kspw hwʾ*)."

If a miscarriage is caused, the offender must pay unlimited ransom to the husband, but it is not clear if it is for his own life or in lieu of vicarious revenge (Exod 21:22). This is *not* the same scholarly problem as in the cuneiform codes and does *not* consider the death of the woman; it is concerned with the identity of the offender and considers the measure of punishment only incidentally (see below).

(2) Lack of Premeditation. Three pentateuchal sources on murder (Exod 21:12–14; Num 35:9–34; and Deut 19:1–6; cf. Jas 20:1–7) are based upon the same scholarly problem (not extant in the cuneiform codes). If A kills B and B's family members immediately take revenge without trial, they can claim on the apparent facts that theirs is justifiable homicide and should not in turn be avenged. If, however, A's act had been unpremeditated, killing him in revenge would be unjustified. But only A can testify to his own state of mind, and killing him without trial frustrates that possibility. Accordingly, A is given the protection of asylum pending trial, either at an altar (Exodus) or in designated cities of refuge (Numbers, Deuteronomy). Exodus and Deuteronomy do not state what happens if A's act is found by the court to have been unpremeditated—presumably it was treated as mitigated homicide. Numbers (P), in this event, converts the asylum into exile until the death of the high priest (35:25); and should A leave that place, he may be killed with impunity ("he has no blood") by the redeemer of blood (vv 26–27). Whether the same system applied in the other sources, or ever in practice, is unclear. Temporary asylum by grasping the altar, as in Exodus, is attested elsewhere (1 Kgs 1:50–53; 2:28); exile measured by the high priest's life is not (but cf. 1 Kgs 2:36–46).

The examples given of unpremeditated acts are of accidents: an accidental push, or the throwing of a weapon or stone without seeing the victim (Num 35:22–23), or the head of an ax flying off during use (Deut 19:5). Premeditated acts are those planned against an enemy (Exod 21:14; Num 35:20–21). The intermediate case of unintentional killing in a fight where blame might be apportioned is not discussed in the biblical codes; but if there were no witnesses, premeditation might be presumed (2 Sam 14:6).

e. Homicide and Pollution. Although it is a private offense, homicide also pollutes. According to a letter from the Hittite king (*KBo* 1.10 Rs. 19–20), if the brothers of the victim accept ransom, they purify the place of the homicide. Likewise in an Assyrian ransom agreement (Kwasman 1988: 393 No. 341), the offender must also wash away the blood. It is possible that a separate purification ritual was needed only when ransom was involved and that killing the offender in revenge was purification in itself. In 2 Samuel 21 Saul's crime leads to a divinely occasioned famine which ended only by David's allowing the Gibeonites to take revenge. The mode of execution is ritualistic: impaling Saul's sons "before Yahweh" (v 9).

The Priestly source takes an uncompromising stand on the issue of purification. Only revenge can purify the land (Num 35:33, cf. Gen 9:6); ransom is inadequate even for mitigated homicide (Num 35:31–32). On the other hand, exile for the latter offense appears to remove the pollution. Whether a purification ceremony was also necessary, as in the banishment of Hittite sexual offenders, is not made clear. Deut 21:1–9 record a ceremony to be performed when the victim's killer is unknown, which has been interpreted as a kind of purification ritual (cf. Deut 22:8).

2. Personal Injury. a. In Cuneiform Sources. This is

dealt with in the cuneiform codes through the medium of three scholarly problems.

First, a list of injuries to various parts of the body is considered. Four codes contain such lists (CU; CE; CH; HL), which overlap to varying degrees. In declining order of frequency, the injuries are: eye, bone, hand, foot, tooth, nose, and ear. All appear to be serious, if not permanent—destruction of the eye, biting off of the nose. No mental element is mentioned, but it is probably intentional injury that is meant, not negligence or accident (Cardascia 1985). An anomalous member of the list (CE 42; CH 202–5) must be intentional: a slap in the face—suggesting that honor was as much at stake as physical integrity.

The Code of Hammurabi distinguishes between an *awīlum*—a member of the upper classes—and a *muškēnum*—a poor man, or perhaps simply an ordinary free citizen. CH 196–97 rule: "If an *awīlum* puts out the eye of the son of an *awīlum*, his eye shall be put out. Here is the famous *talio* (measure for measure), in brutally explicit language. But *talio* was simply part of the system of revenge and ransom. By this means the courts limited the level of revenge exactable, and there was always the possibility of ransom if the parties could come to terms. For the *muškēnum*, the ransom was fixed (CH 198). In CU, CE, and HL there are only fixed payments for the various injuries.

Second, a fight which leads to nonpermanent injury is discussed by CH 206 and HL 10. In both, the offender must pay the doctor's fee; and HL requires in addition that he nurse the victim, supply a man to work in his place until he is well, and pay him a small, fixed sum. These provisions are clearly compensatory in nature (suggesting that the offender was not solely to blame for the fight) and are analogous to damages in tort rather than to criminal punishment.

Third, a fight in which a woman intervenes by seizing a man's testicles is considered. According to MAL A 8 if she crushes one testicle, her finger is cut off; if she crushes both, her nipples (? text broken) are torn out. Merely laying hands on a man is punished by a payment and flogging (7).

b. In the Bible. The treatment of personal injury in the biblical codes is based on these same three problems.

Exod 21:24–25 contain a list: eye, tooth, hand, foot, plus three that are not in the cuneiform provisions: burning, wound, and blow. The context, however, is a scholarly problem not attested elsewhere. A pregnant woman has been caught up in a street brawl and injured by persons unknown (v 23: *ʾswn* = damage by persons unknown). In these circumstances, it is the duty of the local authority to pay (v 23, *ntth* "you shall pay") her compensation appropriate to her injury. In spite of its talionic phraseology, therefore ("eye for eye"), the list here refers to the principles of equitable ransom rather than to revenge. In Lev 24:19–20, on the other hand, the list unambiguously refers to retaliation: "A man who gives a blemish in his fellow: as he did, so shall be done to him—fracture for fracture, eye for eye, tooth for tooth. As he put a blemish on his fellow so shall it be put on him." The rule therefore regulates revenge as in CH. It does not explicitly exclude the alternative of ransom; but it is from the Priestly source, which is hostile to ransom (see above). Possibly considerations of purity are at issue, since the term used here for injury—"blemish" *(mwm)* is the technical term for physical defects that render a priest unfit to offer sacrifices (Lev 21:17–21).

Fixed ransom for injury is set by Exod 21:26 for the maltreated debt slave: "If a man strikes the eye of his slave, male or female, and destroys it, he shall let his slave go free for his eye." (v 27 the same for a tooth). As where the slave died, (v 21), ransom is fixed at the level of the debt owed. The debt is thus canceled and the slave thereby released.

In Exod 21:18–19 nonpermanent injury in a fight leads to tortious damages for loss of work and medical expenses. The offender is "clear" *(nqy)*—not of all liabilities, but of criminal culpability that would give a right to revenge.

Accordingly to Deut 25:11–12 if a wife intervenes in a fight by seizing the genitalia of her husband's opponent, her "hand" (Heb *kp*—female genitalia) is cut off. The facts lie between MAL A 7 and 8, but the punishment is harsher.

3. Rape. a. In Cuneiform Sources. This is considered by the cuneiform law codes in the context of a discussion of adultery. Two main aspects are treated: the status of the victim and her lack of consent.

The laws distinguished between a woman who is unattached, inchoately married, and married. According to MAL A 55, where an unattached girl is raped, her father may demand that the rapist marry her without right of divorce and with payment of a set bride money or demand the bride money without the marriage. If the rapist is married, his wife is to be assigned to the father for sexual abuse.

Where bride money has been paid for the girl, she is inchoately married, a status which aggravates the offense, making it punishable with death (CU 6; CE 26; CH 130). The purpose of this rule, the core of the scholarly problem, is to equate this case with that of a fully married woman, where the rapist's penalty is likewise death (MAL A 12, 23; HL 197). MAL A 12 relies for lack of consent on the fact that the woman was in the street on legitimate business and on testimony to her resistance to the rapist's attentions. HL 197 proposes a mechanical test: if the act took place in the city, consent is presumed; if in the country, it is not, and the offense is rape.

b. In the Bible. Of the biblical codes, only Deuteronomy discusses rape, preserving a fragment of the traditional scholarly problem. Rape of an unattached girl leads, as in MAL A 55, to forcible marriage with no divorce, and payment of a set bride money (22:28–29). (Cf. Genesis 34, where the rape of Dinah is regarded by the offender's family as meriting a similar response, but is met by Dinah's brothers with revenge beyond any normal legal limits. Likewise, Absalom's killing of Amnon in revenge for the rape of his sister Tamar was regarded as unjustified: 2 Samuel 13.) Rape of an inchoately married girl, on the other hand, is punishable with death (22:25). In this case, Deuteronomy relies on the same context for consent as HL 197—city or country—but provides it with a rationale, namely that in the city the girl's cries for help will be heard—and consent is therefore presumed if she does not cry out (22:24–27).

4. Adultery. Illicit sexual intercourse by a wife with a man other than her husband was adultery. The same act by a husband was not considered adultery, unless it was with a married woman. Adultery was an offense against the husband committed by the wife and her lover, but it was also a sin and subject to divine punishment. In Ugarit (Moran 1959) and Egypt (Rabinowitz 1959) it is referred to as the "Great Sin," and in the Bible as the "Great Evil" (Gen 39:9).

a. In Cuneiform Sources. Adultery is discussed in the cuneiform codes in a series of interrelated problems. The general principle is presented in MAL A 13:

> If the wife of a man has gone out from her house to a man where he lives and he has had intercourse with her knowing that she is a man's wife, both the man and the woman shall be killed.

This case is to be distinguished from the seduction of a man who is unaware of the woman's married status, where the man is not liable but the husband may punish his wife as he pleases (MAL A 14b and also CU 7).

If the husband catches the lovers *in flagranti delicto,* there are two possibilities. If he himself kills them on the spot, he is not liable for homicide (HL 197; probably also the meaning of CE 28 and MAL A 15a). If he chooses to bring them before the court, then the death penalty applies (CH 129; MAL A 15b), but according to HL 198, the king has the prerogative of sparing the culprits' lives.

In CH 142 if an inchoately married wife is found not to have kept her chastity during betrothal, it is treated as adultery, and she suffers the death penalty.

If a husband accuses his wife of adultery but has no direct evidence, she must take an oath in order to clear herself of liability (CH 131).

The penalties found in these codes represent regulation of revenge by the husband. Presumably the alternative of ransom existed, but no reference is known from the cuneiform sources. Adultery was regarded as a very grave offense, for which the husband was entitled to demand the death penalty. In his discretion, the husband could demand a lesser penalty, such as mutilation (MAL A 15b) or "treat his wife as he pleases" (14). Since punishment of the wife intersects with marriage law, it is probable that the latter discretion included the right simply to divorce the wife without paying the usual financial compensation (cf. CH 141).

On the other hand, adultery could not be regarded as an offense against the husband if he acquiesced in his wife's conduct, e.g., if he was suspected of sending her out for prostitution (MAL A 14).

Thus all the above provisions emphasize that punishment of the lover is dependent upon punishment of the wife. The husband is not allowed to claim a penalty for the lover while pardoning his wife's offense, and his killing of the lovers caught *in flagranti delicto* is permitted only on condition that he kills both (CH 129; MAL A 14–15, 22; HL 198). MAL A 15b also insists that the lover's penalty be mitigated in step with any mitigation by the husband of the penalty inflicted on his wife.

Where the adulterer goes undetected by the husband, the possibility of divine punishment is still to be reckoned with. Thus the gods will visit with sickness and premature death the man who secretly "entered his neighbor's house, had intercourse with his neighbor's wife" (*Šurpu* 2.47–48; 4.6 [Reiner 1958].

b. In the Bible. The biblical laws contain only fragments of the traditional scholarly problems but with supplementary details from narrative and prophetic passages.

The general principle is presented in Lev 20:10: "A man who commits adultery with a man's wife, who commits adultery with his neighbor's wife shall be killed—the adulterer and the adulteress" and in Deut 22:22: "If a man is discovered to have lain with a married woman, they shall both die: the man who sleeps with the woman and the woman. You shall eliminate evil from Israel."

The seduction of an unwitting man is the subject of three narratives in Genesis (12:10–20; chap. 20; 26:6–11) in which a foreign ruler has (or almost has) intercourse with a patriarch's wife, believing her to be his unmarried sister. The consequence is divine, but not human, punishment.

In Deut 22:20–21, where a wife is found not to have kept her chastity before marriage, she suffers death. It must be presumed that her offense took place during the period of inchoate marriage (cf. Exod 22:15–16 for the case of an unattached girl). Likewise in Gen 38:24, Tamar's unchastity is punishable with death because she was regarded as inchoately married to Shelah. Deut 22:24 extends the scope of the problem on rape of an inchoate wife to consensual intercourse, in which case both she and her lover are put to death.

If a husband accuses his wife without direct evidence, she must take an oath and undergo a ceremony of drinking bitter waters (which will have adverse physical effects if she is guilty) in order to clear herself (Num 5:11–31).

The basis of punishment is explicitly stated to be revenge by the husband, with the alternative right to ransom:

> . . . The fury of the husband will be passionate;
> He will show no pity on his day of vengeance.
> He will not have regard for any ransom;
> He will refuse your bribe, however great
> (Prov 6:32–35—JPSV).

Ransom was therefore unlimited, and in the discretion of the husband. In Gen 38:24, where the inchoate husband Shelah is still young, it is Tamar's father-in-law, Judah, who exercises this right. A kind of limited ransom is prescribed in Lev 19:20: "A man who lies carnally with a wife (*ʾšh),* she being a slave pledged to the man (pointing *neḥrepet lĕʾîš*) . . . there shall be a proprietary claim *(bqrt).* They shall not be put to death because she was not freed." The husband cannot claim the death penalty, but he can reclaim his wife, thus canceling the debt, which thereby represents a limited ransom. The right of the husband to inflict a lesser penalty on his wife is referred to in prophetic passages which use adultery as a metaphor for the nation's apostasy (Hos 2:5, cf. Jer 13:26–27; Ezek 16:37–39). Apparently the wife is stripped naked and driven from the matrimonial home.

As in the cuneiform codes, punishment of the lover depended on the absence of acquiescence by the husband in his wife's adultery. Hence, Lev 20:10 and Deut 22:22 insist on both parties' being killed. The wording of the former law is significant: it is addressed to the lover alone, but adds "the adulterer and the adulteress," showing the former's death to be conditional upon the latter's. Collusion was a well-known factor, as seen in the deception practiced by Abraham and Isaac in representing their wives as their sisters. No human punishment is contemplated (not least because a ruler is implicated), but divine punishment is still a possibility (Gen 12:17; 20:3, 17–18; 26:10). The inclusion of adulterous relationships in the incest categories of Leviticus 20, and the "giving of seed" to one's neighbor's wife in Lev 18:19, suggest collusion and therefore no punishment by the husband. But it remains a sin that will be visited by the divine punishment of childlessness (20:20–21). The context suggests that the Priestly source regarded adultery not merely as a personal sin but as polluting to some extent.

5. Theft. a. In Cuneiform Sources. This category was widely defined, covering fraudulent misappropriation whether by asportation, purchasing stolen property, or retaining lost property. In principle, the owner of the stolen property was entitled to the death penalty as revenge upon the thief, but in practice this was confined to aggravated cases. The courts imposed limited ransom for simple theft, either at a fixed sum or as a fixed multiple of the thing stolen. The severity of the penalty depended sometimes on the circumstances, e.g., a wife stealing from her husband was treated more severely (MAL A 3); the retainer of lost goods, more leniently (cf. HL 57–59, and 60–62). Mostly, it depended on the nature of the thing stolen:

(1) Free persons, i.e., kidnapping—death (CH 14) or a high ransom (HL 19B).

(2) *Res sacra* taken from a temple—death (CH 6; HL 126), but other temple or palace property—30-fold payment (CH 8).

(3) Animals—various multiples, depending on size (HL 59–65).

(4) Other items—various multiples or fixed sums (e.g., CH 254–55, 259–60; HL 121–28). Large sums might be in lieu of death (e.g., CH 256) or mutilation (CH 253; MAL A 5; HL 92), but the smaller sums may represent a simple debt, i.e., ransom of one's freedom.

Apart from simple theft, the cuneiform codes contain two scholarly problems. First, in the case of the owner versus the innocent purchaser of his stolen property, strict liability is imposed on the latter. He must return the goods and make a multiple payment. But the payment is lower than that for theft and probably represented a simple debt, which he could recoup from the thief if he found him (CH 9–12; HL 57–70). Second, in the case of the owner's killing an attempted burglar, if he is killed on the premises at night by the owner, there is no culpability for homicide (CE 12–13). If caught and brought to trial, he must make a very small payment—presumably a simple debt (CL 9; CE 12–13; HL 93).

b. In the Bible. Prov 6:30–31 say of the thief in general that he must pay sevenfold—all the wealth of his house. Elsewhere, the penalty varies according to the thing stolen:

(1) Kidnapping—death, for both the thief and "the one in whose possession he is found" (Exod 21:16).

(2) *Res sacra*—Jacob agrees to the death penalty for whoever is found with Laban's stolen idols (Gen 31:30–32), but this has also been explained as aggravated theft due to the element of hot pursuit (Daube 1947: 236–45).

(3) Bovines—fivefold payment; ovines—fourfold (Exod 21:37—Eng 22:1).

The theft laws of the Covenant Code (Exod 21:37–22:3—Eng 22:1–22:4), combine simple theft with the two scholarly problems. The original thief, identified by his having sold or slaughtered the stolen animal, pays a four- or fivefold penalty, probably ransom for his life. The attempted burglar may be killed with impunity at night but otherwise faces slavery unless he can pay a negotiated ransom. (Unlike the cuneiform counterparts, no limit is imposed.) The innocent purchaser pays only a twofold penalty, probably a simple debt. The innocent finder must pay the same (Exod 22:8—Eng 22:9).

The theft of Joseph's cup provides a rare example of Egyptian law in the Bible. Egyptian procedure allowed an accused to propose his own penalty as the consequences of his oath's (asserting his innocence) being false. The brothers declare that he with whom the cup is found shall die; but the Egyptian official deliberately misunderstands them, to prevent it from becoming Benjamin's death sentence (Gen 44:9–10).

6. Treason. A personal offense against the king, such as disloyalty expressed by deed or word (the latter often associated with blasphemy) is treason. The king was entitled to kill the traitor and confiscate his property (MAL B 3; cf. Wiseman 1953: No. 17). In a trial of conspirators against Rameses III of Egypt (*ANET,* 214–16), the penalties range through enforced suicide for the main protagonists, mutilation for subordinates, and a mere rebuke for an associate not directly involved.

In Exod 22:27—Eng 22:28 it is forbidden to curse a prince (cf. 2 Sam 16:5–10) or blaspheme, and in 1 Kgs 21:10–16 Naboth is executed for "blessing" (euphemism for cursing) God and king, and his vineyard confiscated by the king. Apparently, his sons were also executed (2 Kgs 9:26).

7. Against Parents. Striking one's father is punished according to CH 195 with the loss of a hand, and in Exod 21:15 (father or mother) with death, as is cursing them (Exod 21:17; Lev 20:9; cf. Deut 27:16). All these rules presuppose that the parents' right of discipline is not arbitrary, but subject to legal limits. For a son who is uncontrollably insubordinate and dissolute, the parents may turn to the local court, which can order his public stoning (Deut 21:18–21). In a less extreme case partial or whole disinheritance may have been the practice (Gen 49:3–4; cf. CH 168–69).

8. False Accusation. This act was considered ideal for application of the talionic principle. The accuser bears the very penalty he sought for the accused (CL 17; CH 1–4; cf. CU 26). The principle is applied in a Sumerian document from Nippur, where a son falsely accuses his father, a priest, of cultic offenses (Roth 1984: 9–14). Accusations (by a third party) of adultery are an exception: CU 11 imposes a payment of twenty shekels (MAL A 18), flogging, a payment, and castration.

In Deut 19:16–21 the talionic principle is explicit: "life for life, eye for eye . . . you shall do to him as he schemed to do to his brother." But where a husband accuses his wife of premarital unchastity (which carries the death penalty), his punishment is flogging, a payment, and a bar on divorce (Deut 22:13–19).

E. Offenses Against the Legal System

1. Abuse of Legal Authority. Extraordinary intervention by the ruler, usually on the basis of a petition, was required in cases of abuse since the offender was part of the system and the victim from the weaker strata of society. In the Hittite Instructions to the Border Guard Commander, the latter acts as an itinerant ombudsman for such complaints (*ANET,* 211). The penalty is within the king's discretion and may be death (CH 34). The Bible has two technical terms for such abuses: *gzl,* where property was taken from the victim (e.g., Gen 21:25; Ps 69:5), and *ʿšq,* where he is denied his legal due (Deut 24:14–15). The penalty can be compensation and/or death, at the king's discretion (2 Sam 12:1–6). If the culprit voluntarily confesses, he must restore the property plus a fifth and bring a guilt-offering for sacrifice (Lev 5:21–26). A Hebrew ostracon from the 7th century B.C. (*ANET,* 568) may represent a petition regarding abuse of authority.

2. Contempt of Court. This is punished in Deut 17:8–13 by death (cf. HL 173).

F. Methods of Punishment

1. In Cuneiform Sources. The means by which the death penalty is to be executed is usually not specified. In CH, drowning is mentioned several times (108; 129; 133; 143; 155), burning twice (110; 157) and impalement once (153). MAL has impalement in one case (A 53), while HL mentions single cases of dismemberment by oxteams (166) and beheading (173). No rationale can be discerned behind the choice of method.

Mutilation is often used as a "mirroring" punishment, e.g., severing the hand that strikes (CH 195), the lip that steals a kiss (MAL A 9), and castration of an adulterer (MAL A 15). Note also stinging by bees for stealing a hive (HL 92) and throwing the looter of a burning house into that fire (CH 25). Severing an ear is a characteristic method for punishing slaves (CH 205; HL 95).

The talionic principle is behind most cases of mutilation, where the same injury is inflicted as that which was suffered. A judgment of king Rim-Sin of Larsa applies it to the death penalty: "Because he threw the servant into the oven, do you throw the slave into the furnace" (*BIN* 7.10). Only MAL applies it to sexual violation (A 20, 55). As the talionic principle is usually a limit on revenge, there is no reason to suppose that it was not carried out in practice if no ransom was given. Flogging is used once in CH (202—sixty strokes) and frequently in MAL (between twenty and one hundred), where it is often cumulated with other punishments.

2. In the Bible. Where the Bible specifies the method of execution, the most common is stoning: for apostasy (Lev 20:2; Deut 13:11; 17:5), blasphemy (Lev 24:14, 16, 23; 1 Sam 21:10), sorcery (Lev 20:27), sabbath violation (Num 15:35–36), misappropriating *ḥrm* (Josh 7:25), disobedient son (Deut 21:21), and adultery by an inchoate wife (Deut 22:21, 24; cf. Ezek 16:40; 23:47). It has been suggested that the common element is treason against a superior (Finkelstein 1981: 26–29), but sabbath violation and sorcery fit this category with difficulty, and the male adulterer not at all. All but disobedience and adultery are public offenses. The Deuteronomist may have wished the latter to be so regarded also, but it is not clear why they should have been singled out. Stoning is carried out by the local community except for the Molech cult, where it is the duty of a body called *ʿam hāʾāreṣ* (Lev 20:2). For apostasy, the denouncers must initiate the stoning (Deut 13:10–11; 17:7).

Death is by fire for miscellaneous sexual offenses: incest with a woman and her mother (Lev 20:14), fornication by a priest's daughter (Lev 21:9), and Tamar's adultery (Gen 38:24–26). It is by the sword for an apostate city (Deut 13:15; cf. 1 Kgs 18:40) and is the preferred method of revenge for homicide (Num 35:9; cf. 2 Sam 3:27), for which impalement is also possible (2 Sam 21:9). Dismemberment and being devoured by beasts (Dan 2:5; 6:8) appear in a foreign setting.

Mutilation occurs as a "mirroring" punishment (Deut 25:11–12) and in application of the talionic principle (Lev 24:19–20), also of the corpse of an executed criminal (2 Sam 4:12). Flogging is prescribed once (Deut 22:18) but must have been common, as Deut 25:1–3 restricts it to forty strokes, without mention of a specific offense. For certain types of incest Leviticus imposes special punishments which may be divine rather than human. As punishment for intercourse with a sister (20:17), *karet* may refer to extirpation of the culprit's entire lineage (Wold 1979). Intercourse with an aunt by marriage or a sister-in-law makes the culprits *ʾryry,* usually interpreted as childless (20:19–21).

Hanging, imprisonment, and torture are not generally used as punishments in the ANE legal systems. Hanging is to expose the corpse after death by some other means (CH 21; Deut 21:22–3). Prison is for detention pending trial or for political reasons (e.g., Gen 40:1–22; Lev 24:12; Jer 32:2–3). Torture, such as flaying alive, was used by the Assyrians in warfare against recalcitrant vassals but not in a domestic context.

Of the penalties involving revenge, only death for murder appears to have been personally carried out by the avenger. MAL gives a husband the right to mutilate his wife but under the supervision of an official (A 58).

G. Summary and Conclusions

A crime was conceived of in the ANE as a wrong against a person or a god for which the victim was entitled to revenge. The role of the court was confined to setting a limit on human revenge and to forestalling divine revenge on the society by adopting appropriate measures against the culprit. To determine the proper limit on revenge was the foremost task of Mesopotamian jurisprudence, whose learning was received into the surrounding systems, including that of biblical Israel.

The modern conception of crime as a wrong against society which is to be suppressed by impersonal punishment is derived ultimately from the jurisprudence of classical Greece. In postbiblical rabbinic jurisprudence, where Mesopotamian science gave way to Greek, the adoption of this new conception led in turn to a radical reinterpretation of the biblical texts. The later biblical codes do foreshadow this development with their characterization of certain wrongs against the person also as polluting sins against God. But they are still anchored in the conceptions of the ANE.

Bibliography

Anbar, M. 1974. Le chatiment du crime de sacrilege d'après la Bible et un text hepatoscopique paleo-babylonien. *RA* 68: 172–73.
Bigger, S. F. 1979. The Family Laws of Leviticus 18 in Their Setting. *JBL* 98: 187–203.
Cardascia, G. 1971. Une Justice Infaillible. Vol. 6, pp. 419–31 in *Studi Voilterra*. Milan.
———. 1979. La place du talio dans l'histoire du droit pénal à la lumière des droits du Proche-Orient ancien. Pp. 169–83 in *Mélanges Dauvillier*. Toulouse.
———. 1985. Le caractere volontaire ou involontaire des atteintes corporelles dans les droits cuneiformes. Vol. 6, pp. 163–207 in *Studi Sanfilippo*. Milan.
Civil, M. 1965. New Sumerian Law Fragments. *AS* 16: 1–12.
Daube, D. 1947. *Studies in Biblical Law*. Cambridge.
———. 1986. The Old Testament Prohibitions of Homosexuality. *Zeitschrift der Savigny-Stiftung für Rechtsgeschichte* röm. Abt. 103: 447–48.
Finkelstein, J. J. 1966. Sex Offenses in Sumerian Laws. *JAOS* 86: 355–72.
———. 1981. The Ox That Gored. *TAPhS* 71: 5–47.
Frymer-Kensky, T. 1980. Tit for Tat. *BA* 43: 230–34.
———. 1983. Pollution, Purification and Purgation in Biblical Israel. Pp. 399–414 in *WLSGF*.
Geller, N. 1980. The Šurpu Incantations and Lev V 1–5. *JSS* 25: 181–92.
Greenberg, M. 1960. Some Postulates of Biblical Criminal Law. Pp. 5–28 in *Yehezkel Kaufmann Jubilee Volume*, ed. M. Haran. Jerusalem.
———. 1986. More Reflections on Biblical Criminal Law. Vol. 31, pp. 1–17 in *ScrHier*, ed. S. Japhet. Jerusalem.
Greengus, S. 1969. A Textbook Case of Adultery in Ancient Mesopotamia. *HUCA* 50: 33–44.
Hoffman, I. 1984. *Der Erlass Telipinus*. Heidelberg.
Hoffner, H. A., Jr. 1973. Incest, Sodomy and Bestiality in the Ancient Near East. Pp. 81–90 in *Orient and Occident*, ed. H. A. Hoffner, Jr. AOAT 22. Kevelaer and Neukirchen-Vluyn.
Jackson, B. 1972. *Theft in Early Jewish Law*. Oxford.
———. 1975. Reflections on Biblical Criminal Law. Pp. 25–63 in *Essays in Jewish and Comparative Legal History*. Leiden.
Jacobsen, T. 1970. An Ancient Mesopotamian Trial for Homicide. Pp. 193–213 in *Toward the Image of Tammuz*, ed. W. L. Moran. HSS 21. Cambridge, MA.
Kraus, F. R. 1960. Was ist der Codex Hammurabi? *Geneva* 8: 283–96.
Kwasman, T. 1988. *Neo-Assyrian Legal Documents in the Kouyunjik Collection of the British Museum*. Studia Pohl: Series Maior 14. Rome.
Loweenstamm, S. 1980. The Laws of Adultery and Murder in Biblical and Mesopotamian Law. Pp. 146–53 in *Comparative Studies in Biblical and Ancient Oriental Literatures*. AOAT 204. Kevelaer.
Lorton, D. 1977. Treatment of Criminals in Ancient Egypt. *JESHO* 20: 2–64.
Malamat, A. 1966. The Ban in Mari and the Bible. Pp. 40–49 in *Biblical Essays 1966*. Pretoria.
McKeating, H. 1975. The Development of Law on Homicide in Ancient Israel. *VT* 25: 46–68.
———. 1979. Sanctions against Adultery in Ancient Israelite Society. *JSOT* 11: 57–72.
Milgrom, J. 1976. *Cult and Conscience*. SJLA 18. Leiden.
Moran, W. L. 1959. The Scandal of the "Great Sin" at Ugarit. *JNES* 18: 280–81.
Paul, S. 1983. Daniel 3:29—A Case Study of "Neglected" Blasphemy. *JNES* 42: 291–94.
Petschow, H. P. H. 1973. Altorientalische Parallelen zur spatromischen calumnia. *Zeitschrift der Savigny-Stiftung für Rechtsgeschichte* röm Abt 79: 14–35.
Phillips, A. 1970. *Ancient Israel's Criminal Law*. Oxford.
———. 1977. Another Look at Murder. *JSS* 28: 105–26.
———. 1981. Another Look at Adultery. *JSOT* 20: 3–26.
Rabinowitz, J. J. 1959. The "Great Sin" in Ancient Egyptian Marriage Contracts. *JNES* 18: 73.
Reiner, E. 1958. *Šurpu*. AfO Beiheft 2. Graz.
Roth, M. 1984. A Reassessment of RA 71 (1977) 125ff. *AfO* 31: 9–14.
———. 1987. Homicide in the Neo-Assyrian Period. Pp. 351–65 in *Studies Presented to Erica Reiner*, ed. F. Rochberg-Halton. AOS 67. New Haven.
Weidner, E. F. 1932. Assyrische Beschreibungen de Kriegs-Reliefs Aššurbaniplis. *AfO* 8: 175–203.
Westbrook, R. 1985. Biblical and Cuneiform Law Codes. *RB* 92: 247–64.
———. 1986. Lextalionis and Exodus 21, 22–25. *RB* 93: 52–69.
———. 1988a. *Studies in Biblical and Cuneiform Law*. CahRB 26. Paris.
———. 1988b. The Nature of the Twelve Tablets. *Zeitschrift der Savigny-Stiftung für Rechtsgeschichte* röm Abt 105: 85–97.
Wiseman, D. J. 1953. *The Alalakh Tablets*. London.
Wold, D. 1979. The *Kareth* Penalty in P: Rationale and Cases. *SBLSP* 1: 1–46.
Yildiz, F. 1981. A Tablet of Codex Ur-Nammu from Sippar. *Or* 50: 87–97.

RAYMOND WESTBROOK

PUNITES [Heb *pûnî*]. Clan descended from Puvah, who was a son of Issachar (Num 26:23). The term "Punites" is a gentilic adjective derived from the name "Puvah" used with the article as a collective name. The Sam. Pent., LXX, Syr, and Vg preserve different spellings of these names, which transliterated would be Puah and Puites. While these readings provide a closer correspondence between the names than Puvah and Punites of the MT, this does not mean that they are earlier or better readings (Barthélemy et al. 1979: 253).

Bibliography

Barthélemy, D. et al. 1979. *Pentateuch*. Vol 1 of *Preliminary and Interim Report on the Hebrew Old Testament Project*. Rev. ed. New York.

STEPHEN A. REED

PUNON (PLACE) [Heb *pûnōn*]. A place in the Wadi ʿArabah (Num 33:42–43). The place is generally identified with Gk *Phainô*, the present *Faynân*, the center of copper mining and smelting activities in the Chalcolithic period, the EB Age, the Iron Age, and the late Roman and early Byzantine periods, as well as an Edomite (7th–5th centuries B.C.) and Roman-Byzantine town See also FEINAN, WADI.

Punon is primarily not the name of a settlement, but the name of a district. The name can be interpreted by Arabic *faynân,* "to have long, beautiful hair." Like "Sëir" (literally: "the hairy one"), Feinan refers to a region according to its vegetation: trees, grass, and reed. Typologically, the name may go back as far as to the 4th or 3d millennia B.C. (Knauf 1987). "Punon" derives from **Pônôn* (by dissimilation of the first *ô*), which in turn derives from **Pânân* (by the common "Canaanite" shift *â* > *ô*), which can be regarded as a dialectical variant of **Paynân.* Punon is not a scribal error for Pinon (Gen 36:41; 1 Chr 1:52; and a variant reading in Num 33:42–43; cf. Weippert 1971: 433–434); as early as in the 13th century B.C. Rameses II mentions *pwnw* (that is, **Pûnô* or **Pônô;* cf. for the loss of the final *n* the Gk name *Phainô*) as one of the regions inhabited by Shasu, "nomads" (Görg 1982).

The itinerary through the Wadi ʿArabah, on which Num 33:36–43 is based, may derive from the Persian period (Knauf 1988: 54). In analogy to the Edomite occupation at Buṣeirah, Ṭawîlân, and Tell el-Kheleifeh (Parr 1988: 49), the Edomite settlement at Feinan could have extended into the 5th century B.C.

Bibliography

Görg, M. 1982. Punon—ein weiterer Distrikt der Š3św-Beduinen? *BN* 19: 15–21.

Knauf, E. A. 1987. Supplementa Ismaelitica 9. Phinon—Feinan und das westarabische Ortsnamenkontinuum. *BN* 36: 37–50.

———. 1988. *Midian.* ADPV. Wiesbaden.

Parr, P. J. 1988. Aspects of the Archaeology of North-West Arabia in the First Millennium B.C. Pp. 39–66 in *L'Arabie préislamique et son environnement historique et culturel,* ed. T. Fahd. Leiden.

Weippert, M. 1971. Edom: Studien und Materialien zur Geschichte der Edomiter auf Grund schriftlicher und archäologischer Quellen. Ph.D. diss., University of Tübingen.

ERNST AXEL KNAUF

PURAH (PERSON) [Heb *purâ*]. Servant (Heb *naʿar,* "boy, lad") of Gideon who went with Gideon to spy on the Midianite camp (Judg 7:10–11). His function was probably that of shield and weapon bearer (cf. Judg 9:54; 1 Sam 14:1, 6; Boling *Judges* AB, 146). The meaning of his name is not certain. One suggestion is that it is related to the Ar *furrun,* "to be better, imposing." Another is that it is simply defectively written (i.e., the vowel letter omitted) for *pûrâ,* "winepress trough" (*HALAT,* 908). The LXX and Josephus vocalize the name as Gk *Phara,* with an *a* and not a *u,* possibly indicating the Heb root *prh,* "to be fruitful."

KIRK E. LOWERY

PURIM [Heb *pûrîm*]. See ESTHER, BOOK OF.

PURPLE. The Hebrew and Greek terms underlying the rendering "purple" refer to hues ranging from red to dark purple. Because of this color range and a variety of blending and other techniques involved in the production of "purple" dye, it is necessary to take account of such related renderings as "crimson" (Isa 1:18) and "scarlet." Since it is impossible to attain certainty as to the precise hue that an ancient author had in mind in a particular text, any color specifications here made are merely proximate.

The Hebrew words translated as "purple" in the RSV are *ʾargāmān* (cognate to Aram *ʾargwān* [Dan 5:7, 16, 29; 2 Chr 2:6—Eng 2:7]), *tôlaʿ* (only Lam 4:5; "crimson," Isa 1:18), and *tĕkēlet* (only Ezek 23:6; "blue" [fabric], 2 Chr 2:6—Eng 2:7, 14; 3:14). The RSV reserves the translation equivalent "scarlet" for Heb *šānî* and "scarlet stuff" for the phrase *tôlaʿat šānî* (Exod 25:4, etc.; note Num 4:8, "scarlet").

The word *ʾargāmān* is common to Northwest Semitic (Aram *ʾargwān,* Ug *ʾarmn*) and East Semitic (Akk *argamannu*), and Heb *tŭkēlet* is cognate to Akk *takiltu,* frequently (with *tabarru*) designating blue-purple or violet-blue wool. The Greek equivalent of *ʾargāmān* is *porphyra* (Lat *purpura,* hence "purple"); the equivalents of *tĕkēlet* are *hyakinthos, hyakinthinos* (*phoinikoun* at Isa 1:18); the phrase *tôlaʿat šānî* is rendered by Gk *kokkinon.*

The sources of "purple" dyes included especially marine snails of the class Gastropoda, from which was extracted a rich pigment corresponding generally to Heb *ʾargāmān* (a red purple) and *tĕkēlet* (a violet purple). From the dried bodies of females of the scale insect called the kermes (*Kermes illicis*) was extracted kermesic acid, a bright red dye (cf. Heb *tôlaʿ,* "worm"). See also ZOOLOGY.

Rubia tinctorum, an herbaceous perennial, was the source of a cheaper imitation dye known as madder that found frequent use in Egypt and in the classical world (cf. Pliny *HN* 24.4; Dioskourides 4.46; Strabo 13.4.14 [630], described as competitor with kermes and sea purple; 12.8.16 [578], with special reference to the raven black hue of Laodicean and Colossian wool; Vitruvius 7.14.1–2). Other vegetable dyes in the red-purple color range included henna, alkanet, archil (orseille or litmus), and "dragon's blood" (which was derived from the rattan palm), woad, and indigo.

Displaying nuances of shade from blood red to blue black, with exposure to the sun a principal factor in alteration of the "primitive" hue, the most highly prized was sea purple, extracted from various genera and species of carnivorous marine snails, including *Murex brandaris* (Pliny: "pelagia," common at Tyre), which produced a deep blue violet, isolated by Friedländer (1909) as dibromindigo; *Murex trunculus* (Pliny: "purpura"; a shell common to the Mediterranean region), which supplied a scarlet red; *Helix ianthina,* productive of a violet dye; and *Purpura lapillus.* In Tarentum, Sicily, a hill called Monte Testaccio is composed of brandaris and trunculus shells. Dye produced from the *Murex brandaris* was colorfast and permitted washing of garments; Cicero (*Flac.* 29[70]), snidely notes that Decianus could look the peak of fashion with but one set of garments. Various shades were secured through blending and other processes, many of the details of which belong to the undivulged secrets of the ancient world; but some conception of resources used by imitators for production of cheaper grades can be derived from later recipes that are associated with Bolus of Mendes in the Leyden and Stockholm papyri (see Rostovtzeff 1953: 1225–26 and Ploss 1962: 37–39). The startling alterations in color that took place in dyeing processes induced alchemists to search for mutations in metals, a quest that led to forgeries under the name of Demokritos. That the ancient dyers did not gather the various species haphazardly is confirmed by the fact that numerous shell heaps can be identified in terms of a specific type of murex. Garments dyed with sea purple were termed *conchyliatae vestes* in Rome. Martial sarcastically alludes to a lingering odor in the dyed clothing of one of his targets (*Epigrams* 1.49.32; 2.16.3).

Nuzi texts indicate that purple dye (Akk *kinahhu*) was processed as early as 1500 B.C.E. So prized was sea purple dye for its commercial value that the Hebrew term *ʾargāmān* acquired the sense of "tribute" in both Ugaritic and Hittite. Hittite sources reveal that such payment was made in the form of purple garments for the king, queen, crown prince, and ministers of the court.

The Greek word *phoenix* (red purple) is perhaps cognate with the name Phoenicia. Massive accumulations of shells of the purple-producing murex have been found in the neighborhood of Tyre. The prestige of Tyre in production of the dye was noted by the grammarian Pollux (1.45), who relates a Tyrian legend about its discovery by Heracles. Pliny (*HN* 5.76) and Strabo (16.2.23) report on the city's prestigious reputation for the production of purple. According to 2 Chr 2:3, 7 Solomon asked Huram, king of Tyre, to send skilled workers in purple. An amazing statement in Ezek 27:7 suggests that Tyre had competitors in the purple-textile industry whose wares even graced some of her ships (cf. v 16), and Pausanias (3.21.6) reports that after the Phoenician the best shellfish for purple dye were to be found on the coast of Laconia: at Bulis half of the inhabitants, he states (10.37.3), were involved in the production of purple dye. There is no convincing evidence that purple was a status symbol in Egypt prior to the Greco-Roman period, when its use became widespread during the reign of Ptolemy Philadelphus (283–246).

Apart from its brilliance when exposed to the sun, sea purple was highly prized for its colorfastness; and among the favored hues developed by dyers was the Tyrian shade of congealed blood (Homer's "blood of purple hue"), which at first sight appeared to be black but glistened in the light. According to Pliny the Elder, the most expensive quality of purple garment was Tyrian *dibapha*, "double-dipped," which at one time cost 1000 denarii a pound (*HN* 9.137), apparently not an unreasonable sum; for it is estimated that 12,000 *Murex brandaris* would have been needed to produce 1.4 grams of crude dye (Friedländer 1909: 765–70, but details on probable shortcuts in the ancient technology are lacking). Martial (*Epigrams* 8.10) writes about a Tyrian cloak that sold for 10,000 sesterces. But the *amethystina* grade vied with Tyre's *dibapha* (cf. Martial *Epigrams* 2.57.2). In Aurelian's time the highest quality of purple dye was termed *blatta*, "oxblood." People of average means had to be content with imitations that were made from dyes derived from a variety of animals, minerals, or vegetables. From the text of Acts 16:14 it is not possible to determine that Lydia limited her sale to luxury items or to a specific clientele.

The prestige value of purple garments predates the Exodus. Ugaritic texts point to its importance in international relations as early as the 14th century. In the *Iliad* (8.221) Homer depicts Agamemnon in a purple cloak, and Hector's ashes are deposited in an urn that is covered with purple garments (24.796). According to the *Odyssey* (8.84), Penelope gave her husband a purple cloak when he left for Troy. The writer of Judges (8:26) assumes that the kings of Midian must have worn purple. Ezek 23:6 and 27:24 describe Assyrian governors and commanders as clothed in purple for their military operations. King Solomon's palanquin had a cushion of purple (Cant 3:10). King Belshazzar, frightened by a moving hand writing on his palace wall, promised to clothe in purple and at the same time to put third in command of the empire any one of his wise men who could read and interpret the writing (Dan 5:7). When Xerxes made Mordecai a courtier, he clothed him in purple (Esth 8:15 [LXX]; cf. 1 Macc 10:20, 62, 64; 11:57, of Jonathan's recognition by Alexander Balas, later Antiochus VI; and 14:41–44, of Simon honored by King Demetrius and the Jewish people). Plutarch records that the urn which contained the ashes of Demetrius the Great was "resplendent in its shroud of royal purple" (*Demetrios* 52.2). And Hellenistic monarchs followed the Persian and Macedonian practice of retaining an entourage of advisers whom they honored with distinctive purple garb. Livy appears to echo the custom in his use of the term *purpurati*, "wearers of purple" (see, e.g., 30.42.6). Josephus (*Ant* 14.173) notes that in 47 B.C. Herod wore purple.

Loss of status could be symbolized by stripping a disgraced person, such as Andronicus, one of King Antiochus' nobles (2 Macc 4.38), of his purple robe. Luke's story about the rich man and beggar Lazarus (16:19–31) contains the revealing touch that the former wore purple, and the evangelist dramatizes his loss of status by celebrating the ascent of Lazarus. On the other hand, soldiers make a mockery of Jesus' status by dressing him in purple (Mark 15:17; John 19:2; for which Matt 27:28 uses the term *kokkinē* [*chlamys*], suggesting a cheaper garment).

The popularity of purple extended far beyond royal courts. If the Masoretic Text is to be followed at Prov 13:21, a woman prized for virtue and wisdom clothes her entire household in purple. The Persian custom of wearing purple invaded Greece to such an extent that even philosophers such as Empedocles and the Sophists Hippias of Elis and Gorgias of Leontini adopted purple dress (Aelian, *VH* 12.32; Apuleius, *Flor.* 9). But it remained for Alexander to give the color "worldwide currency as a status symbol" (Reinhold 1970). Plutarch (*Eumenes* 8.7) relates that Alexander's secretary, Eumenes of Cardia, distributed purple felt hats and cloaks to his Macedonian bodyguard. Diogenes Laertius (8.47) reports that a long-haired boxer named Pythagoras wore a garment dyed "sea purple." In Italy the use of purple developed to such an extent from the 3d century on that it became available on the open market (cf. *P. Cairo Zenon* 59069.8.20; 59630.3; 59696.4, in reference to scarlet ribbons, *kokkinai tainiai;* somewhat later, *P. Tebt.* 112, cols. 6–13, 112 B.C.E.; 117.38–39, 99 B.C.E.; 120.3–4, in reference to two veils, *porphyroun* and *kokkinon,* 97 or 64 B.C.E.). A major factor in its spread was the repeal—over Cato's objections—in 195 B.C.E. of the Oppian Law, whose provisions included restriction of the use of purple (Livy 34.1–8). Inexpensive mineral and vegetable dyes (see, e.g., Pliny *HN* 16.77), contributed to the popularity of the color purple. From the time of Cicero, beginning with his *Sest.* (57), reference is occasionally made to "royal purple," but there is no imitation that the use of the color was restricted to royal personages, although Nero limited sale of the two highest grades, *amethystina* and *Tyria* (Suet. *Ner.* 32.3).

As a badge of wealth and luxury spending (cf. Prov 31:22) and because of its association in the popular consciousness with tyranny and decadence, purple became the target of social criticism that crossed centuries and cultures. The comic poet Anaxandrides thought King Cotys' spreading of purple rugs in the Thracian capital for his daughter's wedding was a ridiculous luxury (Athenaios 4.131a). Cicero pilloried Verres for his extravagance in the use of purple (*Verr.* 2.2.72.716; 2.5.31.86, 137; 4.26.59). Lucretius referred to purple and gold in his assault on growing ambition for power and wealth (2.20–36, 51–52, 501 [of Meliboian purple from the coast of Thessaly]; 5.1423–29, 14.27–29; cf. Verg. *G.* 2.495). Affecting simplicity, Horace renounced the wearing of purple (*Carm.* 1.35.12; 2.18.8; 3.1.42). In numerous diatribes against conspicuous consumption by the rich and famous, Seneca decries the wearing of purple, the *color improbus* (see, e.g., *Ep.* 16.8; 76.31; 94.70; cf. Martial *Epigrams* 12.63.4–5; 14.133, 154). Similar garb is attributed in Rev 17:4 to the "great whore" (the ironical point being made that according to Roman law she ought to be wearing a toga, cf. Martial 2.39) and the "great city" (18:16), apparently in contrast to the white garments that are characteristic of God's people. It is of further interest that the whore sits on a "scarlet" beast (17:3). Plutarch (*Lykourgos* 13 = *Mor.* 997d) reminds his public that in the time of Lykourgos Sparta forbade the use of purple. From time to time politicians felt the public pulse. Polybius (10.26.1) observes that Philip of Macedon recognized the hazard in distancing himself from the populace through such apparel, and on a return to Argos after celebrating the Nemean games he laid it aside to "show that he did not consider himself better than the people." In related vein, Judas Maccabeus learned that the Roman Senate, 320 in number, disdained the wearing of purple (1 Macc 8:14–15). Threatened by mutiny of his mercenary troops, Agathocles, the tyrant of Syracuse, doffed his purple and went about garbed as an ordinary citizen (Diodoros of Sicily 20.34.3). But resistance waned in the public domain. So rampant was the desire for the color purple in the 2d century C.E. that people dreamed about purple (cf. Artem. *Oneirokritika* 1.77; 2.3.) Christian leaders joined Greco-Roman social critics in condemnation of enervating luxury. Clement of Alexandria (*Paidagogos* 2.10.108–9, 114–15), in apparent echo of Cicero's tirades in the Verrine Orations, castigated both men and women for their craze for purple robes and veils.

Apart from association of purple with tyranny, Aeschylus' censure of the conqueror of Troy for walking on a carpet dyed sea purple (*Ag.* 946; cf. 910, 957) relates to Agamemnon's guilt of hybris, whereby he invites his own doom. Alexander apparently took heed after his capture of Tyre, for he amazed Darius of Persia by appearing at the time only in white.

Ugaritic texts include the first extant reference to the use of purple in religious ceremony. In Greece, Sappho (66.8–9; 82.8; 87) views gifts of purple garments as a fitting tribute to deities. Artemis Brauronia was the recipient of a variety of such gifts dedicated by women after childbirth (see, e.g., *IG* II^2 1514–18, 1521–25). Purple was featured in Israel's tabernacle (Exod 26:1, 31, 36; 27:16; 36:8). Images of foreign deities were frequently adorned with purple (Jer 10:9). In the *Epistle of Jeremiah* (v 71) idols are satirized for their wearing of rotting purple. Purple was prescribed for the liturgical vestments of Israel's priests (Exod 28:5–8; 39:1–5). The use of purple in sacerdotal garments during the post-Alexander period is documented by Plutarch (*Aratus* 53.4) and Athenaios (7.289c). Concerning a priest of Kybele named Bittaches, from Pessinus in Asia Minor, we are told that he came to Rome about 103 B.C.E. in a bizarre costume of many colors (Diodoros of Sicily 36.13; Plutarch *Marius* (17.5). According to the Dead Sea *War Scroll* (10M 7.10–11), purple was one of the colors in the liturgical battle garb of priests.

Bibliography

Astour, M. C. 1965. The Origin of the Terms Canaan, Phoenician, and Purple. *JNES* 24: 346–50.

Besnier, M. 1877–1919. Purpura. *Dictionnaire des Antiquités Grecques et Romaines* 4: 769–78.

Born, W. 1937a. Purpura Shell-Fish. *Ciba Review* 4: 106–10.

———. 1937b. Purpura in Classical Antiquity. *Ciba Review* 4: 111–18.

Dalman, G. 1937. *Arbeit und Sitte in Palästina.* Pt. 5. Gütersloh.

Dedekind, A. 1898. *Ein Beitrag zur Purpurkunde.* Berlin.

Diels, H. 1920. *Antike Technik.* 2d ed. Tübingen.

Forbes, R. J. 1956. *Studies in Ancient Technology.* Vol. 4. Leiden.

Friedländer, P. 1907. Zur Kenntnis des Farbstoffs des antiken Purpurs aus Murex brandaris. *Monatschrift für Chemie* 28: 991–96.

———. 1909. Über den Farbstoff des antiken Purpurs aus Murex brandaris. *Berichte der deutschen chemischen Gesellschaft* 42: 765–70.

Gallavotti, C. 1939–42. Tre Papiri Fiorentini. *Revista di Filologia,* n.s., 17 (67): 252–60.

Goetze, A. 1956. The Inventory I BoT I 31. *JCS* 10/1: 32–36.

Gradwohl, R. 1963. *Die Farben im Alten Testament.* BZAW 83. Berlin.

Jensen, L. B. 1963. Royal Purple of Tyre. *JNES* 22: 104–18.

Lagercrantz, O., ed. 1913. *Papyrus Holmiensis: Rezepte für Silber, Steine, und Purpur.* Uppsala.

Landsberger, B. 1967. Über Farben im Sumerisch-Akkadischen. *JCS* 21: 139–73.

Leemanns, C., ed. 1885. *Papyri graeci Musei Lugduni-Batavi.* Leiden.

Perkin, A., and Everest, A. 1918. *The Natural Organic Coloring Matters.* London.

Ploss, E. 1962. *Ein Buch von alten Farben.* Heidelberg.

Reinhold, M. 1970. *History of Purple As a Status Symbol in Antiquity.* Collection Latomus 116. Brussels.

Rosa, M. 1786. *Delle porpore e delle materie vestiare presso gli entichi.* Modena.

Rostovtzeff, M. 1953. *The Social and Economic History of the Hellenistic World.* Vol. 2. Oxford.

Rupe, H. 1909. *Die Chemie der natürlichen Frabstoffe.* Pt. 2. Braunschweig.

Schaefer, G. 1941. The Cultivation of Madder. *Ciba Review* 39: 1398–1406.

Schmidt, W. 1842. *Die Griechischen Papyrusurkunden der königlichen Bibliothek zur Berlin.* Berlin.

Schneider, K. 1959. Purpura. *PW* 23/2: 2000–20.

Schunck, E. 1879. Notes on the Purple of the Ancients. *Journal of the Chemical Society* 35: 589–95.

Thureau-Dangin, F. 1934. Un comptoir de laine pourpre a Ugarit. *Syria* 15: 137–46.

Zimmern, H. 1915. *Akkadische Fremdwörter*. Leipzig.

FREDERICK W. DANKER

PUT (PERSON) [Heb *pûṭ*]. According to the genealogies in the Table of Nations (Gen 10:6) and 1 Chr 1:8, Put is the third son of Ham, son of Noah, and brother of Cush (Ethiopia), Mizraim (Egypt), and Canaan. He is the only one of these people without a record of the next generation in these genealogies. Five additional verses refer to Put, being the descendants of Noah's grandson. In each case, they are identified as warriors. Three times they are allies or supporters of Egypt, along with Cush and Lud in North Africa (Jer 46:9), and also Arabia, Cub, and Israel itself ("sons of the land of the covenant"; Ezek 30:5). Nah 3:8 points back to the conquest of Thebes in 668 B.C. This took place, in spite of the combined power of Ethiopia and Egypt, with the support of the men from Libya and Put. Put's soldiers also aided Tyre (Ezek 27:10) and Gog (38:5) but always in vain. The evidence of soldiers from Put in so many armies could indicate that the nation was a well-known source of mercenaries.

The identification of Put is debated. Somalia, Eg *pun.t,* has been suggested (see Westermann 1984: 511; Simons *GTTOT,* 75). The LXX and Vg of the Ezekiel passages, as well as Jer 46:9 (26:9 in the LXX), read Put as Libya. This corresponds to the Old Persian *putiya,* Babylonian *puṭa,* which in Eg was *Tꜣ Ṯmḥw,* Libya (*NBD,* 1003). This identification could cause difficulties in Nah 3:8 if that verse is read as listing two separate peoples, Put and Lub (Libya). Simons suggested that since Cush (Ethiopia) and Mizraim (Egypt) refer to the same people at this period, with Ethiopia dominating Egypt during the 25th Dyn. (ca. 716–664 B.C.), Put and Lub could also be identified. This is grammatically possible since each of the toponymic pairs is joined by the Heb conjunction "and," which can have an explicative function. This is not rare in the OT and would lead to a translation of "i.e." or "that is" (Baker 1980), which would solve the problem in Nahum.

Bibliography

Baker, D. W. 1980. Further Examples of the *Waw Explicativum*. *VT* 30: 129–36.

Westermann, C. 1984. *Genesis 1–11*. Trans. J. J. Scullion. Minneapolis.

DAVID W. BAKER

PUTEOLI (PLACE) [Gk *Potioloi*]. A city visited by Paul on his journey to Rome (Acts 28:13). Puteoli (modern Pozzuoli; 40°49′ N; 14°07′ E) was a port city of ancient Campania on the W coast of Italy located on the N shore of the Gulf of Naples. Puteoli was ringed by a series of volcanic hills, and the name of the city, meaning "sulfur springs," is derived from this geological situation. The volcanic dust (called *pozzolana* in modern Italian), which contributed to the sulfurous atmosphere, produced a cement that resisted seawater when mixed with lime.

The earliest Greek settlement in the W seas was established sometime before the middle of the 8th century on the island of Pithecusae, just N of the Bay of Naples. Pottery confirms that the first colonists were from Chalcis and Eretria. It was not long before many of the settlers moved to a site on an acropolis on the opposite mainland where a native population had been importing Greek pottery. This new foundation was named Cumae after a city of the same name located on the E coast of Euboea. Although the Italian Cumae was a stronghold, the city had no harbor. Ships had to be hauled onto the sand below the acropolis. When trade began to prosper, the citizens of Cumae occupied the harbor just inside the promontory, establishing the town of Dicaearchia (later known as Puteoli) and, farther E, Naples (Strabo 5.4.5f.).

Puteoli was conquered by the Samnites in 421 B.C.E., but there is a paucity of evidence until Campania came under Roman control in ca. 334 B.C.E. The Romans garrisoned the town in 215 B.C.E. and renamed it Puteoli. The following year the Romans defeated Hannibal at Puteoli (Livy 24.7.10–12; 12.1–13.7). In 199 B.C.E. Puteoli received a Roman customs station and was made a Roman maritime colony in 194 B.C.E. Sulla or Augustus may have conferred further colonial status on Puteoli, and Nero and Vespasian certainly did so. Vespasian substantially enlarged the city's territory.

Trade flourished in Puteoli under the Romans, enhanced by a newly fortified harbor and connected with Rome by a series of roads (discussed below). The harbor was protected by a breakwater, the Augustan opus pilarum (115–16 m × 372 m), which carried 15 enormous masonry piers, with at least one triumphal arch, columns topped by statues, a lighthouse, and an architectural ship's prow at the end (Strabo 5.4.6). The remains are embedded in the modern breakwater. The emporium stretched for 1.25 miles along the shore to the W of the mole.

Puteoli was naturally divided into an upper and lower city. Among the remains in the lower city are the great macellum, formerly known as the temple (or baths) of Serapis, and the temple of Augustus. Other monuments of the lower town are depicted on glass vases and engravings produced in Puteoli. The upper town was residential and recreational. A small Augustan amphitheater and a great Flavian amphitheater were situated in upper Puteoli. The Flavian complex was the third largest amphitheater in Italy seating as many as 60,000 spectators. It was constructed at the expense of the citizens of Puteoli during the reign of Vespasian. The baths of Trajan (or Janus), which may have been the same complex as the so-called temple of Neptune (or Diana), were also situated in upper Puteoli. The city was plundered to supply building materials for the cathedrals of Salerno and Pisa.

Oriental goods from Egypt and Palestine and most importantly grain from Egypt were imported through Puteoli (Suetonius *Aug.* 98.1–10; Strabo 17.1.7; Seneca *Epistulae morales* 77.1f.). Export trade included oil, fine wine, glassware, early imperial terra sigillata, and probably Republican black (Campanian) pottery. Alexandria's close trade connections with Puteoli began at the end of the Second Punic War (201 B.C.E.) and lasted until the city's prominence was eclipsed in the 2d and 3d centuries C.E.

Puteoli's population of 65,000 was entrepreneurial and

highly cosmopolitan. A number of oriental cults were found in the city including those of Serapis (105 B.C.E.), Cybele, Jupiter Dolichenus, Bellona, Dusares, I. O. M. Heliopolitanus, in addition to the usual Greco-Roman and imperial worship. Puteoli was also one of the earliest Italian cities to have a sizable Jewish population (Josephus *Ant* 17.328; 18.160; *CIL* 10.1893; 10.1971). There is also an intriguing tombstone of a Puteolian Jewish freedman named Acibas, who was an agent for his master's iron mines and vineyards (*CIL* 10.1931; *CII* 1.75).

There is epigraphical evidence for trade connections between the Greeks of Palestine and Puteoli (*CIL* 10.1746). Jewish merchants were also organized in a closely knit Mediterranean trade cooperative in which Jews from Puteoli and Alexandria played an integral role (cf. *3 Macc.* 3:10). After the battle of Pydna and the decline of Rhodes (167 B.C.E.) a triangular trade developed between Alexandria, Delos, and Puteoli. The extent to which Jewish merchants were involved, specifically in the Alexandrian grain trade, cannot be determined, despite the allegations of Josephus (*AgAp* 2.64). There is evidence, however, that the Jewish alabarchs of Alexandria held credits in Puteoli during the reign of Tiberius (see Josephus *Ant* 18.159–60 for the incident between Agrippa I and the Alexandrian alabarch Alexander).

Sometime after Herod's death, a charlatan called Alexander appeared and deceived Jewish inhabitants of Crete and Puteoli of considerable funds. The imposter claimed to be the son of Herod and Mariamme the Hasmonean in order to finance his trip to Italy (Josephus *Ant* 17.327–28; *JW* 2.103–4). In 39/40 C.E. the Jewish-Alexandrian delegation led by Philo met with Gaius (Caligula) in Puteoli about injustices they suffered in Egypt. It was in Puteoli that the delegation first learned of Gaius' command that a statue of himself was to be placed in the temple in Jerusalem (see Philo *Gaium* 184–348; Josephus *Ant* 18.261–309; and *JW* 2.184–203).

Commerce and travelers went from Puteoli to Naples and then to Capua, where the Via Appia (built ca. 312 B.C.E.) led to Rome, 132 miles away. The Via Latina was a heavily traveled alternative route which went from Casilinum (just outside Capua) to Rome. In order to ease the difficulties of travel on the pre-Sullan road between Puteoli and Naples, the Crypta Neapolitana, a tunnel 750 m in length, was constructed (see Seneca *Ep. Luc.* 57.1–2) and improved by Nerva and Trajan. Nero attempted to join Puteoli with the Tiber by means of a canal. In 95 C.E. Domitian constructed the Via Domitiana, a less costly alternative, which went along the Campanian coast from Puteoli to Sinuessa (modern Mondragone), where it joined the Via Appia.

When Paul's ship landed in Puteoli, he found Christians (probably Jewish converts) living in the city. He stayed with the converts seven days before journeying to Rome by way of Capua and the Via Appia (Acts 28:13–14). A similar journey to Rome is described in the apocryphal *Acts of Peter* 6 and seems to be implied in the *Acts of Paul*.

Although Claudius installed the port at Ostia, Puteoli continued to prosper through the 2d century C.E., followed by a gradual decline until the town was abandoned in the 6th century C.E. Puteoli, like other cities on the Bay of Naples, continued to be a favorite resort area; and the wealth is evident in the magnificence of the columbria, hypogea, and mausoleums in the region. In Christian times some tombs were reused for inhumations. Many of the villas in the region can still be seen, although some are now covered by the sea. Cicero had a villa in this region, as did Nero's mother, Agrippina the younger (see Tacitus *Ann.* 14.5; Seneca *Octavia*).

SCOTT T. CARROLL

PUTHITE [Heb *pûtî*]. One of four families from Kiriath-jearim located on Judah's N border with Benjamin and Dan (1 Chr 2:53). This clan within the tribe of Judah is connected with Shobal, Hur, and Caleb. Shobal is credited with the formation of Kiriath-jearim, earlier called Kiriath-baal (Josh 15:60; 18:14). That the genealogy in 1 Chr 2:50–55 was associated with Ephrathah and the district to the N and SW is clear from the place names mentioned. The three regions connected with the sons of Hur were Kiriath-jearim, Bethlehem, and Beth-gader, plus the surrounding areas, some of which cannot be identified (Myers *1 Chronicles* AB, 16). At least vv 53–55 probably derive from a pre-Chronistic source (Braun *1 Chronicles* WBC, 38, 42). Although a pair of David's mighty men belonged to the Ithrite family (2 Sam 23:38 = 1 Chr 11:40), there exists no further information about the Puthites or for that matter about the other two groups, the Mishraites and the Shumathites. The collective noun *pûtî* is a gentilic form of **pût*.

EDWIN C. HOSTETTER

PUTI-EL (PERSON) [Heb *pûṭîʾēl*]. The father-in-law of Aaron's son Eleazar; hence also the maternal grandfather of Phinehas (Exod 6:25). Earlier scholars tended to connect the name with Syr *pûṭ*, "to scorn or deride." In such a case Puti-el would mean "scorned by God." Most moderns, however, consider it to have originated from Egyptian. Foreign names are attested for Israelites more than once in the OT. One finds, for example, the series of Egyptian names among members of the tribe of Levi. The associated *pwṭyʾl* would be a hybrid form (Noth, *IPN*, 63), built on a pair of Egyptian words (pꜣ dy) plus the Hebrew *ʾel*. One may compare the names Poti-phar and Potiphera and their Egyptian equivalent *pꜣ-dy-pꜣ-Rʿ*, "the one whom Re has given" (Ranke 1935–77: 1.123; cf. Kornfeld 1978: 87–89). "Puti-el" would then signify "the one whom El has given." Since *pûṭ*, "scorn," does not appear elsewhere in Hebrew, and since many names in the Exodus account show Egyptian influence, the Egyptian etymology seems more likely.

Bibliography

Kornfeld, W. 1978. *Onomastica Aramaica aus Ägypten.* SÖAW 333. Vienna.

Ranke, H. 1935–77. *Die ägyptischen Personennamen.* 3 vols. Glückstadt.

EDWIN C. HOSTETTER

PUVAH (PERSON) [Heb *pūwwâ*]. Var. PUAH. PUNITES. The second of the four sons of Issachar (Gen 46:13). Puvah was the grandson of Jacob and Leah, and his name was included in the list of the seventy people who descended with Jacob and his family to Egypt (Gen 46:8–27). According to the second census list mentioned in the book of Numbers, Puvah became the eponymous ancestor of the Punites, one of the clans of Issachar (Num 26:23). However, at this point the Versions depart from the MT. The Sam. Pent., the LXX (Num 26:19 in the LXX), and other versions identify him as Puah (Heb *puʾâ*) and indicate that he became the ancestor of the Punites. In the genealogical list of the descendants of Issachar available to the Chronicler, which was based on the material found in Numbers 26, his name is also listed as Puah (1 Chr 7:1).

CLAUDE F. MARIOTTINI

PYRRHUS (PERSON) [Gk *Pyrros*]. The father of Sopater, who, according to Acts, was a companion of Paul on his final journey to Jerusalem (Acts 20:4).

The name is derived from the Greek word for fire *(pyr)* and means "fiery red." It is not found in some mss, and this led Ropes (1926: 191) to conjecture that it had arisen from a repetition with alteration of *patros* at the end of Sopater's name. Its deletion gives the mention of Sopater a certain symmetry with the other names in the list of Paul's companions, but the weight of textual evidence is for its inclusion.

The mention of personal names and family relationships probably reflects local or personal interest in these people at some stage in the development of a tradition (cf. Mark 15:21). But since this list is pre-Lukan, it cannot be assumed that these people were known by either the final author of Acts or his readers. See also SOPATER.

Bibliography

Ropes, J. H. 1926. *The Text of Acts.* Vol. 3 of *The Beginnings of Christianity,* ed. F. J. Foakes Jackson and K. Lake. London. Repr. 1979, Grand Rapids.

THOMAS W. MARTIN

PYTHAGOREANISM. A philosophical and religious movement founded by Pythagoras of Samos in S Italy in the last quarter of the 6th century B.C. Various claims have been made concerning Pythagorean influence on intertestamental Judaism and the NT, only a few of which can be substantiated by concrete evidence. After a brief description of the Pythagorean tradition, we will examine some of these claims in more detail.

A. The Pythagorean Tradition
  1. Early Pythagoreanism
  2. The Hellenistic Period
  3. Neopythagoreanism
B. Judaism and Early Christianity
  1. Hellenistic and Palestinian Judaism
  2. New Testament
  3. Early Christianity
  4. Conclusion

A. The Pythagorean Tradition

The history of Pythagoreanism can be divided into three periods, namely, Early Pythagoreanism, the Hellenistic period, and Neopythagoreanism.

1. Early Pythagoreanism. Our most important sources for early Pythagoreanism are accounts by Aristotle, his student Aristoxenus, and the historian Timaeus of Tauromenium. Most of these accounts are only extant in texts from late antiquity, especially in the various biographies by Pythagoras that became very popular in the imperial period. Most important of these texts are D.L. 8.1–50, Porphyry *The Life of Pythagoras,* and Iamblichus *On the Pythagorean Life.*

The most helpful and comprehensive recent discussions of early Pythagoreanism are those by Guthrie (1962), von Fritz (PW 47: 171–268), van der Waerden (PWSup; 1979), Burkert (1972; 1985: 296–304), and Kirk, Raven, and Schofield (1983).

a. The Pythagorean Life. The Pythagorean community was famous in later antiquity for its communal living and sharing. This did not apply equally to all members, however. A distinction was made between esoteric and exoteric members: the former shared totally in the Pythagorean life, while the latter kept less strict ritual and dietary observances and were less involved in the esoteric doctrines of the sect. A period of rigorous and extended probation was required before a candidate was accepted as a full member of the community. At that point he had to take a solemn oath not to reveal any of the Pythagorean doctrines.

The esoteric Pythagoreans dressed in white linen and followed a strict daily regimen which included prayer and meditation, physical exercises, discussions of their doctrines, and a common evening meal. They were forbidden to eat beans and certain kinds of meat. Great emphasis was laid on various purificatory rites, which included a daily bath.

b. Pythagorean Doctrine. Pythagoras himself did not leave any writings, and it is therefore difficult to ascertain which teachings originated with him. According to a testimony in Porph. *VP* 18 that probably can be attributed to Aristotle's student Dicaearchus, Pythagoras taught the immortality and the transmigration of the soul, the eternal cyclic recurrence of events, and the kinship of all living things.

Since Pythagorean doctrines were not committed to writing, oral tradition played an important role in the transmission of their teaching. Apart from anecdotes about the life of Pythagoras, teachings were transmitted in the form of *akousmata,* that is, orally transmitted maxims and sayings, also known as symbols because of their allegedly secret nature. The *akousmata* are mainly concerned with a ritual piety, and together they form a catechism that regulated every aspect of the Pythagorean's life (for a comprehensive list see Burkert 1972: 170–73; for discussion, 166–92). In both doctrine and ritual Pythagoreanism shared many characteristics with ORPHISM, and it may indeed be possible to speak of a Pythagorean variant of Orphism (Burkert 1972: 125–33).

c. Pythagorean Science. In keeping with the Presocratic interest in the basic substance of the universe, the

Pythagoreans postulated number as the fundamental principle. The extent of their scientific discoveries and contributions is a matter of dispute; but we know that they studied mathematics, music, and astronomy (Burkert 1972: 299–482; van der Waerden 1979: 323–480).

Both ritualistic and scientific facets of the Pythagorean movement had as their ultimate goal to bring man into closer contact with God under the slogan *hepou theǭ,* "follow God."

2. The Hellenistic Period. We have very little evidence that Pythagoreanism continued after the time of Archytas of Tarentum (ca. 380 B.C.). It is quite probable, however, that there were individuals and perhaps even small groups throughout the Hellenistic period who considered themselves to be Pythagoreans and who preserved the Pythagorean dietary and ritual regulations (PW 47: 268–70; van der Waerden 1979: 269–71).

Be that as it may, during the Hellenistic period a spate of Pseudopythagorean writings made their appearance, most of them under the name of some ancient Pythagorean (Thesleff 1961; 1965). These writings cover a wide variety of subjects and are heavily influenced by Academic and/or Peripatetic doctrines. Most scholars date them at the very end of the Hellenistic period, that is, in the 1st century B.C. and later, although Thesleff (1961) has argued that some of them may be as early as the 4th century B.C. and that few, if any, are later than the 1st century B.C.

3. Neopythagoreanism. From the 1st century B.C. onward there was a revival of interest in Pythagoreanism. The polymath Nigidius Figulus (100–45 B.C.), the philosophers Quintus Sextius (fl. under Augustus), Sotion the younger of Alexandria (a teacher of Seneca), Moderatus of Gades (end of 1st century A.D.), Nicomachus of Gerasa (fl. ca. A.D. 100), Numenius of Apamea (fl. ca A.D. 150), and the wandering prophet and miracle worker Apollonius of Tyana (1st century A.D.) all considered themselves Pythagoreans.

A subterranean basilica, richly decorated with frescoes depicting mythological scenes that symbolize the ascent of the soul, was discovered in 1917 near the Porta Maggiore in Rome; it probably formed the venue of a Roman Pythagorean sect during the reign of Claudius (Carcopino 1927). Further archaeological evidence for the existence of Pythagoreans during this period is furnished by an inscription from Asia Minor dating from the 1st century A.D. Apart from an epigram with a reference to Pythagoras, it also contains a relief depicting a two-way schema, with Virtue *(aretē)* on the right and Dissipation *(asōtia)* on the left (Brinkmann 1911).

The basic features of Neopythagoreanism were an interest in arithmology, a belief in the transmigration of souls, and an emphasis on the need for the purification of the soul, which was accomplished through ascetic and theurgic practices. The doctrine of "following God" had become synonymous with the Platonic ideal of *homoiōsis theǭ,* "becoming like God."

B. Judaism and Early Christianity

Various points of contact between Pythagoreanism, on the one hand, and Judaism and Christianity, on the other, have been suspected.

1. Hellenistic and Palestinian Judaism. Very definite evidence of dependence on Pythagoreanism is to be found in Hellenistic Judaism.

a. Hellenistic Jewish Apologetics. True to the tendency in the apologetic movement to claim the dependence of Greek philosophy on Mosaic Judaism, some Hellenistic Jewish authors asserted that Pythagoras got many of his doctrines from Judaism. As early as the 3d century B.C. Hermippus of Smyrna, a student of Callimachus, cited with approval a tradition that Pythagoras had "imitated Jewish and Thracian doctrines and transferred them to himself." He then referred to three doctrines with somewhat obscure meanings: "Do not pass a place where an ass has defecated," "abstain from waters causing thirst," and "abstain from all blasphemy" (Jos. *AgAp* 1.22 §§162–65; Jacobson 1976; Gorman 1983: 32–36). Later, in the 2d century B.C., Aristobulus (frags. 3 and 4) also cited this tradition.

The few hexameter verses by "Pythagoras" on the unique creator to be found in [Just.] *monarch.* 2 may be still another attempt by a Hellenistic Jew to claim Pythagoras for Jewish concerns.

In traditions used by Iamblichus (*VP* 7–14; 44) which may be associated with Neanthes, attempts were even made to establish geographical links between Pythagoras and Judaism: Pythagoras was depicted as a native of Sidon "who had lived the live of an anchorite and prophet, like Elijah, atop Mt. Carmel in Palestine" (Gorman 1983: 37–40). More importantly, however, dependence can be shown going in the other direction.

b. Aristobulus. The first Jewish "philosopher" in Alexandria, Aristobulus (2d century B.C.), made use of Pythagorean arithmological doctrines to explain the significance of the number 7 (frag. 5; Hengel 1974, 1: 163–69).

c. Wisdom of Solomon. The author of Wisdom may have been influenced by the writings on kingship attributed to the Pythagoreans Diotogenes, Ecphantus, and Sthenidas (texts in Thesleff 1965: 71–75, 79–84, 187–88), although their dates are uncertain (Thesleff 1961: 65–71). Concepts that occur in Wisdom, such as that of God as universal ruler who cares for all men, of the just man as an imitator of the divine ruler, of divine prudence and beneficence, closely parallel ideas expressed in the Pythagorean tracts (Reese 1970: 73–79).

d. Philo. Philo had a very positive evaluation of Pythagoreans, referring to them as "the most saintly company" (*Quod omn* 2). Although there are only a dozen explicit references to Pythagoras or Pythagoreans in his writings (*Quaes Gen* 1.17; 1.99; 3.16; 3.49; 4.8; *Leg all* 1.15; *Op* 100; *Quod omn* 2; *Provid* 1.22; 2.42; *Anim* 62; *Aet* 12), he made extensive use of Pythagorean arithmological doctrines in his exegesis. His lost work, *On Numbers,* was probably dependent on a Pythagorean source text (Moehring 1978).

e. Essenes. Of the Essenes, a Jewish sect which lived W of the Dead Sea and which is nowadays usually identified with the Qumran community, Josephus (*Ant* 15.10.4 §371) explicitly asserted that they "observed the way of life that Pythagoras had taught among the Greeks." A number of scholars, notably Lévy (1927: 264–93), have therefore attempted to demonstrate that the sect was extensively influenced by Pythagoreanism. Since the discovery of theQumran material, there has been less enthusiasm for this hypothesis (Hengel 1974, 1: 245), although Dupont-Sommer has argued that the discovery has only strengthened the hypothesis. According to him the similarities between the Essene/Qumran community and the Pythagoreans can only be explained by direct influence. Some of these similarities are the following: (1) Both communities practiced a communal life with no private property; (2) both groups had a solemn oath of initiation, but prohibited the taking of oaths otherwise; (3) both groups wore white linen exclusively; (4) both practiced asceticism; (5) both seemed to have paid special honor to the sun; (6) the calendar used by the Qumran community probably originated with the Pythagoreans; and (7) there may be an indication in 1QS 10:4 that the sect made use of Pythagorean arithmology (Dupont-Sommer 1955: 86–91). Apart from Dupont-Sommer's last argument, which is indeed based on a scribal error (Hengel 1974, 1: 246), none of the similarities mentioned are necessarily of Pythagorean origin; and all may be attributed to Hellenistic influence in general (Hengel 1974, 1: 243–47). Josephus' statement should therefore be regarded as *interpretatio Graeca.* See also ESSENES.

2. New Testament. Despite Lévy's claim that the Gospels were decisively influenced by legends about Pythagoras' life and doctrines (1927: 295–339), no Pythagorean element can with certainty be discerned in the NT. There are, however, a few cases where Pythagorean influence cannot be excluded completely.

a. Gospels. Much of Jesus' teaching, especially in the Sermon on the Mount, on oaths, marriage, revenge, and prayer, has elements in common with Pythagorean doctrines (Lévy 1927: 310–20). It has been suggested (Schattenmann 1979: 216–19) that the sayings about removing any part of the body that causes one to stumble (Mark 9:45; Matt 5:29–30; 19:11–12) may be directly influenced by a Pythagorean saying: "Banish by all means and cut off by fire and sword and every contrivance, illness from the body, ignorance from the soul, extravagance from the stomach, strife from the city, discord from the home, and likewise, immoderation from all things" (Iambl. *VP* 34). Similarities between other gnomic sayings in the Gospels and Pythagorean symbols relating to dietary laws have been pointed out by Grant (1980: 308–9), although he is careful not conclude that this implies direct dependence on Pythagoreanism.

b. Acts. The early Christian community in Jerusalem described in Acts 2:44–45 and 4:32 approximates the Pythagorean ideal of common property and harmonious friendship, although these characteristics were shared by all political utopias of Greek philosophy and were thus not specifically Pythagorean.

c. Colossians. The philosophy against which the author of Colossians warned his readers (Col 2:8, 16–23) may be a brand of Pythagoreanism. Schweizer has argued that the world view and way of life taught by this philosophy agree in many respects with the doctrine of the *Pythagorean Memoirs* cited by Alexander Polyhistor (D.L. 8.24–33). There is the same emphasis on the importance of the elements of the world, on the worship of heroes/angels, on the flight from this world to the world above, on purification by abstaining from some kinds of food and by baptism, and on mystical visions (Schweizer *An die Kolosser* EKKNT, 103–4, 217–18; van der Waerden 1979: 86–87).

d. "Haustafeln." The "HAUSTAFELN" or lists of household duties in Col 3:18–4:1; Eph 5:22–6:9; and 1 Pet 2:18–3:7 show some similarities to the various Pseudopythagorean *oikonomika* attributed to Bryson, Callicratides, Perictione, and Plinthys, although they do not agree sufficiently for us to postulate a direct dependence (Balch 1977). See also HOUSEHOLD CODES.

3. Early Christianity. Pythagoreanism was very influential among Christians of Alexandria from the 2d century A.D. onward. Its arithmological, metaphysical and ascetic doctrines fascinated not only gnostic Christian sects, but also somewhat more orthodox Christians like Clement of Alexandria and Origen (Grant 1971). A collection of Pythagorean ethical sayings, Christianized and circulating as *The Sentences of Sextus,* remained popular right into the Middle Ages (Edwards and Wild 1981).

4. Conclusion. Although Pythagoreanism had no more than a tangential influence on Hellenistic Judaism and early Christianity, its piety and strict ethics made it attractive to some Jews and Christians. It also bore sufficient resemblance to these movements to be used as a model to describe groups such as the Essenes and the early Jerusalem church.

Bibliography

Balch, D. L. 1977. Household Ethical Codes in Peripatetic, Neopythagorean, and Early Christian Literature. *SBLSP* 11: 397–404.

Brinkmann, A. 1911. Ein Denkmal des Neupythagoreismus. *RhM,* n.s., 66: 616–25.

Burkert, W. 1972. *Lore and Science in Ancient Pythagoreanism.* Trans. E. L. Minar. Cambridge, MA.

———. 1985. *Greek Religion.* Trans. J. Raffan. Cambridge, MA.

Carcopino, J. 1927. *La basilique pythagoricienne de la Porte Majeure.* Paris.

Dupont-Sommer, A. 1955. Le problème des influences étrangères sur la secte juive de Qoumrân. *RHPR* 35: 75–92.

Edwards, R. A., and Wild, R. A. 1981. *The Sentences of Sextus.* SBLTT 22. Chico, CA.

Gorman, P. 1983. Pythagoras Palaestinus. *Philologus* 127: 30–42.

Grant, R. M. 1971. Early Alexandrian Christianity. *CH* 40: 133–44.

———. 1980. Dietary Laws among Pythagorean, Jews, and Christians. *HTR* 73: 299–310.

Guthrie, W. K. C. 1962. *The Earlier Presocratics and the Pythagorean.* Vol. 1 in *A History of Greek Philosophy.* Cambridge.

Hengel, M. 1974. *Judaism and Hellenism.* 2 vols. Trans. J. Bowden. Philadelphia.

Jacobson, H. 1976. Hermippus, Pythagoras and the Jews. *REJ* 135: 145–49.

Kirk, G. S.; Raven, J. E.; and Schofield, M. 1983. *The Presocratic Philosophers.* 2d ed. Cambridge.

Lévy, I. 1927. *La légende de Pythagore de Grèce en Palestine.* Bibliothèque de l'École des hautes études 215. Paris.

Moehring, H. R. 1978. Arithmology As an Exegetical Tool in the Writings of Philo of Alexandria. *SBLSP* 1: 191–227.

Petzke, G. 1970. *Die Traditionen über Apollonius von Tyana und das Neue Testament.* SCHNT 1. Leiden.
Reese, J. M. 1970. *Hellenistic Influence on the Book of Wisdom and Its Consequences.* AnBib 41. Rome.
Schattenmann, J. 1979. Jesus und Pythagoras. *Kairos* 21: 215–20.
Thesleff, H. 1961. *An Introduction to the Pythagorean Writings of the Hellenistic Period.* Acta Academiae Aboensis, Humaniora 24.3. Åbo.
———. 1965. *The Pythagorean Texts of the Hellenistic Period.* Acta Academiae Aboensis, ser. A, Humaniora 30.1. Åbo.
Waerden, B. L. van der. 1979. *Die Pythagoreer.* Zurich.

JOHAN C. THOM

PYTHON [Gk *pythōn*]. See SLAVE GIRL AT PHILIPPI.

Q

Q (GOSPEL SOURCE). "Q" (the abbreviation for German *Quelle,* "source") is the name scholars have given to the hypothetical source that would account for the gospel material (not found in Mark) that Matthew and Luke have in common.

A. Nature of Q
   1. Existence
   2. Language
   3. Unity
B. Theology of Q
C. Sitz im Leben
D. Conclusion

A. Nature of Q

1. Existence. Within the terms of the Two-Source theory as the solution to the SNYOPTIC PROBLEM, the agreements between the three Synoptic Gospels are accounted for in two ways. In most of the passages where all three gospels are parallel (the "triple tradition"), Matthew and Luke depend on Mark's gospel. In other parts of the tradition where Matthew and Luke are parallel (the "double tradition"), the agreements between those two gospels are explained by their dependence on common source material. This material is usually known as "Q."

Some have tried to dispense with Q as part of a wholesale rejection of the Two-Source theory in favor of the Griesbach hypothesis (Farmer 1964; Dungan 1970); others have retained the theory of Markan priority but have questioned whether one needs to posit a lost source Q to explain Matthew's agreements with Luke: Luke's dependence on Matthew might be an adequate explanation (Farrer 1955; Goulder 1978). Nevertheless, the majority of scholars today would favor a form of the Q hypothesis, rejecting for a variety of reasons the theory of Luke's dependence on Matthew. See SYNOPTIC PROBLEM.

For those who would accept some form of the Q hypothesis, the extent of the Q material is reasonably clear. This material covers all the double tradition; it also includes some passages where there is a Markan parallel (the Temptation narrative, the Beelzebul controversy, the parable of the mustard seed and others), so that Mark and Q must have overlapped in places.

Consideration of the Markan tradition in Matthew and Luke shows that at times the latter evangelists omitted material from their Markan source. It is clearly possible that the same has happened with Q: some passages available to both evangelists may have been omitted by one (or both) of Matthew and Luke. Speculation about Q material which is in neither Matthew nor Luke is clearly futile. However, several have argued that in various cases, some passages which occur only in Matthew or Luke might be Q material which the other evangelist has omitted (Schürmann). Nevertheless, such theories must remain slightly speculative. Further, they usually depend quite heavily on a prior understanding of Q as a whole into which the passage in question fits easily. Such additions to Q would then not significantly alter the character of Q as a whole (Vassiliadis 1978). Most are therefore content to work with a fairly minimal definition of Q, i.e., as material common to Matthew *and* Luke, before possibly expanding this with an occasional Sondergut passage. Thus a widely acceptable starting point for discussion of Q would include the following verses: Luke 3:7–9, 16f.; 4:1–13; 6:20–23, 27–49; 7:1–10, 18–35; 9:57–60; 10:2–16, 21–24; 11:2–4, 9–20, 23–26, 29–35, 39–52; 12:2–12, 22–31, 33f., 39–46, 51–53, 57–59; 13:18–21, 23–30, 34–35; 14:16–24, 26–27, 34–35; 15:4–7; 16:13, 16–18; 17:3–4, 6, 23–24, 26–30, 33–37; 18:14; 19:12–27; 22:28–30 with the Matthean parallels (clearly with debates about individual verses, especially in the longer sections). (It has become customary to refer to verses in Q by referring to their Lukan references only; this is in no way intended to prejudge the issue of whether Matthew or Luke has preserved the Q version more accurately.)

2. Language. The problem of the original language of Q has been discussed frequently. Some have claimed that the verbal differences between Matthew and Luke in Q material can often be explained as due to variant translations of an Aramaic original. Hence Q must have been an Aramaic source. Perhaps the most famous example is Matt 23:26/Luke 11:41, where the difference between Matthew's "cleanse" and Luke's "give alms" has been explained as due to a slight misunderstanding/misreading of an original Aramaic *dakkau* (= "cleanse"), being mistakenly read as *zakkau* (= "give alms"). Appeals have also been made to the Semitic nature of much of Q's language (Bussmann 1929; Bussby 1954).

It is doubtful if more than a very few cases of variation between Matthew and Luke can be explained in this way. The Semitic nature of Q's Greek does not demand an Aramaic Vorlage: influence from LXX is quite conceivable in a Greek-speaking Jewish-Christian milieu. Many of the alleged translation variants turn out to be simply cases of synonyms, and the differences between Matthew and Luke can often be explained just as well as due to the redactional activity of the evangelists (Kloppenborg 1987). For example, in Luke 11:41, Luke's "give alms" may well be LkR (Lukan redaction), reflecting Luke's concern for almsgiving. In other parts of the Q material, the verbal agreement between Matthew and Luke amounts to virtual verbal identity in Greek (Luke 3:7–9; 11:9–10 and pars.). In these instances the measure of verbal agreement seems to demand a common Greek source. Further, some features of Q's Greek can be shown to be characteristic of a source originally written in Greek and uncharacteristic of translation Greek (Turner 1969). This suggests that much of the Q material was available to Matthew and Luke in Greek form. This leads to the question of whether the Q material should be regarded as a single source.

3. Unity. Even among those who would deny that Luke knew Matthew and hence would affirm that Matthew and Luke depend on common source material, there has always been dispute as to whether it is appropriate to think of this material as a single source, Q. Some have argued that the Q material never existed as a unified source prior to its inclusion by Matthew and Luke. "Q" may simply represent a mass of oral traditions. (Jeremias; Wrege). Others have pointed to the fact that Q apparently contained no passion narrative. Is it then credible to think of a written source containing a mass of Jesus traditions but no account of the passion? Further, Q seems to lack any formal structure, starting apparently with a strong narrative element but petering out into a mass of unrelated sayings (Farrer 1955). There is also the problem of the measure of verbal agreement between Matthew and Luke. In some instances Matthew and Luke are almost identical in Greek (Luke 3:7–9 and par.); at other times the verbal agreement is minimal (Luke 14:16–24; 19:12–27 and pars.) (Rosché 1960). Hence Bussmann's theory of two sources, one Greek and one Aramaic.

These arguments are not conclusive. The measure of variation in verbal agreement between Matthew and Luke in Q passages has been shown to be statistically comparable to the measure of verbal agreement between these two gospels in Markan passages (Carlston and Norlin 1971). It may be that Q was available to the evangelists in slightly different forms (a Q^{mt} and a Q^{lk}) as it is sometimes not easy to account for all the differences between the gospels as due to MattR or LkR. But it remains uncertain how far it is necessary to make such an appeal. The theory that Q represents a mass of oral traditions does not account for the common order in Q material, which can be discerned once Matthew's habit of collecting related material into his large teaching discourses is discounted (Taylor 1953, 1959). Such a common order demands a theory that Q at some stage existed in written form.

The argument based on the lack of a Passion Narrative in Q, and the apparent formlessness of Q, is also weak. Its strength depends on an a priori assumption of what "must" have stood in a source containing information about Jesus. Q clearly cannot have been a "gospel" of the same nature as the canonical gospels. But the discovery of the *Gospel of Thomas* has shown us that it was possible for some Christians to write a "gospel" with no passion narrative (Robinson 1971, 1986). Further, Kloppenborg (1987) has shown that the form of Q, as a collection of sayings together with some introductory narrative scenes, can be paralleled in several sayings collections in antiquity. The genre of Q is thus not a problem for the theory of its existence.

None of the arguments against the existence of Q as a single source is fully convincing. It is thus best to assume that Q was a single source, available in Greek and probably in written form.

If this is the case, then the source Q is similar to the gospels themselves. It is thus not surprising that many have tried to study Q with techniques similar to those which have been applied to the gospels. In particular, there has been a significant trend in recent years to approach Q from the side of redaction criticism. This involves trying to interpret Q as a unified source in its own right and perhaps with its own distinctive theology. Many have therefore attempted to delineate a "Q theology" and to see what kind of social group of Christians, or "Q community," might have preserved this material and regarded it as significant.

B. Theology of Q

At this point the problem of the unity of Q arises once again, though in slightly different form. Many who would accept that it is appropriate to think of Q as a single written source, with a characteristic theology, would also argue that Q represents the end product of a quite complex tradition history. There may be various strata within Q so that the tradition may have undergone a complex history of expansion and adaptation. Some would claim to be able to identify a single redactional layer in Q (Lührmann 1969; Schenk 1981). Schulz (1972) distinguishes two main strata within Q, corresponding to two distinct stages in the history of the "Q community." Polag (1977), Jacobson (1978), Zeller (1982, 1984), Kloppenborg (1987), and Uro (1987) have all argued for at least three redactional strata in Q (though with little agreement in details). Schürmann (1968) postulates a four-stage growth in the tradition whereby individual sayings were expanded by secondary comments *(Kommentarworte)* which at a third stage were combined to form smaller collections before being incorporated into the larger blocks of Q at a final stage. Many have argued, for example, that the Temptation narrative is quite unlike the rest of Q and hence is probably a relative latecomer into the Q tradition.

It must, however, also be remembered that a division of a text into various strata (whether it be a simple twofold division into "tradition + redaction" or a more complex theory of strata) is not the only key which will unlock the secrets of a writer's theology. A decision to include a tradition, perhaps unaltered, may be just as positive an editorial action as an alteration into a tradition. One should not therefore write off much of the Q material as "merely" traditional and hence having nothing to contribute to Q's theology. One must also beware of making a writer too monochromatic, so that different types of material directed to different audiences, are ipso facto taken as indications of distinct strata within the history of the tradition. So, too, it is perhaps dangerous to assume too readily that we know precisely the way in which the tradition developed from individual sayings to larger complexes. One can sometimes identify ways in which Q material seems to have been redactionally modified, especially in some of the arrangement of the material (Lührmann 1969; Kloppenborg 1984). But the situation is clearly more complex than in the case of Matthew's and Luke's use of Mark since we do not have Q's traditions directly available to compare with Q: we do not even have Q itself directly available. Thus one must be prepared to allow that the substance of the Q material itself, and the choice of which traditions are included, can also help in the clarification of Q's theology (Hoffmann 1972).

A basic presupposition of much contemporary Q study is that the group of Christians who preserved the Q material did so because they believed that this material was still valid and relevant for their own day. The Jesus tradition was thus not a matter of teaching which had been given in the past but was no longer applicable. Rather, the teaching of Jesus was taken up and applied to the present. Further, the preachers of this tradition claimed that in their own preaching, the voice of the present Jesus was to be heard (Luke 10:16 par.). While a verse like Luke 12:10/Matt 12:32 might suggest some awareness of a distinction between the pre-Easter and post-Easter situations, the main bulk of the Q tradition is formulated with the assumption that Jesus' words are still valid. The contemporizing present, "I say to you," predominates as opposed to any historicizing tendencies (Boring 1982).

One theme which is universally recognized as characterizing much of the Q material is that of eschatological warning. A great deal of Q is concerned with this theme of imminent judgment, which may be catastrophic for those who are unprepared and do not "repent." Older views of Q had sought to explain Q as a kind of paraenetic manual, a supplement to fill out the kerygma of the death of Jesus, which was already presupposed (Manson 1949). Such a theory will not explain the note of warning and crisis which dominates so much of Q. Right at the start, this note of warning is sounded in the preaching of John the Baptist (Luke 3:7–9 par.); this continues through the teaching of Jesus in the Great Sermon, bracketed as it is by the eschatologically oriented beatitudes (Luke 6:20–23 par.) and the eschatological warnings against those who fail to obey Jesus' words (Luke 6:46–49 par.); the mission charge repeats the note of the imminence of the Kingdom (Luke 10:9 par.); and toward the end of Q there is the eschatological discourse warning of the End, which may come at any time (Lk. 17; 23ff. par.).

It is probable that Q is aware of a delay in the Parousia. The parables in Luke 12:39–40, 42–46; 19:12–27 par. seem to presuppose such a delay (Lührmann 1969; Schulz 1972). Nevertheless, the very form of Q suggests that Q has not given up the vivid expectation of the End which could come at any minute: the fact that Q includes this material implies that the Q Christians regarded it as still valid. Hence Q is dominated by a vivid hope for an imminent End (Hoffmann 1972).

Integrally related to the note of crisis in Q is the theme of polemic. Q is clearly not just a manual for newly converted Christians. Rather it reflects a situation where the Christian community feels itself to be threatened and to be suffering hostility. Lührmann has shown that the note of polemic against "this generation" dominates Q's arrangement of the material; e.g., in Luke 7:18–35 par., any possible hint of anti-Baptist polemic (Luke 7:18–28 par.) has been overlaid by further material setting Jesus and John the Baptist together against "this generation." So, too, the discourse against the scribes and Pharisees (Luke 11:37–52 par.) is broadened at the end to become an attack on "this generation" (Luke 11:49–51 par.).

In this polemic, use is often made of a model taken from a Deuteronomistic view of history. In this scheme, Israel's history is viewed as one of continual disobedience. God sends the prophets to Israel to call the nation to repent; the response is always negative, and the prophets suffer rejection and violence. As a result, God's wrath has been and will be experienced (Steck 1967). Such a scheme characterizes a significant part of the Q material (Steck 1967; Jacobson 1978; Kloppenborg 1987). Q Christians have evidently experienced rejection of the Christian message; and they interpret this rejection as part of the general violence inflicted on God's prophetic messengers by impenitent Israel (Luke 6:22–23; 11:49–51; 13:34f.). The prophetic self-understanding of the Q Christians may also be indicated by several formal similarities between much of the Q material and the prophetic literature in the OT (Sato 1988).

Another theme closely associated in Q with that of the suffering prophets is the theme of Wisdom *(Sophia).* Late Judaism spoke at times of Wisdom as an almost personified being in her own right, and there are also traditions of Wisdom's preaching being rejected by men (cf. Prov 1:20–33; 8:22–36; *1 Enoch* 42). In Q the two streams of tradition—that of rejected Wisdom and the Deuteronomic theme of the violent fate suffered by the prophets—coalesce so that Wisdom herself becomes the agent who sends out the prophets, all of whom suffer violence (Luke 11:49–51; 13:34f. pars.; and also 6:23; 7:31–35; 9:58). Within this pattern, Jesus appears as one (possibly the last) in the line of the suffering prophets. (Hence it is worth noting that Q does not ignore the death of Jesus. Little salvific significance is attributed to Jesus' death, but the latter *is* implicitly incorporated into a wider interpretative theological scheme.)

Several of Q's warnings of eschatological judgment are couched in terms of the coming of the "Son of Man." The whole question of the Son of Man sayings in Q and the broader question of Q's christology have aroused much discussion. Some have argued that "Son of Man" reveals Q's distinctive contribution to christological development within primitive Christianity (Tödt 1965; Edwards 1971). For example, Tödt claimed that the identification of Jesus with the figure of the Son of Man was due to the Q community. Jesus had spoken of the Son of Man as a figure other than himself. On the basis of the resurrection experience, Q achieved the "christological cognition" of identifying the coming Son of Man with Jesus himself and then undertook to continue the preaching of Jesus as still valid in the post-Easter period.

The place of "Son of Man" within Q's christology is much disputed. Tödt's theory that originally Jesus thought of the Son of Man as someone other than himself would be questioned by many today. More importantly here, many have questioned whether "Son of Man" reflects Q's own interests, or whether it was already part of Q's tradition and hence not relevant for Q's redaction and thus for Q's theology (Lührmann 1969; Schürmann). However, the

Son of Man saying in Luke 11:30 may well be due to Q's redaction (Edwards 1971); and in any case, one cannot dismiss all traditional elements in Q as contributing nothing to Q's theology. It seems therefore best to regard "Son of Man" as a christological "title" of some importance for Q.

Its significance is more debated. It is often thought that "Son of Man" is primarily for Q a reference to Jesus in his capacity as a figure (as judge or advocate) of the end-time (cf. Luke 17:22–37 par.), and it is often pointed out that Q has no "suffering Son of Man" sayings similar to Mark 8:31. Certainly the "eschatological Son of Man" is very strongly represented in Q. However, there are a number of Q sayings referring to the present activity of Jesus as Son of Man (Luke 6:23; 7:34; 9:58; 12:10; and arguably 11:30). Although some have claimed that the use of the term here refers to Jesus as authoritative (Tödt 1965), or to Jesus as returning judge (Hoffmann 1972), it may be relevant that all of these sayings occur in contexts which imply rejection, hostility, and suffering. "Son of Man" is thus a term which seems to be closely linked in Q with these themes (together with the related themes of rejected Wisdom and the suffering prophets). It may be, therefore, that the theme of the "suffering Son of Man" is not so alien to Q as many have claimed (Tuckett 1982).

C. Sitz im Leben

What can be said about the situation of the Christians who preserved the Q material? It is probable that Q reflects a group of Jewish Christians with a fairly conservative attitude to the Jewish Law. It is in Q that we have one of the most conservative statements about the continuing validity of the Law (Luke 16:17 par.); and if, as seems likely, the Lukan context of this saying reflects the Q context, then Q deliberately places 16:17 after 16:16 in order to guard against a possible antinomian interpretation of the latter verse. Elsewhere in Q, the Law is presupposed as still valid and binding on the Christian. The polemic against the scribes and Pharisees in Luke 11:37–52 par. is directed only against their hypocrisy in not obeying the Law themselves. Luke 11:42d may well be a Q-redactional comment to insist that the Law must still be kept. If, as also seems likely, Luke 14:5 par. was part of Q, then Q reflects a sabbath controversy but, unlike Mark, has Jesus operating strictly within the Law to justify his behavior (the rescue of a *man* in a pit would be accepted by all as a legitimate breach of the sabbath law). Further, much of the argument in the woes against the scribes and Pharisees, especially the woes about purity and tithing, seems to operate within Pharisaic presuppositions (Schulz 1972). Given the fact that the Pharisees were probably a relatively small group within pre-70 Judaism, the virulence of the opposition here may indicate a rather close link between the Q Christians and the Pharisaic movement (if they were not close, then each group would probably have ignored the other).

Whether this is still the case at the stage of Q's redaction is not certain. Many have claimed that by the time of this stage, the polemic has sharpened and broadened in scope to be directed against "this generation," a term which refers to the whole Jewish people, not just one part such as the Pharisees (Lührmann 1969; Schürmann 1986). Lührmann has gone further and argued that the sharply polemical tone of Q's redaction means that Israel now only has the threat of judgment; for Q has embraced the gentile mission, and for the Jewish as a whole there is now no hope at all (Lührmann 1969; Kloppenborg 1987).

The meaning of the term "this generation," however, is not absolutely certain. Although some claim that it is a technical term for the nation Israel and lacks any temporal reference (Lührmann 1969), it seems hard to exclude all temporal sense from a saying such as Luke 11:31f, par. Thus others have argued that the term does retain a temporal significance, referring to the people of the final generation before the end (Hoffmann 1972; Schulz 1972). Further, it seems doubtful if one can identify "this generation" with the whole of Israel tout court. At the very least, the term must exclude the Q Christians who, as we have seen, were probably Jewish Christians. It thus seems more likely that Q's polemic is directed against only a part of the Jewish community among which the Q community existed.

The problem of Q's attitude to gentiles and the gentile mission is also disputed. Q does have several sayings which seem to presuppose a friendly attitude to gentiles (Luke 7:1–10; 10:13–15; 11:31f.; 13:28f. pars.), though others have claimed that these refer only to the past or the future: there is nothing in relation to the present (Hoffmann 1972). Many too have argued that Q's rather strict attitude to the Law effectively excludes the possibility that Q had undertaken the gentile mission. (Schulz 1972; Wegner 1985).

These arguments are of varying weight. The relationship between the Law and the gentile mission should not be made too simplistic. A gentile mission is not ipso facto incompatible with a conservative attitude to the Law. Even Paul expected his gentile converts to observe considerable parts of the Law without any questioning. Nevertheless, it must be said that the presence of slighting references to gentiles, almost in passing (Matt 5:47 [Luke's parallel, referring to "sinners," is generally accepted as LkR]; Luke 12:30 par.), make it hard to believe that Q was engaged in a gentile mission. The natural language of Q seems to assume that "gentiles" are those who are outside the sphere of salvation. Thus the terms of reference seem to be wholly Israel-oriented (unless one can assign the slighting references to an earlier stratum in Q: so Kloppenborg—but then why have they been left unredacted by a later stage of Q?). Gentiles seem to be brought into the picture only to shame the Jewish hearers (Meyer 1970), though whether Q holds out any hope for that audience is not clear.

A much discussed feature of Q arises out of Q's version of the mission charge. Here the Q missionaries are told to take absolutely nothing for their journey, not even the basic necessities of life such as food or clothing. Elsewhere, too, Q sayings seem to presuppose an extremely radical break with past personal ties. The Q Christians are told that they must "hate" their own families (Luke 14:26 par.); they are told they must take up their cross (Luke 14:27 par.). They are not to worry about their daily needs (Luke 12:22–34 par.) since God will provide for them. They are to be the followers of the Son of Man, who has nowhere to lay his head; and they are to break with their past in such a radical way that they are not even to go home to bury a member of their own family (Luke 9:57–60 par.). These sayings have led to the plausible theory that behind Q lies a group of Christians who obeyed these instructions to the letter. Hence Q presupposes the existence of wandering prophets or charismatics who made a radical break with their own homes and went about preaching the message of the kingdom (Hoffmann 1972; Theissen 1979). However, the presence of sayings like Luke 10:2 par. may suggest that the final stage of Q also presupposes a group of settled Christians providing backup support for the wandering preachers (Zeller 1982, 1984).

The precise meaning of such a lifestyle depends heavily on the social situation in which such action takes place. Such renunciation could be a voluntary act, similar in kind to the renunciation practiced by Cynic preachers but taken to even more radical extremes (Hoffmann 1972). Schottroff has argued that the "renunciation" implied is simply a reflection of the general extreme poverty which all suffered at the time and Q's preaching is simply a message of how to come to terms with this. Nevertheless, such a theory will not explain all of Q. Q evidently expects other Christians to help the missionaries and provide material support for them: hence some material possessions are assumed. Other sayings only make sense on the same assumption (Luke 16:13; Matt 6:19–21). So too, the sayings about leaving family seem to imply a situation where the Q Christians are in a rather different social situation from that of their neighbors. The lifestyle implied here thus seems to be peculiar to the Christian. In part it is thus a voluntary decision to adopt such a lifestyle and the results are closely connected with the Christian commitment. It is not necessarily something which the Q Christian shares with all his/her contemporaries. This applies particularly in the case of the references to persecution in Q, which are frequently connected with the lifestyle of the wandering charismatics.

Q says much about persecution at a fairly general level. Many have deduced from this that the Q community was suffering very real persecution from its neighbors. At the more "theological" level, it is clear that the Q Christians regard the persecution which they are experiencing as a continuation of the violence suffered by all the prophets in the past. Yet as the latter may be somewhat stylized (not all the prophets suffered violence), the same may be true of Q. Q has a great deal of polemic (against "this generation") for refusing to accept the message of the prophets past and present, but it is hard to infer that such refusal resulted in actual violence against the Q community. Luke 6:22–23 can be interpreted quite naturally as relating to verbal abuse, social ostracism, and perhaps polite indifference, but not necessarily to any physical violence. The precise meaning of the final woes against the scribes and Pharisees is debated, but a strong case can be made for the penultimate woe (against the tomb builders Luke 11:47–48 par.) being directed against those who simply ignore the present prophetic message and try to distance themselves from the past by building tombs for prophets whom "their fathers" killed: the actual violence belongs to the past alone (Steck 1967; contra Hoffmann 1972). If so, the same may also apply to the doom oracle in Luke 11:49–51, where again the period of physical violence seems to be limited to the OT era. Elsewhere in Q, there is violent polemic against apathy (Luke 17:22–37), strong words against waverers (Luke 11:23), against those who seek signs (Luke 11:29–32, but there is no indication that the sign seekers are being physically violent), against those who might give up their Christian allegiance (Luke 12:9—possibly reflecting a persecution situation, but the polemic is *not* directed against the persecutors themselves). Luke 16:16 is probably too vague for the reader to know precisely what is in mind. Only Luke 13:34–35 might imply physical violence in the present, though it is not clear how much is present and how much is past.

If could be that the Q community is *not* suffering a great deal in physical terms. No doubt the Christian message has evoked opposition, some verbal abuse, some polite indifference. So too the wandering preachers have evidently not always found a welcome and been provided with a home (Luke 10:10–11). From the Christian side this was no doubt seen as "persecution," and it has evidently led to a closing of the ranks and some quite violent denunciation of those outside. But such opposition may not have involved any great measure of physical violence.

D. Conclusion

Recent studies have shown how fruitful a redaction-critical approach to Q can be. At first sight such work may appear to be extremely hypothetical, being based on what some would argue is a very questionable presupposition (the very existence of Q as a single document). However, the very distinctiveness of the Q material as shown by recent redaction-critical studies of Q is in itself an indication that this material did exist as a separate entity at some stage in the development of the synoptic tradition. Theories about the theology of Q, if successful, may therefore provide further support for the hypothesis of the existence of Q. Q may also alert us to the great variety within primitive Christianity. It shows us a version of the Christian faith which is perhaps less cross centered than, say, Paul or Mark; but it is nonetheless real for that.

Bibliography

Boring, M. E. 1982. *Sayings of the Risen Jesus.* Cambridge.
Bussby, F. 1954. Is Q an Aramaic Document? *ExpTim* 65: 272–75.
Bussmann, W. 1929. *Synoptische Studien.* Vol. 2 of *Zur Redenquelle.* Halle.
Carlston, C. E., and Norlin, D. 1971. Once More—Statistics and Q. *HTR* 64: 59–78.
Downing, F. G. 1965. Towards the Rehabilitation of Q. *NTS* 11: 169–81.
Dungan, D. L. 1970. Mark—The Abridgement of Matthew and Luke. Vol. 1, Pp. 51–97 in *Jesus and Man's Hope.* 2 vols. Pittsburgh.
Edwards, R. A. 1971. *The Sign of Jonah.* London.
Farmer, W. R. 1964. *The Synoptic Problem.* New York.
Farrer, A. 1955. On Dispensing with Q. Pp. 55–88 in *Studies in the Gospels: Essays in Memory of R. H. Lightfoot,* ed. D. E. Nineham. Oxford.
Goulder, M. D. 1978. On Putting Q to the Test. *NTS* 24: 218–34.
Hoffmann, P. 1972. *Studien zur Theologie der Logienquelle.* NTA NF 8. Münster.
Jacobson, A. D. 1978. *Wisdom Christology in Q.* Ph.D. diss., Claremont.
———. 1982. The Literary Unity of Q. *JBL* 101: 365–89.

Kloppenborg, J. S. 1984. Tradition and Redaction in the Synoptic Sayings Source. *CBQ* 46: 34–62.
———. 1987. *The Formation of Q*. Philadelphia.
Lührmann, D. 1969. *Die Redaktion der Logienquelle*. WMANT 33. Neukirchen-Vluyn.
Manson, T. W. 1949. *The Sayings of Jesus*. London.
Meyer, P. D. 1970. The Gentile Mission in Q. *JBL* 89: 405–17.
Neirynck, F. 1982. Recent Developments in the Study of Q. Pp. 29–75 in *LOGIA—The Sayings of Jesus*, ed. J. Delobel. Louvain.
Polag, A. 1977. *Die Christologie der Logienquelle*. WMANT 45. Neukirchen-Vluyn.
Robinson, J. M. 1971. LOGOI SOPHON: On the Gattung of Q. Pp. 84–130 in *The Future of Our Religious Past: Essays in Honour of Rudolf Bultmann*. London.
———. 1986. On Bridging the Gulf from Q to the Gospel of Thomas (or Vice Versa). Pp. 127–76 in *Nag Hammadi: Gnosticism and Early Christianity*, ed. C. W. Hedrick and R. Hodgson. Peabody.
Rosché, T. R. 1960. The Words of Jesus and the Future of the "Q" Hypothesis. *JBL* 79: 210–20.
Sato, M. 1988. *Q und Prophetie*. WUNT 2/29. Tübingen.
Schenk, W. 1981. *Synopse zur Redenquelle der Evangelien*. Düsseldorf.
Schottroff, L., and Stegemann, W. 1978. *Jesus von Nazareth—Hoffnung der Armen*. Stuttgart.
Schulz, S. 1972. *Q—Die Spruchquelle der Evangelisten*. Zurich.
Schürmann, H. 1968. *Traditionsgeschichtliche Untersuchungen zu den synoptischen Evangelien*. Düsseldorf.
———. 1975. Beobachtungen zum Menschensohn-Titel in der Redequelle. Pp. 124–47 in *Jesus und der Menschensohn: Für Anton Vögtle*. Freiburg.
———. 1982. Das Zeugnis der Redenquelle für die Basileia-Verkündigung Jesu. Pp. 121–200 in *LOGIA—The Sayings of Jesus*, ed. J. Delobel. Louvain.
———. 1986. Die Redekomposition wider "dieses Geschlecht" und seine Führung in der Redequelle (vgl. Mt 23, 1–39 par Lk 11, 37–54). *Studien zum Neuen Testament und seiner Umwelt* A 11: 33–81.
Steck, O. H. 1967. *Israel und das gewaltsame Geschick der Propheten*. WMANT 23. Neukirchen-Vluyn.
Taylor, V. 1953. The Order of Q. *JTS* 4: 27–31.
———. 1959. The Original Order of Q. Pp. 246–69 in *New Testament Essays: Studies in Memory of T. W. Manson*, Ed. A. J. B. Higgins. Manchester.
Theissen, G. 1979. *Studien zur Soziologie des Urchristentums*. WUNT 19. Tübingen.
Tödt, H. E. 1965. *The Son of Man in the Synoptic Tradition*. London.
Tuckett, C. M. 1982. The Present Son of Man. *JSNT* 14: 58–81.
———. 1984. On the Relationship between Matthew and Luke. *NTS* 30: 130–42.
Turner, N. 1969. Q in Recent Thought. *ExpTim* 80: 324–28.
Uro, R. 1987. *Sheep among the Wolves: A Study of the Mission Instructions of Q*. Helsinki.
Vassiliadis, P. 1978. The Nature and Extent of the Q Document. *NovT* 20: 49–73.
Wegner, U. 1985. *Der Hauptmann von Kafarnaum*. WUNT, n.s., 14. Tübingen.
Zeller, D. 1982. Redaktionsprozesse und wechselnder "Sitz im Leben" beim Q-Material. Pp. 395–409 in *LOGIA—The Sayings of Jesus*, ed. J. Delobel. Louvain.
———. 1984. *Kommentar zur Logienquelle*. Stuttgart.

C. M. TUCKETT

QAʿAQIR, JEBEL (M.R. 145103). A mountain (Arabic, "Mountain of the Cairns") situated on a ridge eight miles W of Hebron, near the modern village of Simiyeh, at an altitude of about 400 m. It is located just at the E edge of the Shephelah, where it borders upon the lower slopes of the central hills, in the inner reaches of the Wadi Lachish.

The one-period EB IV cemetery and settlement at Jebel Qaʿaqīr was discovered by tomb robbers in the summer of 1967 and thus came to the attention of archaeologists. It was excavated by W. G. Dever in 1967, 1968, and 1971, sponsored and funded by the Hebrew Union College in Jerusalem. The excavations revealed at least six different shaft-tomb cemeteries all around the base of the ridge near the valley floor. All belonged to the EB IV period, ca. 2300–2000 B.C., a largely nonsedentary interlude between the urban Early and Middle Bronze eras in Palestine. Cemetery B had been extensively robbed, but some 40 tombs were investigated and planned, and nearly 20 undisturbed tombs were excavated. Cemeteries C, D, E, and F produced another 20 tombs, but it is clear that dozens, probably hundreds, of others are present in the vicinity. The tombs were regularly laid out and spaced a few feet apart along several natural rock terraces down the slope, all oriented the same way. Typically, a round elliptical shaft, up to six feet deep, led to a round chamber, the doorway to which was blocked by a single large stone. Several tombs had shallow body shelves, lamp niches, graffiti, and other distinguishing features. Many tombs contained a single human burial; others two to four individuals. Most burials were accompanied by part of a sheep or goat carcass. In every case the burials were secondary, and the bones, even those of the animals, were disarticulated and completely disarrayed. The 47 adult and 2 children's skeletons constitute an exceptionally large and well preserved sample for this period and reveal much about diet, disease, and longevity (Smith 1982). Although many tombs contained a pot or two and occasionally a copper weapon, more than half had no grave goods at all. The disproportionally large number of tombs, the decarnate bones, and the scant offerings all suggest that these are the remains of seminomadic pastoralists who migrated along a seasonal circuit and carried their dead with them for later burial at an ancestral burying ground (Dever 1980). The evidence from similar shaft tombs of numerous EB IV sites in Palestine points to the same conclusion. See JERICHO; DHAHR MIRZBÂNEH; BEER RESISIM.

Evidence of scattered domestic occupation on the nearly milelong S-shaped ridge above the cemeteries consisted only of a dozen or so enigmatic stone cairns (not burials); a rambling low boundary wall; a unique potter's kiln; a single dolmen of the "table top" variety; and a half-dozen or more caves used as shelters. One cave, G26, produced a nearly complete domestic assemblage of some 30 restorable pots, flint blades, and ground-stone implements (Dever 1981). Another, G23, was apparently a pottery dump, which yielded fragments of nearly 1,800 vessels, none restorable (Gitin 1975). The vast domestic ceramic repertoire from Jebel Qaʿaqīr fills out our corpus of EB IV pottery, which was based until recently on the somewhat atypical assemblages from tombs. It helps not only to define further Dever's "Family S" (= "Southern-sedentary"; 1980), but also gives us for the first time sufficient material on which to base an analysis of ceramic technology and decorative design (London 1985).

Bibliography

Dever, W. G. 1972. A Middle Bronze I Site on the West Bank of the Jordan. *Arch* 25: 231–33.

———. 1980. New Vistas on the EB IV ("MB I") Horizon in Syria-Palestine. *BASOR* 237: 35–64.

———. 1981. Cave G 26 at Jebel Qaᶜaqīr: A Stratified MB I Domestic Assemblage. *EI* 15: *22–*32.

Gitin, S. 1975. Middle Bronze I "Domestic Pottery" at Jebel Qaᶜaqīr. A Ceramic Inventory of Cave G 23. *EI* 12: *46–*62.

London, G. 1985. *Decoding Designs: The Late Third Millennium B.C. Pottery from Jebel Qaᶜaqīr.* Diss., Arizona.

Smith, P. 1982. The Physical Characteristics and Biological Affinities of the MB I Skeletal Remains from Jebel Qaᶜaqīr. *BASOR* 245: 65–73.

WILLIAM G. DEVER

QADES, TELL (M.R. 200279). A site in upper Galilee located about 15 km N of Safed. The site comprises a tell at the W edge of the Kadesh Valley and a low hill overlooking the valley some 200 m to the E. It is to be identified with the Kedesh in Naphtali mentioned in both biblical and extrabiblical sources. See KEDESH.

A. History of the Site

The importance of this site in antiquity is attested both by the surface remains strewn over the site and by the numerous references to it in the historical sources. Kedesh was one of the main cities in Upper Galilee during the Canaanite and Israelite periods. The city is probably mentioned in Egyptian sources of the 2d millennium B.C.E. Kedesh is listed as one of the defeated Canaanite towns in Josh 12:22; as one of the levitical cities in Josh 21:32 and 1 Chr 6:61; and as a city of refuge in Josh 20:7. It is also mentioned as one of the strongholds of Naphtali legacy. The Assyrian king Tiglath-pileser III conquered the city in 733/732 B.C.E. together with other Galilean cities which are listed in 2 Kings 15:29. Kedesh is mentioned in one of the Zenon papyri (*PZen. Col.:* 59004), as well as in the account of the battle between Jonathan the Hasmonean and the generals of Demetrius (1 Macc 11:53–73; see also *Ant* 13.154). Josephus (*JW* 4.104) relates that Titus' army set up camp at Kedesh during the campaign against Yohanan of Gush Halav, and that following the massacre of the Jews of Caesarea in 66 C.E., the latter avenged themselves by attacking many Gentile settlements, including *Kadasa (tōn) Tyrion,* "Kedesh (of) the Tyrians," i.e., Kedesh in the region of Tyre (*JW* 2.459). Kedesh was known as one of the strongholds of Tyre in the Galilee and was in constant conflict with the "Galileans" (*JW* 4.105).

According to both the epigraphical and archaeological evidence, Kedesh flourished during the 2d–3d centuries C.E. The town is mentioned also in later historical sources. Thus, Eusebius (*Onomast.* 116.10) note that Kedesh lay 20 miles from Tyre.

B. Research of the Site

Tell Qades—or Tel Kedesh—is one of the largest and most important tells in Upper Galilee (ca. 100 dunams); however, it has not yet been excavated, except for a rescue excavation carried out in the 1950s by Y. Aharoni. On the N part of the tell, on what may have been the ancient acropolis, stood an Arab village. The rescue excavation, the archaeological survey, and the surface remains scattered on the site indicate that the site was continuously occupied from the Bronze Age until the end of late antiquity.

A vast cemetery extends to the NE of the tell. The rock-hewn tombs are dated to various periods and have not yet been investigated systematically, except for a tomb of the MB Age and some from Roman times.

On the hill E of the tell are the remains of a well-preserved monumental temple, and W of this are remnants of mausoleums and decorated sarcophagi. Rock-hewn tombs were discovered at the N and NW fringes of the hill. During the 19th century the site was surveyed in varying detail by E. Renan, V. Guerin, and C. Wilson, and especially by C. R. Conder and H. H. Kitchener of the Survey of Palestine, whose work has been the main source of knowledge of the temple until recently. Since these 19th-century investigations, the site has been explored by only a few scholars, like F. Fenner, G. Dalman, and C. Watzinger. During 1976–77, A. Ovadiah, M. Fischer, and I. Roll made an extensive survey of the site, and in 1981 and 1983–84, they conducted three seasons of excavations.

C. Description of the Temple Complex

The architectural complex at Kedesh, located on the upper part of the S slope of the tell, includes a large *temenos* (sacred enclosure) with a monumental temple at its center. The *peribolos* enclosing the *temenos* is rectangular in plan and measures about 55 × 80 m; because of the topography of the area, its S wall also served as a retaining wall. The E facade of the *peribolos,* only partially preserved, was probably symmetrical in design and had a monumental entrance leading into the *temenos,* similar to the sacred complexes of Helios at Kasr Naus and Zeus at Hosn-Suleiman (Baetocaece) in Syria. The "baroque" characteristics of this design correspond well with the general trend of Roman architecture in the Orient. In view of the parallel walls of the *peribolos* and the temple, it is obvious that the two structures were an integrated architectural complex, although the temple did not stand in the exact center of the *temenos.* The wall of the *temenos,* which is not of uniform construction, stood exposed in a number of places.

The temple consists of a rectangular cella and a portico. See Fig. QAD.01. Its outer dimensions (without the portico) are 20.66 m × 22.63 m; its inner dimensions, 17.60 m × 20.04 m; and its overall length (including the portico), 31.25 m. Only the E facade of the cella remains standing and is preserved to a height of ca. 7.50 m, or 14 courses. Three carved and ornamented entrances pass through the facade: a central opening symmetrically flanked by two smaller ones. The neatly worked ashlars are laid according to the typical Roman dry-wall method, smoothly fitted to each other.

No evidence of columns was found inside the cella to suggest that this inner space was divided into aisles; nor

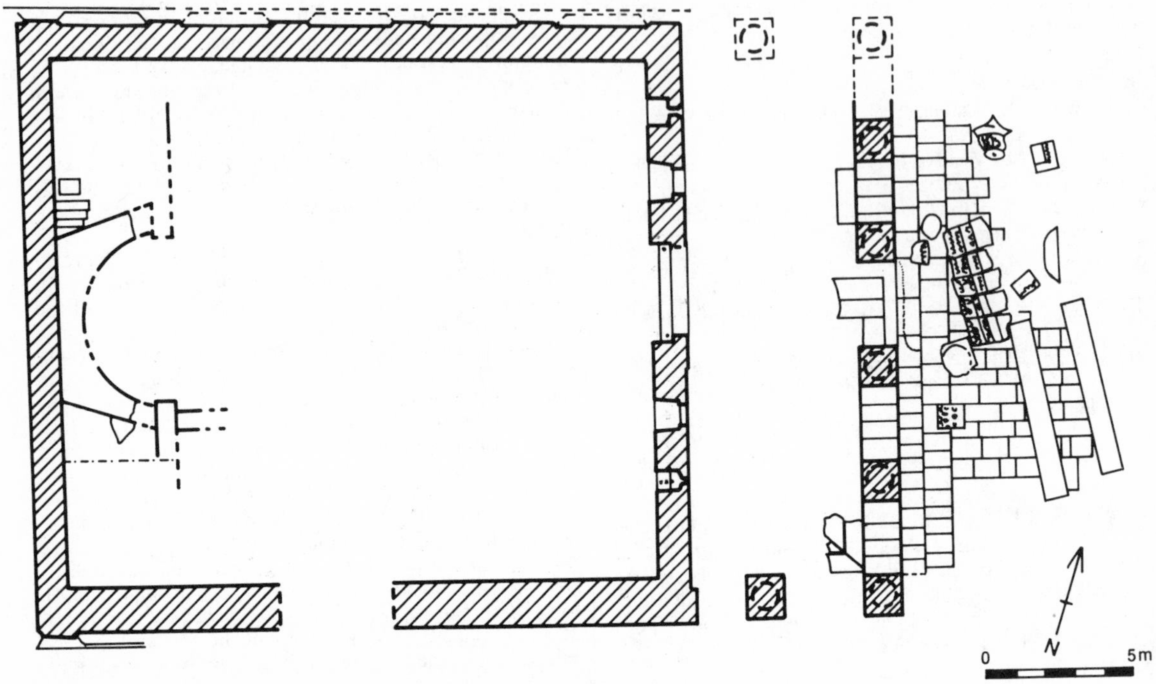

QAD.01. Monumental Temple at Kedesh—Roman Period. *(Redrawn from Fishcher, Ovadiah, and Roll 1984: 150)*

were there traces of any piers against the N and S walls that might have supported the roof. This suggests that the roof, despite the considerable width of the hall (17.60 m), was supported by transverse wooden beams, which, in turn, carried a series of lighter timbers or cross-rafters intersecting and slotted into the transverse beams. It is also possible that in order to reduce the span of the beams, they rested on consoles fitted against the N and S walls of the temple. Similar techniques were probably used to support the roofs in several Roman temples in Syria, such as those at Kasr Naus, Hosn Niha, and Majdal Anjar. Many fragments of terra-cotta tiles were found, both of *solenes* and *kalypteres,* which obviously had been used to cover the roof of the cella.

A paved section of neatly fitted rectangular slabs was found in the E part of the hall, approximately on the same level as both the S entrance threshold and the pavement of the portico. There were also traces of the underpinnings of three steps leading down from the central entrance threshold to the floor of the cella.

An apse, measuring 5.60 m across, abutted the inner side of the W wall of the cella, opposite its central entrance. This was apparently designed to accommodate a statue or relief of the patron deity of the temple, a kind of *adyton,* such as those of the temples at Rahle, Burkush, and Palmyra. This apse was apparently a secondary addition to the temple.

The portico apparently had a hexastyle (six-column) facade, consisting of two groups of three columns each. Parts of the entablature, bases, and capitals also came to light, indicating that the temple probably stood about 12 m high.

To enter the cella the priest probably used the side entrances, which were more or less on the same level as the floor of the portico and the floor of the cella. The approach to the threshold of the central entrance, which was elevated ca. 1 m above the floor of the portico, was probably by a ramp, of which some remains were discovered.

A row of sockets in the threshold in the central entrance implies that it was blocked by a chancel screen which prevented the devotees from entering through it, although they could look inside and see the statue or the relief of the god.

D. Architectural Decoration

The Roman temple of Kedesh exhibits one of the richest collections of architectural features in Israel. Judging by the remains on the surface, and by the items discovered in the excavations, it was a Corinthian temple in the fullest sense.

The fragments of the entablature, the Corinthian capitals, along with the bases and pedestals indicate that the temple was part of a series of "baroque" sites which were built in the E within the framework of Imperial architecture of the 2d century C.E. The character of the architectural decoration, the arrangement of the different items, and their workmanship emphasize the high artistic quality of the temple.

About 10 m of the entablature can be reconstructed. Remaining fragments of the cornices have coffers and consoles, which have been common in the E since the Hellenistic period. They are made up of moldings typical of the Corinthian egg-and-dart *(ovolo)*, coffers, consoles, and astragals motifs. Among other motifs decorating the entablature are a stringed musical instrument (cithara), a basis resting on a tripod, and a crescent with a star.

E. Identification of the Temple Deity and Manner of Worship

It has been suggested that the temple at Kedesh was dedicated to Helios. However, the epigraphical and iconographical data imply a different identification. These include (1) two Greek inscriptions, one of which was found close to the temple and the other in secondary use in the wall of the nearby village police station at Qadis; and (2) two eagles with outstretched wings, one carved on the lintel of the central doorway and the other on the lintel of the N doorway.

The Greek inscriptions refer to Baal-shamin, the "Holy God of the Sky," one of the main gods of the Syro-Phoenician region during the Roman period. This god is mentioned in inscriptions from Palmyra, Damascus, Hosn-Suleiman, and elsewhere. Three of the temples erected in his honor are well known: in Palmyra, in Dura-Europos, and in Seia in S Syria. The two eagles mentioned above support the identification of the deity as Baal-shamin.

To the N and the S of the two side openings of the cella are two kraters carved in stone, with narrow channels leading inside the building. These almost certainly served for libations of wine, oil, or the blood of sacrificed animals intended for the god, in return for which the worshiper received the blessing or oracle from the priest. Possibly the grooves were connected with a religious ceremony facilitating contacts between the world of the living and the world of the dead. The existence of mausoleums to the W of the temple complex and of tombs to the N strengthens this supposition. To the best of our knowledge, these libation channels are unique in the architecture of temples in the Roman world. Above the S krater is an apsidal niche with a sunken, carved relief of a human figure wearing a toga, holding a pear-shaped vessel with basketlike handles in the right hand and a spear in the left. The proximity of the figure to the krater and to the grooves suggests that it depicts the act of libation and symbolizes the worshiper.

F. Summary

The research at Kedesh so far has revealed a rich and elaborate architectural complex consisting of a *temenos* with a temple of the *prostylos hexastylos* type at its center. The architectural decoration is in the Corinthian style with "baroque" characteristics. Its layout and architectural motifs are typical of the decorative context in the Roman East, especially of the Syro-Phoenician region. The temple is the southernmost link in the chain of Roman temples in this region.

In addition to the types of architectural decoration, dated inscriptions discovered previously as well as those from the recent excavations provide evidence for dating the complex. Three Greek inscriptions are dated respectively to 117/18, 189/90, and 214/15 C.E. It may therefore be assumed that construction of the temple complex began around the beginning of the 2d century and continued in stages over a century or so.

Although it is still difficult to determine when the temple was abandoned, it appears that it was destroyed by an earthquake, possibly the one that struck the region on May 19, 363 C.E.

Bibliography

Fischer, M.; Ovadiah, A.; and Roll, I. 1984. The Roman Temple at Kedesh, Upper Galilee: A Preliminary Study. *TA* 11: 146–72.

———. 1985. The Architectural Design of the Roman Temple at Kedesh. *EI* 18: 353–60 (in Hebrew).

———. 1986–87. The Epigraphic Finds from the Roman Temple at Kedesh in the Upper Galilee. *TA* 13–14: 60–66.

———. 1988. Deity and Cult in the Roman Temple at Kedesh. Vol. 2, pp. 168–73 in *Sepher Z. Vilnay*. Jerusalem (in Hebrew).

A. OVADIAH
MOSHE FISCHER
ISRAEL ROLL

QASHISH, TEL

QASHISH, TEL (M.R. 160232). A site located at the foot of Mt. Carmel in the NW end of the valley of Jezreel. It contains ruins dating to the OT period.

A. Location and Identification

Tel Qashish is situated on the right bank of the Kishon river, in one of its meanders, so that it is protected by the river on two sides. Tel Yoqneam can clearly be seen 2 km to the S. The site is elongated, measuring 180 m × 60 m. It slopes steeply in all directions, except in the NE region, where the approach way and gate were located. The site measures some 10 dunams and is clearly divided into two parts, with the W half ca. 5 m higher than the E half. The reason for this is that while the earliest settlement (EB) extended over the entire surface of the mound, subsequent occupation (in the MB and LB, as well as in the Iron Age) was limited to the W part of the site. EB strata are therefore to be found immediately below the present surface in the E part of the site, while MB and LB strata are to be found right below the surface in the center and highest part of the site.

Tel Qashish dominates one of the fords of the Kishon. It also dominates the S exit of the narrow pass, connecting the plain of Acco and the valley of Jezreel. The strategic location, the accessibility of Bronze Age strata, the opportunity to study a small rural site and at the same time to investigate its relationship to a neighboring larger town (Tel Yoqneam) led to the choice of this site for excavation.

Aharoni (*LBHG*, 151) has suggested that the site be identified with "Helkath," no. 112 on the list of Canaanite sites conquered by Thutmosis III, neighboring Jokneam (n. 113 on that same list). Another possibility is to identify the site with Dabbasheth (meaning "camel's hump"), mentioned in the description of the border of the tribe of Zebulun, which "goes up westward, and on to Mareal, and touches Dabbasheth, then the river that is east of Jokneam" (Josh 19:11). Such an identification suits well the order of sites on the border, the immediate vicinity of Jokneam, as well as the general appearance of Tel Qashish (which resembles a crouching camel).

B. The Excavations

The excavation of Tel Qashish is part of a larger, regional archaeological research project—the Yoqneam Regional Project. See JOKNEAM; QIRI, TELL. Eight seasons of excavations have been conducted so far. Two areas are being investigated: "A" on the high part of the site, and "B" in the lower. Together, an area of about 1,100 square meters is being investigated (10 percent of the surface of the site). Fifteen levels of occupation have been noted, spanning EB I through the Persian period.

1. Early Bronze Age. With the exception of a few Neolithic flint tools, found on bedrock, the earliest occupation level of the site is attributed to EB I. The settlement extended beyond the limits of the tel itself, as evidenced by the large amount of pottery and flints scattered all over the area N of the site (some nearly 100 m away). Due to the limited size of the excavated area, only one complete dwelling and a few fragments of others are known so far, with two architectural phases clearly discernible. The houses are small, with their corners rounded on the outside but with 90-degree angles on the inside. This method of constructing corners finds close parallels in the EB I levels of sites such as Megiddo and Byblos. Typical ceramic finds include bow-rimmed pithoi and grey burnished ware. Two cylinder seal impressions on jar fragments are noteworthy, one of which has two close parallels at other sites in the region (Megiddo and Tel-Shadud). In EB II, the site was fortified by a wall 2.5–3.0-m wide, surprisingly massive for a site of that order. The stones were laid in a herringbone fashion, a style also noted in the dwellings. Two major and several subphases of construction were discerned and attributed to EB II–III. The houses are well built, yet in spite of several constructional features common to several of them, no uniformity in plan was observed. Early Bronze Age houses were also excavated in area A. These are of a somewhat different nature than those situated near the fortification wall, even though they are of the same period; the houses there are somewhat larger, and no herringbone construction was observed. The ceramic finds are rather poor and monotonous, comprising mainly platters, cooking pots, and storage jars. In spite of the location of the site in a region where Khirbet Kerak Ware should be expected, the total absence of this ceramic family at Qashish is noteworthy. Cylinder seal impressions on storage jars are relatively common.

In the last phase of the Early Bronze Age settlement—within EB III—the fortification wall went out of use. Following a certain occupational gap, new houses were built, partly superimposed on the derelict fortification. Their standard of construction was inferior compared to that of the previous houses; the walls were built of small rough stones, and the plan consisted of a forecourt behind which was a room serving as living quarters.

2. Middle Bronze Age. Remains of the Middle Bronze Age are confined to the high part of the site and include a fortification system and dwellings. This fortified village may have been preceded by an unfortified phase (stratum X), which is hardly attested. The MB fortifications consist of a 2-m-wide wall, a rectangular tower built against this wall's inner face, and a small glacis of small stones and earth dumped against its outer face. Inside the wall a series of rooms and a courtyard were unearthed. These were built against the inner face of the fortification wall on one side and opened onto a paved alley on the other. Similar arrangements were noted at contemporary sites such as Gezer, Shechem, and Taanach. Three phases of a rather short duration were noted, the final being characterized by infant burials in jars, a phenomenon known from several contemporary sites, including neighboring Tel Yoqneam. Just as at Yoqneam, the transition between the MB and LB ages at Qashish (strata VIII–VII) was peaceful.

3. The Late Bronze Age. This settlement was unfortified, and only fragmentary house walls and a few ceramic assemblages have been found so far. Imported (Cypriote and Mycenaean) pottery is relatively scarce. The settlement suffered two destructions in the course of the period: once in the 14th century and again by the end of the 13th (marking the end of the Late Bronze Age).

4. Iron Age. The remains of the Iron Age settlement are even scantier than those of the previous period: it seems that a small settlement, confined to the higher part of the site, was established in Iron I. A round installation built of stone slabs, probably an oil press, is noteworthy. An exact parallel is known from contemporary Yoqneam. The ceramic assemblage includes collar-rim jars and several Philistine sherds. Remains of Iron II are extremely fragmentary, attesting to some occupation during this period.

5. Persian Period. The final phase of occupation is dated to the Persian period. An impressive building was excavated in the E section of the site. It appears to have been an isolated farmhouse built of extremely large stones, which were still clearly visible on the surface of the mound. A few coins, stray sherds, and glass fragments indicate some kind of activity at the site during the Hellenistic and Mamluk periods.

Stratum	*Period*	
I	Persian	Isolated farmhouse
II	Iron III	Scanty remains
III A–B	Iron II	Scanty remains
IV A–B	Iron I	Farm and agricultural installations
V	LB II A–B	Isolated tower, destruction by fire
VI	LB I B	Unfortified settlement, destruction by fire
VII A–B	LB I A	Unfortified settlement, destruction by fire
VIII	LB II–III	Fragmentary paved areas, ash pockets
IX A–C	MB II	Fortified settlement
X	MB I–II	Occupational surface, sherds
XI	EB III	Unfortified settlement
XII	EB II–III	Fortified settlement
XIII	EB II–III	Fortified settlement
XIV	EB I	Unfortified settlement extending beyond site
XV	EB I	Unfortified settlement extending beyond site
—	Neolithic	Stray flint tools

Bibliography

Aharoni, Y. 1959. Zepath of Thutmoses. *IEJ* 9: 120 (pl. 15b).

Ben-Tor, A.; Portugali, Y.; and Avissar, M. 1981. The First Two Seasons of Excavations at Tel Qashish, 1978–1979. *IEJ* 31: 137–64.

AMNON BEN-TOR

QASILE, TELL (M.R. 130167). A site situated on the N bank of the Yarkon river, about 1 mile from the Mediterranean coast. Two Hebrew ostraca found on the surface of the mound led to systematic excavations of the site, which were carried out under the direction of B. Mazar (1949–51, 1956) and continued under the direction of A. Mazar (1971–74, 1982–84). The 4-acre site is located on a *kurkar* (sandstone) ridge overlooking the Yarkon river and the coastal plain. A permanent settlement was founded on the site in the mid-12th century B.C. The founders were probably Philistines, "Sea Peoples," who settled the S coastal plain of Palestine during the 12th century B.C. Tell Qasile was an important port town, since the Yarkon river was ideal for anchoring the small ships of that time. Seafaring and trade were thus basic factors in the economy of the settlers. Though the ancient name of Tell Qasile is unknown, it is one of the most important sites for studying the material culture of the Philistines during Iron Age I. Three successive occupation levels of the Philistine town were discovered (strata XII–X), covering a span of about 180 years (ca. 1150–980 B.C.). The town was finally conquered and burnt, probably during the conquest of the region by David. The transitions from stratum XII to XI and then from stratum XI to X appear to have been peaceful, and they mark a gradual growth and development of the town.

The buildings of stratum XII are built of mud bricks and are laid on the bedrock, without stone foundations. The two most important structures from this level are the temple and a public building. The temple is a small edifice containing one room, with benches along the walls and a raised platform. A large courtyard in front of the temple accommodated ritual ceremonies and sacrifices. The public building, situated S of the temple, contained a large hall, with benches along the walls and a free-standing hearth, recalling similar hearths in the Aegean and Anatolian worlds. In the following stratum (XI), the city was rebuilt, usually with stone structures. The temple was rebuilt on the remains of the previous one; it was somewhat larger, the entrance was at the NE corner, and a small chamber built inside the main structure served as a treasury, where a large collection of cult objects was found.

In stratum X, the temple was enlarged and redesigned. See Fig. QAS.01. An entrance chamber with a wide opening led to the main hall, the roof of which was supported by two cedar pillar with circular stone bases. Inside the main hall, benches skirted the walls, and a raised platform served as the "holy of holies" in the sanctuary; a narrow room at the back of the temple served as a treasury room. Stone walls surrounded the courtyard of this temple, in which auxiliary rooms and a sacrificial altar were constructed. In both stratum XI and stratum X, a small shrine was built to the W of the main temple. This was a small room with benches along the walls and a raised platform in one corner.

The finds in the successive temples at Tell Qasile are of particular importance, since they contain a unique collection of cult objects made of pottery, as well as of metal, alabaster, and ivory. Some of the cult objects are of particular importance as unique art objects from the period of the Judges. Both the plans of the temples and the shapes of the cult objects reflect a strong Canaanite influence on the local culture. Yet similarities to cultural phenomena in Cyprus, as well as in the Aegean world, point to the origin of the local population, though it can be conjectured that the Philistine newcomers were just the overlords of a local autochtonous population. This is corroborated by the nature of the rich pottery assemblages found in the sanctuary, which show a combination of characteristically Philistine traditions and traditions typical of the Canaanite culture.

A dwelling quarter excavated at the S part of the tell demonstrates the urban planning and the design of private dwellings during the 11th century B.C. See Fig. CIT.05. The houses are arranged in well-planned blocks; each house is square and contains a courtyard divided by a row of pillars. The rich finds in these houses illustrate the wealth of the population on the eve of the Israelite conquest. Imported pottery from Phoenicia, Cyprus, and Egypt implies trade connections.

The destruction of Tell Qasile during the time of David did not end the town. During the United Monarchy, the town was partially rebuilt (strata IX–VIII), though not as densely as in the previous period, and it probably served as a port town for Israel. The town was destroyed at the end of the 10th century B.C., perhaps during Shishak's invasion of the country. A gap in occupation lasted most of the Iron Age, and only in the late 7th century did a small settlement exist on the site, perhaps related to the Judean expansion to the coast during the time of Josiah.

During the Persian period, a large building at the top of the mound perhaps served as an administration building or a farmstead. A rock-cut square well supplied water to the site during this time. During the Hellenistic and Roman periods, there was a small settlement on the site. Isolated structures from the Byzantine period, particularly a large public bathhouse on the mound and a synagogue at the foot of the mound, are evidence for a small town which existed in the vicinity of the tell. An isolated estate, dated perhaps to the time of the Crusaders, was found on the top of the mound.

Bibliography

Mazar, A. 1980. *Excavations at Tell Qasile, Part One.* Qedem 12. Jerusalem.

———. 1985. *Excavations at Tell Qasile, Part Two.* Qedem 20. Jerusalem.

AMIHAY MAZAR
GEORGE L. KELM

QATABANIAN LANGUAGE. See LANGUAGES (INTRODUCTORY SURVEY).

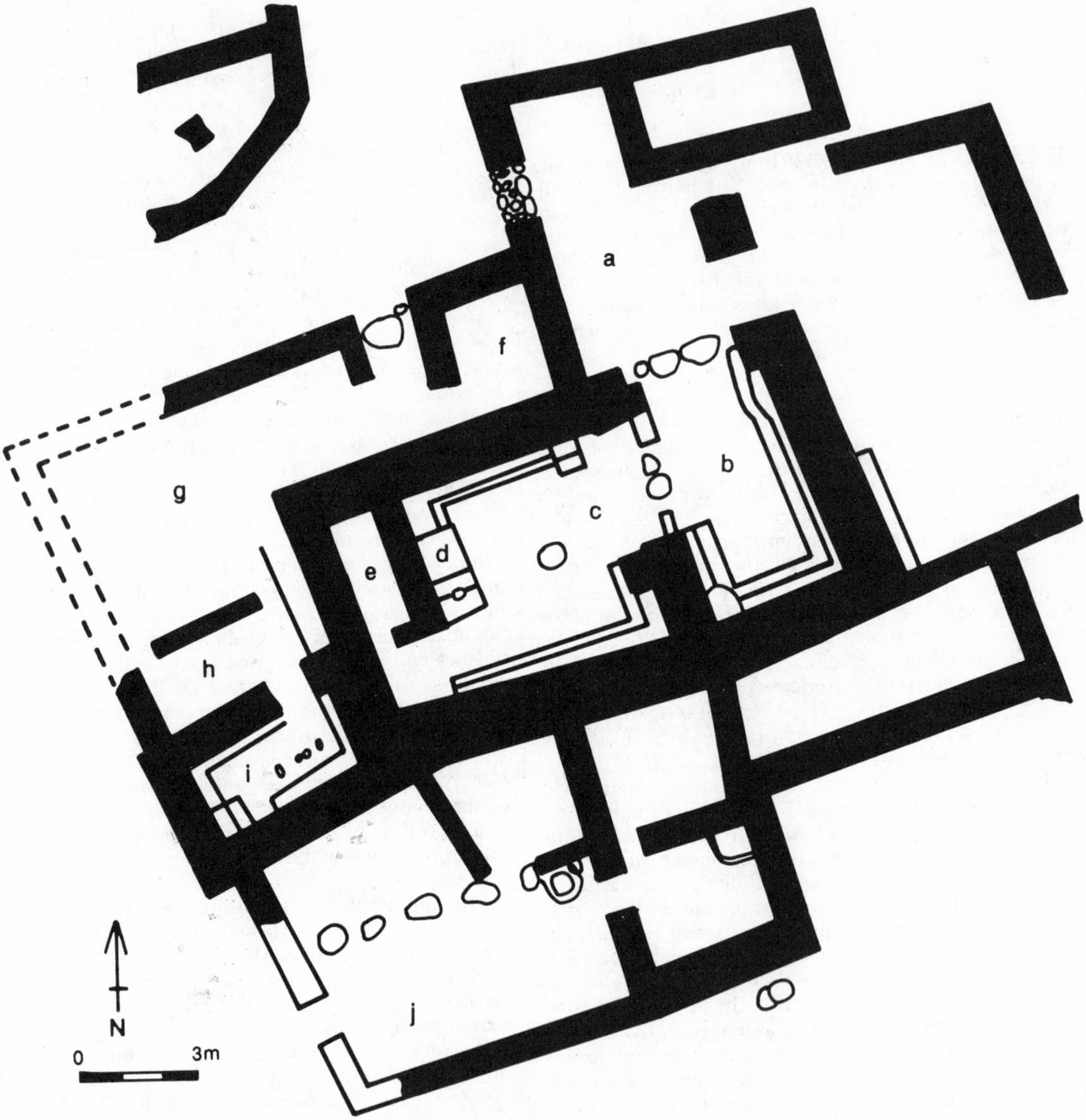

QAS.01. Plan of temple complex in area C at Tell Qasile—Stratum X. (a) courtyard of temple; (b) entrance room; (c) main hall of temple; (d) high altar; (e) storage room for offering vessels; (f) cultic preparation room; (g) courtyard; (h) entrance porch of shrine; (i) shrine; (j) residential quarters (priestly?). *(Redrawn from Mazar 1980: 34, fig. 9)*

QEDAH, TELL EL- (M.R. 203269). A site, located in N Israel between the Sea of Galilee and the Huleh basin, which is certainly to be identified with biblical Hazor. Hazor is first mentioned as the major military power organizing the N coalition against the Israelites (Jos 11:1, 10) and is specifically described as standing on a "mound" (Heb *tēl;* Josh 11:13). The area was later ascribed to the territory of Naphtali (Josh 19:32, 36). The city's military strength is again described when Hazor was able to muster 900 chariots of iron in conflicts with Israel in the days of Deborah (Judges 4). Its strategic importance is further demonstrated when Solomon chose to fortify Hazor along with Jerusalem, Megiddo, and Gezer (1 Kgs 9:15). The environs of Hazor were later targets of a prophetic denunciation by Jeremiah (49:28–33). The name "Hazor" comes from the Hebrew *ḥāṣēr,* "enclosure," which aptly describes the site. Tell el-Qedah (Tell Waqqas) is an imposing mound, with a 180-acre Lower City of the Bronze Age and a 30-

acre Upper City or acropolis at the S end, which dates to the Iron Age. It is strategically situated at the juncture of the E flanks of the Lebanon range and the W edge of the Jordan Valley (4 miles SW of the Huleh basin), on the N border of Palestine and astride the main route N to Syria and beyond. In the Neo-Assyrian annals documenting troop movements S into Palestine, Hazor is always named along with Abel Beth-Maacah and Dan as prominent fortresses on the N frontier.

A. History of Investigations
B. Results of Excavations
   1. Early Bronze Age
   2. Middle Bronze Age
   3. Late Bronze Age
   4. Iron Age
   5. Persian and Later Occupations
C. Other Sites Named Hazor

A. History of Investigations

The mound of Hazor was first investigated in 1928 by J. Garstang, although his soundings remain largely unpublished. It was then excavated in 1955–58 and 1968–72, in a major project carried out by Yigael Yadin and other prominent Israeli archaeologists. Yadin's principal excavation areas were A, B, BA, G, L, and M in the Upper City; and, in the Lower City, areas C, D, E, F, H, K, N, P, and 210. (The Lower City has its own local strata numbering sequence: 4 = XVII; 3 = XVI; 2 = XV; 1b = XIV; and 1a = XIII.)

B. Results of Excavations

1. Early Bronze Age. The site was first occupied in EB II–III (strata XXI–XIX; ca. 2900–2300 B.C.), followed by a break in the EB IV period (scant material of stratum XVIII; ca. 2300–2000 B.C.).

2. Middle Bronze Age. The beginnings of the urbanized city of the 2d millennium B.C. are already seen in the relatively few structures and tombs of MB I (stratum "Pre-XVII"; ca. 1900–1800/1750 B.C.). One tomb, found only in reconstruction work in 1971–72 in connection with the area L water tunnel, contained more than 150 vessels of this and the beginning of the next stratum.

During the MB II period (stratum XVII; ca. 1800/1750–1650 B.C.) there was a substantial buildup of domestic structures, accompanied by rock-cut cisterns (some with numerous scarabs), a system of underground tunnels (originally tombs?), and intramural jar burials, especially of infants. A large, but only partially cleared, mudbrick palace or citadel was found in area K. A jar inscribed with a personal name is the earliest-known Akkadian inscription found in Israel. Most significant are the area-K and multiple-entryway city gates, and the earliest city defenses in areas C, G, H, K, and P. The latter consisted of varying combinations of earthen embankments (the typical MB glacis), fosses, counterscarps, and massive stone and mudbrick ramparts. All these elements were superbly engineered and adapted to the topography and defense requirements of the differing areas of the 180-acre Lower City, which appears to have been entirely developed (local stratum 4). To this horizon belong the earliest-known references to Hazor in the literary sources—the Brussels Execration texts from Egypt (ca. 1825–1775 B.C.) and several references in the Mari texts (ca. 18th century). The Mari texts mention tin-trading caravans plying the routes between Upper Mesopotamia and Hazor (as well as Dan) in N Palestine. This is the period when true tin-bronze technology came into widespread use in Palestine, and Hazor must have played a significant role in the redistribution of the vital element of tin, which had to be imported. At Hazor itself, a fragment of a cuneiform tablet contains part of a Sumerian-Akkadian lexical text of the Mari period.

The zenith of the Lower City was reached in MB III (stratum XVI = local stratum 3; ca. 1650–1550 B.C.), when a population of ca. 15,000–20,000 would have made Hazor probably the largest Canaanite city-state in Palestine. The inhabitants of stratum XVI reused and augmented all of the above domestic features. The extensive rock-cut tunnels of the previous stratum were reused for storage, reservoirs, and even drainage channels. The underground cisterns were also reused (like Cistern 9012). Particularly significant was the reconstruction of the simple area-K gateway into a monumental three-entryway, towered city gate like those known from Shechem and Gezer, as well as prototypes found throughout Syria and Anatolia at this time. This gate was accompanied by a stretch of casemate city wall, one of the earliest known examples of this type of fortification in Palestine (see others at Taʿanach and Shechem). The palace-citadel in area A continued. The first temples appeared in stratum XVI: in area A is a rectangular temple with basalt orthostats at the entrance; a double (or "bilobate") temple is in area F; and in area H is a bipartite temple (the later tripartite "orthostat" temple; below). Stratum XVI ended in a major destruction, as did most sites in Palestine at the end of the MB. These destructions were in connection with Egyptian punitive raids following the expulsion of the Asiatic (or "Hyksos") princes at the end of the 17th and beginning of the 18th Dynasties (ca. 1540–1500 B.C.). An ephemeral post-destruction stratum, "post-XVI," consists mostly of burials and some transitional MB III/LB I pottery. It is probably to this horizon that we should attribute the reference to Hazor on the walls of the temple at Karnak, which lists the sites conquered by Thutmose III.

3. Late Bronze Age. The full developed LB I period witnessed the rebuilding of urban Hazor during the early part of the Egyptian New Kingdom (stratum XV; ca. 1500–1400 B.C.). The city gate in area K was reused, as apparently were some of the earlier city walls. The area-A rectangular temple was slightly altered and reused. The area-H bipartite temple from stratum XVI was reused in its basic form, but it was modified to include a forecourt that featured a stone offering table; a semicircular basin and drainpipe system for animal sacrifices; and a potter's workshop, which was found in situ with many ceramic miniature bowls (votives). Finds of particular significance included bronze figurines; a bronze plaque of a robed priest, which has almost exact Syro-Mesopotamian parallels (one of the finest art objects ever found in Bronze Age Palestine); and a liver model used in divination, which reads in Akkadian (in part): "Ishtar will eat the land; Nergal will . . .; the gods of the city will come back." A new temple was built in area F—a square, "mazelike" structure that has close parallels with the Mt. Gerizim temple at Shechem and with the Amman airport temple.

During the well-known "Amarna Age" in LB IIA, Hazor reached the peak of its recovery (stratum XIV; ca. 1400–1300 B.C.). One tomb contained large quantities of Mycenaean IIIA pottery imported from the Greek mainland. Some of the fortifications appear to have continued along with the temples. The area-H temple was converted from a bipartite into a tripartite structure, and most of the interior was lined with splendid basalt orthostats in the N Syrian style. The newly built "stelae temple" in area C was especially significant. It consisted of a semicircle of ten (?) small monoliths of dressed basalt, with a basalt statue of a seated king or deity. The center stele has a bas-relief depicting a pair of upraised palms, above which is a disk-within-a-crescent. These symbols are often associated with Baᶜal Ḥarmmōn and the Phoenician goddess Tanit (Asherah of the Canaanite pantheon). Near the temple was found a potter's workshop for mass-producing votive vessels; a small, well-modeled terra-cotta cult mask; fine cylinder seals of Mitannian (or N Syrian) style; and a splendid silver-plated bronze cult-standard.

A partially cleared structure below the Iron Age "pillared building" (below) suggests an Amarna Age palace. Its ruins included basalt orthostats; stone columns and bases; a staircase; and the forepart of a magnificent basalt lioness. It is possible that these are remains of the palace of Abdi-Tirshi, a king of Hazor in the 14th century B.C., who is mentioned in the Amarna letters. Some idea of the importance of the city, as inferred from these letters, is the fact that he alone of the Palestinian princes styled himself "king." Abdi-Tirshi presumed to oversee other N cities, seized rival city-states, and connived with the lawless "Habiru" against the pharaoh. An Akkadian fragment from Hazor (unfortunately found out of context) probably belongs to this horizon and concerns litigation over a real-estate transaction, which was brought to the attention of the king of Hazor. Further textual evidence of the importance of Hazor in the LB II period is gained from its mention in topographical lists of Amenophis III (ca. 1400 B.C.), Seti I (ca. 1300 B.C.), and Ramesses II (ca. 13th century B.C.).

The final phase of the Late Bronze Age, LB IIB, is attested by stratum XIII (ca. 1300–1220 B.C.), when Hazor was clearly in decline. While the temples were mostly rebuilt, the area-H temple demonstrates the decline with its misaligned orthostats and generally poor alterations. This phase ended in a massive destruction of the entire Lower City, which was buried under several feet of debris and was never reoccupied. Yadin dated this conflagration to ca. 1250–1230 B.C. on the basis of the presence of Mycenaean IIIB pottery, which ceased to be imported from the Greek mainland by 1220 B.C. Yadin also attributed the destruction to the incoming Israelites under Joshua, who according to Josh 11:10 captured "Hazor . . . the head of all those kingdoms" and killed its king, Jabin. More recently, however, other scholars have pointed out that the destruction was probably too early to allow connection with Israelite invaders (if any) in Joshua's time. Among the most impressive remains from the stratum XIII destruction are those objects connected with the last phase of the area-H orthostat temple. These include basalt offering tables, altars, and basins; a basalt seated figure of a king or deity; a terra-cotta temple model; ceramic votive vessels; cylinder seals; beads and other jewelry; terra-cotta zoomorphic figurines; a bronze bull (probably an El figurine); and bronze figurines representing other deities.

4. Iron Age. Following the massive destruction of the city, there was only a "squatter occupation," consisting mostly of huts and rubbish pits among the ruins (stratum XII; early 12th century B.C.). Yadin supposed this to be the early attempt at settlement by the Israelites after their capture of the city. The following phase (stratum XI; ca. 11th century B.C.) exhibits a more permanent settlement, although it has relatively few structures. A somewhat enigmatic installation was interpreted as a *bâmah,* or "high place." A hoard of bronzes in an associated votive jar included a lugged ax and a seated bronze El/Baal figure. Both, however, are typically LB in design and may be holdovers from earlier levels, and thus are not characteristically "Israelite."

Iron Age Hazor really began as an urban center with the Solomonic era (strata Xb–a; mid-late 10th century B.C.). The large Lower City was abandoned from this point on; the new settlement centered on the 30-acre Upper City. Particularly important for this period is a large citadel complex in area B and the casemate defensive wall and splendid four-entryway city gate, both of which were found in area A. The latter was compared by Yadin with the nearly identical walls and gates found at Megiddo and Gezer, thus confirming the historical footnote in 1 Kgs 9:15–17. Hazor, refortified by Solomon as part of his strongly centralized administrative system, probably served as the regional capital of the district.

The late 10th/early 9th centuries B.C. (strata IXb–a) are characterized by a decline, then a destruction about the time of the rise of the Omrides (ca. 875 B.C.; or perhaps associated with the raids of Ben-Hadad of Damascus in the early 9th century; cf. 2 Chr 16:4). During the Omride dynasty, Hazor (stratum VIII) was again a most impressive site. On the acropolis, the principal building was a multi-roomed citadel, some 70 by 80 ft, constructed with thick walls and ashlar masonry. Several "Proto-Aeolic" (or palmette) capitals found in stratum VII probably originated here. In area G, solid walls were built over the casemates, but in area A the casemate city walls were reused, with the chambers often used as storerooms. In area A, a large three-room structure (the "pillared building"), with a double row of monolithic columns flanking the center aisle, probably served as a storehouse. The most dramatic change in stratum VIII was the construction of the monumental water system in area L. This consisted of a massive stepped shaft, some 50-ft square and about 100-ft deep, cut through the solid rock; from this vertical shaft branched a domed lateral gallery, which sloped downward for some 80 ft to reach a deep underground spring. The ground-level entrance was guarded by a sort of "gatehouse." This marvelously engineered water system, comparable in date and function to the one at Megiddo (and perhaps also at Gezer), was probably constructed in anticipation of the Assyrian advance.

During the late 9th century B.C. (stratum VII), the citadel, pillared storehouse, water system, and other features were reused. This stratum ends in a destruction, perhaps related to the Aramean incursions into the N of Israel ca. 810 B.C.

In the early 8th century (stratum VI), Hazor experienced a renaissance. The area-B citadel continued, but other public areas in the Upper City were converted to residences, workshops, and storage facilities. Near the citadel was a two-story house, with a well-preserved staircase, which may have belonged to an important official or an elite family. Another fine house produced an ostracon with the name "Makbiram" and a carved ivory panel. The destruction that ended stratum VI was probably caused by an earthquake in the time of Jeroboam II (ca. 786–746 B.C.).

Hazor, like all major sites in the N, was destroyed by the Assyrians (strata VB–a), in this case undoubtedly by Tiglath-pileser III in 732 B.C. (1 Kgs 15:29). The citadel, which had been reinforced by an added offsets-insets perimeter wall, was completely destroyed. Among the remains were several objects inscribed in Hebrew, including a storejar "belonging to Pekah, *semadar*" (a kind of wine); another vessel reading "belonging to Delayo"; a bowl inscribed *qodeš*, "holy"; an ivory *pyksis*-box; a carved stone ladle with an embossed hand; stone cosmetic palettes; Asherah figurines; and the skeleton of a partly consumed pig.

Stratum IV (late 8th century B.C.) represents the postdestruction period. It was a temporary, unfortified settlement, which Yadin thought was occupied by the returning Israelite survivors of the Assyrian destruction. The main feature excavated in stratum III was an Assyrian-period citadel. There is no 7th–6th century material that might provide a context for the references to Hazor in Jer 49:28–33.

5. Persian and Later Occupations. Hazor's final days are represented by scattered Persian finds of stratum II (ca. 4th century B.C.), among which were a large citadel on the acropolis, Persian coins, and imported Attic wares. A final, smaller citadel belongs to stratum I (3d–2d centuries B.C.) and may be associated with references in 1 Macc 11:47 to Jonathan's struggles against the Seleucid king, Demetrius II, on the "plain of Hazor." The abandoned site, despite its strategic location and formidable appearance, lay neglected until its rediscovery as biblical Hazor in 1875 in the proposed identification of J. L. Porter.

C. Other Sites Named Hazor

Two other sites named Hazor are found in the Hebrew Bible. In Judah, Hazor-hadattah (so LXX, or "New Hazor"; Josh 15:23) may be located at el-Jebariyeh. In Benjamin, a Hazor (Neh 11:33) has been identified with Khirbet Hazzur, 4 miles NW of Jerusalem. See also HAZOR.

Bibliography

Malamat, A. 1970. Northern Canaan and the Mari Texts. Pp. 164–77 in *Near Eastern Archaeology in the Twentieth Century*, ed. J. A. Sanders. Garden City, NY.

Yadin, Y. 1959–64. *Hazor* I–IV. Jerusalem.

———. 1969. Excavations at Hazor, 1968–1969: Preliminary Communiqué. *IEJ* 19: 1–19.

———. 1972. *Hazor: The Head of All Those Kingdoms*. London.

———. 1975. *Hazor: The Rediscovery of a Great Citadel of the Bible*. London.

———. 1976. Hazor. *EAEHL* 2: 474–95.

Yadin, Y., and Shiloh, Y. 1971. Hazor: Notes and News. *IEJ* 19: 230.

William G. Dever

QEDEIS, AIN. See HEZRON (PLACE).

QEDISH, KHIRBET (M.R. 202237). See KEDESH (PLACE).

QERE. See KETHIB AND QERE.

QIRI, TELL

QIRI, TELL (M.R. 160227). A site about 4 km of Mt. Carmel, where the hill country tapers off into the Jezreel valley. The site contains artifacts dated to the biblical period.

A. Location and Identification

Tell Qiri is situated within modern Kibbutz Ha-Zorea, 2 km S of Tell Yoqneam. It does not have the characteristic appearance of a tell, but instead consists of numerous occupation layers on the E slopes of Mt. Carmel that descend into the Shophet river (the site's water source). Wall fragments, tombs, potsherds, coins, etc., encountered during recent construction activities seem to indicate that the size of Tell Qiri was about 10–12 dunams, which fit well the pattern of other village sites in the region (Qashish, Reᶜala, etc.). These chance finds indicate human activity at the site in almost all periods, from the Neolithic to present times. When excavations started in 1975, about one third of the site was still free of modern buildings; today, the entire site is covered by the houses of Kibbutz Ha-Zorea.

Qiri is the Arabic name of the site. So far no identification with an ancient or biblical place is possible, and it appears that Qiri was a rather insignificant rural site never mentioned in antiquity. Even though a substantial part of the population of the land lived in such small, rural sites, they remain almost unknown and outside the scope of most archaeological investigation. The opportunity to shed some light on this type of settlement provided the impetus for the excavation of the site.

B. The Excavation

The excavation of Tell Qiri is part of a larger, regional archaeological research project—the Yoqneam Regional Project; cf. JOKNEAM; QASHISH, TEL. The site was excavated between 1975 and 1977 by a team from the Hebrew University of Jerusalem, headed by Amnon Ben-Tor. This was the first site investigated in the regional project; excavation techniques and registration and ceramic typology principles developed and tested here were also applied to other sites excavated by the project. Even though sporadic finds indicate some kind of activity in Tell Qiri at almost every period, stratum numbers were assigned only to those periods yielding architectural remains. The earliest settlement (stratum XI), which was reached in a very limited area, is Neolithic. Some walls, a stone silo, a substantial amount of pottery, and flint tools (axes, picks, chisels) were found. The pottery, which includes dark-face burnished ware, correlates well with other assemblages known from the region belonging to the transition from Late Neolithic to Chalcolithic, and dating to the second half of the 5th millennium B.C. Meager remains of houses of an unfortified Middle Bronze II village (stratum X) were encountered on the site's E slope (area E).

The main importance of Tell Qiri lies in the substantial accumulation of the Iron Age strata: four main strata (IX–VI/V), further subdivided into twelve subphases in an uninterrupted sequence, represent an unfortified Iron I–II village (12th–8th centuries B.C.). Gradual changes and development in house plans and ceramic typology can clearly be observed. Dwellings were built of mudbricks on stone foundations, the walls being 0.6-m thick. Since room dimensions never exceeded 2.5 m, the houses could be roofed without supporting pillars. Only once through the entire period—between strata VIII and VII (i.e., between Iron IB and IC)—was there a significant change in the orientation of the buildings. Apparently there was also no major break in the ethnic identity of the village's population during all that time. Botanical remains include olive, wheat, pomegranate, peas, and vetch. Sickle blades represent 45 percent of the lithic assemblage; 80 percent of the animal bones belong to sheep and goats, and 15 percent belong to cattle. Some hunting and fishing was also practiced, as indicated by various fish, gazelle, and fallow-deer bones. This repertoire of finds clearly indicates the rural character of the site, and this is reinforced by the large number of silos and agricultural installations uncovered.

An interesting group of finds includes 10th-century B.C. cooking pots, the rims of which were incised before firing with a sign similar to one of the Phoenician/Hebrew letters of the alphabet, a phenomenon characteristic of sites in the Jezreel Valley at that period (such as Megiddo, Tell Yoqneam, and Tell Qashish). So far, neither the incised signs nor their significance is understood.

A noteworthy ceramic assemblage was unearthed in a dwelling of stratum VIII (= 11th century B.C.), including an incense burner, a double libation vessel, a chalice, a cup and saucer, and a votive bowl. The cultic nature of this assemblage is reinforced by the apparent remains of sacrifices found there. A number of bones belonging to the right foreleg of sheep and goats clearly indicate the practice of sacrificing "the right thigh" (cf. Lev 7:32–33).

From the strata of the Persian period onwards, only fragmentary buildings and some pottery, glass, and coins were found. Some 20 rock-cut tombs of the Persian period were discovered uphill on the W part of the site; the dead were placed in the tombs with their heads pointing north, and the tombs were covered by flat stone slabs. The cemetery, as well as all other remains of strata IV–I, was severely damaged by modern building activities associated with the modern kibbutz.

Stratum	*Period*	
I	Roman–Byzantine	Fragmentary walls, surface finds
II	Early Roman	Fragmentary walls, water installations
III	Hellenistic	Isolated building
IV	Persian	Houses, cemetery
V/VI A–C	Iron II	Public (?) building, house fragments
VII A–C	Iron IC	Rural settlement, agricultural installations
VIII A–C	Iron IB	Rural settlement, agricultural installations
IX A–C	Iron IA	Rural settlement, agricultural installations
X	Middle Bronze II–III	Rural settlement on E slope
XI	Late Neolithic	Rural settlement, agricultural installations

Bibliography

Anati, E., et al. 1973. Hazore'a I. *Archivi* 5. Brescia.

Ben-Tor, A. 1979. Tell Qiri, A Look at Village Life. *BA* 42: 105–14.

Ben-Tor, A., et al. 1987. *The Yoqneam Regional Project: Tel Qiri, A Village in the Valley of Jezreel.* Qedem 24. Jerusalem.

AMNON BEN-TOR

QOHELET. See ECCLESIASTES, BOOK OF.

QOM, KHIRBET EL-. See KOM, KHIRBET EL-.

QOP. The nineteenth letter of the Hebrew alphabet.

QOSEIMEH, AIN. See KARKA.

QUADRATUS. Earliest known Christian apologist, who, according to Eusebius, addressed his work to the emperor Hadrian, presumably when he first visited Athens in A.D. 124–125. His date is known only from Eusebius' *Chronicle* and *Church History,* and the latter work contains the one known fragment of the apology. Eusebius had the whole work, but cited it only to indicate Quadratus' intelligence, "apostolic orthodoxy," and early date. The passage cited contrasts the genuine healings and raisings from the dead of "our Savior" with those of another person whose miracles were only in semblance or had temporary effects, or else with a "seeming" Savior who accomplished no permanent achievements. Quadratus said that those healed or raised from the dead lived on "for a considerable time" after the "departure" of the Savior. In consequence, "some of them survived even to our own day," that is, presumably up to the time of Quadratus' birth (*Hist. Eccl.* 4.3.1–2).

The context of his argument, regrettably not reported by Eusebius, could have lain in philosophical debates over men treated as gods because of fictitious miracles, or in debates over Christ's miracles, or in both at once. About half a century later, Irenaeus may have relied on Quadratus for his own discussions of miracles (*Haer.* 2.31.2 and 2.32.4), later copied by Eusebius (*Hist. Eccl.* 5.7). Irenaeus claimed that in Christian churches there were those who "cure the sick by laying hands on them, and . . . the dead have been raised and remained with us for many years." It is not absolutely certain what time frames either Quadratus or Irenaeus had in view, for the latter spoke of the reign of Domitian, nearly a century earlier, as "not long ago but practically in our own generation" (*Haer.* 5.30.1; a passage known to Eusebius, *Hist. Eccl.* 5.8.6).

Contemporary gnostics used the title "Savior" for their spiritual Jesus, but presumably Quadratus had in mind the more practical "salvation" provided by healings and raisings. In his time, the emperor Hadrian himself was often hailed as Savior, but the apologist would hardly have criticized to his face.

Attempts to identify Quadratus with others of the same name or to connect his work with other writings have not been successful. It is unlikely that Quadratus' apology enjoyed any success, for its theme is not repeated by the later apologists of the 2d century.

Bibliography

Andriessen, P. 1947. The Authorship of the *Epistula ad Diognetum*. *VC* 1: 129–36.

Grant, R. M. 1977. Quadratus, the First Christian Apologist. Pp. 177–83 in *A Tribute to Arthur Vööbus*, ed. R. H. Fischer. Chicago.

———. 1988. *Greek Apologists of the Second Century*. Philadelphia.

Robert M. Grant

QUAIL. See ZOOLOGY.

QUART. See WEIGHTS AND MEASURES.

QUARTER, SECOND (PLACE). See SECOND QUARTER.

QUARTUS (PERSON) [Gk *Kouartos*]. A Christian identified as the brother who sends greetings through Paul to the church at Rome (Rom 16:23). Mentioned after Tertius, the stenographer (v 22); Gaius, Paul's host (v 23); and Erastus, the city treasurer (v 23), Quartus (a Latin name meaning "fourth") is the last person cited by Paul in Romans 16 who sends greetings. The description, "the brother," given to Quartus is generally taken in the figurative sense to indicate membership in the Church, and is usually translated "our brother" (RSV, NEB), meaning "fellow Christian." This interpretation raises the question of why Quartus is singled out with a designation common to all the others in Romans 16. An alternative reading is to take "the brother" in the sense of physical relationship, meaning that Quartus is the brother of the previously mentioned Tertius or Erastus. In support of a link between Tertius and Quartus is an implied connection of siblings based on the meaning of their Latin names: Tertius, the "third" born, Quartus, the "fourth" born (Bruce *Romans* TNTC, 266). The problem with this reading is that the mention of the names Gaius and Erastus between Tertius and Quartus weakens a possible association between the latter two. Also, if Quartus were "the brother in the flesh" of Erastus, the person mentioned immediately before him, the possessive pronoun *autou*, "his," would be expected. Because of these difficulties, it is better to take "the brother" in the sense of spiritual brotherhood. Perhaps Paul included this designation for Quartus because he exhibited the qualities of being a "fellow Christian" in an exemplary way.

John Gillman

QUEEN. The English word "queen" is used to translate three Hebrew words in the OT: *malkâ, šēgal,* and *gĕbîrâ.* The term *malkâ,* the feminine form of *melek* (king), describes foreign queen regnants and consorts, e.g., the queens of Sheba (1 Kgs 10:1ff. = 2 Chr 9:1ff.) and of Persia (Vashti—Esth 1:9; and Esther—Esth 2:22). The term *šēgal* occurs only twice: in Neh 2:6 it refers to the wife of King Artaxerxes of Persia, while in Ps 45:9 it refers to a woman who (clothed) "in gold of Ophir" stands at the right hand of the king. The term *gĕbîrâ,* the feminine form of *gebîr* ("lord" or "master"), is used of a foreign queen (1 Kgs 11:19), but more often it designates the mother of a Judean or Israelite king (1 Kgs 15:13 = 2 Chr 15:16; 2 Kgs 10:13; Jer 13:18; 29:2).

A. ANE Background
  1. Egyptian Queens
  2. Mesopotamian Queens
  3. Hittite Queens
  4. Foreign Queens in the Bible
B. Israel and Judah
  1. Queen as Ruler
  2. Queen as Wife
  3. The Queen Mother

A. ANE Background

1. Egyptian Queens. The 18th Dynasty (ca. 1570–1320 B.C.E.) represents a high point in the history of Egyptian queens. Queen Hatshepsut (wife of Thutmose II and stepmother of Thutmose III) assumed control upon her husband's death and undertook several building projects (e.g., the mortuary temple at Deir el-Bahri; additions to the Temple at Karnak, etc.). Two other queens, Tiy (wife of Amenophis III) and Nefertiti (wife of Akhenaten), are given unusual prominence in both statuary and inscriptional remains.

2. Mesopotamian Queens. Information is scarce concerning the queens of Mesopotamia. At least one woman, Ku-baba, achieved the position of queen regnant. Originally a barmaid, she ruled Kish in the 3d millennium and is the only example of a ruling queen known. Other queens achieved prominence as consorts. Baranamtara (wife of Lugalanda) and Shag-Shag (wife of Urukagina) are mentioned in various temple records. Wives of the last rulers of Lagash (Early Dynastic period), they apparently functioned in a cultic capacity. In addition to these examples, two Neo-Assyrian queens—Sammuramat (wife of Shamshi-Adad V; mother of Adad-nirari III) and Zakutu (wife of Sennacherib; mother of Esarhaddon)—were active as queen mothers. Sammuramat served as queen regnant for her son, Adad-narari III, while Zakutu was probably influential in getting Esarhaddon, the youngest of Sennacherib's sons, appointed his father's heir.

The correspondence of the women at Mari (Old Babylonian period) provides readers with an unusual glimpse into the world of Šibtu, queen of Mari. Daughter of one king (Yarim-Lim of Yamḫad) and wife of another (Zimri-Lim of Mari), Šibtu exerted great influence on the royal court. Though the king retained supreme authority, she often served as his deputy in his absence. As queen, it fell within her duties to oversee the palace, supervise court officials, engage in cultic affairs, and serve as the king's representative in both domestic and state matters. (Batto 1974: 8–21).

3. Hittite Queens. Hittite queens, titled *tawannannas,* occupied positions of great influence. A *tawannanna* served as regnant in the event of the king's death or as his deputy during his absence. She participated in a broad spectrum of activities—political, military, diplomatic—and could on occasion oppose the king. In addition, she had a special relationship with the sun-goddess and played an important role in the cult. One of the more notable *tawannannas* was Paduhepa, wife of Hattusilis III, who had her own seal for state affairs.

4. Foreign Queens in the Bible. Five foreign queens are mentioned in the Bible: the queen of Sheba (1 Kings 10); Taphenes of Egypt (1 Kgs 11:19–20); Vashti of Persia (Esther 1–2); Esther of Persia (Esther 2–10); and Candace of Ethiopia (Acts 8:27). Of these, only the queens of Sheba and Ethiopia are portrayed as sovereign rulers. The two Persian queens—Vashti and Esther—were consorts in whom little power resided. Each was dependent on her royal husband for her position at court.

B. Israel and Judah

1. Queen as Ruler. Neither Israel nor Judah accepted the idea of a female regnant. Only one woman—ATHALIAH of Judah (2 Kings 11)—aspired to and attained the throne. Wife to one king (Jehoram) and mother of another (Ahaziah), Athaliah seized the throne upon her reigning son's death. In spite of her gender, she amassed enough support to sustain a seven-year reign. She was finally killed in a temple-sponsored coup. See also JOASH.

2. Queen as Wife. a. Diplomatic Marriage. Royal marriages in Israel and Judah helped to establish alliances, strengthen treaties, neutralize potential enemies, and generally reinforce relationships between the parties involved. There are four accounts of an Israelite or Judean king marrying a foreign princess: (1) David's marriage to Maacah, daughter of Talmai, king of Geshur (2 Sam 3:3); (2) Solomon's marriage to "pharaoh's daughter" (1 Kgs 3:1); (3) Ahab's marriage to Jezebel, daughter of the king of Tyre (1 Kgs 16:31); and (4) Jehoram's marriage to Athaliah, offspring of the royal house of Israel (2 Kgs 8:18). A fifth possibility is Solomon's marriage to Naamah (1 Kgs 14:21). Although the MT simply describes Naamah as an "Ammonitess," in 1 Kgs 12:24 (LXX) she is called the "daughter of Ana, son of Naash, king of the children of Ammon." If this tradition is correct, Solomon married into the royal house of Ammon as well as the one of Egypt. Each of these wives represented an important diplomatic link between her own country and that of her husband's. Thus, Solomon's marriage to "pharaoh's daughter" was aimed at strengthening relations between Israel and Egypt. The same can be said of Ahab's marriage to Jezebel, which helped ally Israel with Phoenicia. Moreover, Jehoram's marriage to Athaliah may have been responsible for the end of years of hostilities between Judah and Israel. Marriages between royal houses could also give credibility to sovereign claims. David's marriage to Maacah, for example, probably proved helpful in his later bid for Geshur. Domestic policy was another determining factor in the selection of a king's wives. Royal marriages to commoners helped to ensure the allegiance of their powerful families. Since so little information is preserved about these marriages, it is difficult to determine which were politically significant. Information is also scarce about the composition of the king's harem vis à vis his political policies. Only one harem—Solomon's—is described in terms of its ethnic composition: according to 1 Kgs 11:1–2, it included women from Egypt, Moab, Ammon, Edom, Sidon, and Hatti, a wide range of locales which may reflect Solomon's diplomatic agenda, or simply attest to his eclectic taste in women.

b. Royal Harems. Although no technical term is used in Hebrew to designate the king's wives and concubines, there is ample evidence that such a body of women existed. The most notable is the report of Solomon's 700 wives and 300 concubines (1 Kgs 11:3). While these figures are probably exaggerated, it is quite possible that Solomon kept a large number of women in his harem. Nor was Solomon the only king to do so. Rehoboam reportedly had 18 wives and 60 concubines (2 Chr 11:21), while Abijah's wives numbered 14 (2 Chr 13:21). Other kings had harems which are not numbered: Saul (2 Sam 3:7; 12:8), David (2 Sam 3:2–5; 5:13; 11:27; 15:16; 16:21–22; 20:3), Ahab (1 Kgs 20:3–7), Jehoiachin (2 Kgs 24:15), Jehoram (2 Chr 21:14, 17), and Zedekiah (Jer 38:23). The royal harem did not exist without censure; numerous wives were thought to threaten a king's piety: "And he [the king] shall not multiply wives for himself, lest his heart turn away . . ." (Deut 17:17).

Was the king's harem politically significant? There is some evidence to suggest that the harem played a part in the succession process. Whoever possessed the former king's harem also possessed a key to his throne. This conclusion is implied in Abner's quarrel with Ishbaal (2 Sam 3:6–11), in Nathan's oracle to David (2 Sam 12:7–15), in Absalom's capture of Jerusalem (2 Sam 16:15–23), and in Adonijah's request for Abishag (1 Kgs 2:13–25). When Absalom revolted against his father David, David was forced to leave Jerusalem (2 Samuel 15). Upon Ahithophel's advice, Absalom publicly possessed the concubines David left behind (2 Sam 16:20–22). The two events—the possession of the city and the possession of the concubines—are equated with the seizure of David's throne. Twice, in the case of Abner/Ishbaal and Adonijah/Solomon, either the possession of or the desire to possess a former king's woman was interpreted as a bid for the throne. Even Yahweh, through the prophet Nathan, marked David as the future king by giving him Saul's wives (2 Sam 12:8). This function of the harem, however, seems to have been confined to the David/Solomon stories. Perhaps as Israel's succession policy became more defined, the political significance of the harem declined.

c. Influence. It is hard to determine the influence of the king's wife. Although many wives may have been active, information is preserved for only a few. Athaliah of Judah is mentioned briefly in the evaluation of her husband's reign. She is the reason he walked "in the ways of the house of Ahab" (2 Kgs 8:18). More is recorded about Jezebel of Israel. Jezebel is said to have caused the apostasy of her husband Ahab (1 Kgs 16:31), to have persecuted the prophets of Yahweh (1 Kings 18–19), and to have planned the judicial death of Naboth the Jezreelite (1 Kings 21).

As a member of the harem, the king's wife usually gained prominence upon her son's succession. Occasionally she was able to influence dynastic decisions. Although succession in the southern kingdom usually followed the principle of primogeniture (passing from father to the oldest son), two royal wives apparently circumvented convention. The most detailed account focuses upon Bathsheba's intervention on behalf of her son Solomon. Although Adonijah was David's oldest surviving son, Bathsheba convinced David to appoint Solomon as his successor (1 Kings 1). A more implicit instance of a wife's affecting the succession process is found in 2 Chr 11:21–22. While Abijah was not Rehoboam's oldest son, he was nevertheless designated king. Abijah's mother was Maacah, Rehoboam's "favorite" wife. Once again, it would appear, a royal wife stood behind the selection of a king.

3. The Queen Mother. Information concerning the king's mother is often—though not always—preserved in the introductory regnal formula of her son. Of the eighteen mothers who are named, fifteen are of Judean kings, two of Israelite kings, and one is from the period of the united monarchy. See the following table:

KING/SON	MOTHER	MOTHER'S FATHER	MOTHER'S HOME	REFERENCE	
Solomon	Bathsheba	Eliam	?	2 Sam	11:3; 12:24
		ISRAEL			
Jeroboam	Zeruah			1 Kgs	11:26
Ahaziah	Jezebel	Ethbaal	Tyre	1 Kgs	16:31 22:52
Jehoram	Jezebel	Ethbaal	Tyre	2 Kgs	3:2 9:22
		JUDAH			
Rehoboam	Naamah	?	Ammon	1 Kgs	14:21
Abijah	Maacah	Abishalom	?		15:2
Asa	Maacah	Abishalom	?		15:10
Jehoshaphat	Azubah	Shilhi	?		22:42
Jehoram	?	?	?	....	....
Ahaziah	Athaliah	Omri/Ahab (?)	Israel	2 Kgs	8:26
Joash	Zibiah	?	Beersheba		12:1
Amaziah	Jehoaddin	?	Jerusalem		14:2
Azariah	Jecoliah	?	Jerusalem		15:2
Jotham	Jerusha	Zadok	?		15:33
Ahaz	?	?	?	....	....
Hezekiah	Abi	Zechariah	?		18:2
Manassah	Hephzibah	?	?		21:1
Amon	Meshullemeth	Haruz	Jotbah		21:19
Josiah	Jediah	Adaiah	Bozkath		22:1
Jehoahaz	Hamutal	Jeremiah	Libnah		23:31
Jehoiakim	Zebidah	Pedaiah	Rumah		23:36
Jehoiachin	Nehushta	Elnathan	Jerusalem		24:8
Zedekiah	Hamutal	Jeremiah	Libnah		24:18

The queen mothers come from a variety of locations: three are foreign (Jezebel, Naamah, Athaliah); five are from the provinces (Zibiah, Meshullemeth, Jedidah, Hamutal, Zebidah); three are from Jerusalem (Jehoaddin, Jecoliah Nehushta), and seven are named without any mention of their homes.

Did the mother of the king hold specific rank and powers? Since only two Israelite kings' mothers are mentioned, it is difficult to know if the position of "queen mother" existed in the northern kingdom. If it did, no information other than the accounts of Jezebel have survived. The same cannot be said about Judah. All but two Judean kings (Jehoram and Ahaz) have their mothers' names preserved. In at least one instance, the mother of a Judean king (Jehoiachin) possessed her own ceremonial attire and throne (Jer 13:18). Moreover, a Judean king's mother occupied a position from which she could be removed. Asa, for instance, found it necessary to depose his mother/grandmother (?) before he could carry out his cultic reforms (1 Kgs 15:11–13). Another mother, Athaliah, ordered the death of Davidic family members and was obeyed (2 Kgs 11:1). It is difficult to imagine this happening unless she possessed a strong power base.

If the position of queen mother existed in Judah, what was its origin and function? Molin (1954) argued that Judah was originally a matriarchal society which came under the influence of the Hittites. In this context, the queen mother functioned to ensure the succession of the male regent. Donner (1959) also acknowledged Hittite influence, but rejected positing a matriarchy in Judah. Rather than viewing the position of queen mother as an indicator of Judah's social structure, he identified it as part of Judah's political framework. A different approach was taken by Ahlström (1963), who located the position in the cult: as a representative of the goddess, the queen mother would participate in Jerusalem fertility rites. Rejecting the suggested social and cultic origins, Andreasen (1983) turned to the world of politics as the queen mother's original location. For Andreasen, the queen mother was a "lady counselor" whose role was reflected in the motif of "Lady Wisdom" in Proverbs.

a. Influence. The queen mother could and did exercise political and religious power. Her activities, however, were confined to domestic rather than international matters. Bathsheba, for example, mediated (unsuccessfully) between Adonijah and Solomon for the favors of Abishag (1 Kgs 2:13–25). According to the account, Bathsheba enjoyed access to her son's throne as well as a privileged position near it. Another queen mother—Jezebel—was active throughout the reigns of her two sons, Ahaziah and Jehoram (1 Kgs 22:52; 2 Kgs 9:22). Perhaps the most astonishing display of royal influence exercised by a queen mother is found in 2 Kings 11, in which Amaziah's mother, Athaliah, wielded enormous political power when she ordered the massacre of the royal family. Considering the power vacuum which existed after Jehu's murder of Amaziah, Athaliah's move reflected great political acumen (2 Kgs 11:1).

The queen mother also influenced cultic affairs. Maacah supported the worship of Asherah and had a cult object erected in Jerusalem (1 Kgs 15:13). Jezebel actively promoted Baalism and the worship of Asherah, while persecuting the prophets of Yahweh (1 Kings 18–19). Finally, although there is no record of Athaliah supporting either Baal or Asherah, the temple of Baal was destroyed immediately after her death. This action suggests that the temple was protected by Athaliah and could not be eliminated while she was alive. But do these three instances imply the queen mother actually participated in cultic rites? At least two scholars—Ahlström and Terrien—think they do. According to Ahlström (1963), the queen mother was the king's consort in the *hieros gamos* ritual in Jerusalem. Terrien (1970), however, concludes that the position of queen mother was only one cultic element (along with male prostitution, sun rituals, the sacred snake, and chthonian forces) of an omphalos myth in Israelite religion.

b. Literary Treatment. Of all the Israelite and Judean queens named in the book of Kings, only four are given more than cursory mention: Bathsheba, Maacah, Jezebel, and Athaliah. Of these four, all but Bathsheba are portrayed in negative terms. Their characterization employs identifiable narrative elements and casts them into a character "type"—that of the "wicked queen/queen mother." This typecasting of queens warns the reader of the dangers of women in power.

When the stories of Jezebel and Athaliah are analyzed, six elements basic to their character emerge: these women are (1) non-Judean; (2) politically powerful; (3) aggressive; (4) connected with Asherah and/or Baal; (5) liabilities to their husbands and sons; and (6) responsible for the death of others. While elements (1), (4), and (5) are reminiscent of the "foreign woman" character type, the remaining elements each point to an important distinction. The "wicked queen/queen mother" differs from the "foreign woman" in the source of her power. Whereas the foreign woman relies on seductive wiles to achieve her ends, the wicked queen's power resides in her position; she commands rather than charms others into obedience. Maacah's account is much shorter, but contains three (perhaps four) of the "wicked queen/queen mother" elements: (1) she may be foreign (?); (2) she supports the worship of Asherah; (3) she has power and has to be deposed; and (4) she is a liability to her son.

Bibliography

Ahlström, G. W. 1963. *Aspects of Syncretism in Israelite Religion.* Lund.

Andreasen, N. A. 1983. The Role of the Queen Mother in Israelite Society. *CBQ* 45: 179–94.

Artzi, P., and Malamat, A. 1971. The Correspondence of Šibtu, Queen of Mari, in ARM X. *Or* 40: 75–89.

Batto, B. F. 1974. *Studies on Women at Mari.* Baltimore.

Donner, H. 1959. Art und Herkunft des Amtes der Königinmutter im Alten Testament. Pp. 105–45 in *Festchrift Johannes Friedrich zum 65,* ed. R. von Kienle et al. Heidelberg.

Ihromi. 1974. Die Königinmutter und der 'Amm Ha'Arez in Reich Juda. *VT* 24: 421–29.

Ishida, T. 1977. *The Royal Dynasties in Ancient Israel.* BZAW 142. New York.

Lewy, H. 1952. Nitokris-Naqi'a. *JNES* 11: 264–86.

Molin, G. 1954. Die Stellung der Gebira im Staate Juda. *TZ* 10: 161–75.

Sasson, J. 1973. Biographical Notices on Some Royal Ladies from Mari. *JCS* 25: 59–78.

Terrien, S. 1970. The Omphalos Myth and Hebrew Religion. *VT* 20: 315–38.

LINDA S. SCHEARING

QUEEN OF HEAVEN (DEITY) [Heb *mĕleket haššāmayim*].

The epithet of an otherwise unidentified deity worshiped in Judah during the 7th and 6th centuries B.C.E., and possibly in earlier periods as well. The queen of heaven is mentioned only in the book of Jeremiah (7:18; 44:17, 18, 19, 25), where her cult is condemned as one of the defections of the populace of Judah from exclusive worship of the god Yahweh. According to the prophet, the divine wrath provoked by non-Yahwistic observances such as those popularly conducted on behalf of the queen of heaven culminated in the Babylonian conquest of Jerusalem and the deportation of many of the city's inhabitants. After the Babylonian invasion, devotion to the queen of heaven persisted among Judean refugees residing in Upper Egypt ("the land of Pathros" [Jer 44:1]), including the cities of Migdol, Memphis, and Tahpanhes, where Jeremiah had been brought after the Exile, apparently against his will. The prophet publicly denounced veneration of the queen of heaven (Jer 44:1–14, 24–30). The refusal of the Judeans to stop worshiping the queen of heaven is included as a cause of the calamity that befell Judah (Jer 44:20–23); and the transplanted cult of the goddess in Egypt became the subject of a prophetic oracle threatening the extermination of the Judean population resident in Egypt (Jer 44:24–29; cf. Jos. *Ant* 10 §180–82; Wiseman 1956: 94–95; on the political history of this period, see Spalinger 1977, especially pp. 240–41).

The first of the references to the queen of heaven occurs in the context of the "Temple Sermon" (Jer 7:7–15); the others in a third-person prose narrative about Jeremiah's prophetic activities in Egypt. The compositional history of these prose passages is disputed (see JEREMIAH, BOOK OF), but it is widely agreed to be Deuteronomistic in character if not origin.

The Masoretic vocalization of the epithet is *mĕleket haššāmayim,* the first element of which has been distorted as if it were the construct noun *mĕle(ʾ)ket* (from the root *lʾk* "to work") rather than *malkat* (from the base *malkā-,* "queen"). Indeed, the consonantal spelling *mlʾkt* is found in many mss of these verses. The distortion was probably introduced to avoid pronouncing the religiously offensive epithet of the goddess (see Gordon 1978–79). The LXX's *tę stratią tou ouranou,* "the stars of heaven," is evidence of further distortion (or interpretation) of the title, also evident in the Targum to Jer 7:18, which reads (in Aramaic) *kwkbt šmyʾ,* "the stars of heaven." These translations may be intended to avoid the abhorrent title, or they may preserve a midrashic interpretation of the epithet. But there is no doubt that the Hebrew text of Jer 7:18 and 44:17, 18, 19, and 25 originally read "queen of heaven" *(*malkat haššāmayim)*. This interpretation of the epithet is supported by the Greek translations of Symmachus, Theodotian, and Aquila, and in Latin by the Vulgate (Ackerman 1989: 118 n. 2).

Considerable energy has been expended in attempts to ascertain the identity of the queen of heaven more precisely, but only the loosest consensus has emerged from these scholarly efforts. It has long been supposed that the title "queen of heaven" referred to the Mesopotamian goddess Ishtar (so, e.g., Kittel 1927: 86), and this view has frequently been assumed (Bright *Jeremiah* AB, 56; Anderson 1975: 399; Held 1982: 76–77) and defended (Weinfeld 1972: 148–53). Associated with this identification of the queen of heaven is the premise that hers was one among other Mesopotamian cults that entered Israel and Judah as part of the official state religion of the Neo-Assyrian empire imposed after 722 B.C.E. This view gained general acceptance after Ostreicher advanced it in 1923, but reconsiderations of the evidence in its favor (McKay 1973; Cogan 1974) have significantly reduced scholarly confidence in its correctness. See PALESTINE, ADMINISTRATION OF (ASSYRO-BABYLONIAN).

Diminution of emphasis on the Assyrian influence on Israelite religion has been matched by increasing attention to the Canaanite elements. The view that the queen of heaven is to be identified with the Canaanite goddess Ashtoreth, also known by the Greek name Astarte, is relatively recent (du Mesnil du Buisson 1970: 126–27; 1973: 56, 271) but widely accepted (Delcor 1982; Olyan 1987). Most recently it has been argued that the queen of heaven is "a syncretistic deity whose character incorporates aspects of West Semitic Astarte and East Semitic Ištar" (Ackerman 1989: 116–17).

Three activities are mentioned as part of the veneration of the queen of heaven: burning incense to her (if this is the proper interpretation of Heb *qaṭṭēr* [Jer 44:17, 18, 19, 23]; see INCENSE), pouring out libations to her (Jer 7:18 [implied]; 44:17, 18, 19 [2x]), and preparing cakes for her. This third activity is the strongest evidence that the cult is Mesopotamian in origin. The Hebrew word designating the cakes is *kawwānîm*, a loanword from Akk *kamānu*, designating a variety of sweetened cake (CAD 8: 110–11). The cakes called *kamānu* were used frequently in Mesopotamia as offerings to the goddess Ishtar (the evidence is discussed partially and from a primarily archaeological perspective by Rast [1977], more strictly philologically by Delcor [1982: 104-12]). Their Hebrew reflex is found only in Jeremiah (7:18; 44:19), where *kawwānîm* is a technical term associated with the cult of the queen of heaven.

The phonetic shape of Heb *kawwān-* is like that of Aramaic loanwords derived from Akkadian words with medial /m/ (e.g., Aram *nwrʾ*/nawrā(ʾ)/, from Akk *namāru* [Kaufman 1974: 143]; Aram *gwḥ*, borrowed into Mishnaic Heb as *kwk*, from Akk *kimaḫḫu* [O'Connor 1986: 218]). This linguistic fact might indicate that the cult was adopted directly from Mesopotamia by Arameans in Syria, and reached Judah through Aramean mediation.

The only extrabiblical reference to the queen of heaven in a Northwest Semitic text is in the greeting of one of the 6th-century B.C.E. papyrus letters written in Aramaic discovered at Hermopolis (BK 4.1). The letter in question was written by a Syrian residing at Ofi in Egypt to relatives in Syene, and mentions in its opening sentence temples of the god Bethel and the queen of heaven. Several instances of the divine name *ʿnt* (Anat) in compound names of deities and personal names from these and related Aramaic texts are considered by Porten (*ArchEleph,* 176–77; 1969: 120–21) to be evidence that the queen of heaven was the Canaanite goddess Anat. (Vincent made the same identification in 1937 [p. 635] on less secure grounds. It was also considered by Hvidberg-Hansen [1979, 1: 96].) The proposal has the merit of evidence, and it cannot be undermined by alternative etymological explanations of *ʿnt* in the onomastica (as attempted by Olyan 1987: 170).

In Judah, the cult of the queen of heaven was apparently a private observance that could involve entire families (Jer 7:18), but it is particularly associated with women, perhaps economically advantaged women (Jer 44:9, 15, 19, 20). The loyalty of women (and, apparently, their husbands) to this cult in the face of the prophet's denunciation is striking, and raises questions about the marginal status of women in the Yahwistic cultus affirmed in the Law and Prophets of the Hebrew Bible (see van der Toorn 1987: 33–42; 125–27 [cited *apud* van der Toorn 1989: 194 n. 4] and the observations of Ackerman [1989: 110, 117–18]).

Bibliography

Ackerman, S. 1989. "And the Women Knead Dough": The Worship of the Queen of Heaven in Sixty-Century Judah. Pp. 109–24 in *Gender and Difference in Ancient Israel,* ed. P. L. Day. Minneapolis.

Anderson, B. 1975. *Understanding the Old Testament.* 3d ed. Englewood Cliffs, NJ.

Cogan, M. 1974. *Imperialism and Religion.* SBLMS 19. Missoula, MT.

Dahood, M. 1960. La Regina del Cielo in Geremia. *RivB* 8: 166–68.

Delcor, M. 1982. Le culte de la "Reine du Ciel" selon Jer 7, 18; 44, 17–19.25 et ses survivances. Pp. 101–22 in *Von Kanaan bis Karala,* ed. W. C. Delsman et al. AOAT 211. Kevelaer and Neukirchen-Vluyn.

———. 1986. Astarte. *Lexicon Iconographicum Mythologiae Classicae* 3/1 (addendum): 1076–84.

du Mesnil du Buisson, R. 1970. *Études sur les dieux phéniciens hérités par l'empire romain.* EPRO 14. Leiden.

———. 1973. *Nouvelles études sur les dieux et les mythes de Canaan.* EPRO 33. Leiden.

Fitzmyer, J. A. 1966. The Phoenician Inscription from Pyrgi. *JAOS* 86: 287–88.

Gordon, R. P. 1978–79. Aleph Apologeticum. *JQR* 69: 112.

Helck, W. 1971. *Betrachtungen zu Grossen Göttin und den ihr verbundenen Gottheiten.* Religion und Kultur der alten Mittelmeerwelt in Parallelforschung 2. Munich.

Held, M. 1982. Studies in Biblical Lexicography in the Light of Akkadian. *EI* 16: 76–85 (in Hebrew).

Henninger, J. 1976. Zum Problem der Venussterngottheit bei den Semiten. *Anthropos* 71: 139–50.

Hvidberg-Hansen, F. O. 1979. *La déesse Tnt.* 2 vols. Copenhagen.

Kaufman, S. A. 1974. *The Akkadian Influences on Aramaic.* AS 19. Chicago.

Kittel, R. 1927. *Geschichte des Volkes Israel.* Vol. 3, pt. 1. Stuttgart.

McKay, J. 1973. *Religion in Judah under the Assyrians.* SBT n.s. 26. London.

Milik, J. T. 1967. Les papyrus araméens d'Hermoupolis et les cultes syro-phéniciens en Egypte perse. *Bib* 48: 556–64.
O'Connor, M. 1986. The Arabic Loanwords in Nabatean Aramaic. *JNES* 45: 213–29.
Olyan, S. M. 1987. Some Observations Concerning the Identity of the Queen of Heaven. *UF* 19: 161–74.
Ostreicher, T. 1923. *Das deuteronomischen Grundgesetz.* BFCT 27/4. Gütersloh.
Rast, W. E. 1977. Cakes for the Queen of Heaven. Pp. 167–80 in *Scripture in History and Theology,* ed. A. L. Merrill and T. W. Overholt. Pittsburgh Theological Monograph Series 17. Pittsburgh.
Schrader, E. 1886. Die *mlkt hšmm* und ihr aramäisch-assyrisches Aequivalent. *SPAW* 477–96.
Spalinger, A. 1977. Egypt and Babylonia: A Survey (c. 620 B.C.–500 B.C.). *SAK* 5: 221–44.
Stadelman, R. 1967. *Syrisch-Palästinensische Gottheiten in Ägypten.* PÄ 5. Leiden.
Toorn, K. van der. 1987. *Van haar wieg tot haar graf.* Baarn.
———. 1989. Female Prostitution in Payment of Vows in Ancient Israel. *JBL* 108: 193–205.
Vincent, A. 1937. *La religion des Judéo-Araméens d'Elephantine.* Paris.
Weinfeld, M. 1972. The Worship of Molech and the Queen of Heaven and Its Background. *UF* 4: 133–54.
Wiseman, D. J. 1956. *Chronicles of the Chaldaean Kings.* London.

PHILIP C. SCHMITZ

QUEST FOR THE HISTORICAL JESUS. See JESUS (QUEST FOR THE HISTORICAL).

QUESTIONS OF BARTHOLOMEW. See BARTHOLOMEW, GOSPEL OF (QUESTIONS).

QUFIN, KHIRBET. See MAARATH.

QUINTUS MEMMIUS (PERSON). See MEMMIUS, QUINTUS.

QUIRINIUS (PERSON) [Gk *Kyrēnaios*]. When P. Sulpicius Quirinius, who appears to have been born in the fifties B.C., died in A.D. 21, he was one of the most powerful men in Rome. He was noted for his long service as a soldier and his long-standing friendship with the emperor Tiberius (A.D. 14–37). He has also long been the subject of intense controversy. This controversy stems from Luke's statement that the birth of Christ took place while Quirinius was governor of Syria and Herod the Great was on the throne of Judea. The other evidence for Quirinius' career, some inscriptions from Syria (which are not to be confused with the acephelous text from Tibur which has wrongly been thought to provide details of his career), Tacitus' *Annales,* Josephus' *Antiquities of the Jews,* and Strabo's *Geography,* reveal that Luke's statement must be incorrect: Herod died in 4 B.C., but Quirinius was governor of Syria in A.D. 6/7.

Luke wrote (2:1–2), "It happened in those days that a decree went out from Caesar Augustus that the whole world be registered for a tax, the decree first went out while Cyrenius was governor of Syria." Cyrenius is the Greek form of the name Quirinius (*PW* 4: 823), and the fact that he held a census during his term in office is confirmed by an inscription from Apamea (modern Aleppo) in Syria as well as by Josephus. Although it was already recognized in antiquity that there was a problem with Luke's chronology—Tertullian knew that Sentius Saturninus was governor of Syria at the end of Herod's life (*Adv. Marc.* 4.19)—a number of efforts have nevertheless been made by modern scholars to reconcile this statement with Luke's belief that Herod was still alive when the census was held. The most forceful argument has been that Quirinius must have been governor twice and that he must have held two censuses. It is based upon the contention that Quirinius is the officer mentioned on an inscription from Tibur which contains part of the career of a senator in the reign of Augustus.

This inscription does not, however, preserve the name of the man it commemorates, and, indeed, it preserves only part of the career. The surviving section runs, ". . . king, which he brought under the control of Caesar Augustus and the Roman people, the senate decreed two days of thanksgiving to the immortal gods because of the deeds which he had successfully accomplished; as proconsul he obtained the province of Asia and, serving *again* as a legate of the divine Augustus with pro-praetorian power he obtained the province of Syria and Phoenicia . . ." (*ILS* 918). The Latin text of the phrase, ". . . serving again *(iterum)* as legate . . . ," is *legatus pr. pr. divi Augusti iterum Syriam et Phoenicen optinuit.* Many scholars have wanted to translate this as "serving as legate of the divine Augustus with pro-praetorian power he obtained the province of Syria and Phoenicia *again (iterum),*" taking *iterum* with *optinuit* rather than with the words which proceeded it. This has enabled them to claim that this official governed Syria twice, and that he thus must be Quirinius. Aside from an obvious circularity, the most serious objection to this argument is that this is not the proper way to read the Latin. In normal Latin *iterum* is understood with the words that precede it. There is no reason to translate it any other way here, and the phrase should be taken as a reference to the fact that the man in question had held more than one province as a legate of Augustus (Syme 1973: 592–93).

A great number of other arguments have been adduced at one time or another to reconcile Luke's narrative with the facts of Roman history. All of them fail to answer four other basic objections to the historicity of Luke's statement (*HJP*² 399–427). These are:

1. There is no other evidence for an empire-wide census in the reign of Augustus.
2. In a Roman census Joseph would not have been required to travel to Bethlehem, and he would not have been required to bring Mary with him.
3. A Roman census could not have been carried out in Herod's kingdom while Herod was alive.
4. Josephus refers to the census of Quirinius in A.D. 6/7 as something that was without precedent in the region.

In the face of these objections, it is impossible to defend Luke's dating of the Nativity. The easiest explanation for his error is that he wished to provide a synchronism between the birth of Christ and a famous event and so picked upon the census of Quirinius, which caused a great stir throughout the region, as Josephus makes plain. See also CENSUS (ROMAN).

P. Sulpicius Quirinius was a man of considerable importance in the reigns of Augustus (31 B.C.–A.D. 14) and Tiberius. Indeed, Tacitus picked upon his career as a model for that of a *novus homo,* a man without distinguished ancestors in Roman political life, who moved into a position of great influence through his considerable abilities as a soldier and an administrator, and his even more considerable abilities as a courtier.

It may be deduced from the fact that Quirinius held the consulship in 12 B.C. that he must have been born in the early 50s B.C.; as a plebeian he could not have been consul before the age of 42. It is therefore possible that he served in the campaign which ended with Augustus' victory at Actium (31 B.C.), and it is very likely that he served with Augustus' armies in Spain during the following decade. He reached the praetorship by 15 B.C., and in the next year went out to govern the province consisting of Crete and Cyrene. This was not ordinarily an important appointment, but in this case it appears that there was serious trouble in the area. Quirinius distinguished himself by defeating a desert tribe, the Marmarici, which was raiding the area (*PW* 4: 824–27). It was about this same time, if not before, that he married into one of Rome's most distinguished families, the Appii Claudii. We do not know much about this marriage, other than that there were no children and that Quirinius was single again by A.D. 2. Nevertheless, it is clear that Quirinius was moving in very distinguished circles by this point in his life.

Quirinius was *consul ordinarius* in 12 B.C. This meant that he was in office at the beginning of the year, which was a sign of Augustus' particular favor. In the course of this year he must have played an important role in the ceremonies which marked Augustus' assumption of the office of *Pontifex maximus,* high priest of the state religion. In 6 B.C. serious troubles threatened the E part of the empire and the Augustan regime itself. The Parthians appeared to be preparing to go to war in Armenia, and when Augustus appointed his stepson Tiberius to the command, Tiberius opted to retire instead. An expedition could not be mounted for another four years, and in the meantime an experienced soldier was needed to keep an eye on developments in the area. Quirinius went out as governor of Pamphylia/Galatia, the province which bordered Armenia. He served with distinction in that area for at least six years. In 5/4 B.C., he conducted a series of campaigns against the Homonadenses, a tribe on the northern slopes of the Taurus, and was awarded the coveted *ornamenta triumphalia,* the "triumphal ornaments," which had replaced an actual triumph as the highest honor to which a senator could ordinarily aspire as a mark of military success (Levick 1967: 206–14; Syme 1973: 592). In A.D. 2, he was appointed chief adviser to Gaius Caesar, Augustus' grandson, who had been in nominal command of the east since 2 B.C.

Quirinius' appointment marked an important point in the dynastic politics of the reign, for he replaced Marcus Lollius, who had shown considerable hostility toward Tiberius, who was then living in virtual exile on Rhodes. Quirinius had always treated Tiberius with deference (Tac. *Ann.* 3.48), and it was in A.D. 2 that Tiberius' star began to rise once again. Augustus' other grandson, Lucius, had died in that year, and Tiberius was recalled to Rome. At this point, even though Tiberius was not yet restored to his former position, it was clear that he was once again an important factor in political life. When Gaius died after a long illness in A.D. 4, Tiberius emerged once again as the heir apparent, and Quirinius was one of his closest friends. It was at this time that Quirinius married Aemilia Lepida, a woman many years younger than he, who was the daughter of another of the great noble families at Rome and who had previously been betrothed to Lucius Caesar (Tac. *Ann.* 3.23). Even though the marriage was short-lived and unhappy, it was a clear mark of Quirinius' eminence.

Quirinius was therefore one of the most important men in Rome when he was appointed governor of Syria in A.D. 6 to oversee the annexation of the kingdom of Judea; Augustus had previously removed its ruler, Archelaus, a son of Herod the Great, in response to complaints by his subjects (Jos. *Ant* 18 §1–10). A revolt broke out as he seized the royal estates and auctioned them off, but this does not appear to have caused Quirinius great difficulty; he left the area under the administration of a *praefectus* who would be responsible to the governor of Syria in the future. It was also at this time (A.D. 6) that he conducted his census throughout Syria and the newly occupied territory.

The length of Quirinius' term as governor is not known for certain, though he must have returned to Rome by A.D. 12, the year in which Quintus Metellus Creticus is first attested in the province (it is not certain that he was Quirinius' direct successor). He appears to have continued to be a close associate of Tiberius, who became emperor after Augustus' death in A.D. 14. In A.D. 16 his young kinsman by marriage, Scribonius Libo Drusus, asked him to intercede with Tiberius on his behalf when he was charged with treason (Tac. *Ann.* 2.20). Quirinius refused and told him to take his request to the senate, a response which showed Drusus that he had no chance of acquittal since the response could be interpreted as coming from Tiberius himself. In A.D. 20, Quirinius' ex-wife, Aemilia Lepida, was brought to trial on the charges of poisoning, adultery, assailing the imperial house with magical practices, and claiming—falsely—to have had a child by Quirinius. Aemilia was exiled, though not before leading a demonstration of noble women at the theater in which Quirinius was roundly abused (Tac. *Ann.* 3.23). He died in the next year and was granted a public funeral: the last sign of Tiberius' enduring favor.

Bibliography

Levick, B. 1967. *Roman Colonies in Southern Asia Minor.* Oxford.

Syme, R. 1973. The *Titulus Tibertinus.* Pp. 585–601 in *Akten des VI Internationalen Kongresses für Grieschische und Lateinische Epigraphik.* Munich.

D. S. Potter

QUMRAN PESHARIM. See PESHARIM, QUMRAN.

QUMRAN, KHIRBET (M.R. 193127). A settlement near the NW shore of the Dead Sea which was associated with the people who produced the Dead Sea Scrolls. Although noted in various explorations of the area around the Dead Sea since 1851 (de Vaux 1953: 89), Khirbet Qumran attracted the attention of archaeologists only because of the discovery of the Dead Sea Scrolls in caves in the nearby cliffs. See also DEAD SEA SCROLLS.

The area W of the N end of the Dead Sea is given a triangular shape by the convergence of the cliffs and the coast, which come together at Ras Feshkha. About 500 m N of Ras Feshkha, an aquifer surfaces, producing brackish springs, which today nourish reeds, brushwood, and tamarisks. Near the biggest spring, Ain Feshkha, are the ruins known as Khirbet Feshkha. Three km further N, the plain is cut by the Wadi Qumran, which drains the Buqeia, the great valley at the top of the cliffs. The ruins are located on the N bank of the wadi where it cuts through a marl terrace below the cliff, whence the name Khirbet Qumran, "the ruins at Qumran."

The first scrolls were found in early 1947 (de Vaux 1973: vii), but the area from which they came was pinpointed only at the end of January 1949. Official negligence is excused by the turmoil that preceded and followed the withdrawal of British forces in May 1948. But when Captain Philip Lippens, a United Nations Observer from Belgium, approached Major General Lash of the Arab Legion in January 1949, the response was immediate. With the approval of the Jordanian Department of Antiquities, troopers of the legion were sent to the probable area, and within two or three days Captain Akkash el Zebn had found the cave (Harding 1955: 6).

Cave 1 was excavated shortly afterwards by G. L. Harding and R. de Vaux. At that time a surface examination of the nearby ruins indicated no relation to the cave, but the developing controversy regarding the authenticity of the scrolls made it imperative to determine whether the ruins threw any light on the documents, and a thorough investigation was authorized. Responsibility for the excavation was given to de Vaux, who completed the project in five seasons: 1951 and 1953–56. The hiatus in 1952 is explained by the need to follow up new manuscript discoveries by the bedouin. From January 21 to March 3, de Vaux excavated the caves in the Wadi Murabbaat. During March 10–29, he directed a systematic search of the caves in the cliffs 4 km N and S of the Wadi Qumran. Finally, between September 22 and 29, he conducted a careful survey of the marl terrace on which the ruins stand. The last item in the program, the excavation of Khirbet Feshkha, was undertaken in 1958. During these years preliminary reports appeared regularly in *Revue Biblique,* but the closest to a final report that de Vaux produced was his 1959 Schweich Lectures at the British Academy in London. These appeared as *L'archéologie et les manuscrits de la mer Morte* (1961). Just before his death in 1971, de Vaux completed a thorough revision of this book, which was published as *Archaeology and the Dead Sea Scrolls* (1973).

Three km S of Ras Feshkha, R. De Langhe excavated Khirbet Mazin in December 1960 and January 1961 (Stutchbury and Nichol 1962). It appears to have been erected in the Roman period, and was reoccupied in the Byzantine period. There is no evidence that it was related to the installations at Qumran or Feshkha (de Vaux 1973: 88). Some 9 km further S at Ain el-Ghuweir, P. Bar-Adon in 1969 made the first Israeli contribution to the problem of Essene settlement on the coast of the Dead Sea. He brought to light a rectangular building (19.5 m × 43 m), and the pottery of the two levels of occupation showed similarities to that of Periods I and II at Qumran. Some 800 m to the N was a small cemetery. The mode of burial and tomb types were the same as those of the cemetery at Qumran (Bar-Adon 1977). The precise relationship of this settlement to Qumran is still undefined (de Vaux 1973: 89).

A. The Caves

Of the 270 caves, crevices, and holes examined in 1952, 40 contained material ranging from the Chalcolithic to the Arab periods, while 26 of the latter furnished pottery identical to that of Cave 1 (de Vaux 1973: 50–51). The suspicion that the bedouin had planted manuscripts in the caves was negated by the archaeologists' independent discovery of fragments in every cave in which the bedouin reported finds (Caves 1, 2, 4, 6, and 11). The archaeologists themselves discovered Caves 3, 5, and 7–10, which contained manuscript fragments of the same type (de Vaux 1973: 95–97). The pottery found in the scroll caves is of the same type as that found at Qumran (de Vaux 1973: 54), and in one case a manuscript fragment was found still attached to a piece of its linen wrapper and adhering to the neck of a jar (Harding 1955: 7). The scrolls, therefore, must have been placed in the caves when the 1st century A.D. pottery was in use and the settlement occupied. The conclusion that the documents belonged to the inhabitants of Khirbet Qumran is inescapable.

B. Khirbet Qumran

The stratigraphy of Khirbet Qumran revealed eight phases ranging from the 8th century B.C. to the Second Jewish Revolt (Table 1):

	Qumran	Feshkha	Ain el-Ghuweir
ca. 700–600 B.C.	Israelite		
ca. 150–100 B.C.	Ia		
ca. 100–31 B.C.	Ib	I	I
ca. 4 B.C.–A.D. 68	II	II	II
ca. A.D. 69–74	III		
ca. A.D. 74–132		III	
A.D. 132–35	Second Revolt		

1. Israelite Period. The oldest structure at Qumran is a rectangular building. See Fig. QUM.01. A row of rooms bordered the courtyard on the E; there may have been others along the N and S walls. Outside the W wall, but protected by its own enclosure, was a round cistern fed by runoff from the terrace to the N. The pottery shows it to have been in use from the 8th century to the 6th century B.C., when it suffered a violent destruction that is naturally associated with the fall of the kingdom of Judah in 586 B.C. A wall in the plain running S to Ain Feshkha is also dated to this period.

There is general agreement that this structure must be

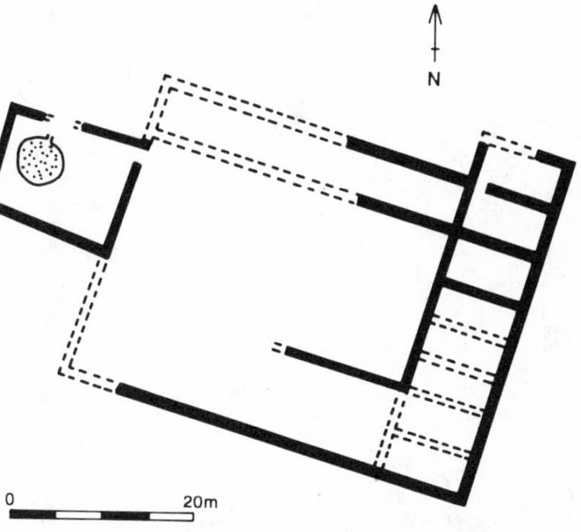

QUM.01. Plan of oldest structure at Qumran—Israelite Period (Iron II). *(Redrawn from de Vaux 1973, pl. III)*

one of the six cities in the wilderness mentioned in Josh 15:61–62. The majority of scholars identify it with Ir-hammelah, the "City of Salt," (references in de Vaux 1973: 91–94), but it has been suggested that the Iron Age buildings near Ain el-Ghuweir (Blake 1966: 565–66) should be identified with the "City of Salt," in which case Qumran would be Sekaka (Bar-Adon 1977: 22–23). This latter hypothesis, however, leaves out of account one of the three Iron Age sites in the Buqeia—Khirbet Abu Tabaq, Khirbet es-Samra, and Khirbet el-Maqari—which were explored by Cross and Milik (1956). These farming installations could have been set up by Jehoshaphat (2 Chr 17:12), but Uzziah (2 Chr 26:10) seems a more likely candidate.

2. Period Ia. Sometime in the 2d century B.C., Qumran was settled by a new group, whose identity is considered in the entry ESSENES. Two rectangular cisterns were dug beside the round cistern, which was brought back into service. Water intake was increased by the provision of two feeder channels that collected runoff from the terrace. The purpose of the small rooms around the cisterns is not clear, but the function of the two kilns in the SE corner is obvious. The pottery of this phase is virtually identical with that of the subsequent period (de Vaux 1973: 5). Hence, the date of the beginning of this settlement cannot be determined with any precision. But if the buildings of Period Ib were occupied from about 100 B.C., the beginning of Period Ia must be placed sometime in the second half of the 2d century B.C. (de Vaux 1973: 5), but exactly when is a matter of some debate (Laperrousaz 1978: 748–52). The number of occupants was small.

3. Period Ib. An influx of new occupants made a building program imperative, and it is in this phase that Qumran acquired what was to be virtually its definitive form. See Fig. QUM.02. The round cistern and the two adjoining ones were retained in service, but the water system was expanded by the addition of two ritual baths and four large new cisterns. The terrace catchment area was too small to fill all of these, so a dam was built across the Wadi Qumran in the cliffs. This directed winter flash floods into an aqueduct that fed the system. The main building block was dominated by a tower that had no entrance at ground level; in times of danger from nomadic mauraders it would have served as a refuge for some of the inhabitants and as a secure place to store essential foodstuffs. The tower was entered via a wooden bridge from the two-story building to the S. The upper floor of this building, which had collapsed into the room below, contained two inkwells plus a plastered table and bench (de Vaux 1973: 29). These suggest a scriptorium, and provide an important link with the manuscripts found in the nearby caves. The bench around the walls in an inner room on the ground floor suggests that the room was an assembly chamber.

The refectory was easy to identify. Not only was it linked to the water system to facilitate cleaning, but the adjoining room contained over a thousand vessels, plates, bowls, beakers, small jars, and jugs (de Vaux 1973: 12). Deposits of bones, carefully buried under potsherds in most of the open areas, indicate that some of the meals had a religious significance that has not yet been adequately explained. The bones also reveal something of the occupants' diet, which consisted of mutton, lamb, goat, beef, and veal (de Vaux 1973: 12–15). The rest of building was given over to a kitchen and workshops, one containing a corn mill. The best preserved of the workshops was the pottery in the SE corner, with its washing basin, storage pit, wheel position, and kilns. It was here that the distinctive pottery found in the ruins and caves was made (de Vaux 1973: 54).

The building contained very few rooms that might have served as living quarters, yet the cemetery indicates a sizable population, which has been estimated at about 200 (de Vaux 1973: 86). The area could certainly have sustained such numbers (de Vaux 1973: 84–86). The inhabitants lived in caves, in tents on the marl terrace, and in underground chambers carved into the marl (de Vaux 1973: 56–57).

The pottery of Period Ib can be dated only very roughly, to the end of the Hellenistic era. The coins, however, permit greater dating precision. According to de Vaux (1973: 18–19), the buildings were certainly occupied during the reign of Alexander Jannaeus (103–76 B.C.) and possibly during that of John Hyrcanus (135–104 B.C.). They were destroyed by an earthquake and a fire, after which the site was abandoned for a generation. De Vaux (1973: 20–23) opted for the simplest hypothesis—the fire was caused by the earthquake—and identified the earthquake with that recorded for the year 31 B.C. by Josephus (*JW* 1.370–80). Others, however, claim that the earthquake merely gave the coup de grace to a building that had already been destroyed by enemy action, but they cannot agree on a date. Laperrousaz (1978: 760) placed it in the context of the struggle between Hyrcanus II and Aristobulus II (67–63 B.C.), whereas Milik (1959: 94) preferred the Parthian invasion of 40 B.C. Neither of these authors has offered an explanation of why a settlement of no strategic importance and far from the war zone should have been the object of military action. Neither do they explain the absence of any destruction level at Khirbet Feshkha. Nonetheless, their hypotheses explain why Qumran was abandoned, whereas de Vaux's does not. Since the

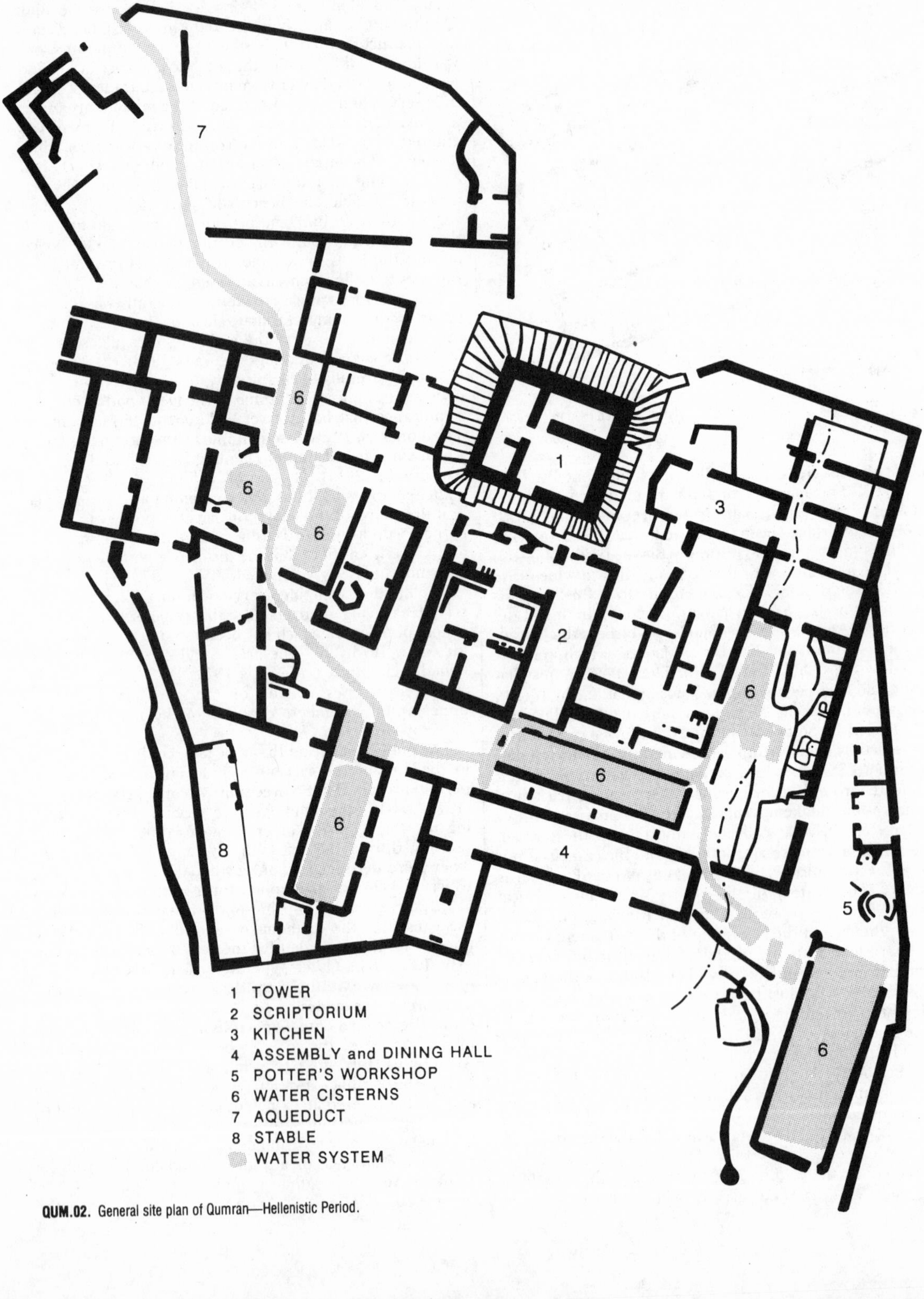

QUM.02. General site plan of Qumran—Hellenistic Period.

majority of the population lived and worked outside the edifice, which had not been badly damaged, it would have been natural for them to rebuild the community center, were the earthquake the only catastrophe.

4. Period II. Continuity both in pottery types and in the function of rooms indicates that the site was reoccupied by the same group that had abandoned it (de Vaux 1973: 24). Rooms that were too badly damaged were left untouched or partially cleared and walled off, while others were brought back into use. The loss of space was compensated for by roofing over, or building in, what had previously been open spaces. The tower was reinforced with a sloping stone girdle. The silted-up decantation basin was abandoned, and the water channel extended to a new smaller decantation pool, which received the periodic flow from the aqueduct.

The beginning of this period is dated by de Vaux (1973: 33–36) to the early part of the reign of Archelaus (4 B.C.–A.D. 6) on the basis of a complex argument based on the coins. It ended in a violent destruction, which is dated to the third year (A.D. 68/69) of the First Revolt by the end of the coin series of this phase (de Vaux 1973: 36–37). The buildings at Qumran would have been visible from the N end of the Dead Sea, which Vespasian visited in the spring of A.D. 68 to test whether the unusually salty water would support bound nonswimmers (*JW* 4.477), and the tower might have suggested a military post. The claim of Laperrousaz (1978: 764–66) that Period II should be divided into two phases separated by another abandonment around A.D. 6 does not seem to rest on solid evidence.

5. Period III. Roman arrowheads found in the destruction level of Period II, and Roman coins discovered in the new occupation level, show that Qumran was occupied by a Roman garrison, presumably until Masada fell in A.D. 74 (de Vaux 1973: 41–44). During operations against this fortress and Machaerus, it was essential for the Romans to control traffic on the Dead Sea. Only the tower and the adjoining areas on the E and S were refurbished for use. The water channel from the aqueduct was modified to serve only the large cistern in the SE corner.

6. Second Revolt. Coins attest the occupation of Qumran by resistance elements during A.D. 132–35, but it must have been of short duration for no structures can be attributed to this level (de Vaux 1973: 45). If Milik (1960: 163–64) is correct in his interpretation of a letter found in the Wadi Murabbaat, the name of the site at this period was Mesad Hasidin, "Fortress of the Pious."

7. Cemetery. The main cemetery of Periods I and II is located 50 m E of the buildings and contains about 1,100 tombs, 26 of which were excavated by de Vaux (1973: 45–48). The bodies were placed with their heads to the S in a cavity under the E wall of a trench, which was 1.2 m to 2 m deep. The tombs in the well-planned section nearest the buildings all contained male bodies, but some of those located in the extension of the cemetery over the hillocks to the E contained bodies of women and a child. Small secondary cemeteries on the terrace N of the buildings and at the foot of the terrace S of the wadi contained about 15 and 30 tombs, respectively. These contained male, female, and infant bodies (de Vaux 1973: 57–58). Very few of the individuals buried in these three cemeteries had passed their fortieth year (de Vaux 1973: 47).

C. Khirbet Feshkha

In terms of pottery and architectural style, the two main occupation levels correspond to Periods Ib and II at Qumran. The period of abandonment between the two phases, however, was marked by neither fire nor earthquake, whereas the end of this settlement was as violent as that of Qumran. Once again Laperrousaz (1978: 773–85) has disagreed with de Vaux's conclusions, and has equated Feshkha I and II with the two subdivisions he discerned in Qumran II, but his reasons are no more convincing. In contrast to Qumran, Feshkha was not reoccupied immediately after Period II, but parts of the ruins were reused in the late 1st century A.D. and early 2d century A.D., and again in the Byzantine period.

The central building, consisting of a series of rooms around a central courtyard, is of less importance for determining the function of Feshkha than the adjoining installations. The principle feature of the enclosure to the S is a long cobble-floored, roofed building which opens to the S; it would have been suitable for ripening dates (de Vaux 1973: 73). Palms were certainly cultivated in this area in antiquity, as the presence of their wood, leaves, and dates at Qumran and in its caves confirms (de Vaux 1973: 74).

The installation to the N is more complex. From a water-control box are run two channels separated by a paved area. The W channel first serves a large basin, and then skirts its edge to serve two smaller ones, whereas the E channel ends in a rectangular pool. All that can be said with certainty is that this complex served an industrial purpose. The initial suggestions that it was used for the preparation of leather or parchment are excluded by the complete absence of any traces of tannin or organic residue (de Vaux 1973: 78–82). Zeuner's hypothesis (1960) that it was a fish farm has encountered no such decisive objections, but in that case one would have expected the installation to have been designed differently. Despite this uncertainty, it is clear that Khirbet Feshkha was a dependency of Qumran, to whose industrial and agricultural needs it catered (de Vaux 1973: 84). The inhabitants also farmed in the Buqeia at the top of the cliffs, to which ancient paths lead from both Qumran and Feshkha.

Bibliography

Bar-Adon, P. 1977. Another Settlement of the Judean Desert Sect at En el-Ghuweir on the Shores of the Dead Sea. *BASOR* 227: 1–26.

Blake, I. 1966. Chronique archéologique: Rivage occidental de la mer Morte. *RB* 73: 564–66.

Cross, F. M., and Milik, J. T. 1956. Explorations in the Judaean Buqêʿah. *BASOR* 142: 5–17.

Davies, P. R. 1982. *Qumran.* Cities of the Biblical World. Guildford.

Farmer, W. R. 1955. The Economic Basis of the Qumran Community. *TZ* 11: 295–308.

———. 1956. Postscript. *TZ* 12: 56–58.

Harding, G. L. 1955. Introductory. The Discovery, the Excavation, the Minor Finds. Pp. 3–7 in *Qumran Cave I.* DJD 1. Ed. D. Barthélemy and J. T. Milik. Oxford.

Laperrousaz, E.-M. 1976. *Qoumrân: L'établissement essénien des bords de la mer Morte. Histoire et archéologique du site.* Paris.

———. 1978. Qumran et découvertes au désert de Juda. 1. Topo-

graphie des lieux et histoire des recherches. 2. Archéologie. *DBSup* 9: 738–89.
Milik, J. T. 1959. *Ten Years of Discovery in the Wilderness of Judaea.* SBT 26. London.
———. 1960. Textes hébreux et araméens. Pp. 67–205 in *Les Grottes de Murabbaʿât.* DJD 2. Ed. P. Benoit, J. T. Milik, and R. de Vaux. Oxford.
Schulz, S. 1960. Chirbet ḳumrān, ʿēn feschcha und die buḳēʿā: Zugleich ein archäologischer Beitrag zum Felsenaquädukt und zur Strasse durch das wādi ḳumrān. *ZDPV* 76: 50–72.
Stutchbury, H. E., and Nichol, G. R. 1962. Khirbet Mazin. *ADAJ* Jordan 6–8: 96–103.
Vaux, R. de. 1953. Fouille au Khirbet Qumran. *RB* 60: 83–106.
———. 1973. *Archaeology and the Dead Sea Scrolls.* Schweich Lectures 1959. London.
Zeuner, F. E. 1960. Notes on Qumran. *PEQ* 92: 27–36.

J. Murphy-O'Connor

QUOTATIONS OF OT IN NT. See NEW TESTAMENT, OT QUOTATIONS IN.

QURAYYA (28°47′N; 36°00′E). An archaeological site (Ar *al-qurayayah*) in NW Saudi Arabia, not mentioned in the biblical texts but possibly associated with the Midianites, and perhaps to be identified with the Ostama of Ptolemy's *Geography.* It is situated ca. 63 km NW of Tabuk and 125 km SE of Aqaba, in a region of broken sandstone and shale hills, cut by innumerable wadis, fringing the W edge of the Tabuk basin. The configuration of the region is such that flash floods flowing eastwards from the Hejaz mountains into the basin during winter and early summer can be utilized for agricultural purposes before they are lost in the gravels, sands, and silts of the basin itself, and it is no doubt this advantageous setting in an otherwise inhospitable environment which enabled the site to be originally settled. It is also close to the main N–S route from Arabia to Palestine and Syria, the route followed by the Mecca pilgrims and by the Hejaz railway.

The existence of ruins at Qurayya was known to a number of early travelers in the region, such as Wallin in 1848 and Burton and Doughty in 1877, though none of them actually visited the site. The first-known European visitor was B. Moritz, in 1906, who recorded a dozen or so examples of Thamudic, Nabatean and Kufic graffiti and published them, with a good description of the ruins (which he referred to as Greje), two years later (Moritz 1908: 399–415). Alois Musil did not visit the site during his journey of 1910, but he was aware of it (as al-Krajje) and tentatively identified it with Ptolemy's Ostama (Musil 1926: 43, 312). In 1951 it was visited by H. St. J. Philby, whose account of the topography and the visible remains was thorough and accurate (Philby 1957: 171–84). The first sketch plans of the site and its immediate surroundings were made in 1968 by a University of London archaeological survey team, who also published the first detailed analysis and interpretation of the remains (Parr, Harding, and Dayton 1970: 219–41). Since then Qurayya has been visited by members of the Saudi Arabian Antiquities Department who have added important details to the description (Ingraham, Johnson, Rihani, and Shatla 1981: 71–75). No accurately measured survey has ever been made, however; nor have proper excavations (apart from a few very minor soundings) been carried out. Knowledge of the site remains inadequate for anything but a superficial description and a tentative understanding of its chronology and its historical significance.

The Qurayya ruins, in their entirety, cover many km^2 and comprise a number of distinct though closely related parts. The most prominent feature is an isolated outcrop of gray-green shale siltstone, about 1 km long and 350 m broad at its widest point; it is oriented approximately E–W. The summit of the outcrop is steeply ridged, with its crest running along the long axis, and its highest point being some 50 m above the level of the broad wadi beds which surround it. It is protected on almost all sides by sheer cliffs, which justify Philby's designation of it as the Citadel Hill. Only at the SW corner is the rock face sufficiently low and broken to provide a means of access, and it was probably here that the original approach was located. The summit is divided into three roughly equal parts by two stone walls, stretching N–S from cliff to cliff. These are built of thin slabs of the local siltstone set in mud mortar and are about 1.40 m thick, surviving in places to a height of over 3 m. A distinctive feature of their construction is the way in which they are composed of separate unbonded sections, each about 3 or 4 m long, perhaps in order to localize any collapse resulting from an earthquake or hostile action. The W wall has a series of semicircular towers projecting from its W face, while there are traces of what may be gateways in approximately the middle of each wall. Other stone structures on the summit include several ruined square towers and what are probably masonry tombs. There can be no doubt that the Citadel Hill served as a fortified place of refuge for the inhabitants of the settlement below.

The ruins of this settlement cover an irregular area of ca. 400 m × 300 m on the level ground some 200 m from the NE foot of the citadel. The line of a surrounding wall is mostly buried beneath debris and windblown sand, but a few traces of its stone and mud-brick structure are visible. It appears to have been provided in places with projecting towers, and there may have been gateways on the N and S. Within the walled area there are considerable mounds of debris, reaching heights of ca. 8 m, and occasional stubs of walls, but there is little indication of the original layout, apart from the presence of a large flat area to the N which may have been an open marketplace.

Arising from the base of the citadel on its N and E sides are a number of long walls similar in general appearance to that which surrounds the settlement. One of them connects the settlement to the citadel, while the others enclose extensive areas of the adjacent flat wadi beds. Still other walls of similar construction can be traced over a wide area to the NE of the settlement, running in relatively straight lines across both wadi beds and the neighboring low hills and ridges, in some cases for distances of several kilometers. Throughout this area are remains of many small rectangular fields, their outlines marked by low single lines of rough stones. Double lines of stones are perhaps the remains of water channels serving the fields, and the remains of a few stone sluices are preserved. A much more substantial water channel, partly in the form of a wide ditch, runs in the direction of these fields from the site of a now-dry spring at the foot of the citadel. This complex of remains clearly suggests an agricultural system based on irrigation, which was protected by enclosure walls from damage by flood and wind and from hostile intrusion.

Finally to be noted are the ruins of three isolated buildings, two just outside the N and E sides of the enclosure wall of the settlement and the third about a km further N in the middle of the fields. They are built of ashlar sandstone masonry, an entirely different material from that employed for the other structures at the site; some of the blocks exhibit the diagonal tooling usually associated with Nabatean craftsmanship, while two of the buildings have among their ruins fragments of typical Nabatean capitals and column bases. The function of these buildings is obscure. Philby (1957) called the two closest to the settlement a nymphaeum and a palace, but there is nothing in their plans to support such a designation. They are clearly of a different date from the rest of the ruins at Qurayya, and perhaps constitute a Nabatean way station on the Arabian caravan route.

With the exception of the three buildings mentioned above, the most striking feature of the Qurayya remains is their homogeneity, reflected in the almost identical style of construction of the walls on the citadel, around the settlement, and encircling the field systems. It is therefore reasonable to suppose that all of these features are more or less contemporary with one another, and are part of one basic design. To provide a date for this complex without a detailed survey and excavation is impossible, but the evidence of the pottery collected from the surface of the site provides some indication. A small proportion of this is of typical Romano-Nabatean ware; it is found particularly in the vicinities of the three isolated buildings described above. The majority of the pottery from the citadel, the settlement, and the fields, however, is very different. A number of types are represented, but only one of these is, with our present state of knowledge, sufficiently diagnostic to help with dating. This is a very distinctive painted ware decorated in various tones of black, brown, red, and yellow applied to a thick buff or cream slip; quite often a bichrome or polychrome effect is produced. The most frequent patterns are geometric (horizontal and vertical bands, triangles, cross-hatching, running broken spirals, etc.), but animal motifs (birds, bulls, and at least one camel) are also reported, and occasional human figures. That this painted ware (and no doubt some at least of the plain wares, which often resemble the painted ware in fabric and shape) was manufactured at the site is proved by the discovery at the N foot of the citadel of a number of ruined kilns, surrounded by spoiled and discarded sherds, some of which were painted. Petrographic analysis of the painted pottery has also indicated that the materials for its production must have derived from Qurayya or from an area of very similar geology (Rothenberg and Glass 1983; 101–13; Rothenberg 1988: 101), and it is possible that two caves cut into the face of the hill near the kilns were quarries for the extraction of claystone for use by the potters.

The dating of this distinctive pottery (for which the term "Qurayya Painted Ware" has been proposed) is still a matter for debate. (For the latest discussion, see Parr 1988). However, that it was in use as early as the 13th and 12th centuries B.C. has been proved by the discovery of identical sherds at a number of archaeological sites in modern Israel, especially at the important copper-mining center of Timna in the S Wadi Araba, where they were found in stratified contexts dated by inscribed Egyptian objects of Dynasties XIX and XX (Rothenberg 1988). This dating is supported by a comparative study of the decorative motifs, some of which—in particular the running spirals and birds—are very reminiscent of those on some LB ceramics from the Aegean and E Mediterranean (Parr, Harding, and Dayton 1970: 238). Other motifs—particularly a lotus design—suggest Egyptian parallels, and it is possible that the immediate source of inspiration for the pottery was Egyptian faience, much of which was found at Timna (Parr 1982: 129–30). Whether the Qurayya Painted Ware was also in production later than about the 11th century B.C. is uncertain; it has been suggested that it was still in vogue in N Arabia as late as the 7th century B.C. (Muhly 1984: 284), but the arguments are by no means convincing (Parr 1988). On present evidence it seems most likely that the pottery dates to the last few centuries of the 2d millennium, and in view of its profusion among the ruins of all parts of the Qurayya site it is reasonable to conclude that these ruins also date in their origin to this period.

As the result of recent archaeological surveys it is now known that this painted pottery is found not only at Qurayya and at Timna but also at a number of other localities in NW Arabia, including the oasis center of Tayma, on the main trade route to the S, and about a dozen sites in the lower reaches of several wadis leading down through the Hejaz mountains to the Red Sea coast near the mouth of the Gulf of Aqaba (Ingraham, Johnson, Rihani, and Shatla 1981: 74–75; Bawden 1983: 42–44). One such site is that of Mughaʾir Shuʿayb (al-Badʿ), almost certainly the oasis known to the classical geographers as Madian and to medieval Arab writers as Midyan, names which derive from that of the biblical Midianites, with which this corner of the Arabian peninsula is traditionally associated (Musil 1926: 278–87). It was because of this association that the Qurayya Painted Ware, when originally reported, was designated "Midianite Ware" (Parr, Harding, and Dayton 1970: 240); and although the more neutral term is certainly now to be preferred, it is hard to avoid the conclusion that the pottery and the people were, in some way, connected.

Regardless, the existence toward the end of the 2d millennium in NW Arabia of settlements of which at least one, Qurayya, is provided with such substantial defensive architecture as to merit the term "urban" requires explanation. In the present state of knowledge, this can be little more than guesswork, but further consideration of the distribution of the painted pottery leads to a reasonable hypothesis. The quantity of Egyptian objects at Timna has been reasonably taken to indicate that the copper mines there were operated under pharaonic control, while the presence of Qurayya Painted Ware at the site shows that its users—presumably workers from the Hejaz—were in contact with the Egyptians. The presence of the pottery at sites close to the Hejaz coast, little more than 150 km across the Red Sea from Egypt, and on routes leading E toward Qurayya and Tayma, is also suggestive of an Egyptian connection. Unlike Timna, however, neither Qurayya nor Tayma have produced evidence to associate them with copper working, and it is much more likely that they were involved with the trade in aromatics. Although it has recently been denied that the land route through Arabia to the incense-producing regions of the S was in use as early as this (Crone 1987: 13–15), there is in fact persuasive evidence that New Kingdom Egypt was obtaining some of its supplies from intermediaries in the NW of the peninsula. It is at least possible, therefore, that it was Egyptian economic involvement, perhaps for the sake of both copper and aromatics, which provided the stimulus toward sedentarization and the establishment of sites such as Qurayya; and it has further been argued that the inhabitants of the region belonged to that vague category of people known to the Egyptians as Shoshu, some of whom at least, according to the Egyptian sources, may have been sedentary (Parr 1988). Whether the inhabitants of Qurayya are also to be thought of as Midianites depends on how the biblical references to that people are interpreted and what view is taken of their territorial, political, and economic status in the 13th and 12th centuries B.C.

Bibliography

Bawden, G. 1983. Painted Pottery from Tayma and Problems of Cultural Chronology in Northwest Arabia. Pp. 37–52 in *Midian, Moab, and Edom,* ed. J. F. A. Sawyer and D. J. A. Clines. Sheffield.

Crone, P. 1987. *Meccan Trade and the Rise of Islam.* Oxford.

Ingraham, M.; Johnson, T.; Rihani, B.; and Shatla, I. 1981. Preliminary Report on a Reconnaissance Survey of the Northwestern Province. *Atlal* 5: 59–84.

Moritz, B. 1908. Ausfluge in der Arabian Petraea. *MUSJ* 2: 399–415.

Muhly, J. 1984. Timna and King Solomon. *BSac* 41: 275–92.

Musil, A. 1926. *The Northern Hegaz.* New York.

Parr, P. J. 1982. Contacts between N.W. Arabia and Jordan in the Late Bronze and Early Iron Ages. Pp. 127–33 in *Studies in the History and Archaeology of Jordan I,* ed. A. Hadidi. Amman.

———. 1988. Pottery of the Late Second Millennium B.C. from North West Arabia and its Historical Implications. Pp. 73–89 in *Araby the Blest: Studies in Arabian Archaeology,* ed. D. T. Potts. Copenhagen.

Parr, P. J.; Harding, G. L.; and Dayton, J. E. 1970. Preliminary Survey in N.W. Arabia, 1968. *Bulletin of the Institute of Archaeology, University of London,* 8–9: 219–41.

Philby, H. St. J. 1957. *The Land of Midian.* London.

Rothenberg, B. 1988. *The Egyptian Mining Temple at Timna.* London.

Rothenberg, B., and Glass, J. 1983. The Midianite Pottery. Pp. 65–124 in *Midian, Moab, and Edom,* ed. J. F. A. Sawyer and D. J. A. Clines. Sheffield.

Saleh, A.-A. 1973. An Open Question on Intermediaries in the Incense Trade during Pharaonic Times. *Orientalia* 42: 370–82.

PETER J. PARR

QUTIAN LANGUAGE.

See LANGUAGES (INTRODUCTORY SURVEY).

R

RA (DEITY). See RE (DEITY).

RAAMAH (PERSON) [Heb *raᶜmâ; raᶜmāʾ*]. A son of Cush and father of Dedan and Sheba (Gen 10:7; 1 Chr 1:9) whose name occurs in the so-called "Table of Nations" (Genesis 10) as a tribal rather than personal name (Westermann 1984: 510–11). Raamah is also named along with Sheba as a commercial partner with Tyre (Ezek 27:22). The biblical contexts point to Arabia; more specifically, the list of delivered products in Ezekiel 27 (best aromatics, precious stones, and gold) suggests a location of Raamah in S Arabia, or at least within the reach of the ancient incense route. An identification which should be considered is *rgmtm* (probably vocalized Ragmatum), the ancient name of the capital of the oasis of Nagrān *(Nağrān)* in what was then N Yemen, today situated in SW Saudi Arabia. Later on, the name of the oasis was also transferred to the town, and the name Ragmatum disappeared. Favoring the equation of biblical Raamah with *rgmtm* are the LXX renderings of the name (1 Chr 1:9; *regma;* Ezek 27:22, *ragma*), as well as a note in the Greek and Ethiopic versions of the *Martyrium of St. Arethas* telling that the meaning of the name of the town of Nagrān is in Hebrew "town of thunder," which can only be explained if one substitutes for Nagrān the name *Raᶜmâ,* since in Aram *raᶜmāʾ* means "thunder" (cf. Müller 1969: 366, n. 103).

The earliest Old South Arabic reference to *rgmtm* is found in the Old Sabean inscription RES 3943,4 from Mārib from the time around 500 B.C. This text is an account of the deeds of a ruler who, among others, destroyed Ragmatum, the town of the king of the Muhaʾmirum, as well as all the towns in the area surrounding Ragmatum and Nagrān. In the Minaean inscription M 247 (= RES 3022,2 from Barāqiš [ca. 340/330 B.C.]), it is mentioned that the Sabeans attacked a Minaean caravan on the route between Maᶜīn and Ragmatum. Another reference to this town is found on a bronze tablet from al-Uhdūd, the ruins of ancient Nagrān, which contains a dedication to D̲ūSamāwī, the lord of a temple in *[r]gmtm;* furthermore, a reference to an inhabitant of the town *d̲r[g]mtm* occurs in the fragmentary text Ja 2132 from Qaryat al-Faw, about 280 km N of Nagrān on the trade route to the Persian Gulf (see Ryckmans 1980: 198, n. 4). In antiquity, Ragmatum in the oasis of Nagrān was an important station on the incense road, the main route of which came from Mārib in Saba and led from there to the N via Dedan until it reached the Mediterranean coast.

An identification of the biblical *raᶜmâ* (or *regma*) with *regma* (or *regama*) *polis* in Ptolemy (*Geog.* 6.7.14) is impossible because that town must have been situated on the Persian Gulf. Likewise, the equation with the *rammanitai* in Strabo (*Geog.* 16.4.24) is out of question, because Raimānites are understood by this gentilic; the inhabitants of Nagrān are designated in the same chapter of Strabo as *negranai.* Already in the 18th century Niebuhr (1772: 248, 293) wanted to compare the biblical Raamah with the region around Ğabal Raima, one of the numerous Yemenite places of that name.

Bibliography

Müller, W. W. 1969. Alt-Südarabien als Weihrauchland. *TQ* 149.

Niebuhr, C. 1771. *Beschreibung von Arabien.* Copenhagen.

Ryckmans, J. 1980. ᶜUzzā et Lāt dans les inscriptions sud-arabes. *JSS* 25: 193–204.

Westermann, C. 1984. *Genesis 1–11: A Commentary.* Trans. J. J. Scullion. Minneapolis.

Winnett, F. V. 1970. The Arabian Genealogies in the Book of Genesis. Pp. 171–96 in *Translating and Understanding the Old Testament,* ed. H. T. Frank and W. L. Reed. Nashville.

Wissmann, H. von. 1964. *Zur Geschichte und Landeskunde von Alt-Südarabien.* Vienna.

W. W. Müller

RAAMIAH (PERSON) [Heb *raᶜamyāh*]. An alternate form of REELAIAH.

RAAMSES (PLACE) [Heb *raᶜamsēs*]. See RAMESES (PLACE).

RABAH, WADI (M.R. 144167). The name of one of the tributaries of the Yarkon river and of a site situated on its S bank, about 1 km E of Tell Ras el-ᶜAin (M.R. 143168). Two Chalcolithic levels and mixed remains of the two Neolithic phases (Jericho IX and Yarmukian) have been identified there.

On the mound of Tell Ras el-ᶜAin itself, no remains earlier than the EB were found; thus, it appears that the earlier Wadi Rabah site was abandoned sometime toward the end of the Chalcolithic period and that settlement resumed further W on virgin soil close to a spring, constituting the earliest settlement at Tell Ras el-ᶜAin. For a discussion of the excavations on the mound of Ras el-ᶜAin, see ANTIPATRIS. The Wadi Rabah site was excavated in November 1952. Stratum I was found to belong to the Ghassulian phase of the Chalcolithic, while stratum II belonged to a pre-Ghassulian phase.

Stratum II is significant in that its pottery is formally similar to that of Jericho VIII; however, there is a larger amount of slipped and decorated ware at Wadi Rabah than at Jericho VIII. Most of the Wadi Rabah pottery is burnished, whereas burnishing appears only on bowls at Jericho VIII, and there is no evidence of burnishing whatsoever at Tuleilat Ghassul, suggesting that the finds associated with Wadi Rabah level II not only antedate the Ghassulian culture of Palestine (which occurred ca. 3500 B.C.) but also that associated with Jericho VIII. In all these three phases of the Chalcolithic age—Rabah II, Jericho VIII, and Ghassulian—the pottery shows uninterrupted development. Finds similar to those of Wadi Rabah stratum II have been found in other excavations, such as those at ha-Bashan Street in Tel Aviv (*EAEHL* 4: 1161), at Lod (area B), in stratum IIIc of Tuleilat el-Batashi (area B), and at ᶜEin el-Jarba. Based on radiocarbon dates of the Wadi Rabah stratum at ᶜEin el-Jarba, it appears that the earliest possible limits for this culture is 4000 B.C. See BATASHI, TULEILAT EL-; JARBA, ᶜEIN EL-; and LOD. The wide geographical horizon of this culture is reinforced by recent surveys in Galilee, where some sites demonstrate close affinities to the Wadi Rabah culture (Frankel and Gophna 1980).

Some of the pottery of these three Chalcolithic phases can be compared with Halafian ware (particularly the Halafian ware and its imitations occurring in strata XVI–XIX at Mersin in Cilicia), and a correlation can be established between the Middle Chalcolithic of Mersin and the Chalcolithic of Palestine (Kaplan 1960). Since, however, certain shapes and ornamentation characteristic of the Wadi Rabah ware were encountered only in Mersin XIX, the Wadi Rabah culture can be placed in the same horizon as that stratum; i.e., it is a Chalcolithic, not a Neolithic culture, even though no copper has been found among the Wadi Rabah repertoire of objects.

Bibliography

Frankel, R., and Gophna, R. 1980. Chalcolithic Pottery from a Cave in Western Galilee. *TA* 7: 65069.

Kaplan, J. 1958. The Excavations at Wadi Rabah. *IEJ* 8: 149–60.

———. 1960. The Relation of the Chalcolithic Pottery of Palestine to Halafian Ware. *BASOR* 159: 32–36.

JACOB KAPLAN

RABBAH (PLACE) [Heb *rabbâ*]. **1.** Also known as *rabbat bĕnê ᶜammôn* (Rabbah of the children of Ammon), the city that served as the capital of the ancient Ammonite kingdom. The site is located on Citadel Hill (Jebel Qalᶜah) in the middle of the modern city of Amman (M.R. 238151) on the N bank of the upper course of the *Nahr ez-Zerqa* (Wadi Zerqa; modern Wadi Amman), where powerful springs serve as the sources of the Jabbok river. See also AMMAN.

According to Deut 3:11, Rabbah is noted as the place where the "iron bedstead" of Og, last of the Rephaim and king of the Amorites at Bashan, was on display. It is possible that the iron bed was taken to Rabbah by the Ammonites as a trophy of their initial conquest, although Landes (*IDB* 1: 109) has suggested that it was preserved because of a special desire to show respect to the powers (human and divine) which controlled and possessed the land prior to the Ammonite emergence. At any rate, this passage shows that Rabbath-ammon was clearly already the capital of the Ammonites by the 13th century B.C.

A reference in Josh 13:25 describes Rabbah's geographical relationship to Aroer. Although some translations locate Aroer "east of Rabbah," a proper rendering should be "in front of [facing] Rabbah" (note the NIV reading of "near"). It would appear from this reference that Rabbah was clearly considered outside of the territory allotted to the Israelites.

The Ammonites were conquered by Israel, after provoking David to war by their humiliation of his messengers (2 Sam 11:1). The account of the siege (2 Sam 12:26–31) appears to provide a small clue to the actual physical layout of the Ammonite capital. Specifically, we are told in 2 Sam 12:26 that after fighting for some time against Rabbah, Joab was finally able to capture the *ᶜîr hammĕlûkâ* ("royal city"). In verse 27, however, Joab informs David that it is the *ᶜîr hammāyim* ("city of waters") which has been taken. The use of these two expressions has raised a long-standing question as to whether Joab was using two different names for the city of Rabbah *at large,* or was intending to describe two different locations *within* the city. Most recent commentators have apparently opted for the second interpretation, suggesting that the *ᶜîr hammĕlûkâ* was a fortified royal citadel located on the top of the mound (acropolis), while the *ᶜîr hammāyim* was a special fortification that guarded the city's water supply in the valley of the Jabbok. Although the two different expressions are attested in both the MT and the LXX, both Syr and Targ have changed the second expression *ᶜîr hammāyim,* to *ᶜîr hammĕlûkâ* in apparent support of the first interpretation. More recent critics have followed a similar approach, although Wellhausen (1871) preferred to alter the text so that *ᶜîr hammāyim* was read in both verses. McCarter, on the other hand, argues that such emendation of the text is unjustified and unnecessary (*2 Samuel* AB, 310–12). He suggests that both verses refer to the same place, but that rather than referring to the entire city at large, both expressions refer to a citadel within the city which both served as the king's royal residence *and* guarded the city's water supply. If the fortified royal residence was located atop that portion of the tell which immediately overlooked the springs of the Jabbok, it could easily have doubled as a fortification for the city's water supply.

At any rate, after the city fell David placed the Ammonite crown on his head and subjected the people to forced labor (2 Sam 12:26–31; 2 Chr 20:1–3). It was during this siege that Uriah the Hittite was sent to his death (2 Sam 11:14–25). Later, when David was forced to seek refuge in Transjordan, Shobi, son of Nahash, from Rabbah, helped supply David (2 Sam 17:27–29).

It appears that Rabbah remained under Israelite suzerainty until the first half of the 9th century B.C., although it is not mentioned again until the mid-8th century B.C. (Amos 1:14). From this time until the fall of the S kingdom, Rabbah received numerous prophetic rebukes as the

Ammonites tried to take advantage of Judah's increasing political difficulties (Jer 49:2; Ezek 21:25 [—Eng 21:20]; 25:5).

Rabbah-ammon became a Hellenistic city when Ptolemy II Philadelphus (285–247 B.C.) rebuilt and renamed the city Philadelphia, although the original name continued to be used by both local officials and contemporary historians. It was later conquered in 218 B.C. by the Seleucid king Antiochus III ("the Great"), who penetrated the city through a water tunnel, the remains of which can still be seen.

Josephus reveals that during the time of Hyrcanus (135–107 B.C.) Rabbah-ammon was ruled by the tyrant Zenon Cotylas and later, by his son, Theodorus. Although Alexander Jannaeus laid siege to the city during this time, he was unable to take it.

In 63 B.C., the Roman general Pompey annexed Philadelphia to the Decapolis. It remained under Arab control until Herod defeated the city in 30 B.C. During the Jewish revolt, Rabbah-ammon joined the fight against the Zealots.

During the time of Trajan, Rabbah-ammon was included in the province of Arabia (A.D. 106). A new road from Elath to Damascus, which ran through Rabbah-ammon, created an economic boom for the city which increased its wealth and importance during the Byzantine period. During the 4th century A.D., it was listed by Ammianus Marcellinus as one of the great fortified cities of Coele-Syria. It eventually became the seat of a Christian bishopric, forming one of the nineteen sees of *Palaestina tertia*.

When the city was conquered by the Muslim Yezid in A.D. 635, it was renamed Amman and made the capital of the Balqa district. During the Crusader period, it was ruled by a Transjordanian prince named Ahamant. It appears that during the Mameluke period Rabbah-ammon was deserted, and remained so until it was resettled by some Circassians in 1876. Amman became the capital of the Emirate of Transjordan in 1921, and today it is the capital of the Hashemite kingdom of Jordan.

The first modern excavation in Amman was conducted by an Italian team led by G. Guidi in 1927. R. Bartoccini took over as director in the years 1929–33. In 1955 G. L. Harding examined the Ammon Airport structure just after it was discovered. It was later excavated by J. B. Hennessy in 1966 and, again, by L. Geraty and L. Herr in 1976. In 1966 R. Dornemann conducted a sounding on the Citadel Hill (Jebel Qalᶜah). Additional work was done at the citadel by C. Bennett (1975; 1979). Jordanian archaeologists (e.g., F. Zayadine, and A. Hadidi) have recently made several important discoveries and conducted many important soundings and excavations at various sites in Amman.

Remains from the Paleolithic, Neolithic, and Chalcolithic periods have been reported from various locations in Amman. Dolmens are also said to have been scattered throughout the area, although none of these survive, the last having been destroyed in the early part of this century. See DOLMEN.

Occupation during the various periods of the EB (ca. 2900–2300 B.C.) is thus far represented only by unstratified pottery from Citadel Hill in Amman (Jebel Qalᶜah).

Middle Bronze I occupation is likewise supported only by sherd material so far, but remains from the MB II–III (ca. 1800–1550 B.C.) have been steadily accumulating. At least four MB II–III tombs have been reported from Amman: one on Jebel Jofeh el-Gharbi, SE of Citadel Hill; one on Jebel et Taj, ESE of Citadel Hill; and two on Citadel Hill, itself. The two tombs on Citadel Hill contained thirty-six scarabs (almost all from the 13th to 17th Egyptian dynasties) and six cylinder seals of types used between 1700 and 1200 B.C. Evidence for occupation of Citadel Hill, itself, comes from a probe conducted on the upper terrace, just N of the Hellenistic-Roman wall, in which a MB II glacis was revealed in association with two walls. Finally, it should be noted that the foundation deposit at the Amman Airport structure contained scarabs from the 17th to 13th centuries B.C., as well as four cylinder seals, two of which may date to MB II–III. Although these scarabs and seals were probably heirlooms and do not date the structure, itself, (which is clearly LB; see below), they do provide additional indirect evidence for MB II–III occupation.

The LB occupation on Citadel Hill is so far supported only by unstratified sherds. More intensive excavation will probably provide new information. The most important find of this period is the Amman Airport structure (Herr 1983a; 1983b). It is almost 15 m square in plan with outer walls 2 m thick. In addition to local pottery, a large quantity of imported Cypriot and Mycenaean ware was found, enabling archaeologists to date the structure to LB IIB (1300–1200 B.C.). Although the structure was initially interpreted as a temple, further excavation and analysis have led to the suggestion that the structure served as a "tower," perhaps for the storage of funerary gifts. The discovery of a large number of burnt human bones as well as a large pile of slightly scorched rocks (which may have served as a pyre for cremation) lends support to the idea that the site served a funerary function. The increasing corpus of MB and LB finds around Amman has forced scholars to reevaluate Glueck's hypothesis that central Transjordan essentially lacked any sedentary occupation during these periods.

Material from Iron I (1200–1000 B.C.) is limited to a tomb on Jebel Nuzha (initially assigned to LB IIB, but more likely represents the earliest Iron I phase; see Dornemann 1983: 31–34) and unstratified sherds from the 1969 sounding of Citadel Hill (Dornemann 1983: 106). The most important finds from Iron Age IB–IIA (10th–9th centuries B.C.) include a wall on Citadel Hill (possibly built by David after his recapture of the city) and the well-known Ammonite Citadel Inscription (dated between 875 and 825 B.C.). Finds from Iron IIB–C (8th–6th centuries B.C.), which are more abundant, include several statues of Ammonite kings—the crowns of which may resemble that which was captured by David (2 Sam 12:30); wall fragments on Citadel Hill from the 7th–6th centuries B.C.—possibly destroyed by the Assyrians; four double-faced stone heads of females, which may have served as ornamental capitals for royal buildings on Citadel Hill; the Siran Bottle Inscription—a 7th-century B.C. dedicatory inscription on a bronze bottle which mentions Amminadab, son of Hisalel, son of Amminadab, king of the Ammonites (this bottle was found at Tell Siran on the campus of the University of Jordan, in Amman); and several Iron IIB–C tombs. (For a more complete summary and bibliography of finds, see Dornemann 1983; Geraty and Willis 1986.)

There has been much discussion about a number of "megalithic towers" which have been assumed to have provided an outer "ring of defense" for Rabbah during the Iron Age. More recent analysis of these structures shows that they were not all contemporary (some date as late as the Roman period), nor did they all serve military functions. Indeed, many appear to have served as agricultural farmsteads and watchtowers.

Clearly, the archaeological evidence shows that during the latter part of the Iron IIB–C period ancient Amman was at the appex of its wealth and political power. This, undoubtedly, reflects the greater independence Amman enjoyed under Assyrian and Babylonian sovereignty as opposed to the greater oppression it experienced when dominated by Israel and Judah.

There is a paucity of archaeological remains for the Persian period, but material from the Hellenistic period has been found, including some walls on the lower terrace of Citadel Hill, various houses with plaster floors, painted pottery, Rhodian jar handles, coins, and an underground reservoir at the N end of the citadel. Two reliefs of gods from the 4th–3rd centuries B.C. were found in the forum area.

The most spectacular ruins, which can be seen on the surface on and around Citadel Hill, are from the Roman period. These remains include the well-known amphitheater, a colonnaded street, the nymphaeum, the odeum, an aqueduct, a bath, a temple complex, and several Roman tombs.

Byzantine and Arabic remains include two large houses on the citadel and a Byzantine church.

Bibliography

Bennett, C.-M. 1975. Excavations at the Citadel, Amman, 1975. *ADAJ* 20: 131–42.

———. 1979. Excavations on the Citadel (al Qalʿa) Amman, 1978. Fourth Preliminary Report. *ADAJ* 23: 161–70.

Dornemann, R. 1983. *The Archaeology of the Transjordan in the Bronze and Iron Ages.* Milwaukee.

Geraty, L. T., and Willis, L. 1986. The History of Archaeological Research in Transjordan. Pp. 3–72 in *The Archaeology of Jordan and Other Studies,* ed. L. T. Geraty and L. Herr. Berrien Springs, MI.

Hadidi, A. 1974. The Excavation of the Roman Forum at Amman (Philadelphia), 1964–1967. *ADAJ* 19: 71–91.

Herr, L. G. 1983a. The Amman Airport Structure and the Geopolitics of Ancient Transjordan. *BA* 46/4: 223–29.

———. 1983b. *The Amman Airport Excavations 1976.* AASOR 48. Cambridge, MA.

Wellhausen, J. 1871. *Der Text der Bücher Samuelis untersucht.* Göttingen.

Zayadine, F. 1973. Recent Excavations on the Citadel of Amman. *ADAJ* 18: 17–35.

———. 1977–78. Excavations on the Upper Citadel of Amman—Area A, 1975–1977. *ADAJ* 22: 20–56.

RANDALL W. YOUNKER

2. A town situated in the N highlands of Judah (Josh 15:60), within the same district as Kiriath-baal/Kiriath-jearim. This settlement, whose name perhaps means "the great one" (fem.), is listed among the towns within the tribal allotment of Judah (Josh 15:21–62). The theory that this list was derived from an administrative roster compiled under the Judean monarchy (Alt 1925) has been widely accepted, although controversy continues over the precise makeup of the districts, the proper context of the town lists of Benjamin and Dan, and the period of the monarchy to which the original roster belongs (Boling and Wright *Joshua* AB, 64–72). It is possible that this town is the same as Rubute of the Egyptian texts, although the difficulties of locating Rubute in the hill country, as Joshua 15 suggests for Rabbah, casts some doubt on this idea. In order to retain the identification of Rabbah with Rubute, Aharoni (*LBHG,* 299) argued that this district consisted of two fortresses guarding each end of the W approach to Jerusalem (M.R. 149137; cf. Rainey *ISBE* 4: 29). However, it seems unnecessarily arbitrary to assume that this district is unique, since all the other districts in this roster form reasonably compact geographical units. If this district is not unique, then we should look for Rabbah in the hill country close to Kiriath-baal/Kiriath-jearim. In this light, it seems best to admit that Rabbah of Judah remains to be identified.

Bibliography

Alt, A. 1925. Judas Gaue unter Josia. *PJ* 21: 100–16.

WADE R. KOTTER

RABBI [Gk *rhabbi*]. Var. RABBONI. An honorific title found in the NT. The Hebrew word *rabbî* is transliterated just over a dozen times in the Greek text of the Gospels. In ten of these cases, the RSV retains the transliteration with the English equivalent "rabbi." In five other instances Gk *rhabbi* is translated "master" (Matt 26:25, 49; Mark 9:5; 11:21; 14:45). In origin a title of authority, Heb *rabbî* became, by the 1st century C.E., a title as well as a mode of address.

A. Literary and Epigraphic Background

1. Biblical and Extrabiblical Evidence. In the OT the word *rab,* "big," "great," occurs only in construct with other nouns: *rab šāqeh,* "chief of officers" (2 Kgs 18:17 = Isa 36:2, etc.); *rab sārîs,* "chief of heads" (2 Kgs 18:17, Jer 39:3, 13; Dan 1:3); *rab māg,* "chief of princes" (Jer 39:3, 13); *rab tabbāḥîm,* "captain of the guard" (2 Kgs 25:8, etc.); Aram *rab ḥartummayyāʾ,* "chief of magicians" (Dan 4:6, 5:1); *rab signîn,* "chief of prefects" (Dan 2:48); *rab ḥôbel,* "chief of sailors" (Jonah 1:6). In two other instances the title *rab* is not connected with a corps of officials (Jer 39:13; [41:1]; Esth 1:8). In extracanonical sources, both Aramaic and Phoenician, *rab* has the sense of "officer" or "chief," and it appears most often in the construct form (*DISO,* s.v.). It is attested in the absolute in Jewish Aramaic texts from Qumran (e.g., 11QtgJob 19:3 [Job 29:4]; 25:1 [Job 34:24]).

2. "Rabbi" as a Jewish Title in the First Centuries C.E. The earliest evidence for "rabbi" as a title attached to a proper name (e.g., Rab Hana) occurs on Jerusalem ossuaries which apparently date from before 100 C.E. (*CIJ* 2: 249; 275–77; 277–79). The inscriptions which date from 100 C.E. to 400 C.E. stem largely from the cemeteries of

Joppa and Beth-sheʿarim (see the annotated list of inscriptions in Cohen 1981: 1–17). These inscriptions indicate that men entitled *rabbî* were probably wealthy, and that many were comfortable with the Greek language and with Greco-Roman artistic and architectural styles (see, e.g., Schwabe and Lifshitz 1973: no. 61). Overall, the inscriptions indicate that the title *rabbî* should be thought of as an honorific roughly equivalent to "sir," with no explicit connection to either teaching or adjudication (much like the colloquial use of Gk *kyrios*). One problematic exception should be noted [Naveh 1978: no. 6]; the inscription cited at Mazar 1974: 46 should not be admitted as evidence.)

B. *Rab* and *Rabbi* in Rabbinic Literature

The use of the term *rab* as a title is not attested before roughly the 1st century C.E. In rabbinic literature, personages associated with the period before 70 C.E. are not referred to with a title (e.g., Hillel, Shammai), while those associated with the later periods are titled (e.g., Rabbi Aqiba, etc.). Of greatest relevance to the present discussion, however, is the absolute use of the term as well as its use as a mode of address (as in the NT). The discussion is based solely on the Mishna and the Tosepta, the two earliest rabbinic collections.

1. "Rab" in the Absolute. In the absolute, the term *rab* is used almost exclusively in two ways: to designate the master of a slave (e.g., *m. Pesaḥ.* 8.1–2; *m. Giṭ.* 4.4 = *m. ʿEd.* 1.3; compare Gk *kyrios*) or to designate a teacher, the more relevant usage for present purposes. In one tradition about a figure associated with the period before 70 C.E. and in two pre-135 C.E. traditions, *rab* designates a link in the chain of authoritative teaching (*t. Pesaḥ.* 4.13–14; *m. Yad.* 4.3; *m. ʿEd.* 8.7).

In traditions attributed to post-135 C.E. figures, obligations to a *rab* are explicitly filial (*m. Makk.* 2.2 with *t. B. Qam.* 9.11; *m. B. Meṣ.* 2.11 with *t. B. Meṣ.* 2.29–30 and *t. Hor.* 2.25; *m. Ker.* 6.9). Similarly, the social relations of a *rab* are the focus of other post-135 C.E. traditions, as well as of anonymous traditions (*m. ʿErub.* 3.5; *m. Meg.* 4.5; *m. Ket.* 2.10; *t. Ber.* 5.7; *t. ʿErub.* 4.1; 5.11; *t. Ket.* 3.3; *t. Sanh.* 3.8).

Two usages characteristic of the Tosepta deserve special mention. First, important biblical figures (Moses, Elijah, Elisha) are described in terms of the relationship of *rab* and disciple (*t. Sot.* 3.7; *t. ʿEd.* 3.4). Second, the plural *rabbôtênû* is used for the collective body of sages, and seems to be characteristic of traditions about Usha (e.g., "*rabbôtênû* were counted [for a vote] in Usha . . ." [*m. Soṭa* 9.14; the only mishnaic tradition of this type]; *t. Ber.* 2.11; *t. Dem.* 1.11; *t. Šeb.* 4.16, 21; *t. Ket.* 5.1; 7.11; *t. Kel. B. Meṣ.* 7.11; *t. ʾOhol.* 16.7; *t. Para* 5.1; *t. Nid.* 3.9; 4.7; 8.3). In this second case, the term *rabbôtênû* at the same time designates "our *teachers*" and members of an authoritative quorum.

2. "Rabbi" as a Mode of Address. A corrupt and apparently late tradition, which assumes that *rabbî* and *rabbān* designate teachers, distinguishes between these titles (or modes of address) on the basis of the success of disciples (*t. ʿEd.* 3.4). Yet another anonymous tradition prescribes greeting the mourning king as *adônênû wĕrabbênû*, "our lord and master" (*t. Sanh.* 4.4), indicating that even in rabbinic literature the older (nontechnical) sense of the term was retained. The remaining examples of the term *rabbî* as a mode of address are in direct discourse; nearly all are about figures associated with the period before 135 C.E. *Rabbî* is used as an address for a judge (*m. Ned.* 9.5; *m. B. Qam.* 8.6; *t. Yeb.* 14.10; *t. Giṭ.* 1.3; *t. Kel. B. Qam.* 1.2–3) and in legal disputes—presumably for the senior member of the dispute (*t. Kel B. Qam.* 1.6; *t. Peʾa* 3.6). Given the earlier usage of the term, these instances are not inexplicable. In still other passages the figure addressed as *rabbî* is so called because he is a teacher (*m. Roš Haš.* 2.9; *t. Ber.* 4.16–18; *t. Maʿas. Š.* 5.16; *t. Ḥag.* 2.11; *t. Giṭ.* 1.3; *t. Zeb.* 2.17; *t. Neg.* 8.6). Finally, in two traditions about R. Gamaliel (II), held to have been the patriarch and one whom we might expect to be addressed as *rabbî* by analogy with a king or a judge, Gamaliel is addressed as *rabbênû* (or *rabbî*) by members of his circle and is challenged on the basis of laws which he *taught* them (*t. Ber.* 4.15; *t. Beṣ.* 2.12; cf. *m. Ber.* 2.5–7).

C. "Rabbi" in the New Testament

1. Mark. Mark uses *rhabbi* three times and *rabbouni (rabboni)* once (10:51); all four instances convey a sense of Jesus' particular greatness (Mark 9:5; 11:21 [Peter]; 14:45 [Judas]; 10:51 [Bartimaeus, who follows Jesus]). In three of the four instances, Jesus is called *rabbi* in response to a miraculous action on Jesus' part: the Transfiguration (9:5), the withering of the fig tree (11:21), and the healing of the blind (10:51). Bartimaeus' reference to Jesus as *rabbouni* is coupled with the address "son of David" (10:47, 48), suggesting that the term should be thought of as meaning "sir" or perhaps "lord," and not "teacher" (cf. 9:17, in which "teacher" is used in a case of healing). *Didaskalos*, "teacher," on the other hand, is used as a more general form of address by both disciples (4:38; 9:38; 10:35; 13:1) and nondisciples (9:17; 10:17, 20; 12:14, 19, 32).

2. Matthew. In Matthew the use of the appellation *rabbi* is polemical. The only person who addresses Jesus as *rabbi* is Judas (Matt 26:25, 49). The other two instances of the word *rabbi* occur in Matt 23:1–12. Although the Matthean material in 23:1–3 does imply some sort of public teaching (as *may* the Q material in v 4 directed in Luke 11:45–46 to lawyers), the immediate context of the address *rabbi* in 23:7 describes a group perceived to enjoy public recognition as well as the outward show of piety, men who wish to be called "sir." In 23:8 the connection between *rabbi* and teacher is made explicitly. Yet the parallelism in 23:9–10 (*patēr/patēr; kathegētēs/kathegētēs*) leads us to expect not *didaskalos*, "teacher," but *rabbi* in the second half of 23:8. This break in parallel structure protects Jesus from being referred to as *rabbi*, a term associated in Matthew with the hateful Pharisees. Moreover, if "teacher" is meant in 23:8, the theme is apparently repeated at 23:10, using the term *kathegētēs* for teacher. It is possible that the author of 23:1–12 has made use of materials in which *rabbi* meant "sir" (Matt 23:7–8), but that for the Evangelist the term had the direct (and negative) connotation of "teacher of the law." This observation may be connected with the development of the term *rab* in rabbinic literature.

3. Luke. *Rabbi* does not occur in Luke. A word needs to be said about the Lukan term *epistatēs*, however (Luke 5:5; 8:24, 45; 9:33, 49; 17:13). This term corresponds once to the Markan *rabbi* (Luke 9:33; Mark 9:5) and twice to *didaskalos* (Luke 8:24; Mark 4:38; Luke 9:49; Mark 9:38). With the exception of 17:13 the address is found only in the mouths of disciples. In LXX, *epistatēs* is used to translate *śārê missîm,* "taskmasters" (Exod 1:11 [RSV]), and elsewhere, *nāgîd,* "chief" (2 Chr 31:12 [RSV]), and apparently it covers some of the same semantic field as *rab* (see also LXX Exod 5:14; 1 Kings 5; 16; 2 Kgs 25:19; Jer 52:25; 2 Chr 2:2). Moreover, in Ptolemaic Egypt and elsewhere the title *epistatēs* designated certain kinds of officials. It is possible that the Lukan term *epistatēs* reflects (as it clearly seems to in Luke 9:33) sources which used the Heb/Aram *rabbî.*

4. John. In John, two disciples address Jesus as *rabbi* after hearing from John that he is the "the lamb of God" (1:36–38); one reports that they have "found the Messiah" (1:41). Nathanael, amazed by Jesus' supernatural vision, addresses Jesus as *rabbi,* son of God and king of Israel (1:49). Even in John 3:2, where Jesus is called "a teacher come from God" in addition to *rabbi,* the use of the term is explained on the basis of Jesus' ability to perform signs. (It should be noted, however, that in John 3:1–5 Jesus does act as a teacher of heavenly things.) When Mary Magdalene perceived Jesus to be a gardener, she called Jesus *kyrios,* "sir"; when she realized that he was indeed the risen Jesus (John 20:15), she called him *rabbouni.* This understanding should inform our reading of John 6:25, in which "the people" call Jesus *rabbi,* as well as of the remaining passages, in which a teacher is called *rabbi* by his disciples (3:26 [John]; 4:31; 9:2; 11:8). It is important to note, however, that in John *rabbi* and *rabbouni* are each glossed as *didaskalos,* "teacher" (John 1:38; 20:16, respectively); it seems to have taken on this meaning exclusively.

The precise connection between early Christian and early rabbinic traditions is unclear. As the term *rabbi* became an honorific title and a mode of deferential address in general, it was taken up by rabbinic literature in particular as a special designator for a teacher. This was accompanied in the Mishna and the Tosepta by the casting of primary figures of authority as "teachers." The semantic shift from "sir" to "teacher" that is reflected in rabbinic literature has left traces in those NT passages in which *rabbi,* used of Jesus because of his greatness, is overlaid with the predominant sense of "teacher."

Bibliography

Cohen, S. J. D. 1981. Epigraphical Rabbis. *JQR* 72: 1–17.
Dalman, G. 1902. *The Words of Jesus.* Trans. D. M. Kay. Edinburgh.
Mazar, B. 1974. *Beth Sheᶜarim.* Vol. 1. *Catacombs 1–4.* Jerusalem.
Naveh, J. 1978. *On Mosaic and Stone.* Tel Aviv (in Hebrew).
Schwabe, M., and Lifshitz, B. 1973. *Beth Shearim.* Vol. 2. *The Greek Inscriptions.* New Brunswick.
Shanks H. 1963. Is the Title "Rabbi" Anachronistic in the Bible? *JQR* 53: 337–45.
———. 1968. On the Origin of the Title "Rabbi." *JQR* 59: 152–57.
Vermes, G. 1973. *Jesus the Jew.* New York.
Zeitlin, S. 1963. A Reply [to Shanks]. *JQR* 53: 345–49.
———. 1968. The Title Rabbi in the Gospels Is Anachronistic. *JQR* 59: 158–60.

Hayim Lapin

RABBINIC HERMENEUTICS, EARLY.

See HERMENEUTICS, EARLY RABBINIC.

RABBINIC LITERATURE AND THE NT.

The discovery of the Dead Sea Scrolls and renewed study, since World War II, of the Jewish pseudepigraphic writings have given new impetus to the study of the NT in its Jewish setting (Saldarini fc.; Vermes 1983: 58–68.) W. D. Davies' studies on Paul and Palestinian Judaism (1955) provided an early model for using rabbinic sources. Most English-speaking NT scholars in the 1950s and 1960s depended on the sketch of normative Judaism worked out by G. F. Moore (1927–30) as a framework for their understanding of Judaism and the topical collection of rabbinic texts by P. Billerbeck as their source for rabbinic literature. The older German evaluations of Judaism as late, legalistic, and inferior to Christianity were less determinative but not entirely absent for the English-speaking world (Klein 1978). Although rabbinic literature dated from the 2d century and later, it was widely used to interpret the NT because it contained material which claimed to be by and about Jewish teachers of the 1st and 2d centuries and also because it presented a wealth of legal, exegetical, and cultural detail about Judaism lacking in the Pseudepigrapha and historical sources. Descriptions of diverse types of prerabbinic Judaism witnessed by the Dead Sea Scrolls and renewed study of the Pseudepigrapha have only gradually eroded the uncritical acceptance of the rabbinic reconstruction of the Second Temple period and provided a more variegated foundation for understanding the NT in its Palestinian context.

A. Problems in the Use of Rabbinic Literature

The use of rabbinic literature (Mishnah, Tosefta, Palestinian and Babylonian Talmuds, midrashic collections, Targums, and mystical writings) as a resource for interpreting the NT has been questioned increasingly in recent years for several reasons. The vision of a coherent and continuous normative Judaism implied by the rabbinic sources and presented by Moore has been shown to be anachronistic for the 1st century. Prior to the destruction of the temple (70 C.E.), Judaism comprised many social groups, including the chief priest and Jerusalem notables, landowners, merchants, Pharisees and Essenes, peasants, and the economically displaced. Among them, many views of how Judaism should be lived and how it should adapt to or resist Hellenistic culture competed for recognition and ascendancy. Serious conflicts separated the governing class, who controlled the wealth and collected taxes for the Romans, from the majority of the people, who were loyal to local customs and the traditional Jewish way of life. The rabbinic way of life and thought had yet to be articulated and certainly was not dominant. The rabbinic sources retrojected their understanding of Jewish life and institutions onto Judaism as far back as Ezra in the 5th century, much as the Gospels retrojected problems and teachings of the early Church into the story of the life of Jesus. Literary and redactional studies of rabbinic sources have shown the later biases of these works and the difficulty of isolating earlier sources and literary strata. Statements and stories attributed to named Jewish authorities, which were previously accepted as historical fact, must now be subjected to the same critical scrutiny applied to the stories and sayings of Jesus (Neusner).

NT scholars who have used rabbinic literature have

often succumbed to "parallelomania," the associative linking of similar words, phrases, patterns, thoughts, or themes, in order to claim the influence or dependence of one text or tradition on another. Many of the earlier studies using rabbinic sources were based on isolated and superficial similarities in very dissimilar texts. Their argument for a relationship between the NT and rabbinic literature was based on the assumptions that the later traditions in rabbinic literature were unchanged from the 1st century, and that the fabric of Judaism was uniform enough for literary and theological details to be related to one another as if deriving from one context (for a review of NT studies using rabbinic literature, see Saldarini fc.). Such fragmentary and uncontrolled use of this complex literature must be replaced by a wholistic grasp of rabbinic life and thought which can then be compared with early Christianity (Sanders 1977: 12–24). The final documents and the traditions within them must be set within their historical, social, and religious contexts, using both literary analysis of the documents' social world and rhetorical goals and historical analysis of their political and social settings.

Rabbinic texts from later centuries have been habitually used as evidence for 1st-century Jewish institutions, leaders, and social structures. Since the rabbinic traditions reached their final forms from about 200 C.E. on, traditions must first be dated before being employed as historical evidence. No rabbinic document or set of traditions can be presumed to be early in its entirety; nor does a late historical reference in a large collection prove that all its traditions are late. The continuity and variations in Jewish and early Christian traditions must be traced by using dated texts and traditions which can be demonstrated by internal criteria to be early. The extensive and repeated redaction of rabbinic materials makes form-critical and redactional dating of texts extremely difficult.

The rabbinic view of earlier centuries is not historically reliable unless verified by 1st-century texts or the general pattern of the culture and empire. The social situation of Palestine in the 1st century was complex in the extreme. Any comparison of Judaism and Christianity must take into account the internal dynamics of the Jewish and Christian communities, their intricate relationships with each other, the divergent developments of both Christian theology and Jewish Talmudic literature, and the external pressure of the Roman Empire, all of which influenced the literature which has survived.

The Palestinian cultural context common to early Judaism and Christianity and the relative stability of traditional society make it probable that the two literatures share traditions, attitudes, and assumptions. However, later rabbinic outlooks and teachings must be separated from more fundamental, traditional, and widespread aspects of Judaism, some of which were foundational for the Jesus movement. The two possibilities of the rabbinic and Christian movements deriving materials from common sources, and of Christianity influencing Jewish literature, must be taken into account. The most likely common source for features of Judaism and Christianity is the Greco-Roman culture, within which both religions developed. For example, the rabbinic exegetical rules, attributed to Hillel, were known to Hellenistic scholars centuries earlier and were part of a common fund of knowledge available to all. Similarities and differences can only acquire significance and promote understanding when placed in a larger social, cultural, historical, and religious context.

B. Problems in the Study of Rabbinic Literature

The use of rabbinic literature in NT interpretation is impeded by a number of problems inherent to the study of rabbinic literature. Rabbinic literature often strikes the Western Christian reader as strange, a perception which has contributed to anti-Semitism. It is a closed, self-referential, elliptical body of literature which is understood only by those fully familiar with it. Fundamental cultural and theological presuppositions, such as a detailed knowledge of biblical law, are assumed. Discussions of legal and exegetical arguments and their solutions often begin without a statement of the biblical or Mishnaic problems to be discussed, because a prior detailed knowledge of the texts and problems is presumed. Legal, logical, and philosophical arguments and minutiae about matters far from traditional Christian or modern concerns fill pages, while multiple, alternative interpretations of each word, phrase, opinion, and consequence are dialectically related to one another. Such discussions, especially prevalent in the Talmuds, take place in a timeless world of academic study and spiritual love for the Torah as God's relevation. The ultimate coherence and meaning of this world of discourse becomes evident only to those persons who enter into the dialogue and adopt the world as their own. Needless to say, such a literature resists both historical analysis and limited use as "background" for the NT. It must be studied on its own and then with the NT as part of the larger history of Judaism (Vermes 1983: 69–71).

Most rabbinic works are collections of earlier material, some of which are consistently and coherently edited with great sophistication (Mishnah, Babylonian Talmud); and others are more like loosely organized compendia (late midrashic collections). Traditions have been added and rearranged in multiple stages in accordance with the presuppositions, purposes, ethos, and interests of the community of scholars which produced rabbinic literature. The views of the final documents can sometimes be determined by literary analysis, but such documents are difficult to place in historical context. Many studies have attempted to determine which traditions are earlier and how they developed. Though some progress has been made in this area, widely differing results and methodological criteria indicate that this type of study is very hypothetical and subjective (see Saldarini 1977, and a review of studies on the Babylonian Talmud in Goodblatt 1979: 281–318). Few of the rabbinic traditions can be securely dated to the 1st century, a result pertinent for NT study.

Most rabbinic documents have yet to be subjected to sustained and extensive higher criticism which seeks to understand the original apart from its later interpretation (e.g., the Mishnah apart from the Talmuds) and the history of interpretation as a mirror of changing Jewish interests and circumstances. All rabbinic documents have received extensive traditional interpretations which treat them as one cultural whole extending over centuries, minutely examine wording and variations in formulation, and attempt to work out a consistent and coherent way of life and thought for the Jewish community. Such traditional interpretations can aid the scholar in understanding the subtleties of the texts and provide a range of possible interpretations, but many of the interpretations reflect the views and interests of later commentators rather than of the original authors.

Finally, few thoroughly scientific critical editions have established reliable texts that do justice to the long and complex manuscript tradition of rabbinic literature. Many passages in the printed editions are corrupt, so Talmudic scholars habitually make use of collections of variants and important manuscripts in precise scholarly studies. Sayings are attributed to various sages in different manuscripts, and blocks of similar or related material are often added or omitted in various manuscripts. Some manuscripts, especially of midrashic and mystical works, differ so greatly from one another as to be independent books rather than variants of one original text (e.g., the traditional Midrash Tanhuma and the Tanhuma manuscript published by Buber).

C. Uses of Rabbinic Literature

Despite the cautions voiced above and the late date of much of rabbinic literature, familiarity with it is helpful for the study of the NT. Rabbinic literature can be used along with other Jewish literature of the Hellenistic-Roman period, including the so-called Apocrypha and Pseudepigrapha, the Dead Sea Scrolls, and Diaspora Greek works, to understand Jewish culture in its breadth and diversity within the Roman Empire. Both the NT and early Church history benefit from insertion into their larger contexts, Near Eastern, Jewish, and Roman. Many assumptions, traditions, practices, and concerns of Judaism either remained constant for centuries or underwent instructive changes already in antiquity. Realistic information concerning Jewish teachings and practices—combined with an empathetic grasp of their fundamental attitudes toward God and humans—will blunt the bias often produced by NT anti-Jewish polemics and will help cure anti-Semitic NT theology which has created the caricature of the spiritually dead and legalistic Jew living a decadent way of life in a proud and hypocritical relationship with God while rejecting the obvious signs that Jesus was Messiah. First-hand knowledge of Judaism as a vital and growing faith and way of life makes clear both the attraction of Judaism in the 1st century and the clear alternative to it offered by Jesus and the early Christian missionaries. Finally, such knowledge provides a stimulus and guidance for taking up the still-unanswered Christian theological problem of the place of Israel in God's plans after the coming of Jesus Christ.

Detailed studies of Jewish beliefs, traditions, and practices in the NT require a comprehensive overview of Judaism and its development in the Second Temple and early rabbinic periods (Vermes 1983: 72–73). Within that context, extended rabbinic commentaries on Scripture, in conjunction with the Qumran and other Jewish interpretative literature, can illuminate hermeneutical procedures used in the NT and can sometimes demonstrate the continuity of interpretative traditions. Though the elegant structure of Mishnaic and Talmudic law cannot be attributed to the 1st century, redactional studies of rabbinic sources and comparison with other sources can sometimes place certain laws and customs in the 1st century and add to the understanding of the Jewish community's inner life. Fundamental affirmations about God and humans which Christianity derived from Judaism, and which are assumed rather than articulated in 1st-century literature, often receive a fuller treatment in rabbinic literature. A comprehensive analysis of the development of Jewish traditions, including early NT traditions and later rabbinic literature, if done with sensitivity to historical development, will yield results which illuminate the Jewish substrate of the NT (Vermes 1983: 84–87) and also reveal, by contrast, the Greco-Roman contributions to NT literature as well.

Bibliography

Alexander, P. 1983. Rabbinic Judaism and the NT. *ZNW* 74: 237–46.

Davies, W. D. 1955. *Paul and Rabbinic Judaism.* 2d ed. London.

Goodblatt, D. 1979. The Babylonian Talmud. *ANRW* 2/19/2: 259–336.

Klein, C. 1978. *Anti-Judaism in Christian Theology.* Philadelphia.

Moore, G. F. 1927–30. *Judaism in the First Centuries of the Christian Era.* 3 vols. Cambridge, MA.

Neusner, J. 1971. *The Rabbinic Traditions About the Pharisees Before 70.* 3 vols. Leiden.

———. 1981. *Judaism: The Evidence of the Mishnah.* Chicago.

———. 1983. *Formative Judaism: Religious, Historical and Literary Studies. Third Series: Torah, Pharisees and Rabbis.* BJS 46. Chico, CA.

Saldarini, A. J. 1977. "Form Criticism" and Rabbinic Literature. *JBL* 96: 257–74.

———. fc. Judaism and the NT. In *The NT and Its Modern Interpreters.* Vol. 3 of *The Bible and its Modern Interpreters,* ed. E. J. Epp and G. W. MacRae. Atlanta.

Sanders, E. P. 1977. *Paul and Palestinian Judaism.* Philadelphia.

Strack H. L., and Billerbeck, P. 1922–28. *Kommentar zum Neuen Testament aus Talmud und Midrasch.* 4 vols. Munich.

Vermes, G. 1983. *Jesus and the World of Judaism.* Philadelphia.

ANTHONY J. SALDARINI

RABBIT. See ZOOLOGY.

RABBITH (PLACE) [Heb *rabbît*]. A town belonging to the territory allotted to Issachar (Josh 19:20). In this sole reference to the name in the Bible, it is listed next to Kishion, which seems to be just S of Mt. Tabor (Kishion = M.R. 187229; Aharoni and Avi-Yonah *MBA,* 53). The LXX B and the Old Latin read the name as "Daberath," which is situated next to Kishion in another list of tribal holdings that were ceded from Issachar to the Levites (i.e., the Gershomites; Josh 21:28; cf. 1 Chr 6:57 [—Eng 6:72]). Daberath is also located near Mt. Tabor, approximately 2 miles NW of Kishion (M.R. 184233; Aharoni and Avi-Yonah *MBA,* 53). Tribal possession of Daberath seems to have been unclear, since it is also allocated to Zebulun (Josh 19:12).

The identification of Daberath with Rabbith is geographically possible, though several critical alterations to the text would need to be accepted. The more difficult reading in this instance appears to be the MT, and an as yet unidentified site of this name in this area is not at all out of the question.

DAVID W. BAKER

RABBONI. See RABBI.

RABMAG [Heb *rab-māg*]. The title of Nergal-sharezer, who was present at Nebuchadnezzar's siege of Jerusalem in 587 B.C. (Jer 39:3, 13). The rabmag (Bab. *rab mugi*) was a high-ranking official in Babylonia.

A. KIRK GRAYSON

RABSARIS [Heb *rab-sārîs*]. The rabsaris (Akk *rab-ša-rēši*) was a high-ranking Assyrian official; the word in Assyrian means literally "chief eunuch." Eunuchs formed a most important part of the Assyrian bureaucracy and were numerous. The rabsaris, together with the rabshakeh and the tartan, played a major role in the siege of Jerusalem by Sennacherib (2 Kgs 18:17). (For further information about officials in the Assyrian administration, see ASSYRIA; see also Tadmor in *WLSGF,* 279–85.) The rabsaris was also the title of a high-ranking official in the Babylonian army, and he, together with the rabmag, played a leading part in the siege of Jerusalem (587 B.C.) by Nebuchadnezzar II (Jer 39:3, 13).

A. KIRK GRAYSON

RABSHAKEH [Heb *rab-šaqēh*]. The title of a high-ranking Assyrian official; the word literally means "chief cupbearer." As a leading Assyrian military officer, the rabshakeh played a prominent role, together with the rabsaris and the tartan, in the siege of Jerusalem led by Sennacherib (2 Kings 18–19 = Isaiah 36–37). Regarding the various high-ranking officers in the Assyrian administration, see ASSYRIA; see also Tadmor in *WLSGF,* 279–85.

A. KIRK GRAYSON

RACA. An expression of reproach used as an example by Jesus in one of his teachings (Matt 5:22). The RSV translates this term as "insult." In Matt 5:22a "raca" (Gk *rhaka*) is basically parallel in meaning to *mōre* (Fool!) in v 22b, and is thus a term of abuse or contempt. The key difference is that while the second of these is a Greek word, the first is not. It seems in fact to be the emphatic state of Aram *r(y)qʾ*, meaning "empty," and hence "worthless," "good for nothing." As a term of contempt, it is found in the Talmud and Midrash, e.g., *b. Ber.* 22b, ". . . she said to him, Numskull! (= *ryqʾ*) . . . ;" and *Eccl. Rab.* to 9:15, "Woe to you, worthless fellows (*rqyyʾ*), tomorrow the Flood is coming . . ." (that is, these are the men of the flood generation). The word was first noticed as a Semitism by John Lightfoot (1684), who gave a series of examples from Talmudic and Midrashic literature. The context in Matt 5:22 supports the identification of "raca" as a Semitism, in that it refers in turn to the person who is wrathful with his fellow, calls him "Numskull" *(raqāʾ)* or "fool," as worthy of "the judgment," "the Sanhedrin," or "the Gehenna of fire." The use of "raca" in Matt 5:22, without any following explanation or translation in Greek, was held by Jeremias to indicate that Matthew's audience could cope with some Aramaic.

MAX WILCOX

RACAL (PLACE) [Heb *rācāl*]. One of the cities listed as places to which David sent spoil following the destruction of the band of Amalekites who had destroyed Ziklag (1 Sam 30:29). The location of Racal is unknown (*IDB* 4: 4). The LXX, however, has "Carmel" at this point (McCarter *1 Samuel* AB, 434), and this reading is to be preferred. Carmel is the town where David met Nabal, who was shearing his sheep and married Nabal's wife, Abigail, upon Nabal's death. Carmel is located about 7 miles S of Hebron (modern Tell el-Kirmil, M.R. 162092; McCarter, 436).

JEFFRIES M. HAMILTON

RACHEL (PERSON) [Heb *rāḥēl*]. Second and favorite wife of Jacob, mother of Joseph and Benjamin, younger daughter of Laban (Rebekah's brother), and sister of Leah (Jacob's first wife). Thus, Rachel and Leah are also first cousins to Jacob, since their father (Laban) and Jacob's mother (Rebekah) are brother and sister. On the father's side, they are second cousins once removed, since Abraham and Nahor are brothers. See Fig. RAC.01.

The story of Rachel is a story of unparalleled love and devotion in the biblical narrative. On Rebekah's suggestion, Abraham sends his son Jacob to Paddan-aram (Haran) to her father Bethuel's house to procure one of the daughters of Laban as his bride (Gen 27:46–28:5). Jacob departs precipitately on this journey because he had incurred his elder brother Esau's murderous hatred for securing the birthright of primogeniture for himself through deception (Genesis 27). However, God reinforces Jacob's blessing in a dream-vision at Bethel, in which God promises to Jacob,

> The land on which you lie I will give to you and to your descendants; and your descendants shall be like the dust of the earth . . . and by you . . . shall all the families of the earth bless themselves (Gen 28:14).

Rachel then appears to Jacob at a well, and here begins Jacob's personal story of deep emotional attachment and love for her. Jacob initiates all the action: he single-handedly rolls away the heavy stone to water Laban's flock, he kisses Rachel, and he weeps, overcome with emotion (Gen 29:9–11). Only then does he introduce himself to Rachel as her father's kinsman (v 12). Rachel remains passively observant until then, and finally runs to tell her father, Laban. The narrative is swift and pointed. The symbolic action of Jacob rolling away the stone at the well is thematically indicative of the numerous obstacles that he must later overcome to obtain the woman he loves (seven years of servitude culminating in the substitution of Leah as first wife, then seven additional years of labor for Rachel). A further obstacle to Rachel's position as wife is her failure to have children for many years. Ironically, she dies at the birth of her second child, leaving Jacob bereft and in sorrow, a sorrow which remains with Jacob, deeply affecting his special relationship with the two sons she bore, and a sorrow which is echoed in later biblical references (Jer 31:15 = Matt 2:18). No other woman is so loved in the Bible.

Jacob's encounter with Rachel at the well (Gen 29:1–12) has some crucial points of difference to an earlier and similar scene of Rebekah's encounter at the well (Genesis 24) There, the betrothal negotiations are between the servant of Abraham (who is not named), as surrogate for Isaac, and Bethuel's household. The emissary bears choice gifts from his master, the patriarch Abraham. His camels kneel at the well outside the city of Nahor in princely fashion. Rebekah approaches and becomes the center of activity as she speaks and gives drink first to the servant and then to the camels. The life-giving water as a fertility symbol is an appropriate introduction to the subsequent betrothal negotiations, which resemble a formal "treaty" between families. Rebekah is sent to her new home with blessings of fertility, and she is received there by Isaac with love. The narrative is formal, repetitious, and oracular, and the impression is that the marriage is preordained by the deity and that it will proceed smoothly. See REBEKAH. By contrast, the well in Genesis 29 is located out in the fields, and it provides a focal point for the pastoral activity against which all of Jacob's life unfolds. Jacob is the poor stranger, his own emissary, a refugee from his brother Esau's wrath, bearing no rich gifts, only his walking staff. He is the initiator of activity when he rolls away the heavy stone by himself to water Laban's flock. Rachel, the younger daughter, is the shepherd who looks after the flock, but she is passive until after Jacob's initial outburst of action culminating in the kiss and his revelation as kinsman. The abrupt betrothal negotiations (vv 18–19) are made directly by the principals themselves and are directed by emotion and sentiment rather than the official decorum of a "family treaty." Jacob readily agrees to seven years of servitude for her, and has, it seems, already served one month for nothing. From the outset the impression is given that the marriage will be less conventional than others because it begins on a note of passion. Jacob's unparalleled love for Rachel is described in very powerful terms: "Jacob loved Rachel; and he said [to her father Laban], 'I will serve you seven years for your younger daughter Rachel' . . . So Jacob served seven years for Rachel, and they seemed to him but a few days because of the love he had for her" (Gen 29:18–20). This love remained undiminished even by her death, when it was transferred to her children, Joseph and Benjamin. Such a description of love is exceptional in the Bible (e.g., Jacob and Rachel's kiss is the only explicit biblical scene of a man kissing a woman); outside the Song of Songs not much is made of love between men and women.

Rachel's beauty is a prevailing motif in the competition between the two sisters. We are not told of her beauty until we meet both daughters of Laban, first the elder, Leah, who is only described as having "weak" or "dull" eyes (which is presumably a flaw) or "tender eyes" (which seems a much more appealing description): the exact meaning of the Hebrew *rakkōt* (29:17) is not clear. By contrast, Rachel is both beautiful and lovely (Heb *yĕpat-tōʾar wîpat marʾeh*), which might seem redundant but is perhaps intended to be an emphatic in aspects of both beauty and character.

After Jacob has labored the agreed-upon seven years, Laban prepares a wedding feast for Rachel. The last-minute substitution of Leah for Rachel is ambiguously interwoven with the prerogative of the elder versus the younger daughter and is contrasted not only in terms of primogeniture but also in terms of appearance, just as Jacob and Esau are similarly contrasted in terms of primogeniture and appearance (Gen 27:11). There is symmetrical "poetic justice" in Laban's deception of Jacob in substituting the veiled Leah for her sister Rachel in the blindness of the night (Gen 29:23), just as earlier Jacob had stolen his blind father's blessing while in disguise as he substituted himself for his brother Esau. Jacob's cry of woe (Gen 29:25) echoes Esau's earlier cry (27:34, 38).

Jacob does receive Rachel to wife at the end of the week of marriage festivities with Leah (Gen 29:27), after which he serves another seven years for Rachel, a total of fourteen years' service for her. We must suppose that both Leah and Rachel were willing parties to the deception, and that Rachel had demanded legitimate compensation for being willing to let Leah precede her in marriage to Jacob. Perhaps she had compassion for her older sister who might otherwise have remained without a husband. But in the bargaining, she would then have insisted that the second wedding not be postponed until the second bridal price was paid. Normally, this was paid to the father of the woman, but since Jacob was penniless, he had to pay in services, the equivalent of seven years' hard labor for a wife. A dowry, however, was paid to the bride by her father and would be hers to control. Later, Rachel and Leah would complain that their father had kept their respective dowries for himself (Gen 31:15–16), which is perhaps a reason for Rachel stealing Laban's household gods (Gen 31:19).

Jacob's greater love for Rachel (Gen 29:30) seems to heighten the competitive mood between the two sisters as they each vie for Jacob's attention and the begetting of children from him. Rachel's barrenness and her desire for children recall other biblical stories, chiefly that of Sarah, who was regarded with contempt by Hagar as soon as Hagar became pregnant with Ishmael (Gen 16:4). Leah had borne four sons to Jacob (Reuben, Simeon, Levi, and Judah) before Rachel's envy finally erupts in a confrontation with Jacob. Now, her jealousy and anger burst forth at Jacob in the impulsive and violent outcry (Rachel's first recorded speech in the Bible): "Give me children, or I shall die!" (Gen 30:1). The demand "give" *(hābâ)* is explosive, and the sense of dying expresses imminence (lit. "I am dead"). Rachel, the barren wife, asks not for one child but for children (plural). Jacob's retort is a rebuke of her anger: "Am I in the place of God, who has withheld from you the fruit of the womb?" (Gen 30:2). The brief exchange of words is extremely effective in conveying Rachel's desperation and Jacob's rebuke, her anger and his controlled response. Rachel's practical solution of offering her maidservant Bilhah to be her surrogate in obtaining sons is intended to build her up. There is a double play on words here, since the verbs meaning "to build up" can also be construed literally as "having sons" (cf. Isa 49:17, where we have a similar allusion on *bōnîm,* which means "builders," and *bānîm,* which means "sons"). Rachel names the children thus conceived, and in the meanings of the names which she gives to the two sons (Dan and Naphtali) she voices her sense of contentment, comfort, and triumph ("God has judged me, and has also heard my voice and given me a son"; and "With mighty wrestlings I have wrestled with my sister, and have prevailed"; Gen 30:6–8).

Leah has borne Jacob six sons and a daughter (Dinah), and her maid Zilpah has borne Jacob two sons (Gad and Asher). Only then does God bless Rachel, the beloved of Jacob, with her first child, whom she names with the expressed wish for a second son: "And she called his name Joseph, saying 'May the Lord add to me another son' " (Gen 30:24). The situation is much the same with Elkanah and his two wives: Peninnah was unloved but bore many children, while Hannah was beloved but barren for many years (1 Samuel 1).

After Joseph's birth, and upon Jacob's decision to leave Laban's household, we see defiance in Rachel's demeanor. In stealing and withholding the household gods (Heb *tĕrāpîm*) from her domineering father, she becomes the unintended object of Jacob's curse: "Any one with whom you find your gods shall not live" (Gen 31:32).

Rachel dies on the journey after giving birth to her second son, whom she names Benoni ("son of my sorrow") but whom Jacob renames Benjamin ("son of the right hand"). He is Jacob's youngest and last child, the object of his great and most tender affection.

Just as Jacob had singled out Rachel for the special love in his life, so he singled her out in death by placing a commemorative pillar on her grave (Gen 35:20) to mark her tomb, where she became revered as mother and matriarch. Actually, there seem to have been two locations for the tomb of Rachel in the folk tradition, one around Bethlehem still known in Saul's day (1 Sam 10:2), and another further N in Benjamin territory. See RACHEL'S TOMB; EPHRAIM (PLACE); see also MARJAMAH, KHIRBET EL- and DHAHR MIRZBANEH. In the NT, Matt 2:16–18 refers to Rachel weeping for her children in connection with Herod's slaying of the infants after Jesus' birth, a reference back to Jer 31:15.

The favorite status and envy engendered by Jacob's special love for Rachel is passed down to the children and becomes evident in the children's interactions with each other. It manifests itself in the hatred of the brothers against Joseph, which is also aggravated, however, by Joseph's dreams of predominance and supremacy over his older brothers (Genesis 37). There is a psychological resonance here to Laban's treachery in substituting Leah for Rachel. In selling Joseph to the Ishmaelites on their way to Egypt (Gen 37:28), the brothers establish their superiority over him, and they punish not only Joseph, but also their father. Additional treachery is perpetrated by Reuben, the firstborn son, who usurped his father's authority in laying with Bilhah, Rachel's maid and conjugal surrogate, soon after Rachel's death, a fact not lost upon Joseph who was still a boy (Thomas Mann elaborates on this narrative in his superb trilogy *Joseph und seine Brüder*). When the ten brothers go down to Egypt as the "sons of Israel" to be emissaries for their patriarchal father, they are called "Joseph's brothers" upon their arrival, a test of the kinship bond to their brother which they tried to deny by selling Joseph into slavery. The designation of Benjamin as "Joseph's brother" has a different impact both emotionally and genealogically, because Benjamin is Joseph's only full brother, the only other one of Rachel's children. Jacob expresses his sorrow poignantly in his own words: "My son shall not go down with you, for his brother is dead, and he only is left. If harm should befall him on the journey . . . you would bring down my grey hairs with sorrow to Sheol" (Gen 42:38). "He only is left," says Jacob, omitting the words "from Rachel," as though only the sons of Rachel count as true sons.

Traditio-historical research into the twelve-tribe system of early Israel led M. Noth and others to postulate that Rachel and Leah were originally "eponymous ancestors" for groups of seminomadic tribes that, at various different times and in various different "waves," settled down in the area that would eventually become Israel (see Weippert 1971: 5–46, esp. 42–46). The "Rachel tribes"—Joseph (Ephraim and Manasseh) and Benjamin—were thus believed by some to have been the final wave of nomads, containing peoples whose traditions included a sojourn in

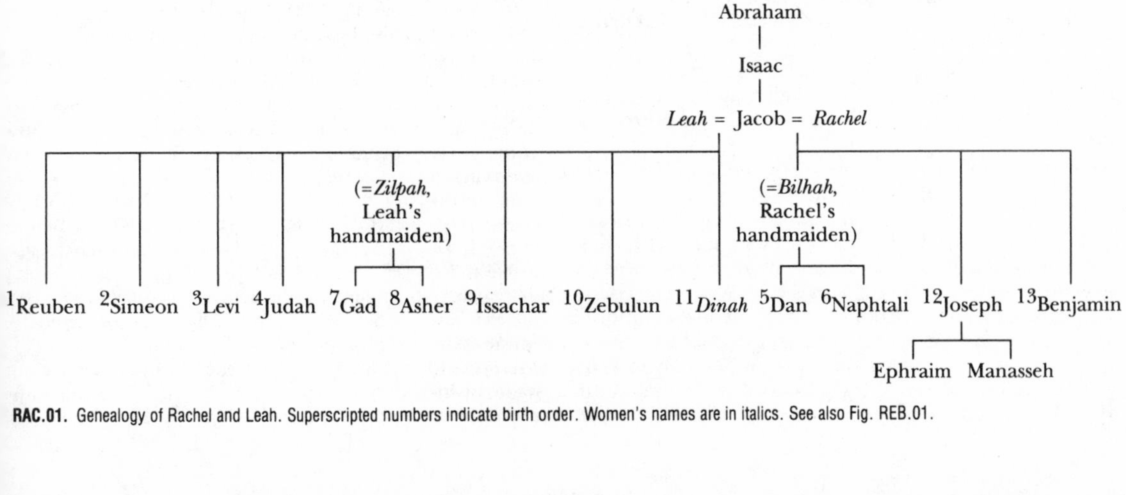

RAC.01. Genealogy of Rachel and Leah. Superscripted numbers indicate birth order. Women's names are in italics. See also Fig. REB.01.

Egypt, the crossing of the Jordan river, the destruction of Jericho and Ai, and the defeat of a coalition of kings near Gibeon, traditions that would later be embraced by all twelve Israelite tribes and find literary expression in the narratives of Exodus and Joshua 1–10. However, more recent study of Israelite origins has tended to reject the notions of seminomadic migrations and to question the merits of applying traditio-historical methods to the question of Israel's origins. See AMPHICTYONY.

In the blessings in Genesis 49, the blessing of Joseph (vv 15–16) is the longest of all the blessings. Yet for all the glory which will accrue to Rachel's firstborn son Joseph, the Davidic kings of Israel will come not from him but from Judah, the fourth son of her sister Leah (although Saul, the first king, was from the tribe of Benjamin).

Bibliography

Alter, R. 1981. *The Art of Biblical Narrative.* New York.
Auerbach, E. 1965. *Mimesis.* Princeton.
Fokkelman, J. P. 1975. *Narrative Art in Genesis.* Assen and Amsterdam.
Mann, T. 1933. *Joseph und seine Brüder.* Frankfurt am Main.
Speiser, E. A. 1964. *Genesis.* AB. Garden City, NY.
Weippert, M. 1971. *The Settlement of the Israelite Tribes in Palestine.* SBT 2/21. Naperville, IL.

ASTRID BILLES BECK

RACHEL'S TOMB (PLACE) [Heb *qĕburat rāḥēl*].

Burial place of the Benjaminite matriarch, Rachel, located in the territory of Benjamin S of Bethel and N of Ephrathah in the vicinity of Ramah (Gen 35:19–20; 48:7; 1 Sam 10:2; Jer 31:15). There are two irreconcilable biblical locations for Rachel's tomb: Bethlehem and Benjamin. Modern scholars are in almost unanimous agreement that she is not buried at Bethlehem. Within the territory of Benjamin, Ramah (M.R. 172140) and Kiriath-jearim (M.R. 159135; see JAAR) are most often suggested by those who attempt to be more specific. See also EPHRAIM (PLACE).

The legends of Genesis record an ancient tradition that Rachel died giving birth to Benjamin during Jacob's journey S from Bethel. This tradition locates the place of her death a short distance N of Ephrathah—a region inhabited by the Judahite clan of the same name located at the N border of Judah. The territory of this clan extended to the E from Kiriath-jearim, which was on the N border, and to the S below Bethlehem. After Rachel was buried, Jacob proceeded into the territory of Judah and camped just beyond Migdal-eder, according to the redacted sources of Gen 35:16–29. Micah 4:8 and *Šeqal.* 7:4 (rabbinic text) seem to identify this place with the Ophel near Zion (but still well N of Bethlehem). Finally, Jacob continues his journey—we assume through Bethlehem—to his S destination of Hebron. The itinerary following the matriarch's burial may not be historical, but it must have been a geographically reasonable one to the redactor. The editorial glosses identifying Ephrathah with Bethlehem represent a tradition from a much later era when the territory of the clan and its most famous village of Bethlehem were assumed to be identical. These glosses are inaccurate with regard to the era of the matriarches and patriarches, but they account for the erroneous tradition which located Rachel's tomb at the N outskirts of Judahite Bethlehem.

Matthew (2:18) appropriated this late Jewish tradition and certainly played a role in focusing attention in the Common Era on a bogus spot. Fourth-century Christian Eusebius mentions a tomb near Bethlehem, as does the 10th-century *Jewish Guide to Jerusalem.* The 12th-century rabbi Benjamin of Tudela and latter pilgrims describe a pyramid of twelve stones, and it was probably in the same century that the Crusaders built a dome supported by four pillars over the monument. In the 18th century, Muslims enclosed the structure, and in 1841 Sir Moses Montefiore added a vestibule. However, the topographical incongruity created by the Genesis glossator was so glaring that LXX omitted Gen 35:21 and made Jacob arrive at Migdal-eder in v 16, as would have been required by a S-moving Jacob were Rachel to be buried at Bethlehem, which she is not (see Tsevat 1962: 109). The Genesis itinerary would also appear to rule out Kiriath-jearim to the W.

The tradition represented in 1 Sam 10:1–6 is consistent with the preglossated legends of Genesis. There, Rachel is buried S of Bethel near the road to Migdal-eder, Bethlehem, and Hebron, but still within the Benjaminite territory, i.e., still some distance N of the old Ephrathite clan territory. The geography of this story is as follows. Saul leaves his home in Benjaminite Gibeah (Josh 18:25; 1 Sam 9:1; 10:5, 10, 26; 11:4; 15:34; 22:6; 23:19), which is S of the Benjaminite Ramah near the N–S route from Bethel to Jerusalem, in order to look for his lost donkeys in the Ephraimite hill country N of Benjamin. He ends up at the Zuphite Ramah, which is the home of Samuel in Ephraim, i.e., Ramathaim, the "two-hilled" Ramah (1 Sam 1:1, 19; 2:11; 7:17; 8:4; 9:5; 25:1; 28:3). Then, from this latter Ephraimite Ramah, which is NW of Benjamin, he returns home to Gibeah. (Some wish to translate Gibeah in 10:5 and 10:10 literally as "hill," but it is clear from the context that everybody knows Saul and from v 26 that he has returned home. There is really no conflict in this part of the narrative, and certainly "Gibeah" was built on or near a "hill.") On his return journey, Saul passes Rachel's tomb, *bĕṣelṣah* (v 2), and finally the Oak of Tabor, which must be S of and near the road to Bethel (v 3). But can we be more specific about these latter two references?

In 1 Sam 10:2, it is said that Rachel's tomb is "in the territory of Benjamin" (RSV). We already know that. But Heb *bigĕbûl* can also be translated as "at the boundary of." We already know, too, that Rachel's tomb is near the Ephrathite border. We are left with the *crux interpretum*—*bĕṣelṣah.* This is almost certainly not a *nomen proprium loci* (RSV, "at Zelzah"). No such place is known in Hebrew, and on the analogy of the other two signs one would expect a modifying phrase rather than a third proper noun: the locus of the sign to be received by Saul is specifically "beside [Heb *ʿim*] Rachel's tomb at the boundary of Benjamin" (cf. Driver *NHT,* 78–79). The Greek witnesses are varied and do little more than attest to the Hebrew letters *ṣlḥ,* "rush," and hence the proleptic wordplay on v 6; or with R. Yose (2nd century C.E., *Midr. Sam.* 14, cited by Tsevat 1962: 111; see Zimolong 1938) and Vg, they redivide the letters *(bĕṣēl ṣaḥ)* to get the curious "at dazzling shade," which they interpreted as "noon." The most appropriate reading seems to be *bĕṣēl ṣĕḥīaḥ* (Hertzberg *Sam-*

uel OTL, 77; haplography), "in the shade of a shiny rock." Genesis relates that Jacob marked Rachel's tomb with a large sepulchral stone," which is there to this day" (35:20) and which likely would have been smooth and shiny after generations of anointing pilgrims (cf. even modern holy spots). This unusual word for rock would have been chosen for reasons of paronomasia to enhance the mysterious nature of the sign as well as to foreshadow the culmination of the third sign when the spirit rushes [*ṣlḥ*] on Saul (v 6). Supporting this pun and forming the connection between signs one and three is the curious employment of *ḥlp* (v 3), not normally used of human transit but more appropriate to the rushing of God or wind, to continue the wordplay in sign two. Finally, if one observes the parallel structure of the three signs, they all state a specific location, with two qualifications, followed by a mysterious activity: Rachel's tomb, at the boundary of Benjamin, in the shade of a shiny rock . . . (v 2); from there, and a bit further, at the Oak of Tabor . . . (v 3); Gibeah, of God (a surprising qualification which occurs only here), where there is a Philistine garrison . . . (v 5). Thus, we have learned nothing more than, but also nothing that is inconsistent with, the traditions of Genesis. Rachel's tomb is in the territory of Benjamin, near the boundary, and is marked by a monumental stone. Again, Kiriath-jearim is all but excluded from Saul's journey since, while it is on the Benjaminite border, it is decidedly S of a path from Ramathaim to Gibeah, especially in light of his following activity near Bethel, N of Gibeah.

Before reaching Gibeah, Saul passes the Oak/Terebinth of Tabor (see Trever *IDB* 3:575). Have we any clues to its location? It is true that sacred trees were common in ancient Israel, but the author of the story assumes the audience will recognize this well-known reference. Some Greek and Latin witnesses read simply the "choice" tree, illustrating confusion surrounding the name "Tabor." The editorial addition in Judg 4:5 mentions the Palm/Post of Deborah (Heb *tōmer dĕbôrâ*) in the context of the great Deborah legend focused at Mt. Tabor (Heb *tābôr*); furthermore, a second parenthetical verse (11) introduces the notorious Oak/Terebinth in Zaananim as a counterpart to Deborah's Palm/Post and paralleled to Mt. Tabor in the following v 12 (Boling *Judges* AB, 96–97). It is highly probable that phonetic similarity, literary parallelism, and geographic confusion have combined to yield two names for the same sacred tree, the Deborah/Tabor tree (*BDB:* 18b). Gen 35:8 mentions the Oak of Deborah is immediately preceding the story about Rachel's tomb, and the narrator employs the definite article "with a title understood and recognized by everyone": the Oak—"the well-known oak which was there" (*GKC,* §126d). That this verse sits loosely in its context has often been noted, and that the tomb of Rebekah's nurse would mark a memorable spot is highly dubious. It is much more probable that Gen 35:8 is a variant etiology for the judgment tree of Deborah/Tabor mentioned above (Vawter 1977: 363). Not only do these names converge on one tree, but the geographical references do so as well. At the tree, Saul meets three men "going up to Bethel" (1 Sam 10:3) and then proceeds to Gibeah (S of Bethel). Deborah is buried "beneath Bethel" (Gen 35:8) just before Rachel dies while journeying from Bethel S to Ephrathah. Deborah's tree is located "between Ramah and Bethel" (Judg 4:5). The latter note is secondary and geographically confused, but almost surely the original tradition meant the Ramah S of Bethel just N of Gibeah (Martin *Judges* CBC, 55–56). Hence, it seems probable that the traditions surrounding a sacred tree of Deborah/Tabor between Ramah and Bethel were focused on the vicinity of Rachel's tomb, where the story of 1 Samuel 10 takes place. An alternate name for the holy place was Oak of Weeping (Heb *bākût;* Gen 35:8), the probable setting of the etiology for the Place of Weepers (Heb *bōkīm;* Judg 2:1–5), which LXX locates near Bethel (Boling [*Judges* AB, 63] correctly notes that *hammāqôm,* v 5, is used in its technical sense to denote a sacred place).

This is the background for Jer 31:15:

> Hark! In Ramah is heard lamentation,
> bitter weeping [*bĕkî tamrûrîm*],
> Rachel weeping [*mĕbakkâ*] for her children.

There is no convincing reason not to translate Ramah as a *nomen proprium loci* as the LXX tradition of Jeremiah, a variant recension from the MT, also attests. Rachel is in synonymous parallelism with Ramah, just S of Bethel and just N of Gibeah, from which height she can peer into Ephraim and weep from her tomb for the exiled northern tribes (vv 15–22; cf. Bright *Jeremiah* AB, 275–87). The poet's use of the word *tamrûrîm* to modify the weeping could be an intentional paronomasiac recall of Deborah's renowned tree (*tōmer,* Judg 4:5; *tābôr,* 1 Sam 10:3; cf. *dĕbôrâ*) to create a triple parallelism. At any rate, the topography is consistent with Saul's rushed journey past Rachel's tombstone in Benjamin, Deborah's oak near Bethel, and on to Gibeah. Hos 5:8 parallels Gibeah, Ramah, and Bethel (Beth-aven; see Amos 5:5), and Isa 10:29 pairs Ramah and "Gibeah of Saul." Near Ramah was the Oak of Weeping (Gen 35:8) and the Weeper's Place (Judg 2:5). Only a few miles S was the border of ancient Ephrathah. In this vicinity, Rachel is most likely buried.

Bibliography

Pearlman, M., and Yannai, Y. 1978. *Historical Sites in Israel.* 4th ed. Secaucus, NJ.

Tsevat, M. 1962. Interpretation of 1 Sam 10:2: Saul at Rachel's Tomb. *HUCA* 33: 107–18.

Vawter, B. 1977. *On Genesis: A New Reading.* Garden City, NY.

Vogt, E. 1975. Benjamin geboren "eine Meile" von Ephrata. *Bib* 56: 30–36.

Zimolong, B. 1938. *bĕṣelṣaḥ* (1 Sam 10:2). *ZAW* n.s. 15: 175–76.

LAMONTTE M. LUKER

RADDAI (PERSON) [Heb *radday*]. One of Jesse's sons and an older brother of David (1 Chr 2:14). Raddai is listed as the fifth son of Jesse, and David is listed as the seventh and presumably the last. In 1 Sam 16:10, 12, David is designated as the eighth and youngest son. In 1 Samuel 16, Raddai does not appear; only Eliab, Abinadab, and Shammah are named. 1 Chr 27:18 refers to one Elihu, another brother of David. The meaning of the name

Raddai is not clear. It is possibly related to the Hebrew root *rdd,* "beat out," or *rdh,* "have dominion, rule," but certainty is not possible.

JAMES M. KENNEDY

RAGES (PLACE) [Gk *Rhagoi*]. Var. RAGAE. A city in NE Media of Persia and the home of Gabael, to whom Tobit entrusted his money (Tob 4:1, 20; 5:5; 6:10—Eng v 12; 9:2). Located 5 miles SE of modern-day Teheran, Rages is identified with the ruins of the city of Rai (35°35′N, 51°27′E; Olmstead 1948: 30). The city is located on a plain which extends from a point one hundred miles NE of the ancient capital of Ecbatana to the mountains of Elburz. Thus located, Rages also gives its name to the region around the Elburz mountains, which is called Ragae *(Rhagau)* in the book of Judith (Jdt 1:5, 15). There, we are told, Arphaxad, an otherwise unknown king of the Medes, was killed in battle. The king, however, is probably a fictional creation, and the reference to Ragae, only symbolic (Moore *Judith* AB, 124, 128–29; Craven 1983: 79–80). Nonetheless, Rages was among the oldest of settlements in Iran and of strategic importance, playing a significant role in the history of Media, the rule of Alexander, and that of his successors (Wikgren *IDB* 4:5).

Bibliography

Craven, T. 1983. *Artistry and Faith in the Book of Judith.* SBLDS 70. Chico, CA.

Olmstead, A. T. 1948. *History of the Persian Empire.* Chicago.

FREDERICK W. SCHMIDT

RAGUEL (ANGEL). According to that part of *1 Enoch* known as the Book of the Watchers (*1 Enoch* 1–36), Raguel is one of the six (Ethiopic mss; seven, according to the Greek ms) archangels. He is identified as "Raguel, one of the holy angels, who takes vengeance on the world and on the lights" (*1 En.* 20:4; Knibb 1984). In *1 Enoch* 21–36, Enoch is accompanied by various angels (Uriel, Raphael, Raguel, and Michael) who interpret what he sees on his journey around the world. At the end of the earth in the W, Enoch sees a burning fire which is interpreted by Raguel as "the fire of all the lights of heaven" (*1 En.* 23:4; Knibb 1984). Milik (1976: 219–20) derives the name of Raguel from Aram *raʿûʾēl* ("shepherd of God") and argues that Raguel was not in charge of punishing stars but was rather their caretaker who supplied them with fire from the reservoir at the W end of the world. The motif of vengeance would have arisen from mistranslation in Greek and Ethiopic.

Bibliography

Knibb, M. 1984. *1 Enoch.* Pp. 169–319 in *The Apocryphal Old Testament,* ed. H. F. D. Sparks. Oxford.

Milik, J. T. 1976. *The Books of Enoch.* Oxford.

CAROL A. NEWSOM

RAGUEL (PERSON) [Gk *Rhagouēl*]. The father of Tobias' wife, Sarah, and the husband of Edna (Tob 3:7; *passim*). Raguel is described as having written a marriage contract giving his daughter to Tobias in marriage (7:14), but also as having dug the young man's grave on their wedding night (8:9ff.). When Tobias survived the encounter with the demon Asmodeus, Raguel blessed God's name and gave the couple half of his possessions (8:20–21).

FREDERICK W. SCHMIDT

RAHAB (DRAGON) [Heb *rahab*]. The name of a mythological sea serpent or dragon, lit. "boisterous one," referred to a number of times in the OT (Ps 87:4; 89:11—Eng 89:10; Job 9:13; 26:12; Isa 30:7; 51:9). The name of this monster has not hitherto been discovered in any extrabiblical text. In the OT, Rahab functions similarly to Leviathan, an originally Canaanite chaos monster, but whether these are to be identified or are separate monsters in origin is not entirely clear.

Rahab appears in two different contexts in the OT. On the one hand, it appears as a sea monster defeated at the time of creation (Ps 89:11—Eng 89:10; Job 9:13; 26:12), and on the other as a metaphorical name for Egypt (Ps 87:4; Isa 30:7). In Isa 51:9 the two usages may be fused.

Ps 89:10–11—Eng 89:9–10 declares to Yahweh, "You rule the surging of the sea: when its waves rise, you still them. You did crush Rahab with a mortal blow, you did scatter your enemies with your mighty arm." The following vv (12–13—Eng 11–12) clearly spell out the creation context of this conflict, so that it is necessary to reject the view of those scholars who see here an allusion to the Exodus or, as some would maintain, to both Exodus and creation. The references to God's conflict with Rahab in both Job 9:13 and 26:12 also appear to be set in creation contexts. Job 26:12–13 reads: "By his power he stilled the sea; by his understanding he smote Rahab. By his wind the heavens were made fair; his hand pierced the twisting serpent *(nāhāš bārîaḥ)*." This expression "twisting serpent" is a term used elsewhere of Leviathan (Isa 27:1 and similarly *bṯn brḥ* in *KTU* 1.5.I.1 = *CTA* 5.1.1), which may indicate that Rahab is being equated with Leviathan. In Job 9:13–14, Job declares: "God will not turn back his anger; beneath him bowed the helpers of Rahab. How then can I answer him, choosing my words with him?" The sentiment here is rather similar to that at the end of the book of Job, where Job is humbled before Yahweh in the wake of the second divine speech in which it is implied that he (Job) cannot overcome the chaos monsters Leviathan and Behemoth, which Yahweh did overcome (cf. Job 40–42:6). As for "the helpers of Rahab," these must be other chaos monsters associated with Rahab. One may compare Tiamat's allies, referred to as "her helpers" in Enuma Elish (4:107).

That Rahab serves as a name for Egypt is explicit in Isa 30:7, where the prophet declares: "For Egypt's help is worthless and empty, therefore I have called her 'the silenced Rahab.'" The translation "the silenced Rahab" is achieved by reading *rahab hammošbāt* for the meaningless MT *rahab hēm šābet,* which seems the most satisfactory emendation (cf. Isa 14:4). Rahab also clearly functions as the name of a country in Ps 87:4: "I reckon Rahab and Babylon as those that know me; behold Philistia and Tyre with Ethiopia—"this one was born there.'" Egypt is the most likely referent for Rahab here, paralleling Isa 30:7.

That the defeated sea dragon Rahab should serve as a metaphor for Egypt is understandable when one recalls the oppressive role which Egypt played with regard to Israel before the Exodus and the location of the heart of the Exodus deliverance at the sea (Exodus 14–15). Compare the allusion to pharaoh as a dragon in Ezek 29:3–5 and 32:2–8 (reading *tannîn,* "dragon," for MT *tannîm,* "jackals").

Isa 51:9–11 is a famous passage, which reads: "Awake, awake, put on strength, O arm of the Lord, awake as in days of old, the generations of long ago. Was it not you who hewed Rahab in pieces, who pierced the dragon? Was it not you who dried up the sea, the waters of the great deep, who made the depths of the sea a way for the redeemed to pass over? So the ransomed of the Lord will return and come to Zion with singing, everlasting joy shall be on their heads; they shall obtain joy and gladness, and sorrow and sighing shall flee away." Verse 10b certainly refers to the Exodus, and v 11 to the new Exodus, the return of the exiles from Babylon. The reference in v 9 to the defeat of Rahab could refer to the chaos monster at the time of creation, to Egypt at the time of the Exodus, or to a fusion of both.

Finally, it should be noted that Gunkel (*Die Psalmen* HKAT) believed that Rahab is mentioned in the plural in Ps 40:5—Eng 40:4, but it is much more likely that *rĕhābîm* there simply refers to proud or arrogant men. See also DRAGON AND SEA, GOD'S CONFLICT WITH.

Bibliography

Day, J. 1985. *God's Conflict with the Dragon and the Sea.* Cambridge.

JOHN DAY

RAHAB (PERSON) [Heb *rāḥāb*]. The story of Rahab is told in the first part of Joshua 2 and the latter part of Joshua 6. In its present context, this narrative is embedded in the account of the Israelite conquest of Jericho. Rahab is introduced as a "harlot" (Hebrew *zônâ*) in Josh 2:1 (so also 6:17, 25; in 2:3 and 6:23, only the name Rahab appears). Two spies, dispatched from Shittim by Joshua, enter her house. She hides them from the ruler of Jericho, thus saving their lives. She acknowledges the power of the Lord and extracts from the spies the promise that she and her family will be saved when the Israelites overwhelm her city. She is told to hang a scarlet cord from her window as a sign that her household is to be spared. Several verses in chap. 6 relate that Joshua kept this agreement. At the time of Jericho's conquest, Rahab and her family, alone of the city's inhabitants, are spared. They were taken outside of the camp. A final note (6:25) records that "she dwelt in Israel to this day."

Rahab's name comes from a root meaning "to be wide or broad." It appears to be the shortened form of a theophoric name (cf., for example, Rehabiah, 1 Chr 23:17; 24:21). The exact nature of Rahab's occupation has been the subject of considerable controversy. Most interpretators now see her as a "secular" prostitute without any cultic or sacred connections. Not only is this in keeping with the biblical description, but there was a Hebrew term *(qĕdēšâ)* available to the author had he wanted to highlight her status as a "sacred" prostitute. The use of the term "innkeeper" in certain Jewish traditions may be seen as an attempt to improve upon her professional standing, but that is not necessarily the case.

The story as it stands contains no indication of what motivated Rahab to risk her life on behalf of the Israelite spies. We are probably meant to connect this action with her affirmation of Yahweh's power. That affirmation, found in Josh 2:8–11 and thoroughly Deuteronomistic in language and theology, is widely regarded as a late element in what otherwise seems to be fairly early material. In a pre-Deuteronomistic stage, Rahab and her family may have been identified with that segment of the Jericho population that opposed the royal establishment and could be expected to respond positively to the invading Israelites.

The survival of Rahab and her family "to this day" suggests that there is an etiological element in the origin and subsequent development of this story. Perhaps, a well-defined group of her descendants could be singled out for some time among the Israelites. That group would obviously have a large stake in preserving Rahab's exploits.

Other elements can also be detected in the diverse traditions that have gone into this account. For example, the narrative concerning Rahab has been identified as one of several spy stories that the OT contains. Moreover, Rahab's role must be seen in light of the type of warfare Israel was waging. It was holy war, under divine command. Rahab's statement was as much an affirmation to Israel as to herself: with God on their side, the Israelites could not fail to be victorious. For her assistance, the absolute ban *(ḥērem)* on Jericho could be waived.

According to some, the essence of the Rahab story is contained in chap. 2, while the verses in chap. 6 form a not wholly consistent afterthought. It is noted, for example, that her house, although "built into the city wall" (2:15), somehow still stood after the walls fell (see 6:22). However, the entire Rahab narrative exhibits many unexpected features—not the least of which is the aid provided by the prostitute herself—and the dramatic and humorous effect of the story taken as a whole survives (and perhaps even thrives on) architectural and other incongruities.

The relatively few verses devoted to Rahab in the OT stimulated an amazingly rich exegetical tradition in both Judaism and Christianity. She was widely depicted as a proselyte or convert to the monotheistic faith of Israel. In Judaism, she could then be portrayed as one of the most pious converts—a worthy wife of Joshua and the ancestor of prophets.

A parallel, but distinctly Christian development, is found in Matt 1:5 where a Rahab is identified as the wife of Salmon and the mother of Boaz. This accords to Rahab a prominent position in the genealogy of "Jesus Christ, the son of David, the son of Abraham." Inasmuch as Matthew does not specifically link "his" Rahab with the harlot of the book of Joshua, and while the Greek text of Matthew preserves a distinctive spelling of the proper name (*rachab, raab* elsewhere), it is possible that this is another Rahab. However, the appearance and identity of three other women from the OT (Tamar, Ruth, and the wife of Uriah [i.e., Bath-sheba]) in the genealogy of Jesus make it virtually certain that we are dealing with only one Rahab in both Testaments. This is clearly the case in the other two NT references to "Rahab the harlot": Heb 11:31, where

Rahab's survival is credited to her faith, and Jas 2:25, in which Rahab exemplifies the dictum that "man is justified by works and not by faith alone" (so v 24).

The role Rahab plays in Jewish and Christian exegetical traditions (many other examples could be cited) is larger than that attributed to her in the OT itself. This is not to say that she is an unimportant figure in the Bible; by her actions, she both preserved her own family and epitomized the sort of faith that the Israelites themselves would have to display to preserve the land and heritage God had promised them. For further discussion, see *DBSup* 5: 1065–92.

Bibliography

Newman, M. 1985. Rahab and the Conquest. Pp. 167–81 in *Understanding the Word,* ed. J. T. Butler. JSOTSup 37. Sheffield.

Tucker, G. M. 1972. The Rahab Saga (Joshua 2). Pp. 66–86 in *The Use of the Old Testament in the New and Other Essays,* ed. J. M. Efird. Durham, NC.

LEONARD J. GREENSPOON

RAHAM (PERSON) [Heb *raḥam*]. The son of Shema and the father of Jorkeam (1 Chr 2:44). Raham, a Calebite and a descendant of Judah, is listed among Caleb's progeny by an unnamed spouse (vv 42–45). Within the genealogy of vv 42–50a, the men are often considered to have been the "fathers" of cities rather than of individuals. The name "Raham" may refer to either an individual, or a city, or both. Jorkeam should perhaps be read here as Jokdeam, a city whose location is unknown (Josh 15:56). Shema was the name of another Judahite city of unknown location (Josh 15:26). And other groups associated with Raham in his line of descent occupied such centers as Hebron, Mareshah, and Ziph. Although "Raham" is not a shortened name with respect to form, a deity is possibly semantically implied in the nature of the name—thus, "(God has shown) compassion" or "(the deity has taken) pity" (*TPNAH,* 168–69). Primarily, this would have signified that the divinity had again remembered a person who was in distress, in order to help him or her. The name has also been taken, differently, to equal Heb *rāḥām* and Ar *raḥam,* "carrion-vulture" or "Egyptian vulture" *(Neophron percnopterus).* Certainly, animal terms were commonly used for personal names in Semitic (Nöldeke 1904: 86).

Bibliography

Nöldeke, T. 1904. *Beiträge zur semitischen Sprachwissenschaft.* Strasbourg.

EDWIN C. HOSTETTER

RAHEL, RAMAT. See RAMAT RAHEL.

RAIN. While the giving or withholding of rain is generally seen in the Bible as a sign of God's favor or disfavor, in the OT (Jer 3:3; Hos 6:3; Joel 2:23; Job 29:23—cf. also Jas 5:7 in the NT) the terminology "early/autumn" rain or the "latter/spring"—or in one case "later/spring" (Deut 11:14)—rain appears. The significance of this terminology lies in the fact that for an agricultural society, it is not just the presence or absence of rain that is important, but its timing as well. Thus, Jeremiah says: "Let us fear the LORD our God, who gives the rain in its season, the autumn rain and the spring rain, and keeps for us the weeks appointed for the harvest" (5:24).

The "early/autumn" rain *(yôreh)* and the "latter/spring" rain (*malqôš,* from the Heb *lqs,* "crops sown late"), are rains which fall in the two transitional periods that mark the beginning and the end of the rainy, winter season in Palestine. The first appreciable rains normally arrive in Palestine in mid-October to early November, with the last significant rains falling in the first half of April. About 70 percent of the rainfall, however, falls from November to February, with January typically being the wettest and coldest month. See PALESTINE, CLIMATE OF.

The early and latter rains are accentuated in the OT because of their critical agricultural role: the early rains preparing the ground for plowing and sowing at the end of the dry season, and the latter rains providing the last bit of moisture which aids the maturation of cereal grains. The critical nature of the timing of these two rains is reflected theologically in the fact that they are seen as one of YHWH's rewards to his people in return for their faithfulness to the covenant: "I will give the rain for your land in its season, the early and the later rain, that you may gather in your grain and your wine and your oil" (Deut 11:14).

FRANK S. FRICK

RAISINS. See FLORA.

RAKEM (PERSON) [Heb *rāqem*]. The Manassite son of Sheresh and brother of Ulam (1 Chr 7:16). He is mentioned only in the genealogy for Manasseh in the MT of 1 Chr 7:14–19 (the LXX omits him from the passage). The name itself is the pausal form of "Rekem," which occurs in 1 Chr 2:43–44 as the name for the Calebite son of Hebron; in Num 31:8 and Josh 13:21 for a Midianite king; and in Josh 18:27 for a town in Benjamin.

M. PATRICK GRAHAM

RAKKATH (PLACE) [Heb *raqqat*]. One of the fortified towns in Naphtali listed in the book of Joshua (Josh 19:35). It is part of an older town list which has been incorporated into the book of Joshua. The Mishnah and the Talmud locate the site of Rakkath beneath modern Tiberias (M.R. 201242), on the Sea of Galilee, but modern scholarship places it somewhere to the N of Tiberias (Tiberias itself was not settled earlier than the Roman period). One suggestion for the site of Rakkath has been Tell Eqlatiyeh, 1.5 miles N of Tiberias, a small site which has EB, MB, and LB remains. W. F. Albright (1926) has suggested that perhaps the Israelite town was situated beneath the Roman village at the foot of the hill, near the spring called Ain el-Fuliyeh. Another suggestion for the location of the site has been Tell Raqqat (M.R. 199245), which is 24 km N of Tiberias, on the shore of the Sea of Galilee. The exact location of Rakkath remains uncertain.

Bibliography

Albright, W. F. 1926. The Jordan Valley in the Bronze Age. *AASOR* 6: 13–74.

SIDNIE ANN WHITE

RAKKON (PLACE) [Heb *raqqôn*]. A village of Dan, which appears in a fragment of a boundary description in the book of Joshua (Josh 19:46). Rakkon must be, according to its descriptions, on or near the river Yarkon, somewhere near the Mediterranean Sea. The place name is omitted by the LXX, suggesting that the word may be a partial dittography of the preceding "waters of the Yarkon" *(mê-hayyarqôn)*. If Rakkon is an actual geographical location, it might be identified with Tell er-Reqqeit, which is 1.6 miles N of the mouth of the Nahar el-Auja. Z. Kallai, in fact, suggests that it actually is a river, not a village (translating the phrase as "the waters of Yarkon and the Rakkon") and identifies it as Nahar el-Barideh (*HGB,* 370). The place, whether a village or a river, is certainly meant to be in the area of present-day Jaffa. The exact location of Rakkon is, however, still uncertain.

Bibliography

Mazar, B. 1960. The Cities of the Territory of Dan. *IEJ* 10: 65–77.

Strange, J. 1966. The Inheritance of Dan. *StTh* 20: 100–39.

SIDNIE ANN WHITE

RAM (PERSON) [Heb *rām*]. A personal name whose meaning is not clear, but it is apparently related to the Hebrew root *rûm* and so possibly means "exalted." To speculate, it possibly is a hypocoristicon of a longer name with a theophoric element *(rmyhw?)*.

1. A descendant of Jacob through the line of Judah and an ancestor of David (1 Chr 2:9, 10; Ruth 4:19). He is listed as a brother of Jerahmeel and Caleb. According to Curtis and Madsen (*Chronicles* ICC, 87) the reference to Ram in 1 Chr 2:9, 10, is suspicious for two reasons: first, the Bible elsewhere knows of no Judean family of Ram coordinate with Jerahmeel and Caleb; second, unlike the cases of Jerahmeel in vv 25–33 and Caleb in vv 42–50, the descendants of Ram are not given in families and cities. The Chronicler possibly added Ram because of the influence of Ruth 4:19. On the other hand, Myers sees no connection between 1 Chr 2:9, 10, and Ruth 4:19. He suggests that both lists go back to a common temple source (*1 Chronicles* AB, 13, 14). At Ruth 4:19, some LXX mss read Arran or Aram. In Matt 1:3, 4, this Ram is listed in the genealogy of Jesus (cf. Arni in Luke 3:33).

2. A son of Jerahmeel and descendant of Jacob (1 Chr 2:25, 27). In the present form of the genealogies of 1 Chronicles 2, he is the uncle of Ram in no. 1 above.

3. The family to which Elihu belongs (Job 32:3). Any identification with the Ram of either 1 Chr 2:9, 10, or Ruth 4:9 is speculative. Nothing in the text of Job necessarily points to an identification. Some LXX manuscripts read Aram instead of Ram.

JAMES M. KENNEDY

RAM (SHEEP). See ZOOLOGY; SHEEP, SHEPHERD.

RAMAH (PLACE) [Heb *rāmâ*]. Var. RAMATHAIM-ZOPHIM. The word means "height" and was a common place name for elevated towns and villages in biblical times.

1. A town in Benjamin (Josh 18:25), usually identified with modern er-Ram (M.R. 172140), situated 7 km N of Jerusalem, though some plausibly suggest Ramallah (M.R. 170146), 12 km N of Jerusalem. Ramah figures prominently in Benjaminite stories relating to the period before the rise of the monarchy in Israel. The village sat on a low hill astride the Palestinian watershed highway extending N from Jerusalem into the hill country of Ephraim. The earliest notices concerning Ramah seem to relate to its position along this highway.

Judg 4:5 notes that the prophetess Deborah used to sit beneath a palm tree somewhere between Ramah and Bethel (Beitin), which lay in Ephraimite territory 8 km to the N. Later in the book of Judges, a Levite couple traveling N from Bethlehem considered stopping for the night at Ramah (19:13), but instead tragically chose another route leading to Gibeah and a subsequent rape-murder.

The narratives relating Samuel's role in establishing the Israelite monarchy locate the great prophet's birthplace, residence, and burial site at Ramah. Some confusion exists, however, as to whether a site separate from Ramah of Benjamin is implied in these stories.

The Hebrew text of 1 Sam 1:1 identifies Samuel's father, Elkanah, as hailing from "Ramathaim-zophim" in the hill country of Ephraim. If the references to "Ramah" which follow in the Samuel stories (cf. 1 Sam 1:19) are short forms of the proper name Ramathaim ("two heights"), then Samuel's home may have existed somewhere in the tribal territory of Ephraim; indeed, a site in Samaria called Ramathaim is mentioned in 1 Macc 11:34. Eusebius' *Onomasticon* identifies the latter site with the Arimathea of NT times (Matt 27:57; John 19:38) and places the village at Remphis (M.R. 151159), 14 km NE of Lod (*NHI,* 378–80). Others have sought Ramathaim at Beit Rima (M.R. 159160), 21 km NE of Lod.

It is more likely, however, that Ramah of Benjamin (er-Ram) was Samuel's home. 1 Sam 1:1 should probably be emended to read that Elkanah was "from Ramah, a Zuphite from the hill country of Ephraim." The territory of Zuph appears to have been adjacent to the land of Benjamin (1 Sam 9:4–5); Ramah, near the border with Ephraim, may therefore have been inhabited by Zuphi tribesmen. Moreover, Samuel's home at Ramah is closely associated with sites within a rather small area in Benjamin: Bethel, Gilgal, and Mizpah (1 Sam 7:16); Rachel's tomb at Zelzah (1 Sam 10:2), which is associated with Ramah in Jer 31:15; and Gibeah (1 Sam 10:10; 19:18; 20:1). The stories concerning the relationship between Samuel and Saul thus arise from a very limited geographical area within Benjamin. These two figures seem to have lived a rather short distance from each other at Ramah (er-Ram) and Gibeah (Jaba), respectively.

Elkanah and Hannah resided in Ramah (1 Sam 1:19) while young Samuel remained at Shiloh in Eli's service (2:11). After leading the Israelites to temporary victory over the Philistines, Samuel based himself in Ramah while traveling as a judge on a yearly circuit to Bethel, Gilgal, and Mizpah (7:16–17). It was to Ramah that the elders of Israel traveled to demand that Samuel appoint a king over them (8:4). Apparently in the same city, Samuel eventually anointed young Saul as prince over Israel, and sent the lad on a mysterious mission to nearby Gibeah (10:1–16). After Saul's brief successes against his enemies, an ill-fated attack on the Amelekites reportedly caused Samuel to reject the king and return in mourning to Ramah (15:34).

Shortly thereafter, Samuel's home at Ramah provided a temporary refuge for the newly anointed David as he fled the danger of Saul's court at nearby Gibeah (19:18–24). The mention in this narrative of an area of Ramah called the Naioth, where the pursuing Saul and his men inadvertently fell into prophetic frenzy, might indicate that there existed in the village a special compound or dwelling place for a band of prophetic disciples of the charismatic Samuel. David reportedly fled the Naioth in Ramah in order to rejoin Jonathan before beginning his temporary career as a renegade (20:1). Samuel's role in the remaining David stories then fades rapidly: two notices of his death and burial at Ramah (25:1; 28:3) bring his earthly mission to a conclusion.

Ramah was left inside Judah very near to the N border with Israel after the division of the kingdom. Shortly after 900 B.C., King Baasha of Israel invaded Judah and fortified Ramah, thereby threatening to cut off or control N access to Jerusalem (1 Kgs 15:17; 2 Chr 16:1). King Asa of Judah reportedly responded by bribing Ben-hadad of Damascus to attack Israel's N territory, forcing Baasha to abandon his occupation of Ramah. Asa then dismantled the Ramah outpost and used its stones and timbers to fortify Geba (Jaba) and Mizpah (Tell en-Nasbeh), sites along the two routes leading into the kingdom of Judah from Israel (1 Kgs 15:21–22; 2 Chr 16:5–6).

In the late 8th century B.C., invasion once again threatened Ramah. The Israelite prophet Hosea sounded a war alarm for the Benjaminite towns of Gibeah, Ramah, and Beth-aven (5:8). Probably shortly thereafter, the Judean prophet Isaiah described panic in Ramah and Gibeah as the invader advanced into the area through the nearby Geba Pass (10:29). Both prophetic oracles probably relate to the Syro-Ephraimite invasion of Judah (cf. 2 Kgs 16:5; 2 Chr 28:5–15; and Isa 7:5–7) around 734 B.C. (Arnold 1987: 237–59).

Following the destruction of Jerusalem in 586 B.C., Ramah seems to have served as a staging point for Jewish groups leaving for exile into Babylon (Jer 40:1). The prophet Jeremiah, taken to Ramah in chains by the Babylonian captain Nebuzaradan, seems to have been freed there at the last minute. Perhaps the sadness of seeing his comrades' exilic departure from Ramah inspired the prophet's oracle in 31:15, which associates the exiles' lamentations with those of Rachel, whose tomb existed nearby at Zelzah (1 Sam 10:2; cf. Gen 35:16–20 and Matt 2:18).

After the Exile, Ramah is mentioned along with Geba in apparent Persian census lists (Ezra 2:26; Neh 7:30; 1 Esdr 5:20). The town also appears in a postexilic list of Benjaminite villages (Neh 11:33) and in a list of Benjaminite towns, now set in the context of the book of Joshua (18:25).

2. A village near the N border of Asher, in the vicinity of Tyre (Josh 19:29). Any identification with modern sites is hypothetical. One commonly accepted candidate is Ramieh (M.R. 180280), 17 km E of Rosh Ha-Niqra. Some have suggested that the town is in fact identical with the Ramah of Naphtali mentioned in Josh 19:36, but in view of the former's association with Tyre, this proposal is unlikely.

3. A fortified village in Naphtali (Josh 19:36), presently sought at modern er-Rameh (M.R. 187259), 12 km SW of Safed.

4. A village in the Negeb desert in the tribal territory of Simeon (Josh 19:8). This text also identifies Ramah of the Negeb by an alternate name, Baalath-beer. In an account describing David's sharing of Amalekite booty with his Judean tribesmen, 1 Sam 30:27 lists a Ramah of the Negeb, undoubtedly the same site, among the favored cities. Neither biblical account gives specific enough geographical information to provide a modern location for the site; however, Aharoni (*LBHG*, 261, 441) suggests identifying it with Horvat ʿUzza (M.R. 165068).

5. Ramah also occurs as a shortened form of the name for the Transjordanian site of RAMOTH-GILEAD (2 Kgs 8:28–29; 2 Chr 22:5–6).

Bibliography

Alt, A. 1927. Die Reise. *PJ* 23: 46.

Arnold, P. 1987. Gibeah in Israelite History and Tradition. Diss., Emory.

PATRICK M. ARNOLD

RAMAT EL-KHALIL

RAMAT EL-KHALIL (M.R. 160107). This site, associated with the biblical Mamre and with the Jewish Bothnah or Beth Ilanim, is located 2 miles N of Hebron. Many scholars believe this is where Josephus located Abraham's terebinth (*Ant* 1.183; cf. Gen 13:18). See also MAMRE. Other scholars locate Mamre either within Hebron or on the Namra hill N of Hebron.

In the postbiblical period, a multitude of Jewish captives were sold into slavery at Mamre after the Bar Kokhba revolt, but the place was always a thriving market in the Roman and Byzantine periods. Constantine ordered the pagan altar of Mamre to be destroyed and to be replaced by a church, which still existed in the 6th century but was in ruins by the 10th century (see also *EAEHL* 3: 776–78; *DBSup* 5: 753–58).

The enclosure of Ramat el-Khalil was first discovered by H. von Schubertine in 1827; excavations were undertaken in 1926–28 by A. E. Mader. The enclosure, or temenos, covers an area of ⅞ of an acre. Although built by Hadrian, it was preceded by two towers outside the N enclosure. These evidently belonged to a temenos of the 9th–7th centuries B.C.E., i.e., during the Judean monarchy. This enclosure was superseded by a Hasmonean pavement probably to be attributed to Hyrcanus I (128 B.C.E.). Remains of a Herodian temenos wall were found along the later S wall; it was composed of huge blocks and supported by external piers, but seems never to have been completed. The later Hadrianic wall contained reused masonry of the early Roman period, and the area so enclosed contained at its E end a shrine apparently dedicated to Hermes and Dionysus.

The Constantinian church, the oldest-known building of its type in Judea, occupied the eastern third of the temenos. It was a "broad house" basilica, oriented E–W, consisting of a nave and an apse flanked by aisles; small sacristies abutted on the N and S of these (see *EAEHL,* 778). The building was entered by a narthex along the W front of the church. An altar marking Abraham's terebinth stood in the atrium, and his well, found in the SW corner, yielded numerous coins of Constantine's time. Other coins found in the area (1,331 in number) ranged from the Hasmonean to the Crusader periods, although coins from the periods of Vespasian to Hadrian were conspicuously absent. A later repair of the church took place, possibly the work of the patriarch Modestus after the Persian invasion of 614.

Bibliography

Mader, A. E. 1957. *The Ergebnisse der Ausgrabungen in Heiligen Bezirk, Ramat el Halil in Süd Palästina.* Freiburg im Breisgau.

SHIMON APPLEBAUM

RAMAT MATRED (M.R. 118020). A series of prehistoric sites on an extensive windswept plateau some 650 m above sea level in the Central Negeb Highlands, bounded on the N and W by a steep escarpment. Drained to the E by Nahal Avdat, a tributary of Nahal Zin, the plateau filled during the Pleistocene with a mantle of aeolian loess sediments. Vegetation on the plateau is sparse, and there are no perennial sources of water today. Prehistoric research in the region was initiated by T. Noy (Yizraeli) in 1964. In 1979 A. N. Goring-Morris and I. Gilead conducted a systematic survey and excavations in the area.

Occasional scatters of Late Acheulian hand axes were recovered from the S and W edges of the plateau, eroding from the basal loess. These indicate that loess accumulation began at the end of the Lower Paleolithic.

Levalloisian cores and flakes were also found at the margins of the plateau, and at the raised W corner a dense scatter, Ramat Matred VI, was noted on the surface, representing a Mousterian occupation.

Upper Paleolithic occupation of the area is well documented. Ramat Matred I is a large surface site of ca. 150 m^2, located at the N edge of the plateau. The abundant lithic tool assemblage was dominated by burins, especially carinated dihedral types. This flake-oriented assemblage may be assigned to the Levantine Aurignacian culture. Ramat Matred IV, Har Lavan IV, and Har Lavan V are smaller in situ occupations, which were occupied later than Ramat Matred I, but while loess continued to accumulate. The lithic assemblages are blade oriented, and the tools are dominated by retouched bladelets, dihedral burins, and scrapers, which can be assigned to the later stages of the Ahmarian tradition.

Epipaleolithic occupations were confined exclusively to the N corner of the plateau, with two adjacent Mushabian occurrences—one, Ramat Matred II, was large (ca. 150 m^2), while the other, Ramat Matred III, was small (ca. 50 m^2). The only other Epipaleolithic assemblage was a Late Ramonian scatter, designated Har Lavan II. Characteristic microliths dominate the tool assemblages.

Neolithic exploitation of the area comprised a site complex of three scatters, Ramat Matred V, VI, and VIII, located at the S end of the plateau. These can be assigned to the PPN B, the lithic assemblages including arrowheads, borers, and massive denticulates. Many burnt stones littered the sites.

All of the sites investigated are open-air camps with no architectural remains. Although no organic materials have been preserved, the composition of the lithic assemblages and the specific site locations (exposed, providing extensive panoramas across the plateau) imply that hunting was probably a major seasonal (summer?) activity.

Bibliography

Gilead, I. 1981a. The Upper Palaeolithic in the Negev and Sinai. Ph.D. diss., Hebrew University, Jerusalem.

———. 1981b. Upper Palaeolithic Tool Assemblages from the Neolithic and Sinai. Pp 331–42 in *Prehistoire du Levant,* ed. J. Cauvin and P. Sanlaville. Colloques Internationaux du C.N.R.S. 598. Lyon.

Goring-Morris, A. N. 1985. Terminal Pleistocene Hunter/Gatherers in the Negev and Sinai. Ph.D. diss., Hebrew University, Jerusalem.

Goring-Morris, A. N., and Gilead, I. 1981. Prehistoric Survey and Excavations at Ramat Matred, 1979. *IEJ* 31: 132–33.

Yizraeli, T. 1967. Mesolithic Hunters Industries at Ramat Matred (The Wilderness of Zin). *PEQ* 99: 78–85.

NIGEL GORING-MORRIS

RAMAT RAHEL (M.R. 170127). An important archaeological site located on a prominent hill almost midway between the Old City of Jerusalem and Bethlehem.

A. Identification

Initially B. Maisler (Mazar 1935) proposed to identify the site with biblical Netophah (2 Sam 23:28). However, a paucity of material from the time of David prompted Y. Aharoni (1978) to suggest that the site was Beth-haccherem (Neh 3:14; Jer 6:1). Two lines of evidence support Aharoni's identification: (1) Jer 6:1 and Jos 15:59 (LXX only) suggest that Beth-haccherem was a fortified site, S of Jerusalem, and (2) Neh 3:14 indicates that Beth-haccherem was an administrative center during the Persian period. Abundant finds from Ramat Rahel date to this period and indicate that the site could have served such a function.

Avi-Yonah, on the other hand, felt that none of these texts, nor the finds at Ramat Rahel, demanded that the site be equated with Beth-haccherem and continued to maintain that the latter place was best identified with ʿAin Karim, ca. 6.5 km W of Jerusalem (1977: 20, 21). Avi-Yonah preferred to retain Maisler's identification of Ramat Rahel with Netophah, although he offered no compelling reason.

Recently, both G. Barkai and D. Tushingham have independently suggested that Ramat Rahel be identified with the elusive *mmšt,* known from the *lmlk* seal impressions. First, it seems clear that all the names on the *lmlk* seal impressions represent administrative centers of some sort which were involved with the distribution of the *lmlk* jars and/or their contents. It is known that during the Persian period the province of Judah was divided into five districts *(pelakim).* At least three of these five districts were subdivided into two halves, including the Jerusalem district (Neh 3:9, 12). It is probable that these divisions reflect earlier administrative districts. Both the location and archaeology of Ramat Rahel make it an ideal candidate for the administrative center for the S half of the Jerusalem district (Avi-Yonah 1977: 20). The reason that *mmšt* is not known from the Bible may simply be that the *lmlk* jar handles, on which the name appears, come from the time of Hezekiah (see below), and none of the biblical city lists date from that period (Franz 1984: 19).

B. Archaeology

The initial work at Ramat Rahel was conducted by B. Maisler (Mazar) and M. Stekelis. This excavation was limited to a Jewish rock-cut tomb from the Second Temple period which had been discovered S of the mound in 1931.

The first excavations on the mound, itself, were begun in the summer of 1954 under the direction of Y. Aharoni. Additional excavations were conducted from 1959 through 1962 for a total of five seasons. In 1984 an additional season was conducted by G. Barkai.

Aharoni dated the earliest occupational phase he found to the late 8th/early 7th centuries B.C. Finds from this level (Stratum V–B) included the foundations of a casemate wall (which Aharoni described as part of an "Early Citadel"), the remains of a private house, and 145 *lmlk* jar handles, mostly of the two-winged type. Most of the pottery from this phase came from a fill used to level the ground for the construction of the citadel of Stratum V-A (see below) and was dated to the 8th–7th centuries B.C. Since Aharoni's excavation, G. Barkay has uncovered a phase in which the pottery was idential to Lachish Stratum III (late 8th century B.C.). This would suggest that Aharoni's Stratum V-B may have been *preceded* by an earlier phase which was terminated in the late 8th century B.C., possibly during Sennacherib's 701 B.C. campaign. An occupation during this period makes sense in view of the fact that so many *lmlk* jar handles, now known to date to the time of Hezekiah, were found on the site.

During the next occupational phase (Stratum V-A) a citadel again dominated the site. It was surrounded by a massive outer wall (the "Outer Citadel") 3–4 m thick. Important architectural elements include ashlars, several Proto-Aeolic capitals, crenellation stones, and balustrades, similar to ones depicted in the "lady-in-the-window" ivories. All of these elements would be expected in an important administrative center or palace. Aharoni believed that this citadel was constructed by King Jehoiakim and destroyed during the time of King Jehoiachin (early 6th century B.C.). However, the architectural elements, which are similar to those found at Samaria, would suggest a construction time closer to the fall of that kingdom—perhaps the builders were even refugees from the N. The presence of Assyrian "palace ware" in this stratum also argues for an earlier date in the 7th century B.C., perhaps during the reign of Manasseh, who was known to be an Assyrian vassal. The "Elyaqim steward of Yokhin" seal found in this stratum, and thought by Aharoni to belong to the steward of King Jehoiachin, has now been redated to the late 8th century B.C., removing one of the main arguments for dating this level to the late 7th/earlier 6th centuries B.C.

Stratum IV-B contained remains from the Persian-Hellenistic periods. Most notable were numerous stamped jar handles of various classes, including *Yršlm* (Jerusalem), *Haᶜir* (the City), *Yhd* and *Yhwd* (Judah), and *Phw* (Pahva, the title of the governor). Other seals portrayed animals or rosettes. Most of the seals probably date from the 4th century B.C. Although the building remains were poorly preserved, the abundance of seals suggests that Ramat Rahel continued as a subdistrict administrative center.

The Herodian period (Stratum IV-A) was represented by a number of houses with small rooms, workshops, burial caves, and a columbarium. It has recently been suggested that the numerous cisterns which Aharoni reported were actually Jewish ritual baths *(miqwâ)*.

After a two-hundred-year abandonment, the site was occupied by the Tenth Roman Legion (Stratum III), indicated by the presence of tiles with the legion's stamp, *LEG(io) X FR(etensis)*. A typical Roman villa, a bathhouse, and various cisterns were recovered from this period.

The site continued to be occupied into the Byzantine period (Stratum II). About A.D. 450, a church, a monastery, and other buildings, collectively known as the Church of the Kathisma, were built on the site. The name is derived from the Gk *kathisma* (seat) and refers to the nearby Well of the Seat (Bir Qadismu), the traditional resting place of Mary, the mother of Jesus, on her way to Bethlehem. The final phase of occupation was during the Early Arab period (Stratum I), during which only a few poorly constructed buildings covered the site.

Bibliography

Aharoni, Y. 1978. Ramat Rahel. *EAEHL* 4: 1000–1009.

Avi-Yonah, M. 1977. *The Holy Land: From the Persian To the Arab Conquest (536 B.C.–A.D. 640).* Rev. ed. Grand Rapids.

Franz, G. 1984. The 1984 Excavation at Ramat Rahel, Jerusalem. Paper read at the ASOR annual meeting, November. Anaheim.

Maisler (Mazar), B. 1935. *Qobes* (Mazie Vol.). Jerusalem (in Hebrew).

RANDALL W. YOUNKER

RAMATH-LEHI (PLACE) [Heb *râmat leḥî*]. An unknown location, mentioned only once in connection with Samson's courageous crushing of many Philistines with an extemporaneous weapon, the jawbone of a dead donkey (Judg 15:17). After singing of his victory with this unique weapon, Samson cast away the "jawbone" (Heb *leḥî*) and named the site *râmat leḥî*. The Vg renders the phrase *elevatio Maxillae,* "lifting of the jawbone"; the LXX *anairesis siagonos* suggests the same meaning, even though it is not definitive; modern translations render "Jawbone Heights" or "Hill of the Jawbone." Some commentators viewed the connection between the "throwing" of the jawbone and the name Ramath-Lehi as incorrect etymology, since there is no connection between *râmat*—derived from the stem *rwm,* "elevate"—and *wayyašlēk,* "he cast away (the jawbone)." However, the verb *wayyašlēk* is identical in meaning with the stem *rmh,* which also means "throw" (cf. Exod 15:1, 21), and this philological explication matches the described event. Indeed, the Targum to Judg 15:17 renders *wayyašlēk* with the biblical Aramaic work *urĕmāʾ* (cf. Dan 3:24; 6:17, 25), a sense identical to the biblical *rāmāh,* thus supporting the theory that the word *rmt* is derived not from *rwm* but from *rmh,* meaning "casting away." However, the Masoretes preserved the *rwm* tradition through the diacritical marks, suggesting instead that the idea of elevation was intended. See LEHI.

The extraordinary weapon, the jawbone (known to cause fatality), is also mentioned in Islamic tradition where a heathen is killed with a jawbone (Ar *laḥy* = Heb *leḥî*), albeit that of a camel.

Râmat Leḥi parallels exactly the Gk name *Onou-gnathon* ("the ass's jaw"), mentioned by Strabo (*Geog.* 8.5.1–2) as "a low lying peninsula . . . which has a harbor" N of the island of Cythera. In this regard it is interesting to note that the phrase "donkey's jaw" is found among two seemingly different groups associated with various forms of the name "Dan." Samson descends from the tribe of Dan (cf. Judg 13:2; 15:20), and the Greeks were known as *Danaans* (*Iliad* 2: 484–86; cf. Gordon 1969: 287–88). The name thus has an E Mediterranean heritage and developed among communities with a maritime tradition (Judg 5:17; *Iliad* 2) during parallel heroic periods.

Bibliography

Gordon, C. H. 1969. Vergil and the Near East. Pp. 267–88 in *Ugaritica VI.* Paris.

Segert, S. 1984. Paronomasia in the Samson Narrative in Judges 13–16. *VT* 34: 454–61.

MEIR LUBETSKI

RAMATH-MIZPEH (PLACE) [Heb *rāmat hammizpeh*]. A border point east of the Jordan River for the land of Jazer, which Moses gave to the families of Gad (Josh 13:26). The exact location is unknown, although Noth (1938) and Gese (1968: 64) guessed that it is *Khirbet eṣ-ṣire* (.5 km NNW of *wadi eṣ-ṣir*), and Kuschke (1965) proposed that it is *Khirbet el-qar'a* (approximately 2.5 km NW of *naᶜur;* M.R. 228142). Wüst (1975: 120–32) was doubtful, and Rowley (1970: 119, 159) speculated that this name is actually a variant upon the Mizpah of Judg 10:17; 11:11, 34; and Hos 5:1 *(Khirbet Jelᶜad).*

Noth suggested that the three place names of Heshbon, Ramath-Mizpeh, and Betonim constitute a N–S boundary line between Reuben and Gad, which was added secondarily to the text. Mittmann (1970: 235–42) dismissed Noth's view as speculative. In a complex literary study, Wüst (1975: 120–32) concluded that in Josh 13:26, Heshbon and Betonim are additions to the report, which is intended to support the larger territorial claims of Gad.

Bibliography

Geze, H. 1968. Ammonitischen Grenzfestungen zwischen *wadi eṣ-ṣir* und *naᶜur. ZDPV* 74: 55–66.

Kuschke, A. 1965. Historisch-topographische Beiträge zum Buche Joshua. Pp. 90–109 in *Gottes Wort und Gottes Land.* Göttingen.

Mittmann, S. 1970. *Beiträge zur Siedlungs und Territorialgeschichte des Nördlichen Ostjordanlandes.* ADPV. Wiesbaden.

Noth, M. 1938. Ramath-Mizpeh und Betonim (Jos. 13.26.). *PJ* 34: 23–29.

Rowley, H. 1970. *Dictionary of Bible Place Names.* Old Tappan, NJ.

Wüst, M. 1975. *Untersuchen zu den siedlugsgeographischen Texten des Alten Testaments.* Vol. 1, *Ostjordanland.* Wiesbaden.

PAUL NIMRAH FRANKLYN

RAMATHAIM-ZOPHIM (PLACE) [Heb *rāmātayīm ṣôpîm*]. See RAMAH.

RAMATHITE [Heb *rāmātî*]. The gentilic identification of Shimei, one of twelve stewards of royal property appointed by David (1 Chr 27:27). His specific charge was oversight of the vineyards. The term is not used elsewhere, and thus it is not known which, if any, of several towns named Ramah might have been his original home.

RICHARD W. NYSSE

RAMESES (PLACE) [Heb *raᶜamsēs*]. Var. RAAMSES. The region of Egypt in which Joseph settled his father and brothers (Gen 47:11), and the name of one of the Egyptian store cities (presumably in the same region) subsequently built by the Hebrew slaves (Exod 1:11). As such, Rameses figures as the starting point for the Exodus trek out of Egypt and into the promised land (Exod 12:37; Num 33:3, 5). According to the book of Judith, when Nebuchadnezzar made war against Arpaxad, he summoned military assistance from various places throughout his empire, including "Tahpanes and Raamses and the whole land of Goshen" (Jdt 1:9).

The biblical city of Rameses/Raamses should be equated with Egyptian Piramesse, the great delta residence of pharaohs of the 19th and 20th Dyns. It is only recently that the location of Piramesse has been clearly established at Khatana-Qantir in the NE delta on the E bank of the Pelusaic arm of the Nile. Earlier attempts to locate Piramesse at Tanis or in the region of Bubastis must be rejected, despite apparent support from biblical evidence. The problems faced by biblical scholars in trying to pinpoint the location of Rameses stem from the nature of the destruction of Piramesse after the New Kingdom, when rulers of the 21st and 22d Dyns. plundered Piramesse for building materials to be reused in constructing edifices at their residences in Tanis and Bubastis. The wholesale deportation of temple blocks, colossal statues, obelisks, and steles from Piramesse was of such magnitude that very little of the grandiose Ramesside temples and palace survives in situ at Qantir. So impressive were the monolithic remains that were transported to Tanis and Bubastis from Qantir that in the Late Period, when there was a conscious attempt to glorify Egypt's past, the Egyptians created anew independent cults to the gods of Rameses at Tanis and Bubastis, quite unaware where Piramesse once lay. As a result, postexilic Jewish scholars in Egypt, seeking to localize events of the Exodus, were misled about the location of Piramesse in assuming that the newly created cults of the gods of Rameses at Tanis and Bubastis could serve to identify the site of the Ramesside capital.

The ancient Egyptian designation of Piramesse in its full form was "The Domain of Ramesses-meramon, great in victories," containing the name of Ramesses II, whose imprint on the development of this large city as a residential capital is unmistakable. He was, however, not the first king to build in this area. In the neighborhood of Qantir there was already considerable building activity in the Middle Kingdom. At the beginning of the Hyksos Period, Avaris at Tell ed-Daba, just S of Qantir, came into prominence as the Hyksos capital. Here, the cult of Seth, an Egyptian god associated with foreigners and adopted by the Hyksos invaders as equivalent to their own god Baal, thrived and continued into the Ramesside Period, when his temple was rebuilt and magnified. Avaris, itself, became incorporated as a part of greater Piramesse. The Ramesside rulers were especially devoted to the cult of Seth, and the Four-Hundred-Year Stele from Ramesses II's reign commemorates the anniversary of the establishment of Seth's cult by the Hyksos.

Although at Qantir there is evidence of building activity by Horemheb and by Ramesses II's father, Sety I, who was responsible for locating the royal residence there, it was Ramesses II who contributed most to the planning and expansion of this vast urban area, which was oriented according to the cardinal points and sprawled over 10 km^2. This was the residential capital where the Ramesside pharaoh normally resided; thus, the palace complex at the core of the city was extensively supplemented by all manner of administrative quarters, and official residences surrounded the palace inner city. The palace area even included a royal zoological garden, as shown by lion and elephant bones found there.

Piramesse was strategically situated, providing excellent defense against possible invasions through the narrow land pass between the Pelusaic branch of the Nile and the Bahr el-Baqar drainage-overflow lakes, and it was an ideal spot for mustering the troops to launch a campaign into Palestine, being relatively close to the beginning of the military road into Asia. To the E of the palace area where extensive military barracks, and some distance to the S was a basin-harbor with easy access to the Mediterranean and to parts of Egypt further S.

In its buildings, Piramesse rivaled Thebes and Memphis. Large temples with huge statues and obelisks were dedicated to the major state gods: Amon, Ptah, Re, and Seth, as well as to Asiatic deities like Astarte, who possessed a temple in the military quarter. The four divisions of the Egyptian army were placed under the protection of these four state gods. Although practically nothing survives of the buildings at Qantir, Egyptian papyri provide glowing descriptions of the city and its monumental temples. It was a place, we are told, to which inhabitants of the rest of Egypt came willingly to take up residence, and where all manner of peoples plied their crafts and occupations. Various waterways and lakes intersected the city, providing some relief to the concentration of settlement. The countryside around Piramesse was noted for its good fishing and agricultural productivity, especially in the vineyards, leading to the designation of Piramesse as the "Sustenance of Egypt."

Of significance to biblical scholars is the statement in Papyrus Leiden 348 that Apiru, a term some scholars equate with "Hebrew," were employed in "hauling stones to the great pylon" of one of Piramesse's temples. There must have been a cosmopolitan air about this city, largely resulting from the presence of foreign mercenaries quartered there. Their weapons and parade grounds have recently been discovered by an expedition of the Pelizaeus Museum.

At Piramesse, the cult of the deified king was much in evidence, particularly in the form of colossal statues of the king, several of which were the object of popular veneration. There is frequent reference to the Amon of Ramesses, Ptah of Ramesses, and others, perhaps expressive of a close personal relationship between the king and the gods. These special forms of the state gods seem to have possessed sanctuaries intended for the king's personal devotion.

The demise of Piramesse at the end of the 20th Dyn. was possibly associated with the silting up of the Pelusaic arm of the Nile, necessitating the transfer of the royal residence to Tanis in the 21st Dyn., when there was also a reaction against the god Seth, who had been so favored at Piramesse. Seth's name and figure were frequently expunged from the monuments prior to their eventual removal to other delta sites. See *LÄ* 5: 128–46.

Bibliography

Bietak, M. 1979. Avaris and Piramesse. *PBA* 65: 225–89.

Uphill, E. P. 1968. Pithom and Raamses: Their Location and Significance. *JNES* 27: 291–316.

———. 1969. Pithom and Raamses: Their Location and Significance. *JNES* 28: 15–39.

———. 1984. *The Temples of Per Ramesses.* Warminster.

EDWARD F. WENTE

RAMESSES II. King of Egypt from 1279 to 1212 B.C., who is considered by many scholars to be the unnamed pharaoh of the Exodus (Exodus 5–15). If so, then his father, Sety I (1291–1279 B.C.), would have been the pharaoh of the oppression (Exod 1:8–2:23).

Ramesses (or Ramses) II was born into a family of military background. His grandfather, Ramesses I, had been a general and vizier under King Horemheb, who, lacking an heir to the throne, appointed Ramesses I as his successor in a move designed to ensure that the supreme leadership remained in the hands of men trained as warriors. Ramesses I's son, Sety I, was well versed in the art of warfare when he came to the throne after his father's brief reign, and it is probable that Sety I's eldest son, Ramesses II, had already been born during the reign of Horemheb. Ramesses II claimed that during his father's reign he was appointed commander in chief of the army at the early age of ten years. While recent research has shown that Ramesses II's princely participation in the early Asiatic wars of Sety I is highly questionable (Murnane 1985: 168–70), he did acquire military experience in some minor warfare in Nubia in the second half of Sety I's reign.

Eventually Sety I appointed his son as coregent. During this brief coregency, lasting two years or less, building projects were carried out in the names of both co-rulers. The elegant raised relief that characterized the interior decoration of temples under Sety I was continued during the coregency, but shortly after Sety I's death, Ramesses II decided to have new temples decorated almost entirely in incised relief. Although this alteration in the technique of carving permitted a more rapid completion of a monument and might be regarded as a lowering of artistic standards, numerous reliefs in the Great Hypostyle Hall at Karnak underwent recutting from raised to incised relief, so that one cannot conclude that the sole reason for the alteration in style was the desire to finish the monument as quickly as possible. The first several years of Ramesses II's sole rule were marked by extensive building activities both at Thebes and at the delta capital named Piramesse (or simply Rameses).

Ramesses II has often been maligned as a usurper of his predecessors' monuments. While it is true that he did not hesitate to replace a previous king's names with his own on temple walls and statuary, nonetheless there was a prodigious amount of building carried out by Ramesses II throughout Egypt and Nubia. Hardly a site exists in the Nile valley that does not preserve some trace of his activity as a builder and enlarger of temples, so that the modern epithet "the Great" is not entirely misapplied to this pharaoh. Indeed, later kings emulated Ramesses II and his long reign of sixty-seven years. The extraordinary amount of building that characterized his reign reflected a healthy economy that prevailed not only because of the productivity of the land and its natural resources, such as gold, but also because of Egyptian dominance in Nubia and a considerable portion of W Asia.

With regard to the Asiatic empire, the major problem faced by the Egyptians in the early 13th century B.C. was the strong Hittite presence in Syria. Sety I's submission of Kadesh, the vital center on the Orontes river, had only been temporary. Instead of launching a major offensive against the Hittites at the start of his reign, as earlier pharaohs were wont to do in their first year, Ramesses II spent his first several years making preparations for a decisive encounter with the Hittites. Thus, his first campaign of victory occurred in Year 4, when a victory stele was set up on the Nahr el-Kalb on the Lebanese coast after he had secured a strong foothold on the Asiatic littoral, a preliminary to the major event of the following year, the famous Battle of Kadesh. Increasing the number of divisions of the Egyptian army from three to four, Ramesses II led the forces overland on an arduous month's march through Palestine toward Kadesh, where the Hittites had amassed a great coalition of chariotry and infantry. En route, Ramesses II was gullibly deceived by false information provided by two bedouin spies (sent by the Hittites) into believing that the Hittite king Muwatallis was too afraid to come S to Kadesh. Because the Egyptian divisions were drawn out in a long line of file at the time Ramesses II reached Kadesh, it was relatively easy for the Hittites in a surprise attack to break into the leading divisions and effectively cut the pharaoh off from the rest of the army. However, during the battle a force of Egyptian troops from the coastal area to the W suddenly arrived, and their prompt action, as well as Ramesses II's own personal valor and skill at shooting from the chariot, saved him from utter defeat. While doubt has usually been cast upon the veracity of Ramesses II's self-serving account of his heroic performance isolated in the midst of the enemy host, it must be remembered that the Hittite king was relying on the effectiveness of a coalition of troops of diverse origins, and it is just possible that a skilled warrior like Ramesses II could, from his chariot, fire upon the commanders of the coalition at close range, creating panic among the enemy chariotry. Ramesses II's prayer to the god Amon in the midst of battle is believable for its imploring of divine aid in a tight situation. On the following day, a more normal battle took place with indecisive results, for while the Egyptians had superior chariotry after the event of the preceding day, the Hittites had more infantry at their disposal. A stalemate prompted both parties to accept a temporary truce.

Although the much publicized Egyptian accounts of the Battle of Kadesh on the walls of several temples, including the famous rock-out temple of Abu Simbel in Nubia, give the impression that the battle was an Egyptian victory, in actuality the Egyptians gained nothing permanent and Kadesh remained in the Hittite sphere. The reliefs of the Battle of Kadesh represent a significant advance in narrative art, with large detailed panoramic scenes portraying the details of the battle in progress. The long texts accompanying the scenes serve to convey what could not be depicted, as, for example, the emotions of the pharaoh in the midst of combat.

During the following decade Ramesses II made several attempts to break the Hittite domination of Syria, occasionally gaining a temporary hold over such places as Tunip and Dapur. With the Hittites facing internal problems and threats from both W Anatolia and Assyria, the time became ripe for them to enter into a formal accord with Egypt. In Year 21, a lengthy treaty was drawn up in Akkadian with copies in Egyptian. It is noted for its cosmopolitan qualities, especially in giving recognition to the gods of both lands as guarantors of the accord, whose terms involved a peace binding unto eternity and included reaffirmation of two former treaties, a common alliance against outside attack and possible internal rebellion, and the extradition of fugitives, who were to be treated humanely (*ANET,* 199–203). In that age of international diplomacy, members of the royal families, including Ramesses II's mother and his wife, exchanged letters of greetings.

Thirteen years later, this peace was further cemented by Ramesses II's marriage to a Hittite princess. This event was treated in Egypt as though Ramesses II's power forced the Hittites into surrender, but lack of rainfall in Anatolia and incipient troubles with the Sea Peoples may have been important factors in this diplomatic marriage, for the Hittite king is made to say, "Our lord Seth (that is, the Egyptian storm god) is angry with us. The sky does not give water before us, and every foreign country is at war fighting us." Later, under King Merenptah, Ramesses II's son and successor, grain was actually sent from Egypt to the Hittites in time of famine.

For Egypt, the second half of Ramesses II's reign was a sort of *pax Aegyptiaca.* The indications are that Egypt maintained a relatively firm control over its Asiatic provinces, where Egyptian garrisons saw to the continued delivery of yearly dues from vassal principalities. A literary text, known as Papyrus Anastasi I, written for a military scribe, demonstrates considerable familiarity with the topography of areas in Syro-Palestine, and there is little doubt that forceful action would have been taken by Egypt to quell insurrection. At home, the king was concerned for the welfare of the Egyptian population, boasting of how well he provided for his artisans and laborers. It is not surprising then that Ramesses II's treatment as a god was accentuated, for he was regarded as the earthly manifestation of the sun-god. For popular worship, there were large statues of the king before which people might address their prayers. Since in theory the king was the sole officiant in the ritual, Ramesses II was even occasionally depicted making offerings to his own image. Beginning with his 13th year, and periodically thereafter, he celebrated a long series of jubilees, with ceremonies designed to reaffirm his vitality as pharaoh.

Ramesses II had a tremendously large number of offspring (45 sons and 40 daughters at least) by his several wives. Prince Khaemwase, who predeceased him, acquired a considerable reputation as a scholar and antiquarian, seeing to the restoration of ancient monuments. Although in the first half of his reign Ramesses II carefully exercised his power of royal appointment of clergy and officials, toward the end of his reign the seeds of inheritance of office are discernible, especially in the Theban priesthood. The rise of powerful families holding important civil and ecclesiastical positions would eventually impinge upon the centrality of royal authority, and the economic strength of the Amon temple at Karnak would come to rival royal wealth. Indeed, the very length of Ramesses II's reign and the size of his family inevitably contributed to problems in the succession of rulers in the second half of the 19th Dyn.

Ramesses II is commonly associated with events of the Exodus and often regarded as the pharaoh of the oppression. Given the fact that already in Year 5 of his son and successor Merenptah, the Israelites are mentioned in a context that indicates their presence in Palestine, it is unlikely that Merenptah was the pharaoh of the Exodus. Since the city of Rameses was already in existence under Sety I, there is the possibility that he was the pharaoh of the oppression and that Ramesses II was ruling when the Exodus occurred, sometime after his Year 15 (Kitchen 1982: 70–71). If, however, the Exodus account contains vague memories of the expulsion of the Hyksos at the beginning of the 18th Dyn., Ramesses II's involvement may have been rather peripheral, perhaps limited to the departure from Egypt of a small group of Apiru Asiatics, who somehow contributed to the collective experience of the Hebrews.

The mummy of Ramesses II, discovered at Thebes, is that of a red-haired octogenarian, who died a natural death at his delta residence, where his body was mummified.

Bibliography

Kitchen, K. A. 1982. *Pharaoh Triumphant: The Life and Times of Ramesses II.* Warminster.

Lalouette, C. 1985. *L'Empire des Ramsès.* Paris.

Murnane, W. J. 1985. *The Road to Kadesh.* SAOC 42. Chicago.

EDWARD F. WENTE

RAMIAH (PERSON) [Heb *ramyāh*]. A descendant of Parosh and one of the returned exiles who was required by Ezra to divorce his foreign wife (Ezra 10:25 = 1 Esdr 9:26). According to M. Noth, the name Ramiah means "Yahweh is exalted" (*IPN,* 145). Ramiah was a member of a family that returned from Babylon with Zerubbabel (Ezra 2:3; Neh 7:8). For further discussion, see BEDEIAH.

JEFFREY A. FAGER

RAMOTH (PLACE) [Heb *rāʾmôt*]. A town of the tribe of Issachar, reportedly granted to the sons of Gershom (1 Chr 6:58—Eng 6:73). The city listed at the same point in the parallel levitical town register in Josh 21:29 is called Jarmuth *(yarmût);* the LXX supports "Ramoth" as the probable original reading. Ramoth is also probably identical with Remeth *(remet)* of Issachar (Josh 19:21).

The location of Ramoth is purely a matter of conjecture. W. F. Albright suggested Kokab el-Hawa, the Crusader castle Belvoir (M.R. 199221), 11 km N of Beth-shean (1926: 231). Its lofty position (over 300 m above sea level) may relate to the possible meaning of Ramoth, "heights."

Bibliography

Albright, W. F. 1926. The Topography of the Tribe of Issachar. *ZAW* 44: 225–36.

PATRICK M. ARNOLD

RAMOTH-GILEAD (PLACE) [Heb *rāmōt gilʿād*]. A fortress-city of Gilead located in the E portion of Gad's tribal territory. Ramoth-gilead is first mentioned in the Bible (Deut 4:43) as a city in Transjordan which Moses set aside for the tribe of Gad as a place of refuge for perpetrators of unintentional homicide (see also Num 35:6–15 for P legislation regarding cities of refuge). In Joshua 20, the Lord commands Joshua to carry out Moses' legislation, including the establishment of Ramoth in Gilead for Gad (Josh 20:8). Though set in the Wandering/Conquest period, the provision for cities to which perpetrators could flee to escape blood revenge from angry relatives of the victim probably reflects a sophisticated innovation of the monarchical period. The Davidic-Solomonic period might provide the earliest such setting for this role.

Ramoth-gilead also appears in the list of forty-eight cities granted to the Levites by Joshua after the Conquest, and is specifically mentioned again as a city of refuge (Josh 21:38 = 1 Chr 6:65 [—Eng 6:80]). The provision for Levitical cities, though set in the premonarchical period, is also widely regarded by scholars as an administrative act of the Davidic or Solomonic reigns (*ARI,* 121–25; Mazar 1960) or even a much later government. Ramoth-gilead's roles as both a Levitical city and a city of refuge are possibly traceable to the same administrative fiat. It is noteworthy that when Solomon reportedly divided his kingdom into twelve local districts (1 Kgs 4:7–19), Ramoth-gilead housed Ben-geber, the governor of Gilead and Bashan (1 Kgs 4:13), indicating the importance of the city during that regime.

After the division of the kingdom in the late 10th century, Israel inherited the tribal territories of the N Transjordan, including Gad and its chief city, Ramoth-gilead. A period of military struggles with Damascus followed (1 Kgs 15:20); Josephus (*Ant* 8.14.1) suggests that the city became a point of contention between Syria and Israel, probably during the mid-9th century. The campaign of Ben-hadad of Syria (1 Kgs 20) may have captured Ramoth-gilead from Israel; certainly 1 Kgs 22 presumes that the city lay in Aramean hands. The intriguing account describes how the king of Israel (Ahab? cf. 22:20) implored Jehoshaphat of Judah to join him in an expedition to recover Ramoth-gilead from Aram (22:3). Though the court prophets encouraged such an attack, Micaiah, son of Imlah, prophesied a resounding defeat at the city (22:15–17); the march went on nevertheless. The attempt failed, and the king of Israel died in his chariot.

Twelve years later (ca. 840), Jehoram of Israel and Ahaziah of Judah reportedly attempted to retake Ramoth-gilead from Ben-hadad's Syrian successor Hazael (2 Kgs 8:28–29). The attack may have succeeded (cf. 9:14), though the Arameans wounded Jehoram in the attempt. While the king of Israel lay wounded at Jezreel, the prophet Elisha dispatched a messenger to the Israelite army at Ramoth-gilead to anoint an Israelite military commander, Jehu, as the new king (9:1–13). This action amounted to a fundamentalist coup d'état, because Jehu returned from Ramoth to exterminate the rest of the liberal Omrides, members of the Judean royal family, and most of the Baal prophets (2 Kgs 9–10). Apparently, the Yahwistic revolt so weakened Israel that Hazael of Aram succeeded in capturing from it the entire Transjordan, including the disputed Ramoth-gilead (2 Kgs 10:32–33). Though not all these prophetically inspired accounts can be taken at face value (see Miller 1966), there is no reason to doubt that Israel and Syria struggled over Ramoth-gilead itself during this period. It is possible that Amos referred to battles in or around the city a century later when he accused Damascus of war crimes: "They threshed Gilead under threshing-sledges spiked with iron" (Amos 1:3).

The modern identification of Ramoth-gilead is hampered by the relative topographical ambiguity of the OT texts. "Gilead" probably refers to an area in modern Jordan S of the Yarmuk River and N of the Jabbok, but there are many ruins in this area. Albright, following Dalman, proposed Tell el Ḥusn (M.R. 232210), some 16 km SW of Ramtha (1929: 11). But N. Glueck later suggested Tell Ramith (M.R. 244210), 7 km S of Ramtha near the modern frontier with Syria (1943: 11–12), and this identification won scholarly approval in view of Ramith's etymological connections with "Ramoth," its commanding location as a "height" over the surrounding plain, and its Iron Age pottery.

Bibliography

Albright, W. F. 1929. New Israelite and Pre-Israelite Sites: The Spring Trip of 1929. *BASOR* 35: 1–13.

Glueck, N. 1943. Ramoth-Gilead. *BASOR* 92: 10–16.

Mazar, B. 1960. The Cities of the Priests and Levites. *VTSup* 7: 139–205.

Miller, J. M. 1966. The Elisha Cycle and the Accounts of the Omride Wars. *JBL* 85: 441–54.

PATRICK M. ARNOLD

RAMPART. See FORTIFICATIONS (LEVANT).

RAMSES (PERSON). See RAMESSES II.

RAPE. See PUNISHMENTS AND CRIMES (OT AND ANE).

RAPHA (PERSON) [Heb *rāpāʾ*]. The fifth son of Benjamin in 1 Chr 8:2. He is not mentioned in the list of Benjamin's sons in Gen 46:21, where Naaman is the fifth.

DAVID SALTER WILLIAMS

RAPHAEL (ANGEL) [Gk *Raphaēl*]. The angel dispatched to restore Tobit's sight and to free Sarah from the dominance of the evil spirit, Asmodeus (Tob 3:17). His name is a play on words, meaning "God heals" (Zimmerman 1958: 66; Lamparter 1972: 108, n. 6). His role in the narrative underlines the writer's belief in both God's transcendence and his involvement in the life of Israel (Zimmerman 1958: 27–28; Nickelsburg 1981: 34). He acts as God's emissary, but is charged with the responsibility of caring for the faithful. In fact, so central to the plot of the book is this angelic intermediary that some scholars have described Tobit as an "extended angelophany" (Nickelsburg 1981: 40, n. 41). Raphael is also described in the book of *1 Enoch* as the second in the hierarchy of the angels (20: 3) and, specifically, as the one who bound Azazel and cast him into a pit (10: 4). Together, both books reflect the impact of Iranian beliefs upon those of Judaism. The emergence of an angelic hierarchy, the view of angels as servants of men as well as God, and the assignment of names determined by function provide evidence of that influence (Gaster *IDB* 1: 132–34). The interest of both writers in the angelic establishes that the gap between the OT and NT on such matters is not as great as it would appear (Metzger 1957: 38; cf. *IDB* 4: 12).

Bibliography

Lamparter, H. 1972. *Die Apokryphen II: Weisheit Salomos, Tobias, Judith, Baruch.* BAT 25/2. Stuttgart.

Metzger, B. 1957. *An Introduction to the Apocrypha.* New York.

Nickelsburg, G. 1981. *Jewish Literature Between the Bible and the Mishnah.* Philadelphia.

Zimmerman, F. 1958. *The Book of Tobit.* Jewish Apocryphal Literature. New York.

FREDERICK W. SCHMIDT

RAPHAH (PERSON) [Heb *rāpâ*]. Var. REPHAIAH. Son of Binea, a descendant of King Saul from the tribe of Benjamin, according to the genealogy of 1 Chr 8:37. The name is an abbreviated form of names such as Rephael, "God has healed" (1 Chr 26:7), and Rephaiah, "YH(WH) has healed," which is a common biblical name in postexilic sources (e.g., 1 Chr 3:21), although the name Rephayahu *(rpyhw)* is attested to in the preexilic bulla corpus (Avigad 1986: 78; Shiloh 1986: 29). The element *rpʾ*, "to heal," is common in biblical names of all periods (Noth *IPN,* 179). The genealogy parallel to 1 Chr 8:37 in 9:43 gives Raphah's name in the form Rephaiah *(rĕpāyāh);* most LXX manuscripts read this longer form in 8:37 as well. The usual shortened form is Rapha *(rāpāʾ),* which is attested to in the Bible (e.g., 1 Chr 8:2), in the Samaria ostraca, and on a preexilic bulla (Avigad 1986: 49), but it is not unusual for a final *ʾalep* to interchange with a final *he* in personal names (Fowler *TPNAH,* 165). Thus, neither the form Rapha of 8:37 nor Rephaiah of 9:43 should be seen as preferable. Raphah's name appears in the section of genealogy (v 37b) using the term *bĕnô,* "his son," in contrast to the preceding section (vv 36–37a), which uses the verbal form *hôlîd,* "begot"; it is therefore possible that they come from different sources and might have been mechanically combined, in which case Raphah is not actually the "son" or "descendant" of Binea. This genealogy is from the end of the First Temple period (Demsky 1971: 20) and was preserved by Benjaminite families that survived the Babylonian Exile (Williamson 1979: 356). The existence and preservation of the Saulide genealogy probably reflect the continued prominence of Saul's family, and perhaps even their hope that they would return to power (Ackroyd *Chronicles, Ezra, Nehemiah* TBC, 42; Flanagan *PWCJS* 8: 25). See MELECH. On the repetition of the genealogy in 1 Chronicles 8 and 9, and its structure within the genealogies in Chronicles, see AHAZ.

Bibliography

Avigad, N. 1986. *Hebrew Bullae from the Time of Jeremiah.* Jerusalem.

Demsky, A. 1971. The Genealogy of Gibeon (1 Chronicles 9:34–44): Biblical and Epigraphic Considerations. *BASOR* 202: 16–23.

Shiloh, Y. 1986. A Group of Hebrew Bullae from the City of David. *IEJ* 36: 16–38.

Williamson, H. G. M. 1979. Sources and Redaction in the Chronicler's Genealogy of Judah. *JBL* 98: 351–59.

Marc Z. Brettler

RAPHAIM (PERSON) [Gk *Rhapain*]. A name given as part of the genealogy of Judith (Jdt 8:1). It should be noted that the Gk text reads Raphain. If this reading is correct, then the name occurs nowhere else in the biblical text. It is often emended, as in RSV, to Raphaim (this follows the Vulgate), or to Rephaiah. If the emendation to Rephaiah is correct, then it is most likely that the author of Judith had in mind the occurrence of the name in 1 Chr 4:42. There, Rephaiah is a leader of the tribe of Simeon, which is, according to the author, the tribe of Judith. The purpose of the genealogy in the book of Judith is to prove the purity of Judith's Jewish descent and to give the story verisimilitude.

Sidnie Ann White

RAPHIA (PLACE) [Gk *Rhaphia*]. The site of the battle between Ptolemy IV Philopater and Antiochus III (*3 Macc.* 1:1; 217 B.C.; see *CAH* 7/22/8: 728–31). It is associated with modern Tel Rafah (M. R. 077079), a city located about 20 miles SW of Gaza and 30 miles N of the Wadi el-ʿArish. This site was important throughout antiquity because of its strategic location on the frontier between Palestine and Egypt. It served as a border station on the main military road which ran from Egypt to Palestine. This road, called the "Way of Horus" by the Egyptians, the "Way of the Land of the Philistines" in the OT (Exod 13:17), and the "Way of the Sea" by the Romans, was the most direct route linking Asia and Egypt and was thus used throughout history for the movement of armies (see *LBHG,* 41–49; Gardiner 1920).

Although Raphia is not mentioned in the OT, there is ample evidence that it dates back to that period. The name is found in both Mesopotamian and Egyptian sources. A Neo-Assyrian annal of Sargon II (721–705 B.C.) claims that "Hanno, King of Gaza and also Sib'e, the *Turtan* of Egypt set out from Rapihu against me to deliver a decisive battle. I defeated them . . ." (*ANET,* 285). Esarhaddon (680–669 B.C.) also passed through Raphia on his way to Egypt: "I removed my camp from Musru and marched directly towards Meluhha (i.e., Egypt)—a distance of 30 double-hours from the town of Apku which is in the region of Samaria as far as the town Rapihu (in) the region adjacent to the 'Brook of Egypt' . . ." (*ANET,* 292).

In Egyptian texts, Raphia is found in the Papyrus Anastasi, a satirical letter dating to the time of Seti I (1294–1279 B.C.). The name (spelled *r-p-h*) is mentioned following *n-h-s* and preceding Gaza (*ANET,* 478; Gardiner 1920: 103). In another list of toponyms from the same period, Raphia follows Hazor (*LBHG,* 166). Ramesses II (1279–1213 B.C.) mentions *r-p-h* in a geographical list preceding Sharu[hen] (Tell el-Farʿah; *ANET,* 292), while in a geographical list from the time of the pharaoh Shishak I (945–924 B.C.), *r-p-h* is associated with Laban (*LBHG,* 290; for a complete listing of Raphia occurrences in Egyptian texts and corresponding bibliography, see *CTAED,* 161–62).

Raphia is next attested in the literature of Hellenistic times. Polybius mentions Raphia as the site of the battle between Ptolemy IV and Antiochus III in 217 B.C. (*Histories* 5.80). Strabo the Geographer, while describing the region, states: "After Gaza one comes to Rhaphia, where a battle was fought between Ptolemaeus the Fourth and Antiochus the Great" (*Geog.* 16.2.31). In the writings of Josephus, Josephus relates how Alexander Jannaeus captured and destroyed Raphia in 97 B.C. (*Ant* 14.5.3) and how it was rebuilt by Gabinius in 55 B.C. (*Ant* 14.5.3; *JW* 1.8.4). Later, Titus passed through Raphia on his way from Nicopolis in Egypt to Jerusalem (70 A.D.; *JW* 4.11.5).

The Talmud (*t. Šeb.* 4.10) mentions the name Raphiah deHagra "Raphia of the wall" as a name of a province located on the border between Egypt and Palestine (*GP* 1: 308–10). For further discussion, see also *IDB* 4: 13; *ISBE* 4: 46; *LÄ* 5: 147–48.

Bibliography

Barag, D. 1973. The Borders of Syria-Palaestina on an Inscription from the Raphia Area. *IEJ* 23: 50–52.

Gardiner, A. H. 1920. The Ancient Military Road between Egypt and Palestine. *JEA* 6: 99–116.

Naʾaman, N. 1979. The Brook of Egypt and Assyrian Policy on the Border of Egypt. *TA* 6: 68–90.

Brian E. Keck

RAPHON (PLACE) [Gk *Rhaphōn*]. A city in Gilead on the banks of a tributary of the Yarmuk River. It is identified with er-Rafeh, 13 km NE of Sheikh Saʿad (Karnaim). It may be the city *nw-r-p-i* in the list of Canaanite cities of Thutmose III.

The Maccabean Revolt met with early success, including the recapture of the temple in 164 B.C., which led to gentile reprisals. Many Jews in Gilead fled to a stronghold at the city of Dathema and sent to Judas for help (1 Macc 5:10), while Jews in other cities were attacked by the gentile citizens (5:26–27). Judas embarked on a highly successful campaign to liberate all of them. The campaign reached its climax when the Ammonite military commander, Timothy, gathered a huge army opposite Raphon (5:37–39), and Judas crossed the wadi swollen with spring rains (Goldstein *1 Maccabees* AB, 303) to attack and defeat him (5:43). Timothy's army retreated to the Temple of Ashtoreth at Karnaim (5:43–44), which Judas captured and burned. Meanwhile, according to 2 Macc 12:24, the retreating Timothy was captured by two Jewish brothers, Dositheus and Sosipater. He persuaded them to free him, thereby avoiding death at Karnaim.

PAUL L. REDDITT

RAPHU (PERSON) [Heb *rāpûʾ*]. A man from the tribe of Benjamin, known only through association with his son Palti (Num 13:9). Palti was one of the twelve tribal representatives who left Kadesh to spy out the land of Canaan.

TERRY L. BRENSINGER

RAPTURE. See REVELATION, BOOK OF; PAROUSIA.

RAQQA, KHIRBET ER-. See JOKDEAM.

RAS ABU TABAT (PLACE). See TABBATH.

RAS ET-TAHUNA (M.R. 170147). See ZEMARAIM.

RAS SHAMRA (PLACE). See UGARIT.

RASSIS (PLACE) [Gk *Rhassis*]. A site mentioned in the book of Judith as one of the scenes of Holofernes' victories (Jdt 2:23). The name occurs only here in the Bible. The author seems to locate the site somewhere in the region of Cilicia, given the context of the passage. The OL text and the Vg give the name as Tharsis (Lat *Tharsis*), leading some to suggest that Rassis is a corruption of the name Tarsus. However, it is much more likely that the Latin is a corruption from the unknown "Rassis" toward the easily identified "Tarsus." Others suggest an identification with a "Rossos" mentioned by Strabo (14.5.19; 16.2.8) and Ptolemy (*Geog.* 5.14). Stummer (1947) thinks this is the most likely identification, and believes it refers to Mt. Rossus (modern Arsus), which was the site of the Battle of Issus in 333 B.C.E. This is possible; the name may have been known to the author of Judith and used to give his story verisimilitude. This identification would also partly depend on the date assigned to the book of Judith; that is, whether or not the author would have been aware of the Battle of Issus.

Bibliography

Stummer, F. 1947. *Geographie des Buches Judith.* Bibelwissenschaftliche Reihe 3. Stuttgart.

SIDNIE ANN WHITE

RAT. See ZOOLOGY.

RATHAMIN (PLACE) [Gk *Rhathamin*]. An administrative district ceded to Maccabean control by Demetrius Nicator of Syria ca. 148 B.C. (1 Macc 11:34). The three "nomes" of Aphairema, Lydda, and Rathamin had formerly been a part of the larger district of Samaria, although their population was largely Jewish. Rathamin, like the other "nomes" associated with it, bordered Judea and had already come effectively under the control of the Maccabees. Demetrius formally annexed Rathamin and other territories to Judea and made further concessions in an attempt to retain Jewish allegiance. This treaty was reported in a letter of Demetrius to Lasthenes concerning affairs in the S portion of the Seleucid empire.

Rathamin is clearly included as one of the three nomes mentioned in the record of Demetrius' earlier attempt to sway Maccabean allegiance from his rival Alexander (1 Macc 10:30, 38). Later, in peace time, Demetrius broke his promises, and his rival Tryphon, in the name of his child-king Antiochus, granted Jonathan Maccabeus control over "the four nomes," which would have included Rathamin (1 Macc 11:57). Josephus uses the toponym Ramatha in his description of these events (*Ant* 13.14.9; cf. LXX ASV Rhamathaim). The change of spelling in early mss may represent a change to a sound more aesthetically pleasing to the Hellenistic ear.

The district of Rathamin is widely accepted as the district surrounding the home of Samuel. This region in the hill country of Ephraim lay along the N approach to Judea. The location is also known as Arimathea (M.R. 151159) and was the hometown of Joseph, one of Jesus' followers (Matt 27:57; John 19:38). The etymological root of this name is Ramah, which refers to a high place. This location is only 11 km N of Modein, the home of the Maccabees. No excavations of the site are reported in current summaries of archaeological activities. According to Avi-Yonah's cartography, the region of Rathamin included ca. 140 square miles and stretched from the foothills near Arimathea in the W to Bethel in the E.

ROBERT W. SMITH

RAVEN. See ZOOLOGY.

RAZIS (PERSON) [Gk *Rhazis*]. One of the elders from Jerusalem who in 2 Macc 14:37–46 is said to commit suicide rather than permit Nicanor to arrest him and use him as an example to the Jews in Judea. While most major translations (RSV, NEB, JB) for the sake of clarity insert the name Razis into the story two or more times, the Gk mss only mention it once at the very beginning (v 37). The mss vary considerably in the spelling of the name, raising questions about its origin. While most commentators accept its Semitic origin, Grimm thinks the Syriac *Ragaš* may preserve the original name (1853: 199). Abel accepts Grimm's other proposal, *Razy,* and argues that it is probably of Persian background (1949: 467), while Goldstein sees the influence of Isa 14:16–18 on *Razy* (*2 Maccabees* AB, 492).

Our knowledge concerning Razis is confined to this account. He is described as one of the *presbyterōn* (elders) from Jerusalem with a good reputation and a love for his fellow citizens. Most commentators think that he must have been among a group of elders assembled by Judas after the revolt (Habicht 1976: 275). While the extent of their power cannot be ascertained (Goldstein *2 Maccabees* AB, 491–92), the use of the title is rather common in 1 and 2 Maccabees. This text also informs us that earlier in the time of *amixia* (separation), risking body and soul Razis had incurred the judgment of Judaism, an apparent reference to the prohibitions under Antiochus IV described in 2 Macc 6:1–6 and elsewhere.

The story of Razis is an independent unit in 2 Maccabees with a limited connection to its surrounding literary context. While in the sequence of events in 2 Maccabees the Razis incident seems to have occurred in the temple, many believe the references in the story are to the courtyard of a house (Grimm 1853: 200; Abel 1949: 469). Since this account seems to stand as an independent literary unit in 2 Maccabees 14, it is very difficult to determine the precise setting.

While the story of Razis is an obvious case of suicide, its parallels with the martyrdoms described in 2 Macc 6:10–7:42 (Goldstein *2 Maccabees* AB, 491) provide some justification for those who regard this story of noble resistance to foreign exploitation as a martyrdom (Schiffman in *HBC* 914).

Bibliography

Abel, F.-M. 1949. *Les Livres des Maccabées.* EBib. Paris.

Grimm, C. L. W. 1853. *Kurzgefasstes exegetisches Handbuch zu den Apokryphen des Alten Testaments.* Leipzig.

Habicht, C. 1976. *2. Makkabäerbuch.* JSHRZ 1/3. Gütersloh.

John Kampen

RE (DEITY). The Egyptian sun-god; a cosmic deity of the greatest importance in the expression and development of Egyptian religious thought. Although the ideogram for the sun—a circle with a central dot—is found in the late Predynastic period (ca. 3000 B.C.), scholars have no solid evidence upon which to date the introduction or development of solar worship in Egypt. What can be determined, however, is that by the end of the Archaic period (ca. 2700 B.C.), the worship of Re was solidly entrenched in mainline Egyptian religion, since the name of Re has been found as a constituent of human names at that time, as was the title "Son of Re," which was to be used in the full titulary of pharaohs from the Old Kingdom through the Roman period.

Re's primary cult center was the city of *Iwnw* (Heliopolis), situated at the apex of the delta, where he was worshipped in the form of a hawk-headed human, and where his most sacred icon—the conically shaped benben stone—was long an object of veneration (Bonnet in *RÄR*, 626). It is from this city that the priests of Re are believed to have developed the highly complex speculative system which influenced much of Egyptian culture, from religious belief and ritual practice to religious and secular literature (Barucq and Daumas 1980: 115; Assmann 1969), and even to architecture, this last providing some of the most stereotypical images of ancient Egypt—the pyramid, obelisk, and sun temple (David 1980: 36).

The three most significant qualities of the sun-god are apparent from his earliest occurrences in the Old Kingdom. Re is a creator god, he is the divine king, and he is the paradigm for the cycle of birth-life-death-rebirth. The sun-god's aspect as a creator god is best described in the Instruction to King Merikare: "Mankind, god's cattle, is well tended. He created the sky and the earth for their sake . . . He made breath for their noses to live . . . He shines in the sky for their sake. He made plants and cattle for them, fowl and fish to feed them . . . He makes daylight for their sake" (Volten 1945: 131; *ANET,* 417).

In this regard, the sun-god is also the dominant creator in many of the various priest-developed cosmogonic systems, such as that of Heliopolis, where Atum-Re generates the first male-female pair through masturbation; Hermopolis, where Re arises from the cosmic egg on the Island of Flames (Brandon 1963: 14); and Edfu, where Re is connected with the origin of sacred places (Reymond 1969: 33).

Perhaps Re's most important characteristic is that he is the king of the gods. This is his most common depiction in the Old Kingdom Pyramid Texts. Re crosses the sky in his great boat which is crewed by the gods who perform various scribal and personal functions, inspecting various districts of his realm, making regal pronouncements (Anthes 1958: 77–89). All of this is so transparently a borrowing of the earthly actions of the pharaoh that, lacking substantial descriptions of pharaonic activities of state during the Old Kingdom, descriptions of Re can be used to supplement our general understanding of royal activities (Firchow 1957: 34–42). We even have one text where Re's royal prerogatives are so unqualified that he is able to call for the destruction of mankind (Piankoff 1955: 26).

As mentioned earlier, one of the standard elements of the pharaoh's titulary was his "Son of Re" name. Some scholars speculated that this was an indication that the primary position of the pharaoh in the Egyptian pantheon was compromised by the rising power of Re and his priesthood during later Old Kingdom times (David 1980: 60). That this Re-king connection was taken seriously throughout the rest of pharaonic history is confirmed by the fact that almost every pharaoh from Dynasty 4 through Dynasty 30, the last native Egyptian dynasty, selected a royal name which was a compound using Re; for example, Khafre, Menkaure, Sahure, Meryre, Kheperkare, Menkheperre, and Usermaatre. Indeed, to the Egyptians, the "Son of Re" title was quite literal, as the Westcar Papyrus relates how the initial kings of the 5th Dynasty were the offspring of the wife of a priest of Re and the sun-god himself (*AEL* 1: 215).

The third major characteristic of Re is that he is the god of resurrection: the paradigm of the birth-life-death-rebirth cycle. The sun is the most dominant of all celestial phenomena, and its daily rising and setting led the Egyptians to regard it as being born each morning and dying each sunset. Connected with this is the vision of the sun sailing across the day sky along the body of the sky-goddess Nut, being swallowed by her at sunset, and traveling through her body by boat at night, to be born again in the morning (Westendorf 1966).

The most commonly held theory is that an afterlife and the otherworld were royal prerogatives in the earlier periods. The best description of this is rendered in the Pyramid Texts, which are thought to represent beliefs originally prepared for and pertaining to pharaohs and the royal bloodline. After death, and through the performance of certain rituals, the pharaoh either became identified with Re or became a member of his official entourage and was, therefore, pulled into the sun's cycle of daily rebirth.

Standard scholarship holds that even in the Pyramid Texts, however, we can detect more "popular" afterlife expressions revolving around the god Osiris, who begins to usurp or at least share in some of Re's prerogatives (Breasted 1933: 109). This process became more pronounced during the First Intermediate Period, when the power of the pharaoh waned substantially and the afterlife became accessible to everyone. This is a very debatable interpretation which is based on the lack of nonroyal funerary literature from the older periods. Even so, the solar influence remained strong in later funerary literature—for example, the Coffin Texts and the Book of the Dead—and was the primary inspiration behind the numerous highly pictorial "books" of the New Kingdom and later, such as the Book of the Day, the Book of the Night, the Book of Gates, the Book of Caverns, and the Book of What Is in the Underworld (Piankoff 1957). All of these texts have as their leitmotiv the inexorable movement of the sun-god through the otherworld, culminating with his rebirth.

Re's influence on the general Egyptian pantheon was profound. As early as the 2d Dynasty, with the occurrence of Re-Horakhty, Re was such a fundamental aspect of the Egyptian religious perspective that he became closely linked with numerous other deities to form new gods, e.g., Re-Atum, Re-Horakhty, Amon-Re, Khepre-Re, and Re-Osiris. Re was easily the most frequently occurring god in these syncretistic associations (Hornung 1982: 86), and one text, the Litany of Re, contains 75 examples of alternate and compound names of Re, many of which are the names of other gods, under which Re's power was manifest (Piankoff 1964: 22 ff.).

This syncretistic technique of Egyptian religious thinkers, particularly as it applied to Re, was responsible for expanding and enriching the character of many originally nonsolar divinities, to the point where, in the New Kingdom, the Egyptian pantheon had a substantially solar flavor.

Bibliography

Anthes, R. 1958. Die Sonnenboote in den Pyramidentexten *ZÄS* 82: 77–89.

Assmann, J. 1969. *Liturgische Lieder an den Sonnengott.* MÄS 19. Berlin.

Barucq, A., and Daumas, F. 1980. *Hymnes et prières de l'Égypte Ancienne.* Paris.

Brandon, S. G. F. 1963. *Creation Legends of the Ancient Near East.* London.

Breasted, J. H. 1933. *The Dawn of Conscience.* New York.

David, R. J. 1980. *Cult of the Sun.* London.

Firchow, O. 1957. Königsschiff und Sonnenbarke. *WZKM* 54: 34–42.

Hornung, E. 1982. *Conceptions of God in Ancient Egypt.* Ithaca.

Piankoff, A. 1955. *The Shrines of Tut-Ankh-Amon.* New York.

———. 1957. *The Tomb of Ramses VI.* New York.

———. 1964. *The Litany of Re.* New York.

Reymond, E. A. E. 1969. *The Mythical Origin of the Egyptian Temple.* New York.

Volten, A. 1945. *Zwei altaegyptische politische Schriften.* Analecta Aegyptiaca 4. Copenhagen.

Westendorf, W. 1966. *Altaegyptische Darstellungen des Sonnenlaufes auf der abschuessigen Himmelsbahn.* MÄS 10. Berlin.

Frank T. Miosi

READER RESPONSE THEORY.

A development within literary studies which focuses on the relationship between text and receiver.

A. Definition
B. Background and Formative Influences
C. Basic Concepts
  1. The Implied and Other Readers
  2. Gaps and the Indeterminacy of the Text
  3. The Wandering Viewpoint
  4. Criticism
D. Reader Response Theory and Biblical Literature
  1. Audience Criticism
  2. New Developments

A. Definition

The communication process by means of texts can be described in terms of the basic relationships between sender, message, and receiver. Historical studies as a general rule tend to concentrate on the relationship between sender and message, structural studies on the text itself, and Reader Response Theory (hereafter RRT) on the interaction between text and receiver(s). Although the approach developed by RRT has its origins in the field of general literary studies, it is becoming increasingly prominent in the interpretation of biblical material.

B. Background and Formative Influences

The interest in reception forms part of a much wider movement toward pragmatics, i.e., the study of the effect of language in use. While syntax has to do with the structure of and the relationship between the different elements of the text, and semantics deals with the meaning of the text, pragmatics is interested in language in action and the effects that can be achieved by language. Because language functions on various levels and in a variety of contexts, pragmatics covers a broad spectrum of investigation. It does not proceed from a unified or universally accepted theory, but draws its inspiration and concepts from diverse methods and traditions. RRT, as a smaller segment within the wider field of pragmatics, reflects the same multifaceted background, and a number of influences can be traced in its development.

In terms of origins, a distinction can be made between RRT and reception theory. The former is a concept prevalent in North America; the latter was developed in a European context. RRT is an umbrella term which brings together literary critics from diverse backgrounds. The common denominator is their opposition to the New Critical emphasis on the "text itself"; that is, on the autonomous status of the text as text, and the concentration on the ways in which the text interacts with readers. In RRT, there is no coordinated attempt to develop a uniform methodological approach; in fact, one of the strengths of RRT claimed by its adherents is that it can accommodate a variety of techniques and methods. Reception theory, on the other hand, is a much more coherent movement, most prominently represented by the so-called School of Constance, with Robert Jauss and Wolfgang Iser as its principal exponents. During the late 1960s and early 1970s, their work was seminal for the exchange of ideas at the biannual colloquia held at the University of Constance in the Federal Republic of Germany. The results of those discussions were eventually published in the series *Poetik und Hermeneutik.*

The rise of reception theory or the "aesthetics of reception" (Jauss) was preceded by four other related developments. First, studies in the sociology of literature emphasized that not only is the production of a work of art or the value of its inherent qualities worthy of investigation, but also, and especially, is its effect on society. Similar ideas came from a second quarter, that of philosophical hermeneutics, where Gadamer developed his concept of the "effective history" *(Wirkungsgeschichte)* of a text. In this concept, an individual does not exhaust the meaning potential of a text, but his or her interpretation is relativized and complemented by other readings of the text. In fact, these different readings form a history of their own which will influence the predisposition of the individual reader even before he or she actually encounters the text—whether the reader is aware of this influence or not. The concept of "effective history" prepared the way for the third influence, namely the idea of writing a history of literature in terms of the reception of texts. Jauss, the major exponent of this concept, understands such an undertaking to be the prerequisite for an "aesthetics of reception." The aim is to provide some explanation for the success or failure of certain texts during certain periods in history, and in doing so to establish a basis for the evaluation of texts. A fourth and very powerful influence came from the ideas of the Prague structuralists. In developing and revising certain concepts of Russian formalism, they maintained a clear distinction between the text as stable structure and the realization of that structure by the reader. They believed that by seeing the work of art as a complex sign which mediated between the artist and the receiver, the social dimension of reception became prominent. This line of thought was taken up and explored further by the School of Constance. From quite a different angle, reception was also influenced by insights deriving from speech act theory. Here, too, the focus was on the effect achieved by language usage.

In its turn, concepts developed by reception theory proved to be fruitful for many other related areas of research, including the following most prominent ones. Theoretical studies have been complemented by a vast amount of empirical work in which the actual reception of texts by various types of readers is monitored under controlled conditions. This has developed into a specialized field of research. Sociology of knowledge has emphasized the historical relativity of knowledge; that is, the effect which the position of the observer—the observer's place in history and in the social network—has on the observer's perception of reality. Critical hermeneutics gave rise to the development of "materialistic" readings of texts, where both production and reception are understood in terms of the interaction of socioeconomic forces. Psychological studies of the reading process have made use of reception insights, while communication theory as a whole has benefited from this interchange. In the earlier stages of development, the work of Iser represented the only significant link between RRT and reception theory. However, as a result of the ongoing exchange of ideas, the different schools and traditions can no longer be separated so easily.

C. Basic Concepts

1. The Implied and Other Readers. Pivotal for all types of reception theory or RRT is the role of the reader. The basic assumption is that every text presupposes a specific reader, whether this is a concrete person or only a hypothetical receiver. This reader influences the way in which the text is structured and framed, and the author of the text assumes that the reader has the ability required to decode and understand what is written.

The reader or readers may be explicitly identified, even addressed by name (for example, Theophilus in Luke 1:3), or their presence may be only assumed. In the course of time a wide variety of readers has been listed, but it was only with the introduction of Wolfgang Iser's concept of the "implied reader" that the reader became an important feature of the methodology for the interpretation of texts. Iser intended this "reader" to serve as a theoretical construct, to account for the presence of the reader in the text without having to deal with the additional complications posed by a real reader. The "implied reader" was devised as a counterpart to the concept of the "implied author." The reason for these distinctions was the recognition that whoever the real author of a literary text might be, the text itself is written from a specific point of view and addressed to a specific reader who shares a certain minimum amount of knowledge with the author, if any communication is to take place via the text.

However, the implied author and the implied reader are not the only participants. Within the text itself, a further set may be introduced in the form of a narrator and an addressee. For example, in the gospel of Mark, the author presupposes that his readers will have a reading knowledge of Greek and will understand references to tax collectors, the book of Isaiah, the Pharisees, and so forth. But within his story he introduces Jesus as a narrator of parables, with Jesus' disciples as audience. On still a further level of embedding, the owner of the vineyard communicates with his servants, who form yet another audience (Mark 12).

Because of this complexity of textual structures, it is important to distinguish between the various receivers. Some are present only "inside" the text—not as real readers, but as possible roles which the real reader might adopt. Examples are the so-called mock reader whose role the real reader is invited to assume, if only temporarily; the addressee who is often explicitly identified; the implied reader who is in possession of the minimum qualities necessary to make sense of the text; and the ideal or model reader who has the competence to follow all the nuances and to realize the potential of the text to its fullest. On the other hand, some readers are clearly "outside" the text. These are real readers like the first or original readers of a text, the past readers who constitute the history of the reception of the text, the composite or communal reader who has accumulated the critical experience of a specific community or of previous generations, or the present reader of the text.

In the long run, however, it becomes problematic to keep intratextual and extratextual readers neatly separated. The "implied reader," as such, illustrates the problem. Although originally conceived as a means of accounting for the presence of the reader without having to deal with a real reader, the implied reader does become the point of entrance for the real reader by representing the stance which the latter attempts to adopt. Iser is therefore forced to define the implied reader both as a textual structure *(Textstruktur)* and as a structured act *(Aktstruktur)*. This dual definition of the concept of the implied reader enables Iser to move to and fro from text to reader, but it has also given rise to the criticism that he can do so only because the relationship between these two aspects remains vague. A clearer understanding of the interaction between the real and the implied reader remains one of the areas in RRT that needs further methodological refinement.

2. Gaps and the Indeterminacy of the Text. Exponents of RRT point out that clues are offered to the reader on various levels of the text. These can come in the form of linguistic indicators, like second-person pronouns, vocative forms, and direct commands. On the rhetorical level, rhetorical questions or other strategies can be used to elicit sympathy or arouse aversion. In the world created by the text, a specific value system can be introduced, offering the reader new possibilities for self-understanding. In Gal 3:28, the "status" of the believer is redefined in contrast to existing norms of the social system. Petersen (1985) has shown how kinship relations play an important role in the symbolic universe developed in the letter to Philemon. Whether the actual reader accepts the role(s) offered by the text is a matter of the appropriation of the text.

Despite these indicators which guide the reader in a certain direction, RRT insists that indeterminacy is a basic characteristic of the literary text. What is revealed in the text is at the same time accompanied by what remains concealed. It is this dialectic between what is explicit and what is implicit, between the known and the unknown, which sets the reading process in motion. According to Iser, the text contains certain deliberate "gaps" or "open spaces." These structured blanks spur the reader to action and entice the reader to supply the missing information in order to make sense of what is said. In this way, the text requires an input from the reader and makes the reader co-responsible for the creation of the text as meaningful communication.

3. The Wandering Viewpoint. The introduction of readers other than the present reader is one way in which the mediating potential of the text comes to the surface. Instead of confronting the reader with only one possible role, the text offers a variety of options. The reader can therefore be present in the text in more than one way. This is what Iser means by the so-called "wandering viewpoint" of the reader. Various textual perspectives are open to the reader—that of the narrator, the characters, the plot, and the implied reader. In moving backwards and forwards between these perspectives, the reader will find that different segments of the text are brought into the foreground, while others become marginal. In presenting these different options to the reader, the text is in fact mediating between the reader's position and where the text would like the reader to be.

4. Criticism. Criticism of both the theory and practice of RRT comes from two opposing quarters. Some maintain that the method destabilizes the text, ignores its constraints, and opens up the gates for all forms of subjectivism. Others object (especially from a deconstructionist perspective) that RRT is not prepared to accept the consequences of its own position. Having recognized the creative input of the reader, it stops halfway by still insisting that the text exercise a decisive control over the reader. RRT proponents have tried to counter this by distinguishing between two stages of reading—the first recognizing the text as a closed system of signs (text-immanent), the second taking the reader's sign system into account (text-transcendent). Even so, the paradox between the constraints of the text and the freedom of the reader remains a methodological challenge.

D. Reader Response Theory and Biblical Literature

Because of the persuasive nature of biblical literature, which presupposes a response from its readers, RRT is of special significance for this type of material. Even before reader reception became a focal point in literary theory, biblical scholars had already addressed many of the issues raised by RRT, even if this did not form part of an overall methodological system. The work already done may be conveniently discussed under the heading "audience criticism" (D.1.). However, recent developments in general literary theory have brought the problems of reception in biblical texts sharply into focus (see section D.2.).

1. Audience Criticism. The question of who the addressees of the various books of the Bible are has always been an important theme in biblical interpretation. Most classical introductions to biblical literature include a standard section on the intended receivers of a prophetic book, a gospel, or a letter. The underlying assumption is that this material is dialogical in nature, and an adequate understanding of the text is therefore dependent on having sufficient information about the circumstances and viewpoints of the receiving party.

It is therefore not surprising that various forms of *audience criticism* have been practiced by biblical scholars. This term was first used in a biblical context by Baird in his study on the Corinthian Church (1969), but as in the case of RRT, it is a concept which has its origin in general literary studies and which in essence is a synonym for RRT (cf. Suleiman 1980: 6).

In the study of biblical literature, a variety of methods, ranging from form criticism to sociological analyses, have been employed to obtain information regarding audiences. A classic example is the case of Paul's opponents, where studies by Schmithals, Wilckens, and Georgi on the Corinthian situation continued along some avenues opened up by the historical-religious work of Bousset and Reitzenstein, and even reached back to the work of F. C. Baur. Techniques employed in this process include the gathering of data from direct and indirect historical references; the use of references based on rhetorical, epistolographic, or sociological grounds; and the application of mirror readings—that is, assuming that the adversaries' viewpoint is the opposite of what is stated in the polemical sections of the writings.

Studies of a sociological nature, exemplified by the work of Theissen, Kee, Malherbe, Scroggs, and others, have further stimulated the investigation of audiences. Many independent studies of individual books have been made, for example John (Brown 1979), Mark (Kee 1977), Hebrews (Jewett 1981), and 1 Peter (Elliot 1981).

2. New Developments. Audience criticism discussed so far remains by and large part of a historical undertaking. The aim has been to obtain reliable data about the real receivers and their circumstances as an aid to a better understanding of the texts. The frequent lack of such data and other methodological problems have led recent researchers to employ RRT primarily as a literary technique. Examples are the work of Crossan (1980) and Du Plessis (1985) on the parables, Culpepper (1983) and Staley (1985) on John, Fowler (1981) on Mark, Petersen (1985) on Philemon, Wuellner (1977) on Romans, and McKnight (1985) on general theory. The text is understood as a literary entity in the first place, with strict adherence to intratextual categories. The focus, inter alia, is on the reader as textual construct and on the world or symbolic universe created by the text. Both narrative and nonnarrative material have been analyzed in this way—the latter analyzation resulting in an interest in rhetorical strategies. The importance of historical issues is not denied, but a literary approach is preferred as the primary means of gaining an understanding of the text. With the growing interest in RRT and its application on biblical material, the challenge remains to clarify the referential potential of these texts and their relationship to extratextual reality.

Bibliography

General Literature

Dijk, T. A. van. 1981. *Studies in the Pragmatics of Discourse.* The Hague.

Eco, U. 1979. *The Role of the Reader.* Bloomington.

Grimm, G. 1977. *Rezeptionsgeschichte.* Munich.

Holub, R. C. 1984. *Reception Theory.* London.

Iser, W. 1974. *The Implied Reader.* Baltimore.

———. 1978. *The Act of Reading.* Baltimore.

Jauss, H. R. 1970. *Literaturgeschichte als Provokation.* Frankfurt.

Suleiman, S., and Crosman, I., eds. 1980. *The Reader in the Text.* Princeton.

Tompkins, J. P., ed. 1980. *Reader Response Criticism.* Baltimore.

Biblical Material

Baird, J. A. 1969. *Audience Criticism and the Historical Jesus.* Philadelphia.

Brown, R. E. 1979. *The Community of the Beloved Disciple.* New York.

Crossan, J. D. 1980. *Cliffs of Fall: Paradox and Polyvalence in the Parables of Jesus.* New York.

Culpepper, A. 1983. *The Anatomy of the Fourth Gospel.* Philadelphia.

Detweiler, R., ed. 1985. Reader Response Approaches to Biblical and Secular Texts. *Semeia* 31. Decatur.

Du Plessis, J. G. 1985. Clarity and Obscurity: A Study in Textual Communication of the Relation between Sender, Parable and Receiver in the Synoptic Gospels. Diss., Stellenbosch.

Elliot, J. H. 1981. *A Home for the Homeless: A Sociological Exegesis of I Peter.* Philadelphia.

Fowler, R. M. 1981. *Loaves and Fishes: The Function of the Feeding Stories in the Gospel of Mark.* SBLDS 54. Chico, CA.

Jewett, R. 1981. *Letter to Pilgrims: A Commentary on the Epistle to the Hebrews.* New York.

Kee, H. C. 1977. *Community of the New Age: Studies in Mark's Gospel.* Philadelphia.

Lategan, B. C., and Vorster, W. S. 1985. *Text and Reality.* Philadelphia.

Lundin, R.; Thiselton, A. C.; and Walhout, C. 1985. *The Responsibility of Hermeneutics.* Grand Rapids.

McKnight, E. V. 1985. *The Bible and the Reader.* Philadelphia.

Meeks, W. A. 1983. *The First Urban Christians.* New Haven.

Petersen, N. R. 1985. *Rediscovering Paul: Philemon and the Sociology of Paul's Narrative World.* Philadelphia.

Staley, J. L. 1985. *The Print's First Kiss: A Rhetorical Investigation of the Implied Reader in the Fourth Gospel.* Diss., Berkeley.

Theissen, G. 1979. *Studien zur Soziologie des Urchristentums.* WMANT 19. Tübingen.

Wuellner, W. 1977. Paul's Rhetoric of Argumentation in Romans. Pp. 252–74 in *The Romans Debate,* ed. K. P. Donfried. Minneapolis.

———. 1987. Where Is Rhetorical Criticism Taking Us? *CBQ* 49: 448–63.

Bernard C. Lategan

READINGS, CONFLATED. See CONFLATE READINGS IN THE OT.

REAIAH (PERSON) [Heb *rĕʾāyāh*]. The name given to three men in the Hebrew Bible.

1. A Judahite, the second generation removed from Judah. He was the son of Shobal and the father of Jahath (1 Chr 4:2).

2. A Reubenite, of the family of Joel. He was the son of Micah and the father of Baal (1 Chr 5:5).

3. The name of a family of temple servants who returned to Palestine with Zerubbabel shortly after 538 B.C.E., the end of the Babylonian Exile. The name appears in Ezra 2:47 in the phrase "the sons of Reaiah" (Gk *Reēa*), where the temple servants are distinguished from the people of Israel, the priests, and the Levites. The parallel passage (Neh 7:50) also lists "the sons of Reaiah" (Gk *Raaia*/*Raea*), as does the later parallel 1 Esdr 5:31 (Gk *Iairos*).

Steven R. Swanson

REAPING. See HARVESTS, HARVESTING; AGRICULTURE.

REBA (PERSON) [Heb *rebaʿ*]. A Midianite king (Num 31:8; Josh 13:21). Historically, the five Midianite kings or chiefs in Numbers 31, also mentioned in Joshua 13, are difficult to date and locate. Albright (1970) assumed that the Midianite war described in Numbers 31 antedated the domestication of the camel (an observation which would now lead into the 3d millennium B.C.; Knauf 1988: 9–10). Knauf suggested interpreting these five "kings" as a list of place names that form an itinerary through N Arabia and S Transjordan in the Persian period (Knauf 1988: 166–67). As a personal name, Reba has parallels in Hadramitic, Lihyanite, Safaitic, and classical Arabic *Rabîᶜ* and *Rubaiᶜ* (Knauf 1988: 90), i.e., from the 5th century B.C. onwards. For Reba as a place name, Râbiġ, a port city of the Ḥijâz, and, more likely, Naqb Rubâᶜî, the main access to Petra from Wadi ᶜArabah, provide possible identifications.

Bibliography

Albright, W. F. 1970. Midianite Donkey Caravans. Pp. 197–205 in *Translating and Understanding the Old Testament,* ed. H. T. Frank and W. L. Reed. Nashville.

Knauf, E. A. 1988. *Midian.* ADPV. Wiesbaden.

ERNST AXEL KNAUF

REBEKAH (PERSON) [Heb *ribqâ*]. Var. REBECCA. Wife of Isaac, mother of the twins Esau and Jacob, daughter of Bethuel (Abraham's nephew), and sister of Laban (Gen 22:23). She is thus also Isaac's cousin once removed, since her grandfather Nahor was Abraham's brother. See Fig. REB.01.

Older etymologies derive the name from the root *rbq,* "to tie fast" (cf. the Heb *ribqâ,* "a looped cord for tying young animals"). It may also constitute a wordplay on the Heb *baqar,* "cattle" (note the metathesis of the *reš*), thus making it analogous to other names in the patriarchal narratives, such as Rachel ("ewe"), or Leah ("cow"), and Zilpah ("short-nosed animal").

The story of Rebekah, beautifully narrated in high literary style, forms the conclusion of the Abraham saga. In his old age, Abraham decides that Isaac, the bearer of Yahweh's promise, should not intermarry with the daughters of the Canaanites (Gen 24:3). This act of securing a bride for Isaac is Abraham's last deed, which is carried out by his most trusted servant. While the servant is not named in this chapter, it is often suggested that he is Eliezer of Damascus, named as Abraham's majordomo in chap. 15. It is noteworthy that the betrothal is to take place by proxy, since Isaac never leaves home. Abraham won't allow Isaac out of his sight, as it were, for several reasons: the lateness of his birth after years of promise, coupled with the strange story of his near-sacrifice (chap. 22). In addition, Abraham has just buried Sarah, his wife, in the cave of the field of Machpelah and is mourning her death. Abraham's reluctance to send Isaac himself on the journey back to the Mesopotamian homeland (24:8–10) is an interesting contrast to Rebekah's later treatment of Jacob: she only too willingly parts with her favorite son and is actually eager to send him back to her homeland because of Esau's anger over the stolen blessing (27:41–45).

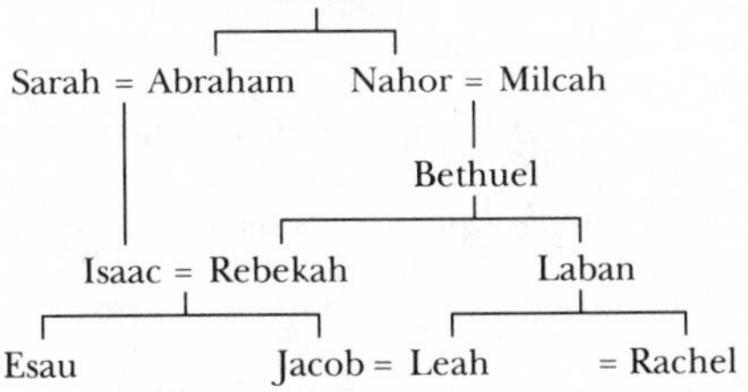

REB.01. Genealogy of Rebekah. See also Fig. RAC.01.

Abraham's servant arrives outside the city of Nahor with his retinue of ten camels, laden with choice gifts for the future bride. It is a princely scene that awaits the maiden as she approaches the well at evening time. Rebekah is beautiful but not passive. She becomes the focal point of purposeful activity. She addresses the servant, draws water, fills her jar, gives drink, draws water for the camels (Gen 24:16–20). She gives consent and determines that she will go with Abraham's servant without delay (Gen 24:58). In later years, she will again become the focal point of purposeful activity in securing the paternal blessing for her favorite son, Jacob. She manipulates the action, devises the plan to fool Isaac, and prepares the savory food. She is the most clever and authoritative of the matriarchs, and yet she epitomizes womanly beauty and virtue, in her conduct (her virginity, her actions at the well), in her energetic speech, in her thoughtful courtesy, and in her self-assurance.

The story assumes that Rebekah has been appointed by the Lord to be Isaac's wife, since events seemingly unfold according to divine providence (Gen 24:11–21, 50–51). Even though Rebekah has never met Isaac, she agrees to the marriage because, in a sense, they are not strangers: both are aware of common family ties and history. The betrothal scene (vv 34–51) is elaborately described in ceremonial language as a formal treaty between two branches of the Terah clan. The bestowal of gifts upon the future bride (v 53) is rendered in detail, and negotiations are couched in diplomatic language (vv 49, 54–58). Laban, keenly conscious of his sister's newfound favor, blessings, and gifts, takes sudden cognizance of her (Gen 24:30–31) as he will also later note that Jacob's herds have multiplied by divine providence and blessing (Gen 30:27–36). Her farewell from her father's household is accompanied by a shower of blessings: "Our sister, be the mother of thousands of ten thousands; and may your descendants possess the gate of those who hate them" (Gen 24:60). The symbolism of the doubling of fertility motifs in the farewell blessing and the offering of life-giving water at the well is intentional. Upon her arrival at her future husband's dwelling place (vv 63–64), their first encounter is poignantly rendered and leaves a powerful visual impression on the reader.

> And Isaac went out to meditate in the field in the evening; and he lifted up his eyes and looked, and behold there were camels coming. And Rebekah lifted up her eyes, and when she saw Isaac, she alighted from the camel.

It concludes (v 67) with the statement:

Then Isaac brought her into the tent, and took Rebekah, and she became his wife; and he loved her. So Isaac was comforted after his mother's death.

Rebekah is barren for the first 20 years of her marriage, and it is only after Isaac's intercessory prayer to God that she conceives (25:21). Barrenness, although exceptional, is a recurrent element in biblical birth stories, and the Bible concentrates on these exceptions. Frequently, barrenness and a son born in advanced age are viewed as proof of divine purpose, such as in the cases of Sarah (mother of Isaac), Rachel (mother of Joseph and Benjamin), the unnamed mother of Samson, Hannah (mother of Samuel), and Elizabeth (mother of John the Baptist). In each case, the offspring is destined to fulfill a special role in the history of Israel. In the case of Rebekah, Yahweh indicates a special purpose concerning the destiny of the two boys who struggle within her womb: "And the Lord said to her, 'Two nations are in your womb, and two peoples, born of you, will be divided, the one will be stronger than the other, the greater the lesser will serve' " (Gen 25:23). This is purposely ambiguous, like the Delphic oracle, and it sets the stage for discord not only between the boys who are to become the eponymous ancestors of two nations, but also between the nations themselves, for Esau is also called Edom and is considered the forefather of the Edomites (Gen 36:8–9), while Jacob is renamed Israel and becomes the forefather of the Israelites (Gen 35:10–12). In point of fact, the prophecy is not fulfilled in the lifetime of either Jacob or Esau, although most scholars think the reference is to the subsequent history of the two peoples, Edom and Israel. Rifts in the family unity are foreshadowed in the womb and are borne out in the selling of the birthright and the stealing of the blessing. The result is that Esau, the father's favorite son, is deprived of his status as firstborn and principal heir. Jacob, who is called "the supplanter," obtains the patriarchal blessing from his aged and blind father, Isaac. It is Rebekah who takes the initial and decisive action by instructing Jacob in deceiving his father, her husband, for in spite of such deception she wants the blessing for her favored son. However, this action is foreshadowed by Esau's abrupt selling of his birthright to his twin brother for a portion of pottage (Gen 25:30–33), and it can be interpreted to demonstrate that Esau is not fit to fulfill divine destiny as the one through whom God's promise to Abraham will move toward fulfillment. The bestowing of the blessing is formulated in legalistic terms and is intended to be a binding pact (Gen 27:28–29). Esau's agonized cry is mitigated by the separate "blessing" which Isaac pronounces upon him (Gen 27:39–40), but which results in his homicidal hatred of Jacob (Gen 27:41), causing the latter to seek refuge among Rebekah's kindred, with her brother Laban, in Haran. Here we have a schematic repetition in Rebekah's charge to seek a wife for Jacob from among her own kindred, just as Abraham had charged his servant to seek a wife for Isaac among his kindred. See RACHEL.

There is no mention that Jacob ever saw his mother again after his sojourn in Haran; rather, he found comfort with Rachel just as Isaac had found comfort with Rebekah. Nor is there mention of Rebekah's death, although Gen 49:31 reports her burial in the family cave at Machpelah, together with Abraham, Sarah, Isaac, Jacob (but not Esau), and Leah. She is revered as the second of the four great matriarchs of the patriarchal age. In the NT, Paul refers to Rebekah to demonstrate God's divine elective purpose and grace, mercy, and compassion (Rom 9:10–11).

Bibliography

Alter, R. 1981. *The Art of Biblical Narrative.* New York.
Auerback, E. 1965. *Mimesis.* Princeton.
Fokkelman, J. P. 1975. *Narrative Art in Genesis.* Assen and Amsterdam.
Speiser, E. A. 1964. *Genesis.* AB. Garden City, NY.

Astrid Billes Beck

RECAH (PLACE) [Heb *rēkâ*]. An as yet unidentified place mentioned in 1 Chr 4:12. Some suggest that Recah should be read Rechab with LXX B, which would ostensibly provide linkage with 1 Chr 2:55.

David Salter Williams

RECHAB (PERSON) [Heb *rēkāb*]. RECHABITE. Name belonging to two individuals in the Hebrew Bible.

A. Biblical Evidence
B. "Nomadic Ideal" and Guilds
C. Rechabite Discipline and Metallurgy
D. Genealogical Lists in Chronicles

A. Biblical Evidence

Biblical references concerning Rechab and the Rechabites are quite limited. There are two individuals named Rechab in the Bible. One of these is Rechab, a Benjaminite, son of Rimmon, who together with his brother, Baanah, was a leader of a raiding band under Saul's son Ishbosheth. Following the death of Abner, Rechab and Baanah killed Ishbosheth and brought his head to David, from whom they expected a reward. Instead, David had them both executed (2 Sam 4:1–3, 5–12). The other biblical Rechab appears either as the father or ancestor of one Jehonadab (Heb *yehônādāb*; or Jonadab [Heb *yônādāb*] in Jeremiah) ben Rechab in 2 Kgs 10:15–17, where he allies himself with Jehu's coup. It is apparently this latter Rechab who became the patriarch of a group who called themselves Rechabites, a group which came to Jerusalem to escape Nebuchadnezzar's invasion and are mentioned in relation to Jeremiah in Jeremiah 35.

Rechabites also appear in genealogical lists in 1 Chronicles. In 1 Chr 2:55, the "house of Rechab" (Heb *bêt-rēkāb*) is associated with the Kenites: "These are the Kenites (or smiths) who came from Hammath, the father of the house of Rechab." In 1 Chronicles 4, which is more than a genealogy in the strict sense of the word, in a part of a list of the sons of Caleb and Ephrathah, who apparently lived in the region between Bethlehem and Hebron, there is the following notice: "Chelub (or Caleb), the brother of Shuhah, was the father of Mehir, who was the father of Eshton. Eshton was the father of Bethrapha, Paseah, and Tehinnah, the father of Ir-nahash. These are the men of Rechab" (reading Rechab with the LXX Vaticanus and the Lucianic text instead of Recah, Heb *rēkâ;* 1 Chr 4:11–12).

Here, the Rechabites appear in a list which refers to the founders of various guilds whose names were associated with localities where they pursued their trade.

It is in Jeremiah that the unique discipline of the Rechabites is described. Here, Jeremiah brings the entire "house of the Rechabites" into a single chamber of the temple in order to use them as a test case in obedience. In response to an offer of wine from Jeremiah, they respond: "We will drink no wine, for Jonadab (= Jehonadab), the son of Rechab, our father, commanded us, 'You shall not drink wine, neither you nor your sons for ever; you shall not build a house; you shall not sow seed; you shall not plant or have a vineyard; but you shall live in tents all your days, that you may live many days in the land where you sojourn'" (Jer 35: 6–7). The Rechabites are then used by Jeremiah as an example of a people which has remained faithful to commandments, in contrast to the people of Israel.

B. "Nomadic Ideal" and Guilds

Because of their peculiar discipline, the Rechabites have often been described as a puritanical, clanlike association which lived a nomadic existence in celebration of a supposed "nomadic ideal" and as a religiously motivated protest against the prevailing way of life in the cities of the divided monarchy. The labeling of the Rechabites as nomads has rested on several assumptions, based on their unique regimen: (1) that abstention from intoxicants is a distinctive trait of a nomadic society; (2) that tent dwelling necessarily suggests nomadism; and (3) that the disdaining of agriculture is a sure sign of nomadism. It is, however, questionable whether these cultural traits can justifiably be interpreted as characteristics peculiar to nomadic groups. The same traits can also fit the description of the way of life of an itinerant guild of craftsmen, probably here a guild of metalworkers involved in the making of chariots and other weaponry.

In the introduction of the group's patriarch, Jehonadab ben Rechab in 2 Kings 10, there is no indication whatsoever that he represented a supposed "nomadic ideal," or even that he lived a nomadic existence. The fact that Jehu met Jehonadab somewhere between Samaria and Jezreel can hardly be used as evidence for the existence of an otherwise unmentioned group of Rechabites. Jehonadab's name (Jonadab in Jer 35) combines a variant of the divine name Yahweh with the triliteral Hebrew root *n-d-b*. The noun *nādîb,* formed on this root, is used in the Bible to denote a member of the ruling class, an administrator or head of a prominent family—in short, a person of position, a member of the urban nobility. All biblical names containing this root belong to such persons, and there is no apparent reason for considering Jehonadab to be an exception (cf. Amminadab [Exod 6:23; 24:19; 28:1]); Nadab, son of Jeroboam [1 Kgs 14:20; 15:25]; Nadab, king of Israel [1 Kgs 15:25]; Nedabiah [1 Chr 3:18]; Abinadab [1 Sam 31:2]; and Ahinadab [1 Kings 4:14]).

There is no way of determining whether the designation of Jehonadab as *ben rēkāb* refers to a actual father-son appellation, or whether *ben* should be understood here in one of the other ways in which it is commonly used in the Bible. It could, for example, mean simply a descendant of Rechab. The designation *ben,* like the Akkadian terms *māru* and *aplu,* could also mean that the person in question is a member of a certain occupational group or guild. Guilds followed the model of the family system from which they originated. The heads of such guilds were given the familial designation "father," while the apprentices were called "sons" (Mendelsohn 1940: 18–19). Prophetic guilds are sometimes designated this way in the Bible (cf. Amos 7:14; 2 Kgs 2:3, 5, 15). In the economic and administrative texts from Late Bronze Ugarit, there is a group in the royal service called *ḥrš-mrkbt,* "chariot makers or wainwrights" (Rainey 1962: 167), and the designation *ben rēkāb* may indicate that Jehonadab was a member of such an occupational group.

One further possibility is to understand *ben rēkāb* as suggesting that Jehonadab was a native of a place called Rechab, which in turn may have derived its name from that of a clan. If Rechab is to be understood as a place name, it could be Beth-marcaboth (Josh 19:5; 1 Chr 4:31), which according to Cohen derived its name from the fact that Solomon selected it as a suitable location for the manufacture and storage of chariots (*IDB* 3: 220; cf. 2 Chr 9:25).

C. Rechabite Discipline and Metallurgy

In his comprehensive study of *Metallurgy in Antiquity* (1964: 64–68), Forbes makes several observations about the smith in antiquity which are pertinent to an assessment of the Rechabite discipline. In a preindustrial society, the smith had to be familiar with many technical procedures, the knowledge of which was handed down and guarded jealously from one generation to the next. When the smith was among agriculturalists, there was emphasis on the guild form of organization, which implied initiation into the technical traditions of the craft, and which in turn retained traits of the original clan organization. Metallurgists in antiquity, as a rule, formed proud endogamous lines of families with lengthy genealogies, which could account for the staying power of the biblical Rechabites, who apparently maintained their discipline at least from the 9th to the 6th centuries B.C. While the smith was characteristically a social outcast among nomads and pastoralists, his social status among agriculturalists was just as typically an honored one.

The nature of his work prevented the smith from establishing a permanent domicile or from engaging in agriculture. Smiths would stay in one general locale from a few months up to several years, or until the supply of ore and/or fuel at that place was exhausted. Whereas other craftsmen might engage in part-time agricultural work, the smith's work required such skill and long practice that he could not farm. The Rechabite discipline might thus be seen as one appropriate to smiths.

The Rechabites' avoidance of intoxicants has often been interpreted as a survival of the nomad's contempt for unnatural fermented beverages. It is, however, questionable whether this is a trait of nomads (Albright 1963: 11–12). Like other measures which were designed to guard the secrets of the trade, such as living apart from urban centers, so too might abstention from intoxicants be yet another safeguard to prevent "loose lips" from "sinking ships." It might also be observed that in the perilous times of Nebuchadnezzar's invasion, the Rechabites, who have commonly been characterized as "antiurban nomads," fled to the "hated" city for protection. If they had been nomadic pastoralists, it seems unlikely that they would have fled to the city rather than move to the desert fringe with their flocks, where they might escape the enemy attack which would focus on the urban centers.

D. Genealogical Lists in Chronicles

The supposition that the Rechabites were a guild of metallurgical craftsmen is also supported by genealogical references in 1 Chronicles 2 and 4. 1 Chronicles 4 is part of a preexilic Judahite list which provides elements missing from the list in 1 Chronicles 2. In the genealogy which can be reconstructed by combining information from these two chapters, the sons of various clans (or members of guilds) are mentioned along with the names of their respective settlements in such a way that one clansman becomes the "father" of a site (cf. *LBHG,* 225–26) In the branch of the list which records the sons of Caleb and Ephrathah, the "men of Rechab" are associated with an Ir-nahash [Heb *ʿîr nāḥāš*], which can be translated either as "the city of Nahash," "the city of copper," or even "the city of smiths or craftsmen," which Myers identifies with Khirbet Nahas, a site at the northern end of the Arabah (1 Chronicles *AB,* 26).

Besides this mention of an Ir-nahash with which the men of Rechab are associated, 1 Chronicles 4 also contains several other references which associate Rechabites with other craftsmen such as Joab, a Kenazite, who is called "the father of Ge-harashim," (i.e., "valley of craftsmen," 4:14); "the families of the house of linen workers at Beth Ashbea" (4:21); and "the potters and inhabitants of Netaim and Gederah," who "dwelt with the king for his work" (4:23).

In 1 Chr 2:55, there is the following notice connected with the sons of Hur who lived in the vicinity of Bethlehem and the northeastern Shephelah around the valley of Elah: ". . . the families (or guilds) of the Sepherites (i.e., inhabitants of Kiriath-Sepher) who dwelt in Jabez: the Tirathites (cf. 1 Chr 4:16), the Shimeathites (cf. 1 Chr 4:17), and the Sucathites (cf. 1 Chr 4:18). These are the Kenites (or 'smiths') who came from Hammath, the father of Beth-rechab." The significance of this verse is that here the name Rechab, or to be specific, Beth-Rechab, "the house of Rechab," is connected with a given location and with a branch of the Kenites, who as early as the 13th century appear to have made their livelihood as metal craftsmen and may well have introduced metallurgical technical skills to the Israelites. Forbes suggests that the Kenites were a group of ironsmiths who came out of the Hittite empire when it was destroyed, and he observes that "the despise in which these 'townsmen' were held by . . . nomads is well expressed in the story of the shepherds and the daughter of Reuel the Kenite" (1964: 98).

It does not appear that the Rechabites can be adduced in evidence of the existence of a "nomadic ideal" in ancient Israel. The lifestyle of the Rechabites does not have to be seen as an idealization of desert life. The nonagricultural mode of life of the Rechabites can just as well be seen as an occupational pattern, not a religiously motivated way of life.

Bibliography

Abramsky, S. 1967. The House of Rechab—Genealogy and Military League. *EI* 8: 255–64 (in Hebrew).

Albright, W. F. 1963. *The Biblical Period from Abraham to Ezra.* New York.

Eliade, M. 1962. *The Forge and the Crucible.* Chicago.

Forbes, R. J. 1964. *Metallurgy in Antiquity.* New York.

Frick, F. S. 1971. The Rechabites Reconsidered. *JBL* 90: 279–87.

———. 1977. *The City in Ancient Israel.* SBLDS 36. Missoula, MT.

Mendelsohn, I. 1940. Guilds in Ancient Palestine. *BASOR* 80: 17–21.

Rainey, A. F. 1962. *The Social Stratification of Ugarit.* Ph.D. Diss. Brandeis.

FRANK S. FRICK

RECHABITES, HISTORY OF. This apocryphon is extant in numerous languages, including Ethiopic, Syriac, and Greek. A 12th-century Syr manuscript in the British Library (BM Add. 12174) may well accurately indicate the transmission of this document: "The History of the Blessed Ones, the Sons of the Rechabites . . . It was Translated from Hebrew into Greek and from Greek into Syriac by the Hands of the Reverend Mar Jacob of Edessa" (fols. 209r–210v).

A holy man, named Zosimus in chapters that appear to be later additions, for forty years prays to God to show him the abode of the Blessed Ones, the Rechabites, who departed from Jerusalem in the time of Jeremiah (Jeremiah 35). His prayer is answered, and with the assistance of an angel, an animal, and two trees he succeeds in crossing over land and sea to the island of the Blessed Ones who recount to him their history.

Despite noting that the Jewish work apparently underlines the extant Greek text, M. R. James (1893), who brought the work to the attention of modern scholars, concluded that the document is Christian and dates from the 6th century C.E. In its present Greek form, the document is clearly Christian; vv 12:9a–13:5c mention the virginal conception of the Word and Lent. Chap. 16:1b–8 is also clearly Christian, as are chaps. 19–23, but the latter are found only in the Greek version. Although it is clear that the document in its present form is Christian, the origin of the work is far from certain. It may be a Christian reworking of Jewish traditions or legends; but most specialists rightly see behind the Christian version an original, and partly preserved, Jewish apocryphon, which is an exegetical expansion of Jeremiah 35 (*OTP* 2: 444–45). If this conclusion is valid, the *History of the Rechabites* contains portions of an otherwise lost Jewish document; it is then similar to the *Ascension of Isaiah,* the *Testaments of the Twelve Patriarchs, 4 Ezra,* and the *Hellenistic Synagogal Prayers.*

It may well be that chaps. 3–15 are originally Jewish. Obviously they are heavily influenced by Jewish traditions. It is conceivable that the original Jewish document, without the redactional and Christian alterations, antedates the 2d century C.E. This apocryphon shows links with numerous non-Jewish cultures, including Roman, Greek, Syrian, Persian, and Egyptian (Charlesworth 1986). The Greek version frequently contains the name of Zosimus in chaps. 3–16; each of these occurrences, except for 7:11, are conspicuously absent in the Syr version (which appears to be earlier and more reliable). Even if the name Zosimus is original, an interest in him is replaced by a preoccupation with the Rechabites in chaps. 7–9 in all versions. These chapters, the core of the document, are an expanded exegesis of Jeremiah 35 and were probably composed by a Jew. Particularly noteworthy are the words the Rechabites write on tablets of stone: "We are called sons of Rechab, we are from you; and behold we departed from your world to this place in which we (are) today. For in the time when Jeremiah, the prophet, announced and prophesied the ravaging and devastation (of) Jerusalem, because of the sins of the sons of Israel, then behold shortly (thereafter) the destroyer came to slay them . . . we lamented with a great lamentation . . . he (God) accepted our petitions, and turned back his fierce anger. . . . King Josiah died and another king ruled after him . . . we answered him, 'We are from your people, and from the city of Jerusalem. We are sons of Jonadab the son of Rechab.' . . . The king raged against us and charged (that) all of us be imprisoned in prison . . . and angels of God . . . appeared to us. They led all of us out of prison . . . brought us to this place (in) which you (now) see (us). . . ." Here we confront interesting traditions often paralleled in early Jewish traditions and documents like the *Lost Tribes.*

Bibliography

Charlesworth, J. H. 1985. History of the Rechabites. *OTP* 2: 443–61.

———. 1986. Greek, Persian, Roman, Syrian, and Egyptian Influences in Early Jewish Theology: A Study of the History of the Rechabites. Pp. 219–43 in *Hellenica et Judaica: Hommage à Valentin Nikiprowetzky*, ed. A. Caquot et al. Leuven-Paris.

James, M. R. 1893. Narratio Zosimi. Pp. 96–108 in *Apocrypha Anecdota.* Cambridge.

McNeil, B. 1978. The Narration of Zosimus. *JSJ* 9: 68–82.

Zanolli, A. 1924. La leggenda di Zosimo secondo la redazione armena. *Giornale della Società Asiatica Italiana* n.s. 1: 146–62.

JAMES H. CHARLESWORTH

RECORDER. See SCRIBES.

RED HEIFER. See HEIFER, RED.

RED SEA (PLACE) [Heb *yam sûp*]. This NW arm of the Indian Ocean, ranging in width from 100 to 175 miles, separates the African continent from the Arabian peninsula and is the reputed body of water through which the Hebrew slaves, led by Moses, escaped from Egypt (book of Exodus). At its northernmost end it splits into two gulfs. The Gulf of Suez, whose width ranges between 20 and 30 miles, separates the Sinai peninsula from Egypt (and Africa) to the W. The Gulf of Aqabah, ranging 10–20 miles in width, separates the Sinai peninsula from the Hijaz (and Arabia) to the E. This entry will focus on two separate aspects of the Red Sea: (1) its appearance in the OT in connection with Israelite traditions about the Exodus from Egypt; and (2) its history of commercial exploitation in antiquity.

OLD TESTAMENT

The term *yam sûp,* usually translated "Red Sea," occurs over 20 times in the Hebrew Bible. It has traditionally been linked to at least three geographical locations: the Gulf of Aqabah, the Gulf of Suez, and the body of water associated with the Exodus crossing. The precise location of the latter—whether sea, lake, or marsh—has been especially problematic for biblical scholars and Egyptologists, both of whom have appealed to extrabiblical evidence (both Canaanite and Egyptian) in support of their positions.

In order to understand more clearly the various issues associated with locating the sea of the Exodus, it is important to examine first those texts that mention *yam sûp* within a context not directly related to the crossing. It should be noted at the outset that certainty of identification is not always possible; thus, some passages must remain ambiguous.

A. Gulf of Aqabah
B. Gulf of Suez
C. The Sea of the Exodus
   1. Character of the Exodus Event (Exodus 13–15)
   2. Other Texts
D. Origin and Meaning of Hebrew *Sûp*
   1. Scholarly Views
   2. Egyptian *Ṯwf*
E. *Yam Sûp* and Mythology
F. Location of the Sea of the Exodus
   1. Raamses
   2. Baal-Zephon
   3. Migdol
   4. Pi-hahiroth
G. Conclusion

A. Gulf of Aqabah

More than a half dozen passages seem to identify *yam sûp* with the Gulf of Aqabah (Exod 23:31; Num 14:25; 21:4; Deut 1:40; 2:1; Judg 11:16[?]; 1 Kgs 9:26; Jer 49:21). Scholars generally agree that the *yam sûp* of 1 Kgs 9:26 refers to the Gulf of Aqabah. Here the sea is said to be "in the land of Edom" and marks the southernmost border of the territory under Solomon. In the same fashion, the idealized description of the land in Exod 23:31, intended to reflect the Solomonic period, sets its southernmost boundary at the *yam sûp* (cf. 2 Chr 8:17 ["the sea"]), which makes sense only as the Gulf of Aqabah (e.g., Simons *GTTOT,* 96, 237; Noth *Exodus* OTL, 193; Childs *Exodus* OTL, 193–94; Davies 1979: 112; Aharoni *LBHG,* 277). With the exception of Jer 49:21, the remaining five passages all relate to the period following the Exodus from Egypt, when the Israelites were instructed by Yahweh to proceed E by way of the *yam sûp* in order to avoid confrontation with the inhabitants of S Canaan and the Transjordan. Judges 11:16 is less clear in this regard, and a case can be made for either of the other two options, i.e., the Gulf of Suez or the Exodus crossing (Davies 1979: 82–83). However, since the immediate context of this episode (11:12–22) concerns Israel's bypassing of Edom and Moab, the Gulf of Aqabah may better suit the geographical situation (de Vaux *EHI,* 377 [tentative]; Bietak in *LÄ* 5: 630). In his oracle against Edom, the prophet Jeremiah (Jer 49:7–

22) asserts that, at their destruction, the cry of its inhabitants shall be heard as far away as the *yam sûp*. The most logical choice here (geographically speaking) would be the Gulf of Aqabah (e.g., Noth 1947: 188; de Vaux *EHI,* 377; Bietak in *LÄ* 5: 630; Sarna 1986: 107). The translation "Sea of Reeds" in this verse (even if that should be the original meaning of the phrase) and its identification with the sea of the Exodus (e.g., Bright *Jeremiah* AB, 331; followed by Thompson *Jeremiah* NICOT, 719, 722, and Caroll *Jeremiah* OTL, 805) is thus not necessary. Bright's apparent assumption that *yam sûp* must in all cases refer to the "Sea of Reeds," i.e., the sea of the Exodus, lacks textual support in the light of passages such as 1 Kgs 9:26 examined above (unless of course one contends that the Gulf of Aqabah was the site of the Exodus event, as was done, for example, by earlier scholars; see Davies 1979: 70, 112 for references). Sayce (1894: 257–59) concluded that all occurrences of *yam sûp* referred to the Gulf of Aqabah, to be distinguished from references to "the sea," which he interpreted as the sea of the Exodus.

B. Gulf of Suez

A few passages (Exod 10:19; 13:18; Num 33:10–11) seem to refer to the Gulf of Suez, although the identification of *yam sûp* in these passages has been a matter of some debate among biblical scholars (general discussion in Simons *GTTOT,* 77–78, 234–64; Davies 1979; and de Vaux *EHI,* 376–81). In Exod 10:12–19, the plague of locusts is brought into the country by an east wind and subsequently removed from it by a strong west wind that had been "turned" (Heb *hāpak*) by Yahweh for that purpose (for interpretations of Heb *rûaḥ-yām,* lit. "wind of the sea," see Simons *GTTOT,* 238; Cassuto 1967: 128; Har-El 1983; Anati 1986: 187). Since the narrator wishes the reader to understand that "not a single locust was left in all the country of Egypt," he probably has in mind a suitably large body of water that borders the country. Thus, the internal logic of the narrative (assuming of course that the writer was concerned with such matters; the question of historicity is irrelevant) may favor either the Gulf of Suez (e.g., Snaith 1965: 396; Hubbard in *ISBE* 4: 59) or even the Mediterranean (note Gardiner 1922: 211, who, for other reasons, identified this *yam sûp* as Lake Menzalah). Cassuto (1967: 129) suggested that this verse "may be a preparatory allusion" to what is later said of Pharaoh and his army in Exod 14:28b (". . . not so much as one of them remained") and thus could refer to the sea of the Exodus; although he admitted that the parallelism would be valid regardless of which sea is meant (note also Bietak 1975: 136, who argues for the sea of the Exodus). Although Simons (*GTTOT,* 238) inclines toward the Red Sea as a possibility, he wisely concludes that the passage as it stands is too vague to support any specific theory on the location of *yam sûp*.

In Exod 13:17–19, traditionally assigned to the E source (e.g., Noth *HPT,* 204, and *Exodus* OTL, 106–8; Childs *Exodus* OTL, 218–21; de Vaux *EHI,* 376–78), the narrator offers an explanation as to why the fleeing Israelites did not take the expected (and most direct) route into Palestine, the "Ways of Horus" in Egyptian texts (see Gardiner 1920; Oren in Rainey 1987: 69–119). While it is true that the Egyptian presence in this area would have been deterrent enough (assuming a 13th-century date for the event), the later writer/redactor instead cites the Philistine threat, a more familiar motif within Israel's early history and one to which his readers could relate. (One may question whether he was even aware of Egyptian presence in this area during this earlier period.) In order to avoid such confrontation, the people are led by Yahweh "around by the Way of the Wilderness (that leads to?) the *yam sûp*" (13:18a). Precisely how *yam sûp* is to be understood here in relation to the "Way of the Wilderness" (Heb *derek hammidbār*) is a problem (see, e.g., Childs *Exodus* OTL, 217). The syntactical apposition of the former phrase has led some to conclude that it is a later addition, possibly for geographical clarification (e.g., Noth 1947: 187; Simons *GTTOT,* 236, 241–42; de Vaux *EHI,* 377). If so, could this addition have been influenced by the similar phraseology in those texts cited above, i.e., Num 14:25, Deut 1:40, and Judg 11:16? The rather vague nature (geographically speaking) of this passage—in contrast, for example, to the P source in 14:1–4—and the lack of any mention of this *yam sûp* as the one crossed by the Israelites would allow the location of *yam sûp* to be at the Gulf of Aqabah or the Gulf of Suez (e.g., Simons *GTTOT,* 242; Snaith 1965: 396; de Vaux *EHI,* 377–78). Walsh's translation (1977) "*Yam Sup* Road" may capture the intended sense here, i.e., that the Israelites took the way named for its ultimate destination. Considering the importance of both gulfs in antiquity, this route could have been named for either one. If one follows the more traditional view of a southern route out of Egypt (e.g., Beit-Arieh 1988), which proceeded along the eastern coast of the Gulf of Suez, then the latter body of water would be the more likely choice. However, this identification depends more upon one's view of the route in general and especially the location of Mt. Sinai (for which there are numerous proposals; see Anati 1986: 161–80; Beit-Arieh 1988: 36–37, for the options).

The list of stations preserved in Numbers 33 is generally considered a late text, attributed to P (Cross *CMHE,* 308–9; Budd *Numbers* WBC, 350–53) or in part a post-JEP redaction (e.g., Noth *Numbers* OTL, 242–46). However, all agree that the creator of this list or itinerary as we now have it made use of another document that included place names not found in the traditional pentateuchal sources. The relevance of this other earlier source to P's placement of *yam sûp* (vv 10–11) *after* the Israelites' passage "through the midst of the sea" (v 8)—thus implying that the sea of the Exodus is not the *yam sûp*—has been debated. Noth (*Numbers,* 243–44) considered the mention of the passage through the sea in v 8 a later addition and the placement of *yam sûp* in v 10 after Elim "an erroneous inference" based on a "misunderstanding" of Exod 15:27b, where the Israelites "came to Elim" and "encamped there by the water." Cross (*CMHE,* 309) has also raised the possibility of corruption in Num 33:10, based on P's omission of *yam sûp* in Exod 16:1. Others, however (e.g., Budd *Numbers,* 253–54; Batto 1983: 28–29), accept vv 10–11 as a valuable independent witness (predating P) attesting to the distinction between the sea of the Exodus and the *yam sûp* later reached by the Israelites. If this is the case, then the most likely location of *yam sûp* according to this itinerary would be the Gulf of Suez. Ezion-Geber and the land of Edom, which would indicate the Gulf of Aqabah, are cited only later in v 36. According to Batto (1983: 29–30), P has deliberately telescoped these two sites in Numbers 33 (the "sea" and the "sea of *sûp*") into one in the Exodus narrative (Exod 14:2 ["the sea"] and 15:22 [the "sea of *sûp*"]), and thus intentionally located the crossing at the Red Sea. (Note also the independent source critical analysis of these narratives by Walsh [1977: 32–33], who reaches similar conclusions concerning the late location of the miracle crossing at the Red Sea [Suez]).

C. The Sea of the Exodus

In a number of passages (Exod 15:4, 22; Deut 11:4; Josh 2:10; 4:23; 24:6–7; Pss 106:7–12, 22; 136:13–15; Neh 9:9–11) *yam sûp* refers to the sea of the Exodus. With the exception of Exod 15:4, the location of the sea crossing at the *yam sûp* in the above passages is thought to represent a later tradition (e.g., de Vaux *EHI,* 377). To be sure, not all have accepted an early date (i.e., pre-10th century) for the "Song of the Sea" in Exod 15:1–18 (e.g., Noth *Exodus,* 123–26; see discussion in Childs *Exodus,* 243–48, and Kloos 1986: 130–35), but even with a 10th-century date (e.g., Day 1985: 100), the poem may contain the earliest textual witness to the *yam sûp* as the sea of the Exodus.

1. Character of the Exodus Event (Exodus 13–15). Much of the debate over what happened at the "crossing" of the sea and the location of the event centers upon the accounts, both narrative and poetic, preserved in Exodus 13–15. In spite of disagreement over the assignment and extent of sources (particularly the role of E and P), scholars have generally recognized the composite nature of Exodus 13–14 and isolated two basic versions within the chapters (discussion in Hay 1964: 398–99; Noth *Exodus,* 102–20; Childs *Exodus,* 215–24; de Vaux *EHI,* 381–88; Ottosson in *TWAT* 5: 797–800). (The dispute over details in this analysis need not imply that the enterprise *as a whole* is faulty or that it should be abandoned, as does Hubbard in *ISBE* 4: 59.)

According to the account normally attributed to J (following the summary of Childs), Yahweh is the main actor: he leads Israel by a pillar of cloud and fire (13:21–22); when the people catch sight of the pursuing Egyptians and cry out to Yahweh, they are instructed by Moses to "stand firm" and "be still" because Yahweh will fight for them (14:5b–6, 10b*a,* 11–14); the pillar of cloud then moves behind the Israelites, cutting off Egyptian pursuit (14:19b). During the night, Yahweh drives back the sea with a strong E wind that blows all night (v 21a*b*); in the morning, the pillar of cloud/fire (= Yahweh) hinders the movement of the Egyptians who, in their panic, flee into the sea as the waters return to their normal course; Yahweh literally "shakes off" (Heb *nāʿar*) the Egyptians into the sea (24–25b, 27b). The Israelites see the dead Egyptians on the seashore and affirm their faith in Yahweh and his servant Moses (30–31). The important element of this account is the passitivity of the Israelites; they are simply witnesses to Yahweh's victory over the Egyptians. No mention is made of their crossing the sea.

The P(E) version, on the other hand, emphasizes the role of Moses; the people are active participants, and precise (for the ancient writer, but difficult for the modern interpreter) geographical locations are provided in the text (e.g., 13:20; 14:1–4, 9b). Yahweh hardens the heart of pharaoh so that the latter might pursue the Israelites, and thus obtain glory (vv 4, 8); at the approach of the Egyptian army, Moses raises his staff over the sea and the waters divide as walls on either side, allowing the people to pass through on dry ground (vv 15–19a, 21b, 22–23). When the Egyptians attempt pursuit, the waters return under Moses' staff and the enemy is engulfed (25a, 26–27a, 28–29). (Certain passages in this account may also point to an actual military encounter; see Hay 1964 for discussion.)

Scholars have long noted the virtual absence of *yam sûp* in this Exodus narrative as a designation for the sea where the deliverance of Yahweh occurred; instead, the writers refer only to "the sea" (Heb *hayyām;* 14:2, 9, 16, 21–23, 26–29). Similarly, Exodus 15 prefers "the sea" to *yam sûp* (vv 1, 4a, 8, 21). As a result, many view the few references to *yam sûp* (= Red Sea) as later additions—attempts to find a body of water suitable (in proportion) to the magnitude of Yahweh's glorious act (such as the Gulf of Suez or Aqabah). A grand miracle deserves a grand setting. However, the mention of *yam sûp* in Exod 15:4—within what many consider to be one of the oldest poems in the Hebrew Bible—is problematic for this view. The parallel position of *yām* and *yam sûp* would seem to indicate that the two are identical. While some view this *yam sûp* as a later Deuteronomistic addition (e.g., Norin 1977: 94), others (e.g., Snaith 1965; Batto 1983; Ahlström 1986) propose another reading (*sôp* instead of *sûp*) in keeping with the mythological language of the poem (see below for discussion).

2. Other Texts. Unlike the account of P presented above, Exodus 15:1–12 lacks any explicit mention of the splitting of the sea or of the Israelites passing through on dry ground (e.g., Cross *CMHE,* 131–32). The poem's relationship to the J account is problematic and largely depends upon the date assigned to the former (see, e.g., Cross *CMHE,* 121–25, and Childs 1970: 411–12 for opposing views and further bibliography). The later prose tradition of the Exodus event tends (with some exceptions) to emphasize these motifs (the splitting of the sea and the Israelite passage through it). Josh 2:10 recounts the drying up of the waters of *yam sûp,* but does not explicitly mention the crossing. The preceding verse (v 9) clearly reflects Exod 15:14–15, but this portion of the Exodus poem relates to the conquest, not the defeat of the Egyptians. Josh 4:24 likens the crossing of the Jordan unto the earlier passage through the *yam sûp.* The close parallels between the two events have produced arguments that the details of the Exodus crossing have been influenced by the Jordan tradition (cf. also, e.g., Pss 66:6; 114:3, 5; Coats 1967: 261; Childs 1970: 414–15; see discussion in de Vaux *EHI,* 384–88). In the speech of Joshua to the tribes of Israel gathered at Shechem (Joshua 24), neither the drying up nor the crossing of the *yam sûp* are mentioned. Verses 6–7 echo for the most part J's version of events (and some portions of E), and the parallel placement of *yām* ("sea") and *yam sûp* may point to a conscious imitation of Exod 15:4. Other passages containing *yam sûp* (Neh 9:9–11; Pss 106:9–12, 22; 136:13–15) generally reflect the tradition of P (but note Neh 9:11b and Exod 15:5).

D. Origin and Meaning of Hebrew *Sûp*

1. Scholarly Views. Particularly since the 19th century, scholars have discussed and debated the meaning of Heb *sûp* (as used in the name *yam sûp*) in the hope that the word's origin may shed light upon the location of the sea miracle. The LXX rendering *eruthra thalassa* could encompass not only our English "Red Sea" (the narrow body of water dividing the NE coast of Africa from the Arabian peninsula) but also the Indian Ocean as a whole, including the Persian Gulf (LSJM 693). The LXX translators apparently intended the term to apply to the two gulfs (Aqabah and Suez) of the Red Sea. This translation is in turn reflected in the Vulgate's *Mare Rubrum,* whence we derive our Red Sea. Earlier exegetes and commentators, both Jewish and Christian, offered varying explanations for the word. Jerome (*Ep.* 78.9; see Labourt 1954: 62–63) resolved the difficulty in Num 33:8, 10–11, by positing two meanings for *sûp:* "red" (Lat *rubrum*) and "rush/bulrush" (Lat *scirpus*). (The latter meaning is attested for *sûp* in Exod 2:3, 5, and Isa 19:6.) Thus, "the sea" *(hayyām)* of v 8—although it lacked *sûp*—indicated, according to Jerome, the "Red Sea," i.e., the sea of the Exodus, while *yam sûp* of vv 10–11 denoted a "marsh/swamp *(palus)* or lake *(lacus)* where sedge *(carectum)* and rushes *(iuncus)* were plentiful." The famous medieval Jewish commentator Rashi (A.D. 1040–1105) explained the *yam sûp* of Exod 13:18 as a "marsh (Heb *ʾăgam)* wherein reeds *(kānîm)* grow," while his near-contemporary Ibn-Ezra (A.D. 1089–1164) interpreted this same *yam sûp* as the name of a place *(hûʾ šēm mākôm),* derived from the fact that reeds grow around it (cf. Deut 1:1 and LXX^B *ziph* in Judg 11:16 [a variant reading which appears to understand Heb *sûp* as a proper name]). All three scholars based their exegesis on other occurrences of *sûp* apart from its use with *yām;* thus, the interpretation of *yam sûp* as "Sea of Reeds" predates later appeals to Egyptian evidence (although this does not imply that this interpretation must be the correct one, only that it has a very long history).

The majority of biblical scholars favor the view that Heb *sûp* is a loanword from Egyptian *ṯwf(j)* "papyrus(-plant)" (Gauthier 2: 43, 139; *AEO* 2, 201*–202*; Lesko 1982–89, 4: 107; see discussion of Egyptian texts in Ward 1974: 339–43). This position is often traced to the 19th-century Egyptologist Heinrich Brugsch's lecture *L'Exodus et les monuments égyptiens,* delivered in London in 1874 (e.g., Cazelles 1955: 323; Batto 1983: 29; see Brugsch 1881). However, a close reading of this lecture reveals that Brugsch in fact believed Eg *ṯwf* was borrowed by the Egyptians from Hebrew *sûp* (Brugsch 1881: 372–73, 376). For him, the meaning of Heb *sûp* as "weeds, reeds, rushes, papyrus-plant" was clear without reference to Eg *ṯwf* (376). Instead, *sûp* was a *translation* of another Egyptian word, *idḥ(w),* "marshes (of the Delta)" (*WbÄS* 1: 155; Lesko 1982–89, 1: 64):

> ". . . this word [Heb *sûp*], I say, contains simply the translation of the Egyptian *Athu* [*idḥ(w)*], which signifies the same as the Hebrew Souph . . . and was applied as a general term to denote all the marshes and lagoons of Lower Egypt . . . The Egyptians, on their part, knew so well the meaning of the Hebrew word [*sûp*], that they frequently adopted the foreign name of Souph, instead of the word *Athu* in their own tongue . . ." (Brugsch 1881: 376).

In a later extended discussion of the question of *yam sûp* and its location, Brugsch (1879: 890–919) further developed his view that the "lakes or marshes of the N Delta" were indicated in Eg texts by both *idḥ(w)* (a "purely Egyptian word") and *ṯwf(j)* ("of Semitic origin") and that the Heb *sûp* represented "the exact translation" of Eg *idḥ(w)* (pp. 906–7). While he did propose translating *yam sûp* as *lac de papyrus,* the origin of the term was for him Semitic, not Egyptian.

In his additions and notes for the second English edition of the lecture (1881) Brugsch cited with approval the conclusion of Schleiden (in his *Die Landenge von Suez*) that the *yam sûp* of Exodus 14 was a "later interpolation" and reiterated his position that "the sea" (Heb *hayyām*) of the Exodus narratives referred to the Mediterranean, particularly Lake Sirbonis (1881: 394–97, 429–30; a position later developed by Eissfeldt 1932).

Others maintained that Heb *sûp* was a loanword from Eg *ṯwf* (e.g., Erman 1892: 122; *BDB* [1st ed., 1907], 693; Gardiner 1918: 186; Naville 1924: 34; Albright 1918: 254; 1934: 35; Lambdin 1953: 153). However, not all have accepted this view (e.g., Simons *GTTOT,* 78, 240). Like Brugsch, some have defended movement in the opposite direction, i.e., Semitic *sp* was borrowed by the Egyptians (e.g., Müller 1893: 101 [modified his view in 1903: 4022–23]; Helck 1971: 525; Wright 1979: 60), while others (Copisarow 1962 and Ward 1974) have posited an earlier Hebrew or Canaanite *sp* (Copisarow: **s[o]p,* "end," with origins in the "patriarchal vernacular"; Ward: biconsonantal Semitic **sp,* "reach, arrive"), whence the various Egyptian and Hebrew meanings ultimately derive. (Ward's article is the more credible of the two and avoids the somewhat naive approach to Israel's early history displayed by Copisarow.) Ward in particular has questioned the validity of Eg *t/č* as Heb *s* in *ṯwf* > *sûp,* contending that Eg *ṯ* was normally reflected as *z* in Semitic (1974: 346–47), but the equation *ṯ* = *s* has been defended by Rainey (1982) with various examples, although he does not mention Heb *sûp.*

2. Egyptian *Ṯwf.* In a number of Egyptian texts, Eg *ṯwf* is found with the definite article *p3.* Of particular interest in this regard are a number of model letters (late 13th century B.C.E.), the first of which is an encomium on Pi-Ramesses-mri-Amun ("House-of-Ramesses-Beloved-of-Amun"), the Delta residence of the Ramesside period (generally equated with the "Raamses" of the biblical text; see discussion below). The texts cited most often are as follows:

Papyrus Anastasi III.2, 11–12 (Gardiner 1918: 185–86; 1937: 22, lines 13–14; translations in Caminos 1954: 74, 79, and Uphill 1968–69: 15–18). In his description of the natural wonders of the Delta residence of Ramesses II (Per-Ramesses, probably Tell el-Dabʿa—Qantir), the scribe asserts that "the papyrus-marshes *(p3-ṯwf[j])* come to it (the residence) with papyrus reeds *(mnḥw),* the Waters of Horus with rushes *(jsw)*." When taken in context, this passage must be viewed against the numerous references throughout the text to various bodies of water (ponds, lakes, marshes, etc.) and the aquatic plants/marine life that thrive in such habitats. While the writer does not hesitate elsewhere to use the determinatives characteristic of lakes, rivers, seas, etc. (see Gardiner *EG,* Sign-list N 35–36), he avoids these determinatives in the various terms for reeds, rushes, marshes, etc., where one finds either the herb or papyrus determinative (or both, as with *p3-ṯwf;* Gardiner *EG,* Sign-list M 2, 15–16).

Papyrus Anastasi IV.15, 6 (Gardiner 1937: 51, line 16; translation in Caminos 1954: 200, 210). In this letter, which lists in general detail the numerous supplies necessary for pharaoh's arrival (e.g., various types of breads, oils, fish, etc.), the recipient is instructed to obtain "*qnj*-birds of the papyrus marshes *(p3-ṯwf[j])*." Here *ṯwf* carries the herb determinative plus the sign denoting a specific place, whether village, town, or city, etc. (Gardiner *EG,* Sign-List 0 49), again in contrast to the various waters mentioned in the lines that immediately follow (Gardiner 1937: 52, lines 1–5).

Papyrus Sallier I.4, 9 (Gardiner 1937: 81; translation in Caminos 1954: 307). In his report concerning the upkeep of the royal residence, the scribe states that the pharaoh's chariot teams *(ḥtrw)* are well taken care of and are fed only with the best grass *(jsw?)* from the *p3-ṯwf.* Here, the term is followed with both the herb and papyrus determinatives, plus the place sign mentioned above.

It is not possible to isolate all occurrences of *p3-ṯwf* in Egyptian texts to one specific area in the Delta; rather, different passages point to varying locations. The use of the city or town determinative may indicate that the scribe had a particular marshy area in mind whose identification and placement were directly relative to the city or town under discussion, e.g., the marshes of or near city X or city Y, etc. Thus, as Ward (1974: 342–43) has shown, *p3-ṯwf* "was a general word for 'marshes' wherever these might occur, a specific marshy area being indicated only when *p3 čwf* is located at or near a particular place." Indeed, other occurrences of the term indicate that it was not restricted to the NE Delta area (Ward 1974: 342), although its placement in the *Onomastica* (*AEO* 2, nos. 417–19) between Tanis *(Ḏʿnt)* and Sile *(Ṯ3rw)* may point—at least in this instance—in this direction (but note Ward 1974: 341, n. 6). Uphill (1968–69: 18), however, has questioned the validity of using such idealized descriptions as geographic guides. In his comments on the first of the above cited texts (Anastasi III.2, 11–12), he remarks, "Any of these items [papyrus marshes, reeds, orchards, etc.] could have been found almost anywhere in the Delta, west as well as east, and are not therefore safe to be used as guides without further details . . . this is a poetical description, and the writer has extended his field far and wide to include all the products that were brought to Per Ramesses or were to be found in the great estates attached to it." In general, the attempt to establish detailed geography based on determinatives is a precarious one, since Egyptian scribes were not always consistent in their employment of these signs.

Even if one accepts Heb *sûp* as a loanword from Eg *ṯwf,* this need not imply that the word must in all respects reflect the precise usage—geographical or otherwise—of the original. Indeed, given the sometimes unpredictable nature of loanwords, it would be unwise to assume such. The question of *yam sûp* = *p3-ṯwf* must be kept separate from *sûp* = *ṯwf.* While the occurrences of *sûp* alone in passages such as Exod 2:3, 5 contextually allow the meaning "reeds" or the like, *yam sûp,* as a proper name, contains no inherent clue as to its (nongeographical) meaning. Proper names may carry a literal meaning that is totally unrelated to their point of reference.

E. *Yam Sûp* and Mythology

In a note on the name *yam sûp,* J. A. Montgomery (1938) expressed dissatisfaction with the then-accepted translation "Sea of Sedge," and called attention to the one passage (1 Kgs 9:26) where the LXX departs from its usual rendering of Red Sea and reads instead *tēs eschatēs thalassēs* "the uttermost sea" or "the sea at the furthermost region," apparently reading *sôp* instead of *sûp.* This translation, which Montgomery referred to as the *Ultimum Mare,* was, he thought, well suited to the Red Sea proper, which, as an arm of the Indian Ocean, could be seen as the *Ultimum Mare* (1938: 131).

As already discussed, Copisarow (1962) rejected the Egyptian derivation of *sûp,* citing passages within the Bible and later versions (e.g., *Tg. Onq.*) which he believed pointed to *yam sôp* as the "End or Border Sea" (1962: 8–11). The *sôp* question assumed new dimensions with the article of Snaith (1965), who introduced the mythological element in his examination of the Song of the Sea in Exodus 15. According to Snaith, terms such as "deeps" (Heb *tehōmōt*) and "depths" (Heb *meṣôlōt*) in v 5 indicated a destruction or annihilation within the mythological primeval sea/chaos known from other biblical texts as having been subdued by Yahweh (e.g., Isa 51:9–11). Thus, the *yam sôp* of v 4 signified the "sea at the end of the land" . . . "that distant scarcely known sea away to the south, of which no man knew the boundary" (1965: 398), which, in mythological terms, represented total destruction or annihilation (in this case for pharoah and his army). Snaith contended that the crossing of "the sea" tradition was later "interwoven with the great Creation-myth" and its *yam sôp* (1965: 398), and he identified the earlier "sea" of the Exodus narratives with the Mediterranean.

The most eloquent spokesman for this interpretation of *yam sûp* has been B. F. Batto (1983), who, like Snaith and others, believes that the presence of *yam sûp* in Exodus 13–15 is the result of the latest redaction, a conscious attempt "to historicize and localize the sea miracle at the Red Sea" (1983: 30). The one exception in the Song of the Sea (Exod 15:4b), which Batto acceps as "one of the most ancient pieces in the Hebrew Bible," is treated as mythological due to its parallel position with *yām,* a word used in other biblical passages (e.g., Ps 74:12–15; Isa 51:9–10) with reference to Yahweh's battle with the sea-dragon/chaos at creation, the so-called *Chaoskampfmythos* (see discussion in Cross *CMHE,* 112–44; Day 1985: 96–100; Kloos 1986: 139–57; and note especially Eakin 1967, who explained the water-separation motif as a reflection of Baal's combat with Yam in Canaanite mythology). Thus, for Batto, "traditional mythical language is used to express the belief that the emergence of Israel as a people during the exodus was due to a creative act by Yahweh equal to that of the original creation of the cosmos itself" (1983: 35). To support his reading of *yam sôp* in Exodus 15, Batto cites the problematic *sûp* of Jonah 2:6 (traditionally rendered as "seaweeds" or the like), where the overall mythological context of the psalm (evident in terms such as the "deep" and the "abyss") makes the reading *sôp* more likely (1983: 32–34; note also his comparison with Psalm 18, esp. vv 4–5). Batto concluded that all references to *yam sûp* fit into either one of two categories: the geographical/historical Red Sea (whether Aqaba or Suez), or the mythological Sea of Extinction or Nonexistence (1983: 35). Thus, he concludes, the existence of a second historical body of water—in addition to the well-known Red Sea—often referred to as the "Reed Sea" is without foundation.

While some have accepted the mythological understanding of *yam sûp,* at least in Exodus 15 (e.g., Eakin 1967; Ahlström 1977: 287; 1986: 49 ["Sea of Destruction"]; de Vaux *EHI,* 377), others have been less than receptive (note especially the critique of Kloos 1986: 153–57). But as scholars have long been aware, one need not assume that the Exodus was either "myth" or "history," as though the two were incompatible, although the precise relationship between these troublesome concepts in the narration of the Exodus—whether "historicized" myth or "mythologized" history—has been a much-discussed topic (see Kloos 1986: 158–214 for summary).

Still others have sought to explain the crossing of the sea in terms of Egyptian mythology (e.g., Towers 1959; Wright 1979; Wifall 1980). According to Towers, the passage through the "sea of reeds" echoes the mythical lake of reeds (Eg *š j3rw*) of the Pyramid Texts. He further contends that this term has survived, albeit corruptly, as *ša(i)ri* in the Coptic (Bohairic) version's *phyom n ša(i)ri* for Heb *yam sûp* (1959: 150–52). However, leaving aside the questionable interpretation of *ša(i)ri* (q.v. Brugsch 1879: 909–12 and Černý 1976: 251 for differing interpretations), the rather large chronological gap between the 3d millennium B.C.E. Pyramid Texts and a later (ca. 4th century C.E.) Coptic version of the Scriptures raises a number of methodological problems, not the least of which is the question of access, especially in the light of recent studies on literacy in ancient Egypt. For example, Towers must assume that the writer "was conversant with the theological terminology of ancient Egypt" (1959: 151), but he offers no explanation as to how (where or when?) the biblical writer may have obtained this information. While he did acknowledge (in a footnote) the parallel *sḫt j3rw* "Field of Reeds" (1959: 151, n. 6), he ignored its occurrences in later Underworld texts such as the Coffin Texts and the Book of the Dead (for the latter, see Allen 1974: 6, 13, 65, 74, 87, *passim;* illustrations in Faulkner 1985: 105, 110–11; and discussion of Leclant in *LÄ* 1: 1156–60). Despite the attempts of Towers and Wright, the overall context of *š/sḫt j3rw* within Egyptian mortuary texts is totally lacking in the imagery or symbolism of the biblical account of the Exodus. The issue of Israel's "passing over" the sea as purification (taken largely from Paul's interpretation in the NT) is not present in those passages mentioning *yam sûp,* and the significance of water as a purifying element is so common that one hesitates to trace its origin here to Egyptian mythology. One might also inquire as to why, in this instance, the biblical writer chose Egyptian over (more easily explained) Canaanite symbolism. Did he have reason to believe that his non-Egyptian readers (or listeners) would correctly perceive the veiled Egyptian reference behind *yam sûp?*

Wifall (1980: 329) escorts the reader through a rather convoluted series of equations in order to demonstrate that lying behind the term *yam sûp* is the biblical concept of Sheol (analyzed as *š el* "Lake of El," which he connects with the mythological "Lake of Reeds" and the geographical "Lake of Horus" [Eg *š Ḥr*]): "Thus, as the geographical *yam sûp* and *Shi-Hor* and the mythological or theological 'lake' and 'field of reeds' and 'Sheol' all seem to be interrelated, so also, perhaps, are the terms *Shi-Hor* and 'Sheol.' " The parallels cited by Wifall concerning the Israelite and Egyptian views of death and afterlife are unfortunately too general to be of any serious use in tracing the influence of particular ideas. Like Towers, he draws attention to what appears to be possible parallels, but he lacks the methodological means to differentiate between broad similarities, which may be common to the ANE as a whole, and specific ideas or motifs that would indicate influence in one direction. While the possibility cannot be ruled out completely, there is no evidence that would identify the *yam sûp* of the Exodus specifically with the Egyptian Lake/Waters of Horus of the NE Delta (for its location, see discussion in Gardiner 1918: 251–52; 1924: 93; Bietak 1975: 129–32 and his article in *LÄ* 5: 623–26; see also Kloos 152–53 for further discussion of Towers and Wifall).

F. Location of the Sea of the Exodus

For over a century, biblical scholars and Egyptologists have been obsessed with the quest of identifying this body of water; virtually every possible site within or near the Delta—and some beyond it, e.g., the Gulf of Aqabah—has at one time or another been proposed as the setting for the grand miracle. The most commonly cited objection to one of the two gulfs of the Red Sea has been the lack of reedy vegetation near these large bodies of salt water (as opposed to the freshwater marshes of the Delta), a necessary element for the *yam sûp* = "*Reed* Sea" position (e.g., Brugsch 1881: 430; Gardiner 1922: 212; Bietak in *LÄ* 5: 630; Anati 1986: 187; Sarna 1986: 107). Those who favor a location within or E of the Delta tend to isolate the area extending N from the tip of the Gulf of Suez up to the coastal site of ancient Pelesium (Tell el-Farama) as the most likely region for the event. Candidates (both past and present) for the sea have included the Gulf of Suez or the Gulf of Aqabah (the older traditional view, see Davies 1979: 70, 112, for references); the Bitter Lakes region (e.g., Davies 1979: 82; Kitchen in *NBD,* 1014; Har-El 1977: 72–73; note also Butzer in *LÄ* 1: 824–25); the Ballah Lakes (e.g., Bietak 1981; 1987; Wilson 1985: 131); Lake Menzalah (Gardiner 1922; Goedicke [as presented by Shanks 1981]); and the Mediterranean/Lake Sirbonis (Sabkhet el Bardawil) (e.g., Brugsch, Eissfeldt, Herrmann, Aharoni *LBHG,* Oren 1981, and Anati 1986). Yet the fact that *yam sûp* clearly refers to the Gulf of Aqabah in at least one case (1 Kgs 9:26) demonstrates that the origin or etymology of the term may be irrelevant to its geographical application. Indeed, context and usage are often much more reliable indicators of a word's meaning, and the older obsession with etymology as the determining factor has largely been abandoned by modern scholars. While some (e.g., Kitchen *NBD,* 1014; Sarna 1986: 107–8) see no problem with the multiple reference of *yam sûp* (i.e., as simultaneously designating the two gulfs, the lakes within the NE Delta region, or even the Mediterranean), others (e.g., Simons *GTTOT,* 237–38; Davies 1979: 74) view such a solution as

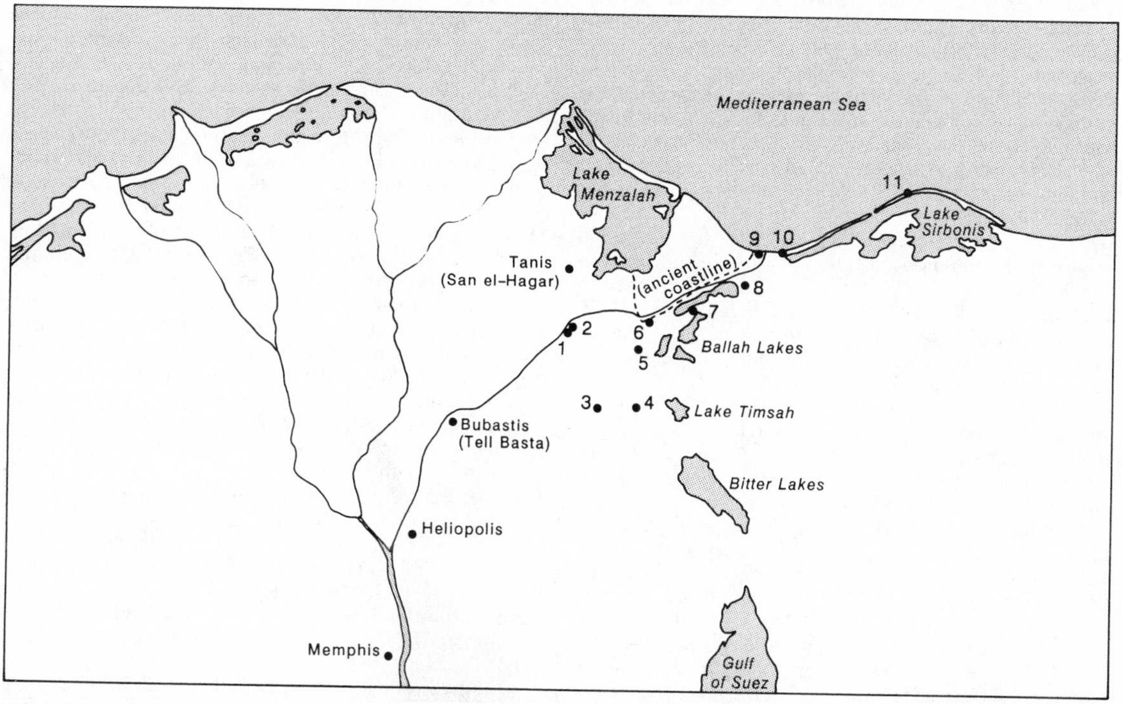

RED.01. Area map of Nile River delta. (1–2) Tell el-Dabᶜa—Qantir; (3) Tell el-Retaba; (4) Tell el-Maskhuta; (5) Tell Hazzob; (6) Tell Defenneh (Daphnae); (7) Tell Abu-Seifeh (Sile); (8) Tell el-Heir; (9) Tell el-Farama (Pelusium); (10) Moḥammedîyeh; (11) Râs Kasrûn.

too ambiguous and thus reject the traditional "sea of reeds" interpretation.

Fortunately, the biblical account does provide the interpreter with a rather precise description of the sea's location in Exod 14:2, where the people of Israel are instructed to "turn back and encamp in front of Pi-hahiroth, between Migdol and the sea, in front of Baal-zephon; you shall encamp over against it, by the sea." Unfortunately, none of the sites mentioned in this text can be identified with certainty, and the various theories concerning their placement are to a great extent determined by one's own view of the general route taken by the fleeing Israelites out of Egypt, whether northern, central, or southern (see Wilson 1985: 154–55 and Beit-Arieh 1988: 37 for the options). The best that one can do is to outline the different proposals for the above-mentioned sites (Pi-hahiroth, Migdol, and Baal-zephon), including also the biblical Raamses, the apparent starting point of the journey. See also EXODUS, THE.

1. Raamses (Exod 1:11; Num 33:5). This biblical name is usually interpreted (with a few notable exceptions; see Redford 1963; 1987; Goedicke [Shanks 1981]; and Oren 1981) as the Egyptian *Piramesses,* the Delta capital of the Ramesside period, generally located at Tell el-Dabᶜa—Qantir on the ancient Pelusiac branch of the Nile (Uphill 1968–69; Bietak 1975: 179–220; 1981; and his article in *LÄ* 5: 128–46; for earlier views concerning the Delta residence, see esp. the articles of Naville and Gardiner; a detailed review of the relevant Egyptian texts may be found in Gardiner 1918). See also RAMESES (PLACE).

2. Baal-Zephon (Exod 14:2; Num 33:7). Attempts to locate this site center upon Egyptian cities where the Canaanite deity of this name was worshiped and thus could have been referred to by the name of the deity. In a highly influential monograph, Eissfeldt (1932) equated Baal-zephon with the later Zeus Kasios and his temple at the Egyptian Mt. Casios, which he placed at *Moḥammedîyeh* on the W edge of Lake Sirbonis (Sabkhet el-Bardawil) facing the Mediterranean, ca. 15 km E of Pelusium. While generally agreeing with Eissfeldt, Cazelles (1955: 333) placed Mt. Casios at *Râs Kasrûn,* ca. 40 km E of *Moḥammedîyeh* between Lake Sirbonis and the Mediterranean (see also Herrmann 1973: 60–64; Aharoni *LBHG,* 196–97; Anati 1986: 186–87; and Redford 1987: 143–44, who favor the Eissfeldt-Cazelles view). (See esp. Simons *GTTOT,* 237–39, 249–50, for criticism of Eissfeldt's theory.) Either site could point to Lake Sirbonis (or even the Mediterranean) as the *yam sûp* of the biblical account, but this N location is rejected by many because the biblical text specifically states that the Israelites did not leave Egypt via this region (Exod 13:17). This objection raises the larger issue of two biblical traditions, a N route (the Elohist) and a S/SE route (the Yahwist). Some have explained these as two different exodoi (e.g., the tribes of Leah followed by the tribes of

Rachel; de Vaux *EHI,* 380–81), while others (e.g., Cazelles 1955: 358–61) have raised the possibility that the N route (through later redaction) has been influenced by or constitutes a later reflection of the well-known tradition of the expulsion of the Hyksos (see also Gardiner 1922: 204; Redford 1987: 148–51). This N location of Baal-zephon poses serious problems for advocates of a S crossing somewhere between the Gulf of Suez and the Bitter Lakes, which, according to some, were physically connected in antiquity (e.g., Finegan 1963: 86; Hubbard *ISBE* 4: 60; Wilson 1985: 131; see Albright 1948: 15–16; Simons *GTTOT,* 247–48; and Davies 1979: 73–74 for discussion and further references; regarding canals in the Delta in the 1st millennium, see Bietak 1975; Butzer in *LÄ* 3: 312–13; Shea 1977; Holladay 1982: 1–3.) This led Davies (1979: 116) to conclude that Baal-zephon was not "an original part of the itinerary" and thus could not be used to reconstruct the earliest route of the Israelites.

Others (following esp. Aimé-Giron 1940; Albright 1948: 15–16; 1950) locate Baal-zephon at Taḥpanḥes (Tell Defenneh [Daphnae]), W of Sile on the S edge of Lake Menzalah (e.g., Bietak 1987: 167; Goedicke [Shanks 1981: 46]). This identification is based on a Phoenician letter (6th century B.C.E.), which mentions "Baal-zephon and all the gods of Taḥpanḥes." According to Bietak, the Ballah Lakes, SE of Tell Defenneh—which he identified with the *p3-ṯwf* of Egyptian texts (1975: 136–39 and maps 23, 45) and Heb *yam sûp* (1975: 217; 1981: 280; 1987: 167)—provided the setting for the sea miracle. Goedicke isolates Tell Hazzob, just S of Tell Defenneh and W of the above Lakes, as the elevated site from which the fleeing Israelites witnessed the destruction of the Egyptian army, due to a massive tidal wave that flooded the low-lying area (following presentation of Shanks 1981 and Wilson 1985). Textual evidence also exists for the worship of Baal-zephon at Memphis (Pap. Sallier IV verso, 1, 6; Gardiner 1937: 89, line 7; Albright 1950: 6–8; Caminos 1954: 333, 337–38). Still others have located the site just N of the Gulf of Suez (e.g., Montet 1968: 49; Finegan 1963). See also BAAL-ZEPHON.

3. Migdol (Exod 14:2; Num 33:7; Jer 44:1). This name occurs a number of times in Egyptian texts, often in compound place names designating forts along the overland route to Palestine. A demotic geographical papyrus (Cairo 31169, iii.20–23) lists four such Migdols, the first of which stands alone (Gardiner 1920: 108; Redford 1987: 143, 154) and was identified by Gardiner as Tell el-Heir (the Magdolo of classical sources), ca. 12 km S of Pelusium (his earlier choice for the Delta residence, which he later abandoned for Tanis; see *AEO* 202*; note also Redford 1987: 143, 153–54). This identification has been used to support a N route for the Exodus, with Lake Sirbonis as the *yam sûp* (e.g., Aharoni *LBHG,* 196–97).

Probably the most widely cited passage mentioning Migdol—and one used to support the early stages of the biblical journey from biblical Raamses (e.g., de Vaux *EHI,* 378, 380; Hubbard *ISBE* 4: 60)—is Papyrus Anastasi V.19, 2–20.6 (Gardiner 1937: 66–67; translations in Gardiner 1920: 109; Caminos 1954: 254–58; *ANET,* 259). This late-13th-century B.C.E. text concerns the pursuit of two escaped slaves and their eventual passage through or around the Migdol (Eg *mktr,* "stronghold, fortification") of Sety I. In addition, their pursuer stops at *ṯkw* (Tell el-Maskhuta of the Wadi Tumilat region, a frequent candidate for biblical Pithom or Sukkoth) and another "fort" (Eg *ḫtm,* often incorrectly equated with Heb *ʾētam;* e.g., Finegan 1963: 84; Montet 1968: 62). But, as Gardiner (1924: 90) and Caminos (1954: 257–58) have noted, this text is difficult and geographically obscure, and thus is of limited use (if any) in identifying the relative placement of these biblical sites. Oren's own archaeological work in the region confirms the identification of Tell el-Heir with the classical Magdolo (1984: 34–35), but he denies that this site was the Migdol of the Exodus, since no evidence of New Kingdom occupation was found. Unlike Redford (1987), Oren and others are not open to the possibility that the biblical writers drew their geographical knowledge from a later period (e.g., the 7th or 6th century B.C.E.), and thus they automatically exclude from consideration any site lacking evidence of a 12th- or 13th-century B.C.E. occupation (the traditional time period associated with the Exodus event).

Others point out that Migdol, the common Semitic word for "tower" or "fortress" (borrowed into Eg as *mktr*), could easily apply to any number of New Kingdom forts along the overland passage to S Palestine (assuming, contra Gardiner and others, that the biblical author was not referring to the Migdol of the prophets), and thus its precise location cannot be established (but note Goedicke [Shanks 1981], who equates both biblical Etham and Migdol with the Egyptian border fortress at *ṯ3rw* (classical Sile, Tell Abu-Seifeh) on the N edge of the Ballah Lakes. See also MIGDOL.

4. Pi-hahiroth (Exod 14:2, 9; Num 33:7). This place name is especially problematic, and no satisfactory site for it has been proposed, although a location in the E Delta is assumed. The name is interpreted in various ways by the LXX, one of which may point to a variant underlying Hebrew text (Exod 14:2, 9; see discussion of Lambdin in *IDB* 3: 810–11). While some (Albright 1948: 16, de Vaux *EHI,* 379) have proposed a type of folk etymology of the Hebrew (e.g., "the mouth of the canals"), others have sought appropriate Egyptian equivalents, e.g., *Pr-Ḥtḥrt,* "House of Hathor," mentioned in Pap. Anastasi III.3,3 and the Nikotris Adoption Stela, somewhere between Tanis and Bubastis (Gardiner 1918: 186; 1922: 213; Caminos 1954: 74, 80; Montet 1968: 64). Another suggestion has been *p3-ḥ3-rti,* a place name in the Wadi El-Arish Naos, apparently interpreted as "Place of the Widow" (Redford 1987: 142, 153, for further possibilities; see also the general discussion of Egyptian derivations in Cazalles 1955: 350–52). See also PI-HAHIROTH.

G. Conclusion

Over the past decade or so, some Egyptologists (e.g., Redford and Bietak) have drawn attention to the question of the biblical writers' geographical sources (note in this regard the earlier comments of Noth 1947 on Eissfeldt's citation of classical sources). According to Redford (1987), the attempt to localize the site of the Exodus in the biblical narrative has drawn heavily from later tradition and represents, for the most part, the writers'/redactors' own knowledge of Egyptian geography as they understood it: ". . . whoever was responsible for the topographic material which now informs the stories of the Sojourn and the

Exodus, be it P or even J, the configuration of the eastern Delta known to them was essentially that of the 26th Dynasty [664–525 B.C.E.] and the early Persian period" (1987: 144). While Bietak is admittedly less pessimistic with regard to the Exodus/Numbers account, he does, however, point to the later attempts of the versions (e.g., LXX and Targum Neofiti), Psalm 78, and the traditions preserved in Manetho, which derived their geographical knowledge from secondary cults of Ramesses at Tanis and Bubastis: "They depended in their search for localization on the Egyptian contemporary opinion" (1987: 164).

Neither scholar, however, is totally pessimistic with regard to a historical event behind the Exodus account. Although Bietak questions the geographical veracity of later texts, he apparently accepts the basic outline of the Exodus account and, based on his own work in the Delta, contends that the Ballah Lakes (as the *p3-twf* of Egyptian texts, 1975: 136–39; 1981: 280; 1987: 167) provided the most likely means of Israelite passage out of Egypt. Redford, on the other hand, traces the ultimate inspiration for the biblical account to the tradition of the occupation/expulsion of the Hyksos (1987: 148–51; for this tradition, see Redford 1970). See also HYKSOS. While the parallels between these two traditions have long been noted (e.g., Gardiner 1922, clarified in 1924), Redford's own exilic/postexilic date for the final version of the biblical account (geographical additions/clarifications at the hands of a later redactor) takes into account the later development and pervasiveness of the Hyksos tradition in the 1st millennium.

As the above evidence illustrates, no consensus has yet emerged on the location of the sea of the Exodus, although the majority opt for an E Delta location. If one contends that *yam sûp* must refer *only* to one of the gulfs of the Red Sea proper, either Aqabah or Suez (e.g., Simons *GTTOT,* 238), then—assuming a Delta site for the crossing—its presence in Exodus 13–14 would constitute a later attempt to connect the miracle at "the sea" with a suitably large body of water such as the Gulf of Suez; while the more frequent references to "the sea" would reflect the earliest tradition (with possible mythological overtones in Exod 15:4). In this case, the question of *yam sûp* as Eg *p3-ṯwf* becomes largely irrelevant, since the biblical writers/redactors did not themselves locate the crossing in the Delta. The now nearly canonical term "Reed Sea" derives ultimately from the modern interpreter's inability to reconcile the geographical problems inherent in the biblical account. Likewise the ancient redactors, perceiving the difficulties within the text, provided geographical roadmaps for their contemporary readers.

On the other hand, if Heb *sûp* and Eg *ṯwf* continue to be correlated, respectively, with *yam sûp* and *p3-ṯwf* as a specific body of water—the "Sea of Reeds"—in the E Delta of Egypt, then the geographically ambiguous nature of *yam sûp* will no doubt occasion further scholarly discussion, and, to be sure, the onomastic quest will continue.

Bibliography

Ahlström, G. W. 1977. Judges 5: 20ff. and History. *JNES* 36: 287–88.

———. 1986. *Who Were the Israelites?* Winona Lake, IN.

Aimé-Giron, N. 1940. Baᶜal Saphon et les dieux de Taḥpanḥès dans un nouveau papyrus Phénicien. *ASAE* 40–41: 433–60.

Albright, W. F. 1918. Notes on Egypto-Semitic Etymology. *AJSL* 34: 81–98, 215–55.

———. 1934. *The Vocalization of the Egyptian Syllabic Orthography.* AOS 5. New Haven.

———. 1948. Exploring in Sinai with the University of California African Expedition. *BASOR* 109: 5–20.

———. 1950. Baal-Zephon. Pp. 1–14 in *Festschrift Alfred Bertholet zum 80. Geburtstag,* ed. W. Baumgartner et al. Tübingen.

Allen, T. G., trans. 1974. *The Book of the Dead or Going Forth by Day.* SAOC 37. Chicago.

Anati, E. 1986. *Har Karkom: The Mountain of God.* New York.

Batto, B. F. 1983. The Reed Sea: Requiescat in Pace. *JBL* 102: 27–35.

Beit-Arieh, I. 1988. The Route Sinai—Why the Israelites Fleeing Egypt Went South. *BARev* 15/3: 28–37.

Bietak, M. 1975. *Tell El-Dabᶜa II.* Vienna.

———. 1981. *Avaris and Piramesse.* Mortimer Wheeler Archaeological Lecture, May 1979. Pp. 225–89 in PBA 65. London.

———. 1987. Comments on the "Exodus." Pp. 163–71 in Rainey 1987.

Brugsch, H. 1879. *Dictionnaire géographique de l'ancienne Egypte.* Leipzig. Repr. 1974, Hildesheim.

———. 1881. *The Exodus and the Egyptian Monuments.* Trans. from French (1875) with additions and notes for 2d English ed. = pp. 357–432 in his *A History of Egypt under the Pharaohs,* 2d ed. Vol. 2. London.

Caminos, R. A. 1954. *Late-Egyptian Miscellanies.* Brown Egyptological Studies 1. London.

Cassuto, U. 1967. *A Commentary on the Book of Exodus.* Trans. I. Abrahams from Hebrew. Jerusalem.

Cazelles, H. 1955. Les localisations de l'Exode et la critique littéraire. *RB* 62: 321–64. [Repr. in his *Author de l'Exode (Études),* Paris 1987.]

Černý, J. 1976. *Coptic Etymological Dictionary.* Cambridge.

Childs, B. 1970. A Traditio-Historical Study of the Reed Sea Tradition. *VT* 20: 406–18.

Coats, G. W. 1967. The Traditio-Historical Character of the Reed Sea Motif. *VT* 17: 253–65.

———. 1979. The Sea Tradition in the Wilderness Theme: A Review. *JSOT* 12: 2–8.

Copisarow, M. 1962. The Ancient Egyptian, Greek and Hebrew Concept of the Red Sea. *VT* 12: 1–13.

Davies, G. I. 1979. *The Way of the Wilderness.* Cambridge.

Day, J. 1985. *God's Conflict with the Dragon and the Sea.* Cambridge.

Eakin, F. E. 1967. The Reed Sea and Baalism. *JBL* 86: 378–84.

Eissfeldt, O. 1932. *Baal Zaphon, Zeus Kasios und der Durchzug der Israeliten durchs Meer.* Halle.

Erman, A. 1892. Das Verhältniss des Aegyptischen zu den semitischen Sprachen. *ZDMG* 46: 93–129.

Faulkner, R. O., trans. 1985. *The Ancient Egyptian Book of the Dead,* ed. C. Andrews. New York.

Finegan, J. 1963. *Let My People Go: A Journey Through Exodus.* New York.

Gardiner, A. H. 1918. The Delta Residence of the Ramassides. *JEA* 5: 127–38, 179–200, 242–71.

———. 1920. The Ancient Military Road Between Egypt and Palestine. *JEA* 6: 99–116.

———. 1922. The Geography of the Exodus. Pp. 203–15 in *Recueil d'études égyptologiques . . . Champollion.* Bibliothèque de l'école des hautes études, Sci. Hist. et Phil. 234. Paris.

———. 1924. The Geography of the Exodus: An Answer to Professor Naville and Others. *JEA* 10: 87–96.
———. 1937. *Late Egyptian Miscellanies.* Bibliotheca Aegyptiaca 7. Brussels.
Gauthier, H. 1925–31. *Dictionnaire des noms géographiques contenus dans les textes hiéroglyphiques.* 7 vols. Cairo.
Goedicke, H. 1987. Papyrus Anastasi VI 51–61. *SAK* 14: 83–98.
Har-El, M. 1977. The Exodus Route in the Light of Historical-Geographic Research. *Ariel* 44: 69–84.
———. 1983. *The Sinai Journeys: The Route of the Exodus.* San Diego.
Hay, L. S. 1964. What Really Happened at the Sea of Reeds? *JBL* 83: 397–403.
Helck, W. 1971. *Die Beziehungen Ägyptens zu Vordasien im 3. und 2. Jahrtausend v. Chr.* 2d ed. ÄA 5. Wiesbaden.
Herrmann, S. 1973. *Israel in Egypt.* Trans. M. Kohl. SBT n.s. 27. London.
Holladay, J. S. 1982. *Cities of the Delta, Part III: Tell el-Maskhuta.* ARCE Reports 6. Malibu, CA.
Kloos, C. 1986. *Yhwh's Combat with the Sea.* Amsterdam and Leiden.
Labourt, J., trans. 1954. *Saint Jérôme Lettres. Tome IV.* Paris.
Lambdin, T. 1953. Egyptian Loan Words in the Old Testament. *JAOS* 73: 145–55.
Lauha, A. 1963. Das Schilmeermotif im Alten Testament. *VTSup* 9: 32–46.
Lesko, L. H. 1982–89. *A Dictionary of Late Egyptian.* 4 vols. Berkeley.
Montet, P. 1968. *Egypt and the Bible.* Trans. L. R. Keylock. Philadelphia.
Müller, W. M. 1893. *Asien und Europa nach altägyptischen Denklmälern.* Leipzig.
———. 1903. Red Sea. Cols. 4022–23 in *EncBib* (1 vol. ed.).
Naville, E. 1924. The Geography of the Exodus. *JEA* 10: 18–39.
Norin, S. 1977. *Er Spaltete das Meer: Die Auszügsuberlieferung in Psalmen und Kult des Alten Israel.* ConBOT 9. Lund.
Noth, M. 1947. Der Schauplatz des Meereswunders. Pp. 181–90 in *Festschrift Otto Eissfeldt zum 60. Geburtstag.* Halle.
Oren, E. D. 1981. How Not to Create a History of the Exodus—A Critique of Professor Goedicke's Theories. *BARev* 7/6: 46–53.
———. 1984. Migdol: A New Fortress on the Edge of the Eastern Nile Delta. *BASOR* 256: 744.
Rainey, A., ed. 1987. *Egypt, Israel, Sinai. Archaeological and Historical Relationships in the Biblical Period.* Tel Aviv.
Rainey, A. 1982. Toponymic Problems (cont.). *TA* 9: 130–36.
Redford, D. B. 1963. Exodus I 11. *VT* 13: 401–18.
———. 1970. The Hyksos Invasion in History and Tradition. *Or* 39: 1–51.
———. 1987. An Egyptological Perspective on the Exodus Narrative. Pp. 137–61 in Rainey 1987.
Sarna, N. 1986. *Exploring Exodus: The Heritage of Biblical Israel.* New York.
Sayce, A. H. 1894. *The "Higher Criticism" and the Verdict of the Monuments.* London.
Shanks, H. 1981. The Exodus and the Crossing of the Red Sea, According to Hans Goedicke. *BARev* 7/5: 42–50.
Shea, W. H. 1977. A Date for the Recently Discovered Eastern Canal of Egypt. *BASOR* 226: 31–38.
Snaith, N. H. 1965. *Yam-Sôp:* The Sea of Reeds: The Red Sea. *VT* 15: 395–98.
Towers, J. R. 1959. The Red Sea. *JNES* 18: 150–53.
Uphill, E. P. 1968–69. Pithom and Raamses: Their Location and Significance. *JNES* 27: 291–316; 28: 15–39.
Walsh, J. T. 1977. From Egypt to Moab: A Source Critical Analysis of the Wilderness Itinerary. *CBQ* 39: 20–33.
Ward, W. A. 1974. The Semitic Biconsonantal Root *SP* and the Common Origin of Egyptian *ČWP* and Hebrew *SÛP:* "Marsh (-Plant)." *VT* 24: 339–49.
Wifall, W. 1980. The Sea of Reeds as Sheol. *ZAW* 92: 325–32.
Wilson, I. 1985. *Exodus: The True Story Behind the Biblical Account.* San Francisco.
Wright, G. R. H. 1979. The Passage of the Sea. *GM* 33: 55–68.

JOHN R. HUDDLESTUN

RED SEA TRADE

The Red Sea has been used as a source of food and maritime transportation since prehistoric times despite the lack of a coastline having good natural harbors and anchorages and the existence of enervating prevailing northerly winds N of 20° N latitude. This has been attested by the discovery of numerous lithic tools (Montenat 1986: 239–55; Prickett 1979: 280–92), a predynastic burial (Murray and Derry 1923: 129–31) along the Red Sea coast of Egypt and lithic tools along the Saudi Arabian Red Sea coast at various points, the existence of numerous prehistoric petroglyphs in the Wadi Hammamat (*LÄ* 6: 1099–1113), dipinti and graffiti elsewhere in the Eastern Desert (Winkler 1938: 18–41; Redford and Redford 1989) and other prehistoric sites (Sodmein Cave), between the Nile and the Red Sea coast (Prickett 1979: 292–93).

In historical times, interest in the Red Sea littoral initially was primarily commercial in nature. Since the desert bordered the entire littoral, few people actually resided on the coast in sizable concentrations except for commercial maritime purposes. Literary sources attest the earliest known exploitation of the Red Sea for commercial purposes in the Egyptian Old Kingdom period (*AESH,* 136; Murray 1950: 14). Literary sources (*AESH,* 137), epigraphic evidence (Tregenza 1958: 181), and archaeological excavation of a Middle Kingdom port at the Red Sea terminus of the Wadi Gawasis (Sayed 1978: 69–71) and of a galena mine at Gebel Zeit (Castel et al. 1984: 45–57) attest activity along the coast at that time. This continued into the Egyptian New Kingdom (Empire) period and was made famous by the expedition sent by the pharaoh Hatshepsut to Punt (*AESH,* 270–71), the precise location of which has been greatly debated. Details of this journey are depicted on Hatshepsut's funerary temple at Deir el-Bahri near Thebes.

Commercial interest persisted in the late pharaonic period (*AESH,* 254; Schweinfurth 1885: *passim*) under Necho II (610–595 B.C.) and after the Achaemenid Persian conquest of Egypt in 525 B.C. under Cambyses (530–521 B.C.) and his successors, especially Darius I (521–486 B.C.). The Ptolemaic dynasty (323–30 B.C.) in Egypt under Ptolemy II Philadelphus (283/282–246 B.C.) and his successors continued and expanded this maritime commerce in the Red Sea and beyond into the Indian Ocean (Thapar 1987: 15–19) by the construction of a number of ports and trade stations on the W coast of the Red Sea to the Bab el-Mandeb (entrance to the Indian Ocean) and, perhaps, beyond (Murray 1967: 24–33; Scullard 1974: 129, fig. 13; Strabo 16.4.7ff.; Pliny *HN* 6.34.170–75). However, Ptolemaic interest in the Red Sea was primarily military (the acquisition of war elephants and gold for the army); commercial considerations were, in the early Ptolemaic period at least, secondary.

The annexation of Egypt by Rome in 30 B.C. brought Rome for the first time into direct contact with the Red Sea. The nature, volume, intensity, and diversity of Roman commerce was different from and greater than that of the Ptolemies (cf. Desanges *ANRW* 2/10/1: 3–43). Roman trade in the Red Sea was motivated by commercial and political interests, not, primarily, by military considerations. Most of the ports the Romans used on the Red Sea had been built earlier either by the Ptolemies or by the Nabateans. Apparently these were subsequently repaired and enlarged (Sidebotham 1986: 48–57)—and one, Leukos Limen on the Egyptian coast, was founded *de novo*—by the Romans (Whitcomb and Johnson 1979; 1982a; 1982b). Egyptian emporia included (1) Clysma-Arsinoë-Qolzoum (near modern Suez; Bruyère 1966: *passim*); (2) Myos Hormos (Diodorus Siculus 3.39.1–2; Strabo 2.5.12; 16.4.5; 16.4.24; 17.1.45; *Periplus Maris Erythraei* 1; 19; Pliny *HN* 6.33.168; Tait 1930: 108–25; Ptol. *Geog.* 4.5.8; Sidebotham 1986: 50–51); (3) Philoteras (Ptol. *Geog.* 4.5.8; Murray 1925: 142; Meredith 1953: 101–3); (4) Leukos Limen (Sidebotham 1986: *s.v.* index "Leukos Limen"); (5) Nechesia (Ptol. *Geog.* 4.5.8; Murray 1925: 142–43; Meredith 1953: 103); and (6) the largest and most important, Berenice (Strabo 17.1.45; *Periplus Maris Erythraei* 1; 19; 21; Pliny *HN* 6.26.103; Tait 1930: 108–25; Ptol. *Geog.* 4.5.8; Murray 1925: 143; Meredith 1957: 56–70; Murray 1968: 49–53; Sidebotham 1986: *s.v.* index "Berenice"). There was a late Roman/Byzantine military installation at Abu Shaᶜar, an area long considered (inaccurately) to have been the location of Myos Hormos (Sidebotham 1989a). Transdesert routes marked with forts, towers, and cairns joined these ports to various emporia on the Nile, such as Edfu (Apollonopolis Magna) in the Ptolemaic period (Bagnall 1976: 35) and Qift (Coptos), Denderah (Tentyris), and Antinoe/Antinoopolis in Roman times (Bernand 1984: *passim;* Bingen 1984: 359–70; Sidebotham 1986: 48–71; Sidebotham 1989c; Sidebotham et al. fc.; Zitterkopf and Sidebotham 1989).

Present scholarship suggests that the economic instability, political chaos, and military turmoil of the 3d century A.D. led to a decline or cessation of this Red Sea commerce. However, literary evidence (*Codex Theodosianus* 12.12.2; Philostorgius *h.e.* 3.4–6; cf. Dihle 1989: 461–68; Procopius *History of the Wars* 1.19.1; 1.19.24–26; 1.20.4; 1.20.9; 1.20.12; 2.3.40; Cosmas Indicopleustes, *top.* I and II; Theophanes *chron.* 6123; cf. Johnson and West 1949: 137–51; cf. Letsios 1988: *passim*) and a growing body of archaeological evidence (Zitterkopf and Sidebotham 1989; Sidebotham 1989b: 222–23) indicate a revival of diplomatic and commercial contacts in the 4th through 6th/early 7th centuries (though this renaissance does not seem to have had the same intensity as activity in the late 1st century B.C.–2d century A.D.).

Red Sea commerce was so important to Egypt that at least as early as the Middle Kingdom period a canal was dug linking the Nile to the Red Sea. Its existence is attested both by ancient writers (Hdt. 2.158–59; 4.39; 4.42; Arist. *Mete.* 1.14.352b25; Agatharchides in Diod. Sic. 1.33.7–12; Strabo 17.1.25–26; Pliny *HN* 6.33.165–66; Ptol. *Geog.* 4.5) and by archaeological evidence (Sidebotham 1986: 67–68, 146, 176). Later rulers—including Necho II, Darius I, Ptolemy II, and Trajan (ruled A.D. 98–117)—were all credited with digging such a canal, and, according to the 9th-century Arab writer al-Maqrizi (Sidebotham 1986: 68), this canal continued to be used in the 9th century. It cannot be determined when it fell out of use or what its exact course was, but remains can still be seen (Redmount 1986: 20).

Less is known about how other regional powers exploited the Red Sea. Solomon's commercial contacts with the Queen of Sheba (Saba) in SW Arabia (Yemen) in the 10th century B.C. are well known (1 Kgs 10:10; Isa 60:6); yet the precise locations of his port of Ezion-Geber and its counterpart in Saba on the Yemeni coast still elude scholars. See EZION-GEBER.

One of the Ptolemaic monarchs (either Ptolemy II or III) is said to have joined the city of Miletus (in Asia Minor) in founding a colony on the Red Sea coast at Ampelone (Pliny *HN* 6.32.158–59; Tarn 1929: 21–22). This city, undoubtedly established for commercial purposes, has never been located. Perhaps it was the site of the later Nabatean/Roman port of Leuke Kome mentioned in the *Periplus Maris Erythraei* (19) as a Red Sea port important enough to warrant stationing there a *hekatontarches* (centurion) and a garrison of unknown nationality. A *paralemptes* collected a 25 percent *ad valorem* customs tax on merchandise imported there (*Periplus Maris Erythraei* 19). Research now suggests that Leuke Kome was located in the Kuraybah-'Aynunah region of NW Saudi Arabia near the Strait of Tiran (Ingraham et al. 1981: 76–77; Kirwan n.d.: 55–61; Sidebotham 1986: 120–26). The nearby island of Iotabe may have superseded Leuke Kome as a customs post later in the Roman/Byzantine period (Abel 1938: 510–33; Letsios 1989: 530; Procopius *History of the Wars* 1.19.3).

Other ports existed along the Red Sea coasts in antiquity, though the dates of their foundation and abandonment are unknown. There was an important port at Aila, near Aqaba (Procopius *History of the Wars* 1.19.3; 1.19.20; 1.19.24), the Islamic section of which is now under excavation (cf. Whitcomb 1988: *passim;* Whitcomb 1989). There were other ports in Sinai (possibly Tor; Murray 1950: 136–38; cf. Gatier 1989: 499–523) and on the African coast (Adulis; Casson 1984: 199–210; Procopius *History of the Wars* 1.20.4) and, undoubtedly, on the Saudi Arabian, Yemeni, and Sudanese Red Sea coasts. The present state of archaeological research has yet to reveal much on pre-Islamic ports in these regions (cf. Crone 1987: *passim*).

Bibliography

Abel, F.-M. 1938. L'île de Jotabé. *RB* 47: 510–38.

Bagnall, R. S. 1976. *The Florida Ostraca.* Durham, NC.

Bernand, A. 1984. *Les Portes du Désert.* Paris.

Bingen, J. 1984. Épigraphie grecque, et latine d'Antioné à Edfou. *CdÉ* 59, 118: 359–70.

Bruyère, B. 1966. *Fouilles de Clysma-Oolzoum (Suez), 1930–1932.* Cairo.

Casson, L. 1984. Rome's Trade with the East. Pp. 182–98 in *Ancient Trade and Society.* Detroit.

———. 1989. *The Periplus Maris Erythraei Text.* Princeton.

Castel, G., et al. 1984. Découverte des Mines pharaoniques au bord de la Mer Rouge. *Archéologie* (Sept.): 45–57.

Crone, P. 1987. *Meccan Trade and the Rise of Islam.* Princeton.

Dihle, A. 1989. L'Ambassade de Théophile l'Indien réexaminée. Pp. 461–68 in Fahd 1989.
Fahd, T., ed. 1989. *L'Arabie Préislamique et son environment historique et culturel.* Leiden.
Gatier, P.-L. 1989. Les traditions et l'histoire du Sinai du IVe au VIIe siècle. Pp. 499–523 in Fahd 1989.
Ingraham, M. L., et al. 1981. Saudi Arabian Comprehensive Survey Program. *Atlal* 5: 58–84.
Johnson, A. C., and West, L. C. 1949. *Byzantine Egypt: Economic Studies.* Princeton.
Kirwan, L. P. n.d. Where to Search for the Ancient Port of Leuke Kome. Vol. 2, pp. 55–61 in *Studies in the History of Arabia,* ed. A. M. Abdalla et al. Riyadh.
Letsios, D. G. 1988. *Byzantium and the Red Sea Relations with Nubia, Ethiopia and South Arabia Until the Arab Conquest.* Athens.
———. 1989. The Case of Amorkesos and the Question of the Roman Foederati in Arabia in the Vth Century. Pp. 525–38 in Fahd 1989.
Meredith, D. 1953. The Roman Remains in the Eastern Desert of Egypt (cont.). *JEA* 39: 95–106.
———. 1957. Berenice Troglodytica. *JEA* 43: 56–70.
Montenat, C. 1986. Un apercu des industries préhistoriques du Golfe de Suez et du littoral égyptien de la mer rouge. *BIFAO* 86: 239–55.
Murray, G. W. 1925. The Roman Roads and Stations in the Eastern Desert of Egypt. *JEA* 11: 138–50.
———. 1950. *Sons of Ishmail.* New York.
———. 1967. Troglodytica: The Red Sea Littoral in Ptolemaic Times. *Geographical Journal* 133: 24–33.
———. 1968. *Dare Me to the Desert.* New York.
Murray, G. W., and Derry, D. E. 1923. A Predynastic Burial on the Red Sea Coast of Egypt. *Man* 23: 129–31.
Prickett, M. 1979. Quseir Regional Survey. Pp. 255–352 in Whitcomb and Johnson 1979.
Redford, S., and Redford, D. B. 1989. Graffiti and Petroglyphs Old and New from the Eastern Desert. *JARCE* 26: 3–49.
Redmount, C. A. 1986. Wadi Tumilat Survey. *American Research Center in Egypt Newsletter* 133: 19–23.
Sayed, A. M. A. H. 1978. The Recently Discovered Port on the Red Sea Shore. *JEA* 64: 69–71.
Schweinfurth, G. A. 1885. *Alte Baureste und hieroglyphische inschriften im Uadi Gasus.* Berlin.
Scullard, H. H. 1974. *The Elephant in the Greek and Roman World.* Ithaca, NY.
Sidebotham, S. E. 1986. *Roman Economic Policy in the Erythra Thalassa 30 B.C.–A.D. 217.* Leiden.
———. 1989a. Fieldwork on the Red Sea Coast: The 1987 Season. *JARCE* 26: 127–66.
———. 1989b. Ports of the Red Sea and the Arabia-India Trade. Pp. 195–223 in Fahd 1989.
———. 1989c. Lure of the Desert Road. *Archaeology* 42/4: 58–60.
Sidebotham, S. E.; Zitterkopf, R. E.; and Riley, J. A. fc. Survey of the 'Abu Sha'ar-Qena Road.
Tait, J. G. 1930. *Greek Ostraca in the Bodleian Library at Oxford and Various Other Collections.* Vol. 1. London.
Tarn, W. W. 1929. Ptolemy II and Arabia. *JEA* 15: 9–25.
Thapar, R. 1987. Epigraphic Evidence and Some Indo-Hellenistic Contacts during the Mauryan Period. Pp. 15–19 in *Indological Studies,* ed. S. K. Maity and U. Thakur. New Delhi.
Tregenza, L. A. 1958. *Egyptian Years.* Oxford.
Whitcomb, D. S. 1988. *Aqaba "Port of Palestine on the China Sea."* Amman.
———. 1989. Coptic Glazed Ceramics from the Excavations at Aqaba, Jordan. *JARCE* 26: 167–82.
Whitcomb, D. S., and Johnson, J. H., eds. 1979. *Quseir al-Qadim 1978 Preliminary Report.* Princeton.
———. 1982a. 1982 Season of Excavations at Quseir al-Qadim. *American Research Center in Egypt Newsletter* 120: 24–30.
———. 1982b. *Quseir al-Qadim 1980 Preliminary Report.* Malibu, CA.
Winkler, H. A. 1938. *Archaeological Survey of Egypt Rock Drawing of Southern Upper Egypt.* Vol. 1. London.
Zitterkopf, R. E., and Sidebotham, S. E. 1989. Stations and Towers on the Quseir-Nile Road. *JEA* 75: 155–89.

STEVEN E. SIDEBOTHAM

REDACTION CRITICISM.

This entry surveys the method of "redaction criticism" as it is applied to the Old and New Testaments.

OLD TESTAMENT

Redaction criticism is a method of biblical study which examines the intentions of the editors or *redactors* who compiled the biblical texts out of earlier source materials. It thus presupposes the results of source and form criticism, and builds upon them.

A. History and Development

Marxsen in his study of Mark's gospel (1st German ed., 1956) appears to have been the first to use the *term* "redaction criticism," but redaction-critical analysis of OT texts is considerably older than this. The discovery of "redactors" in the OT belongs to classical source criticism, as a side effect of the analysis. Once it became clear that the Pentateuch, for example, was compiled from several disparate sources, it followed that someone must have compiled it. But to most source critics of the 19th and early 20th centuries, redactors were not seen as creative editors, still less as literary artists. Redactional *additions* to the text were naturally identified as part of the process of literary analysis, but the redactional *arrangement* of the text was seldom the subject of much interest. This point is sometimes made by saying that redaction was seen in older scholarship as a matter of "scissors and paste." In fact, the picture is less uniform than this suggests. Although the redaction criticism of the Pentateuch attracted much less interest than the study of its original sources, with regard to some other books there has always been more concern among biblical scholars for the finished form of the text and hence for the principles on which it must have been assembled. Even in the 19th century it was common to read Job and Chronicles, for example, from what can now be called a "redaction-critical" point of view.

It was in the years after the Second World War that redaction criticism began to appeal widely to OT scholars. This appeal sometimes resulted from a sense of weariness at traditional source and form criticism, and was part of a desire to move away from what was increasingly thought to be an excessive tendency to fragment the text instead of to read it as it stood. The sense of a renewed respect for the text in its finished shape, and hence for the editors who had worked it into this shape, was often combined with a theological commitment to the Bible in its canonical form (sometimes under the influence of Barthian theology). Gerhard von Rad pioneered this new approach to the OT in a series of articles and books (esp. *PHOE*). In his work on Genesis (*Genesis* OTL), von Rad sought to show that the Yahwist in particular should be seen as a highly creative religious and literary genius, who utterly transformed the materials he used. Beyond that, von Rad even hinted at a possible reading of the Pentateuch as a whole which would attribute a comparable importance to the *final* redactor(s) of the entire work—citing with interest (though not complete approval) a remark of Franz Rosenzweig's to the effect that "R" (see below) ought to be rendered *rabbenu* (in Hebrew, "our Master"), because it is to the redactor that we owe the Bible as it now lies before us (von Rad *Genesis,* 40–42). This may at least serve as a memorable pointer to the renewed respect in which redactors are now held by biblical scholars.

After von Rad, Martin Noth also contributed important works on the redaction of the "Deuteronomistic History" (Joshua-2 Kings) and the work of the Chronicler (Chronicles-Ezra-Nehemiah; see *NDH, NCH,* and *HPT*). Both of these scholars referred to their own work as "traditio-historical." Nowadays, however, this term is more commonly reserved for their contribution to the history of Israel's religious and historical traditions, and the more literary side of their interests would be called redaction criticism.

In Noth's work one can see both the strengths and the weaknesses of redaction criticism. Its strength lies in its minute attention to details of the text, which might strike more casual readers as trivial—small link-passages, tiny changes in wording; and its success lies in explaining puzzling features, such as the sequence in which incidents are related. Noth's work represents what in literary studies is sometimes called a "close reading" of the text, where the reader constantly asks why the particular words or phrases have been chosen in preference to others, and where it is assumed that the authors (or editors) of texts always had a reason for the choices they made. The characteristic weakness of Noth's method is the reverse side of this: a tendency to exaggerate the importance of small details and to foreclose the possibility that some features of the biblical text may be the result of accident or inadvertence. Redaction criticism easily lays itself open to the charge of reading too much significance into the text. Some biblical books may in fact owe much to "scissors and paste" techniques of composition. Though readers should be open to the possibility of finding meaning and theological insight in the way material has been arranged or altered during redaction, they should also not forget that we know very little about the anonymous editors of the OT, and that we do not have the raw materials with which they worked. Redaction critics normally have to reconstruct the redactor's sources from the text as it now stands, and then discover why the redactor changed these (hypothetical) sources to produce the present form. It can easily be seen that it is impossible to check the accuracy of this whole reconstruction against any external controls. This is why the redactional study of Chronicles has always been easier than (and antedates by far) the redaction criticism of the rest of the OT, because we do possess most of the sources with which the redactors of Chronicles worked—namely, the books of Samuel and Kings. Where such external points of reference are lacking, redaction criticism is inevitably rather speculative.

To some extent redaction criticism has been overtaken in the 1980s by newer movements such as canonical criticism and structuralism, which share its interest in the "final form" of biblical texts but are less concerned to derive this from the deliberate intention of one or more redactors and more concerned to read the text as an entity in itself. The "canonical" approach does, however, ask questions about the intentions of the communities responsible for the present form and compass of the entire OT, and so may be said to represent a kind of redaction criticism of the canon as a whole. Thanks to the work of B. S. Childs (e.g., *IOTS*) and others, questions are now asked not only about the significance of the way individual books are arranged but also about the arrangement of whole sections of the OT, such as the Torah (Pentateuch) or the Prophets, and even about the overall organization of the canon. There are still a number of books of the OT, however, which have not been extensively studied by more conventional redaction criticism, and it is therefore probable that the method will continue to be practiced despite these newer approaches.

The history and practice of OT redaction criticism may be studied with the aid of Perrin (1970), Wharton (*IDBSup,* 729–32) and Barton (1984).

B. The Elements of Redaction-Critical Analysis

Strictly speaking, it makes sense to practice redaction criticism only when it is certain that a book is composite in character. For the majority of OT texts, this assumption is fully justified: for example, the Pentateuch and most of the prophetic books are certainly the result of a long process of editing or redaction. Where a text seems to have been composed freely by a single writer, criticism seeks to discover the intentions of this writer, who is an "author" in something like the modern sense of the word, rather than a redactor. Nevertheless, in practice the distinction may be hard to maintain. For example, Ecclesiastes (Qoheleth) has probably undergone several stages of redaction, but the intentions of an original author still shine throughout the whole book; some of the Psalms seem to be freely composed lyrics with no prehistory as a collection of older fragments; and some narrative books (e.g., Ruth, Jonah) probably had a single author from the beginning. Conversely, some of the biblical editors have reshaped the material at their disposal so freely that we might call *them* "authors" rather than mere redactors. For example, the "J" material in Genesis is said by von Rad (see above) to represent such a thoroughgoing reworking of its underlying source materials that "the Yahwist" should no longer be called a redactor at all, but an author, an original writer. See YAHWIST ("J") SOURCE. However, much of the OT is more than a mere assemblage of unrevised fragments, but less than a complete reshaping of old materials into a completely coherent new whole, and it is precisely in relation to such texts that redaction criticism is an appropriate critical tool.

1. Link Passages and the Siglum "R." Source-critical analysis frequently reveals the existence of short passages, individual sentences, or even individual words that cannot be assigned to any of the main sources of a particular passage (J, E, D, or P), but must be assumed to have come into being as part of the process of editing. For example, in Exodus 3:14–15 there are two versions of God's words to Moses at the burning bush: "Say this to the people of Israel, 'I AM has sent me to you,' " and "Say this to the people of Israel, 'The LORD, the God of your fathers, the God of Abraham, the God of Isaac, and the God of Jacob, has sent me to you.' " So that these appear to be successive, rather than alternative, words of God, they are linked by v 15a: "God also said to Moses . . . ," which was not required by either of the original sayings but is needed once they are juxtaposed. Material like this can be ascribed to the redactor, and represents an attempt (sometimes not a very successful attempt) to make the text read smoothly, integrating the original separate sources into a smooth narrative. Source critics use the letter "R" to designate this kind of redactional material.

Sometimes a redactional addition can be identified by the way it integrates into a wider biblical framework a section, for example of narrative, that had an independent existence but in its present context appears to contradict or be inconsistent with something else in the text. For instance, in Genesis 26 there is a story about Isaac and Rebekah at the court of the Philistine king, Abimelech. This story is clearly a version of the same incident related twice of Abraham and Sarah (see Gen 12:10–20 and Genesis 20). Whoever wove together the sources that make up the book of Genesis appears to have realized that the reader might be disturbed if such similar incidents were related without explanation, and accordingly began the story as follows: "Now there was a famine in the land, *besides the former famine that was in the days of Abraham*" (26:1). These words were not required so long as the story formed an independent unit, but they became necessary once it was placed in a continuous narrative containing also the earlier, suspiciously similar story or stories. The effect of the insertion is to make the narrative flow more smoothly than it would otherwise do—though, again, the redactor has been only partially successful, for most readers will feel that the chapter still reads rather awkwardly and will soon suspect that it is in origin an alternative version of one of the other similar incidents, and not genuinely a fresh occurrence.

2. Interpretative Additions. In the examples just discussed, the redactional elements have a minimal function: they merely avoid an awkward break in the text. But redactional additions, even of a few words, can have a profound effect on the meaning of the passage in which they stand. Thus, both Hosea and Ecclesiastes end with what seems to be a proverbial saying. In Hos 14:10—Eng 14:9: "Whoever is wise, let him understand these things; whoever is discerning, let him know them; for the ways of the Lord are right, and the upright walk in them, but transgressors stumble in them." And in Eccl 12:13–14: "The end of the matter: all has been heard. Fear God, and keep his commandments: for this is the whole duty of man. For God will bring every deed into judgment, with every secret thing, whether good or evil." It may be argued that both sayings have an important retrospective effect on the whole book to which they form the conclusion. They tell the reader that the foregoing words (the sayings of Qoheleth; the prophecies of Hosea) are to be read as wise advice on how to please God, and that anyone who does not will suffer punishment. In both cases these redactional additions do not merely serve to shape the book into a finished whole, but they have an *interpretative* function as well. They tell the reader how to understand the book. The redactional addition to Ecclesiastes makes the overall effect of the book much less skeptical and unorthodox than it would otherwise seem, while the addition to Hosea converts a collection of prophecies into a kind of "wisdom" book of generalized advice.

3. Explicit Insertions. So far we have considered types of redactional addition in which there is no question of the redactor addressing the reader in person, but in which the additional material is integrated into the text as though it were original. The OT also contains passages, especially in the narrative books, in which the narrator turns from his source to face the reader directly. For example, twice in the historical books from Joshua through 2 Kings there are summaries of a section of the story that is being told, with comments on its significance from a theological point of view: Judg 2:6–23 and 2 Kgs 17:7–41. Here the compiler of the history offers comments of his own on the story he is telling—for example, "This was so, because the people of Israel had sinned against the LORD their God" (2 Kgs 17:7).

In a similar way, the editors of the prophetic books added headings and indications of the occasions and dates when particular oracles were delivered: e.g., "The words of Jeremiah, the son of Hilkiah . . . to whom the word of the LORD came in the days of Josiah, the son of Amon, king of Judah, in the thirteenth year of his reign" (Jer 1:1). The way in which this is done can sometimes help us to reconstruct the stages by which a book came into its present form. Thus, for instance, the book of Isaiah has *two* redactional "headings," in 1:1 ("The vision of Isaiah the son of Amoz, which he saw concerning Judah and Jerusalem") and in 2:1 ("The word which Isaiah the son of Amoz saw concerning Judah and Jerusalem"). This makes it probable that there was once an edition of Isaiah which began with 2:1, to which chapter 1 was subsequently added, with the result that a fresh heading was needed for the whole book. Here redaction criticism contributes to source criticism and helps it in its task of literary analysis.

4. Changes to the Original Source Material. Ancient editors often had great respect for the material they were assembling and changed very little in it. That is why there are so many inconsistencies in the biblical text. Indeed, it is this that makes it possible for us to reconstruct the sources with which the editors worked, for if they had successfully eliminated all the inconsistencies between the sources, we would not be able to distinguish the sources anyway. The very possibility of source criticism depends on the fact that the redactors so often left alternative versions of incidents unreconciled. Nevertheless, this respect for the original sources did not mean that the redactors *never* changed their raw materials. As well as introducing link passages, marginal comments, and headings, biblical redactors often also make substantial alterations to the documents which they incorporated into their work. In prophetic books, for example, it is common to find comments updating the original prophetic oracles (e.g.,

Isa 16:13–14), and it is probable that the desire to apply the prophet's words to the editor's own situation led to frequent changes in the wording of the original oracles, though this is often hard to prove. The mixture of an extreme respect for an old text and a great freedom in reshaping it to contemporary needs and ideas is one of the most puzzling features of the growth of the Bible for a modern reader, who is used to quite different conventions about the treatment of historical sources. Redaction criticism seeks to clarify how ancient editors went about their work.

5. The Arrangement of the Text. Besides adding new material, the redactors of biblical books also *arranged* existing material into the order in which we now find it. This invisible contribution is probably more important than the individual longer or shorter passages to which we can attach the siglum "R." The effects of arranging older material can be quite varied and may be regarded as forming a sliding scale.

At one end of the scale stands redactional work of a purely *anthological* character. For much of the book of Proverbs, for example, there does not appear to be much significance in the order in which old sayings have been arranged. In the Psalter, there is evidence that some psalms have been grouped together by theme (for instance, Psalms 145–50 form a continuous sequence of psalms of praise) or by form (Psalms 103 and 104 both begin "Bless the Lord, O my soul"); but in many places the order appears random, and in any case the meaning of the individual psalms is not affected by their juxtaposition with each other.

In many prophetic books, there is an element of anthological arrangement, but it is often possible to detect a definite intention in it. For instance, it has been suggested that in placing the particular oracles that form Isaiah 1 at the head of the whole book (see above), the final redactor was providing a short compendium of salient themes from the book as a whole: judgment, mercy, the election of Zion, the remnant, Yahweh's attitude toward sacrifice, and hatred of social injustice (see Jones 1955).

A still more deliberate interpretative intention can be seen in the redaction of the Pentateuch, where material from a wide range of sources, often originally inconsistent with each other, has been arranged so as to tell a single, coherent story running from the creation of the world down to the death of Moses. One may, indeed, speak of many stages in the redaction of the Pentateuch, at each of which such interpretative arrangement must have occurred. Before the four (or more) major sources were combined, each source was itself composed from a variety of older units of tradition. If, as many traditio-historical studies maintain, the stories of the patriarchs (for example) were originally separate stories about unrelated heroes, each used as the cult legend of a particular sanctuary, then the editor we call "J" was already a creative writer who integrated them into a single narrative framework and made each relate to all the others.

Finally, a book such as Judges manifests a highly schematized arrangement of its basic source material where one can scarcely doubt that a redactor is responsible for most of the effect the book now makes on the reader. The stories about various (originally purely local) tribal heroes are arranged schematically, so that each illustrates the same pattern: the Israelites sin, are subjugated by their enemies, cry to God, and are saved by the intervention of a "judge," after which they enjoy a period of "rest" lasting twenty, forty, or eighty years. Indeed, redaction criticism of the other historical books suggests that the same redactor may also have worked on the material in all the books from Joshua to 2 Kings, even though evidence for schematic arrangement is somewhat less marked elsewhere than it is in Judges.

Bibliography

Alter, R. 1981. *The Art of Biblical Narrative.* London.

Barr, J. 1973. *The Bible in the Modern World.* London.

Barton, J. 1984. *Reading the Old Testament: Method in Biblical Study.* Philadelphia.

Clements, R. E. 1977. Patterns in the Prophetic Canon. Pp. 42–55 in *Canon and Authority,* ed. G. W. Coats and B. O. Long. Philadelphia.

Jones, D. R. 1955. The *Traditio* of the Oracles of Isaiah of Jerusalem. *ZAW* 67: 226–46.

Marxsen, W. 1969. *Mark the Evangelist.* Trans. J. Boyce et al. Nashville.

Perrin, N. 1970. *What Is Redaction Criticism?* London.

Porter, J. R. 1979. *Old Testament Historiography.* Pp. 125–62 in *Tradition and Interpretation,* ed. G. W. Anderson. Oxford.

Wolfe, R. E. 1935. The Editing of the Book of the Twelve. *ZAW* 53: 90–129.

JOHN BARTON

NEW TESTAMENT

Redaction criticism is the study of NT texts that concentrates on the unique theological emphases that the writers place upon the materials they used, their specific purposes in writing their works, and the *Sitz im Leben* out of which they wrote. The term is a translation of the German *Redaktionsgeschichte,* which has also been translated "redaction history." Another German term sometimes used to describe this method of study is *Kompositionsgeschichte* or "composition criticism."

A. Origin of the Discipline

Although some scholars had in the past sought to investigate the NT writings from the aspect of their use of various sources, redaction criticism came to the forefront in the mid-1950s with the publication of two major works. The first was Hans Conzelmann's *Die Mitte der Zeit (The Theology of St. Luke),* which appeared in 1954, and the second was Willi Marxsen's *Der Evangelist Markus (Mark the Evangelist),* which appeared in 1956. Conzelmann argued that Luke, in writing his gospel, superimposed over the traditions a "salvation history" scheme in which history was divided into three distinct stages: the period of Israel, the period of Jesus (the "middle" of time), and the period of the Church. He believed that, in so doing, Luke sought to solve the problem of the delay of the Parousia by placing a greater emphasis on realized eschatology. Conzelmann's thesis, which was warmly received at first, has received some telling criticisms, but the interest he generated in the study of how the Evangelists used the gospel traditions was lasting. Marxsen's major contribution lies in his discussion of the relationship of form and redaction criticism. Whereas the form critics spoke of two *Sitz im Lebens* (that of the historical Jesus and that of the early Church), Marxsen pointed out that there existed a third *Sitz im Leben* as well, and this was the situation in life of the Evangelists themselves. In contrast to the interests of form criticism, which were primarily sociological in orientation and sought to discover everything possible about the *Sitz im Leben* of the early Church during the oral period, Conzelmann and Marxsen focused upon the Evangelists and their individual contributions to their works. Whereas form criticism ignored the Evangelists and minimized their contribution in the writing of the gospels, Marxsen pointed out that the Evangelists were not simply collectors or editors of the traditions; they were, on the contrary, theologians. As a result, their works were not to be viewed simply as "Jesus-material collections" but as gospels, and they should be investigated from the perspective of these individual writers. It should not be assumed that before Conzelmann and Marxsen no one had emphasized the theological contribution of the Evangelists to the gospel tradition. Men like W. Wrede, E. Lohmeyer, R. H. Lightfoot, J. M. Robinson, and G. Bornkamm had alluded to this earlier, but it was with the works of Conzelmann and Marxsen that redaction criticism came into its own, and the decades following their works saw this new discipline dominate gospel studies.

B. The Method of Redaction Criticism

Since redaction criticism is primarily interested in investigating how authors used their sources and their unique theological contribution to their sources, it is not surprising that most redaction critical studies of the NT texts have involved the gospels. Whereas at times sources can be discerned in the NT epistles (e.g., Col 1:15–20; Phil 2:6–11; Rom 1:3–4, etc.) or Acts (e.g., the "we sections"), the clearest use of sources is found in the gospels and in particular in the Synoptic Gospels. It is understandable, therefore, that the majority of redaction critical investigations have involved the gospels of Matthew, Mark, and Luke, for behind them lie both written and oral sources of the dominical tradition.

Most redaction critics assume in their investigation of the Synoptic Gospels that Matthew and Luke in composing their gospels used both Mark (or something very much like our present Mark) and a common source or sources which can be designated as Q. The results of most such investigations have tended to support this "solution" of the Synoptic Problem. On the other hand, redactional studies based upon other suggestions of how Matthew, Mark, and Luke are related have tended to be far less successful. Assuming the use of "Mark" by the other two Evangelists, the simplest way of proceeding in the investigation of a Matthean or Lukan redaction criticism is to investigate how they used their source, Mark. Here a synopsis of the gospels is most helpful. By a careful comparison of the additions, the modifications, and the omissions of their Markan source we can detect the theological interests and concerns of Matthew and Luke. Besides investigating the material in the triple tradition, we can also investigate the common material of Matthew and Luke that is not found in Mark and observe the differences we find in the double tradition. By the use of literary and form criticism, we can often determine which of the two traditions is more primitive, i.e., more original, and thus ascertain how the other Evangelist has used the tradition and what this reveals concerning the particular theological emphasis which he seeks to make.

Concerning Mark and the unique material in Matthew and Luke ("M" and "L"), redactional investigation is more difficult, for whereas in the triple and double traditions we either possess their source (Mark) or can reconstruct it (Q) with a reasonable degree of certainty, in the case of Mark, M, and L we have much more difficulty in reconstructing what their sources were like. In the latter instances, we must first—by form critical analysis—attempt to reconstruct what the sources used in these instances were like. This is more difficult, but it is not impossible. With regard to Mark, it would appear that the best areas of investigation for perceiving his redactional emphases are the seams (the "cement" Mark uses to join together different traditions); the explanatory and theological insertions found at various times in the texts (these are often introduced by a *gar*, "for"); the summaries (these are not simply traditions which Mark used but summaries he constructed using various traditional materials); various modifications of individual pericopes and sayings; the selection of the material included; the arrangement of the material; the introduction; and the typical vocabulary of the Evangelist. If we possess the original conclusion of Mark, and if we knew which materials Mark chose not to include in his gospel, this would also be helpful in the investigation of a Mark redaction criticism; but the debate as to the ending of Mark is far from settled, and it is impossible to know what materials Mark possessed but chose to omit. Many of the areas mentioned above are also helpful in the investigation of the M and L materials.

C. The Practice of Redaction Criticism

An example of how a comparison of the triple tradition can lead to insights into the theological emphases of an Evangelist can be found in Luke 4:14. After the baptism and temptation accounts, we read in Matthew and Mark that upon the arrest of John the Baptist, Jesus returned to Galilee. Luke alone, however, states, "And Jesus returned in the power of the Spirit into Galilee. . . ." In comparing the accounts, it becomes clear by this addition to the narrative that Luke wants to emphasize the role of the Spirit in the ministry of Jesus (and, of course, in Acts, in the ministry of the disciples of Jesus). We find similar allusions to the Spirit's ministry in Luke 5:17, where Luke adds to his Markan source the words "and the power of the Lord was with him to heal" (note the connection of the Spirit with "power" in Acts 1:8; 10:38), and in 4:1, where Luke adds to his Markan and Q sources that Jesus, "full of the Holy Spirit," proceeded into the wilderness to be tempted. By carefully observing how Luke handled his sources, it becomes clear that the coming of the Spirit upon Jesus and the disciples and the power to heal associated with this are important Lukan emphases.

In a similar way, when one compares Matt 8:16–17 and 12:15–21 with their parallels in Mark and Luke, and when one compares Matt 13:34–35 with its Markan parallel, it becomes clear that Matthew gives to his source a particular theological emphasis. This is clear in that Mark and Luke never have the expression "This was to fulfill what was spoken by the prophet. . . ." When we compare similar Matthean insertions into his Markan source in Matt 13:14–15; 21:4–5; and 26:54, as well as the frequent occurrence of this theme in the M material (1:22–23; 2:15, 17–18, 23; 4:14–16; 27:9–10) it becomes clear that this is an important theological emphasis on the part of the Evangelist. This is seen most clearly, however, when we compare the occurrences of this emphasis in the material of the triple tradition and note that this emphasis is lacking in Mark and Luke.

With regard to Mark, one of the clearest examples of his redactional activity is found in Mark 8:31–10:45. Assuming the form-critical presupposition that the material in this part of Mark originally circulated as isolated units and that it was Mark who arranged it in its present form, we find a threefold recurring pattern. In this pattern we find a passion prediction on the part of Jesus (8:31; 9:30–32; 10:32–34), followed by an error of some sort by one or more of the disciples (8:32–33; 9:33–34; 10:35–41), which is in turn followed by a collection of teachings on the meaning of discipleship (8:34–9:1; 9:35–10:31; 10:42–45). We also can note the presence of a typically Markan vocabulary throughout this section. It seems quite clear that Mark has arranged this section in order to demonstrate that discipleship involves crossbearing. Even if the situation which caused Mark to emphasize this theme as strongly as he does is uncertain, the emphasis is nonetheless quite clear.

D. The Limitations of Redaction Criticism

The goals and aims of redaction criticism must always be kept in mind. They are in fact quite limited. Redaction criticism is not concerned with the total theology of the biblical writers. A Markan redaction criticism is not concerned with all that Mark believed about God, the authority of the OT, the canon, eschatology, angels, etc. Rather, it is concerned with Mark's unique theological contribution to the gospel traditions he used and his ultimate purpose in writing his gospel. As a result of this emphasis upon the unique element of the Evangelists' writings, there has resulted a strong interest in the "diversity" of the gospels and a corresponding loss of interest in their "unity." If one mistakenly equates these unique theological emphases with the theology of the Evangelists, this problem is further aggravated. Seen in their totality, the theology of the Evangelists possesses a great unity. This is witnessed to by the fact that the early Church incorporated the Evangelists' work side by side into their canon. Placed alongside such works as the Quran, the Vedas, the Tipitaka, the Sayings of Confucius, and the Avesta, the gospels have a tremendous unity. The aim of redaction criticism—which seeks to understand the unique contribution of each Evangelist to the gospel traditions and the *Sitz im Leben* out of which they wrote—is clearly focused upon the "diversity" of these works. The legitimacy of such investigation is undeniable, but it is clearly erroneous to assume that the redactional emphases of the individual Evangelists represent their total theology or to lose sight of their "unity."

E. The Value of Redaction Criticism

Redaction criticism has brought a number of important insights into the study of the NT texts. With regard to the gospels, these insights have shown us that the Evangelists were not mere collectors of the traditions but interpreters of them. As a result, the gospels can and should be studied as wholes in light of the situation of each author. This does not mean that the study of the gospels for the purpose of learning about the *Sitz im Leben* of Jesus or the early Church is illegitimate. It means rather that any study of the gospels is incomplete if it does not take into consideration the unique theological contributions of the Evangelists. Only if redaction criticism is included in the study of the gospels will we be dealing with the total history of the gospel traditions. Another contribution of redaction criticism is that it focuses the attention of the exegete upon the actual meaning of the text. Whereas form criticism and the quest for the historical Jesus used the gospels as sources for their investigations, redaction criticism is concerned with what each author sought to teach and proclaim by his writings. Redaction criticism is therefore concerned with investigating the final canonical product for its own sake, and not simply as a means of gaining historical information about the historical Jesus or the early Church. Redaction criticism sees the meaning of the present canonical text as the final goal of its investigation.

Another value of redaction criticism that can be mentioned is the hermeneutical insight that is gained from such an investigation. By observing how the Evangelists used their sources, we are assisted both in interpreting difficult texts and in grasping their significance for today. An example of the former is seen in Luke 14:26, where Jesus states that to follow him one must "hate" his father, mother, wife, children, brothers, and sisters. By observing the parallel in Matt 10:37, we understand that the Evangelist knew that "hating" was an idiomatic expression for "loving less." Thus, his redactional work enables us to understand better what Luke 14:26 means. With regard to the application of biblical texts, we might refer here to the famous "exception clause" found in Matt 5:32 and 19:9. It is clear that the Matthean sources (Mark and Q) lacked this exception clause. This is also true of the Pauline version of the saying in 1 Cor 7:10–11. By his addition of this exception clause, Matthew reveals that he did not understand Jesus' teaching on divorce as a legal prescription to cover all circumstances but rather as an example of Jesus' use of overstatement. This Matthew clarified for his readers by his addition of the exception clause. How one evaluates this interpretative comment will, of course, vary, but by his redactional activity Matthew reveals his interpretation of this dominical teaching for his reader.

The final contribution of redaction criticism which will be mentioned involves the Synoptic Problem. In seeking to understand the literary relationship which exists between Matthew, Mark, and Luke, redaction criticism has demonstrated that the redactional work of Matthew and Luke can be easily understood if both Evangelists used Mark as their source. On the other hand, the redactional work of Mark and Luke cannot be understood on the basis of their having used Matthew. One of the strongest arguments today for the priority of Mark lies in the success of redactional critical studies based upon this presupposition. Future discussion of the Synoptic Problem will no doubt involve more such redactional investigation.

Bibliography

Best, E. 1965. *The Temptation and the Passion: The Markan Soteriology.* New York.
Bornkamm, G.; Barth, G.; and Held, H. J. 1963. *Tradition and Interpretation in Matthew.* Trans. P. Scott. Philadelphia.
Caird, G. B. 1975. The Study of the Gospels: III. Redaction Criticism. *ExpTim* 87: 168–72.
Carlston, C. E. 1975. *The Parables of the Triple Tradition.* Philadelphia.
Conzelmann, H. 1960. *The Theology of St. Luke.* Trans. G. Buswell. New York.
Edwards, R. A. 1971. *The Signs of Jonah in the Theology of the Evangelists and Q.* Naperville, IL.
Flender, H. 1967. *Luke, Theologian of Redemptive History.* Trans. R. Fuller. Philadelphia.
Gundry, R. H. 1982. *Matthew: A Commentary on His Literary and Theological Art.* Grand Rapids.
Kee, H. C. 1977. *Community of the New Age: Studies in Mark's Gospel.* Philadelphia.
Kingsbury, J. D. 1969. *The Parables of Jesus in Matthew 13: A Study in Redaction-Criticism.* Richmond.
———. 1975. *Matthew: Structure, Christology, Kingdom.* Philadelphia.
Kloppenborg, J. S. 1987. *The Formation of Q.* Philadelphia.
Marshall, I. H. 1971. *Luke: Historian and Theologian.* Grand Rapids.
Martin, R. P. 1981. *Reconciliation: A Study of Paul's Theology.* Atlanta.
Marxsen, W. 1969. *Mark the Evangelist: Studies on the Redaction History of the Gospel.* Trans. J. Boyce, D. Juel, W. Poehlmann, and R. A. Harrisville. Nashville.
Meier, J. P. 1979. *The Vision of Matthew.* New York.
Perrin, N. 1969. *What Is Redaction Criticism?* Philadelphia.
Pryke, E. J. 1978. *Redactional Style in the Marcan Gospel.* New York.
Rohde, J. 1968. *Rediscovering the Teachings of the Evangelist.* Trans. D. M. Barton. Philadelphia.
Smalley, S. S. 1978. *John—Evangelist and Interpreter.* Greenville, SC.
Stein, R. H. 1969. What Is *Redaktionsgeschichte? JBL* 88: 45–56.
———. 1971. The Proper Methodology for Ascertaining a Markan Redaction History. *NovT* 13: 181–98.
———. 1981. *An Introduction to the Parables of Jesus.* Philadelphia.
Talbert, C. H. 1969. Tradition and Redaction in Rom 12:9–21. *NTS* 16: 83–93.
Tannehill, R. C. 1986. *The Narrative Unity of Luke-Acts.* Philadelphia.

ROBERT H. STEIN

REDEMPTION. This entry examines how the notion of redemption is articulated in OT and NT texts.

OLD TESTAMENT

The word "redemption" is the accepted translation of the literal derivative of two Heb roots, *gʾl* and *pdh.* In context, it may have particular nuances. It is also a prophetic, eschatological concept. In the Hebrew Bible, God's interrelationship with nature, humanity, and especially Israel is expressed in metaphors drawn from observable natural and social phenomena (including politics, family, law, etc.). For example, the God-Israel relationship is variously depicted as analogous to that of a king-subject, of a father-son, of a husband-wife, etc. Likewise, the theological dimension of the redeemer-redeemed relationship is also built upon a social and legal foundation.

A. Literal Meaning: Sociolegal Redemption
   1. Land and Houses
   2. Indentured Servants
   3. Cultic Offerings
   4. The Firstborn
   5. The Wife of a Deceased Relative—*gʾl*
   6. The Owner of a Goring Ox
   7. The Blood Redeemer
   8. Ransom
   9. Summary
B. Metaphorical Meaning: The God-Israel Relationship
   1. Redeeming Individuals or Groups from Adversity
   2. Redeeming Israel from Slavery in Egypt
   3. Future Redemption from Destruction and/or Exile
   4. Conclusions
C. Conceptual Meaning: The Eschatological Age of Redemption
   1. Characteristics of the Age
   2. Role of Repentance

A. Literal Meaning: Sociolegal Redemption

In sociolegal contexts, redemption generally refers to the rescue of an individual from a difficult obligation by means of a monetary payment.

1. Land and Houses. Physical property such as land and houses could also be reclaimed through monetary payment. The Israelites were considered tenants on God's land, with the right to produce. Therefore, transfer of property always reverted to the original tenant or his heirs at the jubilee (Lev 25:8–23). If an impoverished Israelite (termed "brother" in Leviticus 25) was forced to sell his land to raise cash, his near redeemer (i.e., kinsman) was supposed to redeem it (v 25, Heb *gʾl*). If the Israelite did not have a redeemer, but had subsequently gained enough wealth, then of course he himself could redeem it (vv 26–27); otherwise, the land would automatically return to him at the jubilee year (v 28). In contrast, Eshnunna #39 states that a man only had the right to redeem his house when the purchaser wished to sell it.

A house in a walled city was not considered "land." If not redeemed within a year, it became the buyer's permanent property (vv 29–30). However, houses outside of walled cities were considered to be redeemable as fields (v 31). Only houses in Levitical cities were always redeemable by the Levites (vv 32–33). Levites were never permitted to sell their land to non-Levites (v 34).

By implication, perhaps, one could sell land in perpetuity to one's own relative. Accordingly, Jeremiah, a priest (and therefore, a Levite), was able to buy the fields of his first cousin Hanamel in the extended family territory of Anathoth (Jer 32:6–15). Jeremiah had the right of redeemer and heir (vv 7–8; cf. Ezek 11:15). Similarly, Boaz was one of Naomi's relatives and redeemers (Ruth 2:20); however, a nearer redeemer-kinsman existed whose claim therefore took precedence over his (3:12–13). Only when that redeemer surrendered his right was Boaz permitted to buy Naomi's land (4:1–9).

It is interesting that if a person was defrauded and then died, the criminal would be required to pay the *ʾāšām* ("guilt") penalty to the *gōʾēl* of the deceased. If there was no redeemer, then the penalty would be paid to the sanctuary (Num 5:8).

2. Indentured Servants. Also, persons could be rescued from servitude by a monetary payment. An impoverished Israelite (again, "brother") who was forced to sell himself into indentured servitude to a resident alien had the same rights of redemption *(gʾl)* as existed with relationship to land. Indentured servitude was not slavery—the resident alien was not allowed to oppress the indentured Israelite (v 53). Israelites could not serve in perpetuity since they were ultimately God's servants whom He had removed from Egypt (v 55). Verses 48–49 indicate that the obligation of redeemer devolved upon the nearest relative.

In the case of a daughter sold to an Israelite as a maidservant/concubine, her master had to permit her to be redeemed (Heb *pdh*) if he was not pleased with her (Exod 21:8; cf. Lev 19:20; for a somewhat similar situation, cf. Hammurabi #119). In Ps 49:8 (—Eng 49:7) notes the refusal of a man to redeem *(pdh)* his brother; perhaps a lamentable reference to those who had the financial means (vv 7, 11, 12) but not the moral inclination to ransom their relatives from servitude.

3. Cultic Offerings. A cultic offering could be reclaimed by substituting a monetary payment. The offering of an unclean animal (Lev 27:9–13, 27), a house (vv 14–15), a field (vv 16–25), and a tithe of the land (vv 30–31) was redeemable by the owner at full monetary value plus 20 percent. Perhaps the case of Jonathan, who was unaware that he was disobeying his father's oath (1 Sam 14:27), is similar. The people redeemed *(pdh)* him (i.e., rescued him) from the death penalty (v 45). In Leviticus 27, redemption (i.e., substitution) of a tithe of animals (vv 32–33) or of a banned object or person was forbidden (vv 28–29).

4. The Firstborn. In commemoration of the tenth plague, all firstborn were sanctified, subject to being sacrificed to God (Exod 13:15). However, under prescribed circumstances, substitutions could be made. Firstborn asses (as unclean animals) were to be redeemed *(pdh)* by sheep (13:13; 34:20; Num 18:15), but the firstborn of unclean animals could not be redeemed (Num 18:17). At the age of one month, all firstborn male Israelites were to be redeemed *(pdh)* by five shekels (vv 15–16; cf. 3:46–51), apparently by the father (Exod 13:13, 15).

5. The Wife of a Deceased Relative—*gʾl*. In an incident with similarities to the law of levirate marriage (Deut 25:5–10) and related to the redemption of land, the book of Ruth assumes that a near kinsman-redeemer was supposed "to raise up the name of the deceased upon his property" by legally acquiring "the wife of the deceased" (Ruth 4:5, 10, with Deut 25:5–6) and siring children who would inherit the property of the deceased. When the near kinsman refused, he signaled this by removing his sandal (Ruth 4:7–8 with Deut 25:9). However, it may also be that the episode in Ruth is connected to the case in Exod 21:8 *(pdh)* of the daughter sold as a maidservant/concubine. In both Exod 21:7–8 and Ruth 3:9 the term *ʾmh* is used. Thus, when Boaz called Ruth "my daughter" in 3:10–11, he may have been saying that "I am adopting you as my daughter, and I will redeem you as one redeems his daughter from servitude." Another perhaps more remote possibility is that Boaz may have been protecting the widow Ruth in consonance with the law in Deut 24:17–18, which emphasizes God's redemption *(pdh)* of Israel from Egypt (see below).

6. The Owner of a Goring Ox. When an ox with a reputation for goring killed a person, its owner was subject to the death penalty. However, the owner was permitted to redeem *(pdh)* himself from the death penalty if a "ransom *(kpr)* is laid upon him" to be given to the deceased's next of kin (Exod 21:29–30). This law may be related to that of the "blood redeemer" below.

7. The Blood Redeemer. The blood redeemer *(gōʾēl haddām)* was the closest male relative of a murdered person, as is indicated by the stories of Gideon's killing of his brothers' slayers (Judg 8:18–21; cf. 1 Kgs 16:11); of Joab's killing of Abner, his brother's slayer (2 Sam 3:27); and of Absalom's killing of Amnon, his sister's rapist (2 Sam 13:28–29). In her parable of Absalom's act, the wise woman of Tekoa specifically used the term "blood redeemer" (Heb *gōʾēl haddām;* 2 Sam 14:11). The case of Absalom is important, since it illustrates broadened parameters of the blood redeemer, who avenged not just murder but severe harm (in this case, rape) inflicted upon a close relative.

In the case of a homicide (Num 35:12–28; Deut 19:4–6, 11–13; Joshua 20; 2 Sam 14:11), the victim's blood redeemer was responsible for putting to death the person who had committed premeditated murder (Num 35:19); the murderer was handed over to the blood redeemer by the elders of his city (Deut 19:12). The accidental murderer found safety in the designated cities of refuge (Num 35:12–15, 22–25; Josh 20:4–6). However, if the blood redeemer killed the accidental murderer before he could reach a city of refuge, or after the accidental murderer had left the city of refuge prior to the death of the high priest, the blood redeemer was guiltless (Num 35:26–28; Deut 19:5–6). In contrast, the Middle Assyrian Laws (A10, B2) proclaimed that the "owner of the life" (parallel to the biblical "blood redeemer") could take compensation in lieu of execution.

8. Ransom. Although not strictly understood as redemption, the Heb root *kpr* ("ransom") is equated to *pdh* in Exod 21:29–30 (see above); thus, "redemption" and "ransom" are not unrelated concepts. The severity and extreme economic cost of ransom, which would at least on occasion be the ransom for a life, is attested by Prov 13:8, "The ransom of a man's life *(kpr npš)* is his wealth" (*EncMiqr* 4: 231–33; cf. Hammurabi #32). The inability to ransom life from the death penalty is reflected in the laws of (a) the murderer, "Do not take ransom for the life of the murderer" (Num 35:31); (b) the blood redeemer, "Do not take ransom from him who has fled to his city of refuge" (v 32); and (c) in the wisdom statement on the husband's reaction to his wife's adulterer, "He will not accept any ransom" (Prov 6:35, see vv 32–34). Of course, there is no ransom which can avert God's decree (Ps 49:8–9—note the connection to *pdh;* Job 36:18), although God can redeem from death (Job 33:24). "Ransom" is paralleled to judicial bribery *(šḥd)* in 1 Sam 12:8 and Amos 5:12. It may be to the latter text that Prov 21:18 relates, "the wicked is the ransom for the righteous." The purpose of the half-shekel ransom given by each adult Israelite in

Exod 30:12 was to save their lives from a divinely sent plague (cf. the plague caused by David's census in 2 Samuel 24).

9. Summary. The *gōʾēl* ("redeemer") was always the nearest adult male relative, responsible for the economic well-being of his kin, inasmuch as the latter lacked sufficient means to redeem his own property. As blood redeemer, the *gōʾēl* avenged murder and, by extension, all severe harm inflicted upon a relative. The passages in Exod 21:8 and Ps 49:8, and the redemption of the firstborn son in Exod 13:13, 15, all indicate that *pdh* is also used primarily in reference to a near male relative (usually the father), or to one's redemption of one's own property (such as firstborn unclean animals). The one exception is the case of Jonathan, who was redeemed from the death penalty by the people. However, it may be argued that the relationship of a people to their prince-leader is here modeled on the familial context. Unlike *gʾl*, which can take an inanimate object, the object of *pdh* is always an animal or human (*TDNT* 4: 328–35). Concerning ransom *(kpr)*, one usually paid it to rescue oneself from an extreme penalty.

B. Metaphorical Meaning: The God-Israel Relationship

1. Redeeming Individuals or Groups from Adversity. The concept that God was the ultimate redeemer-rescuer of the individual and of the collective body from adversity was deeply entrenched in Israelite thought already during the preexilic period. Jacob's blessing of Ephraim and Manasseh (Gen 48:16) provides a good illustration in its reference to "the angel who redeemed *(gōʾēl)* me from all evil" (cf. Isa 29:22, "The Lord who redeemed [*pdh*] Abraham"). God redeems *(pdh)* from unspecified "troubles" (Heb *ṣrh,* 2 Sam 4:9; 1 Kgs 1:29; Ps 25:22).

Specifically, people prayed to God concerning redemption from (a) enemies (*pdh:* Ps 31:5–6 [—Eng 4–5]; 44:27 [—Eng 26]; cf. v 11 [—Eng 10]; 55:19 [—Eng 18]; *gʾl* parallel with *pdh:* 69:19; *gʾl:* 107:2; Job 19:25); (b) the wicked (*pdh:* Ps 26:11; cf. vv 4–10; 34:22–23 [—Eng 21–22]); (c) oppressors (*pdh:* Jer 15:21; Ps 119:134; Job 6:23); (d) death (*pdh:* Ps 49:16 [—Eng 15]; Job 5:20; 33:28; cf. v 24, where *kpr* is paralleled probably to the root *pdh; gʾl:* Ps 103:4); and (e) punishment for sin (*pdh:* Ps 130:7–8).

Furthermore, God redeems *(gʾl)* by prosecuting (Heb *ryb*) enemies (Ps 119:154; Lam 3:58) and those who would steal land and orphans' fields (Prov 23:10–11). Similarly, in Psalm 72, the ideal king, appointed by God and recipient of divine righteousness (vv 1–2), will redeem *(gʾl)* the lives of the poor and needy for their oppressors (vv 12–14; cf. Deut 24:17–18; see below).

2. Redeeming Israel from Slavery in Egypt. The archetypical act of divine redemption was God's saving of Israel from Egyptian bondage. In Exodus, God redeems *(gʾl)* the Israelites from the suffering of Egypt and saves *(nṣl)* them from slavery (6:6) in order to make them His people (v 7) and to bring them to the promised land. In the Song of the Sea, the redeemed *(gʾl)* people are led to God's pasture (Exod 15:13).

In Deuteronomy, *pdh* is always used to indicate redemption from Egypt. The context of 7:8, 9:26, and 13:6 is opposition to idolatry. In 15:5, 21:8, and 24:18, the rescue from Egypt is mentioned in contrast to inhumane behavior. Deut 9:26 and 21:8 are parts of petitions to God to forgive the people, while the other four occurrences are motivations for obedience to the associated laws.

Outside of Exodus, the only place in which *gʾl* is used in reference to the redemption from Egypt is in Psalms. Ps 74:2 ("Remember your community which you acquired long ago, the tribe of your inheritance which you redeemed, Mount Zion, where you dwell") is a call for God to defeat Israel's destroyers as in days of old. Verse 2 probably hearkens back to Exod 15:13, 16–17. Ps 77:16 ("you redeemed your people by your arm") is in the midst of a passage recounting God's mighty acts (vv 12–21). Psalm 78 is a history from Egypt to David; in v 35 God, the *gōʾēl,* is paralleled to "rock," and in v 42, God is said to have redeemed *(pdh)* Israel from Egypt, described as the "enemy." Finally, Ps 106:10, again part of a history, parallels *gʾl* with "save" *(yšʿ)* and refers to the Egyptians as "hating" and "enemy."

Aside from Ps 78:42, *pdh* in the Psalms refers to redemption from Egypt only in Ps 111:9 where it parallels the covenant. *Pdh* in 2 Sam 7:23 (= 1 Chr 17:21) is Deuteronomistic. Mic 6:4 reminds Israel of the redemption from slavery as part of a rebuke; *pdh* is paralleled to *ʿlh,* God's "bringing up" Israel out of Egypt. Finally, in Neh 1:10, Nehemiah mentions the redemption from Egypt in order to beseech God's mercies to permit the return to Zion (vv 4–12); the verse emphasizes Israel as God's people and "servant."

3. Future Redemption from Destruction and/or Exile. The beliefs that God had redeemed Israel from Egypt, and that God had redeemed and would continue to redeem the individual and the group from present distress, were succeeded by the faith that God would redeem Israel from exile at the "end of days." All eight eschatological uses of *pdh* and, with the exception of Ps 107:2, all twenty-eight such uses of *gʾl* (24 of which appear in later portions of Isaiah) occur in prophecy (as is the case with the one such use of *kpr*).

The earliest prophetic intimation of eschatological usages of *pdh* and *gʾl* occur in Hosea. In Hos 7:13, *pdh* indicates God's readiness to redeem the northern Israelites from the destruction that awaits them due to their idolatry (vv 1, 4). Similarly, in Hos 13:14, God would redeem (*pdh* paralleling *gʾl*) Ephraim from death, except for the obstinacy of Ephraim's idolatry (vv 1, 2, 9, 12). In Isa 1:27, the redemption *(pdh)* of Zion from its sinful state will take place through justice and righteousness, i.e., the death of the sinners (v 28; cf. Prov 21:18) and the institution of a just leadership (v 26). The eschatological use of *gʾl* as "return from exile" first appears in Mic 4:10. *Pdh* and *gʾl* are used together in this sense in Jer 31:11 (from one of Jeremiah's prophecies of redemption to Judah). However, Jer 50:34, in which *gʾl* appears, is inauthentic and late exilic (Unterman 1987: 149). The first half of v 34 is nearly identical to Prov 23:11, pointing perhaps to the roots of God's redemption of Israel here in God's care for the unprotected in society.

The exilic and postexilic portions of Isaiah, focusing as they do on the concept of redemption, house the vast majority of the eschatological usages of *gʾl* and *pdh,* and the one such occurrence of *kpr* (43:3, in reference to the redemption of Israel from Egypt). In truth, Isaiah 34–35 and 40–66 draw upon many different themes and images which attached themselves to *gʾl* and *pdh* (and to the general concept of redemption) over the course of time. Some of these elements, such as creation and Israel as God's servant, are distinctive to this collection (Stuhlmueller 1970). These themes and images interweave, overlap, and defy separation—sure testimony to the ability of the author's mind to contain simultaneously a multitude of related images concerning the idea of redemption. Thus, it is extremely difficult, if not impossible, to isolate in this material specific sociolegal roots for the various usages of both *gʾl* (35:9; 41:14; 43:1, 14; 44:6, 22–24; 47:4; 48:17, 20; 49:7, 26; 51:10; 52:3, 9; 54:5, 8; 59:20; 60:16; 62:12; 63:4, 9, 16) and *pdh* (35:10 = 51:11; 50:2).

Some of these themes and images which play significant roles and occur with some frequency are (a) God/parent–Israel/child (Isa 43:1, 6; 44:24; 49:15; 63:16; 64:7; 66:9, 13); (b) God/master–Israel/servant (41:14; 43:10; 44:21; 48:20; 49:3, 5); (c) God/husband–Israel/wife (50:1; 54:5–8; 62:5); (d) God as a furious, vengeful warrior (often with *nqm*) on behalf of Israel (34:1–8; 40:10; 42:13–15; 49:25–26; 51:9; 59:16–20; 62:1–5; 66:15–16); (e) Israel as God's chosen (*bḥr;* 41:8–9; 43:10; 44:1–2; 48:10; 49:7); (f) the new Exodus (35; 40:3; 42:16; 43:2–3, 16, 19; 48:21; 49:9–12; 51:10–11; 52:12); (g) God's saving Israel (primarily, *ysʿ;* 35:4; 43:3, 11, 12, 13; 44:17; 45:8, 15, 17, 21, 22; 46:13; 47:3; 49:8, 25, 26; 50:2; 51:5, 6, 8; 52:7, 10; 59:1, 11, 16, 17; 60:16, 18; 62:1, 11; 63:1, 5, 8, 9); (h) God caring for His poor and needy people (41:17; 49:13; 51:21; 54:11; 58:7; 66:2); (i) God comforting *(nḥm)* Israel (40:1; 49:13; 51:3, 12, 19; 52:9; 54:11; 61:2; 66:13), having mercy *(rḥm)* upon them (49:10, 15; 54:7, 8, 10; 60:10; 63:7, 15), and loving *(ʾhb)* them (41:8; 43:4; 63:9); and (j) God prosecuting *(ryb)* Israel's enemies (41:11, 21; 49:25; 50:8; 51:22) and helping *(ʿzr)* Israel (41:10, 13, 14; 44:2; 49:8; 50:7, 9), so that Israel need not fear *(lʾ tyrʾ;* 35:4; 41:10, 13, 14; 43:1, 5; 44:2; 51:7; 54:4, 14).

The latest prophetic eschatological use of *pdh* is in Zech 10:8—return from Exile. The same meaning appears in Ps 107:2.

4. Conclusions. As time passed, the usages of the roots *gʾl* and *pdh* as verbs and objects (in reference to the Israelites) became theologically synonymous, so that *gʾl* and *pdh* are parallels in Hos 13:14; Isa 35:9–10 (cf. 51:10–11); Jer 31:11; and Ps 69:19. These parallels indicate that lines of distinction between the meanings of the two roots had become blurred in the thinking about God's relationship with Israel. Yet, certain facets of the social and legal roots remained.

(1) The *gōʾēl* was still always the nearest adult male kinsman with the right and the ability of redemption. Thus, God as *gōʾēl* at the very least points to God's close relationship to Israel, probably as father (Isa 63:16) or husband (Isa 54:5–8).

(2) It should be remembered that the enslavement of Israel by Egypt and other oppressions are not comparable to the indentured servitude of Leviticus 25 (vv 3, 53; cf. Deut 15:12–15). In the case of the indentured servant, the redeemer has no animosity toward the temporary master of his kinsman, but rather has the duty to pay off his kinsman's debt or hire (Israel's redemption "without money" from unnecessary enslavement in Isa 52:3 may be in conscious opposition to the circumstances of Leviticus 25; cf. Isa 50:1). Thus, the conditions of Leviticus 25 are not mirrored in the concept of redemption from Exile.

(3) It seems obvious that the divine redemption from Egyptian slavery in order to bring Israel to Canaan became the model for the return from the Babylonian Exile (Jer 16:14–15 = 23:7–8). The most plausible sociolegal root for God's redemption of Israel, whether from Egyptian slavery, Babylonian Exile, or anonymous oppressors and enemies, is the law of the blood redeemer. The *gōʾēl haddām* comes with a sword (Num 35:19, 21) and fury (Deut 19:6) to avenge his beloved relative, a portrait which is similar to the depiction of God as the redeeming, vengeful warrior in Isaiah (e.g., 49:25–26; 51:9–11; 59:16–20).

(4) All sociolegal cases of *gʾl,* with the exception of cultic offerings, concern an impoverished Israelite (Leviticus 25) or one who is severely abused (requiring the intervention of the *gōʾēl haddām*). It is a logical step to include all the deprived members of society. Thus, it is not surprising that God is portrayed as the redeemer of the oppressed, the widow, the stranger, and the poor (Deut 24:17–18; Ps 72:12–14; Prov 23:10–11).

(5) Ultimately, the association of God's redemption with rescue and mercy gives the individual hope that God will redeem one from punishment for sin (Hos 7:13; Isa 44:22; Ps 130:7–8), and even from death (Hos 13:14; Ps 49:16; 103:4; Job 5:20; 33:28).

C. Conceptual Meaning: The Eschatological Age of Redemption

1. Characteristics of the Age. The Hebrew prophets understood destruction and exile as divine punishment for Israel's obstinate, rebellious sins. However, God's love for Israel would eventually compel Him to bring about the age of redemption, which included certain minimal components (cf. *EncMiqr* 2: 388–91): (a) the entire people would be gathered from all the lands of exile in a new exodus which would return them to the land of Israel (e.g., Jer 30:3); (b) once in the promised land, the people would enjoy miraculous agricultural harvests (e.g., Amos 9:13) and increased flocks (e.g., Jer 31:28); (c) the people would dwell securely (e.g., Amos 9:15; Ezek 37:25) and would increase (e.g., Jer 31:27); (d) the Davidic monarchy would be restored (e.g., Amos 9:11; Ezek 37:24) and under just rulers (e.g., Isa 11:1–5; Jer 23:4–5); (e) the cult and priesthood would be reconstituted (Jer 33:18; Zech 3); and (f) all Israel would obey God's Torah—an exilic idea (Jer 31:34; Ezek 36:27).

2. Role of Repentance. Lev 26:40–41 (a confession), Deut 4:29–31, and Deut 30:1–10 all presuppose repentance as a condition for redemption. However, the prophets differed on the significance of Israel's repentance in the redemption process (Unterman 1987).

Amos, the first prophet to predict national destruction and exile, regarded redemption in the context that the sinners would die, leaving a righteous remnant (9:8–10). In this scheme of redemption, repentance is superfluous. Hosea, however, vacillated between prophesying a redemption dependent upon repentance (3:5; 14:2–9) and one that was not (2:16–25; 11:8–11). Sometimes Hosea seems to have felt that Israel did not deserve the benefits of God's love unless it repented, and sometimes it seems that God's love simply overwhelmed His senses. Hosea, more so than Amos, was the first prophet to live on the edge of national disaster. Thus, the need to relate repentance and redemption was more critical with him than with Amos, especially since, unlike Amos, Hosea conceived of no innocent remnant. With no prophetic models to follow, and given the tempestuous times in which he lived and how they must have played upon his psyche, it is not surprising that Hosea's views of the redemptive process fluctuated. It appears that First Isaiah viewed repentance as a prerequisite for redemption (Milgrom 1964: 169).

Jeremiah's thoughts on the relationship of repentance to redemption progress through three stages. First, during Josiah's reign, the young Jeremiah believed that Israel's repentance and God's mercy were the determining conditions for redemption (3:6–13; 3:19–4:2; 31:2–9, 15–22). Second, between 597 and 587 B.C.E., in prophecies of redemption to the Jehoiachin exiles, a subtle shift occurred as the element of divine mercy outweighed that of human repentance (24:4–7; 29:10–14). Jeremiah had begun to despair of the people's ability to return to God of their own accord. Finally, at the time of the destruction of Jerusalem, the aged prophet abandoned the principle of free will and the attendant demand for repentance. On the basis of his tragic experience, yet consumed by his belief in God's eternal love of Israel, Jeremiah concluded that redemption would be solely the work of God, as permanent as creation itself (31:27–37; 32:37–41; 33:1–26; 50:17–20).

Ezekiel never prophesied that repentance was the determinant of national redemption. In 11:17–20 (date 592? cf. 8:1), God promises repentance as part of the redemptive process, reminiscent of Jeremiah's second stage. In later prophecies (chaps. 36–37), much like his model Jeremiah, Ezekiel did not mention repentance. Rather, he said that God would redeem Israel for His name's sake (36:21–23).

The only clear call for repentance in exilic Isaiah is in 44:22c, which is mitigated by the surrounding verses. The main theme in Isaiah 40–54 is unconditional redemption due to God's mercies. The call to repentance in 55:6–7 may refer to individual, not national, redemption, or it may be spurred by the immediacy of the return under Cyrus. In chaps. 56–66, postexilic Isaiah clearly states that God will redeem the repentant (59:20; see also 56:1–2; 58:1–14; 59:9–13; 64:4–6). It appears that the return to the land, presumed in Isaiah 56–66, rejuvenated the old preexilic concept of obedience to God in order to ensure national success.

If Jeremiah, Ezekiel, and Isaiah 40–66 are taken as forming a continuous line from the latter part of the 7th century B.C.E. to the latter part of the 6th, a pattern emerges. As long as destruction had not overtaken Judah, prophecies of redemption still contained the precondition of repentance (dovetailing with the standard prophetic calls for repentance to avoid divine punishment). However, once Jerusalem has been destroyed and the full Exile is under way, redemption is seen as totally dependent upon God's beneficence. It appears that the effect of the cruelty of destruction and the harshness of exile served in large measure to wipe out the need for repentance (e.g., Jer 30:5–17; Isa 47:6). The manifestation of the punishment is a motivation for divine forgiveness and purification of the people. In the exilic situation, the very demand to repent in order to effect national redemption might have been more than the people could have borne.

With the Persian defeat of Babylon and the advent of the actual restoration to the land, the requirement of repentance begins to reappear. Finally, with the people again in their homeland, the demand to return to God regains its preexilic prominence.

Bibliography

Johnson, A. R. 1953. The Primary Meaning of *gʾl*. *VTSup* 1: 67–77.

Milgrom, J. 1964. Did Isaiah Prophesy during the Reign of Isaiah? *VT* 14: 164–82.

Stamm, J. J. 1940. *Erlosen und Vergeben im Alten Testament.* Bern.

Stuhlmueller, C. 1970. *Creative Redemption in Deutero-Isaiah.* AnBib 43. Rome.

Unterman, J. 1987. *From Repentance to Redemption.* JSOTSup 54. Sheffield.

JEREMIAH UNTERMAN

NEW TESTAMENT

In the NT, the notion of redemption carries two meanings. First, it is regarded as the work of God in delivering His people from spiritual bondage unto Himself, usually said to be at the expense of Christ's death. Second, it is also associated with the eschatological deliverance and resurrection of God's people at the Parousia of Christ.

A. Terminology of Redemption
B. Conceptual Background
C. Redemption and Salvation
D. Eschatological Redemption
E. "Redeem the Time"
F. The Doctrine of Redemption in History

A. Terminology of Redemption

There are two word groups which are commonly used to speak of redemption in the NT. Warfield has done a close study of the vocabulary involved (1929: 328–41). It is not possible to assign any particular word to the domain of one author; both word groups are popularly used throughout the literature.

Agorazō is the common word for "to buy" (see Mark 13:44); "to buy" or "to redeem" may also denote the act of redemption (1 Cor 6:20). The compounded form *exagorazō* was taken by Chrysostom with its full etymological force—"to buy away from." This has been taken to unwarranted lengths by those who define the verb, itself, as "to buy out of the agora, never to return." Its etymological roots seem not to have affected its meaning, although in context "redeem" usually implies that God redeems people away from something (Morris 1965: 40).

The other word group, popular in the LXX, is represented by *lytroō* ("to redeem," Titus 2:14; always in the middle or passive in the NT). Its cognates are *lytron* ("ransom," only in Mark 10:45 = Matt 20:28), *antilytron* ("ransom," only in 1 Tim 2:6), *lytrōsis* ("redemption," Heb 9:12), and the popular NT word *apolytrōsis* ("redemption," Rom 3:24). In his commentary on Romans (col. 531), Chrysostom wished to invest *apolytrōsis* with an intensive force based on the compounding of *apo* ("away from") with *lytrōsis*. This led him to conclude that the "redemption of the body" in Rom 8:23 was not merely *lytrōsis*, but being redeemed never to return to the original captivity. The actual use in the NT does not indicate that *apolytrōsis* in itself is an intensive form.

In the OT, redemption normally implies redeeming at a price, although there are exceptions (Marshall 1974: 153 n.1; Murray 1955: 41–42). At times it means generally "to deliver." Leon Morris, therefore, goes a bit too far when he says that OT redemption always comes at a price, even if it is merely the cost of Yahweh's power (Morris 1964: 24). There is no price of redemption in Isa 52:3—"You were sold for nothing, and you shall be redeemed *(lytroō)* without money." The NT writers often used the rare word *apolytrōsis*, which in extant literature almost always signified "obtaining release by payment of ransom" (Morris 1964: 41); an exception is Dan 4:34 LXX.

B. Conceptual Background

The language of redemption was, for the original readers of the NT, familiar and evocative.

The LXX undoubtedly has the weightiest influence on the NT concept of redemption (Warfield 1929: 341–52). *Apolytrōsis*, which is used ten times in the NT, is used only in Dan 4:34 to mean "release." But *lytron* was payment which served as a substitute for a person's life (*TDNT* 4: 329). The cognate verb *lytroō* translated the two Hebrew verbs for redemption, *gāʾal* and *pādâ*. The firstborn was to be redeemed from God by sacrifice (Exod 13:11–16). Family property which had been sold could be redeemed by a near relative (Lev 25:25–34), as could people sold into bondage (Lev 24:47–55). In Exod 15:13, *lytroō* denotes the epitome of God's redemptive work was in the Exodus—"Thou hast led in thy steadfast love the people whom thou hast redeemed" (see also Exod 6:6; Deut 9:26; Neh 1:10). As Warfield notes, "Here there is at least no emphasis placed on the deliverance being in mode a ransoming. The stress is thrown rather on the power exerted in it and the mind is focused on the mightiness of the transaction" (1929: 345). It is "redemption by price and power" (Murray 1955: 78).

The Jews also foresaw that God would redeem them in the future. Isa 52:3 speaks of liberation by the mighty power of God; such hopes also find expression in Luke 24:21—"But we had hoped that he was the one to redeem Israel."

David Hill has suggested that martyr theology has directly affected Paul's theology (1967: 41–48). In *4 Macc.* 17:21, it is speculated that the Jewish martyrs acted as a "ransom" for the whole nation and thus brought about divine deliverance. But this parallel is too remote to serve as the matrix of the whole NT doctrine.

On the other hand, the social background of slave redemption provides a useful key to understanding the NT imagery. The practice of manumission—buying slaves in order to give them their freedom—was extremely widespread. Deissmann (1927: 318–20) went further to locate redemption in the practice of sacral manumission—the emancipation of slaves by a deity. He maintained that Paul drew from that background to contextualize redemption for a Hellenistic audience. A slave would save his earnings and remit to the temple the price of his freedom. The slave owner would then take the slave to that temple, whereupon the "god" would redeem the slave and give him his freedom (although it should be noted that the NT vocabulary of redemption never appears in such transactions; see Lyonnet and Sabourin 1970: 108). The freedman was then the "slave" or devotee of the god. In the record of the transaction the slave was said to have been bought "with a price" (cf. 1 Cor 6:20; 7:23) and given "liberty" (Gal 5:13). Many times, warnings and penalties were attached to the record in the event that the slave was brought again into bondage (Gal 2:4; 5:1).

Deissmann's approach has been criticized by Lyonnet and Sabourin (1970: 107), who claim that the differences between redemption and manumission are more striking than the similarities. We may conclude that if divine manumission was the particular background for some of Paul's teaching on redemption (notably in 1 Corinthians 7), then modifications have been made: God's role in the purchase is active, not symbolic; the "slave" has nothing to contribute to his release; the attachment of the freedman to God is real. Crawford's caution on rooting the NT picture strictly in sacral manumission is against "attempting to trace in the work of Christ an exact conformity to everything that is done in human acts of redemption" (1954: 62).

It is clear that the NT writers used imagery both from the Exodus and from the redemption of slaves (Lyonnet and Sabourin 1970: 110–12). Exodus imagery predominates in Col 1:14; 1 Pet 1:18–19; and Rev 5:9 and 14:3–4. On the other hand, the picture of the redemption of slaves underlies 1 Cor 6:20; 7:23; and Gal 4:5.

This is not to say that there are two or more kinds of redemption in the NT; but the authors were free to choose from two images of liberation to describe the saving action of God in Christ.

C. Redemption and Salvation

Morris (1965) rightly perceives that "redemption" was much more narrowly defined in the 1st century than it is today. While moderns may speak of redemption as a metaphor for the entire saving act, the NT writers used it precisely in the context of well-known social customs.

The first reference to the redemption of the cross is also the most controversial: "For the Son of man also came . . . to give his life as a ransom *(lytron)* for many" (Mark 10:45 = Matt 20:28). The commentaries attest the difficulties that NT scholars have had in attributing this saying to Jesus: it is omitted in the Lukan account, it contains a *hapax legomenon*, it may be based on the *antilytron* saying in 1 Tim 2:6, and it attributes atoning merit to Jesus' death. Marshall (1974: 168–69), on the other hand, cites several arguments to demonstrate its primitive origin, and perhaps its authenticity.

Paul's understanding of the death of Christ as redemption seems to come closest to the custom of manumission. The old man was a slave to a number of masters: sin (Rom 7:14; Titus 2:14), the Law (Gal 3:13; 4:1–7), death (Rom 8:21, 23), false gods (Gal 4:8–9), and Satan's kingdom (Col 1:13; also Heb 2:14–15). Under these deceitful masters, most slaves believed themselves to be truly free—in reality they walked within a limited circle of behavior, which in 1

Pet 1:18 is called "the futile ways inherited from your fathers."

The bare fact of Christ's instrumentality in redemption is brought up in 1 Cor 1:30: "Christ Jesus, whom God made our . . . redemption" and in Titus 2:14: "who gave himself for us to redeem us from all iniquity" (see also *Ep. Barn.* 14:8). Normally, the cross is central to soteriological redemption. Thus, in Rom 3:24 Paul states that "they are justified by his grace as a gift, through the redemption *(apolytrōsis)* which is in Christ Jesus." While this redemption is not explicitly either "deliverance" or "ransom through Christ's blood," the context shows that justification is made possible through his substitutionary death.

The connection between redemption and the blood of Christ is developed in Colossians, Ephesians, and other non-Pauline literature. Col 1:14 says that the past liberation from the dominion of darkness is "redemption," which in part means "the forgiveness of sins." According to its parallel in Eph 1:7, "In him we have redemption through his blood, the forgiveness of trespasses." Col 1:14 does not contain the phrase "through his blood"; Eph 1:7 is best regarded as its expansion. Colossians certainly regards redemption as taking place in Christ's death, God "making peace by the blood of his cross" (Col 1:20).

According to the author of Hebrews, Christ "entered once for all into the Holy Place, taking . . . his own blood, thus securing an eternal redemption" (*lytrōsis;* Heb 9:12). The new covenant means release from legalism and sin: ". . . a death has occurred which redeems *(apolytrōsis)* them from the transgressions under the first covenant" (Heb 9:15). In 1 Pet 1:18–19, it is indicated that redemption is bought with the blood of Christ, who is compared to the Paschal lamb. Revelation also bases redemption in the blood of the Lamb (Rev 5:9; 14:3–4).

If the blood of Christ is the price of redemption, then to whom was the price paid? While the NT does not dwell on the details, it is implicit that Christ offered himself to God to atone for sin. According to Heb 9:12, Christ's work is typified by the priest, who takes the blood of atonement into the Holy Place. Rom 5:10 shows that it is God who must have sacrifice in order to allow people into his fellowship (Marshall 1974: 156). Modern abhorrence of the concept of divine wrath and reconciliation should not allow us to be blind to the NT understanding of Christ's death as atonement.

There are other passages which teach redemption but do not have either of the two word groups for redemption: Acts 20:28—"the church of the Lord which he obtained with his blood" (see also Gal 1:4; 2:20).

In the gospel, the slave is redeemed to serve another master. While Deissmann (1927) has pointed out that sacral manumission bound the freedman only in a loose allegiance to his god, the NT teaches that bondage to God is quite real and exists at one and the same time with Christian liberty (see Rom 6:18).

Bondage to God is more than service; Christian leaders are referred to not only as *diakonoi* but also as *douloi,* a word to which Deissmann (1927: 319) insists we give its full force. Note Paul's insistence on this point in 1 Cor 6:19–20: "You are not your own; you were bought *(agorazō)* with a price. So glorify God in your body."

Paul naturally has an interest in redemption from bondage to the Law, and this is why he tells the Galatians, "For freedom Christ has set us free; stand fast therefore, and do not submit again to a yoke of slavery" (Gal 5:1). But legalism is not the only threat to emancipation: "for you were called to freedom, brethren; only do not use your freedom as an opportunity for the flesh" (Gal 5:13).

Turning away from the freedom of redemption may lead one to false doctrine and abominable moral apostasy. 2 Peter says that Christians "may escape from the corruption that is in the world" (1:4); it describes the false prophets who are "even denying the Master who bought *(agorazō)* them, bringing upon themselves swift destruction" (2:1).

Paul can also describe redemption as adoption. In Gal 4:1–7 he uses *exagorazō* and demonstrates that God has freed us from slavery to be adopted as full-grown children, and thus as heirs. Meanwhile, Revelation describes the redeemed as being freed to participate in God's royal priesthood: "for thou wast slain and by thy blood didst ransom men for God . . . and hast made them a kingdom and priests to our God, and they shall reign on earth" (Rev 5:9–10; also Rev 14:3–4).

D. Eschatological Redemption

The Jews often used *lytroō* to speak of the eschatological deliverance by God or the Messiah. In human history, Israel was delivered from servitude by human instruments; in the future, the people will be delivered by God alone, and undergo servitude no longer (*TDNT* 4: 349–51). This thought appears several times in the NT, and once again the idea of a ransom price does not seem to be present. The final deliverance is analogous to the Exodus from Egypt, which was carried out without payment but through the power of God. Luke, in particular, favors this facet of redemption: "for he has visited and redeemed *(lytrōsis)* his people" (Luke 1:68). The same word appears in Luke 2:38, when Anna speaks "to all who were looking for the redemption of Jerusalem."

Only the Lukan version of Jesus' eschatological message shows a continuity with Jewish convention, in Luke 21:28: "look up and raise your heads, because your redemption *(apolytrōsis)* is drawing near."

Since Deissmann (1927) approached the NT doctrine through its Hellenistic background, he did not appreciate that there is an eschatological aspect of redemption. This side appears most clearly in Eph 4:30: "And do not grieve the Holy Spirit of God, in whom you were sealed for the day of redemption" (cf. Eph 1:13–14; see also *2 Clem* 17:4). Paul relates this eschatological redemption first to creation in Rom 8:21: "because the creation itself will be set free from its bondage to decay." This liberation will take place at the resurrection, otherwise known as "the redemption *(apolytrōsis)* of our bodies" (Rom 8:23) and the "revealing of the sons of God" (Rom 8:19). Here, redemption seems to have the meaning of deliverance from mortal decay rather than of God paying a price to ransom our bodies.

E. "Redeem the Time"

Both Col 4:5 and Eph 5:16 contain the exhortation to redeem the time, using *exagorazō* to describe how Christians should live in this evil age. The opposite of redeeming time seems to be wasting time or letting all the good opportunities go to the devil. The RSV rendering, "making the most of the time," captures the sense of these verses.

F. The Doctrine of Redemption in History

One of the more extreme of ancient theological ideas is that God redeemed his people by paying Satan for their release. Advanced by Irenaeus and developed by Origen, the theory was that the devil possessed the human race by right, but was deceived by taking Christ as a ransom; Christ arose from the dead, thus redeeming the lost and escaping Satan's grasp (Lyonnet and Sabourin 1970: 207–11). This "Ransom to Satan" idea was enormously popular for centuries, but in the 11th century Anselm successfully laid it to rest in his *Cur Deus Homo*. Christian orthodoxy since Anselm has generally held to some form of satisfaction theory of the atonement.

Liberal theology has rejected the idea of Christ's death as a payment for sin (Warfield 1929: 358–61). Redemption becomes deliverance from cosmic alienation (Carré 1914: 100–167) or, in some cases, the redemption of societal structures (Barton 1934: 139–40).

Bibliography

Bandas, R. G. 1925. *The Master-Idea of Saint Paul's Epistles*. Brussels.
Barton, G. A. 1934. *Christ and Evolution*. Philadelphia.
Carré, H. B. 1914. *Paul's Doctrine of Redemption*. New York.
Crawford, T. J. 1954. *The Doctrine of Holy Scripture Respecting the Atonement*. 4th ed. Grand Rapids.
Deissmann, A. 1927. *Light from the Ancient East*. Trans. L. R. M. Strachan. New York.
Hill, D. 1967. *Greek Words and Hebrew Meanings*. Cambridge.
Lyonnet, S., and Sabourin, L. 1970. *Sin, Redemption, and Sacrifice*. AnBib 48. Rome.
Marshall, I. H. 1974. The Development of the Concept of Redemption in the New Testament. Pp. 153–69 in *Reconciliation and Hope*, ed. R. Banks. Grand Rapids.
Morris, L. 1965. *The Apostolic Preaching of the Cross*. 3d ed. Grand Rapids.
Murray, J. 1955. *Redemption Accomplished and Applied*. Grand Rapids.
Warfield, B. B. 1929. The New Testament Terminology of Redemption. Pp. 327–72 in *Biblical Doctrines*. New York.

GARY S. SHOGREN

REED. See FLORA.

REELAIAH (PERSON) [Heb *rĕʿēlāyāh*]. Var. RAAMIAH; REELIAH; RESAIAH. One of the leaders of the group of returnees from Babylonian Exile who is listed along with Zerubbabel in Ezra 2:2 (= Neh 7:7 = 1 Esdr 5:8). One name has apparently been dropped from the Ezra list, for those in Nehemiah and 1 Esdras include twelve leaders in what is probably a symbolic representation of all Israel. The form of the name in Neh 7:7 is Raamiah (Heb *raʿamyâ*), and in 1 Esdr 5:8 it is Resaiah (Gk *Rhēsaias*). The form Reeliah (RSV, 1 Esdr 5:8; Gk *Rheelias*) apparently originates out of confusion between forms of the name Bigvai in various mss of 1 Esdr 2:2 (including *boroliou* and *rheeliou*) and the reading *rheelias* for Reelaiah in the LXX of Ezra 2:2. For discussion concerning the list in Ezra 2, see AKKUB.

CHANEY R. BERGDALL

REFUGE, CITIES OF. Six cities are set aside within Israel as Cities of Refuge (Heb *ʿārê miqlāṭ*). These are places of sanctuary or asylum where a person who unintentionally kills someone may reside, without fear of blood revenge, until a trial can be held. These cities are discussed in Exod 21:13; Num 35:9–15; Deut 4:41–43; 19:1–13; Joshua 20; and 1 Chronicles 6.

The idea of asylum is not unique to the Hebrew tradition. Several ancient peoples, in the ancient Near East and elsewhere, had the idea that fugitives could gain sanctuary by proceeding to or fleeing to certain designated places. Often these places were cultic centers. In the Hebrew Bible we see this tradition in 1 Kgs 1:50–53 where Adonijah, fearing Solomon, seeks sanctuary by holding on to the horns of the altar. In this instance, Solomon observes the idea of sanctuary and allows Adonijah to remain alive, at least for a while (see 1 Kgs 2:23–24). However, in another instance (1 Kgs 2:28–34), Solomon ignores the idea of sanctuary and has Joab, a supporter of Adonijah, killed, even though Joab is clinging to the horns of the altar.

The legislation for the designation of Cities of Refuge is found in Exodus, Numbers, and Deuteronomy. In Exod 21:12–14, which is part of the Covenant Code and thus probably reflects an early tradition, a distinction is made between intentional and unintentional murder. The perpetrator of an intentional murder shall be dealt with immediately, but the person who kills accidentally, or at least without intention, shall have a place to flee. This distinction is continued in Num 35:9–15. Here, the cities are specifically called Cities of Refuge *ʿārê miqlāṭ* (Num 35:11). They are to be places where the unintentional murderer may wait until he can stand for judgment before the community (Num 35:12), without fear from an avenger (see Gen 9:5–6; Num 35:16–21, esp. v 19). In addition, the passage specifies that there will be six Cities of Refuge (Num 35:13), three of which shall be E of the Jordan River and three W of the Jordan (Num 35:14), and that these cities shall be available for the people of Israel, for sojourners and for those who dwell in their (Israel's) midst (Num 35:16).

The passages in Deuteronomy continue the same legislative perspective, with the added specification of particular cities as Cities of Refuge. In Deut 4:41–43, the cities E of the Jordan are mentioned. These are Bezer for the Reubenites, Ramoth in Gilead for the Gadites, and Golan in Bashan for the Manassites (Deut 4:43).

Deut 19:1–13 is concerned with the cities W of the Jordan. While they are not named, three cities are to be set up once the land of Canaan is possessed. This passage also provides an illustration and further specification of the usage of the Cities of Refuge. The example is the accidental slaying of someone with an ax (Deut 19:5). The Cities of Refuge are to be used to prevent the shedding of innocent blood (Deut 19:10), trying to avoid an instance where an "avenger of blood" slays someone who kills unintentionally (Deut 19:6). Furthermore, should someone who hates and then kills intentionally seek asylum in a City of Refuge, the elders of the city are to hand that person over to the "avenger of blood" for execution.

Another explanation of the idea of sanctuary and the actual listing of the Cities of Refuge are found in Joshua 20. Here, after a reference to the prior discussion of Cities of Refuge with Moses, Yahweh explains the idea of Cities of Refuge to Joshua. In addition to repeating the general theory of sanctuary, a procedure for admission to a City of Refuge is mentioned in Joshua 20:4. The killer must explain his case to the elders of the city in the gate of the city. Also, there is an obscure comment that the slayer may return home after a trial or after the high priest has died (Josh 20:6). The reasons behind this amnesty after the death of the high priest are not fully understood.

After this discussion of asylum in general, Joshua sets up the Cities of Refuge themselves (Josh 20:7–9). Kedesh in Galilee, Shechem in Ephraim, and Kiriath-arba (Hebron) in Judah are the three cities W of the Jordan (Josh 20:7). They go with the three cities E of the Jordan—Bezer, Ramoth-Gilead, and Golan (Josh 20:8)—which are also mentioned in Deut 4:43. These cities are for the people of Israel as well as for the sojourner (Josh 20:9).

The Cities of Refuge are also listed among the Levitical Cities in Joshua 21 and 1 Chronicles 6. In the list of Levitical Cities in Joshua 21, all of the Cities of Refuge are mentioned as Levitical Cities (Josh 21:13, 21, 27, 32, 36, 38), and all but one are also specifically designated as Cities of Refuge. This lone exception is that of Bezer; it is listed among the Levitical Cities, but not as a City of Refuge (Josh 21:36). In 1 Chronicles 6, all the Cities of Refuge are also listed as Levitical Cities (1 Chr 6:42, 52, 56, 57, 63, 65—Eng 6:57, 67, 71, 72, 78, 80); however, unlike the list in Joshua 21, only two cities are identified as Cities of Refuge—Hebron (1 Chr 6:42—Eng 6:57) and Shechem (1 Chr 6:52—Eng 6:67). It is thus obvious that some connection was perceived between the Levitical Cities and the Cities of Refuge. Perhaps the Levites were to administer the Cities of Refuge as part of their overall responsibility for the Levitical Cities.

In attempts to date the lists of Cities of Refuge, this connection with the Levitical Cities has often been exploited, and similar arguments for dating have been offered. However, while there is considerable debate over whether the Levitical Cities are historical or utopian, such a debate rarely surfaces in discussing the Cities of Refuge. They are generally seen as historical, reflecting an actual tradition in ancient Israel. It follows then that if the lists represent actual practice, their historical context must be a period when all of the Cities of Refuge fell within the boundaries of ancient Israel. Thus, the dating of the Cities of Refuge is generally argued to be in one of three periods: during the monarchial period of David and Solomon; during the 8th-century expansion of Jeroboam II (2 Kgs 14:23–29); or during the 7th-century reforms of Josiah, when he restored the nation (2 Kgs 23:1–25). However, given the antiquity of the practice of asylum, the long tradition of asylum in ancient Israel, and questions about the arguments which place the city lists in the 8th and 7th centuries, the most likely time period for the origination of the lists is the United Monarchy (10th century). How much earlier the practice of asylum operated is impossible to ascertain.

Bibliography

Albright, W. F. 1945. The List of Levitic Cities. Vol. 1, pp. 49–73 in *Louis Ginzberg Jubilee Volume.* New York.

Auld, A. G. 1978. Cities of Refuge in Israelite Tradition. *JSOT* 10: 26–40.

David, M. 1951. Die Bestimmungen über die Asylstädte in Josua XX. *OTS* 9: 30–48.

Dinur, B. 1954. The Religious Character of the Cities of Refuge and the Ceremony of Admission into Them. *Eretz Israel* 3: 135–46 (in Hebrew); vii–ix (Eng summary).

Greenberg, M. 1959. The Biblical Conception of Asylum. *JBL* 78: 125–32.

Löhr, M. 1930. *Das Asylwesen im Alten Testament.* Halle.

Nicolsky, N. M. 1930. Das Asylrecht in Israel. *ZAW* 48: 146–75.

Smith, W. R. 1889. *Lectures on the Religion of the Semites.* London.

JOHN R. SPENCER

REGEM (PERSON) [Heb *regem*]. One of the six sons of Jahdai (1 Chr 2:47). See JAHDAI. Jahdai was evidently the head of a Calebite family, but the relationship of him and his offspring to Caleb is not actually given. Regem and his brothers should perhaps be included with Caleb's descendants through his concubine Ephah (v 46) on the basis of the overall form of the unit and the occurrence of the name Ephah also among Jahdai's children (Braun *1 Chronicles* WBC, 41). Caleb's line in vv 42–50a is followed through a wife and two concubines, which means that from the writer's point of view it consisted of a main stem with two branches (Myers *1 Chronicles* AB, 15). Some of the names in this unit are those of cities known from the lists of cities allotted to Judah in Joshua 15. The town Beth-pelet of Josh 15:27 may be related to Regem's brother Pelet. The attempt to see in the name Regem the meaning "friend" (namely, of God) seems to be not well founded, relying almost solely on a possible (but if so, rare) significance of the Arabic word *rajm*.

EDWIN C. HOSTETTER

REGEM-MELECH (PERSON) [Heb *regem melek*]. One of two leaders of a delegation that inquired at the rebuilt temple about the continuation of fasting in the fifth month (Zech 7:2). This fast is widely interpreted by scholars to be a commemoration of the destruction of the temple and Jerusalem by the Babylonians.

Melek (melech) is Hebrew for "king." The name Regem is found in 1 Chr 2:47. Other names using "melech," including compounds, occur in the OT; e.g., Ebed-melech (Jer 38:7); Nathan-melech (2 Kgs 23:11); Abimelech (Judg 8:31); and Elimelech (Ruth 1:2).

Meyers and Meyers (*Haggai Zechariah 1–8* AB, 383–84) argue that Regem-melech's part in leading the delegation indicates his high status in the community at Bethel, whence the delegation came, but they deny that he had any royal connections. They find the evidence insufficient to determine whether or not he was an exile returned from Babylon.

Some have questioned whether the name "Regem-melech" is the correct reading for the Hebrew text here. Thomas (*Zechariah 1–8* IB, 1082) and others suggest that the preferred reading—based on the Peshitta—is not a name but a title, "the Rabmag (i.e., the chief officer) of the king" *(rab māg hammelek).* See RABMAG. If this reading is adopted, the title must refer to Sharezer, who is then characterized as a high royal official (see Ackroyd 1968: 209). Since Sharezer's name is Babylonian, such a reading would contribute to the possibility that the delegation was of Babylonian rather than Palestinian origin, although this depends principally on other factors in the verse. See SHAREZER.

Nevertheless, Rudolph (*Haggai Zechariah Malachi* KAT, 138–39) and Meyers and Meyers (*Haggai Zechariah 1–8* AB, 383) correctly argue, albeit along different lines, that the MT (i.e., the name Regem-melech) is the better reading here.

Bibliography

Ackroyd, P. R. 1968. *Exile and Restoration.* OTL. Philadelphia.

RICHARD D. WEIS

REGENERATION. The final stage of creation when God's purposes are fully realized. Regeneration signifies a renovation of all visible things.

A. Extrabiblical Usage

Individual, national, and cosmic regeneration are found in extrabiblical sources. Two examples are Cicero's return from exile (*Att.* 6.6) and Plutarch's writing of "the dismemberment of Osiris and his revivification." Here, regeneration is the "divinity's" return to life (*De Is. et Os.* 35).

The Stoics used the concept to denote cosmic regeneration following the cyclic cosmic conflagration. Philo uses the concept of regeneration to tell about the restoration of Abel after the birth of Seth (*Post* 36) and about renewal after the flood (*Vita Mos* I 11.65). Josephus speaks of "the recovery and rebirth of their native land" in reference to the Jewish return from Babylonian Exile (*Ant* 11.3.9), and Philo speaks of "the conflagration and rebirth of the world" (*Aet* 3.9). Philo also speaks of rebirth following death (*Cher* 32.114).

The Greek mystery religions view the concept of regeneration as the initiate's sharing in "the renewing power of their deity" (Guhrt *NIDNTT* 1: 184). For as the fertility cults became mystery religions, focusing more on the individual, regeneration came to designate salvation through initiation (Robinson *IDB* 1: 25).

B. OT Insights

Though the word *palingenesia* does not occur in the LXX, the concept of regeneration is central to the OT, as circumcision of the heart (Deut 30:6; cf. "changed heart" in 1 Sam 10:9; "pure heart" in Ps 51:10), in Ezekiel's restoration of dead bones (Ezek 37:1–14; cf. Nuelsen *ISBE* 4: 68, 69), and in God's promise to raise Israel from spiritual death (Jer 24:7; Ezek 11:19; 36:26–27) and to return the people from captivity (Ezek 36:24, 25; Mic 4:6, 7; cf. Keil and Delitzsch 1986: 119, 123). This restoration motif is found in the promise of a new covenant (Jer 31:31–34; Ezek 34:25), a new Jerusalem (Zech 14:10ff., 16), and a new heaven and earth (Isa 65:17). It would seem that regeneration is both personal and national in the OT. Nuelsen sees it as eschatological in the earlier portions, becoming personal only after the captivity and Diaspora (*ISBE* 4: 68).

Yet, there is evidence of personal responsibility from Israel's inception. On Passover night of the Exodus from Egypt, each household had to apply the blood on the doorpost and lintel to protect their firstborn from the destroying angel (Exod 12:12, 13). The subsequent tabernacle/temple sin offerings included those for individuals (Leviticus 1–7) as well as those for the nation (evening and morning, 2 Chr 2:4; 13:11; and the day of atonement, Leviticus 16). Personal accountability for sin is seen from the beginning (Gen 3:1–19), and classically in David's plea for renewal (Ps 51:10). It seems that the need for individual regeneration in the OT is given within the context of the need for national regeneration.

C. NT Insights

The noun "regeneration" (Gk *palingenesia,* from *palin,* "new," and *genesis,* "origin, birth") occurs only twice in the NT (Matt 19:28; Titus 3:5). Matthew speaks of "*en tę̄ palingenesią,*" or "in the regeneration." This is a synonym for the Gk word *basileia,* or "kingdom." Literally, it means, in the coming kingdom, after the *parousia,* "at the renewal of all things." The regeneration is the new heaven and new earth (Isa 65:17–25; 2 Pet 3:13; Rev 21:1). "Behold, I make all things new" (Rev 21:5, RSV). Here, regeneration is eschatological.

Titus 3:5 speaks of salvation through the washing of rebirth or renewal by the Holy Spirit. In this instance, regeneration is rebirth/renewal by the Spirit, equivalent to a "new creation" (2 Cor 5:17) or a "new" self (Eph 4:22, 23; cf. Col 3:9, 10). Here, regeneration is existential.

Though these two different aspects of regeneration are given in Matt 19:28 and Titus 3:5, they present individual renewal as but a part of cosmic renewal—the regenerated person is not at the goal but moves toward the goal (cf. Guhrt *NIDNTT* 1: 186). Both terms "new birth" and "new creation" evoke an image of regeneration. Creation of new life or a new world are acts of God. These are acts beyond humanity's capability. Regeneration is the work of God.

The classical definition of regeneration is found in the Johannine pericope—Christ's discourse with Nicodemus (John 3:1–21). Just as proselytes entering Judaism were considered "re-born," so Nicodemus, although a Jewish leader, had to be "re-born" to enter Christ's kingdom. Born "again" (Gk *anōthen,* John 3:3; cf. John 3:31; 19:11, 23) means not only "anew" but also "from above." Nicodemus' birth as a Jew did not count (cf. Ps 87:5, 6): "Neither circumcision nor uncircumcision means anything; what counts is a new creation" (Gal 6:15).

The new-birth discourse (John 3) includes comment on Christ's birth (John 3:13–16). Christ was born of the Spirit (Matt 1:20)—so must be others (John 3:5). Although no one can be born of the Spirit as was Christ (He was *monogenēs,* "one of a kind"; John 1:14, 18; 3:16, 18; 1 John 4:9), yet in the Nicodemus discourse, there is a parallel between these two births—of Christ and of others—by the Spirit. Both are from above (John 3:7, 17), and both are necessary for salvation to take place (John 3:3, 16). For just as Christ entered the world through the Spirit to become the Savior, so each person must be born again to enter heaven and be saved (John 3:3).

To be born again (John 3:3) and to become childlike (Matt 18:3; Mark 10:15) are parallel preconditions for entrance into the Kingdom of God. Being childlike includes receiving and believing in Christ (John 1:12, 13; cf. 3:16). This is effected "through the living and enduring word of God" (1 Pet 1:23). Regeneration is then through the Spirit and through the Word (cf. 2 Pet 1:21). The function of both (Spirit and Word) is to lead individuals to Christ (John 14:26, 15:26; John 5:39; cf. Luke 24:27). These persons are made a "new creation" (2 Cor 5:17) and are referred to as "created in Christ Jesus" (Eph 2:10).

This Christ-centered function of the Spirit finds him in the NT with a new title—"the Spirit of Christ" (Rom 8:9; 1 Pet 1:11; cf. Gal 4:6; Phil 1:19). Regeneration is not a separate work of the Spirit added to the salvific work of Christ; it is the subjective actualization of Christ's work. That actualization includes the dying and rising with Christ (Rom 6:3–14; 1 Cor 15:20–23; Col 3:1), so that the regenerated are spoken of as begotten by Christ's resurrection (1 Pet 1:3, 21).

In summary, as the concept of regeneration passed from Stoicism into Judaism it was "filled with a new religious content" (Büschsel *TDNT* 1: 688). The new meaning had to do with messianic and christological hopes for a final restoration. Renewal was not just a rebirth (return) within a reincarnational cycle, but a historical *telos* at the *eschaton,* with even a "firstfruits" (Rom 8:23) or "deposit" (2 Cor 1:22; 5:5; Eph 1:14) of it in the present. So, regeneration, on the one hand, is the future new eternal life coming into present experience (John 3:36). On the other hand, this existential experience (Titus 3:5) reaches out to its eschatological completion in the coming cosmic renewal (Matt 19:28).

Bibliography

Burkhardt, H. 1978. *The Biblical Doctrine of Regeneration.* Trans. O. R. Johnston. Downers Grove, IL.

Elliott-Binns, L. E. 1957. James 1:18: Creation and Redemption. *NTS* 3: 148–61.

Guthrie, D. 1981. *NT Theology.* Downers Grove, IL.

Kalin, E. 1983. New Birth and Baptism—An Exegetical Study. *Covenant Quarterly* 41: 11–17.

Keil, C. F., and Delitzsch, F. D. 1986. *Commentary on the OT.* Vol 9. Grand Rapids.

Leupold, U. S. 1965. Regeneration in the Theology of Paul. *LQ* 17: 240–51.

Lewis, A. H. 1984. The New Birth under the Old Covenant. *EvQ* 56: 35–44.

Löffler, P. 1965. The Biblical Concept of Conversion. *Study Encounter* 1: 93–101.

Nock, A. D. 1969. *Conversion.* Oxford.

Peters, G. W. 1963. The Meaning of Conversion. *BSac* 120: 234–42.

Selwyn, E. G. 1958. *The First Epistle of St. Peter.* London.

Willoughby, H. R. 1929. *Pagan Regeneration.* Chicago.

NORMAN R. GULLEY

REHABIAH (PERSON) [Heb *rĕḥabyāh(û)*]. Grandson of Moses and father of Isshiah according to 1 Chronicles 23–26, which outlines David's organization of the Levites. Rehabiah is described as *rōʾš* in 1 Chr 23:17. This designated him as a clan leader with respect to levitical duties. His son, Isshiah, is the object of the same term in 1 Chr 24:21. In the larger context, the Levites are grouped according to the families of the three sons of Levi: Gershom, Kohath, and Merari. Rehabiah belonged to the family of Kohath. Kohath's son, Amram, was the father of Aaron and Moses. Moses was the father of Eliezer. Eliezer was the father of Rehabiah. Rehabiah was the grandfather of Shelomoth who, with his brothers, was responsible for the temple treasury kept for maintenance (1 Chr 26:25–26). The duties of Rehabiah and his family are not spelled out in 23:17, although it seems likely that the general responsibilities fell under the heading "charge of the work in the house of the LORD" (23:4). Some specific responsibilities given to this group are listed in 23:28–32: cleaning, assisting with the shewbread, assisting with grain offerings, praying twice daily as well as during burnt offerings, and caring for the temple and the tent of meeting.

It seems unlikely that the name *rĕḥabyāh,* or *rĕḥabyāhû* in its older form, would bear a direct relationship to the office involved. The most likely root of the name—from *rāḥab,* "to be or grow wide"—could be associated with Rehabiah's "many sons," but without further support this association is unconvincing. It is better to consider Rehabiah as a proper name rather than an appellative. It carries the causitive sense of the *Hipʿil,* "Yahweh increases," or "enlarges," although not *Hipʿil* in form (*IPN,* 193).

DONALD K. BERRY

REHOB (PERSON) [Heb *rĕḥōb; rĕḥôb*]. **1.** The father of Hadadezer, king of Zobah (2 Sam 8:3, 12). However, it is possible that Rehob here is actually a place name, and that the Heb *ben-rĕḥōb* identifies Hadadezer as a native of the town of Rehob, being translated loosely as "the Rehobite." In 2 Sam 10:6–8, the Ammonites hire Syrian mercenaries from Zobah and Rehob/Beth-rehob, suggesting that there may have been a preexisting connection between these two cities; indeed, Malamat (1963: 2–3) suggests that Hadadezer first ruled in Beth-rehob and subsequently incorporated Zobah into his domain (just as the Judean David subsequently incorporated Israel). See also BETH-REHOB.

2. One of the Levites who set his seal on the covenant, pledging to walk in God's law (Neh 10:12—Eng 10:11). Rehob and the others mentioned in this verse are not listed in the LXX.

Bibliography

Malamat, A. 1963. Aspects of Foreign Policies of David and Solomon. *JNES* 22: 1–17.

GARY A. HERION

REHOB (PLACE) [Heb *rĕḥōb; rĕḥôb*]. Var. BETH-REHOB. The place name Rehob appears seven times in the OT. At least two separate places, both in Galilee, shared this name. The name "Rehob" also appears in Egyptian documents, suggesting the possibility that in the Galilee-

Jezreel region there may have been as many as three (or even four) places by that name (see *CTAED,* 163–65).

1. A town in the extreme N of Canaan, near the entrance to Hamath (Num 13:21). It was probably the same as Beth-rehob (cf. 2 Sam 10:6, 8). See BETH-REHOB.

2. The fourth city in Asher assigned to the Levites (Josh 21:31 = 1 Chr 6:60 [—Eng 6:75]), but at the time of the conquest Asher was unable to drive out its inhabitants (Judg 1:31). The problem of locating Rehob is compounded by the fact that it is also mentioned *twice* in connection with the border of the tribe of Asher (Josh 19:28, 30). The first citation (v 28) implies that Rehob was in the N of Asher (associated with Cabul, Ebron, Hammon, Kanah, and Sidon), while the latter (v 30) suggests a location in the plain of Accho ("Ummah," *ʿmh,* is probably a corruption of "Accho," *ʿkh;* cf. LXX and Judg 1:31). This has raised the possibility that there may have been two places named Rehob in Asher.

On that assumption, Aharoni (*LBHG,* 162) associated the N Rehob with *rḥb* (no. 87) in Thutmosis III's list (*ANET,* 243), and identified it with Tell el-Balaṭ (M.R. 177280), 10 miles E of Rosh Haniqra and inside the modern border of Lebanon. However, it could also be identified with Tell er-Raḥb (M.R. 180275), 4 miles SE of Tell el-Balaṭ and inside the modern border of Israel (*CTAED,* 164). Because the two sites are almost 20 miles W of the valley of Huleh, neither should be associated with the Rehob/Beth-rehob of Num 13:21 and 2 Sam 10:6–8 (#1 above).

The S Rehob is apparently mentioned in the second group of Execration Texts (*ʾrḥbm,* no. 14); its location in the plain of Accho is supported by its listing after Aphek (no. 9), Achshaph (no. 11), and Mashaal (no. 13). However, because it is also listed immediately before cities further E—Hazor (no. 15), Kedesh (no. 16), and Ijon (no. 18)—Alt (*KlSchr* 3: 166) and Albright (1941: 33) equated this *ʾrḥbm* with Raḥabu (no. 17) in Shishak's list (*ANET,* 243), a town located S of Beth-shean and identified with Tell eṣ-Ṣarem (M.R. 197207; *CTAED,* 164–65; *MBA,* no. 120). Thus, it is unclear whether the *ʾrḥbm* of the Execration Texts refers to a Rehob in the territory of Asher or to yet another one near Beth-shean, although the Raḥabu in Shishak's list is clearly not in the territory of Asher and is apparently not mentioned in the OT.

A topographical list of Ramesses II mentions a Raḥabu in connection with Dor (Mazar 1963), reinforcing a S location for Rehob in the plain of Accho. Thus, the *ʾrḥbm* of the Execration Texts (see above) should probably be identified with the Raḥabu in this Ramesses II text, not with the one in the Shishak text (*CTAED,* 163). Kallai (*HGB,* *362–66) has suggested identifying it with Kh. Dauk, 8 km SE of Accho, a site settled from the MB to the Iron II periods, and again during the Hellenistic period. Most scholars, however, have followed Albright (1921–22: 22–27) and have identified Rehob with Tell el-Bir el-Gharbi (or Tell Birwe; M.R. 166256), located near the edge of the coastal plain of Accho next to the foothills of Galilee. The site had been visited by early-19th-century biblical geographers, including E. Robinson (1841: 88). There have been many surveys and small excavations at the site, and pottery from MB, Iron I–II, Persian, and Hellenistic periods has been recovered.

In summary, it remains unclear whether there were one or two towns named Rehob in Asher, although the biblical and Egyptian records perhaps favor one Rehob located in the Accho plain. Although Tell el-Bir el-Gharbi cannot be identified absolutely with the Rehob listed in connection with the border of Asher (Josh 19:28, 30; cf. Judg 1:31) and with the Levitical cities of Asher (Josh 21:31 = 1 Chr 6:60 [—Eng 6:75]), the evidence in support of this association is strong (Peterson 1977: 56–65).

Bibliography

Albright, W. F. 1921–22. Historical Geography of Palestine. Pp. 22–27 in AASOR 2–3. Cambridge, MA.

———. 1941. The Land of Damascus Between 1850 and 1750 B.C. *BASOR* 83: 30–36.

Mazar, B. 1963. Dor and Rehob in an Egyptian Topographical List. *Yediot* 27: 139–44.

Peterson, J. L. 1977. *A Topographical Surface Survey of the Levitical "Cities" of Joshua 21 and 1 Chronicles 6.* Diss., Evanston, IL.

Robinson, E. 1841. *Biblical Researches in Palestine.* Vol. 3. Boston.

John L. Peterson
Rami Arav

REHOBOAM (PERSON) [Heb *rĕḥabʿām*].

The son of Solomon and Naamah, an Ammonite (1 Kgs 14:21, 31), who succeeded his father to the throne in Jerusalem but failed to win the support of the N Israelites (who formed their own separate nation). Rehoboam ruled the S kingdom of Judah, consisting of the tribe of Judah and the contested territory of Benjamin. His counterpart in the N kingdom of Israel was Jeroboam I.

The chronology of Rehoboam's reign is somewhat uncertain. The claim of a 17-year rule (1 Kgs 14:21; 2 Chr 12:13) is difficult to reconcile with other chronological notations about the early monarchic period. Albright (1945) dated his reign to 922–915 B.C.E., but Thiele (1984) has argued that the full 17 years can be placed in the years 931/30–913. Several other chronological systems have been worked out which also allow for a 17-year reign. Hayes and Hooker, for example, date Rehoboam's reign to 926–910 B.C.E. (1988: 16–20).

A. Sources

The Deuteronomistic Historian (DH) presents the primary account of Rehoboam's reign in 1 Kgs 12:1–24 and 14:21–31. The Chronicler provides a parallel, and somewhat expanded, version in 2 Chronicles 10–12. Each of these accounts is based on sources which contained reliable historical data. The Kings account is drawn, in part, from the annals of the kings of Judah (1 Kgs 14:29), while the latter cites the chronicles of the prophet Shemaiah and Iddo the seer (2 Chr 12:15). Other unnamed sources were perhaps used as well, but it is clear that each biblical historian has stamped his own ideology on the accounts he rendered.

B. The Schism

The dissolution of the United Monarchy began before Solomon's death. The Arameans and the Edomites, both of whom had been conquered by David, successfully rebelled against Solomonic rule (1 Kgs 11:14–25). The N

Israelites, unhappy over Solomon's oppressive policies, attempted a rebellion which Solomon was able to crush. Solomon tried to kill the leader of the revolt, Jeroboam ben Nebat, who fled to Egypt where Pharaoh Shishak gave him asylum (1 Kgs 11:26–28, 40). After Solomon's death, Jeroboam returned to become king over the N Israelites, who rejected the rule of Rehoboam.

According to 1 Kgs 12:1–20 (cf. 2 Chr 10:1–19), the rejection of Rehoboam's claim to sovereignty over the N tribes occurred at a gathering of Israelite leaders in Shechem. Both accounts state that Rehoboam had gone to Shechem for all Israel to make him king. What this indicates about the nature of kingship in the early monarchic period is not clear. Alt (1951: 4–9) maintained that the N Israelites had a charismatic notion of kingship which made them reluctant to follow a principle of dynastic succession when Solomon died (see also Donner, *IJH,* 383–84), and Soggin (1984: 193) proposed that strong democratic tendencies existed in the N to which Rehoboam attempted to answer. But Miller has suggested that Rehoboam's appearance in Shechem may simply have been due to urgent political problems which the new king faced in the N (*HAIJ,* 229–30).

The N Israelites offered to submit to Rehoboam's rule on the condition that he remove the "heavy yoke"—taxation and forced labor—which Solomon had placed upon them. Rehoboam consulted groups of elder and younger advisers (*zĕqēnîm* and *yĕlādîm*), who gave him vastly different counsel. The elders counseled him to offer significant concessions in order to show his intention to serve the people—the language has been compared to royal grants of exemption from taxation and corvée offered to important and sacred cities by various Neo-Assyrian kings (Weinfeld 1982). The younger advisers, however, suggested that he show strength and threaten to increase the burdens which Solomon had placed upon them. When Rehoboam announced that he would pursue the course advised by his younger counselors, the N Israelites broke away from his rule and elevated Jeroboam ben Nebat to kingship over them.

Malamat's proposal (1963) that Rehoboam's two sets of advisers at Shechem point to the existence of "formal bodies of official standing in the kingdom," somewhat parallel to the "bicameral" assembly in the Sumerian epic *Gilgamesh and Agga,* may stretch the evidence, as Evans has cautioned (1966). The two groups of advisers may simply represent a difference of opinion within a single circle of advisers (Evans 1966). It would be natural for the elders *(zĕqēnîm),* who are said to have "stood before Solomon," and the young men *(yĕlādîm),* who are said to have grown up with Rehoboam and "stood before him," to give contradictory advice simply because of the differences in age, experience, and therefore perspective.

In any case, Rehoboam chose to follow the advice given by the younger counselors. The N Israelites responded by declaring their freedom from the rule of Davidic kings. Their cry of independence (1 Kgs 12:16; 2 Chr 10:16) echoed the words of the Benjaminite Sheba, son of Bichri (2 Sam 20:1), who had led an unsuccessful N Israelite revolt against David. Thus the N Israelites, from David's time on, sought opportunities to free themselves from Davidic rule, particularly when policies emanating from Jerusalem became especially burdensome (as they had under Solomon). Apart from the onerous demands of inequitable taxation and forced labor, Solomon's offer of twenty villages in the land of Galilee to Hiram, king of Tyre, to satisfy his indebtedness to the Phoenician king for materials used in the construction of the temple and royal palace in Jerusalem (1 Kgs 9:11), undoubtedly alienated the northerners all the more and precipitated the rebellion (Halpern 1974). Solomon may have used some of these materials for the repair of S fortresses, given the potential for trouble from Pharaoh Shishak, who had come to power in Egypt.

Rehoboam sent Adoram, the commander of the labor forces, to put down the rebellion. The N Israelites displayed their determination by stoning Adoram to death, and Rehoboam hastily returned to Jerusalem. According to 1 Kgs 12:21–24 (cf. 2 Chr 11:1–4), a Judahite prophet, Shemaiah, counseled Rehoboam not to attempt to recapture control of the N, on the grounds that the schism was Yahweh's will. This tradition further claims that the tribe of Benjamin supported Rehoboam along with the tribe of Judah. But the reference to continual warfare between Rehoboam and Jeroboam (1 Kgs 14:30; 15:6; 2 Chr 12:15) no doubt pertains to frequent fighting along their shared border a short distance N of Jerusalem. At stake in these skirmishes was control of the territory of Benjamin.

C. Shishak's Invasion

Shishak, the founder of the 22d Lybian dynasty in Egypt, brought an end to the friendly relations Solomon had once enjoyed with Egypt. This pharaoh displayed hostility toward Solomon by supporting the Edomite and N Israelite rebellions mentioned in 1 Kgs 11:14–25 and 11:26–28, 40. And then, in the fifth year of Rehoboam's reign, Shishak invaded Judah and Israel (1 Kgs 14:25; cf. 2 Chr 12:2). According to Mazar, this campaign was undertaken "to enhance the prestige of his monarchy" and "to enrich his kingdom with spoils" taken from the cities in the path of invasion (1957: 57).

The account in 1 Kgs 14:25–28 mentions only Shishak's attack on Jerusalem. It states that he took the treasures of the temple and the palace and seized the gold shields made by Solomon. The more expansive account in 2 Chr 12:2–12, which is amplified by a prophecy of Shemaiah's, attributes the invasion to Rehoboam's disloyalty to Yahweh. This account claims that Shishak, supported by innumerable troops of Libyans and Nubians, captured the fortified cities of Judah before attacking Jerusalem. The Shemaiah prophecy attributes the sparing of Jerusalem from destruction to the submission of Rehoboam and his officers to Yahweh. Nonetheless, the account allows that Shishak escaped with the spoils mentioned in 1 Kings 14.

Fortunately, the sparse biblical information about these events is augmented by Shishak's hieroglyphic inscription found on the S entrance to the Temple of Amon at Karnak, listing the places he had conquered (*ANET,* 263–64; also 242–43). Mazar (1957) recognized that when the first four lines of place names are read boustrophedon (i.e., the first line should be read left to right; the second line right to left; the third line left to right, etc.), the route of the campaign can be reconstructed. The line of march went from Gaza, to Gezer, to Aijalon, to Beth-horon, and to Gibeon, as Shishak's troops passed N of Jerusalem. From Gibeon, the invading forces moved to Migdal (identification uncertain), then Zemaraim in the S Ephraimite mountains. The troops then proceeded to the Jordan Valley and crossed the Jordan River, where they marched on Adam, Succoth, Penuel, and Mahanaim. They then turned back toward the Jordan and attacked Hapharaim (identification uncertain) before crossing the Jordan and proceeding to Tirzah (reading uncertain). The Egyptian army then turned N and marched on Reḥob, Beth-shean, Shunem, Taanach, and Megiddo before returning to Philistia by the Via Maris.

Curiously, this part of the list does not mention any places in Judah and shows that Shishak's campaign was waged against the cities of the N kingdom of Israel. Mazar suggests that "the rich areas of the Kingdom of Israel were the main object of the expedition" and conjectures that "Shishak intended also to punish Israel, perhaps because after seizing power Jeroboam refused to admit the suzerainty of the Pharaoh, contrary to what he had consented during his revolt and the days he had spent in Egypt" (1957: 62–63).

The second part of the list, actually much longer than the first section, names sites, forts, regions, and families in the Negeb vicinity. Among the sites are Ezem and Arad. Many of the names are difficult to identify, but several names of regions are composed of the Egyptian determinative *pa* (in place of the Heb *ha-*) plus, in some cases, *ḥgr* or *ḥqr* (= fort) and various family or clan names known from the genealogical lists in Chronicles—such as Shuhah (1 Chr 4:11), Hanan and Tilon (1 Chr 4:20), and Peleth (1 Chr 2:33). This concentration of names in the region of the Negeb probably means that Shishak sent a phalanx of his army into this area to protect the troops who were conducting the main campaign into the N from a surprise attack by nomadic or seminomadic tribes from the S desert region (Mazar 1957: 64–66); or perhaps Shishak sought to distract Rehoboam as the main troops advanced N of Jerusalem (Gray *Kings* OTL, 344–45).

D. Rehoboam's Fortresses

The Chronicler supplies a list of 15 towns in Judah and Benjamin (2 Chr 11:5–10; no mention is made of this in the DH) whose defenses were strengthened by Rehoboam. Shishak's campaign probably explains why Rehoboam made the fortifications, although the Chronicler's narrative sequence places Rehoboam's building activity in these towns *before* the account of Shishak's invasion. The list mentions Bethlehem, Etam, Tekoa, Beth-zur, Soco, Adullam, Gath, Mareshah, Ziph, Adoraim, Lachish, Azekah, Zorah, Aijalon, and Hebron. Aharoni observed that these locations "form a logical and continuous line for the defence of [Rehoboam's] kingdom from the west, the south, and the east, with additional forts located at the important road junctions" (*LBHG,* 330). He noted, however, that the southernmost fortifications—at Lachish, Mareshah, Adoraim, Hebron, and Ziph—left the S Shephelah, the Negeb, and even much of the S hill country outside the line of defense. This either means that these regions were taken from Judah by Shishak or that Rehoboam had other fortifications in S Judah which did not need repair at this time and are thus not mentioned in this list.

The Levitical cities in Judah, many of them located in the S hill country, were probably part of Rehoboam's defense system. Many scholars have argued that these cities (cf. the lists in Joshua 21 and 1 Chronicles 6) were established during the period of David and Solomon, and fortified by them, to serve as administrative centers to enforce royal policies and to keep the kingdom secure, especially in regions annexed by David. The cities probably served as cultic centers as well. Rehoboam would have used these strongholds that lay within Judah's borders in addition to the 15 fortresses mentioned in 2 Chr 11:5–10, making for a stronger defense system in the southernmost parts of Judah.

E. Religious Practices

The DH charges that the people of Judah engaged in much religious apostasy during Rehoboam's reign (1 Kgs 14:22–24). The accusations that the people built shrines *(bāmôth),* sacred pillars, and sacred poles, and that cult prostitutes were in the land, are typical of the DH style and polemic and thus must be dismissed or taken with extreme caution. The Chronicler omits these charges, but to explain Shishak's invasion includes a more general accusation that Rehoboam forsook the *tôrāh* of Yahweh (2 Chr 12:1). Perhaps the only hard historical data pertaining to religion under Rehoboam are in the Chronicler's report that priests and Levites came to Judah from the kingdom of Israel when Jeroboam dismissed them and appointed non-Levitic priests (2 Chr 11:13–17). These developments would make sense, assuming that the Levites were administrative and cultic state officials, appointed by David and Solomon, who remained loyal to Rehoboam.

F. Rehoboam's Family and Administration

The Chronicler claims that Rehoboam had 18 wives (only Mahalath and Maacah are named) and 60 concubines and was the father of 28 sons and 60 daughters (2 Chr 11:18–21). The Chronicler further states that Rehoboam appointed Abijah, a son by Maacah, chief *(nāgîd)* among his brothers and designated him as his successor. Rehoboam also assigned his sons to take charge of the fortified towns and granted them generous provisions (2 Chr 11:22–23). When Rehoboam died, he was succeeded by his son Abijah.

Bibliography

Albright, W. F. 1945. The Chronology of the Divided Monarchy of Israel. *BASOR* 100: 16–22.

Alt, A. 1951. Das Königtum in den Reichen Israel und Juda. *VT* 1: 2–22.

Evans, D. 1966. Rehoboam's Advisers at Shechem and Political Institutions in Israel and Sumer. *JNES* 25: 273–79.

Halpern, B. 1974. Sectionalism and Schism. *JBL* 93: 519–32.

Hayes, J. H., and Hooker, P. K. 1988. *A New Chronology for the Kings of Israel and Judah.* Atlanta.

Malamat, A. 1963. Kingship and Council in Israel and Sumer: A Parallel. *JNES* 22: 247–53.

———. 1965. Organs of Statecraft in the Israelite Monarchy. *BA* 28: 34–65.

Mazar, B. 1957. The Campaign of Pharaoh Shishak to Palestine. Pp. 57–66 in *Volume du Congrès, Strasbourg, 1956,* ed. G. W. Anderson et al. VTSup 4. Leiden.

Soggin, J. A. 1984. *A History of Ancient Israel.* Trans. J. Bowden. Philadelphia.
Thiele, E. R. 1984. *The Mysterious Numbers of the Hebrew Kings.* 3d ed. Grand Rapids.
Weinfeld, M. 1982. The Counsel of the "Elders" to Rehoboam and its Implications. *Maarav* 3/1: 27–53.

CARL D. EVANS

REHOBOTH (PLACE) [Heb *rĕḥōbôt*]. The name of three places mentioned in the OT. Literally, the name means "plazas"; as a toponym it means "spacious place" (Borée 1968: 48–49; 49, n. 5).

1. A well in the Negeb, dug by Isaac (Gen 26:22). The location is mentioned within a narrative sequence that could serve as a paradigm for the relationship between agriculturalists and pastoralists, or nomads and the state, in the 2d and 1st millennia B.C. (Matthews 1986: 123–24). Since Robinson and Smith proposed an identification of the site (1841: 289–91), this well has generally been located in Wadi Ruḥaybeh, SW of Beersheba.

2. Rehoboth-Ir, a "place" in Assyria, between Nineveh and Calah (Gen 10:11). The name seems to be based on a mistranslation of Assyrian *rebīt Ninua* ("the streets, or quarters, of Nineveh"; e.g., in Esarhaddon's Nineveh A inscription, III 38; cf. *AHW,* 964). See REHOBOTH-IR.

3. Rehoboth ha-Nahar (RSV "Rehoboth on the Euphrates"), the hometown of the Edomite "king" Shaul (Gen 36:37; 1 Chr 1:48). See SHAUL. The identification of this Rehoboth depends on the interpretation and dating of the "Edomite King List" (Gen 36:31–39). Assuming that this list refers to Edom at the end of the 2d millennium B.C., Zwickel (1985) identifies Rehoboth Nahar with Râs er-Riḥâb (M.R. 208038), overlooking Wadi al-Ḥasâ from the South. Knauf (1987), deriving the "Edomite King List" from the 5th century B.C., interprets Rehoboth ha-Nahar as the designation of a landscape, not a town, and suggests the catchment area of Wadi al-Ghuwayr for an identification. Lemaire (1988) maintains that the "Edomite King List" actually is a list of Aramean kings from the 11th century B.C. This assumption would place Rehoboth ha-Nahar in Syria or Lebanon. In this case, it could well have been the capital of the state of Beth-Rehob. See also REHOB (PLACE).

Bibliography

Borée, W. 1968. *Die alten Ortsnamen Palästinas.* 2d ed. Hildesheim.
Knauf, E. A. 1987. Supplementa Ismaelitica 10. *BN* 38/39: 44–49.
Lemaire, A. 1988. Hadad l'Édomite ou Hadad l'Araméen? *BN* 43: 14–18.
Matthews, V. A. 1986. The Wells of Gerar. *BA* 49: 118–26.
Robinson, E., and Smith, E. 1841. *Biblical Researches in Palestine, Mount Sinai and Arabia Petraea.* 3 vols. Boston.
Zwickel, W. 1985. Rehobot-Nahar. *BN* 29: 28–34.

ERNST AXEL KNAUF

REHOBOTH-IR (PLACE) [Heb *rĕḥōbōt ʿîr*]. The name of a city mentioned in Gen 10:11. The name is a Hebrew phrase meaning "city squares" (the same phrase appears in Lam 2:12). The Yahwistic fragment of the Table of Nations seems to include it in the kingdom of Nimrod, although the translation of the first clause of Gen 10:11 is very unclear. Perhaps the best understanding (although syntactically awkward) is "From that land (Shinar, v 10) he (Nimrod) went to Assyria." (Cf. the RSV; for similar constructions of the verb *yaṣaʾ*, "to go out," with the accusative in the sense of entering a place, see Gen 27:3 and Jer 14:18.) If this interpretation is correct, then Nimrod is to be understood as the builder of Rehoboth-Ir.

The name Rehoboth-Ir is unknown from cuneiform sources. It is probable that it referred originally not to a separate city but rather to some district or attribute of Nineveh. One possibility is that it is an interpretive translation of *rêbīt Ninua,* "Nineveh square," a suburb on the NE side of Nineveh (Cassuto *Genesis* 2: 203). However, the correct reading may be *talbit Ninua,* in which case the comparison must be dropped (Sasson 1983: 96). Alternatively, Rehoboth-Ir may be an epithet describing Nineveh as a city of broad streets. E. A. Speiser (*Genesis* AB, 68) compares it to a similar phrase found in the Gilgamesh epic, *Uruk rêbītu,* "Uruk of the spacious markets." T. Jacobsen (*IDB* 4: 31) has compared it to the cognate Assyrian phrase *rêbīt āli,* "open spaces in a city," used to mean "unbuilt areas on the periphery of Nineveh." J. M. Sasson (1983) proposes that it is a superlative construction meaning roughly "broadest city" (cf. Jonah 3:3; 4:11). In any case, it is generally agreed that Rehoboth-Ir was not a city but rather some appellative or area of Nineveh. At some point in the transmission of the traditions about Nimrod, this descriptive term was misunderstood as a city name itself. See RESEN.

Bibliography

Sasson, J. M. 1983. Reḥōvōt ʿÎr. *RB* 90: 94–96.

JAMES R. DAVILA

REHUM (PERSON) [Heb *rĕḥûm*]. Var. NEHUM. The name of several different persons mentioned in the OT.

1. One of the leaders of the group of returnees from Babylonian Exile who is listed along with Zerubbabel in Ezra 2:2 = Neh 7:7 (where the form is Nehum) = 1 Esdr 5:8. One name has apparently been dropped from the Ezra list, because those in Nehemiah and 1 Esdras include twelve leaders in what is probably a symbolic representation of all Israel. For further discussion concerning the list in Ezra 2, see AKKUB.

2. A Persian civil official (Heb *bĕʿēl ṭĕʿēm* = commander, commissioner) of the province "Beyond the River" who, along with Shimshai and others in Samaria, wrote to Artaxerxes I regarding the Jews' repair of the walls of Jerusalem. When authorized by a return letter to stop the building activity, they did so by force (Ezra 4:8–23 = 1 Esdr 2:16–30). This episode is out of chronological order with the other events of Ezra 4–6. It is inserted there in an apparent summary of incidents in which persons opposed the rebuilding efforts of the Jews.

3. A Levite who assisted Nehemiah in rebuilding the walls of Jerusalem (Neh 3:17). That the list of builders in Nehemiah 3 is a partial one is evident from the references to "second" portions in 3:11, 19, 20, and 30 without previous notations of corresponding first portions (compare 3:4 and 21; 3:5 and 27). There is widespread agreement that the list came from independent archives, perhaps in the temple, and was incorporated into the Nehemiah memoirs by Nehemiah himself or by some other editor. (See Batten *Ezra and Nehemiah* ICC, 206–7; Clines *Ezra, Nehemiah, Esther* NCBC, 149; Williamson *Ezra, Nehemiah* WBC, 199–202.)

4. Head of a clan whose leader affixed the family name to the covenant document of Nehemiah in Neh 10:26—Eng 10:25. Many do not regard the list and covenant of Nehemiah 10 as belonging originally in this context. Williamson (ibid., 325–30) surveys various views about the origins of this list. He concludes that it was compiled from other lists in Ezra and Nehemiah in order to be attached to the terms of an agreement drawn up by Nehemiah following his reforms of Nehemiah 13. This document was then kept in the temple archives until it was inserted into its present position. (See also Clines, 199–200; Myers *Ezra-Nehemiah* AB, 174–75; Jepsen 1954: 87–106.)

5. An alternate form of Harim. See HARIM #3.

Bibliography

Galling, K. 1951. The Gōlā-List According to Ezra 2 and Nehemiah 7. *JBL* 70: 149–58.

———. 1964. Die Liste der aus dem Exil Heimgekehrten. Pp. 89–108 in *Studien zur Geschichte Israels im persischen Zeitalter.* Tübingen.

Jepsen, A. 1954. Nehemiah 10. *ZAW* 66: 87–106.

CHANEY R. BERGDALL

REI (PERSON) [Heb *rēʿî*]. Mentioned with Shimei and others who did not support Adonijah's claim to David's throne (1 Kgs 1:8). The lack of a title or patronym for either Shimei or Rei is unusual. It is possible that the text is corrupt. Lucian reads "Shimei, and his friends, David's mighty men"; Josephus explains the text as "Shimei, the friend of David" (*Ant* 7.14.4). Little is known of the structure of the court in the time of David, but "friend" may have been a title for an official whose role was that of counselor of the king (cf. 2 Sam 15:37; 16:16). See Jones *Kings* NCBC; Gray *Kings* OTL; and DeVries *1 Kings* WBC.

Bibliography

Burney, C. F. 1903. *Notes on the Hebrew Text of the Book of Kings.* New York. Repr. 1970.

Mettinger, T. 1971. *Solomonic State Officials.* ConBOT 5. Lund.

PAULINE A. VIVIANO

REKEM (PERSON) [Heb *reqem*]. The name of three persons in the OT. In all three cases it can be argued that the "persons" were actually places, paralleled by the toponym Rekem in Josh 18:27. See REKEM (PLACE).

1. A "king" of Midian (Num 31:8; Josh 13:21). The names of the five "Midianite kings" in these passages seem to have been taken from an itinerary that led through S Transjordan and NW Arabia and that was composed in the Persian period. See also EVI; HUR; REBA; SUR. Both in the Targum and the Peshitta, Reqem/Rqem renders Kadesh-barnea, which was identified with Petra since, at least, the 1st century B.C. (possibly as early as by the time Gen 14:7 was composed; Knauf 1989: 46, n. 212). *Raqmu (in Nabatean, *rqmw*) was the indigenous name of Petra. Josephus (*Ant* 6.7.1 §161) derives the place name from the Midianite king's name. It is more likely, however, that *Raqam or *Raqm, "the striped one," is a genuine place name, although it does occur as a personal name in Thadmudic and Arabic (it is, however, rarely attested; Knauf 1988: 89 and n. 409). Nor was Petra the only place called Raq(a)m (Knauf 1988: 166 and n. 705).

2. A "son" of Hebron (1 Chr 2:43). In 1 Chr 2:43–44, Rekem is the brother of Tappuah, Shema, and Korah; the son of Hebron, the nephew of Ziph, and the grandson of Mareshah. All of the names of his relatives are also places (Shema recalls *as-Samûʿ*, the present name of Eshtemoa; the abridged form without the *t*-infix may well have originated in the postexilic period), with the only exception being Korah, who was an Idumean clan (a son of Esau [Gen 36:5], and a son of Eliphaz [Gen 36:16]; for Idumean clans among the "sons of Caleb," see MANAHATHITES). Whereas this leaves the possibility open that Rekem was another Idumean family or clan in postexilic S Judea, an interpretation as a place name finds more contextual support.

3. The "grandson" of Gilead and Maachah, both of which are geographical names (1 Chr 7:16; cf. 1 Chr 19:6). The name of his father, Peresh "Fissure," is attested as both a personal and a place name. Because place names frequently lead to the names of clans, and vice versa, and because there is not any external evidence, it cannot be decided whether this Rekem was a Gileadite clan, or a town, or both.

Bibliography

Knauf, E. A. 1988. *Midian.* ADPV. Wiesbaden.

———. 1989. *Ismael.* 2d ed. ADPV. Wiesbaden.

ERNST AXEL KNAUF

REKEM (PLACE) [Heb *reqem*]. A settlement in Benjamin (Josh 18:27). The exact location remains unknown, though the list in which it appears (vv 25–28) generally contains places located in the W half of the territory. Rekem is also the ancient name for Petra. This site is actually never named Rekem in the Bible, though it is possible that the name was somehow associated with the Midianite prince so named in Josh 13:21. See REKEM (PERSON).

ELMER H. DYCK

RELEASE, YEAR OF. See JUBILEE, YEAR OF; SABBATICAL YEAR.

RELIGIO LICITA. A term conveniently coined by Tertullian to designate a religion officially sanctioned by the Roman state. Throughout the Roman world there flourished a rich cultural and ethnic pluralism, and there naturally flourished, alongside this pluralism, an equally rich diversity in cultic practices (often localized in adherence). Roman religion throughout its long history was itself remarkably assimilative and adaptive (and hence showed astonishing powers of survival), and from time to time it might formally absorb by ceremonies of *evocatio,* or by official incorporation into ritual calendars and pageants, the rites and rituals of other nations (cf. Min. Fel. *Oct.* 6.1–3; North 1976: 1–12; 1979: 85–102). But by and large, the Romans were content, with passive acquiescence, to leave others to their own indigenous cultic activities so long as they did not disturb the established boundaries and controls within imperial society, and so long as they did not impinge on imperial policy and security. But there, however, the limits of toleration for the Romans were severely set (Garnsey 1984: 1–27): if in their perception the established social or political order was threatened, the guardians of that social and political order could show themselves fearsomely jealous for the gods of their empire (e.g., Tac. *Ann.* 2.85 [Isis devotees], 14.30 [Druids]; cf. Livy 39.8–19 [Bacchanalians in 186 B.C.])—though what constituted "the gods of the Empire" was an extremely porous list of divinities.

In the case of the Jews, it is clear that religious and ethnic privileges were hard won as *concessions* and needed constant vigilance—as well as polemic—and repetition if they were not to be eroded in practice (Rajak 1984: 107–23): the series of rescripts and edicts as recorded by Philo and Josephus (Philo *Gaium* 309–20, Joseph. *Ant* 14 §185–264, 301–23; 16 §160–73; 19 §280–91) are basically the results of Jewish initiative and efforts to secure for particular cities or provinces the simple rights to pursue without harassment their ancestral laws and customs—and to have, in their perception, what other subject nations enjoyed. (These concessions included the right not to have to appear in court on the Sabbath, to collect and despatch the temple tax, and to congregate and perform the customary ceremonies on the Sabbath and other feast days.) But social friction was inevitable with adherents of a monotheistic religion which could not be assimilated into or be accommodated within the prevailing pluralist religious system. Nevertheless, the Romans fully appreciated the strength of the bond which linked a people to its ancestral cultic traditions and customs, and so, under pressure from Jewish activists who were protecting their coreligionists against social and religious discrimination, the Romans found themselves politically obliged to make formal religious concessions to Jews. Judaism thus became a *religio licita* (= an authorized religion), to use Tertullian's coinage (*Apol.* 21.1). Most nations had no need of such legal sanction in order to maintain their religious observances.

Christians, however, right from their earliest penetration into the Greco-Roman world, found themselves liable to fall foul of official authorities, whether these were local city magistrates or imperial functionaries: charges of magic, of disturbing the peace, suspicion of subversion, or disorder could be leveled at Christian minority groups, some of whom might be given to secret meetings marked by prophetic enthusiasm, who might in millenarian expectation of the Parousia opt out of the routine duties of civic life, or whose vocally expressed views might grate on pagan sensitivities and traditions or outrage Jewish sects and practices. By the time historical evidence from non-Christian sources is specific (e.g., Tac. *Ann.* 15.44 [on events of A.D. 64, written early in the 2d century A.D.], Pliny *Ep.* 10.96, 97 [written ca. A.D. 110]), Christians had already come to belong to a group liable to sporadic and local punishment simply for their general Christian allegiance, based ultimately on the criminal charges that might cohere to their name but which need not be proved in any particular case (de Ste Croix 1963: 6–38; 1964: 28–33). Christians, now including many gentiles, had neither the ancestral traditions nor the racial integrity to which Jews themselves might effectively appeal. The result was (as Tertullian wryly makes much of in his *Apol.* 2.10–18) that Christians might, paradoxically, escape punishment simply by abjuring their present religious adherence—actions of their Christian past were thereby rendered, illogically, irrelevant. No specific legislation against Christianity as such can be established until the time of the emperor Valerian (A.D. 257; Barnes 1968: 32–50), but there is nonetheless ample evidence of rescripts and edicts issued by emperors and provincial governors dealing with particular inquiries or individual provinces (Ulpian could gather such imperial rescripts together in the early 3d century; Lactant. *Div. Inst.* 5.11.19 [listing penalties inflicted upon Christians]).

The tactic in much apologetic Christian writing in the 2d and 3d centuries was therefore to seek tolerant treatment for Christianity similar to that granted other philosophical *sectae,* with emphasis placed on the philosophical pedigree of many of the issues it dealt with and endeavoring to clear the Christian communities of the criminal odium which had come to hover over their religious practices. In effect, in many parts of the Roman Empire Christians enjoyed lengthy periods of that laissez-faire which Rome allowed other cults and alien religious traditions. But unlike those other cults, monotheistic Christianity (like Judaism) laid universal claim to the truth and an exclusive access to the divine (the corollary being rejection of all other gods and all other religious traditions). The orders of the emperor Decius (A.D. 250) for all inhabitants of the Empire to make sacrifice to the gods brought into public view widespread civil disobedience on the part of many Christians (Clarke 1984: 21–39); thus, they could not be left as tolerable religious deviants. The emperor Valerian (A.D. 257–58) followed with more specific attempts to suppress Christian assemblies and clerical leaders, but his capture and death prompted his son Gallienus to rescind those orders and to release sequestered Church properties (Eus. *Hist. Eccl.* 7.13). The effect was to go some way toward decriminalizing Christianity and giving it a quasi-legitimate existence which it had not enjoyed previously.

But it was not until after the bloody persecutions in the first quarter of the 4th century that Christianity won anything like a formally recognized right to coexist, first with the edict of the dying Galerius (A.D. 311: Lactant. *De mort. pers.* 34; Eus. *Hist. Eccl.* 8.17), then with the issuing of the so-called Edict of Milan (A.D. 313: Lactant. *De mort. pers.* 48; Eus. *Hist. Eccl.* 10.5.2–14), and finally after the eventual defeat of Licinius in the east (A.D. 324: Eus. *Vita. C.* 2.56). At long last Christianity had become in fact a *religio licita,* an authorized religion.

Bibliography

Barnes, T. D. 1968. Legislation Against the Christians. *JRS* 58: 32–50.

Clarke, G. W. 1984. *The Letters of St. Cyprian of Carthage.* Vol. 1, *Letters 1–27.* ACW 43. New York.

Garnsey, P. 1984. Religious Toleration in Classical Antiquity. Pp. 1–27 in *Persecution and Toleration*, ed. W. J. Shields. Oxford.
North, J. A. 1976. Conservatism and Change in Roman Religion. *PBSR* 44: 1–12.
———. 1979. Religious Toleration in Republican Rome. *PCPS* n.s. 25: 85–103.
Rajak, T. 1984. Was There a Roman Charter for the Jews? *JRS* 74: 107–28.
Ste Croix, G. E. M. de. 1963. Why Were the Early Christians Persecuted? *Past and Present* 26: 6–38.
———. 1964. Why Were the Early Christians Persecuted?—A Rejoinder. *Past and Present* 27: 28–33.

G. W. Clarke

RELIGION. Articles relevant to the study of religion and religions in the biblical world include CANAAN, RELIGION OF; EGYPTIAN RELIGION; HITTITE RELIGION; MEMPHITE THEOLOGY; MYSTERY RELIGIONS; PHOENICIAN RELIGION; ROMAN RELIGION; SOUTH ARABIA, RELIGION OF—as well as CHRISTIANITY; JUDAISM; and THEOLOGY.

REMALIAH (PERSON) [Heb *rĕmalyāhû*]. Father of Pekah, who was the next to last king of Israel, ca. 736–731 B.C.E. (2 Kgs 15:25). The name appears seven times in 2 Kgs 15:25–16:5 and once each in Isa 7:1 and 2 Chr 28:6 in the phrase "Pekah the son of Remaliah." In Isa 7:4, 5, 9, and 8:6 Pekah is referred to only by the patronym "the son of Remaliah," apparently with derogatory intent. The Bible gives us no other information about Remaliah himself. Pekah, and hence Remaliah, was apparently a native of Gilead (2 Kgs 15:25; Naʾaman 1986: 77–79). See PEKAH. No satisfactory meaning for the first element of Remaliah's name has been found (*IPN,* 257), since the verbal root *rml* does not appear in Hebrew. Two old Hebrew seals contain a name which has been read by some as *rmlyhw* (Diringer 1927: 178–79, 217). However, Diringer (Crowfoot et al. 1957: 21) has argued strongly in favor of reading these seals as *dmlyhw*. One possible explanation of the name depends on a different form of the name than we have in the MT. In the Qumran scroll 1QIsa[a], three passages spell the name *rwmlyh* (Isa 7:1, 5, 9). Since the LXX appears to back up the Qumran text by transliterating the name in these same passages as *Romelia* or *Romeliou,* Beegle (1951: 28) has understood the first element of the name to be derived from the verb *rwm* plus a predicative *la*. Hence, the name would mean "May Yahweh verily be exalted."

Bibliography

Beegle, D. M. 1951. Proper Names in the New Isaiah Scroll. *BASOR* 123: 28.
Crowfoot, J. W.; Crowfoot, G. M.; and Kenyon, K. M. 1957. *The Objects from Samaria.* London.
Diringer, D. 1927. *Le iscrizioni antico-ebraiche palestinesi.* Florence.
Horn, S. 1968. An Inscribed Seal from Jordan. *BASOR* 189: 41–43.
Naʾaman, N. 1986. Historical and Chronological Notes on the Kingdoms of Israel and Judah in the Eighth Century B.C. *VT* 36: 71–92.

John H. Hull Jr.

REMEMBER, REMEMBRANCE. The Scriptures provide no theoretical account of memory, no reflections concerning the nature or psychology or functions of remembering, nothing to compare, for example, with Aristotle's *De Memoria.* J. Pedersen's interesting attempt to construct such a theoretical account of memory based on the so-called "primitive" psychology of the Hebrews (*PI* 1: 99–139) has been rejected by J. Barr (1961: 30–33, *et passim*) and criticized by B. Childs (1962: 17–30).

There may be no theory of memory, but there surely is remembering; indeed, the Scriptures are full of references to memory and remembrance. And it is clear that it will not do to define memory as "the preservation of perception" (Pl. *Phlb.* 34a) or "the permanence of an image regarded as the copy of the thing it images" (Arist. *Mem.* 451a). Such definitions do not do justice to the scriptural usage of Heb *zākar,* Gk *mimnēiskomai,* and their cognates by confining memory to things of the past. In Scripture, things in the present (e.g., Col 4:18)—and even in the future (e.g., Eccl 11:8; Heb 11:22)—can be "remembered." More importantly, such definitions distort the scriptural usage by construing memory as the neutral apprehension of images. In Scripture, however, memory is typically constitutive of identity and determinative of conduct.

A. God Remembers

In great hymns of faith Israel gave praise to God, and a fundamental reason for that praise was that God remembers "his covenant" (Ps 105:8 = 1 Chr 16:15; Ps 106:45; 111:5; also Luke 1:72). The covenant is presupposed when God is said to remember "his steadfast love and faithfulness" (Ps 98:3; cf. 136:23), "his promise" (Ps 105:42), or "his mercy" (Luke 1:54). The covenant is not just something from the past, and remembering it is not merely the neutral apprehension of an image from the past. In the covenant and in remembering the covenant, God establishes an identity and is faithful to it, determines a cause, and acts in accordance with it.

Psalm 105:8 stands at the opening of a long recital of the "wonderful works" which God has done, but it gives this significance to that past: God remembers his covenant "forever" and "for a thousand generations." God's remembering determines conduct and not only the great deeds of the past but also God's works of judgment and mercy in the present and future. That God has remembered the people stands in parallel to the claim that God "will bless" them (Ps 115:12).

God's remembrance of covenant finds its way from the hymns into narrative and especially into the covenantal history of the Priestly narrative, where again and again it is observed that God "remembers" covenant (Gen 9:15, 16; Exod 2:24; 6:5; Lev 26:42 [3×], 45; cf. also Gen 8:1; 19:29).

If the hymns celebrate God's remembering, the laments—and other prayers—plead for it (Ps 25:6; 74:2, 18, 22; 106:4; 119:49; 137:7; also Exod 32:13; Jer 14:21; Lam 5:1; Hab 3:2; Neh 1:8; with respect to the king, cf. Pss 20:3; 89:47, 50; 132:1; 2 Chr 6:42; note also the prayers of Samson, Judg 16:28; of Hannah, 1 Sam 1:11; of Hezekiah, 2 Kgs 20:3 = Isa 38:3). Often the covenant provides the basis for the appeal (e.g., Jer 14:21; Ps 25:6). Sometimes the appeal is simply to the creatureliness and mortality of people (Ps 89:47; Job 7:7; 10:9; 14:13; cf. Pss 8:4; 78:39). Sometimes the appeal is to merit (Ps 132:1; 2 Kgs 20:3 = Isa 38:3; Jer 18:20; Neh 5:19; 6:14; 13:14, 22, 29, 31), but sometimes the plea is simply an appeal to the sheer grace of God, as in the petition that God *not* remember sins, that is, forgive them (Pss 25:7; 79:8; also Isa 64:9).

The prophetic oracles of judgment take this tradition and turn it against the people: God "will remember their iniquity"; that is, punish them (Jer 14:10; Hos 7:2; 8:13; 9:9). The oracles of salvation, however, turn the tradition around again to announce God's mercy on the other side of judgment and repentance (Isa 43:25; Jer 31:20). The astonishing promise of Jer 31:31–34 of a new covenant in which "God will remember their sin no more" is, according to the author of Hebrews, fulfilled in the ministry of Christ (Heb 8:12; 10:17).

B. People Remember

The verb "remember" often has a human subject, and when it does, it can take a wide variety of objects. But whatever the object, memory remains related to the formation of identity and the determination of conduct. David "remembers" Abigail by wooing and marrying her (1 Sam 25:31); he does not "remember" that Shemei was his adversary when he spares his life although he is fully aware of the past (2 Sam 19:19). When the men of Shechem remember that Abimelech is their kinsmen, they are "inclined to follow him" (Judg 9:2, 3). Even Joseph's memory of his dreams (Gen 42:9) is not merely recollection: God's guidance forms him and his conduct.

The most frequent object of human remembering in the OT, however, is God (Deut 8:18; Judg 8:34; Ps 22:7; 42:6; 63:6; 77:3; 78:35; Eccl 12:1; Isa 57:11; 64:5; Jer 51:50; Ezek 6:9; Jonah 2:7; Zech 10:9), including God's works (Deut 5:15; 7:18; 8:2; 9:7; 15:5; 16:3, 12; 24:9, 18, 22; 32:7; Pss 77:11; 78:42; 105:5; 143:5; Ezek 16:22, 43, 61, 63; Mic 6:5) and (less frequently) God's law (Num 15:39, 40; Pss 103:18; 119:52; Mal 4:4; cf. Exod 13:3; 20:8).

Both worship and tradition served this memory. Through the great festivals with their rituals and songs, the people participated in both establishing and remembering the meaningful history of Israel and thus understood themselves better in the light of that meaningful past. Memory provided community and continuity. The Passover, for example, which Israel was to "remember" (that is, observe, Exod 13:3), was itself a "remembrance" (Heb *zikkārôn,* Exod 12:14) of God's deliverance of them from Egypt. By ritual and celebration subsequent generations made that story their own (cf. the Passover Haggadah; *m. Pesaḥ.* 10:4–6). Similarly, the Feast of Unleavened Bread was observed to "remember" the Exodus (Exod 13:8–10; Deut 16:3; consider also the Feast of Booths, Lev 23:43). New Year's Day is also described as a memorial (Heb *zikkārôn;* Lev 23:24), presumably of God's creative activity and sovereignty. Later commemorative festivals might also be mentioned: Purim (cf. Esth 9:28) and Hanukkah (1 Macc 4:52, 59). Even the wearing of phylacteries (Deut 6:8; 11:18; Exod 13:9) and tassels (Num 15:39) served as a memory of God's works and law. Thus Israel "remembered" the Lord. (At the same time, of course, the cultic ceremonies and prayers served to bring the people to God's remembrance.)

The cult was an important context for remembering, but there were others: notably, the instruction of children (Deut 6:20–25; Josh 4:4–7). For the Deuteronomist, memory assumed a special and central importance; the reform depended upon it. There was no greater danger to identity and community that forgetfulness (e.g., Deut 8:11, 19). The remedy for forgetfulness was to tell the old stories, to rehearse the traditions of God's election and grace, to remember. And remembering was never merely "recollecting"; it had the shape of obedience, of covenant faithfulness (8:1, 2; consider also the stereotyped formula in 5:15; 15:15; 16:12; 24:18, 22). The point was not some cultic actualization of the past, already then remote, not some mysterious reliving of it, some of which was painful, but continuity with it, covenant identity and fidelity in a new situation, the reformation of Judah's cult and community.

In the cycles of apostasy, affliction, repentance, and deliverance which the Deuteronomistic Historian used to interpret Israel's history and to call exiles to return, the failure to remember could be used as the equivalent of apostasy (Judg 8:34). The failure to remember was not mere absentmindedness; it was covenant unfaithfulness, the failure to fulfill the obligations of the covenant. Other texts, too, explained God's judgment as being due to Israel's forgetfulness (e.g., Isa 17:10; Jer 3:21; 13:25; 18:15; Ezek 22:12; 23:35; Hos 2:13; 4:6; Pss 78:42; 106:7; Neh 9:17).

Again, however, the prophets finally turned the words of judgment around—but none quite so completely around as Deutero-Isaiah. Alongside the expected admonition "Remember the former things of old" (Isa 46:8) Deutero-Isaiah put the quite astonishing "remember not the former things" (43:18). The eschatological perspective of the prophet looked to a future sovereignty of God over Israel and the cosmos that would completely overshadow the past and provide a new identity, a new community, and a new creation. This "new thing" (Isa 43:19) would stand in both continuity and discontinuity with Israel's memory, and it was done, according to the NT, in Jesus the Christ (e.g. Rev 21:4, 6).

A "new thing" it may have been, confounding as well as fulfilling memories and expectations, but the resurrection of Jesus (or the conviction that he was raised) prompted believers to remember Jesus in tradition and worship.

The tradition of Jesus' words and deeds was by no means merely objective recollection of historical data, and the gospels which gave the oral tradition literary expression were hardly simply retrospective historical accounts. Both were highly interpretive. It was, after all, a living Lord who was remembered, and living communities selected and shaped the tradition even while they received it. When Justin Martyr calls the gospels "memoires," (Gk *apomnemonēumata; Dial* 103:8), one may object against the denotation of an ancient literary form which contained episodes from the lives of famous men and against the connotation of a retrospective historical account; but one at least must appreciate the continuity of the gospels with the Church's memory of Jesus (cf. also Papias in Eus. *Hist. Eccl.* 3.39.15; Luke 1:1–4). At the empty tomb, according to Luke, the disciples were told to "remember" (Luke 24:6, 8), and for the first time they understood (cf. John 2:22; 12:16; 16:4). In John's gospel it is said that the Paraclete, the Holy Spirit, will "bring to your remembrance all that I have said to you" (John 14:26). John's gospel may rework the tradition more than the other gospels, but none of them provides either a recollection of the "life of Jesus" or a timeless existentialist revelation; each gospel is a "remembrance," a literary commemoration of the risen Lord, which situated the lives of their readers in relation to the Christ, forging an identity, a community, and continuity, forming character, and determining conduct.

The epistles, too, served the memory of the Church. Paul explicitly says he writes to the Romans "by way of reminder" (Rom 15:15; Gk *hos epanaminēskōn hymae;* cf. 2 Pet 3:1). The epistles bear the tradition and ask readers to remember it (e.g., 1 Cor 15:1; Rev 3:3). They ask their readers to remember their own conversion (e.g., Eph 2:11, 13) and the ministry of their leaders (e.g., Acts 20:31; Heb 13:7). The later epistles, particularly, are intent upon preserving the tradition (e.g., 2 Tim 2:8, 14; Jude 5; 2 Pet 1:12, 13; 3:1). This "early Catholic" development was based on an understanding of the importance of memory from the beginning and was nurtured by the conviction that Christian identity and community had been put at risk within the congregations. Even here, "remember Jesus Christ, risen from the dead, descended from David, as preached in my gospel" (2 Tim 2:8) is not merely a call to preserve historical data, but a call to identity and community, to fitting thoughts and deeds (cf. Phil 2:6–11).

The epistles frequently remind their readers of the worship of the community (e.g., the hymns of Phil 2:6–11 and Col 1:9–15), and especially of baptism (e.g., Rom 6:1–11; 1 Cor 1:12–13; 12:13; Gal 3:27–28; Eph 2:1–7). It is little wonder, for worship was itself remembrance, and baptism in the name of Jesus and "into his death" (Rom 6:3) established identity, initiated one into a community of common memory, and required fitting conduct. Baptism was remembrance—not merely historical recollection—of the death and resurrection of Christ.

The Lord's Supper is explicitly said to be done "in remembrance" (Gk *anamnēsis*) of Jesus the Christ (1 Cor 11:24, 25; Luke 22:19). Jeremias (1966: 237–55) has argued (partly on the basis of Acts 10:4) that "in remembrance of me" should be translated as "that God may remember me" and should be understood as an eschatological petition for the Parousia. But Jeremias' argument begins with a minimal account of remembering as mere recollection and proceeds by way of a false dilemma between a reference to *either* the past or the future. When believers gathered around this table, they remembered the past, to be sure; they remembered the stories of the suffering and death of the risen Lord—but not merely as a historical recollection. In remembering that past, they owned the stories as their stories (including the story of Peter's "remembering," Mark 14:72). This remembering involved a "pleading guilty" to the death of Jesus but also a sharing in that death and in the new covenant (with its forgiveness) which Christ established. This remembering was constitutive of identity and community and determined conduct in the present. It is said that when the rich humiliate the poor, when community is broken (1 Cor 11:22), then "it is not the Lord's supper that you eat" (v 20), it is an "unworthy manner (v 27), and it is not truly "remembrance." Moreover, precisely because the people composed a community of memory, they were a community of hope, for they remembered the Lord's death as an eschatological event and proclaimed it "until he comes" (v 26). To remember Jesus was to hope for God's cosmic sovereignty—and to plead for God's remembrance, for God to act with covenant faithfulness. So Jeremias' affirmations can finally be accepted, but by way of a different argument, without denying what he denied.

Representatives of various liturgical traditions can agree on seeing *anamnēsis* as the fundamental characteristic of the celebration of the Eucharist. *Anamnēsis* neither prohibits nor requires understanding the sacrament as an "actualization" of the sacrifice of Christ, but it will protest against and protect against any diminishing of the sufficiency of the one death of Christ. *Anamnēsis* will welcome understanding the sacrament as a liturgical "memorial," but it will reject any account which reduces memory to recollection. Remembering remains constitutive of identity and community and determinative for character and conduct.

Bibliography

Barr, J. 1961. *The Semantics of Biblical Language.* London.

Childs, B. S. 1962. *Memory and Tradition in Israel.* SBT 37. Naperville, IL.

Dahl, N. A. 1976. *Jesus in the Memory of the Church.* Minneapolis.

Gerhardsson, B. 1961. *Memory and Manuscript.* Lund.

Jeremias, J. 1966. *The Eucharistic Words of Jesus.* Trans. N. Perrin. New York.

Reisenfeld, H. 1957. *The Gospel Tradition and Its Beginnings.* London.

Schottroff, W. 1967. *"Gedenken" in Alten Orient und in AT.* WMANT 15. 2d ed. Neukirchen.

Allen Verhey

REMETH (PLACE) [Heb *remet*]. A border town in the territory of Issachar (Josh 19:21). Most modern scholars would see Remeth (note LXX^A *Ramath*) as identical with Ramoth in 1 Chr 6:58—Eng v 73 and Jarmuth (LXX *Remmath*) in Josh 21:29, variants of the name of a levitical town in the territory of Issachar. If this identification is correct (for an opposing viewpoint, see W. F. Albright 1926), it is possible to tentatively identify the site of Remeth as Kokab el-Hawa (M.R. 199221), which is an elevated region W of the Jordan River, E of Megiddo, and NW of Beth-shean, the site of the Crusader castle Belvoir. Woudstra (*Joshua* NICOT) notes that in a stele of Pharaoh Seti I, mention is made of an attack by the Habiru from a Mt. Yarmuta, possibly the same location as Jarmuth.

Bibliography

Albright, W. F. 1926. The Topography of the Tribe of Issachar. *ZAW* 3: 32–33.

———. 1942. A Case of Lèse-Majesté in Pre-Israelite Lachish. *BASOR* 87: 36 n. 30.

Sidnie Ann White

REMNANT. What is left of a community after it undergoes a catastrophe. The major Heb terms are derivatives of *šʾr*, *ytr*, *plṭ*, and *śrd;* the major Gk terms, *leimma*, *hypoleimma*, *loipos*, and *kataloipos*.

A. Hebrew Bible

The concept is used most often with reference to Israel/Judah, although sometimes also to other peoples (Josh 12:4; 2 Sam 21:2; Isa 14:30; 17:3; Amos 1:8; 9:12; Zech 9:7), to humankind as a whole (Zech 14:16), or to all living creatures (Gen 7:1–5). It often has a negative connotation: the catastrophe undergone by the community is so great that only an insignificant remnant survives, or none at all (2 Kgs 21:13–15; Isa 17:4–6; Jer 8:3; Ezek 15:1–8; Amos 3:12; 5:3; 9:1–4). In many instances, however, the connotation is positive: despite the greatness of the catastrophe, a remnant survives as the basis for renewed community life (Gen 8:15–19; 45:7; 1 Kgs 19:18; Isa 1:25–26; 28:5–6; Jer 23:3–4; Joel 2:32; Obad 17; Mic 2:12; 4:6–7; Zeph 3:11–13). Because the catastrophe is understood to be an act of divine judgment, the survival of a viable remnant is, correspondingly, an act of divine mercy (Jer 23:3–4; 31:7–9; Amos 5:14–15; Mic 4:6–7). While some passages suggest that a remnant survives despite the fact that all are worthy of destruction (Jeremiah 5, esp. vv 10, 18; Mic 7:18–20), in other places the survivors are described as those who were righteous and faithful (1 Kgs 19:18; Zeph 2:3; 3:12–13). In any case, the catastrophe purges the community of its impurities, and the remnant is called to exemplary life as the people of Yahweh (Ezra 9:13–14; Isa 1:25–26; 4:2–4; 10:20). Thus, the appointment and rescue of the remnant, making possible the continuation of the life of the community, may be viewed as themselves constituting the saving activity of Yahweh (Gen 45:7; Ezra 9:7–9; Isa 1:9). Attention may, however, shift to the future, with the remnant still to be the recipient of new and greater acts of salvation (Isa 11:10–16; 28:5–6; Jer 23:3; 31:7–9; Mic 2:12–13; 4:6–7; 5:7–8; 7:18–20; Zeph 2:7, 9).

Although most often associated with the latter prophets, the concept appears (as already indicated) in some narrative passages as well. It is a motif in Genesis, e.g., the flood story (6:5–8:22), in which the flood is the means of divine judgment on human wickedness, to "blot out . . . man and beast and creeping things and birds of the air" (6:7). The destruction is not to be total, however; Noah, "a righteous man" (6:9; cf. 7:1), is appointed, along with his household, to preserve representative animals from destruction (6:18–21; 7:1–5). After the flood, they become the agents for the repopulation of the earth (8:15–19; 9:1–7).

In the Joseph story (Genesis 37–50), the catastrophe is a famine. It is the descendants of Abraham and Sarah who are threatened, and it is Joseph, a member of that family, who is appointed as preserver. The famine is not said to be the means of divine judgment; nor is Joseph depicted as especially righteous (although his rescue of his brothers in their time of need contrasts favorably with their earlier treatment of him). But when he reveals himself to them, he articulates the divine purpose: "God sent me before you to preserve for you a remnant on earth, and to keep alive for you many survivors" (45:7).

A further narrative instance of the concept is from the Elijah cycle (1 Kings 17–2 Kings 2). Elijah, having fled to Mt. Horeb, complains to Yahweh that "the people of Israel have forsaken thy covenant, thrown down thy altars, and slain thy prophets with the sword; and I, even I only, am left; and they seek my life, to take it away" (1 Kgs 19:10, 14). Yahweh's reply is to send Elijah to anoint those who are to bring the catastrophe, but he also announces his intention to "leave seven thousand in Israel, all the knees that have not bowed to Baal, and every mouth that has not kissed him" (19:18). In this case, the agents of divine judgment are human (two kings and a prophet), and the survivors are those who have been faithful to Yahweh.

Another narrative reference to a remnant appears at the close of Hezekiah's plea to Isaiah to pray for Jerusalem's deliverance from Sennacherib's attack: ". . . therefore lift up your prayer for the remnant that is left" (2 Kgs 19:4 = Isa 37:4). Isaiah's response on this occasion is reassuring. Quite the opposite is the later prophetic word provoked by the situation under Manasseh: ". . . I will cast off the remnant of my heritage, and give them into the hand of their enemies . . ." (2 Kgs 21:14).

The Chronicler views the returned exiles of the Persian period as a remnant left by Yahweh's favor, in spite of sins that merited total destruction. Should they again break the commandments, they would have to expect that even the remnant would be consumed (Ezra 9:8, 13–15).

Among the latter prophets, Amos contains several allusions to the concept. For the most part, these are threatening: all that will remain of Israel are a few artifacts (3:12); only a tenth of the population will survive (5:3); those who escape the initial onslaught will be hunted down one by one (9:1–4). But there is also the possibility that, if Israel changes its ways, "it may be that the Lord, the God of hosts, will be gracious to the remnant of Joseph" (5:14–15; cf. the later gloss, 9:8c).

The references in the book of Micah to a restored remnant of Israel are generally ascribed to postexilic editing. They will be gathered like sheep, and the lame and afflicted will receive special care (2:12–13; 4:6–7); Yahweh's anger will give way to forgiveness, compassion, and love (7:18–20). The remnant will be among the nations like dew and like a lion; that is, as both blessing and curse (5:7–8).

The call of Isaiah of Jerusalem refers to a destruction that is virtually total (Isa 6:11–13), but his son is named Shearjashub ("a remnant will return"). That may well be intended as an expression of doom ("only a remnant"; cf. 10:20–22; 30:15–17); certainly those who oppose Yahweh (including Samaria) will be reduced to a handful of survivors (16:14; 17:1–6; 21:16–17). In other oracles attributed to Isaiah, however, the survival of a few is ascribed to Yahweh's grace (1:9). The destruction is to serve a purifying purpose (1:25–26; 4:2–4). Those who have been scattered will be gathered again (11:10–16) and blessed by Yahweh (28:5–6).

Zephaniah announces a day of Yahweh's wrath, but holds forth the possibility that the humble and obedient, who seek righteousness and humility, may escape (2:3). When the "proudly exultant ones" are removed, there will be left "a people humble and lowly. They shall seek refuge in the name of the Lord, those who are left in Israel; they shall do no wrong and utter no lies, nor shall there be found in their mouth a deceitful tongue. For they shall pasture and lie down, and none shall make them afraid" (3:11–13).

Jeremiah professes to find no one in Jerusalem "who does justice and seeks truth," for the sake of whom the city can be pardoned (5:1–6; 6:9). While some will survive the coming destruction, they will find existence intolerable (8:3). Yet the day will come when Yahweh will gather the remnant of his flock from all the countries where he has driven them, and will provide shepherds for them in their own land (23:1–8); the call will go out, "Proclaim, give praise, and say, 'The Lord has saved his people, the remnant of Israel' " (31:7).

In Haggai and Zechariah, "the remnant of the people" is used as a name for those who have returned from Exile (Hag 1:12, 14; 2:2; Zech 8:6, 11, 12).

B. New Testament

The most explicit NT reference to the remnant is in Romans 9–11. Paul's indebtedness to the Hebrew Bible for the concept is attested by his quotation of such passages as Isa 10:22; 1:9; and 1 Kgs 19:18 (cf. Rom 9:27, 29; 11:4). As he struggles with the fact that most of his fellow-Jews have not accepted his gospel, he observes that "not all who are descended from Israel belong to Israel" (9:6b), and that "it is not the children of the flesh who are the children of God, but the children of the promise are reckoned as descendants" (9:8). Those Jews who accept his gospel constitute the remnant. They and the gentiles who believe have been chosen, not by their own will or exertion, but in divine sovereignty and mercy, as were Israel's first ancestors to whom the promise was given (9:6–33). This does not mean, however, that Israel has been deprived of its heritage (9:4–5) or rejected by God (11:1–2a). Even those who have been excluded for a time will eventually be included (11:11–32). Thus, the existence of the remnant is a temporary phenomenon, to be superseded when God's work is complete.

Allusions to the remnant occur in the Synoptic Gospels. Thus, John the Baptist warns of a judgment coming upon the descendants of Abraham that will leave only the trees that bear good fruit, and will gather the wheat into the granary while the chaff will be burned (Matt 3:7–10 = Luke 3:7–9). Jesus speaks of a wide gate and an easy way that leads many to destruction, while only a few find the narrow gate and take the hard way that leads to life (Matt 7:13–14; cf. Luke 13:23–24). He also tells a parable of a field in which a man sows good seed, after which an enemy secretly sows weeds; both wheat and weeds grow together until the harvest, but then the separation will be made (Matt 13:24–30). When asked about his teaching in parables, Jesus distinguishes between those to whom "it has been given to know the secret of the kingdom of God" and the others for whom parables are intended (Mark 4:10–12 = Matt 13:10–17 = Luke 8:9–10). A proverb, "For many are called, but few are chosen," is ascribed to him (Matt 22:14).

The book of Revelation describes the situation in the churches to which it is addressed in terms that sometimes reflect the concept of remnant (2:24; 3:4). Its portrayal of the destruction to accompany the end time involves a remnant that will survive (11:13; 12:17).

C. Origin of the Concept

No consensus has emerged concerning the origin of the concept of a remnant. It has been held that the motif emerged in the context of eschatology derived from Babylonian mythology and cults. Another view is that the concept has its origins in the civil or political sphere; and, more specifically, that it derives from the Assyrian policy of total warfare, reflected in royal inscriptions boasting of successful military campaigns. A third outlook holds that the remnant idea arose out of existential concern over threats to human survival and the desire to secure life and existence in the face of death.

Bibliography

Campbell, J. C. 1950. God's People and the Remnant. *SJT* 3: 78–85.

Carena, O. 1985. *Il Resto di Israele.* Supplementi alla Rivista Biblica 13. Bologna.

Hasel, G. F. 1974. *The Remnant.* 2d ed. Andrews University Monographs 5. Berrien Springs, MI.

Müller, W. E. L., and Preuss, H. D. 1973. *Die Vorstellung vom Rest im Alten Testament.* 2d ed. Neukirchen-Vluyn.

LESTER V. MEYER

REPENTANCE.

REPENTANCE. The notion of repentance follows from the notion of sin. It suggests that sin is an act or attitude which can be corrected by some change in the person.

A. Old Testament

The basic Hebrew word which is used to express this change is *šwb,* the root of which means simply "to turn." It is a particularly instructive word because it reflects the notion of journeying and pilgrimage, which exemplifies in a very fundamental sense the attitude and relationship between Yahweh and Israel (Deut 26:5–11).

The idea of walking in the way of the Lord is a common metaphor in the Hebrew Bible (Ps 1:1). And in a variety of contexts the way of Israel is contrasted with the way of Canaan, the way of the Lord with the way of evildoers, the way of the righteous with the way of sinners. Israel's religious calendar, too, is built on the core of pilgrim feasts: Passover, Booths, and Pentecost all have pilgrim contexts. It is this notion of walking and journeying, then, that illumines the meaning of *šwb* (or the less common *nḥm;* Exod 13:17). The relationship with Yahweh is envisioned as an ongoing journey requiring constant attention and vigilance, and a sense of purpose. To deviate from the way is, at the same time, to lose sight of the objective.

Three classical passages illustrate this sense of repentance-returning: Amos 4:6–13; Hos 5:15–6:5; Jer 3:12–24.

In Amos the prophetic vision of the coming destruction finds powerful expression. His prophecy cuts through the appearances of prosperity and illumines the hypocrisy and idolatry of self-love. The passage in chap. 4 rehearses the chastisements, punishments, and signs that Yahweh has visited upon Israel. Despite this "parental" admonition, "you did not return *(šwb)* to me." This phrase becomes a refrain in the passage. The general tone of Amos is pessimistic and the repentance which is required seems remote.

In these passages the emphasis is on "Israel," the people. The dire call "Prepare to meet your God" is directed to the nation which "did not return."

In Hosea the great metaphor of the faithless wife is the key to understanding the sense of repentance (Hosea 2–3). Faithless Israel has become a prostitute and abandoned the relationship with the Lord, forgotten the love God showed, and been ungrateful for the Lord's gifts of plenty and prosperity. But the Lord does not (as in Amos) let go. "I will woo her. I will go with her into the wilderness and comfort her: there I will restore her vineyards . . . and there she will answer as in her youth" (Hos 2:14–15). There is in Hosea a real sense of the possibility of repentance. "Come, let us return to the Lord; for he has torn us and will heal us. He has struck us and he will bind up our wounds; after two days he will revive us; on the third day he will restore us, that in his presence we may live" (Hos 6:1–2). Following this consolation, the prophet goes on to enumerate the qualities of repentance: humility and knowledge of the Lord (Hos 6:3–4). And further in chap. 12 he cites "loyalty and justice" (Hos 12:6). Over and over it is the care of the poor, the quality of justice, and the dedication to the Torah that exemplify true repentance.

So in Hosea, while the references are to Israel (2:4–4), the repentance which is required is more personal, more individual than the call to repentance in Amos.

Finally in Jeremiah the prophet's call for a "new heart" provides the context of repentance. In chap. 3 Jeremiah proclaims, "Come back to me, apostate Israel, says the Lord, I will no longer frown on you. For my love is unfailing, says the Lord, I will not be angry for ever" (Jer 3:12). The condemnations of Israel and the apostasy which will bring disaster on the people are offset constantly by the appeal to renewal. "I remember the unfailing devotion of your youth, the love of your bridal days when you followed me in the wilderness, through a land unknown" (Jer 2:2). And the renewal which is required is also specified. "If you will banish your loathsome idols from my sight, and stray no more; if you swear by the life of the Lord in truth, in justice, and uprightness, then shall the nations pray to be blessed like you (Jer 4:1–2).

But one theme that Jeremiah develops more fully than his predecessors is the idea of gleaning out of Israel a faithful few (Jer 6:9). And this faithful remnant may yet survive the disaster if they acknowledge their wrongdoing, confess their rebellion and their promiscuous traffic with foreign gods (Jer 3:13). In this group of confessors, repentant and renewed, the future hope lies because these the Lord loved: "With everlasting Love have I loved you, therefore I have continued my faithfulness to you" (Jer 31:3).

This can only take place, however, when the Lord "will make a new covenant with the house of Israel and the house of Judah." This new covenant will not be external to the faithful, nor a "thing" to be done; rather, the Lord "will write it upon their hearts." The renewed covenant and the renewed heart are essential elements of the future. From the very beginning, the Lord both winnowed and called. And to that call those who heard and repented responded and so became "like a watered garden" (Jer 31:12).

Again in Jeremiah, there is a growing sense of a distinction between the fate of the whole people and the fate of the faithful. So the repentance of the faithful few restores Israel even though the many perish.

It seems clear from the prophetic writings that repentance is eschatological. The final punishment of faithless Israel is withheld. The sword is stayed, the final light is not extinguished, the possibility of repentance remains because the Lord is faithful and full of love and refuses to abandon the covenant (Childs 1986: 226).

Repentance in the prophets, then, is an act of the heart. It is more than mere words. It is defined by clear actions that lead to justice, mercy, and fidelity. But repentance was also a cultic act. It is a liturgical function in Israel. There are a number of passages which point to the liturgical act of repentance (Isa 63:7–64:12; Hos 6:1–3; 7:14; 14:1–3; Joel 2:15–18). These cultic expressions apparently included acts such as rending garments, throwing ashes, wearing coarse garments, and as in the liturgy of the *yôm hakkippurîm*, symbolic acts (Leviticus 16). These cultic acts attest to a widespread belief in both the necessity and the possibility of repentance and forgiveness. Though the prophets often excoriate such rituals because they are performed without a change of heart (Jeremiah 7), they are important indicators of the faith of Israel in the continuous mercy of Yahweh.

Finally, one should note the many references in the Psalms to repentance and forgiveness. Two psalms in particular, Psalm 51 and Psalm 130, express most poignantly the elements of true repentance and its place in the religion of Israel:

If you, Lord, keep count of sins
Who, O Lord, could hold up his head.
But in you is forgiveness
And therefore you are revered (Ps 130:3–4).

Create a pure heart in me, O God,
And give me a new and steadfast spirit. . . .
My sacrifice, O God, is a broken spirit,
A wounded heart you will not despise (Ps 51:10, 17).

Bibliography

Childs, B. 1986. *Old Testament Theology in a Canonical Context.* Philadelphia.

Cody, A. 1969. *A History of the Old Testament Priesthood.* AnOr 25. Rome.

Heschel, A. 1962. *The Prophets.* New York.

Kaufmann, Y. 1960. *The Religion of Israel.* Trans. M. Greenberg. Chicago.

Lindstrom, J. 1962. *Prophecy in Ancient Israel.* Philadelphia.

Sanders, E. P. 1977. *Paul and Palestinian Judaism.* Philadelphia.

JOSEPH P. HEALEY

B. New Testament

The primary Gk term rendered "repentance" in English translations of the NT *(metanoia)* is found 24 times, and its verbal form "to repent" *(metanoeō)* is used another 34 times. In addition, another important word which is sometimes translated "repent" *(metamelomai)* occurs six times. The generally recognized core idea of these words is a "change of mind" (*NIDNTT* 1: 356–57), although *metamelomai* also carries the nuance of "regret" or "remorse"

(*TDNT* 4: 628–29). The English rendering has perhaps been colored by the Latin background of concepts like penance and penitence.

1. OT Background. In the LXX both *metanoia/metanoeō* and *metamelomai* translate the Heb *nāḥam* a total of 35 times, again emphasizing the elements of a change of thinking and regret. It has been commonly held that the NT concept of "repentance" follows the meaning of the frequent Heb verb *šûb* (*TDNT* 8: 989; *NIDNTT* 1: 357). However, such a view cannot be sustained from LXX usage because *šûb,* which is used over 1,050 times, is always translated by *epistrophō* ("to turn, be converted") and its kindred terminology (*TDNT* 8: 726–29; *NIDNTT* 1: 354). Thus, any possible shift in meaning took place during the Intertestamental Period, perhaps under Hellenistic influence (*TDNT* 4: 989), though such a conclusion lacks fully persuasive proof (Wilkin 1985).

2. NT Usage. The noun *metanoia* and its related verb *metanoeō* occur 26 times in the gospels, though not at all in John. They are found eleven times in Acts, five times in the Pauline epistles, three times in Hebrews, once in 2 Peter, and twelve times in Revelation. The minority term *metamelomai* is encountered three times in Matthew, twice in 2 Corinthians, and once in Hebrews.

In the gospels, John the Baptist burst onto the scene in Israel "preaching a baptism of repentance for the forgiveness of sins" (Mark 1:4; Luke 3:3). His urgent message was "Repent, for the kingdom of heaven is near" (Matt 3:2). Those who came to be baptized by John were warned, "Produce fruit in keeping with repentance" (Luke 3:8). Here the basic flavor of intellectual change in *metanoia* is evident. It is also clear that behavioral "fruit" (i.e., a changed life) is expected to flow from repentance (Turner 1975: 63–64).

In his early ministry, Jesus' own message was expressed in similar ways. Like the Baptizer, he proclaimed, "Repent, for the kingdom . . . is near" (Matt 4:17). His mission focused on calling "sinners to repentance" (Luke 5:32). What that meant is clarified in Mark 1:15: "Repent and believe the good news." Any conception of repenting *(metanoeō)* not wedded to faith in the gospel falls short of the full biblical message.

On the other hand, the proclamation of Jesus (Jeremias 1971: 152–58) and his apostles sometimes utilized the idea of *metanoia* to include faith (Mark 6:12). In a real sense, "Repentance and faith are two sides of the same coin" (*IDB* 4: 34). The issue could be sharpened to "repent" or "perish" (Luke 13:3, 5), "repent" or go to "hell" and "torment" after death (Luke 16:23, 28, 30). For those sinners who do repent, however, there is "joy in heaven" (Luke 15:7, 10). Thus, it can be concluded that, in the gospels, *metanoia* stands for the entire response bringing about eternal life, including faith when it is not stated. Accordingly, the Great Commission statement which concludes Luke's gospel reads, "Repentance and forgiveness of sins will be preached in his name to all nations" (24:47).

At the human level, sincere repentance *(metanoeō)* for interpersonal sin demands forgiveness, according to Christ (Luke 17:3–4). Surprisingly, John's gospel contains no reference to repentance in either dimension, the idea apparently being included in John's concept of faith (*IDB* 4: 34).

The three uses of *metamelomai* in the gospels are instructive. In Matt 21:29, 32, it is similar, but not equivalent, to *metanoeō*. In Matt 27:3 the "remorse" of Judas does not have "the power to overcome the destructive operation of sin" (*TDNT* 4: 628). This example "makes it clear that *metamelomai* and *metanoeō* do not have identical meanings in the NT" (*NIDNTT* 1: 356).

Virtually echoing John the Baptist, Peter's sermon at Pentecost in Acts urged, "Repent and be baptized . . . so that your sins may be forgiven" (Acts 2:38). Further usage links repentance not only with forgiveness (5:31) but also with "faith in our Lord Jesus" (20:21) and with "life," as a result of repentance (11:18). In Acts 17:30–31 Paul on the Areopagus states God's command for "all people everywhere to repent" or be justly judged. Parallel to the phenomena in the gospels (*NIDNTT* 1: 359), repentance in Acts may be complementary to faith (20:21) or include faith (17:30) and leads to forgiveness of sins (2:38; 5:31) and eternal life (11:18).

Two other passages bring *epistrephō* alongside *metanoeō* in noteworthy ways. Acts 3:19 records Peter's offer to Israel: "Repent . . . and turn to God, so that your sins may be wiped out." Paul's explanation of his apostolic commission to Agrippa in Acts 26:18 clarifies this turning *(epistrephō):* "from darkness to light," from Satan's power to God to receive forgiveness of sins. The apostle's obedience to that commission meant that he preached that his hearers "should repent and turn to God and prove their repentance by their deeds" (Acts 26:20). Here again is the expectation that the one who changes his mind *(metanoeō)* about the gospel and turns *(epistrephō)* to the Lord will display a "converted" lifestyle (cf. Luke 3:8).

The Pauline literature rarely uses the terms for repentance, and the Johannine epistles not at all. For Paul, like John, repentance is included in faith (*IDB* 4: 34). Besides several standard uses (Rom 2:4; 2 Cor 12:21; 2 Tim 2:25), Paul strongly contrasts *metanoeō* and *metamelomai* in 2 Cor 7:8–10 (*TDNT* 4: 629).

The writer of Hebrews refers to the God who "will not change his mind" (7:21) and Esau, who could not achieve repentance (12:17). He also speaks of foundational initial repentance (6:1) and the utter impossibility of returning to the point of first repentance (6:6). Peter describes the patient God, who desires "everyone to come to repentance" (2 Pet 3:9), apparently including forgiveness and salvation (See 1 Tim 2:4). Again the basic idea of a change of mind is demonstrated in the epistles.

The letters to the churches in the Roman province of Asia in the book of Revelation contain eight uses of "repent" (2:5 [twice], 16, 21 [twice], 22; 3:3, 19). The glorified Christ's command to repent was directed at a lukewarm church in Laodicea (3:19), but also at the great church at Ephesus (2:5), which had "forsaken its first love" (2:4). All these sinful churches needed to change their minds and bring forth the fruit of repentance (Luke 3:8; Acts 26:20), turning again to Christ.

Sadly, the last mentions of "repent" *(metanoeō)* in the NT picture an unrepentant mass of humankind as God's climactic wrath is poured out on the earth (Rev 9:20, 21; 16:9, 11). Instead of turning to the Lord in repentant faith through his longstanding patience (2 Pet 3:9) or to escape his righteous judgment, these sinners continued with their abominable acts (9:20, 21) and cursed God instead of glorifying him (16:9, 11).

In conclusion it can be said that repentance in the NT is always anchored in a change of thinking *(metanoia),* although the psychological and emotional aspects sometimes color or expand the concept (especially the usage of *metamelomai*) (*ISBE* 4: 136–37). Repentance must not be separated from its flip side of faith (Mark 1:15; Acts 20:21), or from the realization that it sometimes stands for the package of human response to the good news of Jesus Christ (2 Pet 3:9; cf. Acts 2:38). True repentance, whether by an unbeliever or a believer (Acts 26:18, 20; Luke 17:3–4), receives the gracious forgiveness that God continually offers all humankind in Christ (Luke 24:47).

Bibliography

Chamberlain, W. D. 1943. *The Meaning of Repentance.* Philadelphia.

Guthrie, D. 1981. *New Testament Theology.* Leicester.

Jeremias, J. 1971. *New Testament Theology.* Vol. 1. New York.

Turner, G. A. 1975. Repentance. *Zondervan Pictorial Encyclopedia of the Bible* 5: 63–64.

Wilkin, R. N. 1985. *Repentance as a Condition for Salvation.* Ann Arbor.

A. Boyd Luter, Jr.

REPHAEL (PERSON) [Heb *rĕpāʾēl*]. Named as the second son of Shemaiah, first son of Obed-edom, Rephael (whose name means "God has healed") is listed among the gatekeepers at the temple in Jerusalem (1 Chr 26:7). The list in which his name occurs (1 Chr 26:4–8) appears to be the contribution of a reviser of the Chronicler's organization of the gatekeepers (Williamson *Chronicles* NCBC, 169–70; Rudolph *Chronikbücher* HAT, 173).

J. S. Rogers

REPHAH (PERSON) [Heb *repaḥ*]. A descendant of Ephraim (1 Chr 7:25). The only other listing of the Ephraimite clan is in Num 26:35–36, but it has no Rephah. The Ephraimite list in 1 Chronicles 7 is a unit that is interrupted in v 21b and resumed in vv 25–27. The antecedent of "his son" before Rephah is unclear. Perhaps the Resheph that follows is partial dittography of Rephah (Braun *1 Chronicles* WBC, 115). There is a repetition of names in vv 20–21 and 25–27 and perhaps some variations in spelling. Hogg (1900–1901: 149–50) argues that the names in vv 25–27 beginning with Rephah are variations or misreadings of the three sons of Ephraim found in Num 26:35–36.

Bibliography

Hogg, H. W. 1900–1901. The Ephraimite Genealogy. *JQR* 13: 147–54.

M. Stephen Davis

REPHAIAH (PERSON) [Heb *rĕpāyāh*]. The name Rephaiah is held by five persons in the Hebrew Bible. The name may mean "Yahweh has healed."

1. In 1 Chr 3:21 Rephaiah is listed as the son of Jeshaiah the son of Hananiah according to the MT. The genealogy in 1 Chr 3:16–24 lists the postexilic descendants of the Davidic line. The MT as it now stands is corrupt in the second half of v 21. If we follow the text as it is, then there is no connection between the first half of the verse and the second and consequently the last recorded descendant of Zerubbabel is Jeshaiah. If we delete the phrase "sons of" and read instead "and," then the list represents further sons of Hananiah. A final possibility would be to change the phrase in the MT "sons of" to "his son" with partial support of the versions. Scholars are in disagreement concerning these possibilities. The solution which is chosen affects how scholars date the work of the Chronicler.

2. Rephaiah was also the name of a chief of the Simeonites, who with a band of five hundred men went to Mt. Seir and destroyed a settlement of Amalekites. The group then settled there. This occurred during the reign of Hezekiah king of Judah (727–698 B.C.).

3. In 1 Chr 7:2 Rephaiah is named as the son of Tola the eldest son of Issachar. He is described as a mighty warrior (Heb *gibbôr ḥayil*).

4. Rephaiah is given as the name of a descendant of Saul of the tribe of Benjamin in 1 Chr 9:43. He is the son of Binea and the father of Eleasah. The list of Saul's descendants in 1 Chronicles 9 is probably adapted from chap. 8 and is intended as an introduction to chaps. 10 and following. Note the variations from that list, for example, the spelling of the name Rephaiah in 1 Chr 8:37 is Raphah.

5. In Neh 3:9 Rephaiah the son of Hur is listed as ruler of half the district of Jerusalem (Heb *śar ḥăṣî pelek yĕrûšālām*). The context in the text is the reconstruction of the walls of Jerusalem under the direction of Nehemiah. There were five administrative units in the Persian "province" of Jehud. The other districts with their rulers are listed in Neh 3:12, 14–18. The intent in this text in listing the rulers of these districts may have been to show the strong support for the rebuilding of the walls within the community.

Russell Fuller

REPHAIM [Heb *rĕpāʾîm*]. A term in the Hebrew Bible whose uses fall generally into two categories: (1) descriptions of the dead in the underworld, or (2) references to a group or nation of giants or warriors.

A. The Rephaim as the Dead

In the OT the Rephaim are frequently described as dead humans who dwell in the underworld. Ps 88:11—Eng 88:10 sets the Rephaim (RSV "shades") in parallelism with "the dead" *(mētîm),* asking if God's love is declared in the grave and if God's wondrous acts are known in "the darkness" and "the land of forgetfulness" (vv 12–13—Eng 11–12). The psalmist implores God not to consign him to death and the grave as well as to the underworld where the dead go after life. The same parallelism between the Rephaim ("shades") and the dead occurs in Isa 26:14, 19. Fifth-century Phoenician inscriptions likewise attest to the Rephaim as those whom the living join in dying (*KAI* 13: 7–8; 14: 8). A Punic-Latin bilingual text renders "the divine Rephaim" with the Lat "the sacred shades," that is, the dead (*KAI* 177: 1; Horwitz 1979: 41; L'Heureux 1979: 112–27; Cooper 1981: 460–67).

References to the Rephaim in the book of Proverbs also indicate that they are the dead dwelling in the netherworld. In Prov 2:18 the house of folly leads (or, sinks down) to death and to the Rephaim. The foolish man does not know that the Rephaim (RSV "dead") are in the underworld, according to Prov 9:18. Prov 21:16 characterizes the Rephaim as a "congregation" or "assembly" *(qāhāl)*.

Further specification of the abode of the dead Rephaim comes from Job 26:5. In this verse the extent of God's power reaches down beneath the waters of the oceans, down to the abode of the Rephaim. There in the underworld the Rephaim (RSV "shades") tremble at God's might. (The final passage of the Ugaritic Baal cycle, *CTA* 6.6.46–52, also juxtaposes the sea with the Rephaim in the netherworld).

Unlike the references to the Rephaim in Psalm 88, references in the book of Proverbs, Job 26, and Isa 14:9 describe the Rephaim as dead kings. This latter passage is a genuine reminiscence of the Rephaim as a line of deceased monarchs. When the Lord relegates the king of Babylon to the netherworld, the netherworld and its inhabitants respond in the following way to the latter's arrival:

> Sheol beneath is stirred up
> to meet you when you come,
> it rouses the Rephaim to greet you,
> it raises from their thrones
> all the kings of the nations.

Unlike any other biblical text, this passage preserves vestiges of a 2d-millennium understanding of the Rephaim. For, while other biblical passages as well as the Phoenician inscriptions and the Punic-Latin bilingual know the Rephaim only as the dead in a general sense, the concept of the Rephaim in Isa 14:9 is similar to the Ugaritic notion of the Rephaim as the ancestral line of dead heroes and kings.

2 Chr 16:12 may contain yet another reference to the dead Rephaim. This passage faults the ailing king Asa for consulting "doctors" *(rōpĕʾîm)*. It has been proposed (Jastrow 1909: 49 n. 23) that Asa did not consult "doctors" but the Rephaim, perhaps much as Saul asked the witch of Endor to consult the dead (1 Samuel 28). It is difficult to criticize Asa for seeking medical aid unless the help was sought from theologically dangerous sources, such as the dead Rephaim.

B. The Rephaim as Giants

The Rephaim are also described in the OT as a people. In Gen 14:5, Chedorlaomer and his cohorts smite the Rephaim in Ashtaroth-karnaim along with peoples called Zuzim and Emim. According to Deut 2:10, the Emim had once lived in Moab. They were as tall as the Anakim, who were giants (Num 13:33). According to Deut 2:11, they were also known as the Rephaim, but the Moabites called them Emim. Deut 2:20 relates that the territory of Ammon, like that of Moab, was known as the land of the Rephaim, but that the Ammonites called them Zamzummim. From the perspective of Deuteronomy, the Rephaim were a legendary race of giants existing in the distant past. See also REPHAIM, VALLEY OF. Unlike Gen 14:5, which describes the Rephaim, Zuzim, and Emim as distinct peoples, Deuteronomy understands them as different names for the same people.

Gen 15:20 lists the Rephaim with various "ethnic" groups which inhabited the areas between the Nile and the Euphrates. Because the term Rephaim lacks the formal grammatical indicator for a people in biblical Hebrew, the Rephaim were likely not an actual nation or people, but a loosely defined group used to fill out this list. (One may compare Josh 5:1 or Num 13:29, where the Rephaim are omitted [Rosenberg 1980: 204].) The Genesis and Deuteronomy 2 passages transformed old traditions about the Rephaim from legendary giants into a people comparable to other nations. In Deuteronomy, the Rephaim serve part of a further theological purpose. In describing the dispossession of the Rephaim by Moab and Ammon, the Horites by Seir, and the Avvim by Caphtor, Israel's dispossession of the Canaanites is shown to be no less moral (Rosenberg 1980: 208).

Other passages in Deuteronomy and Joshua also have a vague view of the Rephaim. Deut 3:11, 13 as well as Josh 12:4 and 13:12 recall Og of Bashan as a remnant of the Rephaim. All of these passages describe the Rephaim as some type of group or nation living in the distant past.

The Rephaim as a line of warriors is apparently preserved in the epithet "the Raphites" (*hārāpâ;* RSV "giants") found in 2 Sam 21:16, 18, 20 and 1 Chr 20:4, 6, 8 (L'Heureux 1976: 83–85). This expression may have derived from an eponymous ancestor named Rapah or the like (cf. Talmon 1983: 237–41). An Ugaritic text (RS 24.252 = *KTU* 1.108) describes a figure named Rapaʾu (Ug *rpʾu,* the vocalization of which is based on the biblical Hebrew *hārāpâ*). This personage has the same address as Og. Both figures are said to dwell in Ashtarot and Edrei (assuming that the Ugaritic words *ʿṯtrt* and *hdrʿy* are place names). Judging from this Ugaritic evidence and Deuteronomy 3, the biblical traditions regarding the Rephaim may have originated in the area of NE Transjordan.

C. Conclusions

How one reconciles these different views of the Rephaim in the OT has been the subject of much scholarly discussion. Fortunately the Ugaritic texts as well as the later biblical and Phoenician texts clarify the process which led to different presentations of the Rephaim in the Bible. In 2d-millennium Ugarit, the Rephaim were the line of dead kings and heroes, as the Ugaritic text, RS 34.126 = *KTU* 1.161 indicates (Pitard 1979; Bordreuil and Pardee 1982; Levine and de Tarragon 1984). Generally this precise understanding of the Rephaim was lost in the course of the 1st millennium (see Horwitz 1979: 41–43). While Isa 14:9 preserves the older understanding of the Rephaim, in other occurrences the older concept of the Rephaim was fractured, bifurcating into various descriptions of the Rephaim. The Rephaim as a line or group of heroes and monarchs at Ugarit corresponds to the biblical view of them as a people or nation. As heroes and monarchs, the Rephaim survived in the Bible as giants or warriors. The royal aspect of the Rephaim is most evident in Isa 14:9. The Ugaritic view of the Rephaim as a dead group has broadened in the biblical texts describing the Rephaim as the dead in general.

The NT also preserves a reference to the Ugaritic god Rapaʾu. In his defense speech before the Sanhedrin in Acts 7, Stephen contrasts the fidelity of Abraham, Joseph, and Moses with the infidelity of their fellow Israelites. As an example of the latter's unfaithfulness, Stephen cites in Acts 7:43 a version of Amos 5:26:

> And you took up the tent of Moloch,
> and the star of the god Rephan,
> the figures which you made to worship;
> and I will remove you beyond Babylon.

The gods Moloch and Rephan are lacking in the Hebrew text of Amos 5:26, and extant in only a few mss of the LXX of the same verse. The deity Moloch was known in Israel and perhaps in Punic Carthage as the god to whom children were sacrificed in fire. This god is also attested in texts from Ugarit. The name Rephan in Acts 7:43 varies a great deal in NT mss. The origin of the name has been attributed to two scribal errors, since the name of the deity in question in the Hebrew text of Amos 5:26 is Kaiwan *(kywn)*. In this case, the Greek form Rephan is assumed to have resulted from the mistaking of Hebrew *kap* for *reš* and the transliteration of Hebrew *waw* by Greek *phi*. With the recent discovery of the Ugaritic god Rapaʾu, it has been suggested as an alternative that Rephan is a vestige of this Ugaritic deity (Pope 1977: 170). Accordingly, Stephen's citation of Rephan with Moloch as examples of Israelite idolatry captures the flavor of Canaanite paganism which the Israelites were said to have enjoyed and the Israelite prophets so zealously condemned.

Bibliography

Bordreuil, P., and Pardee, D. 1982. Le Rituel funéraire ougaritique RS 34.126. *Syr* 59: 121–28.

Cooper, A. 1981. Divine Names and Epithets in the Ugaritic Texts. Vol. 3, pp. 33–469 in *Ras Samra Parallels*, ed. S. Rummel. AnOr 51. Rome.

Dietrich, M.; Loretz, O.; and Sanmartín, J. 1976. Die Ugaritischen Totengeister RPU(M) und die biblischen Rephaim. *UF* 8: 45–52.

Horwitz, W. 1979. The Significance of the Rephaim. *JNSL* 7: 37–43.

Jastrow, M. 1909. *Rôʾēh* and *Hôzēh* in the Old Testament. *JBL* 28: 42–56.

Levine, B., and Tarragon, J. M. de. 1984. Dead Kings and Rephaim: The Patrons of the Ugaritic Dynasty. *JAOS* 104: 649–59.

L'Heureux, C. E. 1976. The *yelîdê hārāpāʾ*—A Cultic Association of Warriors. *BASOR* 221: 83–85.

———. 1979. *Rank Among the Canaanite Gods; El, Baʿal and the Rephaʾim.* HSM 21. Missoula.

Pitard, W. 1979. The Ugaritic Funerary Text RS 34.126. *BASOR* 232: 65–75.

Pope, M. H. 1977. Notes on the Rephaim Texts. Pp. 163–81 in *Essays on the Ancient Near East in Memory of Jacob Joel Finkelstein*, ed. M. de Jong Ellis. Memoirs of the Connecticut Academy of Arts and Sciences 19. Hamden, CT.

Rosenberg, R. 1980. *The Concept of Biblical Sheol Within the Context of Ancient Near Eastern Beliefs.* Diss. Harvard University.

Talmon, S. 1983. Biblical *rĕpāʾîm* and Ugaritic *rpu/i(m)*. *HAR* 7: 235–49.

Mark S. Smith

REPHAIM, VALLEY OF (PLACE) [Heb *ʿēmeq rĕpāʾîm*]. A valley, extending SW of Jerusalem, whose N portion formed part of the boundary between Benjamin and Judah (Josh 15:8; 18:16). It is also the scene of one of the famous exploits performed by the mighty three among the Champions of David (2 Sam 23:13; 1 Chr 11:15). This exploit happened during a major thrust by the Philistines against David at Jerusalem (2 Sam 5:18; 1 Chr 14:9). Whether by military or literary design, the Philistines gathered in the Valley of the Rephaim in preparation for attacking Jerusalem. Militarily the Philistines had cut off access to David's base of strength to the S and to the agricultural productivity of the valley. However, certain literary concerns may have led to the location of the battle.

In the LXX, the valley is called (1) "Valley of the Rephaim (Gk *Raphaim*)" (2 Sam 23:13); (2) "Valley of the *Titans* (Gk *Titanōn*)" (2 Sam 5:18); (3) "Valley of the Giants (Gk *gigantōn*)" (1 Chr 11:15; 14:9). This reflects a tradition in which "Rephaim" is the equivalent of "Giants." It may have been a matter of deliberate choice that the text has the descendants of giants (cf. Hesiod *Theog.* 132–60, 207–10), the Philistines (2 Samuel 15–22), outwitted by the mighty three (2 Sam 23:13–17 = 1 Chr 11:15–19) and ultimately defeated by David's army in the "Valley of the Giants" (2 Sam 5:17–25 = 1 Chr 14:8–17). This tradition of the giants may also have been logical outgrowth of the Ugaritic understanding of Rephaim as the dead royal ancestors. See REPHAIM.

Finally the biblical record (Isa 17:5) also describes the valley as a place of fertile farming. Though the metaphor is one of famine, the implication is left that the valley was a place of rich agriculture. The valley's ancient agricultural productivity has recently been examined quite thoroughly by the Ein Yael Project.

The project involves archaeological survey, excavation, experimentation, research, and reconstruction of ancient agricultural technology. Geographically, the Ein Yael Project is situated in the outskirts of Jerusalem in the Rephaim Valley. As part of the Judean Hills, the Mediterranean climate of this region consists of a short rainy season followed by a long dry summer. Due to the lack of water available during most of the year, inhabitants of the area settled near permanent natural water sources (such as Jerusalem, situated near the Gihon spring) or were forced to develop artificial water supplies. Two artificial methods of water collection are observed at ancient sites in the Rephaim Valley. One system involves the cutting and plastering of a cistern which collects and retains water during the rainy season. The second system involves the cutting of a cave and tunnel into the hillside. Rainwater seeps through the hills and collects in the cave during winter months and flows out through the tunnel during dry seasons. Both systems can adequately supply a small population with water throughout the year.

Serving as the border between Israel and Jordan until

1967, the area of the Rephaim Valley has remained, thus far, free from modern development. This lack of development has allowed for a more extensive study of archaeological remains in the area when compared to other regions. Using topographical maps or aerial photography, one can clearly distinguish the remains of ancient farms as well as the roads which connected each unit and provided access to Jerusalem. The farms consist of distinct terraced units divided by boundary walls, giving each farm its unique shape and defined territory. Outside the agricultural units subterranean tombs, lime kilns for the production of plaster, wine and oil presses are found. Stone quarries from which the rocks were hewn are also recognizable in the vicinity. While it is difficult to date each stone quarry to the time of use, the quarries were undoubtedly used in the construction of the buildings, roads, terraces, boundary walls, and tunnels at these ancient farms.

A major development in the advance of ancient agricultural units in hilly terrain such as the Rephaim Valley is the terrace system of farming. A terrace is an artificial construction used to create a field for farming. Terraces are especially important in hilly areas where erosion of the soil can be problematic. In the Judean Hills, ancient farmers constructed terraces by building a stone wall and filling the space behind it with stones and soil. The terrace system also allows for the retention of moisture throughout the year while the soil is replenished with minerals through the decay of plants. Nutrients provided by plant decay allow the same terrace units to be used for long periods.

Terraces were first used at the beginning of the Bronze Age at sites located near water sources. While the idea of terrace agriculture was known in the EB period, the use of terracing was limited to the spring areas in the valleys, which was sufficient for the limited agricultural needs of a small population. Extensive terracing actually began in the Israelite period as the population increased and continued through the Byzantine period in the 6th and 7th centuries A.D. From the Israelite period onward, the terraced farms in the Rephaim Valley provided Jerusalem with much of its food supply.

The Ein Yael Project—named for a farm in the Rephaim Valley exhibiting remains from the Israelite, Roman, Byzantine, and Ammayad periods—includes an examination and study of agriculture as it developed during the various archaeological periods represented in the valley. Each farming unit in the area depicts a history of occupation exemplifying the varying change in technology over time. Excavation at the site of er Ras, for example, shows that the site was occupied in the Bronze Age (2000–1600 B.C.) before the first terraces were constructed there. The site was later reoccupied in the 8th century B.C. and was rebuilt in the typical size and with installations common to farms of the First Temple period. During this period, the farm at er Ras consisted of four and one-half acres of terraced farmland bordered by stone walls. The site, connected to other agricultural units by a network of paths, exhibits a four-room house and a winepress. The farm at er Ras continued to be used in the Hellenistic, Roman, and Byzantine periods and until 1948, when the area was used as an orchard.

The site at er Ras represents three stages of agricultural development: the first stage of agricultural occupation without terracing in the 2d millennium B.C., the construction of an organized farm unit in the First Temple period, and the reoccupation of the site in subsequent periods through the utilization and reparation of existing terraces and installations.

Aside from the mere excavation and identification of ancient farming units, the Ein Yael Project involves experimentation with raw materials used by ancient inhabitants of the area. Materials to be studied include clay, stone, textiles, and metals. Experimentation is also to be conducted in actual farming practices with the hope that the farm at Ein Yael will be restored and crops will be cultivated in accordance with original technologies.

Connecting biblical descriptions of ancient agriculture to specific farms excavated is difficult. The Bible mentions the organization of the family in several contexts: *bêt ʾab*, *mišpāḥâ*, and *śĕdê hāʿîr* to name three. While these biblical terms undoubtedly relate to some of the agricultural units found in the Rephaim Valley, we cannot specify which term applies to which farm until further research in ancient agriculture is conducted. The ultimate goal of the project at Ein Yael is a combination of knowledge gained from written sources with knowledge acquired from archaeological excavation and practical experimentation. Only through the study of all three of these aspects can one fully understand the nature of life in ancient times.

GERSHON EDELSTEIN

REPHAN (DEITY) [Gk *Rhaiphan*]. A deity whom Stephen claimed that Israel worshipped in the wilderness (Acts 7:43). Greek texts of the OT preserve a variety of transliterations for the name of a deity which appears in the Hebrew text of Amos 5:26 as *kiyyûn* (consonantal text *kywn*). This Greek tradition is the source for the name Rephan in Acts 7:43 where Amos 5:26 is quoted. A common confusion in the text of the OT between the letters *kap* and *reš* accounts for the confusion in the initial letter, and the Greek letter *phi* points to a pronunciation of the Hebrew *waw* as consonant. Although the final vowel is consistently represented in Greek as *alpha*, there is no agreement as to the first vowel, the following forms being attested in Acts and Amos: *rompha(n), rempha(m/n), raiphan, rephan, raphan*. Since there is no deity known who bears such a name, the Hebrew text should be given priority over the Greek transliterations. The Hebrew consonants in Amos 5:26 correspond to an Akkadian name for the planet Saturn, which was recognized as a deity. See SAKKUTH AND KAIWAN.

SAMUEL A. MEIER

REPHIDIM (PLACE) [Heb *rĕpîdîm*]. A station of the Exodus located between the Wilderness of Sin and the Wilderness of Sinai (Exod 17:1, 8; 19:2; Num 33:14, 15). Dophkah and Alush are also mentioned as encampments between the Wilderness of Sin and Rephidim (Num 33:12–14). The location of Rephidim is unknown and dependent upon the identification of Mt. Sinai. Various proposals have been made following a northern route of the Exodus placing Mt. Sinai and thus Rephidim in the Negeb Highlands, N Sinai, or the land of Midian. (For a summary of these views, see Beit Arieh 1988.) Those opting for a southern Exodus route locate Rephidim in the vicinity of Jebul Musa close to the S tip of the peninsula. Wadi Feiran has been traditionally identified as the location of Rephidim dating back to Byzantine times (Perevolotsky and Finkelstein 1985) but Wadi Refayid has also been suggested and was preferred by Abel (*GP* 2: 435).

Three significant events occur while Israel is situated at Rephidim. The Israelites complain of being in a place where "there was no water for the people to drink" so Moses is instructed to provide water by smiting the rock. Rephidim became known as Massah, "testing," and Meribah, "contention," because Israel determined to test the Lord to see if he was among them or not (Exod 17:1–7). The term Massah is used several other times in warnings to Israel not to prove the Lord as they did at Rephidim (Deut 6:16; 9:22; 33:8). Meribah also refers to an incident near Kadesh-barnea involving a challenge to Moses to provide water (Num 20:13, 24; 27:14; Deut 32:51; Ps 81:7). See MASSAH AND MERIBAH.

At Rephidim Israel, led by Joshua (who is mentioned here for the first time), fought Amalek and only prevailed when Moses, assisted by Aaron and Hur, was able to keep his hands and rod raised (Exod 17:8–16). Afterward Moses built an altar to commemorate the victory. From its position in the narrative, the account of Jethro's instruction to appoint judges to relieve the heavy burden on Moses was given at Rephidim (Exodus 18), although some scholars argue that this took place at Mt. Sinai (see Exod 18:5).

A tradition of the sages connected the name Rephidim to the verb *rph* meaning to "relax, weaken, dishearten," because Israel "cast off the commandments of the Torah" and because of this an enemy (Amalek) rose up against them (Vilnay 1978: 341).

Bibliography

Beit Arieh, I. 1988. The Route through Sinai—Why South? *BARev* 14/3: 28–37.

Perevolotsky, A., and Finkelstein, I. 1985. The Southern Sinai Exodus Route in Ecological Perspective. *BARev* 11/4: 26–41.

Vilnay, Z. 1978. *Legends of Galilee, Jordan, and Sinai. The Sacred Land*, vol. 3. Philadelphia.

Jo Ann H. Seely

REPOUSSÉ. See JEWELRY.

REPTILE. See ZOOLOGY.

RESAIAH (PERSON) [Gk *Rēsaiou*]. An alternate form of REELAIAH.

RESEN (PLACE) [Heb *resen*]. A town mentioned in Gen 10:11. The Yahwistic fragment of the Table of Nations seems to include it in the kingdom of Nimrod, although the translation of the first clause of Gen 10:11 is very unclear. See REHOBOTH-IR.

No city Resen is known from the cuneiform sources. It is probable that the name referred originally not to a separate city but to a construction work within the city of Nineveh. Some have identified it with Akkadian *risnu*, understood to mean something like "irrigation system" (Lipinski 1966: 85–86). Another possibility is that Resen is derived from Akkadian *rēš ēni*, "fountainhead" or the like (Speiser *Genesis* AB, 68). Again, the original reference would have been to some kind of waterworks found within the city. If either interpretation is correct, at some point in the transmission of the traditions about Nimrod this descriptive term was misunderstood as a city name itself. See REHOBOTH-IR. It is still possible, however unlikely, that the allusion is to an as yet unknown Assyrian town (cf. Sasson 1983: 95 and n. 3).

The final clause of Gen 10:12, "that is the great city," is ambiguous. It could describe Resen (cf. the punctuation of the RSV) or Nineveh, but it more likely refers to the nearest antecedent, Calah. At the time of the Yahwist (ca. 10th century B.C.E.) Calah was more important than Nineveh and thus merited special mention (Speiser *Genesis* AB, 68).

The LXX reads *Dasem* for *resen*. The latter form is the original. In the tradition behind the LXX *reš* has been confused with *dalet* (the two letters are almost identical in all periods) and the *nun* was misheard as a *mem*. Neither Hebrew nor Akkadian suggests a contextually appropriate meaning for *Dasem*.

Bibliography

Lipiński, E. 1966. Nimrod et Aššur. *RB* 73: 77–93.

Sasson, J. M. 1983. Reḥōvōt ʿÎr. *RB* 90: 94–96.

James R. Davila

RESH [Heb *reš*]. The twentieth letter of the Hebrew alphabet.

RESHEPH (DEITY) [Heb *rešep*]. The god Resheph is attested in documents and personal names from the middle of the 3d millennium B.C.E. to the end of the 1st century B.C.E. The deity is first attested in Syria among the documents of Ebla. Here Resheph is accorded a quarter of the city with a gate named after him (Matthiae 1979: 566); this demonstrates that the deity was already held in high regard.

In the 2d millennium B.C.E. worship of Resheph can be shown to have expanded through Syria-Palestine and into Egypt. It is from Egypt that most of the mythological information concerning Resheph has survived. Amenophis II appears to have introduced the god to Egypt and to have seen himself as adopted by the god (Grdseloff 1942: 2). During the 19th and 20th Dynasties several steles and literary references appear with Resheph. In these Egyptian sources Resheph is a god of war who will lead them to victory. In Egyptian magical inscriptions Resheph appears as a healing deity. The Egyptians picture the god associated with the gazelle, an animal with somewhat ambiguous connotations (Simpson 1953: 88). Resheph always remained a minor Egyptian deity and was not assimilated into the pantheon as were some Syro-Palestinian deities.

In the tablets from Ugarit, Resheph appears as a major deity in the cult ritual texts; however, the mythological narratives provide almost no information on the god. Resheph appears twice in the Kirta Legend, first as the cause of the king's fifth son's death (*KTU* 1.14.i.18–19) and then as a divine guest at the banquet Kirta holds for the gods (*KTU* 1.15.ii.6). Fragmented texts have suggested that Resheph might have been a gatekeeper for the sun deity (Virolleaud 1951: 25–26) and that he may have aided Baal in his battle with Yam (Day 1979: 354), though both are tenuous. The parallel Ug and Akk god lists found at Ugarit pair Resheph with Nergal, usually taken to be the Mesopotamian god of the netherworld, though whether that is the reason for the association of the deities may be debated (Nougayrol 1968: 57). Recently, using the artifacts from Kition on Cyprus, particularly a statue of a deity standing upon an ingot (Karageorghis 1982: 103, fig. 77), Dalley has posited that Resheph was the West Semitic name given to Nergal as the patron deity of metalworking (1987: 62, 65).

Resheph is attested in the 1st millennium B.C.E. in Syrian, Phoenician, and Judean texts; the last known inscription dedicated to the deity is dated 6 B.C.E. and was found at Palmyra (Teixidor 1979: 111). A series of related terms appear with the god. The Karatepe inscription (*KAI* 26.A.ii.10) refers to *rsp ṣprm,* which has been variously translated as "of the birds," "he-goats," or "stag" (O'Callaghan 1950: 360; Simpson 1953: 88). The use of *ḥṣ* with Resheph has been attested at Ugarit and on Cyprus (*KAI* 32.3–4; Fulco 1976: 49); this term has been taken to mean "arrow," "luck," and "outside street" (Irwy 1961: 31; Caquot and Masson 1968: 302), though "arrow" would fit nicely with Resheph as metalworker. Terms taken as divine names (*mkl* and *miqrt,* not to mention Apollo on Cyprus) and places (*gn*) often appear with Resheph, and it has been suggested that all such terms refer to locations which revered the god (Dahood 1981: 47).

The sources do not provide much information about the character of the deity. The inscriptions of Zinjirli and Karatepe listed Resheph among the deities who had placed the ruler on his throne and now sustain him; this only means the god was important. It has been suggested that the connection made between Resheph and Apollo on Cyprus (*KAI* 41:3–4) shows he was a solar deity with responsibilities for justice and law (Conrad 1971: 161–63). Albright (*ARI,* 27) argued that Resheph had to have been a god of the underworld, pestilence, and death; this has become the majority position. The Ugaritic connection with Nergal would seem to confirm this, though it is important to remember the metalworking aspect of the deity as well. The Egyptian vision of a warrior god would fit well with both chthonic and metalworking aspects. The extension of Albright's thesis to see a cult of the dead under the care of Resheph, however, is based on speculation and no data (Spronk 1986: 140, 157, 261); neither at Ebla (Matthiae 1979: 566) nor at Byblos (Gese 1970: 46) is there a temple conclusively dedicated to Resheph upon which such a theory would have to be based (Ribichini 1988: 107).

The biblical references to Resheph have long been taken to be common nouns rather than divine allusions. This may be true in Job 5:7, though, if this is to be taken as "sparks," a clear relation with metalworking may be discerned. However, the poem in Hab 3:5 clearly presents Resheph as an attendant on the God of Judah in a theophanic procession. The context does not define the sphere of the deity, which may, given the rest of the passage, reflect a warrior deity as found in the Egyptian sources or simply describe an attendant deity, such as a smith.

Bibliography

Caquot, A. 1956. Sur quelques démons de l'Ancien Testament (Reshep, Qeteb, Deber). *Sem* 6: 53–68.

Caquot, A., and Masson, O. 1968. Deux inscriptions phéniciennes de Chypre. *Syr* 45: 295–321.

Conrad, D. 1971. Der Gott Reschef. *ZAW* 83: 157–83.

Dahood, M. 1981. Ebla, Ugarit and Phoenician Religion. Pp. 45–57 in *La religione Fenicia.* SS 53. Rome.

Dalley, S. 1987. Near Eastern Patron Deities of Mining and Smelting in the Late Bronze and Early Iron Ages. *RDAC,* 61–66.

Day, J. 1979. New Light on the Mythological Background of the Allusion to Resheph in Habakkuk 3:5. *VT* 29: 353–55.

Fulco, W. J. 1976. *The Canaanite God Rešep.* AOS 8. New Haven.

Gese, H. 1970. Die Religionen Altsyriens. Pp. 1–232 in *Die Religionen Altsyriens, Altarabiens und der Mandäer.* Die Religionen der Menschheit 10/2. Stuttgart.

Grdseloff, B. 1942. *Les Débuts du culte de Reschef en Égypte.* Cairo.

Irwy, S. 1961. New Evidence for Belomancy in Ancient Palestine and Phoenicia. *JAOS* 81: 27–34.

Karageorghis, V. 1982. *Cyprus: From the Stone Age to the Romans.* Ancient Peoples and Places 101. London.

Lipiński, E. 1987. Resheph Amyklos. *StudPhoen 5:* 87–99.

Matthiae, P. 1979. Princely Cemetery and Ancestors Cult at Ebla during Middle Bronze II: A Proposal of Interpretation. *UF* 11: 563–69.

Nougayrol, J. 1968. Textes Suméro-Accadiens des archives et bibliothèques privées d'Ugarit. *Ugaritica* 5: 1–446.

O'Callaghan, R. T. 1950. An Approach to Some Religious Problems of Karatepe. *ArOr* 18/2: 354–65.

Ribichini, S. 1988. Beliefs and Religious Life. Pp. 104–25 in *The Phoenicians,* ed. S. Moscati. Milan.

Schretter, M. K. 1974. *Alter Orient und Hellas.* Innsbrucker Beiträge zur Kulturwissenschaft 33. Innsbruck.

Simpson, W. K. 1953. New Light on the God Reshef. *JAOS* 73: 86–89.

———. 1960. Reshef in Egypt. *Or* n.s. 29: 63–74.

Spronk, K. 1986. *Beatific Afterlife in Ancient Israel and in the Ancient Near East.* AOAT 219. Kevelaer.

Stadelmann, R. 1967. *Syrisch-Palästinensische Gottheiten in Ägypten.* PÄ 5. Leiden.

Teixidor, J. 1979. *The Pantheon of Palmyra.* EPRO 79. Leiden.

Thompson, H. O. 1970. *Mekal: The God of Beth-Shan.* Leiden.

Virolleaud, C. 1951. Les Nouvelles Tablettes de Ras Shamra (1948–1949). *Syr* 28: 22–56.

LOWELL K. HANDY

RESHEPH (PERSON) [Heb *rešep*]. A descendant of Ephraim (1 Chr 7:25). The MT portrays Resheph, along with Rephah, as the sons of Beriah, a son of Ephraim. However, several other Hebrew mss read *bnw,* "his son," after Resheph and so indicate that he is Rephah's offspring (see RSV). The list in which Resheph's name occurs (1 Chr 7:20–29) is curious and difficult to disentangle. It appears to portray Ephraim as living through seven generations of his offspring, finally to see the eighth killed by the men of

Gath. The MT next mentions the birth of Beriah, whose name embodies the misfortune of the death of the eighth generation. The genealogist is possibly listing Ephraim's descendants as brothers and not offering a chronologically descending list. The pronoun "his" in vv 20 and 21 possibly refers to Ephraim and not to the immediately antecedent name. Whatever the textual or chronological problems, the material in 1 Chr 7:20–29 intends to situate the descendants of Joseph firmly in the territory N of but also including Bethel.

JAMES M. KENNEDY

RESURRECTION. This entry consists of two articles. The first surveys the development and articulation of ideas concerning the resurrection of the dead as these are reflected in the OT. The second surveys the development and articulation of these ideas in early Judaism and in the NT.

OLD TESTAMENT

There is little mention of "resurrection" in the OT; this notion does not appear except in texts that are rare, obscure with regard to their precise meaning, and late. On the whole, resurrection—which could simply express Israel's restoration—concerns the dead in only one or two passages, and only Dan 12:2–3, within the apocalyptic context of the 2d century B.C., clearly proclaims that the dead will be snatched from death to experience either "eternal life" or "eternal damnation." Later on the gospel was articulated in a Jewish milieu in which the reality of the resurrection was still debated, notably between the more traditionalist Sadducees, who argued against it, and the Pharisees, the ardent propagators of newer views (cf. Mark 12:18–27 = Matt 22:23–33; Luke 20:27–38; Acts 23:6–9) who would end up imposing their viewpoint after the Jewish Wars against Rome. According to the Mishnah (*Sanh.* 10.1a), denial of the resurrection excludes one from the world to come (see further *DBSup* 10: 481–84, with bibliography).

A. Life and Death According to the OT
B. Some Exceptions to the Common Lot
C. Resurrection-Healings
D. Resurrection-Restorations of the People of God
  1. Restoration of Israel
  2. Restoration of Judah
  3. A Special Case
E. Resurrection of the Dead
  1. Isa 26:19
  2. Dan 12:1–3
F. Conclusion

A. Life and Death According to the OT

When one reads the OT, one fact is striking: that Israel is attached to life—to this life—and in no way dreams of a marvelous life hereafter. Israel considers the world into which she has been placed as the handiwork of her God, and human existence is a divine gift. The Israelite wishes to see his days prolonged in the manner of the patriarchs (Gen 15:15; 35:29), at the heart of the country entrusted to his people (Deut 30:20). Life, the greatest of gifts (Job 2:4; Qoh 9:4), implies piety, success, fecundity, happiness, and peace, under the protection of Israel's God, as Psalm 128, for example, indicates.

Death is associated with everything that comes to disturb this harmony: a setback, injustice, sterility, war, sickness, misery; it can be introduced prematurely into the destiny of individuals who, as the psalms show, then call upon YHWH, ask his intervention, plead their cause which—in their eyes—is identical with that of their God, cry out and lament, or, once their cry has been heard, make their exclamations of joy and their thanksgivings heard (Psalms 6; 13; 22; 30; 32; 38; 88; 130; etc.). Israel's Psalter simultaneously speaks of the importance and the beauty of a life lived in communion with God and his people and of the threatening and hateful character of death, which signifies a rupture of those bonds which united the believer to YHWH, even calling that rupture "excommunication" (Pss 6:6; 86:6, 8, 11–13, 19), and of the contagious joy of someone who is rescued from death's power (Pss 22:22b–24; 30:2–4; 116:1–4).

In general, the human person of the OT thought about death in less dramatic fashion and with a balanced realism: it was self-evident that a creature died, for it was of the "flesh," that is, it was fragile, mortal; the creature possessed within itself no spark of anything divine and destined for immortality (Qoh 12:7: at death the divine breath returned to God, who had loaned it; Ps 104:29–30). However, for death not to be an occasion of scandal and for it not to appear as an unacceptable occurrence, three conditions had to be fulfilled, as far as the Israelite was concerned. First, death had to come at the end of a long and rich existence (Gen 15:15; Job 42:17) and not precociously, "in the middle of one's days" (Ps 102:25; Isa 38:10). Then, the deceased had to leave behind descendants or at least a son (cf. the promises made to the patriarchs: Genesis 15; 17; 18); from this conviction, we can understand the problem posed by a wife's sterility (Genesis 29–30; 1 Sam 1), the special mourning occasioned by the death of an only son (Amos 8:10; Jer 6:26; etc.) and the necessity of mitigating the absence of a descendant by the establishment of the levirate law (Genesis 38; Deut 25:5–10). Finally, funeral rites, especially the burial of the corpse, had to be scrupulously observed (2 Sam 1:11–27; 3:31; Jer 16:1–9; Ezek 24:15–17); woe to the one who was deprived of sepulture (2 Kgs 9:16; Jer 8:1–3; Isa 14:19)! Divine punishment against a guilty person was manifested precisely through a shortened life, the lack of progeny, and a corpse abandoned to wild beasts.

Israel shared with other human groups a representation of the world of the dead, which it generally called Sheol (attested 66 times in the OT, especially in the Psalms [16x] and the book of Isaiah [10x]); Sheol consisted of a vast underground region, dark and dusty ("to return to the dust" means to die [Gen 3:19; Pss 90:3; 104:29] and the "dwellers of the dust" are none other than the dead [Dan 12:2; Job 20:11]). What characterized Sheol was that it was peopled by shades (Heb *rĕpāʾîm*) whose existence—which shares nothing in common with the life that had been led formerly—unfolds without purpose and without communication. The dead are the "forgotten ones" (Ps 88:13; Qoh 3:19–21; 9:5–10); they have no contact with the world of the living and still less with the living God (Pss 6:6; 30:10; 88:6–12).

The world of the dead was a "country of no return" (Job 7:9–10; 16:22), a prison with its own portals and guards (Isa 38:10; Qoh 9:10; etc.); normally one never left it, and although some texts (generally of a sapiential type) affirm YHWH's hold over Sheol (Job 12:2; 26:6; Prov 15:11; Amos 9:2–3), the God of Israel, in general, did not intervene—even on behalf of his own—in this gloomy and pitiful territory, which nonetheless had not yet become a place of judgment and punishment, as hell would become in Christian texts, but rather was the place which awaited the living (Job 30:23).

B. Some Exceptions to the Common Lot

Here and there the OT mentioned the particular lot of individuals who had escaped death not by a resurrection but as the consequence of "translation." First of all, there was the case of the patriarch Enoch (Gen 5:24), whose piety ("he walked with God") brought in its wake an exceptional destiny (a late text, attributed to the Priestly Writer). Another is the prophet Elijah, whose ministry was brought to completion in the same way (2 Kgs 2:1–15). The theme of the transfer of a human creature into the heavenly realms was well known in antiquity; the technical term used in this regard was the Heb verb *lāqaḥ*, which is found in Isa 53:8 where it can have this meaning only with difficulty, as well as in Pss 49:16 and 73:24 where one cannot rule out that it refers to the "transfer/ascension" of a faithful person (see further, *DBSup* 10: 466–68). This theme may perhaps be found also in Hellenistic Judaism, as well as in the book of Wisdom (Wis 2:22–24; 3:1–9; 4:7–11).

C. Resurrection-Healings

Three texts in the books of Kings (1 Kgs 17:17–24; 2 Kgs 4:31–37; 13:20–21) narrate salvific interventions performed by Elijah and Elisha. These were as much instances of resurrections as they were miraculous healings; they served to authenticate the prophetic ministry and to make evident YHWH's power over death: in this way, they confirmed the declarations that one can read in Deut 32:39 and 1 Sam 2:6 about the uncontested sovereignty of the God of Israel (and not of Baal) over the fate of human beings. In the texts from Kings, nowhere is there any mention of a definitive victory over death; the resurrection effected by the prophet consisted in the restoration to health of a patient, and this was characterized by the reintegration of the breath of life into a child's body (1 Kgs 17:21–22; 2 Kgs 4:34–35; cf. also Ps 23:3).

D. Resurrection-Restorations of the People of God

Some other passages in the OT, through the image of a resurrection, evoke the restoration, hoped for or foretold, of the people of God, following a difficult period or even a national disaster. These well-known and easily datable texts are found in Hos 6:1–3 and Ezek 37:1–14. Some exegetes add to these texts those of Isa 53:10–12 and Isa 26:16, but the bearing of these latter units is still debated.

1. Restoration of Israel. Hosea 6:1–3 is a text contemporaneous with the Syro-Ephraimitic War, about 735 B.C.E., in which Northern Israel imprudently became engaged after being pushed to do so by Damascus. The declaration made by the prophet presupposed that his compatriots had endured certain setbacks. The subject matter of these verses constituted a kind of song of repentance in which they expressed their desire to return to YHWH, since they were certain of his help (v 1); they were already envisaging their removal and restoration to normalcy, through the support of their God (v 2). Verse 3 takes up the same schema: it is an exhortation based on the conviction that YHWH would not delay acting in their favor.

The continuation of the chapter shows that Hosea rejected this prayer, however nice it might appear to be (vv 4–6). The prophet denounced a superficial and presumptuous attitude; he condemned the levity of the Israelites, the inconsistency of their piety, and the lack of deference in their outlook toward their God. They treated YHWH as if his pardon would be automatically granted after a few sacrifices which ought to have satisfied him. Hosea said "No" to such hypocritical worship (v 4); he recalled the divine demands (v 6) and invited Israel to be more serious (v 5).

A careful examination of Hos 6:1–3 reveals that the Ephraimites were impregnated with a Canaanite religiosity that was foreign to the Yahwistic tradition; they were making of YHWH a god in the likeness of Baal, which texts from Ugarit allow us to understand better. Several more or less explicit allusions to the theme of the death and resurrection of the deity, whose destiny regularly followed the course of the seasons, are recoverable in the statement reported by Hosea: the formula "in two days, on the third day" could pick up on a naturalistic kind of mythology, unless it meant nothing more than simply "in a little time, after a short delay" (1 Cor 5:4 perhaps implicitly refers to this text; Tertullian was the first to make good use of it [*Ad Marcionem* 4.42.1–2]; a Targum gave it an eschatological meaning); as if by chance, the dawn (*šaḥar*) and the dew (*ṭal*), accompanied by rain, played a not unimportant role at Ugarit. It seems as if Hosea's interlocutors expressed themselves as if they were worshippers of the forces of nature, thereby giving the prophet one more reason to condemn, along with their prayers and their offerings, their hope.

We should note that the idea of resurrection was already attested in Israel in the 8th century, but that then it was scarcely distinguishable either from healing or from salvation of a political kind. It had to do with the fate of N Israel within its history and not at all to do with the final condition of human beings. Its origin, most likely Canaanite, and its ties to agrarian fertility cults rendered this idea suspect to the faithful adorers of YHWH (*DBSup* 10: 444–45).

2. Restoration of Judah. Ezek 37:1–14 is equally concerned with the restoration of the people of YHWH shortly after the tragic events which had preceded, accompanied, and followed the taking of Jerusalem and which marked the downfall of the kingdom of Judah in 587 B.C. To a nation bruised and quasi-moribund, the prophet foretold a resurrection which consisted concretely in the reconstitution of the "house of Israel." Ezekiel's message is composed of a vision (vv 1–10), which acts as a symbolic prophecy and is similar to those which we come across elsewhere (Ezek 12:1; 21:23–27); his vision is followed by an explanation or, better, by a proclamation (vv 11–14; vv 12–13 form a complementary oracle announcing to the deportees the end of the Exile).

Here Ezekiel promises his brothers, rendered hopeless by the misfortunes of Judah (v 11), a renewal as extraordinary as it was unexpected (vv 1, 10, 11, 14): out of bones from which all life has disappeared, God's spirit creates an immense army! This is not an instance of a resurrection, as later Jewish (Pharisaic) and Christian traditions would envision it, but rather a case of Ezekiel, unlike Hosea's contemporaries, describing an event which he had witnessed in his vision, grounded not in a naturalistic kind of mysticism but in the traditional Yahwistic teaching as this stands out in bold relief from Gen 2:7 on (Isa 42:5; Ps 104:29–30; Job 33:4). As was the case with man's creation, so the resurrection would take place in two stages: the scattered bones are first brought back together and then flesh and skin are added to the skeletons to form bodies, which lack only the breath of life (vv 7–8; cf. Gen 2:7a); then, at the summons of the "spirit" or of "the breath," the dead rise up, like an acted-out parable, to testify to the renovation of Israel (vv 9, 10, and 14).

To give his answer to the dread events of 587, Ezekiel in this fashion appropriated the notion of resurrection, but did so within a perspective which fully conformed to the YHWH cult (cf. *DBSup* 10: 445–47).

3. A Special Case. Isa 53:10–12 poses difficult problems and there is no clear evidence that this text can be numbered among those which testify in favor of faith in the resurrection (*DBSup* 10: 447–48).

The servant mentioned in Isa 52:13–53:12 is not with any certitude a human individual, whether of the past, the future, or the present; he might represent Israel in its totality, and the Fourth Servant Song in this case would recount the paradoxical destiny of the people of YHWH, condemned to experience the worst humiliations, restraint, and a condition equivalent to death, only to be, in the end, glorified by its God and hailed by the whole of humanity as the one which bore the faults of the multitudes (the pagans) and secured their salvation. In this communitarian perspective, then, the issue is one neither of death nor of resurrection.

If, however, the referent in this text is an individual, some member of the people of Israel who suffers for others and notably for his brothers, the expressions employed in Isaiah 53 do not automatically imply that the servant is to be put to death, and his final victory (evoked in vv 10–12) does not demand that he be snatched from death. The essence of the message in this chapter consists not in the special lot that awaits the servant after his suffering, but in the fact that God's plan is realized through him and that this is recognized as such.

The author of Isaiah 53 thus does not explicitly proclaim the resurrection of the witness of YHWH; instead, he declares that through the destiny of this individual, and contrary to every expectation, the divine design comes to a successful completion. One finds allusions to the Fourth Servant Song in Jewish texts as diverse as Dan 12:2–4 and Wis 2:12–20.

E. Resurrection of the Dead

Two passages deserve to be mentioned in this paragraph, because they envisage a resurrection of the dead that really is a liberation from death. This is clearly the case with Dan 12:1–3, though the meaning of Isa 26:19 remains a debated instance. One should note that these texts belong to the latest levels of the OT tradition (the end of the Persian period, according to some commentators [Isa 26:19]; the 2d century B.C. [Dan 12:2–3]) and reflect milieus influenced to a greater or lesser degree by apocalypticism.

1. Isa 26:19 is part of a larger unit (Isaiah 24–27) that is complex, postexilic, and characterized as the "Great Apocalypse," the interpretation of which is very difficult. Various exegetes even think that this verse is a late gloss without relationship to its immediate context (Kaiser and Lohse 1977) or else an independent proclamation replying to Isa 26:14 (J. Vermeylen). H. Wildberger (*Jesaiah* BKAT), on the other hand, locates this "Apocalypse" in the 5th century B.C. and sees in Isa 26:19 an oracle of salvation that follows up on the lament of the people articulated in vv 7–18 (discussion and bibliography in *DBSup* 10: 448–52).

Isa 26:19 raises many difficulties; as it is, the Hebrew text possesses little clarity and the versions are divergent. Its author expressed either a vow or a promise (if this verse can be understood as a reply to v 14); thus he either desired or foretold the return to life of the "dead-of-YHWH," an occasion for joy and praise.

Some would call attention to allusions in this brief passage to the "dew," already evoked in Hos 6:1–3, which was a Canaanite motif; with the thunder and the rain it was a pledge of renewal, and so we should not be surprised to find it linked in the rabbinic tradition with the theme of the resurrection of the dead (*Hagiga* 12b). For some specialists, the issue under question, here again, is that of a national restoration after a painful period for the Jewish community during the time of the decline of the Persian period, whereas the majority of critics consider that Isa 26:19 announced a real resurrection of the dead. However, this was not a universal resurrection, but one accorded only to the "dead of YHWH" (cf. v 19, "your dead ones" and "my corpse" understood as "my corpses"; "their corpses" in the Syriac version and in the Targum). Resurrection is promised to those who had died (the martyrs) for the sake of the name of the God of Israel and whom YHWH reclaimed as his own. The resurrection evoked in this passage, when situated in the "Great Apocalypse," was promised not to humanity in general but to those believers who, in an era of troubles and persecutions, had been faithful even to the point of giving their lives for YHWH's cause. This perspective is close to the points of view found in Jewish apocalyptic.

2. Dan 12:1–3 is the one text that precisely points to apocalyptic milieus which came to be expressed at the time of the crisis provoked by the attitude of Antiochus Epiphanes toward Jews opposed to the Hellenization of Jerusalem and of the customs heretofore in effect. Religious persecution was unleashed against the *ḥăsîdîm* (or "Faithful Ones")—from whom the Pharisaic party evolved—in 167 B.C. Dan 12:1–3 can be dated with some precision as part of a complex, a type of historical retrospective (Dan 11:1–45) which antedated by a short time the death of the Seleucid sovereign (in 164 B.C.).

After having evoked the past, the author of the conclusion to the book of Daniel, beginning with 12:1, envisaged the future. In v 1, he foretold a time of anguish that would surpass in horror anything one could have imagined, but simultaneously he promised divine protection to the faithful Yahwists. Then he treated, in vv 2–3, the fate of the dead and in particular that of those who had fallen in the course of the persecutions. No more than was the case in Isa 26:19 do we have here an event that concerns the whole of humanity; the resurrection, as Daniel foresaw it, was a limited one (v 2a, with its use of the partitive *min,* suggests the interpretation "many of . . ." rather than "all of . . ."); it addressed the concrete situation wherein two parties were set against each other within the Jewish community, the partisans of Antiochus and their opponents. The first group was bound for "eternal shame" and the second group was to receive "eternal life" (v 2b); divine justice was thereby vindicated, since retribution, though long delayed, would have become possible "at that time" (v 1), through the resurrection. Several questions remain unanswered: the identity of the ones "punished" (v 2b) remains unclear, if one can believe the exegetes whose opinion on this point remains divergent: are we dealing with great sinners or with renegade Jews or perhaps with pagans hostile to Israel? Questions are also asked whether the condemned will come back to life (v 2a), then to experience an unending opprobrium (v 2b), or whether, in the end, the resurrection concerns only the "just ones."

Verse 3 brings in a new element, for it looks to a certain category of Jews, namely the "wise," whose attitude—that is, their martyrdom—led their brothers to follow the right path and who are called to glory. Here the author alludes to Isaiah 53, to which he gives a communitarian interpretation (cf. also Dan 11:33–34), making use, moreover, of astral symbolism; it is difficult to say whether this should be taken literally or not (see Cavallin 1974; for an opposing viewpoint, Grelot 1971). It seems clear, though, that the resurrection, as it is envisaged here, does not consist simply in a return to the earthly conditions of the past (*DBSup* 10: 452–58).

We draw attention to the fact that the theme of the resurrection asserted itself in the Jewish milieus at the very moment when apocalyptic views were developing in answer to the distress being undergone by faithful Jews. By the victory over death, as this was understood in the 2d century B.C., justice was rendered to the Yahwistic faithful, and those who gave their lives in YHWH's name could thereafter participate in that new age which the God of Israel was preparing for his own. As E. Renan wrote long ago, "the blood of the martyrs was the veritable creator of belief in a second life" (*DBSup* 10: 457). What counted in the eyes of the biblical authors, in the last days of OT times, was not at all the immortality of the soul or even the salvation of the individual, but the possibility that the "dead of YHWH" (Isa 26:19) or the *rabbîm,* that is, "the many," once they had been instructed in justice by their teachers (Dan 12:2–3), would experience, along with those who had been saved in the hour of torment, the triumph of their God and the glory of the age to come.

F. Conclusion

Texts relating to resurrection in the OT are rare and dissimilar; they come from different horizons and we cannot simply examine them in chronological order to retrace the history of this theme in the mind of Israel. Known before the Exile, since it was attested in Hosea's time in the 8th century—and there within a Canaanite context—the return to life of the dead did not really come to the fore until the 2d century B.C.E., in the days of the Maccabean crisis, and from within those quarters deeply attached to the Yahwistic tradition among the hard-pressed *ḥăsîdîm,* who awaited their salvation in their God's final intervention "on the last day."

Between Hosea and Daniel, the resurrection idea cropped up here and there, but chiefly to point toward the political renewal of the people of Israel (Ezekiel).

As was the case with the OT texts themselves, precise vocabulary in the OT which pointed to the resurrection was limited; such terminology was shaped by the ideas that Israel had fashioned about the condition of those who had died. At a person's death, the breath or spirit of life departed; it had to return later on if there was to be any renewal of life (1 Kgs 17:21–22). The dead lie sleeping in their tombs; at the moment of resurrection, they will rise up again (Heb *qûm:* 2 Kgs 13:21; Isa 26:14, 19; Job 14:12 [Ezek 37:10 uses a different verb]). The dead are sleeping now; they will be awakened (2 Kgs 4:31; Isa 26:19; Job 14:12; Dan 12:2) and, finally, they will come back to life (1 Kgs 17:22; 2 Kgs 13:21; Isa 26:14, 19; Ezek 37:3, 5–6, 9–10, 14; Job 14:14 [cf. also Dan 12:2 and, in the Talmud, the rabbinical expression *teḥiyyat hammētîm,* "the resurrection of the dead," which is attested 41 times]).

If the problem of the Israelite's survival beyond his or her earthly existence was scarcely asked about in Israel over the centuries, this was due in the first instance to the traditional anthropological conceptions by the people of YHWH: the human being was composed of body and soul (or breath [Gen 2:7–8]), that formed the organic unity indispensable for life; the person was not constituted of a perishable element (the flesh) and of an immaterial reality endowed with immortality (the soul). Life ceased at that very moment when the breath loaned by God was taken back (Ps 104:29–30; Qoh 12:7) and the body, henceforth inanimate, was destined to return to the earth (Gen 3:19; Ps 90:3). The existence of the shades in Sheol, mentioned many times, noticeably in the psalms, was the total opposite of life—a kind of "nonlife"—out of which no positive element could arise. For Israel there could be no victory over death except that of a state of existence which called for a complete renewal of the human being. The resurrection of the dead, that is, of the body, is etched within the logic of OT concepts.

Secondly, and this might be the chief issue, death which at times signified the total rupture between the dead and the world of the living and, above all, YHWH (cf. the psalms referred to above) had its sting attenuated when the deceased left behind a son or when his body was buried in the tomb of his ancestors. For the Israelite survived in his or her descendants, and they were kept in contact with their own through burial rites which were celebrated in the midst of YHWH's land; the individual Israelite without question died, but Israel was perpetuated and at the same time a certain continuity with the missing ones was assured.

Little by little, under the pressure of the tragic events that the people of YHWH experienced (the disappearance of the northern kingdom in the 8th century; the fall of Jerusalem and the end of the Judean state in the 6th century; the Exile and the difficult and precarious reconstitution of a Jewish community around Jerusalem under the Persians), the condition of the individual in the midst of a national and religious community came to assume the preponderant place and, from this time forward, questions were asked about the fate of the faithful one and in particular of the ultimate future state reserved for him or her. The problem became especially acute during the crises that the Jewish people lived through under the declining Persian Empire and during the time of Antiochus Epiphanes; factions among the people of God were set against each other with passion, with the object of seizing power in Jerusalem, and persecutions raged against those who wished to remain faithful to the law of their God. The Yahwistic cause seemed a lost one, and the martyrs to have died in vain; the prophecy of the resurrection of the dead then allowed people to address the challenge brought on by the circumstances they endured. With the resurrection doctrine, the last word remained with the God of Israel and, with him, on the lips of the faithful. Resurrection, which constitutes the determining backdrop of the NT's gospel, was the fruit of Jewish resistance to the Hellenistic world.

We have mentioned that the notion of resurrection is a foreign body within the OT; it was the result of external influences that came into play in various ways over the course of the history of the people of YHWH. Upon examination, the extent of the contribution from outside Israel, without being denied, needs to be qualified, and one could say that, when some Jews declared that the dead (of their God) would revive, they did so by basing their arguments on Yahwistic principles. The Canaanite or Near Eastern world could have furnished Israel, in this sphere as in others, with themes and a language; but a return to life, conceived in a quasi-automatic fashion and lived out within the framework of an agrarian ritual, was rejected by Yahwism (Hosea) and could not be given free play until it had been subjected to a rigorous purification process (Ezekiel). Much later on, Persian teachings may have served as stimulants to the Jewish visions of the afterlife, but the Persians reckoned the resurrection as but one element in the re-creation of the universe, while the OT texts (Isaiah 26; Daniel 12) envisaged it as an event that concerned all faithful Jews; the universalism of some of these texts contrasts with the particularism, or rather, the pietism of other texts.

It is in the Yahwistic tradition itself that are to be found the roots of faith in the resurrection: the OT proclaimed YHWH's power, one which no force could hold in check; God masters death as God masters life (1 Sam 2:6; Deut 32:39; cf. also a late annotation in Isa 25:8a). God has created and thus can re-create (2 Maccabees 7).

God's justice, affirmed everywhere in the OT, sooner or later had to become manifest, and the resurrection allowed this very thing to happen, as we have seen. Finally, the victory over death, that in the first instance concerned the faithful Yahwists, gave Israel's God an occasion to demonstrate his *ḥesed*, "faithfulness, loyalty, solidarity," toward his own and, in this way, to answer the question already raised by the psalmists about the definitive future of those bonds which actually united YHWH to his *ḥāsîd* (Psalms 6; 16; 22; etc.). Thus, belief in the resurrection of the dead is based on YHWH's power, on his justice, and on his love, as these have been revealed in the course of the history of Israel; in the 2d century B.C.E., at the high point of the Maccabean crisis, the *ḥăsîdîm* drew out the ultimate consequences from the experiences that Israel had lived through over centuries.

Bibliography

Barth, C. 1974. *Die Errettung vom Tode in den individuellen Klage-und Dankliedern des Alten Testaments.* Zollikon.

Cavallin, H. C. C. 1974. *Life after Death.* ConBNT 7/1. Lund.

Cazelles, H. 1961. *Le Jugement des morts.* Sources Orientales 4. Paris.

Collins, J. J. 1974. Apocalyptic Eschatology as the Transcendence of Death. *CBQ* 36: 21–43.

———. 1978. The Root of Immortality: Death in the Context of Jewish Wisdom. *HTR* 71: 177–92.

Grelot, P. 1971. *De la mort à la vie éternelle.* LD 67. Paris.

Greshake, G., and Kremer, J. 1986. *Resurrectio Mortuorum: Zum theologischen Verständnis der leiblichen Auferstehung.* Darmstadt.

Hasel, G. F. 1980. Resurrection in the Theology of the Old Testament Apocalyptic. *ZAW* 92: 267–84.

Hengel, M. 1974. *Judaism and Hellenism.* 2 vols. Trans. J. Bowden. Philadelphia.

Kaiser, O., and Lohse, E. 1977. *Tod und Leben: Biblische Konfrontationen.* Stuttgart.

Maag, V. 1980. Tod und Jenseits nach dem AT. Pp. 181–202 in *Kultur, Kulturkontakt und Religion.* Göttingen.

Martin-Achard, R. 1960. *From Death to Life: A Study of the Development of the Doctrine of the Resurrection in the Old Testament.* Trans. J. P. Smith. Edinburgh.

Nickelsburg, G. W. E., Jr. 1972. *Resurrection, Immortality, and Eternal Life in Intertestamental Judaism.* HTS 26. Cambridge, MA.

Nikolainen, A. T. 1944–46. *Der Auferstehungsglauben in der Bibel und ihrer Umwelt.* 2 vols. AASF B 49/3, 59/3. Helsinki.

Nötscher, F. 1946. *Altorientalischer und alttestamentlicher Auferstehungsglauben.* Würzburg. Repr. Darmstadt, 1970.

Stemberger, G. 1972. *Der Leib der Auferstehung.* AnBib 56. Rome.

ROBERT MARTIN-ACHARD
Trans. Terrence Prendergast

EARLY JUDAISM AND CHRISTIANITY

Resurrection is the eschatological act by which God the judge raises the dead in order to recompense them for their deeds. In the long history of Jewish speculation, the manner of judgment varies: resurrection of the body; revivification of the soul or spirit; eternal life or assumption to heaven immediately upon death or shortly thereafter. In some cases, eternal life or immortality are the present possession of the righteous, while the wicked are thought to be already in the realm of death. Resurrection and its equivalents function variously as recompense for the lack of divine justice in this world, as reward and punishment for one's deeds, or, in special cases, to exalt and glorify the persecuted leaders of the community. NT beliefs about resurrection and its equivalents reflect the variety of their Jewish counterparts, but differ from them uniformly in their christological orientation.

A. Resurrection in Early Judaism

1. Early Developments. Belief in a substantial, meaningful existence after death is a relatively late development in the history of Israelite religion. The usual view expressed in the biblical books is that, upon death, one's shade descends to Sheol, where one remains forever, cut off from God's presence.

Other elements in Israelite religious thought stand in tension with this viewpoint. As creator, God is the Lord of life, who effects and nourishes a covenantal relationship with God's people. As judge, God rewards the faithful and punishes those who rebel against the covenantal commandments. As the Almighty, God can effect what divine justice requires. The tension arises when premature death frustrates this justice.

The origins of resurrection belief are obscure. Authors of the exilic period employ the language of death and resurrection or exaltation as a metaphor for Israel's revival and return from Exile. Although dead in captivity, the people will arise from their Babylonian graves (Ezekiel 37). Kings and nations will view the exaltation of Yahweh's suffering servant (Isa 52:13–53:12). It is doubtful that this metaphorical usage presupposes Jewish speculation on the possibility of substantive life in spite of physical death, but both passages (and Isaiah 65–66) are later used to support such a belief.

At a time and in circumstances that we cannot presently determine, a religious breakthrough occurs. Jews begin to assert that physical death does not nullify God's justice or abrogate the covenantal relationship for individuals. Early texts are ambiguous. Psalms 16, 49, and 73 may point in this direction, but their date and circumstances are unknown. The Isaianic apocalypse (Isaiah 24–27) appears to be the earliest text that envisions a real resurrection of the righteous. God will overcome death forever. The shades of the righteous will arise from Sheol, while their oppressive overlords will remain there (Isa 25:6–8; 26:14–19). Scholars debate this text's precise time and circumstances of origin.

2. Persecution, Oppression, and God's Justice. All of the texts mentioned above deal with the disjunction between human experience and a belief in divine justice. Settings of persecution or oppression trigger further speculation about postmortem recompense.

a. *1 Enoch* 22–27. Chaps. 20–36 of *1 Enoch* (3d century B.C.E.) recount Enoch's journeys through the cosmos. Far to the west, he sees a great mountain with three huge chasms that contain "all the souls of the sons of men," sorted and separated for the purpose of judgment (chap. 22). Dominating the scene is the spirit of Abel, the prototype of the innocent who are persecuted. He accuses Cain "and his descendants" until they are obliterated from the human race. Abel's prominence indicates that violent death and the lack of divine judgment against the perpetrators of this crime are fundamental concerns of this author (cf. chaps. 6–11). The motif of judgment governs the descriptions of the three chasms. In the first of these, the spirits of all the righteous are refreshed by a bright fountain of water. In the second chasm, unspecified sinners already experience the torment to which they will be subjected during their eternal confinement in this place. In the third chasm, the spirits of persons who have been murdered plead for divine vengeance. For these "companions of the lawless," their violent death was ample recompense for their wicked deeds, and so they do not experience the torment of those in the second chasm, nor will they be raised for judgment (22:13).

According to chap. 22, recompense is experienced by the "souls" or the "spirits" or the "souls of the spirits" immediately after death. Nonetheless, the author anticipates a resurrection of some of the dead. Verse 13 suggests that the sinners in the second chasm will be raised for judgment. Almost certainly the righteous in the first chasm will rise to the blessed new life in the new Jerusalem described in chap. 25.

After viewing the realm of the dead, Enoch is carried to the mountain of God (chaps. 24–25) where he sees the tree of life which "will be transplanted to the holy place," where "its fruit will be given to the righteous and the pious . . . and its fragrances will permeate their bones," as they "live a long life upon the earth" as their fathers had, free from "torments and plagues and suffering" (25:4–6). In Jerusalem, Enoch views the holy mountain, as well as the valley of Hinnom, where the blasphemers will suffer forever in the presence of the righteous (chaps. 26–27).

1 Enoch 24–27 is directly or indirectly dependent on Isaiah 65–66 with its descriptions of the New Jerusalem and the blessed and fabulously long life of the righteous and the everlasting punishment of the sinners which will take place there (cf. esp. Isa 65:17–25; 66:14, 24). Different from Third Isaiah, *1 Enoch* 22–27 anticipates a resurrection that will enable some of the righteous and wicked dead to participate in the blessings and curses that result from the great judgment. Reference to the "bones" of the righteous (25:6) indicates a resurrection to some kind of bodily life. The bodily or nonbodily state of those punished in the valley of Hinnom is not specified.

b. *1 Enoch* 92–105. Enoch's "Epistle" (2d century B.C.E.) expounds the implications of Enoch's eschatological visions. Injustice pervades the author's world. The rich and powerful prosper as they oppress the righteous poor, who suffer in spite of their righteousness and piety. The repeated announcement of the coming day of judgment anticipates the adjudication of these circumstances.

The treatment of the problem and its solution reaches its climax in 102:4–104:8, a disputation about postmortem reward and punishment. To "the souls" of the righteous and pious who grieve in Sheol, the author promises that they will "come to life" and receive the reward that their fleshly bodies missed (102:4–103:4). As for the sinners who claim that there is no judgment after death, and act accordingly—their souls will descend to the flaming torture of Sheol (103:5–8). In a pastiche of phrases from Deuteronomy, Enoch quotes the complaint of the righteous and pious that they have received the curses of the covenant (103:9–15). His refutation asserts that their cries for justice have been heard by their angelic patrons, who plead their case before God. Their names are written in the heavenly register. Judgment will come, and the righteous will ascend to heaven and to great joy in the presence of the angels (104:1–6).

c. Daniel 12:1–3. Writing between 167 and 165 B.C.E. to encourage pious Jews during the persecution of Antiochus Epiphanes, the author of Daniel 10–12 composed an apocalypse which describes the events of Israel's history from "Darius the Mede" to Antiochus (11:2–45). When the persecution reaches its climax, the divine Judge will intervene, and the persecutor will be destroyed (11:45). The recitation of past history gives way to a brief description of the judgment (12:1–3) that will adjudicate the injustices just recounted. Michael, Israel's angelic patron and defender, will arise. The book that contains the names of the citizens of people who will be delivered will be opened. Those still alive will be rescued from God's wrath. Then "many of those who sleep in the land of dust will awake, some to everlasting life, and some to everlasting contempt." This is not a universal resurrection; only some of the dead will awake. The author has in mind at least the principal characters in the Antiochan persecution. The righteous whose pious behavior has led to their death will be vindicated. Those who apostasized to save their lives will be raised to suffer the divine punishment they escaped in their lifetime. The author probably also expects that other especially righteous and wicked Israelites will be raised for judgment.

Like *1 Enoch* 24–27, the language of Dan 12:2 recalls Isaiah 65–66. "Everlasting life" is the long life referred to in Isa 65:20–22 (cf. *1 En.* 25:6). "Everlasting contempt" is the fate of the rebels whose bodies will suffer outside Jerusalem (in the valley of Hinnom) according to Isa 66:24 (cf. *1 En.* 27:2–3). The resurrection implicit in *1 Enoch* is explicit in Dan 12:2. The problem of the suffering and persecuted righteous emerges in acute form as the catalyst for resurrection as vindication. The righteous dead, whom Enoch saw refreshed by a bright fountain of water in the realm of the dead, are sleeping in Sheol, the murky "land of dust," according to Dan 12:2. The allusion to Isa 66:14 ("contempt") may indicate that Daniel thinks of a bodily resurrection (cf. *1 En.* 25:4–6), but the brevity of the Danielic passage is elusive.

According to Dan 12:3, the wise teachers of the community, who have encouraged many to follow the path of righteousness, will receive special honor by being gloriously exalted among the stars, the angelic host. Here the author draws on a traditional exposition of the last song of the servant of Yahweh (Isa 52:13–53:12; see below under Wisdom 1–6).

d. *Jubilees* 23:11–31. Written perhaps a year or two before the book of Daniel, as a comment on Abraham's age (Gen 25:7–8), these verses describe the bloody struggle between pious Jews and Hellenizers which culminates in the merciless intervention of the Syrian government. The people's sin has greatly shortened their life spans, but when they return to God's commandments, their life spans will increase to the fabulous length of the first patriarchs (vv 27–28). Again the language of Isaiah 65 informs a description of the end time (cf. esp. 65:20–22). As for the righteous who have died during evil times, "their bones will rest in the earth, and their spirits will have much joy . . ." (v 31). Different from *1 Enoch* 22; 24–25, *Jubilees* contrasts the bones that rest from bodily pain and agony with the spirits that have ascended to the joyous presence of God. The author seems not to envision a future, bodily resurrection; however, vv 30–31 may allude to the righteous viewing the curses that the wicked suffer in the valley of Hinnom.

e. 2 Maccabees 7. This legend about the martyrdom of seven young men and their mother, set in the Antiochan persecution, dates in its present form to the end of the 2d century B.C.E. Central to the story is a conflict of authority and the protagonists' response to it. Pitted against one another are Antiochus Epiphanes, who commands the Jews to eat swine's flesh, and the God of Israel, whose law forbids this. The protagonists choose to disobey the king and obey their God. Condemned to death in a human court, they await vindication in the supreme court of the king of the universe, who will restore the life and limbs that Antiochus has destroyed (vv 9, 11). Bodily resurrection is the counterpart to bodily destruction; vindication is in kind.

To explicate his view of resurrection, this author employs three images from Second Isaiah which originally referred to Israel's return from Exile. (1) The youths are the suffering and vindicated servants of Yahweh. Through their speeches, they are God's spokesmen before the king. They suffer because of this prophetic office, and for this reason they will be vindicated (cf. Isa 50:7–9). (2) God's power as creator, who first gave them life, is the basis of their hope that God will redeem them in the resurrection to a new life (vv 22–23, 27–29). (3) The youths' mother is a personification of Mother Zion, who anticipates the return of her sons, now dispersed in death (v 9).

If the brothers are to be vindicated for their obedience, Antiochus must suffer for his rebellion (vv 14, 17, 19). His judgment is vividly described in chap. 9. The warning that he will have no resurrection to life (7:14) means either that his violent death eliminates the necessity of a postmortem punishment, or that he will be permanently confined to eternal torment immediately after his death.

f. *4 Maccabees*. In this writing from the first half of the 1st century C.E., the stories in 2 Maccabees 6–7 have been transposed into the key of Greek philosophy. In his transformation of the story about the youths and their mother (chaps. 8–17), this author changes the story's eschatology. Future resurrection of the body is replaced by immortality and an eternal life that begins at the moment of death (7:3; 9:22; 13:17; 14:5–6; 15:3; 16:13, 25; 17:12, 18–19). God's creative power is the reason for obedience to the Torah (11:5; 13:13) rather than the guarantee of a resurrection. Eternal life is God's reward for obedience, not the vindicative restoration of the bodies that the martyrs have lost.

g. Wisdom of Solomon 1–6. Written around the turn of the era, Wisdom 1–6 is a disputation on immortality (cf. *1 Enoch* 102–104). The author exhorts kings and rulers to act righteously because the divine judge will hold them accountable for their deeds. By contrast, the rich and mighty comment on the shortness of life and the finality of death (chap. 2). Since death is annihilation, one should enjoy life, even at the expense of others (2:1–11). The special target of abuse is the righteous man who claims to be God's "son" or "servant" and preaches against their "sins." They conspire to bring him to trial and kill him (2:12–20), thus refuting his claims. But the wicked act on a false premise. Death is not the end. The death of the righteous one is an illusion, for "the souls of the righteous are in the hand of God" (3:1–9). The wicked discover this after their death (4:16–5:23), when the exalted righteous one confronts them as judge in the heavenly court. They acknowledge that he stands among the "sons of God" (the angels) and admit that his indictment of their sins was justified. Now they are condemned to the annihilation they had believed in, while the righteous receive the eternal life they had awaited.

In recounting the case of the righteous one, the author of Wisdom 1–6 draws on a type of story found in Genesis 37–45, Ahikar, Esther, and Daniel 3 and 6. See PASSION NARRATIVES. Here, however, the protagonist is exalted and vindicated in the heavenly courtroom, and rewards and punishments are eternal and transcend physical death. The scene of the righteous one's heavenly exaltation has been shaped by Isa 52:13–53:12. As in Second Isaiah (and Genesis 37–45 and Daniel 3 and 6), the protagonist is a spokesman of God. Although his vocation leads to human condemnation, God vindicates him by exalting him to a high position that befits his original status. This Isaianic tradition stands behind Dan 12:3 (see above). In Wisdom 1–6, the case of the persecuted and exalted righteous one is a paradigm for God's judgment of all people, who will be rewarded or punished for their deeds (see esp. 3:10–4:15).

Wisdom 1–6 indicates a belief in immortality, which is not an inherent property of the soul, but God's gift to the righteous. "Death" belongs to the wicked and immortality to the righteous already during their life on earth (see esp. 1:12–16).

3. Reward and Punishment. As postmortem recompense comes to be a fixed topic, it is discussed without particular concern about whether God has rewarded or punished one during one's lifetime.

a. The *Psalms of Solomon*. God's righteous judgment is a repeated theme in this collection of psalms which dates from the 1st century B.C.E. *Pss. Sol.* 3, 13, 14, 15 focus on postmortem recompense. The righteous "will rise to eternal life," while the fate of the sinners is "eternal destruction." Such reward and punishment are dispensed not as compensation for the injustices of this life, but as reward and punishment for piety and sin—apart from one's lot in life. The authors do not indicate whether they anticipate a bodily resurrection or the reviving of one's spirit or soul.

b. *2 Baruch*. Writing in the wake of the destruction of Jerusalem (ca. 100 C.E.), the writer of this apocalypse ponders God's justice and the validity of God's promises. The evils he has experienced are explained by a dualism between the present corrupt age and the incorruptible age to come after God's judgment (21:12–26; 30:2–5; 49–51). He discusses the resurrection in this context (chaps. 49–51). The souls of the dead, presently gathered in the "treasuries" of Sheol (21:23; 30:2–5), will be raised in their original form so that the living may recognize them. Thereafter, the righteous will be freed from the limitations of this age and transformed into glory like the stars and the angels, with whom they will inhabit paradise in the age to come. The wicked will waste away and depart to eternal torment. The heavenly glory that Daniel anticipated for the wise teachers is here the property of all the righteous.

c. *4 Ezra* 7. This writer also writes in response to the destruction of Jersualem. Like his colleague in *2 Baruch,* he discusses postmortem reward and punishment for one's deeds. His focus is on the souls' fate (vv 75–101) as they proceed to the dwellings they will occupy until the resurrection (cf. *1 Enoch* 22). In this universal event of judgment, humanity will enter the glory of paradise and torture of Gehenna, here construed in cosmic proportions rather than as a valley in Jerusalem (vv 26–42).

4. The Presence of Eternal Life and the Two Ways. a. The Qumran Hymn Scroll 3:19–23; 11:3–14. The authors of these hymns give thanks to God for having brought them from death to life. The world outside the sectarian community is described as Sheol. Entrance into the community is construed as resurrection into the realm of eternal life and the presence of the angels. What "traditional" eschatology ascribes to the end time is said to be the present possession of the member of the sect. Although evil will not be eliminated until the consummation, a major eschatological event has occurred.

b. The Qumran *Rule of the Community* 3:13–4:26. Right and wrong actions and their rewards and punishments are discussed according to the organizing principle of the two ways. One's conduct is a journey along the way(s) of light or of darkness, guided by the good or evil angel. Lists of good and evil deeds are given, together with lists of the rewards and punishments dispensed in this life and, mainly, afterward.

The Qumran hymns and the *Rule of the Community* do not specify whether the authors anticipated a resurrection. Several facts are noteworthy, however. The Scrolls rarely refer to physical death. Their radicalization of resurrection language mitigates the importance of a future consummation of the fullness of eternal life. The imagery of the ways stresses continuity between present situation and future recompense. This usage seems most consonant with the idea that at physical death one passes directly to eternal life—even if the world is still subject to a final judgment. On the other hand, the uniform orientation of the graves at Qumran could attest a belief in resurrection.

c. Other Texts. Several non-Qumranic texts espouse views similar to those just discussed. According to *Joseph and Aseneth* (1st century C.E.?), when Aseneth repented of her idolatry, Michael the archangel conferred on her the gifts of immortality and eternal life (chaps. 15–16). In Wisdom 1–6 immortality is also conferred during one's lifetime. In the *Testament of Abraham* 11–12 Rec. A; 8–9 Rec. B and the *Testament of Asher* 6, a theology of the two ways is the vehicle for a belief in final recompense immediately after death.

5. Josephus on the Pharisees, Sadducees, and Essenes. Flavius Josephus twice discusses the beliefs that these groups held regarding postmortem recompense (*JW*

2.8.11,14 §§154, 163, 165; *Ant* 18.1.3–5 §§14, 16, 18). According to him, the Essenes espoused something like immortality of the soul, and the Pharisees resurrection of the body, while the Sadducees did not believe in any postmortem rewards and punishments. Similar views are attributed to the Pharisees and Sadducees in Acts 23:6–8 and Mark 12:18–23.

Of the texts discussed above, only the Qumran Scrolls are widely identified with one of these groups (the Essenes). Josephus' attribution of a belief in immortality could fit the Qumran Scrolls, as well as the book of *Jubilees*, which appears to have been composed in circles ancestral to Qumran. The rich opponents of the author of the "Epistle" of *1 Enoch* 92–105 are not identifiably Sadducean. However, behind the author's polemical rhetoric may be the "conservative" view that prosperity reflects piety and requires no postmortem recompense.

B. Resurrection in Early Christianity

1. Foci and Emphases. Jewish beliefs about resurrection, immortality, and eternal life are presupposed throughout the NT, and these early Christian formulations also mirror the variety in Judaism, as this pertains to the functions, time, scope, and mode of postmortem recompense. The major factor that transforms these beliefs, however, is the Church's universal conviction that God has begun the eschatological process by raising the crucified Jesus from the dead. Every writing of the NT presumes Jesus' resurrection, and the topic of postmortem recompense is rarely treated without reference or allusion to it.

Jesus' resurrection is understood from two perspectives. First, it is God's vindication of the persecuted man Jesus. It makes sense of the humiliation, tragedy, and scandal of the crucifixion. Secondly, the resurrection of Jesus has broader implications, as an act of salvation for humanity and the cosmos. It facilitates Jesus' exaltation as Lord and Judge and promises resurrection and eternal life to all the faithful.

2. Texts and Authors. a. Early Creeds and Hymns. The major NT interpretations of Jesus' resurrection are evident already in the earliest strata of the texts—credal formulas, hymns (or hymn fragments), and other traditions embedded in Paul's epistles. The paradigm of persecution and vindication is basic. Condemned in a human court, the crucified Jesus is vindicated when God raises him from the dead. This emphasis on the resurrection as God's means of reversing the evil of the crucifixion appears in the formulaic "the God [*or* him] who raised him [*or* the Lord Jesus] from the dead" (Rom 4:24; 8:11; Gal 1:1; Eph 1:20; Col 2:12; 1 Pet 1:21; cf. Rom 10:9). The expression is likely a reformulation of the OT formula "The God who brought up Israel out of Egypt" (cf. Heb 13:20 and Isa 63:11). The God of the Exodus has been redefined as the God of the resurrection. Thus, the resurrection is not a private act that simply vindicates Jesus, but a new redemptive act with universal import. Following the familiar pattern, vindication is evident in exaltation. That this exaltation exceeds the conception in Wisdom 5 is shown by the frequent occurrence of the title "Lord" and the stem *pist-*, "believe," and the verb *homologein*, "confess." Jesus' resurrection and exaltation constitute a saving event for those who confess and believe in them.

In the traditional hymn in Phil 2:6–11, the pattern of humiliation and exaltation is extended by prefixing the motif of incarnation. Jesus, the servant of Isaiah 52–53, is the incarnation of a heavenly being (possibly Wisdom), and the self-emptying (*or* pouring out) of Isa 53:12 is applied to the first stage of humiliation, that is, to incarnation, rather than death. Although the hymn makes no reference to Jesus' being "raised," resurrection's frequent function as exaltation is central, and the anticipated universal confession of Jesus as "Lord" reflects the traditional formula in Rom 10:9 (cf. 1 Cor 12:3).

Resurrection is defined as exaltation also in Rom 1:3–4. Jesus is designated "Son of God with power by the resurrection of the dead." A careful parallelism contrasts Jesus' divine sonship with his exalted but human status as Davidic Messiah. His death, as in many of the texts cited above, is not cited as an event of positive, saving significance.

Such a positive evaluation of Jesus' death is, however, not lacking in early formulations. In Rom 4:24, the pattern and the language of Isaiah 52–53 are embodied in the double expression "delivered for our transgressions, raised for our justification" which interprets the crucifixion and resurrection as two facets of one saving act. A similar formulation occurs in 1 Cor 15:3–4, where the dying and resurrected Jesus is identified as "Christ" (cf. also 1 Thess 4:14, "believe, died, rose").

b. The Document "Q." It is necessary to qualify the frequent assertion that the "Q" we can recover from Matthew and Luke had no cross/resurrection kerygma. Although Q evidently had no passion narrative or death/resurrection formulas (an assertion from silence), its christology presumed the pattern. The document preserved the words of Wisdom's spokesman, by definition in this period the persecuted and vindicated righteous one, who stood in the line of Abel and the prophets (Matt 23:34–35; Luke 11:49–51). At some point in the history of the document, Jesus was also identified as the coming Son of Man, whose future judicial status would be the result of the exaltative function of his resurrection. Thus the authority of the logia was tied retrospectively to the one who was crucified for his prophetic mission and prospectively to the exalted one who would judge or witness concerning those who confessed and denied him (Matt 10:32; Luke 12:8).

c. The Apostle Paul. The death and resurrection/exaltation of Jesus are the foundation of Paul's theology, as is evident from his citation of the aforementioned formulas, creeds, and hymns. The first corollary of Paul's resurrection belief is his expectation of an imminent parousia, which sets the keynote for 1 Thessalonians (1:10, etc.) and 1 Corinthians (1:7–8) and is referred or alluded to in Philippians (3:20), 2 Corinthians (5:10), and Romans (2:16). As the latter three passages indicate, the future double function of the exalted one is as savior and as judge of human deeds. Although Paul's favorite term for the exalted Jesus is "Lord," in some texts Paul appears to have imposed this title on Son of Man traditions. See SON OF MAN.

The second corollary of Paul's resurrection belief is his conviction that the Spirit of the risen Jesus presently resides in the Church and enables and prompts right conduct. One means of making this point is the literary form and imagery of the two ways (Gal 5:16–6:8; Romans 6–8). According to Galatians 5–6, these ways are the life according to the flesh and the life according to the spirit. Flesh and Spirit are characterized by catalogues of right and wrong deeds, and the two principals war against one another like the two spirits at Qumran. The punishment and reward of one's conduct will be corruption or eternal life. In Romans 6 Paul identifies baptism as the means to the eternal life made possible in Jesus' resurrection. The Law cannot facilitate such life (*pace* Jewish covenantal theology) because it has been disabled by Sin (the functional equivalent of the evil spirit), which holds human flesh captive (Romans 7). God has resolved the impasse created by this internal battle by sending his Son. Through his incarnation and death, sin is condemned, and through his resurrection his Spirit makes eternal life possible for those who walk according to that Spirit (Romans 8). In 1 Corinthians 15, although he has cited his expectation of the Parousia, Paul cools the Spirit-oriented ardor of some by contrasting one's present fleshly body with the spiritual body that will be a possibility only at the Parousia, which still awaits the final conquering of death.

The third corollary of Jesus' resurrection is the final resurrection of all Christians. Precisely when Paul began to expound this connection is not clear. In both 1 Thess 4:14 and 1 Cor 15:12–19, he argues from traditions about *Jesus'* death and resurrection to the conclusion that *all* will be raised. This suggests that his early preaching in these congregations was oriented around the Parousia. When Christians, who had been given the Spirit and "life" through baptism, began to die, Paul cited the resurrection as God's way of facilitating the continuation of eternal life. Paul's ideas about the state of Christians between death and the Parousia are unclear. In Phil 1:21–25 he speaks of being "with Christ." In 2 Cor 4:16–5:10 he describes the Christian's gradual transformation through the Spirit. He hopes for the Parousia, so that his present body can be "overclothed" with a glorious body, but he seems to anticipate the possibility of death, at which time he would be "naked" (without a body), yet "with the Lord." In both 1 Cor 15:35–57 and Phil 3:21, Paul christologizes Jewish traditions about the eschatological body. Whether one is resurrected or transformed before death, one's body will have the glory of the risen Lord rather than angelic splendor (Dan 12:3; *2 Baruch* 51).

d. The Deutero-Pauline Literature. The resurrection theologies of these texts vary. In 2 Thess 2:8, the Lord will appear as the eschatological messianic antagonist of the Lawless One. Both Colossians and Ephesians stress the present exaltation of Christ. For the latter, Christians already occupy the heavenly realms (2:5–6; cf. the Qumran Hymns), and the Parousia is nowhere evident (contrast 1:22 with 1 Cor 15:25–28), even if sin and temptation are a present reality (6:10–17; cf. 1QH 3). The Pastoral Epistles stress the eschatological character of Jesus' appearing, quoting tradition (1 Tim 3:16; 2 Tim 1:10). Yet they warn against the heresy that the resurrection has already happened (2 Tim 2:18), and they await the Parousia (1 Tim 6:14; 2 Tim 4:8).

e. The Gospel According to Mark. The traditional story of the persecution and vindication of the righteous one probably governed one form of a pre-Markan passion narrative. See PASSION NARRATIVES. The genre still shapes much of the material in Mark 11–16 and is prepared for in the three passion/resurrection predictions, which express the pattern in language drawn from the Isaianic servant songs (8:31; 9:31; 10:33–34, 45). In context, the story of the discovery of the empty tomb (16:1–8) is part of a larger unit (15:40–16:8) which is linked to the centurion's confession. Through the presence of a common set of characters, it attests the death, burial, and resurrection of Jesus (cf. the same elements in 1 Cor 15:3–4). The centurion present at the cross certifies Jesus' death so that Joseph can bury him. The women who see the burial become witnesses of the empty tomb. The young man gives voice to the women's confusion and articulates the fulfillment of the three predictions: "You seek Jesus the Nazarene, who was crucified. He has been raised; he is not here." He then announces a Galilean appearance that Mark will not narrate. The abrupt ending to the story, however, has an equally strange counterpart in 9:2–13. On a mountain in Galilee, after the first passion/resurrection prediction, before Jesus' journey to Jerusalem, the three disciples see Jesus in transcendent glory and are admonished not to speak of the incident until "the son of man is raised from the dead." Mark appears to have displaced an account of the Galilean appearance to which the young man alludes in 16:7. The result of Jesus' resurrection will be his exaltation as Son of Man. As such he will confront his accusers as judge (14:62), and he will gather his chosen ones (13:26–27)—probably an allusion to the resurrection of the dead. This latter is mentioned explicitly only in 12:18–27, which (different from Paul) retains the Jewish idea of an angelic (rather than Christlike) body. In good Jewish fashion, Jesus asserts in 10:17–22 that "eternal life" will be a result of one's obedience to the Torah.

f. The Gospel According to Matthew. In 28:1–10, Matthew combines Mark 16:1–8 with another story about the empty tomb which appears to be independently attested in the *Gospel of Peter* 35–44, which plays up miraculous elements that Matthew has dampened. Perhaps related to this account is the piece of tradition in Matt 27:51–54, which associates Jesus' coming resurrection with the resurrection of "the holy ones." The little epiphany story in 28:11–15 underscores the commission in 28:7 and may epitomize the tradition in John 20:11–18. The story of the guard at the tomb (27:62–66; 28:11–15), also paralleled in the *Gospel of Peter,* gives final expression to Matthew's emphasis on Jewish unbelief in his own time. The Jewish leaders, concerned that the disciples would fabricate a claim that Jesus rose from the dead, concocted their own lie when they were confronted with evidence of the resurrection. The gospel closes with a scene in which Jesus, already invested with the authority of the exalted Son of Man (cf. 26:64; Dan 7:14), commissions the eleven. As God's exalted vice-regent, the risen Jesus assumes the commissioning role that is normally ascribed to God in Israelite tradition. The content of the prophetlike commissioning is that the apostles instruct and baptize the nations according to the authoritative instructions that are epitomized in the gospel. Those who heed their words will belong to the community which the risen Christ identifies as "my Church" (16:18). As in the earlier creeds, salvation is defined christologically. Developing traditions already in

Mark, Matthew envisions the Son of Man's future role as the judge who will dispense eternal life and destruction (25:31–46; 13:24–29, 36–43).

g. Luke-Acts. According to Luke, Jesus is the son of David, born as the Christ and exalted to messianic glory through the suffering that is vindicated in the resurrection. Luke emphasizes this pattern in three insertions in the traditions in 24:7, 26, 46, which reprise and vindicate Mark's three predictions, tying the suffering and resurrection to Scripture (twice by the Greek verb *dei,* "it was necessary"). Like Matthew, Luke elaborates Mark's final chapter by additional stories. Different from Mark 16:7 and Matt 28:16–20, and like John, the appearances are connected with Jerusalem rather than Galilee. The story of the Emmaus disciples has eucharistic overtones (vv 30–31), with the reference to Jesus' body and blood replaced by the disciples' recognition of the presence of the risen Christ. The account of Jesus' appearance in Jerusalem (vv 36–53) allows Jesus to commission his disciples to preach to all nations in his name, as in Matt 28:16–20. Different from Matthew's account, Luke interpolates his pattern of suffering and resurrection and creates or transmits apologetic motifs that emphasize Jesus' bodily resurrection (vv 37–43). Both this story and that of the Emmaus disciples narrate the resurrection appearances in analogy to angelophanies (sudden appearances and disappearances), but the final story breaks with the genre, attributing to Jesus bodily form and functions elsewhere denied to angels in human form. The crucified Jesus must be shown to have risen from the dead. The pierced hands and feet attest the identity of the risen one with the crucified one (cf. 2 Maccabees 7). For Luke the risen Christ has authority to commission apostles. His status as exalted Son of Man is imminent (cf. 22:69 and Stephen's vision in Acts 7:56).

Luke's views on the resurrection of the dead and the intermediate state are not clear. However, he does describe Lazarus enjoying eternal life and the rich man suffering torment immediately after death (16:19–31), and the dying thief will be with Jesus "today" in paradise (23:43). Luke's version of the controversy story in 20:27–40 combines resurrection language with the expression "live to God," used elsewhere of immortality and in two contexts (cf. v 38 with *4 Macc.* 7:19; 16:25; Hermas *Mand.* 1:2; 2:6; 3:5, etc.).

Acts 1:6–11 recounts Jesus' final resurrection appearance to the apostles (but cf. Luke 24:36–51, and esp. v 50). After forty days of instruction, he ascends on the cloud on which he will return as Son of Man (21:27). The apostles return to Jerusalem as witnesses to his resurrection and the forgiveness that is available through repentance and faith in the name of the risen Christ. Repentance is required because the Jewish leaders in particular are guilty of having rejected Jesus. This is emphasized especially in the early chapters of Acts, which are punctuated with formulas that contrast Jesus' persecution by the Jewish leaders and God's vindication of him through the resurrection and exaltation (2:22–24; 3:13–16, 19; 4:10–12; 5:30–31; 10:38–40; cf. 3:27–32, 38). These formulations are epitomized in 2:36. The form and wording of this passage closely parallel 7:35, where the Israelites' rejection of Moses and God's vindication of him are paradigmatic of the kind of rejection and vindication that climax in the crucifixion and resurrection of Jesus and in the persecution of Stephen and his vindicative vision of the exalted Son of Man. In the case of Saul of Tarsus, rejection and vindication take place in Saul's persecution of the Church and the vision of the exalted One which convinces Saul that Jesus is Son of God (cf. esp. Acts 9:20–21 and Wis 5:1–5). In keeping with gospel traditions and Acts 1, this vision functions as a prophetic commissioning. Three times Saul returns to this vision to emphasize the centrality of the resurrection (23:6–8; 24:21; 26:5–8). Twice he ties the future resurrection to (Jesus') judgment of all humanity (17:31; 24:15).

h. The Gospel According to John. One of the most striking features of this gospel is its tension between future and realized eschatology. The latter predominates and pervades in the author's references to resurrection and eternal life. In the case of Jesus, his death is really his departure, the return of the Logos to the Father who sent him. The moment of his death is the time of his glorification (13:31–32); his being lifted up on the cross is his exaltation (3:14; 12:32). Similarly, those who believe in Jesus "will never die" (11:25–26). Death in the Johannine sense is not a possibility for the believer, who by virtue of faith "*has* eternal life and does not come into judgment, but has passed from death to life" (5:24; cf. 3:18; 3:36; 6:47). This radicalization of eschatology is tied to Jesus' function as the revealer who brings life (1:4 and *passim,* also in the many life-related metaphors, e.g., bread and water) and is dramatized in the raising of Lazarus (see esp. 11:25 and compare the story with 5:25). John's realized eschatology is a christologized version of the theologies found in 1QH 3 and 11 (one has been raised) and the Wisdom of Solomon (the righteous one who has immortality only seems to die when he is taken to heaven).

Two sets of Johannine texts stand in tension with the author's realized eschatology. The farewell discourses notwithstanding, the traditional resurrection stories in chaps. 20 and 21 describe Jesus returning from the dead before his departure to heaven (cf. 20:17 and contrast 20:27). Whatever their precise relationship to their synoptic parallels (Luke 24 and Luke 5; Matt 14:22–33; 16:16–19), John 20:19–23 and 21:1–19 recount the foundational apostolic commissionings typical of most other postresurrection appearance stories. In tension with the texts that posit the presence of judgment and eternal life for believers are other texts that speak of a future resurrection and universal judgment on the basis of deeds, over which Jesus will preside (6:39, 40, 44, 54; 5:27–29). See SON OF MAN. Hypotheses of sources, redaction, and recension best explain the origin of most of these tensions.

i. The Epistle to the Hebrews. As in Phil 2:6–11 and the Fourth Gospel, the christology of Hebrews is governed by a combination of the motif of descending and reascending Wisdom and the pattern of suffering and vindication/exaltation (Heb 1:1–3; 5:5–7). Typical of the latter pattern and in keeping with his dualistic world view, the author applies none of the traditional verbs for resurrection to Jesus (see 13:20; but cf. 6:2 of the general resurrection). Departing from the pattern in a related pair of his own emphases, he sees Jesus' death not as persecution but as obedient sacrifice for sin, and he interprets Jesus' messianic exaltation primarily as his installation to the function of heavenly high priest, following the cue of the oft-quoted Ps 110:1, 4 (cf. also Paul in Rom 8:34).

j. The Book of Revelation. The NT apocalypse begins with a commissioning vision of the resurrected Christ (chaps. 1–3). Presumed throughout the book is not only Jesus' resurrection, but his exaltation as Son of Man, Messiah, and perhaps servant of the Lord. The endurance of the persecuted martyrs is vindicated in their exaltation and reign with Christ (20:4–6). Descriptions of the battle between Michael and Satan, the latter's overthrow, and the great judgment (12:7–9; 20:1–3, 7–15) draw on Jewish judgment and resurrection traditions (*1 Enoch* 10; Daniel 7; 12:1–3), while chaps. 21–22 combine traditional interpretations of Second and Third Isaiah (esp. chap. 65) with descriptions of the heavenly Jerusalem rooted in Ezekiel 40–48. The locus of final salvation is the heavenly Jerusalem come to earth.

3. Historical Problems. The early Church's resurrection faith involves a host of unresolved historical problems which we can only sample here. The first problem concerns the experienced mode of Jesus' resurrection. Stories about the empty tomb presume a bodily resurrection or a bodily assumption to heaven. Earlier traditions about post-resurrection appearances are ambiguous. Although in their present form most of these stories posit a bodily presence almost without exception, elements in the stories strain against such an interpretation: Jesus materializes and disappears suddenly; he is mistaken as a mysterious stranger or a gardener; he is thought to be a spirit or ghost; the disciples disbelieve. This suggests an apologetic tendency in the tradition which objectified Jesus' presence by emphasizing bodily features or functions (or, later, by citing neutral or antagonistic witnesses). The tendency may have been a corrective to stories that were originally narrated in the tradition of angelophanies or divine epiphanies and that may have presumed that the exalted Christ appeared from heaven. This viewpoint is amply documented in 2d-century gnostic sources (Robinson 1982).

A second problem is the place, witnesses, and order of the appearances. The earliest list in 1 Cor 15:5–7 is duplicated nowhere. An appearance to James is not documented in any of the canonical gospels. Only Luke mentions the primary, singular appearance to Peter (24:34), although the tradition seems to be reflected in a number of stories set in the historical ministry of Jesus. The appearances are set variously in Galilee (at the sea or on a mountain) and Jerusalem, with Matthew (except for the brief 28:9–10), Mark, Luke, and the original author of John opting for one tradition or the other. Only an uncritical inclusivism can harmonize these disparate traditions.

Finally, there remains the mystery of the genesis of the NT resurrection faith. The earliest credal and hymnic testimonies to this faith simply assert the traditional pattern of suffering, humiliation, persecution, death—vindication, exaltation. However, it is unlikely that belief in Jesus' resurrection or exaltation arose simply as a reasoned application of the pattern to the tragedy of his crucifixion. Different from all the Jewish texts are the primitive assertions of the universal significance of Jesus' exaltation, which is also implicit, and sometimes explicit in the commissioning functions described in the appearance stories. In the earliest available evidence, Jesus' resurrection means his unique exaltation to status and functions hitherto not ascribed to a historical person. As far back as we can go, belief in Jesus' resurrection is the foundation for the Church's speculations and claims about his unique status and role.

Bibliography

Cavallin, H. C. C. 1974. *Life After Death.* ConBNT 7/1. Lund.

Martin-Achard, R. 1960. *From Death to Life: A Study of the Development of the Doctrine of the Resurrection in the Old Testament.* Trans. J. P. Smith. Edinburgh.

Nickelsburg, G. W. E., Jr. 1972. *Resurrection, Immortality, and Eternal Life in Intertestamental Judaism.* HTS 26. Cambridge, MA.

Nikolainen, A. T. 1944–46. *Der Auferstehungsglauben in der Bibel und ihrer Umwelt.* 2 vols. AASF B 49/3, 59/3. Helsinki.

Perkins, P. 1984. *Resurrection: New Testament Witness and Contemporary Reflection.* Garden City, NY.

Robinson, J. M. 1982. Jesus from Easter to Valentinus (or to the Apostles' Creed). *JBL* 101: 5–37.

George W. E. Nickelsburg

RESURRECTION, TREATISE ON THE (NHC I,*4*).

The central teaching of the *Treatise on the Resurrection* (NHC I,*4*) from the Nag Hammadi Library is that "already you (the Elect) have the resurrection" (49,15–16) if you have experienced proleptically death and Christ's resurrection. Such teaching is remarkably similar to that of Hymenaeus and Philetus denounced in 2 Tim 2:18: "that the resurrection is past already." Echoing NT language, couched in a framework of Valentinian gnostic ideas, and revealing the influence of Middle Platonic concepts, the *Treat. Res.* is an important, late 2d-century witness to heterodox development of a key eschatological doctrine outside the mainstream of Great Church teaching.

Treat. Res. occupies only eight pages, 262 lines of text, in Codex I, one of the best-preserved codices in the NHC collection. It is written in Subachmimic, a subdialect of the Coptic language of S Egypt. Its title, found only at the end (50,17–18), seems a composite of statements found in 44,6 ("concerning the resurrection") and 44,11–12 ("let us discuss the matter") and is descriptive of the content of the document.

Though one major study identifies its literary form with the "animated classroom lecture" exhibited in Epictetus' discourses as preserved by Arrian (Layton 1979: 101), most commentators maintain *Treat. Res.* is a didactic letter in which questions raised by a pupil, Rheginos, are answered by an anonymous master (Malinine et al. 1963: 146; Schenke 1968: 125; Krause 1971: 85; Haardt 1969: 1; Peel 1974: 17ff.). Still disputed is whether it is a genuine, personal letter lacking a *praescriptio* (cf. the *Letter of Ptolemy to Flora*), or whether it is a pseudo-epistle whose form was adopted for didactic purposes. Arguments that *Treat. Res.* is either the result of joining two, originally independent letters (Martin 1971: 293ff.) or of a gnosticizing redaction "of an orthodox Christian text" (Dehandschutter 1973: 110) are unconvincing.

Three principal spheres of influence are reflected in the author's teaching. First, Christian belief is manifest in the central conviction that the "Lord, the Savior, Jesus Christ" (43,37; 48,8–10) is the basis of resurrection experience and the ultimate teacher. By raising himself, Christ opened the "way of immortality" (45,14–39), an event in which all believers participate proleptically (45,24–28). Both "Gospel" (48,6–11 = Mark 9:2–8) and "Apostle" (45,24–28 = Rom 8:17 and Eph 2:5–6) attest this truth. Second, the author's Valentinian gnostic background is found in his cosmology, e.g., ideas of a preexistent "Pleroma" of the Elect and "emanations" which fell into a state of "deficiency" when the world was created (46,38–47,1; 45,11–13; 46,35–38; 49,4–5). Third, Middle Platonic ideas are found in the distinction between the heavenly world of immutable realities and this corruptible and changing sphere (48,20–27), in the notion of the preexistence of souls (46,38–47,1; 47,4–6; 49,30–36), and in the exhortation of "practicing" for dying (49,28–33).

Since the Elect have already died and risen to heaven with Christ (49,25–28), the author exhorts the reader to dispel doubt through faith, avoid divisive opinion, and thereby gain certitude about already having the resurrection. Though inevitable, after biological death comes ascension (45,36–38) of one's invisible, inward "members" covered by a new, spiritual "flesh" (47,4–8). Continuity of identity will prevail, as the appearance of Elijah and Moses at Christ's transfiguration attests (48,3–11). This is the "spiritual resurrection" that destroys the "psychic" and "fleshly" forms (45,39–46,2).

Though its place of origin cannot be determined, the text's affinities with later Valentinian, Middle Platonic, late Stoic ideas, as well as with characteristic Christian debates about the resurrection all point toward the late 2d century as its probable time of composition.

Bibliography

Ḍehandschutter, B. 1973. L'Épître à Rheginos (CG 1,3): Quelques problèmes critiqes. *OLP* 4: 101–11.

Gaffron, H.-G. 1970. Eine gnostische Apologie des Auferstehungsglaubens: Bemerkungen zur "Epistula ad Rheginum." Pp. 218–27 in *Die Zeit Jesu: Festschrift für Heinrich Schlier,* ed. G. Bornkamm and K. Rahner. Freiburg.

Haardt, R. 1969. Die Abhandlung über die Auferstehung des Codex Jung aus der Bibliothek gnostischer koptischer Schriften von Nag Hammadi. Teil I: Der Text. *Kairos* N.F. 11: 1–5.

Krause, M. 1971. Die Abhandlung über die Auferstehung. Pp. 85–163 in *Die Gnosis,* vol 2. Ed. W. Foerster. Zurich.

Layton, B. 1978. Vision and Revision: A Gnostic View of the Resurrection. Pp. 190–217 in *Colloque international sur les textes de nag Hammadi (Quebec, 22–25 août 1978).* BCNHE 1. Quebec.

———. 1979. *The Gnostic Treatise on Resurrection from Nag Hammadi.* HDR 12. Missoula.

Malinine, M., et. al. 1963. *De Resurrectione epistula ad Rheginum.* Zurich.

Martin, L. H. 1971. *The Epistle to Rheginos.* Diss., Claremont, CA.

Menard, J.-E. 1975. La Notion de Résurrection dans l'épître à Rheginos. Pp. 110–24 in *Essays on the Nag Hammadi Texts in Honor of Pahor Labib,* ed. M. Krause. NHS 6. Leiden.

Peel, M. L. 1974. *Gnosis und Auferstehung.* Trans. W.-P. Funk. Neukirchen-Vluyn.

———. 1985a. NHC I.4: The Treatise on the Resurrection—Introduction, Text, and Transmission. Pp. 123–58 in *Nag Hammadi Codex I (The Jung Codex: Introductions, Texts, Translations, Indices),* ed. H. W. Attridge. NHS 22. Leiden.

———. 1985b. NHC I.4: The Treatise on the Resurrection—Notes. Pp. 137–215 in *Nag Hammadi Codex I (The Jung Codex): Notes,* ed. H. W. Attridge. NHS 23. Leiden.

Schenke, H.-M. 1968. Auferstehungsglaube und Gnosis. *ZNW* 59: 123–26.

Malcolm L. Peel

REU (PERSON) [Heb *rĕʿû*]. Son of Peleg when Peleg was thirty, father of Serug at thirty-two, Reu lived 239 years (Gen 11:18–21). Unlike many of the figures associated with Abram's immediate family line, Reu cannot be identified with any geographic name in N Mesopotamia (Cassuto 1964: 252; Thompson 1974: 306). The name has the consonants *rʿw,* which may reflect W Semitic *rʿh,* which itself can mean "to pasture," "to associate with," and "to be content." As a noun this expression could mean "shepherd," "friend," and "one who is pleasing" (or adjectival "pleasing"). This element may be compounded with a divine name to describe a characteristic of the deity, or in the case of "friend" to describe the name bearer as "friend of God." See also REUEL. Attestations of this root also appear in extrabiblical Hebrew (*IPN,* 257), Amorite (Gelb et al. 1980: 29, 343), Punic (Benz 1972: 409–10), and possibly in Aramaic names of the 1st millennium B.C. appearing in Akkadian transcription (Zadok 1977: 87, 290). Akkadian personal names with these elements are found in many periods (Clay 1912: 194; Tallqvist 1914: 305, 306; Stamm 1939: 189, 214, 223). Thus the element comprising the name Reu appears in personal names of Semitic origin from a wide variety of times and places.

Bibliography

Benz, F. L. 1972. *Personal Names in the Phoenician and Punic Inscriptions.* Studia Pohl 8. Rome.

Cassuto, U. 1964. *A Commentary on the Book of Genesis. Part II.* Trans. I. Abrahams. Jerusalem.

Clay, A. T. 1912. *Personal Names from Cuneiform Inscriptions of the Cassite Period.* YOS 1. New Haven.

Gelb, I. J., et al. 1980. *Computer-Aided Analysis of Amorite.* AS 21. Chicago.

Stamm, J. J. 1939. *Die Akkadische Namengebung.* 2d ed. MVAG 44. Leipzig.

Tallqvist, K. L. 1914. *Assyrian Personal Names.* AASF 43/1. Helsinki.

Thompson, T. L. 1974. *The Historicity of the Patriarchal Narratives.* BZAW 133. Berlin and New York.

Zadok, R. 1977. *On West Semites in Babylonia during the Chaldean and Achaemenian Periods.* Jerusalem.

Richard S. Hess

REUBEN (PERSON) [Heb *rĕʾûbēn*]. REUBENITE. Firstborn son of Jacob and Leah (Gen 29:31–32; 49:3) and eponymous ancestor of the tribe of Reuben. A number of meanings for the name have been suggested from Arabic, such as "substitute (for another child)" (from Ar *rʾb,* "to restore") or "chief" (Ar *raʾbān*). However the most commonly accepted meaning is "behold a son"—the reaction in Hebrew to the birth of a male child (Nicol 1980: 536, n. 2). The symbolic explanations for the name in Gen 29:32 are related to the circumstances surrounding Reuben's birth—"(Yahweh) has seen my (Leah's) distress" *(raʾā* *bĕʿonyî)* and "now, my husband will love me" *([yeʾĕha]banī)*. Both of these statements refer to Leah's relationship with Jacob and his preference for her sister Rachel (Strus 1978: 62–63).

It was Reuben who collected mandrakes (possibly an aphrodisiac) and gave them to Leah (Gen 30:14ff.). When Rachel demanded the mandrakes, Leah traded them for a night with Jacob, thus leading to the birth of her fifth son, Issachar (also explaining his name "I have hired you," Gen 30:16). After Rachel's death, Reuben had sexual relations with Bilhah, her slave and his father's concubine (Gen 35:22). Using 2 Samuel 16:20–22, in which Absalom takes possession of his father David's ten concubines as a parallel situation, some have seen in this act an attempt on Reuben's part to usurp his father's power and authority. Others have suggested that Reuben's intent was to force Jacob to return to Leah's tent by "spoiling" Bilhah, the last link to Rachel (Unterman *HBD,* 866), and to humiliate his father, which introduced an element of justice into the story (Nicol 1980). Whatever the reason, it was this act which led to Reuben's loss of favor and his birthright to descendants of Joseph and Judah (Gen 49:4; 1 Chr 5:1). In the Joseph story (Gen 37; 42:37), however, Reuben's character was portrayed in a more favorable light and his original position as firstborn was underscored by the role that he played in attempting to save Joseph when the other brothers wanted to kill him and by his offer of his two sons to Jacob as surety for the return of Benjamin from Egypt.

The tribe of Reuben was descended from Reuben through his four sons, Hanoch, Pallu, Hezron, and Carmi (Exod 6:14). The territory assigned to them after the conquest was in the Transjordan, roughly S of Gad/Gilead and N of the Arnon River with the Dead Sea on the W and the Ammonites to the E (Josh 13:15–23). As pastoralists, they and the Gadites coveted this land and were promised it by Moses in return for their assistance in the conquest of Canaan (Numbers 32). There is also some evidence for the existence of a portion of the tribe W of the Jordan (Josh 15:16; 18:17) (Elliger *IDB* 4: 53).

Along with Gad and Manasseh, the Reubenites were accused by the tribes W of the Jordan of setting up an altar for worship in their own territory (Joshua 22). The W tribes were placated and war averted when their Transjordanian brethren swore that this altar was not for cultic use but was a model of the real altar in Canaan symbolizing that the Transjordanian tribes had the right to sacrifice there. Cross (1988: 57), however, sees the story as evidence for "an important and traditional cult and shrine" existing in Reuben's territory.

The subsequent history of the tribe is difficult to construct. In the Song of Deborah (Josh 5:15–16), Reuben was chastised for remaining with its flocks instead of assisting in the conflict with Sisera. In 1 Chr 5:10, 19, however, it was seen as fighting with Gad and Manasseh against the Hagrites in the time of Saul.

There are those who interpret 1 Chr 5:1–10, 26 as indicating that Reuben retained its tribal identity until the deportation of Transjordanian Israelites by Tiglath-pileser III in 732 B.C. Others think that soon after Saul the tribe was absorbed by Gad and Moab. Support for this latter view is derived from new evidence attesting to Ammonite oppressive attacks on the Reubenites and Gadites early in Saul's reign as well as from the fact that in David's census (2 Sam 24:5–6) only Gad is mentioned in the area N of the Arnon (Cross 1988: 48). Also, in the 9th century B.C. Mesha inscription, Gad is described as always having dwelt in that area, but there is no reference to Reuben. Memory of the tribe was retained in Ezek 48:6–7, 31, where it received its portion in the resettlement, and in Rev 7:5, where out of the 144,000 sealed from the tribes of Israel 12,000 were from Reuben.

Scholars assume that the tribe of Reuben must at one time have been extremely important from its eponymous ancestor being Jacob's firstborn and its position of primacy within the various biblical genealogical lists (Cross 1988). The biblical explanation for its weakness and disappearance—Moses' blessing "Let Reuben live and not die" (Deut 33:6)—may be seen either in Reuben's sexual relations with Bilhah or possibly the rebellion against Moses (Numbers 16) instigated by Dathan and Abiram, members of the Reubenite tribe (Unterman *HBD,* 867).

Bibliography

Cross, F. M. 1988. Reuben, First-Born of Jacob. BZAW 100: 46–65.

Nicol, G. G. 1980. Genesis XXIX.32 and XXXV.22a Reuben's Reversal. *JTS* n.s. 31/2: 536–39.

Strus, A. 1978. Etymologies des noms propres dans Gen 29, 32–30, 24, valeurs littéraires et functionelles. *Sal* 40: 57–72.

Gary H. Oller

REUEL (PERSON) [Heb *rĕʿûʾēl*]. Var. DEUEL. The name of various tribes and persons in the OT. Outside the OT, the name occurs in Edomite (Tell el-Kheleifeh Ostracon 6043, 1). Names consisting of *rʿw*- or *rʿy*- and a theophorous element are attested throughout NW Semitic and ancient Arabic (Weippert 1971: 249; Knauf 1988). The name means "The Friend of God" or "God is Friend"; *ʾēl* in personal names does not necessarily refer to the God El (Knauf 1989: 38, n. 170).

1. A son of Esau (Gen 36:4, 10, 13, 17; 1 Chr 1:35, 37). If the list of Gen 36:10–14 reflects the structure of the Edomite tribal system in the 7th century B.C. (Knauf 1989: 10, n. 45; 61–63), Reuel was one of the three major Edomite tribes and had four subtribes (Gen 36:13). The remaining references to this tribe are derived from this entry (Weippert 1971: 437–46). Of Reuel's subtribes, Shammah is attested in Egyptian topographical lists from the 14th century B.C. (*TRE* 9: 292); Zerah probably inhabited the vicinity of Udhruḥ (M.R. 207971), a village, town, and fortress site in S Jordan, located 9 km E of Petra and occupied from the 7th century B.C. through the Ottoman period (Killick 1987). See also ZERAH.

2. The name of Moses' father-in-law (Exod 2:18; Num 10:29). According to another tradition, Jethro was the father of Moses' Midianite wife (Exod 3:1; 4:18 [Jether]; 18:1f., 5f., 12). In the most ancient tradition, Moses' father-in-law seems to have been without a name. He is called Jethro first by the Yahwist (J), and then Reuel by the Jehovist (JE) (Knauf 1988). In Num 10:29, Reuel is the father of Hobab, the eponymous ancestor of a Kenite clan that settled in the Negeb among the tribe of Judah (Mittmann 1977). This clan may well have belonged to the Edomite tribe Reuel before it migrated to the other side of

Wadi Arabah. Therefore, Reuel as Moses' relative is possibly identical with the Edomite tribe (cf. also Albright 1963).

3. The father of Eliasaph, the Gadite tribal leader (Num 2:14; according to the Samaritan and Greek textual tradition). The historical background of the list in Numbers 2 is difficult to ascertain (Kellermann 1970: 155–59). The RSV, following the MT of Num 2:14 reads DEUEL. Barr (1968: 23–25) argues that this form is original; however, the root *dʿw*, "to call," seems to be restricted to S Arabian and Arabic.

4. A Benjaminite family among the inhabitants of Jerusalem (1 Chr 9:8).

5. In Gen 25:3, the LXX adds Reuel to the "sons of Keturah." It is possible that the authors of the LXX knew of an Arabian tribe of this name. It is more likely, however, that they simply wanted to list Moses' father-in-law in their Arabian genealogies in order to emphasize his prominence.

Bibliography

Albright, W. F. 1963. Jethro, Hobab and Reuel in Early Hebrew Tradition. *CBQ* 25: 1–11.

Barr, J. 1968. *Comparative Philology and the Text of the OT.* Oxford.

Kellermann, D. 1970. *Die Priesterschrift von Numeri 1,1 bis 10,10 literarkritisch und traditionsgeschichtlich untersucht.* Berlin.

Killick, A. 1987. *Udhruh. Caravan City and Desert Oasis.* Romsey, England.

Knauf, E. A. 1988. *Midian.* ADPV. Wiesbaden.

———. 1989. *Ismael.* 2d ed. ADPV. Wiesbaden.

Mittmann, S. 1977. Ri. 1,16f und das Siedlungsgebiet der kenitischen Sippe Hobab. *ZDPV* 93: 213–35.

Weippert, M. 1971. *Edom. Studien und Materialien zur Geschichte der Edomiter auf Grund schriftlicher und archäologischer Quellen.* Diss. Tübingen.

Ernst Axel Knauf

REUMAH (PERSON) [Heb *rĕʾûmâ*]. The concubine of Abraham's brother Nahor and the mother of four sons—Tebah, Gaham, Tahash, and Maacah (Gen 22:24). These four were perhaps the eponymous ancestors of Aramean tribes located both N and S of Damascus and related secondarily to the Israelites. Westermann (1985: 367) has drawn attention to the parallel with the Israelite tribes in the division of the names of Nahor's sons: eight were born of the full wife (wives in Jacob's case) and four of the secondary one (again Jacob had two). "Reumah" was evidently a common girl's name, whose meaning nonetheless remains uncertain. Barth (1909: 5) tentatively advocated "Darling," linking it with Akk *râmu* (cf. Ar *raʾima*), "to love." Building on this idea, Coote (1971: 206–7) saw in "Reumah" a shortened form from something like *raʾūmat-ʾili*, "Beloved of El." In a Palmyrene text *rʾwmʾ* shows up as a masculine name and has been compared to the identically spelled Syr word meaning "foster son" and to the Gk name *rhomeos* (Cantineau; Starcky; and Teixidor 1930–65: 6.14).

Bibliography

Barth, J. 1909. Babyl.-assyr. *ra-a-mu* "lieben." *ZA* 22: 1–5.

Cantineau, J.; Starcky, J.; and Teixidor, J. 1930–65. *Inventaire des inscriptions de Palmyre.* 11 vols. Beirut.

Coote, R. B. 1971. Amos 1:11: *RḤMYW. JBL* 90: 206–8.

Westermann, C. 1985. *Genesis 12–36.* Trans. J. J. Scullion. Minneapolis.

Edwin C. Hostetter

REVELATION, BOOK OF. The last book in the NT canon, also known as the Apocalypse of John. The book of Revelation professes to be a record of the prophetic visions given by Jesus to John, who was in exile on the island of Patmos.

A. Title
B. Place in the Canon
C. Summary of Contents
D. Plan of the Book
  1. The Recapitulation Theory
  2. The Source-Critical Theory
  3. Literary Unity and a Linear Design
  4. The Revival of the Recapitulation Theory
  5. Structural and Thematic Theories
  6. A Text-linguistic Approach
  7. Outline
E. Text
F. Authorship
  1. Date
  2. Place
  3. Identity of the Author
G. Literary Character
H. Relation to Other Ancient Literature
I. Theological Perspective and Social Setting
J. History and Methods of Interpretation

A. Title

The oldest textual witness to the opening of the book of Revelation (Codex Sinaiticus) gives "Revelation of John" *(apokalypsis iōannou)* as its title. This title is also found in Codex Alexandrinus (5th century), the best witness, along with Codex Ephraemi (also 5th century), to the text of this work. Other mss contain the titles, "Revelation of John, the one who speaks about God" *(apokalypsis iōannou tou theologou);* "Revelation of Saint John, the one who speaks about God" *(apokalypsis tou hagiou iōannou tou theologou);* "Revelation of John, the one who speaks about God, [the] evangelist" *(apokalypsis iōannou tou theologou kai euaggelistou);* and "The Revelation of the Apostle John, the Evangelist *(hē apokalypsis tou apostolou iōannou kai euaggelistou).* The work may have already been known by the title "Revelation of John" *(apokalypsis iōannou)* in the 2d century. The Muratorian Canon (ca. 200 C.E.) states, "We receive also the apocalyptic works, only [those] of John and Peter" *(scripta apocalypse[s] etiam johanis et petri tantum recipimus;* text cited by Charles *Revelation* ICC, 1: 5). In the 2d century, however, the work may simply have been known as "Revelation" *(apokalypsis;* Swete 1909: 1).

It is likely that the work at first had no separate title and that the opening words aroused the appropriate expectations in the audience by designating the nature of its content: "A revelation of Jesus Christ" *(apokalypsis Iēsou Christou).* The meaning is "a revelation given by Jesus Christ," as the following words show ("that God gave to him [Jesus Christ] to show to his servants"). This is the first time that the Greek word "revelation" *(apokalypsis)* was used to describe a written work or even an explicitly visionary experience (Smith 1983: 14, 18). When the book was copied onto scrolls, a brief title was added at the end of the work, probably "Revelation of John" *(apokalypsis Iōannou).* When the work began to be copied on booklike codices with pages, this title was placed at the beginning (Aune 1987a: 226). In the course of transmission, the older, brief title was expanded in various ways.

B. Place in the Canon

The book of Revelation eventually came to be the last book in the NT. It was in use in Asia and in the West in the 2d century (Swete 1909: cviii). According to Andreas, the archbishop of Caesarea in Cappadocia (who wrote a commentary on Revelation, either around 515 or 620 C.E.; Bousset *Die Offenbarung Johannis* MeyerK, 63, 65), Papias knew and commented on the book of Revelation (Swete 1909: cviii). Papias flourished in the first half of the 2d century. Irenaeus knew and used the work as a sacred text (*haer.* 5.30). Justin used the book to support the belief in the resurrection and the thousand years in a restored Jerusalem, citing it along with Isaiah and a gospel saying (*dial.* 81). The Letter of the Churches of Lyons and Vienne cites Rev 22:11 as Scripture (1.58). Although the events described occurred in 177, this portion of the work may have been added ca. 250 C.E. (Musurillo 1972: xxii and 80.12–14).

The first major figure to challenge the authoritative status of the book of Revelation was Marcion, presumably because of its strong ties to the Jewish Scriptures. Another challenge came from an extreme anti-Montanist group (the "Alogi"), apparently because it, along with the gospel of John, was a favorite text of the Montanists. Taking an anti-Montanist stand, Gaius of Rome (early 3d century), insinuated that the book was written by a certain Cerinthus, not by John the Apostle. This controversy did not seriously affect the acceptance and popularity of Revelation.

In the second half of the 3d century, however, the canonical status of the book was substantially threatened in the course of a conflict over the manner of fulfillment of the promises of the Scriptures. One group, reacting to the allegorical interpretation of Origen and his successors, insisted that the promises would be fulfilled in an earthly reign of Christ. This position was opposed by Dionysius, bishop of Alexandria and follower of Origen. He did not directly challenge the inspiration of the book or its claim to have been written by someone named John, but argued that the gospel attributed to John the apostle and the book of Revelation could not have been written by the same person (Eusebius *Hist. Eccl.* 7.24–25).

The result of Dionysius' work was that the canonical authority of Revelation was greatly weakened in the East. Eusebius did not argue in favor of the book's status as a genuine part of the NT. He simply reported that it was considered genuine by some and spurious by others. Cyril of Jerusalem (also 4th century) omitted Revelation from his list of books in the NT (*catech.* 4.36; cf. 15.13). The Council of Laodicea in Phrygia, held in the mid-4th century, also omitted Revelation from its list of the books of the NT (canon 60; the authenticity of this canon is disputed). Athanasius included Revelation in his list of the books of the NT (*ep. fest.* 39), and Gregory of Nazianzus cited it (*or.* 42.9). Gregory's cousin, Amphilochius of Iconium (ca. 380 C.E.), however, noted that, although some accept the Revelation of John, most call it spurious. The Apostolic Canons, composed in the East in Greek in the 4th century, also omit Revelation from the canon of the NT (canon 85). John Chrysostom, of Antioch and Constantinople (fl. 380), does not cite Revelation. Theodore and Theodoret, also of Antioch, do not cite it.

Athanasius' inclusion of Revelation in his list of books of the NT reestablished it as part of the canon recognized in Egypt (Cyril of Alexandria, for example, accepted it). In Asia Minor it was accepted not only by Gregory of Nazianzus but also by his fellow Cappadocians and contemporaries, Basil the Great and Gregory of Nyssa (so Bousset ibid., 30; but see Swete 1909: cxvi, and Kümmel 1975: 498–99). Epiphanius of Salamis on Cyprus, also of the 4th century, accepted Revelation as canonical.

The book of Revelation was definitively rejected by the Eastern Syrian Church. It was not included in the early Syriac translation of the NT, the Peshitta (Swete 1909: cxvi; Bousset, 26). Ephraem (4th century), Junilius (6th century), and the Nestorians all ignore the book. The Western Syrian Monophysites, however, authorized a new Syriac translation of the NT. It was authorized in 508 by Philoxenus and thus has been known as the Philoxenian version. It was revised in 616 by Thomas of Harkel (Heraclea). The Philoxenian version apparently survives only in the revised form and is now called the Harklean version. This version included Revelation. John of Damascus (fl. early 8th century), who wrote in Greek and admired the Cappadocian fathers, accepted Revelation as Scripture (Bousset, 30). The Peshitta is preserved and revered by the modern Syriac Church in a form lacking the book of Revelation. This version is used by both the Monophysites and the Nestorians (Aland and Aland 1987: 190–93). The older Armenian version, dependent on the Peshitta, lacked Revelation (Bousset, 30). The later Armenian version, dependent on Greek mss, includes Revelation (Aland and Aland 1987: 201).

In spite of the criticisms of Gaius and Dionysius, the support for Revelation in the West never flagged. The oldest complete commentary on Revelation was written in Latin by Victorinus of Pettau (d. ca. 304). Eventually the work was accepted as canonical in the East, but it was a slow process. The Trullan Synod (or Quinisextine [Fifth-Sixth] Council) held by Eastern bishops in 692 affirmed the Laodicean canon that omits Revelation, but they also drew up a list including it (Swete 1909: cxviii; Kümmel 1975: 499). The Byzantine list of canonical scriptures called the Stichometry of Nicephorus (ca. 810 C.E.) omits Revelation. The oldest surviving commentary in Greek was written either by Oecumenius or Andreas (see above). The archbishop of Caesarea in Cappadocia, Arethas, wrote the third surviving Greek commentary ca. 900 C.E. These commentaries apparently won greater recognition for Revelation in the East. In the 10th and 11th centuries Revelation began to be included once again in Greek mss of the NT (Kümmel 1975: 499).

C. Summary of Contents

Revelation opens with a prologue in the third person (1:1–3). It refers to the book as a revelation *(apokalypsis)* that was given through God's angel (or messenger; *angelos*) to his servant *(doulos)* John (v 1). The (content of the) book is also called "the word of God and the testimony of Jesus Christ" (v 2). It is also called "words of prophecy" *(tous logous tēs prophēteias)*, and a blessing is pronounced on the one who reads it (aloud in a communal setting) and on those who keep the things written in it (v 3). The prologue ends with the pronouncement, "for the time is near" *(ho gar kairos engus)*.

The rest of the book (1:4–22:21) has the framework of an ancient letter. This part of the work is in the first person, except for occasional speeches, that seem to be reports of auditions but are unattributed (e.g., 22:12–13). Following the prologue is an epistolary prescript (1:4–7), consisting of a salutation, greeting, and doxology. The salutation is from "John" to "the seven congregations *(ekklēsiais)* that are in Asia" (v 4a). The greeting is a wish for grace and peace upon the addressees from God and Christ (vv 4b–5a). The doxology is addressed to Christ (vv 5b–6). Corresponding to the prescript is an epistolary concluding blessing (22:21). It requests that the grace of Christ be with all the addressees. Attached to the epistolary prescript are two prophetic sayings (1:7 and 8).

The body of this unusual letter (1:9–22:5) consists of the report of a single, but highly segmented, visionary experience. Following this account is a kind of epilogue (22:6–20). The epilogue corresponds formally to the two prophetic sayings placed after the prescript and before the report proper. In part it continues the report ("And he said to me," 22:6). In part it reprises the prologue. The reference to the sending of God's angel or messenger *(angelos)* to show his servants what must happen soon (22:6) recalls the similar statement in 1:1. The blessing on the one who keeps the words of the prophecy of this book (22:7) recalls 1:3. The narrator's allusion to himself as "John" in 22:8 recalls the prescript (1:4) and the opening of the report (1:9). What he goes on to say in 22:8–9 recalls an incident in the report (19:10). There are other connections between 22:6–9 and 19:9–10. The rest of the epilogue contains various prophetic sayings with links to other parts of the work.

The report of the visionary experience is segmented into two formally different parts. The first is an epiphany of the risen Christ in the form of one like a son of man (1:9–3:22). This visionary experience takes place on earth. The manlike figure commands John to record his visionary experience in a book and to send it to the seven congregations. The focus of this first formally distinct part is a series of prophetic messages to the seven congregations that Christ dictates to John (2:1–3:22). The second main part (4:1–22:5) begins like a heavenly journey or ascent (4:1–2). But this formal introduction is not carried through with remarks about John's journeying from place to place in the heavenly world. Such remarks are typical of the widespread literary form of the heavenly journey. At times John seems to be in heaven. For example, he speaks with one of the twenty-four elders (5:5; 7:13–17). At other times, his vantage point seems to be on earth. For example, the mighty angel of chap. 10 seems to come down to John from heaven. John takes the little scroll from the angel while the angel has one foot on the land and one on the sea. The seer's position and vantage point also seem to be earthly in chap. 12. The implication is the same in 18:1, 19:11, and 20:1. The opening of chap. 4 seems deliberately to evoke the tradition of heavenly ascents, but the author did not seem concerned to make such a journey a structuring principle of the work.

The visionary experience recorded in 4:1–22:5 is itself highly segmented. The plan of this portion of the work will be discussed in the next section. It contains a vision of the heavenly court (chaps. 4–5) that introduces several series of symbolic visions.

D. Plan of the Book

A fundamental issue in discerning the plan of the book of Revelation is how to explain the numerous parallel passages and repetitions within it. The book itself suggests that the number seven is an ordering principle by presenting seven messages, seven seals, seven trumpets, and seven bowls. The parallels between the trumpets and bowls are especially close and seem repetitious. Some commentators have explained the repetition as the result of the use of sources. Others have seen the repetition as part of the author's literary design. The literary design has been seen as describing a linear sequence of events within history, including the past, present, and future. Another theory is that the same historical and eschatological events are described several times from different points of view.

1. The Recapitulation Theory. The theory that the book of Revelation describes the same events several times from different points of view is an old and venerable interpretive strategy. This position was taken by Victorinus of Pettau, the author of the oldest surviving commentary (d. ca. 304). He stated that both the trumpets and the bowls predict the eschatological punishment of unbelievers (Haussleiter 1916: 84, line 14–86, line 7). This approach was adopted by Tyconius in his lost, but heavily cited, commentary and by Augustine. It dominated the interpretation of the book for centuries.

2. The Source-Critical Theory. The recapitulation theory endured as the primary solution to the problem of the structure of the work until the fruitfulness of source-critical studies of the Pentateuch and Synoptic Gospels led some critics to apply the method to Revelation. The first such analysis was Daniel Völter's study that appeared in 1882 (Bousset, 128–30). The extreme form of this approach is the theory that the author of Revelation was primarily an editor who simply compiled and superficially edited a number of written sources. Friedrich Spitta's study is an example of this extreme source-critical analysis (Bousset, 135–36). He argued that the seals, trumpets, and bowls each reflect a source based on a sevenfold series.

In the 20th century, the source-critical approach has been adopted by M. E. Boismard, J. M. Ford, and U. B. Müller. Boismard used the repetitions in the work to distinguish two sources, one written under Nero and the other somewhat later (Boismard 1949). Müller used differences in messianic ideas to distinguish sources in Revelation from the minimal editorial work of the author. He found Jewish sources in chaps. 12, 14, 19, and 20, that depicted a national Messiah or Son of Man who would judge or do battle against the powers of the world. To the editor he ascribed the passages expressing a messianism focusing on the redemptive Lamb (Müller 1972). Ford hypothesized that chaps. 4–11 constitute a source consisting of the prophecies of John the Baptist and chaps. 12–22 represent another, later source originating from the disciples of the Baptist. Chaps. 1–3 and several verses in chap. 22 were added by a Jewish Christian. The phrases that mention Jesus throughout the work are taken as interpolations (Ford *Revelation* AB).

3. Literary Unity and a Linear Design. The source-critical studies of the 19th century definitively established that the author of Revelation did use sources. But the discernible sources are few and of limited scope. The theories that argued for extensive sources and reconstructed them were heavily criticized because of the overall unity of style in the book (Bousset, 126; Charles *Revelation* ICC, 1: lxxxviii–lxxxix). Most exegetes following Bousset have taken the position that the repetitions and parallel passages in Revelation are due to the literary design of the author. The recapitulation theory was not revived immediately, however, because it had been used in the attempt to demonstrate that the book prophesied history from the time of its composition to the time of the interpreter (see below). R. H. Charles argued that the literary design of Revelation describes a linear sequence of events (Charles, 1: xxii–xxiii). In this sequence, most of the events are in strict chronological order. There are significant exceptions, however. Chap. 12 does not continue the prophecies of the future associated with the seven trumpets but reverts to the past in order to prepare for the events related in chap. 13. Three "proleptic" visions interrupt the orderly unfolding of events to encourage the audience by reference to the more distant future (7:9–17; 10:1–11:13; chap. 14). The adequacy of this theory was called into question, not only by the need to posit these significant exceptions, but also by the related thesis that the text had been disordered by the activity of an editor after the work left the hand of the author (Charles, 1: xxii–xxiii; l–lv; lix).

4. The Revival of the Recapitulation Theory. As Bousset had already indicated, interpretation of the book of Revelation cannot do entirely without the recapitulation theory (121). The failure of the attempt to interpret the literary design of the work as a linear sequence of events led to the scholarly attempt to retrieve the recapitulation theory for historical-critical interpretation. The first such attempt was that of Günther Bornkamm. His starting point was to ask what portion of the book reveals the contents of the scroll with the seven seals that is introduced in chap. 5. He argued that chaps. 6:1–8:1 could not be an account of the revelation of its contents, since the scroll could not be read until the seventh seal was opened (8:1). He also rejected the theory that chaps. 6:1–11:19 reveal the contents of the scroll. His reasoning was that the unfolding of events connected with the seven trumpets does not exhaust the revelation of the scroll, because of the close parallel structure between 8:2–14:20 and 15:1–19:21. According to his interpretation, the former passage describes the same series of events as the latter, but in a mysterious, fragmentary, and proleptic manner. Because of the relationship between these two passages, he concluded that the revelation of the scroll with seven seals continues from 8:2 to 22:6 (Bornkamm 1937). For a retrieval of the recapitulation theory that leads to a different understanding of the plan of Revelation, see Yarbro Collins 1976: 32–44.

5. Structural and Thematic Theories. E. Schüssler Fiorenza discerned a pattern of inclusion or symmetry in the book of Revelation. The first (A 1:1–8) and the last (A′ 22:10–21) units are related to one another as promise and fulfillment. The second (B 1:9–3:22) and sixth (B′ 19:11–22:9) units correspond because they each have an "inaugural" vision of Christ (1:12–20 and 19:11–16). The third (C 4:1–9:21; 11:15–19) and the fifth (C′ 15:1, 5–19:10) units are related to each other because both evolve out of the scroll with seven seals. The fourth unit (D 10:1–15:4) is the center and climax of the book (Schüssler Fiorenza 1985: 170–75).

C. H. Giblin, building on the work of U. Vanni, argued that the thematic correlations of divine judgment and divine testimony in chaps. 16–22 are articulated in a literary structure of correlated narratives and correlated disclosures (Giblin 1974). The correlated narratives are the seventh bowl (16:17–21) and the elimination of all eschatological adversaries (19:11–21:8). The first describes the negative aspect of divine judgment, i.e., wrath against Babylon. The second is the fulfilled aspect of divine judgment that entails a new creation. The correlated angelic disclosures are the explanation of Babylon (17:1–19:10) and the discourse on the New Jerusalem (21:9–22:6, perhaps extending even further toward the end of the book).

6. A Text-linguistic Approach. David Hellholm has applied methods of text linguistics current in Germany to the structure of the book of Revelation (1986). The analysis has two complementary aspects. The first is the determination of the hierarchy of levels of communication. These levels are of two types, those external to the text and those internal to the text. The external type is between the author and the audience or between a character within the text and the audience. The internal type is between characters in the text. The other aspect is the division of the text into hierarchical text sequences. A shift from one text sequence to another is marked by a change in "world," by indications of or changes in time, by indications of or changes in place, changes in the grouping of characters, reintroduction of a character, or by the use of adverbs or conjunctions.

In the book of Revelation, Hellholm discerned six levels of communication. The lowest level is that between the author and the general Christian audience (Rev 1:1–3 and 22:18–19). The second level is between the author and the more specific group of seven congregations. The third is between otherworldly mediators and the author (e.g., the risen Christ in chaps. 1–3). The fourth is between the "heavenly scroll" and the author (6:1–22:5). The fifth is between the otherworldly mediators and the author within the heavenly scroll. The highest level is communication between God and the author within the heavenly scroll, including the command to write (21:5–8; Hellholm 1986: 43–44). This "highest" level of communication may also be referred to, in text-linguistic terms, as the level of most profound embedment.

Hellholm's preliminary delimitation of the hierarchically ranked text sequences in Revelation indicates that the title (*apokalypsis Iōannou*) is the lowest-ranked text sequence (the double nil grade). The prologue (1:1–3) is the next lowest (the nil grade). On the first grade, he places the epistolary prescript (1:4–8), the visionary part (1:9–22:5), the epilogue (22:6–20), and the epistolary postscript (22:21). The following passages are placed on the second grade: the address (1:4b–5b), the doxology (1:5c–6), motto in the form of a prophetic saying (1:7), God's self-predication (1:8), the revelation without an otherworldly journey (1:9–3:22), revelation with an otherworldly journey (4:1–22:5), attestation of the book (22:6–7) including Christ's statement of the book's motto ("Behold, I am coming soon" in v 7a), verification of the seer (22:8–9), paraenesis (22:10–15), Christ's statement of the revelatory transmission (22:16), prophetic saying (22:17), Christ's canonization formula (22:18–19), Christ's final citation of the motto and a prophetic cultic response (22:20). There are nine grades altogether.

The most striking result of this analysis is that the level of communication most profoundly embedded (the speech of God in 21:5–8) also occurs on the highest grade of the hierarchy of text sequences. According to Hellholm, the reason for this hierarchic embedment is the authorization of the message (1986: 45).

7. Outline. The first key to the plan of the visions of the book of Revelation is the fact that they are, to a great extent, organized in series of seven (Yarbro Collins 1976: 13–16). The second major principle of composition is the technique of interlocking. For example, the seven messages (2:1–3:22) have a dual function in the first major section of the work (chaps. 1–3). On the one hand, they are the logical continuation of the epistolary introduction (1:4–6). They fulfill the literary expectations aroused by the prescript. On the other hand, the messages are part of the account of the epiphanic vision of Christ that begins in 1:9. The seven messages thus contain the personal addresses and remarks that the epistolary prescript leads the audience to expect. At the same time, they are part of a visionary account.

The device of interlocking is used again in the transition from the seven seals to the seven trumpets, this time doubly so. The fact that the appearance of seven angels with seven trumpets is one of the effects of the unsealing of the seventh seal interlocks the entire series of the trumpets with that of the seals. The vision of the angel with the golden censer (8:3–5) also interlocks the seals and the trumpets. It alludes back to the fifth seal ("the altar" is mentioned both in 6:9 and in 8:3) and repeats its action (the praying of the saints) under a different image. At the same time, it foreshadows the trumpets in that the casting of fire on the earth prefigures the catastrophes associated with the trumpets.

The trumpets are not linked to what follows in as clear and firm a manner as the trumpets themselves are linked to the seals. The following series of visions is foreshadowed, however, by the abrupt introduction of the beast from the abyss in 11:7. The audience is not informed about the nature of this beast until chap. 13. Although there is foreshadowing, the compositional techniques seem to indicate a division between 11:19 and 12:1. The unnumbered series of visions beginning in 12:1, however, is again firmly interlocked with what follows, the series of the seven bowls. The last vision of the unnumbered series, the portrayal of the faithful in heaven (15:2–4), is inserted within the introduction to the seven bowls (15:1, 5–8).

The series of the seven bowls (chap. 16) is interlocked with the unnumbered series of visions that closes the visionary report (19:11–21:8) by the parallelism between the explanatory revelations that follow each of these series. The seventh bowl is directly followed by a brief report of the fall of Babylon (16:19). The nature of Babylon and its fall is elucidated in the following vision interpreted by one of the seven angels who had the bowls (chap. 17). The revelations of 18:1–19:10 elaborate on this theme. Similarly, the last vision (21:1–8) of the series that begins in 19:11 includes a brief mention of the new Jerusalem (21:2). The nature of the holy city is then elucidated in a visionary tour of the city led by one of the angels who had the seven bowls (21:9–22:5). The introductions to the two explanatory visions are virtually identical *(mutatis mutandis).* The visions are also linked by antithetical parallelism. Both involve symbolic women, but one is a harlot clothed in scarlet and the other is the pure bride of the Lamb (cf. 21:9 with 19:8).

A final structuring device to be mentioned is the use of two scrolls. The scroll with the seven seals (5:1) characterizes the first half of the book (chaps. 1–11) as mysterious and veiled. A second scroll is introduced in chap. 10 in a way that suggests that it is parallel to the scroll of chap. 5. The angel who appears to the seer in chap. 10 is coordinated with the angel in chap. 5 who asks, "Who is worthy to open the scroll and to break its seals?" (5:2). The latter is called "a mighty angel" *(aggelon ischyron).* The angel of chap. 10 is introduced as "another mighty angel" (*allon aggelon ischyron;* 10:1). A further indication that chap. 10 is meant to be parallel to chap. 5 is the fact that both visions involve a heavenly writing. In both cases the scroll is at first in the hand of a heavenly being. In 5:1 the scroll is in the hand of the deity. In 10:2, 8 the scroll is in the hand of the angel. There also seems to be a deliberate contrast made between the "sealed scroll" *(biblion . . . katesphragismenon)* of 5:1 and the "opened scroll" *(biblion to ēneōgmenon)* of 10:8. The scroll is removed from the hand of the heavenly being in similar ways. In chap. 5 the action of the Lamb is described: "And he went and took [the scroll] from the right hand of him who was sitting on the throne. And when he had taken the scroll . . ." (5:7–8). In chap. 10 the description of the action of the seer is similar: "And I went to the angel. . . . And I took the little scroll from the hand of the angel . . . and when I had eaten it . . ." (10:9–10).

The open scroll of chap. 10 foreshadows the second half of the work and characterizes it as less enigmatic than the first. The fact that it foreshadows 12:1–22:5 is clear in the commission given the seer by the angel, "You must again prophesy about many peoples and nations and tongues and kings" (10:11). The allusion to many kings does not fit what immediately follows (11:1–13), but does describe the content of chaps. 13 and 17. Chaps. 10 and 11:1–13 are accounts of visions that have been inserted between the sixth and the seventh trumpets. Chap. 10 foreshadows 12:1–22:5 by introducing a new heavenly book to characterize that unit and by the command to prophesy about many kings. Chap. 11:1–13 foreshadows 12:1–22:5 by abruptly introducing the character of "the beast from the abyss" who plays a prominent role in chaps. 13, 17, and 19.

The hypothesis that the open scroll characterizes the series of visions beginning in 12:1 is supported by the parallel commissions that John receives from Christ in chap. 1 and from the mighty angel in chap. 10. In the epiphany of Christ in chap. 1, John is told to write what he sees in a scroll and to send it to the seven congregations (1:11). The commission is resumed in 1:19 when he is told to write "what he saw and what is and what is about to take place hereafter." The last clause of this commission is repeated in 4:1. The seer is shown an open door in heaven and he hears the same voice that he heard in the first vision, saying, "Come up here, and I will show you what must take place hereafter." The resumption of the commission of 1:19 in 4:1 shows that the seer was ordered to communicate not just the seven messages but the vision that begins in 4:1 as well. In the vision of the mighty angel in chap. 10, the seer is commissioned a second time. In vv 8–9 he is told to take the little scroll from the mighty angel and to eat it. His compliance is described in v 10. The eating of the scroll here is a symbolic action that expresses in a concrete way the idea that the message communicated by the prophet does not originate with himself but has a divine origin. A similar symbolic action is related in Ezek 2:8–3:3. The commission to prophesy follows the symbolic action in Ezek 3:4–11. So also in Rev 10:11, a command to prophesy follows the eating of the scroll. The image whereby the angel gives the seer a scroll to eat implies that the angel conveys to the seer the message he is to communicate. The wording of the commission in v 11 indicates that the message is embodied in 12:1–22:5. Chaps. 1 and 10 are thus parallel because they each describe the appearance of a revealing figure who commissions the seer to communicate what is about to be revealed to him. They each involve the idea of the reception of revelation in written form. The wording of the commission in 10:11 implies that the first commission is about to be fulfilled and that a new one is being issued: "You must *again* prophesy about many peoples and nations and tongues and kings."

The overall plan of the book of Revelation indicated by the discussion above is as follows:

- Prologue 1:1–3
  - Epistolary prescript 1:4–6
  - Prophetic sayings 1:7–8
    - Visionary report 1:9–22:5
      - Epiphany of the risen Christ 1:9–3:22
        - The seven messages 2:1–3:22
      - Visions in the spirit 4:1–22:5
        - The scroll with seven seals 6:1–11:19
          - The seven trumpets 8:2–11:19
        - The open scroll 12:1–22:5 (cf. 10:1–11)
          - The seven bowls 15:1–16:20
            - Vision of Babylon 17:1–19:10
          - The last things 19:11–21:8
            - Vision of Jerusalem 21:9–22:5
  - Prophetic sayings 22:6–20
  - Epistolary concluding blessing 22:21

E. Text

The textual history of the book of Revelation differs significantly from that of the rest of the NT. The reason for this difference is the fact that the canonicity of the book was contested in the East (see above). In the 26th edition of *Novum Testamentum Graece,* edited by Kurt Aland et al., and referred to as the Nestle-Aland text, certain "constant witnesses" are cited for each canonical book. These are the mss whose importance is so great that their readings are collated for every variant. The most significant are cited explicitly for every variant when they are extant for a passage. Others are cited explicitly only when they differ from the reading of the majority. Because of its differing textual history, the "constant witnesses" for Revelation are different from those of the other books. All available papyri are included among the "constant witnesses" for all books of the NT. In Revelation, not only are all extant papyri included, but also all surviving uncials. In the cases of other books, so many uncials containing those works are available that only a selection can and need be cited. In the case of Revelation, they are so few that all may be cited. Some minuscule mss are also included among the "constant witnesses" for Revelation.

The "constant witnesses" for Revelation in Nestle-Aland^{26} include the following papyri: p^{18} (3d–4th century), p^{24} (4th century), p^{43} (6th–7th century), p^{47} (3d century), and p^{85} (4th–5th century). Since all of these mss are fragments, each represents only a small portion of the work. The following are the uncials: Codex Sinaiticus (4th century), Codex Alexandrinus (5th century), Codex Ephraemi Syri Rescriptus (5th century), 025 (9th century), 046 (10th century), 051 (10th century), 052 (10th century), 0163 (5th century), 0169 (4th century), 0207 (4th century), and 0229 (8th century). Of these only Codex Sinaiticus, Codex Alexandrinus, and 046 are complete. Codex 025 is nearly complete. It is lacking portions of chaps. 16, 17, 19, 20, and 22. Codexes 052, 0163, 0169, 0207, and 0229 are fragments. The minuscules are 1006 (11th century), 1611 (12th century), 1841 (9th–10th century), 1854 (11th century), 2030 (12th century), 2050 (copied in 1107 C.E.), 2053 (13th century), 2062 (13th century), 2329 (10th century), 2344 (11th century), 2351 (10th–11th century), and 2377 (14th century). Several of these mss are lacking large portions of the work.

The earliest witnesses are p^{47} and Codex Sinaiticus, but they are inferior attestations to the text of Revelation in comparison with Codex Alexandrinus and Codex Ephraemi. The latter codexes are of secondary value for other books of the NT but are very valuable for Revelation. Another unusual aspect of the textual history of Revelation is that the majority text-type falls into two groups. Group A consists of a large number of mss that agree with the text of the commentary by Andreas of Caesarea. Group K is constituted by a comparably large number of mss that are of the strictly Koine type. Codex 025 agrees with Group A; Codex 046 with Group K. The minuscules 2053, 2062, and 2344 are related to Codex Alexandrinus and Codex Ephraemi.

There are no ms lectionaries attesting to the text of Revelation, since it was not included in the Greek lectionary system. The Ethiopic version of Revelation is dependent on the text-type represented by Alexandrinus and

Ephraemi, with subsequent influence of the Coptic and Arabic versions. Unlike other parts of the NT, the book of Revelation was not translated into Old Church Slavonic until the 12th century (Aland and Aland 1987: 160, 205, 208). For more information on the textual transmission of the book of Revelation, see the detailed study of Josef Schmid (1955–56). See also TEXTUAL CRITICISM (NT).

F. Authorship

Only the general geographical region in which Revelation was composed is a matter of consensus. The date and the identity of the author have been matters of dispute.

1. Date. The earliest external evidence for the date of the book of Revelation is the statement of Irenaeus that it was seen at the end of the reign of Domitian (*haer.* 5.30.3). Domitian was emperor from 81 to 96, so this witness implies a date ca. 95–96. The wording leaves open the possibility that the work was written somewhat later than the occasion of the visionary experience on which it was based. It is questionable, however, that Irenaeus made such a distinction. Victorinus of Pettau states that John was banished *(damnatus)* by Domitian to a mine or quarry *(metallum)* on the island of Patmos, where he saw the revelation (*in Apoc.* 10:11). In another passage, he explicitly says that the work was written during the time of Domitian (*in Apoc.* 17:10). Eusebius cites Irenaeus and follows him on the date of Revelation. Jerome states that John was banished *(relegatus)* by Domitian to the island of Patmos, where he wrote Revelation (*De Vir. Ill.* 9).

Epiphanius (4th century) states that John prophesied and was on the island of Patmos during the reign of Claudius (41–54 C.E.; *Adv. Haeres.* 51.12,33; Charles, 1. xcii). The source of Epiphanius' opinion is unknown. But, as a date for the work as it now stands, the reign of Claudius is excluded by the internal evidence (see below). The title prefixed to both of the Syriac versions and the 11th-century archbishop of Bulgaria, Theophylact *(praef. in ioann)*, attest to a date under Nero (54–68 C.E.). This dating is probably an erroneous inference from the internal evidence. There are allusions to Nero in the book, but that does not mean that it was written during his reign. In another work, Theophylact implies that Revelation was written under Trajan (98–117 C.E.; *com. in Matt.* 20:22). The dating to the time of Trajan may be an inference from Irenaeus' remark that John lived in Ephesus until the time of Trajan (*haer.* 2.22.5).

The most significant internal evidence for the date of Revelation is to be found in its references to the destruction of a city called Babylon (14.8; 16:19; 17:5; 18:2, 10, 21). It is highly unlikely that the author of Revelation would have been interested in the conquest of the historical Babylon by the Persians in the 6th century B.C.E. or in the occasions on which it was sacked during the period of the wars among the successors of Alexander. It is even less likely that the author hoped for the destruction of a fortified town called Babylon at the head of the delta of Egypt that was the headquarters of a Roman legion during the early empire. The text itself makes clear that the name is not to be taken as a literal denotation. In chap. 17 this city is revealed to John in a vision as a woman. The name "Babylon" is written on her forehead and the audience is told that this name is a mystery (*mystērion;* 17:5). Later the angel who has shown John this vision offers to explain the "mystery" of the woman (v 7). The explanation that follows makes clear that the woman represents the city of Rome. The seven heads of the beast on which she sits are explained as seven hills (*orē;* v 9). Rome as "the city of the seven hills" was a common expression in classical writings. Further, the woman is interpreted as "the great city that holds rule *(basileia)* over the kings of the earth" (v 18). The politically dominant city in the Mediterranean world in John's time was of course Rome.

It is important to note that "Babylon" was not the only symbolic name a Christian of this time familiar with Jewish tradition might choose to designate the city of Rome. "Egypt," "Kittim," and "Edom" appear along with "Babylon" in Jewish sources as symbolic names for Rome. "Kittim" is the most common name in the Qumran literature. "Edom" is the most common in the rabbinic literature (Hunzinger 1965). Most of the occurrences of "Babylon" as a symbolic name for Rome in Jewish literature occur in works with a strong interest in eschatology: the apocalypse of Ezra (*4 Ezra* = 2 Esdras 3–14), the Syriac apocalypse of Baruch *(2 Bar.)* and the fifth book of the *Sibylline Oracles.* In each occurrence, the context makes clear the reason for the choice of this particular symbolic name: Rome's forces, like those of Babylon of an earlier time, have destroyed Jerusalem and the temple (*4 Ezra* 3:1–2, 28–31; *2 Bar.* 10:1–3; 11:1; 67:7; *Sib. Or.* 5:143, 159). Thus, the author of Revelation uses the name "Babylon" for Rome, not only to symbolize the great power, wealth, arrogance, or decadence of the city, but to allude to the events of 70 C.E. The use of this symbolic name is thus an important indication of the date of Revelation. It implies that the work was written after the destruction of the temple by Titus, that is, after 70 C.E.

A passage that seems to offer important internal evidence for the date of Revelation is 17:9–10. Besides the interpretation of the seven heads of the beast upon which the woman rides as seven hills, another interpretation is offered. They are also seven kings *(basileis).* The text then hints at who the seven kings are and at the apparent time of writing: "five have fallen, one is, the other has not yet come, but when he comes, he must remain a short time." The date known from external evidence may be used to solve this riddle, or this riddle may be used to determine the date. If we follow Irenaeus' dating and use it to solve the riddle, then the "one" who "is" must be Domitian. The five who have fallen would be the five emperors immediately preceding Domitian, namely, Galba, Otho, Vitellius, Vespasian, and Titus. The one who has not yet come must be Nerva, who indeed "remained," i.e., ruled, for only a short time (96–98 C.E.). This is the solution of Victorinus (*comm. in apoc.* 17:10). There are two problems with this solution. How did the author know that Nerva would remain a short time? Was this genuine prophecy? Or was it eschatological dogma that happened to be historically accurate? Or was Revelation actually written during the time of Trajan (98–117 C.E.), so that the author was giving the impression of having written during Domitian's reign, but actually wrote under Trajan and thus knew that Nerva had ruled only a short time? Or one could argue that the vision occurred under Domitian but was written down or edited under Trajan. The second problem is that v 11 says that "the beast who was, and is not, is both (the) eighth (king) and one of the seven and he goes to perdition." Victorinus takes this eighth king to be Nero, as do most modern commentators. But if the seven are identified as above, Nero is not one of them. Victorinus "solves" this discrepancy by interpreting "the beast is of the seven" to mean "before those kings Nero reigned."

If one starts with the riddle, appropriate premises are that the kings are Roman rulers and that one should start counting from the beginning of the empire and count consecutively. Contemporary literature indicates that writers of this time, when counting Roman emperors, began with Julius Caesar (Suetonius, *The Twelve Caesars; Sib. Or.* 5:12–51; *4 Ezra* 11–12). Thus, the five who have fallen would be Julius, Augustus, Tiberius, Gaius Caligula, and Claudius. The "one" who "is" would be Nero and the one who has not yet come would be Galba. As we have seen, the work as a whole could not have been written before 70 C.E. A further problem is that "the beast," who is Nero or Nero redivivus, at the time of writing "is not," i.e., is dead.

The solution that best explains the evidence is that the first part of the riddle ("they are also seven kings; five have fallen, one is, the other has not yet come" and possibly also the part stating "and when he comes he must remain a short time") is an older tradition, incorporated and reinterpreted by the author of Revelation. The older tradition may have been formulated in the time of Nero. It is impossible to determine with certainty how the author of Revelation understood the five kings, but it is very likely that Nero was one of them. The second part of the riddle ("and the beast who was and is not, he also is [the] eighth and one of the seven and he goes to perdition") was composed by the author and alludes to the return of Nero as eschatological adversary.

Another passage that seems to provide reliable internal evidence for the date of Revelation is 11:1–2. As we have seen, this vision is part of an interlude in the seven trumpets. John is given a reed like a rod and told to "rise and measure the temple of God and the altar and those worshipping in it." He is told not to measure the courtyard outside the temple, "because it was given to the gentiles, and they will trample the holy city for forty-two months." This passage seems to imply that the earthly, historical temple was still standing at the time Revelation was written. Before source criticism was applied to Revelation, i.e., before 1882, this passage was used to date the entire work before 70 C.E. In the 20th century, J. A. T. Robinson revived the argument that Revelation as a whole was written before 70 (1976: 238–42). Robinson took Rev 11:1–13 as a unity and interpreted the measuring of the temple as a command that the temple be purified. He saw this command as part of the call to repentance issued by the two witnesses whose activity is described in 11:3–13. Robinson argued that vv 1–13 as a unit could not have been composed after 70, since only a tenth of Jerusalem falls after the ascension of the witnesses (v 13) and that destruction occurs because of an earthquake, not an enemy attack.

Contrary to Robinson's premise, 11:1–13 was probably not composed freely by the author of Revelation as a unit. The connection between vv 1–2 and 3–13 is loose and external. The only link is that both are set in Jerusalem. The same period of time is mentioned in different forms in each, but this repetition is an editorial seam. The first unit (vv 1–2) focuses on the temple. The second (vv 3–13) does not mention the temple at all. It is likely that two separate sources stand behind this section. Verses 1–2 seem to be based on a prophetic oracle that circulated in Jerusalem during the war against Rome, before the temple was destroyed. This oracle has been adapted by the author of Revelation in such a way that the earthly temple represents the heavenly temple that cannot be destroyed by Rome.

The most reliable external evidence of the date of Revelation is the testimony of Irenaeus. The clearest internal evidence indicates a date after 70 C.E. Since the internal evidence does not point to a precise date, it seems best to accept Irenaeus' statement and to date the book to ca. 95–96. For a more detailed discussion of the evidence and scholarship on the date, see Yarbro Collins 1984: 54–83.

2. Place. The consensus is that the book of Revelation was composed somewhere in the general region of the W coast of Asia Minor. Some assume that it was composed on the island of Patmos. Others think it more likely that it was written in Ephesus. The text itself says that the revelation contained in it was received on the island of Patmos (1:9). The work is addressed to the Christian congregations in seven cities of W Asia Minor, Ephesus, Smyrna, Pergamum, Thyatira, Sardis, Philadelphia, and Laodicea (1:4, 11). All seven of these cities belonged to the Roman province of Asia in the 1st century C.E.

The likelihood of the work being written on Patmos is linked to the question of why John went there. The text says that he was there "on account of the word of God and the testimony of Jesus" (1:9). A few commentators take this to mean that he went there to proclaim the gospel. This explanation is not impossible, but it is odd that an early Christian missionary would have chosen such a remote and sparsely populated place. The language of Revelation counts against this hypothesis. The Greek preposition translated "on account of" *(dia)* usually designates the cause of an effect in Revelation; it is never used elsewhere in the book to indicate the purpose or goal. Many commentators take seriously some aspects of comments by Victorinus and other early Christian writers and conclude that John was deported to Patmos by the Roman governor of Asia. (In addition to the ancient writers cited in the discussion of the date above, see Hippolytus, *antichr.* 36.) The odd thing about this hypothesis is that most condemned early Christians were executed, not deported. A further problem is that there is no evidence, besides Revelation, that Patmos was used as a place of deportation at this time. The general practice, however, is well attested in non-Christian sources and there is evidence that islands near Patmos were so used. For a more detailed discussion of John's sojourn on Patmos, see Yarbro Collins 1984: 102–4. If John had been sent to Patmos by the Roman governor and was confined there, the use of the letter form to circulate his account of the revelation he had received on the island would readily be intelligible. Confinement, however, is not the only likely explanation for the use of the written medium or the letter form. The classic prophetic oracles had been collected and written down. The written medium is self-consciously chosen and typical of apocalyptic texts in early Judaism. Note in this connection the command issued by the risen Christ to John to write down the revelation. The letter form had been established by Paul as a mode of communication by early Christian leaders.

3. Identity of the Author. The external evidence will be reviewed first. As noted above, the earliest writer known to have been familiar with the book of Revelation was Papias. In the early part of the 2d century, he was bishop of Hierapolis, a city not far from one of the cities to which Revelation was addressed, Laodicea. No clear statement from Papias, however, has been handed down concerning the identity of the author. Justin says that Revelation was written by "John, one of the apostles of Christ" (or "of the messiah"; *heis tōn apostolōn tou christou; dial.* 81). Irenaeus is the first writer to attribute the book of Revelation and the gospel of John to the same author (compare *haer.* 3.11.1 with 4.20.11). He calls this author "John, the disciple of the Lord." That his use of the term "disciple" *(mathētēs, discipulus)* does not exclude the idea that the author was an apostle is shown by his reference to this disciple and "the other apostles" in another passage (*haer.* 2.22.5). Just prior to the latter passage, Irenaeus states that this John was conversant with some elders in Ephesus and remained among them until the times of Trajan. Hippolytus identified John, the author of Revelation, with "blessed John, apostle and disciple of the Lord" (*antichr.* 36). Origen identified the author of Revelation with John, the son of Zebedee (*Jo.* 1.14). It is clear that he considers the author of the gospel of John and the author of Revelation to be the same person; he calls this person "apostle," "evangelist," and "prophet" (*Jo.* 2.4; see also a fragment from the fifth book of Origen's commentary on the gospel of John and its citation in Eusebius *Hist. Eccl.* 6.25). Dionysius of Alexandria, after Origen's death, argued that Revelation and the gospel of John could not have been written by the same person (see above).

Turning to the internal evidence, one notes that the author refers to himself as "John," but not in such a way as to point clearly to John the son of Zebedee or to the anonymous beloved disciple in the gospel of John. The name John (Gk *Iōannēs;* Heb *Yohanan*) was common among Jews from the Exile onward and among the early Christians (Swete 1909: clxxv). The author of Revelation never refers to himself as an apostle or disciple of the Lord. In the vision of the new Jerusalem, the twelve names of the twelve apostles of the Lamb are seen inscribed on the twelve foundations of the wall around the city (21:14). The implication is that the Church in the author's time prefigures the new Jerusalem or that it is the earthly counterpart of the heavenly Jerusalem. The interpretation of the foundations of the wall of the city as the twelve apostles is characteristic of a time in which the age of the apostles is past. It is unlikely that a living apostle would speak in such a way. Rev 21:14 has more in common with the post-Pauline Eph 2:20 than with Paul's own remarks in 1 Cor 3:10–15. The conclusion that best fits the evidence is that the author of Revelation is a man named John who is otherwise unknown to us (for a more detailed discussion, see Yarbro Collins 1984: 25–34).

The historical quest for the identity of the author of Revelation has yielded primarily negative results. A more fruitful line of research has been the attempt to discern the social identity of the author. Considerable research has been done on the relation of the author and his work to the phenomenon of early Christian prophecy (Nikolainen 1968; Hill 1971–72; Müller 1976; Schüssler Fiorenza 1985: 133–56; Aune 1981; Yarbro Collins 1984: 34–49). Most scholars who have written on early Christian prophecy have distinguished community, congregational, or church prophets from wandering prophets. The primary evidence for community prophets is 1 Corinthians 11 and 14. The primary evidence for wandering prophets is the *Didache.* The community prophets are thought of as permanent, settled members of a particular Christian congregation. Wandering prophets are generally defined as translocal leaders, who traveled from place to place, proclaiming their teaching or the revelations they had received. This is a useful distinction but should not be pressed too far, given the great mobility of persons, especially of the nonrural population, that characterized the early empire. At least two types of wandering or itinerant Christian prophets may be distinguished: (1) the prophet who traveled to a particular place to execute a divine commission (Agabus in Acts 11:27–30 and 21:10–14; Hermas in *The Shepherd of Hermas*); (2) prophets whose wandering was an enactment of the ascetic values of homelessness, lack of family ties, and the rejection of wealth and possessions (*Did.* 11–13; prophets of the community reflected in the Synoptic Sayings source [Q]; Peregrinus in Lucian's *The Passing of Peregrinus* [Aune 1981: 18–19, 29]).

John never actually referred to himself as a prophet in Revelation, but he implied that he was one by describing his work as a "prophecy" (*prophēteia;* 1:3; 22:7, 10, 18, 19). Some have argued that the prologue (1:1–3) and the "canonical formula" or curse (22:18–19) were added to the work after it left John's hands. Even if they were, 22:7 and 10 still stand to make this point. Further, John came very close to identifying himself as a prophet when he attributed the following words to the revealing angel, "I am your fellow servant, and the fellow servant of your brothers the prophets" (22:9).

Some have seen the reference to "your brothers the prophets" as evidence for a prophetic circle, school, or guild in one or more of the seven cities. This conclusion goes beyond the evidence. The reference to prophets here is very general, as elsewhere in Revelation, and does not necessarily imply a group of prophets gathered around John. The term "brothers" implies coreligionists, i.e., other Christian prophets (cf. 19:10). This is slim evidence, however, for the hypothesis of a prophetic school led by John.

John was probably not a settled community prophet. His acquaintance with the seven Christian communities in the Roman province of Asia suggests that he was a translocal leader. His rivals, the false apostles who visited Ephesus (2:2), "Jezebel," who evidently was recognized by some Christians as a prophet (2:20), and "Balaam" (2:14), appear to have been translocal leaders also. There is no evidence that John traveled to the seven cities because of a divine commission. Some argue that he went to Patmos by divine order to receive a revelation there, but this theory goes beyond the text. Of the types of known prophet, John fits best the type whose wandering expressed the values of homelessness and the rejection of wealth. The ascetic values associated with that type are expressed in the text of Revelation indirectly (Yarbro Collins 1984: 111–40).

John presented himself indirectly as a prophet. He does not seem to have made a sharp distinction between Israelite and Christian prophets (10:7; 11:3–13; 16:6; 22:6). His self-presentation and the account of the revelation he received are shaped by the records and traditions of the classical prophets of Israel. The evidence suggests that John was a wandering prophet who was familiar with all seven communities because he had visited and instructed each of them. If one of the cities was his primary residence or center of operations, we have no reliable way of determining which of them it was.

G. Literary Character

The terms in Greek meaning "to reveal" *(apokalyptein)* and "revelation" *(apokalypsis)* were probably in common use in the last two or three centuries B.C.E. to refer to the revealing of secrets (Smith 1983: 9–14). Human beings had long attempted to secure guidance from the divine world for personal and public affairs. Eventually, the terms came to be used of heavenly revelations that had to do with cosmic secrets, hidden realities in the present, and with the future. In Luke the verb "reveal" is used to describe the manifestation of the Son of Man to the world in the future (Luke 17:30). Analogously, Paul uses the noun for the manifestation of Christ at the time of his return at the end (1 Cor 1:7). The noun is also used by Paul for a revelatory religious experience (e.g., 2 Cor 12:1).

In Rev 1:1 the noun "revelation" *(apokalypsis)* probably refers collectively to the secrets that Christ has revealed to John (cf. 1 Cor 14:6). In other words, it refers to the content of the book with connotations of a particular kind of revelatory experience. The term in Rev 1:1 is not yet a literary designation or definition of genre, although its use here gave rise to that meaning and use. The situation regarding the opening of Revelation is analogous to the use of "good news" *(euaggelion)* in Mark 1:1. "Good news" in Mark 1:1 was apparently intended as a description of the content of the work: the events associated with Jesus. But the use of the term at the beginning of Mark contributed to the eventual use of "good news" or "gospel" as a literary term.

The 2d-century *Shepherd of Hermas* uses the verb "reveal" *(apokalyptō)* for a religious experience involving the granting of the ability to read a heavenly book (*Herm. Vis.* 2.2.1). The noun "revelation" *(apokalypsis)* is used to describe a vision in which a heavenly being reveals the meaning of another vision (*Herm. Vis.* 2.4.1). The work itself as a whole is not described as an apocalypse, either in the text or in the title, except that Codex Sinaiticus (4th century) gives "The Fifth Revelation" *(apokalypsis ē)* as the title of what is labeled as "The Fifth Vision" *(horasis ē)* in other mss. Like the risen Christ in Revelation, the heavenly shepherd who appears in this fifth vision commands the seer to write down what he is about to reveal to him (commands or mandates and parables or similitudes).

According to Eusebius, Clement of Alexandria considered a "revelation *(apocalypsis)* of Peter" to be canonical (*Hist. Eccl.* 6.14). The work is probably the apocryphal *Apocalypse of Peter,* preserved in fragments in Greek and entirely in Ethiopic. It contains a description of the places of punishment and a vision of paradise. It is probably the same work that is mentioned in the canonical list known as the Muratonian Canon (see above). Although it is not known how the work designated or described itself or whether it had a title, it is at least clear that the Christians who used it called it a "revelation" *(apokalypsis)*. This usage may have been inspired by the opening or title of the book of Revelation. It may, however, have been due in part to a growing interest in the Greco-Roman world in the phenomenon of revelation as a religious experience and a literary form.

Such a growing interest may be reflected in the shift in vocabulary from the Old Greek translation of Daniel to the later translation attributed to a certain Theodotion. In a number of passages the verb "reveal" *(apokalyptō)* is used in the latter, whereas different verbs are used in the former (cf. the two translations of Dan 2:19, 22, 28, 29, 30, 47; 10:1; 11:35). For apparently independent pagan use of the terminology in the 3d and 4th centuries, see Smith 1983: 18.

A Greek work attributed to Baruch *(3 Bar.)* has two superscriptions in the two surviving Greek mss. The first designates the work as "(the) narrative *(diēgēsis)* and revelation *(apokalypsis)* of Baruch." The second simply as "(the) revelation *(apokalypsis)* of Baruch." Although the work was apparently originally Jewish and composed ca. 200 C.E., it was transmitted and edited by Christians. Thus the superscriptions may well be due to Christian hands.

The codices found at Nag Hammadi in 1945 contain five works preserved in Coptic that are designated as "revelations" or apocalypses in their titles. One of these, the *Apocalypse of Adam* (NHC V,*5*), has no explicitly Christian characteristics. It contains no clear indications of date, but may be as early as the 1st or 2d century C.E. This work is a revelation given to Adam by three heavenly beings that he narrates to his son Seth. The other four works are clearly Christian. *The Apocalypse of Paul* (NHC V,*2*) is dated to the 2d century. It describes Paul's ascent to heaven and his journey from the third to the tenth heavens. Following the *Apocalypse of Paul* in Codex V are two works, both of which are entitled "The Apocalypse of James" (NHC V,*3, 4*). These works are also relatively early. *The (First) Apocalypse of James* describes the revelation received by James the Just from the risen Lord. *The (Second) Apocalypse of James* describes revelation given by Christ to James after the resurrection and also the death of James by stoning. *The (Coptic) Apocalypse of Peter* (NHC VII,*3*) was probably written in the 3d century. It is an account of a revelation seen by the apostle Peter that is explained by Jesus.

There are many later Christian works that are designated "revelations" in their titles (see Yarbro Collins 1979 and Himmelfarb 1983). This brief survey of the use of the verb "reveal" *(apokalyptō)* and the noun "revelation" *(apokalypsis)* shows how the literary character of the book of Revelation was perceived in antiquity.

In modern times, scholars have defined a genre "apocalypse," the starting point of which is the book of Revelation. The name of the genre comes from the title and opening word of the book. The scope of the genre likewise has been defined as those ancient works resembling Revelation. These writings include at least the following Jewish works: *1 Enoch,* Daniel, *4 Ezra, 2 Baruch,* the *Apocalypse of*

Abraham, 2 Enoch, and *3 Baruch.* The corpus of Christian apocalypses includes those discussed above as well as the *Ascension of Isaiah,* the (apocryphal Latin) *Apocalypse of Paul* and other, mostly later, works. A number of Greco-Roman, rabbinic, and Persian works resemble these in form and content (Attridge 1979; Saldarini 1979; Collins 1979).

There has been a great deal of debate on what the central characteristics of this genre are. Some scholars emphasize eschatological content and its relation to a social situation of crisis or revolution. Others argue that the term applies to any revelatory text. Others see certain themes as the key, such as theodicy or national restoration. Still others emphasize formal features like pseudonymity or symbolic visions. In the 1970s and 1980s, attempts have been made to define the genre in terms of form and content (Collins, ed. 1979) and in terms of form, content, and function (Yarbro Collins 1986). See also the proceedings of the international conference on apocalypticism held in Uppsala in 1979 (Hellholm 1983).

As noted above, besides its apocalyptic character, the book of Revelation also has affinities with prophecy (Aune 1983) and with early Christian letters.

Revelation has been compared to Greco-Roman drama (Bowman 1955a; 1955b). The most significant insight resulting from such a comparison is that the hymns and acclamations in the book function in a way similar to the choral odes in Greek tragedy.

H. Relation to Other Ancient Literature

A major breakthrough in the scholarly study of Revelation was the recognition of the source and character of its images and narrative patterns. These were not composed freely by the author to comment on the current situation; in other words, they are not primarily allegories invented to comment on current affairs. Further, these images and narrative patterns were not simply borrowed from the "Old Testament" and cannot be understood fully in terms of such borrowing. They can be understood appropriately and in depth only in the context of ANE and Greco-Roman myth. This insight was the contribution of the history-of-religions school to the study of Revelation (Gunkel 1895; Bousset). The approach was sometimes taken to an extreme, with the result that almost all historical allusions were denied (Lohmeyer *Die Offenbarung des Johannes* HNT). But, complemented by other methods, it has become an essential interpretive approach to the work (Charles *Revelation* ICC; Caird *Revelation* HNTC; see also Yarbro Collins 1976).

Gunkel showed that the portions of the Hebrew Bible on which Revelation was dependent ought to be understood in comparison with ancient Mesopotamian mythic literature. He also demonstrated that the mythic elements in Revelation were not fossils but expressions of a living mythic mentality. When examples of Northwest Semitic (Canaanite) mythic literature were discovered at Ugarit, later scholars showed that these provided a more immediate context for the Hebrew Bible (*CMHE*; Hanson 1973; 1975) and for Revelation (Yarbro Collins 1976). The clearest use of Greco-Roman mythic traditions is in the description of the woman clothed with the sun (related to traditions about Isis) and the narrative plot in which the woman about to bear a child is threatened by a serpentine monster (related to the story of Leto's threatened bearing of Apollo) in chap. 12 (Yarbro Collins 1976: 57–85). Other Greco-Roman traditions have influenced the image of Jesus as the morning star in 22:16 (Yarbro Collins 1977a: 379–80), the use of the four elements in chap. 16 (Betz 1966; Yarbro Collins 1977a: 367–79), and the attribution to Jesus of the keys of death and Hades in 1:18 (Aune 1987b: 484–89).

Since the book of Revelation is contemporary with, or perhaps somewhat earlier than, *4 Ezra* and *2 Baruch,* one cannot expect to find allusions to them in Revelation. They have much in common with Revelation in form and content (apocalyptic and eschatological motifs). With regard to canonical Jewish literature, it is well known that Revelation does not cite these older works but uses images and themes from them in a new literary creation. The books of Daniel (Beale 1984) and Ezekiel (Vanhoye 1962) are used extensively in this manner. The book of Revelation is not literarily dependent on any texts from Qumran. Its use of holy war imagery has some affinities with that of the War Scroll (Yarbro Collins 1977b). The description of the new Jerusalem in Revelation 21 is analogous to the description of the eschatological Jerusalem in the fragmentary new Jerusalem text from Qumran (cf. Ezekiel 40–48 and *4 Ezra* 9:26–10:59). The commentary by J. M. Ford (*Revelation* AB) suggests many parallels between Revelation and various documents from Qumran.

The anti-Roman attitude and the use of the motif of Nero's return are shared by Revelation with books 4 and 5 of the *Sibylline Oracles* (Collins 1983).

I. Theological Perspective and Social Setting

God is described near the opening of Revelation as he "who is and who was and who is to come" (1:4). This description is a concrete way of expressing what later theologians would call the eternity of God. The first prophetic saying of the book contains God's self-revelation as "The Alpha and the Omega" and the "Almighty" (1:8). The "Alpha/Omega" epithet expresses metaphorically not only God's eternity but also the notions that God is the source of all things and encompasses all things. The epithet "Almighty," of course, alludes to God's omnipotence. The vision of chap. 4, building on older visions, indirectly presents God as King, enthroned in heaven and surrounded by counselors (the twenty-four elders). The song of the four living creatures emphasizes God's holiness (4:8; cf. Isa 6:3). The song of the twenty-four elders emphasizes God's activity as Creator. In the final series of visions God appears as Judge (20:11–15) and as Creator of the new heaven and earth (21:1, 5). The deepest and most important aspect of the new age symbolized by the new Jerusalem is the dwelling of God with humanity (21:2–4, 6–8). At the beginning and end of the work, it is emphasized that God communicates with humanity through Christ, angels, and the prophets in general and through this book in particular (1:1–3; 22:6–7).

The christology of the book of Revelation is expressed in images, not in philosophical concepts. Like most of the other writings of the NT, Revelation's most basic affirmation is that Jesus is the Christ, i.e., the Messiah (1:1, 2, 5). Jesus is also called "the faithful witness" (1:5). This epithet has two levels of meaning. First, Jesus has communicated faithfully to John the revelation given to him by God (1:1–2; 22:16, 18). Second, Jesus' remembered behavior during his arrest, trial, and execution undoubtedly functioned as a model for the audience who were threatened by persecution (cf. 1:5 with 2:13; 6:9; 12:11; 20:4). Jesus' role in the present, from the point of view of the author, is that, as the firstborn of the dead, he rules the kings of the earth (1:5). The work of Jesus in the past is referred to in the doxology of 1:5b–6. He has freed those who believe in him from their sins by his blood. This affirmation is similar to the summary of the gospel in 1 Cor 15:3 and to Matthew's version of the words of Jesus spoken over the cup at the Last Supper (Matt 26:27–28). The work of Jesus is not yet complete. He is expected to appear in the future as judge or warrior (1:7; 19:11–21).

In the first vision recounted in the book, Christ appears to John as "one like a son of man" (1:13). In terms of form and content, Rev. 1:9–3:22 seems to have been modeled on Dan 10:2–12:4. Both passages describe the epiphany of a heavenly being to a human visionary. In both, the seer identifies himself by name and gives the time and place of the experience. In both texts, the visionary says that he looked and then gives a description of the heavenly being. Following the description, both passages relate that the seer is overwhelmed by the apparition and falls to the ground senseless. The heavenly being then comforts or strengthens the seer. After this exchange, the heavenly being conveys to the seer a long verbal revelation which is associated with a book. In Daniel this book is the heavenly book of truth (10:21); in Revelation it is the book which John is to write (1:11, 19). Significant similarities occur in the descriptions of the heavenly revealer figures. Both are girded with gold; both have eyes of fire; both have lower limbs that appear like metal. Both their faces shine like light.

These similarities suggest that the risen Christ is portrayed in Revelation 1 as an angelic figure. This hypothesis is supported by the angelic character of the "one like a son of man" in Daniel 7:13, to whom allusion is made in Rev 1:13. It is likely that the author of Revelation understood the human figure in Dan 7:13 as an angel. The revealing angel of Daniel 10 is also said to be in human form (v 5). If the author of Revelation identified the "one like a son of man" in Daniel 7 with the revealing angel of Daniel 10, this identification would explain why elements from Dan 7:13 and Dan 10:5–6 are conflated in the description of the heavenly being of Rev 1:12–16.

A striking characteristic of the description of Christ as son of man in Revelation 1 is that it also includes an attribute of the "one that was ancient of days" in Dan 7:9. Like the ancient of days, the son of man has hair like (white) wool (Rev 1:14). How one explains the juxtaposition of the attributes of these two figures has important implications for one's understanding of the christology of Revelation. One possibility is that the author of Revelation understood both the "one ancient of days" and the "one like a son of man" to be manifestations of God. There is evidence that some rabbis read the passage in this way (*Mek. R. Sim. b. Yohai* bashalah 15; see Segal 1977: 35). Such an understanding may imply a christology analogous to the prologue of the gospel of John. The preexistent Christ is a divine being alongside God and apparently equivalent to God in nature. The designation of Christ as "the beginning of God's creation" (Rev 3:14) suggests that the author of Revelation considered Christ to have been preexistent in relation to the human Jesus. Alternatively, the understanding may be that neither the "one ancient of days" nor the "one like a son of man" is identical with God. The transcendent God is beyond the senses and thus the only truly and fully divine being. All the manifestations of God described in the Jewish Bible are to be identified with an angelic being. For the author of Revelation, this being is Christ. The human Jesus could be identified with this high or principal angel in the same way that Enoch was identified with the preexistent Son of Man in the *Similitudes of Enoch.* Given the apparent description of God in Revelation 4 and of the Lamb in God's presence in chap. 5, the former possibility is more likely.

Another issue in the christology of Revelation is whether the image of Christ as Divine Warrior in chap. 19 is transformed by the image of the suffering Lamb in chap. 5 or whether, on the contrary, the image of the suffering Lamb is transformed by that of the Divine Warrior. The character of the book as a whole, as well as the context of the image of the Lamb in chap. 5, suggests that the latter is the case. The death of Christ is affirmed, as we have seen, as the event that freed believers from their sins (1:5b). In chap. 5, the image of the "lamb, standing as if slain" is immediately transformed by the description of the animal as having seven horns (v 6). As is well known, the horn is a biblical and postbiblical image of military might and the horned ram is an image for great military leaders and for a warrior-messiah in the *Dream Visions of Enoch* (*1 Enoch* 85–90). The impression that the older Christian image of the sacrificial Lamb is being reinterpreted in Revelation is supported by the introduction of the figure as the "Lion of the tribe of Judah" (5:5).

This militant christology must be seen in light of the social setting of the book. Several aspects of the work imply that the author perceived a social-theological crisis and was responding to it. One important aspect of this crisis was conflict with the Jews of the synagogues of the province of Asia. The message to Smyrna refers to the Jews of that city as "those who say that they are Jews and are not, but are a synagogue of Satan" (2:9). The context implies that Jewish hostility to local Christians has led the former to accuse the latter before the authorities. These accusations are expected to lead to arrest and interrogation (2:10). Since new religions were frowned upon and the Jewish way of life was approved, rejection by the synagogue meant legal insecurity for local Christians. Similar conflict is reflected in the message to the Philadelphians (3:9).

In the messages to Pergamum and Thyatira, the addressees are warned against eating meat sacrificed to idols and "playing the harlot" *(porneusai).* "Playing the harlot" may be interpreted as idolatry. The two warnings together may refer to social occasions on which food offered to the Greco-Roman gods was consumed and prayers offered to them. Alternatively, *porneusai* may refer to marriages forbidden by the Jewish law. The similarities between these warnings and the "apostolic decree" of Acts 15 support this possibility. In either case the underlying issue seems to be the relations of Christians with gentiles. According to the first interpretation of *porneusai,* the issue would be how much and what kind of socializing was possible. This issue was important for those with non-Christian gentile relatives and for those who belonged to non-Christian voluntary associations. If the second interpretation of *porneusai* is correct, the issue would involve not only socializing but the question whether newly converted Christians should divorce their non-Christian spouses (cf. 1 Cor 7:12–16).

Social tensions resulting from different degrees of wealth and different attitudes toward wealth are reflected in the book of Revelation. The Christians of Laodicea are criticized for relying on their wealth (3:17–18). The Roman Empire is criticized for being a source of wealth, most clearly in chap. 18. There is evidence of tension between rich and poor in Asia Minor at the time Revelation was written (Yarbro Collins 1984: 94–97).

In addition to the tensions between these social groups, Revelation reflects particular events that were traumatic for the author of Revelation and those who shared his point of view. The Jewish War with Rome and the destruction of the temple was a traumatic event, as the use of the name "Babylon" for Rome shows. That Nero's police action against Christians in Rome was perceived in a similar way is indicated by the use of Nero redivivus as the eschatological adversary. We may infer that the enthusiastic performance of the imperial cult in the province of Asia was deeply offensive from the antithetic parallel drawn between worship of God and worship of "the beast." Finally, the death of Antipas and the exile of John, the author of the book of Revelation, were events that emphasized the threatened situation of the Christian communities in the province.

The theology and christology of the book of Revelation are shaped by these elements of crisis and trauma. A new set of expectations had arisen as a result of faith in Jesus as the Messiah and belief that the kingdom of God had been established. If the risen Jesus was enthroned as the ruler of the kings of the earth, the followers of Jesus should share in that rule and glory. The events just described, however, frustrated those expectations. It was the tension between John's vision of the kingdom of God and his social situation that led him to write his apocalypse. The tension is overcome by a revelation of the true, though hidden, state of affairs. God and Jesus do reign in spite of appearances and the Roman Empire is a rule of chaos, not a golden age. It is also overcome by a revelation of the future. In the end, the unjust earthly powers will be judged and the faithful will be rewarded.

J. History and Methods of Interpretation

Dionysius, bishop of Alexandria in the 3d century, wrote that some had set the book of Revelation aside, pronouncing it senseless and without reason. He himself refused to set it aside, because many brothers and sisters valued it highly. But he felt that its subject exceeded his capacity, saying:

> For, though I do not understand, yet I suspect that some deeper sense is enveloped in the words, and these I do not measure and judge by my private reason; but allowing more to faith, I have regarded them as too lofty to be comprehended by me, and those things which I do not understand, I do not reject, but I wonder the more that I cannot comprehend (quoted by Eusebius *Hist. Eccl.* 7.25).

Few interpreters of Revelation have been so modest. Most have felt that they had the key that could unlock its mysteries. For some the key is divine inspiration, analogous to that received by John. For others it is a theory of interpretation or a scholarly method. Yet others believe that their social situation or life experience, which is like that of the original audience, alone makes a sympathetic reading possible (for example, only the oppressed can understand Revelation).

The first great controversy over the book of Revelation was how to interpret the visions involving the binding of Satan for a thousand years and the reigning of the participants in the first resurrection for a thousand years with Christ (20:1–6). Most Christian writers of the 2d century, like Justin Martyr and Irenaeus, read Revelation as prophetic history; that is, as prediction of events in the future. They thus expected an earthly reign of Christ to follow his second coming. Some writers pictured this millennium as a time of eating, drinking, marrying, and producing children. Such views were criticized as overly "sensual" by other Christian writers. By the end of the 2d century, an alternative reading developed, that is usually called "spiritual" or "allegorical." This new reading interpreted Revelation's images as referring to events within history; thus, it may be called an "immanent" reading, as opposed to the older "imminent" reading (McGinn 1987). According to this reading, the binding of Satan had taken place already as a result of Jesus' life and death. The thousand-year reign is the history of the Church.

Augustine of Hippo adopted the immanent or spiritual reading and his authority led to its dominance for seven hundred years. This reading did not eliminate the element of prophecy from Revelation entirely, but it discouraged seeing current events as signs of the end. Revelation was used primarily as a resource for moral teaching against vice and error in the Church.

Prophetic and apocalyptic experiences and concerns, however, never died out and became prominent again in the 12th century. Joachim of Fiore developed a new interpretation that he said was given to him by divine inspiration. Joachim was the first to read the book as a revelation of the entire world-historical process, past, present, and future. World history consisted of three states or ages: the first state was the time of the Law, whose author was God. The second state was the age of the Gospel, brought by the Son. The third state was to come in the near future. It would follow the defeat of the Antichrist and was to be the culmination of history that would involve the reformed and purified monastic Church. This was to be the age of freedom, granted by the Holy Spirit. Thus, the thousand years, although not taken literally, was once again interpreted as a prophecy of a future perfect age.

Martin Luther maintained the old interpretation of the millennium that understood it as the time of the Church within this world and history. But he suggested that other parts of Revelation correlated with events of world history and that some prophesied events of his own time. For example, he identified the papacy with the Antichrist.

The radical Puritan strain in England led to the modern revival of truly millenarian readings of Revelation. Such readings became popular in the 17th century. The expectation of a literal return of Christ to earth to bind Satan and to reign with the saints was revived by Puritan academics in the context of scholastic, if not scholarly, readings.

In the 18th century, the postmillennial view was introduced by Daniel Whitby and others. This position held that the binding of Satan referred to the turning point toward a more just and humane society, one about to occur in their own time. At the end of this new and better age, Christ would return. This perspective had an influence on the first great American commentator, Jonathan Edwards. The term "premillennial" is used to refer to the dogma that Christ will return to earth before the reign of a thousand years. The term "postmillennial" refers to the doctrine that Christ will return after the thousand years. The term "amillennial" is used to refer to those theological traditions that do not take the reign of a thousand years literally.

At the end of the 18th century, historical-critical readings became dominant. These studies raised questions about the sources and traditions used in the book. This approach located the book of Revelation in the time in which it was written. Some images were interpreted as allusions to events in the immediate past and present of the author and the rest to the eschatological future.

The historical-critical approach has evoked two major reactions. One is the aesthetic literary mode of interpretation, that emphasizes the qualities of Revelation that characterize it as a work of art and of the imagination. The other is the fundamentalist approach that insists on the literal truth of Revelation's images, usually as predictions of future events.

The basic issues of interpretation, that still exercise commentators and readers today, are (1) whether the structure of the book is linear, recapitulative, or thematic; (2) how the images and narrative patterns relate to history; and (3) what the goal of interpretation is: whether one should discover and approve only one or multiple meanings and whether one should attempt to discern the author's intention or the reader's response.

Bibliography

Aland, K., and Aland, B. 1987. *The Text of the New Testament.* Trans. E. F. Rhodes. Grand Rapids.

Allo, E.-B. 1933. *Saint Jean: L'Apocalypse.* 4th rev. ed. EBib. Paris.

Attridge, H. W. 1979. Greek and Latin Apocalypses. *Semeia* 14: 159–86.

Aune, D. E. 1981. The Social Matrix of the Apocalypse of John. *BR* 26: 16–32.

———. 1983. *Prophecy in Early Christianity and the Ancient Mediterranean World.* Grand Rapids.

———. 1987a. *The New Testament in Its Literary Environment.* Philadelphia.

———. 1987b. The Apocalypse of John and Graeco-Roman Revelatory Magic. *NTS* 33: 481–501.

Beale, G. K. 1984. *The Use of Daniel in Jewish Apocalyptic Literature and in the Revelation of St. John.* Lanham.

Betz, H. D. 1966. Zum Problem des religionsgeschichtlichen Verständnisses der Apokalyptik. *ZTK* 63: 391–409 = On the Problem of the Religio-Historical Understanding of Apocalypticism. Pp. 134–56 in *Apocalypticism,* ed. R. W. Funk. *JTC* 6. New York. 1969.

Boismard, M. E. 1949. "L'Apocalypse" ou "les apocalypses" de S. Jean. *RB* 56: 507–27.

Bornkamm, G. 1937. Die Komposition der apokalyptischen Visionen in der Offenbarung Johannis. *ZNW* 36: 132–49 = Pp. 204–22 in *Studien zu Antike und Urchristentum: Gesammelte Aufsätze Band II.* BEvT 28. Munich. 1959.

Bowman, J. W. 1955a. *The Drama of the Book of Revelation.* Philadelphia.

———. 1955b. The Revelation to John: Its Dramatic Structure and Message. *Int* 9: 436–53.

Collins, J. J. 1979. Persian Apocalypses. Pp. 207–17 in Collins, ed. 1979.

———. 1983. Sibylline Oracles. Vol. 2, pp. 317–472 in *OTP.*

Collins, J. J., ed. 1979. *Apocalypse: The Morphology of a Genre. Semeia* 14.

Fallon, F. T. 1979. The Gnostic Apocalypses. *Semeia* 14: 123–58.

Farrer, A. 1949. *A Rebirth of Images: The Making of St. John's Apocalypse.* Westminster. Repr. Albany, 1986.

Giblin, C. H. 1974. Structure and Thematic Correlations in the Theology of Revelation 16–22. *Bib* 55: 487–504.

Giet, S. 1957. *L'Apocalypse et l'histoire.* Paris.

Gunkel, H. 1895. *Schöpfung und Chaos in Urzeit und Endzeit.* Göttingen.

Hanson, P. D. 1973. Zechariah 9 and the Recapitulation of an Ancient Ritual Pattern. *JBL* 92: 37–59.

———. 1975. *The Dawn of Apocalyptic.* Philadelphia.

Haussleiter, I., ed. 1916. *Victorini Episcopi Petavionensis Opera.* CSEL 49. Leipzig. Freytag.

Hellholm, D. 1986. The Problem of Apocalyptic Genre and the Apocalypse of John. *Semeia* 36: 13–64.

Hellholm, D., ed. 1983. *Apocalypticism in the Mediterranean World and the Near East.* Tübingen.

Hemer, C. J. 1986. *The Letters to the Seven Churches of Asia in Their Local Setting.* JSNTSup 11. Sheffield.

Hill, D. 1971–72. Prophecy and Prophets in the Revelation of St. John. *NTS* 18: 401–18.

Himmelfarb, M. 1983. *Tours of Hell: An Apocalyptic Form in Jewish and Christian Literature.* Philadelphia.

Holtz, T. 1971. *Die Christologie der Apokalypse des Johannes.* 2d ed. TU 85. Berlin.

Hunzinger, C.-H. 1965. Babylon als Denkname für Rom und die Datierung des I. Petrusbriefes. Pp. 67–77 in *Gottes Wort und Gottes Land,* ed. H. G. Reventlow. Göttingen.

Jörns, K.-P. 1971. *Das hymnische Evangelium.* SNT 5. Gütersloh.

Kümmel, W. G. 1975. *Introduction to the New Testament.* Rev. ed. Trans. H. C. Kee. Nashville.

Lindblom, J. 1968. *Gesichte und Offenbarungen.* Lund.

McGinn, B. 1987. Revelation. Pp. 523–41 in *The Literary Guide to the Bible,* ed. R. Alter and F. Kermode. Cambridge, MA.

Müller, U. B. 1972. *Messias und Menschensohn in jüdischen Apokalypsen und in der Offenbarung Johannes.* SNT 6. Gütersloh.

———. 1976. *Zur frühchristlichen Theologiegeschichte.* Gütersloh.

Mussies, G. 1971. *The Morphology of Koine Greek as Used in the Apocalypse of St. John.* NovTSup 27. Leiden.

Musurillo, H. 1972. *The Acts of the Christian Martyrs.* Oxford.

Nikolainen, A. T. 1968. Über die theologische Eigenart der Offenbarung des Johannes. *TLZ* 93: 162–70.

Robinson, J. A. T. 1976. *Redating the New Testament.* Philadelphia.

Saldarini, A. J. 1979. Apocalypses and "Apocalyptic" in Rabbinic Literature and Mysticism. *Semeia* 14: 187–205.

Schmid, J. 1955–56. *Studien zur Geschichte des griechischen Apokalypse Textes.* 3 vols. Munich.
Schüssler Fiorenza, E. 1985. *The Book of Revelation.* Philadelphia.
Segal, A. 1977. *Two Powers in Heaven.* SJLA 25. Leiden.
Smith, M. 1983. On the History of *APOKALYPTO* and *APOKALYPSIS.* Pp. 9–20 in Hellholm, ed. 1983.
Swete, H. B. 1909. *The Apocalypse of St. John.* 3d ed. London.
Vanhoye, A. 1962. L'Utilisation du livre d'Ézéchiel dans l'Apocalypse. *Bib* 43: 436–76.
Yarbro Collins, A. 1976. *The Combat Myth in the Book of Revelation.* HDR 9. Missoula.
———. 1977a. The History-of-Religions Approach to Apocalypticism and the "Angel of the Waters" (Rev 16:4–7). *CBQ* 39: 367–81.
———. 1977b. The Political Perspective of the Revelation to John. *JBL* 96: 241–56.
———. 1979. The Early Christian Apocalypses. *Semeia* 14: 61–121.
———. 1984. *Crisis and Catharsis: The Power of the Apocalypse.* Philadelphia.
———. 1986. Introduction: Early Christian Apocalypticism. *Semeia* 36: 1–11.

ADELA YARBRO COLLINS

REVOLT, MACCABEAN. See MACCABEAN REVOLT.

REZEPH (PLACE) [Heb *reṣep*]. A town described as having been destroyed by the Assyrians. When Hezekiah rebelled against Assyria (2 Kgs 18:1–7), the king of Assyria, Sennacherib, responded with force. Jerusalem was surrounded (18:17) and the Rabshakeh addressed the people and asked if any of the national gods had delivered their countries from the Assyrians. He then listed Hamath, Arpad, Separvaim, Hena, Ivvah, and Samaria (vv 33–34). A similar follow-up message (19:9–11) added Rezeph to the list. Presumably Rezeph had been destroyed by the Assyrians, along with the other sites; these therefore served to symbolize Assyrian invincibility and to imply that any resistance by the Hebrews would prove futile (a parallel passage appears in Isa 37:12 where Gk versions have several variants—Rapheth, Raphes, Rapheis).

The placement of the name among the other cities suggests that Rezeph was in the area of the Balikh and Khabur rivers, northern tributaries of the Euphrates. Snaith (*IB* 3: 299) notes there are many places called Rezeph *(Ra-sa-ap-pa),* but this one was the Assyrian provincial capital, on the road from Harran to Palmyra, and that it was S of the Euphrates at modern Rezzafeh (35°38′N; 38°43′E). It is also described as E of Tipsah, NE of Hamath (Ptolemy 5.15), and as an important caravan city on the route from Damascus to Raqqa on the Euphrates. Rezeph appears in an Assyrian geographical list (2 R 53, 37a), preceded by Arrapha (Arrapachitis, modern Kirkuk) and Halahhu (Halah), and followed by Tamnunu. The Eponym Canons list as prefects Ninip-kibsi-usur for 839 B.C., Uraseres for 804–775, Sin-shallimanni 747, and Bel-emuranni 737, whose names appear to be Assyrian, but a man named Abda'u or Abda'i, perhaps a native who served later, is mentioned in a list of officials (K. 9921). Records also indicate that Yahutu was *šanû* (deputy governor?) of Rezeph in 673. References to such information in the Assyrian geographical lists imply that Rezeph was a significant trading center (Pinches *ISBE* [1939 ed.] 4: 2588).

The site was conquered by the Assyrians at least by 839 (Shalmanezer III, 858–824 B.C.), though there is some debate about exactly when it was conquered and when it was incorporated into the Assyrian Empire. Some say Sennacherib conquered Rezeph. Since Assyrian victims often rebelled, it would not be surprising if it were conquered in several campaigns, including that mentioned in 2 Kgs 18:33–34 and 19:11–13. However, 2 Kgs 19:12 explicitly has the king saying that his *fathers* conquered these sites.

Others identify Rezeph on the basis of commercial documents as between Tille and Isana between Jebel Sinjar and the Tigris River, 70 miles W of Nineveh (Gray *1 & 2 Kings* OTL, 687–88; Simons *GTTOT,* 367, 441).

HENRY O. THOMPSON

REZIN (PERSON) [Heb *rĕṣîn*]. The name of two individuals in the Hebrew Bible.

1. An Aramean king (RSV: "king of Syria") involved in the Syro-Ephraimite coalition against Judah (2 Kgs 15:37; 16:5, 9). The Masoretic pronunciation of the name is incorrect. The name is attested in Akkadian in the forms *ra-ḫi-a-nu* and *ra-qi-a-nu.* This shows that the second consonant of MT *rṣyn* is Proto-Semitic *ḍ*, and that the *yod* is consonantal. Thus the name was pronounced *raḍyān* in Aramaic (probably written *rqyn*) in the 8th century B.C.E. The name is a hypochoristic (shortened form) and probably means "(The god) is pleased."

Rezin was the last king of Aram-Damascus before it was incorporated into the Assyrian Empire in 732 B.C.E. Rezin is known from biblical and Assyrian sources. He was quite probably a usurper to the throne of Aram, since his hometown is given as Hadara rather than Damascus in the inscriptions of Tiglath-pileser III. The date of his rise to power is not known (there being no information preserved about Aram-Damascus for the period between 773 and 738 B.C.E.). Rezin is, however, listed among a number of Syro-Palestinian kings who rendered tribute to Tiglath-pileser III in 738. An Assyrian stela found in Iran contains a slightly different tribute list that may represent the political situation of Syria-Palestine a year or so earlier than the dated list just mentioned, and it too names Rezin as king of Aram.

Rezin is best known as the leader of an anti-Assyrian coalition which probably developed between 737 and 735, while Tiglath-pileser was involved in affairs on the other side of his empire. Tyre, Philistia and Israel (among others) appear to have joined the coalition, but Judah refused to take part. 2 Kgs 15:37 suggests that even at the end of Jotham's reign Rezin and his ally Pekah of Israel were attempting to force Judah to join the coalition. Shortly after Jotham's death (ca. 735/734), Rezin and Pekah invaded Judah and besieged Jerusalem in an attempt to overthrow the new king Ahaz and install an anti-Assyrian king (one "son of Tabe-el" according to Isa 7:6) who would join the coalition (2 Kgs 16:5–9). This conflict is often called the Syro-Ephraimite War and is the background to the events described in Isaiah 7–8. (The statement in 2

Kgs 16:6 that Rezin captured Elath at this time and settled it with Arameans is highly unlikely. This verse probably referred originally to an Edomite takeover of Elath, but through scribal error [*d* and *r* are very similar in Hebrew] the name Edom was changed to Aram. The explicit identification of the king as Rezin probably occurred only after the earlier corruption took place.) The siege of Jerusalem was broken when the Assyrian army returned to S Syria at that time. Although 2 Kgs 16:7–9 suggests that Tiglath-pileser attacked the anti-Assyrian coalition in response to a bribe from Ahaz, it is probable that the Assyrian king already planned to recapture this area at this time.

Tiglath-pileser spent the year 734 B.C.E. in a campaign along the Mediterranean coast, subduing the rebellious Philistine cities, particularly Gaza. In 733 and 732 he turned his attention to Israel and Aram-Damascus. The attack on Aram and its destruction are described in the rather fragmentary annals of Tiglath-pileser, which state that 591 towns of the land were captured and destroyed. Details of the capture of Damascus and the end of Rezin are not preserved in the annals, but 2 Kgs 16:9 states (rather laconically), "the king of Assyria marched against Damascus, and took it, carrying its people captive to Kir, but Rezin he killed" (2 Kgs 16:9). This was the end of Damascus as the capital of an independent state. Aram was incorporated into the Assyrian Empire and divided into a number of provinces.

Recently Hayes and Irvine (1987: 34–46) have argued for a somewhat different reconstruction of Rezin's reign and his relationship to Israel. They have suggested that Rezin may have been on the throne as early as the 750s and that he recreated an Aramean empire in S Syria and Palestine (similar to that of Hazael a century earlier), annexing all of Israel except the central hill country and dominating Philistia and Transjordan. They argue that Pekah was a "stooge" of Rezin's and probably ruled the E parts of Israelite territory under Rezin's authority as a rival to Menahem. While their reconstruction is generally plausible, note should be made that the evidence for it is extremely slim and that the biblical passages adduced as evidence can be interpreted (often more plausibly) in different ways.

2. Name of one of the families of the temple personnel known as the Nethinim. The sons of Rezin are listed as part of the returnees from the Exile in Ezra 2:48 and Neh 7:50.

Bibliography

Hayes, J. H., and Irvine, S. A. 1987. *Isaiah, the Eighth Century Prophet: His Times and His Preaching*. Nashville.

Pitard, W. T. 1987. *Ancient Damascus*. Winona Lake, IN.

WAYNE T. PITARD

REZON (PERSON) [Heb *rĕzôn*]. An Aramean ruler who appears in 1 Kgs 11:23–25 as an adversary of Solomon. Nothing is known of him besides what is found in this brief passage. Rezon is said to have been an officer of Hadadezer, king of Zobah, who abandoned his position, presumably soon after Hadadezer was defeated by David (2 Samuel 8, 10). Sometime during the reign of Solomon, Rezon gathered a band of malcontents as an army, seized Damascus, which had been under Israelite control, and proclaimed himself king there. There is no evidence that Solomon was able to oppose Rezon's actions, and Rezon thereby became the first in a line of powerful rulers of the kingdom of Aram-Damascus.

It is not possible to date Rezon's rebellion in Damascus with any certainty. While the context of 1 Kings 11 suggests that it occurred late in Solomon's reign, 11:25 states that Rezon "was an adversary all the days of Solomon." This latter statement probably should not be pressed so far as to argue that Damascus withdrew from Israelite control early in Solomon's reign. But it does suggest that Rezon's actions took place well before Solomon's death, and it signals that there was a weakening of the Israelite empire during, and not just after Solomon's reign.

Several scholars over the past century have suggested that Rezon is to be identified with Hezion, the grandfather of Ben-Hadad I of 1 Kgs 15:18. In fact there is no evidence to support this identification (cf. Pitard 1987: 100–4), and the proposal should be dropped.

Bibliography

Pitard, W. T. 1987. *Ancient Damascus*. Winona Lake, IN.

WAYNE T. PITARD

RHEGIUM (PLACE) [Gk *Rhēgion*]. The modern city of Reggio di Calabria, located along the SW coast of the "toe" of Italy (38°06′N; 15°39′E) opposite the Sicilian city of Messina. The Strait of Messina, which separates Sicily and Italy, is only ca. 7 miles wide near Rhegium. During his voyage to Rome, Paul stopped at this city after traveling from Syracuse. He and the others on the ship waited one day at Rhegium for a S wind which allowed them to tack N to the city of Puteoli (Acts 28:13).

The Alexandrian ship which carried Paul to Rhegium had a carved figure of the heads of the "Twin Gods" (Acts 28:11). Rhegium, as found on coins of the city, was noted for the worship of the Dioscuri or the "Twin Gods," namely Castor and Polydeuces or Pollux, who were the "Sons of Zeus" and patron deities of sailors. Rhegium is near two infamous sailing hazards which may have fostered this devotion to the "Twin Gods." These hazards were located just to the N of Rhegium at either side of the Strait of Messina and were identified in Greek mythology with two sisters, Scylla and Charybdis. The dangerous whirlpool of Charybdis was located on the Sicily side of the Strait of Messina while the threatening rock of Scylla was on the Italian side.

The etymology of the name of the city is unclear. Some ancient sources, using the idea that Sicily was separated from Italy by an earthquake, trace it to the Greek term *rhegnymi*, "to split or rend" (Aesch., Fragment 230), while other ancient authors suggest that the city had royal origins. Hence the name is from the Latin term for "royal," *regium* (Strabo 6.258). Many modern scholars believe that the name of the city predated Greek occupation, so they favor the latter interpretation.

Greek colonists from Chalcis founded Rhegium in ca. 720 B.C. (Strabo *Geog.* 6.1.6). Rhegium grew in power during the 5th century (Hdt. 7.165), but its geographical position left it vulnerable to attack. Dionysius, tyrant of

Syracuse destroyed the city in 387 B.C. and he sold many of the inhabitants into slavery (Diod. 14.106ff). Rhegium was partly rebuilt by Dionysius the Younger, who was tyrant of Syracuse from 367 to 343 B.C.

When Pyrrhus attacked Italy in 280 B.C., the inhabitants of Rhegium feared both him and the sea power of the Carthaginians. Rhegium, therefore, requested that a Roman garrison be stationed in the city for protection. The troops soon arrived from Campania under the leadership of Decius, but they quickly realized that the wealth of the city could be easily obtained. The troops, taking advantage of their situation, murdered the men and enslaved the women of Rhegium and thereby made the city their own. The conquering troops were punished by the armies of Rome and the city was returned to the few remaining citizens in 271 B.C. (Polyb. 1.7).

The city, thenceforth, became an ally of Rome and remained loyal to this alliance during the Punic Wars, even when Hannibal nearly captured the city (Polyb. 9.7). In 91 B.C. an earthquake destroyed part of the city and its power waned. Caesar Augustus settled some of the veterans of his army at Rhegium in the early 1st century A.D. The city then became known as Rhegium Julium and its population increased.

JOHN D. WINELAND

RHEIMS VERSION. See VERSIONS, CATHOLIC; VERSIONS, ENGLISH (PRE–1960).

RHESA (PERSON) [Gk *Rhēsa*]. The father of Joanan and son of Zerubbabel, according to Luke's genealogy tying Joseph, the "supposed father" of Jesus, to descent from Adam and God (Luke 3:27). D omits Rhesa, substituting a genealogy adapted from Matt 1:6–15 for Luke 3:23–31. The name Rhesa occurs nowhere else in the biblical documents, including Matthew's genealogy, and falls within a list of seventeen otherwise unknown descendants of David's son Nathan (Fitzmyer *Luke 1–9* AB, 500). Three suggestions have been made regarding reference to Rhesa in the genealogy. First, it could be a personal name (cf. 1 Chr 7:39 with Gk *rasia*), although this son of Zerubbabel is otherwise unknown (Marshall *Luke* NIGTC, 163). Second, in light of the similarity of Rhesa to the Aramaic title *rēʾšāʾ*, meaning "prince," Plummer (*Luke* ICC, 103–4; following Hervey 1853: 111–14, the apparent originator of this theory; cf. Abel 1974: 209) speculates that Zerubbabel, because he was head of the tribe of Judah during the return from captivity in Babylon, was designated as "Prince [Rhesa] of the captivity." But "Zerubbabel Rhesa" or "Zerubbabel the Prince" was mistaken by an earlier copyist of a pre-Lukan version of the genealogy for "Zerubbabel begat Rhesa." Third, Fitzmyer (*Luke* 1–9 AB, 500; following, e.g., Jeremias 1969: 296), believing the word order of the Lukan text does not support Plummer's analysis (but cf. Marshall *Luke* NIGTC, 163, who claims that Plummer's proposal would argue for the genealogy originally being in reverse order), proposes that Rhesa is to be taken with the preceding name, Joanan, thus "Prince Joanan, son of Zerubbabel," referring to Hananiah, son of Zerubbabel in 1 Chr 3:19. This raises the question of the relation of Luke's genealogy to the genealogy in 1 Chronicles (see esp. Jeremias 1969: 295–96).

Bibliography

Abel, E. L. 1974. The Genealogies of Jesus O XPICTOC. *NTS* 20: 203–10.

Hervey, A. 1853. *The Genealogies of Our Lord and Saviour Jesus Christ.* Cambridge.

Jeremias, J. 1969. *Jerusalem in the Time of Jesus.* Philadelphia.

STANLEY E. PORTER

RHETORIC AND RHETORICAL CRITICISM. Rhetoric is the art of composition by which language is made descriptive, interpretive, or persuasive. Related to it is oratory, the art of effective public speaking. The study of rhetoric is a classical discipline that goes back to Aristotle, and insights from the study of rhetoric have been applied to the biblical text. This methodological approach is called "rhetorical criticism." This entry consists of three articles. The first surveys the subject of rhetoric and oratory in the Greco-Roman world; the second examines OT rhetorical criticism; and the third examines rhetoric in the NT and NT rhetorical criticism.

RHETORIC AND ORATORY IN THE GRECO-ROMAN WORLD

A. Greece

Among the Greeks, the expression *rhētorikē technē* (Lat *ars rhetorica*) refers to the theory and practice of "speaking well." The significance of speech was appreciated as early as Homer (9th–8th century B.C.E.). The heroes of his epics often use figures of speech, arrangement, and style to argue and persuade. Kennedy (1980: 9–15) refers to this type of rhetoric as "natural" or "preconceptual," i.e., an unself-conscious use of rhetorical technique. A "conceptualized" rhetoric (Kennedy 1980: 15–17)—or a self-conscious use of technique—is traditionally connected with the 5th century B.C.E. teachers, Tisias and Corax of Syracuse, who wrote handbooks on forensic or judicial oratory for the purpose of helping ordinary citizens argue cases in the law courts of Sicily. It was another Sicilian, however, Gorgias of Leontini, who is credited with introducing the art of rhetoric to Athens in 427 B.C.E. with great success. Gorgias was particularly noted for his florid, emotional style (the so-called "Gorgianic style") with its skillful use of the rhythms, parallelisms, and other figures of poetry. In contrast, his contemporary, Isocrates, emphasized a "pure" rhetoric unencumbered by poetic embellishment. Isocrates, although not a great speaker, was an influential teacher. He was the first to open a school of rhetoric and successfully instruct others in the art. As a result, the study of rhetoric, in both its oral and written forms, soon became the basis of all Greek, and later, Roman education.

A critical reaction to the rhetorical art is most evident in the writings of Plato, notably in the *Gorgias* and *Phaedrus.* In these dialogues, Plato specifically attacks that kind of sophistic oratory or extreme relativism (identified with the Sophists in general) which has no fixed moral purpose but only the goal of winning an argument through any persuasive means. Plato equates this type of rhetoric with deceit and flattery and contrasts it with dialectic, which is concerned with knowledge and universal truths. Plato did admit the value of a "philosophical" rhetoric in the *Phaedrus,* but did not develop this idea in any detail. This task was left to Aristotle, whose *Rhetoric* became an influential source for later developments of the art. In particular, Aristotle developed a practical theory of rhetoric that dealt with the relation of rhetoric to philosophy, the role of the audience, and a general discussion of arrangement and style. His most important contributions included distinguishing three types of rhetoric (judicial, epideictic, deliberative); three modes of persuasion *(logos, ethos, pathos);* and his theory of the rhetorical *topoi* ("topics" or "lines of argument"). The "five parts" of rhetoric (invention, arrangement, style, memory, delivery)—implicit in Aristotle as well as such 4th-century handbooks as the *Rhetorica ad Alexandrum*—would be developed in greater technical detail during the Hellenistic period, notably in the writings of the 2d-century rhetor, Hermagoras. The later Hellenistic period also saw the development of a florid and artificial oratory ("Asianism") reminiscent of Gorgias as well as a renewed hostility between teachers of rhetoric and philosophy. The gains would be made among the rhetoricians, and rhetoric would emerge in Rome as the sine qua non of Roman education.

B. Rome

By the beginning of the 1st century B.C.E., rhetoric and oratory were firmly established in Rome as the primary means by which to advance in public life (judicial oratory was especially emphasized). It was at this time that Cicero wrote his *De Inventione,* the first (and most influential) of his seven books on the techniques of rhetoric. He also composed and delivered numerous speeches (58 are extant). Although clearly dependent on traditional theory and practice, Cicero's mastery of the art made him Rome's greatest orator and most influential writer on rhetorical technique. Cicero's main innovation in terms of technique was his concept of the orator's "three duties": to instruct *(docere),* to delight *(delectare),* to move *(movere).* Each "duty" was connected with an appropriate "style": the "plain" or unadorned style was most suited for instruction and demonstrating proof; the "grand" or lofty style was most useful for stirring up or moving the sublime emotions; the "intermediate" or moderate style was most effective in giving simple pleasure and delight. *Ethos* or character was also stressed by Cicero. May argues (1988: 1–12; 162–69 and *passim*) that this mode of persuasion played a far more significant role in Roman than Greek oratory because of traditional Roman respect for an individual's authority *(auctoritas),* reputation *(existimatio),* honor *(dignitas),* and achievements *(res gestae).* This is particularly evident in Cicero's many speeches. Cicero is also credited with thoroughly integrating the art of rhetoric into the classical *paideia* or "liberal arts": for Cicero, the orator must be a person of wide learning as well as persuasive speech.

Cicero's writings on rhetoric and his own expertise as an orator represent the high-water mark of Roman rhetoric. In the subsequent period of the Empire there is a general decline in oratory, with the noted exception of the late 1st-century teacher and rhetor, Quintilian. His *Institutio Oratoria* is the longest and most complete technical treatise on rhetoric to survive from Antiquity. Its importance lies in its detailed account of how rhetorical training is to be incorporated into every stage of education—from the speech lessons of childhood, to the later mastery of grammar, diction, composition, and enunciation, to the systematic training in adulthood of all the specific techniques and theories of rhetoric under the guidance of a skilled rhetor. The goal of education is to become a "great orator," understood by Quintilian as a "good man" of strong character. Quintilian's treatise was to influence especially the development of rhetoric in the Middle Ages and its later revival in the Renaissance.

During the 2d century, the decline of oratory is most evident in the new importance given to "declamation," a type of school or practice exercise dealing with historical or pseudo-historical themes (e.g., should Caesar cross the Rubicon?) and fictive legal cases (e.g., should a son sue his father?)—or, in the new terminology, *suasoria* and *controversia.* These practice exercises often became so unrealistic and farfetched that they ceased to have any practical purpose and degenerated into mere theatrics and public entertainment. New forms of deliberative oratory are also developed at this time; e.g., formal speeches given on the occasion of festivals, birthdays, marriages, and funerals. A revival of "Asianism" is also characteristic of the period as is the "pure" style of the "Atticists." The orators of the Second Sophistic (as illustrated in Philostratus' *Vita Sophistarum*) are especially identified with these 2d-century developments.

C. Influence on the New Testament

The influence of Greco-Roman rhetoric on the writings in the NT is becoming more widely acknowledged today than in the past, particularly concerning Paul's letters. Galatians, for example, has been analyzed by Betz (1975: 353–79; *Galatians* Hermeneia, 14–25) as an "apologetic letter" which incorporates rhetorical devices familiar to forensic oratory: Paul functions as the defendant, the addressee or the "Galatians" play the role of the jury, and Paul's opponents are the accusers. The structure of the Letter incorporates the standard "parts" of a speech: *exordium* (introduction), *narratio* (statement of facts), *propositio* (main points to be made), *probatio* (proof), and *peroratio* (conclusion). The same pattern of organization is also evident in 2 Corinthians 8 and 9 (Betz, *2 Corinthians 8–9* Hermeneia, 38–41; 88–90). The shorter epistle to Philemon, as analyzed by Church (1978: 17–33), is an example of deliberative rhetoric—divided into *exordium, probatio,* and *peroratio*—and with specific appeals to *ethos* and *pathos.* In the case of Romans, Wuellner (1976: 330–51) argues that this epistle is best understood as an example of epideictic rhetoric with a special appeal to the "*pathos* of love."

Elsewhere in the NT, there is evidence for other examples of rhetorical use, although not strictly in the classical sense. Jesus' preaching in the gospels, for example, is modeled on Jewish traditions of speech: the object is to persuade through divine authority rather than modes of rational proof. The "missionary sermons" in Acts are similar to OT "covenant speeches," and thus are examples of "natural" or preconceptual rhetoric (Kennedy 1980: 120–32). The emphasis here is on warning, repentance, and judgment, not *ethos, pathos,* and *logos.* The so-called "Areopagus Speech" attributed to Paul in Acts 17:22–31 has sometimes been analyzed in classical rhetorical terms, but is again best understood in terms of Jewish speech traditions.

D. Later Christian Developments

The tradition of Greek rhetoric is most apparent in the writings of the 4th-century Cappadocian Fathers—Gregory of Nazianzus, Gregory of Nyssa, and Basil of Caesarea. All three received excellent Greek educations and were well acquainted with the sophistic rhetoric of the period. Their panegyrical orations in particular display a sophisticated use of rhetorical devices, structure, figures of speech, and argumentation. It was Augustine, however—in his *De Doctrina Christiana*—who developed an explicit theory of Christian rhetoric in the Latin tradition, influenced by Cicero. Augustine, for example, accepts Cicero's concept of the orator's three "duties" and their relation to the three "styles." He also underscores the character or *ethos* of the orator as more important than any gifts of style or technique. But the *De Doctrina Christiana* is not simply a reworking of pagan theories and categories but an appropriation of these rhetorical methods with a specific Christian goal in mind; e.g., the Christian orator must confine his subject matter to scriptural themes, he must be concerned with truth and not argument for argument's sake, he must defend the faith, etc. As Kennedy notes (1980: 146), no less than five of the Latin Church Fathers (Tertullian, Cyprian, Arnobius, Lactantius, Augustine) were "professional rhetoricians before they became Christians." Add to this list the number of Greek Church Fathers who were schooled in rhetoric and the "art of persuasion" becomes a significant element in understanding the Christian literature of Antiquity. Recent studies in discourse theory, reader-response criticism, structural linguistics, and the "New Rhetoric" are certain to bring this discussion to new levels of understanding as demonstrated, e.g., by Plank's analysis of 1 Cor 4:9–13 in terms of Paul's "rhetoric of irony" (1987: 33–69). For further discussion see PWSup 7: 1039–1138.

Bibliography

Baldwin, C. S. 1924. *Ancient Rhetoric and Poetic.* New York.
Betz, H. D. 1972. *Der Apostel Paulus und die Sokratische Tradition.* BHT 45. Tübingen.
———. 1975. The Literary Composition and Function of Paul's Letter to the Galatians. *NTS* 21: 353–79.
Bonner, S. F. 1968. Roman Oratory. Pp. 416–64 in *Fifty Years and Twelve of Classical Scholarship.* New York.
Bultmann, R. 1910. *Der Stil der paulinischen Predigt und die Kynisch-Stoische Diatribe.* FRLANT 14. Göttingen.
Church, F. F. 1978. Rhetorical Structure and Design in Paul's Letter to Philemon. *HTR* 71: 17–33.
Clark, D. L. 1957. *Rhetoric in Greco-Roman Education.* New York.
Clarke, M. L. 1953. *Rhetoric at Rome.* London.
Donfried, K. P. 1974. False Presuppositions in the Study of *Romans.* *CBQ* 36: 332–55.
Hudson-Williams, L. 1968. Greek Orators and Rhetoric. Pp. 242–66 in *Fifty Years and Twelve of Classical Scholarship.* New York.
Kennedy, G. 1963. *The Art of Persuasion in Greece.* Princeton.
———. 1972. *The Art of Persuasion in the Roman World (300BC–AD300).* Princeton.
———. 1980. *Classical Rhetoric and its Christian and Secular Tradition from Ancient to Modern Times.* Chapel Hill.
May, J. M. 1988. *Trials of Character: The Eloquence of Ciceronian Ethos.* Chapel Hill.
Plank, K. A. 1987. *Paul and the Irony of Affliction.* Atlanta.
Sider, R. D. 1971. *Ancient Rhetoric and the Art of Tertullian.* London.
Vickers, B. 1988. *In Defence of Rhetoric.* Oxford.
Volkmann, R. 1885. *Die Rhetorik der Griechen und Romer.* 2d ed. Stuttgart. Repr. Hildesheim, 1963.
Wuellner, W. 1976. Paul's Rhetoric of Argumentation in *Romans.* *CBQ* 38: 330–51.

RUTH MAJERCIK

OT RHETORICAL CRITICISM

Although the study of rhetoric is a classical discipline that goes back to Aristotle *(Rhetoric)* and includes works by Cicero *(De Oratore)* and Quintilian *(Institutio oratoria)*, as a contemporary methodology for the study of the Hebrew Bible rhetorical criticism is relatively recent, having first been introduced by James Muilenburg in his 1968 Presidential Address to the Society of Biblical Literature, entitled "Form Criticism and Beyond" (1969: 1–18). The following description of rhetorical criticism will begin with an examination of the work of Muilenburg. The second section will examine the rise of the "Muilenburg School" of rhetorical criticism in the United States during the 1970s and early 1980s. Finally, the essay will conclude by examining recent discussions of rhetorical criticism.

A. James Muilenburg
  1. As a Form Critic
  2. As a Rhetorical Critic
B. The "Muilenburg School"
  1. Similarity to Muilenburg
  2. Contrast to Muilenburg
    a. Extrinsic versus Intrinsic
    b. Diachronic versus Synchronic
    c. Form and Content
    d. Comparison to ANE Literature
C. Classical Rhetoric and Rhetorical Criticism

A. James Muilenburg

In his tribute to James Muilenburg, Bernhard Anderson (1974: xii–xiv) cautions the reader that "rhetorical criticism could easily be misunderstood if it is not seen in the context of [Muilenburg's] whole scholarly career." In order to avoid misunderstanding, Anderson suggested that form criticism and the Biblical Theology movement, the latter with its emphasis on the "historical character of revelation," had to be seen as important influences in Muilenburg's formulation of rhetorical criticism.

1. As a Form Critic. Anderson's caution is most certainly correct. Form criticism plays such a central role in Muilenburg's programmatic statement on rhetorical criticism that he concludes the article "Form Criticism and Beyond" by underscoring how he considered rhetorical criticism to be only a supplement to form criticism (1969: 15). He praised the work of form critics like Gunkel for advances in comparative methodology, which freed biblical literature from the parochialism of the critic's presuppositions; for uncovering the wide range of *Gattungen* (forms) within the Hebrew Bible; and most importantly, for allowing the critic to interrelate biblical literature more closely into the cultural milieu of Israel, which classic source criticism had not been able to do. Thus, Muilenburg praises Gunkel as someone unsurpassed in his ability to "portray the cast and temper of the minds of the biblical narrators and poets . . . [as well as] the ordinary Israelite to whom their words were addressed" (1969: 2).

However, in spite of his praise for Gunkel, Muilenburg was troubled by the legacy of form criticism. He concluded that two problems undercut the goals of form-critical methodology. First, there was a growing tendency to study only similarity in *Gattungen,* with the result that the particularity of the text under study gave way in order to emphasize "pure" forms in biblical literature. Second, because of the movement toward studying "pure" *Gattungen,* form critics were also beginning to read biblical literature intrinsically, which resulted in an "aversion to biographical or psychological interpretations . . . (and a certain) resistance to historical commentary" (1969: 4–5). These two problems, according to Muilenburg, went hand in glove. An overemphasis on similarity in the study of *Gattungen* created an abstraction for the reader so that the uniqueness of the individual text was not sufficiently included in interpretation. The result of such abstraction was that the integral relation between form and content was severed, which not only obscured "the thought and intention of the writer or speaker" but, even more seriously, produced a "skepticism of all attempts to read a pericope in its historical context" (1969: 6).

2. As a Rhetorical Critic. Rhetorical criticism was Muilenburg's response to the way in which particular biblical texts were being severed from their historical context by form criticism. The starting point for rhetorical criticism was the conclusion that most *Gattungen* in the Hebrew Bible are not "pure" but imitations. In view of this conclusion, Muilenburg argued that although each text has to be studied against the backdrop of a "pure" *Gattung,* it should not be reduced to it. This shift in study to the unique features in a given text goes to the heart of rhetorical criticism as it was conceived by Muilenburg, for it gives rise to the study of stylistics of composition in Hebrew prose and poetry (1969: 7–8).

Muilenburg conceived of rhetorical criticism as having two foci: it sought to describe the structure and boundaries of a literary unit and the devices which provide shape and emphasis within a given text. In determining the boundaries of a text, Muilenburg underscored the importance of repetitive motifs and *inclusio;* while the inner structure and movement of a text ("the warp and woof out of which the literary fabric is woven") could be brought to light by studying a variety of literary devices, which included ancient Near Eastern formal modes of speech, techniques of narrative composition, bicola/tricola, strophes, the function of particles (Heb *kî, hinnēh, lākēn*), and repetition.

Muilenburg's treatment of Jer 3:1–4:4 illustrates how he conceived of rhetorical criticism as a method which accentuated the unique features of a given text, even while acknowledging the form-critical background from which a text may have evolved (1969: 5, 9–10). After eliminating the narrative portions of this unit in order to focus exclusively on the poetry, Muilenburg began his interpretation by noting the results of past form-critical research, in which the quest for the smallest literary unit as an instance of a "pure" *Gattung* supported a reading of the poetic units in Jer 3:1–4:4 as being independent of each other. Rhetorical criticism allowed Muilenburg to go beyond the results of form criticism by arguing that none of the poetic units in Jer 3:1–4:4 were "pure" *Gattungen.* Rather they were imitations, which were meant to function as parts of a larger whole. A central criterion for Muilenburg's conclusion concerning the unity of Jer 3:1–4:4 was the *inclusio* of the Heb verb *šûb,* "return," in Jer 3:1 and 4:1a, which marked the boundaries of the larger literary unit. In Jer 3:1 the word occurred in a legal formulation, followed by an indictment:

> If a man sends his wife away,
> and she goes from him,
> and becomes another man's wife,
> will she *return* to him [with correct text]?
> Would not that land
> be utterly polluted:
> But you have played the harlot with many lovers,
> and would you *return* to me?

And in Jer 4:1a the word *šûb,* "return," is repeated in a conditional covenant:

> If you do *return,* O Israel, Yahweh's Word!
> to me you should *return.*

With the boundaries of the poem in place, a closer study of parallelism, repetitive motifs, and the distribution of particles provided Muilenburg with the criteria to describe internal structure. Furthermore, Muilenburg argued that the poetic units in Jer 3:1–4:4 were imitations of a variety of *Gattungen.* In particular, he concluded that the form-critical background was the lawsuit, but that the text also contained elements of a confessional lament and conditional covenant.

The attention to detail within a given text that was required in rhetorical criticism provided the basis for Muilenburg to conclude that there is an inextricable relationship between form and content in the study of any biblical text. In fact, he even went a step further to argue that the two are really one (1969: 5). Muilenburg does not elaborate on this point in his article and consequently two interpretations are possible. One interpretation is that by form Muilenburg means the present structure of a text, in which case content would be the meaning of the text, conceived as author's intent. A second interpretation would focus more on Muilenburg's assessment of form criticism. Form in this case would be the "pure" *Gattung* which provides the backdrop for any given text, while content would be the unique details within a particular text, which provide an avenue to the thought of the author. In either case, the interrelationship of form and content was Muilenburg's way of rescuing biblical literature from its increasing detachment from any historical context at the hands of form critics, who were abstracting every text into "pure" *Gattungen* and thus obscuring the thought and intention of the writer. Muilenburg's response to this was that "prophets do not speak *in abstracto,* but concretely" (1969: 6). Rhetorical criticism was his way of formulating a canon, namely that "a responsible and proper articulation of words in their linguistic patterns and in their precise formulations will reveal to us the texture and fabric of the writer's thought, not only what it is that he thinks, but as he thinks it" (1969: 7).

B. The "Muilenburg School"

The term "Muilenburg School" is being used very loosely to refer to a variety of articles and books that were written primarily (but not exclusively) by students of Muilenburg throughout the 1970s and early 1980s. These writings tend to make reference to Muilenburg's article "Form Criticism and Beyond" as a springboard for further discussion of rhetoric or rhetorical criticism in the Hebrew Bible. The methodology of the "Muilenburg School" will be described through a series of comparisons and contrasts to the work of Muilenburg. These writings are, however, quite diverse and thus they require a degree of generalization.

1. Similarity to Muilenburg. Three points of similarity to the work of Muilenburg frequently appear in the writings of the "Muilenburg School" as being essential features of rhetorical criticism. First, is the affirmation that every text is both typical and unique, and that rhetorical criticism is concerned with the unique features within a given text (Trible 1978: 9; Melugin 1979: 91). Second, is the presupposition that form and content must be interrelated in the interpretation of any text (Greenwood 1970: 419; Trible 1978: 9). Third, there is general agreement with Muilenburg's conclusion that rhetorical criticism has two foci, namely, to determine the boundaries of larger literary units and to describe rhetorical devices which unify particular texts (Kessler 1974: 25–26; Kuntz 1982: 141). Thus, the "Muilenburg School" is in agreement with Muilenburg's original proposal that rhetorical criticism should be the study of stylistics of composition in Hebrew prose and poetry, and that a study of stylistics will underscore the unity of biblical texts.

2. Contrast to Muilenburg. The 1970s ushered in significant hermeneutical changes that are central to the rhetorical criticism of the "Muilenburg School," but which contrast sharply to Muilenburg's original work. The end result of the changing intellectual climate of this decade is that the "Muilenburg School" detaches rhetorical criticism from its original place within form criticism, where it had functioned as a means to counter the intrinsic interpretations of "pure" *Gattungen,* and it was moved, instead, under the umbrella of literary criticism, conceived more specifically as "new criticism," where all literature by definition was interpreted intrinsically (Brooks 1974: 568). This major hermeneutical shift gives rise to a whole series of comparisons with Muilenburg's original conception of rhetorical criticism.

a. Extrinsic versus Intrinsic. The "Muilenburg School" rejects any claims that the interpreter could uncover an author's intention, and that a hermeneutic based on author's intent could provide a basis for interpretation. Consequently, in contrast to Muilenburg's conception of rhetorical criticism as an extrinsic method which would "reveal [to the interpreter] the texture and fabric of the writer's thought . . . ," Trible, for example, concludes that "intrinsic reading is . . . one hallmark of rhetorical methodology." With this starting point, rhetorical criticism must now be seen as a method which "concentrates primarily on the text rather than on extrinsic factors such as historical background . . . authorial intention, sociological setting, or theological motivation and result" (1978: 8–9).

b. Diachronic versus Synchronic. Muilenburg's application of rhetorical criticism took place in the larger context of form criticism. Thus, even though he was concerned with stylistics of larger literary units, rhetorical criticism had a diachronic aspect to it, since a study of stylistics illustrated how particular texts were imitations of "pure" *Gattungen.* Jer 3:1–4:4 provides illustration. Muilenburg had no problem with simply removing the narrative sections of Jer 3:1–4:4 so that he could study the poetic units, which were then evaluated against the backdrop of "pure" *Gattungen.* But, by shifting rhetorical criticism away from form criticism and placing it under literary criticism, the "Muilenburg School" abandons the tradition-historical aspect of Muilenburg's work, so that rhetorical criticism becomes a method which only examines the present or final form of biblical texts (cf. the work of Brevard Childs on canonical criticism, *IOTS*). Thus, for example, in his definition of rhetorical criticism, Kessler argues that the method should be limited to "an exclusively . . . synchronic preoccupation of the text" (1974: 35).

c. Form and Content. The interrelation of form and content is central to rhetorical criticism. Yet the emphasis on intrinsic and synchronic interpretations of biblical texts within the "Muilenburg School" gives rise to a different understanding of form and content from that which Muilenburg had originally proposed. First, it should be noted that the potential ambiguity of this statement by Muilenburg is eliminated by the "Muilenburg School," since form can only mean the present structure of the text and not "pure" *Gattungen.*

A more serious point of contrast arises with the understanding of content. Content may have begun with the configuration of unique details within a given text for Muilenburg, but it ultimately leads to an author's intent. Content, therefore, yielded a singular meaning for Muilenburg. That is no longer true for the "Muilenburg School." Content is not author's intent, but only the unique configuration of details that an interpreter would impose on a text. The result of this hermeneutical stance is that a singular meaning can no longer be the goal of interpretation, since "application . . . may result in multiple interpretations of a particular passage" (Trible 1978: 11). At the same time, however, interpretation for the "Muilenburg School" is not absolutely relative. Thus, Trible, for example, would argue that "the text, as form and content, limits constructions of itself and does, in fact, stand as a potential witness against all readings" (1978: 1). But such an interpretation of form and content has little to do with Muilenburg's quest to recover the historical past through an author's intent.

d. Comparison to ANE Literature. Muilenburg emphasized the important role of comparative analysis of ANE forms of speech as an important aspect of rhetorical criticism. He singled out this aspect of Gunkel's work as having freed biblical literature from the parochialism of the critics' presuppositions, and he suggested that it should also be established as a central tool for studying Hebrew rhetoric (1969: 1, 3–4, 8). Although this call for comparative methodology was echoed in one of the earliest articles on rhetorical criticism (Greenwood 1970: 424–25), comparison has not been a central feature of the "Muilenburg School." Rather, rhetorical criticism has evolved into a method which focuses on "close readings" of singular texts, which are usually studied in isolation.

Nevertheless, in spite of these very basic hermeneutical contrasts that have been outlined, it is important to underscore again that the central point of continuity between the rhetorical criticism of Muilenburg and the "Muilenburg School" is the common concern to study stylistics of Hebrew prose and poetry.

C. Classical Rhetoric and Rhetorical Criticism

Although the most recent discussions that call for a change in rhetorical criticism are taking place in NT studies, they must be included in this essay because these discussions engage the work of Muilenburg and will certainly make their way into the study of the Hebrew Bible. Recent discussion of rhetorical criticism has sought to expand the scope of the method beyond a descriptive study of stylistics, in order to probe the persuasive power of texts to influence action or practice. George A. Kennedy provides illustration when he writes: "The identification of rhetoric with style . . . represents a limitation and to some extent a distortion of the discipline of rhetoric . . ." He then goes on to define rhetoric as "that quality in discourse by which a speaker or writer seeks to accomplish his purpose" (1984: 1). Thus rhetorical criticism, according to Kennedy, is not a descriptive study of style in which a text is viewed intrinsically; rather it is a more historical method, in which texts are studied "from the point of view of the author's or editor's intent, the unified results, and how it would be perceived by an audience or near contemporaries" (1984: 4–5).

The issues motivating this redefinition of rhetorical criticism are both historical and hermeneutical.

The historical reason for the emphasis on persuasion in a definition of rhetorical criticism (rather than simply description) arises from the influence of classical rhetoric, where argumentation for the purpose of influencing action was central (Kennedy 1984). In some respects the influence of classical rhetoric in NT studies fulfills the call for comparative literature that was present in Muilenburg's original proposal for rhetorical criticism, but not pursued by the "Muilenburg School." How such a comparison would apply to ancient Near Eastern literature in general and the Hebrew Bible in particular is yet to be seen.

The hermeneutical reasons are more complex, yet they, too, arise in part from the study of classical rhetoric. In particular, the emphasis on persuasion in the construction of a text raises two hermeneutical questions that are becoming central to recent discussion of rhetorical criticism: First, how is experience organized and presented in a text? Second, how does this organization of the text precondition certain attitudes toward the world and other people in both the writer and the reader? (See Kennedy 1984: 1–38; Wuellner 1987: 448–54.)

When these questions are incorporated into a definition of rhetorical criticism, then texts can no longer be viewed as isolated objects of study in which stylistic features are described. Rather, they are placed back within their historical context, in order to see how "cultural preconceptions" inevitably influence the writers and the readers (Kennedy 1984: 5; Wuellner 1987: 453). The aim of the rhetorical critic, with this more expanded view of the inherent interrelationship of text and world, is to describe the ideology that is embedded in the text (also described as the "argumentative or rhetorical situation" [Kennedy 1984: 34–36]), in order to see how its very construction has preconditioned experience for both the writer and the reader.

Bibliography

Anderson, B. W. 1974. The New Frontier of Rhetorical Criticism. Pp. ix–xviii in *Rhetorical Criticism: Essays in Honor of James Muilenburg,* ed. J. J. Jackson and M. Kessler. PTMS 1. Pittsburgh.

Brooks, C. 1974. New Criticism. Pp. 567–68 in *Princeton Encyclopedia of Poetry and Poetics,* ed. A. Preminger. Princeton.

Greenwood, D. 1970. Rhetorical Criticism and Formgeschichte: Some Methodological Considerations. *JBL* 89: 418–26.

Kennedy, George A. 1984. *New Testament Interpretation through Rhetorical Criticism.* Chapel Hill.

Kessler, M. 1974. A Methodological Setting for Rhetorical Criticism. *Semeia* 4: 22–36. Repr. 1982. Pp. 1–19 in *Art and Meaning: Rhetoric in Biblical Literature,* ed. D. J. A. Clines; D. M. Gunn; and A. J. Hauser. JSOTSup 19. Sheffield.

Kikawada, I. M. 1977. Some Proposals for the Definition of Rhetorical Criticism. *Semitics* 5: 67–91.

Kuntz, J. K. 1982. The Contribution of Rhetorical Criticism to Understanding Isaiah 51:1–16. Pp. 140–71 in *Art and Meaning: Rhetoric in Biblical Literature,* ed. D. J. A. Clines; D. M. Gunn; and A. J. Hauser. JSOTSup 19. Sheffield.

Melugin, R. F. 1979. Muilenburg, Form Criticism, and Theological Exegesis. Pp. 91–102 in *Encounter with the Text, Form and History in the Hebrew Bible,* ed. M. J. Buss. Missoula, MT.

Muilenburg, J. 1969. Form Criticism and Beyond. *JBL* 88: 1–18.

Trible, P. 1978. *God and the Rhetoric of Sexuality.* Philadelphia.

Wuellner, W. 1987. Where Is Rhetorical Criticism Taking Us? *CBQ* 49: 448–63.

THOMAS B. DOZEMAN

NT RHETORIC AND RHETORICAL CRITICISM

A. Rhetoric and the Aim of Rhetorical Criticism
B. The History of Interest in Biblical Rhetoric
C. The Revival of Rhetorical Criticism
D. Contemporary Focus on NT Rhetoric

A. Rhetoric and the Aim of Rhetorical Criticism

For Hyde and Smith (1979: 354), "the showing of understanding by interpretation, such that meaning is made known, is rhetoric in the purest sense." Rhetorical critics, rhetors themselves, attempt to interpret and recreate the past rhetorical phenomena by showing their meaning for the critics' own cultural situations. The rhetorical critics must be cognizant of the rhetors' and their own hermeneutical situations, the parameters of rationality of both their cultures, and the actual and potential consciousness and receptivity in both audience situations in order to make understandable the rhetorical phenomena under investigation.

From a literary perspective, Corbett (1969: xxii–xxviii) sees rhetoric as the art of making judicious choices from among available resources and according to certain norms such as subject matter, genre, occasion, purpose, author, and audience (the principal norm). Rhetorical (or pragmatic) criticism considers a work of art chiefly as a means to an end, as a vehicle of communication and interaction between the author and the audience, and investigates the use of traditional devices to produce an effect in an audience. It is an internal criticism that focuses on the rhetoric of the text itself, but also works outward to considerations of author, audience, and their interrelationships. The critics can detect some idea of the author, real and implied, from the text's rhetorical strategies. The critics can also derive information about the ideal and real reader from the dispositions and desired effects of the work on the reader (implied reader) and from those elements of the work which are capable of producing an effect on certain kinds of audiences. While rhetorical criticism can unfold the communication of aesthetic imagination, it works best where the literary work "has designs on" the audience. While some critics may use versions of classical rhetorical categories (Frye, Booth, Perelman, Winterowd) they will all consider, largely synchronically, the whole piece in an overview: the author, the particular and general circumstances, the literary medium, the particular stance, the individual use of the form, the style, the diction and rhetorical figures, the compositional ratios, and the effectiveness of the communication of meaning.

Adhering closely to classical rhetoric and Aristotle's definition of rhetoric as "the art of discovering the best possible means of persuasion in regard to any subject whatever," Conley (1983: 23–24) notes that rhetoric locates or constitutes the issues, supplies the means for setting out arguments and conclusions, and shows the way toward resolution. A rhetorical hermeneutic is a disciplined sensitivity to the significance of language and the connections between thoughts, an awareness of the originality which uncovers new "facts" by a combination of concepts and terms and by transforming those facts into strategies of argumentation *(topoi)* or relating them to commonplaces, a study of connections among theses and between them and problems of life and action. The rhetorical devices and procedures which carry the argument forward give the critics access to the strategy of the author's text. Thus, rhetorical criticism is a synchronic study of literary texts and their strategies of communication and persuasion. Like "new criticism," rhetorical criticism concentrates on the given text without delving into its sources, historical origins and transmission, or authorship. For Wuellner (1985: 1–2) rhetorical criticism, unlike literary criticism with its focus on content and design, considers the text's language as a social reality by which the author communicates and influences others. It also aims to establish the context of the work, not the historical critics' setting and genre but the complex of conventions and norms which express and shape the author's and audience's attitudes toward their conceptual and social worlds.

B. The History of Interest in Biblical Rhetoric

Alexandria, a center of classical learning, can be considered the founding center of biblical criticism. Philo, who reflects the city's interpretive traditions, sometimes employs fanciful allegorizing, but also considers grammar, rhetoric, etymology, numerology, and other rhetorical techniques.

From Paul on, the allegorical method exerted a pull on Christian interpretation away from a literal reading, which was both a classical and a Jewish interpretive option. Thus, despite Irenaeus' alarm over gnostic allegorical interpretations of Scripture which distorted the text and interpreted out of context and which led him to stress the historical and literal reality of the OT, he still recognized an admixture of OT figures and types of the new covenant and ultimately relied not on a literal-rhetorical method but on the authoritative interpretations of the "rule of faith" *(regula fidei).* Origen, who sometimes found the spiritual meaning in the literal text, advanced the allegorical method, as did his successor Clement.

In the interpretation of the Antioch school, the arbitrary "Platonic" allegorizing of Alexandria gave way to philological, grammatical, literal, "Aristotelian" interests. The Antiochenes' literal sense included the whole meaning of the author, his metaphors and figures, exposition *(theoria),* and grammatical construction and words, along with a spiritual sense achieved through limited typological interpretation. The school lost influence with Theodore of Mopsuestia's condemnation as a heretic, the loss of Antiochene manuscripts and the greater suitability of Alexandrian interpretations to the emotional needs and world outlook of later centuries.

Among the Latin exegetes some, like Jerome, himself a rhetorician and philologist, regarded classical studies as a propaedeutic to the study of the Bible. Inconsistent with his comments on style, clarity, literary genre, and rhetorical form were his allegorical, typological, and moral interpretations even of historical books. Unfortunately, a preoccupation with erudite but curious detail and the decline in knowledge of classical languages and philology eventually left the allegorical method as the only accessible mode of interpretation.

The last major proponent of literal, rhetorical reading was the classically trained Augustine. His *De Doctrina Christiana* prescribed all the "arts," including rhetorical norms, for exegesis. He advocated the literal sense *(locutio propria)* over the allegorical or figurative *(locutio figurata),* but he also applied a spiritual reading *(lectio spiritualis)* to the literal to arrive at the intent of the author.

Smalley (1983: 41–42) finds that medieval exegetes, already inclined toward the moral and spiritual meaning of the texts, tended to discover these through allegorical exegesis, which led to the loss of the literal reading. Consequently, with exceptions like the early school of St. Victor, the widely practiced moral (tropological), figurative (allegorical), and mystical (anagogical) interpretations prevailed over the literary-rhetorically informed literal and historical readings. A more literal and rational interpretive tradition, albeit methodologically deficient, among Jewish scholars like Rashi and Maimonides provided insights into the OT for some of the 12th-century Victorines and 13th-century friars. As the spiritual and moralizing interpretations declined into exaggeration, these Dominican and Franciscan friars, like Bonaventure, Albert the Great, and

Thomas Aquinas, advanced attention to the literal sense and the intent of the sacred authors.

Not until the Renaissance, however, did interpretation according to the literal and historical sense become possible again. Erasmus typifies the Renaissance humanist equipped by classical learning to deal with the text critical, rhetorical, and literary questions. Unlike Erasmus, the Reformation biblical interpreters largely dropped the allegorical and anagogical interpretations, retained but reevaluated the tropological sense and typological analysis, and applied the humanists' rediscovered classical rhetoric to reach the original meaning of the texts. Counter-Reformation biblicists also focused on the literal/historical sense, which sometimes uses figurative language, but retained the possibility of the three traditional spiritual senses where the text requires them. The Augustinian insight of finding the spiritual meaning in the literal reading turned them all to grammar and rhetoric for the rules for a proper textual understanding.

In the 18th century, a realistic sensibility and the Deist challenge to the evidence for revelation led, as Frei (1974: 130–36) explains, to interest in what actually happened and how the accounts achieved their current shape. Tentative efforts at formal analysis on aesthetic grounds, such as Bishop Lowth's *De sacra poesi Hebraeorum* (1753), did not establish a critical alternative to the prevailing historical concerns, and the 19th and 20th centuries saw the development and dominance of the historical critical methodology.

C. The Revival of Rhetorical Criticism

Rhetorical criticism, whose antecedents reach to the origins of biblical study, has only recently regained its place in biblical scholarship. Contributing to its long disuse was the inapplicability of classical critical canons, an assumption for the OT and, if applied, leading to a conclusion of unfavorable literary comparisons for the NT (e.g., the gospels were folk tales to Dibelius, the Pauline Epistles were like nonliterary correspondence to Deissmann). Then, too, classical rhetorical principles no longer necessarily guide the craft of today's writers and literary critics. Moreover, in the post-Enlightenment biblical critical agenda the literary and rhetorical aspects of biblical texts were studied to answer questions of information external to the texts themselves. Finally, the sacred character of the Bible largely discouraged analysis according to secular critical methods.

Frei (1974: 135–36) observes that historical critics look to what the narrative refers to or to the reconstructed historical context outside the text which explains it. Practitioners of the newer methodologies, whether literary, structuralist, or rhetorical, seek the meaning that is found in the text, the narrative structure or sequence. They explicate what Wilder (1971: xxii) calls the "inseparable relation of form and content in all texts." In short, what is said cannot be separated from how it is said, whether in writing or in oral speech.

Rhetorical analyses were carried out in the past (cf. J. Weiss' study of Pauline rhetoric in the 1897 Festschrift for B. Weiss and Cadbury's Lukan studies in the 1920s) but historical criticism's successful results maintained its predominance. Muilenburg's influential assessment of the gains and deficiencies of the then methodologically dominant OT form criticism ended with his proposal of attention to the rhetoric of the biblical writings as a complement to historical criticism. Rhetorical criticism's attention to the texts themselves and to the authors' patterns of words and motifs, to their style, and to the linguistic and rhetorical phenomena they employ would balance form criticism's focus on the typical, both in genre and setting. Nor was the literary focus to obscure attention to the orality behind the texts. His methodological outline specifies: (1) definition of the limits or scope of the literary unit; (2) recognition of the structure of the composition and the configuration of its component parts.

Similarly, the classicist Kennedy proposes to examine the NT text "from the point of view of the author's or editor's intent, the unified results, and how it would be perceived by an audience of near contemporaries." He draws heavily upon classical rhetoric, convinced that rhetoric is "a universal phenomenon which is conditioned by basic workings of the human mind and heart and by the nature of all human society." His brief five-step method specifies: (1) Determination of the rhetorical unit as complete in itself or part of a larger unit. (2) Definition of the rhetorical situation, i.e., the persons, events, objects, and relations, often a single "problem," which call for and in part determine the rhetor's response. Included here is attention to the basic issue *(stasis)*, i.e., whether a matter of fact, definition, quality, or jurisdiction, and to the species of discourse, i.e., judicial or forensic to effect judgment about the past, deliberative or political to urge a future action, epideictic or ceremonial praise or blame which seeks to affect a present evaluation or to persuade decision. (3) Consideration of the arrangement of the material, its subdivisions, the persuasive effects of the parts, and their cohesion in meeting the rhetorical situation, noting assumptions, topics, formal features (e.g., enthymemes), and rhetorical strategy, i.e., to convince by character *(ēthos)* and reasoned argument *(logos)* or to persuade by emotion *(pathos)*. Classical conventions of speech writing and epistolography and the oral character of NT and classical works affect rhetorical analysis. (4) Consideration of devices of style and their rhetorical function. (5) Overview and evaluation of the impact of the entire unit and its details upon the rhetorical situation.

D. Contemporary Focus on NT Rhetoric

NT critics were quick to follow Wilder's groundbreaking theoretical observations on NT rhetoric with studies like Beardslee's on the methodology of NT literary and rhetorical criticism, Via's on the parables, Funk's on the Pauline letters, and Talbert's on the paradigmatic structure of Luke-Acts. Robbins and Patton find that many NT critics (TeSelle, Perrin, Tannehill, Trible, Crossan, Talbert, Funk) apply the theoretical developments of contemporary literary critics and philosophers of language and literature (Black, Brooks, Burke, Frye, Krieger, Langer, Ong, Richards, Wheelwright) to the analyses of the rhetoric of NT literature. Sternberg, for the OT, and Rhoads and Michie, for the NT, employ a mixed literary-rhetorical study relating rhetorical features to other narrative elements to describe the narrative's impact on the reader, ancient or modern. Fowler employs a similar literary-rhetorical methodology in his study of Mark's Messianic Secret. These studies demonstrate the relation of biblical literature to general world literature, thereby securing a place for biblical critics among their secular peers, and they make immediate the impact of the biblical texts on contemporary readers.

Pursuing contemporary questions of audience reaction and social background but with more attention to the classical milieu, Robbins follows Mark's transformations of rhetorical forms to discover the sociorhetorical pattern of the disciple-gathering teacher, common to the Greco-Roman world. Kennedy's treatments, a mixture of thorough analyses and scattered labeling, of rhetorical units from the gospels, Acts, and the Pauline letters find mixed success and even disagreement (with Betz on Galatians and Lahurd on Matthew). More helpful are Dibelius' discussion of the rhetoric and form of the speeches in Acts and more recent studies like those of Wills, Black, and Fiore on the interplay of Greek rhetoric, Jewish and Christian sermons, and NT literature. For the Thessalonian correspondence, Malherbe has delineated the rhetorical situation and Paul's response and Betz's use of Socratic traditions has illuminated Paul's apologetic rhetoric in 2 Corinthians. Church's analysis of Philemon carefully demonstrates the use of deliberative rhetoric. Stowers' study of the classical diatribe clarifies misconceptions of that rhetorical feature in the Pauline letters and establishes it in its literary and instructional context. His introduction to Greco-Roman letter writing updates the work of Doty and White on epistolary form and provides rhetorical critics with a description of classical epistolography to complement the standard discussions of literary and oral rhetoric. Wuellner's studies of Pauline rhetoric demonstrate how the method ought to identify not only rhetorical elements and structure but also their function in the flow of argumentation, how the method can shed light on the function of the epistolary elements identified by form critics, and how misleading a consideration of content (the Law) can be if it is not related to rhetorical aim (epideictic in Romans but forensic in Galatians). The rhetorical criticism based on the principles of classical rhetoric has a historical perspective and thus directly complements traditional historical criticism.

Bibliography

Alter, R., and Kermode, F., eds. 1987. *The Literary Guide to the Bible.* Cambridge, MA.

Beardslee, W. 1971. *Literary Criticism of the New Testament.* Philadelphia.

Betz, H. D. 1972. *Der Apostel Paulus und die Sokratische Tradition.* BHT 45. Tübingen.

———. 1979. *Galatians.* Hermeneia. Philadelphia.

Black, C. 1988. The Rhetorical Form of the Hellenistic Jewish and Early Christian Sermon. *HTR* 81: 1–18.

Booth, W. 1982. *The Rhetoric of Fiction.* Chicago.

Cadbury, H. J. 1968. *The Making of Luke-Acts.* London.

Cecchetti, D. 1976. *L'Esegesi biblica dai padri all'umanesimo.* Turin.

Church, F. 1978. Rhetorical Structure and Design in Paul's Letter to Philemon. *HTR* 71: 17–33.

Conley, T. 1983. *"Philōn Rhētor": A Study of Rhetoric and Exegesis.* Protocol of the 47th Colloquy. Berkeley.

Corbett, E. P. 1969. *Rhetorical Analyses of Literary Works.* New York.

Deissmann, A. 1965. *Light From the Ancient East.* Trans. R. M. Strachan. Grand Rapids.

Dibelius, M. 1927. The Structure and Literary Character of the Gospels. *HTR* 20: 151–70.

———. 1956. The Speeches in Acts and Ancient Historiography. Pp. 138–85 in *Studies in the Acts of the Apostles.* Trans. M. Ling. New York.

Doty, W. 1973. *Letters in Primitive Christianity.* Philadelphia.

Fiore, B. 1985a. "Covert Allusion" in 1 Corinthians 1–4. *CBQ* 47: 85–104.

———. 1985b. The Hortatory Function of Paul's Boasting *PEGLAMBS* 5: 39–46.

Fowler, R. 1985a. The Rhetoric of Indirection in the Gospel of Mark. *PEGLAMBS* 5: 47–56.

———. 1985b. Who Is "the Reader" in Reader Response Criticism? *Semeia* 31: 5–23.

Frei, H. 1974. *The Eclipse of Biblical Narrative.* New Haven.

Frye, N. 1973. *Anatomy of Criticism.* Princeton.

Funk, R. 1966. *Language, Hermeneutics and Word of God.* New York.

Genette, G. 1985. *Narrative Discourse.* Trans. E. Lewin. Ithaca.

Hyde, M., and Smith, C. 1979. Hermeneutics and Rhetoric: A Seen But Not Unobserved Relationship. *Quarterly Journal of Speech* 65: 347–63.

Kennedy, G. 1984. *New Testament Interpretation through Rhetorical Criticism.* Chapel Hill.

Lahurd, C. 1985. Rhetorical Criticism, Biblical Criticism and Literary Criticism: Issues of Methodological Pluralism. *PEGLAMBS* 5: 87–101.

Lausberg, H. 1960. *Handbuch der literarischen Rhetorik.* Munich.

Malherbe, A. 1983. Exhortation in First Thessalonians. *NovT* 25: 238–56.

Martin, J. 1974. *Antike Rhetorik.* Munich.

Muilenburg, J. 1969. Form Criticism and Beyond. *JBL* 88: 1–18.

Patton, J., and Robbins, V. 1980. Rhetoric and Biblical Criticism. *Quarterly Journal of Speech* 66: 327–36.

Perelman, C. 1969. *The New Rhetoric.* Notre Dame.

Pritchard, J. P. 1972. *A Literary Approach to the New Testament.* Norman, OK.

Rhoads, D., and Michie, D. 1982. *Mark as Story.* Philadelphia.

Robbins, V. 1984. *Jesus the Teacher: A Socio-Rhetorical Interpretation of Mark.* Philadelphia.

Smalley, B. 1983. *The Study of the Bible in the Middle Ages.* 3d rev. ed. Oxford.

Sternberg, M. 1987. *The Poetics of Biblical Narrative.* Bloomington.

Stowers, S. 1981. *The Diatribe and Paul's Letter to the Romans.* SBLDS 57. Chico, CA.

———. 1986. *Letter Writing in Greco-Roman Antiquity.* Philadelphia.

Talbert, C. 1974. *Literary Patterns, Theological Themes and the Genre of Luke Acts.* SBLMS 20. Missoula, MT.

Via, D. O., Jr. 1967. *The Parables: Their Literary and Existential Dimension.* Philadelphia.

White, J. 1972. *The Form and Structure of the Official Petition.* Missoula, MT.

Wilder, A. 1971. *Early Christian Rhetoric.* Cambridge, MA.

Wills, L. 1984. The Form of the Sermon in Hellenistic Judaism and Early Christianity. *HTR* 77: 277–99.

Winterowd, W. 1968. *Rhetoric: A Synthesis.* New York.

Wuellner, W. 1976. Paul's Rhetoric of Argumentation in Romans. *CBQ* 38: 330–51.

———. 1978. Toposforschung und Torahinterpretation bei Paulus und Jesus. *NTS* 24: 463–83.

———. 1979. Greek Rhetoric and Pauline Argumentation. Pp. 177–88 in *Early Christian Literature and the Classical Intellectual Tradition,* ed. W. Schoedel and R. Wilken. Paris.
———. 1985. Where Is Rhetorical Criticism Taking Us? Paper read at the CBA national meeting.

BENJAMIN FIORE

RHO. The seventeenth letter of the Greek alphabet.

RHODA (PERSON) [Gk *Rhodē*]. The servant girl of Mary (mother of John Mark) mentioned only in Acts 12:12–17. Hers is not a proper name, but a nickname, a diminutive of the word for rosebud, meaning little rose. Such nicknames were common for household servants (Haenchen 1971: 385). She is called a *paidiskē,* which literally means "little girl" but in the NT is always used of someone of servant class (cf. Matt 26:69; Mark 14:66, 69; Luke 22:56; Acts 16:16; and especially John 18:17).

Rhoda is portrayed as a household servant in charge of (among other things) answering the courtyard gate that opens on to the street. Luke's presentation suggests that Rhoda was a Christian taking part in a prayer meeting when Peter arrived at the house of Mary, mother of John Mark. Rhoda goes to the courtyard entrance, recognizes Peter's voice, and in her excitement returns to the meeting without opening the gate. However, when she announces Peter's presence at the door, she is declared to be "out of her mind." This may reflect prejudice against a woman's, particularly a female servant's, word of witness.

Nevertheless, as Luke tells the story, Rhoda is vindicated by her persistence in claiming Peter's presence. Thus Luke presents Rhoda as an example to his audience that the testimony of a woman, even a female servant, can be trustworthy. He may be intentionally countering tendencies to devalue the word of a woman by showing that even a servant girl like Rhoda can be trusted.

Bibliography

Burton, H. 1881. The House of Mary. *ExpTim* 2d ser. 1: 313–18.
Haenchen, E. 1971. *The Acts of the Apostles.* Philadelphia.
Witherington, B. 1988. *Women in the Earliest Churches.* Cambridge.

BEN WITHERINGTON, III

RHODES (PLACE) [Gk *Rhodos*]. An island 45 miles long and 22 miles wide located in the SE Aegean Sea between Crete and Asia Minor. The capital of the island, also named Rhodes, was a port city on the NE shore of the island. According to Pindar (*Ol.* 7.54–76), the island emerged out of the sea and was a portion of the sun god Apollo (Helios), whose cult continued there throughout antiquity. Three noteworthy ancient foundations were Ialysos, Kameiros, and Lindos, named in honor of the three grandsons of Helios and the nymph Rhodos, daughter of Aphrodite. (For the ancient legends pertaining to Rhodes, see especially Pind. *Ol.* 7; Apollod. *Bibl.* 3.2; Diod. Sic. 5.55–59; Strabo 14.2.6–8; and Ath. 8.360d–61c).

Mt. Atabyrion (1,233 m), once forested with cypress and conifers used for shipbuilding, was a landmark for ancient mariners. Zeus Atabyrios was worshipped on the summit where parts of a walled precinct, which may have been an ancient temple, have survived. A number of dedications to the god have survived, including small bronze bulls. The name of the mountain appears to be the Greek form of the Semitic Tabor.

The island played an influential economic and political role in antiquity and supported a large population. Harbors on the island's E coast were of strategic importance, controlling entry to the Aegean Sea. A number of classical sources (Polybius, Diodorus, Strabo, Dio Chrysostom, and Aristides) extol the achievements of Rhodes in politics, economics, and culture. The island was also ideally situated as a meeting point for the sea routes which converged from the Greek peninsula and islands, from Palestine and Cypress, and from Asia Minor. Considerable quantities of grain, fruit and vegetables, olives, honey, wine, and crafted wares were exported from the island.

A Minoan colony was planted at Ialysos, controlling the entry to the Aegean, around 1600 B.C.E. and flourished until ca. 1425 B.C.E. Evidence for trade with the coastal cities of Syria-Palestine, including Ugarit, exists from the 16th century B.C.E. By 1450 B.C.E. a Mycenean enclave was established which apparently flourished alongside the Minoan foundation. By 1425 B.C.E. the Minoan colonists had abandoned Rhodes, marking a permanent decline in the Cretan thalassocracy in the E Mediterranean. At the time of the fall there is evidence for an acceleration of Greek influence on the island.

The Mycenean settlers on Rhodes traded primarily with the coastal regions of Asia Minor and the Levant, although there is evidence of their ware farther afield. Strong fortifications on Rhodes protected the caravan terminus region. Apparently the Myceneans on Rhodes remained independent of the Myceneans on Knossos, opening new routes for trade and piracy and ultimately supplanting Crete's control of the S Aegean.

From the reign of the Hittite kings Muwatallis and his grandson Tudkhaliyas IV (ca. 1250 B.C.E.), correspondences mention the kingdom of the Ahhiyawa, Hittite for either Achaiwa or Ageiwa. Achaians and Argives are almost interchangeable in Homer for the Greek tribes fighting against Troy. One of the headquarters for the Ahhiyawa was probably Rhodes. These E Myceneans joined forces with the Sea Peoples against Pharaoh Merneptah in his 5th year (1233 B.C.E.). They were ultimately defeated in two large-scale battles at the end of the Bronze Age, the first during the reign of Rameses III (ca. 1187), commemorated on the reliefs from Medinet Habu and the second at the hand of the Hittite king Šuppiluliumas II (ca. 1180) off the coast of Cyprus.

The Myceneans of Rhodes were later listed in Homer's Achean Catalogue. Continuity on Rhodes between the 12th-century Mycenean wares and the proto-geometric wares of the Dark Ages strongly suggests that the Mycenean settlers were not displaced by the Dorian invasions at the close of the Bronze Age. During the ensuing Dark Ages, the island continued to develop as a commercial center, and carved Phoenician and Syrian ivories found on the island illustrate that trade continued with the E.

By 650 B.C.E. Rhodes had completely outstripped Crete for primacy in the E Mediterranean and was second only to Corinth in the W. Rhodian terracotta are found throughout the Greek world after 610 B.C.E. Trade enriched the island as it enjoyed an intermediary position between Egypt and Ionia, and Rhodes planted important and widespread colonies on Sicily, the Adriatic coast of Italy, and the Balearic islands.

From the latter part of the 6th century to the early years of the 5th century B.C.E. Rhodes was under Persian control. After the Persian wars, Rhodes joined the Delian League, further enhancing the island's commercial connections. In 408 B.C.E., Kameiros, Ialysos, and Lindos founded a federal capital on a man-made harbor, naming the city Rhodes. Trade through the newly established portside capital brought great wealth and political power.

The most pronounced symbol of Rhodes' economic and political success was the famous Colossus of Rhodes. The statue portrayed Apollo (Helios), the sun god, and was considered to be one of the seven wonders of the ancient world. The 90-foot-high bronze statue was built between 304 and 292 B.C.E. to commemorate a victory over Demetrius (sarcastically called Poliorcetes, "the sacker of cities") in 304/3, who was unable to sack the capital (Diodoros 20.81–88, 91–100). The Byzantine Philo provides details on the construction of the giant monument. The Colossus did not bestride the harbor mouth, nor was it built on the end of a mole, but rather was probably erected in the center of town. The statue was broken off at the knees by an earthquake in 227/6 B.C.E. and was completely demolished by Arabs in 653 C.E.

The winged Nike of Samothrace was another famous monument dedicated by the citizens of Rhodes to commemorate a victory in 190 B.C.E. over Antiochus III. The statue, which now resides at the Louvre, was reconstructed by Karl Lehman (d. 1960). Other victory prows, not nearly as splendorous, have been excavated on the island.

Rhodes reached a pinnacle of power during the Hellenistic period, subsidizing political and economic activities in other Greek regions. Its preeminence was directly dependent on its relationship with Egypt. As a cultural center during the Hellenistic and Roman periods, Rhodes was the home of the epic poet Apollonius (author of *Argonautica*), a sculptural school which produced the *Laocoön,* and the philosophical schools of Panaetius and Poseidonius. After the Battle of Pydna in 167 B.C.E., Rome undermined Rhodes' economic advantage by declaring Delos a free harbor. The island was further subjugated by Crassus in 43 B.C.E., although it remained a popular resort center throughout the Roman imperial period.

The Hellenistic city of Rhodes had a temple of Aphrodite just W of the harbor and a shrine of Dionysos. On or near the acropolis were at least three more temples, a stadium, and a gymnasium with a theaterlike lecture hall. Toward the N are foundations of the temple of Zeus and Athena and some distance farther S is the Temenos of Pythian Apollo.

The city, renowned by ancients for its beauty, was planned by the famous architect Hippodamus of Miletus, who created a harmonious effect which impressed later writers (Aristides 43.6; Lucian *Am.* 8). The extant remains from Rhodes, however, are comparatively meager. The island suffered disastrous earthquakes in 345 and 515 C.E., and the city was eventually ransacked and fortified by the medieval Knights of St. John.

Rhodes is mentioned several times by Josephus in connection with Herod the Great's travels. On a winter journey Herod passed Rhodes on his way to the Italian port of Brundisium in order to intercede with the Romans on his brother's behalf (*Ant* 14.370–78; and *JW* 1.277–81). After the Battle of Actium in 30 B.C.E. Herod traveled to Rhodes and humbled himself before Octavian, who ratified Herod's kingship over Judea and bestowed further honors upon him. Herod later sailed along the W coast of Asia Minor by way of Rhodes to meet Agrippa, Augustus' chief lieutenant at Sinope in 14 B.C.E. (*Ant* 16.16–26). For his own repute in Rhodes, Herod rebuilt the temple of the Pythian Apollo and made grants to the inhabitants for shipbuilding, probably to enhance the Judean economy.

Rhodes is mentioned among the peoples and nations who traded with Tyre, in a passage describing Tyre's wealth (Ezek 27:15). The RSV and the NEB, following a textual variation (LXX *huoi Rhodiōn* and the Peshitta *bny rdn*), translate the passage "the sons of Rhodes." However, the AV, following the MT and the Vg, translates the passage "the sons of Dedan." If the prophet is listing the peoples from W to E, which seems likely, Rhodes occurs in its proper position in v 15 and Dedan in v 20, as found in the RSV and NEB.

The Roman consul sent a letter in 142 B.C.E. to the city of Rhodes concerning relations between Rome and the Maccabean state, providing the earliest extant testimony for Jewish inhabitants on the island (1 Macc 15:23). Jewish maritime trade probably existed between Alexandrian and Rhodian Jews prior to 142 B.C.E., despite the silence of Hellenistic epigraphic sources. Apollonius Molon (1st century B.C.E.) and Posidonius of Apamea (135–51 B.C.E.) each settled in Rhodes and wrote anti-Jewish works (see Eusebius *Praep. Evang.* 9.19.1–3; and Josephus *AgAp* 2.16, 79–80, 89, 91–96, 145, 148, 236, 255, 258, and 295). Both supplied material for Apion's later attack on the Jews (*AgAp* 2.79).

There is an interesting report of a Jewish *grammaticus* named Diogenus who taught every Sabbath in Rhodes between 6 B.C.E. and 2 C.E. (Suetonius *Vit. Tib.* 32.2). There are also several Jewish inscriptions from the imperial period that bear further evidence of a Jewish community in Rhodes (*IG* 12.1, no. 11; and 12.1, no. 593).

Rhodes is mentioned as one of Paul's stops on his way to Jerusalem (Acts 21:1). Paul may have attempted to convert the Rhodian Jews to Christianity on his journey. According to tradition, Paul landed on an inlet to the S of the main harbor at Lindos.

SCOTT T. CARROLL

RHODOCUS (PERSON) [Gk *Rhodokos*]. Described in 2 Macc 13:21 as a traitor among the Jewish forces who gave Antiochus V Eupator information during the siege of Beth-zur. He is not mentioned in the parallel account of these events in 1 Maccabees. The name, unattested elsewhere in Jewish sources, may be of Iranian origin (Goldstein *2 Maccabees* AB, 466). This collaborationist was sought out, caught and *katekleisthē* (imprisoned). The latter term may be a euphemism for killing him (Abel 1949: 455).

Bibliography

Abel, F.-M. 1949. *Les Livres des Maccabées.* EBib. Paris.

JOHN KAMPEN

RIBAI (PERSON) [Heb *rîbay*]. Mentioned only in 2 Sam 23:29 (= 1 Chr 11:31, where LXX has *Ribai*) as the father of Ithai, one of "the Thirty," David's corps of military elite *(gibbōrim)*. See DAVID'S CHAMPIONS. Ribai was from Gibeah of the Benjamites, the famous "Gibeah of Saul" (1 Sam 11:4), modern Tell el-Ful (M.R. 172136), approximately 3.5 miles N of Jerusalem. "Ribai," shortened from the verbal name form, probably means "May Yahweh plead the case (of the name giver)."

Bibliography

Elliger, K. 1933. Die dreissig Helden Davids. *PJ* 31: 29–75.
Mazar, B. 1963. The Military Elite of King David. *VT* 13: 310–20.

DAVID L. THOMPSON

RIBLAH (PLACE) [Heb *riblâ*]. A city "in the land of Hamath" in Syria (2 Kgs 23:33; 25:21; Jer 39:5; 52:9, 27). Riblah is located 11 km S of Kadesh, between Kadesh and Arnaim (*ANET,* 256) on the E bank of the Orontes River. The ruins of Riblah are located near a modern village, Ribleh, ca. 58 km NE of Baalbek (34°N, 36°12′E), in a wide plain suitable for a large military campsite.

Rameses II records that his troops passed the vicinities of Kadesh, Shabtuna, and Arnaim. The Battle of Kadesh between Rameses (19th Dynasty) and the Hittite king Muwatallis was fought there in the beginning of the 13th century B.C. Shabtuna, between Kadesh and Arnaim, may be identified with Riblah. If the name Riblah is etymologically related to the Aramaic word *ʾarbēlāʾ* "sieve," Riblah may mean "shaken (city)." The shapes of *reš* and *dalet* of the Old Aramaic script from 8th century B.C. to 3d century B.C. are more similar than the *reš* and *dalet* of the Aramaic-Hebrew square script of the MT. Probably for this reason some of the Jews started to call this city Diblah, euphonious to *dĕbēlâ,* "pressed fig cake," the meaning of which is related to Diblathaim in Moab (Num 33:46). Diblah may also be related to a Babylonian word *diblu* (or *dublu*), "foundation platform."

The Riblah of Syria was used as headquarters by Pharaoh Neco II in his military expedition to the N after the battles at Megiddo and Kadesh S of Lake Ḥoms. He killed Josiah in 609 B.C. at Megiddo. Jehoahaz was put on the throne by popular demand, although he was not the eldest son of Josiah. Neco probably feared Jehoahaz' desire for revenge against him for the death of his father. He also feared that Jehoahaz might follow his father's anti-Egyptian policies. Therefore, Neco summoned him to Riblah after a reign of three months "so that he might not reign in Jerusalem." Later he took Jehoahaz with him to Egypt and placed his brother on the throne (2 Kgs 23:33, 34).

Riblah also became the headquarters of Nebuchadnezzar during his third expedition against Jerusalem in 588–586 B.C. After two years of siege, the last king of Judah, Zedekiah, escaped from Jerusalem but was captured near Jericho and brought to Nebuchadnezzar at Riblah. His sons were killed in his presence, his eyes were plucked out, and he was deported to Babylon in chains where he remained a prisoner until the day of his death (2 Kgs 25:1–7; Jer 52:1–11).

If Lebo-Hamath (or the Entrance to Hamath) is located S of Riblah, "Shepham of Riblah" (Num 34:11), which is S of Lebo-Hamath, cannot be identified with the Riblah in Syria. "Hamath" designates both the city of Hamath and the territorial land of Hamath which included the area of the Orontes Valley. So the geographical name "Entrance to Hamath" indicates the area of the source of the Orontes River, not necessarily a city. Likewise, "Shepham of Riblah" (Num 34:11), which is better than the translation "Shepham to Riblah," should be differentiated from the "Riblah of Hamath" and the other Shepham in Gad (1 Chr 5:12). This "Shepham of Riblah" is yet an unidentified point on the NE boundary of the land of Israel. See also *MBA*, map nos. 34, 44, 148, 159, 163; and *EncJud* 14: 151–52.

YOSHITAKA KOBAYASHI

RIDDLES. In the ancient world riddles concealed valuable information from the unworthy while divulging important facts to those deserving them. That simultaneous clue and trap resulted from cipher language, imagery that functioned on two levels, the ordinary meaning and a special sense recognized only by perceptive persons. Often the hidden meaning enabled groups to detect outsiders, who had no idea what the cipher communicated to those who possessed secret data. In other circumstances, less threatening, riddles enlivened ordinary discourse, particularly at weddings, banquets, and intellectual gatherings.

One of the oldest riddles describes the academy as follows: "One whose eyes are closed enters it; one whose eyes have been opened departs from it." This Sumerian riddle uses "eyes" in two senses, ordinary sight and seeing as the equivalent of understanding. Similarly, "opened" and "closed" refer to a literal as well as a symbolic reality. The trap operates on the literal level, tempting the riddlee to offer one of two answers, possibly three: sleep, life, and sex. Astute students who recognize that eyes mirror the soul advance a step further toward solving the riddle. Knowledge acquired through experience opens eyes previously closed by prejudice, inaccurate information, and ignorance.

According to Num 12:6–8, the deity regularly communicated with prophets by means of veiled speech, either visions or dreams, whereas Moses enjoyed preferred status. With him Yahweh spoke mouth to mouth, clearly, and not in riddles (*bĕḥîdōt*). This early tradition implies that Israel's seers and prophets had to interpret their enigmatic visions and oracles in the light of the faith by which they lived. Enigma thus belonged to the essence of prophecy, in this ancient writer's view. One thinks immediately of Amos' visions of ordinary things such as a basket of summer fruit that conveyed to him quite a chilling message of finality, or of Jeremiah's vision of an almond branch that reminded him of Yahweh's watchful eye that overlooks no villainy.

The introduction to the initial collection in the book of Proverbs, and perhaps to the whole book, concludes the goal of instruction with these words: "to understand a proverb (*māšāl*) and a figure (*mĕlîṣâ*), the words of the wise and their riddles (*ḥîdōtām,* 1:6)." The 2d-century teacher, Jesus ben Sira, also emphasizes the hidden meanings and obscurities of parables as the fundamental preoccupation of professional scribes (Sir 39:1–3). Despite such conscious stress on the importance of riddles to the sages, none has survived in the corpus of biblical wisdom literature.

Given the explosive character of riddles, their disappearance occasions less astonishment. They may have persisted as disintegrated riddles, requiring modern interpreters to reconstruct their original form. Numerical proverbial sayings naturally tempt contemporary scholars to seek illumination from riddles, for in many instances one can readily rephrase the sayings in riddle form. Two examples suffice, Prov 30:18–19 and 30:20. The first alludes to movement that leaves no trace; the cipher "way" (*derek*) refers to motion and, in the punch line, dominance. The second example continues the imagery but adds two other cipher words, "mouth" (*pîhā*) and "eats" (*ʾākĕlâ*). Behind this imagery lies the mythic notion of woman as devourer in the sexual act and a widespread understanding of oral sex, easily documented from Egyptian, Mesopotamian, and Greek sources.

Other disintegrated riddles seem to exist throughout the book of Proverbs and Song of Songs. The reference to one's wife as a cistern (= well) and to sperm as streams of water (Prov 5:15–16) can easily be formulated as a riddle. So can the description of a virgin lover as a locked garden and a sealed fountain (Cant 4:12). Other proverbial sayings that possess this ready transferability include the following, among others: Prov 5:15–23; 6:23–24; 16:15; 20:27; 23:27, 29–35; 25:2–3, and 27:20.

Two psalms may preserve riddles, now partially transformed into an unrecognizable form. The description of the sun as a bridegroom on a journey from east to west, and the characterization of day and night as mute messengers could have existed at one time in riddle form. Similarly, Psalm 49 may derive its power from two riddles, one about the resemblance between human beings and animals and the other about the wise person who claims victory over death. Affinities with the pessimistic sayings of Agur in Prov 30:1–4 suggest that a riddle lurks behind the "human revelation" of the sage's ignorance.

Within Israel's narrative literature, riddles play a prominent role in the account of King Solomon (1 Kgs 10:1–5; 2 Chr 9:1–4). The Queen of Sheba came to Jerusalem, so the story goes, to test Solomon with difficult questions (*bĕḥîdôt*). He told her (*wayyagged*) the requisite answers to all her queries, so that nothing was hidden (*neʿlām*) from him that he did not tell her (*higgîd*). Josephus mentions riddle contests between King Hiram of Tyre and Solomon (*Ant* 8.5.3). In neither of these accounts does a single riddle appear, but a Hebrew manuscript compiled in the 15th century associates nineteen "riddles" with the visit of the Queen of Sheba, the first four of which appear in the Midrash to Proverbs. Of the nineteen, only three qualify as riddles by using ciphers. The first refers to the womb, the ten orifices of humans, and the navel ("There is an enclosure with ten doors; when one is open nine are shut, when nine are open one is shut"). The second alludes to a ship that has been constructed out of a tree ("There is something which when living does not move, yet when its head is cut off it moves"). The third points to Jonah's experience in the belly of a huge fish ("The dead lived, the grave moves, and the dead prays: what is that?"). In these three riddles the cipher words are "doors," "head," "grave," and "dead."

The only complete riddles in the Hebrew Bible occur in the Samson narrative, only one of which is actually designated a riddle. During wedding festivities Samson poses a riddle to his thirty companions: "Food came from the eater; sweetness came from strength" (Judg 14:14). In all probability, the riddle antedates its present context and referred to vomit and sperm; both answers served to ensnare unwary Philistines. Samson adapts the riddle to his private experience, specifically the gathering of honey from the carcass of a lion which the young warrior had earlier slain. Unable to solve the riddle, and wishing to escape the consequences of their failure, the companions threaten Samson's beautiful wife repeatedly until she entices him to surrender his well-guarded secret. Equipped with this ill-gotten information, the men give their answer in the form of a question: "What is sweeter than honey? What is stronger than a lion?" and evoke his response: "If you had not plowed with my heifer, you would not have found out my riddle" (Judg 14:18). The Philistines' answer may itself conceal an earlier riddle about love, the emotion that seemed as strong as death (Cant 8:6), and Samson's sharp retort uses the ciphers "plow" and "heifer," erotic imagery that was well known in the ANE.

This story provides valuable information about the vocabulary connected with the act of riddling: *māṣāʾ* for discovering the solution, *pātāḥ* for opening the riddle, *nāgad* in the *Hiphʿil* for posing the riddle. The account in 1 Kgs 10:1–5 suggests that the latter verb also functioned to describe the process of informing the riddler of the correct answer. The two Hebrew words for riddle, *ḥîdâ* and *mĕlîṣâ,* push the symbolic sense of *māšāl* further still. The two Greek words for riddle, *enigma* and *griphos,* capture the twofold nature of riddles, their mysterious clue and hidden trap.

Other biblical texts may contain former riddles. Two examples indicate the possibilities awaiting persistent inquirers. The obscure story of a divine messenger who divulges its name to Samson's father alludes to Yahweh's awesome deeds and demonstrates Manoah's worth when he offers a *minḥâ* sacrifice in addition to the specified burnt offering, thus suggesting a pun on his own name (Manoah and *minḥâ,* Judg 13:18–19). The book of Ecclesiastes preserves a striking observation that "a living dog is better than a dead lion" (9:4). In light of the widespread use of dog for loathsome people such as male prostitutes and lion for royalty, one can offer a sociological interpretation of this saying. It may have been used by a woman to justify remarriage to someone whose social status was decidedly inferior to that of her previous husband.

Two related forms in the ancient world occur also in the Hebrew Bible and in the Septuagint (LXX). The first, difficult questions, has survived in the books of Proverbs and Job. "Can a man carry fire in his bosom and his clothes not be burned? Or can one walk on hot coals and his feet not be scorched?" (Prov 6:27–28). "Can papyrus grow where there is no marsh? Can reeds flourish where there is no water?" (Job 8:11). Sir 1:2–3 has a slightly different form: "The sands of the seas, the drops of rain, and the days of eternity—who can count them? The height of heaven, the breadth of the earth, the abyss, and wisdom—who can search them out?"

The second related form, impossible tasks, became immensely popular in some circles where the deity's mysterious works received emphasis. The poetic exploration of the problem of evil in 2 Esdras uses this form effectively. "Count up for me those who have not yet come, and gather for me the scattered raindrops, and make the withered flowers bloom again for me" (5:36). "Show me the picture of a voice" (5:37). "Go, weigh for me the weight of fire, or measure for me a measure of wind, or call back for me the day that is past" (4:5). Likewise, the wisdom sayings of Ahiqar (see *OTP* 2: 494–507) employ this particular literary device. "Build me a castle in the sky" (5:2). "Sew up for me this broken millstone" (7:20). "Twine me five cables from the sand of the river" (7:17). "If waters should stand up without earth, sparrows fly without wings, ravens become white as snow, the bitter become sweet as honey, then may the fool become wise" (2:62). One can compare Job 11:12 ("But a stupid man will get understanding, when a wild ass's colt is born a man") and Ovid's "Then will the stag fly."

Paradoxical proverbs in Mesopotamia and in Egypt achieved the same result (e.g., see Gordon 1959). Sumerian texts yield the following: "Do not heap up a mountain in the mountains." "Do not cut off the neck of that which has had its neck cut off." "Make the distant side the nearer side." "From 3600 oxen there is no dung." "A scribe without a hand, a singer without a throat." An Egyptian existential proverb attributed to Ptahhotep (see *ANET,* p. 414) refers to "dying while alive every day."

Pseudo-catechisms emerged in Jewish and Christian instruction. These riddlelike questions introduced a playful element into education. "Who was the oldest man on earth, yet he died before his father? Methuselah." "Who was both father and grandfather to two of his children? Lot." "When was the world its narrowest? In Noah's day." Such questions focus on a few unusual circumstances in the Hebrew Bible, especially those surrounding Noah, Lot, Adam and Eve, Jonah, and Elijah.

A third related form, contest literature, has yielded the exquisite discussion in 1 Esdr 3:1–4:41 of what is strongest. The three answers—wine, the king, and women—are supplemented by a fourth, (the Lord of) truth. The Greco-Roman world also explored the strongest things in the world, and riddles were sometimes presented to guests at a party on condition that anyone failing to solve the riddle had to drink salted wine.

Riddles could even dispense with words altogether. Such symbolic or narrative riddles describe actions that convey a particular message to the observant eye. This type of riddle enabled persons to communicate politically dangerous messages without fear of exposure. For example, a young ruler asked his father for advice about improving the government; the father walked into his garden and uprooted older plants, transplanting young ones in their place; *Gen. Rab.* 67 gives a variant of this enacted riddle.

Bibliography

Bal, M. 1987. *Lethal Love: Feminist Literary Readings of Biblical Love Stories.* Bloomington.
Crenshaw, J. L. 1974. Wisdom. Pp. 225–264 in *Old Testament Form Criticism,* ed. J. H. Hayes. San Antonio.
———. 1975. The Samson Saga: Filial Devotion or Erotic Attachment? *ZAW* 87: 470–504.
———. 1978. *Samson.* Atlanta and London.
———. 1981. The Contest of Darius' Guards in 1 Esdras 3:1–5:3. Pp. 74–88 in *Images of Man and God,* ed. B. Long. Sheffield.
Gordon, E. I. 1959. *Sumerian Proverbs.* Philadelphia.
Greenstein, E. L. 1981. The Riddle of Samson. *Prooftexts* 1: 237–60.
Hain, M. 1966. *Rätsel.* Stuttgart.
Hertz, W. 1983. Die Rätsel der Königen von Saba. *Zeitschrift für Deutsches Alterthum* 27: 1–33.
Margalith, O. 1986. Samson's Riddle and Samson's Magic Locks. *VT* 36: 225–34.
Müller, H.-P. 1970. Der Begriff "Rätsel" im Alten Testament. *VT* 20: 465–89.
Nel, P. 1985. The Riddle of Samson (Judg 14,14–18). *Bib* 66: 534–45.
Pepicello, W. J., and Green, T. G. 1984. *The Language of Riddles.* Columbus.
Perdue, L. G. 1974. The Riddles of Psalm 49. *JBL* 93: 533–42.
Porter, J. R. 1962. Samson's Riddles: Judges 14,18. *JTS* 13: 106–9.
Schechter, S. 1890. The Riddles of Solomon in Rabbinic Literature. *Folklore* 1: 349–58.
Taylor, A. 1943. The Riddle. *California Folklore Quarterly* 2: 129–47.
———. 1951. *English Riddles from Oral Tradition.* Los Angeles.
Tur-Sinai, H. 1924. The Riddle in the Bible. *HUCA* 1: 125–49.
Wünsche, A. 1883. *Die Räthselweisheit bei den Hebräern mit hinblick auf andere Völker.* Leipzig.

JAMES L. CRENSHAW

RIDGE OF JUDEA (PLACE) [Gk *ho priōn tēs Iodaias*]. A toponymic designation in the tale of Judith (Jdt 3:9). It was one of the places where Holofernes, Nebuchadnezzar's general, encamped during his invasion of the countries of the West after they had disobeyed Nebuchadnezzar's call to arms against Arphaxad, king of Media. According to the story, Holofernes encamped S of the Plain of Esdraelon, near Dothan (M.R. 172202), between Scythopolis (Beth-shan, M.R. 197212) and Geba. Two towns are possible for the location of Geba, one being 6 km NE of Samaria (M.R. 171192), the other 6 km NE of Dor (M.R. 146228), the former more directly aligned with Dothan and Scythopolis.

Dothan is identified as "fronting the great ridge of Judea" (*tou prionos tou megalou tēs Ioudaias*). Such a description puts this land feature in the hills of N Samaria, and therefore it should not be confused with the hill country of Judah in the S. Thus, the name appears to be a misnomer, and the toponym remains obscure. Some have suggested that the reference is to the Esdraelon Valley. According to this position, the original Hebrew version mentioned "the plain (*mîšôr*) of Judea"; however, the Greek version misread the Heb *mîšôr* as *maśśôr* ("a saw"), thus translating the word by the Gk *priōn,* meaning "jagged row" or "saw." This suggestion has been questioned on the basis that elsewhere the Esdraelon is described only as a "valley" (Heb *ʿemeq*), not a "plain" (*mîšôr*; see Moore *Judith* AB, 143).

While it has been argued that the fictional genre of the

book of Judith might preclude certain geographical accuracies, on the contrary, the nationalistic nature of the tale might, indeed, encourage its realistic setting. However, the difficulty of the ancient versions (e.g., the Vg 3:14 omits this toponym) impedes any certain identification.

JOHN KUTSKO

RIGHT, RIGHT HAND. As in English, the right hand is used in Hebrew to indicate the opposite of the left (Jonah 4:11; Dan 12:7). It quite often is used as a direction, to the right of the person (2 Sam 16:6; 1 Kgs 22:19). When used as a reference to a compass point, right was the direction S, the direction of the right hand when facing E to gain one's orientation (1 Sam 23:19, 24). See also SOUTH.

The Heb *yāmîn,* "right," is paralleled by cognates in several other Semitic languages including Akkadian, Aramaic, and Arabic. The term is also found in Hebrew inscriptions, notably the Siloam Tunnel inscription.

Since right-handedness is most common, one would expect references to the strongest hand and the most skillful hand to refer to the right hand, and such is precisely the case. It is the right hand which holds the arrow, while the left holds the bow (Ezek 39:3). The right hand also apparently played the lyre while the left hand held it (Ps 137:5). The right hand of Yahweh was that which delivered Israel, shattering the enemy (Exod 15:6). Yahweh's right hand gains mighty victories for his people (Pss 20:7—Eng v 6; 44:4—Eng v 3; 98:1). By contrast, not once is Yahweh's left hand mentioned. An unusual phrase, *ʾiṭṭēr yad yāmîn,* literally, "bound of right hand," refers to left-handed warriors. Halpern has argued that the phrase does not refer to those born left-handed, and whose right hands were weaker or less dexterous, but to ones whose right hand had been bound, forcing them to become left-handed or ambidextrous, and, therefore, more skilled as a warrior (Halpern 1988: 41). To have Yahweh at one's right hand virtually assured victory, for it implied that Yahweh was supplying the might for the confrontation: "The Lord is at your right hand; he will shatter kings on the day of his wrath" (Ps 110:5).

Furthermore, the right hand was the hand of special blessing. When Jacob was about to bless his grandchildren, Joseph's sons, Ephraim and Manasseh, Joseph placed the older Manasseh at his grandfather's right hand. Jacob crossed his hands to place the right hand on Ephraim. When Joseph protested, Jacob continued anyway, giving the favored position and the better blessing to the younger Ephraim (Gen 48:13–20).

In a related usage, the position of honor is regularly at the host's right hand. To be at Yahweh's right hand is to be in the position of highest honor (Ps 110:1). Often in the NT (as well as in the well-known formula of the Apostles' Creed), that position is reserved for the resurrected Jesus (Col 3:1, cf. Heb 8:1; 12:2).

The name Benjamin, literally "son of the right hand," may well indicate the special importance or blessing of this child—the second son of the favored wife, and youngest child of Jacob. The name may indicate something like "specially favored."

Only occasonially does right as a direction have a moral connotation. The author of Ecclesiastes does say: "A wise man's heart inclines him toward the right, but a fool's heart toward the left" (10:2). More often the right way is depicted as the straight and narrow, from which one is not to deviate either to the right or to the left (Deut 5:32; 17:11, 20).

Bibliography

Halpern, B. 1988. *The First Historians.* New York.

JOEL F. DRINKARD, JR.

RIGHTEOUSNESS. This entry consists of four articles surveying the concept of righteousness in the OT, in early Judaism, in the non-Jewish Greco-Roman world, and in the NT.

OLD TESTAMENT

The RSV renders the Hebrew *ṣedeq-ṣĕdāqâ* by a variety of words: acquittal, deliverance, honest evidence (Prov 12:17), integrity (Job 31:6), judgment, justice, prosperity, right, righteousness (most common), righteous deeds, righteous help, salvation, saving help, victory, vindication. The JB often translates the Hebrew as "integrity," especially in Isaiah 40–66 and the Psalms. These various renderings endeavor to compass the constellation of nuances that the Hebrew conveys, particularly when in parallelism with other words or when in the context of different word groups.

The meaning of words that derive from the root *ṣdq* cannot be determined *a priori.* There is no basic *ṣdq* notion that must always be present with the three radicals *ṣ-d-q.* The OT texts must not be read through the eyes of the Reformation controversies about "righteousness" and "justification," or even through Paul's letters to the Romans and Galatians. The OT writers were not aware of the problems of the Church of the 1st or 16th centuries. The words and phrases, "righteousness," "justification," "he . . . whose sin is covered . . . to whom the Lord imputes no iniquity" (RSV Ps 32:1–2; cf. JB, NEB, NIV, AB), evoke theological associations which must be laid aside when dealing with the Heb terms *ṣedeq-ṣĕdāqâ.*

A. Cognate Background of *ṣdq*
B. Range and Meaning of Terms
C. Legal Uses and Nuances
  1. The Verb
  2. Nouns in the Pentateuch
  3. Other Uses
D. Proper Order, Proper Comportment
  1. 8th-Century Prophecy
  2. 7th-Century Prophecy
  3. Psalms
  4. Isaiah 40–66
  5. Ezekial, Malachi, Joel
  6. Joshua–2 Kings
  7. Job, Proverbs, Qoheleth
  8. Daniel
  9. *ṣedeq-ṣĕdāqâ* + *mišpāt*

E. God's *ṣedeq-ṣĕdāqâ*: Saving Action
  1. Psalms
  2. Isaiah 40–55
  3. Isaiah 56–66
  4. Hosea, Micah, Isaiah 1–39
  5. Jeremiah, Zechariah, Malachi
F. Plural of *ṣĕdāqâ*
G. Parallels and Word-fields
H. The Just or Righteous One (Heb *ṣaddîq*)
I. Current Research
J. Summary and Conclusion

A. Cognate Background of *ṣdq*

The root *ṣdq* is West Semitic in origin and is well attested in this language group:

1. Akkadian. The CAD has only one entry for *ṣaduq* and describes the word as an adjective meaning "right," "just." Abdu-hepa of Jerusalem (14th century B.C.) writes to the king of Egypt, "See, my Lord, I am right (*ṣa-du-uq*) about the people of GN." Abdu-hepa is acting as he should in the king's interest.

2. Amorite. The word *ṣaduq* occurs as a component of a number of Amorite names in which it is probably a theophorous element; *ṣidq* is rendered "justice," "rightness" by Huffmon (*APNM,* 256–57), who notes that the root is common Semitic, except Akkadian.

3. Old South Arabic. The verb *ṣdq* means "to grant, concede, fulfill an obligation, keep faith with (?)"; the noun means "right, due, truth, reality (?)"; the adjective means "proper, appropriate," with the nuances of "happy and fortunate" (Meyer 1966: 229; *DOSA,* 416–18).

4. Ugaritic. The word *ṣdq* is found in a number of proper names in the Ras Shamra texts (*UT,* 472–73). In the KRT text *ṣdqh* is an abstract noun in parallelism with *yšrh* (Fisher 1972: 320); Gray (1965: 132, n. 7) renders the words as "legitimate wife" (wife of *ṣdqh*), as does Gordon (1949: 67). The king of Ugarit is described as *bʿl ṣdq* (Gray 1966: 175–76), which may mean "legitimate king" or perhaps "lord of order," i.e., the one who brings right order or prosperity into life by giving the rain. Further information is found in Fisher (1981: 132, 203, 406–10).

5. Northwest Semitic Inscriptions. The word *ṣdq* occurs in a number of Aramaic and Phoenician inscriptions the text of which, with German translation and comments, may be found in the three Donner-Röllig (*KAI*) volumes; there is an English translation of some of these in *ANET* (499–505, 653–62). The words *ṣdq* and *yšr* occur together in the 10th-century Yeḥimilk inscription from Byblos describing "a righteous king and an upright king" (*ANET,* 499; *KAI* 1:1; 2:6); Swetnam (1965: 32) argues for "legitimate" instead of "righteous," Herrmann (1958: 22) for "lawful" referring to Jer 23:5, *smḥ ṣdq,* "a righteous, lawful branch." The Jeremiah phrase is found in the Phoenician Lapēthos inscription (*KAI* 1: 10; 2: 60–61) from Cyprus, 3d century B.C. Cooke (1903: 82) proposes "legitimate offspring"; Swetnam (1965: 29–31) "rightful scion"; *KAI* "legitimer Spross." In a bilingual inscription from Karatepe (8th century B.C.), Azitwadda narrates his good deeds and says that "every king considered me his father because of my righteousness (*bṣdqy*) and my wisdom and the kindness of my heart" (*ANET,* 499–500); likewise *KAI* (1: 5; 2: 36); Swetnam (1965: 34) renders "because of my rightfulness" (i.e., legitimacy).

The substantive *ṣdq* occurs five times in the Zinçirli inscriptions (8th century), preceded each time by the preposition *b,* twice without suffix, twice with the suffix of 1st sing., once with the suffix of 3d masc. sing. *KAI* (1: 40–41; 2: 224, 233, 237) renders it as "loyalty," i.e., to the Assyrian overlord. Swetnam (1965: 34–36), following Euler (1938: 278–79), disagrees with the rendering "loyalty" in the Panammuwa and Barrākib inscriptions (Zinçirli) and argues strongly for "legitimate succession," as it is a question of legitimate succession from father to son. In the Barrākib inscription the incumbent says that he was seated on the throne "because of the righteousness of my father (*bṣdq ʾby*) and my own righteousness (*bṣdqy*) . . ." (*ANET,* 501).

On a 7th-century B.C. Aramaic tomb inscription from Nērāb, 7 km E of Aleppo, Agbar, priest of Sahr, has had inscribed "because of my righteousness (*bṣdqty*) before him, he gave me a good name and prolonged my days" (*ANET,* 505; *KAI* 1: 45; 2: 276). The word *ṣdqh* appears with the definite article, *ṣdqtʾ*, in a 5th–4th-century inscription from Tēmā in Arabia. *KAI* renders it "present of allegiance," "Loyalitätsgeschenk" (1: 46; 2: 79–80), Cooke (1903: 196) by "a grant," Jean and Hoftijzer (*DISO,* 243) list as meanings "merit or desert." A 5th-century Phoenician inscription commemorating the foundation of a temple near Sidon records that the king *BDʿŠTRT* and *bn ṣdq* were its founders; *KAI* (1: 3; 2: 25) renders the latter by "heir," "son, who is legitimate heir," referring to Jer 23:5; 33:15. There is also attestation of a West-Semitic god, *ṣedeq* (Rosenberg 1965). Thus, *ṣdq,* in West Semitic apart from Hebrew, covers a range of meanings: proper conduct, order, righteousness, legitimacy of succession, loyalty, favor, concession, grant.

B. Range and Meaning of Terms

Words deriving from the root *ṣdq* occur 523 times in the OT: verbal forms 41 times, the nouns *ṣedeq* 119 times, and *ṣĕdāqâ* 157 times, the adjective-substantive *ṣaddîq* 206 times. Well over half of the occurrences of the nouns are in the Psalms, the poetic sections of the Prophets, and the regular verse of Proverbs. Some scholars make a distinction between *ṣedeq* and *ṣĕdāqâ.* Jepsen (1965: 79, 81), for example, maintains that *ṣedeq* means right order; it is concerned "with a situation that in fact is as it ought or must be"; *ṣedeq* is "an action directed toward the right order of the community and accordingly to its well-being"; *ṣĕdāqâ* is used of human well-being or right behavior; it is that which puts one in order before God. God's *ṣĕdāqâ* is aimed at order in his creation and at leading his community to its goal; it is his salvific will in action. Schmid (1968: 67, 179) follows Jepsen: "*ṣdq* and *ṣdqh* are to be distinguished: *ṣdq* concerns proper order, *ṣdqh* means the proper order of the world, willed by Yahweh, which brings prosperity, *ṣdqh* its appropriate, proper, prosperous state." Others, like Fahlgren (1932), see no essential difference between the two and treat them without distinction. The latter view is favored here. The note of Watson (1980: 335) is pertinent in this context: "I would like to point out that it is not always advisable to draw theological conclusions on the basis of a particular word, differentiating, for example, between *ṣedeq* and *ṣĕdēqâ* [sic], both basically meaning 'justice.' They can have different connotations, but there are texts (e.g., Ps 72:3) where choice has been dictated by poetic convention."

Scholars discern a wide range of meanings, emphases, and directions in biblical *ṣedeq-ṣĕdāqâ*: health of soul, links in a covenant, loyal activity (Pedersen 1926: 336–77); community loyalty (Fahlgren 1932); order, fitting into order, salvific order (Procksch 1950: 568–77); prosperity, saving gift (Cazelles 1951); community loyalty (Koch 1953; 1961; *THAT* 2: 507–30); Yahweh's acts, his loyalty to the covenant, relationship (*ROTT,* 370–83, 392–95); justice (Dünner 1963); a judicial and soteriological process of judging, acquitting, and saving (Justesen 1964); world order (Schmid 1968; 1984); order put into effect by Yahweh, Yahweh's saving action that puts this order into effect (Reventlow 1971); divine covenant activity and conduct that befits the covenant (Ziesler 1972); Yahweh's action toward Israel, toward the individual in distress, his saving action in the future (Crüsemann 1976); legal order, proper order in the community, saving and liberating order (*TRE* 12: 404–11). Many of these scholars underscore the notion of saving action toward the people of Israel and the helpless individual—the poor, the oppressed, the widow, the orphan.

C. Legal Uses and Nuances

1. The Verb. The verb is used predominantly in a forensic sense. The discussion here considers the various Heb verbal stems.

a. Qal. The stative verb expresses how someone stands before the law or God. Judah says of Tamar: "She is more righteous than I" (Gen 38:26); i.e., the law is on Tamar's side (cf. Ezek 36:52). Eliphaz asks Job: "Can a mortal be righteous before (OR more than) God?" (4:17; cf. 9:2, 15, 20; 10:15; 15:14; 25:4; 34:5); Elihu uses the verb in the same sense (33:12; 35:7); and a psalmist declares: "for no one living is righteous before you" (143:2). God challenges Job: "Will you then quash my judgment? condemn me that you may be right?" (40:8). One may render the two passages in the exchange between Job and Zophar: "Shall the glib one be acquitted?" (11:2) and "See now, I set forth my case, I know I shall be acquitted" (13:18), and the objection of Eliphaz: "What good to Shaddai if you are just?" (22:3; Pope *Job* AB, 80, 93, 148).

One psalmist declares that "the ordinances of Yahweh are true, and righteous altogether" (Ps 19:10—Eng v 9); another acknowledges that he has sinned against God, and him alone, "so that you are justified in your sentence" (Ps 51:6—Eng v 4). The forensic sense is clear in the *rîb*-passages in Deutero-Isaiah (43:9, 26), and in the summary verse: "In Yahweh all the offspring of Israel shall triumph (be justified) and glory" (45:25).

b. Hipᶜil. The *Hipᶜil,* causative, is used primarily in the sense of acquit, justify, declare right, vindicate. Those who judge in Israel acquit and vindicate (Exod 23:7; Deut 25:1; 2 Sam 15:4). The one who does the reverse of this, who "justifies the wicked and condemns the righteous," is an abomination to the Lord (Prov 17:15 = Isa 5:23). Solomon calls on God to vindicate the just (1 Kgs 8:32 = 2 Chr 6:23), and the psalmist asks God to "give justice to the weak and fatherless, maintain the right of the afflicted and destitute" (Ps 82:3). The Lord "who vindicates me is near" (Isa 50:8). There are three passages where the forensic sense is weak, if not absent: Job says to Bildad: "Far be it from me to declare you right" (Job 27:5); "my servant, righteous, will bring righteousness to many" (Isa 53:11); "those who turn many to righteousness" (Dan 12:3). There is another possible use of the verb in the *Hipᶜil*: "to defend (lit., and the meekness of) right" (Ps 45:5—Eng v 4) corresponds to MT, *wĕ ᶜanwah ṣedeq*; with no emendations but with a redistribution of the consonants, one may read *wĕ ᶜānāw haṣdēq,* "defend the poor," with a *Hipᶜil* imperative of the verb (Dahood *Psalms 1* AB, 272).

c. Piᶜel. The *Piᶜel* inf. occurs twice in Job, once when Elihu is angry with Job because he "held himself righteous rather (more righteous) than God," (32:2), and again when he calls on Job "to show off your righteousness" (33:32). Ezekiel says that Jerusalem has committed so many abominations that "you have made your sisters appear righteous" (16:51, 52). The Lord said to Jeremiah: "The *nepeš* (life) of faithless Israel is more righteous than false Judah" (3:11).

d. Nipᶜal. Daniel speaks of the sanctuary that shall be restored to its rightful place, *wĕniṣdāq qōdeš* (8:14); i.e., proper liturgical order will be restored.

e. Hitpaᶜel. When the brothers of Joseph are discovered to have the money they paid for the corn in their sacks, Judah replies on their behalf: "How shall we justify ourselves?" (Gen 44:16).

2. Nouns in the Pentateuch. The comparatively few uses of *ṣedeq* and *ṣĕdēqâ* are predominantly legal. The word *ṣedeq* occurs 7 times in Leviticus and Deuteronomy in a juridical sense. The judge shall be impartial in giving judgment; he shall judge *bĕṣedeq* (Lev 19:15), according to what is laid down, without regard to persons (cf. Deut 1:16; 16:18, 20; for remaining uses of *ṣedeq,* see below).

The word *ṣĕdāqâ* is found only in Deuteronomy and Genesis. In the short confession of faith (Deut 6:20–25), the children ask their father about "the testimonies and the statutes and the ordinances which the Lord our God has commanded you" (v 20). The father replies that Yahweh, who led his people from Egypt, gave the commands "for our good" (v 24); i.e., by such ordered conduct, we will be doing what is proper, *ṣĕdāqâ.* In Deuteronomy 9, the people are addressed as having already taken possession of the land. But the possession is the result of Yahweh's action, not theirs; it is not because of their own *ṣĕdāqâ* (vv 4, 5, 6) that they are there, but because of Yahweh's action.

In Gen 18:18–19, Yahweh reflects whether he should reveal to Abraham what he is to do to Sodom and Gomorrah: "I have chosen (known) him, that he may charge his children and his household after him to keep the way of the Lord by doing *ṣĕdāqâ* and *mišpāṭ*." The way of the Lord is the following of his ordinances and commands, and this is *ṣĕdāqâ* and *mišpāṭ*. In the episode of the spotted sheep and goats, Jacob says to Laban: "My *ṣĕdāqâ* will answer for me later" (Gen 30:33). Jacob's honesty or proper conduct will be his vindication.

The accepted interpretation of Gen 15:6 is that Abraham believed in Yahweh and he (Yahweh) attributed it (the act of believing) to him (Abraham) [as] *ṣĕdāqâ.* Following von Rad's important essay (*PHOE,* 130–35), many have seen the *background* to this famous verse in the liturgy of the temple. The priest declares the worshipper righteous "who conducts himself properly with reference to an existing communal relationship, who, therefore, does justice to the claims which the communal relationship makes on him. . . . Man is righteous so long as he affirms the regulations of this communal relationship established by God, say, the covenant and the commandments." The Abraham episode is, of course, not within the realm of cult; "it is transferred to the realm of God's free and personal relationship to Abraham" (von Rad *Genesis* OTL, 185). According to von Rad, the author of Gen 15:6 has Yahweh, not a temple official, priest or Levite, make the pronouncement. And Yahweh pronounces Abraham to have fulfilled righteousness, to share righteousness, *ṣĕdāqâ,* not by an act or a work, ritual or otherwise, but by faith. Von Rad understands the verse less as a polemic than as a revolutionary statement. Faith sets one right with God, and it is God who reckons this internal act to Abraham as *ṣĕdāqâ*.

The MT of Gen 15:6 reads: "And Abraham went on believing (*GKC,* 112e, [a][*a*]) in Yahweh and he [who?] reckoned it [what?] to him [to whom?] *ṣĕdāqâ*." The LXX reads: "And Abraham believed in God, and it was reckoned (*elogisthē,* aor. pass.) to him unto righteousness (*eis dikaiosynēn*). Paul (Rom 4:3; Gal 3:6) and James (2:23) repeat this rendering. However, the text is readily patient of another interpretation: "Abraham went on believing in Yahweh, and he (Abraham) reckoned it (the promise of son and descendants) to him (Yahweh) (as: no prep. in MT) fidelity (*ṣĕdāqâ*)," i.e., Yahweh, who had promised myriads of descendants to Abraham (12:1–3), has, despite appearances to the contrary (15:2–3), remained faithful to himself (15:4–5) (Gaston 1980; Oeming 1983). When Phinehas rose up and interposed and the plague was stayed (Ps 106:30–31), this action was reckoned (*Nipʿal,* pass.) to him *liṣdāqâ*. Phinehas was considered to have done the proper thing.

3. Other Uses. Isa 5:23 heaps "woe" on judges who "acquit (*maṣdîqê,* lit., acquitters of) the guilty for a bribe and reject the right of the just (*ṣidqat ṣaddîqîm*; the case of, the just cause of, the just)." For *ṣĕdāqâ* as claim or right, cf. 2 Sam 19:28–29—Eng 19: 27–28; Neh 2:20; see below.

The word *ṣedeq* is used adjectivally, governed by a noun in the construct state, and often in the sense of legitimate. Priests are to offer *zibḥê ṣedeq,* legitimate sacrifices, i.e., sacrifices according to the liturgical order (Pss 4:6[5]; 51:21[19]; cf. Deut 33:19). The tradesman must have just balances, *moʾznê ṣedeq,* i.e., scales that do not cheat, but weigh as they ought (Lev 19:36; Deut 25:15). In fact, everything dealing with weights and measures must be *ṣedeq* (Lev 19:36; Ezek 45:10). Yahweh's ordinances for one's life are *mišpāṭê ṣedeq,* proper, legitimate ordinances (Ps 119:7, 62, 75). In a royal psalm of thanksgiving the king praises God for his *ḥesed* (loyalty, steadfast love, Ps 118:15). Yahweh, who has stood by him in his distress, is his *yĕšuʿâ* (saving action, v 14); the *ṣaddîqîm* (the just) extoll Yahweh's *yĕšuʿâ*. The king cries out: "Open to me the *šaʿărê ṣedeq*" (the gates of righteousness, v 19) "for this is the gate of Yahweh" (v 20). The king will enter the city, or temple, to the place where Yahweh's order is found. The psalm is framed by Yahweh's *ḥesed* (vv 1, 29), which leads to his *yĕšuʿâ*; his steadfast love embraces his saving action and order. (Could *malkî ṣedeq,* Melchizedek of Ps 110:5, mean "legitimate king," rather than be a proper name? [Dahood *Psalms III* AB, 117]; cf. the Aramaic inscriptions above.) Yahweh leads the psalmist along *maʿgĕlê ṣedeq,* paths of proper, legitimate, order (Ps 23:3[2]). In the blessings of Moses, Gad is said to have executed the *ṣidqat Yahweh* and his *mišpāṭîm* (Deut 33:21), i.e., Yahweh's prescribed order (some understand this in a martial context, Yahweh's prescriptions for war). Other uses of *ṣedeq* governed by the construct noun, *ʿîr haṣṣedeq* (a city where order dwells, Isa 1:26), *yoʿdê ṣedeq* (those who experience Yahweh's saving action, Isa 51:7), *ʾêlê ṣedeq* (oaks of righteousness, Isa 61:3), are considered below.

D. Proper Order, Proper Comportment

The word *ṣedeq-ṣĕdāqâ* is used frequently in coordination with or in parallelism with *mišpāṭ* (order, ordinance, judgment, a regular way of doing something). The combination *ṣedeq-ṣĕdāqâ* and *mišpāṭ* is in essence a hendiadys describing that proper order in the life of the people that is put there and willed by God.

1. 8th-Century Prophecy. In Isaiah 1–39 *ṣedeq* occurs 9 times, 3 times in conjunction with or parallel to *mišpāṭ* (1:21; 16:5; 32:1). Zion was once a faithful city, full of *mišpāṭ* and the dwelling place of *ṣedeq* (1:21); now murderers lodge there; i.e., there was a time when proper order, Yahweh's order, reigned; but no more. When Yahweh acts in the future, it will be the faithful city once more and an *ʿîr haṣṣedeq,* "city of righteousness" (1:26), where Yahweh's order reigns (1:26), with the social disorders of vv 21–23 abolished. When Yahweh's reign finally prevails in Zion, chap. 16, and its oppressors are no more,

> then a throne will be established in *ḥesed* (steadfast love),
> and on it will sit in *ʾemet* (fidelity) in the tent of David
> one who judges and seeks *mišpāṭ,*
> who is quick to do *ṣedeq* (16:5).

Proper order will reign through Yahweh's ideal king. In this ideal time

> Behold, a king will reign *lĕṣedeq,*
> and princes will rule *lĕmišpāṭ* (32:1).

The preposition *l* is rendered "by," as often in Ugaritic and Hebrew. The king rules by a *ṣedeq-mišpāṭ* which is not his own, but Yahweh's (cf. Ps 72:1–3). The shoot from the stump of Jesse, upon whom the Spirit shall rest (11:1–2), shall judge the poor *bĕṣedeq* and decide *bĕmîšôr* (by equity) on the oppressed of the land (11:4). Proper order will be restored, and each will have his due. *Ṣedeq* shall be the girdle of his waist, *ʾĕmûnâ* (fidelity) the girdle of his loins (11:4).

In the late *Apocalypse of Isaiah* (chap. 26), the righteous nation, *goy ṣaddîq,* which keeps faith, is to enter through the gates. When Yahweh's judgments, *mišpāṭîm,* are upon the earth, the inhabitants learn *ṣedeq* from his gracious action, but the wicked never learn *ṣedeq* (vv 9–10).

The word *ṣĕdāqâ* occurs 12 times in Isaiah 1–39, 8 times in conjunction with or parallel to *mišpāṭ* (1:27; 5:7, 16;

9:6[7]; 28:17; 32:16, 17; 33:5). Zion shall be an *ʿîr haṣṣedeq* (1:26, see above) because of Yahweh's action. She shall be redeemed by *mišpāṭ*, and those who repent in her by *ṣĕdāqâ*, i.e., by proper order and conduct resulting from God's action (1:27). In the song of the vineyard (5:1–7) Yahweh looked for *mišpaṭ* and *ṣĕdāqâ*, loyal and proper conduct, but found only *miśpāḥ*, bloodshed (?), and *ṣĕʿāqâ*, a cry (v 7). There was disorder, not order. The glory of God is found in *mišpāṭ* and *ṣĕdāqâ*, in proper order (5:16). The ideal king will rule and administer his kingdom with *mišpaṭ* and *ṣĕdāqâ* (9:6[7]), i.e., according to God's proper order. The foundations of Zion are to be laid with *mišpāṭ* as the line and *ṣĕdāqâ* as the plummet (28:17). Zion is to be founded on proper order.

When the Spirit is poured from on high, then *mišpāṭ* will dwell in the wilderness and *ṣĕdāqâ* in the fruitful field (32:15); God's proper order comes with the Spirit. The effects of Yahweh's action, *ṣĕdāqâ* will be *šālôm*, prosperity, everlasting security, and trust (vv 16b–17a). All will find security (v 18). Yahweh on high answers his people's prayer (33:2); from his throne he will fill Zion with *mišpāṭ* and *ṣĕdāqâ* (v 5), his blessed order;

> and he will be the stability of your times,
> abundance of salvation, wisdom, and knowledge;
> the fear of the Lord is his treasure (33:6).

(Several passages in Isaiah 1–39 in which *ṣedeq-ṣĕdāqâ* occur are regarded by many scholars as coming from hands later than the 8th century [1:27; 5:16; 10:22; 26:9, 10; 32:1, 16, 19; 33:5]. However, they are considered here with the other Isaian passages. Chaps. 32–33 are very close in time, spirit, and language to Deutero-Isaiah, and other sections [26:9, 10] reflect much later expectations.)

In Hosea, Yahweh takes the initiative so as to bring Israel back to him. He will remove the Baals, i.e., false worship (2:19[17]), make a covenant (v 20[18]), and abolish disorder. "I will betrothe you to me *bĕṣedeq û-bĕmišpāṭ û-bĕḥesed û-bĕraḥămîm . . . û-bĕʾĕmûnâ*" (vv 21–22[19–20]). Yahweh will act toward Israel according to his proper, loyal, merciful, and constant way of acting, and Israel, experiencing his steadfast love, will respond with *ṣedeq* and *mišpāṭ*. Later, Yahweh calls on his people to "sow for yourselves *liṣdāqâ* (*l-* means "by means of"), reap the fruit of *ḥesed*," i.e., conduct yourselves toward Yahweh as he conducts himself toward you, "that he may come and rain *ṣedeq* upon you" (Hos 10:12).

Amos attacks those who oppress the just one, *ṣaddîq* (2:6; 5:12). The house of Israel is perverse; it has turned the process of justice, proper order, upside down: "it turns *mišpāṭ* to wormwood, throws *ṣĕdāqâ* to earth" (5:7; cf. 6:12). Yahweh does not want a mere formalized ritual (5:21–23); he wants proper order in every area of life; and so

> let *mišpāṭ* roll on like the waves, *ṣĕdāqâ* like an
> everlasting stream (5:24; cf. Isa 48:18).

Micah calls on the people to look back and experience Yahweh's saving acts in history, *ṣĕdāqôt* (6:5). Yahweh's demand on Israel in response is simple—to do *mišpāṭ*, i.e., to observe proper order, to be constant in *ḥesed*, and to comport oneself humbly (6:8).

2. 7th-Century Prophecy. Zephaniah calls the people to hold an assembly: "Seek Yahweh, all you humble of the land, who do his *mišpāṭ*, seek *ṣedeq*, seek *ʿănāwâ* (humility)" (2:3). The people are to do what is proper in lowly submission before Yahweh.

Jeremiah calls all who enter at the gates of the city, from the king down, to do *mišpāṭ* and *ṣĕdāqâ* (22:3), i.e., to right the wrong done to the oppressed and to give justice to the alien, the fatherless, and the widow. The builder, for example, must not misuse his workmen; he must dispense justice (22:13–17). If he does not act with *ṣedeq* and *mišpāṭ*, then what profit to him? (v 13). His father(s) did act properly and took care of the poor and the needy (v 15b).

Yahweh will raise up a *ṣemaḥ ṣaddîq* (a legitimate branch; cf. above), a *ṣemaḥ ṣĕdāqâ* (33:15, same meaning), who will execute *mišpāṭ* and *ṣĕdāqâ*. This legitimate branch will be the instrument of Yahweh's order in such a way that Jerusalem will be called *ṣidqēnû* (our righteousness, 33:16), the place where Yahweh's proper order is established. Where Yahweh is, there is proper, world order (Schmid 1968: 87–88).

The people must put aside false gods and idols (4:1); they must take their oath, *beʾĕmet, bĕmišpāṭ, biṣdāqâ*, in such a way that their conduct really conforms to proper order. Then the nations shall glory in Yahweh. The wise, the mighty, and the rich are not to glory in what they have, but rather in this, that they know and experience that "I am Yahweh, doing *ḥesed, mišpāṭ, ṣĕdāqâ*" (9:23[24]). Yahweh is a God who acts true to himself and preserves proper order in the world. When Yahweh restores the fortunes of his people, they shall sing: "the Lord bless you, abode of *ṣedeq*, holy mountain" (31:33). The holy mountain is the place where Yahweh's *ṣedeq* (saving order) dwells. The enemies of Israel say that they are not guilty of the destruction of Jerusalem (50:7); it is the people who are guilty; they have sinned against Yahweh, their abode of *ṣedeq* (cf. Job 8:6).

3. Psalms. The words *ṣedeq* and *ṣĕdāqâ* occur 49 and 34 times respectively in the Psalms, for the most part in the context of God's saving action, though often enough compassing proper order and comportment. The psalmist asks God to judge him according to his (the psalmist's) *ṣedeq* and *tōm* (innocence, integrity, freedom from fault), i.e., according to the way in which he has acted (Ps 7:9[8]). Yahweh is a just judge (v 10[9]) who gives judgment in favor of the psalmist, who in turn thanks Yahweh for acting according to his (Yahweh's) *ṣedeq*. God loves *mišpāṭ* and *ṣĕdāqâ* (Pss 33:5; 99:4), i.e., proper order among his people. Those who do *mišpāṭ* and *ṣĕdāqâ* are blessed (Ps 106:3). Psalm 72 is a prayer for blessing on the king. Yahweh is asked to endow the king with his (Yahweh's) *mišpāṭ* and *ṣĕdāqâ* so that he (the king) may be able to judge the people with *ṣedeq* and *mišpāṭ*; i.e., proper order comes from Yahweh through the king (cf. Isa 32:1). As a consequence, the mountains will bring forth *šālôm* (prosperity) and the hills *ṣĕdāqâ* (cf. Isa 32:16–17). Yahweh endows the king with the power to act as he ought, and so the king guarantees God's order, namely *mišpāṭ* and *ṣĕdāqâ*. The psalmist makes explicit what constitutes God's order—deliverance of the needy and poor, freedom from oppression and violence (vv 4, 12–14). To come to the aid of these people is to act *beṣedeq* and to restore *ṣĕdāqâ*. Yahweh also acts *biṣdāqâ* (e.g., Isa 5:16; 96[7]; Pss 119:40; 143:11; Zech 8:8).

The word *ṣedeq* occurs 8 times in the psalm on God's law (Ps 119:7, 62, 75, 138, 142, 144, 164, 172). The psalmist praises the ordinances, *mišpāṭîm*, of Yahweh's *ṣedeq* (vv 7, 62, 164); Yahweh's ordinances, testimonies, and commandments are *ṣedeq* (vv 75, 144, 172); Yahweh has commanded *ṣedeq* (v 138); the psalmist reflects that "your *ṣĕdāqâ* is *ṣedeq* forever (*lĕʿôlām*, or, O Eternal One), your *tôrâ* (law, instruction) is *ʾemet* (truth)" (v 142). Yahweh's saving action *is* divine order, his teaching *is* truth. The whole context of the psalm is proper order in accordance with the prescriptions of Yahweh's law. The one who conducts himself *tamim,* blamelessly, and carries out *ṣedeq,* that which is proper, may sojourn in Yahweh's tent and may dwell on his holy hill (Ps 15:2). The priests are to be clothed with *ṣedeq* (Ps 132:9); i.e., they must comport themselves according to proper liturgical and moral order. Psalm 24 is a liturgical psalm put into a cosmic setting. Yahweh, who has founded the cosmos, will pass judgment on the one who approaches his holy place. He who is the source of cosmic order has also given order to the formal worship of his people. If the worshipper is not guilty of any disorder that would disqualify him from the temple, he will receive *bĕrākâ* (blessing) and *ṣĕdāqâ* (saving grace?) from his saving God (lit., the God of his salvation, v 5). Psalm 118 is a royal hymn of thanksgiving. The king praises Yahweh for his *ḥesed* (vv 1–5); Yahweh has stood by him in his distress; Yahweh is his *yĕšûʿâ*. The king will enter the city, or temple, walking through the gates of *ṣedeq* to the place where Yahweh's order is found (v 19). The psalm is framed by Yahweh's *ḥesed* (vv 1, 29); i.e., Yahweh's steadfast love embraces his saving action and his order.

The psalmist often speaks of "my *ṣedeq*." Psalm 4 is a prayer of one in distress or perhaps a prayer for rain (Dahood *Psalms III* AB, 23). God who is invoked is a God of *ṣidqî* (v 2[1]), God of "my justice" or "my just God," he who restores order; if a prayer for rain, then God who restores the natural order; it is he, not the nature gods of Canaan, who gives rain and fertility. God is called on to act. In an individual lament, the psalmist prays for deliverance from his enemies because of "my *ṣedeq*" and "my *tōm*" (Ps 7:9[8]); i.e., he claims that he is innocent of any breach of proper or liturgical order before God. A plea of the innocent is framed by the inclusio, *ṣedeq* (Ps 17:1, 15):

Hear, Yahweh, my *ṣedeq,* attend to my cry
Give ear to my prayer, destroy deceitful lips.
Let my *mišpāṭ* shine (come from) before you,
  may your eyes gaze upon my *mêšārîm* (equity, integrity).

The psalmist is conscious of his right conduct as he cries to God. He sings in conclusion:

I, *bĕṣedeq,* shall gaze upon your face,
  bĕhāqîṣ, shall be sated with your *tĕmûnâ* (presence, form, being).

Moses alone was allowed to see Yahweh's *tĕmûnâ* (Num 12:8); *hāqîṣ* is the *Hipʿil* inf. of *qîṣ,* to arise, awake; (cf. Isa 26:19 and Dan 12:2, to arise from the sleep of death). He will see God's face in God's vindicating or saving action which awakens him from death. Again, Yahweh has rewarded the singer "according to my *ṣedeq,*" has repaid him according to *bor yāday,* "the innocence of my hand" (18:21[20]). The psalmist has walked in accordance with God's order (words repeated in v 25[24]; cf. 2 Sam 22:21, 25). The psalmist prays that Yahweh will defend "my *mišpāṭ* and my *dîn*" (his just cause and judicial process, Ps 9:5[4]) as he (Yahweh) sits upon the throne *šopēṭ ṣedeq,* dispensing as judge what is proper. Yahweh is the one who gives judgment as it should be given.

Yahweh "rules the world *bĕṣedeq* and judges the people *bĕmêšārîm*" (equity, Ps 9:9[8]). He judges as is proper, according to the order that he has established. The people acknowledge their rebellious acts and approach the temple with confidence (Psalm 65). They petition the God of their salvation to show his wondrous deeds *bĕṣedeq* (v 6[5]). Then follows a series of participles which describe Yahweh as the one who orders and maintains the order of the universe. Yahweh gives order and saves; *bĕṣedeq* describes both actions. He is the creator of the universe (Ps 96:5); hence he is king (v 10). He will judge the peoples *bĕmêšārîm* (with equity), and govern in fidelity to the order he has set up, *bĕṣedeq* and *beʾĕmûnâ,* (v 13).

Yahweh is the restorer of social order who will redress the affliction of the widow, the stranger, the fatherless (Ps 94:6) and will do this through those who are imbued with and respect his *tôrâ* (v 12). The crucial v 15 is difficult, but seems to mean that justice will return to the judicial tribunal; *ṣedeq* and *mišpāṭ* are in the verse, but not in parallelism. Dahood proposes:

But the tribunal (*ʿad*) of justice (*ṣedeq*) will restore equity
  (*mišpāṭ*),
and with it all upright hearts (*Psalms II* AB, 345).

In any case, *ṣedeq* is in the context of proper order in society.

4. Isaiah 40–66. Only once in Deutero-Isaiah (chaps. 40–55) does *ṣedeq-ṣĕdāqâ* denote proper conduct or order. Israel's comportment through the centuries has not been according to *ʾemet* and *ṣĕdāqâ* (48:1a–b). If only Israel had listened to Yahweh's commandments her *šālôm* (welfare) would have been like a river and her *ṣĕdāqâ* (prosperity) like the waves of the sea (48:18).

The oracles, accusations, and laments of Isaiah 56–66 complain that Israel has not followed the path of *ṣedeq-ṣĕdāqâ* and *mišpāṭ*. The people are called on to observe *mišpāṭ* and do *ṣĕdāqâ* (56:1a), i.e., to conduct themselves as is proper because Yahweh's *yĕšûʿâ* and *ṣĕdāqâ,* his saving action, is about to be revealed (56:1b). The *mišpāṭ-ṣĕdāqâ* in v 1a is the people's order; the *yĕšûʿâ-ṣĕdāqâ* in v 1b is Yahweh's action which is salvific and restores his proper order. A series of accusations (57:2–10) concerns cultic aberrations, misguided acts that were thought to set the people in a right relationship with God: "I will tell of your *ṣĕdāqâ* and *maʿăśayik*" (57:12), i.e., your acts of supposed worship which you think make you "just" before God. The people seek Yahweh daily and delight in his ways; they follow the prescribed ritual, like a nation which in fact really did *ṣĕdāqâ* and *mišpāṭ* (58:2b), what is proper. They ask for "ordinances of conduct," *mišpĕṭê ṣedeq* (cf. Ps 119:7, 62, 75). They fast ritually and perform ritual penance, thinking that thus all should go well with them. But mere ritual without concern for the social order is a violation of proper order, of Yahweh's order; it is not *ṣĕdāqâ* and *mišpāṭ* (58:3–7). If, however, the people of Israel do what they should, following the order that Yahweh requires (vv 6–7),

> then shall your light break forth like the dawn,
> and your healing shall spring up speedily;
> your *ṣedeq* shall go before you,
> the *kābôd* (glory) of Yahweh shall be your rear guard (v 8).

Their proper conduct, *ṣedeq,* will be as Yahweh's *ṣedeq,* and will reflect his glory.

A catalogue of the people's sins follows (59:1–8). They look for salvation and God's favor anywhere but in the right area, which is the following of God's proper order, *mišpāṭ* and *ṣĕdāqâ*. This is the reason why God's saving action, *mišpāṭ* and *ṣĕdāqâ* (cf. 56:1b), is far off. Yahweh is not incapable of hearing; the sins of the people are the barrier to his presence (59:2–3); there is no one to speak *bĕṣedeq* (v 4a), no one to recall the community to loyalty to Yahweh (v 4a is usually understood in a legal sense, "no one goes to law honestly," RSV). The people hoped for *mišpāṭ* and *yĕšûʿâ* (v 11b), but it is not there. Why? Because of their many sins (vv 12–13). They lament that *mišpāṭ* is turned back and that *ṣĕdāqâ* is far off (v 14). Why is it so? Because *ʾĕmet* (truth, loyalty) has fallen in the public squares and *nĕkoḥâ* (equity) is no more. Yahweh was displeased that there was no more *ʾĕmet* and *mišpāṭ* (v 15), i.e., no loyalty to his ordinances. There was no one to set the situation right, so Yahweh himself had to intervene. Then his own arm brought salvation (verb *yšʿ*), his own *ṣĕdāqâ* (saving action) sustained him (v 16). Like a leader going out to battle, Yahweh clothed himself with the breastplate of *ṣĕdāqâ* and the helmet of *yĕšûʿâ* (v 17); he clothed himself too with "vengeance" and "fury." There is always the double aspect of Yahweh's saving intervention—judgment for those who remain firm in opposition (v 18), salvation for those "who turn from transgression" (v 20).

5. Ezekiel, Malachi, Joel. The words *ṣedeq* and *ṣĕdāqâ* occur almost exclusively in the context of personal responsibility in Ezekiel and are restricted virtually to passages of hortatory repetition (3:16–21; 18; 33). The leaders of Jerusalem are urged to do (*ʿāsāh*) *mišpāṭ* and *ṣĕdāqâ* (18:5, 19, 22, 27; 33:14, 16, 19; 45:9), i.e., to act as they ought in accordance with Yahweh's precepts and ordinances from ritual observance to care for the poor and needy (chap. 18). This constitutes a person's *mišpāṭ* and *ṣĕdāqâ*. Were Noah, Daniel, and Job living in the midst of this sinful people, they would deliver their own lives by their own *ṣĕdāqâ,* proper conduct (14:14, 20). Ezekiel destroys the traditional proverb: "The fathers have eaten sour grapes, and the children's teeth are set on edge" (18:1–4; cf. Jer 31:29–30). The refrain *ṣĕdāqâ* throughout chap. 18 (vv 5, 19, 20, 22, 24, 26, 27) describes that proper conduct which is each one's personal responsibility; a catalogue of acts lists what the righteous one does (vv 6–9a); this constitutes his *ṣĕdāqâ*. The phrase "to do (observe) *mišpāṭ* and *ṣĕdāqâ*" belongs to the royal ideology; it is the king who, in the first place, must preserve proper order; he does this by virtue of God's *ṣedeq, ṣĕdāqâ,* and *mišpāṭ* (Ps 72:1–3; Isa 32:1). But anyone who does this is *ṣaddîq*. The word *ṣĕdāqâ* carries the same tones and echoes throughout chap. 33 (vv 12, 13, 14, 15, 16, 19). The deeds of the *ṣaddîq* are *ṣĕdāqôt* (pl.) (3:20; 18:14; 33:13).

Malachi, God's messenger, will refine the people until they present their offerings *biṣdāqâ,* as is proper (3:3). Joel cries out: "Be glad, O sons of Zion, and rejoice in the Lord your God because Yahweh *liṣdāqâ,* in accordance with the order that he has established, has given the appropriate rains at their proper time."

6. Joshua–2 Kings. The word *ṣedeq* is not found in the former prophets; *ṣĕdāqâ* only 11 times. When David spares Saul's life at Ziph, he says to the king: "The Lord rewards every man for his *ṣĕdāqâ* and *ʾĕmûnâ*; for the Lord gave you into my hand today, and I would not put forth my hand against the Lord's anointed" (Sam 26:13). David had acted properly. When Mephibosheth meets David on his return from his flight before Absalom, he acknowledges that the king has made a place for him at the royal table: "What futher *ṣĕdāqâ* have I that I should complain to the king" (2 Sam 19:28–29[27–28]). David has observed all propriety so that Mephibosheth has no just claim (for *ṣĕdāqâ* as claim, cf. Neh 2:20; also Isa 5:23, see above). The word *ṣĕdāqâ* in 2 Sam 22:21, 25, is a repetition of Ps 18:21, 25 [20, 24]. David ruled over Israel *ʿośeh* (doing) *mišpāṭ* and *ṣĕdāqâ* (2 Sam 8:15; cf. 1 Chr 18:14). He ruled as king by virtue of *mišpāṭ* and *ṣĕdāqâ* which came from God (1 Kgs 10:9; Ps 72:1–3; Isa 32:1). When Yahweh asks Solomon what he should give him, Solomon replies that Yahweh showed *ḥesed* (steadfast love) to David because he had conducted himself *bĕʾemet, biṣdāqâ, bĕyišrâ,* i.e., loyally, as he ought. At the dedication of the temple Solomon prays that the just be justified according to his *ṣĕdāqâ* (1 Kgs 8:22). If the just man conducts himself according to Yahweh's order, that will justify him. The Queen of Sheba remarks that Solomon's God made him king in love for Israel so that he might do *mišpāṭ* and *ṣĕdāqâ* (1 Kgs 10:9; 2 Chr 9:8), i.e., observe and communicate through his observance Yahweh's order. According to the Chronicler, Solomon requires that the righteous be judged according to his *ṣĕdāqâ* (his proper conduct) (2 Chr 6:23).

Nehemiah said to the governors of the province beyond the river: "It is the God of heaven who will make us prosper, and we, his servants, shall arise and build; but for you, you have no portion, no *ṣĕdāqâ,* no memorial in Jerusalem" (Neh 2:20). Only true Israelites can stake a claim there.

7. Job, Proverbs, Qoheleth. The verb *ṣdq* is used predominantly in a forensic sense in Job (see above). The nouns *ṣedeq-ṣĕdāqâ* move between proper conduct and proper order with legal nuances. Job replies to Eliphaz: "Turn, I pray, let no wrong be done; turn, now, my vindication (*ṣidqî*) is at stake" (or "relent, for my cause is just," AB 6: 29). Job claims: "I put on (my) *ṣedeq* and it clothed me, my *mišpāṭ* was like a robe and a turban" (29:14; cf. Isa 61:10–11). If Job is weighed in a balance of *ṣedeq*; if he is tried according to proper procedure, his integrity will be vindicated (31:6). Bildad asks: "Does God pervert *mišpāṭ,* does Šaddai pervert *ṣedeq*?" (8:3). The implication is that God does not interfere with proper order. Bildad objects that, if Job were pure and upright, God would be on his side and give him *nĕwat ṣidqekā,* a dwelling place or pasture that he deserves because of his conduct (8:3; for the phrase, cf. Jer 3:23; 50:7). Job maintains that he has not sinned; but if that is the case, asks Elihu, does his present state represent his *mišpāṭ* and *ṣedeq* before God? (35:2). Because God observes proper order, Job's state must be the result of his nonobservance of it. Elihu asserts: ". . . to my maker I will give *ṣedeq*" (36:3); he will vindicate God by showing that God observes proper order in punishing Job for his transgressions. Job maintains his claim that he has observed proper order, *ṣĕdāqâ* (27:6; cf. 29:14; 31:6). Elihu speaks of *ṣĕdāqâ* twice in the context of human conduct (33:26; 35:8); he observes too that God will not violate *mišpāṭ* and *ṣĕdāqâ* (37:23).

In Proverbs, *ṣedeq* (9 times) and *ṣĕdāqâ* (18 times), and in Qoheleth, *ṣedeq* (3 times), the idea of proper order predominates. The sayings in Proverbs are directed to knowing wisdom and instruction, to perceiving words of insight, to receiving instruction in discernment and *ṣedeq, mišpāṭ, mêšārîm* (1:2–3). The wise man teaches the proper way to act and how to perceive what constitutes proper order. Yahweh gives *ḥokmâ* (wisdom) and *daᶜat* (knowledge); he guards the paths of *mišpāṭ* (justice, 2:6–8). If you follow Yahweh's way, says the writer, you will come to an insight into *ṣedeq* and *mišpāṭ* (2:9), i.e., you will understand what proper order is. Wisdom herself speaks in chap. 8: all the words of my mouth are *bĕṣedeq*, proper order itself (v 8); by me kings rule and decree *ṣedeq*, my proper order (v 15); by me princes and nobles give judgment (Heb uncertain) in *ṣedeq*, as they ought (v 16); riches and honor are with me, enduring wealth and *ṣĕdāqâ* (prosperity, v 18); I walk in the path of *ṣĕdāqâ*, in the midst of the way of *mišpāṭ*, i.e., as is proper (v 20). A legal proverb says that he who speaks *ʾĕmûnâ* declares *ṣedeq* (12:17), i.e., to speak the truth is to observe proper order. A king's throne is based on *ṣĕdāqâ*, proper order (16:12); lips of *ṣedeq*, i.e., one who speaks what is proper, are a joy to the king (16:13). When the wicked are removed from the presence of the king, this throne is based on *ṣedeq* (25:5). In the words of Lemuel, judging *ṣedeq* means passing just judgment on the poor and needy (31:9). All will go well with the one who comports himself with *ṣĕdāqâ*, according to proper order (11:4, 5, 6, 28, 29; 13:6); *ṣĕdāqâ* guarantees life (12:28; 21:21), prosperity to a nation (14:34), and to the old (16:31); *ṣĕdāqâ* is acceptable to Yahweh (15:9), and he who does *mišpāṭ* and *ṣĕdāqâ* is more acceptable to Yahweh than sacrifice (21:3).

Qoheleth has seen *mišpāṭ* and *ṣedeq*, proper order, overturned (3:16; 5:7[8]). He has even seen the righteous man perishing in his *ṣedeq*, as he does what is right (7:15); the *ṣaddîq*, though he observes proper order, perishes like the rest.

8. Daniel. Daniel confesses to Yahweh that the people have sinned and not listened to the prophets (9:3–6). Yahweh has kept the covenant and shown *ḥesed*, steadfast love; the people have not: "To thee, O Lord, belongs *ṣĕdāqâ*, but to us confusion of face" (v 7). Yahweh has fulfilled his part, but the people have not fulfilled theirs. Gabriel announces to Daniel that the people have been granted seventy weeks to put an end to sin and transgression and to bring about *ṣedeq ᶜolāmîm*, lasting order (9:24).

9. *ṣedeq-ṣĕdāqâ* + *mišpāṭ*. The word pair *ṣedeq* or *ṣĕdāqâ* + *mišpāṭ* occurs in parallelism, in coordinate relationship, and in the phrase to do (*ᶜāśâ*) or to observe (*šāmār*) *ṣedeq-ṣĕdāqâ* and *mišpāṭ*. The pair is a hendiadys and designates the order in Israelite society which God wills and transmits through the king to the people who are required to respond to God's action by living according to that order. The king is the trustee or guarantor of the order.

ṣedeq-ṣĕdāqâ and *mišpāṭ* are the foundation of Yahweh's throne (Pss 85:15[14]; 97:2). His rule is proper order and he sustains it through the throne (i.e., the king). The ideal king will establish lasting peace upon the throne of David and over his kingdom and uphold it *bĕ-mišpāṭ û-biṣdāqâ* (Isa 9:6[7]). Because the throne is based on *ṣĕdāqâ*, the doing of evil is an abomination to kings (Prov 16:12; 25:5). The base of the throne of the Egyptian king takes the form of the sign *m3ᶜ.t*, a hieroglyph standing for justice, order, proper divine order, which can only be rendered in Hebrew by *ṣedeq-ṣĕdāqâ*. By the 19th and 20th Dynasties the throne base, because of its form, was understood as justice, right order (Brunner 1958; Schmid 1968: 61). Much Israelite throne ritual was dependent either directly, or indirectly through Canaanite tradition, on Egypt (cf. 1 Kgs 10:18–20).

E. God's *ṣedeq-ṣĕdāqâ*: Saving Action.

God's *ṣedeq-ṣĕdāqâ* is very often his saving action on behalf of his people, especially in the Psalms and Isaiah 40–66.

1. Psalms. a. God's *ṣedeq*. (Ps 7:9–10[8–9]; cf. above). The heavens proclaim God's *ṣedeq* (Pss 50:6; 97:6), i.e., his action on behalf of his *ḥăsîdîm*, who are bound to him by the obligations that they have assumed in a solemn sacrificial rite (50:5). Yahweh reigns (97:1); he comes in a theophany (vv 2–5) and protects his people (v 10); it is this action that reveals his glory (*kābôd*, parallel to *ṣedeq*, v 6). Yahweh comes to the help of the afflicted and lamenting psalmist who calls for exultant joy from those who desire his (the psalmist's) *ṣedeq*, i.e., his sharing in the effect of God's saving action (35:27). This meaning derives from the second part of the verse, where the community is called to praise God and to say: "Great is Yahweh, who delights in the *šālôm* (welfare, prosperity) of his servant."

The psalmist prays: "Vindicate me, Yahweh, my God, according to your *ṣedeq*" (35:24). The context is Yahweh's *yĕšûᶜâ* (saving action, vv 3, 8); he asks Yahweh to be faithful to himself; because Yahweh is faithful, i.e., acts according to his *ṣedeq*, the psalmist will proclaim this *ṣedeq*, which will be the *tĕhillâ* (praise) of Yahweh: "my tongue shall tell of your *ṣedeq*, of your *tĕhillâ* all day long" (v 28).

The psalmist announces *ṣedeq* in the assembly of the people:

I have told the glad news of (your) *ṣedeq* in the great
  congregation;
 lo, I have not restrained my lips, as you know,
  Yahweh;
I have not hid your *ṣĕdāqâ* within my heart,
 I have spoken of your *ʾĕmûnâ* (faithfulness) and your
  tĕšûᶜâ (salvation);
I have not concealed your *ḥesed* (steadfast love) and
  your *ʾĕmet* (loyalty) from the great congregation.
Do not, Yahweh, withhold your *raḥămîm* (compassion)
  from me,

let your *ḥesed* and your *ʾĕmet* ever preserve me
(40:10–12[9–11]).

God's action has many facets which are described by a variety of words whose meanings are not identical but reinforce each other. Yahweh's *ṣedeq* in these psalms is his action that saves and restores order, thus demonstrating his fidelity.

b. God's *ṣĕdāqâ*. Of the 34 occurrences of *ṣĕdāqâ* in the Psalms, 29 refer to God's *ṣĕdāqâ*.

(1) Psalms of Individual Lament. Yahweh's *ṣĕdāqâ* characterizes the Psalms of individual lament. Though the psalmist is surrounded by evildoers, he is sure that they will not harm him because Yahweh is there with his *ṣĕdāqâ*. He will enter God's house and worship among the God-fearers, relying on Yahweh's *ḥesed* (5:7[6]). He prays that Yahweh will lead him by means of, *bĕ,* his (Yahweh's) *ṣĕdāqâ* (v 9[8]); in paraphrase: "by means of your saving action, that action which preserves proper order, make your way (the observance of your *mišpāṭîm,* instructions) level before me; i.e., remove the obstacles that the wicked may put there to prevent proper order." *Ṣĕdāqâ* is that action of Yahweh which effects this.

Psalm 22 alternates between distress and trust, between prayer for deliverance and praise of God for his intervention. The final prayer for deliverance is that the psalmist may praise God in the midst of the *qāhāl* (assembly, congregation, v 23[22]). Yahweh has remained faithful (v 25[24]); all will acknowledge him as king, and all will bow before him (vv 29–30[28–29]). The psalmist's descendants are to tell of God forever; they are to recount his *ṣĕdāqâ,* his saving action of deliverance, to a people yet unborn, because he has acted, *kî ʿāśâ* (v 32[31]). It is this that the psalmist is to proclaim in the assembly (vv 23, 26[22, 25]). Yahweh's *ṣĕdāqâ* is invoked or praised or declared (Pss 31:2[1]; 51:16[14]; 69:28[27]). The desolate man asks for Yahweh's visible, tangible action:

Is your *ḥesed* (steadfast love) declared in the grave,
your *ʾĕmûnâ* (fidelity) in Abaddon?
Is your *peleʾ* (wondrous, miraculous act) made known in Darkness,
your *ṣĕdāqâ* in the land of Forgetfulness? (88:12–13[11–12]).

A group of words describes God's action seen from various overlapping viewpoints.

In Psalm 71 the psalmist laments and prays for deliverance, recalling Yahweh's *ṣĕdāqâ* 5 times (vv 2, 15, 16, 19, 24). Each time the *ṣĕdāqâ* is God's saving action; twice it is in parallelism with a form of the word "save," *yšʿ,* with the verb *hôšîʿēnî* (save me, v 2), and with the noun *tĕšuʿâ* (saving action, v 15). Yahweh's *ṣĕdāqâ* is without limit; it reaches to the heavens (v 19, cf. Ps 36:6–7[5–6]).

(2) Psalms with Cosmic Dimension. The cosmic dimension permeates Psalm 33. It is a hymn of praise of Yahweh, the creator:

For the word of Yahweh is *yāšār* (upright),
his every deed is *bĕʾĕmûnâ* (fidelity itself),
he loves *mišpāṭ* (justice) and *ṣĕdāqâ,* his *ḥesed* (steadfast love) fills the earth.
By the word of Yahweh were the heavens created,
by the breath of his mouth all their host (vv 4–6).

God's word is act; he is faithful to his created order. Once more, *ṣĕdāqâ* is found amidst a complex of words which describe God in act.

(3) Psalms of the Kingship of Yahweh. Psalms 98, 99, and 145 celebrate the kingship of Yahweh. He is praised because he

has done *niplāʾôt* (wonders), his right hand *hôšîʿāh* (has saved).
Yahweh has made known his *yĕšaʿ* (salvation),
in the eyes of the nation he has revealed his *ṣĕdāqâ*.
He has remembered his *ḥesed* (steadfast love) and his
ʾĕmûnâ to the house of Israel (98:1–3).

The same word group describes Yahweh's action and its effects as in Ps 88:12–13[11–12]. Yahweh, the mighty king, "is a lover of *mišpāṭ* and *ṣĕdāqâ*" (99:4).

Psalm 145 celebrates Yahweh and his kingship. All will praise Yahweh's actions:

They shall pour forth the memory of your *ṭôb* (bounty),
and shall sing aloud your *ṣĕdāqâ*.
Yahweh is *ḥannûn* (gracious) and *raḥum* (merciful), . . .
Yahweh's *ṭôb* (bounty) is to all, his *raḥămîm* (pl. merciful acts) are to all his creation (145:7–9).

Yahweh acts true to himself; he is a gracious God who brings prosperity. (For Psalm 24, see above).

(4) Royal Psalms. These psalms also sing of Yahweh's saving action, his loyalty and fidelity, his steadfast love in act. Psalm 40 is a royal psalm of thanksgiving. Yahweh has raised the psalmist from the pit of desolation, from the miry bog (v 3[2]). The psalmist then tells of Yahweh's *ṣedeq-ṣĕdāqâ* in the assembly of the people (vv 10–11[9–10]). Yahweh's throne is based on *ṣedeq* and *mišpāṭ* and preceded by *ḥesed* and *ʾĕmet.* The people, therefore, will experience Yahweh's radiance and walk in his light, and so rejoice in his *šēm* (name, glory), and exult in his *ṣĕdāqâ*; his *ṣĕdāqâ,* i.e., his intervention, the order that comes from it, and hence his glory, shall be their praise:

ṣedeq and *mišpāṭ* are the foundations of your throne,
ḥesed and *ʾĕmet* go before you;
blessed are the people who know the festal shout,
who walk, Yahweh, in the light of your countenance,
who rejoice in your *šēm* (name) all day,
and exult in your *ṣĕdāqâ* (89:15–17[14–16]).

The *ṣĕdāqâ* of v 17[16] reinforces the *ṣedeq* of v 15[14]. *Šēm* and *ṣĕdāqâ* occur together again in the same word-field in Psalm 143. The king prays to Yahweh to hear him "in your *ʾĕmûna,*" to answer in "your *ṣĕdāqâ,*" and concludes:

for the sake of your *šēm* (name), Yahweh, give me life,
in your *ṣĕdāqâ,* deliver me from strife,
in your *ḥesed,* destroy my foes (143:11–12).

(5) Wisdom Psalms and Hymns. Psalm 36 contains both wisdom and hymnic elements. The psalmist describes the machinations of the wicked (vv 2–5[1–4]), but over against this,

your *ḥesed,* Yahweh, is from the heavens,
your *ʾĕmûnâ* to the clouds;
your *ṣĕdāqâ* like the towering mountains,
your *mišpāṭ* like the great deep;
man and beast you save (*hôšîaʿ*), Yahweh,
how precious is your *ḥesed,* God (vv 6–7[5–6]).

Yahweh is the source of life and light (vv 9–10[8–9]). The psalmist then prays:

extend your *ḥesed* to those who know you,
  your *ṣĕdāqâ* to the upright of heart (v 11[10]).

Yahweh is again acting; his steadfast love and his saving action are different aspects of one and the same action directed to one end.

Psalm 103 is a hymn of praise with elements of individual thanksgiving. A series of active participles (vv 3–6) describe Yahweh in act, moving to a climax: "Yahweh *ʿośeh* (the one effecting) *ṣedāqôt* and *mišpāṭim* for the oppressed" (v 6). Yahweh restores order to the underdogs by his saving actions, pl. of *ṣĕdāqâ.* Yahweh, who "knows our frame, who remembers we are dust" (v 14), is eternal; hence his action is from eternity: "the *ḥesed* of Yahweh is from eternity, and unto eternity . . . his *ṣĕdāqâ* to his children" (v 17). His timeless action, *ṣĕdāqâ,* is underscored again in Pss 111:3; 112:3, 9.

The pious Israelite, meditating on Yahweh's law, muses:

I have longed for your precepts,
By your *ṣĕdāqâ* give me life,
Let your *ḥesed* come to me, Yahweh,
  your *tĕšûʿâ* according to your promise (119:40–41).

Later he reflects: "your *ṣĕdāqâ* is *ṣedeq* for ever (*lĕʿôlām,* or O Eternal One), your *tôrâ* is *ʾĕmet*" (119:142). Yahweh's saving action *is* divine order, his teaching *is* truth.

2. Isaiah 40–55. Yahweh, the God of Israel and the lord of history, has called Cyrus (44:28; 45:1) to victory so that Israel may return home in a second exodus (41:2). He has raised up a savior, *ṣedeq,* from the east; the abstract noun, "saving action," is used for the concrete, "savior," a common device in Canaanite and Hebrew poetry (*ṣedeq* may also be read as the subject of the second colon, "he whom victory accompanies at every step," or as an adverbial accusative with the first colon, "who has raised up from the east [in his] saving purpose"). The context is salvific; Yahweh acts on behalf of his people. The salvific context continues; Yahweh will remain faithful to Israel "my servant," and uphold his people with his saving right hand, lit. "with the right hand of my *ṣedeq*" (41:10).

Yahweh the creator (42:5; 45:11–12) has called both his servant (42:6) and Cyrus (45:13) *bĕṣedeq,* in his saving purpose. Yahweh, "because of his *ṣedeq,*" was pleased to magnify his *tôrâ*; *ṣedeq* takes on nuances of *ḥesed* and fidelity (42:21). *Ṣedeq,* God's saving action, is to drop down from the clouds; *yĕšaʿ,* salvation, is to blossom from the earth, and *ṣĕdāqâ,* prosperity, the result of Yahweh's saving action, is to bud (45:8). Creation, saving action, and prosperity are linked. The prosperity follows on Yahweh's saving action through Cyrus; Yahweh can effect this marvelous response in nature in his ultimate intervention because he is the creator (a polemic against the nature gods of Canaan may lie in the background). Yahweh the creator is not found in pre-creation chaos, *tohû* (45:18–19; cf. Gen 1:2); he is found in the order and stability that comes from his creative word: "I, Yahweh, speaking order (*ṣedeq*), declaring what is proper (*mêšārîm*)."

Each of the three stanzas 51:1–3, 4–6, 7–8, begins with a rousing imperative. The theme is "deliverance" (RSV) or "saving action." *Ṣedeq* is used 3 times (vv 1, 5, 7) and *ṣĕdāqâ* twice (vv 6, 8). The words are parallel to Yahweh himself (v 1a), to *yēšaʿ* and *yĕšûʿâ* (vv 5a, 6c, 8b), and to *tôrâ* (v 7a). The context is salvific; *ṣedeq* and *ṣĕdāqâ* describe God in act toward his people. The word group is extended by *mišpāṭ,* parallel to *tôrâ* (v 4b). Verse 7a speaks of "you who know righteousness (*yodʿê ṣedeq*) . . . in whose heart is my law (*tôrâ*), fear not the reproach of men" (RSV), i.e., you who have experienced God's saving action and have grasped his teaching with all your being (Whitley 1972). The word *ṣĕdāqâ* occurs twice in 54:14, 17 (cf. 51:6, 8 above). Yahweh assures Jerusalem that "you shall be established in *ṣĕdāqâ.*" The city is to be restored *by* his saving action, a promise made in the context of well-being or prosperity (*šālôm,* v 13b). The promise of blessing and the promise of salvation are correlative; they are to introduce a new era. Any attack on Zion must fail because Yahweh has created (*bārāʾ,* twice in v 16) the forgers of weapons and those who seek to destroy. But the citizens of Jerusalem are to enjoy the fruits of Yahweh's saving action because "their *ṣĕdāqâ* is from me" (v 17b). The word *ṣĕdāqâ* has gone out from Yahweh's mouth, a word that will not return (45:23a), and that does not return until it has accomplished its purpose (Isa 55:10–11). It *is* saving action, it *will* effect proper order. Yahweh's *ṣĕdāqâ,* deliverance (RSV), is his saving action which will restore Israel and adorn her (46:12–13, twice). (For Yahweh's saving action in Isaiah 32–33, see above.)

3. Isaiah 56–66. In chap. 62 the prophet assures Zion of salvation through Yahweh's intervention. Then, Jerusalem's *ṣedeq* will shine forth like a light and her *yĕšûʿâ* will blaze like a torch (v 1); nations will see her *ṣedeq* and kings her *kābôd* (v 2). Because Yahweh will intervene, Jerusalem in her *ṣedeq* will reflect Yahweh's *ṣedeq* and *kābôd* (cf. 58:8). Chap. 60 describes Zion in glory after Yahweh has effected his definitive saving action in the city. Zion shall no longer be under foriegn rule; her foremen shall be *šālôm* (peace, prosperity) and her taskmasters *ṣĕdāqâ* (the fruits of Yahweh's action, v 17). Yahweh has countered the harsh oppression; the walls and the gates, now rebuilt, assure *yĕšûʿâ* (salvation) and *tĕhillâ* (praise, v 18). The theme continues in chap. 61. Yahweh has clothed Zion with *yesaʿ* and *ṣĕdāqâ* (v 10). He had already put on these "weapons" to save her (59:17). He will cause the effects of his actions, *ṣĕdāqâ* and *tĕhillâ,* to spring from the earth (v 11; cf. 45:8).

The colorful warrior who intervenes in chap. 63 identifies himself with Yahweh: "It is I who speak: by (my) *ṣĕdāqâ* (saving intervention) mighty to bring salvation (*lĕhôšîaʿ*)" (v 1). The oaks of righteousness, *ʾêlê ṣedeq,* 61:3, may well mean the oaks of the Just One, reading *ṣaddîq* for *ṣedeq* (Rosenberg 1965; Scullion 1971: 345).

It is not easy to determine the meaning of *ṣedeq* in

64:4a[5a] and of *ṣĕdāqâ* in v 5a (6a; pl. with suffix of 1st s.). The passage is part of a communal lament (63:7–64:11[12]). Yahweh has been called on to intervene (63:19b–64:2[64:1–3]). Then: "never have people heard, never has ear perceived, never has eye seen, any God but you (who) act toward those who hope in him" (v 3[4]). Yahweh struck those who were "doing *ṣedeq*"—carrying out the ritual formally, but still sinning (v 4b[5b]). What no one has heard of (v 3[4]) is of a God who punishes those who fulfill formally his ritual instructions (v 3[4]). The pl. *ṣĕdāqôt* (v 5[6]) refers to those external observances by which a sinful people sought to justify itself.

4. Hosea, Micah, Isaiah 1–39. The words *ṣedeq* and *ṣĕdāqâ* occur in Hosea and Micah in the context of saving action. God's intervention effects proper order (Hos 2:21–22[19–20]; 10:12; Mic 6:5, 8; see above). In the lament of chap. 7, Micah acknowledges that he is a sinner; but Yahweh will plead his cause; he will bring him to the light where he (Micah) will see Yahweh's *ṣĕdāqâ,* saving action (7:9).

Only a remnant of Israel will survive (Isa 10:22), even though her numbers are as the sand of the sea; "destruction is decreed, overflowing with righteousness" (RSV; *šotep ṣĕdāqâ*; or "making *ṣĕdāqâ* overflow"). It is *ṣĕdāqâ* to the full; God's action has a punitive as well as a salvific side. Though punishing Israel, God will ultimately preserve it.

5. Jeremiah, Zechariah, Malachi. The oracle against Babylon in Jeremiah 51 tells of Yahweh's deliverance of his people. He has brought forth, or caused to shine out, "our *ṣĕdāqâ*" (v 10). He has acted and saved his people; therefore "let us tell in Zion the work, *maᶜăśeh,* of Yahweh, our God" (v 10). It is God, the savior, deliverer, and vindicator, at work.

Zechariah takes up an old covenant formula when he speaks of Yahweh's saving action: "I will bring them to dwell in the midst of Jerusalem, and they shall be my people and I will be their God *bĕʾemet* and *biṣdāqâ*" (8:8). Yahweh will show that he is true to himself in his saving action.

According to Malachi, the "sun of righteousness," *šemeš ṣĕdāqâ,* will rise with healing wings on those who fear the name of Yahweh (3:20[4:2]). From 2500 B.C.E. through to the late Roman Empire, the winged sun disc, representing the sun as a god, was well known in the ANE. It provided warmth, light, fertility, and general well-being. But it is Yahweh who shines on his people and gives them prosperity.

F. Plural of *ṣĕdāqâ*

The word *ṣedeq* does not occur in the pl. in the OT; *ṣĕdāqôt,* the pl. of *ṣĕdāqâ,* occurs 15 times, designating either the victorious, triumphal, and saving acts of God in favor of his people, or the acts of the people in real or alleged conformity with God's order. Deborah sings of the triumphs of Yahweh after the battle of Kishon (Judg 5:11, twice). Samuel reminds the people of "all the saving deeds (*ṣĕdāqôt*) of the Lord which he performed for you and your fathers" (1 Sam 12:7). "Only in Yahweh . . . are saving acts (*ṣĕdāqôt*) and strength (*ᶜoz*)" (Isa 45:24; cf. Mic 6:5; Ps 103:6; Dan 9:16). Yahweh has effected saving acts in our favor (lit. our righteous acts, Jer 51:10); the *ṣĕdāqôt* are the work (*maᶜăśēh*) of Yahweh our God. Yahweh is the just one who loves *ṣĕdāqôt,* i.e., acts in accordance with his *mišpāṭ* and *ṣĕdāqâ* (Ps 11:7; for Yahweh as a lover of *mišpāṭ* and *ṣĕdāqâ,* cf. Pss 33:7; 99:4). *Ṣĕdāqôt* are the acts of the upright, parallel to *mĕšārîm* (proper acts, Isa 33:15; cf. Ezek 3:20; 18:14; 33:13; Dan 9:18). For Isa 64:5[6], *ṣĕdāqôt* as the external observance of a deluded and sinful people that seeks to justify itself, see above.

G. Parallels and Word-fields

In the Psalms *ṣĕdāqâ* is in parallelism with *tōm* (innocence), *mišpāṭ* (ordinance, right conduct, justice), *tĕhillâ* (praise), *kābôd* (glory), *mĕšārîm* (equity), *ʾĕmet* and *ʾĕmûnâ* (truth, fidelity), *ḥesed* (steadfast love, loyalty), *hāqîṣ* (to wake up); *ṣedeq* with *bĕrākâ* (blessing), *šālôm* (peace, prosperity, well-being), *tĕšûᶜâ* and *yĕšûᶜâ* (salvation, saving action), *peleʾ* (a wonder), *šēm* (name), *ṭôb* (good, prosperity, [in certain context, rain?]). *Ṣedeq* and *ṣĕdāqâ* are not identical with these words; rather the parallels complement and intensify each other or their meanings overlap or both. They describe a reality—the multi-faceted action of Yahweh and its correlative multifaceted effects on the life and land of his people and their response. These 16 words, and others, are often used in groups, creating a word-field, over two or more verses, describing the same reality: Pss 33:5, *ṣĕdāqâ, mišpāṭ, yāšār* (upright[ness]), *ʾĕmûnâ*; 36:1, 11, *ṣĕdāqâ, mišpāṭ, ḥesed, ʾĕmûnâ*; 40:10–12[9–11], *ṣedeq, ṣĕdāqâ, ʾĕmûnâ, tĕšûᶜâ, ʾemet* (2x), *raḥămîm* (compassion), *ḥesed*; 72:1–3, *mišpāṭ* and *ṣĕdāqâ, ṣedeq* and *mišpāṭ, šālôm* and *ṣĕdāqâ*; 85:10–14[9–13], *yēšaᶜ, kābôd, ḥesed, ʾĕmet* (2x), *ṣedeq* (3x), *šālôm, ṭôb, yĕbûl* (produce), *yśm* (v 14[13] beauty ?). These parallels and vast word-fields are used in other books of the OT, especially in Isaiah 40–66 with the additional parallels *maᶜăśeh* (deeds) Isa 57:12; *tôrâ* Isa 51:1; *yēšaᶜ* Isa 45:8; cf. Hos 2:21[19–20].

H. The Just or Righteous One (Heb *ṣaddîq*)

The *ṣaddîq* is the just or righteous one, mentioned so often in Proverbs and in the Psalms. Neither of these two books says what makes one *ṣaddîq,* nor is one exhorted to be *ṣaddîq.* The *ṣaddîq,* the person's conduct and the state resulting from it, is constantly contrasted with the wicked by means of antithetic parallelism. This is especially so in Proverbs 10–15, where the *ṣaddîq* is named 39 times. Virtually every one of the 13 examples in chap. 10 are of this kind (vv 3, 6, 7, 11, 16, 20, 24, 25, 28, 30, 32, with a slight variation in vv 21, 31).

In the Psalms, the righteous (sing. or pl.) will prosper (e.g., 72:7; 92:13[12]), be exalted (e.g., 75:11[10]); the righteous are called to rejoice and cry out, confident in Yahweh's saving action (e.g., 64:10; 68:3); they are contrasted with the wicked (e.g., 1:5, 6; 5:13[12]). However, the *ṣaddîq,* like the wicked, will return to the dust (Qoh 3:16–22).

Yahweh is *ṣaddîq* (e.g., 11:7; 112:4; 116:5; 119:137; 129:4; 145:17). The ideal king to come is described as *ṣaddîq* and *nôšāᶜ* (*Nipᶜal* part. Zech 8:8), "his cause won, his victory gained" (NEB), "triumphant and victorious" (RSV). The nuance of saving action, so prominent with *ṣedeq-ṣĕdāqâ* in the Psalms and Isaiah 40–66, is evident. The *ṣaddîq* elsewhere is the one who is innocent (e.g., Gen 18:22–32), or the one without fault who stands before the court and merits acquittal (e.g., Deut 16:19; 25:1). He is the one who acts on his own responsibility and is guiltless before God (Ezekiel 18). The statutes and ordinances of Israel are *ṣaddîq* (Deut 4:8).

I. Current Research

An outline of scholarly interpretation of *ṣedeq-ṣĕdāqâ* since the 1920s has been given under B above. Reventlow (1971), Ziesler (1972), Reumann (1982), and Mogensen (1984) have synthesized the history of research. Important contributions to the study have been made by Schmid (1968), Reventlow (1971), Crüsemann (1976), and Scharbert (*TRE* 12: 404–11). See also *RAC* 10: 234–360.

Schmid (1968: 166) considers *ṣedeq-ṣĕdāqâ* under the heading of "world order." *Ṣdq* touches order in six areas: (1) law, (2) wisdom, (3) nature, (4) cult, (5) kingship, and (6) war. "The word is constant, the idea, the understanding of the word, is variable. What is 'right', 'in order', does not derive from an inherent 'meaning' of the word, but from the theology of each particular author. It is not the word, with all that is implied in the history of its usage, that defines what order is; rather the word, more or less in accord with its past, is always given new conceptual dimensions so as to formulate what the author wants to express by 'order' " (1968: 169–70). This might be reformulated: the word receives its new conceptual dimensions from its juxtaposition to, its parallelism with, its setting within the context of, other words or groups of words which together describe the reality of God's action and its effects. To say that *ṣedeq-ṣĕdāqâ* looks to cosmic order or to order in nature also requires some modification. It is rather that the creator God, the prime orderer, is the one who restores order in society, who demands proper order in worship, and who acts in his restoring, saving way to effect this. The creator God admits the ritually pure into the temple (Ps 24:1–2, 3–6); he effects ultimate well-being and prosperity (Is 45:8). It is Yahweh, who made the earth and created, *bārāʾ*, *ʾādām* (the human in general) upon it, who also roused Cyrus *bĕṣedeq*, in his saving purpose, (Isa 45:12–13). Yahweh demands and effects order, he is savior and restorer because, as creator, he is the source of order. Schmid writes: "One can say then with a certain simplification: the interpretation of *ṣdq* as 'conformity to a norm' is clearly close to the original meaning and usage of *ṣdq*; the translation, 'community loyalty', however, embraces better the concrete application by the OT in a great number of cases. A survey of the history of scholarship clarifies the basic problem of OT language which comes nicely into focus in the case of 'righteousness': a distinction must be made between the original Canaanite idea and its usage in the OT" (1968: 185–86). But, though the word, or rather *ṣdq*, is West Semitic, we know virtually nothing about "the original Canaanite idea." To speak merely of *ṣdq*, however, comes dangerously close to imposing a "*ṣdq*-Begriff" (concept, notion) on uses of the words deriving from the root, though Schmid does not do this. There is much of value in Schmid's approach, in particular in his emphasis on Yahweh in action, exercising *ṣedeq-ṣĕdāqâ*, and on the individual responding by following Yahweh's order. However it seems too systematic to lay *ṣdq* on a six-point Procrustean bed. Better to say that Yahweh's *ṣdq* touches all areas of life.

Reventlow gives a comprehensive account of the discussion of justification in the OT among scholars in the German-speaking regions and of its ramifications into the NT and systematic theology. He too looks to the divine action: "Justification is centred around *ṣedeq-ṣĕdāqâ*, around something related to the order of the world. But one must bear in mind at the same time that the Old Testament as a whole attests to a divine action that bursts through this order, alters it, renews it" (1971: 37).

Crüsemann (1976) notes that most studies in recent decades have dealt with the meaning and translation of *ṣedeq-ṣĕdāqâ*; attention to "Yahweh's *ṣedeq*" has been a by-product. For Crüsemann, Yahweh's *ṣedeq-ṣĕdāqâ* describes an action of God, but an action that varies in the course of Israel's history:

(1) in the premonarchical period, *ṣedeq-ṣĕdāqâ* describes the military success given by Yahweh to Israel;

(2) in the monarchy, Israel calls *ṣĕdāqâ* (a) the actualization of the normal state of *ṣedeq* in cult, or (b) the rescue of an individual in distress;

(3) in the exilic period, *ṣĕdāqâ* is God's saving action in the future.

That Yahweh's *ṣedeq-ṣĕdāqâ* is an action that saves and restores, commands assent. But one must be cautious in assigning such a definitive and restricted meaning to the word(s) in the premonarchical period; there are at most two examples (Judg 5:11; Deut 33:20–21) in both of which the pl., *ṣĕdāqôt*, is used. The meanings assigned to *ṣedeq-ṣĕdāqâ* in the monarchical period are correct, but too restrictive; Amos, for example, envisages a broader social *ṣĕdāqâ* (5:7, 24); and the Psalms, while often the prayer of one in distress, reach beyond the individual (e.g., Pss 22:32[31]; 50:6; 97:6; 99:4; 103:7[6]; 145:7). Further, the Psalms are notoriously difficult to date, and they contain elements both old and new. Crüsemann's positive contribution is in the area of Yahweh's *ṣedeq-ṣĕdāqâ* as action. But his systematization is too linear and restrictive.

Scharbert has emphasized the aspect of "saving action," particularly in the Psalms, where "Yahweh's righteousness is praised as a saving intervention on behalf of the pious over against persecutors and exploiters, or on behalf of Israel against its enemies" (*TRE* 12: 410). He also makes the important observation: "It is to be noted that the OT regards legal decisions primarily as liberating decisions in favour of the oppressed, exploited, unjustly accused, and less as sentences pronounced on the justly accused. This is important for making any judgment about the righteousness of God" (*TRE* 12: 408).

J. Summary and Conclusion

It is not sufficient merely to determine the meaning of *ṣedeq-ṣĕdāqâ* in isolation and propose an adequate translation in each case. The question arises: whose *ṣedeq-ṣĕdāqâ*? If God's *ṣedeq-ṣĕdāqâ*, then the context, especially in the Psalms and Isaiah 40–66 (cf. E above), is usually God's saving action, directed to the *šālôm* (well-being, prosperity) of the people, where the words are found in word-fields or in parallelism (cf. G above). If Israel's or the person's *ṣedeq-ṣĕdāqâ*, then the words are often in parallelism with *mišpāṭ* (e.g., Pss 37:6; 72:2; 106:2; Isa 1:27; 28:17; 56:1), in coordination with *mišpāṭ* (e.g., Deut 16:18; Pss 72:1; 99:4; Isa 5:16; 33:5; 58:2), or the object of the verbs *ʿāśāh* (to do) and *šāmār* (to observe) *mišpāṭ* and *ṣedeq-ṣĕdāqâ* (e.g.,

Gen 18:19; Deut 33:11; 2 Sam 8:15). This hendiadys describes the conduct of the people in response to Yahweh's saving action, which itself is described by *ṣedeq-ṣĕdāqâ* transmitted through the king who is the custodian of God's *mišpāṭ* and *ṣedeq-ṣĕdāqâ* (e.g., Ps 72:1–3; Isa 32:1). The meaning of the word-pair is proper comportment in every area of life, social and cultic (see D above). *Ṣĕdāqâ,* standing by itself, describes God's action (Deut 6:25) and the people's reaction (Deut 6:25; 9:4, 5, 6); *ṣedeq* by itself means conduct according to what is proper, according to law (Deut 16:29). *Ṣĕdāqâ* also means claim or right (1 Sam 19:28; Neh 2:20), while *ṣedeq* used adjectivally describes what ought to be following what is laid down.

The *ṣedeq-ṣĕdāqâ* of the community and the individual is comportment according to God's order in every area of life, in just and proper social order (justice to the helpless, the poor, the oppressed, the widow, the orphan, the resident alien), in legal procedure, in the ritual of worship, all effected by God's *ṣedeq-ṣĕdāqâ.*

Bibliography

Brunner, H. 1958. Gerechtigkeit als Fundament des Thrones. *VT* 8: 426–28.

Cazelles, H. 1951. A propos de quelques textes difficiles relatifs à la justice de Dieu dans l'Ancien Testament. *RB* 58: 169–88.

Cooke, G. A. 1903. *A Textbook of North-Semitic Inscriptions.* Oxford.

Crüsemann, F. 1976. Jahwes Gerechtigkeit (ṣᵉdāqā/sädäq) im Alten Testament. *EvT* 36: 427–50.

Dünner, A. 1963. *Die Gerechtigkeit nach dem Alten Testament.* Schriften zur Rechtslehre und Politik 42. Bonn.

Euler, K. F. 1938. Königtum und Gottheir in den altaramäischen Inschriften Nord-syriens. *ZAW* 56: 272–313.

Fahlgren, K. H. 1932. *sᵉdaka, nahestehende und entgegengesetzte Begriffe im Alten Testament.* Uppsala.

Fisher, L., ed. 1972–81. *Ras Shamra Parallels. The Texts from Ugarit and the Hebrew Bible.* 3 vols. Rome.

Gaston, L. 1980. Abraham and the Righteousness of God. *HBT* 2: 39–68.

Gloege, G. 1964. Die Rechtfertigungslehre als hermeneutische Kategorie. *TLZ* 89: 161–76.

Gordon, C. H. 1949. *Ugaritic Literature.* Rome.

Gray, J. 1965. *The Legacy of Canaan.* VTSup 5. 2d ed. Leiden.

———. 1966. Social Aspects of Canaanite Religion. Pp. 170–92 in *Volume du Congrès, Genève, 1965.* VTSup 15. Leiden.

Herrmann, W. 1958. Der historische Ertrag der altbyblischen Königsinschriften. *MIO* 6: 14–32.

Jepsen, A. 1965. Ṣdq und Ṣdqh im Alten Testament. Pp. 78–99 in *Gottes Wort und Gottes Land,* ed. H. G. Reventlow. Göttingen.

Justesen, J. P. 1964. On the Meaning of ṢADAQ. *AUSS* 2: 53–61.

Koch, K. 1953. *ṢDQ im Alten Testament.* Diss. Heidelberg.

———. 1961. Wesen und Ursprung der Gemeinschaftstreue im Israel der Königszeit. *ZEE* 5: 72–90.

Krašovec, J. 1988. La justice (SDQ) de Dieu dans le Bible Hebraïque et l'interprétation juive et chrétienne. OBO 76. Freiburg-Göttingen.

Meyer, R. 1966. Melchisedek von Jerusalem und Moresedek von Qumran. Pp. 228–39 in *Volume du Congrès, Genève, 1965.* VTSup 15. Leiden.

Mogensen, B. 1984. ṣᵉdāqā in the Scandinavian and German Research Traditions. Trans. F. H. Cryer. Pp. 67–80 in *The Productions of Time: Tradition History in Old Testament Scholarship,* ed. K. Jeppesen and Benedikt Otzen. Sheffield.

Oeming, M. 1983. Ist Genesis 15,6 ein Beleg für die Anrechnung des Glaubens zur Gerechtigkeit? *ZAW* 1983: 183–97.

Pedersen, J. 1926. *Israel 1–11.* London and Copenhagen.

Procksch, O. 1950. *Theologie des Alten Testaments.* Gütersloh.

Reumann, J. 1982. *"Righteousness" in the New Testament.* Philadelphia.

Reventlow, H. G. 1971. *Rechtfertigung im Horizont des Alten Testaments.* BEvT 58. Munich.

Rosenberg, R. A. 1965. The God Ṣedeq. *HUCA* 36: 61–67.

Schmid, H. H. 1968. *Gerechtigkeit als Weltordnung.* Tübingen.

———. 1980. Gerechtigkeit und Glaube. Genesis 15:1–6 und sein biblisch-theologischer Kontext. *EvT* 30: 396–420.

———. 1984. Creation, Righteousness, and Salvation: "Creation Theology" as the Broad Horizon of Biblical Theology. Trans. B. W. Anderson and Dan. G. Johnson. Pp. 102–17 in *Creation in the Old Testament,* ed. B. W. Anderson. Philadelphia and London.

Scullion, J. J. 1971. *ṢEDEQ-SEDAQAH* in Isaiah cc. 40–66. *UF* 3: 335–48.

Swetnam, J. 1965. Some Observations on the Background of *sadiq* in Jeremias 23,5a. *Bib* 46: 29–40.

Watson, W. G. E. 1980. Gender-Matched Synonymous Parallelism in the OT. *JBL* 99: 321–41.

Whitley, C. F. 1972. Deutero-Isaiah's Interpretation of ṣedeq. *VT* 22: 469–75.

Ziesler, J. 1972. *The Meaning of Righteousness in Paul. A Linguistic and Theological Enquiry.* SNTSMS 20. Cambridge.

J. J. SCULLION

EARLY JUDAISM

The concept of "righteousness" played an important role in the emerging Judaism of the centuries before and at the start of the Common Era, though that role has been variously interpreted (Sanders 1977: xi–xiv, 1–12, 233–38). The concept rests on meanings developed in the Hebrew Scriptures for the root *ṣdq* (see previous article). The applications in Jewish sources—in Hebrew, Aramaic, or Greek—have an importance of their own, as developments within Judaism and for understanding early Christian usage. At times Jewish documents in Greek may exhibit connections with pagan thought of the day (see next article).

A. General Picture
B. Specific Sources and Problems
  1. In the LXX
  2. Jewish Writings (in Greek)
  3. Dead Sea Scrolls
  4. Rabbinic Literature
  5. The "Righteousness of God"
  6. Exegetical Debate

A. General Picture

Terms from *ṣdq* and their Greek translation, usually as *dik*-words, are frequent in the literary remains from Jewish sources in the centuries before and at the beginning of the Common Era. It is possible to combine these together, as Cronbach has done for the period 200 B.C.–A.D. 100, to obtain the following picture of how "righteous(ness)" was spoken of with regard to human beings, above all pious Israelites, and with regard to God (*IDB* 4: 85–91). In this composite, righteousness is identified on the one hand with a host of traits such as mercy, beneficence, and gentleness, and with the absence of avarice or wrongdoing on the other; the righteous person is especially given to prayer (2 Esdr 7:41–42 [111–12]; *1 En.* 47:1–2; 97:1, 3, 5, on earth and in heaven; 39:5–7) and almsgiving (Dan 4:27 [24], RSV righteousness; NEB charity, for Aramaic *ṣidĕqâ;* Sir 3:14, RSV kindness; Heb *ṣĕdāqâ,* Gk *eleēmosynē*). Righteousness is especially looked for in judges. There can, however, be a sense of vindictiveness about justice, even the justice that God works, above all eschatologically (2 Macc 12:40–41; *Ps. Sol.* 4:8).

God's righteousness in this composite description is seen as being "forever" in both judgment (Tob 3:2) and in mercy (2 Esdr 8:36; "to those who have no store of good works"), in turning away God's "anger and wrath" (Dan 9:16). Such righteousness extends especially to Israel (2 Macc 1:25); sometimes the covenant with Abram is mentioned (2 Macc 1:2; *Jub.* 22:15). Upright individuals in the past, from Enoch on, are named, and the righteous will be delivered at the final judgment (2 Esdr 9:13; 7:33–35) into a city "full of all good things," inherited after they endure many sorts of difficulties, including persecution, in this life (7:7–18). "Some authors are persuaded that God alone possesses righteousness" (Cronbach *IDB* 4: 89; cf. Sir 18:2; 2 Esdr 8:32), and so there is in certain texts no appeal to human righteousness (Dan 9:18). It is recognized in some passages (*IDB* 4: 87) that "human righteousness has God as its source (Bar 5:9; *Jub.* 16:26)." To know God is "complete righteousness" (Wis 15:3). Divine justice punishes the unrighteous (Wis 1:8; 12:13, not unjustly; as God had the Egyptians, chaps. 17 and 19, in contrast to the Israelites, chap. 18, though "the experience of death touched also the righteous" during their rebellion in the wilderness, 18:20).

Hence it is important that righteousness be taught, as Enoch (*1 En.* 13:10; 14:1), Abraham (*Jub.* 20:2), and others did. According to Dan 12:3, the wise (cf. 11:33) "who turn many to righteousness" (Isa 53:11) will receive an especial glory (cf. Wis 3:1, 7, on the righteous, who are in the hands of God). The *Psalms of Solomon,* particularly 3 and 9, emphasize how the righteous live—knowing salvation comes from God (3:5–6) and that they stumble (3:5) and sin (3:7–8; 9:6–7), yet that God's righteousness is proven right (3:5; 9:2)—in contrast to sinners (3:9–12). This contrast can also be applied to Israel's enemies (*Ps. Sol.* 17:22) as well as to parties and groups within Judaism; e.g., the "ungodly" of Wis 1:16 who oppose "the righteous man" (2:10, 12, 18).

From this picture of righteousness in Jewish circles, it must be added, there was sometimes dissent (Cronbach *IDB* 4: 91). Alternative opinions are to be seen in the long-standing view that in this "vain life" the righteous often perish in their righteousness, while the wicked prolong life in their evildoing; the conclusion: "be not righteous overmuch" (Eccl 7:15–16; cf. 8:14); "one fate comes to the righteous and the wicked" (9:2). The argument of the Sadducees, who denied a hereafter, surfaces in *1 Enoch*: the righteous die and gain nothing by their deeds; together with sinners, they are equal from now on, neither will see light again (*1 En.* 102:6–8; Wis 2:1–5; Eccl 2:14–16; 3:19–21). At the other extreme is the Jewish author who has one of the LXX translators tell the Egyptian king, Ptolemy II, that he could live harmoniously with all constituencies by "taking justice as your guide, . . . God granting you sound reasoning" (*Let. Aris.* 267); the passage expresses a less supernaturalistic view (*IDB* 4: 87–88) or at least one that accords with Greek ideas of justice.

B. Specific Sources and Problems

Greater precision in some ways can be attained by examining Jewish sources by categories. These include the LXX, Greek and Hebrew writings of the Intertestamental period, including Philo, Josephus, and the Dead Sea Scrolls, and rabbinic materials (Ziesler 1972: 52–127; Sanders 1977: 33–418 for Palestinian Judaism).

1. In the LXX (Ziesler 1972: 52–69). A variety of translators over a number of years sought to put the Hebrew writings (which not all the translators always fully understood) into Greek for use in Diaspora synagogues and possible perusal by Greek inquirers. In general, *ṣdq* words are rendered by those from *dikaioun* in Greek (which indeed has the same range of meanings [Watson 1960]), but on occasion *eleēmosynē* (9 times); *eleos* (3 times), "mercy, pity"; *eusebein,* "be pious"; and various words for judgment (*krisis, krima*) are also employed. On the other hand, *dikaiosynē* is also at times used for *ʾĕmet,* "faithfulness, truth"; *ḥesed,* "kindness, mercy"; and *mišpāṭ,* "judgment, justice" (Hill 1967: 104–9; Ziesler 1972: 59–66). Dodd concluded that the Greek translation narrowed down the broader senses of the Hebrew to a more constricted meaning in Greek of "justice" and impoverished the several aspects of the Hebrew *ṣdq* by polarizing it into now *dikaiosynē,* now *eleēmosynē.* Descamps found that use of the Greek *dikaiosynē* as the noun for *ṣĕdāqâ* distorted its sense in the direction of "distributive justice" ("to each, his own"). Ziesler (1972: 67–69) doubts these findings, giving the LXX translators higher grades on the ground that they sense the covenantal setting.

More recently Olley's investigation, admittedly limited to Isaiah passages, rejects both Dodd's view on "polarization" and the notion that the translators saw covenantal associations, but allows that Greek connotations of justice did enter in. LXX use of *dikaioun* in a positive sense, to "acquit, vindicate, restore to a right relationship," extends the Greek forensic meaning with a personal object, to "do to a person what is necessary to correct an . . . injustice." The classical "forensic sense" continues, with the picture of a judge in mind, but it must be remembered that the role of the judge (and king and God) in Israel—to vindicate the oppressed—was greater than what is often thought of as a "law-court metaphor" (cf. Olley 1979: 12–14, 63–64, 111–17, 125–26; 1980: 71–73). Unlike investigators who believe a *dikaioun* word in the LXX "has the same meaning as MT" Hebrew (p. 12), Olley reaches the conclusion that LXX Isaiah (a book of immense importance for early Christians, who especially cited Isaiah in its Greek form) failed to convey the Hebraic sense of *ṣidqôt-YHWH* as "salvific"; instead, the Greek sense in *dikaiosynē* as "justice" adhered: God "is 'just' and acts according to 'justice' to bring about a state of 'justice' " (Olley 1979: 126–27). This assumes a meaning in Greek of "justice," not Isaiah's "saving righteousness."

If *dikaioun*-terms in the LXX lose this aspect of the Hebrew *ṣdq, adikos* gains more of a religious connotation from the MT associations (Schrenk *TDNT* 1: 150–51, 158). The verb *adikein* comes to mean "to sin against God" as a rendering of *ḥāṭāʾ* (2 Sam 24:17), *māʿal* (2 Chr 26:16, RSV Uzziah "was false to the Lord"), or *ʿāwâ* (Jer 3:21, RSV "perverted").

It is possible that connection of *dik*-terms with faith/faithfulness (*pistis*) in Greek, found in some OT texts (see B.6 below), was abetted in Hellenistic-Jewish literature by Greek linkage of these word-fields (Dobbeler 1987: 114–16).

2. Jewish Writings (in Greek). Ziesler (1972: 73–85) surveys the Apocrypha and Pseudepigrapha and concludes that the verb here remains "almost entirely forensic," the noun and adjective "almost entirely ethical" (a pattern Ziesler seeks then to trace into the NT); righteousness is seen in relation to God, often in legal and covenant-keeping terms, though human righteousness is viewed as nonlegal (p. 85). The analysis of Sanders (1977: 329–418, of Sirach, *1 Enoch, Jubilees, Psalms of Solomon,* and *4 Ezra* [RSV 2 Esdras]) affirms the covenantal emphasis (pp. 332, 341, 361 in 33, 362, 367, 404), in a pattern where "salvation depends on election," but to maintain that state it is necessary then to be righteous, i.e., to continue in "loyalty and obedience to God and his covenant" (pp. 362, 389, 408). In 2 Esdras, however, this covenantal nomism collapses into "legalistic perfectionism" or "works-righteousness" (pp. 409, 418): sin so dominates, according to this document, that even an everlasting covenant (2 Esdr 3:15) and the law cannot preserve nations; only individuals (3:35–36) and then only the few (7:47, 51, 60; 8:1) who are perfectly righteous (7:89) will be found for the world/age to come.

Philo of Alexandria uses *dik*-terms in accord with their Greek, not any Hebraic, sense. The forensic side is absent, the emphasis heavily ethical. Josephus is not theological in his usage (Ziesler 1972: 105–11; Schrenk *TDNT* 2: 183, 193–95, 211–12). But *adikos* takes on a sense of "unjust" with respect to God such as it rarely had in Greek sources (Schrenk *TDNT* 1: 151; Josephus *Ant* 8.10.2 §251 parallel with *asebēs,* scorning the worship of God; 10.5.2 §83 Jehoiakim "was *adikos* and an evildoer by nature and neither reverent [*hosios*] toward God nor kind [*epieikēs*] toward human beings"; 20.2.4 §44 "being guilty [*adikōn*] in the greatest degree against the laws and through these toward God").

The theme of the righteous sufferer can be traced in a variety of writings from this period (Ruppert 1972; Kleinknecht 1984: 85–163). Especially noteworthy is the diptych in Wis 2:12–20 and 5:1–7, where the enemies of the one who is *dikaios* lie in wait for "God's son," to test his gentleness (*epieikeia,* 2:19) by death. But the righteous person, who looks to God for deliverance, finds "unexpected salvation" (5:2, *paradoxǭ tēs sōtērias*), contrary to the plots of those on whom "the light of righteousness" did not shine (5:6), whose "norm for righteousness" (*nomos tēs dikaiosynēs,* 2:11) was their own strength. The contrast in Wisdom of Solomon between the righteous and the ungodly (*dikaioi, asebeis,* 3:1, 10) is also found in martyrdom texts (e.g., *4 Maccabees*). Philo dramatizes it in a way reminiscent of early Greek references to *dikē* when he describes how Flaccus, the anti-Jewish prefect in Egypt (appointed about A.D. 32), is overthrown by God: justice (*dikē*), the "defender of the wronged," opposed him (*Flacc* 104), until he was butchered by assassins, *dikē* willing that his wounds be equal to the number of Jews he had illegally put to death (189)—"an indubitable proof (*pistis*) of the fact that the nation of Jews has not been deprived of God's help" (191).

3. Dead Sea Scrolls (Hill 1967: 110–15; Ziesler 1972: 85–94, 102–3; Sanders 1977: 239–328, esp. 305–12; Przybylski 1980: 13–38). The Dead Sea Scrolls (DSS) present an apocalyptic covenant community of great strictness within Judaism, yet a group deeply conscious of God's grace and election. The sense both of human sin and nothingness compared with God and of God's righteousness appears particularly in the thanksgiving hymns (1QH 1.16; 4.29–31, "there is no *ṣĕdāqâ* with human beings, . . . to God Most High [belong] all deeds [*maʿăśē*] of righteousness"; 12.30–31; 1QS 1.21–2.4; 10.23). There is constant talk in the scrolls of God's grace (e.g., 1QH 11.30–31, "cleanse me by your righteousness, as I have hoped . . . for your grace [*ḥesed*]"), compassion, goodness, and mercy (1QH 1.29–32; 4.36). A number of interpreters have taken *mišpāṭ,* particularly in 1QS 11.5 and 12, to mean "justification" (Grundmann 1968; Ziesler 1972: 102–3), so that one experiences renewal of moral life and can stand in the judgment. The claim is that Paul's teaching is here anticipated (Stuhlmacher 1965: 148–53, 166; Koch *THAT* 2: 530). But more recent treatments take *mišpāṭ* as "judgment," point to the absence of any reference to "faith" (for Qumran treatment of Hab 2:4, see B.6.b below), and blunt such seeming parallels (Sanders 1977: 308–9: *mišpāṭ* and *ṣidqaṭ ʾēl* at 1QS 11.12 are "synonymous parallelism," but mercy [*raḥamîm, ḥasādîm,* 11.13] and goodness [*ṭôb,* 11.14] are also aligned with *mišpāṭ* and related terms; Fitzmyer 1982: 363). Yet it is in the DSS that there appear the closest approximations anywhere in Jewish literature to many items in Paul.

Przybylski differentiates the treatment in different Qumran documents (cf. also Stuhlmacher 1965: 154–65). In general there is a trend to distinguish *ṣĕdāqâ* as "God's saving, gracious activity" (CD 20.20; 1QS 1.21; 10.23, 25; 11.3, 5, 6, 12, 14 [bis]) and *ṣedeq* as the norm for human conduct (CD 20.27–33; 1QS 1.13; 3.1; 4.4), though *ṣedeq* can also refer to God's saving actions (1QS 10.11–12; 1QH 11.2–3, 12, 18; 1QM 18.8) and *ṣĕdāqâ* to human conduct (1QH 4.30; 7.14, 17). The terms occur especially in 1QS and 1QH (where OT influence is strong). God is "my righteousness" (1QS 10.11), to God belongs *ṣĕdāqâ* (1QH 17.20). Chiefly in the *Damascus Document* does *ṣedeq* play "a vital role," as a technical or popular term for "everything that is right in the sight of God," God's righteous norm, as set forth by the Teacher of Righteousness (CD 35–36).

The Teacher of Righteousness in Qumran texts can be seen to stand "in the sequence of the suffering righteous of the Psalter" and in the footsteps of Jeremiah (Ruppert 1972a: 126–27; cf. 1QH 2–8, esp. 5). The one who prays in the *hôdāyôt* is oppressed by enemies (2.20–30) but looks to God for salvation and peace (15.14–17). Similar to this is 1QS 3.20–25, contrasting the children of righteousness (*bĕnê ṣedeq*) with the children of falsehood.

4. Rabbinic Literature (Hill 1967: 115–20). Early rabbinic writings use *ṣdq* (Aram *zakâ*) in a great variety of ways. Ziesler (1972: 112–27) finds the forensic sense in the verb; elsewhere the ethical predominates. Sanders (1977: 33–238, esp. 198–205, who confines his material to the Tannaim or teachers of the first two centuries A.D.; also Przybylski 1980: 39–76) sees a pattern: the "righteous man" is one who obeys the law in order to preserve (not earn) one's place within the covenant. Often *ṣĕdāqâ* means charity—alms, in a human action, or God's charity or mercy toward humanity.

Finkel takes *ṣdq* in Judaism, with both a forensic and an ethical meaning, to be a bridge between interpersonal and intrapersonal areas; that is, among human beings, in a social order (as justice, peace); and within a person (as the starting point toward altruistic kindness). Passages such as Deut 16:20 ("Justice [*ṣedeq*] and only justice, you shall follow") were applied in juridical strife to encourage peaceful compromise (*b. Sanh.* 32b), and almsgiving was institutionalized in the community as a way "leading many to righteousness" (Dan 12:3; *b. B. Bat.* 8b). In the command of Exod 18:20 to make Israel "know the way in which they must walk and what they must do," "the way" was interpreted as the ethical deeds of *ḥesed* and "what they must do" as works beyond the letter of the law (*Mek. Yitro. Amalek* #2; Montefiore and Loewe 1938: 505). The righteous person (*ḥasîd*), such as Ḥanina ben Dosa, was marked by fear before God and love to God.

That righteousness had both judicial and ethical aspects carried over to the transpersonal picture of God as the Righteous One (on God as *ṣaddîq*, see Przybylski 1980: 42–43). Rabbinic thought associated the quality of ordering and judging (*middāt haddîn*) with the biblical name "Elohim," and the quality of mercy (*raḥamîm*) with "YHWH" (*Exod. Rab.* on Exod 3:14). The first aspect suggested God's immanence and a teaching about rewards and punishments, especially for those faithful even to the point of martyrdom who professed God's righteousness. Job exemplified proper fear toward God. Trust in God's mercy was exemplified by Abram (Gen 15:6), who then practiced "the way of the Lord by doing righteousness [*ṣĕdāqâ*] and justice [*mišpāṭ*]" (Gen 18:19); here *ṣĕdāqâ* was taken at times to mean "charity" (*Yal.* 82 on 18:19; *Gen. Rab.* 49 on 18:19). Such passages could in turn lead to a rabbinic type of *imitatio Dei,* walking "in all God's ways" (Deut 10:12), "a God merciful and gracious" (Exod 34:6); . . . as God is called 'righteous' [*ṣaddîq*] and loves righteous deeds [*ṣĕdāqôt,* Ps 11:7], so shall you also be righteous . . ." (*Sipre Deut* 49). Again, Abraham was regarded as the ideal *ṣaddîq,* for whom, indeed, the world was created (*Sipre Deut* 38 on 11:10, 47 on 11:21; *Gen. Rab.* 35 on 9:12). In a debate over the basic form to which the Torah could be reduced, Hab 2:4 was cited as the single form on which all 613 commands can rest: "the righteous shall live by his faith" (*b. Mak.* 24a); thus "the individual *tsaddiq* is a man of faith" (Przybylski 1980: 44).

The judgment aspect of *ṣdq* looms behind rabbinic teaching, so that even the righteous must stand before God the judge (*Pirqe ʾAbot* 4.29; rabbinic comments on Deut 32:4, Zeph 3:5, and Exod 9:27, cited in Przybylski 1980: 42–43). In one passage (*Mek. Exod.* 23:7) a human court case where a guilty party is declared righteous appears in parallel with God's court, though it is not concluded that God so acts (Ziesler 1972: 116–17; Przybylski 1980: 49). Clearly forensic, this emphasis was, however, not merely one of merits and rewards (Str-B 1: 251–52 on Matt 5:20, *dikaiosynē tou nomou*; cf. Odeberg 1964: 30–39, Montefiore and Loewe 1938: 218–22), for one was often instructed to do what is commanded without any thought of reward (*Pirqe ʾAbot* 1.3; *ʿAbod. Zar.* 19a; *ʾAbot R. Nat.* 5, citing Antigonus of Sakho, "[Be] like servants who serve the master not on condition of receiving a reward"). God's judgment could also serve to distinguish among the (7) types of "Pharisees" (Sanders 1977: 61, n. 12; 129, n. 12, gives reasons for thinking that these *pĕrûšîm* were later ascetics or "heretics," not pre-70 Pharisees) enumerated in *b. Soṭa* 22b; *j. Ber.* 9.14b; *j. Soṭa* 5.20c (summary in Montefiore and Loewe 1938: 487–89), including "book-keeping" and reward-oriented types, and the God-fearing and God-loving Pharisees (Job and Abraham, respectively; on "levels of imperfection" in the righteous, cf. Przybylski 1980: 44–46). Even the "perfectly righteous" (*ṣaddîq gāmûr*) is not without minor transgression. Opinions varied on whether gentiles could be righteous; the law served as criterion for righteousness (Przybylski 1980: 48–49, 51–52).

The ideal *ṣaddîq* (Finkel *TRE* 12: 413–14), then, is a rare person who is both loyal servant and loving son (*b. Ber.* 34b; *m. Taʿan* 3.8), exemplified in Onias the rainmaker (about 80 B.C.; *m. Taʿan* 38) or Ḥanina ben Dosa (first generation of Tannaites, ca. A.D. 10–80; *b. Soṭa* 49a). This righteous practitioner of *ḥesed,* prayer, and struggle with the "evil impulse" may, in imitation of God, do works of healing (*Deut. Rab.* 10.3), even awakenings from the dead (*b. Pesaḥ* 68a). Such a person was regarded as living on after death (*b. Ber.* 18b), rewarded with a personal resurrection (*b. Taʿan* 7b). The death of the righteous, especially as a martyr, expiates sin (*b. Moʿed Qaṭ.* 28a, of Miriam's death after the reference to the red heifer in Num 19:1–20:1; Montefiore and Loewe 1938: 225–32; cf. Vermes 1973: 9, 65–82; for later Jewish use, see Jacobs *EncJud* 14: 180–83 [cf. *EncJud* 16: 961] and Mach 1957).

Przybylski (1980: 76) insists that *ṣdq*-language in the Tannaitic literature pertains not to soteriology but to behavior. The *ṣaddîq* follows the norm of righteousness (*ṣedeq*), God's will presented in the covenant laws; righteousness has to do with remaining in the covenant. It is "demand upon men rather than the salvific gift of God for man." To this extent, *ṣĕdāqâ* comes primarily to denote almsgiving, while *ṣedeq* more broadly refers to "all aspects of teaching which are normative for man's conduct" (Przybylski 1980: 75; Stuhlmacher 1965: 181–82). "By living according to the intent and content of righteousness [*ṣedeq*]—and almsgiving [*ṣĕdāqâ*] is included in this—the righteous one [*ṣaddîq*] in effect not only does righteousness [*ṣedeq*] but also shows that he has righteousness [*ṣedeq*]" (Przybylski 1980: 76, cf. 52–66 and 66–74 on the two nouns).

5. The "Righteousness of God." It has been claimed (Käsemann 1969: 172; Stuhlmacher 1965: 142–75, esp. 144–45, 174–75) that the phrase "righteousness of God" was a technical term and a basic theme in the literature of apocalyptic Judaism and Qumran. In early texts it denoted Yahweh's *ṣĕdāqôt* or righteous deeds (Deut 33:21; Judg 5:11; 1 Sam 12:7; Mic 6:5; Ps 103:16—Eng 103:17), in fidelity to covenant and creation. In later apocalyptic texts (Isa 26:8–10; Dan 9:16; *2 Bar.* 5:2) the expectation moves from God's present, delivering power to judgment and a power that will in the future create justice anew. (For correspondence of this righteousness of God with the word as power at creation, see 2 Esdr 9:5–6; *2 Bar.* 14:7; 48:8; for Qumran, note especially *ṣidqaṭ ʾēl* [1QS 10.25, 11.12, 14, 15] and *ṣedeq ʾēl* [1QM 4.6]). Käsemann's appeal to *T. Dan* 6:10, "Forsake, then, all unrighteousness [*adikia*] and cleave to the righteousness of God [*dikaiosynē tou theou*]" (*APOT* 2: 335) is dubious, on the basis both of text (*OTP* 1: 810, "cling to the righteousness of the Law of God") and of context (Soards 1987). Additional material advanced by Berger (1977) served to emphasize the demand and judgment by God subsumed under the phrase (e.g., *T. Ab.* 13:9–14; Philo *Quaest Ex* 1.10; Clem *recogn. suppl.* 3.38.5; 40.3; 41.2, *justitia dei*). In the face of subsequent discussions (Lohse 1973: 216–17; Sanders 1977: 305–10, 494; and Brauch in Sanders 1977: 527; Wilckens *Romans* EKKNT, 212–22; Kertelge *EWNT* 1: 790–91), Stuhlmacher (1986: 82, 91, n. 16) has modified his position: "God's righteousness" is a recurring term suggesting more than one concept: justice and judgment, "God's active work and/or human existence and behavior in accord with that work" (1986: 82, 91, n. 16). There is, however, a certain continuity to OT, Jewish, and Christian apocalyptic texts.

6. Exegetical Debate. Within Judaism disagreement arose over two OT texts which would become important in NT discussions of righteousness.

a. Gen 15:6 (Heidland 1936). This passage is possibly chiastic, not a parallelism:

> And he [Abram] believed Yahweh,
> and he [Yahweh] reckoned it [his faith] to him as righteousness.

Therefore, it is unlikely to have once meant "Abram reckoned it [the promises of son and descendants] to him [Yahweh] as righteousness" in a "covenantal reading" (so Gaston 1980). (Verses 1–6 and 7–21 are separate units, and though the latter has been taken as covenantal because of v 18, *kārat bĕrît* likely means "give solemn assurance or an oath" [Westermann 1985: 212–31]). The effect in this interpretation would be to shift from Abram's subjective believing as righteousness to a view stressing God's objective righteousness. This alternative interpretation where Abram is the subject of 6b seems to appear first in Nachmanides (13th cent.). By rendering 6b with a verb in the passive voice, "it was reckoned to him [Abram] (by God)," LXX (and so NT) and *Tg. Neof.* "rule out an understanding which would attribute the righteousness to God" (Gaston 1980: 42). Of course, God is righteous (Neh 9:8) and acts in righteousness to deliver the descendants of Abraham, God's friend (Isa 41:8–13; 51:1–8), but "Abraham was certainly considered in early Judaism to be the very model of righteousness" (Gaston 1980: 51; Hahn 1971: 94–97). "Abraham believed God and he was held to be righteous" (Philo *Leg All* 3.228; *Heres* 94–95; *Virt* 216), "well-pleasing in righteousness all the days of his life" (*Jub.* 23:10).

Gen 15:6 refers to a response by Abraham to God's call, promise, and election of him (12:1–3; 15:1, 5; Isa 41:8; 51:2). Exactly what Abraham's response was and the salvation that God granted varies considerably enough in texts from Jewish and early Christian sources that one cannot speak of a single tradition of interpretation. See Fig. RIG.01. That Abraham "believed" could be taken to refer to a single event like his hospitality in Gen 18:1–15 (so *1 Clem* 10:6–7) or the offering of Isaac as a sacrifice in Genesis 22 (Jas 2:21) or to a series of events throughout his life (*Jub.* 17:15–18). God's response in terms of righteousness was sometimes identified with the covenant (Sir 44:19–21) or friendship for Abraham with God (*Jub.* 19:8–9, "in the heavenly tablets"; *1 Clem* 9:4–10:2) or even the gift of the Spirit (*Mek.* 40b, on Exod 14:31, tractate *Bešallaḥ* 7:135–41). Participation by Abraham's descendants in the salvation this patriarch enjoyed was the framework for later understandings (Dobbeler 1987: 116–25).

Foremost among "the deeds (*erga*) of the fathers" recited in 1 Macc 2:52 was that "Abraham was found faithful (*pistos*) when tested, and it was reckoned to him as righteousness." To be faithful was here a deed or "work" (Sir 44:19–22, reflecting Genesis 12, 15, 17, 22). Abraham's faithfulness was seen by Philo as his greatest virtue (*Abr* 270, 273: "God, marvelling at the man for his faith in God, repaid him with faithfulness, namely by confirming with an oath the gifts pledged . . ."; *Jub.* 17:17–18; 18:14–16; 23:10). In particular Abraham's believing or faith was seen exemplified in his willingness to sacrifice Isaac upon Yahweh's command (Genesis 22): "When he was tested, he was found faithful" (Sir 44:20; cf. *4 Macc.* 16:19–20; Jdt 8:28). Of Abraham's ten trials (*Pirqe ʾAbot* 5.4; *Jub.* 19:8–9), this was the greatest one (*Midr. Gen. Rab.* 56). An exegetical tradition which thus related Gen 15:6 with Genesis 22 ran through a variety of Jewish texts and appears in Christian writings such as James 2; Heb 11:17; and *1 Clem* 10 (with Genesis 18, "justification by faith and hospitality"; see Dibelius *James* Hermeneia, 168–74). Abraham was also seen as the father of proselytes (*Tanḥuma b. Lekleka* 32a). A much more speculative view is that Abraham was a hero figure for "Hellenistic reformers" among Jews, who early in the 2d century B.C. wished to transform Jerusalem into a Greek city (*polis*) (Betz *Galatians* Hermeneia, 139; Hengel 1974, 1: 277–80, citing Bickermann 1979: 38–42, and Tcherikover 1959: 152–74).

Gen 15:6 is combined with Hab 2:4 in one passage about how Israel "believed in the Lord and in his servant Moses" (*Mek. Exod.* 14:31, tractate *Bešallaḥ* 7:124–64). "As a reward for the faith with which Israel believed in God [at the sea, Exod 14:31], the Holy Spirit rested upon them. . . ." This refrain is also connected with the occasion when Abraham believed the Lord (Gen 15:6) and the statement that "the righteous shall live by his faith" (Hab 2:4). Through use of Ps 118:20 (the righteous shall enter through the gate of the Lord) and Isa 26:2 (the righteous nation that keeps faith will enter the open gate), believers and the righteous are identified. Faith thus characterizes the righteous person (*Bešallaḥ* 7:144–47) and is recompensed by God through salvatory gifts like the Spirit (Dobbeler 1987: 129–30; cf. also *Exod. Rab.* 23 [85a]).

b. Hab 2:4. Textually, this passage has had a more varied history of interpretation than Gen 15:6. The MT likely means that, in contrast to the person whose soul is not "upright" (*yāšrâ*), "the righteous shall live by his faith" (RSV); that is, the *ṣaddîq* in Judah will survive in coming crisis by fidelity (*ʾĕmûnâ*; RSV note, "faithfulness") to Yahweh. That is to construe "by his faith" with "shall live," rather than with "the righteous." Others would take

* indicates verse is cited *o* = mentioned as *not* pertinent	"Abraham believed God" denotes:							"Reckoned as righteousness," God's gift means:							
	Faith	Firmness in Temptation/ Patience	Hospitality	Act, be righteous	Circumcision	Observe commands, law	Conversion	Righteousness	Covenant/ Promise/ Inheritance	"Friend of God"	Blessing	Reward	Delivery/ Protection	Spirit	Faith as a virtue
Neh 9:8 LXX (2 Esdr 19:8)	*x*								*x*						
* 1 Macc 2:52		*x*						*x*					*x*		
Sir 44:19–21		*x*			*x*	*x*			*x*		*x*				
Jub. 18:14–16 (Gen 22)	*x*	*x*							*x*		*x*				
Jub. 19:8–9 (Gen 23)	*x*	*x*								*x*					
ʾAbot 5.3–4		*x*										*x*			
ʾAbot R. Nat. 33		*x*										*x*			
Midr. Teh. 18.25		*x*										*x*	*x*		
Gen. Rab. 55.1		*x*										*x*			
b. Ned. 32a					*x*				*x*						
* *Exod. Rab.* 23.5	*x*							*x*	*x*				*x*		
* *Mek.* 40b	*x*							*x*	*x*					*x*	
CD 3.2						*x*				*x*					
* Philo *Leg. All* 228	*x*							*x*							
* Philo *Heres* 90–95	*x*			*x*				*x*							
* Philo *Mut* 177–87	*x*							*x*							
* Philo *Virt* 211–19							*x*							*x*	*x*
Philo *Praem* 27							*x*								*x*
Philo *Migr* 44	*x*														*x*
* Philo *Abr* 262–76	*x*					*x*				*x*		*x*			*x*
* Ps.-Philo, *de Sampsone*	*x*							*x*						*x*	
Heb 6:13–15	*x*	*x*							*x*						
Heb 11:17–19	*x*	*x*							*x*						
* Jas 2:21–25		*x*						*x*		*x*					
* *Barn* 13:17 (Rom 4:11)	*x*							*x*	*x*						
1 Clem 9:4–10:2	*x*	*x*								*x*					
* *1 Clem* 10:6	*x*	*x*	*x*					*x*							
1 Clem 31:2	*x*			*x*							*x*				
* Just *Dial* 23:3–5	*x*			*x*	*o*			*x*			*x*				
Just *Dial* 27:3–5	*x*				*o*			*x*							
Just *Dial* 44:1–2	*x*				*o*				*x*						
Just *Dial* 46				*x*		*o*							*x*		
* Just *Dial* 92	*x*				*o*			*x*							
* Just *Dial* 119	*x*							*x*	*x*						
Vg Jdt 8:21–23		*x*								*x*					

RIG.01. Interpretations of Gen 15:6 in Jewish and early Christian literature. Cf. K. Berger, *Die Weisheitsschrift aus der Kairoer Geniza* (TANZ 1, Tübingen, 1989), which cites Gen 15:6 with relation to righteousness, faith, and knowledge.

beʾĕmûnātô with its masculine suffix, "by his faithfulness," as referring to vision (masc.) from God in vv 2–3, the "witness" (reading in v 3 *ʿwd* and *wypḥ* for *ʿôd* and *weyāpēaḥ*) from God that does not lie; then 4b means "by God's faithfulness" (Janzen 1980; Fitzmyer *Luke* AB, 236–38). (This has the effect of removing a reference to Judah's faithfulness in favor of one to God's fidelity.)

The LXX mss reflect both interpretations. Regularly the personal pronoun *mou,* "of me, my," is added, but at different points. In Sinaiticus, B, Q, and W, *ho de dikaios ek pisteōs mou zēsetai,* would mean, "The righteous one because of my fidelity shall live." The reading in A and C, *ho de dikaios mou ek pisteōs zēsetai,* would mean, "My righteous one because of fidelity shall live." (The corrector in W omits *mou* after *pisteōs,* in conformity with MT.) The text in the larger number of mss, while open to taking *ek pisteōs mou* with either *ho de dikaios* ("the person who is righteous because of my fidelity") or with *zēsetai* (". . . shall live because of my fidelity"), may in its word order incline to the former, but it is not *ho de dikaios ho ek pisteōs mou* (attributive position for the prep. phrase), and so remains patent to either interpretation. The variant in A and C connects the righteous person more closely with Yahweh ("my righteous one") and is open to connecting "because of fidelity" with either the subject or the verb. The addition of the *mou* depends on confusion of *yōd* and *waw* as suffix with the noun for "faith/fidelity," as also happened with "soul" (*npš*) in 4a (MT his soul; LXX my soul; cf. Fitzmyer *Luke* AB, 239–40). Inclusion of *mou* makes it clearer than in the MT that God speaks here; when attached to *pisteōs, mou* suggests God's fidelity (to covenant), an interpretative line not found for Hab 2:4 elsewhere in early Judaism (Dobbeler 1987: 126–27).

There are also witnesses to other Greek translations of 2:4. One is closer to the MT, in the fragments of the Minor Prophets scroll found at Naḥal Ḥever. It is possible to translate 8ḤevXIIgr, col. 12, "[The right]eous person with his faith/fidelity will live." Aquila had, "And a righteous person in his faith/fidelity will live," and Symmachus, "[But] the righteous person by his own faith/faithfulness will live" (cf. Vg *iustus autem in fide sua vivet*).

The Commentary on Habbakuk (1QpHab 7.5–8.3) presents a Qumran interpretation about the end-time, a prolonged period when the community's "men of truth (*ʾemet*) who do torah" do not grow slack in the service of the truth. While those not upright will not be graciously accepted (*rṣy*; cf. LXX *eudokei*) "at their judgments" (2:4a), the comment on 2:4b (missing here) is, "Its interpretation (*pišrô*) concerns all who do the torah in the house of Judah whom God will deliver from the house of judgment because of their struggle and their fidelity (*ʾemunātām*) to the Teacher of Righteousness." Some have seen here faith in the person of the community's Righteous Teacher; this would be analogous to faith in Moses as faith in God (*Mek. Exod.* 14:31). However, reference to the Righteous Teacher's role as Torah expositor is more likely (Braun 1966, vol. 1: 170–71; vol. 2: 169, 171–72; G. Jeremias 1963: 142–46; Fitzmyer 1981: 242; Grundmann 1968: 97–99 and n. 16; Strobel 1961: 173–202). If "justification by grace" is involved here, it is in order to keep the whole law; " 'sola gratia' corresponds to a 'sola lege' " (Lohse 1973: 218).

The Targum paraphrases 2:4b, "The righteous ones on account of their rectitude (truth, *qûšeṭhôn*) remain alive." The rabbinic story has already been cited above (sec. B.4) where Hab 2:4b is made the most succinct summary of all commands, prized even above Isa 56:1 ("keep justice and do righteousness"), Mic 6:8 ("do justice . . ."), and Amos 5:4 ("seek me and live"). (If from the time of R. Simlai, late 3d century A.D., the story could have a polemical note against Christian use of 2:4: its demand for faith is minimal compared with one that encompasses all 613 Mosaic commands.) *Midr. Qoh.* 3.19 (17b) explains 2:4b to mean the righteous person will live through his "handwork" (*ʾûmmānût,* "workmanship, device(s)," for *ʾĕmûnâ* = faith, fidelity; understood as fulfilling the commandments), as God the Righteous One lives through his handwork, as in Exod 12:29 (Str-B 3: 542–44). Dobbeler (1987: 127) sees an effort to understand Hab 2:4b in terms of ongoing, total lifetime response in the believer, as opposed to faith as response in a particular situation, in the Targum's interpretation as rectitude, or Qumran's fidelity to the expositions by the Teacher of Righteousness, or as fulfilling the commands (*Midr. Qoh.*).

Although these understandings of Hab 2:4 generally suggest that the righteous show themselves righteous through fidelity to God and as such share in the consequence of doing right, namely, life (Wilckens *Romans* EKKNT, 89), a variety of wordings and therefore interpretations of 2:4 existed, among which early Christian writers might choose.

The bibliography for this article is found at the end of this entry.

JOHN REUMANN

GRECO-ROMAN WORLD

The course of development for righteousness terminology—words from the root *dik(ai)-* in Greek (and, in turn, those from *justus* in Latin)—is important not only because the Hebrew terms had in the LXX been put into existing Hellenistic vocabulary which the NT authors would use, but also because audiences that heard or read NT documents may have perceived terms like *dikaiosynē* in Hellenistic ways (cf., for Romans, the references in Stuhlmacher 1986: 92, n. 18; Danker 1982: 347). Moreover, subsequent understandings of righteousness/justice in the NT have sometimes been shaped by Greco-Roman (legal) senses.

A. Early References
B. Plato
C. Aristotle
D. Stoicism
E. Righteousness and Faith

A. Early References

Just as a West Semitic deity *ṣdq* (cf. Egyptian Maat) may lie behind OT use (Gen 14:18; Josh 10:1; *THAT* 2: 509–10), so the figure of Dikē or "Justice" (cf. Acts 28:4), though rarely possessing any cult, served in literature and art to inform Zeus of evils which humans do (*Op.* 248–64) and to punish injustice (Paus. 5.18.2). Hesiod's emphasis on Dikē has, indeed, been compared with the theme of righteousness in Amos the prophet (5:25; 6:12), but the latter's thought is rooted in religion in a way that Hesiod's world of princes and rural citizens is not (Nilsson 1941: 589). Yet Dikē appears also in the Greek tragedians (Nilsson 1941: 714; *RAC* 10: 245–48; Olley 1979: 33–34). The eye of Dikē was said to watch the two ways in Hades, the ways of the righteous and the unjust (Kock frag 246). The scales as symbol of Justice developed relatively late and were probably of Egyptian origin; *Dikaiosynē* with scales appears on Alexandrian coins of the time of Claudius, and on Roman coins as an attribute of *Aequitas,* equality/fairness/justice personified (Nilsson 1941: 341, n. 1).

From *dikē* (etymology disputed; perhaps "instruct, give direction, establish," *NIDNTT* 3: 353; Schrenk *TDNT* 2: 179–80) one can trace in stages the development of the adjective *dikaios;* then, after Homer and Hesiod, the noun *dikaiosynē;* and, in the 5th century B.C., the verb. Schrenk (*TDNT*) and Hill (1967: 98–102) so arrange the data. The verb, as a form ending in *-oō,* ought to mean "cause to be/make *dikaios,*" as happens with adjectives involving a physical sense (*typhloō* = make blind); but those involving a (moral) value judgment, as here, mean "declare (just/righteous)"; cf. *axioō,* "deem worthy" (BDF 148[4]). Hence, "in classical Greek" *dikaioun* "never has exactly" the sense "to make right(eous)" (Hill 1967: 101), but cf. BAGD *dikaioō* 3c, meaning "make free or pure," pass. "be set free," in the LXX; Acts 13:38; 1 Cor 6:11; Rom 6:7; and a noteworthy passage in Corpus Hermeticorum 13.9, where an initiate in a mystery cult experiences rebirth and deification: "This step, child, is the tribunal [or basis] of *dikaiosynē,* [for] behold how[, without a trial,] she has driven out *adikia;* we have been made righteous (or pure) (*edikaiōthēmen* = we have been made *dikaiosynē;* cf. 13.8 as a parallel: knowledge [*gnōsis*] of God came to us . . . ignorance was driven out," and 13.9, "we were deified [reading etheōthēmen]"), O child, *adikia* departing." According to Scott (1924–36, vol. 2: 387–88), the justice of God is involved and the writer passes from the law-court sense of "*pronounce* just" to the cultic sense of the reborn person being "*made* just"; but the writer likely had read Romans or talked to Christians. Less likely is Schrenk's suggestion (*TDNT* 2: 212) that 13.9 is directed against a Jewish-Christian concept of forensic righteousness (on the passage, cf. Grese 1979: 55, 124–26; and John 3:18–19). In classical Greek, *dikaioun* with an impersonal object means "deem it right" (Hdt 1.89) and with a personal object "treat justly, do justice to," usually in the sense of "condemn, punish" (Hdt 1.100, "punish for each offense [*adikēmoi*]").

The earliest Greek use of *dik*-terms in the 8th to 5th centuries B.C. pictures Dikē as a divine principle of "right" in law and society. What is *dikaion* is related to being *hosios* ("approved, lawful, religious") toward the gods and *eusebēs* ("pious, reverent") toward other human beings (*RAC* 10: 240–41, though cf. Danker 1982: 343: "as a rule of thumb, *eusebeia* suggests a vertical relationship, *dikaiosynē* a horizontal one"). Solon of Athens in the 6th century "demythologized" Dikē of any divinity (Hill 1967: 99); now denoting universal law in the cosmos, the term came to refer to "right" in political life and human conduct. Theognis of Megera said that "every virtue (*aretē*) exists collectively (or in sum) in *dikaiosynē*" (147). A sense of equality (*isonomia*), in rights, politically, among colleagues and friends, was often related to it (Danker 1982: 346). Fairness or equity (*epieikeia*) was another concept associated with this emerging view of justice, which became one of the four cardinal virtues, along with prudence or practical wisdom (*phronēsis*), temperance or moderation (*sōphrosynē*), and courage (*andreia*) (cf. Aesch. *Sept.* 610; Dihle 1968). Only at times was there a religious side, e.g., in connection with rewards and punishments for the soul after death (Egyptian influence?) or concerns with how the gods punish for acts contrary to their norms (*RAC* 10: 243–45). By and large, the idea of Dikē's rule, cosmically, over gods and humans took the shape of laws for family, natural and social orders, and norms for justice (*dikaiosynē*) developed in the political and ethical realms.

B. Plato

The Republic (1–4) made *dikaiosynē* the basic virtue for Plato's ideal state, the key for ordering society and educating citizens, the foundation of the *polis.* In the face of varying definitions—that "it is *dikaion* to render to each what is due," benefit to friends or harm to enemies (*Resp.* 1.331e); or that it is "the interest of the stronger" (1.338c–e); or "a mean or compromise between what is best . . . and the worst" (2.359a)—the dialogue moves toward a definition of justice as the excellence or virtue (*aretē*) of the soul (*psychē*) (353d) that helps realize the other virtues. For the city-state, *dikaiosynē* means "that each does his own tasks and is not officious [or meddlesome]" (433a), so that harmony results among the three classes of legislators, warriors, and business people. *Adikia* is meddling or interchange among these classes (434bc). All this is analogous to the harmonious working together of parts in the individual's soul (441c–444e). *Dikaiosynē* is thus "both a having and a doing what is one's own and belongs to oneself" (433e), a quality of soul (*Grg.* 447, 509b–d), "piety" (*Prt.* 330b–333e). To a degree, sanction is provided by rewards or prizes of victory in this life or after death by the gods for the just person (10.612c) and the opposite for the unjust (613b; tenfold retribution [*dikē*], according to the tale of Er, who returned from seeing how *dikaioi* and *adikoi* in the other world were sent by judges heavenward or downward respectively, 614b–615c). Justice for Plato thus involved conformity with a state's laws (*Cri.* 49b), so as to produce the harmonious life (Olley 1979: 22–24; *RAC* 10: 255–58). Ziesler's comparison of Platonic *dikaiosynē* as "activity within the society proper to a man" with "covenantal behaviour" in the OT is admittedly forced (1972).

C. Aristotle

Aristotle dealt with justice in a lost work, *Peri dikaiosynēs,* in Book 3 of his *Politics,* and in Book 5 of the *Nicomachean Ethics* (= *Eudemian Ethics* 5, exact authorship and relation disputed). Justice is contrasted with injustice (*Eth. Nic.* 5.1.1, 1129a): the unjust person is "a law-breaker," unfair, claiming more than his share, while the *dikaios* person conforms to law or custom and is fair (5.1.8, 1129a 17–19). In a general sense, "just" = lawful (*nomimos*), "unjust" = contrary to law (*paranomos*). Things are "just" which produce happiness (*eudaimonia*) in the political community (*koinōnia*), commanding virtues and forbidding wickedness (5.1.13, 1129b). Justice is, then, "perfect (*teleia*) virtue" but one displayed toward other people (5.1.15, 1129b). Besides this general sense there is also a particular meaning (*kata meros*). Justice in this special sense is subdivided into (a) "distributive" justice (*dianemētikon,* from *dianemein,* to distribute honor, wealth, or other goods in the community, equally or unequally) and (b) "corrective" (*diorthōtikon*) justice. The latter is broken down into (b1) voluntary and (b2) involuntary transactions; e.g., voluntary actions like buying and selling, and involuntary actions like theft, adultery, or false witness (5.2.12–13, 1130b–31a). Distributive justice is a mean, that which is equal (*to ison*), between the extremes of "more" and "less"; it involves shares for equal persons, unequal shares for nonequals (as determined by some standard such as birth, wealth, or virtue) (5.3.1–8, 1131a). For corrective justice the virtues or merits of each person do not enter in, but only the damage done or loss, determined before a judge (*dikastēs*) who personifies the right (*dikaion*) and "mediates" (in the middle, *dimeson*) the issue. (An etymology is proposed whereby *dikaion* means *dicha* ["in half"] since the *dikastēs* or judge is said to be a *dichastēs,* one who divides in half [5.4.7–9, 1131b].) The Pythagorean definition that *to dikaion* is simply reciprocity (*antipeponthos*) is rejected (5.5.1, 1132b 21–23). Instead, just conduct (*dikaiopragia*) "is a mean between doing injustice (*adikein*) and suffering injustice (*adikeisthai*)" (5.5.17, 1133b 31; cf. 5.7.7, 1135a 9–13, where *dikaiōma,* as righting an injustice, is distinguished from *dikaiopragma,* "just conduct"; Olley [1979: 31] observes that Aristotle reserves the verb *dikaioun* for correcting unjust acts, not for "doing justice"). Justice (the abstract noun *dikaiosynē*) involves observing the mean; it is the quality "in accord with which the *dikaios* person is said to be disposed by deliberate choice to what is *dikaios,*" so that distribution to others is done in a fair way (5.5.17, 1134a 1–7). While what is just can apply to the domestic realm, between master and slave or father and child (5.6.8–9, 1134b 8–19), its application is developed especially for the political realm, between "free and equal persons" in society, especially through law (5.6.4–7, 1134a; 5.7, 1134b 20–1135a 15).

In the [pseudo-]Aristotelian *Rhetorica ad Alexandrum* these terms reflect more popular usage. Here Schrenk (*TDNT* 1: 157, 161) claims *adikein* means "to do wrong in the sense of transgression," comparing *Rh. Al.* 1427a 36–37, "to act wrongly (*adikein*) is peculiar to wicked persons (*ponērōn*)"; see also 1427a 30, *adikia* is "with forethought to do something wrong," and 1427a 12–15: when making accusation, one should not let a person say he/she has "made a mistake" (*exhamartanein*). But, given the context here of rhetorical devices, one should not strain for ties to a biblical sense of sin (Olley 1979: 31–32). *Dikaion* in the sense of custom (*ethos*)—e.g., honoring parents or doing good to friends—is stressed, as in Plato *Resp* 1 331c–e, 334b.

D. Stoicism

While the Platonic and Aristotelian senses were later influential at many points, especially in patristic and medieval exegesis of righteousness in the NT as "justice" (*dikaiosynē* as *iustitia distributiva*; Stuhlmacher 1965: 11–18; McGrath 1986, vol. 1), the overall picture presented by teachers in the Stoic school probably carried greater popular influence in the Hellenistic and NT worlds. Zeus/nature/fate/necessity—"God" in Stoic syncretism—was occasionally equated with Dikē (Philodemus, *de pietate* 11, ed. von Arnim, cited by page and line, *SVF* 2.315.10). Dihle (*RAC* 10: 266) argues that Chrysippus in the 3d century B.C. took up again the old notion of *Dikaiosynē* as a (virgin) goddess watching in heaven (Aulus Gellius 14.4.1; Menander *Sent.* 179 M). This world soul permeated the universe, so that what is *dikaioun* was given by nature (Porphyry *Abst.* 3.19; *SVF* 1.48.37–49.1 [Zeno]; Plutarch *de Stoic. repugn.* 9, 1035c; *SVF* 3.80.33–38 [Chrysippus]) and through law and reason (Cicero *Nat. D.* 1.36; *SVF* 1.42.35–37 [Zeno]; Diogenes Laertius 7.128; *SVF* 3.76.4–6 [Chrysippus]). It serves as norm (*kanon*) for gods and humans (Marcianus *Instit.* 1.1.11,25 [ed. Mommsen]; *SVF* 3.77.37). Everyone could therefore have knowledge of this virtue, stemming, as it does, from the world order, within the self (Cicero *Leg.* 1.10.28; *SVF* 3.84.12–14). Thus people knew what is enjoined about justice for society. As the virtue concerned with distributing things, *dikaiosynē*—which already in Aristotle had been brought into connection with friendship (*Eth. Nic.* 8.9–12, 1159b 25–1162a 33)—was divided into goodness (*chrēstotēs*), good fellowship (*eukoinōnēsia*), and an accommodating disposition (*eusynallaxia*), which are explained as being disposed toward kindness, fairness in sharing, and blamelessly dealing with the neighbor (Stobaeus *Ecl.* 2.60,9W; *SVF* 3.64. 15–25, 41–43). It could also be expanded to include *hosiotēs* or piety in the sense of observing divine law (Lat *pietas*).

In subsequent syncretism, justice came often to be united closely with piety and also with philanthropy (Dihle 1968). By the latter was intended benevolence toward other human beings. From Hesiod on (*Op.* 213–37), one hears, "Listen to *Dikē*. . . . The better path is . . . towards *ta dikaia*"; those who do not go aside from what is right and who do true justice [*ithydikeis*] are commended; their fields will flourish and earth yield them fruit. There was a tradition in Greek religious thought that from the gods come seeds not only of wheat and barley but also of justice (Aelius Aristides, *Panathenaic Oration* 45) and that the earth "teaches *dikaiosynē*; for the more she is served, the more good things she gives in return" (Xenophon, *Oec.* 5.12). Such a tradition about human righteousness or benevolence and its fruit (Danker 1982: 343–48) perhaps, along with Prov 3:9–10 (LXX), stands behind Paul's use of *dikaiosynē* in 2 Cor 9:10 (Betz *2 Corinthians 8–9* Hermeneia, 115). See RIGHTEOUSNESS (NEW TESTAMENT), F.3.b. In most cases the distributive aspect was stressed in Hellenistic texts; Diogenes Laertius (5.1.2): "*dikaiosynē* is a virtue of soul which distributes in accord with merit."

As rulers and state officials took over what had previously been the civic duties of the average citizen, *dikaiosynē* was no longer the great societal virtue. In Athens, friendship, courtesy, and willingness to aid others, even enemies, came to the fore (Plutarch *Praec. ger.* 3 [799C–D]; Philo *Virt.* 109–15, on the laws in Deuteronomy). But under ruler-cults, justice became a common term among the virtues attributed to the ruler (Dio Chrysostom *Or.* 3.39), as also in lists of virtues attributed to a deity (*dikaiosynē*, of Isis, Plutarch *Is. et Os.* 2 [352B]). Grandjean (1975) has particularly drawn attention to the goddess Isis and *dikaiosynē*. The aretalogy found in Cyme, Asia Minor, dating to the 1st or 2d century A.D., has her speak repeatedly of how she maintains justice: "I have made *to dikaion* strong . . . , stronger than gold and silver. . . . I have handed over the person who plots unrighteously . . . , I established penalties for those who do injustices . . . , I honor those who justly avenge, with me the right prevails . . ." (lines 16, 26, 34–38). In the *Kore Kosmou* (Stobaeus *Ecl.* 1.49.44; Scott 1924–36, vol. 1: 490–93; vol. 3: 552–53) Isis speaks of herself and Osiris as "helpers of the world in its need of all things," who appointed courts of law and "filled the universe with good order and righteousness (*dikaiosynē*)." Solmsen (1979: 57–59) points to "a cult of Isis *Dikaiosynē*, the name of Isis coupled with a personification of Justice," to be explained by the much older Egyptian concept of Maat (Schmid). See also *SIG* 1131 (Delos) and *IG* 3.203 for inscriptions about Isis *Dikaiosynē*. The literary figure of *Dikē* earlier perhaps helped prepare the way for combining "Justice" with Isis Maat. It may be added that there was expectation that the justice of the cosmos would also be brought to expression in human life. The terms are rare in inscriptions and papyri, however, and, when used, refer to legal matters (Olley 1979: 39–40).

Dik-words thus covered a number of things in Greco-Roman use (term-by-term summary most recently in Olley 1979: 40–43). But the OT sense of God's vindicating righteousness was not among them. There is substance to the view that *hē dikaiosynē tou theou* might suggest to the Greco-Roman world God's judgment against it or, from Hellenistic Jewish use, "God's demanding and standard-setting judicial holiness" (Stuhlmacher 1986: 92 n. 18). Use in Roman law was common, especially for distributive justice and fairness (*aequitas*) (*RAC* 10: 280–89).

E. Righteousness and Faith

Reflecting the research by Dihle (1968; *RAC* 10: 238–50), Dobbeler (1987: 102–14) has developed the relation of the word groups *dikē/dikaios/dikaiosynē* with *pisteuein/pistis* ("to believe; faith") in Greek texts as background for Jewish and early Christian usage. Basic are the assumptions that natural right (*physikon dikaion,* what is right as produced by nature, universally) and conventional right (*nomikon dikaion,* resting on law, adopted by a society) intertwine (*Eth. Nic.* 5.7.1, 1134b), i.e., the cosmic and the juridical-moralistic aspects are inseparable (*RAC* 10: 249); and that *dikaiosynē* is the highest virtue, the one with social character, because it deals with others and the community (5.1.15, 1129b). Further, that righteousness includes retribution and equality (see above, and Dobbeler 1987: 104), as well as piety (*eusebeia/hosiotēs,* holiness; Epict. 3.26.32: Heracles was "purifier of injustice and lawlessness, and introducer of righteousness and piety [*dikaiosynēs kai hosiotētos*]"); and finally that what is *dikaion* came to be expressed socially in terms of *epieikeia* (equitableness, reasonableness; *Eth. Nic.* 5.10.1–8, 1137a 31–1138a 3), friendship (*philia*; *Eth. Nic.* 8, 1155a–1163b), and what more and more took the place of *dikaiosynē* in the Hellenistic world, *philanthrōpia* or benevolence toward humanity (Philo described Abraham as *eusebēs* and *philanthrōpos,* i.e., as exhibiting *hosiotēs* toward God and *dikaiosynē* toward human beings, *Abr.* 208).

In Greek texts "righteousness" and "faith" appear in expanded forms of the "two-virtues rule" (*hosios, dikaios*), as in the epitaph of Gorgias (Dihle 1968: 14, n. 21): solemn (*semnoi*) toward the gods with regard to what is *dikaion,* reverent (*hosioi*) toward parents with regard to care (*therapeia*), just (*dikaioi*) toward fellow citizens with regard to equality (*ison*), pious (*eusebeis*) toward friends with regard to fidelity (*pistis*). To be *dikaios* is a sign of faithfulness (Isocrates 3.57.64). *Pistis* and *dikē* endure (Marcus Aurelius 5.33.3; Epict. 3.14.13, *dikaiosynē*). The context for this linking of *pistis* and righteousness was true *philia* (*Eth. Nic.* 8); "indeed, the element of friendliness seems to be characteristic of those who are just in its highest form" (8.1.4, 1155a 28–29). "There is no firm friendship without *pistis*" (*Eth. Nic.* 7.2.40, 1237b 13). For friendship it is necessary "to believe and be believed" (*pisteuein de kai pisteuesthai,* Xen. *Sym.* 8.18). Numerous texts suggest that *philia* is something including righteousness/justice and fidelity/believing in relations between humans, even if what occurs remains imperfect (Dobbeler 1987: 108–11).

In Greek juridical texts *pisteuein tō̧ dikaiō̧* was a regular formula meaning "to rely on, trust in what is right, a lawful claim" about one's case or the court system hearing the case. So Demosthenes (*Or.* 44.4), "If we did not believe, we would not have come to you [judges]." The phrase "to believe nothing to be unjust" (*mēden adikein*) was also used. There could also be a polemical note against the other party and the suggestion that the court not favor the rich over the poor (Dem *Or.* 44.3–4). Andocides (1.2) stressed in one case how he and his client had come not under necessity but "trusting especially in *to dikaion*" and in the judges "to make known *ta dikaia* and not be unjustly overlooked," but "rather to be delivered (*sōzein*) justly in accord with your laws."

The bibliography for this article is found at the end of this entry.

JOHN REUMANN

NEW TESTAMENT

This article will survey the concept of "righteousness" as it is presented in the various texts that comprise the canonical New Testament.

A. Introduction

Derived from Old English *riht,* meaning "right," the noun "righteousness" has come to mean (1) a quality or state of being righteous, upright, in the right, or just; (2) that which is rightful; and (3) that which is in conformity with a standard or in a state of acceptability to God. Although the Latin *rectus,* "straight, right" (cf. *regere,* "to guide, lead, rule"), may be compared with the Anglo-Saxon terms, another Latin root has provided a second family of words in English that intertwines with "righteousness" vocabulary (especially in the KJV and related Bible translations): *justus,* meaning "just, upright," from *jus* ("right, law"). Its related words include *justitia* or "justice," and the verb *justificare* (cf. *facere,* "to make" [*justus*]; passive *fieri,* "be made" [just]), "to justify, be proven just, to vindicate."

Thus those translating biblical or other passages from the Hebrew root *ṣdq* or the Greek *dikaioun* could employ either "just, justice/justification, justify" from the Latin, or "right, righteous(ness)," and the Anglo-Saxon verb "rightwise(n)." Although some commentators, to express the continuity, e.g., in Paul's thought, have recently restored to using the Eng "rightwise" (K. Grobel in translating Bultmann *BTNT,* 253, n. *), this verb, once popular in Middle English, had already been set aside in favor of "justify" in Tyndale's 1535 translation. One cannot, however, accurately treat in English the biblical terms involved without resort to both "righteousness" and "justice/justification." At times, especially in the NT, "righteousness/justification" becomes a more comprehensive rendering. Other languages do not exhibit such a dichotomy; cf. German *recht, Gerechtigkeit, Rechtfertigung, rechtfertigen;* French *juste, justice, justification, justifier;* similarly Spanish.

In the Greek NT, words from the root *dik(ai)-* occur 233 times and those from *adikein* (with an *alpha* privative, meaning "[to be] unjust, [do] wrong") occur 69 times, for a data base of some 300 verses. The Bible sometimes pairs and contrasts "righteousness and unrighteous" (*dikaios* and *adikos;* Matt 5:45; Acts 24:15; 1 Pet 3:18), as classical literature had done (Schrenk *TDNT* 1: 149–51). Behind all these words looms *dikē,* a noun that denotes justice (Homer, *Il.* 16.388, in a Hesiodic passage), judgment, or exposition of the law (*Il.* 18.508); as a mythological personification, it denotes the virgin daughter of Zeus who effects just punishment (Hesiod, *Op.* 256–64). The term can also mean "satisfaction" (*Op.* 712) and "punishment" (Josephus *JW* 7.11.3 §450), as in Acts 28:4 when the Maltese natives, thinking Paul to be a murderer because a viper bit him after he escaped from shipwreck, exclaimed, "Justice *(Dikē)* has not allowed him to live" (cf. also 2 Thess 1:9 and Jude 7).

Greek life was shaped by notions about what is right *(dikaios).* The root yielded the nouns *dikaiosynē,* righteousness, justice, the business of a judge"; *dikaiōma,* "just requirement, act of justice or justification"; and *dikaiōsis,* "setting right, justification, vindication, acquittal." It also yielded the verb *dikaioun,* "set right, deem just, condemn, hold guiltless, justify"; and the adverb *dikaiōs,* "justly, rightly." Related to the verb *adikein,* with its negative prefix, were the nouns *adikia,* "injustice, wrong-doing"; *adikēma,* "wrong done; injury"; the adjective *adikōs,* "unrighteous, unjust"; and the adverb *adikos,* "without right, unjustly." There was often a connection with order and law and a note of judgment implied, clearly in *dikastēs,* a judge, or in a word found only in Jewish sources *dikaiokrisis,* "just judgment" (Rom 2:5).

All these words appear in the LXX except possibly *dikaiokrisia* (*TDNT* 2: 24; Wilckens *Romans* EKKNT, 125–26). For their spread in the NT books, see Fig. RIG.02. About 46% of the NT occurrences appear in the Pauline corpus (which comprises some 22% of the NT). The Gospels and Acts, which make up 60% of the pages of the Greek NT, contain only 29% of the references; the rest of the NT (Hebrews through Revelation, 17% of the NT) contains about 24% of the passages with such vocabulary. One explanation is that terms like *dikaiosynē* are less likely to appear in narratives than in treatments of doctrine and ethics. The gospels of Mark and John especially lack such terms. Romans contains the most examples, twice as many per page as other letters with relatively high frequency of *dik*-vocabulary, e.g., Galatians, Philippians or James.

For *ṣdq* and its derivatives in the Hebrew Scriptures, see the preceding article on RIGHTEOUSNESS (OLD TESTAMENT), where the wide range of RSV renderings is also indicated. In the KJV, "righteousness" was employed far more than "justice" as a rendering, although terms from the Latin root occur especially in Proverbs, Job, and Isaiah. RSV seems to use the verb "justify" less than KJV, but "justice" more.

The importance of the Latin *justus* and related words for English translations has been indicated above. The Rheims NT translation of 1582, based on the Latin, sometimes influenced the KJV in the direction of justice-language; e.g., Rom 2:13 in Tyndale and Geneva Bible (1562) is ". . . righteous . . . justified," but in Rheims and KJV it is ". . . just . . . justified." On the other hand, the KJV often resisted the Latinisms of the Rheims version, especially in its phrase "the justice of God" (Rom 1:17; 3:5, 21, etc.), which has been common in Roman Catholic translations down to NAB Revised NT (1987). But the Latin influence on how *dikaiosynē*-terms were understood in Paul's day and by his congregations could also have been a factor in the 1st century.

In addition to these linguistic influences, in dealing with "righteousness" one must also be aware of the long history of interpretation that *dikai*-terminology has had since NT times, particularly in the West (overstressed by Stendahl; cf. Reumann 1982: ##213, 216; 1985: 632–35) and by no

book	*dikaioun* (verb)	*dikaiosynē* (noun)	*dikaios* (adj)	*dikaiōma* (noun)	*adikein* (verb)	*adikia* (noun)	*adikos* (adj)	*adikēma* (noun)	Totals
Matt	2	7	17		1		1		28
Mark			2						2
Luke	5	1	11	1	1	4	4		28*
John		2	3			1			6
Acts	2	4	6		5	2	1	2	25*
Rom	15	34	7	5		7	1		72*
1 Cor	2	1			2	1	2		9*
2 Cor	8	7			3	1			11
Gal		4	1		1				14
Eph		3	1						4
Phil		4	2						6
Col			1		2				3
1 Thess									1*
2 Thess			2			2			6*
1 Tim	1	1	1						3
2 Tim		3	1			1			5
Titus	1	1	1						4*
Phlm					1				1
(Pauline totals)	(27)	(58)	(17)	(5)	(9)	(12)	(3)		(138*)
Heb		6	3	2		1	1		13
Jas	3	3	2			1			9
1 Pet		2	3				1		8*
2 Pet		4	4		1	2	1		12
1 John		3	6			2			11
2 John									0
3 John									0
Jude									1*
Rev		2	5	2	11			1	21
TOTALS	39	92	79	10	28	25	12	3	302*

*These totals reflect 14 additional occurrences of other less-frequently used *dik-* words: *dikaiōsis* (a noun used twice in Romans); *dikaiokrisia* (used once in Romans); *dikaiōs* (an adverb used once in Luke, 1 Corinthians, 1 Thessalonians, Titus, and 1 Peter); *dikastēs* (a noun used twice in Acts); *dikē* (a noun used once in Acts, 2 Thessalonians, and Jude); and *adikōs* (an adverb used once in 1 Peter).

Note also that *ekdikein* ("avenge, punish") occurs 6 times (twice each in Luke, Pauline writings, and Revelation; *ekdikēsis* occurs 9 times (three times each in Luke and Pauline writings, and once in Acts, Hebrews, and 1 Peter); and *ekdikos* occurs twice in Pauline writings. As exercise of *dikē,* it is also colored by the Heb *naqam* (Schrenk, *TDNT* 2: 442–46; Mendenhall 1973: 69–104).

RIG.02. Distribution of *dik-* words in the NT.

means simply since the Reformation (see Wilckens *Romans* EKKNT, 223–33; McGrath 1986). Several of the recent monographs on righteousness either deal with or have been written in light of ecumenical issues and discussions about righteousness/justification (Ziesler 1972: 1–14, 168–71, 212; Reumann and Lazareth 1967; Reumann 1982).

There have been innumerable attempts to explain most of the biblical references through a single master concept, such as "conformity to a norm," e.g., the law (*TDNT* 2: 174–78); a forensic or law-court setting, where a person is acquitted or vindicated; hence the theme of innocence or not being guilty; the "relationship" approach, above all for Israel the relation to God through the covenant (Ziesler 1972: 36–43). See also previous article on RIGHTEOUSNESS (OLD TESTAMENT), sections C and I, where note is taken of recent research emphasizing "world order," divine actions in that order, and specifically what God does as "saving action." But no single theme has carried the day. In recent NT interpretation there seems a tendency, perhaps not always perceived, to stress grace at the expense of faith with regard to justification, to emphasize God's objective work in Christ over against a subjective appropriation by believers of the results of God's acts in Christ (see below). All such factors and tendencies must be kept in mind when assessing what is, by any reading, a major biblical theme: righteousness/justification.

B. Hebrew Scriptures and Other Backgrounds

The inheritance for NT writers from the OT was enormous in bulk and rich in variety and sense. The terms for righteousness *(ṣedeq-ṣĕdāqâ)* repeatedly express first a forensic, legal sense concerning how one stands before the *tôrâ* or God, or how God acquits, vindicates, or declares people right. Verbs as action words express this more frequently than do nouns. Secondly, especially in the Prophets, the terms—often combined in a hendiadys with *mišpāṭ*, "right, order, justice, judgment"—are used to express proper order, Yahweh's order connected with the reign that is divinely instituted in Israel or the world. From God's just or right reign derives, further, a constant call for right conduct, proper comportment on the part of God's people in accord with what is just. To what extent a cosmic sense of order/kingdom/law/wisdom/nature lies behind this, not only in Israel but in the ANE generally, especially Egypt (Schmid 1968; 1984; Reumann 1982: ##32, 44), remains in dispute (Fitzmyer 1982: ##361, 381).

Thirdly, *ṣedeq-ṣĕdāqâ* as God's "saving action on behalf of his people" comes to the fore, particularly in the Psalms and the Prophets. Indeed, this saving action by God in the context of divine world rule provides the setting for references to proper comportment. One can, with regard to God's acts of deliverance as victory, speak of God's fidelity to Israel (Ps 98:1–3; Isa 41:10), to the covenant (Ps 89:2–3, 5, 8, 19–37, but cf. vv 39, 49), ultimately to the world God created (Ps 33:4–12; 145:6–9; 24:1–2, 5; Isa 45:1–3, 12–13); and to God's own self or name (Pss 35:24; 89:15–17 [—Eng vv 14–16]; 143:11–12; Isa 42:21). As is well known, in Isaiah 40–55 and 56–66 "righteousness" (*ṣedeq;* RSV "deliverance") often comes to parallel "salvation" *(yĕšaʿ)* (Isa 51:5, 6; cf. vv 1, 7; 46:12–13; cf. 45:23–25; 56:1; RSV "deliverance"; 61:10; 63:1c; RSV "vindication"). Hence the plural (literally "righteousness") means "victorious, triumphal, and saving acts of God in favor of his people, or the acts of the people in . . . conformity with God's order" (e.g., Judg 5:11; RSV "triumphs"; 1 Sam 12:7).

God speaks "what is right" (*ṣedeq;* RSV "the truth") and "declares what is just" (Isa 45:19 NEB). Yahweh is the God who "works vindication *(ṣĕdāqôt)* and justice *(mišpāṭim)* for all who are oppressed" (Ps 103:6)—an observation of obvious importance for all theologies of liberation; cf. Scharbert (*TRE* 12: 410), who, concerning God's righteousness, notes that "the OT considers no one completely guiltless and knows always that God in his righteousness does not hold himself to the same rules as a human judge, so that one cannot with God distinguish in the strict sense between *justitia vindicativa* and *distributiva,* and that even human 'righteousness' in the sense of piety is always finally grace given by God." Such a view of God, who works from grace in the name of righteousness, upsets existing notions of what is right, and it will echo in the messages of Jesus and Paul.

One can analyze *ṣedeq-ṣĕdāqâ* references in the OT as applying to (1) Yahweh and (2) Israel and the individual (Hill 1967: 86–98) or to human activity or behavior and to God's activity (Ziesler 1972: 23–32; cf. *TRE* 12: 405–10). However, such analyses must not lose sight of the interrelatedness of the two. Human righteousness for Israel was rooted in God's righteousness, conceived either as gracious saving activity or as a gracious revelation of what is right. God's righteousness must not be seen as a punitive justice, because it also involves God's saving acts. The just or righteous person *(ṣaddîq)*, on whom there is great emphasis especially in Psalms and Proverbs, is not to be isolated from Yahweh as righteous. While later and elsewhere one may be able to speak of relations of human beings with each other as a "secular" or "civil" concept of righteousness/justice and of relations with God as "religious," von Rad has argued that Yahweh's righteousness was "a continuous event directed towards Israel and was consequently a subject of proclamation," indeed "understood in an oddly spatial way, as something like a sphere, or power-charged area, into which men were incorporated and thereby empowered to do special deeds" (*ROTT* 1: 375–76).

The varied senses of the words from *ṣdq* may, in light of such an understanding, be traced out in various situations and types of literature in Israel's long history (*THAT* 2: 512–30; Reumann 1982: ##37–40), noting that, as justice in the world receded for the remnant of Israel, the apocalyptic hope for a righteousness to be revealed from God grew, as did attention to what righteousness and being just meant in a changing world after the return from exile, in the Persian and Greek eras.

The OT terms with which *ṣedeq* and *ṣĕdāqâ* were used, so as to create word-fields, must also be noted, especially the words, "justice" (*mišpāṭ;* Weinfeld 1985, who traces the expression to the realm of social policy; cf. Zech 7:9–10), "truth" and "fidelity" *(ʾĕmet, ʾĕmûnâ)*, "steadfast love" (*ḥesed;* NT "grace"), "blessing" *(bĕrākâ)*, and "peace" *(šālôm)*. Though righteousness is widely spoken of as "a covenant concept" (*IDB* 4: 81–82; Hill 1967: 85–86; Ziesler 1972: 38–39, more precisely, ". . . originally forensic . . . , it has become a covenant word"), it is difficult to find passages that mention *ṣdq* and covenant in the same breath. Genesis 15 provides the most significant example: "Abram believed the Lord, and he reckoned it to him as righteousness" (v 6); "on that day the Lord made a covenant with Abram" (v 18). Generally the connection has been assumed from a more general "biblical theology" of the OT; such a connection remains tenable largely if one begins with covenant as the theme, and it may be undermined either if righteousness indeed has roots in the ANE concept of "order" or if "covenant" is a theological construct that emerged only late in the 7th century B.C. (Perlitt 1969). See COVENANT. The understanding of righteousness/justice could also change as *ṣdq* and other terms in its word-field were discussed in Judaism and put into Greek in the three centuries or so before NT times.

A particular emphasis, of importance for NT usage, involves the righteous person *(ṣaddîq)* who suffers. This motif of the *passio iusti* for the OT and intertestamental literature has been examined by Ruppert (1972a; 1973), particularly with reference to Jesus (1972b), and by Kleinknecht (1984) in terms of tradition history for the OT and Jewish literature, with particular reference to Paul. The data (Ruppert) are in Kleinknecht's "diachronic sketch" traced back to cultic use, as by Stuhlmacher (1965: 131); the relation of the person who prays to Yahweh has been disturbed by oppression (of enemies), and the appeal is for a demonstration of Yahweh's *ṣĕdāqâ* (Kleinknecht 1984: 32–33; cf. Pss 7:9; 14:5–7; 24:4–5; 31:2). The prophets developed this tradition, both before the Exile (Kleinknecht, 33–41; especially by Jeremiah), during, and after it (pp. 42–84). Note "the servant," God's righteous one, who "through his suffering" (reading *bĕrāʿātô*) "will justify many" *(yaṣdîq,* "work righteousness for many"), "and their guilt he shall bear" (Isa 53:11 NAB); or the emergence of a tradition about the violent fate of prophets in Israel (see first in Neh 9:26 and developed in the Deuteronomistic history; cf. 2 Kgs 17:7–20). The righteous sufferer also appears in the wisdom tradition (Job) and in prayers (Lamentations 3), especially psalms reflecting the thanksgiving ceremony or *tôdâ* (Pss 22:25–26; 32:11; 40:10, "I have told the good news of deliverance [*ṣedeq*]"; Psalms 50, esp. vv 6, 14, 23; 64:10–11 [—Eng 9–10]).

A striking reading of the OT evidence is presented by Walsh (1987: esp. 171–73), who invokes the theories on Israel's origins by Mendenhall and Gottwald. In contrast to a Canaanite view of gods, king, and justice *(mišpāṭ),* where *ṣedeq* meant security and abundance, "Elohistic Israel" (coalitions of *ʿapiru* in Canaan) developed a tribal sense of *ṣedeq* as "justice." These marginal outsiders combined with the "refugee slaves from Egypt, proclaiming the good news of Yahweh" (Walsh 1987: 47), to form "Yahwistic Israel." Thereby "the story of deliverance from Pharaoh . . . became the story of deliverance from the power of the Canaanite kings" (p. 47). The Sinai covenant spelled out Yahweh's judgments *(mišpāṭim)* for regulating life justly. The "peasants' revolt" that toppled Canaanite kings can be seen as "acts of *ṣedeq* effected by Yahweh on behalf of, and through, his peasantry" (p. 63; Judg 5:11). So God effects vindication *(nāqām;* Mendenhall 1973: 25–31; 69–104; 194–97). This clash of two different concepts of *ṣedeq*—"bread" versus justice—can be traced through Israel's history. The monarchy threatened to revert to "the Canaanite ideology of kingship" (Walsh 1987: 97) but was checked frequently by prophetic reproof of injustice (pp. 105–9) and later by the Deuteronomistic theology of history, where doing what is right in Yahweh's sight becomes the criterion, and where God acts to vindicate the divine *ṣedeq* and *mišpāṭ* (p. 130). The theme of justice and judgment, revolving around *ṣedeq, mišpāṭ,* and *nāqām,* can be traced forward into the NT, where it is the cross that causes a "sea change" in understanding.

Schulte (1972) in a source critical analysis of J has argued that justice/righteousness *(Gerechtigkeit)* was the theme of the Yahwist about 900 B.C. The OT material was, of course, mediated through developments and interpretations in emerging Judaism. See RIGHTEOUSNESS (EARLY JUDAISM). At times Jewish and Christian usages were influenced by concepts in classical Greek, Hellenistic, and Latin thought. See RIGHTEOUSNESS (GRECO-ROMAN WORLD).

C. Jesus

1. Overview. Judging from the statistical importance and material significance of *ṣdq*-terms in the OT and emerging Judaism, one might expect that Jesus of Nazareth, who stressed the imminence of God's kingdom, would emphasize the concept of righteousness. However, the number of *dik*-words in the four gospels is quite limited. See Fig. RIG.02. The verb occurs only 7 times (twice in Matthew, 5 times in Luke), the noun *dikaiosynē* occurs 10 times (especially in Matthew, once in Luke, and twice in John); *dikē* does not occur at all. The adjective *dikaios* is more common (33 times). Luke also has once each the noun *dikaiōma* (1:6) and the adverb *dikaiōs* (23:41). The verb *adikein* appears only twice in (Matthew and Luke), the noun *adikia* 5 times (4 in Luke, once in John), and the adjective *adikos* also 5 times (4 in Luke, once in Matthew). These statistics become even less impressive when parallel passages are deducted and distinction is made between narrative (which may come from the evangelist) and sayings of Jesus (and even here the wording may not reflect actual sayings of the historical Jesus).

Statistically, therefore, one cannot assert that "righteousness" was a major theme for the historical Jesus, if such an assertion is based on the canonical gospels (and the noncanonical gospels do not change this picture). Like other concepts such as " 'covenant' relationship," which we might expect to be prominent, based on OT data and modern treatments of the Hebrew Scriptures (*IDB* 4: 80, 84–85, 91–93; cf. Ziesler 1972: 38–39, 131–33) or words like "gospel," which are prominent in Christianity after Easter (Fitzmyer 1982: #367), "righteousness" is a term sparsely used in the gospels. It is difficult to force the few references that may come from Jesus' own statements into a "forensic/ethical" pattern (Ziesler 1972: 128, 136: the verb = "vindicate" or has a declaratory sense; as to the noun, "righteousness is always a way of life"). In general, Jesus material will associate the terms with judgment, less commonly, if at all, with saving righteousness. The idea that God is righteous, though to be assumed from the OT picture of God, is rarely stated (cf. John 17:25).

2. The Jewish World of the Gospels. A number of references in narratives do describe righteous persons very much in the sense of the *ṣaddîq* in OT and Judaism. Thus Zechariah and Elizabeth were *dikaioi* before God, "walking blameless in all the commands and statutes *(dikaiōmasin)* of the Lord" (Luke 1:6; cf. Gen 26:5; Num 36:13; Deut 4:40); the point is stressed by Luke possibly to avoid the impression that their childlessness was due to any wickedness on their part (Fitzmyer *Luke 1–9* AB, 323). Similarly Simeon was "upright and devout" (2:25, *dikaios kai eulabēs;* later,

Joseph of Arimathea is described as a Council member who was "just and good" [*agathos kai dikaios*], 23:50). The hope of such people was to live "in holiness and righteousness" (*en hosiotēti kai dikaiosynē,* a pairing common in Greek thought) before God (Luke 1:75). Luke portrays John the Baptist in 1:17 as an Elijah figure who will "turn the disobedient to the wisdom of the righteous" *(apeitheis en phronēsi dikaiōn).* While the verse incorporates Mal 4:5–6, about Elijah, the phrase cited would not be without appeal to Greek as well as Jewish readers; cf. *4 Macc.* 1:16–18, where *phronēsis* and *dikaiosynē,* along with courage and moderation/self-control (the four cardinal virtues), are listed as forms of *sophia,* which, in turn, results from education in the law.

In Matthew, Joseph is described as "a just man" (1:19) when he resolves to divorce Mary quietly and not shame her upon learning of her pregnancy; he is upright because he obeys the law (contrast Judah and David in 1:3, 6, who were not righteous in relations with Tamar and Bathsheba). The passage is complicated, however, by other interpretations that Joseph acted out of mercy, to avoid the punishment of stoning commanded for the woman and her lover (Deut 22:23–27), or that Joseph was showing awe before God's plan of salvation (Brown *John* AB, 125–28).

Herod, it is said, knew John the Baptist to be "holy and righteous" (Mark 6:20). Abel (Gen 4:8) is spoken of as "innocent" *(dikaios),* as is the blood shed by martyrs (*dikaion,* RSV "righteous," Matt 23:35). The centurion, according to Luke 23:47, confessed the dying Jesus to be *dikaios* (RSV "innocent"), as had Pilate's wife (Matt 27:19). Even the confession at Luke 23:47 could fit the "Jesus level" of meaning, though at a later time *dikaios* might have taken on the further sense of the "Righteous One" (Fitzmyer *Luke 10–24* AB, 1520).

3. Sayings of Jesus. Some of Jesus' statements would fit very well with an audience marked by such OT-Jewish piety. He talks of "the just and the unjust" (*dikaious kai adikous,* in parallel with "the evil and the good") on whom God sends rain and sun (Matt 5:45; the verse may also reflect the sense of equality found in Greek thought about justice, and may be "a commonplace throughout the whole of antiquity" on "the cosmic fatherhood of God"; Betz 1985: 120). The parable about the Lost Sheep contrasts the repentant sinner with "the righteous who do not have need of repentance" (Luke 15:7). The parable of the Sheep and the Goats, whatever its origins, speaks of those on the right *(ek dexiōn)* as "the righteous" (*dikaioi,* 25: 37, 46). Reference to "the resurrection of the just" (*dikaiōn,* Luke 14:14) is within the realm of Jewish apocalyptic expectations (beginning with Dan 12:2–3), as is Matt 13:43 ("the righteous will shine like the sun") and 13:49 (the angels separate the evil from the righteous).

Such sayings on the lips of Jesus criticize hypocritical pretensions to righteousness. "Woe to" those who "appear to people righteous outwardly but inwardly are full of iniquity" (*anomia,* lit., "lawlessness"; Matt 23:28); this is paralleled by a woe against scribes and Pharisees who "build tombs for the prophets and adorn the monuments of the righteous" (23:29) but who in their own day continue to murder prophets (who are by implication "righteous" or "innocent"; 23:34–35). Related are narrative references to people who claim to be righteous but do not behave thus (Luke 18:9, despising others; 20:20, pretending to be sincere).

Luke reports a number of phrases, sometimes Semitic in tone, that use *adikos/adikia.* In chap. 16 there is "the dishonest steward" (v 8, *oikonomon tēs adikias,* guilty of "official unfaithfulness" [*TDNT* 1: 157]); "unrighteous mammon" (v 9, *mamōna tēs adikias;* v 11, *adikǭ mamōną*); and a statement that the person "who is *adikos* in the least matter is *adikos* with much"; here "dishonest" is contrasted with being "faithful" (*pistos,* or "trustworthy," 10a). The term also comes up in Jesus' parable of the Pharisee who gives thanks that he is not like others, "extortioners, unjust *(adikoi),* adulterers" (18:11). The term here is general, unless a reference to the Ten Commandments (Exod 20:14–15; Deut 5:17–18) is seen, in which case the term may have the sense of "deceivers" or "cheats" (cf. Lev 19:13, LXX *ouk adikēseis ton plēsion;* 1 Cor 6:9). In a contiguous parable in Luke, also about prayer but linked in the present text with the question of who will be found faithful when the Son of Man comes (18:8, 14b), there is reference to an "unjust judge" (18:6, *ho kritēs tēs adikias*), who "neither feared God nor cared about other human beings."

a. Judgment. Only Luke reports a criticism by Jesus (16:15) of the Pharisees who loved money and scoffed at the principle "God *or* Mammon" (16:13). "You are the ones who (try to) justify (or "vindicate," *dikaiountes*) yourselves in the sight of human beings, but God knows your hearts, because what is exalted among humans is an abomination in the sight of God." The *hoti* clause ("because") sounds like proverbial wisdom (cf. Prov 16:5; 1 Sam 16:7). Their public almsgiving (cf. Matt 6:1–3) masks avarice (Mark 12:38–40 par). The saying threatens judgment on such public-reward-seeking Pharisees. While the statement itself might be traced back to Jesus as an isolated logion, Luke is fond of using *dikaioun* in this sense (cf. 10:29 and 7:24–28).

The note of judgment seen in these passages appears elsewhere in Jesus' message, using *dik*-vocabulary. At 13:27 the Lukan version of a Q statement (about the many who will not be saved once the door is closed) has the householder/*kyrios* saying, "Depart from me, all you workers of iniquity *(ergatai adikias).*" The parallel, Matt 7:23, has, "you who work lawlessness" *(anomian).* The words reflect Ps 6:9 (—Eng 8), where the context is that of a sufferer, whose petition Yahweh has heard, directing his enemies to turn away. Matthew is closer to the LXX. While Luke may have inserted a favorite term, *adikia,* Greek mss of the Psalter elsewhere parallel or use the two words as variants (e.g., 7:14 [LXX 15]). Matthew 12:37 (M) deals with "the day of judgment" (v 36). Then persons, including persecutors who attribute Jesus' deeds to Beelzebub (vv 24, 34), will be either individually justified ("you" sing., *dikaiōthēsę̄*) or condemned *(katatikasthēsę̄)* by their words. Cf. John 16:8–11, where sin, righteousness *(dikaiosynē),* and judgment *(krisis)* are grouped together; judgment by Jesus (John 5:30) or others (7:24) is to be just. On the mood of bliss for the righteous sufferers and woes for sinners hereafter, cf. *1 Enoch* 96–105.

Of course, there are some verses that reflect "everyday use" of the terms. The verb *adikein* at Matt 20:13 means "(not) to wrong" a person, and at Luke 10:19 "(not) to hurt" someone, though the context here is that Satan "will not hurt you in any way." At Matt 20:4 the adjective *dikaion* means simply "that which is right or just."

b. Matthean Emphasis? Though some of the sayings above could go back to the historical Jesus, many of them belong to the thought of the later Church or of a specific evangelist. A test area has often been the 7 examples of "righteousness" in Matthew. All these instances of *dikaiosynē* occur in sayings by Jesus, but they are either unique to Matthew (3:15; 5:10, 20; 6:1; 21:32; M source or redactor) or are shared with Luke (Q) but have the word *dikaiosynē* only in the Matthean version (5:6; 6:33), where it may be redactional. However, several of the sayings could have come from Jesus. Matt 6:1 is very typical of the special sense for *ṣĕdāqâ* and therefore *dikaiosynē* that developed in Judaism: "Beware of practicing your piety (*dikaiosynē;* cf. 5:20) in the presence of other people." The specific example of piety immediately in mind is "almsgiving" (vv 2–5): public ostentation is contrasted with secret giving. The thematic verse at 5:20—that the righteousness of Jesus' followers must exceed that of the scribes and Pharisees in order for them to enter the kingdom of heaven—could also fit an OT emphasis, continued in Judaism, on *dikaiosynē* as ethical response to God in terms of God's will for what is right. The imperative in 6:33, "Seek first the kingdom and the righteousness of him [God]," with the promise, "and all these things shall be yours as well," parallels *dikaiosynē* with Jesus' central message of the kingdom. If the kingdom is God's reign that breaks in by divine action, then God's righteousness here would be a vindicating, saving work of God. But righteousness at 6:33 is better taken as the evangelist's addition (Guelich 1982: 345–57, 371–72) and will be treated below.

The threefold reference to a "righteous man" (RSV) in Matt 10:41b parallels a triple reference to a prophet in 10:41a, the whole being attached to a parallelism in 10:40 that reflects or combines a Q logion (= Luke 10:16) and a Markan statement (9:37 = Luke 9:48 and Matt 18:5). The Matthean context is the close of the address as the Twelve are sent forth to preach and heal, and so the reference is to receiving Jesus' personal emissaries (10:40–41): "The person who receives you receives me, and the person who receives me receives the One who sent me. The person who receives a prophet in the name of a prophet will receive a prophet's reward, and the person who receives a righteous man in the name of a righteous man will receive a righteous man's reward." The phrase "in the name of" means "aware that" or "because he is a (prophet)." The reward the prophet (gen. of origin) gives would be proclamation of God's message, and the reward from a righteous person would then be instruction in understanding that message (Hill [1965; 1967: 137–38] thinks *dikaioi* a quasi-technical term in Matthew's church for "teachers"; cf. 13:17, where "prophets and righteous persons" [*dikaioi* is not in the parallel at Luke 10:24] are said to have longed to see and hear Jesus' day, and 23:29, in light of Dan 12:3 and Qumran, "the Teacher of Righteousness"). The *dikaios* reference could, however, be to "pious, God-fearing upright people of the OT" (Ziesler 1972: 138), or it has been argued that here we have titles for Jesus, in parallel to "me," namely the Prophet (cf. Deut 18:15) and the Righteous One or Messiah (Albright and Mann, *Matthew* AB, 133–34). The last two interpretations of the verse could go back to the historical Jesus. But 10:41 is more likely redactoral (Gundry 1982: 202).

c. Three Passages. The most significant references in what Jesus said are likely (1) Mark 2:17 (and parallels), (2) a Q saying about wisdom, and (3) the parable of the Pharisee and the Tax Collector. The first passage reads: "I did not come to call righteous persons but sinners" (2:17 = Matt 9:13; Luke 5:32 adds "to repentance"). The contrast here between sinners and righteous has been noted above, as at Luke 15:7 (cf. Matt 5:45; 13:49). With regard to the historical Jesus, the reference could have been ironic or could have implied "righteous by the standards of the law, but I have come to call those they despise"; cf. the context (Mark 2:15–17), where scribes and Pharisees scorn Jesus' eating with tax collectors and sinners. The term may even be in response to the self-understanding of the Pharisees, that they were righteous compared with such people (cf. Reumann 1982: #224).

The Q statement (Matt 11:19 = Luke 7:35) in its Lukan form may be attributed to Jesus: "Wisdom is justified (*edikaiōthē,* gnomic aor) by all her children." The context is the response of "this generation" (7:31) to John the Baptist and Jesus. The former in his austerity, the latter in his gregariousness with tax collectors and sinners, are both rejected by the "lawyers and Pharisees." Yet *Sophia* (God) is vindicated and shown right by both John and Jesus and all in a long line of envoys; cf. Wisdom of Solomon 9–11 on how *Sophia,* who sits by God's throne (9:2–4), has punished the *adikoi* (10:3, cf. 20 *asebeis;* 11:20, pursued by *Dikē*) and rescued the *dikaioi* (10:4, 5, 6, 10, 13, 20; 11:14) (Schulz 1972: 386; Schüssler Fiorenza 1984: 132; cf. Luke 11:49–51 [Q], Wisdom sends prophets, whom Israel persecutes and kills, and 13:34–35 [= Matt 23:37–39] as a wisdom lament [Kloppenborg 1987: 139–47, 227–29: a Deuteronomistic concept of history]).

The parable of the Pharisee and tax collector (Luke 18:9–14) tells, in a somewhat overdrawn way, of a Pharisee who in his deeds exceeds the law's requirements and feels far superior to the *adikoi* (vv 11b–12), and of a tax collector whose prayer as a sinner is simply to throw himself on God's mercy. This latter person, Jesus concludes, "went down to his house justified *(dedikaiōmenos)* rather than the other" (v 14). There is considerable agreement (Reumann 1982: ##50, 247) that the parable is Jesus' own, not a Lukanized Paulinism. It provides another example of Jesus' "defense of his attitude toward Pharisees and toll-collectors in contemporary Palestinian society," a critique of Pharisaic "pursuit of uprightness or righteousness . . . by boasting or even by self-confident activity" (Fitzmyer *Luke 10–24* AB, 1184); we glimpse "Jesus' own attitude" that one is "justified" (declared/made upright) before God "by a contrite recognition of one's own sinfulness" and expression of it before God (pp. 1185, 1188). For *dikaioun* in this sense in Jewish texts, cf. 1QS^{b} 4.22 and 2 Esdr 12:7 (to be "accounted righteous" [*iustificatus sum*] is paralleled in a prayer with "find favor" in God's sight); and also note the spirit of Ps 51:1–17. A forensic context is provided by the preceding parable in 18:2–5 (6) about the unrighteous judge *(ho kritēs tēs adikias)* who finally heeds the widow's pleas for vindication (vv 3, 5, *ekdikein*), and by the likely later, allegorical addition in vv 7–8: God will "make vindication" (*ekdikēsis,* vv 7, 8; cf. 21:22, "days of vengeance," from Hos 9:7).

d. Summary. The Synoptic Gospels reflect the Jewish world of Jesus' day with regard to righteousness (Hill 1967: 139). He spoke of the just and the unjust (Matt 5:45) or righteous and sinners (Semiticizing expressions with *adikia* are found especially in Luke). In the style of his day he urged his followers to greater righteousness (Matt 5:20) and spoke of it in terms of piety (Matt 6:1), e.g., almsgiving. Yet Jesus' message about God's kingdom was especially addressed to "sinners" (Mark 2:17 and parallels), and he criticized in no uncertain terms those striving to justify themselves outwardly, hypocritically, and in a way derogatory toward those they termed *adikoi* Matt 23:28–35; Luke 16:15). He reserved praise for sinners who threw themselves on God's mercy; such are vindicated (Luke 18:14). In traditional terms Jesus could speak of the resurrection of the righteous (Luke 14:14; Matt 13:47), but the emphasis was even more on the judgment (Luke 13:27; Matt 12:37), particularly of those who persecute God's prophets and righteous ones (Matt 10:41).

Jesus likely saw John the Baptist and himself in this succession of persecuted prophets (Luke 7:35), but it is nowhere clearly stated that Jesus viewed himself as "the Righteous One" (see above on Matt 10:41). A picture in pre-Christian Jewish sources of a suffering and then exalted Righteous One (Schweizer 1960: 22–31) is a problematical mixture of motifs (Ruppert 1972b: 43–44; see also pp. 44–71 for the possible case that Jesus saw himself as a suffering prophet [like the righteous figure in Wis 5:1–7] who looked to God for vindication, even after a martyr death). That Jesus looked upon his impending death as salvific depends on whether, or how much of, the "ransom saying" (Mark 10:45) or the "passion predictions" (like Mark 8:31) are attributed to the historical Jesus (cf., e.g., Kleinknecht 1984: 167–77). There are only a few possible references using *dik*-terminology that allude to God's righteousness as a gift (Matt 6:33) and to God's justifying (better: vindicating) sinners (Luke 18:14, cf. vv 5 and 8).

4. Extending the Theme. Although many conclude that "righteousness really does not characterize what is new in Jesus' proclamation" (Dihle *RAC* 10: 306), some exegetes, looking ahead to the prominence of the theme in Paul, hold it "likely that Jesus' messianic life of righteousness provided the extent and direction for his community's reflection on this theological concept" (Stuhlmacher 1986: 30). Jungel argued that Jesus' message, especially in the parables, concerned the kingdom of God and its presence as God's grace. Like the righteousness of God in Paul, it has eschatological character: Jesus looked forward to the imminent kingdom, Paul looked back to the eschaton brought "to expression as the revelation of God's righteousness in Jesus' death and resurrection" (Jungel 1962: 282). Both, however, viewed the law basically as the love command (Mark 12:28–31 and parallels; Rom 13:8–10) and gave faith a significant place (for Jesus, in miracle stories where faith is awakened, e.g., Mark 5:34; cf. also Lührmann 1975). It may be that "divine rule" and "right" inevitably go together, as from time immemorial in ancient religion (*Dikē,* Maat), and so "kingdom of God" and righteousness intertwine (Reventlow 1971: 114–15). But gospel passages do not support such a connection.

Different from Jungel's existential hermeneutic is Baird's (1963) stress on "justice" in the teaching of Jesus. The focus is not, however, on righteousness (*ṣdq,* pp. 44–45) but on judgment (*mišpāṭ,* pp. 42–44, 58–62), in terms of equity, love, and wrath. In the crisis that Jesus' coming brings, the righteous and sinners are separated (pp. 185–87). Here Jesus emerges as Judge incarnate. Walsh (1987: 148–49) would understand Jesus against a background of "*ṣedeq* and the belief in Yahweh's *mišpāṭ* found in the Scriptures." Stuhlmacher argues that Jesus brought "a new understanding" of God's righteousness and of righteousness before God (1986: 32). This came by his words and deeds, above all through forgiving sins and inviting sinners to table fellowship. Both Jesus' call to a life of love and his readiness to die a death that is "vicarious life-giving" (Mark 10:45) are involved. But even Stuhlmacher admits it is not until after Easter that Jesus was understood as "personification of God's saving righteousness."

D. Expounding Jesus' Cross

1. Post-Easter Reflection. Reflection on the passion and death of Jesus in light of the assertion that "God has raised him from the dead" (1 Thess 1:10; Gal 1:1; cf. 1 Cor 15:4) led to an understanding of the meaning of the crucifixion in terms at times of righteousness/justification. See also JUSTIFICATION. These early traditions took the form especially of creedal formulae or slogans, sometimes hymnic, to be confessed about the work and person of Jesus the Christ. The starting point here may have been the title "the Just (or Righteous) One," *ho dikaios* (cf. Acts 3:14; 7:52; 22:14; 1 Pet 3:18; 1 John 2:1), applied to Jesus, in contrast to the *adikoi* or unrighteous (1 Pet 3:18; cf. Rom 5:6–7, *hyper asebōn*), to whom he had ministered in life and benefited in death. Jesus also came to be spoken of as "our righteousness *(dikaiosynē)*" (1 Cor 1:30), and verbs from *dikaioun* were employed to tell how he had "vindicated" (1 Tim 3:16) or "justified" (1 Cor 6:11; Rom 3:24) believers, so that one could speak of our "justification" (Rom 4:25) or even our becoming "God's righteousness" in Christ (2 Cor 5:21). OT texts like Gen 15:6 and Hab 2:4 played no direct part, but *ṣdq* as "saving righteousness" and OT cultic concepts did.

2. Background. Williams (1975), focusing on Rom 3:24–26, would trace this understanding of Jesus' death as "saving event" back to Hellenized Christianity, i.e., a congregation of Hellenized Jews and Gentiles (p. 253). He assumes a concept of martyrdom where death purifies the people and the land, a concept mediated through *4 Maccabees* (1:11; 6:28–39; 17:21–22), a document he dates to ca. A.D. 35–40 in Antioch (pp. 183–202; 253). At issue is whether this concept in *4 Maccabees* of atoning, vicarious death can be explained sufficiently from OT and Jewish backgrounds, notably Isaiah 53 and 2 Macc 7:37–38 (*OTP* 2: 539), or whether it shows Greek influence, as is suggested by references in *4 Maccabees* to "divine justice" (*dikē;* 4:21; 8:22; 9:9; 18:22; cf. 8:14; 9:15; 12:12), therefore requiring Greek-Hellenistic ideas as the catalyst, such as "propitiatory sacrifice à la Iphigenia" (cf. Euripides, *Iphigenia at Aulus* 1383–84; 1553–55, the willing sacrifice, to placate the wrath of the goddess Artemis, noting *4 Macc.*

6:28, where the martyr's punishment "suffices" for the people). Most would trace the formulations to Jewish Christianity, relying on OT themes as developed in Judaism (Schweizer 1960: 32–41; Ruppert; Thyen 1970; Stuhlmacher 1965, but cf. 185–88, and 1986: 58–60, 63–65: perhaps a heritage from the circle around Stephen, Acts 7–8). Walsh (1987: 150) finds here a "sea change in the understanding of . . . *ṣedeq*. . . ."

3. Seven Examples from the Epistles. Now embedded in NT letters, these "atonement formulas" or, better, *homologiae* about the meaning of Jesus' death exhibit some variety not only in the range of application for righteousness terms but probably also in backgrounds (Reumann 1982: ##60–75).

(1) 1 Pet 3:18, "Christ once for all *(hapax)* suffered (variant, "died") for *(peri)* sins, the Righteous One on behalf of those who are unrighteous *(dikaios hyper adikōn),*" could have been part of a longer hymn embracing Christ's manifestation (1:20), passion (cf. 2:22–24 = Isa 53:4, 5, 9, 12), death, and exaltation (3:19, 22); it was, in this case, akin to the next example.

(2) 1 Tim 3:16 includes as line 2 of a six-line hymn, likely of Hellenistic-Jewish Christian origin, the statement that Christ, "manifested in the flesh," was "vindicated *(edikaiōthē)* in the spirit." If the first line refers to incarnation, the second could reflect Jesus' baptism (cf. Matt 3:15 where the voice from heaven and the Spirit confirm that he fulfills "all righteousness"). But the hymn may begin with the resurrection. Then, in line 2, Jesus is presented as in the right, as the Justified One, exalted by God.

(3) 1 Cor 1:30 employs the noun *dikaiosynē* as one of several titles for Christ, "who became 'wisdom' for us from God, both 'righteousness' and 'sanctification,' and 'redemption' *(apolytrōsis).*" The last three terms may be formulaic, used by Paul to lay a foundation for the discussion of wisdom that follows. "Christ crucified" (1:23) is "righteousness (from God)" for us. Schnelle (1983: 44–46) sees here "the righteousness marking the community, which has its basis in Jesus Christ," righteousness through baptism.

(4) 1 Cor 6:11 associates Christ as righteousness and sanctification clearly with baptism: "you were washed, you were sanctified, you were justified *(edikaiōthēte)* in the name of the Lord Jesus Christ and in the Spirit of our God." The words would have been spoken over baptized persons as a call to their new existence in Christ (cf. 1 Thess 5:5; Gal 3:26–28; 4:6–7; Rom 8:14–15). In particular, forgiveness of past sins is involved. That "you were justified" (aorist tense) is the climax of the formulation: a single act, declared/made righteous, and (with v 9) called to an ethical life of God's kingdom different from the unrighteous (Schnelle 1983: 38–44).

(5) 2 Cor 5:21, "The One who did not know sin [the sinless Christ], (God) made sin on our behalf, in order that we might become God's righteousness in him," is disputed as to origins. That 5:19–21 is a pre-Pauline hymn (Käsemann 1971a: 52–55) or that at least 5:21 is Jewish-Christian tradition (Kertelge 1967: 99–107; Stuhlmacher 1965: 74–78) has been denied in favor of Paul's own authorship (Hofius 1980a; 1980b; Fitzmyer 1982: #373). Furnish (*2 Corinthians* AB, 351) terms it "a Pauline re-working of traditional, probably Jewish-Christian theological notions." That Christ was "made sin" has been taken to refer either to the sin offering of Lev 4:21 (the bull is the sin offering [*hamartia*] for the assembly) (Wilckens *Romans* EKKNT, 1: 240; Stuhlmacher 1986: 58–60), or to Isa 53:10 (the servant as "an offering for sin") (Hofius 1980a). But the phrase has also been taken to mean no more than that Christ identified with sinful humanity (Furnish). It is possible that vv 18–21 were a "preformed credo," with redaction by Paul in vv 19b and 20c, with v 20 referring to Christ as "sin offering" (Martin *2 Corinthians* WBC, 138–51). In any case, "God's righteousness" is the dominant conclusion. Verse 21 assumes Christ as righteousness (1 Cor 1:30). The goal is that "we in him are righteousness," partaking of the new reality in Christ as new creatures (5:17), through baptism (Schnelle 1983: 47–50).

(6) Rom 3:24–26 (widely held to be a non-Pauline, Jewish-Christian assertion about the meaning of Jesus' death as expiatory) remains debated regarding its perimeters. Käsemann's 1961 proposal (cf. his *Romans* HNT, 95–99), as refined in subsequent discussion (cf. Reumann 1966; 1982: ##70–72; Williams 1975: 5–24), regarded vv 24–26a as (hymnic) tradition:

> [24]Being declared righteous *(dikaioumenoi)* as a gift (*dōrean,* which some assign to Paul along with "by his [God's] grace") through the redemption *(apolytrōseōs)* which is in Christ Jesus, [25]whom God put forward as an expiation *(hilastērion)* in his blood, for a demonstration of his [God's] righteousness, because of the passing over (better: with a view to remission) of former sins, [26a]in the forbearance of God.

Possibly employed in an annual reflection on Jesus' death using Day of Atonement terminology (*hilastērion* = Heb *kappōret*), perhaps used at the Lord's Supper or baptism, the formulation spoke of Jesus' blood demonstrating God's righteousness even as sins are forgiven (v 25) and people being justified/redeemed (24). Williams (1975: 19–56) would include in the formula in v 24 both *dōrean* and "by his grace"; in v 25 "by faith" (understood as Jesus' own faith), as well as in 26c the words *dikaion* and *dikaiounta ton ek pisteōs Iēsou*, i.e., God is "just/righteous and justifies/rightwises the person who shares Jesus' own faith or Jesus-faith." Further, he would understand *dikaioumenoi* in v 24 to refer adjectivally to "all persons" in v 23; in this way the whole formulation pertains to Gentiles. Williams' analysis thus includes in the pre-Pauline text, as most do not, the term "faith," both that of Jesus and that of all who share in it. Pluta (1969: 111) would also include "through faith" in the formula, which expressed "God's justifying fidelity to the New Testament *kappōret* Jesus Christ in the eucharist."

The analysis of Lohse (1955; 1973) has been particularly persuasive to some that v 24 is not part of the formula which Paul cites (so also Wilckens *Romans* EKKNT, 1: 183–84): only *apolytrōsis* in 24 is taken as tradition (cf. 1 Cor 1:30); the quotation then begins, as often, with a relative pronoun in v 25, "whom" *(hon),* not (as can occur) with the participle "being justified" in 24. (If *dikaioumenoi* is included, a subject such as "we" or "you" plus a main verb must be assumed in the original hymn or liturgy; perhaps, "because we are being justified, we await [cf. Rom 8:23] or have [cf. Col 1:14; Eph 1:7] redemption.") Attributing v 24 basically to Paul is supported also by Stuhlmacher (1986: 96) and Schnelle (1983: 67–72), for example.

Still debated also is the sense of *hilastērion* in v 25. Is it the "mercy seat" or ark in the OT (*kappōret,* on the Day of Atonement; Leviticus 16) or "expiatory sacrifice" (Lohse 1955: 152; 1973), stressing *4 Macc.* 17:21–22? (On the OT root *kpr,* see Janowski 1982; in favor of the view that Jesus here is equated with the *kappōret,* the lid of the ark as place of meeting, see Stuhlmacher 1986: 100–3.) Given these difficulties, Schnelle (1983: 70) settles for "means of expiation" as the sense (so also Wolter 1978: 21).

At the least, 3:25–26a associates God's righteousness with forgiveness through Jesus' death. If v 24 is included, justification/redemption is explicitly asserted. If Williams is correct, faith (on the part of Jesus and those justified) was a part of the formula.

(7) Rom 4:25 is less debated as a (Hellenistic-)Jewish Christian formulation. It refers to Jesus, "who was put to death for (*dia,* on account of) our trespasses, and was raised for (*dia,* with the goal of) our justification *(dikaiōsin).*" Jesus' death and resurrection mean sins forgiven and justification/rightwising (cf. Isa 53:11–12 as possible background). The past christological event grounds these soteriological consequences that occur "for us" (*hēmōn,* "our," at the end of each line) in baptism (Schnelle 1983: 72–74). To trace 4:25 (or 3:25) to Jesus via the saying at Mark 9:31 and passion/Lord's Supper material (among others, Popkes 1967: 263–66; cf. Kleinknecht 1984: 187) remains less than convincing to most critics. The connection in 4:25 of Jesus' resurrection with justification, otherwise unparalleled, can be traced thematically in terms of "acquittal by resurrection" and life for believers (Barth 1971: 20; Barth and Fletcher 1964).

4. Significance. The cumulative weight of these texts is to provide a starting point for NT use of righteousness/justification in Christology and soteriology (Reumann 1982: #76). Their appearance in Jewish(-Hellenistic) Christianity is not surprising, given the emphasis on *ṣdq* and the *passio iusti* in the OT and in certain strands of Judaism; but it must also be post-Easter, given the paucity of such terms on Jesus' part. Yet some of the concepts would not have been strange to the Greek world, and from there they had already penetrated Hellenistic Judaism *(4 Maccabees).* The formulations must be early enough—in the thirties or forties—to function as familiar, common tradition in Pauline communities, above all in Rome where the apostle had not labored when he wrote Romans; they were also pervasive enough to appear more broadly than in Paul's own letters (1 Peter; cf. 1 Timothy; "the Just One" in Acts). Thus these formulations can be termed part of early "apostolic Christianity," and they demonstrate that righteousness/justification was not merely a theme Paul picked up in a controversy with opponents in Galatia. The chief line of development will be, however, in Paul's theology, as this Jewish apostle writes to congregations of Jewish and Gentile Christians (see below). These righteousness/justification formulas stressed, among other things, the forgiveness of sins, redemption for the unrighteous, sanctification, and the Spirit, through the death (seen in martyr and cultic terms) and resurrection-vindication of the Righteous One, Jesus, all granted via baptism; however, faith is not mentioned in the formulas themselves (except on Williams' reading on Rom 3:23–26), though justification by faith can be claimed as a commonly held conviction of early Jewish Christianity. See JUSTIFICATION. The ethical demand for righteous living is not explicitly stated in these pre-Pauline statements. Indeed, the starting point for Christian development of righteousness/justification as a theme (Dihle *RAC* 10: 307–13) is not the final judgment and the law's demand for righteousness but Jesus' death and vindication by God.

E. Synoptic Gospels, Acts, Johannine Corpus

While Jesus' passion, death, and resurrection shape the canonical gospels, the evangelists remain true to the fact that Jesus had employed *ṣdq* terminology only sparingly (see above). Most of the examples in the four gospels and Acts reflect OT-Jewish usages. In some cases *dik-*words are used in quite routine ways, without theological significance. Most examples discussed above occur only in one gospel.

1. Q Source. In Q (the sayings material common to Matthew and Luke) the sole example is the statement (in its Lukan form, 7:35; Matt 11:19 shows Matthean rewriting), "Wisdom is justified by her children." As indicated above, Q presented this picture as a statement of how the prophets, sent as representatives of God's own wisdom, are rejected; yet wisdom is vindicated by them, eschatologically. In Q, Jesus, as wisdom's messenger, becomes subordinated to a Son of Man Christology, standing, like his death, in the service of a proclamation of judgment on Israel (Hoffmann 1972: 180–90, 196–98; Kloppenborg 1987: 110–12, 115–17, 166–70).

2. Mark. Mark employs *dikaios* once in a positive sense to characterize John the Baptist as "just and holy" (in the evangelist's description of what Herod thought about him, 6:20) and once in the triple tradition logion (2:17b = Matt 9:13 = Luke 5:32), "I did not come to call righteous persons *(dikaious)* but sinners." This stands parallel with 17a, "Those who are well do not need a physician but those who are ill." Jesus' invitation is for sinners in need of forgiveness, not those self-content in their own rectitude; i.e., he calls tax collectors like Levi, not Pharisees (2:13–16).

3. Matthew. Matthew has a special interest in righteousness (see above for sayings material, narrative, and descriptive references; all except 20:13, "I do you no injustice," are treated in canonical order in Reumann 1982: ##226–43). The cumulative emphasis on righteous (and unrighteous) persons (1:19: 5:45; 13:17, 43, 49; 23:28, 29, 35; 25:37, 46; 27:19) and on what is right (20:4), as well as the sevenfold use of *dikaiosynē,* makes verses from Q and Mark stand out even more in Matthew's context.

Thus at 9:13 the Markan saying of 2:17 is repeated verbatim, though introduced by a connecting word, "*For* I did not come to call righteous persons but sinners." The context is still the call of a tax collector to follow Jesus (9:9–11, here named Matthew, not Levi), but the proverbial statement that preceded 17b in Mark, namely, "Those who are well do not need a physician but those who are ill" (17a = Matt 9:12), takes on added significance in light of the immense collection of miracle stories in chaps. 8–9, about Jesus as healer, who fulfills Isa 53:4 in the way "he took our infirmities and bore our diseases" (8:17). Between what were parallel sayings in Mark (2:17a and b), Matthew has placed an OT citation on Jesus' lips (Matt 9:13a), introduced by a rabbinic exhortation, "Go and learn what it means [in Hos 6:6, where God says], 'I desire mercy and not sacrifice.' " (Matthew repeats this quotation at 12:7; the shift in wording from LXX "mercy *more than* sacrifice" suggests a rejection of temple sacrifices.) The key word "mercy" then explains why Jesus calls "sinners."

The Q saying (Luke 7:35) about wisdom being justified by her children (emissaries like John the Baptist and Jesus) becomes in Matthew 11:19 part of a framework, with 11:2, around material concerning the Baptizer: John heard in prison about "the *works* of Christ" (11:2), and the closing then reads, "Wisdom is justified by her *works*" (11:19). In this way Matthew's version shifts the reference from "all the children" of wisdom, including John, to the miracles ("works") which Jesus as the Christ performs, presented in chaps. 8–9. This is part of Matthew's identification of wisdom as God's plan for salvation (Meier 1980: 124) or even with Jesus himself (cf. 23:34 with Luke 11:49; and 11:28–29 with wisdom's invitation in Sir 51:23–27).

In 10:41, about receiving "a righteous man" (see above), if there is a reference to Jesus as the "Righteous One" this is much more likely on the evangelist's level of meaning than on that of the historical Jesus (cf. 27:19).

The judgment theme mentioned above for the gospels and Jesus in general is, as is well known, especially emphatic in Matthew (cf. 12:37, being justified or condemned at the judgment depends on one's words; 12:7, if opponents of Jesus had known what Hos 6:6 means, they "would not have condemned the guiltless"). (What RSV translates as "justice" at 23:23 and 12:20 [= Isa 42:3] is another Greek word, *krisis.*)

The seven verses where *dikaiosynē* occurs on the lips of Jesus are the prime expression of the righteousness theme in Matthew. While 6:1 might, among others, be authentically from the Jesus level, the claim that all are redactoral or in verses composed by Matthew (e.g., Reumann 1982) finds considerable support (Gundry 1982; Luz *Matthew* EKKNT, 154). That does not mean, however, that the meaning in every passage need be the same. Numerous exegetes do take all of them to mean righteous human actions or relationships, a demand upon disciples to do their just duty (so Luz; Syreeni 1987: 207–11). Others find a varied meaning, sometimes for a divine gift or power, or they see both "God's actions with respect to men and the human actions that spring from God's" (gift and task), perhaps in a covenant setting (Schweizer 1975: 54–55). There is some agreement on the following analysis (Reumann 1982, where earlier literature is cited; Meier 1980: 38; Gundry 1982; Guelich 1982).

The concept of *dikaiosynē* (in the sense of obedient response to Jesus in terms of just and upright conduct) looms over much of Matthew's Sermon on the Mount as the central theme. So 5:20, "Unless your righteousness exceeds that of the scribes and Pharisees, you will never enter the kingdom of heaven," stands over the antitheses of 5:21–48. "Beware of practicing your piety *(dikaiosynē)* before others" (6:1) is the theme for 6:1–18, about almsgiving, prayer, and fasting. While, as in Hebrew, the term at 6:1 could denote almsgiving, it probably has a broader meaning of righteousness before God. The sense in 5:20 and 6:1 is clearly that of human actions, for it is "your righteousness" that is spoken of. Matt 5:10 probably has the same meaning: "Blessed are those who are persecuted for righteousness' sake," i.e., for their righteous conduct. Syreeni, who stresses the sense of demand throughout Matthew (cf. Przybylski), nonetheless speaks of a "defective, transitional conception of covenantal nomism" (1987: 218) in Matthew compared with Tannaitic Judaism (Sanders), for while there has been a break with the Jewish variety, "a new Christian form of covenantal nomism has not (yet?) been conceptualized" (p. 212).

Matt 5:6, however, where the noun *dikaiosynē* is inserted as the object of "hunger" along with the verb "thirst" (contrast Luke 6:21), to yield "Blessed are those who hunger and thirst after righteousness, for they shall be satisfied," may mean "right conduct on God's side"; not human activity but divine exercise of justice, leading to eschatological vindication of the poor, meek, persecuted disciples (Gundry 1982: 70). This soteriological sense is especially likely if, behind the beautitudes at 5:3, 4, and 5 one sees, respectively, Isa 61:1 (good tidings for the afflicted [Heb *ʿănāwîm,* the poor]); 61:2 (all who mourn); and 61:7 (in your land a double portion). Similarly, Isa 61:6 (you shall eat the wealth of the nations) may lie behind Matt 5:6 (the hungry being satisfied). Then Isa 61:10 (where righteousness from God parallels salvation) might even suggest that Matt 5:10 has the further sense of those persecuted for their relationship with God, 5:3 and 10 thus forming an *inclusio* around the 8 second-person beatitudes (Guelich 1982: 84–88, 93, 102–3, 115–18).

The final example in the Sermon on the Mount literally reads, "Seek first the kingdom and the righteousness of him [God], and all these things will be added to you" (Matt 6:33; cf. Luke 12:31, "Seek his kingdom, and these things will be added to you"). The form is an imperative. But usually in Matthew the kingdom is God-given, eschatologically. This is the only instance in Matthew of "*God's* righteousness." And the verse closes with a promise. Hence, this verse also may, like 5:6, refer to the right conduct of God in giving the kingdom and righteousness (Gundry 1982: 118–19) or to "eschatological vindication or salvation by God" as well as "the life lived in keeping with the will of the Father," gift and demand (Guelich 1982: 346–47, 371–72). Involved would be the "imperatival indicative" so characteristic of Matthew (Strecker 1962).

When Jesus urged John to baptize him, "For thus it is fitting for us to fulfill all righteousness" (3:15), we have another example of doing what is right yet also fulfilling the plan of God (Meier 1980: 27: God's "saving activity"). With its reference to "us" (referring to John the Baptist and Jesus), the verse forms a sort of large *inclusio* with 21:35: "John came to you in the way of righteousness." While this could mean demanding an upright life or living in a righteous way, the phrase "way of righteousness" could also have a salvation-history sense (Meier 1980: 241–42): the course of God's plan that culminates in the Baptist and Jesus, who in Matthew often appear in tandem (cf. 3:2 and 4:17).

In summary, Matthew's references to righteousness yield a certain emphasis on God's eschatological gift of salvation (5:6; 6:33), with a definite stress on the response of disciples in terms of righteous living (5:10, 20; 6:1). Two other references (3:15; 21:32) could incorporate both senses (each of which has OT roots), but these may also reflect Matthean salvation history.

4. Luke-Acts. The books of Luke and Acts may be considered together in order to grasp the totality of the Lukan picture. The 53 examples of *dik*-terminology in the two books make this the second biggest grouping of such words in the NT (after Paul). Words from *adikein* also occur with relative frequency in both volumes. See Fig. RIG.02. All examples in Luke's gospel have been noted above except for 12:57 ("Why do you not judge for yourselves what is right?" cf. Acts 4:19). References to righteous people appear with some frequency in Luke 1–2, much as in Matthew. In L material in chap. 16 and 18:6 and 11 *adikos/adikia* appear, the noun often used in the genitive adjectivally ("steward of injustice").

Many of these same uses appear in Acts: "reward of wickedness" (*adikias,* 1:18); "bond of iniquity" (8:23); "resurrection of both just and unjust" (24:15; cf. Luke 14:14); *adikein* at 7:24, 26, 27 (to "wrong" someone) and 25:10, 11 (do wrong); *ekdikēsis* at 7:24 ("avenge"). Cornelius is termed "an upright and God-fearing" centurion (10:22); such a person who "does righteousness" *(ergazomenos dikaiosynēs)* is acceptable to God (10:35, i.e., who lives a devout life and gives alms). In contrast Elymas is an "enemy of all righteousness" (13:10). God's final judgment will occur "in righteousness" (17:31; cf. Pss 9:4; 96:13; 98:9). The ethics and eschatology that Paul is said to argue before Felix and Drusilla, "justice *(dikaiosynē),* self-control, and the coming judgment" (24:25), seem in the first two topics a nod to Greco-Roman understanding (cf. *Aristeas* 278).

Usually it is claimed that Luke-Acts touches on righteousness/justification in a theologically significant way only in the parable of the Pharisee and the Publican (Luke 18:9–14) and in a single verse at Acts 13:38 during Paul's sermon at Pisidian Antioch. One is cautioned against reading the first as more than "generic" roots for Paul's doctrine of justification by faith (Fitzmyer *Luke 10–24* AB, 1185), and the Acts passage is sharply contrasted with Paul's own view as presenting but "partial justification," which is equated with forgiveness of sins (13:38) and occurs "*also* by faith" along with the law (Vielhauer 1966: 41–42).

Luke writes at the intersection of both knowledge about Jesus and awareness of Paul. He is true to the Jesus tradition with its relatively minor emphasis on righteousness/justification (see above, on the Jesus level of meaning for Luke 18:9–14). He probably did not know Paul's letters or appreciate how significant *dikaiosynē* was for the apostle. But his limited references must be read not only in light of a situation (ca. 80–95) that was quite different from Paul's day, but also with respect to the themes of Lukan theology; and with a literary, narrative awareness of Luke's approach. Among the significant theological aspects are a Lukan emphasis on the forgiveness of sins (*aphesis hamartiōn,* Luke 1:77; 3:3; 24:47; Acts 2:38; 5:31; 10:43; 13:38; 26:18; cf. 4:18 "release . . . liberty"; Fitzmyer *Luke 1–9* AB, 223–24) and a sense of the Jewish law (and prophets) as divine prophecies but no longer a theological problem (Vielhauer 1966: 37–43). Further, Jesus dies as an innocent righteous sufferer (cf. the use of "the Righteous One" in Acts 3:14; 7:52; 22:14; the centurion's words at Luke 23:47; contrast Luke 23:41; Schweizer 1960: 32–41), indeed akin to the martyrdom (cf. 23: 34 and 46 with Acts 7:60 and 59) of a Hellenistic *sophos* or wisdom figure (Karris 1985: 23–46; God's prophet of justice, who called for righteousness especially in the sense of almsgiving). There is no association of Jesus' death with expiating sin (Mark 10:45 is omitted; Acts 8:32–33 leaves out of the Isaiah quote 53:6 and 8d; only Acts 20:29 is a counterbalance). But there is no need for this connection, for God has always been forgiving (Luke as "the gospel of great pardons," 7:36–50; 15; 19:1–10; cf. God's grace/graciousness as a theme). Yet "faith" is prominent (e.g., Acts 13:38–39), often along with repentance (Fitzmyer *Luke 1–9* AB, 235–39). Finally, it must be realized that the author of Luke-Acts, stressing such themes a generation after Paul, cannot (by the very genre of these two books) very well *discuss* doctrines: instead, he must teach by means of stories (Schweizer *Luke* NTD).

Thus it is in a ministry by Jesus programmatically described as forgiveness/release from sins (4:18) and exemplified in 5:20–24, that he declares, "I have not come (perfect tense) to call righteous persons but sinners *to repentance*" (5:32). As Levi's conversion (5:27–29) illustrates, this period is "the Lord's acceptable year" (4:19 = Isa 61:2a; cf. Lev 25:10 LXX *eniautos apheseōs,* RSV "a jubilee"). The Pharisees and scribes grumble at the way Jesus eats and drinks with tax collectors and sinners (7:30). The unit 7:29–35, abounding in *dik*-forms, contrasts how "all the people and the tax collectors 'justified God' (*edikaiōsan,* recognized God's justice or accepted divine righteousness) by having been baptized with John's baptism," but the Pharisees and tax collectors rejected God's plan and John's baptism (7:29–30). Whether through John or through Jesus "the friend of tax collectors and sinners" (7:34), "wisdom was justified (*edikaiōthē,* vindicated) by all her children." Simon the Pharisee cannot grasp how a sinful "woman of the city" could be forgiven and saved by faith (7:36–50). The grumbling of opponents continues (15:2; 19:7) in connection with the saving of the lost emphasized both in parables (15:3–32) and in the Zacchaeus narrative (19:1–10). The contrast between "the righteous" and tax collector-sinners is most vividly exemplified in Jesus' story about prayers at the Temple, between "those who trusted in themselves that they were righteous *(dikaioi)*" (18:9) and the sinner who goes home vindicated (*dedikaiōmenos,* 18:14, "justified"). So Jesus is portrayed releasing persons from sins and responding to criticism about this reversal of "righteous" and "sinners" (cf. Tannehill 1986: 37, 65–66, 103–9, 186–87).

In Acts the Lukan version of early Christian and Pauline righteousness that saves through Christ's death cannot be presented as a doctrinal proposition (because of the genre) or in Paul's terms, given Luke's distance from the conflict over whether the law of Moses is the means of salvation, his sense of a distant parousia and future judgment, and his view of Jesus' death. The Pauline word-field of cross and justification is not to be expected. But in the "Council" debate at Jerusalem Peter (not Paul) states what was seemingly a general early Christian position, "We (Jews) believe that we shall be saved (*sōzein,* as also in later Pauline letters, not *dikaioun*) through the grace of the Lord Jesus," as will Gentiles (15:11; cf. Menoud 1978).

It is in the sermon in Acts 13:16–41 that Luke's narrative version of righteousness/justification directly appears. The conclusion, "forgiveness of sins is being proclaimed through this (Jesus) to you" (13:38), is typical of the Lukan kerygma. Somewhat Pauline is v 39: "by him everyone who believes is freed *(dikaioutai)* from everything from which you could not be freed *(dikaiōthēnai)* by the law of Moses." The connection is with Jesus' resurrection (v 37), not his death. Vielhauer has overstressed contrasts with Paul's letters and fails to see Luke's view in its own terms as a later position on Jesus and "rightwising." Faith, to justify or free, appears here together with sin(s) and law. It is Jesus Christ who is proclaiming (cf. 26:22–23) through Paul that all are freed or justified before God from everything that separates from God, not by law but by believing (Weiser 1985: 328, 336–37).

5. Johannine Literature. Together with the six examples of *dik*-terms in the gospel of John may be considered the related and relatively more frequent references in 1 John (11; none in 2 and 3 John), and even the 21 instances in the book of Revelation. In broad terms the Fourth Gospel's one significant passage speaks of Jesus' vindication; 1 John speaks of Jesus the Righteous One who expiates sin and of "doing righteousness" as the proper response; and Revelation speaks of God as just, judging evildoers (Reumann 1982: ##254–65).

In the gospel of John, God is addressed as righteous (17:25). Jesus' judgment is just (5:30), and there is "no falsehood *(adikia,* dishonesty) in him" (7:18). He urges opponents to judge "with just judgment" (7:24, *tēn dikaian krisin*). This language is typical of OT usages and in chap. 7 becomes forensic and polemical. Such a law-court setting also appears in 16:8–11, where *dikaiosynē* occurs twice, in one of the Paraclete sayings in the Upper Room discourse. After departing, Jesus promises to send the Paraclete, who "will convince/convict *(elegxei)* the world concerning sin and concerning righteousness and concerning judgment:

> concerning sin *(hamartia),* because (or that) they do not believe in me;
> concerning righteousness, because (or that) I go to the Father, and you will see me no more;
> and concerning judgment, because (or that) the ruler of this world is judged" (vv 9–11).

The forensic language, including *Paraklētos*—which can mean legal advocate but here seems to be an accuser more than a helper or comforter—suggests a cosmic trial scene, appropriate to the Fourth Gospel's emphasis on judgment. The attempt to take the three nouns in vv 9, 10, and 11 to mean verdicts of guilt or innocence *(dikaiosynē),* in any case a judgment (Lindars 1970), does not fit either the context or John's understanding of what "the world" is (Carson 1979: 556–57). The Paraclete will show the unbelieving world to be wrong both about sin (the opponents' failure to believe in Jesus, 8:21–24, 45–46) and about judgment (for the ruler of this world is already cast out, 12:31–32). It is possible to take the reference to righteousness as referring to Christ's righteousness (Ziesler 1972: 131; Stenger 1979). Carson would take it ironically, of the world's assumed righteousness (1979: 558–60; cf. Rom 10:3; Phil 3:6–9; Matt 5:20). But the statement that Jesus is going to the Father suggests that vindication is meant, when the Righteous One (1 John 2:1) is "justified in the presence of his opponents" (Schnackenburg *John* HTKNT 3: 131, who feels that Jesus' righteousness is a fuller theme in John than this unique occurrence of *dikaiosynē* suggests). The disciples will see Jesus no more (v 10c), but they and the Paraclete will make this threefold witness.

In 1 John, God is (as in John 17:25) described as faithful and righteous (1:9), One who "will forgive our sins and cleanse us from all unrighteousness *(adikia).*" Likewise Jesus is righteous (2:1, 29; 3:7), in whom there is no sin (*hamartia,* 3:5; a term that 5:17 equates with wrongdoing [*adikia*]; cf. John 7:18). This threefold description of Jesus as the Righteous One is closely connected with expiation and forgiveness of sins (2:2; 3:5). Those who believe in Jesus are also termed righteous (3:7) and are characterized as "doing righteousness" (*dikaiosynē,* 2:29; 3:7, 10). Such a person is one who has been begotten/born of God (2:29; *dikaiosynē* is the consequence of being God's child, not the condition for it). See also 3:12, where Abel's deeds were righteous but Cain's were evil (cf. Brown *Epistles of John* AB, 209–10, 383–84).

The book of Revelation shares this pattern in that God (16:5) and God's judgments are described as just (15:3; 16:7; 19:2); Christ is said to judge in righteousness (19:11); and the Christian, described as righteous and holy (22:11), is encouraged to "do righteousness" (22:11), in contrast to the evildoer [*ho adikōn*] who does evil. Hence the holy God's judgments *(dikaiōmata)* have been revealed (15:4). Iniquities *(adikēmata)* are remembered (18:5), but "the righteous deeds *(dikaiōmata)* of the saints" are compared with the fine linen of the Bride (19:8). In the apocalyptic imagery there are several references to hurting or harming *(adikein)* the earth (7:2–3; 9:4, 10, 19; cf. 6:6) or God's witnesses (2:11; 11:5). That God avenges *(ekdikein)* is stated at 6:10 and 19:2.

F. Paul

1. Linguistic Overview. Some 45% of all *dik*-words in the NT occur in the Pauline corpus. Since only 21 (including *ekdikēsis*) occur in letters assigned to Paul late in his career or to other writers in the Pauline school (Colossians, Ephesians, 2 Thessalonians, the Pastoral Epistles, which will be treated separately in section G below), the bulk of the examples are in clearly genuine letters, over half occurring in Romans. A passage-by-passage analysis of all verses with *dik*-terms (Reumann 1982: ##77–162) reveals that the letters other than Romans and Galatians (which has 14 examples in its 6 chaps.) are by no means devoid of the them. In general, Pauline usage exhibits OT-Jewish roots and picks up post-Easter formulas of (Hellenistic-)Jewish Christianity which expounded the meaning of Jesus' death (see above). The lines of development are christological and soteriological, as well as eschatological and ethical.

To add to the picture all the *adikein* references means a further reflection of OT-Jewish usage. For there is the familiar contrast not only of the unrighteous (pagans—a theological, not an ethnic judgment [Dabelstein 1981]) with the saints/those sanctified and justified (1 Cor 6:1, 9, cf. 11) but also of human *adikia* with the truth (Rom 1:18, 29 [RSV wickedness]; 2:8; 1 Cor 13:6) and with God's righteousness (Rom 3:5; 6:13). One does not expect God to be unjust *(adikos),* though the theodicy question is raised at Rom 3:5 and 9:14. The verb can mean "do wrong" (1 Cor 6:8; 2 Cor 7:2, 12; Gal 4:12) and "suffer wrong" (1 Cor 6:7; 2 Cor 7:12). Once Paul uses the noun ironically (2 Cor 2:13; cf. *TDNT* 1: 151–52, 155–56, 160–61).

To bring in another related term: vengeance (*ekdikēsis,* Rom 12:19 = Deut 32:35; 1 Thess 4:6) belongs to God, not to human beings (Rom 12:19). But an earthly ruler is "God's servant, an avenger for (divine) wrath against the evildoer" (Rom 13:4). In the church community, disobedience is to be punished (*ekdikēsai;* 2 Cor 10:6), and the noun can mean punishment produced by godly grief (2 Cor 7:11; cf. *TDNT* 2: 444–46).

2. Underlying Factors. Behind Paul's many references to righteousness/justification are several factors. It is necessary to appreciate these in order to understand his emphases on righteousness/justification.

a. Creedal and Hymnic Formulas. The creedal and hymnic formulas inherited from earlier "apostolic," especially Jewish, Christianity were one such underlying factor. Six of the 7 examples of such formulas cited above appear in Pauline letters, chiefly 1 and 2 Corinthians and Romans. Not Paul's own invention, "justification by faith is part of a Jewish-Christian theology" (Betz *Galatians* Hermeneia, 114, 115, 119). These earlier formulas exhibit a variety of backgrounds, especially in OT cult and sacrifice (2 Cor 5:21; Rom 3:25; 4:25), and reflect a variety of settings for use in congregational life, including baptism (1 Cor 6:11), hymns or creeds employed at worship (1 Tim 3:16 and others), and christological identity (1 Cor 1:30, "for us"). Some elements in the understanding of *dikaiosynē* in these (Hellenistic-)Jewish Christian texts would have been familiar to Paul's audiences through the synagogue; others (like cultic sacrifice) would have had some parallels in Greco-Roman life. If "covenant fidelity" was involved in any of these formulas, that would have been an alien theme to pagan ears and would have required clear explanation. The nuances that Paul's hearers would have brought to "righteousness/justice" language must also be kept in mind, including connections between *dikaiosynē* and faith (Dobbeler 1987: 102–14).

Therefore, much of what becomes the clearly articulated "Pauline doctrine of righteousness/justification" in Galatians, Philippians, and Romans must be accounted part of the inheritance Paul took over from earlier Christians, who created formulas about Jesus Christ and righteousness.

b. "God's Righteousness" *(dikaiosynē theou).* This phrase, which occurs in some of the pre-Pauline formulas (2 Cor 5:21; Rom 3:25, cf. v 26 "his righteousness"; 1 Cor 1:30, *apo theou dikaiosynē*), has, as a supposedly technical term in OT and Jewish apocalyptic literature, been taken as the starting point for Pauline development (Käsemann 1969; Stuhlmacher 1965; Reumann 1982: ##93, 133 [summary]). But reactions to this proposed background for the phrase—which occurs in Paul also at Rom 1:17; 3:5, 21, 22; 10:3; Phil 3:9, as well as in Matt 6:33, Jas 1:20, and 2 Pet 1:1, and possibly 2 Cor 9:8—have denied that the single OT reference (Deut 33:21, a verse Paul never cites) is the origin of Paul's usage (Lohse 1973: 213–14) or that the Qumran data (1QH 4.30–32; 7.28; 17.20; 1QS 10.11–12; 11.2–3, 5, 9–12) are persuasive for fixing the Pauline sense (Lohse 1973: 214–17). The further contentions by Käsemann and pupils about *dikaiosynē theou*—that it means God's power or might (in terms of divine faithfulness to the covenant) and that it takes on a cosmic side (of God's loyalty to the whole creation)—must be taken with caution (Lohse 1973: 222–27). Although this corrective to an individualistic sense of justification should be welcomed, the phrase "righteousness of God" cannot be treated as a fixed apocalyptic phrase, or in isolation from other *dik*-terms in Paul. The genitive *theou,* though most likely one of "authorship"—righteousness that proceeds or goes forth from God (cf. Phil 3:9)—probably varies in sense, at times presenting an attribute or quality of God (subjective genitive, Rom 3:5) and also "righteousness before God" (objective genitive, cf. Rom 1:17; 2 Cor 5:21; cf. also Reumann 1982: #119; Cranfield *Romans* ICC, 95–99; and Wilckens *Romans* EKKNT 1: 86, 91–92, 202–33, who, like Lohse 1955: 227, stresses that in passages such as Rom 1:17, 3:21–26, and Phil 3:9–10, righteousness from God is also righteousness by faith).

c. Apocalyptic Context. A key for grasping Paul's understanding of righteousness is the apocalyptic context in which he wrote. But the concept of Pauline apocalypticism needs definition. Albert Schweitzer (1931) employed eschatology of an apocalyptic sort to construct a logical (but mystical, though non-Hellenistic) Pauline theology. More recently Beker (1980) has made the apocalyptic language of Judaism, interacting with the resurrection of Jesus, the explanation for the coherent theme in Paul, an apocalyptic world view that unites the present triumph and lordship of Christ with the future triumph of God. The "apocalyptic dimension" of righteousness, as "both God's gift of salvation and his power that will encompass his whole creation," provides the basis for "Paul's hermeneutic of the lordship of Christ." The "symbol of righteousness" thus "constitutes the linguistic home of Paul's conversion experience because it was the language in which he received the Christophany and by means of which he broke with the Pharisaic life" and "righteousness under the Torah," though it is not Paul's only hermeneutic or master symbol (Beker 1980: 260–64).

But Paul wrote letters, not apocalypses, even though he incorporates parts of apocalyptic scenarios (1 Thess 4:15–17; 1 Cor 15:23–28) and writes of God's righteousness being "revealed" (*apokalyptetai,* Rom 1:17). He does use apocalyptic motifs, both from Christian tradition and probably directly from his own Judaism, but these he can then interpret through the themes of righteousness/justification (and reconciliation); cf. deliverance from "the wrath to come" in 1 Thess 1:9–10; 5:9, and then Rom 5:9–10; 8:31–39 (Schade 1981: 47–49). Paul's eschatology does not begin with the future parousia but builds toward it, for Christ who justifies already reigns (Schade, 91–104, with regard to 1 Cor 15:20–28). Thus Paul's apocalyptic eschatology is of both the present and the future type, and he preserves "an irreducible tension between the 'already' and the 'not yet,' which is generally absent from apocalyptic theology" (Keck 1984: 240). With regard to righteousness/justification, this means that we should sometimes expect to find "present realization" emphasized (Rom 3:24–28; 5:1), and sometimes its future aspect emphasized (Rom 5:9–10, "justification by faith as anticipation, as prolepsis," Keck 1984: 240; cf. Reumann 1982: ##141, 142, 147, 173). Indeed, one should probably regard as "apocalyptic" not only Käsemann's "cosmological interpretation" of righteousness/justification but also the interpretation of it in individual, anthropological terms: this is "forensic-eschatological" (Bultmann *BTNT* 1: 273–79).

d. The Pauline "Core." Phrases sometimes applied to Paul's notion of righteousness/justification label it the "essence of salvation" (*BTNT* 1: 271), the center of Pauline theology (Reumann 1982: ##192–216), or at least one of its "dominant perspectives" (Fitzmyer 1967: 79, 94–97; contrast 1982: ##403–7). Such prominence has likewise often been disputed, most commonly in preference for mysticisim (A. Schweitzer 1931: "in Christ") or salvation history (Stendahl 1963, but compare 1976: 23–40, 129–32, and Via 1971). Beker has spoken of the "coherent center" in Paul in a multiplicity of ways: as apocalyptic thought (1980: 15–16), the resurrection (p. 171), the lordship of Christ (p. 260), and the triumph of God (p. 355). While all such judgments may be influenced by later theological developments (or reactions to them), and while the quest for such a "center" reflects a desire for coherence amid contingent situations in Paul's varied letters, there is a case for arguing not only that righteousness/justification constitutes Paul's "proper" or "functional" Christology (Bultmann 1933: 262; Lührmann 1976; cf. Käsemann *Romans* HNT, 24; 1971b: 70–76), but also that it represents the center of Pauline soteriology. It rests on the extensive OT roots and pre-Pauline usage of the theme, on Paul's development of aspects of righteousness/justification, on its statistical frequence in a variety of applications, and on preponderance in Philippians, Galatians, and Romans. The endeavor of Sanders (1977: 434–42, 470–72, 543–52) to make "eschatological participation" central in Paul reflects nicely the apostle's eschatological emphasis and rests on a preference for "participatory" rather than "juristic" categories (even though Paul works with the latter and does not make such a distinction, p. 502). Admittedly, however, "righteousness by faith and participation in Christ ultimately amount to the same thing" (p. 506; cf. Reumann 1982: ##217–22, 408).

e. Baptism. The occasion for actualizing righteousness/justification in the lives of believers was baptism. This was true already in pre-Pauline praxis, as 1 Cor 6:11 shows (the aorist passive *edikaiōthēte* indicates the single event of baptism). The sequence in 6:11, "washed, sanctified, justified," may be found also in 1 Cor 1:30 in reverse: Christ is for us "righteousness, sanctification, and redemption" (Hahn 1976: 107–8; cf. Col 1:14; Eph 1:7, 14). Hymnic references with *dik*-terms may reflect at 1 Tim 3:16 Jesus' baptism and at 1 Pet 3:18 (above, a possible *Sitz im leben* at baptism (cf. vv 20–21, "saved through water"). The view of baptism which Paul thus inherited likely maintained that a person was freed from sins through God's power to make righteous, which was connected with Jesus' death and resurrection and which was now available through baptism (1 Cor 6:11; Romans 6; Schnelle 1983: 101). In Hellenistic Christianity, notions that one was by baptism buried and raised with Christ through divine power may show mystery cult influence (Lohse 1965: 233–35).

Paul's particular contribution to baptism, in connection with his understanding of God's righteousness, lay in his emphasis on faith as the means for appropriating the salvatory event in Christ, rather than through transmission of a divine power or life force. To be baptized meant dying to sin's dominion and living obediently "in Christ," i.e., in Christ's body, the community of believers (Lohse 1965: 237–38). In this way baptism links righteousness/justification to ecclesiology. It is baptism which makes present for each individual the justifying righteousness of Jesus' death on the cross as a gift precisely for that person, thus preventing mere vague generalizing. But Paul's proclamation (cf. 1 Cor 10:1–13) also attacked magical interpretations of baptism as a guarantee of security. The use of *edikaiōsen* at Rom 8:30, "those whom God called he also justified . . . and glorified," probably also stems from baptismal tradition, as is suggested by the " 'image' of [God's] son" (v 29), which like "the glory," had been lost (3:23) and is now restored in Christ (cf. 2 Cor 3:18; 4:6; Käsemann *Romans* HNT, 245).

In later writings of the Pauline school (see below), righteousness/justification continued to be associated with baptism (Titus 3:4–7; Eph 4:24; 2:4–10, here with *sōzein,* "save," replacing *dikaioun*). But generally there was no overt connection made with "faith" (esp. in contrast to "law"), though "grace" and "forgiveness of sins" became more prominent (Hahn 1976: 95–104).

That Paul was himself baptized with a baptism involving the (pre-Pauline) understanding sketched above (cf. Rom 6:3; 1 Cor 12:13; Acts 9:18; Lohse 1965: 230–31) suggests that righteousness actualized in the lives of those joined to Christ was a factor in his Christianity from the outset. It is to be assumed in his message—but in varied reflections, not as a uniform and as yet fully developed doctrine (Schnelle 1983: 100–1)—before it becomes a topic of controversy in Galatians as to how one is justified/rightwised. Paul's identification of "righteousness by divine grace" with "righteousness by faith" represented a step beyond the earlier tradition. In some ways the post-Pauline usage was a return to the pre-Pauline view of baptism as a "washing" or rebirth (cf. 1 Cor 6:11; Titus 3:5–6; Hahn 1976: 104–5).

f. The Church (Community). Through baptism, the Christian community becomes apparent as the locus for the life of those justified/rightwised. To be washed/sanctified/justified places one in a group differentiated from the unrighteous (*adikoi,* 1 Cor 6:9–11). For even if some of the "justified saints" still do wrong (*adikeite,* 6:8), those now righteous are not to go on in their wrongdoing (6:7; Rom 6:1–2; Dahl 1977: 103–4). While Paul speaks of those in the Church of God as saints (holy ones, *hagioi*), elect and called (1 Cor 1:2) into the body of Christ, he never applies *dikaioi* ("righteous ones") to them, though he once employs the term for doers of the law who will be justified (= righteous before God, Rom 2:13; Reumann 1982: #124). Is this omission of *dikaioi* for Christians attributable to Paul's view that "no one is righteous" (Rom 3:10), that persons can be reckoned righteous by faith only through God's saving *dikaiosynē* (3:21–26) and thus justified (5:1, 9), and that this is not completed until the final judgment?

Does this explain Rom 5:19, which states that by Christ's obedience "the many will be established as righteous *(dikaioi katastathēsontai)*" (cf. Gal 5:5; Käsemann *Romans* HNT, 157–58; Kuss 1957–78: 239)? Or does Paul's preference for the singular *dikaios* stem from the influence of OT citations (Gen 15:6 and Hab 2:4), as at Gal 3:11; Rom 1:17; and 3:26? The favored term is "believer(s)" *(pisteuōn, -ontes,* 1 Thess 1:7; Gal 3:22; Rom 1:16; 3:22).

An ecclesiology derived from righteousness/justification in Paul (Klaiber) has christology as its basis ("Christ our righteousness," 1 Cor 1:30) and baptism as the step that brings each individual into the corporate body of Christ. Baptism and faith, as complementary sides of the reception of salvation, bring one into a social, egalitarian community (Gal 3:25–29) where all have received the Spirit (1 Cor 12:12–13; Gal 3:1–5; Klaiber 1982: 182–90). This corporate realm or community of the Spirit is the place where believers live out their existence in Christ, with "life because of righteousness" (Rom 8:10; cf. Klaiber, 106–12).

At the heart of Paul's thought is the justification of the ungodly *(asebēs),* which corresponds to the "creation of the church *ex nihilo*" by faith (Klaiber, 121; Romans 4, esp. vv 5, 9, 12, 16, 17, 23–24). Since this new community consists of Jews and gentiles justified by and through their faith (Rom 3:30), in which both groups regard Abraham as prototype (Rom 4:16; Gal 3:6–9), the phrases "seed of Abraham" (Gal 3:29; Rom 4:13, 16, 18) and *hyioi Abraam,* "sons (and daughters) of Abraham" (Gal 3:7) become significant (Klaiber, 29–30). This line of thought is carried further in chap. 5: those justified *(dikaiōthentes)* have peace with God and stand in grace and in the hope of sharing God's glory, even while suffering (5:1–3). The phrases "while still sinners . . . now justified by Christ's blood" and "while enemies . . . reconciled" (5:9–10) indicate the paradoxical contrast of "in the past" and "now" (while also pointing to future deliverance, "we shall be saved"). Also apparent is the universal significance of Christ's death for the entire world (cf. 2 Cor 5:19), a note sounded more fully in 5:12–21 ("for all persons") in terms of Christ's act of righteousness *(dikaiōma)* leading to "acquittal and life" *(dikaiōsis zōēs)* for all (5:18). "We" in this chapter suggests the corporate group of those justified, but the reign of grace "through righteousness to eternal life" (5:21) brings the Church into connection with the world.

There was, on the one hand, a sense of division from, or rejection of, the world in the concept of baptism as separation from those unrighteous who will not inherit God's kingdom (1 Cor 6:9–11). But Paul's development of Christ's act of righteousness in contrast to Adam's trespass, on the other hand, held out a far larger hope, ecclesiologically and cosmically, for the reign of grace through righteousness (Rom 5:16–21; 11:15). In the societal realm, the Church embodied justification and reconciliation by inclusion of Jew and Gentile, male and female, slave and free (Gal 3:28), for God's righteousness had broken down the barriers preventing access to God as well as the barriers separating human beings from one another (Klaiber, 122). Thus "the Pauline . . . doctrine of justification has a clear social relevance; it implies an understanding of what Christian community is, and it provides guidelines to show the members of that community how they ought to relate to one another" (Dahl 1977: 108). Such application precedes the polemical use of the theme in Galatians and can be said to find ecclesiological expression even where the concept does not appear in express words (Dahl, 110; Klaiber, 192). On this view, all offices of leadership and all ministries in the church community stand under the gospel as the experience of righteousness/justification in Christ, as do the gifts of the Spirit, grace for ministering, and concepts of what is right *(dikaion;* Recht, norms in community; members as instruments of righteousness, Rom 6:13–19)—all stand under Christ's lordship and ultimate judgment, in freedom but with responsibility to others (Klaiber, 195–97). In such a way the justification of the ungodly is said to shape ecclesiology.

g. Soteriology and Ethics. The two chief concerns of Pauline passages using "righteousness" terminology are soteriology and ethics (cf. the frequent distinction between God's righteousness and human righteousness [Ziesler 1972: 32–36, 162–63, 212] or between the "forensic" and the "moral" uses). Soteriological and ethical examples of *dik-*vocabulary will constantly be noted below. Paul, of course, also had other ways of expressing his gospel of salvation besides righteousness/justification (Reumann 1982: ##192–216), though these themes interrelate.

His ethic likewise included a variety of emphases, some forms of which, strikingly, do *not* use or only rarely employ terms from *dikaioun.* Such language never occurs, for example, in *Haustafeln* or in virtue lists but does appear in vice lists: Rom 1:29 *(adikia;* cf. 1:32, God's just decree, *dikaiōma*); 1 Cor 6:9 *(adikoi);* possibly Gal 5:22–23, if "fruit of the Spirit" there can be equated with "fruit of righteousness" (Phil 1:11, on which, see below), but even then righteousness is the "umbrella" or "source" term, not one virtue among many; note also Phil 4:8 (*dikaios* in a Stoic listing) and Rom 14:17 (righteousness, peace, and joy, possibly ethical, in a pre-Pauline statement). It is to be emphasized that "for Paul ethics is not a matter of paraenesis for the justified but rather the justification of the ungodly transforms the ethical situation of the doer with respect to the obligatory good [in the law, e.g.] and its ground [God], and with respect to the doer himself and his fellows [the community]"; the "righteousness of God apart from the law altogether" is what frees the believer to act freely (Keck 1976: 209; cf. pp. 206–7; cf. Haufe 1957).

It is now clear that the origins for Paul's extensive use of righteousness terms are not to be sought in a single cause (such as conflict with Judaizers), nor need one choose between the either/or of antithetical use of rabbinic terminology by Paul versus OT (LXX) usage. Rather, influential roles were played by pre-Pauline formulas, OT exegesis by Paul (of Gen 15:6; Hab 2:4; or Ps 143 [LXX 142]:2, at Gal 2:16 and Rom 3:20), Paul's own religious experience (Philippians 3), disputes with "Judaizers" (Galatians, see below), possible Qumran influences (which at the least show how varied were contemporary Jewish views, in addition to those known from rabbinic sources), and even Greco-Roman conceptions of righteousness (as synonymous with *eusebeia*/*hosiotēs;* Rom 1:18, ungodliness [*asebeia*]; Dihle *RAC* 10: 313). Given this many influences and the wide variety of situations addressed in Paul's letters, one should not expect in his writings a monolithic single sense for righteousness/justification. Paul's refinement of this doctrine which he "held in common with others" was to stress faith, not simply Christ, grace, and baptism; he used specific OT texts so as to exclude works of the Law as a condition and to include all, Jews and Gentiles, under his theology-grounding theme (cf. Dahl 1977: 96–97, 108).

3. Paul's Letters Generally. Apart from the three letters by Paul that especially deal with righteousness/justification (Galatians, Philippians, Romans), the other four unquestionably assigned to him by modern scholarship (1 Thessalonians, 1 and 2 Corinthians, Philemon) only occasionally employ *dik*-terms. 1 Thessalonians, that initial experiment in Christian communication by letter between apostle and struggling community, and then 1 and 2 Corinthians (or the fragments of several letters embedded in them; see Reumann 1982: ##86–88, 97, 107, 113 for possible significance of such theories for the topic) are too oriented respectively to specific situations in Thessalonica and Corinth to call for any massive development of the theme of righteousness (but cf. Fung 1980). Philemon is too brief and concerned with the problem of the slave Onesimus to allow such references. As a practice in all his letters, Paul employs the noun *dikaiosynē* in preference to the adjective *dikaios,* and the noun in particular senses, not just the adjectivally derived ones of "being upright" and "doing right" (Wilckens *Romans* EKKNT 1: 209).

a. Pre-Pauline Formulas. Pre-Pauline statements about righteousness are incorporated into significant passages of 1 and 2 Corinthians. In 1 Corinthians the christological sense is found at 1:30, of Christ as *dikaiosynē* for us, and in 6:11, "You were justified." The Corinthians were likely already familiar with both aspects, and the references served as basis for discussion of what was under dispute: Christ as God's wisdom (1:17–3:23) and (in chap. 6) the community's relation to the ungodly (*adikoi,* 6:9, in a set tradition cataloging those who will not enter the kingdom of God).

In 2 Cor 5:21, perhaps the heart of chaps. 1–9, there occurs the earliest of 10 Pauline references to "God's righteousness" (once in Philippians, 8 times in Romans). It deals not only with the basis for appeals concerning reconciliation with God (5:20–6:10) and with the Pauline apostolate (6:11–7:3), but also with the Corinthians' participation in the collection project (chaps. 8 and 9; Furnish *2 Corinthians* AB, 348–49). In its immediate context, this "soteriological credo" with which Paul works (v 21 about rightwising) is expanded not only by use of "new creation" (5:17) and "reconciliation" language (5:18–20) but also by reference to "salvation" (6:2). "Cosmic reconciliation" in vv 18–21 is grounded in Jesus' death for all (vv 14–15), and the mechanics of how the formulation in v 21 is to be explained include identification of God with humankind "through Christ" (18, cf. 19), as "representative" figure ("one . . . for all," 14, 15), with an "interchange" or transference (so that Christ becomes "sin[-offering]" and we become "the righteousness of God," v 21). The reconciliation that results is the message, the content of ministry, and the ground and content of appeal (Martin *2 Corinthians* WBC, 141–51). If in v 19 "not counting (*logizomenos,* reckoning, as in Rom 4:3–12) their trespasses against them" is taken as an insertion by Paul into traditional material (Martin, 139, 142, 145, 154), then there is a reminiscence of OT verses about righteousness/justification (Gen 15:6; Ps 32:2, as at Rom 4:3, 8). Further, Paul has there introduced a "framework of justification," and this "idiom of justification" clarifies how, in reconciliation, " 'righteousness' is God both setting men and women right with himself and justifying himself" (Martin, 149, cf. 139–40).

In the contents of 2 Corinthians as a whole, the description of Christians as "the righteousness of God" (5:21) may be further reflected at 6:14: "What partnership have righteousness and lawlessness?" Whatever the origins of 6:14–7:1 (and the tendency in the commentaries by Furnish [383] and Martin [195] is to see a non-Pauline, perhaps Essene, composition used by the apostle), in the redacted letter this first of five antitheses—which parallel *dikaiosynē* with light, Christ, the person who is faithful *(pistos)* or a believer, and the temple of God (6:14–16), all of which "we," the community, are—seems to have a practical ethical sense. The case for seeing here "God's gracious gift of acquittal" or justification depends on reading in other aspects of *dikaiosynē* from 11:15 and Romans (cf. Martin, 198).

b. OT Background. An OT background for righteousness may thus appear in 2 Cor 5:19. It could also have appeared, but does not, at 1 Thess 5:8. There Paul reflects Isa 59:17 about God putting on "righteousness as a breastplate, and a helmet of salvation on his head." But while the two items of armor are kept, a triad of qualities which have been mentioned at 1 Thess 1:3—faith, love, and hope—are inserted with reference to Christians: "put on the breastplate of faith and love and for a helmet the hope of salvation." God's righteousness in Isaiah becomes in 1 Thess 5:8 the Christians' faith and love. Indeed, at 1 Thess 1:3 it was the Thessalonians' "work of faith *(ergon tēs pisteōs)* and labor of love" that was mentioned. This sense, of "a deed rising from faith," is "studiously avoided" in Paul's later letters, "when the problem of the Judaizers has surfaced," and *pistis* is never again so connected with *ergon* (which came then to imply "deeds of the law," Rom 3:28), but is connected rather with righteousness from God (Fitzmyer 1982: #377).

2 Cor 9:9 is an explicit quotation from Ps 112:9 [LXX Ps 111:9] about the person whose "righteousness abides for ever." In the original Hebrew and LXX, this is a reference to the benevolence or almsgiving of the righteous person (112:6). It may be cited here to characterize how Paul hopes the people in Achaia (9:2) will respond abundantly to the "good work" (9:8) of the collection for the saints in Jerusalem. Use of *dikaiosynē* in this way would also appeal to the Greco-Roman audience in Corinth and Achaia, for it could suggest "equality," a basis for appeal that Paul has used at 8:13 (*isotēs,* "your abundance at the present time supplies their wants, so that [someday] their abundance may supply your want, that there may be equality"; cf. Lührmann *TRE* 12: 417). But v 10 presents God as the subject. If God is also the subject of v 9 (so H. D. Betz *2 Corinthians 8–9* Hermeneia, 111; Martin *2 Corinthians* WBC, 291; cf. Furnish *2 Corinthians* AB, 448–49), then we have a second reference to "God's righteousness" in 2 Corinthians, and a well-documented Hellenistic theme of "God the provider" is in view (Betz, 112–13). Furthermore, 9:10 uses a phrase (here italicized) from Hos 10:12 LXX, God "will multiply your seed and increase *the harvest of your righteousness*" (or "fruits of righteousness," *genēmata*

tēs dikaiosynēs hymōn). Again the OT sense can be paralleled in Greek thought: "the earth willingly teaches righteousness to those able to learn, for to those who serve her better she yields more good things" (Xen *Oec.* 5.12). In context the "produce" would be an abundant collection for Jerusalem. In this "agricultural argument," Paul here employs "God's righteousness" in v 9 to provide the basis for the "human righteousness" of the Corinthians in v 10 "by establishing its economic basis" (Betz, 114). Others have seen in God's righteousness in v 9 a forensic sense so that "Paul is building on God's justifying action," and the response of the Corinthians is a token of their "right relationship to God" (Martin, 291); or "their charitable act is a part of that larger righteousness of God by which they themselves live and in which they shall remain forever" (Furnish, 449, noting that Hos 10:12 LXX reads "sow for yourselves righteousness, gather in the fruit of life," paralleling *dikaiosynē* and "life").

c. Righteousness as Salvation. This notion is indicated in certain of these passages (cf. above on 2 Cor 5:21–6:2; 2 Cor 9:9 in some interpretations; and, less likely, 6:14), based upon Christ (1 Cor 1:30) as righteousness and redemption. In the midrash on Exod 34:29–35 found in 2 Corinthians 3—possibly a sermon Paul gave in synagogues—the *a minori ad maius* contrasts include the ministry (RSV "dispensation") of death, condemnation, and what fades away versus the ministry of the Spirit, righteousness, and what is permanent (3:7–11; Martin, 58–59). This superior "ministry of righteousness" (3:9, subjective genitive, "based on *dikaiosynē*"), embodied here in Paul and colleagues (3:6), offers, according to various interpretations, God's power against death and condemnation, entry into new creaturehood, God's whole intervention in Jesus and its benefits, and forensic righteousness in human lives (Reumann 1982: ##92–94; Martin, 63). Noteworthy are the coordination of righteousness with Spirit (3:8, 17–18) in contrast with Sinai and law (in terms of "old covenant"; *nomos* never occurs in 2 Corinthians), and the connection with apostolic office. Paul's "conception of apostleship is closely tied to his conception of the gospel, at the center of which is Christ's death, interpreted as an act of justification"; in this chapter "Paul's commitment to the idea that justification comes as a gift is fundamental to the argument, and sometimes rises to the surface (e.g., 3:3, 6, 7, 9)" (Furnish, 229, 228). Related is the designation of the opponents in 2 Cor 11:15: they disguise themselves as "ministers of righteousness." This likely reflects their claim to moral rectitude and status as "apostles of Christ" (v 13) and of "Righteousness" (perhaps God or Christ; it is too speculative to try to reconstruct their distinctive teaching, if any, on justification). Paul, with primeval and apocalyptic overtones (the serpent and Eve, Satan as angel of light, vv 3, 14; Kleinknecht 1984: 292–93), rejects these "false apostles."

The phrase at 2 Cor 6:7, "with the weapons of righteousness for the right hand and for the left," depicts the mission of God's true servants in military terms (cf. 1 Thess 5:8, above). 2 Cor 6:4–10, possibly from a source, uses rhetoric familiar to Stoics and the Greek world (v 6, virtues catalogue; 4b–5, list of tribulations) but also akin to Jewish apocalyptic thought (cf. *2 En.* 66:6, virtues and afflictions in which "the righteous" walk). For "weapons of righteousness," appeal has been made to the Cynic philosopher's "weapons of the gods" (Furnish, 346) and to Qumran apocalypticism (battle standards inscribed "Truth of God," "Righteousness of God" [*ʾēl ṣedeq*], and "Right Hand of God," 1QM 4.6–7; Kleinknecht, 264–65, who also [p. 268] sees here the "righteous sufferer" fighting in God's battle). The righteousness phrase at 6:7 marks a turn from 18 items introduced by the Greek preposition *en,* most of them forms of suffering or character traits, to means (now introduced by *dia*) for God's servants to endure in their paradoxical existence (vv 7–10). While a sense of moral strength may adhere to *dikaiosynē* in v 7 (Ziesler 1972: 161), the translation "weapons that God's righteousness has provided" (Furnish, 346) is supported by connection with the Holy Spirit (v 6) and "the word of truth" and "the power of God" (i.e., the gospel) in 7a (cf. Martin, 178–79); this equips the minister for what follows (7b–10). The passage is at least partially autobiographical of Paul.

d. Ecclesiological Applications of Righteousness. These have already been touched on through references in these passages to the apostolic ministry and, through the use of "we" at points, to the community (2 Cor 3:9; cf. vv 6, 12, 18; 6:7; 6:14, cf. 16; contrast 11:15).

e. Apocalyptic Tones. At times such tones can be heard (cf. above, on 2 Cor 11:15 and 6:7; also 5:20–6:2, "now is the day of salvation," present eschatology). Paul's passing remark in 1 Cor 4:4, "I am not aware of anything against myself, but I am not thereby acquitted *(dedikaiōmai)*"—made in the context of a discussion of apostolic ministry—relates justification (v 4) with future judgment (v 5), when God, not human consciences, will pronounce acquittal and commendation.

f. Autobiographical References. Paul's references to himself can be seen in 1 Cor 4:1–4 ("I"), in 1 Thess 2:10 (our conduct toward you believers was "holy, righteous, and blameless [*hosiōs kai dikaiōs kai amemptōs*]," a natural combination in the first two adverbs for a Greco-Roman audience), and in 2 Cor 5:20; 6:3–10 (cf. 1 Cor 4:9–16), 11–13; 7:2–4.

g. Ethical Aspects. The ethical aspects of *dik*-vocabulary stand out most in these letters. 1 Thess 2:10 claims that Paul's own life among converts was "holy and righteous" (*hosiōs kai dikaiōs,* a traditional combination in Greco-Roman morality). He describes the community as "righteousness" in contrast to unbelievers (2 Cor 6:14). "The unrighteous" *(adikoi)* is a term for those outside the Church (1 Cor 6:1; cf. 5:12–13), not as a moral judgment (as if their courts lacked justice) but as a contrast with "believers" who are righteous. Yet *adikoi* can also be the key term in a list of those who practice vices that exclude one from the kingdom (1 Cor 6:9). The verb *adikein* is used by Paul in the sense of "do wrong" (1 Cor 6:8; 2 Cor 7:12), "wrong" someone (2 Cor 7:2; Phlm 18), and in the passive "suffer wrong" (1 Cor 6:7; 2 Cor 7:12). The noun *adikia* can also be employed in the sense of a wrong committed (1 Cor 13:16; 2 Cor 12:13, ironically, "Forgive me this wrong!"). The adverb *dikaiōs* is once used in paraenesis, "Sober up, rightly" (1 Cor 15:34) or "as you ought" (BAGD). The sense of "benevolence" for *dikaiosynē* (2 Cor 9:9–10, RSV note) has been discussed above. Use of *isotēs,* "equality," at 2 Cor 8:13–14 may also reflect the Greek sense of *dikaio-*

synē, though it scarcely suffices (Dihle *RAC* 10: 235); Lührmann (*TRE* 12: 418) would see the *isotēs* theme reflected chiefly in references to "no distinction" between Jews and gentiles (i.e., all are sinners, Rom 3:22; 10:12).

4. Philippians. This epistle is significant for its first-hand description of Paul's personal experience with two kinds of righteousness, that of his own, based on law, and that from God *(tēn ek theou dikaiosynēn),* "which is through faith in Christ" (*dia pisteōs Christou,* 3:9 RSV). The context in chap. 3 is warning against "evil-workers" who are "enemies" of the cross of Christ" (3:2, 18–19). Yet the content is not simply polemical but rather an assertion of true identity for the community in Christ now (3:3) and at the coming of the Savior Jesus Christ (3:20–21). Within the *inclusio* framed by 3:2 ("look out") and 4:1 ("therefore . . . stand firm"), Paul does not employ OT scriptural proof (as in Galatians and Romans) but autobiographical narrative ("I," 3:4–14). This apology presents first his life as a zealous Pharisee (vv 4–6): Saul of Tarsus was "blameless *(amemptos)* as to righteousness under the law (*dikaiosynēn tēn en nomō,* 3:6)." But in a great reversal of values he learned to consider all as loss in comparison with being found in Christ (vv 7–11).

Within this *narratio,* the proposition espoused in vv 9–11 is presented through a doubly chiastic structure (Reumann 1982: ##110–11) that (1) contrasts "my own righteousness based on law" with that from God through faith (v 9), and (2) relates knowing the power of Christ's sufferings and resurrection to Paul's own baptismal experience ("becoming like him in his death"; cf. 1 Cor 6:11; 12:3; Rom 6:4) and to his hope to "attain the resurrection from the dead" (Phil 3:12). It is possible that the background for Paul's use of righteousness in Philippians 3 lies in Jewish proselyte baptism and the *ger ṣaddîq* (or "righteous proselyte") who accepts the covenant, circumcision, and obedience to all the law (Sanders 1977: 200, n. 96, 206), as in the Thirteenth Benediction (in contrast to the Twelfth), as developed by Jewish agitators threatening Philippi (Schenk 1984: 302–3). More debatable is the assertion that ascent of the convert into the heavenly world is involved—compare "resurrection" (3:10 *anastasis, exanastasis*) and "upward call" (3:14) with 1QH 3.19–22; 11.11; 15.17 and *Joseph and Aseneth* 15.4–5 (Schenk, 303–5).

Righteousness/justification in Philippians 3 includes both gift ("from God," v 9) and power (v 10), though Paul makes clear he has not obtained "perfection" or resurrection (3:12–16); hence he directs the implication of his experience in Christ into ethical channels (vv 15–17; 4:1). The passage is emphatic that faith is the way one receives this righteousness from God: "through faith in Christ" (v 9, RSV); it is "righteousness from God that depends on faith to know Christ" (3:9, *dikaiosynēn epi tę̄ pistei*), an "unambiguous instance . . . of a justification 'pronounced' on the basis of the believer's faith" (Cosgrove 1987: 667, n. 34). Although Paul speaks here in first person singular, there is reflection of the corporate aspect of being "in Christ" through address to the brothers and sisters (3:13, 17; 4:1) and use of we/us (vv 15–16, 20 "our commonwealth").

The ethical side of this righteousness/justification is to be seen in 1:10–11, the prayer that the Philippians "may approve what is excellent *(ta diapheronta)* and may be pure and blameless *(aproskoptoi)* for the day of Christ, filled with the fruits of righteousness which come through Jesus Christ *(karpon dikaiosynēs ton dia Iēsou Christou)*. . . ." The fruit (sing.) is ethical, the genitive one either of origin (Ziesler 1972: 151; cf. Prov 11:30; Amos 6:12) or of authorship; indeed "of righteousness" may be equated with "through Jesus Christ" (Schenk, 121–23). Reference to "the day of Christ" suggests the forensic tone of the last judgment. More concretely, 4:8 includes "things righteous" in its list of six virtues, all characteristic of Hellenistic popular morality: "whatever is true, honorable, just *(dikaia),* pure *(hagna),* lovely, gracious, if there is any excellence *(aretē),* any praiseworthiness, continue to take these things into account." But the term are subordinated not to *aretē* as chief virtue (as they would be in Greek thought) but rather to eschatology (4:5, "the Lord is at hand"), the promise of God's peace (vv 7, 9b), magnaminity to all (v 5a NEB), and Paul's own teaching and example as norm (v 9a; cf. the narrative of 3:4–17). Phil 1:7 uses "it is right *(dikaion)*" in the sense of what is proper and just, although it does so in an "I" section (vv 7–9a), "right for me" in Paul's partner-relation with the Philippians in the gospel.

5. Galatians. Some see justification by faith as the predominant theme (Brinsmead 1982: 200–202; Walsh 1987: 156–64; Fung *Galatians* NICNT, 315–20), reflecting the controversy over how righteousness/justification comes about (2:21)—whether by Christ's death and through faith, or in the sphere of law, through "works." It also reflects the controversy over *who* is justified, persons of faith (3:7) or those who perform all things that are in the law, including circumcision (3:10–14; 5:2–4; 6:13–15). At issue for Paul is "the truth of the gospel" (2:5, 14), the proclamation about Christ crucified (1:4, 16; 2:20: 3:1) and about "the faith" (1:23), with which his own status as an apostle or messenger sent by Christ is intertwined (1:1, 15–17, 19; 2:7, 9). In the polemics Paul rebukes Cephas (Peter) for breaking table fellowship with Gentile Christians at Antioch (2:11–14), appealing to the Galatians to stand firm in the freedom they received (5:1, 13) and to live and walk in the Spirit (5:16, 25) that was granted when they responded to Paul's gospel proclamation and were baptized (1:6, 11; 3:1–5, 23–29; 4:8–9, 13, 15). Righteousness/justification is no new topic for those involved in the discussion. After all, "justification by faith is part of a Jewish-Christian theology" (Betz *Galatians* Hermeneia, 114–15, 119) which Paul shared with Peter and other Jewish Christians (2:15–16) and with the Galatians (3:2, 24–29; Fung *Galatians* NICNT, 112–13, 126–27). But how does it now apply to Gentiles, in the face of demands by other missionaries that the Galatians add to faith "works of the law"?

Paul's *propositio* comes in 2:15–21 as part of his address to Peter at Antioch (NIV; Fung)—or more likely an extension of it (RSV; NEB). For the first time in his extant letters Paul fleshes out what "we (Jewish Christians) know" as the gospel, doing so in *dik*-terms: "a person is not rightwised/justified *(dikaioutai)* on the basis of *(ex)* works of law but only (cf. NEB) through faith in Jesus Christ *(dia pisteōs Iēsou Christou)*" (v 16a). This negative, then positive, statement is reiterated twice more. "We too have come to believe in Jesus Christ (*episteusamen* + *eis* + accusative, which Fung [*Galatians* NICNT, 138, n. 30] thinks may be a Christian coinage) in order that we might be rightwised/justified on the basis of faith in Christ *(ex pisteōs Christou)* and not on the basis of works of the law" (v 16b). The final assertion (16c) uses as scriptural proof wording from Ps 143 (LXX 142):2 (italicized here): "for by works of the law *no* human being *(sarx) will be rightwised/justified.*" In this movement from general principle to "our" experience to OT support, it is unlikely that v 16a represents Christian "covenantal nomism" about Jesus as Messiah where only certain laws like circumcision are rejected (so Dunn 1983; contrast Fung *Galatians* NICNT, 116 n. 23). Instead, the implications of OT-Jewish ideas about righteousness and judgment, as reworked in light of Jewish-Christian formulas about Jesus' death and righteousness, are here being applied with regard to Gentiles (Betz *Galatians* Hermeneia, 116–17). Paul insists that for all, Gentiles included, the soteriological medium is Christ, not law (Cosgrove 1987: 661, 664; "the law and the doing of the law are impotent to produce righteousness," 662; cf. 3:11). The particular demands raised by the opponents in Galatia, with regard to observances the law calls for, causes Paul to stress faith (Reumann 1982: #100).

In 2:17–18 Paul defends his position against the charge that such a view of righteousness encourages sinning: "if we, while seeking to be rightwised/justified 'in Christ,' be found, even we ourselves, to be 'sinners' [in the Jewish sense, v 15, of those not observing the law], has Christ then (as opponents charge) become 'an abettor of sin'?" This cannot be, Paul replies. The premise about "gentiles/sinners" is false. The phrase "in Christ" (v 17, *en Christǭ*) introduces the corporate, communal side of righteousness/justification (Betz *Galatians,* 119–20), the new sphere of life for believers. The issue of table fellowship (2:11–14) also shows the social context and issue of church unity. Verses 19–20 bring in the positive point that justification (by God's grace, v 21a) means life. Verse 21 reiterates that *dikaiosynē* (righteousness/justification) results not from law but from Christ's death. In vv 19–20 the result of justification as life is presented autobiographically ("I," though also applicable to all believers), with reference to baptism as background ("died," "crucified with Christ," "I live"; Brinsmead 1982: 73–75, 141, 157, who sees circumcision as a "sacrament" of the opponents, pp. 139–61; Schnelle 1983: 54–56; cf. 3:26–28; more cautiously, Kertelge 1967: 242) or as the principle by which Paul interpreted baptism in Rom 6 (Betz *Galatians,* 123).

Galatians 3, as a *probatio,* presents confirmations of the new status of the justified believers in Galatia. The results of the gospel Paul proclaimed about Christ crucified, about righteousness, and about faith (3:1, 2, 22–25) include the gift of the Spirit (inconceivable without the declaration of "justified," Williams 1987a), divine working of miracles (3:2–5), fulfillment of the covenant promise to Abraham (3:15–18), and status as sons and daughters, heirs and heiresses, "in Christ" (3:25–29). One particular proof is scriptural, from the OT story of Abraham (3:6–14, 16–18, 29). Use of Gen 15:6 by Paul in 3:6 was likely necessitated by his opponents' citation of it. That Abraham "believed God and it was reckoned to him as righteousness" was variously interpreted in Judaism. See RIGHTEOUSNESS (EARLY JUDAISM), and Fig. RIG.01. Those who in Galatia stressed works of the law and circumcision (3:10; 5:2; 6:13) possibly combined Abraham's faith with his deeds (Betz *Galatians,* 139, 141) or viewed his faith in 15:6 as "a meritorious work" (Fung, 135). Paul instead makes "Abraham who had faith" (3:9, *tǭ pistǭ Abraam*) the prototype of all persons of faith (*hoi ek pisteōs,* 3:6, 9), Gentiles also being included in God's blessing on him (3:8, 14).

The negative proposition of 2:16, repeated in 3:11, is contrasted with an OT citation (italicized below) from Hab 2:4, another verse with a varied history of interpretation in Judaism: "No one is justified before God by the law (or "in the sphere of the law," Cosgrove 1987: 662), for '*the person who is righteous by faith shall live.*' " Paul's interpretation, which differs from the several in Judaism and Heb 10:38–39, is marked by his view of faith, *ek pisteōs* (vv 7, 8, 9, contrast 10 *ex ergōn nomou*), which he has defined in 2:16c as "believe in Jesus Christ." Gal 3:24 repeats that "Christ came in order that we might be justified *ex pisteōs,*" in contrast hypothetically to righteousness by law which could bring life (3:21, contrary-to-fact condition). The manner in which Paul employs the Abraham material gives a salvation-history sweep to the gospel that the OT Scriptures proclaimed (3:8) concerning righteousness and faith (Fung, 153, 319–20).

The single use of *adikein* in 4:12 ("you did me no wrong") adds nothing significant on righteousness, but 5:4–5 does. With reference to those in Galatia "trying to get justified/rightwised [conative present, cf. 2:17] in the realm of law," Paul says, "you have become severed from Christ, you have fallen from the sphere of grace" (5:4). In contrast, "we (the believing community) are awaiting (an eschatological term; Phil 3:20; Rom 8:19, 25), by the Spirit (Gal 3:2, 3, 5, 14; 4:6), on the basis of faith (*ek pisteōs;* 2:16; 3:2, 5, 7, 8, 9, 11, 12, 22, 24; cf. 3:14, 26), the hope of righteousness." Out of half a dozen interpretations for *elpida dikaiosynēs* here (cf. Fung, 224–28, who prefers "the hope to which the justification of believers points them forward"; cf. Ziesler 1972: 179–80), a future-eschatological aspect of justification is most likely (Reumann 1982: ##104, 147, cf. 398; Cosgrove 1987: 653–54, 669–70) when those things that God has declared will be fully realized, for righteousness is not at the believer's disposal.

That Paul's gospel of righteousness as salvation has implications for ethical actions is readily apparent in Galatians (5:6–6:10; Haufe 1957), but *dik*-vocabulary is not involved in the ethical sections of this letter.

6. Romans. Paul's epistle to the Romans presents the righteousness of God (1:17; 3:5, 21, 22, 25, 26; 10:3; Williams 1980) as coherent center of a letter in which Paul may reflect on experiences in Greece and Asia Minor, some knowledge of the situation in Rome, and possibly the state of Christianity in Jerusalem. This centrality of righteousness/justification is particularly apparent when eschatological aspects of the phrase are kept in mind (with Beker), and it is regarded as "a code-term for the consistent vision of the salvific triumph of God" (Soards 1985: 108–9). The genitive in *dikaiosynē tou theou* is best taken as one of authorship (cf. Phil 3:9), which shades at times into a subjective genitive, "righteousness as an attribute of God" (3:5), and which functions in other passages so as to provide for human beings a righteousness/justification that holds up at the final judgment (3:22, 24; 10:3; cf. 5:19; 3:20). It is at times spoken of as a "faith righteousness" (*ek* or *dia pisteōs*) apart from works for those who believe (1:17; 3:21, 22; 10:4, 6, e.g.; Wilckens *Romans* EKKNT 1: 204–5). The concept is not simply individualistic (Bultmann 1964, though it addresses individuals [Grässer 1984: 231–33]). It has a corporate, if not cosmic, side (Käsemann 1969), although its depiction as "power," especially as "God's power as Creator" (Stuhlmacher), can be overdone (Lohse 1973: 223–26; cf. Stuhlmacher 1986: 91–92, n. 16, 108–9, nn. 60, 63). In spite of the paucity of covenant references in Paul, the understanding persists of "righteousness in covenantal terms" (*IDB* 4: 91–99; P. Achtemeier 1985: 61–66, "rectitude by trust"). Danker (1972) has sought to show commercial "contract language" in Romans (3:5, God's fidelity to "contractual obligations"; 4:3–5, "put down [righteousness] to one's account").

One can view "the righteousness of God" (8 of the 9 or 10 occurrences of *dikaiosynē theou* in Paul occur in Romans), especially the four examples in 3:21–26, as the basis for the entire letter, or at least for 1:16–5:21 (Wilckens 1: 119–208). Or it has been argued that a chain of phrases, creedal in nature, shapes chaps. 5–8 (Fuchs 1949: 115–18):

> [We believe in] Jesus our Lord,
> who was put to death for our trespasses
> and was raised again for our justification (4:24–25),
> who is at the right hand of God,
> and who intercedes for us (8:34cd),
> through whom we have access to God (5:1–2).

A clear guide is the use of pre-Pauline formulas, likely known at Rome. The formula at 3:24–26 and the phrase *dikaiosynē theou* in the formula at 2 Cor 5:21—as developed in Romans (Wilckens 1: 207–8) and leading to the use of the phrase at 3:5 in the sense of God's own righteousness—account for the outline that emerges: theme (1:16–17); Gentiles and Jews alike under God's wrath (1:18–3:20; "our *adikia* serves to show God's *dikaiosynē*," 3:5); the righteousness of God *(dikaiosynē)* as justification of the ungodly, through faith (3:21–5:21); the effects thereof (chaps. 6–8), especially for Israel (chaps. 9–11) and in believers' lives (12:1–15:13).

The theme of Romans is stated as the gospel in terms of "God's righteousness" and "righteousness by faith" (1:16–17). This gospel about God's Son, and for which Paul is set apart (1:1–3, 9) and which he is eager to preach in Rome (1:15–16a),

> is the power of God for salvation to everyone who has faith, both to the Jew first and to the Gentile. [17]For the righteousness of God *(dikaiosynē theou)* is being revealed in it *(en autǭ apokalyptetai)* through faith for faith *(ek pisteos eis pistin)*. As it is written, "The person who through faith *(ek pisteōs)* is righteous *(dikaios)* shall live" (Rom 1:16b–17).

Apocalyptic eschatology, scriptural fulfillment, universal concern for all people, God's power at work to save, the gospel's content as God's *dikaiosynē*, and the triple emphasis on faith are apparent. Insofar as the gospel is "about God's Son" (1:3–4, 9), "the doctrine of justification" here becomes "the specifically Pauline understanding of Christology" (Käsemann *Romans* HNT, 24). The sense of the genitive "of God" (1:17) remains to be defined by later references, but the salvific sense of God's righteousness as "gospel" is clear. The words *ek pisteōs* in v 17a derive from the same phrase in v 17b (= Hab 2:4, the only example of the phrase in the LXX); in v 17b it goes with *dikaios* (RSV; NEB "justified through faith"; contrast KJV "live by faith"). These words, together with *eis pistin,* have been taken to mean growth in faith; "from the faithfulness of God to the faithfulness of believers"; the obedient faith of believers (Gal 3:2; Rom 3:22) which leads to proclamation of God's righteousness to the world (Rom 1:5; Wilckens 1: 88, 205: reception and address); or as a hendiadys for the sphere of faith (TEV: "faith alone, from beginning to end"; cf. Corsani, [1984], whose evidence suggests an eventual contrast to law and works [4:16; 9:32; 10:5–6]).

Is a part of this gospel also "the wrath of God" which, according to 1:18, "is being revealed *(apokalyptetai)* from heaven against all ungodliness and human wickedness *(adikia)*"? Some find a single process here, either in light of OT oracles about salvation and judgment (Herold 1973) or by understanding *en autǭ* again in v 18 ("in it," i.e., when the gospel is proclaimed; Wilckens 1: 102). But *gar* in 1:18 can be claimed to begin a new section, and the phrase "from heaven" is to be taken as a contrast: divine wrath is revealed not in the gospel proclamation about Christ but by God's apocalyptic actions apart from Christ (Käsemann *Romans* HNT, 35; Schade 1981: 47–48).

A number of *dik*-words are employed in Paul's indictment in 1:18–3:20 of both Gentiles and Jews as sinners before God. A distinction is made between "God's *dikaiokrisia,* 'righteous/just judgment' (2:5), which affects the wicked" and God's "*dikaiosynē,* by which he justifies the sinner" (Fitzmyer 1982: #389). Note *adikia* at 1:18 ("wickedness by persons who by their wickedness suppress the truth"); 1:29 ("filled with all manner of wickedness"); 2:8 (those who "obey wickedness"); and 3:5 ("our wickedness"). Twice the relatively rare word *dikaiōma* is used, for "God's decree" for Gentiles (1:32) and for "the precepts of the law" for Jews (2:26). Both adjective and verb occur at 2:13: "not those who hear the law (are) righteous *(dikaioi)* but the doers of the law will be justified/rightwised *(dikaiōthēsontai)*." But Paul's conclusion, enunciated from Scripture (Ps 14:3; cf. Eccl 7:20), is that before God "no one is righteous *(dikaios)*, no, not one" (3:10); "no human being will be justified in God's sight" (Ps 143:2, LXX 142:2), Paul adding "by works of the law, since through the law comes knowledge of sin" but not salvation (3:20). The law is thus declared impotent to produce salvation (Cosgrove 1987: 664; cf. 7:7–8; 8:3). Words like *adikia, apistia,* and *ethnē* (2:14, 24) represents a theological judgment that includes Jew as well as non-Jew under sin (3:9; Dabelstein 1981).

In 3:1–9 Paul asserts the particular dilemma he sees for the Jew in the face of God's righteousness and righteous judgment. The passage is cast in dialogue form with questions a Jewish opponent might raise and that were likely posed against Paul in Christian circles:

> Jewish faithlessness does not nullify the faithfulness of God (v 3);

our wickedness *(adikia)* serves to show the *dikaiosynē* of God (v 5);
through my falsehood God's truth abounds (v 7);
do evil that good may come (v 8).

Paul dismisses the last item as a slanderous charge (cf. 6:1–2); the condemnation of such people "is just" *(endikon).* In v 5 "the justice of God" denotes an attribute, that God keeps faith to promises made; "covenant fidelity or loyalty" on God's part is thus the common recent interpretation, even if *diathēkē* is not mentioned here (but cf. 9:4; 11:27). Yet the problem is that "the Jew" described in chap. 2 has "broken covenant" by being unfaithful and guilty of wickedness (3:3, 5). Paul's emphasis is, "Let God be true, though every one is false" (3:4), citing Ps 51:4 (LXX 50:6) in 3:5:

That thou [God] mayest be justified *(dikaiōthęs)* in thy words,
and prevail when thou art judged.

Paul's theodicy maintains that God is not unjust *(adikos)* in inflicting wrath on us (v 5), for God will judge the world. The solution is to point to God's *dikaiosynē* as saving righteousness (3:21–26), manifested in the cross of Christ as expiation for sins, establishing God as just and one who justifies even the ungodly who believe.

The heart of the argument is 3:21–31, built around the formula quoted at 3:24–26a, as redacted by Paul: God put forward Jesus as a means of expiation, thereby exhibiting God's righteousness as salvific, remitting sins; thereby people are declared righteous as a gift, through the redemption in Christ Jesus. This righteousness of God is now eschatologically manifested apart from works of the law, although attested in Scripture by both law and prophets (3:21, 28). It is a God-kind of righteousness, available through faith in Jesus Christ, for all who believe in Jesus (3:22; 25 *dia pisteōs;* 26 *ton ek pisteōs Iēsou;* 27 *dia nomou pisteōs;* 28 *pistei;* 30 *ek pisteōs, dia tēs pisteōs;* 31 *dia tēs pisteōs*), everyone, Jew and Gentile alike (3:22–23, 29–30). "Faith" is thus taken up in a massive way for the first time since 1:16–17 (cf. 3:2–3). God has demonstrated his righteousness in this present time, i.e., "he is righteous *(dikaion)* even in (cf. Blackman 1968) rightwising *(dikaiounta)* the person who lives by faith (*ek pisteōs,* Hab 2:4 = 1:17) in Jesus" (3:26). The One God will from now on justify circumcised and uncircumcised by faith (3:30). This momentous paragraph—which uses *dikaiosynē* 4 times, *dikaioun* 4 times, and *dikaios* once—stresses God's action in Christ's death. This saving righteousness is christologically oriented and is received by faith (*pistis, pisteuein* 9 times; see below for further interpretations). It is "righteousness by faith" for sinners before God the Righteous One (Wilckens 1: 199–202).

Does not this view of God as "justifying the ungodly" (4:5) wreck all usual expectations and norms, including that of "covenantal nomism" (cf. Exod 23:7 LXX, *ou dikaiōseis ton asebē;* RSV "I will not acquit the wicked")? Paul turns to Scripture (and in this way upholds the law, 3:31) to support his case that "to the person who does not do works but who believes in the One who justifies the ungodly, his faith is reckoned for righteousness" (4:5). The case of Abraham is cited from Gen 15:6: it is not that he was justified by works (4:2), "but Abraham believed, and it was reckoned to him *eis dikaiosynēn*" (4:3) while he was still uncircumcised, before "works of the law." Abraham exemplifies "righteousness without works" (4:6). His faith was reckoned to him for righteousness (4:5, 9), by God's grace (*kata charin,* v 4; Heidland 1936: 118–28; *TDNT* 4: 290–92). In Abraham's life, circumcision was a later "sign or seal of the righteousness which he had by faith," so that he was father of all "who thus have righteousness reckoned to them" (v 11). "The righteousness of faith" *(dikaiosynē pisteōs)* comes via God's promise, not law (v 13). The point of this parade example is reiterated: Abraham, in all vicissitudes over a promised heir, never weakened in faith but was strengthened in faith (4:19–21); "hence it was reckoned to him for righteousness" (4:22), words written for us "who believe in the God who raised our Lord Jesus from the dead" (4:24). The unit is climaxed by use of the pre-Pauline formula at 4:25 about Jesus "put to death for our transgressions and raised for our justification *(dikaiōsin).*"

In chaps. 5–8 (Reumann 1982: ##142–54) Paul goes on to discuss what the experience of God's saving righteousness as faith-righteousness means in terms of the future and the new life under the Spirit for those rightwised/judgment. *Dik*-terms are as frequent in chaps. 5, 6, (7), 8 as in 3:21–4:25. Because Christians have been justified by faith-righteousness (5:1) through God's rightwising by means of Christ's death (5:9; Christ died for the unrighteous; cf. vv 6–7), believers have peace with God and the hope of future glory (5:1–2). This "eschatological dimension of justification by faith" (Wolter 1978) lets them live amid afflictions, bolstered by the Spirit as representative of God's love. In contrast to Adam, trespass, sin, law, and judgment, Christ means acquittal (*dikaiōma,* 5:16) and life (v 18, *eis dikaiōsin zōēs*), the free gift of righteousness/justification (v 17), through Christ's act of righteousness (*dikaiōma,* 18), so that (v 19) "many" (potentially "all" who believe; cf. vv 18, 12; 11:32) will be established as *dikaioi* (at the judgment; cf. Käsemann *Romans* HNT, 157–58; "will become" [Wilckens 2: 328]; RSV "will be made righteous"). Thus grace reigns, through *dikaiosynē,* resulting in the life of the age to come for them (v 21).

Chaps. 6–8 move logically to "living out the righteousness of God" (Bryne 1981) by those acquitted or "freed *(dedikaiōtai)* from sin" (6:7), who are now (6:18) "slaves to Righteousness" (i.e., of God; Cranfield *Romans* ICC, 322; cf. 8:33, "the God who justifies"). Once " 'free' with regard to righteousness" (6:20, not bound by, devoid of, it) and instruments of *adikia* (6:13), they are now "weapons of and for God's righteousness/justice" (6:13), obedient to *dikaiosynē* (v 16), which results in consecration or sanctification (v 19) as the daily task of living out justification (Käsemann *Romans,* 183). Justification, sanctification, and salvation represent "three effects of the Christ-event," each with "a past, present, and future aspect" (Fitzmyer 1982: #398; contrast Donfried 1976). The contextual setting in Romans 6 for the discussion of ethical aspects of *dikaiosynē* in social life is baptism as means of entry into the Church (6:3–14; Wilckens *Romans* 1: 233; 2: 5–42). The law, though important to save (8:3), remains *dikaios* in its commandments (7:12), and its just requirement (*dikaiōma,* 8:4) is to be fulfilled among Christians, under the Spirit, in terms of love. For "your spirits are alive because of righteousness" (8:10, RSV) or, literally, "the Spirit (means) life (cf. v 6; 10:5) on account of justification" (cf. Wilckens *Romans* EKKNT 2: 132–33). Of all the terms which Paul incorporates in the lyric outburst of 8:29–30 (about those whom God foreknew, predestined, called, justified, and glorified), it is the verb *dikaioun* which covers everything from "call" to final glory and which Paul has discussed the most in Romans. But those vindicated in the judgment will be those conformed to the image of Christ, his cross and suffering (Cosgrove 1987: 667–69).

In Romans 9–11 and its horizon of salvation history Paul returns to the problem of Israel already posed in 3:1–9, in light of the experience of righteousness/justification for all those who believe. The problem is taken up especially in 9:30–10:21 (Müller 1964). Does God's choice, among Abraham's descendants, of Isaac, not Esau, or now of Gentiles, along with some Jews, mean "injustice *(adikia)* on God's part" (9:14)? No, for everything depends on God's mercy (9:16). One may label 9:1–23 a "justification of God" or theodicy (Piper 1983), though *dik*-terms are not used. As in Phil 3:9, two kinds of righteousness are then contrasted, that "from faith" and that involving law, as if based on works (9:32), to which Israel did not attain, though Gentiles did take hold of faith-righteousness (9:30).

Rom 10:3–4 reiterates the contrast: Israel's people, because ignorant of *tēn tou theou dikaiosynēn* and seeking to establish their own righteousness, did not submit themselves (cf. 6:13, 18) to the righteousness of God; Christ, "the end of the law" (in the sense of its temporal end or goal or both), means righteousness (Kertelge 1967: 97–98) for everyone who believes. Thus 10:5–13 contrasts righteousness based on law *(ek nomou)*—about which Moses writes that the person who obeys the law will live by this righteousness (Lev 18:5; cf. Gal 3:12; Rom 2:13)—and righteousness based on faith *(ek pisteōs),* which says, in words reminiscent of Deut 30:11–14, that if you believe God raised Jesus as Lord, you are justified *(pisteuetai eis dikaiosynēn)* and saved. The attempt to make "but" *(de)* in v 5 a connective, so that the two kinds of righteousness are equivalent (Badenas 1985), extends the meaning of *telos* in v 4 as goal only by ignoring Galatians as evidence for Paul's view and for the works/faith contrast here. (On the textual history of 10:5, see Lindemann (1982), who prefers the reading in Nestle-Aland, 26th ed.; cf. KJV, NEB: "For Moses writes of the righteousness which comes from law: 'The person who does these things [which the law demands] will live by them' "; "legal righteousness" [NEB] in v 5 and righteousness-by-faith [vv 6–8] are being contrasted scripturally. Dunn (1988) sees continuity as well as discontinuity in Paul's use of the OT here.

Although 12:1–15:13 provides specific paraenesis for those righteous by faith (cf. Cranfield *Romans* ICC, 592–94, 824), *dik*-terms are few. Rom 14:17 may reflect early (baptismal, catechetical) tradition: the kingdom of God is not food and drink (cf. vv 13–16, on Christian freedom) but righteousness (given in Christ, 3:21–26), which leads to peace (5:1) and joy (5:11), all in the Holy Spirit (see above on 8:4, cf. 8:2). The admonition in 12:19, "Do not avenge *(ekdikountes)* yourselves" but give way to (God's) wrath, rests on Deut 32:35 where God says, "Vengeance *(ekdikēsis)* is mine," which appears here in what is a Christian prophetic application (Käsemann *Romans,* 349; cf. 13:4, in a unit reflecting the political philosophy of the Jewish Diaspora: a ruler is God's servant, an avenger *[ekdikos]* or agent for wrath against the evildoer; Käsemann, 354, 358). Williams (1980: 285–89) suggests that 15:7–13 supports the sense of *dikaiosynē theou* as "God's fidelity to the promise(s) to Abraham" which he finds throughout Romans: Christ is a servant from the Jews to confirm the promises to the fathers for the sake of God's truth (15:8–9), i.e., confirming the fidelity/truthfulness/righteousness of God presented in 3:1–7. Haufe (1957) can speak of "the ethical 'doctrine of justification' in Paul" on the basis of an overall theological analysis, not via use of righteousness/justification language in the ethical sections.

7. "The Faith of Jesus Christ." The Gk phrase *pistis Iēsou Christou,* which is prominent in such passages about righteousness as Gal 2:16, 20; Rom 3:22, cf. v 26; Phil 3:9, has traditionally been interpreted as "faith *in* Jesus Christ" (*objective* genitive), as generally above; so, e.g., Betz *Galatians* Hermeneia, 117; Cranfield *Romans* ICC, 203; Fung *Galatians* NICNT, 114–15. Periodically, however, in a number of recent treatments, the genitive has been taken as *subjective,* "Jesus Christ's faith" but with varying nuances. See JUSTIFICATION; FAITH (OF CHRIST). According to some, it is the faith Jesus exercised historically and now exercises, but including genitives of authorship, origin, and object (Valloton 1960). Taylor (1966) argued that Galatians reflects the Roman legal device of *fidei commissum:* God the testator has given an inheritance to Abraham and to Christ and ultimately to the Gentiles; Christ's faith shows his reliability as trustee (rejected by Hays 1983: 213–18). According to Johnson (1982), this refers to Jesus' obedience, especially his faithful death (but Rom 5:18–21 uses *hypakoē,* not *pistis,* of Jesus). Sometimes both Jesus' faithfulness and human trust/faith in his death and resurrection are included in the phrase.

While grammatically either an objective or a subjective genitive is possible, Hultgren (1980) has reasserted arguments for "faith *in* Christ." In Phil 3:9, alongside *dia pisteōs Christou,* the phrase *epi tę̄ pistei* provides an "unambiguous instance" of "justification 'pronounced' on the basis of the believer's faith" (Williams 1987b: 667, n. 34). Gal 2:16 explains *pistis Iēsou Christou* by "we have believed in *(eis)* Jesus Christ." Similarly at Rom 3:22, "all who believe" is added. Paul never says, "Jesus Christ believed . . ." Theologically, the subjective genitive serves in most of its interpretations to make faith, as well as righteousness, a gift (Thüsing and Rahner 1980: 147–50). Williams (1987b) extends this so that "the faith of Jesus himself" *(pistis Christou)* becomes the way which Christ pioneered that which believers take as their own *(pistis).*

8. The "Pattern of Religion." In Paul's seven acknowledged letters there appears to be a pattern of religion that Sanders (1977) has described as "eschatological participation" in Christ. But this amounts to what Paul himself called "righteousness by faith" (p. 506), true righteousness expressed in participationalist categories. This Pauline pattern was *"an essentially different type of religiousness from any found in Palestinian Jewish literature"* (p. 543, italics in original). In particular, "righteousness terminology" has to do here with "transfer," how one gets into the (Christian) community, not with "maintenance of status," how one *stays* in (p. 544). But Paul's view, Sanders argues, was not sustained, and Christianity became a new form of what Judaism was: "covenantal nomism" (p. 552). This reading of the evidence indicates a uniqueness in Paul's use of *dikaiosynē* and also points to its post-NT fate.

G. Later Pauline Letters

Dik-vocabulary continues in most of the other Pauline documents, but sometimes with changes that augur the widespread loss in the Church Fathers of Paul's distinctive eschatological "righteousness of God" and "justification by faith."

1. 2 Thessalonians (Reumann 1982: #84). This epistle speaks typically of God's righteous judgment (1:5, *dikaias kriseōs*), i.e., when it is right (*dikaios,* 1:6) that God " 'inflict vengeance *(ekdikēsin)* upon those who do not know God' (cf. Isa 66:15 LXX; Jer 10:25) and on 'those who do not obey' (cf. Isa 66:4) the gospel of our Lord Jesus Christ" (1:8). Their punishment (*dikē,* penalty) is described in 1:9. Similar imagery occurs in the parousia passage (2:1–12): Satan will come "with all deceit of wickedness" (2:10, *adikias* is a genitive of origin); but all will be condemned "who did not believe the truth but took pleasure in *adikia*" (2:12). God, gospel, and truth are thus contrasted with Satan and *adikia.*

2. Colossians. In the epistle the vocabulary of righteousness occurs only in the *Haustafeln* section on slaves and masters. The former (and perhaps the latter too) are admonished: "The wrongdoer *(adikōn)* will be paid back for the wrong he/she has done *(ēdikēsen)*" (3:25). Masters are told (4:1), "Grant what is right *(to dikaion)* and equity (*isotēta,* fairness) to your slaves." The language reflects popular Greek moral philosophy.

3. Ephesians. Paul's distinctive themes are preserved far better in Ephesians, but at the loss of the verb "to justify/rightwise"; in the slogan-like statements in the hymnic 2:4–10, the verb *sōzein,* "save," is substituted ("by grace you are saved," 2:5; "by grace you are saved through faith," 2:8). Both verbs are in the perfect tense, reflecting the tendency in Ephesians away from future judgment and toward present salvation in the Church. This outlook frees *dikaiosynē* for use in the area of ethics (Lührmann *TRE* 12: 418): "this is right" (*dikaios;* 6:1); "all that is good and right *(dikaiosynē)* and true" (5:9); "the breastplate of righteousness" (6:14); and "the new person created after the likeness of God in true righteousness and holiness" (*en dikaiosynę̄ kai hosiotēti tēs alētheias,* 4:24, a combination common in Greek ethics). But 4:24 may also reflect baptismal language and thus also the righteousness and holiness given at that "new creation" (cf. 1 Cor 6:11); as may 5:9, an ethical exhortation to the baptized as children of light (cf. 5:8, 14). Eph 6:14 has been taken to refer to *dikaiosynē* as one of the four cardinal virtues or to "being clothed with righteousness" (Isa 59:17; cf. Reumann 1982: ##167–73).

4. Pastoral Epistles. These epistles preserve Paul's sense of justification as a past experience (Titus 3:7) connected with the Christ-event (1 Tim 3:16) and actualized for Christians in baptism with the gift of the Spirit (Titus 3:4–7). As in Ephesians, "saved by grace" or mercy is emphasized (Titus 3:7; 2:11), indeed in antithesis to our deeds (Titus 3:5; 2 Tim 1:9), but it is no longer necessary to say "deeds of the law." "Faith" continues in a Pauline sense (1 Tim 1:16; 2 Tim 1:12), not as *pistis Iēsou Christou* but "*pistis* which is 'in Christ Jesus' " (1 Tim 3:13; 1:14; 2 Tim 1:13), as "what is believed," i.e., the faith of the Church (1 Tim 3:9; 4:1). Righteousness is at times connected with the day of the Lord and judgment (2 Tim 4:8). Above all there is emphasis on Christians' living righteously between their baptism-justification and Christ's future appearance (Titus 2:12–14; 1 Tim 6:11; 2 Tim 2:22; 3:16). Terms from *adikein* are much rarer in the Pastoral Epistles than in the other Pauline letters. Only *adikia* is found: "Let every one who names the name of the Lord depart from iniquity" (2 Tim 2:19; cf. Sir 53:3; *T. Dan.* 6.10).

Basic are the earlier hymns and hymnic passages incorporated in the Pastorals. For 1 Tim 3:16, Christ "was vindicated *(edikaiōthē)* in the spirit." Titus 3:3–7 describes how God our Savior "saved us (cf. Eph 2:4–10), not because of deeds done by us in righteousness" (an LXX phrase; obedient performance of what God commands does not save), but by God's mercy, through baptism, where the Spirit is "poured upon us through Jesus Christ . . . that, having been justified (*dikaiōthentes;* cf. Rom 5:1) by That One's grace, we might become heirs in hope of eternal life." See further 2 Tim 1:9–10; Titus 2:11–14 (God's grace has appeared, training us to renounce irreligion [*asebeian*] and "to live sober, upright, and godly [lives; *dikaiōs kai eusebōs*] in the world"; and the last line in the possible baptismal hymn at 2 Tim 2:13, "If we are faithless, That One remains faithful, for he cannot deny himself" (cf. Rom 3:2–4).

Baptismal paraenesis, perhaps Jewish Christian, from occasions when such hymns are sung, may thus lie behind some of the admonitions, as at Titus 2:12 (live righteously), 1 Tim 6:11 ("Pursue righteousness, godliness [*eusebeian*], faith, love, steadfastness, gentleness" [LXX language; cf. Isa 51:1, RSV "deliverance"; Rom 9:30–31]), and 2 Tim 2:22. While open to many interpretations, 2 Tim 3:16, on one of the purposes of Scripture as "training in righteousness" *(paideian tēn en dikaiosynę̄),* suggests that baptismal instruction (in doctrine and/or ethics) accompanied the gift of righteousness (Titus 3:7). Clearly ethical is Titus 1:8 (the bishop must be "upright"). The statement about "law" *(nomos)* at 1 Tim 1:8–9 is striking: it is "good, if one uses it lawfully," for "it is not laid down for a just person *(dikaiǭ)* but for lawless and disobedient people, the ungodly *(asebesi)* and sinners, those ungodly *(anosiois)* and godless. . . ." The principle that "law is not for the sake of the just or good" reiterates a Pauline theme in Greco-Roman terms (Quinn 1982: #434). The eschatological "crown of righteousness" (2 Tim 4:8) which the "righteous Judge" will award at the day of the Lord may mean a crown that consists of righteousness as God's gift or a crown for an upright life (Quinn, #437).

Hellenistic vocabulary associated with righteousness appears at 1 Tim 2:8 (lift holy [*hosious*] hands in prayer); Titus 1:8 (*hosios,* after *dikaios,* as a quality of character); and in the host of references to *eusebeia,* which may accompany or replace *dikaiosynē* at times in the Pastoral Epistles (1 Tim 2:2; 3:16; 4:7, 8; 5:4 [verb]; 6:3, 5, 6, 11; 2 Tim 3:5; 3:12 [adverb]; Titus 1:1).

The developments in the Pastoral Epistles have been

variously explained (Luz 1976: 367–68, 376–82; Reumann 1982: ##188–91). Most likely involved were the change in eschatological perspective and new deeds as the church settled down in the Hellenistic world.

H. Other New Testament Writings

1. 1 Peter. Written to Christians under persecution, this letter shares many features common to early Christian thought in general and to Paul's letters, though not the verb *dikaioun.* A hymnic, creedlike passage refers in 3:18 to Christ who "once for all died (or suffered) for sins, the Righteous One for the unrighteous" *(dikaios hyper adikōn).* Another verse, 2:24, also possibly from hymn fragments in 2:21–25, tells how "Christ suffered for you" and "*bore our sins himself* in his body on the tree, in order that we might die to sins and live to righteousness *(tē dikaiosynē, zēsomen); by* whose *stripes we are healed*" (italicized words from Isa 53:4, 12). The context, like so much in 1 Peter, is baptismal (cf. Rom 6:10–11, 18–20). Here, "live to righteousness" suggests either a baptismal gift or what is right in God's sight or both soteriology and ethics. The same passage speaks of Christ giving over (himself, his cause) to God, "the One who judges justly" (*dikaiōs,* 2:23). "The eyes of the Lord are upon the righteous" (*dikaious,* 3:12 = Ps 34:17), here interpreted as the Christians, who may "suffer for righteousness' sake" (3:14; cf. Matt 5:10–11). In the latter phrase, *dikaiosynē* can suggest "for God or Christ's sake" (cf. 2:19–21; 3:15; 4:16) but more likely means "for doing what is right" (3:13, literally, "zealous for the good"). The judgment looms over all, both God's household and those who do not obey the gospel of God (4:17); "if the righteous *(dikaios)* is scarcely saved, where will the impious *(asebēs)* and sinner appear?" (4:18 = Prov 11:31). Christian household servants may suffer unjustly (*adikōs,* 2:19). Nonetheless, emperor and governors are affirmed, "who are sent by him for punishment *(ekdikēsin)* of evildoers and praise of those who do good" (2:14).

2. James. Like Paul and Matt 6:33, the epistle of James refers specifically to *dikaiosynē theou* (1:20, RSV "the anger of man does not work the righteousness of God"). But the sense is "the righteousness which God demands" (Ziesler 1972: 135), doing justice (before God); contrast "work/commit sin" (2:9). It is not apocalyptic, covenant fidelity (so Stuhlmacher 1965: 192–93). The usage is OT-Jewish, not via Paul. An isolated wisdom saying at 3:18 speaks of "the harvest of righteousness," i.e., that comes from righteous conduct or consists in righteousness. References to the righteous person *(dikaios)* who prays (5:16) and is condemned and killed (5:6) also reflect OT-Jewish tradition ("the righteous sufferer" theme). The description in 3:6 of the tongue as "an unrighteous world" *(ho kosmos tēs adikias)* remains obscure.

The famous diatribe in 2:14–26 argues against righteousness by faith in favor of justification by works, though Paul's "works of the law" are not mentioned. Involved here are understandings different from those of Paul about works, *pistis,* and even God (2:19). The author of James has also adopted a different exegetical tradition regarding Gen 15:6 (Jas 2:23), which is here combined with Genesis 22 (Jas 2:21; see Fig. RIG.01). Here, he writes, Abraham "was justified by works, by offering up Isaac upon the altar, was he not?" (v 21). In this way faith is seen to be completed by works, so that 15:6 was fulfilled: "it (Abraham's works; or faith and this deed) was reckoned to him as righteousness" (2:23). Hence the conclusion, "A person is justified by works and not by faith alone" (2:24). A further example is given about Rahab (Joshua 2), as developed in Jewish tradition: "the harlot was justified by works, in that she received the Israelite messengers (spies) and sent them on their way" (2:25). The epistle of James may be arguing against a version of Paul's teaching as developed by pupils of his, and may even represent an attempt to defend Paul's own views by stressing that faith inevitably includes obedience and "fruit" from righteousness (Phil 1:11; so Reumann 1982: ## 266–83; 413–14). Laws (*James* HNTC, 4, 16–19, 36–38, 128–34) holds that "law" in James is unlikely "the Jewish Torah in its entirety"; the writer represents a form of Christianity independent of Paul, of a "God-fearer" variety, and opposes quietism which relies on a (misused) slogan about "faith alone." (See Scaer 1983 for the view that James writes as "apostle of faith," prior to Paul in use of Gen 15:6.)

3. Hebrews. With its emphasis on Christ's sacrificial death "once for all" *(ephapax)* and exhortations to lethargic Christians, the epistle to the Hebrews employs *dik*-terms more times than any other General Epistle, though it never employs the verb *dikaioun* (see Fig. RIG.02). If Hebrews can be described as "a word of exhortation" (*logos tēs paraklēseōs,* 13:22), it also calls for skill in "the word of righteousness" (5:13, *logou dikaiosynēs*), i.e., teachings about Christ and faith as well as moral imperatives for life (Reumann 1982: #286 on varied interpretations). Some specific references to "righteous(ness)" come directly out of the OT: 1:9, God's son "loved justice" (*dikaiosynēn,* Ps 45:7, of Israel's king, now applied to Christ); 8:12, under the new covenant, God will be merciful toward iniquities (*adikias;* Jer 31:34); 10:30, God says, "Vengeance *(ekdikēsis)* is mine" (Deut 32:35); and 10:37–38 (where Hab 2:3–4 plus Isa 26:20 [LXX] is quoted). The OT text is here christologized, for it is not "the vision" (2:3) but "the Coming One" (Jesus at the parousia; Heb 10:37, cf. 9:28) who "shall not tarry." This eschatology undergirds the main point, an appeal to those (literally "we") of faith to "live by faith" (Hab 2:4 = 10:38, cf. v 39).

Such a connection between every "righteous one" *(dikaios)* of God and "faith" *(pistis)* sets the stage for the parade of examples of those who, in Israel's past history, lived by faith (chap. 11). Abel (v 4) is specifically said to have "received approval as righteous" (*dikaios,* an interpretation of Gen 4:4, variously taken to refer to his conduct or belief [*Tg. Neof.;* discussion in Reumann 1982: ##290–91]). Noah (v 7) is described as having become "an heir of the righteousness which comes by faith" (*tēs kata pistin dikaiosynēs;* that Noah was righteous is explicitly stated in Gen 6:9). The phrasing in 11:7 is not Pauline. Oddly, Abraham (vv 8–19) is not connected with righteousness, and only in the general summary at v 33 (they "enforced justice" [RSV, *eirgasanto dikaiosynēn* = Heb *ʿāśâ ṣĕdāqâ*]) does a *dik*-word appear in Hebrews 11. The concept of *pistis* in Heb 11:1 remains debated: Luther and RSV see here a reference to a subjective phenomenon, "the *assurance* of things hoped for, the *conviction* of things not seen," while others see a reference to a more objective phenomenon, "the *reality* of goods hoped for, the *proof* of things not seen" (Fitzmyer 1982: #416; contrast Thompson 1982 and O. Betz 1987).

Other references in Hebrews clearly reflect the OT-Jewish tradition. God is not unjust (*adikos*, 6:10). The name Melchizedek is said to mean "king of righteousness" (7:2, *ṣdq*). There were "regulations" (*dikaiōmata*) under the first covenant (9:1, 10), which could not "perfect" worshippers. But now, through Christ, in spite of persecution and the need for discipline, there is a promised yield, "the peaceable fruit of righteousness" (12:11). Among the eschatological expectations at Mt. Zion (12:22–24), with Jesus the mediator of a new covenant, is an intriguing reference to "spirits of just men made perfect" (12:23 RSV, *pneumasi dikaiōn teteleiōmenōn*). If read as referring to the pious of the OT, the phrase could suggest the "perfectly righteous" (*gĕmûrîm ṣaddîqîm*) of rabbinic thought here interpreted apocalyptically. See RIGHTEOUSNESS (EARLY JUDAISM). But since the OT persons of faith were not to be perfected "apart from us" (i.e., the Christians), the reference could be to deceased Christians perfected through Christ's passion (2:10; 5:9), a part of "the assembly of those firstborn enrolled in heaven" (12:23). Hebrews thus achieves a way of using righteousness terminology, against an OT background, different from any other sort of NT Christianity.

4. Jude and 2 Peter. Jude refers once (v 7) to "punishment (*dikēn*) of eternal fire" on Sodom and Gomorrah, but 2 Peter contains a dozen examples of *dik*-root terms (Reumann 1982: ## 306–14). The phrase "righteousness of God," noted in Paul, Jas 1:20, and Matt 6:33, occurs with a new variation at 2 Peter 1:1, in the address to "those who have obtained a faith of equal standing (*isotimon*) with ours in the righteousness of our God and Savior Jesus Christ (*dikaiosynę̄ tou theou hēmōn kai sōtēros Iēsou Christou*)." While this may mean God's justice or fairness (Käsemann 1964: 173), it is here "the righteousness of . . . *Christ.*" The biblical (or Hellenistic) concept may thus be recast more christocentrically. The document further presents "the way of righteousness" (2:21) or truth (2:2) in which walked such figures as Noah, who "heralded *dikaiosynēs* (the righteousness God wills, 2:5)," and righteous Lot, who "was vexed in his righteous soul" (2:7–8). But "the Lord knows how to rescue the godly (*eusebeis*) . . . and to keep the unrighteous (*adikous*) under punishment until the day of judgment" (2:9). Sinners who love "gain (or reward) for wrongdoing" (*adikias*, 2:15) "suffer wrong (*adikoumenoi*) for their wrongdoing" (2:13). God's promise for those who live in holy, godly ways includes "new heavens and a new earth (Isa 65:17; 66:22), in which righteousness dwells" (3:13), a messianic vision of justice. Note also the frequent use of *eusebeia* for "godliness" (1:3, 6, 7; 3:11, with "holy" conduct).

I. After the NT

Amid all its variety in the canonical writings, righteousness/justification achieved its greatest importance in quite early (Hellenistic-)Jewish Christian formulas about the meaning of the Christ event (see D above) and then in the letters of Paul (see F above), who developed the meaning of *dikaiosynē (tou theou)* and of being rightwised/justified to new heights by his use of the Hebrew Scriptures and their sense of God's saving righteousness, now seen in Christ. There were also significant applications of the terminology in Matthew, James, the Pauline school, 1 John, 1 and 2 Peter, and Hebrews (resumé in Reumann 1982: ##336–46, chart #335). Few NT topics exhibit such vitality and widespread linkage with the OT.

The subsequent history of *dik*-terms in Christianity is characterized by (1) loss of the Hebraic sense of *ṣdq* and replacement by the Greco-Roman sense of "distributive justice" and impartiality or equanimity (*aequitas*) and (2) the fortunes of the Pauline doctrine of righteousness/justification. Change in eschatology, as well as loss of OT perspective, meant that the early and Pauline understandings could not be fully sustained. The Apostolic Fathers, for example, preserved some of the sense both of God's redeeming righteousness (*1 Clem.* 32.4; *Barn.* 13.7 and, with future reference, 4.10; Ign. *Rom.* 5.1; *Phld.* 8.2) and of ethical demand (*1 Clem.* 48.4; 31.2; 10.7; and 12.1 [faith and hospitality]; *Barn.* 1.2, 4; 4.11; 5.4; 20.2). Typical of the dominant mixture is *2 Clem.* 19.3, "Let us therefore do righteousness in order that we may be saved at the end" (Reumann and Lazareth 1967: 88–93).

Yet Paul's sense did not totally disappear in the Greek fathers, especially when they commented on Paul. Origen called Christ *autodikaiosynē*, "Himself righteousness" (PG 14. 212B), and Chrysostom on Rom 3:26 spoke of Christ as "the proof of God's righteousness" in that "he makes others who are rotting away in sin suddenly righteous" (PG 59.9 485D). The "gift" character of God's righteousness was widely recognized (Stuhlmacher 1965: 15–16, 18), but, as in fathers like Theodore of Mopsuestia (ca. 350–428), it was held that one makes one's own the righteousness God gives by work and imitation (Reumann 1985: 635). Benz (1951: 291) has claimed that "the East accepted the Paul of the Corinthian Letters, while the West accepted the Paul of the Letter to the Romans." In any case, Augustine and Luther, among others, championed Paul on righteousness/justification. A modern OT theology like von Rad's (*ROTT* 1: 370–83, 392–95) and a NT one like Bultmann's (*BTNT*, 270–85) show why any biblical theology must focus upon *ṣdq/dikaiosynē*.

For the history of righteousness after the NT, see Subilia 1976; Reumann 1985: 632–35, with bibliography in the notes and in 1982: 9, n. 11. For justification, see McGrath 1986 and (after the Council of Trent) Ziesler 1972: 1–16. For *dikaiosynē theou* specifically, Stuhlmacher 1965: 11–73; Müller 1964: 5–27.

Bibliography

Achtemeier, P. 1985. *Romans.* Interpretation. Atlanta.

Arnim, J. von, ed. 1905–24. *Stoicorum Veterum Fragmenta.* 4 vols. Leipzig.

Badenas, R. 1985. *Christ the End of the Law.* JSNTSup 10. Sheffield.

Baird, J. A. 1963. *The Justice of God in the Teaching of Jesus.* Philadelphia.

Barth, M. 1971. *Justification: Pauline Texts Interpreted in the Light of the Old and New Testaments.* Grand Rapids.

Barth, M., and Fletcher, V. H. 1964. *Acquittal by Resurrection.* New York.

Beker, J. C. 1980. *Paul the Apostle.* Philadelphia.

Benz, E. 1951. Das Paulus-Verständnis in der morgenländischen und abendländischen Kirche. *ZRGG* 3: 289–309.

Berger, K. 1977. Neues Material zur "Gerechtigkeit Gottes." *ZNW* 68: 266–75.

Betz, H. D. 1985. *Essays on the Sermon on the Mount.* Trans. L. L. Welborn. Philadelphia.

Betz, O. 1987. Firmness in Faith: Hebrews 11:1 and Isaiah 28:16. Pp. 92–113 in *Scripture: Meaning and Method,* ed. B. P. Thompson. Hull.

Bickermann, E. 1979. *The God of the Maccabees.* SJLA 32. Leiden.

Blackman, C. 1968. Romans 3:26b—A Question of Translation. *JBL* 87: 203–4.

Brauch, M. T. 1977. Perspectives on "God's Righteousness" in Recent German Discussion. Pp. 523–42 in Sanders 1977.

Braun, H. 1966. *Qumran und das Neue Testament.* 2 vols. Tübingen.

Brinsmead, B. H. 1982. *Galatians—Dialogical Response to Opponents.* SBLDS 65. Chico, CA.

Brown, R. E. 1977. *The Birth of the Messiah.* Garden City, NY.

Bryne, B. 1981. Living Out the Righteousness of God. *CBQ* 43: 557–81.

Bultmann, R. 1933. Die Christologie des Neuen Testament. Vol. 1, pp. 245–67 in *Glauben und Verstehen.* Tübingen.

———. 1964. DIKAIOSYNE THEOU. *JBL* 83: 12–16.

Carson, D. A. 1979. The Function of the Paraclete in John 16:7–11. *JBL* 98: 547–66.

Corsani, B. 1984. EK PISTEOS in the Letters of Paul. Vol. 1, pp. 87–94 in *The New Testament Age,* ed. W. Weinrich. Macon, GA.

Cosgrove, C. H. 1987. Justification in Paul. *JBL* 106: 653–70.

Dabelstein, R. 1981. *Die Beurteilung der "Heiden" bei Paulus.* BBET 14. Frankfurt.

Dahl, N. A. 1977. The Doctrine of Justification. Pp. 95–120 in *Studies in Paul.* Minneapolis.

Danker, F. W. 1972. Under Contract: A Form-Critical Study of Linguistic Adaptation in Romans. Pp. 91–114 in *Festschrift to Honor F. Wilbur Gingrich,* ed. E. H. Barth and R. E. Cocroft. Leiden.

———. 1982. *Benefactor.* St. Louis.

Dihle, A. 1968. *Der Kanon der zwei Tugenden.* Cologne.

Dobbeler, A. von. 1987. *Glaube als Teilhabe.* WUNT 2/22. Tübingen.

Donfried, K. P. 1976. Justification and Last Judgment in Paul. *ZNW* 67: 90–110 (cf. *Int* 30: 140–52).

Dunn, J. D. G. 1983. The New Perspective on Paul. *BJRL* 65: 95–122.

———. 1988. "Righteousness from the Law" and "Righteousness from Faith": Paul's Interpretation of Scripture in Rom 10:1–10. Pp. 216–28 in *Tradition and Interpretation in the New Testament,* ed. G. Hawthorne. Tübingen.

Fitzmyer, J. A. 1967. *Pauline Theology: A Brief Sketch.* Englewood Cliffs.

———. 1981. Habakkuk 2:3–4 and the New Testament. Pp. 447–55 in *De la loi au Messie,* ed. J. Doré et al. Paris. (= *To Advance the Gospel,* New York)

———. 1982. The Biblical Basis of Justification by Faith. Pp. 193–227 in Reumann 1982.

Friedrich, J., et al., eds. 1976. *Rechtfertigung.* Tübingen.

Fuchs, E. 1949. *Die Freiheit des Glaubens: Romer 5–8 ausgelegt.* BEvT 14. Munich.

Fung, R. 1980. Justification by Faith in 1 & 2 Corinthians. Pp. 246–61 in *Pauline Studies,* ed. D. Hagner and M. Harris. Grand Rapids.

Gaston, L. 1980. Abraham and the Righteousness of God. *HBT* 2: 39–68.

Gottwald, N. 1979. *The Tribes of Yahweh.* Maryknoll.

Grandjean, Y. 1975. *Une nouvelle aretalogie d'Isis à Maronee.* Leiden.

Grässer, E. 1984. Rechtfertigung des Einzeln—Rechtfertigung der Welt. Neutestamentliche Erwägungen. Pp. 221–36 in *The New Testament Age,* vol. 1, ed. W. Weinrich. Macon, GA.

Grese, W. C. 1979. *Corpus Hermeticorum XIII and Early Christian Literature.* SCHNT 5. Leiden.

Grundmann, W. 1968. The Teacher of Righteousness of Qumran and the Question of Justification by Faith in the Theology of the Apostle of Paul. Pp. 85–114 in *Paul and Qumran,* ed. J. Murphy-O'Connor. London.

Guelich, R. A. 1982. *The Sermon on the Mount.* Waco, TX.

Gundry, R. H. 1982. *Matthew: A Commentary on His Literary and Theological Art.* Grand Rapids.

Hahn, F. 1971. Genesis 15:6 im Neuen Testament. Pp. 90–107 in *Probleme biblischer Theologie,* ed. H. W. Wolff. Munich.

———. 1976. Taufe und Rechtfertigung. Pp. 95–124 in Friedrich 1976.

Haufe, C. 1957. *Die sittliche Rechtfertigungslehre des Paulus.* Halle.

Hays, R. B. 1983. *The Faith of Jesus Christ.* SBLDS 56. Chico, CA.

Heidland, H.-W. 1936. *Die Anrechnung des Glaubens zur Gerechtigkeit.* BWANT 4/18. Stuttgart.

Hengel, M. 1974. *Judaism and Hellenism.* 2 vols. Trans. J. Bowden. Philadelphia.

Herold, G. 1973. *Zorn und Gerechtigkeit Gottes bei Paulus: Eine Untersuchung zu Röm. 1:16–18.* Bern.

Hill, D. 1965. DIKAIOI as a Quasi-Technical Term. *NTS* 11: 296–302.

———. 1967. *Greek Words and Hebrew Meanings: Studies in the Semantics of Soteriological Terms.* SNTSMS 5. Cambridge.

Hoffmann, P. 1972. *Studien zur Theologie der Logienquelle.* NTAbh n.s. 8. Münster.

Hofius, O. 1980a. Erwägungen zur Gestalt und Herkunft des paulischen Versöhnungsgedankens. *ZTK* 77: 186–99.

———. 1980b. "Gott hat unter uns aufgerichtet das Wort der Vorsöhnungen" (2 Kor 5,19). *ZNW* 71: 3–20.

Hultgren, A. 1980. The *pistis Christou* Formulations in Paul. *NovT* 22: 248–63.

Janowski, B. 1982. *Sühne als Heilsgeschehen.* WMANT 55. Neukirchen-Vluyn.

Janzen, J. G. 1980. Habakkuk 2:2–4 in Light of Recent Philological Advances. *HTR* 73: 53–78.

Jeremias, G. 1963. *Der Lehrer der Gerechtigkeit.* SUNT 2. Göttingen.

Johnson, L. T. 1982. Romans 3:21–26 and the Faith of Jesus. *CBQ* 44: 77–90.

Jungel, E. 1962. *Paulus und Jesus.* Tübingen.

Karris, R. M. 1985. *Luke: Artist and Theologian.* New York.

Käsemann, E. 1964. An Apology for Primitive Christian Eschatology. Pp. 169–95 in *Essays in New Testament Themes.* SBT 41. London (repr. 1982, Philadelphia).

———. 1969. "The Righteousness of God" in Paul. Pp. 168–82 in *New Testament Questions of Today.* Philadelphia.

———. 1971a. Some Thoughts on the Theme "The Doctrine of Reconciliation in the NT." Pp. 49–64 in *The Future of Our Religious Past,* ed. J. M. Robinson. New York.

———. 1971b. *Perspectives on Paul.* Trans. M. Kohl. Philadelphia.

———. 1980. *Commentary on Romans.* Trans. and ed. G. W. Bromiley. Grand Rapids.

Keck, L. 1976. Justification of the Ungodly and Ethics. Pp. 199–209 in Friedrich 1976.

———. 1984. Paul and Apocalyptic Theology. *Int* 38: 229–41.

Kertelge, K. 1967. *"Rechtfertigung" bei Paulus.* NTAbh n.s. 3. Münster.

Klaiber, W. 1982. *Rechtfertigung und Gemeinde.* FRLANT 127. Göttingen.
Kleinknecht, K. T. 1984. *Der leidende Gerechtfertigte.* WUNT 2/13. Tübingen.
Kloppenborg, J. S. 1987. *The Formation of Q.* Philadelphia.
Kuss, O. 1957–78. *Der Römerbrief.* 3 vols. Regensburg.
Lindemann, A. 1982. Die Gerechtigkeit aus dem Gesetz. *ZNW* 73: 231–50.
Lindars, B. 1970. *Dikaiosynē* in Jn 16.8 & 10. Pp. 275–86 in *Mélanges Bibliques en hommage au R. P. Béda Rigaux,* ed. A. Descamps and A. de Halleux. Gembloux.
Lohse, E. 1955. *Märtyrer und Gottesknecht.* FRLANT 46. Göttingen.
———. 1965. Taufe und Rechtfertigung bei Paulus. *KD* 11: 308–24 (repr. in Lohse 1973: 228–44).
———. 1973. Die Gerechtkeit Gottes in der paulinischen Theologie. Pp. 209–27 in *Die Einheit des Neuen Testament.* Göttingen.
Lührmann, D. 1970. Rechtfertigung und Versöhnung. *ZTK* 67: 437–52.
———. 1975. Der Verweis auf die Erfahrung und die Frage nach der Gerechtigkeit. Pp. 185–96 in *Jesus Christus in Historie und Theologie,* ed. G. Strecker. Tübingen.
———. 1976. Christologie und Rechtfertigung. Pp. 351–63 in Friedrich 1976.
Luz, U. 1976. Rechtfertigung bei den Paulusschülern. Pp. 365–83 in Friedrich 1976.
McGrath, A. E. 1986. *Iustitia Dei: A History of the Christian Doctrine of Justification.* 2 vols. Cambridge.
Mach, R. 1957. *Der Zaddik in Talmud und Midrasch.* Leiden.
Meier, J. P. 1980. *Matthew.* NT Message 3. Wilmington, DE.
Mendenhall, G. E. 1973. *The Tenth Generation.* Baltimore.
Menoud, P. H. 1978. Justification by Faith according to the Book of Acts. In *Jesus Christ and Faith.* Trans. E. M. Paul. PTMS 18. Pittsburgh.
Montefiore, C. G., and Loewe, H. 1938. *A Rabbinic Anthology.* London (repr. 1960, Philadelphia).
Müller, C. 1964. *Gottesgerechtigkeit und Gottesvolk.* FRLANT 86. Göttingen.
Nilsson, M. P. 1941. *Bis zur griechischen Welterrschaft.* Vol. 1 of *Geschichte der griechischen Religion,* ed. W. Otto. Handbuch der Altertumswissenschaft 5/2/1. Munich.
Odeberg, H. 1964. *Pharisaism and Christianity.* Trans. J. Moe. St. Louis.
Olley, J. W. 1979. *"Righteousness" in the Septuagint of Isaiah.* SBLSCS 8. Missoula, MT.
———. 1980. The Translator of the Septuagint of Isaiah and "Righteousness." *BIOSCS* 13: 58–74.
Perlitt, L. 1969. *Bundestheologie im Alten Testament.* WMANT 36. Neukirchen-Vluyn.
Piper, J. 1983. *The Justification of God.* Grand Rapids.
Pluta, A. 1969. *Gottes Bundestreue.* SBS 34. Stuttgart.
Popkes, W. 1967. *Christus traditus: eine Untersuchung zum Begriff der Dahingabe in Neuen Testament.* ATANT 49. Zurich.
Przybylski, B. 1980. *Righteousness in Matthew and His World of Thought.* SNTSMS 41. Cambridge.
Quinn, J. 1982. The Pastoral Epistles on Righteousness. Pp. 229–38 in Reumann 1982.
Reumann, J. 1966. The Gospel of the Righteousness of God: Pauline Reinterpretation in Romans 3:21–31. *Int* 20: 432–52.
———. 1982. *"Righteousness" in the New Testament: "Justification" in the United States Lutheran-Roman Catholic Dialogue.* Responses by J. Fitzmyer and J. Quinn. Philadelphia and New York.
———. 1985. The "Righteousness of God" and the "Economy of God." Pp. 615–37 in *Aksum—Thyateira* (Festschrift Archbishop Methodius). Athens.
Reumann, J., and Lazareth, W. 1967. *Righteousness and Society: Ecumenical Dialog in a Revolutionary Age.* Philadelphia.
Reventlow, H. G. 1971. *Rechtfertigung im Horizont des Alten Testament.* BEvT 58. Munich.
Ruppert, L. 1972a. *Der leidende Gerechte.* FB 5. Würzburg.
———. 1972b. *Jesus als der leidende Gerechte?* SBS 59. Stuttgart.
———. 1973. *Der leidende Gerechte und seine Feinde.* FB 6. Würzburg.
Sanders, E. P. 1977. *Paul and Palestinian Judaism.* Philadelphia.
Scaer, D. P. 1983. *James the Apostle of Faith.* St. Louis.
Schade, H. H. 1981. *Apokalyptische Christologie bei Paulus.* GTA 18. Göttingen.
Schenk, W. 1984. *Die Philipperbriefe des Paulus.* Stuttgart.
Schmid, H. H. 1968. *Gerechtigkeit als Weltordnung.* Tübingen.
———. 1984. Creation, Righteousness, and Salvation. Pp. 102–17 in *Creation in the Old Testament,* ed. B. W. Anderson. London.
Schnelle, U. 1983. *Gerechtigkeit und Christusgegenwart.* GTA 24. Göttingen.
Schrage, W. 1988. *The Ethics of the New Testament.* Trans. D. Green. Philadelphia.
Schulte, H. 1972. *Die Entstehung der Geschichtsschreibung im Alten Israel.* BZAW 128. Berlin and New York.
Schulz, S. 1972. *Q. Die Spruchquelle der Evangelisten.* Zurich.
Schüssler Fiorenza, E. 1984. *In Memory of Her.* New York.
Schweizer, A. 1931. *The Mysticism of Paul the Apostle.* Trans. W. Montgomery. New York.
Schweizer, E. 1960. *Lordship and Discipleship.* SBT 28. London.
———. 1975. *The Good News according to Matthew.* Trans. D. E. Green. Atlanta.
———. 1982. *Luke: A Challenge to Present Theology.* Atlanta.
Scott, W. 1924–36. *Hermetica.* 4 vols. Oxford.
Soards, M. 1985. The Righteousness of God in the Writings of the Apostle Paul. *BTB* 15: 104–9.
———. 1987. Käsemann's "Righteousness" Reexamined. *CBQ* 49: 264–67.
Solmsen, F. 1979. *Isis among the Greeks and Romans.* Cambridge.
Steck, O. 1967. *Israel und das gewaltsame Geschick der Propheten.* WMANT 23. Neukirchen-Vluyn.
Stendahl, K. 1963. The Apostle Paul and the Introspective Conscience of the West. *HTR* 56: 199–215 (repr. in Stendahl 1976: 78–96).
———. 1976. *Paul among Jews and Gentiles.* Philadelphia.
Stenger, W. 1979. *Dikaiosynē* in Jo. xvi 8.10. *NovT* 21: 2–12.
Strecker, G. 1962. *Der Weg der Gerechtigkeit.* FRLANT 82. Göttingen.
Strobel, A. 1961. *Untersuchungen zum eschatologischen Vergögerungsproblem, auf Grund der spätijüdisch-urchristlichen Geschichte von Habakkuk 2,2ff.* NovTSup 2. Leiden.
Stuhlmacher, P. 1965. *Gerechtigkeit Gottes bein Paulus.* FRLANT 87. Göttingen.
———. 1986. *Reconciliation, Law, and Righteousness.* Trans. E. R. Kalin. Philadelphia.
Subilia, V. 1976. *La Giustificazione per Fede.* Brescia.
Syreeni, K. 1987. *Methodology and Compositional Analysis.* Part 1 of *The Making of the Sermon on the Mount.* AASF Diss. Humanarum Litterarum 44. Helsinki.
Tannehill, R. 1986. *The Gospel according to Luke.* Vol. 1 of *The Narrative Unity of Luke-Acts.* Philadelphia.
Taylor, G. 1966. The Function of PISTIS CHRISTOU in Galatians. *JBL* 85: 58–76.

Tcherikover, V. 1959. *Hellenistic Civilization and the Jews.* Trans. S. Applebaum. Philadelphia.
Thompson, J. W. 1982. Faith in Hebrews. Pp. 53–80 in *The Beginnings of Christian Philosophy: The Epistle to the Hebrews.* CBQMS 13. Washington.
Thüsing, W., and Rahner, K. 1980. *A New Christology.* Trans. D. Smith and Y. Green. New York.
Thyen, H. 1970. *Studien zur Sündenvergebung in Meuen testament und seinen alttestamentlichen und jüdischen Voraussetzungen.* FRLANT 96. Göttingen.
Valloton, P. 1960. *Le Christ et la foi.* Geneva.
Vermes, G. 1973. *Jesus the Jew.* Philadelphia.
Via, D. O., Jr. 1971. Justification and Deliverance. Existential Dialectic. *SR* 1: 204–12.
Vielhauer, P. 1966. On the "Paulinism" of Acts. Pp. 33–50 in *Studies in Luke-Acts,* ed. L. Keck and J. Martyn. Nashville (repr. 1980, Philadelphia).
Walsh, J. P. M. 1987. *The Mighty from Their Thrones.* Overtures to Biblical Theology 21. Philadelphia.
Watson, N. W. 1960. Some Observations on the Use of DIKAIOO in the Septuagint. *JBL* 79: 255–66.
Weinfeld, M. 1985. *Justice and Righteousness in Israel and the Nations.* Jerusalem (in Hebrew).
Weiser, A. 1985. *Die Apostelgeschichte, Kapitel 13–28.* ÖTKNT 5/2. Gütersloh.
Westermann, C. 1985. *Genesis 12–36: A Commentary.* Trans. J. Scullion. Minneapolis.
Williams, S. K. 1975. *Jesus' Death as Saving Event.* HDR 2. Missoula.
———. 1980. The "Righteousness of God" in Romans. *JBL* 99: 241–90.
———. 1987a. Justification and the Spirit in Galatians. *JSNT* 29: 91–100.
———. 1987b. Again *Pistis Christou. CBQ* 49: 431–47.
Wolter, M. 1978. *Rechtfertigung und zukünftiges Heil: Untersuchungen zu Röm 5,1–11.* BZNW 43. Berlin and New York.
Ziesler, J. 1972. *The Meaning of Righteousness in Paul.* SNTSMS 20. Cambridge.

John Reumann

RIGHTEOUSNESS, TEACHER OF. See TEACHER OF RIGHTEOUSNESS.

RIMMON (DEITY) [Heb *rimmôn*]. The name of the Syrian god in whose temple *(bêt)* Naaman the Syrian general goes to worship (2 Kgs 5:18). The text suggests that Naaman, now cured of leprosy and a staunch devotee of Yahweh, is under some compulsion to accompany the Syrian king in worshipping the Syria deity. For this, he begs forgiveness from Yahweh. See HADADRIMMON.

RIMMON (PERSON) [Heb *rimmôn*]. Benjaminite, the father of Baanah and Rechab, the assassins of Ishbosheth (2 Sam 4:2, 5, 9). The identification of his home city Beeroth remains uncertain. It had been one of the Hivite towns which joined the Gibeonites in allying themselves with Israel (Josh 9:17) and was reckoned as part of Benjamin (Josh 18:25; 2 Sam 4:2). Speculation that the murder of Saul's son was somehow a result of his father's atrocity against the Gibeonites (2 Sam 21:2) is undercut by the biblical text's own hints at motivation (2 Sam 4:1, 8–10) and its careful identification of Rimmon as an Israelite.

Richard D. Nelson

RIMMON (PLACE) [Heb *rimmôn*]. Var. EN-RIMMON; RIMMONO; RIMMON-PEREZ. A common place name in ancient Israelite territory.

1. En-rimmon ("pomegranate spring"), a town originally ascribed to the tribal territory of Simeon (Josh 19:7; 1 Chr 4:32), eventually composed part of the Negeb district of Judah (cf. Josh 15:32, where the MT mistakenly distinguishes "Ain" from "Rimmon"). In postexilic times, Jews reportedly settled in En-rimmon and other villages in S Judah (Neh 11:29). The town is mentioned in Zech 14:10, a late apocalyptic oracle promising the exaltation of Jerusalem over the land of Judah. The phrase stating that Judah will be leveled "from Geba to Rimmon southward" seems to imply that Geba and Rimmon were then considered to be the N and S extremes of Judah, respectively.

Eusebius' *Onomasticon* located a town called Erimmon 16 Roman miles S of Eleutheropolis. Since a site named Khirbet Umm er-Rammamin (16 km NE of Beer-sheba) now exists in this vicinity, a number of scholars identified this tell with En-rimmon (e.g., Abel, *GP* 3: 318). Recent excavations, however, have shown that er-Rammamin was not occupied during the biblical period (Kloner 1983: 71). It is quite possible, however, that the toponym "Rimmon" may have shifted to er-Rammamin from nearby Tel Halif, 1 km to the N (Borowski 1988). This site exhibits substantial remains from biblical times (Iron Ages I–II and the Persian period), is in close proximity to two fine springs (hence, the name "Ain"), and has produced a pomegranate-shaped ceramic bowl. Thus, Tel Halif (M.R. 137087) now seems the most promising candidate for the location of En-rimmon.

2. The N village of Rimmon assigned to the patrimony of Zebulun (Josh 19:13. The MT term "Rimmon Hammethoar" is not a place name but should rather be read ". . . Rimmon, and bends toward . . ."). The village seems to have been proclaimed one of the Levitical cities, though the MT of Josh 21:35 reads "Dimnah," an otherwise unknown toponym. Since other manuscripts read "Remmon," it is likely that the Hebrew letter *reš* was once mistakenly written as a *dalet* during textual copying. This idea is supported by the fact that 1 Chr 6:62 (—Eng 6:77), part of a document virtually identical to the Levitical cities list, mentions "Rimmono" as a town of Zebulun. The biblical site is usually identified with modern Rummanah (M.R. 179243), 9 km N of Nazareth.

3. Rimmon-perez. A camping site of the wandering Exodus tribes, located somewhere between Rithmah and Libnah (Num 33:19–20). The modern site is unknown, but seems to lie in the vicinity of the Negeb or the Sinai deserts.

4. The Rock of Rimmon (Heb *selaᶜ harimmōn*—"pomegranate rock"), an outcropping of rock or a cave in the vicinity of Gibeah. After the ambush and massacre of Benjaminite Gibeah by Israelite soldiers, 600 surviving Benjaminite warriors reportedly fled into the desert and found refuge at the Rock of Rimmon (Judg 20:45–47). Four months later, the Israelite tribes successfully reconciled themselves to the exiled Benjaminites by sending messengers to the Rock of Rimmon, where they offered their brother tribesmen women captured during raids on Jabesh-gilead and Shiloh (Judg 21:13).

Generations later, during the Hebrew revolt against the Philistines, Saul and 600 of his men retreated to Gibeah of Benjamin (1 Sam 13:15) and at some stage of the battle camped "on the outskirts of Gibeah under the Rimmon, which is in Migron" (1 Sam 14:2). Most interpreters translate the verse to mean that Saul and his force camped under a pomegranate tree, but this is unlikely for logistical as well as security reasons. It is more likely that the verse refers to the same inaccessible "Pomegranate Rock" near Gibeah as is mentioned in Judges. The fact that each story mentions 600 endangered soldiers finding refuge at Rimmon suggests that the same folklore motif, attached to this geographical feature, has found its way into both stories.

Most commentators identify the Rock of Rimmon with the village of Rammūn, 9 km NE of Jabaᶜ. In view of the close proximity of the Rock of Rimmon to Gibeah implied in each biblical story, a location much nearer to Jabaᶜ (see GIBEAH) than Rammun would seem necessary. Rawnsley (1879: 119) proposed that the "pomegranate tree" might have stood near the el-Jaia cave in the Wadi es-Ṣwenīt, 2 km E of Jabaᶜ. It is more likely that the cave itself, some 30 m high, pitted on the inside with hundreds of small caves and holes and thus resembling a split pomegranate, is the Rock of Rimmon. Its defensible position in the Wadi es-Swenīt (see MIGRON) and its huge size make it an ideal refuge for embattled warriors.

Bibliography

Borowski, O. 1988. The Biblical Identity of Tel Halif. *BA* 51/1: 21–27.

Kloner, A. 1983. The Synagogue of Horvat Rimmon. *Qad* 16/2–3: 65–71 (in Hebrew).

Rawnsley, H. 1879. The Rock of Pomegranate. *PEFQS*, 118–26.

Patrick M. Arnold

RIMMON, HORVAT (M.R. 137086). Known in Arabic as Kh. Umm er-Ramamin, this site in the S Shephelah has been identified with RIMMON mentioned in Josh 15:32; 19:7; 1 Chr 4:32; Neh 11:29. The biblical site is actually Tel-Halif, about one-half mile N of Horvat Rimmon. The present site was first settled in the 2d century B.C.E. and the new settlement took over the name from the tell. Eusebius (Klosterman 1904: 88, line 17; 146, line 25) mentions "Erimmon" as a large Jewish village 16 miles S of Beit Govrin (Eleutheropolis). In the Latin translation, Hieronymus defined its location more precisely in the Darome (i.e., S Judea): the distance of 16 miles ascribed by Eusebius is actually that between Eleutheropolis and Rimmon, 26 km along the ancient road between these two settlements. The name of the site Rimmon is also mentioned by various Jewish sources and sages.

The archaeological results of the excavation correspond to the ancient writings. Excavations on behalf of the Israel Department of Antiquities during 1978–81 revealed a settlement of 7 strata and a synagogue containing 3 principal strata. Remains of the earliest synagogue were fragmentary and comprised patches of a plaster floor dated numismatically to the middle of the 3d century C.E. The size and plan of the building were not clear, but the many decorated architectural fragments found smashed and scattered over the site probably originated from this building.

In the second half of the 4th century, a new synagogue was built. It was rectangular in plan and measured 13.5 m N–S by 9.5 m E–W. This synagogue reused the W wall of the earlier building, but new walls were built along the N, S and E sides. A rectangular *bema* adjoined the N wall which faced Jerusalem. The floor of the synagogue was a layer of plaster laid upon a foundation of small field stones. In some areas this plaster covering was studded with small yellowish pebbles giving a granular effect. This same granular plaster was also found on the walls. The entrance to the building was probably from the S and we can assume the existence of some sort of fore court or narthex adjoining the entrance.

At a later date, sometime at the end of the 5th century or beginning of the 6th century, the synagogue was repaired and the enclosing walls of the complex strengthened. Ten pillar bases were inserted into the floor, dividing the hall into a central nave and two side aisles; the foundation trenches were carefully repaired to match the floor. This synagogue was in use for about 100 years, during which time the space along the W side of the hall became a dump or, perhaps, a storage area for broken and discarded objects no longer used in the synagogue, as well as for objects intended for future use. These pieces included several fragments of different candelabra, jewelry and personal artifacts. Buried among these finds were two small pottery jars containing (respectively) 12 and 35 gold coins which spanned a period from the 4th century to the beginning of the 6th century. Hidden in a wall in the S half of the same area, a third hoard was found containing coins contemporary with the others. Scattered all over the floor were hundreds of bronze coins having fallen, no doubt, from their original hiding places.

Around the year 600 C.E., the synagogue was repaired and brought to the final form we see today. The same architectural plan was retained but the floor of both the synagogue hall and narthex was paved with rectangular slabs of stone. These slabs were laid in straight rows in a N–S direction. This symmetry was broken in the center of the floor where the stones were laid to form a square carpet. Five 6-petaled rosettes were engraved on these stones. Above the rosettes and facing Jerusalem to the N, a seven branched candelabrum (menorah) was incised. This synagogue was abandoned some time at the end of the 7th century C.E.

Bibliography

Kloner, A. 1983. The Synagogue at Horvat Rimmon. *Qadmoniot* 16/2–4: 62–63.

Kloner, A. and Mindel, T. 1981. Two Byzantine Hoards from the Ancient Synagogue of Horvat Rimmon. *Israel Numismatic Journal* 5: 60–68; pls. 14–15.

Amos Kloner

RIMMON-PEREZ (PLACE) [Heb *rīmmōn pāreṣ*]. See RIMMON.

RIMMONO (PLACE) [Heb *rîmmônô*]. See RIMMON; DIMNAH.

RING [Heb *ṭabaʿat*]. A term used most frequently in the tabernacle texts of Exodus in reference to small circular fittings used in various furnishings of the Tabernacle. The movable appurtenances were carried by poles inserted into "rings" attached to the ark (Exod 25:12, 14, 15; 37:3, 5), the golden table (Exod 25:26, 27; 37:13, 14), the golden incense altar (Exod 30:4), and the altar of burnt offering (Exod 38:5, 7). The rings of the ark and the table were gold, in keeping with those golden cultic objects used inside the Tabernacle; and the altar rings were apparently bronze, the material used for the courtyard objects. Also the wooden bars, overlaid with gold, that served as the frames for the Tabernacle were fitted with gold rings for the poles used to carry the frames (Exod 26:29; 36:34). See also TABERNACLE for a discussion of these frames and rings.

The fabrication of the ephod and the breastplate, two special items of the high priestly garb and so made of the most costly materials and highest levels of workmanship, involved the use of gold rings (Exod 28:23, 24, 26, 27, 28; 39:16, 17, 19, 20, 21). The rings were part of the intricate way these two items were joined.

The materials collected to use in making the Tabernacle included signet rings (Exod 35:22), as did an offering made after the defeat of the Midianites (Num 31:50). A similar use involves the earrings collected by Aaron for making the golden calves (Exod 32:2, 3; cf. Gen 35:4). Rings were clearly a luxury item (cf. Esth 1:6; Isa 3:21; Jas 2:2); and signet rings also involved legal or economic transactions (Gen 41:42; Esth 3:10; 8:2, 8, 10). See also JEWELRY.

CAROL MEYERS

RINNAH (PERSON) [Heb *rinnâ*]. A son of Shimon and a member of the tribe of Judah (1 Chr 4:20). Myers states that the list in which Rinnah's name occurs (1 Chr 4:16–20) is preexilic (*1 Chronicles* AB, 29). This is because of the presence of place names such as Ziph and Eshtemoa which are not included the province of Judah in Nehemiah's time. In 1 Chronicles 4, the Chronicler is not concerned to delineate an exact genealogical line from Judah for the listed names. This larger genealogy is an historical detour because it suddenly takes the reader back into the historical period prior to the end of the genealogy of David in chap. 3.

JAMES M. KENNEDY

RIPHATH (PERSON) [Heb *rîpat*]. "Son" of Gomer, and "brother" of Ashkenaz and Togarmah (Gen 10:3). The occurrence of this name in 1 Chr 1:6 as *dîpat,* as attested in a majority of Hebrew manuscripts, reflects a scribal error in distinguishing the similar consonants *dalet* and *reš.* The LXX and Vulgate, however, confirm the reading as *rîpat.* Neither the meaning nor the geographical location of this name have been determined. Josephus (*Ant* 1.126) identifies Riphath with Paphlagonia (Franxman 1979: 105–6). Although there is no evidence for this, the identification with a region in Asia Minor, not unlike that proposed by Josephus, is suggested by Riphath's association with Ashkenaz, who may be identified with the Scythians (Yamauchi 1982: 63), and with Togarmah, who may be identified with the Assyrian Til-garimmu on the border of Tabal (Westermann 1984: 506).

Bibliography

Franxman, T. W. 1979. *Genesis and the "Jewish Antiquities" of Flavius Josephus.* BibOr 35. Rome.

Westermann, C. 1984. *Genesis 1–11: A Commentary.* Trans. J. J. Scullion. Minneapolis.

Yamauchi, E. 1982. *Foes from the Northern Frontier.* Grand Rapids.

RICHARD S. HESS

RISSAH (PLACE) [Heb *rissâ*]. One of the camping sites for the Israelites as they journeyed through the wilderness (Num 33:21, 22); Rissah is part of a list of sites used by the Priestly writer. The location of most of these sites is unknown. It is possible that Rissah is to be identified with the Rasa mentioned in the Peutinger Tables, placed 32 miles NNW of Aila, between Aqabah and Gypsaria. Abel (*GP* 2: 214) identifies Rissah with Kuntilet el-Gerafi, between Qseimé and Aqabah, NW of the mountain Rueisset el-Negin. However, any identification of the site of Rissah is entirely speculative.

SIDNIE ANN WHITE

RITHMAH (PLACE) [Heb *ritmâ*]. One of the camping sites of the Israelites as they journeyed through the wilderness (Num 33:18, 19); Rithmah is part of a list of sites used by the Priestly writer. The location of most of these sites is unknown. Abel (*GP* 2: 214) places Rithmah in an area 30 miles W of the gulf of Aqabah, but its exact location remains uncertain. Gray (*Numbers* ICC) notes that Rithmah is part of a class of names derived from plants, and may be related to the Heb *rōtem,* "broom plant."

SIDNIE ANN WHITE

RIZIA (PERSON) [Heb *riṣyāʾ*]. A descendant of Asher, named in the genealogy of 1 Chr 7:39. Missing in Syriac, this figure appears neither in the parallel genealogies of Asher in Genesis 46 and Numbers 26 nor elsewhere in the Hebrew Bible. Since his father Ulla stands detached from the preceding names in the genealogy, scholars have suggested that Ulla may be a textual corruption of Shua, Shual, Amal or Ara.

While such unique names are often considered as fabrications of the Chronicler, Johnson (1969: 64–66) suggests that they are derived from military census lists, themselves drawn up in genealogical fashion.

Bibliography

Johnson, M. D. 1969. *The Purpose of the Biblical Genealogies.* Cambridge.

JULIA M. O'BRIEN

RIZPAH (PERSON) [Heb *riṣpâ*]. The daughter of Aiah and concubine of Saul ben Kish, first king of Israel. She bore Saul two sons, Armoni and Mephibaal (Mephibosheth). Nothing is known of her life during Saul's reign. During Eshbaal's brief reign, she became the focus of Abner's unsuccessful attempt to depose his inexperienced nephew and rule Israel in his stead (2 Sam 3:7). By having sexual relations with the former king's concubine, Abner tried to lay claim to the throne by virtue of his possession of the royal harem. During the early years of David's joint reign over Israel and Judah, Rizpah's two sons were ritually executed along with the five sons of Merab, Saul's eldest daughter, in an effort to end a three-year famine that had been plaguing the land (2 Sam 21:1–14). See ARMONI. Rizpah is reported to have kept a vigil over the seven dead bodies, keeping away birds and animals of prey until rain fell and ended the drought—from mid-April until October or November. David then is said to have had the bones of the seven victims gathered up, and to have had them buried along with the exhumed bones of Saul and Jonathan, who had been buried in Jabesh-gilead, in the family ancestral tomb located in Benjamin at Zela.

DIANA V. EDELMAN

ROADS AND HIGHWAYS. This entry consists of two articles that survey the ancient road systems that ran through Palestine and that connected Palestine to the larger world of the ANE. The first article covers the pre-Roman period, while the second covers the road system of the Roman period. See also LIMES, ROMAN.

PRE-ROMAN ROADS AND HIGHWAYS

Prior to the advent of Roman technology and political inclinations, it is difficult to differentiate precisely between roads and highways. In Roman terms, of course, "road" denoted the course of local or regional travel, which tended to follow the natural configuration of terrain; which designated a route of communication that normally was not cleared, engineered, or maintained; and which was not specifically constructed to include the conveyance of vehicular traffic and often was incapable of handling vehicles. On the other hand, "highway" denoted the course of travel on an international scale, which traversed terrain of all sorts, which signified a route of communication that was deliberately opened, constructed, and maintained; and which was capable of sustaining traffic of any kind.

Now while some of these points of differentiation were present already in the pre-Roman world, roads and highways cannot so easily be dichotomized before the Romans. Certainly, in addition to countless tracks, paths, and local/regional roads, the ANE possessed transportation arteries capable of conveying travelers over hundreds, even thousands, of miles. Texts from every major section of the Near East attest to the reality and ubiquity of international travel, just as textual and archaeological records of foreign commodities exhumed at numerous ANE sites suggest that international travel was quite extensive. Nevertheless, the same term in a given language may be used to signify an entire range of transportation options, from international arteries to local tracks and winding paths (e.g., Akk *girru, ḫarrānu, urḫu;* Heb *derek, ʾōraḥ;* Gk *hodos*), and the clearing, paving and maintaining of roads is only sparsely attested in the ancient world, and often these references pertain to roads within or in the immediate environs of a particular city.

A. How Ancient Roads and Highways Can Be Reconstructed Today
B. Where Principal Ancient Highways Were Located
  1. Great Trunk Road
  2. King's Highway
  3. Assyrian-Hittite Road
  4. Persian Royal Road

A. How Ancient Roads and Highways Can Be Reconstructed Today

In view of the fact that even a remnant of a paved road or highway connecting ANE towns is practically unknown before the Roman era, and that no map of roads or highways across the Fertile Crescent is attested prior to the Roman period, one may legitimately question whether communication systems from the earliest biblical epochs can be reconstructed at all with any degree of confidence. Though there are extremely diverse and complex issues inherent in responding to this question in any comprehensive manner, scholars who have attempted to trace out ancient highways tend to follow a combination of four lines of evidence. These include (1) geographical determinism, (2) literary documentation, (3) archaeological attestation, and (4) Roman milestones.

By "geographical determinism," scholars mean to suggest that in the ANE, there were certain largely unchanging physiographic and/or hydrologic factors which determined—except where temporarily or partially contravened by geopolitics or in isolated cases of unlawful movement—that routes followed by caravans, migrants, or armies remained relatively unaltered throughout extended periods of time. In general, it would appear that the lowland areas offered the least hindrance to human movement and the most scope for the development of trade networks or the deployment of troops. By contrast, deeply incised canyons cut by sometimes raging rivers were an impediment to travel to be avoided in all periods or, if unavoidable, to be forded at places offering a minimum of difficulty. The quagmire of disease-infested swamps, the sterility and blazing heat offered by desert zones, or the badlands of congealed lava were formidable obstacles to be shunned at any cost. Densely forested mountain slopes, oftentimes with twisting gorges, were consistently navigated at passes, however narrow or hazardous those passes might have been; alternatively, where mountain ridges could be straddled for great distances without the interruption of gorges or valleys, they tended to be employed for travel in all periods. The need to commute between copious sources of fresh water was a prerequisite for travel during all epochs. Accordingly, even though we do not possess an ancient map of the Near East, the location of main roads at least can be logically inferred with a high degree of probability, especially when the principle of geographic determinism is augmented by other lines of evidence.

Literary documentation often enables a scholar to delineate a highway with greater specificity. This documentation may derive from the Bible; the Apocrypha; extrabiblical ancient sources (Egyptian, Assyrian, Babylonian, Persian, Greek, Roman); classical writers (e.g., Herodotus, Ptolemy, Eusebius, Strabo, Josephus, Pliny the Elder); early Christian itineraries (e.g., the Pilgrim of Bordeaux, Egeria, Theodosius, Antonius Martyr, Arculf, Bede the Venerable, Willibald); Arab geographers (e.g., Ibn Khurdadbih, Yaqubi, Istakhri, Ibn Haukal, Mukaddasi, Nasir-i-Khusrau, Idrisi, Yakut, Abulfeda, Ibn Battuta); Crusader and post-Crusader writings (e.g., Saewulf, Daniel the Abbot, Fetellus, Peter the Deacon, John of Wurzburg, Theoderich, Rabbi Benjamin of Tudela, Jacob de Vitry, Burchard of Mt. Zion, Marino Sanuto, Rabbi Eshtori Haparhi, Rabbi Menahem, Ludolph Von Suchem, John Poloner, Felix Fabri); and early modern to modern pioneers or geographers (e.g., Quaresmio, van Kootwijck, Seetzen, Burchardt, Robinsons, Niebuhr, Smith, Thomsen, Ritter, Tobler, Conder, Abel, Musil, Dalman, Albright, Glueck). Some of these literary sources attempt to survey a portion of land or an itinerary route using both distance and direction; these sources may cite in the equivalent of miles or hours/time the distance between two or more known points in a way that can be reconstructed only by presupposing a particular intermediate course (e.g., Old Babylonian itinerary texts; Old Assyrian caravan and *dātum* ["caravan tax"] texts; Hittite itinerary texts; Neo-Assyrian royal annals; Herodotus' or Xenophon's descriptions of the Persian Royal Road; Greek and Roman itineraries; Eusebius's *Onomasticon*). At times these sources may describe a route in terms of intervening natural terrain (e.g., along a certain bank of a given river; near a canyon, ford, tar pit, or oasis; adjacent to a named canal, island, or mountain) or a noteworthy point of interest along the way. Towns along a route may be described as forming part of a certain district or as being contiguous to a given province, sharing common grazing lands, sending communications via fire signals, or coming simultaneously under the control of a certain king. Approximate distances between towns, together with a presumed route, may be inferred from texts which speak of a king or a courier taking his daily rations at point A on one day, at point B on the next, at point C on the third day, and so on. An army or caravan may be given a prescribed number of days' rations in order to undertake a particular journey, or a specific trip is said to have been completed in an expressed number of days. As a group, these sources were not composed for the purpose of enabling someone to trace out absolutely ascertainable highways. They are extremely wide-ranging sources; the geographical details they provide are many, varied and occasionally mistaken; and they do not offer the same degree of detail for all regions within the ANE. Still, the cumulative value of these sources is critical, because they often supply precise details upon which a road or highway can be plausibly reconstructed, or they will give a nuance that can be gainfully employed when combined with other lines of evidence.

In addition to geographical determinism and literary documentation, archaeological attestation can help reconstruct ancient roads and highways. Identifying an archaeological site as a result of unambiguous data exhumed from the ground makes possible a more precise understanding of literary texts which mention the place, and provides a fixed geographical point. For example, because Laish/Dan (Tel Dan) was positively identified from an inscription excavated at the site, greater specificity is automatically conferred upon journeys like those of Abraham (Genesis 14), Ben-hadad I (1 Kings 15; 2 Chronicles 16), and upon texts detailing the itinerary of tin traders which mention this place as a stop along the route (other Canaanite towns identified by this means are somewhat limited [e.g., Arad, Beth-shan, Gezer, Gibeon, Lachish, Taanach], but the phenomenon is rather common in Syro-Mesopotamia). Even where the ancient name of a town is unknown, archaeological remains can bespeak the type of occupation the site may have experienced, which once again could be helpful in reconstructing routes. A palace unearthed on a site, for instance, may allow the inference that a royal or provincial capital was involved (e.g., Tell Brak in the Habur triangle), whereas a small but nevertheless heavily fortified site may suggest a garrison or fortress town (e.g., Tell Barri and Tell Majdal in E Syria). A discernible sequence of a similar type of site, such as the string of New Kingdom Egyptian forts discovered SW of Gaza (Gardiner 1920: 99–116; Oren 1982–83: 20–24; 1984: 7–44; cf. bas reliefs of Seti I [*ANEP,* 106]), may enable one to trace out the probable regional course of a roadway. On a wider scale, archaeology may disclose settlement patterns during particular periods. For example, many MB Age sites within Canaan were adjacent to established transportation arteries, whereas this does not appear to have been the case for EB Age settlements. Similarly, a cluster of MB Age settlements aligned the banks of the Upper Habur River in Syria, whereas no such concentration is known immediately before or after this era. This kind of information is useful if settlement patterns can be linked to causes of movement to the area. For example, should movement to these Middle Bronze sites be ascribable to migrations and should emigration location(s) be known, this might presuppose certain routes which were capable of sustaining domesticated animals with pasturage and migrants with food, while at the same time virtually eliminating other routes. There were, of course, many possible climatological or sociological factors that produced migrations in antiquity, but the point remains that people and animals had to eat off the land as they moved. Or second, should movement to these sites be archaeologically linked to trade—possibly as a result of recovered objects that were foreign to the region (e.g., Egyptian scarabs; cylinder seals in Canaan) or of trading commodities that were not native to the entire ANE (e.g., tin; amber; cloves; cinnamon; spikenard; silk; cotton)—different criteria for reconstructing highways would then obtain. The geographical source of these objects or commodities, and the date(s) for the passage from one point to another, could suggest who was involved, where markets and intermediate *entrepôt* were located, and therefore, what the possible routes were. And where such trade was carried on for extended periods, somewhat fixed commodity routes can be traced (e.g., Baltic amber route from Europe; silk route from SE Asia; spice route from W Saudi Arabia). Often this kind of archaeological evidence can be nuanced by literary documentation, as in the case of tin itinerary texts which spell out itinerary stations across the Fertile Crescent in the MB

Age. Thirdly, should movement to these sites be linked archaeologically to military invasion (e.g., discovery of a monumental victory stele, or of a destruction layer that can be synchronized with an earthen rampart constructed against the exterior of a city wall), yet a third set of criteria might be implied. The demands of military strategy, troop maintenance, and material procurement were such that some areas would be nearly immune to any army. Archaeology most recently has been helpful to scholars who are on a quest to trace out ancient roads and highways by providing aerial photographs that can detect rudiments or even short segments of roadways that have not become completely obliterated.

A fourth line of evidence for reconstructing ancient roads and highways is Roman milestones, though erecting guideposts along roadways predates the Roman period (Olmstead 1964: 271, 334, 555–56; Jer 31:21). For Roman milestones in Canaan, see Thomsen (1917), ʾAvi-Yonah (1936), Goodchild (1948–49), Dar and Applebaum (1973), Isaac and Roll (1976, 1982) and Roll (1983); for Roman milestones in Asia Minor, consult French (1981–88). To date, between 450 and 500 milestones have been found in modern Israel, of which about 120 bear inscriptions. These date as early as A.D. 69 (Vespasian), though specimens dating as early as A.D. 56 are known from modern Lebanon, and early reports of road repairs are recorded on milestones recovered from Jordan. These milestones precisely mark the location of Roman highways, which frequently followed the course of much earlier roads and highways. Locations and inscriptions of milestones give evidence that certain towns were linked in the same sequence as recorded in earlier literature. For example, some 25 milestones representing 20 different mile-stations have been discovered along a stretch of the Roman coastal highway between Syrian Antioch and Ptolemais (OT Acco). Inasmuch as some of the same towns located along that highway were said to have been visited by Shalmaneser III on the return from his campaign in Israel (841 B.C.)—a campaign in which the Israelite monarch Jehu was required to pay tribute (*LAR* 1:243)—the milestones enable one to discern the road employed by the Assyrian monarch. In this case, the correct route of his campaign was confirmed by the discovery of Shalmaneser's victory monument carved into a cliff alongside the mouth of the Dog River (Nahr el-Kalb), just S of Byblos (cf. Astour 1971: 383–89). Similarly, these same milestones enable one to configure the opening phases of Sennacherib's famous 3d campaign (701 B.C.), in which the Assyrian boasts that he "shut up Hezekiah in Jerusalem like a bird in a cage" (*ANET,* 287). Likewise these stones permit one to trace out the course through N Canaan taken by Ramses II, Tiglath-pileser III, Esarhaddon, Alexander the Great, Cestius Gallus, Vespasian, and the Pilgrim of Bordeaux.

B. Where Principal Ancient Highways Were Located

For studies on the location of ancient roads of Babylonia and Assyria, see Sachau (1882), Musil (1927), Stein (1940), Lewy (1952), Goetze (1953; 1964), Jacobsen (1958), Leemans (1960), Hallo (1964), Oppenheim (1970), and Sarianidi (1971); for roads of Syria, consult Dussaud (1927), van Liere and Lauffray (1954–55), Moortgat (1959), Kessler (1980), and Beitzel (1990); for roads of Egypt, refer to Brugsch (1879), Simons (1937), Helck (1971), and Murnane (1985); for roads of Canaan, see Dalman (1916), *WHAB,* Forbes (1965: 131–92), *LBHG,* 43–63, Boraas (*HBD,* 1086–91), and Dorsey (1990); and for roads of Asia Minor, consult Anderson (1897), Gelb (1935), Woodbury (1941), Garstang (1943), Goetze (1957), Calder and Bean (1958), Birmingham (1961), Starr (1963), Mellaart (1968), and Winfield (1977).

1. Great Trunk Road. What was unquestionably the most important highway in the ANE is sometimes referred to as the Great Trunk Road; it passed from Egypt to Babylonia and to frontiers beyond, and vitally linked every part of the Fertile Crescent in all periods. See Fig. ROA.01. This highway began at Memphis (Noph), near the base of the Nile delta, and passed the Egyptian towns of Raᶜamses (Tell ed-Dabᶜa) and Sile (Tell Abu Seifeh?) before arriving at Gaza. Gaza was a fortified emplacement on the edge of Canaan that was an important Egyptian provincial capital and that sometimes served as a launching pad for Egyptian campaigns through Palestine and Syria. This southwestern-most sector of the highway was of paramount importance to Egyptian security: It was called the "way of Horus" in Egyptian literature (e.g., Sinuhe; Merikare; Papyrus Anastasi I, *ANET,* 21, 416, 478, respectively). In the Bible this segment of the road was known as the "way to the land of the Philistines" (Exod 13:17).

From Gaza the highway stretched to Aphek/Antipatris, located at the springs of the Yarkon River; the effusion of these springs constituted a serious obstacle to movement, forcing most traffic to its inland (E) side. See Fig. ROA.02. Continuing in a northward direction and skirting the menacing sand dunes and seasonal marsh of the Sharon plain, the roadway was inevitably confronted by the barrier of Mt. Carmel. Several passes through Mt. Carmel afforded passage from the Sharon plain to the Jezreel Valley on the N. The shortest of these passes, known today as the Aruna pass (Nahal ᶜIron), was the one most frequently used. The N end of this pass, where it opened into the Jezreel Valley, was dominated by the instalation city of Megiddo. This passageway was of major importance in every historical period without exception; it is not an exaggeration to assert that it was one of the most militarily strategic points in all the SW Fertile Crescent.

At Megiddo, the highway broke into at least three branches. One branch led to the Mediterranean Sea at Acco, and then ran northward along the Sea as far as Syrian Antioch (i.e., the highway of the milestones cited above). A second option from Megiddo turned eastward, following the contour of the N flanks of the Mt. Carmel and Mt. Gilboa ranges, before arriving at the strongly garrisoned city of Beth-shan, across the mouth of the Yarmuk River. This section of the highway most likely ran along the edge of the Jezreel Valley during the dry season, but took to the higher ground to avoid the marshiness during the winter months. But at Beth-shan, the highway veered N and proceeded up the Jordan River valley for about 15 miles, before it came to the S end of the Sea of Galilee. It then extended northward along the W shore of the sea as far as Chinnereth/Gennesaret, near Capernaum. (By the NT era, many travelers would have crossed the Jordan River just N of Beth-shan, and made their way across the Yarmuk River valley and the Golan plateau

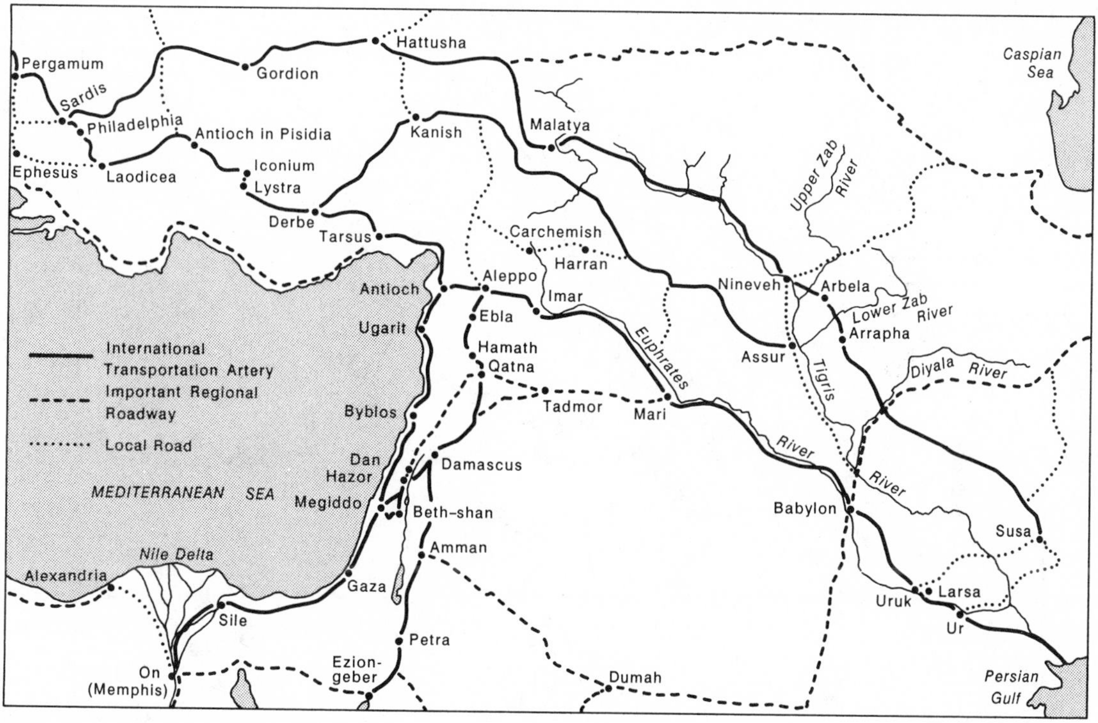

ROA.01. Map of international road system in ANE.

before arriving at Damascus.) A third option from Megiddo stretched diagonally across the Jezreel Valley on a line created by a volcanic causeway. The highway passed between Mt. Moreh and the hills of Nazareth and skirted Mt. Tabor's SE perimeter, before beginning a northward trek as far as the Horns of Hattin. From there, the road veered eastward, traversed the Arbel Pass with its sheer cliffs, finally bursting onto the plain along the NW shore of the Sea of Galilee, where it joined the highway from Beth-shan. This third option may have seen limited usage throughout the rainy seasons of the OT era and, in any event, it underwent a slightly circuitous modification in the Roman period; this branch is not pictured on the Peutinger map, the sole surviving specimen of a road map from the Roman era. See next article.

At Chinnereth/Gennesaret, the highway proceeded up the W flank of the Rosh Pinna dam, a volcanic blockage responsible for creating the Huleh swampland, and approached the preeminent fortress city of Hazor, which guarded Canaan's northernmost sectors. One of the largest tells in all of Canaan, Hazor appears to have served as a provincial capital during the Late Bronze Age; the city figures prominently in Egyptian literature of the period, in the tablets from Tell el-Amarna, and in the Bible (Josh 11:10). From Hazor, the highway turned NE in the direction of Damascus, hugging the outliers of the Anti-lebanon range and attempting to avoid the basaltic land surface of the upper Golan and the Hauran. From Damascus, the road continued its northward trek along the E slopes of the Anti-Lebanon as far as the city of Qatna, from which the highway essentially followed the course of the Orontes River as far as Hamath, where it set off on a N course, passing Ebla and arriving at Aleppo. There the roadway curved sharply to the E and ran to the city of Imar/Emar, located along the W bank of the Euphrates River. The highway then followed the Euphrates River flood plain to a point just N of Babylon, where the river could more easily be forded. Continuing southward through Babylonia, the highway trekked past Uruk and Ur, before finally arriving at the head of the Persian Gulf.

2. King's Highway. Another road that intersected Bible lands was known in the OT as the King's Highway (Num 20:17; 21:22; cf. *CAD* H: 108a *ḫarrān šarri*] for how this expression can be applied to a number of Mesopotamian roads) and outside the Bible as the Sultan's Highway or Trajan's Highway (Via Nova Traiana). It was the Emperor Trajan who converted this route from a road into a bona fide highway in the 2d century A.D. The highway stretched from the head of the Red Sea near Ezion-geber and essentially rode the watershed of Edom and Moab, passing the cities of Bozrah, Kir-hareseth, Dibon and Heshbon, before coming to Amman. See Figs. ROA.01 and ROA.02. It made its way from Amman across the Gilead and Bashan plateaus to Damascus, where it joined the Great Trunk Road.

3. Assyrian-Hittite Road. A highway to carry Assyrian

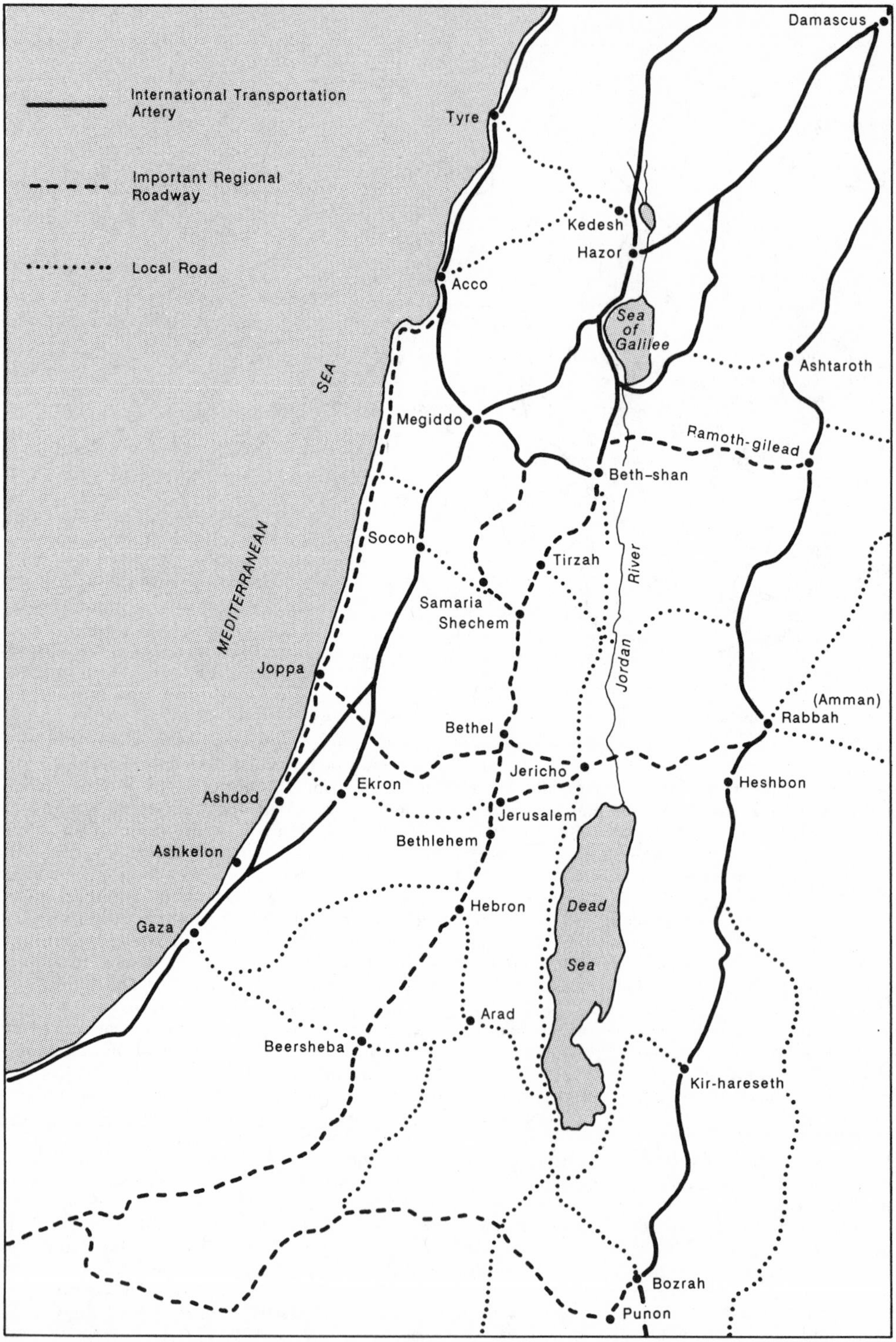

ROA.02. Map of ancient road system in Palestine.

economic and military interests into Asia Minor is known from the early 2d millennium B.C. From any of the cities which alternately served as the Assyrian capital, the highway most likely swept westward as far as the Wadi Tharthar. From there, it essentially followed the contour of the wadi as far as the S edge of the mountain (Jebel) Sinjar, where the highway veered W and went to the Habur River. Following the northwestward course of that river valley past Tell Halaf to a place near modern Samsat, where the Euphrates River was easily crossed, the highway then cut through a major pass in the Taurus mountain range, passed through the Elbistan plain, staying fairly well clear of the headwaters of the Ceyhan River, and eventually came to the strategic Hittite city of Kanish. See Fig. ROA.01. From Kanish, the highway proceeded across the central Anatolian plateau, past the cities of Derbe, Lystra, Iconium, and Antioch in Pisidia, before ending in the direction of the Aegean Sea. Along its descent to the Aegean, the highway intersected Laodicea, Philadelphia, Sardis, and Pergamum. From Pergamum the roadway ran parallel with the Aegean coastline as far as the city of Troy, which was situated on the threshold of Europe.

4. Persian Royal Road. Herodotus (5.52–54) describes a route which he calls the "Royal Road" (cf. *CAD* G: 90b [*girri šarri*] for a similar expression in Akk); his delineation does not always contain sufficient or precise detail as to enable one to trace out a specific course, and in at least one place his account is completely garbled. Nevertheless, he speaks of a road that ultimately linked the cities of Sardis (W Asia Minor) and Susa (Persia), one that was joined by a network of hostelries and some 111 intermediate stages (for Assyrian evidence of such stages, see Ephᶜal 1986: 104, a road that stretched about 1,500 miles and took almost three months to traverse on foot, though the distance could be covered by the rapid courier system in only nine days (Herodotus 8.98; cf. Esth 3:13–15; 8:10, 13–14). From Sardis, with its connection to the Aegean Sea and points W, the road ran through the provinces of Lydia and Phrygia as far as the Halys River where, the historian notes, there was a strong fortress. See Fig. ROA.01. This segment, therefore, is likely to have passed near to Gordium and modern Ankara, before traversing Cappadocia by a loop and arriving at the Euphrates River at modern Malatya. Crossing the Euphrates at the direct ford there, the road then navigated two high passes within the Taurus mountain range and proceeded southeasterly to the city of Diyarbekir, where the Tigris could more easily be ferried. Once on the E side of the Tigris, the road more or less followed the course of that river valley, being hemmed in by the adjacent mountain ranges, past a few other streams which feed the Tigris, as far as the vicinity of Nineveh. Taking advantage there of receding mountains and an extended steppe land to the E, which is really a continuation of the Mesopotamian plain, the road set off on a SE course in the direction of Arbela, crossing the Upper Zab (called the "Tigris" by Herodotus) along the way. Continuing along the W outliers of the Zagros mountains, the roadway passed the city of Arrapha (modern Kirkuk), crossed the Diyala ("Gyndes" of Herodotus) and Kerkha ("Choaspes" of Herodotus) Rivers, and eventually came to the important city of Susa, situated on the W bank of the Karun River.

Xenophon (*Anabasis* 1.1–10; cf. *Cyropaedia* 8.6.17–18) gives the important S branch of this road, which fairly closely followed the course of the westernmost sector of the earlier Assyrian-Hittite road past the cities of Antioch in Pisidia and Iconium, as far as Derbe. From this city, however, the Persian roadway continued eastward and navigated the mighty Taurus range through the slender Cilician Gates, proceeding S past Tarsus and around to Syrian Antioch. The road turned sharply at Antioch, and advanced E to Aleppo, where it joined the Great Trunk Road and ran to points E.

Bibliography

Anderson, J. G. C. 1897. The Road-System of Eastern Asia Minor with the Evidence of Byzantine Campaigns. *JHS* 17: 22–44.

Astour, M. C. 1971. 841 B.C.: The First Assyrian Invasion of Israel. *JAOS* 91: 383–89.

Avi-Yonah, M. 1936. Map of Roman Palestine. *QDAP* 5: 139–93.

Beitzel, B. J. 1990. The Old Assyrian Caravan Road According to Geographical Notices Contained in the Royal Archives of Mari. Pp. 35–57 in *Mari at 50*, ed. G. D. Young. Winona Lake, IN.

Birmingham, J. M. 1961. The Overland Route Across Anatolia in the Eighth and Seventh Centuries B.C. *AnSt* 11: 185–95.

Brugsch, H. K. 1879. *Dictionnaire géographique de l'ancienne Égypte*. Leipzig.

Calder, W. M., and Bean, G. E. 1958. *A Classical Map of Asia Minor*. London.

Dalman, G. 1916. Palästina als Heerstrase im Altertum und in der Gegenwart. *PJ* 12: 15–36.

Dar, S., and Applebaum, S. 1973. The Road from Antipatris to Caesarea. *PEQ* 93: 43–60.

Dorsey, D. A. 1990. *Roads and Highways of Ancient Israel*. Baltimore.

Dussaud, R. 1927. *Topographie historique de la Syrie antique et médiévale*. Bibliothèque archéologique et historique 4. Paris.

Ephᶜal, I. 1986. On Warfare and Military Control in the Ancient Near Eastern Empires: A Research Outline. Pp. 88–106 in *History, Historiography and Interpretation*, ed. H. Tadmor and M. Weinfeld. Jerusalem.

Forbes, R. J. 1965. *Studies in Ancient Technology II*. Leiden.

French, D. 1981–88. *Roman Roads and Milestones of Asia Minor*. 2 vols. London.

Gardiner, A. H. 1920. The Ancient Military Road between Egypt and Palestine. *JEA* 6: 99–116.

Garstang, J. 1943. Hittite Military Roads in Asia Minor. *AJA* 47: 35–62.

Gelb, I. J. 1935. *Inscriptions from Alishar and Vicinity*. OIP 27. Chicago.

Goetze, A. 1953. An Old Babylonian Itinerary. *JCS* 7: 51–72.

———. 1957. The Roads of Northern Cappadocia in Hittite Times. *Revue hittite et asianique* 15: 91–103.

———. 1964. Remarks on the Old Babylonian Itinerary. *JCS* 18: 114–19.

Goodchild, R. G. 1948–49. The Coastal Road of Phoenicia and Its Roman Milestones. *Berytus* 9: 91–127.

Hallo, W. W. 1964. The Road to Emar. *JCS* 18: 57–88.

Helck, H. W. 1971. *Die Beziehungen Ägyptens zu Vorderasien im 3. und 2. Jahrtausend v. Chr.* Wiesbaden.

Isaac, B. H., and Roll, I. 1976. A Milestone of A.D. 69 from Judaea: the Elder Trajan and Vespasian. *JRS* 66: 15–19.

———. 1982. *Roman Roads in Judaea I*. BARIS. Oxford.

Jacobsen, T. 1958. La géographie et les voies de communication du pays de Sumer, *RA* 52: 127-29.

Kessler, K. 1980. *Untersuchungen zur historischen Topographie Nordmesopotamiens.* BTAVO B/26. Wiesbaden.
Leesman, W. F. 1960. *Foreign Trade in the Old Babylonian Period.* Leiden.
Lewy, J. 1952. Studies in the Historic Geography of the Ancient Near East. *Or* n.s. 21: 1–12; 265–92; 393–425.
Liere, W. J. van, and Lauffray, J. 1954–55. Nouvelle prospection archéologique dans la Haute Jezireh syrienne. *Annales archéologiques arabes de syrie* 4–5: 129–48.
Mallowan, M. E. L. 1965. The Mechanics of Ancient Trade in Western Asia: Reflections on the Location of Magan and Meluḫḫa. *Iran* 3: 1–7.
Mellaart, J. 1968. Anatolian Trade with Europe and Anatolian Geography and Culture Provinces in the Late Bronze Age. *AnSt* 18: 187–202.
Moortgat, A. 1959. *Archäologische Forschungen der Max Frhr. von Oppenheim-Stiftung im Nördlichen Mesopotamien.* Cologne.
Murnane, W. J. 1985. *The Road to Kadesh: A Historical Interpretation of the Battle Reliefs of King Sety I at Karnak.* SAOC 42. Chicago.
Musil, A. 1927. *The Middle Euphrates, a Topographical Itinerary.* American Geographical Society, Oriental Explorations and Studies 3. New York.
Olmstead, A. T. 1964. *History of Assyria.* Chicago.
Oppenheim, A. L. 1970. Trade in the Ancient Near East. Pp. 1–37 in *Fifth International Congress of Economic History,* ed. H. Van der Wee, V. A. Vinogradov, and G. G. Kotovsky. Moscow.
Oren, E. O. 1982–83. Ancient Military Roads between Egypt and Canaʿan. *BAIAS* 10: 20–24.
———. 1984. Migdol: A New Fortress on the Edge of the Eastern Nile Delta. *BASOR* 256: 7–44.
Roll, I. 1983. The Roman Road System in Judaea. *The Jerusalem Cathedra* 3: 136–61.
Sachau, E. 1882. *Routen in Mesopotamien.* Leipzig.
Sarianidi, V. I. 1971. The Lapis Lazuli Route in the Ancient East. *Arch* 24: 12–15.
Simons, J. 1937. *Handbook for the Study of Egyptian Topographical Lists Relating to Western Asia.* Leiden.
Starr, S. F. 1963. Mapping Ancient Roads in Anatolia. *Arch* 16: 162–69.
Stein, A. 1940. *Old Routes of Western Iran.* London.
Thomsen, P. 1917. Die römischen Meilentseine der Provinzen Syria, Arabia und Palaestina. *ZDPV* 40: 1–103.
Winfield, D. 1977. The Northern Routes Across Anatolia. *AnSt* 27: 151–66.
Woodbury, R. B. 1941. *Geography and Routes in the Near East.* Unpublished manuscript in the Peabody Museum Library, Harvard University, Cambridge.

Barry J. Beitzel

ROMAN ROADS

Roman roads were constructed for the use of the military organization in the provinces. The economic benefits which may have resulted from their existence were a byproduct rather than a primary aim in their construction. This must be kept in mind when assessing the pattern of the roads in any province. Naturally, various factors determined the course of the roads anywhere. These include the topography, the geography of settlement (itself dependent on natural geography), geopolitical factors within the province and in the larger area, and the means of transportation and level of technology.

Apart from the remains of pavement and the milestones frequently referred to below, the following sources provide relevant information about the Roman road system in Judea, the Negeb, and Arabia: (1) the Peutinger Map (for which see: *Tabula Peutingeriana, Codex Vindobonensis 324, Vollständiqe Faksimile-Ausqabe im Originalformat* [Graz 1976]); (2) various ancient itineraries, including (a) the *Itinerarium Antonini Augusti* (Parthey and Pinder 1840; Cuntz 1929), and (b) that of Theophanes, a member of the staff of the *praefectus Aegypti* who traveled to Antioch (ca. 320; Roberts 1952; Rees 1968), and (3) certain Christian itineraries, including (a) that of the traveler from Bordeaux (Cuntz 1929), (b) that connected with the obituary of St. Paula (Jerome, *ep.* 108), and (c) that of Theodosius (Geyer 1965: 113–25).

A. History of Research
B. The Road Network
  1. Roads in Judea
  2. Roads in the Negeb
  3. Roads in Arabia
C. The Development of the System
D. Wartime Construction
E. General Characteristics of Judean Roads

A. History of Research

During the last century, the surveys carried out by Conder and Kitchener on behalf of the Palestine Exploration Fund resulted in a comprehensive and detailed conception of the network of Roman roads in Palestine. The publications and maps of the British *Survey of Western Palestine* still serve as a source of information for current research, particularly since many of the features which were then recorded no longer exist. As interest in the subject increased, the French scholars Clermont-Ganneau, Germer-Durand, Sejourné, and later Vincent and Abel extended the research to the milestones along the roads and deciphered and published many inscriptions mainly in the periodicals *Echos d'Orient* and *Revue Biblique.* These activities formed the basis of an understanding of the chronological development of the system.

Further fieldwork was carried out by German scholars, Schumacher, Dalman, Kuhl, and Alt. P. Thomsen (1917) assembled all the existing information on roads and milestones in the Roman provinces of Syria, Arabia, and Judea. From the 1930s until the 1960s, Avi-Yonah continued publishing new milestone inscriptions and summarizing the available evidence in various publications and maps (in *QDAP* and *IEJ*). From the 1950s onward comprehensive studies of specific roads were undertaken and published: the Legio-Sepphoris road by Hecker, the Jerusalem-Jericho road by Beauvery and Wilkinson, the Antipatris-Caesarea road by Dar and Applebaum. The studies of Aharoni, Rothenberg, Harel, and Meshel have contributed to the understanding of the Roman road network in the Negeb. Since 1970 the Israel Milestone Committee has been active in the field, affiliated with the International Curatorium of the *Corpus Miliariorum.* The committee carries out a systematic survey of all the extant remains related to the road system and prepares the inscriptions for publication in the *Corpus Inscriptionum Latinarum,* vol. xvii.

B. The Road Network

The road system of Palestine was an integrated system of N–S and E–W routes. Where these intersected there were important junctions which developed into towns such as Caesarea Philippi, Diocaesarea, Scythopolis, Caesarea, Neapolis, Antipatris, Diospolis, Nicopolis, Eleutheropolis, Hebron, Jericho, and the legionary base at Legio. One of the main junctions naturally was Jerusalem, which became the center of the system W of the Jordan because of its political and, hence, military importance, serving as it did as legionary headquarters for two centuries (Kuhl 1928). The system in the Negeb consisted of three routes which ran roughly parallel, following the curving coastline of the Mediterranean and fanning out as they progressed southward. Four other routes running diagonally from NW to SE merged with the former roads and with the system in Transjordan to the E. The natural focus of three of the diagonal roads was the great port city of Gaza. The cities of Berosaba, Elusa, Nessana, Oboda, and Mampsis lay at the nodal points of the network in the Negeb.

1. Roads in Judea. In its fully developed form the road system in Palestine consisted of four N–S arteries intersected by a series of E–W roads. See ROA.03. The N–S arteries include the following:

(1) The coast road from Antioch in Syria to Ptolemais/Acco (Goodchild 1948). From there, via the coastal towns of Caesarea–Apollonia–Jaffa, it continued to Jamnia–Ascalon–Gaza and, finally, to Alexandria in Egypt (Alt 1954).

(2) The Caesarea–Antipatris road (Dar and Applebaum 1973) which continued to Diospolis–Eleutheropolis with branches leading to the Hebron area and to Berosaba.

(3) The road along the watershed: Diocaesarea–Legio (for this section, see Hecker 1961)–Neapolis–Jerusalem–Hebron, with branches heading toward Berosaba and Mampsis (Dalman 1925; Sejourné 1895).

(4) The road through the Jordan valley from Caesarea Philippi, probably along the E bank of the Jordan and the Sea of Galilee, to Scythopolis and thence to Neapolis or, alternatively, to Jerusalem via Jericho (Beauvery 1957; Wilkinson 1975).

The series of E–W roads that intersected those arteries include the following:

(1) Tyre–Caesarea Philippi–Damascus (in Syria).

(2) Ptolemais–Diocaesarea–Tiberias (Roll 1986) and from there to Gadara and the Roman provincial capital of Bostra in Arabia. It crossed the river Jordan over a bridge with ten arches (Irby and Mangles 1844: 90 ff.).

(3) Caesarea–Legio–Scythopolis (Isaac and Roll 1982). It continued to Pella and Gerasa in Arabia.

(4) Caesarea–Sebaste–Neapolis–Coreae (Ilan and Damati 1974–75: 43–53) and from there to Philadelphia on the *Via Nova Traiana.*

(5) Jaffa–Neapolis (Roll and Ayalon 1986).

(6) Diospolis–Neapolis (Roll and Ayalon 1986).

(7) Antipatris–Gophna–Jericho. At Gophna this road crossed the main Neapolis–Jerusalem road.

(8) Jaffa – Diospolis – Beth Horon – Jerusalem – Jericho, and from there to Esbus on the *Via Nova Traiana.* For the Beth Horon road, see Oelgarte 1918.

(9) Diospolis–Nicopolis–Jerusalem (Abel 1925).

(10) Ascalon–Eleutheropolis–Jerusalem (Alt 1929; Kallai 1969).

(11) Gaza–Eleutheropolis, and from there to the mountains S of Hebron.

2. Roads in the Negeb. The road system in the Negeb consisted essentially of (a) four roads generally running NW–SE, and (b) three other roads which ran NE–SW. See Fig. ROA.03.

a. The NW–SE Roads. The four roads running through the Negeb generally from NW to SE include the following:

(1) Gaza–Aila (Arabic: Darb el-Ghaza). It ran S to Quseima, where it turned SE toward Kuntila. It approached Aila either via Ras en-Naqb and the ascent W of Aila or via Maᶜaleh Shaharut and Yotvetah (Meshel 1981).

(2) Gaza–Elusa–Oboda–Petra (Negev 1966; Meshel and Tsafrir 1974–75). This was originally a Nabataean road which continued to be used in the Roman period (Cohen 1982).

(3) Gaza–Moabitis. Passing by Berosaba and Mampsis it reached Charakmoba (Kerak) and Rabbatmoba on the Trajanic road (see B.3; Negev 1969).

(4) The road from Jerusalem to S Transjordan: Jerusalem–Hebron–Mampsis–Tamara (Hazevah), descending to the Arabah in two stages by elaborate stepped ascents (Maᶜaleh Deragot and the Scorpion Pass; Harel 1959). From Tamara the route headed for Aila, with branches heading toward the copper mines at Feinan and Petra (Aharoni 1954; 1963; cf. however, Rothenberg 1967: 109–171; Applebaum 1971: 211–23).

b. The NE–SW Roads. Three roads ran followed this general course: (1) the continuation of the coast road: Ascalon–Gaza–Rhinocorura; (2) the route from Hebron to Sinai: Hebron–Berosaba–Elusa–Nessana; and (3) Mampsis–Oboda–Quseima, crossing the southernmost cultivated area of the Negeb.

3. Roads in Arabia. The caravan routes of the Nabatean kingdom formed the initial basis for the Roman highway system in Arabia. This system was reinforced and enlarged after the annexation of the region in A.D. 106. Over 300 inscribed milestones in Arabia (Bauzou fc.) signify the existence of a complex transportation lattice that was an integral part of the E road system that connected Judea and adjacent territories.

The main artery was the *Via Nova Traiana* constructed between A.D. 111–114 under the emperor Trajan. It connected the capital of the new province of Arabia located at Bostra in S Syria with the port of Aila (Aqaba) on the Red Sea, a distance of 350 km. For much of this distance it presumably followed the old "King's Highway" (Num 20:17) on the Transjordanian plateau from Petra to Charachmoab (Kerak), Rabbathmoba (Rabba), Dibon, Madaba, Esbous, and Philadelphia (Amman) on its way to the N. In the S, the road ran from Petra through Sadaqa and Humayma to Aqaba (Graf 1990). Until A.D. 181, Petra served as the *caput viae* or central point for marking distances; afterwards, it was replaced by the capital city at Bostra (Bauzou 1988). See Fig. ROA.03.

Petra was a major nexus for a number of other routes. The *Darb ar-Rasif* ran along the edge of the al-Sherᶜa escarpment overlooking the Wadi Arabah to the W and past a number of old Nabatean caravanserai on its way to Petra. This road was not paved, but marked by two stone walls still visible between Kh. al-Saᶜud and Qana, an important spring located on the edge of the escarpment above

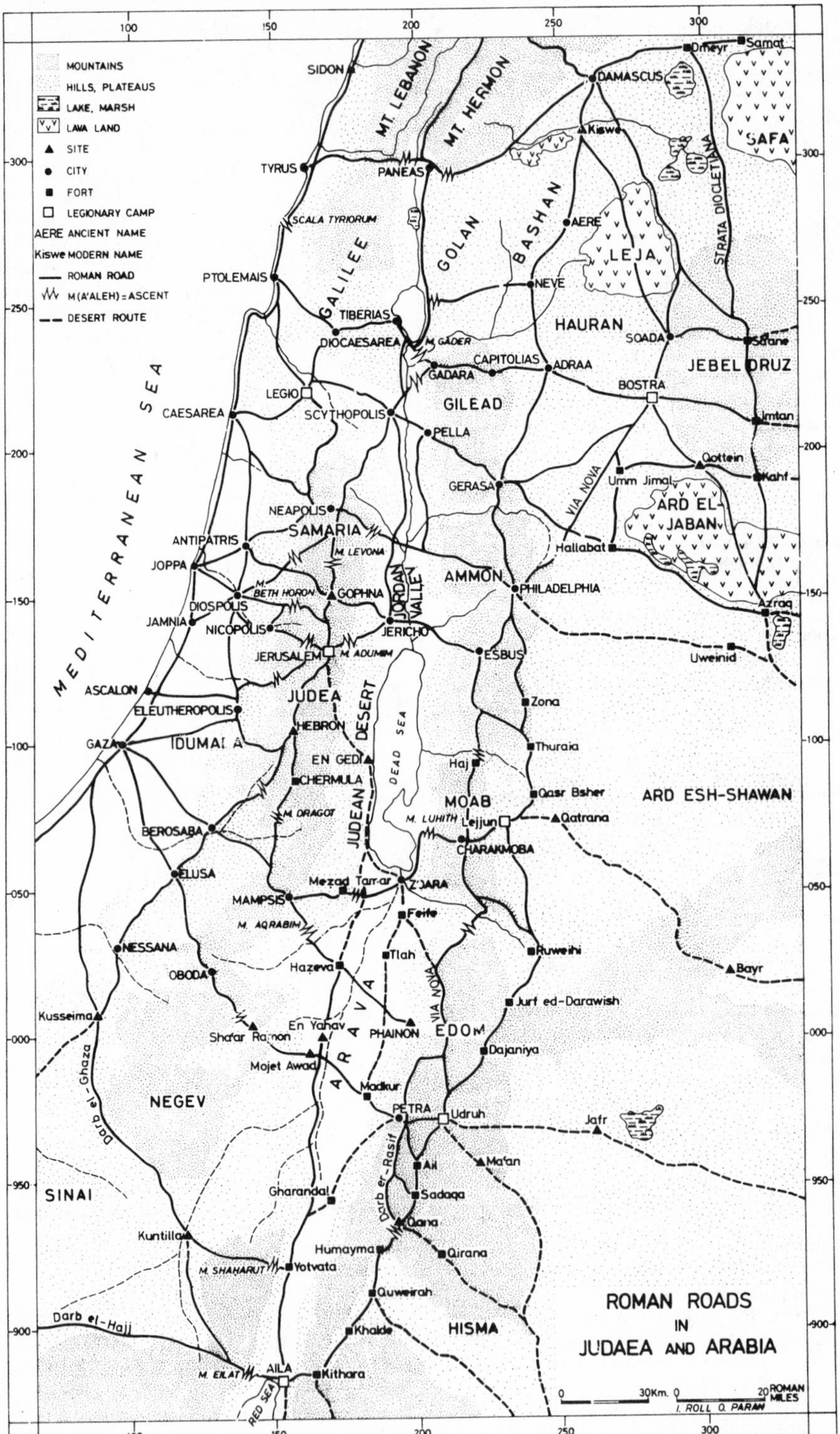

ROA.03. Roman roads in Judea and Arabia. *(Courtesy of I. Roll)*

Humayma. It is without milestones, but appears to have been in use during the Roman period. At least two other routes are marked by milestones between Sadaqa and Petra, one of which must have constituted a segment of the Trajanic road (Graf 1989). Nabataean settlements align all of these routes. Petra was also connected by a number of old E–W Nabataean caravan routes to Gaza on the Mediterranean and the Sinai and the Nile Delta in Egypt (Zayadine 1985).

In the N, the cities of the Decapolis were also interconnected with the Judaean-Arabian road system. Here Gerasa (Jerash) was the major nexus, with branches leading from it to Adraha (Der^{c}a) in the N, Pella to the NW, and Philadelphia in the S (Mittmann 1970: 133–63). The route running from Ptolemais (Akko) across the lower Galilee was connected via Tiberias with the E–W road running to Gadara (Umm Qeis), Capitolias (Beit Ras), Adraha (Der^{c}a), and Bostra, the capital of Arabia (Bauzou 1985). Pella could be reached from Caesarea by the road via Legio and Scythopolis (Isaac and Roll 1982). These routes are best known from the Peutinger Map, which displays the Roman road system of the Antonine period. Philadelphia (Amman) was connected by an E–W route to Neapolis, Caesarea Maritima, and from Esbus a road stretched to Jericho and Jerusalem. In the NE, Bostra, which served as headquarters of the *Legio III Cyrenaica,* was the major crossroads upon which five highways from all directions converged.

The central sector of Moab was also connected with several E–W routes that led to and around the Dead Sea to the W. The Peutinger Map shows a road leading from Rabbathmoba (Rabba) via Zoara to Thamara (Hazeva) at the SW area of the Dead Sea. The so-called "ascent of Luhith" (Isa 15:7) that led up the Jordanian rift to the plateau (Mittmann 1982) could make part of this road.

The S terminus of the Trajanic road was connected with an E–W route between Aila (Aqaba) and Clysma on the Suez. It is known in later sources as the Darb al-Hajj, but may also be identified with "the way to Mount Seir" (Deut 1:2). No traces of the Roman road have been discovered, but it is known from the Peutinger Map (Mayerson 1981). A desert route extended from Aila towards Hejaz and S Arabia.

The important oasis of Azraq was the nexus of several routes even farther to the E. It appears to have been connected to Bostra via a route that ran S from Salkhad to Imtan and Deir el-Kahf, and by two other roads via Umm el-Qottein and via Qasr al-Hallabat (Kennedy 1982: 137–97). It has been assumed that Azraq was also connected with the *strata Diocletiana,* a road connecting Palmyra and Damascus, but there is no evidence it extended as far S as Azraq (Bauzou fc.). A recently discovered milestone at Azraq does suggest that Azraq was connected with a route that ran deep into the desert depression of the Wadi Sirhan at least as far as Dumah (modern al-Jauf), where Roman military activity in the Severan era is known (Speidel 1987).

A N–S road running to the E and parallel to the *Via Nova* has also been proposed on the basis of random finds of milestones beginning S of Lejjun and running on a line toward Jurf al-Darwish and Udhruh (Thomsen 1917: 57–59). Since these finds were made in conjunction with nearby castella and legionary camps, they suggest this route was a military road that ran along the desert fringe that probably was established during the Tetrarchy.

Although these routes were the main arteries of the *provincia Arabia,* numerous other subsidiary routes also existed. Most of these were for local and regional traffic.

C. The Development of the System

The chronological development of the system can be traced insofar as it is reflected by the discovery of dated milestones. Two provisos must be made. First, roads may have been constructed without accompanying placement of inscribed milestones. The problems cannot be discussed fully, and it will be assumed here that the full organization of a Roman road, physically and administratively, is marked by the earliest series of milestones. Second, it cannot always be assumed that specimens of the earliest series have survived. In what follows, emphasis will be laid on obvious patterns which seem to characterize general developments.

No milestones dated before the reign of Claudius have been found anywhere in the E provinces beyond Anatolia. This is also true for Judea.

1. The Time of Claudius-Nero. Veterans of four legions were settled in a new colony in Ptolemais-Acco, in Syria but bordering on Judea. Next the coast road from Antioch to Ptolemais was constructed and marked with milestones "from Antioch to the new Colony of Ptolemais." These are dated A.D. 56. This was the first Roman road marked by milestones in Syria. It was a project apparently undertaken for security reasons: under Claudius there were dangerous troubles between Jews and Samaritans which were investigated on the spot by Ummidius Quadratus, governor of Syria (*WHJP* 1: 458–60, 462ff.; Isaac 1990: 322).

2. A.D. 69. In A.D. 69, M. Ulpius Traianus, commander of the legion X Fretensis is mentioned on a milestone of the Scythopolis–Legio road (Isaac and Roll 1976). As explained elsewhere, the construction of this road, part of a major strategic route, facilitated communication between the legionary winter quarters at Caesarea and Scythopolis. It appears that the road probably continued to Pella and Gerasa, since milestones of A.D. 112 discovered between these cities mention restoration of the road (Thomsen 1917: nos. 215, 216, 218a, 220; Mittmann 1970: 157 f.). The road was built in a period when the Romans were not actively pursuing the war in Judea due to the civil war being fought elsewhere. The army remaining in Judea therefore had nothing else to do and were kept busy on this road project. So far this milestone has remained a unique specimen. This itself is exceptional, since most milestones in Judea belong to a series represented by more than one text. There are no further traces of road construction related to the years of the First Jewish Revolt. As noted below, there are literary references to the activities of legionary road builders, but these must be distinguished from the systematic activity in peacetime which resulted in the placement of milestones.

3. The Flavians, Trajan. There are no milestones of these years (A.D. 72–117) in Judea. This is remarkable, for there are Flavian milestones in Cappadocia and Syria, and in Arabia, Trajan constructed his major road from the N to the S of the new province (see B.3 above). It was often assumed that the First Jewish Revolt was followed by substantial work of this nature. There is no evidence of this, and it may be concluded that Flavian interests focused on the more important province of Syria while the reign of Trajan was marked by activity in the new province of Arabia.

Following the annexation of the new province of Arabia, one legion was stationed at Bostra in the extreme N of the province and a road was constructed from Bostra to the Red Sea. The construction of the road is recorded on milestones of 111 and 114. All milestones known by 1917 are listed in Thomsen 1917: 1 ff., Map 1. For information on the construction of the road to be derived from the milestones, see Pekry 1968: 140–42.

The text emphasizes the connection between the annexation and the construction of the road. The milestones date the completion of the project, not its beginning, and it may be assumed that the construction began immediately after the annexation in 106. A well-known papyrus of March, 107, refers to soldiers cutting building stones not far from Petra (P. Mich. 465–66; text, translation and discussion also in *ANRW* 2/8: 691 f.). This shows that the army was constructing something, probably the road, at the time.

4. Hadrian. In Judea at least twelve roads were first marked by milestones from this period, all dated to 120 and 129/130, well before the outbreak of the Bar Kokhba Revolt. No milestones have been discovered which date to the years of the revolt. The series of 129/130 is contemporary with the emperor's visit to Judea. This shows increased Roman activity in the province. The garrison was doubled and, according to Cassius Dio, the decision was taken to found the Roman colony of Aelia Capitolina at Jerusalem. In Arabia at least one new road was constructed under Hadrian in 120: a road from Gerasa via Adraa to Bostra (the section Gerasa–Adraa [Derᶜa] has been explored by Mittmann 1964: 113 ff.). The section Adraa–Bostra has not so far produced any milestones but only a building inscription recording the construction of a bridge at at-Tayyibeh, dated 163/4 (Bauzou 1985: 151, and map, fig. 1). There is no doubt that the section Adraa–Bostra was part of the road already in Hadrian's time, for the milestones count the distance from Bostra. A road from Caesarea on the coast to Scythopolis and probably onward to Gerasa had already been built in 69 (see C.2 above). The section Gerasa–Scythopolis was repaired in 112 and the section from Scythopolis westward in 129. This provided the legion in Bostra with organized access into the Decapolis. Under Hadrian a legion was based at Legio-Caparcotna, and roads were built to provide an organized link with the legion at Bostra.

5. A.D. 162. This is by far the most extensive series attested in Judea, so far numbering 31 milestones. In Arabia two milestones were set up with identical texts. It has been suggested that there was a connection with the Parthian campaign of Lucius Verus which started in the winter of 161/2. This does not contradict what has been said above: no milestones were set up during times of war inside the province. However these matters are interpreted, there are two complementary facts to be considered about the milestones of A.D. 162: first, an extraordinarily large number of stones in the region dated to this year; and second, milestones of Marcus Aurelius are extremely rare elsewhere. Another such series found in several provinces reflects preparations for Severus Alexander's Persian campaign, in 231–33.

6. Septimius Severus. Milestones of several years during his reign have been found in Judea. There is some evidence that the inscriptions were produced by the citizens of the towns in the neighborhood where they are found. A study of the coast road in Syria has shown that there was a change of organization in 198 (Goodchild 1948). In Arabia there is evidence that the army first moved into the NE desert in the reign of Severus, occupying positions at Uweinid and Azraq and building a road from Azraq to the north (ca. 200–202; Kennedy 1980).

As observed in previous publications, the chronology of the milestone-texts suggests that they are related to events outside of the province of Judea. Apart from the series of 162 there are series which coincide with imperial visits to the area (129/130 and 198). Some series are mere declarations of loyalty, such as that of Perinax or the stones dated to 324–26. There was a short period when milestones were produced as a matter of routine instead of special initiative, from 198 until the death of Caracalla.

There are no milestone inscriptions in Judea later than the reign of Constantine. In Arabia a few inscriptions proclaiming support for Julian the Apostate are the latest in date.

Finally, there are hardly any milestones in the settled area of Judea of the Tetrarchs and their successors. This coincides with the demilitarization of the province in this period. In Syria and Arabia, where the army was not withdrawn but reorganized, there are many inscriptions (Isaac 1990: 162ff.). The Roman road system was originally developed by the army for its own use. It was later maintained for the army by the local population. This road system continued to serve the local population and other armies in later periods, and it was not substantially restored or expanded until the 20th century.

D. Wartime Construction

As observed, there are no milestone inscriptions in Judea clearly related to the major wars between Rome and the Jews in the 1st and 2d century. That certainly reflects the fact that this sort of organization did not belong to wartime activities. Of general interest, however, are two passages in Josephus' *Jewish War* which describe the activities of legionary pioneers who prepared the way in advance of the regular troops on the march (*JW* 3.6.2 §118; 3.7.3 §141).

E. General Characteristics of Judean Roads

In the plains and valleys, roads followed an alignment as straight as possible, familiar from aerial photographs all over the empire. However, when possible the engineers avoided laying out a road through densely wooded lands or marsh-lands. In mountainous areas a route over the watershed or halfway up the slope was preferred to the narrow valleys or river-beds: both for security reasons and because the roads are harder to maintain in low lying terrain which tends to be flooded in winter (representative examples of sections across roads may be found in Roll and Ayalon 1986: 125–29). Passes and ascents were constructed with great care, and were often provided with steps built or cut into the bedrock (notably in the case of roads leading up to Jerusalem). Bridges were constructed where needed.

Milestones were found along the major roads, organized for the use of the army and traveling officials. It goes without saying that there were numerous other roads and some of these have been explored, but only the presence of milestones is unequivocal proof that we are faced with a public highway. They were ideally placed at distances of one Roman mile (i.e., 1482 meters = 4862 ft), but in practice distances appear to vary. In Judea the distances are measured from the main towns, usually from the center. It is to be noted that both in Judea and in Arabia far more milestones have been found in the settled area than in the desert.

Bibliography

Abel, F.-M. 1925. La distance de Jérusalem a Emmaüs. *RB* 34: 347–67.

Aharoni, A. 1954. The Roman Road to Aila (Elath). *IEJ* 4: 9–16.

———. 1963. Tamar and the Roads to Elath. *IEJ* 13: 30–42.

Alt, A. 1929. Römerstrasse Jerusalem–Eleutheropolis. *PJ* 25: 18–23.

———. 1954. Stationen der römischen Hauptstrasse von Agypten nach Syrien. *ZDPV* 70: 154–66.

Applebaum, S., ed. 1971. *Roman Frontier Studies 1967.* Tel Aviv.

Avi-Yonah, M. 1950–51. The Development of the Roman Road System in Palestine. *IEJ* 1: 54–60.

Bauzou, T. 1985. Les voies de communication dans le Hauran à l'époque romaine. Pp. 138–65 in *Hauran I.* Ed. J. H. Dentzer. Paris.

———. 1988. Les voies romaines entre Damas et Amman. Pp. 293–300 in *Géographie historique au Proche-Orient.* Paris.

———. fc. La province romaine d'Arabie et son réseau routier. *IVe Congrès sur l'Histoire et l'Archeologie de Jordanie.* Lyon and Amman.

Beauvery, R. 1957. La route romaine de Jérusalem a Jéricho. *RB* 64: 72–101.

Cohen, R. 1982. New Light on the Petra–Gaza Road. *BA* 45: 240–47.

Cuntz, O. 1929. *Itineraria Romana I.* Leipzig.

Dalman, G. 1925. Die Nordstrasse Jerusalems. *PJ* 21: 58–89.

Dar, S., and Applebaum, S. 1973. The Roman Road from Antipatris to Caesarea. *PEQ* 105: 91–99.

Geyer, P. ed. 1965. *The Topography of the Holy Land.* CChr Series Latina 125. Turnhout.

Goodchild, R. G. 1948. The Coast Road of Phoenicia and Its Roman Milestones. *Berytus* 9: 91–127.

Graf, D. F. 1989. Les routes romaines d'Arabie Pétrée. *Le monde de la Bible* no. 59: 54–56.

———. 1990. The *Via Nova Traiana* between Petra and Aqaba. *ZDPV.*

Harel, M. 1959. The Roman Road at Maᶜaleh Aqrabim. *IEJ* 9: 175–79.

Hecker, M. 1961. The Roman Road Legio–Zippori. *BJPES* 25: 175–86 (in Hebrew).

Ilan, Z. and Damati, E. 1974–75. Ancient Roads in the Samaria Desert. *The Museum Haʾaretz Yearbook* 17/18: 45–55 (in Hebrew).

Irby, C. L. and Mangels, J. 1844. *Travels in Egypt and Nubia, Syria and the Holy Land.* London.

Isaac, B. 1978. Milestones in Judaea from Vespasian to Constantine. *PEQ* 110: 47–60.

———. 1990. *The Limits of Empire.* Oxford.

Isaac, B. and Roll, I. 1976. A Roman Milestone of A.D. 69 from Judaea. *JRS* 66: 9–14.

———. 1982. *Roman Roads in Judaea I, The Scythopolis–Legio Road.* Oxford.

Kallai, Z. 1969. Remains of a Roman Road Along the Mevo–Beitar Highway. *IEJ* 15: 195–203.

Kennedy, D. 1980. The Frontier Policy of Septimius Severus. Pp. 879–87 in *Roman Frontier Studies 1979.* Ed. W. Hanson and L. J. F. Keppie. Oxford.

———. 1982. *Archaeological Explorations on the Roman Frontier in NE Jordan.* Oxford.

Kuhl, C. 1928. Römische Strassen und Strassenstationen in der Umgebung von Jerusalem. *PJ* 24: 113–40.

Mayerson, P. 1981. The Clysma–Phara–Haila Road on the Peutinger Table. Pp. 167–76 in *Coins, Culture and History in the Ancient World,* ed. L. Casson and M. Price. Detroit.

Meshel, Z. 1981. The History of the Darg el-Gaza. *EI* 15: 358–71 (in Hebrew).

Meshel, Z. and Tsafrir, Y. 1974–75. The Nabataean Road from Avdat to Shaᶜar Ramon. *PEQ* 106: 103–18; *PEQ* 107: 3–21.

Mittmann, S. 1964. Die römische Strasse von Gerasa nach Adraa. *ZDPV* 80: 113–36.

———. 1970. *Beiträge zur Siedlungs- und Territorialgeschichte des nördlichen Ostjordanlandes.* Weisbaden.

———. 1982. The Ascent of Luhith. Pp. 175–80 in *Studies in the History and Archaeology of Jordan I,* ed. A. Hadidi. Amman.

Negev, A. 1966. Date of the Petra–Gaza Road. *PEQ* 88: 89–98.

———. 1969. Seal Impressions from Tomb 107 at Kurnub (Mampsis). *IEJ* 19: 89–106.

Oelgarte, T. 1918. Die Bethhoronstrasse. *PJ* 14: 73–89.

Parthey, G. and Pinder, M. 1840. *Itinerarium Antonini Augusti et Hierosolymitanum.* Berlin.

Pekáry, T. 1968. *Untersuchungen zu den römischen Reichsstrassen.* Bonn.

Rees, B. R. 1968. Theophanes of Hermopolis Magna. *BJRL* 51: 164–83.

Roberts, C. H. 1952. The Archive of Theophanes. *Catalogue of the Greek and Latin Papyri* 4: 104ff.

Roll, I. 1983. The Roman Road System in Judea. Pp. 136–61 in *The Jerusalem Cathedra,* vol. 3, ed. L. Levine. Detroit and Jerusalem.

———. 1986. Pp. 297–303 in *Antiquities of Western Galilee,* ed. M. Yedaya (in Hebrew).

Roll, I., and Ayalon, E. 1986. Roman Roads in Western Samaria. *PEQ* 118: 113–34.

Rothenberg, B. 1967. *Negev: Archaeology in the Negev and the Arabah.* Jerusalem (in Hebrew).

Sejourné, P.-M. 1895. Chronique de Jérusalem. *RB* 4: 253–69.

Speidel, M. 1987. The Roman Road to Dumata (Jawf in Saudi Arabia) and the Frontier Strategy of *Praetensione Colligare. Historia* 36: 213–21.

Thomsen, P. 1917. Die römischen Meilensteine der Provinzen Syria, Arabia und Palaestina. *ZDPV* 40: 1–103.

Wilkinson, J. 1975. The Way from Jerusalem to Jericho. *BA* 38: 10–24.

Zayadine, F. 1985. Caravan Routes between Egypt and Nabataea and the Voyage of Sultan Baibars to Petra in 1276. Pp. 159–73 in *Studies in the History and Archaeology of Jordan II,* ed. A. Hadidi. Amman.

DAVID F. GRAF
BENJAMIN ISAAC
ISRAEL ROLL

ROBE. See DRESS AND ORNAMENTATION.

ROCK OF ESCAPE (PLACE) [Heb *selaʿ hammaḥlĕqôt*]. A place in the wilderness of Maon where David escaped from Saul (1 Sam 23:28), often associated with Wadi el-Malaqi (Gold *IDB* 2: 126; Lee *ISBE* 2: 130). Apparently the site featured an unusual rock or cliff foundation. The major discussion about the site, however, concerns the etymology of the Hebrew term *ḥālaq,* its meaning in this passage (Lee *ISBE* 2: 130; Klein *1 Samuel* WBC, 232; BDB, 325), and its relationship to the physical features of the site. Some of the major translations include "Rock of Divisions," "Rock of Slipperinesses," or "Rock of Escape." While the debate concerning the etymology of the term continues, the passage may reflect a popular etymology of that day (Klein *1 Samuel* WBC, 232). Perhaps the context of the passage reflects some hint concerning the intent of the writer. Saul, in pursuit of David and his men, was on one side of the mountain and David on the other (1 Sam 23:26), the setting being perhaps that of a formation with two parallel cliffs so situated that David's escape seemed impossible. However, while Saul was closing in on David, his mission was interrupted by a Philistine raid (v 27) which allowed David to escape.

LaMoine F. DeVries

ROCK OF ETAM. See ETAM, ROCK OF.

RODANIM [Heb *rôdānîm*]. Var. DODANIM. The Rodanim were said to be one of "the sons of Javan," along with "Elishah, Tarshish and Kittim" in 1 Chr 1:7. Were this the only reference to these people, scholars would identify the location with the island of Rhodes. The difficulty arises when one consults Gen 10:4 where the fourth son of Javan is said to be Dodanim. However, even here the Sam. Pent., LXX, and some mss of the MT read Rodanim. It is easy to see how the confusion arose, since Heb *reš* and *dalet* are easily confused. The combined textual evidence for 1 Chr 1:7 is overwhelmingly in favor of Rodanim (with only the Syr Peshitta reading *dûdanîm,* in an obvious harmonistic attempt with Gen 10:4; the Targum to 1 Chr 1:7 does read *wdrdnyʾ*, which looks like a compromise solution of incorporating both readings). So what is the preferred reading? The *lectio difficilior* would favor reading Dodanim for Gen 10:4 and Rodanim for 1 Chr 1:7. However, the principle of the more difficult reading is only valid for intentional errors, such as scribal harmonizations and the like. The accidental substitution of a *dalet* for a *reš* would not be taken into account by the *lectio difficilior.* The most likely external referent for the biblical passages is the island of Rhodes. Some recent attempts to identify them with the *dnn* peoples of various inscriptions of the ANE are marred by the simple fact that the spelling does not correspond to what we would expect from comparative Semitics. Neiman (1973: 121) and Berger (1982: 60) have proposed that we identify the Dodanim with the Greek city Dadona, but this is too obscure to carry much weight. In conclusion, we would read Rodanim for both 1 Chr 1:7 and Gen 10:4, with Rhodes as the referent. The danger of taking "son of" too literally in both the table of nations in Genesis 10 and 1 Chronicles 1 must be pointed out. Both "sonship" and "brotherhood" were terms which could be used very loosely to refer to broader relationships than kinship, such as members of a common treaty (cf. Wenham *Genesis 1–15* WBC, 215; Ross 1980: 344–46). Hence the biblical authors, in listing Rodanim as a "son of" Javan, were describing their perception of some kind of cultural relationship between the Greeks and the inhabitants of Rhodes, in this instance perhaps based on kinship, but not necessarily so.

Bibliography

Berger, P. -R. 1982. Ellasar, Tarschish und Jawan, Gn 14 und 10. *WO* 13: 50–78.

Neiman, D. 1973. The Two Genealogies of Japhet. Pp. 119–26 in *Orient and Occident: Essays Presented to C. H. Gordon,* ed. H. A. Hoffner. AOAT 22. Kevelaer and Neukirchen-Vluyn.

Ross, A. P. 1980. The Table of Nations in Genesis 10—Its Structure. *BSac* 137: 340–53.

H. Eldon Clem

RODENTS. See ZOOLOGY.

ROEBUCK. See ZOOLOGY.

ROGELIM (PLACE) [Heb *rōgĕlîm*]. A town in Transjordan from which Barzillai came to escort the restored king David to the Jordan River (2 Sam 19:31). Rogelim means "treaders," i.e., fullers, people who cleaned, bleached, or dyed wool or cloth, and who may also have traded in textiles. This could indicate Rogelim's local industry, but does not help to locate the site. Judging by the goods the three men (i.e., Shobi, Machir, and Barzillai; 2 Sam 17:27) brought to David, Barzillai was probably wealthy. Since no royalty is implied, his wealth may have come from the local industry or agriculture, suggesting that Rogelim was a fertile area. The food brought to David suggests farmland. The phrase "came down" suggests that Rogelim was in the hills. If one assumes that Barzillai was a Gileadite living in Gilead, Rogelim could have been in that area. Lodebar (2 Sam 17:27) is usually seen as being in Gilead, and Rabbah (2 Sam 17:27; assuming it was the capital city of the Ammonites) was not far away. One might assume, however, that all three men were within some reasonable distance from Mahanaim where David had taken refuge.

Gilead itself has a variety of geographical meanings—Bashan N of the Yarmuk, Transjordan S of the Yarmuk, the area S of the Jabbok, the area between the Yarmuk and Jabbok. Abel (*GP* 2: 437) suggested Rogelim was Tell Barsina on the S side of Wadi er-Rujeileh in E Gilead (M.R. 223215). The site is ca. 5.5 miles SW of Irbid, and ca. 0.5 miles N of Mahanaim. Abel inferred this identification from the similarity of the name, Barsina, with the name Barzillai, and the similarity of the name of the wadi (i.e., er-Rujeileh) with Rogelim.

However, Glueck (1951: 176–77) found no evidence at Barsina of settlement before the Roman period. He instead proposed to identify Rogelim with Zaharet Soq'ah, which was a strong Iron Age I fortress.

Bibliography

Glueck, N. 1951. *Explorations in Eastern Palestine, IV.* Part 1. AASOR 25–28. New Haven.

HENRY O. THOMPSON

ROHGAH (PERSON) [Heb *rohgâ*]. A descendant of Asher listed in 1 Chr 7:34. He is named as the son of Shamer, who perhaps is to be identified with Shomer (7:32). Rohgah does not appear elsewhere in Scripture and is attributed with no offspring. The verse in which this name appears bears several textual problems. First, the consonantal text gives the name as *rwhgh*—perhaps to be pronounced *rôhăgâ*—while the Masoretes have vocalized it as *rohgâ*. Second, the MT reads "Ahi and Rohgah," but subsequent translators have divided the consonants of this phrase differently, to read ". . . his brother, and Rohgah."

JULIA M. O'BRIEN

ROMAMTI-EZER (PERSON) [Heb *rōmamtî ʿezer*]. One of the fourteen sons of Heman who were appointed to prophesy with musical instruments under the direction of their father and the king (1 Chr 25:4). Romamti-ezer received the twenty-fourth lot cast to determine duties (1 Chr 25:31).

Scholars have long suggested that the final nine names in 1 Chr 25:4 can be read as a liturgical prayer. For instance, *rōmamtî* is the first person sing. *Po ʿlel* perf. form of the verb *rûm*. Reading *ʿezer* as the direct object and considering the conjunction attached to *rōmamtî*, one could translate the name Romamti-ezer as "I will exalt [my] helper." It would form part of the third line of the liturgical prayer as reconstructed by scholars. For a reconstruction and translation of the prayer, a summary of interpretative possibilities, and bibliography, see ELIATHAH.

J. CLINTON MCCANN, JR.

ROMAN ARMY. Roman control of Greater Syria (including Judea) lasted for seven centuries, being founded largely on the powerful and effective forces she established in the region. The character, organization, size, and distribution of those forces developed and changed over that long period. The army left by Pompey the Great in his new province of Syria in 63 B.C. was rather different from that of Septimius Severus ca. A.D. 200 and very different from that stationed in the region on the eve of the Islamic invasion and the Battle of the Yarmuk in A.D. 636. The dynamics of change derived from the political and social evolution of the Roman Empire, from developments in military technology, tactics and strategy, and the altered perception of the role of the forces in the region.

The elements of the Roman army with which the inhabitants of the region would have been most familiar were the Legions and the Auxilia; sailors of the Fleet were normally only found along the coast. In addition, for more than a century and half after Pompey, the troops of various client states in the region also had a role to play and were prominent in their own regions or more widely in times of war.

The change in the Roman army from the 1st century B.C. to the 2d A.D. may be summarized in three broad phases of overlapping development. For a generation after Pompey, Roman control was assured by the establishment of a number of Legions in the area which could call upon the armies of allied states in time of rebellion or external war. The next period saw the addition of large numbers of supplementary troops (the Auxilia) serving permanently alongside the Legions and in Roman pay. Finally, progressively from the end of the 1st century B.C. onwards, the various allied states were eliminated, their territory (and armies) brought under direct Roman control. The annexation in A.D. 106 of the last of these allied states, the kingdom of the Nabateans, left military control entirely in the hands of Legions and Auxilia.

In general, the central forces were those permanently based in Greater Syria. From time to time, however, reinforcements were drafted from other provinces; from Cappadocia and Egypt in particular, but also from as distant as the provinces of Africa and Europe.

The subject may now be considered in two parts: the character and organization of the Roman army in general, then the army in the Near East with special reference to the NT period.

A. Late Republic and Early Empire
   1. Legions
   2. Auxilia
   3. Fleets
   4. Forces in Rome
   5. Allied Armies
B. The Roman Army in the East
   1. Background Developments
   2. The Role of the Army
   3. The Military Background to the NT
   4. The Roman Army in the Bible

A. Late Republic and Early Empire

1. Legions. The military success of the Roman Republic had been founded on the effectiveness of her citizen armies, equipped as heavy infantry and organized into legions. The precise numerical strength of the full legion in the Late Republic is disputed, round numbers of 5,000 and 6,000 being found in the literature, but most scholars prefer the former.

During the Republic, by law, all male Roman citizens between the ages of 17 and 46 were liable to be called upon to serve for periods not normally exceeding six years at any one time. Most recruits were conscripted in rotation but increasingly in the 1st century B.C. generals could count on volunteers to form at least a significant nucleus of an army. Troops were required both to provide regular garrisons in distant provinces and to fight in wars. They were equipped by the state but the cost was deducted from their pay. At discharge, men would return to their farmsteads or could hope their general would persuade the Senate to reward them with a grant of land in Italy. The numbers of men under arms varied considerably as circumstances required in the last fifty years of the Republic (80–30 B.C.) but was seldom less than twenty legions.

The end of the Republic brought a change. Augustus, the first emperor, sought to create military institutions better suited to what had become a great Mediterranean-wide power and no longer a small city state. A fully professional, long-service, army was formed, recruited largely from volunteers and gauged more closely to Rome's long-term requirements than had been the case previously. More than half of the legions in service during the civil wars of 44–30 B.C. were disbanded by Augustus and a further three were destroyed in a disaster in Germany in A.D. 9. By the close of Augustus' reign (A.D. 14), there were twenty-five. This number rose to twenty-eight by the end of the century, to thirty in the early 2d century and thirty-three by ca. A.D. 200.

The Republican practice of giving legions numbers and distinctive epithets reflecting characteristics (*VI Ferrata,* "Ironclad"), former service *(IX Hispana),* the emperor under whom they were formed *(III Augusta)* continued in the empire. Increasingly, too, many individual legions remained in the same province—if, indeed, not in the same fortress—over long periods of time (e.g. *Legio III Augusta* was based in the province of Africa from ca. 30 B.C. for at least four centuries and *VI Victrix* was based at York in Britain for three centuries). From the outset, all of these legions were permanently based in the provinces, usually in one of the frontier provinces; not until the end of the 2d century A.D. was one *(II Parthica)* stationed in Italy itself.

Recruits in the imperial period still had to be Roman citizens, but a growing number of replacements in the legions were drawn from provincial sources. Some of these came from the growing numbers of Italians who had settled abroad on their own initiative or in the many colonies established by Julius Caesar and Augustus. Others—after the time of Claudius (A.D. 41–54) in particular—were recruited from the sons of provincial auxiliary soldiers. Still others, especially in the East where there were relatively few Italian settlers, were recruited from natives who were enfranchised to make them eligible. By the end of the 2d century, there were relatively few legionaries of Italian origin. Legions began recruiting within their own region. As a result, the major legionary groupings—Britain, the Rhine, the Danube, the East, Egypt and Africa—took on regional characteristics.

Conditions of service were relatively good. Recruits signed on for a long period—initially sixteen years but soon increased to twenty then twenty-five—but in return received regular pay, periodic bonuses, and a discharge bounty. For most soldiers, everyday service conditions and prospects were far superior to those generally available outside the army. In service, the legionary soldier was usually accommodated in permanent forts (but cf. below) whose timber barracks gave way in the later 1st century A.D. to stone-built ones; forts not only provided basic amenities but even bath houses. Medical care was provided, the soldier was fed well and regularly, and clothing and equipment was charged to him but provided by the state. Outside his military base, the legionary's spending power made him a person of some importance. Moreover, part of his pay and bonuses was compulsorily saved for him which, together with his discharge gratuity, provided the means for him to settle comfortably. Legal privileges and tax exemptions for the veteran gave added status and provided an additional impetus to would-be recruits. A serious disincentive to enlistment was that the state forbid marriage for a serving soldier. The theory, presumably, was that by obliging soldiers to live and work together without any recognized external ties, their esprit de corps and mobility were enhanced. Despite the ban, the state accepted that many soldiers would father children and some would establish families whose status could be legitimized after discharge.

The effectiveness of the Roman legions was due to various factors. As heirs to centuries of steady success their morale was high, but systematic training and harsh discipline played a vital part. Prospective recruits were first screened for suitability—legal status as well as stature and general health. There were regular training sessions with various weapons, parade ground maneuvers, and route marches. Equipment included mail (later segmented plate) armor, a helmet, short sword, dagger, spear(s), and a large curved rectangular shield (replacing an earlier oval one).

The legion itself was internally flexible and efficient on the battlefield. Each probably consisted of ten cohorts of 480. These in turn were divided into six centuries of 80 men (not the 100 implied in the name), subdivided into small units, *contubernia,* of eight men, who roomed and messed together. There were in addition some 120 mounted men attached as scouts and despatch riders for a total of ca. 4,920. Later in the 1st century A.D. the first cohort was reduced to five centuries but each now of double strength (160), giving a paper strength of 5,240.

The handful of most-senior officers were relatively inexperienced. The commander or legate, was an aristocrat, a member of the Roman Senate (except in Egypt, where only equestrian prefects were appointed), most commonly in his thirties and usually appointed for three years. He would probably have seen some previous military service, but at least a decade before and not necessarily for much longer than six months to a year. Subordinate to him were six tribunes, one of whom was of senatorial family, the other five from equestrian families. The latter were commonly in their early thirties, had already gained some experience from the command of an auxiliary regiment for three years and could remain another three years as legionary tribunes. The senatorial tribunes could serve for as little as six months.

The real professionals of the legion were the centurions, sixty of them, one for each century. Most centurions were promoted from the ranks; others came in as direct appointments from the equestrian order or transferred from the elite units in Rome. Promotion over a long career could take a man from junior centurion, *hastatus posterior,* of the tenth cohort to first centurion of the first cohort, *primus pilus.* There was no fixed period of service for a man once he reached the centurionate—he could stay till he died. *Primipilares,* however, served only a year at that rank before proceeding perhaps to be camp prefect *(praefectus castrorum)* (third in command after the legate and senatorial tribune), commanding one of the prestigious cohorts of troops in Rome itself (below), or beginning on an equestrian career with the possibility of governing a small province or even entering the Senate.

The attractions of the army are well illustrated, especially for the officers. Apart from the career prospects, it was financially very advantageous. The first stage in promotion took a man to *sesquiplicarius,* which earned him pay and a half, and next came the *duplicarius* or double pay. The financial attraction of the centurionate, however, was that the pay was probably some 16 times that of the basic legionary salary. In short, a centurion had both considerable military and social status and wealth. Finally, of course, men could move between units, especially if promotion was involved or a reinforcement draft required in an emergency.

2. Auxilia. When the armies of the Roman Republic were called upon to fight outside Italy from the late 3d century B.C. onwards, they came into contact with peoples whose military traditions were rather different from their own. Rather than develop forces to counter the light infantry, mounted troops, archers, and slingers of their new opponents, they preferred rather to employ some of these new peoples as mercenaries. The practice became more common when the mass extension of Roman citizenship in the 80s B.C. integrated many former Italian allies into the legions; it accelerated during the last decades of the Republic, especially the civil wars, with some provincial units remaining in existence for long periods and seeing distant service. Major developments came with Augustus who continued to enroll short-service bodies of auxiliaries under their own tribal leaders, but also many others recruited from among subject provincials as part of the permanent establishment.

The organization of these auxiliary troops differed in some significant respects from that of the legions. The size of each unit was small: cavalry were grouped as *alae* and infantry as *cohortes.* The exact strength of the various types of regiments differed, but all were initially defined loosely as "quingenary," i.e., approximately 500 strong; from the time of Nero onwards a few large military, "thousand strong," regiments appear. Internal organization involved dividing cavalry into sixteen squadrons *(turmae)* of thirty, each commanded by a decurion assisted by NCOs; among the infantry, cohorts were divided as in the legions into six centuries of eighty men each. An innovation was the creation of mixed regiments, *cohortes equitatae,* whose strength was probably made up of 480 infantry in six centuries and 120 mounted men in four squadrons. Auxiliaries were paid less than legionaries, perhaps less than half for an auxiliary infantryman. On the other hand, auxiliary cavalry were better paid, perhaps as much as a legionary. Pay, food, clothing, accommodation, and the improved conditions of everyday life such as the regimental bath buildings available to auxiliaries too, were attractive to those whose warlike instincts needed an alternative outlet after the incorporation of their homeland into a Roman province. Even more attractive was the prospect of Roman citizenship. In the middle of the 1st century, probably under Claudius (A.D. 41–54), the previously occasional practice of rewarding deserving auxiliaries with Roman citizenship was made standard. This usually occurred after about twenty-five years, although service continued indefinitely. By the end of the 1st century A.D., however, the term of service had been fixed at twenty-five years with an automatic grant of honorable discharge together with Roman citizenship for the soldier and, retrospectively, any family he had acquired illegally. There was no gratuity, but the attractions of obtaining Roman citizenship for themselves and their descendants was considerable.

Auxiliary regiments were recruited from throughout the empire. Some such as the Cretan and Syrian archers, Numidian and Gallic cavalry, Balearic slingers, and Raetian spearmen brought prized fighting techniques; most provided simply useful and cheap manpower. Initially, they retained their distinctive equipment and weapons; in time, most infantry and cavalry at least were equipped in a common fashion. More specialized units—archers, slingers, *dromedarii,* and heavy cavalry—inevitably retained a distinctive character. Like legions, auxiliary regiments were given numbers and names, the latter often describing their ethnic origin, particular expertise, or former service; e.g., *Ala I Gallorum, Cohors I Hemesenorum Milliaria Sagittariorum Equitata,* and *Ala I Thracum Mauretana.* Regiments often served at a distance from their homeland; indeed, their loyalty was more assured if they did so. However, through local recruitment to fill vacancies, many such units gradually lost their original ethnic character. Unlike legions, whose personnel after Augustus' time were largely volunteers, auxiliary regiments would often have consisted originally of pressed men and thereafter received drafts of recruits which included some of the same. Like legionaries, auxiliary troops had opportunities for promotion and transfer.

Alongside these permanent formations, Augustus and his immediate successors also made use of regiments brought to their service for fixed periods by native chiefs. Various Gallic regiments in particular served in this way as did units recruited by German chiefs beyond the frontier. With the assimilation of most such warlike elements, this practice died out within the empire but continued beyond the frontiers, not just with German mercenaries but with Thracians and Moors and even with the retainers of Parthian refugees.

With the exception of those units which fought under their own tribal leaders, auxiliary regiments were commanded by Roman officers from Italy or the provinces. Initially, a wide range of men took command, from legionary centurions to the younger sons of senators. By the latter half of the 1st century A.D., however, there was a regular hierarchy of posts for the equestrian class with a sequence of posts as tribunes of cohorts or prefects of cavalry regiments. Such men not only held two or three of these posts but each for as long as three years at a time. As with senatorial officers and generals who were appointed because of who they were, these equestrian officers were not necessarily able, but they did at least gain much more experience of military affairs than senatorial amateurs.

As regards numbers, there is the testimony of Tacitus that such units were both more vulnerable than legions and constantly being formed or disbanded as required. He reports (under the year A.D. 23), however, that their overall strength was about that of the legions, i.e. ca. 125,000, about 250 regiments. Cheaper to maintain and easier to recruit from a much bigger manpower pool, their numbers rose more rapidly than those for the legions. In the mid-2d century there were approximately ninety cavalry regiments (seven of them military) and 300 cohorts (forty of them military and the total equally divided between purely infantry units [*peditata*] and mixed infantry and cavalry [*equitata*]).

Auxiliary units were distributed widely, mainly in the frontier provinces but also in those provinces without legions (e.g., Mauretania). In the Augustan period and for a short time thereafter, some were brigaded along with legions in the same fortresses. Gradually, as legions moved into individual fortresses, auxiliary units were split off too, a few, however, into multiple regiment forts. Their smaller size made it easier to move them, and although some units stayed in particular provinces for several generations, there was far more movement among them.

In peacetime, auxiliaries probably carried out most of the day-to-day patrolling and policing. In time of war, they were no less prominent than the legions, even shouldering the brunt of fighting in battles.

3. Fleets. Under the Republic, fleets had been built as required in time of war or to check piracy. Augustus established permanent fleets, first in Gaul at Forum Julii (Fréjus), then moved to Italy to two great bases at Ravenna and Misenum, which had some 10,000 men each. Subsequently, smaller fleets were created on the English Channel, the Rhine and Danube, the Black Sea, the Levantine coast, at Alexandria, and on the Red Sea. Detachments were certainly outposted to other ports.

Recruits came from noncitizen sources. Like auxiliaries, they were granted citizenship after discharge (finally set at 26 years), and generally enjoyed very similar terms of service. Commanders were drawn from the equestrian order.

With little evidence of piracy after the close of the Republic, the function of these fleets seems mainly to have been to police the seas and convoy transports of grain or troops.

4. Forces in Rome. Under the Republic there had been no troops quartered in Rome. Augustus, however, formed the Praetorian Guard of nine cohorts, each probably ca. 1,000 strong. It was subsequently increased to twelve cohorts and briefly to sixteen before settling at ten in the later 1st century. Finally, at the end of the 2d century, the size of each of the ten cohorts was increased to, probably, 1,600. Initially only three cohorts were based in Rome, but from A.D. 23 all were quartered there in a specially built camp, the *Castra Praetoria*.

Service was highly coveted. Recruitment was restricted not just to Roman citizens but to those from Italy and the older colonies and provinces such as Gallia Narbonensis and Macedonia. Pay was initially twice that of legionaries and later apparently 3 times; service was for twelve (later sixteen) years. Conditions in Rome were highly attractive and men went to war only under the emperor or one of his immediate family. Praetorians could be promoted to centurionates in legions and their tribunes were an elite, too, drawn from former chief centurions of the legions who had progressed up through the tribunates available in the other forces in Rome and who might go on to an equestrian career. The force as a whole was commanded by one, sometimes a pair, of Praetorian Prefects, men who had reached the pinnacle of an equestrian career and enjoyed the trust of the emperor in the sensitive task of providing for his general security. Cohorts took turns at guarding the palace but in practice close protection was provided by the German Bodyguards of Augustus and, later, the provincial troops of the Special Mounted Forces *(Equites Singulares Augusti)* (1,000 men), also based in Rome.

The three Urban Cohorts formed by Augustus were charged with policing the capital. Several others were subsequently formed, and individual cohorts were outposted to Ostia and Puteoli in Italy, and later to Carthage and Lyons. Their strength was initially cohorts of 500 or 1,000—certainly it became 1,000 and, in the late 2d century, probably, 1,500–1,600. Recruits were Roman citizens, serving twenty years, Tribunes commanded cohorts and were responsible to the emminent senator who had been appointed prefect of the city.

Seven cohorts (3,500, perhaps 7,000 men from the outset) of paramilitary fire fighters, the *Vigiles,* recruited from freedmen and serving for periods of six years, were distributed around the city.

5. Allied Armies. From the Late Republic onwards, various petty rulers were recognized by Rome both within the directly administered territories of provinces and around the periphery of the empire as a whole. In time of war, they could be called upon, or expected as a token of friendship, to provide troops at their own expense for the duration of campaigns in their own vicinity. For the period under discussion, the most numerous and best attested of these rulers and their armies are in the East and they may conveniently be discussed now in that context.

Administering the armed forces was a major undertaking. The imperial bureaucracy in Rome oversaw the appointment of provincial governors and the commanders of legions and auxiliary units, and determined their distribution. Troops had to be paid and provision made both for extraordinary payments on state occasions and for gratuities and the regular issuing of discharge diplomas to auxiliaries. Within the provinces the governors oversaw recruitment, inspected troops, and were involved in their payment and discharge. The best known account is that of Hadrian's governor Arrian, who, during his governorship of Cappadocia, carried out an inspection by sea of the coastal forts and garrisons along the Black Sea coast of his province.

Every unit generated a great deal of paperwork ranging from the rosters showing the daily duties of each individual to pay records. Many such documents have survived, especially among the papyri of Egypt, but the largest and most informative single group are the records of the *Cohors XX Palmyrenorum* discovered at their base of Dura Europos on the Middle Euphrates. The language of such documents is Latin, and that was the language of the army as a whole. Nevertheless, most troops were not native Latin speakers. In the East, many legionaries were Greek- rather than Latin-speaking, while auxiliaries everywhere spoke their own tongue—Celtic, German, Thracian, and Aramaic. After 25 years service, even non-Latin speakers will have acquired a considerable familiarity with Latin. The other avenue for Romanization of the non-Italian element was through religion. In practice, Italians and Westerners in general adopted many native deities, not least the mystery cults of the East. Nevertheless, religion was an important element in everyday military routine and it involved for everyone some acquaintance with the old gods of the Classical Pantheon.

The appearance of Roman troops and their campaign practices are known partly from descriptions in the pages of such writers as Polybius, Caesar, and Josephus. A great deal of information, however, is derived from the discovery of pieces of equipment and from artistic representations. Figured tombstones can be useful but relief sculpture is especially valuable, not least the famous representations of campaigning armies of the 2d century A.D. which may be seen on the triumphal arches of the emperors Augustus, Titus, Marcus Aurelius, and Septimius Severus and on the celebrated columns of Trajan (98–117) and Marcus Aurelius (161–80).

B. The Roman Army in the East

1. Background Developments. In 133 B.C., the king of Pergamum in W Asia Minor, bequeathed his realm to Rome. From this gift, Rome created her first province beyond the Aegean—the province of Asia (129 B.C.). During the subsequent century, Roman armies campaigned throughout Anatolia as far as the Caucasus Mountains, then down through Mesopotamia, Syria, and into Egypt. By 30 B.C. much of this region had been brought under Roman control, the political geography of which was a scattering of provinces among and beyond which lay the territories of a number of petty rulers allied to Rome and largely dependent on her support and goodwill. In the same period, the more urbanized and peaceful provinces such as Asia and Bithynia, were demilitarized. A few troops remained, but mainly to assist and protect the governors and their senior officials. The main concentrations of troops moved eastwards, to Galatia, Syria, and Egypt. Major changes followed in the 1st century A.D. as most allied states of Asia Minor and Greater Syria were eliminated, their territory absorbed into an existing or newly created province. Galatia lost its legionary forces at an early stage, but Cappadocia, a new military province, was created on the Turkish Euphrates instead; Syria remained the most-important military province in the entire East, but around it appeared new provinces—Judea in A.D. 6 (renamed Syria Palaestina in the early 2d century A.D.), and Arabia in 106. Provincial boundaries were varied occasionally, and at the end of the 2d century Syria itself was split into two smaller provinces, Syria Coele and Phoenice, and two new provinces were created in northern Mesopotamia, Osrhoene and Mesopotamia.

2. The Role of the Army. Troops were allocated to specific provinces to provide security. The emphasis within that broad definition varied according to local conditions and over time with changing circumstances. Initially, a new region had to be garrisoned to deter rebellion. Later, the size of force would depend on the extent to which the population had to be policed and it had its resources protected from banditry or external threat. In Syria, the large populations of a few great cities certainly represented potential difficulties. Where there were large Jewish elements in the urban population, there was an additional problem arising from the hostility between the "Greek" and Jewish communities. Notable flashpoints in the East were Alexandria and Antioch, but all of the cities of the Phoenician coast from Sidon to Ascalon had such troubles. In the Jewish homelands, deep-seated religious sensitivities and a rapid disillusionment with the realities of Roman rule, made the entire region unsettled. Especially sensitive and requiring close supervision were the occasions of the great festivals of Passover and Pentecost which brought huge numbers of visitors from all over the empire and beyond. Banditry—endemic to the region (see Luke 10:30 and Acts 21:38), could have political overtones and interacted with religious problems to create frequent unrest. In the absence of special forces of police or a regular militia, the task of containing banditry fell to the regular troops of the Roman army or the forces of allied rulers. See BANDITRY. Localized insurrections also were common and there were fierce and bloody rebellions in A.D. 66–70 and 132–35. The numbers and distribution of troops tells the story.

In NE Syria, Rome faced the only other great power on her frontiers, the Parthian Empire. Wars were in fact infrequent, but there was often tension and each was capable of inflicting great harm on the other. Whereas the early province of Syria was allocated only two legions, Augustus greatly increased the army of the E frontier. Syria was now assigned four legions (ca. 20,000 men) and an unknown number of auxiliary regiments. All were now seasoned professional soldiers. After the annexation of Cappodocia in A.D. 18, the dispute between Rome and Parthia over the kingdom of Media (lying between the new province and Parthian Media) became more acute and forced the stationing of an even larger army on the Upper Euphrates.

Many troops would have been stationed around Antioch, and there were detachments—perhaps only temporarily—in various other cities. Apamaea (the Hellenistic military base), Tyre, and Damascus are mentioned, and unrest or insurrection led to Jerusalem being garrisoned by Roman legionaries on various occasions during the generation between Pompey and the victory of Augustus.

Until the late 2d century A.D., the army seems to have consisted of 3 legions, 8 cavalry regiments, and 19 or 20 infantry regiments. The overall total of about 30,000 men was probably little different from the Augustan period, although the proportion of auxiliaries may have been greater.

By this time, most allied states were made into new provinces. Much of the former Herodian territories was transformed into the province of Judea and allowed a garrison of auxiliary troops largely formed out of the army of Herod and his sons. After the First Jewish Revolt (66–71), a legion was established in Jerusalem. After the Second Jewish Revolt (132–35), Hadrian placed a second legion in the Vale of Jezreel. The army in the province in the later 2d century was some 17,000. Finally, in A.D. 106, the Nabatean kingdom was annexed and became the core of the province of Arabia with a legion; the total garrison was probably about 8,000–10,000.

By the death of Hadrian (A.D. 138), there was only one legion more than under Augustus—nine now, but the distribution reflected an altering strategy and preoccupations. The three legions in Egypt under Augustus had been reduced to one, giving a total of ca. 13,000 legionaries and auxiliaries there in the early 2d century; Galatia no longer had a legionary garrison. The East from Aegean to

Egypt had some 90,000 troops, but most were now in frontier provinces. The striking exception was Judea/Syria Palaestina with no frontier but a huge garrison.

Local recruitment had gradually orientalized the legions. In the 2d century, the units which dominate the army lists for the eastern provinces are those recruited in Asia Minor (Phrygians, Galatians, and Paphlagonians) and Greater Syria itself (from Chalcis, Damascus, Palmyra, Arabia Petrea, and the cities of Judea/Palaestina). There seem to have been major recruitment drives in the Syrian region at the time of Nero's wars in Armenia and later in connection with the suppression of the Jewish revolt. Until the First Jewish Revolt, Jews were exempted from conscription, but the practice changed after that time.

In the early Julio-Claudian period the legions were concentrated in N Syria. By the 2d century, they were strung out from north to south and largely along the eastern periphery of the provinces—Satala, Melitene, Samosata, Cyrrhus, Raphanaea, and Bostra; the anomaly is Judea, with legions at Caparcotna and Jerusalem. Few auxiliary units can be located, but if Judea is any guide, in the 1st century many were placed in the towns of the region and a few strongpoints.

Unlike the western provinces, the military camps of the East are difficult to find. Troops were often quartered in the many towns of the region and were billeted directly on households. That was unwelcome and unsatisfactory and the solution was either to construct a camp next to a town or take over an entire quarter. Examples of both practices can be seen at Bostra where the early 2d century legionary fortress was established on the N side of the city, and at Dura Europos, where the late 2d century camp was developed inside a walled off part of the town. The proximity of soldier and civilian would be a mixed blessing. Undisciplined behavior and petty tyrannies by soldiers are a common refrain in ancient documents in general. On the other hand, soldiers brought useful spending power from their regular pay and occasional bonuses. After retirement, relatively few soldiers in the East were established in formal military colonies. Caesar and Augustus founded several in Asia Minor, but in Syria there were only three. Berytus (Beirut) and Heliopolis (Baalbek) were apparently refounded by Augustus after the civil wars. Claudius founded Ptolemais (Akko) in ca. A.D. 53/4. Later, Vespasian made Caesarea a colony but without the introduction of veterans.

3. The Military Background to the NT. In the general absence of community-based forces in the Roman Empire, soldiers were used to maintain law and order. The consequences were predictable. Much petty disorder went unchecked; military intervention, when it came, was heavy handed and often bloody. Inevitably, soldiers were treated warily, with fear, distrust and dislike. Ancient sources in general depict the soldier as despotic. In Syria, and most particularly in Judea, there was an additional factor. Because Jews were long exempted from military service to Rome, they had no family links and few shared values with the troops in the province (but cf. below). The parable of how one should react when pressed to carry a pack for a mile (Matt 5:41) symbolizes the common perception of the petty tyrannies of the military.

The situation was more difficult still in Judea. The Hasmonaean rulers of the region had employed native Jewish troops extensively. Herod the Great had likewise used many Jewish recruits in the civil war in which he had overthrown his Hasmonean rival, Antigonus; his final success, however, was built in part on foreign mercenaries and—not for the last time, on Roman troops. The war was long and bloody, and Herod was subsequently ruthless in consolidating his position. Between 37–30 B.C. his position was underpinned by a legion Antony based at Jerusalem; however, this was withdrawn by Octavian when Roman forces were reassigned in the East.

The elite units in Herod's own pay were foreign mercenaries. Already during the Antonian phase he had recruited non-Jewish troops in Judea as well as Ituraean forces from Mt. Lebanon. Then, in 30 B.C., Octavian made him a gift of 400 Gauls, till recently employed by Cleopatra (Jos. *Ant.* 15 §217; *JW* 1 §397). Such western troops were evidently prized; a generation later, Gallic, German, and Thracian regiments were the principal guards at his funeral (Jos. *Ant.* 17 §198). Within his kingdom, he was able to enroll troops from among his fellow Idumeans, from Samaria and Trachonitis, and from among the "Greek" inhabitants of his cities. There were Jewish troops too, though the best known were not indigenous but the 500 archers who had fled from Babylonia with their chief Zamaris and his family shortly before Herod's death (*Ant* 17 §24). The size of his royal army is not clear: certainly several thousand in addition to military colonists acting as reservists.

Like other allied rulers before and after him, Herod seems to have modeled his forces in part at least on Roman military practices. Units seem to be cohort sized (500), and some of his senior officers—the tribune Volumnius, and the cavalry and infantry commanders, Gratus and Rufus—bear Roman names. The loyalty of these troops was further guaranteed by his generous land grants to them, many being established in colonies to secure themselves and the neighborhood. The largest and best known was Samaria, renamed Sebaste in honor of the Emperor Augustus, to which were allocated 6,000 colonists, many of them veterans. Others were located at Gaba (known as "City of the Horsemen") east of Mt. Carmel, and at Heshbon, beyond the Dead Sea in Perea. Farther afield, at least 2,000 Idumeans were settled in their home territory. Three thousand were settled in Trachonitis and were destroyed in a rebellion in 10–9 B.C.; their successors, the Babylonians of Zamaris, were established as colonists at Bathyra in Batanea.

As well as these secure islands of military colonists, Herod established fortresses to watch over the population. In Jerusalem it was the Antonia fortress and a citadel in the upper city; east of Jerusalem and in the Jordan Valley were strongholds at Cyprus, Herodium, Hyrcania, and Alexandrium; on either side of the Dead Sea were his fortress palaces at Masada and at Machaerus on the borders of the Nabatean kingdom. There were probably other detachments based in his new city of Caesarea and in Idumea, where the likely forts and fortresses were at Arad, Malatha, and Oresa. See HERODIAN ARMY.

After Herod's death in 4 B.C., there were uprisings in his kingdom, and his army split in its loyalties over the succession of his sons, whom the non-Jewish troops—

including 3,000 Sebastenians (from Samaria-Sebaste)—supported. In response, Augustus had a Roman legion from Syria installed in Jerusalem. However, when the rebellion flared up more fiercely, this legion was itself besieged by the rebels and had to be rescued by the return of Quinctilius Varus, the governor of Syria, with much of his provincial army. Just as Herod himself had supplied troops in ca. 25 B.C. to support a Roman campaign into the Arabian peninsula and had gone with a fleet to join a Roman campaign to the Bosporus in 14, Varus now called upon the forces of the various allied rulers in the region to support him in Judea. However, the troops sent by the Nabatean king were more intent on revenging age-old enmities and were soon sent away. The uprising spread from Jerusalem into the Perea, Idumea, and Galilee and required the combined efforts of the loyal Herodian troops and Varus's army. Much of Jerusalem was damaged or destroyed, the city of Sepphoris and numerous towns and villages, especially in Galilee, were sacked. The legion was retained in Jerusalem, probably until the return of Archelaus.

Because of these events, the installation of Herod's sons in various parts of his kingdom was even more dependent on non-Jewish mercenaries. Prominent in Josephus's account of the uprisings of 4 B.C. are the Sebastenians and Trachonite archers; curiously, the European mercenaries are never mentioned again.

Within ten years, the tetrarch Archelaus, who had obtained Judea, Samaria and Idumea, had been removed by Augustus and his territories formed into a province under a prefect. These governors had no legionaries at their direct disposal but relied instead on the Caesarean and Sebastenian regiments formed by Herod. These troops are not actually mentioned under either Archelaus (4 B.C.–A.D. 6), the Prefects (A.D. 6–41), or Herod Agrippa I (A.D. 41–4) when he briefly recovered his grandfather's kingdom. However, at Herod's death in 4 B.C. Josephus reports that Herod's cavalry and infantry commanders, Rufus and Gratus, supported the Romans with "3,000 Sebastenians." They are almost certainly the predecessors of "the regiment of Caesarean cavalry (500 men) and five regiments of Sebastenian infantry (2,500 men)" stationed at Caesarea in 44 (*Ant.* 19 §356–66).

With the creation of a province in A.D. 6, the royal forces were apparently incorporated into the Roman army as auxiliaries. The major force consisted of 3,000 cavalry and infantry originally raised in Sebaste and Caesarea, named now (if not already under their romanophile Herodian masters) *Ala I Sebastenorum* and *Cohortes I–V Sebastenorum.*

The prefects of Judea also removed the seat of government to Caesarea, where at least some of the Sebastenian regiments are later attested. It is at Caesarea too that the *Cohors (II?) Italica* was to be found ca. A.D. 40. An unnamed cohort was based in Jerusalem and the various strongholds probably retained their Herodian garrisons. Extra troops were certainly brought to Jerusalem during the great religious festivals.

The troubles of Judea under these prefects became progressively more severe. Unrest and uprisings caused by provocative action by the governors, required military action. The major forces in Syria, however, were little in evidence. In 37, Vitellius advanced through Galilee on his way to Arabia Petrea. Not until 40, however, when the Emperor Gaius ordered his own statues set up in the Temple at Jerusalem, did troops from Syria intervene in the province of Judea directly.

Virtually nothing can be said of the forces of Herod's other sons in their respective segments of the former kingdom. Since Philip's tetrarchy included the difficult lands beyond the Sea of Galilee, he presumably needed to maintain his father's military arrangements. He died in 37, and his forces would have been briefly under Roman control until given to Herod Agrippa I. Herod Antipas rebuilt and fortified Sepphoris in his Galilean lands and founded and fortified Betharamphtha/Julias in the Perea. That he maintained the frontier fortress at Machaerus and had an army is revealed by the events surrounding the flight of his Nabatean wife and Antipas' defeat in battle by her father. The event provoked a Roman invasion of Arabia Petrea—apparently through Galilee, though it was called off when news arrived of the death of the Emperor Tiberius (A.D. 37). Antipas himself, was deposed in 39.

Herod Agrippa I inherited first the recently annexed territories of Philip (37), then those of Antipas (39), and finally (41) the province of Judea itself. Since he certainly took over the Sebastenian regiments which had been "Roman" for a generation, there is no reason to doubt that he also acquired the forces of his uncles in their former tetrarchies. With a royal army restored, he soon appointed his own commander and was proceeding to refortify Jerusalem when instructed by the suspicious governor of Syria to desist. With Agrippa's death in 44, the new Roman governors, now called procurators, to whom the entire kingdom passed, would have taken charge of the royal forces, converting them into formal auxiliary regiments of the Roman army. Explicit evidence is given in the case of the Caesarean and Sebastenian regiments at Caesarea who, despite the Emperor Claudius' anger at their behavior, were allowed to remain in the province.

The procurators, provocative and violent, used their forces ruthlessly to put down all opposition. A striking feature of both governors and their troops is the extent to which they were anti-Jewish. The procurator Cumanus, for example, took the part of the Samaritans though they appear to have been the aggressors; his successor, Felix, supported the Greeks of Caesarea against their Jewish fellow citizens. Two major affronts to Jewish sensibilities were provoked by soldiers; one when a soldier on duty during Passover exposed himself to the crowds and later when one publicly destroyed a Torah. The regiments are not named, but they were plainly non-Jewish.

The loss of life in disturbances and riots in the cities was considerable and the countryside became ever more lawless. In a deteriorating situation, the governors of Syria had to intervene more frequently both to restore order and curb the procurators. Cassius Longinus went to Jerusalem with troops from Syria in 45/6; in ca. 52 Ummidius Quadratus had to end the Jewish-Samaritan fighting; finally, in 66 there was Cestius Gallus's intervention with a legion and his subsequent disastrous retreat from Jerusalem. The planting of a new Roman colony with legionary veterans at Ptolemais, on the very edge of the Judean province, was another sign of growing concern. It was in this context that the Apostle Paul's imprisonment at Caesarea took place.

The outbreak of the First Revolt in 66 was the occasion of major and protracted intervention by Roman forces. In describing events, Josephus reveals the military arrangements in the province at that moment. In addition to forces at Jerusalem and Caesarea, there were, as might have been inferred, garrisons in Herod the Great's fortresses at Cypros, Masada, and Machaerus. Otherwise unknown are the regiment of cavalry and one of infantry at Ascalon, derived perhaps from forces Salome may have had when the city was given to her after Herod's death.

Immense forces were mustered by Rome to suppress the Revolt. Josephus provides the clearest descriptions. In 67 Vespasian mustered an army at Ptolemais: *Legio X Fretensis* from Syria and *V Macedonica* and *XV Apollinaris* which had been transferred to the East only a few years earlier during Nero's eastern war, from Moesia and Pannonia respectively. The auxiliary units included the Sebastenians from Caesarea, one regiment of cavalry and five of infantry. In addition there were five *alae* and eighteen cohorts from Syria. None are named, but one is otherwise known to have been the *Ala Gaetulorum.* Ten of the cohorts are said to have been "milliary." The neighboring allied kings were there in strength; Antiochus of Commagene, Sohaemus of Emesa, and Herod Agrippa II each provided 2,000 archers and 1,000 cavalry; Malchus, the Nabatean king, sent 5,000 infantry (mainly archers) and 1,000 cavalry. Apparently some 50,000 in total; Josephus says 60,000. In 70, when Titus took command, his forces had been depleted by detachments drawn off by Vespasian to wage his civil wars in the West, but were then augmented by an additional legion, *XII Fulminata* (which had been devastated in Cestius Gallus's retreat in 66), and by further troops from Syria and Egypt. No total is given.

After the war, the province was raised in status and given a major garrison. Henceforth the governors were senators and a Syrian legion, *X Fretensis,* was based in the ruins of Jerusalem, though with a probable detachment at Caesarea. Eight hundred legionary veterans were established as colonists at Emmaus, near Jerusalem. The Sebastenian regiments whose behavior had done so much to cause the revolt, were placed. Most information comes from discharge diplomas, but the earliest is for 86, and names only two *alae* and four cohorts. The two *alae* suggest the composition of the new garrison. The *Ala Gaetulorum,* is known to have fought in the war, presumably now retained; the *Ala I Thracum Mauretana* is thought to have arrived after the war in exchange for the *Ala Sebastenorum* which subsequently appears in Mauretania. Other regiments arrived in later years and some left to go to Egypt or Arabia (created in 106), suggesting a certain amount of mobility. The ethnic character of the new troops is unclear. Spanish and Thracian regiments dominate in the later 1st century, but the 2d century saw many more eastern regiments: Phrygians, Galatians, Damascenes, and Nabateans, and even a regiment of Sebastenians again. Many of the western regiments are likely to have lost their original ethnic character before arriving in Judea/Palaestina, but that is less likely to have been the case with the oriental units. The total is not known, but is unlikely to have been less than the 3,000 Sebastenians removed from the province.

There was a major change in Hadrian's reign (117–135). The status of the province was raised with ex-consuls as governors and a second legion installed. This permanent addition was a Syrian legion, *VI Ferrata,* established at Caparcotna near Megiddo. Initially, however, it may have been preceded by a new legion, *II Traiana.*

The Second Revolt (132–35) again saw huge additional forces drafted in. The garrison of what was now called Syria Palaestina remained at two legions after the war, though the numbers of auxiliary units may have increased. Discharge diplomas of 139 and 186 list three *alae* and twelve cohorts (ca. 7,000 men) and two *alae* and seven cohorts (ca. 5,500 men) respectively. The overall total in the 2d century may have been some 17,000 troops. Units are attested at various times at Hebron, En-Gedi, and Haifa, and possibly at Emmaus and Sebaste.

Beyond the Jordan were further troops. First, with the creation in 53 of a kingdom for Herod Agrippa II over Trachonitis, Batanea, and Gaulanitis (further cities and lands were added later), Judea lost some territory and the king reestablished a royal army. Inscriptions give some clues as to the character of that army, in particular its officers—though plainly native to the region, some the descendants of the Babylonian colonists, often bore Roman names (e.g. Modius Aequus, T. Mucius Clemens, and Lucius Oboulnius). It is tempting to regard this as a consequence of these regiments having been incorporated into the Roman auxilia in 37 and between 44–53. During the First Revolt, Herod Agrippa II contributed 3,000 men, the equivalent of six regiments. Most Hellenistic cities beyond the Jordan were part of Syria, and one at least—Gerasa—had *Ala I Augusta Thracum* in garrison for a time after the First Revolt. After 106, Gerasa and some of these other Hellenistic cities, became part of Arabia, which received a garrison of a legion, *III Cyrenaica,* and several thousand auxiliaries; some transferred from Judea, which apparently received two regiments of the Nabatean royal army (*Cohortes IV* and *IV Petraeorum*), attested on a discharge diploma of 139.

4. The Roman Army in the Bible. The presence and activities of the Roman army are mentioned or implied frequently in the NT. The adoption of the term "legion" to explain large numbers reflects this awareness; thus the man whose name is Legion, from all the devils which possessed him (Luke 8:30), and the observation of Jesus concerning his Father sending a dozen legions of angels to save him (Matt 26:53). Of course, some of the references are to the troops of allied rulers. The Massacre of the Innocents (Matt 2:16), would have been the work of Herod's royal troops—perhaps from Jerusalem or Herodium. Later, Herod Antipas sent a soldier of his guard to behead John the Baptist (Matt 6:27), and it is again Herod's soldiers who mistreated Jesus in Jerusalem after Pilate discovered he was a Galilean and handed him over to the tetrarch's jurisdiction (Luke 23:11). Later, it was the soldiers of Herod Agrippa I who arrested and put Peter under guard in Jerusalem (Acts 12:4). Interestingly, the Herodian soldiers were organized into watches of four men, modelled presumably on a Roman *contubernium* of eight men. We may envisage that when Herod Agrippa II entered the Roman province—as he did when making his courtesy call on the procurator Porcius Felix at Caesarea in ca. 52 (Acts 15:13), he came attended by troops. An interesting royal soldier is the centurion at Capernaum who sought Jesus' aid to cure his servant/son; he is described as being a friend of the Jews and of having built the community's synagogue (Luke 23:11; cf. Matt 8:5–13, John 4:46–53). His rank, centurion *(hekatontarchos)*, further illustrates the Roman model of these forces of the allied rulers. In Jerusalem itself were to be found the Temple Guards. They appear at Gethsemane (John 18:3, 12) and were presumably the force behind Paul's persecution of the early Church (Acts 8:1–3).

It is largely the regular army of the Roman governors which is mentioned in the Gospels and in Acts. The references are at their vaguest in the account of the arrest and crucifixion of Jesus, improve with Peter's ministry in his homeland and are most informative with Paul. Pilate's soldiers flog and mock Jesus in the court of the governor's headquarters (Matt 27:26–37 = Mark 15:21), subsequently crucified him, one of them stabbing him with a spear (Matt 27:35 = Mark 15:24 = Luke 23:36–47 = John 19:17) and later put a guard over the tomb (Matt 27:62–66; 28: 11–15). The location of the flogging is said to be the *praetorium* (Mark 15:16) which was probably the Antonia fortress near the Temple Mount, rather than the Herodian palace in the SW of the city, where the procurators probably took up residence when in Jerusalem. See PRAETORIUM. Pilate's force is described as a cohort *(speires)*, all of which was called together to witness the punishment (Mark 15:16 = Matt 27:27). The only individual identified is an unnamed centurion in charge of the crucifixion (Matt 27:54 = Mark 15:39 = Luke 23:47).

A single passage dealing with the ministry of Peter is useful. "At Caesarea there was a man named Cornelius, a centurion in the Italian cohort, as it was called" (Acts 10). Two *Cohortes Italicae* are attested, but both rather later. This passage gives the earliest reference (A.D. 40) to what is probably the *Cohors II Italica voluntariorum civium Romanorum* and locates it at Caesarea. In the second half of the century—perhaps after the Jewish Revolt—it was part of the Syrian army. In 40 it was evidently part of the prefectural army. The titles suggest that in origin at least it was composed of Roman citizens who were in some sense "Italian"; the only other known soldiers of the regiment are, however, Semites from Philadelphia (Amman). Cornelius himself is described in terms which make it clear that he was not Jewish but was probably one of those Gentiles attached to Jewish communities who were not proselytes but "God-fearers" *(theosebeis)*, Reminiscent, in fact, of the centurion whose servant Jesus had cured at Capernaum. Because Josephus regularly depicts the troops in the province displaying a general insensitivity towards the Jewish religion, indeed, often an open partiality for the non-Jew, the accounts of these two officers provide useful counterbalance. Just as interesting, he has servants, a family, and a home in Caesarea—illustrating how the ban on marriage was widely ignored. Given the apparent origin, the regiment is unlikely to have been inherited from Herod and Archelaus, but, rather, to have been introduced by the prefects of Judea, and as such is evidence that the provincial garrison under the prefects was more than just the former royal troops.

Paul's rescue from a mob in Jerusalem ca. 58 and his subsequent imprisonment and transfer to Rome brought him into close association with the Roman army. In Jerusalem he was rescued by the intervention of the tribune (chiliarch) of the cohort in the city and taken to its barracks (Acts 21:31–23:23). The tribune, Claudius Lysias, astonished to discover that Paul is a Roman citizen by birth, admits that he had had to purchase his citizenship. The obvious inference is that the tribune was a provincial, perhaps an easterner (he speaks Greek), commanding an auxiliary regiment. Paul was subsequently escorted to Caesarea by troops of the Jerusalem garrison. Acts gives their number as 200 infantry, 70 cavalry, and 200 dexiolabois. The meaning of the last is not known; "spearmen" or "light-armed" are guesses. The numbers are interesting, however. The infantry stayed with Paul only as far as Antipatris and he may not have known their exact numbers; the cavalry were with him as far as Caesarea, and the figure may be precise or very close. The overall number is striking, representing the equivalent of an entire cohort. The implication is that Lysias had a force at his disposal which was mixed infantry and cavalry and that he had more than just a single cohort. A possible explanation is that because of the crowds in Jerusalem for Pentecost, the normal modest garrison was reinforced to cope with the turmoil and possible disturbances.

After his long imprisonment at Caesarea, Paul was handed over to Julius, a centurion of the *Cohors Augusta* (*speires* Sebastes), who, together with some other soldiers, escorted him on his sea journey to Rome. Julius is plainly a Roman and his unit is attested serving in the Syrian Hauran in the 80s in the army of Herod Agrippa II. It would seem that the procurator, Porcius Felix, who was then entertaining Herod Agrippa II and his sister Berenice at Caesarea, agreed to send Paul to Rome under escort of some of the king's troops, evidently a very Romanized unit, perhaps with Roman officers. In Rome, these troops will have been housed in the Castra Peregrina. Though uncommon, such exciting journeys to the capital for provincial troops occurred from time to time. For Judea, for example, Josephus twice reports the Syrian governor Quinctilius Varus (7/6–4 B.C.) sending prisoners to Rome who would have required escorts (*Ant.* 17 §303 and *JW* 2 §77, 83). The same would have been true when a later governor, Quadratus (48–52), sent a number of high-ranking prisoners to Rome.

Bibliography

Applebaum, S. 1971. Jews and Service in the Roman Army. Pp. 181–84 in *Roman Frontier Studies 1967*, ed. S. Applebaum. Tel Aviv.

Broughton, T. R. S. 1933. Additional Note XXXIII: The Roman Army. Vol. 5, pp. 427–45 in *The Beginnings of Christianity*, Pt. 1, *The Acts of the Apostles*, ed. F. J. Foakes Jackson and K. Lake. London. Repr. Grand Rapids, 1979.

Campbell, J. B. 1984. *The Emperor and the Roman Army, 31 B.C.–A.D. 235*. Oxford.

Connolly, P. 1981. *Greece And Rome At War*. London.

Davies, R. W. 1974. The Daily Life of the Roman Soldier under the Principate. *ANRW* II/1: 299–338.

Gracey, M. H. 1981. The Roman Army in Syria, Judaea and Arabia. Diss. Oxford.
———. 1987. The Armies of the Judaean Client Kings. Pp. 311–23 in *The Defence of the Roman and Byzantine East,* ed. P. Freeman and D. Kennedy. BARIS 297. Oxford.
Holder, P. 1980. *The Auxilia from Augustus to Trajan.* BARIS 70. Oxford.
Isaac, B. 1984. Bandits in Judaea and Arabia. *HSCP* 88: 171–203.
———. 1989. *The Limits Of Empire: The Roman Army in the East.* Cambridge.
Junkelmann, M. 1986. *Die Legionem des Augustus.* Kulturgeschichte der Antiken Welt 33. Mainz.
Juster, J. 1914. *Les Juifs dans l'empire romain.* Paris.
Kennedy, D. L. fc. The Contribution of Syria to the Roman Imperial Army. In *Eastern Frontier of the Roman Empire Colloquium,* ed. D. French and C. Lightfoot. BARIS 30. Oxford.
Kennedy, D. L., and Riley, D. N. 1990. *Rome's Desert Frontier from the Air.* London.
Keppie, L. 1984. *The Making of the Roman Army.* London.
Redde, M. 1986. *Mare Nostrum: Les infrastructures, le dispositif et l'histoire de la marine militaire sous l'empire romain.* BEFAR 260. Rome.
Speidel, M. P. 1982/83. The Roman Army in Judaea under the Procurators. *Ancient Society* 13/14: 233–40.
Starr, C. G. 1960. *The Roman Imperial Navy, 31 BC–AD 324.* 2d ed. Cambridge.
Wacher, J., ed. 1987. *The Roman World.* Vol. 1/3–4.
Watson, G. R. 1969. *The Roman Soldier.* London.
Webster, G. 1985. *The Roman Imperial Army.* 3d ed. London.

DAVID KENNEDY

ROMAN CHRISTIANITY. See CHRISTIANITY (CHRISTIANITY IN ROME).

ROMAN COLONIES (JUDEA). Roman colonies *(Coloniae civium Romanorum)* were founded as early as the 4th century B.C. Originally they were modest settlements consisting of some 300 families sent to settle in various places in Italy. They remained part of the Roman state, and the settlers retained their citizenship. In the 2d century large colonies of Roman citizens were founded with a population of 2,000 to 5,000 settlers, usually in newly conquered territory. Although still part of the Roman state, they were organized as cities with their own local authorities. In the Gracchan age (163–121 B.C.) and thereafter, Roman colonies were often established outside Italy so as to provide the city proletariat or veteran soldiers with land. The greatest number of veteran colonies were founded in various provinces in the age of Caesar and Augustus. These were planted either on unoccupied sites or imposed on existing cities. The last veteran colonies were founded in the reign of Hadrian (A.D. 117–38). In the mid-1st century a related development took its inception, namely, granting the status of *colonia civium Romanorum* to provincial communities without settlement by Roman veterans. The most important consequence of this was that Roman citizenship was conferred on part of the citizens of such a community—those who had fulfilled certain civic offices in the colony. In the E provinces, grants of colonial status are attested from the second half of the 1st century through the 3d. Acquiring the rank of a *colonia* also considerably enhanced the prestige of a town. The grant might include additional privileges such as the *ius Italicum,* which provided for the same rights as colonies in Italy, including exemption from direct taxation of land or persons.

A. Berytus and Heliopolis

Veterans were settled at Berytus (Beirut) in 14 B.C. by Agrippa, although epigraphic evidence may suggest an earlier date (after Actium and before 27; *CIL* III 14165.6). The legal status of Heliopolis (Baalbek) is a matter of controversy. Either it was founded as a separate colony by Augustus (27 B.C.–A.D. 14), or it was part of the territory of Berytus until the reign of Septimius (A.D. 193–211), when it is on record as a separate colony (references and discussion by Rey-Coquais *IGLS* 6.34, n. 9; and 1978: 51). The Romans were faced with banditry based in the mountains and along the coast, and it has been argued that it was the task of the veterans to suppress it. However, it was quite difficult to solve such problems. While the settlement of retired soldiers in the fertile plain would guarantee a loyal and reliable presence there, military forces would have to operate in the mountains in order to fight within the bandits' own territory and in order to keep the roads safe. This included the difficult road through the mountains which linked Berytus with the Beqaᶜ valley.

A famous inscription originally set up at Berytus honors an equestrian officer who was dispatched by the governor of Syria at the beginning of the 1st century to destroy a fortress of Ituraeans in the mountains of Lebanon (*CIL* III 6687; *ILS* 2683; Gabba 1958: 52–61, Pl. 3). The officer, it may be noted, later became *quaestor, aedilis, duumvir,* and *pontifex* of the colony. Berytus served as base of operations just as the colony of Ptolemais-Acco did in 67. In 4 B.C., Berytus provided Varus, on his way to Judea, with 1,500 infantry troops (*JW* 2.5.1 §67; *Ant* 17.10.9 §287). These were local citizens who formed a militia (there is also evidence of such militias from other towns). In 66, such units from several Syrian cities joined the forces of Cestius Gallus when he marched against the Jews (*JW* 2.18.9 §502, 506). They were very poor fighters. Inscriptions also testify to the presence of soldiers on active service at Heliopolis. The epigraphic material clearly shows the social and cultural impact of the veteran settlement in both centers and in their territory far into the 3d century. Veterans were settled in and around cities and in the Beqaᶜ valley, but not in the mountains. These became crown land, as apparent from numerous Hadrianic inscriptions referring to imperial forests (fully published and discussed in *IGLS* 8.3).

One has the impression that urban and rural development was a slow process. Dated inscriptions are not found in substantial numbers before the second half of the 1st century A.D., almost a century after the foundation. The road system in the region is marked by milestones of the 2d century. Whatever the status of Heliopolis before Septimius Severus, it was taken over by veterans in the time of Augustus. It is therefore of interest to see what the inscriptions from Heliopolis tell us of the urban development of this town and its vicinity (*IGLS,* vol. 6). Here, too, evidence is lacking of an immediate or early development following the settlement of veterans. The earliest imperial texts from the area date to the second half of the 1st century A.D. On the other hand, we are informed that Herod of Judea built exedras, porticos, temples, and forums in Berytus and Tyre (*JW* 1.21.11 §422) Agrippa I built an extraordinarily expensive and beautiful theater at Berytus, where he also built an amphitheater at great expense, as well as baths and porticos. He donated public spectacles and provided great numbers of gladiators for the amphitheater (*Ant.* 19.7.5 §335–37). Agrippa II built (another?) expensive theater at Berytus. He donated annual public spectacles costing thousands of drachmas. He gave grain and distributed olive oil to the citizens and adorned the whole city with statues and replicas of ancient sculptures (*Ant.* 20.9.4 §211). Epigraphical confirmation has been found in the form of an inscription which records the restoration by Berenice and Agrippa II of a building erected by Herod the Great (Cagnat 1928: 157–67; cf. *ANRW* 2:135–63; pl. ii.5).

Public inscriptions set up by the town are in Latin, as would be expected in a Roman veteran colony, even in the East. There is less published material from Berytus than from Heliopolis, but even there inscriptions are in Latin (e.g., Lauffray 1944–45: 13–80, esp. 60; 67f.; 77). There are very few in Greek and none date earlier than the 4th century (*IGLS* 6: nos. 2740, 2827ff., 2830ff.). Inscriptions set up by private individuals tend to be in Latin as well. It is clearly significant that Latin is used by civilians in the surrounding territory (*IGLS* 6: 2894, 2904, 2908ff., 2925, 2955).

There are many inscriptions which show that citizens of the colony combined army careers with local office. Some of them reached very high positions, including membership in the Roman Senate (*IGLS* 6: 2781, 2786ff., 2793–2795). Many citizens of the colony have names which reflect long-standing citizenship (*IGLS* 6: 2714:L. Antonius Silo; 2716:L. Julius Severus; 2781:L. Antonius Naso). On the whole purely Latin names are far more frequent than Greek, Semitic, or mixed names, and this is true for the inscriptions from the town itself as well as for those from the territory.

It is clear that the impact of the settlement of legionary veterans was quite remarkable for its long-lasting intensity. The existence of a distinguished school of Roman law at Berytus has always been seen as an indication of the Latin character of this town. Epigraphical evidence proves that the effects of the settlement of veterans on the social and cultural life of both Berytus and Heliopolis, both in the towns and the surrounding territory, lasted at least until the 4th century.

B. Ptolemais (Acco)

A Roman colony was established at Ptolemais (Acco) in Syria-Phoenicia following serious trouble between Jews and Samaritans in the reign of Claudius (A.D. 41–54; *HJP*² 1: 458–60, 462). An investigation was carried out on the spot by the governor of Syria, and the prefect of Judea was dismissed ca. A.D. 52. Veterans of the four Syrian legions were settled in a new colony at Ptolemais between 51/2 and 54. The last precolonial coin-issue of Ptolemais dates from A.D. 51/2 (Kadman 1961: nos. 86–90; Seyrig 1962: 39; note the founder's coins with *vexilla* [military ensigns] Kadman 1961: no. 92). The foundation by Claudius is mentioned by Pliny (*HN* 5.17.75): "*Colonia Claudi Caesaris Ptolemais, quae quondam Acco* . . ." A new road was constructed from Antioch in Syria to the colony. Milestones of A.D. 56 record the construction of a road "*ab Antiochea ad novam coloniam Ptolemaida*" (Goodchild 1948: 91–123, esp. 126). Together, these items prove the date of the foundation of the veteran colony.

Admittedly, the connection between the troubles in Judea and these measures has not been proven (Josephus does not mention the foundation of the colony); however, the chronological sequence indicates a causal connection. Ptolemais lay just N and W of the boundary of Judea and was situated between the sea and the hills of Lower Galilee which were occupied by Jews. It had the last good harbor N of Caesarea and was the last major town to be passed when traveling from Syria to Judea along the coastal road. Ulpian (*Dig.* 15.1.3) describes it as lying between Palaestina and Syria. "*Ptolemaeensium enim colonia, quae inter Phoenicen et Palaestinam sita est, nihil praeter nomen coloniae habet.*" The last part of this sentence suggests that the colony had no additional financial privileges such as the *ius Italicum* (see above), or the exemptions from taxation enjoyed by Caesarea and Aelia Capitolina. Perhaps it received *ius Italicum* in the reign of Elagabalus (A.D. 218–222), for city coins of his reign show Marsyas (Kadman 1961: no. 163), but this cannot be taken as proof of such a grant.

The town proved useful in A.D. 67, when it served as Vespasian's base of operations. It was precisely such a function which a veteran colony could fulfill. Only after the complete subjugation of Galilee did Vespasian move his headquarters to Caesarea (*JW* 3.2.4 §29; 4.2 §64; 9.1 §409). The veterans at Ptolemais could not possibly fight the rebellious Jews, but they could provide the Roman army with a reliable base. The establishment of a veteran colony at Ptolemais clearly must be distinguished from the granting of privileges, also under Claudius, to several towns including Tiberias, which received the name "Claudiopolis."

The foundation of the colony involved both drastic reorganization of the territory and land grants to veterans. The land, whether bought or confiscated, was taken from its original possessors, and the infusion of veterans entailed the imposition of a new local leadership. Unlike the mere grant of a new name, it was a project to the disadvantage of the existing population. Otherwise, little is known of this city. There are not many inscriptions, but the few that have been found fit the pattern established at Heliopolis. 1946: 85, n. 2). Families of distinction may have lived in the city, since it produced at least one distinguished person: the consul Flavius Boethus, governor of Palestine (A.D. 162–66), known from the works of Galen as a scholar and philosopher with an interest in medicine (Smallwood 1981: 552).

C. Vespasian's Organization of Judea

"About the same time Caesar sent instructions to Bassus and Laberius Maximus, the procurator, to dispose of all Jewish land. For he founded there no city of his own while keeping their territory, but only to eight hundred veterans did he assign a place for settlement called Emmaus . . ." (*JW* 7.6.6 §216 as translated and interpreted by Isaac

1984: 44–50). In this passage, often misunderstood, Josephus wants to emphasize that Vespasian gave instructions to sell all confiscated land in Judea. No Jewish land was granted to foreign settlers, because he did not establish a new Flavian city (i.e., a veteran colony) to replace Jerusalem. Josephus explicitly mentions the modest settlement at Emmaus (Luke 24) as an exception. The site can be identified without doubt with modern Moza. It must be emphasized that this was not a settlement with the status of a *polis*, let alone of a Roman colony. It does not appear in the lists of Roman colonies in the *digest* and did not issue coinage. It is today in one of the most fertile and pleasant valleys around Jerusalem, well watered with ample farm land and situated on the main road from the coastal plain to the city. Even this veteran settlement—it was too small to receive the status of a colony—has left an imprint. The village still bore the name "Qolonia" in the 19th century and the tombstone of a girl with a Roman name was found on the spot, inscribed in Latin (Landau 1967: 369).

Caesarea received colonial status from Vespasian, but it is clear that this was not accompanied by the settlement of veterans in the town (Isaac 1980–81: 39–43). It was a reward for support in the Jewish War and probably commemorated the fact that in Caesarea Vespasian was first proclaimed emperor by his own troops—hence the name of the colony: *Colonia Prima Flavia Caesarea.* The grant of colonial status had a profound impact. It meant that all citizens of the town received Roman citizenship; tax privileges were granted as well, as appears from two passages in the *digest* (Paulus *Dig.* L 15.8.7; Ulp. *Dig.* L 15.1). This, then, was the first "titular" colony established in the E part of the empire.

Another Roman colony which must be discussed here is Aelia Capitolina at Jerusalem, founded in the reign of Hadrian, an act which, according to Cassius Dio, was the cause of the Bar Kokhba Revolt. It is true that veterans of the legion X Fretensis settled in this colony, but the town remained at the same time the headquarters of the legion. It would therefore be futile to claim that veterans who settled there guarded the region, since a proper legion had its base there. The nature of the colony is intriguing. After 70 Jerusalem became a legionary base. Hadrian refounded the city as a Roman colony, and this led to an anomaly: the existence of both an army base and a Roman colony in the immediate proximity. It has been shown that veteran colonies were normally founded at, or alongside, the site of a legionary base only *after* the legion had moved on elsewhere, leaving the military site vacant (Mann 1983: 60–63). What little evidence there is indicates that the citizens of Aelia Capitolina were veterans of the legion X Fretensis. This may be concluded from colonial coinage with *vexilla* and the emblems of the legion (Kadman 1956: nos. 1 [*vexillum*]; 5 [eagle on shaft]; 6 [boar]). The small number of inscriptions of the period suggests the same (see below). Hadrian, therefore, created an anomalous situation.

It is not clear whether Hadrian did anything to build up Aelia as a city, but the establishment of a veteran colony had advantages from a Roman point of view. It would induce discharged soldiers of the legion to settle there, especially since it enjoyed the same exemption from taxation as Caesarea (Ulp. *Dig.* L 15.1.6; Paulus, *dig.* L 15.8.7). The veterans and their descendants would be a focus of loyalty in the middle of Judea, and the latter might, like the citizens of Caesarea, provide the provincial army with recruits.

There are not many inscriptions from Aelia Capitolina, but it is worth observing that all 16 inscriptions datable to the period from the destruction in 70 until Constantine are in Latin. These include two military inscriptions set up before Hadrian (*AE* 1978: 825; *CIL* III:13587), a number of honorary inscriptions for emperors (*CIL* III:116 [6639]), one inscription for a legionary legate (*CIL* III:6641 [12006a]), a few tombstones of veterans (*CIL* III:14155.3; *AE* 1939: 157; Iliffe 1932: 123, no. 4), and, most significant, tombstones of civilians inscribed not in Greek but in Latin with Roman names (Thomsen 1922: no. 179; *CIL* III:14155.4; Thomsen 1941: no. 182a). While the Byzantine inscriptions (far greater in number) are written in Greek, the pattern formed by the pre-Constantinian inscriptions reminds one of that observed in the material from Heliopolis. Aelia Capitolina apparently showed the characteristics of a veteran colony in the East. Its citizens spoke Latin and preferred to be identified with Rome rather than with the Hellenized Orient. The legion was still in Jerusalem in the mid-3d century, as is shown by a city-coin Herennius Etruscus with emblems of the legion (Hill 1914: 100, no. 104). Eusebius (ca. 260–340) mentions the legion as based at Aela on the Red Sea in his time (*Onomast.* 6, 17–20).

D. Septimius Severus

Severus changed the status of many places in the area, often as a reward or punishment for attitudes during the civil war with Niger (*Dig.* L 15, 1 and 8). In Syria-Palaestina Beth Guvrin and Lydda received city status and became, respectively, Eleutheropolis and Diospolis (for city coinage of Eleutheropolis; see Spijkerman 1972: 369–84; for Diospolis, see Hill 1914: 141, nos. 1f.; Rosenberger 1975–77: 2.28–31; 3.80: more than 10 types from Septimius Severus to Elagabalus). Because of the lack of archaeological and epigraphical material from these towns, they cannot be discussed, profitably but there is no reason to assume that more than a change in legal status was involved. Sebaste received the status of a Roman colony (Paulus, *Dig.* L 15.8.7) between 201 and 211, as apparent from the colonial coinage, probably in 201/2 (Hill 1914: xxxix, 80, nos. 12 f.; the latest precolonial coinage dates to 201/2). Nearby Neapolis was temporarily deprived of city status because of its support of Niger in 194. It is possible that there was a connection between the temporary punishment of one city and the enhancement of its neighbor.

At this time Sebaste was splendidly rebuilt. To this period belong the temple in its later form, the forum, colonnades, a basilica, a columned street, the theater, and the stadium. It has been assumed that there was a connection between the grant of colonial status and a subsequent building program. However, the excavators of Sebaste have concluded that several elements of the program were perhaps already in existence, that is to say that they preceded the change in status. The buildings are not dated by any inscriptions. It is quite possible that the prosperity of the citizens of Sebaste gave them the means to carry out a substantial building program for themselves. It is more likely that these circumstances contributed to the decision to grant colonial status than that the latter was accompanied by imperial munificence of which there is no record.

An inscribed architrave block from the basilica mentions *strategoi,* the common Greek term for the *duoviri* (two-person criminal courts) of a Roman colony (Reisner, et al. 1924: 250, no. 7 and Pl. 59c). One military inscription from the area of the temple has been assigned to the Severan period, though it is not clear on what grounds (ibid., p. 20 no. 30).

Severus organized the new province of Mesopotamia. Several cities there received colonial status from this emperor or his successors, including Singara, Rhesaina, Nisibis, and Carrhae. Nothing is known beyond the fact of the grants themselves. Rhesaina may have been the base of the legion III Parthica, because the name of the legion appears on its coins. This colony would then have been organized after the pattern of Aelia Capitolina, being a town with colonial status where a legion was based. The other legionary base, Singara, where the legion I Parthica was stationed, received colonial status at an uncertain date.

Under Severus, Caracalla, and Elagabalus, the status of many cities in the eastern provinces was changed, but there is no evidence that this involved more than formal or administrative measures (Kindler in *INJ* 1982–83: 79–87; Jones 1971). In Judea, for instance, both Emmaus and Herod's foundation of Antipatris received city status from Elagabalus (on Emmaus, see Jones 1971: 279 and n. 72; *HJP*[2] 1: 512–13n; for coins from Antipatris, all from the reign of Elagabal, see Hill 1914: xv.11; Meshorer 1985: nos. 149–52).

In Syria the cities of Sidon, Tyre, Damascus, Laodicea, Emesa, and Palmyra received colonial rank or additional privileges, as recorded in *Dig.* L 15.1.1; 8.7 and on the coinage Hill 1914: 182, 238, 258, 269, 286). The *Digest* explains that in some cases measures were taken by Septimus Severus to reward or punish cities for their role during the war with his rival Niger.

Bibliography

Avi-Yonah, M. 1938–39. Greek and Latin inscriptions from Jerusalem and Beisan. *QDAP* 8: 54–61.

Cagnat, R. 1928. Une inscription relative à la reine Bérénice. *Musée Belge* 32: 157–67.

Gabba, E. 1958. *Iscrizioni greche e latine per lo studio della bibbia.* Milan.

Goodchild, R. G. 1948. The Coast Road of Phoenicia and Its Roman Milestones. *Berytus* 9: 91–127.

Hill, G. F. 1910. *Catalogue of the Greek Coins of Phoenicia.* London. Repr. Bologna 1965.

———. 1914. *Catalogue of the Greek Coins of Palestine.* London.

———. 1965. *Catalogue of the Greek Coins of Arabia, Mesopotamia, and Persia.* Bologna.

Iliffe, J. H. 1932. Greek and Latin Inscriptions in the Museum. *QDAP* 2: 123, n. 4.

Isaac, B. 1980–81. Roman Colonies in Judea: The Foundation of Aelia Capitolina. *Talanta* 12–13: 31–54.

Jones, A. H. M. 1971. *Cities of the Eastern Roman Provinces.* 2d ed. Oxford.

Kadman, L. 1956. *The Coins of Aelia Capitolina.* Corpus Nummorum Palestinensium 2. Jerusalem.

———. 1957. *The Coins of Caesarea Maritima.* Corpus Nummorum Palestinensium 3. Jerusalem.

———. 1961. *The Coins of Akko-Ptolemais.* Corpus Nummorum Palestinensium 4. Tel Aviv.

Landau, Y. H. 1967. Unpublished Inscriptions from Israel. Pp. 387–90 in *Acts of the 5th International Congress of Greek and Latin Epigraphy.* Cambridge.

Lauffray, J. 1944–45. Forums et monuments de Béryte. *Bulletin de la Musée de Beyrouth* 7: 13–80.

Mann, J. C. 1983. *Legionary Recruitment and Veteran Settlement during the Principate.* London.

Meshorer, Y. 1985. *City-Coins of Eretz-Israel and the Decapolis in the Roman Period.* Jerusalem.

Meyer, J. 1983–84. A Centurial Stone from Shavei Triyyon. *Scripta Classica Israelica* 7: 119–28.

Reisner, G. A.; Fisher, C. S.; and Lyon, D. G. 1924. *Harvard Excavations at Samaria (1908–1910).* 2 vols. Cambridge, MA.

Rey-Coquais, J.-P. 1978. Syrie romaine. *JRS* 68: 51.

Rosenberger, M. 1975–77. *City Coins of Palestine.* Vols. 2–3. Jerusalem.

Seyrig, H. 1962. Le monnayage de Ptolemais. *Revue Numismatique* 4: 25–50.

Smallwood, E. M. 1981. *The Jews under Roman Rule.* 2d ed. Leiden.

Spijkerman, A. 1972. The Coins of Eleutheropolis Iudaeae. *LASBF* 22: 369–84.

Thomsen, P. 1922. *Die griechischen und lateinischen Inschriften der Stadt Jerusalem.* Leipzig.

———. 1941. Die lateinischen und greichischen Inschriften der Stadt Jerusalem und ihrer nächsten Umgebung. 1. Nachtrag. *ZDPV* 64: 201–56.

BENJAMIN ISAAC

ROMAN EMPIRE. The final overthrow of the Roman Republic and the inauguration of the Roman Empire, in which power was concentrated in one man, was a process, not a single event, but the culminating event was the victory of Julius Caesar's adopted son, Octavian, over his chief rival for power, Marcus Antonius (Mark Antony), at the Battle of Actium (31 B.C.). Antony fled with his ally Cleopatra, queen of Egypt, to her capital Alexandria, where the following year both committed suicide, and Octavian reorganized Egypt as a Roman province. Moving carefully to avoid alienating Roman upper-class opinion by making his supreme autocratic power too obvious, Octavian restored the outward forms of the Republic, which had virtually ceased to function according to the rule of law over the previous 30 years, but took for himself the title of *princeps,* or 'first citizen', and the name Augustus, which had solemn religious overtones. As a result, the regime which he established (he still had 45 years to live after Actium, and so had time to build strong foundations), and which survived into the 3d century after Christ, was commonly known as the Principate. Augustus himself and his immediate successors did not commonly use the title *imperator,* "emperor," but all adopted the name Augustus, which thus became equivalent to a title.

A. Sources for the History of the Roman Empire
B. Growth and Extent
C. Government
D. Roman and Non-Roman: Citizenship and Law

E. Role of Provincial Governors
F. Social Inequalities

A. Sources for the History of the Roman Empire

For the death throes of the Republic, we have relatively full contemporary sources, particularly in the letters and speeches of Marcus Tullius Cicero, who was however put to death by Octavian and Antony (42 B.C.). Accounts of the next 12 years, until the deaths of Antony and Cleopatra, must be treated with suspicion, as likely to reflect Octavian's propaganda. Thereafter, until his own death in A.D. 14, our sources are uneven, and again one must be aware of possible distortion. We have a year-by-year history by Cassius Dio for most of Augustus' reign, written long after the event in the early 3d century. Suetonius in the 2d century wrote biographies of Julius Caesar, Augustus, and the next 10 emperors, that of Augustus being the longest. The poets of the period, especially Virgil, Horace, and Ovid, testify to the intellectual life of the period and to the climate of opinion at Rome. Augustus himself left his own version of his achievements (the *Res Gestae,* cf. Brunt and Moore 1967) to be set up in front of his mausoleum in Rome, with copies in the principal cities of the empire. But Augustus remains an enigmatic figure, and there are many insoluble problems in the history of his reign, especially chronological. We often cannot ascribe precise dates to his actions or legislation, and the inner workings of dynastic policy and intrigue have fascinated modern scholars (cf. Syme 1939), particularly because Augustus' control of such things ensures that we can never know for sure.

With Augustus' death begins the greatest of Latin historical works, the *Annals* of Tacitus, which continues, with gaps where our manuscripts are defective, to the death of Nero (A.D. 68). Tacitus' *Histories* cover the earlier part of the civil war which followed, but end in 69. Thereafter we lack any good narrative source to serve as a guide, though Cassius Dio survives in an abridged version down to his own day, and we still have Suetonius down to A.D. 96. The continuation of Suetonius, covering the 2d- and 3d-century emperors and known as the *Augustan History* (published in the Penguin translation series as *Lives of the Later Caesars*), is however a late-4th-century historical fiction.

On the other hand, epigraphic evidence (evidence from inscriptions, mostly on stone) becomes increasingly copious until the 3d century, when the breakdown of public order causes a sudden and dramatic collapse of the epigraphic habit (MacMullen 1982). Common types of inscriptions include epitaphs, dedications, building inscriptions, decrees, speeches by the emperor, commemorations of public events, and other official documents. The desert climate of Syria, the Negeb, and above all Egypt has also preserved records, such as personal letters and financial archives, as well as official records, on papyrus. All of this material gives us an insight into the daily life of the empire, and the epitaphs and papyri in particular let us glimpse the lives and concerns of ordinary people, who are not much represented in the literary sources (Jones and Milns 1984). Most surviving writers were senators of their hangers-on, whose view of affairs tends to be upper-class and centered on Rome, although in the 2d century occurs a revival of Greek literature, still upper-class, but based in Greece and Asia Minor rather than in Italy.

Christian writings form a separate category. The NT works show us the underside of Roman administration. We see Roman judicial procedures and punishments from the point of view of those subject to them, not from that of the Roman magistrates who administered them (Sherwin-White 1963). The early Christians, like Jewish writers of the period, are invaluable for insights into many facets, casually revealed, of social and economic life; scholars have become increasingly aware of their value to the historian of the Roman Empire, quite distinct from their value for theology or for the history of the early Church or of Judaism.

So far we have dealt only with verbal sources. Art and archaeology have their own contribution to make. Art historians have shown how sculpture and architecture embody the values of the governing classes. The coinage displays official portraiture and imperial propaganda. Excavation has brought to light buried towns, not only famous sites like Pompeii and Herculaneum, buried in an eruption of Mt. Vesuvius and thus preserved in a time capsule (A.D. 79; cf. Grant 1971), but many other small towns throughout the empire. Much of the center of Rome itself has been laid bare, though some major ancient sites like Alexandria remain inaccessible beneath modern cities. Archaeologists have also excavated country villas, harbor installations, aqueducts, army camps, and many other sites, including cemeteries, both pagan and Christian. In assessing archaeological evidence, however, the scholar needs to be aware of the cultural and financial constraints which make the archaeological record very uneven (Wells 1984: 46–50). What we know may not reflect what once was there, so much as what chance has brought to light or modern political or other interests have chosen to look for.

B. Growth and Extent

After defeating his chief rival, Mark Antony, in 31 B.C., the future emperor Augustus set to work to reorganize the empire so successfully that, when he died 45 years later (A.D. 14), power passed smoothly to his designated successor, the emperor Tiberius, and the Augustan settlement in its essentials survived well into the 3d century, when it collapsed in civil war that pitted the garrison of one frontier province against another in the interest of rival claimants, weakening both the frontier defenses and the economy. Neither the frontiers nor the economy ever fully recovered, although the emperor Diocletian, having fought his way to the top in 284, restored order; divided the empire into E and W halves; and inaugurated a more openly despotic form of rule. His work was continued by Constantine, the first Christian emperor (306–37, at first in partnership, but sole ruler from 324 onwards), who established Constantinople, the ancient Byzantium, as the E capital. The W Empire could not survive the German pressure on the frontiers and by the end of the 5th century had been carved up into Germanic kingdoms; the E Empire survived until 1453, when the Turks captured Byzantium.

Augustus, said the historian Tacitus a century later, left the empire fenced about by the ocean and far-off rivers (*Ann.* 1.9). He completed the conquest of Spain, which the Romans had begun over two centuries earlier, and made the Atlantic, the English Channel, and the North Sea

Rome's boundary in the West, from the Straits of Gibraltar to the Netherlands coast. The invasion of Britain was not begun until nearly 30 years after his death. Across central and eastern Europe, the Rhine and Danube formed a frontier between Rome and the German tribes, although the Roman sphere of influence and often the Roman legions operated beyond them. Asia Minor (modern Turkey) and Syria were Roman up to the river Euphrates, which represented the boundary with the Parthian empire to the East (Millar 1981). Syria was the base for Rome's control of the area, and the governor of Syria was the most powerful Roman general and administrator in the East. Judea, which Augustus had chosen to govern through a client king, Herod, became a province after Herod's death. In any case, client kingdoms were de facto part of the Empire, though with a different juridical status (Braund 1984).

Egypt was made a province after Actium, and Augustus and his successors kept it under close personal supervision, partly because Egypt and the province of Africa (roughly modern Tunisia) were the granary of Rome, without whose wheat the city of Rome itself would have starved. The whole North African coast was under Roman control, and the desert tribes of the Sahara were no threat. The city of Carthage, once Rome's great rival until wiped off the map in 146 B.C., was refounded, and soon rivaled Antioch in Syria and Alexandria in Egypt as the second city of the empire after Rome. The population of Rome was around 1,000,000 in Augustus' day, and perhaps more later; Alexandria, Carthage, and Antioch are commonly estimated to have held between 300,000 and 600,000. It is notoriously difficult to be sure.

The Mediterranean was a Roman lake (*mare nostrum,* they called it, "our sea"), piracy had been suppressed, the tribes beyond the frontier did not come to pose a serious threat until the empire was weakened by civil war and anarchy in the 3d century. In all this time, nowhere but in the East did the Roman Empire face another organized power of similar magnitude, and there the Parthians were constantly weakened by dynastic rivalry. The empire seemed to contemporaries very secure, and the gods willed it so. Horace, Augustus' poet laureate, told the Romans, "Because you are servants of the gods, you rule on earth" (*Carm.* 3.6.5); his friend Virgil stressed Rome's divine mission to rule, "to build civilization upon a foundation of peace, to spare the conquered and destroy proud aggressors" (*Aen.* 6.852–853, trans. R. D. Williams).

By the time when Christ was born, soon after the middle of Augustus' reign, a traveler could go from Jerusalem to Lisbon on the Atlantic, or from the upper Nile to the English Channel, without leaving the empire. Travel was slow (Wells 1984: 150–53), but he needed no passport—a purseful of Roman coins was acceptable anywhere. There was one system of law (different, however, for Roman citizens and noncitizens), and in the towns, at least, and in his dealings with the Roman administration, the traveler needed only two languages: Latin in the West and Greek in the East, where it had been the *lingua franca* since the conquests of Alexander the Great three centuries before. Local languages of course survived: Aramaic and other Semitic tongues in the East, Coptic in Egypt, Punic (also a Semitic language), and Berber in North Africa, Celtic in Western Europe (MacMullen 1966b; Millar 1968). The upper classes in these areas would be bilingual, if not trilingual or multilingual, and the peasants might speak only their own native tongue. Christian bishops, like Irenaeus of Lyon in Gaul and Augustine of Hippo in Africa, make it clear that they needed Celtic or Punic if they were to reach all of their flock.

Not only local languages, however, but many local customs persisted, especially in religion, where local deities continued to be worshipped, often superficially Hellenized or Romanized. The towns and cities, however, and the propertied classes in general for the most part embraced Roman rule, Roman law, Roman nomenclature, Roman architecture and a Roman style of life (Stambaugh 1988). The great line of social cleavage was between rich and poor, not on nationalistic lines. We hear virtually nothing of nationalistic protests against the occupying, colonialist power, such as we are familiar with in the 20th century. The main exception was the Jews, whose fiercely monotheistic religion could not accommodate pagan worship, including the worship of the emperor, which rapidly became almost universal, and whose sense of national and cultural identity made Judea notoriously difficult for the Romans to understand or to govern effectively (Smallwood 1981).

C. Government

The emperor was an autocrat whose word was law and whose relationship with his subjects was highly personalized (Millar 1977). This was obvious to political observers even in Augustus' day, however much he might strive to veil his autocracy in traditional constitutional forms, and by the early 3d century the lawyer Ulpian can state it simply as a legal principle: "What has pleased the emperor has the force of law" (Wells 1984: 232). In normal times, an emperor nominated his successor, and no emperor ever passed over his son, if he had one, though an adoptive son, previously a nephew or stepson, might take precedence of a son by blood. In the first two centuries, the dynastic principle was broken only three times: once on the death of Nero, when civil war and the so-called Year of the Four Emperors (69) ensued; once on the murder of Domitian (96), who left no heir; and again on that of Commodus (193), which led to civil war once again.

Below the emperor was the Senate, which served as his Council of State and increasingly as the organ whereby he caused law to be made. It also acquired important judicial functions (Talbert 1984). By the end of the Republic, it was composed primarily of ex-magistrates, and Augustus systematized the senatorial career *(cursus honorum)* in such a way that 20 men annually were elected quaestor, usually about the age of 25, and thereby entered the Senate. Then they might become aedile or tribune, and at about 30, they could stand for the praetorship (normally twelve posts a year). Quaestors were mostly concerned with financial matters, aediles with municipal administration, praetors with judicial affairs. Ex-praetors might hold various posts, especially in the provinces, including governorships of smaller provinces and appointments in command of a legion.

At the age of 42, or much sooner for those specially favored by the emperor, a man might aspire to the consulship. The two consuls who took office each year on 1

January were the nominal heads of state, and the consulship was eagerly sought, even down into the later empire, when it had become a mere title of honor largely devoid of power. It ennobled one's family: broadly speaking, the descendant of a consul was a *nobilis,* and a man without consular ancestors in the male line, like Cicero or indeed Augustus, was known scornfully as a "new man" *(novus homo).* The consuls gave their name to the year in the official calendar, so that 44 B.C. was dated "in the consulship of Gaius Julius Caesar and Marcus Antonius." If a consul died in office or resigned, a suffect consul *(consul suffectus)* was appointed to complete his term. Suffect consulships were considered less distinguished, but from 5 B.C. onwards it became standard for the consuls of the year to resign halfway through and let suffects take their place in order to increase the supply of ex-consuls for the specifically consular posts in the public service, like the governorships of major provinces and, as the empire went on, an increasing number of administrative jobs at Rome, which were reserved for men of consular rank.

Praetors and consuls possessed *imperium,* as did ex-magistrates holding a special appointment, such as the governorship of a province, which they were considered to hold as a substitute for a praetor or consul (*pro praetore* or *pro consule*). *Imperium* is an untranslatable term signifying the right to command in war, to administer the laws, and to inflict the death penalty (subject to a Roman citizen's right of appeal, originally to the people, later to the emperor). The *imperium* of propraetors and proconsuls was normally restricted to the province to which they were appointed. (A province, *provincia,* originally meant a defined sphere of action, not necessarily geographical, as we might say in English, "the interpretation of the law is the province of the courts"; but by the end of the Republic, it normally meant a specific territory such as the province of Asia or of Gallia Narbonensis, i.e., Provence and Languedoc.) In the Late Republic, it occurred that one proconsul might have his *imperium* defined as greater *(maius)* than another's, so that it was clear who prevailed in case of disagreement.

D. Roman and Non-Roman: Citizenship and Law

Roman law was one of the greatest achievements of Roman civilization, with enormous impact on the legal systems of all countries of W Europe and the Americas, and of other countries and international bodies influenced by them (Crook 1967; Watson 1970). The written record goes back to the Twelve Tables (ca. 450 B.C.), a primitive code for a relatively primitive, largely agricultural society. The body of law then developed through legislation and through magisterial edict. The praetor, i.e., the annually elected magistrate responsible for administering the law, used to publish the principles whereby he intended to be guided during his year of office, and his edict thus came to have the force of law. During the Late Republic the judicial system evolved into one where cases were settled not so much by the sheer forensic brilliance of the rival advocates, as by appeal to precedent and to the interpretations of learned jurists. Under the Empire, and particularly in the 2d and early 3d centuries, the law attracted some of the most able minds in the Roman world, by no means confined to Italy: Salvius Julianus, whom the emperor Hadrian (117–38) commissioned to edit the praetor's edicts, came from Pupput, modern Hammamet, in Tunisia, and Berytus (Beirut) was one of the most famous Roman law schools from the 3d century onwards. By this time, the emperor had become recognized as the ultimate fount of law, but the rules of law prevailed in the courts, and the apogee of Roman law was its codification by the emperor Justinian in 6th-century Byzantium.

Most modern legal systems are territorial and, at least in principle, egalitarian; that is to say, everyone is subject to the law of the place where he or she happens to be, and the law is meant to be the same for everybody. In contrast, Roman law was a law based on personal status, which, as it were, you carried around with you. So there was one law for Roman citizens and a different law for noncitizens, both in criminal and in civil cases, and persons were explicitly awarded different treatment according to their social status (Garnsey 1970). Slaves had no rights in law at all. This can all be exemplified in a famous letter written by the younger Pliny, governor of Bithynia and Pontus in NW Asia Minor about 110, to the emperor Trajan, in which he describes action taken against local Christians who had been denounced to him, action which the emperor approves (*Ep.* 10.96–97). Those of the accused who refused to abjure their religion were summarily executed if they were not citizens, but citizens were remanded for trial in Rome. Two slave women were routinely tortured in the course of the investigation. Pliny admits that he finds the Christians innocent of any crime, except that of being Christians and refusing to worship the gods, including the emperor. The privilege accorded to the citizens and based on a specific law which went back to Augustus (Sherwin-White 1963: 57–70) recalls Paul's successful appeal from arbitrary punishment and from the jurisdiction of the governor of Judea to the emperor in Rome some two generations earlier (Acts 25:11).

The distinction between citizen and noncitizen was gradually whittled down during the 2d century and abolished early in the 3d by the Constitutio Antoniniana, to be replaced by a more-rigid distinction than before between the wealthier classes *(honestiores)* and the rest *(humiliores).* In the early Empire, however, citizenship was important not only because of the right of appeal which it conferred in criminal cases, but because of the status of the citizen in private law. Only children of a valid marriage between two citizens were born citizens, all others normally taking the status of the mother. Citizens came under the provisions of Roman law in all matters concerning personal status, inheritance, property ownership, and business contracts. Citizenship might for various reasons be conferred on those not born with it, such as service to the state or to some individual Roman governor. Paul was a citizen by birth, so that one of his ancestors must have been granted citizenship, perhaps as a large contractor supplying the Roman army in Syria with tents. Sons of legionaries, who could not legally marry, were often granted citizenship on enlistment into the legions themselves (Campbell 1978). Service in auxiliary regiments was rewarded with citizenship on discharge. Many cities had a status which conferred Roman citizenship on municipal magistrates. Slaves formally manumitted by Roman citizens also received citizenship ipso facto. A register of citizens was kept, but

Paul's case suggests that it was not usual for citizens to carry documentary proof of citizenship with them.

E. Role of Provincial Governors

Under the Empire, certain provinces were assigned to the emperor, who governed them through deputies, mostly men of consular or praetorian rank, holding the title of *legatus Augusti pro praetore*, appointed by the emperor for as long as he chose and responsible only to him. Other provinces, of which the most important were Africa and Asia, continued to have proconsuls or propraetors appointed by the Senate for a one-year term. The emperor however always had *imperium maius*, so that he could overrule a senatorial governor at will. The more-important provinces, whether imperial or senatorial, were usually governed by ex-consuls, those of secondary importance by ex-praetors. The governor was also commander-in-chief of any troops stationed in the province. Commanding a Roman legion was normally a job for a senator, but some of the emperors' lesser provinces, which had troops to maintain public order, but not a whole legion, fell into a third category, where the governor was not a senator, but of equestrian rank, with the title of prefect in the early 1st century but procurator later. Syria, for instance, the key to the E frontier, was an imperial province whose legate was always a trusted and experienced soldier. Judea, until Vespasian reorganized the legionary dispositions in the East, had merely an equestrian prefect or procurator, since the forces under him did not amount to a legion, so that he might have to call for help from the legate of Syria and his legions if Judea got out of hand. Egypt was also equestrian, but a special case, because alone of the equestrian provinces in the early Empire it had a legionary garrison; senators were even debarred from entering the country without the emperor's permission.

Except in the great military commands, such as Syria and the provinces along the Rhine and Danube frontier, a governor was more concerned with financial and judicial questions than with military affairs (Garnsey 1968; Burton 1975). He had to maintain public order, but this was not normally a major problem—Judea was exceptionally turbulent. On the other hand, he often had very little force at his disposal; hence the need to step in and suppress disturbances ruthlessly, before they could get out of hand, without too much concern for asking who started the disturbance. The Christians often suffered as disturbers of the peace, not because they started disturbances themselves, but because their enemies did, and a governor might think it prudent to suppress the disturbance by suppressing the cause of it, i.e., the Christians. We see this in what happened to Paul in Jerusalem and in Pliny's treatment of the Christians, referred to above. The governor had the right of *coercitio*—the right to order anyone to stop what he was doing even if there was no specific law against it—if he judged it likely to cause a breach of the peace. Only Roman citizens were exempt from summary punishment and even execution at the governor's discretion for disobeying such an order.

F. Social Inequalities

Not even in theory did the Romans regard all men as equal (to say nothing of the women). Apart from the distinction between citizens and noncitizens already alluded to, birth and wealth counted for a great deal (MacMullen 1974). By the 2d century, the distinction between the propertied classes *(honestiores)* and the rest *(humiliores)* was enshrined in law and recognized by a different scale of punishments for each. This distinction essentially replaced that between citizen and noncitizen after the Constitutio Antoniniana in 212 conferred citizenship on virtually all free inhabitants of the empire. There was a property qualification for office, from membership of the most-insignificant municipal councils up to the Senate itself. The senatorial qualification was set by Augustus at 1,000,000 sesterces, but this was habitually exceeded. The younger Pliny, about whose finances we are reasonably well informed (Duncan-Jones 1965), did not consider himself rich (*Ep.* 2.4), but is estimated to have been worth over 20,000,000. The two largest private fortunes that we hear of are set, in round figures, at 400,000,000.

Membership of the equestrian order, below the Senate, required a capital of 400,000 sesterces, and many men qualified. The cities of Gades (Cadiz) and Patavium (Padua), for instance, each had 500 knights in Augustus' day (Strabo 3.169, 5.213). Also under Augustus (8 B.C.), we hear of a freedman who in his will, despite losses in the civil wars, left 60,000,000, plus 4,116 slaves, 3,600 pairs of oxen, and 257,000 head of other cattle (Pliny, *HN* 33.135). Compare this with the pay of an ordinary legionary, fixed by Augustus at 900 sesterces a year, or the daily wage of a laborer: St. Matthew gives the wage of the laborers in a vineyard as 1 denarius a day, which is 4 sesterces (Matt 20:1), and this may be exaggerated, since a passage in the Babylonian Talmud, for instance, implies that Rabbi Hillel made only half that as a woodcutter in King Herod's day (Wells 1984: 202–5).

The safest investment was land, and probably most rich men, like the younger Pliny, derived most of their income from their estates. Trade was generally looked down on, and senators were prohibited from engaging in it, but even senators participated vicariously by financing others, especially their own slaves and freedmen (D'Arms 1981; Pleket 1983). Freedmen who made their fortunes tended to emulate their social betters by investing in land, as did the fictional Trimalchio (Petron. *Sat.* 76). Only in Italy were slaves used extensively in agriculture, but everywhere they were an accepted part of life, employed not only for the most menial tasks, but for many of what for us are honorable professions, like teaching, accounting, or medicine. Household slaves could usually count on getting their freedom in middle life, and slaves whom their masters hired out or set up in business would expect to buy their freedom out of their savings (Bradley 1984). Once free, since slavery was not based on color, there was nothing to distinguish the ex-slave from the freeborn man or woman.

The urban poor and the peasantry often had a harder life and less chance of bettering themselves than the better sort of slave did. Conditions in the slums of a big city like Rome outdid those in Victorian London, and the 2d-century physician Galen writes vividly of the malnutrition and distress which he had seen in the countryside in time of famine (de Ste. Croix 1981: 14). The magistrates, from the emperor down, combined savagely to repress dissent. Crucifixion, torture, and condemnation to the mines or to the wild beasts in the arena were routine punishments for those who threatened the established order, whether recalcitrant slaves, poor men turned to brigandage, or those deemed subversive, like the Christians (MacMullen 1966a; Hopkins 1983; Wells 1984: 262–78). The Roman order and prosperity were based ultimately on organized terror.

Bibliography

Bradley, K. R. 1984. *Slaves and Masters in the Roman Empire.* Collection Latomus 185. Brussels.
Braund, D. C. 1984. *Rome and the Friendly King.* New York.
Brunt, P. A., and Moore, J. M. 1967. *Res Gestae Divi Augusti: the Achievements of the Divine Augustus.* Oxford.
Burton, G. P. 1975. Proconsuls, Assizes, and the Administration of Justice under the Empire. *JRS* 65: 92–106.
Campbell, B. 1978. The Marriage of Soldiers under the Empire. *JRS* 68: 153–66.
Crook, J. A. 1967. *Law and Life of Rome.* London.
D'Arms, J. H. 1981. *Commerce and Social Standing in Ancient Rome.* Cambridge, MA.
Duncan-Jones, R. P. 1965. The Finances of the Younger Pliny. *Papers of the British School at Rome* 33: 177–88.
Garnsey, P. 1968. The Criminal Jurisdiction of Governors. *JRS* 58: 51–59.
———. 1970. *Social Status and Legal Privilege in the Roman Empire.* Oxford.
Grant, M. 1971. *Cities of Vesuvius.* London.
Hopkins, K. 1983. Murderous Games. Vol. 2, pp. 1–30 in *Death and Renewal: Sociological Studies in Roman History.* Cambridge.
Jones, A. H. M. 1971. *The Cities of the Eastern Roman Provinces.* Oxford.
Jones, B. W., and Milns, R. D. 1984. *The Use of Documentary Evidence in the Study of Roman Imperial History.* Sydney.
MacMullen, R. 1966a. *Enemies of the Roman Order.* Cambridge, MA.
———. 1966b. Provincial Languages in the Roman Empire. *AJP* 86: 1–17.
———. 1974. *Roman Social Relations 50 B.C. to A.D. 284.* New Haven, CT.
———. 1982. The Epigraphic Habit in the Roman Empire. *AJP* 103: 233–46.
Millar, F. 1968. Local Cultures in the Roman Empire. *JRS* 58: 126–34.
———. 1977. *The Emperor in the Roman World (31 B.C.–A.D. 337).* London.
———. 1981. *The Roman Empire and its Neighbors.* 2d ed. London.
Pleket, H. W. 1983. Urban Elites and Business in the Greek Part of the Roman Empire. Pp. 131–44 in *Trade in the Ancient Economy,* ed. P. Garnsey, K. Hopkins, and C. R. Whittaker. London.
Sherwin-White, A. N. 1963. *Roman Society and Roman Law in the New Testament.* Oxford.
Smallwood, E. M. 1981. *The Jews under Roman Rule from Pompey to Diocletian.* Leiden.
Stambaugh, J. E. 1988. *The Ancient Roman City.* Baltimore.
Ste. Croix, G. E. M. de. 1981. *The Class Struggle in the Ancient Greek World from the Archaic Age to the Arab Conquest.* London.
Syme, R. 1939. *The Roman Revolution.* Oxford.
Talbert, R. A. 1984. *The Senate of Imperial Rome.* Princeton.
Watson, A. 1970. *The Law of the Ancient Romans.* Dallas.
Wells, C. 1984. *The Roman Empire.* Stanford.

COLIN M. WELLS

ROMAN IMPERIAL CULT. The Roman imperial cult may be defined as the offering of divine honors to a living or dead emperor. With antecedents in Egypt, Persia, and Greece, the ruler cult developed further in the Republic (Taylor 1931: 35–57), especially under Julius Caesar (Weinstock 1971), and in the time of Augustus (Taylor 1931: 142–246). Beginning with Tiberius, emperor worship played a major role in the origin and spread of Christianity (Jones in *ANRW* 2/23/2: 1023–54).

Tiberius. Tiberius resisted all honors offered to himself (Rostovtzeff 1930) and his mother, Livia (Grether 1946). In 25 C.E. he refused to permit the province of Farther Spain to build a temple in his name, declaring in a famous speech to the Senate: "I am a mortal, and divine honors belong only to Augustus, the real savior of mankind" (Tacitus *Ann.* 4.37–38; Étienne 1958: 420). Suetonius (*Tib.* 26.1) referred to an edict issued by Tiberius which forbade other forms of deification, including swearing allegiance and the erection of statues. Nevertheless, the title *divus* appeared on a denarius of Tiberius and a papyrus from 37 C.E. called him "son of the god" (Cuss 1974: 139).

Caligula. Gaius, nicknamed Caligula because of the "little boots" he wore as a boy, proposed that Tiberius be deified, but the Senate refused, citing strained relations during his last years. Convinced of his own divinity, Caligula demanded that he be worshiped. He believed he was the incarnation of Jupiter, and appeared in the dress of other gods and goddesses. Temples were erected in his honor at Miletus and Rome (Dio Cass. 59.11.12 and 28.1–2). Following his sister Drusilla's death in 38 C.E., Caligula had her deified, aided by a senator who swore under oath that he had seen her apotheosis, or ascent into heaven (Dio Cass. 59.11.3).

When Alexandrian Greeks ordered images of Caligula set up in the synagogues of that city, a delegation of Jews led in 39 C.E. by Philo complained to the emperor. Philo noted that while Jews could not worship Caligula, many of them did regard him as "savior and benefactor" (*Legatio* 75–114 and 349–67; Price 1984b: 184, 209). That same year, Caligula further offended Jewish monotheistic attitudes by ordering Syrian legate Petronius to erect a huge bronze statue of himself in the Jerusalem temple. Fortunately, Petronius' delaying tactics and the intercession the following year of Jewish king Agrippa caused the emperor to abandon the project (Smallwood 1957).

Caligula was not deified following his assassination by officers of the imperial guard—in fact, only the intervention of his successor and uncle, Claudius, prevented the Senate from declaring him "an enemy of the state."

Claudius. Like Tiberius, Claudius generally refused divine honors, but, in a famous letter to Alexandria in 41 C.E. (Barrett 1989: 47–50), while claiming that the establishment of priests and temples is "a prerogative to the gods alone," he did permit the erection of statues to himself and his family throughout the city. In his introduction to this letter, the Egyptian prefect urged reading it in order to appreciate "the majesty of our god Caesar" (Charlesworth 1925). Despite Claudius' stance in the Alexandrian letter with regard to temples, one was erected in his honor in Britain following a Roman victory there (Tacitus *Ann.* 14.31). In addition, there is evidence of

Claudius' being called "lord" (Cuss 1974: 59) and "savior of the world" (Scramuzza 1940).

Nero. Nero had Claudius deified, the first emperor to be so honored since Augustus; but the influential philosopher Seneca, in a clever satire called the *Apocolocyntosis,* ridiculed the idea of Claudius as a god (Altman 1938). From 65 C.E. on, Nero was depicted on coins as "god," and as "Apollo the Lyre Player," and wearing the radiate crown of a deified emperor (Charlesworth 1950). In 55 C.E. the Senate set up a statue of Nero in the temple of Mars Ultor (Tacitus *Ann.* 13.8.1)—the first time since Caesar that an emperor had been directly associated with a god in Rome. In 65 C.E. he rejected a proposed temple to "the divine Nero," citing the tradition that only dead emperors were divine, but he did erect in his place a hundred-foot bronze statue of himself as the sun with a star-shaped crown.

The imperial acclamations by which Nero was greeted had divine overtones, e.g., "Our Apollo . . . by thyself we swear" and "O Divine Voice! Blessed are they that hear you!" (Dio Cass. 62.20.5 and 63.20.5). In a Boeotian inscription from 67 C.E. Nero was called "lord of the whole world" (Deissmann 1927: 354), further evidence that "lord" was a prominent title in the imperial cult (Jones 1974: 85). When the king of Armenia greeted Nero in 66 C.E. as "master" and "god," the emperor agreed that he was indeed close to divinity (Dio Cass. 63.14). Before he committed suicide, Nero had been declared "an enemy of the state" by the Senate. He was never consecrated, although he did deify his wife Poppaea and their infant daughter.

Vespasian. Nero's successor, Vespasian, generally refused divine honors, although on his deathbed in 79 C.E. he joked: "I suppose I am becoming a god" (Suet. *Vesp.* 23.4). He had earlier dedicated a temple to Claudius (Suet. *Vesp.* 9.1) and was regularly called "lord" (Cuss 1974: 61) and "savior" (Scott 1936: 21). Vespasian's son and successor, Titus, had him consecrated, and a temple to the deified Vespasian was erected in Rome.

Titus. Titus was hailed as "savior of the world" (Deissmann 1927: 364) and was consecrated by his brother, Domitian, who succeeded him. As deifying members of the imperial family was becoming a common practice, Titus consecrated his sister Domitilla (Scott 1936: 45–48).

Domitian. Domitian insisted on being recognized as a divine *deus praesens,* an important term in emperor worship (Cuss 1974: 139). Coins show him seated on a throne as "father of the gods" (Abaecherli 1935), and a huge marble statue of himself in Ephesus became the focal point of the imperial cult throughout Asia Minor.

Domitian insisted on being addressed, by letter or in person, as "our lord and god" (Suet. *Dom.* 13; Scott 1936: 88–112) and all who refused were punished. That his persecution extended to Christians is clearly reflected in the book of Revelation (Scherrer 1984). Emperor deification, including offerings of incense, prayers, and vows, was now obligatory and used as a means to identify followers of the Christ. After his death in 96 C.E., statues of Domitian were destroyed by angry senators and he was declared "an enemy of the state." Many of his official decisions were rescinded by his successor, Nerva.

Trajan. Trajan became emperor in 98 C.E. and had his predecessor consecrated. Generally, he rejected divine honors, but he did allow a temple to be erected in his name at Pergamum, and after 100 C.E. his name began to be linked with that of Jupiter. In the year 112 C.E. Christians in Bithynia and Pontus were investigated by the Roman legate Pliny the Younger. In a famous letter to Trajan (10.96) Pliny wrote (Scott 1932):

> This is the course that I have adopted in the case of those brought before me as Christians. I ask them if they are Christians. If they admit it I repeat the question a second and a third time, threatening capital punishment; if they persist I sentence them to death. . . . All who denied that they were or had been Christians I considered should be discharged, because they called upon the gods at my dictation and did reverence, with incense and wine, to your image which I had ordered to be brought forward for this purpose.

Trajan then offered this reply (10.97; Bickerman 1968):

> You have taken the right line, my dear Pliny, in examining the cases of those denounced to you as Christians, for no hard and fast rule can be laid down, of universal application. They are not to be sought out; if they are informed against, and the charge is proved, they are to be punished, with this reservation—that if anyone denies that he is a Christian, and actually proves it, that is by worshiping our gods, he shall be pardoned as a result of his recantation, however suspect he may have been with respect to the past (Bettenson 1947: 5–7).

When Trajan died in 117 C.E., his apotheosis was attested in several traditions, and he was deified by his successor, Hadrian.

Hadrian. Hadrian was frequently identified with the Olympian Zeus and permitted the erection of temples and statues in his honor (Raubitschek 1945). The easy deification of his twenty-year-old Bithynian lover, Antinous, who had drowned in the Nile in 130 C.E., was a scandal for both Jews and Christians. Coins depict Hadrian's apotheosis and that of his empress Sabina who preceded him in death.

Antoninus Pius. Under Hadrian's successor, Antoninus Pius, the demand to offer sacrifice before the emperor's statue had become a test of Christian loyalty to the state. Noncompliance led to the death penalty, as it did in the case of Polycarp, bishop of Smyrna, who, having refused to say "Caesar is lord" and offer incense to Antoninus' image, was sentenced to death by burning (156–57 C.E.; Barnes 1967). Following his death in 161 C.E. Antoninus Pius was consecrated by the Senate and his successor, Stoic philosopher Marcus Aurelius, and coins depicted his apotheosis and that of his empress, Faustina (Mattingly 1948).

Marcus Aurelius. Under Marcus Christians were executed at the Festival of the Three Gauls. A special ruling of the Senate allowed imperial cult priests to use "condemned prisoners" in the arena instead of the more expensive gladiators (Oliver and Palmer 1955). Marcus had no sympathy for Christians. They were brave, but blindly obstinate (*Meditations* 11.3). In 178 C.E. the Platonist philosopher Celsus, in his "True Doctrine," criticized Christians for refusing to offer "due honors," including sacrifice to the emperor, especially since "whatever you receive in this life you receive from him" (Origen *Cel.* 8.55–67). Among the Christian statements of defense was that of Tatian who, in his "Address to the Greeks," ridiculed Hadrian's deification of his lover Antinous and declared that, while he will give human kings human honor, he will worship God alone. Marcus was succeeded by his son, Commodus, who deified his father and struck coins depicting his apotheosis.

Commodus. Commodus, degenerate like Caligula, Nero, and Domitian before him, demanded divine honors (Oliver 1950). He received acclamations and a large gold statue was erected in his honor (Dio Cass. 73.15.3 and 74.2.3). During Commodus' first year (180 C.E.) twelve Christians in Africa refused to swear a loyalty oath to him and were beheaded (Cuss 1974: 61). A few years later, Roman senator Apollonius declared himself a Christian, refused to swear an oath to "our lord Commodus the emperor" or to offer sacrifice to his image, and consequently was sentenced to death by beheading. Commodus died in 192 C.E. and was condemned by the Senate. He was, however, later consecrated by Septimius Severus.

Septimius Severus. Severus accepted the divine title "lord" and married Julia Domna, daughter of the Sun priest at Emesa, thereby bringing the empress into the imperial cult. She was deified following her death in 217 C.E. Tertullian, in his "Apology" (197 C.E.), argued that Christians need not offer sacrifice to the emperor who is only human. They could swear by his health or safety, but if he is ever referred to as "lord," there must be no implication of his divinity. Hippolytus of Rome, in his "Commentary on Daniel," claimed Christians suffered the death penalty for refusing to worship the gods (4.51). Men were burned and their bodies thrown to beasts, children were killed, and women were treated with shame.

Decius. In 249 C.E., Decius restored the worship of consecrated emperors and demanded offerings and oaths in his honor. The following year he issued an edict which resulted in the first general persecution of Christians since everyone in the empire was required to offer sacrifice to the gods and to obtain a certificate from a local commissioner confirming same (Clarke 1969).

Valerian. The persecution of Decius was revived by Valerian who, in 257 C.E., issued an edict ordering Christian bishops, presbyters, and deacons to offer sacrifice to the gods. The following fall Cyprian refused to do so and was beheaded (*Acta proconsularia* 3–4).

Diocletian. Diocletian came to the throne in 284 C.E. and attempted to revive the imperial cult by claiming special protection from Jupiter and demanding that he be called "lord and god." According to both Eusebius (*Hist. Eccl.* 8.7–13) and Lactantius (*De mort. persec.* 15.4–5) all Christians who refused to sacrifice to the gods were sentenced to death or hard labor in the mines.

Constantine. During the time of Constantine, Christianity became the only recognized state religion and enjoyed protection by imperial favor. Christians now comprised half the empire's population and were no longer required to bow to its emperor. Instead, he bowed to their Christ.

Bibliography

Abaecherli, A. 1935. Imperial Symbols on Certain Flavian Coins. *CP* 30: 131–40.

Alföldi, A. 1980. *Die monarchische Repräsentation im römischen Kaiserreiche.* Darmstadt.

Altman, M. 1938. Ruler Cult in Seneca. *CP* 33: 198–204.

Barnes, T. D. 1967. A Note on Polycarp. *JTS* 18: 431–37.

Barrett, C. K., ed. 1989. *The NT Background: Selected Documents.* Rev. ed. San Francisco.

Bettenson, H., ed. 1947. *Documents of the Christian Church.* New York.

Bickerman, E. 1968. Trajan, Hadrian, and the Christians. *Rivista di filologia* 96: 290–315.

Bowersock, G. W. 1983. The Imperial Cult: Perceptions and Persistence. Pp. 171–82 in *Self-Definition in the Greco-Roman World.* Vol. 3 of *Jewish and Christian Self-Definition,* ed. B. F. Meyer and E. P. Sanders. Philadelphia.

Cerfaux, L., and Tondriau, J. 1957. *Un concurrent du christianisme.* Bibliothèque de théologie 3/5. Tournai.

Charlesworth, M. P. 1925. Deus noster Caesar. *Classical Review.* 39: 113–15.

———. 1950. Nero: Some Aspects. *JRS* 40: 69–76.

Clarke, G. W. 1969. Some Observations on the Persecution of Decius. *Antichthon* 3: 63–76.

Cuss, D. 1974. *Imperial Cult and Honorary Terms in the NT.* Paradosis 23. Fribourg.

Deissmann, A. 1927. *Light from the Ancient East.* Rev. ed. New York.

Étienne, R. 1958. *Le culte impérial dans la péninsule ibérique d'Auguste à Dioclétien.* BEFAR 191. Paris.

Fears, J. R. 1977. *Princeps a Diis Electus: The Divine Election of the Emperor as a Political Concept at Rome.* Papers and Monographs of the American Academy in Rome 26. Rome.

Fishwick, D. 1978. The Development of Provincial Ruler Worship in the Western Roman Empire. *ANRW* 2/16/2: 1201–53.

———. 1987. *The Imperial Cult in the Latin West.* 2 vols. EPRO 108. Leiden.

Grether, G. 1946. Livia and the Roman Imperial Cult. *AJP* 67: 222–52.

Herz, P. 1978. Bibliographie zum römischen Kaiserkult (1955–75). *ANRW* 2/16/2: 833–910.

Hesberg, H. von. 1978. Archäologische Denkmäler zum römischen Kaiserkult. *ANRW* 2/16/2: 911–95.

Jones, D. L. 1974. The Title *Kyrios* in Luke-Acts. *SBLSP* 2: 85–101.

Kee, A. 1985. The Imperial Cult: The Unmasking of an Ideology. *Scottish Journal of Religious Studies* 6: 112–28.

Mattingly, H. 1948. The Consecration of Faustina the Elder and Her Daughter. *HTR* 41: 147–51.

Oliver, J. H. 1950. Three Inscriptions concerning the Emperor Commodus. *AJP* 71: 170–79.

Oliver, J. H., and Palmer, R. 1955. Minutes of an Act of the Roman Senate. *Hesperia* 24: 320–49.

Pleket, H. W. 1965. An Aspect of the Emperor Cult: Imperial Mysteries. *HTR* 58: 331–47.

Price, S. R. F. 1980. Between Man and God: Sacrifice in the Roman Imperial Cult. *JRS* 70: 28–43.

———. 1984a. Gods and Emperors: The Greek Language of the Roman Imperial Cult. *JHS* 104: 79–95.

———. 1984b. *Rituals and Power: The Roman Imperial Cult in Asia Minor.* Cambridge.

Raubitschek, A. E. 1945. Hadrian as the Son of Zeus Eleutherios. *AJA* 49: 128–33.

Richard, J.-C. 1978. Recherches sur certains aspects du culte impérial: les funérailles des empereurs Romains aux deux premiers siècles de notre ère. *ANRW* 2/16/2: 1121–34.

Rostovtzeff, M. 1930. L'empereur Tibère et le culte impérial. *Revue historique* 163: 1–26.

Scherrer, S. J. 1984. Signs and Wonders in the Imperial Cult. *JBL* 103: 599–610.

Scott, K. 1932. The Elder and Younger Pliny on Emperor Worship. *TAPA* 63: 156–65.

———. 1936. *The Imperial Cult under the Flavians.* Stuttgart.

Scramuzza, V. 1940. Claudius Soter Euergetes. *HSCP* 51: 261–66.

Smallwood, E. M. 1957. The Chronology of Gaius' Attempt to Desecrate the Temple. *Latomus* 16: 3–17.

Taeger, F. 1960. *Charisma: Studien zur Geschichte des antiken Herrscherkultes.* Vol. 2. Stuttgart.

Taylor, L. R. 1931. *The Divinity of the Roman Emperor.* American Philological Association 1. Middletown, CT.

Turcan, R. 1978. Le culte impérial au IIIe siècle. *ANRW* 2/16/2: 996–1084.

Weinstock, S. 1971. *Divus Julius.* Oxford.

Wlosok, A., ed. 1978. *Römischer Kaiserkult.* Darmstadt.

DONALD L. JONES

ROMAN JUDAISM. See JUDAISM (IN ROME).

ROMAN RELIGION. This article focuses upon the beliefs and practices concerning the supernatural and its place in human destiny found among the ancient inhabitants of the city of Rome, and later in the regions of Europe, N Africa, and W Asia under Roman domination.

A. Religion as a Structural Element of Culture
1. The "Bearers" of Roman Religion
2. The State: Priesthoods
3. Personal Religion
4. Household and Family Religious Observances
B. Elements of Roman Religion
1. Concepts of God
2. The Gods and Their Cults
3. Cult Images and Temples
4. Acts of Worship, Ritual Procedures, Festivals
5. Oversight of Cultic Activity and Religious Policy
6. Mythology
7. Structures of Roman Polytheism: Calendar, Systems, Theology
C. System and History

A. Religion as a Structural Element of Culture

1. The "Bearers" of Roman Religion. A sociological approach to the question of cults and cultic activity might well be organized around the highly practical division found in Festus (284 L), between public and private worship. Public acts of worship (*sacra religionesque publicae,* Cic. *de har. resp.* 14) included not only those performed in the name of the *populus* by magistrates and state priests but also those carried out by local associations, e.g., the *montani* or *pagani,* as part of the total community. Private worship took place in the name of *familiae, gentes* (extended families or clans), and corporations.

Scholars have given relatively little attention to the *gens,* in contrast to the *familia* and the state, as a religious community. Despite this, one should not underestimate the role of the *gens,* especially during the early republic and toward its end. The history of the *gens,* worship, and burial rights are what drew the individual *gens* together, as Cicero explained: "It means much to share in common the same family traditions, the same forms of domestic worship, and the same ancestral tombs" (*de off.* 1.17 §55 [LCL]). *Gens*-oriented special cults are known for, e.g., the *Nautii* (Minerva), die *Potitii* and *Pinarii* (Hercules), the *gens Aurelia (Sol),* and *gens Claudia* (Saturn). Other cults linked the name of the *gens* to a minor deity: the *gens Ancharia* venerated a goddess *Ancharia; Numeria* was honored by the *gens Numeria; Hostia* or *Hostilina* by the *gens Hostilia;* a certain *Domitius* by the *gens Domitia.* As early as 1935, Carl Koch pointed out that Jupiter was the only figure in the Roman pantheon of gods "for whom one can with near certainty say that no *gens*-oriented cult existed" (Koch 1935: 24). The rapprochement between the *gens*-related Italic *Veiovis* cult and the "roman Jupiter" toward the end of the Roman republic probably served to give voice to new claims, the claims of the *Julia* family.

Roman experts on sacred law seem to have distinguished between those public cults in which the community was represented by magistrates and priests and those in which all citizens participated: Antistius Labeo says (Festus 235 L), "Public cults are those which all citizens celebrate, and are not attributed to a particular family: *Fornacalia, Parilia, Laralia, Porca praecidanea.*" The examples given here include both those in which the general populace was represented only in a definite, organized manner (e.g., the *Fornacalia* within the framework of the curial structure) and those in which the citizens participated directly (e.g., the *Parilia*). In the latter case, in the *atrium Vestae* "means of purification" *(suffimenta)* were distributed to all citizens—a *communio sacrorum* in a very material sense. The excerpt from Festus omits mention of the type of ceremony that seems regularly to have encouraged participation by "all" citizens, e.g., the *supplicationes* applied by the Sibylline books are propitiatory rites. It is emphasized by Augustus in his summary account, for example, that ". . . all the citizens . . . have unanimously and continuously offered prayers at all the *pulvinaria* for my health" (*Mon. Ancyranum* 9.2 = Brunt and Moore 1967: 23).

Alongside the large number of religion-oriented groupings to which a Roman belonged by obligation of birth (e.g., *familia, curia*), function (e.g., *miles: religio castrensis*), or home (e.g., *pagus: paganalia; compitum: compitalia*), there were only a few that one could join by choice. Among the latter the *collegia* were most important. These were cult societies (Waltzing 1895–1900) which the *socii cultores* could enter as if entering an "association." The *lex collegii* established the duties and financial contributions expected of members, prescribed the cultic activity, and structured the conduct of members' meetings. Many Greek and oriental cults appear to have established themselves at Rome initially in the juridical form of the cult association. After the affair of the *Bacchanalia,* the Senate repeatedly intervened to control the freedom to organize such associations. Toward the end of the Republic, the *collegia funeraticia* (funerary societies) seem to constitute a special case among the cultic associations. These were self-help organizations of the poor and slaves who, in line with family cults (Gladigow 1985: 126ff.) took as their task the burial of deceased members and the religious observances at their graves.

2. The State: Priesthoods. Priests were the mainstay of the state cult of the Romans. Either as individual priests or as members of priestly *collegia* or *sodalitates* they carried out the liturgy or, in certain instances, advised and assisted magistrates in their liturgical duties (e.g. as augurs or haruspices). The ancient system of Roman religion, oriented toward liturgy and priesthood, can be divided into three areas: "ritual, auspices, and the third additional division consisting of all such prophetic warnings as the interpreters of the Sibyl or the soothsayers have derived from portents and prodigies" (Cic. *de nat. deor.* 3.5 [LCL]). Specific groups of priests corresponded to this part of the Roman state religion: "provisions for priests omit no legitimate type of worship. For some are appointed to win the favour of the gods by presiding over the regular sacrifices; others to interpret prophecies of the soothsayers. . . . But the highest and most important authority in the State is that of the *augurs,* to whom is accorded great influence" (Cic. *de leg.* 2.30 [LCL]). In the Augustan period the term *quattuor sacerdotum amplissima collegia* (i.e., the four significant priesthoods), which virtually comprehended the Roman cult structure, developed. These four were the *pontifices,* the *augures,* the *quindecemviri sacris faciundis* (used from the Sullan period onward; previously the *decemviri,* or *duoviri*), and the *septemviri epulones* (formerly *tresviri*).

With the exception of the *virgines Vestales,* all priestly offices could be held for life and were exempt from military service *(vacatio militiae).* The office of *Rex sacrorum* was considered incompatible with the magistracy; otherwise there was no fundamental prohibition against holding both priestly and magistrate's offices. This meant that no specific priestly class developed at Rome and the political realization of religious ideas could be achieved to a certain degree through the personal union of magistracy and priestly office. Priestly positions were never incorporated in the fixed cycle of offices *(cursus honorum),* although a clear tendency to begin the cycle with a priestly office is visible (*ANRW* 2/16/3: 2328–31). If this was not possible, a priestly office was assumed after having entered the magistracy.

Priests were appointed partly through direct appointment (*captio* of the Vestals by the *Pontifex maximus*), partly through cooptation and, after the end of the 3d century B.C., through limited popular vote. Holding several priestly offices was possible, yet in the republican period this was uncommon: that Caesar was simultaneously *Pontifex maximus* and *augur* was unusual for the Late Republic. The later Empire, especially the 4th century of the Christian era, saw massive accumulation of priestly offices.

Among the great *collegia* the *collegium pontificum* surpassed all others in importance. It consisted of the *pontifices* (9–16 positions), the *Rex sacrorum* (or *Rex sacrificulus*), the *flamines* (3 *flamines maiores,* 12 *flamines minores*), and the *virgines vestales* (6 positions with the *vestalis maxima* at their head). Responsibility for discipline and power of punishment for the entire priestly college rested with the *pontifex maximus* but the old priestly regulations placed the *Rex sacrorum* and the *flamines maiores (Dialis, Martialis, Quirinalis)* ahead of him in rank *(dignatio).* After Augustus assumed the office of *Pontifex maximus* in 12 B.C., it remained firmly attached to the emperor's office. A *promagister* then took charge of the regular administration of the college of priests.

The *collegium augurum* ranked only slightly lower than the priestly college (*ANRW* 2/16/3: 2146–312). Like the priests, the number of augurs grew from 9 to 15 and finally to 16 under Caesar. The augurs played an important role in the self-understanding of the Romans, who considered themselves to be the most religious of all people (*religiosissimi mortales,* Sall. *Cat.* 12.3; cf. Cic. *de nat. deor.* 2.3.8). As guardians of technical matters *(disciplinam tenere)* and interpreters of the entire divination system (in the form of *decreta* and *responsa*), they were closely linked to the magistrates and to all state ceremonies that had to be carried out *auspicato* with augury. As *interpretes Iovis Optumi maxumi* "interpreters of Jupiter the Best and Greatest" (Cic. *de leg.* 2.20) the institution of the augurs constituted the interface between the Roman Jupiter and the Roman state.

3. Personal Religion. Scholars have too-quickly classified Roman religion as the paradigm for a cultic religion, "the 'mere cult acts' view of Roman Religion" (Phillips 1984: 292). This has led them to neglect the limited sources that ascribe individual attitudes, experiences, or even "belief" to the Romans. W. Ward Fowler (1922), who tried to counteract the conventional view, remained isolated and without resonance. Because intimate scenes like the one mentioned by Plautus (*Aulularia,* 24), in which a girl worshipped the *Lar familiaris* out of a sort of heartfelt need (and was rewarded for her devotion) do not fit the conventional portrayal of Roman religion, they have never been set forth in an integrated manner. The meditations that P. Cornelius Scipio regularly carried out, alone in retreat in the temple of the Capitoline Jupiter (Liv. 26.19.5; Gellius 6.1.6), fit this category (Seguin 1974). However so does the well-attested custom of honoring a sacred image by touching one's hand to one's lips *(adorandi gratia manum labris admovere)* not only in a temple but even when passing by a temple (*ANRW* 2/16/1: 579–80). These are scarcely forms of veneration required by proper liturgical practice; rather they are acts of personal religiosity that developed as expressions of religious needs alongside the generally obligatory *sacra privata* and *sacra publica.* A Roman man or woman might also sit in quiet prayer at the feet of a sacred image, remain there for a long time, and tell his or her problems to the deity (as is done in Propertius 2.28.46).

4. Household and Family Religious Observances. The most broadly institutionalized forms of personal religiosity were the household cult *(sacra domestica)* and the family cult *(sacra familiaris).* Domestic gods were the typical "traveling deities" that accompanied people as their living situations changed. In the "founding myth" of Roman religion, Aeneas took, from among all the Trojan deities, only "his" *di penates* with him to Lavinium. Cicero attractively explained the significance of the house for the practice of Roman religion in *De domo sua* in the following way: "Within its circle are the altars, the hearths, the household gods, religion, observances, ritual; it is a sanctuary so holy in the eyes of all, that it were sacrilege to tear an owner therefrom" (109). As part of their daily lives individual Romans practiced and experienced their religion *in the house* (Wissowa 1912: 33–34). Nilsson (1951: 3.285) with a certain appropriateness, described "the domestic religion" as "the most Roman of all cults of the Roman Religion."

At the center of the household religion were the *di penates,* a collective name for all deities honored in the house; the *lar familiaris* (since the Augustan reform, the *lares familiares*), taken from rural settings; the deities connected to the *penus* and hearth of the house; and the *genius* of the *pater familias.* In a Roman house the *lares* and *genius* were normally honored in an *Aedicula (lararium).* Especially the *lares* were incorporated into a form of daily piety observed by all members of the household, they were remembered with small offerings from the table, were involved in family celebrations, and the *bulla* of the eldest son, who put on the *toga praetexta,* was deposited with the *lares.* The consistent separation of household and public cult (Kaser 1955: 51ff.) was blurred by an innovation of Augustus, which ordained that the genius of the emperor be venerated between the two *lares* in the *compita Larum.*

The family cult was also the natural point of departure for the veneration of the dead and of graves (Cumont 1965; Toynbee 1971). At the end of the year, during the *Parentalia* (13–21 February) the dead of the household were collectively honored as *divi parentum* (later *di parentes*). Food, salt, and wine were carried to the graves, which were decorated with flowers and wreaths. It is noteworthy that the Romans never transformed the cult of the *di parentes* into a cult of divine ancestors of the clan. A family's self-portrayal took place at the *pompa funebris,* in which the portrait masks of the ancestors were carried. The close linkage of the cult of the dead with the *familia* seems to have obviated a need for differentiated conceptions of the hereafter among the Romans (Gladigow 1985).

B. Elements of Roman Religion

1. Concepts of God. Based on a special type of Roman gods H. Usener (1896) attempted to set out a theory about the origins of concepts of god. He introduced into the study of the history of religions the terms "momentary gods" *(Augenblickgötter)* and "special gods" *(Sondergötter).* To illustrate the category of "special gods" he used such Roman deities as the *Vervactor* (who was responsible for the first breaking of the soil), the *Raparator* (responsible for the second plowing), all the way to the *Conditor* (responsible for storing the grain). Of Usener's terms only that of the "special god" has survived, often being used synonymously with "functional god," although precisely Usener's examples from Roman religion show that these "special gods" were not "functional gods." What characterized the Roman "special gods" is that they were related to stages in a process, not to logical functions. This may reveal a fundamental property of Roman religiosity: divine activity, for the Romans, was recognizable in specific points in time, in concrete historical actions (Latte 1926–27; Altheim 1937). The deities "revealed" themselves not in time-transcending ontology but through their activity in particular, concrete situations. The institutionalized contact Romans had with their gods took corresponding form: taking place at specific points in time, reacting, keeping a certain distance. For this reason the Roman "special gods" can hardly be interpreted as survivals of an imperfect, undeveloped stage of human conceptions of deity; rather they should be viewed more as distancing and systematizing priestly constructs at the edge of a fully developed and functioning polytheism.

Roman reports of the manifestations of gods, e.g., reports of the appearance of *Aius Locutius* (Liv. 5.32.6; 5.50.6; 5.52.11), shed light on, it seems, a specific model for reacting: one does not try quickly to identify what one has heard (in this instance) with a specific god and relate it to what one knows by means of an epithet; rather, one permits it to stand in its singularity: *Aius Locutius.*

2. The Gods and Their Cults. At the center of the Roman pantheon stood Jupiter, the god of the celestial brightness and at the same time the god who legitimated all important political acts through the auspices and who, under the dual name *auspicium imperiumque* stood behind the power of magisterial lordship. A series of epithets connected him to hills and hilltop cults (*Iuppiter Fagutalis* [on the *mons Oppius*]; *Iuppiter Viminalis, Iuppiter Elicius* [Aventine], *Iuppiter Feretrius* [Capitoline], etc.). To him the Ides, on which it was bright day and night, were dedicated; the dedication days for several of his temples occurred on the Ides *(Iuppiter Optimus Maximus, Iuppiter Victor, Iuppiter invictus).* Celestial events and weather occurrences were connected to Jupiter the god of heaven—the epithets name and swear by him as *Iuppiter Fulgur, Lapis, Summanus, Tonans, Elicius,* as well as *Pluvialis* or *Serenus.* As is often the case, the god of heaven was also linked to the control of oaths, contracts, and legal affairs (Petazzoni 1956). As city- and state-god, *Iuppiter Capitolinus* attracted a number of functions to himself (Fears 1981): the sacrifices required of the consuls upon entering office were directed to him as was the first sacrifice a Roman made when he donned the *toga virilis* (toga of manhood). The *ludi Romani* were devoted to him and the triumphal parade of a victorious general led to *Iuppiter Capitolinus.* In the 3d century a number of temples that describe Jupiter as god of battles were vowed and built to Jupiter: *Iuppiter Victor, Stator,* perhaps also *Propugnator.*

In Rome, in comparison to Jupiter in his role as the central state deity, those deities which otherwise in Latin culture would carry similar political-military characteristics were clearly subordinate—especially *Quirinus* but also Mars. Participants in the liturgies remained aware of Mars as god of war, but the auspices of war themselves proceeded from *Iuppiter Optimus Maximus* and focused the war upon him. Although Mars was responsible for the area *extra pomerium,* the materially significant cultic and legal activities were oriented toward Jupiter: the fact-finding process was understood as undertaken under authority of Jupiter, and even the *ver sacrum,* which was devoted to Mars by the Italic tribes, was promised to Jupiter by the Romans in 217 B.C. (carried out in 195 B.C., but because of a mistake repeated in 194 B.C.).

Of the female deities Juno enjoyed the greatest veneration. Her image stood at first in the left cell of the temple of the Capitoline triad; on the other side of the statue of Jupiter was an image of Minerva. Juno *(Iuno Iugalis, Pronuba, Domiduca, Cinxia, Unxia, Fluvionia, Lucina)* probably developed from a female deity in this grouping to a city goddess and eventually to *Iuno Regina* (*ANRW* 2/17/1: 168 ff.). Minerva took a different route: from what was probably a Sabine goddess who early on was portrayed iconographically as a city goddess, she became the patroness of artisans (*artifices, fabri; ANRW* 2/17/1: 203–32).

Unlike Jupiter, *Vesta,* through her function as *Vesta populi Romani Quiritium,* became a deity who secured the existence of the state (*ANRW* 2/17/1: 276–99). The fire in the visible part of the *aedes Vestae* (temple of Vesta), tended by the vestal virgins, and that in the innermost part of the pledge of Roman rule *(fatale pignus imperii Romani)* guaranteed—insofar as they were maintained and properly dealt with—the continued existence of Rome. Just as the auspices linked Jupiter to political activity, so Vesta was brought into contact with the entire sacrificial process by means of the *mola salsa* (see B.7 below).

Ianus (Janus) seems to have been an ancient god of high rank. Like Jupiter, Mars, *Quirinus,* Neptune, and *Liber,* he was addressed as *pater* (father). In Roman liturgy all that remained were the rules that he should be named first, even before Jupiter, when several deities were addressed, and that the *Rex sacrorum,* the highest ranking priest in the Roman hierarchy, should be his sacrificial priest. In Rome, *Ianus* was connected especially with archways; the *Ianus Geminus* or *Quirinus* between the Forum and the *Argiletum* received the most attention: in time of war the gates were opened; in peacetime they remained closed.

Among the Greek gods one of the first to be taken up by Romans was Apollo (Gagé 1955). When the temple to Apollo located on the *prata Flaminia* but outside the *Pomerium* was constructed is not known; in 431 B.C. it was replaced at the same location by a temple promised in 433 B.C. to Apollo and *Latona* in the wake of a plague. At first Apollo was worshipped as *Apollo medicus.* Only in the 2d century did his character change in the direction of the delphic deity. This process reached a conclusion in 28 B.C. with the construction by Augustus of the temple to Apollo on the Palatine hill. The newly assembled collection of Sibylline books, which had been kept in the temple of the Capitoline Jupiter, were now preserved beneath the image of Apollo.

Greek deities were taken up in Rome from the 5th century B.C. onward as the result of alliances, emergencies, and propitiations of portents. The ancient liturgical and temple religion of Rome was fueled not by conversion and revelation or by triumphant arrival of a god and devout confession, but lived from the transferrence of cult observances in and following emergency situations: plagues, defeats, threats of war, propitiation of portents and omens. A temple was even built on the basis of an aedilistic penalty process. We offer here only a few examples of this specifically Roman form of a sturdily empirical approach to the gods: *Castor* and *Pollux* received a temple in the Roman Forum after the battle at Lake Regillus in 484 B.C. After consulting the Sibylline books, *Ceres* was promised a temple in 496 B.C., together with the *Liber Pater* (erected 493). Mercury was given a temple, outside the *Pomerium,* which had been the place of worship for a *collegium mercatorum* (Combet Farnoux 1980). The oldest datable temple to Venus can be traced to a judgment with monetary penalty handed down against adulterous matrons in 295 B.C. In 293 B.C. the Sibylline books recommended, in the wake of a plague, that the *Aesculapius* cult be brought to Rome; his temple was consecrated in 291 B.C. Hercules, who was first worshipped in the context of a *gens*-oriented cult, was taken under state religious oversight in 312 B.C. and received a temple in 218 B.C. on the basis of instructions from the Sibylline books. In 205 B.C., during the second Punic war, the Sibylline books recommended that the cult of the *Mater deum Magna Idaea* (*ANRW* 2/17/3: 1500–35) be accepted at Rome; she received her temple on the Palatine hill in 191 B.C. In the religious history of Roman warfare *Fortuna* played a special role: as *Fortuna publica populi Romani, Fortuna Equestris, Fortuna huiusce diei,* or *Fortuna Redux,* she received numerous temple dedications as the result of wartime perils or successes.

3. Cult Images and Temples. Only a temple, or at least a sacred image, of the deity could ensure the lasting presence of a god in a city—in the view of Romans and of the ancient world in general. Varro's report that the Romans worshipped the gods without images for 170 years after the founding of the city (fr. 18; *ANRW* 2/16/1: 80–103) probably is best explained as an idealization of Roman origins and can be applied concretely to the appearance of Etruscan terra cotta images on the Capitoline hill. The thesis that early Roman religion was basically aniconic is as unlikely as the parallel thesis that the Romans initially practiced no animal sacrifices. However, it is incontestable that there were some Roman gods that lacked images, even after the historical record begins. Within the historic period a religious image, in some instances a nonanthropomorphic object of worship, was an essential part of a temple (*ANRW* 2/16/1: 568 ff.; general information in *ANRW* 2/17/2: 1032–1199).

The central rites of the temple service, provisioning, showing hospitality, and worshipping all were oriented toward the sacred image in the cult niche or *cella.* The animal sacrifices carried out on an altar in front of the temple (as in Greece) also were directed toward the sacred image inside (Vitruvius 4.9) and as a rule, were probably performed with the doors of the temple standing open.

After the 3d century B.C., a temple building *(aedes)* constructed on a *templum,* erected and maintained for the sake of the state and provisioned and guarded by an *aedituus,* became the dominant form (*ANRW* 2/16/1: 574 ff.). The acceptance of Greek deities on the basis of instructions from the Sibylline books appears to have made a temple into one of the prerequisites for approbation of a cult.

4. Acts of Worship, Ritual Procedures, Festivals. As with nearly all pre-Christian religions, the main element of Roman worship was the sacrifice: *rem divinam facere* "to attend to divine matters" was practically synonymous with "to sacrifice." The actions surrounding the sacrifice, complex in themselves, also involved the most diverse intentions (Gladigow 1984): a gift to the deity "to placate with a gift the wrath of the gods" is the way Cicero described the goal of sacrifice in *de leg.* 2.22); feeding the deity with anything from a portion of the plant and animal sacrifice to a regular meal (Cato *de agr.* 83.131); propitiation *(piaculi gratia);* purification *(lustratio).* Cereal, material, or votive offerings involved relatively little ceremony. In contrast, a properly performed animal sacrifice was a complex ritual with a precisely established sequence of actions that could extend from the purification of the participants and the examination of the sacrificial animal *(probatio hostiae)* through approximately two dozen steps leading up to the *profanare,* the consumption of the meat by the participants in the ritual.

These formal requirements of animal sacrifice and the necessary technical skills soon placed this activity in the hands of specialists. In addition to the priests or lords of the sacrifice there were *victimarii* who, as public servants *(apparitores)* for the state cult, formed their own college. Among the *victimarii* was the *popa,* who stunned the animal, and the *cultrarius,* who opened the jugular vein. *Camilli,* usually eldest sons in the case of private sacrifices, assisted generally. At state sacrifices, flute players were generally present; they also formed a *collegium* (*CIL* VI 2191).

The behavior of the animal immediately before the sacrifice and during the killing was of particular significance as an omen, which provided another reason to entrust the work to specialists. Mistakes and *omina* during the sacrifice could jeopardize achieving the goal of the sacrifice or bring forth negative prognostications. When the animal had been properly *(rite)* killed, its body was opened and an examination of the health of its organs *(extispicium)* carried out. If this examination yielded negative results *(hostia sine litatione caesa),* the entire ritual had to be repeated until a favorable omen was received (Liv. 41.15.4).

Although a sacrifice was an element in nearly all complex rituals, the accentuation and "message" of the ritual shifted with increasing complexity. In the case of the *lectisternia,* a ritual introduced upon the instructions of the Sibyllines, the hospitality and table fellowship of the gods was primary. In the *supplicationes* the fact that the entire populace was called upon to sacrifice in all temples played a growing role. The supplications already had absorbed a processional element, which was also characteristic of the border cults in the form of processions around the fields *(ambarvalia lustratio pagi, amburbium).* Complex rituals like the *Lupercalia* or the *Equus October* integrated nearly all ritual elements in to a composite whole, in which the elements of drama and competition and genuine theatrical productions took center stage. The public games *(Ludi Romani, plebei, Florales, Apollinares, Ceriales, Megalenses)* were rituals that had been expanded in time and content. Their significance as entertainment should not be played off against their religious meaning. At the center of the *Ludi Romani,* the most important Roman games, were the *pompa circensis*—the procession of the images of the deities on *tensa* into the *Circus*—and the games and contests that took place there "before the eyes of the gods." The high degree of religious significance attached to the *Ludi Romani* and *plebei* is indicated by the fact that the rule of *instauratio* applied to them; i.e., in the event of a mistake in the ceremony, the entire process had to be repeated. Livy reports that on one occasion, "the Roman Games in their entirety were repeated three times, the Plebeian Games five times" (38.35.6).

5. Oversight of Cultic Activity and Religious Policy. The Roman state did not interfere in either family or *gens*-oriented religion. However the censors as well as the priests were formally responsible to see that the family cults continued (Cic *de leg.* 2.9.22). Few actual reports of state penalties for neglect of religious responsibilities are known; the most prominent penalty was that which Cato carried out against L. Veturius, ejecting him from the equestrian order. Another, indirect, way to control family rites lay in the priestly implementation of inheritance law. The priests were concerned in cases of *adoptio* and *adrogatio* as well as in the regulation of inheritances that the family cult not die out "so that the memory of them not die out at the death of the father" Cic. *de leg.* 2.19.48).

Overall one can say that legal penalties against Romans who did not participate in *sacra popularia* were unknown in the Roman republic (Mommsen 1899: 567ff.). A report by Dio Cassius (51.19) that nonparticipation in the liturgy for the birthday celebration of the consecrated Caesar was punishable with a monetary fine and the death penalty is unique. Only in the year 249 A.D. was a single, general obligation to religious observance put into effect and enforced—by Decius. In this instance, each Roman citizen was required to sacrifice "to the gods"; the performance of this act was to be certified by a *libellus* (certificate).

The Romans not only established institutionally an openness toward "new" deities that was typical of polytheistic religions, but they also connected it in a characteristic way with the divination and propitiatory system of Roman religion. This was carried out institutionally, under supervision of the Senate, by the *duoviri,* later by the *decemviri,* and finally by the *quindecemviri sacris faciundis* and the *Libri Sibyllini* (Sibylline books). According to a legend of the 2d century B.C. *Tarquinius Superbus,* on the advice of the augurs, bought Greek ritual books offered to him by an old woman (according to Varrio [Lact. *inst.* 1.6.10]; Dion. Hal. 4.62; Gellius 1.19; Gagé 1955). These *libri Sibyllini* were kept in chambers under the temple of Capitoline Jupiter until 83 B.C.; a new collection assembled in 76 B.C. to replace the old books, which had been burned, was placed by Augustus in the temple of Apollo on the Palatine hill in 12 B.C. Only the *viri sacris faciundis* were permitted access to these religious books and then only after approval from the Senate in the wake of a special portent which could not be expiated or appeared not to be capable of expiation (procuration) by the *patrius ritus.* This carefully controlled system (announcing of a portent, a Senate decision, the expert opinion of the *viri sacris faciundis,* and another Senate decision) gave rise to a large number of innovations in Roman religion.

Thus the plague of 399 B.C. was expiated, on advice of the *duoviri sacris faciundis* through a *lectisternium* (reclining feast) for Apollo and *Latona,* Hercules and Diana, Mercury and Neptune. The very ancient custom of entertaining the gods publicly in this way became an established cult form following the *graecus ritus* (Greek rite). These *lectisternia* were repeated in 364, 349, and 326 B.C., and one additional time, for the same reason. In 293 B.C. the cult of *Aesculapius* was brought to Rome, again because of an epidemic and on advice of the Sibylline books. After the defeat at Lake Trasimene, Venus and Ceres appear for the first time in a *lectisternium* commanded by the Sibylline books in 217 B.C. Likewise as the result of consulting the Sibylline books the *Mater Magna* of Pessinus was received in a festive arrival in Rome in 204 B.C. Because of the incest of the Vestals in 114 B.C. a temple to *Venus Verticordia* was established in Rome as a propitiatory measure. The influence of the Sibylline books on the development of Roman religion was considerable, but one should not overlook the fact that these *libri fatales* (Liv. 5.14.4; Cancik 1983: 562 ff.), kept under lock and key, could only affect religious policy by way of the Senate's decision to consult them, interpretation, expert opinion *(responsum),* and a second decision by the Senate. They are a pattern for a religious institution that channeled and clarified anxieties to bring about a religious and political propitiation (Gladigow 1979).

Restrictive measures against cults were not absent from Roman religion. In the most diverse forms and for various reasons limits were placed on the *Mater magna, Bacchus,* and *Isis* cults. Measures taken ranged from prohibition of refinancing and penalties carried out through inheritance law to complete proscription (Vermaseren 1981).

6. Mythology. Only after Wissowa (1912) clearly distinguished Roman from Greek elements in Roman religion was it apparent that Roman religion had no mythology comparable to that of the Greeks, no genealogies of gods, no sexual liaisons of gods, and no offspring of the gods. All evidence indicates that the repression of mythology was a conception of Roman religious policy, a theological program of the leading priesthoods. This, at least, was the way Greek contemporaries viewed it (Dionys. Hal., *Ant. Rom.* 2.19); they admired the basis of Roman religion for that reason (Polybius 6.56). The conditions under which this process of "demythologizing" of the Roman pantheon took place can best be illustrated by the deity that stood in the center of the Roman state cult: *Iuppiter Optimus Maximus.* Through a religiously and politically motivated process of creation the cult of the Roman Jupiter, and with it the cults of the other state deities, was separated from the world of Italic and Greek mythology. Jupiter's cult belonged to the all-encompassing sphere of the state and society, which was kept separate from all other possible links to *gens*-oriented special cults and the privileges and expectations that grew out of them (Koch 1937). The "arena of revelation" for Roman state deities was not a prehistory, not a mythological history predating Rome, but rather the common, obligatory Roman history or the meaningful events of the present.

7. Structures of Roman Polytheism: Calendar, Systems, Theology. The general absence of a Roman mythology—a mythology that would hand down and set forth plausibly a set of inner relationships within the Roman pantheon—meant that other constructive institutions within Roman religion had to carry more weight. The temporal ordering of worship through the calendar was an important aspect of priestly "systematic theology" (Sabbatucci 1988), alongside the spatial organization of religion—temples within or outside of the *pomerium;* within the city at a central, even elevated site (Capitoline, Palatine, Aventine hills); or in a peripheral location. Superimposed on these systems were laws that governed the financing of temples used for worship (state cults took place *publico sumptu* [at public expense], which is why the Senate was very cautious in making *dedicationes*), regulations governing the use of temples (e.g., women were excluded from the worship of Hercules at the *ara maxima* and from the Silvanus cult; men were excluded from the cult of the *Bona Dea*), and rules governing the cooperation and assistances of the priesthoods. In addition to these structuring elements of Roman state religion a very concrete form of "implicit theology" is found in the rituals and ritual instructions, especially in the structure of complex rituals. Thus *Vesta,* the *Vesta*-religion, was linked by the *mola salsa* to all those cultic acts that involved animal sacrifices, i.e., the majority of cultic acts. *Mola salsa* was produced from spelt and brine *(muries)* by the Vestal Virgins in May and was also distributed to the populace three times during the year. This "material systematizing" of the *Vesta* cult corresponded to the ritual prescription that, at all sacrifices, *Vesta* should be named last—and thus with special honor, like *Ianus*'s place at the head of the list—in the series of deities addressed. Similar material cross-referencing is visible in the ashes of the calves slaughtered in the *Fordicidia,* which preserved by the Vestals and distributed at the *Parilia,* formed the bean straw and the blood of the *equus October.*

Non-genealogical connections between the deities were achieved through processions, which linked temples (and gods), e.g., in the procession of 207 B.C. (Liv. 27.37.11; Cancik 1986: 255–56) the temple of Apollo at the *Porta Carmentalis* was linked to the temple of *Juno Regina* on the Aventine hill. *Lectisternia,* ritual entertainments, joined gods and goddesses in a (primarily) public cult act according to Greek models. Apollo and *Latona,* Hercules and Diana, Mecury and Neptune appeared together in a propitiatory ritual mandated by the Sibylline books in 399 B.C.; the same rite with the same conjunction of deities was to be repeated four times. In 217 B.C., as Hannibal stood before Rome, a *lectisternium* with twelve deities was held at the behest of the Sibylline books. It brought together according to the Greek pattern six pairs of gods (Jupiter-Juno, Neptune-Minerva, Mars-Venus, Apollo-Diana, Vulcan-Vesta, and Mercury-Ceres) who later found a place as *Consentes dei* in a portico of the Forum.

Probably the theologically most significant grouping of Roman deities was found in the so-called Capitoline triad of Jupiter, Juno, and Minerva. Here, in a religious and political statement that seems to have had neither Greek nor Etruscan nor Roman prototypes (Radke 1987: 226 ff.), representatives of the Latin and Sabine components of Roman state-building were joined to Jupiter toward the end of the 6th century B.C. The three were found a suitable architectonic setting in a temple with three *cellae* but, as far as the sources reveal, did not received any common worship. As the Roman ideal of the state grew in self-confidence, the Capitoline triad was pushed to the side as *Iuppiter Optimus Maximus* became the integrating center of Roman self-understanding; the two goddesses were gradually given functions separate from the triad.

The triad Ceres, Liber, and Libera provided competition for the Capitoline group in a time of political tension within Rome. At the *secessio plebis in montem sacrum,* the new triad of gods with their temple outside the *pomerium* on the Aventine hill became a political center for the *plebs,* whose temple officials *(aediles)* delivered the point of departure for the plebeian special magistracy of the aedileship.

Alongside these institutionalized results of systematizing, theological conceptions and programs a rich system of documentation, above all by augurs and priests, secured the tradition and professionalism of the interpretations. The archive of the priests was of greatest significance for the general religion (Rohde 1936). It preserved formulas *(carmina),* instructions and documents *(leges),* and ceremonial directions for the entire *ius sacrum.* The records were precise and pragmatic and seem not to have hesitated to regulate the financing of individual cultic acts. Numa, at least, left to the *Pontifex* documents that not only regulated the rites but also their financing (Liv. 1.20.6). From the 2d century B.C. there was an abundance of Roman writings, largely under Greek influence, on the gods, the cult, the sacred laws, and the prehistory of Roman religion. This genre of writings reaches its height in M. Terentius Varro, whose *antiquitates rerum divinarum,* dedicated to the *Pontifex* C. Iulius Caesar, document both the end of the religion of the Roman republic and the restorative themes of the Principate era.

C. System and History

In Roman religion one can trace the development and structuring of a polytheistic system under changing territorial, social, and political conditions. Channeled into *vota, leges templorum, decreta,* and *responsa* and exhibited paradigmatically in historiography, empiricism was incorporated into the religious system. A definite phase of the territorial development of early Rome became part of the ritual of the *Septimontium:* with processions to the *Palatium (Germalus), Velia, Fagutal, Sucusa, Cermalus, Oppius, Cispius* (the names vary in the sources) hills, the status of Rome before the "City of the Four Regions" was recalled. Another phase, the conflicts with the Latin cities, can be detected, for example, in the status of the *Feriae Latinae* with their complicated ceremonial, or, of lesser significance, in the *commune Latinorum templum* of Diana on the Aventine hill.

Up to the end of the republic, both city-building and territorial expansion as well as class tensions remained within Roman religion's range of adaptability and responsiveness. The framework for this adaptability seems to have been the fact that the Romans considered themselves the "most religious of mortals," or, as Cicero put it, *religione . . . multo superiores* "with respect to religious observance . . . for superior" (*de nat. deor.* 2.3.8), when compared with others. Based on this fundamental understanding, empiricism entered Roman religion and did so completely in accord with Roman self-interpretation, something rarely seen in other cultures. Threats, defeats, victories, anomalies of nature, and social conflict were explicit causes for intervention in the traditional status of the cult. Under state regulation, the Romans took up "alien gods" and "experimented" with new forms of worship (e.g. *supplicationes, lectisternia, ludi*), when the occasion arose. The "mythological poverty" of Roman religion did not deprive Roman polytheism of any of its flexibility. Dealing with auspices and portents provided for a steady and clearly conceived interpenetration of state and religious activity, which admitted a wide spectrum of alternatives and innovations.

Bibliography

Altheim, F. 1930. *Griechische Götter im Alten Rom.* RVV 22/1. Giessen.

———. 1937. Altitalische und Altrömische Gottesvorstellung. *Klio* 30: 34–50. Repr. Vol. 1, pp. 99–119 in Altheim 1951–57.

———. 1951–53. *Römische Religionsgeschichte.* 2 vols. Baden-Baden.

Bayet, J. 1969. *Histoire politique et psychologieque de la religion romaine.* 2d ed. Paris.

Bömer, F. 1957–63. *Untersuchungen über die Religion der Sklaven in Griechenland und in Rom.* AAWLM, lit. Kl., 1–4. Wiesbaden.

Cancik, H. 1983. Libri fatales: Römische Offenbarungsliteratur und Geschichtstheologie. Pp. 549–76 in *Apocalypticism in the Mediterranean World and the Near East,* ed. D. Hellholm. Tübingen Repr. 1989.

———. 1986. Nutzen, Schmuck und Aberglaube: Ende und Wandlungen der römischen Religion im 4. und 5. Jahrhundert. Pp. 65–90 in *Der Untergang von Religionen,* ed. H. Zinser. Berlin.

Champaux, J. 1982. *Fortuna dans la relgion archaique.* Vol. 1 in *Fortuna: Recherches sur le culte de la Fortuna à Rome et dans le monde Romain.* Paris.

Clavel-Lévêque, M. 1986. L'espace des jeux dans la monde romain: hégémonie, symbolique et pratique sociale. *ANRW* 2/16/3: 2405–563.

Combet Farnoux, B. 1980. *Mercure romain.* Rome.

Cumont, F. 1965. *Recherches sur le symbolisme funéraire des Romains.* 2d ed. Paris.

Dumézil, G. 1970. *Archaic Roman Religion.* Trans. P. Kapp. 2 vols. Chicago.

Fears, J. R. 1981. The Cult of Jupiter and Roman Imperial Ideology. *ANRW* 2/17/1: 3–141.

Fowler, W. W. 1922. *Religious Experience of the Roman People.* 2d ed. London.

Frier, B. W. 1979. *Libri annales pontificum maximorum.* Papers and Monographs of the American Academy in Rome 27. Rome.

Gagé, J. 1955. *Apollon Romain.* Paris.

———. 1963. *Matronalia: Essai sur les dévotions et les organisations culturelles des femmes dans l'ancienne Rome.* Collection Latomus 60. Brussels.

Gladigow, B. 1979. Konkrete Angst und offene Furcht: Am Beispiel des Prodigienwesens in Rom. Pp. 61–77 in *Angst und Gewalt,* ed. H. von Stietencron. Düsseldorf.

———. 1981. Gottesnamen (Gottesepitheta) I (allgemein). *RAC* 11: 1202–38.

———. 1984. Die Teilung des Opfers. *Frühmittelalterliche Studien* 18: 19–43.

———. 1985. *Naturae deus humanae Mortalis:* Zur sozialen Konstrucktion des Todes in römischer Zeit. Pp. 119–33 in *Leben und Tod in den Religionen,* ed. G. Stephenson. Darmstadt.

Harmon, D. P. 1978a. The Public Festivals of Rome. *ANRW* 2/16/2: 1440–68.

———. 1978b. The Family Festivals of Rome. *ANRW* 2/16/2: 1592–603.

Kajanto, I. 1981. Fortuna. *ANRW* 2/17/1: 502–88.

Kaser, M. 1955. *Das römische Privatrecht.* Munich.

Koch, C. 1937. *Der römische Juppiter.* Frankfurt. Repr. 1968.

Latte, K. 1926–27. Uber eine Egentümlichkeit der italischen Gottesvortellung. *ARW* 24: 244–58. Repr. *Kl. Schr.,* pp. 76–90.

———. 1967. *Römische Religionsgeschichte.* Munich.

Liebeschütz, J. H. W. G. 1979. *Continuity and Change in Roman Religion.* Oxford.

MacBain, B. 1982. *Prodigy and Expiation: A Study in Religion and Politics in Republican Rome.* Brussels.

Michels, A. K. 1967. *The Calendar of the Roman Republic.* Princeton.

Mommsen, T. 1887. *Römisches Staatsrecht.* 3d ed. Repr. Basel, 1963.

———. 1899. *Römisches Strafrecht.* Leipzig.

Nilsson, M. P. 1951–60. Wesenverschiedenheiten der römischen und der griechischen Religion. Pp. 504–23 in *Opuscula selecta.* 3 vols. Lund.

Pettazzoni, R. 1956. *The All-Knowing God.* Trans. H. J. Rose. London.
Phillips, C. R. 1984.
———. 1986. The Sociology of Religious Knowledge in the Roman Empire to A.D. 284. *ANRW* 2/16/3: 2677–773.
Piccaluga, G. 1965. *Elementi spettacolari nei rituali festivi romani.* Rome.
Pohlsander, H. A. 1986. The Religious Policy of Decius. *ANRW* 2/16/3: 1826–42.
Radke, G. 1979. *Die Götter Altitaliens.* 2d ed. Münster.
———. 1987. *Zur Entwicklung der Gottesvorstellung und der Gottesverehrung in Rom.* Darmstadt.
Rohde, G. 1936. *Die Kultsatzungen der römischen Pontifices.* Berlin.
———. 1963. Die Bedeutung der Tempelgrüdungen im Staatsleben der Römer. Pp. 189–205 in *Studien und Interpretationen zur antiken Literatur.* Berlin.
Ryberg, I. S. 1955. *Rites of the State Religion in Roman Art.* Memoirs of the American Academy in Rome 22. New Haven.
Sabbatucci. 1988. *La religione di Roma antica.* Milan.
Schilling, R. 1954. *La religion romaine de Vénus.* Paris.
———. 1972. La situation des études relatives à la religion romaine de la Republique (1950–1970). *ANRW* 1/2: 317–47.
Scullard, H. H. 1981. *Festivals and Ceremonies of the Roman Republic.* Ithaca, NY.
Seguin, R. 1974. La religion de Scipion L'Africain. *Latomus* 33: 3–21.
Szemler, G. J. 1972. *The Priests of the Roman Republic.* Brussels.
Toynbee, J. M. C. 1971. *Death and Burial in the Roman World.* London.
Usener, H. 1896. *Götternamen: Versuch einer Lehre von der religiösen Begriffsbildung.* 3d ed. Bonn. Repr. 1948.
Vermaseren, M. J., ed. 1981. *Die orientalischen Religionen im Römerreich.* EPRO 93. Leiden.
Waltzing, J.-P. 1895–1900. *Etude historique sur les corporations professionelles chez les Romains dequis les origines jusq'à la chute de l'Empire romain d'Occident.* Louvain.
Wissowa, G. 1912. *Religion und Kultus der Römer.* 2d ed. Munich. Repr. 1971.

BURKHARD GLADIGOW
Trans. Dennis Martin

ROMAN TEMPLES. See TEMPLES AND SANCTUARIES (GRECO-ROMAN).

ROMANS, EPISTLE TO THE. The sixth book in the present ordering of works in the canon of the NT.

A. The Author and Name of the Epistle
B. The Place of Romans
  1. In the Christian Church
  2. In the NT Canon
  3. In the Career of Paul
C. The Text of Romans
D. The Epistolary Form and Occasion of Romans
E. The Argument of Romans
  1. Rom 1:16–17
  2. Rom 1:18–3:20
  3. Rom 3:21–4:25
  4. Rom 5:1–8:39
  5. Rom 9:1–11:36
  6. Rom 12:1–15:13
F. The Literary Character and Style of Romans
G. The Relation of Romans to Other Ancient Literature
H. Some "Problem" Texts of Romans Reconsidered
  1. Rom 1:26–27
  2. Rom 13:1–7
  3. Rom 16:1–7

A. The Author and Name of the Epistle

This epistle identifies its author as "Paul . . . [the] apostle" (1:1). Although a few persons in past centuries have questioned the Pauline authorship of the Epistle to the Romans, no one in recent years has successfully challenged the epistle's authenticity. Not only do all agree that the apostle Paul was the actual author of this magnificent letter that bears his name, but this epistle is used as the standard against which the authenticity of other epistles attributed to Paul is measured.

As is the case with all of the Pauline Epistles, this work derives its canonical name from the recipients of the letter and not from the name of its author. According to 1:7a, the apostle Paul addressed this epistle to "all God's beloved in Rome" (NRSV). Although some ancient mss omit the phrase "in Rome" in 1:7, the weight of the ms evidence favors the inclusion of this specific place indicator. The omission of the phrase "in Rome" is probably a later attempt to enhance the universal appeal of this epistle.

B. The Place of Romans

It is difficult to overestimate the significance of the Epistle to the Romans. Coming at a crucial point in the career of the apostle Paul, Romans represents the longest extant Pauline epistle and the most complete exposition of the Pauline gospel. Moreover, this lengthy epistle currently occupies a prominent place in the canon of the NT and has had a profound and lasting impact on the Christian faith. It is little wonder, then, that Romans has received more scholarly attention than any other Pauline epistle.

1. In the Christian Church. Paul's Epistle to the Romans has been first and foremost in the lives of many Christians. The first words that Augustine of Hippo read, after hearing a child next door say, "Pick it up, read it," were from Romans (i.e., 13:13). As a result of this incident, Augustine was immediately converted to the Christian faith (*Confessions* 8.12) and went on to become the most influential theologian of the next millennium. The first NT lectures that Martin Luther gave, after becoming a doctor of theology at the University of Wittenberg, were on the Epistle to the Romans (1515–16). The outcome of Luther's struggle to understand this epistle was the Protestant Reformation, which had a dramatic impact not only on the Christian church but also on all of Western civilization. And the first major writing in the prolific career of the Swiss theologian Karl Barth was a commentary on Paul's Epistle to the Romans (1918) whose impact was like the falling of "a bomb on the playground of the theologians" (Karl Adams). This commentary represented a break with the prevailing schools of theological thought and inaugurated a new era of theological investigation in the 20th century. In a very real sense, then, Romans has been a source of inspiration and reform since its composition.

In the early Church, during the Middle Ages, and on into modern times, Romans has left its indelible mark.

The Epistle to the Romans has also contributed significantly to the history of Christian doctrine. Almost every influential Christian thinker has dealt with Romans. Origen, Thomas Aquinas, and Philip Melanchthon, to mention only a few, wrote noteworthy commentaries on Romans. And numerous theological notions have been derived solely or in part from Romans. Augustine acquired his idea of original sin from Romans 5, Luther gained his understanding of justification by faith alone from Romans 3–4, John Calvin obtained his doctrine of double predestination from Romans 9–11, John Wesley got his distinctive teaching on sanctification from Romans 6 and 8, and Karl Barth learned of the importance of the righteousness of God from Romans 1 and 2. In short, this epistle has exerted a powerful influence on all branches of the Christian Church, and its impact on the lives and thought of prominent Christian thinkers through the years has been second, perhaps, only to the canonical gospels.

2. In the NT Canon. In the current arrangement of NT books, Romans follows immediately after the four gospels (Matthew, Mark, Luke, and John) and Acts. In its present position, therefore, Romans is the first epistle in the NT as well as the first of thirteen epistles in the NT ascribed to the apostle Paul. Because the present ordering of the Pauline Epistles is based roughly on the length of the writings—from the longest to the shortest, first those addressed to churches (Romans to 2 Thessalonians), then those addressed to individuals (1 Timothy to Philemon)—the position of Romans in the canon indicates to the reader that Romans is Paul's longest extant epistle to a church.

But Romans has not always occupied this prominent position, for the order of the epistles within the Pauline corpus has varied throughout the ages. Romans was the fourth of ten Pauline Epistles in the mid-2d century canon of Marcion, and Romans is listed last among the letters of Paul in the Muratorian canon of ca. A.D. 200. In fact, Romans does not appear in canon lists in its present position at the head of the Pauline corpus until the 4th century and later.

But even after it assumed its position of preeminence among the letters of Paul, Romans, contrary to the present English order, was not the sixth book of the NT nor did it follow Acts. In the 4th-century uncial ms cod. Sinaiticus (and also in the 6th-century ms cod. Fuldensis) Romans comes immediately after the four gospels and before Acts, an order that was followed in the Greek NT of the Complutensian Polyglot Bible printed in 1514.

In almost all Greek mss of the NT, however, the seven Catholic Epistles (James; 1 and 2 Peter; 1, 2, and 3 John; and Jude) follow Acts and precede the Pauline Epistles. In these mss, therefore, Romans is the thirteenth book of the NT, and it follows the epistle of Jude. This placement of Romans and the rest of the Pauline corpus may have been due in part to Paul's view that he was "the least of the apostles" (1 Cor 15:9), whereas the Catholic Epistles were associated with the so-called "pillars" of the apostolate (Gal 2:9). But the fact that Paul's writings were addressed to specific churches and persons may also have made them less appealing than the more general address of the Catholic Epistles.

In its present position as the first Pauline work in the NT, Romans serves as an introduction to Pauline thought. Moreover, because of its present position following Acts, the detailed treatment of the missionary career of Paul in the second half of Acts serves as an introduction to the Pauline corpus. In the current arrangement, therefore, Acts ends with Paul in Rome (Acts 28:16–31), then follows the Apostle Paul's Epistle to the Romans.

3. In the Career of Paul. Romans also occupies a significant place in the career of the apostle Paul, for it was written relatively late in the life of Paul. At the time of writing Paul admits that he has completed his mission to the eastern Mediterranean world, having "fully proclaimed" the gospel of Christ "from Jerusalem and as far round as Illyricum" (15:19 NRSV). Paul then informs the Romans that he is heading to Jerusalem with aid for less fortunate believers in that region (15:25).

A relative chronology of the Pauline Epistles can be constructed by means of references in Paul's genuine epistles to the Jerusalem collection. This collection was inaugurated at the apostolic council described in Galatians 2, when Paul agrees to "remember the poor" (Gal 2:10). The collection was introduced to the Corinthians in 1 Cor 16:1–4, where Paul provides directions for collecting money. Then in 2 Corinthians 8-9 (esp. 8:6, 10; 9:1) Paul exhorts the Corinthians to complete what they have begun. When Paul writes Romans, he is ready to travel to Jerusalem with what has been collected among the gentile believers in Macedonia and Achaia (Rom 15:25–26). Prior to the time of writing Romans, therefore, Paul had already written Galatians, and 1 and 2 Corinthians, in addition to 1 Thessalonians (believed to be Paul's earliest extant epistle), and perhaps Philippians as well.

Moreover, Romans is heavily indebted to those epistles that have gone before. As G. Bornkamm (1963: 2–14) has rightly pointed out, a number of topics that are present in Paul's earlier epistles surface in Paul's Epistle to the Romans. Among those topics are justification by faith and not by works of the law (Galatians 3–5; Philippians 3; Romans 1–4); the fatherhood of Abraham (Galatians 3; Romans 4); Adam as the head of the old order of humanity and Christ the head of a new order (1 Cor 15:21–22, 45–49; Rom 5:12–19); the church as Christ's body composed of diverse elements (1 Corinthians 12; Rom 12:4–8); the need to exercise personal freedoms with consideration for the consciences of others (1 Corinthians 8–10; Romans 14–15)—to name only a few. But in Romans, Paul does not merely reiterate these ideas; rather he reformulates and refines them. Romans, therefore, evidences a greater theological maturity than the other Pauline Epistles.

Although we do not know this from Paul's own writings, the visit to Jerusalem that Paul announces in Rom 15:25 results in his being taken into custody briefly in Jerusalem (Acts 21:27–23:30) before being transferred to Caesarea, where Paul remained in prison for no less than two years (23:31–26:32). Having appealed to Caesar (Acts 25:11) Paul is then conducted to Rome (Acts 27:1–28:16), where he remains in custody for two years (Acts 28:17–31) until his execution ca. A.D. 62, a few years before the Neronian persecutions of A.D. 65–68. With this chronology in mind, Romans was written at the height of Paul's apostolic career, ca. A.D. 55–57.

Paul probably wrote this epistle from the city of Corinth. In 2 Cor 1:16, Paul tells the Corinthians that he intends to depart from Corinth for Judea once the gentile offering is complete. Then, at the time that Paul announces to the Romans his impending trip "to Jerusalem with aid for the saints" (Rom 15:25), the collection is complete, and the Roman province of Achaia (whose capital is Corinth) is named as a prominent contributor (Rom 15:26). Moreover, if chap. 16 is accepted as part of the original epistle (see discussion below), then Paul's commendation to the Romans of the deacon Phoebe from Cenchreae (16:1–2), which is the eastern seaport of Corinth, is another reason for believing that this epistle originated in Corinth.

It would appear most likely that Paul composed his Epistle to the Romans during his final three-month stay in Corinth (see Acts 20:2–3) not long before his departure for Jerusalem. The Epistle to the Romans, therefore, is the apostle's last epistle as a free man, and coming at this late stage in his life, Romans represents Paul's mature thought.

C. The Text of Romans

Fragments of the Epistle to the Romans are preserved in a number of ancient Greek papyri. The earliest and most complete is p^{46}, one of the Chester Beatty biblical papyri from about the year A.D. 200, which contains portions of Romans 5, 6, 8, 9, 10, 11, 12, 13, 14, 15, and 16. The complete text of Romans is preserved in the earliest uncial mss that belong to the best ancient text-type (Alexandrian), including the 4th-century codex Sinaiticus, the 4th-century codex Vaticanus (B), and the 5th-century codex Alexandrinus (A), to name only a few.

Although scholars are in agreement that the apostle authored this epistle, there has been much discussion in recent years over exactly what Paul wrote to the Romans and what, if anything, has been added to his work. In other words, while accepting the essential authenticity of Romans, many have questioned the integrity of the epistle.

Several scholars in recent years have argued unsuccessfully that the Epistle to the Romans is actually composed of two or more writings, and its composite nature is the result of post-Pauline redactional activity. Schmittals (1975) perceives in Romans two distinct letters written to Rome at different times, along with some Pauline material not originally addressed to Rome and some later non-Pauline material. Scroggs thinks that Romans is composed of "two self-contained and completely different homilies" (1976: 274). O'Neill (*Romans* PNTC, 11) asserts that the original Epistle to the Romans suffered corruption through the incorporation of brief marginal glosses into the text at an early date and longer editorial sections that were added to supplement the epistle. Nevertheless, none of these scholarly views has been widely accepted.

Another challenge to the integrity of Romans was mounted by Bultmann (1947: 197–202). Because Rom 2:1, 2:16, 6:17b, 7:25b and 8:1, 10:17, and 13:5 appear to disrupt the logic of Paul's argument, Bultmann identified these verses as glosses, or brief marginal notes, that have found their way into the text of Romans. But not everyone has been persuaded by Bultmann's judgment on all of these verses.

The most extensive discussions regarding the integrity of Romans, however, have centered on three somewhat related textual problems. The first problem was mentioned in section A above, namely, the absence in some ancient mss of "in Rome" in 1:7, and the omission in others of the phrase "who are in Rome" in 1:15. Codex Boernerianus (G), a Greek mss with a Latin interlinear version, deletes the name of Rome in both verses. But textual critics agree that neither of these omissions represents earlier readings of the text. Rather these variants are best understood as deliberate attempts by later scribes to eliminate the specificity of the epistle and thereby make its contents more generally applicable.

The chief textual difficulties, however, concern the termination of Romans. At this point the textual history of the epistle is quite complicated. One significant textual problem is the doxology, which many of the best Greek mss (Sinaiticus, B) print at Romans 16:25–27. Other mss include the doxology after 14:23 (L, ms 044), one important witness (p^{46}) places the doxology after 15:33, a few have it at the end of chap. 14 and then again at the end of chap. 16 (A, P), and some mss omit the doxology altogether (G).

The variability in the placement of the doxology, coupled with its distinctive stylistic and theological features, have led most scholars to conclude that these verses were not a part of the apostle Paul's original Epistle to the Romans. But whether the doxology is a fragment from another Pauline work that was added later or simply a non-Pauline insertion cannot be determined conclusively.

The problem of the doxology, however, is related to another textual difficulty in the termination of the epistle. Serious questions about the authenticity and integrity of the rest of chap. 16, as well as chap. 15, have been raised. Evidently, by the 2d century the epistle existed in a 14-chapter version, a 15-chapter version, and a 16-chapter version.

Although the 14-chapter version is not preserved in any extant ms, there is indirect evidence to support its existence. According to Origen (*comm. in Rom.* 7, 453), Marcion used a 14-chapter version of Romans in the 2d century. Moreover, this shortened form of Romans is attested to indirectly in the ms tradition by the varying placement of the concluding doxology. Because of its character and tone, this doxology must have stood at the end of the letter. For this reason, the presence of the doxology after 14:23 in a few mss (L, ms 044, Origen) is indirect testimony to the existence of a short version of Romans, even though those witnesses in their present form contain chaps. 15 and 16.

But although the textual evidence suggests that the 14-chapter version of Romans is early, this version was probably not original. The deletion of chaps. 15–16 may be related in some mss to the practice of omitting the specific addresses in Rom 1:7 and 1:15. The desire to eliminate the specificity of Romans and thereby gain for this work a more universal appeal may also have been the motive behind the elimination of chaps. 15–16, which contain Paul's future travel plans and greetings to individuals.

The original form of the letter, in any case, must have been either the 15-chapter or 16-chapter version. But here the ms evidence is not sufficient to determine conclusively which version is original.

Until relatively recently, the 15-chapter version was conjectured purely on the basis of internal arguments. By Paul's own admission he has never visited Rome (1:10; 15:22), but in Rom 16:3–15 twenty-six persons are greeted by name. Would Paul have known so many people in a place that he had not visited? Moreover, Paul is not in the habit of greeting addressees by name. Paul usually communicates only a general and collective greeting, so would he have greeted specific individuals and groups even if he knew so many?

Finally, some of those on the list are associated more closely with the eastern Church than with the western Church. Prisca and Aquila, who are greeted in Rom 16:3–4a, were in Ephesus (1 Cor 16:8, 19) at the time of the writing of 1 Corinthians. Andronicus and Junia(s) who are greeted in Rom 16:7 Paul describes as having been "in prison with me," most likely at Ephesus. Epaenetus, who is greeted in Rom 16:5b, is called "the first convert in Asia," the capital of which is Ephesus.

Such internal evidence for the 15-chapter version of Romans as the original form of the epistle has also found some external, textual evidence since the discovery in 1935 of the Chester Beatty papyrus of the Pauline letters (p^{46}). This oldest extant mss of the Pauline corpus (from the early 3d century) contains the doxology between 15:33 and 16:1, and from this mss, therefore, one can infer the existence of a tradition that concluded Romans with chap. 15. See CHESTER BEATTY PAPYRI.

Manson (1948), who accepts the 15-chapter version as original explains the existence of the present 16-chapter version by assuming that Paul made two copies of the epistle. While the 15-chapter version was sent to Rome, the 16-chapter version was addressed to a church other than Rome, most likely to the church at Ephesus. Nevertheless, although the 15-chapter version is no doubt ancient, the question remains about whether this version is the oldest tradition.

Prompted by the careful textual study of Gamble (1977; and the insight of Donfried 1970), however, the tide of scholarly opinion is shifting to a renewed appreciation of the integrity of the 16-chapter version of Romans (minus 16:25–27). Gamble's comparison of the style and structure of Pauline epistolary conclusions has shown that all of the elements of chap. 16 are typical of Paul's conclusions. Moreover, without chap. 16 the 15-chapter version lacks a proper epistolary conclusion. In other words, if chap. 16 is not original, then the original ending has either been lost or displaced.

Finally, Gamble has shown that some of the unusual features of chap. 16 can only be understood if chap. 16 was addressed to Rome. One of the most prominent unusual features is the list of explicit greetings to individuals and groups which comprise most of the chapter (16:3–15). But the presence of twenty-six names in chap. 16 does not prove that this chapter is not original. Because Paul had not visited Rome, it was to his advantage to mention the names of those Roman believers who he knew from churches elsewhere. Moreover, Paul describes these persons in laudatory terms, which enhances their position in the community and reflects positively on Paul's status in the church. In this way, Paul presents himself as one who was not unknown to the church at Rome.

This textual difficulty regarding the termination of the epistle, it should be noted, has significant interpretive significance. If the 15-chapter version is the original form of the epistle, then there is no reason to believe that Paul had any accurate information about the church at Rome. If, however, the 16-chapter version is original, then Paul must have known something about the church at Rome through his contact with members of the Roman church elsewhere in the Roman empire.

Although a detailed description of the textual history of the Epistle to the Romans is not within the scope of this article, one additional textual matter is worthy of note, namely, the unusual textual problem found in Romans 5:1. Here the ms evidence strongly favors the subjunctive "let us have" (*echōmen* in Sinaiticus*, A, B*, C, D, Vg, cop^{bo}). The internal evidence, however, supports the less well-attested indicative "we have" (*echomen* in $Sinaiticus^{a}$, B^{3}, P, cop^{sa}), because other verses in this passage (see 5:2, 9–11) offer evidence of an indicative context, and the immediate concern of these verses is clearly with description rather than with exhortation. Because the *o* and *ō* were virtually indistinguishable in pronunciation during the Hellenistic age, the original indicative *echomen* may have been mistakenly understood as the subjunctive *echōmen* at an early stage of dictation, and the repeated use of this text in preaching may also have encouraged a hortatory understanding of the verb. For contextual reasons the indicative *(echomen)* is the preferred reading in 5:1, but the textual evidence for this variant is such that the subjunctive reading has had and continues to have its proponents.

D. Epistolary Form and Occasion of Romans

The uniqueness of the Epistle to the Romans cannot be overlooked. Romans is the only extant epistle written by Paul to a church that Paul did not found. In fact, Paul wrote this epistle to a community that he had never even visited (Rom 1:10f.). Unlike 1 Corinthians, therefore, Romans is not a response to specific questions addressed to Paul by the community. Unlike Galatians, Romans is not a reaction to heretical teaching. And unlike the other Pauline epistles, the body of Romans does not exhibit an obvious "occasional" character. Paul confines his personal remarks largely to the beginning (1:1–15) and the ending of the epistle (15:14–16:23), and the occasional character of "the frame" of the letter appears to have little effect on the central section of Romans (1:16–15:13). The very structure of this epistle, therefore, helps to explain the tendency down through the years to understand Romans as a theological treatise or as "a compendium of the Christian religion" (Philip Melanchthon, *Loci Communes Theologici*), which contains pure, "objective" doctrine (so Nygren 1949: 4–9) untainted by historical circumstances.

Nevertheless, the current scholarly consensus is that Romans is like the Pauline epistles in that it is an actual letter. Although Romans is Paul's longest and most systematic work, it is still an epistle, not a manifesto, or a treatise, or a position paper. As such, Romans exhibits an obvious epistolary form. First comes the salutation (1:1–7) that identifies both the author (1:1–6) and the recipients of the letter (1:7a) and includes the apostle's characteristic greeting ("Grace . . . and peace . . . " [1:7b]). Then, after the thanksgiving (1:8–15) comes the body of the letter (1:16–11:36), which is followed by the paraenetic or hortatory section (12:1–15:13). Finally, Paul relates his travel plans (15:14–33), then he closes with greetings (16:1–16) and a benediction (16:20).

In addition to the epistolary form, however, Romans also has an epistolary occasion. But the question debated by modern scholars is whether the occasion for Paul's Epistle to the Romans is to be found in the situation in Rome or in the life of the apostle Paul. Many scholars, including C. H. Dodd (*Romans* MNTC), T. W. Manson (1948), Nygren (1949), G. Bornkamm (1963), J. Jervell (1971), and C. E. B. Cranfield (*Epistle to the Romans* ICC), argue that Romans was prompted primarily by Paul's own situation in life—his impending journey to Jerusalem, his future visit to Rome, and his eventual mission to Spain. It is not uncommon for these scholars to accept the 15-chapter version of Romans as original. After all, they argue, if chap. 16 was not a part of the original epistle, then we have no evidence that Paul knew much about this community that he had never visited (Rom 1:10). What he did know about was his own situation in life, and that is what prompted his writing to the Romans.

Other scholars, including K. P. Donfried (1970, 1974), P. Minear (1971), J. C. Beker (1980, 1989), and R. Jewett (1986), to name only a few, argue that although Paul had not yet visited Rome (Rom 1:10; 15:23), he did in fact know something about that community. Accepting the 16-chapter version of Romans as the original form of the epistle, these scholars note then Paul apparently had many friends and acquaintances in Rome (some twenty-six, to be exact) who could have informed him of the community situation.

But how would Paul have met these Romans Christians, if he had not visited their city? According to the 1st century historian Suetonius in his *Lives of the Caesars,* the Roman Emperor Claudius in A.D. 49 "expelled from Rome the Jews who were constantly stirring up a tumult under the leadership of *Chrestus*" (*Claud.* 25.4). As a result of Claudius' edict of A.D. 49 some of the Jewish-Christians were expelled from Rome. According to Acts 18:2, Prisca (Priscilla in Acts) and Aquila were among those expelled who Paul met elsewhere.

The fact that good cases can be made for both of these two scholarly views may indicate that each side has an element of the truth. In other words, it could very well be that in addressing the needs of the Roman community Paul finds that his present and future situation in life has applicability to the situation at Rome.

But what was the situation at Rome? Here one must piece together bits of information from the epistle itself. Because Paul directly addresses both gentiles (1:13, 11:13) and those of Jewish background (2:17, 3:9), the Christian community must have been a mixed congregation. Most likely, Jewish Christians founded the church at Rome, and some of these same Jewish Christians, like Priscilla and Aquila (Acts 18:2), may have been expelled from Rome by the Emperor Claudius in A.D. 49. When the ban was lifted after Claudius' death in A.D. 54, many of the exiled Jewish Christians may have returned to Rome. But these returning exiles may have been surprised to find that the small group of gentile Christians that had remained in Rome had grown considerably during their absence. Without a doubt friction between the returning Jewish Christians and the resident gentile Christians must have resulted.

In 15:15 Paul admits that "on some points I have written to you rather boldly by way of reminder . . ." (NRSV). Problems of coexistence with Jewish Christians may have arisen in this largely gentile congregation: the gentile Christians were now in the majority and may have been all too willing to overlook the contribution of the Jewish Christian community. In chap. 14, Paul counsels the gentile Christians to be more tolerant of Jewish believers and their distinctive religious practices (14:3, 5–6, 14). One reason that Paul writes Romans, therefore, is to counsel the church on Jewish-gentile relations in the hopes of establishing the one church of Jews and gentiles. But this does not explain fully Paul's reason for writing this particular letter to this Christian community.

Paul goes on in chap. 15 to say that he has completed his work in the East (15:19), and now he wants to move on to Spain (15:23–24). Rome would be an ideal point of transit (if not headquarters) for his Spanish mission (15:24). Since Paul has not yet visited Rome (15:22), another reason that Paul writes this letter is to introduce himself to the Roman Christians. But the Romans may have already heard about Paul and his law-free gospel (see Rom 3:8), so Paul takes this opportunity to explain his gospel more fully and also to respond to possible objections to it. Although this is another important reason for writing, it is not a sufficient explanation for Paul's writing this letter to the Roman community.

On several occasions in Romans, Paul has stated that he is an apostle whose ministry is directed to the gentiles (1:5, 13, 14; 11:13; 15:16, 18). Because of the large gentile population in the community at Rome, Paul has often longed to visit the imperial city (1:10–15). To date, however, Paul has not paid such a visit (1:13; 15:22), evidently because his mission has involved proclaiming the good news "not where Christ has already been named, so that I do not build on someone else's foundation" (15:20). Since Rome already has an established Christian community, Paul has viewed other areas of the E Mediterranean world as higher priorities. But now that he has finished his work in the East (15:19b) and wants to move on to Spain (15:24a, 28), Paul intends to visit Rome (15:24b).

But Paul again will be delayed, for at the time of writing he is preparing to go to Jerusalem to deliver the gentile collection (15:25). Paul, "an apostle to the gentiles" (11:13), feels compelled to explain to the Romans his reason for doing this, lest they be offended by his decision to go "to the Jew first" in Jerusalem, and only after that "to the Greek" in Rome and beyond. A third reason, then, that Paul writes Romans is to apologize for his further delay in visiting Rome.

Finally, Paul asks the Romans to participate by means of their active intercession in the offering that he is about to deliver: "join me in earnest prayer to God on my behalf . . ." (15:30b NRSV). Paul is concerned about the possibility of persecution, so he asks the Romans to pray "that I may be rescued from the unbelievers in Judea . . ." (15:31a NRSV). Paul is also concerned about the acceptability of the offering, so Paul asks them to pray "that my ministry to Jerusalem may be acceptable to the saints . . ."

(15:31b NRSV). Therefore, a fourth and final reason that Paul writes Romans is to appeal for prayer support.

In short, no single reason accounts for the writing of Romans. Several factors converge, including the situation in Paul's life at the present time and also the situation in Rome. Although Paul does not reveal the factors that prompted his writing until chap. 15, these several factors have in fact influenced the length, scope, and duration of Paul's argument in the first 14 chaps.

E. The Argument of Romans

Although scholars concur that Romans contains the apostle's longest and most systematic argument (1:16–11:36), there has been much discussion about the structure of the argument in this important Pauline epistle. Part of the problem stems from the fact that Romans 1–4 differ considerably from Romans 6–8. The discussion in chaps. 1–4 is carried out primarily in the third person, while the discussion in chaps. 6–8 is in the first and second person. Moreover, in chaps. 1–4 Paul repeatedly refers to the Jews (1:16, 2:9, 10, 17, 28, 29; 3:1, 9, 29) and the gentiles (1:5, 13; 2:14, 24; 3:29; 4:17, 18), but in chaps. 6–8 all such references are absent. And finally, there exist significant lexical differences. Terms prominent in chaps. 1–4 (such as "faith" [*pistis*] and "wrath" [*orgē*]) are lacking in chaps. 6–8 where new terms (such as "life" [*zōē*] and "spirit" [*pneuma*]) predominate.

As a result of these and other differences, most scholars perceive two phases of Paul's argument in Romans 1–8. Traditionally, 5:21 was understood as the conclusion of the initial phase of the argument and 6:1 as the beginning of a new phase (so Sanday and Headlam *Romans* ICC, and most Protestant commentaries from the 16th through the 19th centuries; recently, Wilckens *An die Römer* EKK).

But N. Dahl (1951: 37–48) argues persuasively that the theme of chap. 6 is to be found in the verses that immediately precede in 5:20–21. Therefore, contrary to the traditional understanding of the structure of the epistle, a new phase of Paul's argument does not begin at 6:1. Furthermore, by printing a synopsis of Rom 5:1–11 and 8:1–39 Dahl shows that "chapter 8 contains a fuller development of the themes which are briefly stated in 5:1–11" (ibid., 39), and this fact also argues in favor of connecting chap. 5 with chaps. 6–8. For these reasons, Dahl sees 5:1 as the beginning of a discussion that extends through chap. 8, a conclusion that supported the work of some previous commentators (notably Barth 1933; Dodd; and Nygren 1949) and has been supported by others since (so, e.g., Cranfield; Käsemann 1980; Meyer in *HBC* 1130–67; and Beker 1989).

Another problem in the structure of Romans, however, is a result of the obvious break between the climactic conclusion of chap. 8 and the somber note sounded at the beginning of chap. 9. This raises the question of how chaps. 9–11 are related to chaps. 1–8. Are chaps. 1–8 "the main argument" of the epistle (Sanday and Headlam, 225) to which are appended chaps. 9–11? Or do chaps. 1–8 serve merely as an introduction to the climactic discussion of chaps. 9–11 (Baur 1876: 315; Stendahl 1976: 28–29)? While many contemporary scholars are unwilling to call chaps. 9–11 the "climax" of Romans, most would be even less willing to call these chaps. an "appendix." In these chaps., Paul responds to the questions first posed in Rom 3:1–4 and then answered with a brief "By no means!" The subsequent discussion in chaps. 9–11 shows that Paul's notion of grace, which was the subject of chaps. 3–4, does not invalidate God's promises to Israel. As a result, the discussion in chaps. 9–11 is hardly an afterthought.

These are some of the questions that continue to plague scholars who acknowledge the systematic form of the argument in Romans but who account for this form in different ways. Nevertheless, all agree that the central argument in Romans is without parallel in biblical literature. For that reason, a brief overview of the argument of Romans 1:16–11:36 and its practical application that follows in 12:1–15:13 is in order.

1. Rom 1:16–17. The central argument of the epistle begins with a thematic statement (1:16–17) that picks up on the notion of proclamation from v 15, where Paul has expressed his "eagerness to proclaim the gospel to you also who are in Rome" (NRSV). The theme is introduced by the assertion, "For I am not ashamed of the gospel; it is the power of God for salvation to everyone who has faith, to the Jew first and also to the Greek" (1:16 NRSV). Here Paul acknowledges the salvation-historical priority of the Jews in his remark "to the Jew first," but he also refutes Jewish exclusivism when he adds, "and also to the Greek." The relationship between Jew and Greek in salvation history will be unfolded in greater detail in Romans 9–11.

Paul goes on to say, "For in it the righteousness of God is revealed through faith for faith; as it is written, 'The one who is righteous through faith shall live' " (1:17). That is to say, the gospel reveals exactly how God justifies or puts people right with himself: it is through faith from beginning to end. The OT quote from Hab 2:4 supports this notion that the one who is put right with God by faith shall live.

Romans 1–8 elaborate on the Hab 2:4 quote of Rom 1:17. Chaps. 1–4 treat being put right with God "through faith." This section climaxes in 3:21–30, and the climax is then supported by the example of Abraham in chap. 4. Chaps. 5–8, on the other hand, treat Christian existence in light of God's act of justification. Here Paul considers the life that should be led by one who is righteous through faith.

2. Rom 1:18–3:20. In the first part of the argument in chaps. 1–4, Paul portrays the human dilemma by demonstrating that both Greek and Jew deserve divine condemnation and punishment when judged on the basis of their "works." Paul begins the argument with an indictment of the gentiles (1:18–32). Although Paul does not explicitly identify this group in these verses, the references to idolatry in 1:23, 25, indicate that the gentiles are intended. Paul states that through the creation God has clearly revealed himself to the gentiles as omnipotent and divine Creator (1:18–20). But the gentiles, "though they knew God" (1:21a), did not give God the reverence and thanksgiving due him (1:21b). Instead, they became idolaters (1:21a–23), the result of which was all manner of sordid behavior that violates the divine will (1:24–31) and makes them worthy of divine condemnation (1:32).

In the next section Paul addresses an unspecified "you" (2:1a), although this is identical to the direct address of 2:17 where "a Jew" is named. In any event, the "you" who self-righteously passes judgment on behavior described in 1:24–31 is guilty of self-condemnation, "because you, the judge, are doing the very same things" (2:1c). In other words, the addressee in 2:1–5 stands in the same condemnable position before God as the one judged does in the eyes of the addressee.

But Paul goes on to argue that no one escapes God's impartial and just judgment (2:6–11). God will repay every person for what he or she has done (2:6). People will get exactly what they deserve, either reward (2:7) or punishment (2:8). God judges everyone ("the Jew first and also the Greek," 2:9, 10) alike, "For God shows no partiality" (2:11).

But because God judges "according to each one's deeds" (2:6), the Jew is as deserving of divine condemnation as is the gentile (2:12–29). God revealed his will for his people through the law. Yet mere possession of that law (2:12–24) is not enough to save Jews, because it is only "doers of the law who will be justified" (2:13b). Moreover, mere circumcision (2:25–29) is insufficient unless "you obey the law" (2:25). The failure of Jews to live up to the requirements of the law (2:17–24) annuls their circumcision (2:25) and is grounds for their condemnation. In fact, when redefined in terms of "deeds," traditional Jewish "advantages" are opened up to gentiles, who by keeping the law (2:14–16) can have the benefits of circumcision attributed to them (2:26).

But if the Jew is no better off than the gentile, what benefit is there to being one of God's chosen persons? Of course, the Jew has certain "advantages" over the Greek (3:1), such as possession of "the oracles of God" (3:2). But in light of God's impartial judgment, the Jew is no better off than the Greek (3:9a). The Jew and the Greek are "under the power of sin" (3:9b), and Scripture itself supports Paul's point (3:10–18). Being under the power of sin, therefore, people are unable to put themselves right with God "by works of the law" (3:20).

In 1:18–3:20 Paul has described the impartiality that characterizes all of God's judgments. God is absolutely just and will judge everyone by what they do. God will reward those who do good and punish all who sin, regardless of their ethnic background. But Paul had also demonstrated the universality of sin and the universal inability to be put right with God by means of what one does. The result is the human predicament: being under the power of sin, people are powerless to put themselves right with a just God, and therefore, they are worthy of condemnation and death.

3. Rom 3:21–4:25. In the second part of the argument in chaps. 1–4, Paul presents God's response to the human predicament and begins to discuss the implications of that response. First comes the divine solution to the human predicament (3:21–26); Paul states that God has now revealed the way of being put right with him. It has nothing to do with (works of) the law (= "apart from law," 3:21a), which becomes the topic of 3:22–30. Nevertheless, this way "is attested by the law and the prophets" [= the Scriptures] (3:21b), the topic of 3:31–4:25.

Since no one is able ("all have sinned and fall short of the glory of God," 3:23), God puts people right with himself (3:22a). God puts right with himself all who believe [in Jesus Christ] (3:22b). But being put right with God is not earned; it is merely "by his grace as a gift" (3:24a). Being put right with God was achieved through Jesus Christ, whom God offered up as a sacrifice for human sin (3:25–26a). As a result, God is both just (= "righteous") and the justifier of "the one who has faith in Jesus" (3:25b–26). By judging sin (through the death of Christ) but forgiving the sinner (through faith in Christ), God is shown to be both just and merciful.

Paul then begins to detail the consequences of the divine solution (3:27–30). In the first place, human boasting is excluded (3:27a), for human achievement is denied. God alone puts people right with himself (see 3:22). Persons merely accept by faith what God has done in Christ (3:27b). That is to say, it is through faith in what God has done, not by doing works of the law, that one is put right with God (3:28).

But if a person is put right with God only through faith (3:28b), then, Paul concludes, there can be no distinction between Jew and Greek. God is the God of Jews and Greeks alike (3:29), and God accepts both Jew and Greek on the same basis: through faith (3:30).

Citing the example of Abraham in Rom 4:1–25, Paul demonstrates that being put right with God through faith "apart from (works of) the law" (3:21a) is the clear testimony of "the law and the prophets" (3:21b). Paul's view, then, "upholds the law" (3:30).

In Rom 4:1–15 Paul uses the example of Abraham in Gen 15:6 to prove that divine approval is a gift and is not dependent on circumcision or obedience to the law. Abraham did not earn God's favor. It was granted to him as a gift, and a gift that must be earned is no gift (4:2–8). Moreover, God's acceptance of Abraham came prior to any mention of circumcision, and therefore divine approval cannot be dependent on circumcision and cannot be limited to those who are circumcised (4:9–12). Neither was the promise made to Abraham dependent on obedience to the law, which came much later (4:13–15). Therefore, from the earliest of time people have been put right with God by means of God's grace through their faith!

Paul then goes on to show in Rom 4:16–25 that Abraham's faith is a type of Christian faith. Abraham is "the father of all of us" (4:16), not only of the Jews, because Christian believers share with Abraham a common faith. Abraham believed in a God "who gives life to the dead and calls into existence the things that do not exist" (4:17 NRSV), so he believed that God would keep his promise to make him the father of many nations (4:17, 18), even though Abraham's body "was [already] as good as dead" (4:19 NRSV). Abraham believed in this God (4:20–21), and for this reason was accepted by God as righteous (4:22). Likewise, Christians are accepted as righteous, because they believe in a God who raises the dead, Jesus Christ the Lord (4:23–24).

According to Romans 1–4, both Jew and Greek are confined under sin and both are liberated and united by faith in Jesus Christ. Because distinctions between Jew and gentile are overcome by God's act in Christ, the discussion of Christian life in chaps. 5–8 omits mention of Jews and gentiles. Not until chaps. 9–11 does Paul return to the topic of Jewish-gentile relations.

4. Rom 5:1–8:39. This new life presupposes God's act of justification by grace as a gift (5:1a, which recalls the conclusion reached in 3:28). This act, achieved by God giving up his own son on behalf of those who were "weak" (5:6), "sinners" (5:8), and "enemies [of God]" (5:10), "proves his love for us" (5:8). The result of God's act in Christ, which is received by faith, is "peace with God" (5:1), "freedom from the wrath [of God]" (5:9), and "hope of sharing the glory of God" (5:2).

In 5:12–21 Paul compares Christ with Adam. Adam is the head of the old creation, which has been in bondage to sin and death since Adam's act of disobedience. Christ by contrast inaugurates a new reign of God's grace which "leads to justification and life for all" (5:18) as a result of Christ's act of obedience [unto death] (5:19).

Paul concludes chap. 5 with two radical assertions, the first about the law ("But law came in, with the result that the trespass multiplied . . ." 5:20a) and the second about sin (" . . . but where sin increased, grace abounded all the more . . ." 5:20b). These two statements prompt the discussion of chaps. 6 and 7. In Rom 6:1–7:6 Paul treats the problem of sin, while in Rom 7:7–25 Paul considers the law.

In response to the assertion of 5:20b that grace abounds where sin increases the question naturally arises, "Should we continue in sin in order that grace may abound?" (6:1). Paul responds with an emphatic, "By no means!" then goes on to explain that believers are no longer controlled by sin, because they have "died to sin" (6:2). Through baptism believers have been united with Christ in his death (6:3–5) so that they are no longer enslaved to sin (6:6). Therefore, having been united with Christ in his death, believers "will certainly be united with Christ in a resurrection like his" (6:5) at a future time.

Paul then uses two analogies in 6:15–7:6 to demonstrate that sin and the law have no power over ones who have been "baptized into [Christ's] death." In the slavery illustration of 6:15–23 Paul asserts that a slave is bound to a single master for life. Death, however, discharges one from servitude to one master and thereby allows one to be enslaved to another. The point is that believers, who were at one time "slaves of sin" (6:17), through baptism have "been set free from sin" (6:18) and have now become "enslaved to God" (6:22a), the result of which is sanctification and ultimately eternal life (6:22b).

In the marriage illustration of 7:1–6 Paul notes that the wife is legally bound to one husband for life. With death, however, she is "discharged from the law" (7:2) and may legally marry another. Similarly, believers have "died to the law" (7:4) through baptism into Christ with the result that "now we are discharged from the law" (7:6).

Paul then turns in 7:7–25 to explain the radical claim about the law that he made in 5:20a. Although "law came in, with the result that the trespass multiplied" (5:20a), Paul asserts that the law is not sin (7:7, 12). Rather the law makes obvious the power of sin which manifests itself in "trespass" and "transgression." Sin uses the good law to take advantage of the weak flesh. The function of the law, then, is to drive people to the point of seeing that there is no way out except through the gift of God's grace in Christ (7:24–25).

Having completed in chaps. 6 and 7 his further explanation of the radical comments in 5:20, Paul returns in chap. 8 to the discussion begun in chap. 5 concerning new life. Here Paul characterizes that new life as "life in the Spirit" (8:9). At present, believers live "in the Spirit," if they are controlled by the indwelling of the Spirit of God. According to Paul, "all who are led by the Spirit of God are children of God" (8:14), and as children are "heirs of God and joint heirs with Christ" (8:17), provided that we suffer with him so that we will be glorified with him.

But Paul goes on to show that possession of the Spirit has a twofold function. In the first place, the Spirit makes believers aware that at present they are not what they should be. Present life is characterized by suffering (8:18), weakness (8:26), and decay since Adam's fall (see Gen 3:17). Believers are not above the world order, but rather identify with the rest of creation as they "groan inwardly" (8:22–25). Furthermore, the Spirit intercedes on their behalf, because their prayers are not adequate (8:27).

But possession of the Spirit also assures believers that they have a future. The Spirit is the "first fruits" or down payment of future redemption (8:23) as adopted children of God. When believers themselves (lit., "our bodies" in 8:24) are conformed to the image of God's son (through the resurrection of the dead and the transformation of the living, which will occur at the parousia), then they shall be brethren of the firstborn son (8:29).

The concluding doxology in 8:31–39 serves as a summary of the entire argument in chaps. 1–8. Here Paul asserts that "God is for us." The "us" refers to "the justified," who are "called," who are God's elect (8:33). If God is for this group of "chosen" people, then nothing can be against them. Since God went to great lengths to justify believers, God will not now indict them. And because Christ suffered, died, and intercedes on behalf of believers, he will not condemn them.

Nothing, then, can separate God's chosen ones from his love, absolutely nothing! Or is there something? Can lack of faith on the part of God's chosen ones separate them from the love of God? This one possible exception is the topic of chaps. 9–11.

5. Rom 9:1–11:36. The solemn oath in 9:1–5 stands in stark contrast to the end of chap. 8 where Paul ponders whether anything is able to separate God's chosen people from God's love in Christ (8:35–39). In chaps. 9–11 Paul ponders the one "exception" that threatens to undermine his confidence, namely, the faithlessness of God's chosen people. Paul expresses deep sorrow in these opening verses going so far as to say, "I could wish that I myself were accursed and cut off from Christ for the sake of my own people, my kindred according to the flesh" (9:3 NRSV), because of Israel's unbelief in Christ.

But Paul's sorrow in 9:1–5 is prompted not only by personal sorrow for the unbelieving members of his own race but also by a grave theological consideration, namely, God's faithfulness in the face of Israel's faithlessness. After all, God made promises to his chosen people Israel in the past. In light of Israel's unbelief in Christ, will God now turn his back on Israel and turn to the gentiles instead (as Paul's mission might suggest)? If this is the case, then hasn't God welshed on his (unconditional) promises to Israel? And if he has welshed on his promises to Israel, what is to prevent him from welshing on his promises to Christian believers at some time in the future? Thus, Jewish unbelief is of concern for gentile believers.

Paul begins by arguing that the present unbelieving state of most Jews does not mean that God's promise has lapsed. Paul reconsiders some important OT events, only to discover that human unbelief is unable to thwart the saving purposes of an all-powerful God. The present situation, where many gentiles are included in the people of God and many Jews are excluded, is in accordance with God's revelation in Scripture, Paul says. According to Hosea (2:25; 1:10), gentiles would be called "children of the living God" (Rom 9:25–26), whereas Isaiah (10:22; 1:9) states that only a remnant of Jews will be saved (Rom 9:27–29).

But even though most of Israel suffers from hardness of heart in the present, God continues to reach out to his chosen people. He has made being put right with God (10:6) a simple matter of faith in the resurrection of Jesus Christ and confession of his lordship (10:9). Moreover, he has brought the message of faith near to the Jews (10:8) through the apostles' preaching of Christ (10:15). But even though "not all have obeyed the good news" (10:16), God continues to reach out to Israel to bring about its obedience: "All day long I have held out my hands to a disobedient and contrary people" (10:21).

To the question, "Has God rejected his people?" Paul gives a negative answer (11:1). Paul then goes on to show that the rejection of Israel by God is partial (11:1–10), temporary (11:11–27), and has had a deeper purpose (11:28–36).

Paul points to his own Christian existence as proof that the Jewish people as a whole have not been rejected. Contrary to what many think, there is a remnant of Jews that will be saved. According to 11:7 Israel is composed of "the elect" and "the rest." Surely the elect will be saved (9:27). The real issue is the destiny of "the rest," who are hardened in unbelief (11:8–10).

Next Paul argues that the rejection of Israel is a temporary condition (11:11–24). He begins by asking, ". . . have they stumbled so as to fall" (11:11a). Here the "they" refers to "the [unbelieving] rest" of 11:7, "stumbled" alludes to Jews' rejection of Jesus (see 9:32f), and "fall" means to fall from grace eternally. In short, when the Jews rejected Jesus, was it God's intention to cut them off forever?

Paul's response to the question of 11:11a is an emphatic "By no means!" God turned Israel's stumbling into good. It brought salvation to the gentiles, which in turn will "make Israel jealous" (see Rom 10:19 = Deut 32:21). Therefore, God's promise of salvation has not been taken from the Jews and given to the gentiles. The order of events has merely been reversed: to the gentiles first and also to the Jews.

This fact informs Paul's missionary method. In spite of Israel's unbelief, God can reach the Jew via the gentiles and the jealousy that the gentiles' acceptance of the gospel will cause. Therefore, Paul's mission to the gentiles does not overlook Israel; it is at present the most direct way to get at the Jews.

Paul believes that his mission to the gentiles will have an impact on some of the unbelieving Jews (11:14). Note that the rejection of the Jews by God brought about the preaching of the gospel to the gentiles, which resulted in the reconciliation of the world (11:15). If this tragic event (Israel's rejection by God) brought such good results (gentiles' acceptance by God), what will happen when the Jews are accepted (11:15)? God has rejected unbelieving Israel in the present, but has not cast off Israel forever.

Paul then appeals to the metaphor of the olive tree (11:17–24). Here "some of the branches" (11:17a) refers to "the rest," that is, unbelieving Jews (11:7), while "you, a wild olive shoot" (11:17b) agrees with the direct address of 11:13 and must, therefore, refer to a believing gentile. This metaphor illustrates several points. In the first place, the ingrafting of gentile Christians is something unexpected, unnatural. Gentile Christians are at best "honorary Jews" (so Stendahl 1976: 37) who have become such by adoption. The practical result of this perspective is that gentile Christians must not "boast over the [natural] branches" (11:18), for the gentiles are dependent on the Jews. The gentiles must "not become proud, but stand in awe" (11:20), for God who did not spare the natural branches will surely not spare the wild branches, if they do not continue in their faith. Moreover, God can easily restore the natural branches, if they do not persist in their unbelief (11:23).

In 11:25–32 Paul reveals an eschatological mystery (11:25). The hardening of Israel is limited in extent ("a hardening has come upon part of Israel") and in duration ("until the full number of the Gentiles has come in") (11:25b NRSV). The result is that in the future "all Israel will be saved" (11:26a NRSV). And when will Israel be saved? According to the OT, which Paul cites in 11:26b–27, it will not take place until "Out of Zion will come the Deliverer" (Isa 59:20–21), that is, at the parousia of Christ. At that point Christ "will banish ungodliness from Jacob" (Isa 27:9), which Paul interprets to mean all unbelief on the part of "the rest" of Israel.

In response to the question implied in 9:6a, then, God *is* faithful! God will not take back from his people the gifts of his grace (listed in 9:4f) and their call to salvation (11:29). God's obvious intention is to save all Israel (11:26). Just as the gentiles, who were once disobedient, now have obtained mercy through the disobedience of the Jews (11:30), so too "the rest" of the Jews are now disobedient in order that God may have mercy on all (11:32), both Jew and Greek.

Paul concludes Romans 9–11, and also the whole of Romans 1–11, with a final hymn of praise (11:33–36). Here he states that God's ways of dealing with humankind are miraculous, far surpassing human understanding (11:33–34). Furthermore, no one holds God in his debt. What is received from God is not merited; how God acts is purely according to his will (11:35). Finally, God is creator and sustainer of all, Jews as well as Greeks, and therefore to God alone belongs all glory (11:36).

6. Rom 12:1–15:13. Following the lengthy theological argument in chaps. 1–11 comes the paraenetic section of the epistle which begins in 12:1. Having the paraenesis follow the body of the epistle is not unusual in Paul's writings (see also 1 Thessalonians 3–4 and Galatians 5–6). But this arrangement seems especially appropriate in Romans, for it shows that the saving work of God, which is described in chaps. 1–11, is not dependent on obedience to the injunctions of chaps. 12–15. One does not obey in order to earn God's favor. Rather obedience is the result of gratitude for all that God has already done and will continue to do in Christ for those who believe (understanding the *oun,* "therefore," of 12:1 to refer to all that has gone before).

This paraenetic section falls naturally into two distinct sections. While the first section (12:1–13:14) contains many general injunctions that seem unrelated to particular problems in Rome (but see the discussion of 13:1–7 below), the injunctions of the second section (14:1–15:13) are occasioned by and directed at the specific situation in Rome.

The exhortations of Romans 12–13 begin in 12:3 and end in 13:7. Life within the body of Christ is the subject of the first half of this section (12:3–14 [16a]), whereas relationships with those outside the Church are considered in the second half (12:15 [16b]–13:7). These exhortations are framed by an introductory appeal in 12:1–2, which urges Christians to offer themselves wholly and unreservedly to God as a proper service of worship, and by concluding appeals in 13:8–14, which summarize what has preceded and underscore eschatological urgency.

The present structure of 12:1–13:14 shows that the Christian's present life is radically qualified by the imminence of the New Age (13:11–14). Nevertheless, Paul does not conclude that Christians no longer have any responsibilities in the present age. In fact, according to Paul, life in Christ places special moral requirements on the believer. Gifts with which individuals are endowed (12:3–8) are to be used in the service of God, being the means whereby the believer's faith is enacted in love. As in 1 Corinthians 12, Paul in Romans 12 follows his description of spiritual gifts with an appeal to "let love be genuine" (12:9a). Then in Rom 13:8–10 the love command reappears in the summary appeal of the whole section.

In Rom 14:1–15:13, Paul considers the tensions that are present within the believing community between the "weak" and the "strong." In this section Paul describes those whom he calls "weak in faith" (14:1) as ones who "eat only vegetables" (14:2b NRSV) and also "judge one day to be better than another" (14:5a). The "strong," although not mentioned as such until 15:1, are surely those who "believe in eating anything" (14:2a NRSV) and "judge all days to be alike" (14:5b). While they are never identified as such, the "weak" may refer to overly scrupulous Jewish-Christians, who because of their background, consider diet and festal observance matters of significant religious concern. The very fact that Paul has to council the so-called "strong" not to "despise those who abstain" and the so-called "weak" not to "pass judgment on those who eat" (14:3) reveals the tension between these two parties in the Roman community.

But Paul states that "God has welcomed" (14:1) members of both groups into the fellowship and all are advised to "Welcome one another, therefore, just as Christ has welcomed you" (15:7 NRSV). Unity in the community, however, does not require uniformity of behavior (see 14:3, 5–6). But believers must be "fully convinced in their own minds" (14:5b) that what they do is done "in honor of the Lord" (14:6–9), knowing that one day they will have to account for their actions before God (14:10b, 12).

Believers must recognize that their responsibility to fellow believers does not simply involve tolerating the different practices of others. One's own behavior must not injure or alienate others (14:13–23), even if that means giving up some personal rights, such as eating meat or drinking wine (14:21). If believers are more concerned with pleasing others than with pleasing themselves (15:1–2), then those from different backgrounds in Rome can "live in harmony with one another" (15:5) and thereby "with one voice glorify the God and Father of our Lord Jesus Christ" (15:6).

Ultimately, then, this is the purpose of God's act in Christ: to unite Jew and gentile in the praise of God (15:7–13). And that ultimate purpose explains why Paul writes to the Romans (15:14–17), why Paul wants to go on to Spain via Rome (15:18–24, 28–29), why Paul is about to go to Jerusalem with the gentile offering (15:25–27), and why Paul is concerned about the acceptability of his service for Jerusalem (15:30–31).

F. Literary Character and Style of Romans

The longest of the undisputed Pauline Epistles exhibits a remarkably varied literary character and style. In this 7,094–word epistle Paul uses a relatively large 1,068–word vocabulary, which betrays the author's familiarity with Greek thought as well as his extensive knowledge of the Hebrew Scriptures in their Greek translation (the LXX).

Besides using a varied vocabulary in Romans, Paul employs a wide variety of literary conventions, wider than in any of his other extant writings. Long ago Augustine noted (in *On Christian Doctrine* 4.7) the Apostle's use in Romans 5:3–5 (see also 8:29–30 and 10:14–15) of the rhetorical device known as *climax.* Elsewhere Paul also reveals a familiarity with other ancient rhetorical devices, such as *chiasmus,* a form of parallelism that inverts the order of the elements in the second half of the literary unit (hence, the ABB'A'pattern; see 1:17–18; 2:6–11; 6:3; 11:22; 11:33–36).

The *diatribe* is another important rhetorical device employed by Paul in Romans. In his doctoral dissertation, Bultmann (1910) pointed out the influence of the diatribe on Paul's Epistle to the Romans. But recent studies, particularly by Stowers (1981), have clarified and deepened our knowledge of the subject.

According to recent research the diatribe is actually a form of discourse that was used by teachers in certain philosophical schools to correct students and to refute their objections to the subject being taught. The diatribe, therefore, captures the earnest give-and-take between a pupil and a teacher. With this in mind, one can see that Paul employs the diatribe in Romans when he addresses an imaginary interlocutor (2:1–5; 2:17–24; 9:19–21; 11:17–24; 14:4, 10) and when he responds to objections and false conclusions (3:1–9; 3:31–4:2a; 6:1–3, 15–16; 7:7, 13–14; 9:14–15, 19–20; 11:1–3, 11, 19–20). Paul's conspicuous use of the diatribe in Romans may also indicate something about the original addressees of this epistle. Paul may have known (or at least thought it to be true) that the Romans were a sophisticated, well-educated congregation which would be familiar with this literary device.

In Romans, the longest sustained argument of any extant epistle, Paul skillfully unites the various topics taken up in this lengthy epistle into a single argument. On several occasions, Paul draws together the thought of a longer, more-involved discussion by means of a brief summarizing comment (see 6:11; 7:12; 15:5–6). At other times, the Apostle connects discrete portions of his argument by delaying such summarizing comments until after the next thought-unit has begun. An obvious example of this type of *delayed conclusion* is found in 3:22b–23, where the comment, "For there is no distinction, since all have sinned and fall short of the glory of God," summarizes the discussion of 3:9–20 after a new thought has begun in 3:21 (see also 10:17).

But Paul is also careful to distinguish major sections of the epistle. Thus in 4:25 Paul cites a liturgical fragment to punctuate the discussion begun in 3:21. In 8:31–39 Paul utilizes a hymnlike passage to bring to a close the whole discussion that began in chap. 1 (understanding *tauta*, "these things," in 8:31 as a reference to all that has preceded, at least since 3:21). In 11:33–36 Paul cites a doxological passage to end the discussion of chaps. 9–11, and in 15:13 a blessing serves to round off the previous discussion. In smaller thought-units in Romans, Paul often employs the literary device known as *inclusion*. Here a word or phrase at the beginning of a thought-unit is repeated at the end as a way of concluding the unit (for example, see the phrase "through our Lord Jesus Christ" in 5:11, which recalls 5:1 and rounds out the discussion in 5:1–11).

As a result of these punctuating devices, Romans contains some rather abrupt transitions and sudden changes of mood. But rather than interpreting these abrupt transitions as the result of some post-Pauline redactional activity (so Schmittals 1975; O'Neill *Romans* PNTC; and Scroggs 1976) they are better explained as deliberate attempts to demarcate the various sections of the letter and are not evidence of the composite nature of the epistle. To those who first heard this epistle read aloud these abrupt changes were needed to enable the auditors to distinguish one thought-unit from the next.

Some of the literary style and character of Romans, however, cannot be attributed to the apostle Paul, for there is much tradition cited by Paul in this epistle. In the first place, Paul repeatedly cites the LXX. Romans contains so many quotations from the Greek Bible (some 65 in all) that Martin Luther thought that Paul's intent in writing this epistle was to compose "an introduction to the entire Old Testament" (1522 Preface to Romans).

But in Romans Paul also includes much pre-Pauline and even pre-Christian tradition. For example, Paul cites early creedal fragments (1:3b–4; 4:25), an early Christian hymn (11:33–36), an early Jewish-Christian liturgical statement (3:25), a baptismal tradition (6:4–5), a faith formula and confession (10:9), along with echoes of Christ-sayings (12:14, 17; 13:7; 14:13, 14). Some of the pre-Pauline paraenetic materials, such as the vice list in 1:29–31 and the imperative cluster in 12:9–13, may be pre-Christian. But Paul did not merely cite these traditions. He interpreted what he inherited by adding words and phrases in order to fit the occasion and his audience. The Epistle to the Romans, therefore, is not solely the product of Pauline originality.

All in all, the epistle that has as its theme "the power" of the gospel (1:16) is written in a style that is appropriate for the message. This epistle is forceful, but not angry like Paul's Epistle to the Galatians. Moreover, Romans is argumentative, but not contentious like Paul's Corinthian correspondence. But as is the case in the other Pauline writings, the literary character of Romans is also influenced by the audience that Paul addresses. The more sophisticated and more erudite style of Romans, in comparison to the other Pauline epistles, suggests that the community which Paul addresses is unlike his own congregations. Therefore, Paul wrote this epistle in a manner that he thought would enlighten and also persuade believers in Rome.

G. The Relation of Romans to Other Ancient Literature

Before World War I, Adolf Deissmann published his ground-breaking work (1910). Whereas previous scholars had compared NT works to the literature of Plato, Demosthenes, and other authors of classical antiquity, Deissmann endeavored to compare the literature of the NT with the plethora of nonliterary papyri that had been uncovered of late in Egypt. On the basis of this comparison, Deissmann distinguished between "letters" *(Briefe)*, which were private, unliterary, and clearly occasional communications, and "epistles" *(Episteln)*, which have the outer form of a letter but are actually artful literary products intended for public consumption and written for posterity. According to Deissmann, the writings of the apostle Paul were real letters and not literary epistles (1926: 9–12).

Not all scholars are satisfied with Deissmann's absolute distinction between the letter and the epistle, particularly as it applies to Romans. Although most admit that Romans is occasional in nature, this work is not a casual correspondence written hurriedly and haphazardly. Neither is this work a private, informal communication. On the contrary, Romans is a well-thought-out, authoritative communication that is intended to serve as a substitute for Paul's personal presence (Rom 15:25–27).

The enduring contribution of Deissmann, however, was his awareness of the need to compare the NT writings with the wide variety of Hellenistic literature. This careful comparison has continued to be a vital part of Romans research in recent years, the thought being that the discovery of the rhetorical genre to which Romans belongs may provide some clue about Paul's intention in writing Romans. And a clearer sense of the rhetoric in Romans sheds valuable light on the structure of the argument.

Basing his work on the research of M. L. Stirewalt (1977: 175–206), K. P. Donfried suggests that Romans evidences the characteristics of the "letter-essay" (1977: 143–48). Stirewalt examines fifteen ancient Greek documents that he classified as "letter-essays," because the more personal epistolary features of these writings seem to be giving way to the more impersonal features that characterize an essay. These writings often function as a summary of earlier work, and they seem to assume a third party (not only "I" and "thou," but also "they"). The summary character and the public nature of Romans suggest that this writing may also exhibit characteristics of the "letter-essay," Donfried asserts.

S. Stowers (1986: 114) classifies Romans as a "protreptic letter," a type of letter which is modeled on the protreptic speech that goes back to the Sophists. Protreptic works usually urge one to adopt a new way of life, and to do so they sometimes include a refutation of objections. In Romans, Paul introduces his gospel and himself as an authoritative teacher to the Roman Christians. Moreover, in Romans, Paul answers objections to his gospel and reproaches those who, through arrogance or pretentiousness, will not accept his gospel. All of these features, argues Stowers, are typical of the protreptic letter.

Other scholars have considered the whole of the Epistle to the Romans in relation to ancient Hellenistic literature by means of rhetorical criticism. After determining the conventional parts of a rhetorical composition through a careful examination of the contents of ancient rhetorical handbooks, these scholars (notably W. Wuellner 1976: 152–74; G. Kennedy 1984: 152–54; and R. Jewett 1986: 382–89) then analyze Romans in terms of its rhetoric of argumentation.

Although there is no scholarly consensus at the present time, further comparisons of Romans with other ancient Hellenistic literature is assured. And although this type of scholarly research is still in its infancy, such analysis promises to shed new light on the perennial problems of the author's intent, the structure of the argument, and the climax of the epistle.

H. Some "Problem" Texts of Romans Reconsidered

Several passages in Romans, which down through the years have had a deleterious effect on the social, political, and moral realms, have received special scholarly attention in recent years. Three texts in particular have been the subject of considerable study: Rom 1:26–27, which deals with the subject of homosexuality; Rom 13:1–7, which concerns the Christian's responsibility to the state; and Rom 16:1–7, which provides valuable testimony about the role women played in the first generation of the Christian Church.

1. Rom 1:26–27. In the course of indicting gentile unbelievers in 1:18–31, Paul refers to women who "exchanged natural intercourse for unnatural" (1:26 NRSV) and men who "giving up natural intercourse with women, were consumed with passion for one another." (1:27 NRSV). Rom 1:27 is the clearest statement in the NT regarding the issue of homosexual behavior between consenting adult males, and Rom 1:26 is the only biblical text that addresses the particular issue of homosexual behavior between consenting females. Because of their clarity, these verses have served as a biblical warrant for singling out homosexual behavior as the grossest of sins and for discriminating against those who engage in such behavior.

Greater awareness of the historical context and a greater appreciation of the literary context of Paul's remarks in Rom 1:26–27, however, have forced a reconsideration of these verses. True, homosexual behavior between consenting adult males was a capital offense in ancient Israel (Lev 18:22; 20:13), but so were such "heinous" crimes as consulting a medium or wizard (Lev 20:6), cursing your father or mother (Lev 20:9), and engaging in sexual intercourse with a menstruating woman (Lev 18:19; 20:18).

Apparently, homosexual behavior among consenting males was quite rare among Israelites. Nowhere in the historical literature is this practice mentioned. More importantly, prophetic denunciations of Israel's sins do not include homosexual behavior. The result is that among Jews, homosexual behavior was perceived as a "gentile" phenomenon and practice.

Although homosexual love (usually in the form of pederasty, the love of an older man for a younger) enjoyed a relatively prominent place in ancient Greek social life beginning in the 6th century B.C., homosexuality was viewed differently in the world of the 1st century A.D. To be sure, it was still practiced among some segments of society, but moral philosophers were beginning to question its merit. Homosexuality was viewed as grossly self-indulgent, essentially exploitative, and an expression of absolutely insatiable lust. The same desire that drove men to female prostitutes could, unless kept under control, drive men to seduce other men. Homosexuality was also seen as a violation of the natural order. Since heterosexual intercourse was necessary for procreation, this was "natural," whereas sex between same-sexed partners was "unnatural."

It is vital to note that Paul's presuppositions about homosexuality in Romans 1 are similar to those of his contemporaries. Paul's choice of the active verbs "exchanged" (1:26) and "giving up" (1:27) assumes that homosexuality is an activity freely chosen. Paul's use of the phrase "consumed with passion" (1:27) reveals the belief that homosexual behavior is associated with insatiable lust and unbridled passion. And Paul's remarks concerning the giving up of "natural [heterosexual] intercourse" (1:26, 27) in favor of "unnatural" (1:26) understand homosexuality as a violation of the natural order.

It is also important to note that Paul describes homosexuality as the consequence of idolatry. In 1:18–23 Paul indicates that the source of gentile "ungodliness and wickedness" is their failure to give honor and thanks to God, who has revealed himself to all through the creation. "So they are without excuse" (1:20b). Rather than worshipping the Creator, they worship the creation instead (1:23, 25). And their fundamental confusion regarding the true entity of God ("they exchanged the truth about God for a lie and worshiped and served the creature rather than the Creator . . ." 1:25) results in a basic confusion about their own sexual identity ("they exchanged natural intercourse for unnatural," 1:26). Homosexual conduct (and the other vices catalogued in 1:29–31) is due to the sin of idolatry.

But Paul's description of the gentile world in Romans 1 is not original. As the striking parallels with the Wisdom of Solomon (chaps. 11–15) indicate, Paul is heavily indebted to the traditional Hellenistic Jewish picture of gentile sinners. Homosexual behavior, which was believed to be a typically gentile practice, is understood as a consequence of their refusal to let God be God.

But Paul's argument does not conclude with the description of the gentile world. At 2:1, Paul's indictment of the gentiles' behavior turns to "the man" (the Jewish boaster of 2:17?) who self-righteously judges that behavior. The one passing judgment is not innocent, because no one is guiltless, when judged purely on the basis of what one does before an impartial and just God (2:1–11).

While Paul obviously accepts the description of the gentiles in Romans 1, this is not the point of the initial chapter of Romans. Paul's description of the gentiles is intended to provoke self-righteous Jewish pride, so that Paul can destroy it in chap. 2 by showing them that they sin against the law. Paul is simply leading up to the point that "all people, both Jews and Greeks, are under the power of sin"

(3:9b), so that he can introduce the topic of the reality and power of God's redemptive grace for all (3:21–8:39).

Even within Romans 1, homosexuality is perceived not as one of the "sins" of the gentiles, but as one of the consequences of their root sin of refusing to let God be their God. Therefore, homosexuality cannot be singled out in this chapter, for Paul says that those who do such things (1:32a), or they that approve of others doing them (1:32b), or they that pass judgment on those who do them (2:1) are all worthy of condemnation. In other words, "all have sinned and fall short of the glory of God" (3:23).

2. Rom 13:1–7. The Apostle Paul's admonition to "be subject to the governing authorities" (13:1a) on the grounds that "those authorities that exist have been instituted by God" (13:1c) has caused much needless suffering and much misery even in the 20th century. This passage seems to lend support to any existing government, regardless of how tyrannical or how corrupt, and any governmental policy, however repressive or unjust. This passage has been invoked by Christians to put down revolt, support war, and justify genocide. In fact, many Christians in Hitler's Germany appealed to this text as the decisive biblical warrant for obedience to the Nazi regime. And it has been regret over the Church's alignment with the Nazi regime that has forced a reconsideration of these verses, particularly by German biblical scholars.

Again, a careful reading of the text along with an awareness of the historical context is essential for understanding this problem passage. It must be noted that Paul does not say "obey" or "disobey" governing authorities. He instead speaks of "being subject" (13:1, 5), which can include disobedience.

In Rom 13:1–2, Paul states that the authority of the governing authorities has been granted them by God. Here Paul is indebted to Hellenistic Judaism, which understood that earthly rulers had no authority except what God had given them (see Prov 8:15–16; 24:21; 1 Pet 2:17). But authority was not a license to do whatever one wanted. Tradition also held that earthly rulers were accountable to God for their own actions and were liable to God's judgment (see, for example, Wis 6:1–11).

In Rom 13:3–4, Paul argues that earthly rulers function as servants of God to employ the authority granted them for the common good. According to Paul governing authorities are "God's servants" and not divine representatives. Their authority is recognized, for it is given by God, and their rightful task is to serve. The proper function of governing authorities is to assure the welfare of society by punishing those who do wrong and by supporting those who work for what is good.

In Rom 13:5, Paul advances a third point by repeating the opening admonition to "be subject" not only for fear of punishment but also "for the sake of conscience." Up to this point Paul has argued for being subject to governing authorities, because they are God's servants for the maintenance of law and order. Now he says one must be subject "for the sake of conscience." This refers to the capacity to reflect critically upon what is appropriate given the realities of existence. Therefore, Paul argues that if one thinks carefully and reasonably about it, subjection to the authorities will commend itself as a wise and prudent course. This passage sums up the argument to this point, but the conclusion and real point of the paragraph comes in 13:6–7.

In Rom 13:6–7, Paul states exactly how one should comply with the demands of the governing authorities: by paying taxes. Everything in 13:1–5 has been leading up to the topic of "taxes" in 13:6–7. But the way that the admonition is worded suggests that Paul has a specific issue in mind.

Rom 13:7 is an admonition, which uses two different words (*phoros* = "taxes" in the NRSV, and *telos* = "revenue" in the NRSV) to refer to taxes due, in contrast to 13:6, which is a statement that mentions only "taxes" *(phoros)*. Moreover, the admonition in 13:7 stresses the need to render "to all what is due them" (NRSV).

What Paul apparently refers to in v 6 is direct taxes, which were collected by government officials. The reference to "revenue" in 13:7 is probably a reference to indirect taxes (such as harbor fees, import and export duties), which were collected by Roman citizens known for their exploitation the public. The Roman historian Tacitus (*Ann.* 13.50) says that public displeasure with the corrupt practices of these citizen collectors of "revenues" reached a climax in A.D. 58. As a result of the widespread discontent, Nero almost abolished these taxes, but instead he simply reformed the system.

Paul's letter to Rome was written in ca. A.D. 55–57, while public pressure was building against abuses of revenue collectors. If the Roman church included some well-to-do people, then these would be ones most affected by revenue abuses. If this is true, then Paul is urging Roman believers to continue paying the direct tax (13:6) and also the controversial indirect tax (13:7). Paul urges the paying of whatever taxes are levied. This will prevent punishment for tax evasion, which is a reasonable thing to do as a sign of respect for law and order.

Rom 13:1–7, therefore, was originally directed to a specific situation in Rome during the mid-50s. When these words were composed, several years before Paul's own death at the hands of the Romans and before the Neronian persecutions of the 60s, Paul must have been fairly confident that the Roman government would be just. Nevertheless, Paul's thought about the governing authorities in these verses is not original; he was indebted to the Hellenistic Jewish tradition that he inherited. But Paul uses that tradition to address a specific situation in Rome, because Paul did not believe that Roman Christians should become embroiled in the tax issue. For that reason, the point of the discussion is the concluding admonition: "Pay to all what is due them" (13:7).

3. Rom 16:1–7. The problem with this passage is that it has for so long been overlooked. After all, on the surface these verses appear to be little more than commendations and greetings, material that is hardly worthy of any scholarly scrutiny. Nevertheless, in recent years this passage has been found to contribute some important pieces to a larger puzzle about the role(s) of women in the first generation of the Christian movement.

In Rom 16:1–2 Paul recommends to the Romans (assuming that chap. 16 is a part of the original letter to Rome; see the discussion in section C, above) a woman named Phoebe from the port city of Corinth. Note that she is identified as a *diakonos,* and although at this time "deacon" is not the formal office that it becomes at a later stage in the early Church, the woman Phoebe must have been a prominent figure in the church at Corinth. Moreover, the fact that Paul recommends to the recipients of his letter a woman who comes from the place where Paul wrote Romans suggests that Phoebe probably delivered Paul's letter to the Romans, not an insignificant task.

In Rom 16:3–4, Paul greets Prisca and Aquila, a woman and her husband. According to Acts 18, after this man and his wife (called Priscilla in Acts) were expelled from Rome by the Emperor Claudius, they met Paul in Corinth (Acts 18:1–3). Acts also states that this husband-wife team later "expounded to [Apollos] the way of God more accurately" (Acts 18:26). In Rom 16:3, Paul, contrary to ancient practice, greets Prisca before Aquila, which may indicate that Prisca was the leader of the team. In any event, Paul calls both Prisca and Aquila *synergoi* ("fellow workers"), a title reserved for important leaders (for example, Apollos, 1 Cor 3:9; Titus, 2 Cor 8:23; Timothy, 1 Thess 3:2).

In Rom 16:7, Paul greets two apostles who Paul describes as "prominent among the apostles, and they were in Christ before I was" (NRSV). One of these apostles is a man, Andronicus. But the other apostle, who was an apostle before Paul himself, may be a woman and the spouse of Andronicus. Most English translations merely transliterate the Greek text and render *Ioudian* as "Junias," a male name that is otherwise unattested in antiquity. But the name in the Greek text is in the accusative case, because it is the direct object of the sentence. That same name in the nominative (subject) case could be "Junia," which was the Greek version of a common Roman name for a woman. If "Junia" is the correct name in this verse, and this reading is gaining wider acceptance (so the REB and NRSV), then here is evidence that women were apostles at a very early stage in the Christian movement.

These few verses testify, therefore, that Paul knew of women in positions of leadership in the early Church and that he acknowledged their authority. These verses also reveal that the practice in the first generation of the Church's existence differed from the practice of the later Church, which is reflected in 1 Tim 2:11–3:13. Apparently, in Paul's day women were not denied the right "to teach or have authority over men . . ." (1 Tim 2:12). In Paul's churches, those who led were the ones most-gifted spiritually (see 1 Cor 12:4–11, where Paul's remarks do not bar anyone from participation in the various offices listed). As a result, women had access to prominent roles of leadership in the earliest generation of the Church. Paul's own testimony suggests that in reality women were among his closest associates in ministry and that women were among the most prominent leaders in the early Church.

Rom 16:1–7, therefore, lend additional support for understanding 1 Cor 14:33b–36 as a non-Pauline insertion and for recognizing Paul's remark that "there is neither male nor female; for you are all one in Christ Jesus" (Gal 3:28b) as most expressive of Paul's attitude toward women.

Bibliography

Barth, K. 1933. *The Epistle to the Romans.* Trans. E. C. Hoskyns. London.

Bassler, J. M. 1982. *Divine Impartiality: Paul and a Theological Axiom.* SBLDS 59. Chico, CA.

Baur, F. C. 1875–76. *Paul the Apostle of Jesus Christ.* 2d ed. 2 vols. Trans. A. Menzies. London.

Beker, J. C. 1980. *Paul the Apostle.* Philadelphia.

Bornkamm, G. 1963. The Letter to the Romans as Paul's Last Will and Testament. *ABR* 11: 2–14. Repr. pp. 17–31 in K. P. Donfried, ed. 1977.

Bultmann, R. 1910. *Der Stil der paulinischen Predigt und die kynisch-stoische Diatribe.* Göttingen.

———. 1947. Glossen im Römerbrief. *TLZ* 72: 197–202.

Dahl, N. A. 1951. Two Notes on Romans 5. *ST* 5: 37–48.

———. 1977. *Studies in Paul.* Minneapolis.

Deissmann, A. 1910. *Light from the Ancient East.* London.

———. 1926. *Paul: A Study in Social and Religious History.* 2d rev. ed. Trans. W. E. Wilson. London.

Donfried, K. P. 1970. A Short Note on Romans 16. *JBL* 89: 441–49. Repr. pp. 50–60 in K. P. Donfried, ed. 1977.

———. 1974. False Presuppositions in the Study of Romans. *CBQ* 36: 332–55. Repr. pp. 120–48 K. P. Donfried, ed. 1977.

Donfried, K. P., ed. 1977. *The Romans Debate.* Minneapolis.

Furnish, V. P. 1985. *The Moral Teaching of Paul.* 2d rev. ed. Nashville.

Gamble, H. Y., Jr. 1977. *The Textual History of the Letter to the Romans.* SD 42. Grand Rapids.

Jervell, J. 1971. Der Brief nach Jerusalem: Über Veranlassung und Adresse des Römerbriefes. *ST* 25: 61–73. Trans. and repr. pp. 61–74 in K. P. Donfried, ed. 1977.

Jewett, R. 1986. Following the Argument of Romans. *WW* 6: 382–89.

Käsemann, E. 1980. *Commentary on Romans.* Trans. G. W. Bromiley. Grand Rapids.

Keck, L. E. 1979. *Paul and His Letters.* Proclamation Commentaries. Philadelphia.

Kennedy, G. 1984. *New Testament Interpretation through Rhetorical Criticism.* Chapel Hill, N.C.

Luther, M. 1961. *Lectures on Romans.* Trans. and ed. W. Pauck. LCC 15. Philadelphia.

Manson, T. W. 1948. St Paul's Letter to the Romans—And Others. *BJRL* 331: 224–40. Repr. pp. 1–16 in K. P. Donfried, ed. 1977.

Metzger, B. M. 1987. *The Canon of the New Testament.* Oxford.

———. 1971. *A Textual Commentary on the Greek New Testament.* New York.

Minear, P. S. 1971. *The Obedience of Faith: The Purposes of Paul in the Epistle to the Romans.* SBT 2d ser. 19. Naperville, IL.

Munck, J. 1967. *Christ and Israel: An Interpretation of Romans 9–11.* Trans. I. Nixon. Philadelphia.

Nygren, A. 1949. *Commentary on Romans.* Trans. C. Rasmussen. Philadelphia.

Schmittals, W. 1975. *Der Römerbrief als historisches Problem.* SNT 9. Gütersloh.

Scroggs, R. 1976. Paul as Rhetorician: Two Homilies in Romans 1–11. Pp. 271–98 in *Jews, Greeks and Christians,* ed. R. Hamerton-Kelly and R. Scroggs. SJLA 21. Leiden.

Stendahl, K. 1976. *Paul Among Jews and Gentiles and Other Essays.* Philadelphia.

Stirewalt, M. L. 1977. The Form and Function of the Greek Letter-Essay. Pp. 175–206 in K. P. Donfried, ed. 1977.

Stowers, S. K. 1981. *The Diatribe and Paul's Letter to the Romans.* SBLDS 57. Chico, CA.

———. 1986. *Letter Writing in Greco-Roman Antiquity.* LEC 5. Philadelphia.

Wuellner, W. 1976. Paul's Rhetoric of Argumentation in Romans. *CBQ* 38: 330–51. Repr. pp. 152–74 in K. P. Donfried, ed. 1977.

CHARLES D. MYERS, JR.

ROME (PLACE) [Gk *Rhōmaios, Rhōmē*]. ROMANS. The Italian city-state (Lat *Roma*) which by the 2d century B.C. ruled an empire encompassing the Mediterranean basin and much of its hinterland. References to Rome occur throughout the book of 1 Maccabees and the NT, especially the book of Acts. See also ROMANS, EPISTLE TO THE.

A. Archaic Rome
B. Republican Rome
C. Late Republican Rome
D. The Empire
E. The Late Empire

A. Archaic Rome

The foundation of Rome is obscured by legend and the lack of adequate archaeological material to form substantive hypotheses. Tradition accepts the 753 B.C. founding date proposed by the 1st-century B.C. antiquarian, M. Terentius Varro, and links Rome's origin with the legend of its eponymous founder, Romulus (Bloch 1960: 11–92; Alfoldi 1965: 101–76). That Rome began as a small pastoral, agricultural settlement of Latins at a ford across central Italy's most important river, the Tiber, seems clear enough. Legends of early conflict with a neighboring village of another early Italic people, the Sabines, are also relatively well confirmed by archaeological evidence (Scott 1929: 21–69; Poucet 1967: 5–136). The synoecism of Latin and Sabine villages produced the town, *Roma quadrata,* ruled by kings. The social system there developed was strongly patriarchal and organized on the basis of families and clans, with their headmen forming an advisory council to the kings, known as the Senate. All Roman citizens, *Quirites,* comprised an assembly called the *Comitia Curiata,* as much a religious body as a civic council. The governmental and societal structure of the monarchical period is best elucidated in the works of Palmer (1970: 67–287) and de Francisci (1959: 25–624).

The transformation of Rome from rustic village to city proper must be credited to Etruscans who seized the Tiber crossing around 600 B.C. and proceeded to drain the marshy land between Rome's hills, pave extensive areas, build a city wall, and construct large brick, stone, and masonry public buildings and private edifices. Territorial expansion was effected by its Etruscan rulers and Rome developed into the leading city-state of central Italy. In addition to Rome's physical development as a city, the formulation of its legal and religious systems must in large part be attributed to Etruscans. Etruscan influence continued long past the termination of the Etruscan monarchy as many of the leading men of Rome's new republican government were nobles of Etruscan origin (Alfoldi 1965: 176–419; Scullard 1967: 243–84; Ogilvie 1976: 9–124).

B. Republican Rome

Traditionally established in the year 509 B.C., the Roman Republic, in Latin *res publica* signifying simply "government" or "public thing," was in essence an oligarchy of nobles whose rule continued with little interruption for almost five centuries. After resolving a long protracted struggle between patrician aristocrats and plebeian commoners by temporarily opening in 366 B.C. the ruling oligarchy to the wealthiest and most influential plebeians, an internally unified Rome was able to turn its attention to the rest of the peninsula (Heurgon 1973: 156–221; Raaflaub 1986: 1–377). In rapid succession, Latium, Campania, Umbria, Etruria, and finally an ever resistant Samnium fell to Rome through treaty of alliance or military conquest, and a unified Italian peninsula was prepared to face the growing power in the western Mediterranean of Phoenician Carthage (Salmon 1982: 1–90; Sherwin-White, 3–133).

Rome's conflict with Carthage spanned a century and was resolved in three bitterly contested Punic wars (I, 264–241 B.C.; II, 218–201 B.C.; III, 149–146 B.C.). The system of alliances and citizenship grades established by Rome for its Italian subjects and allies weathered the test of Carthaginian invasion and Hannibal's efforts to foment rebellion. Italian unity and extensive manpower resources overcame Carthage, and at the beginning of the 2d century B.C., Rome possessed an empire in the W Mediterranean including Spain, NW Africa, S Gaul (France), and the islands of Sicily, Sardinia, and Corsica (Scullard 1980: 146–239; Toynbee 1965: 247–82, 505–55).

For administrative purposes these territories were organized into provinces governed by senatorial proconsuls and propraetors, whose responsibilities entailed the maintenance of peace and order, the adjudication of disputes, and the supervision of tax revenue collection (Stevenson 1939: 1–93; Badian 1972: 11–118). This pattern of provincial administration prevailed as the primary mode of organizing Roman territory, including expansive regions acquired by Rome in the E Mediterranean. Some areas were organized into provinces, but others were governed in Rome's behalf by local dynasts who became client kings ultimately subject to Rome's Senate (Badian 1958: 55–115).

Questions related to Rome's involvement in E Mediterranean affairs and gradual domination of the region are complex. Imperial versus economic concerns as cause for Roman expansion continue to be debated (Hatzfeld 1919: 17–50, 192–382; Harris 1979: 54–131). Gruen's recent work (1984) offers a thorough treatment of the Roman conquest of Hellenistic monarchies, providing much useful information on political motivation and the effect exerted by philhellenism initially as a motivating factor and later as a determinant of Roman cultural and societal development. In addition to his discussion of Hellenistic influences on the Near East, Peters (1970) provides an excellent outline not only of Roman conquest and subsequent provincial organization, but also of the Roman cultural impact upon the region.

With the acquisition of the greater part of the Mediterranean and its hinterland, wealth flowed to Rome from its provinces and subject peoples. A cosmopolitan city developed that began to rival even Alexandria as an economic and mercantile center. From throughout Italy individual Romans and Italians, many exposed to the luxuries of the East through soldiering in the campaigns that had brought the area under Rome's dominion, sold farms and property to move to the capital and partake in the "good life" which slowly deteriorated the old-fashioned upright mode of life earlier Romans had practiced and honored as *mos maiorum.* By the mid-2d century B.C., Rome was a city with serious problems that would ultimately prove detrimental to its entire empire (Alfoldy 1988: 29–65). In addition to crime and lawlessness, a new landless proletariat comprised of those who had used up personal fortunes in pursuit of pleasure, constituted for Rome's ruling senatorial order the necessity of a public welfare system to provide for the ever-increasing indigent and unemployed, who without their small farms to work and untrained for other tasks, were unemployable. Indeed, for survival the mob had recourse only to its citizen rights and sold to politicians in exchange for support of social programs or other favors, their one commodity of value: votes and political support. Such goods of trade were welcome to the ruling elite who had not only enriched themselves as a result of overseas conquests and private land acquisition at home, but who had developed among one another intense political rivalries for office, power, and influence (Brunt 1971: 1–73).

C. Late Republican Rome

The nobility's battles for prestige and political preeminence were initially waged in three arenas, the Senate, the electoral and legislative assemblies, and perhaps most importantly in a reorganized court system whose complex structure lent itself more to the manipulation of political factions than to the determination of justice. Here many political careers began and ended as the false accusation was developed as a potent political weapon, while the skilled orator plied the legal trade first as attacker or defender of senatorial nobles, and finally as participant in both the senatorial order and its political combinations (Gruen 1968: 8–278).

During the last century of the Roman Republic, political factions were many and varied. Whether a particular senatorial faction supported increased rights and largesse for the commons and sought to obtain these through legislative means within the popular assembly, or instead opposed the extension of such privileges through obstructing the people's institutions and protecting closed senatorial prerogative, determined inclusion among the broad categories of people's supporters, *populares,* or supporters of the aristocracy, *optimates* (Taylor 1949: 1–70). All segments of Rome's citizen body, whether residents of the city proper or citizens living throughout Italy, took greater interest in public affairs and played a more direct and active role in the politics of the time. Heightened political awareness produced strident demands among particular parts of the population. The urban poor clamored for more government supports; Italian allies claimed citizen rights; soldiers insisted upon mustering out benefits; equestrian businessmen sought a more extensive role in determining fiscal policy, etc. Roman society of the 1st century B.C. was segmented into special interest groups whose dictates threatened to destroy the entire community and nearly did (Alfoldy 1988: 65–93; Brunt 1971: 74–156; Beard and Crawford 1985: 1–87).

Military reform abolished induced military service on the part of land-owning citizens, instituting instead a professional army in which could serve anyone for whom the pay might be sufficient. Soldiers' allegiance underwent transferral from the state to individual commanders who were careful to maintain their troops' loyalty with rewards of money and booty (Gabba 1976: 1–69). Natural results of these changes were greater military involvement in the political arena and the ultimate resort to force as a mode of political determination. Consequently, three civil wars were fought in the last century B.C. to settle political problems or disputes. The first, the so-called Social War or "war of the allies," saw the defeat of a segment of Italian allies (Lat *socii*) who seceded when repeated petition for full Roman citizen rights went unheeded, but were in defeat ultimately granted citizenship as soon as the necessity of politically incorporating the whole of Italy was realized at Rome. The other two conflicts were fought over control of the Roman political system and rule of the Roman world by rival politicians and their followings: Marius versus Sulla in the 80s B.C. and Caesar against Pompey and a few senatorial oligarchs in the 40s (Gabba 1976: 70–130; Taylor 1949: 71–255). The complex historical problems of the era are best analyzed and elucidated in Gruen's thorough treatment of 1st century B.C. politics (1974: 1–596).

The city itself witnessed tremendous growth during the period, both in terms of population increase and in physical structure. Politically motivated government construction projects resulted in a record number of new public buildings and temples. Dudley (1967) and Coarelli (1974) provide the most complete physical description of the city for this period of the late Republic as well as for that of the early empire which accounted for even greater expansion and construction.

D. The Empire

Caesar's military triumphs not only added much of W Europe to Rome's empire and brought to an end the political conflicts and wars of rivalry between *optimates* and *populares,* but more importantly produced a political stability which coincided with Caesar's governance of Rome as *dictator perpetuus*—king in all but name. His reign was a benevolent sort of monarchy that oversaw much needed reform in many spheres, but assassins' knives cut it short and hurled the state once more into political chaos (Gelzer 1968: 102–335).

Leaders of the conspirators, Caesarian political lieutenants, and Caesar's posthumously adopted son and heir, Octavian Caesar, either struggled to succeed to Caesar's power or to protect themselves from those who attempted to do so. After several civil wars the protracted military and political struggle came to an end with the defeat of Antony and Cleopatra by Octavian who remained sole claimant to his father's authority. Hailed as deliverer and restorer of peace and order by a Senate now filled with his own supporters, Octavian established a new government with monarchical powers cloaked in traditional constitutional trappings. In return for sharing power with a grateful Senate happy to oversee peaceful non-military provinces while the *princeps* or emperor retained control of frontier provinces with their troop concentrations, Octavian was rewarded with the title Imperator Augustus Caesar, and received lifetime powers of governance as well as semidivine honors. The empire was thus established and by literary, religious, and artistic propaganda was quickly legitimized and made attractive to Rome's citizens. The much heralded *pax Augusta* did, in fact, provide for an empire at peace for the first time in over a century. Political stability gave rise to economic prosperity, while efficient government in Italy and the provinces won for Augustus the approval of his subjects. Population increased, new cities were established and old cities expanded. In no place was there such a change as in Rome itself where the emperor's building projects transformed the urban area into a beautiful city of marble buildings, monuments, and temples. On a less-extravagant scale the same process occurred not only throughout Italy but also in the provinces where leading citizens were granted Roman citizen rights and romanization was begun in earnest (Syme 1939: 1–568; Jones 1970: 1–189; Taylor 1939: 100–246; Firth 1902: 1–366; Millar and Segal 1984: 1–219).

Through a complicated process of intermarriage among his descendants and his step-descendants, Augustus provided for a succession designed to remain within the family of the Julians and the Claudians. His immediate four successors—the Julio-Claudian emperors Tiberius, Caligula, Claudius, and Nero—were, except perhaps for Claudius, poor administrators more concerned with personal indulgence than the improvement of Rome or its empire. However, save for political unrest in the capital, and that largely between several of these emperors and more independent segments of the senatorial class, the empire continued in an expansion cycle characterized by peace and prosperity, so well had Augustus set the proper course. As a result of Nero's excesses and tyrannies revolution came at last. From this civil war emerged a new dynasty, the Flavians, who would rule almost until the beginning of the 2d century A.D. They in turn were succeeded by five emperors elected by the Senate upon their predecessor's recommendation of high moral character and competence to govern. Because such criteria were applied to the designation of new emperors during most of the 2d century, the empire prospered (Garzetti 1974: 3–861; Salmon 1944: 1–366; M. Rostovtzeff 1926: 38–124).

In the opening lines of his *Decline and Fall of the Roman Empire,* the renowned Gibbon praises the Roman Empire during the era of the 2d century as at the height of its civilization.

> . . . the Empire of Rome comprehended the fairest part of the earth, and the most civilized portion of mankind. The frontiers of that extensive monarchy were guarded by ancient renown and disciplined valour. The gentle, but powerful, influence of laws and manners had gradually cemented the union of the provinces. Their peaceful inhabitants enjoyed and abused the advantages of wealth and luxury. The image of a free constitution was preserved with decent reverence. The Roman senate appeared to possess the sovereign authority, and devolved on the emperors all the executive powers of government. During a happy period of more than four score years, the public administration was conducted by the virtue and abilities of Nerva, Trajan, Hadrian, and the two Antonines.

Gibbon's eloquent prose is only slightly exaggerative. Rather, it is a fairly accurate description of a period of growth during which Britain, Dacia, and the Mesopotamian region were acquired and organized into provinces. The extent of Roman territory would never be greater. The frontier was protected by efficient legions, assisted by local auxiliary troops which functioned to garrison the now fortified borders *(limites)* of the Empire (Luttwak 1976: 7–126). Population growth, thriving industry, and widespread trade insured economic expansion which stimulated urbanization. Not only Italy, but most provinces of the empire were occupied by residents who lived in towns and cities and practiced an urban lifestyle (Rostovtzeff 1926: 125–343; Garnsey and Saller 1987: 43–162; Alfoldy 1988: 94–157). Governmental forms changed little, the emperor continued to rule with supreme authority, though, as previously noted, the 2d century witnessed the rule of emperors who observed constitutional forms and were assisted in their governance by the upper classes of society, the Senate and the equestrian order, members of which occupied high office and filled the roles of provincial governors. Administrative organization was still not too complex. Except for a few equestrian civil servants, most bureaucratic functions were performed by freedmen or slaves of the emperors for whom private and public affairs were frequently mixed (Millar 1977: 59–363; Talbert 1984: 163–493).

Yet despite the material prosperity of the period, individual dissatisfaction with stale Greco-Roman religious forms and increasingly pedantic philosophic discourse questioned traditional ethical and metaphysical systems, embracing instead new salvation-oriented religions arising in eastern sections of the empire or beyond. Mithraism and Christianity were the most popular of the cults that offered a personal religion, and their spread and acceptance, sometimes peacefully but frequently not, occasioned societal changes whose full effect upon the empire would not be realized for a century and a half. It was the chaos of the 3d century A.D. soon to follow, which witnessed the incredible increase of these religions and allowed for the sweeping changes of the 4th century (Ferguson 1970: 88–274; Mattingly 1954: 5–95).

E. The Late Empire

Military and governmental stability was provided Rome by early rulers of the Severan dynasty, but economic woes as well as political, religious, and social dissonance produced strains in the fabric of the empire. Weaknesses and oddities of the last Severan emperors contributed to societal deterioration which by the third decade of this turbulent 3d century A.D. had so declined that the empire was nearly destroyed in a few short years (MacMullen 1966: 163–268; Alfoldy 1988: 157–85). During the fifty years from the death of Severus Alexander in 235 until the accession of Diocletian in 284, twenty men ruled as emperor at Rome, while others ruled elsewhere either as pretenders to the imperial throne or as local dynasts over parts of the empire which had segmented into several separate realms. Civil wars more continuous and intense than those that had gone before devastated population, wealth, and resources. In the East a resurgent Parthia deprived Rome of territories and along the European *limites* the long restrained press of semicivilized humanity poured across borders denuded of legions utilized elsewhere in battle with forces of rival claimants to Rome's once considerable power. To Aurelian and a handful of his successors, all soldier emperors from Illyria, goes credit for reacquiring most of Roman territory (Rostovtzeff 1926: 344–449; Brauer 1975: 3–267; MacMullen 1976: 48–214).

Under the last of these, Diocletian, stability was reestablished and there emerged a new transformed society, more the precursor of the Middle Ages than emulator of classical antiquity. Military reform ended reliance on standing frontier garrisons as the primary defense structure of a realm whose population was too small to support any but the new mobile field armies that accompanied Diocletian and his colleague emperors, each administering a quarter of the empire. The term tetrarchy aptly describes the reformed government that managed a hierarchical system of smaller administrative units, the dioceses and provinces. The balanced and efficient organization of Diocletian gave new life to the empire but functioned less effectively under successors whose rivalries were responsible for initiating Christian persecutions as an aspect of the politics of oppressing or currying favor of a group that had grown to comprise so large a portion of the population. After a decade of civil war a proponent of Christian rights and recipient of Christian support, Constantine, gained supreme power and provided Rome, once more, with but a single ruler (Williams 1985: 24–230; MacMullen 1987: 1–184; Lot 1961: 5–54; Luttwak 1976: 127–94; Jones 1964: 21–76). Many of Diocletian's military and administrative reforms were continued by Constantine in his centralization of authority under a court which accompanied the emperor, wherever he might journey. The reformed mobile army had reestablished the prowess of Roman arms and continued to assist the frontier militia in maintaining the integrity of Roman borders. Administration and society in the era of the late empire is most fully and effectively described in Jones' masterwork *The Later Roman Empire* (1964: 77–1024). Economic problems of inflation and unemployment resulted in price controls and job restrictions which produced hereditary occupation castes and discouraged change of residence. More persons became engaged in farming and individuals became tied to particular parcels of land. Urban society declined and country life flourished in the agricultural economy. Local aristocrats commanded country militias and provided immediate protection to residents against frontier incursions until such time that the emperor's armies could arrive. The seeds of medieval feudalism were thus sown (Lot 1961: 55–127; Claster 1982: 9–57). A repercussion of the struggles between pagan and Christian that characterized the era of Constantine's heirs was the decline of educational institutions and with them the extirpation of classical culture (Smith 1976: 21–144; Lot 1961: 128–87; Dodds 1965: 1–138; Laistner 1951: 1–74). It is perhaps fitting that Constantine had established a new capital for this increasingly Christian empire. The name of Rome's empire remained, but Rome no longer ruled. Rome came to be but another city in the empire of Constantine and his successors, the Senate but a town council. Any authority Rome would possess in the new era ironically derived from the very Christianity which was perhaps ultimately responsible for damaging the preeminent position Rome had occupied in the Mediterranean world for six centuries before Constantine. Moreover, for the first time in over a thousand years Rome had ceased to govern itself, and rather was governed first from Constantinople, later from Mediolanum (Milan) or other seats of the divided empire in the West (MacMullen 1987: 139–240; Lot 1961: 187–309; Smith 1976: 120–250). See also ROMAN EMPIRE.

Bibliography

Alfoldi, A. 1965. *Early Rome and the Latins.* Ann Arbor, MI.

Alfoldy, G. 1988. *The Social History of Rome.* Baltimore.

Badian, E. 1958. *Foreign Clientelae, 264–70 B.C.* Oxford.

———. 1972. *Publicans and Sinners.* Ithaca, NY.

Beard, M., and Crawford, M. 1985. *Rome in the Late Republic.* Ithaca, NY.

Bloch, R. 1960. *The Origins of Rome.* New York.

Brauer, G. C. 1975. *The Age of the Soldier Emperors.* Park Ridge, NJ.

Brunt, P. A. 1971. *Social Conflicts in the Roman Republic.* London.

Claster, J. 1982. *The Medieval Experience 300–1400.* New York.

Coarelli, F. 1974. *Guida Archeologica di Roma.* Rome.

Dodds, E. R. 1965. *Pagan and Christian in an Age of Anxiety.* New York.

Dudley, D. R. 1967. *Urbs Roma.* London.

Ferguson, J. 1970. *The Religions of the Roman Empire.* Ithaca, NY.

Firth, J. B. 1902. *Augustus Caesar and the Organisation of the Empire of Rome.* Freeport, NY.

Francisci, P., de. 1959. *Primordia Civitatis.* Rome.

Gabba, E. 1976. *Republican Rome.* Berkeley.

Garnsey, P., and Saller, R. 1987. *The Roman Empire: Economy, Society and Culture.* Berkeley.

Garzetti, A. 1974. *From Tiberius to the Antonines: A History of the Roman Empire.* Trans. J. Foster. London.

Gelzer, M. 1968. *Caesar Politician and Statesman.* Trans. P. Needham. Cambridge, MA.

Gruen, E. S. 1968. *Roman Politics and the Criminal Courts 149–70 B.C.* Cambridge, MA.

———. 1974. *The Last Generation of the Roman Republic.* Berkeley.

———. 1984. *The Hellenistic World and the Coming of Rome.* Berkeley.

Harris, W. V. 1979. *War and Imperialism in Republican Rome.* Oxford.

Hatzfeld, J. 1919. *Les trafiquants italiens dans l'orient hellenique.* Paris.

Heurgon, J. 1973. *The Rise of Rome.* Trans. J. Willis. Berkeley.

Jones, A. H. M. 1964. *The Later Roman Empire 284–602.* Norman, OK.

———. 1970. *Augustus.* New York.

Laistner, M. L. W. 1951. *Christianity and Pagan Culture in the Later Roman Empire.* Ithaca, NY.

Lot, F. 1961. *The End of the Ancient World and the Beginnings of the Middle Ages.* New York.

Luttwak, E. 1976. *The Grand Strategy of the Roman Empire.* Baltimore.

MacMullen, R. 1966. *Enemies of the Roman Order.* Cambridge, MA.

———. 1976. *Roman Government's Response to Crisis A.D. 235–337.* New Haven.

———. 1987. *Constantine.* London.

Mattingly, H. 1954. *Christianity in the Roman Empire.* New York.

Millar, F. 1977. *The Emperor in the Roman World.* Ithaca, NY.

Millar, F., and Segal, E. 1984. *Augustus Caesar: Seven Aspects.* Oxford.

Ogilvie, R. M. 1976. *Early Rome and the Etruscans.* Glasgow.

Palmer, R. E. A. 1970. *The Archaic Community of the Ancient Romans.* Cambridge.

Peters, F. E. 1970. *The Harvest of Hellenism.* New York.
Poucet, J. 1967. *Recherches sur la legende sabine des origines de Rome.* Louvain.
Raabflaub, K. 1986. *Social Struggles in Archaic Rome.* Berkeley.
Rostovtzeff, M. 1926. *The Social and Economic History of the Roman Empire.* Oxford.
Salmon, E. T. 1944. *A History of the Roman World 30 B.C. to A.D. 138.* London.
———. 1982. *The Making of Roman Italy.* Ithaca, NY.
Scott, I. G. 1929. *Early Roman Tradition in Light of Archaeology.* Rome.
Scullard, H. H. 1967. *The Etruscan Cities and Rome.* Ithaca, NY.
———. 1980. *A History of the Roman World 753–146 B.C.* 4th ed. London.
Sherwin-White, A. N. 1973. *The Roman Citizenship.* 2d ed. Oxford.
Smith, J. H. 1976. *The Death of Classical Paganism.* New York.
Stevenson, G. H. 1939. *Roman Provincial Administration.* New York.
Syme, R. 1939. *The Roman Revolution.* Oxford.
Talbert, R. 1984. *The Senate of Imperial Rome.* Princeton.
Taylor, L. R. 1939. *The Divinity of the Roman Emperor.* Middletown, CT.
———. 1949. *Party Politics in the Age of Caesar.* Berkeley.
Toynbee, A. 1965. *Hannibal's Legacy.* Vol. 2. London.
Williams, S. 1985. *Diocletian and the Roman Recovery.* New York.

JOHN F. HALL

ROME, CHRISTIAN MONUMENTS AT. In Romans 16:4, the apostle Paul refers to a housechurch in Rome, the first of many Christian remains in Rome. One may assume the presence of several other such housechurch congregations (v 15). According to Roman tradition there were twenty-five of these private dwellings *(tituli)* which eventually became the basilicas of Rome. Archaeological studies show there are no extant churches of Rome which unquestionably evolved from a private dwelling of the 1st century, though many of the title churches have incorporated in their structures pre-Constantinian edifices such as a bath (Sta. Pudentiana) or even a Mithraeum (S. Clemente). SS. Giovanni e Paolo may constitute an exception. The foundation of that building incorporates a 1st-century shop complex. One particular room was used by an early Christian community prior to the 4th century. The second and third stories of the shop complex became a meeting hall early in the 4th century. Though not developed from an apparent domicile, SS. Giovanni e Paolo did maintain a continuity of worship from a single room to the present-day basilica.

The earliest extant constructed church in Rome was S. Crisogono in the Trastevere. At approximately A.D. 300, the Christians of that area built a hall 33.8 m long and 19.8 m wide. That first hall lacked furniture, *confessio,* and divisions for laity and clergy. About the end of the 4th century, an apse was constructed, a *confessio* added in front of the apse, and an incipient choir screen inserted, which served as a divider. Within the city proper the first constructed church was S. Giovanni in Laterano. This five-aisled building was started about 313 by Constantine.

Parallel developments occurred with burial edifices. Outside the walls of the city, the Christians of Rome developed an extensive network of catacombs for burial purposes. Often a catacomb developed around a nucleus of special dead. The first monument to appear in such a nucleus was the *martyrium* (e.g., the martyrium for SS. Cassius and Florentius in Bonn). Such a development can be seen at the catacombs associated with Sta. Agnese and S. Lorenzo. Parallel developments occurred at S. Sebastiano and St. Peter's, but the presence of a *martyrium* cannot be ascertained. At these extramural sites, Christians ate meals *(refrigeria)* celebrating the death of the martyr, the special dead and their own family dead. In about the year 240 in the catacomb at S. Sebastiano, they constructed over the original nucleus a larger structure *(triclia)* for eating with the dead. Eventually several such nuclei were honored by large covered cemeteries *(coemeteria subteglata).* Built by Constantine after 313, these edifices were quite long (as much as 100 m), circular at one end with a clerestory supported by an interior columnar structure. All had attached mausolea. Six such structures are discernible: Sta. Agnese, S. Lorenzo, S. Sebastiano, SS. Pietro e Marcellino, St. Peter's, and Tor de'Schiavi. A circular imperial mausoleum attached to Sta. Agnese has survived as Sta. Constanza. SS. Pietro e Marcellino and Tor de'Schiavi, both likely imperial burial sites, exist only as ruins. Sta. Agnese and S. Lorenzo have suffered the same fate, but surviving churches in honor of the saints were built adjacent to the *coemeteria subteglata.* S. Sebastiano still remains while St. Peter's has been greatly altered on its original site.

The site on Via Appia known to us as S. Sebastiano was frequented by early and medieval Christians because it related to the apostles Peter and Paul. Historically there is no known association with the two. The site, a sand pit called the *katakumbas,* first was used by non-Christians until about 200. Only then did Christian symbols appear in the earliest mausolea. By the mid-3d century the *triclia* appeared above the pit and its now Christian mausolea. According to the many graffiti inscribed on the walls of the *triclia,* frequent prayers of petition for family members were made to the apostles Paul and Peter. At some time before the building of St. Peter's, there existed on the Via Appia a site that functioned as the *martyrium* of Peter and Paul. Constantine perpetuated the function of the site by building on it a great *coemeterium subteglatum.* Later the cult of St. Sebastian was transferred to the complex. During the Middle Ages, pilgrims continued to visit it as the location associated with the two apostles. At the same time two separate locations developed in honor of the two apostles. For Paul, it was a great church on Via Ostiense, S. Paulo fuori la Mura, which originated with Constantine. For Peter, it was the Vatican site.

Constantine built St. Peter's over a non-Christian cemetery near the circus of Nero. There is practically no evidence of cultic practices at this site. One family (in mausoleum M) became Christian. The unique green and gold mosaic of Christ Helios decorates their mausoleum. Despite the apparent lack of veneration for Peter, the Vatican has a long association with that apostle. In the poor section of the Vatican necropolis (Campo P), some Christians built a retaining wall (the Red Wall) in about 160. At the time of construction, the wall included a niche which marks a remembrance of Peter. An aedicula was built into the niche by 200 (Eusebius, EH, II, 25:6, 7). In about the year 250, supporting walls were built into the aedicula. In the N wall (wall g), the excavators found a marble box, and on the north side of the same wall they uncovered a number of

Christian graffiti. Nothing about the burials in Campo P or the graffiti on wall g indicate the presence of a martyrium, and there is practically no reference to Peter. Later investigators found a set of bones elsewhere in St. Peter's. The Vatican displays these bones as those of Peter which, it is claimed, were originally found in the marble box of wall g. Constantine encased the aedicula, covered the necropolis and built the five-aisled St. Peter's over the entire complex. The transept allowed worshipers greater access to the aedicula. The present St. Peter's continues that focus on the original aedicula.

Near the end of the 4th century, remains of the special dead were moved into the city and placed in a *confessio* underneath the altar. In this way the practices of the cemetery cult were combined with the traditions of the housechurches and meeting halls. The churches that resulted from this merger were constructed like the *coemeteria subteglata* (e.g., Sta. Sabina) or like St. Peter's and S. Giovanni in Laterano.

The Christians at Rome developed from the original burial nuclei massive networks of catacombs. There are approximately sixty miles of catacombs with about 500,000 burials. They dug the catacombs in a volcanic rock called tufa. The burials consisted of narrow shelves dug out of catacomb tunnels or galleries. Each was covered with a series of plates, often marble. Usually the plates were inscribed with at least minimal epitaphic data and often early Christian symbols such as an anchor, a tree, a dove, a fish, a lamb, a Good Shepherd, an *orante* (praying figure), a branch, a ship, or a cup. Intermittently Christian families cut out a larger burial space called a *cubiculum.* These were decorated with frescoes, especially the space directly over the grave, that is, the *arcosolium.* In Roman Christian art, OT scenes, such as the Jonah cycle, Noah in the Ark, Daniel among the Lions, Susanna and the Elders, and the Three Young Men in the Fiery Furnace, depict deliverance from extenuating circumstances. NT scenes, such as the resurrection of Lazarus and various healing stories, show Jesus as a young wonder worker. This portrayal of Jesus lasted through the Constantinian period until replaced in the 5th century by an older, bearded, majestic type. Several areas of the catacombs are of special value. The Capella Greca in Sta. Priscilla contains the oldest known Christian fresco art (ca. 200). The Crypt of the Popes in S. Callixtus houses the final resting place of six bishops of Rome from the 2d and 3d centuries. More important there are the six early *cubicula* called the Sacrament Chapels. In them are early fresco paintings, especially several related to the agape meal *(refrigerium)* celebrated with the dead. In the same catacomb of S. Callixtus, the double chamber of Lucina contains significant early Christian art. A section of Sta. Domitilla purports to originate as a burial plot of the Flavian family. The hypogeum and gallery contain early examples of fresco art.

The symbolic art of the catacombs shifted to illustrative art after Constantine. Maria Maggiore contains not only an apsidial mosaic honoring Mary, the mother of God, but also extensive mosaics illustrating the OT. Sarcophagi of Rome parallel the catacombs. The sarcophagus of Sta. Maria Antiqua, in the Capitoline, offers Christian pictorial representations as early as the Capella Greca. Not all the catacombs represent mainline Christianity. The newly discovered catacombs on via Latina and the Hypogeum of Aurelii, show, by their selection of artistic subjects, a faith at variance with the rest of Christian Rome. Jewish catacombs have been discovered particularly under the Villa Torlonia (via Nomentana).

The official center of Roman Christianity, S. Giovanni in Laterno, was built by Constantine in the 4th century, ironically and quite significantly, over the barracks of Equites Singulares. Adjacent to this great five-aisled edifice Constantine built an octagonal building used by the bishop of Rome as a baptistry. See also ART AND ARCHITECTURE (EARLY CHRISTIAN).

Bibliography

Apolloj-Ghetti, B. M.; Ferrua, A.; Josi, E.; and Kirschbaum, E. 1951. *Esplorazioni sotto la confessione di San Pietro in Vaticano.* Vatican City.

Brandenburg, H. 1979. *Roms frühchristliche Basiliken.* Munich.

Krautheimer, R. 1975. *Early Christian and Byzantine Architecture.* Baltimore.

Krautheimer, R.; Frankl, W.; Corbett, S.; and Frazer, A. 1937–77. *Corpus basilicarum Cristianorum Romae.* Vatican City.

Mancinelli, F. 1981. *Catacombs and Basilicas.* New York.

Nestori, A. 1975. *Repertorio topografico delle pitture delle catacombe Romane.* Rome.

Snyder, G. F. 1985. *Ante Pacem.* Macon, GA.

Stevenson, J. 1978. *The Catacombs.* London.

Testini, P. 1966. *Le catacombe e gli antichi cimiteri cristiani in Roma.* Bologna.

Vielliard, R. 1959. *Recherches sur les origines de la Rome chrétienne.* Rome.

GRAYDON F. SNYDER

ROME, EARLY CHRISTIAN ATTITUDES TO.

Direct references to Rome are rare in the NT. The authority structures directly encountered by most provincials would be local rather than Roman, although bolstered and supported by Rome in differing degrees. Many commentators assume without question that these would have been seen by provincials simply as extensions of Roman power, but perceptions could vary: while some in the provinces saw Rome as the oppressing power, others identified the empire, and more particularly the emperor, as a protector against more present local exploitation (Millar 1977: 466–67). These complexities must be borne in mind if a serious understanding of Christian attitudes is to be reached.

Methodologically, our problem is that we have no direct access to the "attitudes" of the early Christians, only to their texts. The prime unit of investigation must therefore be the text itself, even though its precise date and historical setting may not be known, and it may be a composite incorporating traditions from many periods. It is the surface narrative itself, not its prehistory, which both forms and reflects the attitudes of the church (Aland 1979: 164–65).

A. Jewish Attitudes
B. The Gospels
C. Acts
D. The Pauline Epistles

A. Jewish Attitudes

The Jewish people had a long experience of life under foreign empires, and the OT already contains a range of texts reflecting a variety of attitudes to the phenomenon. Daniel, Esther, and Nehemiah all provide examples of Diaspora characters who choose to collaborate with the regime in which they find themselves, rising in one way or another to positions of eminence (cf. Tert. *De Idol.* 17). Their stories also show the limits of collaboration: Nehemiah and Esther exploit their closeness to the throne to win concessions for their people, while Daniel and his companions face martyrdom rather than compromise their private religious principles. The book of Daniel also contains the classic expression of theoretical reservations about the world empires in the apocalyptic visions of chaps. 7–12. Only the kingdom of God is eternal (4:3). The empires of the world will meet their fate at the hands of "one like a son of man" (7:13), or of a "stone cut without hands" (2:44–45).

Martyrdom may be described as "passive resistance" (Schaefke 1979: 461–62), apocalyptic perhaps as "theoretical resistance"; but there is no trace in these Diaspora texts of any active resistance to the domination of the world empires. For that we have to turn to the land of Israel and to the literature of the Maccabean period, which produced not only martyrs (2, *4 Macc.*) but also freedom fighters willing and able to take up arms in the cause of independence (1, 2 Macc). The distinction here between the Diaspora and the Land is fundamental: clearly the presence of foreign authority within the Land, coupled with the loss of political independence, raises different ideological problems from those of the individual or community living outside it. It is not surprising, then, that we continue to find a wide spectrum of attitudes in the Roman period: the fanatical opposition of the "Zealots" to the Roman occupation of Palestine, whose rise Josephus charts throughout the 1st century A.D., stands in contrast with the prevailing attitude of Diaspora Judaism, which saw Rome positively as a protective power (*m. Abot* 3:2, cf. Smallwood 1976: 134–43, 235–50, 356–57) or simply advocated a policy of quietism (*m. Abot* 1:10, 2:3; cf. Loewe 1940: 4–37). Even within Palestine there was room for a wide variety of ideological stances in the pre-70 period (Goodman 1987: ch. 4; Stemberger 1979).

B. The Gospels

The pivotal event of the Gospel story (and the one best attested by non-Christian sources) is Jesus' crucifixion by a Roman governor. This immediately raises two different kinds of questions about Christian attitudes: (a) what were its causes? Does Jesus' message inevitably involve conflict with Rome? and (b) what were its results? Did the church perceive Rome as a natural enemy after this cataclysmic event?

The second is easier to answer. All the Gospel narratives, while agreeing that Pontius Pilate was responsible for the order to crucify Jesus, concur in laying the real blame at the feet of the Jewish authorities (Matt 27:1–2, 20; Mark 15:1–11; Luke 23:1–5, 13–25; John 18:38–40; 19:12–16). Thus the Roman governor, in this prototypical martyr-story (cf. 1 Tim 6:13) figures not as the persecutor but as a weak, vacillating (Matt 27:15–24), and basically unwilling tyrant, and the victim's own compatriots are portrayed as the real culprits (Matt 27:25). We must conclude, then, that at the time the Gospels were put into writing, the churches did not wish to pin the blame for Jesus' death on Rome. Despite the manner of Jesus' death, the reader of the Gospels would not assume that Rome was the natural enemy of the Christian movement.

The first question is more challenging. Does the reader of the Gospels gain the impression that following Jesus would inevitably involve conflict with Rome? The problem is that the Gospel message itself allows divergent conclusions to be drawn. Jesus' preaching of the "kingdom of God" (Mark 1:15) echoes the language of Daniel and therefore carries an implicit challenge to all human authority systems, including that of Rome. Moreover the identification of the kingdom with the relief of poverty and hunger (Luke 6:20–21) suggests to modern ears a critique of the Roman tax system which was placing an intolerable burden, at least in Judea, on an already overstrained peasant economy (Rajak 1983: 119–26; Goodman 1987: 60)—although the connection between poverty and Rome is never made explicitly in the text. So the reader is not surprised when both Jesus' supporters (John 6:15; Acts 1:6) and his enemies (Luke 23:2; John 19:12) interpret his mission as a challenge to Rome. Even after the resurrection the disciples' hope of "restoring the kingdom to Israel" is not negated, only postponed (Acts 1:7). Jesus himself, however, is throughout reluctant to accept the title "king" (Mark 15:2), and stresses the radical difference between God's kingdom and the kingdoms of the world (Mark 10:35–45; John 18:36).

Attitudes to more explicitly Roman manifestations are equally ambivalent. Possibly the most striking Gospel comment on the Roman occupation comes in the "Legion" story of Mark 5:1–20. Theissen (1983: 255) argues that Jesus' victory over the demons may be seen as a symbolic victory over the forces of occupation whose name they carry, with the denouement of the story triumphantly symbolizing the expulsion of the "legion" from the country. But elsewhere in the Gospels the tokens of occupation are treated as a much less urgent problem than the spiritual revival of Israel. The centurion of Matt 8:5–13 is simply a foil to Jesus' unbelieving compatriots. Pilate's Galilean massacre (Luke 13:1–3) is treated as a natural disaster calling for theological, not political comment (cf. 13:4–5). In Matt 5:43–48, Jesus goes further: the command to "love one's enemies" must presumably include the Romans, and the instruction to "go the second mile" (5:41) clearly envisages that the demands of an occupying force must not only be met, but be voluntarily bettered. And there is a similar ambiguity about the question of Roman taxes (Mark 12:13–17). Jesus' reply is presented as purposely enigmatic, a wily answer to a question designed to trap. Justin (*I Apol.* 17) quotes it in order to defend the church against a charge of disloyalty, and many commentators see it as an acknowledgment of the authority of the state "and therefore of the obligation to pay taxes" (Taylor *ad loc.*). But there were clearly those who believed that

Jesus forbade the payment of Roman taxes (Luke 23:2), and it is possible to read the passage both as a rejection of the Roman occupation (Belo 1981: 224) and as an ironic pointer to the fact that those who choose to stay "in the world" and participate in its economic system will find it impossible to fulfill their duties both to God and to the system (Wengst 1987: 58–61). What does seem clear is that the problem is not Jesus', but his questioners': by leaving their homes and employment, Jesus and his followers have effectively placed themselves outside the writ of any taxation system (Matt 17:25–26). In many ways it is this radical ideology of withdrawal from the world that is most characteristic of subsequent Christian attitudes.

C. Acts

The narrative of Acts, like that of the Gospels, has a paradoxical stance towards Rome. The book ends with its hero being transported to Rome under a centurion's guard to be tried before Caesar (Acts 27:1), but Paul is portrayed throughout as politically innocent. Attempts to denounce his preaching as contrary to Roman law fail at the tribunal (18:13–15); his final incarceration in Caesarea is for his own protection (23:10, 23–30), and even if its prolongation owes something to the venality of Festus (24:26), Paul's final appeal to Caesar is his own choice, based both on the wish to avoid a trial in Jerusalem and on a belief in a divine vocation (23:11). Caesar here functions not as persecutor but as protector against a more immediate threat; for the author of Acts the problems of the church are caused not by Rome but by "the Jews" (17:5, 13; 18:12; 21:27) or by local troublemakers (16:19; 19:23).

This positive picture of Paul's relationship with Rome should not be dismissed too lightly; it corresponds well with other evidence on the experience of empire in the provinces (Price; Millar; Sherwin-White) and, *mutatis mutandis,* with the Jewish experience of Rome as protector against local hostility (Smallwood). In literary terms the position of Luke's Paul may be compared with that of Daniel in Dan 6:10–15 (cf. 3:8): local denunciation of a religious minority before an impartial higher authority is a common pattern whose persistence into the second century is attested both by Pliny (*Ep.* 10: 96–97) and Melito (*ap.* Eus. *Hist Eccl* 4/26:5–11). But there is also a certain detachment in Paul's attitude to Rome which could be described as a cynical readiness to manipulate the resources of the empire for the furtherance of private religious aims. Paul travels the empire as an "outsider," content to be embroiled in the anonymous world of the streets until it suits him to call on the authorities for protection: his Roman citizenship carries no sense of responsibility, but functions as a "joker" which he exploits only when it suits him to do so (16:37; 22:25). Similarly the "appeal to Caesar" is employed as a stratagem for the spread of the Gospel, and the insistence on the political innocence of Christianity falls well short of active support for the institutions of the empire.

D. The Pauline Epistles

The predominant impression in the Pauline epistles is of a profound lack of interest in either local or imperial politics. The empire and its institutions are hardly mentioned except as metaphors for the religious life (2 Cor 2:14; 2 Tim 2:3–4), and the statement that "our citizenship is in heaven" (Phil 3:20) implies a total disengagement from the authority structures of the Christian's place of residence (Aland 1979: 186–95). This may in part have arisen naturally out of the actual political status of the early Christians; traveling artisans or merchants like Lydia (Acts 16:14) and Priscilla and Aquila (Acts 18:1–3) were often de facto disfranchised, with little political stake in their place of residence. But it must also be linked with a powerful *impulse towards withdrawal* from pagan society, including its law courts (1 Cor 6:1–6) and its social occasions (as evidenced by the problem of "food offered to idols" discussed in 1 Corinthians 8 and Romans 14). The Pauline letter corpus is full of "the language of separation" (Meeks 1983: 94), and Paul's warning against total withdrawal from "the world" (1 Cor 5:10) indicates that such a withdrawal was not inconceivable.

Positive opposition to Rome is harder to document from the Pauline letters. Paul acknowledges that he has been "beaten with rods" as well as receiving "forty stripes save one" (2 Cor 11:24–25): in other words, he has been punished by Roman authorities as well as by synagogue officials. Rome thus stands alongside "the Jews" and Aretas as hindrances to the Gospel, but is not singled out in the list as of any particular significance. In Philemon and Philippians Paul appears as "a prisoner for the Lord's sake" (Phlm 1, 9; Phil 1:7, 13–18), probably but not certainly in Rome; wherever its location, this imprisonment could hardly have taken place without Roman involvement in some way. But what exactly Paul had done to merit either beating or imprisonment is never explained: Paul regards himself as potentially under the death sentence (Phil 2:17), and his imprisonment is "for Christ" (1:13), but it is not clear in what sense, if at all, the two are connected. What is striking again is the lack of overt interest in the exercise of Roman authority as such: the threatened execution is regarded as a way of honoring Christ (1:20), and the imprisonment merely as an opportunity for "the defense of the Gospel" (1:16).

It is in the apocalyptic and eschatological sections of the letters that we come closest to a comprehensive estimate of the role of Rome in God's cosmic plan. The "fashion of this world" is passing away (1 Cor 7:31), and with it the "rulers of this age" who "crucified the Lord of glory" (1 Cor. 2:6–8). Christ's final return in early Christian apocalyptic literature heralds the "subjection" of "all things" to him (Phil 3:21), including the "principalities and powers"; whatever the intended reference of this phrase, it must include in some way the "powers" of the Roman empire. In Paul himself this view is most clearly expressed in 1 Thessalonians. Persecution is a normal experience for the Christian communities (3:3; cf. 2:2, 14–15), and their response is to wait in quietness for the imminent revelation of God's wrath (1:10; 2:16) at the "Day of the Lord" (5:2). The attitude of the persecuted church may thus be described as passive resistance, involving a readiness to accept martyrdom, combined with theoretical opposition to the persecuting powers which are under the wrath of God. There seems to be no distinction between Roman and local persecutors here, and no explicit attack on the institution of empire as such; however, some commentators have seen an ironic rejection of the "Pax" slogans of the empire in 5:3 (Wengst 1987: 77).

There may be a more specific allusion to Rome in 2 Thess 2:3–12. This vividly apocalyptic passage, like the Synoptic apocalypses, concentrates on warning rather than denunciation: the church is not to be "quickly shaken in mind" (2:2), and the "mystery of lawlessness" is at present being restrained (2:6–7). If the "restrainer" is the empire itself (as argued by many interpreters since Tert. *De Resurr. Carn.* 24), it is clear that active resistance to the empire, even if it were a practical possibility, would not be in the interests of the Gospel (Bruce *Thessalonians* WBC, 159–78, 187–88; Trilling *2 Thessalonians* EKKNT, 94–105). On this reading, 2 Thessalonians is consistent with Paul's most explicit statement on the Christian's attitude to authority in Romans 13:1–7. Here the Christian is firmly enjoined to "be subject to the governing authorities" (13:1) which are "instituted by God" (13:4, 6). In a context where "the day is at hand" (13:12), these instructions must be taken as part of the Christian's duty to behave "becomingly" (13:13): good civic conduct, including the payment of taxes (13:3, 6), is simply a part of this wider duty (13:8–10). Conversely, Paul has no conception of a state which may actually *enjoin* "bad conduct" on its citizens (13:3). Paul does not envisage the later Roman practice of requiring Christians to perform a pagan sacrifice as a test of loyalty (Pliny *Ep.* 10: 96), nor does he anticipate the dilemmas faced by later Christians over military service. Like many of his Jewish contemporaries, Paul may have experienced persecution (12:14) only as a local phenomenon, and so might well see the wider and more impartial authority of the empire as a protection rather than a threat. On the history of interpretation of this passage, see Wilckens *Romans 12–16* EKKNT, 43–66.

E. Other NT Epistles

We find a similar combination of themes in the non-Pauline epistles. The impulse to withdrawal from pagan society and its institutions is expressed strongly in the "sojourner" imagery of Hebrews. The heroes of the catalogue of faith in Hebrews 11, like Abraham, are "strangers and exiles on the earth" who "desire a better country, that is, a heavenly one" (Heb 11:13–16); of them, and by implication of the persecuted Christians who follow their example, "the world is not worthy" (11:38). Persecution and the "hostility of sinners" (12:3) are to be accepted as the norm, but the focus is on the disciplinary action of God (12:5–11) rather than on the motives of the persecuting agencies. There may be a hint of civil disobedience in the praise for Moses' parents (11:23; Wengst 141), and Moses' withdrawal from Egyptian society is treated as exemplary (11:24–25); but in general the Christian is to "strive for peace with all men" (12:14).

Similarly in 1 Peter: the Christians are "aliens and exiles" (2:11), set apart by God's election from the society in which they live (2:9); Rome is referred to under the apocalyptic code name "Babylon" (5:13), and persecution is an imminent possibility (4:12). The author is only concerned that none of his flock should justly incur criminal charges (4:15); if they "suffer as a Christian" (4:16) they are to rejoice at the privilege of sharing Christ's sufferings (4:13). Yet the Christian's attitude to authority is to be one of respectful submission (2:13–17). The emperor is not merely to be prayed for, as in rabbinic teaching and in 1 Tim 2:1–2 (cf. *1 Clem.* 61), but actually to be "honored" (2:17). It is interesting to compare this with Pliny *Ep.* 10: 96; the evidence of 1 Peter suggests that it may well have been the sacrifice to the gods, not the reverence shown to the emperor, that was the sticking point for these Bithynian Christians (Price 1984: 221). As in Hebrews, the persecution faced by the church is regarded as God's judgment, a sign of the end and a token of the much more severe judgment which awaits unbelievers (4: 17–19); it is not treated as evidence of the corruption of the political system which produced it. The church's only response is to "seek peace" and keep a low profile (3:8–17).

F. Revelation

Apocalyptic thought, whether Jewish or Christian, does not necessarily entail resistance to the world empires in the practicalities of daily life: it can coexist with collaboration (as in Daniel) or with a counsel of peaceful submission (as in Romans 13). In the book of Revelation, however, the NT's most full-blooded apocalyptic is combined with radical opposition to the empire and all it stands for. Rome for this author is a "great harlot" (17:1) whose name is "Babylon, the great city," i.e., the last of the four world empires of OT history (14:8; 16:19; 17:5; 18:2, 10, 21); in a clear echo of Daniel's visions, the city is also a "beast rising out of the sea, with horns and seven heads" (13:1; cf. 17:3, 7). The precise interpretation of the heads, the horns and other details is disputed, but the description of "the great city which has dominion over all the kings of the earth" (17:18) and the "seven hills on which the woman is seated" (17:9) make the reference to Rome clear.

The beast's authority derives from Satan (13:2, 4; cf. 12:9), but it is "allowed to exercise authority" for a limited period only (13:5). It is widely accepted that the "beast from the land" of chap. 13 refers to the provincial authorities in Asia and their encouragement of the imperial cult (Price 1984: 197); clearly for this author at least the cult was no empty political gesture. But it would be wrong to read John's polemic merely as an attack on one particular excess; it is the empire itself that he sees as demonic, not an individual emperor or policy. There is no indication that he wished to advocate any action against the empire other than the passive resistance of martyrdom. Yet the language he uses is unusually combative: the great city is to be repaid double for her misdeeds (18:6), and the martyrs in heaven are said to have "conquered" the beast and its image (15:2; cf. 2:7, 11, etc.). Although the battle is ultimately fought out in the cosmic realm, there may be a suggestion that human enemies of Rome could play a part in its downfall if 16:12 refers to the Parthian threat on the E frontiers.

John sets out his vision in terms of a series of fundamental oppositions. There is no opportunity for compromise: the saints are called to endure (14:12), to be "faithful unto death" (2:10), and also to separate themselves from the great city (18:4). Since it is impossible to buy or sell without the mark of the beast (13:16–17), this separation must include a withdrawal from the economic life of the empire (cf. the identification of the empire's interests with those of her "merchants and seafarers" 18:11–20). John's tough stance on the issue of "food offered to idols" (2:14, 20) is probably linked with this issue (Schüssler Fiorenza 1984: 195–96). Yet it is clear from the opening letters that not all Christians thought as John did. As Schüssler Fiorenza suggests, there may be a correlation here between theological attitudes and socioeconomic status; "the two communities that deserve Christ's praise and receive no censure are obviously poor and without power. Those communities that receive censure are rich, complacent, and do not experience any harassment" (Schüssler Fiorenza 1984: 196).

G. Conclusion

Early Christian attitudes to Rome thus show as wide a diversity as their Jewish counterparts. The apocalyptic strain of theoretical resistance runs right through the NT from Jesus' preaching of the kingdom of God, with its radical opposition to all human authority structures, to the visions of the book of Revelation. But this theological stance does not necessarily entail active resistance to the empire; allusions to overt political or military activism are virtually unknown in the NT (the puzzling Luke 23:38 is unique). The passive resistance of the martyr is prominent in Revelation, where the apocalyptic enemy of the faithful is clearly identified as Rome. But in 1 Peter even martyrdom is to be avoided as far as possible by law-abiding and submissive behavior (2:13–17; 3:13–17), and in Acts where martyrdom is welcomed (4:19–20; 5:29), it is the priestly authorities of Jerusalem, not the Romans, who figure as the persecutors. Paul's mission is presented throughout Acts as politically harmless to Rome, and the progress of the Gospel is assisted rather than hindered by the timely exploitation of Roman institutions (16:37–39; 18:12–17; 21:31–22:29; 23:11–24:12). If one attitude can be said to predominate in these documents it is not martyrdom so much as radical withdrawal from the political life of the Empire, which is fundamental both in the Gospels and in the Pauline epistles. It is this which must provide the context for understanding the NT recommendation of submission to authority.

Bibliography

Aland, K. 1979. Das Verhältnis von Kirche und Staat in der Frühzeit. *ANRW* 2/23/1: 60–246.

Bammel, E., and Moule, C. F. D. 1984. *Jesus and the Politics of His Day.* Cambridge.

Belo, F. 1981. *A Materialist Reading of the Gospel of Mark.* Trans. M. J. O'Connell, 1975. New York.

Goodman, M. 1987. *The Ruling Class of Judaea.* Cambridge.

Loewe, R. 1940. *"Render unto Caesar."* Cambridge.

Meeks, W. 1983. *The First Urban Christians.* Yale.

Millar, F. 1977. *The Emperor in the Roman World.* London.

Price, S. R. F. 1984. *Rituals and Power.* Cambridge.

Rajak, T. 1983. *Josephus.* London.

Schaefke, W. 1979. Frühchristlicher Widerstand. *ANRW* 2/23/1: 460–723.

Schüssler Fiorenza, E. 1984. *The Book of Revelation: Justice and Judgment.* Philadelphia.

Sherwin-White, A. N. 1963. *Roman Society and Roman Law in the New Testament.* Oxford.

Smallwood, M. 1976. *The Jews under Roman Rule.* Leiden.

Stemberger, G. 1979. "Die Beurteilung Roms in der rabbinischen Literatur". *ANRW* 2/19/2: 338–96.

Theissen, G. 1983. *Miracle Stories in the Early Christian Tradition.* Trans. F. McDonagh, Edinburgh.

Wengst, K. 1987. *Pax Romana and the Peace of Jesus Christ.* Trans. J. Bowden. London.

LOVEDAY C. A. ALEXANDER

ROSETTES. See JEWELRY.

ROSH (PERSON) [Heb *rōʾš*]. Seventh son or grandson of Benjamin (Gen 46:21). The Genesis genealogy is comprehensive including grandsons as if sons. The LXX lists Rosh as a son of Bela and thus Benjamin's grandson. The Genesis list is also obscure, for the genealogies of Num 26:38–39 and 1 Chron 8:1–5 do not list Rosh. The Numbers text records just five sons of Benjamin; the remainder (five in the Genesis account) become grandsons. The LXX credits Benjamin with three sons and seven grandsons. Parallel passages also seem to suggest that the names, "Ehi" and "Rosh" (Gen 46:21), could be read and understood as one name "Ahiram" (Num 36:39; 1 Chron 8:4; Speiser *Genesis* AB, 343). Rosh means "head" or "chief."

JOEL C. SLAYTON

ROYAL JAR HANDLE STAMPS. See STAMPS, ROYAL JAR HANDLE.

ROYAL ROAD. See KING'S HIGHWAY.

RUFUS (PERSON) [Gk *Rhouphos*]. **1.** A Roman Christian who together with his mother received greetings from Paul (Rom 16:13). Paul called him "elect in the Lord" (cf. Acts 9:15). He probably was freeborn: the epigraphical material indicates that the name "Rufus" was not ordinarily a slave name (see Lampe *StadtrChr,* 151–52). Rufus, with his mother, had immigrated to Rome from the East of the Roman empire. Paul called Rufus' mother "also mine," which may mean that she had housed the apostle one or several times in the East. Rufus was probably a gentile Christian. See NEREUS.

2. The brother of Alexander and son of Simon of Cyrene (Mark 15:21). The brothers were Christians and known by Mark's community if not members of it. For the later evangelists, the brothers' names were not worthy of note (Matt 27:32 and Luke 23:26 omit them).

It is possible that Paul and Mark refer to the same Rufus, especially if Mark was written in Rome. But one wonders why Paul did not also mention the "famous" father in Rom 16:13. Also, Rufus in Rom 16:13 was probably a gentile Christian while Mark's Rufus was a son of Cyrenian Jews. For further discussion, see Cranfield, *Romans* ICC.

PETER LAMPE

RUJM EL-HIRI (M.R. 225257). During the archaeological survey of 1967–68 in the central parts of the S

Golan Heights, an outstanding and unique ancient structure was discovered, the Rujm el-Hiri (Kochavi 1972: 277–78). See Fig. RUJ.01. This monument is one of the most enigmatic and disputed subjects of the archaeology of Israel. There is no agreement as to its function or its construction date because of the near total absence of artifacts in its immediate vicinity (Gutman and Drucks 1969). Nevertheless, closer scrutiny might indicate at least a partial answer to the questions that have arisen around this magnificent structure.

A. Description

The Rujm el-Hiri is situated ca. 16 km E of the N shore of the lake of Galilee, and is 515 m above sea level. It consists of a series of concentric circles surrounding a central tumulus (cairn). See Fig. RUJ.01. Its overall diameter varies between 150 m and 155 m. The central tumulus is composed of a core ca. 8 m across, and an enclosing mantle forming a truncated cone of ca. 25 m across at the bottom, and preserved to a height of ca. 10 m. It is built with relatively small stones collected from the surface and from a nearby basalt flow.

This tumulus is encompassed by a semicircular row of medium-sized orthostates, preserved only on the N and the W side. These orthostates form the retaining wall for a low platform around the tumulus, called here wall 5 (as counted from the outside) for convenience. Parallel to wall 5 runs another semicircular wall no. 4 which is 1.2–1.5 m thick. Its two faces can be followed with some difficulty only due to the large amount of fallen stones that cover the site. Whether these two walls were originally full circles cannot be ascertained before excavation.

The next wall, no. 3, is 1.8–2 m thick and forms nearly a full circle. It bulges out in the S and runs under a large heap of fallen stones in the SE; its continuation to the E was probably disturbed by later building activities. However, wall no. 2 forms a closed circle without any perceivable openings or later disturbances. Its thickness is quite consistently 2.6 m all around except in the S where it thickens to 3 m. This wall is connected with wall 3 by two radial walls, one in the NW and the other in the SW. Other

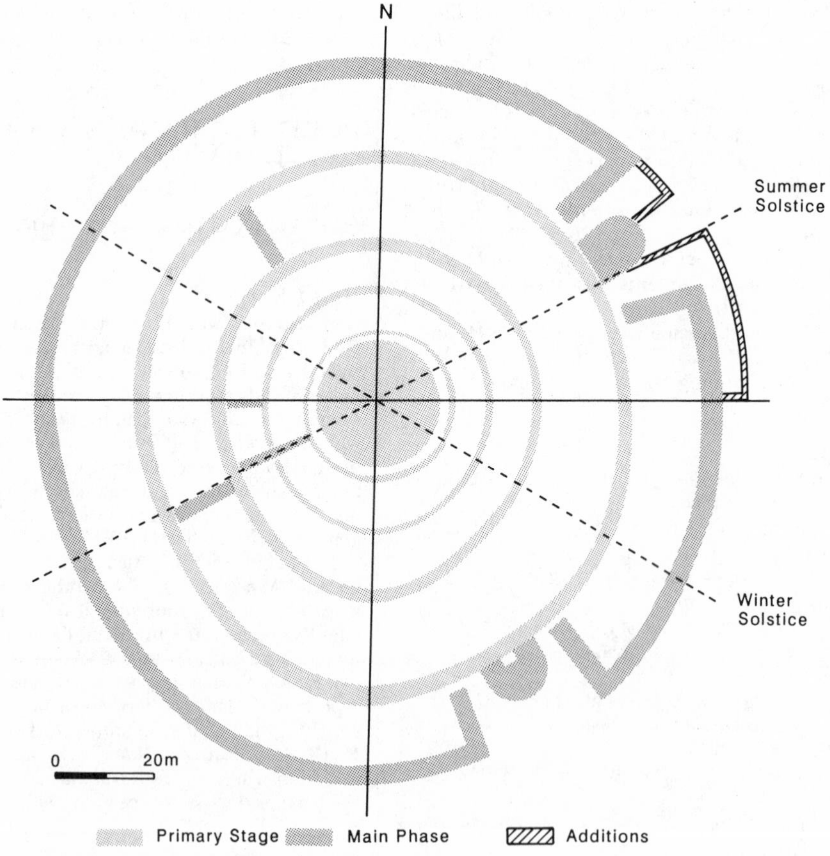

RUJ.01. Site plan of Rujm el-Hiri. *(Redrawn from M. Zohar)*

radial walls can be seen but their relation to the original pattern remains to be clarified; they could be later additions when the site was used as a cattle pen in recent periods.

All these walls are built with medium-sized basalt stones and seem to form a structural unit.

The outermost wall, no. 1, is the most distinctive feature of the Rujm el-Hiri. It is carefully constructed, its thickness being remarkably consistent on all sides, 3.2–3.3 m. Its state of preservation is excellent, in some places up to 2 m in height with 5 or 6 rows of medium-sized to large stones. Some of these stones are true megaliths with sizes 2.5–3 m length, weighing 20 or more tons. The megaliths are found mostly in the E section of wall 1. In the NE and the SE, the line of the wall turns and forms radial walls approaching wall 2. This results in some sort of openings, 29 m and 26 m wide respectively. Both openings are blocked by a mass of large boulders without any clear construction lines. The amount of these boulders seems to indicate that they represent the remains of some structures which were originally higher than the other walls.

Near both openings, and partially blocking them, are fragments of smaller walls. They are rather insubstantial and their relation to the main wall is not clear (called "additions" on Fig. RUJ.01).

B. Discussion

The architectural development of the complex suggests two possibilities. The first is that an older, but seemingly perfect circle underlies the construction as described above. The so-called "additions" could be the remains of this older structure, especially when studied from certain aerial photographs.

The other possibility is that the central tumulus and its circular walls 5 to 2 represent the primary stage. For the time being this seems to be the more convincing theory—a monumental funerary complex which was turned into a sanctuary or ceremonial center with the erection of wall 1. Whether this occurred simultaneously or it entailed a time lapse has yet to be determined. The opening in the NE seems to indicate an orientation towards the summer solstice (azimuth 61°42′9″) of no great precision. When a higher precision was felt to be necessary, the wall "additions" were installed, correcting wall 1. The same wall leads to a point in the E where two large stones indicate the equinoxes. The SE opening, whether it was used for observing celestial phenomena (e.g., midsummer moon rise or the appearance of Sirius), or whether it pointed to some other objects (e.g., a sacred grove or another monument which has disappeared) seems to be a moot point. It is noteworthy, however, that the two radial walls connecting walls 2 and 3 form rather exact back sights to these openings. There is no noticeable indication of the winter solstice (azimuth 118°17′1″).

It is possible that these two openings formed spaces where rituals might have taken place. The only artifacts found were broken flint tools from these open spaces. Perhaps the mass of fallen stones are the remains of elevated altars.

A fairly secure assumption is that the Rujm el-Hiri is oriented towards the summer solstice and the equinoxes. This is a consistent feature of many examples of ANE and Mediterranean sacral architecture. Like other Bronze Age temples, the site also seems to have served, among other things, as a rough timekeeping device.

If we accept the central tumulus as the primary element of the complex, we cannnot dissociate it from the other tumuli and dolmens which cover extensive parts, not only of the Golan, but other areas of the Levant, too. There exists a considerable difference in opinion about their date with an increasing evidence for a MB I date (Epstein 1972; 1973; 1975; Bahat 1972). However, an earlier date, even EB I, cannot categorically be excluded (Yassine 1985).

Undoubtedly, these monuments including Rujm el-Hiri represent the most tangible remains of pastoral cultures on the edge of the desert during most of the 3d and even the 2d millennium B.C.E. Another aspect not to be neglected is the close resemblance of the Rujm el-Hiri, in conception and construction, to certain N African funeral complexes, e.g., those near Djanet in Algeria or in the Nejd in Saudi Arabia. Their date of construction is equally disputed, but a growing number of students assume a date in the 2d millennium as most probable. It is to be hoped that the future excavation of the Rujm el-Hiri will throw more light on the builders of this monument and their relation to other Near Eastern cultures, and will contribute to another aspect of sacral architecture of Israel.

Bibliography

Bahat, D. 1972. The Date of the Dolmens near Kibbutz Shamir. *IEJ* 22: 44–46.

Epstein, C. 1972. Golan Dolmens. *RB* 79: 404–7.

———. 1973. Golan Dolmens. *RB* 80: 560–63.

———. 1975. The Dolmen Problem in the Light of Recent Excavations. *EI* 12: 1–8 (in Hebrew; English summary, p. *17).

Gutman, S., and Drucks, A. 1969. Early Enclosures in the Gaulan. *Qad* 2/3: 91–92 (in Hebrew).

Kochavi, M., ed. 1972. *Judaea, Samaria, and the Golan—Archaeological Survey 1967–1968*. Jerusalem (in Hebrew).

Yassine, K. 1985. The Dolmens—Construction and Dating Reconsidered. *BASOR* 259: 63–69.

Mattanyah Zohar

RULE OF THE COMMUNITY.

See COMMUNITY, RULE OF THE (1QS).

RULERS OF THE SYNAGOGUE

[Gk *archisynagōgos*]. A title of honor for one of several synagogue officials attested in ancient Jewish, Christian, and pagan literary sources and in inscriptions. "Ruler of the synagogue" is the most common Jewish title associated with the synagogue in antiquity. Other titles include "ruler" *(archōn)*, "elder" *(presbyteros)*, "mother of the synagogue *(mater synagogae)*, and "father of the synagogue" *(pater synagogae)*.

Although we have no catalogue of the functions of the "ruler of the synagogue," his or her duties seem to have spanned a range of practical and spiritual leadership roles. The "ruler of the synagogue" chose Torah readers and prayer leaders, invited others to preach, contributed to the building and restoration of the synagogue, and represented the congregation to the outside world. Several inscriptions cite women as "rulers of the synagogue." Children are occasionally called "rulers of the synagogue," which may mean the title was sometimes hereditary.

The sources show no consensus on the practice of selecting an *archisynagōgos.* Some "rulers of the synagogue" were appointed, some elected, and some inherited the office. Some served for one or more terms, while some held the office for life. Certain synagogues had more than one ruler.

The earliest literary evidence for the title comes from the NT. Mark 5:22 and Luke 8:49 tell of the *archisynagōgos* Jairus, whose daughter is healed by Jesus. Luke 8:41 calls him an *archōn tēs synagōgēs* while Matt 9:18, 23 read only *archōn.* However, Roman inscriptions show that *archisynagōgos* and *archōn* were distinct offices, though they could be held by the same person. Other NT references show the "ruler of the synagogue" as regulating worship or acting as representative of the congregation to outside authorities (Luke 13:14; Acts 13:15; 18:8, 17).

Assuming the Hebrew term *rʾš hknst* is equivalent to *archisynagōgos,* we find the earliest Jewish references in the Mishnah (*m. Yoma* 7:1; *m. Soṭa* 7:7, 8). The ruler (or head) of the synagogue is accorded honor in connection with the reading of the Torah. One head is mentioned by name in *t. Ter.* 2:13. The *rʾs hknst* should abstain from reading from the Torah unless no one else is able, according to *t. Meg.* 4:21. Later rabbinic references support the notion that the *rʾs hknst* held a position of esteem as leader of an assembly.

Patristic remarks also portray the *archisynagōgos* as a leader (Just. *Dial.* 137; Epiph. *Pan.* 30.18.2; Pall. *V.Chrys.* 15). Pagan examples show that outsiders were familiar with the term *archisynagōgos* as designating a leader of the Jews (Vopiscus *Life of Saturnius* 8; S.H.A. 3.399). Detractors of Alexander Severus ridiculed him by calling him "the Syrian *archisynagōgos*" (Lampridius, *Life of Alexander Severus* 28, S.H.A. 2.234–35). In the 4th century, laws transmitted in the Theodosian Code suggest that the *archisynagōgos* was one of the leaders who represented the Jewish community (*Cod. Theod.* 16.8.4, 13, 14).

In addition to numerous literary references, over thirty inscriptions from disparate locales, dating from before 70 C.E. and on into the Byzantine era, employ the title *archisynagōgos.*

Bibliography

Brooten, B. 1982. *Women Leaders in the Ancient Synagogue.* BJS 36. Chico, CA.

Horsley, G. 1987. An Archisynagogos of Corinth? *NDIEC,* 213–20.

CLAUDIA J. SETZER

RUMAH (PLACE) [Heb *rûmâ*]. The town of Zebidah, the mother of Jehoiakim, one of the last kings of Judah (2 Kgs 23:36). Rumah is also mentioned by Josephus as the home of two brave Galileans who attacked the Tenth Roman Legion (*JW* 3.7.21). This mention allows us to place Rumah in Galilee, which is evidence of the ties established by Josiah, the father of Jehoiakim, with N Israel. The exact location of the town has not yet been identified. Some scholars would identify Rumah with Arumah, mentioned in Judg 9:41 as the place of residence of Abimelech after he fled Shechem. Aharoni (*LBHG,* 349–50) posits that this Arumah is Khirbet er-Rumeh. (M.R. 177243), by the S border of Battof, to the N of Sepphoris. This place is called Arumah in the annals of Tiglath-pileser III (*ANET,* 283). Cogan and Tadmor (*2 Kings* AB, 305) agree with this as a possible location for Rumah, but also suggest Rumah in the Netophah Valley. The MT of Josh 15:52 has the name Rumah as part of the inheritance of the tribe of Judah, but most of the other witnesses, including the OG, read Dumah. The reading of the MT appears to be an error caused by the confusion of *dalet* and *reš,* a confusion which occurs frequently both in paleo-Hebrew and in the square script.

SIDNIE ANN WHITE

RUTH, BOOK OF. The story of Ruth and Naomi is a tale of human kindness and devotion transcending the limits of national- or self-interest. It is the book of the OT which has long been cited as a perfect example of the art of telling a story.

A. Summary of Plot
B. Composition
C. Date
D. Author
E. Text and Versions
F. Literary-Exegetical Interpretation
  1. Genre
  2. External Design
  3. Internal Structure and Interpretation
  4. Theology
G. Legal Allusions
H. Purpose
I. Canon
  1. Placement
  2. Meanings

A. Summary of Plot

In the days of the judges a family from Bethlehem journeys to Moab because of famine. There the father Elimelech dies, and the two sons, Mahlon and Chilion, take Moabite wives, Ruth and Orpah. After ten years the sons also die, leaving no offspring. Their mother Naomi is bereft. Hearing of food in her native land, she decides to return. When the daughters-in-law resolve to accompany her, Naomi bids them stay. Orpah consents but Ruth clings to Naomi. In Bethlehem the two women seek food. Ruth gleans in the fields of a wealthy man named Boaz who belongs to the extended family of Elimelech. His kindness prompts Naomi to conceive a plan for securing Ruth a home. Obeying her mother-in-law, Ruth goes to the threshing floor at night and asks Boaz to marry her. Though willing, he must first determine if a nearer relative wishes to assume responsibility. The unnamed man refuses, and so Boaz marries Ruth. She bears a son, Obed. A blessing to his grandmother Naomi, Obed continues the family line to become the grandfather of David.

B. Composition

Despite the unity of plot, a few scholars have proposed compositional histories for the book. Utilizing criteria of meter, parallelism, and vocabulary, Myers identifies a poetic nucleus underlying the present text (cf. De Moor 1984). The nucleus bespeaks an oral poem handed down for centuries before the appearance of the prose narrative. Glanzman suggests three stages of development: an old poetic tale of Canaanite origin; a preexilic Hebraized version; and the postexilic final draft. Brenner maintains that the book is composed of two oral tales, one about Naomi and the other about Ruth. Originally independent, these stories shared a geographical and social milieu as well as the theme of the reversal of female fortune. Such compositional theories have not won general acceptance. Most exegetes affirm the unity of the book, though the genealogy at the end (4:18–22) remains a problem as to whether it is an appendix or part of the original story (see McCarthy 1985).

C. Date

Critics diverge widely on the date. Earlier scholars posited an exilic or postexilic time based on alleged Aramaisms, the remoteness of customs (cf. 4:7), discrepancies with the Deuteronomic law, and the theme of universalism over against nationalism. With modified criteria, some contemporary scholars retain this dating. Many others, however, argue for a preexilic composition between the 10th and 7th centuries B.C.E. They detect linguistic features, classical prose, legal and theological perspectives that fit these earlier periods (see Campbell *Ruth AB* and Hals 1969). Still other critics, such as Sasson (1979), find the date altogether elusive.

D. Author

Though Jewish tradition assigned Ruth to the prophet Samuel, scholarship has remained properly silent on the subject. The author is unknown. Nevertheless, commentators have assumed a male gender for the storyteller, an assumption not unchallenged. Subject matter, the dominance of women characters, and point of view suggest a female presence in shaping the narrative (cf. Campbell *Ruth* AB, Brenner 1983).

E. Text and Versions

The Hebrew text has been relatively well preserved. Though variants exist, including those attested in four Qumran manuscripts, they offer few difficulties for interpretation. In general, Gk manuscripts conform to the Hebrew. An incomplete OL text may suggest a different lineage from the known Gk tradition, but the evidence is scant. Differences between Hebrew texts and the Vulgate (e.g., 2:7, 14; 3:15; 4:5) may also indicate another lineage or only show the freedom Jerome exercised in translation. The Peshitta is yet freer. (For discussion of the text and versions, see the commentaries of Campbell *Ruth* AB, and Sasson 1979.)

F. Literary-Exegetical Interpretation

1. Genre. Most form critics call Ruth a *novella.* Closely related is the category of short story, connoting a brief fictional narrative of conscious craftship. With a beginning, middle, and end the plot moves through various scenes to climax and resolution. Words and actions reveal the characters. Sasson (1979) relates Ruth to the folktale as delineated in Russian formalism. Other designations include comedy, saga, romance, and idyll. They all impose modern genres on an ancient story.

2. External Design. A symmetrical design structures the book (Bertman). Three sections in the first half (chapters 1 and 2) match, in reverse order, three in the second (chapters 3 and 4). The first section is the family history (1:1–5). The second, surrounded by the travels of the women (1:6–7 and 1:22), concerns kinship ties (1:8–18) and reports a meeting between the women of Bethlehem and Naomi (1:19–21). The third, after the introduction of Boaz (2:1), contains five elements:

(1) Ruth receives Naomi's permission to glean in the fields (2:2).
(2) Ruth goes to the fields (2:3).
(3) Boaz seeks the identity of Ruth (2:4–7).
(4) Boaz requests that Ruth stay, deems her worthy of blessing, and gives her food. He also orders his men to cooperate (2:8–17).
(5) Returning to Naomi, Ruth reports the meeting and receives counsel (2:18–23).

The second half of the book opens with five analogous elements:

(1) Naomi sends Ruth to the threshing floor (3:1–5).
(2) Ruth goes to the threshing floor (3:6).
(3) Boaz seeks the identity of Ruth (3:7–9).
(4) Boaz deems Ruth worthy of blessing, requests that she stay, and gives her food. He also protects her from other men (3:10–15).
(5) Returning to Naomi, Ruth reports the meeting and receives counsel (3:16–18).

The next section corresponds to section two of the first half. It concerns kinship ties (4:1–13) and reports a meeting between the women of Bethlehem and Naomi (4:14–17). The genealogy of the closing section (4:18–22) returns in theme to the family history at the beginning. Symmetrical design secures the unity of the story, gives balance and rhythm, highlights important motifs, and suggests the richness and complexity of form, content, and meaning.

3. Internal Structure and Interpretation. Sections one and two in the first half constitute scene 1, with an introduction (1:1–7), body (1:8–21), and conclusion (1:22). Throughout, certain motifs prevail. The catchword "return" (*šûb*) occurs 12 times along with the synonyms "go," "come," and "go forth." The struggle between life and death appears on various levels: food and famine, Moab and Judah, Elimelech and Naomi, Mahlon and Ruth, Chilion and Orpah, barrenness and fullness, the names Naomi (Pleasant) and Mara (Bitter). Opening narration presents the characters. The males never speak; after they die, the females talk. Naomi orders Ruth and Orpah to return home. Her words mirror the overall symmetry while emphasizing the themes of kinship and loyalty (1:8–9a):

A Go, return <u>each of you to her mother's house</u>
B *May the Lord be loyal to you*
C as you have dealt with the dead and me.

B' *The Lord grant that you may find a home,*
A' *each of you in the house of her husband.*

Though the young women protest, Naomi insists until Orpah agrees (1:9b–14b). The exchanges among them are enclosed by the words "kissing," "lifting up the voice," and "weeping." Outside this unit lies the extraordinary decision of Ruth (1:14c). She pledges allegiance to Naomi even beyond death (1:16–17). Yet when the two women arrive in Bethlehem (1:19–22), Naomi fails to acknowledge Ruth's presence. Instead, through a chiastic arrangement of the words "Shaddai" and "Yahweh," she convicts the deity of afflicting her (1:20–21). At the close of the scene, the narration counters her sentiments in several ways (1:22). It never calls Naomi "Mara." It observes that Naomi has not returned empty because "Ruth the Moabite her daughter-in-law is with her." And it notes that the women have arrived at the beginning of the barley harvest, a sign of life.

Like the first scene, the second has a narrated introduction (2:1) and conclusion (2:23) surrounding the dialogue (2:2–22). This scene constitutes the third section of the symmetrical design and reflects in its parts patterns of the whole. Three catchwords occur: the verb "glean," *(lqṭ),* the adjective "Moabite," and the phrase, "find favor *(māṣāʾ ḥēn)* in the eyes of." In presenting Boaz, the storyteller gives another sign of life, a male in the family of Elimelech who will endure. Action begins when Naomi grants Ruth permission to seek food. Though Boaz appears to dominate in the ensuing meeting with Ruth, subtleties of language and style indicate that his tremendous power is subservient to the women's story. First, Boaz has not invited Ruth to glean in his fields. She came by choice and chance—perhaps a sign of divine providence (2:3). Second, when Boaz asks the identity of Ruth's owner (2:5), a question that fits his culture, he learns that Ruth does not fit the culture. She has no male lord. Third, though Ruth's first words to Boaz are appropriately deferential (2:10), the reader knows that her deference results from her daring. Boaz is responding to her initiative. Fourth, in seeking a blessing for Ruth, Boaz unwittingly implicates himself. He wishes that her payment be full from Yahweh "under whose wings you have come to seek refuge" (2:12). In time, Ruth will require him to make good on these words. Meanwhile, she reports to Naomi (2:18–22). Their conversation builds on incongruities, each woman having both more and less information than the other. When Ruth finally names Boaz (2:19a), Naomi discloses the kinship: "The man is a relative of *ours,* one of *our* redeemers" (2:20). Thus Naomi reaches out to include Ruth in the family. The old woman also embraces the gift of food. But again the narration counters her by referring to Ruth as "the Moabite" (2:21) and hinting at the return of famine with the "end of the barley and wheat harvest" (2:23).

Corresponding to scene 2, scene 3 begins the latter half of the book (3:1–18). Its catchwords are "threshing floor" *(gōren),* "lie down" *(škb),* and "redemption" *(gʾl).* From the beginning (3:1–5) the characters speak. Naomi initiates a bold, even scandalous, plan to secure Ruth a home. She is to visit the threshing floor when Boaz is sleeping, find his place, uncover his "feet," and lie down. Sexual overtones are clear, even though the extent of intimacy is uncertain. Then, says Naomi, "He will tell you what to do." Ruth agrees to the plan (3:4–5).

This second meeting between Ruth and Boaz constitutes the body of the scene (3:6–15). In contrast to the first encounter, it is private, held indoors at night. Nuances in language and style yield a wealth of meanings. Ruth finds Boaz "at the end of the heap of grain" (3:7). The phrase suggests an accessible area away from the other sleepers—perhaps another sign of the blessed chance (cf. 2:3b) that guides Ruth. When Boaz discovers Ruth lying beside him, he does not ask this time to whom she belongs (cf. 2:5) but rather her personal identity. In answering, Ruth changes the proposed script. Instead of Boaz telling her what to do (cf. 3:5), she tells him. "Spread your wing over your maidservant for you are a redeemer" (3:9c). Once again, she, not he, is in charge. By a play on the word "wing," Ruth asks Boaz to make good on his prayer for her blessing (cf. 2:12). His response is gracious, promising to do "all" that Ruth asks (3:11), even as Ruth has agreed to do "all" that Naomi asked (3:5). Boaz, a "man of worth" (2:1), calls Ruth a "woman of worth" (3:11). Thereupon he introduces information that disturbs the progress of the narrative and heightens suspense. A nearer redeemer must be consulted. In reassuring Ruth, Boaz's speech (3:13) mirrors the symmetry of the story:

A *Remain this night and in the morning*
B if he will do *the redeemer's part,* well and good; let him redeem;
B' but if he is not willing to do *the redeemer's part* for you, then, as Yahweh lives, I will redeem you.
A' *Lie down until morning.*

At the conclusion Ruth reports to Naomi (3:16–18). Her language is guarded, and subtleties persist. Though Naomi asks how Ruth has fared, the answer focuses on "all" that Boaz has done (cf. 3:5, 11) and on food. Ruth says nothing about her own bold speech and action. Naomi, who began the day by plotting a dangerous mission, now closes it by counseling a patient wait. Unlike the endings of scenes 1 and 2, the narration does not counter her words. This tension ceases; the story moves toward resolution.

Yet a different tension emerges in scene 4 (4:1–13). Corresponding to the theme of kinship ties in 1:8–18, it presents a point of view alien to the dynamics of the story. The catchwords "gate" *(šʿr),* "redeem" *(gʾl),* and "buy" *(qnh)* mark the tone. At the gate of the city, where business and legal transactions occur, men gather—the elders, Boaz, and the nearer redeemer whom Boaz addresses as "Mr. So-and-so." Boaz presents the case, again giving new information. In a symmetrical structure he claims Naomi wishes to sell land that belonged to Elimelech and Mr. So-and-so has the responsibility of redemption (4:3). Tension mounts when the unnamed man agrees to the purchase, for he becomes the rival of Boaz. Only then does Boaz present the expected issue, albeit with an unexpected motive. The buying of the land entails the "buying" of Ruth "to restore the name of the dead to his inheritance" (4:5; see Sasson 1979 for a review of the issues implied in this key verse). Upon hearing of this obligation, the nearer redeemer changes his mind. The arrangement would impair his own inheritance for the sake of Elimelech's line. Thus the way opens for Boaz to marry Ruth. But the direction of the narrative has shifted. In scene 1 kinship ties altered radically when Ruth broke with family, country, and faith to commit herself to Naomi rather than to the search for a husband. Now, in the corresponding part of scene 4, kinship ties bind conventionally when restoration for dead males, rather than justice for living females, becomes the motive. Structural symmetry yields semantic dissonance.

Resolution of the women's plight through traditional channels of patriarchy exacerbates tension again. The birth of a son to Ruth (4:13) does not alleviate the problem, but the concluding episode does restore the female perspective. The women of Bethlehem reappear. They call the child a "restorer of life" to Naomi, not a restorer "of the name of the dead to his inheritance," and they exalt Ruth his mother above the ideal number of natural sons (4:15b). When their words converge upon Naomi, she embraces the grandchild. The widow of emptiness is fulfilled. Further, in naming the child Obed, the females of Bethlehem declare, "A son has been born to Naomi!" and not "An inheritor has been born for Elimelech!" Repeatedly, they reinterpret the perspective of the male gathering. As these women spoke for the whole town in scene 1, so now they render its final message in scene 4. Structural symmetry yields semantic harmony.

Poetic analysis finds three conclusions to Ruth, each with its own function (see Berlin 1983). First is the birth of the male child (4:14–16). It completes the events of the story, compensating for the death of the sons at the beginning. Second is the reference to Obed as "the father of David" (4:17). It serves as a coda, moving the time frame into history to forge a link between future and past generations. Third is the genealogy (4:18–22). It provides a larger context for the small family of Elimelech with whom the story began (1:1–5). Yet the androcentric orientation of these endings contrasts strikingly with the distaff life of the story. Such tension opens the narrative to further interpretation.

4. Theology. God never speaks in Ruth or performs miracles, but the story abounds in sacred language and activity. Some commentators uncover the hidden God directing human events (Hals 1969, Campbell *Ruth* AB). Others suggest that human speech and action itself manifests the deity (Trible 1978). Whatever the nuance, the book undercuts dichotomies between the divine and the human and between faith and works.

In the narrated introduction God appears to give food (1:6). This assertion begs the question of who sent the famine (1:2) and so presages the storyteller's perspective throughout. God is the author of life. Accordingly, the deaths of Elimelech, Mahlon, and Chilion are not attributed to the divine (1:1–5), but the birth of Obed is Yahweh's gift (4:13). Contrary to this view sounds Naomi's voice in scene 1. She claims that Yahweh might learn faithfulness from Orpah and Ruth (1:9). She also avers that the Lord's hand has gone forth against her (1:13) and the Almighty has afflicted her with great calamity (1:20–21). For Naomi, Yahweh brings death, not life. Posing the problem of theodicy, her complaints shatter any pat correlation of reward and punishment. The issue resolves as Naomi moves from being a victim to becoming an agent of change and a recipient of blessing. After granting Ruth permission to glean and seeing the successful outcome, Naomi invokes divine blessing upon Boaz, appealing this time to the faithfulness of Yahweh who "has not forsaken the living or the dead" (2:19–20). This altered perspective leads her to propose the plan at the threshing floor and then to advise patience. Eventually she is blessed with the birth of her grandchild. Out of Naomi's pilgrimage comes a theology of providence. God gives life.

The words *ḥesed* and *bārûk/bĕrûkāh* are central. *Ḥesed* connotes faithfulness in action and attitude. *Bārûk* bestows the God-given blessing of life upon another. *Ḥesed* appears alone near the beginning of the story and *bārûk* alone near the end. In the middle they occur together twice. Naomi sees Orpah and Ruth as models of *ḥesed* in their devotion to her and her family (1:8). When she blesses *(bārûk)* the man who took notice of Ruth (2:19), she blesses *(bārûk)* Boaz by Yahweh and cites divine *ḥesed* (2:20). Later when Boaz invokes blessing *(bĕrûkāh)* by Yahweh upon Ruth, he commends her for a second act of *ḥesed* in seeking an heir for Naomi (3:10; cf. 2:12). At last, the women of Bethlehem bless *(bārûk)* Yahweh for goodness to Naomi (4:14).

Even where these words do not occur, their meanings are implicit. Thus a theology of chance emerges. By chance Ruth comes to the field of Boaz (2:3). There she receives the blessing of grain through the faithfulness of Boaz. By chance Boaz lies down at the end of the heap of grain (3:7). The position is the blessing of accessibility for Ruth who dares to request the faithfulness due her. By chance Mr. So-and-so appears at the city gate (4:1) so that Boaz can faithfully settle the issue of redemption to effect blessing upon the widows. Within human luck, then, lies divine intentionality. A faithful God blesses through a faithful people.

Among the book's characters, women predominate. They embody a remnant theology in contrast to patriarchal perspectives. Scene 1 presents Naomi and Ruth all alone; they make their own decisions. This portrayal continues in scene 2, even though the appearance of Boaz complicates the situation. The power of the scene is not, however, transferred to him. The women prevail in their struggle for physical survival. Similarly, in scene 3 they summon an Israelite man to responsibility and thereby secure their cultural survival. At its beginning, scene 4 reverts to a traditional mode when males decide the future of the widows. At the end, the females of Bethlehem reinterpret the occasion. The newborn child symbolizes a new beginning with men. Overall, the book of Ruth shows females working out their own salvation with fear and trembling, for it is God who works in them (cf. Philippians 2:12).

G. Legal Allusions

Three references in chapter 4 evoke comparisons with Pentateuchal laws: the role of the redeemer with laws of redemption (Lev 25:25 and 27:9–33); the right of a widow to inherit her husband's property with the silence of the recorded law (cf. Num 27:1–11); and the remarriage of a childless widow with the law of the levirate (Deut 25:5–10). To reconcile these texts is difficult, though many scholars have tried. One view holds that Ruth belongs to a period after the codification of the law and so reflects modifications of it. A converse proposal maintains that the book precedes the formulation of the law and so reflects its antecedents. Both positions stress the legal credibility of the narrative. (For discussion, see Rowley 1965 and Thompson 1968.) A related approach, not tied to dating, suggests that Ruth demonstrates policy rather than techniques; it appeals to underlying legal principles rather than specific formulations (Campbell *Ruth* AB). Still another perspective finds in the story a metalegal attitude whereby the spirit rather than the letter of the law prevails (Levine 1983).

H. Purpose

Attempts to specify a single purpose falter in light of the book's richness and complexity. Many levels of meaning intertwine—social, political, religious, and aesthetic. A representative list includes: to maintain Israelite customs, inculcate legal duties, integrate law and daily life, legitimate David and his monarchy, tell a good story, encourage proselytes, promote universalism over against nationalism, elevate the virtues of friendship and loyalty, glorify family ties, preserve women's traditions, and witness to God at work. Two approaches, however, are best avoided: to interpret the book as protest literature and to relate its purpose to one specific historical setting. Neither in tone nor content is it polemical, and the date is uncertain.

I. Canon

By the beginning of the 2d century C.E., the canonical status of Ruth was assured (see *Meg.* 7a). Less certain is its place within the canon.

1. Placement. In the Hebrew Bible Ruth appears among the Writings, though its precise location varies. According to the Babylonian Talmud (*B. Bat.* 14b), it comes first, to be followed by the Psalms. This order may be chronological. Set in the days of the judges, Ruth antedates the purported contexts of the other Writings. Ending with the genealogy of David, it prepares the way for the Psalms, most of which are attributed to him.

Another tradition places Ruth within the Megilloth. As one of five festival scrolls, it is read on the Feast of Weeks or Shabuoth (Pentecost) in celebration of the harvest. Two versions of this location exist: (1) a *liturgical* order that puts Ruth second, after the Song of Songs, which is read on Passover, and before Lamentations (ninth of Ab), Ecclesiastes (Succoth), and Esther (Purim); (2) a *chronological* order that has Ruth first, followed by Song of Songs, Ecclesiastes, Lamentations, and Esther. In the latter arrangement Ruth follows Proverbs.

The ordering of the Greek Bible differs. There Ruth comes after Judges and before Samuel. Factors influencing this location include the juridical setting of the story (1:1), the genealogy that prepares for the coming of David (4:18–22), and the ancient ascription of authorship to Samuel.

2. Meanings. Many scholars view canon as a theological issue whereby a single book is interpreted within the whole of scripture. In this light, Ruth elicits numerous observations. When placed after Judges, it contrasts strikingly with the terror story of the unnamed concubine, a tale from which God is absent (Judges 19–21). Ruth shows that in the days of the judges not every man did what was right in his own eyes (cf. Judg 21:25). Some males lived by *ḥesed* and treated females accordingly. Moreover, divine providence guided the affairs of daily life. While contrasted to the concubine narrative, Ruth complements Hannah's story at the beginning of Samuel (1 Sam 1:1–2:21). Also set in the days of the judges, this account continues the theme of providence. Yahweh remembers Hannah and gives her a son. If Ruth is more to Naomi than seven sons (4:15), Elkanah is more to Hannah than ten (1 Sam 1:8). Both stories honor women. This emphasis occurs again in the order that puts Ruth immediately after Proverbs. The latter concludes with an acrostic poem that exalts an *ʾēšet ḥayil,* a woman of worth (31:10–31). The same phrase describes Ruth (3:11) and so places this Moabite in a larger Israelite tradition about women.

Other allusions firmly anchor the narrative to past and future memories. Ruth's decision to follow Naomi recalls Abraham's departure from his country, clan, and father's house to go to an unknown land (Gen 12:1–3). Boaz's words to Ruth confirm the analogy (2:11). Foreigners populate the story of Israel. Among them are the ancient mothers of Rachel, Leah, and Tamar with whom the elders of Bethlehem compare Ruth (4:11–12). Though these names yield fragments for a female genealogical tradition, the reference to Tamar exalts the house of her son Perez. The genealogy at the close (4:18–22) returns to the male line. It traces descendants of Perez through nine generations culminating with Obed, Jesse, and David. Related to the long genealogy of 1 Chronicles 2, this conclusion enlarges the context. Divine activity in the story of Naomi and Ruth belongs to a sacred history that establishes the nation Israel (cf. Merrill 1985).

Finally, in the canonical conversation between the Hebrew scriptures and the NT, genealogies again expand interpretations of Ruth. Though the male line in Luke alludes only to the ending of the book (Luke 3: 31–33), the version in Matthew includes the women Tamar and Ruth (Matt 1:3–6).

Bibliography

Beattie, D. R. G. 1974. The Book of Ruth as Evidence for Israelite Legal Practice. *VT* 24: 251–67.

Berlin, A. 1983. Poetics in the Book of Ruth. Pp. 83–110 in *Poetics and Interpretation of Biblical Narrative.* Sheffield.

Bertman, S. 1965. Symmetrical Design in the Book of Ruth. *JBL* 84: 165–68.

Brenner, A. 1983. Naomi and Ruth. *VT* 33: 385–97.

Carmichael, C. M. 1977. A Ceremonial Crux: Removing a Man's Sandal as a Female Gesture of Contempt. *JBL* 96: 321–36.

De Moor, J. C. 1984. The Poetry of the Book of Ruth (Part 1). *Or* n.s. 53: 262–83.

Dommershausen, W. 1967. Leitwortstil in der Ruthrolle. Pp. 394–412 in *In Theologie im Wandel.* Munich.

Fish, H. 1982. Ruth and the Structure of Covenant History. *VT* 32: 425–37.

Glanzman, G. S. 1959. Origin and Date of the Book of Ruth. *CBQ* 21: 201–7.

Gordis, R. 1974. Love, Marriage, and Business in the Book of Ruth.

Pp. 241–64 in *A Light Unto My Path,* ed. H. N. Bream, et al. Philadelphia.

Green, B. 1982. The Plot of the Biblical Story of Ruth. *JSOT* 23: 55–68.

Hals, R. M. 1969. *The Theology of the Book of Ruth.* Philadelphia.

Hyman, R. T. 1984. Questions and Changing Identity in the Book of Ruth. *USQR* 39: 189–201.

Lacocque, A. 1979. Date et milieu du Livre de Ruth. *RHPR* 59: 583–93.

Levine, B. A. 1983. In Praise of the Israelite *Mišpāha:* Legal Themes in the Book of Ruth. Pp. 95–106 in *The Quest for the Kingdom of God,* ed. H. B. Huffmon, F. A. Spina, and A. R. W. Green. Winona Lake, IN.

Loretz, O. 1960. The Theme of the Ruth Story. *CBQ* 22: 391–99.

McCarthy, C. 1985. The Davidic Genealogy in the Book of Ruth. *PIBA* 9: 53–62.

Merrill, E. H. 1985. The Book of Ruth: Narration and Shared Themes. *BSac* 130–41.

Myers, J. M. 1955. *The Linguistic and Literary Form of the Book of Ruth.* Leiden.

Nielsen, K. 1985. Le choix contre le droit dans le livre de Ruth. *VT* 35: 201–12.

Phillips, A. 1986. The Book of Ruth—Deception and Shame. *JJS* 1: 1–17.

Rauber, D. F. 1970. Literary Values in the Bible: The Book of Ruth. *JBL* 89: 27–37.

Rowley, H. H. 1965. The Marriage of Ruth. Pp. 171–94 in *The Servant of the Lord and Other Essays on the OT.* Oxford.

Sakenfeld, K. D. 1985. *Faithfulness in Action.* Philadelphia.

Sasson, J. M. 1979. *Ruth: A New Translation with a Philological Commentary and a Formalist-Folklorist Interpretation.* Baltimore.

Thompson, T., and Thompson, D. 1968. Some Legal Problems in the Book of Ruth. *VT* 18: 79–99.

Trible, P. 1978. A Human Comedy. Pp. 166–99 in *God and the Rhetoric of Sexuality.* Philadelphia.

Vesco, J. 1967. La date du livre de Ruth. *RB* 74: 235–47.

Wright, G. R. H. 1986. The Mother-Maid at Bethlehem. *ZAW* 98: 56–72.

Würthwein, E. 1969. *Die fünf Megilloth.* HAT 18/1–3. Tübingen.

PHYLLIS TRIBLE

S

SABANNUS (PERSON) [Gk *Sabannus*]. The Greek reading for Binnui (RSV) in 1 Esdr 8:62—Eng v 63. See BINNUI.

SABAOTH [Heb *ṣābāʾôt*]. See HOSTS, LORD OF.

SABBAIAS (PERSON) [Gk *Sabbaias*]. One of the sons of Annan who returned with Ezra (1 Esdr 9:32). He was one of the Israelites who had married foreign wives and had to put them away with their children in accordance with Ezra's reform. He is possibly the same person as Shemaiah, who is identified as one of the sons of Harim in Ezra 10:31.

JIN HEE HAN

SABBATH [Heb *šabbāt*]. The word "sabbath" designates in the Bible the weekly seventh day of festal rest which is a day of abstention from secular work that follows each six-day working week.

A. Sabbath Terminology
  1. Hebrew Terminology
  2. Greek Terminology
B. Modern Research on Sabbath Origins
  1. Babylonian Origins
  2. Kenite Origin
  3. Arabic Origin
  4. Ugaritic Origin
  5. Sociological Origins
C. Sabbath in the OT
  1. Pentateuch
    a. Narrative Texts
    b. Legal Texts
  2. Prophetical Writings
  3. Historical Writings
D. Sabbath in Extrabiblical Texts
  1. Sabbath Attacks on Ancient Israel
  2. Yabneh-Yam Ostracon
  3. Aramaic Ostraca and Papyri
E. Sabbath in Intertestamental Literature
  1. Qumran Literature
  2. Apocryphal and Pseudepigraphical Literature
  3. Historical Literature
  4. Rabbinic Literature
F. Sabbath in the NT
  1. Gospels
  2. Acts
  3. Letters

A. Sabbath Terminology

The discussion of the terminology of the sabbath is in many ways interrelated with the quest for extrabiblical sabbath origins. It will be helpful, however, to describe the terminological evidence for the sabbath in both the OT and NT.

1. Hebrew Terminology. The Heb noun *šabbāt,* "sabbath," occurs 111 times in the OT. Concentrations of usage are in the Pentateuch with 47 times (Exodus 15 times; Leviticus 25 times; Numbers 4 times; Deuteronomy 3 times), the prophetic literature with 32 times (Ezekiel 15 times; Isaiah 8 times; Jeremiah 7 times; Amos and Hosea 1 time each), and the historical books with 30 times (Nehemiah 14 times; 1–2 Chronicles 10 times; 2 Kings 6 times). It appears one time each in Ps 92:1 and Lam 2:6. The noun *šabbātôn,* "sabbath feast," seems to be a derivative of the noun *šabbāt* (GKC §240) and appears eleven times. It is used by itself in Exod 16:23; 31:15; Lev 23:24, 39 in the sense of "sabbath feast" and in Lev 25:6 for "the sabbath of the land," i.e., the sabbatical year. The combination *šabbāt šabbātôn,* "sabbath of complete/solemn rest," appears for the seventh day (Exod 32:5; Lev 23:3), the annual Day of Atonement (Lev 16:31; 23:32), the annual Feast of Trumpets (Lev 23:24) and the sabbatical year (Lev 25:4).

The relationship between the noun *šabbāt* and the Heb verb *šābat,* "to stop, cease, keep (sabbath)" in the *Qal,* "to disappear, be brought to a stop" in the *Nipʿal,* "to put to an end, bring to a stop" in the *Hipʿil,* remains disputed. Scholars have argued that the noun derives from the verb (for example, *AncIsr,* 475–76; *RGG*³ 5: 1259) or that the verb derives from the noun (for example, North 1955: 185–87; KB, 496). While there is no conclusive answer, it seems certain that the noun *šabbāt* cannot be derived from the Akk term *šab/pattu(m)* (see B.1 below). A possible connection of *šabbāt* with the number "seven" has been left open (Hehn 1907, 1909; North *NCE* 12: 780). In this case the Akk feminine form *sibbitîm,* "seventh," may be considered as an ancestor of the Heb noun *šabbāt,* "sabbath," also a feminine form, which, if the relationship holds, may have originally meant "the seventh [day]." On this supposition "the seventh day" in Gen 2:2–3 would receive further light.

2. Greek Terminology. The Gk neuter noun *sábbaton,*

"sabbath," (Mark 2:27–28; 6:2; Matt 12:8; Luke 6:5, etc.) translates the Heb noun *šabbāt.* It corresponds generally to Gk pre-NT usage. Whether the Gk noun *sábbaton* derives from the Aram *šabbāh* by means of the emphatic form *šabbetâ* or is a spontaneous creation seems to be immaterial (Pelletier 1972: 441 n. 2).

The NT has 67 usages of the term *sábbaton* (Synoptics 43 times; John 13 times; the remaining usages appear in Acts and in a few letters). In some usages the plural form (Matt 28:1; Mark 16:2; Luke 24:1; John 20:1, 19; Acts 20:27) or the singular (Luke 18:12; Mark 16:9; 1 Cor 16:2) refers to "week"; otherwise the meaning is always the seventh day of the week, the sabbath.

B. Modern Research on Sabbath Origins

At the end of the 19th century appear the first modern attempts to find the origin of the sabbath outside of the OT. This modern quest for extrabiblical religio-historical sabbath origins was conditioned by the extensive redating of materials in Pentateuchal criticism and the discovery of texts from ancient Babylon.

1. Babylonian Origins. Various hypotheses and theories of Babylonian sabbath origins were put forth some years ago. It was suggested first that the Hebrew noun *šabbāt* and the Akk term *šab/pattu(m),* which were at first thought to be identical, meant approximately the same thing, i.e., "day of rest" (so Lotz 1938). The Akk term was brought into connection with *ûmê lemnûti,* "evil (taboo) days" of the Assyrian calendar, which appeared in approximately seven-day sequences. This hypothesis had to be abandoned when it became apparent that *šab/pattu(m)* was the 15th day of the month, the full moon day, and was never applied to taboo days. In the course of time it also became evident that the *ûmê lemnûti* are the 1st, 7th, 14th, 19th, 21st (added later) and 28th days of the month without fitting into a true weekly cycle. The 19th day was the most important day, but never fits into a seven-day schema.

The Akk term *šab/pattu(m)* cannot be etymologically related to the Heb term *šabbāt* and the latter cannot be directly derived from the Akk term. The Heb term has its middle consonant (radical) doubled, whereas the Akk term has its last consonant (radical) doubled. Comparative Semitic linguistics cannot adequately account for connections between the two terms because of the differing doubling of letters.

Beginning in 1905, J. Meinhold argued that the OT sabbath was originally a monthly full-moon day and as such was borrowed by Israel from ancient Babylon. His hypothesis has found sporadic support. It is recently defended by G. Robinson (1988) who argues that the sequence of "new moon—sabbath" in preexilic sabbath texts (Amos 8:4–7; Hos 2:11–15—Eng 2:9–13; Isa 1:10–14; 2 Kgs 4:22–23) shows that the sabbath after the monthly "new moon" is a monthly "full moon" day just as the sequence in Babylonian texts has *arḫum-šapattu,* "new moon–full moon." In postexilic times the monthly (full moon) sabbath is said to have been transformed into the weekly sabbath. However, this alleged parallel has serious problems: (1) The sequence in all currently known Babylonian (and Sumerian) texts is *arḫum-sebutu-šapattu,* "1st (new moon), 7th, and 15th (full moon) days," which is totally unaccounted for in the OT. (2) The 8th-century text of Hos 2:13—Eng 2:11 (cf. Amos 8:5; Isa 1:13) manifests the sequence of "feasts–new moons–sabbaths," three festal celebrations in the order of increasing frequency of "yearly (feasts), monthly (new moons), and weekly (sabbaths)" celebrations. The sequence also appears in reversed form of decreasing frequency of "weekly (sabbaths), monthly (new moons), and yearly (feasts)" celebrations (Ezek 46:1, 3, 9; 1 Chr 23:31; 2 Chr 2:3—Eng 2:4; 31:3; cf. Ezra 3:5). Both sequences are unknown outside of Israel. (3) New moon and sabbath continue to stand next to each other in later and particularly postexilic texts (Ezek 45:17; 46:1; Neh 10:33; cf. 1 Chr 23:31; 2 Chr 2:3—Eng 2:4) where *šabbāt* refers clearly to the seventh day of the week. (4) The respective contextual settings are so distinct that they cannot be related to each other (Hasel 1988: 37–64; Kutsch 1986: 71–77). Furthermore, there is no compelling evidence in the OT for an alleged transfer from a preexilic monthly sabbath to an exilic/postexilic weekly sabbath.

Other Babylonian hypotheses hold that an early Semitic pentecontad calendar was used, based on the *ḫamuštu(m)* unit of Babylon, meaning "fifty days" ("pentecontad") as first suggested. The sabbath is said to have been the 50th day of such a period (Morgenstern 1947: 1–136; *IDB* 4:135–41) or an alleged last day of a reconstructed Babylonian seven-day week (H. and J. Lewy 1942: 1–152) or one-fifth of a month of a sexagesimal calendar system (Tur-Sinai 1951: 1, 14–24). These menological hypotheses have not received much support in scholarly circles, because (1) there is no clear evidence for a pentacontad calendar, and (2) *ḫamuštu(m)* is typically a five-day period and does not stand for fifty or six days respectively.

2. Kenite Origin. The Kenite hypothesis holds that the Israelites adopted the seventh-day Sabbath through Moses in the Sinai region from metal-working nomads known as the Kenites. The sabbath was supposedly Saturn-day of the nomadic Kenites (Eerdmans 1925: 79–83; Rowley 1951: 81–118). There is no documentary evidence in support of this hypothesis, and the biblical texts cited in its favor (Exod 35:3; Num 15:32; Amos 5:26) are highly disputed in their precise meaning. Accordingly this hypothesis has had only few followers and is hardly supported today.

3. Arabic Origin. D. Nielsen (1904: 52–88) suggested that the sabbath originates through the linguistic link with the Akk *šabattu* which is supposedly derived from the Ar verb *ṯabat,* "sit," a word used for the four monthly phases where the moon "sat." Ancient Arabs worshipped the moon on the four days of the "sitting" of the moon each month, and thus provided the background for the seven-day intervals which in Israel were turned into weekly cycles. This lunar hypothesis has the same difficulties as the ones mentioned previously. The Akk term *šap/battu(m)* is never used for a seven-day cycle or for the four monthly stages of the moon and thus cannot provide a link. The lunar month has 29 days, but weekly sabbath cycles never harmonize or coincide with the phases of the moon. It is not surprising that this hypothesis has not attracted any supporters.

4. Ugaritic Origin. Texts from ancient Ugarit (Ras Shamra) have divisions of "seven years" in the Danel cycle and "seven days" in the *Krt* legend. These days have to do with a festival week and it is maintained that "it is only a short step to the assumption that the origin of the seven-day week was the festival week, which was carried over . . . from the cultic festival and from the cultic week to the reckoning of time as a whole" (Kraus 1966: 87). There is no direct or indirect evidence in support of this connection. Some scholars build on the supposition that there was a universal "seven" structure on the basis of which the origin of the sabbath is to be explained (Negretti 1972, and earlier, Hehn 1907: 59–61, 115–20).

5. Sociological Origins. Several scholars have suggested a variety of sociological contexts out of which the seventh-day sabbath is said to have evolved. H. Webster (1916: 188–92, 101–23) sees the sabbath rooted in "special days" or "rest days" of primitive agriculturalists. Some suggest that the sabbath had its beginning in the "market days" (Jenni 1956: 7–16). However, there is no evidence for a seven-day cycle of market days from the ancient Near East or anywhere else. The development from a market day to a regularly recurring cycle of weekly sabbath celebration remains likewise unaccounted for.

In spite of the extensive efforts of more than a century of study into extra-Israelite sabbath origins, it is still shrouded in mystery. No hypothesis whether astrological, menological, sociological, etymological, or cultic commands the respect of a scholarly consensus. Each hypothesis or combination of hypotheses has insurmountable problems. The quest for the origin of the sabbath outside of the OT cannot be pronounced to have been successful. It is, therefore, not surprising that this quest has been pushed into the background of studies on the sabbath in recent years.

C. Sabbath in the OT

The sabbath appears in a variety of texts in OT literature and in varied contexts of historical and theological import.

1. Pentateuch. The Pentateuch has been considered traditionally to contain the earliest references to the sabbath in the OT. Historical-critical redating of many Pentateuchal strata and traditions has called this into question for many modern scholars. However, there is no unanimity of scholarly opinion on matters of dating and caution remains in order. Also new methods of research throw new light on old questions.

a. Narrative Texts. There are two narratives in which the sabbath plays a prominent role. The creation account of Gen 1:1–2:4a climaxes in the creation sabbath (2:1–3). This pregnant passage reveals that God had finished his creative activity in six days after which he "rested" *(šābat)* on the "seventh day," i.e., ceased from his creative activity (v 2). The "seventh day" means the sabbath even though the noun *šabbāt* is not used. The phonetic linkage between *šābat* and *šabbāt* is generally perceived to indicate sabbath-rest. This seems supported by other typical sabbath terminology which Gen 2:1–3 has in common with the fourth commandment of the Decalogue: "seventh day" (vv 2–3; Exod 20:10), "bless" (Heb *bārak,* v 3; Exod 20:11), "sanctify/make holy" (Heb *qiddaš* [*Piʿel*], v 3; Exod 20:11; cf. 31:14), "make" (Heb *ʿāśāh,* vv 2–3; Exod 20:9–10; cf. 31:14–15), and "work" (Heb *melāʾkāh,* v 3; Exod 20:9–10; cf. 31:14–15). The "seventh day" sabbath is "blessed" as no other day and thereby imbued with a power unique to this day. God made this day "holy" by separating it from all other days. Rest-day holiness is something God bestowed onto the seventh day. God manifested himself in refraining from work and in rest as the divine Exemplar for humankind. The sequence of "six working-days" and a "seventh [sabbath] rest-day" indicates universally that every human being is to engage in an *imitatio Dei,* "imitation of God," by resting on the "seventh day." "Man" *(ʾādām),* made in the *imago Dei,* "image of God," (Gen 1:26–28) is invited to follow the Exemplar in an *imitatio Dei,* participating in God's rest by enjoying the divine gift of freedom from the labors of human existence and thus acknowledging God as his Creator.

Exodus 16 reveals "that through a miraculous rhythm in the provision of the manna Israel was both shown the keeping of the sabbath rest on each seventh day and was obliged to keep this divine ordinance" (Noth *Exodus* OTL, 132). The noun "sabbath" *(šabbāt),* the expression "sabbath feast" *(šabbātôn),* the explicit identification of sabbath as "seventh day," the "sixth day" as preparation for the sabbath, the idea of "rest" on the sabbath for human beings, the notion of the sabbath as a feast and not a day burdened with fasting, and the sabbath being based on YHWH's "commandments and laws" appear in Exod 16:22–30 for the first time. In Noth's view this is "presumably the oldest Old Testament passage about the sabbath" (*Exodus* OTL, 136). For Childs "the existence of the sabbath is assumed for the writer" (*Exodus* OTL, 290). The idea that sabbath keeping is part of "laws and commandments" (v 28) has led Buber to say that the sabbath "is not introduced for the first time even in the wilderness of Sin, where the manna is found. Here, too, it is proclaimed as something which is already in existence" (1958: 80). The nature ("holy"), function ("sabbath feast"), and purpose ("rest") of the sabbath reveals religious, social, and humanitarian significance already in this wilderness setting.

b. Legal Texts. The fourth commandment of the Decalogue (Exod 20:8–11; Deut 5:12–15) is dated late in form-critical and traditio-historical study and is reconstructed into a supposedly short early (Mosaic?) commandment which was formulated either positively according to some scholars or negatively according to others. However, no scholarly consensus has emerged from these endeavors (Meesters 1966: 84–111; Negretti 1972: 173–224; Robinson 1988: 143–54). The Mesopotamian tradition of old ANE law codes reveals that long and short laws can stand next to each other (*ANET,* 160–61, 162–63, 166–77) without necessarily involving a long development of either. Later Hittite laws (14th century B.C.) manifest that a later version of a law can be shorter or longer than the original version (Hasel 1982a: 28–29).

The sabbath commandment has a literary structure shared in common in the versions of Exod (siglum E) and Deut (siglum D): A–Introduction (E, v 8; D, v 12), B–Command (E, v 9; D, v 13), C–Motivation (E, v 10a; D, v 14a), B1–Command (E, v 10b; D, v 14b), C1–Motivation (E, v 11a; D, vv 14c–15a), D–Conclusion (E, v 11b; D, v 15b). It reveals that aside from the minor changes between the two versions the most noticeable change in wording appears only in the C1–Motivation. In Exod 20:11a the C1–Motivation grounds the sabbath in YHWH's creation (Gen 2:2–3), whereas in Deut 5:14c–15a it is grounded in the redemptive Exodus experience. The soteriological and freedom-from-slavery emphasis in Deut 5:14c–15a and the creation freedom-from-labor emphasis in Exod 20:11a indicate that one is dependent on the other and that both are humanitarian in essence. Man is to rest on the seventh day because YHWH, as rest-providing Creator, sets an example of rest for human beings and because YHWH, as liberating Redeemer, sets an example of rest from slavery so that all are able to rest (Exod 5:5). Thus the covenant community is called upon to "remember/observe" (both infinitive absolutes functioning as strong imperatives). The command to "remember" points to the origin of the sabbath prior to Mt. Sinai, an obligation (cf. Exod 16:28) going back to the beginning (Childs *Exodus* OTL, 416), and Deuteronomy uses an equivalent expression in the term "observe."

The Book of the Covenant (Exod 20:22–23:33) contains various covenant statutes and ordinances and among them an ordinance of sabbath rest on the "seventh day" (23:12) similar to Deut 5:14. The sabbath commandment of Exod 34:21 indicates that sabbath celebration shall not be interrupted even in times of plowing and harvest. The instruction for sabbath keeping in Exod 31:12–17 reiterates most of the known aspects of the sabbath. However, several major thoughts appear here for the first time: (a) "Whoever does any work on the sabbath shall be put to death" (v 14), (b) sabbath observance is a "perpetual covenant" (v 16), and (c) the sabbath is a "sign between me and you" (v 13). The death penalty is enjoined upon a member of the covenant community for sabbath disobedience (cf. Exod 35:2b; Num 15:32–36). There is no indication that such punishment should be inflicted outside of the realm of ancient Israel. As the Noahic covenant has a "sign" (Gen 9:13, 17) in the rainbow and the Abrahamic covenant has a "sign" (Gen 17:11) in circumcision, so the Sinai covenant has a "sign" in the sabbath. Its "sign" signification is *commemorative* of God as Creator and Redeemer where the sabbath-keeping community confesses its continuing relationship to its covenant Lord; it is also *prospective* in signification in that it is a "sign" of the covenant history moving forward to its appointed goal; it is at the same time a "sign" signifying the believer's *present* posture vis-á-vis God with physical, mental, and spiritual renewal taking place in each sabbath celebration.

2. Prophetical Writings. The weekly sabbath appears in Amos, the oldest of the classical prophets. Amos 8:5 affirms the knowledge of the seventh-day sabbath in the N Kingdom (Israel). Greedy merchants could hardly wait for the sabbath to end, presumably at sundown, on which the sabbath began and ended as any other day (Gen 1:5, 8, 13, etc.; Lev 23:32; Ps 55:18—Eng 17; Neh 13:19). The sabbath is a day on which no business activities took place. The social-humanitarian aspect is present in the idea of rest, and the moral aspect manifests itself in the control of avarice and greed by refraining from commercial interests.

The widely discussed sequence of "new moon and sabbath" in Amos 8:5; Hos 2:13—Eng 2:11; and Isa 1:13, which are universally accepted 8th century sabbath passages, have been understood to occur "at equal intervals" and "that we have here an institution parallel to the Babylonian *šab/pattú* with monthly occurrence" (Robinson 1988: 55, cf. pp. 59–60; see above on the alleged Babylonian parallel). The full sequence in Hos 2:13—Eng 2:11 is "feasts *(ḥag)*, new moons *(ḥōdeš)* and sabbaths *(šabbāt)*" followed by an appositional phrase "and all her appointed festivals *(môᶜēd)*." The term "feasts *(ḥag)*" stands in the OT only for the annual feasts, the designation "new moons *(ḥōdeš)*" is a monthly celebration, and "sabbaths *(šabbāt)*" are accordingly weekly celebrations. The sequence is clearly one of an increasing number of celebrations in the order from least frequent to most frequent, i.e., yearly–monthly–weekly, celebrations (Hasel 1988: 38–45). Evidently the sabbath was celebrated weekly as a day of rest in both the Northern (Amos 8:5; Hos 2:13—Eng 2:11) and the Southern kingdoms (Isa 1:13; cf. 66:23) in the 8th century B.C. Isa 1:13 even indicates that the seventh-day sabbath institution was one of both rest and worship and could be abused, if it regressed into formal ritualism when emptied of a true relationship with God.

Later sections of the book of Isaiah contain pregnant sabbath passages (Isa 56:1–8; 58:13–14; 66:23). The sabbath belongs to YHWH (56:4), sabbath-keeping means holding fast "my covenant" (v 6; cf. Lev 26:42, 45), Israelite and non-Israelite sabbath-keepers receive divine blessings (Isa 56:2, 6).

Isa 58:13–14 is a most profound OT sabbath passage not to be separated from its context in this chapter. Three prohibitive injunctions protect the believer from having human and secular affairs diminish the sabbath, because the sabbath is a day of "delight" *(ᶜonēg)* and enjoyment on which humans are set free to experience liberation from everyday pursuits. The sabbath is not a legalistic, ritualistic, and burdensome institution, but one that creates "delight" in all spheres of human existence. The sabbath-keeper will be the recipient of such superb divine promises as being fed with the heritage of Jacob and riding on the heights of the earth. Isa 66:23 has the context of the new creation, in which universally "all flesh" will worship YHWH "from sabbath to sabbath."

Jeremiah's prose sermon about the sabbath (17:19–27) keeps sabbath-breaking and sabbath-keeping within the confines of the covenant and the instruction given to the "forefathers" (v 22). The sabbath is a day of rest on which no commercial enterprises are to be enacted. The idea that sabbath-keeping is the condition for the survival of Jerusalem (and Judah) is rooted in the notion of obedience to the covenant stipulations contained in the Decalogue, the breach of which had profoundest concern for Jeremiah (7:8–10; cf. Lam 2:6).

The book of Ezekiel has a high concentration of references to the sabbath (20:12–24; 22:8–26; 23:38; 44:24; 45:17; 46:1–4, 12). The sabbath belongs to YHWH (20:12–13, 20–21, 24; 22:26; 23:38; 44:24) and is a covenant "sign" (20:12, 20) between YHWH and his people. Its profanation is cited among infractions of God's law (20:13, 16, 21, 24, 26; cf. 22:8–26; 23:38). The exile did not come because of sabbath profanation. The latter is but an external sign for covenant breaking, a key theme in Ezekiel, of which the sabbath is the "sign." The sabbath is to be "sanctified/hallowed" (20:20; 44:24; cf. Gen 2:3; Exod 20:8, 11). The sabbath "may well have become a touchstone of loyalty to YHWH from the time of the assimilatory reforms of Manasseh onward" (Greenberg *Ezekiel 1–20* AB, 367) and therefore is singled out by Ezekiel (and

Jeremiah, as also in the later parts of the book of Isaiah) as a special sign of faithfulness to the covenant God.

3. Historical Writings. 2 Kgs 4:22–23 indicates that there was no travel restriction for visiting a man of God on "the new moon or sabbath." The sequence of the two festivals is here also one of increasing frequency of celebration. The new moon arrived monthly and the sabbath weekly. This text may be safely dated to the 9th century B.C. and gives evidence of knowledge of the seventh-day sabbath in the Northern kingdom at that time.

In 2 Kgs 11:4–12 (= 2 Chr 23:4–11) the sabbath is the day of the week on which the ruling monarch was overthrown, presumably since he visited the temple for religious purposes. 2 Kgs 16:17–18 mentions the removal of a structure "for the sabbath" in the time of Ahaz (735–715 B.C.).

The sabbath has a variety of connections in the work of the Chronicler (1 Chr 9:32; 23:31; 2 Chr 2:4; 8:13; 31:3; 36:21) with reference to temple, land, covenant, rest, redemption, and restitution.

Sabbath observance was lax in the time of Nehemiah. The sabbath was "profaned" (Neh 13:17–18) and there was need to bring the sabbath back to its rightful place (9:6–37; 10:31–34; 13:15–22) as a day of rest, worship, and enjoyment from sunset Friday to sunset Saturday (13:19).

D. Sabbath in Extrabiblical Texts

There are various archaeological discoveries that have been linked directly or indirectly to the sabbath in biblical times.

1. Sabbath Attacks on Ancient Israel. Sennacherib's letter written on his Judean campaign in 701 B.C. refers to his capture of Lachish on Hezekiah's "seventh time" (*ina 7-šu,* lit. "in his 7th (time)," Naʾaman 1974: 26). Shea (1988: 178) has suggested that Hezekiah's "seventh time" refers to the sabbath, the day when its defenders rested and the Assyrians captured Lachish. If this suggestion is correct, this cuneiform text from Sennacherib "becomes the earliest extrabiblical reference to the Sabbath" (Shea 1988: 179; cf. Shea 1989: 22–23). It corresponds to such passages as Amos 8:4; Hos 2:11—Eng 13; and Isa 1:13 where the weekly sabbath is also depicted as a day of rest.

The publication of the Chronicles of the Babylonian Kings by Wiseman in 1956 provided the date for the capture of Jerusalem "on the second day of the month of Adar" (Wiseman 1956: 72–73), i.e., March 16, 597. The day was a sabbath (Johns 1963: 483–84). Also the day for the first assault against Jerusalem on January 15, 588, is again a sabbath, based on the synchronism of the biblical date (2 Kgs 25:1; Jer 52:4; Ezek 24:1–2) with the Babylonian records. Again the fall of Jerusalem on the 9th day of the 4th month of Zedekiah's 11th year (Jer 52:5–8) is calculated to fall on a sabbath (Johns 1963: 485). Based on these calculations, it appears that the military strategy of the Assyrians and Neo-Babylonians utilized the seventh-day sabbath rest of the Israelites to accomplish their military-political goals.

This strategy was again used later by the Seleucids at the beginning of the Maccabean period when Jews were attacked on the sabbath but refused to resist on this day (Josephus *Ant* 12.6.2; 1 Macc 2:33–38).

2. Yabneh-Yam Ostracon. The so-called Yabneh-Yam (Meṣad Ḥashavyahu) ostracon, discovered in 1960 by J. Naveh and dated to about 625 B.C., contains in lines 5–6 the Heb phrase *lpny šbt,* "before sabbath" (Cross 1962: 45 n. 45; Albright *ANET,* 568; Delekat 1970: 455; Lemaire 1977: 261). Some scholars have emended *šbt* into *šbty* and vocalized it as *šibtî,* "I stopped" (Robinson 1988: 91), but there is no reason to emend the text of the ostracon. The term *šbt* seems contextually best rendered "sabbath" (Shea 1989: 22). In this case, the Yabneh-Yam ostracon provides extrabiblical evidence for a seventh-day sabbath in preexilic times, the time of the reign of Josiah of Judah.

3. Aramaic Ostraca and Papyri. The Aram Elephantine ostraca, dated to the 5th century B.C., contain four ostraca which refer to the sabbath. A certain Jedaniah who was imprisoned makes reference to "the [d]ay of the sabbath" ([*y*]*wm šbh CAP* 44); a Uriah refers to a shipment which needs to take place before "the day of the sabbath" (*ywm šbh CAP* 186); another ostracon refers to someone who will arrive at "the eve (of the sabbath) [*ʿrwbh*])" (*CAP* 204); and the fourth ostracon is addressed to a woman urging, "Meet the boat tomorrow on sabbath *(šbh)* lest they [vegetables] get lost/spoiled" (Porten 1969: 116; cf. Dupont-Sommer 1949: 31). These brief remarks in private letters seem to indicate that the sabbath as special day was important to the Jewish community at Elephantine in Upper Egypt.

The personal name Shabbethai, meaning "born on the sabbath," appears a number of times in the Elephantine ostraca as it does in the OT (Ezek 10:15; Neh 8:7; 11:16). Porten (1969: 117) believes that in some instances in Elephantine this name is used also by non-Jews, indicating that they had apparently adopted sabbath observance.

An Aram papyrus from Saqqâra (not later than 5th-4th century B.C.) mentions the words *šbtʾ* and *šbt,* which may refer to the "sabbath" or perhaps be interpreted as the personal name Shabbatai (Segal 1983: 95). In either case it seems to give evidence for the sabbath at Saqqâra in Egypt.

The Aram name *šbty,* "Shabbatai," appears on a sarcophagus in Assuan, Upper Egypt, presumably belonging to a non-Jew (Kornfeld 1967: 9–16).

E. Sabbath in Intertestamental Literature

The development of the sabbath in intertestamental times shows variance in observance and reveals significant intensifications.

1. Qumran Literature. The recent publication of the Shabbath Songs (4QShirShabb), a fragmentary liturgical composition from Qumran in thirteen sections, one for each of the first thirteen sabbaths of the year, describes the heavenly priesthood of angels serving in the heavenly sanctuary each sabbath, supposedly corresponding to sabbath worship on earth (cf. *Jub.* 2:30). 4Q403 1 i 30 is translated by Newsom, "Song of the sacrifice of the seventh Sabbath on the sixteenth of the month" (1985: 211), followed by a call to praise addressed to angels.

The Damascus Document (CD), dated to ca. 100 B.C., enjoins strict sabbath observance (VI, 18), but does not call for the death penalty for sabbath profanation (XII, 3–4). A long section outlines appropriate sabbath observance (X, 14–XII, 5). Sabbath prohibitions include such things as walking further than 1,000 cubits (X, 21), eating that which is prepared on the sabbath (X 22), drinking outside of the camp (X 23), drawing water up into any vessel (XI 2), voluntary fasting (XI 4–5), opening of a sealed vessel (XI 9), wearing of perfume (XI 9–10), lifting of stone or dust at home (XI 10b–11a), aiding a beast in birthing (XI 13a), lifting an animal that has fallen into a pit (XI 13–14), lifting a person that has fallen into a place full of water (XI 16–17), and having sexual relations in the city of the sanctuary (XII 1). These rigid demands are more or less like the sabbath *halakhah* of normative Judaism outside of the Qumran community (cf. Kimbrough 1966: 498–99).

The Temple Scroll (11QTemple), dated not later than the third quarter of the 2d century B.C., makes it clear how the Qumran community took the famous expression "on the morrow after the sabbath" (Lev 23:10–11; cf. 23:15–16), which has caused the so-called Pentecost controversy that divided Jewish sects in pre-NT times and ever since. The rabbis and normative Judaism took "sabbath" in this context to mean Passover. The Sadducees, the Samaritans, and other sects took it to mean a regular seventh-day sabbath. The Temple Scroll changes Lev 23:15–16 to read, "And you shall count seven full sabbaths from the day you brought the sheaf of the wave offering; you shall count to the morrow after the seventh sabbath, counting fifty days" (11QTemple 18, 11–12). Based on the 364-day and 52-week solar Qumran(-Jubilees) calendar and beginning the year on Wednesday Nisan 1 (March/April), the Temple Scroll takes the "sabbath" under dispute as the first sabbath after the entire Feast of Unleavened Bread, which is dated to the 25th of the 1st month so that the "morrow of the seventh sabbath" was the 15th of the 3rd month, a Sunday, the 50th day after Pentecost (Yadin 1983: 2.76). In this way these festivals always fall on a Sunday, the day after the seventh seventh-day sabbath of the year (Maier 1985: 71–73).

2. Apocryphal and Pseudepigraphical Literature. The author of *Jubilees* (ca. 150 B.C.) has the sabbath fall regularly on the seventh day of each week according to its calendar of 364 days. In *Jub.* 2:17–33 the sabbath is depicted as a specially holy day to be observed only by Israelites and not made for any other people (*Jub.* 2:30). The author strongly maintains the death penalty for any transgression of the sabbath (*Jub.* 2:25–27). The list of sabbath *halakhah* in *Jub.* 50:6–13 corresponds in many aspects with the ones in the Damascus Document (see E.1 above). The following section is typical, "And (as for) any man who does work on it [sabbath], or who goes on a journey, or who plows a field either at home or any (other) place, or who kindles a fire, or who rides an animal, or who travels the sea in a boat, and any man who slaughters or kills anything, . . . or who fasts or who makes war on the day of the sabbath, let the man . . . die so that the children of Israel keep the sabbath . . ." (*Jub.* 50:12–13, trans. Wintermute, *OTP* 2: 142).

Fragment 5 of the work of Aristobulus (ca. middle of 2d century B.C.) explains the sabbath in relationship to cosmic orders, also linking the sabbath to wisdom (Frag. 5.9–10) and the sevenfold structures of all things (Frag. 5.12). This work is an attempt to bring the sabbath into relationship with Hellenistic thought similar to that of Philo.

3. Historical Literature. In earlier times Israelite enemies captured Jerusalem on the sabbath (see D.1 above). In *Jub.* 50:13 fighting is still prohibited on the sabbath. Ptolomy I Soter (323–283/82 B.C.) took Jerusalem on a sabbath unopposed and ruled it harshly (Joseph. *Ant* 12.1.1). Apollonius, a commander of an army corps of Antiochus IV Epiphanes, in 168 B.C. "waited until the holy sabbath day" to "rush into the city with his armed men and killed great numbers of people" (2 Macc 5:25–26), because Jews did not fight on the sabbath. Sabbath attacks continued (1 Macc 2:38), and Mattathias and his followers decided that they needed to defend themselves on the sabbath (vv 39–41) in order to avoid annihilation. According to Josephus this practice continued (*Ant* 12.6.2). By the time the Romans engaged in war against the Jews, the latter would even attack viciously on sabbath (Joseph. *JW* 2.17.10; 18.1).

4. Rabbinic Literature. Rabbinic literature is filled with sabbath regulations and detailed instructions that go far beyond anything found elsewhere in Jewish literature. The most extensive regulations are gathered together in the Mishnah (*Šabb.* 7.2; *Beṣa* 5.2; and in *ʿErubin,* cf. *TDNT* 7: 12–14). Many of these instructions are aimed at protecting the sabbath from profanation. In cases of emergency, however, particularly as regards threats to life, one could flee on sabbath (*Tanḥ.* 245a), act as a midwife on sabbath (*Šabb.* 18.3) to preserve life, and put out a fire on sabbath (*Šabb.* 16.1–7). These are exceptions and sabbath sacredness is to be maintained in cases of doubt (*Tanḥ.* 38b). The rabbis followed the thought that the sabbath was made for the Jews and not for anyone else (*Midr. Exod.* 31.12 [109b]; *Exod. Rab.* 25.11; *Deut. Rab.* 1.21). A Gentile who keeps the sabbath, according to Rabbi Simeon b. Laqish (mid 3d century A.D.), "deserves death" (*Sanh.* 58b). Sabbath-keeping and Jewish identity were one concept in normative Judaism.

F. Sabbath in the New Testament

The sabbath appears in the teachings of Jesus, in his conflicts with religious leaders, and in the later NT church.

1. Gospels. Jesus, at the beginning of his ministry in Galilee, "went to the synagogue, as his custom was, on the sabbath day" (Luke 4:16). The phrase "as his custom was" indicates that Jesus continued to worship on the sabbath. He remained a faithful disciple of OT scripture following his established custom of attending the synagogue each sabbath (cf. Mark 1:21, 29; 3:1; Luke 4:44; 13:10; etc.).

The four Gospels record among eight sabbath incidents six controversies in which Jesus "rejected the rabbinic sabbath *halakah*" (Jeremias 1973: 201), i.e., two are recorded in the three synoptics (Matt 12:1–8 = Mark 2:23–28 = Luke 6:1–5; Matt 12:9–14 = Mark 3:1–6 = Luke 6:6–11), one is recorded in two synoptics (Mark 1:21–28 = Luke 4:31–37) and the remainder are found in Mark (1:29–31), Luke (13:10–17; 14:1–6) and John (5:1–18; 9:1–41) only. The authenticity of these pericopes seems well established (Rordorf 1968: 54–74; Lohse *TDNT* 7: 21–30; Goppelt 1981: 94). Only Jesus' inaugural sabbath sermon in Nazareth (Luke 4:16–30) and the healing of Peter's mother-in-law on the sabbath (Mark 1:29–31) are outside of explicit controversy contexts. All except two (Luke 4:16–30; Mark 2:23–28) of the nine sabbath pericopes involve sabbath miracles.

After Jesus had started to preach in the synagogue in

Capernaum a man with an unclean spirit interrupted him. Jesus drove the unclean spirit out of this demon-possessed man (Mark 1:21–28 = Luke 4:31–37). Subsequently, Jesus healed Peter's mother-in-law from a fever on the sabbath (Mark 1:29–31). Jesus continued to preach in the Galilean synagogues presumably on the sabbath and cast out demons (v 39).

At times Jesus is interpreted to have abrogated or suspended the sabbath commandment on the basis of the controversies brought about by sabbath healings and other acts. Careful analysis of the respective passages does not seem to give credence to this interpretation. The action of plucking ears of grain on the sabbath by the disciples is particularly important in this matter. Jesus makes a foundational pronouncement at that time in a chiastically structured statement of antithetic parallelism: "The sabbath was made for man and not man for the sabbath" (Mark 2:27). The disciples' act of plucking grain infringed against the rabbinic *halakhah* of minute casuistry in which it was forbidden to reap, thresh, winnow, and grind on the sabbath (*Šabb.* 7.2). Here again rabbinic sabbath *halakhah* is rejected, as in other sabbath conflicts. Jesus reforms the sabbath and restores it to its rightful place as designed in creation, where the sabbath is made for all mankind and not specifically for Israel, as claimed by normative Judaism (cf. *Jub.* 2:19–20, see D.3). The subsequent logion, "The Son of Man is Lord even of the sabbath" (Mark 2:28; Matt 12:8; Luke 6:5), indicates that man-made sabbath *halakhah* does not rule the sabbath, but that the Son of Man, not man, is Lord of the sabbath. It was God's will at creation that the sabbath have the purpose of serving mankind for rest and bring blessing. The Son of Man as Lord determines the true meaning of the sabbath. The sabbath activities of Jesus are neither hurtful provocations nor mere protests against rabbinic legal restrictions, but are part of Jesus' essential proclamation of the inbreaking of the kingdom of God in which man is taught the original meaning of the sabbath as the recurring weekly proleptic "day of the Lord" in which God manifests his healing and saving rulership over man.

The seven miraculous sabbath healings of Jesus indicate once again that Jesus restores the sabbath to be a benefit for humankind against any distortions of human religious and/or cultic traditions. The healing of the man with the withered hand (Mark 3:1–6 = Matt 12:9–14 = Luke 6:6–11) brought about another confrontation with Pharisees and scribes, because healing on the sabbath was only permitted in case of danger to life (*m. Yoma* 8.6) which obviously was not the case here (cf. Luke 14:1–6) or elsewhere in sabbath healings (John 5:1–18; 9:1–41). Jesus maintained here as always, against the rabbinic position, that "it is lawful to do good on the sabbath" (Matt 12:12).

In his eschatological discourse (Matthew 24), Jesus urged his followers to pray that their flight "may not be in winter or on the sabbath" (Matt 24:20; Mark 13:18 omits "on the sabbath"). Jesus anticipated that his followers would continue to regard the sabbath as holy in the future. His request for them was that they be spared from having to flee on the sabbath, but he presupposes that they would flee if they had to. Lohse maintains, "Mt. 24:20 offers an example of the keeping of the Sabbath by Jewish Christians" (*TDNT* 7: 29). A society governed by many rabbinic sabbath laws would make it rather difficult for Christians to flee on the sabbath.

In short, Jesus declared himself Lord of the sabbath. He consistently rejected man-made sabbath *halakhah.* He freed the sabbath from human restrictions and encumbrances and restored it by showing its universal import for all men so that every person can be the beneficiary of the divine intentions and true purposes of sabbath rest and joy. Carson has concluded, "There is no hint anywhere in the ministry of Jesus that the first day of the week is to take the character of the Sabbath and replace it" (1982: 85).

2. Acts. Aside from two casual references to the sabbath (Acts 1:12; 15:21), the sabbath is mentioned in connection with the establishment of churches in Pisidian Antioch (13:13–52), Philippi (16:11–15), Thessalonica (17:1–9), and Corinth (18:1–4). The Western text includes Ephesus (18:19). Paul, as Jesus before him, went to the synagogue on sabbath "as his custom was" (Acts 17:2; cf. 24:14; 28:17). There is silence on the subject of sabbath abolition at the Jerusalem Conference (15:1–29). There is also no evidence for the abrogation of the sabbath after the Jerusalem Council in the apostolic age or by apostolic authority in the early church (Turner 1982: 135–37). Early Jewish and non-Jewish Christians continued to worship on the seventh day as far as the evidence in the book of Acts is concerned.

The single reference to "the first day of the week" in Acts 20:7–12, when Christian believers broke bread in a farewell meeting at the imminent departure of Paul is debated in its meaning. Some scholars suggest that Roman reckoning is used so that "the first day of the week" means Sunday night (Rordorf 1968: 200–2; Turner 1982: 128–33) and other scholars suggest that Jewish reckoning is used and in that case it means Saturday night (Bacchiocchi 1977: 101–11; Mosna 1969: 14–17). This passage hardly supports Sunday-keeping on the part of the apostolic church, since this was an occasional farewell meeting lasting till after midnight (v 7) and the breaking of the bread is hardly the Lord's Supper.

3. Letters. The meaning of the term "sabbath" in Col 2:16 is controversial. Among the major suggestions are those that take it to refer to the seventh-day sabbath which is thought to be done away with; ceremonial sabbaths of the Jewish cultic year; some Jewish aspect of the sabbath without denying true sabbath-keeping; perverted sabbath-keeping in honor of the elemental spirits of the universe; weekdays that were designated to be sabbaths; or sabbath sacrifices prescribed in Num 28:9–10. Within the context of the Galatian Judaizing heresy, "sabbath" seems to refer to something other than wholesome weekly sabbath-keeping as the majority opinion holds.

Hebrews 4:9 states, "There remains therefore a Sabbath rest for the people of God." The words "sabbath rest" translate the Gk noun *sabbatismos,* a unique word in the NT. This term appears also in Plutarch (*Superst.* 3 [*Moralia* 166a]) for sabbath observance, and in four post-canonical Christian writings which are not dependent on Heb 4:9 (Justin *Dial.* 23:3; Epiph. *Panar. haer.* 30, 2.2; Martyrdom of Peter and Paul, chap. 1; *Const. Apost.* 2.36.2) for seventh-day "sabbath celebration" (Hofius 1970: 103–5). The author of Hebrews affirms in Heb 4:3–11, through the joining of quotations from Gen 2:2 and Ps 95:7, that the promised "sabbath rest" still anticipates a complete realization "for the people of God" in the eschatological end-time which had been inaugurated with the appearance of Jesus (1:1–3). "Sabbath rest" within this context is not equated with a future, post-eschaton sabbath celebration in the heavenly sanctuary; it is likewise not experienced in the rest that comes in death. The experience of "sabbath rest" points to a *present* "rest" *(katapausis)* reality in which those "who have believed are entering" (4:3) and it points to a *future* "rest" reality (4:11). Physical sabbath-keeping on the part of the new covenant believer as affirmed by "sabbath rest" epitomizes cessation from "works" (4:10) in commemoration of God's rest at creation (4:4 = Gen 2:2) and manifests faith in the salvation provided by Christ. Heb 4:3–11 affirms that physical "sabbath rest" *(sabbatismos)* is the weekly outward manifestation of the inner experience of spiritual rest *(katapausis)* in which the final eschatological rest is proleptically experienced already "today" (4:7). Thus "sabbath rest" combines in itself creation-commemoration, salvation-experience, and eschaton-anticipation as the community of faith moves toward the final consummation of total restoration and rest.

Bibliography

Andreasen, N.-E. 1972. *The Old Testament Sabbath.* SBLDS 7. Missoula, MT.

Bacchiocchi, S. 1977. *From Sabbath to Sunday.* Rome.

———. 1985. *The Sabbath in the New Testament.* Berrien Springs, MI.

Buber, M. 1958. *Moses: The Revelation and the Covenant.* New York.

Carson, D. A., ed. 1982. *From Sabbath to Lord's Day.* Grand Rapids.

Cross, F. M. 1962. Epigraphic Notes on Hebrew Documents of the Eighth–Sixth Centuries B.C., II. *BASOR* 165: 34–46.

Delekat, L. 1970. Ein Bittschriftentwurf eines Sabbatschänders (KAI 200). *Bib* 51: 453–70.

Dupont-Sommer, A. 1949. L'ostracon araméen du Sabbat. *Sem* 2: 29–39.

Eerdmans, B. D. 1925. Der Sabbat. Pp. 79–83 in *Vom Alten Testament, Festschrift für Karl Marti,* ed. K. Budde. BZAW 41. Berlin.

Goppelt, L. 1981. *Theology of the New Testament.* Vol. 1. Trans. J. E. Alsup. Grand Rapids.

Gruber, M. 1969. The Source of the Biblical Sabbath. *JANES* 1: 14–20.

Hasel, G. F. 1982a. The Sabbath in the Pentateuch. Pp. 21–43 in *The Sabbath in Scripture and History,* ed. K. A. Strand. Washington, D.C.

———. 1982b. The Sabbath in the Prophetic and Historical Literature of the Old Testament. Pp. 44–56 in *ibid.*

———. 1988. "New Moon and Sabbath" in Eighth Century Israelite Prophetic Writings (Isa 1:13; Hos 2:13; Amos 8:5). Pp. 37–64 in *"Wünschet Jerusalem Frieden": Collected Communications to the XIIth Congress of the International Organization for the Study of the Old Testament, Jerusalem 1986,* ed. M. Augustin and K.-D. Schunck. Frankfurt am Main.

Hehn, J. 1907. *Siebenzahl und Sabbat bei den Babyloniern und im Alten Testament.* Leipzig.

———. 1909. Der israelitische Sabbat. *Biblische Zeitfragen* 12: 463–96.

Hofius, O. 1970. *Katapausis: Die Vorstellung vom endzeitlichen Ruheort im Hebräerbrief.* WUNT 11. Tübingen.

Jenni, E. 1956. *Die theologische Begründung des Sabbatgebotes im Alten Testament.* ThStud 46. Zollikon-Zurich.

Jeremias, J. 1973. *Neutestamentliche Theologie.* Pt 1, *Die Verkündigung Jesu.* 2d ed. Gütersloh.

Johns, A. F. 1963. The Military Strategy of Sabbath Attacks on the Jews. *VT* 13: 482–86.

Kimbrough, S. T. 1966. The Concept of the Sabbath at Qumran. *RQ* 20: 483–502.

Kornfeld, W. 1967. Aramäische Sarkophage in Assuan. *WZKM* 51: 9–16.

Kraus, H.-J. 1966. *Worship in Israel: A Cultic History of the Old Testament.* Trans. G. Buswell. Richmond, VA.

Kutsch, E. 1986. Der Sabbat—ursprünglich Vollmondtag? Pp. 71–77 in *Kleine Schriften zum Alten Testament. Zum 65. Geburtstag herausgegeben,* ed. L. Schmidt and K. Eberlein. Berlin.

Lemaire, A. 1977. *Inscriptions Hébraïques.* Vol. 1, *Les ostraca.* Paris.

Lewy, H. and J. 1942. The Origin of the Week and the Oldest West Asiatic Calendar. *HUCA* 17: 1–152.

Lotz, W. 1938. *Questiones de Historia Sabbati.* Leipzig.

Maier, J. 1985. *The Temple Scroll.* Trans. R. T. White. Sheffield.

Meesters, J. H. 1966. *Op zoeg naar de oorsprong van de sabbat.* SSN 7. Assen.

Meinhold, J. 1905. *Sabbat und Woche im Alten Testament.* Göttingen.

Morgenstern, J. 1947. *The Chanukka Festival and the Calendar of Ancient Israel.* Hebrew Union College Annual 20: 1–136.

Mosna, C. S. 1969. *Storia della domenica dalle origini fino agli inizi del V secolo.* AnGreg 170. Rome.

Naʾaman, N. 1974. Sennacherib's "Letter to God" on His Campaign to Judah. *BASOR* 214: 25–39.

Negretti, N. 1972. *Il Settimo Giorno.* Rome.

Newsom, C. 1985. *Songs of Sabbath Sacrifice.* HSS/HSM. Atlanta.

Nielsen, D. 1904. *Die altarabische Mondreligion und die mosaische Überlieferung.* Strassburg.

North, R. 1955. The Derivation of the Sabbath. *Bib* 36: 182–201.

Pelletier, A. 1972. *Sabbata*: Transcription grecque de l'arameen. *VT* 22: 436–47.

Porten, B. 1969. The Religion of the Jews of Elephantine in Light of the Hermopolis Papyri. *JNES* 28: 116–21.

Robinson, G. 1988. *The Origin and Development of the Old Testament Sabbath.* BBET 21. Frankfurt am Main.

Rordorf, W. 1968. *Sunday: The History of the Day of Rest and Worship in the Earliest Centuries of the Christian Church.* Trans. A. A. K. Graham. Philadelphia.

Rowley, R. R. 1951. Moses and the Decalogue. *BJRL* 34: 81–118. Repr. pp. 1–36 in *Men of God,* London, 1963.

Segal, J. B. 1983. *Aramaic Texts from North Saqqâra with Some Fragments in Phoenician.* Texts from Excavations 4. London.

Shea, W. H. 1988. Sennacherib's Description of Lachish and of Its Conquest. *AUSS* 26: 171–80.

———. 1989. The Sabbath in Extra-Biblical Sources. *Adventist Perspectives* 3/2: 17–25.

Turner, M. M. B. 1982. The Sabbath, Sunday, and the Law in Luke/Acts. Pp. 99–157 in Carson 1982.

Tur-Sinai, N. H. 1951. Sabbat und Woche. *BiOr* 8: 14–24.

Webster, H. 1916. *Rest Days: A Study in Early Law and Morality.* New York.

Wiseman, D. J. 1956. *Chronicles of the Chaladean Kings (626–556 B.C.) in the British Museum.* London.

Yadin, Y. 1983. *The Temple Scroll.* 2 vols. Jerusalem.

GERHARD F. HASEL

SABBATH SACRIFICE, SONGS OF THE

(4QShirShabb). See SONGS OF THE SABBATH SACRIFICE.

SABBATICAL YEAR. The term applied to the seventh year in Israel, in which a variety of significant religious and civil events took place.

A. Definitions
B. Fallow Year for the Land
C. Release of Debts or Pledges
D. Release of Slaves
E. Historical Evidence
F. Theological and Ethical Significance

A. Definitions

Strictly speaking, the term "sabbatical year" is only found in Lev 25:2–7, where the expressions "sabbath of rest" and "sabbath to Yahweh" are applied to the seventh year, as the year in which the land is to be left fallow. However this law in Leviticus is clearly an expansion of the simpler and earlier fallow law of Exod 23:10f., and there are other laws concerning what was to take place in that year. Deut 15:1–3 is concerned with the release of debts (or of pledges for debt) in the seventh year. Exod 21:1–6 and the parallel Deut 15:12–18 prescribe the release of Hebrew slaves after seven years. Furthermore, Deut 31:10–13 specifies this year as the time when the whole law was to be read to the whole community. According to Lev 25:8ff., the seventh sabbatical year either was, or was followed by, the year of jubilee in which any land which had been sold was returned to the original owner and any Israelites who had entered slavery as a result of poverty or debt were released to return to their patrimony.

The question of extrabiblical parallels to Israelite sabbatical cycles (both the weekly sabbath and the sabbatical year) is problematic. Attempts to find direct parallels for either in the Babylonian calendars have not been successful. On the other hand, the existence of a seven-year cycle of nature is found in the Ugaritic texts (Gordon 1953). Its purpose was connected with the victory of Baal over Mot, and was to ensure agricultural prosperity. So while it is probably mistaken to think that Israel simply took over their sabbatical institutions from outside (particularly for the weekly sabbath), there are some parallels (particularly for the seventh year) which indicate the close association of religious belief and agricultural practices—an association that is common in all human societies. Certainly we can say that in Israel, as was the case in so many areas of life where it exhibited similarities with the customs of its contemporaries, the theological rationale and the historicizing of the motivation for sabbatical institutions were unique.

Leaving aside the matter of the reading of the law to the whole community in the seventh year, three major aspects of the sabbatical year can be distinguished: legislation concerning land, debt, and slaves. It is thus clearly a primarily socioeconomic institution. The fact that it receives such heavy religious significance as well simply underlines how central was the economic dimension to the faith of Israel. We shall return to this in the paragraphs below on theological and ethical significance. For the sake of clarity, it will be best to deal with each of these three aspects of the year separately.

B. Fallow Year for the Land

1. Exodus 23:10f. This law allows six years of normal agriculture, but in the seventh there was to be no plowing. Whatever grew by itself was treated as common, available to the poor and wild animals. The law applied to vines and olives as well as crops. Coming in the Book of the Covenant (Exodus 21–23), this is the earliest of the OT laws concerning the seventh year and may well reflect very ancient and pre-Israelite custom. Though the text of the law itself does not contain any religious rationale or theological motivation, its inclusion within the Book of the Covenant certainly gives it the same overall orientation as the rest of the law within that corpus. It is seen as part of Israel's wider obligations to Yahweh himself within the framework of their covenant relationship to him. Whatever the precise redactional history of the Book of the Covenant, the laws which were included in it, or its constituent sections, by their incorporation as laws of *Israel,* took on the distinctive religious perspective of all Israel's law and life.

While the religious aspect of the law may be implicit, then (especially in view of the deep religious significance of anything to do with the land and agriculture), the humanitarian or social aspect is quite explicit: The fallow year was to be for the benefit of the poor, meaning specifically those without land of their own. In the seventh year the natural produce of the land was common and free. The humanitarian motive for the law fits it in with its surrounding context: the preceding laws concern judicial integrity and fair treatment of foreigners; the following law prescribes weekly rest for the benefit of the slave and domestic animals.

It may be questioned whether a fallow year once in seven years would be of much real benefit to the poor. What did they eat in the other six years? For this reason, some scholars reckon that this earliest form of the law was not prescribing a universal fallow over the whole land of Israel in a single sabbatical year for all. Rather the law meant that individual farmers must operate their own fallow year on their land, as and when they cultivated it, or in some kind of rotation. While it is certainly possible that this was the meaning of the law in its earliest formulation, the question of how the poor survived for six years need not arise when this sabbatical law is set in the context of other laws concerning assistance for the landless poor (see Mason 1987). There was the annual right of gleaning, in the fields, vineyards, and olive groves (Lev 19:9f.; 23:22; Deut 24:19–22). And there was the triennial tithe which was to be stored and used for distribution to the poor, and was expected to suffice for their "satisfaction," presumably for the intervening two years (Deut 14:28f.). These laws, of course, are in later legal collections than the Book of the Covenant, but it is very probable that they witness to early practices in Israel concerning benefit rights for the landless poor, of which the fallow year was one.

2. Leviticus 25:2–7. When this text is carefully compared with Exod 23:10f., the number of verbal parallels shows that it is obviously dependent on it, and an expansion of it. Several points emerge from the comparison.

Whether or not the law in Exodus was intended as a universal fallow or a seven-year rotation for individual farms, the Leviticus formulation clearly intends a single universal year. "Your land" (Exod 23:10) has become, repeatedly, "the land." The sabbatical year is here more clearly linked to the theology of the land itself.

Two additional phrases, not used in Exodus, intensify the religious aspect of the year: *šabbat šabbātôn* and *šabbat layhwh* (twice). However, it is improbable that this is introducing for the first time a religious rationale. Rather it is making explicit what was always understood. "This sacramental reason . . . might well be the more original one . . . in point of content" (Noth, *Leviticus* OTL). For this reason it is unnecessary to see the religious addition in the text itself as evidence for a late date.

The humanitarian dimension is somewhat modified. Whereas the Exodus law specified the poor in a general sense as the beneficiaries of the fallow year, Leviticus homes in on the domestic world of the slaves, hired workers and resident alien workers (25:6). These would have had primary access to the produce of the fallow ground in the households to which they belonged, without ruling out other groups of landless people. The humanitarian concern for the poor is in any case expressed by other laws within the same legal corpus—i.e., the gleaning rights in Lev 19:9f., and 23:22.

The combination of the religious and the humanitarian can also be seen by comparing the Leviticus law with the immediate context of its Exodus predecessor. In describing the seventh year as a "sabbath to Yahweh," Leviticus is linking it to the sabbath-day law which, in Exod 23:12, immediately follows the fallow-year law. In the decalogue the sabbath day is explicitly referred to as a "sabbath to Yahweh" (Exod 20:10). Thus the seventh year is interpreted in the same way as the seventh day. The land is to enjoy rest after six years of being worked. Interestingly, however, in the Book-of-the-Covenant formulation of the weekly sabbath (just as in its formulation of the seventh year fallow), the religious or theological rationale is taken for granted and it is the humanitarian motivation that is explicit: "so that your ox and donkey may rest and the slave born in your household, and the alien as well, may be refreshed." The same classes of beneficiary are listed in the sabbatical year law in Leviticus (25:6f.), including even the last—the *gēr*, i.e., the non-Israelite, residential laborer. While the sabbatical institutions of Israel were at one level symbolic of their special relationship with Yahweh (the sabbath was a covenant sign), they were not exclusive or narrow in the benefit they gave. The landless alien is included along with the landless Israelite in weekly sabbath rest, septennial access to the fallow produce, as well as his express entitlement to the annual gleaning and the triennial tithe.

C. Release of Debts or Pledges

The opening sentence of the law of release in Deut 15:1–3 undoubtedly picks up the phrasing of the fallow year law in Exodus: "you shall make a release" *(šĕmiṭṭâ);* "you shall release it (i.e., the land)," using the same root verb, in Exod 23:11. In fact, some scholars suggest that the opening sentence of the law in Deuteronomy was an ancient formula in Israel prescribing precisely the fallow year—which Deuteronomy has then expanded in vv 2f. into a law concerning debt. It seems best, therefore, to treat this as a law primarily concerned with debt, i.e., agrarian debt related to the use of the land, rather than linking it with the laws concerning the release of slaves.

If the Deuteronomic *šĕmiṭṭâ* presupposes, then, the fallow year law of the Book of the Covenant, the question arises as to its relation to the sabbatical year law of Leviticus. The common critical source division, of course, assigns Leviticus 25 to the "Holiness Code," or the Priestly compilation (H or P), much later than Deuteronomy. However, it is generally agreed that the sociological date of origin of a law or institution may be quite unrelated to the date of its inclusion in a literary compilation, so that the traditional documentary classification of texts cannot really provide an answer to the question of historical precedence among the laws. (Weinfeld 1972 cites the sabbatical and *šĕmiṭṭâ* laws as examples of his contention that some of the laws in P are earlier than those in Deuteronomy.)

On two grounds it seems arguable that the Deuteronomic *šĕmiṭṭâ* law is the latest of the three. First, the verbal parallels are much closer between Leviticus and Exodus. Secondly, and more important, it is easy to suppose that the Deuteronomic law has simply presupposed the existence of the seventh year fallow, as prescribed in Exodus and Leviticus, but it is very difficult to explain why Leviticus should have omitted reference to the release of debts in the seventh year if the Deuteronomic law had already been in existence. Leviticus 25 is throughout concerned with economic arrangements, including problems of debt and poverty, so that the omission of a sabbatical debt release, if it had existed, would be baffling. It seems to make much better sense to see Deuteronomy as expanding the scope of the original fallow-year law so that it is not only a year when the land is released, but also when humans are released from the burden of debt. And certainly for Deuteronomy, the seventh year is universal (as in Leviticus), and has the same sacred significance (it is "to Yahweh," as in Lev 25:2, 4). But it has recaptured and intensified the humanitarian aspect of the original law.

Several exegetical difficulties face us when we try to ascertain precisely what the *šĕmiṭṭâ* law actually prescribed. These cannot be treated in detail here, but it is a well-argued view (see Horst 1930; North 1954; Weil 1938; Wright 1984) that the law commands the release of *pledges* given for debt, not simply the debt itself. Verse 2 reads *šāmôṭ kol-baʿal maššēh yādô ʾăšer yaššeh bĕrēʿēhû*. Taking *maššeh* as the pledge given in security for a loan, this can be translated, "Every owner of a pledge within his power *(yādô)* shall release what has been pledged to him by his neighbor." A person in debt would offer a pledge to his creditor. This might be some valuable possession, but more likely was a part of his land, or even a dependent person (child, slave), who would be put at the disposal of the creditor. Probably this pledge would function not merely as a security until the debt was paid, but would actually serve to repay it in what is known as an "antichretic" arrangement. That is, the produce of the pledged land, or the labor of the human pledge, would belong to the creditor and serve to pay off the debt. What this law prescribes, then, is that in the seventh year, all such pledged land or persons should be released by the creditor from his control, and returned to the debtor.

Lev 25:25ff. and Neh 5:3–5 show the kind of circumstances in view, and also make it clear that the pledging of dependent *persons* was the last extremity for a debtor, preceded by several stages in which *land* (or vineyards, etc.) would have been mortgaged first. In any period of seven years there would be many more people who had surrendered parts of their landed property to secure loans than had yet begun to hand over children or slaves as pledges. So the *šĕmiṭṭâ* law can be seen as aimed primarily at the release of *land* pledges for agrarian loans. It should not therefore be confused with the laws concerning the release of "Hebrew" slaves, who were sociologically in a quite different category.

The wording of the law leaves open the question of whether it prescribes a complete cancellation of the debt, or a one-year suspension of repayment. Either could be textually justified. Jewish exegesis and practice has always assumed that the law required complete cancellation of debts in the seventh year. As Wacholder (*IDBSup,* 762–63) points out, this would have meant that in Israel loans were never to be treated as business or profit-making transactions, but exclusively a temporary form of assistance to the needy. Hence, in later, developed forms of financial arrangements, ways were found to avoid the sabbatical cancellation in the fixing of loans. Such radical legislation would not be impossible, in the context of the radical nature of other Israelite practices and ideals—such as its astonishing laws concerning slaves (astonishing in the context of established ANE customs). But several considerations point to the possibility that the original law intended a suspension rather than a cancellation.

The wording of the second half of v. 2 is literally "He (i.e., the creditor) shall not *press* his neighbor, his brother, for Yahweh's *šĕmiṭṭâ* has been proclaimed." It could be said that this implies that there was to be no pressing for repayments for the duration of the *šĕmiṭṭâ* itself. That is, the creditor was required to do two things: not to press for any repayments on the loan in that year; to release any pledges back to the debtor, which would mean that the debtor would have the use of his land and the labor of his family or workers—even in a reduced form, since it was a fallow year. Since repayments were probably linked to harvests, this would mean the creditor would receive nothing after whatever was repaid in the sixth year, until the autumn of the eighth year. Thus the impact of a one-year suspension of repayment should not be minimized, either as a relief to the debtor, or as a surrender by the creditor.

A suspension rather than a cancellation would also enable the law to fit more easily with the jubilee arrangements. Of course, as has been pointed out, the relationship between the laws in different sections of the Pentateuch is problematical, and complete harmonization may always elude us. However, it is obvious at least that if all debts were totally cancelled every seven years, and all mortgaged lands returned to debtors, there seems to be little point in a special year of jubilee apparently with the same intention. If, however, the seventh year was a suspension of repayment combined with release of pledged land for that year, the fiftieth year was a year of complete freedom (*dĕrôr*—a word not used in the *šĕmiṭṭâ* context), for families who in the course of two or three generations—even with the assistance of sabbatical and redemption procedures—had been unable to avoid the final consequences of poverty and debt. It was a fresh start, not a temporary respite.

In the end, however, one has to accept the uncertainty and acknowledge that either cancellation or suspension could have been the intention of the law. Either way, it is clear from the law itself and reinforced in the "preaching" which characteristically follows it (4–11), that its dominant motif is humanitarian concern for the impoverished. And this concern has been extended now not only to the landless poor (as in the original fallow), but also to land*owners* threatened by burdens of poverty and debt.

D. Release of Slaves

The laws pertaining to the release of slaves (Exod 21:2–6; Deut 15:12–18) are not, strictly speaking, concerned with the sabbatical year, because they prescribe that slaves were to be freed after six years of service from the time of their purchase or acquisition, not necessarily in a universal seventh year. Some scholars have argued that the freeing took place in the sabbatical year. It has been suggested that they had to be freed in order to attend the great reading of the law in the year of *šĕmiṭṭâ,* as prescribed in Deut 31:10ff. But in view of the explicit inclusion of slaves in the other great cultic occasions of Israel's life, this seems unnecessary. And the natural reading of the law in both Exodus and Deuteronomy is that the slave was to be offered his freedom after six years of service, regardless of what year it was. Nevertheless, the principle of the law—six years of work, then freedom—is clearly "sabbatical," and it may therefore be appropriately included along with the other septennial requirements.

The beneficiary of the law was the "Hebrew" slave. It is widely (though not universally) agreed among scholars that the term "Hebrew" is in some way related to the various forms of *ʿapiru* found in many ANE documents, where it apparently has a social rather than an ethnic meaning. That is, the term is not simply equivalent to Israelite, but denotes a class of people in ancient society. They appear to have been landless, and in some cases "stateless," surviving by selling their services, sometimes as mercenary soldiers or as laborers. They were therefore a dependent class, potentially troublesome, as some extra-biblical texts show, but also vulnerable to exploitation. See also HEBREW; HABIRU, HAPIRU.

The Book of the Covenant sets a limit to that potential exploitation by giving the Hebrew slave the option of freedom after six years of service to one employer. If he took it, he joined the ranks of the *ḥopšîm* (Exod 21:2b; Deut 15:12b), a term also found throughout the ANE to describe a class of people, technically and legally free, but still without land, and therefore needing to hire themselves out as laborers, or settle as tenant farmers. For the Hebrew slave, therefore, release after six years was probably more a change of employment than any significant rise in social status. Not surprisingly, therefore, this may not have been an attractive option. So the law allows for the fact that some Hebrew slaves may prefer to remain in the permanent service of benevolent landowners.

The Deuteronomic development of the law (Deut 15:12–18) is characteristic of its humanitarian ethos. It extends the benefit of the law explicitly to female slaves (who were excluded in the Exodus legislation), and it tries to encourage slaves to take the option of freedom by requiring the owner to provide a substantial endowment of livestock, grain, and wine to the departing slave. Presumably this was not merely a parting gift, but an attempt to help him become economically viable.

Recognizing that the law of seventh-year release applied to Hebrew slaves helps us to understand the significant difference between this pair of laws and the jubilee law concerning release in the fiftieth year. The apparent discrepancy is not to be solved by literary critical manipulation of the texts, nor by arguing that Leviticus is a repeal or a modification of the earlier law. Rather it can be seen that the two laws are directed at two quite distinct groups in society: on the one hand the *landless* "Hebrews," for whom slavery was the only way of life; and on the other hand, Israelite *landowners,* who for various reasons had had to mortgage part or all of their land, but who still retained legal title to it, and could return to it in jubilee (see Ellison 1973; Wright 1984).

E. Historical Evidence

There is no direct reference to a sabbatical year being observed in the OT period itself, but there is plenty of evidence to affirm that it was an ancient institution, and not, as has been thought, a postexilic invention. Deut 31:10 prescribes the reading of the law at the end of the *šĕmiṭṭâ* year. Jer 34:8–16 reports a freeing of Hebrew slaves, which was subsequently revoked. Since this happened in a time of national emergency (the siege of Jerusalem, when all available manpower was needed) it was probably not an actual sabbatical year; but the account shows clearly that the institution, though neglected, was known. Lev 26:34f., 43 includes among its reasons for the exile of Israel their neglect of the land-sabbaths—i.e., the sabbatical years. The predictions that the exile would last seventy years (Jer 25:12; 29:10; cf. Dan 9:2), also seem to presuppose the use of sabbatical cycles. Finally, the terms of the solemn agreement initiated by Nehemiah, with the priests, Levites, and people, included the keeping of the sabbatical year. In Neh 10:32b (—Eng 31b) they undertake to "leave" (the produce, cf. BHS) of the seventh year, and "pledges of the hand" (same phrase as in Deut 15:2). Their promise thus encompasses both the fallow law of Exodus and the *šĕmiṭṭâ* law of Deuteronomy, showing that this is a restoration, not the invention, of sabbatical requirements.

In the post–Old Testament and early Christian eras, there are some explicit references to sabbatical years. These occur in the Maccabean period (163/2 B.C.), at the time of the murder of John Hyrcanus' father (135/4 B.C.), in the reign of Agrippa I (A.D. 41/2), and in the second year of Nero (A.D. 55/6). For these and further details, see Wacholder (1973), who argues that "the sabbatical year remained a living institution in Palestine until the period of the Crusades."

F. Theological and Ethical Significance

In conclusion we may pick out several themes which have been touched on in the above analysis.

1. God's Lordship over Time and History. Israel's sabbatical concept in its different manifestations is related to their view of time as having been created by God and therefore, in a sense, "owned" by him. The seventh day, and the seventh year, being alike "holy to Yahweh," symbolized God's claim on all time, from a creation perspective. But Israel's concept of time was dominated by its awareness of history, and that in turn was shaped by its experience of redemption in history. Thus it is the historical redemption from Egypt which forms the motivation for the weekly sabbath in the Deuteronomic decalogue (Deut 5:15). By its sheer proximity the Exodus dominates the Book of the Covenant, and it is also explicitly used as motivation in the immediate context of the fallow year law (Exod 23:9). The *šĕmiṭṭâ* law and the Hebrew-slave release in Deuteronomy 15 are both commanded on the basis of God's historical generosity in Exodus and the gift of the land. The same motif is present in the sabbatical arrangements of Lev 25:38, 42, 55. As was the case with several other festivals and practices in Israel, whatever extra- or pre-Israelite roots there may have been, the sabbatical institutions of Israel were unique to them in terms of their historicized theological rationale.

2. God's Ownership of the Land. "The land is mine and you are my guests and tenants" (Lev 25:23) is the principle at the heart of the economic arrangements of Leviticus 25. The land was a fundamental part of Israel's faith: included within the promise to Abraham; the explicit objective of the Exodus from Egypt; the focus of the major historical traditions of Israel from Joshua to David. It was the land of divine promise and gift, but also a land still divinely owned. Thus everything to do with the division, tenure, and use of the land was ethically significant because it fell within the mainstream of Israel's covenant relationship with Yahweh. The sabbatical year, therefore, was one among many dimensions of a total economic system that was intended to reflect not only the sovereignty of Yahweh, but also his moral demands (see Wright 1983: chaps. 3 and 4).

3. Humanitarian Ethics. The moral aspect of the institution has already been seen clearly. We noted that whatever religious or sacral meaning attached to fallow years or septennial cycles outside Israel, and even allowing for the implicit religious significance within Israel, the dominant motivation or explanation of the sabbatical arrangements was humanitarian. As in other areas of Israel's life and customs, one fulfilled one's duty to God by practical care for fellow humans—particularly in care for the poor, the vulnerable, and the alien, for they were God's special concern. Much sociological analysis of ancient Israel has demonstrated that not only in principle but also in reality their economic system was geared to the needs of the lowest in society, with the immediate goal of giving maximum assistance to the poor, and the ultimate ideal that there should be no poor (Deuteronomy 15). The sabbatical year fits within this overall framework of ethical objectives.

4. Eschatological Hope. The combination of a sense of time and history with an awareness of ultimate ideals generated a future orientated perspective. At the very least the sabbatical year and the jubilee gave the poorer section of Israelite society something to look forward to—a hope, in a purely economic sense. But beyond that, concepts like rest, release, and (from the jubilee) return and restoration could easily fit metaphorically into the vocabulary of the hoped-for new age of God's unhindered blessing on a perfectly obedient people. Thus we find that future hope in the prophets sometimes draws allusively from the sabbatical milieu (e.g., Isaiah 35, 58, 61).

It is possible that the ministry of John the Baptist coincided deliberately with a sabbatical year (see Wacholder 1975), which would fit both with the radical ethical challenge of his call to repentance and also with the messianic implications of his mission which were traditionally high in sabbatical years. Sabbatical and jubilary influence on the teaching of Jesus is seen in the "Nazareth manifesto" of Luke 4:16–20 and also in his explicit teaching on actual remission of debts (see Sloan 1977). Luke's interest in the eschatology of sabbatical texts is probably reflected in his descriptions of the way the early church in Acts, under the control of the eschatological spirit, voluntarily solved the problem of poverty in itself. His observation in Acts 5:34 that "there was not a needy person among them" is almost certainly an echo of the virtually identical LXX wording of Deut 15:4, which expressed the hope and ideal that underlay the sabbatical law. Finally, Hebrews 4 uses the concept of sabbatical rest (which derives from the sabbatical year, not just the weekly sabbath, since the context has to do with rest in the land particularly), as an eschatological picture of the heritage of God's people that yet awaits those who will enter it by faith and obedience.

Bibliography

David, M. 1948. The Manumission of Slaves under Zedekiah (A Contribution to the Laws about Hebrew Slaves). *OTS* 5: 63–79.

Ellison, H. L. 1973. The Hebrew Slave: A Study in Early Israelite Society. *EvQ* 45: 30–35.

Gordon, C. H. 1953. Sabbatical Cycle or Seasonal Pattern. *Or* n.s. 22: 79–81.

Horst, F. 1930. *Das Privilegrecht Jahves.* Munich.

Kessler, M. 1971. The Law of Manumission in Jeremiah 34. *BZ* 15: 105–8.

Lemche, N. P. 1975. The Hebrew Slave. *VT* 25: 129–44.

———. 1976. The Manumission of Slaves—the Fallow Year—the Sabbatical Year—the Jobel Year. *VT* 26: 38–59.

Mason, J. 1987. Biblical Teaching and Assisting the Poor. *Transformation* 4/2: 1–14.

Neufeld, E. 1958. Socio-Economic Background of *Yōbēl* and *Šᵉmiṭṭā*. *RSO* 33: 53–124.

North, R. 1954. Yâd in the Shemitta-law. *VT* 14: 196–99.

Phillips, A. 1970. *Ancient Israel's Criminal Law.* Oxford.

———. 1973. Some Aspects of Family Law in Pre-exilic Israel. *VT* 23: 349–61.

———. 1984. The Laws of Slavery. *JSOT* 30: 51–66.

Sarna, N. 1973. Zedekiah's Emancipation of Slaves and the Sabbatical Year. Pp. 143–149 in *Orient and Occident,* ed. H. A. Hoffner, Jr. AOAT 22. Kevelaer and Neukirchen-Vluyn.

Siker-Gieseler, J. S. 1981. The Theology of the Sabbath in the Old Testament: A Canonical Approach. *SBT* 2/1: 5–20.

Sloan, R. B., Jr. 1977. *The Favorable Year of the Lord: A Study of Jubilary Theology in the Gospel of Luke.* Austin, TX.

Wacholder, B. Z. 1973. The Calendar of Sabbatical Cycles during the Second Temple and Early Rabbinic Period. *HUCA* 44: 153–96.

———. 1975. Sabbatical Chronomessianism and the Timing of Messianic Movements. *HUCA* 46.

Weil, H. M. 1938. Gage et cautionnement dans la Bible. *Archives d'histoire du droit oriental* 2: 171–241.

Weinfeld, M. 1972. *Deuteronomy and the Deuteronomic School.* Oxford.

Wright, C. J. H. 1983. *An Eye for an Eye.* Downers Grove, IL.

———. 1984a. The Ethical Relevance of Israel as a Society. *Transformation* 1/4.

———. 1984b. What Happened Every Seven Years in Israel? Old Testament Sabbatical Institutions for Land, Debt and Slaves. *EvQ* 56: 129–38, 193–201.

CHRISTOPHER J. H. WRIGHT

SABEANS. There are three references to "Sabeans" in the OT; in each passage the name may refer to a different group of people. In the book of Isaiah, the Sabeans (Heb *sĕbāʾîm*) are identified as a tall race of people (45:14), which probably refers to an African people which Josephus (*Ant* 2.10.2) locates in Nubia (modern Ethiopia; cf. Isa 43:3). See SEBA.

In Joel 3:8, the Sabeans (Heb *šĕbāʾî*) are identified as a far-off nation to whom the Judeans will sell peoples captured from Tyre, Sidon, and Philistia. The reference here is probably to the inhabitants of the S Arabian kingdom of Sheba (modern Yemen). See SHEBA (PERSON); SHEBA, QUEEN OF. It is possible that there is some historical connection between the S Arabian Sabeans and the African Sabeans, the latter originating as a trade colony of the former sometime before the 6th century B.C. See SEBA.

In the book of Job, Sabeans (Heb *šĕbāʾ*) steal Job's oxen and asses and kill some of his servants (1:14–15). The peoples here are a N Arabian group in the vicinity of Tema (Job 6:19), an oasis city which is often associated with Dedan (Isa 21:13–14; Jer 25:23; cf. Gen 10:7 and 25:3). Pope (*Job* AB, 13) suggests that these N Arabian Sabeans are probably the *Saba* mentioned in the inscriptions of Tiglath-pileser III and Sargon II, that memory of them may be preserved in the toponym Wadi esh-Shaba in the vicinity of Medina (200 miles S of Tema), and that these Sabeans should be viewed as distinct from the S Arabian and African Sabeans. However, it is possible that a Sabean presence in the vicinity of Tema and Dedan in N Arabia attests to the expansion of the S Arabian Sabeans N along the major trade route shortly after the middle of the 8th century B.C. See also TEMA; DEDAN.

GARY A. HERION

SABTAH (PERSON) [Heb *sabtâ; sabtāʾ; śabtāʾ*]. A son of Cush (Gen 10:7; 1 Chr 1:9) and hence the name of a tribe or place located somewhere in South (in Gen 10:7 several mss) Arabia or Ethiopia. The attempts to identify the biblical name either with the Ethiopian harbor *Sabat* (Ptolemaios, *Geog.* 4,7.8) or with *Saba* (Strabo, *Geog.* 16,4.8) respectively or even with *Sabai* (Strabo, *Geog.* 16,4.10) at the coast of the Red Sea (see, e.g., Gesenius 1883: 566) or with the place *D̲ū s-Sabtaʾ* at the shore of the Persian Gulf (Glaser 1890: 252–53) are not convincing.

Tuch (1871: 176) was the first to propose identifying it with the capital of Ḥaḍramaut (see HAZARMAVETH), whose name appears in classical sources as *Sabata* (Strabo, *Geog.* 16,4.2 according to Eratosthenes), *Sabbatha* (variant *Sabatha;* Ptolemaios, *Geog.* 6,7.38), *Sabbatha* (variant *Saubatha; Periplus maris Erythraei* 27), and *Sabota* (Pliny, *HN* 6,155; 12,52). In the Old S Arabian inscriptions the name of that town is attested in the form *šbwt,* Shabwat. It has been argued that for phonetic reasons Shabwat cannot be combined with the biblical *sabtāh,* since one would expect in the corresponding Heb form the consonantal sequence *šbwt.* However, it should be mentioned that there are in fact mss variants (of Gen 10:7) with an initial *š* in Hebrew; furthermore, the forms of the LXX (Gk *Sabatha; Sabata*) are identical with the names by which the capital of Ḥiḍramaut is designated in the above-mentioned classical sources.

Shabwat is located at the E border of the desert Ramlat as-Sab'atayn on a hill at the mouth of the Wadi ᶜAṭf, the lower course of the Wadi ᶜIrma. Already in the middle of the 2d millennium B.C. a settlement existed there, and its inhabitants practiced agriculture dependent upon seasonal irrigation by flash floods. In spite of its geographical position in the utmost W part of Ḥaḍramaut, Shabwat became the capital of that ancient kingdom and was, according to the testimony of the classical authors, a center of the incense trade. The frequent mention of Shabwat in Ḥaḍramitic inscriptions found outside of the capital (*hgrhn šbwt;* e.g., RES 4912,1; Khor Rori 1,2; etc.) as well as in Sabean texts reporting on military campaigns (*hgrn šbwt;* e.g., Iryānī 13 §10; Fakhry 75,3; etc.) give evidence to the importance of the town. Beginning in the 5th century A.D. the town began to decay, and the Arabic geographers of the Middle Ages knew on the ruins of the former metropolis only an insignificant place still called Shabwa, a name which has survived to this day. At any rate, the reference to Shabwat (i.e., Sabtah) in the table of nations (Genesis 10) seems to point to an active traffic on the incense road already in the 7th century B.C.

Another less-plausible explanation for Sabtah is the assumption of an old writing error for *sbkh,* i.e., for *Shabako* or *Shabaka* (Gk *Sabakōs*), the name of the first ruler of the 25th ("Ethiopian") Dynasty of Egypt, who reigned about 715–702 and who, like his successor Shebitku (see SABTECA), is supposed to be mentioned among the sons of Cush (see Astour 1965: 422–25; Yurko 1980: 221–40).

Bibliography

Astour, M. 1965. Sabtah and Sabteca: Ethiopian Pharaoh Names in Genesis 10. *JBL* 84: 422–25.

Breton, J.-F. 1987. Shabwa, capitale antique du Ḥaḍramaut. *Journal Asiatique* 275: 13–34.

Gesenius, W. 1883. *Hebräisches und chaldäisches Wörterbuch über das Alte Testament.* 9th ed. Leipzig.

Glaser, E. 1890. *Skizze der Geschichte und Geographie Arabiens.* Vol. 2. Berlin.

Philby, H. St. J. B. 1939. Shabwa. Chap. 4 of *Sheba's Daughters; Being a Record of Travel in Southern Arabia.* London.

Tuch, F. 1871. *Commentar über die Genesis.* 2d ed. Halle.

Wissmann, H. von, and Höfner, M. 1953. Shabwat. Pp. 106–22 in *Beiträge zur historischen Geographie des vorislamischen Südarabien.* Wiesbaden.

Yurko, F. J. 1980. Sennacherib's Third Campaign and the Coregency of Shabaka and Shebitku. *Serapis* 6: 221–40.

W. W. MÜLLER

SABTECA (PERSON) [Heb *sabtĕkāʾ; sabtĕkâ*]. The youngest son of Cush (Gen 10:7; 1 Chr 1:9) and hence the name of a tribe or place located somewhere in S Arabia or Ethiopia. The peculiar enumeration of the five sons of Cush as "Seba and X and Sabtah and Y and *Sabteca,*" however, gives rise to doubts about the correct transmission of the form of the last name in the MT. Bochart (1674: 246) had identified Sabteca with *Samydakē* (Ptolemaios, *Geog.* 6.8.7), a town in Carmania, the present province of Kerman in SE Iran, not far from the mouth of the coastal river Samydakos. For that reason he was even inclined to change the vocalization of the Heb form of the name *Sabtheca* to *Sabithace.* This equation was accepted by other scholars in spite of the fact that it is highly improbable to search for sons of Cush from the table of nations on the NE side of the Persian Gulf.

In connection with the biblical name Sabteca, von Wissmann and Höfner (1953: 109) mention two places named Shabaka and Shubaika in the region of al-Ḥāḍina in Ḥaḍramaut, a journey of two days to the S of the ancient capital Shabwat (see SABTAH), at the W slope of the plateau of the Djōl. These localities are situated on the ancient trade route coming SE from the harbor Qana' via Maifaᶜat and Ḥabbān and then continuing from here N to Shabwat. The names Shabaka and Shubaika are still unattested in the Old S Arabian inscriptions, and the area of these two places has not yet been investigated by archaeologists. It cannot, however, be entirely excluded that Shabaka might be related to Sabteca, all the more since the form of the name in the LXX, *Sabakatha,* corresponds exactly to an ancient *šbkt,* Shabakat. Philby (1939: 338–39) has described the settlements Shubaika and Shabaka as consisting of fort-dwellings scattered among trees; Shabaka belongs to the Ahl Ḥumaiyir which is a diminutive form of Ḥimyar.

Already Glaser (1890: 331) had written that the name of the Ethiopian Pharaoh Shabataka reminds one immediately of the Sabteca in the book of the Genesis. In fact, that biblical name has been compared to Shebitku or Shabataka (Gk *Sebichōs*), the name of the second ruler of the 25th ("Ethiopian") Dynasty of Egypt, who reigned about 702–690 B.C. and who, like his predecessor Shabaka (see SABTAH), perhaps because of his Cushitic name, is supposed to be mentioned among the sons of Cush (see Astour 1965: 422–25; Yurko 1980: 221–40). During the siege of Jerusalem by Sennacherib in 701 B.C., Shebitku was Pharaoh of Egypt to whom the Bible (2 Kgs 18:21; Isa 36:6) refers (his name, however, is not given). As a contemporary of Hezekiah, on the contrary, Shebitku's brother and successor Taharqo or Taharka (Heb *tirhāqâ*) is mentioned by name as "king of Cush" (2 Kgs 19:9; Isa 37:9), who at that time was commander of the Egyptian army in Palestine fighting against the Assyrians.

Bibliography

Astour, M. 1965. Sabtah and Sabteca: Ethiopian Pharaoh Names in Genesis 10. *JBL* 84: 422–25.

Bochart, S. 1674. *Geographia sacra: Pars prior Phaleg.* Frankfurt am Main.

Glaser, E. 1890. *Skizze der Geschichte und Geographie Arabiens.* Vol. 2. Berlin.

Philby, H. St. J. B. 1939. *Sheba's Daughters; Being a Record of Travel in Southern Arabia.* London.

Wissmann, H. von, and Höfner, M. 1953. *Beiträge zur historischen Geographie des vorislamischen Südarabien.* Wiesbaden.

Yurko, F. J. 1980. Sennacherib's Third Campaign and the Coregency of Shabaka and Sehbitku. *Serapis* 6: 221–40.

W. W. MÜLLER

SACHAR (PERSON) [Heb *śākār*]. **1.** According to 1 Chr 11:35 Sachar the Hararite was the father of Ahiam, one of David's mighty men. In the parallel at 2 Sam 23:33 he is called Sharar the Hararite. It is difficult to decide which of the two forms is the more original; the likelihood of confusion of the letters *kap* and *reš* is very great, but it is not possible to tell in which direction the confusion might have gone. It is worth noting that the textual tradition in 1 Chronicles is much more unified than that of 2 Samuel 23 here. In 1 Chr 11:35 Gk B, along with a few mss, reads *achar* while the vast majority of Gk mss have *sachar.* In 2 Sam 23:33 several Heb mss have *šrd* instead of *šrr* while in Gk we find *arad* (A), *sacharō* (Lucianic mss), *arai* (B), *saraia* (MN). For Heb *hărārî* at 1 Chr 11:35, Gk ms S has *sararei,* but the others follow the Hebrew. At 2 Sam 23:33, for Heb *ʾarārî* the majority of Gk mss have *arathuritēs,* with the variants *arareitēs* (A) and *saraoureitēs* (B).

2. At 1 Chr 26:4 Sachar is mentioned as one of the gatekeepers of the temple. He is listed as the fourth son of Obed-edom. 1 Chr 26:15 tells us that in the casting of lots for the assignment of watches in the service of the house of the Lord, the S side fell to Obed-edom, and to his sons the storehouse.

STEPHEN PISANO

SACHIA (PERSON) [Heb *śākĕyâ*]. A Benjaminite, whose father was Shaharaim and mother was Hodesh (1 Chr 8:10). The only occurrence of this name is in a Chronicler's list of Benjaminites. Many mss, supported by the LXX and Targums, read the more common *šibĕyâ* ("captivity" or "captive"). The same root is found in the dubious *śĕkîyâ* (ships?) in Isa 2:16.

TOM WAYNE WILLETT

SACKCLOTH. See DRESS AND ORNAMENTATION.

SACRAL KINGSHIP. An expression used by contemporary scholars to bring into focus the different aspects of the relationship "God–King–People" as it underlies the different monarchic systems of the ANE. "Sacral kingship" is not a biblical term, and its two elements would, at best, have ambiguous equivalents in the ANE. The word "sacred" (from a W Semitic base *qudš-*) had different values at the beginning and the end of the period during which the Hebrew Bible was composed. "Kingship" (Heb *malkût*) had roughly the same meaning in Israel as among the "other nations" when the Israelite monarchy was established (1 Sam 8:5, 20), but under the impact of the prophets its religious connotations changed (Hos 8:4; 13:10–11).

A. Ancient Near East
  1. Mesopotamia
  2. Egypt
B. Monarchic Israel
C. The Desacralization of Sacral Kingship in the Bible
  1. In the Narratives
  2. By the Prophets

A. Ancient Near East

With the development of sedentary civilization in the ANE, trade networks complexified and urbanization fostered social stratification. Kin-based social organizations were no longer fully effective for meeting the increasingly complex demands of urban and political development. Leadership passed on to certain officials responsible for military, economic, and civil administration. The invention of writing at the end of the 4th millennium B.C. gave rise to texts in which can be found the various titles of political leaders. The precise meanings of terms designating civil and political authorities are not always known.

1. Mesopotamia. The head of a Sumerian city in the first half of the 2d millennium B.C. bore the title *ensi.* The Sumerian word can be roughly translated "lord" (CAD 7: 262–65); often, in relation to a god, it can refer to some sort of a *sangû,* "priest" (CAD 7: 263b). Apparently the *ensi* was in charge of the land of the god of the city (Seux 1965). In addition to the *ensi* there was a set of notables, counselors, and sometimes a general assembly (Akk *puḫru*), although there is no indication that lesser dignitaries had the power to vote; they seemed to have gathered to approve the decisions of the "director" (Garelli 1974: 182). In the absence of a system of suffrage, it seems inappropriate to speak of "primitive democracy"; Sumerian society was "democratic" only in the most general sense.

The strength and shrewdness of the *ensi* led him to be called a *lugal,* or "great man" (cf. 1 Sam 10:23). According to the Sumerian King List (*ANET,* 265), Etana, a member of the postdiluvian Kish dynasty, reigned as *lugal;* also, a *lugal* named Lugalzaggizi, king of Uruk, established an empire extending from the Persian Gulf to the Mediterranean Sea.

The Semitic equivalent of Sum *ensi* was *šarru.* At Mari, for example (which was under West Semitic influence), the term was applied not only to the rulers of Mari itself but also to various tribal heads (Anbar 1986). In time, the East Semitic *šarru* would be identified with the West Semitic *malku* (Heb *melek*), but earlier (e.g., at Ebla) there is a lexicographic problem. Even if *malku* (Sum *en*) was not a dynastic "king" but rather appointed for a limited time, he nevertheless ruled as a king (Gregoire 1981: 385), and it was the *lugal* (Akk *šarru*) who acted as an official (cf. Heb *śar;* Charpin and Durand 1986). The word *mlk* prevailed at Ugarit and Phoenicia, and is attested as well in Aramaic and Hebrew documents. Even in Mesopotamia, the word *malku* was used not only for foreign kings but also for the kings of Assyria and Babylonia (CAD 10: 168a), even though it seems to have been associated more with giving counsel and advice than with military activity; indeed, a *māliku* was a counselor (CAD 10: 162b).

In mesopotamian cities a ruler might also be a priest. Rulers bearing the Akk titles *išakku* (Sum *ensi*), *šarru* (Sum *lugal*), and *malku* could receive the Sumerian title of priestly office *sangû.* A priest-king was "pure" or "sacred" (Akk *ellu*) and "august" (Akk *ṣiru;* Seux 1967: 287; van Driel 1969: 80; *AHW* 1163b; *RLA* 6: 169). As such, he was not a cult specialist but rather a possessor of special gifts from the national and dynastic god. From the god he received scepter, crown, throne, and royal staff (*RLA* 6: 167). He also received his name *(nibitu)* from the gods. He might be said to have been created by them, or even fashioned by them in the womb of his mother (Labat 1939: 58). He is not only the "servant" of a divinity (Seux 1967: 360–62), but also "vicar" (*išakku*, very often), messenger, and even "son" of a divinity (*RLA* 6: 170). (These expressions have no precise dogmatic significance; anyone might be said to be a "son" of a god, and the title seems to have become obsolete in the 1st millennium B.C.)

The names of kings of the Akkad dynasty (ca. 2300 B.C.), of the Ur III dynasty, and of some members of the 1st dynasty of Babylon prior to Hammurabi are written in cuneiform with the divine determinative. In plastic representations, kings are sometimes depicted wearing the horned helmet, a symbol of deity. But there were many types of gods in the polytheistic world of Mesopotamia, and the practice of divine determination of royal names disappeared during the 2d millennium B.C. In Ebla, in the Hittite empire, and in the Ugaritic kingdom kings were not deified until after their deaths (Archi 1986: 215; Gurney in Hooke 1958: 115; del Olmo 1987: 48–50; Xella 1981: 288–91; *KTU* 1: 113).

According to what we know about Babylonian cultural influence in the West Semitic area during the 2d millennium B.C., it is not surprising that Ugaritic and Canaanite kingship also exhibited a sacral character. The king, who was "just and fair," participated not only in administrative affairs but also in cultic rites (*DBSup* 9: 1335). Tabnit, king of Sidon, and his father are said to have been "priests of Ashtart" (*KAI* 13: 1–2).

2. Egypt. Canaan and Israel were confronted with another type of sacral kingship, that of pharaonic Egypt. Etymologically, "Pharaoh" (Eg *Pr-ᶜ3*) was an administrative title meaning "great house," the palace where the king (Eg *neswt*) of Upper and Lower Egypt lived. In Egyptian texts, "pharaoh" is not used metonymically of the king before the 1st millennium B.C. The king of Egypt possessed additional names which revealed his relationship with the gods. He is one of the two deities (of Upper and Lower Egypt), the living Horus, the son of Re, and priest in all temples of the country. With respect to Egypt, we can speak not only of sacral kingship but of divine kingship (Frankfort 1948). The teaching of Sehetep-ib-Re (*ANET*, 431) is one of the most eloquent and concise statements on the topic. In Egypt, concepts of the divine were rich and complex (Posener 1960), and any simplistic schematization of divine kingship is vitiated by the evidence. In addition, the relative cultural influence of Mesopotamia and Egypt on Israel is impossible to measure in any comparative sense.

B. Monarchic Israel

Kingship was established in Israel ostensibly according to the pattern found in other nations (1 Sam 8:5–20). The king was the military chief and primary decision maker *(špt)*, enjoying the benefits of the "way of the king" enumerated in 1 Sam 8:10–17 (Mendelsohn 1965). But what can we say about the "sacral" character of the Saul-David-Solomon monarchy?

The institution of human (i.e., political) kingship was understood to have been granted by Yahweh, the god of Israel, who himself had previously been considered Israel's "king" (see Judg 8:22–23), but the prophetic and Deuteronomic redactors of these traditions were not fully favorable toward the institution of kingship. Paying great attention to the fidelity of the biblical authors in the premonarchic Israelite tradition, a number of scholars have denied the "sacral," much less the "divine," character of the Israelite monarchy (Irwin in Frankfort 1948: 337–44; de Fraine 1954; Bernhardt 1961). Others hold that Israelite kingship was sacral in character from the beginning of the monarchy (Mowinckel 1922; 1956; Hooke 1933; Bentzen 1955; Johnson 1955; for complete bibliography, see Cazelles 1984: 1065–66). See also KING AND KINGSHIP. Hooke became gradually more cautious (compare 1958 with 1933), and de Vaux insisted that the data requires a more-balanced resolution of the problem (*AncIsr* 1: 175), concluding that "the king, consecrated by anointment and adopted by YHWH, is a sacred personality and consequently entitled to religious office" (p. 174). The two issues that are important for us to consider are (1) the role the king played in the religious cult according to the historical narratives, and (2) the prophetic and Deuteronomistic response to this role.

The king is the "anointed of the God of Jacob" (2 Sam 23:1) or the one "anointed" by Yahweh. On this concept, see CHRIST; KING AND KINGSHIP. In the ancient Orient, unction is a sign of dependency: an emancipated slave toward his master, a bride toward her father-in-law, a Syrian prince toward the Pharaoh (EA 51: 5–6; cf. Cazelles 1978: 68–71 and notes). The king is "elected" *(bḥr)* by the national God (1 Sam 16:9; cf. 9:15ff.; Ps 78:70). Solomon is called *Jedidiah*, "beloved of YHWH" (2 Sam 12:25), just as Naram-sin was the beloved of Sin, and Rameses II the beloved of Amon. The king is the servant of the national God (2 Sam 7:19; cf. v 5; Pss 18:1—Eng title; 36:1—Eng title; 89:4—Eng v 3; Zech 3:8) as had been the kings of Mesopotamia (Seux 1967: 360–63), the Pharaoh (Eg *hm.f:* his servant), King Keret in Ugarit (*KTU* 1.14 III 49 = *ANET*, 144, line 153), and Azitawadda in Karatepe (*ANET*, 653).

Infrequently in the historical books (2 Sam 7:14), but more clearly in the Psalms (2:7; 89:27–28—Eng vv 26–27; cf. Ps 110:3), the king is considered to be "the son" of God. The Bible, however, has no developed concept of theogamy (as in Egypt; Brunner 1964), nor allusion to suckling by goddesses (as in Ugarit), or fashioning in the womb of the mother (as in Mesopotamia). In the texts of Psalms 2 and 110 the divine sonship of the king is expressed in a context of rites of royal investiture (110:1) and accession (Heb *hayyôm* "today" [Ps 2:7]). This type of sonship has been called an "adoptive" sonship (de Boer 1955); in other words, it is not by birth but by accession to kingship that the king shares the duties of the national God as savior and ruler. He sits at the divine "right hand" (Ps 110:1). He is endowed with supernatural power: not the symbolic crowns as in Egypt (even if he was crowned: 2 Sam 1:10; 2 Kgs 11:22; Jer 13:18) but the Spirit *(ruaḥ)* of YHWH, either directly bestowed (1 Sam 11:6, 14; 2 Sam 23:2) or obtained by the mediation of prophets (1 Sam 10:10; 16:13). Unction in the ancient Orient was a gift of health and strength; *ruaḥ* is life (in a Ugaritic text) and wonderful strength (Samson in Judg 14:6, 19; 15:4).

Although the biblical authors appear to have understood intimations of divine sonship as evidence of a king's legitimacy, it is possible that earlier in the monarchy the official ideology of the royal court construed the metaphor more literally. Pss 2:7 (in its syntax) and 110:3 (in the text itself) disclose a recasting of older sentences. The Anointed of YHWH is a consecrated man. People are forbidden to touch him (1 Sam 24:7, 11; 26:9, 11, 23; 2 Sam 1:14, 16). A woman of Tekoa regards him as a *mal*ʾ*ak* ("messenger," but also "angel") of God (2 Sam 14:17–20). He was recognized as possessing "divine wisdom" (1 Kgs 3:28), and very probably was himself called ʾ*elohîm* ("God") in Ps 45:7–8—Eng vv 6–7 (on this passage, see KING AND KINGSHIP). In Prov 16:10 the sentence given by the king is called an "oracle" (Heb *qesem*). In Lam 4:20 the anointed of YHWH (as in Egypt) is said to be "the breath of life" of the people protected under his shadow. When he is crowned and receives the scepter he receives a new name, and in Isa 9:5 one of those names is ʾ*el gibbôr*, "God hero."

Elected by the national God, the king is mediator between God and his people. He must pray for the people and their welfare (1 Kings 8) and offer holocausts and sacrifices (*šelâmîm*) so as to protect the country from plagues whenever the people (1 Sam 14:33), he himself (2 Sam 24:25), or any of his predecessors (2 Sam 21:14) have sinned. Even if he does not perform the slaughtering himself, he is nevertheless the one who commissions it. This was the role of, for example, Saul at Gilgal (1 Sam 13:9–10), David at Jerusalem after the transfer of the Ark to the new capital (2 Sam 6:13, 18), and Solomon after his accession (1 Kgs 8:5, 62–64) and at the three great feasts of the year (1 Kgs 9:25). He "mounts the steps" of the altar (1 Kgs 12:33; 2 Kgs 16:12), and he blesses the people in the name of the Lord after the installation of the ark (2 Sam 6:18) and the dedication of the Temple (1 Kgs 8:56). David danced before YHWH during the transfer of the ark (2 Sam 6:14).

Like the Pharaoh, an Israelite king builds temples (2 Sam 7:2–3; 1 Kings 6), changes the cultic rules (2 Kgs 16:12–18; cf. 1 Kgs 12:31–33), selects priests (Heb *kōhănîm*) for the cultic service (2 Sam 8:18; 1 Kgs 12:31) and is able to remove them (1 Kgs 2:27). According to Ps 110:4, a king's enthronement invested him not only as king but also as priest (Heb *kōhēn;* priestly titles were likewise given to the kings of Egypt, Mesopotamia, and Phoenicia). Although Psalm 110:4 mentions only a royal priesthood ("after the order of Melchizedek") and not the specific levitical priesthood (as defined in the Pentateuch), the Israelite kings' activities with respect to religious and cultic affairs justify the assumption that they legitimately bore the title "priest." Some scholars (even those who would date Psalm 110 late) still regard the psalm to be more "royal" than "messianic."

C. The Desacralization of Sacred Kingship in Israel

1. In the Narratives. 1 Samuel 8–10 recounts opposition to an Israelite kingship patterned after that of other nations. It is possible that Saul's opponents (1 Sam 10:27) are more politically than religiously motivated. The privileges of the king are described in 8:10–18 as an arbitrary oppression of the people. The bestowal of the divine spirit on Saul produces manifestations similar to those found among the ecstatic prophets (1 Sam 10:10–13).

The long narrative of David's succession is intended to demythologize the king's succession, especially with regard to the sexual potency of the king (1 Kgs 1:1–4; 2 Sam 16:21–22), the value of the king's political wisdom (2 Sam 13:3; 14:2; 15:35; 20:16), and his ability to practice justice (2 Sam 15:3–4). Even the praise of Solomonic wisdom in matters pertaining to judgment, politics, and sacred architecture conclude (1 Kings 11) with sharp criticism.

2. By the Prophets. In biblical narrative are found prophetic interventions against the king: Nathan against David's adultery (2 Samuel 12), Gad against his census (2 Samuel 24), Ahijah of Shiloh against Solomon (1 Kings 11) and afterwards against Jeroboam (1 Kings 14), Shemaiah against Rehoboam's war with Israel (1 Kgs 12:24). The Elijah-Elisha cycles (1 Kings 17–2 Kings 2), even when they retain old features reflecting the sacrosanct quality of kings (1 Kgs 18:46), criticize the decisions made by the kings. The kings are condemned for being unfaithful to YHWH, the national God, and for travesties of justice (e.g., Naboth in 1 Kings 21). In short, kings do not save Israel; the word of YHWH is given to (and by) the *prophets,* who are the only reliable counselors of the kings.

As far as Hosea is concerned, there is no sacral kingship in N Israel. The kings are victims of the court (7:3–7). The Israelites "set up kings without my consent" (8:4). They say: "We have no king because we didn't revere YHWH; but even if we had a king, what could he do for us?" (10:3). And comes the word of God: "Where is your king that he may save you? Where are your rulers in all your towns of whom you said: 'Give me a king and princes'? So in my anger I gave you a king, and in my wrath I took him away" (13:10–11). At the same time, in Bethel, Amos had condemned the "house of Jeroboam" (7:9, 11).

In Judah, the S kingdom, the prophets Micah and Isaiah are less critical of kingship as an institution, largely because of their faith in the election of the house of David, a Bethlehemite and thus a southerner (Mic 5:1; Isa 9:6). But these prophets show no special recognition of the sacral character of kingship. Micah does not apply the title "king" to the ruler coming from Bethlehem. In the text as it stands, Isaiah criticizes the unfaithfulness of Ahaz (Isa 7:13) and the reluctance of Hezekiah to correct the injustices committed by the judges (10:1–4); he also criticizes the stubbornness of the king's "sages" (29:14). A century later Jeremiah not only condemned the sages (Jer 8:8–9) and the government in Jerusalem, as had Micah (Jer 26:17–19; cf. Mic 3:9–12), but also the kings who didn't change (as Hezekiah had done; Jer 22:10–30). The name "YHWH our justice" (23:6) will be no more given to the king but to the city (Jer 33:16).

The Deuteronomic movement further diminished regard for the sacral character of kingship. The law of the king in Deut 17:17–20 subordinates the king, "a brother" (vv 15, 20), to the Law; as such, he is himself subject to the Levites and the prophets. In the Deuteronomistic history (esp. 1–2 Kings) the king is never called "Messiah." In fact, the Davidic promises are made to a "prince" (Heb *nāśî;* Ezek 34:34; 37:25; cf. Ezra 1:8). From the time of Ezekiel on, the "prince" is distinguished from the "priest," and only the latter retains a sacral character.

Bibliography

Anbar, M. 1986. The Kings of the Bini-Yamina Tribes in the Mari Texts. Pp. 13–18 in *IXth World Congress of Jewish Studies (1985).* Jerusalem.
Archi, A. 1986. Die ersten zehn Könige von Ebla. *ZA* 76: 213–17.
Bentzen, A. 1955. *King and Messiah.* London.
Bernhardt, K. H. 1961. *Das Problem der altorientalischen Königsideologie im A.T.* Leiden.
Boer, P. A. H. de. 1955. "Vive le roi!" *VT* 5: 225–31.
Brunner, H. 1964. *Die Geburt des Gottkönigs.* Wiesbaden.
Cazelles, H. 1974. De l'idéologie royale. In *The Gaster Festschrift.* JANES 5. New York.
———. 1978. *Le Messie de la Bible.* Paris and Tournai.
———. 1984. Royauté sacrale. *DBSup* 10: 1056–77.
Charpin, D., and Durand, J. M. 1986. "Fils de Simʾal": les origines tribales des rois de Mari. *RA* 80: 141–83.
Coppens, J. 1954. Les origines du messianisme. Pp. 31–38 in *L'attente du messie.* Paris.
———. 1968. *Le messianisme royal.* LD 54. Paris.
Driel, G. van. 1969. Review of Seux 1967 in *BiOr* 26: 80–81.
Engnell, Y. 1943. *Studies in Divine Kingship.* Oxford.
Fraine, J. de. 1954. *L'aspect religieux de la royauté israélite.* AnBib 3. Rome.
Frankfort, H. 1948. *Kingship and the Gods.* Chicago.
Gadd, C. J. 1948. *Ideas of Divine Rule in the Ancient Near East.* London.
Garelli, P., ed. 1974. *Le palais et la royauté.* XIXe Rencontre assyriologique internationale. Paris.
Gregoire, J. M. 1981. Remarques sur quelques nomes de fonction et sur l'organisation administrative dans le royaume d'Ebla. Pp. 383–99 in *La Lingua di Ebla,* ed. L. Cagni. Naples.
Hooke, S. G., ed. 1933. *Myth and Ritual.* Oxford.
———. 1958. *Myth, Kingship and Ritual.* Oxford.
Johnson, A. 1955. *Sacral Kingship in Israel.* Cardiff.
Klausner, J. 1955. *The Messianic Idea in Israel.* New York.
Labat, R. 1939. *Le caractère religieux de la royauté assyrobabylonie.* Paris.
Mendelsohn, I. 1965. Samuel's Denunciation of Kingship in the Light of the Akkadian Documents from Ugarit. *BASOR* 143: 17–22.
Mowinckel, S. 1922. *Psalmenstudien.* 6 vols. Amsterdam.
———. 1956. *He That Cometh.* Trans. G. W. Anderson. Oxford.
Olmo Lete, G. del. 1987. Los nombres "divinos" de los reyes de Ugarit. *AulaOr* 5: 39–70.
Pettazoni, R., ed. 1957. *La regalitá sacra.* Leiden.
Posener, G. 1960. *De la divinité du Pharaon.* Paris.
Seux, M. J. 1965. Remarques sur le titre royal assyrien *iššakki Aššur.* *RA* 19: 101–9.
———. 1967. *Epithetes royales akkadiens et sumériennes.* Paris.
Talmon, S. 1986. *King, Cult and Calendar.* Leiden.
Widengren, G. 1955. *Sacrales Königtum im Alten Testament und in Judentum.* Stuttgart.
Xella, P. 1981. *I testi rituali di Ugarit.* Vol. 1, *Testi.* SS 54. Rome.
Zandee, J. 1971. Le Messie: Conception de la royauté dans les religions du Proche Orient ancien. *RHR* 180: 3–28.

HENRI CAZELLES

SACRED MARRIAGE.

The term "sacred marriage" is a translation of the Gk term *hieros gamos,* which originally referred to the marriage between Zeus and Hera. It is nowadays applied to marriage or sexual union between a god and a goddess, in ancient or primitive religions, an act which is usually connected with some form of fertility cult. The present discussion will include the phenomenon of sacred marriage in ancient Mesopotamian religions, and the question of whether or not it was consummated between a god and a goddess, or between a human pair representing a god and a goddess, having some form of relation to the cult.

A. The Sacred Marriage Rite in Sumerian Religion
 1. Sources
 2. Origins
 3. The Nature and History of the Ritual
 4. Frequency and Purpose of the Ritual
 5. Vestiges of the Cult of Dumuzi in the Post-Sumerian Period
B. The Sacred Marriage Rite in Babylonian and Assyrian Religion
 1. Nature and Origins
 2. Allusions to the Sacred Marriage in the 2d Millennium B.C.E.
 3. Allusions to the Sacred Marriage in the 1st Millennium B.C.E.
C. Other Fertility Cults in the Ancient Near East

A. The Sacred Marriage Rite in Sumerian Religion (ca. 2700–1800 B.C.E.)

1. Sources. The sacred marriage rite in Sumerian religion and mythology almost exclusively revolves around the goddess Inanna (Akk *Ištar;* Semitic *ʿAṯtar;* Heb *ʿAštōret*) and her divine spouse Dumuzi (Akk *Duʾūzu;* Heb *Tammūz*). Information as to the relationship between these two deities is furnished mainly by three groups of literary sources: (1) cultic love-songs and royal hymns, describing the love, courtship, and marriage between Dumuzi and Inanna; (2) Sumerian (and some Akkadian) mythological compositions, describing Dumuzi's rejection by Inanna, his death and descent to the netherworld; and (3) dirges and laments bewailing Dumuzi's tragic death. For the reconstruction of the sacred marriage rite, it is the love-songs and the royal hymns which provide the most pertinent information (Sefati 1985).

2. Origins. Direct evidence for the sacred marriage in Sumer can be found only in the Ur III and Old Babylonian (OB) literary texts. Sumerian epic literature, however, attributes statements concerning the performance of the sacred marriage rite with Inanna, already to Enmerkar, the second king of the First Dynasty of Erech (Berlin 1979: 40, 58). Furthermore, the god Dumuzi, who is the central male figure in the sacred marriage rite, seems to be either the deified shepherd-king Dumuzi who, according to the Sumerian King List, ruled over Bad-Tibira, in the Early Dynastic (ED) period, or the deified fisherman, his namesake, who ruled over Erech three generations after Enmerkar (or perhaps a mixture of these two ancient royal figures; cf. Heimpel 1972: 290–91). Hence, it is quite possible that the sacred marriage rite originated in ED (or even prehistoric) Uruk, where it was customary for the priestly-king (EN) to marry the city-goddess, Inanna, the Sumerian goddess of love and fertility. However, it is not clear whether the sacred marriage, in this early period, was consummated only symbolically or, as in later periods, was performed carnally with a priestess representing the goddess (Falkenstein 1954: 41–45; Kramer 1969a: 57–62; *RLA* 4: 257–58). Later, in Sumerian mythology, Dumuzi was identified with the god Amaushumgalanna, becoming a fertility god, conceived as the power of growth in vegetation and animal life (cf. Jacobsen 1970: 74–82), and his human origin was forgotten (or ignored). However, several facts still attest to his origin: throughout the history of Sumerian religion, Dumuzi appears as a passive, minor deity, a shepherd-king always inferior to his mate, Inanna, who chose him to be her husband. Furthermore, all the kings of the Third Dynasty of Ur and the Isin Dynasty impersonate him in the sacred marriage rite. Finally, in contrast to his central role in the literary sources related to the sacred marriage, his actual worship in Sumerian cult was rather limited; and by the late 2d millennium, his role in the sacred marriage rite was altogether forgotten (see below). His female counterpart, Inanna/Ishtar, on the other hand, not only kept her prominent position in the Mesopotamian pantheon but, toward the 1st millennium, was even promoted to the status of the divine consort of An, the heaven god, in Uruk; whereas in Babylon she became the mistress of the chief god, Marduk, with her cult having spread to many important Mesopotamian religious centers.

3. The Nature and History of the Ritual. In the Ur III and Early OB periods (ca. 2100–1800 B.C.E.), the performance of the sacred marriage was a royal prerogative: throughout these periods, the king used to represent Dumuzi/Amaushumgalanna in the sacred marriage rite. To the king's central role in this rite attest not only the numerous references in the royal inscriptions and royal hymns to him as the "beloved spouse of Inanna" (Hallo 1957: 140–41; Römer 1965: 147–48; Klein 1981: 49 n. 112); but also a number of royal hymns, devoted wholly or partly to the description of the sacred marriage ceremony (see below). Furthermore, some Dumuzi laments list the Ur III and Isin kings as Dumuzi figures, beside other deities of Inanna's circle (Jacobsen 1975: 67, 90–93).

The identity of the female partner in the sacred marriage rite is still a mystery, although it is generally assumed that she was a priestess (cf. Bottéro 1983: 215). The possible candidates could be the NU-GIG (hierodule), the LUKUR (concubine, *RLA* 4: 256), the NIN-DINGIR ("the divine lady," Hallo 1987: 49), or the EN (high priestess, Frayne 1985: 12–22). Since the female partner in the sacred marriage rite is consistently referred to as the goddess Inanna, it is not impossible that the goddess in the sacred marriage rite was represented merely by her statue, and the whole ceremony was performed only symbolically. According to the Old and Neo-Sumerian Lagash inscriptions, this particular form of sacred marriage was not celebrated in Lagash. Hence, it may be assumed that the kings of the Third Dynasty of Ur, and most probably Shulgi himself (ca. 2094–2047 B.C.E.), borrowed this cultic practice directly from the Uruk tradition, among other religious and political ideas and institutions. The Ur III kings apparently celebrated their sacred marriage with Inanna in Uruk, the original cult center of the goddess. This follows from a Shulgi hymn, describing the pilgrimage of the king to Inanna of Uruk, perhaps on the occasion of his coronation. Inanna, upon seeing Shulgi dressed in his ceremonial priestly garment and carrying with him sacrificial animals, utters a sumptuous love song, in which she recalls or anticipates the physical pleasures of her sacred union with the king, and subsequently blesses him (lit. "decrees his fate"). In her blessing, she promises him support in battle and administration, and declares him suitable for all prerogatives of kingship (cf. van Dijk 1954: 83–88; Klein 1981: 124–66). In another Shulgi hymn, Inanna complains about the total absence of vegetation, whereupon Shulgi invites her to his fields, gardens, and orchards, to fructify them in some way (cf. Kramer 1969b: 18–23). Another Ur III king who is the subject of three love-dialogues (Sum BAL-BAL-E) is Shusin, the grandson of Shulgi (*ANET*, 496; Kramer 1969a: 92–95). Although the female protagonists in these love songs are LUKUR-priestesses, according to their subscripts· these hymns are dedicated to the goddesses Inanna and Baba of Lagash. Hence, no doubt, these hymns were sung in the sacred marriage rite. As to the kings of the Isin Dynasty, these seem to have celebrated the sacred marriage in their capital with a priestess representing the city-goddess Ninisinna, whom they identified with Inanna. This follows from a royal hymn, which gives a detailed description of the sacred union between king Iddindagan (ca. 1974–1954 B.C.E.) and Inanna-Ninisinna on New Year's day. The New Year celebrations in Isin, according to this hymn, involved the following major events: various priests and cultic personnel pass before Inanna and pay homage to her; the cult-places and the roofs are purified; incense is burned, and animal and food offerings are presented there (probably at night, when the goddess is visible as the Venus star); a bed is set up for the goddess and she bathes for the ritual; the king goes to the goddess and they unite on the bed. After the sacred union the people enter the Egalmaḫ temple with their incense and food offerings, and the ceremony ends with a joyful banquet, sponsored by the king in honor of the goddess (Römer 1965: 128–49; Reisman 1973: 185–97). The only other Isin king who is referred to in a fertility prayer, dedicated to Inanna, is Ishmedagan (ca. 1953–1935 B.C.E.). In this prayer, Inanna is asked to bless the stalls and sheepfolds with fertility and abundance for the sake of the king, as well as to grant the king, her spouse, a long life. A duplicate of this prayer substitutes the name of Dumuzi-Amaushumgalanna for Ishmedagan, which shows that the same hymn could be used in connection with a number of kings who represented Dumuzi in the sacred marriage (Römer 1965: 21–22; Hallo 1966: 244–45). In another royal hymn, dedicated to an anonymous king, Ninshubur, Inanna's maiden, leads the royal bridegroom to Inanna's bosom and he requests the goddess to bless him with long life, a stable kingship, and fertility for his land (Kramer 1963: 501–3; 1969a: 81–84; *ANET*, 640–41). From these and other Dumuzi-Inanna love songs, we can reconstruct an approximate procedure for the Neo-Sumerian sacred marriage rite: priests and other cultic personnel (such as, e.g., transvestites and musicians) pass and do homage before Inanna, and offerings and gifts for the (later) banquet are brought. A (canopied) dais is erected for the goddess in the temple (more specifically in the *giparu*, an ancient storehouse, which later became the residence of the high priestess), and a bed, covered with halfa grass and other greenery is set up for her therein. Inanna then bathes and anoints herself. The king, impersonating Dumuzi/Amaushumgalanna, is led to her dais or chamber, carrying with him customary marriage gifts (NÍG-MU$_{10}$-ÚS-SÁ). Inanna opens the door for him, he enters, and the holy nuptials take place. Thereafter, the goddess decrees a good fate for the king and the land. The ceremony ends with a banquet, wherein the king and the goddess sit together, and the goddess is celebrated in hymns accompanied with sacred music.

4. Frequency and Purpose of the Ritual. Earlier it was generally held that the sacred marriage was celebrated in Sumer annually, during the New Year festival, and its primary purpose was to guarantee abundance and fertility in nature and human society for the coming year. According to this hypothesis, the divine pair itself became the power of fertility in nature, and the sexual union between them was believed to have produced new life and prosperity everywhere (cf. Labat 1939: 163–65, 247–49; Frankfort 1948: 286–99; Kramer 1969a: 49–84). This hypothesis has been recently questioned on the grounds that, apart from the Inanna-Iddindagan hymn from Isin, no source mentions New Year's eve as the date of the ritual, and the blessings put in the mouth of the goddess in the various sources include not only the fertility theme, but also the themes of long life and a firm reign for the royal bridegroom. Accordingly, some scholars assume that the main purpose of the sacred marriage rite was the legitimation and deification of the Sumerian king, and hence the ritual took place usually on the day of his coronation (*RLA* 4: 256–57). Still another opinion holds that at least on the real (if not the symbolic) level, the sacred marriage in its classical phase served to engender the crown prince, who thereby was assured of divine parentage (J. Klein in Durand, ed. 1987: 97–106). According to a recent hypothesis, the sacred marriage was consummated between the king, in his role as an EN-priest, and an EN-priestess of Inanna, both of whom impersonated the divine couple of the Sumerian city. The occasion for the celebration of the ritual, according to this opinion, was the installation of the priestess in her office, and its main purpose was the promotion of fertility (Frayne 1985: 12–22). In conclusion, it should be pointed out that the overwhelming stress and main concern, both of the Dumuzi-Inanna love songs and the Dumuzi laments, is the theme of fertility. Accordingly, the main purpose of the sacred marriage rite in Sumerian religion must have been to assure fertility for the land. Since the only date ever alluded to in the literary texts dealing with this ritual is New Year's day, it is this date on which this ritual most probably took place.

5. Vestiges of the Cult of Dumuzi in the Post-Sumerian Period. Up to the OB period, Dumuzi had two temples where he was worshipped as a minor deity: one in Girsu and another in Bad-tibira. Surprisingly, there is no indication that the sacred marriage rite was practiced in any of these two cultic centers. The sources point only to Uruk and Isin, as the loci, where this rite was performed. After the OB period (i.e., from ca. 1800 B.C.E. to 100 C.E.) the Dumuzi-Inanna sacred marriage rite was apparently abandoned, and Dumuzi lost the character of the young bridegroom and god of fertility, in parallel to the decline of the institution of divine kingship. From now on, Dumuzi is only Inanna's tragic husband, killed and carried down to the netherworld by its "bailiffs," as a substitute for the goddess (for this motif, see the epilogue of "Ishtar's Descent to the Netherworld"; *ANET:* 52–57). Whereas Dumuzi's official cult fell into oblivion, his death continued to be mourned annually in the fourth month (i.e., the month of Duʾūzu/Tammuz), or in the fifth month, throughout the 2d and 1st millennia. The absence of any temples of Dumuzi in this period, as well as Ezekiel's reference to the "women bewailing Tammuz" in the Temple (Ezek 8:14), suggest that in the late periods the mourning of Dumuzi/Tammuz was an unofficial, popular cult practiced mainly by women and perhaps also by GALA-cantors (Kutscher 1990: 41–44).

B. The Sacred Marriage Rite in Babylonian and Assyrian Religion (ca. 1800 B.C.E.–100 C.E.)

1. Nature and Origins. Parallel to the Dumuzi-Inanna type of sacred marriage, there seems to have existed another type of sacred marriage in Sumer, namely one which was conceived as having taken place between deities only, and did not involve human protagonists. This type of ritual seems to have been practiced already in the cult of Lagash, since its ruler, Gudea (ca. 2143–2124 B.C.E.), refers in his inscriptions to customary "marriage gifts" (NÍG-MU$_{10}$-ÚS-SÁ), presented on "New Year's day during the Festival of Baba," (Stat E 5:1–6:4; G 5:5–6:19; cf. Lambert and Tournay 1952: 82–83). Similarly, the Ḫendursanga Hymn praises Nindara of Lagash for presenting the "marriage gifts" to his wife Nanshe "every New Moon and New Year's day" in her temple (cf. Edzard and Wilcke 1976: 144–47). This type of sacred marriage was presumably performed in a symbolical way, such as, e.g., by bringing the god's statue into the "bedchamber" of the goddess. It was probably practiced in other cultic centers also, from times immemorial, ever since the gods were thought of as anthropomorphic figures, and its purpose was likewise to secure prosperity and fertility for the land during the ensuing year. It is this type of sacred marriage that survived and continued to be practiced after the Isin-Larsa period, when the Dumuzi-Inanna type of sacred marriage was totally abandoned.

2. Allusions to the Sacred Marriage in the 2d Millennium B.C.E. The only source explicitly dealing with the sacred marriage (Akk *ḫašādu*) in the OB period, is a divine love-song from the time of Abiešuḫ, king of Babylon (ca. 1711–1684 B.C.E.). It contains a love dialogue between Nanaya of Babylon/Uruk and her lover, Mu'ati (a divine figure of the Tammuz type), in which Nanaya is requested to bless king Abiešuḫ with a long life. The poem also quotes the actual blessing, which the goddess granted the king and his city, Babylon (Lambert 1966: 12–41). An entirely different source which also seems to be related to the sacred marriage, is a Middle Babylonian ritual text from Emar (modern Meskene, a recently excavated Syrian city), which describes the consecration of an *entu* priestess to the storm god, Ishkur. During the ceremony, the priestess is given a bridal hairdo and lies down on a bed, which indicates that we are dealing here with her marriage to the deity (Arnaud 1986: 1.100–101; 1986: 3.326–27). This unique ritual, attested in a West Semitic milieu, recalls the relationship of the *entu*-priestess of Ur to the moon god Nanna, during the Old and Neo-Sumerian periods.

3. Allusions to the Sacred Marriage in the 1st Millennium B.C.E. There is a Neo-Assyrian catalogue, from the beginning of the 1st millennium, furnishing the incipits of about 275 Sumerian and Akkadian love songs, divided into a number of groups, with each group provided with a generic subscript. Two groups of these incipits, subsumed under the generic terms *rēʾî rēʾî* ("My Shepherd, My Shepherd") and *māruma rāʾimni* ("The Little One, Our Lover"), are explicitly concerned with love between Ishtar and "the shepherd" Dumuzi. However, it is not clear what purpose these Akkadian songs served, and hitherto only one of them, entitled "Come in, Shepherd, Ishtar's Lover!" was found inscribed on a tablet, dated approximately to the Middle Babylonian period. In this poem, which resembles the earlier Sumerian Dumuzi-Inanna songs, Ishtar invites Dumuzi to spend the night with her in her parents' house, and later she visits Dumuzi in his sheepfold (Black 1983; cf. Loretz 1964: 191–203). Sporadic references to actual practices of sacred marriage within the temple cult in this period can be found mainly in ritual texts and texts of historical nature. These references, however, are usually laconic and quite obscure. There are direct and indirect references in Neo-Assyrian texts to a periodical sacred marriage between Nabu (the tutelary deity of Borsippa) and his spouse Tashmetu, on the third day of Addaru. There is also a liturgical calendar, which describes how Nabu, "in status of a bridegroom (Akk *ša ḫadaššūtu*)," was led to Nanaya of Babylon, his divine mistress, in order to perform with her a six-day sacred-marriage ritual. As to the sacred marriage between Marduk and Ṣarpanitu, Ashurbanipal, king of Ashur, tells in one of his inscriptions that during his restoration of Babylon he fashioned a luxurious bed for Bel and Beltiya, "to perform (their) marriage and make love," and that this bed was set up in the Kaḫilisu, the residence of Ṣarpanitu (Matsushima 1988: 99–100). From another text describing the material and the size of this bed we learn that, during the sacred marriage, the goddess was expected to intercede for the king, her protégé, before her husband, and the divine couple was expected to bless the king with long life and firm kingship (Matsushima 1988: 107–108). A most peculiar source, connected only indirectly with the sacred marriage rite, is a late ritual-tablet of Ishtar of Babylon, containing a liturgical "Love Song," which was used in the context of "rites against a rival mistress" (Akk *qinayyātu;* cf. Lambert 1975a). It contains a discourse between Marduk, his wife Ṣarpanitu, and his mistress-lover Ishtar of Babylon, with whom Marduk makes love and betrays his "lawful" wife (cf. Edzard 1987). Finally, there are ritual texts from Uruk, from the Seleucid period (Thureau-Dangin 1921: 61–125) which describe, among others, the New Year festival *(akitu)* during the first eleven days of Tishre. These texts indicate that the "sacred marriage rites" (Akk *parṣē ḫašādu*), whose main protagonists were Anu and his wife Antum, were an integral part of the *Akitu*/New Year festival of Tishre (for further details as to the sacred marriage rite according to Akkadian sources, see Matsushima 1985; 1987; 1988).

C. Other Fertility Cults in the Ancient Near East

Some students of religion and anthropology believe that there was a common fertility cult in the ANE which included (1) the worship of a Great Mother goddess, who was the personification of fertility, and (2) the worship of a young god, her spouse, who was believed to have died and resurrected, embodying the yearly growth of vegetation, which whithers away in the summer and reappears again in the winter or in springtime. These mythological beliefs and cultic practices were assumed to have been shared by all peoples of the ANE, with local variations of minor importance, and traces of them were deemed to be found in the Bible. According to this theory, the dying god Dumuzi/Tammuz, who is lamented by his spouse Inanna/Ishtar, and semiannually resurrects, is to be identified with the Syrian Adonis, the Egyptian Osiris, and the Ugaritic Baal (cf. Pope in *IDB* 2: 265). Recent scholarship, however, based on a more sound philological approach and a more careful methodology, rejects these identifications as superficial and misleading. It is becoming evident that the ancient cultures and religions do not follow a common pattern, as it was formerly assumed, but greatly differ from each other. In any case, it is not clear whether the Mesopotamian Ishtar can be characterized as a "mother goddess"; and since the Dumuzi/Inanna type of fertility cult was abandoned after 1800 B.C.E., this cult could not have exerted any significant influence on Western or biblical religion. Accordingly, careful distinction should be drawn between Mesopotamian fertility cult on the one hand, and seemingly similar cultic phenomena in other ANE cultures (cf. *RLA* 4: 253–55).

Bibliography

Arnaud, D. 1986. *Textes sumeriens et accadiens.* 3 vols. EMAR 6/4. Paris.

Berlin, A. 1979. *Enmerkar and Ensuhkešdanna.* Philadelphia.

Black, J. A. 1983. Babylonian Ballads: a New Genre. *JAOS* 103: 25–34.

Bottéro, J. 1983. La hierogamie après l'époque sumérienne. Pp. 175–214 in Kramer 1983.

Buren, E. D. van. 1944. The Sacred Marriage in Early Times in Mesopotamia. *Or* 13: 1–72.

Dijk, J. J. A. van. 1954. Le fête du nouvel an dans un texte de Šulgi. *BiOr* 11: 83–88.

———. 1964. Le motif cosmique dans la pensée sumérienne. *AcOr* 28: 1–59.

Durand, J.-M., ed. 1987. *La femme dans le Proche Orient.* Paris.

Edzard, D. O. 1987. Zur Ritualtafel der sog. "Love Lyrics." Pp. 57–69 in *Languages, Literature and History,* ed. F. Rochberg-Halton. AOS 67. New Haven.

Edzard, D. O., and Wilcke, C. 1976. Die Hendursanga-hymne. Pp. 139–76 in *Kramer Anniversary Volume,* ed. B. Eichler. Kevelaer.

Falkenstein, A. 1954. Tammuz. *CRRA* 3: 41–67.

Frankfort, H. 1948. *Kingship and the Gods.* Chicago.

Frayne, D. R. 1985. Notes on the Sacred Marriage Rite. *BiOr* 42: 5–22.

Hallo, W. W. 1957. *Early Mesopotamian Royal Titles.* New Haven.

———. 1966. New Hymns to the King of Isin. *BiOr* 23: 239–47.

———. 1987. The Birth of Kings. Pp. 45–52 in *Love and Death in the Ancient Near East,* ed. J. H. Marks and A. M. Good. New Haven.

Heimpel, W. 1972. Review of *The Sacred Marriage Rite,* by S. N. Kramer. *JAOS* 92: 288–91.

Jacobsen, T. 1970. *Toward the Image of Tammuz and other Essays on Mesopotamian History and Culture.* Cambridge, MA.

———. 1975. Religious Drama in Ancient Mesopotamia. Pp. 65–77 in *Unity and Diversity*, ed. H. Goedicke and J. J. M. Roberts. Baltimore.
Klein, J. 1981. *Three Šulgi Hymns.* Ramat-Gan.
Kramer, S. N. 1963. Cuneiform Studies and the History of Literature: The Sumerian Sacred Marriage Texts. *PAPS* 107: 485–527.
———. 1969a. *The Sacred Marriage Rite.* Bloomington.
———. 1969b. Inanna and Šulgi: A Sumerian Fertility Song. *Iraq* 31: 18–23.
———. 1983. *La mariage sacré à Babylone.* Paris.
Kutscher, R. 1990. The Cult of Dumuzi/Tammuz. Ramat-Gan.
Labat, R. 1939. *La caractère religieux de la royauté assyro-babylonienne.* Paris.
Lambert, M., and Tournay, J.-R. 1952. Les statues D, G, E et H de Gudéa. *RA* 46: 75–86.
Lambert, W. G. 1966. Divine Love Lyrics from the Reign of Abi-ešuh. *MIO* 12: 41–56.
———. 1975a. The Problem of the Love Lyrics. Pp. 98–135 in *Unity and Diversity,* ed. H. Goedicke and J. J. M. Roberts. Baltimore.
———. 1975b. The Cult of Ištar of Babylon. *CRRA* 17: 104–6.
Loretz, O. 1964. Zum Problem des Eros in Hohenlied. *BZ* 8: 191–216.
Matsushima, E. 1985. Le lit de Šamaš et le rituel du mariage à l'Ebabbar. *AcSum* 7: 129–37.
———. 1987. Le rituel hiérogammique de Nabû. *AcSum* 9: 131–75.
———. 1988. Les rituels du mariage divin dans le documents Accadiens. *AcSum* 10: 95–128.
Meek, T. J. 1924. Babylonian Parallels to the Song of Songs. *JBL* 43: 245–52.
Moortgat, A. 1949. *Tammuz: Der Unsterblichkeitsglaube in der altorientalischen Bildkunst.* Berlin.
Reisman, D. 1973. Iddin-Dagan's Sacred Marriage Hymn. *JCS* 25: 185–202.
Römer, W. H. P. 1965. *Sumerische "Königshymnen" der Isin-Zeit.* Leiden.
Sefati, Y. 1985. *Love Songs in Sumerian Literature: Critical Edition of the Dumuzi-Inanna Songs.* Diss. Bar-Ilan (in Hebrew).
Thureau-Dangin, F. 1921. *Rituels Accadiens.* Paris.

Jacob Klein

SACRED MEALS (GRECO-ROMAN).

See MEAL CUSTOMS (GRECO-ROMAN SACRED MEALS).

SACRED STONE. The "sacred stone which fell from the sky" (Acts 19:35) was an object of worship in the temple of Artemis at Ephesus. The Greek is one word, *diopetēs,* lit. "fallen from the sky," and the meaning of the passage is therefore somewhat obscure. It probably refers to a meteorite to which the Ephesian worshippers of Artemis attached significance and which they worshipped in their temple.

Although no ancient source mentions such a meteor in the Artemis temple at Ephesus (Munck *Acts* AB, 196), meteorites were often venerated by the Greeks and Romans. A meteorite which had been brought to Rome from Pessinus was worshipped as a symbol of the Great Mother, Cybele (Lake and Cadbury 1979: 250), and a meteorite called the Palladium was venerated at Troy (ibid.). Meteorites are attested as part of the Artemis cult itself, as one was present in the temple of Artemis at Tauris (Eur. *IT* 87, 1384).

The reference in Acts 19 is in the speech of the "town clerk" of Ephesus in his calming of a crowd which threatens to riot against Paul. The clerk argues that Paul is not offending Artemis when he denounces images "made with hands" (Acts 19:26). As a meteorite, the Artemis sacred stone was not man-made, but could claim superhuman workmanship (Williams *Acts* BHNTC, 224). In addition, the meteor need not have been viewed as an *image* of Artemis; the meteorite in the temple of Cybele at Rome was actually a quite small stone (Gk *baitylos;* Lake and Cadbury 1979: 250).

Bibliography

Lake, K., and Cadbury, H. J. 1979. *Commentary.* Vol. 4 of *The Acts of the Apostles,* ed. F. J. Foakes Jackson and K. Lake. Beginnings of Christianity 1. Grand Rapids.

Robert D. Miller II

SACRIFICE AND SACRIFICIAL OFFERINGS. This entry consists of two articles: the first surveys the Israelite practices of sacrificial offerings as outlined in the OT, and the second focuses upon how those sacrificial practices were understood and adapted in the NT writings.

OLD TESTAMENT

The main biblical references to cultic sacrifice are found in the Priestly (P) section of the Pentateuch, especially in Leviticus and Numbers. This cultic practice was also the subject of harsh prophetic critique.

A. The Problem of Sacrifice
  1. General Concerns
  2. Social Science Explanations
  3. Social Science and Biblical Scholarship
  4. Biblical Sacrifice as Cultic Realia or Textual Phenomenon
B. Sacrifice and Offering: Some Basic Distinctions
C. Development of Terminology
  1. The Problem of P
  2. The Development of Cultic Vocabulary
D. Sacrifice in P
  1. The Animals
  2. The Technique of Sacrifice
  3. Literary Genres in P
  4. The Basic Types of Animal Sacrifice
    a. Burnt Offering *(ʿôlâ)*
    b. Peace Offering *(šĕlāmîm)*
    c. Purification Offering *(ḥaṭṭāʾt)*
    d. Reparation Offering *(ʾāšam)*
E. Prophetic Critique
F. The Scripturalization of the Cult
  1. Biblical Sacrifice in the Second Temple Period
  2. Example: The Interpretation of the Purification Offering in Second Temple Jewish Sources
  3. The Sacrificial System in Canonical Perspective
  4. Biblical Sacrifice in Jewish and Christian Tradition

A. The Problem of Sacrifice

1. General Concerns. The concept of sacrifice is at the root of both Christian and Jewish tradition. Though neither religion practices animal sacrifice any longer, the legacy of those practices perdures. Yet this legacy is not always so easy to understand, for the two traditions have been both attracted to and repelled by the image of slain animals being offered up within the sacred precincts of the holy temple. There is perhaps no better reflection of this ambiguity than the work of M. Maimonides (1135–1204). On the one hand, Maimonides was an assiduous systematizer of every detail of the sacrificial system as it was reflected in Jewish tradition. In his *Mishneh Torah,* Maimonides organized all the legal decisions that had accumulated rather haphazardly about sacrifice in biblical and rabbinic literature. No other compiler of Jewish law gave sacrifice this type of attention. Yet in his *Guide for the Perplexed,* Maimonides speaks discursively about the sacrificial system, nearly condemning it. In his evaluation he cites the standard prophetic critique of sacrificial worship (1 Sam 15:22; Isa 1:11; Jer 7:22–23) and says that sacrificial worship was never God's primary desire for humankind (Twersky 1972: 332–34). The laws were given to Moses because the people needed them to counteract the attractions of contemporary paganism.

Scholars have long been perplexed over this double-mindedness on the part of Maimonides. Yet his perplexity strikes at the very root of what most modern readers of the Bible at least implicitly believe about the sacrificial system. On the one hand there is the feeling of responsibility toward the sacrificial material in the Bible—it must be organized, systematized, and understood—yet on the other hand there is the constant uncertainty as to its true religious significance. This uncertainty was very nicely summarized by Origen in a remark he made in a homily on the book of Numbers (*Homilia* 27). He noted that if you took a person whom you wished to instruct in the fundamentals of piety and faith and proceeded to instruct him in the laws of sacrifice, he would turn away from such teaching and react as one "who refuses food that is not fitting *(et tanquam non sibi aptum cibum recusat).*" Sacrificial practice remains a foreign and obtrusive element to the present-day interpreter. This problem is compounded by the fact that sacrificial practice constitutes a good portion of the Torah, the first five books of the Bible. Even more telling is its redactional placement; it is at the very heart of the Sinaitic legislation (Leviticus 1–9 *et passim*). Unlike other oddities of the biblical narrative that can be avoided because of their infrequency, the large corpus of sacrificial lore demands the interpreter's attention.

For many students of the Bible, the motif of sacrifice finds religious value in its symbolic role: the act of animal sacrifice is understood to reflect *the bond* between God and humanity. But such a general observation of symbolic value fails to satisfy. One wishes to know more concretely why *animal* sacrifice? Could not the bond between humankind and God be represented in another ritual form?

2. Social Science Explanations. The mystery of sacrificial practice also troubled early anthropologists and prompted the opening of a whole new era of comparative research. The problem with the earliest theorists is that they often desired to account for this particular cultic practice, and religion in general, in severely reductionistic, evolutionary models. Indeed, a strong undercurrent in the thinking of one such theorist, Sir Edward Tylor (1871), was to expose the false premises of all theological thought in his exploration of social evolution. Tylor claimed that sacrifice was "a gift made to a deity as if he were a man" (1871, 2: 375). Thus, Tylor reduced all sacrifice to a primitive formula of self-aggrandizement, *do ut des* ("I give so that you will give in turn"). This ritual process was devoid of moral value in its original setting because for Tylor all religions developed from a very primitive animism that viewed the spiritual world as indifferent to morality. Only at a far later stage did a more moral and spiritual meaning surface. On a similar level is the theory of Frazier (1890) that all sacrifice arose out of a ritual of slaying a "divine king." His ritual murder was thought to aid the crops. Frazier believed that this magical impulse was only at a later date spiritualized, and substitutes for the divine king were developed.

One other thinker we might include in this group is Robertson Smith (1889). His work can be distinguished from that of Tylor and Frazier on the grounds that Smith saw the religious impulse behind sacrifice in positive terms. For Smith, sacrifice began as an act of slaying the totemic animal that represented both the tribe and its god. The tribe's consumption of the flesh of this animal provided a means of experiencing a communion between the god and the tribe; thus the life of the community was sustained. The primary goal of the sacrifice was communal and mystical: it enhanced the feeling of unity among the tribe and provided a moment of communion between the tribal folk and their god. Only far later in the development of human culture, under the influence of the state, did sacrifice come to be thought of as a gift to a god. Smith's theory, like those of Tylor and Frazier, is an evolutionary one. Like other anthropologists from the late 19th century, Smith believed that religious sacrifice could be broken down to one original impulse from which all later permutations could be traced.

The gift theory of Tylor was subject to radical revision at the hands of Hubert and Mauss in their famous essay (1899). This work continues to command considerable respect among anthropological theorists and constitutes the starting point for all modern discussion of the problem. Hubert and Mauss argued against the crudely mechanistic theory of Tylor *(do ut des).* On the one hand they agreed with Tylor in seeing sacrifice as a form of a gift to the deity. Yet, on the other hand, they argued that sacrificial victims fashioned a link between the profane and sacral worlds. The animal becomes a mediating vehicle because it partakes of both realms: its body belongs to the physical world whereas its life belongs to the spiritual realm. This mediator, the sacrificial victim, became identified with the sacrificer (Hubert and Mauss' term for the individual who makes the sacrifice) during the moment of consecration. As Valeri notes (1985: 65), "the gift ceases to be a commodity, a mere utilitarian object; *it is the subject in an objective form.*" Certainly one of the strengths of the work of Hubert and Mauss is their emphasis on the *entirety* of the sacrificial rite. The process begins with rituals which sacralize the time, place, and officiants. Then the victim is killed and consumed. Finally rituals of desacralization must be carried out to ensure an undisturbed entry to the profane world.

One problem with the gift theory is that it fails to account for the asymmetry of the sacrificial process. How is it that the human being can give so little (a single animal) and receive so much (the promise of divine blessing in its many varied forms)? Here one is greatly aided by recent anthropological theories of gift giving: the gods establish their superiority by giving more than they receive. But there is another level of meaning here as well. There is a degree of equality in the exchange because "the value of the thing given is inversely proportional to that of the giver. In other words, for a god, giving much is giving little; for man, giving little is giving much. Hence man's small gift to the god is as valuable as god's big gift to man, but at the same time this equivalence of the gifts signifies and establishes the nonequivalence of the givers, of god and man. It is in this way that reciprocity can coexist with hierarchy and that the sacrificial exchange can represent the gods' superiority over men" (Valeri 1985: 66).

3. Social Science and Biblical Scholarship. Our survey of anthropological scholarship has to be severely curtailed for the purposes of this essay, but the reader should know that much work still remains to be done here by the biblical scholar. We have only surveyed those theories which have directly affected past biblical research. More recent conceptualizations have not been discussed (e.g., Girard 1977; Burkert 1983; Valeri 1985). By and large, biblical scholarship has not kept up with the theoretical work of recent anthropology. The handbooks on biblical sacrifice generally do one of two things: they either dismiss all or most of previous research as not applicable to the special case of the Bible or take up an evolutionary model such as that of Tylor or Frazier and apply the lower forms to Israel's ANE neighbors and the higher forms to Israel. The second strategy is especially dangerous. Such apologetic tendencies, besides being historically suspicious, are of marginal value theologically. The presumption of such thought seems to be that the biblical cult is odd on its own terms, and only in comparison to a clearly inferior *Vorlage* can any theological value be extracted.

One prominent evolutionary model that has been popular in biblical handbooks is the motif of sacrifice as food for the gods. God is portrayed in this model as an anthropomorphic being who requires daily sustenance like any human being. Against this primitive mode of religious thought, some scholars have chosen to juxtapose the more evolved form of religion found in the Bible:

> If I am hungry, will I not tell you?
> For the earth and what fills it are mine.
> Do I eat the flesh of bulls,
> the blood of goats do I drink?
> Sacrifice to God praise!
> Fulfill, to the Most High, your vows! (Ps 50:12–14)

To be sure, this psalm explicitly says that YHWH needs no food. But before quickly concluding that the Bible's account of sacrifice is on a higher evolutionary level, one must account for the enormous amount of evidence that portrays Israelite sacrifice as food for YHWH. Countless texts from every period describe YHWH's sacrifices as food. The altar itself is called "the table of YHWH." The sacrifices can be called "YHWH's food." The aroma of the burnt offerings is said to be "a sweet savor to YHWH." All of this is dismissed by some biblical scholars as ancient relics of Israel's pagan past. No account of the fact is made that these terms and phrases are *freely* introduced into *all genres* (cultic and epic narratives, psalms, and more) of Israel's literature in all periods.

The boldness of such an argument is clear. While one can point to a few isolated poetic texts that speak of YHWH's freedom from human needs such as food, one must dismiss dozens of other texts from a variety of genres as unrepresentative, or as relics from an archaic past. Moreover, even the presumption that all non-Israelite conceptualizations of sacrifice uniformly presumed that the gods required food needs to be rethought. Tigay's work on the development of the Gilgamesh Epic has provided damaging evidence for the simplistic comparisons made by some biblical scholars (1982: 224–28, 293–96). The late Assyrian reworking of this epic shows a decided tendency to downplay, if not altogether delete, all references to the gods' need for food. What are we to make of this shift? Is this late text representative of a new Mesopotamian perspective on sacrificial rites? If so, what do we make of all the subsequent Mesopotamian material (like the Neo-Assyrian and Babylonian ritual texts) wherein sacrifices are still described as food for the gods? Are these subsequent descriptions simply ancient relics? The most we can say with any certainty is that in Mesopotamia certain literate groups inveighed against an overly anthropomorphic characterization of the deity. *Mutatis mutandis* for the biblical material. The likelihood that this immediately became a generalizable philosophical principle in either civilization is very remote.

It would be preferable to see sacrifice as a *multivalent entity*. Various explanations of its function could coexist, and what a given writer enunciates is also affected by the literary needs and genre of the writer in question. Even in the rabbinic period the notion that the deity consumed sacrifices could find a literary setting in spite of the rabbinic tendency to avoid anthropomorphism. There exist halakic discussions which explicitly compare human consumption of the sacrificial fare to that of the deity (*Mekhilta of R. Ishmael ad* Exod 23:15). What this type of material demonstrates is that even the Rabbis of the Tannaitic era could say both that sacrifice was food for God and that God needed no food. *Mutatis mutandis* for the biblical Israelites and the Babylonians. The crucial variable is not an evolutionary development from magical, prelogical thinking to a more spiritual and ethical form of religion, but rather the literary genre in which a particular concept was found (myth, hymn, liturgical formula, etc.). Each of these linguistic forms or language games, to use the terminology of Wittgenstein, had its own particular ideology of sacrifice. This *multivalency* need much more attention than has been hitherto provided. Too much theoretical discussion of sacrifice is dependent on the assumption that sacrifice can be reduced to one essential concept. In the course of the present essay, we will attempt to develop further this notion of multiple levels of explanation.

4. Biblical Sacrifice as Cultic Realia or Textual Phenomenon. All treatments of sacrifice by biblical scholars have focused on the historical *realia* of the cultus. The dominant question concerns just what happened in the temple when animals were slain and what did it mean to the particular practitioners. This research paradigm involves two distinct but interrelated programs of investigation. First would be the construction of a history of Israel's cultic worship from its origins in the patriarchal period to its conclusion in the beginning of the Second Temple period under Ezra and Nehemiah. Having established this historical grid, the various data from the P source and from other ritual materials scattered throughout the former and latter prophets (especially Ezekiel 40–48) are then placed in their proper temporal setting. This method has produced significant results in terms of assessing the function of biblical sacrifice in ancient Israelite culture. But the cost of this methodology has been that the role of sacrifice in the final form of the biblical text, or the canonical function of the material, has received scant (one could say almost no) attention. The effects of this are manifold. As one enters the Second Temple era, sacrifice becomes as much a textual enterprise as one of actual practice; the study of the sacrificial system begins to develop a level of significance independent, though not inseparable, from cultic practice. Evidence of this approach to sacrifice as a textual phenomenon is already present, *in nuce,* in some pieces of what has come to be called "inner biblical exegesis" (Toeg 1974; Fishbane 1985). It becomes a full-blown reality in such documents as *Jubilees* and the Temple Scroll, not to mention the fifth division of the Mishnah, "sacred (offerings)." All of these sources seek to reconstruct a model of sacrifice that is not simply reflective of actual practice, but results from learned exegesis of the Bible in its final canonical form. This creation of an ideal, exegetical model of sacrifice we prefer to label "the scripturalization of the cult" and it will be discussed below (section F).

B. Sacrifice and Offering: Some Basic Distinctions

Thomas Aquinas defined the distinction between offering and sacrifice as one of "genus" and "species." Offering constitutes the more general category of gift or oblation, while sacrifice is a specialization of this category which entails a more specific means of delivery to the deity. For Aquinas, the act which separated sacrifice from offering was "immolation." In Latin, *immolare* does not mean "to destroy" as its English cognate would suggest, but "to sprinkle with sacrificial meal." For Aquinas, though, what constitutes "immolation" varies with the substance being offered: whereas an animal may be killed, liquids are poured out and foodstuffs such as grains and fruits are burnt (Turner 1977: 190). As Turner observes: "In Scholastic terminology, oblation can be taken as the matter, immolation as the form of sacrifice."

This is a useful typology for biblical sacrifice as well, though one should note that such a distinction is not explicitly made in the biblical vocabulary. The Bible does have two basic terms for offering: *minḥâ* (in the non-P materials) which means simply "gift," and *qôrbān* (in P) which implies something "brought near" (namely, to the altar). These words are generic terms which include every type of sacrifice or oblation. There is no single term which defines how, or in what manner, an offering becomes a "sacrifice." The basic term for sacrifice in the Bible is *zābaḥ,* which means "to slaughter." In Phoenician this root develops the broader sense "to prepare food" in general, but nowhere does it become a generic term for sacrifice. Because blood sacrifice was such an important category in Israelite religion, this term for animal slaughter assumed the technical meaning of sacrifice.

The root *zbḥ* also appears in the Hebrew word for altar, *mizbēaḥ.* Although the term literally means "the place of slaughter," it functions in the OT to designate the spot where each sacrifice is formally offered. It is at this spot that animals are slaughtered, liquids are poured out, and grains are burned. Indeed, we might define sacrifice in the Bible as those oblations which are burned (wholly or partially) at the altar *(mizbēaḥ).* These would include the burnt offering *(ʿôlâ),* the "peace offering" *(šĕlāmîm),* and the grain offering *(minḥâ),* as well as the purification *(ḥaṭṭāʾt)* and reparation offerings *(ʾāšām).* Other types of sacred donations, though brought to the sanctuary and even sometimes presented at the altar, are not burned in any way at the altar and so are not sacrifices. These would include the tithe *(maʿăśēr),* firstfruits *(bikkûrîm),* the wave-offering *(tĕnûpâ),* and the heave-offering *(tĕrûmâ).* In general, those offerings we have designated sacrifices are of higher sanctity ("most holy") than the more general category of offerings ("holy").

C. Development of Terminology

Every modern study of biblical sacrifice begins with an attempt to define the development and usage of various biblical terms for sacrifice. Indeed, the problems of definition can be so acute in respect to certain terms that many studies begin and end with nothing more than a purely philological discussion. Though the particular problem of definition of individual sacrifices is a difficult one, the more general problem of understanding their distribution in the Bible is also not easy to understand.

1. The Problem of P. Ever since the beginning of critical biblical studies scholars have noted the uniqueness of the sacrificial terminology of the P source as compared with the rest of the OT. We could summarize the distinctiveness of P's sacrificial vocabulary along 3 axes: (1) P has an immense technical vocabulary that vastly exceeds the other narrative sources; (2) much of P's vocabulary—indeed vocabulary that is central to the P system—is either absent from the rest of the Bible or used in a very different fashion; and (3) P's sacrificial vocabulary is heavily weighted toward rituals of atonement. Wellhausen *(WPHI)* used these data to derive very distinctive, if not pejorative results about the value of the P code in general. First, for Wellhausen, the vast technical vocabulary of P reflects the "externalization" of the cult. For P, a product of the Exile, sacrifice is no longer a *spontaneous* act of individual piety as it was in JE, but rather a *prescribed* ritual of the community (*WPHI,* 103). Second, the fact that these prescribed rituals and their distinctive vocabulary appear nowhere in the preexilic narrative and historical sources was one of Wellhausen's strongest arguments that P was a late product of the postexilic period. Finally, P's emphasis on rituals of atonement, in a manner that is unprecedented in earlier biblical narrative, indicated to Wellhausen the heavy sense of guilt Jews of the early Second Temple period felt and the tremendous efforts that were made to purge the community of its sin.

Each element of Wellhausen's system has come under attack. Dussaud (1941), on the basis of comparing Phoenician cultic tariffs from the early 1st millennium, demonstrated that an elaborate list of technical sacrificial vocabulary was not sufficient grounds for labeling the Priestly system as late or unique in the ancient world. Such lists were present among Israel's nearest neighbors. Weinfeld has carried this argument even further, noting that Wellhausen was "unaware of the existence of ordered, institutionalized cultic centers in the great cultural centers of the ancient Near East. All cult was based on ceremonial precision" (1983: 96). As to the problem of P's "unique" interest in rituals of atonement, Thompson's (1963) study showed that atonement is also an operative sacrificial category outside of P. Even more important is Weinfeld's demonstration that the great cultural centers of the ancient world (1983: 105–6) had appropriate terminology for sacrifices of purification and atonement. These types of sacrifice were an accepted norm for ancient ritual, and thus P's interest in them is hardly extraordinary. The fact that only P records these sacrifices tells us more about P's interest than P's date. We might add that Weinfeld's point can be strengthened by noting how the technical cultic vocabulary of Ugaritic is distributed among its various literary genres. Here, too, as Tarragon (1980) and Anderson (1987) have noted, the technical sacrificial terminology of the sacrificial texts is quite variant from the terminology of the epic and mythic materials. Not only do the meanings of various sacrificial terms vary from one genre to another, but each genre has its own unique terminology. Just as P's vocabulary stands out in relation to J, E, and D, so also the Ugaritic sacrificial tariffs stand out from the Baal myth or the epic of King Kirta. The differences cannot be explained on purely historical grounds; the nature and genre of the text in question is an equally if not more important conditioning factor.

2. The Development of Cultic Vocabulary. The development of cultic terminology in the Bible must be seen in a broader perspective than simply the distinctions between P and non-P usage. To be properly appreciated it must be seen in its overall NW Semitic (or Canaanite) context, that is, in relation to Israel's closest cultural relations (Ugarit, Phoenicia, Aramea, Ammon, and Moab). To illustrate how Israel's cultic terminology is related to these contiguous cultures, we will trace the development of the cultic term *minḥâ*.

The Heb word *minḥâ* has two very different meanings in the OT. On the one hand it can refer to the specific "cereal offering" (so the P source, so Leviticus 2) or it can simply mean "gift," including even noncultic donations. In Phoenician, the term only appears in cultic tariffs, and like the usage in P refers to the cereal offering. At Ugarit the specialization proceeded in another direction. The term occurs at least three times in economic texts referring to some type of secular payment (*CTA* 14.1; KTU 4.91; and in the Ras Hani materials).

In the past, it has been typical to explain the different levels of meaning for *minḥâ* in the Bible in historical terms. The specialization of the term in the P source (cereal offering) is seen as a postexilic development. Inherent in this view is an implicit Wellhausenian bias: because P is a postexilic document, its technical terminology reflects postexilic origin. This view has a number of problems, the most severe being the widespread usage of the term *minḥâ* meaning "cereal offering" in the preexilic period in both Phoenicia and Israel (*AncIsr* 2:430). In other words, it seems safe to say that the meaning "gift" and "cereal offering" could coexist.

How can we account for these variant meanings existing side by side? It is well known in anthropology that societies which possess religious specialists also have very technical explanations of ritual and mythic motifs. These learned explanations are often very different from those of the nonspecialist. In cultures where these specialists are able to write, the extensive recording of temple revenues further contributes to the development of elaborate classification schemes (Goody 1977: 74–111). These classification schemes were necessary for temple revenues and expenditures being accounted for. This ability to classify allowed for more precise conceptual and lexical boundaries and gave much greater visibility to categories of items. Though these classification schemes were very important for the development of a sophisticated social structure, they were not generally relevant to the daily affairs of the common citizen.

How is this relevant for *minḥâ*? For the common Israelite, the term *minḥâ* meant a "gift," most often a gift given to the temple. Because the economic base of Israelite society was dependent on grain, the *minḥâ* payment given to the temple was usually grain. This basic datum was further refined by priestly specialists. A typical Judean farmer need not be specific regarding these matters; he simply contributed a tenth of whatever it was he produced. But the priests—who had to deal with a variety of agricultural and pastoral gifts and revenues—needed a more elaborate taxonomy so to order their experience. No doubt a large impetus for this ordering came from temple lists and tariffs (Levine 1963; 1965). In order to deal meaningfully with the income of the temple, a precise lexicon of cultic contributions had to be in place. This would explain the need to specialize further a term like *minḥâ* from "a gift" (which was most often grain) to "a cereal offering."

The development of a specialized meaning for *minḥâ* should be seen as both an inner-Israelite and broad NW Semitic phenomenon. In its early proto-NW Semitic form, the root had the broad generic connotation of "gift." During the Iron Age, or perhaps a bit earlier, the cultic specialists in Phoenicia and Israel used this word to express the most basic cultic offering, the cereal offering. But this specialization was uneven: its earlier generic usage survived even into postexilic literature in Israel. While in Ugarit, already in the Bronze Age, the prose material showed a limitation of meaning to a secular economic sense.

The specialization of meaning for cultic terms has important ramifications. In any one particular dialect the terms for sacrifice can become quite specific and technical. As a result of this learned procedure of classification which occurs within the cult the priestly vocabulary becomes quite idiosyncratic. This idiosyncratic and complex classification system is paradigmatic of all mature cultic centers in the ancient world. It does not reflect a crudely materialistic view of the cult; rather it reflects the attempt of each and every cultic center to provide order and meaning to the wide variety of gifts and offerings which it receives. The special usages of any one cult center cannot be predicted on the basis of the archaic meanings of the pertinent cultic terms. The specialization of *minḥâ* from "gift" to "cereal offering" is paradigmatic of this.

In summary, we can say that the P code's interest in classifying the broad array of sacrificial donations made to the temple does not reflect a crudely materialistic view of the cult as Wellhausen and von Rad (*ROTT* 1: 259–60) believed. Instead it represents the maturation and individuation of the biblical cult. Each cultic center in the ANE developed its own very intricate system of sacrificial categories and terminology. In the realm of Canaanite culture, what separates each center from the other is the *unique configuration* of the various sacrificial offerings. Thus the development of the Priestly vocabulary is part of a larger movement to develop a specialized and unique cultic identity that one sees in other cultic centers in the Iron Age.

D. Sacrifice in P

1. The Animals. As a general rule, the sacrifices can be broken down into two categories in regard to which animals were used: those sacrifices which specifically required a particular animal for each and every sacrificial occasion, and those which required a range of different animals depending on the social standing or economic status of the individual offerer. In the former class we can place the burnt offering, the peace offering, and the reparation offering, while in the latter class we would place the two forms of purification offering.

It would not be accurate to say that the requirements for the burnt offering, peace offering, and reparation offering were rigidly fixed; there was room for variability, but the variability was not similar to that reserved for the purification offering. For the burnt offering one had to offer a male animal from the herd or flock, or a bird (turtledove or pigeon). The peace offering could be either a male or female from the herd or flock. The reparation offering was always a ram, except for the Nazirite who became impure, who had to bring a lamb. The reparation offering was also unique in that most of the time this sacrificial requirement could be converted into an equivalent in silver. In contrast to these requirements, the laws for the purification offering in Lev 4:1–23 conform strictly to the *social standing* of the offerer. The priest, community, ruler, and individual had their own requirements that could not be varied. The additional situations for the purification offering listed in Lev 5:1–13 articulate a separate system altogether. In this material, the requirements for the purification offering are graded in accord with the *economic standing* of the offerer.

The animals used for sacrifices were domestic animals. Even though there were wild animals that were fit for consumption according to the laws of *kašrut* (e.g., the hart, gazelle, roebuck, wild goat, ibex, antelope, and mountain sheep; Deut 14:5) these animals were never used for sacrifices. What was fit for game was evidently not suitable for the altar.

2. The Technique of Sacrifice. Before beginning our formal discussion it is worth noting that since the P code made the setting of the Sinaitic revelation the primal location of Israel's cultic commandments, all of the sacrificial law was given in reference to the tent of meeting or tabernacle that was erected there (Exodus 35–49). In the eyes of the P source, all this material was thought to be equally applicable to the domain of the temple.

The sacrificial act consisted of six basic steps which can be divided into two groups: those which were performed by the layperson who offered the animal and those which were restricted to the priests. Laypersons were responsible for (1) bringing the animal to the sanctuary, (2) laying hands on the animal, and (3) slaughtering the animal (included cutting up the animal and washing or cleaning the insides, see Lev 1:6, 9). The priests were responsible for (4) tossing the blood, (5) burning the animal (or part of the animal), and (6) disposing of the remains. The first three actions of the layperson took place at the opening of the tent of meeting, a spot where the laypeople could also witness the Lord's "consumption" of the sacrifice (Lev 9:23–24). The fact that the laypeople were responsible for actions 1–3 can be seen from the diction of Leviticus 1. Those actions which the layperson was to perform, the P writer identifies with the third person singular: "he shall lay his hand . . ." (Lev 1:4). Those actions which the priest was to perform are rendered: "and Aaron's sons, the priests, shall present the blood . . ." (Lev 1:5). The meaning of the hand-laying rite, which is so basic to understanding the process of atonement in the expiatory sacrifices, has long been obscure to scholars. It has recently been suggested that the rite of hand-laying merely signified that the animal belonged to the owner (Wright 1986). This theory pertains to the generally prescribed law of laying *one hand* on the animal. The exceptional act of laying on *two hands* on the day of atonement must be explained differently. In this case, the act of laying on hands identified a particular animal as the recipient of the ritual action.

The actions which only the priest could perform (tossing blood and burning the animal) were actions which had to occur at the altar. Because only the priests were given access to this location, the responsibility naturally was theirs. Blood manipulation varied from sacrifice to sacrifice. With the burnt, reparation, and peace offerings, the blood was tossed around the altar. In contrast to these, the purification offering required that the blood be first daubed on the horns of the altar and then the rest poured out at the base of the altar in the case of a ruler or commoner. For the priest or the entire congregation the blood was first sprinkled seven times before the veil of the sanctuary and then put on the horns of the inner incense altar. The remainder was poured out at the base of the outer altar. In certain cases the priests were also required to eat the sacrifice (cereal offering and reparation offering).

Disposal rites were different for each sacrifice. The burnt offering, of course, had no disposal rite: the entire sacrifice was burned on the altar. For the other sacrifices, disposal rites varied, seemingly in accord with sanctity. Thus the peace offering, which was of lesser sanctity ("holy"), could be eaten for two days and burned only on the third, whereas the purification sacrifice ("most holy") had to be eaten on the same day (Wright 1987). Special laws (Lev 7:16–18) of disposal also pertained to utensils used in preparing expiatory sacrifices (Lev 7:28). On the disposal rites in general, see Wright (1987).

3. Literary Genres in P. a. General Matters. The P source has brought together a variety of materials into its sacrificial program from different time periods and perhaps even variant sacred sites. Scholars often argue that because certain of these sources can be shown to be preexilic, the P source as a whole can be safely anchored in the preexilic period. See PRIESTLY ("P") SOURCE. One should not be so quick to reach such a solution. The date of the final redaction of the P source is an issue independent of the date of its constituent materials.

Scholars have noted the variety of materials that are found within the P source. The most basic source division, which all are agreed upon, is that between the Holiness Code (Leviticus 17–26) and the rest of P. It has been generally assumed that H is earlier than P, but recently Knohl (1988) has offered weighty arguments for presuming the reverse. Within the P source itself there is further evidence of different layers of source material. One may wish to compare the classic doublet regarding the purification offerings in Leviticus 4 and Num 15:22–31 (see below); other doublets can also be found. One stream of scholarship has taken the evidence of the doublets as a starting point for reconstructing the complex tradition history of the OT sacrificial materials (Rendtorff 1967; Elliger, *Leviticus* HAT). Although this method worked very well in narrative sources of the Pentateuch and has achieved a rather high degree of consensus, the same cannot be said for the sacrificial material. There simply is not enough data within these sources or in extrabiblical sources to reconstruct with any certainty the question of literary history. In proof of this, one need simply to compare the vastly different reconstructions found in the work of Elliger, Rendtorff, and Noth (*Leviticus* OTL). Perhaps the most convincing treatment of the tradition history of the P source and its variant sources is that of Knohl.

Another method of analyzing the sacrificial material in P has been employed by J. Milgrom. Working from the assumption that the source material of P cannot be reconstructed, and that the material presents itself, on the whole, as a complete system, Milgrom has opted to interpret OT sacrifice on the basis of the final redactional form of the P source. Thus, when Milgrom investigates the meaning of the purification or reparation sacrifices, he does not ask which treatment of it in the Bible is earliest, nor does he look for inconsistencies or contradictions as signs of literary seams in a particular pericope. Rather, Milgrom assumes that the P material as a unit has sufficient integrity to be treated as a whole. Thus, the meaning of the purification or reparation offering, for example, can only be grasped when each pericope is read and explained as though it was part of a complete system.

Milgrom's method has achieved some remarkable results, especially in regard to the purification and reparation offerings. His work is especially helpful to those working in Second Temple sources because his emphasis on how the P material presents itself in its final redactional shape provides a smooth transition to the type of interpretation one finds in Second Temple sources. Others, though, have been critical of Milgrom's perspective on the grounds that it is not sufficiently historical in its outlook.

The 1988 study of I. Knohl has called into question some of Milgrom's assumptions about the homogeneity of the P material. As mentioned above, Knohl dates H earlier than P. But just as important, Knohl finds new evidence for the H source outside of Leviticus 19–26. He argues that H material can be readily identified and contains an understanding of sacrifice that is quite different from P. If Knohl is correct (and he marshals a good deal of evidence in support of his thesis), many of the integrative readings of Milgrom will have to be rethought.

In summary, one can say that the sacrificial matter in P is approached in very different ways and that no consensus has emerged as to what the most appropriate method might be. Readers of this literature must be careful to note what the operative assumptions are of a particular interpreter before assessing his particular understanding.

b. Descriptive and Prescriptive Ritual Texts. Although the exact stratification of P's source material remains a matter of debate, significant work has been done on the variant *Sitze im Leben* of some of this material. One scholar, B. Levine, has distinguished himself as an especially sensitive interpreter of OT sacrificial ritual against the ANE environment. He advanced the thesis, which has since been widely accepted, that sacrificial instruction could be broken down into one of two types: the descriptive and the prescriptive (1965). Working from sacrificial material found in Mesopotamia, Ugarit, and the Bible, Levine argued that descriptive texts describe what transpired at a specific cultic occasion. As a result these texts exist in a narrative format. Prescriptive texts, on the other hand, do not describe an actual ritual; rather they legislate what must be brought for a certain ritual. In the biblical material good examples of prescriptive texts can be found in Numbers 7; 28–29, while Leviticus 8–9 is descriptive in nature. Levine argued that behind the narrative of Numbers 7 was an actual archival record of cultic offerings which, "in its simplest terms, is an account of sanctuary income resembling numerous similar accounts from Mesopotamia" (1965: 317); whereas the origins of Leviticus 8–9 were actual reports of ritual occasions that were "subsequently adapted into narrative accounts" (1965: 324).

A. F. Rainey (1970) took Levine's results one step further and noted that such a form-critical distinction could account for the different order of sacrifices found in OT ritual texts. Rainey notes that the order of sacrifices in Leviticus 8–9 is different from Numbers 7; 28–29. The former includes a progression from the purification offering to burnt offering while in the latter the reverse order is found. Rainey argues that the proper administrative procedure is that found in the descriptive texts. Rainey's thesis finds resounding support in the narrative regarding the leper: "And on the eighth day he shall take two male lambs without blemish, and one ewe lamb a year old without blemish, and a cereal offering . . ." (Lev 14:10). Because the burnt offering must be a male animal (Lev 1:10), whereas the purification offering for the individual is a female (Lev 4:32), the order of this *prescriptive* text is: burnt offering and then purification offering. But when the actual performance of the ritual is *described,* a different order is found: the purification offering is offered before the burnt offering (Lev 14:19–20). A similar contrast can be found between the *descriptive* list of sacrifices that the Nazir was to furnish (Num 6:14–15) and the *prescriptive* text which describes their execution (Num 6:16–17).

The results of this form critical distinction between descriptive and prescriptive lists is also important for understanding the meaning of OT sacrifice. The purification sacrifice is first because it prepares the way for full sacrificial communion: it deals fully with any tinge of sin that may separate the divine presence from the worshipper. Once the rite of purification had been completed, the burnt offering, which was an offering given over totally to God, could be offered. Only then could peace offerings be given wherein the people at large would rejoice before their Lord (Deuteronomy 12).

c. Redaction of Sacrificial Material in P. When one first looks at the P source in its entirety, the laws of sacrifice seem to be ordered in a rather haphazard way. Beginning in Exodus 25 and continuing to the end of Numbers the sacrificial laws of P are interwoven among the various narrative materials of J and E. It is difficult, especially in Numbers, to understand what was the editorial function of this structure. Yet there are clear signs of editorial design within this larger framework. One might note the structure of Exodus 25–Leviticus 9. Exodus 25–40 is the narrative which describes the delivery of the architectural plans for the tabernacle to Moses (Exodus 25–31) and the subsequent execution of those plans (Exodus 35–40). This particular section comes to a climax with the appearance of the divine presence ("glory of the Lord") in the Tabernacle (Exod 40:34–38). After the tabernacle has been revealed, the laws of sacrifice are laid out in a very general way (Leviticus 1–7). Concluding this section is the narrative of the ordination of Aaron and the ceremony of the eighth day (Leviticus 8–9). This final section concludes with the first appearance of the Lord to the entire gathered throng of Israelites:

> Moses and Aaron then went inside the Tent of Meeting. When they came out, they blessed the people; and the Presence of the Lord appeared to all the people. Fire came forth from before the Lord and consumed the burnt offering and the fat parts of the altar. And all the people saw, and shouted, and fell on their faces" (Lev 9:23–24).

The importance of this narrative has been underestimated by biblical scholars. In many respects it reflects the very center of the P document. Whereas prior to the revelation at Mt. Sinai, God had appeared to his chosen only sporadically, now this divine presence could be routinized and made available on a regular basis: "An altar of earth you shall make for me and sacrifice on it your burnt offerings and your peace offerings, your sheep and your oxen; *in every place where I cause my name to be remembered I will come to you and bless you*" (Exod 20:24).

The climax of the P narrative in the completion of the worship rites commanded at Mt. Sinai contrasts rather sharply with the climax of the epic narratives of the Pentateuch. In the Israelite epic, the climax of the narrative is found outside the Pentateuch in the settlement traditions. Whereas JE was interested in highlighting the role of the settlement, P chose to subordinate this theme to the inauguration of a regular, routinized temple-service in the desert. The inauguration of the priesthood and the sacrificial altar, and as a consequence, the appearance of the "glory of the Lord" (Lev 9:23) to all Israel constituted the very heart of Israel's relation to its God. It was here that the drama of Israel's relationship to God was consummated. So important was this moment of "consummation" that rabbinic midrash retold this moment using sexual imagery (*Sifra ad* Lev 9:23).

In summary one can say that the Torah has both *general rules* for the performance of individual sacrifices and *particular applications* for the individual sacrifices or sets of sacrifices. General rules for all of the sacrificial types are primarily found in one location, Leviticus 1–7. These general rules tell everything one needs to know about *how* to administer the burnt offering. It tells one where to bring the animal, how to lay on hands, where to kill it, how to handle its blood, how to prepare the altar, and what to burn on the altar. The section closes with the statement: "This is the law of the burnt offering, of the cereal offering, of the purification offering, of the reparation offering, of the consecration offering, and of the peace offering which the Lord commanded Moses on Mt. Sinai" (Lev 7:37–38).

In its present canonical shape, the laws of Leviticus 1–7 are viewed as the basic rules for how each sacrifice is to be performed. One must be careful to note though that these rules, on their own, are very artificial and do not constitute a complete system of sacrificial ritual. Leviticus 1–7 takes up each sacrificial type individually and treats it as an isolated entity. It is only rarely that an Israelite offered only a burnt offering or cereal offering. It was not the individual offering on its own terms that had meaning, but its particular combination within a given ritual. Thus the rest of the laws of sacrifice in the Pentateuch can be viewed as the specific ritual application of the rather abstract and general rules of Leviticus 1–7 (excluding the doublets to Leviticus 1–7, such as Num 15:22–31 and Num 5:5–8). The specific applications of the general rules of Leviticus 1–7 can be grouped into three categories: (a) foundational sequences (ordination of priests and Levites [Leviticus 8–9, Numbers 8], dedication of the tabernacle [Numbers 7]); (b) festival laws and the *tāmîd,* "daily burnt offering" (Leviticus 16; 23; Numbers 28–29); and (c) specific rituals pertaining to the life cycle of the individual: childbirth (Leviticus 12), "leprosy" (Leviticus 13–14), vows of the Nazir (Numbers 6), impurity from discharge (Lev 15:13–15), corpse defilement (Numbers 19), and so forth.

4. The Basic Types of Animal Sacrifice. a. Burnt Offering (*ʿôlâ*). The Heb term for "burnt offering" is *ʿôlâ,* literally, "an offering of ascent" or "an ascending offering" (Levine 1974: 6). The noun is used with its cognate verbal root *haʿăleh ʿôlâ,* "to make ascend an *ʿôlâ.*" It is not difficult to guess why this name is appropriate for this particular offering. The *ʿôlâ* sacrifice was one which was entirely burnt on the altar and so its smoke—or better, its scent—was directed toward the heavenly realm, wherein the deity was thought to have "inhaled" it. The *ʿôlâ* was generally offered along with accompanying cereal and drink offerings (Num 15:1–10). In Ugarit this sacrificial type was called *šrp,* that is "(totally) burnt."

The sacrifice was a widely used one in ancient Israel. Indeed the phrase "burnt offerings and peace offerings" (e.g. Exodus 20:24) could be used as a merism for the entire sacrificial system (Levine 1974: 21). Once in the book of Ezra, the term *ʿôlâ* describes both the purification and the burnt offerings that were offered by the returning exiles (8:35). Levine has argued that the *ʿôlâ* sacrifice should be understood as one which attracted the deity's attention and invoked the deity's presence for a particular ritual occasion. Such a theory would nicely explain the usage of the *ʿôlâ* for the purposes of divination when the deity's response to an urgent plea was desired, as in the case of Balaam's oracles (Numbers 21–24), or the usage of the *ʿôlâ* by Elijah as a means of testing which prophetic group truly "had YHWH's attention" so to speak (1 Kings 18). It would also explain the usage of the *ʿôlâ* as a term for child sacrifice, which was thought in some circles to show one's consummate devotion to the deity (2 Kgs 3:26–28) and hence worthiness of divine assistance. Milgrom has argued that the *ʿôlâ* was the earliest form of atonement sacrifice in the biblical materials (*EncBib* 7: 243). Job 1:5 is good evidence of this: "Job would rise early in the morning and offer burnt offerings according to the number of (his sons) for he said: 'It may be that my sons have sinned and cursed God in their hearts.' " The atoning function of the *ʿôlâ* survives vestigially in the P source itself. Although P generally holds that only the purification and reparation offerings deal with sin, in Lev 1:4 it is said that the burnt offering "shall make atonement" for the offerer. We say this is a vestigial usage because nowhere else does P spell out how this atonement would work. All subsequent discussion of atonement revolves around the purification and reparation offerings. In Milgrom's view, the development of these specialized offerings brought about a restructuring of the role of the more general *ʿôlâ*. One must be careful, though, not to presume that this restructuring of the system and refinement of the typology of atoning sacrifices was late simply because they do not appear in preexilic sources. They probably did exist, but nonpriestly sources took no interest in the more exacting taxonomy of the priestly system.

Another level of meaning present in the *ʿôlâ* is that of a gift to the deity. Of course the gift is not just any type of gift but a gift that the deity consumes, a "soothing odor." The consumable gift was thought to be in many respects the food of the deity. Just as the temple was conceived to be the deity's home, complete with furniture and other appurtenances, so this divine home had its hearth, the altar. The daily sacrifices for the deity are described in Exod 29:38–42 (cf. Num 28:3–8 and Ezek 46:13–15). These sacrifices took place both in the morning and the evening and consisted of the *ʿôlâ* (lamb) along with a cereal and drink offering. It was called the *tamid* offering in rabbinic sources because scripture says it was to be offered "continually *(tāmīd)* . . . throughout your generations" (Exod 29:42). It is no accident that Exod 29:42 continues to require the sacrifice "at the door of the tent of meeting before the Lord, where I will meet you, to speak there to you." This *tāmīd* sacrifice was symbolic not only of the deity's meal, but by extension, of the deity's presence among the people. No greater cultic calamity could be imagined than the loss of this sacrifice, since it symbolized the severing of the divine-human relationship (Dan 8:11).

b. Peace Offering *(šĕlāmîm)*. The translation and interpretation of this sacrifice has bothered scholars for many years. It seems clear that at least three terms can refer to this sacrifice: *zebaḥ, zibḥê-šĕlāmîm,* and *šĕlāmîm.* This history of the development of these terms has been treated by Rendtorff (1967). The *šĕlāmîm* seems to be a special type of an earlier *zebaḥ* sacrifice. One should not infer that *zebaḥ,* "slain sacrifice," refers to any slain sacrificial animal. In spite of its name, which is quite general, this sacrifice designation often occurs in the pair *zebaḥ* and *ʿôlâ.* In this type of usage there can be no doubt that *zebaḥ* refers specifically to the *šĕlāmîm* offering.

The sacrifice has commonly been translated as "peace offering" but this is certainly an unhappy rendering. It tells us precious little about the nature of the sacrifice. Just what is peaceful about this sacrificial rite? Some say the peace refers to a harmonious relationship between humanity and God. R. Smith went even further and said it symbolized a communion between them (1889). Others have argued that the peacefulness refers to a covenantal pact, either between God and humanity or simply between different peoples. Of course the lexical root of the term *šĕlāmîm (šlm)* does mean "peace," and in certain cases nouns formed from this root in Hebrew and Akkadian refer to covenantal relations. Yet each one of these attempts to locate the function of the *šĕlāmîm* in terms of etymology has not been persuasive. In the case of the *šĕlāmîm,* Gray's dictum that usage is a more important determinant of meaning than etymology is certainly true (1925: 1–20).

(1) Types. In the P source the *šĕlāmîm* sacrifice is broken down into three subtypes (Lev 7:11–18): the *tôdâ* or "thanksgiving" sacrifice, the *neder,* "vowed sacrifice," and the *nĕdābâ,* "freewill offering." All of these sacrifices played a very important role in the life of the individual. Besides constituting the basic form of sacrifice brought on feast days (1 Sam 1:3–4; Deut 12:11–12), the *šĕlāmîm* also played an important role in the ritual of lamentation and thanksgiving that is so prominent in the Psalms. Very similar to the *šĕlāmîm* are the *pesaḥ,* "passover," and *millûʾîm,* "ordination" sacrifices. Although the *pesaḥ* sacrifice is prepared in a different manner (it is roasted and not boiled according to Exod 12:9), it is a sacrifice that all Israel must consume. The *millûʾîm* sacrifice is prepared almost exactly like the *šĕlāmîm,* the significant difference being that the blood is applied to the ear, thumb, and toe of the Aaronid priest (Exod 29:19–34).

The *pesaḥ, millûʾîm,* and *tôdâ* sacrifices were all to be eaten on the very day they were offered, unlike the other *šĕlāmîm* types. This is certainly due to the fact that the former rites are all obligatory ones. The fact that their flesh must be consumed within one day points to a higher level of sanctity. The other *šĕlāmîm* rites were not obligatory and so the prescriptions for consumption and disposal of the remains were more lax.

(2) Usage. One negative conclusion that emerges from even a cursory look at the *šĕlāmîm* material in the Bible is that the sacrifice had nothing to do with atonement. Though the fat and certain other organs of the sacrifice were burnt on the altar as a "pleasing odor" and the blood was sprinkled on the altar, nowhere do we hear of these acts as atoning for any sin. It seems that the peace offering, in this exceptional circumstance, was nothing more than an accepted manner for slaughtering any animal that was to be used for human consumption (Lev 17:1–7) in the P system.

The role of human consumption constitutes the primary level of meaning for this sacrifice and helps to explain why the *ʿôlâ* and the *šĕlāmîm* are routinely paired in biblical (and Ugaritic) ritual. The *ʿôlâ* was the sacrifice that constituted the basic nourishment for the deity, while the *šĕlāmîm* in turn nourished the people. This was recognized by the rabbis (see the discussion of the *Mekhilta* cited in A.3 above), who explicitly compared these two offerings on exactly this point. Indeed so formative was the notion of celebratory eating to the *šĕlāmîm* that the rabbis even labeled one application of the *šĕlāmîm* sacrifice the "celebration sacrifice" *(šalmê-śimḥâ)*.

The celebrative role of the *šĕlāmîm* is certainly its most prominent feature. If we define the *šĕlāmîm* as a celebrative sacrifice we not only can explain its presence in the rituals of thanksgiving and fulfillment of vows but we can also understand its role on feast days. In many texts in the Bible the command "to celebrate" *(liśmōaḥ)* can only refer to the obligation to consume the *šĕlāmîm*. So prominent is this association that the rabbis themselves say: " 'celebration' means nothing other than consuming the flesh (of the *šĕlāmîm*)." Rabbinic materials also further subdivided the *šĕlāmîm* to include both the *ḥăgîgâ* sacrifice, the sacrifice that all Israelite males were obligated to consume during the three pilgrimage festivals, and the *śimḥâ* sacrifice *(šalmê-śimḥâ)* which all Israelites, male and female, were to consume therein (*Sifre* 138).

Because the *šĕlāmîm* were emblematic of moments of joy or celebration, the *šĕlāmîm* could be, in certain circumstances, banned for days of public mourning. This appears to be the logic of Isa 22:12–14. Isaiah reports that the Lord had called for public mourning, yet Israel was slaying her fatlings and rejoicing. Such a practice does not seem to have been uniform in Israel, for on other occasions *šĕlāmîm* were offered at times of public mourning. In regard to these latter examples, though, one should note that the *šĕlāmîm* were offered in conjunction with the burnt offering and, as Milgrom (*EncBib* 7: 244) has demonstrated, it was the *ʿôlâ* that held the primary role in these rites.

c. Purification Offering *(ḥaṭṭāʾt)*. Lev 4:1–5:13, Num 15:22–31, *et passim* refer to this offering. The traditional translation of this term has been "sin offering." This translation, followed by the LXX, is based on etymological considerations. The Hebrew root *ḥṭʾ* means "to miss the mark, to sin." Yet as Milgrom (1983a: 67) and others have noted, the term would better be understood as referring to the process of purification. This seems clear from the verb used in conjunction with *ḥaṭṭāʾt*, *lĕ-ḥaṭṭēʾ*. This verbal form is best understood as a *Piʿel* privative which conveys the sense of "cleansing, purging," or purifying an object. Even more important is the fact that the *ḥaṭṭāʾt* offering oftentimes is used in situations that have no relation to sin. For example, consider the cases of the parturient (Leviticus 12), the person suffering from a discharge (Leviticus 15), the Nazirite who completes a vow of abstinence (Numbers 6), or the installation of a new altar (Leviticus 8). In each of these cases, the act of sacrifice serves to purge or purify something rather than to remove sin. This is not only logically reasonable, but the biblical text explicitly says this is the function of the sacrifice. For example, in the case of the parturient instead of the ritual closing with a formula of forgiveness we read: "and the priest shall perform purgation for her *(kippēr)* and she shall be clean" (Lev 12:8). The rabbis also noted this: "The sacrifices [the parturient] brought, are nevertheless, for the purpose of permitting her to partake of consecrated food and are not expiatory" (*Ker.* 26a).

(1) Purification and atonement. The purificatory function of the *ḥaṭṭāʾt* challenges us to reconsider the role of the *ḥaṭṭāʾt* in rituals that seem to have an atoning function. Can these rituals also be understood in a purificatory sense? Milgrom has argued the affirmative on the basis of the atonement rituals found in Leviticus 4:1–5:13 and Leviticus 16. Milgrom pays particular attention to the role of blood manipulation in each of the rituals described here, for it is the blood itself which acts as the purging agent. In light of this fact, it is significant to note that the blood is never placed upon the individual. If the individual himself was being cleansed, one would expect the blood to be placed on him or her. Instead, the blood is placed on various cultic appurtenances. Even more telling is the variability of this blood ritual with respect to the status of the sinner. Leviticus 4 makes very careful distinctions between the status of various classes of people. The inadvertent sins of the priest and community as a whole are more serious than the sins of the individual, be he a commoner or a ruler. Most serious of all are the advertent offenses of any kind. In each of these cases, as the seriousness of the sin becomes more pronounced, the blood is brought closer to the very inner sanctum of the holy of holies. Thus the blood used for the commoner is placed on the altar of the burnt offering *outside the sanctuary* per se (Lev 4:30). The blood used for the sin of the priest or of the community as a whole is placed *within the sanctuary* itself, sprinkled on the veil separating the holy of holies from the outer chamber and placed on the incense altar. Finally, the blood of the purification offering on Yom Kippur, which atones for advertent sins (so would seem the sense of *pešaʿ* in Lev 16:16), is sprinkled "in front of the mercy seat" within the holy of holies itself (Lev 16:14).

Milgrom has argued that this sequence of the graded usage of blood in respect to the grid of the sacred shrine shows that what is being purged is not the sin from the sinner, but the effects of sin, i.e. cultic impurity, from the sanctums within the sanctuary. Since the blood is understood to be a purging agent, one would expect the sinner to receive this material if the primary intention of the ritual were to eliminate his/her sinful condition. Such an understanding would accord well with what is said about the purificatory role of the *ḥaṭṭāʾt* blood in the case of those suffering from discharge: "Thus you shall keep the people of Israel separate from their uncleanness lest they die in their uncleanness by defiling my tabernacle that is in their midst" (Lev 15:31, cf. Num 19:13). Impurity, conceived in this fashion, becomes "a physical substance, an aerial miasma which possessed magnetic attraction for the realm of the sacred" (Milgrom 1983a: 77). The purification offering is designed to remove this maleficent material from the sanctuary itself. If the impurity is allowed to accumulate, the deity will be forced to leave the sanctuary. This understanding of the process of atonement is quite distinct from previous theories (Gese 1981; Janowski 1982) which hold that the process is primarily concerned with removing sin from the sinner. Whereas the latter stress the role of substitutionary death in the atoning process, Milgrom stresses the role of purification.

Stated in this general way, Milgrom's argument is very persuasive. Things become more difficult when Milgrom attempts to argue that the purification offering has no role whatsoever in removing human sin. Indeed scripture itself says that the purification rite is performed so that the sinner may be forgiven (Lev 4:20, 26, 31). Yet Milgrom contends that the forgiveness is not for the sinful act per se but rather for the *consequence* of the act, the contamination of the sanctuary. How then is the actual act of the individual sinner forgiven? Milgrom argues that the forgiveness of the original sin itself is accomplished by a feeling of remorse. This feeling is indicated in the biblical text by the use of the verb *ʾāšēm* (Lev 4:13, 22, 27), which Milgrom translates "to *feel* guilty." But there are problems. If such an important atoning function is present in the act of feeling remorse, why is this term absent in Num 15:22–31? Or why is it absent in the case of the priest (Lev 4:1–12)? This situation is complex and does not offer any easy solution. Certainly Milgrom's work is an important contribution, but loose ends still abound.

(2) The Performance of the Purification Offering. The purification offering varies across four classes of individuals: priest, congregation, ruler, and individual. (Lev 5:1–13 constitutes a special case which we will not have room to discuss.) Not only does the act of blood manipulation vary over these four classes, but so do other elements of the ritual. The four classes can actually be reduced to two groups: (1) priest and congregation, and (2) ruler and individual.

The performance of the purification offering has six discrete steps: (1) the animal is brought to the tent of meeting; (2) the offerer lays on hands; (3) the animal is slain; (4) the blood rites are performed; (5) the animal's remains are disposed by burning or are eaten; and (6) a forgiveness formula is cited which formally closes the atonement process. Within this schema there are two elements which serve to highlight and distinguish the offerings of the priest/congregation from those of the prince/individual. First, the blood and disposal rites are performed differently depending on whether one is handling the animals of the priest/congregation or the prince/individual. For the priest/congregation the blood is brought into the sanctuary and sprinkled seven times on the veil that stands in front of the holy of holies and then is daubed on the horns of the incense altar (Lev 4:5–7a; 16–18a). The remainder of the blood is poured out at the base of the altar reserved for the burnt offering which is outside the tent proper (Lev 4:7b; 18b). The fat of the bull as well as certain organs are burned at the altar of the burnt offering (Lev 4:8–10; 19–20); the remainder of the animal, including its edible flesh, is burned outside the camp (Lev 4:11–12; 21). For the prince/individual, the rite is quite different. The blood is applied to the horns of the outer altar and then poured at its base (Lev 4:25; 30). The fat is burned on the altar, but the remainder, that is, the edible flesh, is eaten by the priests (cf. Lev 6:17–23—Eng 6:24–30). It is difficult to know how to interpret the act of eating the meat. Is this an act of disposal parallel to the burning of the bull, or is the consumption simply a perquisite of the priesthood?

This asymmetry has been noted by Levine, who uses these data to reconstruct two originally separate offerings that lie behind our present text. The rite of the priest/congregation, he believes, is a "purification rite intended to safeguard the sanctuary and its ministering priesthood from contamination" (1974: 103). The other rite is similar to the peace offering and originally had nothing to do with the process of purification; rather, its function was "to expiate certain of the offenses of the 'people,' of Israelites, individually, and even of their *nĕśîʾîm,* the tribal chiefs." A later redactor artificially fused two independent pieces of tradition. Levine's hypothesis is quite different from the theory of Milgrom. Though several aspects of Levine's hypothetical reconstruction are weak and have been correctly criticized by Milgrom, his basic description of the problematic posed by the present form of the text holds and has not been adequately addressed by Milgrom's own integrative reading.

(3) Order. The purification offering is generally brought in conjunction with other sacrifices. It is always the first sacrifice to be offered when it is offered in conjunction with other sacrifices such as the *ʿôlâ* and the *ʾāšēm.* The reasons are quite obvious: the purification offering cleanses the sacred appurtenances so that they are able to receive the subsequent sacrifices. In some lists the purification offering is listed after the *ʿôlâ* (Numbers 28–29). This is not an exception to the general rule. Rather this phenomenon results from the particular literary genre of the sacrificial list. Descriptive lists often put the purification offering in the second position, whereas prescriptive lists which describe the actual order always put the purification offering first (see D.3.b above).

d. Reparation Offering (*ʾāšam*). This offering has generally been translated "guilt offering." This translation was predicated on etymological considerations; the root *ʾāšēm* can often mean "to be, feel guilty." Yet as Milgrom has shown (1976), though feelings of guilt are integral to the atonement process, the basic feature of the sacrifice is its function as a means of reparation. Unlike other sacrifices which one "offers" *(hiqrîb),* the *ʾāšām* can "be payed" *(šillēm, hēšîb).* Also, unlike other sacrifices, the *ʾāšām* can be converted into a monetary equivalent and simply paid.

Of all the offerings in the P system, the *ʾāšām* is the most difficult to understand. Indeed some scholars have claimed that even the P school no longer appreciated the distinctiveness between the *ʾāšām* and the *ḥaṭṭāʾt.* Almost every imaginable historical reconstruction for the relationship of the reparation offering and the purification offering has been posed. Needless to say, no overwhelming consensus has emerged.

The most detailed recent study of the reparation offering is that of Milgrom (1976). In many respects his work represents a major advance over previous studies. He offers a persuasive hypothesis as to how the reparation and purification offerings should be differentiated, but one should be aware that his proposal cannot account for every single example in the P source. Before presenting his theory, those conditions which call for the reparation sacrifice should be listed: (1) the act of misappropriating or misusing an item of sacred value (Lev 5:14–16); (2) sinning inadvertently and not knowing it (Lev 5:17–19); (3) swearing falsely in regard to damages done to another person (Lev 5:20–26—Eng 6:1–7); (4) the rite of purification of the leper; (5) the rite of renewing the vow of the Nazirite who has become unclean (Num 6:10–12); (6) having sexual relations with a slave who has been betrothed to another man (Lev 19:20–21).

Milgrom sees a thread of continuity between cases 1, 3, and 5. In each case something sacred to the deity has been violated. The first case is most obvious; it explicitly says the person has misused a sacred item. As Milgrom observes, this text is very similar in function to the problem of desanctifying an animal that is unfit for sacrifice which is discussed in Lev 27:9–13. Lev 27:9–13 charges a penalty for this desanctification, a penalty equaling the value of the animal plus one-fifth. Milgrom believes that it is not coincidental that Lev 5:14–16 charges the same penalty for misusing a sacred item. In both cases we are dealing with a situation where an item's sacred status has been profaned. Lev 25:9–13 stipulates the *charge* imposed for the *right* to do this, whereas Lev 5:14–16 stipulates the *penalty* imposed for the *crime*. The case of swearing falsely can also be grouped here because a false vow necessarily entails a misuse of the divine name which was originally invoked by the person in question. Indeed as Milgrom demonstrates, violation of vows and desecration of sacred items are treated as parallel phenomena in ANE legal materials. Finally, the case of the Nazirite who has become unclean also represents a case in which a sacred item has been sullied. In this case it is the Nazir himself who had become like a priest himself and hence "holy to the Lord" (Num 6:8). As Milgrom shows, the example of the Nazir has a formal parallel with the case of land dedicated to the sanctuary (Leviticus 27). Both are a result of a vow; both are for a limited period of time; but most importantly both vows can be prematurely terminated and have similar penalties for doing so. Whereas the Nazir brings an *ʾāšām,* the donor of the land must provide the equivalent of the entire value of the land plus an additional 20 percent (in other words, the equivalent of the *ʾāšām*).

The example of the leper and the betrothed slave girl are the most difficult for Milgrom's theory. Neither are said to have violated a sacred item in any way. Milgrom tries to explain the case of the leper on the grounds that elsewhere in the ANE and in the Bible leprosy is often the result of a serious sin against the sancta of a particular deity. On these grounds Milgrom suggests that the leper must bring an *ʾāšām* because he *suspects* he may have so offended the deity. The slave girl cannot be accounted for in this theory (Schwartz 1986).

The case of a person sinning and not knowing it also provides some problems. The text in question (Lev 5:17–19) is so similar in wording to the material in Leviticus 4 that some scholars have suggested that this material is a doublet of the purification rite that has been misplaced by the P editor. Milgrom presumes that the P source knew what it was doing when it put this narrative here. The crucial feature that separates Lev 5:17–19 from the purification offering in Leviticus 4 is that the individual in question sins and *does not know it.* Leviticus 4, on the other hand, deals with cases where inadvertent sin is later realized or made known to the offender. Lev 5:17–19, then, appears to presume a case wherein an individual suffers from either a guilty conscience or, perhaps like Job, suffers the effects of divine retribution but cannot pinpoint the cause. In the ANE there are many cultic and ritual materials that deal with this exact problem. In each case, when an individual felt the effects of some divine chastisement, the presumption was that the individual had offended the deity in some way. On the basis of this comparative model Milgrom suggests that Lev 5:17–19 functions in the very same way. In this regard its redactional placement after Lev 5:14–16 is quite understandable: whereas vv 14–16 dealt with a known infraction against sancta, vv 17–19 deal with a supposed or alleged infraction.

In summary, one could say that the basic distinction between the purification and reparation offerings is that the purification offering deals with the issue of impurity while the reparation offering deals with profanation of sacred items. Though not every example in the P source can be explained this way, the overwhelming majority can.

E. Prophetic Critique

It has been common for Christian scholars of the past to denigrate the entire enterprise of biblical sacrifice. One scholar went so far as to describe the system as a means of "self-help." This obvious importation of an Augustinian-Lutheran reading of a Pauline soteriology into the OT is unacceptable to biblical critics of the most recent past (Stendahl 1963). In any event, there can be no doubt as to why Christian treatments of biblical sacrifice spend as much time as they do on the issue of the OT prophetic critique of the sacrificial system: it calls into question one of the fundamental tenets of Mosaic law. For Christian interpreters, these prophetic criticisms suggest that routine observance of the law in all its particularity is not as important as a more general stance of obedience toward one's God. If one can thus find a foothold in the OT itself for questioning the validity and perhaps timelessness of OT law, then the Pauline imperative that law was only given as a temporary measure (Galatians 3) will not seem so out of line with the OT itself.

Perhaps it was just this type of thinking that prompted Milgrom to read at least one prophetic critique in a very different manner (cf. other examples such as 1 Sam 15:22–23; Isa 1:11–14; Amos 5:21–23; Micah 6:6–9). Milgrom contends that the prophetic critique, at least in Jeremiah, is not a radical questioning of the cult's very foundation (1983a: 119–21). Milgrom's hypothesis is all the more intriguing when one realizes that the particular text in Jeremiah which he addresses is perhaps the most thoroughgoing cultic critique in the Bible:

> Thus says the Lord of hosts, the God of Israel: "Add your burnt offerings to your sacrifices, and eat the flesh. For in the day that I brought them out of the land of Egypt, I did not speak to your fathers or command them concerning burnt offerings and sacrifices. But this command I gave them, 'Obey my voice, and I will be your God . . .' " (Jer 7:21–23).

The text appears to call into question the very foundation on which the sacrificial system rests: the Mosaic legislation. Weinfeld argued (1976) that this prophetic text was a "slap in the face of the Priestly Code." It seemed to overturn the priestly notion that all cultic laws had been part of Mosaic law. Weinfeld also notes that this text was adopted by Maimonides as a proof of the secondary importance of sacrificial practice in the first place. Milgrom, though, reads the text quite differently. He notes that Jeremiah's rebuke only specifies the burnt offering and the peace offering (here called *zebaḥ*). In the P code, these two sacrifices only occur together in the context of voluntary offerings of the individual. The *zebaḥ* never occurs in any cultic calendar of public sacrifice; it is not a statutory offering. The primary staple of the fixed temple cultus was the *tāmîd*. In regard to this offering, Milgrom argues, Jeremiah has nothing to say. "Rather he turns to the people and urges them to renounce their individual offerings because their ritual piety is vitiated by their immoral behavior" (1983a: 274).

One problem with Milgrom's argument, besides its being an argument from silence, is the context of Jeremiah 7 itself. Jeremiah's indictment of the cultus in vv 21–23 occurs within Jeremiah's temple sermon which itself seeks to undermine the grounding of the mythic nature of the temple. Hyperbole against the sacrificial cultus is just what one would expect here. Another problem is Milgrom's attempt to overspecialize the meanings of *ʿôlâ* and *zebaḥ* in this prophetic context. There is no evidence that Jeremiah is dependent on an overly specialized priestly sense here. Rather, the pair *ʿôlâ* and *zebaḥ* are better understood as a merism, a cliche indicating the sacrificial cultus in general. Levine has shown how this pair functions in exactly this way (1974: 21).

In summary, one should not mistake the prophetic critique of the cult for systematic theology. Prophetic discourse occurs in a highly charged atmosphere. It is a mixture of hyperbole, exalted rhetoric, and even polemic. A more balanced view of the prophet's criticism of the cult can be found in the work of A. Davidson (1904). He argues that the Bible contains two models for dealing with human sin. The most prominent would be that of the P code. In P, sins are forgiven through a system of sacrificial atonement. The sins envisioned to fall within this framework are those acts of disobedience which are committed within the context of a larger covenantal bond. The prophets, on the other hand, are concerned with sins of a vastly different nature: sins that represent advertent, gross rebellion against the very fabric of the covenant charter. So heinous are these deeds, that the whole covenant framework is called into question. It is not a question of rejecting P, but rather finding oneself in such a radically new context that P's norms are no longer believed to apply.

A. Toeg (1974) and B. Childs (1986) have recently argued that this "prophetic" understanding of human sin is also to be found in the P code itself. Both scholars point to Leviticus 26, a chapter that lists the curses and blessing that will accrue to Israel depending on her response to the covenant. This chapter moves beyond the concerns of purification and atonement found in Leviticus 1–25. Israel's wanton disobedience, which is foreshadowed here, calls for measures of divine punishment that cannot be altered by the sphere of the cult. The language of judgment found in Leviticus 26, especially the threat to terminate the cultic order itself, is very close to prophetic thought. Toeg goes further and even claims that in one sacrificial law found in P, Num 15:22–31, one also can find evidence of a quasiprophetic critique. In this text, the P writer indicates that not only will all advertent sins be unforgivable in terms of any cultic procedures, but the penalty will also be severe, banishment from the community. The threat of banishment is very close conceptually to the prophetic warning of exile. But perhaps more striking is the P writer's extension of this penalty to *all who sin* in this fashion. Elsewhere in the P code this penalty is used very sparingly and only for the most heinous of sins. Here, however, any advertent sinner is to be banished. Toeg argues that this text, which presents itself as simply another religious law, ought to be understood as a form of prophetic rhetoric, this time employed by the P writer to exhort his community to obedience. Fishbane (1985) has picked up Toeg's argument and has provided additional support for the homiletic nature of this text and its role in a context of preaching rather than strict legal enforcement.

Whether the specific points of Toeg's and Fishbane's theories are accurate need not detain us here. What is important to note is that within the P code itself there are allusions to the type of criticism of the cult that one finds within the prophetic materials. This evidence, in and of itself, should call into question any overly rigid typological distinctions which would isolate priestly concepts of the cult from those of the prophets. The difference has to do with emphasis and rhetorical purpose rather than with outright contradictory evaluations of Israel's spiritual heritage.

F. The Scripturalization of the Cult

1. Biblical Sacrifice in the Second Temple Period. The Israelite sacrificial system has a long and far more expansive existence outside of its brief textual witness in the books of Leviticus and Numbers. It receives extensive attention in pseudepigraphical books that originate in Palestine (*Jubilees*, Temple Scroll) and in Hellenistic sources both within and without Palestine (Josephus, Philo). Of course its most extensive development is to be found in the rabbinic literature beginning with the foundational statement, the Mishnah, the contemporaneous supplementary material of the Tosefta, and culminating in the Palestinian and Babylonian Talmuds, the massive rabbinic commentaries on the Mishnah. Biblical scholars have tended to react to this material in one of two ways. In certain instances the material is conjectured to reflect actual practice in the Second Temple that is then claimed to have certain lines of continuity with First Temple practice (so Milgrom). On the other hand, many scholars have cast aspersions on the utility of this material for the biblical scholar. In this perspective, these Second Temple sources are understood as operating in a world that is sharply distinguished from the biblical one with very few clearly reconstructible lines of continuity. Furthermore, this attitude toward Second Temple writings precludes their having any bearing on biblical exegesis per se; they are understood to have meaning only in relation to the history of Second Temple thought. In other words—to exaggerate a bit for the purpose of clarity—Philo's writings on the biblical sacrificial system can teach us a lot about Philo and Alexandrian Judaism, but precious little about biblical sacrifice. Similarly, the Temple Scroll can teach us a lot about the sect at Qumran and its sectarian outlook, but very little about the nature of biblical sacrifice.

On the one hand, there is no doubt that such a statement contains a good bit of truth. There is a wide gap between Hellenistic philosophical circles in Alexandria and the ritual of blood sacrifice practiced in Solomon's Temple in Jerusalem. Yet the emphasis on the realia of blood sacrifice within the temple of Solomon as the sole determinant of what constitutes biblical sacrifice is a bit odd and tendentious. Behind this emphasis is the mistaken notion that biblical sacrifice is, in its truest form, the historically reconstructed entity of critical scholarship and archaeology. One may construe the matter in a very different manner altogether. Perhaps what is *biblical* about biblical sacrifice is not only the historical *realia* presumed by the texts, but also the interpretation of sacrifice in the *present canonical form of the texts themselves.* After all, it is this canonical form which presented itself to the earliest interpreters of the Bible.

But there is more at stake here than simply taking care to note the final canonical form and its impact on early biblical interpreters. As is becoming increasingly self-evident, the boundary that separates the postbiblical from the biblical period is becoming increasingly hard to draw (Fishbane). The transition from what constitutes the "biblical" to the "postbiblical" period is an extended and, to a degree, overlapping one (VanderKam 1984). In other words, the sharp distinction made by Stendahl (*IDB* 1: 418–32) between what a text *meant* (in the biblical period, by its original author) and what it *means* (to subsequent interpreters) must be blunted on purely historical grounds.

OT scholars are increasingly familiar with the fact that as scripture is being redacted and set in its final form, there is already significant interpretative work being done by the compilers of that literature. Both at the level of gross organization of the antecedent tradition into biblical books and at the more refined level of textual transmission, important hermeneutical shaping of the biblical tradition is taking place. Materials have ceased to be malleable oral traditions, or even written traditions that can be discarded or reworked at will; instead what is evolving are fixed written corpora that are interpreted by a variety of techniques ranging from such simple means as framing them between introductory or concluding formulae (Fishbane 1985) to full scale proto-midrashim (Toeg 1974). In between these poles we might place the phenomena of ascribing various literary works such as the Psalms or the Wisdom material to various biblical figures. What this tells us is that attention to the methods of early exegesis may give us insights into the very methods used by the compilers of the canon.

The interchange between the final composition of the Bible and its early interpretation is becoming increasingly well known for narrative and poetic material. It has not been so readily recognized in the sacrificial material. One obvious reflex of this movement has been the expansion of the Deuteronomistic History by the hand of the Chronicler so as to reflect priestly sacrificial concepts that were absent in the Deuteronomistic History. Sometimes these expansions are unmarked and only noticeable by comparing the Chronicler's expansions with similar material in P. Other times, the expansions are formally marked by the formula "as it is written in the Torah of Moses." More subtle forms of exegetical harmonization can be found in such texts as the Chronicler's treatment of the manner by which the passover sacrifices should be prepared. In this text, the Chronicler says Israel should eat this sacrifice "cooked in water" (2 Chr 35:13). This odd text is translated "roasted in fire" in the JPSV. But what it reflects is the uneasy disjunction between the commandments found in Exod 12:8 and Deut 16:7. The former requires roasting, the latter boiling. What is important to note for our purposes is not simply that the Chronicler has harmonized two conflicting traditions, but the manner in which he appropriates this sacrificial law. No longer are we dealing simply with the realm of temple realia (the Chronicler is not reading back Second Temple practice into his First Temple text) but the *inner-biblical, exegetical formulation of a cultic ideal.* The exegesis is being performed on materials that no longer function as simple prescriptions for the cult. These materials are viewed at a second level of remove from the cultic realia. They have now become contradictory sacrificial prescriptions which must be rectified by exegetical artifice.

2. Example: The Interpretation of the Purification Offering in Second Temple Jewish Sources. A good example of the "scripturalization of the cult" can be seen through the exegetical development of the purification offering in the P code. This general description of this offering exists in two different places in P (Leviticus 4 and Num 15:22–31), and thus constitutes a classic example of what literary critics have labeled a doublet. Leviticus 4 describes the purification offering in terms of four different social groups (priest, congregation, prince, and individual); Numbers 15 in terms of two (congregation, individual). The most important difference is that Leviticus 4 requires that the congregation bring a bull for its purification offering while Numbers 15 requires a calf for the purification offering and a bull for a burnt offering. Conventional scholarship has attempted to see one of these texts as historically primary and the other as a secondary development. Toeg (1974) has correctly criticized this methodology. Though such methods have been used with considerable success in the narrative portions of the Bible where the data for comparative historical analysis can be quite abundant, they often fail in the cultic material precisely because of a paucity of comparative data. In the particular example of the purification offering, Toeg offers an ingenious solution to the problem of the relationship of the two texts which has in turn been picked up and somewhat expanded by Fishbane. Instead of seeing one as reflecting a later *historical* practice than the other, he suggests that the text of Num 15:22–31 is a systematic *exegetical reworking* of Leviticus 4. No longer are we speaking of *development of cultic practice* but rather of *learned reflection on a developing canon of textual material.*

Toeg's argument is predicated on the assumption that the author of Numbers 15 recognized a problem with the formulation of Leviticus 4. In this text—which is a general rule for the purification offering—the congregation is required to bring a bull (4:13–21). Yet, if one looks at all the other examples of how this general rule is applied, one notes that in every case, the congregation brings a goat. Toeg argues that this would have struck the author of Num 15:22–31 as odd. As a result, this writer assumed that the biblical text of Leviticus 4 was an abbreviated one which had to be filled out by a skilled interpreter. Toeg believes that the law of Leviticus 4, which commands the congregation to bring "a bull as a purification offering," was understood to really mean "a bull [for a burnt offering and a goat] for a purification offering." As Toeg shows, such exegetical "expansions" are very common in both midrash halakah and in some of the versions, such as the Samaritan Pentateuch. If Toeg is correct, Num 15:22–31 constitutes an inner-biblical example of this well-attested postbiblical phenomenon. Perhaps more important for the purposes of our argument is how the author of this piece of inner-biblical exegesis has understood the laws of sacrifice. No longer is sacrifice simply a matter of what takes place in the temple; it is also a matter of recovering what a *textual* law requires. And this manner of recovery is not that of observing what happens in an actual ritual of the temple but rather of interpreting what appears to be a problematic biblical text.

Though the treatments of Toeg and Fishbane are significant in their own right, and do provide witness to an early example of the "scripturalization of the cult," they do not address the question of how the data of the canon present themselves to the earliest readers of the Bible. The question we should address is: just how does canonical shaping effect the interpretation of the purification offering? Though Toeg may be correct that Num 15:22–31 constituted an inner biblical interpretation of Leviticus 4, for the readers of the Torah in its final form the two texts would have provided an exegetical problem. They would have assumed that the Torah was a seamless whole and taken the canonical shape of the Torah seriously. Rather than speak abstractly, let us look at how the rabbis and the Temple Scroll (TS) resolved this problem. By reconstructing how the TS read this text and comparing it to rabbinic exegesis we will see how the laws of biblical sacrifice were viewed in their final canonical form.

The basic problem regarding the purification offering, as stated above, is that the Bible contains two sets of general rules regarding its performance: Leviticus 4 and Num 15:22–31. Moreover, these general rules are contradictory about what the congregation must bring: bull or goat. In addition to these two general rules, there are over a dozen examples of particular applications of the rite. When one presents the data this way, the issues facing the early interpreter of scripture are quite clear: one of the general rules had to be shifted into the category of specific application. No halakic system could allow two contradictory sets of general rules to stand. What is the congregation to bring as its purification offering, a bull (Leviticus 4) or a he-goat (Numbers 15)? This is no small matter for a covenantal religion centered on the keeping of commandments.

For the rabbis the choice is very easy to discern. They chose to understand Num 15:22–31 as a specific application. Num 15:22–31 was understood to refer to the sin of idolatry (*m. Hor.* 2:6). Thus the danger of having two sets of general prescriptions was defused. One should note that this exegetical decision is a very prominent feature in the Mishnaic system of sacrificial atonement. It is not a matter of its being found in just a few *halakhoth.* Indeed, the entire tractate of *Horayot* depends on this exegetical decision, as do whole sections of other tractates.

The TS, on the other hand, has understood Leviticus 4 as a special application of the purification offering and Numbers 15 as the general rule (Anderson fc.). Two features of the TS make this clear. First, on the basis of a midrashic reading of Num 15:24b the author of the TS concluded that each purification offering must include a cereal and a drink offering. This exegesis of Num 15:24b was then applied to every application of the purification offering in the TS. Second, the TS understood the peculiar detail of Lev 4:14 which required that the congregation bring a bull as a special application that pertained to the rite of ordination. This fact can be proven by the manner in which the TS expresses the laws with respect to the ordination sacrifices of the priest and congregation. In both cases the TS expresses its laws of ordination on the basis of the distinctive diction of Lev 4:2–12 (the case of the priest) and 4:13–21 (the congregation). One may ask why the day of ordination was chosen as a particular application of the ritual found in Lev 4:1–21. Perhaps because of the unusual summary statement of Lev 7:37:

> This is the law of the burnt offering, of the cereal offering, of the purification offering, of the reparation offering, of the consecration, and of the peace offerings.

This verse summarizes what has just been itemized in detail over Lev 1:1–7:36. However, the careful reader will note that no mention of *the consecration offering* is found in the previous seven chapters. To be sure, there is a brief mention of how Aaron and his sons are to perform the cereal offering at the ordination rite, but no mention of how the animals in particular are to be treated. This textual anomaly has been explained as being due to a faulty transmission of the text. Again, one must note that though this explanation may be fine historically, it does not do justice to the meaning of the text in its final canonical form. For one canonical reader, the author of the TS, this tiny clue in Lev 7:37 pointed to the existence of an ordination rite hidden somewhere in Lev 1:1–7:36. Only with considerable exegetical skill could this rite be discovered.

3. The Sacrificial System in Canonical Perspective. It should be emphasized that what the TS has done is very closely paralleled in the rabbinic materials. The only difference is that the rabbinic sources understood the relationship of Leviticus 4 to Numbers 15 in a contrary fashion; for the rabbis Numbers 15 was the special application (for the sin of idolatry) while Leviticus 4 was the general rule (so the mishnaic tractate *Horayot*). What is common to both of these sources is the attempt to solve a puzzle left in the canonical shaping of the sacrificial material. The type of exegesis that is practiced by the author of the TS and the rabbis might be labeled *holistic* in the sense that these authors use the entire textual tradition of the Sinaitic revelation as the basis for constructing an exegetical system. Though modern critical scholarship has noted many of the irregularities that caught the eye of the author of the TS, its method of understanding those irregularities is quite different. The differences in detail which arise in the Torah's presentation of the purification offering are attributed to variant historical levels of the tradition, artificial fusings of disparate sacrificial lore, and even occasionally faulty transmission of the biblical text. This method of analysis presumes that the present state of the text is not the starting point for analysis, rather that the earlier hypothetically reconstructed levels of the tradition constitutes the most valid entry point for the biblical scholar to begin his or her work.

A more appropriate model of exegesis that would allow the biblical scholar to move from the biblical text to a document like the TS or the mishnaic tractate *Horayot* must presume a mode of analysis that understands the Torah as a systemic whole. Perhaps the closest analogy to the type of exegesis would be the model of canonical exegesis advocated by Childs *(IOTS)* and others. Childs' own formulation of the task of biblical exegesis demands that the reader take seriously the final canonical form of the text as a way of recovering what the earliest shapers of the Bible intended. We would argue that the mode of analysis that Childs' presupposes, which seeks to understand the text in categories that are not purely historical, is the best starting point for understanding the conceptual horizon of early exegetes like the author of the TS. It is not a fact that the author of the TS was paying particular attention to the process of canonical shaping as much as he was working within the constraints of the canonical product. What modern scholars dismiss as textual accidents of omission are details of highest significance to early readers of the Bible.

It is most important to note the legacy of biblical sacrifice in its final canonical form. There is a certain tension in this form which must be appreciated. On the one hand, we can see as a result of historical criticism that the canonical shapers were selective in regard to what they put in the text. At no time in Israel's cultic history did this book as a collective whole function as a priest's manual. Or, to put it another way, the canonical shapers did not choose one particular historical expression of Israel's cultic experience as normative. In a very real sense this selectivity demonstrates that the cultic material of the Torah is "one step removed from the actual historical activity of the cult" (Childs 1986: 160). But, on the other hand, these statutes are presented, in their final literary or canonical form, as *perpetual laws that cannot be periodized.* We could summarize this dilemma in the following manner: biblical sacrifice in its final canonical form consisted of disparate and fragmentary cultic materials which were presented en masse as a perpetual coherent system. Nowhere can this be better illustrated than in the example of Leviticus 4 and Num 15:22–31. Here we have materials that are one step removed from the cult and thus make any systematic historical reconstruction very difficult. Witness the many varied and often self-contradictory solutions of modern scholarship regarding their historical priority, none of which can claim an overwhelming consensus. Yet for the earliest readers of the Bible, this text presents itself as a perpetual statute, not a law that can be historically cordoned off into a particular epoch of history, nor a law that simply represents a mode of demonstrating covenantal obedience. Rather, this is a commandment that calls for actualization in the present. For the reader of the Bible in the Second Temple period the question had a particular edge: just which animal does the congregation bring for a purification offering? The author of the TS provided one answer, the rabbis another. As is true for the material on the purification offerings, so also for the other sacrifices. Removed historically on the one hand, yet commanding on the other—this is the legacy of biblical sacrifice in its final canonical form.

4. Biblical Sacrifice in Jewish and Christian Tradition. It has recently been argued that most of the Mishnah's treatment of the sacrificial system is a response to the destruction of the temple in 70 C.E. The ideological and exegetical superstructure of the tractate on sacred offerings has been explained as an attempt to recreate the world of the *destroyed* temple. No doubt there is much truth to such a suggestion. Indeed the exegetical reconstruction of the temple in the Mishnah was so successful that one can find the rabbis, in the context of interpreting the text, speaking of the sacrificial cultus as if it were still in operation (Bregman 1978). This "as if" quality of rabbinic speech continues to influence readers of rabbinic literature until the present day. As the anthropologist S. Heilman notes, the textual details of the temple cultus are still discussed in the present tense in contemporary Talmudic study groups *(haburoth).* Moreover, the discussion is not limited to rote citation of divergent textual traditions or rabbinic opinions, but rather the whole sacrificial complex is, in part, composed afresh (Heilman 1984: 65) by each *haburah.* He writes: "As we reviewed each move the ancient priests would make in their ritual preparation of the sacrifices, I could begin to see all that rush of activity a bit more clearly. It was evident my partners [in the *haburah*] around the table were walking into the page and onto the Temple Mount with all the assurance of old hands. When they came to a discussion of the sprinkling of blood on the altar and wondered aloud whether or not the priest bent his wrist in that act, it took only a quick look back into their own memory to see precisely how the ritual was carried out. But this memory was of course not theirs in origin; it was a memory acquired from the text. Their many years of review had allowed them to construct that ancient Temple and altar in their minds and people it with priests and worshippers" (p. 62). In the circle of these *haburoth* the transformation of biblical sacrifice from temple-practice to exegetical artifice is complete. The cultus has been "scripturalized."

The movement by the rabbis to transform the sacrificial system from that of a physical reality into an exegetical reality was enormously successful. But one must question whether this project is to be understood *solely* as a reaction to the events of 70 C.E. If the data we have compiled from the TS reflect a more general phenomenon of the pre-70 period era, then we can safely assume that the exegetical refashioning of the sacrificial system was already well underway in the pre-70 period. For Christians, this refashioning of the cultic system led to the denigration of much of the particularities of the books of Leviticus and Numbers.

Not only were the details of Leviticus understood to be tedious, but the very fact that Jesus had predicted the actual destruction of the temple (Matt 24:1–3) seemed to call for a depreciation of the intrinsic value of the sacrificial cult. Indeed in the Byzantine city of Jerusalem the entire area of Temple Mount was left in a very conspicuous state of destruction as a physical sign and symbol of the fall of the first covenant. The sacrificial material of the OT had value only insofar as it pointed allegorically or typologically to the atoning death of Jesus of Nazareth and the new covenant his resurrection occasioned. Even OT materials that had little or no relation to the process of atonement, like the Passover rite, were made to conform to this Christological pattern (cf. 1 Cor 5:7).

For Jews, though, the cultic details of Leviticus and Numbers and the sometimes conflicting and incomplete laws found therein became the subject of intensive exegetical study. The final shaping of the Torah had put the diverse and, at times, fragmentary cultic materials of the First Temple period into a unitary framework: they now comprised the complete Torah which the Lord delivered to Moses at Mt. Sinai. The tension that resulted from the presentation of this fragmentary and diverse material as a complete revelation provided the impetus for subsequent interpreters creatively to refashion this Torah through carefully derived exegetical principles. Such is the legacy of biblical sacrifice in its canonical form; all the rest is commentary.

Bibliography

Anderson, G. A. 1987. *Sacrifices and Offerings in Ancient Israel: Studies in their Social and Political Importance.* HSM 41. Atlanta.

———. 1989. Celibacy or Consummation in the Garden? Reflections on Early Jewish and Christian Interpretations of the Garden of Eden. *HTR* 82: 121–48.

———. fc. The Interpretation of Leviticus 4 and Numbers 15:22–31 in the Temple Scroll. *RQ.*

Bourdillon, M. 1980. *Sacrifice.* New York.

Bregman, M. 1978. Past and Present in Midrashic Literature. *HAR* 2: 45–59.

Burkert, W. 1983. *Homo Necans: The Anthropology of Ancient Greek Sacrificial Ritual and Myth.* Berkeley.

Childs, B. 1971. Psalm Titles and Midrashic Exegesis. *JSS* 16: 137–50.

———. 1986. *Old Testament Theology in a Canonical Context.* Philadelphia.

Davidson, A. 1904. *Theology of the Old Testament.* New York.

Dussaud, R. 1941. *Les origines Cananéenes du sacrifice Israélite.* Paris.

Fishbane, M. 1985. *Biblical Interpretation in Ancient Israel.* Oxford.

Frazier, J. B. 1890. *The Golden Bough.* 13 vols. London.

Gese, H. 1981. *Essays on Biblical Theology.* Trans. K. Crim. Minneapolis.

Girard, R. 1977. *Violence and the Sacred.* Baltimore.

Goody, J. 1977. *The Domestication of the Savage Mind.* New York.

Gray, G. B. 1925. *Sacrifice in the Old Testament.* Rep. New York.

Haran, M. 1978. *Temples and Temple-Service in Ancient Israel.* Oxford.

Heilman, S. 1984. *The Gate Behind the Wall.* New York.

Hubert, H., and Mauss, M. 1899. *Essai sur la nature et la fonction du sacrifice. L'année sociologique* 2: 29–138.

Janowski, B. 1982. *Sühne als Heilsgeschehen: Studien zur Sühnetheologie der Priesterschrift und zur Wurzel KPR in Alten Orient und im Alten Testament.* WMANT 55. Neukirchen-Vluyn.

Knohl, I. 1988. *The Conception of God and Cult in the Priestly Torah and in the Holiness School.* Diss., Jerusalem.

Köhler, L. 1957. *Old Testament Theology.* London.

Kraus, H. J. 1965. *Worship in Israel.* Richmond.

Levine, B. 1963. Ugaritic Descriptive Rituals. *JCS* 17: 105–11.

———. 1965. The Descriptive Tabernacle Texts of the Pentateuch. *JAOS* 85: 307–18.

———. 1974. *In the Presence of the Lord.* Leiden.

Milgrom, J. 1976. *Cult and Conscience.* Leiden.

———. 1983a. *Studies in Cultic Theology and Terminology.* Leiden.

———. 1983b. The Two Pericopes on the Purification Offering. Pp. 211–15 in *WLSGF.*

Rainey, A. F. 1970. The Order of Sacrifices in Old Testament Ritual Texts. *Biblica* 51: 485–98.

Rendtorff, R. 1967. *Studien zur Geschichte des Opfers im alten Israel.* Neukirchen-Vluyn.

Schmid, R. 1964. *Das Bundesopfer in Israel.* Munich.

Schwartz, B. 1986. A Literary Study of the Slave-girl Pericope—Lev 19:20–22. Pp. 241–55 in *Studies in Bible,* ed. S. Japhet. Jerusalem.

Smith, W. R. 1889. *Lectures on the Religion of the Semites.* Repr. New York, 1969.

Snaith, N. 1957. Sacrifices in the Old Testament. *VT* 7: 308–17.

Stendahl, K. 1963. The Apostle Paul and the Introspective Conscience of the West. *HTR* 56: 199–215.

Tarragon, J. M. de. 1980. *Le cult à Ugarit d'apres les textes de la pratique en cunéiformes alphabétiques.* Paris.

Thompson, R. J. 1963. *Penitence and Sacrifice in Early Israel outside the Levitical Law.* Leiden.

Tigay, J. 1982. *The Evolution of the Gilgamesh Epic.* Philadelphia.

Toeg, A. 1974. Numbers 15:22–31—Midrash Halakha. *Tarbiz* 43: 1–10.

Turner, V. 1977. Sacrifice as Quintessential Process: Prophylaxis or Abandonment? *HR* 17: 189–215.

Twersky, I. 1972. *A Maimonides Reader.* New York.

Tylor, E. B. 1871. *Primitive Culture.* 2 vols. New York.

Valeri, V. 1985. *Kingship and Sacrifice.* Chicago.

VanderKam, J. 1984. *Enoch and the Growth of an Apocalyptic Tradition.* CBQMS 16. Washington.

Weinfeld, M. 1976. Jeremiah and the Spiritual Metamorphosis of Israel. *ZAW* 88: 17–55.

———. 1983. Social and Cultic Institutions in the Priestly Source against Their ANE Background. Pp. 95–129 in the *Proceedings of the Eighth World Congress of Jewish Studies.* Jerusalem.

Wright, D. 1986. The Gesture of Hand Placement in the Hebrew Bible and in Hittite Literature. *JAOS* 106: 433–46.

———. 1987. *The Disposal of Impurity: Elimination Rites in the Bible and in Hittite and Mesopotamian Literature.* Atlanta.

Yadin, Y. 1983. *The Temple Scroll.* Jerusalem.

GARY A. ANDERSON

NEW TESTAMENT

When the NT was in the process of formation, any religion without the practice of sacrifice would have been almost inconceivable. As far as Judaism is concerned, the sacrifices described by the law continued to be offered daily in Jerusalem right up to the destruction of the temple in A.D. 70. Following that event the rabbis continued to discuss the sacrificial system as prescribed by the Torah and in fact laid even greater emphasis upon it (cf., e.g., *Zebaḥ*). In the gentile world the practice of sacrifice continued into late antiquity (cf. Rudhardt and Reverdin 1981). On the other hand, signs of a reaction against the practice began to appear. There was precedent for this in the OT with the prophetic critique of the cultus (e.g., Amos 5:21–27) and in the metaphorical use of sacrificial terms for interior religious dispositions (Ps 50:23; 51:19). There are further examples of this in postbiblical Judaism, e.g., Philo of Alexandria and the Qumran sect. Philo was a Diaspora Jew with no direct contact with the temple cult. He interpreted the OT references to sacrifice in allegorical terms and took them to refer to inward processes of the soul (cf. *Vita Mos* 2.106–8). As a result of its historical circumstances the Qumran sect found it impossible to take part in temple worship even though in principle they would have liked to have done so. They found a way out of their dilemma by interpreting their whole communal life, their very existence, their organization, and their prayer life in cultic terms (cf. 1QS 8:5–10; Klinzing 1971: 50–166). In any case the centralizing of worship in Jerusalem made it increasingly necessary, even before the debacle of A.D. 70, for those living outside the holy city to worship in the synagogue. Here holiness in everyday life provided a substitute for the sacrificial system. In Greek philosophy since pre-Socratic times there had been a strong tradition advocating a more appropriate view of God and humanity. This led to a polemic against blood sacrifice which reached its climax in the hermetic literature, with its fundamental antagonism toward the cultus (cf. *Ascl.* 41). We find the same thing in Porphyry (Ferguson 1980: 1152–65).

Such was the world into which Christianity was born. In general it may be said that Christianity succeeded in bringing the problem of sacrifice into association with the Christ event and working it out from that perspective. To be specific, the following questions arise in connection with the various levels of historical tradition and the respective documents: What was the Christians' attitude to the sacrificial practices of Judaism and pagan religion? Are the death of Jesus on the cross and, in close connection with it, the Lord's Supper, interpreted in sacrificial terms? In what way was sacrificial imagery employed as a metaphor for the Christian life?

A. Jesus and the Synoptic Tradition

1. Attitude to Sacrifice. There is surprisingly little about the actual performance of sacrifices in the Jesus tradition. We are never told that Jesus took an active part in them. In the infancy narratives (Luke 1:8–11; 2:22–24) temple sacrifice is mentioned merely as part of the necessary background. There is one authentic Jesus saying which is relevant, viz. Matt 5:23. Here the practice of sacrifice is taken for granted. The same is true in Mark 1:44 and Luke 17:15; cf. 13:1. On textual grounds Mark 9:49 is to be regarded as secondary and so may be left out of the account. There is no trace of any direct polemic against sacrifice. At the same time, however, Jesus does expect the worshipper, if necessary, to stop what he is doing in the middle of a sacrifice in order to seek reconciliation with a neighbor. Here we have a paradoxical and provocative perspective. Jesus takes up the requirements of OT liturgy and Jewish admonitions about approaching sacrifice in the proper frame of mind and enhances them in a significant way (Kertelge 1983: 349–51). The redactional insertion of the prophet's critique of the cultus (Hos 6:6) in Matt 9:13 and 12:7 is along the same lines. Mark 12:33 (cf. 1 Sam 15:22) gives a similar precedence to the love commandment over burnt offerings *(holokautōmata)* and other sacrifices *(thysiai)*. The same point is made indirectly in Luke 10:25–37 with the two figures of the priest and Levite in vv 31 and 32 (cf. also Mark 7:9–13; 12:41–44). Jesus introduces an unmistakably new emphasis in the cleansing of the temple (Mark 11:15–19), as he does with the difficult saying about the temple's destruction (Mark 14:58 par). In an act of prophetic symbolism Jesus shows explicitly that the temple is first and foremost a place not for the sacrificial cultus—which is so easily open to corruption—but for prayer to God (cf. Isa 56:7). In line with the apocalyptic hope for a new temple in the end time Jesus sets before his people the prospect of a complete renewal of worship in the kingdom of God. Such things as the forgiveness of sins (Mark 2:5) and festive table fellowship (Mark 2:15), which in Judaism had sacrificial associations, Jesus transforms, with supreme messianic authority, into profane occasions of everyday life.

2. Suffering and Death. It can hardly be denied that Jesus had a premonition of his impending suffering and death. The question is, What categories did he use to interpret these events? And which of them belong to the pre- or post-Easter strata of the tradition? (Gubler 1977: 206–334; Hengel 1981: 65–75). Sacrificial images should not be given too much prominence in a one-sided way. Nor should they be entirely eliminated. After all, it was customary in Judaism to use such terms for the deaths of human beings. The innocent death of the Servant of God on behalf of the many, i.e., the nations of the world (Isa 53:12), was regarded as a sin offering (Isa 53:10; cf. 53:6f; *T. Ben.* 3:8 may have undergone Christian reworking). The martyrdom of the Maccabees was believed to be a means of atonement for the sins of the people (*4 Macc.* 6:29; cf. 2 Macc 7:37). This means that the Jews considered the vicarious surrender of life to have sacrificial significance. This was partly, though by no means entirely, a result of Hellenistic influence. True, the personal dimension remains primary; the ritual allusion is added more by way of illustration. In any case, this opens up the way as far as it goes for the interpretation of Jesus' death as a fulfillment of the OT sacrifices and their atoning effect. Of course it is difficult to prove how much of this goes back to the historical Jesus himself. We cannot be sure whether he used Isaiah 53 as Mark 10:45 suggests. This logion probably has its *Sitz im Leben* in the eucharistic tradition and must be judged accordingly.

3. The Last Supper. In the eucharistic tradition we find a great variety of motifs concentrated in a remarkably small space. The following elements may be mentioned as suggesting a sacrificial interpretation (cf. Cooke 1960: 15–38; Aalen 1963: 147–52). (a) In our texts the Lord's Supper is set in the framework of the Passover. Now, in Judaism the Passover was interpreted as a sacrifice because of the killing of the lambs in the temple and the shedding of blood which accompanied it. (b) The cup-word in Mark 14:24 includes the phrase "the blood of the covenant which was shed. . . ." This is an allusion to the covenant sacrifice and to the sacrificial meal in which it culminated (Exod 24:1–10). (c) In the same cup-word the phrase "for the many *(hyper)*" is a reminiscence of Isa 53:12. Here we have a connecting link with the martyrological interpretation of the Servant Song. Matt 26:28 makes the specific point that its purpose was "the forgiveness of sins," an idea associated in Judaism with the sin offering. (d) Various attempts have been made to classify the Lord's Supper as a *tōdā meal,* another type of OT sacrifice. But this suggestion cannot be taken as proven (cf. Klauck 1986: 17f.). We must reject the thesis that "body" and "blood" in the words of interpretation were technical terms associated with sacrifice, referring to the division of the sacrificial animal into its component parts (Klauck 1986: 305–61). Rather, the word "body" stands for the entire person of the speaker, while "blood" points to his violent end.

The expansion of the eucharistic words with sacrificial notions is the result of a theological development which was as rapid as it was intensive. The source of it seems to lie in the gestures and words which Jesus used at his farewell meal to interpret his death as a voluntary act of self-giving. After Easter all this could be brought out and made explicit with the help of sacrificial terms derived from Jewish martyrology and covenant theology. It was an attempt to express the uniqueness of Jesus' death and its universal validity, and to show how it was the ultimate fulfillment of the ancient sacrificial cultus. The rending of the temple veil in Mark 15:38 points in the same direction. The death of Jesus opens up access for all to the holy of holies which only the high priest hitherto could enter once a year on the Day of Atonement.

B. The Primitive Christian Community

In Acts 2:46, 3:1, and 5:42 we see the early Jerusalem community regularly attending the temple. But they only went there for the times of prayer, thus agreeing with the cleansing of the temple in Mark 11:17 ("house of prayer"). Whether they occasionally took part in the daily sacrifices is not entirely clear. From Acts 2:46 we gather that the breaking of bread in private homes replaced the temple sacrifices. This rite formed a nucleus from which distinctive Christian forms of worship were developed (Hahn 1983: 69–71). The canonical texts do not make it clear whether the strict Jewish Christians associated with James took a more favorable view of sacrificial practice or whether such an attitude developed over the course of time. The apocryphal evidence is equally vague. It is typical that the Hellenists, Diaspora Jews who had already drifted away from temple worship, were critical of the temple itself and the sacrificial cult, as can be seen from Stephen's speech (Acts 7:41–43, 48–49). It is obvious that in circles such as these the view prevailed that Christ's death had an exclusive saving significance. This was realized through the resurrection and the descent of the Holy Spirit. Hence the earlier cult became superfluous. The development of the eucharistic tradition and the concomitant formation of creedal statements belong to this phase. We can trace these developments in the older formulae of the epistolary literature.

C. Paul

1. Attitude to Sacrifice. As a result of his origins and the sphere of his missionary activity Paul was on the one hand familiar with the temple sacrifices of Judaism. On the other hand he found himself face-to-face with the sacrificial cults of paganism (cf. the telling description in Acts 14:11–15).

a. Jewish. In arguing for his right as an apostle to receive financial support Paul refers in 1 Cor 9:13 to the privilege of the priests to have a share in the sacrifices (cf. Lev 6:9 etc.). In 10:18 he speaks of the table fellowship in which "Israel according to the flesh" became partners in the sacrifice. It is an open question whether Paul is simply giving an objective description or whether he is continuing the polemical invective of 10:7—the golden calf, Exod 32:6—as an instance of idolatry. In Acts 22:17 Paul visits the temple only for prayer, whereas in 21:26 he offers a sacrifice to discharge the dues for four Nazarites (cf. Num 6:13–21). The reliability of this piece of information has often been questioned. It becomes more plausible when we take Paul's missionary policy enunciated in 1 Cor 19:20 seriously.

b. Pagan. Paul discusses the sacrificial practices of paganism in a debate about meat sacrificed to idols in Corinth (cf. Acts 15:29). For Christians, participating in a sacrifice or worshipping in a pagan temple (1 Cor 8:10) is strictly prohibited. Paul believes that pagan sacrifices are offered not to God but to demons (10:20) as was already the case in the OT (cf. Deut 32:17). He is familiar with the technical details of sacrifice as we can see when he refers in 10:21 to the cup of libation and to the table which was a special feature of the *theoxenia* (a banquet given to the gods) and of the cult of the dead (Klauck 1986: 264–71).

2. Christological Use. It would be wrong to suppose that everything Paul has to say about atonement (e.g., Gal 2:20; 1 Cor 15:3; 2 Cor 5:14–15; Rom 5:8–9; 8:3, 32) has sacrificial implications. But the idea of atonement, with its related images (e.g., ransom and reconciliation), includes the metaphor of sacrifice (Hengel 1981: 34–54). When Paul says Christ was offered as our paschal lamb (1 Cor 5:7) he is borrowing from early tradition. In this instance the death of Jesus has already affected Christian perspective on Jewish ritual and has accentuated already latent ideas of sacrifice and atonement. In Jewish thought the killing of the lamb, though a necessary preliminary to the Passover meal, had no intrinsic significance of its own (Schmitz 1910: 51, 161). When Paul says in 2 Cor 5:21 that "he made him to be sin who knew no sin," this is best taken as an allusion to the OT sin offering (*hamartia,* e.g., LXX Lev 4:8, 20–21). Such sacrifices are now overshadowed by the death of Christ (Lyonnet and Sabourin 1970: 187–289). In Rom 3:25 Paul cites a fragment of tradition which probably comes from the Hellenistic circle in Jerusalem. It shows their critical attitude to the temple and was probably connected with the Lord's Supper (Gubler 1977: 224–30). The focal points in it are "place of atonement" *(hilastērion)* and "in his blood." The LXX uses *hilastērion* to translate *kappōreth.* This is the golden plate on the ark of the covenant in the holy of holies, which the high priest sprinkles with the blood of the animal sacrificed as a sin offering on the Day of Atonement (Lev 16:14–16; cf. *4 Macc.* 17:22). The final stage of the atonement ritual takes place concealed within the innermost shrine of the temple, one of a series of sacrifices performed on that occasion. Now, however, the atonement has taken place on Golgotha for all to see. The Deutero-Pauline saying in Eph 5:2 makes the same point. Here we have a formula which speaks of Christ's self-surrender ("he gave himself for us"), expanded with sacrificial language from the OT: "as a fragrant offering and a sacrifice to God" (cf. Ps 40:7; Num 15:24, etc.). The context here is parenetic. It is an appeal to Christians, bidding them to show the same kind of love to one another (Hahn 1983: 75–76).

3. The Lord's Supper. The Lord's Supper appears to be connected with sacrifice in 1 Cor 10:14–22, where Paul places the two entities side by side and draws a comparison between them (Fiebig 1911: 272–73). But Paul is not thinking of *thysia,* the actual performance of a sacrifice, but of *koinonia,* the fellowship which is formed by participation in the common meal and which forms the climax of the sacrifice. The Christ community created by the Lord's Supper is exclusive in character and rules out any further participation in pagan sacrifices (Klauck 1986: 284–85). In 1 Cor 11:27 sacral terminology is used in connection with the eucharistic tradition (Aalen 1963: 143–46). Again, in the explanation given at 11:30 Paul uses the idea of taboo, which comes from the sacrificial cultus. Such ideas are certainly not dominant in the text taken as a whole. It is arguable that, for Paul, Jesus' self-offering on the cross becomes a present reality in the Lord's Supper (cf. 1 Cor 11:26), but in no way can it be said that the Church itself offers any sacrifice in the supper except perhaps in a metaphorical or ethical sense.

4. Metaphorical (Ethical) Use. There is ample evidence for a metaphorical or ethical use of sacrificial language. Such terms describe concrete Christian behavior exhibited in everyday life in the world or in the missionary activity of the apostle himself (Klauck 1989: 349–56).

Temple imagery is used to describe the community in 1 Cor 3:16–17 and the individual in 6:19 (cf. 2 Cor 6:16; Eph 2:19–22; 1 Pet 2:5–6; Klinzing 1971: 167–96). In Phil 4:18 Paul gives a symbolic meaning to the material gifts provided by the Philippians: they are a "fragrant offering" (cf. Gen 8:21, etc.) and an "acceptable sacrifice" (Rom 15:31). The cultic language in 12:1 is colored much more by the Hellenistic milieu. The closest parallels to *logikē latreia* ("reasonable service") are to be found in *Corp. Herm.* 1.31; 13.18. Yet in one respect Paul does transcend the Hellenistic critique of the cultus with its spiritualizing tendency (Seidensticker 1954: 17–43, 256–63). He can charge the Romans to offer their own bodies *(sōmata)* as a living sacrifice. Here Paul rises to new heights of existential relevance and ethical responsibility. In this connection we may also add 1 Pet 2:5. Here the community is pictured as a priestly body which offers spiritual sacrifices *(pneumatikas thysias)* in a life consistent with its faith (cf. 1:15).

In 2 Cor 2:14–16 Paul borrows two sacrificial terms, "savior" and "aroma," and applies them to the preaching of the gospel. The content of the gospel is Christ, with the apostle as his personal representative. In Rom 15:16 Paul calls himself a "liturgist" or "priest" of Christ Jesus. He is performing a "priestly sacrifice" *(hierogounta)* and making the gentiles into an "acceptable sacrifice" by converting them. In Phil 2:17 the two trains of thought converge. Alongside "sacrifice" *(thysia)* and cultic service *(liturgia),* Paul introduces the image of "drink offering" (*spendomai;* cf. 2 Tim 4:6). He pictures his own life, which he is likely to lose (cf. Rom 8:36), as a libation accompanying the main sacrifice, which is the Philippians' faith. See APOSTLE.

In conclusion let us mention the term *aparchē,* which is derived from the offering of the firstfruits and is applied by Paul in several different ways. He uses it for Christ (1 Cor 15:20, 23), for the Holy Spirit (Rom 8:23), for Israel (Rom 11:16), and for the first converts to be baptized in a particular city (1 Cor 16:15; Rom 16:5).

D. The Johannine Writings

1. The Gospel of John. According to the gospel of John Jesus travels several times to Jerusalem in order to celebrate the principal Jewish feasts (2:13; 5:1; 7:14; 10:22–23; cf. 12:1, 12, 20). He suffers death on the cross on the day before the Passover (18:28; 19:14, 31) at the same hour the lambs were being slaughtered for the Passover meal in the forecourt of the temple. How far this rests on historical reminiscence we need not now inquire. The gospel's intention is to say that Jesus invests the Jewish lamb cult with entirely new content. He gives himself (3:16; cf. Horvarth 1979: 74–77) as the Passover lamb of the new covenant (cf. 19:36) for *(hyper)* his own (10:15; cf. 13:1) and for the life of the world (6:51; cf. 11:50, 52; 18:14). John 6:51 serves as a bridge to the tradition of the Lord's Supper. The Johannine redaction carries this further in the eucharistic discourse of 6:52–58, which is remarkable for its brutal language about "flesh" and "blood" and "chewing" *(trōgein)* the flesh. Whether this language is sacrificial in origin (Betz 1964: 180–81) is open to question. According to 1:29 (cf. 1:36) the Baptist calls Jesus the "Lamb who takes away the sin of the world" (cf. also 1 Pet 1:19). But the matrix of this concept was more likely the Servant of Yahweh of Isa 53:7, even though further connotations (paschal lamb; the lamb of the daily Tamid-sacrifices) cannot be excluded. The saying about Jesus consecrating himself in 17:19 should most likely be connected with the activity of the high priest on the Day of Atonement (Schmitz 1910: 256–57). The theological basis for the new evaluation of the Jewish sacrificial cult is laid down by the Evangelist in 4:20–24. Earthly places of cultic worship lose their significance when the eschatological hour dawns. The need is for a new form of worship "in spirit and in truth." The *pneuma,* i.e., the reality of God, makes the renewal of worship possible. Jesus Christ is an essential factor in such worship for he is the One in whom God's *truth* is personally revealed. Such worship of God in the spirit is not therefore to be construed as a purely spiritual affair which only takes place in the human psyche. Rather, it is located in the worship of the Johannine community.

2. 1 John. In 1 John 1:7 we read that the "blood of Jesus" cleanses us from all sin. This assumes that blood has an atoning effect (Lev 17:11) brought about by the sprinkling of the blood of the sacrificial animal on the horns of the altar or suchlike manipulations. Later on in 2:2 (cf. 4:10) we read that Jesus, our advocate in heaven (2:1) is in person the atonement *(hilasmos)* for our sins. Atonement according to the OT is accomplished through bloody sacrifice. In Lev 25:9 the great day of reconciliation is called the "Day of Atonement" (LXX: *hilasmou*). 1 John applies the terms of sacrifice strictly to Jesus. They serve to explain 3:16: He gave his "life for us *(hyper)*." The conclusion drawn from this is that we must therefore do the same for our brothers and sisters. The Christians' existence is incorporated into the self-giving of the Lord. The concept of sacrifice can also be applied to the Christian life, although 1 John does not make this point directly.

3. Revelation. The heavenly sanctuary the seer speaks of is modeled after the temple at Jerusalem. The heavenly ritual is patterned on the liturgy of the temple. This provides a starting point for the development of many points of contact with the sacrificial cults. We will select only the most important ones.

The preeminent christological title is the "Lamb" (28 times). There are several references to "the blood of the Lamb" and also to the fact that this lamb was slaughtered (e.g., 5:6, 9, 12; 13:8). The lamb figures in early Judaism as a sacrificial animal par excellence. It serves as a sacrificial element in the daily Tamid. Alongside of this the Passover rites and Isa 53:7 may also be influential. In any case the author uses the Lamb as a code word for the crucified and exalted Lord, who is now enthroned in heaven but bears the signs of his sacrificial death upon his person (Wenschkewitz 1932: 149–52).

Revelation reflects the persecution which provides the immediate context of the work. In 7:14 the author speaks of those who have washed their robes and made them white in "the blood of the Lamb," and in 12:11 of those who have conquered "through the blood of the Lamb." The reference here is to the Christian martyrs who have given up their lives for the sake of their beliefs. In 6:9 their fate is interpreted theologically in sacramental terms. The souls of those who were "slain" for the word of God are under the altar in the heavenly sanctuary. They are the firstfruits *(aparchē)* who were redeemed for God and for the Lamb (14:4).

In the OT the incense offering is by no means unimportant (e.g., Lev 16:13). In Rev 8:3–4 it is transferred from the temple cult on earth to the heavenly liturgy. In Rev 5:8 the incense offering acquires a metaphorical meaning symbolizing the prayers of the saints (Daly 1978: 64–69, 301–3).

E. The Letter to the Hebrews

Of all the writings in the NT the Letter to the Hebrews provides the most systematic treatment of the sacrificial cultus of the OT. But it does so not for its own sake but because it wants to make a theological statement for mainly parenetic purposes. Christians who are unsure of themselves and are unduly impressed by certain Jewish rites (cf. 9:9–10; 12:16; 13:9) are told that they enjoy in full (4:14; 8:1; 13:10) what was only partially available in the worship of the old covenant. The paradox of this work is that it uses a thoroughly cultic language to make a deeply uncultic statement. In sacramental terms it announces the end of all sacrifice (10:18). The author succeeds in using the thought forms of apocalyptic and Platonism (8:5; 9:23; 10:1) to describe the permanent effect of the Christ event—how it fulfills and transcends all previous sacrifices.

1. High Priest and Sacrifice. Christ stands at the center of the argument as the One who is both priest (2:17) and victim (9:14). The author is relatively free in his handling of his OT sources. He uses as his archetype not the temple but the tabernacle in the wilderness (9:1–5). The ritual he has in mind is the liturgy of the great Day of Atonement (9:7). But the covenant sacrifice of Exod 24:3–8 also figures in the discussion (9:18–20; cf. 12:18-21; 13:20), and elsewhere he even mentions the daily sacrifice (7:27; 10:11). The main purpose of all sacrifice was to make atonement for one's own and other people's sins (5:1–3), which is accomplished by the shedding of blood (9:22). But the effects were only temporary (10:1–4, 11). Jesus, the sinless One (7:26), however, offered himself as a victim on the cross and was raised to the right hand of God (12:2). Thus he removed the burden of sin from humanity once and for all (7:27; 9:12, 26, 28; 10:10) by a single sacrifice (10:12, 14) and opened up access to God for them for all time (1:3; 4:16; 10:19). One aspect of this self-sacrifice is the obedience to God which he showed during his earthly life and suffering (5:7–8; cf. 10:9–10). Now he is continuing his priestly work by making intercession in heaven (7:25; 9:24). As we can see from 13:11–12, his death on the cross was basically a noncultic affair despite all the cultic terms employed in 13:11–12. The unclean cadavers of the animals sacrificed on the Day of Atonement were burnt outside the city gates, their blood having already been used in the atonement rites of the temple (Lev 16:27). In this noncultic place Jesus shed his redeeming and atoning blood for all (2:9).

2. The Christian Life. In the parenetic part of the letter (from 10:19 onward) the meaning of this theology of sacrifice for the Christian life of the recipients is set forth. Now that the sacrifice of Christ has freed them from their sins (10:22) they are henceforth enabled and obligated to hold fast to the confession (10:23), to show brotherly love to one another, and to join in the assembly (10:24–25). They must guard against lapsing into sin a second time—if they do so there can be no atoning sacrifice (10:26)—and they must stand firm in suffering (10:32–39; cf. 12:1–11). As the cultic community of the new covenant which takes part in the heavenly liturgy (12:18–24), God finally honors them for their faith and for the gratitude they show in their lives (12:28). The shameful death of Jesus in that unholy place (13:13) should inspire them to face hostility outside of existing religious conventions. Their ongoing sacrifice according to 13:15 consists of prayer and the confession of faith, which the author calls "the fruit of the lips" (cf. Ps 50:14, 23; 1QS 9:26; 10:6, 8, 14, 22). As stated in 13:16, to do good and to maintain fellowship *(koinōnia)* is the only sacrifice pleasing to God. It is a matter of scholarly discussion as to whether these injunctions might be susceptible in part at least to a sacramental interpretation, in other words whether they allude to the celebration of the eucharist (Betz 1964: 144–66). But this is highly questionable since there are no clear indications of that in the text. The expression "blood of the covenant" in 9:20 (cf. 10:29; 13:20) could just as well come directly from the OT, thus bypassing the eucharistic tradition entirely. The term "altar" *(thysiastērion)* in 13:10 serves as a summary description of Christ's saving work as a whole and should not be interpreted in isolation as a reference to the Lord's Supper. It would seem that the primary focus of the community's worship was the Word. The expositor should not be led astray by the sacrificial language.

3. The Binding of Isaac. One of the heroes of the faith cited in Heb 11:17–19 was Abraham, who was ready to sacrifice his only son at God's behest (Gen 22:1–18; cf. esp. v 9 quoted again at Jas 2:21, with a possible allusion in Rom 8:32). Isaac plays a central role in the Jewish Haggadah. He willingly accepts a sacrificial death, and in fact the sacrifice is regarded as actually accomplished. It has the effect of atonement for Israel (Gubler 1977: 336–75; Daly 1978: 175–86). The main evidence for this belief is to be found in the Palestinian Targums. But in view of the late date of their written form we have here a major chronological problem. It may be that it was only after the destruction of the temple that the sacrifice of Isaac came to be interpreted as an archetype of the Tamid-offering and its atoning function (Davies and Chilton 1978). We should therefore be cautious. Heb 11:17–19 shows no sign that this interpretation of the sacrifice of Isaac had already been developed.

F. Conclusion

It is impossible to do justice to the NT evidence if it is judged in the light of a general concept of sacrifice as a phenomenon in the history of religion. Otherwise the novelty and originality of the Christian appropriation of the concept would be decidedly shortchanged. Equally, the favorite notion that sacrifice was "spiritualized" (Wenschkewitz 1932: 6–10) does not really fit the bill. It would be better to speak of its being "christologized" and "pneumatized." Jesus' saving death gives an entirely new meaning to sacrifice as a consequence of his resurrection and the sending of the Holy Spirit. He opened up a new dimension of reality. As a result sacrifice is reduced to its personal core from which ethical consequences can be drawn for Christian faith and life.

Here is the unbroken thread in the early Church's understanding of sacrifice (Daly 1978: 311–508). We can see this, for instance, in the use of sacrificial language in connection with martyrdom (*Ign. Rom.* 2.2; 4.2; Young 1979: 223–33). There is a parallel development in the application of sacrificial language to the new worship of the Christian community. The liturgy comes to be increasingly interpreted in the categories of the OT cultus (1 *Clem.* 40–45). This has an important effect on the understanding of the eucharist (cf. *Did.* 14.1–2), although to begin with it was only the prayer of thanksgiving plus the material gifts of charity that were regarded as the Church's offering. This tendency is enhanced from another angle. The absence of real sacrifices in the ancient sense led to accusations that the early Christians had no cultus of their own and were therefore atheists. The apologists replied by seeing the "pure offering" of Mal 1:11 as a reference to the eucharist. It was the sacrifice of the new covenant (Just. *Dial* 41.1–3; 117.1–3; cf. also Iren. *Haer.* 4.17.5; 4.18.4–5). Much of this development is perfectly understandable from a historical point of view (Young 1979: 239–84), but it has only a limited justification in the NT.

Bibliography

Aalen, S. 1963. Das Abendmahl als Opfermahl im Neuen Testament. *NovT* 6: 128–52.

Betz, J. 1964. *Die Eucharistie in der Zeit der griechischen Väter.* Vol. 2, pt. 1, *Die Realpräsenz des Leibes und Blutes Jesu im Abendmahl nach dem NT.* 2d ed. Freiburg.

Cooke, B. 1960. Synoptic Presentation of the Eucharist as Covenant Sacrifice. *TS* 21: 1–44.

Daly, R. J. 1978. *Christian Sacrifice.* Studies in Christian Antiquity 18. Washington, D.C.

Davies, P. R., and Chilton, B. D. 1978. The Aqedah: A Revised Tradition History. *CBQ* 40: 514–46.

Ferguson, E. 1980. Spiritual Sacrifice in Early Christianity and Its Environment. *ANRW* 2/23/2: 1151–89.

Fiebig, P. 1911. Das kultische Opfer im Neuen Testament. *ZWT* 53: 253–75.

Gubler, M. L. 1977. *Die frühesten Deutungen des Todes Jesu.* OBO 15. Freiburg and Göttingen.

Hahn, F. 1983. Das Verständnis des Opfers im Neuen Testament. Pp. 51–91 in *Das Opfer Jesu Christi und seine Gegenwart in der Kirche.* Ed. K. Lehmann and E. Schlink. Dialog der Kirchen 3. Freiburg and Göttingen.

Hengel, M. 1981. *The Atonement.* Trans. J. Bowden. Philadelphia.

Horvarth, T. 1979. *The Sacrificial Interpretation of Jesus' Achievement in the New Testament.* New York.

Kertelge, K. 1983. Die "reine Opfergabe": Zum Verständnis des "Opfers" im Neuen Testament. Pp. 347–60 in *Freude am Gottesdienst, Aspekte ursprünglicher Theologie.* Ed. J. Schreiner. Stuttgart.

Klauck, H. J. 1986. *Herrenmahl und hellenistischer Kult.* 2d ed. NTAbh n.s. 15. Münster.

———. 1989. Kultische Symbolsprache bei Paulus. Pp. 348–58 in *Gemeinde-Amt-Sakrament,* ed. H. J. Klauck. Würzburg.

Klinzing, G. 1971. *Die Umdeutung des Kultus in der Qumrangemeinde und im Neuen Testament.* SUNT 7. Göttingen.

Lyonnet, S., and Sabourin, L. 1970. *Sin, Redemption, and Sacrifice.* AnBib 48. Rome.

Rudhardt, J., and Reverdin, O., eds. 1981. *Le sacrifice dans l'Antiquité.* Entretiens sur l'Antiquité classique 27. Geneva.

Schmitz, O. 1910. *Die Opferanschauung des späteren Judentums und die Opferaussagen des Neuen Testaments.* Tübingen.

Seidensticker, P. 1954. *Lebendiges Opfer (Röm 12,1).* NTAbh 20/1–3. Münster.

Wenschkewitz, H. 1932. *Die Spiritualisierung der Kultusbegriffe Tempel.* Angelos Beihefte 4. Leipzig.

Young, F. M. 1979. *The Use of Sacrificial Ideas in Greek Christian Writers from the New Testament to John Chrysostom.* Patristic Monograph Series 5. Cambridge, MA.

Hans-Josef Klauck
Trans. Reginald H. Fuller

SADDLE. See ZOOLOGY.

SADDUCEES [Gk *Saddoukaios*]. One of the major groups constituting Palestinian Judaism in the late Hellenistic and early Roman periods.

A. Sources
B. Name
C. Beliefs and Doctrines
D. Social Status
E. History

A. Sources

Contemporary references to the Sadducees are found in Josephus, the NT, and in the rabbinic corpus. Josephus first mentions the Sadducees as the second of the schools of thought (Gk *haireseis*) among the Jews of his day (*JW* 2 §119; 164–65; *Ant* 13 §171). The chronologically earliest appearance of them is in connection with events at the time of John Hyrcanus (135–104 B.C.E.; *Ant* 13 §293, 297). Their doctrine differed from Pharisaic teaching (*Ant* 13 §297–98) and was of great antiquity (*Ant* 18 §11); it primarily concerned personal immortality (which they denied: *Ant* 18 §16), determinism (which they rejected: 13 §173), and the validity of tradition (which they ignored, though inconsistently: 18 §17). Sadducees appear infrequently as a contemporary group with much the same doctrines in the NT (Matt 3:7; 16:1, 6, 11, 12; 22:23, 34; Mark 12:18; Luke 20:27; Acts 4:1; 15:17; 23:6–8).

Mention of the Sadducees in rabbinic literature is rather more abundant in the Mishnah (e.g., *m. ʿErub.* 6.1; *Mak.* 1.6; *Yad.* 3.7; 4.6, 7; *Nid.* 4.2; 5.2, 3; *Para* 3.7, 8), the Babylonian Talmud (e.g., *ʿErub.* 68a; *Yoma* 2b, 4a, 19b; *Ḥag.* 16b, 23a; *B. Bat.* 115b; *Sanh.* 33b, 52b; *Mak.* 8b; *Hor.* 4a–b; *Zebaḥ.* 65a; *Nid.* 33b), the Palestinian Talmud (*B. Bat.* 8.1), and in the Tannaitic Midrashim (*Sipra* 81b; *Sipre Num.* 112; *Sipre Deut.* 190). In many instances the word "Sadducees" in later rabbinic texts proves to be ambiguous, the intended reference in some contexts being to "heretics" and "gentiles" (i.e., Christians) in avoidance of medieval censors.

It is clear that anyone wishing to study the Sadducees faces a major obstacle, for all of the extant information about this sect must be culled from documents written by people who were not members of the sect and who often opposed them.

B. Name

Some of the Church Fathers (e.g., Epiphanius [*Haer.* 1.14] and Jerome [*Comm. in Matt.* 22:23]) thought that the term was derived from the adjective "righteous," *ṣaddîq*. However, modern scholarship connects it with the name Zadok, *ṣādôq*. Although a story in *ʾAbot R. Nat.* A.5 states that the term "Sadducees" derives from Zadok, a disciple of Antigonus of Soco (who is said to have flourished early 2d century B.C.E.), current scholarly opinion connects the term to the name of Zadok, the high priest at the time of David (1 Sam 8:17 and 15:24) and of Solomon (1 Kgs 1:34 and 1 Chr 12:29). Stern (1976: 561, 567) states that from the beginning of the Persian period until the wake of the Maccabean revolt, the priestly house of Zadok, descended from Joshua son of Yehozadak, controlled the high priesthood in Jerusalem. Thus, Mansoor (*EncJud* 14: 62) claims that the term "Sadducees" refers to "anyone who is a sympathizer with the Zadokites." Kohler stated that "in the course of time" the term became "a party name applied to all the aristocratic circles connected with the high priests by marriage and other social relations" (*JEnc* 10: 630–33). However, as we shall see, the actual connection between the Sadducees and the priests is unclear.

C. Beliefs and Doctrines

Josephus identifies the Sadducees as one of the major varieties of Judaism which came into existence during the Maccabean period. In *JW* 2 §162 he refers to the Sadducees' rejection of the concept of fate and their acceptance of the idea of man's free will. He implies that they held these ideas so that God could not be held responsible for evil. Furthermore, the Sadducees did not believe that the soul continued to exist after death or that people suffered punishments or received rewards after they died. In *Ant* 13 §293 Josephus refers to only the Sadducees' belief in free will, and in *Ant* 18 §16–17 he refers to their claim that the soul perished along with the body at death. The most striking feature about these lists is that no single belief appears in all of them. When Josephus enumerated the Sadducees' doctrines not one element of their system of beliefs so impressed Josephus or his source(s) that it immediately came to mind when he set down his descriptions of their concepts.

The NT considers the Sadducees' rejection of resurrection as their primary characteristic, for the issue of resurrection was of central importance to the early Church. *Abot R. Nat.* A.5 claims that Zadok's followers broke away from Antigonus of Soco over the issue of resurrection; therefore, the evidence suggests that the Sadducees were known for their rejection of the idea of resurrection.

Josephus consistently emphasizes the opposition between the Sadducees and the Pharisees. In *Ant* 13 §297 we first encounter the Sadducees' rejection of the Pharisaic law "not recorded in the Laws of Moses," and in *Ant* 18 §17 Josephus says that the Sadducees observed nothing apart from the Law. Thus, the claim that the Sadducees considered valid only those regulations and traditions written down in the Law appears just twice, and only in the latter books of the *Antiquities*. The NT does not draw a consistent picture of the opposition between the Sadducees and the Pharisees. In Acts 23:6–8 the Sadducees sit in the council along with the Pharisees. The gospel of Mark does not place the Sadducees in opposition to the Pharisees, and Matthew often places them together, as if they were two similar groups. Only in Acts do we find the two groups disagreeing; however, here the disagreement centers only on the issue of resurrection. One gains the impression from reading the Gospels that their authors did not have a clear idea of the differences between the Pharisees and the Sadducees. To the Christian writers, they merely represented two leadership groups within the Jewish community, and their disagreements over issues, with the exception of resurrection, were either unknown or of little importance.

In the rabbinic material we find the most extensive discussions about the differences between the Sadducees and the Pharisees. The earliest rabbinic texts in which these discussions appear are the Mishnah and the Tosefta (Lightstone 1971: 206–17; Rivkin 1969/70: 205–49). The Mishnah, edited ca. 220 C.E. (Neusner 1981), contains several passages in which the Sadducees disagree with the Pharisees; in most of these texts, the two groups dispute over matters of purity: *Yad.* 4.6, whether or not Scripture renders the hands unclean; whether or not the bones of an ass or the high priest are clean; *Yad.* 4.7, whether or not certain types of water are unclean; *Para* 3.7, the importance of the setting of the sun in rendering one clean; *Nid.* 4.2, the state of cleanness of Sadducean women. The Sadducees and Pharisees also disagree about matters of civil law: *Yad.* 3.7, whether or not a slave's master is responsible for the damage caused by the slave; *Mak.* 1.6, whether or not a false witness is executed only when the one against whom he testified is executed. Lastly, *ᶜErub.* 6.1 discusses a matter of Sabbath law and suggests that the Sadducees held their own views concerning the establishment of the Sabbath limit. Similarly, in the Tosefta, a document edited ca. 250 C.E., the major issue between the Sadducees and the other Jews is purity; the other topics found in the Mishnah do not even appear in the Tosefta in the context of a reference to the Sadducees. *T. Para* 3.8 reflects *m. Para* 3.7; *t. Nid.* 5.2 is the same as *m. Nid.* 4.2; *t. Nid.* 5.3 states, as does *m. Nid.* 4.2, that the Sadducean women do not follow their own laws concerning menstrual purity. The Tosefta informs us that all Sadducean women followed the rulings of sages on this matter. One woman did not consult a sage, and she died soon after her failure to check with a sage. *T. Ḥag.* 3.35 presents the Sadducees and the Pharisees disagreeing about the purity of the menorah in the temple.

We find three references to the differences between the Sadducees and the Pharisees in three early midrashic collections. *Sipre Num.* 112, a midrash on the book of Numbers which was edited some time in the latter half of the 3d century C.E., interprets Num 15:31, "for he despised the word of YHWH," as a reference to the Sadducees. This is our earliest reference in the rabbinic texts to the view that the Sadducees did not follow the Word of God as interpreted by the rabbis/Pharisees. *Sipre Deut.* 190, part of a midrash on the book of Deuteronomy which appears to have been edited sometime in the 3d or 4th century C.E., contains a story about a Sadducean high priest who did not burn the incense on the Day of Atonement in accordance with the rules of the sages; compare this passage with *Sipra* 81a.

The Babylonian Talmud contains a number of references to the Sadducees; however, the censorship which this document has undergone makes some of these references suspect, for the word "Sadducees" often replaced reference to "gentiles" or "heretics" (Le Moyne 1972: 97–99).

B. ᶜErub. 68b is the Amoraic discussion of *m. ᶜErub.* 6.1. In *b. Yoma* 19b we find a version of the *Sipre* and *Sipra* story about the Sadducean high priest who offered incense on the Day of Atonement. In this version we learn that the Sadducees were afraid of the Pharisees and that the former generally followed the rulings of the latter. We are further told that the high priest who offered the incense in a manner different from the way in which the Pharisees ruled soon died. *B. Nid.* 33b, which is the Amoraic discussion of *m. Nid.* 4.2, informs us that if the attitude of a Sadducean woman is unknown, she is considered to have followed the rules concerning her menstrual period to which all other Israelite women adhere, that is, the Pharisaic/rabbinic injunctions. These are clearly examples of rabbinic propaganda, attempts to make everyone into a Pharisee. The Gemara contains a version of *t. Nid.* 5.3; however, the version in the former pits the Sadducees against the Pharisees rather than against the "sages" as we find in the Tosefta. The Sadducean view concerning the importance of the sun's setting in matters of cleanness is discussed in *b. Yoma* 2b, *b. Ḥag.* 23a, and *b. Zebaḥ* 21a. In *b. Yoma* 4a the Sadducees are excluded from the "students of the sages" and the "students of Moses." This is probably a reference to the fact that the Sadducees, who did not follow the Pharisaic/rabbinic traditions, were seen as rejecting the complete revelation given to and transmitted by Moses. *B. Ḥag.* 16b and *b. Mak.* 8b refer to the matter of the execution of false witnesses. In *b. B. Bat.* 115b we learn that the Sadducees and the Pharisees differed concerning a daughter's right of inheritance in certain circumstances. In *b. Sand.* 52b, R. Joseph, a third generation Babylonian Amora, refers to a Sadducean court; however, Joseph lived after the Tannaitic period and in a land which probably had not seen a Sadducee. From *b. Menaḥ.* 65a we learn that the Sadducees believed that individuals, and not the community, should pay for the daily offering. *B. Hor.* 4a and *b. Sanh.* 33b discuss a court which incorrectly ruled according to Sadducean law, a suspect reference, given the date of the collection in which they appear.

When we review the rabbinic evidence, we discover that the basic issue separating the Sadducees and Pharisees/rabbis was purity. This is not surprising, given the importance of the idea of purity in the Judaism of this period (Smith 1960/61: 7; Neusner 1973). Curiously, virtually no one, with the exception of Lightstone, points to the purity laws as a major area of disagreement between the Pharisees and the Sadducees. Rather, scholars such as Bowker (1973: 18), Sandmel (1969: 39), Guttmann (1970: 127), Mansoor (*EncJud* 14: 621), Meyer (*TDNT* 7: 63), and Le Moyne (1972: 378–79) argue that the essential element of Sadducean belief was their rejection of the oral law and their literalist interpretations of the Bible. While there are a few references in Josephus and the later rabbinic texts to support this claim, this disagreement must be put into its proper perspective. Both Josephus and the rabbis/Pharisees had something to gain by claiming that they had the correct interpretation of revelation, that those who disagreed with them or rejected their ideas were incorrect, and that everyone followed the Pharisaic/rabbinic teachings anyway. Furthermore, if Judaism around the turn of the era was based on interpreting God's revelation to Moses, it stands to reason that each group would have its own set of interpretations which it favored, while rejecting those of the other groups. Lastly, it is unlikely that any group in the 1st century would have claimed that they were not in fact offering the "literal," or correct, interpretation of the Mosaic revelation. Each group would claim that it alone was faithful to the Law and that it taught only things contained in the Law. To claim that the Sadducees rejected the Pharisees' "oral law" is merely to state that Pharisees were not Sadducees (Blenkinsopp 1981: 1).

D. Social Status

Josephus offers us limited information concerning the Sadducees' social status. In the context of his description of the split between John Hyrcanus and the Pharisees (*Ant* 13 §297), Josephus states that the Sadducees did not have the support of the masses; they enjoyed only the "confidence of the wealthy." In *Ant* 18 §17 only a few men of the "highest standing" know the Sadducean doctrines; however, we also discover that the Sadducees follow Pharisaic teachings. This "sociological information" appears only in these two contexts, and it is clearly connected with Josephus' attempt to prove that one cannot rule Palestine without the Pharisees (Smith 1956: 75–76). In *ʾAbot R. Nat.* A.5 we read that the Boethusians and/or the Sadducees used silver and gold vessels, "not because they were ostentatious, but because it was the Pharisaic tradition to afflict themselves in this world, hoping to receive a reward in the world-to-come." The *b.* version of *ʾAbot* contains a shorter version of this story and omits the reference to the gold and silver vessels. Thus, the evidence for the patrician nature of the Sadducees is based on Josephus' polemical passages and a text in one version of *ʾAbot* which points to the Sadducees' acting as rich people for theological reasons. Ignoring the polemical side of Josephus' description and the curious nature of *ʾAbot*'s description, Mansoor (*EncJud* 14: 621), Jeremias (1977: 230), Le Moyne (1972: 349), and Baron (1952: 35) argue that the Sadducees were the Palestinian aristocracy.

In *Ant* 18 §16–17 Josephus states that the Sadducees considered it a virtue to dispute with their teachers. In *Ant* 20 §163 he tells us the Sadducees were "boorish," and in *Ant* 20 §199 he describes them as "more heartless" than other Jews.

In *Ant* 20 §199 Josephus tells us that *one* high priest, Ananus, was a Sadducee. While the NT sometimes pictures the Sadducees' working in concert with the high priest (Acts 4:1–4; 15:17–18), it does not equate the priests and the Sadducees. Similarly, the rabbinic texts speak of Sadducean priests, especially in the discussions of how one is to burn the incense on the Day of Atonement, but the rabbis also believed that there were Pharisees who were priests and identified many of the early rabbis, such as Ishmael and Tarfon, as priests. Therefore, none of our texts allow us to claim that all priests were Sadducees or that all Sadducees were connected to the priesthood. For this reason, we must look with suspicion when Goldstein (*1 Maccabees* AB, 57), Sundberg (*IDB* 4: 160–61), Baumbach (1973: 208), and Jeremias (1977: 230) see a close relationship between the Sadducees and the priesthood.

The problem of the hellenization of Jewish groups during this period is difficult. The complexity of this situation is reflected in the scholarly discussion of the hellenization of the Sadducees. Mansoor (*EncJud* 14: 622), Baron (1952: 236), and Farmer (1956: 189) suggest that the Sadducees were highly hellenized, while Sundberg (*IDB* 4: 162) claims that the Pharisees were as hellenized as the Sadducees. Meyer (*TDNT* 7: 44), Zeitlin (1961: 125–26), and Sundberg (*IDB* 4: 162) have argued that the Sadducees were the most nationalistic of the Jewish population. Baron (1952: 36) seems to believe that the Sadducees were at the same time the most hellenized and the most nationalistic of the Palestinian Jews, without seeing any contradiction between the two positions. The problem is that our sources simply do not give us any information with which we could decide on the hellenization of the Sadducees or their political and nationalistic views.

E. History

Just as we cannot draw a clear picture of the political, theological, or nationalistic views of the Sadducees, we are also unable to clearly delineate the history of the group. Mansoor (*EncJud* 14: 620) argues that the sect originated ca. 200 B.C.E., while Sundberg (*IDB* 4: 160–61; cf. Baumbach 1973: 240) places its origin "not long before the reorganization of Judaism under Maccabean leadership." Le Moyne (1972: 331) merely states that in the 1st century B.C.E. "the Sadducees constituted a complete group inserted into Jewish life." Jeremias (1977: 243), Bowker (1973: 10), Davies (1967: 19), Meyer (*TDNT* 7: 31), and Sandmel (1969: 58) tie the end of the Sadducees in with the destruction of the Second Temple in 70 C.E. This view rests on the assumed close relationship between the Sadducees and the priesthood; however, we have seen that that relationship is far from firmly grounded in our sources. Sundberg (*IDB* 4: 161–62) argues that the end of the Sadducees did not come about simply with the destruction of the temple, for the Jews anticipated the rebuilding of the temple; "probably," he writes, "the Sadducees, concentrated about Jerusalem and being implicated in the war, suffered heavily with the fall of the city." Eppstein's suggestion (1966: 213–23) that the end of the Sadducees is related to the Pharisaic doctrines concerning the waters of the Red Heifer is based on a naive reading of the rabbinic texts. Virtually all we know about the history of the Sadducees is that Josephus first mentions them in the Maccabean period at the same time that he first discusses the Pharisees and the Essenes. Furthermore, with the Pharisaic/rabbinic rise to power after 70 C.E., the Sadducees play a small role in the Jewish documents which have come down to us from that period.

Bibliography

Baron, S. 1952. *A Social and Religious History of the Jews.* Vol. 2, *Christian Era: The First Five Centuries.* New York.

Baumbach, G. 1973. Der sadduzaische Konservativismus. Pp. 201–3 in *Literature und Religion des Frujudentums*, eds. J. Maier and J. Schreiner. Würzburg.

Blenkinsopp, J. 1981. Interpretation and the Tendency to Sectarianism: An Aspect of Second Temple History. Vol. 2, pp. 1–26 in *Jewish and Christian Self-Definition*, ed. E. P. Sanders. Philadelphia.

Bowker, J. 1973. *Jesus and the Pharisees.* Cambridge.

Davies, W. D. 1967. *Introduction to Pharisaism.* Philadelphia.

Eppstein, V. 1966. When and How the Sadducees Were Excommunicated. *JBL* 85: 213–23.

Farmer, W. R. 1956. *Maccabees, Zealots, and Josephus.* New York.

Guttmann, A. 1970. *Rabbinic Judaism in the Making.* Vol. 1. Detroit.

Jeremias, J. 1977. *Jerusalem in the Time of Jesus.* Philadelphia.

Le Moyne, S. 1972. *Les Sadducceens.* Paris.

Lightstone, J. 1971. Sadducees versus Pharisees: The Tannaitic Sources. Vol. 3, pp. 206–17 in *Christianity, Judaism, and Other Greco-Roman Cults*, ed. J. Neusner. Leiden.

Neusner, J. 1973. *The Idea of Purity in Ancient Judaism.* Leiden.

———. 1981. *Judaism: the Evidence of the Mishnah.* Chicago.

Rivkin, E. 1969/70. Defining the Pharisees: The Tannaitic Sources. *HUCA* 40–41: 205–49.
Sandmel, S. 1969. *The First Christian Century in Judaism and Christianity.* New York.
Smith, M. 1956. Palestinian Judaism in the First Century. Pp. 67–87 in *Israel: Its Role in Civilization,* ed. M. Davis. New York.
———. 1960/61. The Dead Sea Sect in Relation to Ancient Judaism. *NTS* 7: 347–60.
Stern, M. 1976. Aspects of Jewish Society: The Priesthood and Other Classes. Vol. 2, pp. 561–630 in *The Jewish People in the First Century,* eds. S. Safrai and M. Stern. CRINT 1/2. Assen and Philadelphia.
Zeitlin, S. 1961. The Pharisees: A Historical Study. *JQR* n.s. 52: 97–128.

GARY G. PORTON

ṢADE. The eighteenth letter of the Hebrew alphabet.

SAFAITIC INSCRIPTIONS. See INSCRIPTIONS, SAFAITIC.

SAFAITIC LANGUAGE. See LANGUAGES (INTRODUCTORY SURVEY).

SAFFRON. See PERFUMES AND SPICES; FLORA.

SAFI (M.R. 195147). A large EB and Byzantine period cemetery site in the Ghor es-Safi, S of the Dead Sea. The location of a town connected with the cemetery remains uncertain. The name "Safi" was assigned to the site in lieu of a traditional local name. The cemetery is located on the slopes of a descending series of limestone foothills, between 300 and 330 m below sea level, at the SE edge of the Wadi el-Hesa delta on its SE edge. The visible ruins of a medieval sugar mill, Tawahin es-Sukkar, mark the N and lowest limits of the cemetery area just above the valley floor.

Safi must be viewed in the context of the Ghor es-Safi region which today is the largest, best-watered, and most extensively farmed area in the SE Ghor area (Harlan 1981: 157–59). There is evidence for a wetter climate during the Late Chalcolithic–Early Bronze ages and the Byzantine period (Neev and Emery 1967) which must have made the region even more attractive during these periods. Despite these features the area is comparatively poor in archaeological remains.

During the 19th century, a series of explorers (Irby and Mangles in 1823; De Saulcy in 1853; Tristam in 1865; Hayne in 1873; Tristam in 1873; Klein in 1880; Kitchener in 1884; Hart in 1885; Hill in 1896) visited the Safi area. Most noted the low tell area of Sheikh Isa (500 m NW of the Safi cemetery), the ruins of the sugar mills of Tawahin es-Sukkar, and recorded vivid descriptions of the flora and fauna of the region. Kitchener also describes a large walled site with a tower and scattered *nawamis* called Kh. Labrush, located 500–600 m SE of Tawahin es-Sukkar high above the Wadi Hesa (1884: 216). In 1924 a survey team led by Albright (1924) explored the Safi region and carried out soundings at Kh. Sheikh Isa. Subsequent published surveys in the area include Frank's (1934), Glueck's (1935), and Rast and Schaub's (1974). More recent unpublished surveys have been carried out by McCreery in 1979, King in 1982, and Macdonald in 1987.

The Ghor es-Safi appears to have been most extensively utilized in the EB I, Roman, Byzantine, Early and Late Arabic periods. The first evidence for an early history of the area came from a tomb group from Safi published by Frank (1934: 204). This group was recognized by Glueck as belonging to the early phases of the EB (1935: 8). Amiran has also published EB IB pots from the Safi region (1969: 49; photos 44, 45). The source of these artifacts was further determined by the survey of Rast and Schaub, which recorded an extensive area of EB and Byzantine tombs on the slopes of Safi (1974: 9–11, 15–17). Iron Age, Late Roman, and Byzantine sherds were also found. Some wall foundations were noted during the survey on one of the upper plateaus of the site, but subsequent visits have been unable to confirm the presence of a town site in this area, which has been considerably disturbed by recent trenching and the construction of a town site on the upper plateau regions. Sauer has mentioned the recovery of intact MB vessels at Safi (1982: 207). The site of Sheikh Isa was described by Albright as belonging to the Byzantine and early Arabic periods, mostly to the latter. Most recently MacDonald has identified the site of Labrush, called Umm Tawabin, as a large Nabatean fort dating from the last decades of the 1st century B.C. to the mid 2d century A.D. Tawahin es-Sukkar is probably the last surviving remnant of the medieval "Zugar" which is mentioned frequently by Arabic geographers as a commercial center for sugar, dates, and indigo.

It seems unlikely that the scarcity of earlier archaeological remains in the Wadi el-Hesa delta region is due to major changes in the water levels. Donahue (Donahue and Beynon 1988) has suggested the possibility of severe downcutting near the mouth of the Wadi Hesa since the EB, but this is difficult to maintain since the EB I tombs are at approximately the same level as the present wadi mouth. Klein (1982: 90–93) has also argued that there was a dramatic rise in the Dead Sea level during the 1st century B.C. to 330 m below sea level or to the very edge of the N limits of the cemetery, but archaeological remains have survived below that level in other areas of the Dead Sea.

The discovery of the cemetery at Safi, contemporary with other EB cities (Bab edh-Dhraᶜ, Numeira, Feifeh, and Khanazir) in the SE Ghor has renewed discussion about the location and identity of the Cities of the Plains (Gen 13:12; 19:29). The region of the Ghor es-Safi has been favored by many scholars (Albright, Aharoni, Abel, Lagrange, Harland, Glueck, Howard) as the location of the biblical site of Zoar (Gen 13:10; 14:2, 8; 19:22, 23, 30; Deut 34:3; Isa 15:5; Jer 48:4 (LXX), 34). Arguments in favor of this location have been drawn from the global geographical indications of the biblical texts and the strong Byzantine tradition culminating in the placement of Zoar at the S end of the Dead Sea on the Madeba Map. Other scholars (Mallon, Powers) have argued for a N location using the same texts and a late Byzantine tradition that places Byzantine Segor (Zoar) within site of Mt. Nebo.

Noth, tracing the Lot traditions, also favors a N location (*HPT,* 151–54). Recently Shea has attempted to trace the geographical routes of the Ebla texts and has argued for Adamah as a site in the Safi region (1983: 608–10). Although the cemetery site at Safi remains the only candidate for early presence in the area and the original existence of a town site nearby seems likely (on the analogy of the other EB sites in this region) the identification of this site with the Zoar of the Genesis texts remains uncertain.

Bibliography

Albright, W. F. 1924. The Archaeological Results of an Expedition to Moab and the Dead Sea. *BASOR* 14: 2–12.

Amiran, R. 1969. *Ancient Pottery of the Holy Land.* Jerusalem.

Donahue, J., and Beynon, D. E. 1988. Geologic History of the Wadi El Hasa Survey Area. Pp. 26–39 in *The Wadi el Hasa Archaeology Survey 1979–1983, West-Central Jordan,* ed. B. Macdonald. Waterloo, Ontario.

Frank, F. 1934. Aus der Araba I: Reiseberichte. *ZDPV* 57: 191–280.

Glueck, N. 1935. *Explorations in Eastern Palestine, II.* AASOR 15. New Haven.

Harlan, J. R. 1981. Natural Resources of the Southern Ghor. Pp. 155–64 in *The Southeastern Dead Sea Plain Expedition: An Interim Report of the 1977 Season,* ed. W. E. Rast and R. T. Schaub. AASOR 46. Cambridge, MA.

———. 1985. The Early Bronze Age Environment of the Southern Ghor and the Moab Plateau. Pp. 125–30 in *Studies in the History and Archaeology of Jordan, II,* ed. A. Hadidi. Amman.

Howard, D. M., Jr. 1984. Sodom and Gomorrah Revisited. *JETS* 27: 385–400.

Kitchener, H. H. 1884. Major Kitchener's Report. *PEFQS.*

Klein, C. 1982. Morphological Evidence of Lake Level Changes, Western Shore of the Dead Sea. *Israel Journal of Earth-Sciences* 31: 67–94.

Neev, D., and Emery, K. O. 1967. *The Dead Sea: Depositional Processes and Environment of Evaporites.* State of Israel, Ministry of Development Geological Survey Bulletin 41. Jerusalem.

Rast, W. E., and Schaub, R. T. 1974. Survey of the Southeastern Plain of the Dead Sea, 1973. *ADAJ* 19: 5–53.

Sauer, J. A. 1982. Syro-Palestinian Archaeology, History and Biblical Studies. *BA* 45: 201–10.

Shea, W. H. 1983. Two Palestinian Segments from the Eblaite Geographical Atlas. Pp. 589–612 in *WLSGF.*

R. THOMAS SCHAUB

SAFIYEH, WADI ES-. See ZEPHATHAH.

SAFUT, TELL (M.R. 229160). A site named after the modern village W of the tell, it has been identified by Mallon as ancient NOBAH of Judg 8:11 (LXX: Nabai), which is not to be confused with Nobah (LXX: Naboth) of Num 32:42 (cf. de Vaux *EHI,* 590).

A. Location and Topography

Tell (es-) Safut is located on the edge of the modern Amman-Jerash highway, 1.5 km N of Suweileh, at the point where the road enters the 5-km-wide × 10-km-long BAQᶜAH VALLEY, which the tell overlooks from the S. Covering 17.73 dunams, the tell rises 300 m above the valley floor to a fairly flat oval top which is oriented E–NE by W–SW and measures approximately 18 × 70 m. At 927 m above sea level, it is 200 m lower than the Suweileh hills behind it.

Tell Safut guarded one of the principal roads leading from the interior of Gilead through the valley toward Rabbath-ammon (modern Amman), which it undoubtedly served at key moments in Amman's history. Ottosson (1969: 188) connects Tell es-Safut with the Kings' Highway in a way that also suggests that Nobah of Judg 8:11 corresponds with Safut.

B. History of Exploration

First reported in 1877 as one of four important regional sites near Amman, in 1881 it was placed by R. Meyer on the Map of the American Palestine Exploration Society. Tell Safut was surveyed by N. Glueck and R. de Vaux in the 1930s.

A 1950s cut into the tell by road-building bulldozers led Maᶜayeh (1960a: 114; 1960b: 228) to report finding an MB glacis, a report which Sauer (1986: 6) simply accepts; Dornemann (1983: 19) calls the finding "highly likely," but Landes (1961: 67) is clearly uncertain. Ottosson (1969: 188), on the other hand, goes so far as to call it a Hyksos fortification, "probably not unique for southern Gilead." However, a further sectioning of the area shows the alleged glacis to be sterile and nothing more than a natural geological formation.

C. Current Excavations

In 1982, a cooperative effort between the Department of Antiquities and Seton Hall University, with assistance from ACOR, undertook the first of (currently) four seasons.

Three definite stages were adopted in the strategy. The first (in 1982) required exposing sufficient architecture to help persuade authorities to preserve as much of the tell as possible. A close examination of the general configuration of the acropolis and its corresponding perimeter defense wall indicated that the tell was not as severely damaged as had at first appeared. In the second stage (in 1982 and 1983), three probes were cut to bedrock or virgin soil to determine the range of occupation. The lowest strata in each case yielded only LB sherds. In stage three (1985, 1987), horizontal exposure, which sought clarification of successive historical phases, disclosed that the latest significant occupation was during the Iron IIC/Persian period, with traces of a Late Byzantine presence on the very top of the tell.

D. History of the Settlement

1. The Middle Bronze Age. An MB presence cannot be denied on the basis of the pottery, but neither can it be posited conclusively.

2. The Late Bronze Age. A major perimeter defense wall attests that Transjordan, at least in this region, was heavily enough occupied by a sedentary society in the LB Age to require protection with a substantial perimeter defense wall. Inside the city was probably a sanctuary in which was found a bronze figurine deity (see Fig. SAF.01), a footed bowl or chalice, and a large amount (over 600 cm^3) of charred two-row barley. The seated figurine is unique in that it is clearly smiling and its crown is flat. Both forearms are extended and wrapped in gold, as are the hands; one is open, the other is closed—neither holds

SAF.01. Bronze deity from Tell Safut with gold wrappings on forearms and hands. *(Courtesy of D. Wimmer)*

anything. The crown boasts a motif not unlike a seashell, a conch, or perhaps a feather. The eye sockets were probably inlaid. The nose and left arm are enlarged by thick erosion. Two bronze pegs protruding from the seat and feet suggest that the figurine was attached to a chair or throne of some other material. Whether this figurine is a S Gilead form of the Canaanite Baal, an Ammonite deity, or simply the tutelary god of Safut remains an open question.

3. Iron Age I. To date, a comparatively light Iron Age I occupation is evident from both ceramic and architectural finds.

4. Iron Age II. Occupation in Iron Age II is attested in every square. Most pottery types represent 8th–6th century forms, with some almost certainly from the Persian period. The Late Iron Age population overflowed the earlier LB boundaries, enclosing an area easily ten times the size of the LB settlement.

By the end of the 8th century, several rooms on the S exposure were enclosed in a 1 m thick Iron IIB casemate wall which was subsequently buttressed by a dirt-filled battered wall of glacis. One of the casemate rooms contained a destruction layer sealing an excellent collection of Iron IIC pottery. Finds included figurine heads, pilgrim flasks, Assyrian bottles, a miniature ceramic horse, and a series of cooking pots smashed in situ. From elsewhere on the tell came a late Assyrian seal and a late Babylonian seal.

5. Late Byzantine. A population decrease in the Late Byzantine period is evident in that associated architecture is found only on the very summit. Classical and Islamic evidence from nearby shows that protection of the region shifted from the tell to other sites.

Bibliography

Burrows, M. 1931. News from the School of Jerusalem. *BASOR* 44: 10–12.

Dornemann, R. 1983. *The Archaeology of the Transjordan.* Milwaukee.

Glueck, N. 1937. Explorations in the Land of Ammon. *BASOR* 68: 13–21.

———. 1939. *Explorations in Eastern Palestine, III.* AASOR 18–19. New Haven.

Landes, G. M. 1961. The Material Civilization of the Ammonites. *BA* 24: 66–86.

Maʿayeh, F. 1960a. Recent Archaeological Discoveries in Jordan. *ADAJ* 4/5: 114–15.

———. 1960b. Safout; Quailbe (ancienne Abila). *RB* 67: 228, 229.

Ottosson, M. 1969. *Gilead: Tradition and History.* Lund.

———. 1980. *Temples and Cult Places in Palestine.* AUU 12. Uppsala.

Sauer, J. 1985. Ammon, Moab and Edom. Pp. 206–14 in *BibAT.*

———. 1986. Transjordan in the Bronze and Iron Ages: A Critique of Glueck's Synthesis. *BASOR* 263: 1–26.

Vaux, R. de. 1938. Chronique: Exploration de la Region de Salt. *RB* 47: 398–425.

Wimmer, D. H. 1985. The Third Archaeological Expedition to Tell Safut. *LASBF* 35: 408–10.

———. 1987a. The Excavations at Tell Safut. Pp. 279–82 in *History and Archaeology of Jordan, III,* ed. A. Hadidi. Amman.

———. 1987b. Tell Safut Excavations, 1982–85: A Preliminary Report. *ADAJ* 31: 159–74.

Donald H. Wimmer

SAHAB (M.R. 245142). A site in a high plateau (873 m above sea level) 12 km SE of Amman and ca. 15 km W of the E Jordanian desert. It was probably one of the last major settlements on the road to Saudi Arabia and was possibly the largest pre-Roman site on the borders of the E Jordanian desert. It is situated on the present and ancient road to the desert castles of the early Islamic period.

A. Geography
B. Exploration
C. Preliminary Survey Results
D. Excavations at Tell Sahab

A. Geography

The tell occupies an area of about 500 dunums, the highest point of the mound being some 22 m above the W plains. Its location affords the benefits of being a transitional zone between the highlands and the desert, thus producing a pleasant combination of varying climate and good agricultural conditions. Geologically, the hilly area consists of Mesozoic limestone with chert, while the plains are of Cenozoic sediments. Rainfall is within the 200–300 mm isohyet, making dry farming possible and extensive land use viable. Natural water resources have been supplemented by rock-cut cisterns over the entire survey area.

These agreeable conditions were attested by the long occupation of both the site and the surrounding region. The 1983 survey results show settlement from the Paleolithic, while the tell has occupation from the Late Neolithic and Chalcolithic periods (5th–4th millennia B.C.) to the late Iron Age (ca. 600 B.C.). After the 6th century B.C. the site was apparently abandoned until the 11th to 13th centuries A.D.

The modern town of Sahab is built on the ancient tell and has spread from there to the surrounding area, thus destroying major parts of the ancient settlement. However, much of this modern development has been responsible for revealing earlier occupational material; such activity discovered the tomb which led to the first season of excavations.

The mild environmental conditions combined with the archaeological evidence of steady occupation within this region indicates Sahab's probable importance over a long period of time. While one might, therefore, expect references to the site in historical records, to date no identifications have been made.

B. Exploration

Surveys around this area have only recently been undertaken and until 1972 little was known about the archaeology of the area. A few sites were visited in the region and reported in *Die Provincia Arabia,* Band 2, by R. E. Brunow and A. von Domaszewski at the turn of the century. Otherwise the area was known only through occasional tomb finds reported to the authorities.

The first of these was reported in 1929 and published later by W. F. Albright (1932). The second was excavated and findings published by G. L. Harding in 1948. Both tombs were dated by the authors to the Iron II period (i.e., 9th–7th centuries B.C.). Two other tombs have been officially excavated; one by R. Dajani in 1968 (1970) and the other soon to be published by M. Ibrahim. Apart from these, no attention was given to the tell of Sahab until an MB tomb was accidentally discovered in 1972. The Jordanian Department of Antiquities excavated and recorded the tomb which initiated further investigations and a 6-month rescue operation. The Sahab excavations have been directed by M. Ibrahim.

A survey was carried out in 1983 to determine the occupational history and settlement patterns of this area on the fringes of the E desert, and to establish the position of Sahab within its environment. The survey area was 15 × 13 km, with Sahab in the center of the W border of the region.

C. Preliminary Survey Results

The survey identified many sites from different stages of the Paleolithic (almost half of the 131 recorded), and also showed that the area was continuously occupied throughout the Hellenistic, Roman, Byzantine, and Umayyad periods.

Neolithic and Chalcolithic settlements with material similar to the evidence from Sahab were identified at Tell es Suwwan (25), Salbud (27), Wadi el Qattar (104) and Hweytan Abu Snesle West (125). Eight pre-Pottery Neolithic sites were identified, twelve from the MB period (el-Qattar being the largest), and five from the LB but none with as extensive an occupation as Sahab. The only tell site within the area apart from Sahab is el-Rajib (SS 83 91). The Iron Age is well represented with 45 sites recorded, many of which were fortified and were possibly watchtowers. Most of these were located on hilltops and may possibly have been part of a defense system for the town of Sahab.

D. Excavations at Tell Sahab

To date, the Sahab excavations have identified six main periods of settlement. The earliest evidence dates from Late Neolithic–Early Chalcolithic, with some EB. A continuous occupation exists throughout the MB, LB, and Iron II period, at the end of which there appears to be a period of abandonment of town occupation.

During the 1983 survey several other Neolithic/Chalcolithic settlements around Sahab were located, but Sahab was the largest of these and probably represents a typical large village farming community from the 5th–4th millennia B.C. The large number of storage facilities discovered both inside and outside domestic structures suggests a period of extensive agriculture. Some of these courtyard storage pits were huge, spanning 4 m in diameter. The presence of such large storage pits suggests anticipated long periods of agricultural yield. One particular occupational unit, in area E, implies a large family occupation—it consists of several rooms, mostly of unhewn stone, surrounding a courtyard in which storage pits were cut into virgin soil. These contained large amounts of seed, and were lined with small stones. The extensive occupation of Sahab is also evident by the combination of cave and rock shelters with rectangular domestic structures which were used for habitation. This simultaneous combination of housing at Sahab is fairly logical given the climatic range of the area. Cave shelters were excavated over the entire area. In area A, a cave was found with a pebble-and-plaster floor and ash deposits. Area B had a large cave complex subdivided by well-built stone walls and hard-packed floors. It seems clear that these cave dwellers coexisted alongside the occupants of the constructed domestic structures described above. Many of the caves had several occupation surfaces, the uppermost of which date from the EB. Most of the caves were reused as tombs in the MB (1800–1600 B.C.), LB (1400–1300 B.C.) and early Iron I (ca. 1200 B.C.) periods.

Toward the end of the 4th millennium B.C. there is a suggestion of seasonal settlement. In area E above the Neolithic/Chalcolithic levels several fragmentary walls were discovered without any clear architectural plan. In the cave sites occupational floors above the earlier levels yielded pottery similar to area E. Related to this phase were two burial jars containing human skeletons, a continuation of the Ghassulian burial tradition, and in area E was a reused pit containing 7–9 animal burials.

Evidence of the EB at Sahab is witnessed by the presence of some sherds in the uppermost levels of caves and by a number of sherds in area B, though so far there are no associated structures.

The MB evidence derives from two caves used for burials in areas A and B. Area G II, near the center of the site, yielded part of the MT fortifications connected to a typical MB glacis rampart; however, the excavation area has been too limited for more definite information. In area H III, a massive MB wall was excavated. Unfortunately the distance between this and the MB rampart is covered by modern housing and thus impossible to explore.

The fortified site, possibly indicating a move from the large-scale agricultural community to a smaller fortified settlement, was probably the closest of the MB II fortified settlements to the E desert.

In 1968 a rich LB-Iron Age tomb was discovered (Dajani 1970), but no other LB tombs have been found. The major evidence for LB occupation comes from a partially uncovered 13th-century building and the town wall. The LB town, the interior part of which is largely unexplored because of modern construction, appears to have covered an area of about 20 dunums; thus it was a town much larger than the MB fortification limits.

In area E, a large public building was discovered under an accumulation of Iron Age and modern structures. Four walls appear to be associated with this building, the largest of which continues for more than 17 m in an E–W direction. Associated with this is an almost square, towerlike structure on the E end of the exposed length of the wall.

The major excavated portion of the town wall is in the W part of the LB settlement (areas G II, III, IV) where nearly 75 m of wall has been exposed. Soundings in the S and SE (H III and IV), in the E (H II), and in the N (H II and BO19) allow some reconstruction of the course of the town wall. The complete enclosure seems to have been symmetrical and oval in shape, along a N–S axis. The wall remains are largely foundations sunk in a deep trench lined on both sides with large and medium stones.

The pottery associated with the wall includes imports and imitations of Mycenaean vessels as well as local ware. Examples of bichrome simple and carinated bowls, jugs, kraters, goblets, and pyxides imply that the site, along with other central Jordanian sites, had ties with Cyprus and the Mediterranean, as did sites in coastal Syria and those W of the Jordan.

The LB town had an apparently long occupation, from the 15th to 13th centuries B.C. The earlier date is based on a seal impression found on an LB storage jar handle discovered in the foundation trench of the town wall. The scene on the seal is typical of the period of Thutmose III and depicts a combination of three signs, possibly a cryptogram of the god-name Amon.

Sahab's unbroken occupation from the beginning of the MB to the late Iron II, with massive fortifications during most, if not all, of these major periods, strengthens the inference that it was recognized as an important regional center.

As is common in Palestine and Jordan the transition from LB to the beginning of the Iron Age is still unclear. In this respect Sahab resembles other major tell sites, such as Amman, Tabaqat Fahil, Tell Deir Alla, and Tell Irbid. The evidence shows no occupational gap, but a general cultural continuity in terms of burial practices; there are, however, gradual changes in the pottery and metalwork.

The site was heavily occupied during both Iron Ages I and II. Tombs from both periods have been found, as well as clear occupational and architectural material. On the W and N faces, the Iron Age material extends beyond the LB town; though the walled town during the Iron II became smaller, it was better planned.

Domestic architecture has been identified from Iron I, but the evidence is fragmentary. A clear picture of the Iron I settlement is hard to form. The area A structure had two architectural phases, though the purpose of the building is yet uncertain. The plastered room in area A had a large number of collared-rim storage jars. Some of these 12th-century jars bear seal impressions. One example, found on the rims of two jars, shows an animal with long horns followed by a human figure with raised hands. Another seal, repeated three times on a single jar, depicts two seated animals, an ibex on the top, with a lioness below.

Separating Iron Age I from Iron II is some evidence of destruction on the site. Apparently, scattered houses were built after the destruction of the major Iron I town, as indicated by the material from area D and some trial trenches on the E slope.

The excavations in the Iron Age II period have revealed a complex series of rooms with multiple architectural phases. Several of these rooms contained large amounts of stone mortars and pestles, complete and broken pottery vessels, and large amounts of seed. The largest and most interesting of these rooms was the rectangular "pillared-room" from area B.

This room, measuring 7.5 × 4 m, had two entrances in the SW corner of the room. Inside were four stone pillar bases set into a plastered floor running the central length of the room. The center of the floor contained a circular fireplace constructed of stones and mud. Finds from this area included a number of basalt and limestone tools, half a steatite scarab, a large number of loom weights (conical and round), and weights in at least three units. There are at least two adjoining rooms on the W side that form one unit, which in turn is separated from another unit by a corridor.

Another, smaller "pillared-room" was excavated in area G II. The function of these buildings is not certain but they may have had some industrial purpose, e.g., a textile workshop. Parallels are common in Palestine such as those found in Tell Bir es-Sabᶜ, Ain Shems, Tell Beit Mirsim, Tell el-Farah (N), Tell el-Qidah, and Tell el-Mutasallim. In Jordan similar rooms are found at Tell es-Saᶜidiyeh, Tell Deir Alla, Tell el-Khalifah, and Tawilan.

The pottery from area B is typical of the Iron II period, especially in the Amman region. The types include ovoid storage jars with two handles and thickened overlapped rims, bowls and platters with red and black highly burnished slip and band slips inside and outside, and profile-rimmed bowls with shallow disc bases.

The small finds, the pottery, and the stone implements

are typical of the 8th–7th centuries B.C., and confirm the prosperity of the site during the first half of the 1st millennium B.C. They also indicate close contacts with Palestine and Syria. After the 7th and 6th centuries B.C., Sahab appears to have been abandoned until the 11th to 13th centuries A.D.

Bibliography

Albright, W. F. 1932. An Anthropoid Coffin from Sahab in Transjordan. *AJA* 36: 295–306.

Brunow, R. E., and Domaszewski, A. von. 1902. *Die Provincia Arabia.* Vol. 2. Strasbourg.

Dajani, R. 1970. A Late Bronze–Iron Age Tomb Excavated at Sahab, 1968. *ADAJ* 15: 29–34.

Harding, G. L. 1948. An Iron Age Tomb at Sahab. *QDAP* 13: 92–102.

Horn, S. 1971. Three Seals from Sahab Tomb C. *ADAJ* 16: 103–6.

Ibrahim, M. 1972. Archaeological Excavations at Sahab. *ADAJ* 17: 23–36.

———. 1974. Second Season of Excavations at Sahab, 1973. *ADAJ* 19: 55–61.

———. 1975. Third Season of Excavations at Sahab, 1975. *ADAJ* 20: 69–82.

———. 1978. The Collared-Rim Jar of the Early Iron Age. Pp. 116–26 in *Archaeology of the Levant,* ed. P. R. S. Moorey and P. Parr. Warminster.

———. 1983. Siegel und Seigelabdrücke aus Sahab. *ZDPV* 99: 43–53.

———. 1984. Sahab. *AfO* 29: 256–60, Figs. 8–12.

———. 1987. Sahab and its Foreign Relations. Pp. 73–82 in *Studies in the History and Archaeology of Jordan* III, ed. A. Hadid. Amman.

MOAWIYAH M. IBRAHIM

SAᶜIDIYEH, TELL ES-

SAᶜIDIYEH, TELL ES- (M.R. 204186). Most plausibly identified as ancient ZARETHAN (Josh 3:16; 1 Kgs 4:12; 1 Kgs 7:14; and possibly 1 Kgs 11:26 and 2 Chr 4:17), Tell es-Saᶜidiyeh lies in the central Jordan Valley, 1.8 km E of the Jordan river, on the S side of the Wadi Kufrinjeh. The two elements of the site comprise an upper tell to the E, rising to a height of some 40 m above present plain level, and covering an area of about 10,350 m^2 at its summit, and a low, benchlike mound to the W, measuring approximately 90 × 40 m, and about 20 m lower than the upper tell.

In 1943, the site was visited by N. Glueck during his survey of E Palestine. His surface collections indicated a long history of occupation from EB I–II to Iron Age II, with extensions into the Roman and Byzantine periods (Glueck 1951: 290–95). To the W of the low mound, and separated from it by a gap of about 40m, Glueck identified an additional site with sherds not only of EB I–II, but also of the Chalcolithic period (1951: 293). It was this low mound, described as "Tell es-Saᶜidiyeh el-Tahta," which was investigated in 1953 by H. de Contenson. In a number of small soundings, a very thin occupation deposit was revealed, associated with pottery and lithics of the Middle Chalcolithic period (de Contenson 1960: 49–56).

Large-scale systematic excavations were undertaken at the main double mound between 1964 and 1967 directed by J. B. Pritchard, and have resumed since 1985 under J. N. Tubb.

The earliest remains reached by the end of the 1987 season were of the EB Age. In area DD, on the SW side of the low mound (see Fig. SAI.01), two superimposed occupation phases of EB II have been found, both characterized by well-constructed and carefully planned buildings of mudbrick on stone foundations. In the lower phase, stratum L3, part of a pebble street has been uncovered with entrances into two houses. The most completely excavated of these has a small semicircular courtyard giving access to a long narrow rectangular room with a row of roof supports along its central axis, and five large store jars sunk into the beaten earth floor. In stratum L2, many of the walls of the previous phase were reused as foundations, but a radical change in plan took place which involved a 90 degree shift in orientation. Part of a multiroom complex has been excavated, including a quite elaborate stepped entranceway. Stratum L2 ended in a destruction, which sealed a rich and varied corpus of pottery and other finds. The pottery, in particular, shows evidence of a distinctively local and yet innovative tradition, characterized by red-on-cream "ribbon painted" wares and thin-walled, highly burnished fine wares. Noteworthy is the presence in the assemblage of four-spouted lamps, types more usually associated with the much later EB IV period.

No evidence has been found of defensive walls at any point on the lower tell; the impression is that the EB II was a period of relative stability in this area. This view is enhanced by the discovery in the region W of the site of a series of small contemporary undefended settlements—single housing units or farmsteads.

With the destruction of stratum L2, habitation on the lower tell ended. During the 13th century B.C., its entire area became an extensive cemetery. The graves cut into the substantial silt layer which covered the EB ruins, and disturbed some of the ruins as well. The cemetery, which can be related to contemporary occupation on the upper tell (see below, stratum XII), seems to have been used intensively over a period of little more than 150 years (ca. 1300–1150 B.C.). By the close of the 1987 season, 285 graves had been excavated, 45 by Pritchard on the N side (now published as Pritchard 1980), and most of the remainder in Tubb's area BB toward the center of the mound. The graves exhibit a bewildering variety of construction types, practices, burial customs, and grave goods. Some are simple subrectangular or oval pits, often incorporating elements of the preexisting EB architecture—foundation stones or even mudbrick. Others consist of neatly dug rectangular trenches, lined and roofed with mudbrick slabs. In addition, there are mudbrick tombs, often built in rows, which were intended to be partially visible aboveground.

Numerous infant jar burials have been found; the jars had been broken off at the shoulder to allow for insertion of the deceased. The most important type of burial, however, was the so-called "double-pithos" type, in which the deceased was interred in a coffin composed of two extremely large store-jars, of which the necks had been removed; these were then joined shoulder-to-shoulder. The double-pithos "coffin" was set into a grave large

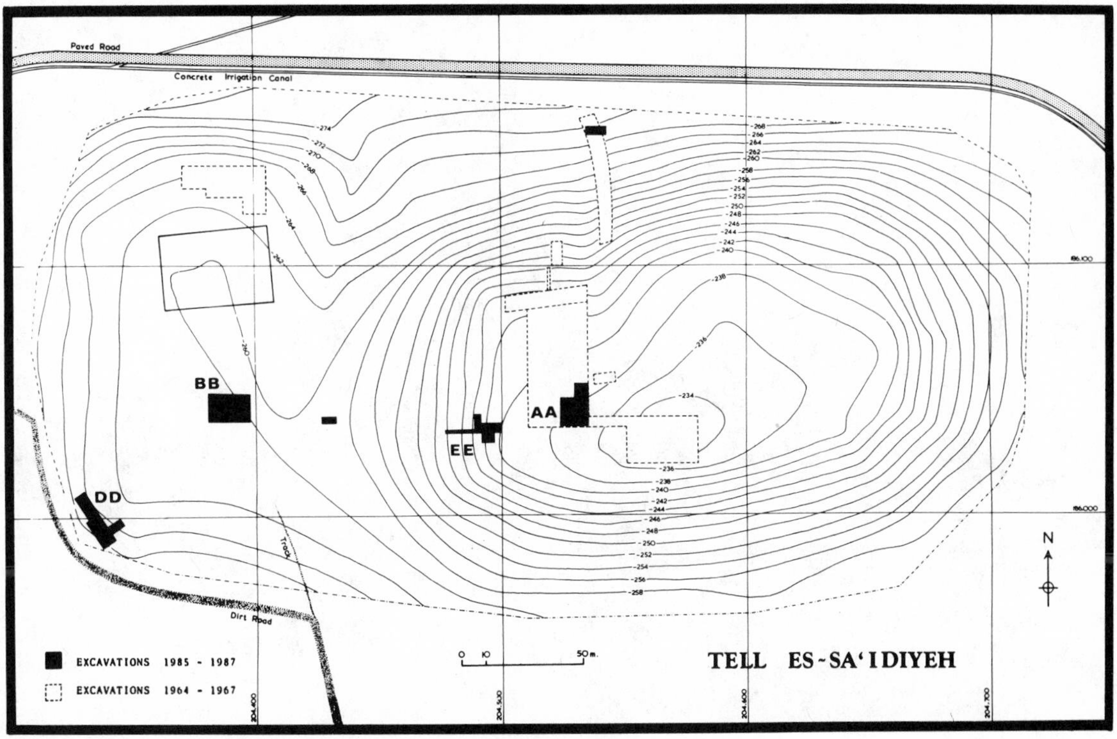

SAI.01. Contour plan of Tell es-Saᶜidiyeh, showing excavated areas. *(Courtesy of J. N. Tubb)*

enough to allow offerings to be deposited around, as well as inside the pithoi. This type of burial, extremely rare elsewhere in Palestine, clearly anticipates the slightly later anthropoid coffins well known from sites such as Beth-shan and Deir el-Balah. A somewhat poorer expression of the same practice was encountered in a number of the pit graves, where the deceased had been covered with sherds of store jars, and in two cases, the deceased's head had been inserted inside complete vessels.

Generally, the burial practice was single and primary. Only a few clear examples of secondary burial have been recorded, but a third type of practice, which may be described as "derived secondary," is quite common. As a result of the continuous reuse of the same cemetery area, earlier burials were frequently disturbed by later interments, and, to show some degree of repect, some of the major remains (e.g., the skull and perhaps two of the long bones) were collected, and were either reburied in a small circular pit, or were carefully placed within the later grave.

Considerable variation has been found with regard to the disposition of the deceased, but most commonly the individual was extended on his or her back. In many instances the legs were crossed and the hands had been brought together to meet at the pelvis. In several cases a bronze bowl had been placed over the face or genitals, and from textiles preserved by the corrosion products of the metal, it is clear that the bodies had been wrapped or bound. In all cases where this textile has been analyzed, it has been found to be Egyptian linen.

The cemetery has produced a rich assemblage of grave goods. In addition to pottery, many of the burials contained bronze vessels, tools and weapons of both bronze and iron, ivory and bone ornaments, alabaster vessels, seals, scarabs and amulets, and items of personal adornment including a varied collection of beads of different styles and materials. Many imported objects have been found, principally from Egypt and the Aegean, and many of the bronzes in particular show strong Aegean influence. Among the bronzes have been found two three-piece sets consisting of bowl, strainer, and juglet, and on the basis of an illustration on an ivory box from Tell Farᶜa, these have been interpreted as wine sets. See Fig. SAI.02.

The great variety of burial types and practices within the Saᶜidiyeh cemetery suggests a mixed population during the 13th–12th centuries B.C., and certain features, most notably the double-pithos burials, the large number of bronzes—many of Aegean type—the practice of binding the deceased in linen, and the very high proportion of imitation Mycenaean wares within the pottery repertoire, may imply the presence of a Sea Peoples element within the community.

The use of the cemetery appears to have ended around

SAI.02. Bronze wine set from Tell es-Saᶜidiyeh—Grave 32, 13th century B.C. *(Courtesy of J. N. Tubb)*

the middle of the 12th century B.C., coinciding with a major destruction of the settlement on the upper tell. Stratum XII in area AA (see Fig. SAI.01) shows a tightly packed complex of houses, streets, and stepped passageways which had been subjected to an intense conflagration. Large numbers of complete pottery vessels were recovered from the rooms, and many of these conform closely to types found in the latest graves of the cemetery. It is nevertheless clear that the destruction had been anticipated. Very few luxury items were found, and some rooms had been emptied completely. In addition, most of the external doorways had been blocked from the outside with large stones, suggesting a carefully planned departure of the residents.

Architecturally, stratum XII is of interest because the generally substantial mudbrick walls had been built without foundation trenches; instead they had been laid on a superbly prepared construction surface of pisee. Further, the external walls had been built as pairs with a channel of about 15 cm width between them, perhaps as a precaution against earthquake damage, or more likely to provide a system of drainage.

Remains of the city wall of stratum XII have been excavated in area EE on the W slope of the upper tell. This consisted of a massive casemate defensive wall, constructed of mudbrick on a foundation of pisee, which was laid over an earlier, apparently solid wall. The casemates were filled with brick rubble, producing a formidable defensive structure which was in excess of 13 m thick.

Belonging also to stratum XII, at least in its latest phase, was an impressive water system. Built on the N side of the tell, it consisted of a stone-built staircase, contained within substantial walls, cut into the slope. The upper part of the staircase had along its central axis a mudbrick wall, suggesting that it had been roofed over to provide a means of concealment from the outside. At the base of the tell, the steps turned 90 degrees to the E, and continued down at a somewhat steeper inclination, reaching water at a depth of approximately 6 m below present plain level. The water, from an underground spring, was fed into the system by means of a conduit in the S containing wall, and there was probably an overflow through the N wall to prevent stagnation. The system was enclosed by the joining of the side walls to form a semicircular pool, and within the curve a platform had been placed to provide access to the E end of the system at times of high water level.

Following the destruction of stratum XII, there appears to have been an ephemeral phase of squatter occupation (stratum XIB). Both in the ruins of the houses in area AA, and also in the burned-out casemates of the city wall in area EE, remains of beaten earth floors and hearths have been found. Whether this phase represents the temporary occupation of the attackers or the return of the refugee population is unknown, but it is unlikely to have lasted very long. It was followed by a major leveling of the site which involved in area AA the importation of a large quantity of fill. This became, in stratum XI A, the foundation of a small bipartite temple. Constructed of rather narrow but substantially founded walls, it measured 7.9 × 4.7 m. The slightly offset entrance on the S side gave access to a roughly square antechamber which in turn led to a much smaller rear sanctuary. This room had a low bench against its N wall, and a small semicircular niche, at the base of which was set a circular, perfectly flat stone, presumably to serve as the base for a cultic installation. In front of the niche was found a burned area containing the bones of sheep and gazelle, and immediately in front of this was a basalt incense burner.

Almost certainly related to this building, there was found in area EE, deeply cut into the remains of the casemate wall, a large rectangular, plaster-lined bin which contained two additional basalt incense burners, a pottery trough, and a large square basalt altar. All of these items appear to have been broken in antiquity, and it seems likely that the bin was a type of *favissa.*

Stratum XIA, on the basis of the small quantities of pottery recovered, should be dated to the late 11th century B.C. There is no evidence to suggest that the stratum was destroyed, and it must be assumed that the temple simply fell out of use. In stratum X, which followed without any break, the function of the area had clearly changed, and was no longer religious in nature. The temple was leveled to within one course of its foundations, and above it was laid a large open courtyard composed of rough cobbles. This courtyard extended over the entire excavated area without any associated walls, but at irregular intervals several shallow, stone-lined depressions were constructed. Roughly rectangular, with a circularity at one end, these depressions were associated with a horizon of decayed animal manure. The large quantities of pig bones found in this stratum suggests that the area had been given over to the keeping of pigs, the depressions being best interpreted as types of pens.

No evidence for stratum X nor of strata IX or VIII, was found in area EE. Apparently the settlement shrank during these phases. Certainly there was no evidence for defensive walls belonging to these strata.

Elsewhere on the tell, in stratum IX, which followed X without a break, remains of a large but insubstantially constructed building were found, together with an adjacent courtyard. Two subphases were recognized, the upper IXA yielded evidence that it had been abandoned. The mudbrick walls were heavily eroded, and the whole stratum was covered by a layer of natural silt. Stratum IX is dated to the early 9th century B.C.

Following the abandonment of stratum IXA, which may have lasted for no more than 20 years, the area examined in the excavation appears to have become a dump for an industrial process. Stratum VIII was characterized by a dense layer, up to 40 cm thick, of finely divided ashy material containing bands of brown, blue, pink, black, and predominantly white. The nature of the industry has not yet been established, but the presence of copper slag in the deposit suggests some metalworking.

Strata VII–IV have been examined in a much larger exposure than the earlier levels. Stratum VII, divided into two subphases (VIIA the later) represents the city of the late 9th–early 8th centuries B.C. The excavated plan of some 12 building units shows clusters of dwellings separated by pebble-paved streets. Although rather irregularly constructed, the houses appear to have been carefully planned with provision for drainage. On the N side of the mound, evidence has been found of a city wall of mudbrick, about 3.5 m wide, and separated from the settlement by a stone-paved walkway. Perhaps following a short gap in occupation, stratum VI was built on a new plan. The houses in this phase, dated 790–750 B.C., were more regular and slightly larger, but generally followed the same pattern as those of the previous stratum.

Stratum V, dated 750–730 B.C., is characterized by regular and uniform planning. Houses were larger, neatly constructed, and carefully laid out on a grid of intersecting streets. A block of 12 houses has been excavated, all showing identical plans with a single doorway opening from the street into a large front room which was divided into two parts by a row of columns or roof supports. On one side of these columns the room was paved with large stones, and on the other side, which was left unpaved, there was an entrance into a smaller back room which had a floor of beaten earth. The houses in the block were arranged as two rows of six, placed back to back. Despite the extreme regularity of the plan, there is nothing to suggest that the building represents anything more than purely domestic occupation, and its construction in this form testifies to an effective city plan in the Iron Age.

Stratum V was destroyed toward the middle of the 8th century B.C. Within the excavated area, stratum IV, which followed, was devoid of buildings. Instead it consisted of a floor surface into which 98 circular pits and two rectangular mudbrick lined bins had been cut. A number of postholes dug into the surface suggest that temporary coverings had been erected from time to time, and a number of circular ovens indicate that baking also took place. From botanical remains recovered from the pits, it would seem probable that the area was for storing grain.

No stratigraphic relationship exists between strata IV and III, the latter having been investigated in a different area of the tell, some 20 m farther E, on the highest point of the mound—the so-called "acropolis." A massively constructed square building stood on the acropolis. It consisted of seven rooms built around a paved courtyard with a drain and tower at the SE corner. Dating to the Persian period, it contained a limestone incense burner decorated with geometric designs, a horse and a human figure, and bearing the inscription *lzkwr,* "belonging to Zakkur."

Over this building was constructed in stratum II a rectangular building, 21.2 × 13.3 m. The substantial nature of the external walls, approximately 90 cm in width, suggests that it was probably a type of fortress. An unusual feature of the construction was the placement of a layer of reeds between the foundation course and the mudbrick superstructure. This building, which should be dated to the Hellenistic period (4th–2d century B.C.) was destroyed by fire.

The latest building remains on the upper tell (stratum I) are foundations for a rectangular building, 9.25 ×

10.40 m, best interpreted as a watchtower. Together with two plastered cisterns, these remains belong to the Roman period. The latest remains on the entire site, however, are to be found on the N side of the lower tell. Here was built, during the 7th–8th century A.D., a large rectangular enclosure, 40 × 30 m, with a block building, 18 × 5.0 m set in the SW corner. The enclosure had a number of partitions, and was entered through an extremely large gateway. It seems likely that this building was a type of khan, a staging post for caravans passing W from Ajlun across the Jordan River.

Bibliography

Contenson, H. de. 1960. Three Soundings in the Jordan Valley. *ADAJ* 4–5: 12–66.

Glueck, N. 1951. *Explorations in Eastern Palestine IV.* AASOR 25–28. New Haven.

Pritchard, J. B. 1980. *The Cemetery at Tell es-Saʿidiyeh, Jordan.* University Museum Monograph 41. Philadelphia.

———. 1985. *Tell es-Saʿidiyeh: Excavations on the Tell, 1964–1966.* University Museum Monograph 60. Philadelphia.

Tubb, J. N. 1988. Tell es-Saʿidiyeh: Preliminary Report on the First Three Seasons of Renewed Excavations. *Levant* 20: 23–88.

Jonathan N. Tubb

SAKKUTH AND KAIWAN (DEITIES) [Heb *sikkût* and *kiyyûn*]. A name and epithet, respectively, of the planet Saturn (Amos 5:26). Because Saturn was the most distant of the planets known to the ancients, and hence the planet was the slowest and steadiest movement across the sky, it was described in Mesopotamia by the adjective *kayamānu,* meaning "the steady one." Learned speculation enhanced Saturn's connection with stability, justice, and truth such that it even became identified with the Sun, who was perceived to have the same qualities in Mesopotamian tradition (Parpola 1983: 343). Since Akkadian *m* may appear as *w* in loanwords into Hebrew, the Akkadian consonants *kymn* would appear in Hebrew as *kywn,* as in fact occurs in Amos 5:26. Frequent references to *kywn* when the planets are invoked in Aramaic and Mandaean texts in the 1st millennium A.D. (Obermann 1940) affirms the longevity, popularity, and cross-cultural transfer of this title for Saturn.

The pronunciation of the Sumerian logogram SAG.KUD as *sakkud* in Akkadian has been confirmed (Hallo 1977: 15), permitting its appearance as a loan into Hebrew as *sakkût.* But since there is no cuneiform evidence to connect this name with Saturn (Borger 1988), the possible occurrence of both name and epithet in Amos 5:26 is at best hypothetical. 2 Kgs 17:30 is equally problematic in this regard.

Although Amos 5:26 may therefore make a double reference to the planet Saturn worshipped as a deity under its Mesopotamian names, such a reading is not without its problems. The Hebrew actually reads *sikkût* and *kiyyûn,* and Gevirtz has demonstrated that these unexpected vowels cannot be explained (as is commonly attempted) from the influence of the vowels of *šiqqûṣ,* "detestable thing." Equally respectable alternative interpretations result when the possibility of different vowels is considered, especially the evidence of early texts that do not interpret the consonants *skt* as a divine name at all but instead translate the word as a singular common noun, "tent of, tabernacle of," *sukkat* (LXX, Acts 7:43, Vg; Damascus Rule 7.14–19 provides a plural form but explains it as singular). A similar problem with uncertain vocalization is encountered with the name Kaiwan. See REPHAN.

Bibliography

Borger, R. 1988. Amos 5,26, Apostelgeschichte 7,43 und Šurpu II,180. *ZAW* 100: 70–81.

Gevirtz, S. 1968. A New Look at an Old Crux: Amos 5:26. *JBL* 87: 267–76.

Hallo, W. H. 1977. New Moons and Sabbaths: A Case Study in the Contrastive Approach. *HUCA* 48: 1–18.

Isbell, C. D. 1978. Another Look at Amos 5:26. *JBL* 97: 97–99.

Obermann, J. 1940. Two Magic Bowls: New Incantation Texts from Mesopotamia. *AJSL* 57: 1–31.

Parpola, S. 1983. *Letters from Assyrian Scholars to the Kings Esarhaddon and Assurbanipal.* Part 2. AOAT 5/2. Neukirchen-Vluyn.

Samuel A. Meier

SALA (PERSON) [Gk *Sala*]. See SALMON.

SALAMIEL (PERSON) [Gk *Salamiēl*]. A personal name given as part of the genealogy of Judith (Jdt 8:1). The name is almost certainly to be identified with Shelumiel (Heb *šĕlumîʾēl*) the son of Zurishaddai, the descendant of Simeon, who was a leader of the tribe of Simeon during the time of Moses (Num 1:6; 2:12; 7:36, 41; 10:19). The purpose of the genealogy is to provide proof of the purity of Judith's Jewish descent, and to give the story verisimilitude.

Sidnie Ann White

SALAMIS (PLACE) [Gk *Salamis*]. An important commercial city on the E shore of the island of Cyprus (35°10′N; 33°55′E). It is often confused with a Greek island of the same name, which is near Athens. Even though Paphos was the capital in the NT era, Salamis was still arguably the most important city. Josephus (*Ant* 13.284–87) as well as Acts 13:5 seem to indicate a large Jewish population, with several synagogues, dating perhaps to pre-Roman times.

Salamis was the 1st stop on the initial missionary journey of Paul, who went there with Barnabas (who was from Cyprus; Acts 4:26) and John Mark (perhaps also a Cypriot; Col. 4:10). From Salamis, the missionaries traveled overland to the Roman administrative capital, Paphos, at the other end of the island. The so-called *Acts of Barnabas* (22–23) allege that the eponymous missionary was later martyred in Salamis by a mob encouraged by Jews visiting from Syria.

In retaliation for a Jewish-led rebellion of the island during the reign of Hadrian, Trajan in A.D. 117 dealt severely with Salamis and many Greek Cypriotes were killed. Following this, Jews were forbidden to set foot on the island (Dio Cassius 68.32.2). After an earthquake in the reign of Constantine, the city was rebuilt by Constantius II and renamed Constantia. This new city became capital of Cyprus in the 4th century only to be decimated by an invasion in A.D. 647, and has remained abandoned since that time. Parts of the city wall and the ancient harbor, a number of public buildings, and a Roman villa have been recovered through the excavations at the site of Salamis/Constantia, about 3 miles N of the modern port of Famagusta.

CONRAD GEMPF

SALATHIEL (PERSON) [Lat *Salathihel*]. See SHEALTIEL.

SALECAH (PLACE) [Heb *salkâ*]. A town reportedly captured from Og, king of Bashan (Deut 3:10), as part of territory given by Moses to the tribes of Gad and Reuben (Josh 12:5). Salecah is apparently an outer limit ("all of Bashan as far as Salecah") for the 60 cities of Bashan. As the southeasternmost point, it is given equal weight with Mt. Hermon at the NE tip of the region of Bashan (Josh 13:11 and 1 Chr 5:11). Thus it is suggested by the Deuteronomistic Historian, through a genealogy and a deed recorded during the days of King Josiah or perhaps Jotham, that Selecah may ideally represent the farthest reach S and E of the Israelite expansion in Transjordan. Kallai (*HGB*, 486, 491) concludes that this outer limit, Salecah, refers to the actual expansion of territories during the reign of David, which were restored in the 8th century B.C.E. through a partnership between Jotham and Jeroboam II against the Ammonites. The modern location is usually identified as Salkhad (M.R. 311212), at the top of an imposing basalt cone, though this link is probably only due to phonetic similarity in the names.

PAUL NIMRAH FRANKLYN

SALEM (PLACE) [Heb *šālēm*]. The city of Melchizedek in Gen 14:18. Psalm 76:3—Eng 76:2 uses "Salem" in parallelism with "Zion," thus equating it with Jerusalem. The *Genesis Apocryphon* from Qumran (1QapGen 22:13) glosses *šlm* with *hyʾ yrwšlm*, "that is, Jerusalem," and *Tg. Onq.*, *Tg. Neof.*, and *Tg. Ps.-J.* render it outright by *yrwšlm*, "Jerusalem." This is certainly a correct tradition in view of the role of Melchizedek as the symbolic archetype of the high priests of Jerusalem in the Hellenistic and Hasmonean ages who combined sacerdotal and secular authority. The author of Genesis 14, who modified most of the place names he mentioned in order to give them an antiquarian sound, took the second half of *Yerûšālēm* (the actual form of the name before the Masoretes revocalized it). Whatever the original semantics of the city name may have been, the element *šālēm* could be construed as meaning "peaceful," alluding to the messianic "prince of peace" in Isa 9:5—Eng 9:6.

There were attempts, since antiquity, to separate Salem from Jerusalem. Eusebius (*Onomast.* no. 152) equated Salem with Salumias, a village 8 Roman miles (ca. 12 km) S of Scythopolis. Jerome adhered for a time to that location. Another identification proceeds from the translation of Gen 33:18 in LXX, Vg, and Syr as "and Jacob came to Salem, a city of Shechem." Hence the suggestions that Salem was the old name of Shechem itself (Landersdorfer 1925), or that it corresponds to the modern village Sālīm (M.R. 181179), ca. 5 km E of Balaṭa (ancient Shechem; Dhorme 1956: 45; Milik 1972: 137; cf. *GP*, 2:441–42). The grammar of the sentence is awkward no matter how it is understood, but the translation, "And Jacob came safely to the city of Shechem," as in RSV and other modern versions, makes better sense. Shechem bore its historical name as early as the time of the Egyptian 12th Dynasty.

Both villages proposed as sites of Salem were too insignificant to have been depicted as a royal temple city. In particular, the one near Shechem is not attested in ancient sources; the "valley Salem" in the assemblage of disparate place names in Jdt 4:4 is borrowed from Genesis 14, along with Choba in the same verse and Arioch in Jdt 1:6. The name *Sālīm* is frequent in Arabic anthroponymy and toponymy. The position of Salem on Abram's return route from Damascene to the Hebron area, and the proximity to it of the Valley of Shaveh also apeak in favor of its identity with Jerusalem.

Bibliography

Dhorme, E. 1956. *La Bible: L'Ancien Testament.* Vol. 1. Bible de la Pléiade 139. Paris.

Landersdorfer, S. 1925. Das Priesterkönigtum von Salem. *JSOR* 9: 203–16.

Milik, J. T. 1972. Milkî-ṣedeq et Milkî-rešaʿ dans les anciens écrits juifs et chrétiens. *JJS* 23: 95–144.

MICHAEL C. ASTOUR

SALIM (PLACE) [Gk *Salim*]. A town near Aenon where John the Baptist preached repentance during the latter half of his ministry and baptized converts since there was a copious supply of water (John 3:23). Salim appears to have been located W of the Jordan River (John 3:26; 1:28; 10:40).

The identification of this site is further assisted by its association with Aenon, which means "place of springs." The number of major spring sites along the W side of the Rift Valley is limited. Three of these locations have been identified as the Aenon near Salim.

Eusebius *(Onomast.)* and Jerome *(De situ et nom. loc. heb. 165)* in the 4th century locate the site 8 Roman miles S of Scythopolis (Beth-shan, M.R. 197212) near the Jordan River. The Medeba Map affirms this tradition by locating springs in that region. Modern advocates of this position point to Tell Sheikh Salim as retaining the ancient name and also to Umm el-Umdan (M.R. 199199).

W. F. Albright (1924: 193) and others have argued for a site which retains the name "Salim," located 4 km away from springs named Ainun in the Wadi Farah. This site in ancient Samaria is rejected by some scholars as it is argued that John the Baptist would have avoided the area.

A proposed S site of Salim in Judea is located 10 km NE of Jerusalem in the Wadi Saleim near an important water source.

Bibliography

Albright, W. F. 1924. Some observations Favoring the Palestinian Origin of the Gospel of John. *HTR* 17: 189–95.

ROBERT W. SMITH

SALLAI (PERSON) [Heb *sallay*]. **1.** A Benjaminite and provincial leader who agreed to settle in Jerusalem (Neh 11:8). Used in this way, the name (along with Gabbai) occurs only here. The differences between this list and its parallel in 1 Chronicles 9 suggest that there is no direct literary relationship between them (contra Kellermann 1966 and Mowinckel 1964: 146–47). Some, however, have conjectured that both writers were dependent upon common archival materials (Schneider in *HSAT,* 42–43; Brockington 1969: 187; cf. Myers *Ezra, Nehemiah* AB, 185). This singular reference to Sallai and other factors have also prompted some scholars to argue that the text is corrupt and should read *gbwry ḥyl,* meaning "mighty men of valor." Sallai, it is argued, was then supplied, either because it was a variant of Sallu *(slwʾ),* mentioned in v 7, or because of the rhyming effect achieved with the name "Gabbai" (Brockington 1969: 189–90; Williamson *Ezra, Nehemiah* WBC, 343). Less likely is the suggestion that together Gabbai and Sallai constitute a rare instance of a double name (cf. Batten *Ezra, Nehemiah* ICC, 268–69). Notwithstanding the widespread support for an emendation of the text, others continue to argue that the text should read as it stands (Myers *Ezra, Nehemiah* AB, 184).

2. The name of a levitical household (*IDB* 4: 166) or the head of one (Myers *Ezra, Nehemiah* AB, 198) in the days of Joiakim (Neh 12:20). The name appears again in a parallel list as Sallai *(sly)* in 12:7 and the difference may be due to a corruption of the text (Brockington 1969: 189–90; cf. *IDB* 4: 166). Others regard the two names as variants of one another (Myers *Ezra, Nehemiah* AB, 198).

Bibliography

Brockington, L. 1969. *Ezra, Nehemiah and Esther.* Century Bible. London.

Kellermann, U. 1966. Die Listen in Nehemia 11 eine Dokummentation aus den letzten Jahren des Reiches Juda? *ZDPV* 82: 209–27.

Mowinckel, S. 1964. *Studien zu dem Buche Ezra-Nehemiah.* Skrifter utgitt av Det Norske Videnskaps-Akademi i Oslo. Oslo.

FREDERICK W. SCHMIDT

SALLU (PERSON) [Heb *sallûʾ, salluʾ, sallû*]. **1.** A Benjaminite and provincial leader who agreed to settle in Jerusalem (Neh 11:7). Sallu's line is referred to in Nehemiah 11 and 1 Chronicles 9 (v 7). The differences between the two lists suggest that there is no direct literary relationship between them (contra Kellermann 1966 and Mowinckel 1964: 146–47). Some, however, have conjectured that both writers were dependent upon common archival materials (Schneider in *HSAT* 2: 42–43; Brockington 1969: 187; cf. Myers *Ezra, Nehemiah* AB, 185). The meaning of the name is obscure. Tracing it to the Arabic root, *salaʾa,* some scholars believe the name means "(God) has restored" (Dahlberg in *IDB* 4: 166).

2. One of the twenty-two priests (Brockington 1969: 197–98) or families of priests (Myers, 196), who returned to Jerusalem with Zerubbabel (Neh 12:7). The name appears again in a parallel list as Sallai *(sly)* in Neh 12:20; the difference may be due to a corruption of the text (Brockington 1969: 189–90); cf. Dahlberg in *IDB* 4: 166). Others regard the two names as variants of one another (Myers *Ezra, Nehemiah* AB, 198).

Bibliography

Brockington, L. 1969. *Ezra, Nehemiah and Esther.* Century Bible. London.

Kellermann, U. 1966. Die Listen in Nehemia 11 eine Dokummentation aus den letzten Jahren des Reiches Juda? *ZDPV* 82: 209–27.

Mowinckel, S. 1964. *Studien zu dem Buche Ezra-Nehemiah.* Skrifter utgitt av Det Norske Videnskaps-Akademi i Oslo. Oslo.

FREDERICK W. SCHMIDT

SALMON (PERSON) [Heb *śalmôn*]. Var. SALMA; SALA. The name of two persons in the Bible. The name possibly means "mantel"; see Noth *IPN,* 232.

1. The father of Boaz, the husband of Ruth, and the son of Nahshon, tracing the line of David (Ruth 4:21). He appears again in Chronicles (1 Chr 2:11) and in both NT genealogies of Jesus Christ (Matt 1:4–5; Luke 3:32 [Gk *salmōn*]. His name is spelled *śalmâh* (with a final *he* instead of *-ôn*) in Ruth 4:20. In each case, a few LXX or Hebrew manuscripts support the opposite variant. This final *he* is a vowel letter which was used in the text to represent *ā* before the full Masoretic vocalization system was developed in the Middle Ages. The variant spelling *śalmāʾ* uses the final *ʾalep* to represent the same sound. The presence of variant spellings has suggested differing traditions to scholars (Campbell *Ruth* AB, 172; Myers *I Chronicles* AB, 13–14).

2. Founder of Bethlehem, whose descendents settled that general region (1 Chr 2:54–55; Rudolph *Chronikbücher* HAT, 23). He was the son of Hur (1 Chr 2:50), eldest son of Caleb (not one of the twelve spies of Numbers 13; Myers, 14).

KIRK E. LOWERY

SALMONE (PLACE) [Gk *Salmōnē*]. A promontory on the easternmost point of the island of Crete (35°19′N; 26°18′E), the modern Cape Sidero where once stood a temple to Athena. Paul, guarded by Julius the centurion, and other prisoners boarded a large Alexandrian grain ship at Myra which was bound for Rome. The ship reached Cnidus with difficulty and strong winds forced it to seek protection by sailing to the lee side of the island of Crete. When the vessel sailed to the S of Crete it passed by the Salmone (Acts 27:7) and made its way to the port of Fairhavens. The pilot and the owner of the ship decided to bypass Fairhavens and set sail for the port of Phoenix, where they intended to spend the winter. The ship, however, was forced off of its course by a wind of hurricane force called Euroquiloa, or "northeaster," and it was later shipwrecked near the island of Malta.

JOHN D. WINELAND

SALOME (PERSON) [Gk *Salōmē*]. **1.** One of Jesus' female followers in Galilee who traveled with him to Jerusalem and witnessed his death and the events that followed (Mark 15:40; 16:1). It is possible that she was the mother of the

Zebedees (Matt 27:56). If so, then Matthew tells us that she was ambitious for her sons and sought for Jesus to give them the chief seats on either side of him when he came into his kingdom (20:20–28).

2. The daughter of Herodias who beguiled Herod Antipas with her dancing (Mark 6:14–29; Matt 14:1–12). She is identified by Josephus as Salome, the daughter of Herodias and Herod Philip (*Ant* 18.136). To confuse matters further, Josephus also tells us that Salome first married another Philip who was also a son of Herod (the Great?), and later Aristobolus, yet another Herodian relative. See HEROD PHILIP. Salome's dance is said by the gospel writers to have led to John the Baptist's beheading. In the gospels she is depicted as a young woman who is totally compliant with her mother's wishes. She passes on her mother's request for John the Baptist's head to her stepfather. Indeed, in the Markan account, it is Salome herself who adds the grotesque touch of requesting the head *on a platter*. The NT says nothing about her later life.

Bibliography

Hoehner, H. W. 1980. *Herod Antipas: A Contemporary of Jesus Christ.* Grand Rapids.

Witherington, B. 1984. *Women in the Ministry of Jesus.* Cambridge.

BEN WITHERINGTON, III

SALT SEA (PLACE) [Heb *yām hammelaḥ*]. One of the designations of the DEAD SEA, due to its high content of salts (25 percent, the highest salinity in the world). This name occurs in Gen 14:3 (identified with the valley of Siddim); Num 34:3, 12; Deut 3:17; Josh 3:16; 12:3 (in this and the previous two passages, gloss to sea of the Arabah); Josh 15:2, 5; 18:19.

MICHAEL C. ASTOUR

SALT, CITY OF. See CITY OF SALT.

SALT, VALLEY OF (PLACE) [Heb *gêʾ hamelaḥ*]. Two Israelite battles, each from a different period of Israel's history, were won in this valley against the Edomites. The first occurred during the time of David under the command of his lieutenant Abishai (2 Sam 8:13). The second was conducted ca. 200 years later by King Amaziah and opened the way for him to reconquer a large part of Edom (2 Kgs 14:7; 2 Chr 25:11). Opinions are varied on the location of this valley. Some prefer to identify it with the Wadi el-Milḥ (Arabic "salt") E of Beer-sheba, because of the similarity of names and because of its location on a natural frontier of Canaan. However, since Israel was clearly the aggressor in these two campaigns, it seems more likely that the battle occurred closer to Edomite territory. Therefore, other scholars have preferred to identify the valley with the salt-encrusted lowlands of es-Sebkah, S of the Dead Sea, although this area seems unsuitable for military activity. B. Mazar (see Cogan and Tadmor, *II Kings* AB, 155 n. 7) has suggested that the Valley of Salt is identical with *gêʾ ḥărāšîm,* the "Valley of Craftsmen" (cf. 1 Chr 4:13–14).

RANDALL W. YOUNKER

SALU (PERSON) [Heb *sālûʾ*]. The head of a family of the tribe of Simeon (Num 25:14). Salu's son, Zimri, placed the very life of Israel in jeopardy by cohabiting with a Midianite woman and thereby bringing about a plague. Zimri, the son of Salu, was therefore killed in order to save Israel from the plague (Num 25:6–9). A name similar to Salu but belonging to a Benjaminite named Sallu is found in the later books of the OT. See SALLU. The LXX transliteration of the Simeonite Salu is identical in one instance to that of the Benjaminite Sallu. Salu appears in the LXX as Gk *salō,* as does Sallu in LXX 1 Chr 9:7. For the author of 1 Maccabees, Zimri, son of Salu (Gk *salōm*), represented those Jews whom Mattathias the Hasmonean killed, owing to their disobedience to the Law. 1 Macc 2:26 clearly demonstrates the author's dependence upon the LXX rather than the MT by referring to the Simeonite Salom.

MICHAEL E. HARDWICK

SALVATION. Even if it does not always use a formally salvific terminology, the Bible introduces on practically every page the theme of salvation (or its absence). To express the comprehensive nature of salvation, the OT and NT employ a rich variety of terms with different nuances according to their contexts. To organize the material, particular attention will be paid to the recipients, agents, nature, and mediation of salvation.

A. The Hebrew Bible/OT
   1. The Recipients
   2. The Agents of Salvation
   3. The Nature of Salvation
   4. The Mediation of Salvation
B. The NT
   1. The Recipients
   2. The Agents of Salvation
   3. The Nature of Salvation
   4. The Mediation of Salvation
C. Issues of Interpretation
   1. Salvation-History
   2. The Kingdom of God
   3. Covenant

A. The Hebrew Bible/OT

Hebrew words for salvation include *nāṣal* ("deliver"), *pālaṭ* ("bring to safety"), *pādāh* (var. *pādaʿ,* "redeem") and *mālaṭ* ("deliver"). Two major salvific terms are *gāʾal* ("redeem," "buy back," "restore," "vindicate," or "deliver") and *yāšaʿ* ("save," "help in time of distress," "rescue," "deliver," or "set free"). The LXX translates *yāšaʿ* as *sǭzō* ("save") 138 times.

1. The Recipients. Personal, group, and national needs indicate those who need to be saved and why they need to be saved.

a. Personal Needs. Individuals find help and deliverance in the face of very specific problems. Barren women receive the gift of a son (Judges 13; 1 Sam 1:1–2:11). Jacob seeks and receives the blessing from his father (Gen 27:1–29).

The Psalms pray for deliverance from wicked people (Ps 12:1; 43:1; 86:16), victory for the king (Ps 20:9), and deliverance from personal enemies (Psalms 7, 109). The

Psalms also offer thanksgiving when the individual is delivered from trouble (Psalm 34), from dangers in battle (Psalm 18), and from death (Ps 86:13).

b. Groups. The Abraham cycle and the patriarchal narratives present groups of people who receive saving blessings. In Genesis 37–50 Joseph's family escapes starvation and Joseph is reconciled with his brothers. The story of the great flood (Gen 6:5–9:19) portrays a situation of general perversion and consequent destruction from which God saves a just man (Noah) and his family; they form a holy remnant from which the entire human race will be regenerated.

It is above all the whole people of Israel who receive salvation. The Israelites in Egypt are poor slaves (Exod 1:11, 13, 16; 2:23–25; 5:1–21; 20:2) who are threatened with genocide (Exod 1:8–22). It is especially through the miraculous deliverance at the sea (Exod 14:1–15:21) that God brings the people out of Egypt (Judg 6:8–9; 1 Sam 10:18; Isa 63:7–14; Hos 11:1; 13:4). The cult of the Passover preserves the memory of the Israelites being delivered from their heavily armed persecutors through the crossing of dangerous waters (Exod 12:1–28).

The Scriptures also enshrine the conviction that God has continued to save Israel from other peoples (1 Sam 11:13; 14:23, 39; 2 Sam 8:14). The Psalms pray that God will continue to deliver his people (Pss 28:8–9; 60:5; 108:6). The Lord of history will save Israel from famine and death (Ps 33:19).

Through Deborah and Barak, God delivers the Israelites from the Canaanite oppression of Jabin and Sisera (Judges 4–5). The cycle of stories from the northern kingdom about the prophets Elijah and Elisha show God's power at work in a salvific way (1 Kings 17–2 Kings 10).

Postexilic literature (Esther, Tobit, and Judith) presents the Israelites as a minority in a Diaspora situation. God intervenes to save this oppressed people.

At times God's salvation seems restricted to a holy remnant (Isa 7:3–4; 10:20–23). Other prophetic voices attest to the Lord's steadfast love for the people as a whole and desire to renew the saving covenant with Israel (Hos 2:14–23).

Both preexilic (Amos 1–2; Isaiah 13–23) and exilic prophecy (Jeremish 46–51; Ezekiel 25–32) contain oracles against foreign cities and nations. Yet such negative utterances imply the Lord's concern with these peoples. Through that comic caricature of a prophet, Jonah, God's message (Jonah 3:1–10) brings the people of Nineveh to repentance. What seems a prophecy of doom ("yet forty days, and Nineveh shall be overthrown") is not a final rejection but a last call to conversion. Significantly, Jonah is sent to warn the Ninevites about the consequences of their sins, but not to call on them to accept the faith of Israel. It is moral conversion that the prophet has to proclaim, not a change of religion.

The sense that divine salvation is for all people turns up in Isaiah and Second Isaiah, even though this universalism takes a centralist form. The gentile nations must turn toward Jerusalem, as center, to find salvation (Isa 2:1–4; 49:6, 22–23; 60:1–14). The Hebrew Scriptures frequently denounce pagans and their idolatry, yet even preexilic prophecy maintains a certain universalism in God's saving activity (Amos 9:7). Add, too, the holy pagans like Melchizedek (Gen 14:18–22; Ps 110:4), the queen of Sheba (1 Kings 10), Ruth, and Job, who enjoy God's friendship and favor. Finally, through its covenant theme the flood story affirms God's good will toward every living creature on the face of the earth (Gen 9:1–19).

2. The Agents of Salvation. Self-salvation is not a typically biblical perspective. Deliverance comes through others. Some texts (Psalms 77 and 78) emphasize divine action with virtually no mention of human actors. Other texts (Exodus 1 and 4; Psalm 105) highlight human actors. Reconciling divine and human action was not a biblical problem.

a. Human Deliverers. The just man Abraham intercedes for the people of Sodom (Gen 18:16–33). Through him Israel and all humanity will be blessed by God (Gen 12:1–3; 15:1–6; 17:1–8; 22:15–18). A political leader and mystic, Moses delivers Israel from the Egyptian oppression, interprets God's saving activity, and mediates the Sinai covenant (Exodus). The book of Judges recognizes the salvific role of various "judges" (Judg 2:16) such as Othniel (Judg 3:9), Ehud (Judg 3:15), Shamgar (Judg 3:31), Gideon (Judg 8:22; 9:17), and Samson (Judg 13:5). David saves Israel (2 Sam 3:18; 9:19); kings have the task of saving the people (Hos 13:10) and of defending the helpless (Ps 72:4). The everlasting dynasty promised to David will make him an agent of salvation for his people (2 Samuel 7; Psalm 89; Ezek 37:24–25). In the four Servant Songs of Second Isaiah (Isa 42:1–4; 49:1–6; 50:4–11; 52:13–53:12), the Servant—whether understood as a representative individual, the entire people, or both—will restore justice and light to the nations, so that God's "salvation may reach to the end of the earth" (Isa 49:6).

b. God the Savior. Whether or not human deliverers are portrayed, God's role is preeminent. It is the divine warrior—not Moses primarily—who saves the people at the sea (Exod 15:1–21). Judges and kings have the task of delivering the Israelites. Yet the Scriptures acknowledge that God took the initiative in raising up these deliverers for the people (Judg 2:16, 18; 3:9, 15). It is God who saved and saves both individuals (2 Sam 12:7; 22:18, 44, 49; Pss 25:5; 27:1) and the nation as a whole (Exod 6:6; Deut 7:8; 13:5; 32:15; 33:29; Isa 41:14; 43:14; 44:24; Psalm 78; 1 Macc 4:30). Hence the Psalms pray for deliverance (Pss 69, 77, 79, 80) and praise the Lord as the God who has kept and will keep Jerusalem safe (Psalms 46, 48, 76, 87).

The names of Joshua (Num 13:8, 16) and others make them living witnesses to the saving power of God, Israel's faithful protector. The Lord heals the people like a doctor (Exod 15:26; Num 21:4). He feeds them in the desert (Exodus 16) and miraculously supplies them with water (Exod 15:22–25; 17:1–7). "The Day of the Lord" is above all a day when the Lord works some striking deed of salvation in favor of Israel.

3. The Nature of Salvation. There is a strong emphasis on the this-wordly nature of salvation. Material and national prosperity is prominent. Yet it would be false to contrast an OT, very earthly salvation with a NT, spiritual and thoroughly other-worldly salvation. Even a brief examination of the language of "peace," "blessing," "life," "law," "justice," and "promise" would seriously modify any such sharp contrast.

a. The Earthly Dimension. Salvation involves being delivered from slavery (Deut 24:18), separation from one's family, and the threat of death. It means victory in battle, the freedom to marry, the gift of descendants, a long life, and the protection needed to enjoy one's rightful patrimony. The final blessing attributed to Moses before his death sums up Israel's sense of being a uniquely favored nation, saved by God to live freely in a fertile land of its own (Deut 33:28–29). The oracles of Balaam celebrate God's saving acts and purposes for the people delivered from actual or threatening oppression at the hands of Egypt or other nations (Num 22:41–24:25).

In Isaiah's terms, salvation means Israel enjoying earthly peace with other peoples (Isa 2:1–5). The messianic king will not only rule with wisdom and justice, but will also restore a proper harmony with nature (Isa 11:1–9).

b. The Spiritual Dimension. One cannot overlook the spiritual, other-worldly elements involved in the making of the Sinai covenant, the giving of the law, the building of Solomon's temple, the role of ideal kings, and much else in Israel's history. The redemption and restoration of Israel (Isa 43:14–44:5) after the Babylonian Captivity illustrate strikingly the spiritual aspect of salvation.

Like a valley of dry bones, the people will be raised to life, brought back from Exile, and given a new beginning (Ezek 37:1–14). God will cleanse the people from their sins, to give them a new heart and spirit (Ezek 36:22–32). Jerusalem will be rebuilt, and the temple and the land will be restored (Ezekiel 40–48). These visions of a salvific future go beyond the merely political and social to involve a new religious relationship with God. They hold out the hope of enjoying the Lord's intimate presence in the temple, and as renewed people freely living again with God in their own country (Jer 31:17).

To depict the fidelity and intensity of that divine love, which the people should once again experience, Second Isaiah uses the most powerful images available; the Lord loves his people like a spouse or a mother (Isa 49:14–16; 54:1–8; Hos 2:14–23; 11:1–9).

c. Future Salvation. As many Psalms testify, the Israelites experienced God's salvific power in situations that regularly recurred, such as pilgrimages to Jerusalem and worship in the temple. Yet the same people were also called to await and accept new and extraordinary interventions from God.

Amos expected Israel's present existence to end through some new divine action (Amos 7:1–9; 8:1–2). Hosea proclaimed a renewal which would let the people experience a fresh start (Hos 2:6–7, 14–15; 3:4–5). Isaiah announced the coming of a new Davidic king (Isa 9:2–7; 11:1–10), Jeremiah a new covenant (Jer 31:31–34), Ezekiel a new life for the people (Ezek 37:1–14), and Second Isaiah a new exodus as God comes to restore the people (Isa 40:1–11).

These prophetic expectations assume more and more an eschatological dimension (Isa 43:5–44:5; Psalms 46, 76; Zechariah 14). In the book of Joel a catastrophic locust plague leads the prophet not only to call the people to repentance (1:2–2:27) but also to speak of the judgments and blessings to come at the end (2:28–3:21). In the last days, "all who call upon the name of the Lord shall be saved" (Joel 2:32). Eventually the expectations of future salvation takes the form of apocalyptic hopes for the resurrection of the dead and a new life with God in a transformed world (Isa 26:19; 65:17–25; 66:22; Dan 12:1–3).

4. The Mediation of Salvation. Over and over again the Hebrew Scriptures testify to the conviction that God's saving self-communication was mediated through events that the people experienced, interpreted, remembered, and reenacted. Various episodes effected salvation, above all the Exodus from Egypt. Several covenants, in particular the Sinai covenant, promised salvation. It is worth highlighting certain points about the means, signs, places, and conditions of human deliverance.

a. The Means of Salvation. At crucial stages in the Exodus story, theophanies reveal God's saving presence (Exodus 3, 19, 33). There is a strong earthly dimension to divine deliverance, yet the means for saving the people are not to be reduced to saving on an ordinary military level (Hos 1:7; 1 Macc 3:18–19). Through a providential plague Jerusalem and Judah are saved from Sennacherib (Isa 37:33–37). As creator and lord of history, God controls the destinies of the nations whose deliverance is not to be found in armies, great heroes, and war horses (Ps 33:10–19). Salvation comes through the gift of wisdom (Prov 1:20–2:22; 8:1–36; Wis 8:2–9:18). It is mediated through a new covenant to be written in the human heart (Jer 31:31–34; Ezek 11:19).

b. Signs and Places. Visible signs and places are repeatedly understood to convey the promise and power of divine salvation. The signs often take a "living" form, like the rainbow in the story of the universal covenant after the Flood (Gen 9:12–17), the three visitors who appear to Abraham at the noontime siesta (Genesis 18), the child in the Immanuel sign (Isa 7:10–17), and the food which is provided day by day in the wilderness.

At times it is in the fields and countryside that God mediates help or promises deliverance. Thus the Lord appears to Abraham by the oaks of Mamre, an ancient sacred place slightly north of Hebron (Gen 18:1). Gideon is visited by the angel of the Lord under the oak of Ophrat (Judg 6:11). In the days before the monarchy, the shrine of Shiloh is a place where God hears prayers, grants saving blessings, and calls the prophet Samuel (1 Samuel 3).

But it is above all the temple in Jerusalem which from the time of David was seen as the place par excellence for receiving God's help and blessing. After the Babylonian Captivity the prophet Haggai, assisted by Zechariah, encourages the building of the new temple, the place where God will give full and final prosperity (Hag 1:1–2:9).

c. The Conditions for Salvation. On the human side, certain conditions are required. God responds to those who exhibit a trusting faith (Ps 22:4). He delivers those who fear him and hope in his steadfast love (Ps 33:18–19).

In particular, those who care for the poor, the stranger, and the weak will not lose God's covenanted protection (Exod 22:20–27). The law of holiness brings not only cultic requirements but also ethical obligations toward such defenseless people as strangers (Lev 19:33). The Deuteronomic Code stresses the people's responsibility toward the legally helpless, the object of God's special concern: "He executes justice for the fatherless and the widow, and loves the sojourner, giving him food and clothing. Love the sojourner therefore; for you were sojourners in the land of Egypt" (Deut 10:18–19). Echoing a ceremony of covenant renewal, Deuteronomy presents salvation as a choice of divine blessing rather than divine judgment, a choice of the way which promises to bring life, peace, and freedom: "Behold, I set before you this day a blessing and a curse: the blessing, if you obey the commandments of the Lord your God . . . and the curse, if you do not obey the commandments of the Lord your God" (Deut 11:26–28; 28:1–68; 30:15–20).

In a classic passage Micah sums up the appropriate human response to God's offer and gift of salvation: "What does the Lord require of you but to do justice, and to love kindness, and to walk humbly with your God?" (Mic 6:8).

B. The NT

The NT uses the very *sǭzō* ("save," "keep from harm," "rescue," "heal," or "liberate") 106 times, and its compound *diasǭzō* 9 times. The corresponding nouns *sōtēria* ("salvation"), *sōtēr* ("savior") and *sōtērion* ("salvation") turn up 45, 24, and 4 times respectively. We find the very *ruomai* ("rescue") 15 times in the NT, which also uses many other terms ("freedom," "justification," "life," "reconciliation," "redemption," "resurrection," and "rule of God") to express salvation.

1. The Recipients. a. Personal Needs. At times, "save" involves some individual being delivered from physical danger. Thus Paul is rescued from various perils, including shipwreck, on his way to Rome (Acts 23:24; 27:20, 31, 34, 43, 44; 28:1, 4). God "delivered" Paul from an unspecified danger in the province of Asia (2 Cor 1:10). The ark meant that Noah and his family "were brought to safety through the water" (1 Pet 3:20). In this context "save" carries baptismal overtones as well (1 Pet 3:21).

According to the Synoptic Gospels, sin (Luke 15:18), sickness (Luke 8:48; 17:19), deformity (Mark 3:4; Luke 18:42), demonic possession (Mark 1:34), the threat of death (Mat 14:30), the power of wealth (Mark 10:25–26 par.; Luke 19:1–10), and the constant and pervasive domination of "evil" or "the evil one" (Matt 6:13 par.) put people in need of deliverance. Elizabeth's problem is very specific: her infertility (Luke 1:7, 18, 25). The gift of a son leads her husband Zechariah to make his prophetic prayer of thanksgiving for God's saving interventions (Luke 1:67–79).

The Synoptics report Peter (Matt 14:30) and the core group of disciples (Matt 8:25 par.) crying out to be "saved" from drowning. In both cases the stories symbolize for the hearers and readers of the gospels various problems (that go beyond mere physical danger) and a corresponding salvation which they can receive from the risen Lord. Likewise "save" in the context of Jesus' crucifixion (Mark 15:30–31 par.) is used in the sense of "rescue from death," yet the overtones suggest much more than mere deliverance from physical death (Matt 27:49; John 12:27; Heb 5:7).

b. Collective Needs. Like the Hebrew Scriptures, the NT highlights the general rather than the individual needs that make people candidates for salvation. Where Mark 10:45 par. does not specify from what "the many" will be rescued, other passages make clear the common need to be delivered from the power of sin (Matt 1:21; Mark 1:5 par.; Acts 2:38; 3:19, 26; 10:43) and death (Luke 1:79).

"All have sinned," Paul writes, "and fall short of the glory of God" (Rom 3:23). Sin and death are personified forces which enslave Jews and gentiles alike (Rom 5:12–7:25). Cosmic powers hold human beings in bondage (Gal 4:3, 9; Col 2:8, 20; 1 Cor 15:24). In a sense, those under God's good and holy law need to be delivered from it, as they resist it, break it, or use it in a misguided attempt to justify themselves (Rom 5:20, 10:4; 1 Cor 15:56; Gal 3:10–25). In a classic passage, Hebrews sums up the condition (from which Jesus delivered us) as a bondage to sin, the devil, death, and the fear of death (Heb 2:14–18).

Luke uses Isaiah to portray our presalvation state as that of poverty, captivity, blindness, and oppression (Luke 4:18). Elsewhere this common state is called that of being "strangers to the covenants of promise, having no hope and without God in the world" (Eph 2:12). It is the condition of those who live "in darkness and the shadow of death" (Luke 1:79; Col 1:13).

2. The Agents of Salvation. a. Human Deliverers. In a variety of ways human beings serve as agents of salvation. Through an encounter with the risen Lord (1 Cor 9:1; 15:8) which he describes as "a revelation of Jesus Christ" (Gal 1:12), Paul knows that he has been called to proclaim God's Son "among the Gentiles" (Gal 1:16). He is "eager" to visit Rome and preach "the Gospel" which is "the power of God for salvation to everyone who has faith" (Rom 1:15–16; 1 Cor 1:18; 15:1–2). Paul's missionary activity helps to bring about salvation (Rom 11:14). He lists the spiritual gifts which Christians "appointed" by God use in the saving service of others (1 Cor 12:28).

From the wider group of his disciples Jesus appoints "twelve" to preach and cast out demons (Mark 3:13–19 par.). They are sent out to preach, heal, and deliver people from diabolic powers (Mark 6:7–13 par.). In the post-resurrection situation "the eleven disciples" receive a missionary mandate to "make disciples of all nations" by bringing them baptism and the teaching of Jesus (Matt 28:16–20).

Acts describes the beginnings of the Church in Jerusalem and its outward movement which eventually brings Paul to Rome (Acts 28:15–31). Through Peter and others, people receive salvation in the form of conversion, the forgiveness of sins, baptism, and the gift of the Spirit (Acts 2:38; 3:18–19; 5:31–32; 10:43–48).

b. God the Savior. The NT applies the term "Savior" to God 8 times (for example, Luke 1:47; 1 Tim 1:1) and to Jesus 16 times (for example, Luke 2:11, John 4:42; Acts 13:23; Phil 3:20). No one else is called "savior." It is the same with *ruomai* ("to rescue" or "deliver"): when the agent of deliverance is named, it is always God (for example, Matt 27:43; 2 Cor 1:10; Col 1:13; 2 Pet 2:7) or Jesus (1 Thess 1:10).

Mary's son is to be called "Jesus" ("God is salvation"), because he will save "his people from their sins" (Matt 1:21). Luke makes it clear that the true bringer of peace and salvation is not the emperor Augustus but only "Christ the Lord" (Luke 2:1, 10–11). It is exclusively in the name of Jesus that salvation comes (Acts 2:38; 5:31): "there is salvation in no one else, for there is no other name under heaven given among men by which we must be saved" (Acts 4:12).

Through the crucified and risen Jesus comes the "forgiveness of sins" (Acts 13:38). Acts makes the universal and absolute claim that all, both Jews and gentiles, are to be "saved through the grace of the Lord Jesus" (Acts 15:11).

The Pastoral Epistles are rich in the explicit vocabulary of salvation, speaking both of "God our Savior who desires all men to be saved" (1 Tim 2:3–4; Titus 2:11) and "Christ Jesus" who "came into the world to save sinners" (1 Tim 1:15). When "the goodness and loving kindness of God our Savior appeared, he saved us . . . through Jesus Christ our Savior" (Titus 3:4, 6). The alignment of "God" and "Jesus" as Savior reaches its climax in the phrase about the object of "our blessed hope," which can be translated as either "the appearing of the glory of our great God and Savior Jesus Christ" or "the appearing of the great God and our Savior Jesus Christ" (Titus 2:13).

3. The Nature of Salvation. The Synoptic Gospels present salvation in terms of "entering" the kingdom of God (Mark 10:23–26 par.), "accepting" it like a child (Mark 10:15 par.), or "sitting at table" in God's kingdom (Luke 13:23–30 par.). Let us see what this entails.

a. The Earthly Dimension. Unlike the OT, the motif of a political oppression (from which Christians and others wish to be delivered) turns up comparatively rarely (Luke 13:1–5; Acts 12:1–17; Rev 16:17–19:3).

Luke and Acts reflect some "national" expectations of salvation. The hymn of Zechariah draws on OT traditions to speak of God's fidelity to the covenant in saving his people from their enemies (Luke 1:68–79). Cleopas and his companion on the Emmaus road express a similar hope for national salvation to come through Jesus (Luke 24:21). The disciples' question in Acts 1:6 ("Lord, will you at this time restore the kingdom to Israel?") seems to reflect a similar nationalistic interpretation of salvation. In these last two cases Jesus himself corrects an inadequate view of salvation (Luke 24:25–27; Acts 1:7–8).

At the same time, Jesus' message of repentance calls on the financially secure to care for the poor, the maimed, the lame, and the blind (Luke 14:12–14). The judgment to come encourages "all the nations" to attend now to the earthly needs of the hungry, strangers, the naked, the sick, and prisoners (Matt 25:31–46). The present experience of salvation leads Zacchaeus to give half of his goods to the poor (Luke 19:8–10). Jesus invites a rich man to sell his possessions and give the proceeds to the poor (Mark 10:21–22). Before Jesus begins his ministry, John the Baptist preaches a message of justice and aid for the needy (Luke 3:10–14). After Jesus ascends into heaven, Jerusalem Christians share their wealth and take care of the poor (Acts 4:32–5:11). In short, the NT version of salvation includes a practical concern here and now for needy people (Rom 12:8; 1 Cor 13:3; Heb 13:16; 1 John 3:17; Jas 1:27; 2:14–17).

b. The Spiritual Dimension. In the Synoptic Gospels, through his words, deeds, and presence Jesus proclaims "the rule of God" and "the kingdom of heaven," which are reverent circumlocutions for divine salvation. He is "Emmanuel, which means 'God with us' " (Matt 1:23), who calls people to change their way of life, believe in the good news, and enjoy a new relationship with God (Mark 1:15).

Jesus' miracles not only physically heal men and women but also symbolize what he ultimately wants to do—namely, bring salvation to their whole person. He tells Bartimaeus, "Your faith has made you well" (Mark 10:52; see 5:34; Matt 9:22, Luke 7:50; 8:48). A paralytic is healed, but the assurance "Your sins are forgiven" shows that the cure is spiritual as well as bodily (Mark 2:1–12).

Jesus' preaching, teaching, and healing (Matt 4:23, 9:35) initiated the final saving intervention of God (Matt 12:28), that was expressed in particular through the divine concern to forgive sinful men and women. Jesus proclaimed God's compassion to those who were marginalized by respectable people: "I came not to call righteous, but sinners" (Mark 2:17 par.). Tax collectors and other close collaborators with the occupying Roman army, women of bad reputation, tanners and those whose occupations made them ritually unclean, socially powerless and disadvantaged people, lepers, and others whom religion and society had left in some depressed condition found Jesus promising them happiness: "Blessed are you poor, for yours is the kingdom of God" (Luke 6:20). Some people were scandalized when Jesus set out to communicate the divine compassion by dining with sinners and so taking them into God's company. These critics derided him as "a glutton and a drunkard, a friend of tax collectors and sinners" (Matt 11:19). Through the parable of the prodigal son (Luke 15:11–32) Jesus defended his conduct in receiving and forgiving those who had been "dead" and "lost" through sin. His visit to a chief tax collector meant that "salvation" had come to that house (Luke 19:9).

Unlike the Synoptic Gospels, Acts does not so much use the image of God's rule to express the present reality of salvation. It speaks directly of being "saved": the day Pentecost fulfills the promise, "whoever calls on the name of the Lord shall be saved" (Acts 2:21; 15:1, 11). Through conversion and baptism in the name of the crucified and risen Jesus, people are saved through the forgiveness of sins and the gift of the Spirit (Acts 2:38; 3:18–19; 5:31–32; 10:43ff.). Healings effected in the name of Jesus manifest the present reality of salvation (Acts 3:6; 4:9–10).

In a rich variety of ways Paul's letters speak of what "the day of the salvation" (2 Cor 6:2) or "the gospel" of salvation (Eph 1:13) means. It brings a new freedom from sin (Rom 6:1–23), from the law (Rom 7:4; Gal 2:15–21), from death (Rom 6:21), and from the cosmic powers (Gal 4:8–10; Col 2:16–23). Salvation means life "in Christ" (Rom 8:1; 16:7; 1 Cor 15:22), the gift of the Holy Spirit (Rom 5:5; 8:9, 11), "peace with God" (Rom 5:1), "justification" (Rom 4:25), being a "new creation" (2 Cor 5:17), and enjoying "reconciliation" (Rom 5:10–11; 2 Cor 5:18 + 20) and existence as "adopted" sons and daughters of God (Gal 4:4–7).

For John, salvation characteristically means being "born again" (John 3:3–6) to become "children of God" (John 1:12) who through the Holy Spirit share in the life of Christ. Here *zōē* (used 36 times in John's gospel) goes beyond mere *bios,* or biological existence, to mean life that will never end.

c. Future Salvation. We have just sampled major ways in which the NT witnesses to and describes the present experience of salvation. At the same time, it indicates that at best, human beings experience only a fragmentary anticipation of the full and final salvation to come from God.

The Synoptics record Jesus' promise of eschatological salvation: "Whoever loses his life for my sake and the gospel will save it" (Mark 8:35); 10:29–30). Those who persevere under persecution and suffering "will be saved" (Mark 13:13). An eschatological discourse on the coming of the Son of Man lists various signs of the end and adds: "When these things begin to take place, look up and raise your heads, because your redemption is drawing near" (Luke 21:28).

In the main Pauline Epistles the futurity of salvation is especially prominent. Apropos of the final destiny of Israel, Paul passes from a negative quotation from Isaiah ("Though the number of the sons of Israel be as the sand of the sea, only a remnant of them will be saved" [Rom 9:27]) to maintain, on the authority of the same prophet, that "all Israel will be saved" (Rom 11:26). In his own case Paul is sure that sufferings will bring his "deliverance" (Phil 1:19). He tells the Philippians to look to the future: "Our commonwealth is in heaven, and from it we await a Savior, the Lord Jesus Christ" (Phil 3:20). He exhorts the Thessalonians to put on "for a helmet the hope of salvation. For God has not destined us for wrath, but to obtain salvation through our Lord Jesus Christ" (1 Thess 5:8–9; see also 1 Thess 1:10); the Romans are encouraged "to wake from sleep," since "salvation is nearer to us than when we first believed" (Rom 13:11). This coming salvation will mean sharing in Christ's glory (Rom 8:17; 1 Cor 15:49–57; Phil 3:20–21). It will free from corruption the whole of creation; even in hoping for this fullness of redemption, believers already experience something of that full salvation (Rom 8:18–24).

The future vision is reflected in Hebrews. Through suffering, Christ became "the pioneer" of human salvation (Heb 2:10). It is at his second coming that he will "save those who are eagerly waiting for him" (Heb 9:28). In its own way the letter of James shares this eschatological version of salvation (Jas 4:12; 2 Tim 4:18). Only once (Jas 5:15) does *sǭzō* refer to a present experience of salvation. 1 Peter comforts believers with the hope that they are "guarded through faith for a salvation ready to be revealed in the last time" (1 Pet 1:5). The NT ends with the vision of that consummation of salvation when the Lord Jesus comes and God makes all things new (Rev 21:1–22:5).

4. The Mediation of Salvation. The classical NT statement on the universal mediation of salvation declares: "There is one God, and there is one mediator between God and men, the man Christ Jesus, who gave himself as a ransom for all" (1 Tim 2:5–6). Let us see some details.

a. The Means of Salvation. Paul clearly appreciates the role of God's free and loving initiative in effecting human salvation: "God shows his love for us in what while we were yet sinners Christ died for us . . . if while we were enemies we were reconciled to God by the death of his Son, much more, now that we are reconciled, shall we be saved by his life" (Rom 5:8–10). John is equally clear about this divine initiative: "God so loved the world that he gave his only Son, that whoever believes in him should not perish but have eternal life. For God sent his Son into the world, not to condemn the world, but that the world might be saved through him" (John 3:16–17). Paul, too, speaks of Christ being "sent" to bring salvation (Rom 8:1–4; Gal 4:4–5). The Synoptic Gospels express the climactic and salvific intervention of God by speaking of the kingdom of God being "at hand" (Mark 1:15), "coming" (Mark 11:10; Matt 6:10 par.; Luke 17:20), or "appearing" (Luke 19:11).

Christ's obedience brought him to crucifixion, resurrection, and exaltation (Phil 2:8–9; Heb 5:8). Through dying and rising he won the victory over "the principalities and powers" (Col 2:12–15). Being thus "made perfect he became the source of eternal salvation to all who obey him" (Heb 5:9). Christ's obedience brought "the free gift of righteousness" and "life for all men" (Rom 5:17–21). He "was put to death for our trespasses and raised for our justification" (Rom 4:25; see 1 Pet 1:18–19).

Through his blood Christ expiated human sin (Rom 3:25) and established a new covenant (Mark 14:24; 1 Cor 11:25). In a range of high-priestly categories, Hebrews presents the sacrificial and saving deed of Christ (Heb 8:1–10:18). Through his offering made once and for all (Heb 10:11–12), he entered into the heavenly sanctuary (Heb 9:11–12:24), and remains forever the living way into that sanctuary and to God (Heb 10:19–22).

b. Signs and Places. In Luke's infancy narrative an angel of the Lord announces the birth of "a Savior who is Christ the Lord" (Luke 2:10–11) and adds: "This will be a sign for you: you will find a babe wrapped in swaddling cloths and lying in a manger" (Luke 2:12). Later in the same gospel Jonah's successful preaching (the sign of Jonah) which saved the Ninevites is contrasted with the failure of "this generation" to repent and be saved when faced with the preaching and "greater" sign of salvation: the Son of Man's presence (Luke 11:29–30, 32). In Matthew, "the sign of Jonah" is understood to refer also to the "three days and three nights the Son of man will spend in the heart of the earth" between his death and resurrection (Matt 12:38–41; 16:1–4).

Mark's eschatological discourse about the signs of the end opens with Jesus announcing the destruction of the temple buildings and four disciples asking him, "when will this be, and what will be the sign when all these things are to be accomplished?" (Mark 13:3–4). In Matthew's version the question about the sign becomes more personal: "When will this be, and what will be the sign of your coming and of the close of the age?" (Matt 24:3). Luke writes of the cosmic "signs" (Luke 21:11, 25) that will accompany the glorious and redemptive coming of the Son of Man (Luke 21:27–28).

Right from the story of the marriage in Cana, John calls Jesus' miraculous deeds "signs" (John 2:11). The gospel reaches its conclusion by explaining its saving purpose in presenting various signs worked by Jesus: "These [signs] are written that you may believe that Jesus is the Christ, the Son of God, and that believing you may have life in his name" (John 20:30). Paul (2 Cor 12:12) and Acts (5:12; 6:8; 14:3) designate as "signs" the miraculous deeds that effectively accompanied the spread of the saving message.

As with these visible signs, many places reveal and mediate salvation in the NT. In Luke's infancy narrative shepherds are "out in the field" when "the glory of the Lord" shines around them and an angel announces the birth of "a Savior" (Luke 2:8–11). That gospel of salvation moves from the sign of a baby in a manger (2:12) to the ambiguous sign of an open and empty tomb which the words of Jesus and two angels interpret in terms of the new life of resurrection (24:1–9). The same gospel begins and ends with the temple, the place par excellence of prayer and divine blessing (1:8–23; 24:52–53). At the same time, whereas Luke's gospel reaches its climax in the neighborhood of Jerusalem when Jesus is "taken up" and enters into his glory (Luke 9:51; 24:26, 50–51; Acts 1:2, 6–11), the salvific geography of Acts eventually takes Paul from Jerusalem to Rome (Acts 21:15–28:16), where the book ends with him "preaching the kingdom of God and teaching about the Lord Jesus Christ quite openly and unhindered" (Acts 28:31).

In Mark's gospel it is at the place of the skull (15:22 par.) that Jesus "gives his life as a ransom for many" (10:45). The fact that "Jesus suffered outside the gate in order to sanctify the people through his own blood" becomes the basis for an exhortation that relativizes the salvific significance of Jerusalem: "Therefore let us go forth to him outside the camp, and bear the abuse he endured. For here we have no lasting city, but we seek the city which is to come" (Heb 13:12–14). The NT closes with the vision of "the holy city, new Jerusalem" where God's people will enjoy a new life forever (Rev 21:2–22:19).

Jesus' dialogue with the Samaritan woman likewise relativizes the importance of sacred places, even Jerusalem (John 4:20–24). John's gospel climaxes with a search for the presence of Jesus (John 20:2, 13, 15). The risen Lord is to be found in the worshipping community (Matt 18:20; 1 Cor 12:3) and in the presence of suffering humanity (Matt 25:35–40). Even the whole cosmos becomes the place of reconciliation through Christ who died on the cross and became "the first-born from the dead" (Col 1:18–20).

c. The Conditions for Salvation. Through God's "own purpose and grace" and not by virtue of their "works," human beings are "saved and called with a holy calling" (2 Tim 1:9). This calling leads them to be saved through repentance (Acts 2:38), the "regeneration" of baptism and "renewal in the Holy Spirit" (Titus 3:5; see 1 Pet 3:21). Often the NT sums up the conditions for salvation by speaking of the need to be "justified" through faith (Rom 1:16–17; 3:21–26) or "saved" through faith (Eph 2:5–8; Acts 16:31). At times this salvation through faith rests on a knowledge of the Scriptures (2 Tim 3:14–15).

The gift of salvation is understood to put the baptized under an obligation to live in holiness and persevere in their struggles with suffering (1 Pet 4:1, 13–14). They are to "work out" their salvation (Phil 2:12) and "strive to enter" God's "sabbath rest" (Heb 4:9–11). They should see the delay of the Parousia "as salvation" (2 Pet 3:15), since they thus have time for improvement (2 Pet 3:14–18), as they wait for "new heavens and a new earth in which righteousness dwells" (2 Pet 3:13).

C. Issues of Interpretation

A number of important biblical themes are intertwined with that of salvation. Research and debate on those other themes affect, to a greater or lesser extent, the interpretation of what the Bible says about salvation. To illustrate this briefly I want to recall some points in the 20th-century discussion of salvation-history, kingdom, and covenant.

1. Salvation-History. In his two-volume *Old Testament Theology* (1962–65), G. von Rad presents the story of Israel's salvation-history as first confessed in ancient creeds like those of Deut 26:5–9 and Josh 24:2–13 and then expanded in various ways. This history of salvation is a story of ever-increasing expectations as divine promises point to future fulfillments. While many prefer von Rad's overall interpretation to that of R. Bultmann (who dismisses OT history as a history of failure and miscarriage), they find serious problems in von Rad's version of salvation-history. He appears, for instance, to separate the "facts" of salvation-history from the actual events of public history.

For O. Cullmann, in *Christ and Time* (German original, 1946), and *Salvation in History* (German original, 1965), the reality of external historical events is central to salvation-history. God's saving acts in history reach their climax in Jesus Christ. Hence Luke's scheme of salvation-history, which presents Christ as the center of time, is no aberration, but the heart of NT theology. Critics believe that Cullmann has not sufficiently clarified the relationship of salvation-history to ordinary history. They have other objections to his scheme of saving history: they point, for instance, to the fact that the wisdom books and other sections of the Bible are not always clearly oriented to a historical way of thinking.

In his two-volume *Theologie des Neuen Testaments* (1948–53), R. Bultmann does not present salvation in terms of the external facts of past history (not even that of Jesus) but as the authentic existence to which the proclamation of the cross calls me and which puts an end to my old world, with its sin and false securities. The salvation event is the eschatological "now" that challenges me to the decision of faith and the chance of a new life "beyond" the world. E. Käsemann and many others have criticized Bultmann for neglecting the theological significance of the Jesus of history, the genuinely futurist eschatology of Paul, and the public and cosmic nature of salvation expressed by the NT.

This brief look at von Rad, Cullmann, and Bultmann can serve to illustrate a crucial issue. Any interpretation of the biblical account of salvation will be deeply affected by the view one holds of history, time, and the historical mediation of salvation.

2. The Kingdom of God. Turning away from contemporary presentations of Jesus as a supreme teacher of ethics, J. Weiss (1863–1914) proposed a different key for the reading of the gospels: Jesus proclaimed the kingdom of God as imminent—a view that A. Schweitzer popularized and developed. In *The Quest of the Historical Jesus* (1968) Schweitzer portrayed Jesus as the disappointed herald of a divine consummation which did not come.

The enduring contribution made by Weiss and Schweitzer was to establish the common consensus that eschatology is not peripheral but central to a correct understanding of the kingdom of God in Jesus' teaching. But what did Jesus mean by the kingdom? Against Schweitzer, C. H. Dodd maintained a realized eschatology: for Jesus the kingdom was not some eschatological climax approaching in the immediate future, but had already come. The emphasis was on a kingdom of God that was accessible here and now. In the aftermath of Schweitzer and Dodd, many scholars have argued for a mediating interpretation of Jesus' preaching of the kingdom: an inaugurated eschatology in which the promised kingdom had already come but was not yet fully operative. This scheme of "already" but "not yet" proposed that Jesus allowed for some interval between his death and the final consummation of the kingdom.

There have been these and other changes in the interpretation of what the kingdom of God meant in Jesus' own preaching and for the evangelists. All such shifts and debates about the kingdom obviously influence any understanding of what the NT indicates about the salvation offered by God through Jesus Christ.

3. Covenant. There are three major approaches to salvation which are interconnected but distinct: salvation as (a) deliverance from evil, (b) ritual purification from sin, and (c) the formation of a new relationship with God. W. Eichrodt serves to illustrate this point. In his three-volume *Theology of the Old Testament* (German original, 1933–39), Eichrodt argued for an underlying unity in the OT. Its central theme he found in the divine covenant with Israel and God's desire to establish a covenantal fellowship with all peoples. Whatever we hold about particular details in Eichrodt's argument, his thesis would encourage us to approach salvation in terms of salvation as a new covenant-relationship with God.

Besides the issues of salvation-history, kingdom of God, and covenant, many other areas of research can modify what we understand the Bible to say about salvation. These would include: the OT messianic expectations; the saving function of the message of the prophets; the contribution of wisdom literature; the nature and value of apocalyptic; beliefs about the afterlife; the social environment of Israel and emerging Christianity; Jesus' understanding of his identity, role, and imminent death; his resurrection, exaltation, and the coming of the Holy Spirit; the nature of justification by faith; the effect on early Christians of the delay in God's final manifestation. Beyond question, the interpretation of biblical salvation is radically influenced by one's view of the relationship between the OT and the NT. For those of Jewish faith the Hebrew Bible constitutes the complete scriptural account that shapes their understanding of the nature of salvation.

Bibliography

Bright, J. 1976. *Covenant and Promise.* Philadelphia.

Bultmann, R. 1948–53. *Theologie des Neuen Testaments.* Tübingen.

Conzelmann, H. 1960. *The Theology of St. Luke.* New York.

Cullmann, O. 1950. *Christ and Time.* Trans. F. V. Filson. Philadelphia.

Eichrodt, W. 1961. *Theology of the Old Testament.* Trans. J. A. Baker. Philadelphia.

Flender, H. 1967. *St. Luke Theologian of Redemptive History.* Philadelphia.

Fuller, R. H. 1981. Jesus Christ as Savior in the New Testament. 35: 145–56.

Goppelt, L. 1981–82. *Theology of the New Testament.* 2 Vols. Grand Rapids.

Hanson, P. D. 1975. *The Dawn of Apocalyptic.* Philadelphia.

Käsemann, E. 1980. *Commentary on Romans.* Grand Rapids.

Kümmel, W. G. 1973. *The Theology of the New Testament According to Its Major Witnesses—Jesus, Paul, John.* Nashville.

Lohfink, N. 1973. *Heil als Befreiung im Israel: Erlösung und Emanzipation.* Freiburg.

Murphy, R. E. 1981. Israel's Wisdom: a Biblical Model of Salvation. *Studia Missionalia* 30: 1–43.

Nicholson, E. W. 1986. *God and His People: Covenant and Theology in the Old Testament.* New York.

Perlitt, L. 1969. *Die Bundestheologie im Alten Testament.* Neukirchen-Vluyn.

Perrin, N. 1963. *The Kingdom of God in the Teaching of Jesus.* Philadelphia.

Reventlow, H. G. 1986. *Problems of Old Testament Theology in the Twentieth Century.* Philadelphia.

Sawyer, J. F. A. 1972. *Semantics in Biblical Research.* London.

Schnackenburg, R. 1968. *God's Rule and Kingdom.* New York.

Schweitzer, A. 1968. *The Quest of the Historical Jesus.* Trans. W. Montgomery. New York.

Terrien, S. 1978. *The Elusive Presence.* New York.

Westermann, C. 1978. *Theologie des Alten Testaments in Grundzügen.* Göttingen.

GERALD G. O'COLLINS

SAMARIA

SAMARIA (PLACE) [Heb *šōmrôn*]. The place name "Samaria" has a twofold sense. First, it refers to the capital city of the N kingdom of Israel, from the time of its construction by Omri in the early 9th century B.C. (1 Kgs 16:23–24) to its conquest by the Assyrians in the late 8th century (probably 721 B.C.; attributed to Shalmaneser V in 2 Kgs 17:1–6, but to Sargon II in Assyrian records). This city has been identified with the ruins of Sebastiya (M.R. 168187).

Second, after the destruction of the city the name "Samaria" (Assyrian *Samerina*) was applied to the larger district in which the city had been situated, following the Assyrian practice of naming a province after its capital or principal city. The natural borders of this region were defined by the valleys of Jezreel and Aijalon on the N and S respectively, by the coast to the W, and by the Jordan river valley on the E. In pre-Assyrian times this region and its population had been referred to after the old Israelite territorial/tribal name Ephraim (in Hosea 36 times and Isaiah 12 times; cf. Jer 31:5–6). Sometimes the name Ephraim was reserved only for the hill country of S Samaria, while the hill country of N Samaria was called Manasseh. Later, however, the area was repopulated by heterogeneous populations from throughout the Assyrian empire, whom the Judeans of Jerusalem generally regarded with contempt. See SAMARITANS.

This entry consists of four articles that treat the history and archaeology of Samaria. The first focuses exclusively on the history and archaeology of the city itself, while the second focuses on important ostraca that were discovered during the excavations of the city. The third article focuses on archaeological survey work that has been done within the larger region, while the fourth focuses on papyri that have been discovered in this region. See also EPHRAIM (PERSON) and DALIYEH, WADI ED-.

SAMARIA THE CITY

A. Biblical Overview
B. Name, Topography, Location
C. History of Excavation
D. History during the Israelite Period

E. History during the Assyrian-Hellenistic Periods
F. History during the Roman-Byzantine Periods

A. Biblical Overview

References to Samaria in biblical writings relating to the Israelite kingdom are to the city and not the district, with only a few exceptions—e.g., "cities of Samaria" in 1 Kgs 13:32 (an anachronism inasmuch as the city of Samaria had not yet been built and named); 1 Kgs 21:1 (where Ahab is called "king of Samaria" [read "king in Samaria"]); and perhaps also 2 Chr 22:9 (where Ahaziah is said to have been "captured while hiding in Samaria"; the earlier account in 1 Kgs 9:27–29 had stated that he was wounded at the ascent of Gur near Ibleam and died in Megiddo). The MT reference to "mountains of Samaria" in Amos 3:9 should be read "mountain of Samaria" along with the LXX.

The Assyrians did not completely destroy Samaria, although a large part of it was burned. It was rebuilt and became an administrative center which appears to have maintained hegemony over much of the Judean territory during the Babylonian and early Persian periods. With the coming of the Macedonians in 332 B.C., and after the suppression of a local uprising, Samaria was rebuilt as a Greek city. This city was destroyed by the Jewish ruler John Hyrcanus in 108/107 B.C. and later rebuilt by Herod the Great, ca. 30 B.C. Herod renamed the city Sebaste (Gk *Sebasté*), in honor of Caesar Augustus (Gk *Sebastós* = Lat *Augustus*). After the rebuilding and renaming of the city, Samaria was used as a name only for the region, a usage which is seen in the NT. Samaria continued to be known as Sebaste throughout the period of Roman and Byzantine rule. The name survives in the modern Arab village of Sebastiyeh.

The gentilic "Samaritans" (Heb *šoměrōnîm*) is not used in the Hebrew Bible for residents of the city of Samaria. The term appears only in 2 Kgs 17:29, where it is used for the people of mixed ethnic and religious background who were settled in the region by the Assyrians. This designation is used by Josephus (Gk *Samaritai*) not only for these colonists but also, and primarily, for a people of the region of the Hellenistic and Roman periods who constituted a distinct religious community based at Mt. Gerizim and Shechem (whom he regarded as descendants of the Assyrian colonists). It was the members of this religious community who are the "Samaritans" of the NT—a people who at that time had no relationship with the pagan city of Sebaste. The contemporary, surviving Samaritan community explains the origin of its name as deriving neither from the city nor the district, but from the Heb *šōměrîm* [Sam Heb = *šāměrîm*], "observers, keepers" (i.e., of the Torah).

B. Name, Topography, Location

The Deuteronomistic Historians utilized a local folk etymology to explain the naming of Samaria. Omri is said to have purchased the "hill of Samaria" from a man named Shemer for two talents of silver: "and he fortified the hill, and called the name of the city which he built, Samaria, after the name of Shemer, the owner of the hill" (1 Kgs 16:24). The name is more readily explained, however, as "watch-mountain," from the root *šmr* (to watch, guard, observe) and from the topography. Samaria was built on a hill rising over 300 feet above the valleys on the N, W, and S, with a commanding vista of a long sloping ridge to the E (of which the hill was the summit). It was strategically located (M.R. 168187) near the crossroads of the major N–S, E–W highways—leading to Shechem and the Jordan valley on the E, the coastal plain on the W, Megiddo and the Jezreel valley on the N, and Jerusalem on the S.

The site was thus one of considerable military and commercial advantage, although it had a limited water supply. It was more easily defended than the earlier capital at TIRZAH (modern Tell el-Farᶜah), which was especially vulnerable on its W approach. Tirzah, for example, was taken by Omri in the brief (one-week) military infighting that followed Zimri's assassination of Baasha (1 Kgs 16:15–18). Samaria, on the other hand, was able to withstand a siege of three years prior to its conquest by the Assyrians (2 Kgs 17:5).

C. History of Excavation

There were major archaeological campaigns in 1908–10, under the direction of G. Schumacher (1908) and G. A. Reisner and C. S. Fisher (1909–10), and from 1931–35 under the direction of J. W. Crowfoot, E. L. Sukenik, and with major publication responsibilities by K. M. Kenyon and G. M. Crowfoot. Minor campaigns were undertaken in 1965–67, directed by F. Zayadine, and in 1968 by J. B. Hennessy.

The initial campaign excavated the W portion of the acropolis, where royal buidings and a casemate wall of the Israelite period were uncovered. See Fig. CIT.06. Three building phases were distinguished: a palace was attributed to the time of Omri; the casemate wall and a storehouse to the time of Jehu; and buildings on the W of the casemate wall to the time of Jeroboam II. [But see below on the clarification of building phases and the attribution of constructions to kings, based on the campaigns of the 1930s.] Also excavated on the acropolis were Hellenistic remains, including round towers and a wall, mistakenly attributed to the Israelite and Babylonian periods respectively, and the remains of an Augustan temple built by Herod. In the area to the W of the summit, a city wall of the Roman period and a gate were uncovered, and, on the E, a theater, a basilica, a forum, and a stadium. Of epigraphic significance was the discovery in 1910 of 63 ostraca (plus 44 additional illegible sherds), uncovered in a building to the W of the palace (the so-called "Ostraca House"). A number of ivory objects were also found. An even larger number of ivories were uncovered during the excavations of the 1930s. See SAMARIA (OSTRACA) below.

The campaigns of the 1930s extended the areas excavated in the first expedition, including the royal buildings of the Israelite period on the acropolis and the round towers of the Hellenistic period. A third, extremely well-preserved Hellenistic tower was excavated on the NE of the acropolis. This tower has been called "the most impressive remnant from the Hellenistic period to have survived in Israel." A colonnaded Roman street to the S of the acropolis was cleared and, on the N, the remains of a Roman temple dedicated to Kore were discovered. Some EB I pottery was also found, attesting to an earlier, pre-Israelite settlement. Also, pottery found in the fill of buildings identified by K. Kenyon as belonging to *Periods I–II* of the Israelite period, the times of Omri and Ahab, has been identified by some (W. F. Albright, G. E. Wright, Y. Aharoni, R. Amiram, and N. Avigad) as being of a type from the 10th to early 9th centuries. This suggests that a small settlement had already existed on the hill of Samaria before Omri built his capital there, although Kenyon maintained that the site was unoccupied from EB I to the time of Omri.

The campaign of 1965–67 was initiated to provide better access to the acropolis and viewing of the theater and colonnaded street for visitors. It was discovered that the market area of the colonnaded street remained commercially active in the Byzantine period, but was destroyed in the early-to-mid 6th century (either during the suppression by Justinian of a local revolt in 529, or by an earthquake in 551). The 1968 excavations concentrated on the residential section (including a rock-cut water system) to the N–NW of the summit. This area was found to have been developed only during the Hellenistic and Roman periods, suggesting a concentration during the earlier Israelite period nearer to the citadel on the E and S of the hill, and closer to the original, natural water supply.

The stratigraphy of Samaria is complicated by the fact that the builders usually recycled the stones of earlier structures and cut their foundation trenches down to bedrock, resulting in foundations of buildings of different periods located side by side, rather than superimposed on one another. Kenyon established a stratigraphy of nine building phases and pottery periods for pre-Hellenistic Samaria, of which the first six were from the time of the Israelite monarchy. Differences of opinion exist, however, on the attribution of construction activities to specific rulers and on the relationship between the building periods and the ceramic phases (see Wright 1959). As already noted, some have interpreted the pottery of Kenyon's *Period I* as belonging to a time earlier than the buidings of *Period I.* Non-correlations between the pottery and buildings of other periods have also been suggested (notably, *Periods II–IV*). The pottery of Israelite Samaria was of high quality, especially the red burnished vessels popularly known as "Samarian ware."

For purposes of standard reference, Kenyon's six building/ceramic phases of the Israelite period were as follows: *Period I,* the time of Omri (inner wall of acropolis and palace); *Period II,* time of Ahab (casemate wall and east gate); *Period III,* time of Jehu and his successors (repair of casemate wall and earlier buildings, new buildings); *Period IV,* time of Jeroboam II and his successors (repair of casemate wall and alteration of earlier buildings, new buildings); *Periods V–VI,* time of Assyrian hegemony and destruction of the city (alterations to existing buildings, burned layer). The building phases of post-Israelite Samaria were: *Period VII,* time of Assyrian administration; *Period VIII,* time of Babylonian rule; *Period IX,* time of provincial status within the Persian Empire.

The masonry of Samaria of the Israelite period was of extremely high quality. Foundation stones were laid in rock-cut trenches in rows of headers with upper courses of headers and stretchers (two headers alternating with one stretcher). The ashlars for the courses set below ground level were cut with marginal drafts on three sides and irregular bosses. The stones for the upper courses were dressed smooth. They were laid without mortar and dressed on the site for precise setting in their courses. This style is characteristic of Phoenician masonry. The influence of Phoenician design on the Israelite architects is not surprising, considering the observations of the biblical historians on Phoenician cultural influence in the N kingdom in the mid 9th century (e.g., 1 Kgs 16:29–34). See *EAEHL* 4: 1032–50; *IDBSup,* 771–72.

The design of some of the ivory plaques, inlays, and toilet articles found in Samaria, especially those in high relief, also indicate Phoenician and other Syrian influence. The ivories of this type are similar to 9th century ivories discovered at Arslan Tash and are attributed to the time of Ahab (cf. 1 Kgs 22:39, on the ivory houses which Ahab built). The largest of these ivories was found in situ with a jar-inscription which enabled dating to the 9th century. Other ivories, those in low relief with gold foil and glass and stone inlays, are characterized by Egyptian motifs. These are similar in design to ivories found at Nimrud, which have been dated to the 8th century (cf. Amos 3:15; 6:4, on the "houses of ivory" and "beds of ivory" of Samaria during the reign of Jeroboam II). The ivories found at Arslan Tash and Nimrud were probably of Syrian, Phoenician, and Israelite origin, plundered by the Assyrians in the western campaigns. See IVORY.

D. History during the Israelite Period

The selection and development of Samaria as the capital of the N Israelite kingdom by Omri invites comparison with the action of David in establishing Jerusalem as the capital of the united monarchy, over a century and a quarter earlier. Each move represented a venture, the adoption of a new base of operation for the monarchy, and each selection involved a place not previously associated with the nation and its history. In each case the move was associated with the building of a fortress and palace and resulted in the strengthening of the king's rule and the stability of the ruling house (but lasting a much shorter time in Omri's case). A significant difference between the two moves was that Jerusalem was a city of some antiquity (the city wall had been built ca. 1800 B.C.) and Samaria was a place with no urban history (even if settlements had existed there earlier). This meant that Omri would have to create those civil and cultic institutions necessary for a capital city.

But first Omri needed a city. He had come to power following the death of king Baasha by besting his rival Zimri, Baasha's assassin, who had established himself in the (then) capital, Tirzah. When it became evident that Omri had taken the city, Zimri set fire to the citadel "and burned the king's house over him with fire, and he died" (1 Kgs 16:15–18). Omri thus inherited a burned capital city, an inauspicious beginning for a monarch. Nor was his reign secure politically. There followed a civil war of four years in which it was necessary to suppress yet another claimant of the throne, Tibni the son of Ginath (1 Kgs 16: 21–23). In the excavations at Tirzah (Tell el-Farᶜah) by the École Biblique of Jerusalem, R. de Vaux uncovered two distinct phases of occupation of the 10th–8th centuries, each of which ended with a destruction: the first was a city of the 10th century, destroyed in the early 9th century, evidently by Zimri, and the second a city of the 8th century, destroyed by the Assyrians. Between these two clearly distinguished levels, and set in the debris of the 10th-century city, were walls of unfinished buildings. De Vaux proposed that these belonged to the uncompleted work of Omri, who abandoned the rebuilding of Tirzah to establish his new capital at Samaria. According to the Bible, Omri reigned six years in Tirzah before he moved the capital to Samaria (1 Kgs 16:23).

Unlike David and Jerusalem, the establishment of Samaria by Omri was not associated with an attempt to relate the new capital to Israel's historic cultic traditions (in the case of David, the ark of Yahweh and the tent sanctuary). Nor does the biblical record indicate that Omri patronized the Yahwistic cult centers of Bethel and Dan, as the Israelite kings had before him. In fact, the Deuteronomistic Historians offer very little information about Omri. But we are given some information on the cultic situation during the reign of Omri's son Ahab, which may have been a continuation of his father's policy. According to 1 Kgs 16:32, Ahab "erected an altar for Baal in the house of Baal, which he built in Samaria." This was seen as part of the general apostate character of the king following his marriage to the Phoenician princess Jezebel, a worshipper of the Sidonian Baal. It is Jezebel who is said to have been the patron of the functionaries of the Baal cult (1 Kgs 18:19). Ahab is otherwise represented as a Yahwist (1 Kgs 21:28–29; 22:1–8), or as a disloyal Yahwist who had "forsaken the commandments of Yahweh and followed the Baals" (1 Kgs 18:18). Nonetheless, the cult of Baal was officially established in Samaria during the time of Ahab, if not earlier, under Omri. The temple of Baal remained active in Samaria throughout the reigns of Ahab's two sons, Ahaziah and Joram, until it was desecrated and converted into a public latrine by Jehu, in the purge of baalism which accompanied his ascent to the throne (2 Kgs 10:18–27).

Although the story of the rise and fall of the Baal cult during the reign of the house of Omri begins and ends with the temple of Baal in Samaria (1 Kgs 16:29–2 Kgs 10:27), much of the principal action of the story takes place elsewhere—notably on Mt. Carmel (1 Kgs 18:19–45; 2 Kgs 2:25; 4:25) and in Jezreel (1 Kgs 18:45–46; 21:1–29; 2 Kgs 8:28–10:11). Jezreel is represented as a second capital of the kingdom of Israel in this story (see 1 Kgs 21:1, "Now Naboth the Jezreelite had a vineyard in Jezreel, beside the palace of Ahab king of Samaria"). A. Alt argued that the two capitals were the result of the deliberate policy of Omri and Ahab in establishing Samaria as a capital city after the Canaanite city-state model: Samaria was to be the capital of the city-state, the site of the (Canaanite) temple of Baal, with Jezreel being a traditional Israelite capital, with a Yahwistic cult on nearby Mt. Carmel. This opinion was recently reversed by Y. Yadin, who argued that the temple of Baal in Samaria was actually in Jezreel, i.e., in the district of, not the city of, Samaria: Jezreel and Mt. Carmel were the centers of Jezebel's baalistic campaigns, not the centers of traditional Israelite cultic and political traditions. Yadin cited what he believed to be a parallel phenomenon in the case of Athaliah, the daughter of Ahab and Jezebel who seized the throne in Jerusalem at the time of Jehu's coup in Israel (2 Kgs 11:1–20). According to Yadin, Athaliah established a baalistic center at Ramat Rahel, while allowing the sanctuary of Yahweh to remain in Jerusalem. Yadin's argument is not, however, very convincing, and of the two positions, that of Alt appears to be a better model for understanding the development of Samaria as the new capital under Omri and Ahab.

Nothing remained of the temple of Baal in Samaria at the time of the writing of the Deuteronomistic History, nor was a temple uncovered in the excavations. What were discovered from the time of Omri and Ahab (Kenyon's building *Periods I–II*) were fragments and foundation trenches of a royal quarter with a palace and a defense system of two walls, a casemate wall (a double wall with cross-walls and fill between) and an inner wall. The inner wall (ca. 5 feet broad) encompassed an area of ca. 5,840 feet E–W and 292 feet N–S. The much stronger casemate wall, not all of which was uncovered, extended the secured area by ca. 54 feet to the N and 98 feet to the W. The casemate wall on the N side was ca. 32 feet across, with an exterior face 6 feet thick, an interior face 3 feet thick, and a filled space between of ca. 23 feet. It was less broad on the W side (ca. 16 feet) and on the S and SE, where for topographical reasons it became a single wall set up against the inner wall. The inner wall was originally attributed to Omri and the casemate wall to Ahab, but it seems more likely (following Avigad) that Omri would not have occupied his new capital until after the stronger fortification had been completed.

A pool ca. 33 × 16.5 feet was found within the casemate wall at the NW corner. This would have been "the pool of Samaria" mentioned in 1 Kgs 22:37–38, in the story of Ahab's death in battle at Ramoth-gilead and the return of his body and chariot to Samaria: "So the king died, and was brought to Samaria; and they buried the king in Samaria. And they washed the chariot by the pool of Samaria, and the dogs licked up his blood, and the harlots washed themselves in it, according to the word of the Lord which he had spoken." Also uncovered, on the middle terrace level of the summit, about 500 feet to the E of the casemate wall, were remains of a building, tower, and wall which were probably part of a gate system. This has been attributed to Ahab (building *Period II*), and would have been the "gate of Samaria" which was the site of the grain market during the time of Joram (2 Kgs 7:1) and the "threshing floor at the entrance of the gate of Samaria," where kings Ahab and Jehoshaphat received counsel for war from the Yahwistic prophets (1 Kgs 22:10). All in all, the city was extremely well fortified and was able to withstand two sieges mounted by the Syrians, one in the time of Ahab (1 Kgs 20:1) and the other during the reign of Joram (2 Kgs 6:24). In fact, the city was not taken by a besieging army until the time of the Assyrian conquest in 721 B.C.

There is evidence of some destruction in the royal quarter during building *Period III*, which may have resulted from Jehu's coup d'état, or from some natural situation such as accidental fire or earthquake. But the time of Jehu was one in which earlier buidings and the casemate wall were repaired and new buildings were constructed. These appear to have been modest in comparison to the repairs and new constructions of building *Period IV,* the time of Jeroboam II.

The reign of Jeroboam II (ca. 786–746 B.C.) would have to be considered the time of Samaria's greatest prosperity, due to the influx of wealth from the Israelite king's hegemony over neighboring lands, including Syria (2 Kgs 14:23–29). A picture-window of the cultural history of Samaria of this time is given in the oracles of the prophet Amos, who carefully noted the signs of power and affluence he saw there: strongholds, defenses (3:10–11), couches, beds (3:12; 6:4), winter houses, summer houses, houses of ivory, great houses (3:15; 6:11), wine (4:1; 5:12; 6:6), houses of hewn stone, vineyards (5:11–12, 17), beds of ivory, choice meats, musical instruments, drinking bowls, and fine oils (6:4–6). These impressed him, but negatively. What caught his eye especially was the indolence and spiritual insensitivity of Samaria's nobility and their oppression of the poor (3:9–12; 4:1–3; 5:11–12; 6:1–7; 8:4–6).

During the reign of Jeroboam II, the temples of Dan and Bethel were the Yahwistic shrines of the N kingdom, notably Bethel (Amos 7:13, "for it is the king's sanctuary, and it is a temple of the kingtom"). The "calf of Samaria" of Hos 8:5–6 ("I have spurned your calf, O Samaria / The calf of Samaria shall be broken to pieces [or, go up in flames]") is a reference to one of the bull calves set up by Jeroboam I in the sanctuaries of Bethel and Dan (1 Kgs 12:28–30). The particular referent is to the calf of the temple of Bethel, as is evident from a parallel oracle in Hos 10:5, "the inhabitants of Samaria tremble for the calf [following Gk and Syr; Heb reads "calves"] of Beth-aven." Beth-aven is clearly a contemptuous surrogate for Bethel. The incorporation of calf iconography into the Bethel cult paralleled Canaanite iconography, in which El was venerated as a bull calf and the storm god Hadad was sometimes depicted riding on the back of a bull. In this connection, reference should be made to a proper name found on one of the Samaria ostraca (Ostracon 41), which appears to read Egelyau, "Calf of Yahweh," or "Yahweh is Calf."

That Bethel (so too Gilgal) was the site of pilgrimage by the nobles of Samaria is seen also in the juxtapositioning of the oracles of Amos 4:1–3 and 4:4–5, the former heaping contempt on the rich women "in the mountain of Samaria" and the latter urging them (in ironic speech) to "come to Bethel, and transgress; to Gilgal, and multiply transgression." A parallel oracle in Amos 5:4–5 (cf. also 8:14) suggests that there was a pilgrimage route for the people of Samaria connecting the sanctuaries of Bethel, Gilgal, and Beer-sheba: "Seek me and live; but do not seek Bethel, and do not enter into Gilgal or cross over to Beer-sheba; for Gilgal shall surely go into exile, and Bethel shall come to nought."

The royal patronage of the historic Yahwistic sanctuaries of Bethel, Dan, and Gilgal does not preclude the possibility of pagan cults in Samaria during the time of Jeroboam II. Amos rebuked those who took oaths by a goddess of Samaria (8:14, "Ashimah of Samaria"), although he did not indicate that her veneration included a temple. That pagan worship characterized Samaria in the time after Jeroboam II, shortly before its destruction, is indicated in Micah 1:6–7: "Therefore I will make Samaria a heap in the open country, a place for planting vineyards; and I will pour down her stones into the valley, and uncover her foundations. All her images shall be beaten to pieces, . . . and all her idols I will lay waste." The idolatry of Samaria and its subsequent destruction were cited by Isaiah as a warning for the people of Jerusalem: "Shall I not do to Jerusalem and her idols as I have done to Samaria and her images?" (10:11).

The power and prestige of Samaria declined rapidly following the death of Jeroboam II, as the nation not only lost the tribute of neighboring vassals, but became itself a vassal of the Assyrians (building *Periods V–VI*). King Menahem paid a heavy tribute to Tiglath-pileser III rather than risk a siege of his city (2 Kgs 15:17–22; Assyrian Annals). An ill-fated alliance of Samaria with Damascus against Tiglath-pileser during the reign of Pekah, with an unsuccessful military campaign against Jerusalem (2 Kgs 16:1–9; Isa 7:1–8:4), resulted in the loss of a considerable amount of Israelite territory to the Assyrians and a deportation of the population (2 Kgs 15:29–31). Samaria appears to have been spared at that time only because of the assassination of Pekah by Hoshea, whom Tiglath-pileser claimed as a confederate/puppet ("they overthrew their king Pekah and I placed Hoshea as king over them"). But with the death of Tiglath-pileser, Hoshea rebelled against the new Assyrian monarch Shalmaneser V—i.e., he refused to pay tribute and sought to forge a counteralliance with Egypt (2 Kgs 17:1–6). Assyria responded and Samaria is said to have withstood a siege of three years after the capture and imprisonment of the king. But the city was finally taken by the Assyrians, in spite of its strong defences, either by Shalmaneser V in 722 or Sargon II in 721.

E. History during the Assyrian-Hellenistic Periods

Of the conquest of Samaria, Sargon wrote: "I besieged and conquered Samaria, led away as booty 27,290 inhabitants of it, I formed from among them a contingent of 50 chariots and made remaining inhabitants assume their social positions. I installed over them an officer of mine and imposed upon them the tribute of the former king." He also boasted, "I conquered and sacked . . . Samaria, and all Israel [literally, Omri-Land]." Of the rebuilding of Samaria, Sargon wrote: "The town I rebuilt better than it was before and settled therein people from countries which I myself had conquered. I placed an officer of mine as governor over them and imposed upon them tribute as is customary for Assyrian citizens." The reports of deportation and settlement of foreign peoples correspond generally with the biblical history (2 Kgs 17:6, 24). It is also known, from recent excavations in the upper city of Jerusalem, that the Judean capital expanded considerably in the late 8th century (perhaps to four times its previous size), evidently due to the influx of refugees from Samaria and the territories annexed by Assyria.

The excavations of Samaria reveal few remains from the Assyrian and Babylonian periods *(Periods VII–VIII)*. Material objects uncovered include a portion of an Assyrian stele attributed to Sargon II and a fragment of a Babylonian cuneiform tablet with the name of the local governor, Avi-ahi. Among the scanty remains of the Persian period *(Period IX)* were found remnants of a throne which had belonged to one of the governors.

Knowledge of the political status of Samaria during the early Persian period is derived primarily from what is reported of the power and activities of Samaria's governors in the Jewish accounts of the Judean restoration (i.e., in the biblical books of Ezra and Nehemiah). From these it is learned that the development of Judah as a functional entity within the Persian province "Beyond-the-River" was severely restricted by Judah's neighbors until the time of Nehemiah, who came to Jerusalem as governor in the 20th year of the reign of Artaxerxes (445/444 B.C.). Even then the rebuilding of Jerusalem's wall was resisted (unsuccessfully) by Sanballat, governor of Samaria, and Tobiah and Geshem, his Ammonite and Arab confederates (Neh 4:1–23). In his memoirs, Nehemiah refers to the oppressive policies of the governors who were before him (Neh 5:14–15). A. Alt argued that the governors of reference could not have been Nehemiah's Jewish predecessors, Sheshbazzar and Zerubbabel, but would have been the governors of Samaria who had exercised hegemony over Judah prior to Nehemiah's appointment. Alt further maintained that Samaria had exercised hegemony over Judah from the time of the collapse of the Jewish state following the destruction of Jerusalem, most particularly after the assassination of the puppet governor Gedaliah and the failure to establish an effective administrative center at Mizpah (582 B.C., see Jer 40:1–41: 3). Recent epigraphic discoveries (seal impressions and bullae of the Persian period which appear to bear the names of Judean governors before the time of Nehemiah) may necessitate the modification of Alt's position, but his assessment of Samaritan authority over Judah in the early Persian period appears to be valid. It should be noted also that when the Jewish colonists of Elephantine sought permission to rebuild their sanctuary (which had been destroyed in the 14th year of Darius II, 410 B.C.), they wrote not only to Bagohi, governor of Judah, but also to Delaiah and Shelemiah the sons of Sanballat, who had succeeded their father as (co-) governors of Samaria.

Other governors of the family of Sanballat down to the beginning of the Hellenistic period are known from the papyri of Wâdī Dâliyah and Josephus (*Ant* 11. 304–47), from which it may be surmised that there were two subsequent governors who also bore the name Sanballat. It was the last of these (Sanballat III) who was governor at the time of Alexander's conquest of the region. He was probably the last of this illustrious family to govern in Samaria. During (or shortly after) his administration, a revolt against Macedonian rule broke out. The revolt was quashed by the general Perdiccas and Samaria was rebuilt as a Greek city. At the time of the revolt, some of the Samaritan nobility fled to the wilderness of Wâdī Dâliyah, where they perished. The remainder of the disenfranchised citizenry of Samaria appear to have taken up residence in nearby Shechem, which was rebuilt at this time. It was also at this time that a "Samaritan" temple was built on Mt. Gerizim, above Shechem. This was not a temple of the Hellenistic city of Samaria, but of the Yahwists of the Samaritan district (based at Shechem) who desired a sanctuary of their own.

It is to the Hellenistic city of Samaria that the massive towers excavated in the first and second campaigns belong. In addition, a new wall (with insets and towers, enclosing an area of ca. 750 × 400 feet) was built following the fortification lines of the old Israelite casemate wall, and perhaps also a second wall on the lower terrace. This extensive wall is now attributed to the 2d century B.C., sometime after Samaria had been taken by the Seleucid king Antiochus the Great, ca. 198 B.C. (*Ant* 12. 133)—it had previously been a city with municipal rights under Ptolemaic rule. The need for a new wall to secure the city was occasioned by the rising power of the Maccabees and the Hasmonean rulers who succeeded them. It was a legitimate concern. The wall was destroyed and the city was taken by John Hyrcanus and his sons Aristobulus and Antigonus in 108/107 B.C., after a siege of one year. This was part of Hyrcanus' campaign to take the Hellenistic cities (Strato's Tower, Samaria, and Scythopolis) which blocked his control of the territory between Judea and the Galilee. (He had previously subdued the "Samaritans" of Shechem by destroying their city and their sanctuary on Gerizim in 128 B.C.) According to Josephus, the fortifications of Samaria were so undermined by tunneling that their collapse and subsequent destruction by erosion "removed all signs of its ever having been a city" (*Ant* 13. 280–81; cf. *JW* 1. 64–66, where Aristobulus and Antigonus are credited with having "confined its people within the walls, captured the town, razed it to the ground, and reduced the inhabitants to slavery").

The city Hyrcanus destroyed included a temple of Serapis-Isis, remnants of which were found in the fill beneath the Roman temple of Kore. In addition to architectural discoveries, small finds from the Hellenistic period at Samaria have been especially rich, including coins, inscriptions, sculpture, pottery, and stamped jar handles—all of which attest to the commercial prosperity of the city at this time.

F. History during the Roman-Byzantine Periods

Samaria was among those Greek cities wrested from Jewish control by Pompey (63 B.C.). It was rebuilt in 57–55 B.C. by Gabinius, after whom the city was renamed, and given independent status under the proconsul of Syria (*Ant* 14. 74–76, 86–88). The city was further repaired by Herod, ca. 37 B.C. (*Ant* 14. 284), who used it as a base in his campaigns against Antigonus Mattathias. It was rebuilt on a grand scale by Herod after it was ceded to him by the emperor Augustus, ca. 30 B.C. (*Ant* 15. 217, 292–98; *JW* 1. 403). Herod renamed the city Sebaste (Gk *Sebasté*), in honor of his imperial patron (Gk *Sebastós* = Lat *Augustus; Sebasté* = Lat *Augusta,* used as an honorific title, sometimes of military legions; the port of Caesarea was named *Sebastós,* i.e., the port city of Augustus, see *Ant* 17. 87 and *JW* 1. 613).

Josephus relates that Herod surrounded Sebaste with a strong wall (strengthening also its outer walls) and built in the center a sacred area with a massive temple consecrated to Augustus. He then repopulated the city with six thousand colonists, to whom he gave apportionments of the rich farmland round-about. Save for the dimensions of the wall (a circumference of 20 stades, about 2 miles), Josephus does not offer many details about the city—except to note that the Augustan temple "in size and beauty was among the most renowned," and that the city itself, although smaller than the previous city at the site, "did not fall short of that of the most renowned cities."

The excavations at Sebaste reveal that it was indeed a splendid city, although most of the impressive remains visible today belong to the time of Septimius Severus (A.D. 193–211), when the city was known as Lucia Septimia Sebaste. Also excavated were remnants of the city of the time of Gabinius, to whom the street grid and the design of the forum are attributed. The wall of which Josephus wrote (not all of which was uncovered) enclosed an area with a diameter of ca. ½ mile E–W and ½ mile N–S. The city gate was on the W, where two round towers were found dating to Herod's time (ca. 46 feet across and preserved to a height of ca. 33 feet). Remnants of the Augustan temple built by Herod (and later modified by Septimius Severus) have been uncovered, including a monumental staircase leading to an altar on a 14-feet-high platform (with an area of ca. 272 × 236 feet), a fragment of a statue of Augustus, and sacristy buildings. See Fig. SAM.01. The temple itself had a base of ca. 79 × 115 feet. In addition to the imperial shrine, the cult of Kore was also represented in Sebaste. Her temple (base of ca. 118 × 51 feet; octagonal altar with dedicatory inscription; sacred precinct of ca. 275 × 147 feet) stood to the N of the Augusteum. Her cult was associated also with the stadium (statue and dedicatory inscription to the goddess). Statues of Apollo, Dionysus, and Hercules were found in addition to those of Augustus and Kore. Both the Augustan and Kore temple complexes were damaged when Sebaste was burned by

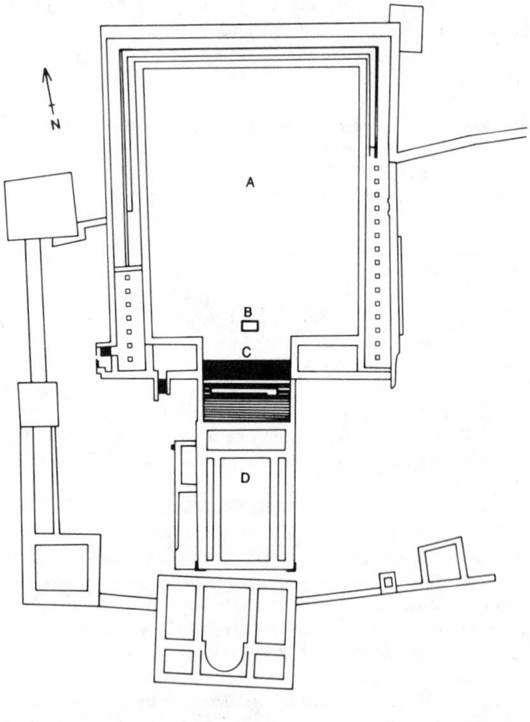

SAM.01. Augustan temple at Sebaste, built by Herod and remodelled by Septimius Severus. (A) forecourt on raised platform; (B) altar; (C) monumental staircase ascending to temple; (D) temple of Augustan. *(Redrawn from* EAEHL *4: 1045)*

Jewish insurgents during the first revolt against Rome, A.D. 66. These and other structures were rebuilt and expanded by Septimius Severus in the late 2d–early 3d centuries (the height of Sebaste's prosperity). Remains of this later period include the west gate, the reconstructed stadium (ca. 755 × 197 feet), the colonnaded street (2,625 feet long, 41 feet wide, with ca. 600 surviving columns, 18 feet high), the forum (ca. 420 × 238 feet), a theater (external diameter of ca. 213 feet), a basilica (ca. 223 × 107 feet), tombs, and an aqueduct.

Sebaste is not referred to at all in the NT, at least not by name. References to Samaria are to the district only and not to the city of that former name. Some hold that "the city of Samaria" visited by the evangelist Philip was Sebaste, i.e., "the (principal) city of Samaria" (Acts 8:5; KJV), and that Simon Magus (Acts 8:9–13) may have been a functionary of the cult of Kore. However, the reading "a city of Samaria" is preferred (so most modern translations).

Sebaste became a bishopric during the Byzantine period and a site of Christian pilgrimage. The latter phenomenon was due to the identification of local tombs as the burial places of John the Baptist and the prophets Elisha and Obadiah (identified/confused with the associate of the prophet Elijah, 1 Kgs 18:3–16). Pilgrims also venerated two nearby caves as the places where Obadiah hid the Yahwistic prophets during the time of Ahab and Jezebel (1 Kgs 18:4). A tradition later developed (by the 6th century) that John the Baptist had been beheaded in Sebaste (*contra* Josephus, *Ant* 18. 119, who located the incident at the fortress of Machaerus).

The bishops of Sebaste were present at the major ecumenical councils of Nicea, Constantinople, and Chalcedon and at the Synod of Jerusalem. But the classical pagan tradition of the city was not easily extirpated. During the time of Julian II ("the Apostate," A.D. 361–363), the pagans of Sebaste desecrated the tombs and relics of the saints (Philost. *h. e.* 7. 4–80; Rufinus, *Eccl Hist* 2. 28–1034). The restored holy places were seen by Egeria and Paula and Jerome in the late 4th century. Jerome mentions strange, appalling religious rites in front of the tombs, which may have been vestiges of pre-Christian pagan customs.

The suppression of paganism following the death of Julian appears to have resulted in architectural changes in the city, including the eradication of the old temples and the conversion of the Roman basilica on the E of the summit into a cathedral church. A church of John the Baptist was built in the 5th century, on the E side of the city, over the alleged tomb. Five capitals which had probably belonged to this church were found in the remains of a Crusader cathedral church of the 12th century. Also, remnants of another 5th-century basilica church were found to the S of the summit, in the excavation of a medieval monastery marking the site where Herodias received the head of John the Baptist (Matt 14:3–12; Mark 6:17–29).

Sebaste declined rapidly in the 6th century, probably as the result of an earthquake in 551. As previously noted, the market area of the colonnaded street was destroyed at this time and not rebuilt. The reduced city came under Muslim Arab control in the following century, ca. 634.

When the Christian pilgrim Willibald visited Sebaste in 726, he referred to it as a village.

Bibliography

Alt, A. 1931. Judas Nachbarn sur Zeit Nehemias. *PJ* 27: 66–74.
———. 1934. Die Rolle Samarias bei der Enstehung des Judentums. Pp. 5–28 in *Festschrift Otto Procksch zum 60, Geburtstag.* Leipzig.
———. 1954. *Der Stadtstaat Samaria.* BSAW. 101/5. Berlin.
———. 1956. Archäologische Fragen zur Baugeschichte von Jerusalem und Samaria in der Israelitischen Königszeit. *Wissenschaftliche Zeitschrift der Ernst-Moritz-Arndt-Univerität Greifswald* 5: 33–42.
Cross, F. M. 1966. Aspects of Samaritan and Jewish History in Late Persian and Hellenistic Times. *HTR* 59: 201–11.
Crowfoot, J. W., and Crowfoot, G. M. 1938. *Early Ivories from Samaria.* London.
Crowfoot, J. W.; Crowfoot, G. M.; and Kenyon, K. M. 1957. *The Objects from Samaria.* London.
Crowfoot, J. W.; Kenyon, K. M.; and Sukenik, E. L. 1942. *The Buildings of Samaria.* London.
Hennessy, J. B. 1970. Excavations at Samaria-Sebaste, 1968. *Levant* 2: 1–21.
Kenyon, K. M. 1971. *Royal Cities of the Old Testament.* London.
Mallowan, M. 1978. Samaria and Calah-Nimrud: Conjunctions in History and Archaeology. Pp. 155–63 in *Archaeology in the Levant,* ed. P. R. S. Moorey and P. Parr. Warminster.
Oppenheim, A. L. 1955. Babylonian and Assyrian Historical Texts. Pp. 265–317 in *ANET.*
Parrot, A. 1958. *Samaria, the Capital of the Kingdom of Israel.* SBA 7. London.
Reisner, G. A.; Fisher, C. S.; and Lyon, D. G. 1924. *Harvard Excavations at Samaria.* Cambridge, MA.
Tadmor, H. 1983. Some Aspects of the History of Samaria during the Biblical Period. *Jerusalem Cathedra* 3: 1–10.
Tadmor, M. 1974. Fragments from an Achemenid Throne from Samaria. *IEJ* 24: 37–43.
Vaux, R. de. 1967. Tirzah. Pp. 371–83 in *Archaeology and Old Testament Study,* ed. E. W. Thomas. Oxford.
Wright, G. E. 1959. Israelite Samaria and Iron Age Chronology. *BASOR* 155: 13–29.
Yadin, Y. 1978. The "House of Baᶜal" of Ahab and Jezebel in Samaria, and that of Athalia in Judah. Pp. 127–35 in *Archaeology in the Levant,* ed. P. R. S. Moorey and P. Parr. Warminster.
Zayadine, F. 1967–68. Samaria-Sebaste, Clearance and Excavations (October 1965–June 1967). *ADAJ* 12–13: 77–80.

James D. Purvis

SAMARIA OSTRACA

The Samaria Ostraca were discovered by G. A. Reisner in 1910 in the excavation of Samaria, capital of the ancient N kingdom of Israel. They comprise the earliest corpus of ancient Hebrew writing extant today, consisting of 66 pen-and-ink inscriptions on potsherds which record delivery of quality wine and fine oil to the capital city during the 9th, 10th, and 15th years of the king who was, in all probability, Jeroboam II (786–746 B.C.E.). Reisner published a few of his many photographs of the ostraca along with 63 hand-drawn facsimiles (1924, 2: pl. 55; 1: 239–43). There are also about 40 unpublished fragments, listed by register number (1924: 246), including a few whole pieces which are fairly legible. All are part of the collection of the Archaeological Museum in Istanbul.

Studies of the ostraca have been continuous since the Reisner, Fisher, and Lyon publication of 1924. Significant early works are Noth (1927; *IPN;* and 1932), Albright (1931), Diringer (1934), Maisler [Mazar] (1948), Moscati (1951), and Birnbaum (1954–57). Renewed interest in the ostraca followed Yadin (1959), Cross (1961), and *LBHG.* Extensive studies of the ostraca since that time by Rainey, Kaufman, and Lemaire are included in the bibliography below. Bibliography down to 1968 may be found in Gibson (*TSSI* 1), Teixidor (1967–81), and Lawton (1984).

A. Importance of the Ostraca
B. Samples of the Text
C. Archaeological Data
  1. Locus of the Ostraca
  2. Pottery Typology
D. Paleography
E. Hieratic Year Number
F. Function of the Ostraca
G. Place Names and Personal Names

A. Importance of the Ostraca

In brief, the ostraca are important for the following reasons: They contribute to the development of a relative typology of early Hebrew scripts. They provide a reasonably accurate absolute date on other than paleographical grounds, namely their locus in the fill of the foundations and floors of a building complex which was used for a considerable time prior to the destruction of the city, and also because a number of the ostraca bear the Egyptian hieratic numerals which indicate the 15th year. Moreover, many samples of letters of the alphabet written by a number of scribes increase our knowledge of how the letters were formed. The ostraca shed light on administrative record keeping. They provide the geographical location of clan districts within the tribal area of Manasseh. They give us new place names and personal names. They suggest a possible sociological distinction between persons whose names are formed with a Baal element and those whose names are Yahwistic or non-Baalistic. Orthographically, the ostraca indicate contracted diphthongs which, along with some other variations, reflect a dialectical difference from the Hebrew of Judah at that time (Cross and Freedman 1952: 48–49). Three main issues have been debated recently: the date of the ostraca, whether the ostraca belong to one reign or two, and whether the significant person whose name is preceded by the letter *lamed* (*l*-man) was a tax collector, or an owner and sender, or a recipient of the product.

B. Samples of the Text

The ostraca may be classified in two groups for the recognition of similarities and differences between ostraca of different years. Only selected ostraca are presented here.

1. Type 1. Three examples of this include the following:

(a) No. 4 (as reconstructed from duplicates 5–7)

bšt · htšᶜt · mq	In the ninth year from Qo-
ṣh · lgdyw · nbl	soh to (credit of) Gaddiyaw, a jar
yn · yšn ·	of old wine.

	(b) No. 1
bšt · hʿśrt · lšm	In the tenth year to (credit of) Shem-
ryw · mbʾrym · nbl [· *yn* ·]	aryaw from Beerayim, a jar of
yšn ·	old [wine.]
grʿ · ʾlyšʿ · II	Gera Elyasha 2
ʿzʾ · q[d]b[?] · I	Azza Qadbesh (Lemaire 1973: 83) 1
ʾlbʾ [·] [I]	Eliba 1
bʿlʾ · ʾlyš[*ʿ* ·] [I]	Baala Elyasha [1]
ydʿyw [·] [I]	Yadayaw [1]

	(c) No. 13
bšt · hʿśrt · mʾbʿ	In the tenth year from Abie-
zr · lšmryw · nbl ·	zer to (credit of) Shemaryaw, a jar of
yn yšn · lʾṣḥr ·	old wine to (credit of) Etshar
mtwl	from Tawil

2. Type 2. Note the following

	No. 22
bšt · XV mḥ	In the 15th year from He-
lq · lʾśʾ · ʾh	leq to (credit of) Asa Ahi-
mlk ·	melek.
ḥlṣ · mḥṣrt	Heles from Haserot

3. Comparison. These two most common types shown above (1 a–c and 2) may be compared graphically as follows:

1.	2.
year (ninth or tenth)	year (15th)
from a town (or clan district in Nos. 3 and 13)	from a clan district
(credited) to a person with a single name	(credited) to a person with two names
commodity (not named in No. 2)	commodity not named
secondary personal names (Nos. 1 & 2)	secondary personal names (one name plus town or two names and no town)

Types 1 (b and c) manifest all of the characteristics of type 2 but in a less strict form. Aharoni (*LBHG,* 366) and Lemaire (1977: 80) argue that the difference between types 1 and 2 suggests that they belong to different reigns.

C. Archaeological Data

1. Locus of the Ostraca. The commonly held view that the ostraca were found in the surface destruction debris on the floor of the Ostraca House, which was demolished with the fall of the city in 722/721 B.C.E., stems from Reisner's published report in which he states that the ostraca were found on the "living floor" of the courtyard. He goes on to report, however, that they were found in "the lowest part of the debris of occupation." Beneath the identified top surface of the floor, the ostraca were found in packed layers of dirt 20 to 40 cm. thick (1924: 63, 223, 401). In his field diary he states that a number of the ostraca were found in dirty yellow debris that lay below the black surface debris. (Reisner, unpublished: 593). Clearly, ostraca dating only a few years apart could not find their way into widely varying depths of so-called occupational debris. The ostraca were, then, part of the makeup fill of the foundation walls and floor, and must be considered to be as old or older than the building to which later structural modifications were made including different kinds of doors and additional walls (Reisner 1924: 116; Kaufman 1982: 231–33). In several of the room and corridor areas where the ostraca were unearthed, both 9th- and/or 10th-, and 15th-year ostraca were found together as if, before being thrown out, they were in a common cache. With the possible exception of the jar label (no. 63), bearing a number probably between 12 and 14, no years other than 9th, 10th, and 15th are reported among the ostraca (Kaufman 1966: 140; Lemaire 1977: 37).

2. Pottery Typology. Pottery evidence is ambiguous due to the difficulty of dating the bowls and jars of Pottery Period IV accurately (Holladay 1966: 69; 1976: Chart 2: 269). It is clear, nevertheless, that at least one period of pottery existed between that of the ostraca and the fall of Samaria (Kaufman 1982: 233). K. Kenyon and G. Crowfoot examined the ostraca in Istanbul, and concluded that most of them were written on Period IV pottery. Kenyon stated that none were later; Crowfoot believed that a few also resembled pottery of Period V. In their view both periods lay within the first half of the 8th century (Crowfoot et al. 1957: 203, 470). At any rate, Period VI contains water decanters which do not appear in Reisner's levels associated with the ostraca, and a few samples of inscribed Period VI pottery from the Joint Expedition (Crowfoot et al. 1957: 2, 470), bear a script which is clearly later typologically than that of the Samaria Ostraca. The evidence would indicate that the ostraca are no later than the penultimate pottery period before the destruction of the city, and this fits with the evidence that they were part of the fill of a substantial building project.

D. Paleography

The script of the Samaria Ostraca is a broad sampling of early cursive writing by skilled scribes using cut reed pens and ink. They wrote fairly rapidly with broad and thin strokes. A number of letters bear reflexes or tics which result from the readiness of the hand to proceed to the next horizontal of a letter or to the next letter itself. An intriguing question for which there is no ready answer is what the relationship might have been between this scribal tradition and that of the scribes of Egyptian hieratic writing. The technique is similar, and the Samaria scribes, who used the hieratic numerals, may well have been influenced by Egyptian scribal style even if indirectly through international relations with Egypt or Phoenicia. Incidentally, all of the letters of the alphabet are present on the ostraca with the exception of the letter *ṭeṭ*.

In typological development, the script of the ostraca is considerably later than that of the Mesha Inscription (ca. 840 B.C.E.). Between Mesha and the Samaria Ostraca in time are the ivory plaque found in Nimrud (probably taken there from Israel by the Assyrians) (Millard 1962: 45) and the inscriptions from Kuntillet ʿAjrud (Meshel 1978: figs. 10–12). On the other hand, the script of the Samaria Ostraca is clearly earlier typologically than that of the several ostraca discovered at Samaria by the Joint Expedition inscribed on pottery from Period VI and dated by S. Birnbaum to the third quarter of the 8th century (Crowfoot et al. 1957: 2, 24). Detailed description of the characteristics of individual letters and comparison with their counterparts in several other inscriptions has been done by Kaufman (1966: 4–100; 1982: 238).

The alphabet of the Samaria Ostraca shows some variety within the corpus, as we might expect from the number of scribes, but these variations are within the limits dictated by the formal shapes of the letters. See Fig. SAM.02. Special attention is drawn to the reflexes or tics on the horizontals of the letters *ʾalep, zayin, yod, samek,* and *ṣade. Qop* is uniformly written with a closed circular head. The so-called "S-headed" open *qop* should be excised from all charts of the Samaria Ostraca. Reisner may have been influenced in seeing this form because he read the combined letters *pe* and *reš* in ostracon no. 16a as *qop.*

Defending the two-reign theory, Y. Aharoni (*LBHG,* 366) and A. Lemaire (1977: 80) date the 9th- and 10th-year ostraca to the reign of Joash (801–786 B.C.) and the 15th-year ostraca to the reign of Jeroboam II (786–746 B.C.). By this theory, the two groups of ostraca are separated by 21 years. Apart from the question of why the ostraca would have been kept for so long in close proximity as indicated by their being scattered together in the fill, the paleographical data does not appear to demand two periods, nor does the change in form of the notation on the 15th-year ostraca demand a different king as an explanation.

The paleographical argument against the two-reign theory is the fact that the characteristics described as advanced in the 15th-year ostraca are found as well in the 9th- and 10th-year ostraca. These would include the reflexed *ʾalep,* the two-horizontal *ḥet,* and the *lamed* with an angular hook. Other letters singled out in support of the two periods are *waw* and *qop.* Lemaire (1973: 44–54; 1977: 41) interprets some examples of *waw* as having been written with a single continuous stroke of the pen, a style which would fit better in the second half of the 7th century as in the Mesad Hashavyahu letter. The so-called "S-headed" *qop* which Lemaire cites as advanced is found in Reisner's inexact hand-drawn facsimiles of 15th-year ostraca nos. 22–24 and 26, but not 27 (1924, 1: 240). It appears to be indefensible as a form as stated above, and even Reisner's published photograph of no. 22 (1924: 2 pl. 55e5) does not substantiate the form, although the closed circular head will break open, being written with two strokes, in roughly another generation at Samaria as is shown by the script of the ostraca of the Joint Expedition (Crowfoot et al. 1957: 14; pl. 1).

E. Hieratic Year Number

In concert with the paleographical and archaeological data, the year number 15 on many of the ostraca demands a reign of at least that many years, and the period of Jeroboam II seems right. Reisner had no doubt that the numerals were hieratic ten and five (undated: 13; 1924: 1. 229–30). Yadin's series of numbers from 1–9 enabled him to claim that the figures in question were five and four (1961: 9–25). The result for a while was that the 15th-year ostraca became 9th, and the whole corpus was assigned to the reign of Menahem (746–736 B.C.). Soon, however, interest in hieratic numerals in the Arad inscriptions (Aharoni 1966: 17) and on weights (Scott 1965: 137) and fractional weights (Kaufman 1967: 39–41) demonstrated that the numerals were to be read at face value.

F. Function of the Ostraca

The ostraca functioned in an accounting system, perhaps as temporary records. They were written in Samaria, since sherds broken from a common bowl or jar bear different place names, and the same scribal hand on ostraca such as 17a, 17b, 19, and 21 records different personal and place names (Yadin 1962: 65; Kaufman 1966: 155). Therefore they are not waybills from the source of the product. Some ostraca bear identical notations (16a and 16b, 17a and 17b and 4–7). Each would appear to record a separate jar of oil or wine. All 9th-year ostraca and three of the 10th record wine. All of the oil notations are written on thin gray jar sherds of Reisner's type I-3, and all but one of the wine notations are written on reddish bowl sherds of type I-14 (1924: 1. 232–38). None of the 15th-year ostraca are written on the hard gray ware; most are written on bowl sherds, and half of these are of the I-14 type. Since the 15th-year ostraca mention no product, the pattern suggests that the unnamed product may have been wine.

The main issue in determining the function of the ostraca is the role of the men whose names are preceded by the preposition *lamed.* Its range of meanings, "to," "belonging to," "for," or even "to be credited to," are explained in three ways: (1) the *l*-men were tax officials to whom tax in kind was delivered (Shea 1977: 26); (2) the *l*-men were owners or important officials who sent the commodity to the royal city as tax in kind (Yadin 1959: 186; Cross 1975: 10; Kaufman 1966: 159; 1982: 236–37); (3) the *l*-men were important officials who received the commodity from lands given to them by the crown, they being resident in Samaria "eating at the king's table," but providing their own subsistence from their land (Rainey 1962: 62; 1967: 32–41; 1979: 91–94; Lemaire 1977: 76; Aharoni *LBHG,* 322). According to the third theory, the ostraca would be directives, written at the royal storehouse in Samaria, assigning the commodity to the *l*-man who lived in the city.

The *l*-man can be associated with as many as four towns or three clan districts. No two *l*-men are related to the same town. Other persons without *lamed* are associated with only one *l*-man and one town, although several of these secondary men can be related to the same *l*-man and the same town as in ostraca nos. 1 and 2. The non-*l*-man would appear to work for the *l*-man, and is taken to be a tenant or servant responsible for delivery.

Rainey's theory (3) is based both on a land grant system operative in Ugarit in the Bronze Age in which the *lamed* refers to recipients of goods, and on biblical references (1 Sam 8:14; 22:7; 2 Sam 9:7–13). Rainey's Ugaritic references are directives ordering the giving of something, a tithe, tribute, or grain, to a person or persons. Whether the function of these texts is precisely parallel to that of the Samaria Ostraca is open to question. The latter contain no wordings that would indicate that they were directives.

Another hypothesis set forth recently in support of the second theory is as follows: Inscribed jars bearing personal and place names and content were not uncommon in Egypt and Israel (Lemaire 1977: 68, 135; Avigad 1972: 3).

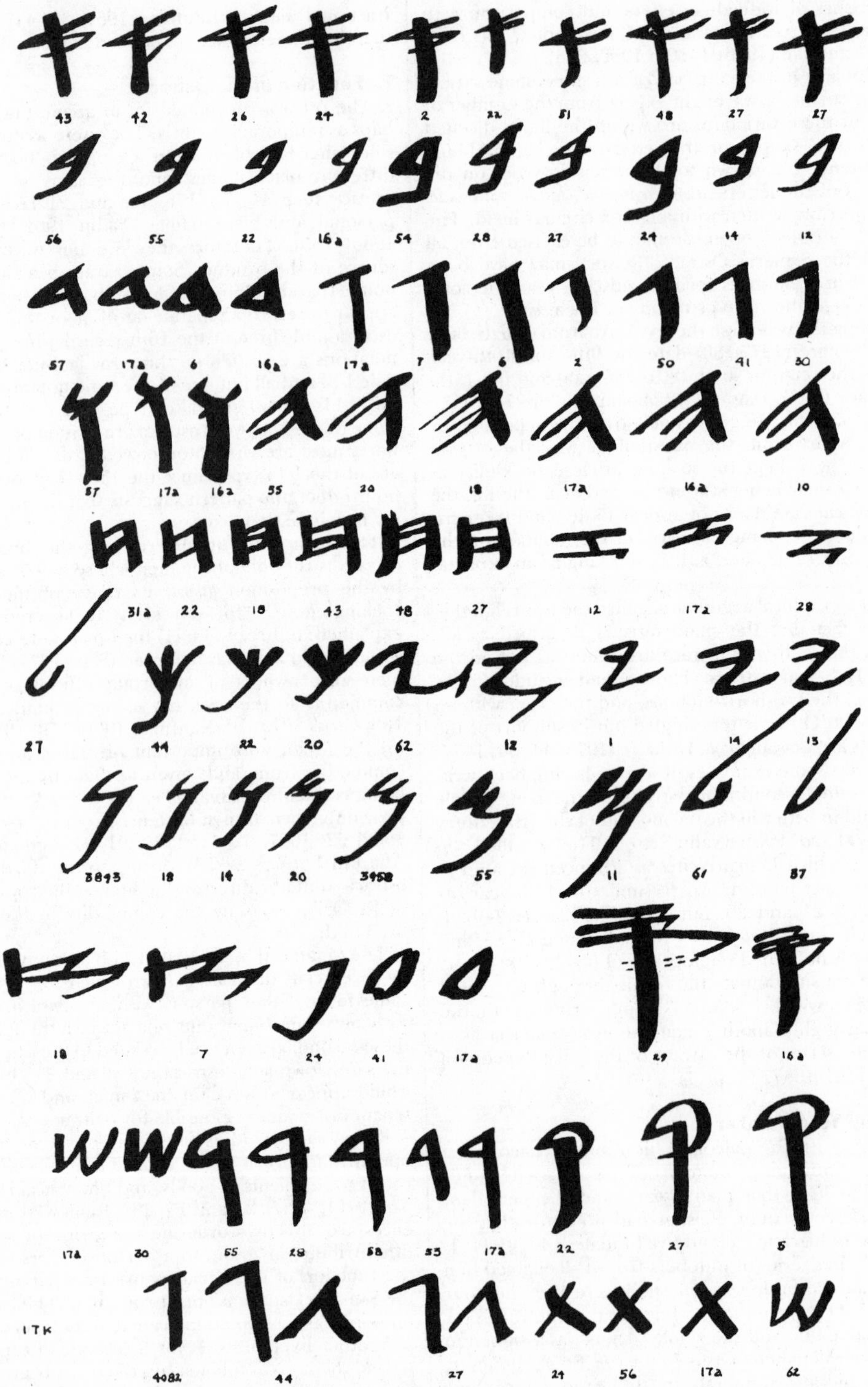

SAM.02. Paleographical chart of Samarian ostraca. Ostraca identified by numbers.

If jars of wine or oil delivered to Samaria bore inscriptions, as has been suggested by Yadin (1959: 186) and by the presence of ostraca nos. 61–63, which are partial jar labels (unlike the other ostraca inscribed on prebroken sherds) the data contained on the label might have been the primary source of information used for writing the ostracon for a given transaction. The scribe at Samaria might not have needed any other data than the deliverer's name, which appears on the 15th-year ostraca at the end, often discontinuous with the rest of the notation by half a line. If that were the case, the scribe would be crediting the delivery to the owner whose name appeared on the jar. The *lamed* of ownership would become the *lamed* of "to the credit of," and the *l*-man would be a sender (Kaufman 1982: 237). While the identity of the *l*-men has not been ascertained indisputably, we should expect evidence that the palace in the time of Jeroboam II was taxing its subjects, probably in kind, for the maintenance of high living noted for its lavish use of wine and fine cosmetic oil (Amos 6:6; Diringer 1934: 38).

G. Place Names and Personal Names

The place names provide valuable geographical data. Town names corresponding with modern village names serve to locate clan divisions such as Asriel and Heleq. While Reisner had not recognized the name Asriel on ostraca nos. 42 and 48, new photographs confirm that reading by Albright (1931: 249) and Cross (1962: 36). The town name Yashub now locates Asriel in the S part of Manasseh. Similarly, Reisner's town *sq* on ostraca nos. 16a and 29, is to be read as *spr* (Sepher), and its identification with Saffarin, W of Samaria locates the clan Shemida (Cross 1961: 14; Michaud 1958: 58). Albright believed that the town name *ttl* on ostraca nos. 13 and 21 was to be identified with modern Till (1931: 250). This is supported by a new reading of the place name as *twl* (Kaufman 1966: 136). Another probable reading is *gt prʾn* (Gat Paran) for Reisner's *ʾztprʾn* on ostracon no. 14 (Michaud 1958: 57; Kaufman 1966: 136). The reading, *bʾrym,* on ostracon no. 1, is preferable to Mazar's *pʾrym* (1948: 129).

The towns of the ostraca lie in a cluster around the city of Samaria at a distance of 4 to 8 miles, except for Yashub, at 12 miles, and Gat Paran, at 10. With the exception of Shechem they belong to the tribal area of Manasseh. None are from N Manasseh, which may have extended to the Esdraelon Valley. None are from Ephraim. The ostraca do not appear to represent nationwide taxation but rather convenient local sources of wine and oil. For distributional patterns see map-chart (Kaufman 1982: 236). See also HEPHER (PLACE).

Personal names on the ostraca reflect the piety of the namers in keeping with the biblical practice. Albright's calculation (*ARI,* 160–61) that the ratio of Baal names to Yahwistic or non-Baal names in the ostraca is 7:11 appears now to have some sociological implication: only one *l*-man has a Baal name, while all of the rest of the Baal names belong to secondary men who work for the *l*-men. While Baalism was a force to be dealt with in the 8th century, the owners and senders of the wine and oil appear on the whole to be Yahwistic or at least non-Baalistic as far as their names are an indication. Recent photographs provide new readings for some of the personal names published by Reisner in the following ostraca: (1) *grʿ,* (9) *ʾdnʿm,* (13) *ʾṣhr,* (42) *ʾdnyw,* (50) *lʾ ryw,* (57) *ʿbdʾyw,* (58) *pdyw* (Kaufman 1966: 141–44). The personal names on the ostraca have been examined by Noth *(IPN),* Diringer (1934), Lemaire (1977: 47–55), and Lawton (1984: 332–46).

Bibliography

Aharoni, Y. 1962. The Samaria Ostraca—an Additional Note. *IEJ* 12: 67–69.

———. 1966. The Use of Hieratic Numerals in Hebrew Ostraca and the Shekel Weights. *BASOR* 184: 13–19.

Albright, W. F. 1931. The Site of Tirzah and the Topography of Western Manasseh. *JPOS* 11: 241–51.

Avigad, N. 1972. Two Hebrew Inscriptions on Wine-Jars. *IEJ* 22: 1–9.

Birnbaum, S. A. 1954–57. *The Hebrew Scripts.* London.

Cross, F. M. 1961. Epigraphic Notes on Hebrew Documents of the Eighth–Sixth Centuries B.C.: I. A New Reading of a Place Name in the Samaria Ostraca. *BASOR* 163: 12–14.

———. 1962. Epigraphic Notes on Hebrew Documents of the Eighth–Sixth Centuries B.C.: II: The Murabbaʿat Papyrus and the Letter Found Near Yabneh-Yam. *BASOR* 165: 34–46.

———. 1968. Jar Inscriptions from Shiqmona. *IEJ* 18: 226–33.

———. 1975. Ammonite Ostraca from Hesbon. *AUSS* 13: 1–20.

———. 1980. Newly Found Inscriptions in Old Canaanite and Early Phoenician Scripts. *BASOR* 238: 1–20.

Cross, F. M., and Freedman, D. N. 1952. *Early Hebrew Orthography: A Study of the Epigraphic Evidence.* AOS 36. New Haven, CT.

Crowfoot, J. W.; Crowfoot, G. M.; and Kenyon, K. 1957. *The Objects from Samaria.* London.

Diringer, D. 1934. *Le iscrizioni antico-ebraiche palestinesi.* Florence.

Holladay, J. S., Jr. 1966. *The Pottery of Northern Palestine in the Ninth and Eighth Centuries B.C.* Harvard.

———. 1976. Of Sherds and Strata: Contributions toward an Understanding of the Archaeology of the Divided Monarchy. Pp. 253–93 in *Magnalia Dei: The Mighty Acts of God,* ed. F. M. Cross et al. Garden City, NY.

Kaufman, I. T. 1966. *The Samaria Ostraca: A Study in Ancient Hebrew Palaeography, Text and Plates.* Diss. Harvard.

———. 1967. New Evidence for Hieratic Numerals on Hebrew Weights. *BASOR* 188: 39–41.

———. 1982. The Samaria Ostraca: An Early Witness to Hebrew Writing. *BA* 45: 229–39.

Lawton, R. 1984. Personal Names on Pre-Exilic Hebrew Inscriptions. *Bib* 65: 330–46.

Lemaire, A. 1973. *Les Ostraca Hebreux de l'Époque Royale Israelite.* Texts and Plates. Diss. Paris.

———. 1977. *Inscriptions Hebraiques, Tome I, Les Ostraca.* Paris.

Maisler [Mazar], B. 1948. The Historical Background of the Samaria Ostraca. *JPOS* 21: 117–33.

Meshel, Z. 1978. *Kuntillet ʿAjrud: A Religious Centre from the Time of the Judean Monarchy on the Border of Sinai.* Jerusalem.

Michaud, H. 1958. *Sur la Pierre et l'Argile.* Neuchatel.

Millard, A. R. 1962. Alphabetic Inscriptions on Ivory from Nimrud. *Iraq* 24: 41–51.

Moscati, S. 1951. *L'epigrafia ebraica antica.* Rome.

Noth, M. 1927. Das Krongut der israelitischen Koenige und seine Verwaltung. *ZDPV* 50: 211–44.

———. 1932. Der Beitrag der samarischen Ostraka zur Loesung topographischen Fragen. *PJ* 1932: 54–67.

Rainey, A. F. 1962. Administration in Ugarit and the Samaria Ostraca *IEJ* 12: 62–63.
———. 1967. The Samaria Ostraca in the Light of Fresh Evidence. *PEQ* 99: 32–41.
———. 1970. Semantic Parallels to the Samaria Ostraca. *PEQ* 102: 45–51.
———. 1979. The *Sitz in Leben* of the Samaria Ostraca. *Tel Aviv* 6: 91–94. Appears also as editor's insertion in *LBHG*, 363–65.
Reisner, G. A. undated. *Israelite Ostraca from Samaria.* Boston.
Reisner, G. A.; Fisher, C. S.; and Lyon, D. G. 1924. *Harvard Excavations at Samaria 1908–10.* Vol. 1, Text; vol. 2, Plans and Plates. Cambridge.
Scott, R. B. Y. 1965. The Scale-Weights from Ophel. *PEQ* 1965: 128–39.
Shea, W. H. 1977. The Date and Significance of the Samaria Ostraca. *IEJ* 27: 16–27.
Teixidor, J. 1967–81. Bulletin d' épigraphie semitique. *Syria* 44–58.
Yadin, Y. 1959. Recipients or Owners, a Note on the Samaria Ostraca. *IEJ* 9: 184–87.
———. 1961. Ancient Judean Weights and the Date of the Samaria Ostraca. Scripta Hierosolymitana 8: 9–25.
———. 1962. A Further Note on the Samaria Ostraca. *IEJ* 12: 64–66.

IVAN T. KAUFMAN

ARCHAEOLOGICAL SURVEY OF THE REGION

A. Borders
B. Roads
C. Archaeological Periods
   1. Early Bronze Age
   2. Middle Bronze Age
   3. Late Bronze Age
   4. Iron Age I and II
   5. Persian Period
   6. Hellenistic Period
   7. Roman Period

A. Borders

Samaria's N border extends W from the Gilboa mountains along the juncture of the mountains and the Plain of Jezreel, and from there to the mountains of Um el-Fahm and Nahal ᶜEiron (Zertal 1986: 12–15; Karmon 1980: 349–60). Its E border extends along the escarpment of the hills leading down to the Jordan Valley. Its W border is along the junction connecting the foothills and the Sharon Plain. Its S border is somewhat controversial, but most researchers consider it to be in the region of Mt. Baal-hazor, along the streams of ᶜAuja and Shiloh, which are tributaries of the Yarkon River (Ziv 1983: 10–27).

The area of Samaria is estimated to be some 2250 km^2, and is rectangular in shape, having sides 50 km long and 45 km wide. The city of Nablus lies at its center. Geographers divide the district into three main units: Central Samaria, W Samaria, and E Samaria.

Central Samaria includes the area N of the Qalqilya-ᶜAzun-Nablus road. This region on the slope of the mountains readily lends itself to agriculture, and is thickly settled. The Nablus Mountains, with some of the highest peaks in Samaria, are in this area: Jebel Hureish (764 m above sea level), Mt. Ebal (940 m above sea level), and Mt. Gerizim (881 m above sea level).

The Nablus Mountains region is surrounded by valleys that have attracted man since ancient times: the Dothan Valley, the Jaba Valley, the valleys of Nahal Shekhem, ᶜAskar, Farᶜah, Tubas, and Bezeq (Zababida). The Sanur valley lies at their center. The area of the valleys is some 15 percent of the total area of the region.

W Samaria consists of offshoots of mountain ranges extending from E to W and descending toward the Sharon Plain. South of Tulkarm they are composed of hard dolomite limestone, which creates a stony, dissected landscape.

From N of Tulkarm to Nahal ᶜEiron the landscape is less rugged, consisting of chalk hills compatible to settlement. It ranges 100–500 m above sea level.

E Samaria consists of mountain ranges extending S–SW from the anticline of Farᶜah. In this area the landscape consists of alternate ridges and valleys: Ras Jadir (712 m above sea level) and the Bukeia Valley; Jebel Tamun (539 m above sea level) and the Tirzah Valley; Jebel Kabir (792 m above sea level) and the Beit Dagan Valley.

Several of the peaks in the E are more than 900 m above sea level. Because of the limited rainfall in E Samaria (an average of 200 to 400 mm per annum), there have been no permanent settlements at any time throughout history.

Modern archaeological and geographical research contains studies in which Samaria is divided in a more detailed and discriminating manner than in this three-region division. A. Zertal divides the N part of Samaria, the hill country of Manasseh, into 23 geographic units, in accordance with landscape and geomorphological considerations (1986: 12–15). I. Finkelstein divides S Samaria, the hill country of Ephraim, into six landscape units, each of which, in his opinion, is an independent geographic and settlement region (1986b: 117–19).

For the most part, Samaria has a Mediterranean climate. The average annual rainfall is from 550 to 700 mm, dependent on the altitude of any particular locality. Dew is plentiful in the mountains. In E Samaria there are various types of desert lithosols.

B. Roads

Two main historical routes extend the length of Samaria: the way through the slopes of the mountains in Central Samaria, and the way that follows the foot of the mountains, parts of which coincide with the well-known Via Maris, in the W. In the Classical periods, there were additional parallel routes, which were located between the two mentioned above (Dar 1981: 376–82).

More than a dozen historical roads crossing the width of Samaria have been discovered. The most important passes through Nahal Shechem and Wadi Farᶜah and connects the coastal plain, the slopes of the mountains, and the Jordan Rift. The city of Nablus, which is situated at the juncture of the two branches of this road, attained its important status because of its strategic command of the route.

Other roads across Samaria pass through the beds of wadis, and some pass over mountain ranges that rise from W to E.

The archaeological research conducted in the area has proved that Samaria's road network preceded the Roman-

Byzantine period, and that parts of it were appropriated into the Roman system, which also set up milestones along them (Zertal 1986: 183–94; Dar 1986: 126–41).

C. Archaeological Periods

During the last 20 years, Samaria has been the object of intensive field research, which has revealed the character of the settlement distribution in the region. More than 1,000 archaeological sites are known in Samaria. The foundations for the renewed research were laid by the Emergency Survey of 1967 and 1968 conducted by groups led by Z. Kallai, R. Gophna, and Y. Porat (Gophna and Porat 1972: 196–202). Y. Porat conducted a supplementary survey of the region, but it was not published. The surveys have revealed that ruins are typical of Samaria, and are usually situated on top of domes or at the tips of spurs. Tels are also prevalent, and as a rule they are situated near the internal valleys of the region.

1. Early Bronze Age. Some 80 sites of the EB were surveyed, and ceramics from periods I and II were discovered. In addition, strata of settlements of this period were unearthed in the well-known excavated sites of Tel el-Far^cah (Tirzah), Samaria-Sebaste, and Tel Dothan.

Most of the sites are situated in the internal valleys, near conveniently available sources of water. They may have hewed out catch basins in the chalk rock, which holds water well. The mountain settlers preferred the soft rendzina soils, which are easier to cultivate. Not many archaeological sites were found in the stony terra rosa areas. In some W Samarian sites, evidence of EB agricultural activity was discovered. The researchers believe that Mediterranean viniculture and olive growing began developing during this period (Gophna 1982: 105). Study of the settlement pattern in the mountains of Samaria during the Bronze Age reveals central fortified sites (cities) and subsidiary unwalled villages spread out among them. The fortified settlements may have controlled the agricultural and pasture lands in their surrounding areas.

In the mountains of Nablus and in Wadi Far^cah, A. Zertal has explored six fortified enclosures dating from EB I and II. They are remarkable for their location and their command of the region.

Some 15 sites dating from the EB IV were explored. Some of them were walled settlements such as Bir Hassan, on the outskirts of the Dothan Valley, and Bab a-Naqb in Wadi Far^cah. In Nablus, as well, evidence of settlement from this period was found. Black ceramics dating from the EB IV, of the type found by N. Glueck on the E side of the Jordan, were found in several sites in the mountains of Samaria.

It is customary to think of this period as a combination of local and newly arrived populations. The settlements are small and spread out, and they were not long-lived (Gophna 1982: 122–23).

2. Middle Bronze Age. The Emergency Survey of 1967 and 1968 revealed for the first time the wide distribution of sites from the MB in Samaria (Gophna and Porat 1972: 197–98). Today we know of some 170 sites in Samaria; 120 of them are in the area of Manasseh in the N, and about 50 are in the less settled area of Ephraim in the S (Zertal 1986: 175–79; Finkelstein 1986b: 169).

Seventy percent of the MB settlement sites were established on virgin soil, especially in the 18th century B.C. Researchers noted the following characteristics of these sites: (1) most were on the edges of the inner valleys; (2) they depended on sources of flowing water; (3) most of the settlements were small and unwalled, and were originally established in this period; and (4) in difficult-to-settle regions, such as the desert frontier and the NW portion of Samaria, there were almost no settlements. The residents of Samaria began during this period to clear the forests in Samaria, to hew cisterns and seal them against seepage, and to develop advanced mountain agriculture based on orchards, field crops, and cattle.

In the internal valleys, fortified cities (e.g., SHECHEM, which became a center for its surrounding rural settlements) began to emerge. Each fortified mound became a center for 10–20 rural settlements (Zertal 1986: 197). Only in Iron Age II and in the Persian period were there more sites in Samaria than there were in the MB. According to Zertal's calculations, the population was less than 50,000 (Zertal 1986: 214).

3. Late Bronze Age. There was a sharp decrease in the number of settlements in Samaria during the LB. Only 36 sites were surveyed, indicating that there were 70 percent fewer settlements than there had been in the MB. In the area of Manasseh, the reduction in the number of settlements was not as sharp as in the land of Ephraim (Finkelstein 1986b: 169; Zertal 1986: 201–10). Settlements concentrated on the larger central mounds of Samaria. Their reduced number may have been a result of the military campaigns of the pharaohs of the 18th Dynasty against the land of Shechem or, possibly, of temporarily diminished water sources.

According to Zertal's calculations, 80 percent of the cultivated lands in the region of Manasseh were abandoned, and the woodlands expanded again. In contrast to the sharp reduction in the number of unwalled settlements at that time, Shechem became the capital of a principality ruled by Bani Lebaya. The principality of Shechem, which is well known from the documents of el-Amarna, ruled most of Samaria under the patronage of the New Kingdom in Egypt.

4. Iron Age I and II. During the Iron Age I, the process of the Israelite settlement in Samaria took place. Small rural de novo settlements began to appear. Today we know of ca. 200 settlement sites in the mountains of Samaria, indicating a large-scale settlement process, which is attributed to the tribes of Ephraim and Manasseh. These settlement sites shared many common geographical and archaeological characteristics: most were small unwalled settlements whose area was from 2–4 dunams which relied upon rainwater collected in hewed cisterns. They were established in stony mountain areas, all the way to the frontier of Samaria. A small number of settlements were established on ruins of settlements and mounts from the MB or LB periods. Ceramic storejars with distinguishing collared rims, trench silos dug into the ground, and four-room houses are considered characteristic of the Israelite settlement in the mountains of Samaria. On the basis of various considerations, archaeologists have concluded that the process of Israelite settlement in the mountain regions took place during the last half of the 13th and the beginning of the 12th centuries B.C.

On the basis of extensive surveys and excavations carried out by Finkelstein and Zertal at ᶜIZBET SARTA and SHILOH (Finkelstein 1986a and 1986b) and at Mount EBAL (Zertal 1986: 225–75), several proposals concerning the settlement process in the mountains of Samaria were suggested; settlement was not uniform throughout the region. See also SEILUN, KHIRBET. Some sites show a continuity from the LB to the Israelite settlement. Additionally, the settlement pattern tends to shift from E to W into the areas that are void of crowded Canaanitic settlement, thus indicating that there was coexistence between the Canaanitic and Israelite populations.

Researchers propose the following sequence in the development of the settlement economy: from a pasture economy on the edge of the desert, to a pasture-and-field crops economy in the internal valleys, to, finally, a plantation economy in the mountains.

The site excavated by A. Zertal on Mount Ebal, above Nablus, is an interesting find dating from the settlement period (Zertal 1986: 224–74; 1986–87). Zertal has identified a large two-layered ritual site dating from the period of 1250–1150 B.C. He also found bones of kosher animals and ceramic and archaeological evidence that admirably establish the date of the site.

Most of the sites established in Iron Age I continued to exist into Iron Age II, when many new settlements were also established. The total number of Samarian mountain settlements yielding pottery from Iron Age II is ca. 320. This process of accelerated settlement continued from the period of the kingdom until the Assyrian conquest of Samaria.

In Iron Age II, even marginal agricultural areas at the edge of the desert were settled. Also, various branches of agriculture were developed and many technical innovations introduced during that period. D. Eitam has identified W Samarian settlements whose populations supported themselves by producing olive oil (Eitam 1987: 16–36). Kh. Jemeʾin, a walled rural settlement dating from Iron Age II, operated a communal olive press, a wine press, and a wine cellar (Dar 1986: 13–73). In Iron Age II, for the first time in Samaria, farmhouses of the type prevalent particularly in the W of the region made their appearance. A single-period farmhouse of this type was explored in Qoren Liqrana, 2 km E of Kafr Tult. The dimensions of the farmhouse were 27.10 × 29.30 m, and it was built of stone (Dar 1986: 2). It included an internal quadrangular tower and an external round tower. It is possible that the farmhouse served as a center for an extended family, which was normal in Iron Age II and lasted into Roman times. To the best of our knowledge, these farmhouses are the most ancient that have been found in the E Mediterranean region.

The first archaeological indications of solutions for the security problems of Samaria in Iron Age II were found during a survey of W Samaria. Approximately a dozen enclosures and strongholds were located. They formed a defensive line on the slopes of the mountains of Samaria and defended the main passes from the coastal plain to the center of the mountains. These enclosures and strongholds included Tel Qaᶜada and Shufa near Tulkarm; the enclosures of Beit Lid, which defended the approach to Shechem and Samaria; Kur, Qarnei Shomron, the stronghold of Nahal Qanah, Haris, and Qarawat Bani Hassan (Dar 1986: 213–17). It is probable that in E Samaria, there was a defense and stronghold network similar to that explored in W Samaria.

5. Persian Period. The history of the mountains of Samaria during the Persian period has not yet been fully understood, but archaeological surveys have found ceramic evidence at ca. 300 sites of widespread Persian influence. Despite the political changes in Samaria from the end of the Iron Age and into the Persian period, many sites show a continuity, and apparently the population did not decline.

The major settlements of Samaria, (e.g., Shechem and the city of Samaria) have yielded archaeological finds from this period (Stern 1973: 31–34), but the evidence is scanty. Only a few excavations at Persian sites have been carried out in the countryside of Samaria, and the general picture is not yet clear. At Qedumim decorated pottery was found in a cistern, in addition to imported Attic pottery from Greece (Magen 1982). The excavator believes that the settlement is situated on a previously Samaritan site. Remnants from the Persian period were found in agricultural towers near Qarnei Shomron, in SW Samaria, and at Um Rihan in NW Samaria (Dar 1986: 108).

The distribution of the Persian period farms in the mountains of Samaria is an interesting phenomenon. In two regions, more than 20 farmhouses dating from Iron Age II and the beginning of the Persian period were explored. A large concentration was found in SW Samaria between Nahal Qanah in the N and Nahal Natuf in the S (Finkelstein 1981: 331–48), and a smaller concentration was found in the region of Um Rihan in NW Samaria (Dar, Safrai, and Tepper 1986: 105–14). The distribution of the farmhouses indicated agricultural activity on marginal and stony lands in the Persian period and before it. Some of these farms were established in Iron Age II, but continued to be active in the Persian and Hellenistic periods.

It should be noted that the enclosures and military strongholds from Iron Age II, which were investigated in W Samaria, continued into the Persian period. Ceramic evidence from that period was found in Tel Qaᶜada, in Shufa, in the enclosures of the Beit Lid region, in Kur, and in Qarnei Shomron.

The Persian authorities of Samaria may have reactivated part of the defense line of their predecessors. The well-known documents of Wadi Daliyeh have indicated security problems at the end of the Persian period, and the recent discovery of an Aramaic economic document in the caves of Ketef Yeriho have added to our knowledge. It contains a list of money borrowers, all of whose names are Jewish (Eshel 1988: 18–23). It is attributed to the years 300–335 B.C., and may relate to the rebellions against Artaxerxes III, which took place at that time in Palestine. See DALIYEH, WADI ED-.

6. Hellenistic Period. As many sites can be attributed to the Hellenistic period in Samaria as to the Persian period. However, complete data on the latest investigations have not yet been published.

In the principal settlements of Samaria, such as Shechem and the city of Samaria, substantial finds from the Hellenistic period were discovered, but little excavation has taken place in the rest of the region. A fortified city from the Hellenistic period was recently excavated on Mt. Gerizim, and covers ca. 300 dunams (Magen 1986: 91–101). A defense wall, a gate, and a stronghold measuring 23 × 25 m were among the finds. The splendor and the high quality of the construction of the dwellings are striking. They were evidently built according to a uniform plan, which consisted of a stone-paved courtyard surrounded by rooms. The two-story houses had toilets and bathrooms, and their walls were well-plastered. In light of the unearthed ceramics and coins, the excavator proposed that the city was built at the beginning of the 2d century B.C. and was destroyed during the military conquests of John Hyrcanus.

We lack sufficient data on the city's founders and its inhabitants in the Hellenistic period. The residents were probably members of the Samaritan community who separated themselves from their fellow Jews in Jerusalem, and consequently suffered from the Hasmonean conquests. However, another plausible assumption is that the settlement on Mt. Gerizim was part of the Ptolemaic or the Seleucid settlement in the region, and that its conquest by John Hyrcanus was part of the Hasmonean rulers' activities against the foreign population in the mountains of Samaria.

During the Hellenistic period, widespread settlement activity took place, and its distinguishing feature was field towers, hundreds of which have been surveyed in both N and S Samaria. A typical field tower is a small stone structure whose dimensions average approximately 4 × 4 m. These towers were used in the processing of agricultural produce, especially in grape growing and wine production. In many instances the tower is situated in an enclosed agricultural area, probably the estate of the farmer who operated it (Dar 1986: 88–125). Some of the towers were built in the Hellenistic period, and in the opinion of S. Applebaum, they are evidence of the Hasmonean dynasty's settlement project in Samaria (Applebaum 1986: 257–69). There is also a possibility that parts of the settlement areas in W Samaria were property of the king in the Hellenistic period and that they became Kings Mountain Country from the Hasmonean period and thereafter.

The fortifications network of W Samaria, which was put into operation in Iron Age II and continued to operate in the Persian period, was not entirely abandoned in the Hellenistic period. In most of the enclosures, Hellenistic ceramics were found in quantities that testify to continued activity. The outstanding site is the acropolis of Kh. Firdusi, N. of Qarawat Bani Hassan (Dar 1986: 218–21). An investigation was carried out there on a fortified area covering approximately 35 dunams, leading to the discovery of a wall, a fortified tower, and large storage areas reminiscent of Hellenistic Pergamum and Herodian Masada.

7. Roman Period. Several hundred sites from the Roman and Byzantine periods were explored in Samaria. The line of archaeological differentiation between these two periods is not yet clearly drawn, so the distinction between them is primarily historical. This was a peak period of settlement in the region, from the point of view of the number of settlements, and evidently the number of residents also peaked at that time. All the marginal stony lands, including those on Samaria's desert frontier, were settled and cultivated by the local population, which included indigenous elements of Samaritans and Jews who were joined by settlers of pagan origin. The Hellenistic and Roman governments first seized important settlements such as Shechem and Samaria-Sebaste, but subsequently they spread their rule to the rural settlements.

In Shechem-Neapolis, excavations revealed important parts of the Roman city, including the theater, the hippodrome, the amphitheater, a section of the street of the cardo, and the stairs leading to the temple of Zeus-Jupiter, which was located at er-Ras on Mt. Gerizim. An approximately 3-m-thick section of the city's wall was also discovered.

In addition, a mosaic floor of a citizen's luxurious dwelling from the 3d century A.D. and a number of magnificent mausolea were found at the foot of Mt. Ebal.

The theater was found at the foot of Mt. Gerizim, and part of it is built into the side of the mountain. It is one of the largest theaters in W Palestine, with a diameter of approximately 110 m (Magen 1984: 269–77). The orchestra is colorfully tiled, and along the row of stone seats belonging to the community's dignitaries, are engraved the names of the families for whom the seats were reserved. Parts of statues of dolphins and of women were found among the ruins. The theater was probably built in the 2d century A.D.

Between Mt. Gerizim and Mt. Ebal, where Roman Neapolis once stood, parts of the hippodrome were unearthed. It is approximately 320 m long and 80 m wide. In the E part of the hippodrome, a section of the amphitheater, elliptical and with dimensions of some 80 × 100 m, was unearthed. Magen estimates that it could seat 10,000 spectators.

In the center of the Casbah of Shechem part of the Roman cardo was discovered. Underneath it is an impressive sewage canal. Several mausolea were discovered at the foot of Mt. Ebal. The names of the buried are carved on some of the sarcophagi; they were Jews or Samaritan citizens of the polis (Damati 1973: 118–20). In the W part of the city, another magnificent mausoleum was found. It has three complete burial caves (Magen 1987: 72–91). The agricultural area of the polis was investigated by Z. Safrai, who detected systematically arranged plots of land on the mountains surrounding the city (Safrai 1986: 83–126). He found that the average size of the plots was about 13 to 17 dunams, and believes that they belonged to the settlers of the Roman polis of Neapolis. The archaeological findings of Samaria-Sebaste have been well-known for some time, and no new excavations that changed the picture have been carried out there.

A. Zertal carried out excavations in NW Samaria at Kh. al-Hammam and discovered a siege defense system from the early Roman period (Zertal 1981: 112–18). The system includes a dike, camps, and a rampart. A branch of the Roman Caesarea-Ginei (Jenin) road passes near the site. Archaeological evidence from the time of the First Temple through the Early Roman Period (1st and 2d centuries A.D.) was discovered at Kh. el-Hammam. Zertal identifies this site as Arruboth of the Bible, and Narbatha of the time of the Second Temple, the place to which the Jews of Caesarea fled when the rebellion against Rome broke out (in 66 A.D.). This sophisticated siege defense system is attributed to the campaign of the Roman Governor Cestius Gallus, who hastened to suppress the rebels in Judea.

Extensive field studies of the rural landscape of Samaria in the Roman period have been carried out. In addition, a number of excavations were made in villages and towns of the region. The population of the region was mostly rural, and lived in clusters of villages or in towns of unstable size. The archaeological difference between a village and a town is strictly physical. A village has a small number of houses and families, whereas in a town, the built-up area covers approximately 20 to 40 dunams. On the other hand, the social differences between town and village are considerable.

A rural Samaritan settlement was excavated in Qedumim, but its total area was not investigated. It contained two fine olive presses, stone dwellings, and ritual purification baths. Also discovered were iron agricultural tools including a plowshare, and axe, and chisels (Magen 1982). The village of Qedumim, whose origins are in the Persian period, was destroyed in the Samaritan insurrection against the Byzantines in the 5th and 6th centuries A.D.

Kh. Buraq is a medium-sized town whose well-preserved condition enables measurement of its developed area (some 25 dunams), its crafts area, and its overall agricultural area. This settlement had some 60 or 70 houses with courtyards and a population of 1,000 to 1,500 (Dar 1986: 51–76). The overall agricultural area of Kh. Buraq is estimated to be 1,800 dunams, and each family theoretically held about 25 dunams on the average. In the agricultural area, some 70 field towers, corresponding to the number of houses in the settlement, were investigated. The agricultural installations of the village indicate that its residents made their living from vineyards, from olive orchards for the production of olive oil, from grains, from flocks, and from crafts such as hewing stones. In the Roman period, the residents of Buraq produced more than they needed for their own consumption, and sent large quantities of wine and oil to market. With the proceeds they could afford a higher standard of living, as indicated by the material finds in their settlement.

Um Rihan is a large town whose built-up area covers approximately 36 to 40 dunams. Similar to its sister settlement, Kh. Buraq, it is almost completely preserved. The town had some 100 houses (Dar, Safrai, and Tepper 1986). A well-made network of narrow streets linked the parts of the town. This network served, among other things, to collect runoff water into hewn cisterns. The houses are built of hewn stone, and have cellars and upper levels.

The town was defended by a network of watch- and lookout towers, and the outside walls of houses were arranged to form an enclosing line around the settlement. The remnants of a Roman bath house and the Latin inscription of a public building were found, along with 8–9 oil presses, and a considerable number of wine presses. Some 100 field towers were surveyed—and some of them were excavated—in the agricultural area of Um Rihan. Reconstruction of the economic basis of the town in the Roman period shows that olive oil, wine, cereals, sheep, and livestock were the mainstays of its agricultural economy. Evidence of local iron-tempering and glass-blowing was also found in the excavations. It is estimated that the town had 3,000–3,500 residents—Jews or Samaritans who abandoned it after the revolts of the 5th century A.D.

Farmhouses which had originated in Iron Age II were still prevalent in the Roman period. One, in N Samaria, was still intact. The farm, called Qasr e-Lejah, is located on a stony spur E of Um Rihan (Dar 1986: 10–12; Dar, Safrai, and Tepper 1986: 109–13). It measures 26.5 × 36.0 m, and contains a tower in which the master lived, living quarters for the workers, storehouses, and a fine olive press. Surrounding the farm are cisterns for winepresses, which are carved into the rock. The finds indicate that olive oil and wine were among its basic agricultural products. Evidently its owner was well-to-do, and perhaps was close to the Hellenistic-Roman authorities.

In the Roman period the number of field towers reached its peak, but it was then that they also lost their important position in the agricultural system. More than 1,200 towers were surveyed in Samaria, and from them, we learn of developed plantation agriculture, especially viniculture and wine production (Dar 1986: 88–125). The towers were widespread in Samaria in the early Hellenistic and Roman periods, and they served as centers of the agricultural estates of the farmers of the region. Evidently, in wake of the events of the Jews' rebellions against Rome, they lost this function in the 2d century A.D. The field towers did not disappear from the landscape of Samaria in the Late Roman and Byzantine periods, but their use and importance in the agriculture of the region diminished, and they became ordinary field structures.

In the Roman period, the road network in Samaria attains its widest scope and distribution. The network, some of which existed in the earlier biblical periods, encompassed all of Samaria, linking its settlements, and linking the farmer to his fields. Until the Roman period, the road network was organic and adapted to the settlement distribution of the region. A rural road network that served the agro-economic needs of the villagers was detected in Samaria. Thus, for example, 18 roads from the center of the village Qarawat Bani Hassan were found, with a total length of about 35 km (Dar 1986: 126–46).

In addition to the rural roads, a network of roads connected settlements, irrespective of size. An enormous amount of work went into constructing the roads system, which included quarrying, making the shoulders, and hewing water cisterns for the use of travelers and animals.

Evidently in the Roman period, the main ancient routes became Roman Kings Highways, and milestones were set up along them. In W Samaria, I. Roll and E. Ayalon found Roman roads that connected the polis cities on the coastal plain with the polis cities in the hill country (Roll and Ayalon 1986: 113–34). Other surveys have discovered milestones along the routes connecting Sebaste and Apollonia; Neapolis and Joppa; Neapolis and Apollonia; Neapolis and Lod; and Gophna and Antipatris.

The rural and state road network of Samaria is an indication of organized administration, of social and economic openness, and of extensive commerce.

Bibliography

Applebaum, S. 1986. The Settlement Pattern of Western Samaria from Hellenistic to Byzantine Times: A Historical Commentary. Pp. 257–69 in Dar 1986.

Damati, I. 1973. A Roman Mausoleum at ʾAskar. *Qadmoniot* 6: 118–20 (in Hebrew).
Dar, S. 1981. Roads and Forts in the Beth Lidd Region of Samaria. *EI* 15: 376–82 (in Hebrew).
———. Ed. 1986. *Landscape and Pattern An Archaeological Survey of Samaria 800 B.C.E.–636 C.E.* BARIS 308. Oxford.
Dar, S., Safrai, Z., and Tepper, Y. 1986. *Um Rihan: A Village of the Mishnah.* Tel-Aviv (in Hebrew).
Eitam, D. 1987. Olive-Oil Production During The Biblical Period. Pp. 16–36 in *Olive-oil in Antiquity,* ed. M. Heltzer and D. Eitam. Haifa (in Hebrew).
Eshel, H. 1988. Finds and Documents from a Cave at Ketef-Yericho. *Qadmoniot* 21: 18–23 (in Hebrew).
Finkelstein, I. 1981. Israelite and Hellenistic Farms in the Foothills and in the Yarkon Basin. *EI* 15: 331–48 (in Hebrew).
———. 1986a. *ʿIzbet Sartah an Early Iron Age Site, near Rosh-Haʾayin, Israel.* BARIS 299. Oxford.
———. 1986b. The Archaeology of the Period of Settlement and Judges. Tel Aviv (in Hebrew) [English *AIS*].
Gophna, R. 1982. The Early Bronze Age and Intermediate Bronze Age (3300–2000) B.C.E. Pp. 95–120 in *History of Eretz Israel,* vol. 1, ed. I. Ephʿal. Jerusalem (in Hebrew).
Gophna, R., and Porat, Y. 1972. The Land of Ephraim and Manasseh. Pp. 196–202 in *Judea Samaria and the Golan Archaeological Survey 1967–1968,* ed. M. Kochavi. Jerusalem (in Hebrew).
Karmon, J. 1980. *Eretz Israel, Geography of the Country and its Regions.* Tel-Aviv (in Hebrew).
Magen, I. 1982. *The Archaeological Discoveries at Qedumim, Samaria.* Qedumim (in Hebrew).
———. 1984. The Roman Theater at Shechem. Pp. 269–77 in *Z. Vilnay Volume 1,* ed. E. Schiller. Jerusalem (in Hebrew).
———. 1986. A Fortified Town of the Hellenistic Period on Mount Gerizim. *Qadmoniot* 19: 91–101.
———. 1987. The Western Mausoleum at Neapolis. *EI* 19: 72–91 (in Hebrew).
Roll, I., and Ayalon, E. 1986. Roman Roads in Western Samaria. *PEQ* 118: 113–34.
Safrai, Z. 1986. Shechem in the Days of Mishnah and Talmud 63 B.C.E.–637 C.E. Pp. 83–126 in *Shomron Studies,* ed. S. Dar and Z. Safrai. Tel-Aviv (in Hebrew).
Stern, E. 1973. *The Material Culture of the Land of the Bible in the Persian Period 538–332 B.C.E. Jerusalem (in Hebrew; in English from Warminster).*
Zertal, A. 1981. The Roman Siege-System at Khirbet el-Hammam (Narbata) in Samaria. Qadmoniot 14/3–4: 112–18.
———. 1986. The Israelite Settlement in the Hill-Country of Manasseh. Ph.D. diss., Tel-Aviv University (in Hebrew).
———. 1986–87. An Early Iron Age Cultic Site on Mt. Ebal. *TA* 13–14: 105–65.
Ziv, J. 1983. The Landscape in Judea and Samaria. Pp. 10–27 in *The High Mountains of Israel,* ed. J. Levite. Tel-Aviv (in Hebrew).

Shimon Dar
Trans. Menachem Erez

PAPYRI

The Samaria papyri are a group of fragmentary remains of legal papyri once belonging to wealthy patricians of Samaria. In the early spring of 1962, Taʿâmireh Bedouin came upon them in a cave in the Wâdī ed-Dâliyeh (about 14 km N of Jericho, on the W rim of the Jordan rift), along with the bones of their owners—men, women, and children. See also DALIYEH, WADI ED-.

F. M. Cross suggests a likely explanation. After an abortive revolt in 331 B.C.E., Samaritans fleeing Alexander's forces hid in these caves with their title deeds in hand. But Alexander's forces found them out and built a fire at the mouth of the cave to suffocate them. There the papyri and skeletons remained undisturbed for nearly 23 centuries.

The earliest dated papyrus comes from sometime between the 30th and 39th year of Artaxerxes II (Mnemon), therefore between 375 and 365 B.C.E. The latest is from 335 B.C.E. in the reign of Darius III (Codomannus). Most of the papyri were probably written during the reign of Artaxerxes III (Ochus; 358–337 B.C.E.). Whenever the place of execution is extant on the papyrus, it is "Samaria."

There are 18 fragments large enough to call "papyri," and about 9 other pieces of some size. Various types of deeds are represented among the papyri, but by far the most prevalent type is the slave sale. The first 9 papyri—all deeds of slave sale—can be reconstructed rather fully despite their fragmentary character because they adhere so closely to a common formula. There is less hope for reconstructing those papyri that fall into other categories. For instance, there are two documents that look like pledges of a slave in exchange for a loan, a sale of a house, a sale of living quarters or storerooms in a house, a sale or antichretic pledge of a vineyard, manumission or release of a pledged slave, a receipt for a payment associated somehow with a pledge, and one small fragment that looks like a judicial settlement by oath.

The Samaria papyri afford the paleographer rare and valuable examples of 4th-century Aramaic script, filling in the gap between the better documented Aramaic scripts of the 5th and 3rd centuries. The documents are written in a conservative form of Official Aramaic—the standard Aramaic used by scribes in the Persian period (from Darius I to Darius III) to draft documents of an official nature (e.g., legal documents and administrative correspondence). The language shows very little Persian influence. Otherwise, it is essentially indistinguishable from the Aramaic of the 5th-century Arsames correspondence and Elephantine legal papyri.

The greatest importance of the Samaria papyri lies in their contribution to the history of law. The formulary for selling slaves exemplified in the Samaria papyri seems to derive in its basic structure from the formulary used for the sale of movables in the late Neo-Babylonian period (from the time of Darius I on). Aramaic scribes appear to have adopted this basic structure and then freely modified it, in part by drawing on formulas from other types of late Neo-Babylonian documents and in part by assimilating it to their own native legal traditions. A comparison between the law of the Samaria papyri and cuneiform law contributes to a growing awareness of an extensive and ongoing symbiosis between Aramean and Babylonian scribal traditions throughout the Persian and Hellenistic periods. Further, the evidence of the Samaria papyri both clarifies and expands our picture of the role of Aramaic scribes as creative intermediaries of cultural traditions throughout the ANE.

The Syria papyri also give us a peephole on the political and social life of 4th-century Samaria. For instance, we learn that Samaria was then a city within the Persian province of the same name administered by a governor and prefect. Several names of governors and prefects are attested in the papyri, including one Sanballat. The vast majority of sellers, buyers, and slaves alike bear Yahwistic names. Further, the slaves sold become slaves for life, directly violating the regulations of Lev 25:39–47.

Bibliography

Cross, F. M. 1963. The Discovery of the Samaria Papyri. *BA* 26: 110–21.

———. 1966. Aspects of Samaritan and Jewish History in Late Persian and Hellenistic Times. *HTR* 59: 201–11.

———. 1969. Papyri of the Fourth Century B.C. from Dâliyeh. Pp. 41–62, figs. 34–39 in *New Directions in Biblical Archaeology*, ed. D. N. Freedman and J. Greenfield. New York.

———. 1974. The Papyri and Their Historical Implications; Other Finds: Coins; Scarab. Pp. 17–29; 57–60 in *Discoveries in the Wâdī ed-Dâliyeh*, ed. P. W. Lapp and N. L. Lapp. AASOR 41. Cambridge, MA.

———. 1985. Samaria Papyrus 1: An Aramaic Slave Conveyance of 335 B.C.E. *EI* 18: 7*–17*.

———. 1988. A Report on the Samaria Papyri. Pp. 17–26 in *Congress Volume: Jerusalem 1986*, ed. J. A. Emerton. VTSup 40. Leiden.

Greenfield, J. C. 1982. Babylonian-Aramaic Relationship. Pp. 471–82 in *XXI Recontre Assyriologique Internationale Berlin July 3–7, 1978*, ed. H.-J. Nissen and J. Renger. Vol. 1, pt. 2. Berlin.

Gropp, D. M. 1986. The Samaria Papyri from the Wâdī ed-Dâliyeh: The Slaves Sales. Ph.D. diss., Harvard.

Lapp, N. W. 1974. The Late Persian Pottery. Pp. 30–32 in *Discoveries in the Wâdī ed-Dâliyeh*.

Lapp, P. W. 1974. An Account of the Discovery. Pp. 1–6 in *Discoveries in the Wâdī ed-Dâliyeh*.

Lapp, P. W. and Lapp, N. W. 1974. The Cave Clearances. Pp. 7–16 in *Discoveries in the Wâdī ed-Dâliyeh*.

Douglas M. Gropp

SAMARITAN PENTATEUCH. The Samaritan Pentateuch (Sam. Pent.) is the Samaritan version of the first five books of the Hebrew Bible, which constitute the entire canon of the Samaritan community. The renewed interest in the Sam. Pent. by biblical scholars has focused on its importance as a source for the history and origins of this community, which still exists at Nablus and at Ḥolon; as a valuable textual witness to an early recension of the Hebrew Bible and to the antiquity of the text preserved in the MT; and as empirical evidence of a documentary hypothesis for the composition of literatures in the ANE.

A. History of Investigation
B. History of the Samaritan Pentateuch
  1. Prehistory of the Sectarian Recension
  2. Origination as a Sectarian Recension
  3. History of the Sectarian Recension
C. Character of the Samaritan Pentateuch
D. Value of the Samaritan Pentateuch

A. History of Investigation

The history of research into the Sam. Pent. can be grouped into five periods: early Jewish and patristic writers; J. Morinus to G. Gesenius; Gesenius to P. Kahle; Kahle to P. Skehan and F. M. Cross; and the present state of the study.

Whereas patristic writers accepted the Sam. Pent. as a viable text, early rabbis did not because it was written not in Aramaic script but in paleo-Hebrew. However, this early period is obscure, and little is known of the use and value of the Sam. Pent. outside the Samaritan community.

It was not until the 17th century that a rediscovery of the Sam. Pent. by European scholars led to a renewed interest in the text and its tradition. In 1616 Pietro della Valle acquired a complete codex of the Sam. Pent. and forwarded it to Europe. In 1631 J. Morinus pronounced the new codex infinitely superior to the MT, and published its text in the Paris Polyglot of 1645. B. Walton corrected that edition in the London Polyglot of 1657, to which Cassellus appended in vol. 6 the famous collation of 6,000 variants between the MT and Sam. Pent., 1,900 of which agreed with LXX.

In the period from Morinus to Gesenius theological bias informed attitudes toward the Sam. Pent. Roman Catholics, wanting to embarrass Protestants, who had recently replaced the authority of the Church with the original Scriptures, preferred the Sam. Pent. and found support in its ancient script. Morinus also observed that the two translations authorized by the Roman Catholic Church, the Vg and LXX, often agreed with the Sam. Pent.

Gesenius' classic study in 1815 of the Sam. Pent.'s origin and age, and of its character and critical value, dominated the field for the next century. He thought the Samaritan sect and its text began when Alexander the Great allowed the Samaritans to build their temple on Mt. Gerizim. Consequently, Samaritan priests introduced sectarian readings into the Jewish text they received. Concerning the agreement between the Sam. Pent. and LXX, Gesenius (1815: 14) drew the conclusion: "The Alexandrian translation and the Sam. Pent. came from Judean codices which were similar to each other." He refers to this common source as "*the Alexandrino-Samaritanus* recension," in contrast to the Judean recension, which obtained authority among the Jews. The Alexandrino-Samaritan recension, he argued, was a vulgar text, received by the Jews in Alexander and by the Samaritans in Palestine, who further simplified and popularized the text by correcting its difficulties and adding glosses and conjectural emendations. The Jews of Jerusalem, by contrast, Gesenius argued, "because of their piety . . . tried to preserve the ancient text unchanged though it was harder to understand, more obscure, and not completely free from defects" (1815: 14). According to him both the history and character of the Sam. Pent. unite in their testimony that it has no critical value. Gesenius was followed with slight modifications by Z. Frankel, S. Kohn, and J. Nutt. While A. Geiger held the same view toward the Sam. Pent. as Gesenius, he introduced much new material, recognized that most variants antedate the Samaritans, and was more critical of the MT. Although Gesenius' work is a masterful tour de force, it is often arbitrary.

In 1915 Kahle inclined scholars to look more favorably

toward the Sam. Pent. with his theory that the Sam. Pent. was very old, the LXX was derived from many old translations and standardized by the Church, and the MT was a late creation from older sources. Therefore, even though Kahle conceded that the Sam. Pent. was a vulgar text, because of its antiquity he asserted it must preserve many more genuine readings than the four allowed by Gesenius. Kahle also judged that the text was much older than the time of the schism. He argued for the early character of the "pre-Samaritan text" based on the agreement of the Sam. Pent. with the book of *Jubilees,* the book of *1 Enoch,* the *Assumption of Moses,* the LXX, and the NT. J. E. H. Thomson, out of a desire to refute the documentary hypothesis, dated the Sam. Pent. to the age of Ahab, and M. Gaster, taking an uncritical attitude toward the Sam. Pent., accepted as genuine even Gesenius's "most desperate" sectarian readings. J. Hempel in 1934 accepted Kahle's reconstructed history of the recensions of the Pentateuch, but after carefully collating, comparing, and weighing texts having Samaritan readings against the MT, he concluded that the MT was a much better text than the Sam. Pent. R. H. Pfeiffer, B. Roberts, F. G. Kenyon (1975) and F. F. Bruce, ignored Gesenius and, following Kahle, stressed its antiquity and implied authority, especially where it agrees with LXX. O. Eissfeldt, A. Weiser, and E. Würthwein, though following Kahle, are more cautious, and B. Roberts (1969; cf. 1951: 188) became more cautious after the discovery of the Qumran literature (QL).

The discovery of the QL enabled scholars to view the Sam. Pent. more clearly in its textual and historical horizons. In 1955 P. Skehan announced that 4QpaleoExod^{m} (Q^{m}) belonged to the Samaritan recension with its paleo-Hebrew script, full orthography, and lengthy repetitions. In 1959 he noted that this recension, which stood behind the Sam. Pent., lacked the "sectarian readings" of the Sam. Pent. from which it derived.

In 1964 R. Hanson dated Q^{m} on paleographic grounds to 225–175 B.C., which antedates the existence of the Qumran community (ca. 150 B.C.–A.D. 68). However, on the same grounds, M. McLean (1982) revised its date from 100 to 25 B.C. J. Sanderson (1986: 308) essentially confirmed Skehan's study but found that "all of the characteristics of that 'sectarian' expansion about Gerizim had their precedent in those shared expansions." Note, however, that Q^{m} itself does not have room for the Sam. Pent.'s inclusion about the altar on Gerizim as part of the Decalogue. She (1986: 189) also found "very little evidence . . . to support the notion of a relationship between the Sam. Pent. and the LXX, whether or not Q^{m} is included," but she did not interact with the evidence presented in Waltke's unpublished dissertation (1965) which suggested such a relationship. Finally, on text critical grounds Sanderson suggested that Q^{m} "represents a somewhat earlier stage in the development of the tradition than Sam. Pent." (189).

Following W. F. Albright (1955: 27–33), from 1956 on F. M. Cross revised Kahle's notion of the development of the Torah text by his theory of three local texts, each developing naturally in isolation from the other. According to this model, the LXX originated in Egypt, proto–Sam. Pent. in Palestine, and proto-MT in Babylon. According to Cross, the Sam. Pent. diverged as a sectarian recension ca. 100 B.C., and proto-MT became the standard text of the rabbis ca. A.D. 100. In 1965 Waltke sought (1) to establish on the basis of Gerleman's earlier study (1948) that the proto–Samaritan text-type reached back at least to the time of the Chronicler; (2) to reestablish on the basis of later research Gesenius' classifications of the Sam. Pent.'s secondary readings; and (3) to suggest on the basis of collating Exodus 1–10 in the Sam. Pent., LXX, and MT that proto-MT influenced proto–Sam. Pent. at a later stage before its adaptation by the Samaritan sectarians.

In 1975 Talmon rejected both limiting the number of text-types to three and, more importantly, the notion of an Urtext from which others diverged. In his view the text was known from the beginning in a variety of forms. In 1978 Albrektson rejected the theory that the rabbis consciously produced a standard text; instead, he argued, the MT emerged as the standard text because it was the text of the Pharisees who supplanted other religious groups. From 1980 on, E. Tov has argued in the direction pioneered by Talmon against both the notions of an Urtext and of grouping QL mss into fixed text-types. Instead, he (1981: 247) argued, they relate to each other "in an intricate web of agreements, differences and exclusive readings," although he does grant that Q^{m} is close to the Sam. Pent. (1982: 22–23). Even though Cross' theory of local texts may have to be modified, QL confirms the internal evidence of the Sam. Pent.'s readings that the text-type of the MT is older than the Sam. Pent.

B. History of the Samaritan Pentateuch

The history of the text can be analyzed as consisting of three phases: its prehistory, its origination as a sectarian recension, and its later history.

1. Prehistory of the Sectarian Recension. The prehistory of the Sam. Pent. can be surmised from the relatively direct evidence of QL and from the indirect evidence of early Jewish literature, NT, LXX, the book of *Jubilees,* and the canonical book of Chronicles. Geiger (1876: 67) recognized that the variant readings of the Sam. Pent. derive from a nonsectarian recension.

a. Sam. Pent. and QL. An important group of relatively early texts unearthed at Qumran is the one characterized by harmonistic expansions and linguistic simplifications like those found in the Sam. Pent. These texts include one in paleo-Hebrew script, 4QpaleoExod^{m} (Sanderson 1986); others in Aramaic square script, 4Q158, 4QTestim (Allegro 1956; Skehan 1957); and unpublished texts, 4QNum^{b} (Cross 1961: 186; 1963 newsletter), 4Q364, and 4QDeut^{n}. Scholars refer to these texts, which themselves show a complex pattern of agreements and disagreements with one another and with known recensions, as proto-Samaritan because it was the type of text which the Samaritan sectarians adapted by slight alterations for their Torah. Sanderson (1986: 308) draws the conclusion that "the Samaritans used a biblical text that is a very natural descendant of texts that other groups also used at that time," including "sectarian" readings. Furthermore, the Sam. Pent. "appears to represent a very close collateral line of the Sam. Pent. textual family and/or a slightly later representative than Q^{m}." By collating the Sam. Pent. with the MT, LXX, and the fragment of 4QTestim containing the extended interpolations from Deut 5:28–29 and 18:18–19 (= Sam. Pent. Exod 20:21b), Waltke (1965: 218–24) found that the Sam. Pent. stood closer in its orthography and linguistic tradition to the MT than 4QTestim. The second fragment containing Num 24:15–17 cannot be identified uniquely with any text-type, and its third fragment, containing Deut 33:8–11, shows definite affinities with the earliest form of the LXX (Skehan 1957: 435). According to K. Matthews (1986: 198–99), although 11QPaleoLev is written in paleo-Hebrew script, it does not fit the pattern of such scrolls in 4Q, for it is not characterized by "Samaritan" readings.

b. Sam. Pent. and NT. Speakers in the NT depended on a text-type similar to the Sam. Pent. in several passages. Stephen's statement that Abraham went to Canaan *after* the death of Terah (Acts 7:4), comports with the chronology in the Sam. Pent. that Terah died at 145 (cf. Gen 11:26; 12:4) and not with the statement in the MT that he died at 205 (Gen 11:32), 60 years after Abraham left. In 7:5 Stephen quotes Deut 2:5b using the word *klēronomia,* whose Hebrew equivalent *yršh* appears only in the Sam. Pent., but not in the MT or LXX. In that same sermon (7:32) Stephen quotes from the Sam. Pent. of Exod 3:6 and not from the LXX or MT. In v 37 he unexpectedly interpolates a passage from Deut 18:15 in a way similar to the Sam. Pent. Finally, the writer of Hebrews (9:3) probably locates with the Sam. Pent. against the MT and LXX the golden altar of incense behind the veil of the holy of holies. These agreements between the NT and the Sam. Pent. are best explained as the use of the proto-Samaritan text-type in some NT literature (Pummer 1976: 441–43).

c. Sam. Pent. and LXX. We already observed that according to Cassellus, the Sam. Pent. agrees with the LXX against the MT in 1,900 readings, and that according to Gesenius this is best explained as a dependence upon an earlier common recension. Waltke's (1965: 226–56) collation of the first ten chaps. of Exodus led him to agree with Gesenius that the Sam. Pent. and the LXX stem from an earlier common tradition, and with Wiener (1911: 217) that the Sam. Pent. is nevertheless more closely related to the MT. He found no contact between the MT and LXX. These conclusions, however, must be reevaluated in the light of Tov's criticisms (1981: 267–71) and Sanderson's findings to the contrary. Sanderson (1986: 189) found that the LXX shows "itself to be much further removed from the other three witnesses than any of them is from each other." However, Cross found the contacts of 4QNum with LXX "striking" (1961: 138–39). If they ultimately stem from an early, yet secondary source, as we suggest, the closer agreement of the Sam. Pent. with the MT than with some earlier mss of QL may be due to the influence of proto-MT on that collateral line of text from which the Sam. Pent. derives. Proto-MT may have been adopted by the Pharisees as early as 175 B.C., allowing time for its influence on the proto-Samaritan text-type before the emergence of the sectarian recension at 100 B.C.

d. Sam. Pent. and the Book of Jubilees. The book of *Jubilees* was dated by R. H. Charles between 135 and 105 B.C.E. (1917: xxix–xxx), but by Zeitlin (1939: 3–8), with Albright's approval (*FSAC,* 346–47), "in the early time of the Second Jewish Commonwealth in the pre-Hellenistic period." According to Charles' statistics (1917: xxxiii–xxxix) it has affinities with the Sam. Pent. and even more striking affinity with the LXX against the MT. In sum, its affinities are similar to those of 4QNum, suggesting once again that the earlier proto-Samaritan text-type had more affinity with the LXX and less with the MT than the Sam. Pent.

e. Sam. Pent. and The Book of Chronicles. The similarities between Chronicles and the LXX, and QL of Samuel in contrast to MT of Samuel put beyond reasonable doubt that the Chronicler did not revise his sources but relied on sources already differing from the MT (cf. Gerleman 1948: 34; Cross 1964: 293). Gerleman (1948: 9) found that the genealogies and lists of names in 1 Chronicles 1–9 "show greater resemblance to the Samaritan Pentateuch than to the Massoretic." Elsewhere he wrote: "It is . . . not only in morphological and syntactical details that the textual tradition of the Chronicler shows affinity with the Samaritan Pentateuch. The resemblance extends also to the actual composition, the arrangement of the material, the form of the narrative" (1948: 21). Finally, he observed that the correspondence pertains to the LXX as well: "We have seen that the texts from which the lists of names in 1 Chronicles 1–9 have been taken show remarkable correspondence not only with Samaritanus, but also with the Septuagint" (28). If Gerleman's analysis is valid, one finds in the light of QL and other Jewish literature strong evidence for positing a very early, though already modernized, recension from which the LXX and proto–Sam. Pent. independently developed.

f. Conclusion. Collateral lines of the text-type known as proto-Samaritan, characterized by widespread glosses, expansions from parallel passages, modernizations, and smoothings spanned the time of the Chronicler to the 1st century of the Christian era. Some lines of this text-type show affinity with the LXX probably because of an earlier common source. Shortly before the creation of the Sam. Pent. as a sectarian recension (ca. 100 B.C.), a collateral line of proto-Samaritan texts was probably influenced by the developing proto-MT.

2. Origination as a Sectarian Recension. In 1968 J. Purvis, following the lead of W. F. Albright (*FSAC,* 346 n. 12), chiefly on grounds of script, orthography, and text-type, demonstrated that the Samaritan text diverged as a sectarian recension in the Hasmonean era (ca. 100 B.C.E.). "A comparison of archetypal forms of the Samaritan letters with the late history of Paleo-Hebrew writing indicates that the Samaritan script began to diverge from Paleo-Hebrew as it was used among the Jews at a comparatively late date (late Hasmonean and early Roman times)" (Purvis *IDBSup,* 774). At this time also internal *matres lectionis* were at their height as attested in the oldest evidence of the Sam. Pent., and its text-type reflects a developed stage of Cross' Palestinian (= proto-Samaritan) recension. Cross, who supervised Purvis' thesis, agrees (1969: 65). Other scholars, such as M. Smith (1971: 182–92), R. J. Coggins (1975), R. Pummer (1976–1977), and F. Dexinger (1981) reached similar conclusions about the origin of the Samaritans. Coggins (1969) and B. Roberts (1969) found Purvis' arguments about script and orthography more convincing than his argument about text-type, whereas J. Macdonald (1970) was more persuaded by the last argument than the first two. In sum, the Sam. Pent. probably originated ca. 100 B.C. However, we need not necessarily conclude with Purvis and others that the Samaritan sect began at this time. Ben-Ḥayyim (1971: 225) justly asks "whether one can really come to . . . the time of the formation of the Samaritan sect according to the orthographic form and the script of its Holy Writ. Can the Jewish version of the Torah with its square script testify as to the time of the crystallization of Judaism? Does the existence of the Dead Sea Scrolls, with the differences in the writing even in the Torah, teach us the opposite of the supposition of the author [Purvis]?"

3. History of the Sectarian Recension. The text of the Sam. Pent. is found in three kinds of sources: manuscripts of the Hebrew text, translations, and Samaritan literature. The manuscripts give direct evidence of the Sam. Pent.'s text but they are medieval. The other sources, although secondhand, indirectly bear witness to the Samaritan text during the first millennium, and, more importantly, interpret obscure passages in the Sam. Pent.

a. Manuscripts. The manuscript purchased by P. della Valle was written in A.D. 1345/46 and is the basis of the polyglots and Blayney (1790). It is Codex B, a reliable ms, in von Gall's critical, eclectic text (1918). His eclectic text, however, is based on questionable canons of criticisms (such as preference for defective orthography), and it contains errors, relies too heavily on the MT, and lacks important sources such as the ʾAbishaʿ Scroll. Hempel (1934: 256) justly urges caution in its use. Von Gall's best ms in Exodus is *E* (A.D. 1219).

Samaritan manuscripts are dated by their cryptograms and/or by scribal techniques as identified by R. Gottheil (1906), E. Robertson (1938), and S. Talmon (1963). By collating manuscripts extending from the 13th to 16th centuries, Waltke (1965: 42–64) documented that the Sam. Pent. is a uniform tradition drifting away from the MT through scribal error. Kahle (1915: 402–3) earlier reached the same conclusion.

The sacrosanct text preserved by the Samaritans as the palladium of their religion is the *Sefer ʾAbishaʿ* scroll. According to its cryptogram, labeled as "a planned deception" by E. Robertson (1962: 235), it was written by "ʾAbishaʿ, son of Phineas, son of Eleazar, son of Aaron . . . in the 13th year after the Israelites ruled the land of Canaan in its borders round about." F. Pérez Castro (1959) distinguished nine hands in its composition and dates the oldest portion to A.D. 1149. This manuscript is the basis for the edition of the Sam. Pent. edited by Ṣadaqa (1961–65); they supplemented it with a manuscript written by Abu al-Barakat, a scribe of the 12th to 13th centuries.

L. F. Giron-Blanc (1976) offered the text of codex Add. 1846 University Library Cambridge (A.D. 1100) and variants from fifteen unpublished manuscripts. Oral readings of the Sam. Pent. by contemporary Samaritans have been made by several, especially Ben-Ḥayyim.

Although Samaritan scribes were not as careful as the Massoretes, they preserved a uniform text. Von Gall (1918: lxviii) questioned whether all the manuscripts go back to one archetype, but Kahle (1915: 402–3), who is famous for his theory that vulgar texts precede a standardized *textus receptus,* on the basis of manuscripts and translations drew the conclusion that "the Samaritan Pentateuch at 200 A.D. could not have read essentially otherwise."

b. Translations. The Samaritans translated their Torah into Greek, Aramaic, and Arabic. These translations, although lacking complete critical editions of their often corrupt texts, prove that the Sam. Pent. survived as a uniform tradition from the earliest period. Their main value, however, is not in restoring the original text of the Sam. Pent. but in interpreting some of its unusual readings.

The Greek translation is known as *Samareitikon* from Origen's reference to it in his Hexapla. Its only extant form is found in the Giessen fragments preserving the text of Deuteronomy 24–29, including the Samaritan sectarian readings in Deut 27:4, 12. Glaue and Rahlfs questionably argued that though the Giessen fragments do not overlap with Origen's *Samareitikon* readings, both share an affinity with the Samaritan Targum, and therefore belong to the same translation. On firmer ground they claimed that though it is independent and more accurate than the LXX, nevertheless the Samaritan translator used the LXX. It contains three readings that agree with MT against the medieval Samaritan manuscripts.

The Samaritan Targums *(Sam. Tg.)* are written, according to G. Dalman, in a dialect of West Aramaic. Its readings, which never gained recognition because of its misunderstanding of the Hebrew language and text, became debased in the hands of scribes ignorant of Aramaic (J. Montgomery 1907: 271). P. della Valle brought the first manuscript of the *Sam. Tg.* to Europe. This text, published in the Paris and London polyglots and by Brüll (1873–76), according to Kahle, is "the worst known ms of the Samaritan Targum" (1959: 53; cf. Kohn 1865: 24–30). A. Tal in his critical three-volume edition juxtaposes ms Or 75623 of the British Museum on the right-hand page and ms 3 of the Shechem Synagogue on the left because these two manuscripts represent two stages of development in the history of Samaritan Aramaic, two different linguistic strata; only in a few cases do they reflect changed exegesis (1980–83: 1.vi). Kahle (1898), followed by L. Goldberg (1935), validated that the various manuscripts represent a number of independent translations from the end of the 1st millennium B.C. to the 11th century A.D. The *Vorlage* of *Sam. Tg.* is the same as that represented by the extant manuscripts of the Sam. Pent. L. Goldberg showed that *Tg. Onkelos* secondarily influenced the *Sam. Tg.,* and Kahle (1959: 191–95) dated this influence to between A.D. 800 and 1000.

Kahle in 1904 contended that the Samaritans in the 10th century first used the Arabic version of the Pentateuch prepared for the Jews by Saʿadia Gaon (ca. A.D. 1000), and shortly thereafter began to adapt this text to the Sam. Pent. About the middle of the 13th century, Abu Saʿid revised the translation(s), producing a text that became the recognized version for the Samaritans. Abu Saʿid's *Vorlage* agreed with various codices and translations. Moreover, it can be demonstrated that he himself does not always adhere faithfully to his *Vorlage* for theological reasons and due to his own negligence and inconsistency. A partial, critical edition of it with extensive notes in Hebrew is given by H. Shehadeh (1977).

c. Quotations of Samaritan Pentateuch in Samaritan Literature. Quotations attesting the Samaritan text at an early period can be found in Samaritan inscriptions, the Samaritan Chronicles, the Samaritan liturgy, Samaritan commentaries, and other religious treaties. For further discussion, see Stenhouse 1989 and Tal 1989. A comparison of these sources with Samaritan manuscripts, the MT, and LXX yield the following conclusions about the text after A.D. 200: (1) the Sam. Pent. was transmitted as a uniform tradition; (2) the earlier text had a much higher percentage of *plene* readings; (3) the earlier text stood closer to the MT but gradually drifted away from it through scribal errors; (4) similar variants are found in all stages of the text; (5) the uniform tradition is not influenced by either the MT or LXX.

C. Character of the Samaritan Pentateuch

Essentially following Gesenius, secondary variant readings of the Sam. Pent. can be classified into eight groups (see secondary variant readings of the Sam. Pent. can be classified into eight groups (see also Waltke 1965).

1. *The Samaritan text has been corrupted by scribal errors.* All traditions have suffered in the hands of scribes. Several errors are peculiar to the Sam. Pent. (a) Confusion of gutturals; e.g., *ʾdwrm* in the Sam. Pent., *hdwrm* in MT (Gen 10:27). In the light of the Sam. Pent.'s prehistory, the widespread confusion of gutturals in the text is not surprising for, as Goshen-Gottstein (1958: 107) says: "the system of four separate laryngeal and pharyngal phones has collapsed in QS [= QL], probably under the impact of Aramaic—direct or indirect." (b) Confusion of labials; e.g., in Gen 31:40, the Sam. Pent. unintelligibly reads *ḥrp* "harvest-time, autumn" for *ḥrb* "scorching heat" (MT; LXX). (c) Confusion of dentals; e.g., in Exod 37:22 the masc. *ʾḥd* modifies the fem. *mqšh,* in the Sam. Pent. instead of *ʾḥt* in MT. (d) Confusion of palatals; e.g., in Gen 14:23 MT reads *śrwk* "thong, sandal" from the root *śrk* "twist," whereas the Sam. Pent. reads *śrwg* whose root is unattested. (e) Confusion of *d* and *r;* e.g., *ś/šmʾbd* in the Sam. Pent., versus *šmʾbr* in MT and *symbor* in LXX (Gen 14:2). (f) Confusion of the letters *ʾalep, he, waw, yod;* e.g., *gaʾoh gaʾa* in MT, but *gwy gʾh* in Sam. Pent. (Exod 15:1).

2. *The Samaritan text preserves a linguistic tradition which differs from the linguistic tradition preserved by the Tiberian grammarians.* It is beyond the scope of this article to write a grammar of Samaritan Hebrew though several observations are in order. Before the discovery of the QL, Gesenius (1815: 26) though the Sam. Pent. reflected "the norms of an unlearned and inaccurate grammar," Kahle thought it represented a relatively older tradition than the MT (1921: 230–39; 1947: 97), and Sperber (1939: 153–247) followed by R. H. Pfeiffer (1941: 103; cf. D. W. Thomas 1951: 240) thought it represented a North Israelite dialect. In the light of the QL, Ben-Ḥayyim (1957–62: 3.vii) drew the conclusion that Samaritan Hebrew "generally represents a later stage of development than that denoted in the Tiberian vocalization. However, this does not mean that no elements older than those of the Tiberian Hebrew, esp. in morphology, are not to be found in it. Preservation of ancient elements in a later stage is a well-known phenomenon in the history of languages."

3. *The Samaritan text has been modernized by replacing archaic Hebrew philology with a later tradition.* Ben-Ḥayyim observed and demonstrated that "on the whole the Samaritan tradition . . . is closer to Mishnaic Hebrew than is the Tiberian [= MT] tradition" (1965: 208). In orthography the Sam. Pent. systematically alters the *he* for final *ō,* a feature of early Hebrew orthography (Cross and Freedman 1952: 69), to the later *waw* (cf. Gen 9:21; 49:11; Exod 22:26). The internal *matres lectionis yod* and *waw* are used more extensively than in the MT, and it even employs *ʾalep* as an internal *mater.* In morphology the earlier short form of the prefix conjugation with *waw*-relative is often replaced in Sam. Pent. with the long form of the prefix conjugation, probably under the influence of Aramaic, which lacks the distinction. Sperber cites many examples of this phenomenon (1939: 187, 193), but he is not always careful to distinguish an inner Sam. Pent. variant from an original variant (cf. *Hipʿil* of 3d weak verbs in Gen 31:42; Num 16:10; 31:50, and of inclusion of its final *he* in Gen. 41:22; Deut 3:1; 10:3). The Sam. Pent. also frequently introduces "pseudo-cohortative" forms, an archaizing practice in late Hebrew writing (Gerleman 1948: 15), whereas the MT rarely has this form (cf. Exod 6:5; Deut 2:13; 3:4; 10:2, 3). The earlier *waw*-relative with the suffix conjugation is sometimes replaced by the Sam. Pent. (Moran 1961: 64–65) with the normal prefix conjugation. The Sam. Pent. systematically replaces the earlier inf. absol. (Moran 1961: 61) found in the MT with finite verb forms, imperatives, and adverbs (A. Kropat 1909: 23; Gerleman 1948: 18; cf. Gen 8:3, 5, 7; Num 15:35; 25:17; Deut 31:26). The inf. constr. after a particle is replaced with a finite tense constr. (cf. Gen 46:30; Num 3:13; 9:15 and Deut 12:30). The rare and early indefinite pronouns are replaced with later and more customary forms (e.g., *zû* in Exod 15:16 with *zh,* and *nḥnw* with *ʾnḥnw* in Gen 42:11; Exod 16:7, 8; Num 32:32). The earlier enclitic *mem* construction (H. Hummel 1957) is replaced with the construct form (cf. Deut 33:11). Even as Chronicles has a tendency to use *Hipʿil* for both *Qal* and *Piʿel* in Samuel-Kings (Kropat 1909: 14), so also the Sam. Pent. sometimes prefers *Hipʿil* (cf. *Hipʿil* for *Qal* in Gen 22:23; Deut 20:8, and for *Piʿel* in Num 33:52). A Geiger (1876: 58) says the Sam. Pent. "treats *he* locale rather roughly." Both the textual evidence and the Jewish ridicule of the Samaritan exegetes indicate Samaritan ignorance of this archaic suffix, well-established already in Ugaritic (cf. Gen 37:24; Exod 10:19). The Samaritan text-type is clearly modernized relative to the MT.

4. *The Sam. Pent. presents an exegetically and linguistically more straightforward text than the MT by removing grammatical difficulties, and replacing rare constructions with more frequently occurring constructions.* The Sam. Pent. has a more consistent orthography than the MT. Talmon (1951: 147) observed: "But whilst the MT might use the same word in the same sentence once in *plene* and once in defective spelling, S is more consistent and harmonizes such instances as, for example in Gen. 1:14, 15, 16; 7:2; 8:20." The Sam. Pent. replaces the asyndetic constructions of the MT with the smoother syndetic constructions (cf. Gerleman 1948: 10–12). The Sam. Pent. corrects discrepancies in syntax by correcting verb or attribute to agree with the customary gender of the noun (cf. Gen 13:6; 49:15, 20), or with the number of the subject (cf. Gen 10:25; 30:42; 46:27; Exod 4:29; Num 9:6), or with other verbs (Exod 39:3; Lev 14:42; 19:27; Num 13:2; 21:32). Lack of syntactical agreement is a feature of early Canaanite (Moran 1950: 60–61). The Sam. Pent. tends, with the Chronicler (Gesenius 1815: 28 and Kropat 1909: 9–10), to discard the collective form in favor of plurals. Talmon (1951: 147–48) noted: "Collective nouns are treated somewhat haphazardly by the Massoretes. The number of verbs and adjectives connected with them is flexible and apparently influenced by the context. S, on the other hand, strives to establish a more consistent treatment and, in most cases, deliberately chooses between given possibilities. Once accepted, a definite number will be used predominantly in connection with the collective noun concerned." The Sam. Pent. replaces passive constructions with active constructions (cf. Gen 10:1; Exod 27:7; Num 3:16; 28:17; Lev 4:35; 6:23; 11:13; 25:34), rare forms with more customary forms (e.g., with inf. constr. of *tertiae infirmae* verbs *ʿswt* is substituted for *ʿsh* in Gen 50:20; with *Pe-waw* verbs *yld* replaces *wld* in Gen 11:30), and rare and lively expressions with customary and prosaic expressions. Geiger (1876: 58) observed: "For him [the scribe of Sam. Pent.] the lively expressions are no longer fitting, and so he chooses the more sober, and seemingly more regular expressions" (cf. Gen 7:2; 17:17; 21:28; Exod 25:20).

5. *The text of the Samaritan tradition has been supplemented and clarified by the insertion of additions and interpolations of glosses from parallel passages.*

Small additions have been added to the text of SP to achieve greater clarity. Clarifying smaller additions include: subjects (cf. Gen 2:24; 21:33; 29:23; Exod 2:16; 15:25); appositives (cf. Gen 26:5; 38:13; 48:7); various nouns (cf. Gen 48:14; Exod 15:22 [Blayney 1790]; Lev 5:24; Num 23:26), various prepositions (cf. Gen 48:5; Exod 2:14; 12:28 [Blayney], 43), the particle *ʾt* (cf. Gen 44:26; Exod 2:9; Lev 4:17; Num 22:41 [Blayney]; Deut 2:2), and various other particles (cf. Gen 2:12, 19; Exod 18:21; 21:8; 29:33).

The Samaritan text has been harmonized and supplemented by parallel passages. An outstanding characteristic of the "Samaritan" tradition, stretching back to at least the time of the Chronicler, is its predilection for duplicates and supplementations of the text with the aid of parallel passages.

Sometimes the Sam. Pent. has harmonized and supplemented one passage by another with little alteration of the text. Concerning this class of variant readings see the detailed discussion in Gesenius (1815: 45). Geiger (1876: 59) notes that the Sam. Pent. also changes the borders in Gen 10:19 exactly as it alters the text of Deut 34:1–3 from Gen 15:18 (cf. Exod 23:31). The latter is the only case where the Sam. Pent. has been reduced.

Other times the Sam. Pent. expanded the text by larger interpolations. In Genesis, Geiger (1876: 59) notes that the Sam. Pent. added to the text of Gen 30:36 from 31:11–13 (that an angel appeared to Jacob in a dream revealing his portion in Laban's herds), and to Gen 42:16 using the text of 44:22 (that Benjamin could not leave his father). "A large harvest of these examples," says Gesenius (1815: 45), "is offered in Exodus where you have interpolations either from the same book or from Deuteronomy"; see 6:9 (cf. 14:12); 7:18 (cf. vv 16–18); 7:29 (cf. vv 26–28); 8:1 (cf. v 1); 8:19 (cf. 16:19); 9:5 (cf. vv 1–5); 9:19; 10:2; 11:3 (cf. 4:22, 23); 18:25 (cf. Deut 1:9–18); 20:17 (cf. Deut 27:2, 5–7); 20:21 (cf. Deut 5:26, 28; 18:18–22; 5:27, 28). In some of these passages the narrative is filled out by the repetition of God's speeches to Moses for Aaron, indicating that they were delivered as commanded, or that the delivery corresponded to God's speech. Additions to the decalogue deserve separate treatment. Similar additions to Numbers, paralleling Deuteronomy 1–3, are also found: Deut 1:6–8 preceding Num 10:11; Deut 1:20–23 preceding Num 13:11; Deut 1:27–33 following Num 13:33; Deut 1:42 preceding Num 14:41; Deut 2:2–6 following Num 20:13*b;* Deut 2:9 following Num 21:11; Deut 2:17–19 following Num 21:12; Deut 2:24–29, 31 following Num 21:20 and included in 21:21–23; Deut 3:21–22 following Num 27:23; Deut 3:24–28 following Num 20:13. Likewise, Deut 2:8 and 10:6–7 are based respectively on Num 20:17–18 and Num 33:31–38*a*.

J. Tigay astutely observes that the hand of a redactor is at work in these interpolations to achieve a smooth text. For example, in the interpolations of Deut 1:9–18 in Samaritan Exod 18:21–27, Tigay (1975: 334–35) notes that the redactor-scribe "preserves the version of Deuteronomy and drops that of Exodus," and changes persons from first to second or to third where necessary "as suits the narrative context of its new home in the Samaritan Exodus." He recognizes the same editorial activity in Samaritan Exod 20:18–26 with its interpolations from Deuteronomy 18 and 5, and in Samaritan Exod 20:17ff. with its additions from Deuteronomy 27.

6. *The Sam. Pent. has been corrected to remove historical difficulties and objectionable passages.* In Gen 50:23 the Sam. Pent. changes the phrase *ʿl brky ywsp,* "upon the knees of Joseph," to *bymy ywsp,* "in the days of Joseph," because it seemed improper that Joseph's grandchildren should be born upon his knees. In Deut 25:11 MT's *mbšyw,* "his private parts," is changed to *bśrw,* "his flesh," because it seemed too obscene to mention that in a fight a woman would grab a man's private parts. In Deut 28:30 *šgl* was deemed too vulgar for public use and so changed to *yškbn* in *Qere* and the Sam. Pent. It is beyond the scope of this article to debate the issue of original text with reference to the well-known differences in pentateuchal recensions concerning the genealogical tables of Genesis 5 and 11:10–26, as well as the addition of "in the land of Canaan" in Exod 12:40. Regarding the former, Cross (1969: 86) notes that recalculated chronologies are one of the special characteristics that are found in texts that "develop over a long span of time in geographical isolation." Regarding the latter it is noteworthy that the LXX reads "in the land of Egypt and in the land of Canaan," whereas the Sam. Pent. reverses them, "in the land of Canaan and in the land of Egypt," a well-known inconsistency with glosses. König (*HDB* extra volume, 70) noted that the MT of Exod 12:40 existed in Ezekiel's times because the 390 plus 40 years in Ezek 4:5–6 is "nothing else than a reflection of the 430 years of the Egyptian bondage of Egypt."

7. *The Samaritan text has been interpreted as well as clarified by small changes.* The Sam. Pent.'s tendentious exegesis, like its other changes, have the one purpose of bringing the text closer to the people. This tendency, which was present among exegetes during the Sam. Pent.'s formative period, found complete expression in the later Midrashic literature. For a detailed discussion of one example of this kind of variant, see Gesenius' observations concerning Gen 22:2, where the MT reads *hmryh* but the Sam. Pent. reads *hmwrʾh* (1815: 30–31).

8. *The Samaritan text has been adapted to Samaritan theology. It is evident, for example, that the Sam. Pent. has been adapted to* *defend the honor of God.* It avoids any suggestion of polytheism; e.g., the plural predicates with *ʾĕlōhîm* in the MT (Gen 20:13; 31:53; 35:7; Exod 22:8) are changed to the singular. It also avoids anthropomorphisms; e.g., "my own people" for "my first-born son" (Exod 4:22), "breath from you" for "breath of your nostrils" (Exod 15:8), and "he forgave" for "he repented" (Deut 32:6). Similarly, the Sam. Pent. transcendentalizes the concept of God; e.g., wherever in the MT God is said to deal directly with man without a mediator, or to descend to earth, the Sam. Pent. substitutes the angel of God (cf. Num 22:20; 23:4, 5, 16).

Secondly, the Sam. Pent. has been adapted to defend the honor of Moses and other great persons of antiquity. In Gen 49:7, in order not to allow a curse to fall upon the most holy men, Levi and Simeon, in place of *ʾrwr ʾpm,* "their anger is cursed," the Sam. Pent. reads *ʾdyr ʾpm,* which, according to *Sam. Tg.* and Abu-Saʿid means, "their anger is beautiful." In Deut 34:10 instead of "there arose not again a prophet like Moses in Israel," the Sam. Pent. reads "there will not arise again. . . ."

Thirdly, the Sam. Pent. preserves legal differences from MT. Geiger (1857: 467; 1866: 527–73) and Heller (1923: 203–8) pointed out many differences between the Samaritan interpretation of the law; occasionally these differences influence the text. For example, whereas any kind of work is prohibited in many biblical passages on holy days and sabbath days, the Bible allows an exception on passover, which disallows work "save that which every man must eat, that only may be done by you" (Exod 12:16). But the parallel passage in Deut 16:8 lacks this exception in the MT. The LXX resolves the problem by inserting the addition from Exod 12:16, and the Sam. Pent. resolves it by changing *kl mlʾkh* "all work" to *kl mlʾkt ʿbdh,* "any kind of servile work."

Lastly, the Samaritan text has been adapted to defend Mt. Gerizim as the cultic center of YHWH. The Samaritan creed is: "My faith is in Thee, Yhwh; and in Moses, son of Amram, thy servant; and in thy Holy Law; and in Mount Gerizim Bethel; and in the Day of Vengeance and Recompense" (Montgomery 1907: 207). Only the point about faith in Mt. Gerizim distinguishes them from other Jewish sects such as the Sadducees and the Qaraites. The last Halaka of the Talmudic tractate, *Masseket Kutim,* reads: "When shall we [Jews] take them [the Samaritans] back? When they renounce Mount Gerizim and confess Jerusalem." This difference explains why they restricted their canon to the Torah, which according to the MT was theologically neutral in this matter, and rejected the Prophets and Writings, both of which celebrate Jerusalem/Zion. By Occam's razor, all other explanations for their limited canon, such as that the Torah had not as yet become canonical by the time of the Samaritan schism, can be rejected as unnecessary.

In part, the Samaritan controversy with the Jews involves the interpretation of text, such as the identification of Salem in Genesis 14, of Moriah in Gen 22:2, and of Luza in Gen 28:19. Sometimes, however, the text has been altered. In Deut 11:30 the Sam. Pent. reads "opposite Shechem" after *mwrʾ*. More significant differences in the text, some of which antedated the Samaritans, favor their theology. Following Exod 20:17, as part of the Decalogue, Sam. Pent. includes a lengthy passage composed from Deut 11:29–30 and 27:2b–3a, 4–7, commanding the Israelites to build an altar on Mt. Gerizim. In Exod 20:24 the Sam. Pent. reads "in *the* place where I *have caused* my name to be remembered," as opposed to the MT, "in *every* place where *I will cause* my name to be remembered." Similarly, Deut 27:2–7 is found after Deut 5:21, also as part of the Ten Commandments, as well as in twenty other passages (Deut 12:5, 11, 14, 18, 21, 26; 14:23–25; 15:20; 16:2, 6–7, 11, 15–16; 17:8, 10; 18:6; 26:2; 31:11). In Lev 26:31 "your sanctuaries" takes the place of "your sanctuary." Finally, in Deut 27:4, whereas the MT prescribes building an altar on Mt. Ebal, the Sam. Pent. dictates Mt. Gerizim. The effect of these differences is that the Sam. Pent.'s Torah prescribes only one sanctuary and altar in the land, Mt. Gerizim, and elevates that law to the status of the Ten Commandments. Pummer (1987: 3), citing Coggins, Kippenberg, and Dexinger, says: "the Samaritans in all probability, like other groups, began to adapt certain passages in the Pentateuch to their particular theology." The Sam. Pent.'s additions to the Decalogue have all the earmarks of interpolated glosses, and their interpretation of the first commandment as part of the introduction is strained. The general character of the Sam. Pent. and MT inspires more confidence in the latter with reference to these theologically biased readings.

D. Value of the Samaritan Pentateuch

The Sam. Pent. is of little value for establishing original readings. Out of eighty-five readings where Sanderson thought she could assign preferable readings involving the MT, LXX, Sam. Pent., and Q^m, she found no variants where the Sam. Pent. uniquely or even with LXX preserves the preferable reading (1986: 85, 88). She found two preferable readings where the Sam. Pent. agreed with Q^m, "both representing small errors on the part of MT" (1986: 58), and four preferable readings where the Sam. Pent., LXX, and Q^m agreed, revealing errors or lapses on the part of MT (1986: 75). The chief textual value of the Sam. Pent. is its indirect witness that MT is "a superb, disciplined text" (Cross 1964: 271).

The Sam. Pent. is of greater interest for literary criticism. First, as Tigay (1975) noted, the supplemented proto-Samaritan texts and Sam. Pent. give indirect empirical evidence for the documentary hypothesis. More accurately, it validates a documentary hypothesis. The phenomenon of sewing formerly independent documents into a new, unified whole can be observed from the Gilgamesh Epic through Tatian's *Diatasseron.* Before his very eyes the critic can observe the redactor at work splicing texts together. The resulting work is not a "crazy patchwork" of sources, as once thought, but a unified whole. Second, and this has not been previously noted, the modernized Sam. Pent. along with early Jewish sources suggests that the Pentateuch was begun to be modernized before the time of the Chronicler, entailing that the archaic text-type of the Pentateuch preserved in MT must be much older.

The Sam. Pent. is also of interest for canonical criticism, because alongside QL it bears witness to texts being adapted to meet the needs of the living community. We are not suggesting, however, that sectarian differences merely represent varying ideologies of equal worth.

Rather, we suggest, one should guard against absolutizing confessions and relativizing truth.

The Sam. Pent. has intrinsic value for the study of religion in general and for the understanding of the Hebrew Bible and its interpretation in early pre-rabbinic Judaism in particular. Its preservation as a uniform tradition makes it especially valuable in this respect.

Finally, as noted by Pummer (1987), the Sam. Pent. assisted the Samaritans in preserving themselves as a unified community for over two millennia. In this respect it is of indirect value and interest to sociologists and anthropologists. For further discussion of these issues, see SAMARITANS.

Bibliography

Albrektson, B. 1978. Reflections on the Emergence of a Standard Text of the Hebrew Bible. VTSup 29: 49–65.

Albright, W. F. 1955. New Light on Early Recension of the Hebrew Bible. *BASOR* 140: 27–33.

Allegro, J. M. 1956. Further Messianic References. *JBL* 75: 182–87.

Ben-Hayyim, Z. 1957–62. *The Literary and Oral Tradition of Hebrew and Aramaic among the Samaritans,* 3 vols. Jerusalem (in Hebrew).

———. 1958. Traditions in the Hebrew language with Special Reference to the Dead Sea Scrolls. Pp. 200–14 in *Aspects of the Dead Sea Scrolls,* ed. C. Rabin and Y. Yadin. Vol. 4 of *ScrHier.* Jerusalem.

———. 1971. Review of *Purvis 1968. Bib.* 52: 253–55.

Blayney, B. 1790. *Pentateuchus Hebraeo-Samaritanus charactere Hebraeo-Chaldico.* Oxford.

Bruce, F. F. 1953. *The Books and the Parchments.* Westwood, NJ.

Brüll, A. 1873–76. *Das samaritanische Targum zum Pentateuch.* Frankfurt. Repr. 1971.

Charles, R. H. 1917. *The Book of Jubilees.* New York.

Coggins, R. J. 1969. Review of *Purvis 1968. JSS* 14: 273–75.

———. 1975. *Samaritans and Jews: the Origins of Samaritanism Reconsidered.* Atlanta.

Cohen, M. 1976. The Orthography of the Samaritan Pentateuch. *Beth Mikra* 64: 54–70; 66: 361–91 (in Hebrew).

Cross, F. M., Jr. 1961. *The Ancient Library of Qumran and Modern Biblical Studies.* Rev. ed. Garden City, NY.

———. 1963. Newsletter of Hebrew Union College—Jewish Institute of Religion, and Biblical and Archaeological School. Jerusalem.

———. 1964. The History of the Biblical Text in the Light of Discoveries in the Judean Desert. *HTR* 57: 281–99.

———. 1966. The Contribution of the Qumran Discoveries to the Study of the Biblical Text. *IEJ* 16: 81–95.

———. 1969. Papyri of the Fourth Century B.C. from Daliyeh. Pp. 41–79 in *New Directions in Biblical Archaeology,* ed. D. N. Freedman and J. C. Greenfield. Garden City.

Cross, F. M., and Freedman, D. N. 1952. *Early Hebrew Orthography.* AOS 36. New Haven.

Crown, A. D. 1975–76. The Abisha Scroll of the Samaritans. *BJRL* 58: 36–65.

Dalman, G. 1960. *Grammatik des jüdisch-palästinischen Aramäisch.* Darmstadt.

Dexinger, F. 1977. Das Garizimgebot im Dekalog der Samaritaner. Pp. 111–33 in *Studien zum Pentateuch,* ed. G. Braulik. Vienna.

———. 1981. Limits of Tolerance in Judaism: the Samaritan Example. Vol. 2, pp. 88–114 in *Jewish and Christian Self-Definition,* ed. E. P. Sanders. Philadelphia.

Eissfeldt, O. 1934. *Einleitung in das Alte Testament.* Tübingen.

Frankel, Z. 1841. *Vorstudien zur den Septuaginta.* Leipzig.

———. 1851. *Über den Einfluss der palästinischen Exegese auf die alexandrinische Hermeneutik.* Leipzig.

Gall, A. F. von. 1914–18. *Der hebräische Pentateuch der Samaritaner,* 5 vols. Giessen. Repr. 1966.

Gaster, M. 1925. *The Samaritans: Their History, Doctrines and Literature.* London.

Geiger, A. 1857. *Urschrift und Übersetzungen der Bibel.* Breslau.

———. 1866. Über died gesetzlichen Differenzen zwischen Samaritanern und Juden. *ZDMG* 20: 527–73.

———. 1876. Einleitung in die biblischen Schriften. *Nachgelassene Schriften* 4: 54–67, 121–32.

Gerleman, G. 1948. Synoptic Studies in the Old Testament. *LUÅ* 44: 3–35.

Gesenius, G. 1815. *De pentateuchi samaritani origine, indole et auctoritate commentatio philologico-critica.* Halle.

Giron-Blanc, L. F. 1976. *Pentateuco hebreo-samaritano, Genesis.* Madrid.

Glaue, P., and Rahlfs, A. 1911. Fragmente einer grieschischen Übersetzung des samaritanischen Pentateuchs. Vol. 1, pt. 2, pp. 29–68 in *Mitteilungen des Septuaginta-Unternehmens.* Berlin.

Goldberg, L. 1935. *Das samaritanische Pentateuchtargum: Eine Untersuchung seiner handschriftlichen Quellen.* Bonner Orientalische Studien 11. Stuttgart.

Goshen-Gottstein, M. H. 1958. Linguistic Structure and Tradition in the Qumran Documents. Pp. 101–37 in *Aspects of the Dead Sea Scrolls,* ed. C. Rabin and Y. Yadin. Vol. 4 of *ScrHier.* Jerusalem.

Gottheil, R. 1906. The Dating of Their Manuscripts by Samaritans. *JBL* 25: 29–48.

Hanson, R. 1964. Paleo-Hebrew Scripts in the Hasmonean Age. *BASOR* 175: 26–42.

Heller, C. 1923. *The Samaritan Pentateuch.* Berlin.

Hempel, J. 1934. Innermasoretische Bestätigungen des Samaritanus. *ZAW* 12: 254–74.

Hummel, H. D. 1957. Enclitic *Mem* in Early Northwest Semitic, Especially Hebrew. *JBL* 76: 87–107.

Kahle, P. 1898. *Textkritische und lexikalische Bemerkungen zum samaritanischen Pentateuchtargum.* Leipzig.

———. 1904. *Die arabischen Bibelübersetzungen: Texte mit Glossar und Literaturübersicht.* Leipzig.

———. 1915. Untersuchungen zur Geschichte des Pentateuchtextes. *TSK* 88: 399–439.

———. 1921. Die überlieferte Aussprache des Hebräischen und die Punktation der Masoreten. *ZAW* 39: 230–39.

———. 1947. *Cairo Geniza.* London.

———. 1959. *Cairo Geniza.* Rev. ed. Oxford.

Kennicott, B. 1776–80. *Vetus Testamentum Hebraicum cum variis lectionibus.* Oxford.

Kenyon, F. G. 1958. *Our Bible and the Ancient Manuscripts.* Revised by A. W. Adams. New York.

———. 1975. *The Text of the Greek Bible.* 3d ed. rev. and augmented by A. W. Adams. London.

Kippenberg, H. G. 1971. *Garizim und Synagog.* Berlin.

Kohn, S. 1865. *De Pentateucho Samaritano eiusque cum versionibus antiquis nexu.* Leipzig.

Kropat, A. 1909. *Die Syntax des Autors der Chronik verglichen.* BZAW 16. Giessen.

Macdonald, J. 1970. Review of *Purvis 1968. JSS* 21: 69–72.

Matthews, K. 1986. The Leviticus Scroll (11QpaleoLev). *CBQ* 48: 171–207.
McLean, M. D. 1982. *The Use and Development of Palaeo-Hebrew in the Hellenistic and Roman Periods.* Ph.D. Diss. Harvard University.
Montgomery, J. A. 1907. *The Samaritans, the Earliest Jewish Sect: Their History, Theology and Literature.* Philadelphia. Repr. 1968.
Moran, W. L. 1950. *A Syntactical Study of the Dialect of Byblos as Reflected in the Armana Tablets.* Ph.D. Diss. Johns Hopkins.
———. 1961. The Hebrew Language in its Northwest Semitic Background. Pp. 54–72 in *BANE.*
Morinus, J. 1631. *Exercitationes ecclesiasticae in utrumque Samaritanorum Pentateuchum.* Paris.
Nutt, J. W. 1874. *Fragments of a Samaritan Targum.* London.
Pérez Castro, F. 1959. *Sefer Abisha.* Madrid.
Pfeiffer, R. H. 1941. *Introduction to the Old Testament.* New York.
Pummer, R. 1976–77. The Present State of Samaritan Studies. *JJS* 21: 36–61; 22: 24–47.
———. 1976. The Samaritan Pentateuch and the Old Testament. *NTS* 22: 441–43.
———. 1987. *The Samaritans.* Leiden.
Purvis, J. D. 1968. *The Samaritan Pentateuch and the Origin of the Samaritan Sect.* HSM 2. Cambridge, MA.
Roberts, B. J. 1951. *The Old Testament Texts and Versions.* Cardiff.
———. 1969. Review of Purvis 1968. *JTS* 20: 569–71.
Robertson, E. 1938. *Catalogue of the Samaritan Manuscripts in the John Rylands Library.* Vol. 1. Manchester.
———. 1962. Review of Castro 1959. *VT* 12: 228–35.
Ṣadaqa, A., and R. 1961–65. *Jewish Version Samaritan Version of the Pentateuch.* Tel Aviv (in Hebrew).
Sanderson, J. E. 1986. *An Exodus Scroll from Qumran: 4QpaleoExod and the Samaritan Tradition.* HSS 30. Atlanta.
Shehadeh, H. 1977. *The Arabic Translation of the Samaritan Pentateuch, Prolegomena to a Critical Edition.* Jerusalem.
Skehan, P. W. 1955. Exodus in the Samaritan Recension from Qumran. *JBL* 74: 182–87.
———. 1957. The Period of the Biblical Texts from Khirbet Qumran. *CBQ* 19: 435–40.
———. 1959. Qumran and the Present State of Old Testament Text Studies: The Massoretic Text. *JBL* 78: 21–25.
Smith, M. 1971. *Palestinian Parties and Politics that Shaped the Old Testament.* New York.
Sperber, A. 1939. Hebrew Based Upon Biblical Passages in Parallel Transmission. *HUCA* 14: 153–247.
Stenhouse, P. 1989. Samaritan Chronicles. Pp. 218–265 in *The Samaritans,* ed. A. D. Crown. Tübingen.
Tal, A. 1980–83. *The Samaritan Targum of the Pentateuch.* 3 vols. Tel Aviv.
———. 1989. Samaritan Literature. Pp. 413–67 in *The Samaritans,* ed. A. D. Crown. Tübingen.
Talmon, S. 1951. The Samaritan Pentateuch. *JJS* 2: 144–50.
———. 1961. Synonymous Readings in the Old Testament. Pp. 335–83 in *Studies in the Bible,* ed. C. Rabin. Vol. 8 of *ScrHier.* Jerusalem.
———. 1963. Some Unrecorded Fragments of the Hebrew Pentateuch in the Samaritan Version *Textus* 3: 60–73.
———. 1964. Aspects of the Textual Transmission of the Bible in the Light of Qumran Manuscripts. *Textus* 4: 95–132.
———. 1975. The Textual Study of the Bible—a New Outlook. Pp. 321–400 in *Qumran and the History of the Biblical Text,* ed. F. M. Cross and S. Talmon. Cambridge, MA.
Thomas, D. W. 1951. The Textual Tradition of the Old Testament. Pp. 238–63 of *The Old Testament and Modern Study,* ed. H. H. Rowley. London.
Thomsen, J. E. H. 1919. *The Samaritans: Their Testimony to the Religion of Israel.* London.
Tigay, J. H. 1975. An Empirical Basis for the Documentary Hypothesis. *JBL* 75: 327–42.
Tov, E. 1980. Determining the Relationship between the Qumran Scrolls and the LXX: Some Methodological Issues. Pp. 45–76 in *The Hebrew and Greek Texts of Samuel,* ed. E. Tov. Jerusalem.
———. 1981. *The Text-Critical Use of the Septuagint in Biblical Research.* Jerusalem.
———. 1982. A Modern Textual Outlook Based on the Qumran Scrolls. *HUCA* 53: 11–27.
Ulrich, E. 1984. Horizons of Old Testament Textual Research at the Thirtieth Anniversary of Qumran Cave 4. *CBQ* 46: 613–36.
Waltke, B. K. 1965. *Prolegomena to the Samaritan Pentateuch.* Ph.D. Diss. Harvard University.
———. 1970. The Samaritan Pentateuch and the Text of the Old Testament. Pp. 212–39 in *New Perspectives on the Old Testament,* ed. J. B. Payne. Waco, TX.
Walton, B., ed. 1657. *Biblie Polyglotta.* 6 vols. London.
Weiser, A. 1961. *The Old Testament: Its Formation and Development.* Trans. D. M. Barton. New York.
Wiener, H. M. 1911. Samaritan Septuagint Massoretic Text. *Expositor* 8th ser. 2: 211.
Würthwein, E. 1979. *The Text of the Old Testament.* Trans. E. F. Rhodes. Grand Rapids.
Zeitlin, S. 1939. *The Book of Jubilees.* Philadelphia.

BRUCE K. WALTKE

SAMARITANS [Heb *haššōmĕrōnîm*]. The people who dwelt in Samaria, particularly in the tribal regions of Manasseh and Ephraim, and who have maintained a unique identity to the present. Subsequently the form of Israelite religion that developed in the area centered around Mt. Gerizim.

A. Introduction
  1. Problems
  2. Name
B. Origins
  1. Samaritan Version
  2. Old Testament Version
C. History
  1. Persian Period
  2. Hellenistic Period
  3. Roman Period
  4. Byzantine Period
  5. Middle Ages
  6. Modern Period
D. Literature
  1. Pentateuch
  2. Targum
  3. Memar Marqah
  4. Liturgical Works
  5. Asatir
  6. Joshua
  7. Chronicles
  8. Chronicle II

E. Beliefs and Practices
   1. Monotheism
   2. Torah
   3. Moses
   4. Mt. Gerizim
   5. Day of Vengeance and Recompense
   6. Festivals

A. Introduction

1. Problems. The Samaritans are not easily brought into sharp focus. Sources are often contradictory, sketchy, or nonexistent. It is problematic how distinct the Samaritans are from the Jews of different periods, what constitutes the basic distinguishing focus, or how much interaction existed between the Samaritans and other sects based on the Mosaic Pentateuch. The geographic origin of the people called Samaritans has been seen in Mesopotamia and both N and S Palestine, raising the question whether their basic characterization is geographical, ethnic, or doctrinal.

2. Name. As a cultural designation of a particular people the term Samaritan *(haššōmĕrōnîm)* appears biblically only in 2 Kgs 17:29 where it is associated with idolators. The Samaritan Chronicle seems to accept usage of that term as a designation of the inhabitants of the city of Samaria. The Samaritans derive their name not from this geographical designation, but rather from the term *šāmĕrîm,* "keeper [of the law]" (Coggins 1975: 10–12).

B. Origins

1. Samaritan Version. The Samaritans have insisted that they are direct descendants of the N Israelite tribes of Ephraim and Manasseh, who survived the destruction of the N kingdom of Israel by the Assyrians in 722 B.C.E. The inscription of Sargon II records the deportation of a relatively small proportion of the Israelites (27,290, according to the annals [ANET, 284–85]), so it is quite possible that a sizable population remained that could identify themselves as Israelites, the term that the Samaritans prefer for themselves.

Samaritan theology of history would place the basic schism at the time Eli moved the sanctuary from Shechem to Shiloh, establishing both an illegitimate priesthood and place of worship. From the time of Moses until that move was the Era of Divine Favor. With that move began the Era of Disfavor, which would exist until the coming of the Taheb or savior (Macdonald 1964: 15–21).

2. Old Testament Version. Jewish accounts, characterized by 2 Kings 17 and Josephus (*Ant* 9.277–91) claim that the Samaritans are descendants of colonists brought into the region of Samaria by the Assyrians from other lands they had conquered, including Cuthah, and thus the Jewish designation of Samaritans as Cutheans (*Ant* 9.290). The Jews have argued that the veneer of Israelite religion displayed by the Samaritans is the result of instruction by an Israelite priest repatriated from Assyria after the colonists had been attacked by lions sent by God (2 Kgs 17:25–26).

C. History

1. Persian Period. Ezra 4, the earliest source of information on relations between Jews and Samaritans during this period, reports opposition by the Samaritans to both the building of the temple (4:4–5, 24) and the building of the walls (4:17–23) of Jerusalem. Since Haggai and Zechariah are silent on any Samaritan obstruction to the temple and Ezra 4:7–23 seems to be an intrusion reflecting the troubles during Nehemiah's time, it is likely that the city wall was the real issue and the earliest breach between the two communities was expressed in political rather than religious terms. The Tobiads of Transjordan, who also claimed descent from Israelite tribes, had close ties with the Samaritans during this period (Spiro 1951) and likely joined them in their opposition to the building of the city walls. The identity of the opposition is not obvious and various identifications have been made (Coggins 1975: 65–68).

The 5th century B.C.E. Elephantine papyri include letters requesting help to build a temple from both the Samaritan and Jewish priests (*CAP,* 30), implying an already existing schism. Indeed the Samaritan Chronicle of Abu'l Fath claims that Zerubbabel and Sanballat, subsequent leaders of the Jewish and Samaritan communities, were already feuding about the appropriate location of the restored temple while still in Babylon (Stenhouse 1985: 89–95). The Persian king, "Surdi," likely Darius spelled backward, ruled in favor of Sanballat and sent him home to Mt. Gerizim with funds to construct the altar and by implication the temple.

Josephus agrees that Sanballat, whom he calls a "Cuthean," was appointed as a political leader by Darius and subsequently promised a temple to his son-in-law, Manasseh, son of a Jewish high priest who had murdered his brother and married a Samaritan woman. In Josephus' account, Manasseh renounces Darius and transfers his loyalty to Alexander the Great, who supports the building of the Samaritan temple.

The accounts pose several serious questions. The first is chronological: how to account for Sanballat's apparent longevity if he ruled from the time of Darius to that of Alexander the Great? A second question is the issue of the Samaritan temple. Was there such a structure and, if so, when was it built? Lastly, what was the origin of the Samaritan priesthood?

There are basically three possible explanations for Sanballat's apparent long tenure. Some argue that Josephus incorrectly brought the event down to the period of Alexander (Montgomery 1907: 68), while some say that the Alexandrian dating is correct and Josephus was incorrect in associating Sanballat with the temple (see list in Purvis 1968: 11). A compromise allows that on the basis of papponymy there could have been two different Sanballat's involved (Wright 1965: 170ff.).

Some scholars believe that the Samaritan temple was built in 388 B.C.E., during the Persian period (Spiro 1951: 312). The basis is the 260 years that constitute the Samaritan "Era of Favor," supposedly the time from the entry into Canaan until the days of Eli when the sanctuary disappeared on account of the sin of Eli (MacDonald 1969: 115–18). It is assumed that the Samaritans projected their own experienced era of favor, the life-span of their temple, onto the ancient story. We know their sanctuary was destroyed in 128 B.C.E. (Josephus *Ant* 13.254–56); 260 years earlier would be 388.

Most scholars accept Josephus' implicit Hellenistic date late in the 4th century, mainly on the basis of Josephus alone. The archaeological evidence is minimal. There was a resettlement of Shechem at that time (Wright 1965: 167ff.). Robert Bull had some expectation that Building B at Ras el Tin would prove to be the Samaritan temple (Bull 1967: 393), but in the light of Magin's more recent excavations reported by R. Pummer (1989: 169–74) that hope now seems unlikely and the remains of the temple still elude us. Perhaps there never was a temple on the scale implied by Josephus, but rather a more modest tabernacle. In the postexilic period, Samaritans probably had neither the political nor financial need for a temple.

The turmoil that led to the resettlement of Shechem may also account for the nucleus of the Samaritan priesthood, if not the Samaritan people themselves. Fossum speculates that as the N shrine at Bethel was desolated, priests may have migrated from that site to Shechem and the designation of Mt. Gerizim as Bethel may be a vestige of that move (Fossum 1985: 41).

The chronicles of Abu'l Fath concur that relations between Samaritans and Jews worsened throughout the Persian period (Stenhouse 1985: 81), and this emerging schism benefited the Persians by diminishing the likelihood of any broadly based Palestinian rebellion.

2. Hellenistic Period. The arrival of Alexander the Great polarized the political loyalties of Samaritans and Jews, at least temporarily, because the Samaritans initially gave support to Alexander by contributing 8,000 Samaritan troops to his Egyptian campaign. While Alexander was in Egypt, the Samaritans revolted and killed their newly appointed governor, Andromachus. In retaliation, Alexander destroyed the city of Samaria and established a garrison of 600 troops there. Many of the Samaritans fled to ancient Shechem at the base of the mountain, and this became their chief religious center. The city they rebuilt at Shechem in 331 B.C.E. survived for more than 200 years, until it was destroyed by the Jewish king John Hyrcanus in 107 B.C.E. (Wright 1965: 172).

By contrast, the Jews remained loyal to Persia and did not support the Greeks. In time, the Samaritans, sobered by Alexander's destruction of Samaria and subsequent conflicts between Ptolemies and Seleucids, shared Jewish wariness of the Greeks. However, the issue of Jerusalem versus Mt. Gerizim became a major factor separating Samaritans from Jews.

The latter site may or may not have included a temple. The rather limited documentary and archaeological evidence is ambiguous. The primary source is Josephus, whose stories related to the Samaritan temple suspiciously duplicate his own and other familiar stories of temple building (Anderson 1989). Samaritan sources seldom mention a temple or provide specific information about one. Archaeological remains are at best suggestive (see above); no local tradition corroborates it, and the Samaritan chronicles are vague (Montgomery 1907: 36). Their focus was the place rather than the structure, and the structure was likely quite modest.

Descriptions of Samaritan response to the reign of the Seleucid tyrant Antiochus IV (175–164 B.C.E.) are varied. 2 Macc 6:2 implies that the Samaritans unwillingly renamed their sanctuary Zeus Xenios. But Josephus claims they quite willingly renamed it Zeus Hellenios (*Ant* 12.257–64). The more resistant Jews were unhappy with the Samaritan position, as is evident in Jewish polemics of the time: Sir 50:26 and portions of the LXX version of Joshua.

John Hyrcanus, Jewish governor and high priest, focused and expressed the deepest Jewish bitterness toward the Samaritans, and inspired by such anti-Samaritan stories as Genesis 34 (recalled in *Jubilees* 30; Judith 9; and *Testament of Levi* 5–7), destroyed the Samaritan sanctuary in 128 B.C.E. Shechem was also destroyed, and during the next decade most Samaritans drifted back to Samaria, leaving behind only a residual community at the foot of Gerizim.

3. Roman Period. In NT times Samaritans struggled with their own schisms and shared practices and beliefs with a variety of Jewish groups. Simon Magus (Acts 8:9ff.) was the leader of an unorthodox, possibly gnostic-influenced Samaritan group that continued to play a role in Samaritan history, and was particularly visible in the 4th century (with the movement of Dusis) and 14th century C.E. (through the writings of the Samaritan chronicler Abu'l Fath). The Dositheans, whom some of the Church Fathers associated with Simon Magus, were more likely an alternate contemporary sect, perhaps in part derived from the Sadducees. For further discussion, see Fossum 1985: 45–55; 1989.

The Qumran community evidences some beliefs and practices shared with the Samaritans. Both sects were exclusive and used the imagery, "sons of light," to affirm their special chosen status. Both were critical of the Jerusalem Temple, though for quite different reasons, and they shared a unique emphasis on Deut 18:18 in their messianic expectations. Each group had a Nazarite movement and a purification ritual using the ashes of a red heifer. Each used a complex calendar combining both solar and lunar designations, perhaps going back to Zadokite reckoning, although the Samaritan calendar was influenced by later Byzantine and Islamic calendars as well. Neither group celebrated Purim or Hanukkah. Some Qumran texts, particularly 4QEx$^{\alpha}$ (Skehan 1955: 182–87; currently designated as 4QpaleoExod^{m}, see Sanderson 1986: 11), preserve a "Samaritan" text type leading some to conclude that these two groups had unique ties. However, most critics assume that these texts demonstrate the fluidity of texts at this period and not necessarily any special affinity between these two sects.

According to Acts 8, Samaria was one of the first missionary fields for the disciples, and there has been considerable discussion of the role of the Samaritans in the formulation and orientation of parts of the NT. The most concentrated debates focus on the gospel of John (Bowman 1958 and Purvis 1975), Stephen's speech in Acts (Spiro 1967 and Lowy 1977), and the Epistles to the Hebrews. Bowman contends that John consciously addresses a Samaritan audience. Attention to the Samaritan woman in chap. 4, reference to "other sheep" in 10:16, and the use of Samaritan imagery such as "light" and "word" is cited as evidence. Spiro argues that the speech in Acts 7:22ff. reveals Stephen's Samaritan origin since he, like the Samaritans, challenges the Jerusalem Temple and priesthood, refers to the key Samaritan biblical verse, Deut 18:18, and when he quotes from the OT cites a recension akin to the Samaritan text. Lowy, however, argues that there was sufficient variety of text among all groups to account for such idiosyncratic readings.

Less convincing is the thesis that the Epistle to the Hebrews was addressed to Samaritan Christians. "Hebrews" would have been a tactful term with which to address the Samaritans (the title they preferred for themselves, see Josephus *Ant* 11.344), and the focus on the tabernacle rather than the Jerusalem Temple, the list of the faithful in Heb 11:32–40 (all of whom would be acceptable to Samaritans), and the strong argument for the superiority of Jesus over Moses are all relevant issues.

Whether or not they were recipients of NT writings, the Samaritans were often part of the NT story. Usually they were objects of scorn rather than serious obstacles to the NT mission, much the same role they had played in the time of Ezra and Nehemiah. John 4:9 simply states that the Jews had no dealings with the Samaritans. Jesus himself instructed the Twelve not to enter any town of the Samaritans, but rather to go only to the lost sheep of the house of Israel (Matt 10:5–6; cf. John 4). On other occasions, Jesus used that very antipathy to shame his hearers in the stories of the Good Samaritan (Luke 10:29–37) and the Ten Lepers (Luke 17:11–19).

In the next few centuries the gospels were influential in shaping Samaritan thinking: sometimes in opposition, as in the strong Samaritan affirmation of monotheism in response to the developing Christian Trinity; other times expanding upon the Christian conceptualizations of Moses.

Samaritan fortunes initially improved under Roman rule. Pompey (63 B.C.E.) ended the Jewish persecution of Samaritans, and Herod the Great 37–4 B.C.E. carried out an extensive building program in Samaria. Samaritans were emboldened to harass Jews, notably during the period from 6–9 C.E., when they created disturbances at the Jewish Passover, and in 52 when they slaughtered Jewish pilgrims at En-gannim in the border town of Galilee. These actions earned a series of reprisals from both Jews and Romans. As a result of one such action, the Samaritans were successful in having Pontius Pilate deposed, but generally they paid dearly. Samaritans fleeing Roman oppression under Vespasian gathered by the thousands at Mt. Gerizim and held the Romans at bay for a month before their water ran out and more than 10,000 men were slaughtered.

Hadrian, the Roman emperor from 117 to 138 C.E. usurped the Samaritan holy place and constructed a large temple to Zeus Hypsisto (Bull 1967; 1968). Features of that temple are preserved on coins dating to between 138 and 253 C.E. (Bull 1968: 58–60). The metal doors he used in his new temple purportedly were taken from the ruined Jerusalem Temple. Centuries later they were to adorn two Samaritan synagogues before being taken off by the Ottoman Turks.

Early in the Christian era, waning Roman control facilitated a flowering of Samaritan theology and hymnody represented in the work of Marqah, Baba, and the hymn writer Amram Darrah. Generally scholars have followed Montgomery (1907: 294) in placing these figures in the 4th century; however Crown (1986: 104) and Stenhouse (1988: 246–53) argue effectively for a 3d century date. Marqah's son, Nana, and Amram Darrah contributed richly to the growing liturgical tradition. The Samaritans had been strongly influenced by Judaism and continued to be, but as Christianity grew in strength and influence, it, too, played a role in the growing heterodoxy of Samaritan thought.

The Samaritan recension of the Pentateuch was widely available: there is evidence that the scribes of Codex Alexandrinus made some use of a copy; Origen, Eusebius of Caesarea, Epiphanius and Cyril of Jerusalem among other Church Fathers referred to it; Jerome used it in his translation of the Vulgate; and the Talmud reflects awareness of it, if only in a generally critical sense.

Synagogues were built in the vicinity of Nablus and in such remote places as Rome, Thessalonica and possibly Delos, and under the leadership of Baba the apparently Dosithean influenced laity party gained in power over against the priests, perhaps as a compromise to strengthen the Samaritan community in the face of adversity. Marble remnants of Samaritan synagogues preserved with the few surviving Samaritan inscriptions (for example at Imwas), suggest reasonable prosperity within the community.

4. Byzantine Period. Under Byzantine domination the Samaritans experienced three centuries of severe repression. The primary community remained anchored to Nablus, the town at the foot of Mt. Gerizim, throughout the Byzantine period, despite an uninterrupted Diaspora responding to the frequent military operations in Palestine. The almost continuous presence of a place of worship at Gerizim until 484 C.E. offered a primary focus for the community through the upheavals and it is estimated that half a million Samaritans remained in Palestine. When they did leave Palestine, they tended to convert to Christianity and become assimilated into the local culture. Nevertheless, there was a Samaritan Diaspora estimated at 150,000 that maintained its religious identification with communities in such key centers as Cairo, Rome, Constantinople, and Thessalonica (remains of Samaritan synagogues have been found in the latter two cities).

They became targets of Byzantine wrath on two major counts: their theology, which the Christian Byzantines felt was influenced by gnosticism, and their claim to such holy places as Jacob's well and Joseph's tomb. Unlike the Romans, the Byzantines more frequently distinguished between Jew and Samaritan and treated the latter much more harshly. When the Samaritans rebelled against repressive legislation, particularly in 526 and 529, they were decimated by Byzantine forces.

5. Middle Ages. The increased political turmoil encouraged migration to other Middle Eastern centers. Communities developed at Aleppo, Tyre, Caesarea, Ascalon, Gaza, Damascus and Cairo. In 636, all of these cities came under Muslim rule. The Samaritans were not badly treated and assimilated the Arabic language and Muslim ideas. The Pentateuch probably was translated into Arabic in the 11th century, with its classic formulation attributed to Abu'l Said in the 13th century. By the time of the advent of Islam, the Samaritans were too diminished to significantly influence the Muslims, although some motifs, like depictions of the day of judgment that appear in the *Memar Markah,* have notable parallels in the Quran. The Samaritans were affected very explicitly by Islam: *Elah,* a close parallel to *Allah,* became a preferred term for God; they began using part of the Muslim creed, "There is no God, but God"; and they introduced prayers and other statements with the Muslim form, "In the name of God."

In 1099 the Crusaders arrived and left their mark by converting the Samaritan synagogue at Nablus into a church, the tower of which still survives. When the Muslims returned to power in 1244, they made the building into a mosque, and in subsequent centuries the Samaritans had varying degrees of access to their central city.

The 14th century witnessed a new surge of theological and literary activity growing out of a reconciliation among several Samaritan sects, particularly the priestly-centered orthodox and the more lay-oriented Dositheans. The revered Abisha Scroll of the Pentateuch was discovered in 1355. Much of the manuscript dates from prior centuries, but it is likely that some portions were written in the 14th century to restore and link ancient fragments. In the same year, Abu'l Fath drew from several previous sources to write in colloquial Arabic a history of the Samaritans commissioned by the high priest Phineas. Another work, *Joshua,* an historical commentary with parallels to the biblical book, was also completed in this century. From this accumulated base of authority, the priests maintained control but were more open to heterodoxy (Crown 1967).

In response to a series of hardships during the following century, the Samaritans migrated among the major cities of the Diaspora, reaching a peak in the years 1474–85, during which they copied and exchanged a substantial number of Pentateuchs. The end of the 15th century witnessed some building restoration in Nablus.

Muslim oppression drove Jews, Christians, and Samaritans into quite congenial relations at this time. Jews and Samaritans accepted each other's authority in local communities. Samaritans in Cairo accepted the authority of the Jewish rabbi and Jews in the region of Nablus accepted the authority of the Samaritan high priest. Samaritans were in direct relationship with Christians, as well. For example, in 1497 the sale of a Pentateuch (von Gall 1914–18 vol. 2) was witnessed by two Christians.

6. Modern Period. The 16th century set the stage for a continuous diminution of the Samaritans and the unrelated birth of Samaritan studies in Europe. The invasion of the Ottoman Turks early in the 16th century led to greater oppression of the Samaritans provoking many Diaspora Samaritans to return to Nablus. The high priest at Nablus was exiled to Damascus, where the Samaritan leaders came into contact with the Jewish community. The Samaritan scholar Abraham ha-Qabasi wrote a book, *Sayr al Qalb,* containing a second list of the 613 precepts (the number of Pentateuchal commandments based on the numerical value of the word "Torah"), undoubtedly influenced by Jewish scholarship. This was one of the treasures brought back to Nablus in 1538 when the author returned with the high priest. Within a century, the Samaritan community at Damascus had disappeared and the demise of the Egyptian community was not far behind. A mid-16th-century traveller notes that Nablus was *the* city of the Samaritans and that they were located nowhere else in the world. Persecution of non-Muslims continued throughout the century.

Concurrently, European scholars became aware of the Samaritans and their literature. In 1537 Guillaume Postel acquired a Samaritan grammar and included comments on it and the Samaritans in his work *Ce Traite des douze langues,* published the following year. It was the first western information published on the Samaritans since Jerome's prologue to the book of Kings (de Robert 1988; 15–21). By the latter half of the 16th century Joseph Scaliger, a self-taught Semitist, had begun a correspondence with the Samaritan communities at Nablus and Egypt in an attempt to secure a copy of their Pentateuch. In 1584 he did receive some materials including a copy of the Samaritan *Joshua* which had been written in 1362–63 by Abd-el Ghani. He also received letters, some of which arrived after his death, but no copy of the Pentateuch was sent. The Samaritans may have been reluctant to entrust their sacred text to outsiders, although some speculate they were holding out for money or perhaps a text was sent and lost at sea.

The opportunity for Westerners to study the Pentateuch had to await the early 17th century, when Pietro della Valle did find a Pentateuch (von Gall's Codex B, dated 1345/46 C.E.) in Damascus. It arrived in Paris in 1623, where it was studied and published by Jean Morin. Morin remained at the center of all discussion of the Sam. Pent. for three decades, from the arrival of the della Valle codex through its publication in the Paris polyglot of 1645 until the rather incomplete catalogue of Samaritan texts that he published in 1657.

After the publication of the Walton or London polyglot of 1657, a flurry of interest in the Sam. Pent. sent emissaries to the Middle East in search of more copies. Because the Samaritan text seemed to support the Roman Catholic–favored LXX version of the OT against the MT which Jews and Protestants considered the "original" text, an extensive polemical literature developed between Roman Catholics and Protestants. No thorough, systematic examination and comparison of the text was accomplished.

Within a year of the receipt of Codex B in Paris, others began to appear in the British Isles, solicited mainly by Archbishop Usher in his quest for accurate dating of biblical events. He received a total of six pentateuchal manuscripts dating the next decade, of which von Gall's N, dated 1362/63 C.E. is the most easily identifiable.

The Samaritans for their part became confused about the European interest and concluded that a community of Samaritans were living in Europe, particularly in England. A few Englishmen encouraged this delusion as a strategy to elicit more Samaritan writings and as a tool for proselytizing.

When the priestly line of Aaron came to an end in 1623–24, the Samaritans sent two letters to their "brethren" in England hoping to reinstitute the line. Samaritans have given particular importance to the priest, Phineas, who is assumed to be the grandson of Aaron. Since the *Taheb,* or Messiah, was expected to descend from this line, it was urgent that the line not be broken. In practice, the priesthood resorted to the Levitical family.

French scholars used the same deception for similar ends. A fascinating sidelight to the story of French Samaritans is the evidence that there may have been some such presence. Two Arabic Samaritan Pentateuchs completed in

1685 were copied from a text brought to Paris by Capucin "rabbis" in 1684 (Anderson 1978: 45).

During the 19th century, European scholars were intrigued with the possible links between the Samaritans and the Karaites, an antirabbinical sect of Judaism that emerged late in the 1st millennium C.E. Both groups used complex calendars that required specialists to establish the feast days for a particular year, and even the formula for some feasts, like Pentecost, differed from orthodox Judaism. In response to direct questioning the Samaritans affirmed their distinctiveness (de Sacy 1831: 52–63). Many of their mutual practices can be traced back to Zadokite traditions at Qumran and may help establish the family tree of a particular style of Judaism.

During the 19th century the Samaritans were denied access to their sacred Mount, their literary efforts had long since dwindled, and in the early 20th century their total population was less than 200. That number has more than doubled with the community equally divided between Nablus and Holon, a suburb of Tel Aviv.

Historical tensions between Rabbinic Judaism and Samaritanism are minimal. Both are heirs of traditions and festivals authorized in the Pentateuch. Samaritans were legally considered a form of Jew during much of the history of occupation in Palestine, and often Samaritan and Jew recognized each other's authorities. Yet Samaritans do not consider themselves Jews and this distinction can be noted in both religious and social practices. They do not celebrate Purim or Hanukkah or the four minor fasts that are rooted elsewhere in Jewish tradition. They are reluctant to marry Jews; although, as a modern expediency, Samaritan men may marry Jewish women. For their part, Jews still have reservations about Samaritans and will not allow Samaritan burials in the Jewish cemetery at Tel Aviv.

D. Literature

1. Pentateuch. Only the Torah is canonized and it is read and revered in all services of worship. The unique artifact of the Samaritan community is the Abisha Scroll, a copy of the Pentateuch, housed in the synagogue at Nablus and attributed to Abisha, the great grandson of Aaron, the brother of Moses. It signifies both the scope and reverence accorded to Samaritan scripture.

About 150 pentateuchal manuscripts survive, some in a fragmentary state. They date from about the 9th century C.E. to the present century, with the largest production coming from the 14th and 15th centuries. The Sam. Pent. evolved somewhat independently from Judaism beginning or following the Hasmonean period (142–53 B.C.E.), although all text types remained quite flexible for at least a couple of centuries as evidenced by the discoveries at Qumran. Samaritan texts reflect awareness of later Jewish versions as well. The major points of explicit and intentional difference between the Samaritan and Jewish Torah relate to the Samaritan concern to establish the priority of Mt. Gerizim, witnessed most dramatically in the addition of the commandment to build an altar at the site (added to Exod 20:17) and the reading of "Gerizim" for "Ebal" at Deut 27:4.

While most of the pentateuchal manuscripts are written in Hebrew, it is not uncommon for Aramaic or Arabic or both to appear in adjoining columns, and there are exclusive Arabic and Aramaic texts.

Attempts have been made to cluster pentateuchal manuscripts into families of texts with sufficient common characteristics to indicate geographical, chronological, or scribal relationship (Anderson 1988). Punctuation, for example, is more likely influenced by geography, while the time period has more effect on the text choices. The majority of manuscripts come from four primary centers: Damascus, Egypt, Shechem, and Zarephath. For further discussion, see SAMARITAN PENTATEUCH.

2. Targum. The *Sam. Tg.* (a paraphrase of the biblical text in the vernacular Aramaic often found in a column paralleling the Hebrew text) offers remarkable parallels to the *Tg. Onq.* A. Tal has done significant study of the *Sam. Tg.* in several works, including the editing of a critical edition (1980–83).

3. Memar Marqah. This work, "Sayings of Marqah," a series of sermons expressing Samaritan theological beliefs, is attributed to the 3d or 4th century theologian Marqah, but examination of the language betrays several periods of Aramaic linguistic style, and the work was obviously enriched over the centuries. It is divided into six parts. The first five parts expand on biblical stories and develop homilies on biblical verses. The last section is a midrash on the letters of the Hebrew alphabet, though essays on only twelve letters remain. (For a summary of these sections, see Tal 1989: 462–65.) Marqah is the most highly venerated of all nonbiblical personages by the Samaritans, and in later tradition he is described as a priest. Macdonald (1963: xvii–xix) notes the assimilation of Christian concepts in Marqah, particularly the attribution to Moses of traits John uses to describe Jesus.

4. Liturgical Works. The earliest part of the liturgy is called the Defter, a collection of Marqah's compositions, hymns composed by his father, Amram Darah, and by his son, Nanah. With subsequent additions, it constitutes the prayer book of the Samaritan community (Tal 1989: 450–62). More than one hundred liturgical manuscripts appear in catalogues of various Samaritan collections. They cover a wide range of festivals (Sabbaths, Passover, Unleavened Bread—separated from Passover by the Samaritans—Weeks, Booths, and Atonement) and special occasions such as circumcision, marriage, and burials. Much of every service is devoted to hymns, the longest of which are usually acrostics in which each succeeding verse or stanza begins with the subsequent letter of the Hebrew alphabet. Cowley has written the standard treatment of the liturgy (1909).

5. Asatir. In Islamic times a wide diversity of literature developed. *Al-Asatir* ("Stories") of Moses, an Aramaic work of about the 11th or 12th century C.E., preserves ancient traditional stories paralleled in the OT pseudepigrapha. E. Robertson (1938–62: 2. xxxi–xxxii) describes it as a haggadic supplement to the Pentateuch. It was held in high regard by the Samaritans, since they assumed it had been written by Moses. A translation and modern commentary has been published by Z. Ben-Hayyim (1943–44).

6. Joshua. The Samaritan *Book of Joshua,* quite independent of the OT book, was written in Arabic and contains legendary material describing the period from Joshua until the 4th century C.E. Crown (1967) has suggested that the Dosithean sect of the Samaritans had a book of Joshua that is no longer extant, but which may have been included in some part in this extant work during the reconciliation of priestly and lay movements in the late Middle Ages.

7. Chronicles. In Islamic times a wide diversity of literature developed. Chief among them was a series of Chronicles. *Ha-Tolidah* ("Genealogy") was composed in Hebrew in 1346 and contains genealogical lists to the time of the entry into Canaan. Another chronicle, The Shalshalah ("Chain"), is a genealogy of the high priests from Adam to the present, begun by Eleazar ben Phineas and brought up to date by Jacob ben Harun in the 20th century C.E. The *Kitab al-Taʾrikh* ("Annals"), the "great chronicle" composed by Abu'l-Fath in the 14th century is an account from Adam to Muhammad (Stenhouse 1985). For further discussion, see Stenhouse 1989.

8. Chronicle II. Another Chronicle, which Gaster referred to as a continuation of Abu'l Fath, has been described by Macdonald (1969) and Cohen (1981). Apparently originating in the 14th century C.E., it seems to draw on several Jewish writings, possibly even a pre-MT, various Samaritan priestly sources, and the chronicles of Abu'l Fath to create material which is in part parallel to the biblical books of Joshua, Judges, Samuel, Kings, 2 Chronicles, and Psalms. It is quite critical of several biblical heroes, including David, Solomon, and Elijah.

E. Beliefs and Practices

The Samaritan creed has been succinctly stated in letters from the Samaritans to inquiring Western scholars (Montgomery 1907: 207): "We say: My faith is in Thee, YHWH; and in Moses son of Amram, Thy servant, and in the Holy Law; and in Mount Gerizim Bethel and in the Day of Vengeance and Recompense."

1. Monotheism. The Samaritan concept of God has shaped itself in the direction of the rigorous monotheism of Islam rather than the dispersal suggested by the Christian Trinity or the emanations of Gnosticism. They borrow the Muslim slogan, "There is no God, but God" for use in their services and writings. *El* or *Elah* is most commonly used for God (akin to Islamic Allah). The tetragrammaton, YHWH, is in regular use. Samaritans, like Jews, avoid making images and are even reluctant to apply the anthropomorphic concept of "Father" to God, whom they see as the ineffable and incorporeal creator and sustainer who has entered into unique covenant with Israel.

2. Torah. Torah, the Law of God, emanates from the divine fire as part of the covenant. Its verses are carved in stone to decorate synagogues, inscribed on amulets for personal protection, and carefully copied by hand on parchment or good paper. Wealthy families owned beautifully hand-printed copies which were passed down through many generations and now reside in the collections of such institutions as the Bibliothèque Nationale, the British Museum, the John Rylands Library at the University of Manchester, and Michigan State University. The practical and legal aspect of Torah has been emphasized to define the location of the altar and the services to be performed there, elevating its interpreters, the priests, to unique authority.

3. Moses. Moses as mediator of the Torah deserves adoration as the third focus of Samaritan faith. Blessings are offered "in the name of Moses the faithful," the last and most exalted of the prophets. Little is made of his death, but his birth is exalted in a treatise, *Molad Mosheh.* He is depicted as a preexistent primordial light who came to illuminate the world. The restorer who will come as the agent of God will be one like Moses.

4. Mt. Gerizim. The Samaritan version of Moses commanding the building of an altar on Mt. Gerizim (Deut 27:4) is probably earlier than the MT citation of Mt. Ebal. On the other hand, the Samaritans themselves presumably inserted the commandment in the Decalogue (after Ex 20:14 and Deut 5:18) ordering the building of an altar for sacrifice on Mt. Gerizim. It is, in their view, the navel of the world where Abel built the first altar, and where God told Abraham to sacrifice Isaac. The *Memar Marqah* enumerates thirteen honorific names for the mountain. Tradition calls it the oldest and highest mountain in the world, and its peak survived the flood in the time of Noah. Here the Samaritans have built a series of altars and sanctuaries at three major sacred spots and continue to celebrate their festivals. The mutually exclusive claims of Gerizim and Jerusalem define a very tangible distinctive difference between Jew and Samaritan, though some caution against overstating its significance (Purvis 1986: 88 and Coggins 1975: 113).

5. Day of Vengeance and Recompense. The eschatology of the Samaritans is not unlike that of other heirs of the Israelite tradition. A coming Day of the Lord will be ushered in by a Messiah and characterized by a long period of peace and security before the final end. The Samaritan periodization of the history of salvation includes an Age of Disfavor preceding Moses, an Age of Grace lasting 260 years after Moses, a second Age of Disfavor initiated by the evil priest, Eli, and the New Age of Grace to be initiated by the Messiah. The designation of the Messiah as *Taheb,* a cryptic term, whose role is to be modeled after Deut 18:18, is also unique to the Samaritans.

6. Festivals. The calendar by which the feasts are determined originated with the Jewish calendar. However, it has become so complex through influence of Byzantine and Arab usages that only the priest can calculate the appropriate feast days for any given year. On the Day of Simmuth, 60 days before Passover, each member of the community pays a half shekel and receives the calendar in which the priest has calculated the festivals for the next six months. During the year, the Samaritans celebrate Passover, the Feast of Unleavened Bread, The Feast of Weeks, the Feast of the Seventh Month, Yom Kippur, the Feast of Booths, and "the eighty days of solemn assembly." The Festival of Unleavened Bread, the Feast of Weeks, and the Feast of Booths are celebrated on Mt. Gerizim. Although Passover is distinct from the Feast of Unleavened Bread, the Samaritans remain on the mountain through the days of each.

Regular services of Sabbath are celebrated in the synagogue. On the Day of Atonement, the main festival of the synagogue, the law is read and the Abisha Scroll is displayed for adoration. All services use extensive readings from the Torah, hymns, and prayers.

Bibliography

Anderson, R. T. 1978. *Studies in Samaritan Manuscripts and Artifacts: The Chamberlain-Warren Collection.* Cambridge, MA.

———. 1988. Clustering Samaritan Hebrew Pentateuchal Manuscripts. Pp. 57–65 in *Études samaritaines Pentateuque et Targum, exégèse et philologie, chroniques,* ed. J. P. Rothschild and G. D. Sixdenier, Louvain and Paris.
———. 1989. Josephus' Accounts of Temple Building: History, Literature or Politics. *PEGLAMBS* 9.
Ben-Hayyim, Z. 1943–44. The Asatir. *Tarbiz* 14: 104–25, 174–90; 15: 71–87 (in Hebrew).
Bowman, J. 1958. Samaritan Studies I. The Fourth Gospel and the Samaritans. *BJRL* 40: 298–308.
Bull, R. J. 1967. A Preliminary Excavation of an Hadrianic Temple at Tell er Ras on Mt. Gerizim. *AJA* 71: 387–93.
———. 1968. The Excavation of Tell er-Ras on Mt. Gerizim. *BA* 31: 58–72.
Coggins, R. J. 1975. *Samaritans and Jews.* Atlanta.
Cohen, J. A. 1981. *A Samaritan Chronicle.* Leiden.
Cowley, A. E. 1909. *The Samaritan Liturgy.* Oxford.
Crown, A. D. 1967. Some Traces of Heterodox Theology in the Samaritan Book of Joshua. *BJRL* 50: 178–98.
———. 1984. *Bibliography of the Samaritans.* Metuchen, NJ.
———. 1986. The Samaritans in the Byzantine Orbit. *BJRL* 69: 96–138.
Crown, A. D., ed. 1989. *The Samaritans.* Tübingen.
Fossum, J. E. 1985. *The Name of God and the Angel of the Lord.* WUNT 1/36. Tübingen.
———. 1989. Samaritan Sects and Movements. Pp. 293–389 in Crown 1989.
Gall, A. von. 1914–18. *Der hebräische Pentateuch der Samaritaner.* 5 vols. Geissen. Repr. 1966, 1 vol.
Lowy, S. 1977. *The Principles of Samaritan Bible Exegesis.* Leiden.
Macdonald, J. 1963. *Memar Marqah.* Vol. 1. Berlin.
———. 1964. *Theology of the Samaritans.* London.
———. 1969. *The Samaritan Chronicle II.* BZAW 107. Berlin.
Montgomery, J. A. 1907. *The Samaritans, the Earliest Jewish Sect.* Philadelphia. Repr. 1968.
Pummer, R., 1989. Samaritan Material Remains and Archaeology. Pp. 135–77 in Crown 1989.
Purvis, J. 1968. *The Samaritan Pentateuch and the Origin of the Samaritan Sect.* HSM 2. Cambridge, MA.
———. 1975. The Fourth Gospel and the Samaritans. *NovT* 17: 161–98.
———. 1986. The Samaritans and Judaism. Pp. 81–98 in *Early Judaism and Its Modern Interpreters,* ed. R. A. Kraft and G. W. E. Nicklesburg. Philadelphia and Atlanta.
Robert, P. de. 1988. La Naissance des études samaritaines en Europe aux XVIe et XVIIe siècles. Pp. 15–26 in *Études samaritaines Pentateuque et Targum, exégèse et philologie, chroniques,* ed. J. P. Rothschild and G. D. Sixdenier. Louvain and Paris.
Robertson, E. 1938–62. *Catalogue of the Samaritan Manuscripts in the John Rylands Library Manchester.* 2 vols. Manchester.
Sacy, S. de. 1831. *Correspondence des Samaritains de Nablouse.* Vol. 12 of *Notices et extrait des manuscrits de la Bibliothèque du Roi.* Paris.
Sanderson, J. E. 1986. *An Exodus Scroll from Qumran. 4QpaleoExod*[m] and the Samaritan Tradition. HSS 30. Atlanta.
Skehan, P. 1955. Exodus in the Samaritan Recension from Qumran. *JBL* 74: 182–87.
Spiro, A. 1951. Samaritans, Tobiads, and Judahites in Pseudo Philo. *PAAJR* 20: 279–355.
———. 1967. Steven's Samaritan Background (condensed by W. F. Albright and C. S. Mann). Pp. 285–304 in J. Munck, *The Acts of the Apostles.* AB. Garden City.
Stenhouse, P. 1985. *The Kitab al Tarikh of Abu'l-Fath.* Sydney.
———. 1988. The Reliability of the Chronicles of Abu'l-Fath. Pp. 235–53 in *Études samaritaines Pentateuque et Targum, exégèse et philologie, chroniques,* ed. J. P. Rothschild and G. D. Sixdenier. Louvain and Paris.
———. 1989. Samaritan Chronicles. Pp. 218–65 in Crown 1989.
Tal, A. 1980–83. *The Samaritan Targum of the Torah: A Critical Edition.* 3 vols. Tel Aviv (in Hebrew).
———. 1989. Samaritan Literature. Pp. 413–67 in Crown 1989.
Wright, G. 1965. *Shechem.* London.

ROBERT T. ANDERSON

SAMEK. The fifteenth letter of the Hebrew alphabet.

SAMGAR-NEBO (PERSON) [Heb *samgar-nĕbô*]. One of the Babylonian military officers who (along with Nergal-sharezer, Sarsechim the Rabsaris, and Nergal-sharezer the Rabmag) was charged with the disposition of the city of Jerusalem after it had been captured by the Babylonians in 587 B.C. (Jer 39:3). Some perplexities occur in the passage (39:1–13) containing the names of these (and other) officers: the LXX presents a garbled version of the first three vv (LXX Jer 46:1–3), omits vv 4–15, and then resumes the narrative in Jer 52:4–16.

The name of the ranking Babylonian officer, Nabuzaradan, "the captain of the guard," appears four times in the passage and itself presents no difficulties. He functioned as the liaison between King Nebuchadnezzar and the Babylonian forces in Jerusalem, supervising the deportation of Judeans to Babylon, apportioning Judean lands to the indigent, and carrying out royal orders concerning the prophet Jeremiah (39:9–14). However, there are numerous problems associated with the other four Babylonian officers listed in 39:3. Apparently this same group is referred to again in v 13, but there only two officers are mentioned: Nebushazban the Rabsaris (not mentioned in 39:3) and Nergal-sharezer the Rabmag (a name which also occurs twice in 39:3; is it possible that all three occurrences of the name Nergal-sharezer refer to one and the same individual?).

The names Nebu-shazban, Nabu-zaradan, and Nergal-sharezer are all theophoric with a divine name in the initial position. The names Samgar-nebo and Sarsechim are different, however, in that they do not begin with a theophoric element (the god Nebo/Nabû appears in the final position in Samgar-nebo's name). A major problem has been that despite the thousands of Babylonian names known to us, none exhibit any affinity to the Samgar- element in Samgar-nebo's name. A dramatic breakthrough transpired when E. Ungar (1930: 36, 290) pointed out an entry in the court- and state-calendar of Nebuchadnezzar mentioning the name Nergal-šarri-uṣur (Neriglissar) prince of Sin-magir. The name was immediately recognized to be that of Nebuchadnezzar's son-in-law and eventual successor. The province of Sin-magir was identified as being located N of Babylon, an area that was well-known as early as the Isin dynasty (ca. 2100 B.C.). Nergal-šarri-uṣur was identified with Nergal-sharezer in Jer 39:3, and it was suggested (Bewer 1925) that the first name in v 3 should be read "Nergal-sharezer [prince] of Sin-magir, the Rabmag." Bright (*Jeremiah* AB, 243), following Rudolph

(*Jeremia* HAT, 208) and appealing to v 13, reconstructs v 3 to read "Nergal-sharezer, lord of Sin-magir, the Rab-mag; Nabushazban the Rab-saris." Thus, the first element in the name Samgar-nebo is seen to contain an actual reference to the province of Sin-magir (Akk *simmāgir*), while the theophoric element and the next name *(nbwśrskym)*—which may be a corruption of *nĕbûšazbān śar sāsîs*, "Nabushazban the Sar[variant of Rab]-saris"—as well as the second reference to Nergal-sharezer, are essentially deleted. Another approach is to read *nbwśrskym* as another proper name, Nebusarsekin. Of course, all proposed emendations can be rejected in toto, and one can hope that future discoveries will help to clarify the serious difficulties that remain in Jer 39:3.

Bibliography

Bewer, J. A. 1925. Nergalsharezer Samgar in Jer. 39:3. *AJSL* 42: 130.

Ungar, E. 1930. *Babylon.* 2d ed. Berlin.

EDWARD R. DALGLISH

SAMLAH (PERSON) [Heb *śamlâ*]. The sixth ruler mentioned in the Edomite king list, Gen 36:31–39 (v 36; also 1 Chr 1:47). Opinions vary concerning the date of this list. Suggestions range from the 11th century B.C. (Weippert 1982: 155) through the 8th to 6th centuries B.C. (Bennett 1983: 16) to the 6th/5th centuries B.C. (Knauf 1985). Scholars tend to agree, however, that the succession scheme of this list is artificial, and that, in all likelihood, the rulers mentioned were contemporaries (Bartlett 1972: 27; Weippert 1982: 155). The name has parallels in ancient N Arabian epigraphy, in classical and contemporary Arabic. It may signify "cloak" (Arabic *šamlah*). If the consonants alone are taken into account, the name can also be derived from **Śām'allāh*, "The God has placed" (Knauf 1985: 248). Because of the form *'al-* for the definite article, Samlah would then represent one of the earliest attestations for Nabateans in Edom. Samlah's place or region of origin, Masrekah, cannot be identified.

Bibliography

Bartlett, J. R. 1972. The Rise and Fall of the Kingdom of Edom. *PEQ* 104: 26–37.

Bennett, C.-M. 1983. Excavations at Buseirah (Biblical Bozrah). Pp. 9–17 in *Midian, Moab and Edom.* Ed. J. F. A. Sawyer and D. J. A. Clines. Sheffield.

Knauf, E. A. 1985. Alter und Herkunft der edomitischen Königsliste Gen 36, 31–39. *ZAW* 97: 245–53.

Weippert, M. 1982. Remarks on the History of Settlement in Southern Jordan during the Early Iron Age. Pp. 153–62 in *Studies in the History and Archaeology of Jordan I,* ed. A. Hadidi. Amman.

ERNST AXEL KNAUF

SAMMUNIYEH, KHIRBET. See SHIMRON (PLACE).

SAMOS (PLACE) [Gk *Samos*]. One of the most important islands of the Aegean, located one mile from the W shore of Asia Minor (modern Turkey) SW of Ephesus and NW of Miletus (37°45′N; 26°49′E). Samos is a mountainous island, hence its name, which means "height" or "mountain"; it is 14 miles in width and 27 miles long.

Samos is mentioned in 1 Macc 15:23 as one of the recipients of a letter sent by the Roman consul Lucius. The passage in 1 Maccabees records a letter, which instructed rulers of various regions to treat the Jews with favor. This request was prompted by the gift of a shield made from 1,000 minas (1 mina equals about 1.25 pounds) of gold which the Jewish ambassadors brought to the Roman ruler. The inclusion of Samos on this list attests to its large population of Jews during the 2d century B.C.

Paul, after visiting Macedonia, traveled to Troas and then went cross-country to Assos. There he joined his companions on the ship and sailed S to Chios and Samos, eventually traveling on to Jerusalem. It was common for ships to overnight at convenient harbors and set sail early in the morning to take advantage of favorable morning winds. The ship carrying Paul during his third missionary journey may have "touched at" Samos and anchored there overnight (as in the RSV), or perhaps the vessel "came near" to the island and set anchor at the nearby promontory of Trogylium (Acts 20:15). The confusion comes from variant textual evidence, but the earliest manuscripts omit the phrase "and having remained in Trogylium" (cf. KJV). This phrase may have been added to the later texts as gloss to explain the Greek word *paraballo,* which technically means "to touch land" and therefore does not require the ship to make an actual landing.

Samos was inhabited in the Early Bronze Age by the Late Mycenaeans. The Ionians established settlements on the island during the early Iron Age. Samos was a great naval power and established several colonies throughout the Mediterranean, including Dicaearchia (Puteoli) in Italy, and Zanucle (Messana) in Sicily. During the 6th century B.C., the island was ruled by tyrants, of which the most powerful was Polycrates, whose death is recorded by Herodotus (3.39ff.). Samos participated in the Ionian rebellion and joined the Athenian League after the Greeks defeated the Persian fleet at the Battle of Mycale, which was fought in the narrow strait that separates Samos from Ionia (Hdt. 9.100ff.). Samos was a loyal ally of Athens for many years.

During the First Mithridates War, Samos joined the rebellion against Rome and at the conclusion of that uprising in 84 B.C., Rome joined the island to the province of Asia.

Samos became prosperous due to the benefits of Cicero, and through its one-time residents, Antony and Cleopatra. Later, Augustus made the island a free state (Dio Cassius 54.9; Pliny *HN* 5.37). Both Herod and Marcus Agrippa visited the island and gave many gifts to the inhabitants (Josephus *Ant* 16.2.2; *JW* 1.21.11).

Samos, the chief cultural center for Ionia, was the home of the famous moralist Aesop and the philosopher Pythagoras. Samos also had the largest temple of its day (built in 569 B.C.)—an Ionic style building which was dedicated to Hera (Hdt. 3.60; Paus. 7.4). This temple was located in the capital city of the island, which was also known as Samos.

JOHN D. WINELAND

SAMOTHRACE (PLACE) [Gk *Samothrąkē*]. A small island located in the NE Aegean Sea (40°27′N; 25°32′E). It lies approximately 20 miles S of Thrace (Samos of Thrace, or the Thracian Samos) on a sea route between Macedonia and the Hellespont (Dardanelles) in Asia Minor. The name Samos, meaning "height" or "mountain," reflects its mountainous topography. With a summit more than one mile above sea level, Samothrace represents the highest point on all of the Aegean Islands. It is in view of the Trojan coast and represents the most conspicuous landmark for ships on the sea route. In the *Iliad* (13.12), Homer called Samothrace Poseidon's island, because Poseidon surveyed the plains of Troy from the top of its mountains.

Few people lived on the island before the 7th century B.C. During Greek and Roman history, Samothrace remained relatively insignificant, probably due to its rugged coastline and lack of a satisfactory harbor. In 190 B.C., Samothrace became independent after the Romans defeated Antiochus the Great at Magnesia (1 Macc 15:23). The island later came under Roman rule in 133 B.C., though Romans permitted autonomy on Samothrace after 19 B.C.

Although unsuitable as a trade center, ships would anchor on the N shore of Samothrace near a town by the same name. The mountains provided a relatively safe place to shelter ships at night from SE winds, and ancient sailors preferred to anchor overnight when convenient or possible. The mountains also made it possible to locate Samothrace easily from sea. Consequently, the N shore of the island became an anchorage for many ships.

After receiving the vision of a man beckoning to him from Macedonia, Paul left Troas in order to set sail for Europe across the Aegean Sea (Acts 16:9–10). With the benefit of good wind conditions, Paul sailed as far as Samothrace on the first of a two-day voyage (Acts 16:11). The ship undoubtedly anchored on the N shore of the island before continuing to Neapolis, the port of Philippi (Acts 16:12). There is no record of Paul going ashore at Samothrace, though some speculate that he did during a later voyage E which took several days longer to complete (Acts 20:6).

In the ancient world, Samothrace was best known as a center for the worship of the pre-Greek deities known as the Cabiri. The Cabiri were twin fertility gods, possibly of Phrygian or Phoenician origin. The gods were supposed to protect people in danger, particularly at sea. Many sailors revered them as navigational guides and protectors. Thus, Samothrace became a center of worship for this mystery cult, which involved an initiation ritual to secure the favor of the gods for this life and the next. Philip of Macedon and Olympias his wife, the parents of Alexander the Great, became initiates on the island. The popularity of the Cabiri rivaled the cults of Demeter and Persephone at Eleusis, which represented the principal religious mysteries of ancient Greece. Upon receiving financial support from Macedonian and Egyptian kings, the people of Samothrace built magnificent buildings and monuments to their gods.

Beginning in the 19th century, archaeologists excavated a number of buildings, including a sanctuary for the gods and the largest round classical building before Hadrian's pantheon in Rome. In the Nike Fountain was found the *Winged Victory,* also called *Nike of Samothrace,* a statue probably built to commemorate a naval victory by the Rhodians in ca. 190 B.C. Today the statue is displayed prominently in the Louvre and considered one of the greatest Greek sculptures.

DONALD A. D. THORSEN

SAMPSAMES (PLACE) [Gk *Sampsamēs*]. One of the cities in the area of Asia Minor to which the Roman consul Lucius wrote a letter in support of the interests of the Hasmonean kingdom under Simon (1 Macc 15:23). The name Sampsames is unknown and probably corrupt (unfamiliar names lead to scribal confusion; most of the geographical names in chap. 15 are otherwise unknown). It might perhaps be identified with Samsun (41°17′N; 36°22′E), a port city on the Black Sea in modern Turkey. Samsun is built on the ancient Hellenistic city of Amisus, a trading port of the independent kingdom of Pontus. It was a large and wealthy city, and therefore possibly able to influence foreign policy as regarded the fledgling Hasmonean kingdom over against the disintegrating Seleucid empire. Another possible identification might be the city of Samosata (37°31′N; 38°30′E), to the N of Edessa, again part of the kingdom of Pontus. However, the location of Sampsames has not yet been satisfactorily identified.

Bibliography

Rostovtzeff, M. 1941. *The Social and Economic History of the Hellenistic World.* 3 vols. Oxford.

SIDNIE ANN WHITE

SAMRA, KHIRBET ES- (M.R. 221086). The Arabic name means "The Black Ruin," as does the site's less common name, Kh. es-Sauda. A third name is sometimes used: Qalaʾat es-Samra, "The Black Castle." This site should not be confused with Kh. es-Samra in Judah (M.R. 187125). See SECACAH. The site is in fact built of black basalt, which gives the area a somber look. The ruin was often visited by those who were following the Roman road *(Via Nova Trajana).* M. Germer-Durand (1902) identified it with Hatita, mentioned on the *Tabula Peutingeriana,* and H. C. Butler (1904) identified it with Gadda, listed in the *Notitia Dignitatum* (where Hatita is also referred to as Aditha). The distances between the sites, compared with the Roman miles written on the *Tabula Peutingeriana,* favor Hatita, while a Greek inscription recently found near the site features the Greek form *Adeitha.*

The basalt outcrop on which Samra is situated stands 15 m above the bend of a little wadi. The site measures only 200 × 250 m. Without springs and enjoying only a light rainfall, it was habitable because of the construction of large cisterns, aqueducts, and birkeh (pools), one of which, 1 km from the site, measures 50 × 50 m. Owing to the scarcity of water and the poverty of the soil, agriculture was neither prosperous nor sufficient. The economy had to rely upon other factors. The remains, which have been seriously damaged by robbery, present a close network of structures relatively well organized. The École Biblique et Archéologique de Jérusalem has excavated there since 1981 under the direction of J.-B. Humbert.

This site, which could not subsist on agriculture, obtained its livelihood as a staging post on the caravan route linking the Red Sea with the rich cities of Syria (Palmyra). In addition, its position on the edge of the desert made it a junction between the Decapolis and routes passing up the Wadi Sirhan to Arabia. At first a Nabatean post halfway between Philadelphia (Amman) and Bostra, Samra became a strategic point on the great road which the Romans built after annexing the province in A.D. 106 and was eventually integrated into the *limes Arabicus.* Under Diocletian (ca. 300) the Nabatean guard post was replaced with a fortress. Measuring 60 × 60 m, it has towers at each corner and in the center of each side. The main gate on the E side was flanked by two towers and permitted the passage of vehicles. The building was restored under Valentinian, Valens, and Gratian (Latin inscription ca. A.D. 375), but was abandoned in the Byzantine period and given over to domestic use. Eventually, the little town was surrounded by a wall.

It is difficult to know how the town which grew up around the fort became Christian. The seven churches excavated could have been built under Justinian or just after his reign (A.D. 565), when Bostra and its district were undergoing extensive redevelopment. The mosaic floors were laid when the buildings were being reconstructed, which the inscriptions date ca. 630/640. This is, of course, when Islam was sweeping through the region. The mosaics were defaced by iconoclasts, but it is noteworthy that the sanctuaries remained in use almost until the end of the Ummayad period (750).

The special interest of Samra lies, however, in its cemetery. Cemeteries from this period are rare (Umm el-Jimal, Kerak) and Samra is the only one to yield monuments written in Syro-Palestinian. These testify to the existence of a community speaking this language, which is Palestinian in origin and written in a script derived from the Syrian Estrangelo of Mesopotamia. The translation of the Bible into Syro-Palestinian was made by Christians of the Chalcedonian faith who firmly opposed the Monophysites of Syria. The cemetery was first non-Christian and had gravestones in Greek (notable is one for a veteran of the Roman army at the end of the 4th century). It then became overwhelmingly Christian, as indicated by more than 600 rough stones and simple slabs which have been found engraved with crosses of various styles. About 100 stones bear the name of the deceased in Greek or Syro-Palestinian. The list of names is extremely varied: there are those of the local (pagan) stock with Nabatean, Palmyrene, and Arab names; there are names which show acquaintance with the Old and New Testaments, and there are a few Latin names. That these varied cultures should be found in such an association may be explained by the need for soldiers, merchants, and missionaries to use the main route from inland Syria to Aqaba.

After destructions caused by repeated earthquakes and the ravages of plague throughout the 8th century, Samra was completely abandoned before 800.

Bibliography

Desreumaux, A., and Humbert, J.-B. 1981. Hirbet es-Samra. *ADAJ* 25: 33–83.

———. 1982. La première campagne de Fouilles Khirbet es-Samra 1981. *ADAJ* 26: 173–82.

JEAN-BAPTISTE HUMBERT

SAMSON (PERSON) [Heb *šimšôn*]. A warrior-deliverer whose personal vendetta against the Philistines, resulting from sexual encounters, cost him sight and life (Judges 13–16).

A. Introduction
B. Literary Components of the Narrative
C. Motifs
D. Rhetorical Features
E. Function of the Story
F. Postcanonical Readings of the Story

A. Introduction

Judges 13–16 records the story of Samson, a *šōpeṭ* (warrior-deliverer) from the tribe of Dan. Samson's heroic exploits approximate a private vendetta against the Philistines, arising from his amorous adventures with three women. The narrative, however, interprets these incidents as motivated by a religious factor, God's desire to vex the uncircumcised neighbors of the Danite clan. Samson's erotic liaisons with foreign women led to his enslavement and eventual death by his own hands.

The name Samson appears to be a diminutive form of *šemeš* (sun), hence "little sun." Various features of the story suggest a connection at some stage with solar worship: e.g., *Šamaš* the sun god; the city Beth-shemesh (lit. "house/temple of the sun [god]"); the blinding of Samson, analogous to a solar eclipse; the similarity between Delilah's name and the Hebrew word for night *(laylâ).* The prominence of fire in the episodes further strengthens the hypothesis of solar mythology, as does the incident of the foxes, which recalls a ritual for preventing mildew reported to have taken place during the Roman festival of Cerealia.

The present form of the story resembles a saga, which recounts the amazing deeds of a single individual, exploits that greatly affected the course of events for the Danites. Its component parts, although unrelated, mesh nicely, largely the result of the overarching Deuteronomistic framework and two themes: Samson's inability to guard the secret of his strength and his failure to keep the Nazirite vow, imposed on him by divine mediation and reinforced by his mother, throw into focus the Deuteronomistic conviction that disobedience brings certain retaliation from on high (see, e.g., Boling *Judges* AB, 252f.).

The narrative draws on literary conventions that find expression in various parts of the canon. Its motifs appear also in the Torah, Prophets, Writings, and the Deuterocanon. Moreover, the story weaves an intricate tapestry from separate strands of Hebrew rhetoric. Familiar themes, motifs, and rhetoric unite in a suspense-filled tale about squandered potential. The mighty Samson fell victim to his own fascination for foreign women; his plight provided a lesson very much needed in Israelite society, which harbored exclusive ideas about pure religion.

Christian interpretation of this story quickly recognized some startling similarities between Samson and Jesus, despite significant differences. Resemblances between Samson and Heracles also occasioned comment. In the 17th century John Milton reinterpreted the Samson narrative as an epic psychological and spiritual struggle against primal evil. Artists, musicians, and poets testify to the emotive power of the biblical story about Samson, and the movie industry has exploited its sexual features.

B. Literary Components of the Narrative

The Samson narrative features prayers, etiologies, victory songs, riddles, heroic deeds, a birth story, and a recognition account. Elements such as these originated in oral tradition and circulated for a considerable time before being incorporated into the Deuteronomistic rendering of Israel's early existence. At least one item in the account, the riddles, may antedate inclusion in the story of Samson's wager on the occasion of his wedding at Timnah.

Three prayers rise to heaven in the raucous story, one generated by Manoah, Samson's father, and the other two by the warrior-judge in dire circumstances. Although the divine messenger gave clear and specific instructions to Samson's mother about her diet prior to his birth and about the intended life-style for her son, Manoah entreats the deity to return and instruct both parents on the rearing of their child. "O Lord, let the man of God whom you sent come again to us and teach us what we ought to do for the boy who will be born" (13:8). The verb that describes Manoah's actions belongs in cultic contexts. No such language escapes Samson's lips, nor does the narrator introduce the vocabulary of the cult when describing the fervent requests of a weakened fighter. An exceedingly thirsty Samson calls on the Lord as follows: "You have given this great victory into the power of your servant, but now I am about to die with thirst, and I shall fall into the grasp of the uncircumcised" (15:18). Samson's penultimate words address the Lord in a similar manner: "O Lord God, remember me, I pray, and strengthen me just this time, O God, that I may avenge myself a vengeance from the Philistines for one of my two eyes" (16:28). The narrative emphasizes the deity's readiness to answer prayer, even prayer inspired by selfish motives.

Samson's initial prayer occurs in the context of two topographical etiologies. One explains the origin of the name Partridge Spring (En-hakkore), the other identifies the locale in which Samson used an unconventional weapon against some Philistines (Ramath-lehi). In all probability, the name "Spring of the Caller" is secondary, and the original sense of calling had nothing to do with humans or prayer. The usual formula for an etiology occurs here: "Therefore its name was called . . . which is at . . . until this day" (15:19). This formula does not appear with the other etiology in the Samson narrative. In this instance certain features of the hill probably resembled the jawbone of an ass (15:17).

Two victory songs stand in juxtaposition, one celebrating the slaughter of Samson's enemies and the other praising the god Dagon for delivering Samson into the hands of the Philistines. After slaying a thousand enemies Samson announces—he does not sing (*ʿanah* or *šîr*) like Miriam and Moses—that "With the jawbone of the ass, ass upon asses, with the jawbone of the ass, I have slain a thousand men" (15:16). Nine words suffice for Samson (actually five, since the word for "ass" occurs four times and "jawbone" twice). The Philistine victory song excels in repetition of a single sound, the first person plural ending *-ēnû* punctuating the joyous shout eight times. "*Our* god has given into *our* control Samson *our* enemy . . . *Our* god has given *our* enemy into *our* grasp, and the ravager of *our* land, who has killed many *of us*" (16:23b, 24b).

Samson's song breathes the spirit of braggadocio, whereas the Philistine song acknowledges a higher power as vanquisher. The Israelite hero attributes the victory to himself, despite his innate strength and a handy weapon. The Philistines obtained their foe through bribery and deceit, but in a solemn assembly they acknowledge divine assistance.

Samson's victory over a young lion and subsequent discovery of honey in its carcass provided private information that he used to formulate a six-word riddle on the occasion of his wedding to the beautiful Timnite woman: "Food came from the eater; sweetness came from strength" (14:14). Four cipher words furnish a clue for opening the riddle: food, eater, sweetness, strength. Only one word lacks initial *m,* the twice-used verb *yāṣāʾ*. The Philistine's response, acquired through threat of death from Samson's bride, takes riddle form: "What is sweeter than honey, and what is stronger than a lion?" (14:18a). Like Samson's riddle, this one has only six words, five of which begin with the letter *m.* The only exception derives from his riddle (*ʿaz,* strength). The parallelism in Samson's riddle is synonymous, but the response has ascending parallelism. Samson's closing retort includes a riddle-like accusation: "Had you not plowed with my heifer, you would not have found out my riddle" (14:18b). The metaphor of plowing, widely used for sexual experience in the ANE, seems here to have a more general sense of exploiting someone's vulnerability.

Riddles often have several answers, and Samson's may actually have antedated its incorporation in the Samson narrative (Gunkel 1913). It could have described an erotic relationship between "eater" and the "eaten," sweetness and strength, with reference to both sexes as eater, strong, and eaten. Alternatively, the riddle could allude to soldiers' gorging themselves on delicacies at the wedding until they vomit.

The heart of the story consists of five heroic exploits perpetrated on the Philistines, the first one resulting from the lost wager. Bristling from the thought that his bride has betrayed his trust, Samson kills thirty hapless citizens from Ashkelon and removes the clothes from their corpses to pay his wager (14:19).

Later in a fit of rage over being denied admission to see his bride, who has been given to his best man, Samson catches three hundred foxes, ties their tails together, sets them on fire, and turns the frightened animals loose in the grainfields of the Philistines (15:4–5).

One grievance leads to another, steadily escalating in magnitude. The aggrieved Philistines pursue Samson, whose flight into the land of Judah endangers this tribe and prompts them to bind him for his pursuers. Snapping the ropes, he grabs an ass's jawbone and kills a thousand of his pursuers (15:9–17).

Seeking respite from his hostile engagements, he visits a prostitute for a different kind of game. Somehow, news of his whereabouts reaches the citizens of Gaza, who stealthily surround her house and lie in wait, anticipating the emergence of an exhausted Samson after a full night of loveplay. Their intended victim departs unexpectedly, tearing down the door to the city and ripping up its posts, depositing door and posts near Hebron far away in the hill-country (16:1–3).

His final heroic exploit wipes out more than three thousand mocking Philistines, but Samson also dies in the process. Called to make sport at a celebration honoring Dagon, Samson invokes divine remembrance in order to heap revenge on the people who had put out his eyes. Then he pulls down the two columns supporting the weight of the sacred edifice, filled with jubilant worshippers (16:23–30).

Only two of these exploits (14:19; 15:14) are attributed to the power of the spirit, and they involve the killing of Philistines. The final episode (16:28) *implies* special power external to Samson, the gift of prayer. It follows that only two episodes, those involving foxes and Gaza's gate, accord with the understanding of Samson's strength as a permanent possession dependent on keeping the Nazirite vow.

Such a view of his strength resides in the story of his unusual birth. An angel appears to Samson's barren mother and informs her that she will give birth to a wondrous son (13:3–5). Both she and the son must abstain from strong drink, according to the divine messenger, and the boy will be a Nazirite from birth.

This birth announcement stands alongside a recognition story in which the messenger conceals its identity until Manoah demonstrates worthiness. The return of the messenger, a response to prayer, implies divine acceptance of the childless couple. The angel's subtle hint as to its true identity evokes mystery, recalling a divine epithet about the one who does wonders (13:19). Manoah perceives the secret, offers an appropriate sacrifice, and cowers in terror as the visitor departs in the flame. A perceptive wife, however, calms her husband's fears. Her intuition tells her what Manoah must learn through question and answer.

C. Motifs

Several motifs occur in the Samson narrative: a barren wife who gives birth; a helpless hero in the power of a woman; a quest for the deity's name; a hero's death wish; loss of charisma; and terror in the presence of theophany. The author varies the motifs, selecting only individual elements that contribute to the total purpose of the story. A religious ethos permeates most of these subplots.

Like her predecessor Sarah, Manoah's wife received a divine visitor who communicated news of a forthcoming birth. Unlike Sarah, she was still capable of giving birth, hence her response was thoughtful silence rather than disbelieving laughter. Sarah's husband repeatedly asked for a son, whom God had already promised, but no such request from either Manoah or his wife surfaces in this story. Missing also is any allusion to mockery of the barren woman by a rival wife, which occurs elsewhere in tales about Rachel and Hannah. Neither of these women learned of her pregnancy from a divine messenger, although Hannah heard from the priest Eli that God had responded favorably to her fervent request for a son. The NT accounts of Elizabeth and Mary alter the components of the motif radically, particularly the latter, which involves an unmarried woman. Manoah's wife alone received two visits from an angel.

The story about a mighty hero falling helpless before a designing woman takes place in several biblical narratives. The Canaanite warrior, Sisera, succumbed to the treacherous hands of Jael, wife of Heber the Kenite (Judges 4–5). Another foreigner, Haman, paid at Esther's hands for plotting to eradicate the Jewish population in Persian captivity (Esther) and Holofernes lost his head to the lovely but merciless Judith (Judith). In all these instances the women feigned friendship or love, and the hero let down his guard and forfeited his life. Lust dominated in the episode involving Holofernes and possibly in the story of Haman, although both he and Sisera had less cause to abandon suspicion. In Samson's case, tearful imploring led him to reveal vital information that set into motion his conflicts with the Philistines and eventually led to his capture and eventual death. Delilah's teasing adds a new dimension to this motif.

Because knowledge of a deity's name was thought to convey power over that god in the ancient world, such information was guarded closely. At times a hostile deity begrudgingly provided a name to a persistent combatant, and at other times a willing deity nevertheless was evasive. Jacob used his own changed name (Israel) to conclude that he had striven with God, hence the deity's essence is striving and the place is Peniel. Moses received enough hints in the name "I am who I am" to conclude that the use of the Tetragrammaton, YHWH, was being avoided. Manoah gained vital knowledge about "one who does wonders," a clue that came amid faltering syntax but that resulted in a worthy counter-clue that echoed Manoah's own name (v 19, *minḥâ;* "cereal offering").

The death wishes of Elijah, Jonah, Tobit, and Sarah (Tobias' future wife) came when they found themselves in miserable circumstances, like Samson's captive existence without sight. All of them, including Samson (16:30), requested death from God, and three of them chose to live longer after listening to divine arguments. Jonah sat and waited for Nineveh to disintegrate before his eyes, and the story leaves him there. Both Tobit and Sarah obtained vindication for the loss of sight and honor. Neither Elijah nor Samson enjoyed public exoneration. The prophet anointed a successor and journeyed into the heavens, borne on a fiery chariot, according to tradition. Samson fell under the debris of a crowded temple.

Pro-Davidic circles interpreted Saul's collapse as loss of charisma, despite similarities with David's own fall from favor. In this account, the hero betrayed his high calling, prompting God to withdraw the blessing that accompanied his special vocation. That departure of favor opened the door to adversity, which stalked Saul until his enemies destroyed Israel's first king. Samson, too, turned his back on the Nazirite profession, treating it lightly when gathering honey from the carcass of a lion and when selecting the jawbone of an ass as a weapon. His behavior at the wedding may also have involved use of strong drink, but that is not explicitly stated. Clearly, he toyed with cutting his hair until it became reality (16:6–19). At that point loss of charisma took place, for Yahweh's spirit departed, at least temporarily (vv 20–22).

Whenever the deity manifested itself in the OT, humans naturally reacted with appropriate dread. Jacob expressed astonishment over seeing God and surviving; Moses stood in awe, barefoot and stammering; and Isaiah experienced *mysterium tremendum et fascinans.* Notably, Samson felt no such terror before anyone. His father and mother knew terror before God's emissary, having to muster their confidence in the presence of a perceived danger from a holy one.

D. Rhetorical Features

The Samson narrative uses many different kinds of rhetorical devices: anticipation and repetition, retardation and restraint, assonance, contrast, double entendre, humor, hyperbole, dialogue and monologue, suspense. The narrator looked forward to coming attractions and glanced backward at what had already taken place; slackened the pace of the story and heightened suspense; invoked laughter and tears, both from the sublime and the ridiculous; painted contrasting pictures; achieve intimacy by dialogue and distance by monologue.

The story opens in the context of Israel's surrender to the power of the Philistines and an envisioned emancipation as a result of Samson's actions. The identity of the divine visitor is intuited and subsequently disclosed, and Delilah's gradual mastery of her lover anticipates the departure of the spirit of the Lord. Even a sparse reference to the renewed growth of Samson's hair promises ill for the uncircumcised. Normally, anticipation serves to hasten the flow of the narrative while repetition serves to slow it down. The angel's instructions to Manoah's wife occur twice, the second time on her lips and with significant variation (as in Eve's report on the initial divine prohibition in Gen 3:3). Often the repetition consists of a refrain or a formula, although slight changes occur from time to time. The episode with Delilah contains several repetends concerning the source of Samson's strength and the way to conquer him, the consequences of such victory over him, the proximity of the Philistines in another room and the announcement that they were attacking him, the reiteration that the source of his strength still remains unknown, and the declaration that Samson told her all his mind. The language of enticement, vexing, and ignorance spans the whole story.

Several observations function to slow down the story to a crawl or to relieve tension at crucial junctures: the narrator's comment that Manoah did not know the identity of the angel (13:16), the remark that Samson's parents did not recognize Yahweh's hand in Samson's fascination with the Timnite beauty (14:4), the reminder that young men used to celebrate differently during weddings (14:10), and the identification of two sites in the story as currently locatable (15:17, 19). The pace is virtually suspended in air by the twice-mentioned report that Manoah and his wife watched the angel vanish in fire.

Wordplays abound in the story: e.g., puns on the Hebrew word for "ass"; clever plays on sibilants *(wayyaᶜas šam šimšon mišteh);* frequent initial *mems*; and puns on "thirst" and "find" *(wayyimṣaʾ; wayyiṣmaʾ; baṣṣamaʾ).* "Philistines" and "I shall fall" *(pilištîm; wĕnapaltî)* as well as rare rhymes indicate that the narrator appreciated the niceties of language.

Contrast contributes to the delineation of character. Pairings such as love and hate, friend and foe, strength and weakness, knowledge and ignorance, joy and sorrow fill the narrative. The verbs *yārad* (to go down) and *ᶜālāh* (to go up) feature prominently in the story, giving the words symbolic weight. As the flame and angel ascend to heaven, Manoah and his wife fall to the ground. The transcendent and the merely human are thereby effectively distinguished.

Certain expressions in the narrative are filled with implication for the future. For example, the word *yaḥel* (to begin) occurs four times in crucial contexts, each time with a different infinitival object: Samson will begin to deliver Israel (13:5), the divine spirit began to stir the lad (13:25), Delilah began to afflict her lover (16:19), and his hair began to grow back (16:22). Only the second and third activities referred to by the verb *yaḥel* actually come to completion: the lad was certainly stirred up, and Delilah afflicted Samson mightily. The first and last activities do not reach successful conclusion, i.e., Samson does not deliver Israel from the Philistines and his hair does not grow back to full length.

Identifying humor in ancient texts proves difficult, but some features of the Samson narrative must surely have evoked raucous laughter. Samson's method of starting a fire (15:4) and his postcoital activity (16:3) fall into this category, as does, perhaps, the side trip to visit the carcass of a lion while on his way to marry the Timnite woman (14:8).

The story has hyperbole from start to finish. Exaggeration of numbers, distances, and deeds takes place, for anything can happen in legends. The heightening of numbers (thirty Ashkelonites, three hundred foxes, a thousand Philistines, three thousand Judahites, three thousand-plus Philistines) lends suspense, turning Samson into a hero of magnificent proportions and thus magnifying even more his eventual fall to a woman.

Lively dialogue provides balance for the violent activity reported in the story. The conversation, always brief and to the point, offers characterization and brings readers more directly into the movement of the story. A woman talks to an angel, a man to his wife, parents to their son, lover to lover, enemy to enemy, Judahite to Danite, Samson to God, a prisoner to his youthful servant. In the story monologue inevitably aborts. Samson expressed his intention to visit his bride, to get one final revenge and quit, and to shake off his ropes and go out as usual. Similarly, the Gazites uttered a collective monologue ("At the crack of dawn we will kill him") that failed to materialize.

The episode with Delilah is full of suspense, whether by use of the refrain ("The Philistines are upon you, Samson") or by the gradual disclosure of Samson's vital secret. The allusion to the beginning of the regrowth of Samson's hair creates eager expectation, a suspense-creator that the narrator for some reason failed to follow up.

E. Function of the Story

The powerful story about a secret betrayed and a vow ignored addressed a difficult problem in Israelite society: the attraction to foreign women. Early proverbs in Egypt and in Israel attest to the desirability of foreigners, whose ways were different and whose sexual appeal was great. The Samson narrative juxtaposes an ideal Israelite wife (and mother) with three foreign women: the beautiful Timnite represents an erotic attachment based on physical attraction, the harlot illustrates a detached type of sexual relief; and Delilah depicts the dangers of unreciprocated love. Samson's inability to emerge unscathed from such liaisons stood as a warning for lesser beings. The message could scarcely be missed: if the mighty Samson could not manage relationships with foreign women how could ordinary Israelites succeed in such ventures? The attraction of exogamy persisted as late as the Exile, making the Samson story timely long after its original composition.

F. Postcanonical Readings of the Story

Josephus (*Ant* 5.8) embellished the account by commenting on the beauty of Manoah's wife and introducing the theme of jealousy. This Jewish historian also toned down Samson's waywardness by having him stay at an inn in Gaza. The early Church described Samson as a saint, despite his pride, immoral conduct, and suicide. Resemblances with Christ occurred to some interpreters: both had wondrous births; both freed Israel; both defeated a lion (in Jesus' case, Satan); the spirit departed from both; each struggled alone and succumbed to foes as a result of a bribe; both were bound; both broke down gates (Jesus destroyed the gates of hell); both achieved victory in death.

Milton's *Samson Agonistes*, an autobiographical epic treatment of primal temptation, transforms the hero into a thinker. Milton freely adapts the plot, having Manoah and Delilah confront the enslaved Samson, introducing a champion of the Philistines, Harapha, and adding a chorus and public messenger. Samson defends God's justice and grieves over the dishonor he brought to the Lord. Manoah questions answered prayer, which had reversed the role of father and son, making the old father look after his son, but he will gladly hand over his possessions to obtain his son's release. Delilah tries various ploys to get Samson back, defending her actions as (1) natural feminine curiosity and weakness; (2) an attempt to keep him at home; (3) love for State and God; and (4) love for Samson. Harapha, no match for Samson, accuses him of murder, theft, and betrayal of country. In Milton's eyes, Samson suffers faithfully in a battle with Dagon, achieving catharsis. Samson symbolizes everyone's struggle against sin and ultimate victory; his defeat was only a temporary tragedy of spiritual suffering resulting from failure in a high calling.

Bibliography

Blenkinsopp, J. 1959. Some notes on the Saga of Samson and the Heroic Milieu. *Scripture* 11: 81–89.

———. 1963. Structure and Style in Judges 13–16. *JBL* 82: 65–76.

Carmy, S. 1974. The Sphinx as Leader: A Reading of Judges 13–16. *Tradition* 14/3: 66–79.

Crenshaw, J. L. 1974. The Samson Saga: Filial Devotion or Erotic Attachment? *ZAW* 86: 470–504.

———. 1978. *Samson: A Secret Betrayed, a Vow Ignored.* Atlanta and London.

Greenstein, E. L. 1981. The Riddle of Samson. *Prooftexts* 1: 237–60.

Gunkel, H. 1913. Simson. Pp. 38–64 in *Reden und Aufsätze.* Göttingen.

Krouse, F. 1949. *Milton's Samson and the Christian Tradition.* Princeton.

Maragalith, O. 1986. Samson's Riddle and Samson's Magic Locks. *VT* 36: 225–34.

Nel, P. 1985. The Riddle of Samson. *Bib* 66: 534–45.

Rad, G. von 1974. Die Geschichte von Simson. Pp. 49–52 in *Gottes Wirken in Israel: Vorträge zum Alten Testament,* ed. O. H. Steck. Neukirchen-Vluyn.

Selms, A. van. 1950. The Best Man and Bride—from Sumer to St. John with a New Interpretation of Judges, Chapters 14 and 15. *JNES* 9: 65–75.

Wharton, J. A. 1973. The Secret of Yahweh: Story and Affirmation in Judges 13–16. *Int* 27: 48–66.

JAMES L. CRENSHAW

SAMSON, WIFE OF. Samson's determination to marry a Philistine woman from Timnah is surprising in view of his mission—to deliver Israel from Philistine oppression (13:5). Samson's parents object (14:1–3), but unknown to Samson or his parents, it is all part of the divine plan (14:4). The fact that the Danite Samson can marry a Philistine suggests that the Israelites and Philistines managed to live side by side in the Shephelah with some measure of harmony; his parents' objection to the marriage and its disastrous consequences (Judges 14–15) illustrate the extent of hostilities between the two peoples.

The Bible does not record the woman's name. The story of Samson and the Timnite (14:1–15:8) is modeled on the account of Samson and Delilah (16:4–22). In both accounts the Philistines rely on a woman's help to discover Samson's secret: in 16:4–22 the source of his great strength; in 14:15–18 the answer to his riddle. Whereas they bribe Delilah (16:5), they threaten the Timnite (14:15). Both women wear down Samson's resistance by harassing him (14:17; 16:16); the Timnite relies on tears whereas Delilah uses words. Both use love to cajole Samson into revealing his secret (14:16; 16:15).

When Samson, having been outwitted by the Philistines, angrily returns to his father's house, his father-in-law apparently takes it as a sign that Samson has renounced any claim to his daughter, and the Timnite becomes the best man's wife. Thus when Samson reappears, the woman is denied to him (15:1–2). Reprisals and counter-reprisals in chap. 15 allow Samson to wreak more havoc among the Philistines, thereby fulfilling God's purpose (14:4). The Timnite is a victim of their hostility. The threat she sought to avert by revealing the answer to Samson's riddle comes to pass: the Philistines "burned her and her father with fire" (15:6).

J. CHERYL EXUM

SAMUᶜ, ES-. See ESHTEMOA (PLACE).

SAMUEL (PERSON) [Heb *šĕmûʾēl*]. The Hebrew Bible portrays Samuel in a variety of roles: priest, prophet, judge, and "seer." Moreover, at a critical juncture in the history of the Israelite people, Samuel appears very instrumental in the establishment of the monarchy. In the words of one writer, "all the great predicates which Israel had to bestow in the period before the growth of the monarchy have been heaped on this man—and in spite of this, or more accurately, because of this, it is difficult to classify the historical Samuel" (Möhlenbrink 1940–41: 65; cf. Weiser 1962: 93–94).

A. Historical Studies

The first block of material relating to Samuel (1 Samuel 1–3) portrays him as an aspiring priest (note 1 Chronicles 6 connects his lineage with Levi; 1 Samuel 1 with Ephraim), serving under Eli at the sanctuary of Shiloh (1 Sam 2:11, 18; 3:1). Later passages in 1 Samuel report his performing sacrificial functions often associated with priests (7:9; 9:13; 10:8; 16:1–5). The stories of young Samuel are commonly classified as legend or idyll, and Samuel's associations with the priesthood have been widely questioned (Press 1938: 222–23; Wildberger 1957: 462; Cody 1969: 72–80; for a different view, see Willis 1972). The biblical text never applies the label "priest" to Samuel. At the time of Samuel, the offering of sacrifices did not require that one be a priest (*AncIsr,* 355). After the ark of the covenant was captured and the shrine of Shiloh apparently destroyed by the Philistines (cf. 1 Samuel 4) there is no report that Samuel sought to rebuild Shiloh or restore the ark of the covenant to a prominent position in Israelite cultic life, or that he moved to the sanctuary at Nob, as did other priests from Shiloh (cf. 1 Sam 14:3; 22:11–12). It is quite conceivable that, at a time when levitic ancestry was not a prerequisite for priestly service (*AncIsr,* 361–62), Samuel was apprenticing for the priesthood, but the calling of the Lord turned him to other forms of ministry. Later Israelites, assuming a priestly role for Samuel, assigned to him a levitic ancestry (1 Chr 6:7–13; contrast the lineage in 1 Sam 1:1).

1 Sam 9:5–14, 18–21 refers to Samuel as a *seer,* one who has the gift of clairvoyance (note also 1 Chr 9:22; 26:28; 29:29). The prevailing historical-critical position is that a folktale about Saul meeting an anonymous local seer was at some point reworked to identify the seer with Samuel and to insert the account of his anointing of Saul as prince (Bardtke 1968: 301–2; Mayes 1978: 13–14, 17–18; McCarter *1 Samuel* AB, 26, 186; for a different analysis of this pericope see Robertson 1944: 180–83; Willis 1972: 49).

1 Sam 3:20 explicitly labels Samuel a prophet. This is the epithet which later tradition commonly used for him (2 Chr 35:18; 1 Esdr 1:20; Sir 46:13–20). According to 1 Sam 8:10–18, 10:17–19, and 15:1–2, Samuel delivers messages from the Lord, even employing the prophetic formula, "Thus says Yahweh," (10:18; 15:2). In 7:8–9 and 12:23 he exercises the prophetic function of intercession (cf. Jer 7:16; 27:18; *3 En.* 48A:5). 1 Sam 9:1–10:16 and 16:1–13 cast Samuel in the role of king-designator in a fashion similar to Ahijah and Elijah (1 Kgs 11:29–39; 19:15–17; cf. 2 Kgs 9:1–12). As Saul begins to fall out of favor with God, Samuel announces God's words of judgment to the king (13:13–14; 15:17–19, 22–23). Even in the séance scene in 1 Samuel 28, Samuel acts as a prophet, announcing doom upon the ill-fated king (Beuken 1978). A number of recent works have suggested that the mantle of prophecy was cast upon Samuel by later handlers of the tradition. Prior to the composition of the final (Deuteronomistic) version of 1 Samuel, it is hypothesized, there was an edition prepared by prophetic circles, which developed the character of Samuel into a figure who speaks and behaves like the prophets of a later era (Fohrer 1968: 223–25; Birch 1976: 140–47; McCarter *1 Samuel* AB, 18–23).

The role with which the greatest number of scholars associate the historical Samuel is that of *judge.* 1 Sam 7:15 declares that "Samuel judged Israel all the days of his life," an expression akin to that used of the so-called "minor judges" who are mentioned briefly in the book of Judges (10:1–5; 12:7–15) and whose activity is usually assumed to have been primarily judicial. This aspect of Samuel's "judgeship" is credited by a number of commentators as rooted in historical fact (Hertzberg *1 and 2 Samuel* OTL, 67; Bardtke 1968: 294; Willis 1972: 50–53; *BHI,* 186). The language in 1 Sam 7:13–14 about the subduing of enemies and peace in the land is reminiscent of statements made in connection with the accomplishments of the "major judges" such as Ehud, Gideon, and Jephthah (Judg 3:30; 8:28; 11:33), whose fame rests on military exploits. 1 Sam 12:11 mentions Samuel in the same breath with Jerubbaal, Barak, and Jephthah, whom the Lord raised up as deliverers for Israel's sake. The fact that 1 Sam 9:16 and chaps. 13–14 contradict the statement of 7:13–14 that the Philistine threat was subdued at this time makes the report of Samuel's military activity dubious. Scholarly consensus considers the portrayal of Samuel as a military deliverer to be a late fiction created by the Deuteronomistic editors (*NDH,* 55; McKenzie 1962: 14; Mayes 1978: 8).

Since virtually all of the accounts surrounding the establishment of Saul's kingship assign Samuel an instrumental role, it is hard to avoid the conclusion that he was a major figure in the transition to monarchy, but scholars are divided over where in these accounts genuine historical recollections are to be found.

Although 1 Sam 8:1–5 is often adjudged to contain reliable information (Wildberger 1957: 457; Weiser 1962: 29–33; Mayes 1978: 11), many critics believe that the description of Samuel's activity in the rest of chap. 8 reflects later generations' unhappy experiences with the Israelite kingship (McCarter *1 Samuel* AB, 161–62; Van Seters 1983: 251–52). Some, however, do attribute the speech (vv 10–18) to Samuel, who feared the imitation of exploitative governmental practices common among Canaanite kings and a jeopardizing of Yahweh's kingship, as well as encroachment on his own prerogatives (Mendelsohn 1956; Bardtke 1968: 294–95; Halpern 1981: 186, 216–24).

As noted above, the references to Samuel in 9:1–10:16 are widely thought to have been inserted at a secondary stage of the tradition by prophetic editors. Some have suggested that the foreign origin of the anointing ritual, with its magical connotations, makes it unlikely that Samuel would have utilized the practice (Bardtke 1968: 302; cf. Weiser 1962: 52–57).

Several traditions of varying historical value seem to have been combined in 10:17–27. There is no reference elsewhere in the OT to choosing a king by lot, which is an unlikely way to select a king (Wildberger 1957: 455; McKenzie 1962: 11; Weiser 1962: 65). It seems more reasonable that Saul was identified via an oracle from God specifying the tallest man to be the divine nominee. Although 10:25 is often attributed (with reference to Deut 17:14–20) to later redactors, a fairly widespread interpretation is that this refers to a constitutional document spelling out royal regulations negotiated by Samuel with the popular assembly (Halpern 1981: 222–35; Ishida 1977: 45–46, 53; cf. McCarter *1 Samuel* AB, 193–94). The prophetic oracle in vv 18–19 is usually regarded as an addition by prophetic or Deuteronomistic editors (Birch 1976: 47–51).

Most scholars agree that chap. 11 has substantial historical value, but that the references to Samuel in vv 7, 12–14 are secondary additions (Irwin 1941: 113–14, 129; Birch 1976: 54–56; Mayes *IJH,* 325). Chap. 12 is generally conceded to be a composition of the Deuteronomistic writers of the 7th or 6th centuries (Fohrer 1968: 225; Mayes 1978: 10–11; Van Seters 1983: 258).

With regard to the two accounts which relate Saul's rejection by Samuel (13:7b–15; 15:1–35), the usual conclusion is that the present stories are revisions of traditions originally sympathetic to Saul, seeking to explain two historical phenomena: Saul's failure to establish a dynasty and the final rupture between the king and Samuel (Press 1938: 209–10). Prophetic circles responsible for the present shape of the stories were seeking to enhance the concept of prophetic authority vis-à-vis the king (Birch 1976: 74–85, 95–108; McCarter *1 Samuel* AB, 230, 269–71; Mayes *IJH,* 330).

The parlous times following the events related in 1 Samuel 4 called for a figure whose authority was recognized on a relatively wide front within the league of Israelite tribes to assist them in making the transition to a new system of governance, while not abandoning the sacral traditions. At a time when "offices" such as priest, prophet, and judge were not precisely and finally defined, Samuel apparently engaged in activities which tradition eventually associated with one or another of these roles. Subsequent generations very reasonably enhanced the portrait of Samuel with features common to these various functionaries (cf. Weiser 1962: 9–16; Willis 1972: 41).

B. Literary Studies

In contrast to historical-critical and traditio-historical studies, which attempt to distinguish the diverse sources underlying 1 Samuel and the different social and historical situations which produced these sources and their redactions, literary critics of the Bible attempt to read the final text as a single coherent narrative. These scholars perform a "close reading" of the narrative, carefully scrutinizing narratalogical features of the text—features such as plot arrangement, quoted speech, repetition of key words, parallels of situations, contrasts, and ambiguity—which may assist the reader in construing the character of the dramatis personae (cf. Alter 1981; Sternberg 1985).

The contrast achieved, in 1 Samuel 2, by juxtaposing references to Samuel's growth and faithful service with reports of the wickedness of Eli's sons—separated by some historical critics into separate narrative cycles—prompts an understanding of Samuel as a worthier holder of the priestly office than the family of Eli (Willis 1979: 208n; Eslinger 1985: 119–20, 127–28). This impression is fortified further in chap. 3 by several literary devices, such as the contrast of Samuel sleeping in the temple of Yahweh, while Eli sleeps "in his own place" (Fishbane 1982: 195–200). The opposing parallelism between 3:1 and 3:20 conveys the great significance of Samuel's activity (Simon 1981: 122). The remark in 3:19 recalls the motif from Deut 18:15–22 of the prophet like Moses whose word comes true (Miscall 1986: 44–45).

Instead of taking the absence of Samuel from 1 Samuel 4–6 as an indication that these chapters originated in a different socio-historical situation than the Samuel material, the literary critics read this as a deliberate authorial technique to help characterize Samuel. The nonmention of Samuel in connection with the events which proved so tragic for Israel is a narrative device to represent the difficulties which the nation experiences without the presence of Samuel (Willis 1979: 212; Polzin 1989: 58–60). This is underscored by the marvelous success which Israel enjoys vis-à-vis the Philistines as soon as Samuel reenters the narrative in 1 Samuel 7.

The chapters surrounding the inauguration of the monarchy (1 Samuel 8–12) may be read as an account of a very human and ambivalent Samuel who is pressed into service as a kingmaker against his will. Out of loyalty to the kingship of God (1 Sam 10:18–19; 12:12) Samuel resists the move to human kingship, but finally yields to the instruction of God (8:7, 9, 22; 9:16–17) and makes Saul king. When God repents of making Saul king, Samuel again exhibits ambivalence: he shows sympathy for the king (1 Sam 15:11, 35; 16:1) and, instead of delivering a frontal accusation, gives Saul a chance to supply an explanation for his disobedience (15:19). Exemplifying his own declaration that a human may repent though God will not (15:29), Samuel yields to the importuning of the repentant Saul (15:31) and continues to grieve (16:1) over the fallen king (Sternberg 1985: 503–15).

In contrast to the aforementioned examples, other readers have discovered in the narrative clues which suggest that Samuel is to be construed as imperceptive, insensitive, self-seeking, and manipulative. (This usually accompanies interpretations of Saul as a more heroic figure than has traditionally been the case and of God in rather unflattering terms: see especially Gunn 1980 and Eslinger 1985; Polzin 1989).

1 Samuel 2 and 3 predispose the reader to expect that Samuel will be the "faithful priest" for whom God will build a "sure/faithful house" (2:35), but this turns out to be a feint on the author's part. Why did Samuel not turn out to be the promised priest? Perhaps the explanation lies in 8:1–3, which relates what Buber (1967: 76) refers to as "the delinquency of Samuel." The wickedness of Samuel's sons recalls the motif of Eli's evil sons. From that earlier experience Samuel should have learned of the dangers of filial corruption. Like Eli, Samuel hears of his sons' wickedness from others, but the narrator makes no mention that Samuel sought to rebuke his sons (contrast 2:23–25); in 12:2, he blithely ignore their wickedness.

In various ways the narrator appears to raise doubts about Samuel's prophetic credentials. Does 1 Samuel 3 depict a Samuel who goes to the priest Eli repeatedly because he is a humble and devoted servant of the elderly clergyman (Simon 1981: 125), or is the repeated trip to Eli a reflection of Samuel's dullness and lack of perception (Polzin 1989: 49–51)? Although in 1 Samuel 9 Samuel is called a "seer," it is only after he *hears* God's instruction (vv 15–17) that he comprehends who this Saul is: even when he "sees" Saul (v 17) he does not really see, until the Lord speaks. Samuel's affirmation about God's nonrepentance in 15:29 seems to place him in direct contradiction to both the narrator (15:35) and the Lord (15:11). In the scene of David's anointment, Samuel blunders and needs

God's correction (16:6–7; see also Alter 1981: 149; Sternberg 1985: 94–97; Polzin 1989: 95, 140, 153–55).

Analysis of the rhetoric in Samuel's speeches in 1 Sam 8:10–18 and 12:1–17 reveals him to be petulant, truculent, and ungracious (Good 1981: 65). The speeches depict Samuel manipulating the audience through a one-sided description of kingship (8:11–17), threats (8:18), and meteorological pyrotechnics (12:16–18). He is selective in what he recalls of the facts and in what he reveals of God's will: no mention in 8:10–18 of the Lord's principal objection to kingship (on theocratic grounds) nor of the Lord's willingness, in spite of this, to grant the people a king (cf. 8:7–9); no recognition in either speech of the wickedness of Samuel's sons, a basic motivating factor in the people's request for a king (cf. 8:3–5; see also Gunn 1980: 64; Preston 1982: 33–34; Eslinger 1985: 386).

Even in the closing scene in which Samuel appears, the story of his being summoned from the realm of the dead by the witch of Endor (1 Samuel 28), he is made to appear cold and insensitive in contrast to the tender hospitality which the witch extends to the desperate king Saul (Preston 1982: 36).

An imaginative retelling of the Samuel material, much in the fashion of the writings of Josephus, is found in *Pseudo-Philo* 50–59, 64 (Harrington *OTP* 2: 364–73, 376–77).

Bibliography

Alter, R. 1981. *The Art of Biblical Narrative.* New York.

Bardtke, H. 1968. Samuel und Saul. Gedanken zur Entstehung des Königtums in Israel. *BiOr* 25: 289–302.

Beuken, W. A. M. 1978. I Samuel 28: The Prophet as "Hammer of Witches." *JSOT* 6: 3–17.

Birch, B. C. 1976. *The Rise of the Israelite Monarchy: The Growth and Development of I Samuel 7–15.* SBLDS 27. Missoula.

Buber, M. 1967. *Kingship of God.* Trans. R. Scheiman. New York.

Cody, A. 1969. *A History of Old Testament Priesthood.* AnBib 35.

Eslinger, L. 1985. *Kingship of God in Crisis: A Close Reading of 1 Samuel 1–12.* Bible and Literature 10. Sheffield.

Fishbane, M. 1982. 1 Samuel 3: Historical Narrative and Narrative Poetics. Vol. 2, pp. 191–203 in *Literary Interpretations of Biblical Narratives,* eds. K. R. R. Gros Louis and J. S. Ackerman. Nashville.

Fohrer, G. 1968. *Introduction to the Old Testament.* Trans. D. Green. Nashville.

Good, E. M. 1981. Saul: the Tragedy of Greatness. Pp. 56–80 in *Irony in the Old Testament.* Sheffield.

Gunn, D. M. 1980. *The Fate of King Saul.* JSOTSup 14. Sheffield.

Halpern, B. 1981. *The Constitution of the Monarchy in Israel.* HSM 25. Decatur.

Irwin, W. A. 1941. Samuel and the Rise of the Monarchy. *AJSL* 58: 113–34.

Ishida, T. 1977. *The Royal Dynasties in Ancient Israel.* BZAW 142. Berlin.

Mayes, A. D. H. 1978. The Rise of the Israelite Monarchy. *ZAW* 90: 1–19.

McKenzie, J. L. 1962. The Four Samuels. *BR* 7: 3–18.

Mendelsohn, I. 1956. Samuel's Denunciation of Kingship in the Light of Akkadian Documents from Ugarit. *BASOR* 143: 17–22.

Miscall, P. 1986. *1 Samuel: A Literary Reading.* Bloomington.

Möhlenbrink, K. 1940–41. Saul's Ammoniterfeldzug und Samuels Beitrag zum Königtum des Saul. *ZAW* 58: 57–70.

Noth, M. 1963. Samuel und Silo. *VT* 13: 390–400.

Polzin, R. 1989. *Samuel and the Deuteronomist.* San Francisco.

Press, R. 1938. Der Prophet Samuel. *ZAW* 56: 177–225.

Preston, T. R. 1982. The Heroism of Saul: Patterns of Meaning in the Narrative of the Early Kingship. *JSOT* 24: 27–46.

Robertson, E. 1944. Samuel and Saul. *BJRL* 28: 175–206.

Simon, U. 1981. Samuel's Call to Prophecy: Form Criticism with Close Reading. *Prooftexts* 1: 119–32.

Sternberg, M. 1985. *The Poetics of Biblical Narrative.* Bloomington.

Van Seters, J. 1983. *In Search of History.* New Haven.

Weiser, A. 1962. *Samuel: seine geschichtliche Aufgabe und religiöse Bedeutung.* FRLANT 81. Göttingen.

Wildberger, H. 1957. Samuel und die Entstehung des israelitischen Königtums. *TZ* 13: 442–69.

Willis, J. T. 1972. Cultic Elements in the Story of Samuel's Birth and Dedication. *StTh* 26: 33–61.

———. 1979. Samuel versus Eli. *TZ* 35: 201–12.

George W. Ramsey

SAMUEL, BOOK OF 1–2.

This entry consists of two articles. The first examines the critical problems associated with the text, composition, and content of 1–2 Samuel, while the second article focuses on the narrative and theological aspects of the text.

TEXT, COMPOSITION, AND CONTENT

The books of Samuel, two of the Former Prophets, are named either for the prophetic figure who dominates chaps. 1–3 and 7–15 of 1 Samuel, or because 1 Chr 29:29–30 credits the seer with recording the acts of David. The text, considered one of the most disturbed in the Hebrew Bible, was initially a single story. The division into the eighth and ninth books in the MT, but ninth and tenth in English, derives from the LXX, where Samuel and Kings each have two parts that together comprise the four "Books of Kingdoms" *(basileiōn A-D).* The apportionment may have been introduced because of the length of the manuscript and the desire to conclude a first unit with the account of Saul's death. Although the separation detached the figure Samuel from episodes in 2 Samuel, the tradition continued in Latin versions and in the 15th and 16th centuries C.E. began to make its way into the Hebrew text where it influenced the Jewish canon, first in hand-copied manuscripts (1448) and then through printed editions. The first Rabbinic Bible, the "Bomberg Bible" published by Daniel Bomberg in Venice in 1516–17, accepted the division, and it was retained when the Second Rabbinic Bible was published in 1524–25.

Textual and source critics expend considerable effort in trying to recover an elusive "original" text of Samuel. Any attempt to summarize their contributions or that of other scholars who study the composition or content of the books must be sketchy and correspondingly arbitrary. The descriptions can only identify major currents and turning points that have brought scholarship to its present state. In the case of composition and content, the choices affect not only impressions regarding the tradition of scholarship, but also an understanding of the Bible itself. Assertions about the book's composition and content are controlled in part by the questions asked, methods and approaches taken, and theories projected by researchers. The stance represented in this article assumes that 1–2 Samuel are religiously motivated cultural artifacts that originated and have been transmitted by human agents in physical space and historical time. It presumes also that the books reflect early attitudes about the social world(s) of Yahwists, Israelites, and others who lived relatively customary lives in the E Mediterranean basin sometime between the beginning of the Iron Age I (ca. 1200 B.C.E.) and the beginning of the Common Era.

A. Text Tradition
B. Composition
  1. Early Approaches
  2. Early 20th Century Criticism
  3. Recent Criticism
C. Content
  1. Presuppositions
  2. Overview
  3. Principal Cycles
  4. Unity of the Cycles

A. Text Tradition

In the last century, critics such as Thenius (*Samuels* KEHAT), Wellhausen (1871), Driver (1890, *NHT*), and others sought to emend the MT and recover a Hebrew original by relying heavily on the ancient versions, especially the LXX. Imbued with the evolutionist, diffusionist, and comparativist enthusiasms of their day and lacking early Hebrew manuscripts, they were attracted by the fullness and antiquity of the Greek and other versions. In them, they sought their own and the Bible's origins. A more accurate original Hebrew text could be restored, it was hoped, that would reflect a pristine religion against which later developments might be judged. The versions examined by comparative methods offered grounds for improved readings, but new primary data were needed before certainty about the Hebrew text tradition could be attained. By the time Driver's notes were revised in 1912, knowledge of Hebrew orthography, philology, and idiom, and of Palestinian topography had increased greatly, as had familiarity with characteristics of the versions and text families. Kittel's *Biblia Hebrica,* Kautzch's revision of Gesenius' grammar, and the lexicon of Brown, Driver, and Briggs had been published. These stood together with an expanding list of critical commentaries as witnesses to the growing interest and confidence in the details of biblical scholarship and comparative methods.

Although certainty about the relationship between the LXX and the MT remained in doubt during this century (de Boer 1938, 1949), the LXX remains an indispensable source for the text of Samuel. New confidence in the version was restored following the discovery of three Hebrew Samuel manuscripts in Cave IV at Qumran ($4QSam^{a,b,c}$) in the 1950s. The fullest, $4QSam^a$, written in the first half of the 1st century, ca. 50–25 B.C.E. (McCarter *1 Samuel* AB, 6), holds the greatest promise for textual criticism. The fragmentary $4QSam^c$ preserves only portions of 1 Samuel 25 and 2 Samuel 14–15, but also dates from the early 1st century B.C.E. The second principal manuscript, $4QSam^b$, dates from the late 3d century B.C.E. but witnesses only to portions of 1 Samuel (Cross 1961; Ulrich 1978: 10).

Comparisons with the QL first seemed to confirm the proximity of an early Hebrew tradition to the *Vorlage* of the LXX. Later, however, critics surmised that the QL stands closer to the Lucianic manuscripts (LXX^L) than to the Codex Vaticanus (LXX^B). This suggests that the Lucianic tradition, which draws on the OG, represents a move toward a Palestinian Hebrew text tradition represented by the QL. Today, at least eleven early witnesses to Samuel (besides the fragmentary $4QSam^c$) must be weighed in the search for primitive traditions. In addition to the $4QSam^{a,b}$ and $LXX^{L,B}$ they are Codex Alexandrinus (LXX^A), the MT, the OL, *Tg. Jon.* (Jewish Aramaic version), Syr Peshitta, Vg, and Josephus *Ant.*

The delay in publishing the QL diminished its expected impact. Bible translators have been able to use the material occasionally, and for Samuel, McCarter's commentary and Ulrich's study are particularly valuable contributions. As a result of these publications, however limited, critics now tend to accept fuller versions of stories where several forms exist. For example, the expansive description of Nahash's disfiguring of peoples from the eastern tribes ($4QSam^a$, 1 Sam 10:27b–11:1), previously known only through Josephus *Ant* (6.68–71), is no longer considered secondary (McCarter *1 Samuel* AB, 199). Implicit in such choices, however, is a lingering evolutionary hope for an "original" Samuel.

B. Composition

During the 20th century, continental, British, and American scholarship continued to seek original meanings of Samuel texts by separating portions of the books according to literary units. Individual sections were divided according to authorship, form, source, redactor, or other phenomena that had left their mark in the text. As philological, archaeological, historical, and comparative skills improved, many forms of biblical criticism developed. Many were modeled on textual criticism and archaeology and sometimes were described as excavative methods. They were used in order to identify discrete textual units and to trace the trajectories through which they had passed on their way to becoming the Hebrew canon. The approaches became virtual "subspecialties" within biblical studies. Paradoxically, however, they inspired doubt as well as confidence: doubt because the methods tended to fragment the text and suggest a religious evolution that challenged the historical certainties of the 19th century; certainty because the methods presumed to resolve contradictions and obscurities in the texts.

Critical scholarship held its own, but studies on 1–2 Samuel were influenced and overshadowed by contemporary discussions of other portions of the Hebrew canon, particularly the Pentateuch. Full and independent attention was given to Samuel only after many of the issues raised in those units had been argued. The tendency to treat the Pentateuch, especially Genesis, first, and Samuel later affected the way the composition of the books was examined and described. Interest in Samuel increased gradually and eventually independently as history was abandoned in Genesis studies and thought to survive in

Samuel, but no sharp division marks clearly defined chronological phases in Samuel criticism. Several fundamental hypotheses were proposed at the beginning of the ventures, and until recently much of the subsequent discussion was refining or reacting to earlier expositions. Nevertheless, two phenomena deserve mention. The first is the important study of Leonhard Rost (1982), first published in 1926. Although itself derivative, the work was exceptionally influential, especially after the 1960s, when works by von Rad (*PHOE,* 166–205) and Weiser (1948) that were based on it became available in both German and English. The second is the increasing role that archaeology played in biblical studies, especially Samuel studies, in the postwar era. Then, Iron Age archaeologists and biblical specialists showed renewed interest in the Davidic and Solomonic eras because they assumed that the texts were solidly historical, and comparative philological studies advanced, especially under the influence of the Ras Shamra texts, in ways that provided greater access to the culture of Syro-Palestine.

1. Early Approaches. Repetitions, doublets, contradictions, breaks, and uneven seams in the narrative led critics as early as Eichhorn (1780–83) to abandon the synagogue tradition of a unified text in order to look for parallel traditions within and outside Samuel that linked seemingly isolated literary units. Thenius followed this direction in his commentary on Samuel (*Samuels* KEHAT), but it was Wellhausen's revision of Bleek's introduction (1878) that laid the groundwork on which many later Samuel studies were built. Wellhausen developed the first elaborate multisource explanation of parallel strands. He identified 2 Samuel 9–20 and 1 Kings 1–2 as distinctive, and, without returning to the synagogue tradition, he credited the section with critical literary unity and historical accuracy. But Kittel (1892) and others argued somewhat contrarily that similarities between Samuel and other materials were due to a common background of thought and that Samuel, including the succession story, should be investigated in its own right. It would be for Rost eventually to reconcile these two positions, but the bases for his analysis of the succession narrative were already in place.

2. Early 20th Century Criticism. Much of the debate during the first half of the 20th century centered around three questions inherited from the century before: Were the books compiled from repetitious narrative strands or independent literary blocks? What was the relationship between the Samuel traditions, on the one hand, and the Pentateuch, Deuteronomistic History (DH), and their sources on the other? Did the authors of Samuel write history?

a. End of the Quest for Parallel Literary Strands. Contemporary pentateuchal criticism led many early 20th century scholars to continue the search for extensions of the sources J and E in Samuel and for Samuel parallels in the books of Joshua and Judges. Budde (*Samuel* KHC) divided the narrative into parallel strands J and E, but in Samuel these were substantially redacted by the Deuteronomist. Thus, he proposed that a pre-Deuteronomic Samuel was redacted first by the Deuteronomist who introduced Deuteronomic views and excised sections that were objectionable. Eventually, the excluded sections were reintroduced by other editors who misplaced them, thereby confusing the original order.

Alternative documentary and fragmentary hypotheses followed (Gressmann 1921, Caspari *Samuelbücher*). Each assumed an integral original story, inferred compilation over time, and credited repetitious sections of the books to early writers and later redactors, such as Elohists, who introduced redundant and inconsistent sections. Owing to the evolutionary presuppositions of the day, the later materials were usually described as "additions" and thought to be historically less reliable than earlier sources. This approach continues until today, but the search for literary strands that extend beyond the books of Samuel reached its zenith when Eissfeldt (1931) proposed three parallel sources (I, II, and III) as continuations of presumed Heptateuchal traditions L, J, and E.

b. Rost's Succession Narrative (SN). The quest for parallels abated gradually. In his 1926 work, Rost expanded Kittel's proposal *contra* various documentary and fragmentary hypotheses, but he did so by examining a unit Wellhausen had already delineated, 2 Samuel 9–20 and 1 Kings 1–2. On the basis of style, themes, literary devices, and, to a lesser extent, content, he presumed to identify not only the narrative's limits but also its relationship to other sections of Samuel, including 2 Samuel 7 (the Dynastic Oracle) and 2 Sam 6:16, 20–23 (that signals the end of Saul's line). The SN was, Rost argued, the longest unit in Samuel and the work of a single writer close to the events who may have written the early account from experience. He insisted that the writer, who was more author than compiler, used literary techniques such as foreshadowing to weave an integral account of Solomon's succession to the throne. The compiler of Samuel, on the other hand, arranged preexisting sources, including literary units, sequentially and not in parallel.

The study had enormous influence on Samuel studies and, although now seriously out of date, still stands as a starting point for investigations of the SN and other sections of 1 and 2 Samuel. The thesis or portions of it gradually made their way into introductions and interpretative studies. Weiser (1948) argued for a pre-Deuteronomistic compilation of Samuel that reflected the theological viewpoint of prophetic circles and the Elohist (but earlier than E) and that was assembled from heterogeneous literary compositions. These independent fundamental units—the ark narrative, the story of Saul's rise, and the SN—were brought together with others from disparate sources by an awakening national consciousness inspired by David's successes. The consciousness and Samuel tradition continued together so that the Deuteronomistic revisers who inherited them saw little to emend or change. Weiser's insistence, against Noth, on the earlier pre-Deuteronomic layer has been more widely accepted (Birch 1976) than his claim for Deuteronomic unity (Cross 1967; Würthwein 1974; Veijola 1975; Langlemet 1976).

Von Rad (*PHOE,* 166–205) focused attention on the SN as history writing. By insisting that the document was nearly contemporary to the events it described, he inferred both an early date, perhaps Solomonic, and a high degree of historical accuracy. These and other factors led him to interpret the narrative as theological history that demonstrates how the deity intervenes in human affairs. See also COURT NARRATIVE (2 SAMUEL 9–1 KINGS 2).

c. Noth's Deuteronomistic History. The relation of the

Samuel traditions to materials beyond the books of Samuel took another turn when Noth (*NDH*) proposed that the narrative, Deuteronomy through 2 Kings, was a unified history produced by a single compiler during the Exile. This was to deny an earlier unified Samuel stratum and to reopen questions regarding early Israel's historical consciousness. Responses were predictably varied. Those who continued to argue for the existence of literary strands recognized an exilic or postexilic Deuteronomistic redactor but denied that the individual was a purposeful historian (see Hölscher 1952; Eissfeldt 1947). Others accepted the fundamental hypothesis of a DH but saw it as a work by more than one person and believed that it had passed through two or more redactions before, during, or after the Exile (Pfeiffer 1948; Carlson 1964; Cross 1967; Dietrich 1972; Veijola 1975). The discussions tended to cut Samuel free from its early monarchic moorings and to allow sections to be examined apart from the SN. See DEUTERONOMISTIC HISTORY.

3. Recent Criticism. During the 1970s and 1980s, the composition of Samuel was linked to other historical, literary, archaeological, and sociological realia. Interpreters continued to rely upon the standard critical methods of the preceding decades, but these gradually gave way to or were used in conjunction with new approaches and forms of analysis borrowed from disciplines outside biblical studies. Earlier concerns for isolating units and tracing compilation and redaction processes were displaced by interest in thematic and final form readings of the canonical text and in the social worlds that yielded and were envisaged in the texts. The shifts were accompanied by surges of interest in orality, narrative, literacy, monarchy, ecology, canon, and other elements of the ancient social environment that demanded 1–2 Samuel and their contexts be reexamined even though no consensus about their date and interpretation could be expected. The prominence of Jerusalem and centralization in the stories, the presence of extended narrative units, and the long history of scholarship that blurred distinctions between literary and historical criticism made Samuel an important testing ground for new hypotheses about the literature and its setting. After several generations of preoccupation with details and particulars, scholarship began to emphasize holistic settings and texts.

a. Transition from Traditional Approaches. The standard forms of criticism endured and were used to examine the composition of Samuel, but the sections placed under scrutiny became longer and were often chosen because of thematic unity. In this, the influence of Rost can be seen again. Sections of Samuel that deal with specific themes such as the ark (Campbell 1975), the rise of Saul in 1 Samuel 7–15 (Birch 1976), and David in 1 Samuel 15–2 Samuel 5 (Gronbaek 1971) were treated, but much of the work was still done on the SN or portions of it. Studies on individual character roles (Conroy 1978) and themes (Brueggemann 1972) were typical ways of defining units of composition and bringing differing historical, literary, and religious questions to them. See following article on Narrative and Theology.

On the basis of theme and literary structure, Flanagan (1972) challenged the unity of Rost's SN by suggesting that it contained an earlier Court History that did not include 1 Kings 1–2 and portions of 2 Samuel 11–12. Although the study seemed to move against the thrust toward analyzing longer literary units, it had originally been part of a treatment of the entire 1–2 Samuel. Moreover, it opened the path leading to a totally Davidic Samuel, as suggested by the canonical division of the books, and toward treating the entire Samuel corpus, including the so-called appendices in 2 Samuel 21–24, as an integral composition (Flanagan 1988: 236–72). With the Solomonic succession theme removed, the focus of the books shifted to the legitimation of Jerusalem and tensions between Saul and David that are amply described in the narrative (Flanagan 1979).

A number of investigations followed Rost's definition of the SN but sought different readings (Whybray 1968; Clements 1976; Fokkelman 1981). Gunn's study (1978), however, was transitional and managed to encompass, on the one hand, the excavative and literary approaches and, on the other hand, fragmenting and holistic interests. Although offered as a study on the SN, not only did it extricate the narrative from the exclusive realm of history writing that Rost and many since had prided themselves in demonstrating, but it also treated the unit as a section in a larger integral whole and pointed away from the 19th century preference to isolate "original" units as a first step toward interpretation. Gunn achieved his ends by insisting on one of Rost's own observations, namely, the difficulty in determining an absolute thematic beginning for the SN. Rost had noted connections with 2 Samuel 6–7 particularly. On the same grounds, Gunn strengthened these and other associations, argued that an early date for the SN was not ensured, and suggested that its purpose might be entertainment.

b. Return of the Biblical Guild. For Gunn and the discipline, the work was not radical, but it signaled development. Its timing and the fact that he had recently founded a journal and press (1976) devoted to innovative approaches to biblical scholarship marked it as a turning point in Samuel studies. Many works with a similar approach followed shortly, some published under Gunn's editorship and others appearing in *Semeia,* an American journal for experimental approaches to biblical studies begun in 1974.

Gottwald's monumental study on Yahwist tribalism (1979) centered on materials in Joshua and Judges, but affected studies on the composition of Samuel enormously. While writing the volume, the author co-chaired a social world research group within several learned societies. By linking the endeavors—a forum for deliberation and a published statement that reflected the discussions—he applied the model being explored in *Semeia.* Again, the work's impact derived not from the fact that it was radical, which it was, but because it built on a hypothesis proposed by Mendenhall nearly two decades before and because a cross-section of biblical specialists was prepared to accept its sociological approach and conclusions. The work restated issues that Mendenhall had raised and that had been pondered ever since, and the biblical guild had already begun to reflect on the book's problems and advantages. Indeed, Gottwald relied heavily upon traditional source criticism and only secondarily applied a Marxist critique to conclusions drawn from those approaches. By eroding the historical tribal roots of centralization in Israel in the books of Joshua and Judges, however, Gottwald forced reevaluation of the stories of Saul and David which had now lost their presumed beginning. The reasons, modes, and structures of Samuel's composition were threatened.

The pathways toward new literary and social world studies widened when Gunn inaugurated a monograph series devoted to areas of research in a second press he founded in 1980 (Almond). One series nurtured ahistorical literary critical approaches while the other hastened the advance of comparative historical social world studies. Both evoked scholarship that moved beyond the standard source criticisms. Because the editors of each simultaneously chaired research seminars in learned societies, the research and publication model was applied again. By happenstance, the series provided outlets for the research presented in the seminars so that the two approaches were quickly defined and legitimated.

Rejoining scholarship to the crafts of communication reunited orality and literacy, this time in the service of biblical scholarship. Now, individuals were forced to engage peers' review at every step of the research and communication process. The sociology of biblical knowledge was altered substantially, and as a consequence, the temporal lag between proposal and consent was lessened. Plurality and simultaneity of hypotheses and interpretations became the hallmarks of scholarship on Samuel. These displaced the uniformity and consecutiveness of 19th and early 20th century scholarship just as Darwin's treelike variability had displaced Spencer's chainlike progressivism as an explanatory model for change. Scholars represented and could choose among options, and they could no longer trace their intellectual pedigree by listing a series of prominent, but mostly dead, mentoring or institutional ancestors. Because of the rapid and intense sharing of ideas across disciplines and at every level in scholarship, it became increasingly difficult to trace scholarly traditions by citing a few authors' names or dominating theories. Consensus regarding the composition and meaning of Samuel that had been gradually evolving suddenly devolved, and differing sets of questions and priorities moved to the fore.

In the classical sense, the *opus magnum* on Samuel during this period was still McCarter's two-volume Anchor Bible commentary. Its size and attention to detail guaranteed it prominence in the continuing discourse on Samuel. Drawing upon traditional archaeological and philological approaches developed within the Albright school, the author introduced readings derived from the QL and offered cautious interpretations that continued to see the texts as primarily historical and compiled over time.

c. Influences from Other Disciplines. Biblical studies in general and Samuel studies in particular continued to adopt insights and approaches from literary studies, comparative sociology, and archaeology. These had affected the critical understanding of the composition of Samuel along three trajectories. One branch led increasingly toward literary studies and away from history, and historical and source critical interests. The other continued to lead toward critical historical and archaeological interests, but this branch subdivided according to methods and approaches. One offshoot continued to perceive Samuel as historical, compiled over time from earlier smaller literary sources, and literally representative of a physical world that could be confirmed by successful archaeology. The other offshoot shared the first's concern for history, archaeology, and traditional forms of criticism but was less confident in its ability to discover literal or detailed historical referents to match episodes and characters in the biblical text. Instead, those who shared these views accepted wider use of heuristic models—iconic, sociological, and statistical—as aids for understanding the social world in the Samuel text and the early Iron Age that the texts purport to reflect. For this as for the literary branch, the social sciences offered the greatest hope for new understandings. The difference separating the first and third group, however, was interest in history and the confidence placed in texts as a means for reaching the past.

Because of their preference for holistic and final form readings, literary and canon critics of this era showed little concern for the composition of Samuel, at least as the issue was previously defined. Historical critics—those who relied on traditional methods as well as those who followed social world approaches—continued to examine the date and setting of individual units, accept the existence of earlier and later sections, and propose groups or circles as "authors."

C. Content

To discuss the content of Samuel is to choose among the levels of signification in the richly multivalent text and to select one of the approaches outlined above. The orientation here is toward social world criticism and the information the books hold regarding the human ecology in ancient Israel during Iron Age I. The exposition is limited by data within the books, i.e., 1 Samuel 1–2 Samuel 24, and for the most part does not exploit relevant but external information from archaeological or comparative studies that would be weighed in a different mode of analysis. Similar restraint excludes comparisons with Psalms 132 and 89, other portions of the DH, and 1 Chronicles.

1. Presuppositions. a. Extent of the Narrative. This summary presumes that 1–2 Samuel represents the views of Jerusalemite writers who, among other things, seek to reconcile and integrate a spectrum of attitudes and beliefs that spread among diverse peoples. Differences and contradictions in the stories have ecological, political, social, economic, and religious bases. By their existence, the texts signal continuing hope for social unity grounded in belief. The unifying force of Yahwist religion is central to the stories. Tensions among factions and perspectives that can be felt, for the most part, follow from contemporary differences rather than successive revisions of the texts. Hence, 1–2 Samuel, although formed from separate traditions, cycles, and stories, is a unified account that captures the urgency of the compilers' time, whether it is a pre-Deuteronomic or Deuteronomic era. From its beginning, the text is complete more or less as it now stands. The completeness extends throughout 1–2 Samuel and includes the so-called appendices in 2 Samuel 21–24, but does not include the material now in 1 Kings 1–2 that Rost makes part of the SN.

b. Social Structure in the Stories. Many commentators continue to envisage the centralizing processes that lead to

Davidic kingship and full statehood. In fact, they presume that the books describe and promote this development. Social world critics, however, argue against this historical interpretation of monarchy in favor of chieftaincy (Flanagan 1981; Frick 1985). In this summary, the role of a paramount tribal chief is assumed as the image of leadership that suits Saul and David because it offers greater potential for understanding the narrative and its parts. A tribal ethos controls the character roles and plots that fill the narratives' drama.

2. Overview. Three distinct but overlapping cycles of stories unfold in 1–2 Samuel: (1) a Samuel cycle (1 Samuel 1–25); (2) a Saul cycle (1 Samuel 9–2 Samuel 2); and (3) a David cycle (1 Samuel 10–2 Samuel 24). Interlaced ark, Jerusalem, and house themes run through the stories giving them continuity and vibrance. Thematic advances and fulfillments alternate with reversals and displacements. The story unfolds so that Saul (1 Samuel 7–15), then Jerusalem (2 Samuel 6), then David (2 Samuel 7), then David and Jerusalem, i.e., Davidic Jerusalem (2 Samuel 20, 24) are legitimated. In the process, however, the ark, which looms as the sign of the deity's presence in the beginning of the books (1 Samuel 4–6), recedes and is displaced by David who carries out the deity's will in the absence of the ark (2 Samuel 24). The pressure toward high centralization heard in requests for a king (1 Samuel 7–10), plans to build a temple (2 Samuel 7), and a census that would provide for taxation and conscription (2 Samuel 24) are juxtaposed with scenes showing resistance to the centralizing processes. Statements about the dangers of centralizing (1 Samuel 8), denial of the temple plans (2 Samuel 8), and the plague sent in punishment for the census (2 Samuel 24) signal socio- and religio-political displeasure with plans and maneuvers leading toward Jerusalemite power.

The stories are also economic. They illustrate a world reconciling ideals and beliefs with material realities. By linking religion and resources in a check and balance relationship, overcentralizing is resisted and centralized chieftaincy legitimated. Statehood with its temples, taxes, *corveé*, and militia drains away surplus and essential resources so that a subsistence economy such as that in Iron Age Syro-Palestine is depleted. Excesses would lead to exploitation and social stratification that victimize peoples, to religious and economic imbalance, and to politico-economic schizophrenia that would inspire religious schism. In Samuel, such maladaptation is avoided by having David be leader in Jerusalem, but forcing him to lead without the symbolic and technological advantages of kingship.

Genealogies and lists of family members and officers provide an outline for the books. The patronage networks and real and fictive kinship relationships typical of segmented societies can be seen in the materials (1 Sam 14:49–51; 2 Sam 2:2–3; 3:2–5; 5:13–16; 8:15–18; 20:23–26). The fluidity of the genealogies and lists, i.e., the manner in which names change and move about, also indicates on one plane that rural and independent tribal roles are giving way to urbanized and administrative bureaucracies. Although a number of factors no doubt contributed to the changes, the genealogical patterns suggest a sociopolitical metamorphosis. The decreasing concern for wives' and mothers' patronymics (compare 2 Samuel 2–3 and 3:2–5 with 5:13–16, 8:15–18, and 20:23–26) reflect interests that are turning increasingly from politics based on marriage and affiliation to administrative concerns for consolidation and succession. But the process is not complete, as comparisons with ethnographies of societies with a chieftaincy indicate (Flanagan 1988: 325–341).

On another plane, David's journey is charted from his position as member of Saul's house, to northern outcast, to southern fugitive warrior and overlord, and finally to centralist leader of two tribal moieties in Jerusalem. The momentum toward centralizing leadership controls the genealogies and lists, but in order to grasp the individual and communal human drama in the stories, that thrust must be measured against the religious restraints visible elsewhere in the narratives.

3. Principal Cycles. The complexity and richness of the stories make every person and episode important for appreciating the narrative in its entirety or parts. The role and status of outsiders, whether women or men, cannot be ignored. Abigail (1 Samuel 25), Michal (2 Samuel 6), Tamar (2 Samuel 13), the woman from Tekoa (2 Samuel 14), and wives (cf. genealogies) for instance, are essential to the storyline, as are Samuel's sons (1 Samuel 8), the crippled Mephiboseth (2 Samuel 9), and others. Nevertheless, in another era and genre, the account might be classified as "Great Person" stories because of the way the course follows decisions and actions of the principal figures, Samuel, Saul, and David.

a. Samuel Cycle. The figure Samuel dominates the opening chapters of 1 Samuel and sets the stage for the drama that continues through 2 Samuel 24. Only at the end of the second book are the problems outlined at the beginning resolved. Samuel, who portrays at least four social roles in the narratives (priest, judge, prophet, and seer [McKenzie 1962]), looms as a representative of a charismatic, prophetic tradition that values the deity's immediacy and spontaneity in human affairs. Samuel's responsibilities as one who articulates the deity's will, discerns and anoints preferred leaders, and awakens religious consciences are loosely interwoven with stories of the ark. Samuel's inexplicable birth and early years are reported (1 Samuel 1–3), only to be interrupted by the religio-political tragedy symbolized by the Philistines' capturing of the ark (chaps. 2–4), before his life as chief-maker is taken up again (chap. 7).

Samuel's apparent ambiguous and indecisive responses to the northern crisis reflect differing opinions and modes of social organization among the Yahwists (chaps. 7–15). A portion of the stories' participants and audience resists a segmented ethos in which problems are solved and order maintained by competition among equals. And yet, according to the storyline, that system is being threatened by marauders and warriors from the outside—the Philistines—who promise to dominate the peoples and their land. In light of this, the story portrays the Yahwists as being simultaneously pushed by the Philistines and pulled by survival instincts toward leadership which is organized as a centralized monopoly of force, and it credits the story's ultimate monopolizer, David, with the slaying of a symbolic enemy giant, Goliath (1 Samuel 17–18).

Stripped of Western and modern evolutionary presuppositions and political preferences, the stories portray

Samuel and the Philistines in contrasting but complementary roles. Both are mediators who absorb social hostility and thereby allow the divided Yahwists to transfer their frustrations out of their midst and into other realms. In the case of Samuel, the transfer is toward a holy man who is not socially, politically, or economically a member of any party. Like "marginal" religious figures and shrines in other societies, his paradoxical involvement/non-involvement roles allow him to adjudicate and resolve conflicts that otherwise would destroy the community.

In the case of the Philistines, the transfer of responsibility is accomplished by having an enemy to blame, one who is portrayed negatively as a motley band of outsiders, disturbers, and aggressors. A closer examination of the group's role, however, reveals similarity with mediators in other societies. Mediating individuals and groups are often craft specialists and traders whose services are essential to their neighbors. Their skills are especially important where ecologically diverse groups interact. Marginal and transitional areas that are populated simultaneously by pastoralists and cultivators, nomads and sedentaries, are typical examples. But the mediators are looked down upon socially and despised personally by the very people who depend on them. In spite of this, they, like the Philistines, often yield great power and enjoy considerable status as overlords of expansive holdings. Future leaders for the warring factions who consider them as mutual enemies are sometimes chosen from their midst (Flanagan 1988: 300–304).

In Samuel, the mediation of the most holy Samuel and least holy Philistines is inadequate. In the end, only one person can provide the needed service: David whom Samuel has chosen and who will serve Saul, the Philistines, and Judah.

b. Saul Cycle. But before the problems would pass, the community had to suffer Saul's phobias and incompetence (1 Samuel 9–31). Although the narrative portrays matters sequentially, and therefore presents Saul as a Yahwist attempt to resolve the difficulties, in the story his inadequacies compounded the troubles. The reader has the impression that Saul's regime is ended almost as it begins. In their hindsight perspective, the compilers include several traditions of Saul's emergence (1 Samuel 9–11). Quickly his role is recognized as transitional and his fate tragic (13:7–15; chap. 15). As a result, the destiny of Saul's family and David's involvement with it is as important as the consequences that befall Saul personally. The legitimacy of David, an outsider/insider, over against Saul's house is a fundamental theme in the Samuel narrative. David becomes a member of the inner circle, befriends Saul's son Jonathan, and marries Saul's daughter Michal. The inclusion with the royal house will be essential when David seeks legitimacy as leader of the northern tribes (2 Samuel 5–6). Then his former affiliation with Saul, institutionalized by political marriage, gains him acceptance through optative affiliation. This is a tribal practice whereby the husband of a daughter succeeds vicariously in lieu of the daughter/wife when the father has no legitimate male heirs (Flanagan 1981: 55, 57). The situation describes Saul's because elsewhere in Samuel, virtually all his male heirs in the first and second generation, except for the crippled Meribaal, are killed (1 Samuel 31; 2 Samuel 21). The presumption would be that the grandfather/chief's lineage would continue *via* offspring from the ruling daughter and her husband. But Michal's childlessness prevents this and makes it possible for the line to pass to the house of David (2 Sam 6:23).

Saul's animosity also serves the interests of David. In terms of the story, the suspicions are unfounded and unprovoked (1 Samuel 19–20). David is victimized and pursued by Saul and consequently is forced to seek refuge with the Philistines (chaps. 21–27) and to build a personal power base among the Judahites (1 Samuel 30–31; 2 Samuel 2). Again the strategy is typical. A losing contender for succession withdraws to a remote marginal region and begins again to weave a fabric of alliances that will satisfy his immediate urge to lead, even if the followers are fewer, and stand him in good stead in the next campaign for paramountcy. On the surface, however, because of Saul's paranoia David appears innocent of culpability and intrigue and is fully justified in his rather passive rise to power.

Regardless of the independent meaning of the Saul stories, together as a cycle within the Samuel narrative they depict the worsening conditions of the Yahwists. Samuel's initial judgment must be reversed, Saul's actions are misguided, and Philistine power, the indirect cause for Saul's election, continues to grow. The Yahwists obviously need new blood and fresh leadership. The stage is set for the shepherd David to begin his ascent from pasture to palace.

Modern interpreters' propensity for seeing continuity and ignoring the discontinuities in the stories has obscured an important distinction that the ancients would have recognized. It is the separate socio-political systems in the N and S, i.e., in Israel and Judah. Saul appears only as leader of a northern confederation of tribes. The Samuel stories indicate clearly that a separate southern confederation is led by David before he leads all Israel. He seeks refuge in the S, the house of Judah act independently in electing him (2 Sam 2:4), and he exercises leadership in Judah while Saul's son, Ishbaal, leads a separate confederation (2 Samuel 3–4). There are signs of continuing hostility dividing Saul's and David's houses (2 Sam 3:1). As in the Samuel cycle, divisiveness threatens the Yahwists and poises David to be the solution.

c. David Cycle. Although the David cycle reaches into Samuel's and Saul's careers, readers have a sense of relief and anticipation when the hero is finally on his own in 2 Samuel. His first years were lived on the run and in the shadow of Israel's two biggest problems, Saul and the Philistines. With the former's demise and the latter's blessing, he is free to unite the Yahwists first by becoming paramount chief in Hebron, an ancient Yahwist city (chap. 2), then by succeeding the incompetent Ishbaal, leader of the N (chap. 4), and finally by combining centers of religious and political alliance in Jerusalem (chap. 5).

The relocation is accomplished by a ritual marking the final displacement of Saul's house and the transfer of legitimacy to David personally (but not his house) in Jerusalem (2 Samuel 6). The scene depicts a rite of passage, a primary social act that both symbolizes and enacts the transfer (Flanagan 1983). Role reversals typical of such rites are manifested: David dances nude before the ark, Michal looks down on and chastises him, the lowly hold him in esteem while the royalty despise him. The popular and divine bases for his leadership are at one, and only his predecessor's family and their allies are at odds.

The relocation of the ark also marks another step in the displacement of the sacred symbol. Its value as a unifying force for the N tribes and sign of the deity's presence among them is now affixed to the new capital and leadership. Placing the ark in the custody of David recalls and revives its traditional religious, political, military, and social power while suggesting David's authority over both the people and their traditions. Structurally, however, the arrangement cannot last. It can only be a phase in the course of events that ultimately will require David to submit his leadership to divine control. In the view proposed in this summary, the submission, accomplished in 2 Samuel 21–24, is part of the storyline of the David cycle, whereas the Solomonic succession scene in 1 Kings 1–2 is not. Accordingly, the appendices in chaps. 21–24 demonstrate that Yahweh will be custodian of David, not David of Yahweh.

The route to this fuller transformation is cluttered with trials and tribulations for David. It leads through the court story (chaps. 9–20) and the appendices (chaps. 21–24). After establishing himself and the sacred chest in Jerusalem (chap. 6) and arranging for the house arrest of Meribaal, the only surviving Saulide and potential contender (chap. 9), difficulties erupt within his own house. First Ammon, then Absalom demonstrate their ineptitude, the former by risking his life for a passing moment of pleasure with his sister (chap. 13), the latter by attempting premortem succession, capturing the royal harem, and pursuing his father during his flight into exile (chaps. 13–18). The rebellion of one and the deaths of two sons and successors reveal David's tenuous hold on leadership. As in other tribal societies, his ascendancy marks only a pause in the continuing struggle among competitors for paramountcy.

David's return to his house in Jerusalem (20:3) witnesses to the deity's favor and moves the story toward David's full submission. At David's request the ark is left in Jerusalem during his exile (15:24–29), as are ten concubines in the harem (15:16). Ironically, David sets up a concubine-test for Absalom (16:20–23) and an ark-test for Yahweh (15:25–26). Will custody over the royal harem be the sign of David's political authority as it is in other ANE societies, or will David's forced departure but willful leaving of the ark and his return to Jerusalem, again without the ark's companionship, be the sign of his political and religious legitimacy? The court story unfolds to show that the ancient customs and their symbols are displaced. David returns according to Yahweh's will, and the ark is not mentioned.

Further tests, however, are still ahead (chaps. 21–24). David's paramountcy must be submitted to the deity. This is accomplished by a ritualistic, as it were, cosmic duel in which a census and plague are set off against each other as instruments in the hands of a combating human and God. David proclaims a census—according to the story, at divine urging—that in ancient practice provides the basis for taxation and conscription. The maneuver bespeaks the motives of a would-be king, in this case a person who seeks to advance his leadership to another level of bureaucracy and control. The divine response is a plague, a direct attack on the economic base that could support the taxes and conscription. The information from David's census is immediately eradicated and its value depleted. David loses and submits. He buys an altar place and offers sacrifices. Yahweh remains the sole ultimate authority in Jerusalem.

4. Unity of the Cycles. Examined as a continuous but self-contained story without the additions in 1 Kings 1–2 that Rost attached to his SN, the contents of Samuel are a story of David, his rise, and his survival. This image is linked to others in the Hebrew Scriptures by the story of David's covenant, i.e., the dynastic oracle in 2 Samuel 7. As it stands, the deity's election of David's house anticipates the court story as well as Solomon's ascendancy in 1 Kings 1–2, and with minor editing, it legitimates the construction of a temple. The pro-temple revision stands in opposition to the anti-centralizing thrust of the narrative exposed here. In terms of the structure of the story as it now stands in the DH, the divine election of David's house over that of Saul is ritually confirmed in chap. 6 and finalized and further sanctified in chap. 7. In terms of the structure of the David myth, however, readers would expect the oracle later in the cycle, perhaps in conjunction with the purchase of the temple site in 2 Samuel 24. Then, for the first time the possibility of a Davidic dynasty is a serious but paradoxical issue. Saul's forces and the ark's power are suppressed; with two sons already dead, David's own lineage is becoming threatened; and divine assurance for Jerusalem—a major theme of the myth—is needed and welcomed. It seems probable that the oracle was once the final assertion in the religious myth in 1–2 Samuel, and that the episode moves ahead in the cycle when the stories are integrated with others in order to make David and the stories the center of later religio-political claims.

On many planes, the narratives are simultaneously the story of the emergence of Jerusalem as the place of Yahweh's presence, the story of Israel's affiliation with Judah, the story of a nomadic cult object settling in a sedentary urban center, and the story of a religion's adaptive ability in the face of economic and political necessity. The list could be much longer, and one of the contributions of recent critical scholarship has been to increase its length by exposing the rich polyvalence of this classical text.

By opening onto multiple meanings in the story, the new criticisms have challenged modern scholars' ability to describe the "content" of the text. The challenge, in effect, denies the goal of earlier criticisms insofar as they are directed toward the authentic "original" statements and events of the past. Instead, the newer literary and social world critics agree that the stories' mutability testifies to their enduring meaning and power and that these are first sought in the texts rather than in the tracing of their parts. The texts witness to the cosmologies and beliefs that are ancient Israel's.

The shifts in understanding the Samuel texts, their composition, and their content draw attention to the question of their historicity. No unanimous consent can be expected, but the self-consciousness that modern critics bring to the question are made explicit in ways that the source criticisms begun in the 19th century ignored. Literary critics state the limits of their interests and hypotheses and are clear when these do not include questions of history. Social world critics, on the other hand, express continuing concern for the past and the means whereby it is examined and understood, but they also are aware of the limits that the partiality of information, passage of time, and accidents of discovery place on their endeavors. Many assume that the texts of Samuel do not correspond statement for statement in one to one relationships with historical referents that existed in Iron Age I or later. Instead, the words woven into stories reflect and depict ancient social worlds that can be known generally by drawing together literary and archaeological information and illuminating that information, its congruences, and its contradictions by comparative materials found in ancient and modern societies, especially those where similar ecologies and social systems can be expected.

Bibliography

Birch, B. 1976. *The Rise of the Israelite Monarchy: The Growth and Development of I Samuel 7–15.* SBLDS 27. Missoula, MT.

Bleek, F. 1878. *Einleitung in das Alte Testament.* 4th ed. rev. by J. Wellhausen. Berlin.

Boer, P. A. H. de 1938. *Research into the Text of I Samuel i–xvi.* Amsterdam.

———. 1949. Research into the Text of I Samuel xvii–xxxi. *OTS* 6: 1–100.

Brueggemann, W. 1972. On Trust and Freedom. A Study of Faith in the Succession Narrative. *Int* 26: 3–19.

Campbell, A. 1975. *The Ark Narrative (1 Sam 4–6; 2 Sam 6): A Form-Critical and Traditio-Historical Study.* SBLDS 16. Missoula, MT.

Carlson, R. A. 1964. *David, the Chosen King.* Stockholm.

Clements, R. E. 1976. *Abraham and David.* SBT 2d ser. 5. Naperville, Il.

Conroy, C. 1978. *Absalom Absalom! Narrative and Language in 2 Sam. 13–20.* AnBib 81. Rome.

Cross, F. M. 1961. *The Ancient Library at Qumran.* 2d ed. Garden City, NY.

———. 1967. The Structure of the Deuteronomic History. Vol. 3, pp. 9–24 in *Perspectives in Jewish Learning.* Chicago.

Dietrich, W. 1972. *Prophetie und Geschichte.* Göttingen.

Eichhorn, J. G. 1780–83. *Einleitung in das alte Testament.* Göttingen.

Eissfeldt, O. 1931. *Die Komposition der Samuelisbücher.* Leipzig.

———. 1947. Die Geschichtswerke im Alten Testament. *TLZ* 72: 71–76.

Flanagan, J. W. 1972. Court History or Succession Document? A Study of 2 Samuel 9–20 and 1 Kings 1–2. *JBL* 91: 172–81.

———. 1979. The Relocation of the Davidic Capital. *JAAR* 47: 223–44.

———. 1981. Chiefs in Israel. *JSOT* 20: 47–73.

———. 1983. Social Transformation and Ritual in 2 Samuel 6. Pp. 362–72 in *The Quest for the Kingdom of God,* ed. H. B. Huffmon, F. A. Spina, and A. Green. Winona Lake, IN.

———. 1988. *David's Social Drama. A Hologram of Israel's Early Iron Age.* SWBA 7. Sheffield.

Fokkelman, J. P. 1981–. *Narrative Art and Poetry in the Books of Samuel.* 2 vols. SSN. Assen.

Frick, F. 1985. *The Formation of the State in Ancient Israel.* SWBA 4. Sheffield.

Gellner, E. 1973. Introduction to Nomadism. Pp. 1–10 in *The Desert and the Sown,* ed. C. Nelson. Berkeley.

Gressmann, H. 1921. *Die älteste Geschichtsschreibung und Prophetie Israels.* SAT 2. 2d ed. Göttingen.

Gottwald, N. 1979. *The Tribes of Yahweh.* Maryknoll, NY.

Gronbaek, J. 1971. *Die Geschichte vom Aufstieg Davids (1. Sam. 15–2. Sam. 5): Tradition und Komposition.* ATD 10. Copenhagen.

Gunn, D. 1978. *The Story of King David.* JSOTSup 6. Sheffield. Repr. 1982.

Hölscher, G. 1952. *Geschichtsschreibung in Israel.* Lund.

Khazanov, A. M. 1984. *Nomads and the Outside World.* Trans. J. Crookenden. Cambridge.

Kittel, R. 1892. Die pentateuchisch Urkunden in den Büchern Richter und Samuel. *TSK* 65: 44–71.

Langlemet, F. 1976. Pour ou Contre Salomon? La Rédaction Prosalomonienne de I Rois, I–II. *RB* 83: 321–79, 481–528.

McKenzie, J. 1962. The Four Samuels. *BR* 7: 3–18.

Pfeiffer, R. 1948. *Introduction to the Old Testament.* 2d ed. London.

Rost, L. 1982. *The Succession to the Throne of David.* Trans. M. D. Rutter and D. M. Gunn. Sheffield.

Ulrich, E. 1978. *The Qumran Text of Samuel and Josephus.* HSM 19. Missoula, MT.

Veijola, T. 1975. *Die ewige Dynastie: David und die Entstehung seiner Dynastie nach der deuteronomistischen Darstellung.* Helsinki.

Weiser, A. 1948. *Einleitung in das alte Testament.* Göttingen. ET 1961. New York.

Wellhausen, J. 1871. *Der Text der Bücher Samuelis untersucht.* Göttingen.

Whybray, R. N. 1968. *The Succession Narrative.* SBT 2d ser. 9. Naperville, IL.

Würthwein, E. 1974. *Die Erzählung von der Thronfolge Davids-theologische oder politische Geschichtsschreibung?* ThStud 115. Zurich.

James W. Flanagan

NARRATIVE AND THEOLOGY

As a unified whole, the corpus of 1 and 2 Samuel figures significantly in the narrative presentation of Israel's memory and faith. This narrative complex, which encompasses Joshua through 2 Kings, is central in the canon as well as in the study of Israel's history and theology. Moreover, the received form of 1 and 2 Samuel reflects specific narrative concerns such as the juxtaposition of human power and divine authority, and frames these with theological intentionality and literary ingenuity. Finally, a survey of the narrative elements of the books brings into focus how the literary form accomplishes the narrative intent.

A. Literary Context
   1. In the Canon
   2. In Critical Scholarship
B. The Literature in its Full and Final Form
   1. Historical Transformation
   2. Narrative Concerns
   3. Frame of the Narrative
C. Survey of the Narrative Elements
D. Some Important Texts

A. Literary Context

1. In the Canon. Canonically, these books are reckoned as part of the "Former Prophets" in combination with the books of Joshua, Judges, and 1 and 2 Kings. They are peculiarly linked to 1 and 2 Kings and in the LXX, these four books are named 1, 2, 3, and 4 Kingdoms, suggesting that the real subject matter of the literature is the monarchy. While our more familiar designation "Samuel" relates this literature to the person of Samuel, who looms so large as "kingmaker," the connection to 1 and 2 Kings correctly reflects the overriding theme of the literature, namely

Israel's venture toward and experimentation with monarchy.

The general canonical grouping, "Former Prophets," serves notice that this literature is not to be regarded as "historical" in the sense that it simply narrates "what happened." The word "Prophet" indicates that this literature expresses a peculiar view of the ongoing historical process, one which is open to and shaped by the rule of God through the (usually verbal) interventions of God's authorized speakers. That is, prophetic speech is not incidental to this view of history, but is constitutive to the meaning and course of historical experience. As we shall see, in much of 2 Samuel this direct intervention is subdued, but even there it is the active engagement of Yahweh, the God of Israel, which decisively influences the outcome of events.

2. In Critical Scholarship. Under the influence of Martin Noth (1981), the canonical corpus, "Former Prophets," has come to be regarded as "the Deuteronomistic History." That is, the literature of Joshua, Judges, Samuel and Kings is reckoned on this hypothesis to be one sustained historical-theological effort (Fretheim 1983: 97–133). It is named "Deuteronomistic" because the theological presuppositions and impetus for the perspective of the literature derives from the book and tradition of Deuteronomy. This corpus in its present form, according to scholarly consensus, is dated sometime around the destruction of 587 B.C.E. and the Exile, though scholars are divided on a more precise dating. Cross (*CMHE,* 274–89) has proposed two editions of the material, before and after 587, and Smend (1971: 494–509), Veijola (1977), and Dietrich (1972) have attempted a more refined distinction between three layers of the material. In its present form, this entire literature is a reflection upon (not a report of) Israel's historical experience as that experience relates both to the actual demands of historical realism and as it relates to the dominant theological claims of Israel's covenantal tradition. Indeed, it is a major achievement of this literature to hold together in a coherent way the demands of historical realism and the claims of the covenant traditions, so that they are perceived as intimately and integrally related to each other.

The literature of 1 and 2 Samuel seems less directly involved in the Deuteronomistic program than the rest of that larger corpus. Nonetheless it cannot be understood apart from that larger enterprise. In its present articulation, the narrative data concerning Samuel, Saul, and David is offered for reflection at the end of the monarchal period, when this great ambition of Israel had come to a sorry end. The narrative uses older materials of many kinds in the service of this reflection. At the same time, scholars are agreed that this "end-time" utilization has not severely distorted the earlier memories, nor has it muted the courage and vitality of the earlier period reflected in the material itself. In the literature of 1 and 2 Samuel (more than anywhere else in the Deuteronomistic corpus) the claims and intentionality of the earlier material have been respected on their own terms. Interpretation, then, must take into account both the early intentionality and the later reflective utilization of that early intentionality. One need not choose between the two, as they come together in this carefully and artistically crafted presentation.

B. The Literature in its Full and Final Form

The canonical nomenclature of "Former Prophets" and the critical consensus concerning "Deuteronomistic History" require us to begin our analysis by asking about the shape of the literature of 1 and 2 Samuel in its full and final form. To begin in this way is to acknowledge an important shift in scholarly approach. The long-standing critical practice has been to analyze the sources and traditions which have gone into the making of the corpus (see *IDBSup,* 777–81; *IDB* 4: 202–9; for the more recent analysis of layers of sources in Dtr, see McCarter *1 Samuel* AB, 14–17 and *2 Samuel* AB, 4–8). Both the older source analysis and the newer fragmentation of sources in Dtr share a concern to start with the lesser units. Our approach is to begin at the other end with the completed form of the text. This approach is reflective of the developing direction of scholarly procedure.

1. Historical Transformation. It is helpful to see what Israel accomplished in the course of this literature by considering the condition of Israel at the beginning and at the end of the corpus. That is, we inquire about the historical transformation wrought through this literature. Preceding this corpus, in Judges 17–21, Israel reflects a loose tribal organization in which "there was no king in Israel; every man did what was right in his own eyes" (Judg 17:6; cf. 18:1; 19:1; 21:25). That is, there was no viable, reliable social order and no legitimated public structure of governance. The result, as characterized in these materials, was a chaotic, barbaric social practice and a correspondingly doubtful religion which is presented as image-generating and idolatrous (Judges 17–18). That is where the book of Samuel opens. (The placement of the book of Ruth at this point in our English Bible is a departure from the Jewish order of books which is assumed in this and parallel analyses.)

At the other end of our literature, when 2 Samuel ends and we move from 2 Samuel 24 to 1 Kings 1–2, we are confronted with a situation completely contrasted with that of Judges 17–21. Now, at the end of David's life, the narrative 1 Kings 1–2 focuses on the question of succession to the throne and the rivalry of David's sons, Adonijah and Solomon. By this time the dynastic principle has been fully established and is unquestioned, at least in the circles adhering to this literature. Now the social issue is not chaos and barbarism, but bureaucratic ruthlessness and rival claims to legitimacy.

The books of Samuel are the narrative rendering of Israel's move from tribal chaos and barbarism to monarchic legitimacy and bureaucratic ruthlessness. The historical achievement of Israel in the course of this decisive and irreversible transition is a remarkable one and should not be underestimated. Israel has been in the process of building public structures of legitimacy and institutions of accountability and order. While the narrative tends to focus on personalities, this larger public agenda is crucial.

2. Narrative Concerns. With reference to this historical transformation, we may identify three dimensions of narrative concern in the books of Samuel.

a. Social Analysis. The basic course of development in

this literature generally reflects the course of events. To be sure, the literature is cast imaginatively with considerable legendary accretion. However, that legendary propensity is not accidental but instead represents sophisticated artistic ability. What might be missed because of this particular narrative quality is the historical realism, the political finesse and the capacity for critical and sober assessment that is present in the text. Not only is the alien principle of monarchy introduced into Israel through a series of deep conflicts, but additionally there is a shift in economics, so that a community of economic marginality begins to move toward affluence and an accumulation of surplus wealth which requires new social forms. The debate over the temple in 2 Sam 7:1–7, which parallels the debate over monarchy in 1 Samuel 7–12, indicates an awareness of how radically the shifted political and economic realities impinge upon theological notions and liturgic practices. The narrative shows a discernment of the interrelatedness of economic-political and theological-liturgic matters, and it is this interrelatedness that embodies the practice of social criticism.

b. Legendary Imagination. Historical realism in this corpus is mediated through literature that exercises the freedom of artistic legend concerning the major personalities. The literature is focused in turn on the persons of Samuel, Saul, and finally David. We are unable to and uninterested in sorting out every factual element, but there can be little doubt that the birth story of Samuel, the call narrative of Samuel, David's triumph over Goliath, and many other narratives take important liberties of imagination in the presentation and portrayal of the main characters. This literary freedom is no cause for suspicion, nor are we mandated to purge the material so that we might get to "the facts," for the only facts available to us are mediated in these imaginative forms, and the very engagement of this imagination is crucial to the facts which are mediated to us. The narrative intends that we experience the historical memory in this freighted imaginative mode. We are required to recognize exactly the kind of literature this is, and to see that "the facts" are precisely these inventive, imaginative portrayals without which this literature would lose its power, its significance, and its interest for us. This is not scientific-factual, scholastic literature, but it is nevertheless exactingly artistic literature of a quite sophisticated kind. It understands that the narrated historical transformation of Israel is to be understood as wrought precisely through these "larger-than-life" characters. Without the formidable persons, the move from Judges 17–21 to 1 Kings 1–2 would never have been accomplished.

c. Involvement of God. The literature then partakes of legendary imagination and of discerning social analysis. A third factor is perhaps most decisive, with particular reference to the term "Former Prophets." This literature is intensely theonomous. It understands that ultimately the historical process is not shaped by political-economic factors, nor by inventive personalities, but by the purposes and governance of Yahweh, which may operate visibly or unnoticed. The literature is committed to this perception of reality and neither apologizes for it nor explains it. The modern reader is not free to regard this central motive as an intrusion or an embarrassment. Yahweh is a central character in the narrative, a quite expected presence in the drama, and a proper agent of historical events. Insofar as this factor is a problem for interpretation, it must be remembered that it is not a problem for the narrative or the narrators, but only for modern "scientific" interpreters.

3. Frame of the Narrative. We may notice how the literature is framed. At the outset, in 1 Samuel 1, the presenting problem (as so often for Israel) is the matter of barrenness. The narrative method of dealing with this crisis is that Hannah makes a vow and speaks a prayer (1:11). The issue is resolved in vv 19–20, when a son is born and identified in the narrative by the formula, "Yahweh remembered her" (cf. Gen 30:22). The son, Samuel, is identified with the beginning of Israel's new historical process. In vv 21–28 the reference to Yahweh as history-maker is clear: Elkanah awaits Yahweh keeping his word (v 23); Hannah credits Yahweh with the gift of a son (v 27); the narrative ends with the worship of Yahweh (v 28). The historical drama and the legend of personalities is here overridden by the decisive power of Yahweh to cause a beginning for barren Hannah, for hopeless Elkanah, for oppressed Israel. Consequently, this new history is underway.

The issues are framed similarly at the end of the corpus in 2 Samuel 24. This chapter offers a remarkable statement concerning the relation between David, the well-established king, and Yahweh, who actually governs. The substance of the narrative consists in the prayer of David and a response from Yahweh. Twice David confesses sin (vv 10, 17), and once he pleads for Yahweh's mercy (v 14). The answer which then completes the Samuel corpus (v 25) is that Yahweh heeded the supplication and lifted the curse. The situations of Hannah and David, at the beginning and end of this literature, are very different, but the dramatic moment is the same. In both there is petition and in both there is a transformative divine response:

> The Lord remembered her (1 Sam 1:19).
> The Lord heeded the supplication for the land (2 Sam 24:25).

The two framing narratives take into account the course of events and the cruciality of major personalities, but they attest to the confiction that finally it is Yahweh's remembering and heeding which shapes Israel's life. It is Yahweh's attentive engagement which moves Israel from chaotic, barbaric social practice (Judges 17–21) to a legitimated monarchic structure (1 Kings 1–2). The narrative of 1 and 2 Samuel traces the ways in which this move is made, albeit with fits and starts of human anguish, historical uncertainty, and moral ambiguity. While the narrative celebrates the achievement, it does so without obscuring the problematic of the achievement.

In assessing the theological tenor of the canonical form of 1 and 2 Samuel, Childs (*IOTS,* 263–80) has placed particular emphasis upon the two poems of the Song of Hannah (1 Sam 2:1–10) and David's psalm of praise (2 Sam 22:2–51). Again, the placement of these two poems as a second level of envelopes (inside the two narratives ending in prayer) cannot be accidental. Both are undoubtedly independent poems which have been intentionally placed where they are. 1 Sam 2:1–10 relies on a poetic tradition reflected in Psalm 113; 2 Sam 22:2–51 also utilizes a liturgic tradition, as is reflected in Psalm 18. The Song of Hannah ostensibly celebrates Samuel's birth, but in fact the poetry lauds the readiness of Yahweh to perform transformative acts in the public life of Israel. Childs (*IOTS*, 273) regards the poem as "an interpretive key for this history which is, above all, to be understood from a theocentric perspective." If, as seems clear, the narrative traces the fall of Saul and the rise of David (cf. 1 Sam 18:7; 21:11; 24:17, 20; 25:28; 26:25; 28:17; 2 Sam 3:1), then the affirmation that God "brings low and exalts" (1 Sam 2:7) asserts Yahweh's irresistible sovereignty and anticipates David's emergence and dominion in the literature. Likewise, 2 Samuel 22 is a recital of the ways in which David's remarkable achievements are to be referred to the power of Yahweh. This psalm is a well-crafted combination of reference to Yahweh's sovereignty and deep appreciation of the activity of David as the bearer of Israel's history on its way from chaos to order.

Carlson (1964) has offered a very different attempt to understand the present shape of the literature. While he has focused exclusively on 2 Samuel, it is not difficult or unreasonable to extrapolate how his analysis might comprehend 1 Samuel as well. He sees 2 Samuel as juxtaposing "David under the blessing" (2 Samuel 2–5) and "David under the curse" (9–24). Under this rubric, part of 1 Samuel would likely be a longer narrative statement of David under blessing, because in that literature, everything that happens to David moves toward his final triumph.

In Carlson's analysis, 2 Samuel 11–12 is singled out as the pivotal passage wherein the mood, direction, and intentionality of David's narrative is inverted. From that point forward, David's family and throne are under assault, and each episode develops further the dimension of the tragic which is countered only by Yahweh's resilient promise which is still operative. Humphreys (1982; 1985) has characterized the Saul narrative in 1 Samuel as "tragic," but that tragic quality does not touch the character of David until the latter part of the narrative. Such a delay in the articulation of the tragic no doubt serves the narrative intention of the text.

By a very different route, Alter arrives at a judgment about the David material that is oddly parallel to that of Carlson:

> Indeed one of the most striking aspects of the entire David story is that until his career reaches its crucial breaking point with his murder-by-proxy of Uriah after his adultery with Bathsheba, almost all of his speeches are in public situations and can be read as politically motivated. It is only after the death of the child born of his union with Bathsheba that the personal voice of a shaken David begins to emerge (1981: 119).

Alter is interested in literary, not theological questions, but as Carlson identified 2 Samuel 11–12 as the point of transition from blessing to curse, so Alter identifies that text as the move from a public to a personal David, and we may say, from a triumphal to an anguished David, from an opaque to a transparent David.

Through all these different analyses with attention to literary and theological issues, we may conclude that the Samuel corpus is composed with great literary finesse and with theological intentionality. It is aimed at presenting the character of David as the bearer of Israel's historical possibility and as the vehicle for God's purposes in Israel. This entire literary, theological assertion about Israel's possibility and God's purposes hinged on the narrative events of 2 Samuel 11–12 (see Brueggemann 1985: chap. 3).

C. Survey of the Narrative Elements

Wide scholarly consensus holds that the present books of Samuel have been formed by joining together independent literary pieces which in and of themselves are important literary achievements. Alter, who asks a very different set of questions than is usual among biblical scholars, dissents from this view, ". . . the evidence for a unified imaginative conception of the whole David story seems to me persuasive" (1981: 119 n. 1). However, Alter's view is against the consensus, and in any case "a unified imaginative conception" does not necessarily preclude earlier independent elements. On the whole, most scholarly analysis has been preoccupied with efforts to identify and/or reconstruct those earlier pieces. The most that can be said with confidence is that this literature, which now moves from poem (1 Sam 2:1–10) to poem (2 Sam 22:2–51), from the prayer of Hannah (1 Samuel 1) to the prayer of David (2 Samuel 24), is formed as it stands by a long traditioning process working with extant materials. That long process is not completely visible to us, but with the aid of a rough scholarly consensus, we may identify several narrative elements.

1. 1 Sam 1:1–4:1a. The early Samuel materials of 1 Sam 1:1–4:1a present the historical problem of Israel in crisis. These materials, drawn from a variety of sources, focus on the birth, authorization, and establishment of Samuel as a key leader in premonarchic Israel. The centrality of the Song of Hannah assures one that the narrative does not have an excessive interest in the person or personality of Samuel. It is clear that the person of Samuel is early placed in the service of the liberation of Israel from historical oppression. Thus Samuel is of interest as he is included in the anticipation of Israel's social well-being under the new organization of life wrought by David.

2. 1 Sam 4:1b–7:2. The second element of the text is 4:1b–7:2 (with a conjectured continuation in 2 Samuel 6). This narrative reflects the situation of a vulnerable tribal organization, though the narrative is stunningly silent on the leadership role of Samuel. The central subject here is the ark of the covenant which is taken as a rallying symbol of the tribal confederation and as a mark of God's powerful, effective presence. Scholars have concluded that this narrative at one time circulated independently. In terms of the overall move from chaotic tribal organization to an ordered monarchy, this narrative serves (congruent with Judges 17–21) to indicate that the old organization and the old modes of trust in Yahweh were not adequate for the Philistine threat. Indeed, the books of Samuel make sense only if one recognizes that there is a social, political, and therefore theological issue about the adequacy of old forms of public life. The capture of the ark is not only a religious failure, but it also bespeaks an organizational and institutional crisis which is present throughout this literature.

Miller and Roberts (1977) have seen that the Ark Narrative is shaped, not unlike the Plague Narrative of Exodus 5–11, as a battle between the gods which culminates in the triumph of Yahweh over rival gods and their images. Thus the debacle of the image of Dagon is a liturgic, narrative assertion of the power of Yahweh. That is, the repeated retelling of this narrative functioned in ancient Israel as a paradigmatic statement concerning the sovereignty of Yahweh vis-à-vis all other religious claims. The "Ark Narrative" (as this piece is named) no doubt is quite distinct, but when it is juxtaposed with 1 Samuel 1–3, and particularly the Song of Hannah, the combined narrative asserts the power of Yahweh to govern the history of Israel in irresistible ways. It is probable that the Ark Narrative, because of its ties to the tribal order, also attests to the validity of leadership embodied in Samuel as the last of the judges. Samuel, however, is not mentioned by name in the narrative, which means that enhancement of Samuel's leadership here is at best only by inference. The more important point is that Yahweh is the real governor of the historical process. The same point is made in the Succession Narrative (cf. 2 Sam 11:27; 12:24; 17:14) in a very different mode. Israel here sees its narrative history, an implementation of the powerful themes of the Song of Hannah.

3. 1 Sam 7:3–15:35. The emergence of monarchy is the theme of 1 Sam 7:3–15:35, which is particularly linked to the person of Saul. There is no doubt that this narrative is the result of an intensive redactional process, but the exact features of this are impossible to determine. While the story is cast around the disputed leadership of Samuel and the emergence of Saul, the real debate does not concern personalities. Rather, it concerns the relationship between the faith of the community and public forms of power and how the trust Israel has in Yahweh should be implemented in institutional forms.

The narrative discloses to us opinions which believe not only that monarchy is required to cope with historical threats, but that monarchy is a gift from Yahweh to Israel for the securing of the community. A counter opinion, more forcefully expressed, argues that monarchy is a departure from faith in Yahweh even as it is a departure from the old tribal organization. Both opinions are expressed in this complicated narration of chaps. 7–15. It is a truism of scholarship that the narrative contains two sources reflecting two strongly held political opinions which judge the institution of monarchy positively and negatively. Scholarship moreover has held that the pro-kingship source is from the period itself, whereas the anti-kingship sources are later, reflecting disillusionment with the tyranny of Solomon.

It seems more probable that the two opinions were in fact alive at the same time. The two opinions reflect a genuine dispute and a genuine probe of a serious issue upon which the theological answers were not yet clear. As Mendelsohn (1956) has shown, Israel could appeal to models of tyrannical kingship very early in its existence. The debate was not an artificial or simply pragmatic one. Instead, the issue turned (as it frequently does) on the concrete institutional form that is to be given to zealous faith.

The two voices in the text need to be assessed not only as serious theological offers, but also in terms of sociopolitical reality. It is common to say that kingship arose in response to the external threat of the Philistines. But Gottwald (1983) has suggested an alternative. As economic prosperity developed in Israel and some group(s) came to be affluent, Israelites in the community developed an accumulation of wealth (surplus value) that needed to be defended and legitimated. The institution of monarchy emerged, on this reading, to defend and maintain the social inequity in Israel. From the outset (on this reading), monarchy was sponsored by and in the interest of the affluent, dominant class. As the monarchy defended such a disproportion, so monarchy was accompanied within one generation by the temple which served to legitimate the economic monopoly which might earlier have received a harsh critique, but now is given religious sanction. Thus the debate about kingship is not an isolated theological question about the will of Yahweh, but the debate contains within it a covert discussion of social power, social theory, social organization. It is a debate about egalitarianism and social inequity in institutionalized forms. The yearning "to be like the nations" (1 Sam 8:5, 20) is a yearning to abandon the radical egalitarian social vision of covenantal, tribal Israel (as portrayed in Joshua-Judges) and to embrace the economics and politics of surplus that other cultures practiced and other religions legitimated. The dispute thus is for the heart of Israel, but with a keen awareness that Israel's heart is not far distant from its treasure. (Notice the embodiment of this shift as it is portrayed in Solomon, with reference to his heart from 1 Kings 3:9, 12 to 11:4.) As the narrative now presents the monarchy issue, 1 Samuel 12 is a sober rejection of monarchy by a voice not disinterested, and 1 Sam 13:8–15 and 15:1–35 are strongly critical voices against monarchy. The precise intent of these latter narratives, however, is unclear. It appears in 13:14; 15:10, 35 that what is rejected is not the institution and principle of monarchy, but only Saul as the appointee.

Gunn (1978) and Humphreys (1978) have shown that the Saul narrative is a portrayal of tragedy, marked by ambiguity, darkness, and fate. It may be that the tragic character of Saul in this narrative is a portrayal from the perspective of Davidic interests. That is, Saul's fate is the counter-theme of David's success and so the Saul portrayal is not disinterested. But it is also plausible, as Gunn and Humphreys suggest, that taken on its own terms and without reference to David, the great artistic achievement of the narrative is to see and articulate that Saul's public life was indeed a tragedy, the end of which is not found in sin and judgment, but in a hidden, irrevocable destiny that is beyond understanding. What is offered then, is not an imposed philosophy of history, but simply a discerning study of how the historical process has worked in this one case. It is indeed true that the sword devours one and now another (2 Sam 11:25). Saul is indeed devoured by the historical process in an inexplicable, inscrutable way.

The analyses of Humphreys and Gunn, contrasted, e.g., with those of Birch (1976) and Campbell (1975), reflect an important shift in scholarly perspective away from technical to artistic sensitivity. The newer scholarship is not so much interested in source analysis and dissection of the material, as it is in an attempt to grasp the artistic construction that is offered when the narrative is taken as a whole. When so viewed, Saul is the character in the drama who is sacrificed around the inescapable public question of faith and power. The narrative does not linger over Saul, but recognizes that the issue of faith and power is on its way to a new resolution at the severe cost of Saul's person, reputation, and destiny.

4. 1 Sam 16–2 Sam 5:10. The central character of the books of Samuel does not appear until 1 Sam 16:1. It is as though the literature has withheld this character as long as possible, in an intentional attempt to enhance the drama. It is generally held that with the appearance of David in 1 Sam 16:1–13, we have a new piece of literature, referred to as "The Narrative of the Rise of David," which extends through 2 Sam 5:10 (though Gunn [1978] divides the material differently).

This material is marked by (1) a narrative quality that allows for playfulness and a kind of naïveté which likely is quite artistically crafted, (2) intense redactional activity so that there is some evidence of traditions which are often repetitious and occasionally contradictory, and (3) an intense fascination with David that is celebrative and uncritical. The combination of narrative mode and the celebrative presentation of David suggests that this material is free from (and perhaps prior to) the disputes concerning monarchy. This material presents the emergence of the institution of monarchy under David as an unmitigated good.

The narrative moves from an idyllic picture of the shepherd boy (1 Sam 16:1–13) to the establishment of the shepherd (king) over Israel (2 Sam 5:3). The central subject of the narrative is the conflict between Saul and David, which of course comes to an end in 1 Samuel 31 with the death of Saul. (It is clear from 2 Sam 9:3 that David and the literature continue to be haunted by the Saul legacy and cannot put its reality and danger to rest.) The break in the narrative between 1 and 2 Samuel is organized around Saul's death and is marked by the exquisite poem of lament in 2 Sam 1:19–27.

Jobling (1978: 4–25) and Humphreys (1978; 1980) have shown that notwithstanding all the redactional activity and the fact that old narratives have been secondarily employed, there is indeed an intentional literary design to the construction of the whole. The story line concerns the unhindered advance of David and the corresponding demise of Saul. The intent of the story line and the artistic skill of literary design are matched by the theological intentionality of the story, for it is clear that David's heroic buoyancy is held in close relation to the purposes of Yahweh. This theological affirmation of David is evident in the initial transitional episode of 1 Sam 16:1–13 and is reaffirmed in the concluding formula of 2 Sam 5:10: "And David became greater and greater, for the Lord, the God of hosts, was with him." The formula perhaps appeals to the old slogans of holy war ("I am with you,") and is the basis of the claim of Immanuel ("God with us,"), a programmatic claim of the Davidic dynasty (see also 1 Sam 25:28). The narrative is able to discern and articulate in a seemingly unreflective mode the powerful and resilient purpose of Yahweh, so that the very shape of the narrative makes the assertion of God's will for this dynasty. As the narrative presents it, the person of David overrides the misgivings and disputes of 1 Samuel 7–15. Those issues simply are not present to a Davidic purview of reality.

5. 2 Sam 5:11–8:18. The materials in 2 Sam 5:11–8:18 clearly reflect a very different literary tone, a different set of sociological presuppositions, and a different theological sensitivity. This literature may indeed be a miscellaneous collection of materials lodged between the two great narratives of "The Rise" (1 Sam 16:1–2 Sam 5:10) and "The Succession" (2 Samuel 9–20). Within this section there is surely a different mode of literature, largely lacking the free narrative style of "The Rise" and being much more preoccupied with technical data concerning lists of officers, indices of victories and logs of battles. The material also contains a narrative about the ark (2 Samuel 6) which has been reckoned to be a continuation of 1 Sam 4:1–7:1. Finally, there is the formidable oracle of legitimacy in 2 Samuel 7, which has no parallel elsewhere in this literature.

The entire unit breathes the air of an established, legitimated royal apparatus, having the tone of ideology, propaganda, and justification for the state. In that regard it is clear that the uncritical enthusiasm and amazement of the tale of "The Rise" have been displaced and overcome by a self-assured and seemingly self-serving order. What had been amazing in prospect is self-serving in reality. As the social reality changes, so the literary form changes with it.

The "in between" chapters are conventionally regarded as miscellaneous. However, Flanagan (*WLSGF,* 361–72) has shrewdly observed that there is a possible three-tiered structure of older materials:

Transfer of Ark (6:1–20)	Dynastic Oracle (7:1–29)
Philistine War (5:17–25)	Battles of the Empire (8:1–14)
Children of David (5:13–16)	Officers of David (8:15–18)

Such an analysis not only suggests a quite intentional arrangement, but Flanagan proposes that the order of materials in this way makes a statement of social and theological transition from tribe to state, from Saul to David, indicating that the "social, political, economic, and religious center of Israel's world had shifted" (*WLSGF,* 369). That shift was the work of David, but the text is uncompromising in its conclusion that the work wrought by David is in fact the work of Yahweh, who wills the change in Israel's life. Such a juxtaposition of David and Yahweh cannot fail to legitimate the entire enterprise.

6. 2 Samuel 9–10. In 2 Samuel 9–20 (1 Kings 1–2), we consider the second major collection, which stands architecturally over against the long narrative of "The Rise." This narrative has been designated by scholarship as "The Succession Narrative" because it seems to concern the crisis of identifying the successor to David on the throne (1 Kgs 1:20). But that designation is at most a scholarly convention. Given the complex nature of the book, a simple structural design of the Samuel material is not feasible. However, 1 Sam 16:1–2 Sam 5:10 can be viewed as the "Rise" to power (ascent), 2 Sam 5:11–8:18 the "Establishment" of power (plateau), and 2 Samuel 8–9 the "Succession" of power (descent). These three literary blocks concerning David are cast in very different modes, make very different theological assertions, and reflect very different sociological realities and experiences.

The Succession Narrative is divided into five episodes: 2 Samuel 9–10, 11–12, 13–14, 15–19 (20), and 1 Kings 1–2. Scholars have recognized that this is a distinctive mode of literature not met elsewhere in Samuel, rarely elsewhere in the OT or in the ANE. It is a self-conscious literature that focuses upon human agents as history-makers and presents God in subdued and indirect ways. This theological perspective, which reflects a new historical self-consciousness, is matched by a literary style especially marked by its artistic style and sensitivity. Various analyses by Gunn (1978), Conroy (1978), Alter (1981), Ridout (1971), and Fokkelman (1981) have illuminated the artistry of the unit.

It is generally recognized that 2 Samuel 11–12 is the key element in the narrative. In this episode David breaks the Torah, violates Uriah and Bathsheba, and is denounced by Nathan the prophet. Although David repents and is rescued from death, the dynasty of David is placed perpetually under the threat of the sword (2 Sam 12:10). With consummate skill, this vague threat works its way through the narrative, until in the concluding episode, Solomon assumes his father's throne through the use of the sword, which works havoc. Note the repeated use of Heb *pāgaᶜ*, "strike down" (1 Kgs 2:29, 31, 34, 46; cf. v 9). Thus, it seems plausible that the governing episode of 2 Samuel 11–12 and the concluding events of 1 Kings 1–2 are held together by this common reference to the sword.

What emerges is a very different disclosure of David, a personal account of the interiority, ambiguity, and pathos of the man that is absent in the early narrative sections. This narrative characterizes the struggle of David to hold together personal reality and public office. Gunn has seen how this portrayal of David, without any didactic effort, functions as a mirror and disclosure of the same brokenness that is present in all of human life.

The narrative celebrates and focuses on David in a most remarkable way, as von Rad (*PHOE,* 176–204) has noted. Nonetheless, even here the narrative shows clearly that David is not an independent, free agent. Even David's life is encompassed in the rule of Yahweh, who is both faithful and demanding.

7. 2 Samuel 21–24. Finally, 2 Samuel 21–24 is commonly reckoned as a miscellaneous collection of old materials inserted in the Succession Narrative before the concluding episode of 1 Kings 1–2. This material is much more like the narrative style of "The Rise," but we cannot assign it to any particular corpus of material. Two comments must suffice. First, it is generally recognized that these chapters of miscellaneous notes have a structure of two narratives, two lists, and two poems, a sequence in parallel to what Flanagan has found in 2 Sam 5:11–8:18 (McCarter *2 Samuel* AB, 18). One may at least conclude that this unit is not without some intentionality.

Second, as suggested above, that these materials may function for canonical purposes so that the concluding episode of 2 Samuel 24 may be a counterpart of 1 Samuel 1, even as 2 Samuel 22 is a poem in relation to the Song of Hannah in 1 Samuel 2. These "appendices" evidence a much less sophisticated reading of historical reality. They affirm in more direct fashion that Yahweh's governance is overriding, even of David's capacity. The whole of Samuel in the service of David is to legitimate and enhance the monarchy. Yet it is noteworthy that in 2 Samuel 24 as in 2 Samuel 11–22, the narrative articulates a theological Yahwistic foil to rapacious royal power. Moreover, David as a king is not free from Yahweh and Yahweh's Torah. Thus the ambiguity so painfully articulated in 1 Samuel 7–15 persists here. In the end even the chosen and much-celebrated David stands rebuked and under judgment. The narrative seems not to know how (or chooses not) to resolve this issue, but calls the reader to participate in this ambiguity which characterizes Israel's relation with Yahweh.

D. Some Important Texts

It may be helpful to identify and comment briefly on texts in Samuel which are structurally important for a sense of the whole, both literarily and theologically. Though the identification of such texts requires an interpretive judgment, the judgments made here reflect a general interpretive consensus.

1. 1 Sam 2:1–10. This hymn likely dates to the 10th century, i.e., to the time of David. It asserts some of the governing themes of the Samuel corpus, namely the inversion of the historical process through the activity or governance of Yahweh. The poem is reflective of the hymnic pattern of Israel's liturgy, which sings about the distinctiveness of Yahweh known in Yahweh's powerful transformative interventions.

In its present setting, this poem functions to signal the destiny of Israel as it will be presented in the ensuing narrative of Samuel. At the beginning of the narrative, in the face of the Philistines, the Israelites are the low (v 7), the poor (v 8), but the course of Davidic history is one of exalting, lifting, raising up (vv 7–8). Thus the older independent hymn has been made a fundamental element in the larger account.

2. 1 Sam 8:11–17. This text is bounded in the narrative (vv 5, 20) with a yearning to be "like the nations." It is the urging of the narrative (even in 2 Samuel 11–12, 24) that Israel, even under a king, is not and cannot be like the nations. In these verses the narrative presents a sober and realistic analysis of the way of kings. According to Gottwald's model (1979), Israel in the tribal period is a radical social experiment in organizing social power in egalitarian ways. This text discerningly asserts that to embrace monarchy is to embrace the very exploitative, rapacious power of a legitimated state from which Moses and Joshua had emancipated Israel.

The characterization of monarchy in this text may be reflective of Solomon, but also of neighboring kings of the period before Solomon. This characterization is dominated by the Heb verb *lāqaḥ,* "take." Israel has seen and knows that the primary social function of legitimated central power is "to take," to develop concentrations of wealth and power at the expense of some for the benefit of others. The text is important because it makes clear that Israel's theory of public life is deeply opposed to the conventional systems available, and that for Israel justice issues are paramount religious and social matters.

3. 1 Sam 12:1–25. This valedictory oration by Samuel

provides a general theoretical statement about history from the perspective of the old tribal organization and from Israel's old covenantal tradition. As such, it is consistent with 8:11–17. This text is most unambiguous in regarding monarchy as a violation of the will of Yahweh. While the passage is highly stylized, it no doubt reflects an old and deep conviction in Israel.

In terms of literary structure this passage is important because it marks the culmination of a view and practice of history best known in the book of Judges. Thus some scholars propose that Samuel follows the pattern of the old judges and that 1 Samuel 1–12 is in fact an extension of the literature known in the book of Judges. While 1 Samuel 13–15 provides a transition toward David, in terms of dramatic power the literature moves directly from the verdict of chapter 12 to the appearance of David in 16:1–13. The emergence of David has the literary effect of rendering the old dispute irrelevant. All of that is forgotten in the face of Israel's fascination with David.

4. 1 Sam 16:1–13. This passage may not be as important structurally as others cited. Yet there is no doubt that it marks a decisive shift of the flow of historical power from Saul to David. What is perhaps most interesting and important is the "innocent" quality of the narrative in which Yahweh is a direct, unexplained voice who participates in and governs the events of the narrative. No doubt the purpose of the narrative is to legitimate David by means of presenting David as a direct, divine choice. David is chosen by no human agent or process, only by the voice of God. Yet it is clear that such a narrative would not persuade anyone not already committed to the cause of David. This narrative has a legitimating function and is effective because it claims David's authority, in the most naive and direct way possible, as an act of simple designation by Yahweh, without pleading, justification, or explanation. This is the voice for "true believers."

5. 2 Sam 7:1–17. This is the hinge point between "The Rise" and "The Succession," or as Carlson (1964) has it, between blessing and curse. The chapter begins with a dispute concerning "presence," (vv 1–6), in the form of a discussion of "tent" and "temple." But the heart of the chapter is vv 7–17 which is a decree of Yahweh in the mouth of Nathan, giving divine legitimacy to the Davidic dynasty. This chapter is decisive for all of biblical faith in shifting both the political and theological ground of Israel's life with God.

The most remarkable move made is in vv 14–16, whereby Yahweh is now fully, firmly, unconditionally, and perpetually committed to the Davidic line. Clearly the unconditional terms were not everywhere embraced (cf. Ps 132:12), and it is obvious that in history the promise was not kept in the face of disobedience (cf. Jer 22:18–20). But in this moment the hazards of Israel's disobedience is fully overcome, and for the first time the God of Israel is unreservedly committed to a specific historical arrangement. While we may rightly regard such a claim as ideology or propaganda, the decree was in fact accepted in the Bible as a genuine disclosure. That God should be so committed to an historical arrangement reflects the scandal of particularity in biblical faith. That sort of theological thinking in terms of the historical concreteness of God adumbrated in this text becomes the source for theological messianism in both Judaism and Christianity.

6. 2 Samuel 11–12. This remarkable narrative achievement is one of the most exquisite in the Bible. The narrative does not present a full-bodied theological proposition as most of the other texts we have cited. Rather, with a very different mode of disclosure and a different set of epistemological assumptions, this narrative made its own case for the inscrutable governance of Yahweh. It asserts that David, the embodiment of Israel's new social power and new monarchic history, is not adequately committed to the Torah and perhaps does not fully understand the claims of the massive decree of 2 Sam 7:1–17. The narrative traces in an artistic and well-paced manner the several attempts at cover-up by David, until the voice of the prophet is sounded. The move from artistic delight in chapter 11 to theological clarity in chapter 12 is unmistakable, a move not unlike that from Genesis 2 to Genesis 3. The possibilities facing this powerful, gifted man are resolved in terms of prophetic judgment and covenantal curse.

This text is important because it marks a transition in the portrayal of David and seems to set in motion the destructive events that accompany the transition in power. From this moment on, the monarchy is a scarred social reality in Israel and will continue to be so, until its end.

7. 2 Sam 22:2–51. This poem has already been mentioned in relation to the canonical position of 1 Sam 2:1–10. This Davidic hymn of praise belongs to the general, familiar liturgic corpus of royal songs as attested by Psalm 18 in the Psalter. The Psalm refers the king's success and well-being completely to the fidelity and power of Yahweh, and claims nothing for the king himself.

The placement of the Psalm in this narrative gives it a quite specific function. While David in both "The Rise" and "The Succession" takes a great deal of initiative and is the key agent, this Psalm acknowledges precisely that the reality of history is found in Yahweh's action. It is as though this Psalm is now used to acknowledge the theonomous cast of life, even of royal life, as it is anticipated in 1 Sam 2:1–10.

If one traces the contours of the entire story of Samuel through this set of texts (1 Sam 2:1–10; 8:11–17; 12:1–25; 16:1–13; 2 Sam 7:1–17; 11–12; 22), one sees that the juxtaposition of human power and divine authority is the pervasive issue.

The books of Samuel are Israel's subtle effort to resolve this question in a theologically sensitive fashion that neither concedes too much nor claims too much. History is known to be an arena of human freedom and responsibility, of divine authority and governance. David in his restlessness and fidelity is the carrier of that troublesome settlement which never stays finally settled.

Bibliography

Ackroyd, P. R. 1981. The Succession Narrative (So-Called). *Int* 35: 383–96.

Alter, R. 1981. *The Art of Biblical Narrative.* New York.

Birch, B. C. 1976. *The Rise of the Israelite Monarchy.* SBLDS 27. Missoula, MT.

Brueggemann, W. 1985. *David's Truth.* Philadelphia.

Campbell, A. F. 1975. *The Ark Narrative.* SBLDS 16. Missoula, MT.

Carlson, R. A. 1964. *David The Chosen King.* Uppsala.
Conroy, C. 1978. *Absalom, Absalom: Narrative and Language in II Samuel 13–20.* Rome.
Dietrich, W. 1972. *Prophetie und Geschichte: eine redaktionsgeschichtliche Untersuchung zum deuteronomistischen Geschichtswerk.* FRLANT 108. Göttingen.
Flanagan, J. W. 1972. Court History or Succession Document. *JBL* 91: 172–81.
Fokkelman, J. P. 1981. *Narrative Art and Poetry in the Books of Samuel.* Assen.
Fretheim, T. E. 1983. *Deuteronomic History.* Nashville.
Gottwald, N. K. 1979. *The Tribes of Yahweh.* Maryknoll, NY.
———. 1983. Social History of the Monarchy. Paper delivered at the annual meeting of the Society of Biblical Literature, seminar on Sociology of Monarchy.
Gunn, D. M. 1978. *The Story of King David.* JSOTSup 6. Sheffield.
———. 1980. *The Fate of King Saul.* JSOTSup 14. Sheffield.
Halpern, B. 1981. The Uneasy Compromise: Israel between League and Monarchy. Pp. 59–96 in *Traditions in Transformation,* ed. B. Halpern and J. D. Levenson. Winona Lake, IN.
Humphreys, L. 1978. The Tragedy of King Saul: A Study of the Structure of I Samuel 9–31. *JSOT* 6: 18–27.
———. 1980. The Rise and Fall of King Saul: A Study of the Ancient Narrative Stratum in I Samuel. *JSOT* 18: 74–90.
———. 1982. From Tragic Hero to Villain: A Study of the Figure of Saul and the Development of I Samuel. *JSOT* 22: 95–117.
———. 1985. *The Tragic Vision and the Hebraic Vision.* Philadelphia.
Jobling, D. 1978. *The Sense of Biblical Narrative.* JSOTSup 7. Sheffield.
Mendelsohn, I. 1956. Samuel's Denunciation of Kingship in Light of Akkadian Documents from Ugarit. *BASOR* 143: 17–22.
Miller, P. D., Jr., and Roberts, J. J. M. 1977. *The Hand of the Lord.* JHNES. Baltimore.
Noth, M. 1981. *The Deuteronomistic History.* Trans. J. Doull. JSOTSup 15. Sheffield.
Ridout, G. P. 1971. Prose Compositional Techniques in the Succession Narrative (II Samuel 7, 9–20, I Kings 1–2. Ph.D. diss., Graduate Theological Union.
Rost, L. 1982. *The Succession to the Throne of David.* Trans. J. W. Rogerson. Sheffield.
Smend, R. 1971. Das Gesetz und die Völker; Ein Beitrag zur deuteronomistischen Redaktionsgeschichte. Pp. 494–509 in *Probleme biblischer Theologie,* ed. H. W. Wolff. Munich.
Sternberg, M. 1983. The Bible's Art of Persuasion. *HUCA* 54: 45–82.
Veijola, T. 1977. *Das Konigtum in der beurteiling der deuteronomistischen Historiographie.* Helsinki.

WALTER BRUEGGEMANN

SANBALLAT (PERSON) [Heb *sanballaṭ*]. An individual whose name means "Sin (the moon-god) gives life" (cf. Akk *sin-uballiṭ*). He is mentioned in Neh 2:10, 19; 3:33—Eng 4:1; 4:1—Eng 4:7; 6:1, 2, 5, 12, 14; and 13:28 as the leading figure in the opposition which Nehemiah encountered in his rebuilding of the walls of Jerusalem, and in the Aramaic documents from Elephantine as the "governor of Samaria" (*paḥat šmryn;* cf. *CAP,* 30:29). There are also references to a Sanballat in the Samaria Papyri from Wadi ed-Daliyeh and in Josephus *Ant* 11, though the precise relationship of these to the character in Nehemiah is disputed (see below).

Nothing is known for certain of his origins and background. Because of his foreign name, it is generally believed that he was a descendant of one of the settlers whom the Assyrians deported to Samaria after the fall of the northern kingdom of Israel in 721 B.C. (cf. 2 Kgs 17:24–41; Ezra 4:2, 10; see most recently Zadok 1985: 569–70). While this is not at all unlikely, it must nevertheless be remembered that it was by no means unusual for Jews (and therefore presumably descendants of the inhabitants of the old N kingdom also) to adopt Babylonian names at this time (e.g., Zerubbabel). At any rate, he gave his sons Yahwistic names (Delaiah and Shelemiah; *CAP,* 30.29), suggesting that he regarded himself as an adherent of the Israelite cult.

Instead of giving Sanballat a title, Nehemiah regularly calls him "the Horonite," again a designation of uncertain significance. Among the main proposals are (1) that he came from, or was a resident of, either upper or lower Beth-horon (Josh 16:3, 5), some five miles N of Jerusalem. Because of its strategic position, Zadok has maintained that it is not unreasonable to assume that this might have been an administrative center near the SW border of the province of Samaria, and he further points to parallels for designating hostile rulers in this manner. The absence of *bêt* from the designation is no problem in view of the analogy with *happalṭî,* "the Paltite" (2 Sam 23:26), generally assumed to come from *bêt peleṭ,* "the house of Pelet" (Josh 15:27). It has been argued against this view that we expect some term of abuse here to parallel that for "Tobiah the Ammonite," and to explain why Nehemiah preferred this designation to that of "governor of Samaria." Both points carry some weight, but they are not sufficiently conclusive to eliminate this possibility. It remains the most probable explanation, and is certainly the most widely held view; cf. Torrey 1928; Rudolph *Esra und Nehemia* HAT; and Rowley 1963b: 246. (2) In response to the difficulties just mentioned, other scholars (most recently Kellermann 1967: 167) link the name with Horonaim in Moab (cf. Isa 15:5; Jer 48:3). This would make Sanballat a Moabite, just as Tobiah was an Ammonite, consequently excluding both from "the assembly of God"; cf. Neh 13:1–3 with Deut 23:4–7—vv 3–6. Nehemiah's action in 13:28 also implies that Sanballat was of foreign origin, although for Nehemiah that might have applied to any non-Judahite and especially to the possible descendant of an originally foreign settler. While this proposal has obvious attractions, it fails to explain why Sanballat was not simply called "the Moabite." Would contemporary readers have readily understood the allusion? In addition, Zadok objects that we should expect retention of the *m* suffix in a gentilic. (3) Other less plausible suggestions include revocalizing to *heḥārānî* and so linking Sanballat with Harran in Mesopotamia, a center for the worship of the god Sin (Feigin 1926–27 and Galling *Chronik, Esra, Nehemia* ATD), associating him with Hawan, E of Galilee (Kraeling *BMAP,* 107–8) or even that he was a devotee of the god Horon (Williamson *Ezra, Nehemiah* WBC, 183).

It would seem from the use of the description "the Horonite" that Sanballat was the first in his family to act as governor of Samaria, it being known now that he was followed in this office by his direct descendants through four generations until the start of the Hellenistic rule (see below). It is possible, therefore, that his appointment reflects part of an administrative "shake-up" in the W of the Persian Empire. This would have been due to an attempt by the Persians to reassert their control of the region after some fifteen years of turbulence, starting with the Egyptian revolt, which lasted for several years from 460 B.C. on, and continuing with the revolt of the W satrapies under the leadership of Megabyzos in ca. 449 B.C. (cf. Williamson fc). From the Persian point of view, Nehemiah's appointment a few years later (445 B.C.) may reflect part of the same policy.

At any rate, by the time Nehemiah arrived in Jerusalem Sanballat was clearly the dominant partner in a loose federation of neighboring provincial leaders (cf. especially Neh 4:1—Eng v 7). In the light of Nehemiah's highly partisan account of events, we can only speculate as to the motives for Sanballat's determined, but ultimately unsuccessful, opposition to Nehemiah's mission. In an influential article, Alt (1934 = *KlSchr* 2: 316–37) argued that until this time Judah was included within the province of Samaria and that his opposition was thus due to pique at the diminution in his sphere of influence. While this theory still has eminent adherents, it has attracted increasing criticism in recent years in view of a reexamination of the biblical data and fresh epigraphical data (for a survey and evaluation, cf. Williamson 1988) so that it becomes necessary to propose alternative reasons. One attractive speculation is that following the debacle of the Jews' slightly earlier attempt to rebuild the walls of Jerusalem (recounted out of its chronological setting in Ezra 4:8–23, on which cf. Rowley 1963a) Judah was placed temporarily under the supervision of Samaria, with Tobiah (on this view a subordinate of Sanballat) acting as a caretaker administrator in Jerusalem until such time as Artaxerxes could find a reliable replacement. This would at least explain why Tobiah had close ties with some of the population in Jerusalem (Neh 6:17–19; 13:4–9). If this were the case Sanballat may have regarded Nehemiah's appointment as a personal slight.

Broader commercial and political considerations no doubt also played a part and may have been used by Sanballat to justify his opposition to Nehemiah among his associates if not to the imperial court itself. It seems certain that between the landed classes and those who had not returned from exile of both provinces there was a good deal of trade and social interaction (see, for example, Neh 5:8; 6:17–19; 13:4–9, 15–28), while if our earlier speculation about Tobiah is correct there would also have been excellent relations between Judah and the neighboring provinces. All this, Sanballat would have reasonably supposed, would have been very much to the liking of the imperial authorities. Nehemiah's policy of pursuing a rigid isolation of Judah from all outsiders, typified by his rebuilding of the walls of Jerusalem, would have been regarded as detrimental to the stability of the region, and it would not have been difficult even to represent it as treasonable (cf. Neh 2:19; 6:6–7). In such circumstances Sanballat's personal opposition to Nehemiah may readily be understood.

We have little other information about Sanballat the Horonite except that by the year 408 B.C. he was still in office but had delegated effective power to his two sons, Delaiah and Shelemiah, presumably because of his advanced age (cf. *CAP,* 30:29). Finds of papyri and seals from the Wadi ed-Daliyeh, however, have revealed more information about his descendants, who continued to hold the office of governor, and at least one who was also called Sanballat. According to Cross (1966: 204), they show that a Sanballat (II) became governor sometime early in the 4th century B.C.E., and that he was therefore probably the son of Delaiah and so the grandson of Sanballat the Horonite. They further refer to a *yšʿyhw* (or *ydʿyhw;* the name is damaged and therefore the precise reconstruction is hypothetical) and a Hananiah, both sons of Sanballat II and both governors after him. Because Josephus refers to a Sanballat at the start of Hellenistic rule, and because the practice of papponymy (naming a child after his paternal grandfather) was not uncommon at this period, Cross further suggests that Hananiah may have been succeeded by a Sanballat III.

While nothing is known of these men, the reconstruction is of considerable significance because of the light it may shed on the account in Josephus *Ant* 11.306–12 concerning the founding of the Samaritan temple. According to this source, Manasseh, a brother of the Jerusalem high priest Jaddua, was married to Nikaso, a daughter of Sanballat. When "the elders of Jerusalem" obliged Manasseh to leave Jerusalem rather than divorce his wife, he found consolation in that his father-in-law had a temple built for him on Mt. Gerizim. All this took place at the time of Darius before the advance of Alexander the Great.

There is a somewhat similar account of this in Neh 13:28, which states, "Now one of the sons of Jehoiada, son of Eliashib, the high priest, was a son-in-law of Sanballat the Horonite, so I (Nehemiah) banished him from my presence." Many earlier scholars thought that the coincidence between these two accounts was too great for them both to be true and therefore concluded that Josephus had fabricated his account from the incident in Nehemiah and dated it a century later. Cross, however, has suggested that the probability that there was a Sanballat III in Samaria puts the issue in a new light and that it is therefore no longer reasonable to doubt the essential accuracy of Josephus' account. We should reckon with the possibility of repeated intermarriage between the leading families of Jerusalem and Samaria (1966: 202–5; 1975: 5–6).

In assessing this proposal, several points need to be remembered. First, the fact that the Samaria Papyri show that there was a Sanballat II as governor may make plausible the suggestion that there was also a Sanballat III at the end of the Persian period. Nevertheless, this remains conjectural, the only direct evidence for it being the account in Josephus, and concerning the latter many other problems still remain. Secondly, therefore, with regard to Josephus it must be remembered that he clearly made the impossible identification of the Sanballat of his account with the enemy of Nehemiah (cf. *Ant* 11.302). Thirdly, we also now know that Josephus was confused about the chronology of the last century of Persian rule and so reduced the period by two whole generations (cf. Williamson 1977); it is therefore likely that he regarded his account as an alternative version of Neh 13:28, and this is reinforced by the fact that he omitted a parallel reference at the point where the story should appear in his retelling of the career of Nehemiah (cf. *Ant* 11.182). Finally, there are many internal incoherences in Josephus' story when taken as a whole. These have been frequently rehearsed (e.g., by Rowley 1963b and Mowinckel 1964: 104–18), and the recent discoveries and discussions have done nothing to remove them. It is clear that the narrative of Josephus cannot simply be accepted at face value (cf. Grabbe 1987), and the most probable view remains that which sees in Josephus a garbled variant of Neh 13:28, even if he himself derived it from some other source, subsequently lost to us (cf. Williamson *Ezra, Nehemiah* WBC, 401).

Bibliography

Alt, A. 1934. Die Rolle Samarias bei der Entstehung des Judentums. Pp. 5–28 in *Festschrift Otto Procksch zum 60. Geburtstag.* Leipzig.

Cross, F. M. 1966. Aspects of Samaritan and Jewish History in Late Persian and Hellenistic Times. *HTR* 59: 201–11.

———. 1975. A Reconstruction of the Judean Restoration. *JBL* 94: 4–18.

Feigin, S. 1926–27. Etymological Notes. *AJSL* 43: 58.

Grabbe, L. L. 1987. Josephus and the Reconstruction of the Judean Restoration. *JBL* 106: 231–46.

Kellermann, U. 1967. *Nehemia.* BZAW 102. Berlin.

Mowinckel, S. 1964. *Studien zu dem Buch Ezra-Nehemia II: Die Nehemia-Denkschrift.* Oslo.

Rainey, A. F. 1969. The Satrapy "Beyond the River." *AJBA* 1: 51–78.

Rowley, H. H. 1963a. Nehemiah's Mission and its Background. Pp. 211–45 in *Men of God: Studies in Old Testament History and Prophecy.* London.

———. 1963b. Sanballat and the Samaritan Temple. Pp. 246–76 in *Men of God: Studies in Old Testament History and Prophecy.* London.

Torrey, C. C. 1928. Sanballat "the Horonite." *JBL* 47: 380–89.

Williamson, H. G. 1977. The Historical Value of Josephus' *Jewish Antiquities* xi. 297–301. *JTS* n.s. 28: 49–66.

———. 1988. The Governors of Judah under the Persians. *TynBul* 39: 59–82.

———. fc. Early Post-Exilic Judaean History. In *The Bible and the Ancient Near East,* ed. J. A. Hackett.

Zadok, R. 1985. Samarian Notes. *BiOr* 42: 567–72.

H. G. M. Williamson

SANCTUARIES. See TEMPLES AND SANCTUARIES.

SANHEDRIN. The sanhedrin in Jerusalem, as it appears in the gospels, Josephus, and rabbinic literature, has been understood alternately as the high priests' political council, the highest legislative body in Jewish Palestine, the supreme judicial court, the grand jury for important cases, the council of the Pharisaic school, and the final court of appeals in deciding halakic questions. Even the number of assemblies properly called "the sanhedrin" has been debated.

A. Introduction
B. Meanings of "Sanhedrin"
C. Josephus
D. New Testament
E. Origin and Development
F. Rabbinic Literature
G. Leadership Bodies in Palestine
H. Theories
I. Synthesis

A. Introduction

The confusion concerning the number and character of the sanhedrin(s) is related to uncertainty about the structure and leadership of 1st century Jewish society in Palestine. The biblical Hebrew terms for leadership groups *(sôd; ʿēdâ),* and the later Hebrew term *bêt dîn,* give no clear indication of the composition, jurisdiction, or powers of the assemblies so designated. Likewise, the Greek political terminology adopted as words for Jewish governing bodies, especially *boulē, gerousia, symboulion, synedria,* and *synedrion* (all translated "council" in RSV), is general and imprecisely used.

Most theories of the sanhedrin have been developed with seriously flawed methods or assumptions. Many scholars have made uncritical use of the sources, especially rabbinic literature, treating every statement as historically reliable, with the result that very diverse and often irreconcilable sources have been harmonized to produce hypothetical and improbable legislative and judicial bodies. The various sanhedrins and other bodies mentioned in the texts must be understood as part of the whole political and social structure of Palestinian Judaism, set within a larger Hellenistic or Roman empire.

Jewish leadership underwent many organizational changes in response to the imperatives of outside powers and the changing balance of power within. The membership, leadership, powers, and functions of the Jerusalem Sanhedrin and other councils, regional assemblies, and courts varied with the strength of external rulers, such as the Romans, and with internal leaders, such as Alexander Jannaeus and Herod. Consequently, neither the sanhedrin nor any other institution can be treated as unchanging and continuous.

The theory of two sanhedrins, one political, led by the high priest and concerned with secular matters, and the other religious, dominated by the Pharisees and concerned with halakic matters, is based on a modern and artificial separation of religion and state, on an unhistorical retrojection of the 2d- and 3d-century rabbinic academies and courts on the Second Temple sanhedrin, and on an exaggeration of the Pharisees' role and power in Jewish society. Religion was so thoroughly embedded in political society that any ruling body had to deal with political, religious, legislative, and judicial issues. The laws which governed Jewish society derived from the Bible as interpreted through later laws and custom. Ritual, civil, and criminal law, moral imperative and social mores were inextricably intertwined. The struggle to control or influence this Jewish way of life fills the pages of all the sources. It is likely that there were many assemblies and councils attached to various Jewish groups, but only one supreme council in Jerusalem, made up of the most powerful and influential leaders at any given time.

B. Meanings of "Sanhedrin"

The Greek word *synedrion,* "sanhedrin," literally a "sitting down with," is widely attested in Greek literature, Ptolemaic Egypt, and elsewhere. It is one of a number of general words for meetings and assemblies. It is used of the meetings of city councils, the Areopagus council in Athens, meetings of representatives of allied cities, the assembly of the Roman senate, and meetings of high officials. In later Hellenistic Greek, *synedrion* denotes various kinds of law courts and this is the sense given the term in the NT and Mishnah (*HJP*[2] 2: 205). In the Roman period it was used of provincial assemblies (Kennard 1962), a usage which also fits Josephus and the NT. Finally, it is used for the councils of smaller, less official groups such as private associations and boards of trade (Hoenig 1953: 3–11; Mantel *IDBSup,* 784).

C. Josephus

Josephus uses the term "sanhedrin" in its several meanings, but only when writing of the Roman period. The five districts into which the Roman governor Gabinius divided Palestine in 57 B.C.E. are called sanhedrins in the *Antiquities* (14.5.4 §91), but synods in the *Jewish War* (1.8.5 §170), an indication that the terms were not technical and fixed. These sanhedrins were regional assemblies of traditional leaders whose primary responsibility was tax collection and civil order in their districts (Kennard 1962). The many councils of family, friends, and officials summoned by Herod to settle disputes within his family (e.g., *JW* 1.27.1 §537) are called sanhedrins. These ad hoc bodies both advised Herod and rendered judgment concerning his adversaries' culpability (subject to his approval). "Sanhedrin" is used for other ad hoc meetings of advisors, such as Titus' meeting with his officers during the siege of Jerusalem (*JW* 6.4.3 §243) and Josephus' strategy sessions with his friends in Galilee (*Life* §368). It is also used for meetings of permanent bodies, such as the Roman senate (*JW* 2.2.4 §25). It is not certain that the council of leaders in Jerusalem, headed by the high priest Hyrcanus, which put Herod on trial (*Ant* 14.9.3 §167 ff.) and the group of Jerusalem leaders directing the initial stages of the war against Rome (*Life* §62) were a permanent assembly of Jewish leaders. They may have been ad hoc gatherings for specific purposes. A sanhedrin (nature not specified) was convened in Jerusalem by Agrippa II, at the request of the Levites, to grant them permission to wear linen robes like those of the priests (*Ant* 20.9.6 §216–17).

The evidence from Josephus shows that the term "sanhedrin" did not refer exclusively to a fixed assembly of the highest Jewish leaders in Jerusalem, nor does it reveal the nature of that body unequivocally. "Sanhedrin" was used in a variety of nontechnical senses to refer to legislative, judicial, and advisory bodies assembled by rulers. Josephus may refer to the sanhedrin under Hyrcanus as a permanently organized judicial body, but it is not clear that the sanhedrin which directed the early stages of the war against Rome was that same permanent body. When the Levites wished to wear linen robes, they requested that Agrippa convene *a* sanhedrin, not *the* sanhedrin. It is very probable that the leading citizens of Jerusalem, priests and nonpriests, had a permanent city council which had power or influence over Judea and the rest of Palestine, depending on political circumstances. Josephus does not give the technical name for this body consistently, nor does he describe its membership or powers, perhaps because they varied greatly over time. Most probably the powerful social leaders at any time were members of it. The functions of this council most probably covered whatever was important to society, including legislative, judicial, temple, and civil matters.

The highest council or senate of a Hellenistic-Roman city was often called the *boulē,* and some scholars have tried to separate the Jerusalem political *boulē* from the Pharisaic sanhedrin (or in the case of Rivkin, vice versa). However, Josephus' use of the term *boulē* is as varied as his use of sanhedrin. He uses it often for the Roman senate (*Ant* 18–19) and in its related meanings of "plan, policy." He uses it occasionally for the supreme council of cities and peoples, for example, Tiberias' council of 600 (*JW* 2.21.10 §639–41), Antioch's city council (*JW* 7.5.2 §107) and the Samaritans' supreme council (*Ant* 18.4.8 §88). He also speaks occasionally of a council in Jerusalem: the chief priests and council (*JW* 2.15.6 §331), the priests with the powerful citizens and the council (*JW* 2.16.2 §336), the secretary of the council (*JW* 5.13.1 §532), and leaders, council, and people of Jerusalem (addressed in a letter by Claudius) (*Ant* 20.1.2 §11). Since the council is usually mentioned alongside the leading citizens, such as the chief priests, it seems to refer to a body larger than and advisory to the rulers. However, Josephus does not use the term with a specific technical meaning nor does he relate it to sanhedrin. (The use of *koinon* for city and provincial assemblies is relevant here also.) In general, *boulē* refers to a permanent governing body in a city which meets regularly. Since Jerusalem was not a Hellenistic city in the technical sense (Tcherikover 1964), the Jerusalem *boulē* or sanhedrin was not an independent governing body, but probably a variable assembly (or series of assemblies) of leading citizens, subject to the wishes of those in power and the needs of the society at different periods and called by different names by Josephus and the other sources.

D. New Testament

The Greek term *synedrion* has a general and specific use in the NT. In its general meaning it refers to local courts or councils which keep order and administer punishment (Matt 5:22; 10:17; Mark 13:9). Most often sanhedrin refers to the supreme council in Jerusalem which acts as a judicial court, as the political link to the Roman governor, and as the guardian of public order. The high priest presided over this sanhedrin, and its members included the chief priests, elders, scribes, and other members, presumably leading citizens (Mark 15:1). The Pharisees are not active in Jerusalem in the Synoptic Gospels nor, according to the primitive passion accounts, are they members of the sanhedrin. (John's claim that the Pharisees along with the chief priests summoned the sanhedrin [11:47] is historically unreliable because John turns all Jesus' non-priestly adversaries into Pharisees. Luke puts Pharisees in the sanhedrin in Acts.) In Mark and Matthew the sanhedrin condemns Jesus to death (Mark 14:64; Matt 26:66), but then must approach the Roman governor to have Jesus executed. In Luke no formal condemnation is made before the governor is approached (22:71). John attributes a political role and motive to the sanhedrin, which fears that Jesus will cause unrest and stimulate the Romans to destroy the nation (11:48–50). Luke, a gentile Christian, describes the sanhedrin as if it were a typical Hellenistic-Roman city council: "The elders-council [*presbyterion*] of the people gathered together, both chief priests and scribes, and led him away to their sanhedrin" (22:66). The chief priests and scribes made up the council of elders, and they plus other citizens made up the sanhedrin or larger assembly. Note that Luke refers to it as "their," not "the" sanhedrin, implying that every city and people had some sort of assembly. In the case of Jesus the sanhedrin is composed of the leaders of the Jews, takes action against Jesus to preserve public order, uses its judicial power to condemn his teaching and activities, and represents the nation before the Roman administration.

In Acts the sanhedrin functions as it does in the gospels, guarding community order against the early Jerusalem community, meting out punishment to them, keeping order in the Temple (chaps. 4–6; 23), and representing the nation to the Roman authorities (22:30). Luke portrays the sanhedrin as composed of Sadducees and Pharisees, including Gamaliel (5:34), and led by the high priest (5:21). It controls temple officials, guards, and a prison, and thus is a typical Hellenistic-Roman regional or city council charged with the deliberative, judicial, and ritual tasks necessary for social order and efficient administration.

Because the condemnation of Jesus by the sanhedrin has been used as an excuse for anti-Semitism, many controversies have arisen concerning the nature of the Jewish judicial process against Jesus and the authority ultimately responsible for his death. Such controversies are misdirected. The regional leaders of the Jewish community, meeting in an assembly (sanhedrin or *boulē*), were held responsible for keeping order in their society by the Romans. In the case of Jesus, and in many other similar cases, they exercised their authority with the assistance of the Roman government in a normal way by neutralizing a troublesome teacher and threat to public order.

E. Origin and Development

Both 1st-century Greek sources (Josephus and the NT), which mention the Jerusalem sanhedrin in a Jewish context, assign it to the Roman period and attribute it to the usual range of legislative, judicial, and executive tasks found in sanhedrins, councils, and assemblies elsewhere. Josephus refers to a supreme council of Jewish authorities in Jerusalem, but does not explain its composition, exact functions, or place within Jewish government, probably because all of these changed frequently according to political circumstances and because the presence of such an aristocratic council was normal and presumed. The NT writers see the sanhedrin as an opponent of Jesus and his movement, and assign it a membership and functions to fit that role. Generally, the NT agrees with Josephus' perceptions of the sanhedrin in Jerusalem as a central council of the highest leaders with broad powers.

The usage of the term "sanhedrin" for Jewish assemblies is attested only in the Roman period and may reflect Roman usage of the term for regional assemblies (Kennard 1962; Schürer *HJP*² 2: 205). Another less probable suggestion is that the use of the term "sanhedrin" for the council derived from Ptolemaic Egypt during the 3d century where sanhedrins were high councils and courts (Mantel 1961: 786). It is very likely that the presence of such a council, under other names, in varied forms and with shifting functions, goes far back into Jewish history.

F. Rabbinic Literature

Rabbinic literature uses "court" *(bêt dîn)* often and "sanhedrin" relatively infrequently for assemblies which varied in size, composition, location, and function. Because the literature does not provide a coherent and consistent account of Jewish judicial and legal institutions, conflicting theories of the sanhedrins differ in their assessment of the historical reliability of sources and individual texts, in schemes for arranging the fragments of conflicting information into an intelligible whole, in assumptions about the roles and power of the Pharisaic organization in society and in the sanhedrin, and in their understanding of the social and political institutions and relationships which bound Jewish society together. Since the dozens of pertinent rabbinic texts derive from Palestine and Babylon over several centuries, emphasis will be placed on the Mishnah, which is the earliest and most subject to historical control. Special attention will be given to the Great Sanhedrin/Court, made up of seventy-one members, which met in the Chamber of Hewn Stone on the Temple Mount. Parallels from the Bible and Josephus suggest that supreme councils traditionally consisted of seventy to seventy-two members (Schürer *HJP*² 2: 210–11).

The Mishnah uses the word "sanhedrin" in a variety of senses. Tractate *Sanhedrin* is concerned with judicial courts, especially those which try capital cases, but for the most part uses the term "court" *(bêt dîn)*, not "sanhedrin." A number of overlapping uses of these two terms suggest that they are used as equivalents in the Mishnah (*Sanh.* 1.5 and *Šebu.* 2.2; *Sanh.* 11.2 and *Mid.* 5.4; cf. Mantel 1961: 1). Attempts to show that the two words refer to separate institutions or derive from separate eras (Zeitlin 1942; Rivkin 1975) do not explain either Josephus' or the rabbinic usage. The term "sanhedrin" is used for bodies appointed for the tribes by the courts of seventy-one, for the Great Sanhedrin of seventy-one itself as well as for lesser ones of twenty-three (*m. Sanh.* 1.5–6), for the judicial court (size not stated, but probably the court of seventy-one) which sat in a half-circle (*m. Sanh.* 4.3), for a judicial court which has competence to try capital and other cases (*m. Mak.* 1.9–10), for a council of seventy-one with competence over expanding the temple (*m. Šebu.* 5.4) and finally, for the Great Sanhedrin of Israel, housed in the Chamber of Hewn Stone, which used to judge whether priests had blemishes (*m. Mid.* 5.4). Most theories of the sanhedrin attempt to sort these functions into categories and assign them to one or more legislative, religious, or judicial bodies, including the court of the priests, the kings' council, and the like.

"Court" *(bêt dîn)* is the normal mishnaic word for a judicial court and also for a quasi-legislative body which decides the meaning of the law and issues decrees and laws based on Biblical and traditional law (Mantel 1961: 64, 80–85, 227–35). *M. Sanhedrin* (1.1–6; 3.1) defines the competences of courts with three, twenty-three, and seventy-one judges. The rabbis envisioned courts in every city and a sanhedrin (of twenty-three) with power to try capital cases in any city with 120 men. In Jerusalem, according to the mishnaic system, there were three courts at the temple, in the gate to the Temple Mount, the gate to the Temple Court, and the Chamber of Hewn Stone (*m. Sanh.* 11.2). The center of the legal system was the Great Court of seventy-one members which met in the Chamber of Hewn Stone in Jerusalem. It tried tribes, false prophets, and high priests; sent the people forth to voluntary wars; approved additions to Jerusalem and the temple; set up tribal sanhedrins; and declared cities apostate (*m. Sanh.* 1.5–6). It also was the final court of appeals concerning the legitimacy of laws (11.2), and it executed rebellious elders (11.4). It had to be composed of Israelites with pure descent (*m. Qidd.* 4.5) and in the rabbinic ideal all were scholars (*m. Sanh.* 4.4). Most interpretations of rabbinic literature envision a great court or sanhedrin presided over by the rabbinic patriarch (*nāśîʾ*), dominated in the 1st century at least by Pharisees and in control of the laws and activities of the priests.

The legal system set forth in *m. Sanhedrin* and elsewhere is an ideal which does not describe the pre-70 sanhedrin. Many of the competencies of the Great Court in Jerusalem are drawn from the monarchic period of the Bible and do not fit Jewish society in the Hellenistic-Roman period (*m. Sanh.* 1.5–6). An assembly of scholars deciding how Israelite life should be lived (*m. Sanh.* 4.3) fits the 2d- and 3d-century rabbinic assemblies which guided the rabbinic movement and competed for control of Palestinian Jewish life, not the political ferment of the Roman Empire. Texts concerning the Great Sanhedrin in the Tosefta and Talmuds support and expand the mishnaic presentation of the Sanhedrin as an assembly of scholars ruling Israel under the direction of the heads of the Pharisaic schools before 70 and the patriarchs after 70. When the details of the patriarch's office are gathered from the Talmuds, a complex network of roles and powers devolve upon the patriarch and his office emerges as a dominant institution in Jewish society along with the rabbinic assembly (Mantel 1961: 174–253). Such an account fits the Talmudic, not the Second Temple period. Traditional accounts of the Sanhedrin, which make uncritical use of the rabbinic sources (e.g., Mantel 1961), accept isolated statements as historical facts and assemble them into an intricate social edifice, harmonizing conflicts in a very subjective way.

G. Leadership Bodies in Palestine

Before treating various theories which seek to reconcile the data on the sanhedrins, they must be put in their Palestinian social context. The city council (*boulē*), the assembly of elders (*gerousia*), the regional assembly of leaders, and the city assembly of all the citizens were common in the Hellenistic-Roman period, as was pointed out above. The bodies served mixed legislative, judicial, and executive functions which varied with time and place. The underlying pattern was common in all periods, though precise terms and powers varied. The notables, traditional leaders, wealthy citizens, hereditary aristocrats, and leading priests in ancient society ruled over the much more numerous lower classes, using a variety of institutional structures and traditional relationships. These leaders existed at every level and were usually represented by one or more councils like those described as the council (*boulē*), Great Sanhedrin, Great Court, or court of seventy-one. Duties covered anything pertaining to the overall welfare of the state, including political affairs, religious conflicts, disputes over laws and customs, and important judicial cases. For example, in the Maccabean period the council or senate is called a *gerousia* and the members of it are elders (2 Macc 4:44; 1 Macc 12:6; 11:23; 12:35). The term "sanhedrin" comes into use only in the Roman period and probably reflects changing official terminology and distribution of powers. Hoenig's neat division of social functions into the priesthood represented by the court of the priests, the political by the *boulē*, and the interpretation of the law by the Great Sanhedrin is artificial and improbable (Hoenig 1953: 163–68), as are two and three sanhedrin theories to be treated below. It seems that there were many city and regional assemblies and courts, controlled by local leaders and guided by traditional law and custom, as well as by the wishes of the political authorities of the day. (See Büchler [1909: 21–33] for the presence of lay courts in contrast to the rabbinic vision of scholars as judges.)

The highest assembly and court was in Jerusalem and met on the Temple Mount in the *liškat haggazît*, usually translated as the "Chamber of Hewn Stone." But *gazît* is translated into Greek as *Xystos* and refers to a part of the old western wall of the Temple Mount next to the council chamber (*boulē*), north of the western portico, according to Josephus (*JW* 5.4.2 §144; see Schürer *HJP*^{2} 2: 223–24). Thus the high court was not an assembly of scholars meeting inside the inner forecourt (*m. Mid.* 5.4), as imagined by the Mishnah, but the supreme legislative, judicial, and executive body of leading citizens meeting in a council chamber at the center of the city, near the temple.

H. Theories

The disagreements between the Greek and rabbinic sources have produced three streams of interpretation. (See Hoenig 1953 and Mantel 1961 for exhaustive reviews of the many positions on the sanhedrin dating back more than 100 years.) Some favor the Greek sources in which the sanhedrin is the supreme political body. This approach is taken here. It interprets the rabbinic sources as retrojecting Talmudic rabbinic institutions onto the 1st century, a contention which dates back at least to Geiger (1857: 114–21). Another approach favors the rabbinic sources and harmonizes them with the Greek sources by hypotheses of joint leadership, separate divisions of the sanhedrin, or committees with special powers. The third approach, initiated by Büchler (1902) and defended by Zeitlin, Mantel, and others, acknowledges the contradictions and differences between the Greek and Hebrew sources and proposes two sanhedrins, one political, reflected in the Greek sources, and the other religious, described in the rabbinic sources.

The sanhedrin theories which accept the rabbinic sources as historically reliable vary greatly in details of how the sanhedrin developed, who led it, how it was constituted, who controlled it, what its functions were and its role in the development of Talmudic law. The following are common variations. The sanhedrin is usually treated as an authoritative, continuous institution dating from the time of Ezra, or, more often, the Hellenistic period. In its early period it was led by the high priest and consisted of priests and other community leaders. In the Hasmonean period conflicts between Sadducees, Pharisees, and high priest caused splits in Jewish leadership. Some hold that the Pharisees gained control of the sanhedrin and others the Sadducees; those who hold the two-sanhedrin theory often argue that the Pharisees withdrew from the unified Sanhedrin to form a religious sanhedrin because it was too political and hellenized or because they lost power under Hyrcanus, Jannaeus, or Herod. Many grant to the Pharisees great political power over domestic affairs, the courts, and the temple ritual, and great influence with the people. Those who hold that there was one sanhedrin often argue for a Pharisaic takeover of the sanhedrin, but also for a separate political council (*boulē* or *gerousia*) which advised the high priest or king. For these scholars the leaders of the Pharisaic movement led the unified sanhedrin, whether they had the title *nāśîʾ* or not. Some proponents of the two-sanhedrin theory envision the Pharisaic religious sanhedrin as the ruling body of the private Pharisaic association, not as a public body with control over Jewish life, and others picture it as a more publicly active and powerful body. Many scholars nuance their one- and two-sanhedrin theories by distinguishing various governmental and religious functions and assigning them not just to the sanhedrin, but to a *gerousia, boulē,* or various types of *bêt dîn.*

Fundamental to any theory of the sanhedrin is the author's stance on the development of Jewish law during the Second Temple period. Traditional interpretations of the rabbinic evidence have attributed many mishnaic and Talmudic laws and practices to the Hasmonean and Roman periods and have assumed popular acceptance of Pharisaic-rabbinic practice among the people. Such views attribute various mishnaic laws and customs to the Hellenistic and Roman periods and postulate the development and collection of laws at an early date. The Pharisees and later the rabbis are pictured as engaged in the labor of studying and developing the law and applying it with authority to Jewish life, so that the halakic, Talmudic way of life was essentially known and accepted in the Second Temple period, though it was only codified at the end of the 2d century C.E. The history of the sanhedrin, then, becomes entwined with the history of the implementation of Pharisaic law and their quest for power over Jewish society.

I. Synthesis

Both textual and wider historical evidence indicates that there was a central council in Jerusalem, but its membership, structure, and powers are not clear in the sources and probably varied with political circumstances. Typically in the Greco-Roman world, the leading citizens according to heredity, wealth, power, and position met in a body which had legislative, executive, and judicial functions relative to the welfare and control of the whole nation. The sanhedrin in Josephus, the gospels, and some rabbinic texts fits this pattern. In contrast, the rabbinic vision of an assembly of scholars and learned judges, debating points of law and establishing halakic policy for the Jewish community, fits the social and political situation of the Talmudic period; its highly articulated version of Jewish law and life bears the marks of intensive thought and effort in the aftermath of the destruction of the temple. Attribution of such a pattern to the Hellenistic-Roman period is anachronistic.

The theory of two sanhedrins, one political and one religious, during this period is improbable in the extreme because political and religious life were one. However, it is probable that the Pharisees, Sadducees, and many other groups in Jewish society had their own organizations, including executive and legislative and disciplinary assemblies and bodies, and that such groups intermittently exercised influence, and even power, in Jewish political and social life. Whether they called their assemblies by the terms "sanhedrin," *bêt dîn,* or *boulē* is not known. Diversity and change in Palestinian Jewish life must constantly be kept in mind. The forms and structure of government evolved in response to the conflicts among the Hasmoneans, the hegemony of the Romans, and the civil unrest during the Herodian period. The powers of traditional leaders waxed and waned and governmental offices, taxation districts, judicial arrangements, and laws were changed in complex ways only dimly glimpsed in the sources. Traditional laws, local customs, new adaptations, colonial impositions, and sectarian rules vied with one another for control of Jewish society. Only in the relative power vacuum after the two wars with Rome did the rabbinic version of Jewish life take hold and the rabbinic court *(bêt dîn)* become the central and authoritative council of the Jewish community. The mishnaic and Talmudic vision of a community founded on biblical law, understood through the oral Torah, guided by learned scholars and judges, and made holy by fidelity to God and obedience to the sages, only became apparent and accepted after the temple was destroyed and the priesthood failed to retain leadership of the Jewish community. While the temple stood, the traditional priestly and aristocratic leaders met in council to rule, guide, supervise, and judge the Jewish community in its internal and external social relations.

Bibliography

Büchler, A. 1902. *Das Syndedrion in Jerusalem und das Grosse Beth-Din in der Quaderkammer des jerusalemischen Tempels.* Vienna.

———. 1909. *The Political and Social Leaders of the Jewish Community of Sepphoris in the Second and Third Centuries.* London.

Ephron, Y. 1967. The Sanhedrin as an Ideal and as Reality in the Period of the Second Temple. Pp. 167–204 in *Doron sive Commentationes . . . Benzioni Katz . . . dedicatae.* Tel Aviv.

Geiger, A. 1857. *Urschrift und Übersetzung der Bibel.* Breslau.

Hoenig, S. B. 1953. *The Great Sanhedrin.* Philadelphia.

Kennard, J. S. 1962. The Jewish Provincial Assembly. *ZNW* 53: 25–51.

Mantel, H. 1961. *Studies in the History of the Sanhedrin.* Cambridge, MA.

Rivkin, E. 1975. Bet Din, Boule, Sanhedrin: A Tragedy of Errors. *HUCA* 46: 181–99.

Saldarini, A. 1988. *Pharisees, Scribes, and Sadducees.* Wilmington, DE.
Tcherikover, V. 1964. Was Jerusalem a "Polis?" *IEJ* 14: 61–78.
Zeitlin, S. 1942. *Who Crucified Jesus?* New York.

ANTHONY J. SALDARINI

SANSANNAH (PLACE) [Heb *sansannâ*]. The name (literally, "fruit-stalk of date," see also Cant 7:9) suggests that a grove of palm trees was once located in the vicinity of this site. Sansannah has been identified with Kh. esh-Shamsaniyat (M.R. 140083), SW of Kh. Tatrit (Madmannah) in the Negeb plains at the foot of the Hebron hills. This town was in the Negeb administrative district of Judah, according to Josh 15:31, the only place this site is mentioned in the Bible. However, there is some question as to whether the list of Simeonite towns in Josh 19:5 (Hazar-susah) and in 1 Chr 4:31 (Hazar-susim) contain variations of the name Sansannah because their location in these lists appears to be parallel. See discussion in MADMANNAH for a similar problem in interpretation.

HAROLD BRODSKY

SANT, WADI ED-. See ELAH, VALLEY OF.

SAPARDIANS. See IVVAH.

SAPH (PERSON) [Heb *sap*]. Var. SIPPAI. Notorious Philistine warrior, slain by one of David's soldiers in a battle at Gob (2 Sam 21:18 = 1 Chr 20:4). His name is written as Saph in 2 Samuel and Sippai (Heb *sippay*) in the parallel account in 1 Chronicles. In 2 Samuel, he is described as one of the descendants of Rapha *(yĕlīdê hārāpâ),* and the account of his demise is placed alongside that of three of his relatives at the hands of David's men (2 Samuel). Saph was killed by Sibbecai the Hushathite, a member of "the Thirty" (1 Chr 11:29). See DAVID'S CHAMPIONS. The location of the battle, Gob, where the death occurred, is unknown. 1 Chronicles has "Gezer" (M.R. 142140) for Gob, a town near the border of Philistia on the coastal plain, a probable location.

Saph and his relatives have been traditionally understood as the last of the Rephaim, the legendary race of giants which inhabited pre-Israelite Canaan. Note that *yĕlīdê hārāpâ* is written *yĕlīdê hārĕpāʾîm* in 1 Chronicles and this, in turn, is translated *tōn huiōn tōn gigantōn* in the LXX. Some modern scholars have proposed an alternative explanation of the group to which Saph belonged. It is argued that the translation "descendant" for Heb *yālîd* is inaccurate since the word does not primarily indicate membership in a class due to heredity. For example, Willeson concludes that it refers only to children born to slaves in an Israelite household, and can be extended to include slaves dedicated to a deity who was regarded as the head of their social unit (1958a). Moreover he interprets Heb *hārāpâ* as a Greek word *(harpē)* which means "scimitar." Consequently, Saph was a member of a distinguished guild of Philistine soldiers whose emblem was a scimitar (1958b).

L'Heureux (1974) and McCarter reject Willeson's conclusions regarding Heb *hārāpâ* and explain it in terms of other biblical and extrabiblical evidence in which the Rapha/Rephaim can signify underworld deity/deities. It is concluded that Saph belonged to an elite class of Philistine warriors devoted to a deity named Rapha, whose cult center was in Gath (McCarter *II Samuel* AB, 449–50).

Although these theories are stimulating, they do not adequately explain the biblical data. There is insufficient evidence to make firm conclusions about the meaning of *yālîd* (cf. also Josh 15:14 where *yālîd* is parallel to *bēn*). As far as the biblical text is concerned, Saph and his relatives descended (*yullĕdû,* 2 Sam 21:22) from Raph, probably the eponymous ancestor of the Rephaim. The plain language indicates physical descent. Far more satisfying is the explanation that the account of the defeat of the Rephaim in 2 Samuel 21 demonstrates that David and his warriors finished that which Israel had failed to do under Joshua during the Conquest (Hertzberg *Samuel* OTL, 388).

Bibliography

L'Heureux, C. 1974. The Ugaritic and Biblical Rephaim. *HTR* 67: 265–74.
Willeson, F. 1958a. The Yalid in Hebrew Society. *ST* 12: 92–110.
———. 1958b. The Philistine Corps of the Scimitar from Gath. *JSS* 3: 327–35.

STEPHEN G. DEMPSTER

SAPPHIRA (PERSON) [Gk *Sapphira*]. Convert to Christianity who, along with her husband, Ananias, is miraculously killed after lying to the apostles about turning over all their money (Acts 5).

The name is from the Aramaic *šappîrāʾ*, "good" or "beautiful," and both Aramaic and Greek forms of the name are found on ossuaries discovered near Jerusalem (*BAGD,* 742). Although there is no solid proof that Luke knew Aramaic and used the name for its meaning, Lake (1979: 140) believes it is almost certainly historical that Ananias, at least, died suddenly, under circumstances which led the Church to see in his death the punishment of some offense. Lüdemann (1987: 71) believes that the parallel to 1 Cor 5:1–8 demonstrates an earlier analogous story and thus an historical kernel for Acts 5:1–11. But neither of these positions nor the general tendency to doubt the historicity of Acts 5:1–11 explain the presence of the name "Sapphira."

Sapphira appears along with her husband, Ananias, in this narrative of miraculous divine judgment which results in sudden death and fear (Weiser 1979: 156–58). Noorda (1979: 480–81) rightly advises us to take Acts 4:32–5:16 as a unit and to see at the level of literary composition by the final author a mixture of summary style and narrative scenes (4:36–37 on Barnabas; 5:1–11 on Ananias and Sapphira; 5:15–16 on Peter's miraculous power which attracts wide attention). On the other hand, a number of scholars feel that the exact nature of the sin of Ananias and Sapphira is not easily determined.

To be sure, there is a lack of realism in the portrayal of Sapphira. She does not even know of her own husband's death and burial, and Peter and the others sit and wait three hours for her arrival. Moreover, Luke in Acts 5:1–11 (cf. v 14) portrays a woman as he portrays a man, thus suggesting an appropriate equality (O'Toole 1984: 118–26). Naturally this also allows him to stress his ideas through repetition. Consequently, Sapphira appears much like Ananias. She knew and had agreed to the unjust use of the money. However, handing over of the money was not part of an entrance rite for Christians as it was at Qumran (Klauck 1982: 78). Sapphira does go beyond Ananias in that she tells Peter a lie about the price paid for the field, and both she and Ananias, in trying to deceive Peter, have acted against the Spirit. In fact, Mettayer (1978: 419) sees a play of opposites in the text between Spirit and Satan, life and death, truth and lies, love and aggression, necessity and freedom, and confidence and fear. Luke 12:10, ". . . but he who blasphemes against the Holy Spirit will not be forgiven," may well apply here since Ananias and Sapphira were already Christians, and if so, the harshness of the penalty would be explained (Brown 1969: 106–8). Peter's prophetic statement is fulfilled when Sapphira falls dead at his feet where Ananias had earlier laid the money. Likewise, the Christians and Barnabas had laid the proceeds from the sale of their properties at the apostles' feet in recognition of their authority (v 10; cf. 4:34, 37; 5:1–2). This irony continues that of Sapphira's ignorance of her husband's fate, despite her previous knowledge of everything else, and of her joining him in the grave (Johnson 1977: 204–9). Her miraculous punishment and that of her husband recalls the threatened damnation of Simon (Acts 8:20–23) and the Lord's blinding of Elymas (13:11). Sapphira's death brings great fear on the whole Church and on everyone who hears of the incident. This is the first time Luke uses "church," and that fact, joined with the first verse of the unit (Acts 4:32; "Now the company of those who believed were of one heart and soul, and no one said that any of the things which he possessed were his or her own"), reveals the centrality of community to the pericope. The immediate reference would be to the Jerusalem Church, but more obviously, it would be the whole Christian Church whose very unity was threatened by actions such as that of Sapphira and her husband.

Everyone calls attention to the contrast Barnabas presents by laying the true price of his field at the apostles' feet. But Sapphira would likewise share in the parallel between her husband and Judas; in both cases Satan is the transcendent cause of the sin, the root cause of the sin is "unrighteous mammon," the act is free, somehow property is involved, and the sin is punished with sudden death (Brown 1969: 106–9).

Through his story about Sapphira and her husband, Luke reflects on a number of concerns. God and the Spirit work in the community and through Peter (and the apostles), and to sin against the community is to sin against them and expose oneself to divine judgment. Christians are encouraged to respect this reality: be fearful. Of course, God and the Spirit are opposed to Satan (cf. Acts 26:18). To suggest an appropriate equality, Luke pictures women as he does men, and, finally, he also presents a lesson in the Christian use of wealth.

Bibliography

Brown, S. 1969. *Apostasy and Perseverance in the Theology of Luke.* AnBib 36. Rome.

Johnson, L. T. 1977. *The Literary Function of Possessions in Luke-Acts.* SBLDS 39. Missoula, MT.

Klauck, H. J. 1982. Gütergemeinschaft in der klassichen Antike, in Qumran und in Neuen Testament. *RevQ* 11: 47–79.

Lake, K. 1979. Note XII: The Communism of Acts ii. and iv.–vi. and the Appointment of the Seven. Pp. 140–51 in *The Beginnings of Christianity,* vol. 1/5. Ed. K. Lake, H. J. Cadbury. Grand Rapids.

Lüdemann, G. 1987. *Das frühe Christentum nach den Traditionen der Apostelgeschichte.* Göttingen.

Mettayer, A. 1978. Ambiguïté et terrorisme du sacré: Analyse d'un texte des Actes des Apôtres (4,31–5,11). *SR* 7: 415–24.

Noorda, S. J. 1979. Scene and Summary, A Proposal for Reading Acts 4,32–5,16. Pp. 475–83 in *Les Actes des Apôtres,* ed. J. Kremer. BETL 48. Gembloux.

O'Toole, R. F. 1984. *The Unity of Luke's Theology: An Analysis of Luke-Acts.* GNS 9. Wilmington, DE.

Weiser, A. 1979. Das Gottesurteil über Hananias und Saphira: Apg 5, 1–11. *TGl* 69: 148–58.

Robert F. O'Toole

SARAH (PERSON) [Heb *śārâ*]. Var. SARAI. The name of two women in the Bible.

1. The wife of Abraham and mother of Isaac. In Genesis 11, 12, and 16 Sarah is called Sarai, an older form of the name which in Hebrew means "princess." In Gen 17:15, the Priestly version of God's covenant with Abraham, Sarai's name is changed to Sarah, just as Abram's name becomes Abraham. Name changes signify a new reality. Thus, the barren Sarah is brought into God's covenantal promise as the mother of many nations and kings (17:16). Over and against Hagar and Ishmael, she is the lawful wife who will bear the son through whom God's promises to Abraham will be realized.

The stories of Genesis 12–50 focus on the threefold promise to the patriarch Abraham that he would have land, descendants, and a great name (Gen 12:1–3); how this promise is passed on from father to son becomes the central plot. The narratives about the matriarchs, then, are not primarily about the women themselves as individuals, but rather about their roles as the legitimate or "correct" wife and mother of the male successor. The question of who is the correct wife, mother of the heir, should be seen in the context of marriage and kinship systems of the Israelite society. Marriage alliances here are endogamous, i.e., within one's own tribe or social group. Lines of descent are patrilineal, traced through the father instead of the mother. Sarah and Abraham are closely related endogamously. They are, in fact, siblings, having the same father but different mothers (Gen 20:12). For this reason, Abraham is able to claim that Sarah is his sister as well as his wife in Gen 12:13 and 20:2, 12. See Wander (1981) and Donaldson (1981) regarding the complexities of such endogamous patrilineal relationships, which are used to control women in the self-interests of their men.

Several recent studies show that the biblical stories of the matriarchs follow a literary paradigm whereby the legitimate wife is paired with a rival co-wife who possesses certain characteristics that the other lacks (Brenner 1985; 1986; Cohen 1983). The competition and jealousy between the two are the destructive consequences of the patriarchal and polygamous society where the narratives are played out. Both sides represent incomplete womanhood, shadowy reflections of the other. Because of the asymmetry of both entities, the two women are locked in conflict until one can expel the other. The person of Sarah, therefore, must be discussed in conjunction with her complementary pair, her maid Hagar.

Sarah far outstrips Hagar on several levels. She is Abraham's only beloved wife, a free woman who exerts considerable control over Abraham's household affairs. Her beauty attracts the attention of pharaohs and sheikhs. However, she is barren and her advanced age seems to preclude any hope for a son. Sarah's barrenness is a twofold stigma. On one level, it represents a loss of status in a patriarchal, labor-intensive society with a high mortality rate. Here, a premium is placed on the ability to bear many sons. On another level, it seems to be an impediment to the fulfillment of God's promise of posterity to Abraham.

In contrast to the freeborn Sarah, Hagar is a slave, one with a particularly lower status in the household. Having no immediate relationship to Abraham, she is subject directly to her mistress, Sarah. Even when she is given to Abraham to produce a child, she is accountable to Sarah in the end. Hagar is also a foreigner from Egypt. Her foreignness creates a foreboding tension in the story. If she bears the child of the promise, it will be a product of an exogamous union in conflict with the endogamous practice of the Hebrews. Hagar is also younger than Sarah. Yet, in contrast to Sarah, whose beauty is highlighted, the text is silent about Hagar's appearance. Finally, where Sarah is barren, Hagar is fertile and she ultimately conceives the child that Sarah so desperately wants. The pregnancy and Hagar's disdain toward her mistress evoke in Sarah jealousy and a shocking cruelty. Sarah abuses her subordinate, forcing Hagar to flee, and ultimately engineers her expulsion from the household along with her son, Ishmael.

Both women are victims and victimizers within the patriarchal system in which they live; the narrative structure itself sets limits on the role each character can play (Exum 1985). Sarah is a victim of the patriarchal system which defines her in her capacity to bear sons and of a narrative structure that spotlights the promise of a son. Hagar is a double victim by virtue of her class as well as her sex. She is exploited by a privileged woman for her fertility. Yet she is victimizer in regarding Sarah and her barren condition not with compassion but with contempt. This elicits another round of oppression, whereby Sarah mistreats her servant and ruthlessly cuts her and her son off from the source of their economic well-being. The insinuation of the text is that women cannot collaborate or bond, even when they are engaged in a common goal. They allow their own self-interests to consume them and to compete with and abuse the other. However, the text is silent about the patriarchal society in which this tragic drama is performed, a society which defines for women what is of value and the social role they are to play.

The NT contains several traditions regarding Sarah. In Rom 4:19 her barrenness highlights Abraham's faith in God's promises. Heb 11:11 shifts the focus from Abraham to Sarah's own faith in conceiving in her old age. Nevertheless, Sarah is used to legitimate patriarchy and women's submission to their husbands: 1 Pet 3:6 states that "Sarah obeyed Abraham, calling him lord." Rom 9:6–9 alludes to the conflict between Sarah and Hagar by insisting that not all are children of Abraham because they are his descendants. God chose Isaac over Ishmael to be the heir of God's promises. In Gal 4:21–31, a text with much supersessionist anti-Semitic potential, Hagar allegorically represents those in slavery under the law, "the present Jerusalem." Sarah, on the other hand, is the "Jerusalem above" who is "free," the mother of the Christian community.

2. The daughter of Raguel destined to become the wife of Tobias in the book of Tobit. Her seven husbands were killed by the evil demon Asmodeus on their wedding night. There is an interesting parallel between Sarah of the book of Tobit and Sarah of Genesis that emphasizes the conflict between women in a patriarchally defined society. Just as Sarah in Genesis mistreats her maid Hagar when Hagar becomes pregnant and lords it over her mistress, so does Sarah in Tobit apparently beat her maids for chiding her inability to keep a husband (Tob 2:8–9).

Bibliography

Brenner, A. 1985. *The Israelite Woman.* Sheffield.

———. 1986. Female Social Behaviour: Two Descriptive Patterns within the "Birth of the Hero" Paradigm. *VT* 36: 257–73.

Cohen, N. J. 1983. Sibling Rivalry in Genesis. *Judaism* 32: 331–42.

Donaldson, M. E. 1981. Kinship Theory in the Patriarchal Narratives: The Case of the Barren Wife. *JAAR* 49: 77–87.

Exum, J. C. 1985. "Mother in Israel": A Familiar Story Reconsidered. Pp. 73–85 in *Feminist Interpretation of the Bible,* ed. L. M. Russell. Philadelphia.

Wander, N. 1981. Structure, Contradiction, and "Resolution" in Mythology: Father's Brother's Daughter Marriage and the Treatment of Women in Genesis 11–50. *JANES* 13: 75–99.

GALE A. YEE

SARAPH (PERSON) [Heb *śārāp*]. An individual of the tribe of Judah, identified as a ruler over Moab. The Vg rendering of 1 Chr 4:22 reflects a rabbinic tradition of a partial or total conquest of Moab by the men of Bethlehem.

DAVID CHANNING SMITH

SARASADAI (PERSON) [Gk *Sarasadai*]. See ZURISHADDAI.

SARDIS (PLACE) [Gk *Sardeis*]. A city in Asia Minor located some 100 kms (38°28′N; 28°03′E) inland from Smyrna and Ephesus, most famous in antiquity as the capital of the Lydian empire (ca. 680–ca. 547 B.C.) and for the legendary king Croesus (ca. 560–ca. 547 B.C.). Following the Lydian empire, the city served in turn as the seat of a Persian satrap, as an administrative center for the Seleucids, and as a leading city of the Roman province of Asia. Its only explicit reference in the Bible is in the book of Revelation (Rev 1:11; 3:1, 4).

Obad 20, however, remarks on the exiles of Jerusalem who are in Sepharad (=Sardis: Kraabel 1969: 81 n. 2) which introduces the question of the Jewish community in the city. The enlargement of this community may have been encouraged in Seleucid times by Antiochus (Josephus, *Ant* 12.148–49). Josephus also (*Ant* 16.171) records that the Jews in Asia Minor successfully appealed to the Roman emperor Augustus against the decisions of the city administrations, and more specifically relays Caesar's instructions to the proconsul, Gaius Norbanus Flaccus, to the effect that the Jewish community at Sardis is not to be prevented from subscribing funds to be sent to Jerusalem. He also reports (*Ant* 14.235) that the propraetor, Lucius Antonius, informed the Sardians that the Jews were to be allowed to congregate privately in accordance with their own customs. Striking confirmation of the size and influence of the Jewish community in the Roman period may be seen in the large synagogue excavated in the city, now handsomely restored thanks to Turkish and American support.

Originally used as a synagogue in the early 3d century A.D. (though evidently built for a different purpose—perhaps a basilica, since that is the building's shape), this structure underwent several phases of change (Seager in Hanfmann et al. 1983: 163), and remained in full operating condition, alongside the burgeoning Christian church, until the devastation wrought by the army of Chosroes II in A.D. 616; at that moment, the city, and the Jewish community with it, vanished. The synagogue is notable for its huge size and its setting. It forms an integral part of a major urban complex in the heart of the city; this complex comprised a gymnasium and a bath building in use in the time of the emperor Lucius Verus (epigraphic evidence), and a *Kaisersaal* (place for the imperial cult: Yegul 1986: 6–7). Since synagogues are normally found on or close to the periphery of ancient cities, the location of the Sardis synagogue is unusual, and speaks eloquently of the continuing strength and wealth of the Jewish community.

The building consisted, in its final stage, of a forecourt and a main hall, measuring some 85 m long and 20 m wide. The forecourt was surrounded by a peristyle and adorned by a large central fountain; this fountain was probably open to the general public since there is mention of "the Fountain of the Synagogue" in an epigraphic description of public fountains at Sardis. Three doors gave access to the main, oblong hall (ca. 60 m long) with an apse at the W end, i.e., pointing away from Jerusalem. Two shrines, one of which would have protected the torah, the OT scrolls, were raised on platforms against the E wall of the hall, while a large marble table stood in front of the apse at the W. There was no sign of benches installed along the walls, features thought to be characteristic of synagogues, nor of a staircase or balcony for the separation of the sexes at their devotions. It is thought that the hall could have accommodated up to one thousand people. Inscriptions in Greek from the interior (Robert 1964: 37–57) announce dedications made by prominent members and reveal the professions of some (goldsmiths, etc.) and the status of others (city councillors, etc.). Mosaic pavements, some again inscribed as dedications, embellished the floors, while decorative panels of *skoutlosis,* mosaic-like designs made up of shaped fragments of colored marbles and other stones (Robert 1964: 40; Seager in Hanfmann et al. 1983: fig. 264, 265), decorated the walls. Several representations of menorahs in or on stone, on brick, metal, and pottery shards, some again with inscriptions, came to light, though there were only a couple of terse inscriptions in Hebrew, among many in Greek. Incorporated in the building are many reused blocks, some whose function had originally been structural, and others of a more religious nature. Notable among these is a rectangular block of the 6th century B.C. sculpted in relief (Hanfmann and Ramage 1978: 43–51) with a representation of a temple of Cybele, the goddess herself, and members of her retinue. In the synagogue, this block was used as part of a pier, its imagery invisible. Also of interest are free-standing 6th century B.C. sculpted stone lions, originally the lions of Cybele, reused in this changed context as the lions of Judah.

The discovery of this building has shed new light on two important topics, the architectural history of the synagogue, and the place of Jewish communities in the Roman cities of Asia. The building is by far the largest example of an ancient synagogue so far discovered, and there are no clear parallels. Inscriptions testify to the existence of other synagogues in W Asia Minor—at Acmonia, Apameia, Aphrodisias, Hierapolis, Laodicea, and Miletus—but only at Priene has another been excavated (Kraabel in Hanfmann et al. 1983: 180–82), which is small in size, unobtrusive, and bears no similarity to Sardis. Sardis is unusual for the absence of balcony and benches along walls, and for the presence of the seating in the apse, the marble table opposite the apse, the pair of shrines (where only one is needed), and the *skoutlosis* decoration. In terms of apsidal synagogues, the general arrangement of colonnaded forecourt plus apsidal hall on axis is found sparingly elsewhere (e.g., at Beth Alpha in Israel), but the Sardis evidence suggests that there was no canonical plan either of shape or decoration or placement of features and furnishings, and that flexibility was the main criterion. The size, the setting, and the richness of decoration and paraphernalia bespeak a Jewish community, not only flourishing but entirely at home in the Roman city. The confident statements of the piety of donors reveal the generosity of members of the congregation, while the identification of some as participants in the administration of the city and indeed of the province (one a *procurator,* another a *comes*), speaks to the integration of the Jewish peoples into the Roman populace. The theory of the ghettoization of Jews in Roman cities may now be challenged, at any rate with respect to Sardis; and if the religion of Christ was on the move, at Sardis it prospered alongside of, not in place of, that of the Jews.

Evidence of an early Christian community is found in Rev 1:11 where Sardis is mentioned along with Ephesus, Smyrna, Pergamum, Thyatira, Philadelphia, and Laodicea as one of the seven churches of Asia; while Rev 3:1–6 records, at some length, promises and warnings to Christians in Sardis. A well-known bishop of Sardis in the 2d century is Melito, who substantiates accounts of the persecution of Christians recorded in a letter from Antoninus Pius to the council of Asia in A.D. 161 (Eusebius, *Hist. Eccl.,* 4.13.1–8). A prolific writer, Melito produced tracts, treatises, and homilies, of which the *Homily on the Passion* is the only one to survive almost in its entirety (Kraabel 1971: 76–85; Bonner 1940). Melito was a Quartodeciman, i.e., he celebrated Easter on the same day as Jews celebrated Passover, on whatever day of the week Passover fell. In spite of this "Judaizing" practice, later pronounced a heresy by the Church, Melito attacked the Jews vigorously as being responsible for the death of Christ; almost a third of the text of the *Homily on the Passion* is preoccupied with the condemnation of "Israel." Yet Melito was faced not only with a prosperous and large Jewish community in the city, but also by other Christian sects and pagan survivals; it is in this context of the struggle for adherents that his outbursts may be explained.

Churches began to be constructed as the Christianization of the city gathered pace following the conversion of Constantine. In the middle years of the 4th century, a large basilican complex was built outside the city walls to the W, and a small chapel was constructed against the SE corner of the Temple of Artemis before A.D. 400. The latter was evidently thought of as hallowing the sanctuary of Artemis and providing a chapel for the large cemetery nearby (Hanfmann et al. 1983: 195). The remains of a huge domed basilican structure, unexcavated, lie to the E of the gymnasium–synagogue complex; this is thought to be of Justinianic date and to have been the cathedral of the city.

The late Antique city came to an end with the Persian attack of A.D. 616. Even during the period of obscurity which followed, however, it seems that metropolitan bishops continued to be appointed: we hear of Marinus in A.D. 680 and Euthymius from ca. A.D. 787–805 (Foss 1976: 135), and these appointments suggest that Christianity was still a force to be reckoned with. The list of bishops of Sardis continues until the 14th century, the last attested being Gregory (ca. A.D. 1315–1343). In the first half of the 13th century, a new church was built on the site of the earlier basilican complex of the 4th century; this new church was smaller than its predecessor, but vaulted, domed, and richly decorated. It may well prove to have been the final confident gesture of Sardis Christians prior to the Turkish onslaughts in the second half of the century.

Bibliography

Bonner, C. 1940. *The Homily on the Passion by Melito, Bishop of Sardis.* London.

Foss, C. 1976. *Byzantine and Turkish Sardis.* Archaeological Exploration of Sardis. Monograph 4. Cambridge, MA.

Hanfmann, G. M. A., and Ramage, N. H. 1978. *Sculpture from Sardis. The Finds through 1975.* Archaeological Exploration of Sardis. Report 2. Cambridge, MA.

Hanfmann, G. M. A., et al. 1983. *Sardis from Prehistoric to Roman Times: Results of the Archaeological Exploration of Sardis 1958–1975.* Cambridge, MA.

Kraabel, A. T. 1969. *Hypsistos* and the Synagogue at Sardis. *GRBS* 10:81–93.

———. 1971. Melito the Bishop and the Synagogue at Sardis: Text and Context. Pp. 77–85 in *Studies Presented to George M. A. Hanfmann,* ed. D. G. Mitten, J. G. Pedley, and J. A. Scott. Monographs in Art and Archaeology 2. Mainz.

Pedley, J. G. 1972. *Ancient Literary Sources on Sardis.* Archaeological Exploration of Sardis. Monograph 2. Cambridge, MA.

Robert, L. 1964. *Nouvelles inscriptions de Sardes.* Archaeological Exploration of Sardis. Fascicle 1. Paris.

Seager, A. R. 1972. The Building History of the Sardis Synagogue. *AJA* 76: 425–35.

Yegul, F. K. 1986. *The Bath-Gymnasium Complex at Sardis.* Archaeological Exploration of Sardis. Report 3. Cambridge, MA.

JOHN GRIFFITHS PEDLEY

SAREA (PERSON) [Lat *Sarea*]. One of the five scribes whom Ezra was instructed to take with him in restoring the Scriptures (2 Esdr 14:24). See DABRIA for further discussion.

JIN HEE HAN

SARGON (PERSON) [Heb *sargôn*]. In Assyrian the name is spelled *Šarru-kīn* and means "legitimate king." It is clearly a throne name adopted by the king at the time of his accession. Three kings in Mesopotamian history bore this name—Sargon of Akkad (ca. 2334–2279 B.C.), Sargon I of Assyria, who ruled about 2000 B.C., and Sargon II (721–705 B.C.). Only the last is mentioned in the Bible (Isa 20:1).

Although Sargon is mentioned by name only once in the Bible, in the aforementioned passage he played a more significant role in biblical history than this might suggest. It was probably this king who led the Israelites into exile after the fall of Samaria, a subject which has been discussed under SHALMANESER. In fact, the transportation of the Israelites and the settlement of new peoples in Israel to replace them probably stretched over several years at the beginning of Sargon's reign.

To understand better Sargon's dealings with Samaria and the kingdom of Israel it is necessary to look at Assyrian records and the whole context of Assyrian history during this period. Sargon came to the throne as the result of a rebellion against his predecessor, Shalmaneser V. It is reasonably certain that Sargon was a usurper and not in the direct Assyrian royal line. Thus the fighting was bitter and lasted for some time. The internal confusion in Assyria was an excellent opportunity for a major rebellion by states in Syria and Palestine against Assyrian control. This rebellion was led by the king of Hamath and included among others Samaria, Arpad, and Damascus. Once Sargon had secured his hold over the Assyrian throne he launched a campaign into Syria to put down the rebellion. He met the allied forces at Qarqar in 720 B.C. and defeated them. The Assyrian army then marched south right through Israel and Judah and down to Gaza, and defeated an Egyptian army on the border of Egypt. In the wake of this successful march, Sargon launched a massive campaign against the various rebel states. The offending rulers were punished and large numbers of people transported to Assyria (*ANET,* 284–85). This punitive operation included Samaria.

As remarked above, Sargon is mentioned by name only once in the Bible (in Isa 20:1). In this passage reference is made to the year in which the commander-in-chief of Sargon, the king of Assyria, attacked and captured Ashdod. Once again we must look to Assyrian records for a fuller understanding of this event. Ashdod, a major city in Philistia, was independent of Assyria in the first part of the reign of Sargon II. According to the royal inscriptions of Sargon, however, the king of Ashdod made an anti-Assyrian alliance with his neighboring rulers. Therefore Sargon launched a campaign against Ashdod (ca. 713 B.C.) and replaced the offending ruler, Aziru, with his brother Ahimetu. The moment the Assyrian troops withdrew, the people of Ashdod rebelled against Ahimetu and replaced him with Yamani. Sargon therefore led a second campaign against Ashdod (712 B.C.). Yamani fled to Egypt, but the Egyptians put him into irons and sent him to Assyria as a goodwill gesture. Sargon laid siege to Ashdod and two other cities in Philistia. All three cities were captured, their populations were carried off into exile, and they were replaced with peoples from the E (*ANET,* 285–87). For more details about the reign of Sargon, see MESOPOTAMIA, HISTORY (ASSYRIA), and also *CAH* 3/2/22.

A. Kirk Grayson

SARID (PLACE) [Heb *śārîd*]. A town in the territory of Zebulun, the starting point for the description of the borders of the territory (Josh 19:10, 12). The town has been identified with Tel Shadud (M.R. 172229), in the N Jezreel Valley. This identification is supported by LXX manuscripts which render *sedoud* for Heb *śārîd* (Aharoni *LBHG,* 117). The site has yielded sherds of the LB and Iron Ages, as well as of later periods (Aharoni *EncMiqr* 8:392).

Raphael Greenberg

SAROTHIE (PERSON) [Gk *Sarōthie*]. Forefather of a family included under the heading the "sons of Solomon's servants," which returned with Zerubbabel (1 Esdr 5:34). However, this family is not included in the parallel lists in Ezra 2 and Nehemiah 7.

Bibliography

Haran, M. 1961. The Gibeonites, the Nethinim and the Sons of Solomon's Servants. *VT* 11: 159–69.

Craig D. Bowman

SARSECHIM (PERSON) [Heb *sarsĕkîm*]. A Babylonian official, included in the list of officials in Jer 39:3, who participated in the invasion of Jerusalem in 587 B.C.E. However, the list of names in Jer 39:3 is widely held to be confused (cf. Bright *Jeremiah* AB, 243; Thompson *Jeremiah* NICOT, 644; Carroll *Jeremiah* OTL, 691), and it is not certain that Sarsechim is in fact the name of an official, or even an official title. Ward (*IDB* 4: 224) has suggested that Sarsechim may be the title "Chief of the Slaves." However, Ward and most modern interpreters understand the word division of the MT to be confused, and Jer 39:3 needs to be reconstructed on the basis of Jer 39:13. The MT consonantal text reads, *nrgl śr-ʾṣr smgr-nbw śr-skym rb-srys nrgl śr-ʾṣr rb-mg,* "Nergal-sharezer, Samgar-nebo, Sarsechim the Rabsaris, Nergal–sharezer the Rabmag, . . ." However, Jer 39:13 reads "Nebushazban the Rabsaris, Negal-sharezer the Rabmag. . . ." The proposed solution includes both a revocalization of *smgr* to *simmāgir,* a district governed by Nergal-shar-ezer (Bright AB, 243), and a redivision of the text from *smgr-nbw śr-skym* to *nbw śr-skym.* The latter, according to Bright, is a corruption of *nĕbûšazbān śar sārîs,* with Sar-saris the equivalent of Rab-saris. Therefore the reconstructed part of the verse would read as follows: "Nergal-sharezer, prince of Simmagar, the Rab-mag; Nebushazban, the Rab-saris . . ." See NEBUSHAZBAN.

John M. Bracke

SARTA, ʿIZBET. See ʿIZBET SARTA (M.R. 146167).

SATAN. The purpose of this article is to provide a summary of the occurrences and an objective analysis of the various uses of the term "Satan" throughout the Bible, as well as within deuterocanonical, pseudepigraphical, and early rabbinic literature.

A. In the Old Testament
  1. Meaning of Satan
  2. Terrestrial Satans
  3. Celestial Satans
B. In the Apocrypha and Pseudepigrapha
C. In Rabbinic Sources
D. In the New Testament

A. In the Old Testament

1. Meaning of Satan. There is little doubt that the noun *śāṭān* is related to the verb *śāṭan.* The verb occurs only six times (Ps 38:21—Eng 38:20; 71:13; 109:4, 20, 29; Zech 3:1). The problem arises when one attempts to select the best English equivalent for Heb *śāṭan,* especially since *śāṭan* lacks a cognate in any of the Semitic languages. The choice appears to be between "accuse," "slander," and "be an adversary." Thus Ps 38:21—Eng v 20 may be rendered "those who repay me good with evil accuse/slander me when I seek what is good." (LXX's rendering of *śāṭan* by *endieballon* would suggest slander.) Ps 71:13 reads "may my accusers/adversaries/slanderers perish." Similarly, in Ps 109:3, 20, 29 the writer speaks to God about his accusers/slanderers and the duress they have brought into his life. And last of all, and the only occurrence of the verb outside of a lament Psalm, is Zech 3:1, in which the prophet sees *śāṭān* standing at the right hand of Joshua the high priest to "slander/accuse" him.

There is a good deal of overlap in meaning between "accuse" and "slander," but they are not synonyms. To accuse means to find fault and bring charges, falsely or accurately, against another. Thus, an accusation may be valid or inaccurate. By contrast, slander is always false, a statement of claim that is both inaccurate and damaging to the character and reputation of another.

It is clear from the six passages cited above, and from especially the five from the Psalms, that the enemies of the writer are defaming his character and thus are slanderers. What they are saying about the writer is palpably false, and therefore their mouths must be shut, one way or another. But does the fact that *śāṭan* = "to slander" suggest that the noun *śāṭān* should always be translated as "slanderer"? Not necessarily so. There are some instances where a *śāṭān* engages in activities that are patently slanderous (for example, Job 1 and 2). However, there are other places where a *śāṭān* engages, or is urged to engage himself, in activities that are clearly non-slanderous (e.g., 2 Sam 19:23 = Eng 19:22 [Abishai's charge of blasphemy against Shimei is legitimate]; Ps 109:6). On the basis of the actual uses of *śāṭān* (see A.2 and A.3), we would suggest that *śāṭān* means "accuser," with the added nuance of either "adversary" or "slanderer," depending on context.

2. Terrestrial Satans. The first human called a *śāṭān* in the OT is David. Philistines rulers, observing the presence of David and his supporters in their camp as they prepared for war with Israel, complained that David would in fact become their "adversary" (1 Sam 29:4), and thus win the favor of his own king, Saul.

The second instance involves Shimei, a Benjaminite who had earlier cursed and humiliated David as the king fled Jerusalem (2 Sam 16:5–14). Subsequently a repentant Shimei sought David's forgiveness (2 Sam 19:19b–21—Eng 19:18b–20). Abishai, a member of David's court, pushed for Shimei's execution for blaspheming the king. David, however, opted for leniency, and branded Abishai (and his brothers) as an "adversary" for even suggesting such a thing (2 Sam 19:23—Eng 19:22). Killing Shimei, while legally permissible, would seriously diminish David's chance of effectively ingratiating himself with the Saulide Benjaminites. David will decide who, if anybody, shall die for any crime.

The third instance involves Solomon. He wrote to Hiram, king of Tyre and friend of his late father, stating that David had been unable to build a temple because he was so preoccupied with war in expanding and defending his empire. Now, however, Solomon is free to pursue that project, for his era is one of relative peace, one in which Solomon is without any kind of an "adversary" (1 Kgs 5:18—Eng 5:4). Clearly *śāṭān* here designates military enemies, those who threaten the well-being of others.

Perhaps Solomon, in speaking of the absence of satans on his borders, spoke prematurely. Some years later Yahweh raised up two satans against Solomon, whose relationship with Yahweh was in disarray. The first was Hadad from Edom (1 Kgs 11:14), and the second was Rezon from Syria (1 Kgs 11:23, 25). Here again, the meaning of *śāṭān* is military rival who lives outside one's empire.

The last reference to a human *śāṭān* is Ps 109:6. The writer of this Psalm has been on the receiving end of verbal and physical abuse. His request to God is that God will, in response to such vilification, "appoint a wicked man against him; let an 'accuser' bring him to trial" (RSV) [understanding many enemies as one individual]. Only with the help of such a prosecutor will the culprits be brought to justice. The verb and preposition for "stand at" are *ʿāmad ʿal,* the same words used to describe the activity of a celestial *śāṭān* against Israel (1 Chr 21:1) and against Joshua the high priest (Zech 3:1). In the latter two *ʿāmad ʿal* conveys sinister work by a *śāṭān* (inciting one to do something illicit, or falsely condemning someone), while the first example speaks of truthful accusation against one who is clearly in the wrong.

We have included Ps 109:6 under the category of terrestrial satans. Among modern Psalm commentators only Dahood (*Psalms III* AB, 101–102) argues for a celestial *śāṭān* in this passage. He translates the verse "Appoint the Evil One *(rāšāʿ)* against him; and let Satan stand at his right hand." So understood, vv 6–7 would refer to the psalmist's wish for judgment on his enemies after death, while vv 8–19 would be his wish for their terrestrial misfortunes. Dahood's translation, if supportable, would challenge the idea, frequently advanced, that Satan as an Evil One is not an OT teaching, but rather a later development of the intertestamental period.

3. Celestial Satans. There are four passages in the OT that talk of a celestial *śāṭān*. These are Num 22:22, 32; Job 1 and 2; Zech 3:1–2; and 1 Chr 21:1. The noun *śāṭān* occurs 26 times in the OT. Seven of these (discussed above) refer to terrestrial satans, thus leaving 19 references to celestial satans. Three of these 19 use *śāṭān* without the definite article (Num 22:22, 32; 1 Chr 21:1). The remaining occurrences in Job 1 and 2 (14 times) and Zech 3:1, 2 employ the noun with the article *(haśśāṭān)*, literally "the *satan*." Leaving aside Num 22:22, 32, because there the Angel of Yahweh is a *śāṭān,* we note that 16 of 17 references to the celestial *śāṭān* use the expression "the" *śāṭān*. The lone exception is 1 Chr 21:1. This would seem to indicate that only in 1 Chr 21:1 is *śāṭān* possibly a proper name. In the remaining passages, with the definite article, it is a common noun, to be translated something like "the Accuser." GKC, §126e and Joüon 1923, §137m–o cite this as an instance of the definite article prefixed to a noun when a term normally applying to whole classes is restricted to particular individuals. As such, the definite article could be translated "a certain one of." It is not without significance that consistently the LXX does not transliterate *śāṭān* in Job (or elsewhere) as *ho Satanas* (a term used six times in the *Testament of the Twelve Patriarchs* as a synonym for the diabolical Beliar), but translates with *ho diabolos,* a term used in the LXX for both a celestial being (Zech 3:1–2) and a human adversary (Esth 7:4; 8:1). Even as late as 1 Macc 1:36, around 100–50 B.C., Antiochus IV is referred to as a *diabolon ponēron,* "an evil foe." This shows that *diabolos* needed the adjective *ponēros* to make it clear that the *diabolos* was wicked. Gammie states (1985: 18–19), "Instead of having a clear demonic overtone, the choice of translation *ho diabolos* on the contrary probably represents the translator's desire to utilize a term still relatively neutral and not yet associated in the public mind with a leader of forces in opposition to the divine intentions."

The one instance where *śāṭān* describes a celestial figure who is not in any way hostile to God is Num 22:22, 32. The Angel of Yahweh is sent to be a satan to sinning Balaam. The angel performs his task first by blocking the path so that Balaam's ass may not proceed, then by rebuking Balaam. Only when Balaam's eyes are opened does the angel *śāṭān* become visible to Balaam. The angel is both adversary to and accuser of Balaam, and is dispatched on his mission by Yahweh.

It is in the first two chapters of Job that "the satan" *(haśśāṭān)* is most prominent (but that name is not mentioned again after 2:7). The sons of God, i.e., the divine council, present themselves before Yahweh, and the satan is among them. The question arises whether he is with the assembly as a legitimate member or whether he is an intruder. In favor of the latter interpretation is the fact that the satan alone is asked "from where have you come?" But possibly he is a heavenly agent whose responsibilities have taken him to earth, and the question comes not from surprise in the deity at an outsider's presence, but rather from the deity's questioning of the agent's faithful expediting of his chore.

Job 1 and 2 provide the only instance in the OT where God and the *śāṭān* converse with each other, and twice God initiates the dialogue by asking the *śāṭān* a question about his whereabouts (1:7; 2:2). The question answered, God proceeds to bring Job and his impeccable spiritual credentials to the satan's attention (1:8; 2:3). The satan is not impressed. On the contrary, he suggests that Job's motives for serving God are selfish ones; i.e., Job serves God to get what he really wants, which is prosperity. Thus the satan directly impugns Job's motives for service to God and indirectly accuses God of divine patronage (Day 1988: 76). The satan's question to God is a thoughtful, legitimate, and profound one: "Does Job fear God for nothing?" To disprove or substantiate that question, God grants to the satan carefully circumscribed destructive powers (1:12; 2:6). The satan may not act independently, but only with divine permission.

The second reference to an antagonistic celestial *śāṭān* is found in Zech 3:1–2. In the fourth of eight visions the prophet observes Joshua, the high priest, in front of the Angel of Yahweh, and the *śāṭān* standing by his right side to accuse him. It is not clear exactly what the nature of the accusation against Joshua is. Unlike Job's *śāṭān*, Zechariah's *śāṭān* does not talk. But he is rebuked, not by the Angel of Yahweh, but by Yahweh himself. In his rebuke, Yahweh reminds the satan that he has chosen Jerusalem. That Yahweh draws attention to his choice of Jerusalem, and not of Joshua, would seem to indicate that Joshua not only represents himself, but in some way also represents the restored postexilic community. Neither the iniquity of Joshua nor the sins of the Judeans are such that they bar the way to the investiture of the high priest or the forgiveness of the community, much to the dismay of the prosecuting satan.

The third and final appearance of a malevolent celestial *śāṭān* is in the Chronicler's account of David's census of Israel. That version informs the reader that it was *śāṭān* who rose up against Israel and incited David to number his people (1 Chr 21:1). Two items are of special import here. First, this is the only place in the OT where the Hebrew word *śāṭān*, when referring to a celestial diabolical being, is used without the definite article. This has suggested to most commentators that *śāṭān* is here a personal name. GKC §125f. refers to this instance of *śāṭān* (as opposed to *haśśāṭān*) as an illustration of an original appellative that has assumed the character of a real proper name and is therefore used without the article. The passage, however, might as justifiably be translated "and a *śāṭān* stood up against Israel, and provoked David to number Israel."

The second issue focuses on the question of why the account in 2 Samuel 24 attributes the stimulus for David's census to Yahweh (2 Sam 24:1), while the Chronicler attaches blame to a *śāṭān*/Satan. There are three possible explanations for this shift. The first is that the Chronicler was bothered by the attribution of morally questionable activities to Yahweh; i.e., he incited David to take a census, then punished David for doing so. To that end the Chronicler deleted Yahweh's part in the story as a stimulating factor and replaced him with *śāṭān* (Kluger 1967: 159). But if the Chronicler was concerned with saving Yahweh's image from tarnish, why did he leave unmolested other stories in which Yahweh was responsible for Rehoboam turning his back on the wise counsel of his advisers (2 Chr 10:15), or in which Yahweh sends a deceiving spirit into the mouths of Ahab's prophets? Closely related to this explanation is the suggestion that the Chronicler downplayed Yahweh's complicity in this event with his substitution of *śāṭān*, primarily because he was concerned to paint as beautiful a picture as possible of the relationship between Yahweh and David, Yahweh's chosen servant (Day 1988: 136–37). Accordingly, the Chronicler omitted any reference to Yahweh's arbitrary anger with his people during David's reign and told the story simply as a temptation episode. A third possible explanation is that the contrast between 2 Sam 24:1 and 1 Chr 21:1 (Yahweh/*śāṭān* illustrates a development in how OT thought explains evil. Most of the earlier literature of the OT explained evil in terms of a primary cause (Yahweh). Later OT literature, such as Chronicles, expanded on this by introducing the concept of a secondary cause in its explanation of evil (*śāṭān*).

To summarize, so far we have seen that (the) *śāṭān* is a maligner of character (Job 1 and 2), an accuser of God's servant (Zech 3:1), and a seducer of Israel's royal leader (1 Chr 21:1). Clearly in the OT *śāṭān* (and other demons) is not connected with some primordial realm, but with sin. As Kaufmann (KRI, p. 65) has stated, "Biblical religion was unable to reconcile itself with the idea that there was a power in the universe that defied the authority of God and that could serve as an antigod, the symbol and source of evil. Hence, it strove to transfer evil from the metaphysical realm to the moral realm, to the realm of sin."

B. In the Apocrypha and Pseudepigrapha

Setting aside 1 Chr 21:1 and Ps 109:6, one observes that the earliest evidence for *śāṭān* as a personal name appears in *Jub.* 23:29 and *Assum. Mos.* 10:1, both of which date to the period of the pogroms of Antiochus IV against Jews in Palestine (ca. 168 B.C.). Actually, however, the majority of these deuterocanonical texts refer to other demons by name, but seldom use the name *śāṭān*. For example, in Tobit, one called Asmodeus is the archdemon. He has already slain the seven bridegrooms of Sarah even before any of those marriages is consummated (Tob 3:8), and only when Asmodeus is exorcized from Sarah by Raphael, the protecting angel, will Sarah be happily married to Tobias (Tob 3:17). Asmodeus may be connected with the Hebrew verb *šāmad*, "to destroy," or possibly even with Aeshma, a demon of violence and wrath in Persian religion. The possible connection of Asmodeus with Hebrew *šāmad* is heightened by the reference to the demon Shimadon in the midrash, *Gen. Rab.* 36. Shimadon is explicable as deriving from *šāmad*, but not from Iranian Aeshma. Additionally there are major philological problems in connecting Asmodeus and Aeshma, as Barr (1985: 214–16) has shown. Again, in 1 *En.* 6–11 (3d century B.C.), the ringleader of the angels who were punished because of their sexual activity with the daughters of men is called Shemihazah (chap. 6) or Azazel (8:1–2).

In the book of *Jubilees* the name of the devil is primarily Mastema, a Hebrew word *(maśṭēmâ)* that occurs in Hos 9:7,

8 with the meaning "hatred, hostility, enmity." Scattered references to Mastema throughout *Jubilees* (10:1–14; 11:1–5; 19:28) identify him as the chief of evil spirits, who, after the flood, received permission from God for one-tenth of his spirits to expedite his will on humanity. *Jubilees* also tends to attribute to Mastema certain actions of a questionable nature which the OT attributed to Yahweh. For example, *Jub.* 17:16 says it was Mastema who caused Abraham's testing (Gen 22:1), and *Jub.* 4:2 states that it was Mastema who attacked Moses on his way to Egypt (Exod 4:24).

In the Qumran literature *śāṭān* occurs only three times (1QH 4:6; 45:3; 1QSb 1:8), and never as a proper name. Rather, in this literature the leader of the forces of darkness was Belial, i.e., "the Worthless One." This word is also used in the OT in apposition with son (Deut 13:14—Eng 13:13; 1 Sam 2:12), daughter (1 Sam 1:16), man (1 Sam 30:22), witness (Prov 19:28), and counselor (Nah 1:11). In time Belial became a proper name in Qumran and in some other pseudepigraphical writings. In these sources, and even in the NT the name appears mostly as Beliar (2 Cor 6:15). He is the spirit of darkness (*T. Levi* 19:1; 1QM 13:12), who exercises control over the world (1QS 1:18, 24; 2:5, 19; 1QM 14:9; *Mart. Is.* 2:4). He controls evil people (*T. Levi* 3:3; *T. Jos.* 7:4; *T. Dan.* 1:7; *T. Benj.* 6:1). Ultimately he will be chained by God's Holy Spirit (*T. Levi* 18:12), and cast into a consuming fire (*T. Jud.* 25:3).

To summarize, it is clear that references to *śāṭān*, either by that name or by a surrogate, are much more extensive in apocryphal/pseudepigraphical literature than in the OT. More than likely, exposure to Persian religion and its Zoroastrian-based dualism provided some of the stimulus for the more pervasive demonology in these Jewish writings. Rather than viewing the world as the canvas on which one God sketched his unique will for his world, the world was now viewed as a battleground fought over by both benevolent and malevolent deities. It is difficult, of course, to trace exactly how this borrowing or influencing worked, or even why such a concept would have appealed to exiled Jews in Mesopotamia. Are there, for example, other Persian religious emphases to which the exiles were attracted besides Iranian dualism, and if so, what were they? The evidence is slim to nonexistent. Books of the OT that would be expected to show most awareness of Persian religion—Nehemiah, for example—are conspicuously silent about it. It is also debatable whether or not the proliferation of demons and the demonizing of the world represents post-biblical Judaism's attempt to come to grips with a world so grim and hostile that not all phenomena could no longer be placed under the umbrella of divine sovereignty. Rather, it may be that the demonizing of the cosmos, as reflected in the Apocrypha and Pseudepigrapha, represents the emergence of Israel's quasi-mythology that was widely embraced throughout the OT period. Such ideas, inimical as they were to orthodox monotheism, would have been repressed by the prophets.

C. In Rabbinic Sources

Although *śāṭān* does not appear in Genesis 3, later rabbinic sources identified satan with the serpent in Eden (*Soṭa.* 9b; *Sanh.* 29a). He is identified in a more impersonal way with the evil inclination which infects humanity (*B. Bat.* 16a). In a more personal way, he is the source behind God's testing of Abraham (*Sanh.* 89b). Additionally, *śāṭān* is responsible for many of the sins mentioned in the OT. For example, it is *śāṭān* who was responsible for the Israelites worshipping the golden calf because of his lie that Moses would not return from Mount Sinai (*Šabb.* 89a). He is the driving force behind David's sin with Bathsheba (*Sanh.* 107a), and it is he who provokes the gentiles to ridicule Jewish laws, thus weakening the religious loyalties of the Jews (*Yoma* 67b). The sounding of the horn on the New Year is to confuse *śāṭān* (*Roš. Haš.* 166). Only on the Day of Atonement is *śāṭān* without power. This is suggested by the numeral value of *śāṭān*, 364; i.e., there is one day in the year he is powerless (*Yoma* 20a).

D. In the New Testament

The NT also makes frequent references to Satan. He is mentioned by name 35 times. The breakdown of these references is: (a) the Synoptics, 14 times; (b) gospel of John, once; (c) Acts, twice; (d) Epistles (all Pauline and half of which are in the correspondence with Corinth), 10 times; and Revelation, 8 times (5 of which [2:9; 2:13; 2:13; 2:24; 3:9] are in the letters to the churches and not in prophetic portions [chaps. 4–22]). As popular as the designation Satan is, the name *ho diabolos* appears 32 times.

There are additionally a number of titles given to him. For example, while John uses Satan only once (13:27), the preferred Johannine term for Satan is the "prince of this world" (12:31; 14:30; 16:11). This phrase parallels Matthew's "the prince of the demons" and Paul's "the god of this world" (2 Cor 4:4), "the prince of the power of the air" (Eph 2:2), and "rulers of the darkness of this age" (Eph 6:12) (but not "rulers of this age" in 1 Cor 2:6–8, which refers to human rulers [Carr 1976]). A Johannine parallel appears in 1 John 5:19 where the claim is made that the whole world is in the power of the Evil One. These references teach at least a modified dualism which is close to the Qumran picture of a titanic struggle between the Angel of Darkness and the Prince of Light.

John can claim, on the one hand, that Satan has already been judged (John 16:11), and that the prince of the world will be cast out when Jesus is crucified (John 12:31, 32), and on the other hand, that the world is in the power of the Evil One (1 John 5:19). These are not self-contradictory ideas. Rather, they suggest that for John, Jesus' death and resurrection constitute a victory over Satan in principle; yet the implementation of this victory will be gradual, and yet awaits a climactic conclusion.

If there are titles describing Satan's power, there are also a number of titles that describe him pejoratively. He is an enemy (Matt 13:39); the evil one (Matt 13:38); a tempter (Matt 4:3; 1 Thess 3:5); an adversary (1 Pet 5:8); the father of lies (John 8:44); a murderer (John 8:44); a liar (John 8:44); a deceiver (Rev 10:9); an accuser (Rev 10:10); and one disguised as an angel of light (2 Cor 11:14).

Both John 13:27 and Luke 22:3 speak of Satan entering *(eisēlthen ho satanas)* Judas. The same vocabulary is used for the "entering in" of evil spirits in Mark 5:12, 13 and Luke 8:30–32. Compare with this concept the reference in *Mart. Is.* 3:11: "Beliar dwelt in the heart of Manasseh and in the heart of the princes of Judah and Benjamin, and of the eunuchs, and of the king's counselors."

Luke speaks not only of Satan entering Judas, but also of Satan's desire to have Peter, that he may sift him as wheat (Luke 22:31). (Satan's asking permission to "have" Peter is reminiscent of the satan's request to God to remove the protecting hedge around Job.) Jesus, however, is Peter's advocate (Luke 22:32) pleading against Satan the accuser. It is of interest that apart from John 13:27, Satan occurs in the passion narrative only in the Lukan account. Luke speaks of Satan the "enterer" and Satan the "sifter" in his gospel, and speaks of Satan "filling the heart" of Ananias and thus fomenting deception by Ananias in Acts (5:3).

In several ways the NT makes it clear that Satan is not without limitations. First, the intercession of Jesus stalls his designs on Peter (Luke 22:32). Second, he is a fallen being (Luke 10:18). Third, he is judged (John 16:11). Fourth, his power over a person's life may be broken (Acts 26:18). Fifth, God may use Satan to chasten an apostate believer (1 Cor 5:5; 1 Tim 1:20). Sixth, his temptations, however potent, may be overcome and his ruses exposed (Matt 4:1–11, and the only incident in the NT in which any of Satan's words are recorded). Seventh, he may be resisted, just as Jesus resisted him (Eph 4:27; Jas 4:7; 1 Pet 5:8, 9). Eighth, the NT never refers to Satan as simply the prince/ruler (*ho archon*), but as "prince of devils" (Matt 9:34) or "prince of the world" (John 12:31). Ninth, at God's discretion he is bound (Rev 20:2), released (Rev 20:7), and incinerated (Rev 20:10).

Bibliography

Barr, J. 1985. The Question of Religious Influence: The Case of Zoroastrianism, Judaism, and Christianity. *JAAR* 53: 201–35.
Carr, W. 1976. Rulers of this Age. *NTS* 23: 20–35.
Day, P. L. 1987. Abishai the *śāṭān* in 2 Sam 19:17–24. *CBQ* 49: 543–47.
———. 1988. *An Adversary In Heaven. Satan in the Hebrew Bible.* HSM 43. Atlanta.
Ferguson, E. 1985. *Demonology of the Early Christian World.* New York.
Forsyth, N. 1987. *The Old Enemy: Satan and the Combat Myth.* Princeton.
Gammie, J. G. 1985. The Angelology and Demonology in the Septuagint of the Book of Job. *HUCA* 56: 1–19.
Gaylord, H. E. 1982. How Satanel lost his "-el." *JJS* 33: 303–309.
Haag, H. 1974. *Teufelsglaube.* Tübingen.
Hanson, P. 1975. *The Dawn of Apocalyptic.* Philadelphia.
Jacobsen, R. 1981. Satanic Semiotics, Jobian Jurisprudence. *Semeia* 19: 63–71.
Joüon, P. 1923. *Grammaire de l'hébreu biblique.* 2d. ed. Rome.
Kluger, R. S. 1967. *Satan in the Old Testament.* Trans. H. Nagel. Evanston.
Kruse, H. 1977. Das Reich Satans. *Bib* 58: 29–61.
Oppenheim, L. 1968. The Eyes of the Lord. *JAOS* 88: 173–80.
Russell, J. B. 1977. *The Devil: Perceptions of Evil from Antiquity to Primitive Christianity.* Ithaca.
———. 1981. *Satan, The Early Christian Tradition.* Ithaca.
Tremmel, W. C. 1985. Satan—The Dark Side. *The Iliff Review* 42: 3–12.
Wernberg-Møller, P. 1961. A Reconsideration of the Two Spirits in the Rule of the Community. *RevQ* 3: 413–41.
Yadin, Y. 1962. *The Scroll of the War of the Sons of Light against the Sons of Darkness.* London.
Yates, R. 1980. The Powers of Evil in the NT. *EvQ* 52: 97–111.

VICTOR P. HAMILTON

SATHRABUZANES (PERSON) [Gk *Sathrabouzanēs*]. An official of the Persian bureaucracy governing the province "Beyond the River." He was among those who wrote Darius, king of Persia concerning the rebuilding of the Temple in Jerusalem by the Jews (1 Esdr 6:3, 7, 27; 7:1). The name "Sathrabuzanes" is clearly a linguistic variant for the Aramaic SHETHAR-BOZENAI, the name used for this official in the parallel text of Ezra (5:3, 6; 6:6, 13).

SATRAP. The governor of a province or satrapy of the Achaemenid empire. Herodotus (3.89 ff) informs us that Darius I (521–486 B.C.) reorganized the empire into a total of twenty satrapies and placed a satrap (Old Persian *xsacapaban* = satrap = "protector of the kingdom/kingship") in charge of each province, in order to bring more rigorous method to taxation and control throughout his vast empire.

The satrap, often a close relative of the king, was generally appointed and removed by him. The satrap's court was modeled on that of the great king. Usually a wealthy man in his own right, he regularly spent of his own resources in the service of government while also having command over royal government resources within his satrapy.

Generally the satrap's power of command extended over both civil and military affairs, but in some cases major fortresses and their garrisons were under commanders who reported directly to the Great King. Other means were available to the king for independently monitoring the satrap's activities. The "king's scribes" for example, regularly reported back to the court. There were also officials called "the eyes and ears of the king," who are assumed to have provided the central government with information on events in the provinces.

In the 4th century B.C. some satrapies (most notably in Anatolia) became semi-independent hereditary fiefdoms, with the satrap no longer appointed by the king. Also, as might be expected, from time to time individual satraps or coalitions of satraps rebelled against central authority. In the main, however, the system of provincial organization re-structured under Darius served the empire well for some two centuries. See also PERSIAN EMPIRE.

T. CUYLER YOUNG, JR.

SAUL (PERSON) [Heb *šāʾûl*]. Two persons in the Bible bear this name. The first, Saul, son of Kish, became the first king of Israel (1 Samuel 9–31); he is the subject of this entry. The second, Saul of Tarsus, is discussed under the entry on PAUL.

A. Name and Family Background
B. The Saulide Narratives in Literary Perspective
C. Models of Saul's Role in the History of Israel
  1. The Permanent Judge
  2. The Self-Appointed Protector
  3. The Chieftain
  4. The State-Builder
D. History and Saul's Story
  1. The Late Iron I Period
  2. Chronology

3. Saul's Coronation
4. Saul's Military Career
5. The State of Israel under Saul

A. Name and Family Background

The name Saul is a *Qal* passive participle from the Heb root *šʾl,* meaning "the one asked for, requested." It perhaps is an abbreviated name form, because Semitic names frequently contained multiple elements, some of which consisted of a verbal element followed by a divine name. This name occurs elsewhere in the Bible as the name of a purported king of Edom (Gen 36:37); a Simeonite (Gen 46:10); and a Levite (1 Chr 6:9—Eng 6:24. See SHAUL (PERSON). In Assyrian texts, *ša-u-la-nu* occurs (Tallquist 1914: 219), and an Aramaic honorary inscription from 3d cent. A.D. Palmyra contains the form *šʾylʾ* (Šaʾîlaʾ); Cooke 1903: 283).

Saul the son of Kish was a member of the Benjaminite clan of Matri (1 Sam 10:21). 1 Sam 9:1 traces his ancestry back five generations, from his father Kish, through his grandfather Abiel and forebears Zeror and Becorath, to Aphiah. Saul's choice of Abner as Israel's military commander was based on family solidarity, because Abner's father, Ner, was Saul's paternal uncle. As Saul's wife, Ahinoam the daughter of Ahimaaz bore seven children: five sons and two daughters. According to 1 Sam 14:49, the firstborn child was Merab, a daughter; then Jonathan, the eldest male heir; Ishvi, a son who either died as a youth or is to be identified with Eshbaal; Malchishua, a son; and Michal, a second daughter. 1 Chr 8:33 and 9:39 name Abinadab and Eshbaal as two additional sons, although Eshbaal may be named in 1 Sam 14:49 under the variant name form Ishyo. Merab bore five grandsons (2 Sam 21:8) and Jonathan a single grandson, called variantly Merib-baal (1 Chr 8:34; 9:40) and Mephibosheth (2 Sam 4:4; 9:6, 13; 16:1, 4; 19:25, 26, 31; 21:7). The Saulide family line continued through Jonathan's grandson Micah (1 Chr 8:34–40; 9:40–44). No names of possible granddaughters have been preserved. Saul fathered two additional sons with his concubine Rizpah—Armoni and Mephibosheth (2 Sam 21:8).

B. The Saulide Narratives in Literary Perspective

The career of Saul is described in 1 Samuel 8–2 Samuel 1 and is part of the so-called Deuteronomistic History (DH), which includes Deuteronomy–2 Kings. The DH divides its account of Israel's development into five successive periods: the Mosaic period; the occupation of Cisjordan; the period of the Judges; Saul, David, and Solomon (the United Monarchy); and the period of the kings of Israel and Judah *(NDH).* 1 Samuel 9–12 form a concluding subsection to the period of the Judges, which is anticipated by a speech in chap. 8. After narrating Saul's election as king, this section concludes with Samuel's farewell speech in chap. 12. 1 Sam 13:1, with its characteristic Deuteronomistic accession and regnal formula (see below), marks the formal beginning of the new period of the United Monarchy, which ends with the death of Solomon. Thus, Saul's career bridges two of the larger subdivisions within the DH, emphasizing his pivotal position within the ancient scheme.

Various structuring techniques have been used to make the account of Saul's career a coherent, unified narrative. Three main overlapping patterns are discernible. The first is the three-part kingship ritual, consisting of the designation of the candidate as *nāgîd,* "king-elect," through anointing; his testing by performance of a military deed; and his subsequent confirmation as king by coronation upon successful completion of the test. This pattern is used three times within the 1 Samuel narrative: to describe Saul's elevation to kingship (9:1–11:15); to describe the heir-elect Jonathan's rejection as Saul's successor (13:2–14:46); and to describe David's progression to the kingship as Saul's successor (16:13; 30:1–31; his final coronation is recounted in the succeeding narrative in 2 Sam 2:4; 5:1–6). The repetition of the pattern emphasizes the writer's desire for it to be viewed as normative from the very founding of the monarchy.

The second pattern is the standard regnal account. It consists of an initial accession formula, including the name of the king, his age at accession, and the length of his reign (13:1); an account of some of his accomplishments (13:2–14:46); a summary of his deeds (14:47–48); and a report of his death, burial, and succession (1 Samuel 31; 2 Sam 2:8–11). In the case of Saul's reign, the customary DH reference to the Book of the Chronicles of the Kings of Israel (or Judah) does not appear in the summary of deeds, and the final stage does not immediately follow the summary of deeds, as is the pattern. The deviation from the normal sequence seems to have been done by the writer for two reasons: (1) so that he could use Saul's career to depict the consequences a king would face for disobeying the central principle of the pre-existent Horeb covenant, obedience to Yahweh's revealed command; and (2) so he could prepare the way for David's unusual succession to the throne of Israel in place of a legitimate Saulide.

The third pattern divides Saul's career into two segments: his life under Yahweh's "good spirit," and his life under Yahweh's "evil spirit" (16:14). The pattern is closely associated with the previous regnal pattern and shares with it the same purpose. It emphasizes that the king, as Yahweh's anointed, remains in office and in possession of some form of divine spirit throughout his life, but that disobedience to God will result in the king's divine rejection and his inability to continue to serve his nation adequately as God's earthly vice-regent during the remainder of his reign. His loss of the ability to be guided by God's benevolent spirit will inevitably result in his failure to be able to discern the divine will and act appropriately.

An additional structuring device in the Saulide narrative is the theme of David's covenant with Jonathan, the heir-elect to the throne. It complements the use of the three-part kingship ritual pattern, which establishes a progression from Saul's legitimate coronation to David's "legitimate" coronation, after Jonathan's failure to pass the test for coronation. The theme is developed progressively through scenes that alternately center on Jonathan (18:1–5; 19:1–7; 20:1–21:1—Eng 20:1–42; 23:15b–18) and ones that involve David and Saul (16:14–17:58; 18:6–30; 19:8–25; 21:2–23:15a [with other material]; 23:19 onward [with much other material]) (Jobling 1978). It continues into 2 Samuel, in sections depicting David's dealings with Jonathan's son Merib-baal/Mephibosheth (see MERIB-BAAL). The covenant theme stresses Jonathan's immediate acceptance of David as Saul's divinely chosen successor, and Saul's reluctant but gradual acceptance of David's status.

Two of these covenant theme scenes serve the additional and overlapping function of stressing the king's lifelong inviolability, regardless of his stance vis-à-vis God, by progressively intensifying the message through repetition and alteration. David refuses to harm Saul on two separate occasions because he is Yahweh's anointed, who must die naturally, in battle, or by God's own hand (24:1–15; 26:1–11).

Scholars view the nature and extent of source material underlying 1 Samuel 9–31 in different and conflicting ways (cf. Hertzberg *1–2 Samuel* OTL, 130–34; McCarter *1 Samuel* AB, 18–23; Klein *1 Samuel* WBC, xxx–xxxii). Often, Saul's career is limited to 1 Sam 9:1–15:34. When this is done, the chaps. are generally thought to be based either on the juxtaposition of blocks of material from a pro-monarchic and an anti-monarchic source or to be a collection of individual traditions. In the latter case, the stories are often associated with the sanctuaries of Gilgal, Ramah, and Mizpah, and are generally thought to have already been organized into complexes detailing Saul's career before their incorporation into the DH. In the former case, the two strands are likewise commonly considered to predate the DH. Chaps. 16–31 are frequently thought to be part of a larger, pre-Deuteronomistic narrative called the History of David's Rise, which is thought to span 1 Samuel 15 (or 16)–2 Samuel 5 and to be an early literary attempt to justify David's accession to the Saulide throne (see Grønbaek 1971). The latter understanding is rejected by a small but growing group for varying reasons. One faction attempts to trace within the 27 chapters the so-called Pentateuchal sources "J" and "E" or "J" alone and therefore denies the existence of a separate early literary composition beside these two complexes (i.e. Eissfeldt 1965: 271–80; Shulte 1972: 105–80; contrast Halpern 1981: 149–74, who traces two sources but does not link them to "J" and "E"). The other faction questions the existence of Israelite historiography at such an early date and sees the themes, structuring patterns, and historical presuppositions within the Saulide narrative to reflect concerns and techniques that are more plausibly associated with the late 7th century (i.e. Van Seters 1983: 217; 270; Edelman 1990).

C. Models of Saul's Role in the History of Israel

Four conceptions of Saul's political role within Israel have been proposed. All make use of the same biblical and extrabiblical materials, but each assesses the reliability and relevance of the materials differently, thereby yielding divergent views of Saul and his career. Each theory is summarized below using details taken from the discussion of its main proponent. Subsequent modifications to the seminal study that have gained acceptance are included.

1. The Permanent Judge. In 1930 A. Alt argued that Saul's leadership represents a transitional stage within Israel's political existence, between pre-monarchic tribal league and nationhood (1967: 223–309). Due to the constant threat of Philistine dominion and expansion, the tribes are thought to have united and subsequently "institutionalized" the existing charismatic office of "judge." The latter was to have been a temporary office of military commander which lasted only as long as the immediate crisis that necessitated intertribal leadership. Saul's appointment, by contrast, was a permanent one, intended to cope with the ongoing Philistine threat, even though (according to 1 Sam 11:1–11) the Ammonite siege of Jabesh-gilead led to Saul's elevation to office. It is argued that his only role was to have been that of commander of the tribal levies, and that internal affairs continued to be managed by the older tribal groupings. Saul's authority was limited to military concerns; it was not to have been hereditary; unlike his successor David, Saul was not a true "king." His office is seen to have evolved naturally out of Israel's tribal, nomadic heritage, rather than to have been "borrowed" from the Canaanite state system or the Philistine political system. Saul's introduction of a rudimentary professional army in addition to the tribal levies is seen to be the only institution adopted from the latter systems.

Alt's model of permanent judge is based on the presupposition that the Bible provides a reliable witness to the political situation and institutions of the pre-monarchic period. It is the oldest and most widely accepted understanding of Saul's role. Its most commonly disputed points are the proposed non-hereditary nature of Saul's office and subsequent kingship; and the origin and uniqueness of eventual Israelite kingship—whether it was indeed a unique, native development within tribal Israel, or whether it was modeled after Canaanite city-states or the newly formed neighboring "nation states" of purported tribal origin, like Moab and Ammon.

2. The Self-Appointed Protector. The second characterization of Saul is one of a self-proclaimed protector/ruler. It has been developed by M. Miller as the first challenge to the permanent-judge model (1974; *HAIJ* 120–49). According to this view, the Bible's depiction of the pre-monarchic era is not entirely dependable. In this period, Israel was not a unified tribal league or a chiefdom headed by a single, recognized "judge" or "chief." Rather, it was a time when the various autonomous tribal groups were segmented, and when self-styled military leaders who controlled private armies were able to establish themselves through force as protector-rulers over portions of the population in a limited area.

Saul, like the traditional "judges" Jephthah and Abimelech, and David in his early career, is viewed as such a opportunistic leader, who, unlike the first two examples, was able gradually to extend his initial realm of influence in Benjamin to include large portions of the eventual Israelite state. Saul is assigned the title "king" with the caveat that he was not the head of a full-blown state. He is credited with the creation of a rudimentary administration and military bureaucracy, but is denied the establishment of a state religion and the existence of precisely defined state boundaries. His main base of support is seen to have been obligatory "gifts" made by those to whom he offered his protection and military services.

3. The Chieftain. Borrowing terminology used in social anthropology, and assuming the reliability of the biblical depiction of pre-monarchic Israel, this view argues that Saul's political role constituted the transitional, intermediate step of chieftaincy within Israel's natural growth from an "egalitarian" or segmented (i.e., village-based) society to statehood. As a "chief" or "paramount chieftain," Saul was in a political office that fell short of kingship. The model is grounded on E. Service's three-stage model of "pristine" state evolution (1975), which was developed to describe the predictable path of increasing political complexity that civilizations undergoing their first development would have taken to reach statehood. As presented by J. Flanagan (1981), Saul and David are to be understood as competing chiefs within Israel, on the eve of its move to full-fledged statehood.

4. The State-Builder. The final model, developed by D. Edelman (fc.), proposes that Saul should be viewed as the monarchic founder of the Israelite state. This view assumes that Israel's political development must be viewed from the perspective of secondary rather than primary state formation, within the framework of the disintegration of the LB empire system of Syria-Palestine (see also Ahlström fc.). The position therefore on principle rejects the use of models for the formation of *pristine* states, challenging those interested in applying models from social anthropology to Israelite state formation to employ ones designed to account for the formation of *secondary* states. This final model does not espouse the use of comparative models that use analogy to fill in informational gaps in reconstructing the rise of statehood in Israel. Instead, it seeks to reconstruct to the extent possible the specific events that led to Saul's rise to power, to chart the progress of his political career, and to evaluate the nature of his realm on the basis of critically evaluated textual and artifactual material. As in the "Self-Appointed Protector" model (see above), the reliability of the biblical depiction of the pre-monarchic era as a time of a unified, twelve-tribe league is rejected. A political unit bearing the name Israel is seen to have been associated with groups living in a limited portion of the central Ephraimite hill country, but not to have included all twelve tribes or all of the territory that would be encompassed during its statehood, nor to have been itself structured as a sacred league.

According to this model, Saul was a full-fledged king responsible for uniting the various geographico-political units in the Samarian and Ephraimite hill countries, Benjaminite plain, and central Transjordan to create the territorial state of Israel. He was the founder of Israelite statehood and its first king. The term "territorial state" is used to describe Israel under Saul in contrast to the two other types of statehood commonly applied to the ANE, "city-state" and "nation-state" (Buccellati 1967). By definition, a territorial state includes some non-centralized administrative units. The administration of the centralized portion of the Israelite state is viewed in terms of what M. Weber has called "decentralized patrimonialism" (1947: 341–58).

D. History and Saul's Story

1. The Late Iron I Period. On the eve of Saul's political career, the ANE was still recovering from the effects of the decline of the LB political configuration. The traditional powers of Egypt, Hatti, Assyria, and Babylonia were all preoccupied with domestic problems. While they probably were participating in international trade, none was strong enough to attempt to conquer and control Syria-Palestine. The Aegean world was in the midst of a dark age, a period of isolation, and was unable to reestablish its former role as an international maritime trade power. Syria-Palestine was home to a number of polities of limited territory and of varying degrees of centralized power. In S Syria, Aramean groups were coalescing into states. The Golan heights appear to have contained the states of Geshur and Maacah. In Transjordan, the states of Ammon and possibly Moab appear to have arisen. The territory of Edom may have contained some independently governed towns or regional centers, but it does not appear to have reached territorial or national statehood at this time.

In the desert fringe adjoining Judah, another state of Geshur was established, alongside Girzite and Amalekite groups. The Cisjordanian coastal strip was home to the Philistine pentapolis, while a few city-states controlled the Megiddo Plain–Jezreel Valley corridor, inland valleys, and the ghor. Recent archaeological surveys in the hill country regions of both Transjordan and Cisjordan have established that these areas witnessed a significant growth in population during the course of the Iron I period and became dotted with small villages (i.e., Finkelstein *AIS*; Mittmann 1970; Zertal 1986). Settlement in the Judahite hill country was not as pronounced as in the other areas. The new settlements were usually only a few acres in size and often did not have protective walls, although in most cases houses were arranged to form a contiguous encircling belt that would have eliminated the labor-intensive task of building a separate encircling wall but would still have provided some measure of protection from outside attack.

The political constituency within the hill country is extremely difficult to determine. The traditions concerning the so-called judges, once stripped of their idealized, twelve-tribe orientation, tend to indicate that the mountain areas were fragmented into a number of smaller polities which had varying degrees of centralized power, ranging from village-based governments to probable chiefdoms. In theory, *in situ* remains from the past can chronicle the presence or absence of social stratification through varying house size, diet, and material remains, and can document levels of political complexity by the presence or absence of public buildings. Nevertheless, only a small number of hill country sites have been excavated, and of those, no more than 30 percent of the total area has been uncovered, thus it is not possible at present to reconstruct the political configurations of any of them with certainty.

2. Chronology. The accession formula for Saul in 1 Sam 13:1 is corrupt; consequently, Saul's age at the time of his coronation and the length of his reign are unknown. Most LXX manuscripts lack v 1 altogether. A few minor mss that contain the verse give 30 as the age at accession, which is a figure representing responsible adulthood; the Hebrew mss have no number, but read "son of ____ year(s) was Saul when he became king." Both the MT and LXX give 2 years as the regnal length.

General parameters for the length of Saul's reign can be deduced from narrative details. Since it was the standard ancient practice to undertake military campaigns annually in the spring, at least six years of reign are needed to accommodate a single battle against each enemy recorded in 1 Sam 14:47–48. Details of three separate battles involving the Philistines are preserved in the Bible (1 Samuel 13–14; 17; 29–31), so a minimal reign of 8 to 10 years would seem required for Saul. Bearing in mind the successful coronation of Saul's surviving young and inexperienced son Eshbaal as the dynastic successor to the throne—in spite of critical circumstances of the day that would have favored the appointment of a seasoned military commander (see ESHBAAL)—it seems likely that Saul would have enjoyed an even longer and more successful reign than the deduced minimum. Such an acceptance of a weak dynastic successor presumes that Saul had been able to establish among the court and the citizenry at large his respect and authority as head of state.

If one is willing to assume that the number 2 in 1 Sam 13:1 is part of the original regnal figure that was subsequently corrupted, which is a possible but not necessary inference, it would seem most appropriate to restore either 12 or 22 as the length of Saul's reign. The second figure is more probable in light of the succession issue. A figure of 32 seems too great if one bears in mind two factors. First, Saul's youngest son by Ahinoam apparently survived the battle of Gilboa because he was too young to fight in it, and hence he was probably under 20 years of age at the time of Saul's death. Second, Jonathan, Saul's eldest son, is reported to have had only a single son not more than five years of age at the time of his death at Gilboa. By implication, Jonathan was not more than about 30 when he died. Although the Bible provides no firm indication for marriage ages for males and females in ancient Israel, it would be a reasonable guess to posit an age within the 20s for males and within the teens for females, particularly in light of the low life expectancy. With one child older than Jonathan, Saul should have been in his mid to late 50s when he died at Gilboa.

Since Saul probably would not have been able to gain the support and respect of the people as king if he had not been an experienced soldier proven in battle, it is reasonable to suspect that he must have been at least 30 when he became king. In light of Saul's deduced age at death, a reign lasting upwards of 25 years seems indicated.

3. Saul's Coronation. According to 1 Sam 11:1–11, Saul's rescue of the citizens of Jabesh-gilead from Ammonite threats of oppression and disfigurement was the event that prompted Saul's coronation over Israel. The inclusion of Saul's successful execution of a military deed in the account of his elevation to king has been dictated in part by the use of the literary pattern of the tripartite kingship ritual to structure the presentation (Edelman 1984; see C above). A military testing deed was the necessary second step before the king-elect could be confirmed by official coronation (11:14–15). While it is likely that a military feat was the historical stimulus that led to Saul's being made king, the patternistic nature of the present depiction allows room for the possibility that Saul's rescue of Jabesh-gilead may not have been the actual deed that led to his elevation to kingship. Although its authenticity has been widely accepted, in recent years different military deeds have been connected with Saul's initial coronation.

Saul's ability to have been able to lead his fellow untrained Benjaminite countrymen in a successful rout of the national Ammonite army as currently depicted is historically implausible. Such a battle almost certainly would have had to have taken place after Saul had become an established king who commanded a national and professional militia strong enough to take on the Ammonite state's army with some hope of success. Thus, while 1 Sam 14:47 indicates that the king successfully fought against the Ammonites at some time during his reign, it is likely that the encounter took place in the later part of his reign, not as a prelude, or even in the opening years.

Confirmation of the historical unreliability of the Jabesh-gilead incident as the founding event of Saul's career is found in 2 Sam 2:4b–7. The passage uses the ancient technical treaty language "to do goodness" (Heb *ʿāśâ haṭ-ṭôbâ* to describe Jabesh-gilead's status under Saul. David is reported to have approached the citizens of the town and to have offered to "do goodness" toward them as Saul their former lord had done. The statement indicates that during Saul's reign, the town had not been part of the Israelite state, but instead, had been linked to the state by treaty. David is depicted to have been encouraging the town to revolt against Eshbaal, Saul's successor, and instead to enter into a treaty with him as king of the newly established state of Judah. 2 Sam 2:4b–7 indicates that Jabesh-gilead was not Israelite before or during Saul's reign, so the depiction in 1 Sam 11:1–11 of the town appealing to its fellow Israelite "brethren" for deliverance cannot be historical. When it is further observed that the story exhibits one of the fullest uses of the pattern commonly found in the Judges stories, the historical character of the account becomes even more suspicious (Edelman 1984).

Two alternative military deeds have been associated with Saul's initial coronation: (1) Saul's overthrow of the Philistine prefect at Gibeah and the related capture of Michmash; and (2) Saul's overthrow of the Philistine prefect at Gibeon. According to the first proposal, the natural continuation of the old folktale underlying 1 Sam 9:1–10:16 was an account of Saul's repossession of Gibeah and Michmash from the Philistines, now described in expanded form and associated secondarily with Jonathan in 1 Samuel 13. It is argued that the killing of the Philistine prefect at Gibeah is the military deed that originally was the third part of the sign described in 1 Sam 10:2–7, which was to confirm Saul's anointment by Samuel as king-elect. The original popular account is thought to have been fragmented and rearranged into the present, artificial order by the person responsible for the material's inclusion in the DH (Miller 1974). This proposal has the advantage of having as its basis an attested Saulide battle. A potential drawback is its need to explain why Saul's overthrow of Gibeah has been displaced by the Ammonite incident as the deed that led to his coronation.

The second proposal, like the first, postulates that the old folktale underlying 1 Sam 9:1–10:16 originally included an account of a military deed that served as the third part of the sign in 10:2–7 and was the historical deed that led to Saul's coronation, but that the deed in question has been deliberately excised from the account and replaced with the secondary account of the rescue of Jabesh-gilead. Following the lead of the extant plot in 9:1–10:16 it is suggested that the story went on to tell how Saul returned home to Gibeon (cf. 1 Chr 8:29–40; 9:35–44) and overthrew the resident Philistine prefect by posing as a member of the prophetic train during a religious procession in order to gain access to the official. The abrupt reference to Saul's visit to his "uncle" (Heb *dwd*) is understood to be a vestige of an account of Saul's visit to the resident Philistine *dwd,* "prefect," whom he killed, thereby liberating his hometown from Philistine dominion.

The present arrangement of the text is seen to have resulted from the deliberate "censure" of the Gibeon incident by the creator of the DH. The historian's bias toward Jerusalem as the sole, legitimate place of worship during the monarchic period is seen to have led to his elimination of clear references to Gibeon as Jerusalem's precursor as the first national sanctuary and state capital of the Israelite state (Edelman fc.). A negative attitude toward the Gibeonites has been noted to exist throughout the History (Kearney 1973). This proposal has the advantage of explaining the present arrangement of the text, but it also has the disadvantage of reconstructing an otherwise unattested and unverifiable incident as the basis for Saul's coronation.

4. Saul's Military Career. One of the few positive evaluations of Saul's accomplishments as first king in the biblical portrayal of his career is that of his military prowess. 1 Sam 14:47–48 summarize his deeds as king in terms of his military victories over his enemies on every side: Moab, the Ammonites; Edom, the kings of Zobah; the Philistines; and the Amalekites. Details of a few of these battles have been preserved in 1 Samuel 11; 13–14; 15; 17; 28–31. Careful literary analysis can help separate fictional embellishment from likely historical fact in many instances, and reveals that Saul was a masterful military tactician.

The battle of the Michmash Pass, currently recounted in 1 Samuel 13–14, is probably the earliest extant Saulide battle. If one follows Miller, it would have been Saul's first battle, which led to his coronation by fellow Benjaminites and his establishment of the site of Gibeah as his capital. If one follows Edelman, it would have taken place within the early years of Saul's kingship, after his establishment of Gibeon as his capital. Saul would have needed to eliminate the two Philistine outposts at Gibeah and Michmash, which together controlled the Michmash Pass through the Wadi Suweinit and an important, internal E–W route from the Philistine Plain to the ghor, to have been able to have created a defensible E flank and to have prevented periodic Philistine traversal of his home base territory to man the garrisons.

Jonathan's reported capture of Gibeah in 1 Sam 13:3 is probably literary fiction; he would have been a child in his early teens at the time, assuming a 22- to 25-year reign for Saul. See JONATHAN SON OF SAUL. The military strategy reportedly used by Saul, which involved the division of the army into two batallions that were to attack both posts simultaneously from the rear and force a retreat into the pass, where escape was impossible (13:2), also seems to be unreliable. It is likely that the hill country on the north side of the Wadi Suweinit, in the vicinity of Michmash and Bethel, was part of the political domain of Saul's rival Samuel (1 Sam 7:15–17; Edelman 1989: 57). Saul would not have been free to deploy troops on the north side of the wadi. It seems plausible to suggest that Saul's strategy led him to capture the Philistine fortress at Gibeah, on the Benjaminite side of the wadi, and then to have tricked the Michmash fortress into an unwanted battle before reinforcement troops could arrive from the Philistine homeland. It is possible that the depiction of Jonathan and his weapons bearer pretending to be deserters in order to gain access to the Michmash post (14:1–16) is based on Saul's actual use of a small squadron of men feigning desertion to draw the Michmash post into premature battle. As a result of this two-step offensive, Saul would have eliminated Philistine control to his E, gained control over the E half of the E–W road to the ghor, and gained a foothold among Samuel's constituents, paving the way for his eventual takeover of Samuel's domain as he began to build a territorial state.

The logical goal of the battle against the Philistines in the valley of Elah (1 Samuel 17; 2 Sam 21:19) would have been to secure the S Gibeonite flank and the next most southerly E-W route from the Philistine homeland to the ghor. The latter road ran W from Jerusalem along the Sorek Valley into the Elah Valley before reaching the Philistine Plain. The actual confrontation took place in the form of representative combat in the Elah Valley, the natural point of entry into the hill country. Tradition now names the Israelite champion as the young David, but the actual hero seems to have been a certain Elhanan, son of Jarreoregim, from David's home town of Bethlehem (2 Sam 21:19) (Stoebe 1956).

Saul's battle against the Amalekite stronghold, Ir Amalek, is presently associated with the traditional Amalekite region in the desert S of Judah (1 Samuel 15). Ir Amalek has been identified with the site of Tel Masos in the Beersheba basin (Kochavi 1980: 27), which appears from excavations conducted there to have been a regional trade center in the Iron I period (Str. II) (Finkelstein 1988: 247–52). Saul's interest in gaining control over such an economic base provides a logical motive for both the proposed identification and the purported battle recorded in 1 Samuel 15.

Although the story contains direct allusions to other S Amalekite traditions in the DH, there are a few hints scattered throughout the Bible that an Amalekite enclave also had once been located in the hill country S of the Jezreel Valley (Exodus 17; Judg 5:14; 6:3–7:20; 12:15; 2 Sam 1:2–2:26), which raises a potential question as to the identity of the Amalekite group with whom Saul fought. The only probable historical details that can be gleaned from chap. 15 are the name of the city against which Saul launched his offensive (v 5); that it was located near a wadi (v 5); that Saul may have employed an ambush to take the city (v 5); and that he erected a "stele" (Heb *yad*) after his victory in Carmel, probably as a commemorative marker (v 12). The well-known N Carmel promontory had a long history of such monument erections by Mesopotamian rulers, while the S Carmel region did not (Edelman 1986).

Saul's historical campaign against Ir Amalek could have taken place against the N Amalekite enclave, in response to the group's escalating raids against segments of the central Ephraimite hill country population that had become part of Saul's expanding state, rather than against the more well-known S pastoral groups who would have been raiding the few settlements that existed in the S Judahite hills. Saul's control over any portion of the latter region, which was geographically separated from his core territory by the Jerusalemite city-state and a band of no-man's-land, is disputed. This is the region that David raided as a Philistine mercenary and which he subsequently welded into his Hebron-based state of Judah. The editorial attempt to include Judah within the Saulide state in the DH is perhaps best understood to have been motivated by the use of the idealized twelve-tribe scheme for the pre-monarchic era, which then required its continued use into the early monarchic period.

The Saulide rescue of Jabesh-gilead (1 Sam 11:1–11) has been discussed briefly above. What is noteworthy is the report that Saul used the strategy of surprise attack in order to catch the Ammonite forces off guard and gain a military advantage (v 11). The story is presently structured as a judge-style narrative, to depict Saul's successful completion of a military "testing" after his designation as king-elect and prior to his confirmation as king. The actual battle probably took place in the second half of his reign and may have been prompted by Saul's preexisting treaty obligations to supply Jabesh with military support upon request. Although the present account tends to suggest that Jabesh voluntarily sought to enter into a treaty with Saul to avoid the vassalship that Nahash was intending to impose upon them by force, the report of Saul's overnight march to surprise the Ammonite forces and lift a preexisting siege against the city suggests that a treaty may already have been in effect.

The final battle of Saul's career appears to have been an offensive attack against the city-state of Beth-shean, aimed at securing access to an important trade route. Without control of the corridor that descended through the Jezreel and Beth-shean Valleys to the lower end of the Sea of Galilee and then N to Damascus, it was not possible to carry on commerce directly and freely at the international exchange center of the times. The account of the battle spans 1 Samuel 28–31, and is a highly polished, nonchronological, episodic narrative that parallels Saul's final defeat and death with David's successful routing of the remnant of the Amalekites (whom Saul failed to exterminate), confirming Saul's untransmuted divine rejection from the kingship (1 Samuel 15). David's Amalekite battle provides him with an alibi for his whereabouts during the Battle of Gilboa while deliberately depicting him as Yahweh's champion who carries out the commands of his heavenly regent, in contrast to Saul. The historicity of the incident is questionable.

Chap. 28 sets the entire battle within the larger context of a personal crisis facing David, the king-elect. As a Philistine mercenary, he is told he must accompany the Philistine troops into battle against Saul (28:1–2) and muster with them at Aphek. Immediately, the scene jumps forward in time to the eve of the actual battle, to reveal Saul's destined death via the medium of En-dor (28:3–25). The result is to heighten suspense about David's actions and deepen his dilemma: on two previous occasions he has refused to harm Yahweh's anointed agent, even though he had been in a position to do so (1 Sam 24:1–22; 26:1–25); now, he is put in a situation where, as a Philistine servant who cannot control the upcoming conflict with Saul, he may potentially become the unwilling agent of the Israelite king's certain death. Chap. 29 resolves the suspense and dilemma by moving the scene back a few days earlier to the Philistine mustering ground and recounting David's dismissal from the Philistine forces. With the outcome of the impending battle already revealed in chap. 28, chap. 30 recounts David's successful completion of Saul's earlier divinely ordered task of eliminating the Amalekites, so as to make his victory contemporaneous with Saul's death. Chap. 31 briefly portrays the battle sequence outside Beth-shean that leads to Saul's preordained death.

The Bible reports that Saul took the initiative in his final campaign by encamping by the fountain in the Jezreel Valley. In response, the Philistines are said to have mustered their forces at Aphek in the Philistine Plain (29:1) and then marched N to the Megiddo Plain-Jezreel Valley and encamped opposite the Israelites at Shunem (28:4). Their move supposedly resulted in the Israelites' moving camp further E, to the foot of the Gilboa mountains (28:4). The site of the actual battle is not specified, but seems to have been in the Jezreel Valley between the two camps. The Philistines are reported to have routed the Israelites, and pressed them into the Gilboa mountains, where they were able to wound Saul mortally, kill his three sons (Jonathan, Malchishua, and Abinadab), and gain a decisive victory (31:1–7). The next day, the Philistines are said to have gathered booty and to have beheaded Saul's corpse, nailed it to the walls of Beth-shean, along with the bodies of his sons, and to have sent Saul's armor home to Philistia, to be kept in the temple of Ashtaroth (31:8–10). The citizens of Jabesh-gilead are to have retrieved the bodies and to have taken them home and cremated them. Cremation was an established Aegean and Anatolian burial practice that was used especially to honor fallen warriors and royalty.

The report that Saul was the aggressor in the battle of Gilboa is probably historically reliable, as is his reported encampment in the Jezreel Valley, near the local water source, below the Gilboa spur. His apparent target was the city of Beth-shean, which becomes clear from the detail concerning the displaying of the royal family's bodies on the walls of that city, after the Israelite defeat. This was a gesture of victory. Both Saul's position in the Jezreel Valley to the W of Beth-shean and the disposition of his body by the citizens of that city after his defeat confirm that Saul's intended goal was the conquest of the Canaanite city of Beth-shean (Koizumi 1976).

1 Samuel 28–31 portrays the Philistines as Saul's enemies on this occasion. Many scholars have concluded that Beth-shean was a Philistine city at this time to explain its role in the battle. However, excavations at the site have yielded only one sherd of Philistine pottery, in a disturbed locus, after eleven seasons of excavations, while demonstrating that the city was a prosperous and powerful fortified center during Saul's reign. In the LB period, it had been an important Egyptian garrison city, and Egyptian influence appears to have continued as late as ca. 1075 B.C. (James 1966: 150–53). In light of the predominance of local Canaanite pottery in the city and the lack of any evidence of partial destruction layers in the course of Lower Level V, which spans the period ca. 1100–1000 B.C., it seems best to conclude that the city became an independent Canaanite center after the disappearance of the Egyptian presence and that it voluntarily entered an alliance with the Philistines at some point in the Late Iron I period. The Philistines would have wanted to have secured access to the same important trade routes that Saul appears to have been interested in. The Philistine presence at the battle almost certainly is to be explained in terms of

its status as Beth-shean's ally, and not in terms of its direct control over Beth-shean.

The course of Saul's campaign against Beth-shean remains uncertain. The strong literary shaping of the account leaves its historicity open to challenge. It is possible to conclude from the depiction that Saul planned to attack the city from the E, but perhaps planned to lay squadrons in ambush in the Gilboa hills to the S of the city and to rely on additional Israelite and allied troops from Gilead to join the battle from the east by marching up the ghor. It is not clear if Saul had set a siege against the city or not. In view of the absence of details concerning the actual encounter with the Philistines that led to the rout of the Israelites in the Gilboa hills, it might be possible to suggest that allied Philistine troops arrived unexpectedly from the W, threw the Saulide camp into confusion, and were able successfully to defeat the men as they fled up into the hills in retreat. The current report that the Philistines had encamped opposite the Israelites at Shunem could well be fictional embellishment, created by the author to facilitate his scene of Saul's visit to the witch of En-dor on the eve of the battle.

5. The State of Israel under Saul. Although the Bible devotes some 25 chapters to Saul's career as king, it provides little information about the process of state formation in Israel or about the nature of the early state under Saul. Nevertheless, the list in 2 Sam 2:9 of the areas over which Eshbaal, Saul's son, was crowned provides the historian with crucial data about the nature of the early Saulide state by recording its territorial boundaries and administrative divisions. The list appears to be derived from an old administrative document that could have been included in the Davidic state archives as an enumeration of the territories to which David gained title as Eshbaal's successor. In view of the latter's troubled reign, it is unlikely that he would have made sweeping administrative innovations, so the list should be seen to reflect both the administrative structure and territorial domain of Saul's state.

Although it is possible that Eshbaal could have lost firm control over some former Saulide areas, the reported prolonged war with David in 2 Sam 3:1a tends to suggest that his experienced general Abner was able to maintain Israel's holdings, to the embarrassment of David and the probable anger of the other surrounding states. This situation has resulted in the literary depiction of Eshbaal as a seasoned veteran of 40 when he became king rather than the inexperienced youth other texts indicate he was, to make him a more formidable enemy capable of fending off David's attacks (2 Sam 10:2). It also seems to have led to his assignment of a brief 2-year reign (2 Sam 2:10) to indicate that in spite of his strength and experience, David was able to overpower him quickly and gain the support of the Israelite state leaders.

The list names five areas that together comprised "all Israel": the Gilead, the Ashurites, Jezreel, Ephraim, and Benjamin. The five are further grouped into two subcategories by the use of two different Heb prepositions, *ʾel,* "to," and *ʿal,* "over." The first three were regions "to" which Eshbaal was made king, while the last two, which included his home territory of Benjamin and the area where the premonarchic entity Israel had been located, were regions "over" which he was made king. It has been suggested that the alternation of the two prepositions is attested elsewhere in the Bible and carries no significance in v 8 (*NHT,* 186). However, the verb "to be made king" in all of its attested conjugations never appears in the Bible outside of this verse or in other extant East or West Semitic writings followed by the preposition *ʾel;* the prepositions *ʿal* and *b* are idiomatic. It is unlikely then that the preposition *ʾel* would have been secondarily introduced into the text, creating an unknown idiom. On the other hand, the deliberate use of the preposition in contrast to the idiomatic *ʿal* would be understandable in the context of an incipient and evolving state administration to create a contrast between two types of districts. The idiomatic *ʿal* category probably can be seen to have designated districts with a centralized administration, while the nonidiomatic *ʾel* category would have designated noncentralized districts. The latter perhaps would have been outlying areas where Saul's sovereignty would have been recognized and in which the people would have paid taxes and performed military duty, but areas that would not have had state-built and state-run fortresses established at strategic crossroads and along borders (Edelman 1985: 88–90).

The district of Gilead probably was not identical with the hill country of Gilead. See Fig. SAU.01. The administrative base was Mahanaim (2 Sam 2:8), which apparently was established to gain an Israelite monopoly over the iron ore in the Ajlun region. See MAHANAIM (PLACE). The Manassite settlements in the hill country N of the Wadi ez-Zerqa, as far as the Wadi Yabis, can probably be included within the district of Gilead. Jabesh-gilead's status as an ally tends to limit Saulide holdings to the region S of the Wadi Yabis. The settlements associated with the "judge" Jair, which lay N of the Yabis, appear to have been incorporated into the state by David. 1 Chr 5:10 and 7:8–16 indicate that some portions of the areas of Reuben and Gad were within Saulide control. The W hill country S of the Wadi ez-Zerqa, the adjoining land of Jazer in the Salt region, the hilly territory around Heshbon, and perhaps the Hagrite territory in the desert steppe in the vicinity of the Arnon River (Wadi Mujib) can probably be included within the southern limits of Saulide Gilead.

The Ashurite district seems best associated with the SW Ephraimite hill country, in the area surrounding the Beth-horons. See ASHURITES and Fig. SAU.01. The Jezreel district should probably be confined to the Gilboa hills, with the Wadi Faria perhaps serving as the natural S boundary and the Dothan Valley as the W boundary. It would not have included the Jezreel Valley proper, which would have been controlled by the city-state of Beth-shean. Recent archaeological surveys have determined that there were no settlements on the N side of the Valley, in the traditional tribal allotment of Issachar, at this time (Gal 1982).

The district of Ephraim probably would have included the bulk of the central Ephraimite hill country land mass, which would have included the regions of W Samaria, central Samaria, E Samaria, and the hill country of Ephraim. See Fig. SAU.01. The NW boundary might have been the Dothan Valley; the NE boundary, the Wadi Faria; the E boundary, the ghor; the SE boundary, the Wadi Suweinit; the SW boundary, the Ashurites; and the W

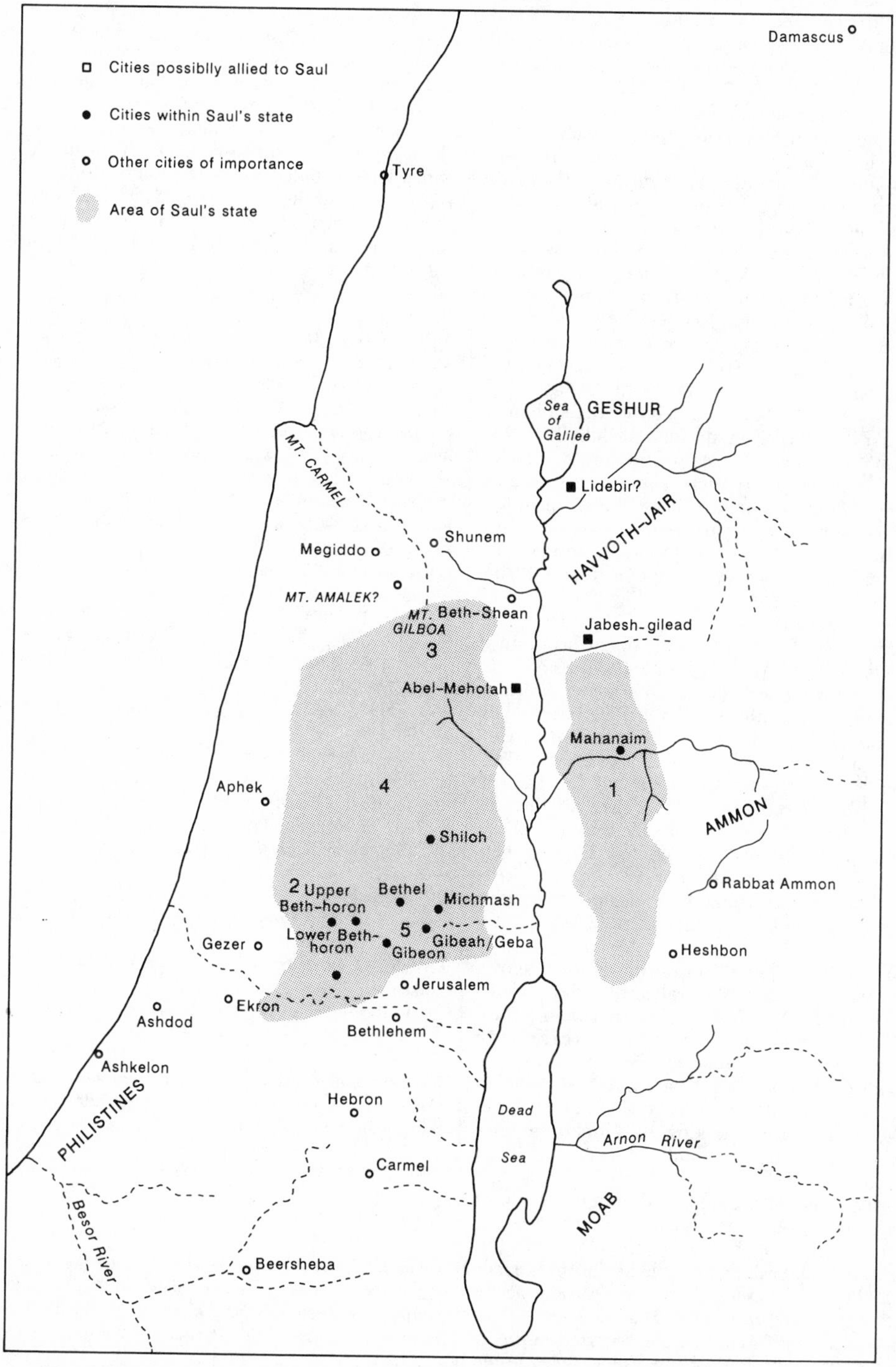

SAU.01. Area map of the kingdom of Saul. Numbers 1–5 within the territory of Saul's kingdom denote the districts named in 2 Sam 2:9. Mahanaim = Telul edh-Dhahab el-Garbi; Lidibir = Tell Dover; Abel-meholah = Tell abu Sus; Gibeah/Geba = Jabaʿ; Jabesh-gilead = Tell Maqlub.

boundary the Sharon Plain. Included within the district of Ephraim would have been Manassite, Ephraimite, and Issacharite clans (i.e., Judg 10:1), and the former political domains of Israel, Samuel, and possibly, the Abiezerites (Judges 6–8).

The district of Benjamin would have included the hills S of the Wadi Suweinit and N of Jerusalem; the plain to their W and the hills to the E of the plain, bordering the Philistine lowland. In the E hills, Israelite settlements would have been confined to the northernmost hills, N of Tell el-Fûl. It seems likely that the latter site, if it indeed housed a fortress at the end of the Iron I period, which is not clear from the archaeological evidence (Finkelstein *AIS*, 56–60), was a Jebusite outpost. From the site one can see Gibeon and Geba, but not Jerusalem, so Saul would not have gained any advantage in fortifying it. However, Tell el-Fûl may have been merely a farmstead, in which case it could have been part of the Saulide district of Benjamin. It is likely that Nob was a Jebusite dependent at this time, given its location on an adjacent hill. The NW boundary would have been the Ashurites, and it is likely that the Sorek Valley and Jerusalem would have served as the S boundary. The Gibeonite enclave, which included the cities of Gibeon, Chephirah, Beeroth, and Kiriath-jearim, appears to have been incorporated into the centralized Benjaminite district at some point during Saul's administration (2 Sam 4:2–4; 21:5).

2 Sam 2:9 indicates that Saul's state did not include the Galilee or Judah. David was responsible for incorporating the former region into the Israelite state. It is possible that Saul had been able to assert control over some segments of Judah, but that he lost these areas to David in the last years of his reign, when David established the rival state of Judah at Hebron (2 Sam 2:10–11). In view of the relatively sparse settlement in the Judahite hills and the lack of additional agricultural commodities that were not already available from other districts, it is possible that Saul chose to control limited portions of Judah by alliance rather than through incorporation, even as a noncentralized district. The Ziphites, for example, may have become associated with Israel by such an alliance arrangement (2 Sam 23:19–24).

In addition to the corporate state land outlined above, Saul appears to have established alliances with various foreign city-states. Besides his treaty with Jabesh-gilead, which may have been struck in order to secure access to the internal N–S hill country road in Gilead, the existence of treaties with Lidebir (var. Lo-debar) and Abel-meholah can be discerned from the extant narratives. The willingness of Machir ben Ammiel, king of Lidebir, to give political asylum to Jonathan's infant son after the Gilboa disaster strongly implies that some form of treaty had existed between Israel and Lidebir. Although the site of Lidebir is uncertain, it seems to have been located N of the Yarmuk River, perhaps at the foot of the Golan heights. Saul's interest in establishing an alliance with the city almost certainly would have been to secure trade access through the upper ghor, en route to Damascus.

A probable treaty with Abel-meholah, located in the W ghor at the S edge of the Beth-shean Valley, is suggested by two pieces of information. The marriage of Saul's eldest daughter Merab to Adriel ben Barzillai the Meholathite (1 Sam 18:19; 2 Sam 21:8) might well have reflected the common ANE practice of sealing a political alliance by marriage. The inclusion of the city in the subsequent fifth Solomonic district strongly indicates that Abel-meholah had remained an independent, Canaanite city-state until the reign of David or Solomon. The district encompasses the former Canaanite domains located in the Megiddo Plain-Jezreel Corridor and the Beth-shean Valley extension, which included the N portion of the W ghor (1 Kgs 4:13). Access to the W ghor road may have motivated this alliance, particularly since Abel-meholah appears to have been located at a commonly used ford of the Jordan (Judg 7:22).

Bibliography

Ahlström, G. fc. *The History of Ancient Palestine.* Winona Lake, IN.

Alt, A. 1967. *Essays on Old Testament History and Religion.* Trans. by R. A. Wilson. Garden City, NY.

Birch, B. 1976. *The Rise of the Israelite Monarchy: The Growth and Development of 1 Samuel 7–15.* SBLDS 27. Missoula.

Blenkinsopp, J. 1975. The Quest for the Historical Saul. Pp. 75–99 in *No Famine in the Land,* ed. J. W. Flanagan and A. W. Robinson. Missoula, MT.

Buccellati, G. 1967. *Cities and Nations of Ancient Syria.* SS 16. Rome.

Cooke, G. A. 1903. *A Textbook of North Semitic Inscriptions.* Oxford.

Coote, R., and Whitelam, K. 1987. *The Emergence of Early Israel in Historical Perspective.* SWBA 5. Sheffield.

Edelman, D. 1984. Saul's Rescue of Jabesh-Gilead (1 Sam. 11:1–11): Sorting Story from History. *ZAW* 86: 195–209.

———. 1985. The "Ashurites" of Eshbaal's State (2 Sam 2:9). *PEQ* 117: 85–91.

———. 1986. Saul's Battle Against Amaleq (1 Sam. 15). *JSOT* 35: 71–84.

———. 1989. Saul's Journey through Mt. Ephraim and Samuel's Ramah (1 Sam. 9:4–5; 10:2–5). *ZDPV* 104: 44–58.

———. 1990. The Deuteronomist's Story of King Saul: Narrative Art or Editorial Product? Pp. 207–220 in *Pentateuchal and Deuteronomistic Studies.* BETL 94. Leuven.

———. 1991. *King Saul and the Historiography of Judah.* JSOTSup. Sheffield.

———. fc. *Saulide Israel: A Literary and Historical Investigation.* Winona Lake, IN.

Eissfeldt, O. 1965. *The Old Testament, an Introduction.* New York.

Finkelstein, I. 1988. Arabian Trade and Socio-Political Conditions in the Negev in the Twelfth–Eleventh Centuries B.C.E. *JNES* 47: 241–52.

———. 1989. The Emergence of the Monarchy in Israel: The Environmental and Socio-Economic Aspects. *JSOT* 44: 43–74.

Flanagan, J. W. 1981. Chiefs in Israel. *JSOT* 20: 47–73.

Fokkelman, J. P. 1986. *Narrative Art and Poetry in the Books of Samuel.* Vol. 2, *The Crossing Fates (I Sam 13–31 & II Sam 1).* Assen.

Frick, F. 1985. *The Formation of the State in Ancient Israel.* SWBA 4. Sheffield.

Gal, S. 1982. The Settlement of Issachar. Some New Observations. *TA* 9: 79–86.

Grønbaek, J. H. 1971. *Die Geschichte vom Aufstieg Davids (1 Sam 15–2 Sam 5). Tradition und Komposition.* ATDan 10. Copenhagen.

Gunn, D. M. 1980. *The Fate of King Saul.* JSOTSup 14. Sheffield.

Halpern, B. 1981. *The Constitution of the Monarchy in Israel.* HSM 25. Chico, CA.

Hauer, C., Jr. 1986. From Alt to Anthropology: The Rise of the Israelite State. *JSOT* 36: 3–15.

Humphreys, W. L. 1978. The Tragedy of King Saul: A Study of the Structure of 1 Samuel 9–31. *JSOT* 6: 18–27.
———. 1982. From Tragic Hero to Villain: A Study of the Figure of Saul and the Development of 1 Samuel. *JSOT* 22: 95–117.
James, F. 1966. *The Iron Age at Beth Shan.* Philadelphia.
Jobling, D. 1978. Jonathan: A Structural Study in 1 Samuel. Pp. 4–25 in *The Sense of Biblical Narrative.* JSOTSup 7. Sheffield.
Kearney, P. 1973. The Role of the Gibeonites in the Deuteronomistic History. *CBQ* 35: 1–19.
Kochavi, M. 1980. Rescue in the Biblical Negev. *BAR* 6: 24–27.
Koizumi, T. 1976. On the Battle of Gilboa. *AJBI* 2: 61–78.
Langlamet, F. 1970. Les récits de l'institution de la royauté israélite (1 Sam VII–XII). *RB* 77: 161–200.
Miller, J. M. 1974. Saul's Rise to Power: Some Observations Concerning 1 Sam 9:1–10:16; 10:26–11:15 and 13:2–14:46. *CBQ* 36: 157–74.
Miscall, P. 1986. *1 Samuel: A Literary Reading.* Bloomington, IN.
Mittmann, S. 1970. *Beiträge zur Siedlungs- und Territorialgeschichte des nordlichen Ostjordanlandes.* ADPV. Wiesbaden.
Polzin, R. 1989. *Samuel and the Deuteronomist.* San Francisco.
Preston, T. R. 1982. The Heroism of Saul: Patterns of Meaning in the Narrative of Early Kingship. *JSOT* 24: 27–46.
Schulte, H. 1972. *Die Entstehung der Geschichtsschreibung im Alten Israel.* BZAW 128. New York.
Service, E. 1975. *Origins of State and Civilization.* New York.
Stoebe, H. J. 1956. Die Goliathperikope 1: Samuel XVII 1–XVIII 5 und die Textform der Septuaginta. *VT* 6: 397–413.
Tallqvist, K. L. 1914. *Assyrian Personal Names.* AASF 43/1. Helsinki.
Van Seters, J. 1983. *In Search of History.* New Haven.
Weber, M. 1947. *The Theory of Social and Economic Organization.* Trans. by A. M. Henderson and T. Parsons. New York.
Zertal, A. 1986. *The Israelite Settlement in the Hill-Country of Manasseh.* Ph.D. Diss. Tel Aviv (in Hebrew).

DIANA V. EDELMAN

SAVIOR, DIALOGUE OF THE. See DIALOGUE OF THE SAVIOR (NHC III,*5*).

SAWEH, TELL ES-. See JESHUA (PLACE).

SAYINGS OF JESUS, OXYRHYNCHUS. Dominical sayings that appear in four texts found in rubbish mounds at Oxyrhynchus, a city which flourished in Middle Egypt principally during the Roman period. Now part of the modern town Behnesa, the site stood between the W bank of the Nile and the Baḥr Yusuf (Canal of Joseph) about 125 miles S of Cairo. Along with an extensive number of documents written on papyrus and parchment, which date from the 1st to the 9th century A.D., the texts were recovered by Bernard P. Grenfell and Arthur S. Hunt over a series of archaeological seasons beginning in 1897. Actually, only three of the pieces—Oxyrhynchus papyrus nos. 1, 654, and 655—are cast in the strict form of collections of independent sayings of Jesus. The fourth, papyrus 840, exhibits the character of a continuous gospel account, as this form is known in the four NT gospels. Unfortunately, all four—along with possibly a fifth, poorly preserved text (no. 1224) which may be a gospel account—are brief and, for the most part, very fragmentary. Since only a few lines can be made out on most of them, this has provided seeming invitations for commentators to attempt restorations of the texts. Significantly, the discovery of the Coptic *Gospel of Thomas* near Nag Hammadi in Upper Egypt has now shown both that numbers 1, 654, and 655 all derive from a Greek version of that text, and that prior attempts at restoring lacunae in the Oxyrhynchus texts were largely misguided. In this connection, it is also important to note that even though all three texts bear an obvious literary connection both with the *Gospel of Thomas* and therefore with one another, they are not from the same scribe, but came from different hands.

1. This papyrus leaf of a codex was found in 1897. Containing seven sayings attributed to Jesus that are reasonably legible, three of which parallel the Synoptic Gospels, the verso of this text as it was first published by Grenfell and Hunt has now been shown to precede the recto; for the proper order can be demonstrated from the Coptic text of the *Gospel of Thomas.* The seven sayings, plus one word from an eighth, which stands in the broken portion at the bottom of the verso, are paralleled by the nine sayings numbered 26–30, 77, and 31–33 in the Thomas document. The reason for the expanded number of sayings in the latter text is because the long fifth saying in the Oxyrhynchus document was split in the Coptic version, becoming saying 30 as well as the latter part of saying 77 in Thomas. Adopting Marcovich's readings (1969), one has the following:

Oxyrhynchus Papyrus 1, lines 24–31 (verso):

> [Jesus sa]ys: [Wh]erever there are
> [three,] th[ey are] gods; and
> [wh]ere there is o[ne] only
> [or tw]o, I am with
> th[em.] Lift [u]p the rock
> and there you will find me;
> cleave the wood and I
> am there.

These words of Jesus are arranged in the *Gospel of Thomas* as follows:

> Jesus said: Where there are three gods, they are gods; where there are two or one, there I am with him (logion 30).
>
> Jesus said: I am the light that is above them all. I am the All. The All came forth from me, and the All has attained to me. Cleave wood, I am there. Lift up the stone and you will find me there (logion 77).

The sense of the first part of the Oxyrhynchus passage and Thomas's logion 30 seems to recall Matthew 18:20 where Jesus says that "where two or three are gathered in my name, there am I in the midst of them." The implication in the two non-canonical sayings is that Jesus makes up the second or third person, in company with one or two disciples, for the purposes of worship. The second part of the Oxyrhynchus piece links to the last segment of logion 77, though the order of lifting the rock and cutting the wood is reversed. As with other readings, it is impossible here to determine which arrangement of the sayings was prior.

654. During the second season at Oxyrhynchus in February 1903, Grenfell and Hunt found a survey list on papyrus whose reverse side preserved a text of 42 lines, broken off on the right side, which consisted of a series of sayings, all apparently attributed to Jesus. Because of lacunae, it is only in sayings 3, 5 and 6 that we find the introductory phrase "Jesus says." The similarities between lines 1–39 of text 654 and the prologue and first six logia of the *Gospel of Thomas* are unmistakable. In the last three damaged lines of the Oxyrhynchus piece, enough can be made out to connect the saying lost here to logion 7 of Thomas. Even so, one significant difference is to be found in the second saying of these two texts. Recalling Matthew 7:7–8 (= Luke 11:9–10), one reads:

Oxyrhynchus Papyrus 654, lines 5–9:

[Jesus says:]
Let not him who see[ks] cease [seeking until]
he finds. And when he fin[ds he will be amazed, and being]
amazed he will reign; and [reigning he will]
rest.

Logion 2, *Gospel of Thomas:*

Let him who seeks not cease seeking until he finds; and when he finds he will be troubled; and when he has been troubled, he will marvel and will reign over the All.

The version that appears in 654 is also attributed by Clement of Alexandria to the *Gospel of the Hebrews* (*Stromateis* 5.14.96), and the two doubtless preserve the original version of this saying as well as the original order of the chain (seek-find-marvel-reign-rest). The principal difference between 654 and logion 2 lies in the final outcome of the person's spiritual quest: to reign or to rest. Since both are well-attested motifs in scripture and elsewhere (see Marcovich 1969: 56f.), it is impossible to determine which was the prior reading in the texts quoted above, that is, whether one or the other was "corrected" by a copyist to its current reading.

655. Eight fragments of two columns of a text dated no later than A.D. 250 by Grenfell and Hunt were found in 1903. Written in a small, skilled hand in uncial letters, the document comes from a papyrus roll whose fibers and sense of the text have allowed an accurate placement of the fragments. As in the case of nos. 1 and 654, the discovery of the *Gospel of Thomas* has demonstrated that 655 is from a copy of a Greek version of this collection of individual sayings. Indeed, it is possible to determine that logia 36–39 and possibly 24b were written in the two columns.

The freedom felt by a copyist to alter a reading in a text can be seen from a comparison between the first saying and logion 36, its parallel in Thomas.

Oxyrhynchus Papyrus 655, lines 1–17:

[Take no thought] from early un[til late or]
from even[ing until] morning, neither [for your food]
what you may ea[t, nor] for [your
clot]hing what you should put on. [You are]
much better than the [li]lies which [nei]ther
card nor spi[n. But] since you have one
[gar]ment, what in fact do you la[ck]? Who can
add to your stature? He himself shall give to
(each of) you your garment.

In an apparent effort to minimize the seeming contradiction between this saying, in which one's special garment was to be supplied by the Lord, and the following one, in which a person is expected to take one's garment off and trample it in the dust before being able to associate with "the Son of the Living One," the redactor [?] of the Coptic text purposely dropped most of the saying, leaving only the following.

Gospel of Thomas, logion 36:

Jesus said: Take no thought from morning to evening and from evening to morning for what you should put on.

840. Found in December 1905, this partial text consists of a small vellum leaf (8.8 × 7.4 cm.) written on both sides in a tiny, rather regular hand. The writing is dated by its discoverers to the 4th century, and the copyist exhibits an inclination for using red ink in specific instances such as the first letters of sentences, dots of punctuation and—twice—accent marks.

The opening seven lines of the text introduce the reader to the end of an address by Jesus—consistently referred to as "the Savior"—in which he warns his hearers against the sort of overconfidence which leads to punishment both in this life and in the next. He then leads his disciples into the temple, apparently going within the "court of Israel," where they meet a Pharisaic high priest, possibly named Levi. The priest reproaches them for entering without properly purifying themselves and for not changing into white clothing, hence desecrating the sacred precinct. In response, Jesus inquires about the state of cleanness of the priest, who in turn affirms that he has performed the necessary purificatory rites. Against this Jesus delivers a sharp criticism, which recalls Jesus' harsh condemnation of the "tradition of the elders" in Matt 15:1–20 and Mark 7:1–23, contrasting the shallow character of external purity with the deeper inward cleansing in which he and his disciples had been immersed from above at "the waters of life" (line 43).

The absence of connections in this piece to special interests within the early Christian community as well as the presence of both numerous Semitisms and an informed view on temple matters lead naturally to a high estimate of this text as a virtual companion piece to the Synoptic Gospel accounts. Further, it is likely that the original document was composed at least by the early 2d century, since it shares none of the uncontrolled fantasies about Jesus and the disciples that 2d and 3d century apocryphal accounts typically exhibit.

Bibliography

Grenfell, B. P., and Hunt, A. S. 1898. *The Oxyrhynchus Papyri.* Part I. London.

———. 1904a. *New Sayings of Jesus and Fragment of a Lost Gospel from Oxyrhynchus.* New York.

———. 1904b. *The Oxyrhynchus Papyri.* Part IV. London.

———. 1908. *The Oxyrhynchus Papyri.* Part V. London.

Hennecke, E., and Schneemelcher, W., eds. 1963. *New Testament Apocrypha.* Vol. 1. Philadelphia.

Marcovich, M. 1969. Textual Criticism on the Gospel of Thomas. *JTS* 20: 53–74.

S. Kent Brown

SCAB. See LEPROSY; SICKNESS AND DISEASE.

SCALLOPS. See ZOOLOGY.

SCANDINAVIAN SCHOOL. The designation "Scandinavian school," regardless of whether it is used to refer to OT or NT studies (or both), should be used cautiously, since those normally designated by this term have not thought of themselves as belonging to a "school." The fact that several Scandinavian scholars in both OT and NT studies have held views explicitly different from German exegetes in particular may explain why English-speaking colleagues, mainly in North America, have come to regard them as a "school."

OT STUDIES

It is fair to say that, without constituting a "school" in the strict sense of the word, certain trends especially since the 1920s have put a distinctive stamp on OT scholarship in Scandinavian countries. The point of departure was the work of the Danish historian of religions Vilhelm Grønbech, who between 1909 and 1912 published the Danish original of his *The Culture of the Teutons* (1931) and in 1915 a brief introduction to "primitive religion." In the former he tried to reconstruct the thought-world of the ancient Teutons, using their own expressions and trying to understand them on their own conditions; in the latter he explained primitive cult as a creative drama with the aim of renewing the conditions that were the result of the myth reproduced in the ceremonies.

The former approach was applied by Johannes Pedersen to ancient Israel (1926). He analyzed the thought-world of the OT, letting the texts speak for themselves without the introduction of modern categories. Especially important was his explanation of *nepeš,* "soul," as the vital principle in man, and his interpretation of *berākâ,* "blessing," as a concept very much like the *mana* of primitive peoples. This volume was followed in 1934 (Eng 1940) by a second one in which the institutions of the OT were dealt with in terms of holiness, holy persons, holy places, and holy actions. At the same time, Pedersen was a heavy opponent of literary source criticism; some of his ideas in this respect were set forth when he argued that the exodus story was the cult legend of Passover (1934).

On the other hand, Grønbech's theory of the cult as creative drama became decisive for the Norwegian Sigmund Mowinckel in the 2d volume of his work on the Psalms (1921–24). Following up Gunkel's idea of the cult as the *Sitz im Leben* of the OT psalms, he launched the theory that certain psalms (47, 93, 95–99) were connected with an Israelite festival in which Yahweh's enthronement as the king of the world was celebrated (*YHWH mālak,* "Yahweh has become king"). Other elements of this festival were Yahweh's defeat of the powers of chaos, the creation of the world, and his "judging" the enemies. The aim of the festival was to convey supernatural blessing to the worshippers. Other volumes of this study dealt with cultic prophecy and with the "evildoers" who were explained as sorcerers causing the suffering of the psalmists.

These ideas gained wide acceptance in the Scandinavian countries. A new slant was given to this approach by Ivan Engnell of Uppsala with additional inspiration from the English "myth-and-ritual" school. Hooke, in collaboration with other British scholars, had published a collection of essays under the title *Myth and Ritual.* His original intention was to contribute to the discussion between evolutionism and diffusionism in comparative religion. In favor of the latter theory, Hooke and his followers introduced the idea of a common myth and ritual pattern in the ANE. Since this pattern appears in its purest form in Mesopotamia, Hooke concluded that it originated there and spread to the W Semites (including Israel) and Egypt but at the same time disintegrated. Among the elements of this pattern was the New Year Festival, in which the defeat of the powers of chaos and the death and resurrection of the god were reenacted, the king being the main actor of the cultic drama. Engnell accepted this theory and developed it further in 1943 in his dissertation, which was meant to be a preliminary study to be followed by a treatment of divine kingship in the OT (Engnell 1960).

Engnell combined the idea of the myth-and-ritual pattern with the theory that most of the OT texts had for a long time been transmitted orally, which meant, first, that the documentary hypothesis in Pentateuchal research was wrong, and second, that literary criticism in the prophetic writings was impossible and that the *ipsissima verba* of the prophets could not be retrieved. In this emphasis on oral tradition Engnell developed a suggestion made by another Uppsala scholar, H. S. Nyberg, whose study of the book of Hosea (1935) was devoted primarily to proving the reliability of the Masoretic text. This latter point became another cornerstone in Engnell's so-called traditio-historical method.

Engnell's opposition to source criticism was also combined with criticism of Wellhausen's view of the development of Israelite religion, which was deemed evolutionistic. Here Engnell joined hands with his colleague G. Widengren, who was fighting the evolutionistic theory in comparative religion (note his treatment of sacral kingship); this again related to Hooke's position in the question of diffusionism versus evolutionism. Engnell devoted much of his time to a Swedish biblical encyclopedia, in which he set forth his ideas in numerous articles (some of them were translated into English as *A Rigid Scrutiny* [1969], and so he never had the opportunity to develop his ideas in detail on a scholarly level. Some of his suggestions were followed up by Ahlström (1959), focusing on sacral kingship, and Carlson (1964), who intended to present a traditio-historical analysis of 2 Samuel but dealt more with questions of the composition of the final text. Also to be mentioned is Haldar, a student of Widengren's, who directed much of his work to the study of the prophets (1945; 1947). These were sometimes referred to as the "Uppsala School."

Engnell's views were partly accepted, partly opposed by other Scandinavian scholars. The theory of oral transmission was opposed by Widengren, who on the basis of Arabic material stressed the importance of written tradition; this led to a modification by Engnell, who in the prophetic literature introduced the differentiation between the *diwan* type, which was oral, and the liturgy type, which was written (e.g., Deutero-Isaiah). Mowinckel took a compromise stand, arguing that in spite of oral transmission, literary criticism was possible. The idea of "divine" or sacral kingship was taken up and modified by Mowinckel (1956) and by A. Bentzen (Copenhagen) in several minor works. Mowinckel continued his works on the Psalms and published a comprehensive work (1962), partly in discussion with Engnell and also with his compatriot Birkeland, who had argued that the enemies of the Psalms were primarily political (1955). Bentzen also published commentaries on the Psalms and Isaiah in which he utilized the results of Pedersen and Mowinckel.

A number of other scholars should be mentioned. Kapelrud, Mowinckel's successor on the chair of Oslo, studied the book of Joel (1948), a study which reveals strong influence by Engnell. His works on Ugaritic religion are independent studies of the texts within the framework of a myth-and-ritual view. Another noteworthy scholar is F. F. Hvidberg, whose *Weeping and Laughter* (1938) was a source of inspiration for Engnell's treatment of Ugaritic texts in his dissertation. Nielsen was initially interested in oral tradition (1954) but later (1959) developed Engnell's ideas in an independent way. Mettinger's work (1976) tries in new ways to interpret the central theme of the Uppsala school. Finally, Lindblom, for many years professor of Lund, took a positive stand to Pedersen and Mowinckel, but represented in many respects a more traditional approach. Ringgren, in his study of Israelite religion (1966), confesses his debt to the Uppsala school but also endeavors to pay due attention to new findings.

In summary, it can be said that the main importance of the "Scandinavian school" in OT studies seems to be its history-of-religion, or comparative religion, approach to the religion of Israel, including the emphasis on the cult and on the central role of sacral kingship.

Bibliography

Studies on Scandinavian Scholarship:

Knight, D. *The Traditions of Israel.* SBLDS 9. Missoula.

Ringgren, H. Les récherches d'AT en Scandinavie. *ÉTR* 46: 419–28.

Works by Scholars Associated with the School:

Ahlström, G. *Psalm 89: Eine Liturgie aus dem Ritual des leidenden Königs.* Lund.

Birkeland, H. 1955. *The Evildoers in the Book of Psalms.* ANVAO 2/2. Oslo.

Carlson, R. A. 1964. *David the Chosen King.* Trans. E. Sharpe and S. Rudman. Stockholm.

Engnell, I. 1960. *Studies in Divine Kingship in the Ancient Near East.* 2d ed. London.

Haldar, A. 1945. *Associations of Cult Prophets.* Uppsala.

———. 1962. *Studies in the Book of Nahum.* Uppsala.

Hooke, S. H. 1933. *Myth and Ritual.* London.

Kapelrud, A. 1948. *Joel Studies.* Oslo.

Mettinger, T. 1976. *King and Messiah.* Lund.

Mowinckel, S. 1921–24. *Psalmenstudien I–IV.* SNVAO. Oslo.

———. 1956. *He That Cometh.* Trans. G. Anderson. Oxford.

———. 1962. *The Psalms in Israel's Worship.* Oxford.

Nielsen, E. 1954. *Oral Tradition.* Trans. A. Lange. SBT 11. London.

———. 1959. *Shechem: A Traditio-Historical Investigation.* 2d ed. Copenhagen.

Nyberg, H. S. 1935. *Studien zum Hoseasbuche.* Uppsala.

Pedersen, J. 1926. *Israel, its Life and Culture.* Vols. 1–2 (vols. 3–4 in 1940). Copenhagen.

———. 1934. Passahfest und Passahlegende. *ZAW* 52: 161–75.

Ringgren, H. 1966. *Israelite Religion.* Trans. D. Green. Philadelphia.

HELMER RINGGREN

NT STUDIES

In NT studies, the contours of the so-called "Scandinavian school" are much less vague, with considerable differences among its various members even in what could be regarded as principal matters.

Two Scandinavian NT scholars exerted a particular influence on their doctoral students and thus decisively inspired the scholarly work and outlooks which characterized the school. They were Anton Fridrichsen (Uppsala University, Sweden, [1928–1953]) and Hugo Odeberg (Lund University, Sweden, [1933–1964]). Of these, Odeberg published relatively little during his tenure as professor, but had a decisive influence on his students through his lectures.

Of Norwegian birth, Fridrichsen received most of his postgraduate education in Germany and France. As a scholar he was constantly on the move and open to new impulses. In his dealings with doctoral students, his openness meant that he never acted as a teacher to whose program the students should conform in order to gain his acceptance. Rather, he encouraged work on topics which were new to him or approaches which differed from his own. Behind most of his work, however, lay a particular understanding of history and of historical research. For him, scholars were to dismiss the sort of "historicism" which "above all wants to find 'authentic' material, reliable biographical data that make it possible to draw a picture of the persons' lives, characters and ideas, . . . their milieu and the creative factors therein" (Fridrichsen 1953: 54). One should rather regard the gospels in the same way as other oriental texts, which have a divine man as their main character, i.e., a figure surrounded by adherents who are inspired by him and in whom he continues to live after his death. This does not preclude the possibility of differentiating between older and younger layers of tradition, but "to him who has liberated himself from historicism's narrow view and meagre experience of reality, precisely the tradition in all its abundance, diversity and multiplicity becomes the mirror in which historical reality is reflected"

(1953: 56). There was a fundamental unity of the NT, indeed of the whole Bible; one could "discern history, the continuity of events, reality working and being transformed—in short, eschatological fulfillment in preparation under the old Israel, in realization through Jesus Christ, and in interpretation in his Church" (1953: 59–60). Similar ideas are also encountered among some of Fridrichsen's students, while among others only faint echoes of them are heard.

Naturally, an outlook of this kind signaled a serious departure from radical form-criticism. It may also explain why the demythologization program had little success among people influenced by Fridrichsen. On the other hand, the study of NT texts or of their motifs was often made from a history of religions perspective; approaches like "myth-and-ritual" and "patternism" or complexes like "sacral kingship" or "corporate personality," which were important to the neighboring OT scholars, could be brought in (see above). Much more than "Hellenism," one stressed the relevance of Judaism for the understanding of the NT, and often, in many ways, one underlined the importance of the OT both for the preaching of Jesus and for the thinking of the early Church. Thus it was common that the Messiah concept was central to the manner in which one understood Jesus and his self-consciousness, as well as his eschatological preaching. The Son-of-Man idea was taken as containing the thought of a heavenly Messiah, incorporating God's people. A kingly Messiah was easily connected with his people, and so not only the Church found a natural place in the study of some members of the school, but the ministry and the sacraments did as well.

Largely independent of Fridrichsen and his seminar, Hugo Odeberg promoted a NT study with abundant recourse to Judaism, himself a specialist in the area with special linguistic competence and a deep acquaintance with Jewish mysticism. He did not publish programmatic or wide-embracing articles, as Fridrichsen did, but he had an outstanding ability in, so to speak, taking his students with him into the Jewish texts. Thus exegetes who have worked with Odeberg very often go deeply into Jewish, not least Rabbinic material, in order so to shed light on NT texts.

Obviously much of what was done in the school during the 1950s agreed with general tendencies in the world of theology, such as "Heilsgeschichte" and "neo-orthodoxy." But the perspectives intimated above give the school, insofar as one can talk of a "school" at all, a profile of its own.

The successors of Fridrichsen (Riesenfeld) and Odeberg (Gerhardsson) became involved in a development at Swedish universities which meant that "theology" became "science of religion." This cooled down some of the earlier readiness among the exegetes to pursue biblical theology. However, features from the preceding decades still were there, e.g., the suspicion of "uncritical" criticism, the interest in the historical Jesus, and the study of Judaism as a natural frame of reference for Jesus and the early Church. This was also the background against which Riesenfeld (1957) and Gerhardsson (1961) suggested that the gospel tradition and its transmittance were comparable with Rabbinic tradition and its transmission.

One reason behind the discernment of a school may have been that, relatively seen, so many of its members held university teaching positions in Scandinavia and abroad. The following men had all studied under Fridrichsen: C.-M. Edsman (History of Religion, Uppsala), B. Gärtner (NT, Princeton Seminary), G. Lindeskog (NT, Turku/Åbo), B. Reicke (NT, Basel), H. Riesenfeld (NT, Uppsala), K. Stendahl (NT, Harvard), Å. V. Ström (History of Religion, Lund), and B. Sundkler (Missiology, Uppsala); O. Linton (NT, Copenhagen) only finished his thesis under Fridrichsen. Others were not long-time members of his seminar, but spent some time with him and are sometimes regarded as representing the School, e.g., P. Nepper-Christensen (NT, Aarhus) and B. Noack (NT, Copenhagen). N. A. Dahl also studied with Odeberg for a period of time and, after his dissertation in Oslo, spent a couple of years with Fridrichsen. He then returned to teach in Oslo, moving later to Yale. E. Lövestam (NT, Lund) also studied under Odeberg, as did S. Aalen (NT, Oslo). Among other Odeberg students, sometimes mentioned as School-representatives, are E. Percy and E. Sjöberg. A younger generation began their BD studies under Fridrichsen, but completed their doctorates under Riesenfeld, e.g., B. Gerhardsson (NT, Lund) and E. Larsson (NT, Oslo).

One may doubt whether there still is a "school." Some of its original features are still found in Scandinavian NT scholarship, such as a marked readiness to study the NT in the light of the OT and of Judaism (P. Borgen, L. Hartman), but, at the same time, research has moved in new directions, and generally, the tendency to group people into clearly demarcated "schools" has diminished. Consequently, the contours of the "school," already blurred, may be said to have faded away.

Bibliography

Studies on Scandinavian Scholarship:

Dewailly, L.-M. 1977. Quelques récentes études suédoises sur les Évangiles. *Les Quatres Fleuves* 7: 111–19.

Hartman, L. 1976. New Testament Exegesis. Pp. 51–65 in *Faculty of Theology at Uppsala University.* Vol. 1 of *Uppsala University 500 Years,* ed. H. Ringgren, Uppsala.

Lindeskog, G. 1950. Nordische Literatur zum Neuen Testament 1939–1949. *TRev* 18: 216–38, 288–317.

Stendahl, K. 1951–52. Neutestamentliche exegetische Dissertationen in Uppsala 1937–50. *VF* 46–56.

Works by Scholars Associated with the School:

Aalen, S. 1951. *Die Begriffe 'Licht' und 'Finsternis' im Alten Testament, im Spätjudentum und im Rabbinismus.* Det Norske Videnskaps-Akademi i Oslo. Skrifter, II. Hist.-Filos. Kl. 1951: 1. Oslo.

Dahl, N. A. 1941. *Das Volk Gottes. Eine Untersuchung zum Kirchenbewusstsein des Urchristentums.* Det Norske Videnskaps-Akademi i Oslo. Skrifter, II. Hist.-Filos. Kl. Oslo.

Fridrichsen, A. 1947. *The Apostle and His Message.* Uppsala Universitets Årsskrift 1947: 3. Uppsala.

Fridrichsen, A., et al. 1953. *The Root of the Vine.* London.

Gärtner, B. 1955. *The Areopagus Speech and Natural Revelation.* ASNU 21. Copenhagen.

Gerhardsson, B. 1961. *Memory and Manuscript.* ASNU 22. Copenhagen.

Larsson, E. 1962. *Christus als Vorbild.* ASNU 23. Copenhagen.

Lindeskog, G. 1973. *Die Jesusfrage im neuzeitlichen Judentum. Ein*

Beitrag zur Geschichte der Leben-Jesu-Forschung. ASNU 8. Darmstadt.
Linton, O. 1932. *Das Problem der Urkirche in der neueren Forschung. Eine kritische Darstellung.* Inaugural-Dissertation. Uppsala.
Lövestam, E. 1961. *Son and Saviour.* ConBNT 18. Lund and Copenhagen.
Noack, B. 1948. *Satanás und Soteria.* Copenhagen.
Odeberg, H. 1929. *The Fourth Gospel.* Uppsala.
———. 1939. *The Aramaic Portions of Bereshit Rabba with Grammar of Galilaean Aramaic* 1–2. LUÅ n.s. 1/36: 3–4. Lund and Leipzig.
Percy, E. 1942. *Der Leib Christi (sōma Christou) in den paulinischen Homologoumena und Antilegomena.* LUÅ n.s. 1/38: 1. Lund and Leipzig.
Reicke, B. 1946. *The Disobedient Spirits and Christian Baptism.* ASNU 13. Copenhagen.
Riesenfeld, H. 1947. *Jésus transfiguré.* ASNU 16. Copenhagen.
———. 1970. *The Gospel Tradition.* Trans. M. Rowley and R. A. Kraft. Philadelphia.
Sjöberg, E. 1946. *Der Menschensohn im äthiopischen Henochbuch.* Kungliga humanistiska vetenskapssamfundet, skrifter 41. Lund.
Stendahl, K. 1954. *The School of St. Matthew and Its Use of the Old Testament.* ASNU 20. Copenhagen.

LARS HARTMAN

SCARAB. See JEWELRY.

SCEVA (PERSON) [Gk *Skeyas*]. A man identified as "a Jewish chief priest" (Acts 19:14), whose seven "sons" (possibly disciples) were itinerant exorcists. In response to the fame achieved by Paul's miracles during his time in Ephesus, other Jewish exorcists began to use the name of Jesus as a magic spell in the hopes of having the same effects (cf. also Simon Magus, Acts 8:18–24). But when Sceva's seven sons (disciples?) attempted the feat, "like an unfamiliar weapon wrongly handled it exploded in their hands" (Bruce *Acts* NICNT, 368). The demon-possessed man reacted so violently to their attempted exorcism that they ran for their lives. According to Acts, the impact of this event had a profound influence in the city whose fame for its magical practices was widely celebrated (Bruce *Acts* NICNT, 269–70, with refs. and bibliog.; Hemer 1989: 121): soon many of those who practiced the magic arts were confessing their errors and burning the scrolls with their magic incantations. The author of Acts uses the event to underline the unrivaled power of God working through the life of his servant Paul and also the fact that Jesus' name should not be used as a magic formula (cf. the words of a Jewish magical papyrus in the Bibliothèque Nationale in Paris: "I adjure you by Jesus, the God of the Hebrews;" and the forbidding of the use of Jesus' name in magic by some rabbis [Bruce *Acts* NICNT, 368n]).

The origin and meaning of the name "Sceva" is uncertain. It may be a Greek rendering of the Latin cognomen *Scaeva* rather than a Jewish name, but this would not necessarily mean that the bearer was a Roman citizen (Hemer 1989: 234). There is an inscriptional reference to a slave by this name (*CIG* 2889) and also to a gladiator by the same name (*IGRR* 1.701). If Latin in origin it would mean "left-handed," perhaps literally, or possibly used in a metaphorical sense of the word as "favorable omen" (so Hemer). The suggestion has been made (Bruce 1952: 358, but not *Acts* NICNT, 368) that the name is derived from the Hebrew *šebaʾ* ("seven"), but this is unlikely.

It is not even certain that Sceva was, strictly speaking, Jewish; and it is quite certain that he was never a "high priest" *(archiereus)* in Jerusalem, since that name is never found on the existing lists. It seems likely that he had simply adopted the title as a public relations gimmick—who in Ephesus could disprove the claim?—and what was the role of the Jewish high priest but to enter into "the holy of holies" and to utter the sacred name (Lake and Cadbury [quoting F. C. Burkitt] 1933: 241)? Maston suggests that the title was used to authenticate the activity of the "sons" as "*bona fide* exorcists" (1976: 405). It is unlikely also that he was a member of a family with Jewish high priestly connections or a former head of the courses of temple priests, of which the term was more broadly applied (Jeremias 1969: 175–81; BAGD). As far as the use of the term itself is concerned, Sceva may have been "an apostate and a high priest of the imperial or some other cult" (Williams *Acts* GNC, 327), but it is just as possible that the Greek prefix *archi* ("high" or "chief") is merely a typical example of the Koine tendency to compound words with *archi* (*NDIEC* 2: 18). However, it seems more likely that he was simply a professional exorcist with entrepreneurial skills, and that his sons or associates—the text does not actually say that Sceva himself lived in Ephesus—plied their trade in the congenial setting. As Bruce comments: "Luke might have placed the words between quotation marks, had these been invented in his day" (*Acts* NICNT, 368). In spite of its strangeness to modern ears, the story has the earmarks of historicity.

Bibliography

Bruce, F. F. 1952. *The Acts of the Apostles.* [Greek Text]. Grand Rapids.
Hemer, C. J. 1989. *The Book of Acts in the Setting of Hellenistic History,* ed. C. Gempf. WUNT 49. Tübingen.
Jeremias, J. 1969. *Jerusalem in the Time of Jesus.* Trans. F. H. Cave and C. H. Cave. London.
Lake, K. and Cadbury, H. J. 1933. *The Beginnings of Christianity.* Pt. 1, *The Acts of the Apostles.* Vol. 4, *English Translation and Commentary,* ed. F. J. Foakes Jackson and K. Lake. London. Repr. Grand Rapids, 1979.
Maston, B. A. 1976. Scaeva the chief priest. *JTS* n.s. 27: 405–12.
———. 1978. A Note on Acts 19:14. *Bib* 59: 97–99.

W. WARD GASQUE

SCHOLARSHIP, BIBLICAL (JAPAN). See BIBLICAL SCHOLARSHIP, JAPANESE.

SCHOOL OF SHAMMAI. See SHAMMAI, SCHOOL OF.

SCHOOLS. See EDUCATION.

SCHOOLS, HELLENISTIC. The Hellenistic schools are important for the understanding of the NT in two respects: it has long been recognized that their social structures provide a partial analog to the early Christian groups; and they produced a large body of literature (much of it still extant) which needs to be taken into account in any study of the literary background of the NT. But in order to utilize this material properly, it is essential to examine the Hellenistic schools as institutions in the widest possible sense: an integrated picture must include not only the better-known areas of philosophy and rhetoric, but also training for the professions and crafts.

A. The Nature of the Schools
  1. The Individual Level
  2. The Secondary Level
  3. The Tertiary Level
  4. The Movement
B. The Functions of the Schools
C. Training in the Crafts
D. Rhetoric
E. Philosophy
F. Medicine
G. Mathematics and Technical Subjects
H. Philo

A. The Nature of the Schools

1. The Individual Level. The fundamental relationship lying behind any "school" is that between a teacher and an individual student, normally a non-symmetrical relationship between leader and led, between age and youth. It is important to remember that most teaching in antiquity operated on just this individual basis; teachers were specialists (Clarke 1971: 7), and a father who wished his son to achieve the full *enkuklios paideia* or "all-around education" could not enroll him in a school where this curriculum was centrally administered but had to find him a different teacher for each subject. (Women participated in the higher levels of Greek and Roman education, but only to a very limited extent.) This basic pattern may be extended beyond the one-to-one teaching relationship in two ways. First, loyalty to the teacher, and imitation of the teacher as a model, might well extend into adult life, and thus by extension teacher-disciple language may be used metaphorically of any individual following the precepts of a particular teacher (or belonging to a particular "school"), even where there has been no physical contact between the two. Adherence to Stoicism tended to work in this way, and Philo's references to the "school of Moses" (see below) may also be understood in this sense. Second, the basic teacher-student relationship in itself can be sufficient to set up an institutionalization of tradition, if the student in his/her turn becomes the teacher of the next generation and passes on what s/he has learnt from the teacher. It seems thus perfectly proper to use the term "school" in any context where we have a "chain of tradition" (Bickerman 1952), even though we have no evidence of any social structures beyond the basic "one teacher plus one student."

2. The Secondary Level. A social relationship can come into being between fellow students at a secondary level, especially where (as often happened in antiquity) one teacher could have a number of students or apprentices living in his house in a modified "family" atmosphere. In these conditions, where the natural camaraderie of the young was often intensified by feelings of loyalty to one teacher and rivalry with the students of other teachers, the development of a lateral, peer-group community spirit was almost inevitable. Such a development, with its attendant language of friendship *(philoi, hetairoi),* is often seen as particularly characteristic of the philosophical schools, but in fact it is just as common in rhetoric or medicine.

3. The Tertiary Level. Less common in antiquity is the development at a tertiary level of groups of teachers and/or researchers engaged in a common enterprise. A wide degree of variation is possible here, from the high-powered research organizations of the Theophrastus or the Alexandrian Museum to the religiously committed brotherhood of Pythagoras or Epicurus; both could rightly be called "schools." Generally speaking, however, the combination of a number of teachers into a single administrative unit (as in a modern "high school") seems to have been rare in antiquity (Marrou 1956: 264–65): the great teachers, like the lesser ones, operated as individuals, and where we speak of a "university atmosphere" this was simply a function of the large number of individual teachers working in major centers such as Athens, Alexandria, or Tarsus. It is only under the later Roman Empire that we find anything like the modern university system, resulting from increasing state intervention in the organization of education (Clarke 1971: 130). Where we do hear of teachers operating as a group in the earlier period, it is where a flourishing teacher has co-opted a number of subordinates (sometimes slaves, though this was frowned on) to act as his assistants (Clarke 1971: 27, 33).

4. The Movement. Finally, the most complex kind of school structure in antiquity comes into being where a number of small groups in different localities are conscious of belonging to the same sect or movement: the "school" here means an agglomeration of geographically scattered groups professing adherence to the same ideals and teaching tradition. This kind of grouping is mainly associated with certain philosophical schools, particularly that of Epicurus; but a similar phenomenon at a less self-conscious level may be observed wherever a number of individual teachers in different places profess to follow a particular teaching tradition, such as the "dogmatist" and "empiricist" schools in medicine.

B. The Functions of the Schools

Most of the functions of the Hellenistic schools can be plotted on a grid summarizing four major consumer needs:

I: professional training in a particular skill or "art" (Gk: *technē*)	III: intellectual inquiry as an end in itself
II: liberal education of a gentleman (Gk: *paideia*)	IV: moral training and the quest for a life-style

Of these, I and II are the most obviously "educational," and on this side our subject forms part of the tertiary or "higher" level of the ancient educational system. Schools serving either of these functions were ministering to a need which was at the same time *recurrent,* in that society provided a constant stream of the young requiring one or the other, and *transient,* in that they belong to a certain stage in the life of the individual student. Typically, the student would engage in his or her chosen course of study as a preparation for adult life and would therefore pass out of the school when the training or education was complete.

However, the 5th century B.C. also saw the emergence of two other subsidiary demands which could persist into adult life and therefore provide a greater degree of permanency, III and IV. On this side we have to see the Hellenistic schools not just as something pertaining to youth, but as an integral part of Greek (and later Roman) cultural life. The Ionian appetite for intellectual inquiry (Gk *theoria*) for its own sake flourished in Pericles' Athens and persisted right through the Hellenistic age; it saw a notable renaissance in the 2d century A.D., but had never ceased to be a feature of the public life of the Greek cities. This phenomenon created the conditions for two classic features of Hellenistic culture, both (interestingly) described with the same group of *philo-*compounds *(philomathēs, philiatros, philotechnos).* On the one hand, there is a constant market for public lectures attended by leisured adults as well as by the young; given the semi-public conditions in which many teachers operated, in fact, it is often difficult to determine whether a discourse is given primarily for the benefit of the disciples who cluster round the master or for the interested passers-by who pause to listen and question (Clarke 1971: 33; Bonner 1977: 116–17). On the other hand, the patronage of the Hellenistic courts was vital to the financial survival of many scholars and teachers; such a *chorēgia* was often by tradition coupled with some sort of educational duties towards the monarch's children, but antiquity's most famous example of royal patronage, the Museum of Alexandria, was apparently founded solely to support research and did not carry any teaching obligations (Marrou 1956: 261; Fraser 1972: 1.318). In the Roman period this kind of intellectual patronage could be found in the households of wealthy Romans (including, but not exclusively, that of the imperial family).

Moral training and the search for a lifestyle, finally, in Greco-Roman culture fall under the province of philosophy rather than religion (Clarke 1971: 85–99). Many fathers sent their children to a philosopher for a basic moral education (Clarke compares the atmosphere of a philosopher's school to that of a catechism or confirmation class, 1971: 96), but it was the philosophical schools above all which demanded, and often got, a lifelong commitment which has been likened to the effect of a religious conversion (Nock 1933).

C. Training in the Crafts

Training for any of the multitudinous craft or technical skills falls under the first of these four categories. This kind of professional training is the oldest and also the least documented area in Greek education. Plato, writing in the 4th century B.C., sees it as the norm that professional skills are passed down within families from father to son (*Protagoras* 328a1–6), and there is no lack of evidence that this was in fact the case (Burford 1972: 82–87). But Plato also speaks of students attaching themselves, for a fee, to teachers of such crafts as medicine or sculpture (*Prt.* 311b2–c8), and he implies that this was a well-established and widely-known phenomenon, as presumably it was. It is evident that some sort of apprenticeship system developed: we know little of its detailed working (Burford 1972: 87–91), but the dominance of the general pattern is clear. In order to learn how to be a sculptor, or a nail maker, or a flute player, you had either to be born into a family which possessed those skills or to attach yourself to a practitioner who could pass them on to you. A famous teacher might have had more than one such apprentice at any given time, but the fundamental pattern remains that of individual tuition, achieved largely through the age-old method of watching the expert at work and performing any tasks he might entrust to you.

When we use the word "school" in this context, we may mean either the group of pupils attached to any practitioner at one time or the continuity of the teaching tradition passed down in this way, as pupils eventually became practitioners and teachers, passing on to the next generation the accumulation of theoretical knowledge and practical experience which made up their particular *technē.* This teaching was fundamentally oral and practical in character, placing a high premium on personal contact with the teacher and on immersion in the living tradition of the craft (Burford 1972: 69): "learning out of a book" came a poor second to the "living voice" of the teacher (Galen *De comp. med. sec. loc.* VI pref.).

D. Rhetoric

The rhetorical schools, by contrast, fall largely under the second category: although a few in any school might go on to become professional rhetors, the vast majority of students would have enlisted solely because they were persuaded that a training in rhetoric was indispensable to a liberal education. In a suggestive discussion on the nature of the education offered by the sophist Protagoras, Plato explicitly contrasts the *paideia* of a gentleman with the professional training of the craft: "Why may you not learn of him in the same way that you learned the arts of the grammarian, or musician, or trainer, not with the view of making any of them a profession *(epi technē),* but only as a part of education *(epi paideia),* and because a private gentleman or a free man ought to know them?" (*Prt.* 312a1–b6, Jowett's translation). The idea of a non-professional "higher education" for the sons of the wealthy appears quite suddenly in Athens at the end of the 5th century B.C. Up to that time a general education (involving literacy skills, music, gymnastics, and mathematics) was seen as part of childhood, which finished at 14 with puberty and the passing into adulthood. The next stage was the (all-male) *ephebia,* essentially a kind of military service concentrating on physical education. Encouraged by Pericles, the Sophists came to Athens offering a new kind of teaching aimed not at those who needed a professional skill in order to earn a living, but at citizens of independent means. Their arrival and immediate success sparked an intense debate which in turn was responsible for the major 4th-century developments in the fields of rhetoric and philosophy. The distinction between this liberal education and the professional training already described was always carefully maintained. Thus music, a traditional part of a gentleman's education, gradually declined in importance amid fears that it was becoming a professional skill (Clarke 1971: 52–54). The debate between Socrates and the Sophists was partly over the issue of fees and the need to maintain the "amateur" status of rhetoric surfaces at intervals throughout antiquity (Clarke 1971: 28–32).

Following the success of the Sophists, rhetoric quickly emerged as the central component in the higher education of the free-born, and was to keep its place right through antiquity and on into the Middle Ages. The details of ancient rhetoric and its role in education are well documented: cf. Marrou 1956: Pt. 2 chap. 10 and Pt. 3 chap. 6; Clarke 1971: 28–45, 130–51. The content and systematization of rhetoric teaching grew rapidly in complexity, but in terms of school structures, rhetoric seems to have maintained the relatively archaic pattern seen in the activities of the Sophists. These were non-citizens, dependent on patronage for a welcome into the city and for introductions to potential clients (Kerferd 1981: 18–19). Protagoras, in Plato's dialogue of that name, is shown as using the house of his patron to make his initial contacts and to hold semi-public debates and instructional sessions (*Prt.* 314b6–316b6; see further Kerferd 1981: 17–23). Right through antiquity the sophist traveled from place to place, attracting attention first of all as a "star performer" of display rhetoric on his first arrival in a city (Philostr. *VS* 2.8). In this sense the "apprenticeship" model of the crafts is still basic here, in that the teacher first and foremost offers himself as a model to his pupils and claims to teach skills of which he himself is a practitioner. Clearly the most successful performer could expect to attract the most students (and charge the highest fees); it appears that a core of students would attach themselves to the sophist and move from place to place with him, while others would simply attend a course while he was in residence in a given city (Plato, *Prt.* 314e3–315b2).

Fourth-century rhetoric sees a huge explosion in the numbers seeking this kind of teaching, but fundamentally the same pattern continues of the individual teacher attracting a group of fee-paying pupils. The sources speak of phenomenonally large numbers attending the classes of some 4th-century rhetorical teachers (Isocrates is said to have had 100 pupils, though scholars debate whether this was a career total or the number attending at any one time [Marrou 1956: 494 n.11; Clarke 1971: 29 + n.128]). Either way, this may be a peculiarity of the period when Athens was the educational mecca for the whole Mediterranean world; as rhetoric established itself invincibly at the core of the educational system, what we see is not so much a growth in the size and complexity of rhetorical schools as a proliferation of small schools coupled with a gradual expansion of the "higher" forms of rhetorical training down the educational ladder to successively younger and younger children (Marrou 1956: 223–24). The tradition of mobility continues, but as time goes on we see a strong tendency for teachers to congregate in certain cultural centers, notably Athens, Alexandria, and Tarsus (Strab. 14.5.13 / C673–74): mobility thus became characteristic of students as much as of teachers (Bonner 1977: 90–96). This tendency may well have contributed to a "university" atmosphere for the young men involved without implying any collegiate structure, or even any concerted action, by their teachers, who operated essentially as private individuals conducting a commercial enterprise and competing for clients. Students lived in lodgings and could move from one teacher to another, listening to their display speeches or to semipublic teaching sessions, before making their choice of teacher or even when enrolled with one particular teacher.

E. Philosophy

The position of the philosophical schools on the grid is more complicated, ranging at different times and in differing degrees over categories II, III, and IV. Plato's portrayal of Socrates' dispute with the Sophists reflects his own struggle to establish philosophy, not rhetoric, as the central element in higher education (Marrou 1956 Pt 1, chaps. 6 and 7). The time when this ideal most nearly achieved success was the period of the flourishing of the Academy at the end of the 4th century, when a wide variety of subjects were taught to the thousands of wealthy young men who came to Athens from all over the Mediterranean world to finish their education there (we may compare the social appeal of "Oxbridge" or the "Ivy League" schools in England or the USA). Although philosophy eventually lost out to rhetoric on this front, it was not before the subject had achieved a lasting influence on the ancient ideal of a liberal education, to the extent that many would expect to spend some time with a philosopher during their studies. But philosophy had come into existence as an adult intellectual pursuit in Ionia and in the Greek colonies of the western Mediterranean, and even though its popularity in education waned in time, and the political upheavals of the Hellenistic age curtailed Athens' position as the major "university" city of the civilized world, the philosophical schools survived as communities of adults dedicated to the maintenance of the philosophic lifestyle and to the preservation and elaboration of the teachings of the founder.

The flowering of Ionian science and philosophy in the 6th and 5th centuries B.C. has left us the names of many famous teachers and their followers or companions *(hetairoi)*—e.g. Plato, *Soph.* 216a3. It has thus become customary to speak of the "schools" of Democritus or Parmenides; but virtually nothing is known of the organization of these "schools." The major exception is Pythagoras, who according to the traditional account "founded at Kroton in southern Italy a society which was at once a religious community and a scientific school" at the end of the 6th century B.C. (Burnet 1962: 39). This school had many of the characteristics later associated with monasticism (though it was open to women as well as to men): members lived in "lodges" and followed a strict dietary and mental discipline (*D.L.* 8.22). Even though the school did not last beyond the 4th century B.C., the community ideal it stood for exercised a profound influence on Greek thought about the nature of the philosophic life, reemerging as a conscious ideal in the 1st century B.C.; this can be seen most clearly in Iamblichus' treatise *On the Pythagorean Life,* which dates from the 4th century A.D. Nevertheless the very fame of this "Pythagorean" lifestyle suggests that it was not the normal pattern for the early philosophical schools.

A clearer picture emerges when we turn to the philosophers of Athens in the 5th and 4th centuries B.C. Socrates is portrayed in the dialogues of Plato as conducting purely informal instruction sessions in the streets of Athens and in the private houses of friends, as in *Resp.* 327a–c, 328b–c (although if we were to take seriously Aristophanes' description of Socrates' "*Phrontisterion*" or "Thinking-shop" [*Nub.* 94] we should have to assume with Burnet [1962: 147] that he actually had a school of the Ionian type). This apparent lack of social structure actually presupposes the restricted social world of the leisured youth of the Athenian upper classes. Unlike the Sophists, whom he castigates for charging fees for teaching "virtue" (Plato, *Prt.* 311–14, 318–20; *Soph.* 223–32), the Platonic Socrates refuses to regard the teaching of philosophy as a profession or trade on a par with the teaching of medicine or flute playing. This stance was only possible, however, in so far as both teacher and taught had independent means: Socrates' personal asceticism was famous, but he was not, like the later Cynics, a beggar.

The situation is very different when we come to the Academy of Socrates' most famous pupil, Plato. Possibly influenced by his knowledge of the Pythagorean communities, Plato created an institution which was to outlast its founder by almost a thousand years. The "Academy" proper was a gymnasium in a public park on the outskirts of Athens, where Plato bought land (*D.L.* 3.7) for a house and garden. Here he set up his school, constituting it legally as a *thiasos* or cultic community dedicated to Apollo and the Muses. Like the Pythagoreans, students at the Academy were expected to embrace a frugal lifestyle, and in later years the founder's birthday was celebrated as a festival with offerings, a festal meal, and a public disputation. The philosophical education which Plato offered was thus no longer conducted amidst the public life of the streets of Athens: the Academy is said to have had an inscription over the entrance reading "Let no-one enter who is not a geometer" (Elias in *Arist. Cat.* 118.18). There was a later tradition that Plato had charged no fees for his instruction, and that the financial strength of the Academy rested either on Plato's own wealth or on the accruing of legacies (Clarke 1971: 101). For the later Academy, see especially Dillon (1977).

This closed, institutionalized structure had certain clear advantages in the Hellenistic world that emerged after Alexander and was copied by the schools of Aristotle and Epicurus and, ultimately, by the great Museum of Alexandria. Thus when Aristotle came to Athens in 335 B.C. with the express purpose of setting up a second school to rival the Academy (and with the backing of Alexander), he too set about acquiring land as a permanent base for the school. As a non-Athenian he could not own land, and the Athenian authorities assigned him the "*Lyceum,*" a grove already sacred to Apollo and the Muses where a complex of buildings (including the famous covered walk or *peripatos* from which the school takes its name) soon grew up to house the growing numbers of students who flocked to the Lyceum (Grayeff 1974: 38). Like the Academy, the Peripatetic school bore a strong resemblance to a "society possessing a cult-center with buildings" (Fraser 1972: I.314), but legally speaking, the house, grounds, and other buildings were the property of the head of the school and his legal heirs: hence the importance of establishing the "succession" of heads (Theophrastus, Straton, Lykon), each of whom left a will detailing the property to be passed on to the next in line (*D.L.* 5.11–16, 51–57, 61–64, 70–74). By the time of Straton this includes such "collegiate" details as the dinner plates and glass for the common table (Fraser 1972: 2.314).

Stoicism has the name of being "the only philosophical school which taught in a public building" (*KlPauly* 5: 377–78). In one sense this is not entirely accurate (both the Academy and the Lyceum were public places), but it does convey accurately one important difference between the Stoics and the other philosophical schools. Stoicism never became a closed institution. To be a Stoic was to profess adherence to a set of doctrines and a body of wisdom passed down from Zeno and the great masters, perhaps to have studied with a teacher who made the same profession, but not necessarily to join—or ever to have joined—a body or group with a communal existence. Despite this, Stoics had a great feeling of "fellowship" with other Stoics and a profound loyalty to the accumulated body of wisdom associated with the school. Significantly, Seneca, one of the school's most influential adherents, still shows the traditional school preference for "personal converse and daily intimacy with someone" over the reading of philosophical books (Sen. *Ep.* 6.4). Arrian's *Discourses of Epictetus* provide us with a valuable picture of the operation of one Stoic school (in Nicopolis, Bithynia) at the end of the 1st century A.D. (Culpepper 1975: 135–40).

Epicurus, by contrast, seems to have set out deliberately to create a community withdrawn from the world: unlike Plato and Isocrates, he did not encourage his pupils to prepare themselves for public life, and even participation in the earlier stages of encyclic education was derided as unnecessary. Epicurus bought himself a house and a garden in Athens to serve as a base for the school, and his followers lived a communal life there in the pursuit of moral excellence, encouraged (perhaps by means of some sort of hierarchical system: cf. De Witt 1936) to correct and discipline each other in striving toward the ethical ideal. Devotion to the founder and his words was an integral part of this process; communal meals, the celebration of the founder's birthday, and other modes for reinforcing a communal identity were known in other philosophical schools, but this aspect of the life of the school was particularly marked among the Epicureans, who even had the founder's image on their rings and cups (Cic. *Fin.* 5.3). Since the school professed no interest in the training of its students for public life, women could be and were accepted as members (Culpepper 1975: 110–11). The house and garden survived as the center for an Epicurean community for many centuries, but Epicurus had also, unusually, assured the survival of his school by missionary activity in the eastern Aegean, which was enthusiastically taken up by his followers. The school of Epicurus was thus conscious almost from its inception of being a "sect" or "movement" broader than the individual group: each group of *philoi,* "friends," was part of a network which by Cicero's day was regarded as worldwide (Fin. 2.15.49). See further Clarke 1971: 69–82; Culpepper 1975: 101–21.

The Cynics in many ways represent a return to a "Socratic" anti-structure. Financial independence was achieved by begging: many Cynics were known as poor men of little education (Lucian, *Bis. Acc.* 6; Dio Chrys. *Or.* 32.9), but the Cynic's begging-bowl and staff were also an expression of a philosophic ideology which preached indifference to the goods of the cultured life. Like Socrates, the Cynics taught in the streets, engaging in debate with anyone, rich or poor, who would listen; hospitality also played a part in their teaching activity, since an invitation to join a rich man at dinner could mean an opportunity for further discussion and further spiritual therapy for the host (Diog. *Ep.* 38.3–5; Malherbe 1977: 163). Most Cynic teaching activity seems to have been of this casual variety, though we do hear of long-standing associations with Cynic teachers, such as that between the 1st-century Roman senator Thrasea Paetus and Demetrius the Cynic (Tac. *Ann.* 16.34). Nevertheless Cynicism was recognized in antiquity as one of the philosophical schools with its own distinctive teaching tradition and means of operation, and it is probable that, because of their non-elitist teaching methods, the Cynics would have been among the best-known philosophers in the Empire at large. See further Malherbe 1977; Clarke 1971: 84–85.

F. Medicine

Medical studies could be pursued in a wide variety of ways. On the grid suggested above, medicine belongs principally in categories I and III; but there was a (largely unsuccessful) lobby which would have liked to have seen medicine taught also under II, and when Galen argues that the best doctor is really a philosopher (Temkin 1953: 224; Galen 1.53–63/*Scripta Minora* 2.1–8), we are reaching into IV as well. Despite the abundance of Greek medical literature, however, it is not easy to draw up a clear picture of school structures in this area. The evidence we have points to a wide diversity (Drabkin 1944: 333), but overall it seems clear that the main medium of instruction was attachment to an individual teacher, sometimes at parental choice (e.g., Galen *Libr. Propr.* 4), so that essentially there was no structural difference between medicine, rhetoric, and other subjects.

Medicine in Greece was an ancient and revered craft or *technē*, passed down traditionally from father to son. The doctor "carried his skill from town to town, establishing in each a workshop or surgery *(iatreion)*" (Singer *OCD*: 549–50; Sigerist 1961: 306–307). Doctors, like other craftsmen, operated as individuals, but "what united them and gave them standing was that they belonged to a guild based on the fictitious assumption that physicians were descendants of Asclepius the hero: they were Asclepiads just as minstrels were Homerids" (Sigerist 1961: 57). See ASCLEPIUS, CULT OF. Whatever the mythic origins of this pattern, however, doctors, like other craftsmen, began at an early date to take pupils or apprentices into the "family" to learn the craft; Hippocrates, according to Plato, took fees for this instruction (*Prt.* 311b5–c2). It is interesting, however, that the so-called "Hippocratic oath," dating possibly from as late as the 1st century A.D., still places great stress on the archaic "family" pattern of instruction: the swearer promises "to hold him who has taught me this art as equal to my parents and to live my life in partnership with him, and if he is in need of money to give him a share of mine, and to regard his offspring as equal to my brothers in male lineage and to teach them this art—if they desire to learn it—without fee and covenant; to give a share of precepts and oral instruction and all the other learning to my sons and to the sons of him who has instructed me and to my pupils who have signed the covenant and have taken an oath according to the medical law, but to no one else" (Sigerist 1961: 301–4).

The classic pattern of medical instruction in antiquity was thus a matter of apprenticeship to an individual doctor who would train students while using their services as assistants in the sickroom and workshop. Numbers could be large: Marital's epigram (5.9) speaks of "a hundred" students accompanying the doctor on his rounds (Drabkin 1944: 335–36). It seems clear that this craft-based system of instruction remained the basic staple of medical training right through antiquity (Drabkin 1944: 333–38; Temkin 1953); even in Alexandria, where some of the most eminent physicians of the period had "research fellowships" at the Museum, students are described as being "of the house of" a master, which suggests that the old apprenticeship pattern survived alongside the more rarefied intellectual activity of the Museum (Fraser 1972: 1.357–58). As in rhetoric and philosophy, certain centers (like Cos, Cnidus and, later, Alexandria and Ephesus) came to be especially famous for medical teaching. Even so, Marrou (1956: 264–65) believes we have no warrant for speaking of "schools" in these places in the sense of a modern teaching "faculty": the individual teacher-pupil relationship was still the primary one, intensified by the "family" fiction and externalized through the passing down of oral and written tradition from one generation to the next.

But the inclusion of medical authorities among the beneficiaries of the Museum at Alexandria is a reminder that there was always a lively interest in the study of medicine among "amateurs," i.e., those who wished to pursue it not as a profession but as a matter of intellectual interest. There were a few lone voices who argued that some medical teaching should be included in the adolescent studies of every *pepaideumenos* (Drabkin 1944: 343), but generally speaking, lay interest in medicine was pursued at an adult level. Much of what we call "science" was included under "philosophy" by the Greeks, and the physical basis of medicine was among the subjects discussed by the philosophical schools of Ionia (Drabkin 1944: 342–43). The Hippocratic corpus contains polemic against such "philosophical" medicine (Temkin 1953: 217), and both Plato and Aristotle imply a distinction between the medical craft as craft and the more "scientific" investigation of the subject (Plato, *Leg.* 720d–e; Arist. *Pol.* 1282a3; Temkin 1953). Third-century B.C. Alexandria saw the birth of two major medical schools whose debates on the theoretical basis of medicine became well known outside professional circles (Deichgräber 1930); Galen in the 2d century A.D. bears witness to public interest in these "sects" *(haireseis)*, e.g., in *Libr. Propr.* 1–2. There is in fact ample evidence for a lively intellectual interest in the theory of medicine, catered for by public lectures and debates, not only among the "iatrosophists" of the 4th century A.D. (Drabkin 1944: 344–45), but by the activities of earlier lecturers like Galen (Bowersock 1969: chap. 5).

G. Mathematics and Technical Subjects

Information about schools in mathematics, architecture, engineering and other technical subjects is even harder to come by than in medicine. For most of these subjects, we possess a substantial amount of technical literature but virtually no information about its production. Mathematics had been securely established as an element in *paideia* since classical times, and the individual geometer, like the rhetor or grammarian, earned his living from the pupils who were sent to him to complete this part of their "encyclic" education (Marrou 1956: 243–55; 378–79; Clarke 1971: 45–54). Mathematics had also been regarded since Pythagoras as a component in philosophy. But for the major mathematical achievements of the Hellenistic world, either patronage or financial independence seem to have been a prerequisite: the correspondence of the great names of the 3d century B.C., Archimedes, Eratosthenes, and Apollonius of Perga, breathes the atmosphere of the leisured intellectual rather than that of the schoolroom, and their writings are individual compositions rather than school texts. Eratosthenes certainly felt the benefit of Ptolemaic patronage as head of the Library in Alexandria; Archimedes had a close (but undefined) relationship with King Hiero of Syracuse, to whose son he dedicated one of his books; the Attalus to whom Apollonius dedicated some of his books may have been (but is not certainly) the king of Pergamum. Unlike these three, Euclid is known as the head of a school (also in Alexandria), but little is known of its structure (Fraser 1972 1.376–425).

Architecture, like medicine, was regarded as a "liberal" profession, i.e., one that could be practiced without loss of social status (Cic. *off.* 1.150), and Vitruvius in the 1st century B.C. did his best to argue that the subject should form part of the *enkuklios paideia.* Nevertheless most of the pupils of the *architectus magister* were probably destined for the profession, and it appears that the teacher would rely as much on the exercise of his profession for financial survival as on the fees he received from teaching (Clarke 1971: 113–14). Essentially, we have here the same pattern as we have observed in medicine, where instruction is gained by a form of apprenticeship to a practicing master.

As Marrou points out (1956: 263), "the same absence of documentary evidence forces us to the same conclusion in the case of all the other technical experts—the engineers (civil and military), surveyors and sailors who are so familiar in Hellenistic society and yet so strangely absent from its education. . . . The technician, like the scientist, learned his job in a very simple, archaic way, the way of personal relationship between master and pupil, craftsman and apprentice." It is significant that we have a number of texts in this area which must derive from a teaching situation, without any ancient evidence as to their social context: papyrus exercises in practical calculation and mensuration (Marrou 1956: 263) and textbooks like those of Hero of Alexandria, which contain a kind of practical mathematics derived ultimately from Babylonian tradition and distinct from the philosophical mathematics of Euclid (Neugebauer 1969: 80; 157–58). We do know, however, that patronage played some role in the development of Hellenistic technology, particularly in the field of siege warfare (Philo of Byzantium, *Belopoeica pref.* Th50.24–26). One of the few names in the field of technology to achieve fame is that of Ctesibius, who is connected with Alexandria and appears to have founded a school there (Fraser 1972: 1.431–32).

H. Philo

Any survey of the Hellenistic schools must also ask questions about the social milieu of the Philonic corpus. Was Philo's vast exegetical output simply the expression of an individual literary whim? (And if so, who preserved it?) Bousset's hypothesis of an "exegetical academy" in Alexandria has now been "either rejected or carefully qualified by most Philonists" (Culpepper 1975: 197, 204–205). Nevertheless, it is now clear that Philo's exegetical activity must be placed within a "scholastic tradition" (Culpepper 1975: 205–206) and equally clear that Philo himself located the bulk of this scholastic activity within the sabbath-day teaching of the synagogues, which he describes (in an intentional comparison with the Greek philosophical schools) as "schools of Moses" (*Vita Mos* II 215–16; *Spec Leg* II 62; *Hypothetica* 7.12–14). It is less clear whether the whole of Philo's expository work can be satisfactorily accounted for in the context of normal synagogue teaching and preaching; Culpepper suggests that "his writings were probably used in a synagogue-school where Philo taught the higher vision of scripture to a select group of initiates whose ears were purified" (1975: 211–12). Whatever the merits of this suggestion, it is worth noting in this context the structural importance of the dominant "individual tuition" pattern which we have already observed in the Hellenistic schools. This pattern explains why we often have "school" texts surviving where nothing is known of any school structures beyond the basic presumption of a teacher and a succession of students. As we suggested above, this in itself is sufficient to create the conditions for a "school" tradition which may be concretized in written form: there is no need to postulate "school" structures where we do not know of their existence. Galen provides a useful parallel to Philo in this respect: despite the enormous volume of his writings, and despite his vigorous activity as a teacher and public lecturer, Galen's name is not associated with the founding of any "school."

Bibliography

Bickerman, E. 1952. La chaîne de la tradition pharisienne. *RB* 59: 44–54.
Bonner, S. F. 1977. *Education in Ancient Rome from the elder Cato to the younger Pliny.* London.
Bowersock, G. 1969. *Greek Sophists in the Roman Empire.* Oxford.
Burford, A. 1972. *Craftsmen in Greek and Roman Society.* London.
Burnet, J. 1962. *Greek Philosophy: Thales to Plato.* London.
Clarke, M. L. 1971. *Higher Education in the Ancient World.* London.
Culpepper, R. A. 1975. *The Johannine School.* SBLDS 26. Missoula, MT.
Deichgräber, K. 1930. *Die griechischer Empiririkerschule.* Berlin.
De Witt, N. 1936. Organization and Procedure in Epicurean Groups. *CP* 31: 205–11.
Dillon, J. 1977. *The Middle Platonists.* London.
Drabkin, I. E. 1944. On Medical Education in Greece and Rome. *Bulletin of the History of Medicine.* 15: 333–51.
Fraser, P. M. 1972. *Ptolemaic Alexandria.* 3 vols. Oxford.
Grayeff, F. 1974. *Aristotle and His School.* London.
Kerferd, G. B. 1981. *The Sophistic Movement.* Cambridge.

Malherbe, A. 1977. *The Cynic Epistles.* SBLSBS 12. Missoula, MT.
Marrou, H. I. 1956. *A History of Education in Antiquity.* Trans. G. Lamb. 3d ed. New York.
Neugebauer, O. 1969. *The Exact Sciences in Antiquity* 2d ed. New York.
Nock, A. D. 1933. *Conversion.* Oxford.
Sigerist, H. E. 1961. *A History of Medicine.* Vol. 2: *Early Greek, Hindu and Persian Medicine.* New York.
Temkin, O. 1953. Greek Medicine as Science and Craft. *Isis* 44: 213–25.

LOVEDAY C. A. ALEXANDER

SCORPION. See ZOOLOGY.

SCREEN [Heb *māsāk*]. A word that denotes three items used in the construction of the Tabernacle according to the priestly accounts in Exodus. The Hebrew noun is derived from the root *skk,* which means "to screen, cover." All three screens are used at entrances to various parts of the Tabernacle and its compound.

The innermost screen, also called the *pārōket,* or "veil," was used to divide the innermost sacred space from the outer sanctum (Exod 35:12; 39:34; Num 3:31; 4:5). This screen, supported by four pillars, thus shielded the ark from the view of priests ministering to the items in the outer sanctum (Exod 40:3, 21). The splendid features of this screen are presented in the description of the veil (Exod 26:31–35; 36:35–36): it used the best textiles (colored wools mixed with twined linen) and the most elaborate workmanship, which included decorations of cherubim. But see TABERNACLE for another view of the nature of the "veil."

The next important passageway, dividing the Tabernacle itself from the surrounding court, was covered with a screen that used the same fine textiles, but was not decorated with cherubim, as was the inner screen (Exod 26:36–37; 35:15; 36:37–38; 39:38; 40:5, 28; Num 3:25). This screen was supported on five pillars made of acacia and covered with gold.

The third screen was placed at the gate to the courtyard (Exod 27:16; 35:17; 38:18; 39:40; 40:8, 33; Num 3:26; 4:26). This screen was twenty cubits long and was hung on four pillars with silver fittings. Its workmanship and fabric were the same as for the screen at the door to the Tabernacle.

These fabric dividers are not mentioned in the descriptions of the Jerusalem Temple, where wooden doors marked the divisions between the various chambers of the Temple and courtyard, that is, between zones of holiness. The mention of the *pārōket* veil by the Chronicler (2 Chr 3:4) may be the result of the influence of P materials. It is also possible that, unlike the First Temple, the Second Temple may have used such a veil, a fact perhaps known to the Chronicler. Herod's Temple almost certainly had the inner veil, but the presence of the two other screens is less likely (see Matt 27:51; Heb 6:19; 9:3). See also VEIL.

CAROL MEYERS

SCRIBAL EMENDATIONS. This title refers to a tradition that the Hebrew text of the Bible has been changed in a number of passages. The two earliest sources (ca. 400 C.E.), both midrashic, are the *Mek.* of R. Ishmael, which lists eleven cases, and *Sipre,* which lists seven. Later midrashic and masoretic sources list more cases. The masorah states that such change has occurred in eighteen cases, but the lists vary somewhat in composition, so that altogether some two dozen cases are mentioned. In many manuscripts the *masorah parva* marks each case as "one of the eighteen cases of emendation," but this is not done in the Aleppo or the Leningrad Codex.

The terminology describing the change is *tiqqûn sōpĕrîm,* "emendation of the scribes" (some lists replace "scribes" with "Ezra" or "The men of the Great Synagogue") or *kinnâ hakkātûb* "the text has substituted (one wording for another)." The changes are said to have been made to avoid language which might seem disrespectful to God.

In most cases, the change suggested involves only a single letter representing a pronoun, as in Ps 106:20, where "They exchanged their glory *(kbwdm)* for the likeness of an ox that eats grass" is said to have read originally "my glory" *(kbwdy).* A similar change is suggested in Jer 2:11. In a few cases, a more extensive change is suggested, as in Gen 18:22, where "Abraham was still standing before God" is said to have read originally "God was still standing before Abraham." In the majority of cases (as in these two), the Greek translation does not reflect the text said to have been original. This also appears to be the case with the Habbakkuk commentary from Qumran (1QpHab) for the case in Hab 1:12.

In a few cases the Greek translation may reflect the original text, as in 1 Sam 3:13, where the received Hebrew texts reads "His sons brought a curse on themselves" *(mqllym lhm),* and the Greek reads "His sons spoke evil of God." This passage, however, exemplifies the considerable problem of evaluating this tradition. The standard Hebrew text is considered problematic, because the verb in the case is elsewhere used with a direct object (not the preposition *l-,* as here), and means simply to "curse." The same problem occurs with the text which the tradition gives as the original: "cursed him" *(mqllym lw).* Moreover, in the context, the pronoun "him" must refer to Eli, so no disrespect to God would have been involved. There is also a problem if, as many modern critics argue, the original text read "cursed God" *(mqllym ʾlhm),* as is suggested by the LXX. The cursing of God, which is forbidden in Exod 22:27 and Lev 24:15, would be excellent justification for the punishment of the house of Eli with which the passage is concerned. However, if the original text did have this reading, the received text is much more likely to have arisen through the accidental omission of *ʾalep* from *ʾlhm* than from a deliberate change. Such considerations lead some scholars to argue that the tradition of "emendation" is merely a form of midrashic interpretation, intended to supply a reason for an apparent illogicality in the text.

On the other hand, there is no good reason to suggest that such changes could not have been made, especially if they were made at an early period, as the evidence of the Greek translation suggests. Only 3 verses in the Torah are affected: Gen 18:22 is not included in the early lists, whereas Num 11:15 and 12:12 are included (in Num 12:12

ʾ*mw* and *bśrw* are counted separately). Even here changes would be justified, according to some Talmudic sages, who argued that a change in one letter of the text was justified to avoid profanation of the name of God. Most modern scholars would agree that the inclusion of a passage in this list of emendations may well show that the text was changed in ancient times to avoid some problem, but they would not necessarily accept as authentic the wording identified by the tradition to be original. No doubt the best approach is to treat each case on its own merits.

The Talmud uses the term *ʿiṭṭûr sōpĕrîm,* "omission by the scribes," of five passages, in most of which the conjunction is expected but does not occur, as in Gen 18:5, where ʾ*ḥr* appears, but *w*ʾ*ḥr* is expected. The term *miqrāʾ sōpĕrîm,* "reading of the scribes," is the title given to a list composed of the words ʾ*rṣ, šmym, mṣrym* (earth, heaven, Egypt). The significance of the title and list is wholly uncertain. In the case of the "omissions," it is difficult to see why the conjunction should have been omitted in the instances named. It is equally difficult to see why the term should not have been used in the many other cases in which the conjunction is expected but does not occur, if the term is just a means of explaining its absence.

It is quite possible that these traditions of "emendation," "omission," or "reading" reflect a partially forgotten period of editorial activity. During this time, some biblical passages may have been modified, with no support from earlier tradition, in accordance with some view held at that time. However, the available evidence suggests that any such activity was sporadic, and antedated the Greek translation. The many anomalies in wording, spelling, and vowel pointing which have been carefully preserved in the text show that any suggestion that "the scribes" ever made a systematic attempt to "normalize" some feature of the text is untenable. See also BIBLE, EUPHEMISM AND DYSPHEMISM IN THE.

Bibliography

McCarthy, C. 1981. *The Tiqqunê Sopherim.* OBO 36. Göttingen.

McKane, W. 1974. Observations on the *tikkûnê sôperîm.* Pp. 53–77 in *Language, Culture, and Religion: Essays in Honor of Eugene A. Nida,* ed. M. Black and W. A. Smalley. The Hague.

E. J. REVELL

SCRIBES. The Hebrew word for scribe *(sôpēr)* comes from the Semitic root *spr,* originally meaning a written message which was sent, then meaning "writing," and finally meaning "writer." The Greek word for scribe *(grammateus)* comes from the word *gramma,* which means something drawn and, most commonly, written letters. In various combinations this root in Greek refers to all aspects of writing and education. The word "scribe" in Hebrew, Greek, and other languages had a wide range of meaning that changed over time and could denote several social roles. The closest English equivalent is the term "secretary," which refers to roles from that of a typist to a cabinet officer at the highest level of government. In both Semitic and Greek usage, the scribe was commonly a middle-level government official, for example, a "secretary" in charge of the town council (Acts 19:35). Major political bodies in Athens each had a scribe as one of their officers (see Kraeling 1958: 94–102).

A. The Near East
B. Old Testament
C. Greco-Roman Period
D. Jewish Literature
E. Diaspora
F. New Testament
G. Rabbinic Literature
H. Inscriptions

A. The Near East

Egypt and Mesopotamia provide detailed information on the social position, roles, and education of scribes. From the 3d millennium on scribes were situated in the royal court and in the temples. Their duties included administrating and keeping records of tax collection, forced labor, military activities, commodities, and building projects. For example, in Egypt they supervised land measurement after the annual Nile flood; drafted correspondence, contracts, and treaties; and at the highest level kept the royal annals, collected laws, preserved scared traditions, and were experts in astronomy, omens, and other religious rites and activities. Scribes occupied high posts as royal secretaries in charge of royal correspondence and as such functioned as counselors and high officials.

In Egypt boys were brought to the court or temple and trained to read and write. Practice ostraca found behind one temple testify to an open-air school, and one text suggests that initial training took four years (Williams 1972: 216). After training in a school, a young man was apprenticed to a scribe; more advanced young scribes were sometimes apprenticed to high officials as potential replacements. Training seems to have consisted of copying, reciting, and memorizing various traditional materials. Advanced students had access to grammatical treatises, lists of idioms, catalogs of natural phenomena, and didactic treatises which taught them how to write, speak, and behave in a correct way. It is likely that scribes in high office had to know more than one language. Students were exhorted to learn their difficult lessons both by corporal punishment and the threat that they would be transferred to a more arduous and less pleasant manual occupation (see Williams 1975: 238–41).

B. Old Testament

The first scribe in the OT appears in the Song of Deborah as a muster officer (Judg 5:14). The chief scribe at the Jerusalem court was a high cabinet officer concerned with finance, policy, and administration (2 Kgs 22; Jer 36:10), and Baruch, who recorded Jeremiah's words, was a scribe (Jer 36:32) who moved among the highest government officials. Though there is little direct evidence for scribal schools in Israel, their presence is very probable, especially in major cities (LeMaire 1981). In addition, the Wisdom literature reflects scribal and school activity similar to that found in Egypt and Mesopotamia.

In the postexilic period the most well-known scribe in the Bible is Ezra, a priest and a "scribe skilled in the Law of Moses" (Ezra 7:6), who asked the Persian king Artaxerxes for permission to lead a party of exiled Jews back to

Jerusalem. The king ordered various officials to give Ezra the resources he needed for the return and the resumption of worship (7:21–22). The king commissioned Ezra to appoint magistrates and judges who knew the law of God and the king (7:25–26). In Ezra 8–10, Ezra the scribe functions as the leader of the returnees in conjunction with leading priests, Levites, and families. Though Ezra is of high priestly stock, he does not officiate at the cult but is a religious leader, while Nehemiah is governor (Nehemiah 8–9). As such he exercised the office of teacher and priest by reading from the Law to the people while a group of Levites helped the people understand the law and led the people in prayer and sacrifice (Ezra 8).

Because of confusion in the chronology and sources of Ezra and Nehemiah, Ezra's exact office and power is a matter of dispute. Schaeder argued that "scribe" was the title of a Persian official appointed to govern Judea and that Ezra was the governor. Galling disputed him and understood "scribe" as an office in the Jewish Diaspora community, but this view depends on a number of controversial textual interpretations. Some recent archaeological evidence suggests that Ahzai was governor when Ezra arrived in 458, and this leads Talmon (*IDBSup,* 317–28) to deny that Ezra was a Persian official. It is very questionable, therefore, whether Ezra was governor. He was certainly a recognized authority in the Jewish community because he was of high priestly descent and also learned in the law. He had enough access to the Persian court to obtain a favor from the king and enough community standing to lead a group to Jerusalem and establish himself there. The continuing problems with intermarriage and the opposition to Ezra indicate that he was one of a number of influential and powerful forces in the Jerusalem community but that his views did not immediately predominate.

One other scribe appears in Ezra and Nehemiah—Zadok, who was appointed with a priest and Levite to be a treasurer of the storehouses where the tithes were brought (Neh 12:12–13). This text suggests that scribes were part of society and its leadership in Jerusalem. In the postexilic Jewish community the roles of priests, Levites, scribes, and other Jewish leaders overlapped. Ezra was a priest, scribe, and community leader, and possibly a government-appointed leader (Ezra 7). The Levites taught (Nehemiah 8), and in the view of the Chronicler, which probably reflects the postexilic situation, some Levites served as scribes (1 Chr 24:6; 2 Chr 34:13). Even though the Chronicler is promoting the rights of the Levites, his advocacy shows that scribal activity was consistent with priestly and levitical activities (see *IDBSup,* 317–28).

Scribal activity by a variety of groups (priests, prophets, visionaries, scribes, and other community leaders) must be postulated in order to account for the composition and editing of the biblical collection during the exilic and postexilic periods. Fishbane (1985: 78–84) has isolated the activities of scribes who copied the biblical text and engaged in unsystematic interpretation by making comments and clarifications, some of which have been incorporated into the text. It is not clear whether the scribes also belonged to the circles which produced the biblical traditions, but certainly they had responsibility for its transmission. Scribes or people with scribal skills must have been part of priestly, prophetic, and leadership circles at all times. While it is difficult to prove historical continuity, the nature of the biblical materials in their Near Eastern cultural setting makes the hypothesis of a continuous and diverse scribal tradition very likely.

C. Greco-Roman Period

The Greeks had a lively scribal tradition and often appointed learned individuals, scribes, sophists, and teachers to government offices and councils. The first evidence for scribal officials in Hellenistic Palestine is contained in a letter of Antiochus III to his governor of Coele-Syria, Ptolemy, in which he exempted the senate *(gerousia),* priests, temple scribes, and temple singers from several taxes (Josephus *Ant* 12.3.3 §§138–44). Scribes appear once in 1 Maccabees and are somehow associated with the Hasideans. During the Maccabean revolt (167–164 B.C.E.) a group of "pious ones" or "Hasideans" *(ḥasîdîm)* joined the Maccabees in their struggle against Antiochus IV: "Then there united with them [Mattathias and his friends] a company of Hasideans, mighty warriors of Israel, everyone who offered himself for the law" (1 Macc 2:42). After the death of Antiochus and the accession of Demetrius I "a group of scribes appeared in a body before Alcimus [the new high priest, appointed by the king] and Bacchides [the king's governor] to ask for just terms. The Hasideans were the first among the sons of Israel to seek peace from them, for they said, 'A priest of the line of Aaron has come with the army, and he will not harm us' " (1 Macc 7:12–14). Eventually Alcimus killed sixty of those who made peace (1 Macc 7:16). The two sentences mentioning the scribes and Hasideans follow one another awkwardly and the relationship between the two is not clear. The scribes may have been a part of the Hasideans or the Hasideans part of the scribal class. The motive for the pietists' actions, that a priest of the line of Aaron would not harm them, bespeaks a great confidence in the traditional institutions and laws of Israel and perhaps a certain interpretation of Israel's history which stressed confidence in God and the sanctity of the priesthood. It is clear that the scribes are associated with the pietists and with defense of the Jewish way of life. Because they could come to Alcimus as a group and were the object of an assassination plot, they probably had some influence or power and were perceived as a threat by the government. They were part of the political leadership of Judaism but in a subordinate position where they were open to the kind of oppression they suffered at the hands of Alcimus. In 2 Maccabees, Eleazar, a leading scribe (6:18), dies for the law and as an example to younger Jews. The author conceived of scribes as prominent leaders in Jewish Palestinian society, notable for their nobility, virtue, and community responsibility.

Josephus uses "scribe" in the usual Greco-Roman way for officials at all levels from village to royal court. He does not use the term for an organized social group, nor does he use it for groups especially devoted to the law, like the Pharisees. In the first half of the *Antiquities,* when Josephus is summarizing the Bible, he retains scribes where they appear as royal officials or as individuals (Baruch, Ezra) and occasionally adds them to the biblical account as mid-level officials serving the king. For example, when the Israelites defeated the Philistines in battle (1 Sam 14:31–35), they began to kill animals and eat them without observing the laws for slaughter of animals. The Hebrew says someone ("they") told Saul about it; Josephus says that the scribes told him (*Ant* 6.6.4 §120). Scribes are community officials with access to the king and responsibility for supervising observance of the law. According to 1 Chr 23:1–6, just before his death David organized the Levites according to tasks with six thousand assigned to be officers (*šoṭerîm*) and judges. Josephus translates "officers" as "scribes" (*Ant* 7.14.7 §364), since he understood scribes to be government officials. Scribes are also government record keepers. When David took a census of the people (2 Sam 24:1) he sent Joab and the commanders of the army to take the census. Josephus understood census-taking as a scribal and not a military activity, so in his account Joab takes the chiefs of the tribes and the scribes with him (*Ant* 7.13.1 §319). In the story of Esther, scribes are twice added to the story by Josephus as keepers of records (Esth 6:1; *Ant* 11.6.10 §§248, 250; Esth 9:3; *Ant* 11.6.13 §287). Josephus refers to temple scribes in the letter of Antiochus III above and in his version of Ezra 7:24, where the Persian king exempts from "tribute, custom or toll" the following groups: priests, Levites, singers, doorkeepers, temple servants, and other servants of the house of God. The last two repetitious and vague terms are translated by 1 Esdras (8:22), Josephus' source, as temple servants (*hierodouloi*) and temple functionaries (*pragmatikoi*). Josephus replaces 1 Esdras' unclear category *pragmatikoi* with "scribes of the Temple" (*Ant* 11.5.1 §128).

While writing of the Herodian period, Josephus refers to village scribes of very low status (*JW* 1.24.3 §479), Diophantes a scribe and high official of Herod (*JW* 1.26.3 §529), and Aristeas, priest and scribe of the council (*boulē*), killed during the siege of Jerusalem (*JW* 5.13.1 §532). Josephus understands scribes to be both high and low officials associated with king, temple, and village.

D. Jewish Literature

The presence of scribes in the Hellenistic period is witnessed by Jewish literature whose very abundance testifies to scribal traditions and efforts. The Enoch tradition, with its early interest in calendar and astronomical matters (*1 Enoch* 72–82), the Wisdom books and stories (Qoheleth, Daniel 1–6, Ecclesiasticus), and the variety of literary products of this period testify to intense authorial activity and educational support for such activity. The scribal activity and separatist tendencies in the Enoch traditions were intensified later in the Qumran community's traditions and in those of many other nameless groups of the Greco-Roman period. During the Hellenistic period Judaism produced a vast amount of literature, and this authorial activity argues for a strong core of educated Jews and an educational establishment, including scribes fulfilling their normal range of duties.

The most famous description of the scribe in Jewish literature is given by Ben Sira in the early 2d century (38:24–39:11). He attributes to the ideal scribe all areas of knowledge, high government station, and lasting fame. The wisdom of the scribe is closely linked with and dependent on God because his main source of knowledge is the "law of the Most High," the study of which leads him "to seek out the wisdom of the ancients" and "be concerned with prophecies." He will also "preserve the discourse of notable men and penetrate the subtleties of parables; he will seek out the hidden meanings of proverbs and be at home with the obscurities of parables" (39:1–3). Ben Sira conceived of the scribe as an expert in what had by then become the three parts of the Hebrew Bible, the law (Torah), prophets, and writings. The scribe is not simply a scholar or teacher in the modern mold, but a high official, advisor to the governing class, and international ambassador and traveler (39:4; 38:32–33). The foundation for the scribes' social leadership is not birth or wealth but knowledge of discipline (*paideia,* education, culture), judgment, and proverbs (*parabolais,* parables, similitudes). In Ben Sira the understanding of scribe has been widened so that it is almost equivalent to that of the wiseman. Ben Sira also seems to have conceived of himself as a scribe (39:9–10) and he may have been a teacher with a school in Jerusalem (51:23; if the hymn in chap. 51 is original to Ben Sira and the description of his situation correct, and if *bet midraš* is correctly translated as "school").

Scribes are also mentioned in other Jewish literature. In the first section of *1 Enoch* (1–36), which dates from before the Maccabean revolt, Enoch is twice referred to as a scribe of righteousness (12:3–4; 15:1) and sent as a messenger to the Watchers, a group of angels who have sinned against God. At the beginning of the *Epistle of Enoch* (92:1), which dates from the latter part of the 2d century or earlier, Enoch appears as the scribe who has written this part of the book: "Written by Enoch the scribe—this complete wisdom teaching." In *2 Baruch,* an apocalypse written after the destruction of the temple in 70 C.E., the scribe Baruch appears as a community leader whose authority now exceeds that of the prophet Jeremiah (2:1; 9:1–10:4) contrary to the biblical text. He carries out traditional scribal tasks of writing to the exiles and also prophetic tasks of receiving revelation. The community looks to him for guidance and for knowledge of God's will in a time of crisis. It seems that the author and his community understand scribes as heirs to the prophets, interpreters of the Bible, and visionaries. Such an understanding of the scribal office fits well an apocalyptic group because apocalyptic literature has strong links with traditional and mantic wisdom. For example, Daniel, an archetypical apocalyptic seer, is a wise man and an official in Babylon.

E. Diaspora

The Palestinian use of "scribe" for an official, wise man, and religious leader may have differed from that in the Diaspora. In the *Letter of Aristeas to Philocrates* the translators of the Hebrew Bible into Greek are presented as highborn Jews distinguished by education or scholarship (*paideia*) and knowledge of the literature of the Jews and Greeks. They have some specifically Greek accomplishments, including a talent for talking about the law (the ability to speak well was an essential Greek virtue for the educated person). They seek the "mean," an Aristotelian ideal of virtue, they are not uncouth, nor conceited in dealing with others and they can listen and comment appropriately. In addition, they are also qualified for embassies. While in Egypt on an embassy they discuss kingship with the king, a typical concern of both wisdom literature and Greek philosophy. The description of this group fits the wisdom ideal of the scribe attached to the highest levels of the ruler's court and has much in common with the scribe as depicted in Ben Sira. The translators and the scribe are wise men who know the whole tradition, can function in international situations, and have the talent to be leaders, judges, and scholars. In the Hellenistic age the international ideal of the wise man endured in the Near East and Israel, both in Palestine and in the Diaspora, and continued to adapt and evolve to meet changing circumstances and the development of the Jewish tradition. The use of the term "scribe" in Ben Sira and its absence in *Aristeas* may reflect Palestinian and Diaspora usage. The Alexandrian Jewish community was led by educated, wealthy, highborn people of the type depicted in *Aristeas*. Since the Jewish community had very limited independence and Jews were not Alexandrian citizens, the community may not have had an official class of scribes, in contrast to Jerusalem. Similarly the Greek prologue to Ben Sira, written by his grandson in Alexandria, does not refer to Ben Sira as a scribe, even though Ben Sira implies that he is a scribe in the book. The Greek term scribe *(grammateus)* does not seem to have been used for a learned wiseman or teacher or translator but for a government official or copiest. Further evidence for this view is found in Josephus who refers to teachers of the law as *sophistai* (*JW* 1.33.2 §648) and characterizes them by descriptive expressions such as most learned (*Ant* 17.6.2 §149) but not as scribes. Josephus is probably following the Greek usage of his audience rather than Palestinian usage. One other indication of this usage can be found in *4 Macc.* 5:4, a Diaspora work where Eleazar, called a scribe in 2 Macc (above), is identified as a priest, presumably because the leadership role attributed to him is more proper for priests than scribes in the Greek world.

F. New Testament

More than in any other source the scribes are seen as a unified group in the NT, but this view may not be historically accurate. The Synoptic Gospel writers see the scribes as a group opposed to Jesus but say very little about their other characteristics. In Mark the scribes are associated with Jerusalem and the chief priests as part of the government of Judaism. Though their roles are not specified, their close association with the chief priests means they functioned as high officials and advisors. Some scribes who appeared in Galilee were identified as coming from Jerusalem (3:22; 7:1). Their teachings are referred to in an offhand way, which suggests that they were recognized as authoritative teachers of Jewish law and custom (1:22; 9:11). Mark presents them as a unified political group because for him their salient unifying characteristic is opposition to Jesus. Actually, the scribes probably stand for a plethora of Jewish community officials, many of them actual scribes, who opposed Jesus' claim to authority and his growing popularity.

For Matthew both the scribes and Pharisees had many interests in common and were the learned groups par excellence in Judaism. The scribes were connected both with village life and the leaders in Jerusalem and were part of the middle leadership of Judaism. Matthew approves of scribes because he recognizes the scribal role in the new Christian community (13:52; 23:34). His quarrel is not with the role of scribes as learned guides of the community and guardians of the tradition, but with the Jewish scribes' opposition to Jesus. It is very likely that Matthew's view of scribes as community leaders in the Galilean villages reflects more the situation of his church, in which he himself was a scribe (13:52; cf. 23:34), than conditions in Palestine before the war.

In Luke-Acts the scribes are less distinct as a group and more like an appendage of the Pharisees, united to them by belief in resurrection. At the time of Jesus' death the scribes are associated with the chief priests in Jerusalem as they are in Mark and Matthew. In Acts the scribes continue to appear as learned leaders in Jerusalem who are active in protecting Judaism. Luke also inserts a new category of leader, the lawyer. "Lawyer" replaces "scribe" in one instance (10:25; cf. Mk 12:28), and lawyers are similar to scribes and Pharisees (7:30; 11:45; 14:3). Luke adds no new evidence for 1st century Palestine. His understanding of the scribes is either vague (he conflates them with the Pharisees) or guided by the general functions of scribes in the Greco-Roman world.

The scribes presented in the Synoptic Gospels are best understood as bureaucrats and experts on Jewish life. They could have been low-level officials and judges both in Jerusalem and in the towns and villages of the country. Mark, possibly the most reliable of the gospels, which may reflect conditions in Palestine just before or after the war and which most probably has traditions from the middle of the 1st century, places scribes mainly in or from Jerusalem and only twice simply in Galilee (2:6; 9:14). The presence of scribes in Jerusalem as officials and in Galilean villages as copyists and low-level officials is very probable. The gospels testify most reliably to scribes connected to the government in Jerusalem, and their role there seems to be as associates of the priests, both in judicial proceeding and enforcement of Jewish custom and law, and ongoing business in the Sanhedrin. It is likely that the scribes did not constitute a unified social organization or class, as the NT claims, but rather fulfilled a number of roles in different parts of society. The gospel traditions about scribes may reflect the opposition of many scattered local officials to early Christian communities before and after the war and perhaps opposition to Jesus also.

"Scribe" is used once in Paul's letters, where he contrasts the wisdom of the world with the foolishness of the cross and claims that the cross is true wisdom. In the course of his attack he cites scripture and then asks rhetorically, "Where is the wise man *(sophos)*, where is the scribe *(grammateus)*, where is the debater *(suzētētēs)* of this age?" (1 Cor 1:20). Paul seems to be referring to well-known terms for educated intellectual leaders in the Greco-Roman world.

G. Rabbinic Literature

The Mishnah and other rabbinic collections refer sporadically to the scribes *(sôperîm)* as early authoritative teachers to whom a number of rulings and legal interpretations are attributed. Modern historical reconstructions of the development of Jewish law have usually identified the scribes as the Jewish scholars who had great influence on Judaism from the time of Ezra down to the time of the pairs (*m. ʾAbot* 1:5–11) in the 2d century (Lauterbach 1973: 27–29; 163–94). The scribes are often identified as members of the Great Assembly, the legendary ruling body of

Judaism during this period. See SANHEDRIN. Scholars have differed concerning whether or not they were priests, when their influence ceased, and the scope of their teachings. Some attribute certain anonymous teachings of the Mishnah to them, but no clear critical method has been constructed for isolating these traditions. Lauterbach holds that they first commented on Scripture in midrash and then developed the Mishnaic form of teaching, but this view has been challenged. All these interpretations of the scribes have treated them as a cohesive body with a well-defined agenda and independent power, but the evidence for this position is very weak.

That the scribes were not an organized group with its own teaching can be seen in the rulings explicitly attributed to the scribes in rabbinic literature. Rules which are designated the "words of the scribes" *(dibrê sôperîm)* are scattered in the sources and so form no coherent body of teaching. In the Mishnah the scribes are used as the source for teachings which are thought to be ancient or for rulings which are not fully accepted or are of less authority than Scripture. For example, the restrictions concerning eating the fruit of young trees are said to apply outside the land of Israel as well as inside as a matter of halaka, that is, biblical law which is generally accepted as such in rabbinic teaching (*m. ʿOr.* 3:9). On the other hand, the restrictions concerning growing diverse crops together are also binding outside the land of Israel, but only by authority of the "words of the scribes," which may mean a supposed ancient enactment or simply rabbinic teaching. In view of the fact that other passages which refer to the words of the scribes seem to imply that the traditions derive from older and reliable authorities, this passage probably invokes their authority, which is less than Scripture but greater than any recent rabbinic teacher.

The rabbis' desire to circumscribe the authority of the teachings of the scribes is most clear where the authority of the laws in Scripture is sharply distinguished from the teachings of the scribes (*m. Yad.* 3:2). Though the Mishnah circumscribes the authority of the teachings of the scribes, it does not contemn or annul it. *M. Sanh.* 11:3 decrees that those who deny that one must observe some part of the words of the scribes are to be treated with greater stringency than those who deny that one must observe some point of scriptural law, probably because a direct challenge to scriptural law is unthinkable.

Many of the passages in Mishnah which mention the words of the scribes are concerned with purity. Certain rules which seem to defy the general principles of uncleanness are attributed to the scribes (*m. Kelim* 13:7) in an effort to ground them on early authority. Secondary rules concerning marriages between relatives are also attributed to the scribes (*m. Yebam.* 2:3–4). The words or teachings of the scribes can function as a general category for classifying different types of rules. Reference is made to a class of unclean persons, those who require immersion according to "the words of the scribes" (*m. Para* 11:5–6). Elsewhere the words of the scribes and the teaching of the sages are distinguished (*m. Ṭohor.* 4:7).

The authority of the scribes is less obvious and well established than that of the Bible as can be seen in the preceding Mishnaic passages. The references to the scribes in the Tosefta are similar to those in Mishnah where they are used as a source for certain teachings. Later Talmudic literature also mentions the scribes from time to time and sometimes in a way congruent with the passages cited above and sometimes with other meanings. In the Talmudic lexicon, "scribe" can refer to a copyist who produced Torah scrolls, to a literate person who writes letters and documents, and to a teacher and interpreter of scripture. In addition, the teachings of the scribes function as they do in the Mishnah, as an ancient source of authority for Jewish traditions.

The figure of the scribe in rabbinic literature is consistent with scribes in other literature. However, the historical role assigned the *sôperîm* in passing on part of the legal tradition and the implication that they were a cohesive "rabbinic-like" group fits the later rabbinic view of its own origins rather than the known historical facts.

H. Inscriptions

Some of the Diaspora literature reviewed earlier suggested that "scribe" was not used for the Jew learned in the law. One other body of evidence from the Diaspora needs to be assessed. The Greek title "scribe" *(grammateus)* appears over twenty times in the inscriptions from the Jewish community in Rome (Leon 1960). The Roman community had at least eleven separate congregations from the 1st century B.C.E. to the 4th C.E. "Scribe" or "Secretary of the Congregation" is the second most common title, after "*Archōn*" ("leader," "president"; Leon 1960: 183). The limited evidence of the inscriptions shows that the scribe was not the leader of the congregation but a subordinate official, probably the keeper of records and writer of marriage contracts or similar documents. Misspellings in an inscription by a scribe suggest that the average scribe was not greatly learned (Leon 1960: 184–85). Since there probably would not have been enough work as a maker of scrolls and contracts to keep a scribe busy full time, the role of community scribe would have been a part-time occupation often filled by a person with minimal training. The slim evidence gathered by Leon fits the Greco-Roman pattern which was alive in some Jewish communities of the Roman Empire. The scribe was a literate person who might not be greatly educated and who fulfilled limited but essential functions in the community.

Bibliography

Fishbane, M. 1985. *Biblical Interpretation in Ancient Israel.* Oxford.
Galling, K. 1964. Bagoas and Ezra. Pp. 149–84 in *Studien zur Geschichte Israels im persischen Zeitalter.* Tübingen.
Kraeling, C., ed. 1958. *City Invincible.* Chicago.
Lauterbach, J. Z. 1973. *Rabbinic Essays.* New York.
LeMaire, A. 1981. *Les Ecoles et la formation de la Bible dans l'ancien Israël.* OBO 39. Fribourg and Göttingen.
Leon, H. J. 1960. *The Jews of Rome.* Philadelphia.
Olivier, J. P. J. 1975. Schools and Wisdom Literature. *JNSL* 4: 49–60.
Schaeder, H. H. 1930. *Esra der Schreiber.* BHT 5. Tübingen.
Williams, R. J. 1972. Scribal Training in Ancient Egypt. *JAOS* 92: 214–21.
———. 1975. "A People Come out of Egypt": An Egyptologist Looks at the Old Testament. Pp. 231–52 in *Congress Volume. Edinburgh 1974.* VTSup 28.

ANTHONY J. SALDARINI

SCRIPT, ARAMAIC. See ARAMAIC SCRIPT.

SCRIPTURAL AUTHORITY. This entry consists of eight separate articles, all of which address some aspect of the history of biblical authority. However, each focuses on one particular aspect of this subject. The first three provide general overviews of how this notion developed within the particular confessional contexts of Judaism, Eastern Orthodoxy, and Roman Catholicism. Two other articles focus on the idea of scriptural authority in the formative period of the early Church and in the Middle Ages. An article on the authority of the Bible in the Reformation and Post-Reformation periods provides an introductory overview of the notion in the context of early Protestantism. The two final articles survey how the authority of Scripture was affected by Enlightenment and Post-Enlightenment developments, and how it is now being articulated by religious communities in a modern, "post-critical" environment.

BIBLICAL AUTHORITY IN JUDAISM

The issue of biblical authority has never been a question which bothered Jews. The issue of authority indeed has bothered non-Jews, especially since the period of the Reformation. Judaism ceased relying on the written scriptural law as the ultimate source of authority in tannaitic times (about the 1st century C.E.), and ever after the oral law—*verba divina non scripta*—became decisive. This does not mean that the written law was relinquished or ignored. In theory all authority flows from the word of written Scripture, but that only in the way interpreted by the rabbis or "sages."

Hence we must ask, What actually is regarded as "biblical" in Judaism? Who fixed the borderlines, and who was bound by the definition? It is at this first juncture that Judaism stands apart from Christianity. The problem here is the biblical canon. Again this leads us to the era of the Tannaites: what did make that time so special? Apparently there were various reasons. On the one hand, the central legal authority had collapsed following the destruction of the Temple in Jerusalem and the subsequent cessation of sacrifices. Thus the need for fixing rules binding every Jew had become imperative, and those rules were the ordinances as laid down in the Torah.

On the other hand, although "officially" prophecy had ceased after the time of the return from the Babylonian exile (see HOLY SPIRIT), certain texts circulated in Jewish circles which were taken by some to be inspired. We learn specifically from Josephus that men acknowledged as prophets arose towards the end of the Second Temple period, and some attracted followers. See JOHN THE BAPTIST. We cannot know in what precise sense Josephus used the term "prophet."

Our generation has learned how the Qumran covenanters were particular in expounding Scripture. No one can say for sure whether they were more or less extreme in expounding Scripture than their opponents—whether Pharisees, Sadducees, or another group. The fact that this was a Jewish sect which we know about does not mean that this sect was the only one which felt that its interpretations of the Bible were the correct ones. Different sects had "sacred" literature in their possession, books such as Jubilees, Enoch, and Ecclesiasticus. Hence authoritative steps had to be taken to decide which writings should be considered "sacred" or inspired. After the First Jewish War, in mainstream Judaism the authority was in the hands of the Tannaim or "Sages." As far as we can tell, for Judaism there never was an official act of introducing certain writings *into* the canon. The issue was rather which of the various writings which groups had regarded as "inspired" should be left *inside* the canon. See also CANON (HEBREW BIBLE).

Each term we use may lead to misconceptions. "Inspired" means conceived under the influence of *rûaḥ haqqôdeš,* "holy spirit." The expression used in rabbinic literature in discussions regarding canonical status is "books that defile the hands." The writings regarded as inspired are among those things which "defile the hands." That very discussion in rabbinical literature is extremely complicated, but one may be sure that the canonical Scriptures were those which "defiled the hands" in contrast to "profane" literature. (The prolonged discussions as to how that term came to signify what it did cannot be gone into here.)

Since many writings were considered inspired by the common crowd—who were not particular in regard of keeping their hands "undefiled"—it can be understood how this equation of sacredness and defilement could become a token of canonical status in speaking of sacred writings. To be sure, the books of the Torah were regarded as the core of the canon at least since the time of the return from the Babylonian Exile. The books known as prophetic as well as the Psalms had a somewhat lesser degree of sacredness, although we cannot state at which point in history the Psalms (and other writings) were already part of the sacred corpus.

Certain verses of writings which are not considered part of the Hebrew canon are quoted in rabbinic literature by the same introductory formula—"as it is said"—normally reserved for canonical writings. Also, there were traces in rabbinic literature of tannaitic disputes as to whether certain books should indeed be considered inspired. Such discussions may reflect uncertainty about the authoritative status of the book in question. Specifically the character of three books of Scripture was questioned: (a) Ezekiel, because it included legal ordinances contrary to those of the Torah (which in the end were clarified through rabbinic ingenuity; (b) Ecclesiastes, because it expresses doubts regarding the divine order—yet finally the author retracts his doubts; (c) "Song of Songs," the most questionable of all because of the lewd associations it arouses. Even the fact that this book too was attributed to Solomon could not assuage all doubts. Only after a leading tannaite of the 2d century found a way to declare that the catchy superscription should be interpreted symbolically as referring to the relationship between God and Israel as "holiest of poems" was it so recognized.

All this is mentioned to show that not only the legal parts of the Torah—which were the body prescribing practical observation—served as the major authority of biblical writings, but that each book had to pass the test for canonicity. The choice of the books for possible invalidation may help us answer the question why other books were never regarded as authoritative. The criterion seems not to have been the alleged authorship but rather certain parts of the contents which raised doubts.

On the other hand we cannot say for sure whether assumed time of authorship played any role. Contrary to what modern critics may state, there is no book in the Hebrew Bible canon fixed at a time much later than the return from the Babylonian exile. This is not meant as a statement regarding the time of the redaction of the so-called P source, a problem which has raised many disputes. But it means that no part of the prophets or Psalms can for instance be pushed down to the Maccabean era. Jewish tradition holds that no later prophecies from other sources were admitted into the canon.

Concerning the book of Daniel, the issue of its provenance from Hellenistic times, as claimed by many scholars, does not concern us here. Daniel is not reckoned as part of the prophetic literature in the Hebrew canon, contrary to the Greek. Its content did not raise theological problems and thus its position was never queried.

On the other hand, the book of Esther might have caused difficulties because of its contents, which can hardly be said to be edifying literature. Yet our moral considerations have nothing to do with the question of biblical authority. Questions may be raised why a book which lacks any explicit mention of the divine name altogether should have entered the canon and why no scroll containing Esther was recovered at Qumran. But these are different issues.

The last question brings us to the twilight period between biblical and post-biblical literature. The attitude of the Qumran covenanters toward Scripture is of special importance for our subject. First, their life was totally Bible-centered. Their way of understanding the Bible may seem to us somewhat distorted, just as their very attitude to life did. They felt that they understood the Bible better than other groups of Jewry. The group claimed that it was they who knew the exact historical meaning of a given prophetic text. Their self-understanding as "sons of light" in contrast to the "sons of darkness" may raise the impression that this group felt itself driven to the brink. But none of that can belittle their absolute loyalty to the biblical authority.

If "inspiration" is a criterion for judging a group, it can be stated for sure that the leaders of that sect drew a clear dividing line between the prophetic text and themselves as authoritative interpreters. Just as rabbinic Judaism coined the phrase "a sage (Heb *ḥakām*) is superior to a prophet" so the authors of a Qumran *pešer* (interpretation of prophecy) felt that the prophecy was a dead letter without their authoritative interpretation. Speaking of the term *pešer* used by the Qumran interpreters, that term is easily understood, though previously unknown. We do not know whether it was coined especially for the Qumran type of exegesis. But one point is clear: that sect spent such an effort to achieve correct interpretation that for them the Bible must have played an outstanding role.

However, we should not ignore an argument from silence. While the Qumran writings deal with the correct interpretations of various passages of the Torah, no Torah-*pešer* has been found. What could that mean? Is it purely an accident, or does it mean that regarding the Torah the *pešer*-technique of interpretation was inapplicable, especially for passages with legal implications?

Having talked about Torah and prophets, let us now look at the Psalms. Also here issues of text-type and redaction are intertwined. In this case there is no dearth of texts. Some are practically identical with the MT, while others include odes previously known only from non-Hebrew sources.

A further example of overlap between MT and non-masoretic rephrasing is the so-called Temple Scroll. That text retells the laws of the Torah mainly regarding sacrifices and festivals. But it rephrases ordinances, mainly from Deuteronomy. To us this may seem like an infraction of biblical authority. But this might be the way the covenantors acted out the way they understood the Torah.

Before the discovery of the Dead Sea Scrolls, rewritings of biblical stories in Aramaic were known. Since every translation amounts to a retelling of the original, all Aramaic Targums amount to so many retellings.

It is one of the old prejudices of biblical studies that only the Onqelos-type of targum is usually reckoned as a proper targum. However, if one studies the Palestinian targums, one realizes that their literary technique in retelling and embellishing the story is much richer. See also TARGUM.

In this case of viewing the power of biblical authority it becomes clear that the *meturgeman*—similar to the midrashist—does not allow any biblical text to stand without embellishment of details. Such facts show the importance of biblical authority in post-biblical Judaism. There hardly exists a biblical text without midrashic elaboration, mainly amoraic. However, midrashic elaborations occur atomistically, not in verse-by-verse fashion, as in medieval commentaries.

The part of the Bible which is the most authoritative is the ordinances of the Torah. Regulations as worked out by oral law have achieved an autonomous status, even if they are theoretically only "fences" erected by the sages. A simple example of legal regulations might help. Deuteronomy 25:2 specifies the procedure of punishment by lashes by order of the court. The Torah is quite explicit regarding the number of lashes: i.e., forty, no more. However, rabbinic law reduces that number, based on the fact that "forty" is preceded in the text by the construct "in number," which is construed as "coming near in number." We may assume that the real justification for the rabbinic reduction was the injunction of Deuteronomy "lest your brother be humiliated."

While it may seem that rabbinic law has overruled biblical law arbitarily, in fact no legal statement is made without a basis in the biblical text. Let us now look at the typical run of a legal argument in midrash halakhah or a Talmudic statement. All rulings regarding halakhah must be deduced from an explicit biblical ordinance in the Torah. If the halakhah is a prohibition, two proof-texts are usually required. For this purpose generally a verse from Deuteronomy serves as additional proof. The execution of the law needed two proof-texts to be declared based on the Torah, and sometimes rather crooked exegemes had to be used. To be sure, the rabbis had power to enact "fences," and those laws are based on the consensus of rabbinic opinion.

Another category which shows the need for a basis in the Bible was termed "halakhah revealed to Moses at Sinai." For post-biblical legislation these were ordinances of two different degrees. In some instances the rabbis realized themselves that the proof from the Torah-text was rather feeble, and might regard it as a "legal prop."

All this is mentioned here to show how carefully the rabbis had to proceed to regulate practical obervance, and they took special pains to stress that "it is the statements of the Sages that need enforcement" (e.g., *Roš Haš.* 19a; *Yebam.* 36b). The general ruling is that any condition appended contrary to an express ordinance in the Torah is not binding (e.g., *Ketub.* 84a). Prophets had no authority to lay down the law (*Šabb.* 104a).

We intentionally stressed the issue of the absolute authority of the Torah. No ruling could be based on pronouncements by prophets if they ran counter to the Torah. Only if a prophet decided in a special emergency—such as Elijah's sacrificing outside the Jerusalem Temple—could their action be regarded as valid. To be sure, prophets had to exhort the people to act justly and morally. But this was not legal enactment. The prophets had to get across a message which became part of the theological heritage of subsequent generations. Issues of ethics and morals are not part of the enacted law.

To finish with a rather extreme statement we may mention the saying "The words from prophets and writings will be abolished in the future, but those of the Torah will not" (*j. Meg.* 1:9). On the other hand the Talmud states (*Taʿan.* 17b), "This point we do not know from the Torah but by prophetic tradition."

Traditional interpretation also had to account for linguistic change. Biblical law was phrased in prose, and most of the Hebrew Bible is written in Classical Hebrew or Late Biblical Hebrew. There are various theories concerning how biblical Hebrew gave way in literary use to rabbinic Hebrew. In general the rabbis had no doubts concerning the sense of words in biblical Hebrew. But sometimes the exact sense of a biblical word was queried. Such discussions are not transmitted for the benefit of the historical linguist, but they originated from practical need. In deciding the sense of a biblical law no linguistic uncertainty was permissible. On the one hand, the Torah uses normal language of humans. On the other, the language of the Torah is one thing and the language of the sages another. Since the understanding of biblical law depended on the exact interpretation of all key words, this issue comes up rather often in the period of post-biblical and Aramaic diglossia.

Up to now we have dealt only with Hebrew and Aramaic. But there also was Greek. Rabbinic sources contain some snide remarks on renderings of the Bible into those languages. Nowhere do we find a remark that the Bible rendered into another language was as authoritative as the Hebrew original. But we see what contortions in Greek Aquila had to make so as to render the slightest nuance of the Hebrew sentence in proper Greek garb.

We can draw conclusions with regard to the authority of the Bible not only from the pseudepigrapha composed in the period of the Second Temple—most of which can be understood only if one assumes the Bible as authoritative—but even more from two contemporary authors, neither of whom specialized in biblical law. One was Philo—the first Jewish philosopher, the predecessor of medieval Jewish and European philosophy. Philo left us a long list of what he felt his readers should know regarding the teaching of the Bible. The list is included in his *Hypothetica,* which are in fact an apology for Judaism. It was meant for Hellenistic pagans who, as is well known, started many pogroms against Alexandrian Jewry. In this treatise Philo tells how the Bible describes the creation of the world—contrary to Greek mythology—then continues with the laws and their allegorical meaning *(De legum allegoria),* then with the fate of the first representatives of the human race, summing up with a theological essay how "the worse attacks the better" and the unchanging nature of God, then the story of Noah and the confusion of tongues, then to Abraham and who the proper heir of divine matters is *(Quis rerum divinarum heres),* then to "flight and findings," on to the decalogue and certain specific laws and virtues, on "reward and punishment," and in the very end *De vita contemplativa* and *De aeternitate mundi.*

This is not mentioned as an exhaustive index but as an indication of what this early philosopher thought important for his non-Jewish compatriots to know about the contents of the Bible.

Since we can judge the treatise only from what we have of it, it could well be that Philo tried to convey to his readers some points on why and how biblical teaching is authoritative for Jews. But since he was a Hellenistic philosopher writing for other Hellenistic Egyptians, we can only deduce his ideas on the authority of the Bible from these pronouncements.

While Philo, as a philosopher, never let his feelings get the better of him, his slightly younger contemporary Flavius Josephus dealt with the important issue of biblical authority in this polemical treatise *contra Apion* (1.7). This treatise is the first Jewish counter-polemic treatise written by a descendant of Jerusalem priests who was a military leader as well as a historian. It deals specifically with the reverence with which the Bible is regarded by all Jews and thus teaches us something about its authority. Josephus sums this up thus: "We have given proof of our reverence for our scriptures." This statement is based expressly on the interpretation of Deut 4:2 "do not add or subtract anything," which was a standard proof-text from early tannaitic writings till today. Josephus adds "No one has ventured to either add or subtract a syllable. It is an instinct (!) with every Jew to regard them as decrees of God, to abide by them and—if need be—cheerfully to die for them" (*AgAp* 1.42). To be sure, Josephus made his statements in a polemical framework, but we cannot doubt that he tried to present the attitude of mainstream Jewry at his time.

All testimonies from the tannaitic era indicate that the Bible was regarded as absolute authority not only by mainstream Jewry but also in a sect such as the Qumran covenanters. But we cannot gauge the actual type of differences and possible idealizations.

Scholars ask, why the laws of the Torah were regarded so highly when, in fact, they were mainly the background for daily life regulations by the sages or sectarian leaders. Was there perhaps a polemic undercurrent against disparagers? What really is the meaning of the strong interpretation of the phrase "he has despised the word of the Lord" (Num 15:31) and the rabbinic interpretation "This refers to someone who claims that the Tora was not given from heaven" (*Sanh.* 99a).

We have already learned of doubts uttered by some of the sages regarding the canonical status of certain books of what finally became the canon. But some statements were even stronger: "There are many verses which actually should be burned, but these may be the very texts on which the Torah is based (*Ḥul.* 60b). To be sure, the modern scholar often feels that the rabbis in their statements must have left their critical acumen at home; therefore such statements should be viewed with double attention. On the other hand, we should not minimize the feelings expressed by the rabbis. They held that often laws of the Torah should not be adhered to literally, basing themselves on their interpretation of Ps 119:126, "there is a time to act for God even if one sets aside your Torah." The authority of the Torah is not diminished even if necessity forces one to break its ordinances.

Biblical authority could also be tackled on esoteric bases. We do not know who the first group was to produce in ancient time the *hekālôt* (lit. "[divine] chariot") esoteric literature or whether there was a direct connection between them and the medieval Kabbalists. To be sure, tradition has it that the leading talmudic sages were also masters of esoteric teaching and practice. But since there is more than a trace of suspicion that there was also a group which held on to some kind of Jewish Gnosticism, one should be careful in trying to identify the different expressions of esoteric knowledge and action. But one point should be stressed: whatever the exact shade of reliance on the Torah, its authority was uppermost even if the exegetical approach was esoteric. The Torah had hidden meanings, and the expositor had to search for them.

Up to now we have dealt mainly with what can be called mainstream Judaism, this is to say the heritage of ancient pharisaic ideology. But at the time when normative Judaism gained ascendance there was at least one non-mainstream group apart from the Qumran sect: the Sadducees. Since rabbinic literature developed from Pharisaic sources, it presents a slanted picture. Sadducees differed from Pharisees at certain points of theology, such as bodily resurrection, in regard to the status of oral law, and in practical observance. The Sadducees were stricter in observing biblical law to the letter. Whether the Essenes mentioned in ancient sources were indeed identical with the Qumran covenanters remains an open question.

Mainstream Judaism developed from the Pharisees; no known remnants of the Sadducees survived in Judaism. But because there was no persecution of Sadducees, their disappearance from the scene remains a riddle. The question has been raised what relationship there is between the Sadducees and the splinter group called the Karaites, which developed in Babylonia around the 8th century C.E. as a clear alternative to rabbinic Judaism. That group or sect denied the validity of rabbinic hermeneutics and maintained that the rabbis had strayed from the correct meaning of the biblical law by substituting their legal understanding for that found in the Bible.

The likeliest group that may have kept—or revived—Sadduceean teaching indeed seems to be the 7th–8th century Karaites, which arose as a splinter group of dissatisfied followers of rabbinic Judaism in Babylonia. But the main point of that group is rather stricter adherence to the biblical text according to the slogan of its founder, "search very exactly in the Torah." Since the time the Samaritans had split away from developing Judaism during the period of the Second Temple, there had not been a schism of such magnitude as the Karaitic denial of rabbinic authority. Karaites were enjoined to learn every part of the law by searching the details of the biblical text; and because soon after their schism the vowel and accent signs came into use in writing Torah manuscripts, scholars claimed for some time that the invention of these graphemes was due to Karaite influence, and only afterward was taken over by Rabbanites. See MASORETIC TEXT.

Without going into more details we can only say that if mainstream Judaism had the highest regard for the Bible, the Karaites outdid them. One may possibly compare the relationship to that between normative Catholicism and the claims of the 16th-century Reformers who fought under the banner of *sola scriptura.* Whatever the suitability of that comparison, the fact that Catholicism followed the tradition of the Church Fathers does not at all imply their disregard for the authority of the Bible.

We have spent the major part of this discussion on the early post-biblical period because that was the decisive time when attitudes to the Bible took shape. By the time the Talmud was finally redacted, attitudes had already become frozen. All later Jewish activity regarding the Bible involved exegetical differentiations of philological or philosophical or esoterical character. Esoteric (Kabbalistic) attitudes towards the Bible may seem rather odd to modern scholars, but the Kabbalists were also part of the main body of Jewry and felt that their dealing with the Bible text actually was the most correct, since they tried to uncover the hidden meaning.

Biblical authority was first called into question by European Jewish thinkers in early modern times. Through the new spirit which arose in Europe after the Middle Ages, the authority of the Bible was challenged. It was first challenged by Benedict (Baruch) de Spinoza (1632–1677), who was no longer a member in good standing of the Jewish community of Amsterdam when he wrote his *Tractatus.* Spinoza attacked the authority of the Torah, giving explicit expression to the hesitant doubts of his medieval predecessor Abraham ibn Ezra. As a matter of fact his compatriot and contemporary Manasse ben Israel composed at that very time his treatise concerning the internal contradictions in the Bible. Neither of those two dealt habitually with the Bible, and in the long run Spinoza's attack was more powerful than Manasse's apology. See further SCRIPTURAL AUTHORITY (IN THE WAKE OF THE ENLIGHTENMENT). One might suggest that the previous sharp division regarding the authority of the Bible between Jews and non-Jews came to an end in the first generation of Enlightenment.

All this happened as part of Western European intellectual development. Jews in other parts of the world took no part in this development, and their attitude did not change from earlier tradition. The first western Jew who lived as a conscious "modern" Jew in the evolving twilight world was

Moses Mendelssohn (1729–1786). Mendelssohn tried to bring his German coreligionists nearer to an aesthetic appreciation of the Bible but did not dare to get involved with the rabbinic authorities on issues of its authority. None of this changed until the political and intellectual life of German Jews underwent changes. English Jewry had little to contribute, and American Jewry did not yet exist as an intellectual force. Only once German Jewry had digested the impact of Mendelssohn's program and had come into intellectual contact with the surrounding non-Jewish world did the issue of biblical authority become a problem.

By the middle of the 19th century the religious life of European Jewry had undergone major changes, and the nascent *Science of Judaism* had begun to revolutionize Jewish thinking. Whereas previously traditional orthodox attitudes were the only recognized forms of Jewish worship, now a new type of schism had divided the Jewish world. To be sure the main issues in daily life were the way rabbinic regulations were kept and how religious services were conducted. But, as we have already stressed, such issues were never divorced from the issues of biblical authority, even if the actual biblical laws only stood in the background.

Starting from the second half of the 19th century, western Jewry was split into three streams regarding halakhic observance and custom. The old stream strictly adhered to "orthodox" traditional halakha, which automatically entailed recognition of biblical authority, which then was taken as identical with rabbinic interpretation. The contrasting stream was that of liberal or "Reform" Judaism, which did not adhere any longer to the teachings as they had developed from tannaitic times through the Middle Ages. By its own logic, that "liberal" attitude also affected practical expressions of biblical authority. Since those "modernists" also followed trends of liberal views in general, all this worked in the same direction of despoiling Judaism from its age-old heritage. Some of the ideologies of the liberal wing saw their task in justifying their anti-rabbinic program.

Between these two groups stood the "conservative" or traditional wing, which tried to steer a middle course, claiming that present-day Judaism must be viewed as the product of its historical development. In theory, biblical authority was recognized as in earlier times, and nobody dreamt of denying it. But for daily life the issue remained the degree of observing rabbinic halakha rather than worrying about the biblical statements without their rabbinic elaboration.

These three streams today form the major subdivisions common to all parts of Jewry (leaving aside the ultra-orthodox wing, which often calls forth comparisons to the opinions expressed by Protestant or Islamic "fundamentalists"). While all such differences inside Judaism address pragmatic concerns over the degree of observance of rabbinic regulations, they cannot evade reflection on attitudes toward biblical authority.

This picture was correct until a generation ago, before the American scene found its own new expression for its Judaism. At present the so-called "reconstructionist" group officially still is a subdivision of traditional conservative Judaism. This group has tried to sever connections to biblical authority in its attempt to understand Judaism as a matter of "peoplehood," civilization, and common custom. For the first time since the Karaite schism all validity of rabbinic observance is regarded only as a matter of custom and convenient expression of one's feeling of belonging.

In Judaism biblical authority was never absent from the minds of believers. But in daily life the important factor was the way the sages did interpret the law of the Bible. In practical terms, the Bible dwindled to those parts of biblical ordinances which were applicable after the destruction of the Temple. What the prophets had admonished also played a part, but since they could not lay down the law, they remained rather unimportant regarding the issue of biblical authority. Therefore our subject should be approached not as the reading of clear writing, but rather as a palimpsest, which is there for those who spend the effort of studying it, but which otherwise fades practically into the background.

MOSHE GOSHEN-GOTTSTEIN

BIBLICAL AUTHORITY IN EASTERN ORTHODOXY

Biblical authority connotes a broad concept embracing revelation, inspiration, canonization, and interpretation as well as the ongoing work of the Spirit. The authority of the Bible is concretely engaged, whether consciously or not, in the actual uses of Scripture, e.g., liturgical, homiletical, catechetical, apologetic, doctrinal, devotional, and academic. In Eastern Orthodoxy a historical review of biblical authority may be presented under three periods: classical, traditionalist, and modern.

A. The Classical Period (1st–5th Centuries)

Extending roughly up to John Chrysostom and Theodore of Mopsuestia, the classical period (1st–5th centuries) marked not only the gradual formation of the Christian Bible as the norm of Christian life and thought but also the accompanying development of a hard-won and theologically coherent exegetical tradition guided by fundamental credal insights of the Catholic Church. This double achievement established a classic unity among Scripture, tradition, and church, while allowing significant variety and creativity, and thus raised a normative claim on all subsequent Christian generations.

The first struggle over biblical authority involved the Church's christological appropriation of the Hebrew Scriptures whose authority as the revealed oracles of God (Rom 3:2) embodied in sacred writings (Luke 24:44) was assumed by early Christians. However, in the early Church, "though the Old Testament was God's word, it was not in fact God's final word" (Lamb *CHB* 1: 585). The direct revelation of Christ and the Spirit decisively qualified the authority of the Hebrew Bible, and also gave impetus to a whole new process in which Christian writings bearing the authority of Christ, the apostles, and the prophetic Spirit began to gain authoritative status. Jesus himself exemplified interpretive freedom in the Spirit and set the new dynamics in motion by proclaiming the immediacy of the reign of God (Mark 1:15), challenging the authority of the Mosaic Law (Matt 5:21–48), and seeing in his own ministry the end time fulfillment of prophecy (Luke 5:21). It was no longer the Mosaic Law but Christ who formed the salvific center of divine revelation, and consequently Christ became the new hermeneutical key of God's saving activity in history. Diverse Christian writers such as Paul, Matthew, the author of Hebrews, and the author of the *Epistle of Barnabas* all shared the christological hermeutical principle but gave various unsystematic answers to the question of how the new revelation was related to the traditional Scriptures (see, e.g., Gal 3:19–26; 1 Cor 10:11; Matt 5:17–18; 23:1–3, 23; Heb 7:18–19; 10:1–5; *Ep. Barn.* ix.4).

A sharper struggle over biblical authority was occasioned by the confrontation with various 2nd-century gnostic teachers who severely compromised and at times rejected the authority of the OT. While interpretive freedom in the Spirit led the Church to seek its own rightful christological integrity and mission over against the Jewish biblical tradition, the radical interpretive freedom claimed by Marcion, Valentinus, Ptolemaeus, and others now risked a dissolution of both the church's moorings in salvation history and its distinctive identity amidst the syncretistic sea of Hellenistic religions and sects. In part against them, Justin developed the first signs of a conscious doctrine of Scripture (von Campenhausen 1972: 88–102). He simultaneously held to the authority of the OT, while he qualified its unity by discerning it in a tripartite stratification of prophecy, ethics, and historical legislation for the Jews, which was no longer valid in view of a Christocentric hermeneutic (Stylianopoulos 1974: 51–53). Irenaeus is a richer witness, not only for the advanced stage of the canonization of the NT along with the OT, but also for the new awareness of the hermeneutical function of credal insights (rule of faith) of the living tradition of a now worldwide Great Church (Greer 1986: 109). Armed with these teachings, the ongoing church reasonably refuted various claims about secret doctrines, apocryphal books, and new revelations by gnostics and later by Montanists.

The crucial questions in the 3d and 4th centuries focused not on biblical authority as such, now reinforced through the completion of the canon (A.D. 367 by Athanasius), but rather on exegetical methodology. A tremendous exegetical output based on allegory, typology, and grammatical exegesis was produced by Alexandrian and Antiochene interpreters whose approaches, despite some sharp differences, should be viewed as complementary rather than antithetical (Froehlich 1984: 20, 22; Trigg 1988: 31, 34). Regarding biblical authority, however, it was the Arian controversy of the 4th century, fought extensively on exegetical grounds and necessitating ecumenical councils for resolution, that yielded additional profound implications. The unbiblical Athanasian term Gk *homoousios* ("of one essence,"), adopted by the First Council (A.D. 325) under protest, was meant to safeguard what was in fact considered biblical truth regarding the Son's relation to the Father. The adoption of this term was official vindication of the exegetical tradition's insight that a contextual search for the *skopos* ("central aim" or "unifying purpose") of Scripture, rather than a literalist approach to the canonical text, was decisive for the correct interpretation of its meaning. The Second Council's (A.D. 381) promulgation of the Spirit as the Third Person of the Trinity, despite recognized exegetical ambiguity on the matter, yet following Basil's and Gregory the Theologian's liturgical and pneumatological arguments (Pelikan 1981: 339, 345, 359–60), underlined the hermeneutical role of the conciliar authority of the Church. It could go beyond mere exegetical deductions and could rely on the inspired integrated insights of the living tradition (Santer 1975: 110) for final decision on crucial, universally disputed matters of faith.

B. The Traditionalist Period (6th–18th Centuries)

The traditionalist period (6th–18th centuries) emerged organically from the previous one, but also developed new features and emphases which distinguish it. Biblical authority continued to have an impact especially on worship where a phenomenal development of biblical lectionaries and liturgical hymnology occurred by the end of the 1st millennium. Although not of the same quality, commentaries also continued to be written by Oecoumenios (6th century), Euthymios Zigabenos (11th century), Nicodemos of the Holy Mountain (17th century), and others. The devotional reading of Scripture especially in monastic circles continued to influence Orthodox spirituality and much later Russian piety. The authority of the biblical canon remained formally supreme and yet did not totally eliminate a certain freedom for Nicephoros of Constantinople (9th century) to list the books of Revelation, 1–3 Maccabees, Wisdom of Solomon, and many others outside the narrower canon (*NTApocr,* 50).

What particularly distinguished this period, however, was an archaizing loyalty to the Church Fathers and a maximalist devotion to tradition placed on a level of authority formally equal to but virtually higher than Scripture. Already the 5th century christological controversies marked a shift from direct argument from Scripture to appeal to the witness of the fathers (Santer 1975: 100), an appeal compromised by a plethora of forgeries between the 5th and 7th centuries (Grant 1960: 23). Maximos the Confessor (6th century), despite his own creative mind, held that an exegete depended on the God-inspired fathers more than on one's very breath (Pelikan 1974: 18–19). The Council of Trullo (A.D. 692), while enjoining biblical teaching to lay people and clergy alike by church leaders, prohibited new interpretations apart from the patristic ones. Significant examples of direct use of the Bible, accompanied by powerful calls for evangelical renewal, such as in the case of Symeon the New Theologian (10th century) and Kosmas Aitolos (18th century), were exceptions swallowed up by the massive authority of tradition.

The traditionalist features reached their sharpest formulation in the 17th century when Eastern Christianity became more conscious of the proselytizing threat of Protestantism. Against Patriarch Cyril Lucaris, who was influenced by Calvinism and advocated the authority of Scripture over the Church as well as the narrower OT canon, the local councils of Constantinople (A.D. 1638) and Jerusalem (A.D. 1672), as well as doctrinal statements by Peter Mogila and Dositheos of Jerusalem, wedded biblical authority to the authority of the Church with new precision (Pelikan 1974: 284–87). The inseparability of Scripture from patristic exegesis, the validity of liturgical additions to the biblical text, and the absolute authority of conciliar decrees were all ultimately grounded by the Orthodox on notions of Church "infallibility" and of Scripture and tradition as "two sources" of revelation, echoing Latin theology (Pelikan 1974: 288–89). In this context, not only was the wider biblical canon (including the "readable" or "deuterocanonical" books) affirmed, but the reading of Scripture by the ordinary faithful was on one occasion prohibited in imitation of Latin measures against Protestant influence.

C. The Modern Period (19th–20th Centuries)

The modern period (19th–20th centuries), too, has unfolded in organic continuity with the past, and basic traditionalist positions have been maintained to the present. However, the birth of an independent Greek State (1830) as well as the establishment of Athens University as a state academic institution (1837) created conditions in which the "new learning" of Western liberal ideas and critical methodologies began to exercise greater impact on traditional thinking.

A major case in point was the heated controversy over the translation of Scripture into modern Greek. No Orthodox theological principle militates against the translation of Scripture into the vernacular of any people. Sporadic attempts at such translations had in fact been made among Greeks since the early 16th century and seemed to be welcome except when explicitly associated with Protestant proselytizing interests in the Near East. But the complete translation of the Bible during the first half of the 19th century, sponsored by the British Bible Society and supported by a liberal and influential Greek minority, generated traditionalist furor and official disapproval. Preference for the MT over the authoritative LXX version of the OT was rejected. A translated Bible, and one without patristic commentary, could in no way be thought of as part of the tradition, and it was thus stigmatized as Protestant (Vaporis 1970: 235). But official condemnations did not necessarily impede use of the translation until very recent times when new ones superceded it. Reaction to the new translations, especially from official circles, has remained mixed.

A deeper creative tension pertaining to biblical authority was introduced through academic critical and historical studies which have raised the problem of history for Orthodox theology (Stylianopoulos 1967: 394–400). For one thing, the new approach has put into historical relief the old problem of the wider OT canon, which for many Orthodox has yet to be resolved by the church as a whole. For another and far greater thing, historical studies have opened up the possibility of rediscovering the witness of Scripture as a means of valid critique and renewal in the Church, while at the same time risking an historical relativization of biblical authority. This new problem regarding the authority of the Bible has not been faced directly by Orthodox theologians (Agourides 1976: 8). Some continue to hold that Scripture derives its validity from the church and that tradition contains nothing contrary to the Bible (Bratsiotis 1951: 21–22). Others stress the ecclesiastical context of Scripture but also advocate the corollary principle that everything in the Church should be judged by Scripture (Hopko 1970: 66–67). Still others favor the development of biblical studies as a field in its own right (Stylianopoulos 1972: 83–85). The challenge is to define an appropriate balance among Bible, tradition, and Church, a challenge that can possibly be met by a "neopatristic synthesis" (Florovsky 1960: 45), including a hermeneutical model derived from the classical period which would avoid both stifling traditionalism and barren historicism (Trigg 1988: 55).

Bibliography

Agourides, S. 1976. *The Bible in the Greek Orthodox Church.* Athens.

Bratsiotis, P. 1951. The Authority of the Bible: An Orthodox Contribution. Pp. 17–29 in *Biblical Authority for Today,* ed. A. Richardson and E. Schweitzer. London.

Breck, J. 1986. *The Power of the Word in the Worshiping Church.* Crestwood, NY.

Campenhausen, H. von. 1972. *Formation of the Christian Bible.* Philadelphia.

Florovsky, G. 1960. The Ethos of the Orthodox Church. Pp. 36–51 in *Orthodoxy: A Faith and Order Dialogue.* Faith and Order Paper 30. Geneva.

———. 1972. *Bible, Church, Tradition: An Eastern Orthodox View.* Vol. 1 in *The Collected Works of Georges Florovsky.* Belmont, MA.

Froehlich, K. 1984. *Biblical Interpretation in the Early Church.* Sources of Early Christian Thought. Philadelphia.

Grant, R. M. 1960. The Appeal to the Early Fathers. *JTS* 11: 13–24.

Greer, R. A., and Kugel, J. L. 1986. *Early Biblical Interpretation.* Library of Early Christianity 3. Philadelphia.

Hopko, T. 1970. The Bible in the Orthodox Church. *SVTQ* 14: 66–99.

Kesich, V. 1972. *The Gospel Image of Christ: The Church and Modern Criticism.* Crestwood, NY.

Pelikan, J. 1974. *The Spirit of Eastern Christendom (600–1700).* Vol. 2 in *The Christian Tradition.* Chicago.

———. 1981. The "Spiritual Sense" of Scripture: The Exegetical Basis for St. Basil's Doctrine of the Holy Spirit. Pp. 337–60 in *Basil of Caesarea: Christian, Humanist, Ascetic: A Sixteenth-Hundredth Anniversary Symposium,* ed. P. J. Fedwick. Toronto.

Santer, M. 1975. Scripture and the Councils. *Sobornost* 7: 99–111.

Stylianopoulos, T. 1967. Historical Studies and Orthodox Theology or the Problem of History for Orthodoxy. *GOTR* 12: 394–419.

———. 1972. Biblical Studies in Orthodox Theology: A Response. *GOTR* 17: 69–85.

———. 1974. *Justin Martyr and the Mosaic Law.* SBLDS 20. Missoula, MT.

Trigg, J. W. 1988. *Biblical Interpretation.* Message of the Fathers of the Church 9. Wilmington, DE.

Vaporis, N. M. 1970. *The Controversy on the Translation of the Scriptures into Modern Greek and Its Effects, 1818–1843.* Diss. Columbia.

THEODORE STYLIANOPOULOS

BIBLICAL AUTHORITY IN ROMAN CATHOLICISM

Roman Catholicism is a Church of sacraments as well as of the Scripture, of the living experience of Christ preserved in a visible hierarchical structure. As the Second Vatican Council expressed it in 1964, "the Church, in Christ, is in the nature of a sacrament" (Flannery 1975: 350). Roman Catholicism, therefore, places the authority of Scripture within the broader context of the Church. In 1546, the Council of Trent defined that the gospel which Christ promulgated and ordered to be preached was "the source of all saving truth and rule of conduct" and "that this truth and rule are contained in the written books and unwritten traditions which have come down to us, having been received by the apostles from the mouth of Christ Himself or from the apostles by the dictation of the Holy Spirit, and have been transmitted as it were from hand to hand" (Neuner and Dupuis 1982: 73). Trent was formulating Catholic doctrine against the Reformers, but it was reflecting an ancient Catholic and Orthodox belief in the relationship between Scripture and traditions, between inspired writings and the Church's experience.

Scripture for the apostolic Church meant the OT as it was now fulfilled in Jesus Christ. The Church and its preaching of Christ was the norm for interpreting the Scripture. With Paul, the apostolic Church began to produce its own writings. One of the earliest problems was to determine what writings were suitable for usage in the Church—the issue of the canon of Scripture that was not definitively settled for Roman Catholicism until Trent (Kelly 1960: 52–60). Irenaeus (fl. 190) repudiated the claims of the gnostics that they were the heirs to teaching communicated by Jesus only to his most intimate disciples. Instead, he appealed to the teaching of the apostles, Jesus' closest followers, and preserved through their successors. Even if the apostles had left nothing in writing, he asserted, the Church would have been able to follow "the structure of the tradition which they handed on to those to whom they committed the churches." The gnostic writings were therefore unsuitable for liturgical use. Origen (ca. 185–ca. 254), too, argued that the norm of faith was more than Scripture—it was "the doctrine of the church, transmitted in orderly succession from the apostles and remaining in the churches to the present day" (Pelikan 1971: 115–6).

Only gradually did the Church determine the canon of the NT books, but there still remained the problem of the proper interpretation of Scripture. Arius interpreted the gospel of John to mean that the Word (Gk *logos*) was subordinate to the Father—"there was when he was not," to use his famous dictum. Nicaea, the first ecumenical council, condemned Arius' heresy. It believed itself divinely assisted to preserve the Church from heretical interpretation of Scripture and to determine the correct one. In the process, it adopted the language current in the day but not found in Scripture to formulate its creed—the Son was consubstantial (Gk *homoousios*) with the Father (Kelly 1960: 226–37). By itself, then Scripture was not an infallible guide to the total Gospel of Christ. It needed some other authority not only to recognize its inspiration but also to preserve its interpretation from error. Like Nicaea's, the creeds and definitions of subsequent councils took on an authority parallel to Scripture, not in proclaiming new revelations, but in preserving the revelation that had been handed down. The theologians who had helped shape the great conciliar definitions, the Fathers, came to be seen as the principal commentators on Scripture.

In the early Middle Ages, the "sense of the Fathers" provided the key to understanding the Scripture. Their exegesis became almost synonymous with tradition, whose distinguishing characteristics were antiquity, universality, and consensus. Tradition was static, and the medieval commentator was to hand on what he received or, in the words of Pope Stephen I, "*nihil innovetur nisi quod tranditum est*" ("nothing is to be introduced except that which has been received") (McNally 1959: 31). But in the West, the Fathers meant primarily Augustine, and few commentators even sought to refer to the Greek Fathers except in translation. Few scholars were even familiar with the Greek NT or Hebrew OT. The Latin Vulgate, originally translated by Jerome, replaced the study of Scripture in the original languages. Commentators appealed beyond the literal to the threefold spiritual sense of Scripture: tropological, anagogical, and allegorical. The Scripture became more of a guide for scriptural life than a source of dogmatic theology (McNally 1959: 54–63). In the later Middle Ages, many of the great scholastics, notably Albert the Great and Thomas Aquinas, wrote commentaries on Scripture, but still they were unfamiliar with the original texts. Moreover, the development of the papal office now added a source of doctrinal authority complementary to that of councils.

The Renaissance return to original sources paved the way for the Reformation which challenged the Catholic understanding of revelation and the rule of faith. Trent's decree, cited above, was purposely vague about what "traditions" meant, since many of the bishops present were themselves divided on the question, but it also avoided making Scripture and tradition separate sources (Jedin 1961: 2.86–94). The council, moreover, formally defined the canon of Scripture—the same books listed at the Council of Florence in 1442. Trent attached an anathema to "anyone [who] does not accept all these books in their entirety, with all their parts, as they are being read in the Catholic Church and are contained in the ancient Latin Vulgate edition, as sacred and canonical, and knowingly and deliberately rejects the aforesaid traditions." Trent, therefore, contrary to the Reformers, accepted as canonical those books contained in the LXX that Jerome had translated in the Vulgate, the so-called "deuterocanonical" books. The council, furthermore, declared that "the ancient Vulgate version . . . is to be regarded as the authentic translation in public readings, disputations and expositions." This decree, intended only for the Western Church, did not affirm that the Vulgate was inspired, but only that it did not contain errors in matters of faith and morals and was to be used in the Western Church. Finally, the council decreed that no one was to interpret the Scripture "contrary to the meaning that holy mother the Church was held and holds—since it belongs to her to judge the true meaning and interpretation of Holy Scripture—and that no one dare to interpret the Scripture in a way contrary to the unanimous consensus of the Fathers, even though such interpretations be not intended for publication" (Neuner and Dupuis 1982: 74–75). Contrary to some popular misconceptions, the council did not prohibit private reading of Scripture, but only a private interpretation different from that of the Church.

Trent thus rejected the Protestant tenet *sola scriptura*, "Scripture alone," and reasserted the Church's role in preserving apostolic teaching. Yet, its formulation about Scripture and traditions would undergo several developments. During the Counter-Reformation debates, some Catholic theologians began arguing that tradition was a source of revelation, separate from Scripture, but their position was not universal. In the late 18th century, John Carroll (1735–1815), who became the first Catholic bishop in the United States in 1789, considered tradition to be the "living doctrine" of the Church. Writing against a former Catholic priest, he stated "that we have always asserted, that the *whole* word of God, unwritten, as well as written, is the christian's rule of faith." For Carroll, the whole authority of Scripture depended on the testimony of the Church throughout the ages, "for if the catholic rule of faith could be proved unsafe, what security have we for the authenticity, the genuineness, the incorruptibility of Scripture itself: How do we know, but by the tradition that is, by the living doctrine of the catholic church, which are the true and genuine gospels?" (Hanley 1976: 111). "Tradition," he concluded, was "*the word of God* delivered down to us by the testimony of the fathers, and in the public doctrine of the catholic church" (Hanley 1976: 137–38). He thus saw Scripture and tradition closely related.

A generation later, Carroll's fifth successor as Archbishop of Baltimore, Francis P. Kenrick (1793–1863), also argued for the inadequacy of Scripture alone being the rule of faith. In 1838, he wrote that "a full and adequate rule of faith within the Christian economy must necessarily be referred to the time of Christ and the Apostles, and then suit the condition of men through all ages." The NT, however, could not "be referred to the age of Christ, nor to the beginning of the apostolic preaching: for it is evident that many years elapsed before anything was consigned to writing," and only gradually were the apostolic writings collected and recognized by the churches (Kenrick 1858: 1.282–83). Recommending Johann Adam Möhler's *Symbolik,* he concluded that tradition was essentially the preservation of Christian teaching from apostolic times. The "*tradition,* which is the rule for our faith," he declared, "is contained in the greatest part in Scripture, and celebrated back through the ages in the monuments and documents of Christian antiquity, and the custom and public worship of the Christian faithful throughout the world" (Kenrick 1858: 289). Kenrick relied heavily for his treatment on the Fathers of the Church, with only a rare citation from St. Thomas or the other scholastics . In this, he was similar to Carroll before him and to John Henry Newman, his own contemporary.

But other theological schools soon overshadowed this close association of Scripture and tradition. The First Vatican Council (1869–1870) issued a constitution on faith. Seriously truncating Trent's decree on Scripture and traditions, Vatican I now stated that "supernatural revelation" was "contained in the written books and unwritten traditions" (Neuner and Dupuis 1982: 75). The council further declared that "all those things are to be believed with divine and Catholic faith which are contained in the word of God, written or handed down *(verbo Dei scripto vel tradito),* and which the Church, either by a solemn judgment, or by her ordinary and universal magisterium, proposes for belief as having been divinely revealed" (Neuner and Dupuis 1982: 43). The "doctrine of faith," the council continued, "is like a divine deposit handed on *(tradita)* to the Spouse of Christ, to be faithfully guarded and infallibly declared" (Denzinger-Schönmetzer 1976: 3020). The conciliar statement, reflecting the theology of Johann Baptist Franzelin, S.J., shifted tradition from the dynamic preservation of apostolic preaching to a static deposit and implied that it was a source of revelation separate from Scripture. Moreover, by "Spouse of Christ," as Yves Congar, O.P., noted, "the council understands here above all the magisterium, especially that of the Roman Pontiff" (Congar 1966: 196–98).

The council also addressed the relatively new question of inspiration, then surfacing as Catholics began entering the arena of biblical criticism. It declared that the books of Scripture were "canonical and sacred" not because they were "composed by mere human industry" and "were afterwards approved by her [the Church's] authority," "but because, having been written by the inspiration of the Holy Spirit, they have God for their author and have been delivered as such to the Church herself" (Neuner and Dupuis 1982: 75–76). For certain theologians, this statement precluded multiple authors or redactors of a sacred book in its present form—the precise point that historical criticism was making. The theological viewpoint, flowing from the council, rendered the Church incapable of grappling with some of the issues arising from biblical criticism. It was ironic and tragic that the Church, which so adhered to tradition, would founder on the crisis of Modernism. The older, more dynamic understanding of tradition would have opened the Church to some of the new developments. One American Catholic theologian, John B. Hogan, S.S. (1829–1901), put it succinctly when he stated that Protestants might regard the findings of historical criticism with "dismay," but Catholics could "contemplate it with perfect equanimity. Their faith is based, not on the Bible, but on the Church" (Hogan 1898: 480–81). Unfortunately, the form of neo-Thomism, then rising, could not grapple with some of these issues.

Catholic theologians took two general approaches to the new challenge of historical criticism. Some equated inspiration with revelation and attributed to God as the author of Scripture everything known of a human author. Hence, despite the findings of historical critics, there could be no error in Scripture, for this would be incompatible with divine authorship. Others, notably M.-J. Lagrange, O.P., sought to distinguish between inspiration and revelation—while everything in the Scripture was inspired, not everything was revealed; what appeared to be error was the divine accommodation to the human mode of expression proper to the age of the particular human author of Scripture. According to their critical method, they admitted that some books of the OT, especially the Pentateuch, had multiple authors and that the gospels had undergone several redactions. The opposing theologians, however, appealed not only to their theory of inspiration but also to their understanding of tradition. Some interpreted Trent's reference to the "five books of Moses" in the canonical list, for example, as meaning that the council had pronounced on the Mosaic authorship of the Pentateuch (Fogarty 1989: 99–100, 122). This interpretation contributed to the Pontifical Biblical Commission's assertion in 1906 that Catholic scholars had to hold that Moses was substantially the author of the Pentateuch (Denzinger-Schönmetzer 1976: 3394).

In the Church's combat against Modernism in the 20th century, it came close to adopting biblical fundamentalism. Although the Church never formally condemned evolution, for example, the Biblical Commission did declare in 1909 that the Catholic exegete had to uphold the historical character of the first three chapters of Genesis in what pertained to Christian doctrine, the special creation of man by God, and the formation of woman from man (Denzinger-Schönmetzer 1976: 3513–4). These decisions, however, were intended not so much to adhere to a literal interpretation of Scripture as to preserve the doctrine of original sin.

Catholics were isolated from the world of biblical scholarship until 1943, when Pope Pius XII issued his encyclical *Divino Afflante Spiritu,* calling for Catholic scholars to apply the historical method held so suspect at the beginning of the century. Yet only seven years later, the same pope published *Humani Generis* warning scholars not to go beyond the magisterium, particularly in regard to the interpretation of the creation of Adam to mean a "plurality of ancestors." While Pius did not condemn such a theory outright, he did state that "it is not all apparent how such a view can be reconciled with the data which the sources of revealed truth and the documents of the Church propose concerning original sin, namely that it originates from a sin truly committed by one Adam" (Neuner and Dupuis 1982: 126). Dogmatic considerations flowing from the traditional interpretation of Scripture, then, were still to be the guiding norms for Catholic scholars.

On the eve of the Second Vatican Council, and through the first session in 1962, some biblical scholars were accused of denying official teaching or the magisterium and were on the defensive. The council's first draft of the constitution on revelation was entitled "Sources of Revelation"—Scripture and tradition were separate. Although the bishops failed to muster enough votes to reject the document, John XXIII withdrew it. In 1964, biblical scholars received further encouragement from an instruction of the Biblical Commission on the historicity of the gospels. Scholars were to investigate the development of the gospel traditions from the sayings and events in the life of Jesus through the apostolic preaching to the formation of the gospel traditions themselves (Fitzmyer 1964: 134–36). The way was now paved for a fuller appreciation of Scripture and of Scripture scholarship within the Church.

The council's final constitution, promulgated in 1965, declared that "sacred tradition and sacred Scripture make up a single sacred deposit of the Word of God, which is entrusted to the Church." It belonged to "the living teaching office of the Church alone," however, to give "an authentic interpretation of the Word of God, whether in its written form or in the form of tradition." But the constitution made it clear that "this magisterium is not superior to the Word of God, but is its servant. It teaches only what has been handed on to it" (Flannery 1975: 755–56). While to many Catholics, Vatican II's treatment of Scripture and its relation to tradition was revolutionary, it was in fact a return to an older theology and one quite compatible with the teaching of Trent.

In the post-conciliar Catholic Church, Scripture has assumed a larger role in the lives of the people. Prior to the council, for example, there were only four major liturgical feasts that had readings from the OT. The council provided for a three-year cycle of readings for Sundays, with the first reading, except for the Easter season, taken from the OT. The homily was made an essential part of the liturgy or Mass and was usually to address the meaning of the biblical texts. Of equal significance, Catholic biblical scholarship came to be accepted in most circles not as a threat to traditional teaching, but as a means of uncovering the richness of the original Scripture message.

Bibliography

Congar, Y. M. J. 1966. *Tradition and Traditions: An Historical and a Theological Essay.* New York.

Denzinger-Schönmetzer. 1976. *Enchiridion Symbolorum.* Rome.

Fitzmyer, J. A. 1964. The Biblical Commission's Instruction on the Historical Truth of the Gospels. *TS* 25: 386–408.

Flannery, A., ed. 1975. *Vatican Council II: The Conciliar and Post Conciliar Documents.* Collegeville, MN.

Fogarty, G. P. 1989. *American Catholic Biblical Scholarship: A History from the Early Republic to Vatican II.* San Francisco.

Hanley, T. O., ed. 1976. *The John Carroll Papers.* 3 vols. Notre Dame.

Hogan, J. B. 1898. *Clerical Studies.* Boston.

Jedin, H. 1961. *A History of the Council of Trent.* Trans. by E. Graf. St. Louis.

Kelly, J. N. D. 1960. *Early Christian Doctrines.* New York.

Kenrick, F. P. 1858. *Theologia Dogmatica.* 4 vols. 2d ed. Baltimore.

McNally, R. E. 1959. *The Bible in the Early Middle Ages.* Westminster, MD.

Neuner, J., and Dupuis, J., eds. 1982. *The Christian Faith in the Doctrinal Documents of the Catholic Church.* New York.

Pelikan, J. 1971. *The Christian Tradition.* Vol. 1, *The Emergence of the Catholic Tradition (100–600).* Chicago.

GERALD FOGARTY

BIBLICAL AUTHORITY IN THE EARLY CHURCH

In speaking of scriptural authority in the early Church we may focus attention upon the gradual emergence of an ecumenical Church out of the diversity of earliest Christianity. This development marks the formative period of the early Church, and its completion is reflected in the writings of Irenaeus (fl. 180). While all the many different forms of earliest Christianity assumed the importance and authority of sacred writings, the mainline development was obliged to wrestle with the question which writings were to be regarded as sacred and authoritative. Initially, then, the problem of scriptural authority coincided with the emergence of a Christian Bible and with the arguments for the canonical status of the writings included in it. As a result, the question was not so much how to understand the character and function of scriptural authority as which writings were to be accepted as authoritative.

If by "early Church" we mean the mainline development during the formative period and the ecumenical Church from Irenaeus to the collapse of the Roman Empire in the West (5th century), two general points can act as rubrics for discussion. First, the early Church did not think of the authority of Scripture apart from its relation to the theological tradition expressed in the rule of faith or apart from the use of Scripture in Christian worship. The authority of Scripture was bound to the life of the Church. Scripture, the theological tradition, and the worship of the Church were not treated as alternative points of departure for articulating the meaning of the faith, nor were they regarded as alternative authorities to be played off against one another. Second, the authoritative meaning of these norms of belief and practice was designed to establish unity for the Church, but not a unity involving uniformity. The development of the liturgy preserved regional and even local variations that by no means presented themselves as obstacles to unity. No uniform text of the rule of faith or even of the creeds appears in the Church before the latter part of the patristic period. With respect to Scripture we find not only no uniformity of interpretation, but also no uniform canonical list. To be sure, the rule of faith, the creeds, and Scripture ruled out certain opinions and practices as incorrect. But it did not follow that ruling out error implied the establishment of a single correct view. Instead, the Church remained content with diversity; and we may speak of valid interpretations of Scripture. Only when differing interpretations became contradictory did conflict arise, and the resolution of conflict by no means pretended to eliminate diversity.

A. Scripture, Theology, and the Church

It is obvious from the NT that Christians initially understood Scripture to mean what only later was called the OT. When Paul repeated the tradition about Christ's death and resurrection, the "Scriptures" by which the Christian preaching was demonstrated were the sacred books of Israel (1 Corinthians 15). Scripture in this sense demonstrated the truth of the Christian claim in a number of different ways: by prophecy, by type and foreshadowing, by testimony lists, by allegory, and by simple proof-texting. No one method prevailed for employing the authority of the OT. Moreover, it began to be clear that final authority rested in the Christian preaching and not in the sacred writings thought to demonstrate it. The authority of the OT was neither rejected nor accepted in simple and absolute terms. Instead, it was only a Christianized OT that remained authoritative in the mainline development, which eliminated Judaizing forms of Christianity and excluded gnostic and Marcionite forms of Christianity that rejected the OT and its God.

The authority of the OT, then, was made subservient to the authority of the Christian preaching. The next step was the transition from an oral form of that preaching to a written one. In other words, we must speak of the rise of a NT canon. The writings that eventually constituted the NT canon are, of course, older than the canon itself. And even at a time when the four gospels and a collection of Pauline epistles were regarded as authoritative, the oral form of the Christian preaching still functioned. Papias, for example, in the early 2d century tells us that he prefers a "living voice" to writings. It is also clear from the writings of Justin Martyr in the middle of the 2d century that the Synoptic tradition was still living apart from its incorporation in the written gospels. In the long run, however, the written form of the Christian preaching prevailed; and by the time of Irenaeus at the end of the 2d century we can speak confidently of a Christian Bible. For further discussion, see CANON.

The sort of authority vested in this Christian Bible can best be understood by speaking of the motives for regarding Christian writings as canonical. While the Church Fathers were agreed that canonical books are inspired, inspiration alone did not in their view constitute sufficient grounds for their inclusion in Scripture. The reason for this is quite simply that inspiration was thought to attach to other writings and was also required for the correct reading of Scripture. Instead, the chief criterion for canonical status was apostolicity. The Christian preaching was identified with the apostolic faith and came to be embodied in the writings of the NT. There were, of course, difficulties. Mark's apostolic credentials were vindicated by arguing that he preserved the preaching of Peter; Luke's, that of Paul. And writings purporting to be those of apostles but not widely accepted and demonstrably to one side of the theology of the greater Church had to be regarded as spurious.

What this means is that two further criteria for the authority of canonical books came into play. First, wide currency and acceptance in the churches played a role. Second, the Church's rule of faith increasingly determined the acceptability of the NT writings. Thus, apostolicity was required; acceptability was a factor; but orthodoxy became the central issue. The development that led to Irenaeus' definition of a Christian Bible at the end of the 2d century and Eusebius' list at the beginning of the 3d depends upon these three criteria. We must also reckon with the impact of the struggle with heresy that forced the greater Church to make the decisions that led to a biblical canon and to a rule of faith. The gnostics and Marcion forced the Church to decide which writings were apostolic and orthodox, and to widen the list of authoritative writings. The Montanists, who treated their inspired writings as authorities taking precedence over those of the apostles, forced the Church to develop the idea of a limited canon. The final step was to decide upon the details of the canon.

What is remarkable about this development is the role played in it by the theological tradition. While the rule of faith was identified with the message of Scripture and was authoritative because it cohered with the message of the Christian Bible, from another point of view it was the developing rule of faith that actually created a Christian Bible and that was posited as an authoritative norm for interpretation. Just as the authority of the OT had been available to earliest Christianity only when properly interpreted by the Christian preaching, so the Christian Bible had authority only when rightly read in accordance with the rule of faith. Scripture and tradition went together. There were, however, different views of what this meant in practice. For Tertullian (fl. 200) the rule set limits to the interpretation of Scripture and no meaning could be given Scripture that took one beyond the confines of the rule. On the other hand, for Origen (d. 254) the rule merely established the authoritative beliefs required of simple Christians, while it supplied both a point of departure for and a limit upon the flights of speculation appropriate for the "more perfect" Christians. In both cases Scripture, understood in accordance with the rule of faith, was authoritative. But its authority functioned for Tertullian to establish a doctrinal standard and for Origen to encourage speculations that moved toward the truth without pretending to have arrived at it.

The authority of Scripture was united not only with the developing theological tradition, but also with the liturgical life of the Church. From the earliest times Christians followed the practice of the Jewish synagogue in reading and commenting upon Scripture in their worship (Luke 4, Acts 13). Lectionary systems began to develop in relation to the development of the liturgical year. And we gain the clear impression that preaching was based upon the lessons used in the liturgy. Melito of Sardis' *Paschal Homily* (late 2d century) explained the narrative of the Exodus in a Christian fashion. John Chrysostom (late 4th century) asked his flock to read ahead of time the lessons that were to be read and explained. The liturgical rites themselves, as they began to be fixed and organized, appropriated Scriptural language and themes. It is here that we should probably speak most confidently of the authority of Scripture in the early Church. Scripture in the liturgy did not so much decide theological and moral questions as shape the minds and hearts of worshippers. Such authority is persuasive, subtle, and hard to define. But it was central to the authority of Scripture in the early Church.

B. Authority and Validity

Implicit in arguing that the authority of Scripture in the early Church was always associated with the theological tradition and with the liturgical life of the Church is the conclusion that diversity obtained at every level. It is not going too far to say that no uniform canon of Scripture ever obtained during the first 600 years of the Church's history. A synod at Carthage in 419 established the canon of the NT as we have received it, but there are much later manuscripts that sometimes omit Hebrews and sometimes include the *Epistle to the Laodiceans.* In the East there long remained a tendency to reject Revelation. And the Syrian church's Bible at the beginning of the 5th century omitted not only Revelation but also 2 Peter, 2 and 3 John, and Jude. A second sign of diversity has to do with differing translations of the OT and with problems of textual variants in the whole of the Bible. The LXX took pride of place, but writers like Theodore of Mopsuestia (ca. 350–428) and Augustine (354–430) took seriously other Greek translations and the Hebrew original. Jerome (ca. 342–420), of course, turned to what he called the "Hebrew truth." Neither the absence of a uniform canonical list nor the existence of differing texts and translations seems really to have troubled the fathers of the Church. For them diversity did not prevent the recognition of a Christian Bible and of a unity of faith found in it.

The same recognition of diversity as no obstacle to unity characterized the way Scripture was interpreted. Even the decisions of the ecumenical councils should be understood this way. For example, at Chalcedon in 451 the Church arrived at an interpretation of Christ that would be true to Scripture and to the Nicene Creed. The Definition of Chalcedon, however, more clearly ruled out error than it defined truth. The views of Arius, Apollinaris, Nestorius, and Eutyches were excluded from orthodoxy; but the council in one way or another ratified the three strikingly different Christologies of Cyril, Theodoret, and Leo. We can only conclude that Chalcedon imposed no correct reading of the Scriptural account of Christ, but instead accepted three valid interpretations of Scriptural authority.

One particular problem revolved around the kind of interpretation that had authority. In general, the early Church assumed the authority of Scripture both at the level of the "letter" (the *historia,* or narrative meaning) and at that of the "spirit" (the *theoria,* or spiritual meaning). Nevertheless, after Origen's time we find an increasing emphasis upon retaining the narrative meaning not only in the Antiochene school but also in the exegetical work of figures like Augustine and Jerome. We also find a tendency to codify the various sorts of spiritual meanings that have authority. It is John Cassian, writing in the early 5th century, who first established the fourfold distinction of the narrative, tropological, allegorical, and anagogical meanings which became standard in the West during the Middle Ages. Despite certain tendencies towards standard and uniform views of Scripture and its authority, the early Church understood the authority of Scripture both as one that functioned within the theological and liturgical life of the Church and as one that allowed for considerable diversity. Scriptural authority was not so much a matter of propositions or of the application of principles to cases as a question of the way in which the lore of the church's past persuasively shaped the corporate life of Christians. (See further, *CHB* vol. 1.)

Bibliography

Grant, R. M., and Tracy, D. 1984. *A Short History of the Interpretation of the Bible.* 2d ed. Philadelphia.

Hanson, R. P. C. 1962. *Tradition in the Early Church.* London.

Metzger, B. M. 1987. *The Canon of the New Testament.* Oxford.

ROWAN A. GREER

BIBLICAL AUTHORITY IN THE MEDIEVAL CHURCH

The Church in the Middle Ages lived in and by the Bible (Congar 1967: 86, Schüssler 1977: 1). As the ultimate source of divine truth, Scripture set norms for society through nearly a thousand years (600–1517) of European history (Kropatschek 1904; Rost 1939). As the standard of literacy, it shaped Latin letters and intellectual life, and gave rise to one of medieval Europe's dominant groups, clerics who could read Scripture and who ordinarily learned their letters by way of the Psalms. As "the book," the Bible became paradigmatic for the handwritten codex and for early print, and as "the holy book," its sacred character attracted to it rich ornamentation and illustration, together with sacral functions in processions, oaths, and the like.

The conviction that Scripture formed both the source and the content of divine revelation underlay the whole of medieval European civilization. The ordinary function and influence of this authority require at least cursory attention before turning to questions of biblical authority in a narrower theological sense. Scriptural texts were invoked at almost every point in medieval civilization. Kings, princes, and prelates were understood to rule by the grace of God; subjects were expected to submit to authorities ordained by God (Rom 13:1) and to honor kings and governors (1 Pet 2:13–14, 17). These principles were combined with OT stories and prophetic oracles to produce a full range of teaching on the political and social order (Ullmann 1963; Schramm 1963; see Riché 1984b: 399–400 for a list of the most commonly cited texts). Institutions fundamental to medieval social and economic life, such as a tithe on all people, the anointing of kings, and the proscription of usury, derived their authority as well from OT texts (Chydenius 1965; Kottje 1965; Little 1984).

Canon law, which governed the church and included such social matters as marriage and wills, drew equally upon principles enunciated in Scripture (Gaudemet 1984, with a tabulation of preferred texts; Izbicki 1984; Tierney 1967). Professed members of religious orders, the first order of medieval society and the chief exemplars of the Christian life, pledged themselves to observe the way of life set out in their respective rules and customs, documents understood to implement concretely the teachings of the gospel and the apostles, almost literally so in the case of Saint Francis (Chartier 1984; Leff 1985). Public conflict, whether it concerned church and state in the Investiture Struggle (Leclercq *CHB* 2: 183–97; Robinson 1985) or religious poverty in the later medieval religious orders (Leff 1985), invariably drove all participants to seek out the support of biblical texts.

In two areas the text of Scripture dominated entirely. Public worship, the prayers said every day all across medieval Christendom by monks and clerics, were comprised largely of scriptural materials. Priests read through and preached from the gospels and epistles appointed for all the ordinary and special days of the church year, making the language of the Latin Scriptures second nature to most of them. Canons in cathedrals and collegiate churches were to sing the psalms and canticles of Scripture at appointed hours. Benedictine monks prayed the entire psalter each week and read through the entire Bible at least once a year in an evening cycle. Monastic life in particular came to be defined largely in terms of reading and meditating upon Scripture (Gy 1984, Leclercq *CHB* 2: 183–97; Dubois 1984). In the later Middle Ages, the laity increasingly emulated these forms of public prayer by way of private "books of hours." Whether for show or for devotion, these books, which thousands of later medieval laypersons thought it fitting to own and sometimes to use, contained an accepted set of prayers derived directly from Scripture (for instance, the seven penitential psalms), or indirectly in the form of petitions and meditations that borrowed heavily from the language of the Bible.

Outside public and private worship, Scripture represented the endpoint of a clerical education, and from the 12th century onward the set textbook for what became the faculty of theology. In late antiquity, Augustine's *On Christian Learning* and Cassiodorus' *Introduction to Divine and Human Readings (Institutiones)* established the understanding and preaching of Scripture as the goal of a Christian education; by the 8th century, churchmen were nearly the only educators left in Europe, and the programs of Augustine and Cassiodorus therefore became paradigmatic for all of learning. The cultural revivals associated with Carolingian Europe (750–900) aimed, in the first instance, at acquiring a better text and a better understanding of Scripture. This goal was enunciated already in Charlemagne's *Admonitio generalis,* as well as in his document on letters *(De litteris colendis),* and restated throughout the 9th century. Patronage from the court and from important churchmen promoted biblical scholarship in the 9th century, though most of it remained centered still around compiling commentaries based upon the fathers (Contreni 1983; Riché 1984a).

It was the revival of learning in the 12th century that conferred upon Scripture an authoritative role beyond that of sourcebook for divine revelation and public worship. Scripture now emerged as the textbook for an academic discipline, the *raison d'être* for a separate faculty of theology (Smalley 1983; Châtillon 1984; Verger 1984). Masters of theology were to teach the "sacred page." This way of designating the Bible, rooted in usage going back to the fathers, came to dominate in university circles, distinguishing the "sacred textbook" used by theologians from the texts in grammar, logic, and law taught by artists and lawyers (de Ghellinck 1947). Masters of theology were expected to teach "ordinarily" the text of some book of the Bible, often choosing one from the OT and another from the NT in the same year, after bachelors of theology (modern–day graduate assistants) had first led students through a "cursory" reading of the entire text of Scripture (Glorieux 1968). Masters commonly focused their attention on the Psalms and the Pauline epistles as those books richest in doctrinal content, though the Wisdom books and the Gospels likewise drew attention as fruitful for elucidating the moral dimensions of the Christian way of life (Smalley 1985; Smalley 1986). To facilitate understanding of the "sacred page," 12th-century masters, first in Laon and then in Paris, prepared an "ordinary gloss," an abbreviated standard commentary written in margins and between lines, which armed masters and students with the essential interpretations laid down by the fathers and earlier masters. To facilitate the use of the "sacred page," another master (usually said to be Stephen Langton, d. 1228) divided the text into chapters for ease of reference, while still others organized alphabetized glossaries and concordances to access key terms. Basic to this entire scholastic enterprise was the persistent conviction that all of "theology" (or "God-talk"), however philosophical or speculative in character, was only introductory to and derived from the study of the "sacred page." Every medieval master of theology, be it Thomas Aquinas or Martin Luther, took these convictions and methods for granted.

All the foregoing examples of Scripture's authoritative place in medieval society beg a prior question: the accessibility of its text. Throughout the Middle Ages in the west, the accepted text was Jerome's translation of the Bible into Latin, widely known therefore as the *Vulgate* (Vg), though readings from older Latin translations (the *Vetus Latina* [VL]) circulated by way of earlier commentaries. Despite notions about three sacred languages, occasional forays into Greek by a few extraordinary intellectuals, conversations and disputes with Jews from time to time about the Hebrew original, and a mandate at the Council of Vienne in 1311 that schools appoint language instructors, the Latin Bible remained the norm for both religious and intellectual life. Humanists in the late Middle Ages (Lorenzo Valla, Erasmus of Rotterdam, and Reuchlin), who generally found themselves at odds with the Latinate masters of theology, first promoted a return to the Greek and Hebrew originals and a philological approach to the text. It was the protestant reformers who successfully imported these humanist aims and approaches into faculties of theology.

The Bible is a large book and the reproduction of it by hand costly and time consuming. It was only in the 9th century that the whole of it was commonly contained in a single great codex, in a corrected and legible script. This revision in format was accompanied by an attempt (usually associated with the names of Alcuin and Theodulf) to establish an accurate text (Loewe *CHB* 2: 102–54). Twelfth century schoolmen produced the glossed Bible, a format preserved in early modern printed editions, but whose origins remain unclear and poorly investigated. Theologians at Paris in the early 13th century oversaw the production of Bibles more uniform in format, with divisions into chapters and aids such as glossaries of Hebrew terms. It was the second third of the 13th century that witnessed the production at Paris of complete Bibles in formats small enough to be called "pocket editions" (Light 1984)—possibly products indirectly of the new university (this still disputed), certainly indicators of a new emphasis upon pastoral education and preaching.

Translations into the vernacular languages were numerous and proceeded apace from the 12th century. This was a matter of cultural importance for the Middle Ages, not a product solely of the reformation; but its history belongs properly to the study of the individual vernaculars (useful orientation in *CHB* 2: 338–491; *Lexikon des Mittelalters* 2: 88–106). For the question of authority, the issue of vernacular translations is confusing and often misrepresented. The Church insisted throughout that the Latin text employed in public worship and in the schools represented the only authoritative version, a point made strongly over against Slavic missionary inquiries already by Pope Nicholas I (858–67). But vernacular versions were permitted for private devotional purposes, an attitude presumed by Pope Innocent III in 1198 (Boyle 1985) and defended on later occasions, for instance, by Gerard Zerbolt of Zutphen in behalf of the Brothers of the Common Life around 1400 (Jellouschek 1935). This became problematic only when certain groups (Waldensians, Lollards) claimed the right to preach from vernacular versions without ordination, or used them to defend doctrinal positions contrary to receive orthodoxy (Lollards, Hussites, see Hurley 1960). For the great majority of medieval people, access to Scripture was not a matter of vernacular translation—they remained largely illiterate—but of vernacular preaching and still more of illuminated, sculpted, and painted representations of the biblical stories. Toward the end of the Middle Ages, a kind of structured "picture Bible" *(Biblia pauperum)* became very popular in manuscript and early print.

The more focused question of biblical authority came to discussion, and increasingly to debate, in the context of a European-wide church where the divinely conferred primacy of Scripture was taken altogether for granted. Throughout the Middle Ages churchmen said, with Isidore of Seville (d. 637) or Henry of Ghent (d. 1297), that the Holy Spirit (Beumer 1968: 33) or God himself (Schmaus 1960) was the author of Holy Scripture. Despite a small dispute in the 9th century over how "error-free" Scripture had been transmitted and some ambiguous remarks in the prologue to Peter Abelard's *Sic et Non,* the question of how this worked, how inspiration took place and to what effect, was rarely raised (Beumer 1968: 33, 35). While Thomas Aquinas apparently saw and explored some of the potential difficulties, it was Henry of Ghent who first tried to account for the process by distinguishing primary (divine) and secondary (human) agents in the writing (Beumer 1968: 39–40). But this problem was little explored: most churchmen and masters contented themselves with general, and usually forceful, declarations on the divine authorship of Scripture.

Yet that same Spirit of God they also saw at work in the interpretation of Scripture offered by the fathers, the councils, and the prelates of the Church (Congar 1967: 125–37). Writers would place the four gospels in parallel to four fathers of the church, and treat the latter as an extension of the former (de Lubac 1959: 1.56–57 and passim). Duns Scotus could explain that the same Spirit responsible for the recorded words of institution at the Lord's Supper inspired the prelates at Lateran Council IV to settle on the difficult term "transubstantiantion" as their proper meaning (Congar 1967: 131). Theologians generally understood the difference between a divinely authored "canon" and inspired Church Fathers, a distinction found prominently in Rupert of Deutz (d. 1129) and very commonly in the later Middle Ages (Oberman 1963). But it came to expression more often in polemical circumstances, where a master was attempting to defend from Scripture a position contrary to another affirmed elsewhere by fathers or doctors of the Church. The reigning assumption was that one God and one Spirit worked continuously both in Scripture and in the subsequent interpretative traditions of the Church.

Medieval churchmen, in sum, rarely or never imagined Scripture coming to them "alone"; Scripture came by way of the explanations of the fathers (hence the gloss), the teachings of prelates and masters, and the practices of the church. It was possible therefore to affirm the divine authority of Scripture while assuming the framework through which it was transmitted. Canonists did this when they alluded to the singular authority of Scripture, but focused primarily on the Church's laws: Gratian (the textbook for medieval canon law), for instance, conceded Scripture this primary position but never included a Scriptural text as a "canon" in its own right, though he cited it fifty times in explanatory passages. So too, all the masters of theology (Thomas Aquinas, for instance, in the opening arguments of his *Summa*) did the same when they described theology as a "science" (a coherent body of knowledge, or scholarly discipline) derived from and built upon Scripture. Bonaventure, among 13th-century masters, was particularly insistent upon the authority and fullness of Scripture (de Voogt 1954: 17–22).

Questions pertinent to Scripture's "primacy" and scope arose in different ways in the later Middle Ages. The first concerned its rank in a series of authoritative sources. All medieval thinkers, including jurists and philosophical theologians from the time of Abelard (Tierney 1967; Schüssler 1977) consistently placed it first. Bonaventure, Thomas Aquinas, and numerous other theologians declared at times that nothing was truly binding if not authorized by Scripture. But at the end of the 13th century, theologians began to separate out the different strands that went into the making of Christian revelation. This raised two questions common to 14th and 15th century writers. First, was Scripture a "sufficient" source of divine revelation? Nearly all masters held that it was "materially sufficient," meaning all that was required for divine truth and human salvation was contained in some sense in Scripture (de Voogt 1954: 148ff and passim; Schüssler

1977: 73–75). Canonists in particular, such as Panormitanus (d. 1445), held to the traditional declarations of Scripture's primacy and sufficiency, and Luther was later to draw specifically from him for his early apologetic (Schüssler 1977: 172ff).

The essential question in later medieval discussion concerned the relations between "Scripture" and "Church" (meaning tradition, authority, and practice). Henry of Ghent raised the question explicitly (Schmaus 1960), as did Gerard of Bologna (d. 1317), Ockham, and nearly all subsequent theologians (de Voogt 1954: 356–60; Schüssler 1977: 92–130). All sought in some way to underscore their mutuality: Scripture came to humankind by way of the Church, even was authorized by the Church; yet Scripture alone was the source of the divine truths taught by the Church. Some, like Ockham, emphasized the primacy and infallibility of Scripture over against fallible prelates; others, like Jean Gerson (d. 1429), declared Scripture binding as the Church interpreted and transmitted it. A greater sense of distinction between the "canon of the Bible" and the "teachings of the fathers or the church" emerged, thus in Gabriel Biel (Oberman 1963), even when no tension was presumed. In the late Middle Ages, tensions between the two surfaced more often. Wycliff and Hus set the authority of Scripture over against Church and tradition (de Voogt 1954: 168–99, 218–232); conciliarists deployed an infallible Scripture against fallible popes (Schüssler 1977: 184–224); and certain churchmen (especially Franciscans) isolated more clearly "apostolic" or "oral" traditions to authorize non-Scriptural teachings, especially on Mary (Oakley 1979: 148–57; Beumer 1962: 62–73). But the assumption that Scripture was divinely authored, uniquely authoritative, and transmitted by way of the Church and her traditions prevailed, despite inherent tensions, to the time of Luther and the Reformation.

Bibliography

Beumer, J. 1962. *Die mündliche Uberlieferung als Glaubensquelle.* Freiburg.

———. 1968. *Die Inspiration der Heiligen Schrift.* Freiburg.

Boyle, L. 1985. Innocent III and Vernacular Versions of Scripture. Pp. 97–107 in *The Bible in the Medieval World,* ed. K. Walsh and D. Wood. Oxford.

Chartier, M. C. 1984. Presence de la Bible dans les Règles et Coutumiers. Pp. 305–25 in Riché and Lobrichon 1984.

Châtillon, J. 1984. La Bible dans les écoles du XIIe siècle. Pp. 163–97 in Riché and Lobrichon 1984.

Chydenius, J. 1965. *Medieval Institutions and the Old Testament.* Helsinki.

Congar, Y. M. J. 1967. *Tradition and Traditions: An Historical and a Theological Essay.* New York.

Contreni, J. 1983. Carolingian Biblical Studies. Pp. 71–98 in *Carolingian Essays,* ed. U.-R. Blumenthal. Washington, DC.

Dubois, J. 1984. Comment les moines du Moyen Age chantaient et goûtaient les Saintes Écritures. Pp. 261–98 in Riché and Lobrichon 1984.

Evans, G. R. 1984. *The Language and Logic of the Bible: The Earlier Middle Ages.* Cambridge.

———. 1985. *The Language and Logic of the Bible: The Road to Reformation.* Cambridge.

Gaudemet, J. 1984. La Bible dans les collections canoniques. Pp. 327–69 in Riché and Lobrichon 1984.

Ghellinck, J. de. 1947. "Pagina" et "Sacra Pagina": Histoire d'un mot et transformation de l'objet primitivement désigné. Pp. 23–59 in *Mélanges Auguste Pelzer.* Louvain.

Glorieux, P. 1968. L'enseignement au moyen age: Techniques et méthodes en usage à la Faculté Théologie de Paris, au XIIIe siècle. *Archives d'histoire doctrinale et litteraire du moyen age* 43:65–186.

Gy, P.-M. 1984. La Bible dans la liturgie au Moyen Age. Pp. 537–52 in Riché and Lobrichon 1984.

Hurley, M. 1960. "Sola Scriptura": Wycliff and his Critics. *Traditio* 16:275–352.

Izbicki, T. 1984. La Bible et les canonistes. Pp. 371–84 in Riché and Lobrichon 1984.

Jellouschek, C. J. 1935. Ein mittelalterliches Gutachten über das Lesen der Bibel und sonstiger religiösen Bücher. Pp. 1181–99 in *Aus der Geisteswelt des Mittelalters.* Münster.

Kottje, R. 1965. *Studien zur Einfluss des alten Testament auf Recht und Liturgie.* Bonn.

Kropatschek, F. 1904. *Das Schriftprinzip der lutherischen Kirche.* Vol 1, *Das Erbe des Mittelalters.* Leipzig.

Leclercq, J. 1979. Usage et abus de la Bible au temps de la réforme grégorienne. Pp. 89–108 in *The Bible and Medieval Culture,* ed. W. Lourdaux and D. Verhelst. Louvain.

Leff, G. 1985. The Bible and Rights in the Franciscan Dispute over Property. Pp. 225–35 in Walsh and Wood 1985.

Light, L. 1984. Versions et révisions du texte bibliques. Pp. 55–93 in Riché and Lobrichon 1984.

Little, L. K. 1984. Monnaie, commerce et population. Pp. 555–79 in Riché and Lobrichon 1984.

Lubac, H. de. 1959–64. *Exégèse Médiévale.* 4 vols. Paris.

Oakley, F. 1979. *The Western Church in the Later Middle Ages.* Ithaca, NY.

Oberman, H. A. 1963. *The Harvest of Medieval Theology.* Cambridge, MA.

Riché, P. 1984a. Instruments de travail et méthodes de l'exégète à l'époque carolingienne. Pp. 147–61 in Riché and Lobrichon 1984.

———. 1984b. La Bible et la vie politique dans le haut Moyen Age. Pp. 385–400 in Riché and Lobrichon 1984.

Riché, P., and Lobrichon, G., eds. 1984. *Le Moyen Age et la Bible.* Bible de tous les temps 4. Paris.

Robinson, I. 1985. The Bible in the Investiture Contest: the South German Gregorian Circle. Pp. 61–84 in Walsh and Wood 1985.

Rost, H. 1939. *Die Bibel im Mittelalter.* Augsburg.

Schmaus, M. 1960. Die Schrift und die Kirche nach Heinrich von Gent. Pp. 211–34 in *Kirche und Uberlieferung.* Freiburg.

Schramm, P. E. 1963. Das alte und das neue Testament in der Staatslehre und Staatssymbolik des Mittelaters. Pp. 229–55 in *La bibbia nell'alto medioevo.* Spoleto.

Schüssler, H. 1977. *Der Primat der Heiligen Schrift als theologisches und kanonistisches Problem im Spätmittelalter.* Wiesbaden.

Smalley, B. 1983. *The Study of the Bible in the Middle Ages.* 3d ed. Oxford.

———. 1985. *The Gospels in the Schools, ca. 100–ca. 1280.* London.

———. 1986. *Medieval Exegesis of Wisdom Literature: Essays.* Atlanta, GA.

Tierney, B. 1967. "Sola Scriptura" and the Canonists. *Studia Gratiana* 11:347–66.

Ullmann, W. 1963. The Bible and Principles of Government in the Middle Ages. Pp. 181–227 in *La bibbia nell'alto medioevo.* Spoleto.

Verger, J. 1984. L'exégèse de l'Université. Pp. 199–232 in Riché and Lobrichon 1984.
Voogt, P. de. 1954. *Les sources de la doctrine chrétienne*. Paris.
Walsh, K., and Wood, D., eds. 1985. *The Bible in the Medieval World*. Studies in Church History Subsidia 4. Oxford.

JOHN VAN ENGEN

BIBLICAL AUTHORITY AND THE PROTESTANT REFORMATION

The doctrine of Scripture was a significant theological issue in the Reformation and post-Reformation periods. The polemical writings of Protestants and Roman Catholics make it clear that disagreement over the nature of Scripture's authority in the Church was at the root of many other theological conflicts. The authoritative status of Scripture, its relation to the tradition of the Church, to human reason, Christian experience, and the proper means of Scripture's interpretation formed a cluster of concerns that fostered intense debates in these periods. The ongoing implications of these disagreements have continued to affect the Christian Church through the subsequent centuries.

A. Luther
B. Calvin
C. Post-Reformation Protestant Theologians

A. Luther

The first generation of Protestant Reformers did not write systematic treatises on their views of Scripture. Martin Luther (1483–1546), who broke decisively from the Roman Catholic Church and its medieval theological formulations did, however, stand in continuity with Catholicism in recognizing the Bible's divine authority and inspiration. Yet Luther did not share the Roman Catholic view of the nature and purpose of Scripture and its appropriate interpretation.

Luther looked to the early church theologians and agreed with them that the Bible is inspired by God for the purpose of proclaiming the gospel of salvation in Jesus Christ. It further serves as the Christian's normative guide for living a life of faith. For Luther, salvation is found in the message of Scripture itself rather than, as with the Roman view, through the teachings of the Church and the pronouncements of the church hierarchy, including the Pope. As Luther stated in his 1519 Leipzig debate with the Catholic theologian Johann Eck: "By divine law we are forbidden to believe anything which is not established by divine Scripture or manifest revelation." The authority of Scripture was primary for Luther since "the Scripture is the womb from which are born theological truth and the Church." It is "the Word of God" that "preserves the Church of God" (WA 3.454; 259). The Bible is the "touchstone," "ruler," and "plumb line" or "Lydian stone by which I can tell black from white and evil from good" (See Rogers and McKim 1979: 76). For Luther, all authorities—including the early church theologians and the apostles themselves—must be tested according to their fidelity to Scripture. For "their authority is worth most when it has clear scriptural support."

Luther found Scripture authoritative because of its content: Jesus Christ. In Jesus Christ, God had graciously condescended to be revealed to humankind as a human being. The Christian Gospel as found in Scripture presents Jesus Christ to the world. Luther's view of Scripture rested on the analogy he drew between the Bible and the person of Christ. He wrote that "the Holy Scripture is God's Word, written, and so to say 'in-lettered,' just as Christ is the eternal Word of God incarnate in the garment of his humanity. And just as it is with Christ in the world, as he is viewed and dealt with, so it is also with the written Word of God" (WA 48.31).

Luther's christological focus in his theology took on special importance as he made this connection between the two natures of Christ and Scripture. For as "the divinity and power of God are embedded in the vessel of Christ's incarnate body, so the same divinity and power of God are embedded in Scripture, a vessel made of letters, composed of paper and printer's ink. In order to grasp the biblical revelation in its fullness it is necessary to conceive of Scripture in terms of the divine-human nature of Christ" (WA 3.515; 403–4).

This meant for Luther that the limitations and "humanity" of Scripture were no barriers to its conveying God's divine Word of salvation. By adopting an incarnational means of communicating with humanity, God used human beings to speak to other human beings. Luther could exercise scholarly criticism in dealing with apparent discrepancies and even "errors" in Scripture. His stress was on the central articles of the Christian faith conveyed by Scripture—centering in the message of the Gospel.

B. Calvin

John Calvin (1509–1564) shared with Luther the emphasis on Scripture as the Word of God and the supremely authoritative source for Christian guidance on what to believe and how to live. Calvin's understanding of God's revelation in Scripture was enhanced by his training as a Christian humanist and the insights he gained into the nature of communication and how to study ancient documents (Rogers and McKim 1979: 89–96; McKim 1984: 44–50).

Calvin's views on the need for Scripture are intimately connected with his views on the knowledge of God. Scripture is needed to reveal God's will since human sin has smothered *(suffocari)* and corrupted *(corrumpi)* the true knowledge of God that is implanted within all persons as a "seed of religion" or "sense of divinity" (Calvin 1536: 1.3–4). The will and mind reject the true knowledge of God and become "puffed up and swollen with all the more pride" so the mind is "like a labyrinth." No natural theology or human reasoning can cause the sinner to come to a true knowledge of God.

God has provided "another and better help" to direct humans "aright to the very Creator of the universe" (1.6.1). God has given the Bible to bring people to a true knowledge of God. Scripture functions as "spectacles" by "gathering up the otherwise confused knowledge of God in our minds, having dispersed our dullness" so it "clearly shows us the true God," according to Calvin. Thus the Scriptural revelation is necessary to communicate what God's revelation in nature cannot communicate because of human sin. Scripture is a gift of God's grace to fallen humanity.

Calvin's background training as a Christian humanist affected his way of studying the ancient biblical texts. He understood Scripture as "the Word of God" (1.7.1) that has "flowed to us from the very mouth of God" by the ministry of the biblical writers (1.7.5). Scripture is superior to all human wisdom. In it, "the sublime mysteries of the Kingdom of Heaven came to be expressed largely in mean and lowly words" (*contemptibili; humilitate* 1.8.1).

Calvin recognized that Scripture communicated a true knowledge of God and that this divine message came through human words. Of help for his understanding of these two dimensions was the concept of "accommodation" *(accommodare)*, a term drawn from the Latin rhetoricians and jurists which Calvin learned through his humanist studies. Ancient rhetoricians "accommodated" the content of their speeches to the "capacities" *(captus)* of their hearers. So, in Scripture—God's divine speech to humanity—God has accommodated God's self to human capacity by communicating with humans in a way (through words) adapted to their limited understandings. The divinely appointed human authors of Scripture express God's divine message in human words and thought forms. Thus the infinite distance between God and humanity has been overcome. The "uncultivated and almost rude simplicity" of Scripture was not a barrier to God's revelation. The simple, human style was the very *means* of God's revelational communication. For Calvin, Scripture's content and function was more decisive than the form of its language. God's condescension and accommodation to human capacity in Scripture is an expression of God's love for humanity. The supreme example of God's accommodation is God's incarnation in Jesus Christ.

The authority of Scripture for Calvin flowed from this understanding of Scripture's nature. He rejected the Roman Catholic view that the authority of Scripture is conferred by the Church (1.7.1). For Calvin, "the church is 'built upon the foundation of the prophets and apostles' (Eph. 2:20)." Thus, "if the teaching of the prophets and apostles is the foundation, this must have had authority before the church began to exist" (1.7.2). The Scriptures have authority when humans "regard them as having sprung from heaven, as if there the living words of God were heard" (1.7.1). Scripture is "God's Sacred Word" (1.7.4), "set down and sealed in writing" (4.8.6).

Scripture's authority is recognized only through the work of the Holy Spirit. The internal testimony of the Holy Spirit *(testimonium Spiritus sancti internum)* is the means by which the origin and authority of Scripture become certainties. Calvin wrote: "We ought to seek our conviction in a higher place than human reasons, judgments, or conjectures, that is, in the secret testimony of the Spirit" (1.7.4). For the "highest proof of Scripture derives in general from the fact that God in person speaks in it." The prophets and apostles did not "dwell upon rational proofs" as they spoke. Instead, "the testimony of the Spirit is more excellent than all reason" and "the same Spirit, therefore, who has spoken through the mouths of the prophets must penetrate into our hearts to persuade us that they faithfully proclaimed what had been divinely commanded."

While Calvin recognized there are "human testimonies" that point to Scripture as coming from God (miracles, prophecy, etc.; 1.8), but he believed these "arguments" for the credibility of Scripture were insufficient or "vain" in themselves. External arguments are only "secondary aids to our feebleness" (1.8.13) and are useful to believers who had already accepted Scripture's authority. But "Scripture will ultimately suffice for a saving knowledge of God only when its certainty is founded upon the inward persuasion of the Holy Spirit." This faith in Scripture's authority is intimately related with faith in Jesus Christ since it is only through Scripture that we know of Christ. Faith for Calvin was personal and relational, "a firm and certain knowledge of God's benevolence toward us, founded upon the truth of the freely given promise in Christ, both revealed to our minds and sealed upon our hearts through the Holy Spirit" (3.2.7). Believers are "more strengthened by the persuasion of divine truth than instructed by rational proof." So "the knowledge of faith consists in assurance rather than in comprehension" (3.2.14). Thus for Calvin, Word and Spirit belong inseparably together. The Holy Spirit does not witness apart from the Word; and the Word has no power or effect apart from the work of the Holy Spirit.

Calvin's emphasis on the divine origin of Scripture's message led him to stress Scripture's inspiration. He wrote of "the mouth of the Lord" and "God speaking in Scripture," and in some commentaries he used the term "dictation" to describe this action. Most interpreters agree that Calvin rejected the idea of mechanical dictation since he much more frequently stressed the involvement of the biblical writer's whole personality in the composition of Scripture. His predominant emphasis in using the term "inspiration" is on the divine doctrine or gospel message that humans have expressed in their own words, thought forms, and contexts (see 1.6.2).

In sum, for Calvin, the authority of Scripture lies in its power as God's Word, centered on God's promise and revelation in Jesus Christ, and made known fully through the work of the Holy Spirit.

C. Post-Reformation Protestant Theologians

The followers of Luther and Calvin developed more fully the thought of their mentors on many theological topics. Faced with the Counter-Reformation of Roman Catholicism and later in the 17th-century with new developments in science and philosophy, post-Reformation Protestant theologians were concerned to secure the foundations of their doctrinal views. This concern led to an increased emphasis on establishing the authority of the Bible.

Insofar as the second-generation Reformers sought to use the approaches of the Aristotelian philosophy developed in the medieval universities, they have been termed "Protestant scholastics." These theologians were drawn to the resources of Aristotelianism in order to counter the arguments of their opponents by using the same methods. Of importance here was a heavy reliance on the use of reason as a means of establishing proof. Eventually, Protestants attempted to prove the authority of the Bible by using the same type of Aristotelian arguments put forth by Roman Catholics who sought to prove the authority of the church.

A key dimension of the post-Reformation Protestant theologians' approach to biblical authority was the doctrine of inspiration. The Bible gained its authority because it was divinely inspired by God. Scripture is God's Word, and as God's self-communication, Scripture can be expected to share in God's own characteristics. Chief among these for the scholastic theologians were attributes of Scripture such as its complete truthfulness or inerrancy. In particular, these theologians wished to affirm that Scripture's inspiration was completely under God's control and that biblical writers wrote under God's specific, definite command and impulse; that the complete contents of Scripture were the product of God's "breath" or "inspiration" *(theopneustos)*, so there is a "plenary inspiration" of Scripture; and therefore, the words of Scripture themselves are directly inspired by God (verbal inspiration). If the inspiration of Scripture is established in this way, these theologians believed Scripture then carried with it God's own truthfulness, power, and authority (Preus 1970: 263–65).

For these dogmaticians, the Holy Spirit suggested to the authors of Scripture what they were to write and how it should be written so that as the Lutheran theologian Abraham Calov (1612–1686) wrote: "There is no word of Scripture, not even a jot, that does not occur by divine inspiration" (*Biblia Novi Tesatmenti Illustrata,* II, 1034 in Preus 1970: 281). Both the content and "the words also, which are placed in their mouth and dictated to their pen by the Holy Spirit, were communicated to the individual amanuenses, or men of God" (*Biblia* II, 1547). At the same time, these theologians wished to say that the differing temperaments *(ingenia),* feelings *(studia),* and differences in background *(nationes)* of the biblical writers are reflected in Scripture as well (Preus 1970: 290–91). The heavy emphasis on verbal inspiration has led a number of scholars to view the post-Reformation theologians as teaching in essence a "dictation" theory of inspiration in which there is no real room for the human personalities of the biblical authors to hold a significant place (Preus 1970: 291–92).

Post-Reformation Reformed theologians also grounded Scripture's authority in its inspiration. Francis Turretin (1632–1687) stressed the necessity of establishing Scripture's authority, which he saw as "the primary foundation of faith" (*Institutio* 2.12.1 in Rogers and McKim 1979: 176). Amandus Polanus (1561–1610) wrote that "The authority of Holy Scripture is the dignity and excellence pertaining to Holy Scripture alone, above all other writings, by which it is and is held to be *authentic,* i.e., infallibly *certain,* so that by absolute necessity it must be believed and obeyed by all because of God its Author" (*Particiones theologicae* 1:16; Heppe 1950: 21).

Since Scripture is God's Word and is inspired directly by God, it gains its authority solely from God and not, as in the Roman Catholic view, from the church's acknowledgment of the canon of Scripture. Yet for Turretin and other Reformed theologians of this period, the function of the Holy Spirit in regard to the composition of Scripture was to lead the Apostles "into all truth so that they might not err" (Turretin, *Inst.* 2.4.24 in Rogers & McKim 1979: 176). Turretin argued that "unless unimpaired integrity characterize the Scripture, they could not be regarded as the sole rule of faith and practice" (*Inst.* 2.5.7). This approach led Reformed scholastics to a great concern with establishing rational proofs for Scripture's inspiration and inerrancy. For Turretin, "Before faith can believe, it must have the divinity of the witness, to whom faith is to be given, clearly established, from certain marks which are apprehended in it, otherwise it cannot believe" (*Inst.* 2.4.13). Turretin proposed a number of "external marks" such as Scripture's "antiquity" and "duration" to testify to Scripture's inspiration and inerrancy.

This in turn led to a strong concern to establish the purity of the biblical texts and the original autographic texts of Scripture. Turretin argued that God had providentially preserved the books of the canon so that they accurately reflected the original manuscripts of Scripture. He acknowledged that errors in biblical manuscripts "crept into the books of particular editions through the negligence of copyists or printers." Yet, these "corruptions and errors" could be "restored and corrected by any collation of various copies, or of Scripture itself and of parallel passages" (*Inst.* 2.5.4).

The implication of this approach for Turretin was to insist on the divine character of even the vowel points of the Hebrew OT (which Turretin believed had been part of the original autographs of Scripture). This view was given confessional status in the Helvetic Consensus Formula (1675) which in answer to the rising tide of textual criticism of the Old Testament, asserted that the inspiration of the "Hebrew Original of the Old Testament" is found "not only in its consonants, but in its vowels—either the vowel points themselves, or at least the power of the points." The Bible was described as inspired "not only in its matter, but in its words" (see Rogers and McKim 1979: 184).

In the Protestant scholastic doctrine of Scripture, the perfection of Scripture was the most crucial dimension of Scripture's authority. The doctrine of the "inerrancy" of Scripture was a way of asserting Scripture's authority on the basis of its complete truthfulness and accuracy in all details. As Calov wrote, "Inasmuch as Scripture has been written by a direct and divine impulse and all the Scriptures recognize as their author Him who cannot err or be mistaken in any way (Heb 6:18), no untruth or error or lapse can be ascribed to the God-breathed Scripture, lest God Himself be accused" (*Systema,* I, 462; Preus 1970: 341). The Lutheran Johann Quenstedt (1617–1688) spelled it out fully:

> The holy canonical Scriptures in their original text are the infallible truth and are free from every error. That is to say, in the sacred canonical Scriptures there is no untruth, no deceit, no error, not even a minor one, either in content or words, but each and everything presented to us in Scripture is absolutely true whether it pertains to doctrine, ethics, history, chronology, topography, or onomastics, and no ignorance, no lack of understanding, no forgetfulness or lapse of memory can or should be ascribed to the amanuenses of the Holy Spirit in their writing of the Holy Scriptures (*System,* P.I, C.4, S.2, q.5; Preus 1970: 346).

Some scholars have seen the precision and systematization of the post-Reformation doctrine of Biblical authority as an elaboration and clarification of directions initially spelled out by the first generation Reformers, Luther and Calvin. Other have argued that Protestant scholasticism with its emphasis on the place of reason in theology and stress on verbal inspiration and the inerrancy of Scripture as the basis of biblical authority deviated significantly from the views of the early Reformers and set the basis of Biblical authority on a footing that was not consistent with the contents of Reformation theology. This was to lead to increasing difficulties as the further impacts of 17th-century revolutions in science and philosophy coupled with the later development of biblical criticism raised new questions about the nature and authority of the Bible.

Bibliography

Battles, F. L. 1977. God Was Accommodating Himself to Human Capacity. *Int* 31: 19–38.

Calvin, J. 1536. *Institutes of the Christian Religion* [facsim.]. ed. J. T. McNeill. Trans. F. L. Battles. 2 vols. LCC. Philadelphia. 1960.

Gerrish, B. A. 1957. Biblical Authority and the Continental Reformation. *SJT* 10:337–60.

Heppe, H. 1950. *Reformed Dogmatics.* Rev. ed. by E. Bizer. Trans. E. T. Thomson. London.

McKim, D. K., 1984. Scripture in Calvin's Theology. *Readings in Calvin's Theology.* Grand Rapids.

Preus, R. D. 1970. *The Theology of Post-Reformation Lutheranism.* Vol. 1. St. Louis.

Rogers, J. B., and McKim, D. K. 1979. *The Authority and Interpretation of the Bible.* San Francisco.

Donald K. McKim

BIBLICAL AUTHORITY IN THE WAKE OF THE ENLIGHTENMENT

A. The Period of Orthodoxy
1. Protestant Orthodoxy
2. Reformed Positions
3. Puritanism
4. Spiritualism
5. Millenarianism
6. Roman Catholic Exegesis
B. Humanism and Early Enlightenment
1. Humanistic Anglicans
2. Latitudinarians
3. Arminianism
4. Outsiders
5. English Deists
C. The Age of Pietism
1. German Pietism
2. Awakening in Britain and America
D. The Period of Enlightenment
1. French Enlightenment
2. German Neology
3. New Developments

A. The Period of Orthodoxy

1. Protestant Orthodoxy. In continental Protestantism of the post-Reformation period the orthodox theologians developed systems of a scholastic type in which the loci (dogmatic themes) were arranged in analytical manner, starting from the causes and progressing to the effects. Already in J. Gerhard's *Loci theologici* (1610–25) the system is fully developed (Hägglund 1951). Holy Scripture occupies in it a prominent place. Of the two sorts of revelation, natural and supernatural, the last mentioned is the decisive. And "divine revelation, as it is handed down in the revealed word, is the effecting cause of supernatural theology" (*Loci theologici,* Prooemium §18). Scripture itself is the instrumental cause. The principle of the Reformation that "Scripture alone" is the source of faith in this way is brought into an (Aristotelian) system. The equation "Scripture = Word of God" is also preserved. Gerhard maintains that "between the word of God and holy Scripture as such there is no real difference" (*Loci theologici,* 1.1, §7). Therefore the Bible is inerrant in matters of faith. In all this, however, an important shift from Luther's understanding of Scripture has happened: whereas for Luther the Bible becomes the living word of God in being preached and heard, in the orthodox systems (see also Hutter 1961) Scripture in its written form is identified with revelation (Ratschow 1964–66). Against the spiritualists, the orthodox theologians defended the efficiency of the written word. Against the Catholic propaganda which claimed that the Bible cannot be understood without the authority of tradition, the Protestants maintained that it is perspicuous to everybody and unequivocal in itself (Ratschow 1964–66: 1.123ff). The inner testimony of the Holy Spirit insures its effectiveness (Kirste 1976). The analogy of faith (cf. Rom 12:6) is the guiding principle for understanding the sense of a biblical sentence in the light of the whole canon. In its late phase, orthodoxy defended the integrity of the Bible by the dogma of verbal inspiration (e.g., J. B. Carpzow: every word is directly dictated to the biblical writers by the Holy Spirit) against the rising criticism. Even the vowel points of the Masoretes were taken for inspired (J. Buxtorf). Orthodoxy lost its predominance on the continent by the end of the 17th century, though it still found its defenders in the 18th. But one may not undervalue orthodox Lutheran piety even in the late phase. An example is J. S. Bach, who in his music shows himself as a believing interpreter of the Bible in the way of Luther (Besch 1950; Petzold 1985; Voigt 1986).

2. Reformed Positions. The reformed wing of orthodoxy shared the principles regarding the authority of the Bible with the Lutherans. The Consensus Helveticus (1675) is the most rigid defense of the inerrancy of Scripture. But the reformed dogmatic tradition also knew some special doctrines which had a far-reaching influence on the understanding of the Bible and its authority in England, the Netherlands, Scotland, and (later) the United States. One of the most important was *federal* (or covenant) theology, which originated in Switzerland with the reformers Zwingli and Calvin but was dogmatically developed by dogmatists like P. Melanchthon, H. Bullinger (Baker 1980), Zwingli's successor in Zürich, and C. Olevian in Heidelberg. Later it spread over all reformed territories and was shared by the Puritan W. Perkins and the Dutch theologians F. Gomarus and, above all, J. Coccejus. The Westminster Confession (1647), art. 7, made innerancy a part of the official doctrine of the church (Schrenck 1923; Harinck 1986). The federal theology distinguished two covenants: the general or natural covenant between God and Adam/Noah (which is destroyed by the Fall), and the covenant of grace (which God renewed with Abraham and fulfilled in Christ). Important for its understanding is

Melanchthon's theory of mutual obligation: the believer who by baptism belongs to the covenant is obliged to fulfill its commandments. Another reformed doctrine, the theory of double predestination (the greater part of mankind is predestined for doom, the smaller one is elected to be saved by grace), aggravated the problem for the believer how he might know that he would be saved. A legalistic understanding of the Bible crept in—against the intentions of both Luther and Calvin. Legalism was partially reinforced by the continuance of pre-Reformation attitudes to the Bible which took it as a book containing rules of conduct. There was also a deep-rooted conviction—which originated with Zwingli and Calvin—that the whole life of the church, starting with the liturgy and ecclesiastical organization, but including the daily behavior of every believer, had to be molded on the model of Scripture.

3. Puritanism. Puritanism, as it originated in England in the 16th century, reached its largest political influence during the period of the Commonwealth (1649–60), was repressed under the Restoration, and found a late working field in America far into the 18th century. It was the most rigid movement impressing the reformed rules of life upon church, state, and people. It became the more vigorous as it encountered a strong opposition and repression from the Anglican state church and its hierarchy under Queen Elizabeth I, King James I, and King Charles I's archbishop Laud.

At its best, the Puritan movement was a party of clergymen and laypeople in the Church of England striving to carry into effect the reformation program of "scripture alone" (Ryken 1986: 137–54) and to live a spiritual life according to the Bible (Watkins 1972). In the Westminster Confession, art.1, the reformed doctrine of Scripture is preserved (Rogers 1966–67: 257–455). At its worst, it was strictly legalistic, as can be seen in the narrow rules for Sabbath observance (Solberg 1977; Wagner 1982). The Puritans were inclined to use the Bible (especially the OT; Selbie 1953) as a book of laws, culminating in the decalogue. For the separatist groups, the NT delivered the direct model of church organization. But Puritanism did much for spreading knowledge of the Bible in England. The famous Geneva Bible (a work of the Marian exiles in Geneva, 1560; Wilson 1976: 122–25), which strongly influenced the officially competing KJV (1614; Wilson 1976: 145–48), was a Puritan work (*CHB* 3:141ff). That every layman—even the soldier in Cromwell's army with his pocket Bible—could read the Bible himself and became, at least partially, independent from the sermons in which his parson explained it to him, was a Puritan achievement.

Since 1630, the date of the Puritan-sponsored migration to the Massachusetts Bay, the Bible played a decisive role as the basic authority for developing an ideology of the New World. Whereas the spiritualist Quakers failed to build up durable theologico-social structures in their settlement in Philadelphia, the Puritans in Boston developed the concept of the New England people as the people of the covenant and God's chosen nation (Miller 1933, 1937). Millennial expectation, which was impressed in everybody's mind by reading the Bible, helped to form the conscience of a messianic nation (Bercovitch 1978; Stout 1982). The OT supplied the figure in ancient Israel of the New Israel, to be identified with the American Puritans. For the individual was reserved a personal salvation by grace which could be "prepared" for by listening to the preached Word and being a loyal citizen.

4. Spiritualism. From the beginnings of the Reformation, orthodox Protestant theology fought a continuing struggle against spiritualism. Whereas for the reformers the Word itself, as contained in the letter of the Bible, was the bearer of the Holy Ghost and capable of effecting belief in the heart of the hearer, for the followers of the mystic-spiritualist tradition, the "dead letter" lacked any force; the Spirit was kindled like a candle in the heart of the believer. Such spiritualism was to be met with in different degrees: from the mild, Lutheran type of a K. von Schwenckfeld or H. Rahtmann to the radical form of a S. Franck or G. Fox, the founder of Quakerism, who denied to the Scripture any independent authority and relied on the "inner light" as the only saving power in man. The mild spiritualism—to which the Lutheran type of mysticism such as J. Boehme's is related (Pältz 1965)—did not devalue the Bible, but maintained that the utter word cannot be efficient unless the Holy Spirit is opening the heart of the hearer (cf. Grützmacher 1902). Radical spiritualism could sometimes slip into secular revolutionary activity, as with T. Müntzer in the time of the Reformation, or the Ranters and Diggers in England during the Commonwealth. In the main, spiritualism did not win very many followers in the 17th century, and its radical wing had not the power to endanger the high authority of the Bible in the Protestant countries.

5. Millenarianism. A phenomenon that for a long time escaped notice in modern scholarship is the apocalyptic trend in the 17th century which can be observed in different countries. On the continent theologians like J. V. Andreae (1586–1654) J. H. Alsted (1588–1638) and J. A. Comenius (1592–1670) had millenarian ideas (Firth 1979: 204–13). Later in the century the mystic spiritualists (A. von Franckenberg, P. Felgenhauer, C. Hoburg, F. Breckling, J. G. Gichtel, Q. Kuhlmann, E. and J. W. Petersen) spread their visions of a coming millennium (eschatological reign of Christ of a thousand years) according to Revelation 20 (Wallmann 1986: 338ff). Paracelsus, V. Weigel, and J. Böhme had had the same expectations. In England (Ball 1975) during the civil war eschatologically oriented sects like the Fifth Monarchy Men and the Muggletonians (Hill 1972; Hill, Reay and Lamont 1983; Hill 1986: 253–300) searched the book of Daniel and feverishly expected the imminent coming of the glorious reign of Christ. But still an Anglican theologian like J. Mede could write an influential chiliastically oriented commentary on Revelation (Firth 1979: 213–28; Oberdieck 1985: 138ff), the Puritan R. Baxter was likewise a millenarist (Lamont 1979), and even Isaac Newton took a lively interest in the topic in his private religious studies (Manuel 1974; Jacob 1976: 100–142; Westfall 1981: 309–30, 815–30). The contemporary "scientific" endeavors for a universal chronology relied totally upon the OT. J. Ussher's *Annales Veteris Testamenti* (1650) is the best known example (Barr, 1984–85), but W. Ralegh in his *History of the World* (1614; Fussner 1962: 191–210) also relied completely on biblical chronology. Joseph Scaliger in his *Opus novum de emendatione temporum* (1583) and later Newton used astronomical calculations to support the biblical data.

6. Roman Catholic Exegesis. For Roman Catholic exegesis the decisions of the Council of Trent (1545–48) remained obligatory. The Vulgate was declared the official version for dogmatic purposes in the church; it included the apocryphal books of the OT as contained in the LXX. In contrast to the reformed churches, the Bible was not the only authority; the oral ecclesiastical ("apostolical") tradition gained the same, if not a higher doctrinal importance (F. J. Crehan in *CHB* 3: 199ff). The reading of the Bible among laypeople was in no way furthered by the official church; during the Counter-Reformation it was even suspected as indicating a hidden Protestantism. But the dissemination of Protestant translations in the vernacular languages gave impetus to the production of dogmatically inoffensive Catholic translations in different countries. Only part of them received official recognition (because Pope Paul V in 1559 had forbidden publication of a vernacular edition without formal allowance of the Holy Office). In contrast to the Protestant stress on the literal sense of Scripture, the Roman Catholic tradition preserved the fourfold sense. Patristic exegesis was held in high esteem. In the Jesuit universities founded in the period of the Counter-Reformation, biblical exegesis had a certain, if not prominent, place. The most influential commentator in the Baroque age of nearly the whole Bible was C. a Lapide (van den Steyn). In the wake of L. Molina, Catholic exegetes were inclined to a less strict theory about verbal inspiration. Textual criticism gained a certain place in the work of J. Morin, who held (in defense of the LXX) that the Hebrew text of the OT is corrupt. In other ways, the standpoint of Catholic apologetics was similar to protestant orthodoxy. A good example is D. Huet's *Demonstratio evangelica* (1679), in which the OT was defended as prophecy upon Christ. Critical outsiders, such as R. Simon, were relentlessly persecuted by censorship. The popularizing of the Bible took place in Germany (Valentin 1983–84), in France (Sayce 1955; Rougemont 1986) and in other countries in the Jesuit drama, mostly on OT stories. Besides, several long poems on biblical topics were produced. But all in all, the role of the Bible in Catholic countries was restricted.

B. Humanism and Early Enlightenment

1. Humanistic Anglicans. In the Church of England, different currents struggled against one another. A thoroughgoing reformation like that in the Protestant countries had never taken place. Henry VIII's anticlerical measures were exclusively motivated by personal and political interests. Nevertheless, first Lutheran, then reformed theological influences altered the situation. Broadly speaking, the Anglican church can therefore be reckoned among the churches of the Reformation. Whereas the Puritan party followed a narrowly biblicistic program, the Anglicans (this is a 19th-century term, but it adequately describes the majority trend in the Church of that time) steered a middle course *(via media)*. They also held the Bible in high esteem (Reedy 1985), but gave reason its place. The rationalism of the Enlightenment was not yet dominant, but the mildly rational temper of humanism used reason for establishing a moral way of life and for apologetic purposes. R. Hooker, in his *Laws of Ecclesiastical Polity* (1594–97), ascribed to natural reason an important role as a basis for positive law, arguing that it is sufficient for reaching moral perfection. Supernatural revelation as codified in the Scripture is needed to lead man by redemption to the goals of faith, love, and hope (for Hooker, Hillerdale 1962; Marshall 1963). Reason and Scripture in that way supplement one another in a dualism, the impact of which was important for the whole following development.

In the Church of England in the late 16th and early 17th centuries, biblical typology was used as well by Puritans as by Anglicans for establishing royal prerogatives and duties in church and state. OT kings such as David and Hezekiah became the models for English monarchs (*ABRMW*, 135ff). The divine right of kings was defended from OT hereditary rights in the patriarchalism of R. Filmer, whose *Patriarcha* was published posthumously in 1680 by the Jacobites in support of the legitimate succession of King James II.

In Anglicanism, the high-church ceremonialism of Archbishop Laud could go hand in hand with broad mindedness in doctrinal matters. The representative work on the Bible from the perspective of liberal Anglicanism was W. Chillingworth's *Religion of Protestants* (first published in 1638). Against Roman claims to infallibility, Chillingworth set the principle that the Bible alone is the complete rule for faith and action (Orr 1967; *ABRMW*, 147–52). Chillingworth also employs the Erasmian distinction between fundamental and non-fundamental doctrines; he is ready to reduce doctrinal obligations to a minimum—that Christians should believe on Christ. The central content of Scripture (especially the NT and in it the moral teaching of Jesus) is the will of God that is visible in it and can be understood by everybody with the help of reason. The Bible is just a means of conveying this will; alongside Scripture, natural reason can help to judge right from wrong.

One of the most famous liberal Anglicans was Thomas Hobbes (1588–1679). Often falsely stamped as an atheist, Hobbes, a lay philosopher, developed his political theory from a liberal Anglican standpoint. He combined anti–Roman polemics, a moral understanding of the Bible, and dogmatic minimalism (it is enough to believe "that Jesus is the Christ") with a royalist state-church idea, which induced him to give in his theory of an ideal government (Hobbes 1839a; 1839b) the sovereign the right to decide on all outward ceremonies in the church and the public creed, including also which books of the Bible should be canonical. Scriptural proof by typological arguments for these comprehensive rights on one side and historical criticism of the Bible (especially against Moses' authorship of the Pentateuch) on the other show the ambivalence of an old-fashioned thinker who also tries to use new methods for a political theory developed *more geometrico*: according to the rules of modern natural science.

2. Latitudinarians. The Latitudinarians were the successors of the liberal Anglicans in the last decades of the 17th century. Their attitude was the same: no objections against the basic contents of the Christian creed, but with some of them a tendency to minimalism, the whole energy directed to improving the moral behavior of believers. The most famous latitudinarian was archbishop J. Tillotson (1630–94) who in innumerable catechizing sermons was extremely influential in that direction. The Bible again was taken mainly as a book of moral rules. In a similar vein John Locke (1632–1704), who had refuted Filmer's patriarchalism on its own basis, the OT (*Two Treatises of Government* [1690]) in his *Reasonableness of Christianity* (1695) took the NT as the basis for his two closely connected goals: to demonstrate that the minimal confession that Jesus is the Messiah is enough for salvation and that Holy Scripture provides the only reliable authoritative morality. Locke distinguishes between a law of works (including the law of nature and the law of Moses), which has to be done by everybody, and the law of faith (Rom 3:27), which compensates for the gaps in fulfilling the law. The teaching of Jesus was needed, not because reason is principally unable to attain a natural knowledge of God and human duties, but because in practice, humankind did not use it. The gospel, therefore, has above all a pedagogical purpose. The Bible is held in high esteem, but Locke's rationalism prepared the way for the deistic criticism.

3. Arminianism. The followers of Jacob Arminius (1560–1609) opposed the strict Calvinist dogma of predestination. They were also called Remonstrants (after the Remonstratio they had presented to the General States of Holland in 1610). To the Remonstrant community belonged the famous Bible exegetes Hugo Grotius and Johannes Clericus (Jean Leclerc). Grotius, humanist, lawyer, and politician (*TRE* 4: 277–80), was also an able exegete (Reventlow 1988a). He wrote *Annotations* to both Testaments (1679). Besides philological exegesis and text-critical research, Grotius offers the first historical explanation of the whole Bible. But he does not criticize the Scriptures. In his apologetic work *De veritate religionis Christianae* he even defends the truth of Christianity by the truthfulness of the Bible. Biblical authority is not yet called in question. Leclerc (Barnes 1938; Reventlow 1988b) goes a step further: he formulates a basic hermeneutical rule requiring that to understand a biblical book one has to detect the intention of the author in writing it, the circumstances of its having been written, and the meanings and events mentioned in it (*Sentiments de quelques théologiens de Hollande* [1685]). Dogmatically Leclerc is a minimalist: he stresses (against R. Simon) that the Bible contains all that is essential for a right religion. Leclerc also wrote several mainly philological and historical OT and NT commentaries (Pitassi 1987).

4. Outsiders. Benedict de Spinoza (1632–1677), a Jewish philosopher who was excommunicated by his community, consequently separated the realms of reason (on which he founded his holistic philosophical system) and religion (Strauss 1965; Zac 1965 and 1979; Malet 1966; Heimbrock 1981; di Luca 1982). For his philosophy he demanded complete freedom from any external authority, including the Bible. Faith and philosophy are to be severed (Spinoza 1670 chap. 14). Truth belongs to the realm of philosophy, subjective piety and obedience to the realm of faith and theology (cf. Sandys-Wunsch 1981). Faith is defined (according to Jas 2:17) as obedience. In his *Tractatus theologico-politicus* (1670), which he also wrote for the political purpose of vindicating typologically from the Bible the rule of the regent J. de Witt's party in Holland (Meinsma 1896; Frances 1937; Breton 1973; Greschat 1980), he gave a definition of the historic-critical method (Spinoza 1670 chap. 7): (1) the aim is to give a history of Scripture, which must not be seen on one level; (2) the intention of the biblical writers is decisive; (3) everything is to be drawn out of Scripture itself and must not be taken from dogmatics. He refuses the allegorical method of the Aristotelian Jewish interpreter Maimonides and restricts exegesis to the verbal sense. From his historical standpoint Spinoza is able to detect many mistakes in the orthodox opinions about, e.g., the authorship of the Pentateuch and the historical books (which are not from Moses and the other authors mentioned in their headings, but presumably from Ezra), about the biblical text and the OT canon, and about contradictions between the four gospels and other passages in the NT (Spinoza 1670 chaps. 8–10). All this is no problem for faith, because the Bible has reached us unfalsified as far as the Word of God is concerned (chap. 12). Spinoza's immediate influence was not large, as he was everywhere proscribed as an atheist. But his works were read secretly in opposition circles.

In 1655, the French reformed thinker Isaac de la Peyrère (McKee 1944; Klempt 1960: 89–96; Popkin 1979: 214–28) anonymously published his book on the Pre-Adamites (Peyrère 1655). In a way this book was revolutionary, as de la Peyrère put in doubt the hitherto commonly accepted biblical picture of the world and of a history of humanity which started with Adam as the first man. He could no longer reconcile the increase of knowledge about the development of early cultures, such as the Babylonians and the Egyptians, or the ancient and still flowering civilization of China, with the outmoded biblical theory. Therefore he postulated the existence of a pre-Adamite humanity; Adam was the father of the Jews only. The new cosmology was a greater danger to the authority of the Bible (see Popkin 1987).

Catholic orthodoxy regarding Scripture was in principle monolithic, especially because the Inquisition suppressed any independent utterance. But there were some who went their own ways.

Best known is Richard Simon (1638–1712), a French Oratorian who was ousted by his order and prosecuted by the ecclesiastical censorship because of his heterodox opinions, but died as a Catholic priest (Bernus 1869; Margival 1900; Stummer 1912; Steinmann 1960; Auvray 1974; Reventlow 1980). His main work, the *Histoire critique du Vieux Testament* (1678, 2d ed. 1685), intended according to his own declaration (Preface, fol. 3c) to shake the foundations of the Protestant Scripture principle by showing the unreliability of the Bible. Therewith he also invoked a Catholic principle in questioning the correctness of the Hebrew text, which he showed to be corrupted in the long process of textual transmission. Only the originals were inspired (see Le Brun 1982). Simon makes clear that the biblical chronology is not trustworthy (Simon 1685: 5.38.204–11)—a very important step for the time—and that profane sources have to be taken into consideration. In these respects he is one of the founders of modern historical scholarship. Whereas his statement that Moses cannot be the author of the Pentateuch is not new, a new method can be observed in his hypothesis that Moses installed "public scribes" who had to write down the minutes of the most important public affairs, which in abbreviated form served as a pattern for the historical books of the OT (Simon

1685: 3–5.15–21). In this way tradition attains a position prior to Scripture (though Simon, who sees in the hypothetical scribes inspired prophets, ascribes inspiration to these minutes as well). Simon also wrote several works on NT textual criticism (Simon 1689 a–b; 1695) and on the history of NT exegesis (Simon 1693), in which he also referred to such already acceptable critical observations as the spuriousness of the last section in Mark (Simon 1689a: 77–85), the presumably non-pauline origin of Hebrews (Simon 1689a: 120–30), and the pseudonymous authorship of the so-called Catholic Epistles, especially James (Simon 1689a: 130–42). Though Jean Leclerc strongly opposed Simon's theses (1685) and the supposed scribes were nowhere accepted, Simon was later acknowledged by Protestant Bible criticism as an important precursor.

5. English Deists. Deism (see especially Lechler 1841; Gawlick 1972, 1973) is a widespread phenomenon of diffuse appearance. Under the common denomination of believers in God it comprised adherents of Epicureanism (who knew only a remote, motionless God and who disputed revelation) and followers of the Stoic tradition (who were prepared to acknowledge natural revelation). In calling themselves Christians they were quite sincere, because they were even ready to accept a biblical revelation, though revelation adapted to their ideas.

The deists as a movement carrying this name are first mentioned in France in the second half of the 16th century (Betts 1984). But the repression in that reactionary Catholic country forced them into the underground. An open (though still restricted) discussion about deistic principles was only possible in England after the Glorious Revolution of 1689. The first name to be mentioned is that of Edward Herbert of Cherbury (1582–1648), who is commonly regarded as the founder of English deism (Rossi 1947; Bedford 1979; *ABRMW,* 185–93), though that characterization has been disputed (Pailin 1983). Cherbury in his *De Veritate* was proud to have detected five "common notions" or "catholic truths" concerning religion which are innate ideas and everywhere the same in all mankind: (1) there is a God; (2) to him worship is due; (3) virtue combined with piety is the most important part of the service owed to God; (4) sins have to be expiated by penance; (5) there will be reward or punishment after this life (Cherbury 1645a = 1966:1.210–222). The same "catholic truths" he also had detected in the Bible insofar it contains God's Word (*Religio Laici,* Cherbury 1645b = 1966: 135). But the Bible also hands down the words of criminals, women, beasts, even the Devil (ibid.)! This utterance shows Herbert to be a moralist influenced by stoic thought who is prepared to acknowledge the Bible insofar it conforms with his system, but also measuring it with the yardstick of preconceived ideas to which he ascribes universal validity. This is fundamentally the same position taken by later "Christian" deists.

After a long interval the works of Charles Blount (1654–93) appeared. (Bonante 1972; Walber 1988). Though Blount referred to Cherbury, he was in fact opposed to natural religion. It is debated how far he was completely against religion, but in the main he was a skeptic. In his work *Great is Diana of the Ephesians* (1695) Blount criticizes the whole cult (rites, ceremonies and sacrifices) as an invention of the priests. His translation of Philostratus' life of the ancient miracle worker Apollonius of Tyana (1680) contains many concealed opinions about the miracles of Christ and other biblical matters. In the letter of a correspondent of Blount whose initials are given as "A. W." (*Oracles of Reason* [1695]) Deism is for the first time defined as faith in the adequacy of natural religion without the need of an additional revelation. *A Summary Account of the Deists' Religion* (1695), also an anonymous pamphlet (Walber 1988: 41f) and the first Deist manifesto, proclaims the same creed as Cherbury's without mentioning revelation. J. Toland (Sullivan 1982; Daniel 1984) in his early career—later he became a pantheist—wrote the famous book *Christianity not Mysterious* (1696) in which he used the epistemology of Locke to show that Christian religion and all of its fundamental doctrines as revealed in the Bible are not contrary to or above reason. As human knowledge is gradually progressive it may be that we do not understand everything at the present, but in religion we know all that is useful and necessary to know. These are the "concepts and doctrines of the Gospel" (Toland 1696: xiv). The "plain convincing instructions of Christ" (XXI). Toland's concept is apologetic—he takes "the Divinity of the New Testament for granted" (XXVI)—and near to Anglican moral rationalism. But his step to making reason the measure for deciding about the contents of the Bible is important for the following development of criticism.

The third Earl of Shaftesbury, Anthony Ashley Cooper (1671–1713), is important for having formulated a theory of ethics independent of any outward authority, including the Bible (for Shaftesbury, see esp. Aldridge 1951; Zani 1954; Grean 1967; *ABRMW,* 308–21). In his *Inquiry Concerning Virtue or Merit,* first published in 1699, he asserted that in every person, even the most primitive, has a natural feeling of good and evil and a friendly attitude, or a "moral sense." As virtues are "natural," "instinctive," or "innate," they are independent from revelation, even in the form of natural law, and all the more of a divine will communicated in the bible. Because moral action has its rewards in itself, the promise of future rewards and punishments in the beyond is superfluous. On the other hand, if there exists a god, he must be just, righteous, and true; he is bound by the pre-existing moral order. The God of the Bible is partly in contradiction to this, as he sometimes acts cruelly, revenges himself, is friendly to only a minority of humanity.

With Shaftesbury we also encounter a moral criticism of the OT figures Moses, Joshua, and the Patriarchs, as well as the people of Israel as a whole. Any critically thinking Christian must be sceptical about the biblical tradition: Shaftesbury is the first to develop this principle as a methodological postulate. Reason can reflect only about things which are perceived by the senses. Shaftsbury also rejects miracles as a proof for the divinity of Jesus' mission, because they are reported by merely human tradition. His personal religion is "enthusiasm": the love of the good and the beautiful; in outward forms he is willing to subject himself to the official church.

In his *Christianity as Old as the Creation* (1730), usually said to be a key work of Deism, M. Tindal (1657–1733) sets natural religion, which is based on the law of nature and adequate for everyone, because it is rational and moral, as the scale on which the doctrines of revelation are to be measured. Basically Christianity is identical with natural religion as pure morality; therefore it can be called its "republication" (for Tindal, see Lechler 1841: 326–42; *ABRMW,* 374–83).

A special topic is the debate about the role of prophecy. In orthodox apologetics, OT prophecies (according to 2 Pet 1:19) were one of the most important proofs for Jesus' Messiahship. W. Whiston, mathematician and (eccentric) theologian (Farrell 1981; Force 1985) had postulated that all prophecies apply to Jesus in their literal sense. As that is not everywhere the case, both the MT and LXX texts of the OT are regarded as corrupted (allegedly altered by the Jews in the 2d century) and in need of restoration (Whiston 1722). A. Collins, who had already demanded the right of free-thinking in all religious matters, including the Bible (Collins 1713; Redwood 1976: 209–11; Horstmann 1980), answered Whiston (Collins 1724). Asserting that in fact the fulfillment of OT prophecies in Jesus is the only touchstone for the truth of Christianity, and that Whiston's hypothesis is fantastic and easy to refute, Collins concludes that there is really no other proof for Christianity than the usual typological and allegorical one. But OT prophecies (for instance Isa 7:14) were fulfilled literally in OT times. Collins leaves it open what conclusions follow from that (Lechler 1841: 269–75; O'Higgins 1970: 155–99; Frei 1974: 66–85; *ABRMW,* 362–69).

There is also wholesale rejection of the OT: T. Morgan (1738–40 = 1969) acknowledged neither the ceremonial nor the moral law of Moses as divine. The instructions of Jesus, which are identical with natural law, are binding. The prophets also find favor as proclaimers of morality. For Morgan, a pure primal religion stands at the beginning, which the patriarchs to some degree represent. The priests, who introduced the cult, are the main corrupters of OT religion. David, Samuel, and the kings are sharply critized for their immorality (Lechler 1841: 370–87; Gawlick, in Morgan 1969: 5*—36*; *ABRMW,* 396–404).

Another chapter in the history of biblical authority is the debate about the miracles in the NT (for the whole discussion see Burns 1981, Brown 1984). For the moderate Anglicans, including the empirical scientists as J. Glanville and R. Boyle, and also Locke, it was no problem that the miracles had really happened. There was a realm of the supernatural above the empirical world. Even some of the Deists were prepared to accept the possibility of miracles. A critical discussion between the apologist T. Sherlock (1729) and the radical deist P. Annet (1744) focused on the central miracle, the resurrection of Jesus (Lechler 1841: 312–14; Craig 1985). Sherlock tries to demonstrate by "eye-witness testimony" that the resurrection has in fact happened. Annet acknowledges reason as the sole criterion, if fact cannot be demonstrated. As proofs cannot be given that the witnesses were not deceived—and a detailed examination of the decrepancies in the gospels, etc., shows the contrary—the evidence is not sufficient to convince anybody but believers. Annet's conclusion goes further: he asserts "that an historical faith is no part of true and pure religion, which is founded only on truth and purity. That it does not consist in the belief of any history, which . . . makes no man wiser nor better" (Annet 1744: 72). This is the basic weakness of the enlightenment.

The discussion on miracles culminated in David Hume's "Essay on Miracles" (chap. 10 of *An Enquiry Concerning Human Understanding,* 1748) According to Hume miracles are extraordinary events which infringe the laws of nature and are contrary to daily empirical experience. Belief in miracles means to consider them more probable than the laws of nature. The moderate empiricists criticized Hume's arguments because they were not prepared to subsume the whole of reality under the laws of nature (Burns 1981: 176–246).

The apologists of the period attempted to defeat the Deists on their own territory and thereby furthered the development of Deism against their will. In the wake of Newton, the Physico-Theologians tried to demonstrate the existence of God and his freedom to act from the origin of matter and the perfection of creation. S. Clarke in his Boyle Lectures of 1704 and 1705 wanted to develop his ethics from his natural philosophy and his doctrine of God. But the notion of the freedom of God and the theory that the present order of the world is created by his arbitrary decrees is contradicted by the principle that God must be infinitely good, and that all his actions must be determined by this goodness. In correspondence to God, all subordinate rational beings must act for the good of the whole. The biblical revelation in principle becomes superfluous. Clarke proves its necessity on pedagogical grounds: humankind was in such a corrupted state that it needed special instruction by divine revelation. Personally Clarke believed firmly in the Bible: in his book on the Trinity (1712) he showed that the doctrine of the Church is contradicted by NT evidence. The seeming contradictions are caused by diverging traditions (natural-right theory, aversion against "mysteries") in Anglican rationalism.

Also very popular was J. Butler's *Analogy of Religion* (1736). His method (Mossner 1936; Jeffner 1966; Ramsay 1969) is a double one: (1) he shows the analogy between natural and revealed religion—natural religion taken in the usual understanding of Anglican ethical rationalism; (2) he owns that certainty is not to be gained in both areas—but if not certainty, at least probability (in the scheme of Locke's epistemology). Revealed religion is a "republication of natural religion," but it also contains supernatural truths. As those are above reason, miracles and prophecies serve as proofs. Butler demonstrates their reliability by showing that they are a "matter of fact," historical events which can be demonstrated as such. Though Butler's arguments made a great impression and seemed to stop the deistic debate, he actually opened the way for historical criticism of the Bible to sap the foundations of scriptural belief which took the Bible as a report of historical facts and would collapse when they were disproved as such.

C. The Age of Pietism

1. German Pietism. In 1675 P. J. Spener published his *Pia Desideria,* the famous program for a renovation of the Church. The Bible stands in the center of his proposals (M. Schmidt 1970): the deplorable state of spiritual life in the communities could only be bettered, if "the word of God would be brought more abundantly among us." Toward reaching this aim, some concrete advice is uttered: above all that the Bible (mainly the NT) should be read in every household and therefore be distributed in cheap copies everywhere, that meetings (*collegia pietatis;* the first in Frankfurt in 1670) should be arranged for reading biblical texts and meditating together about them in order to edify one another, and that the syllabus of theological studies for ministers should be altered from scholastic to biblical topics (Brecht 1986).

Spener's program found an unexpectedly broad echo among the youth and part of the clergy. In Leipzig, a collegium philobiblicum of young masters of theology studied the Bible in the original languages, among them A. H. Francke; biblical lectures *(collegia biblica)* were held at the university with great concourse of students. Later the center of Pietism moved to Halle (Aland 1960), where Francke became pastor and professor in the newly founded university (opened 1694). The intensive study of the Bible, based on the literal sense read in the original languages, but leading to Christ in the scriptures, was the basis of this study; dogmatics and philosophy were pushed to the background. Historical criticism was not involved. Spener had no interest in critical exegesis (though he inquired into the historical situation of a text); as a former student of the younger J. Buxtorf (1599–1664; see Wallmann 1986: 134–39) he even defended verbal inspiration (for his method, M. Schmidt 1970: 27–54). Francke's position was similarly orthodox (see Peschke 1970). The pietists deemed the assistence of the Holy Spirit central to understanding the Scripture. Spiritual experience, leading to rebirth, was regarded as most important (Stroh 1977). The spiritualistic and mystic heritage (Tauler) played an important role. Also, eschatological expectations were nourished (Spener; Francke). The Orphanage (founded 1695) became the place of education for many young Prussian gentlemen, but also a locus of world mission and international connections. The v. Canstein Bibelwerk (founded 1710) printed and distributed Bibles and NTs in many languages in large numbers (Aland 1960: 30–39; 1970a: 90–92; Köster 1984: 100–135; Köster also on other pietist Bible editions). Pietism spread in all German-speaking territories. A special group was the Brüdergemeine (Moravian Church), founded by Count N. L. von Zinzendorf and still in existence in many countries. Zinzendorf (on his Bible knowledge, see Dose 1977) in 1728 invented the "Losungen" (watchwords), which contain for each day a verse of the OT and the NT and are the best-known German books of devotion to this day.

All in all, Pietism promoted an individualistic or group-oriented piety, above all in laypeople. An example is the Reformed pietistic poet G. Tersteegen, who found in the Bible an everflowing spring of spiritual life (Zeller 1970). The NT especially was read and understood as a book of instruction for pious life. Basic is the demand of a spiritual rebirth of every Christian which has to bear visible fruit.

The best known representative of Wurttemberg pietism was J. A. Bengel (1687–1752). His work on the Bible (Brecht 1967; 1970; Aland 1970a) was divided between philological and historical research on the text of the NT (he was author of a critical edition of the NT, 1734, and a commentary of the whole NT, the *Gnomon,* published in 1742) and his theological interest. Theologically he was orthodox (he believed in verbal inspiration), spiritualist (for understanding the Bible, one needs the help of the Holy Spirit) and apocalyptist (he wrote several works about the calculation of the approaching end of the world on the base of biblical chronologies; Sauter 1966).

Radical pietism (Schneider 1983–4) showed a growing tendency toward spiritualism, mysticism, and eschatological expectations, combined with a separatist criticism of all outer forms in the church. For the Berleburger Bible (1726–42) the "inner word" (Christ indwelling in the soul) is decisive; it is the key for understanding the threefold sense of Scripture: the verbal, spiritual-moral, and secret-mystical senses. The aim is to gather the dispersed communities of the elected ones who are living at the end of the times and serve God in the Spirit, not in the letter. So the outer word loses its normative character (cf. Hofmann 1937; Urlinger 1969; Brecht 1982). From this position it was just one step to the equation of spirit with reason and the rationalistic rejection of Scriptural authority, which we find in the work of J. C. Edelmann. Edelmann equated the living God, reason, and conscience (see Grossmann 1976), and found reason in the Logos of John 1:1. Both before and after having read Spinoza's *Tractatus,* Edelmann opposed the orthodox doctrine of verbal inspiration and separated God's word (which is spirit and reason) from the Scriptures, which as a human product he found to be full of errors.

2. Awakening in Britain and America. Awakening in England is a child of German pietism. Spener's pupil A. Horneck, who in 1660 emigrated to England and from 1670 worked as a parson in London, effected ca. 1678 the founding of the "religious societies" which struggled for a spiritual renovation of the church. The Society for Promoting Christian Knowledge (founded in 1698) accrued from this movement. Its main endeavor was the printing and distribution of Bibles, Bible excerpts, and devotional literature. There were also relations to Halle and A. H. Francke. But most influential for the outbreak of the awakening (for the movement, see Watts 1978: 394–490) were the brothers John and Charles Wesley (on John, Cannon 1946; Outler 1964; M. Schmidt 1953–66; Tuttle 1978; Ayling 1979; on Charles, Tyson 1986). Both happened to meet German Moravians and were introduced by them to Luther's doctrine of justification, but with the pietists' emphases on conversion, spiritual rebirth, and above all, sanctification (which they also found in their zealous reading of Eastern theology and with the Church Fathers, but above all understood as "imitation of Christ"; see Källstad 1974: 57–81). These themes gained the most important place (Lindström 1980) in their sermons and hymns (Rattenbury 1941). Like the Puritans, they lived by the Bible and built their theological system out of its verses (see Watson 1984), placing stress on the NT. This biblical orientation was born in their studies at Oxford, where close examination of the Bible was part of the program of the "methodist" group (Resembling the *Collegium philobiblicum* at Halle). Another independent revivalist movement arose in Wales.

Methodism separated from the Anglican church late in the century, and related varieties of revivalism were also to be found among the Anglicans (Balleine 1951; Davies 1961: 210–40; Walsh 1966). In the New England colonies the Calvanist Puritan Jonathan Edwards (1703–1758) was one of the centers of the "First Great Awakening" (1734–44). His own preaching, and that of George Whitefield

(1714–1770), initiated and invigorated the movements of revival which were formative for American Protestantism (see Carse 1967; Miller 1949; on his theology of God's self-communication, Elwood 1960; on Whitefield, Dallimore 1970. On the awakening, Sweet 1944; Gaustad 1957; Weisberger 1958; Hudson 1973: 59–82; Rutman 1970 is a sourcebook).

Revivalism was a phenomenon that crossed denominational borders. A personal Bible-oriented piety is characteristic of the whole movement. Everywhere the Bible was taken at face value. Historical criticism is lacking or was explicitly rejected. There was also revivalism in other countries (for the Netherlands cf. van den Berg and van Dooren 1978), but mostly later (*TRE* 10: 205–20); later movements showed similar characteristics. Edwards also renewed the Puritan millenarian typology for the spiritual awakening in New England: his followers were more inclined to equate the beginning of millennium with the New World political and social reality (Bercovitch 1978: 92–118; Noll 1982: 46–48; Heimert 1968: 59–94). When later the black population of the American South found its religious folk identity (Genovese 1972: 161–284), it was the same topos of the chosen people, now that of the Exodus with Moses as leader, together with the eschatological expectations of Revelation that formed the black consciousness (see Levine 1977: 33–55).

D. The Period of the Enlightenment

The English Deists, beginning with Herbert of Cherbury, are the forerunners of theological enlightenment, so the period overlaps with the age of pietism, and even late orthodoxy. The impact of the deistic works which became known to foreigners by travel or from reviews in scientific periodicals (for S. J. Baumgarten, see Schloemann 1974) was an important factor in the development of enlightenment theology and Bible criticism in other countries. But also rational apologetics, natural theology, empiricism (Locke), and rational philosophy played a significant role. Its development in the various countries was different according to the political and confessional circumstances; the role of the Bible was more central in Protestant countries, and therefore the interest in critical exegesis more basic. In Catholic territories the Inquisition forced the opposition into the underground.

1. French Enlightenment. This was obviously the case in 17th- and early 18th-century France. Several pamphlets containing sharp criticism of the official church and the Bible circulated as clandestine manuscripts (Wade 1938; Bloch 1982; Betts 1984: 157–183). Moral criticism of the habits of OT heroes in the manner of Bayle (see below), and even of God's behavior in the stories of the OT, was frequent. A. Calmet's apologetic commentaries on the literal sense of both OT and NT (1707–1716) in refuting the objections against the Bible even gathered a storage for the later adversaries. Such orthodox defenders of the Bible as Bossuet, who declared in the wake of Cartesian rationalism that the Bible must be infallible in every detail, inadvertently prepared the way for the critics. The objections against the Bible were summarized by Voltaire in his *La Bible enfin expliquée* (1776; see Schwarzbach 1971; Cotoni 1986: 780–88) and for the NT in his *Histoire de l'etablissement du christianisme* (1777: 407–526). Voltaire was anti-Christian but believed in God (Mailhos 1983). Denis Diderot (1713–1784), a psychomaterialist and sceptic, rejected the divinity of the Bible completely. Only Rousseau, who was educated as a Protestant and knew the Bible very well, avoided a wholesale rejection of Christianity. In his *Confession of a Savoyard Vicar* (1762), which relied primarily on natural religion, Rousseau managed to preserve a high esteem for what he found elevating in the life and teaching of Jesus in spite of his skepticism toward the authority of the Bible (Grimsley 1968; Jacquet 1985; Cotoni 1986: 788–95). The anti-Catholic intellectual climate in enlightened France hindered a positive evaluation of the Bible, although positive approaches can be observed among the French Catholic moralists of the first half of the century (Vauvenargues; Duclos; Toussaint; cf. Mydlarski 1986).

2. German Neology. A decisive step in the evaluation of the bible was the transition to a historical exegesis which slowly developed in the 18th century in Germany and neighboring Protestant countries. Already in the late "rational" orthodoxy a trend toward a philological and historical exegesis of the Bible can be observed (for Budde and Pfaff, see Stolzenburg 1926). It was P. Bayle, a reformed fideist opposed to taking reason as the measure for ethics and faith (Labrousse 1963–64; Rex 1965), who first liberated historical research from dogmatical and philosophical premises. Faith accepts God's word in the Bible, but in its historical form it is a human book and its heroes can be morally criticized (cf. the famous article on David in Bayle's *Dictionnaire historique et critique* (1738; 13; Rex 1965: 197–255). J. A. Turretini in Geneva (Merk 1988) formulated the basic principle that the biblical scriptures have to be interpreted in the same way as other human books (1728). The philological work in Pietism (for instance, the Institutum Judaicum in Halle, founded 1728, for instruction in Hebrew and oriental languages) partially prepared the way. The textual criticism of the NT showed that innumerable variants exist, thereby shaking belief in the integrity of the known manuscripts and dealing a deadly blow to the doctrine of verbal inspiration. R. Simon (1689), J. Mill (1710; see Fox 1954), J. A. Bengel, K. F. Houbigant (1746), J. J. Wettstein (1751–52; see Hulbert-Powell 1938; Merk 1988) worked on this field. Their critical editions of the NT provided the basis for further research.

In Germany, the effects of the Enlightenment on theology increased as the 18th century progressed. Neology (as the theological thought of this period is referred to; see Bianco 1983, Sparn 1985) was subject to a number of influences. An infusion of natural theology and philosophy of religion came from the writings of C. Wolff, who in his *Theologia naturalis* (1736) developed rational rules for differentiating genuine from spurious revelation. (Genuine revelation cannot contradict the nature of God, must have a moral character, cannot contradict itself, and must contain no mysteries which are against reason.) The process of "enlightenment" was viewed as a spiritual power capable of forming the human heart for philanthropic "love."

For Spalding, who wrote a very popular anti-materialist manual entitled *Bestimmung des Menschen* (1748), the feeling of harmony and beauty and the striving for knowledge, virtue, religion (the tasting of God's infinity and benevolence), and immortality are natural gifts in man

(Bourel 1978: 137–46). The optimistic anthropology of humanism gains preponderance. G. W. Leibniz's cosmology of a "prestabilized harmony" which leads back to the creator of a well-ordered universe stands in the background. The theologians of neology try to reconcile reason and revelation. For J. J. W. Jerusalem the Bible is authentic as a source of morality and the basic truths of religion (Müller 1984: 50–66). His position allows doubts about the historicity of biblical stories. The theory of accommodation (Müller 1984: 66–76) explains why the contents of biblical revelation are not yet on the level of a higher development of human reason only reached later. But the religion of Jesus is on the highest level of simplicity and thereby understandable by everyone (Müller 1984: 76–88). On the other side, reason in the field of natural theology is able to arrive at knowledge of God out of the order and existence of the world (Müller 1984: 88–104). In the realm of ethics the biblical teachings (original revelation; Moses; Jesus' teaching to love one's neighbor) are stages in the moral progress of humans (Müller 1984: 104–109).

In the period of neology, basic steps in historical criticism of the Bible were taken. Two names are especially important: J. D. Michaelis (1717–1791) and J. S. Semler (1725–1791). Michaelis (Smend 1987; 1989: 13–24; Löwenbrück 1986), who was a prolific writer on many fields, worked on Hebrew and Semitic philology, lexicography, and grammar (he gave up the doctrine of the inspiration of the Masoretic vowel points) and on the environment of the Bible. His famous work on the Mosaic Law (Michaelis 1770–75; studied by Smend 1983) intended to explain the circumstances of its origins and to defend it against the deists and atheists. Michaelis intended to show that the Mosaic law becomes understandable as wise and of divine authority for its immediate addressees if one sees it before the background of the time of "childhood" of the Israelite people. Childhood having passed, it is no longer obligatory for Christians. The orthodox opinion of the authority of the Bible is abandoned, the idea of a religious development born. J. S. Semler's best-known work on the canon (1771–73) refuted the doctrine of the inspiration of the canon as a whole, demanded a historical-critical exegesis of the biblical scriptures, but emphasized that the word of God is contained in the Bible (Hornig 1961; Hess 1974; Kaiser 1984a; H. Schulz 1988). He distinguished between theology and religion and stressed the importance of historical knowledge for theology. The distinction between official (Dogmatic) and private (practical-moral) Christian religion resembles latitudinarism. J. A. Ernesti in his *Institutio* (1761) restricted his hermeneutics to the NT; he demanded a grammatical (literal) exegesis of the human sense free of dogmatic interests, but did not doubt the authorship of the inspired authors of the NT books (*NTHIP*, 68–70).

The most radical criticism of the Bible came from the pen of H. S. Reimarus (see Stemmer 1983; Gawlick 1983; Walravens 1986; Reventlow 1988c). Reimarus, who as an orthodox Lutheran initially defended the traditional understanding of the OT as prophecy upon Christ (1731), changed his standpoint under the influence of J. L. Schmidt's "Wertheimer Bibel" (1735; cf. Hirsch 1951: 2.417–31; Stemmer 1983: 102–112). Schmidt was an adherent of C. Wolff's rationalism and followed in his translation of the Pentateuch (the other parts of the OT translation are preserved in manuscript form) his maxim that nothing in revelation can be contrary to reason. He also knew the English deists and like them rejected miracles and predictions (typology) as proof for the truth of revelation. He therefore translated the respective sentences "for themselves," "according to the intentions of the authors." But his goal (like Wolff's) was apologetic: the natural world is a closed system following the rules of reason. In it nothing that is against reason can be accepted. But revelation, like any historical event, is "above reason": that it happened cannot be disproved unless it is against reason. Therefore Christian religion needs no proof.

Reimarus followed Wolff as an adherent of natural religion (physico-theology), which he defended in a series of systematic works (1754, 1756, 1760). He never published the critical parts of his *Apology* of which Lessing printed fragments in 1734 and again in 1777. Reimarus brought the biblical criticism of the Enlightenment to the summit of radicalism: the messianic predictions of the NT do not mean Jesus; OT and NT are to be divided. The receivers of revelation in the OT lack an adequate moral qualification. The narrations about wonders (for instance, about the exodus in Exodus 14) are contradictory. The OT does not teach saving revelation, because it does not know the immortality of the soul. In the NT the doctrine of the apostles, which taught a supernatural religion, is to be separated from Jesus' teaching of a "natural, rational, and practical religion." But Jesus also announced the approaching realm of God and himself as its political messiah. Only part of Jesus' teaching is acceptable; the other contents of the NT are falsifiable.

For Immanuel Kant, the moral religion of reason, which can be defined as "knowledge of all our duties as divine commands" (*Religion within the Bounds of Pure Reason* [1793]), is in principle something other than the "faith of revelation" (on Kant, see Bohatec 1938; Bruch 1968; Lötzsch 1976; Kaiser 1984b; Bayer 1988: 33–36). In the famous formulation: "the starry sky above me and moral law within me" (*Critique of Practical Reason* [1788]) Kant describes this moral faith as founded in a transcendent-immanent certainty in man himself. This religion in principle does not need revelation, for anyone can verify it by reason. Moral reason is also the scale on which to measure the Bible (*Conflict of the Faculties* [1798]); for instance the command to Abraham to offer Isaac (Genesis 22) cannot come from God. But as in practice the empirical abilities of men are insufficient, the existence of a church, which is an assembly for teaching moral sensibility, is unavoidable. Such a church needs a holy Scripture which can ground moral teaching in revelation and provide the rules for its statutory faith. For Kant it is the NT, which, however, has to be interpreted according to the rules of a pure religion of reason. As such he holds the NT in high esteem. He remarks that the Bible has proved its divinity by the homiletical and catechetical influence it has on the heart (*Conflict of the Faculties*).

With G. E. Lessing (1729–1781) the Bible criticism of the Enlightenment reaches its climax. His much-debated position (as rationalist: Aner 1929: 343–361; as believing in revelation: Thielicke 1957) is to be seen in the context and in opposition to dominant opinions of his time. Against the orthodox apologetic endeavor to prove the truth of Christian religion by messianic prophecies and wonders he formulates the famous sentence "casual truths of history can never become the proof of necessary truths of reason" (Lessing 1886–1907: 8.12). He does not deny that Jesus performed wonders, but they could impress only persons then present. Secondhand reports do not lead to faith. The historical Jesus himself was not more than human (8.538f). Between historic certainty and actual truth there is the "nasty broad ditch," which he cannot get over (8.14). But there is another certainty for belief: "the proof of spirit and power" (8.9f). Lessing means an immediate personal experience of revelation (standing in the tradition of spiritualism; cf. Schultze 1969: 110–116; Gericke 1985: 13–35; 49–51). In his "Axiomata" (8.164) he differentiates between letter and spirit, Bible and religion, and declares that Christian religion is not totally dependent on the Bible. In the time of the apostles the Christian message was proclaimed without a letter (7.813; 8.176f). "The letter is not the spirit, and the Bible is not religion (= revelation)" (7.173; 8.813). That makes Bible criticism possible: "Therefore objections against the letter, and against the Bible, are not in the same way objections against the spirit and against religion" (7.813; 8.174). But there is an "inner truth" (7.813; 8.189) which furnishes the authority of revelation. It means spirit, reason, love.

But the Bible (OT and NT) has also a positive purpose. In the pamphlet "The Education of Mankind," Lessing understands the Bible as a book of education which conducted its readers to the highest steps of enlightenment. Education does not give more than humans could have reached by unassisted reason, but advances humanity faster (§4). At first God chose a single "rough" people for special education (§8) with the OT as "elementary book" (§§26–53). Later, when a part of mankind had reached a greater capacity for reason and morality (§55), Jesus Christ came as a teacher (§53) who taught the immortality of the soul (§57f). Lessing is original in applying the idea of education (which was a common motif in the enlightenment period) to history (on his theology of history, Schilson 1974), but of course this is not yet historical understanding. Morality and reason remain abstract ideas. Lessing saw that the doctrines of the apostles (§63) contain certain supernatural truths (Trinity, §73; hereditary sin, §74; atonement through Christ, §75), which are also useful to know (§§76–80). Lessing preserves elements of orthodox doctrine. But the expected completion, when people will "do the good, because it is good" (§85), will make even the NT superfluous. This reminds one of Shaftesbury and Kant. The Bible has no independent continuing authority.

3. New Developments. In 1753 R. Lowth published his lectures on Hebrew poetics in which he treated the poetic style of the OT from a purely aesthetic viewpoint, but also regarded it as parabolic expression of its contents (see Hartlich and Sachs 1952: 6–10; F. Meinecke 1965: 243–52 saw in Lowth a prominent representative of "English preromanticism"). In Göttingen, the classical philologist C. G. Heyne explained Greek mythology as the manner of thinking and speaking characteristic of the childhood of humanity. Because primitive thinkers do not know the real causes of things, they understand everything extraordinary in nature, history, or the human soul as immediate intervention of gods. There are two sorts of myths: historical myths founded on real occurrences, and philosophical myths containing cosmogonical and theological speculations. Myth research has the task of finding but the historical facts behind the myths (Hartlich and Sachs 1952: 11–19). Heyne's pupil (Sehmsdorf 1971: 125–28) J. G. Eichhorn adapted his method to the explanation of Genesis 1–3 (1779); the re-edition by J. P. Gabler (1790–93) set the new method of understanding the Bible on the basis of its historical circumstances and modes of expression on a theoretical foundation and applied it also to the NT (Merk 1972: 52–54). Myth research observed that the primeval history of Genesis 1–3 does not contain historical facts (Hartlich and Sachs 1952: 20–38). Here and in other places the aim is also rationalistic-apologetic: to explain away the supernatural element in the OT. G. L. Bauer developed the theory of the "mythical school" in the direction of a historical-critical exegesis (1799): the verbal sense as intended by the author is the only object of interpretation. Eichhorn (see Smend 1989: 25–37) was also the author of a famous introduction to the OT (1780–83), in which he defended the thesis of two narrative sources in Genesis and detected the late date of Is 40–52 (see Sehmsdorf 1971: 52–54). Eichhorn also wrote introductions to the apocryphical books of the OT (1795), and to the NT (1811–35). An important step was taken by Gabler in 1787 by his separation of Biblical theology, as an historical enterprise, from dogmatics (*NTHIP*, 115–18; Merk 1972: 31–45.81–113.273–84; Smend 1962).

Against the ideology of Enlightenment, J. G. Hamann, the "magus from the north," fought with zeal (O'Flaherty 1979; *TRE* 14: 395–403). He went through a conversion, was influenced by the awakened J. Hervey (Gründer 1958: 51f; Jørgensen 1988), and gained a personal relation to the Bible, which he read in a *sensus plenior* meaning as typologically relating to his own existence (Gründer 1958: 116–58; Jorgensen 1980). Against the optimism of the Enlightenment he stressed the Lutheran standpoint of sin and redemption. Against Kant (Bayer 1988) he showed (using Hume's epistomological skepticism) that reason is history-bound and not absolute as a criterion for evaluating the Bible. In the Bible, according to Hamann, are united the word of God, who in humility has bound himself into human history, and the traditions of human weakness. In reading the Bible correctly—that is, with attention to its symbols—as "the language of God," the pious interpreter is able to communicate with God as well as with other people (German 1981) and to detect God as "author of his life-story" (Bayer 1980).

The idea of humanity *(Humanität)* is leading in the work of J. G. Herder (biography: Haym 1880–85; survey of work and bibliography: *TRE* 15: 70–95). In history, in which mankind is moving step by step—though not without retrogressions—to an ever greater perfection in its destiny as humanity, it is aided by revelation, which for Herder is already given in the existence of human beings as created by God. In their ability to become acquainted with the world and with history by feeling, understanding, experience, "spirit," conscience, language, but also in the testimony of those who report their own experience of revelation in nature and history, such as patriarchs, prophets, Jesus, humans encounter biblical tradition and the Christian church as institutional bearers of such revelation. But the revelation in nature and in conscience is only understandable in the light of tradition (Herder 1877–1913: 10.295). The content of the "documents" of tradition is nothing other than the human, human origins and human destiny as the image of God. Revelation is the "education of humankind" (13.345) to ward the goal of humanity. The Scripture gains its authority by being a testimony of true humanity, reaching its summit in the life of Jesus (20.165–80). Jesus' humanness as a model of conduct, not his divinity, is the object of belief.

The understanding of the Bible as a human document makes historical exegesis possible and necessary. "One has to read the Bible in a human way, for it is a book written by men for men" (10.7). Characteristic for Herder's exegesis of the OT (on which see Willi 1971; Kraus 1973) is the approach from language and "Hebrew poetics" (*Songs of Love* 8.845–588.589–656; *Spirit of Hebrew Poetry* 11.213–466); the authority of the OT as a historical document rests on its antiquity and poetic power (*The Most Ancient Document of Mankind* 6.193–511; 7.1–172). In the NT (see *NTHIP,* 94–98; Bunge 1988) he treated the Synoptic Gospels (19.135–252) and the gospel of John (19) separately and developed the theory of a protogospel standing behind both.

Herder's exegesis of the Bible represents a transitional stage to the historical view as developed in the 19th century. For him, revelation is the precondition of human existence and understanding as such, but by making human beings the genuine subject of his world view and also of the Bible, and by declaring humanity to be the goal of history, he opened the way for more thoroughly secular types of biblical criticism and a diminishment of biblical authority. It was the Second Great Awakening in the first half of the following century that opened again another way, where the Bible regained its former value.

Bibliography

Aland, K. 1960. Der hallische Pietismus und die Bibel. Pp. 24–59 in *Die bleibende Bedeutung des Pietismus: Zur 250–Jahrfeier der von Cantsteinischen Bibelanstalt,* ed. O. Söhngen. Witten.

———. 1970a. Bibel und Bibeltext bei August Hermann Francke und Johann Albrecht Bengel. Pp. 89–147 in Aland 1970b.

Aland, K., ed. 1970b. *Pietismus und Bibel.* Arbeiten zur Geschichte des Pietismus 9. Witten.

Aldridge, A. D. 1951. Shaftesbury and the Deist Manifesto. *TAPhS* 41: 297–385.

———. 1964. *Jonathan Edwards.* Great American Thinkers W 881. New York.

Aner, K. 1929. *Die Theologie der Lessingzeit.* Halle. Repr. Hildesheim. 1964.

Annet, P. 1744. *The Resurrection of Jesus Considered.* 3d ed. London.

Auvray, P. 1974. *Richard Simon (1638–1712): Étude bio-bibliographique avec des textes.* Paris.

Ayling, S. 1979. *John Wesley.* London.

Baker, S. W. 1980. *Heinrich Bullinger and the Covenant.* Athens, OH.

Ball, B. W. 1975. *A Great Expectation: Eschatological Thought in English Protestantism to 1660.* Leiden.

Balleine, G. R. 1951. *A History of the Evangelical Party in the Church of England.* London.

Barnes, A. 1938. *Jean Leclerc (1657–1736) et la république des lettres.* Paris.

Barr, J. 1984–85. Why the World was Created in 4004 B.C.: Archbishop Usher's Biblical Chronology. *BJRL* 67: 575–608.

Bayer, O. 1980. Wer bin ich? Gott als Autor meiner Lebensgeschichte. *Theologische Beiträge* 11: 245–61.

———. 1988. Vernunftautorität und Bibelkritik in der Kontroverse zwischen Georg Hamann und Immanuel Kant. Pp. 21–46 in Reventlow, Sparn, and Woodbridge 1988.

Bedford, R. D. 1979. *The Defence of Truth: Herbert of Cherbury and the 17th Century.* Manchester.

Belaval, Y., and Bourel, D., eds. 1986. *Le siècle des Lumières et la Bible.* Bible de tous les temps 7. Paris.

Bercovitch, S. 1978. *The American Jeremiad.* Madison, WI.

Berg, J. van den, and Dooren, P. P. van. 1978. *Pietismus und Réveil.* Kerkhistorische Bijdragen 7. Leiden.

Bergsträsser, A. 1951. Religiöse Motive des universalgeschichtlichen Denkens. Pp. 315–36 in *Deutschland und Europa,* ed. W. Conze. Düsseldorf.

Bernus, A. 1869. *Richard Simon et son Histoire critique du Vieux Testament.* Lausanne. Repr. Geneva, 1969.

Besch, H. 1950. *Johann Sebastian Bach: Frömmigkeit und Glaube.* Vol. 1, *Deutung und Wirklichkeit.* 2d ed. Basel.

Betts, C. J. 1984. *Early Deism in France: From the So-Called 'déistes' of Lyon (1564) to Voltaire's "Lettres philosophiques" (1734).* International Archives of the History of Ideas 104. The Hague.

Bianco, B. 1983. Vernünftiges Christentum: Aspects et problèmes de la néologie allemande du XVIIIe siècle. *Archives de Philosophie* 46: 179–218.

Bloch, O., ed. 1982. *Le Matérialisme du XVIIIe et la littérature clandestine.* Paris.

Bohatec, J. 1938. *Die Religionsphilosophie Kants in der "Religion innerhalb der Grenzen der bloben Vernunft".* Hamburg. Repr. Hildesheim, 1966.

Bonante, U. 1972. *Charles Blount: Libertinismo e deismo nel Seicento inglese.* Florence.

Bourel, D. 1978. *La vie de Johann Joachim Spalding: Problèmes de la théologie allemande au XVIIIe siècle.* Diplome de l'École Pratique des Hautes Études. Sciences religieuses. 2 vols. Paris.

Brecht, M. 1967. Johann Albrecht Bengels Theologie der Schrift. *ZTK* 64: 99–120.

———. 1970. Johannes Albrecht Bengel und der schwäbische Biblizismus. Pp. 193–218 in Aland 1970b.

———. 1982. Die Berleburger Bibel: Hinweise zu ihrem Verständnis. *Pietismus und Neuzeit* 8: 162–200.

———. 1986. Philipp Jacob Spener und die Erneuerung des Theologiestudiums. *Pietismus und Neuzeit* 12: 94–108.

Breton, S. 1973. *Politique, religion, écriture chez Spinoza.* Lyon.

———. 1977. *Spinoza: Théologie et politique.* Paris.

Brown, C. 1984. *Miracles and the Critical Mind.* Grand Rapids.

Bruch, J.-L. 1968. *La philosophie réligieuse de Kant.* Paris.

Bunge, M. 1988. Johann Gottfried Herders Auslegung des Neuen Testaments. Pp. 249–262 in Reventlow, Sparn and Woodbridge 1988.

Burns, R. M. 1981. *The Great Debate on Miracles: From Joseph Glanville to David Hume.* Lewisburg.

Cannon, W. R. 1946. *The Theology of John Wesley.* Nashville.

Carse, J. 1967. *Jonathan Edwards and the Visibility of God.* New York.

Collins, A. 1713. *A Discourse of Free-Thinking.* London.

———. 1724. *A Discourse of the Grounds and Reasons of the Christian Religion.* London.

Cotoni, M.-H. 1986. Voltaire, Rousseau, Diderot. Pp. 779–803 in Belaval and Bourel 1986.
Craig, W. L. 1985. *The Historical Argument for the Resurrection of Jesus during the Deist Controversy.* Lewiston, NY.
Dallimore, A. A. 1970. *George Whitefield.* London.
Daniel, S. H. 1984. *John Toland: His Methods, Manners and Mind.* Montreal.
Davies, H. 1961. *Worship and Theology in England.* Vol. 3, *From Watts and Wesley to Maurice, 1690–1850.* Princeton and London.
Dose, K. 1977. *Die Bedeutung der Schrift für Zinzendorfs Denken und Handeln.* 2 vols. Diss. theol. Bonn.
Eichhorn, J. G. 1779. Urgeschichte. Pp. 129–256 in Vol. 4 of *Repertorium für biblische und morgenländische Literatur.* Leipzig.
———. 1780–83. *Einleitung ins Alte Testament.* 3 vols. Leipzig.
———. 1795. *Einleitung in die Apokryphischen Schriften des Alten Testaments.* Leipzig.
———. 1811–35. *Einleitung in das Neue Testament.* Leipzig.
Eichhorn, J. G., and Gabler, J. P. 1790–93. *Joh. G. Eichhorns "Urgeschichte." Hg. mit Einleitung und Anmerkungen.* Altdorf and Nürnberg.
Elliot-Binns, L. E. 1961. *The Early Evangelicals: A Religious and Social Study.* 1st ed. 1953. London.
Elwood, D. J. 1960. *The Philosophical Theology of Jonathan Edwards.* New York.
Farrell, M. 1981. *William Whiston.* New York.
Firth, K. R. 1979. *The Apocalyptic Tradition in Reformation Britain: 1530–1645.* Oxford.
Force, J. E. 1985. *William Whiston, Honest Newtonian.* Cambridge.
Fox, A. 1954. *John Mill and Richard Bentley: A Study of the Textual Criticism in the New Testament 1675–1729.* Oxford.
Frances, M. 1937. *Spinoza dans les pays néerlandais de la seconde moitié du XVIIe siècle.* Paris.
Frei, H. W. 1974. *The Eclipse of Biblical Narrative.* New Haven.
Freiday, D. 1979. *The Bible: Its Criticism, Interpretation and Use in 16th and 17th Century England.* Catholic and Quaker Studies 4. Pittsburg.
Fussner, F. S. 1962. *The Historical Revolution: English Historical Writing and Thought 1580–1640.* London.
Gaustad, E. S. 1957. *The Great Awakening in New England.* New York. Repr. Gloucester, MA. 1965.
Gawlick, G. 1972. Deismus. Vol. 2, pp. 44–47 in *Historisches Wörterbuch der Philosophie,* ed. G. Ritter. Basel and Stuttgart.
———. 1973. Der Diesmus als Grundzug der Religionsphilosophie der Aufklärung. Pp. 15–43 in *Hermann Samuel Reimarus (1694–1768) ein "bekannter Unbekannter" der Aufklärung in Hamburg.* Göttingen.
———. 1983. Hermann Samuel Reimarus. Vol. 8, pp. 299–311 in *Gestalten der Kirchengeschichte,* ed. M. Greschat. Stuttgart.
Genovese, F. D. 1972. *Roll, Jordan, Roll: The World the Slaves Made.* New York.
Gericke, W. 1985. *Sechs theologische Schriften Gotthold Ephraim Lessings.* Berlin.
German, T. J. 1981. *Hamann on Language and Religion.* Oxford.
Grean, S. 1967. *Shaftesbury's Philosophy of Religion and Ethics.* Athens, OH.
Greschat, M. 1980. Bibelkritik und Politik: Anmerkungen zu Spinozas Theologisch-politischem Traktat. Pp. 324–43 in *Text-Wort-Glaube. Studien zur Überlieferung, Interpretation und Autorisierung biblischer Texte K. Aland gewidmet,* ed. M. Brecht. Arbeiten zur Kirchengeschichte 50. Berlin.
Grimsley, R. 1968. *Rousseau and the Religious Quest.* Oxford.
Grossmann, W. 1976. *Johann Christian Edelmann: From Orthodoxy to Enlightenment.* The Hague.
Gründer, K. 1958. *Figur und Geschichte: Johann Georg Hamanns "Biblische Betrachtungen" als Ansatz einer Geschichtstheologie.* Freiburg.
Grützmacher, R. H. 1902. *Wort und Geist.* Leipzig.
Hägglund, B. 1951. *Die heilige Schrift und ihre Deutung in der Theologie Johann Gerhards.* Lund.
Harinck, C. 1986. *De Schotse verbondsleer: Van Robert Rollock tot Thomas Boston.* Utrecht.
Hartlich, C., and Sachs, W. 1952. *Der Ursprung des Mythosbegriffes in der modernen Bibelwissenschaft.* Schriften der Studiengemeinschaft der Evangelischen Akademien 2. Tübingen.
Haym, R. 1880–85. *Herder: Nach seinem Leben und seinen Werken.* 2 vols. Berlin. Repr. 1958.
Heimbrock, H.-G. 1981. *Vom Heil der Seele: Studien zum Verhältnis von Religion und Psychologie bei Baruch Spinoza.* Erfahrung und Theologie 4. Frankfurt am Main.
Heimert, A. 1968. *Religion and the American Mind.* 2d ed. Cambridge, MA.
Herbert of Cherbury, Edward Herbert, Baron. 1645a. *De Veritate.* 3d ed. London. Repr. Stuttgart, 1966.
———. 1645b. *De Causis errorum. De Religione laici.* London. Repr. Stuttgart, 1966.
Herder, J. G. 1877–1913. *Sämtliche Werke.* Ed. by B. Suphan. Berlin. Repr. Hildesheim, 1967–68.
Hess, H.-E. 1974. *Theologie und Religion bei Johann Salomo Semler.* Diss. theol. Kirchliche Hochschule Berlin.
Hill, C. 1972. *The World Turned Upside Down.* New York.
———. 1986. *The Collected Essays.* Vol. 2, *Religion and Politics in 17th Century England.* Brighton.
Hill, C.; Reay, B.; and Lamont, W. 1983. *The World of the Muggletonians.* London.
Hillerdale, G. 1962. *Reason and Revelation in Richard Hooker.* LUÅ n.s. 1/54/7. Lund.
Hirsch, E. 1949–51. *Geschichte der neueren evangelischen Theologie.* 2 vols. Gütersloh.
Hobbes, T. 1839a. *De Cive,* in *Opera philosophica,* ed. G. Molesworth. Opera Latina, vol. 2. London. = Pp. 157–432 in repr. Aalen, 1966.
———. 1839b. *The English Works of Thomas Hobbes,* ed. W. Molesworth. Vol. 3, *Leviathan.* London. Repr. Aalen, 1966.
Hofmann, M. 1937. *Theologie und Exegese der Berleburger Bibel (1726–1742).* BFCT 39. Gütersloh.
Hornig, G. 1961. *Die Anfänge der historisch-kritischen Theologie: Joh. Salomo Semlers Schriftverständnis und seine Stellung zu Luther.* Göttingen.
Horstmann, U. 1980. *Die Geschichte der Gedankenfreiheit in England: am Beispiel von Anthony Collins "A Discourse of Free-thinking".* Meisenheim.
Hudson, W. S. 1973. *Religion in America.* 2d ed. New York.
Hulbert-Powell, C. L. 1938. *John James Wettstein, 1693–1754, An Account of His Life, Work, and Some of His Contemporaries.* London.
Hutter, L. 1961. *Compendium locorum theologicorum.* Ed. W. Trillhaas. Berlin.
Jacob, M. C. 1976. *The Newtonians and the English Revolution: 1689–1720.* Hassocks, Sussex and Ithaca, NY.
Jacquet, C. 1975. *La pensée religieuse de J.-J. Rousseau.* Louvain.
Jeffner, A. 1966. *Butler and Hume on Religion.* AUU 7. Stockholm.
Jorgensen, S.-A. 1980. Hamanns hermeneutische Grundsätze. Pp.

219–231 in *Aufklärung und Humanismus,* ed. R. Toellner. Wolfenbütteler Studien zur Aufklärung 6. Heidelberg.

———. 1988. Hamann und Hervey: Zur Bibellektüre während Hamanns Londoner Krise. Pp. 237–248 in Reventlow, Sparn, and Woodbridge 1988.

Källstad, T. 1974. *John Wesley and the Bible: A Psychological Study.* Stockholm.

Kaiser, O. 1984a. Johann Salomo Semler als Bahnbrecher der modernen Bibelwissenschaft. Pp. 59–74 in *Textgemäss: Festschrift E. Würthwein.* Göttingen, 1979 = Pp. 79–94 in id., *Von der Gegenwartsbedeutung des Alten Testaments.* Göttingen.

———. 1984b. Kants Anweisung zur Auslegung der Bibel: Ein Beitrag zur Geschichte der Hemeneutik. Pp. 75–90 in *Glaube, Geist, Geschichte.* Leiden, 1967 = *Neue Zeitschrift für systematische Theologie* 11 (1969): 126–38. = Pp. 47–60 in id., *Von der Gegenwartsbedeutung des Alten Testaments.* Göttingen.

Kessler, M. 1986. *Kritik aller Offenbarung.* Tübinger Theologische Studien 26. Mainz.

Kirste, R. 1976. *Das Zeugnis des Geistes und das Zeugnis der Schrift.* GTA 6. Göttingen.

Klempt, A. 1960. *Die Säkularisierung der universalhistorischen Auffassung.* Göttingen.

Köster, B. 1984. *Die Lutherbibel im frühen Pietismus.* Texte und Arbeiten zur Bibel 1. Bielefeld.

Kraus, H.-J. 1970. *Die Biblische Theologie.* Neukirchen-Vluyn.

———. 1973. Herders alttestamentliche Forschungen. Pp. 59–75 in *Bückeburger Gespräche über J. G. Herder 1971,* ed. J. G. Maltusch. Bückeburg.

———. 1982. *Geschichte der historisch-kritischen Erforschung des Alten Testaments.* 3d ed. Neukirchen-Vluyn.

Labrousse, E. 1963–64. *Pierre Bayle.* 2 vols. The Hague.

Lamont, W. M. 1979. *Richard Baxter and the Millennium.* London and Totowa, NJ.

Le Brun, J. 1982. De la spéculation à la morale—la Bible dans le catholicisme français au XVIIe siècle. *Esprit* 9.

Lechler, G. V. 1841. *Geschichte des englischen Deismus.* Stuttgart and Tübingen. Repr. Hildesheim, 1965.

Lessing, G. E. 1886–1907. *Sämtliche Werke,* ed. K. Lachmann and F. Muncker. 3d. ed. Berlin. Repr. 1968.

Levine, L. W. 1977. *Black Culture and Black Consciousness.* Oxford.

Lindström, H. 1980. *Wesley and Sanctification.* Grand Rapids.

Lötzsch, F. 1976. *Vernunft und Religion im Denken Kants.* Böhlau Philosophica 2. Cologne.

Löwenbrück, A.-R. 1986. Johann David Michaelis et les débuts de la critique biblique. Pp. 113–128 in Belaval and Bourel 1986.

———. 1988. Johann David Michaelis' Verdienst um die philologisch-historische Bibelkritik. Pp. 157–70 in Reventlow, Sparn, and Woodbridge 1988.

Luca, G. di. 1982. *Critica della religione in Spinoza.* L'Aquila.

Mailhos, G. 1983. *Voltaire, témoin de son temps.* Europäische Hochschulschriften 13/87, Frankfurt am Main.

Malet, A. 1966. *La Traité théologico-politique de Spinoza et la pensée biblique.* Paris.

Manuel, F. E. 1974. *The Religion of Isaac Newton.* Fremantle Lectures 1973. Oxford.

Margival, H. 1900. *Essai sur Richard Simon et la critique biblique au 17e siècle.* Paris. Repr. Geneva, 1970.

Marshall, J. S. 1963. *Hooker and Anglican Tradition.* London.

Mauthner, F. 1921–23. *Der Atheismus und seine Geschichte im Abendlande.* 4 vols. Stuttgart. Repr. Hildescheim, 1963.

McKee, D. R. 1944. Isaac le Peyrère, a Precursor of Eighteenth-Century Critical Deists. *PMLA* 59: 465–85.

Meinecke, F. 1965. *Die Entstehung des Historismus.* Ed. by C. Hinrichs. Vol. 3 in *Friedrich Meinecke Werke.* 4th ed. Munich.

Meinsma, K. O. 1896. *Spinoza en zijn Kring.* The Hague. = *Spinoza und sein Kreis: Historisch-kritische Studien über holländische Freigeister.* Trans. L. Schneider. Berlin, 1909.

Merk, O. 1972. *Biblische Theologie des Neuen Testaments in ihrer Anfangszeit.* Marburg.

———. 1988. Von Jean-Alphonse Turretini zu Johann Jakob Wettstein. Pp. 89–112 in Reventlow, Sparn, and Woodbridge 1988.

Meyer, G. W. 1802–09. *Geschichte der Schrifterklärung seit der Wiederherstellung der Wissenschaften.* 5 vols. Geschichte der Künste und Wissenschaften 11/4. Göttingen.

Michaelis, J. D. 1770–75. *Gründliche Erklärung des mosaischen Rechts.* 6 pts Frankfurt am Main.

Mill, J. 1710. *Novum Testamentum Graecum cum lectionibus variantibus . . .* Amsterdam.

Miller, P. G. E. 1933. *Orthodoxy in Massachusetts 1630–1650.* Cambridge, MA. Repr. Gloucester, MA 1965; New York, 1970.

———. 1937. The Marrow of Puritan Divinity. *Publications of the Colonial Society of Massachusetts* 23: 247–300 = Pp. 48–98 in *Errand in the Wilderness.* Repr. New York, 1956, 1964; 3d ed. Cambridge, MA. 1970 = Pp. 12–42 in *The New England Puritans,* ed. S. V. James. New York, 1968.

———. 1939. *New England Mind: The Seventeenth Century.* New York, Repr. 1954; 3d ed. Cambridge, MA, 1967.

———. 1949. *Jonathan Edwards.* New York. Repr. Westport, CT. 1975.

Morgan, T. 1969. *The Moral Philosopher.* 3 vols. London, 1738–40. Repr. ed. and introd. G. Gawlick. Stuttgart-Bad Cannstatt. 1969.

Mossner, E. C. 1936. *Bishop Butler and the Age of Reason.* New York.

Müller, W. E. 1984. *Johann Friedrich Wilhelm Jerusalem: Eine Untersuchung zur Theologie der "Betrachtungen über die vornehmsten Wahrheiten der Religion."* Theologische Bibliothek Töpelmann 43. Berlin.

Mydlarski, H. 1986. Les moralistes des Lumières et la Bible. Pp. 625–47 in Belaval and Bourel 1986.

Noll, M. A. 1982. The Image of the United States as a Biblical Nation, 1776–1865. Pp. 39–58 in *The Bible in America: Essays in Cultural History,* ed. N. O. Hatch and M. A. Noll. Oxford.

Oberdieck, W. 1985. Henry More und die Frage nach Gott im 17. Jahrhundert. Diss. Göttingen.

O'Flaherty, J. C. 1979. *Johann Georg Hamann.* Boston.

O'Higgins, J. 1970. *Anthony Collins: The Man and His Works.* International Archives of the History of Ideas. The Hague.

Orr, R. R. 1967. *Reason and Authority: The Thought of William Chillingworth.* Oxford.

Outler, A. C. 1964. *John Wesley: A Representative Collection of His Writings.* Oxford.

Pailin, D. A. 1983. Herbert of Cherbury and the deists. *ExpTim* 94: 196–200.

Pältz, E. H. 1965. Zum pneumatischen Schriftverständnis Jakob Böhmes. Pp. 119–27 in *Kirche-Theologie-Frömmigkeit.* Berlin.

Peschke, E. 1970. August Hermann Francke und die Bibel. Pp. 59–87 in Aland 1970b.

Petzold, M., ed. 1985. *Bach als Ausleger der Bibel.* Göttingen.

Peyrère, I. de la. 1655. *Praeadamitae sive exercitatio super versibus duodecimo, decimotertio et decimoquarto capitis quinti epistolae D. Pauli ad Romanos.* Paris.

Pitassi, M. C. 1987. *Entre croire et savoir: Le problème de la méthode critique chez Jean Le Clerc.* Kerkhistorische Bijdragen 14. Leiden.

Popkin, R. H. 1979. *The History of Scepticism from Erasmus to Spinoza.* Berkeley.

———. 1987. *Isaac La Peyrère (1593–1676): His Life, Work and Influence.* Leiden.

Ramsay, I. T. 1969. *Joseph Butler 1692–1752.* London.

Ratschow, C.-H. 1964–66. *Lutherische Dogmatik zwischen Reformation und Aufklärung.* 2 vols. Gütersloh.

Rattenbury, J. E. 1941. *The Evangelical Doctrines of Charles Wesley's Hymns.* London.

Redwood, J. 1976. *Reason, Ridicule and Religion: The Age of Enlightenment in England 1660–1750.* London.

Reedy, G. 1985. *The Bible and Reason: Anglicans and Scripture in Late Seventeenth-Century England.* Philadelphia.

Reimarus, H. S. 1731. *Vindicatio dictorum Veteris Testamenti in Novo allegatorum.* Ed. P. Stemmer. Göttingen, 1983.

———. 1754. *Die vornehmsten Wahrheiten der natürlichen Religion in 10 Abhandlungen. = Gesammelte Schriften,* ed. G. Gawlick. 2 vols. Göttingen, 1985.

———. 1756. *Vernunftlehre.* Ed. F. Lötzsch. Munich, 1979.

———. 1760. *Allgemeine Betrachtungen über die Triebe der Thiere, hauptsächlich über ihre Kunsttriebe.* Ed. J. von Kempski. 2 vols. Veröffentlichungen der Joachim-Jungius-Gesellschaft 46. Repr. of ed. Hamburg 1760. Göttingen, 1982.

———. 1972. *Apologie oder Schutzschrift für die vernünftigen Verehrer Gottes.* 2 vols. Ed. G. Alexander. Frankfurt am Main.

———. 1979. *Handschriftenverzeichnis und Bibliographie.* Comp. W. Schmidt-Biggemann. Göttingen.

Reventlow, H. Graf. 1973. Das Arsenal der Bibelkritik des Reimarus: Die Auslegung der Bibel, insbesondere des Alten Testaments, bei den englischen Deisten. Pp. 44–65 in *Hermann Samuel Reimarus (1694–1768), ein "bekannter Unbekannter" der Aufklärung in Hamburg.* Göttingen.

———. 1980. *Bibelautorität und Geist der Moderne.* Göttingen.

———. 1988a. Humanistic Exegesis: The Famous Hugo Grotius. Pp. 175–91 in *Creative Biblical Exegesis,* ed. B. Uffenheimer and H. Graf Reventlow. JSOTSup 59. Sheffield.

———. 1988b. Bibelexegese als Aufklärung: Die Bibel im Denken des Johannes Clericus. Pp. 1–19 in Reventlow, Sparn, and Woodbridge 1988.

———. 1988c. "Sullo Scopo di Gesù e dei suoi disepoli": Il contributo di Hermann Samuel Reimarus all' indagine del Nuovo Testamento. Pp. 97–110 in *"Gesù storico": Problems della modernità,* ed. G. Vermès. Casale Monferrato.

———. 1988d. Wurzeln der modernen Bibelkritik. Pp. 47–63 in Reventlow, Sparn and Woodbridge 1988.

Reventlow, H. Graf; Sparn, W.; and Woodbridge, J., eds. 1988. *Historische Kritik und biblischer Kanon in der deutschen Aufklärung.* Wolfenbütteler Forschungen 41. Wiesbaden.

Rex, W. E. 1965. *Essays on Pierre Bayle and Religious Controversy.* International Archives of the History of Ideas 8. New York.

Rogers, J. B. 1966–67. *Scripture in the Weestminster Confession.* Kampen and Grand Rapids.

Rogerson, J.; Rowland, C.; and Lindars, B. 1988. *The Study and Use of the Bible.* History of Christian Theology 2. Basingstoke and Grand Rapids.

Rossi, M. M. 1947. *La vita, le opere, i tempi di Edoardo Herbert di Chirbury.* 3 vols. Florence.

Rougemont, M. de. 1986. Bible et théâtre. Pp. 269–287 in Belaval and Bourel 1986.

Rousseau, J. J. 1762. *Oeuvres complètes.* Vols. 3–5, *Émile ou de l'éducation.* The Hague, 1762. Repr. Paris, 1825–28.

Rupp, G. 1986. *Religion in England 1688–1791.* Oxford.

Rutman, D. R., ed. 1970. *The Great Awakening.* London.

Ryken, L. 1986. *Wordly Saints: The Puritans As They Really Were.* Grand Rapids.

Sandys-Wunsch, J. 1981. Spinoza—the First Biblical Theologian. *ZAW* 91: 327–41.

Sauter, G. 1966. Die Zahl als Schlüssel zur Welt: Johann Albrecht Bengels "prophetische Zeitrechnung" im Zusammenhang seiner Theologie. *EvT* 26: 1–36.

Sayce, R. A. 1955. *The French Biblical Epic in the Seventeenth Century.* London.

Schilson, A. 1974. *Geschichte im Horizont der Vorsehung: G. E. Lessings Beitrag zu einer Theologie der Geschichte.* Mainz.

Schloemann, M. 1974. *Siegmund Jacob Baumgarten: System und Geschichte in der Theologie des Übergangs zum Neuprotestantismus.* FKDG 26. Göttingen.

Schmidt, M. 1951. Speners *Pia Desideria:* Versuch einer theologischen Interpretation. *ThViat* 3: 70–112. Repr., pp. 129–68 in *Wiedergeburt und neuer Mensch.* Witten, 1969.

———. 1953–66. *John Wesley.* 2 vols. Zürich.

———. 1970. Philipp Jakob Spener und die Bibel. Pp. 9–58 in Aland 1970b.

———. 1972. *Pietismus.* Stuttgart.

Schneider, H. 1983–84. Der radikale Pietismus in der neueren Forschung. *Pietismus und Neuzeit* 8: 15–42.

Scholder, K. 1962. Herder und die Anfänge der historischen Theologie. *EvT* 22: 425–40.

———. 1966. *Ursprünge und Probleme der bibelkritik im 17. Jahrhundert.* Munich.

Schrenck, G. 1923. *Gottersreich und Bund in älteren Protestantismus, vornehmlich bei Johannes Cocceius.* Gütersloh.

Schultze, H. 1969. *Lessings Toleranzbegriff.* Forschungen zur systematischen und ökumenischen Theologie 20. Göttingen.

———. 1978. Religionskritik in der deutschen Aufklärung: Das Hauptwerk des Reimarus im 200. Jahre des Fragmentenstreits. *TLZ* 103: 750–13.

———. 1988. *Johann Salomo Semlers Wesensbestimmung des Christentums.* Würzburg.

Schwarzbach, B. E. 1971. *Voltaire's Old Testament Criticism.* Geneva.

Seckler, M. 1980. Aufklärung und Offenbarung. *Christlicher Glaube in moderner Gesellschaft* 21: 5–78.

Sehmsdorf, E. 1971. *Die Prophetenauslegung bei J. G. Eichhorn.* Göttingen.

Selbie, W. B. 1953. The Influence of the Old Testament on Puritanism. Pp. 407–31 in *The Legacy of Israel,* 3d. ed. Ed. E. R. Bevan and C. Singer. Oxford.

Siegfried, C. 1867. *Spinoza als Kritiker und Ausleger des Alten Testaments.* Naumburg.

Simon, R. 1685. *Histoire critique du Vieux Testament.* 1st ed., Paris, 1678. Repr. of 1685 ed. Frankfurt am Main, 1967.

———. 1689a. *Histoire critique du texte du Nouveau Testament.* Repr. of 1689 ed. Frankfurt am Main, 1967.

———. 1689b. *Histoire critique des versions du Nouveau Testament.* Repr. of 1689 ed. Frankfurt am Main, 1967.

———. 1693. *Histoire critique des principaux commentaires du Nouveau Testament.* Rotterdam. Repr. Frankfurt am Main, 1969.

———. 1695. Nouvelles observations sur le texte et les versions du Nouveau Testament. Repr. Frankfurt am Main, 1973.

Smend, R. 1962. J. Ph. Gablers Begründung der biblischen Theologie. *EvT* 22: 345–57.

———. 1983. Aufgeklärte Bemühung um das Gesetz: Johann David Michaelis' "Mosaisches Recht." Pp. 129–39 in *Wenn nicht jetzt, wann dann?,* ed. H.-G. Geyer. Neukirchen-Vluyn.

———. 1987. Johann David Michaelis und Johann Gottfried Eichhorn - zwei Orientalisten am Rande der Theologie. Pp. 58–81 in *Theologie in Göttingen,* ed. B. Moeller. Göttingen.
———. 1989. *Deutsche Alttestamentler in drei Jahrhunderten.* Göttingen.
Solberg, W. U. 1977. *Redeem the Time: The Puritan Sabbath in Early America.* Cambridge, MA.
Sparn, W. 1985. Vernünftiges Christentum: Über die geschichtliche Aufgabe der theologischen Aufklärung im 18. Jahrhundert in Deutschland. Pp. 18–57 in *Wissenschaften im Zeitalter der Aufklärung,* ed. R. Vierhaus. Göttingen.
Spinoza, B. de. 1670. *Tractatus Theologico-Politicus.* Hamburg. = Vol. 3 in *Opera,* ed. C. Gebhard. Heidelberg, 1925; repr. 1973.
Steinmann, J. 1960. *R. Simon et les origines de l'exégèse Biblique.* Bruges.
Stemmer, P. 1983. *Weissagung und Kritik: Eine Studie zur Hermeneutik bei Hermann Samuel Reimarus.* Veröffentlichungen der Joachim-Jungius-Gesellschaft 48. Göttingen.
Stolzenburg, A. F. 1926. *Die Theologie des J. Franc. Buddeus und des Chr. Matth. Pfaff.* Berlin.
Stout, H. S. 1982. Word and Order in Colonial New England. Pp. 19–38 in *The Bible in America,* ed. N. O. Hatch and M. A. Noll. Oxford.
Strauss, L. 1965. *Spinoza's Critique of Religion.* Trans. E. M. Sinclair. New York.
Stroh, H. 1977. Hermeneutik im Pietismus. *ZTK* 74: 38–57.
Stummer, F. 1912. *Die Bedeutung Richard Simons für die Pentateuchkritik.* Münster.
Sullivan, R. E. 1982. *John Toland and the Deist Controversy.* Cambridge, MA.
Sweet, W. W. 1944. *Revivalism in America.* New York. Repr. Gloucester, MA.
Thielicke, H. 1957. *Offenbarung, Vernunft und Existenz: Studien zur Religionsphilosophie Lessings.* 4th ed. Gütersloh.
Tracy, P. J. 1980. *Jonathan Edwards, Pastor.* New York.
Tuttle, R. G., Jr. 1978. *John Wesley: His Life and Theology.* Grand Rapids.
Tyson, J. R. 1986. *Charles Wesley on Sanctification.* Grand Rapids.
Urlinger, J. 1969. Die geistes—und sprachgeschichtliche Bedeutung der Berleburger Bibel. Diss. Saarbrücken.
Valentin, J.-M. 1983–84. *Le Théatre des Jésuites dans les pays de langue Allemande.* 3 vols. Bern.
Voigt, M. 1986. *Johann Sebastian Bach als Ausleger der Heiligen Schrift.* Hannover.
Wade, I. O. 1938. *The Clandestine Organization and Diffusion of Philosophic Ideas in France from 1700 to 1750.* Princeton. Repr. New York, 1967.
Wagner, H.-P. 1982. *Puritan Attitudes Towards Recreation in Early Seventeenth-Century New England.* Frankfurt am Main.
Walber, K.-J. 1988. *Charles Blount (1654–1693), Frühaufklärer: Leben und Werk,* ed. J. Klein. Vol. 15. Frankfurt am Main.
Wallmann, J. 1986. *Philipp Jakob Spener und die Anfänge des Pietismus.* 2d ed. BHT 42. Tübingen.
Walravens, E. 1986. La Bible chez les libres penseurs en Allemagne. Pp. 579–97 in Belaval and Bourel 1986.
Walsh, J. D. 1966. Origins of the Evangelical Revival. Pp. 132–62 in *Essays in Modern English Church History in Memory of Norman Sykes,* ed. G. V. Bennett and J. D. Walsh. London.
Watkins, O. C. 1972. *The Puritan Experience.* London.
Watson, P. 1984. *The Message of the Wesleys.* Grand Rapids.
Watts, M. R. 1978. *The Dissenters.* Vol. 1, *From the Reformation to the French Revolution.* Oxford.
Weisberger, B. A. 1958. *They Gathered at the River: The Story of the Great Revivalists and Their Impact upon Religion in America.* Boston.
Westfall, R. S. 1981. *Never at Rest: A Biography of Newton.* Cambridge.
Wettstein, J. J. 1751–52. *KAINE DIATHEKE: Novum Testamentum Graecum.* 2 vols. Amsterdam.
Whiston, W. 1722. *An Essay towards Restoring the True Text of the Old Testament; and for Vindicating the Citations made thence in the New Testament.* London.
Willi, T. 1971. *Herders Beitrag zum Verstehen des Alten Testaments.* Beiträge zur Geschichte der biblischen Hermeneutik 8. Tübingen.
Wilson, D. 1976. *The People and the Book: The Revolutionary Impact of the English Bible, 1380–1611.* London.
Zac, S. 1965. *Spinoza et l'interpretation de l'Écriture.* Paris.
———. 1979. *Philosophie, théologie, politique dans l'oeuvre de Spinoza.* Paris.
Zani, L. 1954. *L'Etica die Lord Shaftesbury.* Milan.
Zeller, W. 1970. Die Bibel als Quelle der Frömmigkeit bei Gerhard Tersteegen. Pp. 170–92 in Aland 1970b.

HENNING GRAF REVENTLOW

BIBLICAL AUTHORITY IN THE POST-CRITICAL PERIOD

Each generation of believers and scholars must answer its own particular form of the question of the authority of scripture, for the question is posed differently for different communities in different intellectual and cultural circumstances. The Jewish and Christian religious communities have characteristically accepted the scriptures as revelatory, but have been mostly unclear and largely uninterested in stating precisely in what ways this literature is authoritative. It has been enough to affirm that this literature provides norms and permits for the abundant life intended by God for the creation. Specificity beyond that affirmation has been only hard and tenuously won. The problem is that the articulation of any formal criteria concerning authority or revelation turn out to be in tension with the actual concrete practice of the communities affirming the authority (Kelsey 1975). In most circumstances, the actual concrete practice is to be taken more seriously than is the formal statement which tries to objectify and intellectualize that practice.

A. The Modern Discussion
B. The Cultural Context for the Question of Authority
C. Originary Power and Practice
D. Authority as "Classic"
E. Spheres of the Question of Authority
  1. Church and Synagogue
  2. The Academy
  3. The Public Arena
F. Authorization and Communities of Praxis
  1. Biblical Authority as Requirement
  2. Biblical Authority as Permit
G. Strange Authorization for Newness

A. The Modern Discussion

The governing categories for the questions that have dominated the modern discussion of biblical authority for the last two centuries need to be assessed and appreciated in their own cultural context. The question of the authority of scripture as understood in the Euro-American context has been framed in response to the rise of science, the emergence of scientific method, and the dominance of historical-critical modes of handling literature (Richardson *IDB* 4: 248–51; Barr *IDBSup,* 794–97). Prior to this development in the 17th and 18th centuries, there was in the West a sufficient cultural consensus concerning the nature of Scripture. Thus, even critical questions were set within the secure framework of well-established and widely held convictions about the religious authority of the Bible. Prior to the rise of scientific consciousness, questions of authority were indeed an enterprise of "faith seeking understanding" (Barth 1985; Cushman 1981).

The above changed, however, with the introduction of new thought patterns that shattered the theological consensus and paved the way for the study of the Bible as an autonomous piece of literature—a literature that was increasingly understood in relativizing ways. This suggestion of relativity concerning the Bible in turn evoked an urgency with respect to its certitude and absoluteness, a phenomenon new to biblical studies. Thus the "Battle for the Bible" (Lindsell 1976) forced extreme positions, radical and reactionary, concerning such matters as inspiration, revelation, inerrancy, and infallibility. It must be recognized that the very posing of the question in terms of revelation and scientific criticism is reflective of a cultural crisis which challenged every settled authority and which defined the debate in terms of relativity and absoluteness. The above categories of discussion unfortunately skewed the matter in a number of ways. The controversial discussion from the 18th century until now (which is roughly coterminous with the practice of Enlightenment criticism) has a strange quality to it, in that the categories of the conversation have been more or less imposed from external sources such as scientific accuracy or historical precision—categories essentially alien to the material itself. This is just as true of radical views which jeopardized the authority of Scripture as it is of reactionary views which submitted the claims of Scripture to the canon of modern scientific certitude. On the one hand, radical criticism provided a sense of autonomy and freedom within the literature, i.e., now the Bible need not be taken with such heavy authoritarianism when understood to be historically conditioned in all its parts. On the other hand, reactionary scholasticism provided a sense of intellectual control and technical assurance; the Bible was understood as a lone champion of unbending reality in a situation marked by "change and decay." "Change and decay" is one important perception of the rise of science, technology, secularization, and individual freedom, and its corollary, the demise of the old hegemony in its intellectual, moral, economic, and political dimension. "Change and decay" is one experience of the emergence of modernism. But neither such autonomy and freedom, nor such control and assurance, seems particularly germane to the biblical literature itself; nor are they finally satisfying as responses to the religious thirst for truth as mediated by the Bible. The Bible does not mediate the *kind* of certitude sought in these categories.

In retrospect, the recent controversial discussion which opposed criticism and scholasticism now appears to have been misguided. Since the controversy failed to mediate the faith-claims of the text itself, it proceeded on both sides in alien, inappropriate categories. That particular conversation has now become somewhat obsolete because our present-day culture no longer excessively trusts nor fears such scientific methods. These scientific-critical methods, whether willingly embraced or vigorously resisted, really do not touch the issue of the authority of scripture as a theological problem.

The modern polemical conversation concerning faith and criticism, now so well documented in the handbooks (e.g., Rogers and McKim 1979), has distorted the character of the Bible. On the side of literalism, the truth of God's power was cast in Enlightenment categories of script, document, authorship, and historical accuracy of written reports. In response to this, on the side of liberalism, resistance was offered to such scribalism, which was viewed as authoritarian. Scholars distanced themselves from the religious claims of the text through an appeal to (1) personal experience which judged the text, (2) cultural values held over against the text, and (3) events which happened outside and behind the text. Neither literalism nor liberalism faced the theologically dangerous character of the text, i.e., both articulations of authority became defenses against yielding to the potentially dangerous, upsetting, and subversive power of the text that speaks characteristically against our settled, constructed worlds on behalf of a world yet to come.

B. The Cultural Context for the Question of Authority

Ours is a religious and cultural situation in which the question of authority must be posed anew, because the categories of the conversation have shifted. Ours is a post-modern, post-scientific, post-Enlightenment, post-positivistic situation (Gilkey 1981; Harrington 1983). It will not do to frame the question of authority as a scholastic one of proof, or as a romantic one of experience, or as a probe into scientific categories. The question now becomes one of what it means to be a community of interpretation and action called into existence by a text that remains distant and of less utility in the pursuit of certitude. Thus it appears that the question has been wrongly cast as one of *authorship,* a question we might expect from a book-oriented society preoccupied with questions of copyrights, sources, documentation, and scientific facts. The Bible itself has almost no interest in such modern questions of authorship which result in hopeless and misguided investigations of claims of inspiration and revelation.

Rather, authority has to do with *issues of authorization,* i.e., how, in a pluralistic world like ours, concrete communities can be authorized to live, act, and hope in a manner which may at times oppose the accepted norm, a manner which can be justified neither scientifically nor experientially. It is this authorization of a community's obedience and praise that is the real issue in the question of the authority of Scripture. In order to answer this question of authorization, we must attempt to free ourselves of the immobilizing influence of the Enlightenment categories of certitude. An increasing number of people draw the conclusion that communities created and authorized by these texts are summoned and permitted to live, act, and hope in different and dangerous ways, and authorized by a different "voice" which is heard in the text, even if that voice cannot easily be accommodated in the conventional categories of academic investigation. The "authorizing voice" of scripture "heard" in the community needs to be understood as a theological reality mediated through the biblical literature. That is, the authorizing voice heard in the text, albeit mediated through social institutions and more immediate experiences, is indeed the voice of the Holy God. That is the voice communities of faith heard in the text, a voice which authorizes in odd and unsettling ways.

Communities of faith around the world, and especially in the West, where the old "Battle for the Bible" has been largely conducted, are now in deep crisis. Questions of authority cannot be considered apart from this crisis which concerns believers and nonbelievers alike.

The overarching crisis of Western culture (within which the authority of Scripture must be articulated) is that the values and institutions of society are mostly organized against the "prospect of humanness" (Heilbroner 1980). Two articulations of this crisis may be cited. Robert Bellah (1982) has characterized the mood of conventional modern life (largely shaped by the social sciences) by the terms "positivism, reductionism, relativism, and determinism." Bellah further observes that such values are inherently anti-human. Moreover, the live alternative to this practice of society lies only with the religious community which is authorized to preserve values and practices of humanness:

> To the extent, however, that real religious communities can retain or recover a sense of being in but not of this world, can live, at least to some extent, in patterns of voluntary simplicity and mutual concern, then they may act as genuine alternatives to the prevailing current . . . it is more than ever necessary that there be demonstration communities where elementary decencies can be maintained and handed down, humanizing a bad situation as long as it exists, and providing seedbeds for larger amelioration when that becomes possible (pp. 21–22).

In a more recent, extended treatment, Bellah and his colleagues have concluded that American society has lost or neglected those acts and gestures that make sustained human community possible (Bellah et al. 1985). They propose that the religious community has a responsibility and an opportunity to foster and encourage more fully human possibilities.

In a much more abrasive analysis, Richard Rubenstein (1983) has proposed a reading of the economic history of the West as a history of triage. Legitimated practices of land management and use of money and power have as their social result the devaluation and elimination of marginal and useless people. Rubenstein proposes that only the biblical-based religious community can hope to terminate such destructive values and practices, i.e., the social vision of the Bible is the only effective alternative to this triage:

> Only a religious faith radically polemic to magic and to belief in earth's indwelling spirits could have brought about the cultural revolution in which an entire civilization came to reject what men and women had revered as sacred from time immemorial. . . . Perhaps the most influential example of a congery of strangers forming a community by adopting a common faith is that of the Hebrews of Sinai. . . . Neither unending growth nor unending movement offers a solution. . . . That is why a religious transformation is crucial. . . . The call for religious transformation is in reality a call to conversion, a call to change ourselves. Our preachers have rightly told us that we must be converted, that we must be born again. Unfortunately, what has been understood as conversion has all too often been devoid of the inclusive social component our times demand. In truth, we must be born again as men and women blessed with the capacity to care for each other here and now (pp. 230–40).

The question of biblical authority is too urgent to be reduced to a parlor game of conventional scholastic categories. It is not a mechanistic question of proof and certitude for intramural debate within the religious community. It is now a public question of energy, courage, and freedom to act. The larger question is, what will provide energy, courage, and legitimacy for action against the destructive tendencies embedded within our civilization?

C. Originary Power and Practice

Against such settlements which reflect the intellectual climate and needs of the modern world, it must be recognized that the biblical text is in an odd way "originary," i.e., it has the capacity to generate real newness. This text contains the power to work a newness that is indeed an act *creatio ex nihilo,* to call into being that which does not exist until brought to speech (Rom 4:17). This "originary" character of the texts means that the text cannot be shackled by theories of inspiration, cannot be domesticated by archaeological proofs, and cannot be assessed by religious antecedents drawn from surrounding cultures. This power to articulate newness shatters all our cherished presuppositions and in turn pushes the question of authority outside the realm of explanation, leading into the world of testimony.

It is necessary, for that reason, to find new modes of articulation of the matter of authority. It is clear that an Enlightenment notion of technical-scientific explanation (either of literalism or of critical scholarship) is irrelevant to this question. One recent attempt with much to commend it is a literary approach that draws attention to the artistic power of the text, that is, authority is located in the speech of the text itself and not in something behind the speech of the text. Such an artistic approach, however, fails to face the ethical demands imposed by the text. It tends, instead, to remain preoccupied with the aesthetic dimensions of the literature.

The authority of scripture must ultimately be articulated in confessional terms by communities which assert that they have discerned the truth of power and the power of truth precisely in this text. (In his shrewd analysis Chilton [1984] has argued that this is true for individuals in their experience as well as for communities.)

This confessional claim is what is meant by the "self-authenticating authority of Scripture" (Raschke 1985). It is the readiness to act that keeps a confessional claim honest. This way of putting the matter is honest in not claiming that this authority can be objectively demonstrated, even though authority is claimed to be objectively grounded in the character of the classic. This way of making a claim is honest in asserting that there is a compelling power we have discerned and upon which we are prepared to act. Such a statement of authority will not claim less. But it will not claim more, as though the claim were objectively provable. It is finally the readiness of a confessing community to stake its life on the summons of the text which is its only credible authentication. Both the Church, with its excessive penchant for dogmatic certitude, and the academy, with its fascination with objective rationality, characteristically stop short of the evidence of communal obedience. The question of authority is and must be shaped around the issue of obedient practice at the end of the Enlightenment period.

D. Authority as "Classic"

David Tracy (1981) has offered a fresh perspective on scriptural authority centered around the theme of "classic." In that term he proposes a category of authority that is not the special pleading of a partisan community, but a claim submitted to the criterion of public conversation. Tracy understands a text as a "classic" when:

> its "excess of meaning" both demands constant interpretation and bears a certain kind of timelessness—namely the timeliness of a classic expression radically rooted in its own historical time and calling to my own historicity. . . . The classic text's real disclosure is its claim to attention on the ground that an event of understanding proper to finite human beings has here found expression. . . . Every classic lives as a classic only if it finds readers willing to be provoked by its claim to attention (p. 102). If, even once, a person has experienced a text, a gesture, an image, an event, a person with the force of the recognition, "This is important! This does make and will demand a difference!" then one has experienced a candidate for classic status (pp. 115–16).

It is the text and not the community of the text which has authority. Tracy nonetheless understands that the response of the community of the text is important in determining the classic character of a text.

> At the very least, we will be willing to listen to that wider community of enquirers and readers who have found and find this text a classic. We will listen to them and then return to our dialogue with the subject matter of this "formed" text. After that second exposure, we may still decide that the community of enquiry in this instance has been mistaken. . . . At that point, tentativeness must cease. For in those instances where a matter of importance is at stake—and the assignment of the status "classic" to any text is a matter of singular importance—then we must insist. But where tentativeness ceases, listening never does. The wider community of readers, living and dead, must continue to be heard as all return to the struggle of finding some appropriate response (from some initial sense of import to a formed judgment) to this possibly classic text (p. 116).

For Jews and Christians this tentativeness has ceased concerning the Bible. The decision that the Bible is a classic which mediates power and truth is a settled question for those communities. The church and the synagogue have found here "a certain kind of timelessness" which "demands constant interpretation."

With this characterization, Tracy hopes to avoid the circular argument of establishing the authority of the text by quoting the document itself. This practice satisfies only those who are already predisposed to accept the internal testimony of the text. Tracy also avoids the claim to authority which appeals to inspiration, revelation, or the work of the Spirit. Claims of this type may be valid, and are not here denied, but they bear the marks of special pleading as traditionally formulated. Moreover, Tracy eschews any notion of authority imposed externally through declaration, promulgation, or canonization. Circular argument, special pleading, and external imposition are not finally persuasive in such an urgent matter. Rather, authority is recognized (not given) by a public judgment that this text bears authority in its powerful offer of truth which has been recognized over time as having an inescapable claim upon us. The other dimension of tracy's characterization is that, since the text is distant in time, it requires interpretation which both discloses and conceals, so that the affirmation of authority requires and invites interpretation rather than resisting it. Understood in this way, interpretation is not a threat to the initial claim of the text, but is appropriate to its character and intention.

E. Spheres of the Question of Authority

The power of the Bible as a classic as norm and authorizer is operative in three realms. In each of these we may observe the way in which the Bible authorizes.

1. Church and Synagogue. The classic is peculiarly linked to the synagogue and church out of whose memory the text has come. There is no doubt that text and community are dialectically related, i.e., that community forms text and text evokes community. The formal claim of canon asserts that this literature is normative, functioning as a norm for life and faith. It functions in the church (in the language of Ricoeur) to permit an imaginative rereading of reality, so that the believing communities can discern and respond to the world in ways different from those dominant responses described by Bellah and Rubenstein. Indeed this text mediates "truth" to these communities, truth about God, truth about self, truth about human history, and truth about the world as God's creation. Gilkey has summarized this "rereading of reality" in ways that show the distinctiveness of this mediation:

> . . . in the Old Testament understanding of history there are three distinct moments or stages characterizing historical passage. . . . First of all, there was the divine constitution or "creation" of the people and their cultural life. . . . The second moment . . . is the appearance of estrangement or alienation, of the fallen character of even the life of a chosen people. . . . The final moment is also prophetic. . . . This is the promise of a new

covenant beyond the destruction of the old . . . the promise of new possibilities in historical life. . . . [In the New Testament] divine constitution, divine judgment, and new creative acts become incarnation, atonement and resurrection/*parousia,* aspects of history, to be sure, but not of *ordinary* history (1984: 12–13).

The problem with this classic in the religious communities is its possible subjugation to the "tyranny of the church," i.e., it is made to conform to ideological claims of the religious community. Traditionally this tyranny has been especially evident when the Bible has been interpreted only as a reinforcement for patterns of dogmatic formulation. For a very long period the Bible was used in the Christian tradition primarily to support such creedal formulations and it was precisely the rise of historical-critical methods that rescued the Bible, so that it could have its own liberated way, apart from these dogmatic categories. Thus the truth of the Bible cannot in good faith be accommodated to such tyranny, nor can it legitimately be made to serve ideological, partisan, or sectarian ends. Moreover, the truth given in this classic does not concern every kind of question that might be asked—scientific, astronomical, psychological, biological—but it is truth of a theological kind having to do with God's sovereign graciousness and gracious sovereignty.

The urgency of the Bible as authorization for the community of faith is its potential to release from false notions of absoluteness and certitude, and to unite a community currently beset by partisan and divisive pluralism. In the latter regard, the classic would gather disparate communities of faith together around a truth that is larger and more majestic than any similar partisan "truth" claimed by a particular community.

2. The Academy. This classic is also historically and culturally linked to the academy. Ebeling (1980) has shown how the Bible has played a key role in the origin of the Western intellectual and educational tradition. In the United States, the Bible has been crucial in forming the school tradition now so much taken for granted (Lynn 1980; Westerhoff 1978). However, the posture of the academy toward the text differs greatly from that of the Church (Childs 1982). Whereas the community of faith has characteristically bowed before the authority of the text, the academy has sought to analyze and understand the text, believing that clear understanding according to the best canon of reason poses no threat to biblical authority, but is a practice natural and congenial to the nature of the texts.

We can, however, speak of the "tyranny of the academy" over the voice of the Bible. The rise of historical criticism which freed the Bible from tyranny of the Church has led in turn to an autonomous reason which fundamentally resists the claims of the text. In contrast to the older discussion of reason and revelation, the academy has taken up a form of reason not only in tension with revelation, but deeply hostile to the claims of the text. Analytic methods have been joined to rationalistic categories of interpretation so that dimensions of mystery, awe, and inscrutability have been denied the text. Scientific or pseudoscientific norms of knowledge have been imposed on the Bible which have reduced it to an archaic book emptied of its power to transform or to authorize.

An example of the above tyranny is found in the well-articulated article of Smith (1969), who candidly observes that the perceptual field of scholars is in contradiction to the claims of the text. Smith fails to notice, however, that the problem does not lie with the claims of the classic, i.e., the text, but with the methods and questions of the scholarly guild. This type of tyranny of reason has been dramatically identified by Wink (1973) and more programmatically articulated by Childs (1979). The issue has yet to be connected, however, with the larger crisis of technical reason which largely dominates the conversation of the academy (Horkheimer and Adorno 1972).

The function of the classic, i.e., the Bible, in the academy concerns epistemological questions and the nature of knowledge. The academy in the modern world practices a form of knowledge aimed at control and which characteristically tends to domination. Lamentably, too many discussions about biblical authority have assumed such theories of knowledge and technique. Against that, however, the Bible is concerned with modes of knowledge that are relational, convenantal, and interactional, believing that knowledge should not dominate, but should serve to liberate and transform communication (Palmer). Modes of knowledge which tend toward domination cannot offer genuinely "new truth," i.e., they cannot be revelatory, but can only rearrange old patterns of power. "New truth" comes where imagination challenges, where spirit blows against letter (2 Cor 3:6), and where yielding replaces control.

3. The Public Arena. Lastly, the classic is culturally available in the public arena. It is a remarkable and enduring fact that the Bible has authority in the Western world far beyond the limits of its proper confessing communities. Indeed the dominant images and metaphors still governing public life are largely and powerfully shaped by the Bible (Frye). Bellah has shown that while civil religion in America may be distorted ideology, it nonetheless still partakes of echoes and sentiments derived from the Bible (Bellah 1975; see also Marty 1982).

To be sure, the Bible in our society has been utilized in coercive, oppressive, and ideological ways, e.g., as a law to keep minorities and women in their respective places, and as a lever against all sorts of "objectionable" people in the public arena (e.g., homosexuals). Nonetheless, it has been the Bible and its derivative traditions that have provided impetus and power for restorative notions of personal health and social humanness. Characteristically, liberation movements in our time have found their central images in the Bible (Walzer 1985). A striking example is Martin Luther King, Jr., a child of this text, who had the imagination and the ability eloquently to articulate the issues of racial discrimination through biblical metaphors that mobilized both public and secular responses (Smylie 1970).

The key to public issues in our society, as in every society, concerns access to power and the processes of decision making. It is obvious that a monopoly of access exists and that many are voiceless and excluded from decision making. Access is characteristically arranged in the interest of certain notions of order and merit. In the public conversation, against such a destructive commitment to an order which opposes egalitarianism in politics and economics, the Bible powerfully insists that questions of justice, questions of abundant life for the marginal, and questions of social access, social goods, and social power cannot be silenced.

The issue of biblical authority in our time, then, may be understood as an issue of the juxtaposition of *the crisis of inhumaneness* (Bellah 1982; Rubenstein 1983) and *the classic* (Tracy 1981) which has enduring authority. Without this classic, it is probable that the church and synagogue would settle for distortions of truth in partisan forms of absolutism or divisive forms of pluralism. The classic, however, summons the church to a *truth that liberates* us from our certitudes and *frees* us from our private and partisan commitments. Without this classic, it is probable that the academy would settle for distorted modes of knowledge, aiming at control and eventually leading to domination. This classic, however, invites the academy to practice *knowledge which heals, reconciles, and mobilizes power* in the service of human dignity, while simultaneously it provides a broad definition of what constitutes human dignity. Without this classic, it is probable the public domain would distort justice, pursue an oppressive order, and practice economic and political inequality. This classic urges those public practices of power to be *concerned with questions of justice,* so that marginal and powerless persons can be included in the formation of public policy. Thus the classic invites the church and synagogue to consider a truth that liberates, invites the academy to consider a knowledge that reconciles and heals, and invites the public arena to practice a form of justice which provides equal access to all, irrespective of privilege, power, or accomplishment.

The fact does, however, remain that some wield the authority of Scripture as a sponsor of sectarian truth, of ideological knowledge, and of a social order indifferent to issues of justice. To such an alternative and distorted reading of the Bible, one may respond in two ways: first, that it is on the issues of truth, knowledge, and justice (in the ways here characterized) that the Bible has established its claim as a classic. The Bible would not anywhere, at any time, have arrived at the status of classic, if it had been a text characteristically in the service of oppressive truth, technical knowledge, of partisan injustice. It is the largeness of its vision and its promise of a viable alternative that determines its functional power. The Bible is recognized in its classic proportion because it attempts to mediate and make available that which we judge most definitional for human life.

Second, we insist that the question of authority should not concern authorship, but authorization. As soon as the question of authorization is posed, one must ask, authorization to what? To what are the church and synagogue, the academy, and those in public life authorized? Within the scope of the biblical texts, the inescapable answer is the substantive disclosure of the Bible on all three counts, namely, there are (1) a God committed to liberation, unity, healing, knowledge, and justice; (2) an ongoing conflict within the course of public history precisely over these matters; and (3) a vision of the eventual triumph of these commitments of God.

F. Authorization and Communities of Praxis

The test of the authorizing power of the Bible is not, however, to be settled according to intellectual formulation. The test in this time of need for human possibility is in praxis, i.e., in the emergence of communities which embody and implement the rereading of the world that is voiced in the text. These communities of obedience bear witness to the authorizing power of the book as well as to the spirit which blows through that book. The text gives them not only advice and guidance but also the energy and courage for a life of obedience. It is staggering evidence of the authority of Scripture that even in the face of harsh, systemic brutality there have been and still are communities of faith who have demonstrated this alternative vision in the public arena. We may identify these communities under the rubric of those authorized by *biblical requirement* and those authorized by *biblical permit.*

1. Biblical Authority as Requirement. The Bible gives authorization to *communities of requirement* in its voice as the norm of commandment. The Bible, as the classic in which tentativeness is ended, is heard as the voice of summons and command which can be answered only with obedience. There is a stringent insistence in the Bible concerning expectations and demand for the community which it authorizes. Such communities ask in the face of this text, "What is required?" (cf. Deut 10:12; Mic 6:8). The answer, given in a variety of ways, is justice and mercy (Sider 1977).

This authorization *as requirement* is evident especially in communities of radical obedience in contexts of affluence, satiation, and accommodation. This has been true through the history of the church and the synagogue. In such contexts, the biblical text authorizes communities of the faithful who, in obedience to the text, order their lives in ways distinct from the dominant value system so as to disengage from those practices of power and well-being advocated by the society in which they find themselves placed. Such communities of obedience are given over to acts of mercy, strategies of justice, and visions of peace peculiarly authorized by this text.

2. Biblical Authority as Permit. The Bible reciprocally gives authorization to *communities of permit* in its voice as the norm of deliverance (Schreiter 1985). In quite parallel fashion, we may speak of "communities of permission." These communities are located not in contexts of affluence but in contexts of oppression and marginality where people hear the voice of liberation and acceptance, a voice which can be answered only in energy, freedom, and trust.

These are communities of faithful individuals who are authorized and permitted by this text to stand against oppression and to refuse marginality in the name of justice and liberation. Such communities are characteristically found in Third World situations where the dominant value structures preclude justice, legitimize marginality, and invite docility and passive acceptance of the status quo. Within such contexts, this text acts as an impetus to new life through the assertion of one's dignity, rights, worth, and power (Walzer 1985).

These communities of requirement and permission clearly concern public values of justice and dignity. But these same communities also have an intense pastoral concern in that individual persons are called to be obedient and are invited to assert and enact their own dignity, worth, and self-respect.

The authority of Scripture can be understood only in relation to and in terms of the communities it authorizes.

The authorizing power of the text is evident through both its demand for obedience and its grant of permission to act in new ways against both accommodation and oppression (Levinas 1969). The force of such authorization implies that the book and its authorized communities cannot wait for the resolution of scholastic arguments concerning inspiration or revelation, nor can they wait upon the academy to formulate properly its own intellectual stance on the matter. The authorizing power of the text is of another order.

In communities of requirement and permission, the Bible does not offer strategies or advice. What it does offer is energy, courage, vision, and hope. Historically, we have spoken of these matters in the text as "the inspiration of the Holy Spirit," and that is indeed what they are. But "Holy Spirit" needs to be understood apart from literary questions of authorship. Rather, the spirit has to do with faith questions of authorization, imagination, and life. The power of the spirit functions to permit communities to discern, imagine, and appropriate life differently, as it is mediated, remembered, and hoped in this text. The work of the spirit is the liberation of the community's imagination mediated through the text. These communities of requirement and permission find such liberation mediated in these texts in ways that permit a new life in the world. The text is "in-spirited" in the sense that it is "peopled" with the force of God's power to permit new communities to emerge in the world. It is "infallible" in the sense that it authorizes a way of living and believing that without fail leads to the fruits of the spirit (Gal 5:22-24). It is "revelatory" in the sense that it discloses a new way of living in the world that was not previously known and that seemed heretofore prohibited by the structures of coercion and domination.

The central thrust of this classic which mediates new life is its offer of an alternative reality of governance which is sure but not dominating, producing new modes of certitude, power, and knowledge. The "otherness" of the text is the disclosure of a "secret" (cf. Luke 10:23–24). In the scripture of Israel, that "secret" is about a transcendent governance rendering all other imperial power inoperational (Exod 8:18), confounding spear and sword with a power name (1 Sam 17:45), and opening the world against might and power by the spirit (Zech 4:6). In the NT that same secret concerns "the impossible" being made possible (Mark 10:27), weakness in obedience which turns out to be triumphant strength (cf. 2 Cor 11:30; 12:5, 9).

G. Strange Authorization for Newness.

Martin Buber, in a voice of faithful Judaism, and Karl Barth, in a voice of faithful Christianity, both understood that the Bible is a strange voice and a strange book which gives life. Buber writes:

> The modern person must read the Jewish Bible as though it were something entirely unfamiliar, as though it had not been set before him ready-made, as though he has not been confronted all his life with sham concepts and sham statements that cited the Bible as their authority. He must face the Book with a new attitude as something new. He must yield to it, withhold nothing of his being, and let whatever will occur between himself and it. He does not know which of its sayings and images will overwhelm him and mold him, from where the spirit will ferment and enter into him, to incorporate itself anew in his body. But he holds himself open. He does not believe anything a priori; he does not disbelieve anything a priori. He reads aloud the words written in the book in front of him; he hears the word he utters and it reaches him. Nothing is pre-judged. The current of time flows on, and the contemporary character of this man becomes itself a receiving vessel.
>
> In order to understand the situation fully, we must picture to ourselves the complete chasm between the Scriptures and the man of today (1968: 5).

Barth (1957) asserts in parallel fashion:

> Within the Bible there is a strange, new world, the world of God. This answer is the same as that which came to the first martyr, Stephen: Behold, I see the heavens opened and the Son of man standing on the right hand of God. . . . We must openly confess that we are reaching beyond ourselves. But that is just the point: if we wish to come to grips with the contents of the Bible, we must dare to reach far beyond ourselves. The Book admists of nothing less. . . . A new world, the world of God (pp. 33–34).
>
> Once more we stand before this "other" new world which begins in the Bible. In it the chief consideration is not the doings of man but the doings of God—not the various ways which we may take if we are men of good will, but the power out of which good will must first be created (pp. 39–40).
>
> It is not the right human thoughts about God which form the content of the Bible, but the right divine thoughts about men. The Bible tells us not how we should talk with God, but what he says to us; not how we find the way to him, but how he has sought and found the way to us; not the right relation in which we must place ourselves to him, but the covenant which he has made with all who are Abraham's spiritual children and which he has sealed once and for all in Jesus Christ. It is this which is within the Bible. The word of God is within the Bible (p. 43).

The Bible is fundamentally alien to modernity, even as it is fundamentally alien to every dominating mode of rationality in every age of the synagogue and the church. It is for this reason that the Bible and its authority can never be articulated or summarized in dominant modes of rationality. The book can be received and its authority evidenced only in communities of obedience and praise which, with marvelous indifference to categories of explanation, act with power, courage, freedom, and energy toward a new world envisioned, imagined, and promised in this text. To try to reduce such liberated imagination either to the categories of literalism or to the more respectable but equally problematic categories of liberalism is a sorry, mistaken assessment of this book. The practice of literalism is to hope for a kind of control that this inspirited book will never countenance. To practice liberalism is to hope for a kind of benign distancing that this restless book will never tolerate. In the face of such ill-conceived control or distance, genuinely authorized communities regularly find the book more terrifying than that, and more dangerously healing. Any formulation of authority which alleviates the terror or domesticates the healing is inadequate for the book. Such a reduction in either direction is an attempt at domination, whereas the book insists upon yielding as the point of access to its truth and power. This yielding means that truth and power, with all their terror and healing, are yet to be granted in new forms. That is what the theories of "*Sensus Plenior*" (Brown 1955), "The New Hermeneutic" (Fuchs 1964; Ebeling 1964), and "world-making speech" (Wilder 1983) have attempted to articulate. The authorized communities will continue in obedient interpretation, in obedience which in itself is an act of interpretation. In the midst of interpretation and obedience, there is a waiting (Hab 2:3) and a watching (Mark 13:37) for what will soon be given by God through this text.

Bibliography

Barr, J. 1980. The Bible as a Document of Believing Communities. Pp. 25–47 in Betz 1980.
———. 1980a. *The Scope and Authority of the Bible.* Philadelphia.
———. 1983. *Holy Scripture: Canon, Authority, Criticism.* Philadelphia.
Barth, K. 1957. *The Word of God and the Word of Man.* Trans. D. Horton. New York.
———. 1985. *Anselm: Fides quarens intellectum.* Trans. I. W. Robertson. Pittsburgh.
Bartlett, D. L. 1983. *The Shape of Scriptural Authority.* Philadelphia.
Barton, J. 1984. *Reading the Old Testament.* Philadelphia.
Bellah, R. 1975. *The Broken Covenant.* New York.
———. 1982. Biblical Religion and Social Science in the Modern World, *NICM Journal for Jews and Christians in Higher Education.* 6/3: 8–22.
Bellah, R. et al. 1985. *Habits of the Heart.* Berkeley.
Betz, H. D. ed. 1980. *The Bible as a Document of the University.* Chico, CA.
Brown, R. E. 1955. *The Sensus Plenior of Sacred Scripture.* Baltimore.
Buber, M. 1968. The Man of Today and the Jewish Bible. In *On the Bible,* ed. N. N. Glatzer. New York.
Childs, B. S. 1979. *Introduction to the OT as Scripture.* Philadelphia.
———. 1982. Some Reflections on the Search for a Biblical Theology. *HBT* 4: 1–12.
Chilton, B. 1984. *A Galilean Rabbi and His Bible.* Wilmington, DE.
Curran, C. and McCormick, R. A. 1984. *The Use of Scripture in Moral Theology.* Readings in Moral Theology 4. New York.
Cushman, R. 1981. *Faith Seeking Understanding.* Durham, NC.
Ebling, G. 1964. Word of God and Hermeneutic. Pp. 78–110 in *The New Hermeneutic,* ed. J. M. Robinson and J. B. Cobb, Jr. New York.
———. 1980. The Bible as a Document of the University. Pp. 5–23 in Betz 1980.
Frye, N. 1982. *The Great Code: The Bible in Literature.* New York.
Fuchs, E. 1964. The New Testament and the Hermeneutical Problem. Pp. 111–45 in *The New Hermeneutic.* ed. J. M. Robinson and J. B. Cobb, Jr. New York.
Gese, H. 1981. The Biblical View of Scripture. Pp. 9–33 in *Essays on Biblical Theology.* Minneapolis.
Gilkey, L. 1981. *Society and the Sacred.* New York.
———. 1984. Scripture, History and the Quest for Meaning. Pp. 3–16 in *History and Historical Understanding.* ed. C. T. McIntire and R. A. Wells. Grand Rapids.
Grant, R. M. and Tracy, D. 1963. *A Short History of the Interpretation of the Bible.* Philadelphia. Repr. 1984.
Greenspahn, F. E. ed. 1982. *Scripture in the Jewish and Christian Traditions.* Nashville.
Harrington, M. 1983. *The Politics at God's Funeral.* New York.
Heilbroner, R. L. 1980. *An Inquiry into the Human Prospect.* New York.
Horkheimer, M. and Adorno, T. W. 1972. *Dialectic of Enlightenment.* New York.
Kelsey, D. 1975. *The Uses of Scripture in Recent Theology.* Philadelphia.
Knight, D. A., ed. 1982. *Humanizing America's Iconic Book.* Chico, CA.
Levinas, E. 1969. *Totality and Infinity.* Pittsburgh.
Lindsell, H. 1976. *The Battle for the Bible.* Grand Rapids.
Lynn, R. 1980. *The Big Little School.* Birmingham, AL.
Marty, M. 1982. America's Iconic Book. Pp. 1–23 in Knight 1982.
Palmer, P. J. 1983. *To Know As We Are Known.* San Francisco.
Raschke, C. A. 1985. On Reading Romans 1–6 or Overcoming the Hermeneutics of Suspicion. *Ex Auditu.* 1: 147–55.
Reventlow, H. G. 1985. *The Authority of the Bible and the Rise of the Modern World.* Trans. J. Bowden. Philadelphia.
Ricoeur, P. 1975. Biblical Hermeneutics. *Semeia* 4: 29–148.
Rogers, J. B. and McKim, O. K. 1979. *The Authority and Interpretation of the Bible.* New York.
Rubenstein, R. 1983. *The Age of Triage: Fear and Hope in an Overcrowded World.* Boston.
Schreiter, R. J. 1985. *Constructing Local Theologies.* Maryknoll, NY.
Sennett, R. 1981. *Authority.* New York.
Sider, R. L. 1977. *Rich Christians in an Age of Hunger.* Downers Grove, IL.
Smart, J. 1970. *The Strange Silence of the Bible in the Church.* Philadelphia.
———. 1977. *The Cultural Subversion of the Biblical Faith.* Philadelphia.
Smith, M. 1969. The Present State of OT Studies. *JBL* 88: 19–35.
Smylie, J. H. 1970. On Jesus, Pharaohs, and the Chosen People. *Int* 24: 74–91.
Tracy, D. 1981. *The Analogical Imagination.* New York.
Walzer, M. 1985. *Exodus and Revolution.* New York.
Westerhoff, J. H. 1978. *McGuffey and His Readers.* Nashville.
Wilder, A. 1983. Story and Story World. *Int* 37: 353–64.
Wink, W. 1973. *The Bible in Human Transformation.* Philadelphia.

WALTER BRUEGGEMANN

SCULPTURED STONES. See IDOL, IDOLATRY.

SCURVY. See SICKNESS AND DISEASE.

SCYTHE. See WEAPONS AND IMPLEMENTS OF WARFARE.

SCYTHIANS [Gk *Skythēs*]. The term "Scythians" is used both to describe specific tribes which inhabited the area N and E of the Black Sea beginning in the 7th century B.C. and as a generic word for horse-riding pastoralists who lived during the mid-1st millennium B.C. on the steppes which extend from the Black Sea to S Siberia (Jettmar 1967: 21–23). Biblical scholars sometimes associate the Scythians with ASHKENAZ and with the bringers of destruction in the prophecies of Jeremiah (4:29; 5:15–17; 6:22–26; 50:41–42) and Zephaniah (Malamat 1950/51: 154–59). Outside the Hebrew Bible their reputation for savagery is alluded to in 2 Macc 4:47; *3 Macc.* 7:5; *4 Macc.* 10:7; and Col 3:11.

The Scythians, called "Ashguzai" by the Assyrians (cf. Heb *ʾaškĕnaz*), apparently first appear in written history in the annals of Esarhaddon (681–668 B.C.), and seem to be centered at that time in what is today NW Iran. According to Herodotus (1.103–6) the Scythians ruled over all of the Near East for 28 years after entering the area from the N; traditionally this period of rule is assigned to the 7th or 6th century B.C. The Scythians continue to be mentioned in texts of the Babylonians, Persians, and Greeks as allies and as enemies through the 4th century B.C. By the 3d century B.C., Scythian presence in the Near East is restricted to the Crimea and the shores of the Black Sea. Ovid records Scythian life in the 1st century A.D., by which time their power is spent; the Scythians shortly after fade from history (Piotrovsky et al. 1987: 12–15).

The Scythians did not have a writing system; what textual references we have for them are recorded by outsiders. The principal discussion of Scythian life is by Herodotus (book 4), many details of which have been confirmed by archaeological finds from across the Eurasian steppe.

The Scythian economy was based on their herds of sheep and goat and on their horses. On horseback and in carts, they moved from one seasonal pasture to another, ranging over a wide area. Trade with settled peoples provided grain, metalwork, and luxury goods to the nomads. The Scythians were famed for their military prowess and served as mercenaries for the Babylonians and other Near Eastern kingdoms, and as policemen for the Athenians.

The Scythians mastered fighting on horseback, as Herodotus records, and it is their special military skills which recommended them as mercenaries. This reputation may be why the Scythians are associated with Jeremiah's and Zephaniah's prophecies. Whether the Scythians were meant to be invoked as "the enemy from the north" in these writings is a matter of some debate (Yamauchi 1982: 87–97). The precise chronology of Scythian presence in the Levant is based on spotty documentary evidence, primarily Herodotus' (1.105). If in fact the Scythians reached that far W, then it would have been sometime in the second half of the 7th century B.C. (Malamat 1950/51: 155). Yamauchi's suggestion that the Scythians were mercenaries in the Chaldean army (1982: 99) is based on the excavation in Jerusalem of a few specimens of an arrowhead type called "Scythian." However, this kind of arrowhead was used by many different peoples in this period (Muscarella 1988: 107–108), and Yamauchi's argument is not conclusive. Whether Beth-shan was called Scythopolis because the Scythians were once present in the area cannot be determined (Smith 1897: 362–64).

In the Black Sea area, the so-called Royal Scythians were buried in grave pits under large mounds of earth and stone, often accompanied by sacrificed horses and people. Grave chambers were at first constructed of timber, though by the 4th century B.C. some were made of stone. The grave goods demonstrate economic interaction with the local settled populations, in the 7th and 6th centuries with Urartians and other Near Eastern groups and in the 5th and 4th centuries with Greeks. Large amounts of gold preserved in some tombs testify to the great wealth of Scythian rulers.

Scientific excavations of Scythian tombs began in the 18th century and continue today. The graves in the Black Sea region had often been robbed in antiquity, but nevertheless contained many objects when they were excavated, and some burials have been found intact (Piotrovsky in Metropolitan Museum of Art n.d.: 26–31).

The objects display art styles of the Near East, Greeks, and Scythians. Scythian art is often called "animal style," since the principle motifs are animals, often in characteristic curled up poses or with folded legs. Felines, stags, and griffins are favored motifs, and animal combat scenes are often depicted. The role of Near Eastern art in the development of the Scythian "animal style" is problematic, though the roots clearly lie earlier in the Caucasus, Central Asia and S Siberia (Bunker, Chatwin, and Farkas 1970: 24).

Greek-made objects in the Black Sea tombs, dating primarily to the 4th century B.C., depict scenes of Scythian life. From these objects we can learn more about Scythian clothing, customs, warfare practices, and pastoral life. Details include the typical Scythian costume of tunic, trousers, and boots, often covered with small gold plaques; Scythian weaponry, including the bow and arrow case known as *gorytus,* the shield, spear, and battle ax; and activities of animal husbandry, including the breaking of horses and the milking of sheep (Artamonov 1969: pls. 147–50, 162–76; Metropolitan Museum of Art n.d.: pls. 31, 33).

Although the Scythians primarily lived in tents, there is some evidence in the N steppe of settlements dating to the 7th or 6th century B.C. which may have been occupied only seasonally. By the end of the 5th century B.C., some of the Scythians in the Black Sea region had become permanently settled, although nomadism continued among the Scythians in the Black Sea area until at least the 3d century B.C. (Rolle 1980: 124–38).

Bibliography

Artamonov, M. I. 1969. *Treasures from Scythian Tombs.* London.

Bunker, E.; Chatwin, B.; and Farkas, A. 1970. *"Animal Style" Art from East to West.* New York.

Jettmar, K. 1967. *Art of the Steppes.* New York.

Malamat, A. 1950/51. The Historical Setting of Two Biblical Prophecies on the Nations. *IEJ* 1: 149–59.

Metropolitan Museum of Art. n.d. *From the Lands of the Scythians: Ancient Treasures from the Museums of the U.S.S.R. 3000 B.C.–100 B.C.* New York.

Muscarella, O. W. 1988. *Bronze And Iron.* New York.

Piotrovsky, B.; Galanina, L.; and Grach, N. 1987. *Scythian Art.* Oxford.

Rolle, R. 1980. *Die Welt der Skythen.* Luzern.

Smith, G. A. 1897. *The Historical Geography of the Holy Land.* London.

Yamauchi, E. 1982. *Foes from the Northern Frontier.* Grand Rapids.

Karen S. Rubinson

SCYTHOPOLIS (PLACE) [Gk *Skythōn polis*]. A name applied to the town of Beth-shan during the Maccabean period and later (Jdt 3:10; 2 Macc 12:29, 30). See BETH-SHAN.

SEA [Heb *yām;* Gk *thalassa*]. The Hebrew noun *yām* occurs 390 times in the OT and refers to bodies of water of various sizes, whether lakes or oceans. While Greek aquatic vocabulary is far more diversified, the standard Greek noun for sea, *thalassa,* is usually used in both the LXX and the NT in the same general manner as the more limited Hebrew noun.

A. Sea as a Natural Phenomenon

Biblical authors applied the word "sea" to specific bodies of water known today as the Mediterranean Sea, the Sea of Galilee, and the Dead Sea. In addition, they often spoke about the Reed Sea (Red Sea, KJV and RSV), identification of which is not certain. See also RED SEA. With but few exceptions, during the reigns of Solomon (1 Kgs 9:26–28; 10:22) and Jehoshaphat (1 Kgs 22:49—Eng 22:48), the Hebrews were not navigators of the Mediterranean, which they often called the "great sea" or the "western sea." The coastline of Palestine is remarkably straight, with no natural harbors, and from the 11th century B.C. the Philistines controlled it. (Hence the land was named Palestine, the land of the Philistines.) These two facts explain the Hebrews' lack of maritime activity. Their Phoenician and Canaanite neighbors to the N, however, were active traders. Hiram I, king of the Phoenician city of Tyre, was a major ally of Solomon and was responsible for outfitting the ships that every third year (1 Kgs 10:22) sailed the Mediterranean, and ventured as far as Ophir (Somalia?) on trading expeditions.

The Sea of Galilee, also referred to in the OT as the Sea of Chinnereth (Num 34:11; Josh 13:27) or Chinneroth (Josh 12:3), and in the NT as the Lake *(limēn)* of Gennesaret (Luke 5:1) or the Sea of Tiberias (John 6:1; 21:1), is actually a large freshwater lake in N central Palestine. It was frequently navigated, especially by fishermen. Because of its size and situation it is subject to sudden, violent storms similar to those associated with the ocean itself. See also GALILEE, SEA OF.

The Dead Sea is located in the Arabah region of S Palestine and has no outlet. Its waters, fed by the Jordan river, have a high concentration of salt and other minerals; hence it is often called the Salt Sea (Gen 14:3; Num 34:12; Deut 3:17; Josh 3:16, etc.). Alternatively, it is known as the "Sea of the Plain" (Deut 3:17; 4:49; Josh 3:16) or the "Eastern Sea" (Ezek 47:18; Joel 2:20; Zech 14:8). See also EASTERN SEA; SALT SEA.

The Red Sea *(yām sûp)* figures prominently in the story of the Exodus (Exod 10:19; 15:4, etc.). Its precise location is uncertain, but it is generally considered unlikely that the term refers to what is today known as the Red Sea, despite the fact the Hebrew is so translated by KJV, RSV, and others. Many scholars therefore prefer to translate it "Reed Sea." There is also reference to the "sea of Egypt" in Isa 11:15.

B. Sea as a Cosmic Element

Like other peoples in the ancient Mediterranean community, the Hebrews thought of water as one of the basic elements from which the universe was formed. In the Priestly account of creation (Gen 1:9–10), God separates the waters from land, and calls the former "seas."

More specifically, the Hebrews conceptualized the universe as constructed of three storeys: the earth; heaven above the earth; and waters beneath the earth (e.g., Exod 20:4). The last, which included the oceans of the world and everything underground, was sometimes called *tĕhôm,* the abyss or the deep (e.g., Ps 135:6). Gunkel defines it as *Urmeer,* "primordial ocean." The "deep" was considered the cosmic ocean, whose waters completely surrounded the universe. It was the source of the waters of every ocean, lake, river, and spring on the earth's surface, and also of precipitation from heaven. Rain or snow would fall to earth when the "windows of heaven," apertures in the firmament dome which enclosed the atmosphere and separated it from the heavenly ocean, were opened (Gen 7:11; 8:2; Mal 3:10).

Because the sea figured so prominently as an element within the created order, many ancient cultures personified it. The Mesopotamian sea monster Tiamat is one important example. Canaanite literature includes reference to others: Lady Athirat of the Sea, consort of the high god El (*UT* 49, 51, *ʿnt*); Prince Sea, a chaotic challenger of Baʿal the creator god (*UT* 129, 137, 68); and Lôtan (*UT* 67), a sea monster vanquished by Baʿal and widely held to be identical with the biblical Leviathan (Job 40:25—Eng 41:1; Ps 74:14; 104:26; Isa 27:1).

C. Sea as a Cultic Object

A large bronze basin (over 7 feet high and over 14 feet across) stood outside Solomon's temple in Jerusalem and was referred to as the "brazen (bronze) sea" (2 Kgs 25:13; 1 Chr 18:8; Jer 52:17), the "molten sea" (1 Kgs 7:24; 2 Chr 4:2), or "the sea" (1 Kgs 7:24; 2 Kgs 16:17). It was designed and cast by Hiram, a Phoenician craftsman from Tyre (1 Kgs 7:13–14) and was supported by twelve bronze bulls. The basin was full of water, and was probably used by the priests in connection with the animal sacrifice carried out on the great altar which stood across from it at the temple entrance. Apart from its practical function as a place to wash, the bronze sea probably symbolized the cosmic ocean, even as the temple itself represented the created order of the universe. The sea was dismantled when the Babylonians destroyed the temple in 586 B.C. See SEA, MOLTEN.

D. Sea in Symbolic Imagery

As part of creation, the sea was under the control of Yahweh; but it was also a consistent threat, pushing against the shores which held back its potentially violent force. The Hebrew writers viewed the sea with distinct ambivalence. They saw its waves as symbolic of fullness and regularity (Isa 48:18), its dimensions as expansive (Job 11:9), and its waters as the home of countless small animals (Ps 104:25). But they also spoke of its depths and the entangling vegetation therein as entrapment (Jonah 2:6—Eng 2:5). The sea, with its roaring and churning (Ps 93:3–4), had a dangerous power, so much greater than that of mankind that the Hebrews sometimes used marine imagery to speak of their enemies' attacks which they felt helpless to withstand without divine intervention (e.g., Jer 6:23). Accordingly, when describing their greatest victory in the tradition of the Exodus, the Hebrews referred to a parting of waters—specifically, the waters of the Red Sea. In this parting, Yahweh showed his ultimate authority over insurgent forces, both in nature and among men, an authority celebrated in the Song of the Sea in Exodus 15.

The theme of *Chaoskampf*, a battle between a creator god and a sea monster, appears in literature throughout the ANE. The Babylonian epic poem *Enuma Elish* presents one version of it. Whether remnants of it also appear in the OT is widely debated. The conquest of the Egyptians at the Red Sea is sometimes held to be a historicized version of *Chaoskampf*, "mythology come to life" (*CMHE*, 112–44). Also significant in this regard are references to Leviathan (particularly in Isaiah 27, which may quote an ancient Canaanite poem about the sea monster *Lôtan*), Rahab (Job 26:12) and the dragon (Isa 27:1). See also DRAGON AND SEA, GOD'S CONFLICT WITH.

The book of Revelation refers to a "sea of glass mingled with fire" (15:2). Bowman sees this as a multifaceted reminiscence of OT traditions, including those of the cosmic sea, the temple's bronze sea, and the Exodus tradition of the victory at the sea, coupled with the fires of purification. See SEA OF GLASS, GLASSY SEA. Additionally, the Revelator speaks of a new order with "no more sea," (21:1), probably best understood as no more threat, even potentially, to God's authority and harmonious government of the universe.

Bibliography

Anderson, B. W. 1967. *Creation Versus Chaos.* New York.

Follis, E. R. 1976. *Songs of the Sea: The Sea in the Poetry of Israel, Ugarit, Greece, and Rome.* Diss. Boston University.

Gunkel, H. 1895. *Schöpfung und Chaos.* Göttingen.

Kaiser, O. 1959. *Die Mythische Bedeutung des Meeres in Agypten, Ugarit und Israel.* Berlin.

Reymond, P. 1958. *L'Eau, Sa Vie, et Sa Signification Dans L'Ancien Testament.* Leiden.

Stadelmann, L. J. 1970. *The Hebrew Conception of the World.* Rome.

Wakeman, M. K. 1973. *God's Battle with the Monster.* Leiden.

ELAINE R. FOLLIS

SEA GULL. See ZOOLOGY.

SEA OF GLASS, GLASSY SEA [Gk *thalassa hyalinē*]. The Sea of Glass is mentioned only in Rev 4:6 and 15:2. The context of the former is the vision of the throne of God and the Lamb (chaps. 4–5). The context of the latter is the vision of the victorious martyrs before the throne of God (15:1–4) which prefaces the vision of the seven bowls (chaps. 15–16). In both instances the Sea of Glass is an apocalyptic symbol used to describe a heavenly wonder. It is a simile, for what is envisioned is "like" a Sea of Glass, but not actually such a sea.

Although it lends majesty and awe to the description of the visions, the symbol of the Sea of Glass is not merely a stylistic device. The symbolism of a heavenly sea before the throne of God originates from diverse Jewish traditions of the creation, Exodus, and apocalyptic throne visions. The waters that were above the firmament, the counterpart of those below the firmament, were considered to be in heaven (Gen 1:7; Ps 148:4; *Jub.* 2:4; *T. Levi* 2:7; *2 Enoch* 3:3 [J]; Str-B 3.798–99), and God's chambers and his throne to be above the waters above the firmament (Ps 104:3; Ezek 1:26). The symbolism may also originate in the molten sea which stood before Solomon's Temple and was used for priestly purification, for it may have represented the waters above the firmament (1 Kgs 7:23–26; cf. Exod 30:17–21). The same may be represented by the ten bronze lavers around Solomon's temple used for the purification of sacrifices (1 Kgs 7:38–39; 2 Chr 4:6).

In 4:6 the Sea is described as being like crystal, a description having several possible origins. The seventy elders of Israel on Mt. Sinai saw God standing on "a pavement of sapphire stone, like the very heaven for clearness" (Exod 24:9–10, RSV). Ezekiel's throne chariot vision describes a firmament "shining like crystal" over the heads of the four living creatures (Ezek 1:22). *1 Enoch* describes God's throne as being like crystal and the floor beneath as crystal (14:12, 18). The Quran (27) relates that there was a glass floor before the throne of Solomon so clear that it was mistaken for water by the Queen of Sheba.

In 15:2 the Sea is described as "mingled with fire" (not to be confused with the lake of fire—Rev 19:20; 20:14). This description, too, has several origins. "Mingled with fire" may describe the reflection of the lightning which plays above the throne of God (Rev 4:5). Ezekiel's throne chariot vision describes the loins of God and below his loins as fire (Ezek 1:27; cf. 1:4, 13). Daniel's vision describes "his throne as fiery flames, its wheels were burning fire. A stream of fire issued and came forth from before him" (7:9–10). Enoch's vision relates that a stream of flaming fire issued from under God's throne (*1 Enoch* 14:19).

The context of 15:2 provides an important association for the Sea of Glass. The martyrs are singing the Song of Moses sung by Moses and the Israelites after their deliverance from Pharaoh at the Crossing of the Red Sea (Exod 15:1–18). The vision of the seven bowls (chaps. 15–16), of which 15:1–4 is a preface, describes plagues very similar to those of Egypt prior to the deliverance of Israel (Exodus 7–12). Rabbinic tradition assumes that the Israelites beheld the Shekinah while crossing the Red Sea (*Mek. Širah* 3,37a to Exodus 15). The fiery sea may thus be an allusion to the deliverance at the Red Sea and the judgment of the enemy by water. The fiery sea may symbolize God's deliverance of his people in time of persecution and the judgment of their enemies that is about to be inflicted (cf. Rev 8:5).

Bibliography

Caird, G. B. 1962/63. On Deciphering the Book of Revelation: IV. Myth and Legend. *ExpTim* 74: 103–05.

McNamara, M. 1966. *The New Testament and the Palestinian Targum to the Pentateuch.* AnBib 27. Rome.

DUANE F. WATSON

SEA PEOPLES. A modern term referring to nine seaborne peoples mentioned in Egyptian sources (see

Helck in Müller-Karpe 1977 and in Deger-Jalkotzy 1983) from the reigns of Merneptah (1212–1202 B.C.) and Rameses III (1182–1151 B.C.); the Egyptian consonantal spellings can be vocalized in some of the names with the help of cuneiform sources: *Šerdani, Lukka, Šklš, Trš, ʾq(y)wš* (perhaps *Aḫḫiyawa*), *Sikila, Danuna, Wšš,* and Plšt (the Philistines). Some of these warlike bands already occur in Hittite sources (see Güterbock 1981 on the Madduwatta text) and in the Amarna correspondence of the 14th century B.C. (on the Šerdani see Lehmann in Deger-Jalkotzy 1983; on the Lukka see Bryce 1974), both as pirates raiding the shores of Cyprus and Egypt and as mercenaries recruited to the Egyptian and other armies. However, the main thrust of the Sea Peoples to the Levantine coasts occurred in the late 13th and early 12th centuries B.C.

Several groups *(Šerdani, Trš, Šklš, ʾqywš, Lukka)* fought within the ranks of the Libyan armies in the W delta and were defeated by Merneptah in 1207 B.C. There are no pictorial representations, but according to the textual descriptions some of these Sea Peoples were circumcised, others were not.

About the turn of the 12th century (for the chronology see Singer 1987) seaborne raiders invaded the coasts of Cyprus (Karageorghis and Muhly 1984), Cilicia (Bittel in Müller-Karpe 1977 and in Deger-Jalkotzy 1983) and N Syria (for Ugarit see summaries in Young 1981) and eventually brought about the collapse of the Hittite Empire. Cuneiform sources from Ugarit (Astour 1965; Lehmann 1970) and from Hattuša (Otten in Müller-Karpe 1977 and in Deger-Jalkotzy 1983; Singer 1983 and 1985b) portray a situation of total confusion and inability of the imperial fleet and armies to cope with the "enemy," who, with one exception, are not mentioned by name. "The Sikila people, who live on ships" in an Ugarit text (Lehmann 1979) are probably identical with the *Skl* of the Eygptian sources (or else, with the *Šklš*).

After the collapse of the central Hittite government, some of the Sea Peoples settled along the shores of the N Levant and Cyprus, while others gradually continued to move farther S, toward Canaan (Schachermeyr 1982). In 1174 B.C., Rameses III attempted to block their advance at the N end of the Egyptian Empire, near the land of Amurru; the ensuing battles, both on land and in sea, are depicted on reliefs in the mortuary temple of Rameses III in Medinet Habu (Nelson 1930; 1932; Sandars 1978: 117 ff.). In the sea battle two different types of Sea Peoples are shown on distinctive ships: the *Šerdani* wear horned helmets, whereas the Philistines and related groups *(Šikila, Danuna)* wear feathered headdresses. Only the latter are portrayed on the scene of the land battle; the fighters, three on each chariot, carry long spears, rounded shields, and swords. Their families follow in heavy carriages drawn by oxen. Despite the boastful descriptions of his victory (in the Medinet Habu inscriptions and in the Great Papyrus Harris), it is obvious that Rameses III was unable to stop the advance of the Sea Peoples. To make the best out of the inevitable, he settled them as mercenaries in Egyptian strongholds along the coast of Palestine (Alt 1944; Singer 1983). The Philistines settled on the fertile coast of Philistia, the Sikila seized the region of Dor in the Sharon Plain, and a third group, probably the Šerdani, settled in the Plain of Acco (Lehmann in Müller-Karpe 1977; Singer 1988). In addition to 11th-century Egyptian sources (the report of Wen-Amon and the Onomasticon of Amenope), abundant evidence for the settlement of the Sea Peoples is supplied by excavations (for recent summaries see Dothan 1982; Dothan and Gitin 1987; Brug 1985) in Philistia (Ashdod, Ashkelon, Ekron, Timnah, Tel Seraᶜ, etc.) and N of it (Tell Qasile, Tell Jerishe, Tel Aphek, Tel Zeror, Dor, Akko, etc.). One of the distinctive features is a monochrome pottery (Mycenaean IIIC) of Aegean origins, found along the Levantine coast, from Cilicia to Philistia, and in Cyprus (Schachermeyr in Deger-Jalkotzy 1983; Kling in Karageorghis and Muhly 1984). This early pottery of Aegean origins gradually adopted local traditions and developed into the characteristic Bichrome Philistine ware (A. Mazar 1985; Singer 1985a).

Of the Sea Peoples who settled in Palestine, only the Philistines are mentioned in the OT, probably because the other groups were already fully assimilated with the local populations by the end of the 11th century B.C. The Philistines, organized in five city-kingdoms, gradually became the leading force in Palestine and dominated the land until the reign of David (B. Mazar 1971 and 1986: 63–82; Malamat 1971). They still kept their political autonomy and their national identity after the Israelite takeover, until the Babylonian exile.

Clear evidence for the origins of the Sea Peoples is still missing (survey of views in Singer 1988). Disregarding some farfetched theories, the admissible views may be roughly classified according to three main geographical zones. (a) The N Balkans, particularly Illyria on the Adriatic coast; the "Illyrian theory" is related with the identification of the Philistines (**Palaisti* may be the original form of the name) with the Pelasgoi (sometimes spelled Pelastoi) of the classical sources, a pre-Hellenic people who inhabited the Balkans and the Aegean regions (Lochner-Hüttenbach 1960). (b) The W Aegean region, i.e., Greece, the Aegean islands, and Crete; this theory relies on archaeological (mainly ceramic) comparisons and on the biblical tradition, which brings the Philistines from the island of Caphtor, i.e., Crete. (c) The E Aegean, i.e., Anatolia and the offshore islands. This view, which is gaining increasing acceptance, is supported by the most solid and diversified evidence. (1) At least two out of the nine Sea Peoples mentioned in the Egyptian sources are undoubtedly located in Anatolia—the Lukka in Lycia and the Danuna in Cilicia; a third group, the *Trš,* is probably related to the Tyrsenoi (and biblical Tiras), who, according to Herodotus, migrated from Lydia to Etruria. (2) The few traces of Philistine words *(seren, q/kobah)* and names (Goliath, Achish) appear to be etymologically connected with Anatolian languages. (3) The Hittite texts provide ample evidence for serious upheavals in SW Anatolia (the Lukka lands) in the second half of the 13th century B.C., which can clearly be related with the emergence of the Sea Peoples (Singer 1983). (4) Some of the classical traditions on W Anatolian heroes who trekked eastward and eventually settled in Cyprus and the Levant (Teucros, Mopsus) may reflect dim echoes of the migratory movements of the Sea Peoples (Schachermeyr 1982).

Although the focal point of the turbulence appears to have been in SW Anatolia (still a poorly explored region), the 'tidal waves' soon affected the neighboring regions and disrupted the authority of the Hittite and the Mycenaean empires. The major cause for the economic and political breakdown, which motivated large populations to migrate, was probably the severe food shortage, amply documented in contemporary Near Eastern texts and also echoed in the classical and biblical sources. Whereas some of the Sea Peoples poured down along the Levantine coast in search of land and food, others turned westward and sailed as far as Sardinia *(Šerdani), Sicily (Sikila* or *Šklš),* and Etruria *(Trš/ Tyrsenoi).* Archaeological evidence from the central Mediterranean, particularly from Sardinia, confirms the classical traditions on these movements (Sandars 1978, chap. 4). Quite extensive in itself, the diaspora of the Sea Peoples represents only a fraction of much larger population drifts, which encompassed vast territories in the E Mediterranean, the Balkans, Asia Minor, and the Levant, and radically changed the face of these regions in the transition from the Bronze Age to the Iron Age (see summaries in Deger-Jalkotzy 1983). Contrary to traditional views which conceived of the Sea Peoples as barbarian raiders spreading ruin and chaos, modern historical and archaeological research increasingly appreciates their cultural role in the merging of the Indo-European civilizations of the Aegean realm with the Semitic cultures of the Levant.

Bibliography

Alt, A. 1944. Ägyptische Tempel in Palästina und die Landnahme der Philister. *ZDPV* 67: 1–20. Repr. *KlSchr* 1: 216–30.

Astour, M. C. 1965. New Evidence on the Last Days of Ugarit. *AJA* 69: 253–58.

Barnett, R. D. 1975. The Sea Peoples. *CAH*³ 2: 359–70.

Brug, J. F. 1985. *A Literary and Archaeological Study of the Philistines.* Oxford.

Bryce, T. R. 1974. The Lukka Problem—and a Possible Solution. *JNES* 33: 395–404.

Deger-Jalkotzy, S., ed. 1983. *Griechenland, die Ägäis und die Levante während der "Dark Ages" vom 12. bis zum 9. Jh. v. Chr.* Wien.

Dothan, T. 1982. *The Philistines and their Material Culture.* Jerusalem.

Dothan, T., and Gitin, S. 1987. The Rise and Fall of Ekron of the Philistines: Recent Excavations at an Urban Border Site. *BA* 50: 197–222.

Güterbock, H. G. 1981. The Hittites and the Aegean World: Part 1. The Ahhiyawa Problem Reconsidered. *AJA* 87: 133–43.

Karageorghis, V., and Muhly, J. D., eds. 1984. *Cyprus at the Close of the Late Bronze Age.* Nicosia.

Lehmann, G. A. 1970. Der Untergang des hethitischen Grossreiches und die neuen Texte aus Ugarit. *UF* 2: 39–73.

———. 1979. Die Šikalayu: Ein neues Zeugnis zu den "Seevölker" Heerfahrten im späten 13. Jh.V.Chr. (*RS* 34.129). *UF* 11: 481–94.

Lochner-Hüttenbach, F. 1960. *Die Pelasger.* Vienna.

Macalister, R. A. S. 1911. *The Philistines.* London. Repr. Chicago, 1965.

Malamat, A. 1971. The Egyptian Decline in Canaan and the Sea Peoples. *WHJP* 3: 23–38; 294–300.

Mazar, A. 1985. The Emergence of Philistine Culture. *IEJ* 35: 95–107.

Mazar, B. 1971. The Philistines and Their Wars with Israel. *WHJP* 3: 164–79; 324–25.

———. 1986. The Philistines and the Rise of Israel and Tyre. Pp. 63–82 in *The Early Biblical Period. Historical Studies.* Jerusalem.

Müller-Karpe, H., ed. 1977. *Geschichte des 13. und 12. Jahrhunderts v. Chr. (Jahresbericht des Instituts für Vorgeschichte der Universität Frankfurt A.M. 1976.).* Frankfurt.

Nelson, H. H. 1930, 1932. *The Earliest Historical Records of Ramses III, Medinet Habu.* 2 vols. Chicago.

Sandars, N. K. 1978. *The Sea Peoples.* London.

Schachermeyr, F. 1980. *Griechenland im Zeitalter der Wanderungen.* Vienna.

———. 1982. *Die Levante im Zeitalter der Wanderungen.* Vienna.

Singer, I. 1983. Western Anatolia in the Thirteenth Century B.C. According to the Hittite Sources. *AnSt* 33: 205–17.

———. 1985a. The Beginning of Philistine Settlement in Canaan and the Northern Boundary of Philistia. *TA* 12: 109–22.

———. 1985b. The Battle of Niḫriya and the End of the Hittite Empire. *ZA* 75: 100–23.

———. 1987. Dating the End of the Hittite Empire. *Hethitica* 8: 413–21.

———. 1988. The Origin of the Sea Peoples and Their Settlement on the Coast of Canaan. Pp. 239–50 in *Society and Economy in the Eastern Mediterranean (c. 1500–1000 B.C.),* ed. M. Heltzer and E. Lipinski. OLA. Louvain.

Strobel, A. 1976. *Der Spätbronzezeitliche Seevölkersturm.* Berlin.

Young, D. Y., ed. 1981. *Ugarit in Retrospect.* Winona Lake, IN.

ITAMAR SINGER

SEA, MOLTEN [Heb *yām mûṣāq*]. Var. BRONZE SEA; SEA. Designations for a spectacular bronze appurtenance that is said to have stood in the courtyard of Solomon's temple. It is described in the temple text of 1 Kings (1 Kgs 7:23–26) and in the parallel account in Chronicles (2 Chr 4:2–5). Both 2 Kings (25:13) and Jeremiah (52:17) list the Sea among the temple vessels that were broken into pieces and carried off to Babylon when the temple was destroyed in 587.

The bronze Sea (Heb *yām hannĕḥōšet*), like the other bronze vessels of the temple, was crafted by Hiram of Tyre, an expert in bronze work. The Chronicles preserves a tradition that the requisite metal for the sea and other vessels was part of spoils acquired by David (1 Chr 18:8; cf. 2 Sam 8:8). It apparently was made by casting, since the term "molten" derives from the Hebrew root *yṣq,* "to cast, pour" (as metal). According to the Kings account, it was a vessel of huge proportions: 10 cubits in diameter (ca. 15 feet), 5 cubits high (ca. 7.5 feet), and 30 cubits in circumference. When empty it would have weighed between 25 and 30 tons. Although it is not certain whether it was a hemisphere or a cylinder, its capacity would have been enormous. The Bible has two conflicting traditions about how much it held: 2000 baths in 1 Kgs 7:26, and 3000 baths in 2 Chr 4:5. Furthermore, it is not certain how baths were reckoned, and some have suggested that 1000 baths would be a better figure (Scott 1958: 209–12). In any case, it can be estimated to have had a capacity of about 10,000 gallons of water (Paul and Dever 1973: 257).

Just as spectacular as its size was its ornamentation. Under its rim was a series of cast decorations: two rows of "gourds." The rim ("brim") itself was made of lily work. Most amazing of all was the way it was supported on four sets of bronze oxen, with three oxen in each set. Each set of oxen faced a direction of the compass, with their "hinder parts" facing inward and supporting the basin.

The cultic purpose of this elaborate item among the

courtyard appurtenances of the temple is not specified, except for a rather peripheral notation in 2 Chr 4:5 that it was "for the priests to wash in." Its use as a laver is dubious, since ten bronze lavers, also large and spectacular in design, were also part of the courtyard furnishings. See LAVER. Furthermore, its height makes it difficult to imagine how it was used for lustrations. The cultic purpose of the Sea may lie more in its symbolic nature rather than as a ritual vessel. See also SEA.

One of the features of ANE temples was their utilization of artistic and architectural elements relating to the idea of the temple as the cosmic center of the world. The great deep, or cosmic waters, is one aspect of the array of cosmic attributes of such a holy spot. The temple of Marduk at Babylon, for example, had an artificial sea *(ta-am-tu)* in its precincts; and some Babylonian temples had an *apsû*-sea, a large basin. Such features symbolize the idea of the ordering of the universe by the conquest of chaos; or they represent the presence of the "waters of life" at the holy center. Ancient Israel shared in this notion of watery chaos being subdued by Yahweh and of the temple being built on the cosmic waters. The great "molten sea" near the temple's entrance would have signified Yahweh's power and presence. Furthermore, the bronze courtyard furnishings (including the large pillars Jachin and Boaz [1 Kgs 7:21]) were the only temple appurtenances visible to the public, which included both Israelites and foreigners in the cosmopolitan days of Solomonic reign. The role of these elaborate objects in providing visual messages about Yahweh's availability and power thus helped establish the legitimacy of the monarchy.

The great Sea did not survive intact until the Babylonian conquest. At the end of the 8th century, Ahaz partially dismantled it, an action that was one of several changes he made in the temple precincts. These changes can be seen as part of his political maneuvering with the Assyrians.

Bibliography

Paul, S., and Dever, W. G., eds. 1973. *Biblical Archaeology*. Jerusalem.
Scott, R. B. Y. 1958. The Hebrew Cubit. *JBL* 77: 205–14.

Carol Meyers

SEALS, MESOPOTAMIAN. Seals take two forms in Mesopotamia: stamp and cylinder. The earliest seals are small geometric pieces of stone, bone, or fired clay, one surface engraved with a design and a back by which it can be handled (Buchanan 1984). Cylinder seals are short tubes (avg. 20 mm) of stone drilled through the center and engraved around their circumference. Both stamps and cylinders are engraved in intaglio to produce a positive impression when rolled or stamped on a receptive surface. Seals may bear either design or inscription or both. Designs include scenes of everyday life, warfare, sport, gods, legends, myth, and ritual activities. Such scenes provide information on activities poorly recorded in texts or archaeological deposits as well as evidence of a monumental art no longer extant (Amiet 1973). Seal inscriptions most commonly refer to the owner's name, but also may include his patronymic, office or profession, political allegiance, and/or religious affiliation (Gelb 1977). Thus seal inscriptions are excellent sources of information on onomastics, administrative hierarchies, political history, and religious preferences. Seal impressions on clay documents or their envelopes both protected the integrity of the contents and served to identify the sealer as author, witness, agent, buyer, or seller, depending on the contents and purpose of the text (Leemans 1982).

A. Materials and Manufacture

Different materials for seals were used during the successive periods in Mesopotamian history, depending on accessibility and technical ability to work them. In the earliest period bone, shell, soft stone (serpentine and limestone), and fired clay are used to make stamp and cylinder seals. Harder stones are introduced in the late 3d and 2d millennium when quartz, hematite, carnelian, and lapis lazuli become popular.

Valued as amulets and ornaments as well as administrative devices, seals often are set in gold, silver, or bronze for rings or pendants, or attached by string to toggle pins. Occasionally a seal inscription will indicate that it was given as a votive gift to a god. The "seal cutter," Sum BURGUL or Akk *purkullu*, both cut and set seals. While most of our information comes from official archives and refers to seal cutters employed in large institutions, the number and variability of seals extant indicate that access to seals usually is not restricted to any particular class or institution in Mesopotamian society (Porada 1977).

B. History and Use

The earliest evidence for the use of engraved devices as seals dates from the 4th millennium B.C. During this period stamps are used to impress the wet clay applied to secure the closures of various types of containers. Sealing served both to protect the contents and identify the responsible individual or institution. Increasing social and political complexity during the late 4th millennium resulted in the need for more precise methods of accounting and accountability.

Initially hollow clay balls containing tokens representing various commodities were sealed to maintain the integrity of their contents, just as seal impressions on containers secured the commodities themselves (Le Brun and Vallat 1978). Over time cuneiform writing on clay tablets developed as a more efficient means of recording and conveying information, and these were also sealed. Cylinder seals appear at the same time, perhaps because rolling the seal over wet clay tablets or jar closings was a more efficient means of sealing a large surface than stamping it (Frankfort 1939: 1–4). Designs on 4th millennium B.C. cylinder seals include scenes of hunting, herding, battle, storage of grain, and ritual activities. Recent research suggests that these motifs refer to the activities of various departments in early administrative centers (Brandes 1979). Other contemporary designs show mythical beasts and geometric patterns. Jemdet Nasr style seals are contemporary with those of the late Uruk period but smaller in size and made of harder stones. Many of the designs show women at work spinning, weaving, and making pottery or participating in ritual activities (Asher-Greve 1985).

Cuneiform inscriptions appear on seals at the beginning of the Early Dynastic period (2900–2300 B.C.). Seal size and design becomes more standardized, and seal impressions can be found on a few tablets as well as jar, box, bag, and door sealings. Two scenes that recur throughout the Bronze Age are formalized during the ED period: the contest between lion and bull or bull-man, and the banquet (Selz 1983). Banquet scenes show female and male figures eating or drinking, sometimes in the company of musicians, and it has been suggested that this represents the sacred marriage ceremony or the Near Year Festival known from later texts (Collon 1987: 27).

Around 2300 B.C. Sargon of Akkad created the first Mesopotamian empire, and a number of innovations in art and administration are credited to this period of unification and expansion. Often created for the court and of very high artistic quality, Akkadian seals demonstrate a new, more naturalistic style and greater use of hard semiprecious stones. One of the most important innovations of the Akkadian period is the portrayal of deities with attributes that permit their identification with gods known from texts (Amiet 1980). From this period on seal design is one of the primary sources of information on the Mesopotamian pantheon and activities associated with its gods (Frankfort 1939). As in the earlier periods, seals continue to be used to secure closures and to impress administrative and legal tablets.

Much of the Akkadian iconography persists after the fall of Akkad and throughout the Ur III period (2250–2000 B.C.), although the quality of the engraving declines (Porada 1980: 10). The presentation scene, however, remains an important source of information on political ideology and administration in this period (Winter 1986). In this design a human figure accompanied by a god or goddess approaches a deity seated on a throne. The seated figure in the Ur III presentation scene may be either deity or king, the distinction apparent in the form of the headdress. When the king appears in such a scene the inscription often refers to its ownership by a royal official, usually at a very high level. Used primarily within administrative contexts, official seals are commonly found on orders, letters and receipts, and the series of seals and impressions remains one of the few instances where iconography, inscription, and function are clearly related. During the Ur III period, seals are used predominantly in administrative contexts on both objects and texts.

Old Babylonian (OB) period (2000–1500 B.C.) seals retain much of the Akkadian and Ur III iconography, albeit in a more simplified and occasionally schematic form, particularly at the end of the period (Collon 1986). Around 1700 B.C. new techniques for drilling and cutting designs were introduced and resulted in a "drilled style" of seals (Buchanan 1970). These techniques probably aided the mass production of seals evident in the identical scenes found on a great number of them. Throughout the OB period private seals are widely owned and used to impress the various legal documents that required witnesses or personal acknowledgment. "Burgul" seals, simple clay cylinders inscribed with the owner's name, are produced for single transactions for individuals who did not regularly require a seal.

In the last half of the 2d millennium B.C., in the kingdom of Mitanni in N Mesopotamia, sintered quartz ("faience," composition, or frit) made its appearance as a material for cylinder seals (Porada 1947). Easily made out of locally available materials, frit seals were produced in quantity for internal use and for export. Rarely inscribed, "common-style" frit seals were probably meant to be jewelry or amulets, although occasionally they were used as seals. "Elaborate style" seals were more carefully produced, and are often found impressed on legal and government documents. While Assyria was under the political domination of Mitanni, Assyrian seals were produced in the Mitannian style. As Assyria grew more powerful at the beginning of the 1st millennium B.C., they developed their own style reflecting Assyrian interests and ideology. However, the use of seals on documents and containers followed OB tradition (Porada 1979).

The rise of the Neo-Assyrian empire in the 9th and 8th centuries B.C. was accompanied by the reappearance of stamp seals which quickly replaced cylinders as the preferred method of sealing. Long the most widespread form of seal in the rest of the ANE, its reintroduction and popularity in Iron Age Mesopotamia has been tied to expansion of the Assyrian Empire and forced resettlement of large numbers of people from W Asia and W Iran (Parker 1962: 27). As papyrus became a common vehicle for written documents during the 1st millennium B.C., a small sealed lump of clay (bulla) served to fix the string binding the rolled document, and replaced the impression of stamp or cylinder on a clay tablet as means of authorizing, witnessing, or securing the text. Stamp seals continued to be used throughout the Persian period. The Persepolis Fortification tablets indicate that impressions still served to acknowledge receipt and disbursement of goods in complex administrative systems (Hallock 1977).

C. Bibliographic Sources

A good introduction to cylinder seals as well as a full bibliography of published collections and current scholarship can be found in Collon 1987, while Frankfort 1939 remains a basic, though dated, resource. A good introduction to stamp seals and review of the current literature on the subject can be found in Buchanan 1984, and Buchanan and Moorey 1988. The art of Mesopotamian seals is a vast subject most recently reviewed by Porada in her introduction to *Ancient Art in Seals* (1980). Brief articles on seal use in various periods can be found in the symposium volume edited by Gibson and Biggs 1977.

Bibliography

Amiet, P. 1973. *Bas-reliefs imaginaires d'après les cachets et les sceaux-cylindres.* Paris.

———. 1980. The Mythological Repertory in the Cylinder Seals of the Agade Period (ca. 2335–2155 B.C.). Pp. 35–59 in *Ancient Art in Seals*, ed. E. Porada. Princeton.

Asher-Greve, J. M. 1985. *Frauen in altsumerischer Zeit.* Malibu.

Brandes, M. 1979. *Siegelabrollungen aus den archaischen Bauschichten in Uruk-Warka.* Wiesbaden.

Buchanan, B. 1970. Cylinder Seal Impressions in the Yale Babylonian Collection Illustrating a Revolution in Art ca. 1700 B.C. *The Yale University Library Gazette* 45: 53–65.

———. 1984. *The Prehistoric Stamp Seals.* Vol. 2 in *Catalogue of Ancient Near Eastern Seals in the Ashmolean Museum*, ed. P. R. S. Moorey. Oxford.

Buchanan, B., and Moorey, P. R. S. 1988. *The Iron Age Stamp Seals.*

Vol. 3 in *Catalogue of Near Eastern Seals in the Ashmolean Museum.* Oxford.
Collon, D. 1986. *Isin-Larsa and Old Babylonian Periods.* Vol. 3 in *Catalogue of the Western Asiatic Seals in the British Museum, Cylinder Seals.* London.
———. 1987. *First Impressions.* Chicago.
Frankfort, H. 1939. *Cylinder Seals.* London.
Gelb, I. 1977. Typology of Mesopotamian Seal Inscriptions. Pp. 107–26 in Gibson and Biggs, eds. 1977.
Gibson, M., and Biggs, R., eds. 1977. *Seals and Sealing in the Ancient Near East.* Malibu.
Hallock, R. T. 1977. The Use of Seals on the Persepolis Fortification Tablets. Pp. 127–33 in Gibson and Biggs, eds. 1977.
Le Brun, A., and Vallat, F. 1978. L'origin de l'écriture à Suse. *Cahiers de DAFI* 8: 11–59.
Leemans, W. F. 1982. La fonction des sceaux apposés à des contrats vieux-babylonians. Pp. 219–44 in *Zikir Šumim,* ed. G. van Driel et al. Leiden.
Parker, B. 1962. Seals and Seal Impressions from the Nimrud Excavations. 1955–1958. *Iraq* 24: 26–40.
Porada, E. 1947. *Seal Impressions of Nuzi.* AASOR 24. New Haven.
———. 1977. Of Professional Seal Cutters and Nonprofessionally Made Seals. Pp. 7–14 in Gibson and Biggs, eds. 1977.
———. 1979. Remarks on Mitannian (Hurrian) and Middle Assyrian Glyptic Art. *Akkadica* 13: 2–15.
———, ed. 1980. *Ancient Art in Seals.* Princeton.
Selz, G. 1983. *Die Bankettszene.* Wiesbaden.
Winter, I. J. 1986. The King and the Cup: Iconography of the Royal Presentation Scene of Ur III Seals. Pp. 253–68 in *Insight Through Images,* ed. M. Kelly-Buccellati. Malibu.

BONNIE S. MAGNESS-GARDINER

SEASON. See CALENDARS.

SEBA (PERSON) [Heb *sĕbāʾ*]. SABEANS. The firstborn son of Cush (Gen 10:7; 1 Chr 1:9) and hence the name of a people or region located either in Ethiopia or in South Arabia. According to Ps 72:10 the kings of Sheba in Arabia (LXX *Arabōn*) and of Seba came with presents, which is an indication of wealthy kingdoms. In Isa 43:3 God is ready to give the rich countries of Egypt, Cush, and Seba as ransom for Israel; the listing of Seba after Egypt and Cush points to NE Africa, which is confirmed by the LXX, which reads here *Soēnē* (for Syene) instead of Saba. A further passage in Deutero-Isaiah gives the same sequence: "The Egyptians with their produce, the Cushites with their profit, and the tall Sebaites (MT *sĕbāʾîm,* LXX *Sebōin,* Vg *Sabaim*) shall come to you" (Isa 45:14); in the light of the comparison with the Cushites noted for their stature (Isa 18:2), this likewise points to an African people.

Already Dillmann (1892: 180–81) proposed locating biblical Seba at the coast of Erythraea and consequently seeing in Sheba and Seba the two present countries Yemen and Abyssinia on the E and W shores of the S part of the Red Sea. This would be a reference to the colonization of the Ethiopian littoral by Sabaean settlers from S Arabia which started toward the end of the first half of the 1st millennium B.C. Beginning with the end of the 6th century B.C., however, Abyssinia existed no longer as a Sabaean colony, but came under the control of native sovereigns; Sabaean epigraphic texts with dialectal peculiarities have been discovered on Ethiopian soil bearing witness to this fact. In the inscription JE 4 from Maqalle king Rabāḥ designates himself as "*mukarrib* of Daʿmāt and Sabaʾ," which probably means ruler of the highland and of the coastal plain, and his son Lammān similarly designates himself in the inscriptions JE 1384+1370 from Melazo and Abuna Garimā 2 from Adde Kaweh in Tigre.

Furthermore, a few topographical names with Sabaean foundations testify to the immigration from S Arabia to Africa and also to the relations between ancient Yemen and Abyssinia; these include the harbor Saba (Strabo, *Geog.* 16,4.8) on the Ethiopian coast of the Red Sea to the N of Adulis; Sabat (Ptolemaios, *Geog.* 4,7.8), most probably to be identified with the harbor Saba; *Sabai* (Strabo, *Geog.* 16,4.10) NW of the straits of Bāb al-Mandab; and the *Sabaïtikon stoma* (Strabo, *Geog.* 16,4.8 on the authority of Artemidor), a place at the mouth of a river on the coast of the Trogodytice in the region of present-day Suakin. Possibly Soba on the river Atbara can also be connected with Seba, especially since the Ethiopic translation of the Bible offers in Gen 10:7 *Sobā* for *Seba.* Less trustworthy, on the other hand, is the remark given by Josephus (*Ant* 2.10.2) that Saba is said to be the ancient name of the kingdom of Meroë, to which this name was supposedly given only by Cambyses; therefore the connection of Meroë with biblical Seba is surely wrong. Consequently, the Heb name *sĕbāʾ* is finally identical with the name *šĕbāʾ;* while, however, the latter is the correct phonetic rendering of South Arabic *sbʾ,* the form *sĕbāʾ* might reflect the Ethiopic variant of the pronunciation of that name.

Caussin de Perceval (1847: 42–46) held the view that the people of Cushite Seba are to be identified with the prehistoric ʿĀdites of the Arabian Peninsula, who later on were expelled from there by the immigrating Joktanide Sabaeans, emigrated to Abyssinia, and possibly became the founders of the Axumite kingdom. Glaser (1890: 387–91) looked for Seba at the Djabal Shammar in N Central Arabia, and likewise Hommel (1926: 577) believed that Seba is to be counted among the Arabian Cushites and is the name of a people in Central Arabia. Occasionally it has been suggested that while *šĕbāʾ* designates Sheba in SW Arabia, *sebāʾ,* which is mentioned besides *šĕbāʾ* in Gen 10:7 and Ps 72:10, refers to a Sabaean colony on the incense road in the NW part of the Arabian Peninsula. This view, however, is also hardly acceptable.

Bibliography

Caussin de Perceval, A. P. 1847. *Essai sur l'histoire des Arabes avant l'Islamisme.* Paris.
Dillmann, A. 1892. *Die Genesis.* KEHAT. Leipzig.
Glaser, E. 1890. *Skizze der Geschichte und Geographie Arabiens.* Vol. 2. Berlin.
Hommel, F. 1926. *Ethnologie und Geographie des Alten Orients.* HAW 3/1/1. Munich.
Wissmann, H. von. 1976. Abessinien als sabäische Staatskolonie. Pp. 41–49 in *Die Mauer der Sabäerhauptstadt Maryab. Abessinien als sabäische Staatskolonie im 6. Jh. v. Chr.* Istanbul.

W. W. MÜLLER

SEBAM (PLACE) [Heb *śĕbām*]. Variant spelling of SIBMAH.

SEBAOTH. See NAMES OF GOD IN THE OT.

SECACAH (PLACE) [Heb *sĕkākâ*]. A town situated in the wilderness of Judah (Josh 15:61), within the same district as En-gedi. This settlement, whose name perhaps means "protection" or "cover," is listed among the towns within the tribal allotment of Judah (Josh 15:21–62). The theory that this list is derived from an administrative roster compiled under the Judean Monarchy (Alt 1925) has been widely accepted, although controversy continues over the precise makeup of the districts, the proper context of the town lists of Benjamin and Dan, and the period of the monarchy to which the original roster belongs (Boling and Wright *Joshua* AB, 64–72). Recent archaeological work in the Buqeiah valley has uncovered three Iron Age fortress-farms which may be associated with the towns of this district (Stager 1976). If the list in Josh 15:61–62 runs N to S, then ancient Secacah is probably to be identified with the largest of these three fortresses, Khirbet es-Samrah, located approximately 7 km SW of Khirbet Qumran (Boling and Wright *Joshua* AB, 392; M.R. 187125).

Bibliography

Alt, A. 1925. Judas Gaue unter Josia. *PJ* 21: 100–16.
Stager, L. E. 1976. Farming in the Judean Desert During the Iron Age. *BASOR* 221: 145–58.

WADE R. KOTTER

SECOND COMING. See PAROUSIA.

SECOND DEATH. See DEATH, SECOND.

SECOND QUARTER (PLACE) [Heb *mišneh*]. A district within the city of Jerusalem in which Huldah the prophetess resided toward the end of the 7th century B.C. (2 Kgs 22:14 = 2 Chr 34:22). The Heb *mišneh,* in the usual ordinal sense, indeed means "second," but it can also have the nuance of "expansion/increase as a result of doubling"; thus one could translate *mišneh* as "annex" (cf. Zeph 1:10; perhaps also *haʿîr mišneh* in Neh 11:9). The texts attesting to the "Second Quarter" are all late, and it has long been suspected that this new addition to Jerusalem was constructed opposite the Tyropoeon Valley on the hill W of the old city of David and SW of the Temple Mount sometime during the reign of Hezekiah (late 8th–early 7th centuries B.C.). This expansion would have been designed to handle the increasing number of Israelite and Judean refugees fleeing the devastations of the Assyrian army.

Archaeological confirmation of this "Second Quarter" emerged during Avigad's excavations (beginning in 1969) in the center of the Jewish Quarter in the Old City of Jerusalem. Beneath Byzantine, Herodian, and Hasmonean levels, evidence of Israelite occupation in the 8th–7th centuries was found, including a portion of an Israelite defensive wall (Avigad 1983; *EAEHL* 2: 597). Although the complete line of this fortification is unknown, the addition of this new quarter seems to have approximately quadrupled the area of Jerusalem's residential neighborhoods, accommodating a swollen population of perhaps 25,000 (compared to an estimated population of ca. 7,000 in Solomonic Jerusalem). See also DAVID, CITY OF; JERUSALEM.

Bibliography

Avigad, N. 1983. *Discovering Jerusalem.* Nashville.

GARY A. HERION

SECOND TREATISE OF THE GREAT SETH. See SETH, SECOND TREATISE OF THE GREAT (NHC VII,*2*).

SECRET, MESSIANIC. See MESSIANIC SECRET.

SECU (PLACE) [Heb *śekû*]. A site on the route between Gibeah and Ramah which Saul visited while pursuing David (1 Sam 19:22). Secu, commonly thought to be a village, is otherwise unknown. It is questionable whether Secu is a place name at all; some LXX and Latin mss read "on the bare hill." The well at the site mentioned in the passage was apparently a common meeting place.

TOM WAYNE WILLETT

SECUNDUS (PERSON) [Gk *Sekoundos*]. A gentile Christian from Thessalonica mentioned in Acts 20:4. He accompanied Paul from Macedonia to Jerusalem during his 3d missionary journey. He and the others in Paul's party were probably the delegates delivering the special collection to the church at Jerusalem (cf. Acts 24:17; 2 Cor 8:23). Secundus and his fellow Thessalonian traveler Aristarchus were probably representing the church at Thessalonica in the presentation of their portion of the contribution to the collection. Ambiguities in the text of Acts 20:5–6 create two possibilities. Either Secundus and the others crossed the Aegean Sea to wait for Paul at Troas, or they celebrated the Festival of Unleavened Bread at Philippi with Paul and then sailed with him to meet Trophimus and Tychicus, who alone had gone on ahead to Troas, possibly to procure a ship.

JOANN FORD WATSON

SEDHEQ (DEITY) [Heb *ṣedeq*]. The god Sedheq appears in West Semitic proper names from the 2d and 1st millennia B.C.E. The deity appears on a god list from Ugarit (*KTU* 1.123.14) where it is half of the dual divinity form *ṣdq mšr*. The other source of information about this god comes from a pair of classical writers. The major information derives from the *Phoenician History* of Philo of Byblos (fragments of which are preserved in Eus. *Praep. Evang.* 1.10.13, 14, 25, 38), while a note appears on Sedheq's sons in Damascius, *Vita Isidori,* 302 (Attridge and Oden 1981: 92 n. 140; Baumgarten 1981: 228).

The fact that both the Ugaritic text and the Philo of Byblos references pair Sedheq with the god *mšr/misōr* (*Praep. Evang.* 1.10.13) has led to the reasonable conclusion that these two divinities may have been the West Semitic variants of the Babylonian pair of gods Kittu and Mešaru. The Mesopotamian pair are sons of the god Šamaš and represent two aspects of the sun god's role as the deity of justice (Rosenberg 1965: 161; Astour 1966: 282; Liverani 1971: 58). This association would imply that the god Sedheq was seen as an attendant deity to some other, more powerful divinity; it would not necessitate that the god was associated with a solar deity cult (Rosenberg 1965: 164–65; Baumgarten 1981: 231). The root *ṣdq* supports the connotation of the divine sphere of the deity as having been justice; this understanding is recorded by Philo of Byblos, who explained the name as *dikaion.* Both in Mesopotamia and Syria-Palestine the gods may reflect deified characteristics of divine qualities (Troiani 1974: 135).

What mythological information exists about Sedheq comes from classical sources. In these works it is posited that Sedheq and his brother Misor discovered how to use salt; this has been related to the legal aspect of the gods (Baumgarten 1981: 176), but Philo of Byblos has treated these divinities as humans, and it is unlikely that a clear rendition of myth has been retained in the narrative, though it is possible that salt played a part in some myth told about these gods. What the classical writers were more interested in when dealing with Sedheq was his offspring. Sedheq not only was credited with fathering the Dioskouri and Kabeiri, but his eighth son was the renowned Asclepius, born to the god by one of the Titanids. The descendants of Sedheq are credited with inventing the boat, devising medicines, and beginning the noble art of historiography.

Names containing a Sedheq element have been acknowledged for a long time as divine references (Wood 1916: 271–72). Among the Phoenicians Sedheq appears commonly among the royal names (Masson and Sznycer 1972: 98–99). In biblical texts three names often are cited for bearing the divine name Sedheq: Melchizedek (Gen 14:18; Ps 110:4), Adonizedek (Josh 10:1), and Zadok (2 Sam 15:24, etc.). Since all of these men are related in the narratives to the city of Jerusalem, two as kings and one as priest, it has been suggested that Sedheq was a major deity in the Jerusalem cult. This would explain the consistent use of Sedheq and variants in biblical names and names found in Hebrew inscriptions, though Tigay (1986: 79) doubts such names refer to the deity. Sedheq does appear as a constant characteristic of Yahweh and may even be taken as an attendant minor deity to the Israelite/Judean deity (Rosenberg 1965: 170–75); which might raise a mythological background to the constant pairing of the priests Zadok and Abiathar as with *ṣdq* and *mšr* (Cody 1969: 89). At least such a pairing has been suggested for the use of the words *ṣdq* and *yšr* as used in the Bible (Liverani 1971: 67).

The god appears in Syria-Palestine, perhaps in Judah, and among the Phoenician colonies. Sedheq would appear to have been a minor god, one who was seen to stand in attendance on the major deity of a given pantheon. "Justice" and "Rectitude" seem to have been a pair of gods recognized as members of the divine hierarchy in Mesopotamia and the West Semitic pantheons.

Bibliography

Astour, M. C. 1966. Some New Divine Names from Ugarit. *JAOS* 86: 277–84.

Attridge, H. W., and Oden, R. A., Jr. 1981. *Philo of Byblos The Phoenician History.* CBQMS 9. Washington, DC.

Baumgarten, A. I. 1981. *The Phoenician History of Philo of Byblos: A Commentary.* EPRO 89. Leiden.

Cody, A. 1969. *A History of Old Testament Priesthood.* AnBib 35. Rome.

Liverani, M. 1971. *SYDYK* e *MISŌR.* Vol. 6, pp. 55–74 in *Studi in Onore di Edoardo Volterra.* Milan.

Masson, O., and Sznycer, M. 1972. *Recherches sur les Phéniciens à Chypre.* Hautes Études Orientales 3. Geneva.

Rosenberg, R. A. 1965. The God Ṣedeq. *HUCA* 36: 161–77.

Tigay, J. H. 1986. *You Shall Have No Other Gods.* HSS 31. Atlanta.

Troiani, L. 1974. *L'Opera storiografica di Filone da Byblos.* Biblioteca degli studi classici e orientali 1. Pisa.

Wood, W. C. 1916. The Religion of Canaan from Earliest Times to the Hebrew Conquest. *JBL* 35: 1–133; 163–279.

LOWELL K. HANDY

SEDRACH, APOCALYPSE OF. Extant in only one 15th-century Gk manuscript (Bodleian Library, Cod. Misc. Gr. 56, fols. 92–100), this pseudepigraphical work attributed to Sedrach has not been adequately researched. James (1893: 127–37), Shutt (1984), and Diez Macho (1984) rightly contend that "Sedrach" does not refer to one of Daniel's companions, according to the Greek spelling; it is a corruption of "Esdras." The document certainly belongs with the apocryphal works attributed to Ezra.

The work begins with a sermon on love by Sedrach, who is subsequently taken up as far as the third heaven by an angel, the hypostatic Voice. Sedrach stands before the Lord and questions him.

P. Volz (1934) and C. C. Torrey (*JEnc* 1: 674) thought that the pseudepigraphon was a Jewish work. P. Riessler claimed it was a Christian redaction of a Jewish document (1928: 1274). The apocalypse may be a compilation of many documents (Denis 1970), many of them Jewish, but it is Christian in its present form.

James (1893) incorrectly divided the work into two separate and unrelated documents: the sermon and the apocalypse. The connection between these two—specifically that God's actions are motivated by love—suggests that the sermon is a Christian preface to a much older work, the apocalypse. This portion may be a Christian reworking of much older Jewish traditions (and perhaps even a Jewish work). The author (or compiler) was influenced especially by Job, Paul, the gospel of John, the *Testament of Abraham, 2 Baruch,* and especially the *Greek Apocalypse of Ezra* and *4 Ezra.* Agourides (*OTP* 1: 606) contends that the apocalypse was composed by a Jew between 150 and 500 C.E., and that the sermon was added by a Christian shortly after 1000 C.E. Diez Macho (1984) suggests that the Jewish document, if one can be isolated, dates from the 2d century C.E., and that the Christian additions date from the 5th century. Sparks (in Shutt 1984: 953) attributes the sermon on love to Ephraem Syrus. The Greek is close in some passages to modern Greek, suggesting that the present form of the work is late; but the original language is probably an earlier form of Greek (Agourides). There are sections with Byzantine and even patristic syntax and words.

As in *4 Ezra* the theme of the *Apocalypse of Sedrach* is God's compassion for the sinner. Here are some significant excerpts: "And Sedrach said, 'What (is it), my Lord?' And the Voice said to him, 'I was sent to you that I may carry you up into heaven. . . . the angel, having stretched out his wings, took him and went up into the heavens, and took him as far as the third heaven, and the flame of the divinity stood there" (2:2–5). Sedrach urges the Lord to make it impossible for Adam to sin, and to "hold onto his foot" so that he will not stray. Then, "God said to him, 'If I hold his foot, he says, "You have given me no grace in the world," and so I left him to his own desires because I loved him' . . ." (8:1).

Bibliography

Charlesworth, J. H. 1981. Apocalypse of Sedrach. *PMR,* pp. 178–82.

Denis, A.-M. 1970. L'Apocalypse de Sedrach. Pp. 97–99 in *Introduction aux pseudépigraphes grecs d'Ancien Testament.* SVTP 3. Leiden.

Diez Macho, A. 1984. Apocalipsis de Esdras (griego). Apocalipsis de Sedrac. Vision de Esdras. Vol. 1, pp. 281–83 in *Apocrifos del Antiguo Testamento.* Madrid.

James, M. R. 1893. *Apocrypha Anecdota.* Cambridge.

Riessler, P. 1928. *Altjüdisches Schrifttum ausserhalb der Bibel.* Augsburg.

Shutt, R. J. H. 1984. The Apocalypse of Sedrach. Pp. 953–66 in *The Apocryphal Old Testament,* ed. H. F. D. Sparks. Oxford.

Volz, P. 1934. *Die Eschatologie der jüdischen Gemeinde im neutestamentlichen Zeitalter.* 2d ed.

Wahl, O. 1977. *Apocalypsis Esdrae, Apocalypsis Sedrach, Visio Beati Esdrae.* PVTG 4. Leiden.

James H. Charlesworth

SEFUNIM CAVES (M.R. 238148). A set of three prehistoric sites in the Carmel range just S of Haifa. Nahal Sefunim is one of the rivers draining Mt. Carmel westward toward the Mediterranean, about 5 km S of Haifa. Three prehistoric sites are known along this river, all located on its S bank. Whereas most of the prehistoric sites of the Carmel range are located on the mountain edge overlooking the plain, the Sefunim sites are unique with their hidden, inland position. They are, from E to W, the "Brecchia Cave," the "Sefunim Cave," and the "Sefunim Shelter."

A. The Brecchia Cave

This is a large mass of brecciated sediment about 1 m thick which covers the floor of a small cavity and the slope outside it. It apparently constitutes the rear part of a collapsed cave. The stone-hard sediment contains abundant animal bones and a few flint artifacts. The site has never been studied nor dated, but the breccia indicates the Middle Paleolithic (90,000–40,000 years ago) as the latest possible age.

B. Sefunim Cave

This cave (formerly "Iraq el-Barud") is located about 1 km from the coastal plain. Stekelis briefly tested the cave in 1941, and A. Ronen excavated it between 1965 and 1970. It is a vast cave, 50 m x 24 m, with two chambers. Cultural remains were found only in the front chamber and on the terrace, yielding a sequence (from bottom to top) of Middle Paleolithic, Upper Paleolithic, Neolithic/Chalcolithic, and modern remains.

1. The Middle Paleolithic. A small area near the present cave entrance (layers 13 and 12) and on the terrace (layers VII–VI) yielded Middle Paleolithic remains. These were embedded in a light brown silty clay, with abundant calcareous concretions on the terrace. The lithic industry, mostly of Levallois technique, is governed by points and scrapers. Tool making took place on the terrace, where almost all the cores were found. Faunal remains include forest dwellers such as wild boar and deer, and open-country species such as hippopotamus, gazelle, and cattle.

2. The Upper Paleolithic. This period consists of several occupations of Levantine Aurignacian (layers 10–8 in the cave), including one floor made of chalk (layer 10). The cave area occupied by the Upper Paleolithic is slightly larger than that of the Middle Paleolithic; the terrace had no remains of the Upper Paleolithic. The lithic industry includes the typical steep and end-scrapers, burins, various blades, and two bone points. The remains of boar, deer, gazelle, cattle, and antelope were found.

A small Kebaran occupation existed after the Aurignacian, and was almost completely removed by Stekelis' excavations.

3. The Neolithic/Chalcolithic. The Neolithic and Chalcolithic remains (cave layer 7; terrace, V–III) are found in a thick (0.2–2 m) stone layer. The entire front chamber and terrace were occupied. The lithic industry includes mainly cores, indicating that the site served primarily as a workshop, which produced celts of various types, scrapers, burins, retouched blades, and knives. A few arrowheads and a dagger were found on the terrace. A hearth 1 m x 1.3 m and 0.2 m deep was dug on the terrace, which was filled with ashes and burnt stones. A stone anvil was carefully placed on the edge of the hearth. This structure may have been used to heat-treat stone artifacts. The charcoal was C_{14} dated to the end of the 8th millennium B.C.E., which begins the Neolithic/Chalcolithic occupation. Its estimated end was in the 5th millennium.

The faunal remains contain wild species—gazelle and deer—with domestic goat and donkey. Cattle and boar are present, but it is unclear whether they were wild or domesticated. Marine mollusks are relatively abundant here compared with older layers.

4. The Modern Period. The site was used to corral flocks and to exploit saltpeter for gunpowder manufacture during the last few centuries. Several plaster-and-ash floors were built in the cave during this period.

C. The Shelter

Located midway between Sefunim Cave and the coastal plain, Sefunim Shelter was discovered by A. Ronen and excavated by Lamdan in 1975 and 1976. The site is at the foot of a high vertical cliff where the river terrace is the widest (ca. 10 m) along its entire course. Two periods are represented: Middle Paleolithic and Neolithic.

1. The Middle Paleolithic. This phase is embedded in the top part of a red *terra rose,* 0.5–1.0 m thick, which lies on bedrock. The remains were concentrated in a 6 m × 5 m area, and included a pavement 2.5 m × 3.5 m made of thin stone slabs—the only architectural feature known in the Middle Paleolithic of the Levant.

The lithic industry is represented by a small assemblage, indicating a limited occupation both in time and in number of occupants. This fact apparently contrasts with the significance of the slab floor. Possibly each occupation cleaned the remains of the former, so that the remains of the latest use of the Mousterian site are what were preserved. This involved local manufacture of stone tools, inferred from the relatively numerous cores. Levallois products, points, and scrapers form the bulk of the small assemblage, a composition similar to that found in Sefunim cave. The fauna includes deer, boar, and few gazelle. A few mollusks were also found, both marine and sweetwater, but these could have come from the overlying Neolithic occupation. No sediments were found between the Mousterian and Neolithic layers.

2. The Neolithic. The Neolithic layer is gray and humic, clearly distinguishable from the underlying red clay. The Neolithic inhabitants built a 13 m long, slightly curved wall parallel to and near the cliff; it was constructed of large boulders. At the W end of the wall a structure made of smaller stones was added which extended the wall another 5 m. It might originally have been a circular structure, but the N part has completely eroded. The Neolithic remains were scattered mainly in the W part of the structure and in the narrow space between the wall and the cliff. Only sparse finds were in the central and E parts of the structure, where had been the Mousterian site.

The lithic assemblage includes very few cores, so that tool manufacture clearly took place outside the area of excavation, perhaps at another site. There are celts, sickles, and arrowheads, along with scrapers, burins, borers, and various retouched items. Faunal remains include primarily cattle (which was absent in the underlying Mousterian), boar, deer, and a horse. Abundant sweetwater and marine mollusks were brought to the site, both for consumption and ornament.

The Sefunim shelter can only be understood as coexisting and cooperating with the cave inhabitants. From the shelter, both the cave and a narrow portion of the coastal plain are visible. Signals could have been transmitted between the sites, and communal hunting could have taken place in the Sefunim valley during the Middle Paleolithic. The shelter's function in the Neolithic, with its long and massive wall, remains unclear. Possibly the tools were brought to the shelter from the workshop in the cave, but this is yet to be demonstrated.

Avraham Ronen

SEGUB (PERSON) [Heb *śĕgûb*]. **1.** The younger son of Hiel who was responsible for the refortification of Jericho during the days of Ahab (1 Kgs 16:34). Scholars debate what is implied by the note that Hiel rebuilt Jericho "at the expense of" (Heb *bĕ*) his two sons, Abiram and Segub. It is obviously intended by DH to be the working out of Joshua's curse pronounced against Jericho in Josh 6:26, thereby bringing the entire reign of Ahab under the judgment of the divine curse.

Several possibilities exist, however, for understanding the nature of the curse. Some see in this text the fated working out of a curse, whereby Segub and Abiram died of natural causes. Blake (1967: 86–97), for example, argued that the entire family (inclusive use of "elder" and "younger") was wiped out due to radiation contamination of the spring. Others argue that the two sons may indeed have been buried in the foundations or gates, but only because they died in childbirth or of other natural causes.

Commentators more commonly assume that the note may be referring to the practice known elsewhere in the ANE and in Israel itself as the offering of a "foundation sacrifice." The association of Abiram with the rebuilding of the foundations and of Segub with the setting of the gates certainly suggests that one son's death marked the beginning of the project and the other son's the conclusion. The question hinges on whether the sons died of natural causes and were therefore buried in the foundation and at the gate, or whether they were offered as a sacrifice in order to ensure the future of the fortifications. If the latter was the case, did Hiel himself take the curse so seriously that he offered his own sons as a sacrifice, or was he compelled to give his sons over to be killed out of popular superstition? Already the Targum understands the text to mean that Hiel "killed" his two sons.

Most probably, the motif of the "fated curse" is due to the literary interest of DH. An early legendary tradition concerning the offering of a foundation sacrifice by Hiel was taken up by DH and reworked for polemical interests. By composing the tradition of Joshua's curse, the note in 1 Kgs 16:34 was thereby made to serve as prophetic fulfillment of a curse, with the literary effect of bringing the reign of Ahab under this divine curse.

2. Listed in 1 Chr 2:21–22 in the genealogy of Hezron. The genealogical information given is as follows: Judah > Perez > Hezron > Segub > Jair. The displacement of Hezron's genealogy in vv 21–23 to a position following that of his sons Ram and Caleb, together with the fact that the names presented in these verses represent geographical territories (Jair, Gilead, Aram), suggest that this material is a fragment cemented into the larger genealogy of Judah for certain interests. In this genealogy Judah is linked through Hezron to the family of Machir, whose daughter (Gilead's sister) becomes Hezron's wife. The families of Judah and Machir are nowhere else related, and in Num 32:39–41 both Machir and Jair are considered sons of Manasseh.

The editor of Chronicles has evidently used old genealogical information in order to further Judean claims of prominence. In spite of the territory of Gilead clearly being linked to the eponymous figure of Gilead, a later Judean claim to Gileadite sites (the 23 cities in Gilead) was effected by grafting Hezron into the genealogy by extending it back one generation to Machir and by coupling Hezron with Gilead's sister (to whom some give the name Abijah). Such Judean claims on Gileadite territory may go back to the era of David, who was allied through marriage to the territory of Geshur (2 Sam 3:3).

Braun (*1 Chronicles* WBC, 40) suggests that the name Segub is a corrupted form of the name Argob, since elsewhere Argob is connected with Jair.

Bibliography

Blake, I. M. 1967. Jericho (Ain Es-Sultan): Joshua's Curse and Elisha's Miracle—One Possible Explanation. *PEQ* 99: 86–97.

Rod R. Hutton

SEILUN, KHIRBET (M.R. 177162). Khirbet Seilun, in the heart of the territory of Ephraim a short distance E of the main road leading from Jerusalem to Shechem, is identified with the biblical town of Shiloh. Throughout the ages its location was not forgotten. In the Middle Ages, Eshtori ha-Parhi described its ruins, and the American explorer, E. Robinson, reidentified the site with Shiloh in 1838, according to the detailed biblical description of its location (Judg 21:19), "north of Bethel, on the east of the highway that goes up from Bethel to Shechem and south of Lebonah" (the Arab village Lubban-Sharqiya), and on the basis of the Onomasticon of Eusebius, which states that Shiloh is 12 miles from Neapolis in the district of Acrabattene. He also relied on the fact that the name is preserved by the ruins and nearby spring.

A. Biblical Shiloh

Shiloh, where the Ark of the Covenant was kept in the first half of the 11th century B.C.E., was the sacred center of the Israelite hill country tribes. See SHILOH. According to the Bible, it was in Shiloh that the land was apportioned among the tribes (Josh 18:10) and the Levitical cities were allocated (Josh 21:2). The population assembled there both in times of distress (Josh 22:12) and times of celebration (Judg 21:19–21). The importance of Shiloh as a religious center and the seat of leadership of the Israelite tribes reached its zenith in the days of Eli the priest, when it became a focus of pilgrimage (1 Sam 1:3, 24). The town figured prominently in the battle of Ebenezer (1 Samuel 4); after defeating the Israelites, the Philistines apparently took advantage of their victory to press up into the hills and to put Shiloh to the torch. The Bible does not explicitly report the destruction of the site at the hands of the Philistines, but its fiery demise is alluded to in a number of passages (Jer 7:12, 14; 26:6, 9; Ps 78:60). Shiloh remained deserted for some time thereafter, but by the reign of Jeroboam I, settlement had been renewed (1 Kgs 14:2, 4), and the town still existed when Jerusalem was destroyed (Jer 41:5). The site is also mentioned in rabbinical sources and by Byzantine pilgrims.

C. Excavations

The mound of Seilun is located at the northern end of a fertile valley surrounded by hills. At a distance of 900 m to its NE there is a copious spring, providing water to supplement the runoff water that was collected in cisterns on the mound. The tell, which rises 714 m above sea level, covers an area of about 30 dunams (7.5 acres). Since its E, W, and N slopes are very steep, its most convenient approach is from the S. Three considerations thus determined the location of the settlement: proximity to the fertile valley, availability of a permanent water source, and an easily defensible topographical location.

The first archaeological soundings at Seilun were made by A. Schmidt in 1922. Between 1926 and 1932 a Danish expedition headed by H. Kjaer undertook three seasons of excavations, and an additional probe was made by S. Holm-Nielsen in 1963. The 1981–1984 expedition of the Department of the Land of Israel Studies, Bar Ilan University, headed by I. Finkelstein, conducted four seasons of excavations at the site. Eight strata were exposed by this expedition.

Period	*Stratum*	*Description of remains*
MB II	VIII	Pottery in the glacis and earthen fills of Stratum VII.
MB III	VII	Elaborate defense system consisting of a solid city wall and glacis, adjoined by a row of rooms; earth and stone fills.
LB	VI	Deposits of pottery of a cultic nature, ash and bones.
Iron I	V	Pillared buildings; numerous silos.
Iron II	IV	Scanty architectural remains.
Hellenistic	III	Scanty architectural remains.
Roman and Byzantine	II–I	Remains of village on upper part and S slope of the mound.
Middle Ages	Surface	Ruins of medieval village.

The first settlement at Seilun (Stratum VIII), apparently a small unwalled village, was established in the MB II. The evidence for this occupation consists solely of pottery found in the glacis and earthen fills of the following stratum; the builders of Stratum VII evidently used the debris from the previous settlement as fills in their earthworks.

During the MB III (Stratum VII) the site, probably about four acres in size, was surrounded by massive fortifications consisting of a solid city wall reinforced by an earthen glacis, whose remains were discovered in five places on the perimeter of the tell. The city wall, founded on bedrock and constructed of large fieldstones, was 3.0–5.5 m wide. In several of its segments its state of preservation is very impressive; in the sectional trench cut near its outer face in the NE sector (Area D), it was found standing to a height of almost 8 m. Following its destruction, it became a quarry for building material, and its stones were robbed throughout the ages. Since the wall was designed to conform to the contours of the mound, its standard of construction was not uniform. The glacis was also constructed of segments of differing size, density and structural components. In the large section cut into the steep NE slope it was found to be 25 m long and to be composed of five different elements. Against the fortification wall it is 6.3 m thick. A wall 3.2 m high is incorporated into it, and two masses of large rough boulders were laid at the base in order to stabilize the earthworks and to prevent them from sliding down the slope. The glacis was especially strong wherever the slope is the steepest, while on the more moderate slopes it was less thick and of lesser complexity. Hence it is obvious that the principal motivation for laying the glacis was as a reinforcement rather than an attempt to hinder an enemy's approach to the fortification wall.

In the N sector of the site (Areas F–H) a row of rooms 115 m long was built against the inner face of the city wall. Their walls are preserved to a height of 2.5 m. Behind these rooms, in the direction of the center of the tell, and on a higher level, are stone and earth fills, giving the rooms the character of basements; judging by the large quantities of storage vessels found in them, they probably served as storerooms. In addition to these vessels, a unique hoard of silver and bronze objects was discovered, includ-

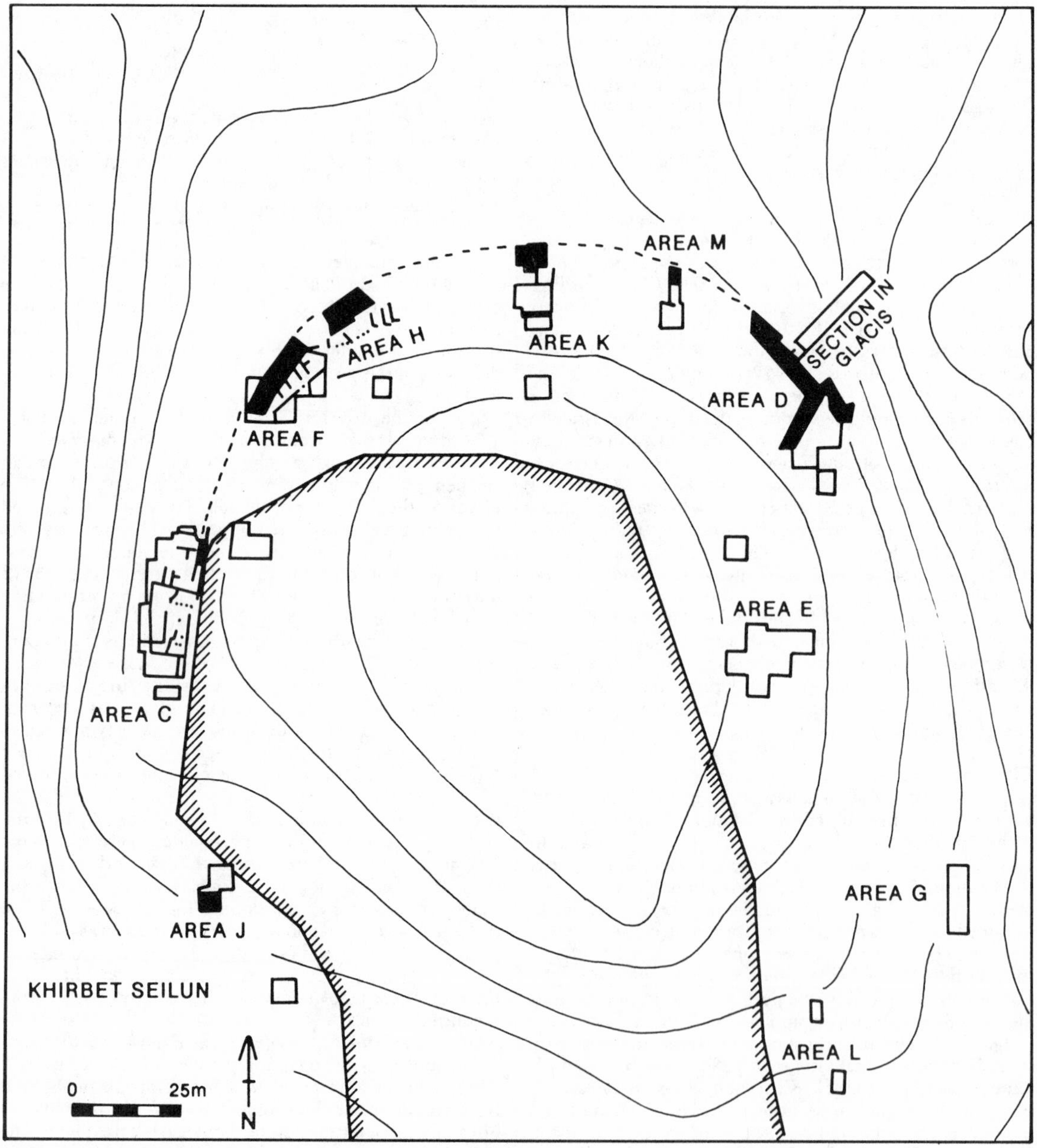

SEI.01. Contour plan of Tell Seilun (Shiloh), showing excavated areas. Shaded border indicates limits of Roman-Byzantine village remains. *(Redrawn from Finkelstein 1985: 126, fig. 2)*

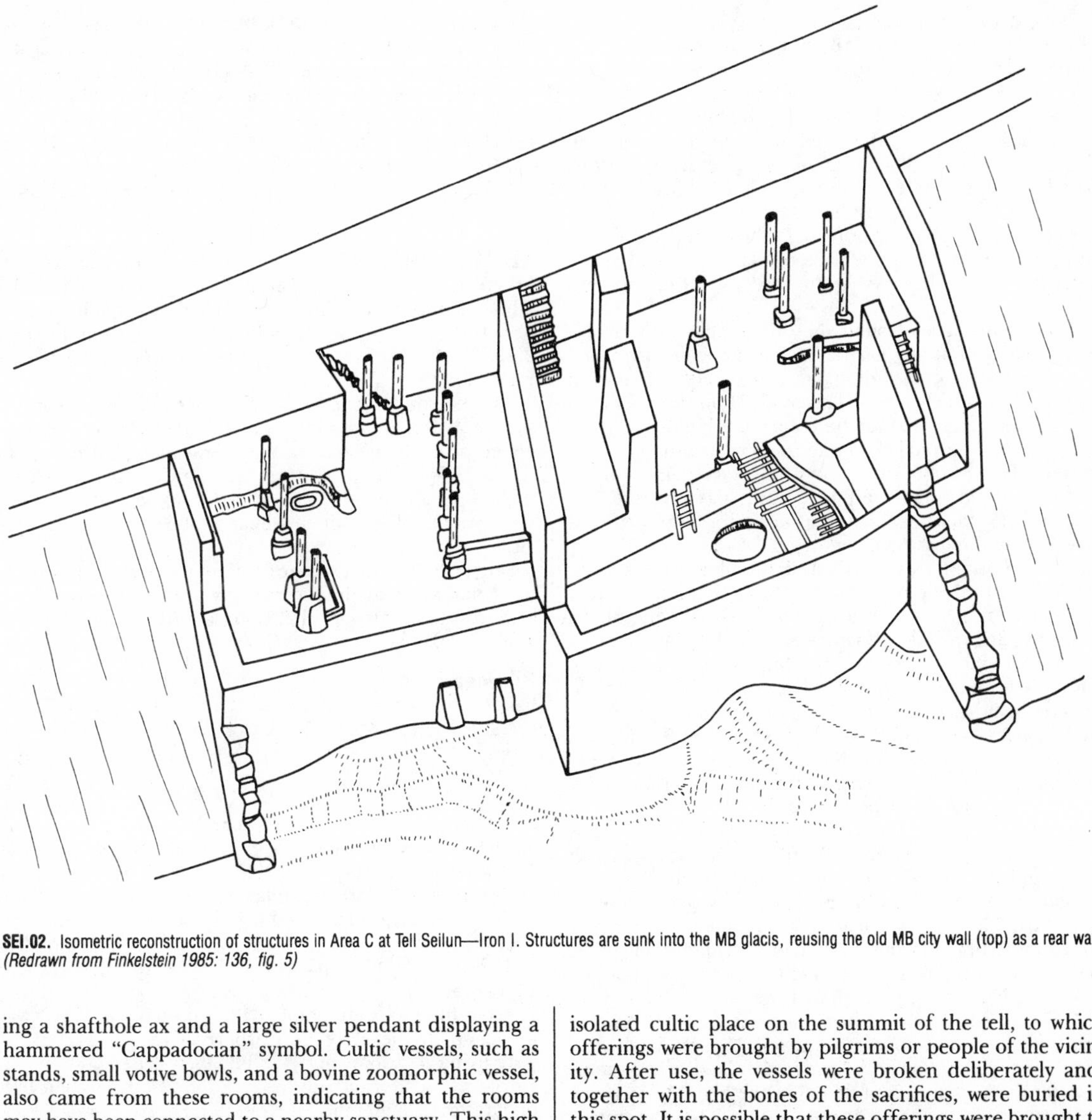

SEI.02. Isometric reconstruction of structures in Area C at Tell Seilun—Iron I. Structures are sunk into the MB glacis, reusing the old MB city wall (top) as a rear wall. *(Redrawn from Finkelstein 1985: 136, fig. 5)*

ing a shafthole ax and a large silver pendant displaying a hammered "Cappadocian" symbol. Cultic vessels, such as stands, small votive bowls, and a bovine zoomorphic vessel, also came from these rooms, indicating that the rooms may have been connected to a nearby sanctuary. This high place may have stood on the top of the tell, supported by the stone and earthen fills uncovered above the above-mentioned rooms. Stratum VII was destroyed at the end of the MB III (16th century B.C.E.).

It was not long, however, before activity was renewed on the site. The LB level (Stratum VI) was exposed only in one part of the mound—Area D. No architectural remains came to light, but there was a thick accumulation of earth, ashes, and stones extending over an area of about 200 square meters inside and on top of the MB fortifications. A large quantity of broken pottery (mainly bowls and chalices) and animal bones was retrieved from this deposit. Several vessels containing ashes and bones were found intact, or nearly so. There were no other signs of activity in LB Seilun. The site may have consisted solely of an isolated cultic place on the summit of the tell, to which offerings were brought by pilgrims or people of the vicinity. After use, the vessels were broken deliberately and, together with the bones of the sacrifices, were buried in this spot. It is possible that these offerings were brought to the sacred location of the former (MB III) sanctuary. Most of the pottery is of the LB I horizon; from the ceramic evidence, it appears that the activity slowly decreased and finally ceased completely long before the end of the LB Age.

After a period of abandonment, the site was resettled in the 12–11th centuries (Stratum V). Iron I remains were found almost everywhere on the mound: more than 20 silos were unearthed in the N and NE sectors, and a group of pillared buildings was exposed on the W slope (Area C). These are the most important building remains of Iron I Seilun/Shiloh, indicating developed construction techniques and architectural concepts already at this early stage of "Israelite" settlement. The buildings adjoined the outer side of the former MB city wall, which was well preserved here and served as their rear wall. See Fig. SEI.02. A segment of the MB glacis was removed, and the Iron I structures were actually "sunk" into the glacis. The steep slope necessitated two building levels which were divided by a terrace wall. Two pillar buildings, separated by a corridor, stood on the upper level and a large hall on the lower level. The S building on the upper level had four parallel aisles separated from each other by three rows of pillars, while the N upper building consisted of a courtyard set off by pillars from each of its three side units, which were neatly paved with stone slabs. The hall of the lower level probably served as the basement of the upper S building.

The ceramic assemblage from this complex, the richest ever discovered at any early Israelite site, consists mainly of storage vessels, including more than 20 collared-rim jars (seven of which were found by the Danish expedition in 1929). Among its other functions, the building apparently served as a public storehouse. The buildings of the western slope were destroyed by a fierce conflagration. As suggested by Albright and Kjaer, this was probably the work of the Philistines in the aftermath of the battle of Ebenezer in the mid-11th century B.C.E.

The excavation results shed light on several aspects concerning the role of Shiloh in the Israelite Settlement process. First, it is now clear that in the beginning of the Iron Age Seilun/Shiloh was the outstanding candidate to become the sacred center of the hill-country population, since it was an ancient cult site that now stood deserted in an area with only a sparse Canaanite population and a high concentration of "Israelite" sites. See EPHRAIM (PERSON). The exact date Shiloh was first settled by the Israelites is not yet clear; however, it seems that major construction did not begin before the middle of the 12th century B.C.E. The important role played by Shiloh is reflected in the density of the Iron I sites around it, which is two and even three times greater than that of the other regions in the land of Ephraim. The size of the settlement was about 2.5–3 acres. Since a considerable part of it was probably occupied by the shrine complex and other public buildings, the possibility that Shiloh was primarily a sacred *temenos* rather than an ordinary village should not be ruled out. According to the data from the excavations, the shrine was probably at the summit of the tell. Unfortunately, this area was badly eroded and destroyed by later occupation.

After the destruction of Shiloh in the mid-11th century B.C.E., the site lay in ruins for some time. The resumption of settlement in Iron II is represented by scanty village-typed remains found in various places on the mound (Stratum IV). Shiloh of the Roman and Byzantine periods was a large village (Strata II–I). The two Byzantine churches with ornamental mosaic floors uncovered by the Danish expedition S of the mound show that Shiloh still retained its religious association.

Bibliography

Andersen, F. G. 1985. *Shiloh: The Danish Excavation at Tall Sailun, Palestine, in 1926, 1929, 1932 and 1963.* Vol. 2, *The Remains from the Hellenistic to the Mamluk Periods.* Publication of the National Museum, Archaeological Historical Series 23. Copenhagen.

Buhl, M. L., and Holm-Nielsen, S. 1969. *Shiloh: The Danish Excavation at Tall Sailun, Palestine, in 1926, 1929, 1932 and 1963.* Vol. 1, *The Pre-Hellenistic Remains.* Publications of the National Museum, Archaeological Historical Series 12. Copenhagen.

Finkelstein, I., ed. 1985. Excavations at Shiloh 1981–1984: Preliminary Report. *TA* 12: 123–80.

Finkelstein, I., and Brandl, B. 1985. A Group of Metal Objects from Shiloh. *Israel Museum Journal* 4: 17–26.

ISRAEL FINKELSTEIN

SEIR (PERSON) [Heb *śēʿîr*]. Ancestor of people living in Edom (Gen 36:20–21; 1 Chr 1:38). Seir belonged to the ethnic group of the Horites who lived in the hill country of Seir (Gen 14:6). See SEIR (PLACE). According to Deut 2:12, 22 the Horites were defeated and displaced by the Edomites.

The personal name Seir is always found in the expression *běnê śēʿîr*, "descendants of Seir." Seir is also used as a geographical name and for the people living in this region (Ezek 25:8; Num 24:18). It is sometimes unclear whether the people identified as *běnê śēʿîr* should be understood as descendants of Seir or inhabitants of Seir (2 Chr 25:11, 14).

Seir, Edom, and Esau are closely connected in biblical texts, and are sometimes seemingly used as synonyms. For a thorough discussion of their relationships, see Bartlett 1969: 1–20.

Bibliography

Bartlett, J. L. 1969. The Land of Seir and the Brotherhood of Edom. *JTS* n.s. 20: 1–20.

STEPHEN A. REED

SEIR (PLACE) [Heb *śēʿîr*]. **1.** The biblical name for part of the country of Edom (Gen 14:6; 36:20–21, 30; Deut 1:2, 44; 2:1; 33:2; Josh 11:17; 12:7; Judg 5:4; Isa 21:11; 1 Chr 1:38; 4:42) and, secondarily, a synonym for Edom, both in the geographical and the political sense (Gen 32:4; 33:14, 16; 36:8–9; Num 24:18; Deut 2:4–5, 8, 12, 22, 29; Josh 24:4; Ezek 25:8; 35:2–3, 7, 15; 2 Chr 20:10, 22–23; 25:11, 14).

According to Gen 36:30, "the country of Seir" was inhabited by the HORITES, whereas "the sons of Esau" were living in Edom. In Gen 36:20, Seir is personified as a Horite whose descendants live in Edom. In the archaic text of Judg 5:4, "Seir" and "the field of Edom" parallel each other. Seir is frequently referred to as "the mountain," or "mountains of Seir" (Gen 14:6; 36:8–9; Deut 2:1, etc.). Combined, these references suggest that Seir was a mountainous region which became part of the Edomite state. Etymologically, Seir means "hairy," whereas Edom signifies "red." There are three possibilities to circumscribe the pertinence of the toponym "Seir" more closely:

(a) "Edom" was originally connected with the Transjordanian plateau between Wādī al-Ḥasâ and Râs en-Naqb (because of its reddish soil; cf. the "field of Edom" in Judg 5:4). "Seir," accordingly, was originally connected with the wooded precipice leading from the plateau down to the Wādī al-ʿArabah (Weippert 1971; Knauf 1988b). This is the most likely interpretation.

(b) "Edom" meant the region between Wādī al-Ḥasâ and

Wādī al-Ġhuwayr (which is called in Arabic *el-Jibâl*), and "Seir" referred to the S part of the Edomite state, the area between Wādī al-Ġhuwayr and Râs en-Naqb (in Arabic, *eš-Šarâh*). One argument in favor of this distinction is the fact that the formation of the Edomite state started in the north, in el-Jibâl. In addition, eš-Šarâh, "the mountain range," may have replaced eš-Šarâ, "the wooded rocky mountain with springs," since the region was probably known in Nabatean times when the Nabatean god Dhû Sharâ had his central sanctuary in its center, at Petra. Arabic *šarâ* refers to the same geographic features, rocks and trees, as does Seir, although there is no etymological connection between the two similar sounding words. The slight change from eš-Šarâ to eš-Šarâh may be due to post-Nabatean deforestation, or Islamic shunning of the memory of an "idol."

(c) "Edom" signified the area of eš-Šarâh because of the Nubian sandstone which is dominant along the precipice, especially in the Petra area, and "Seir" referred to el-Jibâl, "the mountains" (hence, the frequent mentioning of "mountains of Seir" in the OT). A ruin in the vicinity of et-Tafīlah may have preserved the ancient regional name: *Khirbet Umm Šaᶜīr*.

Hypothesis (c) is irreconcilable with the epigraphic and archaeological evidence concerning the evolution of the Edomite state; hypothesis (b) is based on more assumptions than are needed for hypothesis (a). Furthermore, both Khirbet Umm Šaᶜīr ("Seir" in hypothesis c) and Petra ("Seir" in hypothesis b) are situated on the upper terraces of the precipice, well below the plateau, i.e., both places are comprised in "Seir" (hypothesis a).

After Seir had become part of Edom (Gen 36:21), "Edom" and "Seir" became synonyms. Thus, Deut 2:12, 22 concluded from the "Horites in Seir, the inhabitants of the country" (Gen 36:20, 30) on the one hand and the "sons of Esau, this is Edom" (Gen 36:19) on the other that the Edomites conquered Seir and annihilated its previous inhabitants. Deut 1:44; 2:1 seems to presuppose Seir on both the W and the E side of Wādī al-ᶜArabah (cf. Deut 2:3), a geographical extension due to Edom's penetration of the Negeb, and the subsequent establishment of Idumaea S of Judah from the late 7th century B.C. onward.

If "Edom" and "Seir" were originally distinct geographic units, the undoubtedly ancient text of Judg 5:4, which has Yahweh come from Edom and Seir to do battle for his people, already betrays a rather vague knowledge of the precise location of the "mountain of god" (Ahlström 1986: 58–59; *HAIJ,* 111–12). Deut 33:2 ("Yahweh . . . dawned upon us from Seir") seems to be an evocation of various places connected with Yahweh's seat in different traditions which, in a geographic context, do not lead to a coherent itinerary. Egyptian topographical lists from the 14th and 13th centuries B.C. do, however, list a "country of *Yhw*-nomads" under the heading "country of Seir-nomads" (another possible translation would be "country of nomads: *Yhw,*" "country of nomads: Seir"). The most ancient references, both biblical and extra-biblical, connect Yahweh and Seir, i.e., the region SE of Canaan (Knauf 1988a: 50–51; Görg 1989 *pace* Astour 1979, who tried to locate the nomads of *Yhw* and Seir in S Syria).

2. The name of a mountain in Judah (Josh 15:10). Because the geographical features (land formation, vegetation) which determine the majority of Semitic place-name formation are nearly ubiquitous in the Near East, place names also reoccur frequently. Because the mountain mentioned in Josh 15:10 is situated on the W slopes of the Judean range, it must have been heavily wooded in antiquity. This or a third Seir is mentioned in the Amarna letters (No. 288, line 26; Knauf 1988b: 64; cf., however, Görg 1989, who argues for the identity of the Amarna Seir with the Edomite Seir). Similarly, a Seirah was located in either Benjamin or Ephraim (Judg 3:26). See also SEIRAH.

Bibliography

Ahlström, G. W. 1986. *Who Were the Israelites?* Winona Lake, IN.

Astour, M. C. 1979. Yahweh in Egyptian Topographic Lists. Pp. 17–34 in *Festschrift Elmar Edel,* ed. M. Görg. Wiesbaden.

Axelson, L. E. 1987. *The Lord Rose up from Seir.* ConBOT 25. Stockholm.

Görg, M. 1989. Zur Identität der "Seir-Länder." *BN* 46: 7–12.

Knauf, E. A. 1988a. *Midian.* ADPV. Wiesbaden.

———. 1988b. Supplementa Ismaelitica 13. Edom und Arabien. *BN* 45: 62–81.

Weippert, M. 1971. *Edom.* Diss., Tübingen.

Ernst Axel Knauf

SEIRAH (PLACE) [Heb *śĕᶜîrâ*]. The name of either a city or a topographical feature to which the Benjaminite judge Ehud fled after he assassinated Eglon, the Moabite king and oppressor of Israel, in the vicinity of Gilgal (Judg 3:26). So far Seirah has not been located, and the name does not appear to be mentioned apart from this reference.

Simons believes that by analogy with *happĕsîlîm* ("the quarries" or "the idols" in Judg 3:19, 26) *haśśĕᶜîrātâ* is best understood as a topographical feature with the meaning "the woody hills" (*GTTOT,* 288).

On the understanding that Seirah designates a specific place name, it has been variously located E of the river Jordan, in the Jordan Valley, at Mount Seir, or in the hill country of Ephraim. A location E of the Jordan seems questionable, as it is less likely that Ehud would have found his countrymen in the Transjordan region than in the hills of Ephraim. The identification of Seirah with Mount Seir on the boundary of Judah (Josh 15:10) is unlikely, as it would have been too distant for Ehud to rally the Israelites and return in time to thwart the retreat of the Moabite soldiers across the river Jordan (Judg 3:28–29). A location in the Jordan Valley would account for the rapid deployment of Israelite forces to the fords of the Jordan River, but the identification of Seirah with some place in the hill country of Ephraim is best supported by the context and especially v 27.

Arthur J. Ferch

SELA (PLACE) [Heb *selaᶜ*]. The word occurs about 65 times in the MT, though not usually as a proper name. In six passages it does appear as a place name—2 Kgs 14:7; 2 Chr 25:12; Isa 16:1; 42:11; Jer 49:16; Obad 3; and Judg 1:36. The name means "rock."

1. An Edomite fortress city conquered by Amaziah King

of Judah and renamed Joktheel (2 Kgs 14:7). Usually this city has been identified with the Nabatean rock-city of Petra (M.R. 192971) halfway between the Dead Sea and the Gulf of Aqaba. Umm el-Bayyârah is the rocky peak that dominates the Wadī Mûsā on which Petra was built and towers 300 m above the level of Petra and 1,130 m above sea level. This may have led to the description of the Edomites as living "in the clefts of the rock" (Jer 49:16; Obad 3). However, another site has been proposed for Sela (see *IDBSup,* 800): the modern Sela^c (M.R. 205020), which is 4 km NW of Buseira (biblical Bozrah). Excavations show that this site was a fortified city from the 9th to the 7th centuries B.C., whereas at Umm el-Bayyârah there are no remains earlier than the 7th century. It could be that both sites served as capitals of Edom at different times but with the same name. Isa 42:11 may refer to the same city.

2. An unidentified place on the Amorite border during the time of the judges (Judg 1:36). Apparently it was situated within Judah. This site is mentioned alongside the ascent of Akrabim (lit. "scorpions"), which lies to the SW end of the Dead Sea.

3. A place in Moab cited in Isaiah's prophecy against that nation (Isa 16:1). The site has not been identified. Some have proposed that this Sela is the same as that of Sela in Edom (#1 above) and that the Moabite fugitives fled there for refuge. However, the oracle is concerned only with Moab (Isa 15:1) and the fugitives fled S only as far as Zoar (15:5), S of the Dead Sea. Furthermore, references are made to Moab's borders, the "Brook of Willows" (15:7), which is identified with Wadī el-Ḥesā, and the "waters of Dibon" (15:9), which probably refers to the Arnon river. Petra lies yet 80 km farther S of Wadī el-Ḥesā and even farther from Dibon.

Bibliography

Hart, S. 1986. Sela: The Rock of Edom? *PEQ* 118: 91–95.

Lindner, M. 1986. *Petra: neue Ausgrabungen und Entdeckungen.* Munich.

WANN M. FANWAR

SELBIT (M.R. 148141). See SHAALBIM.

SELED (PERSON) [Heb *seled*]. A leader in the tribe of Judah, the firstborn son of Nadab without male issue (mentioned twice in 1 Chr 2:30), and a descendant of Jerahmeel through his wife Atarah. Seled is the brother of Appaim through whose line the Jerahmeelites are traced another 16 generations to Elishama (the apparent interest of the genealogy). Variant spellings of Seled are found in the LXX (B *alsalad* and *salad*), although many scholars consider those genealogies corrupt (especially codex Vaticanus). However, the genealogies of Jerahmeel in the MT are viewed by most contemporary commentators as being in good order. For further discussion of the provenance and authenticity of the genealogies in 1 Chronicles 2, see MAAZ.

Many commentators note the sense of loss apparent in the OT for the lack of male issue and conclude that aspects of immortality were perpetuated through one's descendants. The meaning of this name is very uncertain, although it appears to come from the root *sld,* possibly meaning "to spring" or "to beat the ground in running"; some suggest the meaning for Seled is "exultation."

W. P. STEEGER

SELEMIA (PERSON) [Lat *Selemia*]. One of the five scribes whom Ezra was instructed to take with him in restoring the Scriptures (2 Esdr 14:24). See DABRIA for further discussion.

JIN HEE HAN

SELEUCIA (PLACE) [Gk *Seleukia; Seleukeia*]. A name given to several cities established during the Hellenistic period. These cities are named after Seleucus I Nicator, one of the Diadochi who gained control of a large portion of Alexander the Great's empire and founded what is known as the Seleucid empire. As many as ten such cities have been identified within his domain. This article will discuss four of these which are of particular interest in biblical studies, including the Seleucia in Syria which is mentioned in 1 Macc 11:8 and Acts 13:4.

Other cities named Seleucia include those in the Anatolian districts of Pisidia, Pamphylia, Caria, and Phrygia. There were also other cities by this name, including one in the Orontes Valley and two others in Mesopotamia in addition to the more significant one on the Tigris. In Coele-Syria, the Decapolis cities of Abila and Gadara, although first mentioned in 217 B.C., have Seleucia added as a prefix in some inscriptions. The port city of Gaza also was given the dynastic name for a brief time while it was under Seleucid control.

The Seleucid state spanned an arc from the Persian Gulf across the Plain of Babylon to the Valley of Aleppo to the Mediterranean coast and up that coast to the Plain of Cilicia. The regions of Mesopotamia, Cilicia, and Syria formed the economic, strategic, and political nucleus of the empire. Seleucus I built important cities named after himself in each of these regions. The first of these to be established was in Mesopotamia.

1. Seleucia in Mesopotamia was founded by Seleucus Nicator in 312 B.C. as his E capital, replacing Babylon as the political and cultural center of Mesopotamia. It is variously known as Seleucia-on-the-Tigris, *Seleucia Babylonia, Seleucia Assyriae,* and *Seleucia Parthorum.* It was located on the W bank of the Tigris, at the Babylonian town of Opis, just N of the Royal Canal which provided access between the Tigris and Euphrates river systems (ca. 20 miles SE of modern Baghdad). Its strategic location on navigable waterways (Strabo 16.739) and on caravan routes to E Asia promoted trade and population growth. As the hub of the new Hellenistic culture in the region, its population was principally Greek and Syrian. Seleucus also built extensively in N Syria, but this did not mean the end of Seleucia-on-the-Tigris as a political and cultural center. It is true that N Syria became the unique center of Seleucid power in the second half of the 2d century B.C., but is a mistake to believe that the Seleucid empire had a single "capital" before that time. The empire had several capitals to house the royal administration, the army, and the court.

The central authority in the Seleucid empire was peripatetic, although the Seleucids recognized Babylonia as the heart of their empire.

Archaeological evidence indicates that Seleucid occupation of the site ended ca. 143 B.C. Even after the fall of the Seleucid empire the city continued to flourish. The new autonomous city was made up of a mixture of peoples including large Jewish and Greek populations. Pliny the Elder reports that in the 1st century A.D. there were 600,000 inhabitants (*HN* 6.122). The large numbers of Diaspora Jews in eastern cities like Seleucia in time became a concern for the Romans who desired to maintain control in the Levant.

Successive Parthian campaigns by Trajan, Avidius Cassius, and Septimius Severus during the 2d century A.D. devastated the city. Excavations from 1927–32 at Tell Umar, the site of Seleucia-on-the-Tigris, produced less spectacular results than might have been expected (see reports by Waterman 1931; 1933). Many of the architectural fragments appear to have been reused at the Parthian capital of Ctesiphon on the opposite bank of the Tigris.

2. Seleucia in Cilicia was founded by Seleucus I in 300 B.C. on the W bank of the Calycadmus River, 6 km from the Mediterranean coast. This city, also known as *Seleucia Tracheotis,* lay along a coastal highway as well as a route that penetrated deep into Anatolia. Its location suggests that the purpose of the city was to protect the region against attacks from the sea. It served in this capacity very well. It did not capitulate even though the rest of E Cilicia fell to Ptolemy III Euergetes in 245 B.C. during the Third Syrian War. This city was of regional cultural significance because it was the location of an oracle of Apollo, and annual athletic competitions. Architectural remains at the site include ruins of temples, porticoes, aqueducts, and a fortification on a nearby height. The site is located near modern Silifke.

3. Seleucia in Palestine was a Hellenistic city in Gaulanitis, what is known today as the Golan. The city eventually came into Jewish control under the leadership of Alexander Janneus (103–76 B.C.), who seized it from the Syrians (Josephus *Ant* 13.15.4). Under Roman control, Seleucia never regained her former importance. Josephus later fortified the site against the Romans during the First Jewish Revolt (*War* 2.20.6). Agrippa II, however, persuaded the city to come to terms with the Romans (*Life* 187, 358). Modern Seluqiyeh (M.R. 222267), 16 km NW of the Sea of Galilee, is believed to retain the ancient name of this Seleucia.

Bibliography

Jones, A. H. M. 1971. *The Cities of the Eastern Roman Empire.* Oxford.
Streck, M. 1917. Seleukeia und Ktesiphon. *AO* 16/3.
Waterman, L. 1931. *Preliminary Report upon the Excavations at Tel Umar, Iraq.* Ann Arbor.
———. 1933. *Second Preliminary Report upon the Excavations at Tel Umar, Iraq.* Ann Arbor.

ROBERT W. SMITH
LESLIE J. HOPPE

4. Seleucia in Syria was the most important city founded by Seleucus I; it was also known as *Seleucia Pieria.* The name Seleucia honors Seleucus I as the founder of the city, while the name Pieria derives from Mt. Pierius, on whose S slope the city was built. Seleucia was one of four cities that Seleucus I built in N Syria. Apparently he considered it the most important of the four, since he named this one after himself. The three other cities were Antioch-on-the-Orontes (named for Seleucus' father), Laodicea-on-the-Sea (named for his mother), and Apamea (named after his wife). These four cities, known as the "Syrian Tetrapolis," became centers for propagating Hellenistic cultural ideals throughout the region. Coins minted in these cities called them "brother townships."

Although Seleucus I defeated Antigonus and so acquired hegemony over Syria for himself, he did not convert the latter's capital to his own use but built a new city, Seleucia Pieri, 4 miles N of the mouth of the river Orontes, in the N coastal region of Syria, at its frontier with Cilicia. It was 16 miles W of Antioch-on-the-Orontes and served as the seaport of that city. The southern slope of Mount Pierius, which rises 4,000 feet above the Mediterranean, was an ideal location for a fortified city. The city included three areas. The lower part of the city was the port and commercial center. Above the lower city to the NE were terraced cliffs that supported the residential area. At the summit of Mt. Pierius was the acropolis, where the city's monumental public buildings were located. Surrounding the city on three sides were the cliffs of Mt. Pierius, which made Seleucia nearly invulnerable from land-based attacks. By 220 B.C. the population was 6,000 adult male citizens (Polybius *Histories* 5.61.1). This means that about a century after its founding the total population of the city—including women, children, and slaves—was approximately 30,000.

Seleucus' building program in Syria was evidence of his intention to orient his empire to the W and to press his claims on Palestine, which Ptolemy I Soter controlled. Although Antioch-on-the-Orontes eventually became the capital of the Seleucid empire, it is likely that Seleucus himself considered Seleucia more important. It was the first city he built following his victory over Antigonus at the battle of Ipsus in 301 B.C. He established a mint there and chose it as his burial place.

Seleucia's importance was not simply a matter of imperial vanity. Its location on the sea made it a communications and commercial center. Its acropolis was almost impregnable. The city's most serious disadvantage was that it was too far from the intersection of the major land routes that connected the Euphrates, Asia Minor, and central and S Syria. The need to control these land routes led to the emergence of Antioch-on-the-Orontes as the capital of the Seleucid empire after the death of Seleucus I.

Seleucia Pieria was the site of the tomb of Seleucus I. Antiochus I, his son and successor, deified his father by identifying him with Zeus. Antiochus built a temple in his father's honor called the Nicatorium. The city became the center of the private cult that honored Seleucus I.

Under Antiochus I Seleucia became a flourishing commercial center and formidable fortress protecting Antioch-on-the-Orontes. The commercial importance of the region encircled by the Syrian Tetrapolis goes back to the 3d millennium B.C., as attested by the discoveries at Ebla (Tell Mardikh). This region served to connect the Tigris with the Mediterranean and was at the axis of intersecting trade routes.

Seleucia also had strategic military importance. Seleucia and Ephesus were the two principal naval bases of the Seleucid empire. During the Third Syrian War, Seleucia Pieria fell to Ptolemy III. The Egyptians controlled the city from 245 to 219 B.C. Mastery of Seleucia Pieria was central to any military strategy that aimed to control the Seleucid empire. Dan 11:7–9 does not refer by name to the battle for Seleucia or the principals involved, but the text clearly refers to the events of Seleucia's capitulation to the Egyptian forces. The fortress of the "king of the north" that Dan 11:7 mentions is probably Seleucia.

Seleucia remained under Egyptian control until the reign of Antiochus III ("the Great"). He retook the city at the beginning of his war with Ptolemy IV Philopater. Antiochus III thus eliminated Ptolemaic presence in Seleucia just a few miles from his capital at Antioch. The Ptolemies made no serious effort to retake Seleucia since the city was too far from Egypt for them to exercise meaningful control over it. Also it made diplomatic sense for the Egyptians to end their provocative presence near the heart of the Seleucid domains.

This did not mean that the desire of the Ptolemies to control Syria-Palestine ended with their departure from Seleucia. This city was the key to political, military, and economic domination of the region. In the middle of the 2d century B.C. when the Egyptians wanted to retake Syria-Palestine from the Seleucids, they had to move against Seleucia. According to 1 Macc 11:8, Ptolemy VI Philometor succeeded in taking Seleucia and several other cities along the Mediterranean coast in 146 B.C. (1 Maccabees refers to the city as "Seleucia by the sea.") Later Ptolemy VI entered the Seleucid capital at Antioch and had himself proclaimed king of the Seleucid empire. Ptolemaic control continued until 138 B.C., when Antiochus VII Sidetes landed in force at Seleucia and there had himself proclaimed king.

Seleucia remained under Syrian control until the Roman period. Pompey granted Seleucia the status of a free city because it resisted the kings of Armenia and Pontus who challenged Roman hegemony in the ANE by invading Syria-Palestine. The anti-Roman coalition got as far as Jerusalem before Pompey defeated them and brought everything W of the Euphrates under the jurisdiction of Rome.

The role of Seleucia Pieria as a port is apparent from several references in the NT. In A.D. 49, Paul, Barnabas, and Mark sailed from Seleucia on the first Christian missionary journey (Acts 13:4). When the missionaries returned, Acts 14:26 says that they "sailed back to Antioch." Though the latter text does not mention Seleucia, it is probable that the three landed at the port from which they began their journey. It is less likely that they continued sailing up the Orontes to Antioch. It is likewise probable that it was at the port of Seleucia that Paul and Silas parted company with Mark and Barnabas at the beginning of the second missionary journey (Acts 15:39–41).

Seleucia continued to have strategic importance throughout the Roman period. It was the home base of an imperial fleet in the 1st century A.D. so the Roman emperors maintained the port at Seleucia. This was a costly project since the area was not a natural harbor. Contemporaneous with the First Jewish Revolt against Rome in Palestine (A.D. 66–70), the Romans under Vespasian and Titus built a canal in solid rock to divert the waters from a mountain stream that caused regular flooding in the harbor area. At the beginning of the 4th century A.D., Roman soldiers who worked on deepening the harbor mutinied. Although the civilian population of Seleucia and Antioch helped put down the mutiny, the Roman authorities blamed the Christians for inciting the rebellion (Libanus *Antiochikos,* 158–62; Eusebius *Hist. Eccl.* 8.6.8). This became an excuse for a persecution of the city's Christian community. In A.D. 346 Constantius completed a new harbor to improve the movement of military supplies. This brought the city new economic prosperity. The port at Seleucia required regular maintenance. When the eclipse of its harbor took place in the Byzantine period, maintenance ceased, the harbor silted up, and it became a swamp, as it remains today.

The site of ancient Seleucia Pieria was excavated along with Antioch-on-the-Orontes between 1937 and 1939. The most impressive structure found on the acropolis was a large (36 by 19 m) Doric temple. Excavation of the upper city revealed Roman-period villas that were decorated with polychrome mosaic floors. Surrounding the lower city were ramparts made of polygonal Hellenistic ashlars. At the entrance of the lower tower there is a Hellenistic period monumental gate to the market area that was reused in the Roman period as a fortress. Little remains of the theater built in the Roman period. The most significant remains in the lower city is a Byzantine period cross-shaped martyrion with an adjoining choir and baptistery. Just N of the site 1,300 m of Vespasian's canal is visible. Also outside the lower city were several cemeteries with sarcophagi from the Roman period. The more modest tombs of Roman sailors occupy the area between the canal and the port.

Bibliography

Downey, G. 1961. *A History of Antioch in Syria.* Princeton.

———. 1963. *Ancient Antioch.* Princeton.

Finegan, J. 1959. *Light from the Ancient Past.* 2d ed. Princeton.

Millar, F. 1987. The Problem of Hellenistic Syria. Pp. 110–33 in *Hellenism in the East,* ed. A. Kuhrt and S. Sherwin-White. Berkeley.

Seyrig, H. 1968. Seleucus I and the Foundation of Hellenistic Syria. Pp. 53–63 in *The Role of the Phoenicians in the Interaction of Mediterranean Civilization,* ed. W. A. Ward. Beirut. Repr. 1970. Antiquités Syriennes, 92: Séleucus I et al fondation de la monarchie syrienne. *Syr* 47: 290–311.

Stillwell, R., ed. 1941. *Antioch-on-the-Orontes* III. *The Excavations, 1937–1939.* Princeton.

LESLIE J. HOPPE

SELEUCIDS. See SELEUCUS; PALESTINE, ADMINISTRATION OF (SELEUCID). See also ANTIOCHUS.

SELEUCUS (PERSON). Name of the founder of the line of Greek-speaking kings of Syria and adjacent areas after the death of Alexander the Great. Hence the line, which lasted more or less continuously from ca. 321 B.C. to 64 B.C., is known as the Seleucid dynasty, the rulers as the Seleucidae. It is of biblical interest because the kings' policies of Hellenization, while bringing them into conflict with the Jews (particularly during the reign of Antiochus Epiphanes, 175–164 B.C.), nevertheless prepared the ground in which Christianity was eventually to flourish, the city of Antioch among others being a Seleucid foundation. The Seleucid era, beginning 1 October 312 B.C. in Syria and on New Year's Day, 1 Nisan (=3 April) 311 B.C., in Babylonia, is also important for chronological purposes.

1. *Seleucus I Nicator* ("victor") (312/311–281 B.C.). Born ca. 358 B.C., son of the Macedonian Antiochus, a general of Philip. After distinguished service as one of the generals of Alexander the Great, he was made chiliarch (commander of 1000 men) under Perdiccas, protector of the kingdom, on the first division of Alexander's empire (323 B.C.). In the second division made after Perdiccas' murder (321 B.C.) he became satrap of Babylon, but subsequent struggles among the Diadochi (successors to Alexander) saw him forced by Antigonus to flee to Egypt (316 B.C.). With Ptolemy's help (Dan 11:5 refers to Seleucus as "one of his princes"), he regained Babylon in 312 B.C. after Ptolemy's victory over Antigonus' forces at Gaza. He soon added Media and Susiana to his domains and between 311 and 306 B.C. continued to expand to the E, eventually reaching as far as NW India (his territories there were ceded to Chandragupta, ca. 304 B.C., in exchange for 500 elephants).

After the assassination of Alexander's sons (310–309 B.C.), the Diadochi declared themselves kings and Seleucus followed suit in 305 B.C. In 301 B.C., in alliance with Lysimachus, he defeated Antigonus at Ipsus and so gained control of Syria, much of Asia Minor and, more important, access to the Mediterranean. His policy now became oriented more to the west, with the establishment of Antioch (300 B.C.) as a new W capital (although Seleuceia, the E capital, was to remain important) and the foundation in Asia Minor of several other great cities designed to foster the spread of Hellenism. The Jews whom he settled in them were also granted citizen rights (Appian, *Syr.* 57; *Ant* 12.3.1 §119).

In 281 B.C. Seleucus consolidated his hold on Asia Minor by the defeat of Lysimachus at Corupedium. He was now poised to take over the Macedonian throne and thus reunify most of Alexander's empire, but en route to Europe he was murdered at Lysimacheia in Thrace by Ptolemy's exiled elder son, Ptolemy Ceraunus.

2. *Seleucus II Callinicus* ("glorious in victory") (246–225 B.C.). Born ca. 265 B.C., the oldest son of Antiochus II and Laodice. His reign saw a disintegration of the Seleucid empire that, despite his efforts, was reversed only under his son Antiochus the Great. Bactria and Parthia became independent, while in the W, Asia Minor was temporarily lost as a result of an invasion by Ptolemy III of Egypt in reprisal for Laodice's murder of his sister Berenice (Third Syrian [or Laodicean] War, 246–241 B.C.; Dan 11:7–9 alludes to this). Seleucus soon regained control of Antioch, but his attempts to recapture all the territory seized by Ptolemy in the E were further hampered by a rebellion in Asia Minor by his younger brother Antiochus Hierax, supported by Laodice. He died in 225 B.C. of a fall from his horse.

3. *Seleucus III Soter* ("savior") (225–223 B.C.). Elder son of Seleucus II, he attempted to recover Asia Minor but was murdered by conspirators while on campaign against Attalus I of Pergamum. He was succeeded by his brother Antiochus the Great; Dan 11:10 alludes to them ("his sons").

4. *Seleucus IV Philopator* ("father loving") (187–175 B.C.). Son of Antiochus the Great and co-ruler with him after the Romans defeated Antiochus at Magnesia in 190 B.C. The terms of the treaty of Apamea (188 B.C.) imposed by the Romans had not only prevented him from pursuing any Seleucid claims to Asia Minor W of the Taurus but had also imposed a huge indemnity. Seleucus had plans to pay this by confiscating the funds in the treasury of the High Temple, but his minister Heliodorus is said to have been prevented from entering the sanctuary by the monstrous apparition of a mounted rider (2 Macc 3:7–39; 5:18; there is also an allusion in Dan 11:20). After a comparatively peaceful reign Seleucus was murdered by Heliodorus in an unsuccessful coup d'état. He was succeeded by his younger brother Antiochus IV Epiphanes.

Bibliography

Bevan, E. R. 1902. *The House of Seleucus.* 2 vols. London.

Bouché-Leclerq, A. 1913–14. *Histoire des Séleucides (232–64 avant J.-C.).* 2 vols. Paris.

Préaux, C. 1978. *Le monde hellénistique.* 2 vols. Nouvelle Clio 6. Paris.

Seyrig, H. 1968. Seleucus I and the Foundation of Hellenistic Syria. Pp. 53–63 in *The Role of the Phoenicians in the Interaction of Mediterranean Civilizations,* ed. W. A. Ward. Beirut.

Will, E. 1979. *Histoire politique du monde hellénistique (323–30 avant J.-C.).* Vol. 1. 2d ed. Nancy.

JOHN WHITEHORNE

SEMACHIAH (PERSON) [Heb *sĕmakyāhû*]. This name, which means "Yahweh has supported," occurs once in the OT. It also appears in a shortened form, *smky,* in the Elephantine correspondence (*CAP,* 49.1). (Compare also AHISAMACH.) Named as the sixth and last son of Shemaiah, firstborn of Obed-edom, Semachiah is listed among the gatekeepers at the temple in Jerusalem in 1 Chr 26:7. The list in which his name occurs (1 Chr 26:4–8) appears to be the contribution of a reviser of the Chronicler's organization of the gatekeepers (Williamson *Chronicles* NCBC, 169–70; Rudolph *Chronikbücher* HAT, 173).

J. S. ROGERS

SEMANTICS. The scientific study of the meaning of linguistic signs.

A. Lexical Meaning of Words
B. Contextual Meaning of Words
C. Phrases and Sentences
D. Grammatical Categories
E. Ethnological and Sociological Categories

A. Lexical Meaning of Words

Although linguistic signs apply to all levels of language from morphemes and words to paragraphs and total discourses, it has long been assumed that semantics is primarily the study of the meaning of words. Earlier writings on semantics were even more restricted; they were concerned mainly with the historical development of words and their meanings. Within such a framework it was believed that *words* were the basic semantic elements, each having an inherent original meaning underlying all later developments. Words were thus said to have a "basic" or "real" meaning to be recognized for the proper understanding of an utterance. This approach to meaning, called etymology, was for many centuries the core of semantics. During the 20th century, however, etymology became restricted to the mere history of words and their change of meanings, while semantics emerged as the study of the relationship between meaning (defined as the content of what people intend to communicate) and the linguistic signs used to express such meanings.

This new perspective is based on the insight that "the meaning of a word" is not a statement about something a word "has" as a "possession," but merely that meaning is conveyed by *using* words as conventional linguistic signs to convey certain features of meaning. It further involves the implication that meaning is primary, words secondary. This shift in orientation from "word" ⟶ "meaning" to "meaning" ⟶ "word" had a significant implication for semantics in suggesting that the meaning of a word cannot be properly expressed merely by substituting another word. Therefore, *paradidōmi* in Greek does not "mean" *betray* in English, but is a Greek term denoting a meaning for which the English term *betray* can be used in certain contexts.

The relevant meaning for which *paradidōmi* is used in Greek comprises a set of semantic features, namely, (1) an interpersonal activity, (2) involving the handing over of someone (either of the in-group or the out-group) to an authority, (3) to deal with such a person according to will or jurisdiction, and (4) usually implying punishment. In English this same set of semantic features can be largely expressed by terms such as *betray, hand over, turn over to,* etc. The term *betray* will not signify an out-group person, while *hand over* or *turn over to* usually do not pertain to an in-group person though it could be used of such a person in certain contexts. *Betray* is semantically more marked than *hand over* or *turn over to. Betray* also involves a component of lack of loyalty which is not signified by *paradidōmi.* The meaning denoted by *paradidōmi* is closer in semantic space to that of *hand over* than to that of *betray.* Nevertheless, the English terms are close enough to be used to translate *paradidōmi* in particular contexts. They are not "meanings" of *paradidōmi;* they are "translational equivalents."

The semantics of words is based upon the fact that the position of a word in an utterance is restricted by its lexical environment. The meaning of *bank* in "go to the bank and cash this check" is different from *bank* in "bank more earth along the fence" or "you can bank on him to do the job" or "she banked the plane to avoid the tower." The same word may be used to signify quite different meanings.

On the contrary, one may use different words to communicate the same meaning. For "bank more earth" one may say "pile (up) more earth" or "heap (up) more earth." Though there may be some subtle difference in meaning between *pile, heap* and *bank,* it is a remarkable characteristic of language that semantically there is much more in common between different words used to convey essentially the same meaning than between the so-called different meanings of a single word. This fact implies that words function within semantic "fields" or "domains."

In the domain of interpersonal activities involving helping and taking care of, the meaning "to assist someone in supplying what may be needed" (often rendered in English by "help") is conveyed in the Greek NT by *paristamai* (Rom 6:2), *antilambanomai* (Acts 20:35), *epilambanomai* (Heb 2:16), *antechomai* (1 Thess 5:14), *eparkeo* (1 Tim 5:10), *boētheo* (Mark 9:22) and *boētheia* (Heb 4:16), *sumballomai* (Acts 18:27) and *hupolambano* (3 John 8). Though many native speakers undoubtedly would have sensed some subtle contrastive features of meaning, even if these were only of a connotative type or pertained to different levels of formality (since absolute synonyms are not a regular feature of language), the use of *paristamai* in Rom 6:2 is so close in semantic space to the use of the other terms occurring for this same meaning that one can hardly, on the basis of our limited contexts and distance in historical and cultural space, determine any significant contrastive semantic features.

On the other hand, *paristamai* in Rom 6:2 differs considerably in semantic space from *paristamai* in John 19:26, "to stand near or alongside of someone" or in Acts 27:23, "to come to be present at a particular place." The etymological approach to semantics would have tried to find some underlying core connection between these meanings. Such a connection, however, is generally quite artificial and misleading in that it tends to emphasize issues that are very remote and even petty. In semantics it is not so much a matter of comparing the same words, but rather the same meanings. Exegetically this implies that the same word in different passages is no true guide for equating the contents of the passages. Rather, the same meaning expressed, even by different words, should be pursued, and those passages will have a shared semantic feature.

Though in some instances it seems difficult to define the difference in meaning between terms belonging to the same semantic domain, it is important to be alert to possible differences, since in many other instances a semantic domain will highlight the significant contrastive features. For example, in the domain of forgiveness, Greek can use *aphiēmi* for the meaning "to remove guilt resulting from wrongdoing," while *charizomai* denotes "to remove guilt resulting from wrongdoing," but on the basis of one's gracious attitude toward the guilty individual. In both instances one may translate by using English words such as *pardon, forgive, overlook, condone,* etc. Yet the Greek terms differ, not with respect to the difference in meaning of the English translational terms, but in at least one crucial component, namely, that *aphiēmi* is a generic term, while *charizomai* focuses on the attitude of the person doing the forgiving.

The type of semantic relationship exhibited by the foregoing examples may be called contiguous. They are similar in meaning, though they differ mainly in one crucial semantic feature. Other semantic domains may have a hierarchical relationship as in animal-mammal-canine-dog-poodle. Terms such as alienate/reconcile, lend/borrow, hot/cold, and old/young constitute complementary sets in which the semantic components are very similar though reverse in sequence or orientation. A fourth type of relationship involves overlapping in that the terms are maximally similar in meaning and can be used almost interchangeably, as in the set involving *paristamai* above. These differ only in subtle issues of usage or association.

B. Contextual Meaning of Words

What has been discussed above may be called the lexical meanings of words, that is, what a particular word in and of itself contributes to the understanding of an utterance. This type of meaning should be distinguished from a further level of meaning, namely, contextual meaning involving the reference, usage, and inference of lexical meanings in a context. The Hebrew term *bĕʾēr* means lexically a deep hole in the ground, such as a well or pit, but in Ps 69:16 it occurs in a figurative context, "let not the pit close its mouth over me," in which the reference is probably to the underworld. In Greek *skeuos* is a highly generic term for any kind of container, but in the context of Luke 8:16 the reference seems to be to a bowl or bucket, while in Acts 10:11 it is a sheet used as a container. Closely related is the difference between meaning and usage. The Hebrew *tôʿēbâ* means "something that is highly offensive, to the extent of being abominable." It may be used of various activities such as Egyptians eating with Hebrews (Gen 43:32), homosexual relations (Lev 18:22), unclean animals (Deut 14:3), foreign gods (Deut 32:16), unaccepted customs (1 Kgs 14:24), etc. Yet, it still means "something abominable," the usages are merely examples of abominable entities or activities and are not part of either the lexical or the contextual meaning of the term. Usage is thus much more generic than reference. Yet another distinction should be made, namely, the difference between meaning and inference. In Jer 31:39, "the measuring line shall extend straight forward over the hill," the Heb word *neged* can be translated by "straight forward" or "straight ahead," though its lexical meaning is merely "a position in front of something." In Jer 31:39 the inference of a surveyor's line extending before a person is that it runs straight ahead. One should carefully avoid reading into a word's lexical meaning features derived from other items in a context. Contextual meaning, whether reference, usage, or inference, can be expressed in translating a passage, but not in defining the meaning of a word as such.

C. Phrases and Sentences

Semantics extends beyond the lexical and contextual meanings of words. Phrases and sentences also have multiple meanings and as such they comprise all the distinctions made with regard to the meaning of words. Paragraphs and even total discourses can exhibit similar distinctions. Phrases such as "the book of Moses" may be understood as "the book belonging to Moses" or "the book Moses wrote" or even "the book about Moses." The same phrase may thus have different meanings, and each meaning can be semantically expressed by other phrases or sentences, e.g., "Moses owns a book" or "the book which is in the possession of Moses" or "the book Moses has," etc. Phrases, sentences, paragraphs, etc., can also have reference, usage, and inference. Their meanings can also be defined componentially, but though a larger stretch of language is constituted by the combined data of its members, the meaning is not the sum total of the units. A sentence such as "it is going to rain" can, on the basis of its word level, be understood as meaning that water will fall from clouds onto the ground. Yet a person may pronounce such a sentence to communicate various other meanings in addition to what the word level signifies, e.g., "there will be no tennis today" or "the crops might be saved" or "shelter should be sought." These are inferential meanings of the above sentence, and they function as speech-acts to prompt behavior. The same applies to the meanings of paragraphs and larger discourses. Each level of linguistic structure adds its features to eventually communicate a specific notion.

What makes semantics so extremely complex is that each structure may allow multiple combinations. A sentence such as "I saw his children in Boston" may be interpreted as "I was in Boston and saw his children there" (linking "in Boston" more closely with "I saw") or "I was in Boston and saw his children who live there" (linking "in Boston" more closely with "his children"). Meaning, therefore, is also expressed by the structural arrangement of an utterance.

The syntax of a sentence may allow for different linkages. Some may be as overt as in the above sentence. Others may have a semantic structure that seems somewhat obscure. In Ps 48:2, "the mountain of his holiness," the term "holiness" is syntactically linked to "his," though semantically it pertains to "mountain," meaning "his holy mountain." In Acts 9:36 it is said of Tabitha that she was "full of good works." The term "full" is syntactically linked to "she," yet semantically it designates the quantity of her deeds—"she did many good works." Syntax and semantics are not necessarily related in a direct one-to-one correspondence.

As with words, sentences may not only have more than one meaning, but practically the same meaning may also be conveyed by a number of different sentences. Because sentences are more complex than words, the different sentence structures a speaker may use to communicate almost the same idea can be rather numerous. To reprimand a person, several stylistic choices may be employed, depending on the foci and the harshness of the reprimand. One might say "do not ever be late again," or "I see you tried to be on time," or "I am glad you could make it." The responses elicited by these utterances may be quite varied, depending on the context in which they are used. Yet from the practical context the receptor will know that primarily a reprimand is communicated. The multiple choices are essentially a matter of style.

The semantics of style is extremely varied and complex since it also relates to the communication functions of language, often termed expressive, informative, emotive, imperative, phatic, etc. A phatic statement such as "how do you do" has meaning in the sense of communicating goodwill and acceptance to a certain extent, though its word-level meaning may be zero. One may say "do this" as a direct command, but the imperative function may also be expressed by "may I ask you to do this for me?"—a question used not to elicit information, but to give a command. Though the function may be the same, the meaning of the command can have quite different inferential semantic components, such as authoritarian versus cordial, or advice versus pleading. Informative speech may often use present tenses of the verb to foreground statements while narrative tenses are used to supply background information. These semantic features are quite subtle and depend largely on the wider discourse structure. Nevertheless, they have important semantic content.

Discourses are semantically arranged by the clustering of units into structural patterns. The theme may occur at the beginning and be explained by enlarging on the same topic. Or one may develop various aspects of a theme and then present the theme as a summary statement. It is also possible to combine these by having the theme in the center of a paragraph. What is important is not so much the types of structural patterns of a discourse, but the extent of its semantic unity in contrast with preceding and following thematic units. The relationships between the constituent units have considerable semantic implications for a receptor's understanding of a passage.

D. Grammatical Categories

Semantics also involves grammatical meaning, such as word order conventions which in some languages may mark the subject of a sentence, conventions of concord marking the immediate constituents in a sentence, or the use of coordination and subordination marking the relationship between nuclear structures. In a sentence such as "she did not respond; she remained silent" the two synonymous expressions are coordinated into one utterance for the sake of emphasis. Coordinate grammatical constructions may also involve different expressions to highlight the range of a discourse setting, to contrast, or to compare. Subordinate grammatical constructions are even more complex and, therefore, semantically more varied in their effect. In "there were many reports of how he has bribed the officials," the subordinate construction involves the content of the report. Likewise, one may have clauses of manner, setting, cause, reason, result, condition, or concession expressed by different subordinate constructions. All these relations are utilized by receptors to analyze and interpret an utterance, and to sense any important semantic implications.

Grammatical categories also involve a number of communication strategies, such as speech perspectives and registers (or levels) of language. One may view a past event from the perspective of its *occurrence* at a particular point in time, as in "Christ died for us," or from the perspective of what happened as a *state of affairs,* e.g., "Christ has died for us." Semantically such a state highlights the present reality of an event. The meaning of tense forms is often a matter of speech perspectives, but nominalization as a stylistic alternative may also focus on a state; for example, "his reputation is impeccable," nominalizes "what people have reported about him." Speech registers are likewise important strategies. Formal speech differs in many ways from casual speech. Frozen language, as in some legal documents or in religious ritual, may have little denotative content, but they contribute significantly to the solemnity of the occasion and as such can influence the understanding of the receptor by means of impact and appeal.

E. Ethnological and Sociological Categories

Semantics also involves ethnological and sociological concerns. People often tend to think of words or sentences wholly in terms of psychological entities, especially the relationship between the referent and the concept. An expression taken at face value may be interpreted quite differently within a particular ethnological and sociological framework. In Acts 14:8–18, where Paul and Barnabas were mistaken for gods, they "tore their clothes." The significance of this action was once misinterpreted by people from a particular culture as indicating that Paul and Barnabas were happy because they were regarded as gods; but in the cultural context of the text of Acts, Paul and Barnabas were expressing their utter indignation with the total misunderstanding of the people they were trying to preach to.

The ethnological and sociological framework within which language is used has a considerable impact on the semantic interpretation of an utterance in a given situation. Linguistic semantics cannot be studied apart from the semiotics of cultures and customs. Therefore, though semantics is primarily concerned with linguistic signs, the interpretation of linguistic utterances cannot be disassociated from ethnological and sociological concerns. The same applies to psychological attitudes peculiar to particular individuals or cultures. Likewise, logical considerations play an important part in semantics insofar as they focus on the validity of propositions. An expression such as "this man is a woman" may be interpreted logically as a contradiction, while in a particular sociological context it may be understood as meaning "the person you are referring to as a man is in fact a woman," or in another context, "this man is very effeminate."

These issues are very important for the response of receptors to linguistic discourses. People generally understand utterances in terms of their personal presuppositions. A person's ideological beliefs, especially political or religious convictions, have a direct bearing on how language is interpreted. In fact, the mere words and sentences often contribute much less to people's final reaction to a stretch of language than do their presuppositions.

Semantics is essentially an interpretative procedure. Though one may say that semantics primarily has to do with the meaning of linguistic items, the interpretive acts performed by receptors assign meaning to an utterance in terms of an extremely complex network of interrelated features. Every use of language by someone has to do with meaning and understanding, and as such, semantics is perhaps the most crucial component of language.

Bibliography

Barr, J. 1961. *Semantics of Biblical Language.* Oxford.

Basso, K. H., and Selby, H. A., eds. 1976. *Meaning in Antropology.* Albuquerque.

Chafe, W. 1970. *Meaning and the Structure of Language.* Chicago.

Chomsky, N. 1972. *Studies on Semantics in Generative Grammar.* The Hague.

Cruse, D. A. 1986. *Lexical Semantics.* Cambridge.

Davies, E. C. 1979. *On the Semantics of Syntax.* London.

Fillmore, C. J., and Langendoen, D. T., eds. 1971. *Studies in Linguistic Semantics.* New York.
Hervey, S. G. J. 1979. *Axiomatic Semantics.* Edinburgh.
Katz, J. J., and Fodor, J. A. 1963. The Structure of a Semantic Theory. *Language* 39: 170–210.
Kempson, R. M. 1977. *Semantic Theory.* Cambridge.
Landman, F., and Veltman, F., eds. 1984. *Varieties of Formal Semantics.* Dordrecht.
Leech, G. 1981. *Semantics.* New York.
Lehrer, A. 1974. *Semantic Fields and Lexical Structure.* New York.
Louw, J. P. 1982. *Semantics of New Testament Greek.* Philadelphia.
———, ed. 1985. *Lexicography and Translation.* Cape Town.
Miller, J. 1985. *Semantics and Syntax.* Cambridge.
Nida, E. A., 1975a. *Exploring Semantic Structures.* Munich.
———. 1975b. *Componential Analysis of Meaning.* The Hague.
———. 1986. Meaning vs. Reference—The Touchstone of Lexicography. *Language Sciences* 3: 51–57.
Pulman, S. G. 1983. *Word Meaning and Belief.* London.
Raskin, V. 1975. *A Concise History of Linguistic Semantics.* Jerusalem.
Weinrich, U. 1980. *On Semantics.* Philadelphia.
Wierzbicka, A. 1980. *Lingua Mentalis: The Semantics of Natural Language.* Sydney.

JOHANNES P. LOUW

SEMEIA SOURCE. See SIGNS/SEMEIA SOURCE.

SEMEIN (PERSON) [Gk *Semein*]. The father of Mattathias and son of Josech, according to Luke's genealogy tying Joseph, the "supposed father" of Jesus, to descent from Adam and God (Luke 3:26). Codex D omits Semein, substituting a genealogy adapted from Matt 1:6–15 for Luke 3:23–31. Although there are names similar in form in the Hebrew Bible and the LXX (e.g., Exod 6:17: Heb *šmʿy,* Gk *semei;* 1 Chr 5:4: Heb *šmʿyh* and *šmʿy,* Gk *semei*), the only use of significance is in 1 Chr 3:19, where a Heb *šmʿy* and Gk *semei* is said to be the son of Pedaiah and brother of Zerubbabel. Kuhn (1923: 212), however, claims that a number of the names in the list in 1 Chr 3:19ff. were transposed in transmission. Kuhn's proposal has not gained adherents, not least because it is questionable on other grounds how closely Luke follows 1 Chronicles (Jeremias 1969: 295–96). Most scholars believe that reference to Semein as an ancestor of Jesus occurs nowhere else in biblical documents, including Matthew's genealogy, and that he falls within a list of seventeen otherwise unknown descendants of David's son Nathan (Fitzmyer *Luke 1–9* AB, 500).

Bibliography

Jeremias, J. 1969. *Jerusalem in the Time of Jesus.* Philadelphia.
Kuhn, G. 1923. Die Geschlechtsregister Jesu bei Lukas und Matthäus, nach ihrer Herkunft untersucht. *ZNW* 22: 206–28.

STANLEY E. PORTER

SEMITIC LANGUAGES. See LANGUAGES (INTRODUCTORY SURVEY).

SEMITIC OSTRACA. See OSTRACA, SEMITIC.

SEMITICISMS IN THE NT. A "semiticism" (or "semitism") in the NT is an aberration of language or style which suggests influence, direct or indirect, of Aramaic or Hebrew upon the Greek. The category includes elements of diction which (1) deviate from known Greek usage so as to conform with natural Aramaic or Hebrew idiom or style, or (2) though attested in Greek are relatively more frequent in the NT, possibly because they happen to coincide with normal Aramaic or Hebrew use.

A. Introduction
B. Identification of Semiticisms
  1. Linguistic Criteria
  2. Dialect Models for Aramaic and Hebrew
  3. Aramaic or Hebrew?
C. Types of NT Semiticisms
  1. Lexical
  2. Syntactic
D. Interpretation

A. Introduction

The detection of semiticisms in the Greek (or Latin) texts of certain noncanonical works (e.g., *1 Enoch*) led scholars to posit Aramaic or Hebrew originals for them, and in a number of cases Semitic originals were subsequently discovered. The better a Greek translation of a Semitic original, the harder it will be to detect as such: only stray traces of the Semitic prehistory may remain. Translation need not be the only explanation of semiticisms: bilingualism would give many similar effects. Both possibilities must therefore be kept in view.

It has also been fashionable to look for another cause of NT semiticisms: imitation (conscious or unconscious) of the Greek style of the LXX. While this may have been a factor, it is of little explanatory help except where the semiticisms in question (1) reflect biblical Hebrew idioms, (2) occur with fair frequency in the LXX as we have it, and (3) are not allusions to some specific OT passage. (Septuagintisms in the gospel of Luke are discussed by Fitzmyer *Luke I–IX* AB, 114–18.) A subtler variant of this explanation is that the NT author involved may have sought to impart realism to his work by making his characters speak the kind of Greek which his prospective readers might recognize as "Jewish." But that still means that the semiticisms need to be noticed as such. Such theories really relate to the manner of composition of a writer and tend to presuppose what they seek to prove. Interpretation of semiticisms should follow, not precede, their identification.

The essential problems of the semiticisms of the NT are thus how to isolate and identify them, and how to interpret them.

B. Identification of Semiticisms

1. Linguistic Criteria. The Hebrew and Aramaic texts from Qumran, Masada, Murabbaʿat, and Naḥal Ḥever, along with coins and inscriptions, reveal that in the first two centuries C.E. (and probably earlier also) Aramaic, Greek, and two types of Hebrew (akin to classical and Mishnaic Hebrew respectively) were in use in Palestine. The vital role of Aramaic in the language and life of Jesus and his early followers appears from the various transliterated Aramaic words and sentences attributed to him or to the early church in the NT, usually followed by a Greek translation or explanation. Examples include *Talitha koum(i)* (Mark 5:41), *ephphatha* (Mark 7:34), *abba* (Mark 14:36 = Rom 8:15, Gal 4:6), and *eloī eloī* (or: *ēli ēli* Matt) *lama sabachthan(e)i* (Mark 15:34, Matt 27:46 = *Tg. Ps* 22:1a). It is natural that Jesus should have uttered his cry of distress on the cross in his native language, and that he should have addressed the comatose daughter of Jairus in hers (Wilcox 1982: 470, 476). Hebrew words also occur. Among these is *hosanna* (Mark 11:9, 10; Matt 21:9; John 12:13; *Did.* 10:6; cf. Ps 118:25), while *korban* (Mark 7:11) may be either. These tiny scraps of evidence give valuable clues to the type of Aramaic (and/or Hebrew) spoken by Jesus and his circle, but they do not mean that he or they spoke only Aramaic or only Hebrew.

The linguistic data thus favor the presumption that the influence of Aramaic (and/or Hebrew) upon Greek is reflected in at least some parts of the NT. This presumption will be all the stronger where the material or traditions in question appear to have emerged from circles in which Aramaic or Hebrew was the native language.

However, a particularly intractable problem is that of knowing just what was not grammatical in Greek. Many expressions once thought due to Aramaic or Hebrew influence have been traced in the nonliterary Greek papyri and other sources more or less contemporary with the NT. However, even if an apparent semiticism in the NT does happen to coincide with an expression attested in such Greek material, that does not mean that *in its NT context* the linguistic element involved is not a semiticism. In some cases the Greek of the papyri may have been affected by another local language, such as Aramaic or Coptic (Lefort 1928: 152–60; *DBSup* 3: 1353). But then some of the NT material or its basic tradition did in fact emerge from Aramaic- or Hebrew-speaking circles. However, where an apparent semiticism does turn up in the Greek papyri, it is probably wise to allow it no more than a supporting role in the argument, and then only where Semitic influence in the NT context is indicated on other grounds.

Next, the fact that Biblical Hebrew was in use in the NT period means that apparent "septuagintisms" must be examined carefully, for they may indeed be genuine cases of Hebrew influence after all. The use of the term "Heaven" in Luke 15:18, 21 as a substitute for the Divine Name can hardly be a septuagintism, while the language of Luke 1–2 has striking links with that of 4Q246 and related texts (Fitzmyer 1979: 93). Expressions like *kai egeneto* (= Hebrew *wyhy*) and *en tō* with the infinitive are very frequent in the LXX; although basically Hebraisms, they may, in the NT, be septuagintisms. Whether, say, in Luke or Acts, they are due to the author's choice or were taken over ready made from earlier material is an open question. These doubts mean that such expressions should not be used as evidence of direct Semitic influence.

A serious problem is what in fact constitutes a septuagintism. Thus, appeal is sometimes made here to expressions of a Semitic type which appear only a few times in the LXX. Such cases may indeed be allusions to the OT, but if not, their very rarity makes it highly questionable whether they could have been used by an author to give a work a "biblical" atmosphere. If they are not due to reflection of underlying Semitic tradition or material, they may possibly have crept into the author's style or text from liturgical or other ecclesiastical sources (Wilcox 1965: 65–86).

A suspected semiticism must of course be shown to be grammatical in Aramaic or Hebrew. But criteria must be established to determine (1) what kind of Aramaic or Hebrew is the source of the semiticism, and (b) how these languages can be distinguished from one another beneath the present Greek mask.

2. Dialect Models for Aramaic and Hebrew. Texts from which comparative data should be drawn ought ideally to meet certain conditions, namely:

1. They should be as close as possible to the NT in date and place (Fitzmyer and Harrington 1978: 420)
2. They should be extensive enough to give statistically reassuring samples of the language
3. They should embody literary forms akin to those in the NT
4. They should be free compositions, not translations
5. They should reflect spoken forms of the language.

The material from Qumran, Masada, Murabbaʿat, Naḥal Ḥever, and the contemporary epigraphic data may meet conditions (1), (2), and (4), and the apocalyptic texts may also help with cases like Mark 13 and Revelation. The Palestinian Targums, and parts of Talmud Yerushalmi and the Midrashic literature, satisfy (2), (3), (4), and (5), but not (1). An examination of the linguistic affinities of the transliterated Aramaic words in the NT shows coherence with the 1st and 2d century C.E. Aramaic texts, and also a suprisingly high correlation with the language of the Palestinian Targums. Indeed, a check of the Aramaisms claimed by Matthew Black (1967) for the Gospels and Acts showed that in the majority of cases where the early texts could be used, their evidence supported the arguments he had built on Targumic Aramaic (Wilcox 1985: 101; *ANRW* 2/25/2: 988–1007).

3. Aramaic or Hebrew? Two main problems arise here. First, where Mishnaic Hebrew differs from biblical Hebrew, it is often very close to Aramaic, especially in syntax but also in vocabulary. Examples of this include: (1) absence of the "consecutive" verbal construction; (2) use of the participle to express the present (far commoner in Aramaic and Mishnaic Hebrew than in biblical Hebrew); (3) the periphrastic tenses, use of the verb "to be" with a participle to form frequentative and iterative meanings; (4) use of 3d person plural of a finite verb or plural of a participle to indicate an indefinite subject (that is, "they" do x = "one" does x); (5) the relative particle *š*- or Aramaic *d-*, *dy*, to introduce circumstantial, causal, and (with prepositions) temporal clauses; (6) the ethic dative with *l-*; (7) the "proleptic pronoun": use of a personal pronoun either in the nominative or, with a preposition, in the oblique cases to anticipate a following noun (*ANRW* 2/25/2: 993). Second, there is now known to be a real possibility that biblical-type Hebrew may be involved. How are the two types of Hebrew to be distinguished? Aramaic can at times be distinguished from Hebrew (of either sort) through the presence of cognates in vocabulary: e.g., *ʿbd* in Hebrew is "to serve," in Aramaic "to do, make." But this raises the problem of supposed "mistranslations" as signs of semiticism. Of course, such "mistranslations" may in fact be due to bilingualism rather than to actual translation.

C. Types of NT Semiticisms

Apart from transliterated Aramaic and Hebrew, the following is a list of the more convincing examples of semiticisms in the NT.

1. Lexical. *alla* = *ei mē* or *ean mē*, "except." This use of *alla* has been traced in the Greek papyri (MM, 22), but in Mark 4:22, a saying of Jesus, may it not reflect an underlying *ʾlʾ* (Wellhausen 1911: 16–17)? Now *ʾlʾ* "except" does not seem to be attested in early Palestinian sources, but it is common in Targumic Aramaic, Samaritan Aramaic, Christian Palestinian Aramaic and in Mishnaic Hebrew. Semitic influence seems probable, but whether Hebrew or Aramaic is an open question.

anastēthi epi tous podas sou, "stand up upon your feet" (Acts 14:10). 4 Kgdms 13:21 is the only case of this in the LXX and Acts 14:10 does not seem to allude to that passage. The Aramaic idiom occurs in a number of mss of the Palestinian Targums to Gen 38:26 (or 38:25, *Tg. Neof.*), as A. J. Wensinck saw (unpublished note). The Hebrew form (with *ʿmd,* not *qwm*) is found in 1QS 6:13 = "to stand up," as also in *Sipra* (Emor, 14:3).

ginōskein eis, "to be aware of." Luke 19:44 (D it^{d}) has the strange form *ouk egnōs eis kairon episkopēs sou,* "you did not know (of) the time of your visitation," where the usual text reads *ton,* not *eis*. Black (1967: 115–16) looked to Aramaism; but the idiom he examined *(ydʿ b-)* occurs not only in 1QH frag. 1:3, 3:4, and 10:3 (?), but also in Mishnaic Hebrew with the meaning "to realize, know of, be aware of" (*m. B.Qam.* 10:8 "if its owners knew neither of its theft *[bgnybtw]* nor of its return *[bḥzyrtw]*"). It may thus be a Hebraism. The passage is in material peculiar to Luke.

eklegesthai en, "to choose from among." This construction in Acts 15:7 may reflect Aramaic *bḥr b-* (Torrey 1916: 7, 22). The Greek construction does occur in the LXX some 11 times, but the idiomatic translation (without *en*) predominates by far. The Hebrew idiom occurs at Qumran (1QS 4:22, 10:12, etc.) and in Mishnaic Hebrew. The Greek may be explained as either an Aramaism or a Hebraism.

einai/prostithenai epi to auto. The Qumran texts provide several examples of the Hebrew expressions *lhywt lyḥd* "to be in the fellowship" (1QS 5:2, 6:23, 8:12), and *lhwsyp lyḥd* "to join the fellowship" (1QS 5:7, 8:19, CD 13:11, 16:14). This may well explain the difficult words of Acts 2:47, giving the meaning "the Lord was daily bringing into membership of the fellowship" (Wilcox 1965: 93–100).

heuresthēnai eis, "to be found at." Wensinck saw this expression in Acts 8:40 as an Aramaism; cf. *y. Maʿas. Š.* 5:2, Pal. Tg. Gen 28:1 (MS Paris BN hebr. 110): *wʾskḥ bḥrn* (unpublished note; see Wilcox 1965: 100). Both passages (interestingly) narrate a miraculous event.

heuriskein, "to be able." The use of Aramaic *ʾskḥ,* "to find" in the sense "to be able," was noted by Wensinck (see Black 1967: 134) as a possible Semitic idiom behind the alternate replacement of the Greek verbs *dynasthai* and *ischyein/katischyein* with *heuriskein* in Codex Bezae (cf. Wellhausen 1911: 17). Wensinck cited the Targumic Tosefta to Gen 4:7. Aram *ʾskḥ* also occurs in the meaning "to be able" in 1QapGen 21:13 (the ordinary meaning "to find" being attested in 1QapGen 21:19; Fitzmyer and Harrington 1978: 423). Wellhausen and Wensinck are supported by Qumran Aramaic, and the Targumic data shown to be of greater value than sometimes held.

idou before expressions of time and number. The Greek evidence for this construction is somewhat late (papyri of the 4th–5th century C.E.), and there does not seem to be any Aramaic support for it. Connolly thought its use in Luke 13:16 due to Syriac influence (1936: 378–81). The Mishnaic Hebrew use of *hry* "lo" before totals of numbers and times (especially, months, years, etc.) may be relevant: see *m. B. Bat.* 3:1, *m. Sanh.* 1:6.

polis, "province." Torrey's solution of the problem of Luke 1:39, where *eis polin Iouda,* "to the city of Judah," would make better sense as "to the province of Judah," hinged upon the double meaning possible for Hebrew *mdynh* (or Aramaic *mdynʾ*) (1912: 290–91). The Aramaic case is now supported by documentary material from the NT period, for example, 1QapGen 20:28, 22:4, 5, where the word means "province," and *Meg. Taʿan.* 12, where it probably means "city" (*ANRW* 2/25/2: 1014). Interpretation of the passage as a semiticism is opposed by Fitzmyer (*Luke I–IX* AB, 363).

2. Syntactic. a. Verbal. (1) Participle as Simple Indicative. In Aramaic and later Hebrew (especially Mishnaic) the participle frequently acts as a finite verb, especially in the present tense. 4QAmram^{b} frag. 1:10 reads: "Lo, two were (lit: are) passing judgment (Aram *dʾnyn*) on me and saying (Aram *ʾmryn*)." NT examples include Acts 10:19, *idou andres (duo) zētountes se* "lo, (two) men are looking for you," 14:3 (D), Rev 1:16; 6:5 (Wilcox 1965: 122–23; *ANRW* 2/25/2: 1016). The idiom does occur in the papyri occasionally, but in the NT it may be a semiticism; whether it calques Aramaic or Hebrew is not clear.

(2) Periphrastic Tenses. The use of the participle with the verb "to be" to represent a continuous aspect (especially the imperfect) is known in Greek, though the construction is not a major feature of Hellenistic Greek. It is found in Hebrew, but is quite usual in Aramaic, Syriac, and Mishnaic Hebrew, and is common in the texts from the NT period from the land of Israel. NT examples include Rev 1:18 "and lo! I am alive *(zōn eimi)* for evermore" (Beyer 1961: 199).

(3) Impersonal 3d Person Plural. The 3d person plural active of a finite verb may be used in Hebrew and Aramaic to represent an indefinite subject or the passive voice. Wellhausen noted the impersonal plural as a NT semiticism (1911: 18). Examples include: Mark 15:27: "and with him they crucify two robbers"; Acts 3:2: *hon etithoun* "whom they used to put" = "who used to be put"; Acts 19:19; and Rev 16:15: "lest he go naked and they see his shame" (i.e., "lest . . . his shame be seen").

(4) Redundant Auxiliaries. Aramaic and Syriac at times use certain verbs, for example, *qwm* ("to stand"), *nsb* ("to take"), *ʿny* ("to answer") and *srʾ* ("to begin"), as auxiliaries. These verbs introduce the action of the main verb, or, in the case of *qwm,* add an existential predicate. The great difficulty in identifying this construction in the NT is determining whether any given instance is truly pleonastic (Black 1967: 125–26).

b. Substantival. (1) Pronouns. (a) The Resumptive Pronoun. The use of a resumptive pronoun after a relative particle is very common in Aramaic and Hebrew (on the phenomenon in biblical Hebrew, Gross 1987; as a syntactic feature of Semitic languages, Khan 1984, 1988). Similar use of pronouns in the Greek of the NT may indicate the influence of Aramaic or Hebrew. The following may be cited as examples: Rev 3:8, "an opened door, which no-one can close *it* (Gk *autēn*)"; 7:22, "to the four angels, to whom it was given *to them* (Gk *autois*)."

(b) The Ethic Dative. In Aramaic and Syriac (but also in Hebrew) the preposition *l-* ("to, for") with pronominal suffixes is often used with the verb superfluously as an "ethic dative." The use may be documented from 1QapGen 21:19 (*wtbt wʾtyt ly lbyty bšlm,* "and then I returned and came [for myself] to my house in peace"); it also occurs in the Palestinian Targums. Arnold Meyer (1896: 124) and Black (1967: 104) detected it in John 20:10, where *apēlthon . . . pros autous hoi mathētai* might represent an Aramaic *ʾzlw lhwn tlmydyy,* "the disciples went (them) away." See also Acts 14:2(D) (Wilcox 1965: 132), Luke 10:11 (Joüon 1928: 353).

(2) Adjectives. Aramaic and Hebrew typically use the positive (plus the preposition *min*) for the comparative and the superlative. In the NT, compare Matt 22:36, "Which is the *great* (i.e., the greatest) commandment . . . ?"; John 1:15 (cf. 1:10), "He who comes after me is ranked ahead of me, because he was *prior* (lit. "first") to me."

Another variant of the matter may be the expression of the superlative by the positive followed by *en* (= Aramaic or Hebrew *b-*): Luke 1:42, "Blessed art thou among women *(en gynaixin)*" = "Most blessed are thou of women" (cf. Cant 6:1, *hyph bnšym* "most beautiful of [lit.: among] women").

(3) Numerals. In Mur 19 recto 1:10, the Aramaic idiom *lrbʿyn* "fourfold" occurs. There may be an interesting resemblance here with Mark 4:8, *en hekaton,* "one hundredfold," if the Aramaic preposition *l-* can be translated by Greek *en.* The form *eis hekaton,* found for example in Codex Sinaiticus and some other mss at this point, corresponds even better. However, if the Greek text of Mark be read with *hen,* "one," we must allow with Metzger that another Aramaic idiom for "x-fold" employing the noun *ḥd,* "one" (e.g., *ḥd šbʿa,* "sevenfold" [cf. Dan 3:20]), may underlie the Greek of Mark 4:8 (Metzger 1975: 83).

(4) Indefinite Article. Use of Greek *heis, mia, hen,* "one," to represent an indefinite article in certain NT passages may reflect the corresponding Aramaic idiom attested, for example, in 4QTLevi ar^a 2:18, *wmlʾk ḥd,* "and an angel"; Lam R. 1:51, *ʿbr ʿlwy ḥd ʿrby,* "an Arab passed by him." NT cases may be found in Rev 8:13, "and I heard an eagle (Gk *henos aetou*) flying in mid-heaven," and 19:17, "and I saw an angel *(hena aggelon).*" Moulton and Milligan (MM, 187) argue that such a use is found in the papyri, but it seems more likely here in the NT to be due to semiticism.

c. Sentential. (1) Subordination. Subordinate clauses introduced by the Aramaic particle *d-, dy,* or the Hebrew particle *š-* may be ambiguous sometimes, due to the range of meanings which these particles possess, which include:

(a) relative particle = "who" "which"
(b) conjunction introducing a statement of fact = "that" = Gk *hoti*
(c) conjunction = "in order that" = Gk *hina*
(d) marker introducing direct speech = Gk *hoti*
(e) "for" "because"
(f) possibly also "so that" = Greek *hōste* (Black 1967: 70)

In addition, the Aramaic particle is used to express possession indirectly in a form which partly replaces the construct state.

Black noted an interesting example of possible confusion of meanings for *d-, dy,* in Mark 8:24, "I see the people, *hoti hōs dendra peripatountas:* because I see them as trees walking." Codex Bezae and some other mss omit *hoti* and *horō* ("I see," second use), reading simply "like trees, walking." W. C. Allen (*Mark* ICC, 330) saw an original Aramaic *d-* here, read as *hoti* ("that") instead of *hous* ("whom"): "whom I see like trees walking" (Black 1967: 53–54).

(2) Conditional Clauses. Beyer (1961: 271–78) documents complex Aramaic sentences in which the logical relationship "if . . . then" is expressed by simple coordination of two clauses with the conjunction *w,* "and." NT examples include Matt 11:17, "We piped for you *and* you did not dance, we wailed for you *and* you did not lament"; the implicit logical structure might be paraphrased, "If we pipe for you, you do not dance, if we wail for you, you do not lament" (Beyer 1961: 280; see also John 7:4, 21; 9:30). The fact that Matt 11:17 is a saying of Jesus and in synonymous parallelism heightens the chance of its having been influenced by Aramaic (or Hebrew).

(3) Indefiniteness. Aramaic and Hebrew use *k(w)l* to express indefinite countable quantities ("all") or nonspecific selection from definite sets ("any"). The construction occurs especially in generalizing statements. Thus an Aramaic writ of divorce dated to 111 C.E. (Mur 19 ar recto 1:5–7) reads: "you are authorized on your part to go and become a wife of *any/whatever (kwl)* Jewish man that you wish." Matt 19:3 [RSV] has: "Is it lawful to divorce one's wife for *any* cause?" The Greek *kata pasan aitian* means literally "for *every* cause," suggesting a semiticism.

(4) Negation. The negation of statements involving indefiniteness is sometimes accomplished in NT Greek by use of the negative particles *ou* or *mē* with the pronoun *pas* in the order *ou/mē . . . pas* or *pas . . . ou/mē.* Turner (1963: 196–97) notes that extrabiblical examples of this construction are rare. It occurs in both Aramaic and Hebrew, thus: 1QapGen 11:17, "you may not eat blood at all" *(kwl dm lʾ tʾklwn);* 20:6, etc. See Matt 24:22; Mark 13:30; Luke 1:37; Acts 10:14; Rev 9:4; 18:22; 21:27; 22:3 (LXX Zech 14:11).

(5) Focus. A constituent noun phrase or clause may be moved so that it precedes the verb, and its expected position in the sentence may be occupied by a copy pronoun. This syntax, traditionally called *casus pendens,* is frequent in biblical Hebrew (Gross 1987) and in Semitic languages generally (see Khan 1988). Sentences in the Greek NT exhibiting focus construction may be semiticisms. Matt 5:40 (D) is a clear case: "He who wishes to sue you and take your tunic, leave to him *(autō)* your mantle."

Generalizing statements (see (3) above) may employ focus construction, copying an initial relative clause with a pronoun. Thus, John 6:39: "everything *(pan)* which he has given me, I have not lost any of it *(ex autou),* and I shall raise it *(auto)* up on the last day."

D. Interpretation

Evaluation of the semiticisms in the NT, like much ancient historical and linguistic work, is very dependent on circumstantial evidence. The case for any given example will be strengthened if (1) it occurs in close contiguity with other suspected semiticisms, (2) its context is properly Jewish, and (3) its wider context also reflects knowledge of Jewish exegetical traditions. It may lead to a source theory, but must not presuppose one. Torrey's argument was tied to a documentary theory, which laid it open to needless question. The complex linguistic situation of the land of Israel in NT times requires other possible explanations, such as bilingualism, to be kept in view. Further, after form-criticism and redaction-criticism, not to mention common sense, a multiplicity of routes may have been taken by any piece of material which ended up in the text of the NT, and correspondingly, perhaps more than one different linguistic medium may have affected its transmission. Indeed, the very complexity of the apparent linguistic affinities of NT semiticisms coheres well with what is known from the contemporary Aramaic, Hebrew, and Greek texts, and warns against easy solutions. Every case must be judged on its merits and against its contexts, immediate and wider alike.

Bibliography

Beyer, K. 1961. *Semitische Syntax in Neuen Testament,* vol. 1/1. SUNT 1. Göttingen.

Birkeland, H. 1954. *The Language of Jesus.* Avhandlinger utgitt av Det Norske Videnskaps-Akademi i Oslo, II, Hist.-Filos. Kl. 1. Oslo.

Black, M. 1967. *An Aramaic Approach to the Gospels and Acts.* 3d ed. Oxford.

Burney, C. F. 1922. *The Aramaic Origin of the Fourth Gospel.* Oxford.

———. 1925. *The Poetry of Our Lord.* Oxford.

Cadbury, H. J. 1919–20. *The Style and Literary Method of Luke.* HTS 6. Cambridge, MA.

———. 1920. Luke—Translator or Author? *AJT* 24: 436–55.

Chaine, J. 1927. *L'épître de saint Jacques.* EBib. Paris.

Chase, F. H. 1893. *The Old Syriac Element in the Text of Codex Bezae.* London.

———. 1895. *The Syro-Latin Text of the Gospels.* London.

Colwell, E. C. 1931. *The Greek of the Fourth Gospel.* Chicago.

Connolly, R. H. 1936. Syriacisms in St. Luke. *JTS* 37: 374–85.

Dalman, G. H. 1902. *The Words of Jesus Considered in the Light of Post-Biblical Jewish Writings and the Aramaic Language,* vol. 1. Trans. D. M. Kay. Edinburgh.

———. 1929. *Jesus-Jeshua: Studies in the Gospels.* Trans. P. E. Levertoff. London.

Deissmann, G. A. 1909. *Bible Studies.* 2d ed. Trans. A. Grieve. Edinburgh.

Dupont, J. 1967. *Études sur les Actes des Apôtres.* LD 45. Paris.

Emerton, J. A. 1961. Did Jesus Speak Hebrew? *JTS* n.s. 12: 189–202.

———. 1967. Maranatha and Ephphatha. *JTS* n.s. 18: 427–31.

———. 1973. The Problem of Vernacular Hebrew in the First Century A.D. and the Language of Jesus. *JTS* n.s. 24: 1–23.

Fitzmyer, J. A. 1971. *Essays on the Semitic Background of the New Testament.* London.

———. 1979. *A Wandering Aramean.* SBLMS 25. Missoula, MT.

Fitzmyer, J. A. and Harrington, D. J., eds. 1978. *A Manual of Palestinian Aramaic Texts.* BibOr 34. Rome.

Greenfield, J. C. 1972. Review of *An Aramaic Approach to the Gospels and Acts,* 3d ed, by M. Black in JNES 31: 58–61.

Grintz, J. M. 1960. Hebrew as the Spoken and Written Language in the Last Days of the Second Temple. *JBL* 79: 32–47.

Gross, W. 1987. *Die Pendenzkonstruktion im biblischen Hebraisch.* ATAT 27. St. Ottilien.

Jeremias, J. 1948. Die aramäische Vorgeschichte unserer Evangelien. *TLZ* 74: 527–32.

———. 1966. *Abba: Studien zur neutestamentlichen Theologie und Zeitgeschichte.* Göttingen.

Joüon, P. 1927a. Notes philologiques sur les évangiles. *RSR* 17: 537–40.

———. 1927b. Quelques aramaismes sous-jacents au grec des Évangiles. *RSR* 17: 210–29.

———. 1928. Notes philologiques sur les évangiles. *RSR* 18: 345–59; 499–502.

———. 1930. *L'Évangile de Notre Seigneur Jésus-Christ.* Paris.

———. 1932. Mots grecs de l'araméen d'Onkelos ou de l'hébreu de la Mishna qui se trouvent aussi dans les évangiles. *RSR* 22: 463–69.

Kahle, P. E. 1949. Das palästinische Pentateuchtargum und das zur Zeit Jesu gesprochene Aramäisch. *ZNW* 49: 100–16.

———. 1956. Das zur Zeit Jesu in Palastina gesprochene Aramäisch. *TRu* 17(49): 201–16. Repr. Pp. 79–95 in *Opera Minora,* ed. M. Black. Leiden.

Khan, G. 1984. Object Markers and Agreement Pronouns in Semitic Languages. *BSOAS* 47: 468–500.

———. 1988. *Studies in Semitic Syntax.* London Oriental Series 38. Oxford.

Kutscher, E. Y. 1961. Das zur Zeit Jesu gesprochene Aramäisch. *ZNW* 51: 46–54.

———. 1976. *Studies in Galilean Aramaic.* Trans. M. Sokoloff. Ramat-Gan.

Lancellotti, A. 1964. *Sintassi Ebraica nel Greco dell'Apocalisse.* Vol. 1, *Uso delle forme verbali.* Collectio assisiensis 1. Assisi.

Le Deaut, R. 1968. Le substrat araméen des évangiles: Scolies en marge de l' "Aramaic Approach" de Matthew Black. *Bib* 49: 388–99.

Lefort, L.-T. 1928. Pour une grammaire des LXX. *Mus* 41: 152–60.

Lieberman, S. 1963. How much Greek in Jewish Palestine? Pp. 123–41 in *Biblical and Other Studies,* ed. A. Altmann. Cambridge, MA.

———. 1965. *Greek in Jewish Palestine.* 2d ed. New York.

Maloney, E. C. 1980. *Semitic Interference in Marcan Syntax.* SBLDS 51. Chico, CA.

Martin, R. A. 1974. *Syntactical Evidence of Semitic Sources in Greek Documents.* SBLSCS 3. Missoula, MT.

———. 1987. *Syntax Criticism of the Synoptic Gospels.* Studies in the Bible and Early Christianity 10. Lewiston, NY.

McNamara, M. 1972. *Targum and Testament.* Shannon, Ireland.

———. 1978. *The New Testament and the Palestinian Targum to the Pentateuch.* 2d printing, with Suppl. AnBib 27A. Rome.

Metzger, B. 1975. *A Textual Commentary on the Greek New Testament.*

Meyer, A. 1896. *Jesu Muttersprache.* Freiburg i. B.

Mussies, G. 1971. *The Morphology of Koine Greek as used in the Apocalypse of St. John.* Leiden.

Schlatter, A. 1902. *Die sprache und Heimat des vierten Evangeliums.* BFCT 6/4. Gütersloh.

Schulthess, F. 1917. *Das Problem der Sprache Jesu.* Zurich.

———. 1922. Zur Sprache der Evangelien. *ZNW* 21: 216–36, 241–58.

Schwarz, G. 1986. *Jesus "der Menschensohn." Aramäistische Untersuchungen zu den synoptischen Menschensohnworte Jesu.* BWANT 6, 119. Stuttgart.
———. 1987. *Und Jesus sprach: Untersuchungen zur aramäischen Urgestalt der Worte Jesu.* 2d ed. BWANT 6, 118. Stuttgart.
Scott, R. B. Y. 1928. *The Original Language of the Apocalypse.* Toronto.
Segal, M. H. 1908. Mišnaic Hebrew and its Relation to Biblical Hebrew and to Aramaic. *JQR* 20: 647–737.
———. 1927. *A Grammar of Mishnaic Hebrew.* Oxford.
Segert, S. 1957. Aramäische Studien, II. Zur Verbreitung des Aramaischen in Palastina zur Zeit Jesu. *ArOr* 25: 21–37.
Sevenster, J. N. 1968. *Do You Know Greek?* NovTSup 19. Leiden.
Silva, M. 1975. Semantic Borrowing in the New Testament *NTS* 22: 104–10.
Sparks, H. F. D. 1943. The Semitisms of St. Luke's Gospel. *JTS* 44: 129–38.
———. 1950. The Semitisms of Acts. *JTS* n.s. 1: 16–28.
———. 1951. Some Observations on the Semitic Background of the New Testament. *SNTS Bulletin* 2: 33–42.
Thackeray, H. St. J. 1900. *A Grammar of the Old Testament in Greek, according to the Septuagint.* Vol. 1. Cambridge.
Thompson, S. 1985. *The Apocalypse and Semitic Syntax.* SNTSMS 52. Cambridge.
Torrey, C. C. 1912. The Translations made from the Original Aramaic Gospels. Pp. 269–317 in *Studies in the History of Religions, Presented to Crawford Howell Toy,* ed. D. G. Lyon and G. F. Moore. New York.
———. 1916. *The Composition and Date of Acts.* HTS 1. Cambridge, MA.
———. 1922. The Aramaic Origin of the Gospel of John. *HTR* 16: 305–44.
———. 1941. *Documents of the Primitive Church.* New York.
———. 1958. *The Apocalypse of John.* New Haven.
Trudinger, P. 1972. 'O AMHN (Rev. III:14), and the Case for a Semitic Original of the Apocalypse. *NovT* 14: 277–79.
Turner, N. 1963. *Syntax.* Vol. 3 of *A Grammar of New Testament Greek,* ed. J. H. Moulton. Edinburgh.
———. 1974. Jewish and Christian Influence on New Testament Vocabulary. *NovT* 16: 149–60.
Vazakas, A. A. 1918. Is Acts i.–xv. 35 a Literal Translation from an Aramaic Original? *JBL* 37: 105–10.
Wellhausen, J. 1911. *Einleitung in die drei ersten Evangelien.* 2d ed. Berlin.
Wensinck, A. J. 1936. *Un groupe d'aramaismes dans le texte grec des évangiles.* Mededeelingen der koningklijke Akademie van Wetenschapen, Afd. Letterkinde 81, Serie A, 5. Amsterdam.
———. 1937. The Semitisms of Codex Bezae and their Relation to the Non-Western Text of the Gospel of Saint Luke. *Bulletin of the Bezan Club* 12.
Wilcox, M. 1965. *The Semitisms of Acts.* Oxford.
———. 1972. The Judas-Tradition in Acts I. 15–26. *NTS* 19: 438–52.
———. 1982. *Talitha koum(i)* in Mk 5,41. Pp. 469–76 in *LOGIA: Les Paroles de Jesus—The Sayings of Jesus.* Memorial Joseph Coppens, ed. J. Delobel. BETL 59. Leuven.
———. 1985. Review of *Die Muttersprache Jesu. Das Arämaisch der Evangelien und der Apostelgeschichte.* Trans. by G. Schwarz. *TLZ* 110: 100–02.
Williams, C. B. 1909. *The Participle in the Book of Acts.* Chicago.
Zimmerman, F. 1979. *The Aramaic Origin of the Four Gospels.* New York.

MAX WILCOX

SENAAH (PERSON) [Heb *sĕnāʾâ*]. Name of a family of Babylonian exiles who are listed as returnees under the leadership of Zerubbabel and others (Ezra 2:35 = Neh 7:38 = 1 Esdr 5:23 [Gk *Sanaas*]). The presence of Senaah in a section with many geographical names (Ezra 2:21–35) raises the possibility that this family's name was derived from the place 8 miles NE of Jericho which was later known as Magdalsenna (*IB* 3: 582). If the names Hasenaah (Neh 3:3) and Hassenuah (Neh 11:9; 1 Chr 9:7) are alternate forms of Senaah, it is better understood as a clan of Benjamin whose name was derived from a personal name. Because of the unusually large number associated with an otherwise unknown place or clan, some have suggested that Senaah is a collective term, perhaps derived from the verb "to hate," which refers to lower classes or to persons unattached to any clan in Judah and Benjamin. (See discussion in Batten, *Ezra and Nehemiah* ICC, 81, and Clines *Ezra, Nehemiah, Esther* NCBC, 53.) For further discussion concerning the list in Ezra 2, see AKKUB.

CHANEY R. BERGDALL

SENATE [Gk *gerousia*]. In origin a council of nobles organized as an advisory body to the kings of the city-state of Rome, the Senate survived the monarchy to become the de facto ruling body of the Roman Republic. Under the Empire, the Senate largely reverted to its advisory role, though functioning at times as a high court and as an electoral assembly.

The Senate was originally comprised of the heads of the Roman *gentes* or clans, known as *patres* or fathers, along with other individuals appointed by the kings and known as *conscripti.* This small group of nobles functioned in religious and civil capacity as lifelong advisors to a monarch whose selection they proposed. Under the Republic the same advisory function was fulfilled in relation to annually elected consuls who had replaced the kings as heads of state. In the second century of the Republic, after a protracted political struggle, the normally tightly closed ranks of the senatorial patricians opened to admit a large influx of wealthy and talented plebeian families to form an expanded senatorial aristocracy which again closed ranks to protect its elite status as Rome's rulers (de Francisci 1959: 546–96, 760–73; Palmer 1970: 189–288).

By the era of Rome's conquest of the Mediterranean, the Senate was the single most important component of the government. Elected magistrates, themselves members of the Senate, though not compelled by law to do so, nevertheless always abided by senatorial recommendations or *senatus consulta,* formally enacted opinions of the house. Through this method of giving advice which was invariably taken, the Senate in effect ruled Rome and the empire; it had guided Rome to win by its setting of policy and through military leadership provided at its direction by individual senators. Senatorial leadership deteriorated in the last century B.C. as a result of political factionalism which resulted in civil war and the termination of senatorial governance of Italy and the provinces (Scullard 1959: 1–9; Taylor 1949: 1–75). The history of the Senate of the Roman Republic is long, and its procedures varied and complicated. The best brief treatment is Momigliano's

(*OCD*, 973–74) and the most complete, though somewhat dated, is that of Willems (1878).

Under the Empire, the Senate reverted in large measure to its former role as advisory body to a powerful ruling monarch. As an assemblage its powers were curtailed and its prestige diminished. Individual senators if favored by the emperor continued to exert tremendous influence, however, and were full participants in the governance of empire as agents of its ruler. The Senate as a body retained direct governance of provinces where troop concentrations were unnecessary. New powers, none threatening to imperial rule, were bestowed by Augustus and other early emperors seeking senatorial service in the administration of the empire. Direct legislative authority, appellate judicial powers, and electoral authority for self-perpetuation were among the most important (Talbert 1984: 341–491).

The RSV uses the word "senate" exclusively as a translation of Gk *gerousia,* and only with reference to the governing council in Jerusalem from the Hellenistic period on. This is true of both the Apocrypha (Jdt 4:8; 11:14; 15:8; 1 Macc 12:6; 2 Macc 1:10; 4:44; 11:27) and the NT, which has a single reference to "the senate of Israel" (Acts 5:21). See SANHEDRIN.

Bibliography

Francisci, P. de. 1959. *Primordia Civitatis.* Rome.
Palmer, R. E. A. 1970. *The Archaic Community of the Romans.* Cambridge.
Scullard, H. H. 1959. *From the Gracchi to Nero.* London.
Talbert, R. J. A. 1984. *The Senate of Imperial Rome.* Princeton.
Taylor, L. R. 1949. *Party Politics in the Age of Caesar.* Berkeley.
Willems, P. 1878. *Le Senat de la république romain.* Paris.

JOHN F. HALL

SENATOR [Gk *gerōn*]. The informal title by which members of the Roman Senate were addressed was senator; the technical term *patres et conscripti,* fathers and enrolled members, was the more formal mode of address for senators.

In the Senate of the ancient kings of Rome, membership was by royal appointment and was for life. Senators were the heads of Rome's clans, and addressed as *patres.* Additional members were appointed as *conscripti,* also for lifelong terms. With the advent of the Republic, first consuls and then censors appointed members of the Senate. The monarchical practice of lifetime appointment was continued, and new members were regularly adlected from sons of senators. In this fashion membership in the Senate came to be a hereditary right. Moreover, from the Senate membership, state magistracies and priesthoods, military commands and other offices of distinction were filled. From 367 B.C. men from non-senatorial families, *novi homines,* had access to the Senate through election to state offices. Henceforth both election and adlection would stand as legitimate modes for attaining the rank of senator. Distinction between senators was based on elected office held. The highest ranking senators, and those with the greatest privilege within and without the Senate, were men who had served as consuls and were thereafter titled *consulares,* or consular senators. All senators were ranked by censors in an order of seniority based on the attainment of office. Adlected senators who had not yet held office were lowest in rank and known as *pedarii,* foot senators, because their only prerogative was to vote, accomplished by walking from one side of the chamber to the other. Under the emperors membership continued to be based on election to office which in imperial times was conducted by the senate itself, as well as by adlection through the individual appointment of the emperor who had assumed the powers of the censors. The senatorial class became in effect a court aristocracy without real power but privileged to honors and status. To control the action of senators imperial restrictions stipulated the travel, the service, the expenditure, the marriage and family activities of senators and family members (*OCD* 973–75; Gruen 1974: 121–211; Talbert 1984: 9–112).

In the RSV, the word "senator" is used once to translate Gk *gerōn* with reference to an Athenian senator (2 Macc 6:1), and in another passage is supplied to complete the implications of the verb *bouleuō* "deliberate" (1 Macc 8:15).

Bibliography

Gruen, E. 1974. *The Last Generation of the Roman Republic.* Berkeley.
Talbert, R. J. A. 1984. *The Senate of Imperial Rome.* Princeton.

JOHN F. HALL

SENECA, EPISTLE OF. See PAUL AND SENECA, EPISTLES OF.

SENEH (PLACE) [Heb *senneh*]. One of two crags at the pass of Michmash, which Jonathan crossed in defiance of the Philistine garrison located there (1 Sam 14:4). The pass is 7 miles NE of Jerusalem, along the Wadi es-Suweinit. The first crag, which v 5 places to the N, was named Bozez. Seneh is the second crag, on the S. The etymology of the name Seneh is uncertain; it may be from *šēn,* "tooth," which would relate to the crag itself, or from *snh,* "thorn bush," which implies the difficulty of crossing.

SIDNIE ANN WHITE

SENIR (PLACE) [Heb *śĕnîr*]. An alternative name applied to Mt. Hermon. Deut 3:8 locates the range of Israel's conquests in Transjordan between the Arnon Valley (Wadi Mujib at a mid-point on the Dead Sea) on the S and Mt. Hermon to the N. The latter is stated in a note (v 9) to be called Senir by the Amorites and Sirion by the Sidonians. Hermon and Senir are collocated also in Cant 4:8, where the lover is allured to come down from the "summit of Senir and Hermon" (cf. 1 Chr 5:23 concerning the land allocation of half of the Manasseh tribe). The Hebrew "and" in this verse should probably be read as explicative, "that is, i.e." (Baker 1980), indicating the identity between the two names rather than suggesting two different locations (Kallai *HGB,* 310).

In an oracle against Tyre, Ezekiel mentions the import of wood, more particularly fir, from Senir, as well as other woods from Bashan and Lebanon (27:5–6). Both of the latter are also located in N Transjordan. This designation appears less precise, and could be an example of synecdoche in which the whole (the entire Anti-Lebanon mountain range) is identified by one of its parts (Senir/Hermon).

Senir *(saniru)* is known from Akkadian sources dating from the 9th to the 7th centuries B.C. In Shalmaneser's 18th year (841 B.C.), he defeated Hazael of Damascus despite the latter's resorting to his fortress on Mt. Senir "facing the Lebanon" (*ANET,* 280). Sennacherib also associates Senir with Lebanon, calling it its entrance and in another text placing it at the S of the Anti-Lebanon range (see Parpola 1970: 304).

Bibliography

Baker, D. W. 1980. Further Examples of the *Waw Explicativum. VT* 30: 129–36.

Parpola, S. 1970. *Neo-Assyrian Toponyms.* AOAT 6. Neukirchen-Vluyn.

DAVID W. BAKER

SENNACHERIB (PERSON) [Heb *sanḥērîb*]. The king of Assyria (704–681 B.C.) mentioned in connection with the invasion of Judah during the reign of Hezekiah (2 Kgs 18:13–19:37 = Isa 36–37; 2 Chr 32:1–23). In Assyrian the name is spelled *Sîn-aḫḫē-erība* and means "the god Sin has substituted the dead brothers." The name therefore tells us that Sennacherib was at least the third son to be born to his father Sargon II, but the first one to survive childhood. The reign of Sennacherib (704–681 B.C.) is described in more detail under MESOPOTAMIA, HISTORY OF (ASSYRIA). The biblical narratives about Sennacherib concern two major events, Sennacherib's invasion of Judah and Judah's involvement in a rebellion against Sennacherib led by Merodach-baladan of Babylonia.

A. Sennacherib's Invasion of Judah

The invasion of Judah by Sennacherib has been the subject of much debate among modern historians since the biblical narratives seem to describe the events rather differently from the Assyrian sources. In the Bible, the main narrative is found in 2 Kgs 18:13–19:37 and essentially the same narrative is found in Isaiah 36–37. In brief we read here that Hezekiah, king of Judah, was allied to Egypt, but when Sennacherib invaded Palestine and laid siege to Lachish, Hezekiah sent a valuable amount of treasure to Sennacherib at Lachish in an effort to buy off the Assyrian. Nevertheless, Sennacherib sent an army S under the leadership of his Tartan, his Rabsaris, and his Rabshakeh. Upon arrival the Rabshakeh approached the walls and addressed a speech to the inhabitants of Jerusalem who were sitting on the walls. In this eloquent speech he attempted to persuade the citizens to turn against their own king Hezekiah and their ally Egypt and surrender the city to the Assyrians without a fight. He pointed out that other cities of Syria and Palestine had had no success in withstanding Assyrian might and the Egyptians had not lifted a finger to help them. He called Egypt a "broken reed" which pierced the hand which leaned upon it. Hezekiah sent out emissaries to negotiate with the Rabshakeh and in particular to try and persuade him to stop speaking to the men on the wall in "the language of Judah." They pleaded with the Rabshakeh to speak in Aramaic since they did not want the common citizens to understand what was being said. The Rabshakeh however refused. The officials returned to Hezekiah reporting that their mission had been unsuccessful. Hezekiah asked the prophet Isaiah for advice. Isaiah counselled him not to submit to the Assyrians and predicted that they would withdraw of their own accord.

In the meantime the Rabshakeh returned to Sennacherib, who was now besieging Libnah, to report. At the same time a second report came in to Sennacherib that an army led by Tirhakah of Ethiopia was marching against the Assyrians. Curiously nothing further is said about this invasion. In response to the report of the Rabshakeh, Sennacherib sent a second message to Hezekiah which was essentially the same as the first. Hezekiah again consulted Isaiah, and Isaiah gave the same advice, do not submit for the Assyrians will withdraw of their own accord. The biblical narrative then proceeds to say that the "angel of the lord" descended upon the Assyrian camp at night and slew 185,000 warriors. When the survivors woke in the morning and saw their dead comrades, they retreated quickly to Assyria. The narrative concludes with a statement that Sennacherib was assassinated in Nineveh while worshiping in the temple of his god Nisroch. The assassins were two of his sons called Adram-melech and Sharezer, who subsequently fled to "the land of Ararat" (Urartu). Another son of Sennacherib, Esarhaddon, then ascended the throne in Nineveh.

The narrative in 2 Chr 32:1–23 is much shorter but similar to that of 2 Kings and Isaiah already summarized. The version of 2 Chronicles has one extra interesting piece of information, however. It describes how Hezekiah prepared for an Assyrian siege by building fortifications and arming his troops.

B. Judah and Merodach-baladan

The second major event in the Bible concerning the relations between Hezekiah and Sennacherib is described in 2 Kgs 20:12–19; 2 Chr 32:31; Isaiah 39. Once again the fullest version of the events is found in 2 Kings and Isaiah; only a brief summary is given in 2 Chronicles. In these passages we read that ambassadors were sent from Merodach-baladan of Babylonia to Hezekiah. Hezekiah received them cordially and showed them over his palace and treasury. Isaiah castigated Hezekiah for receiving them and predicted that in the future Babylonia would conquer Jerusalem.

To understand these two major events in the context of Assyrian affairs it is necessary to look at the Assyrian sources. From consideration of these it is reasonably certain that Merodach-baladan's ambassadors were sent to Jerusalem early in the reign of Sennacherib. From Assyrian sources it is known that Merodach-baladan led a major alliance against Sennacherib when the latter first came to the throne. This alliance consisted of Chaldeans, Aramaeans, and Elamites. If one dates the Babylonian embassy to Hezekiah to this time, it indicates that Merodach-baladan attempted, perhaps successfully in view of Hezekiah's attitude, to persuade the kingdom of Judah to join in the alliance against Assyria. This would certainly account for Sennacherib's later aggressive action against Hezekiah. The anti-Assyrian alliance was, after many years of fighting, finally defeated and Merodach-baladan eventually disappeared.

Sennacherib's invasion of the kingdom of Judah, as stated earlier, presents problems to modern historians since the Assyrian records and the biblical narratives do not seem to be very close in detail. Both concern an invasion of Palestine by Sennacherib during the reign of Hezekiah and both mention an Assyrian siege of Jerusalem but apart from these essentials they have little in common. According to Sennacherib's annals (*ANET,* 287–88), this king directed his third campaign (701 B.C.) against Syria. After Sidon and Ashkelon were taken by force a large number of other cities and states submitted without a fight and paid tribute. However, the people of Ekron (Amqarruna) were afraid of the Assyrians since they had sent their former king, an Assyrian vassal, as a prisoner to Hezekiah at Jerusalem. Egypt and Ethiopia now came to the aid of Ekron. The allied forces met the Assyrians at Eltekeh and the Assyrians claimed a victory. The king of Ekron was released by Hezekiah but nevertheless Sennacherib laid siege to Jerusalem. During the siege various surrounding towns were plundered.

Surprisingly, the Assyrian records do not tell us the result of the siege but simply go on to say that Hezekiah sent a large amount of booty to Sennacherib at Nineveh. This concludes the relevant narrative for the campaign of 701 B.C. The only other pertinent Assyrian information is the portrayal of the sack of Lachish on sculptured reliefs found at Nineveh (and now in the British Museum), which is undated, and a broken text in which reference is made to the capture of the Palestinian town Azekah.

C. Historical Reconstruction

It seems that the biblical and Assyrian narratives are so different that they represent two different events. The first was the campaign of 701 B.C. and the second probably took place late in the reign (688–681 B.C.), a period for which no Assyrian annals are preserved. Sennacherib's first Palestinian campaign could have taken place more or less as he described it in his annals. The siege of Jerusalem came to an end when Hezekiah paid a huge tribute to Sennacherib (see 2 Kgs 18:14–16). In subsequent years, Hezekiah, encouraged by the absence of the Assyrian army, must have allied himself to Egypt. At the same time he took the precaution of fortifying Jerusalem to face a siege as narrated in 2 Chronicles. Sennacherib, late in his reign after he had dealt with other problems, was in a position to deal with Hezekiah. Thus, he probably led a second campaign into Palestine which involved among other things the siege of Lachish. It was possibly on this occasion that the Rabshakeh made his vain efforts to persuade Hezekiah to give up without a fight. Tirhakah led an Egypto-Ethiopian force into Palestine to raise the siege. Before the two armies met however a catastrophe befell the Assyrian camp and Sennacherib retreated in haste (cf. Herodotus 2.141). This is a hypothetical reconstruction of the events but it accepts the biblical narrative as essentially accurate while at the same time reconciling it with the Assyrian records. See also Cogan and Tadmor *2 Kings* AB; *CAH* 3/2/23.

Bibliography

Clements, R. E. 1980. *Isaiah and the Deliverance of Jerusalem.* Sheffield.

A. KIRK GRAYSON

SENTENCES OF SEXTUS. See SEXTUS, SENTENCES OF (NHC XII,*1*).

SEORIM (PERSON) [Heb *śĕʿōrîm*]. Head of a priestly family appointed to service by David according to 1 Chr 24:8. Aside from this mention, nothing is known of Seorim. In 1 Chr 24:1–19 twenty-four families of priests are chosen by lot for temple service. They were chosen from the descendants of the sons of Aaron, Ithamar and Eleazar. According to the passage, David was assisted by representatives of the family lines. One of these was the priest, Zadok. The other was Abiathar. The lots were chosen without discrimination, however, Zadok's lineage (Eleazar) contained more heads of families. For this reason, sixteen of the families came from Zadok's side and only eight from Abiathar's. Seorim was elected to the fourth course. Priestly duties rotated among the families according to the order of election.

DONALD K. BERRY

SEPHAR (PLACE) [Heb *sĕpār*]. One of the boundaries, described as the mountain or hill country of the E, to which the territory of the sons of Joktan extended (Gen 10:30). The other boundary, Mesha, is usually located somewhere in N Arabia. Because of similarities between the names of most of Joktan's progeny and the names of many towns and regions in S Arabia, a location for Sephar in that area has been sought. Two places bearing the name Zafar, one, the site of the Himyarite capital near Sana in the interior of Yemen, the other, in the Hadramaut on the coast near Shihr, have been proposed. While some scholars are dubious about either equation because of the discrepancy in the initial sibilants of the Arabic and Hebrew names, others have felt that the appropriateness of the equation outweighs that discrepancy. Cohen (*IDB* 4: 272) has noted that in post-biblical Hebrew *sĕpār* has the meaning "border country" and suggests that perhaps the phrase in Genesis does not refer to a locality but could better be rendered as: "as far as the border country, that is, the hill country of the east." Without a firm location for Mesha or additional evidence, no conclusive identification is possible.

GARY H. OLLER

SEPHARAD (PLACE) [Heb *sĕpārēd*]. The place where some inhabitants of Jerusalem were exiled (Obad 20). The biblical text gives no indication of the location of Sepharad, but at least three possible locations have been suggested: a city in Spain, possibly Sefarad; a city located in Media; and the city Sardis, located in Lydia of Asia Minor.

The least plausible suggestion originates from the *Targum of Jonathan* which placed Sepharad in Spain. Neiman (1963) suggests that there were at least two cities with the name Sepharad: one designated Sardis in Asia Minor and one called Sefarad in Spain. Jewish tradition preserves the name by calling the Jews from Spain (Sepharad) the "Sephardim" and thereby distinguishing them from the Ashkenazim Jews of Central Europe.

The second possibility comes from several Assyrian inscriptions which record a city named Saparda. One locates this city to the E of Assyria in Media. This location has been determined from a mention of Saparda in the Assyrian annals which record the campaign of Sargon II along the Lower Zab. Other Mesopotamian inscriptions, however, indicate that Saparda was located in Asia Minor. Saparda is mentioned as an ally of the Cimmerians, Medes, and the Minni in their attack on Assyria during the reign of Esarhaddon. This would then locate Saparda, if it is near its allies, to the NW of Assyria. More evidence of a possible Asia Minor location comes from the Behistun inscription which notes that Saparda is between Egypt and Ionia. While another inscription from the same period found at Naksh-i-Rustam, locates it between Cappadocia and Ionia.

The location of Sepharad is also identified with the capital city of Lydia, Sardis, which is located in Asia Minor and is near the modern village of Sart in Turkey (38°28′N; 28°02′E). An Aramaic-Lydian inscription was found at Sardis which preserves the Aramaic name of the city as the same four letters, *sprd,* as the text of Obadiah 20. The date of the inscription is debated (455, 394, or 349 B.C.), but it certainly attests that Sardis is a good candidate for Sepharad. Some have argued that Sardis was too distant to be a possible location of an early Jewish settlement. The city was, however, an important center of trade which would have far reaching contacts. If Sardis is Sepharad it would certainly indicate an early settlement of Jews in Asia Minor. Archaeological evidence at Sardis demonstrates a significant Jewish population in the 2d century A.D. as attested by a large synagogue.

Bibliography

Neiman, D. 1963. Sefarad: The Name of Spain. *JNES* 22: 128–32.

JOHN D. WINELAND

SEPHARVAIM (PLACE) [Heb *sĕparwayim*]. Sepharvites. One of the places from which the Assyrians, perhaps under Sargon II (722–705 B.C.E.), brought settlers to the cities of Samaria according to 2 Kgs 17:24. The taunting messages from Sennacherib (705–681 B.C.E.), king of Assyria, to the people of Jerusalem in 2 Kgs 18:34 (= Isa 36:19) and 2 Kgs 19:13 (= Isa 37:13) emphasize that the gods and the king of Sepharvaim were unable to resist the Assyrian onslaught.

Albright (*ARI,* 220), among others, located it at Sabarain, a city conquered (ca. 722 B.C.E.) by Shalmaneser V according to the Babylonian Chronicle 1:28 (TCS 5:73). However, Tadmor (cf. Cogan and Tadmor *2 Kings* AB, 199) argues that this place should be transcribed as *šamaraʾin,* and is to be identified with Samaria. Citing the dual ending on Sepharvaim, Driver (1958: 18*) proposed identification with Sippar, an ancient Mesopotamian city (modern Abu Habbah some 20 miles SW of Baghdad, Iraq) which apparently consisted of two towns. The fact that Sippar did not have a king during the Assyrian period and other difficulties militate against Driver's suggestion. Zadok (1976: 115) argues for identification with Sipraani, the Chaldean name of a city mentioned in the Murashu documents (5th century B.C.E.) from Nippur in S Mesopotamia, but more data is needed to render this conclusive. Identification with Sepharad by Astour (*IDBSup,* 807) has met with little acceptance. Albright (*ARI,* 220) and other scholars view the Sibraim mentioned in Ezek 47:16 as a variant spelling of Sepharvaim, while others (e.g., Zadok 1976: 116) argue that these were two distinct places.

A related problem is the identification of the gods worshiped by the Sepharvites. According to 2 Kgs 17:31, the people of Sepharvaim worshiped Adrammelech and Anammelech by burning children. Following A. Ungnad, Deller (1965) made the strongest case for equating Adrammelech with Adad-milki, a deity associated with the burning of children in texts from, among other places, Tell Halaf, an ancient town near the Turkish-Syrian border. However, Kaufman (1978) argues that the cuneiform signs read as *Adad-milki* may also have other interpretations. Anammelech has been identified with the enigmatic Anatmelek by some scholars (e.g., Weinfeld 1972: 149), and with An(u), the Mesopotamian sky-god, by others (e.g., Cogan and Tadmor *2 Kings* AB, 212).

Bibliography

Deller, K. 1965. Review of *Les sacrifices de l'Ancien Testament,* by R. de Vaux. *Or* 34: 382–86.

Driver, G. R. 1958. Geographical Problems. *EI* 5: 16*–20*.

Kaufman, S. A. 1978. The Enigmatic Adad-Milki. *JNES* 37: 101–9.

Weinfeld, M. 1972. The Worship of Molech and of the Queen of Heaven and its Background. *UF* 4: 133–54.

Zadok, R. 1976. Geographical and Onomastic Notes. *JANES* 8: 113–26.

HECTOR AVALOS

SEPPHORIS (M.R. 176239). Sepphoris was one of the leading cities of Lower Galilee from the early Roman period. Yet much of its history extended back into the OT period. It lay scarcely 4 miles NW of Nazareth on a high hill in a mountainous plain at an elevation of 286 m above sea level. The territory of Sepphoris extended 10 miles NW to the territory of Acco-Ptolemais and 9 miles SE to Mt. Tabor, which suggests that Nazareth belonged to the territory of Sepphoris.

The rabbis believed that Sepphoris was founded by Joshua the son of Nun, and some identified Sepphoris as biblical Kitron (Judg 1:30) or even Rakkath (Josh 19:35; *b. Meg.* 6a). The name of the city means "bird," and one rabbi explained that it got its name because it perched on a hill like a bird (*b. Meg.* 6a).

Pottery sherds of the Iron Age II and perhaps earlier appear on the surface at Sepphoris. A beautifully molded rhyton or drinking vessel of the Persian period found at Sepphoris may hint at the importance of the city during that period. The priestly family of Amok may have settled there after the return from the Exile (Neh 12:7 and 20; *Mishmaroth* 2). Scant remains of the Hellenistic period are known, but the city clearly reached its peak beginning in the Early Roman period.

Sepphoris entered recorded history for the first time in

103 B.C.E. Ptolemy Lathyrus, the King of Cyprus, was at war with King Alexander Jannaeus of Israel. Ptolemy besieged Acco-Ptolemais, then successfully besieged Asochis hardly 5 miles from Sepphoris. He then besieged Sepphoris itself on a Sabbath, but with no success (*Ant* 13.12.5).

If Sepphoris was already a secure, walled city at this period, then it was likely Greek in character, as was Ptolemais, Shikmona, Dora, Strato's Tower, Joppa, Azotus (Ashdod), and other coastal cities. Since Ptolemy besieged Sepphoris on the Sabbath in order to gain advantage, it is likely that it had a large Jewish population.

There is no historical information about the city at the coming of Rome in 63 B.C.E. However in 55 B.C.E. Gabinius, Proconsul in Syria, recognized the strategic importance of Sepphoris and located one of the five Roman Synedria or Councils there, and the only one for Galilee (*Ant* 15.5.4 §91; *JW* 1.8.5 §170). During the winter of 39/38 B.C.E., Herod the Great took Sepphoris during a snowstorm immediately after Antigonus abandoned it (*Ant* 14.15.4; *JW* 1.16.2). Herod retained the city as his N headquarters for the remainder of his reign.

Judah the son of Hezekiah led the Sepphoreans in revolt immediately upon the death of Herod the Great in 4 B.C.E. The Roman governor of Syria, Varus, responded swiftly. He dispatched to Sepphoris a portion of his legions and auxiliary troops under his son and under Caius, a friend, while Varus marched on to Sebaste. His legions sacked Sepphoris, reduced the city to ashes, and sold its inhabitants as slaves (*Ant* 17.10.9; *JW* 2.5.1).

Herod Antipas, son of Herod the Great by the Samaritan wife Malthace, inherited Galilee and Perea (Transjordan) at the death of his father. Antipas immediately set to work to rebuild Sepphoris and its wall, employing craftsmen from villages all over Galilee. It was Sepphoris that Josephus called the "ornament of all Galilee" and "the strongest city in Galilee" (*JW* 2.511; *Ant* 18.27). Evidently it surpassed Tiberias and Julias in beauty and opulence (*Ant* 18.2.1). Antipas probably granted Sepphoris the rank of capital of Galilee (*Ant* 18.2.1).

The works of Herod Antipas at Sepphoris included a theatre that seated 3000, a palace, and an upper and lower city with an upper and lower market. The upper city was predominantly Jewish by the time of the Second Revolt and likely earlier (*b. Yoma* 11a). There was also an "old fort" (*m. ʿArak.* 9.6), which was under the command of a hyparch. There was an archive (*m. Qidd.* 4.6), and certain archives were brought from Tiberias to Sepphoris in the days of Nero (*Life* 38). The Romans later replaced the "old archives" with the "new archives." Excavations at Sepphoris show that workmen quarried stone on the site itself for Antipas' rebuilding of the city.

Other information about the appearance of this Roman city of mixed population comes from the rabbis. They knew the upper and lower market (*b. ʿErub.* 5b), a fortified upper city, a colonnaded street in the middle of the city (*j. Ketub.* 1.25d), a city wall that required repairs from time to time (*b. B. Bat.* 7b–8a), a city gate (*Eccl. Rab.* 3), many shops (*Bar. B. Bat.* 75a), inns, synagogues, schools or academies (*j. Peʾa* 20b, 27–31), private dwellings with upper stories and sometimes with a Roman-style dining room (*Lev. Rab.* c.16.2), and "the wheels of Sepphoris," evidently referring to water wheels that lifted water to the upper city (*Eccl. Rab.* 12.6). There was a flowing spring below the city (*m. Ketub.* 1.10). The territory of Sepphoris extended 16 miles in every direction, according to the rabbis, and flowed with milk and honey (*b. Ketub.* 111b, *b. Meg.* 6a). Water ran down to the city on two aqueducts from springs at Abel 3 miles to the E (*m. ʿErub.* 8.7). The road from Tiberias to Sepphoris was marked by stadia with castra and a "Syrian monument" (*j. ʿErub.* 6.31b).

The destruction of Sepphoris by Varus and its rebuilding by Antipas seems to mark its transition from a Greek city to a loyalist Roman city of Jewish and gentile population. Certainly the rabbis referred to the "old government" of Sepphoris (*m. Qidd.* 4.5), which suggests they remembered the change. After this period many Latin and Greek names appear in the record, including the names of Jews (*Sipre Dt.* 13; *Mid. Tannaim* 7.2; *t. Bab. Metzia* 3.11).

Pharisaic families are scarcely mentioned in the 1st century in Sepphoris. Instead we find references to those with some sort of priestly connection. Sepphoris was therefore likely a priestly or Sadducean city. For example, Jose ben Illem of Sepphoris served as substitute for the High Priest Matthias in Jerusalem on the Day of Atonement, and Arsela of Sepphoris led the scapegoat from the temple into the desert on the Day of Atonement (*m. Yoma* 6.5; *j. Ber.* 3.6b; *t. Taʿan.* 1 end; *j. Yoma* 6.43c; *j. Maʿas. Š* 5.56a). In this regard it is important that, after 70 C.E. and the destruction of the Second Temple, the second priestly course of Jedʿaiah settled at Sepphoris (*Mishmaroth* 2).

R. Halaphta was a city official and religious leader in Sepphoris during the second half of the 1st century C.E. (*b. Taʿan.* 16b). The beginnings of Pharisaic Judaism at Sepphoris lie in the meeting of R. Halaphta, R. Eleasar ben 'Asaria the smith, R. Huspith the interpreter, R. Jeshebab, and R. Johanan ben Nuri. They met in the smith's shop to decide a religious question (*t. Kelim B. Bat.* 2.2).

Sepphoris did not figure directly in the ministry of Jesus, though it is worth noting that one logical route from Nazareth to Cana of Galilee ran through Sepphoris.

In the course of the devastating First Revolt against Rome, Sepphoris, a Jewish city, remained mainly pro-Roman. Even when the temple was in danger, the Sepphoreans refused to send aid (*Life* 65). The Sepphoreans met the Roman commander Vespasian at Ptolemais and petitioned him for help against their countrymen, who resented it that the city had already made peace with Cestius Gallus and received a Roman garrison (*JW* 3.2.3). Vespasian responded willingly, supplying the city with one thousand cavalry and six thousand infantrymen under Placidius the Tribune (*JW* 3.4.1). These forces successfully withstood an attack of Josephus himself (*JW* 3.4.1). The city responded by depicting Vespasian on one of their coins in the 14th year of Nero (or 68 C.E.), the year before Vespasian was proclaimed emperor. The pro-Roman attitude of the city also helps explain the special titles for Sepphoris on the same coins. The full inscription reads "In the time of Vespasian, City of Peace, Neronia, Sepphor[is]." That is, the city was named for Nero (a name which did not stick) and was granted a peace title, while the city specifically honored Vespasian.

Hadrian visited Palestine in 130 C.E. In preparation for

the *adventus Augusti,* the road from Legio to Sepphoris was built, though there is no record that he visited Sepphoris. There is also very little notice of the city during the Second Revolt of 135 C.E. However, it is said that R. Johanan ben Nuri read the Esther scroll at Purim at night "in the time of danger." (*t. Meg.* 2.4). R. Eleasar ben Perata of Sepphoris was sentenced to death, but escaped punishment through his clever answers (*Midr. Tanhuma, misʾai* 23). During the Bar Kokhba Revolt every house in the Upper Market was examined for a *mezuzah* on the doorpost. If found, the owners were fined 1000 denarii (*b. Yoma* 11a).

The religious and political complexion of Sepphoris changed after the Second Revolt. Although the *boule* or council of Sepphoris had received permission from Trajan to mint coins before 117–118 C.E. (Sepphoris coin inscription: "Trajan Gave Authority"), no Sepphorean coins of the period of Hadrian are known. Hadrian may have denied Sepphoris the right to mint coins as punishment for the Second Revolt, simply holding responsible one of the largest Jewish cities in the province. When the right to mint coins resumed under Antoninus Pius, the city was known by its new, Roman name, Diocaesarea (the "Divine Caesar").

The 2d century saw the rise of the rabbis at Sepphoris/Diocaesarea. These sages perpetuated and participated in the reconstruction of Pharisaic attitudes and ideals. R. Jose bar Halaphta was a leather-worker and leading Tannaʾ of the third generation, active from around 120 C.E., and teacher of Judah I. He is the chief authority for the accepted Jewish chronology as fixed in *Seder Olam Rabba.* R. Jose reported that the priestly courses mourned during the week in which they were supposed to serve in the temple (*t. Taʿan.* 2.3). The names of nineteen other rabbis in Sepphoris/Diocaesarea are known in the 2d century as the city came into its own as a great Jewish intellectual center.

It is also in the second half of the century that we have the first encounters between the rabbis and Jewish Christians at Sepphoris, including Jacob of Kfar Sakhnin (*Eccl. Rab.* 1.8.3). They debated proper interpretation of scripture (*b. Sanh.* 38b; *Ber.* 10a), though the rabbis also debated among themselves whether one should save the scriptures of the heretics, which seems to include Jewish-Christians, should a fire break out on a Sabbath (*m. Sabb.* 16.1).

Near the end of the century Sepphoris was famous as the residence of the Sanhedrin and of Judah the Prince, who compiled and redacted the Mishnah at his school in the city. This dazzling literary and religious development occurred during a period of increased urbanization and yet during a period of agricultural decline (*Gen. Rab.* 90.5).

It was in this period that the legends of the idealized relationship between the emperor and Judah the Prince emerged. These tales may reflect the life and times of the emperor Caracella (198–217 C.E.). Coins of Sepphoris/Diocaesarea from the reign of Caracella bear the legend "Diocaesarea the Holy, (city of) Shelter, Autonomous, Loyal, Friendship and Alliance (between the) Holy Council (of the city) and the Senate of the Romans." This inscription assumes a treaty between Rome and Sepphoris, a treaty as yet unattested in the ancient literature.

At the death of Judah the funeral train stopped at 18 synagogues in Sepphoris/Diocaesarea. This reflects a very strong Jewish population in the city at the beginning of the 3d century C.E. (*Eccl. Rab.* 7.11–12).

The 3d century was a time of major changes for Sepphoris/Diocaesarea. For example the Sanhedrin moved to Tiberias, perhaps even before the death of Judah (*t. Holin* 1). At this time R. Hanina, who lived in the (upper) market of the city (*j. Taʿan.* 3.4) became Judah's successor in the Academy at Sepphoris. Severe drought also troubled the land, but it persisted longer in the N. The city coinage of Sepphoris/Diocaesarea stopped under Elagabalus, 218–222 C.E.

During the 3d century the problem of liturgies and excessive taxation became acute. Liturgies were levied both on the Council of the city, which was still Jewish, and on guilds (i.e., on the flax [or linen] guild of Sepphoris/Diocaesarea; (*j. Peʾa* 1.1). Economic problems were growing serious enough that Jewish land around the city was passing into non-Jewish hands (*j. Dem.* 5.8; *j. Giṭ.* 4.9). Yet Sepphoris/Diocaesarea remained an important commercial center (*j. B. Mezia* 5.6).

In 4th century sources we read of the synagogue of the people of Gophna (*j. Sanh.* 10.28a) and the synagogue of the Babylonians (*j. Sabb.* 8a). A "Great Synagogue" of Sepphoris is also mentioned (*Pirqe R. Kahana* 18).

During the 1st half of the 4th century Eusebius claimed that all of Diocaesarea was Jewish (*m.P.*, p. 29). Epiphanius reported that Count Joseph of Tiberias built a church at Diocaesarea with special imperial permission, since there was as yet no large Christian population (*Adv. Haeres.* 1.30). In the same half century R. Jose ben Hanina and R. Abbahu debated about the books of the heretics, which seems to refer to the Jewish-Christians at Sepphoris/Diocaesarea. They certainly knew of a written gospel (Hebrew Matthew?: *b. ʿErub.* 53b; *j. Soṭa* 16b).

A synagogue inscription from a mosaic floor at Sepphoris likely dates to this period. It refers to R. Judan bar Tanhum bar [Buta], who also dedicated the mosaic floor in nearby Cana. Burial inscriptions from tombs S of the city mention a Hoshayah bar Tanhum, a Rabbi Yaakob, a Rabbi Nahum, and a certain Crispina. A Greek inscription is likely from the lintel of a synagogue or school. It mentions a certain Gelasius son of Aetios, Head of a Synagogue, whose family was from Tyre.

In 351 C.E. a man named Patricius led the city in revolt (Aur. Vict., *Caes.* 42.9–12). Gallus Caesar, an Arian Christian responded by destroying the city and selling the survivors into slavery (Socrates, *Hist. Ecc.* 11.33; Sozomen, *Hist. Ecc.* 4.7). The city was immediately rebuilt, and archaeology shows that the top of the city was dominated by a huge military enclave that included the fortress visible on the site to this day. The burn layer associated with Gallus extends everywhere in the 4th century layer at the site.

In 374 the emperor Valentinius exiled to the territory of Diocaesarea Orthodox Christians from Egypt (Palladius, *h.Laus.* ch. 117). This suggests that the city was no longer a cultural force to be reckoned with, as far as the emperor was concerned.

In the 5th century a bishop with a Greek name presided in Diocaesarea. This bishop, Doretheus, took part in the council of Chalcedon in 451 C.E. (Mansi 6.1091E). Probably gentile Christianity had finally gained a secure foothold. During the same century, in Bethlehem, Jerome thought that the tomb of the prophet Jonah was at Diocaesarea. He also believed that the Gath of 2 Kgs 24:25 was in the city territory of Diocaesarea (*Preface to the book of Jonas* 25.1119). The names of prominent rabbis from Diocaesarea are no longer to be found in the tradition.

During the 6th century Christians took the lead politically. In the year 512 C.E. Marcellinus, bishop of Diocaesarea, intervened in the Council of Jerusalem against Severus and the monophysites (Mansi 8.1071C). After 518 C.E. Theodosius reported—wrongly—that Simon Magus was from Diocaesarea (*Topo.* 4.139). The name of the city appears in a tax decree of the emperor Justinian dated 531–32 C.E. In this decree, posted in Beer-sheba, Diocaesarea is taxed 60 gold solidi per year. Its comparatively high tax assessment suggests that it had recovered from the poor economy of the 3d and 4th centuries. In 570 the Pilgrim of Piacenza visited Diocaesarea and other venerated relics of Mary the mother of Jesus, the first mention of this tradition at the city (*Travels* 161). By the 12th century the city was practically empty (Benjamin of Tudela, *Itinerary* 43). In the same period the name "Diocaesarea" had disappeared from memory, and the Arab village that remained was called "Saffuriyeh." This name survived to the early 20th century.

Bibliography

Buchler, S. 1909. *The Political and Social Leaders of the Jewish Community of Sepphoris in the Second and Third Centuries.* London.

Freynem, S. 1980. *Galilee from Alexander the Great to Hadrian, 323 B.C.E. to 135 C.E.* Notre Dame.

Hecker, M. 1961. The Roman Road Legio-Zippori. *Yediot* 25: 175.

Klein, S. 1909. *Beitrage zur Geographie unt Geschichte Galilaas.* Leipzig.

Meshorer, Y. 1978. Jewish Symbols on Roman Coins Struck in Eretz Israel. *Israel Museum News* 14: 61–63.

Schurer, E. 1979. *HJP*² 2: 172–76.

Waterman, L., et. al. 1937. *Preliminary Report of the University of Michigan Excavations at Sepphoris/Diocaesarea, Palestine, in 1931.* Ann Arbor.

Wilkinson, J. 1977. *Jerusalem Pilgrims Before the Crusades.* Warminster.

JAMES F. STRANGE

SEPTUAGINT. The most widely accepted designation for a diverse collection of Greek literature encompassing: (1) translations of the contents of the Hebrew Bible; (2) additions to some of its books; and (3) works written originally in Greek (or in some instances in Hebrew) but not included in the Hebrew canon. The word "Septuagint," (from Lat *septuaginta* = 70; hence the abbreviation LXX) derives from a story that 72 (other ancient sources mention 70 or 5) elders translated the Pentateuch into Greek; the term therefore applied originally only to those five books. That story is now acknowledged to be fictitious, yet the label persists by virtue of the tradition. The precise referent of the term Septuagint in modern discussions, and especially of "the Septuagint" is neither consistent nor clear.

A. Terminology
1. The Problem of Terminology
2. Definition of the Term
B. Witnesses to LXX
1. Primary Witnesses
2. Secondary Witnesses
C. Theories of Origins
1. Aristeas
2. Kahle
3. Lagarde
4. Tov
5. Other Theories
D. History of the LXX Text
1. Revisions
2. Recensions
E. LXX as a Translation
F. Importance of LXX
G. Bibliographic Resources
1. Collections
2. Selected General Bibliography
3. Modern Printed Editions

A. Terminology

1. The Problem of Terminology. Some scholars use Septuagint (often in quotation marks) to refer only to the Pentateuch while others intend the term to include the entire collection of Jewish-Greek scriptures (1–3 above), reserving the rubric Old Greek (OG) for those books which are translations from Hebrew. Others, recognizing that all the extant Greek mss are corrupt and probably only partially representative of what the original translators intended, use the terms "Ur-Septuagint," "Original Septuagint" or "Proto-Septuagint" to describe the text as it presumably left the translators' hands. Septuagint for some scholars describes a "critical text," i.e., one chosen after careful reading and evaluation of all the available witnesses to the book(s) in question, and determined to be the "nearest approach" to the original translation. Where such critical texts are not established, these scholars would contend that it is inappropriate to speak of Septuagint, only of mss, papyri etc. Still other scholars, viewing the critical process as artificial, cumbersome, time-consuming and subjective, select one or two well-known uncial mss—Codex Alexandrinus (A) and Codex Vaticanus (B) being the most common—as sufficiently representative of the Greek translation. Citations such as LXX^A, LXX^B, or LXX^{AB} appear in their work—the last being considered more authoritative than either of the first two. Many other scholars, having subjected the matter to little or no critical scrutiny, use Septuagint to refer to any printed edition so labelled, which may be used to correct/adjust readings in the printed editions of the Hebrew Bible. There are also scholars who dispute the idea of a single original translation to which all deviant witnesses could theoretically be traced. For them it is pointless to speak of Septuagint as a single enterprise since there were multiple translations each reflecting the concerns of specific communities.

The first desideratum concerning Septuagint then is some agreement, if not consensus, on the way the word is being or should be used. What relationships do the diverse Greek witnesses to the books of the Hebrew Bible have to each other on the one hand, and to the various Hebrew witnesses to those very books on the other? It is not sufficient to identify "Old Greek" in contrast to Septuagint (with or without quotation marks) as is so often done, unless one indicates the precise mss or editions in which either may be found.

2. Definition of the Term. For convenience, it is assumed throughout what follows that a single set of original translations of the Hebrew scriptures into Greek was effected in several stages, and in locations not known for sure; that the earliest parts (most likely the Torah) of the translation took place in the 3d century B.C.E. (perhaps in Egypt) and the last parts were completed by the first part of the 1st century B.C.E.; that, in the absence of "hard copy" of these translations, we can recover from the extant witnesses, texts sufficiently reliable to be considered equivalent to the originals, if carefully controlled text-critical principles are employed. This process is being carried out with extreme care in the editions of the Göttingen Septuaginta-Unternehmen (on which see below). It is to the printed texts of these editions (as distinct from readings in their apparatuses), that the term Septuagint as used herein primarily applies. Secondarily, in those books for which full critical editions have not yet been established, Septuagint is considered equivalent to the partially critical texts found in A. Rahlfs' manual edition (Rahlfs 1935). However, despite the long-established contrary practice (such as found in Rahlfs' manual edition), whole books without known Hebrew equivalents are not considered Septuagint. They are usually listed also as Apocrypha and even Pseudepigrapha, and again, since much of LXX discussion concerns translation technique, that question is moot in such books. Where, as in parts of Joshua and all of Judges, Rahlfs prints two lemmata, the LXX is deemed to have not yet been established.

B. Witnesses to LXX

1. Primary Witnesses. a. Papyri. Several papyri containing mostly parts of the Pentateuch and dating from the 2d century B.C.E. to the 1st century C.E. constitute the earliest and most important of the primary witnesses to LXX. Equally important are certain fragments from Qumran. Given their value, these early witnesses are listed below. Only by their number in Rahlfs' numeration (i.e., the number by which they are cited in the Göttingen Septuagint) are their contents, and approximate dates given.

Rahlfs' number	*Contents*	*Date*
957	about 20 verses from Deut 23–28	early 2d B.C.E.
942	fragments from Gen 7 and 38	late 1st B.C.E.
847	parts of Deut 11 and 31–33	early 1st C.E.
848	parts of Deut 17–33	late 1st B.C.E.
819	Deut 11:4	2d B.C.E.
801	Lev 26:2–16	late 2d B.C.E./ early 1st C.E.
805	Exod 28:4–7	ca. 100 B.C.E.
802	Lev 2–5 with lacunae	1st B.C.E.
803	Num 3:30–4:14, with lacunae	1st B.C.E.
943	Minor Prophets fragments	late 1st B.C.E./ early 1st C.E.

Other unpublished fragments found at Qumran and several papyri, more complete in some instances but later than those listed above, are extant. The most important of these are the Chester Beatty papyri IV and V (Rahlfs 961 and 962) containing with lacunae substantial portions of Genesis 8–46 and dating from the 4th and 3d centuries C.E. respectively. Chester Beatty VI (Rahlfs 963) contains Numbers and Deuteronomy with lacunae and dates from the 2d or early 3d century C.E. (Pietersma 1977). See also CHESTER BEATTY PAPYRI. Detailed treatments of LXX and Qumran (particularly the witness of the scrolls) are found in *QHBT;* Klein 1974; Ulrich 1978, 1987, 1989; and Jeansonne 1988.

b. Uncials and Cursives. A few fine uncial and hundreds of cursive mss from the 16th century C.E. and earlier, witness to all or parts of LXX. The oldest of these mss (Codex Vaticanus = B, Codex Alexandrinus = A) were printed as texts in some of the early editions of LXX (see below). Full references to these and other mss are found in any modern critical edition and in several Introductions. The definitive descriptions of LXX mss are found in A. Rahlfs, *Verzeichnis der griechischen Handschriften des Alten Testaments* (MSU 2, Berlin, 1914). Critical editions published by the Göttingen Septuginta-Unternehmen provide documentation of the mss, papyri and other witnesses used in each instance, and the reader is directed to these for specifics. Jellicoe has also provided tables of mss collated in the Göttingen and larger Cambridge editions, with cross references to the older edition of Holmes-Parsons in the appendices to his *The Septuagint and Modern Study* (Jellicoe 1968: 360–69). The tools for Septuagint study—concordances, grammars, dictionaries and the like—are listed and discussed in the standard Introductions and surveys, and in several modern works (e.g., Tov 1981: 142–44; Harl 1988: 223–66; Brock, Fritsch, and Jellicoe 1973: 23–28).

c. Printed Editions. The first printed text of the complete Septuagint was included in the Complutensian Polyglot prepared in the years 1514–1517 under the auspices of Cardinal Ximenes de Cisneros, of Spain. The Greek text of this Bible, produced with care from selected mss including some sent to the Cardinal from the Vatican Library, formed the basis for LXX columns of four other great polyglots—the Antwerp (1569–72) the Heidelberg (1586–87), the Hamburg (1596), and the Paris (1645). After the printing of the Complutensian but before its publication, Andreas Asolanus issued in 1518–19 a completed edition of the Greek Bible in Venice. That edition, issuing as it did from Aldine press, is usually referred to as the Aldine and seems not to have been based on as wide a selection of mss as the Complutensian. The third and most influential of the older editions of LXX appeared in 1587 under the auspices of Pope Sixtus V. This Sixtina Romana was based primarily on the great Vatican Codex B with its lacunae being supplied from other mss. Numerous editions of LXX have been based on Sixtina and it is to the publication of this great uncial that the practice of identifying LXX with the B text is to be traced.

The fourth major edition of LXX appeared in England in the 18th century (1707–1720). Based on Codex Alexandrinus and produced initially by John Grabe at Oxford, it was completed on his death by able assistants. While in the main the edition was a presentation of the readings of a single codex, it utilized the Hexaplaric symbols (see below) to mark those portions which did not correspond with Masoretic Hebrew. Additions of any kind to the printed text of A were printed in smaller type.

The first attempt to provide what we would call today a critical edition was made under the direction of Robert Holmes of Oxford in the years 1788–1827. The first decade of that period was spent collecting support and collating mss for the project with the aid of scholars both from England and the continent. The first volume, *Genesis,* appeared in 1798, seven years before Holmes' death; the remaining volumes were completed by James Parsons. The printed text was the Sixtine edition but the apparatus included readings of some 300 mss (including 20 uncials), evidence from the Old Latin, Coptic, Arabic, Slavonic, Armenian and Georgian versions as well as patristic citations. The notes included readings from the great editions-Complutensian, Aldine, Grabian and others. While the edition of Holmes and Parsons has been the object of criticism it still remains an invaluable and certainly the largest storehouse of materials concerning LXX.

The 19th-century edition which has had the most lasting impact was begun at Cambridge in 1883. Initially the Syndics proposed to present an edition of LXX and Apocrypha with a critical apparatus containing the variations of all the Greek uncial mss, of select cursives, of the more important versions, of quotations made by Philo and the earlier and more important ecclesiastical writers. As a first step, they produced, between 1887 and 1894, a portable text (edited by the well-known Henry Barclay Swete) using B as text and two or three other uncials as supplements. In time the larger edition of the Cambridge LXX appeared, the early volumes being edited by A. E. Brooke and N. McLean, the later ones by H. St John Thackeray. Though not as wide in scope as the Holmes and Parsons edition, the Cambridge LXX was executed with greater care. The larger Cambridge LXX also printed the text of B, listing several other witnesses in an apparatus. Its citations, especially of the versions and the patristic citations, have not always proven to be accurate. The project was arrested in 1940 and shows no sign of being resumed.

Modern LXX studies owe much to the work of Paul A. de Lagarde (1827–1891) who, despite his failings, was an exceptionally accomplished scholar by any standard. His primary conviction—the basis for his own activities and the school of LXX thinking to which his name is attached—was that all mss of the LXX present mixed texts, the result of an eclectic process. Thus, the process of arriving at the *Urtext* of the Septuagint must likewise be eclectic. To restore the text, one: (1) needs to be acquainted with the style of individual translators; (2) should give preference to a free translation rather than the slavishly exact one, all other things being equal; (3) should give preference to readings pointing to a Hebrew original other than the MT. Although Lagarde never produced any critical edition, he had hoped, using principles like these, to arrive in due course to the original LXX.

While one may quarrel with the specific results of Lagarde's approach, it is difficult to fault his principles in view of the subsequent history. On Lagarde's death in 1891, his task was taken over by his able student A. Rahlfs. By the beginning of the 20th century, Rudolf Smend and Julius Wellhausen initiated a program to provide the necessary resources for the maintenance and extension of Lagarde and Rahlfs' work, resulting in the establishment of the Göttingen "Septuaginta-Unternehmen" in March, 1908. With this support Rahlfs was able to produce the first critical editions based on his mentor's principles. *Ruth* appeared in 1922, followed by *Genesis* in 1926 and *Psalms* in 1931. His popular edition of the Septuagint based on three major uncials was edited just before his death in 1935 and is perhaps still the most widely used edition of LXX today. From then till now the "Septuaginta-Unternehmen" has produced with unfailing determination the most reliable editions of LXX arranged on Lagardian principles (see below).

2. Secondary Witnesses. Secondary witnesses to the text of LXX consist of: (1) scripture quotations and allusions in Greek preserved in Jewish and Christian authors; and (2) the texts of various versions based on early mss of LXX.

a. Versions. The most valuable of the versions made from Greek are the Syro-Hexaplar, the Coptic, Armenian, Georgian, Arabic, Ethiopic, and Old Latin. The autographs of some versions would have been made from mss that predate considerably our oldest complete extant Greek mss. Vaticanus, for instance, is only a 4th century C.E. ms, whereas versions such as the Coptic and the Old Latin were known to have been prepared in the 2d or 3d century C.E. Thus, the accurate editing and evaluation of the versions illuminate our understanding of the textual history of LXX, if only because in each case their texts, when carefully established and retroverted into Greek, would provide a record of at least one Greek ms from the period of their composition.

Just as the translation from Hebrew into Greek produced changes reflective of the concerns of the Greek translators, so in each of the versions one finds further evidence of local coloring. And just as it is difficult to determine for sure whether a deviant reading in Greek reflects the translator's idiosyncracy or a different Hebrew parent text, so in the versions it is not always clear whether variance is due to the translator or to the text being translated. Likewise, the grammatical and syntactical limitations of each of the target languages affect the translation from Greek and by extension, the interpretation of the value of that version for text criticism.

The relationship of the various secondary witnesses to LXX is only now beginning to become clear. Earlier printed editions of LXX which collated the versions often culled their readings from an easily accessible ms, or from printed editions (of the versions) themselves often based on one or two convenient mss. Thus in many instances the full witness of the secondary version had not been utilized. Critical studies of the Armenian, the Ethiopic and the Coptic (Bohairic and Sahidic) of specific books of LXX have been concluded in recent times and their results would not be reflected everywhere in the Göttingen editions. The present writer's own work on the Bohairic has shown that while in the main the translation follows LXX, there are instances when the relatively late mss that are available retain deviant readings which, while probably the result of inner Coptic developments, could also point to the existence of a Greek ms now no longer extant. Each of the other versions reflects its own idiosyncracies and the reader is urged to consult the individual studies on them (Fernández-Marcos 1985: 15–80; Nagel 1985; 1987; Clear 1973).

b. Patristic Evidence. In addition to the versions made from Greek, the witness of the early Christian writers provides a valuable LXX resource. Though many writers are known to have flourished in a period contemporary with and antecedent to our oldest Greek mss, the record of their writings—commentaries, sermons and the like—comes to us in mss that are themselves much later. Our ability to determine what exactly was said is affected by this historic fact, and also by the fact that well-intentioned copyists often corrected the biblical patristic citation with that of a version of the Bible current in their time. To complicate matters further, the early Christian writer may merely allude to a text or may quote from memory or, what is most frustrating, may quote one form of a biblical text in one instance and a different version of the same text in another. Some fathers consistently quote accurately, others are rather cavalier. Thus recording and evaluating this evidence presents its own challenges.

In summary, the total witnesses to LXX have been estimated to be well over two thousand. Several mss contain only a single book or a small section of a book, other books are witnessed to by hundreds of mss and several are in between these extremes. But together all these sources provide a complete, if somewhat complex picture of the textual backdrop against which LXX studies must be executed.

C. Theories of Origins

1. Aristeas. As suggested above, the best known story of the origin of the Greek translation of the Hebrew Bible is the story of Aristeas, sometimes referred to as the Letter of (pseudo-) Aristeas. The details of this story are so often repeated that only its broadest outline and some of the reasons for its implausibility as history need be mentioned.

The Epistle of Aristeas describes how a King Ptolemy, probably Ptolemy II Philadelphus (285–247 B.C.E.), desiring to collect if possible all the books in the world, and having been informed by his librarian, Demetrius of Phalerum, that the royal library was lacking a copy of the laws of the Jews, sent a letter to Eleazar the high priest in Jerusalem (by the hand of the Aristeas and others) requesting six learned elders from each tribe to perform the translation. The letter is full with details seemingly extraneous to a modern reader—descriptions of the temple, qualifications of the translators, questions by the king to the translators, the nature of the High Priest's garments, and so on. On the arrival of the translators in Egypt, they are received immediately by the king, given the best accommodations and invited to a royal banquet. In due course, Demetrius conducts them to comfortable secluded quarters by the sea where they completed the work in 72 days—precisely as many as the number of the translators. The finished work is highly praised by the Alexandrian Jewish community and it was determined to be so final that a curse would be on any one who, by omission, transposition or addition, would change any part of it. The Egyptian king is impressed with the mind of the Lawgiver and comments on the divine origin of the Law. He dismisses the translators with gifts for themselves, for the High Priest, and with invitations to return.

The story has been augmented and retold by several subsequent writers—Aristobulus, Philo, Josephus, and in various patristic sources. (Extensive discussions of and references to it are found in Jellicoe 1968: 29–58; 1974: 158–225; Harl 1988: 40–68.) It seems to be the product of an unknown Jewish writer in Alexandria writing in the last half of the second, or the first part of the 1st century B.C.E. The narrative contains a number of inconsistencies and inaccuracies, a condition unlikely to have been the case had the writer been a contemporary of the events being described. Most notable is the mention of Demetrius of Phalerum as chief librarian—a position he never held in the court of Ptolemy II since the latter, on his accession had banished him to exile. Another error is the mention of Menedemus of Eritria as being present at the banquet held in honor of the translators when he had already been dead two years before the end of Ptolemy I Soter's reign. Several other points of detail suggest the improbability of the story being historical, among which is the matter of a Greek king being so interested in the Hebrew scriptures, to go to great lengths to secure them. In fact the idea of Greeks translating the religious scriptures of such a minority of their population is highly improbable.

The dating of pseudo-Aristeas's work and the historical circumstances to which it points have generated intense scholarly discussion. Opinions on the date run the gamut from 200 B.C.E. to 50 C.E. As to the real purpose of the work, it has been variously considered as: (1) an apology for the Greek translation of the Torah; (2) a propaganda piece directed at Greeks to show them the superiority of Jewish religion and law; (3) a work which is intended to defend the literary activities of Alexandrian Jews against the attacks of other Jews in Palestine or elsewhere in Egypt; and (4) a propaganda for the original Greek translation against a contemporary revision.

Despite questions about dating and purpose, a broad consensus has emerged concerning the *Letter of Aristeas* on the following points. First, the events described in it relate only to the Pentateuch which was the first part of the Jewish scriptures to be translated into Greek. Second, the translation was an official undertaking supported by Jewish authorities possibly for synagogue and instructional use, and done in Egypt probably in the middle of the 3d century or earlier. Third, the number of translators is not certain.

2. Kahle. While the Aristeas story is the most popular, it is by no means the only theory of LXX origins. Much discussed in recent times is the explanation of the Aristeas account and of the origins of LXX identified with Paul Kahle. Using the analogy of Aramaic Targumim, Kahle suggested (first in 1915 and often thereafter) that the diversity of witnesses to the text of the Greek points to the fact that there was never one original translation but rather several designed to meet the needs of specific communities. The Aristeas story is propaganda for an official revision of earlier translations, not a description of a new one. Kahle finds evidence for his position in the Aristeas text itself, section 30 of which he believed (contrary to most scholars) alludes to the existence of other translations in Greek not in Hebrew; in the differences in the A and B texts of Judges; and in the existence of the different early papyri. For him, the task of scholarship in this field is not to reconstruct or even attempt a hypothetical reconstruction of the original text of the version, but to assemble and examine with the greatest care all the fragments and traces of the earliest forms of the Greek Bible we can discover. It is fair to say that while some reputable scholars found Kahle's thesis appealing if not persuasive, the majority of Septuagintalists have not been convinced by it.

3. Lagarde. More representative of the mainstream of contemporary scholarship is the theory of LXX origins identified with Paul de Lagarde and the Göttingen school. This *Urtext* theory as it is sometimes called, suggests that all mss of LXX can ultimately be traced to one prototype. In order to achieve this, Lagarde theorized that one needed first of all to attempt to reconstruct the original forms of each of the three main recensions of LXX—the Origenian, the Lucianic and the Hesychian—and from them to work back to the *Urtext.* No one, not even Lagarde himself, succeeded in the reconstruction of the *Urtext* conceived in this way. The recension of Hesychius has never been identified with any certainty and much controversy surrounds the Lucianic text. However the basic idea of an original translation for each of the books of LXX is accepted by the vast majority of Septuagintalists and constitutes the working hypothesis of the Göttingen Septuaginta-Unternehmen—the only active institute involved in the preparation of LXX texts.

4. Tov. Recently, a median position between Kahle and Lagarde has been articulated with some vigor by Tov (1981: 42, and often elsewhere) who traces it back to Bickerman. Essentially, Tov identifies four stages in the development of the text of LXX: (1) the original translation; (2) a multitude of textual traditions resulting from the insertion of corrections (mainly toward the Hebrew) in all known individual scrolls; (3) textual stabilization in the 1st and 2d centuries C.E.; and (4) the creation of new textual groups and the corruption of existing ones through the influence of the revisions of Origen and Lucian in the 3d and 4th centuries C.E.

Attractive as this position seems in theory, it is problematic on two practical counts. First it assumes that the "original translation" was different from some identifiable "Hebrew" and thus was immediately in need of "correction." A corollary of this assumption is that the original translation was free of human failings so that no traceable "corrections" of any kind would have been present from the start. Second it implies that there was homogeneity in the Hebrew traditions from the earliest times. If we take for granted the possibility that the original translation may have included what to us might seem to be corrections of and insertions in MT (and this seems eminently plausible), there is no need to make a distinction between (1) and (2) above, and the position is not a median position at all but rather a refinement of the Lagardian hypothesis.

5. Other Theories. Other theories have been posited but none has gained widespread acceptance; some have been rejected outright. The following are only representative not exhaustive. Originated by O. G. Tychsen (1734–1815) and revived by F. X. Wutz (1883–1938) is the so-called transcription theory. It suggests that the LXX translators used a Hebrew text translated into Greek characters. Moses Gaster is identified with a theory which places the milieu of the Greek Pentateuch not in Alexandria as is broadly accepted but rather in Palestine, because only a Palestinian origin could have generated sufficient prestige for the new translation. The decision to produce the Greek OT was a means by which Jews could assert their superiority and antiquity to the Greek speaking world. With H. St. John Thackeray has been identified the liturgical approach, which in its essence suggests that the LXX translation originated from the needs of the Jewish community of Alexandria, which required a translation of the Pentateuch for synagogue reading. In time, the Latter Prophets, a partial version of the Former Prophets, and then gradually the Writings were all translated. Thackery's position, though speculative, seems plausible enough especially for the Pentateuch.

Several modern scholars have seen the LXX translation as arising out of Jewish community needs other than liturgical—educational, apologetical, proselytizing, and so on. It has even been proposed that Greek Torah received the official sanction because it was a part of the judicial system of the Ptolemies intended to govern the activities of the Jews (Harl 1988: 66–78).

D. History of the LXX Text

1. Revisions. Even though the circumstances surrounding the original production of what has become known as LXX are disputed, its subsequent history is much clearer. If Tov is correct, revision of the translations began almost as soon as they were copied for the first time but we can only speculate about the nature of such revisions. We know for sure that by the 2d century C.E., Jewish scholars, reacting to the widespread co-opting and polemical use of the LXX by Christians, began to produce editions intended to correct mistranslations, expunge Christian additions and to conform to the Hebrew text that had by then become normative in Palestine.

a. Aquila. One of these editions was done in 128 C.E. by a certain Aquila, a Jewish proselyte of Pontus and disciple of the famous Rabbi Akiba. Aquila's version was based on strict principles of Jewish interpretation and was slavishly literal to the Hebrew text, even though it is clear that he had a good knowledge of Greek. Aquila's literalism and precision even to the point of using words with similar sounds made his work particularly attractive to his Jewish contemporaries. The version of Aquila was respected for many years. Both Origen and Jerome were impressed with it, the latter even borrowing from that version's readings in the case of a few rare words. Aquila is considered in some circles to be identical with Onqelos, the compiler of a Targum of the Pentateuch and there is virtual unanimity in Septuagintal circles that the extant text of the Greek of Qoheleth is to be identified in some way with him.

The text of Aquila's translation is preserved in a number of different places. The longest text available is a palimpsest containing some 141 verses of the Psalms. In addition we have several other fragments of Origen's Hexapla (see below), the third column of which contained Aquila's translation. Several mss preserve in the margins readings not only from Aquila but also the other two well known revisers Symmachus and Theodotion. Finally, the Church Fathers (especially Eusebius, Theodoret and Jerome) cite the three Jewish revisers in their discussions and commentaries. See AQUILA'S VERSION.

b. Symmachus. Another revision is identified with Symmachus, who produced it toward the end of the 2d century C.E. The edition is distinguished for its literal accuracy and use of good Greek idiom. That is to say, the revision is very precise in some places, whereas in others it translates in keeping with the sense. Some sources identify Symmachus as an Ebionite and thus a Christian; others contend that he was a Samaritan convert to Judaism. See SYMMACHUS, SYMMACHUS' VERSION.

c. Theodotion. The third reviser of the Septuagint, Theodotion, presents one of the more intriguing problems in modern LXX studies. According to early Christian writers, there was a historic Theodotion variously identified as an Ephesian proselyte to Judaism (Irenaeus), and an Ebionite (Jerome) who worked toward the end of the 2d century C.E. The text on which he worked as a reviser seems however to have been different from the standard LXX and to have been in existence since the early part of the 1st century B.C.E. For instance, NT citations from the book of Daniel, where a version generally considered to be Theodotion has supplanted LXX in all but two mss, are drawn from the former not the latter. Early Church Fathers—Clement of Rome, Justin Martyr, Irenaeus—cite Theodotion's text of Daniel. This situation has led many scholars to postulate an Ur- or a proto-Theodotion in order to explain the presence of Theodotionic readings before the time of Theodotion. See THEODOTION, THEODOTION'S VERSION.

d. Proto-Theodotion. The discovery in 1953 of a Greek Scroll of the Minor Prophets (Rahlfs 943 above) at Naḥal Ḥever (and its subsequent edition by D. Barthélemy) led to a rethinking in some circles of the Theodotion problem. Some scholars have been persuaded completely by Barthélemy, and now argue that a 2d century Theodotion is no longer necessary, suggesting that Ur-/proto-/*kaige*- Theodotion was all there was, and that this reviser flourished toward the end of the 1st century B.C.E., his work being the basis for both Aquila's and Symmachus' in light of the demonstrable similarity of all three in so many instances. Other scholars, recognizing that Barthélemy's thesis and assumptions raised as many problems as they solved, have been more cautious and maintain that the historic Theodotion may have worked as a reviser within the tradition reflected by the earlier so-called Ur-Theodotion. Questions have also been raised as to whether or not the so-called Theodotion text in Daniel is to be attributed to Theodotion, or whether the sixth column of Origen's Hexapla—traditionally considered to be Theodotion—is indeed what it has been claimed to be.

Whether or not one accepts a proto-Theodotion, there seems to be agreement on the following characteristics of the revision as per Barthélemy and his followers: (1) the use of *kaige* to translate Hebrew *gam* and *wĕgam;* (2) the use of *anēr* rather than *hekastos* to represent Hebrew *ʾîš;* (3) a tendency to use *ep/apanōthen* as a translation of Hebrew *mʿl* in contrast to LXX, which uses *apo* or *epanō;* (4) the elimination of the historical present in favor of the aorist as a translation of the Hebrew *waw*-consecutive with the imperfect in narration; (5) tendency to stress the atemporal nature of Hebrew *ʾên* by translating it as *ouk estin;* (6) use of phrase *egō eimi* as a translation of Hebrew *ʾānōkî* and to distinguish it from *ʾănî;* (7) avoidance of *eis apantēsin* as a translation of Hebrew *lqrʾt;* (8) a tendency toward transliteration, especially of unknown words; (9) a tendency to systematize the Greek equivalents of specific Hebrew words or roots. Further refinements and characteristics of this recension have also been proposed.

Barthélemy identified the work of the Reviser (who has been later called *kaige*-Theodotion) in the other parts of LXX—Lamentations, Ruth, the B text of Judges, the Theodotionic text of Daniel, the Theodotionic supplements to LXX Jeremiah and Job, and in the Quinta of the Psalter.

It is regrettable that the portion of the LXX—the books of Samuel-Kings—on which so much energy has been spent is not yet available in a truly critical edition. Many conclusions which seem valid with the state of the text that we now possess, may well be adjusted in the future. It is highly likely that several of the readings attributed to revisers of one kind or another would, on careful scrutiny of all the available evidence (not merely that listed in Brooke, McLean, and Thackeray), be determined to be original LXX.

2. Recensions. a. Origen's Hexapla. Next to the story of Aristeas, that of Origen and the Hexapla is perhaps the best known in the history of the LXX text. A native of Egypt and a Christian, Origen was one of those persons with an enormous capacity for detailed and hard work. He also had the benefit of a wealthy benefactor who provided the means to facilitate his voluminous publications. The Hexapla, a massive six-columned work estimated to have been about 6,500 pages long, was completed between 230 and 240 C.E. Origen's chief purpose was to equip Christians for their discussions with Jews, who frequently appealed to the original Hebrew. To this end he arranged in parallel columns the following texts: (1) the Hebrew of his day; (2) the Hebrew text transliterated into Greek; (3) Aquila; (4) Symmachus; (5) LXX, and (6) Theodotion. In some books of the Bible it is reported that Origen added even more columns which he called Quinta, Sexta and Septima; there is also evidence that a version consisting of only the last four columns, a Tetrapla was in use, though some have argued that the Tetrapla was merely another name for the Hexapla.

Origen's main concern was the fifth column, LXX, which he hoped to link with the Hebrew of his day. To this end he borrowed from Aristarchus (217–145 B.C.E.) certain sigla, well known and used in Alexandrian philological studies, and incorporated them into his work. Words in his LXX without Hebrew counterparts were placed between an obelus and a metobelus. Words and passages in Hebrew without LXX equivalent were copied from another version (most often Theodotion) and inserted into the LXX column between an asterisk and a metobelus.

That would have been an acceptable condition had the

Hexapla been retained in its original form, or if Origen did only what he claims to have done. But he seems in fact to have adjusted his text without always indicating where he did, and also the extant witnesses to the Origenian recension do not everywhere retain the hexaplaric signs. Equally problematic was the situation Origen faced when there was variance between the Greek and the Hebrew necessitating a choice from one of the three versions, and when those versions themselves were divergent from each other. His tendency to choose the version closest to the Hebrew meant that in effect the final form of the fifth column was conservative, mixed, and in the last analysis, not much more than a Greek version of Origen's Hebrew. As a result, the work of Origen, rather than helping to clarify a problem, has in many ways created one. The responsible modern text critic tries to get behind Origen—to identify pre-Hexaplaric readings—in order to approach in some reasonable way what might have been original LXX. Because Origen mistakenly believed that the Hebrew text available to him was identical with that from which the Greek translators worked, he unwittingly perpetuated the very confusion he tried to remove.

The Hexapla was not easily duplicated, but its fifth column was copied and widely circulated during the 4th century. A new recension was thereby created consisting of a mixture of Origen's Septuagint with random readings from Theodotion, and Aquila. In addition, the word order of this Hexaplaric Septuagint differed in places from that of the LXX on which Origen worked because he, believing in the primacy of the Hebrew, had deliberately changed the Greek word order to conform to the Hebrew. The copying of the fifth column in isolation from the Hebrew resulted in the gradual misapprehension of the meaning of the Hexaplaric symbols and in the tendency of scribes to omit them. As a result, many extant mss show the influence of Origen's work but do not retain the Hexaplaric signs.

b. The Syro-Hexaplar. Fortunately, the fifth column was translated into Syriac by Paul, Bishop of Tella (618–19) and is known as the Syro-Hexaplar. The translation was made in a monastery not far from Alexandria between 613 and 617 (Baars 1968: 1). Opinions vary as to the fidelity and accuracy of the copying of the Hexaplaric signs retained in this Syriac work, but few question its importance.

c. Hesychius. While the Hexapla was copied in Caesarea for use in Palestine, two other revisions were in circulation, so Jerome informs us, one for use in Egypt and the other in Antioch. These recensions are identified with Hesychius and Lucian respectively. So little is known for sure about the Hesychian recension that it can only be mentioned in passing. In recent times Jellicoe (1963: 409–18) has argued that the B text reflects this recension. Others have mentioned various witnesses including the Coptic (Bohairic) of the minor Prophets or even the A text.

d. Lucian. The more important revision is identified with a martyr who died in 312 C.E. The nature and person of Lucian and his activity can be established in a number of ways. Eusebius, in his *Church History,* refers favorably to Lucian, commenting on his competence in sacred learning. Jerome makes the most famous comment about the Lucianic revisions in his preface to the books of Chronicles: ". . . Constantinople to Antioch approves the copies [containing the text] of Lucian the martyr . . ." (Metzger in Jellicoe 1974: 273). According to the description of Pseudo-Athanasius in his *Synopsis sacrae Scripturae,* Lucian, "Using the earlier editions [i. e., of Aquila, Theodotion and Symmachus] and the Hebrew, and having accurately surveyed the expressions which fell short of or went beyond the truth, and having corrected them in their proper places, he published them for his Christian brethren" (Metzger in Jellicoe 1974: 274). The ancient witnesses thus attest to the life and activity of Lucian, but give no clear indication of the range of his revision or the sources he may have used.

Modern scholars have identified certain mss in which the text of Lucian is believed to appear. Seminal work in that area was carried out by Ceriani, Field, and Lagarde. Two devices assisted in this attempt: (1) the frequent agreement of the presumed Lucianic text with biblical quotations in the works of early Christian writers especially Chrysostom and Theodoret, both trained in Antioch and likely to have been influenced by the Lucianic revision; and (2) the presence of a siglum *kai "lambda"* (the Greek letter "l") in the marginal readings of several Greek mss, and of the Syriac letter "lomadh (L) marking variants in certain Syriac mss. These sigla, although open to other interpretations, were thought to confirm the existence of Lucian's revision and work. The mss 19, 82, 93 and 108 (Brooke and McLean's boc_2e_2) were identified in the historical books as Lucianic by Ceriani and Field, while Lagarde came to a similar conclusion on his own.

Thus began a detailed investigation for the past 100 years into the Lucianic recension. Rahlfs refined and extended the work of his mentor and confirmed the Lucianic nature of the four codices in the books of Kings. Several attempts were made by other scholars to identify Lucian outside Samuel-Kings; none of these has proven conclusive. In fact it has been shown that in much of the Pentateuch there is no evidence of Lucian at all.

e. Ur/Proto-Lucian. What has been of greater interest, however, is the so-called Ur/proto-Lucian debate. Many have observed the similarity of certain texts known to have existed before the time of the historic Lucian, to what was determined to be "Lucianic" readings. Among these "pre-Lucianic" readings according to Metzger (in Jellicoe 1974: 285–88) are parts of the Old Latin version dating from the 2d century C.E., the Peshitta version of the OT, a papyrus fragment of Ps 77:1–18 dating from the 3/2d century C.E., quotations from Justin Martyr (mid 2d century), certain NT quotations, biblical quotations by Josephus of Samuel-Kings, and 2d-century papyrus fragments of Deuteronomy.

The debate on Lucian and proto-Lucian has proceeded into the modern period. Several of these witnesses to a pre-Lucianic text, especially in the Pentateuch (Wevers 1973, 1977; Fernández-Marcos 1978) and the Psalms (Pietersma 1978 and Perkins 1978), have been seriously questioned in recent discussions. Tov (1988: 186–87) summarized the four main positions on Lucian research in Samuel-Kings in the following terms:

Rahlfs: Lucian brought the OG in conformity with the Hebrew and at the same time removed the OG from the

MT by revising its language and style. Rahlfs also recognized that Lucian reflected ancient elements.

Barthélemy: Lucianic mss (19-82-93-108) in 2 Sam 11:2–1 Kgs 2:11 are the OG and the other mss (formerly considered OG) contain the *kaige*-Theodotion.

Cross: The Lucianic mss in the same passages consist of two layers: (1) a substratum consisting of a text (proto-Lucianic and) revised toward a Hebrew similar to that found in 4QSam[a]; (2) a layer consisting of the historical corrections of Lucian.

Tov: Data do not support Cross' proto-Lucianic revision. Lucian mss contain two layers both containing revisional elements made in the time of the historic Lucian.

One of the clearest syntheses of the issues involved in the Lucianic debate is given by N. Fernández-Marcos (1984: 163–74). There he adds an element that should augment Tov's categories above. Marcos would locate the work of Sebastian Brock (1966) between Rahlfs and Barthélemy. Two of Brock's discoveries concerning Lucian in 1 Samuel deserve stressing: (1) the desire to improve the LXX text stylistically by eliminating Hellenistic forms and terms; and (2) the adaptation of the text to the needs of the public reading (e.g., by the insertion of proper nouns instead of pronouns, translation of transliterated words, etc.).

E. LXX as a Translation

The real value of LXX resides not so much in its function as a corrective to some Hebrew text of which we have a copy, but rather as a record of the way in which a group of Jews in the 3d century and for some time thereafter understood their traditions. In the pre-Christian centuries, there was wide textual variety as is evidenced in the discoveries of materials both in Palestine and Egypt, and thus it is well established that the parent texts (and certainly the translators) for each book of the LXX were probably different. It is also quite clear that the revisional activity which took place after Origen was in fact taking place long before his time, both on the Hebrew and Greek texts. Thus, while it is convenient to use *BHS* or *BHK* as a starting point for understanding what undergirded the LXX translations, it is dangerous, dishonest and wrong to assume that Leningradensis B 19A (MT) lay before the pre-Christian translators (cf. Ulrich 1988). Even more reprehensible is the widespread practice of assuming that the text of one uncial represents LXX. It has been shown that the character of B, the ms most often mistaken for LXX, is by no means consistent throughout. In Daniel, for instance, it witnesses to the text of Theodotion.

In order to evaluate properly the value of LXX as a translation, it is necessary first of all to ensure that the Greek text in use is as close as possible to the original. The process by which this is achieved is not well known nor often discussed, and so the end products of the Göttingen Septuaginta-Unternehmen are mistakenly referred to as eclectic texts. The choice of the word eclectic, while appropriate for some kinds of literature, is misleading and to some degree pejorative in LXX criticism because it suggests that "bits and pieces" from "pure" mss are blended to create a product, the sum of which is less desirable than its parts. In point of fact, as any one who has worked with LXX mss will attest, and as Lagarde himself pointed out long ago, all extant LXX mss (including the great uncials) are corrupt, in view of the complicated history of LXX. (Equally corrupt, for that matter, is the so-called MT.) The task of the modern editor of LXX is thus not one of picking from equals but rather of sorting and making, at every stage, critical judgments about a vast array of uneven witnesses, following well established principles which only sometimes can be clearly articulated. In some rare instances the reading which appears in the text may not even be present in a Greek ms.

An editor gets that kind of confidence only after years of working intimately with the extant materials and reflecting not only on the grammatical and syntactical principles of Hellenistic Greek, classical and post-biblical Hebrew, and Aramaic, but also and especially on the tendencies present in each of the mss in question, and on the complicated textual history of LXX's relationship with the Hebrew traditions.

The process of establishing the critical text begins in Göttingen, where assistants with several years of classical Greek are employed to collate completely and then recollate each of the more than 120 (at least for the Pentateuch, more or less in other books) mss—uncial, cursive, and some fragments—cited in the apparatus. The collations are rechecked before the books are sent to the respective editors, who in turn establish textual groupings, and also identify unaligned mss. For most of the Pentateuch some 17 textual groups and subgroups with varying numbers of *codices mixti* have been shown to exist. The precise relationship of these textual groups to the critical text, to each other and to the unaligned mss is yet to be determined fully, although descriptions of the individual characters of each of these groups are given the Text Histories of the various editions.

The first task of the editor is to augment the collation books by adding the readings of the papyri; the readings of early versions known to have been based on the LXX—Arabic, Ethiopic, Armenian, Old Latin, etc.; other important witnesses to LXX such as the Syro-Hexaplar and the older printed editions—Complutesian, Aldine, Sixtina; the newer printed editions, especially Rahlfs and of course the Hebrew of *BHS*, the Samaritan Pentateuch and, where extant, fragments from Qumran.

One critical part of the editor's task is to address demonstrably Hexaplaric readings—both pluses and minuses—*en route* to determining the critical text. In this regard the readings of the early papyri are scrutinized carefully and given due consideration but not automatic preference, since they too may be corrupt. The dates and format of mss do not necessarily always indicate accurately the level of their reliability; cursive mss, though later than uncials and papyri, often preserve early traditions. Nor is the equation of Leningradensis (MT) with some segment of the Greek textual tradition taken automatically as indicative of original LXX. The governing principles are much more nuanced than that: readings are everywhere "weighed" not counted. When the final text (and detailed apparatus) has been established, it is then returned to Göttingen for careful checking and publication.

This means that it is not possible for average scholars with only the text and apparatus before them to understand fully all of the factors which entered into the textual judgment in every instance. It means also that unless the scholarly community wishes to perpetuate widespread confusion, the judgment of each editor with respect to the critical text should be respected.

Once the critical text is chosen, the techniques of the translator in, and if possible, the textual character of the witnesses so that book should be examined carefully before any final statement is made about it. Each modern critical edition is accompanied with a textual history prepared by the editor, which attempts to explain the relationships of the various textual families to each other and also to describe particular tendencies in that book. Erroneous assertions about LXX have been published because scholars fail or are unwilling to compare the translation patterns in an entire book and thus confine their observations to isolated readings. Equally dangerous is the widespread practice in scholarship of making comparisons between words found in different books of LXX (or in critical and diplomatic editions) on the unexamined assumption that translators were acquainted with each other's work.

The last point is particularly apposite in view of the diversity of translation styles and textual anomalies which present themselves when one compares the critical LXX text with the text in *BHS.* Although critical texts have not been completed for the whole of LXX and thus any conclusions should be considered tentative, certain patterns of translation have begun to appear. The Pentateuch, it is fair to say, is in the middle of a continuum with wooden/mechanical/literalistic on the one extreme and free paraphrase on the other. On the wooden end is the translation of Ecclesiastes, on the other end is Proverbs and Job. Specific studies of particular books have been done and their conclusions are generally helpful (cf. Tov 1988: 168 n. 22). In addition, it has been shown that several types of "exegesis"—theological, midrashic, actualizations and so on—are present in the various books of LXX. Thus, the nature of the LXX translations as a whole, the kinds of techniques and interpretational principles in specific parts, shape our view of the LXX books as translations. The textual anomalies of LXX vs MT are equally significant. Some of the more obvious are listed below:

Exodus: Chaps. 35 to 40 differ considerably from the MT. Some details in the Hebrew are absent, others abridged, and others transposed in the Greek text. Several theories have been proposed to explain the situation as it stands.

Deuteronomy: At the end of the Song of Moses (32:43) the LXX is longer by six verses than the Hebrew; the Greek version of the Shema is different also.

Joshua: Two different descriptions of the territory of Benjamin, Judah and Simeon (15:21–62 and 18:22–19:45) are attested in the main uncials A and B. The discussion of the institution of the cities of refuge (20:4–6) is present in the MT and not in LXX. There is also variance in the ending of Joshua and the beginning of Judges where the Greek contains fifteen lines unattested in MT.

Judges: Rahlfs prints two texts because the main uncials A and B differ so widely. It has been suggested that the B text reflects an early revision (possibly *kaige*-Theodotion?) whereas the A text reflects the Origenian recension. In both texts there are elements not paralleled in the MT. Despite the differences there seems not to be sufficient reason to postulate two translators but rather only two witnesses to a complex textual tradition.

1–2 Samuel: The Greek text is longer in general than the Hebrew, often providing smoother reading. There are also elements in the Hebrew that are not in the Greek. One of the more notable details is the portrayal of David in relation to the Goliath story (1 Samuel 17–18). The Greek text is shorter by 50 verses than the Hebrew.

1–2 Kings: The LXX portrayal of Solomon, Jeroboam, and Ahab differs considerably from the MT. In general the LXX text is more extensive, often giving two accounts of narratives attested only once in the MT. Some of these seem to point to the existence of two textual traditions concerning the schism between Israel and Judah.

1–2 Chronicles: There are differences in the listing of the genealogies of the descendants of Ham, the Greek in general shortening the list found in MT. The Greek text of 2 Chronicles 35 contains readings which, while absent in the MT, are attested in the same form in 2 Kings, 23 and 24.

Psalms: The numbering of the Greek Psalms from 9–147 is generally less by one than that of the MT. Hebrew psalms 9 and 10 and also 114 and 115 are, in both instances, combined in the Greek. Psalm titles in the Greek tend to be longer and more numerous than in the Hebrew.

Proverbs: Several verses in MT have no Greek equivalent and vice versa. Many of the Greek additions may be explained as fusions of two readings or additions from other known contexts, but some suggest that they were drawn from collections different from those reflected in the MT.

Job: The Greek text is shorter by approximately one sixth than the MT. The differences do not everywhere consist of abbreviations. There is a long final addition and alternate rendering of some passages.

Esther: Of the 270 verses in the Greek text of Esther, 107 find no parallel in the MT. The additions are widely distributed.

Jeremiah: The variance between the Greek and the MT is extensive and often observed. The Greek text is shorter by some 2700 words than the MT. It now seems assured that the shorter Greek version is based upon a different Hebrew text than the MT and is not merely a shortening of the latter. The "oracles against the nations" are situated in another place and in a different order than the MT. Chaps. 46–51 in the MT are placed in the LXX following 25:13 and there are significant differences in the contents of Chaps. 10 and 23.

The Minor Prophets: The order of the books differs in the two sources.

Ezekiel: The Greek version differs from the MT in many ways. The difference most often discussed is 36:23–38, the oracle of a new heart. The Greek text seems to have been based on a Hebrew original much shorter than that represented in the MT.

Daniel: Two Greek texts are available for this book, one a revision called Theodotion, the other LXX. Both of these differ with the MT in a variety of ways. In Chap. 4, for example, the LXX text is clearly longer than the MT even though it omits several elements present in the Hebrew. In addition to these differences there appear the well-known additions *Bel and the Dragon, The Prayer of Azariah and the Three Young Men,* and the *Story of Susanna.*

F. Importance of LXX

That the LXX is an important document in biblical studies has long been recognized, but the reasons why have not always been uniformly or clearly expressed. Mainline biblical scholars have therefore tended to use it primarily as a means to correct the MT where the latter is perceived to be corrupt. The foregoing discussions should make clear that the Greek version, although translated from Hebrew, was not necessarily translated from a text accessible to us. The most important reason for studying the LXX then is to read and understand the thought of Jews in the pre-Christian centuries. In the process we may obtain insights into the textual history of the Hebrew Bible. On the purely formal level, any Hebrew text retroverted from the Greek Bible will in fact predate by several hundred years the complete ms on which our Hebrew Bible is based. Septuagint studies are thus important for textual, canonical, and exegetical purposes.

A second reason western scholars especially specialists in Christianity, should consider the LXX, is that it was the Bible of the early Christian Church. It was not secondary to any other scripture; it was Scripture. When a NT writer allegedly urged his audience to consider that all scripture given by divine "inspiration" is also profitable for doctrine, it was to the LXX not the Hebrew that attention was being called. The LXX also provides the context in which many of the lexical and theological concepts in the NT can best be explained. Excellent syntheses of the relationships between LXX and NT have been made. Summaries and evaluations of these discussions and issues appear in Smith (1972 and 1988).

Before and after the adoption of the LXX by Christians—most of whom were former Jews—it was an important document in Hellenistic circles. Early Jewish writers in Greek, such as Philo (ca. 30 C.E.), Paul (ca. 50 C.E.), and Josephus (ca. 80 C.E.) allegorized, expanded and quoted it extensively. The sermons and commentaries of Greek and Latin Church Fathers show evidence that they were using a Greek not a Hebrew Bible; serious study of the early Christian writers cannot proceed without a secure Greek text.

A third reason the LXX is important is that it explains the way the Hebrew Bible was understood and interpreted in antiquity. To the degree that every translation is a commentary, the LXX, as the first translation of the Hebrew Bible, provides insight into the art of translation of a sacred text and the subtle (and at times blatant) way in which it was re-interpreted in the process.

The Septuagint is also important as a reminder to all who would wish for simplistic answers to scriptural and canonical questions, or shortcuts around the complexity surrounding most human endeavors. Some religious movements have sought uniformity of thought and action by destroying or curbing the propagation of dissenting voices. It is to the credit of Judaism and Christianity that the LXX and other materials—Pseudepigrapha, Apocrypha, Targumim, and recently discovered materials such as those found at Qumran and elsewhere—have been freely transmitted.

G. Bibliographic Resources

The International Organization for Septuagint and Cognate Studies (IOSCS) is the ongoing body dedicated to research on the Septuagint. The monograph Series of this group, *SBLSCS,* contains some 24 items all of which are relevant in some way to the Septuagint. In addition, its annual *Bulletin (BIOSCS)* records work published or in progress relating to the Septuagint, and also includes technical articles. The reader is urged to consult that publication for detailed current bibliographies. Many fine overviews on the Septuagint have already appeared and are recommended (Wevers *IDB* 4: 273–78; Kraft *IDBSup,* 811–15, and Tov *IDBSup,* 807–11; Tov 1986a and 1988). Some of the more seminal discussions about Septuagint matters have been gathered in the essay collections, festschriften and bibliographies listed in part 1 below. Of these the Brock, Fritsch, and Jellicoe 1973 is the most comprehensive Bibliography to date. In part 2, M. Harl et al. (1988) is especially useful because it lists current extensive bibliographies following the discussions of specific topics.

1. Collections.

Brock, S. P.; Fritsch, C. T.; and Jellicoe, S. eds. 1973. *A Classified Bibliography of the Septuagint.* Leiden.

Cox, C., ed. 1986. *VI Congress of the International Organization for Septuagint and Cognate Studies.*

Fernández-Marcos, N. 1985. *La Septuaginta en la Investagacion Contemporanea.* Madrid.

Jellicoe, S. 1974. *Studies in the Septuagint.* New York.

Pietersma, A., and Cox, C., eds. 1984. *De Septuaginta.* Mississauga, Ontario.

Wevers, J. W. 1954. Septuaginta Forschungen. *TRu* 22: 85–138; 171–90.

———. 1968. Septuaginta Forschungen seit 1954. *TRu* 33: 18–76.

2. Selected General Bibliography.

The works listed below are only some of the more valuable discussions (mainly in English) of the issues raised, alluded to or cited directly above.

Allen, L. C. 1974. *The Greek Chronicles.* 2 vols. VTSup 25, 27. Leiden.

Baars, W. 1968. *New Syro-Hexaplaric Texts Edited, Commented upon and Compared with the Septuagint.* Leiden.

Barr, J. 1968. *Comparative Philology and the Text of the Old Testament.* Oxford.

———. 1979. *The Typology of Literalism in Ancient Biblical Translations.* MSU 15. Göttingen.

Barthélemy, D. 1953. Redécouverte d'un chainon manquant de l'histoire de la Septante. *RB* 70: 18–29.

———. 1963. *Les Devanciers d'Aquila.* VTSup 10. Leiden.

———. 1974. "Qui est Symmaque?" *CBQ* 36: 451–65.

Bickerman, E. J. 1950. Some Notes on the Transmission of the LXX. Pp. 149–78 in *Alexander Marx Jubilee Volume,* ed. S. Lieberman. New York.

———. 1959. The Septuagint as a Translation. *PAAJR* 28: 1–39.

Bodine, W. R. 1980. *The Greek Text of Judges: Recensional Developments.* HSM 23. Chico, CA.

Brock, S. P. 1966. The Recensions of the Septuagint Version of I Samuel. Ph.D. diss. Oxford.

———. 1972. The Phenomenon of the Septuagint. *OTS* 17: 11–36.

———. 1979. Aspects of Translation Techniques in Antiquity. *GRBS* 20: 67–87.

Clear, J. 1973. The Ethiopic Text of 2 Paralipomenon. *Textus* 8: 126–32.

Cox, C. 1977. Cyril of Alexandria's Text for Deuteronomy. *BIOSCS* 10: 31–51.

———. 1981. *The Armenian Translation of Deuteronomy.* Chico, CA.

Fernández-Marcos, N. 1978. Theodoret's Biblical Text in the Octateuch. *BIOSCS* 11: 27–43.
———. 1979. *Introduccion a las versiones griegas de la Biblia.* Textos y estudios "Cardenal Cisneros" 23. Madrid.
———. 1984. The Lucianic Text in the Books of Kingdoms. Pp. 163–74 in Pietersma and Cox 1984.
Gooding, D. W. 1963. Aristeas and Septuagint Origins. *VT* 12: 357–79.
———. 1976. An Appeal for a Stricter Terminology in the Textual Criticism of the OT. *JSS* 21: 15–25.
Goshen-Gottstein, M. H. 1963. Theory and Practice of Textual Criticism: The Text-Critical Use of the Septuagint. *Textus* 3 130–58.
———. 1983. The Textual Criticism of the Old Testament: Rise, Decline, Rebirth. *JBL* 102: 365–99.
Greenspoon, L. 1983. *Textual Studies in the Book of Joshua.* Chico, CA.
———. 1987. The Use and Abuse of the Term "LXX" and Related Terminology in Recent Scholarship. *BIOSCS* 20: 21–29.
Harl, M.; Dorival, G.; and Munnich, E. L. 1988. *La Bible Grecque des Septante.* Paris.
Jeansonne, S. P. 1988. *The Old Greek Translation of Daniel 7–12.* CBQMS 19. Washington, DC.
Jellicoe, S. 1963. The Hesychian Recension Reconsidered. *JBL* 82: 409–18.
———. 1968. *The Septuagint and Modern Study.* Oxford.
Kahle, Paul. 1947. *The Cairo Genizah.* London.
Klein, R. W. 1974. *Textual Criticism of the Old Testament.* Philadelphia.
Kraft, R. 1972. *1972 Proceedings of IOSCS II.* Missoula, MT.
Lee, J. A. L. 1983. *A Lexical Study of the Septuagint Version of the Pentateuch.* Chico, CA.
Nagel, P. 1983–84. Studien zur Textüberlieferung des sahidischen Alten Testaments. *ZÄS* 110: 51–74; 111: 137–64.
———. 1985. Aufgaben und Probleme einer kritischen Edition der sahidischen Version der Septuaginta. Pp. 215–24 in *Acts of the Second International Congress of Coptic Studies,* ed. T. Orlandi and F. Wisse. Rome.
———. 1987. Sahidische Pentateuchfragmente. *ZÄS* 114: 134–66.
O'Connell, K. G. 1972. *The Theodotionic Revision of the Book of Exodus.* HSM 3. Cambridge, MA.
Orlinsky, H. M. 1952. Origen's Tetrapla—A Scholarly Fiction? *PWCJS* 1: 173–82.
———. 1969. The Hebrew Vorlage of the Septuagint of the Book of Joshua. Pp. 187–95 in *Congress Volume: Rome, 1968.* VTSup 17. Leiden.
———. 1975. The Septuagint as Holy Writ and the Philosophy of the Translators. *HUCA* 46: 89–114.
Perkins, L. J. 1978. The So-called "L" Text of Psalms 72–82. *BIOSCS* 11: 44–63.
Peters, M. K. H. 1986. Why Study the Septuagint? *BA* 49: 174–81.
Pietersma, A. 1977. *Chester Beatty Biblical Papyri IV and V.* Toronto.
———. 1978. Proto-Lucian and the Greek Psalter *VT* 28: 66–72.
———. 1985. Septuagint Research: A Plea for a Return to Basic Issues. *VT* 35: 296–311.
Rabin, C. 1968. The Translation Process and the Character of the Septuagint. *Textus* 6: 1–26.
Rahlfs, A. 1914. *Verzeichnis der griechischen Handschriften des Alten Testaments.* MSU 2. Berlin.
Seeligmann, I. L. 1948. *The LXX Version of Isaiah.* Leiden.
Smith, D. M. 1972. The Use of the Old Testament in the New. Pp. 3–65 in *The Use of the Old Testament in the New and Other Essays,* ed. J. M. Efird. Durham, NC.
———. 1988. The Pauline Literature. Pp. 265–91 in *It is Written: Scripture Citing Scripture,* ed. D. A. Carson and H. G. M. Williamson. Cambridge.
Swete, H. B. 1968. *An Introduction to the Old Testament in Greek.* Repr. New York.
Thackeray, H. St. J. 1921. *The Septuagint and Jewish Worship.* London.
Tov, E. 1972. Lucian and Proto-Lucian: Toward a New Solution of the Problem. *RB* 79: 101–13.
———. 1980. *1980 Proceedings IOSCS: The Hebrew and Greek Texts of Samuel.* Jerusalem.
———. 1981. *The Text Critical Use of the Septuagint in Biblical Research.* Jerusalem.
———. 1982. *Lexical and Grammatical Studies on the Language of the Septuagint and its Revisions.* Jerusalem.
———. 1986a. Jewish Greek Scriptures. Pp. 223–237 in *Early Judaism and its Modern Interpreters,* ed. R. A. Kraft and G. W. E. Nickelsburg. Atlanta.
———. 1986b. The Growth of the Book of Joshua in the Light of the Evidence of the LXX Translation. Pp. 321–39 in *Studies in Bible,* ed. S. Japhet. ScrHier 31. Jerusalem.
———. 1988. The Septuagint. Pp. 161–87 in *Mikra.* CRINT 2/2. Assen and Philadelphia.
Ulrich, E. 1978. *The Qumran Text of Samuel and Josephus.* HSM 19. Missoula, MT.
———. 1987. Daniel Manuscripts from Qumran. Part 1: A Preliminary Edition of 4QDan[a]. *BASOR* 268: 17–37.
———. 1988. Double Literary Editions of Biblical Narratives and Reflections on Determining the Form to be Translated. Pp. 101–16 in *Perspectives on the Hebrew Bible,* ed. J. Crenshaw. Macon, GA.
———. 1989. Daniel Manuscripts from Qumran. Part 2: Preliminary Editions of 4QDan[b] and 4QDan[c]. *BASOR* 274: 3–26.
Vööbus, A. 1975. *The Pentateuch in the Version of the Syro-Hexapla.* CSCO 369. Louvain.
———. 1983. *The Book of Isaiah in the Version of the Syro-Hexapla.* CSCO 449. Louvain.
Wevers, J. W. 1973. A Lucianic Recension in Genesis? *BIOSCS* 6: 22–35.
———. 1974. *Text History of the Greek Genesis.* MSU 11. Göttingen.
———. 1977a. The Attitude of the Greek Translator of Deuteronomy towards his Parent Text. Pp. 498–505 in *Beïtrage zur alttestamentlichen Theologie,* ed. H. Donner, R. Hanhart and R. Smend. Göttingen.
———. 1977b. *Das Göttinger Septuaginta-Unternehmen II: Die Methode.* Göttingen.
———. 1977c. The Earliest Witness to the LXX Deuteronomy. *CBQ* 39: 240–44.
———. 1978a. Text History and Text Criticism of the Septuagint. Pp. 392–402 in *Congress Volume, Göttingen 1977.* VTSup 29. Leiden.
———. 1978b. *Text History of the Greek Deuteronomy.* MSU 13. Göttingen.
———. 1982. *Text History of the Greek Numbers.* MSU 16. Göttingen.
———. 1985. An Apologia for Septuagint Studies. *BIOSCS* 18: 16–38.
———. 1986. Translation and Canonicity: A Study in the Narrative Portions of the Greek Exodus. Pp. 295–303 in *Scripta Signa Vocis: Studies about Scripts, Scriptures, Scribes and Languages in the Near East,* ed. H. L. Vanstiphout et al. Groningen.
———. 1988. Barthélemy and Proto-Septuagint. *BIOSCS* 21: 23–34.

Würthwein, E. 1979. *The Text of the Old Testament.* Repr. Grand Rapids.

3. Modern Printed Editions.

Septuaginta, Vetus Testamentum Graecum. 1931– . Auctoritate Academiae Scientiarum Göttingensis editum. Göttingen. Twenty volumes have appeared to date. *Genesis* (1974, ed. J. W. Wevers); *Leviticus* (1986, ed. J. W. Wevers); *Numeri* (1982, ed. J. W. Wevers); *Deuteronomium* (1977, ed. J. W. Wevers); *Isdrae liber I* (1974, ed. R. Hanhart); *Esther* (1966, ed. R. Hanhart; 2d ed. 1983); *Judith* (1979, ed. R. Hanhart); *Tobit* (1983); *Maccabaeorum liber I* (1936, ed. Kappler; 2d ed. 1967); *Maccabaeorum liber II* (1959, ed. Kappler and R. Hanhart; 2d ed. 1976); *Maccabaeorum liber III* (1960, ed. R. Hanhart; 2d ed. 1980); *Psalmi cum Odis* (1931, ed. Rahlfs; 2d ed. 1979); *Iob* (1982, ed. J. Ziegler); *Sapientia Salomonis* (1962, ed. J. Ziegler; 2d ed. 1980); *Sapientia Jesu Filii Sirach* (1965, ed. J. Ziegler; 2d ed. 1980); *Duodecim Prophetae* (1943, ed. J. Ziegler; 3d ed. 1984); *Isaias* (1939, ed. J. Ziegler; 3d ed. 1983); *Jeremias, Baruch, Threni, Epistula Jeremiae* (1957, ed. J. Ziegler; 2d ed. 1976); *Ezechiel* (1952, ed. J. Ziegler; 2d ed. 1977 supplemented by D. Fränkel); *Daniel, Susanna, Bel et Draco* (1954, ed. J. Ziegler). [*Exodus* is expected in 1989 and *2 Esdras* in 1990.]

Rahlfs, A. 1935. *Septuaginta, id est Vetus Testamentum Graece iuxta LXX interpretes.* Stuttgart.

Brooke, A. E.; McLean, N.; and Thackeray, H. St. J., eds. 1906–1940. *The Old Testament in Greek according to the Text of Codex Vaticanus Supplemented from Other Uncial Manuscripts.* Cambridge. The following books have appeared: *Genesis* (1906); *Exodus, Leviticus* (1909); *Numbers and Deuteronomy* (1911); *Joshua, Judges, Ruth* (1917); *1 and 2 Samuel* (1927); *1 and 2 Kings* (1930); *1 and 2 Chronicles* (1932); *I Esdras, Ezra, Nehemiah* (1935); *Esther, Judith, Tobit* (1940).

MELVIN K. H. PETERS

SEPULCHRE, HOLY. See HOLY SEPULCHRE, CHURCH OF THE; GOLGOTHA.

SERAᶜ, TEL (M.R. 119088). See ZIKLAG (PLACE).

SERAH (PERSON) [Heb *śeraḥ*]. The daughter of Asher (Gen 46:17; Num 26:46; 1 Chr 7:30). Serah also was the granddaughter of Jacob and Zilpah, the maid whom Laban gave to his daughter Leah on the occasion of Leah's marriage to Jacob (Gen 29:24). Serah's name is included in every genealogical list of Asher and she was counted as one of the seventy people who descended to Egypt with Jacob at the time of the severe famine in the land of Canaan (Gen 46:8–27). Because her name also appears in the census list of the clans of Asher (Num 26:46), it is possible that she became the ancestress of one of the prominent clans of Asher. The presence of her name in all of the genealogical lists of Asher gave rise to many stories and legends to explain her prominence among the Asherite clans.

CLAUDE F. MARIOTTINI

SERAIAH (PERSON) [Heb *śĕrāyāh*]. Name of eleven individuals in the Hebrew Bible and Apocrypha. The name is a Qal perfect form of the Heb root *śrh* "to persevere, persist." On rare occasions, the root may mean "to rule." With the divine element, *yah(û),* the name probably means "Yahweh has persevered or persisted" (Fowler, *TPNAH,* 108).

1. The son of Neriah, and a high-ranking official in the government of Judah's last king, Zedekiah (597–587 B.C.E.), who also played a direct role in furthering the ministry of Jeremiah the prophet and lent his hand to help preserve the Jeremiah legacy among exiled Jews in Babylon. According to Jer 51:59–64, Seraiah accompanied Zedekiah on a trip to Babylon in the king's fourth year, i.e. 594/3 B.C.E. The purpose of the royal mission was apparently to reaffirm Judah's loyalty to Nebuchadnezzar following the rebellions in Babylon and Judah earlier that year. Before making this trip Jeremiah instructed Seraiah to take with him a scroll or oracles announcing doom on Babylon (Jeremiah 50–51). Upon arrival he was to read the oracles aloud, then roll up the scroll, tie a stone to it, and cast it into the Euphrates with the words of a curse also provided by Jeremiah. Seraiah's title at the time of the mission was *śar mĕnûḥâ* (Jer 51:59), commonly thought to mean "commander of the caravan," "general quartermaster," (Hitzig 1866: 399) or something similar. The LXX has *archōn dōrōn* "officer of the gifts."

Seraiah was brother to Baruch the scribe who figures so prominently in the book of Jeremiah (note the same double patronyms in Jer 32:12 and 51:59). Both no doubt descend from a family of Judean scribes. The biblical tradition does not assign the title "scribe" to Seraiah as it does to Baruch (Jer 36:26, 32), nevertheless Seraiah can be assumed to possess the requisite skills of a scribe and can be considered competent to perform a range of scribal functions. A seal impression has been found which reads, "Belonging to Seraiah, (son of) Neriah" (Avigad 1978a: 56; 1978b), and the probability is high that the seal's owner is the biblical Seraiah ben Neriah. If so, the bulla confirms Seraiah's scribal competencies, while at the same time corroborates the biblical tradition of not labelling him a "scribe" (a seal impression found with Baruch's name on it does contain the title "scribe"; Avigad 1978a).

Jeremiah 51:59–64 is a colophon which Seraiah wrote originally for the scroll of Babylon oracles (cf. LXX 27–28), a scroll which had to be copied also by him before it was thrown into the Euphrates (Lundbom 1986). In the MT, where the foreign nation oracles are relocated to the end of the book, this colophon has an expanded role of concluding the entire book (less chapter 52). Seraiah may thus have been the one who, in Babylon, shaped the final form of the book of Jeremiah (or at least the form underlying our present MT). However, we have no independent evidence that Seraiah was exiled to Babylon, only that he went there on the mission of 594/3. However much Seraiah did help preserve the Jeremiah legacy, his role in any case was not as significant as that of his better-known brother Baruch.

Bibliography

Avigad, N. 1978a. Baruch the Scribe and Jerahmeel the King's son. *IEJ* 28: 52–56 [Repr. in *BA* 42 (1979): 114–18].

———. 1978b. The Seal of Seraiah (Son of) Neriah. *EI* 14: 86–87 (in Hebrew).

Hitzig, F. 1866. *Der Prophet Jeremia.* Leipzig.
Lundbom, J. R. 1986. Baruch, Seraiah, and Expanded Colophons in the Book of Jeremiah *JSOT* 36: 89–114.

JACK R. LUNDBOM

2. High-ranking government official who held the position of *sōpēr* (royal secretary) during the reign of David (2 Sam 8:17). In two other lists of David's ministers of state, he is called Sheva (2 Sam 20:25) and Shavsha (1 Chr 18:16). In a similar list of officials of the Solomonic period (Mettinger 1971), he is called Shisha (1 Kgs 4:3 (LXX reads "Sheva"); according to 1 Kgs 4:3, two of Shisha's sons held the office of royal secretary). What the original form of the name might have been is disputed. See Rüterswörden (1985).

3. One of the sons of Kenaz and member of the tribe of Judah (1 Chr 4:13).

4. A Simeonite (cf. 1 Chr 4:24–33) mentioned in a list of those who were "princes in their clans" in the time of Hezekiah (1 Chr 45:34–43). He is the son of Asiel and the father of Joshibiah (v 35).

5. Son of Azriel and officer at the court of Jehoiakim (Jer 36:26). Seraiah was one of those sent by Jehoiakim to arrest the prophet Jeremiah and his secretary Baruch following the reading of Jeremiah's scroll in the fifth year of Jehoiakim's reign (604/3 B.C.E.). Seraiah is named together with Jerahmeel "the king's son" and Shelemiah son of Abdeel (Shelemiah's name is omitted in the LXX [Jer 43:26]). Both Jeremiah and Baruch escaped (Jer 36:26).

6. Chief priest of Jerusalem, and one of the Judean royal officials put to death in Riblah by the Babylonians in 587/6 B.C.E. (Jer 52:24–27; 2 Kgs 25:18–21). Seraiah was the son of Azariah and the father of Jehozadak (1 Chr 6:14; alternately Jozadak [Ezra 3:2]). The Chronicler reports that Jehozadak was taken into exile by the Babylonians (v 15). Seraiah's grandson Jeshua, a contemporary of Zerubbabel, was high priest following the exile (Ezra 3:2; 1 Esdr 5:8). According to Ezra 7:1 (= 1 Esdr 8:1), Ezra was "the son of Seraiah, son of Azariah, son of Hilkiah." Although it is not possible that Ezra's father was the Seraiah under consideration here (whereby he would be the brother of Jehozadak), it is possible that Ezra was a direct descendant of Seraiah.

7. One of the Judean troop commanders who, following the destruction of Jerusalem in 587/6 B.C.E., chose to join Gedaliah, the ruler of Judah, at his administrative center at Mizpah (Jer 40:8; 2 Kgs 25:23). He is identified as the son of Tanhumeth, a Netophathite—in the parallel passage (2 Kgs 25:23), the words "the sons of Ephai" (Jer 40:8) are omitted. Presumably Seraiah and his men were among those who, fearing Babylonian reprisals for the assassination of Gedaliah (Jer 41:18; 2 Kgs 25:26), fled to Egypt (Jer 43:5–7).

8. One of the leaders who returned to Jerusalem and Judah with Zerubbabel (Ezra 2:2; 1 Esdr 5:8). He is called Azariah in Neh 7:7.

9. One of the twenty-two "chiefs of priests" (Neh 12:7) who accompanied Zerubbabel out of exile (12:1). In Neh 12:12–21—closely connected with 12:17—Meraiah is named as head of the priestly family of Seraiah at the time of the high priest Joiakim (12:12), Jeshua's successor (cf. Neh 12:10).

10. One of the priests who was signatory to a legal document of reform associated with Ezra or Nehemiah (Neh 10:30—Eng 10:29). Although the term "covenant" is not used in Neh 10:1–40—Eng 9:38–10:29, the account probably relates to a covenant-making ceremony (cf. 10:30—Eng 10:29) which addressed itself to various concerns of the postexilic community. It would appear that the priests (unlike the Levites) are listed by their family names, and not as individuals. The individual signing under the name of Seraiah—the first name to appear in this list of twenty-one priests—does so as a representative of the high-priestly family (cf. 2 Kgs 25:18 [= Jer 52:24]; 1 Chr 6:14; see #6 above). In Neh 10:1–2, the LXX places "son of" following the name Zedekiah and before the name Seraiah, thereby removing Seraiah from the list of signatories (see Myers *Ezra, Nehemiah* AB; Rudolph *Esra und Nehemia* HAT).

11. A priest who is listed among those who resided in Jerusalem after the exile (Neh 11:3–24). According to the MT, Seraiah is named as "ruler of the house of God" (11:11). However, there is good reason to believe that the MT is to be emended. One possible reading of Neh 11:10–11 is "Jedaiah son of Joiarib, son of Seraiah, son of Hilkiah. . . ." (NEB; JB emends the text to read "Jedaiah son of Joiakim, son of Seraiah. . . ."). With this reading, vv 10–11 provide the genealogy of Jedaiah, the high priest—the names of Jeshua and Jehozadak (Jozadak) are missing. In the similar list in 1 Chr 9:2–34, Seraiah's name fails to appear in 9:11; instead, Azariah is named as the son of Hilkiah. It is very possible that two different individuals are intended (cf. 1 Chr 5:39–40—Eng 6:13–14 and Ezra 7:1 [=1 Esdr 8:1], where it is stated that Hilkiah is the father of Azariah and Azariah the father of Seraiah; see #6 above).

Bibliography

Mettinger, T. N. D. 1971. *Solomonic State Officials.* ConBOT 5. Lund.
Rüterswörden, U. 1985. *Die Beamten der israelitischen Königszeit.* BWANT 117. Stuttgart and Berlin.
Herr, L. G. 1980. Paleography and the Identification of Seal Owners. *BASOR* 239: 67–70.
Peterson, R. M. 1984. Reinterpretation in the Book of Jeremiah. *JSOT* 28: 37–46.
Schmidt, K. W. 1982. Prophetic Delegation: A Form-Critical Inquiry. Bib 63: 206–18.

JOHN M. BERRIDGE

SERED (PERSON) [Heb *sered*], SEREDITES. The oldest of the three sons of Zebulun (Gen 46:14). Sered was the grandson of Jacob and Leah. His name appears in the list of the seventy people who descended with Jacob and his family to Egypt at the time of a severe famine in the land of Canaan (Gen 46:8–27). Nothing is known about Sered. In the census list mentioned in the book of Numbers he is listed as the ancestral head of the family of the Seredites, one of the clans of the tribe of Zebulun (Num 26:26).

CLAUDE F. MARIOTTINI

SEREK HAYYAHAD. See FLORILEGIUM (4QFLOR).

SERGIUS PAULUS (PERSON). See PAULUS, SERGIUS (PERSON).

SERMON ON THE MOUNT/PLAIN. The customary designation for the discourse of Jesus recorded in Matthew 5–7 and Luke 6:20–40.

A. Name
B. The Addresses
C. Present Situation of Scholarship
D. Origin and History of Tradition
E. Literary Genre and Function
F. Composition
  1. The Sermon on the Mount
  2. The Sermon on the Plain
G. Theology
  1. The Sermon on the Mount
  2. The Sermon on the Plain
H. Literary Influences
  1. Within the NT
  2. In the Post-NT Period

A. Name

The name "Sermon on the Mount" (henceforth abbreviated SM) designates the first programmatic speech Jesus delivered according to the gospel of Matthew (5:3–7:27). The name SM (*sermo in monte*) was used by Augustine (A.D. 354–430), who in his early commentary (written ca. 392–396 [Mutzenbecher 1967: ix]), most probably the first ever written on SM alone, highlighted the famous text as a literary entity in itself. Since then, the name not only designates the particular text in Matthew, but, for the public mind and especially in the present debate, stands also for the text that sums up the uncompromising ethics of the historical Jesus as distinct from the post-Easter theology of the Christian Church. This simplification, however, proves untenable in the light of scholarship past and present.

Since "mountain" refers to the place where Jesus is said to have presented his sermon (Matt 5:1), the parallel speech in Luke 6:20b–49 was called after the place where it was delivered (6:12, 17), of the "Sermon on the Plain" (henceforth abbreviated SP).

B. The Addresses

The sources are unclear concerning the question of the original addresses of SM and SP. According to Matt 5:1, SM is addressed to the disciples of Jesus after he had separated them from the crowd and moved to the mountain. In 7:28, however, Matthew says that all, disciples and crowds, praised the sermon because of its authoritative power. Further, who are the disciples? According to Matt 4:18–22, only four have so far been called: Simon Peter and his brother, Andrew, and the two sons of Zebedee. Matthew can hardly have believed that only four disciples were present on the mountain, however, for he certainly holds that Jesus spoke to all the disciples and, indeed, to all the people as well. Similar ambiguity is found in connection with SP: in Luke 6:12–16, Jesus goes up to the mountain in order to elect the Twelve, and in 6:17–19, all come down to the plain and meet with the people, so that according to 6:20a, disciples and people are present. Yet Jesus makes his speech "fixing his eyes on his disciples." Mark 3:13–19 also reports that Jesus went to the mountain to elect the Twelve, but of course there is no parallel to SM and SP in Mark. This situation would indicate that the gospel writers are certainly interested in having Jesus address both the disciples and the people, probably because the disciples (then and in their own time) have been called from the people who represent the general readership of the gospels. The address to the disciples only appears to have come from the earlier sources, SM and SP, and perhaps the Q-versions, Q[Matt] and Q[Luke], into which they were integrated before their inclusion in the gospels (see Strecker 1984: 26). In terms of the history of tradition, therefore, both SM and SP serve as instructions given to disciples, a function that is borne out as well by their literary genre and composition.

C. Present Situation of Scholarship

The present situation in scholarship regarding SM and SP shows little consensus. All the fundamental problems are debated: authorship, textual transmission and history of tradition, literary genre, composition and function, historical origin, location in early Christian theology, and relationship to other NT and extra-NT sources (gospels and epistles in the NT, Christian apocrypha, Jewish writings, Greco-Roman philosophy, ethics, and religion). Wide differences regarding the meaning of SM for the modern world characterize the present debates inside and outside the Christian churches. In comparison, SP has attracted little attention until recently.

D. Origin and History of Tradition

According to the gospel authors, both SM and SP go back to Jesus of Nazareth. The authors are historically correct in the general sense that the main theological doctrines expressed in SM and SP point back to Jesus; but their thesis is hardly demonstrable concerning the written texts, which are in Greek and which cannot be shown to be simple translations from the Aramaic. Both SM and SP were conceived in Greek by whoever composed them.

That SM and SP are parallel texts was recognized and debated in the patristic literature. Perhaps Origen (*fr. in Mt.* 79) and certainly Chrysostom (*In Matth. Hom.* 15) believed that the same sermon of Jesus was transmitted twice; but Augustine took the differences between them seriously, regarding them as two different speeches, one (SM) given before the apostles only and the other (SP) addressing all the people (*De consensu evangelistarum* 2.19). Both options have been held through the entire history of exegesis, up to the present time (see Lambrecht 1985: 35–40).

Most scholars today assign the composition of SM to Matthew (Guelich 1982; Strecker 1984; Lambrecht 1985; Luz *Matthäus* EKKNT) and that of SP to Luke (Schürmann *Lukasevangelium* HTKNT, 385–86; Marshall *Luke* NIGTC, 243–45; Fitzmyer *Luke I–IX* AB, 627–62). For these scholars, Matthew received the basic material from Q and expanded it with other sources he found in his tradition or which he made up himself; he also made editorial changes in the material. Concerning the basic Q-material, some assume that it was, on the whole, identical with SP, while others hold that Q is represented in Matthew and Luke in two recensions (Q^{Matt} and Q^{Luke}) and that SM and SP were transmitted to the gospel writers as part of these two recensions (see Moffatt 1918: 194–204; Streeter 1930: 249–59; Kümmel 1975: 63–80; Lindemann 1984: 251–63, 335–39; Strecker 1984: 9–12). Some scholars have attempted to reconstruct from SM and SP an earlier Q-Sermon (see, e.g., Schenk 1981; Polag 1982); but it is still uncertain whether SM and SP were part of Q, and if they were, whether there ever was *one* Q-Sermon, and if there were, whether it can be reconstructed from the two recensions. Wrege (1968: 1–4, 57, 108–9, 131, 172), however, does not subscribe to the hypothetical Q-source but has Matthew compose SM from sayings clusters in the oral tradition of the sayings of Jesus. Yet Wrege cannot explain—and does not treat—the parallel literary integrity of SP. Betz (1985b) regards both SM and SP as presynoptic compositions older than Q. Constructed for specific purposes, they took their form from the literary genre and function. As the evolving collection Q—really a collection of earlier collections and clusters of sayings *(gnomologium)*—was expanded, SM and SP ended up in the two recensions.

Over the past decades, some scholars have assumed that SM originated in early Jewish Christianity (Streeter 1930: 254–59; Dibelius 1953: 97: ca. A.D. 50; so also Betz 1985b:1). Accordingly, SM continues the teaching of Jesus, looking back at it from a later perspective and making a critical and pointed selection of what was then recognized as essential (see G below). More precise data are hard to ascertain, but the central position of Jerusalem, the only place ever named in SM, is conspicuous (5:14, 34b–35; 7:13–14); and an allusion to the Peter-rock tradition in 7:24–25 is conceivable. In later Jewish Christianity, SM exerted an extraordinarily strong influence (*Didache*, Jewish Christian gospels, *Pseudo-Clementines;* Elchasaites).

There are no clues to the origin of SP as a presynoptic source. The text is apparently designed from a Jewish-Christian perspective, although written for gentile Christians.

E. Literary Genre and Function

The literary genre and function of SM was investigated by Betz in 1978 (see Betz 1985b: 1–16), who proposes that SM conforms to the genre of the epitome, which he describes thus (p. 13):

> As a literary work, the epitome is secondary in nature. It is a condensation of a larger work, made by a redactor (who may of course be the same person as the author of the larger work) for a specific purpose. Its characteristics include brevity and precision in selection and formulation. But the epitome is not simply a collection of selected passages. Rather, the author has systematic goals and looks at the work to be epitomized as a whole. What he or she selects and composes into the new literary unit is intended to be a systematic synopsis. In composing the epitome, the author has considerable freedom to be creative, to reformulate, to transpose, to add and omit as necessary in view of the overall demands of the genre and purpose.

Applied to SM, that text conforms to the genre in this way: "The literary genre of the SM is that of an epitome presenting the theology of Jesus in a systematic fashion. The epitome is a composition carefully designed out of sayings of Jesus grouped according to thematic points of doctrine considered to be of primary importance. Correspondingly, its function is to provide the disciple of Jesus with the necessary tool for becoming a Jesus theologian. 'Hearing and doing the sayings of Jesus,' therefore, means enabling the disciple to theologize creatively along the lines of the theology of the master" (p. 15).

The text of SP also falls into the category of epitome and serves the same function. That SP on the one hand is composed in a similar way but on the other hand differs so greatly from SM is due not to a different genre or function but to the different addressees. SM is designed for Jewish Christians, SP for gentile Christians.

F. Composition

Careful literary analyses are indispensable for the question of the literary composition of both SM and SP. These analyses consider form and redaction criticism as well as rhetorical and argumentative strategies. Thus far such analyses have been proposed only in experimental form, but even on that basis one can say that both texts are exceedingly well constructed. Each in its own way is a textual unit with its own form, composition, and theological thought world, similarities notwithstanding. Number symbolism is one of the major elements in the composition of both.

1. The Sermon on the Mount. The number three is of great importance to the composition of SM. As a whole, SM falls into three parts: the exordium (5:3–16), the central section (5:17–7:12), and the concluding section (7:13–27).

a. The Exordium (5:3–16). The exordium begins with an impressive and highly complex series of ten beatitudes (macarisms), whereby the number ten is hardly fortuitous but corresponds to an ordering principle, frequently encountered in Jewish literature, which symbolizes perfection. See BEATITUDES. But matters are still more complicated, for in 5:3–12 two strata can clearly be distinguished. In 5:3–10, a series of eight macarisms, largely parallel in form, have been brought together. Each consists of a distich in the third person plural, the second line of which is invariably introduced by *hoti* ("that"). In patristic exegesis, the number eight (according to other reckonings, the number seven) symbolizes perfection as well. In 5:9–10, two further macarisms have been added secondarily. These secondary expansions bring about changes in form, though it is not clear for what reason. In any case, the symbolism remains constant, since both the number eight (seven) and the number ten express perfection. As a *theologumenon,* perfection itself plays an important role in the SM (5:48).

The phenomenon of the series of macarisms raises the problem of how individual macarisms are related to one another. Again there are wide-ranging discussions among the Church Fathers on this point. They noticed that the first in the series of macarisms speaks of the basic virtue of humility, while the last deals with the vision of God and deification. Thus some patristic expositors interpreted the design as a step-ladder for the ascent of the soul from the elementary virtue of humility to mystical union with God. Though one may be skeptical toward such speculative ideas, it remains necessary to find an explanation more appropriate to the text for why the Beatitudes are arranged in their present order.

In itself, the series of macarisms is by no means uniform, but is made up of four distinct types, each of two lines, with the exception of v 12, which is a tristich. The first and no doubt the "leading" macarism is found in v 3. It has its counterpart in v 10. The first line contains the macarism as such, "Blessed are the poor in spirit," formulated in the third person plural. The designation of those addressed is unusual (see below). The second line constitutes a *hoti*-clause, in which the grounds for the macarism are stated. However, the *hoti*-clause belongs to the macarism in only a qualified sense. The phrase "to them belongs the kingdom of heaven" was originally a verdict that had its place in the last judgment and is anticipated here (cf. Matt 25:34).

The second type is found in vv 4–9. Again the first line contains the macarism, cast in the third person plural, together with the designation of those who are addressed, while the second line is a *hoti*-clause giving the basis for the blessing. But in this instance the *hoti*-clause consists of an eschatological promise, formulated in the future passive. These promises arise through an eschatological interpretation of the *ius talionis* (law of retribution). The series comprised by vv 4–9 contains macarisms that correspond to individual scenes in which the fate of the righteous in paradise is described. Thus one can see in this section a greatly abbreviated apocalyptic vision of the world to come.

The third type is found only once (v 11). The macarism is now formulated in the second person plural and is not connected with a designation of those addressed. The second line takes the form of a *hoti*-clause. It presents three situations of persecution that the addressees must be prepared to undergo.

The fourth type is a tristich, represented by v. 12. Also formulated in the second person plural, it begins with a double summons to "rejoice and be glad," then passes over into a *hoti*-clause in the second line, which provides the necessary justification. This line consists of a Jewish dogmatic judgment: "Great is your reward in heaven." This verdict is then furnished with its justification in the third line: "for so they persecuted the prophets who were before you." In other words, an historical verdict is rendered by which the present persecution of the community is equated with the persecution of the prophets, that, in accordance with Jewish thought, results in eschatological reward. One must read the argument in reverse, so to speak. The historical verdict rendered in v 12c leads to the dogmatic judgment in v 12b, and both together constitute the basis for the macarism in v 12a.

The beatitudes are followed by a commission of the "Church" (if at this point one can call the Christian community a church), stated as two declarations, each claiming a traditional metaphor of Jewish self-description: the salt of the earth (5:13) and the light of the world (5:14–16).

b. Central Section (5:17–7:12). The main body of SM (5:17–7:12) sets forth what is called in 7:14 "the way to the (eternal) life" (7:14), i.e., guidelines for a way of life. It consists of three parts, the first of which is devoted to the interpretation of the Torah (5:17–48).

This interpretation is introduced by a set of four *hermeneutical principles* (5:17–20) which are regarded as underlying all of the teachings of Jesus. The first principle (5:17) assesses the intention and purpose of Jesus as a Torah teacher and refutes the idea that he had come to abolish the Torah. The second principle (5:18) affirms the authority of the written Hebrew text of Scripture. The third (5:19) defines the status and authority of Jesus' interpretation of the Torah in the Christian community. The fourth (5:20) specifies what is to be understood by righteousness in distinction from Pharisaism.

These principles are then applied in six cases of *halakah,* the so-called *antitheses* (5:21–48). Taken together, all six cases comprise legal issues exemplifying the commandment of Lev 19:18, "Love your neighbor" (5:43). There are two sets of three "neighborly" conflicts, the first set dealing with family conflicts, second with friends and foes, thus covering in principle all interpersonal relationships.

The first antithesis is on murder and focuses on the brother, understood here also in the wider sense of the term (5:21–26). The second antithesis treats adultery (5:27–30), the third divorce (5:31–32). The second set is based on the assumption that broken friendship is the root cause of enmity, and it opens with the fourth antithesis on oath-taking as the opposite of speaking the truth, the mark of true friendship (5:33–37). The fifth antithesis then deals with retaliation (5:38–42), while the sixth leads up to the climax and the role diametrically opposed to treatment of the brother, treatment of the enemy (5:43–48).

The arrangement of the entire series is worked out with great skill down to the smallest detail, and as a whole it amounts to an interpretation of Jesus' love command in terms of Jewish Torah exegesis (cf. also Betz *Galatians* Hermeneia, 274–76). Each antithesis is carefully constructed as a legal and ethical argument interpreting in a parallel pattern Torah prohibitions and prescriptions. The argument proceeds by first refuting a false interpretation of the Torah in order then to submit the right interpretation of the same Torah and to argue the latter rhetorically with the help of illustrative examples, images, and metaphors. Each argument leads up to a conclusion justifying Jesus' interpretation as ethically valid.

The second section of the body (6:1–18) contains *cultic instruction* (see Betz 1985b: 55–69). After a general exhortation (6:1), three subsections deal with the improper and proper performance of the rituals of almsgiving (6:2–4), prayer (6:5–15), and fasting (6:16–18). Analysis shows (see Betz 1985b: 57–59) a highly stylized parallel structure of the three sections and also reveals the insertion of a separate instruction on prayer after 6:5–6 (6:7–15). Composed somewhat differently from the rest of the section, this insertion presents as well different theological ideas. It polemicizes against assimiliation with the "heathen" and presents a Jewish (-Christian) doctrine of prayer (6:7–8), for which the Lord's Prayer (6:9–13) serves as the authoritative example; to this is joined a "sentence of sacred law" regarding forgiveness (6:14–15).

The third section of the body (6:19–7:12) is composed of seven compositions of *sententiae,* varying in length and character and concluded by their underlying hermeneutical principle, the Golden Rule (7:12). The collection begins with a piece on gathering treasures (6:19–21) and continues with a very succinct composition on vision (6:22–23; see Betz 1985b: 71–87). Next comes a short saying on serving two masters (6:24), followed by two long and highly developed arguments, one on worrying (6:25–34; see Betz 1985b: 89–123) and another on judging (7:1–5). A concise yet cryptic *sententia* on profaning the holy (7:6) is followed by a longer argument on giving and receiving (7:7–11), often thought to refer to petitionary prayer (see Luz *Matthäus* EKKNT, 382–87). While the arrangement appears to be somewhat loose, as is often the case in collections of *sententiae,* the Golden Rule (7:12) is assumed to underlie all components and, indeed, SM as a whole.

c. Concluding Section (7:13–23). The last major part of the SM consists of *eschatological warnings;* again there are three subsections. Indicating the importance of the Two-Way schema for SM, the first exhortation (7:13–14) combines the image of the narrow and the wide gates with that of the rough and the smooth roads: one leads to the eternal life and the other to everlasting destruction. The disciples of Jesus must struggle on the rough road and find the narrow gate, images describing the difficulties of a life lived in obedience to the SM itself.

The second exhortation (7:15–20) is a warning to be alert in view of false prophets invading and subverting the community. There is no identification as to who these "wolves in sheepskin" are, except that ways of detecting them are indicated.

The final exhortation (7:21–23; see Betz 1985b: 125–57) against self-delusion is cast in the form of a scenario of the Last Judgment. Jesus is shown to act as the advocate of his faithful and to reject those who are deluding themselves by claiming to have prophesied, cast out demons, and wrought miracles in his name but who have failed to observe his teaching of the Torah and are therefore in a state of "lawlessness" and unrighteousness.

The *peroration* (7:24–27; see Betz 1985b: 3–7) takes the form of a double parable describing success and failure in discipleship through imagery of the prudent builder who builds his house on the rock in contrast to the foolish one who builds on the sand.

2. The Sermon on the Plain. Falling into the same literary category, using much of the same tradition, and showing a similar arrangement in composition, SP is nonetheless very different from SM. SP has three parts: an exordium (Luke 6:20b–26), a main body containing rules for the conduct of the disciples (6:27–45), and a peroration (6:46–49).

a. The Exordium (6:20b–26). The exordium combines four beatitudes (macarisms) with four contrasting threats ("woes"). The former describe the poor as hungry and weeping and the rich as stuffing their stomachs and laughing indecently (6:20b–21, 24–25b). This description conforms to a social typology, used here to identify the Christian experiences of discrimination and harrassment of the faithful and to warn against seeking the approval of opportunists and flatterers (6:22, 26). Between the beatitudes and the threats lies a call for joy (6:23), formulating a doctrine of reward in the Last Judgment for sufferings endured.

b. Main Body (6:27–45). The rules for the conduct of the disciples in the body of SP can be divided into two subsections, the first dealing with the outside world (6:27–38) and the second with specific guidelines for education (6:39–45).

The first subsection (6:27–38) comprises a lengthy argument concerning Jesus' fundamental command to love the enemy. The command is given in the form of four parallel ethical maxims, the first of which is Jesus' love command, while the others provide interpretations through variations (6:27–28). This set is followed by an elaborate argumentation designed to prove that Jesus' commandment makes sense in terms of Greek ethical discourse. First, critical objections are taken into account through a set of four examples demonstrating the seeming absurdity of the commandment (6:29–30). The Golden Rule is introduced (6:31) as the principle which makes the command intelligible. Since the Golden Rule can be misinterpreted, however, a commentary follows that refutes its erroneous interpretation (6:32–34) and sets forth the correct one (6:35) and concludes with a maxim (6:36) stating the imitation of God as the theological doctrine undergirding both the Golden Rule and the commandment of Jesus. Finally, there is paraenetical application in the form of four maxims (6:37–38).

The second subsection (6:39–45), contains the guidelines for education and opens with a demonstration of the need for and a formulation of a doctrine of Christian education. Christian education is needed as a means to prevent ignorance: "Can the blind guide the blind?" (6:39). Three rules for the learning community follow: first a rule concerning relationships between students and teachers, including their status both before and after graduation (6:40); second, a rule concerning the relationship between students, demonstrating the need for self-criticism and self-correction (6:41–42); and third, a rule concerning the relationship to oneself (6:43–45), proving the need for self-knowledge and spelling out the elements of an anthropology ("the good person" versus "the bad").

c. The Peroration (6:46–49). The concluding section begins with a rhetorical question describing the typical behavior of immature students (6:46), and concludes with the double parable of the two builders portraying the successful and the failed disciple. Although elaborated somewhat differently, the double parable is the same as in SM.

G. Theology

In theological concepts, both SM and SP are at the same time characteristically similar and different. Both show dependency on presuppositions coming from the teachings of Jesus, but these have been developed into independent and coherent theological concepts of faith (the term faith, however, is not used by either SM or SP). While doctrinal presuppositions are frequently stated, the whole of the theologies must be inferred from the arguments presented in the texts. These theologies are characteristically different from, although not irreconcilable with, the secondary contexts (Q [?], Matthew, Luke) into which they have been integrated. As compared with other NT texts, both theologies appear archaic insofar as that they show christology and ecclesiology at relatively early stages of inception, and their soteriology is essentially Jewish. Their views on God, the world, and eschatology although in many ways peculiar, do not go beyond what is conceivable in Judaism (see Betz 1985a). Apart from these general agreements, the theologies of SM and SP are strikingly different.

1. The Sermon on the Mount. "*The message of Jesus* is a presupposition for the theology of the New Testament rather than a part of that theology itself" (*BTNT* 1:1; for the current state of the question, see Sanders 1985: 1–58). The position of SM is that Jesus' teaching was orthodox in the Jewish sense (5:17–20; see Betz 1985b: 37–53), but that this view is contested and must be defended against adversaries. There are those, apparently other Jews, who say that Jesus was a heretic, one who came to abolish the Torah (5:17). In fact, SM must admit that there are Christians who say this and who disregard Jesus' teaching of the Torah. These seem to be gentile Christians, probably adherents of Paul (cf. Gal 3:23–25; Rom 10:4). SM warns that they will surely fail in the Last Judgment (7:21–23). However, even Jewish Christian teachers must be strongly warned against such thinking (5:17–20). Not to be overlooked are his warnings against assimilation (5:47; 6:7, 32) and self-doubt (6:30). SM, therefore, presents Jesus' teaching as decidedly Jewish, and it contains no trace of what we know from contemporary (e.g., Q or Paul) or later NT sources as Christian theology. Conspicuous is the absence of the kerygma of the crucifixion and resurrection of Jesus Christ, even in places where one would expect it (e.g., Matt 5:11, 12, 44; see Betz 1985b: 151). Jesus has no salvific function apart from the obedience to the Torah (5:17, 18; 7:12: *hō nomos*) that he teaches through his commandments (5:19: *hai entolai*) and sayings (7:24–27, 28: *hoi logoi*; see Betz 1985b: 48–49). His eschatological function is understood entirely in Jewish terms as the advocate for his faithful in the Last Judgment (7:21–23; see Betz 1985b: 151–54). Because of this role, Jesus is able to pronounce the beatitudes in the here and now (5:3–12). Constituting a complicated literary creation in themselves, these beatitudes anticipate the eschatological verdict to be rendered by God in the Last Judgment. Such anticipation is based on the knowledge of the legal and doctrinal terms according to which that Judgment will be conducted. Since every Jewish teacher of the Torah ought to possess that knowledge, no "messianic" consciousness or "higher" christology is needed for pronouncing the verdict (differently, of course, when Matthew is considered as the redactor of the Gospel who is followed by most modern commentators; e.g., Guelich 1982: 27; Strecker 1984; 27 Luz *Matthäus* EKKNT, 189). The promises made in 5:3–12 are, of course, conditional upon verification in the Last Judgment, from which the disciples of Jesus are not exempt (see 7:21–23 and Betz 1985b).

The soteriology of SM, however, is not based simply on observance of the Torah. Both this soteriology and the teachings of the Torah are based on the notion of "the kingdom of the heavens" (*hē basileia tōn ouranōn,* i.e., of God), the interpretation of which is unique in the NT (see Betz 1985b: 89–123). The kingdom of God is otherworldly and eschatological (5:19, 20; 6:10, 33; 7:21), but is simultaneously at work in the present world. The faithful disciples participate in it during their life on earth. In fact, all creation participates in it, consciously or unconsciously, but the disciples do so knowingly. Jesus taught his disciples the Torah as the way revealed by God which corresponds to his kingdom and which leads one into it (7:13–14). The Torah has salvific force, therefore, because of its coordination with God's reign. The disciples who study and practice this Torah can count upon eschatological reward (5:12, 46; 6:1, 5, 16). With the help of the Torah as taught by Jesus, righteousness (5:6, 10, 20; 6:1, 33: *dikaiosynē*; 5:45: *dikaios*) can actually be produced; its opposite is lawlessness (7:23: *anomia*; see Betz 1985b: 52). The task of the disciples in this life, therefore, is "to seek after the kingdom [of God] and his righteousness" (6:33), guided by the Torah as Jesus taught it.

Salvation in SM is thus primarily identical with the kingdom of God. Drawing upon an archaic mythology (5:45: God "makes his sun rise on the evil and the good, and he rains upon the just and the unjust"), SM describes God's reign as that of the Father of the cosmos (6:9 [Lord's Prayer]; 5:16, 45, 48; 6:1, 4, 6, 8, 14, 15, 18, 26, 32; 7:11, 21). His reign stands in stark contrast to that of the political despots (cf. also 5:35, where God is given the title, "the great king," *ho megas basileus*). Unique in the NT is the concept of the divine Fatherhood as *creatio continua,* the evidence of which is observable in the natural order (6:25–34; see Betz 1985b: 108–18, 121–23) by those whose eyes function properly (6:22–23; see Betz 1985b: 71–87). The heavenly Father treats Jesus' disciples as his own sons, and they in turn are called to understand themselves and act as "sons of God" (5:9, 45; 7:9–11; see Betz 1985b: 122–23). Like all sons, the disciples of Jesus must mature to perfection (5:48: *teleios*). To provide the necessary guidance for this learning and maturing is the aim of SM. Its goal is to teach the disciples to imitate their heavenly Father in their daily lives, even as they themselves are fathers (7:11). In this sense the entire Christian existence as taught by SM is imitation of God *(imitatio Dei)*.

2. The Sermon on the Plain. Although SP is designed from a Jewish-Christian perspective, its addressees were in all likelihood disciples of Jesus coming from a Greek cultural background. None of the material in SM concerned with matters of Jewish religion is found in SP. The language, conceptuality, and ideas, as well as the construction of the arguments, conform to Greek presuppositions. The teaching of Jesus is centered in the maxim, "Love your enemies" (Luke 6:27b), without prooftext as in SM/Matt 5:43) and, argued in terms of Greek ethical discourse, dispels all doubts about its absurdity (6:29–30). Salvation comes to these disciples (the notion of "disciple" occurs in 6:40) as an extension of Jewish eschatological promises, very similar to but not identical with those in SM. As disciples of Jesus, the addressees can expect great reward "on that day," that is, the day of the Last Judgment (6:23). The verdict will be admission to the "kingdom of God" (6:20: *hē basileia tou theou*), when they will be made "sons of the Most High" (6:35). Then there will be the traditional celebrations: good food, fun and games, and wild dances. Hence there can be joy even now (6:21, 23) in anticipation.

What are the theological grounds for extending these promises? They are not based, as one might expect, on the kerygma of the death and resurrection of Jesus Christ; there is no doctrine of "grace" and no concept of "faith in Jesus Christ." The great reward which is said to be stored in heaven (6:23b) will be given to the faithful disciples "on that day" because of the sufferings they have endured "on account of the Son of Man" (6:22). These sufferings seem to be discriminations coming primarily from Jews (6:23c, 26c; note "*their* forefathers" instead of "the prophets before *you*" in SM/Matt 5:12c), and are said to be the same as those endured by the prophets of old and hence deserve the same reward. Since their reward was great, so will be that of Christians who suffer (6:23, cf. 26). Discipleship of Jesus, however, does not consist primarily of ugly sufferings. SP conceives of that discipleship in terms of Greek education *(paideia),* by which the ethics of Jesus is learned as a way to realize one's humanity and as a means of survival in an evil and dangerous world.

Like Greek ethics, SP is primarily concerned with the realization of one's humanity. How such realization is to be accomplished is explained in clear, extremely concise terms. Basic is the Greek ethical concept of "the good person" *(ho agathos anthrōpos):* "The good person brings forth the good out of the treasure of the heart, but the bad produces the bad out of the bad" (6:45). Notably, the bad is denied the honorific term, "human person" *(anthrōpos).*

The central ethical demand of Jesus is to love one's enemies (6:27b–28). Properly understood, this demand conforms to God's philanthropy and mercy, both of which are key terms of Greek religion and ethics. God is "kind to the ungrateful and the evil" (6:35d). He is "your Father who is merciful" (6:36). Therefore, the proper human response can only be that one is both generous and merciful and thus imitates God (6:35–38). Love of the enemy, however, not only corresponds to divine philanthropy but also exemplifies the Golden Rule (6:31) rightly understood (6:32–35). Loving the enemy (6:27c–28) means taking the initiative in turning the enemy into a friend, a theory rooted in Greek ethics. Later, Polycarp (*Phil.* 12:3) can rightly comment: "Love those who hate you, and pray for those who curse you, and you will have no enemy." Therefore, a life of generosity and mercy in every respect is the proper response to divine generosity and mercy.

This message was common in both the Greek and the Jewish world, especially in the Hellenistic-Jewish diaspora (see Betz *2 Corinthians 8–9* Hermeneia on 2 Cor 9:6–15). As a presupposition, it is also the basis for the rules of Christian education (6:40–45). Salvation can thus be experienced even now in overcoming ignorance (6:39), in improving one's relationship within the community (6:37–38, 41–42), in becoming a good human person (6:43–45), and in surviving the hazards of life in general (6:47–49). This life of discipleship is, however, threatened from within at every point, so that constant self-examination and self-correction remain indispensable (6:41–46).

H. Literary Influences

The literary influences of SM have been and continue to be immense. Comprehensive studies do not exist and probably never will because of the number of sources involved. Bibliographies, despite their efforts, remain incomplete. In comparison, SP has been far less influential. In fact, until recently not much attention has been devoted to it, apart from the gospel of Luke (see Wellhausen 1911: 59–60; Knox 1957: 9–17; Kahlefeld 1962; Schürmann *Lukasevangelium* HTKNT, 323–86; Robinson 1982: 391; Worden 1973; Lambrecht 1985: 206–32).

1. Within the NT. Literary dependencies and influences exerted by SM and SP upon other NT writings is a problem recently investigated by many scholars. There is a multitude of hypotheses and methodologies, and most questions remain open. What were the relationships between SM, SP, and Q, or versions of Q? Whatever these were, what was their influence *upon* Q? If Matthew and Luke included these texts in their gospels, did they influence these gospel writers elsewhere? Why do Mark and John have no knowledge of either SM or SP? Did Paul know of SM or SP? The parallels in his letters are too close to be accidental, but the significant differences have so far prevented any agreeable solution; see especially 1 Thess 4:2, 3–12 (cf. SM/Matt 5:16, 27–32; 6:33); 5:15 (cf. SM/Matt 5:38–42); 1 Cor 4:12 (cf. SM/Matt 5:44; SP/Luke 6:28); 7:10–16 (cf. SM/Matt 5:31–32); Gal 5:14 (cf. SM/Matt 5:43–48); Rom 2:1–3 (cf. SM/Matt 7:1–5, 37–42); 12:9–21; 13:8–10 (cf. SM/Matt 5:43–48; SP/Luke 6:27–28, 32–36). Did Paul obtain access to these texts through SM, SP, a version of Q, or from the oral tradition? One of the greatest puzzles remains the literary and theological relationship between SM and the Epistle of James (see Shepherd 1956; Dibelius and Greeven *James* Hermeneia, 28–29; Davies 1966: 401–14), but also 1 Pet 3:14; 4:14 appears to be familiar with the beatitudes (cf. SM/Matt 5:10; SP/Luke 6:22; see also 1 Pet 2:19, 20, 23; 3:16; and Best 1969–70: 95–113).

2. In the Post-NT Period. As Koester, Robinson, and many others have pointed out, early collections of Jesus' sayings developed side by side with the Gospels well into the 2d century (see Robinson 1982: 389–94 with references). Evidence of such collections has surfaced in papyrus findings such as Papyrus Egerton and the Oxyrynchus Papyri nos. 1, 654 and 655, both of which contain important parallels to SM and SP (noted in Aland 1982: nos. 51–75, 78–83, and pp. 584–85; *NTApocr.* 1: 97–116). Such sayings collections are also related to the Nag Hammadi texts, especially the *Gospel of Thomas* (see Koester 1980: 238–61; Robinson 1982: 393–94). As some of the sayings collections made their way into the NT (notably SM, SP, and Q), others did not, which may account for many similarities and differences among all sources concerned. These developments may also be responsible for the parallels to SM and SP in the Apocryphal Gospels and the Apostolic Fathers, where clusters of sayings can be found (see especially *1 Clem.* 13:2; *2 Clem.* 4:1–7:7; 13:2–4; Polycarp, *Phil.* 2:3; 6:2; 7:2; 12:3; see Koester 1957).

Strongly reminiscent of the Two Way schema in SM/Matt 7:13–14 is its appearance in the *Doctrina apostolorum,* probably originally a work of great proximity to *Did.* 1:1–6:3 and *Barn.* 18–20 (see Rordorf and Tuilier 1978: 22–34, 206–10; Wengst 1984: 13 with references and bibliography). The relationship of SM and SP to the *Shepherd of Hermas* is as yet unexplored. For Justin Martyr and the Pseudo-Clementine literature, doctoral dissertations have been published but they do not deal explicitly with the problem of SM and SP. All Christian writings of the post-NT period up to and inclusive of Justin Martyr contain numerous references and allusions to SM and SP with most of them textually different and independent from the canonical gospels as we have them. Even after the gospels of Matthew and Luke became generally accepted, this process of transmission may have continued for some time, especially in the Sayings of the Desert Fathers, the monastic rules (e.g., the *Regula Benedicti*), and the liturgical, martyrological, hagiographical, and mystical literature of the East and West. Specialized studies on most of these aspects are lacking. For preliminary surveys, see Massaux 1950; Mees 1975; Beyschlag 1977; Grant 1978; and the indexes of passages in *Biblia Patristica* 1–3 (1975–1980).

Bibliography

Aland, K. 1985. *Synopsis Quattuor Evangeliorum.* 13th ed. Stuttgart.

Bauer, B. 1841. *Kritik der evangelischen Geschichte der Synoptiker.* Leipzig. repr. Hildesheim, 1974.

Berner, U. 1985. *Die Bergpredigt. Rezeption und Auslegung im 20. Jahrhundert.* 3d. ed. GTA 12. Göttingen.

Best, E. 1969–1970. I Peter and the Gospel Tradition. *NTS* 16: 95–113.

Betz, H. D. 1985a. Eschatology in the Sermon on the Mount and the Sermon on the Plain. Pp. 343–50 in *SBLSP.* Atlanta, GA.

———. 1985b. *Essays on the Sermon on the Mount.* Trans. L. L. Welborn. Philadelphia.

Beyschlag, K. 1977. Zur Geschichte der Bergpredigt in der Alten Kirche. *ZTK* 74: 291–322.

Billerbeck, P. 1926, 1928. *Kommentar zum Neuen Testament aus Talmud und Midrasch.* Vol. 1: 189–470, 470–74. Vol. 4/1: 1–22. Munich.

Davies, W. D. 1966. *The Setting of the Sermon on the Mount.* Cambridge.

Delobel, J., ed. 1982. *Logia. Les paroles de Jésus. The Sayings of Jesus.* BETL 59. Louvain.

Dibelius, M. 1940. *The Sermon on the Mount.* New York.

———. 1953. Die Bergpredigt. Pp. 79–174 in *Botschaft und Geschichte.* Vol. 1. Tübingen.

Dupont, J. 1954. *Les béatitudes.* 3 vols. Bruges and Louvain.

Feine, P. 1885. Ueber das gegenseitige Verhältnis der Texte der Bergpredigt bei Matthäus und bei Lukas. *Jahrbücher für protestantische Theologie* 11: 1–85.

Grant, R. 1978. The Sermon on the Mount in Early Christianity. *Semeia* 12: 215–31.

Guelich, R. 1982. *The Sermon on the Mount.* Waco, TX.

Heinrici, C. F. G. 1900–1905. *Die Bergpredigt (Matth. 5–7; Luk 6, 20–49) quellenmässig und begriffsgeschichtlich untersucht.* 2 vols. Leipzig.

Holtzmann, H. J. 1863. *Die synoptischen Evangelien.* Leipzig.

Kahlefeld, H. 1962. *Der Jünger. Eine Auslegung der Rede Lk 6,20–49.* Frankfurt.

Kilpatrick, G. D. 1946. *The Origins of the Gospel of Matthew.* Oxford.

Kissinger, W. S. 1975. *The Sermon on the Mount: A History of Interpretation and Bibliography.* Metuchen, NJ.

Knox, W. L. 1957. *The Sources of the Synoptic Gospels 2: St. Luke and St. Matthew,* ed. H. Chadwick. Cambridge.

Koester, H. 1957. *Synoptische Überlieferung bei den apostolischen Vätern.* TU 65. Berlin.

———. 1980. Gnostic Writings as Witness for the Development of the Sayings Tradition. Pp. 238–61 in *The Rediscovery of Gnosticism.* SHR 1/1. Leiden.

Küchler, M. 1979. *Frühjüdische Weisheitstraditionen. Zum Fortgang weisheitlichen Denkens im Bereich des frühjüdischen Jahweglaubens.* OBO 26. Freiburg.

Kümmel, W. G. 1975. *Introduction to the New Testament.* Rev. ed. Trans. H. C. Kee. Nashville, TN.

Lambrecht, J. 1985. *The Sermon on the Mount.* GNS 14. Wilmington, DE.

Lindemann, A. 1984. Literaturbericht zu den Synoptischen Evangelien 1978–1983. *TRu* 49: 223–76, 311–71.

Loisy, A. 1907. Le discours sur la montagne. Pp. 534–645 in *Les évangiles synoptiques.* Vol. 1. Ceffonds, Près Montier-in-Der (Haute-Marne).

———. 1924. *L'évangile selon Luc.* Paris.

Massaux, E. 1950. *Influence de l'évangile de Saint Matthieu sur la littérature chrétienne avant Sainte Irenée.* Louvain.

McNeile, A. H. 1915. *The Gospel according to St. Matthew.* London.

Mees, M. 1975. *Ausserkanonische Parallelstellen zu den Herrenworten und ihre Bedeutung.* Quaderni di "Vetera Christianorum" 10. Bari.

Moffatt, J. 1918. *An Introduction to the Literature of the New Testament.* 3d ed. Edinburgh.

Mutzenbecher, A. 1967. *Sancti Aurelii Augustini de sermone domini in monte libros duos.* CChr Series Latina 35. Turnholt.

Polag, A. 1982. *Fragmenta Q.* 2d ed. Neukirchen-Vluyn.

Robinson, J. M. 1982. Early Collections of Jesus' Sayings. Pp. 389–94 in *Logia. Les paroles de Jesus. The Sayings of Jesus.* BETL 59. Louvain.

Rordorf, W., and Tuilier, A. 1978. *La Doctrine des Douze Apôtres (Didachè).* SC 248. Paris.

Sanders, E. P. 1985. *Jesus and Judaism.* London.

Schenk, W. 1981. *Synopse zur Redenquelle der Evangelien.* Düsseldorf.

Shepherd, M. H. 1956. The Epistle of James and the Gospel of Matthew. *JBL* 75: 40–51.

Soiron, T. 1941. *Die Bergpredigt Jesu.* Freiburg.

Strecker, G. 1984. *Die Bergpredigt.* Göttingen.

Streeter, B. H. 1930. *The Four Gospels.* London.

Tholuck, A. F. 1869. *Commentary on the Sermon on the Mount.* Trans. L. Brown. Edinburgh.

———. 1872. *Die Bergrede Christi.* 5th ed. Gotha.

Wellhausen, J. 1911. *Einleitung in die drei ersten Evangelien.* 2d ed. Berlin.

———. 1914. *Das Evangelium Matthaei übersetzt und erklärt.* 2d ed. Berlin.

Wengst, K. 1984. *Didache (Apostellehre), Barnabasbrief, Zweiter Klemensbrief, Schrift an Diognet.* Schriften des Urchristentums 2. Darmstadt.

Wernle, P. 1899. *Die synoptische Frage.* Freiburg.

Worden, R. D. 1973. A Philological Analysis of Luke 60:20b–49 and Parallels. Diss., Princeton University.

Wrege, H. T. 1968. *Die Überlieferungsgeschichte der Bergpredigt.* WUNT 9. Tübingen.

Zeller, D. 1983. *Die weisheitlichen Mahnsprüche bei den Synoptikern.* FB 17. 2d ed. Würzburg. Verlag.

Hans Dieter Betz

SERON (PERSON) [Gk *Sērōn*]. A commander of a unit of the Syrian army, which he led against Judas Maccabeus. He was the second Syrian commander to oppose Judas on the battlefield. See also APOLLONIUS. He is mentioned only in 1 Macc 3:13–14, with the parallel passage in Josephus (*Ant* 12.288).

The information these sources give about Seron is minimal and his position is thus far from clear. He is described as "commander of the army of Syria" (1 Macc 3:13), which Josephus turned, wrongly, into "governor of Coele-Syria." This could not have been so, since the governor of Coele-Syria at that time was Ptolemy son of Dorymenes. "Commander of the army of Syria" is meaningless in this context and was coined after biblical phrases.

It was suggested that he might have been an official of higher rank than Apollonius, and that he commanded some unit of the Syrian army not far from Judea. Its location was suggested at Dora by Goldstein (*1 Maccabees* AB, 246), and at Gazaro or Jammia by Bar-Kochva (1989: 133). Bar-Kochva also suggested, according to his name, that he was Thracian by origin, and so might have been a commander of a garrison of Thracian mercenaries (Ibid.). Seron was defeated by Judas Maccabeus, sometime in the spring of 165 B.C.E. at the Ascent of Beth-Horon.

Bibliography

Bar-Kochva, B. 1989. *Judas Maccabaeus*. Cambridge.

URIEL RAPPAPORT

SERPENT (RELIGIOUS SYMBOL). In comparative religions the term "serpent" refers to a number of creatures, real and imaginary, distinguished by physical serpentine characteristics. Serpents play a major role in mythological and religious traditions throughout the world from arctic peoples (where snakes are rare or nonexistent) to equatorial cultures (where snakes are plentiful). The diversity of serpent figures within a culture may be demonstrated by N European traditions where this category includes, in addition to snakes, such beasts as sea serpents (usually huge, scaley ocean monsters), dragons (snake-like reptiles with four legs), wyverns (two legged dragon-like creatures with wings), cockatrices and basilisks (rooster-headed wyverns), and hydras (multi-headed serpents). Though each religious tradition views its own serpent symbols within its own world-view, certain correspondences may be found in several widely separated cultures. The ANE peoples shared in the use of serpentine symbolism, though the extant artifacts often leave an imprecise understanding of the snake images. Serpents do appear in literary texts, however, so some idea of their significance to the culture may be determined.

The creation of the universe arising from a titanic struggle of deities, monsters, or both is a fairly common motif. In Enuma Elish the monster Tiamat is defeated by Marduk; with her defeat the cosmos can be designed. It has often been posited that Tiamat was a dragon or some form of serpent; though the text is quite unclear on her nature, it is certain that monstrous serpents aided her in her battle with the gods. In the Bible, God is pictured as struggling with sea serpents, which are controlled, and such texts have been interpreted as examples of creation myths. Serpents aid other deities in the creation of the cosmos in certain Indian, African, South Pacific, and South American religious traditions (Ions 1967: 108; Parrinder 1982: 25; Poignant 1967: 94; Sullivan 1988: 297); yet in some cultures the serpents are themselves the creators. Wollunqua, an Australian rainbow serpent, set out the souls of humanity (Butterworth 1970: 189) and for various peoples in Angola it is claimed that the python is the creator of all life (Mundkur 1983: 260), a notion which finds its parallel among the Warao of Venezuela (Wilbert 1975: 168). Moreover, serpents may be representations of both chaos and creation simultaneously (Sullivan 1988: 58; Roe 1989: 16–17) or the benevolent side of creation which saves people from the chaotic events of creation itself (Reichel-Dolmatoff 1971: 26).

In cosmic terms the universe always sits on the threshold of relapse into chaos. In numerous cultures the ordered cosmos includes serpents as central figures in the vision of the created world. Often it is the serpent which holds the universe together by lying in the sea surrounding the land, tail in mouth, physically containing the ground (Parrinder 1982: 24; Roe 1989: 12; Wilbert 1975: 164–65; Davidson 1964: 32, 34–35). In this form the serpent symbolizes both the boundaries of the created world and the notion of eternity. By holding the universe together tightly in coils, any movement by the snake will cause ground to buckle and quake; therefore the serpent is both protection against chaos and a potential danger. The fact that the serpent surrounding the land is clearly enormous and powerful provides for a cosmic sea serpent; not unlike *Itn* from Ugarit's myths or the biblical Leviathan.

Also common in world mythology is the notion of the world tree which forms the center of the created universe. This is understood to reach from heaven to the netherworld forming a natural pillar on which all levels of the cosmos exist. Either at the roots or around the trunk of the tree there is usually a serpent which appears contrasted with an eagle in the branches above (Butterworth 1970: 49–50, 85, 149; Davidson 1964: 26–27). Both the Etana myth and the story of Gilgamesh and the Huluppu tree reflect these notions (Kramer 1938: 5). The serpent may either be guarding the tree or destroying it. The eagle and serpent as a symbol of perpetual animosity appears to be a common motif portraying the eternal battles between good and evil or, more properly, order and chaos, which are then represented as the extremes of the cosmos (Jordan-Smith 1989: 64).

In some traditions the central axis of the world is a serpent, either transversing the planes of existence or upholding the center of the earth (Ions 1967: 25, 108; Wilbert 1975: 164–65; Paper 1978: 28). Common among Indian and American religious traditions, it has been argued to have been represented as early as the 5th millennium B.C.E. in the Ukraine (Gimbutas 1982: 101–13). Within the cosmic realm serpentine beings form bridges from the area of human habitation to other abodes; most common is the perception of the rainbow as a snake bridging this land with heaven, a pervasive belief throughout Oceana, South Asia, Africa, and the Americas. Serpents also convey souls to the land of the dead for the Ojibwa and Dauavani (Paper 1978: 29; Sullivan 1988: 532). As with certain serpentine deities who are related to rivers in Mesopotamia (and possibly with Ug *ṯpṭ nhr*), snakes create, inhabit, and are rivers in various cultures (McEwan 1983: 226–29; Parrinder 1982: 25; Roe 1989: 9).

The final area of the cosmos in which serpents play a significant role is the underworld. In western Christian tradition the serpent as a sign of evil belongs to the realm of hell, but long before Christian iconography the ancient Egyptians could use the serpent Apophis as the very underworld through which Re had to travel; not to mention the myriads of snakes which could destroy the soul of the dead on the way to the afterlife should the departed not know the correct spells for getting by them. Among the Dinka of the Sudan there is some notion of a world beneath the earth inhabited by cobras which act as humans; in India the nagas, who appear in both human and cobra forms, also exist as a counterpart to human life (Lienhardt 1961: 117; Rawlinson 1986: 137). In South America such python-people are thought to live on an island (Roe 1989: 27).

If there are human-like serpents, it is natural that for several peoples around the earth their own ancestors are seen as snakes. In these situations the particular species of snake becomes a symbol for the group. In Oceana the snake is one of four animals from which all people derive (Poignant 1967: 90–91); in Africa and the Americas particular snakes (python, cobra, anaconda, rattlesnake, etc.) commonly are held to be the direct ancestors of tribes who then hold the serpents in honor (Mundkur 1983: 57, 91, 96; Lienhardt 1961: 118; Luckert 1976: 124; Voth 1903: 352). For these people snakes can be very much like humans and may breed with them.

Serpents have been connected to the destruction of life in several cultures. As in Gen 3:1–15, ANE and African narratives tell how serpents diverted a form of immortality meant for humans. This usually refers to a plant or extra skin which is taken by or given to a snake before the humans could make use of it; therefore snakes may become young again but people may not, a motif which may be seen in the tales of Gilgamesh and Adapa (Joines 1974: 70–71; Parrinder 1982: 56–59; Wrigley 1988: 375). Serpents appear in several fashions with the dead. In Africa, classical Greece and South America the souls of the dead may appear in the form of snakes (Mbiti 1970: 216; Cole 1982: 61; Küster 1913: 67; Burkert 1985: 195; Sullivan 1988: 544). Pythons convey messages between the dead and God in Turu belief (Mbiti 1970: 91), but more often poisonous serpents are sent as messengers of death by sorcerers (Mbiti 1970: 255–56; Sullivan 1988: 485). Of course chthonic deities and deities of death may take the form or attributes of snakes (Hultkrantz 1979: 63; Burkert 1985: 201: Lawuyi and Olupọna 1988: 2). Finally, the shed skins of snakes have been taken as symbols of immortality of the soul and the mortality of the flesh in Hinduism (*Brihad-Aranyaka Upanishad* 4.4.7 and *Prasna Upanishad* 5.5).

The serpent as the end of life is also found in cosmic scope. Those serpents which surround the earth may also destroy it. In Norse mythology this is a certain fate, for the Midgard serpent eventually will destroy the universe and kill the god Thor in the process (Davidson 1964: 37). In the same vein, the Fon believe that if the serpent around the earth is not properly fed it will consume itself, destroying the universe (Parrinder 1982: 27). In an Oaxacan myth of Mesoamerica gigantic snakes attempt to devour the earth (Vázquez 1983: 9, 13) while South American traditions see periodic cycles of destruction in the universe precipitated by the slaying of two mythical anacondas (Sullivan 1988: 197).

Serpents clearly are used for symbols of both good and evil. Few serpent symbols are as unambiguously positive as the use of the boa constrictor among the Tukano to reflect the joy of dancing (Reichel-Dolmatoff 1971: 103). Yet as ancestors of various peoples serpents appear as positive symbols. They also are beneficent as signs of gods and royalty. Deities may appear as serpents or have aspects of snakes and still be good gods; this is especially true in East Asia where serpents (dragons in particular) are perceived as beneficial (Paper 1978: 29; Faure 1987: 338). Buddha may, in fact, be represented by the Naga Mucilinda which had protected him (Rawlinson 1986: 136). Among the Elamites serpent figures are common and may reflect divine attributes reflected in "Master/Mistress of the animals" representations, often with snakes, and in the thrones, which appear to have held deities, composed of entertwined serpents for a base and with four hooded serpents crawling up the back, for which comparisons with the Naga thrones of Indian tradition should be made (Amiet 1966: 58, 310–11 fig. 233 A-B, 378–79 fig. 286 A-C). Mesopotamia had several minor serpent deities, the exact realms of which are largely unknown (Joines 1974: 70–71; Frayne 1982: 512; McEwan 1983: 215). Major deities of Latin America have been portrayed as serpents, including Tlaloc, Cihuacoatl, and the reknowned Quetzalcoatl (Luckert 1976: 49; Delhalle 1982: 130; Carrasco 1982: 79, 96–98). The terror or power of serpents may also be ascribed to deities in the form of serpent attributes, as with Athena (Burkert 1985: 229), where in Greek myth some serpents may slay with a glance.

Serpents also serve as royal symbols. In Egypt the uraeus was worn by the ruler as part of the crown and serpent-shaped sceptres have been found in Elam (Amiet 1966: 382). In China the dragon was a standard royal symbol into the 20th century and the sword, one of three symbols of emperorship, in Japan is said to have come from a dragon, probably representing lightning (Paper 1978: 29; Holtom 1972: 24). Moreover, the poison of serpents may give mortals an invincibility in battle if bathed in or drunk in European and South American traditions (MacCulloch 1973: 139–40; Sullivan 1988: 444). In some cultures of Africa and America the first ruler of the world, the origin of royalty itself, was a serpent (Wrigley 1988: 375; Carrasco 1982: 79).

Serpents have been used as representations of lightning throughout the Americas and often are associated with rain throughout the world. In China it is the dragon which causes or witholds rainfall and this is a common belief across Asia including India where the nagas hold such power (Cohen 1978: 255; Vogel 1926: 4). In Latin America and Oceana the great gods of rain are the celestial serpents (Roe 1989: 9; Mountford 1978: 23–24). In Africa the same serpent who may "be" a river or the rainbow also can supply rain (Wrigley 1988: 372). With this symbolic use of the serpent, however, the snake creatures become ambiguous figures, for drought also is caused by the serpent and hail, flooding, and ruination of crops may come with the rains if the serpents in charge wish to punish people.

The most ambiguous function of the serpent as symbol is as killer/healer. The naga serpents of India are often evil and bite people, causing death; but they may also use their poisons to save lives (Vogel 1926: 17–18). Similar attributes are found concerning serpents in South America (Sullivan 1988: 444) and Europe in the healing cults of Asclepius and Glycon. The caduceus has become the symbol of medicine in European tradition. The story of the firey serpents sent to kill and the serpent image used to heal in Num 21:8–9 may reflect this aspect of serpent symbolism. It may be noted that in some cultures the serpent only brings disease not a cure (Walker 1980: 91).

In some cultures serpents play the role of the villain. Pali belief allows no nagas to grow in dharma and the Lakota believe that snakes are not allowed into the spirit world (Rawlinson 1986: 137; Walker 1980: 71). As symbols of chaos and gluttony, snakes are a constant threat to the existence of the universe and humans. In Asia and Europe dragons are often seen as killing people, consuming vast amounts of livestock, and holding young women captive or eating them. Evil spirits, monsters, and demons come in the shape of snakes throughout Europe, Asia, Africa, and the Americas. Classical mythology has a number of serpentine chaos monsters, including Hydra, Typho, Echidna, and Skylla; Illuyanka, the vast serpent of the Anatolian myth falls into this chaotic vision of the serpent (Beckman 1982: 11). Volcanoes can be seen as monstrous destructive serpent mouths (Luckert 1976: 44–46; Burkert 1985: 127–28). Finally serpents are presented as examples of slyness, lying, and seduction all of which would conform to the serpent which appears in Eden (Ions 1967: 113; Hultkrantz 1979: 63; Walker 1980: 122).

Snakes may be used for sexual symbols. In Europe and the ANE there seems to be reason sometimes to view serpents as symbols of sexuality (Mundkur 1983: 180–208). Clearly the serpent has been a symbol for fertility in many cultures among the Oceanic peoples, Africans, and Latin Americans (Poignant 1967: 91; Hauenstein 1978: 529; Luckert 1976: 46; Hultkrantz 1979: 236). But there is no universal gender distinction in the use of serpents. While Moor (1988: 111) has seen serpent references in the ANE as masculine symbols, it must be noted that in East Asia and Japan serpents are more apt to represent women (Mundkur 1983: 176–77); this is true also in Borneo and West Africa (Davidson 1964: 193; Hauenstein 1978: 530) while Celtic tradition seems to use serpents for a male symbol (Mundkur 1983: 180). The Tukano of South America use one snake, the anaconda, to represent women and another, the boa constrictor, to symbolize men (Reichel-Dolmatoff 1971: 102). So while serpents are related to gender, they are multivalent symbols with regard to sexuality.

Serpents also appear consistently as guardians and as companions to the divine realms. As guardians they are perhaps most noted for protecting pools and wells (Vogel 1926: 4; Poignant 1967: 92; Ross 1967: 348; Mountford 1978: 23; Paper 1978: 29; Roe 1989: 12), though they also protect territory and can stand guard at boundaries (McEwan 1983: 221–22). Serpents as guards for people are attested in the Eastern Mediterranean and South America (Burkert 1985: 30, 130; Sullivan 1988: 493); in the same manner, serpents guard the deities and their dwellings (Grimm 1888: 1491; Butterworth 1970: 80; McEwan 1983: 219). Buddhist monks, from the time Mucilinda protected Buddha, have had guardian serpents (Faure 1987: 339, 356). In the heavenly realm fire-spitting snakes protected the divine drink in Indian tradition (Ions 1967: 102) in much the same manner that beings interpreted as fire-serpents stand in the presence of God in Isa 6:2. Finally, serpents are renowned for guarding treasures of gold and jewels in both East Asian and European traditions.

As companions of the deities serpents usually serve as a means of transportation. Vishnu floats along on the cosmic sea on his snake raft (Ions 1967: 108); Mawa, the Fon creator deity, rides about in the mouth of a snake (Parrinder 1982: 25); the Japanese goddess of fortune, Benten is conveyed on the back of a dragon (Piggott 1969: 132); while in South America the boa may carry a deity on its back (Sullivan 1988: 143). The Elamite representations of serpents with deities mounted on them may reflect the same traditions (Amiet 1966: 286). In Hindu mythology the serpent Vasuki is used by the gods and the demons to churn the milk ocean into amrita, the sacred drink and then becomes a constant companion of Shiva. The Fon of Africa perceive snakes to be the intermediaries of the ritual experts and the gods (Mbiti 1969: 91).

This relationship between the gods and humans through serpents is perhaps best represented by the serpent as symbol of wisdom. In Japan, Siberia, Africa, and South America one becomes a shaman through the intermediary of snakes (Kitagawa 1969: 318; Mundkur 1983: 77; Mbiti 1970: 91; Sullivan 1988: 282, 444). Wisdom may be conveyed to humans through serpents either as oracles or through the consuming of parts of the serpent (Grimm 1888: 1491; MacCulloch 1973: 140). Magic is a particular form of wisdom which serpents can impart to humans (Piggott 1969: 93; Rawlinson 1986: 137). However, culture itself may be a product delivered to humans by a serpentine agent. This is clearly the case with Quetzacoatl in Mesoamerica, but in South America as well anacondas bring culture and art (Roe 1989: 27); even the snakes which are evil by nature may be forced to impart valuable information for the culture as with the Algonkian tradition that snakes taught humans about poison and medicine (Hultkrantz 1979: 63). Within the various Buddhist traditions, in fact, serpents, especially the nagas, can be used as examples of the devout followers of the Buddha, filled with wisdom.

Finally, serpents appear as regular objects of omens. For the most part a snake is an ill omen, but not always. Among the ANE omen texts the sighting of snakes often reflects an impending death or ill fate (Whiting 1984: 208); this is a common notion with the sighting of snakes, especially pythons, in Africa, where the snake is taken to be the soul of an elderly man who is about to die (Cole 1982: 61, 202). Messages may be sent to humans by the gods through the intermediaries of common snakes and these then will tell the future or diagnose illness (Kitagawa 1969: 319; Piggott 1969: 132; Hauenstein 1978: 532).

For further discussion of the biblical tradition, see Schlüter 1982 and SERPENT, BRONZE.

Bibliography

Amiet, P. 1966. *Elam.* Auvers-sur-oise.

Beckman, G. 1982. The Anatolian Myth of Illuyanka. *JANES* 14: 11–25.

Burkert, W. 1985. *Greek Religion.* Trans. J. Raffan. Cambridge, MA.

Butterworth, E.A.S. 1970. *The Tree at the Navel of the Earth.* Berlin.
Carrasco, D. 1982. *Quetzalcoatl and the Irony of Empire: Myths and Prophecies in the Aztec Tradition.* Chicago.
Cohen, A. P. 1978. Coercing the Rain Deities in Ancient China. *HR* 17: 244–65.
Cole, H. M. 1982. *Mbari: Art and Life among the Owerri Igbo.* Bloomington.
Davidson, H. R. E. 1964. *Gods and Myths of Northern Europe.* Harmondsworth.
Delhalle, J. C. 1982. Le serpent a plumes des Olmèques a Teotihuacan. *RHR* 199: 123–30.
Faure, B. 1987. Space and Place in Chinese Religious Traditions. *HR* 26: 337–56.
Frayne, D. R. 1982. Naram-Suen and the *Mušḫuššu* Serpents. *JAOS* 102: 511–13.
Gimbutas, M. 1982. *The Goddesses and Gods of Old Europe 6500–3500 B.C.* Rev. ed. Berkeley.
Grimm, J. 1888. *Teutonic Mythology.* Trans. J. S. Stallybrass. 4th ed. London.
Hauenstein, A. 1978. Le serpent dans les rites, cultes et coutumes de certaines ethnies de Côte d'Ivoire. *Anthropos* 73: 525–60.
Holtom, D. C. 1972. *The Japanese Enthronement Ceremonies with an Account of the Imperial Regalia.* Tokyo.
Hultkrantz, Å. 1979. *The Religions of the American Indians.* Trans. M. Setterwall. Hermeneutics: Studies in the History of Religions 7. Berkeley.
Ions, V. 1967. *Indian Mythology.* London.
Joines, K. R. 1974. *Serpent Symbolism in the Old Testament.* Haddonfield.
Jordan-Smith, P. 1989. The Serpent and the Eagle. *Parabola: The Magazine of Myth and Tradition.* 14/3: 64–71.
Kitagawa, J. M. 1969. Ainu Myth. Pp. 309–23 in *Myths and Symbols,* ed. J. M. Kitagawa and C. H. Long. Chicago.
Kramer, S. N. 1938. *Gilgamesh and the Ḫuluppu-Tree: A Reconstructed Sumerian Text.* AS 10. Chicago.
Küster, E. 1913. *Die Schlange in der griechischen Kunst und Religion.* Religionsgeschichtliche Versuche und Vorarbeiten 13/2. Giessen.
Lawuyi, O. B., and Olupọna, J. K. 1988. Metaphoric Associations and the Conception of Death: Analysis of a Yoruba World View. *Journal of Religion in Africa.* 18: 2–14.
Lienhardt, G. 1961. *Divinity and Experience: The Religion of the Dinka.* Oxford.
Luckert, K. W. 1976. *Olmec Religion: A Key to Middle America and Beyond.* The Civilization of the American Indian Series. Norman.
Lurker, M. 1983. *Adler und Schlange: Tiersymbolik im Glauben und Weltbild der Völker.* Tübingen.
MacCulloch, J. A. 1973. *The Celtic and Scandinavian Religions.* Westport.
Mbiti, J. S. 1970. *African Religions and Philosophy.* Garden City.
McEwan, G. J. P. 1983. ^{d}MUŠ and Related Matters. *Or* 52: 215–29.
Moor, J. C. de 1988. East of Eden. *ZAW* 100: 105–11.
Mountford, C. P. 1978. The Rainbow-Serpent Myths of Australia. Pp. 23–97 in *The Rainbow Serpent,* ed. I. R. Buchler, and K. Maddock. The Hague.
Mundkur, B. 1983. *The Cult of the Serpent.* Albany.
Paper, J. 1978. The Meaning of the "T'ao-T'ieh." *HR* 18: 18–37.
Parrinder, E. G. 1982. *African Mythology.* Rev. ed. New York.
Piggott, J. 1969. *Japanese Mythology.* London.
Poignant, R. 1967. *Oceanic Mythology: The Myths of Polynesia, Micronesia, Melanesia, Australia.* London.
Rawlinson, A. 1986. Nāgas and the Magical Cosmology of Buddhism. *Religion* 16: 135–53.
Reichel-Dolmatoff, G. 1971. *Amazonian Cosmos: The Sexual and Religious Symbolism of the Tukano Indians.* Trans. G. Reichel-Dolmatoff. Chicago.
Roe, P. G. 1989. Of Rainbow Dragons and the Origins of Designs: The Waiwal and the Shipibo Ronin Ehua. *Latin American Indian Literatures Journal* 5: 1–67.
Ross, A. 1967. *Pagan Celtic Britain.* London.
Schlüter, M. 1982. *"D^{e}rāgōn" und Götzendienst: Studien zur antiken jüdischen Religionsgeschichte.* Bern.
Sullivan, L. E. 1988. *Icanchu's Drum: An Orientation to Meaning in South American Religions.* New York.
Vázquez, J. A. 1983. The Cosmic Serpent in the Codex Baranda. *Journal of Latin American Lore* 9: 3–15.
Vinycomb, J. 1906. *Fictitious and Symbolic Creatures in Art with Special Reference to their Use in British Heraldry.* London.
Vogel, J. P. 1926. *Indian Serpent-Lore or the Nāgas in Hindu Legend and Art.* London.
Voth, H. R. 1903. *The Oraibi Summer Snake Ceremony.* Field Columbian Museum Publication 83: Anthropological Series 3/4. Chicago.
Walker, J. R. 1980. *Lakota Belief and Ritual,* ed. R. J. DeMallie, and E. A. Jahner. Lincoln.
Whiting, R. M. 1984. Six Snake Omens in Babylonian Script. *JCS* 36: 206–10.
Wilbert, J. 1975. Eschatology in a Participatory Universe: Destinies of the Soul among the Warao Indians of Venezuela. Pp. 163–89 in *Death and the Afterlife in Pre-Columbian America,* ed. E. P. Benson. Washington, D.C.
Wrigley, C. 1988. The River-God and the Historians: Myth in the Shire Valley and Elsewhere. *Journal of African History* 29: 367–83.

LOWELL K. HANDY

SERPENT'S STONE (PLACE) [Heb *ʾeben hazzōḥelet*]. A symbolic landmark at En Rogel where Adonijah, a rival of Solomon for King David's throne, made sacrifices during his abortive attempt to become king (1 Kgs 1:9). The Hebrew word, *zōḥelet* is derived from a verb that means "to shrink back, crawl, glide." The LXX translation, *lithou tou Zōeleth,* where serpent is simply transliterated, would seem to support that the stone was a recognized landmark near En Rogel. This landmark was most likely a sacred stone dedicated to a deity whose symbol was a serpent—frequently a sacred symbol on objects in Palestine—and thus a logical place for Adonijah to legitimize his attempt to seize the throne with sacrifices and feasting.

Various attempts have been made to locate the landmark geographically. The most frequently recognized location is En Rogel at the S end of the Kidron Valley near its confluence with the Hinnom Valley. Another interpretation attempts to locate more precisely the Serpent's Stone with reference to the Serpent (Heb *tannîn,* "serpent, dragon") or Jackal (Heb *tan*) Well mentioned in Neh 2:13. This well is outside the city in the vicinity of the Dung Gate. This would place the well (identified by many with Job's Well at En Rogel [Myers *Ezra, Nehemiah* AB, 104, 118]) most likely near En Rogel and the sacred Serpent Stone. Some link the word *zōḥelet* with a modern Arabic word *zahueileh,* "a slippery rock slope." This has been identified with a rocky slope at the modern village of Silwan, opposite Gihon. This interpretation has two difficulties. First it changes the meaning from a stone to a rocky slope. Second it places the location too far N at Gihon, the location where Solomon legitimized his right to the throne (1 Kgs 1:38–39). Locating the Serpent's Stone farther S at En Rogel fits the biblical description that Adonijah could hear but not see the royal enthronement of Solomon (1 Kgs 1:41; Smith 1907: 109–11; Simons 1952: 160–62).

Bibliography

Simons, J. 1952. *Jerusalem in the Old Testament.* Leiden.

Smith, G. A. 1907. *Jerusalem.* Vol. 1. London.

W. HAROLD MARE

SERPENT, BRONZE. Serpent figures crafted from copper alloy or bronze have been found throughout the ANE. Some fine examples have been recovered on plaques with deities or as independent figurines (Yadin et al. 1960: 117, pl. 181; Macalister 1912: 399, fig. 488; Speiser 1935: 111–12, pl. 50; Loud 1948: pl. 240, no. 1). To date, the most exquisitely wrought of these serpentine figures is the copper alloy snake with gold foil overlay found at Timna (Rothenberg 1972: 159, pls. 19, 20). These objects have been assumed to be cultic images and the appearance of the serpent in artwork in the hands of a god or goddess would seem to confirm this. The serpent appears to have been a stock religious character in Syria-Palestine from the middle of the 2d millennium through the 1st millennium B.C.E. (Joines 1974: 62–63) often appearing on pottery or pendants of various types, more attested than in bronze. See also SERPENT (RELIGIOUS SYMBOL).

The most famous bronze serpent, however, is the one called Nehushtan which Hezekiah is recorded as having destroyed (2 Kgs 18:4). It has long been recognized that this object stood for a deity (Kittel *Die Bücher der Konige* HKAT, 278–79; Lods 1930: 469), but exactly which one is uncertain since the name of the god is not given. The MT states that the name *nĕḥuštān* (LXX *neesthan*) was given to the object by Hezekiah; it clearly is a play on the words bronze/copper *(nĕḥōšet)* and serpent *(nāḥāš)*. It has been suggested that the deity represented by the snake figure was the little known Horon and was related to the Greek Asclepius who was represented by a snake symbol (Gray 1949: 32). Exactly where this object was revered in Judah is unclear, but it has often been assumed that it had a place in the pantheon of the temple of Yahweh in Jerusalem; wherever it was maintained, it was worshiped as a deity since the people sacrificed to it.

Rowley (1939: 136) believed Nehushtan was a deity from the Jebusite cult of Jerusalem which David retained after having taken the city; the god would then have no relation to the cult of Yahweh. In Num 21:8–9, however, the story of the fashioning of the image is recorded; this story is alluded to in the Hezekiah passage so it is clear that the cult assumed that there was a relationship between Yahweh and this god. According to the Numbers narrative the image was created to cure snakebites. This intermediary between God and the people reflects the divine world of the ANE where an important deity would produce a lesser deity to handle mundane matters such as curing the sick (Levine and Tarragon 1988: 518); such an incident is recorded in the Kirta Legend from Ugarit (*KTU* 1.16.V.10–VI.14) where El creates Shatiqatu to save the king's life.

The bronze serpent which Hezekiah destroys was clearly part of the Judean pantheon and almost certainly a deity of healing. The fact that snake divinities which can heal are also capable of killing should be kept in mind (Pardee 1988: 213); it is often the very god who harms people who is needed to protect them. This god had a very specialized sphere of expertise (curing those bitten by poisonous snakes) and therefore would have been on a lower level of divine rank than most deities, what Smith (1984: 359) has given as the third level, which might be called "craft-gods." This deity appears to be the only biblical example of a Judean god of this level of deities. There is no evidence from the biblical text or, as of yet, from ancient Syro-Palestinian sources to connect this bronze serpent image with fertility cults rather than healing, though this has been a popular interpretation of the snake figure (Joines 1974: 74).

Bibliography

Gray, J. 1949. The Canaanite God Horon. *JNES* 8: 27–34.

Joines, K. R. 1968. The Bronze Serpent in the Israelite Cult. *JBL* 87: 245–56.

———. 1974. *Serpent Symbolism in the Old Testament.* Haddonfield.

Levine, B. A., and Tarragon, J. M. 1988. "Shapshu Cries Out in Heaven": Dealing with Snake-bites at Ugarit (KTU 1.100, 1.107). *RB* 95: 481–518.

Lods, A. 1930. *Israël des origines au milieu du Ville siècle.* Paris.

Loud, G., ed. 1948. *Megiddo II: Seasons of 1935–1939: Plates.* OIP 62. Chicago.

Macalister, R. A. S. 1912. *The Excavation of Gezer 1902–1905 and 1907–1909.* Vol. 2. London.

Pardee, D. 1988. *Les textes para-mythologiques de la 24e campagne (1961).* Memoire 77. Paris.

Rothenberg, B. 1972. *Timna: Valley of the Biblical Copper Mines.* London.

Rowley, H. H. 1939. Zadok and Nehushtan. *JBL* 58: 113–41.

Smith, M. A. 1984. Divine Travel as a Token of Divine Rank. *UF* 16: 359.

Speiser, E. A. 1935. *Excavations at Tepe Gawra, Volume I: Levels I–VIII.* Philadelphia.

Yadin, Y. et al. 1960. *Hazor II: An Account of the Second Season of Excavations, 1956.* Jerusalem.

LOWELL K. HANDY

SERUG (PERSON) [Heb *śĕrûg*]. Son of Reu when Reu was 32, father of Nahor at 30, Serug lived to be 230 (Gen 11:20-23). The name has been related to URU *sa-ru-gi* appearing in texts from the region W of Harran in the 7th century B.C. (Johns 1901: 29, 33, et passim). Attempts to identify this with a *ṣe-er-ki* on an Old Babylonian itinerary from Harran to Emar (Hallo 1964: 64, 78–79) must now be discounted and the site's name read as *ṣe-er-di/-da* (Dossin 1974: 28; Beitzel 1978: 212). However, *sa-ru-gi* may be named in a broken context in the annals of Shalmaneser III. It is also possible that *sa-ru-gi* is to be identified with the site described by the later place names Batnai and

Sürüç (Kessler 1980: 197–202). A Neo-Assyrian place name *Šá/Še-ri-gu-ú* (Zadok 1977: 325–26) and an Ur III period personal name *ša-ru-gi* (Barton 1909: plate 94; Schneider 1952: 521) have also been compared with Serug. The root thus appears primarily in place names of the 1st millennium B.C. Like others in the ancestry of Abram in Genesis 11, it is possible to relate the name to a geographical location in N Syria. See also HARAN (PERSON), NAHOR (PERSON). However, the occurrence of a similar form in a 3d millennium B.C. personal name, implies that the 1st millennium attestations of the place name cannot be used to date its occurrence. In Hebrew the root *śrg* means "to intertwine" and can refer to a twig or a tendril (Wenham, *Genesis 1–15* WBC, 251–52).

Bibliography

Barton, G. A. 1909. *Haverford Library Collection of Cuneiform Tablets or Documents from the Temple Archives of Telloh.* Pt 2. Philadelphia.

Beitzel, B. J. 1978. From Ḫarran to Imar Along the Old Babylonian Itinerary. Pp. 209–219 in *Biblical and Near Eastern Studies. Essays in Honor of William Sanford LaSor,* ed. G. A. Tuttle. Grand Rapids.

Dossin, G. 1974. Le site de Tuttul-sur Balīḫ. *RA* 68: 25–34.

Hallo, W. W. 1964. The Road to Emar. *JCS* 18: 57–88.

Johns, C. H. W. 1901. *An Assyrian Doomsday Book or Liber Censualis of the District Round Ḫarran: in the Seventh Century B.C.* Leipzig.

Kessler, K. 1980. *Untersuchungen zur historischen Topographie Nordmesopotamiens nach keilschriftlichen Quellen des 1. Jahrtausends v. Chr.* BTAVO B26. Wiesbaden.

Schneider, N. 1952. Patriarchennamen in zeitgenössischen Keilschrifturkunden. *Bib* 33: 516–22.

Zadok, R. 1977. *On West Semites in Babylonia during the Chaldean and Achaemenian Periods.* Jerusalem.

RICHARD S. HESS

SERVANTS. See SLAVERY.

SESTHEL (PERSON) [Gk *Sesthēl*]. A descendant of Addi who was required by Ezra to divorce his foreign wife (1 Esdr 9:31). In the parallel text of Ezra 10:30, the name Bezalel, son of Pahathmoab, appears in the position that Sesthel holds in 1 Esdr 9:31. However, whether they are identical cannot be determined, and any grounds for identification are based solely on the order of these two lists.

SETH (PERSON) [Heb *šēt*]. Var. SHETH. Third son of Adam, born when Adam was 130 years old (Gen 5:3–8). At 105 years of age, Seth sired Enosh, and subsequently lived to the age of 930. Eve explained the name of her son as the divine "establishing" of a replacement for the murdered Abel (Gen 4:25). Seth establishes the line of righteous antediluvians culminating with Noah in Genesis 5 and continuing to Jesus according to the NT (Luke 3:38). Sir 49:16 describes Shem and Seth as highly honored among humanity. The expression, "children of Seth" (*bĕnê šēt;* RSV SHETH) appears in Num 24:17 in what may be a reference to humanity in general (from the perspective of Genesis, Seth through Noah was the ancestor of all of postdiluvian humanity) or more particularly to the nomadic tribes known as the Sutu (attested in the Egyptian Execration texts and in the Amarna texts, but never located in the region of Moab where Numbers 24 occurs [Rouillard 1985: 438]). Later Jewish, Gnostic, and Christian writings assigned a special significance to Seth and his righteousness (Klijn 1977).

The paronomasia on the name of Seth in Gen 4:25 has evoked some discussion in the commentaries. Although the *kî* particle introducing the second half of the verse may be understood as explaining the meaning of the name, this is not necessary. It may simply mark the beginning of a statement (whether as an emphatic *kî* or otherwise) which includes wordplay on the name Seth, with a loose, unspecified relationship to the name itself (e.g., She called his name Seth, "God has (indeed) provided another seed for me in place of Abel whom Cain slew."). The assonance of the proper name Seth and the verb *šāt* serves to emphasize the sense in which Seth's birth brings to an end one line and begins a new line of descent (Strus 1978: 66). Attempts to assign the Seth of Genesis 4 to a J source and that of Genesis 5 to a P source prove of little value in understanding the traditions underlying the figure. In both chapters he is the "son" of Adam and Eve, and in no case does the text assign Seth to the Cainite line of Genesis 4. Reconstructions of such an association (*GHBW,* 158–66) are conjectural. Also speculative and discredited are suggestions relating Seth to the figure of Alalgar, second name in the antediluvian line of the Old Babylonian king list (cf. Zimmern 1924: 24; Westermann 1984: 348–52).

Bibliography

Klijn, A. F. J. 1977. *Seth in Jewish, Christian and Gnostic Literature.* NovTSup 46. Leiden.

Rouillard, H. 1985. *La péricope de Balaam (Nombres 22–24): La prose et les 'oracles'.* EBib n.s. 4. Paris.

Strus, A. 1978. *Nomen-Omen.* AnBib 80. Rome.

Westermann, C. 1984. *Genesis 1–11: A Commentary.* Minneapolis.

Zimmern, H. 1924. Die altbabylonischen vor-(und nach-) sintflutlichen Könige nach neuen Quellen. *ZDMG* 78: 19–35.

RICHARD S. HESS

SETH, SECOND TREATISE OF THE GREAT (NHC VII,*2*). This Christian-gnostic treatise is the only one of all the Nag Hammadi tractates which has been perfectly preserved. It occupies pp. 49.10–70.12 of Codex VII. *Treat. Seth,* which almost certainly was translated from the Greek, is written in pre-classical Sahidic Coptic. It is likely that many of its serious grammatical and syntactical difficulties are due to the ineptitude of the translator. The title which is found at the end (70.11–12) retains the Gk case endings and appears to be secondary. Already during its transmission in Gk someone must have added this subscript in the belief that the work was another treatise by the heavenly revealer Seth. This is surprising in view of the fact that Seth is nowhere mentioned in the tractate. The likely reason for the mistake is the fact that the speaker in *Treat. Seth* is identified only near the end as Jesus Christ (65,18 and 69,21–22). Someone already familiar with a treatise of Seth, e.g., *The Gospel of the Egyptians* (NHC III,*2* and IV,*2*), might on the basis of a brief look at the beginning have considered it a second one by the same author.

The genre of *Treat. Seth* is that of a revelation discourse, but the pattern is often broken due to what appear to be traditional blocks of material which the author has incorporated. The lack of transitions, unexpected shifts in personal pronouns, and apparent doublets give the work a disunited and confusing appearance. Two main parts can be distinguished. In the first one (49,10–59,19), which is didactic, the speaker asks and receives permission from the heavenly "Church" to descend to the world and reveal "the glory" to "my fellow spirits." He takes over a human body and causes great consternation among the archons. Only one archon, Adonaios, also known as Sabaoth, joins the side of the savior; the others are put at ease by the boast of the cosmocrator, Yaldabaoth. The cosmological framework which is assumed in the account is similar to the one found in *The Apocalypse of John* (NHC II,*1*; III,*1*; IV,*1* and BG 8502,2), *The Hypostasis of the Archons* (NHC II,*4*), and *On the Origin of the World* (NHC II,*5*). In 54,14 a doublet begins which repeats in different words the descent myth and adds the plan of the archons to kill the savior. The passion account (55,15–56,13) at first appears typically docetic in that Christ's suffering and death are not real but only in appearance. This, however, is followed by the claim that Simon of Cyrene was crucified while the savior looked on from on high laughing at the ignorance of his enemies (56,4–19). This interpretation of the passion, based on Mark 15:21–22, is attributed to Basilides by Irenaeus (*Haer.* 1.24.4) and Epiphanius (*Pan.* 24.3.2–4). In 58,17–59,11 there is a third passion account which consists of an allegorical reading of Matt 27:45–53. Though the interpretation is gnostic, it does not appear to be docetic in origin. The profundity and literary quality of this piece is far beyond the vulgar level of most of the rest of the treatise.

The last part of *Treat. Seth* is homiletical and polemical (59,19–70,10). The gnostic readers are exhorted to live in unity with each other and Christ in the face of persecution by Christians who "proclaim a doctrine of a dead man" (60,20–21). A similar anti-orthodox polemic is found in *The Apocalypse of Peter* (NHC VII,*3*) and *The Testimony of Truth* (NHC IX,*3*). The section includes also a dramatic litany in which Adam, Abraham, Isaac, Jacob, David, Solomon, the twelve prophets, Moses and John the Baptist are called laughingstocks and counterfeits of the Hebdomad, i.e. the cosmocrator, since "none of them knew me nor my brethren" (62,27–64,1). The litany may have been borrowed from a Marcionite source. The theme of the heavenly wedding, which is the model for union among the gnostics, appears to be dependent on Valentinian speculation (57,7–27 and 65,33–68,16).

Treat. Seth gives striking evidence of the eclectic nature of gnostic literature. It is able to borrow freely from other traditions and writings without much concern for theological or literary unity. It is unlikely that such writings reflect the doctrines of specific sects. The author and intended readers of *Treat. Seth.* in contrast to their orthodox opponents, were not discriminating readers. Evidently they found comfort and inspiration in a wide variety of esoteric sources. What makes *Treat. Seth* of special interest is that the conflict with orthodox Christianity has become open and confrontational. The rejection of the OT and of the death of Christ have become unambiguous, even though there is no standard formulation for this. Persecution may have brought some clarity and unity in what Christian Gnostics denied, but it appears that they remained individualistic and eclectic in what they affirmed. The polemical nature and dependence on other gnostic traditions makes it unlikely that *Treat. Seth* was written before the 3d century, and it could be as late as the early 4th. Nothing in the tractate betrays the identity and provenance of the author.

Bibliography

Bullard, R. A., and Gibbons, J. A. 1988. The Second Treatise of the Great Seth (VII,2). *NHL* 362–71.

Krause, M. 1973. Der zweite Logos des grossen Seth. Vol. 2, pp. 106–51 in *Christentum am Roten Meer,* ed. G. Altheim and R. Stiehl. Berlin.

Painchaud, L. 1981. La polémique anti-ecclésiale et l'exégèsede la passion dans le 'Deuxième traité du Grand Seth' (NH VII,2). Pp. 340–51 in *Colloque international sur les textes de Nag Hammadi (Québec, 22–25 août 1978)*, ed. B. Barc. BCNHE 1. Quebec.

———. 1982. *Le deuxième traité du Grand Seth (NH VII,2): Texte établi et présenté.* BCNHT 6. Quebec.

Tröger, K.-W. 1975. Der zweite Logos des grossen Seth, Gedanken zur Christologie in der zweiten Schrift des Codex VII. Pp. 268–76 in *Essays on the Nag Hammadi Texts in Honour of Pahor Labib,* ed. M. Krause. NHS 6. Leiden.

FREDERIK WISSE

SETH, THREE STELES OF (NHC VII, *5*). The fifth and final tractate of codex VII (pp. 118–127) of the Nag Hammadi codices. The well-preserved text is a Coptic translation of a Greek original and represents the only surviving witness to this document. The dialect is Sahidic with the presence of some non-Sahidic forms.

Steles Seth presents itself as a revelation received by a certain Dositheos, probably the obscure Samaritan teacher of Simon Magus (Schenke 1981: 592–93; Tardieu 1973: 551; Claude 1983: 3). The revelation consists of the contents of three steles composed by Seth in the distant past and now, through the agency of Dositheos, being transmitted to a latter-day Sethian gnostic community. The single reference to Dositheos at the beginning of the text, however, together with the limitation of the term revelation (used twice) to the opening and closing lines of the tractate betray the apocalyptic imagery or genre as part of a secondary redaction (Robinson *NHL,* 362; Claude 1983: 9–13).

In its present form, *Steles Seth* is divided into three sections or steles which preserve three hymns addressed to a divine triad presented in Neoplatonic terms. The original form of the hymns, however, has been corrupted by the secondary redaction which integrated them with the Sethian gnostic conception of four races (Adamas, Seth, Proto-Sethians or Dositheos, and latter-day Sethians or elect) (Claude 1983: 9–12). The original three hymns are addressed to the divine figures of the Self-begotten *(Autogenes),* Barbelo, and the Unbegotten Father. The triad expresses the relationship between the unknowable god and the perceptible world of humanity. Barbelo, the mother (though never so named in the text) of the divine triad, is the active nature of the stationary Father (the divine as non-being), and the Self-begotten is the vehicle through which that activity is expressed in the perceptible world. This functional relationship of the triad betrays its strong indebtedness to Neoplatonic thought. Numenius, for example, speaks of a movement from the stationary unity of the primordial god through a motion or energy expressed first in the noetic realm and then in the perceptible world (Numen. *Fragment* 15; Tardieu 1973: 560–61). The prevalence of Neoplatonic vocabulary in *Steles Seth* (e.g., the existence-life-mind triad; 122, 20–23) is extensive (Tardieu 1973: 560–67; Claude 1983: 20–31; Robinson 1977).

Steles Seth, which presupposes this ontological system, is best understood in its present form as a liturgical document. The three redacted hymns, addressed in ascending order to the triadic nature of the divine, represent a mystery of ascension (Schenke 1981: 601–602). In *Steles Seth* one encounters the members of a community in the act of appropriating salvation through liturgical participation in the primordial ascent of their spiritual ancestor Seth. The hymns were likely recited as part of a liturgical process through which the individual ascended and descended from the vision of the divine.

The date and provenance of the original work is difficult to determine. The strong Neoplatonic influence on the text together with Porphyry's mention of Plotinus' confrontation with sectarians whose books apparently included the related Sethian texts of *Zost.* (8.1) and *Allogenes* (11.3) suggests a date in the first half of the 3d century C.E. (Robinson 1977: 132–33; *NHL* 362–63). The speculative nature of the text and the survival of the only copy in Coptic translation support Alexandria as the most likely place of composition (Claude 1983: 31–33).

The text is an extremely important witness to the interaction of Neoplatonic and gnostic ideas in the latter 2d–3d centuries. It offers also a rare opportunity to look into the social or worship setting of a gnostic community.

Bibliography

Böhlig, A. 1975. Zum 'Pluralismus' in den Schriften von Nag Hammadi. Pp. 19–34 in *Essays on the Nag Hammadi Texts in Honor of Pahor Labib,* ed. M. Krause. NHS 6. Leiden.

Claude, P. 1981. Approche de la structure des trois stèles de Seth. Pp. 362–73 in *Colloque international sur les textes de Nag Hammadi (Québec, 22–25 août 1978),* ed. B. Barc, BCNHE 1. Quebec.

———. 1983. *Les trois stèles de Seth. Hymne gnostique à la triade (NH VII, 5).* BCNHT 8. Québec.

Krause, M., and Girgis, V. 1973. Viertes Kapitel: Die drei Stelen des Seth. Vol. 2, pp. 178–99 in *Christentum am Roten Meer,* ed. F. Altheim and R. Stiehl. Berlin.

Layton, B. 1987. *The Gnostic Scriptures.* New York.

Robinson, J. M. 1972. The Three Steles of Seth (CG VII, 5). *American Research Center in Egypt Newsletter* 81: 24.

———. 1977. The Three Steles of Seth and the Gnostics of Plotinus. Pp. 132–42 in *Proceedings of the International Colloquium on Gnosticism. Stockholm, Aug. 20–25, 1973,* ed. G. Widengren. Filologisk-filosofiska serien 17. Stockholm.

Schenke, H.-M. 1981. The Phenomenon and Significance of Gnostic Sethianism. Vol. 2, pp. 588–616 in *The Rediscovery of Gnosticism: Proceedings of the Conference at Yale March 1978,* ed. B. Layton. Leiden.

Tardieu, M. 1973. Les trois stèles des Seth. Un écrit gnostique retrouvé à Nag Hammadi. *RSPT* 57: 545–75.

Wekel, K. 1975. "Die drei Schriften des Seth." Die fünfte Schrift aus Nag-Hammadi-Codex VII. *TLZ* 100: 571–80.

———. 1977. Die drei Stelen des Seth (NHC VII, 5). Diss., Humboldt-Universität. Berlin.

James E. Goehring

SETHUR (PERSON) [Heb *sĕtûr*]. One of the twelve individuals sent from Kadesh in the wilderness of Paran to spy out the land of Canaan (Num 13:13). Mentioned only in this list of scouts, Sethur was the son of Michael and a representative of the tribe of Asher. He is numbered among the ten who returned from their adventure with a negative report.

Terry L. Brensinger

SETTLEMENT OF CANAAN. The biblical account of how Israel took possession of the land of Canaan presents at first glance a deceptively straightforward picture. The Conquest fulfills Yhwh's promises to the patriarchs and to the generation of the Exodus. It marks the beginning of that period in which Israel, liberated by Yhwh from bondage, enters fully into a treaty-partnership with him, responsible to abide by his ordinances. It ratifies and proclaims Israel's passage into nationhood through her passage from the limbo of landlessness to a franchise in the soil; from a protected, but bereft, perambulation in the wasteland to a fruitful, settled possession of the land. The Conquest is the capstone of Israel's national epic. See also ISRAEL, HISTORY OF (PREMONARCHIC PERIOD) and (ARCHAEOLOGY AND THE ISRAELITE CONQUEST).

Nevertheless, biblical narratives concerning the Conquest take an inferior place to those of the Exodus. Joshua does not tower, Moses-like, over the consciousness of biblical authors. Indeed, no text outside the book that bears his name explicitly attributes the Conquest to him.

Except as a conclusion foregone from the moment of the Exodus, or from the crossing of the Jordan, the Conquest plays only a small role in Israelite literature outside the book of Joshua. Hosea, Isaiah, and Deutero-Isaiah utilize the Exodus as a conceptual model for Israel's return from exile, but never come to grips with the concrete historical, strategic details of its sequel. Micah (6:1–4) recalls the conflict with Balaam and Balak that threatened Israel's initial entry into Cisjordan: the implication is that the transition from the wilderness to the Promised Land was the moment of peril, the Conquest itself a mere corollary; the Conquest, like the seizure of Troy, demanded the powers of an Apollodorus to describe it, but on it those of a Homer would be sadly squandered. The same attitude suffuses the Pentateuchal account, and informs the notion that one should divide off the first five books of the Bible as a Torah, "the five books of Moses." Only a philistine would demand, after the climactic vision of Moses surveying from a Moabite crag the Promised Land denied to him, an explicit, literal account of Canaan's reduction. That there had been a Conquest was self-evident: Israel possessed the land. Describing the Conquest after Moses' death could be nothing more than belaboring the aftermath.

Nevertheless, Israel's historians have indeed provided us with a reconstruction of the Conquest. The tale itself they have confected from the ingredients of old traditions, an occasional written source, and surmise; it is mounted as a component of the Deuteronomistic History, the historical work putatively stretching from Deuteronomy through 2 Kings, a work in large measure assembled in the 7th century B.C.E. In this setting, the tale of the Conquest furnished a crucial link between the prose epic that described the nation's birth, in the Torah, and the history of Israel's life in the land until the twin catastrophes of subjection and exile overtook it—for Israel, the north, at Assyria's hands, and, for Judah, the south, at Babylon's.

A. The Biblical Presentation
  1. The Transjordanian Conquests
  2. The Cisjordanian Conquest
  3. After Joshua: The Nations Remaining
B. Scholarly Treatments of the Conquest
  1. The Beginnings of Modern Criticism
  2. The Sociological View
  3. The Internal Conquest
  4. Résumé
C. The Emergence of Israel in Canaan
  1. Canaan Before Israel
  2. Canaan in the Earliest Israelite Eras
  3. Israel on the Ground
  4. Israelite Traditions in the Light of Modern Knowledge
  5. The Israelite Conquest

A. The Biblical Presentation

The accounts of this fateful epoch in Israel's historical odyssey deserve to be read not just singly, but as an organic reconstruction. Discrepancies in the Israelite view of the Conquest, with the possible exception of Ezekiel's (if Ezekiel 16 comments on the Conquest), are less significant than scholars have generally claimed. In any event, the treatment of the theme begins in the Pentateuch.

Yhwh had promised Canaan to Israel's ancestors, starting with Abraham (Gen 15:18–21; 26:3; 28:13; 48:6, 16, 21f.; Exod 3:8, 17; 13:5, 11; 23:23, 28–33; 33:1–3; 34:11; Gen 17:8; 28:4; 35:12; Exod 6:8). Scholars have quibbled over the unanimity of these texts concerning the dimensions of the territory vouchsafed—the Priestly source (P), at least, does not reckon Transjordan as part of the land. But the prolusory promise is consistent: Yhwh affirms it in both major Pentateuchal narrative strands (P [Priestly] and J [the Yahwistic source]) to each of the patriarchs and to the generation of the Exodus.

The Exodus follows, of course, its goal, i.e. the Conquest and settlement. Yet a lack of faith, when Israel's spies have reconnoitred Canaan's landscape, leads to the abortion of the appointed day (Numbers 13–14). Condemned to delay, the Israelites ultimately invade not from the south, the most natural and quickest route from Egypt, but from Transjordan. The "wanderings" determine the geographical sequence and the extent of Canaan's vanquishment: the Israelites must brand Transjordan with destruction, under the leadership of Moses, before proceeding to capture the prize Yhwh had promised them.

1. The Transjordanian Conquests. The Mosaic accessions in Transjordan are recalled in two somewhat different recensions in the books of Numbers and Deuteronomy. In the Deuteronomic resumé, Israel avoids contact with the Transjordanian powers—Edom, Moab, and Ammon—and purposefully engages the Amorite kingdom of Sihon, centered on Heshbon (Deuteronomy 2). The succeeding episode recounts the overthrow of Og. Here, Og is king of the Bashan and a region stretching to the Hermon; the operation, thus, entails a daunting detour from the primary objectives of Israel's military thrust in Cisjordan (Deut 3:1–11; 29:6f.). But according to Deuteronomy, Transjordan is an integral part of the land pledged to the patriarchs (see 2:24f.,31). So like Joshua's, Moses' conquests must envelop everything up to the Hermon (Deut 3:8).

The tradition of Transjordanian confrontations in Numbers is of a different cast. Sihon's subjection is incidental, a by-product of his refusal to permit Israel passage through his territory to its promised land, Cisjordan. It leaves Israel master of the land from the Arnon, Moab's border, to Ammon's border at the Jabbok. Northward expansion embraces the districts of Jaazer, Gilead, and, in the southern Bashan, Kenath (Num 21:21–32; 32:39–42). All these areas were traditionally understood to have been peopled by Amorites—the race whose sin, in the theology of Gen 15:16; Deut 9:4f., laid the moral foundation for its extirpation of Yhwh's hands.

The Amorites are consistently portrayed (Amos 2:9) as the aborigines of the Cisjordanian interior, particularly its highlands (Num 13:29; Deut 1:7, 19f.; Josh 10:6). Their rightful successors, apart from the Philistines on the coast of S Canaan, are the *Hebrews.* Biblical ethnography links the *Hebrews* to an eponym, Eber, who is an ancestor of Abraham (Gen 10:21, 25; 11:14). Thus, the *Hebrews,* Abraham's descendants and collaterals, comprise in Transjordan Israel, Edom, Moab, and Ammon, as the delimitations of Num 20:14–21; 21:13–15, 24 (and Deut 2:4f., 9–11, 19–23) make clear.

In sum, Israel's historians identified the kin-based, territorial kingdoms of the Iron Age as Yhwh's avengers against an autochthonous population organized politically into individual city-states. Possibly, the identification of Sihon as an Amorite rather than a *Hebrew* contributed to the Deuteronomic notion that Transjordan was doomed to Israelite conquest from the first. This corollary is absent in Numbers.

Num 21:33–35 does recount the digressive expedition against Og in the Bashan. This text stems from a tradition more closely related to that infusing Deuteronomy. But it does not press the claim that Og was an Amorite (as Deut 3:8; cf. v 11). It conflicts with the more modest reports about Israel's initial penetration only into the southern reaches of the Bashan. And, since Wellhausen observed that Judg 11:22f., Num 22:2, and Josh 24:8 reflect no knowledge of the Og tradition in Bashan (1963: 109), scholars (e.g., Noth *ÜgS,* 35) have widely regarded the notice as an accretion. One sees the tendency for Og to be attached to Sihon secondarily also in 1 Kgs 4:19, where territory S of the Bashan is associated with him (as against 1 Kgs 4:13).

The ideological profile of the reports in Numbers is most distinctive when silhouetted against their attitude toward Transjordan. This substantiates the thesis that the text concerning Og is a late correction of the tradition. As opposed to Deuteronomy, where Transjordan is the first object of Israel's ambitions, Numbers regards any territorial acquisitions in Transjordan as incidental. The sole value of Transjordan is as a springboard for invading the western bank.

Indeed, of the generation that had balked at invading Canaan when the spies returned (Numbers 13–14), only Caleb, in J (Num 14:23f.), or Caleb and Joshua, in P (Num 14:35, 38; 26:65; cf. the layered Deut 1:34–39), are accorded the privilege of entering that consecrated zone plighted to the patriarchs: Moses' death, thus, preempted his entry into this region (P in Num 27:12–14; Deut 32:48–52). This view even underlies some Deuteronomic pronouncements (e.g., Deut 19:1–10; 31:20–23), despite Deuteronomy's otherwise consistent insistence that the Conquest of the Promised Land had begun in earnest in Transjordan (esp. 2:24, 30–31; 3:24, 26f.; 34:1–4). Similarly, the Mosaic legislation of Deuteronomy is phrased as though it is to come into effect in the future, "when you come to the land that Yhwh your god is giving you" (as Deut 17:14; cf. 6:1, 3; 7:1; 11:10–12, 23, 29; 30:18; 31:13; esp. 31:21). Yet the legislation is proclaimed at the brink of the Jordan crossing; the implication is that the Canaan of the patriarchal promises did not include Transjordan. The stratification of this perspective inside Deuteronomy indicates that it is the older view, on which the authors of Deuteronomy's historical recitations imposed a revisionist position (contrast Weinfeld 1983).

This old view of the Transjordanian occupation comes to most lucid expression in Numbers 32. Here, P portrays the decision by Reuben and Gad to dwell across the Jordan as a betrayal of faith—a refusal to take possession of the allotted inheritance—potentially equivalent to the sin of the spies (32:7–15). These tribes must help master Cisjordan before returning to the portions they have selected on their own. The text also has a reflex in Joshua 22. On returning from the Conquest, the Transjordanian tribes erect an altar, purely for symbolic purposes. Again, the idea that Transjordan is not a part of the land of the promise colors the narrative. Transjordan is impure, profane, and its Israelite inhabitants have the option—even the duty—of abandoning it for "the land of Yhwh's possession, where the Tabernacle of Yhwh abides" (22:19).

Much of this material stems from P, and may have no origin earlier than the 6th century B.C.E. The same probably applies to Num 34:1–15, which define "Canaan" as the Cisjordanian entity, though one stretching to Hamath (Hama) in N Syria (cf. Num 35:14). Still, Deuteronomy's pre-conscious ambivalence on the issue, the occasional reference in J, and the invariable description of Moses' achievements as "bringing Israel up from Egypt," but not as enfranchising her in the land, all indicate that P here followed traditional lines of thought: the Mosaic conquests, across the Jordan (and in the far south, at Hormah; Num 21:3) were supererogatory; the terminus of Israel's migration was west of the Jordan only. This was the region whose subjugation Joshua ben-Nun engineered.

Both the Deuteronomic and the more traditional scenarios locate the Cisjordanian conquest in a clearly defined chronological sequence. Moses' death marks the end of Israel's circuitous migration from Egypt. It rings in a new epoch, in which Yhwh will redeem his second pledge to the Israelites in their Egyptian thrall, and give to them the land of the Amorites, Canaanites, and other residents of Cisjordan (Exod 3:8; 6:8). The transfer of authority from Moses to Joshua takes place amid intermittent action and legislation (Num 27:15–23; Deut 3:28; 34:9). It provides the only tangible continuity from the first era to the next.

2. The Cisjordanian Conquest. a. The First Movement: Emblematic Victories. (1) The Crossing. The book of Joshua opens with two cycles of tradition concerning the entry into Canaan, deftly interwoven and partially rephrased by the ("Deuteronomistic") historian. The first focuses on the miraculous and ceremonious fording of the Jordan at Gilgal (Joshua 1:3–5), a site whose location is uncertain, but which lay most probably in the vicinity of the Adam[ah] (Damiya) crossing (B. Mazar 1985). As the narrative unfolds, Israel waits encamped by the Jordan near Shittim from the 8th until the 10th day of Nisan. On the 10th day, the Levites bear the ark into the riverbed: the current upstream comes to a halt, and the people pass dryshod. They pitch camp at Gilgal, where Joshua circumcizes them—responding, apparently, to the P (Genesis 17) and possibly E traditions that circumcision was introduced earlier (Gen 34:13–24; Exod 4:25f.), the narrator explains that the practice was in hiatus during the wanderings (Josh 5:4–7). So fortified, in accordance with the specifications of Exod 12:43–48 (P), Israel celebrates her first Passover in the land (5:9–12). It is at this point that Joshua encounters the "commander of Yhwh's army", at Jericho (5:13–15), though this tradition may conceivably belong to the Jericho cycle (Josh 2:6).

This impressive foundation legend for the shrine at Gilgal figures the Conquest in a miraculous river-crossing. The marvel deflates "all the kings of the Amorites", reducing them to that state of fatalism whose tactical reflex is rout (5:1). An identical reconstruction of events surfaces in the Song of the Sea (Exodus 15), one of the earliest extant Hebrew lyrics: awe at Yhwh's might struck the peoples and leaders of Trans- and Cisjordan dumb, until Yhwh's people had passed over Jordan, into the land of the inheritance (vv 13–16). In Joshua 5 (vv 13–15), as in Exodus 15 (v 17), there follows the consecration of Yhwh's sanctuary. This occasion, and the concomitant appearance of the captain of Yhwh's hosts, foreordains, for the second time, the Amorites' destruction.

The tradition that transformed the Jordan crossing into Israel's proleptic triumph probably negotiated the gap between the time when Exodus 15 was written and that of Joshua 1;3–5's composition in the form of an annual ritual. Such a ritual progress from Shittim to Gilgal is alluded to in Micah 6:5; the prophet associates it with commemoration of the Exodus, and with the story of Balaam (Numbers 22–24). Joshua 24 juxtaposes the same events with a sudden and miraculous Conquest (in the Pentateuch, a number of P texts separate Balaam from the fording) in a (Deuteronomistic) framework that presents

Moses' work in Transjordan as the start of, not the prelude to, the settlement (vv 8–12): it represents this historical rehearsal as a history of salvation, the reason for Israel at Shechem (not Shiloh) to make fast its commitment to Yhwh. Interestingly, Hos 6:7–9, in the context of 6:1–10, suggests that both Mic 6:5 and Joshua 24 reflect a single ritual: Hosea refers to a ritual movement from Adam in Transjordan (through Gilgal? Hos 9:10, 12, 15; 12:12; B. Mazar 1985) to a climax at Shechem (cf. Deut 11:29–32; 27:1–13; Josh 8:30–35). This unopposed processional march furnishes the basis for later prophetic transformations of the motif (esp. Isa 11:14–16; see Cross *CMHE,* 99–111).

It is no coincidence that the narratives of Abraham's (Gen 12:5–7) and Jacob's (Genesis 32–34) arrival in Canaan both recapitulate the pattern—the pattern of Israel's entry after the Exodus. The processional route is triply enshrined in the nation's ancestral lore. All these indications concur on the point that the materials reformulated in Joshua 1:3–5 constitute one of Israel's oldest, most carefully preserved traditions concerning the Conquest. They are the fruit of a sanctuary's foundation legend and a ritual hallowing it. In fact, liturgical elements associated with the ritual may survive in Exodus 15, Deuteronomy 33, Psalm 114, and, in embedded form, in Psalm 68 and Hab 3:3–6 (Cross *CMHE,* 99–105). An association with royal ritual seems also to have taken hold, sometime early in the era of the monarchy. 1 Sam 11:12–14; 2 Sam 19:16, 32, 40–44; and, probably 2 Sam 2:8–9, 12 all situate confirmations of the king's accession at Gilgal after a crossing from Transjordan.

(2) Jericho and Ai. The second narrative cycle in Joshua chronicles the overthrow of Jericho and Ai (chaps. 2; 6–8). It begins with a reconnaissance of the former town, an act that is set (in the present edition) during the three days Israel encamped by the river in Transjordan (2:22f.): Israel's spies in Jericho find themselves in the home of Rahab, a prostitute, who barters their abetment for immunity from the Holy War. Rahab recounts how Israel's experience at the Reed Sea and victories over Sihon and Og in Transjordan had demoralized "all the inhabitants of the land" (2:9–11). This information the spies carry back to Joshua; it leads, as the opening cycles are edited, to the fording of the river (2:24).

The narrator resumes this strand after Joshua's encounter with Yhwh's divine commander (5:13–15). Jericho is invested. The ark and the army circle the city over the course of a full week; on the seventh day, down fall the walls. Joshua annihilates the population, Rahab and her family excepted, and the livestock. Captured metal is dedicated to Yhwh, in accordance with the precepts of the Holy War (ch. 6).

Joshua 24 portrays this event as the decisive confrontation, as an emblematic victory over all those groups with which later generations understood pre-Israelite Canaan to have been peopled (24:11f; correspondingly, the Clementine liturgy breaks off at just this point). Conceivably, the reference in Josh 24:12 to "the two kings of the Amorites", an expression elsewhere applied to Sihon and Og (Deut 3:8; 4:47; 31:4; Josh 2:10; 9:10), twins the account with that of the siege of Ai. This is uncertain, however. The LXX of Josh 24:12 refers to twelve Amorite kings instead of two. And v 12 may in fact allude to a rout of the Amorites derivative from and not identical with the battle at Jericho (v 11). But even if Joshua 24 did once preserve a tradition focused on Jericho alone, the narrative in chaps. 6–8 will now allow no dismemberment: the spectacular dismantling of Jericho leads without discontinuity to Ai's storming by subterfuge.

The direct link between events at Ai and Jericho is Achan ben-Karmi of the tribe of Judah (Josh 7:18). His peculation from the consecrated booty of Jericho forestalls the first attempt on Ai. Only his stoning permits the successful renewal of the assault (7:1–8:29). Hos 2:16f. (in the Valley of Achor, as Josh 7:25f; cf. 1 Chr 2:7; and note Hosea's play on Karmi) plainly associate the Achan incident with the first check encountered in Israel's advance from the wilderness into Canaan. This part of the Conquest cycle, like that surrounding Gilgal, had already been constructed, thus, in the oral or written sources that antedated the Deuteronomist's work.

At this juncture, the historian lowers the curtain on the first movement of the Conquest. He does so by taking the Israelites to Mt. Ebal, in fulfilment of the command of Deut 11:29f; 27:1–14 that they write the law mediated by Moses on stones there, and recite the blessing and curse associated with that law. Deut 27:2, 4 assign this duty to "the day when you cross the Jordan." One might suspect that the delays at Jericho and Ai were not envisioned by the authors of the Deuteronomic texts. But "the day when" in Hebrew can mean, "the time when." Too, the narrative as it stands brings Israel past Jericho and directly into the central hills, in a path that intersects the road from Ai or Bethel to Shechem: from Jericho, no other debouch would be more swift. It is to Shechem, in any event, that the historian draws his subjects for the climactic confirmation of their loyalty to Yhwh, in preparation for the practical part of their penetration of the land. That is, significantly, the last point in Joshua at which the ark, a regular element in the narrative from chap. 1 on, plays a role.

b. The Second Movement: The Big Battalions. A different sort of history begins in chap. 9. Instead of being dispirited, or magically expelled by hornets, the Amorites fashion formidable coalitions and engage Israel in pitched battles. 9:1, originally placed before 8:30–35 (with G), introduces this shift as a consequence of the foregoing action. It describes an assembly of "all the kings that were across the Jordan" (cf. 5:1), "in the highlands and in the lowlands and in all the shore of the Great Sea opposite the Lebanon—the Hittite, Amorite, Canaanite, Perizzite, Hivite, and Jebusite—. . . to war with Joshua and with Israel, with one accord" (for the resemblance to EA 366, see C.5.c below). Through the succeeding three chapters, the details of this extraordinary engagement, differing somewhat from the expectations this exordium evokes, unfurl compellingly.

The first palpable step in the plot takes place at Gilgal. Edified by the fate of Jericho and Ai, the Hivites of Gibeon and three other towns, located N and NW of Jerusalem, persuade Israel that they dwell in a "distant" land. By this ruse, they lure Israel into a treaty guaranteeing their lives. Only later, when they have already been rendered powerless to act by their leaders' sworn oath, do the Israelites learn where Gibeon really lies (chap. 9).

On the heels of Jericho's and Ai's devastation, the alliance with the Gibeonite tetrapolis creates a cordon in the central hills separating Jerusalem from the north. This strategic situation impels the king of Jerusalem into action. He forms an alliance with the other Amorite city-states of the southern hills and Shephelah (with Hebron, Jarmuth, Lachish, and Eglon), whose joint field force then beleaguers Gibeon. Joshua relieves the town after a night march from Gilgal and scores a resounding rout down the Aijalon Pass. During a two-day period when "the sun was still, and the moon stayed" for illumination, he pursues his antagonists, already enfiladed by hailstones, past Azekah to Makkedah (10:1–14). There, Joshua hangs his royal adversaries (10:16–27; v 15 is to be omitted, with G).

The next segment portrays Joshua as reducing systematically six strongholds in the Shephelah and hills—Makkedah, Libnah, Lachish (where he eradicates as well a field force led by the king of Gezer), Eglon, Hebron, and Debir—all according to the precepts of the Holy War (10:28–39). The historian summarizes: Joshua had taken the mountain, the S, the Shephelah and the "declivities" (*ʾăšēdôt*), establishing an ascendancy from Kadesh-barnea to Gaza in the S to Gibeon in the N. The rather extreme claim that Joshua had eliminated all life within these borders (except on the plain) also appears (10:40–42). The inheritance of Judah had been gutted.

The logical sequel to the southern clash is, of course, a northern one. The king of Hazor organizes a coalition similar to that in the S, but embracing his royal colleagues from the Hermon to the Jordan Valley, from the coast to the Chinnereth. They risk battle at "the waters of Merom," where Joshua annihilates them in a rout stretching to Sidon. Joshua again sets about reducing fortresses, but the only one named or burned is Hazor. Of the rest, Joshua destroys the population, but spares the architecture. The summary discloses that Joshua captured all the territory from the Negeb to the Hermon (the coasts and Jezreel Valley are not explicitly named), ridding the country of all its former inhabitants (Anakim) except in the Philistine littoral. "And the land was tranquil from war" (11:1–23).

This observation marks the juncture of the Conquest with the implementation of Yhwh's plans for the Israelite settlement. The historian provides two reviews, one of the areas conquered (chap. 12), the other of those unsubdued (Philistia, the southern Lebanon, the coast, and the region from the Hermon to Lebo Hamath: 13:1–6). Joshua assigns the tribes' territories (13–19), designates cities of refuge (20; responding to Num 35:9–34; cf. Deut 4:41–43; 19:1–13; Exod 21:12f.) and Levitical cities (21; responding to Num 35:1–8), and dismisses the Transjordanian contingent (22; following Num 32). Thus, the Conquest effectively closes with the confrontation at Merom. At the end of the book of Joshua, two final orations (chaps. 23; 24) punctuate it definitively.

3. After Joshua: the Nations Remaining. Joshua's military activity winds down over the course of "many years" with the consolidation of his gains at Merom (11:18). Israel's borders are extended to Lebo Hamath and the Euphrates much later: it is under David (2 Samuel 8) that Israel first fulfills its ultimate territorial destiny. More germane to earlier times are local traditions, which emerge in something of a tangle in Joshua and Judges.

One encounters the first of these traditions in the tribal allotments in Joshua. Manasseh cannot displace the inhabitants of the Jezreel fortresses; Ephraim does not take Gezer. More confusing, Josh 15:13–19 impute the conquest and settlement of Hebron and Debir to Caleb and Othniel, respectively; yet, the towns are already reduced in Josh 10:36–39 (Joshua deeds Hebron to Caleb five years after crossing the Jordan in 14:6–15). Judges 1 seems to place Caleb's conquest after Joshua's death (1:1, 10–15, 20). This text may in fact be drawn from Josh 15:13–19. In it, Hebron is taken by Judah, but Debir by Othniel; Debir is handled similarly in Josh 15:15–17. Yet even Hebron, it is implied in 14:11f., may have succumbed specifically to Caleb's arms (see further C.4).

The border lists assert that Judah (15:63), Ephraim (16:10), and Manasseh (17:11–13) failed to "supplant" (*hôrēš*) some inhabitants of their territories (cf. also 13:13). A comparable note in 19:47 about Dan's taking Laish glosses over the action's roots in Dan's failure to supplant the population of its allotment (Judg 1:35; 18:1, 27). But the primary repository of such recollections is Judges 1, an old text adapted for its present use by the Deuteronomistic Historian (Halpern 1983: 179–182; Soggin *Judges* OTL, 26–27). This Cisjordanian compendium is peculiar in two respects: first it claims that Israel's task after Joshua's demise was not the extension of the collective borders, as Joshua 10–13 might suggest, but making exclusive their grasp on the territories already theoretically in their possession; and, secondly, the chapter presumes that in this stage of the Conquest, the tribes fought singly for mastery within their allotments.

Judges 1 reports victories only for Judah (1:2–16, 20), Simeon (1:17), and Joseph (1:22–26), precisely the tribes concerning whom the Joshua border lists present notices of failure. For Ephraim and Manasseh (Joseph), Judges 1 preserves these notices (1:27 = Josh 17:11–13, Manasseh; 1:29 = Josh 16:10, Ephraim). Judah's failure notice, concerning Jerusalem, is transferred to Benjamin in Judges 1 (Josh 15:63; Judg 1:21). A Judahite sack of Jerusalem is supplied (Judg 1:8). The only mitigation of Judah's success is the remark in 1:19 that the Judahites were unable, because of the "iron chariotry" there (see Sawyer 1983: 130–32), to supplant the inhabitants of the coastal lowlands.

Some scholars discover inconsistencies in Judges 1. These are chimerical: one produces them only by equating capture with "supplanting," between which the chapter distinguishes carefully. Joshua had taken the country; Israel must settle it. Judah had burnt Jerusalem (1:8); its inhabitants were not supplanted (1:21). Judah conquered (*lkd*) Gaza, Ashkelon, and Ekron (1:18; read MT), but could not supplant (*yrš*) the denizens of the lowlands (1:19, read with G); in this instance, only the distinction between conquest and supplanting dissolves an outright contradiction between two adjoining verses.

The logic of the chapter, like that of Joshua 13–19, is that military domination does not translate mechanically into supplanting Amorites. Victory at war, however sweet, is merely a preface to the work of rooting out the existing population and colonizing the land. As in Joshua, in short, de- and repopulating the country are two separate steps. This distinction permits the historian to explain how Israel came into political control of parts of Canaan (or, under David, of all of it) without discharging Yhwh's injunction to blot out the memory of the indigenous peoples (Deut 20:16–18; Num 33:52–56; Deut 7:24–26; 12:2f).

Between Judges 1 and Joshua there may seem to be a certain tension, which in some respects cannot be denied. Thus, the summary in Josh 10:40–42 maximizes the achievements recorded earlier in the same chapter, where no activity outside the hills region is described. It interprets the detailed campaign reports to imply Joshua's thorough execution of Yhwh's plans. Nevertheless, it differentiates between highlands and lowlands, just as the segment on Judah in Judges 1 is so careful to do. Joshua smote both (v 42), but destroyed all life only inland (vv 40f.). The summary reflects a desire to inflate Joshua's achievements without violating the limits of historical possibility as the historian perceived it. It is the urge, not the formulation, that creates a sense of tension or contradiction.

More problematic is the relationship between Judges 1 and Joshua 11. Josh 11:16–20 mentions Joshua's "taking" the land from the Negev to Baal Gad, as though without exception. Judges 1 lists the exceptions. But if the historian in Judges 1 relates Josh 11:16–20 (whether or not he wrote them) only to the cities whose forces Joshua met at the battle at Merom (11:1–9), there is no necessary conflict. Alternatively, the historian in Joshua may have distinguished between eradication and Israelite colonization. This would explain the exaggeration of 10:40–42 as well, though it would not altogether relieve the tension occasioned by Joshua 12 (below).

Josh 11:21f. confirms that the text demands such a nuanced reading. These verses must be consistent with Josh 10:40ff. That they rehearse 10:40–43 suggests that they take 11:16–20 not to describe Joshua's ousting the populations of the southern hills. Indeed, this represents a sharp reading: 11:16–20 speak of "taking" territory, of capturing the cities of specific kings (those of vv 1–15), but not of "supplanting" the indigenous populations either in whole or in part. It does not, in the reading of 11:21f. or of Judges 1, present the Conquest as fully accomplished.

The final segment of the Joshua narrative, the list of kings in Joshua 12, corresponds to Josh 11:10–15 in the sense that it enumerates which towns Israel depopulated. The list includes Taanach, Megiddo, and Dor, whose populations were not supplanted, according to Judges 1. It is to be remembered that Judges 1 is placed deliberately after Joshua's death. The chapter presumes that Joshua's campaigns established a generalized control of the countryside; it remained for the several tribes to carry through the settlement thereafter, each in its own territory. This is the meaning of the sequence in Joshua as a whole: one proceeds from Israel's irruption from Transjordan to the overcoming of indigenous resistance (chaps. 10–12) to the distribution of tribal territories (chaps. 13–22). That individual areas were left unmastered or unsettled may be a tradition alien to some of the sources subsumed in the account. In the presentation as a whole, however, it is a consistent element, one with which the account of the tribal allotments in fact begins (Josh 13:1–6). In all, the qualification of Israel's success at colonizing Canaan may represent the historian's overlay on traditions (like that of the Amorite giants) that were more schematic, and more self-aggrandizing.

At issue in Judges 1 are the nations remaining. Unlike Joshua 13, Judges 1 focuses on interstitial regions, areas within the confines of Israelite control. It denies Israelite dominance in the Jezreel and the Aijalon Pass as well as on the coast, and points to Canaanite enclaves in areas under Israel's heel. Further, where those earlier texts, in which Yhwh's "hornet" is the medium of expulsion, speak of the "remaining peoples" as Yhwh's deliberate provision against the countryside's collapse into uncontrolled wilderness (Exod 23:29f.; cf. Deut 7:22; Josh 24:18), Judges 1 furnishes grounds for the verdict that Israel had willfully failed to execute the command to expunge the former population (2:1–5).

Consistent with this view, where Josh 15:63; 17:11–13, 18 spotlight the invaders' *inability* to expel their foes ("they *could* not supplant"), Judges 1 reserves this excuse for Judah (v 19, the formulation taken from Josh 17:18). Otherwise, it reports only that individual tribes "*did* not supplant" certain antagonists. And what appears as a Danite success in Josh 19:47, Judges 1 translates into a consolation prize, unworthy of mention, for the tribe's failure (vv 34f.). Other than Judah, thus, Israel has turned its back on Yhwh's command: Yhwh ceases, in the remarkable theology of the chapter, to subjugate Israel's (peripheral) foes for them, because Israel had failed, after subjugating them, to eradicate them (2:1–5).

The materials after Judges 1 develop this view. Judg 2:6–10 present an epanaleptic account of Joshua's death (after Josh 24:28–31). This synchronizes the events reported in 2:11ff. with those of Judges 1 (and especially 2:2–4), developing in parallel with Judges 1 an account of Israel's infidelity during what amounts to an interregnum. Thus, there remain (Judges 1) Canaanites whose presence the Israelites suffered after Joshua's death. After the demise of Joshua's generation, who "knew" Yhwh and his acts, Israelites unfamiliar with the wondrous Exodus and entry begin to worship the gods of the peoples around them—the influence of and Israel's fraternization with the Canaanite remnant here asserts itself, as predicted in Josh 23:13; Num 33:55.

In retaliation for Israel's infidelity, Yhwh repeatedly subjects them to the power of aliens. But when they repent, he relents, raising up "judges" (*šôpĕṭîm*) to save them. Yet, at the "judge's" death, the Israelites revert to cultivating gods of "the peoples who were around them." Yhwh therefore resolves against "supplanting" those nations Joshua has left (2:11–21).

By this expedient, Yhwh exploits the "nations remaining" to "test" Israel's fidelity—to wage war on Israel when it is necessary to reprove Israel for its waywardness, to instruct those who "did not know the wars of Canaan" (with G), who could not draw on first-hand experience of Yhwh's intervention for Israel, in wars over Canaan of their own (2:22f.; 3:1f,4). The nations in question are the peripheral powers enumerated among the unconquered in Josh 13:2–6 (cf. Judg 3:3). This presentation, then, links an interpretation of the book of Judges—in which the cycle of apostasy, oppression, and salvation plays itself out (Judg 3:7–11; 3:12–15, 30; 4:1–3, 23f. + 5:31c; 6:1–6, 11–17 + 8:28; 10:6–18 + 11:1–11, 33)—to the major historiographic framework in Joshua, specifically that recounting Joshua's complete subjugation of the interior (as chap. 23; contrast Weinfeld 1967; Kaufmann 1966: 632–44).

Both Judg 1:1–2:5 and Judg 2:6–3:6 ascribe Israel's failure to capture and depopulate all the appointed lands to infidelity to Yhwh after Joshua's death. How Judg 1:1–2:5 defines this territory is uncertain (Cisjordan to the Hermon?). Judg 2:6–3:6 defines Canaan after the manner of Joshua 12–13; 23, as embracing all of Syria up to Lebo Hamath (roughly congruent with the dimensions of Egypt's Ramesside empire, and of David's). Both concede that Joshua's death left the Conquest incomplete, effectively confined to the central highlands. Even when David repaired this defect, an indigenous population remained (Judg 1:21, 28, 30, 33), the process of their extirpation having been irrevocably suspended (2:1–5; 2:20–3:6; 1 Sam 7:14). It is to their presence that Joshua 23–Judges 3 traces Israel's failure to fulfill her divinely appointed destiny.

B. Scholarly Treatments of the Conquest

1. The Beginnings of Modern Criticism. Even in the 19th century, by which time source-criticism and the inroads of Enlightenment historical method had compelled most scholars to abandon the Pentateuch as a historical record, the book of Joshua continued to command a healthy respect. As late as 1909 a scholar as eminent as Paul Haupt was speculating in print as to the seismic character of the events at Jericho (Haupt 1909: 361f.). Moreover, historians of Israel uniformly reconstructed the Conquest as a concerted Israelite entry from Transjordan, climaxing a migration aimed from the first at the overthrow and colonization of the country. Often, they thought of this migration as ending a period of nomadic wanderings, on the model of Numbers 13ff.

Judges 1, taken, it must be said, out of context, furnished the first focus of skepticism about this view. E. Meyer ushered in the new era by arguing (1881) that this chapter recorded a series of triumphs by individual tribes rather than a united invasion, as in Joshua 10–12. The former type of Conquest he assigned to the J source of the Pentateuch, the latter to the Elohist (E). Meyer stressed that the two traditions were not to be harmonized by being placed sequentially (as in the present recension), that they represented contradictory historical variants touching different tribal groups.

Meyer's *tour de force* bore the encumbrance of all the 19th-century biases about the patriarchal narratives. Especially from the time of Ewald's *Geschichte des Volkes Israel* I (1843), students of Genesis looked to these narratives as troves of information concerning mass population movements and other early, national history. Thus, the patriarchal life-style reflected Israelite nomadism in the pre-Conquest period. Genesis 34, relating Dinah's ravishment and the curse of Simeon and Levi, memorialized an early Israelite settlement at Shechem and the expulsion of the tribes (not individuals) accursed. The Rachel tribes could be linked to the stories of Conquest in the central hills; the Leah tribes were southern, tied to a penetration from Kadesh (below). Scholars mined the eponymic lore as though it were a mathematical notation of pre-Occupation history. Assuming that the tribes had existed discretely and in perpetuity, they sought to explain their coalescence outside Canaan. Most assumed it had taken place in Transjordan.

Not unnaturally, this posture among the pundits threw the relative chronology of the Exodus and Conquest out of whack. Which tribes belonged to what stages of each? Many scholars chose to harmonize, as they thought, the cacophony of Judges 1 and Joshua. Wellhausen (1894) and Guthe (1900) resolved it into two invasions from the east in the post-Mosaic era. Kittel (1888) and Procksch (1906) read the relative sequence of the patriarchs and Exodus to imply one invasion was pre-Mosaic. Still others (Paton 1900, Steuernagel 1901, Gressmann 1913) posited an early onslaught from the S by the Leah tribes: they unearthed traces of it, now buried beneath the literary structure of a unified incursion from Transjordan, in Israel's reconnaissance from Kadesh (Numbers 13–14; tellingly, J takes the spies only as far as Hebron), and in Num 20:14–21 (confrontation with Edom); 21:1–3 (the defeat of Arad). They also appealed to the fact that in Judges 1, Judah and Simeon proceed first of all the tribes. These scholars associated the later intrusion of the Rachel tribes with a movement of the Exodus-community from Transjordan after Moses' death (Joshua 9–11; Judg 1:21–27). The Leah invasion had been piecemeal (associated with Judges 1 and J); the Rachel invasion (Joshua, E) was unified.

The appearance of the *ḫa-bi-ru* (Eg *ʿapirū*) in the archive from the 14th-century court of Akhenaten at El Amarna undergirded these speculations. The Habiru were identified with the Hebrews (*ʿibrîm),* and the latter, even more speculatively, with the Israelites. The Amarna letters from Egyptian vassals in Canaan were taken to reflect the first stage of Israelite occupation (some in fact exploited them to date the Conquest as a whole to the 15th or 14th century, citing also the problematic 1 Kgs 6:1). A number of scholars identified the Habiru of Amarna with the Leah tribes. A 13th-century allusion to a "chief of Asher" being treed by a bear somewhere in the neighborhood of Megiddo ratified the hypothesis: Israel, or elements of it, had been in the land from the 14th century on. These were the Hebrews who had destroyed Jericho, the fall of which before Late Bronze IIB (ca. 1300–1200 B.C.E.) had embarrassed the dominant school of thought, which placed the Exodus in the 13th century. The Exodus, by contrast, involved only Rachel.

These analyses all coordinated three dichotomies: between Judah (the south) and Israel (the north), between Leah and Rachel, and between Judges 1 and Joshua. None of these was indissoluble, and that between Judges 1 and Joshua was forced. The theories further attached great weight to the peregrinations of the patriarchs, and to traditions of Israel's wilderness wanderings, even though these were now viewed as a literary device to connect the southern to the northern thrusts. They relied, ironically, on the details of these sources, including their insinuations of the tribes' discrete existence, all the while they rejected the sources' overall historiographic framework; no real inquiry into the interrelationship between the details and the framework was essayed. To anchor all this surmise, though, the traditions of "nomadism" had to mirror authentic conditions in the era before Israel's invasions: how else could diverse groups of Israelites keep sweeping in off the desert? Testimony as to these nomadic origins thus emerged as a nodal point for inquiry. At the same time, these reconstructions affirmed in essence the value of the reports in Joshua 1–11.

2. The Sociological View. This consensus was first restructured by Albrecht Alt in 1925. Alt observed that the sources in Joshua portrayed the events from a considerable chronological remove, and that they were insufficiently extensive to permit on this basis alone a detailed reconstruction. He saw that the translation of patriarchal legend from eponymic folklore into national history was arbitrary, and the use of its results solipsistic. He also understood that the reconstruction of pre-Conquest Israel as a medley of marginal nomads had implications for the history of the settlement incompatible with the conclusions at which his colleagues had arrived. Heavily under the influence of Max Weber, he therefore reframed the problem as one of historical geography and political structures: instead of concentrating on the airy problem of the intentions of a people, Israel, immune from historical scrutiny in a sort of wilderness limbo—instead of asking what "tribes" were where in the twilight of Israel's prehistory—Alt asked what it was that the Conquest had meant on the ground.

His answer: in the coastlands and Jezreel, where in the LB Age Egypt's empire had flourished, the old city-states continued to dictate the shape of Canaan's political divisions. Even those city-states vanquished by the Philistines and other Sea Peoples retained their traditional territories; the territories continued to be named after the towns. Conversely, the interior initially occupied by the Israelites lay outside the lowlands system—in the Amarna texts, Shechem, and Jerusalem were the only city-states of the central and southern hills. These Israelite zones, defined by Judges 1 and roughly coincidental with the shape of Saul's kingdom (2 Sam 2:9), took the name not of a town, but of a nation. Their political culture was national, ethnic rather than local and territorial. Indeed, Israel achieved *geographical* continuum only when David took the Jezreel Valley: this was the first era in which the lowland city-state was broken down and subordinated to a national structure, that of a territorial state.

Alt concluded that Israelites had first entered and occupied those hinterlands least fitted to withstand their penetration. Their movement into Canaan resembled that of semi-nomads fixed on a course of sedentarization, a model contoured to the paradigm of Israel's wandering in the wilderness. Yet Alt's scenario incorporated the healthy qualification, based on the model of Bedouin sedentarization, that such a people could have entered the land only by infiltration: they could have mastered territory only outside close political and military control, which is to say, in regions not systematically tesselated with city-states; even here, they must at first have cooperated with the city-state system. The destruction of the city-states was a second stage in the process. Even the coalescence of Israelite ethnicity into articulated peoplehood (which Alt identified with statehood) took place in the land itself.

Alt's emphasis on bedouin infiltration capped the trend focusing on Israelite nomadism as a formative historical and cultural element. Fresh was the element of sociological theory applied almost formally in picturing the nature of sedentarization and the complex interdependence between the pastoral and urban populations, and in emphasizing the development of the state as a measure of meaningful transition in political history. Alt further diverted scholarly attention from Joshua's exploits in storied battles to Israel's and David's achievements across historical Canaan. The issue was not what Joshua had done so much as what measurable benefits had accrued from his and from any other hypothetical early efforts. Correspondingly, the question of the character and composition of the original incursion into Canaan paled into virtual invisibility beside the issue of what territories Israel in her early years secured: the consciousness of the incoming Israelites ceased to be material, in line with Alt's conviction that they grew together as a political unit only on Canaanite soil. The notion of "conquering" Canaan evolved only slowly out of the gradual consolidation of Israel's ethnopolitical condition there.

Alt's position entailed evaluating Israel's conquest literature as a telescoped compendium of subsequent honors, devoid of direct or literal value. He himself stressed its etiological character, and drew strength from the fact that excavations at Ai showed the site to have been vacant during the LB Age (ca. 1570–1200 B.C.E.), when the Israelites should have been destroying it. Subsequent exploration at Jericho disclosed, too, that the walls did not "come a-tumblin' down" because there were no walls to have tumbled in LB II (though Garstang's "city wall" section has never been relocated and reinterpreted). Stressing that Judges 1 and the record of Hazor's undoing in Judges 4–5 contradicted Joshua's personal association with the struggle against the northern city-states, Alt and his followers dissociated Joshua from any action other than that in the Aijalon Pass (Josh 10:1–15).

The more conservative scholarly positions that antedated Alt did not altogether wither under Alt's attack. In the 1930's, William Foxwell Albright and his disciples emerged as the staunchest advocates of the older constructions, with Israel howling in off the desert and sweeping Canaan before it (Albright *ARI*). The wrinkle of the double-entry (once from the south) was retained from the 19th century. And the concession was made, against the most extreme claims of the text, that the Conquest confined itself to the hills, and even there was only partially successful. Alt's crucial distinction, thus, between the lowlands in the hands of the Canaanites and the hills controlled by Israel, prevailed, though no clear correlation of this point to the distinction between conquest and supplanting in Joshua and Judges was essayed. But Albright pointed to destructions at LB II Lachish and Tell Beit Mirsim, and, later, at LB II Hazor as evidence of a violent entry. He proposed, somewhat more feebly, that the story of Ai's destruction had been displaced from Bethel. Finally, Albright's partisans observed that Judges 1's tribe-by-tribe reportage could not be used to buttress Alt's scenario, as the latter claimed in 1939. Judges 1 was a list, not a narrative, and therefore necessarily presented a fragmented view: further, "tribe-by-tribe" was not a normal process of sedentarization, which takes place at the individual or expanded family (*hamula*) level (Wright 1946).

This whole vantage-point must be seen today as something of a rearguard action. Proponents of Alt's *"Landnahme"*—"occupation," a term that embraces the process through to David's time—retorted that destructions did not imply Israelite action: Egyptians and earthquake, fire and Philistines all had to be reckoned as possible causes. Even where Israelite settlement succeeded the destruction (Bethel, Hazor, and in the Albrightian brief, Lachish, Tell Beit Mirsim), one had evidence only of occupation, not of the identity of the attacker.

Further, they contended, biblical historiography concerning the Conquest took its shape from various concerns—etiological, ideological, political—not all historical, that worked in cumulative synergy from the era of the events to that, much later, of the writing. One could not match textual claims to archaeological results from LB sites without analyzing the claims diachronically: the literature, like the sites, needed to be approached as a stratigraphic cipher. Thus, Jericho (Bienkowski 1986) and Ai (Callaway 1968) were unpopulated in the Late Bronze, so that those elements of the Conquest account were incorrect. At Gibeon, the only signs of a "great" LB city were a few rather inconsequential tombs—so the tradition of alliance had to be called into question or dated later. Debir, probably to be identified with Khirbet Rabud, not with Tell Beit Mirsim, apparently experienced no interruption in occupation (Kochavi 1974). And there are no signs, to date, of LB IIB settlements either at Hebron or at Tell Yarmut. Indeed, epigraphic data from Lachish places the end of the Canaanite city there around 1150 (Ussishkin 1985), some half century after the Israelites are known—from the Merneptah stele—to have established themselves in Canaan. Archaeology does as much to disprove the Joshua narratives as to support them: those who use it to buttress a theory of a unified Conquest must use it, and the texts, very selectively.

As to the issue whether the Israelites entered united, bent on war, or in smaller groups, Alt's disciples observed that one had only to note how exiguous their early impact had been on the city-states. Indeed, the logistics and coordination of the venture imagined by Albright defied rational reconstruction (as Weippert 1979: 31–32); and, why the supposedly centralized Israelites dispersed after vast victories into the undesirable hinterlands and the plight of powerlessness seemed puzzling.

3. The Internal Conquest. These strictures had great force, and for 40 years the "infiltration" hypothesis furnished the dominant paradigm for reconstructing the Occupation. "Conquest" advocates more or less accommodated to it by debating, as they had since the 19th century, which tribes came to Canaan when. But upon this asymptotic movement, a new model supervened. In 1962, G. E. Mendenhall turned the flank of Alt's position by calling its strongest, yet least defended bulwark into issue.

Mendenhall denied that the Israelites had been desert nomads at all, or underwent any collective transformation from wanderers in the steppe to farmers in the Canaanite interior; he found Alt's supporters at a disadvantage, for the biblical text affords evidence of migration, even of pastoral pursuits inside Canaan, but none of nomadism. Moreover, the model of nomadism with which Alt's supporters most often worked was not that of transhumant communities or transhumant pastoral specialists inside agricultural communities, but one of the groups of wanderers with no special territorial affiliation. It agreed with no known ANE reality, but leaned heavily on the model of Arabian camel-nomads, only superficially understood. This defect, of course, was one inherited from the bedouin ideal of the 19th and 20th centuries (Budde 1895; Flight 1923), an ideal concretized in the popular imagination by the exploits of Colonel Lawrence.

Mendenhall proposed instead that Israel conquered Canaan through a "peasants' revolt." Stressing the importance of the Habiru as an element in Amarna Canaan, Mendenhall defined the term to denote those disenfranchised from a role in the city-state system. He regarded this as a phenomenon more widespread than the case of Israel alone, just as the "gentilic" (his social class) "Hebrew" comprised a group of people of which Israel was only one part. In the Amarna era, he claimed, such alienation was progressing apace: the peasants of the villages yearned for relief from the oppressive cities; they made common cause with the Habiru to this end. Ultimately, he suggested, these peasants must have withdrawn from the city-state structures, drifting off to a refuge in the highlands. Galvanized by a radical new religion, Yahwism, carried across Jordan by a few survivors of the Exodus, these "Hebrews" carved out for themselves a community, ecumenical (Gottwald 1979 adds "egalitarian"; cf. Mendenhall 1983) in character—as reflected in Israelite covenant law—and radically opposed to the feudal despotisms of Canaan. The list of kings killed in Josh 12:9–24 testified powerfully to the zeal with which the Habiru prosecuted their mission to liberate all the prisoners of pagan autocracy.

Mendenhall's "ideal model" stood off against earlier efforts in two respects. Against the Conquest model, it posited no sizable invasion from Transjordan. Against the Occupation model, it restored the element of an early, collective Conquest, repudiating the unteleological notion of nomadism Alt's followers had fostered. It represented a sort of Internal Conquest hypothesis (see further esp. Gottwald 1979; Chaney 1983).

Scholars were not wanting (esp. Weippert 1967) who applied their ingenuity to confute the arguments toward the Internal Conquest. The arguments have been various. The most important of the contentions may be reduced to six.

First, Mendenhall's characterization of the situation at Amarna is misleading. It is true, there are cases in which Canaanite townsmen kill their kings. But uniformly, where the evidence permits us to say anything at all, the old king is replaced with a new one. There is, in short, no evidence of a reaction against the institution of monarchy itself. Indeed, most of the evidence on which Mendenhall, and his defenders, Gottwald and Chaney, draw comes from the Byblos correspondence. Here, the Habiru are allegedly present in greatest number, and the party that deposes the king of Byblos, Rib-Addi, is the Habiru party. Yet these supposedly disaffected ruffians immediately set Rib-Addi's brother on the throne—a development no doubt more reassuring than disconcerting to the pillars of the social order. Similarly, the letters furnish no evidence whatever of peasant flight from the city-states. The only population withdrawal at Byblos occurs when siege conditions result in a shortage of grain; and the deserters take refuge not among a community of disenfranchised fugitives, but at the next city-state, not under siege, down the coast. The disaffection of which Mendenhall speaks is nowhere in evidence (Halpern 1983: 56–88). Unattested in Canaan either before or after the era of Israel's entry, it was, if it ever existed, a cut-flower phenomenon without textual reflex.

If the peasantry does not exhibit the restiveness on which Mendenhall bases his case, the Habiru are positively discouraging. There are a few unequivocal references to real—ethnic or sociological—Habiru in the archive (EA 195; Edzard et al 1970: 1,2; possibly EA 71:20–22, 28–31; 76:17–20; 288:25–33, etc.). And scholars frequently stress the fact that Amarna vassal kings complain loudly that their lands, towns, or people are controlled by or have linked hands with the Habiru (Helck 1968: 473; Chaney 1983: 72–81). But when one asks, what does this mean concretely, the answer is, the lands, towns, or people have fallen into the hands of royal political opponents. Rib-Addi complains loudest and longest about the Habiru: but by "Habiru," he usually means the king of Amurru—another vassal king of the pharaoh—and its allies, i.e., the party that enthroned Rib-Addi's brother. This is the situation in the letters from other vassals as well. Whatever Habiru were, there is absolutely no textual evidence of a large number of them in Amarna Canaan. Almost always, Habiru is a term of opprobrium, denoting rebels against the pharaoh's authority (Halpern 1983: 55–56; Naʾaman 1986: 276–278). One "joins the Habiru" but does not become one (Moran 1988): They are "the brigands," people accused of subversion against Egyptian overlordship; not coincidentally, the same nomenclature is used by the Romans for restive elements (including, retrospectively, Brutus and Cassius).

This understanding of the Amarna evidence finds stark corroboration in the archaeological and historical record. If the Canaanite peasantry in the 14th century was seething with anti-monarchic activism, as Mendenhall supposes, one would expect that large numbers of the disaffected took refuge in the hill country, out of reach of the plains city-states with their Egyptian-supported armies. Likewise, if there was a significant, powerful, and militarily active population of Habiru, locked in an unceasing struggle with the kings of the city-states, they must have settled off the plains. Yet the hill country of Ephraim in LB II was all but devoid of settlements outside the city-states (Finkelstein 1983; *AIS*). The more fertile hills of Manasseh have revealed only exiguous levels of occupation (Zertal 1986b). That is, there is no sign of organized or settled Habiru even in the land of Shechem, notorious for being the stretch of Canaan whose king "gave it to the Habiru" (EA 289: 23–24). The Galilean uplands, too, seem to have been bare (Gal 1990; Amir 1980). The simplest explanation for this situation is that there was no significant Habiru population, and no significant flight from the city-states.

Gottwald (1979: 296–97, 655–58) has attempted to shore up this soft spot in Mendenhall's armor. He suggests that the peasantry shunned the hills because without lime-slaked cisterns and iron tools for terracing, the hills could not be settled. But the uplands were heavily settled in the MB II—the cisterns must have been lined effectively wherever the bedrock was permeable, though the bedrock did not require this in all places (as Callaway 1976: 30). And there is little evidence of iron in the hills in Iron I (Waldbaum 1978; Stager 1985a). Moreover, in LB II-Iron I, Assyrian kings still preferred bronze pickaxes for cutting roads through mountain country (Grayson 1987: 272. 40–46; *ARI* 2: 7.13). This preference actually lasts into the late 8th century (Thureau-Dangin 1912: 3:24): iron implements from this era suggest that quality control remained a serious problem (Pleiner 1979). In light of this difficulty, Chaney has suggested that the kings of LB Canaan deprived their cultivators of all metal (1983: 64–65). This, however, is sheer conjecture; the widespread representation of bronze in LB sites, including even relatively simple burials (note Khalil 1984), speaks compellingly against it. The weight of the evidence is that the peasants of the Amarna-era had the means to domesticate the hills. What they lacked was the motive.

One further consideration should be added. The designation, Habiru, may originally have had an ethnic connotation. This interpretation is difficult to disprove if one identifies, as Mendenhall did, the Habiru with the Hebrews: early biblical texts see the latter as an ethnological designation, embracing in one tradition the Israelites and their Transjordanian, south Arabian and south Syrian neighbors (J in Gen 10:25–30; 16:10–14; 19:30–38; 22:20–24; 25:25). If so, early Israel was not, as Mendenhall supposes, ecumenical (see below), but rather an ethnic entity.

In sum, conditions in Canaan in the LB Age do not resemble Mendenhall's characterization: the peasants are not on the verge of withdrawal; the Habiru are not present in any great number; and, there is no evidence of a population of disaffected anti-royalists. Mendenhall's view of the Amarna era is a conjecture whose accuracy is an aleatory matter, not a case argued on the basis of firm evidence and probability.

Mendenhall's position on early Israel is no more apt. Mendenhall's supporters are quick to point out that there are lines of continuity between Canaanite and Israelite material culture. The "collared-rim" style for ceramic ware so characteristic of Israelite settlements is found also in Canaanite strata, stretching back into the 14th century at Beth-shan, Megiddo, Tell Abu Hawam, and Tell Beit Mirsim. Collared-rim storage jars, which are particularly typical of Israelite pottery repertoires, appear in some number at Megiddo VI, an Iron-Age layer the identity of whose inhabitants is disputed (but see Fritz 1987: 97). However, only one appears in a LB context, at Canaanite Aphek, and this one occurs at the very end of the period, and in a site with Israelite neighbors close nearby (Beck and Kochavi 1983). Further, there is a change in Iron I from pottery "thrown" on a fast wheel to pottery coil-built and hand-made. There is also discontinuity between Israel and Canaan in the relative frequency of collared-rim ware in the pottery finds of Iron I, and especially in housing stock, where the dominant architectural types and the village plans are entirely divorced (below, C.3).

Too, the settlement pattern in Iron I contradicts Mendenhall's model. The manpower of urban LB Canaan was depleted (Gonen 1984). Yet, the hills population burgeons in Iron I, at a rate far exceeding that of natural increase. Nor were the settlers fugitive peasants: they first homesteaded regions suited to an economy based on pastoralism; only later did settlement extend to regions suited to an autarkic or cash-crop economy (Finkelstein 1983: 110–77). So the settlers were not refugees, but migrants, who had converted their assets into livestock, and entered the hills with established herds: this is why 65–80% of the hills villages' area consisted of enclosure space (Finkelstein 1986b: 116–21). They were of recent agrarian background (Callaway 1976: 29; Stager 1985b: 60*), but they certainly had not withdrawn from local city-states, which did not have the spare manpower to sustain such an extensive population movement, and whose rulers would not have tolerated the nomadization of their agrarian population.

This point, too, has confirmation. Merneptah's "Israel stele" contains a portrait of "the people, Israel" (Stager 1985b: 59*–60*). However, this portrait actually stems from the artists of Ramesses II, when it functioned as a depiction of Shasu (Redford 1986: 192–200). Shasu is the Egyptian term for the pastoralists of Transjordan (Weippert 1974: 270–71). In short, the Merneptah stele identifies Israel with pastoral elements from outside Cisjordan. Its record, thus, conforms to that of Israel's own ethnography, for it is with Edom, Moab, Ammon, and Aram, in Transjordan, that Israel claimed the closest affinities—claims that in turn reflect the authentic relations of the Israelite language (see below). All this is what the pattern of settlement leads us to expect, and both contradict the Internal Conquest model.

Mendenhall's cultural arguments are equally unconvincing. The case for Israelite king-killing boils down to the list in Josh 12:9–24—a text that is composite and late, and integrally bound up with the presentation in chaps. 1–11 (above A.3). Even if the text were early, it would constitute evidence of activity not against kings, but against *enemy* kings, a distinction lost on Mendenhall. The distinction is important from all viewpoints: Israel identified the interest of the king with that of the people (Judg 3:15–30; 4; 6–8; Josh 10:1–39). The role of the list in Joshua 12 in the Conquest narratives bears witness only to this prejudice: how does one separate the commemoration of kings killed in Joshua 12 from that of populations extirpated in Joshua 10–11? Further, early Israel was precisely xenophobic, as Judges 5 (esp. v 19) and Exodus 15 (esp. vv 13–17) testify, and as Saulide policy confirms (2 Sam 21:1–14; 4:3). Maintenance of the ethnic distinction between allied Hivites (Joshua 9; 2 Sam 21:1–14), or other local groups within the compass of Israelite territorial ambitions (Judg 1:27–36), and Israelites, reflects a long consciousness and defense of ethnic or national distinction. If early Israel killed kings, it did so not because kings defended the privilege and social stratification of an *ancien regime,* but because the kings were Canaanites.

This is a major blow to Mendenhall's thesis. That Israel was not egalitarian is a state of affairs Mendenhall acknowledges (1983). But his whole theoretical structure comes crashing down if Israel was not ecumenical. Nevertheless, not only is the early poetry characterized by extreme xenophobia, but the Israelites actually practiced mutilation (male circumcision), the function (although not necessarily the origins) of which is to inhibit connubium with neighbors, such as the Philistines, and perhaps non-Hivite (Genesis 34) Amorites (see Goody 1969). Statistical evidence is also accumulating (Wapnish and Hesse fc.; Hellwing and Adjeman 1986: 145–46, 151) for a distinctive Israelite dietary profile, which included the avoidance of pig even in zones bordering on Canaanite and Philistine centers where pig-consumption was regular (Hesse 1986, forty percent of the meat diet in a Philistine site, eight percent in a Canaanite). In the dietary evidence, Israelite xenophobia leaves a firm archaeological reflex.

Here, again, Alt enjoys a firm purchase on the high ground. Israel was first a consanguinary and only secondarily a territorial entity. It afforded no refuge for outgroups. Early Israel may have been, as Mendenhall's adherents claim, egalitarian. Its egalitarianism, however, embraced Canaanite elements roughly under the conditions and in the proportions in which Spartan egalitarianism extended to the Helots. That is a lesson that the reduction of Canaanites to forced labor under Solomon firmly teaches. This xenophobic posture is incommensurable with the view that Israel was ecumenical in origin and disposition. Correspondingly, there exist records of local accommodation to the invaders (Joshua 9; Judges 1), but none of active connivance with them. The implication is not necessarily that no such cases occurred; but the circumstance reflects the hostile attitudes toward such allies that governed the course of Israelite memory. Mendenhall's scenario, again, consists of more imagination than inference.

Had its exponents to labor under none of these considerable disabilities, the Internal Conquest would nevertheless suffer from a fundamental flaw. Unlike either the Conquest or the Occupation hypothesis, it draws no direct support from Israelite sources: Mendenhall (1962) cites such texts as Joshua 12; the Song of Heshbon (suppositiously preserved by defectors to Israel); and links between Reubenites and Gileadites and places in Judah and Ephraim (uninhabited in LB) respectively. All these hints are based on the decontextualization of particular claims. The literature not only contains no recollections of Israelites swarming out of Canaanite villages, but explicitly affirms the opposite. Israel's distinction from Canaan, blemished only by the pact with Gibeon, persisted until the era of the entry had ended. In Mendenhall's case, "the ascent of reason was aided by the wings of imagination." The model can never therefore amount to anything but one among innumerable possible scenarios. Its inherent probability is low.

4. Résumé. Each of the reconstructions reviewed above is coherent within the context of the facts. The Conquest scenario responds both to the claims of Joshua 9–11 and to the archaeological data especially from Hazor and Tell Beit Mirsim. The Internal Conquest model focuses on conditions in pre-Israelite lowlands Canaan. One should note that neither model dispenses with the element of invasion from abroad: The Yahwistic invader is reduced, at best, from an agent of radical change, or, in Alt's case, of gradual change, to a catalyst of reactionism; even in this case it remains the fulcrum of historical development.

The Occupation model, however, is methodologically most mature. By asking first what change Israel's entry effected, it sets out from facts immediate to Israel's early life in Canaan. It involves no necessary recourse to the history of Israel before the Occupation. The Internal

Conquest presupposes that Israel existed latently among disaffected lowland peasants; the Conquest model presumes that Israel arrived on the brink of Canaan ready-formed, and intent on broad conquests (it effectively presupposes the Exodus). The Occupation model's explanatory power consists in its narrow adhesion to palpable fact: early Israel peopled the hills and backwaters of Canaan.

This very strength proved in the end the theory's Achilles' heel. Alt's view presumed that there was outside Canaan's confines a fund of potential settlers, who fitfully drifted in to homestead the empty hills. Left to him was the 19th-century model of the Bedouin as a means to construe the pre-community community; no doubt the texts in Genesis and Numbers that portray Israel and its progenitors as migrants encouraged him to exploit the legacy. Here, Alt, too, left the firm ground of historical geography and political structures on the wings of sociological typology. Although his recourse avoided the historically sterile issue of the connection of Israel's Hebrews to the Habiru, and relegated to abeyance the destruction and repopulation by Israelites of Bethel, Hazor, and Tell Beit Mirsim, its implications for Israelite history in an eking existence on the steppe, strike discordantly on the register of verisimilitude: pastoralism is an activity intimately connected with settled culture, with markets for meat, with material plenty. Pastoralists in Canaan belong not to the untamed wilds of the land, but to the fringes of the most heavily cultivated districts. Even a neo-Altian scenario, like that offered by I. Finkelstein, must acknowledge that the failure of archaeological surveys to locate any significant Israelite presence in the hills prior to 1200 contradicts the thesis that a large population could have been engaged in pastoralism there.

C. The Emergence of Israel in Canaan

The variables whose isolation is an assault on the Conquest demands are daunting in their diversity. One must mate evidence biblical and extra-biblical, textual and archaeological, intrinsic and ideal. One must distinguish pre-Israelite Canaan from that of subsequent eras. One must distinguish pre-Canaanite Israel from Israel in the land. Finally, one must justify in historical terms the attested condition of pre-monarchic Israel, holding parts of Canaan, on the basis of the process of occupation. In all these enterprises, Alt is to be emulated. The unknown should be approached through the medium of the concrete. Otherwise, guided by "ideal models" and prejudices, the quest after the Conquest is merely a blind groping toward origins—lent a superstitious significance—that lie beyond the glimmer of measurable historical circumstance.

1. Canaan Before Israel. Israel's emergence as a people in Canaan coincides with the end of the LB Age (LB II, ca. 1400–1200 B.C.E.) and the beginning of the Iron Age (Iron I, ca. 1200–1000). Various textual sources illuminate the former time: Egyptian monuments deposited at Megiddo and Beth-shan document the pharaoh's domination, and periodic internal and external challenges to it. Hittite archives corroborate them in regard to Canaan's periphery. The diplomatic correspondence from El Amarna (and letters found in a few Canaanite tells) elucidates brilliantly the petty "politicking" of the mid-14th century, during the reigns of Amenhotep III and Akhenaten. To the N, the Ugaritic tablets afford a glimpse of a great kingdom approaching the end of its days in the 13th/12th century. And, starting at about this time, Assyrian texts commemorate campaigns to the West and to the Sea. The archaeological record mirrors the textual record closely, a circumstance rather different from those surrounding Israel's origins, though whether this means that the Sea Peoples or Achaeans caused the collapse of Asian civilization is a difficult question (see Tadmor 1975; Millard 1981, on the age as a whole). Relatively, the era basks in a liberal light.

Late Bronze II Canaan was fashioned from the rich block of the Middle Bronze IIC by the chisel of the Egyptian pharaohs. From the mid-16th to the mid-15th centuries, monarchs from Ahmose to Thutmosis IV, perhaps in common with their local competitors, cut a swath of destruction across SW Asia, reducing the hollow shell of Hyksos Canaan to ash. What Israel later inherited these forces denuded of its numerous, prosperous settlements; they left behind an empire of ruins. In all the Late Bronze Age, Canaan never recovered the density of settlement it enjoyed in the Middle Bronze II.

In the 14th century, a renewed city-state system represented the means of administering the empire, which Amenhotep III's armies consolidated against threats from Hatti and Mitanni. The empire consisted of a series of petty kingdoms, governed by local dynasts whose positions were dependent on the pharaoh's confirmation; it embraced all the land from Gaza to the doorstep of Ugarit. The disruptive element in this conglomerate were the mountain states, territorially extensive entities inland from the coast. Controlling them was difficult at the best of times—logistics and communications considered—and uneconomical at all. Sparsely populated, they remained rugged and refractory. In the plains and valleys, at the same time, a drama of dubious allegiances, alliances with foreign powers (Hatti, Mitanni), and reliance on pharaonic support played itself out. Distance vaccinated the southern lands against the ambitions of Hittite overlords. In the S, the region of later Israel, purely local ambitions dictated the course of the political maneuvers. In the N, however, in collusion now with this, now with that restive Egyptian vassal, Hatti gradually wrested dominion from the decline of the 18th dynasty.

The landmark development in the relationship between the twin contestants was the battle of Qadesh. Fought early in the reign of Ramesses II, it arrested the erosion of Egyptian control in northern and central Syria, and on the coast south of Hatti. It led to a formal Egypto-Hittite condominium in Canaan. Yet this ratification of the *status quo* by coequal partners was not fated to endure. By the end of the 13th century, the Peoples of the Sea were a third force crashing onto the shores of Egypt and Canaan, and associated developments engulfed hapless Hatti, which beneath their tide sank helplessly from view, affording scope to Assyrian vigor west of the Euphrates, from the mid-13th century onward.

2. Canaan in the Earliest Israelite Eras. At the close of the LB Age, a series of new nations crystallized in Syria, Transjordan, and Canaan. For the first time, Egyptian sources during the interminable reign of Ramesses II surely speak of Moab and Edom. The celebrated reference to Israel in the Merneptah stela occurs only slightly later, around 1220–1207. Ammon's development cannot have lagged far behind. These are the nations that J in Genesis classifies as *Hebrew* (*ʿibrî*)—descendants of the eponym Eber (**ʿi/abr*), a group that includes proto-Arameans in S Syria—which emerged in the Cisjordanian interior and along the line of the King's Highway in Transjordan at the end of LB II. While Egyptian reports of Shasu in Transjordan antedate this era (see Helck 1968), the names later adopted by Iron-Age *Hebrew* kingdoms appear only in the 13th century.

Egypt in adversity maintained a grip on Canaan. This land weathered the Sea-People onslaught and mastered or possibly even installed their colonies on the Canaanite coast (see Singer 1988). Ramesses III, in particular, in the first half of the 12th century consolidated this domination. Locked in a martial struggle with the Sea-Peoples, he memorialized his campaigns against them in Canaan from Megiddo to Medinet Habu.

Ramesses III left his mark on Canaan's architectural complexion with public works at Beth Shean, Megiddo, and Lachish. Yet Egyptian control, like Egyptian interest, centered on the lowlands and trade-routes; even there, it was insouciant and sporadic (cf. Weinstein 1981: 22). Just before Ramesses III's reign, the Philistines in the south and the Tjekker at Dor thus began to dislodge earlier Egyptian vassals or were settled in their place (as by Merneptah at Ashkelon?) on the coast. They were unceremoniously absorbed as new vassals into the old empire by the pharaoh (see Ussishkin 1985: 222 on the date). Off the trade routes, the *Hebrew* nations appeared. Egypt could tolerate or adapt to considerable flux in its Asiatic possessions.

It is ironic that Israel retained no recollection of Egyptian domination in the land. Egyptian armies went calling in Canaan's valleys through the middle of the 12th century (Ussishkin 1985: 218–19, 221, 224–26; Oren 1985: 188), at a time when Israel was certainly at home in the hills (the Merneptah stela). We see the indirect influence of Egyptian dominion in Israel's adopting as its national myth an account of liberation from Egyptian bondage: slaves were one of LB Canaan's major exports to Egypt, and this practice probably continued into the 12th century. Famine, occasioned either by political turmoil or by drought, inevitably intensified the level of traffic. Thus, the Joseph story was based on conditions with which all inhabitants of Canaan were conversant. Servitude in Canaan and slavery in Egypt were the Canaanite lot: a story of a slaves' revolt and the overlord's overthrow at the Reed Sea was calculated to comfort all those still under the pharaoh's iron heel in Canaan. All the more, though, should the Canaanite subjects recall an era of Ramesses' revenge.

This conundrum has its key in the nature of Egyptian administration. Israel encountered it as exercised through the medium of local chieftains. Even when the Egyptian army itself appeared, it most often operated under the command of local commissioners (Sisera?) and in close cooperation with the vassals. An Israel subsumed within the territories of the city-states, not itself an administrative unit of the empire, would have had no reason to remember an Egyptian oppression, along the lines of those described in Judges; still less would an Israel in the hills have cause to recall participating in the Egyptians' expulsion. In other words, an ethnic Israel not recognized as a political unit by the pharaoh—because its demography violated the administrative lines of the Asiatic empire—and an Israel whose communal political influence was confined to the topographic backwaters of Canaan could have encountered and remembered only the demands of local suzerains. The aggregate of these figures Israel claimed to have bested in a melee by the waters of Megiddo (Judges 5).

The Canaan that Israel settled at the start of the 12th century was a land in intermittent turmoil. On the chaos, Egyptian arms imposed a superficial order. It was an order against which Israel could not prevail. Indeed, during Israel's earliest years in Canaan, it was positioned neither politically nor geographically to offer a challenge to the pharaoh's forces. The Merneptah stela portrays Israel as an ethnos, not as a geographical entity. Its representation matches the bulk of the textual evidence as Alt construed it. It also fits precisely the contours of the archaeological data.

3. Israel on the Ground. Archaeological data adduced in defense of the Conquest model proved in the end a "recoiling bow." Results were mixed or negative at Jericho, and wholly falsified the claims of Joshua concerning Ai. But these setbacks affect only the symbolic portion of the Conquest, and it is natural to withdraw, as the Albright school did, to the more defensible line of Joshua 9–11. Here, after all, one could take cover behind the bulwark of an Israelite occupation succeeding that of the Canaanites at Hazor and, theoretically, Lachish (contrast Ussishkin 1985) and Tell Bet Mirsim (contrast Greenberg 1987), the two occupation levels divided by a violent destruction. The same was true at Bethel, whose defeat is recorded in Judg 1:22–26. Similar claims have been lodged regarding Beth Shemesh, Tell Zeror, Beth-shan, and, in Transjordan, Tell Deir Alla.

The pungency of this corroboration, however, is neutralized by two factors. Most of the destructions are not at sites to whose conquest Joshua 9–11 lay claim (Gezer, another case, is re-occupied by Philistines). And, at Lachish (V) and Hazor, Israel occupies the post-destruction site only after a gap in occupation. This is a quibble, since Joshua presumes, as noted, only destruction, not necessarily resettlement. But the gaps, even more than the late destruction of Lachish, are embarrassing. Further, if Khirbet Rabud is indeed ancient Debir, there is a flat contradiction: Rabud suffered no discontinuity in the period in question.

Second, as noted above (B.3), several towns named in Joshua 9–12 were either completely or virtually unoccupied at the end of LB IIB; others exhibit no sign of Israelite takeover in this era. The most embarrassing instance is that of Gibeon, hardly "a great city" (Josh 10:2). Jerusalem's ally in the same chapter, Jarmuth (10:3; no destruction is reported), was wholly or partly deserted. Taanach seems to have been devoid of LB IIB remains, despite Josh 12:21. And Arad (Josh 12:14, after Num 21:1–3) was abandoned from EB II until Iron I. Conversely, Lachish, whose destruction Josh 10:31f. describes, survived intact into the mid-12th century under Egyptian control (Ussishkin 1985). Tell Beit Mirsim was not occupied by Israelites until the 11th century (Greenberg 1987). The case of Bethel may be similar. All this poses more serious a difficulty, insofar as the testimony of the book of Joshua is concerned, than the paucity of early Israelite settlement.

The prize cases of exaggeration in Joshua 9–12 come in summaries claiming that Canaanites were uniformly annihilated (10:40–43; 11:12–23). This has precipitated the inclusion of such kings as those of Taanach, Aphek, and Megiddo in Josh 12:18, 21. If one takes this to imply the envelopment and capture of these towns, as scholars have usually felt Josh 11:12, 14 licensed them to do (but see above, A.3.), the archaeological record is damning: LB Aphek fell into non-Israelite hands, thence to the Philistines (note Beck and Kochavi 1983); Megiddo VIIA remained Canaanite into the second half of the 12th century, and it is unclear that Megiddo VI was held by Israel. Yet, discounting for slight exaggeration in the telling, the only specific town whose sack Joshua 11 asserts is Hazor (for whose fall ca. 1200 see the argument of Yadin 1972: 108 [Yadin holds for 1230]). Nor can archaeological investigation falsify claims that Joshua met and routed enemy kings in the field.

As noted, the main danger in applying excavation results against the text is identical with that in applying them for it: the textual problems are in the process apt to be oversimplified. The case of Lachish has been cited. One might take the gap in occupation after Lachish VI to contradict the claim of Josh 10:31 that Israel took the town. But the text explicitly distinguishes Conquest from colonization as chronologically separate phases—a distinction presupposed by and indispensable to a sensible reading of Judges 1. Israel did ultimately gain control of the town. Like that of Jerusalem in Judg 1:8, Lachish's role in Josh 10:31f. probably reflects only the natural telescoping of gradual achievements and their attribution to the emblematic Conqueror, Joshua.

Individual archaeological results are more likely to cast doubt on the biblical testimony than to confirm it. Where destruction and resettlement occur at times and places that coincide with those for which we might expect Israelite activity, the conqueror's identity and the timing of reoccupation can be called into question. Where excavations contradict biblical evidence—at Heshbon, for example, no remains antedating the Iron Age except a tomb (Harding et al. 1953: 27–41) have been found (cf. Num 21:21–32)—the evidence can be devastating (though the ongoing settlement at Rabud or Lachish is perhaps more damning). The passage in point must be abandoned as an accurate record, and attempts to explain its origins elaborated without prejudice to surrounding records. Here, however, there is a lesson to be learned: in reconstructing the history, the issue is neither solely what is in the ground nor solely what is in the text; the object of research is the genetic relationship between them, their common, collateral antecedents.

In this connection, the most important archaeological data are not those directly related to textual claims. In a defense of a neo-Altian view, Finkelstein (1983; *AIS*) has adduced the data concerning Israelite population distribution in Iron I; he draws particularly on surveys conducted by Israeli archaeologists of settlement in the fringe areas (including especially mountain ridges and the intermontane valleys). The picture is instructive: the earliest Iron Age saw the multiplication of small villages especially in the central hills, with minor development in the mountains of Judah and the Galilee (on the Galilee, see Aharoni 1970: 264; Gal 1990). The picture in the hills of Manasseh is similar (22 sites in toto), and cult sites are among the remains (Mazar 1982; Zertal 1986a: 43–53). By the 11th century, this trend toward cultivation and squatting in the central hills had grown feverish. For example, where the hills of Ephraim sustained 4–5 settlements in LB II, they hosted something like 125 in Iron I (Finkelstein 1983: 110–77). Barren areas, earlier abandoned, such as the Beersheba basin (Cohen 1985; note Finkelstein 1984) and the lower Galilee, began somewhat later to attract pioneers as well, and the countryside swelled with extensive and intensive agriculture and pastoralism.

Transjordan yields up a picture that is, generally speaking, comparable. Surveys tend to confirm that the Wadi Hasa region (to et-Tafileh) and the territory north of it to the Yarmuk experienced significant increases in settlement early in Iron I (Mittmann 1970; Weippert 1979: 28–30; MacDonald 1983). Here, it may be added, evidence may be accruing that the process of settlement began effectively in LB, continuing into and snowballing in Iron I (see Miller 1982: 172; Ibrahim, Sauer, and Yassine 1976: 55–56; Sauer 1986: 4–14). Finkelstein has linked this process hypothetically to the expulsion of the settled population from their various domiciles in MB IIB, which propelled them into pastoral nomadism in the fringes of Canaan. The process of resettlement reflects, then, their sedentarization some centuries later.

Archaeologically, however, the settlement increase in Iron I (or Late Bronze and Iron I) does not suffice to distinguish a sudden, massive influx from a slower stream of immigration from abroad, or the stream of outsiders from peasant flight to the hills. Still, when excavated, the Iron I sites in the hills and in Transjordan yield characteristic early Israelite pottery, particularly the "collared rim" ware ubiquitous in Israel's Iron I settlements. Like the rest of the Iron I pottery repertoire (esp. Kempinsky 1985; Albright 1932: 53–54; Albright and Kelso 1968: 63–65), this has been shown to have clear antecedents in LB II (Ibrahim 1978: 121–22; above, B.3). Nor is it necessarily limited in Iron I to Israelites alone: it is heartily represented in Transjordan, for example (Ibrahim 1978). That is, it is a feature of early Israelite culture (the relative proportions of the pottery being particularly diagnostic, with roughly a third of rim fragments at Israelite sites composed of collared-rim store jars, and, at Giloh, another thirty percent of cooking pots—Mazar 1981b: 31). Insofar as this resembled that of the Transjordanian "Hebrews" (esp. Ammon, Moab, Edom; see Sauer 1986: 10–14), and of elements inside Canaanite society, it also characterizes the cultures of other, associated peoples—whose settlements and states developed in parallel with Israel's.

The settlements also disclose either the prototypes or the realized form of a characteristic house-plan, that of the "four-room house," in which three rooved rectangles form a U about a courtyard; the parallel rooms (the sides of the U) are separated from the courtyard sometimes only by pillars; the entrance, normally, is through the courtyard. Again, there is a possible prototype of the plan in LB IIA—an elegant building whose first floor was dedicated to industry was recently unearthed at Tell Batashi (Mazar 1981b: 91). Possibly, therefore, the housing stock is no more discontinuous with that of LB Canaan than is the pottery. Again, however, the common Canaanite house is not identical with the common Israelite: the Canaanite house is a square with a courtyard at its center. Speaking broadly, collared-rim ware and the four-room house characterize Israelite settlements of the Iron Age in Cisjordan, and some Transjordanian "Hebrew" sites (Sauer 1979). They are not characteristic of LB Canaanite centers.

There has been a controversy whether the four-room house was Israelite, and whether it developed from the pastoralist's tent (Fritz 1981: 65; Fritz and Kempinski 1983: 31–34); this, by definition, reaches beyond our historical grasp. But Israelite settlements also manifest a tendency to erect their housing in a ring, kept hollow in the Negeb, an arrangement convenient for pastoralists. Finkelstein linked the pattern of village planning to the exigencies of hills architecture (1983: 192–94); but both factors probably played a role (see Finkelstein 1984: 193–95; 1986b: 116–21). The four-room house itself is designed to accommodate small-scale family animal husbandry: the stock sleep under the areas parallel to the courtyard (the sides of the U, which can also serve as storage areas); the cross-room (the bottom of the U) stores feed and provisions for or sleeps the family. See HOUSE, ISRAELITE. Indeed, troughs are often found between the pillars separating the side-rooms from the courtyard (Holladay fc.). And the storage jars and other items of the household economy appear regularly in the cross-room. This design must have disseminated because of its functional advantages. Like the shape of the village, it implies a specific socioeconomic dynamic inside—what the common shape of the pottery shows is a shared economic microcosm. The predominance of this dynamic in its context weighs heavily against a theory that the Israelites originated as peasants in the plains. The Iron I hills pioneers were pastoralists, not peasants, first—a point corroborated by Merneptah's equation of Israelites with Shasu.

Finkelstein's survey (1983; *AIS*) stressed other impinging factors as well. Most of the Iron IA Israelite villages appear in the northern and central reaches of the central hills, clustering alongside the five established Canaanite centers in that region: the earliest settlers did not choose to establish themselves in the least populous and most isolated regions, such as Judaea. It does seem to be the case that the earlier settlements concentrate primarily on the eastern (wilderness) side of the mountain ridges, which afford adequate pasturage for their established herds of sheep. Still, the inhabitants of Izbet Sartah, possibly along with those of several nearby villages, set up shop on land suited to a mixed farming-pasturing strategy within shouting range of Aphek, which they no doubt supplied with meat in exchange for processed goods (see Finkelstein 1986).

The earliest Israelite pioneers thus brought their herds to regions suited to pastoralism. As they expanded their encampments, and erected permanent, agricultural dwellings, they deliberately exploited less densely forested patches in the uplands (thus near towns). This would have helped them avoid some of the intensive capital investment reclaiming the land involved; by the same token, the earliest settlements in the central hills were located in inland valleys (though no excavation results are yet available to determine how these compare to the hilltop villages), where terracing could be kept to a minimum (Finkelstein 1983: 161–62; 1986: 179).

All this is only to be expected. The new elements seem to have thought their settlements relatively secure—inadequately defended and often unwalled (Callaway 1976: 29) as they were—whether because they were negligible or because prevailing conditions were relatively peaceful—as in the case of Izbet Sartah III–II. And, although they depended to some extent on the market for meat in the hills and plains towns of Canaan, many of them, especially the later ones, invested long years of hard labor clearing the farms of trees and rocks, terracing them, planting olive trees and vines, and cutting cisterns and grain silos into the hillsides. These pioneers also built enclosures to protect their property from their neighbors'; they planed the wood of their houses, built pillars and troughs, and participated in public works.

The nature of these projects was such that the families involved required labor for clearing, for improvements, and for harvesting. They needed labor exchange for the herds and fields, which involved a certain critical mass of population involvement. Allowing that half of the Iron I population was present in Iron IA, the minimum influx into the region of the central hills, (the net Israelite population of which can be estimated at 40,000–80,000; Finkelstein *AIS*, 330–35), must have been something on the order of 15,000 people. That is, the total immigration into the hills of Cisjordan will, minimally, have reached the vicinity of 25,000: the influx simply must have continued over the course of the whole 12th century (and note the two waves of settlement at Ai—Callaway 1976: 29–30 and the alterations from unstructured pastoral to a hierarchical, probably patriarchal, agricultural village at Izbet Sartah—Finkelstein 1986: 5–23). The immigrants elected to clear, to cut, and to work the rock and the forest.

These are not in the end choices one would expect of peasants fleeing to an uncertain refuge from the plains. Indeed, as noted above, the historical behavior of such peasants had been to seek haven in other plains communities, not in a strange environment. It is difficult to imagine that the massive gamble of labor and materials involved in settling the hills would have come naturally to a plains population, or that marketing meat in the lowlands—and failing to fortify themselves against military constabularies sent to repatriate them (Finkelstein *AIS*, 313)—was a natural course for lowlands fugitives. Whether this movement reflects the sedentarization of peoples uprooted at the end of MB, or simply the influx of migrants from outside Cisjordan (and outside Transjordan), it suggests less the flight of urban peasantry than the homesteading of pastoral elements already integrated in economic interdependence with the plains. The continuity in pottery forms coupled with the distinction in the frequency of pottery types and in the dominant form of domestic (and public) architecture, and the settlement history of Transjordan, are consistent with this reconstruction (see Kempinski 1985). The clearing of trees and the clearing of stones, the building of terraces and the cutting of cisterns, the cutting of silos and the building of enclosures all stand in this tradition.

Still, it must be observed that neither the architectural evidence, which answers to function rather than style, nor the pattern of settlement, decisively contradicts the peasants' revolt. It is rather the textual evidence (above) that disqualifies that theory. One may add, in contrast to the Hivites, Kenites, and others who were absorbed as cohesive ethnic communities distinct from Israel—the list of Judges 1 furnishes numerous examples—whatever fugitive peasants took to the hills could have assimilated to Israel only singly. These would have had the characteristics of clients, at best, among the Israelite kin-groups (see, for example, Khazanov 1983: 152–64). That they made a material contribution either to the culture or to the manpower of the hills communities seems unlikely.

4. Israelite Traditions in the Light of Modern Knowledge. Attention to archaeology and the history of the tradition has made it plain that the key to interpreting the Joshua traditions as history lies in critical distance and felicitous judgment. The narratives concerning the Jordan crossing, Jericho and Ai must be altogether discarded. The first reflects an annual ritual crossing, whose survival both attested to and re-shaped the traditions of earliest times (A.2.a.(1)); the latter attest the process whereby the sight of an Israelite settlement, or of no settlement at all, atop a noble tell inspired Israelite storytellers and historians to deduce that Joshua had taken the place. The participation of Yarmuth in the coalition of southern kings (10:3) reflects this sort of thinking, as does the confrontation with Arad in Num 21:1–3; 33:40; Josh 12:14. If Tell Hesi proves to be Israelite Eglon (10:34f.), it would represent another instance: the massive EB tells became the objects of Israelite romance.

All this damages the testimony of Joshua 9–11, for this cycle is intimately connected in the historian's presentation with that of Jericho and Ai (esp. 9:3, central to the nuance of vv 10, 24; 10:28, 30; 12:9). Nor does the historian distinguish the "symbolic" Conquest from that in Joshua 9–11 in terms of genre—the two are equally historical. Possibly, diverse sources underlie the account: the narrative in Josh 9:3–10:15 understands itself to focus on a battle against the kings of the southern hill country (esp. 10:6); even the continuation, in 10:16–39, does not exceed the confines of the Shephelah. One might go so far, since the distinction between "smiting" and "supplanting" corresponds to that between lowlands and hills, as to claim that the summary in 10:40–43 goes no further itself (so above, A.3.).

Conversely, 11:1–23 depict Israel as conquering everything Canaanite that moved, except on the coastal plain and in Syria N of the Hermon. This latter material stands in close continuity with chaps. 12–13; 23; Judg 2:6ff., where it is the peripheral nations who remain unsubdued. Again, it should be noted that Josh 11:16–20 reports the "taking" of the land, not the supplanting of all indigenous populations. "Taking" in 11:23 is a prelude to tribal allotments, which (as Judges 1) precede the "supplanting" of the Canaanites; 11:23 can claim that the whole land was "taken" even though v 22 cites an ongoing Amorite presence in the Philistine region. Still, even the more modest interpretation of the chapter's assertions entails the conclusion that it exaggerates, telescopes, distorts the historical process beyond recognition.

Nor does detaching the southern campaign of chap. 10 from the northern of chap. 11 produce a separate, reliable account. The Albright school appealed to the destruction of Hazor XIII as support for Joshua 11. But the identification of Deborah's opponent in Judg 4:1–3 as the same Yabin, king of Hazor (Josh 11:1) illustrates that later Israel believed pre-Israelite Hazor to be the leading power in northern Canaan (Josh 11:10), the key to the Galilee.

This tradition is probably founded in a hazy combination of historical recollection and geopolitical reality; whether it was in fact Israel that overthrew Hazor remains obscure. Certainly, the more exaggerated claims that the historian suspends from this peg (11:1–4, 12) reflect only his hardened conviction that Joshua's victory was total, his prosecution thorough (11:18–20, 23). Even the locus of Joshua's supposed northern decisive battle, "by the waters of Merom/the height (*ʿal mê mērôm*)" (11:5, 7) reads as though it hatched from a conflation of Judg 5:18–19: these verses locate the other big battle joined by Sisera, identified in Judges 4 as the general of Jabin, king of Hazor, "by the waters of Megiddo" (*ʿal mê mĕgiddô*)" and "on the heights of the field" (*ʿal mĕrômê śādeh*)".

The story of the southern confrontation has been incorporated into the framework of 9:1f.; 11–13. No doubt, the historian received this tradition already partly shaped. Yet *it* is the one in which deserted LB Gibeon, the abiding LB settlement (to 1150) at Lachish, and probably unoccupied Jarmuth play prominent roles. The key to understanding the historian's reconstruction may lie in his use of a quotation from "the book of the Jashar": " 'Sun, be still in Gibeon, and, Moon, in the Aijalon Valley!' And the sun was still, and the moon stood, so that the nation acquitted itself of its foes" (10:12–13).

This old couplet had been attributed to Joshua before the historian of chaps. 9–10 laid his hands on it. 10:12 heads it with a superscription closely resembling those of some psalms, "when (lit., on the day when) Yhwh delivered up the Amorites before the children of Israel" (cf. Ps 3; 7; 9; 18; 34; 51f.; 54; 56f.; 59f.; 63; 142). This is redundant in context, and must have been drawn from a written source. It sufficed to place the apostrophe to the luminaries in Joshua's mouth. Moreover, Isaiah cites the incident in connection with an oracle against Jerusalem, as a case of Yhwh's wrath consuming his foes (28:21). His allusion presumes that his hearers recognized the historical reference in all its bearings.

It is around this notion of a decisive confrontation at Gibeon that Joshua 9–10 were built. 2 Sam 21:1–14, in which David decimates the Saulide establishment in expiation of that king's attacks on the Gibeonites, appeals explicitly to old traditions of a hoary alliance between Gibeon and Israel. It was not unnatural for those who wove the narratives of Israelite antiquities, then, to relate the battle at Gibeon to the ratification of Israel's treaty there. That any early Israelite community really contracted such a formal pact with the Hivite tetrapolis is unlikely, and there could have been no such pact at the start of Iron IA, with Gibeon yet to be reoccupied. What seems probable is that Gibeon's role in the literary formulation of the confederates' common history grew as the fortunes of the site waxed during Iron I. After Shechem's destruction in the mid-12th century (Judg 9:45–49), Gibeon seems to have blossomed into one of the larger and more strategically placed towns in Israel (2 Sam 2:12–16 after 2:8–11), and one of the most prestigious (1 Kgs 3:4–14; 2 Sam 21:1ff.). Its eminence among the Hivites by David's time led traditionists thereafter to regard Gibeon's residents as having been the leading element in all earlier Hivite transactions.

Against an Israelite-Hivite axis in the Aijalon Pass, the Amorite opponents mentioned in the Book of the Jashar had to be sought in the S hills. Isa 28:21 may already reflect the view that Jerusalem was the head of the anti-Israelite front: as noted above, it threatens a repetition of Yhwh's "strange deed" in the context of an oracle against the Jerusalem establishment. Certainly, the geopolitical logic of the reconstructed league with Gibeon (above, A.2.b) demanded such a deduction. The old poetic snatch in Josh 10:12–13 also defined tolerably the extent of the hostile community: "Amorite" is a term deployed primarily to designate denizens of the hills. The enemy thus consisted of city-states in the Judean uplands and in the Shephelah. The knowledge that Israelite settlement did not overflow such areas until the time of David must have informed the tradition and corroborated the reconstruction.

Originally, the song in Josh 10:12 comprised an appeal for the bestowal of a favorable omen—that the sun should be visible in the east and the moon in the west. The omen and its significance are known from Babylonian sources. The granting of the omen and the confirmation of its efficacy are the subject of v 13 (Holladay 1968). But the historian (or his sources) interpreted the text literally to mean that the sun and moon stood still, extending the time in which Joshua could pursue the broken foe. This defined the course and length of the rout—down the defiles of the Aijalon Pass, spilling out into the Shephelah. For the purposes of integrating this reconstruction with that of Joshua's sweeping triumph, the logical sequel was a campaign in the Shephelah and an incursion from the S Shephelah into the hills (10:28–39).

Extensive portions of this concept of the Conquest must have been antique. The association of the old song with "the day in which Yhwh delivered up the Amorites"—and references to the climactic battle in Isa 28:21, and to the confrontation with towering Amorites in Amos 2:9—already contain the skeleton of the treatment in Joshua, even if none mentions Joshua himself by name. The idea that the Amorites were giants implies that they were obliterated—at least in the popular imagination—since the titans did not survive to be examined by later Israel. Similarly, the Gilgal and Jericho cycles derive from old traditions, here reinterpreted in line with the 'Deuteronomist's" theology of history. The tradition of a treaty with Gibeon also stems from antecedents in the time of David (2 Sam 21:1f.). Though David's treatment of the Hivites merely implies the prior existence of a traditional *modus vivendi,* it was natural enough for folklorists to concretize the relationship by reconstructing a formal pact (cf. also 1 Sam 7:14; Genesis 34). For the most part it is impossible to date the growth of the traditions on which the historian depends (though Judges 1 probably stems from the time of Solomon, as Halpern 1983: 179–82). Still, a good deal of the treatment originates in traditional perspectives on Israel's entry into the land.

Nevertheless, nothing in the literary evidence suggests that the details of the reconstruction antedate the Deuteronomistic History. The Shephelah campaign of 10:28–39 probably represents the historian's systematization of different claims concerning local victories in that region, or his extrapolation, based on a strategic reconstruction, from such claims in the tradition elsewhere (Hazor?). This is the campaign that establishes Joshua's control over the borders he is said to have secured. One might say that he had "conquered" the country from the S up to Gibeon (10:41f.). The appropriation of credit for the conquest of Hebron and Debir (10:36–39; 11:21f. vs. Josh 14:6–15; 15:13–19; Judg 1:10–15, 20; cf. A.3.) may represent either a normal accretion to Joshua of victories dated later elsewhere (cf. Hazor) or an adumbration of his consolidation of the Conquest within the territory whose perimeters he had seized. (The contrast between Joshua's and Judah's or Judah's and Caleb's taking Hebron is a matter of emphasis, partly on conquest or supplanting, and partly on the identity of the groups named.) Conversely, the actual choice of specific Shephelah forts has no plain motivation. Significant towns are excluded. However, since three of the four sites are not yet positively identified, no hypothesis should be advanced on this point.

In light of all this, and with the exception of the confrontation of Gibeon, the most fruitful approach to Israelite traditions may be to note what they do *not* claim, rather than what they do. For example, even the author of Joshua 11–12 does not assert an Israelite colonization of Megiddo and the Jezreel: traditions such as those encapsulated in Josh 17:11–13; Judg 1:27 inhibited the historian from such overweening hyperbole. Thus, Josh 12:21–23 can reflect a success in the field, or at most a raid (born of braggadocio), not the supplanting of lowlands populations. Monarchic Israel generally understood that its forebears in Canaan stuck to the hills.

On this basis, the geographic extent of Joshua's victories could be identified with that of Canaan S of the Hermon. He could be said to have bested opponents from all regions of the land (11:2; 12). And attributing to him some later regional successes, he could be said to have left Israel ascendant in a Canaan it claimed, but alone, as Israel aspired to be, only in parts of it. The territorial framework and nationhood of a later Israel is thus retrojected to the first moment of Israel's intrusion into the land. The process by which this occurred was no doubt entirely innocent, one of historical reconstruction, based in part on reifications of embellished cultic confessions, in later times, not willful or wholesale invention.

The texts' reluctance to claim that Joshua made permanent gains in the lowlands matches the archaeological and extra-biblical materials from the LB-Iron I transition. There is, beside it, another rather loud silence in the text, the one surrounding Israel's movement into the central hills. It is true that Judg 1:22–26 record a sack of Bethel—typically, for early Israel, by strategem rather than direct assault; the death of Bethel's king is toted up in Josh 12:16. In the Ephraimite hills between Gibeon and Shechem, this is the only conflict any record of which survives (of a town, it should be noted, that was indeed occupied in LB II). And the record itself places the accession after Joshua's time, in the era of internal consolidation.

Outside of Bethel, Josh 12:17 (Tappuah, Hepher), 24 (Tirzah) contain the only assertions that Joshua killed kings of towns in the Manassite hills. In the scheme of Joshua 11–12, the kings in question would have fallen "by the waters of Merom/the height" (11:8). The same scheme dictates that Joshua should have depopulated their towns, though, in accordance with a suspicious proviso (11:13), without doing injury to the buildings. Yet the presentation posits that Joshua fought a battle in the Aijalon Pass that enabled him to encircle the southern hills, then fought another in the north, giving Israel control of the Galilee. The idea of a battle for the central hills, or of extensive operations to gain a foothold there, is alien even to the latest strata of the history. It is unclear whether any tradition ever envisioned these areas as subject to conquest in the same sense that Judea and the Galilee were.

This argument is susceptible to the objection that the historian responsible for the Conquest accounts concerned himself with Israel's mastery only over a large territory, from the far south to the Hermon; he did not imply systematic eradication of the Amorites in Joshua's lifetime (or thereafter). This, after all, is the view presupposed in Judges 1. In accordance with it, one may imagine the central hills, as the history now runs, as a region encircled, awaiting the detailed attention reserved for the period after Israel had stilled the sound of opposing armies, marching in concert against Israel in the field. The objection, however, is vulnerable to the counterstroke that the historian claims that Joshua cleared Israel's hills territory of foreign elements (11:16–23). It also ignores the most piercing hush of all: there is no conquest of Shechem.

In LB IIA, Shechem was the dominant town of the central hills: its king, Lab'aya, had reduced all the region from Jerusalem in the south to Megiddo in the N to his sway. Shechem *was* the central hill country in that era. Yet confrontation with the power fails Israel's memory. Genesis 34 assigns a treaty with the town and Israel's violation of it to the patriarchal era. Judges 9 conversely sets Shechem's sowing with salt in the time after Gideon, in the middle of the era of the "judges." Between the two, Josh 8:30–35; 24 locate ceremonies of covenant confirmation at Shechem, responding in part to Deut 11:29f.; 27. There is a broad tradition of activity at Shechem, but none of siege and capture (cf. Toombs 1979).

The Joshua narratives contain other lacunae, in the northern hills and even in Judah. But in the context of an account of securing perimeters, the omissions are no surprise. The extent to which exaggeration might accrue to accounts of Joshua's time is clarified in Judg 1:8, assigned to the years after his death: in the face of pre-Davidic reality, the verse affirms a Judahite destruction of Jerusalem (but no occupation). No comparable claims concerning Shechem appear. The silence is loud indeed.

Overall, it seems legitimate to speak of a Conquest tradition that stems at least from the 10th century B.C.E.—the time when the ritual crossing of the Jordan to Gilgal is first clearly attested, when the earliest compilation of Judges 1 was made, and when a violation of a "treaty" with Gibeon was remedied. The story of Abimelech (Judges 9) attests incidentally that ambivalence as between local and national or ethnic administration rent the early Israelite community: would the city-state or the nation become the articulated political musculature of Canaan? A central government, like that of the United Monarchy, would have seized on and fostered national traditions—the J source of the Pentateuch may have originated in this concern (its final form is, however, later). The later historian responsible for the Conquest accounts that survive today overlaid and reinterpreted the sources such elements had mediated to him.

5. The Israelite Conquest. a. The Earliest Phases. The absence of traditions of violent entry into the central hills so dovetails with the archaeological evidence of Israelite coexistence in that region with the scattered Canaanite remnants of LB II (and Toombs 1979) that it affords one of the few footholds in the morass of the Conquest. It complements the tradition of Israelite coexistence with the Hivites of the Gibeonite tetrapolis. It resonates harmoniously with the tradition of early (and originally pacific) relations with Hivite Shechem. One may justifiably infer a peaceful Israelite presence among the Hivites of the central hills in general, whose expansion into the region N of Jerusalem was coeval with the Israelite influx.

Israel's early cultic community at Shechem may have centered on the ratification of this relationship (Judg 8:33; 9:4, 46). In any event, the "covenants" in Josh 8:30–35; 24 and Genesis 34 presumably reflect ongoing cultic activity at Shechem during the monarchic era. This would have been inherited and reinterpreted from the time before Abimelek; after his destruction of Shechem, the focus of the action there would have shifted, perhaps from the town to the surrounding hills (as in Deuteronomy 27). It is not impossible that the Iron I installation unearthed in 1983 on the N slope of Mt. Ebal was associated with this displacement, and with pilgrimage coming from the Jordan up the Wadi Far'ah, then down from the N. But this is a matter of speculation; the excavator places the Ebal pottery at the outset of Iron I (Zertal 1986a), which would rule it out.

The character of the earliest Israelite hills villages is consonant with this general understanding. Though the Negev sites, starting in the 11th century (such as Tell Esdar, Arad, Beer-sheba, and, earlier, arguably, Tell Masos) exhibit a stronger predilection for pastoralism and more architectural variety, they differ more in the proportion than in the identity of their constitutive elements. The pioneer study in the socioeconomics of uplands settlements is that of L. E. Stager (1985a), which focuses particularly on the close-knit structure of the sites, uniformly modest in scope. The tendency in them is for houses to cluster together in a few small groups, representing no doubt two or three generations in the life of a nuclear family. The whole of a site might thus consist of only a few families, probably all related within the context of an "expanded" family (see Cohen 1965: 56), along the lines of the Arabic hamula (so Izbet Sartah III and II): working, breeding, and relating to the outside world in common.

In the courtyard of the four-room house stood the oven and industrial installations for agricultural and animal produce. In the early settlements this included small, inefficient grain pits, often lined with stone, or storage jars sunk into the earth. The stables underneath the rooved areas parallel to the courtyard (the verticals of the U; see Holladay fc.) indicate that most nuclear families had herds. If the stable space is a guide, the flocks were rarely extensive. See STABLES. Indeed, some of this physical plant may have been given over to draught animals (Gen 49:14?) and fatlings (1 Sam 28:24; 2 Sam 12:3; Amos 6:4). The family, that is, kept a small flock (Judg 6:4, 11; 1 Sam 17:28) while cultivating the soil; no doubt this provided an occupation for young boys (as 1 Sam 16:11) and other unemployables (Amos 7:15). However, occasional large flocks were probably bred by some families, who would have exploited the village commons and supplementary, makeshift enclosures, as well as more distant pastures (e.g., 1 Sam 9:3–5; 25:2–8; 2 Sam 13:23f.). The Negeb settlements, where pastoralism (and, at Tell Masos, as at Izbet Sartah, large cattle) loomed larger, reflect this fact unmistakably. The reference in the Song of Deborah to (large?) Reubenite flocks bedded at home (Judg 5:16; cf. Gen 49:14; Ps 68:14, both with verbs meaning "to lie down") may refer to a similar situation early on in Transjordan.

Overall, the flocks were a significant component of the village economy; but the Israelite family as a whole did not *specialize* in pastoralism. The elements of their extensive cultivation have been touched on above (C.3). The olive and the vine—their exploitation solidly attested later, in the Samaria ostraca—and cereals required some clearing, planting, terracing, provision for processing, storage arrangements that would minimize spoilage, and other capital investments (including defense against freebooters). The suggestion, corroborated by the location of the earliest settlements in the vicinity of Canaanite towns, and by the integration of Shechem into the Israelite economy as witnessed by its Iron I pottery repertoire (Toombs 1979: no conquest need be posited), is that the first Israelite homesteaders dwelled in peaceful symbiosis with their local Canaanite neighbors. The pastoral component of Israelite industry demanded such markets for meat and wool, and one presumes that this produce was welcome enough among the hills' few tenants, who offered processed goods in exchange (see Rosen 1986: 180–81). For the herders in particular, open communications were vital, razzias a catastrophe (Judg 5:6; 1 Sam 25:2–8). Except for royal caravans, hill country commerce may have depended wholly on their wanderings.

All indications thus point toward cooperation between the Israelites and the earlier population from Shechem to (newly-settled) Gibeon (with similar patches in the upper Galilee and along the virgate ridge of the Judaean highlands; in the Negev, assuming Tell Masos was an Israelite settlement, there were no nearby Canaanite towns [as Gen 21:22–34; 26:16–33]), but the inhabitants of Tell Masos, and, later, those of Beer-sheba VII, were no doubt suppliers of meat to the Philistine coast and mediators of the Egypto-Philistine caravan trade with Arabia. This sort of symbiosis is precisely what the earliest Israelite traditions concerning relations with the Hivites N of Jerusalem have led us to expect. Nor would it come as a surprise if, in line with the old song in Josh 10:12f., an Israel so distributed fought one of its earliest memorable battles—one of its earliest battles as "Israel," instead of as a collection of highlands families—in the Aijalon Pass, against a bloc led by Jerusalem.

b. Where They Came From. The archaeological situation does not unequivocally demand that the Israelites should have entered Canaan from Transjordan. However, the textual situation does. In no way is Israelite insistence on Israel's ethnic distinctiveness—from the earliest times on (Judg 5:11–19, 31; Exod 15:14f.)—compatible with the hypothesis of an Internal Conquest. As noted above (B.3), despite long coexistence and ongoing life with the Israelites, the Hivites remained ethnicly distinct into the monarchy (2 Sam 21:1–14), as did other indigenese (Judges 1). The monarchy itself arose in part as a result of this xenophobia (Halpern 1983: 12–16). From at least the 12th century, Israel understood itself as a people allochthonous and apart in Canaan. Merneptah's equation of Israel with Shasu—otherwise unattested in Cisjordan north of the desert—corroborates the Israelite view.

No precise point of origin outside Canaan can be stipulated with any confidence. Some indications are, however, present. The emergence of the Iron I nations of Canaan—the Philistines and other Sea-Peoples in Cisjordan and the "Hebrew" kingdoms across the river—was an event never lost to Israel's memory. Later historians wrote that the Transjordanian "Hebrew" nations had dispossessed inhabitants there who were "Amorite," that the Philistines had done the same in their territory, just as Israel had done in Cisjordan and in the region from the Arnon to the Jabbok (Deut 2:9–12, 19–23; Judg 11:16–26; Num 21:24–26). All these Iron I peoples Israel regarded as rightful successors to the Amorites (A.1): Amos 9:8 memorializes their migrations in Yhwh's work, bringing "Israel from the land of Egypt, and the Philistines from Caphtor, and Aram from Kir" (Amos 1:5 threatens Aram with a return to Kir).

It is to the "Hebrews" of Transjordan that the Israelites felt themselves most closely related, and, in terms of language (Halpern 1987), forms of social organization, material culture, and religion (each people its own god—Mic 4:5), rightly so. The narratives of Genesis extend both this sense of kinship and the term "Hebrew" also to the peoples of the neo-Hittite kingdoms in Syria (Aram), whose crystallization dates to the same general time (Genesis 24, J; 29f., JE). These Aramean elements fell heir to the remnants of the Hittite empire. Their languages, in this era, were not discontinuous with those of the southern Hebrews; though certain differences, largely phonological, already obtained, they were inconsiderable compared with those that afterward developed. Nor should the tradition of Israel's ultimate origins among these groups be neglected (Gen 11:28–31; 12:1), especially as it embraces (patrilateral parallel cousin) connubium (Genesis 24; 29).

Altogether, the evidence suggests that Iron I "Hebrew" elements were in the ascendant in areas peripheral to the great empires during the last decades of the LB Age. In the Iron I period settlement in Transjordan, as in Canaan, snowballed. Some of these "Hebrews"—a term whose basic meaning is best explained as an ethno-linguistic one (cf. Eber, their eponym, in Gen 10:21, 24; 11:14)—had long been in contact with Canaanite civilization (as Kempinski 1985; from a slightly different perspective, Finkelstein *AIS*).

Scholars misled by exorbitant rhetoric and the use of the term, *ḫabiru,* in an extended sense ("traitor," "outlaw") have significantly overestimated the role "Hebrews" assumed in Amarna Canaan; in reality, the only "Hebrews" attested are bit players, working for minor figures in the political landscape (Halpern 1983: 55 & nn. 24). But there is no denying that small "Hebrew" bands were present (EA 195). Seti I commemorates a campaign against some ʿPR.W (*ʿ*abirū*?) in the Beth-shan region at the end of the 14th century; most likely, he uses the term in its basic, not its extended sense. In any event, the Iron Age newcomers *were* Habiru, "Hebrews," crystallizing from band- into regional organization wherever the parallel administrative structures of the empire and the city-states weakened. Israel is most plausibly viewed as an instance of this contemporary phenomenon.

Some of the "Hebrews" may have been propelled into Transjordan by the stick of Assyrian expansion at the end of the 13th century, then again in the 12th. Under Adad-Nirari I, Shalmaneser I and Tukulti-Ninurta, Asshur extended its control over the western bank of the Euphrates and the Habur basin. The initial deportations, followed by a routinization of Assyrian taxation and the imposition of a harsh bureaucratic commercial control (see Machinist 1982), will have created migrants; these elements can have transported their property only in the form of livestock. The relatively effete rule of Egypt might represent a carrot, drawing the migrants on. By the end of the 13th century, these had congealed into ethnic communities.

The route by which the Cisjordanian elements came is thus recorded both in the patterns of "Hebrew" national development and in the patriarchal narratives (Genesis 12; 24; 31–35; Halpern 1983: 91–92; B. Mazar 1985). Some time after the process halted, it was ritualized skeletally in the pilgrimage linking Succoth, Penuel, Gilgal (?), Shechem, and Bethel (see A.2.a). Like their Ammonite, Moabite, and Edomite counterparts across the Jordan River, such migrants would have developed a close set of kinship ties and a sense of communal identity, reinforced both by their habitation in a limited territory and by the characteristics (religion and a shared historical identity among them) that divided them from the administrative units and populations near which they settled: "a fugitive Aramean was my father" (Deut 26:5; Millard 1980).

Even on this scenario, one must posit that an early, important constituent of later Israel came from the direction of Egypt. This component furnished the national myth, and conceivably the god, of the Cisjordanian "Hebrews." This group cannot be identified as the ancestor of an individual tribe or set of tribes, for the "tribes" took their shape in the land. We may justifiably suppose nevertheless that its members occupied some of the earliest Israelite villages in Transjordan, and in the hills of Judah, Ephraim, and the Galilee. The possibility that this group originated with "Hebrews" engaged in commerce with Edom in Transjordan and the Negeb, and ended in bondage to Egypt, is an attractive one. The appeal of their historical identity to other "Hebrews" has been canvassed briefly above (C.2). It can be added that the persistence, until the time of the United Monarchy, of a dichotomy between the Israelites of the hills (whose god was thought to be a god of the hills—1 Kgs 20:23) and the Canaanites of the valleys (and some in the hills) illustrates that the appeal of the new identity did not extend to much of the local population.

c. How They Came. A problem that has persistently plagued proponents of a gradual- or multiple-entry hypothesis is that of Israelite solidarity, of common subscription to the Yahwistic-Israelite syndicate. Authors reasoning to northern and southern or to southern and eastern entries repeatedly wrestled with the question, how did their groups come together. Israelite texts furnish an explanation. The homesteaders maintained an ethnic and perhaps even a religious identity distinct from that of their previously-settled neighbors. They maintained, too, a culture, a style of life, alien to that of LB Canaan. Not that intermarriage and commerce played no part in their lives, nor yet that in the pre-Saulide era fraternization was forbidden; only, the settlements and economy and customs of the Israelites were distinctively Israelite ("Hebrew"), those of their neighbors Amorite. For one thing, Israelites ate no pork (though no pig was found at Lachish VI, either). For another, they practiced the mutilation of circumcision. No doubt conservative and endogamous marriage patterns directed against property-alienation helped to perpetuate the distinction (except, probably, at Shechem). Highlands Canaan—such as it was—was a mosaic, not a melting-pot.

Other data sustain this view. The scattered villages in the highlands and in the hitherto empty Negeb, with their heavy capital investment but without fortification, betoken an atmosphere of toleration, not of strife. This is inconsistent with a mass, unified migration. Even to the S of LB Jerusalem, isolated Israelite communities took root (Giloh, just outside Jerusalem, Beth Zur, probably Hebron, the Negeb sites), contradicting the notion that a threat from a whole body of newcomers was perceived. Most likely, the "invaders" came not in waves, but in tiny bands, as Alt divined, intent on taming intractable lands beyond the grasp, if not beyond the reach (Judg 5:6), of the plains city-states, in the relative freedom of the backwaters. The lords of Shechem may finally have "given [their land] to the Habiru," as the king of Jerusalem precociously accuses them of doing in the Amarna letters (EA 289: 23f.); inviting "Hebrew" settlement enhanced capital accumulation and manpower. Local authorities had less of an interest in resisting the migrants than in subjecting or coopting and regulating them.

Again, Judges 9 implies that much the same concerns applied shortly afterward in Iron I: this chapter reflects local nervousness about fealty to a king located outside one's own town in an Israelite community that must antedate the 10th century. Though kingship is desirable over against oligarchy (9:2), an absentee kingship is intolerable (9:28). The local competition of the Israelite era is nothing more than an extension of the lie of the land in LB. Under the circumstances, contests for the loyalty of incoming populations, and especially of pastoral elements and bandits, may have raised the stakes in the bidding to very attractive levels.

It is appropriate, in short, to speak of the stick (the advance of hostile or predatory powers in Syria) and the carrot in connection with Israel's emergence. The pattern of early Israelite settlement, in thinly populated regions, but in the vicinity of LB settlements there, is suggestive. The dwindling of settlements in LB Canaan left land available for pasturing, and, ultimately, farming, that was not closely regulated (as the pastoralists at Mari were—at least in theory—by the Mari regime). As the "Hebrews" spread down from northern Transjordan, they tended to migrate to such areas, their common culture leading ultimately to political crystallization based on the development of an infrastructure of villages (below). One might almost envision the operation of a territorial corollary to Parkinson's Law here. But it is important to recall that the wealth of urban LB II Canaan—or of Egypt's vassals there—may have had an important influence in creating markets for meat and for cereals and cash-crops raised in small lots in the relative security of the upland valleys.

It is tempting to suppose that the "Hebrew" pastoralists were present in number in LB II Canaan (so Finkelstein *AIS*). This would account for the overlaps in material culture between Israel and the earlier Canaanites. Since surveys in the hills have not, however, turned up any evidence of pastoralist encampments (in the form of sherds), this notion should be played diminuendo. Herders were doubtless present in the valleys, but not necessarily in large groups. Instead, the more recent model, which sees the "Iron I" settlement of the hills as coincidental with the last era of "LB II" in the city-states, should be adopted (Kempinski 1985; Ussishkin 1985). The pastoralists *migrated* to LB II Canaan, bringing with them the culture that would become characteristic of Iron I. Their settlement in the hills was gradual; it did not result from the transhumance of herders based in the plains, but from the attempt of alien elements to penetrate new markets.

Two factors accelerated the "Hebrew" inroads into Cisjordan. The first was the economic and political success of the pioneers in diversifying types of production and avoiding fatal conflicts. This would have enticed further homesteaders (as at Izbet Sartah and at Ai). Particularly if the migration was accompanied by a transition in the families concerned (not of their earlier social world) from medim-scale pastoralism (flocks fluctuating from about 10–30) to a mixed economy partly rooted in cereals and cash crops, this impulse could only have been enhanced by Assyrian pressure, and especially by the accommodation of local authorities. These incentives would have remained substantial even if the "Hebrews" migrated without fundamental changes in their economic order (and this is difficult to believe of those who came to Cisjordan). They would have been self-perpetuating: human and material capital accumulation would create a pool of collaborators for labor-exchange, wife-exchange, and common defense. Simultaneously, economic success would have issued in natural increase, resulting again in a multiplication of settlements, an ongoing, leapfrogging movement into contiguous areas. To this process over the course of Iron I, the archaeological record, and the history of Israel and the other "Hebrew" nations bear unanimous witness.

The Shasu connection, and Merneptah's identification of Israel with the Shasu, warrant that a similar process characterized the arrival of the "Hebrews" in Transjordan, probably in LB IIB. The terrain and textual traditions (as Judg 5:16) suggest that pastoralism was relatively more important there. Still, the success of Iron Age elements penetrating early into the framework of existing LB society encouraged others to come; it reinforced itself, too, with a flourishing of the population. Again, the incoming elements were probably those who had formed part of the pastoral component of Syrian society until the upheavals of LB II (Idrimi 15f.); at any rate, all must have converted their capital into stock when undertaking the trek SW. This process produced the Transjordanian nations and kingdoms of Iron I; it is not to be distinguished from that that produced those kingdoms' Cisjordanian counterparts (Philistines and other Sea-Peoples excepted). In Cisjordan, where Egyptian control was not so early or so carelessly withdrawn, the process of political unification was more extended and more gingerly. One could effectively pyramid the band-structure of the immigrants regionally only when the Egyptian-supported city-states lapsed into a natural, insolvent, internecine chaos, desperate for money and laborers.

At some point, the confrontation between Canaanite city-states and a force that Josh 10:1–15 attributes to Joshua must have taken place in the Aijalon Pass. It is unnecessary to assume that the "Hebrews" had just arrived by way of Shittim, but a substantial body of them (in the hundreds, at least) should be assigned to this encounter. The most significant historical characteristics of the collision are its apparent direction against those domiciled in Judea, and its coordination (if one may extrapolate) with the Hivite elements north of Jerusalem. Here is a reprise of the antagonism between Shechem and Jerusalem so familiar from Amarna. Indeed, as if foreshadowing Josh 9:1; 10:40–43; 11, EA 366 reports a coalition of Jerusalem and S and N allies against "the Habiru-man": the term perhaps refers to Lab'aya, ruler of Shechem, and the principle, of the coordination of peripheral city-states against the center, remains constant.

As the occasion of the engagement by Gibeon, one must not think of a challenge to locally-delegated Egyptian authority. In Iron I, as in LB IIA, pharaonic imperium inhered, in theory, as much in Shechem as in Jerusalem; the contretemps between these towns were local, within the context of formal submission to Egypt. Still, the "Hebrews" of the long, uneven LB II—Iron I transition eventually comprised a threat. In the ridges, they created consternation among the southerners, then worsted them in the Pass marking the southern off from the central hills. It is likely that these Israelites made common cause with the Shechemite state in the enterprise, and that the outcome permitted the Hivite towns that dominated the interior routes of trade to flourish at the expense of their southern neighbors over the course of Iron IA (poorly attested in Jerusalem; see Shiloh 1984: 26f.)—this was the strategic thrust of the Hivite settlements in the Gibeonite tetrapolis in the first place. Until Abimelech's destruction of Shechem (Judg 9:45–49), the Israelite "Hebrews" probably represented a parallel sociopolitical structure within the city-state's territory. Like the older Habiru, they had no natural attachment to the city-state system; their political relations with the Shechemite state, like their economic, consisted less of competition than of connivance, but fell short of undifferentiated social integration. In all, the reconstruction of Joshua 9–10 does not seem too wide of the mark.

Even if the success in the Aijalon Pass was a victory for a whole bloc of highlands dwellers, Israelite and Hivite, it would have had two ramifications for the "Hebrews." First, it would have buttressed their political position and prestige in the highlands, enabling them to augment the territory and markets available for their exploitation. Second, it would have promoted still further immigration from Transjordan, from Syria, from other "Hebrews." If the Hivites of the central hills had "given all the land of Shechem to the Habiru," the "Hebrews" had not been patient, passive partners in the process. Nor had they restricted themselves solely to the "land of Shechem."

d. The Development of Israelite Identity. Of two things regarding Iron I we may be certain: that an explosion in population not explicable on the basis of natural increase transformed conditions in the areas of Israelite habitation (predicted in Halpern 1983: 98–99 and confirmed in Finkelstein 1983; Gal 1990; Zertal 1986), registering particularly in an expansion in area cultivated and the number of villages; and, that the burgeoning population had a sense of unity, however loose, which they expressed in the name Israel, in their common devotion to a god, Yhwh, and in their general assimilation of a national history, of ancestral lore, embracing them as one and articulating their identity (compare the American myths of Jamestown and the Mayflower). Just as the Edomites, Moabites, and Ammonites had crystallized into national units transcending the bournes of individual towns, so Israelite identity evolved across older territorial boundaries based on endogamy, religion, and culture.

Propinquity and natural obstacles lent this concept nuance. The inhabitants of the central hills, themselves divided into three districts (tribes, lit. "staves") corresponding to differences in location and terrain, constituted a distinct *ʾummâ*, or mother-unit (the etymology of Ar *hamula:* Cohen 1965: 2f.), Rachel, in the eponymic folklore. The tribes of this *ʾummâ* were all full brothers, expressing their close relation to one another. But the tribesmen outside the central hills, conceived of, like the Rachel-tribes, as children of the father Israel, had other eponymous matriarchs (Leah, Zilpah, Bilhah): to these tribes' eponyms, the eponyms of the Rachel-tribes were only half-brothers, that is, more distant relations. The ancestral lore thus functioned to express economic, ecological, geographic, and political relationships. Yet it could do so only approximately: the tribal divisions themselves represented no more than a mode of organizing discussion and thought about the components of the basic unit, Israel. In the early period, "tribes" were not programmatic, mutually exclusive administrative entities, as the relationship between Simeon and Judah, or between Joseph and the Joseph tribes, or between the clans of Reuben and those of Judah, illustrates (de Geus 1976: 124–80; Gottwald 1979: 295–318).

How soon this sense of identity came to be shared by those who frequented the territory between the Arnon and the Jabbok is unclear. Here, geographic discontinuity had led local "Hebrews" to dissociate themselves from the national networks of Ammon to the N and of Moab to the S. Already by the time of Deborah (Judg 5:15–17), they had declared themselves, linking their destinies probably through commerce and kinship to those of their Cisjordanian neighbors. The choice may reflect a desire to elect looser, less organized "protectors" over against more structured ones. Though Gilead was a source or channel for Cisjordanian homesteaders, it might have developed affinities for Moab or Ammon instead of for Israel, and the fact that it did not, merits consideration.

The Song of Deborah (Judges 5) affords a chronological framework for these developments. Under no circumstances can the events described in the song be placed later than the 12th century B.C.E., and a situation in the middle of the century suits them best. The ode already gives vent to a vision of Yhwh as setting forth on his march to war from Edom (v 4), an element typologically infusing or extracted from the Exodus-Conquest cycle (as Deut 33:1–3; Ps 68:8–9). Under the circumstances, it is probable that elements in Transjordan had also had experience of the Exodus. This conclusion sustains and draws support from the opinion that the "Mosaic" community consisted of "Hebrew" migrants through Transjordan down to the periphery of Egyptian control.

As noted above (B.3; note C.4.), the Song of Deborah, the Song of the Sea (Exodus 15) and all of subsequent tradition testify that these "Hebrews" distinguished themselves ethnicly from their neighbors. Even the Hivites of Gibeon and Shechem, alongside whom the Iron I community dwelt, remained distinct into the monarchic era. Only as Egyptian power waned, however, and its own demographic fortunes waxed, was Israel able to exercise its ambitions to revise the political map of Canaan. Egypt's decline drew into the N part of its Asian empire Assyrian as well as "Hebrew" elements—the Assyrian in the shape of Tiglath-Pileser I's foray to the Mediterranean. Egyptian withdrawal precipitated a struggle for the succession, a wolfpack's fierce fighting over scraps and over dominance.

The parties to this affray were the old city-states of the Canaanite lowlands, the Philistines and other Sea-Peoples, and the highland-dwelling Israelites. Their fortunes varied over the succeeding century, often called "the period of the Judges." What is significant, if natural, is that it is at this point—the start of the clamor for Canaan—that Israel emerges, in the Song of Deborah, from the mists of her proto-history (and the Merneptah stela) to the light of day. It was in the aftermath of imperial Egypt's demise that Israel developed into the grand entity on which David's dominions would be based. Like those of the Transjordanian powers, like that of the Philistines, Israel's path into Canaan was slow and rocky. Like theirs, Israel's "Conquest" was in any conventional sense the consequence of the melee among Egypt's successor states. The war for the succession lasted a century. It culminated in the rise of the Davidic Empire, which reconstituted that of the Ramessides in Asia. In this respect, as in so many others, Alt's understanding of the *Landnahme* has proved prescient and compelling to many scholars.

Bibliography

Aharoni, Y. 1970. New Aspects of the Israelite Occupation in the North. Pp. 254–67 in *Near Eastern Archaeology in the Twentieth Century*, ed. J. A. Sanders. Garden City.

Albright, W. F. 1932. *The Excavation of Tell Beit Mirsim.* Vol. 1. AASOR 12. Cambridge, MA.

———. 1939. The Israelite Conquest of Canaan in the Light of Archaeology. *BASOR* 74: 11–23.

Albright, W. F., and Kelso, J. L. 1968. *The Excavation of Bethel (1934–1960).* AASOR 39. Cambridge, MA.

Alt, A. 1925. *Die Landnahme der Israeliten in Palästina.* Leipzig.

———. 1930. *Die Staatenbildung der Israeliten in Palästina.* Leipzig.

———. 1936. Josua. Pp. 13–29 in *Werden und Wesen des Alten Testaments,* ed. P. Volz et al. BZAW 66. Berlin.

———. 1939. Erwägungen über die Landnahme der Israeliten in Palästina. *PJ* 35: 8–63.

Amir, D. 1980. The Galilee in the Canaanite Period and Israelite Settlement. Diss., Hebrew University.

Beck, P., and Kochavi, M. 1983. The Egyptian Governor's Palace at Apheq. *Qad* 16: 47–51.

Bienkowski, P. 1986. *Jericho in the Late Bronze Age.* Warminster.

Budde, K. 1895. The Nomadic Ideal in the Old Testament. *New World* 4: 726–45.

Callaway, J. A. 1968. New Evidence on the Conquest of Ai. *JBL* 87: 312–20.

———. 1976. Excavating Ai (et-Tell): 1964–1972. *BA* 39: 18–30.

Chaney, M. L. 1983. Ancient Palestinian Peasant Movements and the Formation of Premonarchic Israel. Pp. 39–90 in *Palestine in Transition,* ed. D. N. Freedman and D. F. Graf. SWBA 2. Sheffield.

Cohen, A. 1965. *Arab Border-Villages in Israel.* Manchester.

Cohen, R. 1985. La Fonction du Réseau/des Fortresses. *MB* 39: 45–48.

Cross, F. M. 1979. *Symposia Celebrating the Seventy-fifth Anniversary of the Founding of the ASOR.* Cambridge, MA.

Edzard, D. O., et al. 1970. *Kamid el-Loz—Kumidi.* Saarbrücker Beiträge zur Altertumskunde 7. Bonn.

Ewald, H. 1843–55. *Geschichte des Volkes Israel bis Christus.* 5 vols. Göttingen.

Finkelstein, I. 1983. The ᶜIzbet Ṣarṭah Excavations and the Israelite Settlement in the Hill Country. Diss., Tel Aviv.

———. 1984. The Iron Age "Fortresses" of the Negev Highlands: Sendentarization of the Nomads. *TA* 11: 189–209.

———. 1986a. The Israelite Settlement. The Sociological School and the Test of the Archaeological Evidence. *Iyyune Miqra ve-Parshanut* 2: 175–86.

———. 1986b. *ᶜIzbet Ṣarṭah, An Early Iron Age Site near Rosh Ha'ayin.* BARIS 299. Oxford.

Flight, J. W. 1923. The Nomadic Idea and Ideal in the Old Testament. *JBL* 42: 158–226.

Fritz, V. 1981. The Israelite "Conquest" in the Light of Recent Excavations at Khirbet el-Meshâsh. *BASOR* 241: 61–73.

———. 1987. Conquest or Settlement? The Early Iron Age in Palestine. *BA* 50: 84–100.

Fritz, V., and Kempinski, A. 1983. *Ergebnisse der Ausgrabungen auf der Ḥirbet el-Mšāš (Tel Masos) 1972–1975.* Wiesbaden.

Gal, Z. 1983. The Settlement of the Lower Galilee. Diss., Tel Aviv.

———. 1990. *Ha-Galil ha-Tahton.* Tel Aviv (in Hebrew).

Geus, C. H. J. de. 1976. *The Tribes of Israel.* SSN 18. Assen.

Gonen, R. 1984. Urban Canaan in the Late Bronze Period. *BASOR* 253: 61–73.

Goody, J. R. 1969. *Comparative Studies in Kinship.* London.

Gottwald, N. K. 1979. *The Tribes of Yahweh.* New York.

Grayson, A. K. 1987. *Assyrian Rulers of the Third and Second Millennia BC.* Royal Inscriptions of Mesopotamia Assyrian Periods 1. Toronto.

Greenberg, R. 1987. New Light on the Early Iron Age at Tell Beit Mirsim. *BASOR* 265: 55–80.

Gressmann, H. 1913. *Mose und seine Zeit.* FRLANT n.s. 1. Göttingen.

Guthe, H. 1900. *Geschichte des Volkes Israel.* Grundriss der theologischen Wissenschaft 2/3. Leipzig.

Halpern, B. 1983. *The Emergence of Israel in Canaan.* SBLMS 29. Chico.

———. 1987. Dialect Distribution in Canaan and the Deir Alla Inscriptions. Pp. 119–39 in *"Working with No Data."* Ed. D. Golomb and S. Hollis. Winona Lake, IN.

Harding, G. L., et al. 1953. *Four Tomb Groups.* Annual of the Palestine Exploration Fund 6. London.

Haupt, P. 1909. The Burning Bush and the Origin of Judaism. *Proceedings of the American Philosophic Society* 48: 354–69.

Helck, W. 1968. Die Bedrohung Palästinas durch einwandernde Gruppen am Ende der 18. und am Anfang der 19. Dynastie. *VT* 18: 472–80.

Hellwig, S., and Adjeman, Y. 1986. Animal Bones. Pp. 141–52 in Finkelstein 1986b.

Hesse, B. 1986. Animal Use at Tel Miqne-Eqron in the Bronze Age and Iron Age. *BASOR* 264: 17–28.

Holladay, J. S., Jr. 1968. The Day(s) the Moon Stood Still. *JBL* 87: 166–78.

———. fc. The Stables of Ancient Israel. In *The Archaeology of Jordan and Other Studies,* ed. L. T. Geraty.

Ibrahim, M. M. 1978. The Collared-Rim Jar of the Early Iron Age. Pp. 117–26 in *Archaeology in the Levant,* ed. R. Moorey and P. Parr. Warminster.

Ibrahim, M. M.; Sauer, J. A.; and Yassine, K. 1976. The East Jordan Valley Survey, 1975. *BASOR* 222: 41–66.

Kaufmann, Y. 1962. *The Book of Judges.* Jerusalem.

———. 1966. *History of the Israelite Faith.* Jerusalem and Tel-Aviv.

Kempinski, A. 1985. The Overlap of Cultures at the End of the Late Bronze Age and the Beginning of the Iron Age. *EI* 18: 399–407.

Khalil, L. 1984. Metallurgical Analyses of Some Weapons from Tell el-ᶜAjjul. *Levant* 16: 167–70.

Khazanov, A. 1983. *Nomads and the Outside World.* Cambridge.

Kittel, R. 1888. *Geschichte der Hebräer.* Vol. 1. Handbücher der alten Geschichte 1/1. Gotha.

Kochavi, M. 1974. Khirbet Rabûd = Debir. *TA* 1: 2–34.

MacDonald, B. 1983. The Late Bronze and Iron Age Sites of the Wadi el Ḥasā Survey 1979. Pp. 18–28 in *Midian, Moab and Edom.* Ed. J. F. A. Sawyer and D. J. A. Clines. JSOTSup 24. Sheffield.

Machinist, P. 1982. Provincial Governance in Middle Assyria and Some New Texts from Yale. *Assur* 3/2.

Malamat, A. 1955. Doctrines of Causality in Hittite and Biblical Historiography: A Parallel. *VT* 5: 1–12.

———. 1971. The Egyptian Decline in Canaan and the Sea-Peoples. Pp. 23–38 in *Judges,* ed. B. Mazar. WHJP 1/3. Rutgers.

———. 1978. *Early Israelite Warfare and the Conquest of Canaan.* 4th Sacks Lecture. Oxford.

Mazar, A. 1981a. Canaanites, Philistines and Israelites of Timnah/Tel Batashi. *Qad* 51/52: 89–96.

———. 1981b. Giloh: An Early Israelite Settlement Site near Jerusalem. *IEJ* 31: 1–36.

———. 1982. A Cult Site in the Samaria Mountains from the Period of the Judges. *EI* 16: 135–45.

Mazar, B. 1985. Biblical Archaeology Today: The Historical Aspect. Pp. 16–20 in *BibAT.*

Mendenhall, G. E. 1962. The Hebrew Conquest of Palestine. *BA* 25: 66–87.

———. 1983. Ancient Israel's Hyphenated History. Pp. 91–103 in *Palestine in Transition,* ed. D. H. Freedman and D. F. Graf. SWBA 2. Sheffield.

Meyer, E. 1881. Kritik der Berichte über die Eroberung Palästinas (Num. 20,14 bis Jud. 2,5). *ZAW* 1: 117–46.
———. 1906. *Die Israeliten und ihre Nachbarstämme.* Halle.
Millard, A. R. 1980. A Wandering Aramean. *JNES* 39: 153–55.
———. 1981. Events at the End of the Late Bronze Age in the Near East. Pp. 1–15 in *The Trojan War,* ed. L. Foxhall and J. K. Davies. 1st Greenbank Colloquium. Liverpool.
Miller, J. M. 1982. Recent Archaeological Developments Relevant to Ancient Moab. Vol. 1, pp. 169–73 in *Studies in the History and Archaeology of Jordan,* ed. A. Hadidi. Amman.
Mittmann, S. 1970. *Beiträge zur Siedlungs- und Territorialgeschichte des nördlichen Ostjordanlandes.* ADPV. Wiesbaden.
Moran, W. L. 1987. Join the ʿApiru or Become One? Pp. 209–212 in *"Working with No Data."* Ed. D. M. Golomb. Winona Lake, IN.
Naʾaman, N. 1986. Habiru and Hebrews: The Transfer of a Social Term to the Literary Sphere. *JNES* 45: 271–88.
Noth, M. 1930. *Das System der zwölf Stämme Israels.* BWANT 4/1. Stuttgart.
Oren, E. D. 1985. The Architecture of Egyptian "Governors' Residencies" in Late Bronze Age Palestine. *EI* 18: 183–99.
Paton, L. B. 1900. *The Early History of Syria and Palestine.* The Semitic Series 3. London.
Pleiner, R. 1979. The Technology of Three Assyrian Iron Artifacts from Khorsabad. *JNES* 38: 83–91.
Procksch, O. 1906. *Das nordhebräische Sagenbuch.* Leipzig.
Redford, D. B. 1986. The Ashkelon Relief at Karnak and the Israel Stele. *IEJ* 36: 188–200.
Rosen, B. 1986. Subsistence Economy of Stratum II. Pp. 156–85 in Finkelstein 1986b.
Sauer, J. A. 1979. Iron I Pillared House in Moab. *BA* 42: 9.
———. 1986. Transjordan in the Bronze and Iron Ages: A Critique of Glueck's Synthesis. *BASOR* 263: 1–26.
Sawyer, J. F. A. 1983. The meaning of *barzel* in the Biblical expressions 'Chariots of Iron,' 'Yoke of Iron,' etc. Pp. 129–34 in *Midian, Moab and Edom.* Ed. J. F. A. Sawyer and D. J. A. Clines. JSOTSup 24. Sheffield.
Shiloh, Y. 1984. *Excavations at the City of David.* Vol. 1. Qedem 19. Jerusalem.
Singer, I. 1988. Merneptah's Campaign to Canaan and the Egyptian Occupation of the Southern Coastal Plain of Palestine in the Ramesside Period. *BASOR* 269: 1–10.
Stade, B. 1881a. Lea und Rachel. *ZAW* 1: 112–16, 146–50.
———. 1881b. *Geschichte des Volkes Israel.* Vol. 1. Berlin.
Stager, L. E. 1985a. The Archaeology of the Family in Ancient Israel. *BASOR* 260: 1–35.
———. 1985b. Merenptah, Israel and Sea Peoples. *EI* 18: 56–64.
Steuernagel, C. 1901. *Die Einwanderung der israelitischen Stämme in Kanaan.* Leipzig.
Tadmor, H. 1979. The Decline of Empires in Western Asia ca. 1200 B. C. E. Pp. 1–14 in Cross 1979.
Thureau-Dangin, F. 1912. *Une relation de la huitième campagne de Sargon (714 av. J.-C.).* TCL 3. Paris.
Toombs, L. E. 1979. Shechem: Problems of the Early Israelite Era. Pp. 69–83 in Cross 1979.
Ussishkin, D. 1985. Levels VII and VI at Tel Lachish and the End of the Late Bronze Age in Canaan. Pp. 213–30 in *Palestine in the Bronze and Iron Ages,* ed. J. N. Tubb. London.
Vaux, R. de. 1971. *Histoire ancienne d'Israël.* Paris.
Waldbaum, J. C. 1978. *From Bronze to Iron: The Transition from the Bronze Age to the Iron Age in the Eastern Mediterranean.* Studies in Mediterranean Archaeology 54. Göteberg.
Wapnish, P., and Hesse, B. fc. *Philistine/Israelite Animal Use in Iron Age Canaan.*
Weinfeld, M. 1967. The Period of the Conquest and of the Judges as Seen by the Earlier and the Later Sources. *VT* 17: 93–113.
———. 1983. The Extent of the Promised Land. Pp. 59–75 in *Das Land Israel in biblischer Zeit,* ed. G. Strecker. Göttingen.
Weinstein, J. M. 1981. The Egyptian Empire in Palestine: A Reassessment. *BASOR* 241: 1–28.
Weippert, M. 1967. *Die Landnahme der israelitischen Stämme in der neueren wissenschaftlichen Diskussion.* FRLANT 92. Göttingen.
———. 1974. Semitische Nomaden des zweiten Jahrtausends. über die š³św der ägyptischen Quellen. *Bib* 55: 265–80.
———. 1979. The Israelite "Conquest" and the Evidence from Transjordan. Pp. 16–34 in Cross 1979.
Wellhausen, J. 1894. *Israelitische und jüdische Geschichte.* Berlin.
———. 1963. *Die Composition des Hexateuchs und der historischen Bücher des Alten Testaments.* 4th ed. Berlin.
Wood, B. G. 1989. *The Late Bronze II/Iron IA Pottery Transition in Palestine.* ASORDS. Baltimore.
Wright, G. E. 1946. The Literary and Historical Problem of Joshua 10 and Judges 1. *JNES* 5: 105–14.
Yadin, Y. 1972. *Hazor.* London.
Zertal, A. 1986a. How Can Kempinski Be So Wrong! *BARev* 12: 43–53.
———. 1986b. *The Israelite Settlement in the Hills of Manasseh.* Diss., Tel Aviv.

BARUCH HALPERN

SEVEN CHURCHES [Gk *hai hepta ekklēsiai*]. The seven churches are those in seven cities of the Roman province of proconsular Asia on the west central coast of Asia Minor. They are the addressees of Revelation (1:4, 11, 20), and individual letters are addressed to each of them in Revelation 2–3. The use of the article indicates that the seven churches were a recognized group: Ephesus, Smyrna, Pergamum, Thyatira, Sardis, Philadelphia, and Laodicea.

The question arises, "Why does the author only write to seven churches when there were others in the province of Asia?" These other churches include Troas (Acts 20:5–12; 2 Cor 2:12), Colossae (Col 1:2; 2:1), and Hierapolis (Col 4:13). Ignatius addressed letters to Magnesia *(Magn.)* and Tralles *(Trall.)* less than two decades later. More fanciful explanations are that these seven churches are symbolic of the types of churches to be found during the church age, or of seven sequential periods of church history. A more accepted explanation takes into account that seven is a number of completeness. The seven churches are representative or heads of all the churches in the region with which the author is familiar and expects his letter to reach, or are representative of the Church at large.

The explanation of William Ramsay (1904: 171–96) has received wide support. He proposed that these church cities were selected because, in their given order, they are the postal and judicial districts which a courier from Patmos would encounter and from which his letter could be distributed most effectively throughout the province of Asia. From Patmos, the letter courier would arrive at Ephesus, travel N to Smyrna and Pergamum, and then turn SE to Thyatira, Sardis, Philadelphia, and Laodicea. This forms a circular route through the west central portion of the province. Other church cities not mentioned are located beyond the main circular route and could easily be reached on a secondary route from one of these seven cities.

Ramsay's explanation has the advantages of fitting the geographical positioning of the seven cities, maintaining the sequential order in which they are presented, and explaining why other church cities are not mentioned. It also corresponds to what we know of early Church communication elsewhere. For example, if Ephesians is an encyclical, then it may have been similarly distributed to neighboring churches. Also, when Paul sent his letter to Colossae, the Colossians were to send it on to Laodicea, and Laodicea was to reciprocate with their letter from Paul as well (Col 4:16).

Bibliography

Hemer, C. 1986. *The Letters to the Seven Churches of Asia in Their Local Setting.* JSNTSup 11. Sheffield.

Ramsay, W. 1904. *Letters to the Seven Churches.* London.

Yamauchi, E. M. 1980. *The Archaeology of New Testament Cities in Western Asia Minor.* Grand Rapids.

DUANE F. WATSON

SEX AND SEXUALITY. Sex is at once much-discussed and ignored in the Bible. In the narrative portions of the Bible, sexuality appears only occasionally as a motive or force for actions and history. The beauty of women may set them up as victims of men who abuse their superior strength and position in order to possess them: the Pharaoh desired and took Sarah because she was beautiful (Gen 13:10–20), as did David with Bathsheba (2 Samuel 11). Similarly, the beauty of Tamar induced Amnon to rape her (2 Samuel 13). In the Bible, women are not depicted as being in control of this erotic attraction: the Hebrew Bible has no story in which a woman exploits her beauty or erotic attraction as a weapon by which to control or manipulate men. Granted, Tamar (Genesis 38) and Ruth maneuver men into sexual liasons, but they do so not to weedle something else from them as much as to attain the direct benefits of the liason itself: family and progeny. Unlike the later Judith of the Apocrypha, who uses her sexual charms to seduce and murder Holofernes, Jael defeats Sisera with her deceptive nurturing (Judges 4). Unlike the Delilah of modern Western lore who likewise weakens Samson's resolve by toying with his sexual passions, the biblical Delilah instead simply nags him into revealing the secret of his strength (Judges 16).

A. Sex, Marriage, and Family
  1. Adultery
  2. Chastity
  3. Rape
  4. Incest
B. Commingling: Bestiality and Homosexual Practices
C. Sexuality and Purity
D. The Metaphysics of Sexuality

A. Sex, Marriage, and Family

The lack of a *femme fatale* figure in biblical narrative might suggest that the Bible had a cavalier attitude about sexuality. However, the mythological and legal portions of the Bible show a deep concern for sex and its proper manifestations. In the Bible, the appropriate locus of sexuality is the monogamous nuclear family, the ideal human relationship. The creation account of Genesis 2 emphasizes the fundamental nature of such marriage, for God created woman to be the suitable companion to man. The message is reinforced by an interruption in the narrative, a direct aside to the reader: "therefore a man leaves his father and mother and cleaves to his wife and they become one flesh" (Gen 2:24). Marriage in the real world was somewhat problematic, particularly for the wife, who was economically dependent on her husband and at least nominally under his control, and who faced the danger and difficulties of childbirth and child-rearing. The glue that held marriage together and caused women to accept these conditions was sexual attraction: "your desire will be for your husband and he will rule over you" (Gen 3:16).

The Bible considers a strong marital unit essential to societal well-being, with sex cementing the marital bond. The societal interest in conjugal sex is reflected in Deuteronomy's provision that new bridegrooms be exempt from military campaigns for a year in order to cause the wives to rejoice (Deut 20:7; 24:5). Intact families demand sexual fidelity, and the best way to ensure this is to find sexual satisfaction in marriage: "find joy in the wife of your youth . . . let her breasts satisfy you at all times, be infatuated with love of her always" (Prov 5:18–19).

1. Adultery. Israel viewed extra-marital sexuality in the severest light, prescribing death for adultery. As in the rest of the ANE, there was a double standard: males could have sex outside marriage, most notably with prostitutes: "adultery" meant copulation with a *married* woman. Beyond concern for property rights or clear paternity, the demand for sexual exclusivity for wives sought to prevent married women from establishing bonds that could weaken the family unit. Women's sexual behavior increasingly became a matter of public interest rather than the sole jurisdiction of the head of the household. In the Middle Assyrian laws, husbands had the right to pardon or determine the penalty for his adulterous wife and, with her, her partner in adultery. Biblical laws demand the death penalty absolutely. A hint of husbandly jurisdiction is nevertheless found in the book of Proverbs, in which the young man is warned against adultery for "the fury of the husband will be passionate; he will show no pity on his day of vengeance. He will not have regard for any ransom; he will refuse your bribe, however great" (Prov 6:34–35). This passage indicates, perhaps, an awareness that the husband had (by custom) the right to pardon the adulterer, but an expectation that irate husbands would not do so. See also ADULTERY.

2. Chastity. A lessening of father's disposition over daughter's sexual behavior may be detected within the biblical period. In premonarchic times, the head of household had great authority. Lot's offering his daughters to the men of Sodom (Genesis 18–19), the Levite's offering his concubine to the men of Gibeah, and the Ephraimite's offering his daughter to them (Judges 19) were responses to emergency rather than normal actions. Nevertheless, the narratives do not condemn their actions; Lot, in particular, is considered righteous for offering his virgin daughters in order to save wayfarers. The laws of Exodus reflect this parental authority. At all periods, girls living in their father's house were expected to be chaste. In the laws of Exodus (22:14–16), a man who seduced a single girl had to offer to marry her and pay the proper brideprice. But the father had the option to refuse this offer of marriage and determine the fate of his daughter. The father's right of determination seems weaker in the Deuteronomic laws: if a man grabs an unbetrothed girl he must pay the father 50 shekels, and he *must* marry her, without the possibility of divorce (Deut 22:28–29). No mention is made of father's right of refusal. The Deuteronomy section deals with rape, rather than seduction, but the difference between Exodus and Deuteronomy does not seem due to this, but rather to the emergence in Deuteronomy of *public* concern and control over sexual behavior: in Deuteronomy, the entire community has an interest in assuring the chastity of young girls.

A similar example of Deuteronomy's *public* concern for female chastity is the rule of the non-virgin bride (Deut 22:20f). If her unsuspecting bridegroom accused her, with proof, of being non-virgin, she was to be stoned, a communal form of execution reserved in the Bible for offenses that upset the order of the universe and thus threaten the entire community. The mode of "proof" reveals this law as, an object lesson in public concern. If the parents of the girl produced the bloody nuptual sheet before the elders, then the accusing bridegroom was flogged and fined and had to remain married to her for life. If they did not produce a bloody sheet, then she would be stoned. She and her parents would have to be ignorant not to find blood for the sheets, and knowing this, it is unlikely that a bridegroom would make such a charge. But the rule clearly indicates that the elders as judges and the people as executioners have an interest in the girl's chastity and will act to protect their interest.

3. Rape. Deuteronomy also prescribes stoning when a man "comes upon" a betrothed girl in town and sleeps with her. The girl is stoned because she did "not cry out," meaning that the sex was consensual (Deut 22:23–24); the man because he had illicit sex with his neighbor's wife. The term used for the man's behavior is *ʿinnâ,* normally translated "rape," but *ʿinnâ* is generally "statutory" rather than forcible rape. A man who has sex with a woman without proper arrangements is said to "rape" (*ʿnh;* cf. *BDB,* 776) the woman even if she consents. This usage is found in the story of Dinah and Shechem (Genesis 34). Dinah had gone out and Shechem, seeing her, lay with her and had illicit sex *(ʿnh)* with her. In this way he treated her as a "whore" (Gen 34:31) rather than as a proper woman whose parents have to be consulted. Forcible rape is punishable by death and is explicitly linked to murder, a realization that rape is a crime of aggression and violence rather than sex, and that the girl is a victim (Deut 22:25–27).

4. Incest. The Bible defines the parameters of sexual behavior by forbidding intolerable relationships. Sexual relationships may not infringe on another family; they may also not blur the lines in one's own family through incest. Leviticus 18 and 20 and Deuteronomy 27 detail strong incest prohibitions. In one's parent's generation, sex with parents, step-mother, paternal uncle and wife, and both maternal and paternal aunts was prohibited. One's mother's brother and wife are not mentioned: were they considered from a different family (and therefore not prohibited)? One's father's brother's children (first cousins) and one's brother's and sister's daughters (nieces) are also not mentioned; but since one's paternal uncle is prohibited, we might infer that his daughter is also. In one's own generation, both sister and brother's wife were prohibited. In the succeeding generation, one's daughter-in-law is prohibited, as are one's granddaughters. One's wife's lineage is also off limits: mother-in-law, wife's sister (while wife is alive), wife's daughters and granddaughters.

There is a difference in the amount of control that Israel could exert to forbid these incestuous relationships. In Leviticus 20, adultery, homosexuality, bestiality, and copulation with step-mother, mother-in-law, and daughter-in-law are all punishable by death. However, sex with sister, sister-in-law, aunt, uncle's wife, and menstruant, although equally prohibited, are beyond societal control. They are to be punished by God. The startling omission of "daughter" from the list of forbidden women may be an indication that paternal position was still considered so strong in the family that the text hesitated even to list an absolute prohibition. From the expectation that an unmarried girl would be virgin, it is clear that father-daughter incest at least was not expected.

Taken together, the incest laws define and clarify family lines. Since marriage creates a family, sexual intercourse with one's father's wife, father's brother's wife, and brother's wife is explicitly prohibited because the *ʿerwâ* (normally translated "nakedness," perhaps meaning exposed genitalia) of the woman is tantamount to the *ʿerwâ* of her husband. So, too, the wife's bloodlines *(šĕʾēr)* are parallel to his own and prohibited. The use of a special term, *zimmâ,* for incest with mother-in-law, wife's sister, wife's daughter and granddaughter, indicates that this intercourse, which is not with blood kin, is a special category of incest. Another term, *tebel,* "(improper) mixing," used for sex with daughter-in-law, demonstrates the biblical concern that sex within the family could blur and collapse family structures.

B. Commingling: Bestiality and Homosexual Practices

Israel's intense interest in regulating sexual behavior is an aspect of its concern to prevent intermingling between individuals and groups who should be separate. The commingling of divine beings and human women threatened to blur the distinction between divine and humans and thereby eradicate "humanity" as a distinct species (Gen 6:1–4). Bestiality contains the same potential, and is strongly forbidden for both males and females (Exod 22:28; Lev 18:23; 20:15–16; Deut 17:21). Like sex with a daughter-in-law, sex with an animal is also called *tebel,* "(improper) mixing." Homosexual intercourse is not labeled *tebel,* but the extreme prohibition of homosexuality by the death penalty (Lev 29:13, cf 18:22), not inherited from other ANE laws, is best explained as a desire to keep the categories of "male" and "female" intact. Anything that blurs the lines, such as cross-dressing, is also prohibited (Deut 22:5). Lesbian interaction, however, is not mentioned, possibly because it did not result in true physical "union" (by male entry). The biblical view of creation is one of organization and structure; collapsing the categories of existence is a return to chaos. See also PUNISHMENTS AND CRIMES.

C. Sexuality and Purity

This ability of sexuality to blur existential categories makes it a cosmic national issue. Like murder, aberrant sexuality could pollute the land and endanger the very survival of Israel. Israel felt that its right of occupation was contingent upon its preserving the purity of the land: if Israel indulged in the same behavior as the people before it, the defiled land would spew them out as it spewed out the nations before Israel (Lev 18:28). The people had to guard the land by not permitting murderers to go free or accidental homicides to leave the cities of refuge (Num 35:31–34) and by not leaving unburied the corpses of those who had been executed (Deut 21:22–23). Similarly, they had to refrain from forbidden sexual relationships, and to observe more technical regulations of sexuality, such as not allowing a man to remarry his divorced wife who had since remarried (Deut 24:1–3; Jer 3:1–4). There were no rituals to purify the land, but two rituals sought to prevent imminent pollution. One, the ritual of the decapitated heifer, was concerned with the pollution of murder. When a corpse was found and the murderer could not be identified, the elders of the city nearest the corpse went to a wadi and decapitated a heifer. They declared their lack of culpability and prayed to avert the blood-pollution of the land (Deut 21:1–9). The trial of the suspected adulteress was concerned with the pollution of adultery. A suspicious husband brought his wife to the temple, where she drank a potion made from holy water, dust from the floor of the sanctuary, and dissolved curse words. At the same time, she answered "amen" to a priestly adjuration that the water would cause her grave consequences if she was guilty. She can then return to her husband, and they can continue normal marital relations.

D. The Metaphysics of Sexuality

In these laws of social control over sexuality and its consequences, we can detect a respect for the power of sexual attraction. Controlled and confined within the marital system, it reinforced the social order. Allowed free reign, it might destroy social arrangements and threaten the existence of civilization. This metaphysics of sex, however, only finds explicit statement once in the Bible: "for love is fierce as death, passion is mighty as Sheol, its darts are darts of fire, a blazing flame. Vast floods cannot quench love, nor rivers drown it" (Song of Songs 8:6–7). Otherwise, there is no explicit reflection on the meaning of sexuality nor its place in the cosmic order.

The reason for this absence may be monotheism itself. There is no sexuality in the divine sphere. God, usually envisioned as male in gender, is not phallic; God does not represent male virility, and is never imaged below the waist. The prophets use a powerful marital metaphor for the relationship between God, the "husband," and Israel, the "wife," but the relationship is not described in erotic language. God neither models nor grants sexual potency or attraction. This absence of sex from the divine realm and of God from the sexual realm is accompanied by a separation of sexuality from the realm of the holy. Moses and the people had to abstain from sexual activity for three days before the revelation at Sinai (Exod 19:15). So too, David assured Ahimelech that he and his men could eat hallowed bread because they had been away from women for three days (1 Sam 21:4–5). The priests of Israel were not a reflection of God, and celibacy was a totally foreign idea; yet they modelled controlled sexual behavior. When the sons of Eli slept with the women who came to worship, they forfeited their family's right to be priests (1 Sam 2:22–24). The priest could not marry a prostitute or a divorcee (Lev 22:7), and if his daughter was not chaste, she was to be burnt for profaning her father (Lev 22:9).

All hints of sexuality were to be kept far away from cultic life and religious experience. People had to wait a day after sexual intercourse or nocturnal emission before coming to the temple (Lev 15:16–18), and the wages of a prostitute could not be given to the temple as a gift. There were *qědēšôt* in the temple until the time of Josiah. Until recently, these were understood as temple prostitutes, implying sacred prostitution. However, more recent studies have revealed that there is no basis for finding sacred prostitution in Israel. See PROSTITUTION; PROSTITUTION (CULTIC). Similarly, previous theories about Canaanite orgiastic rites or pagan sexual fertility rituals cannot be substantiated. The separation of sexuality from the realm of the holy should not be seen as a polemic against pagan religion but as a result of the lack of sexuality in the conception of the divine. This created a vacuum in thinking about sex, one that was ultimately replaced by the negative Greek ideas about women and sexuality which entered Israel in the Hellenistic period.

Bibliography

Cosby, M. R. 1985. *Sex in the Bible.* Englewood Cliffs, NJ.
Dubarle, A. M. 1967. *Amour et Fecondité dans le Bible.* Toulouse.
Finkelstein, J. J. 1981. *The Ox that Gored.* TAPhS 71. Philadelphia.
Frymer-Kensky, T. 1983. Purity, Pollution and Purgation in Biblical Israel. Pp. 399–414 in *WLSGF.*
———. 1984. The Strange Case of the Suspected Sotah (Numbers 5:11–31). *VT* 34: 11–26.
———. 1989. Law and Philosophy: The Case of Sex in the Bible. *Semeia* 45: 89–102.
———. fc. *In the Wake of the Goddesses.*
Larue, G. 1983. *Sex and the Bible.* Buffalo.
Oden, R. 1987. *The Bible Without Theology.* San Francisco.
Perry, F. L. 1982. *Sex and the Bible.* Atlanta.
Van Seters, J. 1987. Love and Death in the Court History of David. Pp. 121–24 in *Love and Death in the ANE,* ed. by J. Marks and R. Good. Guilford, CT.

TIKVA FRYMER-KENSKY

SEXTUS, SENTENCES OF (NHC XII,*1*). A collection of Greek wisdom sayings assembled by a Christian redactor probably near the end of the 2d century C.E. A 4th century Latin translation by Rufinus enjoyed popularity in the West. Also copies in Syriac, Armenian, and Georgian are extant. In the nineteenth century two mss of the Gk *Sent. Sextus* were discovered. Codex XII from Nag Hammadi adds to these a fragmentary copy of a version in Sahidic Coptic. No title or page numbers survive; of the estimated original 39 pages only 10 are extant and all have suffered considerable loss. They represent maxims 157–180 and 307–397 of the 451 maxims known to Rufinus.

The value of the Coptic *Sent. Sextus* is textual. It proves to be a faithful, consistent translation which lends significant support to the critical Greek text established by H. Chadwick (1959). The only differences are the omission of maxim 162a and two minor changes in sequence. No attempt was made by the translator to change the theological or ethical outlook of the Greek text. Since the Coptic text predates the Syr mss by two and the Gk mss by five centuries, it is an important witness to the text, order and the divisions of the Gk maxims known to the Coptic translator near the beginning of the 4th century or perhaps even earlier.

Sent. Sextus are not gnostic in origin. Most of the maxims appear to have been drawn from Stoic and Pythagorean collections. Their appearance among gnostic writings is not more surprising than the popularity they enjoyed in Christian orthodoxy. The gnostic tractates in the Nag Hammadi collection contradict the belief that gnostics put no value in the virtuous life or that they tended towards libertinism. Evidently their spiritual elitism was matched by a profound asceticism for which the heavenly life was the model. This is also the preoccupation of the *Sent. Sextus* as well as such other non-gnostic, Nag Hammadi tractates as *The Exegesis on the Soul* (NHC II,*6*), *The Book of Thomas the Contender* (NHC II,*7*), *The Acts of Peter and the Twelve Apostles* (NHC VI,*1*), *Authoritative Teaching* (VI,*3*), and *The Teaching of Silvanus* (VII,*4*). The ascetic outlook is the only obvious link between this diverse collection of texts. It lends support to the conclusion, based on the waste papyrus in the cover of Codex VII, that the Nag Hammadi codices were produced and used in a Pachomian monastery before they were buried in a jar near Chenoboskia.

Bibliography

Chadwick, H. 1959. *The Sentences of Sextus.* TextsS. Cambridge.
Poirier, P.-H. 1983. *Les sentences de Sextus (NH XII,3).* BCNHT 11. Quebec.
Wisse, F. 1975. Die Sextus-Sprüche und das Problem der gnostischen Ethik. Pp. 55–86 in *Zum Hellenismus in den Schriften von Nag Hammadi.* ed. A. Böhlig and F. Wisse. Göttinger Orientforschungen 6/2. Wiesbaden.
———. 1988. The Sentences of Sextus (XII,1). *NHL,* 503–8.

Frederik Wisse

SEXUAL IMPURITIES. See DISCHARGE.

SHAALBIM (PLACE) [Heb *šaʿalbîm*]. Var. SHAALABBIN. A city within the tribal territory of Dan (Josh 19:42 note var. spelling Shaalabbin [Heb *šaʿălabbîn*]), probably to be identified with Selbit (M.R. 148141), about 3 miles NW of Aijalon. It was one of the cities where the Danites failed to dislodge the old Amorite population, but the Ephraimites later succeeded in suppressing the Amorites and putting them to forced labor (Judg 1:35). Shaalbim also appears in the list of cities that made up Solomon's second administrative district (1 Kgs 4:9). Possibly one should also identify Shaalbon, the home of one of David's thirty mighty men (2 Sam 23:32; 1 Chr 11:33), as the same city.

Excavations carried out at Selbit in 1949 uncovered the foundation of a building which was identified as a Samaritan synagogue constructed in the 4th or 5th century C.E. The building was built to face in the direction of Mount Gerizim, the holy mountain of the Samaritans. Its mosaic floor was decorated with two seven-branched menorahs with fragments of a Greek inscription appearing above them. The mosaic also contained two fragmentary Samaritan inscriptions, one of which was the Samaritan version of "The Lord shall reign for ever and ever" (Exod 15:18). See D. Barag in *EAEHL* 4: 1070–71.

Wesley I. Toews

SHAALBON (PLACE) [Heb *haššaʿalbōnî,* lit. "the Shaalbonite"]. Apparently the hometown of Eliahba, one of David's elite warriors (2 Sam 23:32 = 1 Chr 11:33). The town should probably be identified with SHAALBIM, a town which is spelled either *šʿlbym* or *šʿlbyn* in various Heb mss.

SHAALIM (PLACE) [Heb *šaʿălîm*]. An area crossed by Saul as he searched for his lost asses (1 Sam 9:4). Shaalim appears to be a specific territory in the land of Ephraim, mentioned nowhere else in the Bible, between Oprah and Rimmon. It is possible that Shaalim is an error for Shaalbim (Judg 1:35; 1 Kgs 4:9) or Shual (1 Sam 13:17). Both of these are geographical names which are in the same general location as Shaalim. Shual is mentioned in relation to the Philistine camp at Michmash; it is near Oprah, in the region N of Bethel in the central hill country. Shaalbim is an Amorite city given to the tribe of Dan, which becomes part of Solomon's second administrative district. It is identified with modern Selbit (M.R. 148141), 3 miles NW of Aijalon.

Sidnie Ann White

SHAAPH (PERSON) [Heb *šaʿap*]. **1.** The youngest of the six sons of Jahdai (1 Chr 2:47). Shaaph was the name of a Judahite, who descended from Jerahmeel's brother Caleb. It should be noted, however, that the precise relationship of Jahdai and his children with any of the individuals mentioned in v 46 is not stated. "Shaaph" was apparently a non-theophoric name, meaning "balm" (as does also the Jewish Palestinian Aramaic term *šaʿăpāʾ*). The name gave expression to the parents' joy over the child (*IPN,* 223).

2. The third son of Maacah, Caleb's second concubine (1 Chr 2:49). Shaaph founded the town of Madmannah (Josh 15:31), which has been identified with Khirbet Tatrît in the N Negeb/S Judean hill country (*LBHG,* 353, 439). Pace (1976: 146) thinks a name was omitted in 1 Chr 2:49 before "father of Gibea"; the missing person would be parallel to Shaaph and Sheva as descendants of Caleb. Sheva, incidentally, carries the same name (*šwʾ*) as that of a few Jews recorded in Aram correspondence from Elephantine (*TAD* A, 38; *BMAP,* 284). The rather abrupt beginning of v 49 might reflect a textual displacement.

Some suggest changing the verb from *wattēled,* "she (Maacah) bore," to *wayyôled,* "he (Shaaph) begot" (cf. Vg). This would solve as well the problem of the absence of an expected "and" before "Sheva" (though it is present in the LXX). Under this view Shaaph here would be identical with Jahdai's son of v 47 but would merely have been called the son of Caleb and his concubine.

Bibliography

Pace, J. H. 1976. The Caleb Traditions and the Role of the Calebites in the History of Israel. Ph.D. Diss. Emory University.

EDWIN C. HOSTETTER

SHAARAIM (PLACE) [Heb *šaʿărayim*]. **1.** A town in the Shephelah district of Judah (Josh 15:36). It is listed after Soco and Azekah, and before Adithaim and Gederah. After the defeat of Goliath by David, the Philistines fled "on the Shaaraim road" on their way to Gath and Ekron (1 Sam 17:52). Although its location has not been identified, it has been sought in the region N and W of Azekah in the Elah Valley (Wadi es-Sant; Rainey 1983: 6–7; for a discussion of possible sites see Galil 1985: 61–62). The mention of *Saraein* in Eusebius' *Onomast.* does not aid in identifying the site. Some scholars have advocated following LXX B in reading Shaaraim as a regular noun "gates" (Wellhausen 1871: 109–10) or as corresponding to the town of Tarʿin in the environs of Ashkelon (Tosefta *Ahilot* 18:15; Abel *GP* 2: 439; but see Smith *Samuel* ICC, 165 and Rainey *EncMiqr* 8: 244).

2. A town in the tribal inheritance of Simeon in the Judean Negeb (1 Chr 4:31). In the parallel Simeonite list in Josh 19:6 Sharuhen appears in its place, whereas in the list of towns in the Judean Negeb Shilhim is mentioned (Josh 15:32). Albright (1924: 134–35 n. 6) speaks for the majority of scholars in viewing this mention of Shaaraim as a later scribal error for Sharuhen (but see *CTAED,* 173).

Bibliography

Albright, W. F. 1924. Egypt and the Early History of the Negeb. *JPOS* 4: 131–61.
Galil, G. 1985. The Administrative Division of the Shephelah. Hebrew. Vol. 9, pp. 55–71 in *Shnaton: An Annual for Biblical and Ancient Near Eastern Studies,* ed. M. Weinfeld. Jerusalem.
Rainey, A. F. 1983. The Biblical Shephelah of Judah. *BASOR* 251: 1–22.
Wellhausen, J. 1871. *Der Text der Bücher Samuelis.* Göttingen.

CARL S. EHRLICH

SHAASHGAZ (PERSON) [Heb *šaʿašgaz*]. A eunuch in charge of one of the two harems of king Ahasuerus (Esth 2:14; note vocalization in *BHS, šaʿăšĕgaz*). His specific office "the keeper of the concubines" (Heb *šōmēr happîlagšîm*), entailed the oversight of the harem of Ahasuerus' married wives as opposed to the harem of virgins waiting to be wed to the king under the care of Hegai (Esth 2:3). The LXX confuses these two individuals giving them both the name *Gai* (cf. LXX of Esth 2:8 and 2:14). Shaashgaz is an incidental character in this story being mentioned only in the context of how Ahasuerus selected a new queen. Each prospective wife would leave Hegai's harem and spend just one night with the king at which time she became one of his lesser wives and was sent to Shaashgaz's harem—unless the king liked her enough to make her queen in place of Vashti (Esth 2:13–14). Esther would have been sent to this second harem had she not been chosen as the new queen (Esth 2:16–18). Several scholars have noted similarities between this subplot in the story of Esther and the harem tale of king Shekriya in *1001 Arabian Nights* (Moore *Esther* AB, 23–24, Clines *Ezra, Nehemiah, Esther* NCBC, 266). Shaashgaz's name may be the Heb equivalent of Old Bactrian *saskšant,* meaning "one anxious to learn" (Paton *Esther* ICC, 69).

JOHN M. WIEBE

SHABBAT [Heb *šabbāt*]. See SABBATH.

SHABBETHAI (PERSON) [Heb *šabbĕtay*]. A Levite who was present when Ezra enacted the edict against having foreign wives (Ezra 10:15; 1 Esdr 9:14). The accompanying Hebrew phrase *ʿāmĕdû ʿal-zōʾt* can be translated as either "they supported this" or "they opposed this." However, the introductory particle *ʾak* ("only") in Ezra 10:15 suggests an exception, and the fact that overwhelming support for the edict did exist further indicates a minority opposition. In other words, Shabbethai was among the few who apparently voiced disapproval of the edict. Such opposition, however, was perhaps not directed against the edict itself, but against its perceived leniency. Shabbethai, it must be noted, is not listed among those who had such a wife to give up, so he might very well have sought stricter measures. Furthermore, if we can assume that additional occurrences of the name refer to the same person, then Shabbethai was a man of deep religious convictions. He is described elsewhere as a chief Levite who was responsible for external business pertaining to the temple (Neh 11:16), and he also provided interpretive assistance during the great reading of the Law (Neh 8:7; 1 Esdr 9:48). Shabbethai's opposition to the edict, therefore, quite likely indicates that he was a member of a more rigid or demanding minority (Blenkinsopp *Ezra-Nehemiah* OTL, 194).

TERRY L. BRENSINGER

SHADDAI [Heb *šadday*]. See ALMIGHTY; GOD IN THE OT.

SHADOW [Heb *ṣel;* Gk *skia*]. Both the Hebrew and the Greek word for shadow are used in the Bible in a literal and in a metaphorical sense.

In the literal sense it is used for the place where the (sun)light cannot penetrate, especially the shadow of a tree (e.g., Jonah 4:6; Judg 9:15, Ezek 31:6, 12, 17; Hos 4:13; Ps 80:10; Mark 4:32); also of a rock (Judg 9:36); of a cloud (Isa 16:3; 25:5); of a roof (Gen 19:8); etc. Since shadow protects against the heat of the sun, the word develops the metaphorical meaning of "protection," e.g., by a man (Cant 2:3); by a city (Jer 48:45); by a rock (Isa 32:2); but especially—this is the most frequent usage—by God (e.g.,

Ps 17:8 "Hide me in the shadow of thy wings;" Ps 36:8 "The sons of men seek refuge in the shadow of thy wings;" Ps 57:2 "I will take refuge in the shadow of thy wings;" Ps 63:7 "I am safe in the shadow of thy wings"), the image being here that of God as a mighty eagle; see also Exod 19:4 and Deut 32:11. For other images in connection with God's shadow see Hos 14:7; Isa 49:2; 51:16.

Another metaphorical use of "shadow" is found in its application with the negative sense of "transience" and "vanity" (e.g., Ps 102:11 "My days dwindle away like a shadow;" Ps 109:23; 144:4; Job 8:9 "Our life on earth passes away like a shadow;" Job 17:7; Qoh 6:12 "Who knows what is good for man in those few days of his empty life which he spends as a shadow?"; *IDB* 4:302).

Traditionally, the Hebrew *ṣalmawet* (Amos 5:8; Jer 13:16; Ps 44:20; Job 3:5; etc.) was translated as "shadow of death" (already in the LXX), because popular etymology wrongly divided the word into *ṣl* (shadow) and *mwt* (death), but it is now certain that it has the meaning of "deep darkness" (Thomas 1962).

In the NT the word has an additional metaphorical meaning, which has its background in Hellenistic ideas. In Col 2:17 the Mosaic commandments are called "no more than a shadow of what was to come" and are posited over against the "body" which is Christ. This opposition of shadow and body is ultimately of Platonic origin. The same applies to Heb 8:5 and 10:1, where the author says that the earthly sanctuary of the Jews is only a copy and shadow of the heavenly, and that the Law contains but a shadow and no true image of the good things to come. The Platonic antithesis between heavenly reality and earthly adumbration is at the background of these passages (*TWNT* 7: 400–01).

There are two passages in the work of Luke, one with a literal and one with a metaphorical use of "shadow," that belong together and have a different background than other passages in the Bible, namely Luke 1:35 and Acts 5:15. In the first passage Mary is told by Gabriel that the power of the Most High will overshadow her (the verb *episkiazein* is used) so that she will become pregnant. In the second, the same author tells that the inhabitants of Jerusalem carried out their sick into the streets in order that the shadow of Peter might fall upon them (again *episkiazein* is used) so that they would be healed. Here the person's shadow is equivalent to his soul or vital power or *alter ego* (Frazer 1911: 77–100). This soul-concept is well-known from anthropological study of primitive peoples and medieval Western societies (Rochholz 1867; Negelein 1902; Pradel 1904; Bieler 1940; van der Leeuw 1933; Fischer 1965).

The idea that the shadow was a vital part of a human being or an animal (or even of a tree) was also widespread in antiquity and is attested for Mesopotamia, Egypt, Greece, Rome, and Israel (George 1970; Cook 1914; Röscher 1892; Frazer 1911; van der Horst 1976–77; 1979). Humans and animals are liable to be injured if violence is done to their shadows. If the shadow is trampled or urinated upon, struck or stabbed, one will feel the injury as if it were done directly against the person (Pliny the Elder, *HN* 28.69; *Defixionum tabellae* 190:4–13, ed. Audollent). It is dangerous to let one's shadow fall upon particular persons or objects because one's soul might then be purloined by them; to lose one's shadow meant to die within the very near future (Cook 1914: 66–68). Certain trees have beneficial, other ones noxious shadows (Pliny *NH* 17.18; Lucr. *de Rerum Natura* 6.783–85; Verg. *Ecl.* 10.75–76). To be touched by the shadow of a criminal will have a very harmful effect upon the person touched (Ennius in Cic. *Tusc.* 3.12, 26). Very famous and much discussed in Hellenistic-Roman times were stories about the extremely powerful and dangerous shadow of hyenas (Arist. *Fr.* 369 Rose = Ael. *NA* 6:14; Pseudo-Aristotle, *Mir. Ausc.* 145; Pliny *HN* 8.106; Solin. 27:24; *Gp.* 15.1, 10; see further van der Horst 1979: 28–30), and about the loss of one's shadow when one entered Zeus' sanctuary on Mount Lycaeus in Arcadia (Polyb. 16.12, 7; Paus. 8.38, 6; Plut. *Quaest. Graec.* 39, 300C; further Röscher 1892; Cook 1914: 66–68), which meant that death was soon to follow.

That these magical ideas were current also in Jewish circles is proved by several texts in the LXX (Job 15:29; Exod 40;35; Ps 139:8) in Targums (e.g., *Tg. Ps.-J* on Num 14:9), in the Mishna (*ʿAbod. Zar.* 3:8; *Ohol.* 2:1–2), and the Talmud (*b. Hor.* 12a; *b. Ker.* 5b–6a; *b. Pesaḥ.* 11a–b; see van der Horst 1979: 34–35).

The idea that a shadow could have a powerful positive or negative effect upon another person is the background of the story about the miraculous healing of the sick Jerusalemites by Peter's shadow in Acts 5:15 (van der Horst 1976–77). Egyptian texts prove that a god's shadow could even be thought so powerful as to fertilize a woman (George 1970: 112–13; the texts speak about the ejaculation of the god's shadow). A similar conception is probably the background of the otherwise enigmatic passage in Luke 1:35 about the overshadowing of Mary by the Most High (van der Horst 1976–77: 211–12).

Bibliography

Bieler, M. 1940. Schatten. Pp. 126–42 in *Handwörterbuch des deutschen Aberglaubens* 9.

Cook, A. B. 1914. *Zeus, A Study of Ancient Religion.* Vol. 1. Cambridge. Repr. 1964.

Drexler, W. 1897. Meridianus Daemon. *Ausführliches Lexikon der griechischen und römischen Mythologie* 2: 2832–37.

Fischer, H. 1965. *Studien über Seelenvorstellungen in Ozeanien.* Munich.

Frazer, J. G. 1911. *The Golden Bough II: Taboo and the Perils of the Soul.* 3d ed. London.

George, B. 1970. *Zu den altägyptischen Vorstellungen vom Schatten als Seele.* Bonn.

Hölzer, V. 1965. *Umbra. Vorstellung und Symbol im Leben der Römer.* Diss. Marburg.

Horst, P. W. van der. 1976–77. Peter's Shadow. The Religio-Historical Background of Acts 5:15. *NTS* 23: 204–12.

———. 1979. Der Schatten im hellenistischen Volksglauben. Pp. 27–36 in *Studies in Hellenistic Religions,* ed. M. J. Vermaseren. Leiden.

Leeuw, G. van der. 1933. *Phänomenologie der Religion.* Tübingen.

Negelein, J. von. 1902. Bild, Speigel und Schatten im Volksglauben. *ARW* 5: 1–37.

Pradel, F. 1904. Der Schatten im Volksglauben. *Mitteilungen der schlesischen Gesellschaft für Volkskunde* 12: 1–36.

Rochholz, E. L. 1867. Vol. 1, pp. 59–130 in *Deutscher Glaube und Brauch im Spiegel der heidnischen Vorzeit.* Berlin.

Röscher, W. H. 1892. Der Schattenlosigkeit des Zeus-Abatons auf dem Lykaion. *Jahrbücher für classische Philologie* 38: 701–09.
Thomas, D. 1962. *Ṣalmawet* in the Old Testament. *JSS* 7: 191–200.

PIETER W. VAN DER HORST

SHADRACH, MESHACH, ABEDNEGO (PERSONS) [Heb; Aram *šadrak, mêšak, ʿăbēdnĕgô*]. Babylonian names given to a special group of Jewish noblemen by Nebuchadnezzar's chief eunuch Ashpenaz in the exilic period. Along with Daniel, who was similarly named (see BELTESHAZZAR), they constitute the central heroes of the series of court tales recorded in the 1st half of the book of Daniel (chaps. 1–5). Shadrach appears to be a deliberate perversion in spelling of Marduk, the patron deity of the city of Babylon, and likewise Abednego is a clever deformation of Abednebo which corresponds to Akk *arad - nabu* "servant of (the god) Nabu." Meshach has all the appearance of a further disfigurement of a Babylonian original no longer recognizable. The changing of names, on this occasion from the familiar sounding Hebrew Hananiah, Mishael, and Azariah (see Dan 1:7), was a familiar practice in the ANE, signifying a change of destiny *(nomen est omen)*. Parallels may be seen within the OT in Pharaoh's renaming Joseph (Gen 41:45) and Nebuchadnezzar's new name for Judah's last crowned head (2 Kgs 24:17).

Shadrach, Meshach, and Abednego are first mentioned in a list which is headed by the principal hero whose name is given to the canonical book of Daniel (Dan 1:6–7). It has been argued that Daniel alone was the protagonist in the oldest tradition of the court tales and only in the later stages of the book's composition were the heroes incorporated into the narrative as Daniel's companions (*Daniel* AB, 131). It is possible that in the tale of the colossal statue mention of Daniel's companions could be a later addition (2:17–49) but they are not intrusive here or when they are introduced in the first chapter, although Daniel is given a certain prominence. Chap. 3 does not fit happily with this view since only the three companions are the heroes.

From a literary standpoint the Hebrew names and their Babylonian counterparts do not appear at random in the texts. In fact they are subtly woven into the narrative fabric in order to reflect the cultural and religious dichotomy which existed between the Jewish people and their Babylonian overlords. In the introductory chapter the authorial voice uses Hebrew nomenclature in referring to the three companions (1:6, 11, 19) and it is left to Nebuchadnezzar's chief of the eunuchs to change their names (1:7). In the story of the colossal statue it is Nebuchadnezzar who bestowed high office on Shadrach, Meshach, and Abednego (1:49) even though in their personal relationship with Daniel they keep their Hebrew names (2:17). In the tale of the furnace of burning fire the Babylonian names are declaimed 13 times within the space of 19 verses (3:12, 13, 16, 19, 20, 22, 23, 26 (twice), 28, 29, 30). Such reiteration seems to be a rhetorical rather than a structural device but it is worth noticing that the sonorous repetition is set firmly in the context of the confrontation between the Jewish heroes and Nebuchadnezzar, the king himself declaiming the Babylonian names 5 times (3:14, 16, 28, 29). Babylonian nomenclature thus provides an authentic local touch to the narratives while at the same time the deft deformation of the spelling satirizes Babylonian cultural values.

PETER W. COXON

SHAGEE (PERSON) [Heb *šāgēh*]. At 1 Chr 11:34 Shagee the Hararite is the father of Jonathan, one of David's mighty men. In place of "Jonathan son of Shagee the Hararite" we find two separate names in the parallel at 2 Sam 23:32b–33a: "Jonathan; Shammah the Hararite." It is difficult to reconcile the two texts. Wellhausen (1871: 216) prefers Shagee (or Agee; see 2 Sam 23:11) at 1 Chr 11:34, saying that Jonathan was a brother of Shammah (2 Sam 23:33) as both of them were Hararites. For 2 Sam 23:33 many suggest that an original *ben* has fallen out of the text and restore it to "Jonathan son of Shammah the Hararite" (NAB; NEB). According to Elliger (1935: 31 n. 3) "Shagee" might be a cross between the names Shammah and Agee, the father of Shammah in 2 Sam 23:11. Wellhausen, while pointing out that either the name in v 11 should be *šgʾ* or that of v 33 should be *ʾgʾ*, prefers *šgʾ*. In the Gk mss the form of the name in the Lucianic text of 1 Chr *(samaia[s])* reflects the variant at 2 Sam 23:33 MT and may indeed be a modification based on it. The reading in the Vaticanus and Sinaiticus codexes *sōla*, can be explained by a confusion of the Greek letters *gamma* and *lambda*. Codex Alexandrinus, which reads *sagē*, reflects the MT.

While the possibility of textual confusion may be a factor in seeking the original form of this name, it seems best nevertheless to accept the MT reading "Jonathan son of Shagee the Hararite" for 1 Chr 11:34 as the authentic reading of the Chronicler's tradition here.

Bibliography

Elliger, K. 1935. Die dreissig Helden Davids. *PJ* 31: 29–75.
Wellhausen, J. 1871. *Der Text der Bücher Samuelis*. Göttingen.

STEPHEN PISANO

SHAHAR (DEITY) [Heb *šaḥar*]. The Hebrew word meaning "dawn," often personified in the Bible as a reflection of its status as a god in the ANE (Ps 139:9). Although spelled *šahar* in Hebrew, the second *a* vowel *(pataḥ)* is a later Hebrew development; its original pronunciation is preserved in Akkadian syllabic spellings as *šaḫru* (Emar #369, 371). The frequent absence of the definite article with this noun in Hebrew (i.e., instead of "the dawn" simply "Dawn" in Isa 14:12; Hos 6:3; Amos 4:13; Ps 57:9—Eng 57:8; 108:3—Eng 108:2; 139:9; Job 3:9; 41:10—Eng 41:18; Cant 6:10) points to the awareness within the biblical tradition of the personification of this natural phenomenon. In addition, the title "Hind of the Dawn" (Heb *ʾayyelet haššaḥar*) occurs in the context of a Psalm title (Ps 22:1—Eng title), presumably indicating the melody to which the psalm was sung.

Many details concerning this deity surface from widely separated cultures over a period of two millennia, and one must be cautious in assuming that the resulting picture represents what was recognized at any one time. The Syrian environment of the 2d millennium is most appropriate as a background for the biblical text, and this also provides the most detail. An entire mythical/ritual text from Ugarit (*KTU* 1.23) is devoted to describing the birth of this god along with his half-brother Shalim. The father of these two "gracious gods" is the chief god, El, who impregnates two of his wives (perhaps Athirat and Rahmay). Shahar nurses at the breasts of the Mother-goddess, but his voracious appetite remains unsated, depicted graphically as "one lip to earth, one lip to heaven, the birds of the sky and the fish of the sea entering their mouths." As time passes, Shahar and Shalim are found frequenting the wilderness where—when the text breaks off—the issue remains one of satisfying the needs of their diet.

Shahar is the divinity of the dawn while Shalim is that of the evening, bearing the appropriate epithet "sons of day" in *KTU* 1.23. Wherever the two brothers appear together, Shahar is named first before Shalim, pointing to the sequence dawn-dusk in contrast to the biblical sequence "evening and morning" (Genesis 1).

Dawn's moral place in the cosmos is fraught with ambiguity. Although Dawn brings light and dispels darkness (note the phonetic correspondence with the root for "dark" *šḥr*), it is also the begetter of the rebel morning star (Isa 14:12–13), a star which is associated with the underworld (*KTU* 1.6; Isa 14:15). God acknowledges that the daily commissioning of Dawn is a Herculean task with moral consequences (Job 38:12–15), a task described between the apparently comparable effort required to tame a rebellious Sea and survey the Abyss and the Gates of Death. Sharing contexts with the chaos monster Leviathan places Dawn in a morally charged environment (Job 3:8–9; 41:10—Eng 41:18). Outside the Bible, sacrifices for Shahar are accompanied by offerings to underworld deities (Emar #369.24–25). Appropriately in this regard, the most common verb which describes the dawn's activity in Hebrew is that it "rises" (*ʿlh*), probably echoing the old notion of the underworld connections of Dawn.

An astral orientation of Shahar is suggested in his juxtaposition with other celestial elements (sun and moon in Cant 6:10; one may favorably compare Eos, the Greek goddess of the dawn, and her brother and sister sun and moon). A connection with the sun is frequently made at Ugarit where after Shahar's birth in *KTU* 1.23, offerings are made specifically to the sun and the stars (1.54). Elsewhere, Shahar and Shalim along with eight other pairs of deities assist the sun goddess (*KTU* 1.107), while the sun goddess in another text is the central deity around which Shahar and Shalim with eleven other deities (or pairs of deities) are mustered in an incantation to neutralize a snake's venom (*KTU* 1.100). In this text, Shahar's characteristic location is said to be the heavens (*šmmh*). The astral divinity Athtar (identified with Venus) also appears in conjunction with Shahar at Ugarit (*KTU* 1.123) and even more regularly in Epigraphic South Arabic (ESA) texts where the two are invoked as a pair. Allusion to Shahar's offspring is so far known only from biblical texts such as Isa 14:12 where he is depicted as the father of Hellel (RSV "Day Star;" Vg *lucifer*), the morning star, again connecting Shahar with the heavens.

A further biblical text which identifies the offspring of Shahar is Ps 110:3, but it raises the problem of Shahar's gender. Like the Greek goddess Eos, along with Moabite which preserves the feminine form Shahrat (*KAI* 181.15), Psalm 110 explicitly personifies Shahar as a female, for the offspring of Dawn's womb is the dew, Ṭal (consistently masculine in Hebrew; Dawn as the bestower of the dew also may lie behind the imagery of the parallelism in Hos 6:3). The goddess of the dew, Ṭallay, is a female at Ugarit where her progenitor is identified as Shower (*rb; KTU* 1.3–4); Syrian and Hittite rituals juxtapose the storm god with Shahar although the gender of the latter in this case is not clear (Emar #369.24, 52). In spite of this feminine imagery, wherever gender marking is observable in Hebrew, the noun Shahar is masculine. Therefore, one must be prepared to see variable gender in the deity associated with the dawn, a fluctuation observable with other gods and goddesses (e.g., the masculine sun in Hebrew is feminine at Ugarit and in ESA, just as Dew is masculine in Hebrew but feminine in Ugaritic). Note also the Babylonian comment: "Venus is seen in the west, she is male. . . . Venus is seen in the east, she is female" (*Enūma Anu Enlil* 50/4.6–7).

A gargantuan mouth with corresponding appetite seems to place this creature in the company of giants, as does the comparison with Leviathan (Job 41:10—Eng 41:18; cf. Job 3:8–9). The eyelids of Dawn are a characteristic feature (Job 3:9; 41:18), no doubt a reference to the gradually spreading rays of sunlight which presage the sunrise, again pointing to the gigantic stature of Dawn whose eyelids spread over all the earth. Shahar is also winged to allow him to fly as other supernatural beings (Ps 139:9). Although the symbol of Shahar in ESA is a horned dragon, this may not represent the god himself but the animal with which he was associated.

The prominent place of this deity in popular religion is confirmed by its appearance in personal names in Hebrew (e.g., Ahi-Shahar 1 Chr 7:10), Phoenician, Ugaritic and Akkadian. A pious attraction to this deity may be explained by the general perception of the dawn as an envigorating moment, anticipated as the sign of renewal of strength, the realization of vindication and victory (Isa 58:8), and the expeller of darkness and the forces of evil (Gen 32:25, 27—Eng 32:24, 26; Job 38:12). Just as other astral elements are traditionally cited as the most stable features of creation (Ps 72:5, 17; 89:37, 38—Eng 89:36, 37; cf. Jer 33:25), so the dawn is included in this class as a certainty which can be trusted to recur (Hos 6:3).

Bibliography

Arnaud, D. 1986. *Recherches au pays d'Aštata—Emar VI.3: Textes sumériens et accadiens*. Paris.

Gese, H.; Höfner, M.; and Rudolph, K. 1970. *Die Religionen Altsyriens, Altsudarabiens, und der Mandäer*. Stuttgart.

McKay, J. W. 1970. Helel and the Dawn-Goddess. *VT* 20: 451–64.

SAMUEL A. MEIER

SHAHARAIM (PERSON) [Heb *šaḥărayim*]. A Benjaminite (1 Chr 8:8). Shaharaim is listed by the Chronicler as the progenitor of a clan of Benjaminites who lived in Moab. This mention of Shaharaim by the Chronicler, however, has no connection to what precedes it, and there is no hint of the source of the list headed by Shaharaim. The mention of Israelites living in Moab is rare, though not unheard of (see Ruth and 1 Sam 22:3–5). Shaharaim's descendants are said to have built Ono and Lod, though the names Ono and Lod are not found outside the Chronicler's work; see further Myers (*1 Chronicles* AB, 52–53).

Noth (*IPN,* 223) classified the name as part Hebrew and part Aramaic, and therefore postexilic. The name could be a copyist's error for Shehariah (1 Chr 8:26) or Ahiram (Num 26:38), though neither option has any textual support.

TOM WAYNE WILLETT

SHAHAZUMAH (PLACE) [Heb K *šaḥăṣûmâ; Q šaḥăṣ-îmâ*]. A border town in Issachar, located between Tabor and the Jordan River (Josh 19:22). The location of the town is uncertain, as is its correct name. Naʾaman (1986) notes that the name is non-Semitic in appearance. Albright (1926) suggests that the name may be a conflation of the elements *šḥṣ* and *ymh* (reading with the Qere), that is, "Shahaz-which-is-toward-the-sea" (of Galilee, contrary to *yammâ*'s usual sense of "westward"). A possible location for the site was found by Alt (1928), among others, at Tell Mukharkhash (M.R. 194228), at the confluence of the wadis Sirin and esh-Sherrar, 5 miles SE of Tabor. This site was occupied in the MB, LB, Iron I, and Byzantine periods. However, Mukharkhash has since been more convincingly identified with Anaharath (*HGB,* 195–96; *LBHG,* 155). Another possibility is to locate Shahazumah at Tell el-Hadatah, in the district between Tabor and Beth-shemesh, or according to Kallai (*HGB,* 195), at el-Karm, a tell near el-Hadatah. Kallai (ibid., 196) also suggests a third possibility: if Shahazumah is part of a town list of Issachar and not part of the border document, then it may be identified with Shekh el-Muzegit, below Beth-shemesh. However, the exact location of Shahazumah remains uncertain.

Bibliography

Albright, W. F. 1926. The Topography of the Tribe of Issachar. *ZAW* 3: 32–33.
Alt, A. 1928. Die Reise. *PJ* 24: 51.
Naʾaman, N. 1986. *Borders and Districts in Biblical Historiography.* Jerusalem Biblical Studies 4. Jerusalem.

SIDNIE ANN WHITE

SHAKERS. See MUSIC AND MUSICAL INSTRUMENTS.

SHALEM (DEITY). Shalem is attested as a West Semitic minor deity in the 2d millennium B.C.E. The god appears in the mythological and ritual texts from Ugarit; however, these documents provide little information by which the divine function of Shalem might be determined. The provenance of the cult of the god is unknown, though both Mesopotamia and South Arabia have been posited as the original area of the deity. While evidence for the existence of the god is clear, how widely the divinity was revered and for how long is impossible to determine. Personal names among the West Semitic peoples may suggest that the god was worshipped into the middle of the 1st millennium B.C.E. Among these personal names are several biblical names which have been construed as containing the divine element Shalem, which makes the deity important for the study of biblical religious history.

Among the myths from Ugarit is one in which the two deities *šḥr w šlm* appear as the offspring of the god El and a pair of "women" whom he impregnates on a beach (*KTU* 1.23). The myth then seems to imply that other gods are sired by El with these women (Caquot and Sznycer 1980: 8). The ambiguity of the intent of this myth (del Olmo 1981: 437–39) precludes any certainty as to whether the gods mentioned at the end of the narrative include Shalem or not. These latter deities are sent by El into the desert to live for seven, even eight, years; after this period of time there is a reference to imbibing wine. The only characteristic provided for these deities is that of insatiable consumption, presented in the manner used of Mot. Clearly the text assumes a knowledge of the principal deities and therefore does not define or distinguish them.

Because Shalem appears with *šḥr,* not only in the mythological text, but in some of the ritual offering lists (Xella 1981: 391), it has been generally taken for granted that the two gods are related to "dawn" and "twilight" either as the divine representations of the two times of day (Gaster 1946: 54; Xella 1973: 107) or as two aspects of the planet Venus appearing as morning and evening star (Gray 1949: 73; *IDBSup,* 821). For this it has been necessary to define Shalem with respect to the slightly better known Saḥar and, to the extent that these two gods appear together in the Ugaritic texts, such an interpretation is possible; however, Shalem also appears on the ritual tablets from Ugarit without *šḥr* which should mitigate against too facile an integration of the two deities such as the interpretation which has declared them the astrological Gemini (Gaster 1946: 70; Gibson 1977: 29). See also SHAHAR (DEITY).

If evidence of the divine name Shalem is not pervasive in the West Semitic world of the 1st millennium B.C.E., personal names containing the divine element Shalem can plausibly be identified in the period (Tigay 1986: 67–68). However, the god's name is written with the root *šlm* which is a common verbal and noun form and might be used in personal names without referring to a god as the meaning "wholeness" or "well-being" (Eisenbeis 1969: 50–51) carries a positive connotation. This makes using the personal names containing a *šlm* element for evidence as the worship of Shalem uncertain, though by no means improbable (Tigay 1986: 80).

The god Shalem has been correlated with the city of Jerusalem since it was observed that the final element in the city's name could be read as a divine name. It was then proposed that the city must have been named after the deity and therefore Shalem must originally have been the major deity of the area. Support for Jerusalem having been named for Shalem is derived from the story of Melchizedek, who is called the "king of Shalem" (Gen 14:18). In Ps 76:3—Eng 76:2 Shalem is used in a parallel construction with Zion thereby locating it in Jerusalem. It is clear that the biblical text is not using an early Judaic tradition, because already in the Egyptian execration texts, from the early 2d millennium B.C.E., the name Jerusalem was known; though this might suggest a double tradition of the city's name known to the psalmist. Julius Lewy (1934: 62) argued that Shalem and Yahweh had originally reigned together in the city of Jerusalem and the town was named for the former. At some time after the Davidic capture of the city Yahweh replaced Shalem as the major deity and then ruled alone. He later (1940: 519–21) expanded on his theory and posited that the Mesopotamian deity Shulmānu, in the guise of Ninurta, was the patron god of "*Bêt Šulmān*," the Jebusite Jerusalem.

The relation of Jerusalem to the god Ninurta led other scholars to posit that the original cult in Jerusalem was dedicated to Saturn; this theory was derived from Mesopotamian astrological reflection on Ninurta (Lewy 1950: 353). A continuation of this trajectory produced a vision of Shalem as a deity of violence, destruction, and death (Curtis 1957: 168). Rosenberg (*IDBSup,* 820–21) assumes that the identification of Shalem with Saturn is correct, but also wishes to accept the Ugaritic evidence for a possible "evening star" equation, and declares that the deity is a solar god. These theories must be seen as failures. There is little, if any, reason to presume Mesopotamian influence on the origins of the city of Jerusalem. Moreover, the West Semitic Shalem serves sufficiently as a source for the name of the city, even if the nature of the deity is obscure.

Further evidence for the early, and continuing, interest in the cult of Shalem in Jerusalem is seen in the names David gave his sons; both Absalom and Solomon have been argued to have been named after the god. The fact that Absalom is supposed to have been born in Hebron (2 Sam 3:2–3), before David captured Jerusalem, precludes a facile use of the name to show David's veneration for the god of Jerusalem (*IDBSup,* 820). If Solomon was named after Shalem, which is less than certain, it would appear to have been his throne name, used more often in the Bible than the Yahwistic Jedidiah. Proper names containing *šlm* continue throughout the monarchical periods in the biblical texts which may reflect a continuing cult of Shalem; it is unlikely that they reflect aspirations of the populace for peace (Coogan 1976: 85). One last name has been suggested as related to the cult of Shalem in Jerusalem; the Shulamite maiden (Cant 7:1) has been suggested as the consort of Shalem (*IDBSup,* 820) and a fertility cult has been suggested for her in the city (Ahlström 1963: 84). Neither the identification nor the intent of the poems is clear and therefore any connection between Shalem and the Shulamite remains speculation.

Bibliography

Ahlström, G. W. 1963. *Aspects of Syncretism in Israelite Religion.* Trans. E. J. Sharpe. Horae Soederblomianae 5. Lund.

Caquot, A., and Sznycer, M. 1980. *Ugaritic Religion.* Iconography of Religions 15/8. Leiden.

Coogan, M. D. 1976. *West Semitic Personal Names in the Murašû Documents.* HSM 7. Missoula.

Curtis, J. B. 1957. An Investigation of the Mount of Olives in the Judaeo-Christian Tradition. *HUCA* 28: 137–80.

Eisenbeis, W. 1969. *Die Wurzel* šlm *im Alten Testament.* BZAW 113. Berlin.

Gaster, T. H. 1946. A Canaanite Ritual Drama: The Spring Festival at Ugarit. *JAOS* 66: 49–76.

Gibson, J. C. L. 1977. *Canaanite Myths and Legends.* 2d ed. Edinburgh.

Gray, J. 1949. The Desert God *ʿAṯtr* in the Literature and Religion of Canaan. *JNES* 8: 72–83.

Lewy, H. 1950. Origin and Significance of the *Mâgên Dâwîd. ArOr* 18/3: 330–65.

Lewy, J. 1934. Les textes paléo-assyriens et l'Ancien Testament. *RHR* 110: 29–65.

———. 1940. The Šulmān Temple in Jerusalem. *JBL* 59: 519–22.

Mackay, C. 1948. Salem. *PEQ* 80: 121–30.

Olmo Lete, G. del. 1981. *Mitos y leyendas de Canaan segun la tradicion de Ugarit.* Fuentes de la Ciencia Biblica 1. Madrid.

Tigay, J. H. 1986. *You Shall Have No Other Gods: Israelite Religion in the Light of Hebrew Inscriptions.* HSS 31. Atlanta.

Xella, P. 1973. *Il mito di ŠḤR e ŠLM: Saggio sulla mitologia ugaritica.* SS 44. Rome.

———. 1981. *I testi rituali di Ugarit—I: Testi.* SS 54. Rome.

LOWELL K. HANDY

SHALISHAH (PLACE) [Heb *šālišâ*]. A region through which Saul passed on his search for his father's lost donkeys (1 Sam 9:4). The context implies that the region is outside Benjamin, presumably in Ephraim to the N. It is probable that the settlement known as Baal-shalishah (2 Kgs 4:42) was located in that region and that the one will have suggested the name for the other.

ELMER M. DYCK

SHALLECHETH GATE (PLACE) [Heb *šaʿar šalleket*]. An inner gate of Jerusalem that was part of an enclosure that surrounded the sacred temple precincts and the royal residences (1 Chr 26:16). The name of the gate possibly means "Gate of Departing." This gate was known at different periods by several other names: the "Foundation Gate" (2 Chr 23:5, LXX "Middle Gate") and the "Sur Gate" (2 Kgs 11:5, LXX "Gate of Departing or Turning Aside"). In Hebrew, *sûr* and *šalleket* share similar indicative meanings and the LXX renders both of these words with *ekspan* "draw out" (Isa 6:13 and Ezek 11:19 in Codex Alexandrinus) and with *ekpiptein* "go forth" (Isa 6:13 and Job 15:30 in Codex Vaticanus and Codex Sinaiticus).

When King David assigned gatekeepers for the Temple complex (1 Chr 26:16), Shuppim, Hosah and their sons were assigned the W gate of the sacred Temple precincts as well as the Shallecheth Gate of the outer royal enclosure, the walls of which stood between (hence the LXX "Middle Gate" of 2 Chr 23:5) the Temple precincts and the outer defensive wall that was W of the city. The area between the W gate of the Temple enclosure, (possibly the mysterious Parbar or Parvar Gate of 1 Chr 26:18 [BDB, 826] and the Shallecheth Gate may have been a forum or "Priests' Chambers" as suggested by the Septuagint's use of *pastophoriou* "priest's chamber," and it may have been in this forum that the guards were stationed as mentioned in 1 Chr 26:16. This forum apparently exited (through the Shallecheth Gate) onto a roadway that "ascended" or "went up" (Heb *lamsillah* [1 Chr 26:18]) to the Fish Gate on the NW corner of the city.

The Shallecheth Gate (and the possible forum associated with it) may have functioned much like the later "Kaiaphon Gate" of Josephus or the "Kiphonas Gate" of the Mishnah (*Mid.* 1:3) as an entrance for priests who were entering the area for Temple service (Mackowski 1980: 131–32, 194 n. 4).

Bibliography

Mackowski, R. 1980. *Jerusalem, City of Jesus.* Grand Rapids, MI.

DALE C. LIID

SHALLUM (PERSON) [*šallûm; šallūm*]. Some fourteen individuals bear this name, which may mean "the requited" or "he for whom compensation has been made" (Gray *1 and 2 Kings* OTL, 621; *IPN,* 174). In the so-called Barley Letter (Samaria ostracon C1101) the form of this name is attested (*ANET,* p. 321; *KAI,* # 188; *TSSI,* pp. 14–15). Shallun in Neh 3:15 may be a variant spelling; Myers (*Ezra, Nehemiah* AB, 111) compares Ug *bn ṯlln* (*KTU* 4.63:I:16).

1. A son of Jabesh, probably a reference to a clan or district rather than to his father, and may be translated, "a man of Jabesh." This might indicate that opposition to Jehu's dynasty came from Jabesh-gilead in Transjordan (Jones *1 and 2 Kings* NCBC, 521) for he gained the throne of the northern kingdom over which he ruled for one month about the year 750 B.C. (2 Kgs 15:10, 13–15) by assassinating Zechariah, the last king of Jehu's house, before being himself murdered by his successor Menahem. The prophets Amos and Hosea allude to these events. Amos foretells Zechariah's murder (7:9, 11) and Hosea speaks of royal assassinations (7:6–7, 16). Both see them as signs of the corruption that will take Israel into exile. These strokes plunged the country into civil war shortly before the renewed advance of Assyria into the West.

2. Son of Tikvah and husband of Huldah the prophetess (2 Kgs 22:14; son of Tokhath in 2 Chr 34:22).

3. The fourth son of Josiah, king of Judah. He succeeded his father in 609/608 B.C. (Jer 22:11; 1 Chr 3:15) and took the throne-name Jehoahaz by which he is usually called.

4. An uncle of the prophet Jeremiah (Jer 32:7). His son Hanamel sold a field at Anathoth to Jeremiah during the siege of Jerusalem.

5. The father of Maaseiah, a keeper of the threshold of the temple in the time of the prophet Jeremiah (Jer 35:4).

6. Son of Sismai and father of Jekamiah; a descendant of Jerahmeel of Judah (1 Chr 2:40–41).

7. Son of Shaul and father of Mibsam; a descendant of Simeon (1 Chr 4:25).

8. The fourth son of Naphtali by Bilhah (1 Chr 7:13). In Gen 46:24 and Num 26:49 he is called SHILLEM (Heb *šillēm*). See also SHILLEM.

9. Son of Zadok and father of Hilkiah; a high priest (1 Chr 5:38–39—Eng 6:12–13; Ezra 7:2; 1 Esdr 8:1; 2 Esdr 1:1; Bar 1:7). Ezra is descended from him. He is perhaps identical with MESHULLAM in 1 Chr 9:11; Neh 11:11; 12:13.

10. A gatekeeper in the camp of the Levites (1 Chr 9:17). He was the head of a family of gatekeepers in postexilic Judah (Ezra 2:42 = Neh 7:45; 1 Esdr 5:28) and one of the first to return from exile in Babylon. He occupied an especially honored position as the gatekeeper of the east gate through which the king usually entered (cf. Ezek 46:1–8) and the one which faced the entrance to the sanctuary. He is perhaps identical with Shallum the Korahite, son of Kore, mentioned in 1 Chr 9:19, 31. He is called SHELEMIAH in 1 Chr 26:14, MESHULLAM in Neh 12:25, and MESHELEMIAH in 1 Chr 9:21. According to Ezra 10:24 (= 1 Esdr 9:25) he was one of those who had married a foreign wife while in exile but by the law of the postexilic community he was compelled to put her away.

11. The father of Jehizkiah and a member of the tribe of Ephraim (2 Chr 28:12).

12. An Israelite who had married a foreign wife while in exile (Ezra 10:42).

13. The son of Hallohesh; head of one of the eight groups working to repair the wall of Jerusalem between the Jeshanah Gate and the Valley Gate in the time of Nehemiah (Neh 3:12). He administered half of the district of Jerusalem, postexilic Judah being divided into five districts.

14. Son of Colhozeh (Neh 3:15). He administered the district of Mizpah in the time of Nehemiah and repaired the Fountain Gate as well as the wall of the Pool of Shelah at the King's Garden as far as the steps going down from the City of David.

ROBERT ALTHANN

SHALMA [Heb *šlmh*]. A N Arabian tribe which is probably mentioned in Cant 1:5: "Black I am, but beautiful, O daughters of Jerusalem, like the tents of Kedar, or the tentcloths of Shalma." The MT has vocalized this "tentcloths of Solomon" (Heb *šĕlōmōh*). What, however, connects the luxurious textiles of King Solomon with the rough goathair of bedouin (Kedarite) tents? Wellhausen (*WPG1,* 227, n. 1) suggested, therefore, reading *šlmh* as *šalmâ* or *śalmâ*. The tribe lived in the vicinity of Hegra/Madāʾ in Ṣāliḥ S of the Nabataeans. "Kedar" may in Cant 1:5 actually refer to the Nabataeans. See KEDAR. Shalma is mentioned in the Targums under the name of *šalmāʾā* and *šlmyʾ*, in Nabataean as *šlmw*, in Safaitic as *slm*, in Greek as *Salámioi* (Knauf 1989: 107, and n. 586). Part of the tribe may have immigrated into S Palestine in the exilic or early post-exilic period, if *śalmāʾ* (1 Chr 2:51, 54) can be linked to *šlmh*. See also EPHAH; MENUHOTH.

Bibliography

Knauf, E. A. 1989. *Ismael.* ADPV. Wiesbaden.

ERNST AXEL KNAUF

SHALMAI (PERSON) [Heb *šalmāy*]. Var. SHAMLAI. Head of a family of NETHINIM (Temple Servants) who returned from the Babylonian exile to Jerusalem with Zerubbabel and Jeshua, between 538 and 520 B.C.E. (Ezra 2:46; Neh 7:48; 1 Esdr 5:30). Written Shamlai in Ezra 2:46, the correct form is Shalmai as in Neh 7:48 (see also 1 Esdr 5:30, LXX and the Qere in MT notations to Ezra 2:46). The name is one of the few among the Nethinim to have a Semitic root. It is noteworthy that this name appears in a 4th century B.C.E. seal which had been transcribed as "Shalmi the messenger" (Becking 1986: 446), although no connection between the bearers of the names can be supposed.

As members of the guild of Nethinim (Levine 1963), the family of Shalmai would have had a special role in the Temple cult, perhaps assisting the Levites. Although some scholars consider the Nethinim to be foreigners or of foreign origin, it appears that during the postexilic period the Nethinim, as cultic personnel, were considered neither foreigners nor slaves. Rather, like the Levites, they had been devoted to cultic service the precise nature of which can not longer be identified. The size of Shalmai's family, its origins and specific role are no longer discernible. Together with thirty-four other families of Nethinim and ten of families of Solomon's servants, the group included 392 members (Ezra 2:58; Neh 7:60) or 372 (1 Esdr 5:35). See also Blenkinsopp *Ezra-Nehemiah* OTL; Williamson *Ezra, Nehemiah* WBC.

Bibliography

Becking, B. 1986. A Remark on a Post-Exilic Seal. *UF* 18: 445–46.
Levine, B. A. 1963. The Netinim. *JBL* 82: 207–12.

TAMARA C. ESKENAZI

SHALMAN (PERSON) [Heb *šalman*]. The person who ransacked Beth-arbel (Hos 10:14). Shalman's destruction of Beth-arbel must have been both particularly brutal and well-known. The prophet Hosea cited the event as a warning to Israel of the utter devastation God was about to bring upon it.

Both Shalman and Beth-arbel are mentioned only in Hos 10:14; neither can be identified with confidence. Many scholars interpret "Shalman" as a hypocoristic form of Shalmaneser, the name of several Assyrian kings. Common proposals include Shalmaneser V, who died while besieging Samaria (722 B.C.E.) and Shalmaneser III, whom Astour (1971: 383–89) believes invaded Israel in 841 B.C.E. However, elsewhere Shalmaneser is fully spelled out. Other scholars identify Shalman with Salmanu, a Moabite king contemporaneous with Hosea, who is listed among those paying tribute to Tiglath-pileser III (*ANET,* 282).

Bibliography

Astour, M. C. 1971. 841 B.C.: The First Assyrian Invasion of Israel. *JAOS* 91: 383–89.

CAROLYN J. PRESSLER

SHALMANESER (PERSON) [Heb *šalmanʾeser*]. In Assyrian the name Shalmaneser is spelled *Šulmānu-ašarēd* and means "the god Šulmānu is the foremost." There were five kings in Assyrian history who bore this name but only the fifth and last such king is mentioned in the Bible. Of the preceding four kings only Shalmaneser I (1273–1244 B.C.) and Shalmaneser III (858–824 B.C.) were important. See MESOPOTAMIA, HISTORY OF (ASSYRIA) for a discussion of their reigns.

Shalmaneser V (726–722 B.C.), although a relatively insignificant king in Assyrian history, played an important role in biblical history since he laid siege to Samaria, capital of the kingdom of Israel, as narrated in 2 Kgs 17:1–41; 18:1–12; cf. 2 Esdr 13:40. According to this narrative Hoshea became a vassal of Shalmaneser, king of Assyria, but then changed his mind and made friendly overtures to the pharaoh of Egypt. When Hoshea withheld tribute from the king of Assyria, the latter shut him up in prison. Eventually the king of Assyria laid siege to Samaria and after three years the city fell.

The Israelites were carried off to live in exile in Assyria, along the River Habur, and in the cities of the Medes. In their place the king of Assyria settled in Israel people from various cities such as Hamat in Syria and Babylon and Cutha in Babylonia. The exiles from Syria and Babylonia continued to practice their own religions and these practices were condemned by the biblical narrative as evil.

The passage in 2 Kings is the most detailed narrative of the fall of Samaria to the Assyrians which has been preserved. In Assyrian records the event is scarcely mentioned. This is not due to lack of interest on the part of the Assyrians but rather to the lack of Assyrian sources in general for the reign of Shalmaneser V. Samaria's fall is given due prominence in the *Babylonian Chronicle* which singles this out as the only significant event in Shalmaneser V's reign. Given the paucity of our sources there has been much debate among modern historians about the exact date of the fall of Samaria, and some historians have even suggested that it was Sargon II rather than Shalmaneser V who captured Samaria (see *ANET,* 284–87). The most attractive solution to the problem is that Samaria fell in 722 B.C., the year of Shalmaneser V's death and the accession of Sargon II. Thus the leading of the Israelites into exile by the Assyrians was probably carried out during the reign of Sargon II (721–705 B.C.). Consequently, references to Shalmaneser (Gk *Enemessaros*) in the book of Tobit (1:2, 13, 15, 16), in connection with events during the exile of the people of Samaria at Nineveh, actually relate to the period of Sargon II. See also SARGON.

A. KIRK GRAYSON

SHAMA (PERSON) [Heb *šāmāʿ*]. A son of Hotham the Aroerite and one of the Reubenites associated with King David's chief military men (1 Chr 11:44). The name means "(YHWH) has heard" or "May (YHWH) hear." The Chronicler's expansion (1 Chr 11:41b–47) of the parallel lists of David's military elite (1 Chr 11:10–41a = 2 Sam 23:8–39) includes Shama and fifteen other men from the Transjordan, suggesting that Moabite AROER (1 Chr 5:8) is more likely Shama's hometown, although Judean Aroer (1 Sam 30:28) is also possible. There is general agreement that these expanded verses were not part of the original list. The addition of the sixteen names may have been inspired by 1 Chronicles 12 (Myers, *1 Chronicles* AB, 90), while Williamson (*1 & 2 Chronicles* NCBC, 104) and others (Mazar 1986: 101–102; Rudolph *Chronikbücher* HAT 1st ser., 101) have argued that the Chronicler or a later redactor did not fabricate these names.

Bibliography

Mazar, B. 1986. The Military Élite of King David. Pp. 83–103 in *The Early Biblical Period,* ed. S. Aḥituv and B. Levine. Jerusalem.

RUSSELL FULLER

SHAMGAR (PERSON) [Heb *šamgar*]. One of the early saviors of Israel in the premonarchy period, according to one prose statement (Judg 3:31). In Shamgar's days caravan trade came to a virtual standstill, according to one line of poetry (Judg 5:6). In both the prose and the poem Shamgar is further identified in Hebrew as *ben-ᶜănāt,* "son of Anath" or "Anathite." In the prose Shamgar is credited with single handedly disabling an entire Philistine brigade. The figure "six hundred" is probably not to be taken literally. "Six hundred" is a unit of military organization, an optimum figure rarely reached in practice (cf. Judg 18:11; 20:47) and often, presumably, deliberately kept below strength. Even so, Shamgar's achievement is impressive. His weapon is a metal-tipped pole, some eight feet long.

The name Shamgar is non-Semitic and probably of Hurrian origin, occurring in texts from Nuzi. That he was "Anathite" has long been thought to relate Shamgar to the town of Beth-anath in Galilee (Josh 19:38 Albright 1921). But the Hebrew label *ben ᶜănāt* may be a military designation involving the name of the goddess Anath, who was consort of Baal and warrior-goddess in her own right. Analogical evidence connecting Anath with the seminomads known as Ḫaneans in Mari texts, who on several occasions provide the king of Mari with sizable military contingents, lends support to the identification of Shamgar as a mercenary (Craigie 1972). (Another "Ben Anath" is known as a Syrian sea captain with whom Pharaoh Rameses II was allied, a century earlier than Shamgar.)

In the Song of Deborah and Barak, the "days of Shamgar" are seconded in parallelism as being also the "days of Jael" (Judg 5:6). The mention of disruption of the caravan trade, together with the modern opinion that 1125 B.C.E. is too early for Philistine presence in the N, has meant to some interpreters that Shamgar was, rather, one of the causes of hard times for Israel. On such a view, Shamgar was a Canaanite chieftain, perhaps a Hurrian newcomer menacing the entire countryside. On this view, Shamgar could perhaps be said to have "saved Israel" (3:31) in some less direct sense. There is, however, no longer any difficulty in understanding Shamgar, Jael, Deborah, and Barak as contemporaries in one period of success and achievement.

The *pĕlištî* were only one of the Sea Peoples, for whom "Philistine" became the generic label in Israel. It is likely that Sisera (another non-Semitic name), who commands the Canaanite forces in Judges 4–5, had a "Sea People" origin. What the Song of Deborah and Barak celebrates is disruption of the caravans by Israelites living in the highlands, so that Israel prospered to the point that it was able to defeat (thanks to a timely cloudburst and flash flood) the mercenaries sent against them by the N coalition. The activities of Shamgar and Jael lent support.

The brief mention of Shamgar's rescue work, killing six hundred Philistines, may be secondary in the prose, which lacks the familiar formulas about judging and giving the land rest for a number of years. The verse appears to be awkwardly inserted, for the beginning of the Deborah and Barak story (4:1) implies direct continuation of the Ehud story. Some LXX recensions have the Shamgar notice following the conclusion of the Samson cycle at 16:31, taking the reference to "Philistines" at face value. Some interpreters consider the Shamgar notice in 3:31 to be entirely a late piece of creative writing, based on 5:7 and perhaps a supplementary oral tradition. This is conceivable but unlikely.

Bibliography

Albright, W. F. 1921. A Revision of Early Hebrew Chronology. *JPOS* 1: 49–79.

Craigie, P. C. 1972. A Reconsideration of Shamgar ben Anath (Judg 3:31 and 5:6) *JBL* 91: 239–40.

ROBERT G. BOLING

SHAMHUTH (PERSON) [Heb *šamhût*]. One of twelve commanders supervising monthly courses of 24,000 men, or possibly 24 "units," rather than "thousands" (Myers *Chronicles* AB, 183, 53, 98), in the armed service of the king (1 Chr 27:8). Shamhuth was in charge of the course of the fifth month (v 8). This list of commanders and their functions is possibly a construct of its author/redactor, since (1) no such monthly, conscripted, civilian army is mentioned elsewhere during David's reign; (2) the large number of 288,000 men, if the term is understood correctly, seems improbable; and (3) one of the commanders, Asahel (v 7) was dead before David had rule over all Israel (Williamson *Chronicles* NCBC, 174–75). However, the author/redactor's thesis that David made preparations for the proper ongoing cultic and national life of Israel, as illustrated throughout chaps. 23–27, draws on the fact that David took a census (cf. vv 23–24; chap. 21) which could have been utilized for designing a monthly plan of conscription, a plan which would have been analogous to Solomon's monthly courses for his provision (1 Kgs 4:7–19).

Because the names of the other eleven commanders appear again in the list of David's Champions in 1 Chr 11:10–47 (= 2 Sam 23:8–39), it is probable that Shamhuth is to be equated with Shammoth of 1 Chr 11:27 and Shammah of 2 Sam 23:25 and, therefore, was a member of this select class of warriors directly attached to the king for special assignments. The form, "Shamhuth," can be explained as a combination of the variant spellings of "Shammah" and "Shammoth" (*IPN*, 259; Allen 1974: 190). Shamhuth, however, is not to be confused with the Shammah of 2 Sam 23:33 (= SHAGEE of 1 Chr 11:34), for the latter is probably to be equated with SHAMMAH, the son of Agee listed in 2 Sam 23:11–12 (see Driver *NHT,* 371 who reconstructs 2 Sam 23:33: "Jonathan, son of Shammah the Hararite").

Shamhuth is identified as an Izrahite, which is probably intended to be a gentilic designation for one from the place "Izrah," a place which is otherwise unknown. However, since variants of this designation occur with the other forms of "Shamhuth," it appears that this form has arisen through textual corruption.

Bibliography

Allen, L. C. 1974. *The Greek Chronicles.* VTSup 25. Leiden.

RODNEY K. DUKE

SHAMIR (PERSON) [Heb Q *šāmîr*]. The son of Micah in the levitical genealogy in 1 Chr 24:20–31. Shamir's descent was traced to Levi through his grandfather, Uzziel, son of Kohath, son of Levi. The mention of Shamir in 24:24 is one of several additions to the genealogy in 23:6–23. Due to the absence of Gershon in the list in chap. 24, some consider it secondary. The family of Gershon was probably not active at the time of the composition of the book. Also, the passage does not seem to fit the context in which it is placed. Shamir, as a personal name, occurs only in 24:24. The K, *šmwr,* denotes a passive participle based on the triliteral *šmr*. The meaning of the name is uncertain, but the word *šāmîr* means "thorns" and may carry the connotation of hardness as well as sharpness.

DONALD K. BERRY

SHAMIR (PLACE) [Heb *šāmîr*]. **1.** A town situated in the SW hill country of Judah (Josh 15:48), within the same district as Debir. This settlement, whose name perhaps means "thorn bush," is listed among the towns within the tribal allotment of Judah (Josh 15:21–62). The theory that this list is derived from an administrative roster compiled under the Judean monarchy (Alt 1925) has been widely accepted, although controversy continues over the precise make-up of the districts, the proper context of the town lists of Benjamin and Dan, and the period of the monarchy to which the original roster belongs (Boling and Wright *Joshua* AB, 64–72). The ancient name appears to be reflected at Khirbet es-Sumara, approximately 20 km SW of Hebron (Boling and Wright *Joshua* AB, 388; M.R. 143092). Although the location seems correct, archaeological confirmation of occupation during the appropriate periods is lacking.

2. A town in the hill country of Ephraim which became the home and burial place of Tola, first of the so-called "minor" judges (Judg 10:1–2). Mentioned only once in the OT, the precise location of this ancient town remains unknown. Based on the similarity between their names, Shamir has often been associated with Samaria, better known as capital of the N kingdom (*IDB* 4: 307; *LBHG,* 223). However, such an association is difficult to reconcile with 1 Kgs 16:24, where we are told that Omri named his new royal city after Shemer, the man from whom he had purchased the hill. If Samaria was the home and burial place of a famous Israelite hero, it seems unlikely that this would have been forgotten or ignored in later generations. On the other hand, 1 Kgs 16:24 does not necessarily rule out prior occupation on the hill.

Bibliography

Alt, A. 1925. Judas Gaue unter Josia. *PJ* 21: 100–16.

WADE R. KOTTER

SHAMLAI (PERSON) [Heb *šamlay*]. The variant for the name Shalmai used in Ezra 2:46. It is also the RSV rendering of the Gk name *Sybai* in 1 Esdr 5:30. See SHALMAI (PERSON).

SHAMMA (PERSON) [Heb *šammāʾ*]. One of the eleven sons of Zophah listed in the Asherite genealogy in 1 Chr 7:37. Shamma is descended from Helem (perhaps to be identified with Hotham) and hence falls within the dominant line of the clan. This name does not appear elsewhere in the Hebrew Bible and its etymology is uncertain. While some scholars consider such unique names as fabrications of the Chronicler, Johnson and others suggest that they derive from military census lists, themselves drawn up in genealogical fashion (Johnson 1969: 64–66).

Bibliography

Johnson, M. D. 1969. *The Purpose of the Biblical Genealogies.* Cambridge.

JULIA M. O'BRIEN

SHAMMAH (PERSON) [Heb *šammâ; šammāʾ*]. Var. SHIMEA; SHIMEAH; SHIMEI; SHAMMOTH? **1.** The third son of Reuel and the grandson of Esau (Gen 36:13, 17; 1 Chr 1:37). According to Gen 36:17, he was one of the Edomite "tribal chiefs" (Heb *ʾallûpîm*), and as such the name probably represents a clan within the Esauite-Edomite tribe of Reuel.

2. The third son of Jesse of Bethlehem, and older brother of David the king (1 Sam 16:9; 1 Chr 2:13, MT *šimʿāʾ*, RSV "Shimea;" cf. 1 Chr 20:7). Shammah took part in the battle against the Philistines (1 Sam 17:13). Apparently the son of Shammah (MT *šimʿâ,* RSV "Shimeah"), Jonadab, was the crafty friend (and cousin) who helped Amnon concoct a plan to lure the unsuspecting Tamar to Amnon's bed (2 Sam 13:3), and it was also he who subsequently reported that Tamar's brother Absalom had murdered Amnon in revenge (13:32–33). This same Jonadab eventually distinguished himself in battle (21:21, MT *šimʿay,* RSV "Shimei").

3. The son of Agee the Hararite, and one of David's elite fighters (2 Sam 23:11). He may also be listed after Jonathan in 2 Sam 23:33, although the parallel text 1 Chr 11:34 reads "Jonathan the son of Shagee the Hararite."

4. A man from Harod, and one of David's elite fighters (2 Sam 23:25). The orthographic similarities between Heb *d* and *r* mean that this soldier from Harod could be the same as the Hararite mentioned above (#3). The parallel text 1 Chr 11:27 reads Shammoth (Heb *šammôt*) of Harod.

With respect to Shammah #3–4, one should not put too much weight on the attestations in 1 Chronicles 11, which represent a later attempt to harmonize the parallel attestations in 2 Samuel 23. The meaning of the name "Shammah" and its variants is not clear. See also SHAMMA; SHAMHUTH. It is most probably a variant or a shortened form of a theophoric personal name containing the verb *šmʿ*, "hear," although derivations from **šmm* or *ṯmm* are also possible. See *IPN,* 38–39, 185.

ULRICH HÜBNER

SHAMMAI (PERSON) [Heb *šammay*]. **1.** The son of Onam, a descendant of Jerahmeel (1 Chr 2:28, 32).

2. The son of Rekem, a descendant of Caleb (1 Chr 2:44, 45).

3. The son of Mered, who married Bithiah, the daughter of Pharaoh (1 Chr 4:17).

H. C. LO

SHAMMAI, SCHOOL OF. Talmudic tradition (collected in Neusner 1971) describes the 1st-century Pharisees and their early rabbinic successors as having been divided into two wings or schools, called "houses" in Hebrew; these were named after the two great sages Hillel and Shammai, who flourished toward the end of the 1st century B.C.E., about 100 years before the Jerusalem temple was destroyed by the Romans. The very existence of such division in the movement of the Sages was a cause of some perplexity among later authorities, who explained (*t. Ḥag.* 2.9) that it arose among students paying inadequate attention to their teachers, but since Hillel and Shammai themselves are reported to have disagreed on occasion this explanation must be understood as homiletical.

A very large proportion of early Tannaitic and pretannaitic rabbinic traditions take the form of disputes (Neusner 1981: 19–21 considers many of them pseudepigraphic) between the two "houses." Most of these disputes concern details of halakhic practice, and in general the School of Shammai is reported to have held a view more restrictive or more stringent than that of its rival (*ʿEd.* 4 offers a catalogue of exceptions to this rule). Numerous modern scholars have attempted to explain this "conservative" tendency by reference to the Shammaites' social standing (Ginzberg 1962) or theory of law (Safrai *EncJud* 4: 737–41), but all such attempts rest on a very narrow base and must therefore be considered speculative. It should also be noted that not all reported disputes between the schools concerned legal matters; they are described as having argued for two and a half years over the question whether it would have been better for Adam never to have been created, only to agree that now that Adam has been created he ought to examine his deeds.

Later traditions do not agree in their descriptions of the relations between the two schools. *Yebam.* 1.4 reports that despite their serious differences over matrimonial law members of the two "houses" did not refrain from marrying women who belonged to the other, but *b. Šabb.* 17a contains a story that in the days of Hillel and Shammai themselves a dispute over purity law got so out of hand that "a sword was planted in the Study House . . . and that day was as hard for Israel as the day the golden calf was made."

At a later time the rulings of the School of Hillel were adopted as normative and those of the School of Shammai in most cases set aside. This decision was remembered as having been authorized by explicit heavenly instruction (*b. ʿErub.* 13b; *j. Soṭa* 3.4 19a). The fact, however, that in the great majority of cases the Shammaite opinion is reported first in extant traditions and often gets the last word as well suggests that at an earlier time the size and influence of the two factions was rather more balanced. The general impression is that the Pharisaic/rabbinic movement eventually came under the domination of the School of Hillel but preserved the memory of a time when the School of Shammai was the equal of the other in all respects. Later mystical teaching (*Zohar, Raʿva Mehemna* 3:245a) held that in the "World to Come" the present situation would be reversed and the rulings of the School of Shammai would become law. Thus in the end the original parity of the houses would be restored.

Bibliography

Ginzberg, L. 1962. The Significance of the Halakhah for Jewish History. Pp. 77–124 in *On Jewish Law and Lore.* Cleveland.

Goldenberg, R. 1986. Hillel/Hillelschule (Schammaj/Schammajschule), *TRE* 15: 326–30.

Neusner, J. 1971. *The Rabbinic Traditions about the Pharisees before 70.* Vol. 2. Leiden.

———. 1981. *Judaism: The Evidence of the Mishnah.* Chicago.

ROBERT GOLDENBERG

SHAMMOTH (PERSON) [Heb *šammôt*]. According to MT 1 Chr 11:27 Shammoth the Harorite is one of David's mighty men. In the parallel at 2 Sam 23:25 he is called Shammah the Harodite. Greek ms B for 1 Chr 11:27 reads *samaoth ho hadi,* reflecting MT for the personal name but perhaps indicating an attempt to modify the gentilic according to MT for 2 Sam 23:25 (*ḥărōdî*). In any event, between 1 Chronicles *hărôrî* and 2 Samuel *ḥărōdî* there appears to be some confusion between the Heb letters *he* and *ḥet* and *dalet* and *reš*. Because of the similarity of these names, there is either textual confusion or a confusion of the persons and the places themselves. As Driver (*NHT,* 362) remarks concerning the list of David's men as found in 2 Samuel and 1 Chronicles, "the names in several instances vary, nor is it always possible to determine which form is original, or whether both may not be corrupt."

It has been suggested (e.g., Curtis *Chronicles* ICC, 191) that Shammoth here is identical with Shamhuth, the fifth army commander for the fifth month, mentioned in 1 Chr 27:8, and/or with Shammah, son of Agee the Hararite, one of David's soldiers mentioned in 2 Sam 23:11 (*HDB* 4: 901).

STEPHEN PISANO

SHAMMUA (PERSON) [Heb *šammûaʿ*]. Var. SHIMEA. **1.** One of the twelve spies—one from each tribe—sent out by Moses to survey the land of Canaan (Num 13:4). He was the Reubenite representative chosen, the son of Zaccur.

2. A son of David born in Jerusalem (2 Sam 5:14; 1 Chr 14:4). According to 1 Chr 3:5 (where his name is Shimea), his mother was Bathsheba (Bathshua) and he had three full brothers: Shobab, Nathan, and Solomon. In addition, his father had six sons born in Hebron to six different wives, and nine born in Jerusalem to unnamed wives, as well as many sons born to his concubines in Jerusalem (1 Chr 3:9). See also DAVID, SONS OF.

3. A Levite in postexilic Jerusalem (Neh 11:17), one of 284 in the holy city (11:18). He is called Shemaiah in 1 Chr 9:16. He was father of Abda (Obadiah), and son of Galal, a descendant of Jeduthun, who was one of three musicians appointed by David to oversee the musical service of the Temple (1 Chr 25:1; 2 Chr 5:12).

4. A priest, son of Bilgah, in postexilic Jerusalem (Neh 12:18). Despite their identical names, similar occupations, and contemporary status, it is probable that this Shammua and the one in #3 above are different persons, since their fathers' names are different and especially since Shammua #3 is clearly listed as a Levite and not a priest.

DAVID M. HOWARD, JR.

SHAMSHERAI (PERSON) [Heb *šamšĕray*]. One of the Benjaminites who dwelt in Jerusalem in postexilic times, a son of Jeroham (1 Chr 8:26). The name Shamsherai is only found here in the OT. Noth (*IPN,* 259) suggested Shamsherai was a combination of *šāmray* and *šimšay,* and that *šimšay* should be read at 1 Chr 8:26, following the Lucianic recension of the LXX. The name *šimšay* is found several times in an Aramaic portion of Ezra (4:8, 9, 17, 23).

TOM WAYNE WILLETT

SHAPHAM (PERSON) [Heb *šāpām*]. A Gadite, who was one of four (or three; see SHAPHAT) tribal leaders named in the genealogy (1 Chr 5:12). He was designated "the second" after Joel, who was called "the head" or "chief." The translator of the LXX probably interpreted "the second" to refer to Shapham's birth order, after Joel "the firstborn" (Gk *prōtotokos*). At any rate, these leaders and their seven brethren are presented as sons of Abihail. The LXX mss that give spelling variants for Shapham's name (Sabat and Saphan) probably attest scribal confusion of two Hebrew letters that were written similarly (*pe* with *bet*) and the name "Shapham" with the more common "Shaphan."

1 Chronicles 5 notes that Shapham and the other Gadites lived opposite the Reubenites in "Bashan as far as Salecah" (v 11) and "in Gilead, in Bashan . . . and in all the pasture lands of Sharon to their limits" (v 17). While Num 13:24–28 assigns Gilead to Gad, too, it does not mention Bashan and Sharon, probably because the former is too far N and the latter too far W. It may be that the reference in 1 Chronicles 5 to Bashan reflects confusion about the N boundary of the tribe or about the extent of Bashan (cf. Deut 3:10). The inclusion of Sharon within Gad's inheritance may be correct in light of reference in the Mesha inscription (line 13; *ANET,* 320) to an otherwise unknown city or region by that name in Transjordania.

While 1 Chr 5:17 notes that Shapham and the other sons of Abihail were enrolled "in the days of Jotham . . . and . . . Jeroboam," it is likely that several years separated their reigns (unless Jotham's co-regency with his father Azariah/Uzziah is counted).

Neither Shapham nor the others named in the Chronicler's genealogy for Gad (1 Chr 5:11–17) appear in other lists of Gadites (Gen 46:16; Num 26:15–18; 1 Chr 12:9–16—Eng 12:8–15).

M. PATRICK GRAHAM

SHAPHAN (PERSON) [Heb *šāpān*]. **1.** A person bearing the title of "secretary" or "scribe" (Heb *hassōpēr*) who served under Josiah, king of Judah (2 Kgs 22:3, 8, 9, 10, 12 = 2 Chr 34:8, 15, 16, 18, 20; 2 Kgs 22:14). In his eighteenth year (621 B.C.), Josiah commissioned Shaphan to distribute temple funds to workers for the repairing of the temple in Jerusalem. While the temple was being repaired a document referred to as "the book of the law" was found and presented to Shaphan. Shaphan then read it to Josiah. Upon hearing the book, Josiah instituted reforms which cleared Judah of the elements of traditional Canaanite religion and which centered sacrifice to Yahweh in the Jerusalem temple.

2 Kgs 22:12 (= 2 Chr 34:20) refers to one Ahikam as a son of Shaphan (see also 2 Kgs 25:22; Jer 26:24; 39:14; 40:5, 9, 11; 41:2; 43:6). Whether or not this is Shaphan the scribe is a debated question. That Ahikam the son of Shaphan is mentioned in 2 Kgs 22:12 (= 2 Chr 34:20) before Shaphan the scribe seems to argue against a father-son relationship (Cogan and Tadmor *2 Kings* AB, 282).

Jer 29:3 mentions one Elasah the son of Shaphan by whom Jeremiah sent a letter—along with Gemariah the son of Hilkiah—to the Babylonian exiles of 597 B.C. In all likelihood, this is Shaphan the scribe of 2 Kings 22. This identification seems appropriate in light of the reference to Hilkiah in Jer 29:3. Hilkiah and Shaphan the scribe were closely associated in the Josianic reform movement. Shaphan the scribe is explicitly mentioned as the father of one Gemariah in Jer 36:10–12.

2. The father of Jaazaniah (Ezek 8:11). Jaazaniah is portrayed as participating in a cult conducted in a secret room with various kinds of animals engraved on the wall. The nature of this cult is not clear and several possibilities exist for its source (Greenberg *Ezekiel 1–20* AB, 168). Whatever the nature of the secret ritual, it clearly would not have involved Shaphan the scribe himself. If the former is Jaazaniah's father, Jaazaniah has departed from his father's perspective.

JAMES M. KENNEDY

SHAPHAT (PERSON) [Heb *šāpāṭ*]. The name derives from the perfect form of the verb *šāpaṭ* ("to judge") and occurs both in the short form (Shaphat), as well as in theophoric forms (e.g., Elishaphat) (see *IPN,* 22, 187).

1. A Simeonite, the son of Hori, who was sent by Moses with eleven other tribal leaders to spy out the land of Canaan before Israel began her assault (Num 13:5). They entered Palestine from the wilderness of Paran in the S, passed through the Negeb, and traveled throughout the land. After 40 days, the spies returned, and ten of them, including Shaphat, reported that the land was bountiful but its inhabitants were giants, dwelling in strongly fortified cities. They recommended that Israel not attempt to assault the land (Num 13:3–29, 31–33). Only two spies, Caleb and Joshua, urged the people to attack the land (Num 13:30). The narrator calls the report of the ten spies "evil" and notes that they all died of plague before the Lord (Num 14:36–37).

2. The father of Elisha, who dwelt with his son in Abel-meholah (1 Kgs 19:16), a city which has been located by some on the E bank of the Jordan (Tell el-Maqlub, according to Cohen *IDB* 1: 5), but by most on the W bank (e.g., Tell Abû Ṣûṣ, according to Aharoni *LBHG,* 313). Shaphat may have been a man of some means, since twelve yoke of oxen were used to plow his land. Gray, though, sees the plowing as a community effort and so does not attribute such prosperity to Shaphat (*1 and 2 Kings* OTL, 413). When Elijah called Elisha to leave the plowing and follow him, Elisha asked and received permission to kiss his parents first (1 Kgs 19:19). Shaphat is mentioned again only in the designation of his son "Elisha son of Shaphat" (2 Kgs 3:11; 6:31).

3. A descendant of Zerubbabel mentioned only in 1 Chr 3:22. The text of this section of Solomon's genealogy (1 Chr 3:10–24) is corrupt at several points. Apparently, "the sons of Shemaiah" arose through dittography and should be deleted (Rudolph *Chronikbücher* HAT, 31). This allows the number "six" at the end of v 22 to be correct (otherwise only five names precede it) and makes Shaphat the sixth son of Shecaniah, a descendant of Zerubbabel.

4. A Gadite mentioned only in 1 Chr 5:12. He was the son of Abihail and the fourth tribal leader named in the genealogy. It may be, however, that *šāpāṭ* should not be translated as a personal name but as the noun "judge." In this case, Joel was the leader of the tribe, Shapham the second in authority, and Janai a judge in Bashan (Rudolph *Chronikbücher* HAT, 47). The Targum and LXX support this interpretation. An alternative is to vocalize *špṭ* as a verb *(šāpaṭ)* and translate "Janai judged in Bashan." (Braun *1 Chronicles* WBC, 69–71.)

According to 1 Chronicles 5, Shaphat and the other Gadites lived opposite the Reubenites in "Bashan as far as Salecah" (v 11) and "in Gilead, in Bashan . . . and in all the pasture lands of Sharon to their limits" (v 17). Although Num 13:24–28 assigns Gilead to Gad, neither Bashan, which is too far N, nor Sharon, which is too far W, is mentioned. It may be that the reference in 1 Chronicles 5 to Bashan reflects confusion about the N boundary of the tribe or about the extent of Bashan (cf. Deut 3:10). The inclusion of Sharon with Gad's allotment coincides with a reference in the Mesha Inscription (line 13; *ANET* 320) to an otherwise unknown city or region by that name in the Transjordan.

The claim (1 Chr 5:17) that Shaphat and the other sons of Abihail were enrolled "in the days of Jotham . . . and . . . Jeroboam" is problematic, since several years separated their reigns (unless Jotham's co-regency with his father Azariah/Uzziah is counted).

Neither Shaphat nor the others named in the Chronicler's genealogy for Gad (1 Chr 5:11–17) appear in other lists of Gadites (Gen 46:16; Num 26:15–18; 1 Chr 12:9–16—Eng 12:8–15).

5. An official who managed David's herds in the valleys. He was the son of Adlai and is named as the ninth of twelve officers over the king's possessions (1 Chr 27:29). The list is without parallel in 1–2 Samuel and may derive from a period after David's reign (Rudolph *Chronikbücher* HAT, 184).

6. One of the family heads listed as "the sons of Solomon's servants" (1 Esdr 5:34). The name is rendered as Shaphat by the RSV according to LXX A *(Saphat)*, which is the usual representation of the Heb *šāpāṭ*, while Myers (*1 and 2 Esdras* AB, 61) renders it as Shaphag according to LXX B *(Saphag)*. However, this individual does not occur in the parallel texts in Ezra 2:57 and Neh 7:59.

M. Patrick Graham

SHAPHIR (PLACE) [Heb *šāpîr*]. A village in the Shephelah, otherwise unknown (Mic 1:11). Shaphir ("beautiful"), like Maroth, is mentioned by Micah in his paronomastic lament over Jerusalem's "daughters," towns in the Shephelah which were to have formed a bulwark for her defense. LXX A reads *Saphir* for Shamir (Heb *šāmîr*) which Josh 15:48 locates in the hill country of Judah (cf. Judg 10:1–2); and Eusebius' *Sapheir* between Eleutheropolis and Ashkelon (*Onomast.* 156) has been identified by some with modern es-Suwafir (SE of Ashdod) which would have been in ancient Philistia. Both are improbable locations within the context of Mic 1:10–16. More possible is Tell ʿEitun (M.R. 143099) and most likely of all is Khirbet el-Kôm (M.R. 146104) W of Hebron (Dever *EAEHL* 4: 976–77). Micah's pun stems from his personification of Shaphir as a beautiful woman who, in the expected (or recent) military disaster, will be stripped/violated and led away into exile. Hence, v 11: "Move on, 'Lady Fairfax,' in shameful nakedness" (Luker 1985: 89, 115). See also Hillers *Micah* Hermeneia, 26.

Bibliography

Dever, W. G. 1969–70. Iron Age Epigraphic Material from the area of Khirbet El-Kôm. *HUCA* 40–41: 139–204.

Luker, L. M. 1986. Doom and Hope in Micah: The Redaction of the Oracles Attributed to an Eighth-Century Prophet. Diss. Vanderbilt University.

Lamontte M. Luker

SHARAI (PERSON) [Heb *šārāy*]. Presumably a descendant of Binnui and one of the returned exiles whom Ezra required to divorce his foreign wife (Ezra 10:40). Sharai's name does not occur in the parallel list of 1 Esdr 9:34. According to Noth, Sharai is a shortened form of *(šērēbyāh)*, but the meaning of the first element *(šrb)* is unknown (*IPN*, 259–260). However, Noth also argues that the name Machnadebai, which occurs earlier in the verse, is a corruption of the phrase "from the sons of" (*IPN*, 249). If that is true, this would introduce the next family from which offenders come, and Binnui would not be the ancestor of Sharai. See also MACHNADEBAI. Assuming Binnui was Sharai's ancestor, Sharai was a member of a family who returned from Babylon with Zerubbabel (Neh 7:15; note that Bani replaces Binnui in Ezra's list [2:10]). See also BEDEIAH.

Jeffrey A. Fager

SHARAR (PERSON) [Heb *šārār*]. Father of Ahiam, one of "The Thirty," an elite group of King David's warriors (2 Sam 23:33). See DAVID'S CHAMPIONS. In the parallel reference in 1 Chr 11:35 his name reads "Sachar" (Heb *śākār*). It is difficult to decide with certainty the original name. The LXX is not that helpful, essentially reflecting MT in each text (Luc reads *Sarachō* in 2 Samuel, possibly suggesting *śakar* through substitution of the *kap* for the *reš*). The list of David's warriors extant in 2 Samuel 23 is generally regarded as textually superior to the parallel list in 1 Chronicles 11, in which case Sharar would be preferable (Elliger 1966: 72 n. 1). See SACHAR.

Bibliography

Elliger, K. 1966. Die dreissig Helden Davids. *KlSchr*, 72–118.

Stephen G. Dempster

SHAREZER (PERSON) [Heb *śarʾeṣer*]. There is one undisputed occurrence of this name in the Hebrew Bible;

another is open to question. The name seems to be a form of Akk *šarra uṣur* "may (the god X) protect the king!"

1. According to 2 Kgs 19:37 (= Isa 37:38), one of the sons of the Assyrian king Sennacherib who, along with his brother Adrammelech, assassinated their father. As yet no son of Sennacherib bearing this name has been attested in Assyrian sources.

2. One of two emissaries sent by the people of Bethel in 518 B.C.E. to inquire of the temple priests and prophets in Jerusalem concerning continuation of the practice of fasting in the fifth month (Zech 7:2). The Hebrew text is difficult, and susceptible to more than one analysis. Wellhausen was among the first to suggest that the word *byt ʾl* "Bethel" preceding the name might be its theophoric element, and that its proper form is Bethelsharezer "may (the deity) Bethel protect the king." This interpretation has been adopted in several modern English translations (NEB, NJPS, NAB). For discussion, see BETHEL (DEITY).

A. KIRK GRAYSON

SHARON (PLACE) [Heb *šārôn*]. Name of two places in the Bible. The etymology of the name is unclear (cf. *GP* 1: 414; *LBHG*, 22; Rudolph *Chronikbücher* HAT, 48).

1. A coastal plain, skirting the Mediterranean on the W and the central highlands on the E, which extends from the Yarkon River in the S to the Tanninim (Crocodiles) River in the N—about 32 miles in length with an average width of 11 miles. In the OT, the Sharon is a metaphor both for splendor and desolation (Cant 2:1; Isa 33:9; 35:2) as well as a place for pasture (1 Chr 27:29; Isa 65:10). In the NT, it is the location for the early ministry of the apostle Peter (Acts 9:35).

a. Geography. The Sharon has geographical features that have determined its socioeconomic and political history (Karmon 1961: 43–46). The features consist of three distinct corridors that run parallel to each other from S to N. These three corridors are intersected by several rivers flowing E-W to the Mediterranean. The W corridor, extending E about 2.5 miles, is a series of three N-S sandstone ridges with two intervening lowland areas. The W lowlands are dry most of the year, but are filled with temporary lakes during the rainy season. The E lowlands have extensive swamps due to lower elevation. The central corridor consists of red sand hills with an average height of 160–190 feet. In the N part of this corridor, the rivers, hindered by the sandstone ridges, have created broad river valleys with frequent marshlands. The soil of the area is too poor for agriculture; therefore, in antiquity, extensive oak woodlands were formed (for ancient descriptions: Strabo 16.2.27; Pliny *HN* 4.18; cf. Josephus *JW* 1.13.2; *Ant* 14.13.3; for modern analysis: Liphschitz and Waisel 1985: 139; Liphschitz, Lev-Yadun, and Gophna 1987). The E corridor is the only level area—one to four miles in width—of the Sharon Plain, consisting of well-drained alluvial soil suitable for agriculture. In the W along the sea, there is a beach of 65–100 feet abutting the W sandstone ridge, forming a coastal cliff of 130 feet in height. From the mouth of each river breaking through this cliff, sand dunes extend inland for several miles. In the E where the mountain slopes rise quickly above the plain, the S and central portions of those slopes consist of hard limestone allowing little access to the central highlands. However in the N, intermittent hard limestone and soft chalk permits access through valleys extending deep into the mountain slopes.

b. Settlement and Transportation. In antiquity, these geographical features determined both the settlement patterns and the transportation systems of the Sharon. Settlement of the area seemed to be determined by two factors: (1) access to agricultural resources and (2) strategic control of the transportation systems. In the S, the alluvial soil suitable for farming stops abruptly just N of the Yarkon River. Therefore the settlement patterns based on archaeological surveys show clusters of settlements around the Yarkon River and to the S. This same clustering is true also for the N, beyond the Hadera River, where well-drained alluvial soil permits farming in large areas of the hinterland (MB II: Broshi and Gophna 1986; earlier periods: Gophna and Portugali 1988; N Sharon in the Hellenistic period: Roller 1982). In all periods until the late 1st century B.C.E., the central Sharon from the Mediterranean to the edge of the central highlands was largely uninhabited because the land was unsuitable for agriculture.

However the second factor, transportation, also gave impetus to settlement in other areas of the Sharon. In order to understand this impetus, attention needs to be given to the influence of geography on the various trade routes. The Sharon in antiquity had a double orientation: first by land to the routes between Egypt and Syria, and second by sea toward Egypt, Cyprus, Lebanon, and, at various periods, the whole Mediterranean world. There were only two inland routes running N-S. One was along the coast using both the beach and the lowlands just E of the coastal cliffs. From the Yarkon River to the Hadera River, access from the coast to the E corridor was impossible. Therefore the armies and caravans of the ancient world only could have moved toward the Jezreel and the central highlands after they reached the Hadera River in the N (Roller 1982: 43). However, this coastal route was impassable in the rainy season and was hindered by rivers and the coastal cliff in the dry season.

The second inland route through the Sharon was part of the *Via Maris* "The Way of the Sea," a route extending N out of Egypt. It was used by the Egyptians as they moved N to control the Levant and later by other countries as they moved S to gain access to Egypt. Due to the lack of E-W routes noted above, the *Via Maris* had to leave the sea, ascend the Yarkon River to Aphek at its headwaters, then go either directly into the central highlands or N along the level ground of the E corridor to one of the passes in N Sharon. The strategic importance of these geographical limitations was readily recognized in antiquity and gave impetus to settlement along this route. Archaeological surveys of the E corridor show that settlements were clustered at strategic points of access to the highlands and the Jezreel (in the N: Socho [M.R. 153194] and Tel Zeror [Migdol?, M.R. 147203]; in the S: Aphek [M.R. 143168]).

The possibility of commerce by sea also gave impetus to settlements along the coast. These, however, are mainly single sites (Tel Mevorakh [M.R. 143215], Hepher [M.R. 141197], Tel Poleg [M.R. 135185], Tel Qasila [M.R. 130167], and Tel Michal [on the coast, M.R. 131174]) located usually on the rivers beyond the sand dunes. These port cities used the rivers for protection since the coast afforded no safe harbors except at Dor (M.R. 142224) in the N and Joppa (M.R. 126162) in the S. These settlement patterns and transportation routes remained constant until the Roman period and the reign of Herod the Great.

Under Herod and the Romans, a major change occurred in the Sharon which was accomplished by a remarkable feat of engineering. In a span of just twelve years, Herod built the artificial port of Caesarea (M.R. 140212) on the Mediterranean. This necessitated a new network of roads running both N-S and E-W. The Roman technology of paved roads with causeways and bridges allowed commerce to travel through the formerly inaccessible central Sharon. This network of roads also made the Sharon—even in the central region—the most densely populated area of the coastal plain (Karmon 1961: 53–57).

c. History. The issues of history for the Sharon that have been raised thus far have been those of the *longue durée*. These have been presented in order to raise the possibility of alternative interpretations that may be missed if one only deals with the political issues of the written sources. The synthesis needed to correlate all the data is beyond the scope of this article. However, the analysis stated above provides insight into the importance of the Sharon as (1) a strategic point of control of overland commerce, (2) a reservoir of economic resources both for farming and herding (for an analysis of the food and animal economy at Tel Qasile see Kislev and Hopf 1985; Davis 1985), and (3) an access to the maritime commerce of the Mediterranean (Roller 1982: 50; Hohlfelder 1983: 67).

The history of the Sharon gleaned from written texts and other archaeological sources beginning with the 18th Dyn. of Egypt illuminates the interplay of the above three factors. The annals and especially the letters of Amarna show that even though the Egyptians sought to control the trade routes to Syria, still they left the settlements of the Sharon under the control of the local population. These settlements, located largely in the areas of agricultural resources, became the source of supplies for the "colonial administration and Egyptian military forces in Palestine" (Weinstein 1981: 15). An illustration of this comes from the annals of Amenhotep II of the 18th Dyn. (*ANET,* 245–47). From the list of booty taken from the Sharon, including horses, large and small cattle, weapons, chariots, and prisoners, it would seem that Amenhotep was exploiting the rich agricultural region of N Sharon and not some semi-nomadic settlement as suggested by Aharoni (*LBHG,* 155) and Aḥituv (*CTAED,* 136). Also the names of the towns taken by Amenhotep such as Aphek, Socho, Yaham (M.R. 153197), and Eg *Migdalēn* (= Tel Zeror? [Aḥituv *CTAED,* 142)—each at a strategic point leading to the central highlands and the Jezreel—would indicate that Amenhotep had a vital interest in the trade routes leading to Syria. However, with the close of the LB age under the 19th Dyn. and the onset of Iron I with the 20th Dyn., the involvement of Egypt in S Palestine intensified politically, culturally, and militarily. Evidence of this intensification is seen in administrative centers such as the governor's residence at Aphek (Oren 1984: 49–50, 52). It appears that at least the S portion of the Sharon was under the control of an Egyptian province whose center was at Gaza (M.R. 099101) (Oren 1984: 54; cf. Singer 1988).

With the fall of the 20th Dyn. in the mid-12th century, our written sources become very meager. There is evidence of the presence of "Sea Peoples" at the two centers of agriculture: the Peleset/Philistines in the S at Tel Qasile on the Yarkon River, and the Tjeker at Dor in the N (Sandars 1985: 164, 170, 174). The complexity of the issues on the status of the Sharon during the emergence of Israel up to the early monarchy has created much diversity in scholarly opinion. Did the Sharon continue its earlier Canaanite development; was it absorbed by the emerging Israelites; or were other forces at work? The diverse conclusions about the biblical evidence (Josh 12:1–24; 17:1–13; Judg 1:27–28) proposed by Alt, Albright, and others are summarized succinctly by Kallai (*HGB,* 3–15, 50–61; cf. Gottwald 1979: 174–87, 484–85, 583–87 for a different approach).

The evidence for the history of Sharon until the Roman period consists mainly of the names of the administrative districts or provinces that controlled the area. Under the united monarchy, most of the Sharon seems to have been in Solomon's third district (1 Kgs 4:10). The fourth district (1 Kgs 4:11) according to Kallai (*HGB,* 60–61) was the region of Dor, the coastal plain S of Mt. Carmel and N of the Tanninim River. The exact extent of these districts is a matter of debate. After the divided monarchy, the Sharon fell under the jurisdiction of the N kingdom with only the port city of Joppa remaining under the control of Judah. Dor in the N then became the principle port for Israel (*LBHG,* 23). Under the Assyrians, administrative control of the Sharon was switched to the province of Dor (Akk *Dūʾru*), thus breaking the connection with the central highlands which existed during the monarchical period. The exact time of this change is open to discussion. Some suggest that it was established by Tiglath-pileser III as early as 734 B.C.E. so he could have direct access to Philistia (Donnor in *IJH,* 425). Another factor might have been the need for the agricultural resources of the N Sharon as well as direct access to the maritime commerce. This Assyrian administrative structure was maintained into the Hellenistic period. At that time the whole coast of the Levant became the district of Paralia (*GP* 2, map 8). Under Herod, the Sharon was divided into four districts: Antipatris, Apollonia, Caesarea, and Dora (*GP* 2, map 9).

d. Nature of Biblical Evidence. The biblical texts that do mention the Sharon convey little information. 1 Chr 27:29 is part of a list of royal officials that most scholars agree goes back to the time of David (Myers *I Chronicles* AB, 181; Rudolf *Chronikbücher* HAT, 184). In this list, Shitrai the Sharonite has been appointed supervisor of the royal herds of large cattle (Heb *bāqār*) in the Sharon. Rudolph notes that the persons supervising the royal herds and flocks were experts in animal husbandry. Therefore the use of the gentilic "Sharonite" not only gives his place of origin, but also intimates that persons from this area were trained in the care of animals. The other OT passages are metaphorical and care must be exercised in extracting issues of realia. However they do give a picture both of the agricultural (Cant 2:1; Isa 33:9; 35:2) and pastoral (Isa 65:10) value of the Sharon. Even though these metaphors seem to reflect actual conditions of the Sharon, one can never be sure of the exact referent of the writer.

The situation of Acts 9:35 is quite different. In place of a rustic rural area suitable for grazing, the passage reflects an area of dense population. "All the residents of Lydda and the Sharon" accepted the Christian faith as proclaimed by the apostle Peter because of the healing of Aeneas, a paralytic for eight years. "All the residents" probably is reflective of the new settlement patterns and network of roads that were the result of the building of Caesarea.

The Sharon played a strategic role in the history of the Levant. Its geography made it an important link on the trade routes between Egypt and Syria. Its geography, however, also hindered its natural orientation toward the sea. It is an area that remained basically the same—rustic and rural—until the technology of an outside culture allowed it to expand by sea to the doorstep of Rome. See also Gophna in *EAEHL* 4: 1071–74.

2. An unidentified site in the Transjordan region of Bashan (1 Chr 5:16). The context would identify this name with a place somewhere in Bashan rather than with the coastal plain of Sharon. Since the exact location is unknown, scholars have attempted to connect it with other texts that mention Sharon. Some have suggested a reference in the Mesha Stela (Myers *I Chronicles* AB, 34; cf. Rudolph *Chronikbücher* HAT, 48 who locates it further S). Another suggestion comes from the name of a place called *Sārūna* in an inscription of Amenhotep II (*CTAED,* 170; = Šarūna of EA 241:4). The context of the Amenhotep inscription is sufficiently unclear so that any identification remains uncertain.

Bibliography

Broshi, M., and Gophna, R. 1986. Middle Bronze Age II Palestine: Its Settlements and Population. *BASOR* 261: 73–90.

Davis, S. 1985. The Large Mammal Bones. Pp. 148–50 in Mazar 1985.

Gophna, R., and Portugali, J. 1988. Demographic Processes in Israel's Coastal Plain from the Chalcolithic to the Middle Bronze Age. *BASOR* 269: 11–28.

Gottwald, N. K. 1979. *The Tribes of Yahweh.* Maryknoll, NY.

Hohlfelder, R. W. 1983. Appendix: The Caesarea Maritma Coastline Before Herod: Some Preliminary Observations. *BASOR* 252: 67–68.

Karmon, Y. 1961. Geographical Influences on the Historical Routes in the Sharon Plain. *PEQ* 93: 43–60.

Kislev, M. E., and Hopf, M. 1985. Food Remains from Tell Qasille. Pp. 140–47 in Mazar 1985.

Liphschitz, N., and Waisel, Y. 1985. Analysis of Wood Remains from Tell Qasile. Pp. 139–40 in Mazar 1985.

Liphschitz, N.; Lev-Yadun, S.; and Gophna, R. 1987. The Dominance of *Quercus Calliprinos* (Kermes Oak) in the Central Coastal Plain in Antiquity. *IEJ* 37: 43–50.

Mazar, A. 1985. *Excavations at Tell Qasile: Part Two.* Qedem 20. Jerusalem.

Oren, E. 1984. "Governors' Residencies" in Canaan under the New Kingdom: A Case Study of Egyptian Administration. *JSSEA* 14: 37–56.

Roller, D. W. 1982. The Northern Plain of Sharon in the Hellenistic Period. *BASOR* 247: 43–52.

Sandars, N. K. 1985. *The Sea Peoples.* Rev. ed. New York.

Singer, I. 1988. Merneptah's Campaign to Canaan and the Egyptian Occupation of the Southern Coastal Plain of Palestine in the Ramesside Period. *BASOR* 269: 1–10.

Weinstein, J. M. 1981. The Egyptian Empire in Palestine: A Reassessment. *BASOR* 241: 1–28.

HARRY R. WEEKS

SHARUHEN (PLACE) [Heb *šārûḥen*]. A site in SW Palestine mentioned in Josh 19:6 in a list of cities belonging to Simeon (Josh 19:2–8). In pre-Israelite times, Sharuhen must have been a major town, since it is mentioned a few times in Egyptian texts (Aḥituv *CTAED,* 171). When Pharaoh Ahmose (ca. 1552–1527 B.C.) ended the more than a century-long domination of the foreign Hyksos by conquering their city of residence, Avaris (Tell ed-Dabᶜa) in the E Nile Delta, he also acquired their S Palestinian bastion, Sharuhen (*šrḥn*). In a burial inscription, a ship's captain with the name Ahmose records that the town was besieged for three (perhaps not uninterrupted) years (*ANET,* 233).

Having been influenced by the Hyksos, a time of Egyptian imperialism began with Ahmose and his successors, among them Thutmose III (ca. 1490–1436) who, in his first campaign (1468) into Palestine engaged a coalition of Canaanite and Syrian petty princes. His achievements are recorded in his annals in his temple at Karnak (*ANET,* 234–38). The beginning of the account records that the lands from Yurza (Eg *jrḏ* = Tell Jemmeh) and northward had rebelled; only Sharuhen (*šrḥn*) remained in Egyptian hands (Helck 1971: 119). This strategically important site (seen from Egypt's point of view) is mentioned again in a list of places in the temple of Amon in Soleb which dates from the time of Amenhotep III (ca. 1402–1364), and also in a list in a temple in Amara West (Nubia), which Rameses II (ca. 1290–1224) had inscribed. Sharuhen is always mentioned with other sites which are situated along the coastal road (Giveon 1964: 247–48; Kempinski 1974: 149–50).

After Pharaoh Sheshonq I (ca. 950–929) campaigned in Palestine (mentioned in 2 Kgs 14:25–28), he inscribed the names of the sites he conquered in the temple of Amon in Karnak. Sharuhen is probably among the Negeb sites mentioned, if the text in question is to be read *šrḥn* (Ahituv *CTAED,* 171 n. 499), and not *šlḥm* (Mazar 1957: 65, cf. *šilḥîm* Josh 15:32).

Here the vocalization in question is possible, since, in connection with foreign names, the vowelless Eg system of writing prefers a syllabic orthography. In the case of Sharuhen we should read either *s3-r3-h3-n3* or *š3-r3-[ḥ3]-nw,* that is, Šarahna or Šaraḥanu (Aḥituv *CTAED,* 171). Albright (1924: 134–35; 1934: 53) read *Š3-ra-ḥu-na,* thus connecting the word with Canaanite Šarḥôn, later Širḥôn. He regarded the Hebrew vocalization šārûḥen as erroneous. Noth (*Josua* HAT²[1953], 88) agreed on this point and postulated the reading "Sirhon."

In the OT, Sharuhen is mentioned only once. The Vg reads Saroen, while LXX, which reads *hoi agroi autōn* must have read or understood Heb *śdyhn* or *śdwtyhn.* There are two lists which may be compared with Josh 19:2–8, namely Josh 15:21–62(63), a list of towns belonging to the tribe of Judah, and 1 Chr 4:28–32, which is, like Josh 19:2–8, a list of sites belonging to Simeon. The names correspond at least in part in both lists; for this reason the sites *šilḥîm* (Josh 15:32) and *šaʿărāyim* (1 Chr 4:31) are usually taken to be variants of *šārûḥen*. However, this contradicts the principles "of scribal tradition regarding the patterns noticeable in the composition of the lists. Names peculiar to a given version are inserted in place of others that dropped out of a previously known list" (Kallai *HGB*, 353, n. 46).

A variety of name forms might reflect changing geographico-historical circumstances. Thus it has been suggested that the list in 1 Chronicles 4 (not yet containing Sharuhen), the oldest, and the list in Joshua 19 (containing Sharuhen) date from the time of David, whereas the one in Joshua 15 (no longer containing Sharuhen) is to be assigned to the time of Hezekiah or Josiah (Kallai *HGB*, 353–54).

To the extent that scholars have reckoned with a locality associated with the tribe of Simeon, they have sought to place it in S Palestine, though as far W as possible, to make the extension into Philistine territory appear plausible (Aharoni *LBHG*, 299). If, on the other hand, it has been assumed that the Simeonites were semi-nomadic until around the 8th century, then the list in 1 Chronicles 4 has been taken as the frame of reference of the migrations of the clan; in consequence of this, Sharuhen has been sought even further to the E (Kempinski 1974: 150–52).

As a conceivable locality, the W Negeb has long been under consideration (Aharoni *LBHG*, 26–27). Albright's suggested identification (1929: 7) of Sharuhen with Tell el-Farʿah ("the high ruin-mound," M.R. 100076) on the W bank of Wadi Ghazze, about 20 km SE of Gaza and about the same distance from the Mediterranean coast, was unchallenged for a long time. This tell, which covers approximately 15 acres and is about 15 m high, was the site at which Flinders Petrie thought to find Beth-pelet (Josh 15:27; Neh 11:26). It contains occupation remains dating from MB IIB until the Roman period (*EAEHL* 4: 1074–82). Like other MB II sites (Aharoni *LBHG*, 148), the complex at Tell el-Farʿah was well protected by walls, a glacis, and trench-moats. The single feature found at the tell which best exemplifies MB IIB design is the three-piered gate flanked by two towers. In the LB II period a residence was constructed whose models date from the 19th Dyn. (*EAEHL* 4: 1077; plans of both gate and residence). The small finds which were discovered, particularly in the graves, reveal both Egyptian and Egyptianizing stylistic features (Keel and Küchler 1982: 129–31). The Philistines settled at the site during the Iron Age; the lack of finds in the necropolis may indicate that the site was either uninhabited or only sparsely populated between the 9th and 7th centuries (Cohen 1977: 170). It is first with the Persian and Roman periods (extending to the 1st century B.C.) that evidence of settlement again becomes clearer.

An objection against Albright's identification of Sharuhen with Tell el-Farʿah is that the site is too modest to explain Ahmose's three-year siege (Rainey *ISBE* 4: 454). Another objection is even more pertinent: the fact that a ship's captain was a participant in Ahmose's undertaking shows that Sharuhen must have been close to the coast (Kempinski 1974: 149). The suggestion to identify Sharuhen with Tell Abû Hurêre (M.R. 112087; Rainey *ISBE* 4: 454), is even further away from the coast than is Tell el-Farʿah, rendering this identification improbable. Admittedly, the surface finds, which date from MB II and the LB period, do show that this site could have been important at the time in question.

To be preferred is another tell situated about 6 km SE of Gaza and near the coast: Tell el-ʿAjjûl (M.R. 093097), just N of the mouth of the Wadi Ghazze (Kempinski 1974: 145–52; Stewart 1974: 63). Measuring 300 m × 500 m, this tell, of which only a tiny fraction was excavated by Petrie, is one of the largest in S Palestine. Because of its name ("ruin-mound of the calf") the tell was previously identified with Beth-ʿeglaim ("house of the two calves"; cf. Ezek 47:10), which is attested for the Byzantine period (Maisler 1933: 186–88). This identification is, however, just as improbable as the attempt to locate MB Gaza there (Keel and Küchler 1982: 97).

As at Tell Farʿah, ʿAjjul was both fortified and protected by a deep moat and flourished during the MB Age (Tufnell *EAEHL* 1: 55–56). During the course of MB I (12th Dynasty) a town arose which was expanded in MB II and was supplied with a palace. Destroyed in the 17th century, the town was renovated during the Hyksos period. Evidence of this renascence is provided by the architecture, red and black pottery with depictions of birds, fish, and cattle, numerous gold ornaments containing the image of the Syrian goddess, and the largest collection of scarab seals with figural motifs yet discovered in Palestine (*EAEHL* 1: 57–60; Stewart 1974). Of interest for historians of culture are the joint burials of men and horses (*EAEHL* 1: 55, 57), which reflect the significance of the horse for the Hyksos, who had brought the horse to Palestine.

A feature which perhaps helps to date the destruction of the Middle Bronze Age town is the presence of scarabs bearing the name Apopi (Eg *ʿ3 wsr rʿ*), one of the last of the Hyksos rulers; these may be seen in relation to the destruction of Sharuhen by Ahmose (Kempinski 1974: 147). The time of Thutmose III is also epigraphically attested on the tell: fragments of a storage jar display two cartouches bearing the names of Hatshepsut and Thutmose (Keel and Küchler 1982: 99–100). See ʿAJJUL, TELL EL-.

After its destruction, the inhabitants of the town seem to have moved to Gaza, which probably became the new Egyptian administrative center for Palestine. The site of Tell el-ʿAjjul continued as a fortress with a harbor at the mouth of the Wadi Ghazze (Kempinski 1974: 148). The tell was completely abandoned when the Philistines appeared on the scene. Only some individual finds form subsequent periods have been found (*EAEHL* 1: 60).

Bibliography

Albright, W. F. 1924. Egypt and the Early History of the Negeb. *JPOS* 4: 131–61.

———. 1929. Progress in Palestinian Archaeology during the Year 1928. *BASOR* 33: 1–10.

———. 1934. *The Vocalization of the Egyptian Syllabic Orthography.* AOS 5. New Haven.

Cohen, R. 1977. Tell el-Farʿa (South). *IEJ* 27: 170.

Giveon, R. 1964. Toponymes ouest-asiatiques à Soleb. *VT* 14: 239–55.

Helck, W. 1971. *Die Beziehungen Ägyptens zu Vorderasien im 3. und 2. Jahrtausend v. Chr.* ÄA 5.2. Wiesbaden.

Keel, O., and Küchler, M. 1982. *Orte und Landschaften der Bible. Ein Handbuch und Studienreiseführer zum Heiligen Land. Band 2: Der Süden.* Zürich.
Kempinski, A. 1974. Tell el-ᶜAjjûl—Beth-Aglayim or Sharuḥen? *IEJ* 24: 145–52.
Kitchen, K. A. 1973. *The Third Intermediate Period in Egypt (1100–650 B.C.).* Warminster.
Maisler, B. (= Mazar, B.) 1933. Der antike Name von tell ᶜaddshcūl. *ZDPV* 56: 186–88.
Naʾaman, N. 1980a. The Shihor of Egypt and Shur that is before Egypt. *TA* 7: 95–109.
———. 1980b. The Inheritance of the Sons of Simeon. *ZDPV* 96: 136–52.
Stewart, J. R. 1974. *Tell el ᶜAjjūl. The Middle Bronze Age Remains,* ed. H. E. Kassis. Studies in Mediterranean Archaeology 38. Göteborg.

RÜDIGER LIWAK

SHASHAI (PERSON) [Heb *šāšay*]. Presumably a descendant of Binnui and one of the returned exiles whom Ezra required to divorce his foreign wife (Ezra 10:40 and 1 Esdr 9:34). According to Noth, Shashai is a short "pet name" which originated in early childhood and completely replaced the full name (*IPN,* 40–41). However, Noth also argues that the name Machnadebai, which occurs before Shashai, is a corruption of the phrase "from the sons of" (*IPN,* 249). If that is true, this would introduce the next family from which offenders come. However, Shashai is not named as the head of a family in the lists of Ezra 2 or Nehemiah 7. This is further indicated by the parallel text of 1 Esdr 9:34 in which the phrase "of the sons of Ezora" replaces the name Machnadebai, perhaps preserving a name dropped from Ezra 10:40. This would mean that Binnui was not Shashai's ancestor. See also MACHNADEBAI. Assuming Binnui was Shashai's ancestor, Shashai was a member of a family who returned from Babylon with Zerubbabel (Neh 7:15; note that Bani replaces Binnui in Ezra's list [2:10]). See also BEDEIAH.

JEFFREY A. FAGER

SHASHAK (PERSON) [Heb *šāšāq*]. A Benjaminite, the son of Elpaal (1 Chr 8:14, 25). The Chronicler makes no connection between Shashak, son of Elpaal in 1 Chr 8:14, and Shashak, head of a household in 8:25. The two could be different people but there is not enough evidence to determine this, even though Curtis and Madsen (*Chronicles* ICC, 160) believed Shashak was misplaced in 8:14. Noth (*IPN,* 64) believed Shashak was an Egyptian name from the post-exilic period. The last verse of this section (1 Chr 8:28) states that the preceding men, presumably including Shashak, lived in Jerusalem.

TOM WAYNE WILLETT

SHASU. A term appearing only in Egyptian that designates both a people encountered by the Egyptians in the period 1500–1100 B.C., and the territory which they inhabited. Since we see the Shasu only through Egyptian eyes, and this view is often obscure, modern interpretations vary as to their origin and identity. The derivation of the word is uncertain: it is related either to the Egyptian verb "to wander" or Semitic "to plunder" (Giveon 1971: 261–63; Ward 1972: 56–59; Weippert 1974: 433). An Egyptian origin seems more likely. It is clear that the Shasu-people were not an ethnic group but rather a social class.

It has been proposed that "Shasu" appears both as a people and a land before the Egyptian Empire period, but this early material is not clear and is best left aside until more conclusive evidence is known (Helck 1971: 17–18; Görg 1976: 425–26). The first clear reference to the Shasu is found in the biography of an Egyptian army officer who records the taking of prisoners from "Shasu-land" in the reign of Thutmosis II (Giveon 1971: Doc. 1). References to the Shasu land or people which can be used as historical sources continue to appear until the 20th Dynasty.

Though most references to the Shasu are in lists of conquered towns or important enemies, there are enough specific statements to locate these people geographically. In his N campaign undertaken in his first year, Seti I went through Shasu territory before he reached S Palestine. The area concerned lies between the E border of the Egyptian Delta and the town of Gaza (Giveon 1971: Doc. 11; Weippert 1974: 270; Spalinger 1979: 30).

To the N, Egyptian texts place the Shasu in N Palestine and S Syria-Lebanon. "Two Shasu of the Shasu-tribes" brought false information to the Egyptian king Ramesses II during the Battle of Kadesh in 1300 B.C.; these tribes were allies of the Hittite ruler (Giveon 1971: Doc. 14). Certain of the topographical lists are important in this respect since "Shasu" is included among N districts, for example in a short list of Thutmosis IV (Giveson 1971: Doc. 4). This list has six names: Naharin (N Mesopotamia), Babylonia, Tunip, Shasu, Kadesh, and Takhsi, the latter in the Lebanese Beqaᶜa Valley (Edel 1966: 11). A similar list of King Amenhotep III places ᶜAin-Shasu, "the well of the Shasu," among places in N Palestine such as Dothan and Shamkhuna (Giveon 1971: Doc. 5a). ᶜAin-Shasu, the Enshasi of the Amarna Letters, is probably to be located in the Beqaᶜa Valley (Helck 1971: 261; Weippert 1974: 273).

Another group of texts places the Shasu in S Transjordan. Short lists of place-names in Nubian temples of Amenhotep III and Ramesses II record six toponyms located in "the land of Shasu" (Giveon 1971: Docs. 6a, 16a). Those that can be identified are in the Negeb or Edom (Kitchen 1964: 66–67; Weippert 1974: 270–71). One of the six, Seir in Edom, is found elsewhere in connection with the Shasu. A monument of Ramesses II claims that he "has plundered the Shasu-land, captured the mountain of Seir;" a 19th Dynasty model letter mentions "the Shasu-tribes of Edom;" Ramesses III declares that he has "destroyed the Seirites among the tribes of the Shasu" (Giveon 1971: Docs. 25, 37, 38). From the Egyptian viewpoint, then, the Shasu were a prominent part of the Edomite population. These references indicate that there must have been Egyptian military activity in Transjordan, born out by the claim of Ramesses II that he plundered Dibon in Moab (Kitchen 1964: 53; 1976: 313–14) and possibly the enigmatic Balu'a Stele (Ward and Martin 1964). This stele portrays a local king receiving his kingship from a god with a goddess in attendance. All three figures are in Egyptian costume though the king is bearded and wears the bag-like head-cloth particularly associated with the Shasu. The panel is surmounted by a six line inscription which remains undecipherable. This stele may show Egyptian influence in Moab in the Empire period but its interpretation is extremely difficult. Only two Egyptian royal monuments of the period have been found locally, both of no value in assessing Egyptian relations with Transjordan since they were not found *in situ:* a stele fragment of Seti I from Tell el-Shihâb on the Yarmuk River (Giveon in *LÄ* 4: 245) and a rock stele, the so-called "Job Stone," of Rameses II at Sheikh Sa'id in the Hauran (Schumacher 1891).

In another direction, an important geographical reference is found in a 20th Dynasty letter from the High Priest of Amon in Thebes to Nubian officials in the district of *'Ikt.* "The Shasu of the land of *mw-ḳd* who live in *ḳḥḳḥ* on the sea-coast" are mentioned three times as being hostile to Egyptian expeditions sent to mine gold in the area (Helck 1967: 140; on the gold mines, Vercoutter 1959). While *ḳḥḳḥ* is unknown and there is still some controversy over the meaning of *mw-ḳd* in this context (see Kitchen in *LÄ* 4: 1201, n. 32), the district of *'Ikt* is the area of the Wadi Allaqi E of Kubân (Zibelius 1971: 95–96). There is thus no doubt that the Egyptians met people known to them as Shasu in Nubia though, as Giveon (1969–70) suggests, they may have moved in from Transjordan and were not native to the area. Other evidence for Shasu-people in Africa is ambiguous (Goedicke 1968; Ward 1972: 38–40).

In general, the more specific geographical evidence from the texts suggests an origin for the Shasu in Transjordan though other proposals have been made (e.g., Lorton 1971–72: 149; Görg 1976). The question is basically whether the term "Shasu" was originally geographic and was then applied to a people, or vice-versa. The latter seems most likely. The "land of the Shasu" from whence the Shasu came was in Transjordan, the term then being used to refer to any district further W where they were encountered.

Apart from the textual evidence, one must also consider the numerous pictoral representations in Egyptian reliefs said to portray the Shasu, though few of these figures are identified as such by accompanying texts. In general, the Shasu were bearded and wore either a short, often tassled, kilt or an ankle-length garment as well as a peculiar bag-like head-cloth. They fought with axe and spear, but not bow and arrow, and are sometimes shown with a round medallion suspended from the neck. However, all these elements of costume, with the possible exception of the head-cloth, are seen in representations of other foreigners as well. This is due to the somewhat casual conventions of Egyptian artists who carefully distinguished foreigners from general regions such as the Aegean, Syria, and Nubia, but were not so careful about more detailed ethnic definitions. Unidentified foreigners in the reliefs must therefore be interpreted with caution; some "Shasu" in the reliefs may not belong to that group at all (Ward 1972: 46–47).

While there are few references to the nature of the Shasu-people, these seem clear enough. They were divided into tribes with tribal chieftains and are described as rebellious, quarrelsome, and unfriendly highwaymen who are "ignorant of the laws of the palace" (Giveon 1971: Docs. 11, 36). The latter expression can refer to Egyptian law or, more probably, to the legal institutions of the Asiatic city-states among which the Shasu lived. The Shasu appear as mercenaries in both Asiatic and Egyptian armies and, following Egyptian practice, we find them resident in Egypt, undoubtedly as retired mercenaries allowed to settle there when their military service was over (Giveon 1971: Docs. 46, 50; Helck in *LÄ* 4: 134–35).

But fighting and robbery were not the only aspect of Shasu life. In the reign of Merneptah we find them driving their herds across the frontier into the pasture-lands of the Delta, and the campaign of Ramesses III against the Shasu in Edom netted him animal-herds as well as property and prisoners (Giveon 1971: Docs. 37, 38). The latter reference also notes that the Shasu lived in tents and another text is generally taken to mean that some Shasu lived in towns (Giveon 1971: 114–15, n. 5).

This description, sparse though it may be, indicates that the Shasu represent a social class, partially nomadic and partially sedentary, members of which regularly left the Transjordanian homeland to hire out as mercenaries or engage in free-booting. Since the texts speak of "tribes" of Shasu and there are differences in their costume (e.g., either long dress or short kilt), we can speak somewhat confidently of a social class made up of several tribal groups at least partially, perhaps only seasonly, uprooted from their tribal areas. An analogy to the well-known Hapiru-people is obvious, though the analogy is not a complete one.

The Egyptians themselves seem to have recognized that the Shasu and Hapiru had separate identities as shown by a stele of Amenhotep II which lists prisoners from both groups taken in his N campaign (Giveon 1971: Doc. 3). Two texts of Seti I suggest that the Egyptians believed the Shasu and Hapiru to be of the same social class. One speaks of Shasu in N Sinai, the other of Hapiru in the Beth-shan region (Giveon 1971: Doc. 1; Albright 1952; Helck 1968: 475–78). The two groups are described in much the same terms as trouble-makers among the sedentary population of Palestine. See also ḪABIRU, ḪAPIRU.

Both groups are best understood in the framework of Rowton's studies on the dimorphic social and political structure of society, prevalent throughout W Asia in the 2d millennium B.C. This embraced both the sedentary and the nomadic (urban and tribal) so that there was continuous economic and political interaction between two groups of rather different social structure (Rowton 1973: 202–4). The nomadic element in this dimorphic structure is termed "enclosed nomadism," a type of nomadism, which itself may be partially sedentary, in constant touch with urban life (Rowton 1974).

On the margin of urban and tribal society there was a third group: "a social element consisting of detribalized labor, mercenaries, predatory bands, and tribal splinter groups, all impelled from tribal society into urban society by lack of food, sometimes amounting to genuine famine, and also by intertribal warfare and disputes" (Rowton 1976: 14). Such outcasts came also from urban society. This third social group injected a considerable element of unrest in the midst of city-states which had limited political and military control. Even under the Egyptian Empire, the

Asiatic provinces were administered rather than ruled so that Egyptian provincial governors were not militarily strong.

If we view the Shasu from this standpoint, the Egyptian texts describe a social class quite similar to the Hapiru. It would appear that in their Transjordan homeland, the Shasu lived in an "enclosed nomadism" type of society, but wherever else they were found, they are very much like Rowton's third element of society—the uprooted, detribalized element which has taken to brigandage and fighting for pay. This seems to be a better definition than the more general terms "transmigrant" or "transhumance" previously used (Ward 1972: 54; Weippert 1974: 274). The Shasu thus fit into the general pattern of the dimorphic structure of society in W Asia which existed as long as the city-state system prevailed. It can be no coincidence that both "Hapiru" and "Shasu" ceased to have any historical meaning toward the turn of the 2d millennium B.C. when the appearance of nation-states brought stricter political control (Greenberg 1955: 88; *LÄ* 5: 534). The social class these terms designated had disappeared.

Several parallels have been noted between the Shasu and the biblical Hebrews, but these are of a general rather than a specific nature (Giveon 1971: chap. 5; Weippert 1974: 279–80). Such parallels are to be expected if, as many claim, the patriarchal Hebrews belonged to the same widespread social class as the Shasu. If the early Hebrews are to be identified with any other known group, it would be with the Hapiru (Weippert 1967: 101–3; Cazelles in *POTT,* 1–28; Rowton 1976: 18–20).

Bibliography

Albright, W. F. 1952. The Smaller Beth-Shan Stela of Sethos I (1309–1290 B.C.). *BASOR* 125: 24–32.

Edel, E. 1966. *Die Ortsnamenlisten aus dem Totentempel Amenophis III.* BBB 25. Bonn.

Giveon, R. 1969–70. The Shosu of the Late XXth Dynasty. *JARCE* 8: 51–53.

———. 1971. *Les bédouins Shosou des documents égyptiens.* DMOA 22. Leiden.

Goedicke, H. 1968. Papyrus Lansing 3,9–3, 10. *JARCE* 7: 128–30.

Görg, M. 1976. Zur Geschichte der *Š3sw. Or* 45: 424–28.

———. 1979. Tuthmosis III und die *Š3sw*-region. *JNES* 38: 199–202.

Greenberg, M. 1955. *The Ḫab/piru.* AOS 39. New Haven.

Helck, W. 1967. Eine Briefsammlung aus der Verwaltung des Amuntempels. *JARCE* 6: 135–51.

———. 1968. Die Bedrohung Palästinas durch einwandernde Gruppen am Ende der 18. und am Anfang der 19. Dynastie. *VT* 18: 472–80.

———. 1971. *Die Beziehungen Ägyptens zu Vorderasien im 3. und 2. Jahrtausend v. Chr.* 2d ed. ÄA 5. Wiesbaden.

Kitchen, K. A. 1964. Some New Light on the Asiatic Wars of Ramesses II. *JEA* 50: 47–70.

———. 1976. Two Notes on Ramesside History. *OrAnt* 15: 311–15.

Lorton, D. 1971–72. Review of Giveon 1971. *JARCE* 9: 147–50.

Rowton, M. B. 1973. Urban Autonomy in a Nomadic Environment. *JNES* 32: 201–15.

———. 1974. Enclosed Nomadism. *JESHO* 17: 1–30.

———. 1976. Dimorphic Structure and the Problem of the ʿAPIRÛ-ʿIBRÎM. *JNES* 35: 13–20.

Schumacher, G. 1891. Der Hiobstein, Sachrat Eijub, im Hauran. *ZDPV* 14: 142–47.

Spalinger, A. 1979. The Northern Wars of Seti I: An Integrative Study. *JARCE* 16: 29–47.

Vercoutter, J. 1959. The Gold of Kush. *Kush* 7: 120–53.

Ward, W. A. 1972. The Shasu "Bedouin." Notes on a Recent Publication. *JESHO* 15: 35–60.

Ward, W. A., and Martin, M. 1964. The Balu'a Stela: A New Transcription with Palaeographical and Historical Notes. *ADAJ* 8–9: 5–29.

Weippert, M. 1967. *Die Landnahme der israelitischer Stämme in der neueren wissenschaftlichen Diskussion.* FRLANT 92. Göttingen.

———. 1974. Semitische Nomaden des zweiten Jahrtausends. Über die *Š3sw* der ägyptischen Quellen. *Bib* 55: 265–80, 427–33.

Zibelius, K. 1972. *Afrikanische Orts- und Völkernamen in hieroglyphischen und hieratischen Texten.* BTAVO B/1. Wiesbaden.

William A. Ward

SHAUL (PERSON) [Heb *šāʾûl*]. The name means "The One Asked-For." In addition to being the name of the very first king of Israel (see SAUL), it was also the name of various tribes and persons in the OT. Names with the same consonants (and related meanings) are attested in Iron Age Syrian epigraphy (*šʾl,* KAI 24,4), in Palmyrene (**Šaʾīlā),* and in ancient North Arabian epigraphy (*sʾl,* possibly to be vocalized **Saʾʾāl*).

1. The seventh ruler mentioned in the Edomite King List (Gen 36:37; 1 Chr 1:48). Opinions vary concerning the date of this list. Suggestions range from the 11th century B.C. (Weippert 1982: 155) through the 8th to 6th centuries B.C. (Bennett 1983: 16) to the 6th/5th centuries B.C. (Knauf 1985). Scholars tend to agree, however, that the succession scheme of this list is artificial, and that, in all likelihood, the rulers listed in it were contemporaries (Bartlett 1972: 27; Weippert 1982: 155). According to Gen 36:37, this ruler originated from Rehoboth ha-Nahar (RSV translates "Rehoboth on the Euphrates"), which may be a place or a region. See REHOBOTH (PLACE).

2. A clan of Simeon (Gen 46:10; Exod 6:15; Num 26:13; 1 Chr 4:24). According to Genesis 34 and Genesis 49:5–7, Simeon (and Levi) were tribes of the central Palestinian hill country and were dispersed after a conflict with the city of Shechem. All other references to the tribe of Simeon are, therefore, highly doubtful.

3. A Levite (1 Chr 6:9).

Bibliography

Bartlett, J. R. 1972. The Rise and Fall of the Kingdom of Edom. *PEQ* 104: 26–37.

Bennett, C.-M. 1983. Excavations at Buseirah (Biblical Bozrah). Pp. 9–17 in *Midian, Moab and Edom,* ed. J. F. A. Sawyer and D. J. A. Clines. Sheffield.

Donner, H. 1984. *Geschichte des Volkes Israel und seiner Nachbarn in Grundzügen.* Vol. 1. Göttingen.

Knauf, E. A. 1985. Alter und Herkunft der edomitischen Königsliste Gen 36, 31–39. *ZAW* 97: 245–53.

Weippert, M. 1982. Remarks on the History of Settlement in Southern Jordan during the Early Iron Age. Pp. 153–62 in *Studies in the History and Archaeology of Jordan I,* ed. A. Hadidi. Amman.

Ernst Axel Knauf

SHAVEH, VALLEY OF (PLACE) [Heb *ʿēmeq šāwēh*]. In Gen 14:17, the place in which the king of Sodom (and implicitly, Melchizedek in v 18) met Abram as he returned from his defeat of Chedorlaomer and his allies. The word *šāwēh,* which occurs as an adjective only here, and as a noun only in v 5 of the same chapter (see SHAVEH-KIRIATHAIM), is derived from the root *šāwah* "to level, make even, smooth." The author of Genesis 14, following his usage, explained "the Valley of Shaveh" by the current appellation "that is, the King's Valley" (Heb *ʿēmeq hammelek*). The latter is mentioned in 2 Sam 18:18 as the place where Absalom set up a pillar for himself. According to Jos. *Ant* 7.10.3 §243, that monument was two stadia (350 to 400 m) distant from Jerusalem (presumably, from its outer walls). This seems to point to the identity of the King's Valley with the Valley of Kidron E of old Jerusalem. Other ancient sources corroborate it. *Tg. Onq.* has here *mēšar mēpannā hūʾ bêt rêsā dĕmalkā* "the leveled valley, that is the race course of the king." According to Jer 31:39—Eng 31:40, the Horse Gate was in the E wall of Jerusalem, adjacent to the Kidron (cf. also its context in Neh 3:28); *Tg. Jon.* translates it *tĕraʿ bêt rêsā* "the Race Course Gate." Neh 3:15 mentions "the King's Garden" in Jerusalem (which included the Pool of Shelah) in a location near the junction of the Tyropoeon with the Kidron (Allegro 1960: 90–91; *IDB* 2: 10–11; *IDB* 4: 310); cf. *Tg. Neof.* of Gen 14:17: *bmyšr prdsyʾ h[w]ʾ mšrh dmlkʾ* "in the valley of the gardens, that is the King's Valley." The Genesis Apocryphon (1QapGen 22: 13–14) adds to *bʿmq šwh whwʾ ʿmq mlk* (equivalent to the definition in Gen 14:17) the further specification *bqʿt byt krmʾ* "the valley of Bet-karma (or, of the house of the vineyard)." Aharoni (*IDBSup,* 97) saw in it the Aramaic form of Beth-haccherem, a Judean city which he identified with the excavated site of Ramat Raḥel, 3.4 km S of Jerusalem (Aharoni 1956: 152). This identification may be correct, but it does not entail the transfer of the Valley of Shaveh to the area of Ramat Raḥel. In the Copper Treasure Scroll from Qumran (3Q15), a detailed list of the spots where hoards of silver, gold, and precious objects had been buried, *hšwʾ* (*haššāwēʾ* "the plain") is listed twice (Allegro 1960: 47, items 37 and 38) immediately after the Kidron. Further in the Treasure Scroll, item 47, "the reservoir which is in *byt hkrm*" is listed after a certain "cistern which is fed from the Great Wadi *(mhnḥl hgdwl)*" (probably the Kidron, cf. *hannaḥal* in that meaning, 2 Chr 33:14), and before "the vat of the olive valley (?)" (or "olive press (?)," cf. Allegro 1960: 99–101, who connects it with Gethsemane, directly E from the Kidron) and "Absalom's Pillar" which, as mentioned above, stood in the Kidron Valley. It appears thus that the *byt hkrm* in question is the same as *byt krmʾ* of 1QapGen and is, most likely, a synonym of the King's Garden (which possessed indeed a reservoir—the Pool of Shelah). The Valley of Shaveh can thus be definitely located as the little plain formed by the junction of the valleys of Hinnom, Tyropoeon, and Kidron (see Allegro 1960, fig. 9; *GP* 1: 402–3; Milik 1961).

Bibliography

Aharoni, Y. 1956. Excavations at Ramath Raḥel, 1954: Preliminary Report. *IEJ* 6: 102–11; 137–57.

Allegro, J. M. 1960. *The Treasure of the Copper Scroll.* Garden City, NY.

Milik, T. J. 1961. "Saint-Thomas de Phordêsa" et Gen. 14,17. *Bib* 42: 77–84.

MICHAEL C. ASTOUR

SHAVEH-KIRIATHAIM (PLACE) [Heb *šāwēh qiryātāyîm*]. The place in which Chedorlaomer and his allies defeated the Emim (Gen 14:5). *Šāwēh* (construct of **šāweh*") refers to the level terrain, or plain (see SHAVEH, VALLEY OF), near the city of KIRIATHAIM in Moab. According to Deut 2:10–11, the Emim were the aboriginal population of Moab. Strangely, LXX, 1QapGen, and *Tg. Neof.* did not recognize *qiryātāyîm* as a geographical name and translated it "city" or "cities." *Tg. Neof.,* moreover, did not understand *šāwēh* either and rendered the passage in question "and the Powerful Ones who dwelt inside the city," thus assigning the Emim (as well as the Zuzim) to the same city (Ashteroth-karnaim) as the Rephaim.

MICHAEL C. ASTOUR

SHAVSHA (PERSON) [Heb *šawšāʾ*]. Var. SERAIAH; SHEVA; SHISHA. A scribe in the political administration of King David (1 Chr 18:16, 2 Sam 8:17, 20:25, 1 Kgs 4:3). The name is probably foreign in origin, perhaps Egyptian (de Vaux 1939; *AncIsr* 1: 129–32) or Hurrian (Mazar 1946–47). A non-native Israelite would have been ideal for the profession of scribe, one in which foreign documents would have been handled. The foreign character of the name is the reason for its various spellings in the text: *šĕyāʾ* (2 Sam 20:25 Q: *šĕwāʾ*), *śĕrāyâ* (2 Sam 8:17), *šîšāʾ* (1 Kgs 4:3), *šawšāʾ* (1 Chr 18:16). The weight of the evidence, when the LXX is also considered (see SHEVA), points to the originality of Shavsha, although certainty is not possible.

Shavsha's sons, Elihoreph and Ahijah, performed the same scribal function as their father in the political bureaucracy of Solomon (1 Kgs 4:3). The B text of the LXX in 1 Kings suggests that Shavsha did not retire from his position until after the beginning of Solomon's reign, since his name occurs but not those of his sons. It may be, however, that their names have been accidentally omitted. See *HDB* 4: 478–79.

Bibliography

Mazar, B. 1946–47. The Scribe of King David and the Problem of the High Officials in the Ancient Kingdom of Israel. *BJPES* 13: 105–14 (in Hebrew).

Vaux, R. de. 1939. Titres et fonctionnaires égyptiens à la cour de David et de Salomon. *RB* 48: 394–405.

STEPHEN G. DEMPSTER

SHAVUOTH [Heb *šābûʿôt*]. See WEEKS, FESTIVAL OF.

SHEAL (PERSON) [Heb *šĕʾāl*]. A descendant of Bani and one of the returned exiles who was required by Ezra to divorce his foreign wife (Ezra 10:29 = 1 Esdr 9:30). Noth believes this name should be read *yišʾāl* (with *kethib apud Orientales*), meaning "May he (God) make a request of him" or "May he (God) use him" (*IPN* 209, 257). Sheal was a member of a family that returned from Babylon with Zerubbabel (Ezra 2:10; note that Binnui replaces Bani in Nehemiah's list [7:15]). For further discussion, see BEDEIAH.

JEFFREY A. FAGER

SHEALTIEL (PERSON) [Heb *šĕʾaltîʾēl, šaltîʾēl*]. Var. SALATHIEL. The son of Jeconiah (= Jehoiachin), king of Judah (1 Chr 3:17; Matt 1:12). In the genealogy of Jesus found in the gospel of Luke 3:27 he is made the son of Neri. This differs markedly from the Matthean genealogy (Fitzmyer *Luke* AB, 488–505).

Shealtiel is listed as the father of Zerubbabel in all occurrences in the Hebrew Bible (Ezra 3:2, 8; 5:2; Neh 12:1; Hag 1:1, 12, 14; 2:2, 23; see also 1 Esdr 5:5, 48, 56; 6:2) except in the list of postexilic Davidic descendants in 1 Chr 3:17 where Zerubbabel is listed as the son of PEDAIAH. Compare that entry for a discussion of scholarly views on this matter.

In 2 Esdr 3:1 Shealtiel (RSV Salathiel) is equated with Ezra which is probably the result of an attempt by the author/editor to link the two figures in his/her sources (see discussion of "4 Ezra" in *APOT* 2: 549–50; *OTP* 1: 517–569).

RUSSELL FULLER

SHEAR-JASHUB (PERSON) [Heb *šĕʾār yāšûb*]. A son of Isaiah named in Isa 7:3. (The phrase *šĕʾār yāšûb* occurs twice again in 10:21–22, though the authenticity of both verses is disputed.) The occasion of 7:3 is the Syro-Ephraimite invasion of Judah in 735 B.C.E. Isaiah is told to take the child with him while he tells Ahaz not to fear the attackers. The significance of the name, which means "a remnant will return," is ambivalent. If the emphasis is that *only* a remnant will return, a threat is implied; if the emphasis is on the certain return of some, it is a promise of sorts. The "return" intended is also disputed. The verb (*šûb*) can mean "return" in the physical sense, as survivors from battle or exile (as in 10:22). But it can signify, as often in the prophets, conversion or repentance, and that sense is to be preferred here, as in 10:20–21. In 8:16–18 Isaiah refers to himself and his sons, which would include Shear-jashub, as "signs and portents in Israel." If his name speaks of the conversion of a remnant, which is the better interpretation, it finds its fulfillment already in Isaiah's little group of disciples (v 16) and sons, who have accepted Yahweh's message through Isaiah, clinging to it in faith and awaiting its fulfillment (v 17). On Isaiah's use of symbolic names, see also Immanuel in 7:14, Maher-shalal-hash-baz in 8:1–4, and names he bestows on the ideal king in 9:5.

JOSEPH JENSEN

SHEARIAH (PERSON) [Heb *šĕʿaryāh*]. Son of Azel, one of the latest descendants of King Saul from the tribe of Benjamin listed in the genealogy in 1 Chr 8:38 and 9:44. The meaning of the element *šʿr* in the name is unclear. Some relate it to the noun *šaʿar*, "gate," and understand it as "YH(WH) has opened" (Bordreuil and Lemaire 1976: 45), but *šʿr* is unknown as a verbal form in this sense. More likely, *šʿr* should be taken as "to reckon," and the name should be interpreted "YH(WH) has reckoned" (Fowler *TPNAH,* 90). The name is attested to twice on a Hebrew seal from the 8th or 7th century (Bordreuil and Lemaire 1976: 45–46). The section of the Saul genealogy mentioning Sheariah was probably composed during the time of Azel (Demsky 1971: 19), who according to the current structure of the genealogy lived eleven generations after King Saul. The genealogy is from the end of the First Temple period (Demsky 1971: 20), and was preserved by Benjaminite families that survived the Babylonian exile (Williamson 1979: 356). The existence and preservation of the Saulide genealogy probably reflects the continued prominence of Saul's family, and perhaps even their hope that they would return to power (Ackroyd *Chronicles, Ezra, Nehemiah* TBC, 42; Flanagan 1982: 25). See MELECH. On the repetition of the genealogy in 1 Chronicles 8 and 9, and its structure within the genealogies in Chronicles, see AHAZ.

Bibliography

Bordreuil, P., and Lemaire, A. 1976. Nouveaux Sceaux Hébreux, Araméens et Ammonites. *Semitica* 26: 45–63.

Demsky, A. 1971. The Genealogy of Gibeon (1 Chronicles 9:35–44): Biblical and Epigraphic Considerations. *BASOR* 202: 16–23.

Flanagan, J. 1982. Genealogy and Dynasty in the Early Monarchy of Israel and Judah. *PWCJS* 8: 23–28.

Williamson, H. G. M. 1979. Sources and Redaction in the Chronicler's Genealogy of Judah. *JBL* 98: 351–59.

MARC Z. BRETTLER

SHEARING. See ZOOLOGY.

SHEATH. See WEAPONS AND IMPLEMENTS OF WARFARE.

SHEBA (PERSON) [Heb *šĕbāʾ; šebaʿ*]. SABEANS. **1.** The descendant of Ham and Cush and the "son" (Heb *bēn*) of Raamah and brother of Dedan (Gen 10:7; 1 Chr 1:9). The name appears again in Gen 10:28 (1 Chr 1:22), where Sheba (Heb *šĕbāʾ*) is listed as a descendant of Shem and among the "sons" of Joktan. The name is also found in Gen 25:3 (1 Chr 1:32) as a descendant of Abraham and Keturah, the son of Jokshan, and the brother of Dedan. The similarity or identity of certain of the names in these genealogies has led some to conclude that the name Sheba refers to the same person or tribe, most probably related to the kingdom of Sheba in SW Arabia (referred to in native sources as Saba—Sabaean *sbʾ*) (Westermann 1984: 511). See SHEBA, QUEEN OF. If the occurrence of the name Sheba in these instances does represent the same person or tribe, or closely related persons or tribes, it indicates that the Israelites viewed Sheba and his descendants as related both to themselves and to the peoples of Africa. However, such wideranging relationships are understandable, given the extensive trade links of the peoples of the S Arabian littoral (Simons 1954: 159; *IDB* 4: 511). Alternatively, this passage may be understood to mean that descendants of Ham as well as descendants of Shem lived in SW Arabia (Ross 1981: 25–26, 29).

However, the name Seba (Heb *sĕbāʾ*) the son of Cush, also mentioned in Gen 10:7, is found in the topography of ancient E Africa and should be kept distinct from Sheba. See SEBA (PERSON). The "kings of Seba and Sheba" are found together in Ps 72:10, while in Isa 43:3 and 45:14 Seba is mentioned together with Egypt and Cush. Josephus (*Ant* 2.249) identifies it with Meroē, a city (or country) between the White Nile and the Blue Nile, and calls it the capital city of the Ethiopians that Cambyses had named Meroē after he had captured the city. Strabo (*Geog.* 16.4.8, 10) also knows of the cities Saba and Sabai on the African coast (PW 2/1: 1511–13, 1515–20; Winnett 1970: 174; Westermann 1984: 511).

Bibliography

Ross, A. P. 1981. The Table of Nations in Genesis 10—Its Content. *BSac* 138: 22–34.

Simons, J. 1954. The "Table of Nations" (Gen. X): Its General Structure and Meaning. *OTS* 10: 155–84.

Westermann, C. 1984. *Genesis 1–11: A Commentary,* trans. J. J. Scullion. Minneapolis.

Winnett, F. Y. 1970. The Arabian Genalogies in the Book of Genesis. Pp. 171–96 in *Translating and Understanding the Old Testament: Essays in Honor of Herbert Gordon May,* ed. H. T. Frank, and W. L. Reed. New York.

STEPHEN D. RICKS

2. A Benjaminite, son of Bichri, from the hill country of Ephraim, who led a rebellion against David (2 Samuel 20). When David finally finished his mourning for Absalom and began his return to Jerusalem, components of the armed forces of Judah and Israel quarreled over who would accompany David. The forces of Judah gained the upper hand and Sheba (Heb *šebaʿ*), who is termed a "troublemaker," initiated a rebellion of the forces of Israel. Sheba's words foreshadowed the eventual split of the kingdom: "We have no share in David and no estate in the son of Jesse" (2 Sam 20:1 and 1 Kgs 12:16). Absalom's rebellion had threatened the king personally, but Sheba's rebellion was a threat to the kingdom itself (2 Sam 20:6). Amasa, whom Absalom had made the leader of the army but whom David had later forgiven, was selected by David to muster the men of Judah in order to quell the rebellion. Amasa did not accomplish the task soon enough and David dispatched Abishai with personal forces, but Joab quickly assumed control. While they pursued Sheba, Amasa caught up with Joab at Gibeon only to be killed by him. Sheba passed through Israel but in the end seems to have gathered no more than his own clansmen to his cause (2 Sam 20:14). He took his stand in Abel of Bethmaacah, a fortified city. Joab began seige of the city, but, before he destroyed the fortifications, a woman intervened and agreed to trade Sheba for Joab's withdrawal. She persuaded the inhabitants who then decapitated Sheba and threw his head over to Joab (2 Sam 20:14–22). On the possibility that Saul's clan, the Matrites, and Sheba's, the Bichrites are the same, see Gottwald 1979: 259–60.

3. A head of a family in the tribe of Gad. Sheba (Heb *šebaʿ*) is the name of one of seven families listed for the tribe of Gad in 1 Chr 5:13. None of the seven family names are otherwise known, and their genealogical connection to those mentioned in subsequent verses is not clear (see Braun *1 Chronicles* WBC, 74). The genealogy containing his name is said to have been recorded during the reigns of Jotham and Jeroboam (1 Chr 5:17).

Bibliography

Gottwald, N. K. 1979. *The Tribes of Israel.* Maryknoll, NY.

RICHARD W. NYSSE

SHEBA (PLACE) [Heb *šebaʿ*]. A city in the territory allotted to Simeon (Josh 19:2). In Josh 19:6 the sum of the cities in Simeon's allotment is given as thirteen, yet fourteen names are listed. Several scholars, noting that the name Beer-sheba immediately precedes Sheba, assert that Sheba is the result of a scribal error known as dittography; that is, it is assumed that the second element in Beer-sheba was accidentally repeated (Soggin *Joshua* OTL, 187). Thus, there never was a place named Sheba, and the discrepancy in the city count is resolved. In a parallel passage (Josh 15:21–32), however, a list of Judahite cities includes nine of the fourteen cities mentioned in Josh 19:2–6, and the name Shema is found in the place of Sheba. In view of this fact, some scholars maintain that Sheba does represent an actual city, though its real name (Shema) has been corrupted in Josh 19:2 (Cooke 1918: 173). Cohen (*IDB* 4: 311) suggests a third position: Shema is a corruption of Sheba. According to Cohen, Sheba and Beer-sheba ("the well of Sheba") were two parts of the same city.

Bibliography

Cooke, G. A. 1918. *The Book of Joshua.* Cambridge.

DAVID SALTER WILLIAMS

SHEBA, QUEEN OF (PERSON) [Heb *malkat-šĕbāʾ*]. An otherwise anonymous person who visited the courts of king Solomon (1 Kings 10; 2 Chronicles 9). According to these accounts, the queen of Sheba heard of Solomon's fame and came to test him with hard questions (1 Kgs 10:1; 2 Chr 9:1a). She came to Jerusalem with camels loaded with spices, gold, and precious stones (1 Kgs 10:2a; 2 Chr 9:1a). She quizzed Solomon, who was able to answer all of her questions (1 Kgs 10:2b–3; 2 Chr 9:1b–2). She was thoroughly impressed by the king's wisdom and the splendor of his court and temple (1 Kgs 10:4–5; 2 Chr 9:3–4), expressed to Solomon her amazement at his wisdom, achievements, and wealth (1 Kgs 10:6–8; 2 Chr 9:5–7), and praised Solomon's God for the king's happy state (1 Kgs 10:9; 2 Chr 9:8). Thereupon she gave the king an enormous amount of gold, spices, and precious stones (1 Kgs 10:10; 2 Chr 9:9. King Solomon gave her an even greater amount in return, whereupon she left with her retinue for her own country (1 Kgs 10:13; 2 Chr 9:12).

It is likely that another significant reason for the queen of Sheba's visit to Solomon was to strengthen trade relations. Solomon had just constructed a fleet at Ezion-geber at the head of the Gulf of Aqaba (1 Kgs 9:26–27; 2 Chr 8:17), and his ships were plying the length of the Red Sea, thereby affecting the profitability of the overland trade routes in which the rulers of Sheba had an interest as well as threatening Sheba's lucrative trade with East Africa. Further, Israel's wide control of land routes north of the Gulf of Aqaba posed a potential roadblock to caravans bound for either Gaza on the Mediterranean or Damascus (Gray *Kings* OTL, 241). On a visit such as the one described in 1 Kings 10 and 2 Chronicles 9, the queen of Sheba could have secured important trade concessions and prevented potential conflicts between the two powers.

The most plausible location for Sheba is in the SW corner of the Arabian peninsula. This area, known in the native sources as Saba, already had an advanced culture by the early 1st millennium B.C. (and perhaps earlier), with urban complexes equal in size to other parts of the Near East, a sophisticated irrigation system to support agriculture, and important trade links N and W toward the Mediterranean basin and Mesopotamia and E to India (van Beek 1974: 40–63). The merchants of Sheba were renowned in Israel and elsewhere in the ANE as traders in gold (Ps 72:15; Isa 60:6; Ezek 27:22; cf. Ezek 38:13), gems (Ezek 27:22), and incense (Isa 60:6; Jer 6:20) and myrrh—products grown in various locations near the South Arabian littoral (Nielsen 1986: 19–24).

The queen of Sheba is mentioned twice in the NT, and extensively in subsequent Jewish, Ethiopian, and Muslim traditions. In Matt 12:42, Jesus contrasts the energy of the "Queen of the South" in coming "from the ends of the earth to listen to Solomon's wisdom" with the relative complacency of his contemporary Jews, though "now one greater than Solomon is here" (cf. Luke 11:31). Josephus mentions the queen once, calling her the "Queen of Egypt and Ethiopia" (*Ant* 8.6.5–6). She is mentioned twice in the Talmud—both times in connection with Job 1:15—while the story of her visit to Solomon's court and especially the "hard questions" that she posed and Solomon answered formed a part of later traditions and embellishments (Silberman 1974: 65–84).

According to the *Kebra Nagast,* the national saga of Ethiopia, the queen's visit resulted in her conversion to Solomon's religion. Solomon had a son by her, Menelik, who was born following the queen's return to Ethiopia. When Menelik had grown up, he went to Israel to visit his father. When he returned to Ethiopia, he took with him the Ark of the Covenant, thereby transferring God's presence from Israel to Ethiopia (Ullendorf 1974: 109–12). In Quran 27:15–45, the queen of Sheba is described as a sun worshipper. She visited Solomon, who tested whether she was "rightly guided" and tricked her into baring her legs. Later, she and Solomon submitted to Allah. In Quranic commentaries and subsequent Muslim legends, the queen is identified as Bilqīs and is sometimes described as being endowed with supernatural powers (Watt 1974: 85–103).

Bibliography

Nielsen, K. 1986. *Incense in Ancient Israel.* Leiden.
Silberman, L. H. 1974. The Queen of Sheba in Judaic Tradition. Pp. 65–84 in *Solomon and Sheba,* ed. J. B. Pritchard. London.
Ullendorf, E. 1974. The Queen of Sheba in Ethiopian Tradition. Pp. 104–14 in *Solomon and Sheba,* ed. J. B. Pritchard. London.
Van Beek, G. W. 1974. The Land of Sheba. Pp. 40–63 in *Solomon and Sheba,* ed. J. B. Pritchard. London.
Watt, W. M. 1974. The Queen of Sheba in Islamic Tradition. Pp. 85–103 in *Solomon and Sheba,* ed. J. B. Pritchard. London.

STEPHEN D. RICKS

SHEBANIAH (PERSON) [Heb *šĕbanyāh; šĕbanyāhû*]. Four individuals in the Hebrew Bible bear this name.

1. One of the priests who played musical instruments before the ark during the time of David (1 Chr 15:24). Given his extreme interest in the installation of temple musicians (Braun *1 Chronicles* WBC, 186), the Chronicler informs us that Shebaniah's specific role was to blow the trumpet before the ark as it was brought into Jerusalem.

2. One of the Levites who led worship in the public ceremonies prior to the establishment of the new covenant under Ezra (Neh 9:4). According to Neh 9:5, Shebaniah and other selected Levites specifically called the assembly to join in a liturgical blessing of Yahweh before Ezra's prayer. This individual may possibly be identified with one of the two Levites mentioned in #4 below.

3. The head of a priestly family in the postexilic period (Neh 12:14) and one of the priests who "sealed" the new covenant of Ezra (Neh 10:5—Eng 10:4). By examining the related list in Nehemiah 12:3 as well as other manuscripts, Shebaniah in this case should probably be equated with the Shecaniah of 12:3 (Blenkinsopp *Ezra-Nehemiah* OTL, 334; Williamson *Ezra, Nehemiah* WBC, 362). Given the similarity between the Hebrew letters *bet* and *kap,* such a misreading is easily understandable.

4. Two Levites who joined in with other officials and laity in supporting and "sealing" the new covenant of Ezra (Neh 10:11, 13—Eng 10:10, 12). One of them may possibly be identified with the Levite discussed in #2 above.

TERRY L. BRENSINGER

SHEBARIM (PLACE) [Heb *haššĕbārîm*]. The place to which the routed Israelites were first pursued by the men of Ai (Josh 7:5).

In the MT of Josh 7:5 the world *haššĕbārîm* appears as a masc. pl. noun formed from *šeber* ("a break or fracture"). A number of the early versions depart from the Hebrew text by replacing the noun *haššĕbārîm* with a verb formed from *šbr* ("to break"). Targum Jonathan preserves the root *šbr* (Aram *t̠br*) as an element in the verbal clause, "until they broke them," while the LXX similarly translates, *kai synetripsan autous,* "and they crushed them."

Several factors suggest that the reading of the MT is preferable to that of the Targum and the LXX. The context and structure of Josh 7:5 favors the presence of a noun over a verb; the phrase, *ʿad-haššĕbārîm,* "as far as the *šĕbārîm*" provides a suitable compliment to the preceding phrase, *lipnê haššaʿar,* "from the gate." The presence in Josh 7:5 of a noun bearing the prefixed definite article is also consistent with the style of the chapter as a whole. Indeed, in Joshua 7–8 the preponderance of topographical nouns bearing the definite article (e.g., *hāʿay,* "the ruin," 7:2, 4, 5, 8:12, 14, 18, 19, 20, 23, 24, 29; *hāʿēmeq,* "the plain," 8:13; *bammôrād,* "the descent," 7:5; *hammidbār,* "the wilderness," 8:15, 20; *hāʿărābâ,* "the desert," 8:14) seems to represent the author's attempt to convey a vivid sense of the geography of the battle.

While a noun may best suit the context of Josh 7:5, a variety of opinions exist as to how this noun should be interpreted. Although most English translations (KJV; RSV; NASB; JPSV) have followed the Vulgate in simply transcribing *haššĕbārîm* as a proper noun "Shebarim" (Vg *Sabarim*), the presence of the definite article would suggest that such a rendering is not what the MT intends. Others (NIV; NEB; Keil 1857: 183; Boling *Joshua* AB, 218) translate "the quarries," but the fact that *haššĕbārîm* occurs only here in the Hebrew Bible makes such a specific translation too interpretive. It seems best, therefore, to translate *haššĕbārîm* as simply as possible while paying close attention to its context within the story of the attack on Ai.

A few scholars have attempted to preserve the awkwardness of the MT by translating *haššĕbārîm* simply as "the Breaks" (Woudstra *Joshua* NICOT, 123) or "the Breaking Points" (Butler *Joshua* WBC, 77). Monson (1983: 168, 169), in a discussion of the geography of Joshua 7–8, suggests that "the breakings" of 7:5 may well be identical with the deep fissures caused by the Wadi Makkuk as it carves its way toward the hill country E of Khirbet et-Tell (M.R. 174147). Just W of the cliffs caused by the Wadi Makkuk, the natural route between et-Tell and the Jordan Valley passes N of the Makkuk and continues eastward along the ridge which separates the Wadis Makkuk and ʿAuja. It may have been at the pass across the Wadi Makkuk (5 km E of et-Tell) that the men of Ai were able to overtake and slaughter the Israelites.

Bibliography

Keil, K. F. 1857. *Commentary on the Book of Joshua*. Edinburgh.

Monson, J. M. 1983. *The Land Between: A Regional Study Guide to the Land of the Bible*. Jerusalem.

BRIAN P. IRWIN

SHEBAT [Heb *šĕbāṭ*]. The eleventh month of the Hebrew calendar, roughly corresponding to January and February. See CALENDARS (ANCIENT ISRAELITE AND EARLY JEWISH).

SHEBER (PERSON) [Heb *šeber*]. A son of Caleb and his concubine Maacah (1 Chr 2:48). Sheber was a Judahite listed among genealogies containing ancestors and descendants of David. The extra Calebite material in vv 42–50a (alongside the other version of the family tree in vv 18–24, 50b–55) suggests either that the Chronicler had access to more information from the source which included the Calebite genealogy than from elsewhere or that a great many families of Judah in the Chronicler's day claimed descent from Caleb (Coggins *Chronicles* CBC, 22). Many of the names listed as those of individuals are really of cities—Hebron and Maon and Bethzur being several of the best known. "Sheber" could mean "breach" or the like, in some way maybe reflecting circumstances surrounding the child's birth. Noth (*IPN*, 230) opposed this idea and preferred to see an animal name, "lion" (Ar *sabr*). He did, however, entertain the notion that *šeber* might signify "young" or "child" (similar to *šabrāʾ*—in Syriac, "little boy"; in Aramaic, "naive").

EDWIN C. HOSTETTER

SHEBNA (PERSON) [Heb *šebnāʾ*, *šebnāh*]. An important civil servant during the reign of Hezekiah of Judah (715–687 B.C.E.). His original position was "royal steward" (Heb *ʾăšer ʿal habbāyīt*) (Isa 22:15), but he was eventually demoted and replaced by Eliakim ben Hilkiah (Isa 22:20), presumably because of some scandal. He accompanied Eliakim in the lesser role of scribe as part of the delegation which met with the Assyrian Rabshakeh at the conduit of the Upper Pool of Jerusalem during Sennacherib's siege of the city in 701 B.C.E. (2 Kgs 18:13–19:7).

Although the Hebrew title (*ʾăšer ʿal habbāyīt*) is regularly translated as "royal steward," there is no firm agreement on what the term exactly means. Mettinger (1971: 71–110) compares the title to the Egyptian *mr-pr-wr*, who was an overseer of the royal estates, similar to the role of Joseph (Gen 41:40), and suggests that the Judaean and Israelite equivalent performed a similar function. On the other hand, Avigad (1988: 9) regards the person holding this title as ". . . the top ranking senior officer in the official hierarchy of the monarchy, some kind of prime minister." In the biblical and non-biblical sources, the status of the office is assumed and never explained, although it is to be noted that in 1 Kgs 4:6 Ahishar is not listed first in the new monarchical bureaucracy. Known holders of the office were Ahishar, under Solomon (1 Kgs 4:6), Arza under Elah (1 Kgs 16:9), Obadiah under Ahab (1 Kgs 18:3), Jotham, under his father Uzziah (2 Kgs 15:3), Azrikam, under Ahaz (2 Chr 28:7), and Shebna and Eliakim. Non-biblical sources offer Gedalyahu whose name appears on the Lachish seal (*TSSI* 1: 62–63), Adoniyahu and Natan, whose names appear on the Jerusalem bullae #1–2, 3 (Avigad 1986: 21–23), and the unknown owner of the Silwan tomb (*TSSI* 1: 24).

It is clear from Isa 22:15–25 that some time during the reign of Hezekiah, Shebna was publicly removed from office because of some scandal. He had become "the shame of his master's house," by some public misdeed, and had to suffer a public humiliation in return. This act of public humiliation is described in detail in the oracle. He will be stripped of all symbols of office and demoted. His replacement will receive these symbols, assume duties over the royal house and be called a "father" by the inhabitants of Jerusalem. Exactly what Shebna's sin was is not clear, although the impression is given in the oracle that he had dishonored his master by committing it. The maintenance of a proper balance in such patron-client relationships in the ANE, in which the patron is revered, is fundamental to social relationships of this kind, and at the basis of the understanding of covenant. As known covenant texts show, the breaking of that relationship carries with it severe penalties. Likewise, to bring dishonor to one's superior carries with it severe sanctions which often override long-standing relationships. A clear example of this is David's treatment of Joab, who, by killing in peace time to avenge a death in war, had brought shame to his master (1 Kgs 2:5–6).

Shebna had built a tomb near Jerusalem, "on the height" (Isa 22:16), and Isaiah's oracle against him indicates that he will not die in Jerusalem so that he may be buried in this tomb. Instead, he will be thrown like a slingstone, into a foreign land. How much of this is to be taken literally, and how much of it is to be taken as prophetic hyperbole is not clear. Such comments made by prophets to royal officials do have a similar, rather stereotyped ring to them, as is seen in Amos' comments to Amaziah (Amos 7:16–17) and Jeremiah's comments about Pashhur (Jer 20:1–6). Common to both is the threat of exile and foreign burial. If the language of the Isaiah oracle is formal, then it might well have played a part in the demotion ritual which Shebna underwent, and it can be treated as a standard denunciation of high officials. This formal nature of the language might also explain why Shebna reappears later as a scribe, accompanying his successor, Eliakim to meet the Assyrian delegation (2 Kgs 18:8–37). He still has an important role to play in the bureaucratic structure of Hezekiah's court, albeit a slightly diminished one.

There has been much speculation on whether the tomb discovered on the slopes of Silwan, and bearing part of a name and the title *ʾăšer ʿal habbāyīt,* is the tomb referred to in Isa 22:15–16. It is certainly regarded so by Avigad (1953; 1979), but the evidence is lacking. If it was Shebna's tomb, then it certainly takes the sting out of Isaiah's words, because it once contained the owner's bones and those of his maidservant (*TSSI* 1: 24). All that is left of the owner's name is the theophoric ending ". . . *yhw,*" an element which is never found on Shebna's name in the Bible. Of course, it is possible to add the element, and Aharoni has suggested (*AI,* 53) that the Arad inscription #27 be reconstructed as *"Ydnyhw bn Šbn[yhw] . . ,"* but this is speculative. The origin of the name is unknown, and no verbal root *šbn,* exists in biblical Hebrew.

Bibliography

Avigad, N. 1953. The Epitaph of a Royal Steward from Siloam Village. *IEJ* 3: 137–52.

———. 1979. A Group of Hebrew Seals from the Hecht Collection. Pp. 119–26 in *Festchsrift for Reuben R. Hecht.* Jerusalem.

———. 1986. *Hebrew Bullae from the Time of Jeremiah: Remnants of a Burnt Archive.* Jerusalem.

———. 1988. Hebrew Seals and Sealings and Their Significance for Biblical Research. *VTSup* 40:7–16.

Katzenstein, H. J. 1960. The Royal Steward. *IEJ* 10: 149–54.

Lipinski, E. 1988. Royal and State Scribes in ancient Jerusalem. *VTSup* 40: 157–64.

Mettinger, T. N. D. 1971. *Solomonic State Officials.* Lund.

Millard, A. R. 1982. In Praise of Ancient Scribes. *BA* 45: 143–53.

T. R. Hobbs

SHEBUEL (PERSON) [Heb *šĕbûʾēl*]. Var. SHUBAEL. **1.** One of the fourteen sons of Heman who were appointed to prophesy with musical instruments under the direction of their father and the king (1 Chr 25:4). When the lots are cast to determine priestly duties (1 Chr 25:9–31), the name Shubael (1 Chr 25:20) appears where the name Shebuel would be expected, suggesting that the two names are variants. Shubael receives the thirteenth lot cast. Petersen (1977: 92) suggests that Shebuel in 25:4 is a misreading of Shubael in 25:20; he finds support in the LXX reading in 25:4, *Soubaēl.* For further discussion of the relationship between the lists in 1 Chr 25:2–4 and 1 Chr 25:9–31, see ASHARELAH; IZRI.

2. The son of Gershom and the grandson of Moses (1 Chr 23:16, 26:24). In 23:16, Shebuel is identified as "the chief;" and the Levites in question are assigned "the service of the house of the Lord" (23:24). In 26:24, Shebuel's duties are more specific; he is identified as "chief officer in charge of the treasuries." In 1 Chr 24:20, a person called Shubael is apparently the same person as the Shebuel of 23:16 and 26:24. Shubael is identified as one of the "sons of Amram." According to 23:12, Amram should be Shubael's great-grandfather; however, "sons" in 24:20 may mean more loosely "descendants." The LXX supports the reading Shubael in 23:16, 26:24 as well as 24:20, suggesting the possibility that Shebuel in 23:16, 26:24 is a misreading of an original Shubael; see above.

Bibliography

Petersen, D. L. 1977. *Late Israelite Prophecy: Studies in Deutero-Prophetic Literature and in Chronicles.* SBLMS 23. Missoula, MT.

J. Clinton McCann, Jr.

SHECANIAH (PERSON) [Heb *šĕkanyāhû*]. The name Shecaniah is held by eight persons in the Hebrew Bible, six of whom lived in the 6th–5th centuries B.C.E. All of our information about persons holding this name is taken from material redacted in the postexilic period.

Note that there is textual evidence which may indicate that Shebaniah (Heb *šĕbanyāhû*), a person mentioned in Neh 10:4 and 12:14, may be identical to the Shecaniah of #3 below. This apparent identity of the two is due to the confusion of the letters *bet* and *kap* which were very easily confused in the Aramaic scripts of the 5th century B.C.E.

It is also not surprising that the name Shecaniah should be so popular in the period after the return from the Babylonian Exile. The root, *škn,* is a favorite of the Priestly tradent who played an important role in shaping the Pentateuch; it is also used in Ezekiel to indicate the dwelling, actually "tenting," of Yahweh with the community. The names formed with this root, such as Shecaniah, are expressive of the desire and perhaps the conviction, that Yahweh again dwell among the people.

1. In 1 Chr 24:11 Shecaniah is the name of a priest in the time of David to whom fell the tenth lot for taking charge of the service of the sanctuary. On this list see Myers (*1 Chronicles* AB, 162–168) and Williamson (*1 and 2 Chronicles* NCBC, 162–164).

2. Shecaniah is the name of one of the assistants of Kore the son of Imnah the Levite who was in charge of apportioning the freewill offerings during the reign of Hezekiah, king of Judah. Shecaniah helped distribute the portions in the cities of the priests (2 Chr 31:15).

3. In Neh 12:3 Shecaniah is listed as a priest who returned to Jerusalem along with Zerubbabel and Jeshua (= Joshua). In v 7 the preceding names are labeled as those of the chiefs of the priests (cf. also Ezra 2). As noted above, this priest may be the same as Shebaniah in Neh 10:4 and 12:14.

4. Shecaniah is mentioned in 1 Chr 3:21, 22 as a descendant of Zerubbabel. The verse has some textual problems. Williamson (*1 and 2 Chronicles* NCBC, 58) delineates the major possibilities. If we follow the reading chosen by RSV and NEB then Shecaniah was the son of Obadiah in the 7th generation after Zerubbabel. He is also probably to be identified with the Shecaniah mentioned in Ezra 8:3 (and

1 Esdr 8:29), the father of Hattush (cf. 1 Chr 3:22) although the text of this passage also has textual difficulties (Myers *1 Chronicles* AB, 67n).

5. In Ezra 8:5 Shecaniah is listed as the son of Jahaziel of the sons of Zattu, if we include the reading in 1 Esdr 8:32. He was apparently a family leader (Ezra 8:1).

6. A layman mentioned in Ezra 10:2 (also 1 Esdr 8:92) who suggested that those in the postexilic community who had married foreign women send them and their children away. This led to the formation of a covenant among the men of Judah and Benjamin to do just that. This covenant is the topic of the entire last chapter of the book of Ezra.

7. The father of Shemiah, a priest who was the guardian of the East Gate and who helped repair the wall in the time of Nehemiah (Neh 3:29).

8. The son of Arah and the father-in-law of Tobiah the Ammonite (Neh 6:18). Tobiah was one of the ring leaders in opposition to Nehemiah's successful attempt to rebuild the walls of Jerusalem in the Persian period.

RUSSELL FULLER

SHECHEM (PERSON) [Heb *šĕkem; šekem*]. SHECHEMITE. **1.** Hamor's son, who raped Jacob's daughter Dinah (Gen 34:2). After the sexual encounter Shechem came to love Dinah and wanted to marry her (v 3). He proceeded to speak feelingly to the girl to persuade her to become his wife. Dinah seems to have remained in Shechem's house (v 26) while he and his father obtained from her family its consent to a marriage (vv 8–17). Hamor proposed that his people and Jacob's intermarry and offered to let the Israelites settle in his territory. The sons of Jacob countered by requiring that all of the city's males be circumcised. Davidson (*Genesis 12–50* CBC, 195) says circumcision for the Shechemites would have been a mark that they now belonged to Yahweh's chosen community. Von Rad (*Genesis* OTL, 333) however believes that only at a much later period did circumcision receive conscious theological significance and that the acceptance of faith in the God of Abraham was not suggested in the demand of Jacob's sons. See also CIRCUMCISION. In either case Shechem and his fellow citizens regarded circumcision as a trivial price to pay for an alliance which would have potentially increased their own power and wealth (v 23). But on the third day Simeon and Levi massacred the town's men, who lay incapacitated with fever, and fetched their sister (25–26). According to Von Rad (p. 335) the narrative depicts a prehistoric conflict of the tribes Simeon and Levi in the region around the town Shechem, which means "shoulder of mountain." The Shechemites appear anomalously in Jdt 5:16 in a list of peoples dispossessed from the Promised Land. This inclusion may represent the author's hostility to Samaritans and especially to Shechem, which Samaritan refugees rebuilt in the Hellenistic period and which John Hyrcanus I may have taken by the time the book was written (Moore *Judith* AB, 160). Or the addition of Shechem could be in anticipation of Judith's denunciation (9:2) of him for raping Dinah and recollection (vv 3–4) of the subsequent taking over of his territory (Enslin 1972: 90).

2. A son of Gilead, son of Machir, son of Manasseh (Num 26:31—LXX 26:35). Shechem's descendants formed the Shechemite clan within the tribe of Manasseh. Noth (*Numbers* OTL, 207) thinks that the reference to Shechem was to the well-known town of that name—an indication that it had been incorporated as a clan into the Manassite tribe. It should not be overlooked that contrary to Numbers 26, which calls Shechem the fourth of Gilead's six sons, Josh 17:2 considers Shechem to be one of Manasseh's sons, on a par with Machir. This latter arrangement might possibly have arisen to more neatly explain the division of Manasseh on the E and W sides of the Jordan River.

3. A son of Shemida, who was a descendant of Joseph's son Manasseh (1 Chr 7:19). If however this Shechem is the same as the preceding one, he is here listed incorrectly as Shemida's second-born son rather than his brother. Fellow siblings Likhi and Aniam may be equal to Helek of Num 26:30 and Noah of v 33, respectively (Braun *1 Chronicles* WBC, 111). The names of Shechem and Shemida as well as Noah and Helek appear along with relatives, Abiezer and Hoglah, as names of persons, tribes, or places in the Samaria ostraca (Myers *1 Chronicles* AB, 54–55).

Bibliography

Enslin, M. S. 1972. *The Book of Judith.* Jewish Apocryphal Literature 7. Leiden.

EDWIN C. HOSTETTER

SHECHEM (PLACE) [Heb *šĕkem*]. A city and its environs in the central highlands of Israel.

A. Modern and Ancient Name
B. Topography
C. Archaeological Excavations
  1. German Expeditions
  2. American Excavations
D. Archaeological History
  1. Earliest Settlement
  2. Middle Bronze Age
  3. Late Bronze Age
  4. Iron Age
  5. Persian and Hellenistic Periods

A. Modern and Ancient Name

About 65 km N of Jerusalem, in the territory occupied in biblical times by the tribes of Ephraim and Manasseh and known as Mt. Ephraim, is a low, flat-topped mound called Tell Balâṭah (M.R. 176179) with a surface area of about 2.4 hectares. It takes its name from the Arab village of Balâṭah, which covers most of the S half of the mound. The site stands at the end of a narrow pass between the two highest mountains in central Palestine, Mt. Gerizim (881 m) on the S and Mt. Ebal (940 m) on the N.

In 1903, Hermann Thiersh and a party of German scholars examined the mound and found along its NW face a wall of massive stone construction, 3 m in height, which they traced for over 37 m. It was obviously part of a powerful defensive wall appropriate to a major city. Prior to this discovery, there had been considerable controversy as to whether the site of ancient Shechem was identical with that of Neapolis (modern Nablus), or was situated some distance from it. Jerome's statement, "Shechem, which is now called Neapolis," apparently equated the two sites, but Eusebius stated that Shechem was "in the suburbs of Neapolis," and the Madaba mosaic map, which depends on Eusebius' *Onomasticon,* shows Shechem a short distance SE of Neapolis. Thiersh's discovery of a major ancient fortification system at Tell Balâṭah seemed to establish Tell Balâṭah, rather than Nablus, as the site of ancient Shechem, and the identification has not since been seriously questioned.

The Hebrew word *šěkem* probably means "back" or shoulder," referring to the location of the ancient city on the col between Mt. Ebal and Mt. Gerizim. Fifty-four of the 67 occurrences of the word in the OT refer to the city or its surrounding district. The remaining thirteen are the personal name of a prince of that city, the son of Hamor, its reputed founder. See SHECHEM (PERSON). The Gk equivalent *(Sychem)* appears twice in the NT (Acts 7:16), both times in the speech of Stephen, where the martyr refers to the burial of Joseph's remains near the city. There are also a substantial number of references to Shechem and its inhabitants in the Apocrypha and Pseudepigrapha, as well as a smaller number in non-biblical sources. The biblical passages and the non-biblical material will be discussed in the context of the archaeological period which provides their background. Passages in which the word Shechem is the personal name of the son of Hamor will be mentioned only in passing.

B. Topography

Ancient peoples built their cities in militarily strategic locations where there was an abundant supply of water, sufficient agricultural land to meet the basic needs of the population, and access to roads or other channels of communication. These requirements are all met at the site of ancient Shechem.

Shechem had a guaranteed water supply. The water table is far beneath the surface, but can be reached by deep, hand-dug wells, such as Jacob's Well about 400 m SE of Shechem. In the village of Balâṭah, approximately where the S wall of the ancient city would have been, there is a copious spring. It is the best of many such springs in the plain of ʿAskar, and provides water not only for the village of Balâṭah but also for neighboring communities in times of drought when their own springs have dried up.

The Shechem area possesses agricultural potentialities favorable to the development of a major city. The underlying rock is limestone, formed about seventy million years ago when the region was at the bottom of the Tethys sea. Subsequent periods of folding and uplifting of the land produced the mountains and the network of flat-bottomed valleys which characterize the Shechem area today. Limestone weathers at the rate of about one centimeter in 1000 years to form a fertile red-brown soil, *terra rosa.* Erosion brought soil down from the hills and left a deep deposit of rich earth in the valleys. Vineyards and fig and olive orchards flourish on the slopes, especially when they are terraced. Grain and vegetables grow well in the valleys. The annual rainfall of about 50–60 cm is sufficient to sustain these crops.

At Shechem both valley-bottom land and hillsides were available for cultivation. See Fig. SHE.01. A broad fertile valley, the Plain of ʿAskar, runs E from Shechem toward the Jordan. It was probably on this plain that Abimelech ambushed the Shechemites who came out to do battle with him (Judg 9:42–44). The Plain of ʿAskar, together with the et-Tahtani and el-Gharbi Plains, provide the city with an area of valley-bottom land about ten km long and 2.4 km wide. The Plain of Mukhna, actually a long rift valley, enters the ʿAskar Plain from the S. Along it runs the road from Jerusalem.

The mountain slopes and valleys not only served the purposes of agriculture, they also provided grass for the pasturage of sheep and goats. Jacob sent his sons from Hebron to Shechem to pasture their flocks, but they preferred the still more luxuriant grassland near Dothan, about a day's journey N of Shechem (Gen 37:12–14).

A network of roads converges on and funnels through the pass between Ebal and Gerizim. See Fig. SHE.01. A N–S highway from Egypt through Beer-sheba and Hebron runs from Jerusalem along the watershed to Shechem. A N extension of this road passes through the Wadi el-Abrad to the Wadi Fariʿa where it connects with the main road to the Jordan Valley and so reaches the principal trans-Jordanian throughfares leading to Damascus and Phoenicia.

In Judg 21:19 the Jerusalem-Shechem section of the road provides a reference point for the location of Shiloh and in Jer 41:5, it is the route by which pilgrims from the N reached Jerusalem. Along its course the road runs through a number of dark, narrow defiles where robbers often lay in wait for unwary travelers (Hos 6:9).

The road which emerges from the W end of the Shechem pass divides and subdivides giving access to most of the main centers of population in the country and to the great coastal highway, the Way of the Sea *(Via Maris).*

The location of Shechem at the E entrance to the pass thus allows it to dominate and control all commercial and military traffic through the region.

C. Archaeological Excavations

1. German Expeditions. Just ten years after Thiersh's identification of the site, full-scale excavations began at Shechem. A German expedition under the direction of E. Sellin, who had previously excavated at the important sites of Taanach and Jericho, conducted its first season of excavation in 1913, followed by a second campaign the following year.

World War I brought this first phase of the excavations to an end, and the post-war economic conditions in Germany prevented resumption of the work until 1926. Between the spring of 1926 and the spring of 1928, Sellin directed five additional seasons of excavation at the site. During the spring season of 1926, G. Welter, an archaeologist with considerable experience in Greece, joined the expedition. His work in the summers of 1926 and 1927 drew praise from Sellin, but evidently tensions were building beneath the surface. Welter came to be regarded as the "archaeological expert" and Sellin as the "theological" director. Sellin's critics accused him of bad excavation techniques, inadequate recording, poor reporting, and dubious interpretation of the finds. In the summer of 1928, the German Archaeological Institute, which was responsible for the scientific integrity of the expedition, removed Sellin from the directorship and replaced him with Welter.

The move was a near disaster. Welter carried out two

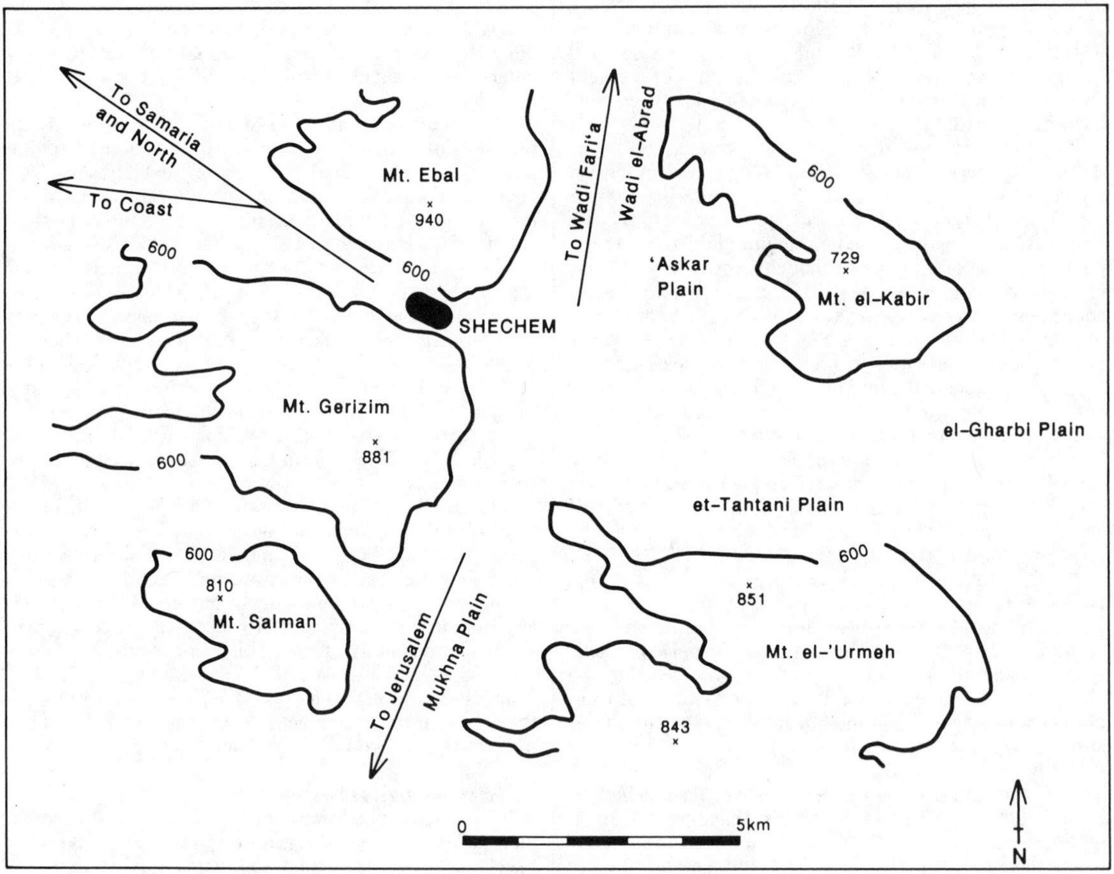

SHE.01. Area map of Shechem indicating the mountain and valley system and the principal roads. *(Courtesy of L. E. Toombs)*

campaigns, each of about three months duration, in the summers of 1928 and 1931, but the pace of the work slowed dramatically. Welter's reports were brief and lacking in precision and detail, and his revisions of Sellin's conclusions were in most cases unfortunate. It is to Welter's credit, however, that he prepared excellent plans of the principal remains uncovered by the German expedition and drew the first sections produced at the site.

In 1933, Sellin was reinstated as director and given the assistance of an architect with Egyptian experience, Dr. Hans Steckeweh. What Sellin aptly called the expedition's "unlucky star" continued to shine. After a summer season in 1934, a shortage of funds and the troubled political scene in Palestine prevented resumption of the work until the Second World War made it completely impossible. Sellin had faithfully published informative, though brief, preliminary reports for each season, but the manuscript of the final report together with the field records of the expedition were destroyed when Sellin's home in Berlin was demolished by a bomb in 1943.

Under Sellin's direction the German expedition employed three excavation methods; exploratory trenches, tracing of fortification walls, and area clearances.

Four huge trenches were dug into the tell. A N–S trench 52 m long by 5 m wide (1 on Fig. SHE.02) was cut into the mound near the center of its N side. In the search for the city wall this trench was extended and widened at its N end. Two N–S trenches were laid out to explore the area S of the wall observed by Thiersh. These were later swallowed up in the large area clearances around the NW gate and the Temple (IV, V and VI on Fig. SHE.02). A fourth trench (3 on Fig. SHE.02), later widened at its S end, ran from a building called "the house of Sheik Selim" NW at a width of 5 m for a distance of about 80 m. The fifth trench (4 on Fig. SHE.02), 5 m wide, ran from the slope of the mound on the NE side westward for about 60 m. These

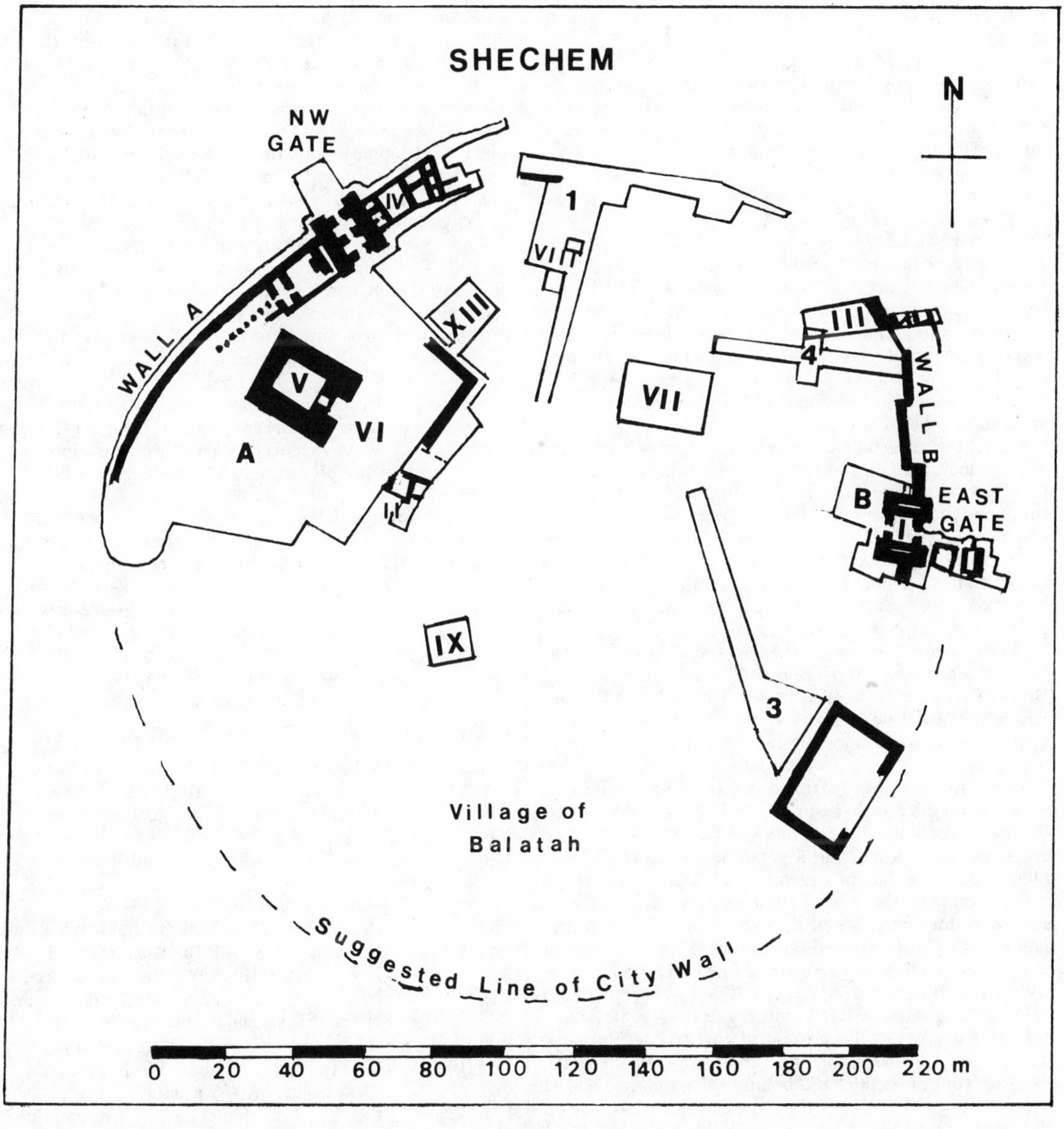

SHE.02. Site plan of excavations at Shechem. The German excavations are shown in capital letters and Arabic numbers; the American fields are indicated by Roman numerals. *(Courtesy of L. E. Toombs)*

trenches were too narrow to reveal the full extent of any structures encountered, and were dug without cross balks along their lengths to provide stratigraphic control.

The tracing of the major defensive walls naturally began with the exposed portion of Thiersh's cyclopean wall. See Fig. SHE.02, wall A. This led to the discovery of the NW Gate, and what Sellin called the W and E "palaces," abutting the gate on either side. A later wall, with offsets and insets along its length (Wall B), appeared in Trench 4, and tracing it southward led to the discovery of the E Gate of the city.

The discovery of the NW gate with its associated structures led to a huge area clearance in that sector of the mound (A on Fig. SHE.02). A smaller area clearance at the E Gate uncovered the N two thirds of the structure (B on Fig. SHE.02).

Numerous other trenches and small area clearances yielded rich and important finds, but the reports of these are given only in very general terms.

2. American Excavations. In 1954, G. E. Wright and B. W. Anderson planned renewed excavation at Shechem. They believed that the important advances in the knowledge of Palestinian pottery chronology, in field method, and in recording and interpretative techniques which had taken place in the twenty years since the last German expedition would make possible the recovery of much of the lost information and would add new dimensions to the archaeological history of the site.

Under the direction of Wright the Drew-McCormick Archaeological Expedition (later called the Joint Expedition) went into the field in the summer of 1956, and continued with approximately six week seasons in the summers of 1957, 1960, 1962, 1964, 1966, and 1968. In 1968, R. Boling reexamined a large building on the N slope of Mt. Gerizim about 300 m from the tell which had been excavated by Welter in 1931. In the summer of 1969, J. D. Seger directed an investigation of the MB remains adjacent to the Temple area. Sellin's "palaces" were the focus of a summer campaign in 1972 conducted by W. G. Dever. Extensive cemeteries of the LB and the Roman-Byzantine Period were discovered on the S slopes of Mt. Gerizim by persons unconnected with the Joint Expedition.

The Joint Expedition planned its work with two aims in view; to reevaluate and supplement the results of the German expedition by excavation adjacent to or within areas already exposed, and to open new areas in order to fill in gaps in the data provided by the earlier expedition.

To accomplish the first of these aims seven fields were excavated during the life of the expedition. (In the terminology used by the expedition a "Field" is a system of interconnected 5 m by 5 m squares. The individual squares within a Field were called "Areas".) The Fields referred to below are indicated by Roman numerals on Fig. SHE.02.

Field I uncovered the portion of the E Gate not excavated by the German Expedition and examined the structures in front of, beside, and behind the gateway. Field II was sited on the SE edge of the huge German clearance on the sacred area. See A on Fig. SHE.02. Field III was a trench over the fortification system on the E side of the tell, just to the N of Trench 4 of the German Expedition. The exploration of the massive temple found by the Germans in Area A on the NW side of the tell constituted Field V.

Less extensive excavations designed to clarify the German results were Field IV in one of the rooms of Sellin's Eastern Palace, Field VI.2 on the NE side of German Area A, and Field VIII on the bottom and S side of German Trench 1.

Of the new excavations, Field VI penetrated below the levels reached in the German Area A to expose and elucidate the earlier structures in the citadel area. Field VII, near the center of the tell, explored the housing of the city from the latest remains to the MB III period. In an effort to determine the overall stratigraphy of the site an 11 × 11 m area (Field IX), located about 40 m S of the citadel area, was excavated from the preserved surface to bedrock. Field XIII, adjacent to the NE side of the citadel area, reached LB levels and exposed rich Canaanite remains. Field XV attempted (with ambiguous results) to locate the MB city walls on the S side of the city.

The expedition undertook some work in the environs of the tell. The most important projects were a survey of the Shechem region, conducted by E. F. Campbell, Jr., and the excavation of a Roman and Byzantine temple site on Tell er-Ras, a spur projecting from the N slopes of Mt. Gerizim (Field XII). Field X designated a largely futile search for tombs on the S slopes of Mt. Ebal. Field XI was a salvage operation to investigate a Byzantine building partially exposed when municipal workers dug a trench to lay a water pipe. Field XIV, an exploratory trench in the compound of the Tomb of Joseph, produced entirely negative results.

D. Archaeological History

Combining its own findings with those of the German excavators, the Drew-McCormick Expedition isolated 24 strata of occupation (from latest to earliest Strata I–XXIV). The accompanying table gives these results in a simplified form. The dates are, of course, approximate.

The Stratigraphy of Shechem
(dates approximate)

Period	Strata	Dates	Characteristics
Chalcolithic	XXIV–XXIII	4500–3200	Village occupation
[Gap in occupation during Early Bronze Age]			
MB I	XXII–XXI	1900–1750	Earliest urbanization
MB II	XX–XVII	1750–1650	Hyksos Period
MB III	XVI–XV	1650–1550	Prosperous urban center
[Gap in occupation during LB IA]			
LB IB	XIV	1450–1400	Complete rebuilding
LB IIA	XIII	1400–1310	Amarna Period
LB IIB	XII	1310–1200	Post-Amarna decline
Iron IA	XI	1200–1125	Israelite dominance
["Abimelech" destruction and gradual resettlement]			
Iron IB–IIA	X–IX	975–810	Early monarchy
Iron IIB	VIII–VII	810–724	Divided monarchy
[Destruction by Assyrian armies]			
Iron IIC	VI	724–600	Assyrian domination
Persian	V	600–475	Cultural decline
[Abandonment 475–331]			
Hellenistic	IV–I	475–331	Samaritan sacred city

1. Earliest Settlement (Strata XXIV–XXIII). During the Chalcolithic Period (ca. 4500–3200 B.C.), settlers, attracted by the abundant water supply, moved into the area later occupied by the city, which was then virtually a level valley floor (Stratum XXIV). They built roughly circular huts with cobblestone floors and superstructures probably of hides or compacted earth. Field IX contained the remains of three such huts in close proximity to one another. The compact nature of the occupation suggests an agricultural village of the type common in the Chalcolithic era. In Field VI a beaten earth surface, covered by occupational debris and fragments of pottery represents a second phase of occupation, still within the Chalcolithic Period.

2. Middle Bronze Age. a. MB I (Strata XXII–XXI). Urban occupation at Shechem began in Middle Bronze I (ca. 1900–1750 B.C.). Because of deep excavation for later construction the remains are disappointingly scanty, but are sufficient to show the presence of a large and well-organized community. The period began with a massive leveling and filling operation, designed to prepare the site for subsequent building operations. No fortification walls can be assigned to the period. In the interior of the city, there were two levels of housing (Strata XXII–XXI) with a period of temporary abandonment between. The buildings are substantial structures with mudbrick walls on stone foundations and typical furnishings and artifacts of domestic occupation.

The most imposing structure belonging to the period is an earthen platform held in place by a sloping stone wall. A scree of stones and pottery had fallen down the outer face of the platform, but whatever structure surmounted it had been removed by later construction. The W wall of the platform was traced for a distance of 10 m when it turned at right angles to the S. Excavation in 1964, which located the NE corner of the platform fill, discounted earlier suggestions that the structure was the corner tower of a city wall or an altar analogous to the large stone-supported structure at Megiddo. Probably the platform was a rectangular podium near the N limits of the city, topped by a large public building (sacred or secular).

Two Egyptian texts mention the city just described. An inscription on the stele of Khu-Sebek, a noble of the court of King Sesostris III (ca. 1880–1840 B.C.), describes how the king campaigned in a foreign country of which the name was Sekmem (Shechem), and how "Sekmem fell, together with the wretched Retenu (a general Egyptian term for the inhabitants of Syro-Palestine)." The Execration Texts were devices by which the Pharaohs of the 12th Dyn. (20th–19 centuries B.C.) guaranteed the overthrow of their enemies by placing their names and appropriate curses on potsherds or clay figurines which were then ceremonially broken. One of the texts gives the name of Ibish-hadad of Shechem. These texts indicate that by the mid–19th century Shechem was an important strategic and political center, a leader of resistance against Egyptian expansionist policies and probably the head of a city-state confederacy.

b. MB II (Strata XX–XVII). The second phase of the MB began in Stratum XX with the city enclosed within a simple, free-standing mudbrick wall 2.5 m wide, set on a stone foundation, a direct continuation of the defensive concepts of the 1st period of urbanization in Palestine (the EB Age, ca. 3300–2400 B.C.). A 43 m long segment of this wall was uncovered on the NW side of the city. See Wall D on Fig. SHE.03.

As the period developed (Stratum XIX), the fortifications underwent dramatic change, due partly to the introduction of the battering ram in seige warfare and partly to the appearance in the area of a new people, the HYKSOS. The city was surrounded by a huge mound of earth over 30 m wide at the base with a slope of between 30 and 40 degrees and surmounted by a defensive wall, the typical "Hyksos rampart."

In Stratum XX a large rectangular area on the inner (W) side of the defensive wall was isolated from the rest of the city. An especially massive wall formed the S side of the enclosure nearest the city. See Wall 900 on Fig. SHE.03. The walled-off area served a double purpose: it provided an enclosed space for public buildings, and a fortified last line of defense in case the outer walls were breached.

Along the inner face of Wall 900 ran a cobbled street with a drain along its edge. Beyond the street lay two groups of buildings, a S and a N block, separated at some stages by a heavy wall and at others by a paved corridor. The S block was dominated by several large courtyards with adjacent smaller rooms. The N block had for most of the period a residential and storage function. This general plan of the citadel area continued throughout the period, but the layout of the individual rooms and courtyards underwent four distinct phases of modification and rebuilding.

In the earliest of these phases (Stratum XX, Fig. SHE.03A) the N block, approached through a pillared entryway, contained two groups of small rooms, one for storage (Rooms 21–24) and one for domestic purposes (Rooms 25–28). The principal features of the S block were two large courtyards (34 and 35) with a range of three smaller rooms (31, 32 and 33) on the N side.

In the 2d phase (Stratum XIX, Fig. SHE.03B), a corridor separated the two parts of the complex. A courtyard replaced the storage chambers of the previous phase. Three courtyards (Rooms 10/11, 12, 14) dominated the S block. Around these open spaces on the E and S sides lay a range of small rooms. Judging by the number of silos and ovens, most of these subsidiary rooms were cooking or grain storage areas. However, one of them (Room 16) had a low partition in its center and was provided with a drain. Copper slag on the floor of the room suggested the possibility that it was used for casting bronze objects.

Extensive modifications during the third phase of the citadel (Stratum XVIII, Fig. SHE.03C) resulted in the elimination of the small industrial rooms, and the production of four courtyards; a large L-shaped courtyard to the S and E (Room 5), a central court with a small, rectangular room provided with a drain in its SW corner (Room 6), a W court with a small room similarly located (Room 4), and a N court (Room 2).

The N court had a row of column bases stretching across its N end, and an isolated column base near its center. The colonnade probably supported the (wooden?) columns for a canopy. An isolated column base was found near the center of the court. If the complex was a palace, this room probably served as the audience hall, with the throne

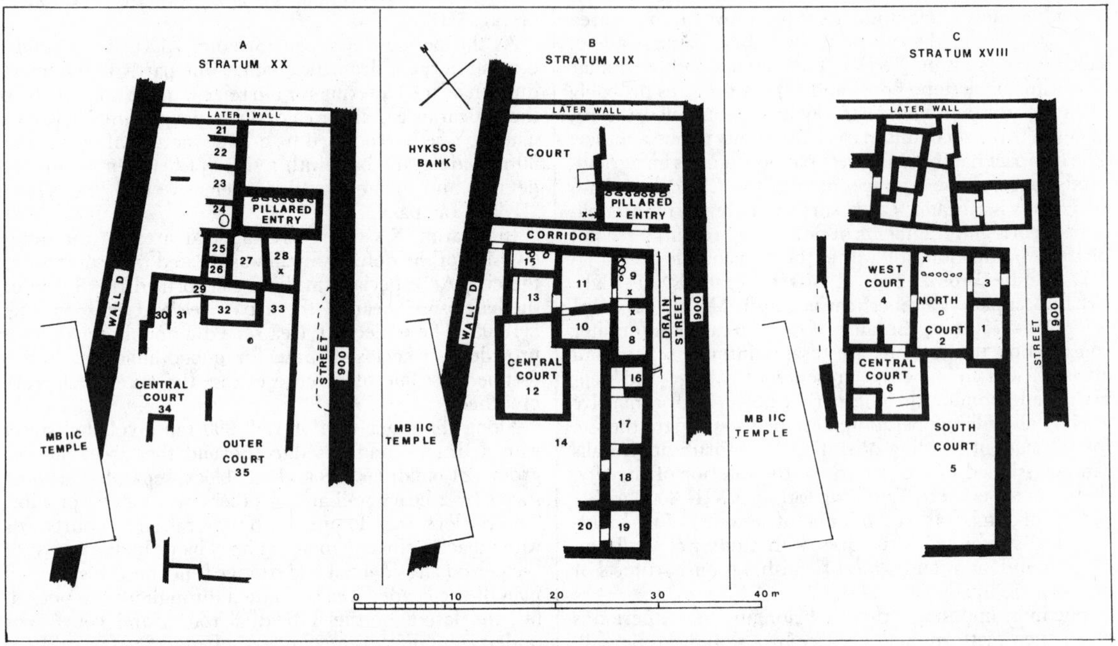

SHE.03. Schematic of the three main phases of the acropolis building at Shechem—MB IIB. This building has been variously identified as a "Courtyard Temple" or a royal palace. The subfloor burials are marked *x. (Courtesy of L. E. Toombs)*

placed under the protection of the canopy. The W court would then have been the waiting room for those seeking an audience and their retainers. The central court may have been the palace shrine with the cult room tucked away in the corner.

The final phase of the citadel (Stratum XVII) is poorly delineated, because most of its structures and all of its floors were removed by the German excavators. It extended beyond the W limits of the earlier phases, over the stump of the disused Hyksos embankment.

Considerable debate has centered around the function of this important complex. Its isolation from the rest of the city, the size and solidity of its buildings, the numerous courtyards, and the frequent use of solidly-founded pillars demonstrate that the area served a public function. At first the expedition tentatively identified it as a palace (Toombs and Wright 1961: 16, 22–28). In 1962, G. E. Wright suggested that the structures had a religious function, and called the complex the "Courtyard Temple" (Toombs and Wright 1963: 11–18; G. E. Wright 1965: 104–9). Paul Lapp argued that the identification of the complex as a temple was "dubious" (1963: 129–30). The evidence and the arguments based on it were later summarized and evaluated by L. E. Toombs (1985: 42–60). The most likely conclusion seems to be that the complex was a palace in all its phases, and that its central courtyard, located throughout the history of the structures almost directly beneath the later altar of the MB IIC period, may have been the palace shrine.

Special interest attaches to a series of burials within the complex. The earliest is the skeleton of a child, lying in a flexed position on the Stratum XX floor of Room 28 (Fig. SHE.03A), without burial jar or grave furnishings.

The best preserved of the series was found beneath the floor of the Stratum XIX pillared entryway (Fig. SHE.03B). The body of a six or seven year old child lay inside a large storage jar, placed on its side in a shallow trench, protected by flat stones. The skeleton, flexed on its right side, wore a necklace of crystal and agate beads. Pottery vessels, probably once containing grave offerings, and scattered bones of an indeterminate nature were found inside the jars and in the trench. A very similar jar burial, with the bones in disarray, was found under the floor of Room 9. Beneath the floor of the adjacent room (Room 8) was the deliberate burial of a sheep or goat on a bed of small stones. Under the W wall of the entryway (Fig. SHE.03B) a deposit consisting entirely of pottery, a storage jar with two smaller vessels inside, came to light.

A Stratum XVIII burial under the floor of the N courtyard was somewhat different. A jumble of bones, including fragments of at least four skulls, rested within an upright storage jar, protected by fragments of a second jar. The jar stood in a specially prepared shallow niche in the base of the wall. Two smaller vessels were associated with the burial.

The burials (human, animal, and ceramic) were made just prior to the laying of the floors or in conjunction with the construction of the walls with which they were associated. They seem clearly to have been foundation offerings, but the evidence is not sufficient to establish whether or not the human burials were child sacrifices.

c. MB III (Strata XVI and XV). Extensive building activity, high quality construction in both domestic and public architecture, and an abundance of luxury items among the artifacts show that Shechem reached a peak of prosperity in the last phase of the MB. But the presence of three major destruction levels, the last a veritable holocaust, indicates the troubled and dangerous nature of the times.

At the beginning of the period (ca. 1650 B.C.), the defensive system of the city was completely rebuilt on a new plan. The outer revetment wall of the Hyksos embankment was used as the base for a massive wall of huge boulders. See Wall A on Fig. SHE.02. Earth obtained in the main from cutting down the embankment was deposited behind the wall, so that it backed up against solid earth and was virtually impregnable to the battering ram. Eight m inside this outer wall ran a slighter circumvallation. The two walls were connected at intervals by cross walls to form a casemate system, the chambers of which were used for domestic and storage purposes.

On the NW side of the city a monumental gateway, 18 × 16 m, pierced the two walls. See Fig. SHE.02. Massive towers, projecting beyond the entryway both inside and outside the city, flanked the paved roadway through the gate. Three pairs of projections jutting out from the towers narrowed the roadway to only half its width and effectively divided it into two chambers. Each projection consisted of two huge flat stones (orthostats) set on the long edge 75 cm apart. Three gates, swung between the orthostate pairs, probably closed off the entry in time of war or disorder.

Enigmatic structures, which Sellin identified as the two wings of a palace (1926b: 304–7), stood between the outer and inner walls on either side of the gate. G. E. Wright (1965: 61) identified the structures as storage rooms. Dever's reexcavation of the buildings (1974) raises the strong possibility that Sellin was correct. Immediately S of the gate, Dever identified a tripartite temple, probably the oldest example in Palestine. It consisted of an antechamber leading into a shrine room with a podium at the N end and through the shrine room to a small chamber abutting the gate. Access to the temple could only be had through a long, narrow room with a colonnade along its central axis. The layout suggests an audience hall and a palace shrine. A substantial building, consisting of a central court with a range of rooms at each end, situated N of the gateway, may have been, as Dever suggests, a barracks for troops. Alternatively, it may have constituted the living quarters of the palace.

The effect of this construction was to shift the palace to the space between the walls in order to leave room for a great public temple and its courtyard. Indeed, the public temple seems to have been built *before* the palace, since the E wall of the palace was inset to avoid the NW corner of the temple. The acropolis of the MB II city was filled over to a depth of almost 4 m to create a level platform. On this filling, a building with walls 5.1 m thick made of well-dressed masonry with a mudbrick superstructure and with its entrance flanked by two large towers was erected. See Fig. SHE.02, building V. The massive nature of the structure has earned it the name "fortress temple." The long axis of the building ran NW to SE, and the entrance, with a standing stone *(maṣṣēbāh)* on either side, was in the SE wall, where it would catch the rays of the rising sun.

The open area in front of the building was occupied by an altar and a huge limestone slab set in a stone socket, but sufficient space remained to accommodate a large gathering of worshippers.

The temple can hardly have been involved in the visits of Abraham (Gen 12:6) and Jacob (Gen 35:4) to the sacred place at or near the city, nor in Jacob's purchase of a piece of ground from the "sons of Hamor" on which to pitch his camp. The temple had a clear function in relation to the urban population, and the oak and altars referred to in the text, if they existed at all, must have stood outside the city. An intriguing possibility is that the compilers of Genesis were attempting to appropriate the site of the Canaanite shrine on Mt. Gerizim as an Israelite sacred place (see below).

The Wall A fortification system seems to have provided inadequate backup defenses behind the great outer wall, and survived for only about 25 years. The new fortifications used the lower courses of Wall A as a stone scarp for the outer face of the mound, a precaution against sappers and the battering ram. On the relatively level area 11 m back of the scarp a powerful new wall of mudbrick on stone foundations 3.5 m wide was constructed with offsets and insets to permit enfilade fire along the wall. See Wall B on Fig. SHE.02. A new gateway (the East Gate, Fig. SHE.02) gave access to the fertile plain, the breadbasket of the city. It conformed to the plan of the Northwest Gate, but had only four pairs of orthostats, forming a single chamber within the gateway. From inside the city a flight of five steps led up to the roadway through the gate. In its initial phase the gate had a cobbled entranceway between the flanking towers. Toward the end of the city's life the surface of the roadway was raised and the orthostats were moved up to the new level and placed on rather flimsy foundations of smallish stones. The public temple and the Northwest Gate remained in use, but what happened to the "palaces" beside that gate is uncertain because most of the relevant evidence was removed during the German excavations.

If the identifications proposed above are correct, the MB city possessed at least two sacred structures, a public temple and a palace shrine. A third building, possibly also of a sacred nature, stood on the N slope of Mt. Gerizim about 300 m from the city. It was first excavated by Welter in 1931 and reexcavated by Boling in 1968. It is a square structure 18 × 18 m, consisting of an unroofed court 9 × 9 m surrounded on all four sides by smaller chambers, probably used for storage. The court had in its center a stone pedestal, which may have served as the base for a sacred pillar, and in its SE corner an altar-like platform of stone. Incense burners, a libation bowl, and a foundation deposit of bronze weapons were found near the "altar" and, in a side chamber, a stone phallus. Campbell and Wright (1969: 111) suggested that the building was a shrine used by semi-nomadic clans in covenant unity with one another. However, the shrine could hardly have functioned in plain sight of the city without the approval and support of its governing authorities. If the building was indeed a tribal shrine, its presence indicates a cordial relationship between the urban and rural populations.

The nature of the domestic structures at Shechem is not well known. In Field XIII a large, multi-roomed building, probably the house of a nobleman or extremely wealthy citizen, yielded many luxury items including numerous fine scarabs and the ivory inlay for two boxes. Such houses as were excavated in Fields VII and IX were well constructed of mudbrick on stone foundations and the fine pottery and artifacts, including several scarabs, confirm the impression of a high level of prosperity.

The final destruction of MB III Shechem displays a calculated ferocity and an intent to cause complete destruction of the city. Everywhere there is evidence of intense fire. Half-destroyed buildings were looted and then deliberately pulled down and the bodies of their inhabitants thrown into the street. When the destruction was complete a layer of debris covered the city to a depth of up to 1.6 m. There is little doubt that the Egyptian armies of Ahmose I or Amenhotep I brought this disaster upon the city as they followed up the triumph of Egyptian arms over the Hyksos. Shechem lay in ruins for about a century until its rebuilding in LB IB as a Canaanite city under the domination of the Egyptian Empire.

3. Late Bronze Age. a. LB IB (Stratum XIV). The LB engineers who reconstructed Shechem seem to have done the entire rebuilding in a single, well-planned operation, using the surviving stumps of the walls of major structures as a guide for their work. The old Wall A still served as the facing of the slope of the mound. Behind it, the main defensive wall of mudbrick on a stone foundation followed the line of the Wall B system. A rebuilt Northwest Gate probably remained in use, although the evidence for this is not conclusive. The East Gate was reconstructed with a significant modification. A building, consisting of two chambers, the outer of which had a paved floor, was built on the S side of the gateway, probably to accommodate the guards on duty at the gate. The corresponding guardroom on the N side of the gate, if it existed, was removed by the German excavations.

Under the lowest floor of the outer guardroom the body of a quadruped, probably a donkey, had been buried. The head was missing. It had been severed from the body prior to the burial. Near the neck was a clump of bones from a smaller animal. The deposit appears to be a foundation sacrifice. It is particularly interesting since Gen 33:19 refers to the Shechemites as *bĕnē ḥămôr,* "sons of a donkey."

In the acropolis area (Fields V/VI) a shrine, of which only portions of the cella were preserved, stood on massive foundations of the MB III temple. Its walls were only about one third the width of those of its predecessor. The cella was a room 16 × 12 m with the entrance on the long E side. The axis of the building was shifted five degrees to the S, possibly to bring it more accurately into line with the rising sun at the summer solstice. A cement covered podium, approached by a flight of steps, occupied part of the W wall of the cella opposite the entrance. It probably provided a base for the statues of the deities worshipped in the temple. A large altar stood in the broad forecourt. This temple, which continued in use throughout the LB and into Iron I, is a strong candidate for the Temple of *ēl-bĕrît* where the Shechemites made their last stand against Abimelech (Judg 9:46).

The broad room temple was not the only sacred structure in LB Shechem. In Field IX, part of a building with substantial walls, contained a brick platform (altar?) and a monolith, the base of which had been dressed to fit into a stone socket. This building went through several stages of reflooring during the LB Age. It may have been a satellite of the main temple or a private shrine associated with a large tripartite house adjacent to it.

An impressive LB structure filled the whole of Field XIII and extended beyond it in all directions. The W side of the complex consisted of two large courtyards. The E side was occupied by a range of three rooms used for cooking and storage, and E of these rooms the edge of what appeared to be a large courtyard disappeared tantalizingly out of the excavated area. The function of the complex is unknown. Its exceptional size and its location next to the temple area raise the possibility that it was a royal palace, but it may have been the residence of an exceptionally wealthy citizen.

The historical occasion for the LB rebuilding of Shechem was probably the establishment of the Egyptian Empire. The earliest 18th Dyn. Pharaohs would have had a vested interest in keeping the hill country depopulated and without fortified cities. The overwhelming interest of these Pharaohs would be to avoid recurrence of the Asiatic intrusions which had put the Hyksos in control of the Delta region and had cost the Pharaohs blood and treasure to repel. Fear of the Asiatics would urge the creation in the Palestine area of a defenseless buffer zone against the still powerful states to the N. However, to create such a zone would run counter to another vital Pharaonic interest, that of holding the coastal strip as an advance line into Asia and as an artery of trade. A workable compromise of these conflicting interests would be to hold the coastal road by means of a chain of fortified bases and, at the same time, to discourage the rebuilding of strong points in the hills, which would be potential threats to communication along the coast.

With the warrior king Thutmose III, Egyptian obsession with defense gave way to imperialist ambition, and an empire without cities is a contradiction in terms. When, after his victory at Megiddo, Thutmose felt that he was master of Asia he may have encouraged the rebuilding of the hill cities, Shechem among them, ruled, of course, by his puppets. A tentative date for the founding of LB Shechem is, therefore, shortly after the battle of Megiddo (i.e., about 1465 B.C.). It ended with the decline of Egyptian control in Palestine and the establishment of the mini-empire of Lab'ayu, king of Shechem (ca. 1400 B.C.).

b. LB IIA (Stratum XIII). This stratum is the high point of LB culture at Shechem. The rising level of prosperity is best seen at the East Gate, where the guardrooms were strengthened and paved with flagstones. Just S of the gateway an open area, also paved with flagstones, provided a place for the mustering of troops and for public meetings.

The building complex in Field XIII underwent alterations and improvements. The W courtyard was subdivided into four interconnecting chambers where domestic activities took place. The range of rooms to the E followed the lines laid down in the previous phase, but their functions became more clearly defined. The S chamber was a cooking area and contained an oven and a pantry equipped with storage pits. Under the central room was a sub-floor storage chamber 2 m deep and surrounded by heavy stone walls. Toward the end of the period, this chamber was filled in with material taken from a midden. The fill contained a great many restorable pottery vessels which constitutes a unique ceramic collection, datable to LB IIA. The N room housed a plaster lined silo. The houses in Field VII are of excellent construction.

The flourishing of LB IIA Shechem can be associated with the slackening of Egyptian control over its Asiatic empire in the latter years of Amenhotep III and during the reign of Amenhotep IV (Ikhnaton). Taking advantage of the power vacuum, Lab'ayu, king of Shechem extended his control from the Valley of Jezreel to the environs of Jerusalem. The Amarna Letters show him as a shrewd, calculating ruler, skilled at setting his sails to the prevailing wind. He professed allegiance to the Pharaoh, but his neighbors refer to him as the ring-leader of opposition, the head of a coalition of rebels and a predator on his neighbors. Lab'ayu was captured by his enemies and killed, but for a time his two sons continued the policy of their father. The fruits of conquest and the profits from the caravan trade would account well for the prosperity of Shechem during the Amarna period.

In the end, the enemies of Lab'ayu's family, whether the Canaanite cities which he had threatened or despoiled, troops sent from Egypt, disgruntled allies or some combination of these, evidently had their way. Destruction by fire brought an end to the city of Lab'ayu. Its debris covers almost every quarter of the city.

c. LB IIB (Stratum XII). The city, quickly rebuilt, retained most of the features of its forerunner. The defensive system, the temple on the acropolis, the shrine in Field IX, and the housing in Field VII underwent little modification. The guardrooms at the East Gate remained, but the paved courtyard behind them went out of use and a narrow alley separated the guardrooms from the houses of the city. The principal feature of the period is a marked decline in the prosperity of the city. Walls founded in this period and rebuilds of surviving walls are of shoddy construction.

Two interesting finds are associated with this phase of the city's life. A figurine of the god Baᶜal in cast bronze overlaid with silver came from the floor of a house in Field VII. See Fig. SHE.04. The deity, wearing a conical crown, strides forward on his left foot and holds some object (now lost) in each hand. Figurines of the fertility goddess found in several of the houses show that the consort of the Baᶜal was an even more popular object of veneration than her male counterpart. The second object, recovered from the fill under an Iron I wall in Field XIII, is a fragment of a cuneiform tablet which contains part of the opening lines of an Amarna period letter.

If the story of the rape of Dinah and the subsequent plundering of Shechem by Simeon and Levi (Genesis 34) is not the vague memory of a tribal skirmish inflated and attached to the city of Shechem and the family of Jacob, there seem to be only two points at which it could conceivably fit into the archaeological history of Shechem. While the powerful walls of MB and LB Shechem stood, two semi-nomadic tribes would have been powerless to breach the defenses of the city. The period of abandonment after

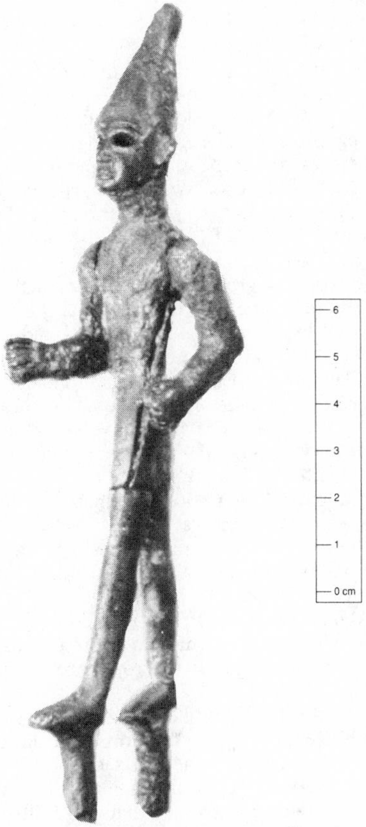

SHE.04. Figurine of the god Baᶜal found on the floor of a house at Shechem—LB. *(Courtesy of L. E. Toombs)*

the destruction of the MB Age city, when the ruins may have housed a small village or have been the headquarters of a tribal group, or the period of decline at the end of the LB Age are the only likely contexts for the story.

A persistent tradition associated with Shechem is that Jacob bought a piece of land near the city from Hamor, the king of Shechem (Gen 33:19), and that in fulfillment of Joseph's death bed command (Gen 50:25, 26), the Hebrews on leaving Egypt carried with them the bones of Joseph (Exod 13:19) and buried them in this plot of ground (Josh 24:32). A garbled form of this tradition appears in Stephen's defense before the Sanhedrin (Acts 7:16). The martyr states that Abraham bought the land from Hamor, and that, not only Joseph, but all who had died in Egypt were brought to Shechem for burial. This is the only reference to Shechem in the NT.

4. Iron Age. a. Iron I (Stratum XI). No general destruction layer marks the end of the LB at Shechem. The temple on the acropolis, the defensive walls, and the East Gate with its guardrooms remained in use. This evidence indicates a relatively peaceful passage of the city into Israelite hands, and may account for its absence from the list of cities conquered by Joshua (Josh 12:7–23). Shechem is named as a "city of refuge" (Josh 20:7; 1 Chr 6:67) and as a lLevitical city in the "hill country of Ephraim" (Josh 21:21).

Shortly after the initial intrusion of the Israelites into the region, the city was the scene of a covenant-making ceremony, conducted by Joshua (Judges 24). The ceremony took place in or near a shrine (v 26) where the representatives of the people "presented themselves before the Lord" (v 1). G. E. Wright has argued convincingly that the shrine was the temple on the acropolis, called in Judg 9:4 the "Temple of El-Berith," the God of the Covenant (1965: 134–36).

During Iron I, a great deal of building activity of poor quality went on in the city. In Field XIII the LB complex was replaced by several less impressive buildings. Poorly-constructed houses crowded up against the guardrooms of the East Gate. Many of the buildings in Fields VII and IX show traces of destruction by fire. The impression of disorder and economic decline conveyed by the archaeological remains supports the picture of political unrest and turmoil provided by Judg 8:23–35.

The instability of the period culminated in the brief and abortive reign of Gideon's son, Abimelech (Judges 9). Boling (1969: 103) makes the interesting suggestion that Jotham stood on the site of the ruined tribal shrine on Mt. Gerizim when he uttered the parable of the trees and cursed Abimelech (Judg 9:7–21). It would have been an appropriate place from which to protest in the name of the tribal tradition against the royal pretentions of Abimelech.

When the Shechemites rebelled against the upstart king, Abimelech's revenge was swift and complete. The topography of the region and the archaeological remains illuminate his four-stage campaign against the city. The following reconstruction assumes that the Beth-millo ("the building on the artificial fill," Judg 9:20) and the Tower of Shechem (Judg 9:47, 49) are one and the same and refer to the temple and its ancillary buildings on the acropolis. The rebel chief Gaal, deceived and taunted by Abimelech's agent Zebul, brought his troops out of the city into the Plain of ʿAskar. See Fig. SHE.01. Abimelech's forces, which had slipped down from Mt. el-ʿUrmeh during the night, ambushed the rebels and drove them back into the city through the East Gate with heavy losses. Abimelech then feigned withdrawal, and the Shechemites, thinking themselves safe came out to work in the fields in the ʿAskar Plain. Abimelech's troops cut them off from the city and massacred them in the plain. Following up this success, they breached the East Gate and in a day of street fighting captured the lower city, burning and looting as they went. The surviving defenders made a last stand in the temple, but their defenses were burned to the ground and they themselves were slaughtered. The heaps of debris covering the Iron I city are silent witnesses to the completeness of Abimelech's vengeance.

The city recovered only slowly from the disaster. The beginning of the recovery was marked by the digging of unlined, bag-shaped pits through the acropolis and adjacent areas. Because of the absence of a lining the pits were unsuitable for storage. Their fill was rich in organic matter and destruction debris, containing pottery of the 12th century B.C. The pottery indicates that the pits were filled soon after the Abimelech destruction. Their most obvious use was to dispose of some of the masses of debris which covered the site. The organic matter may have come, as Campbell suggests (unpublished communication), from garments and utensils burned to prevent the spread of disease.

After the pitting phase, the most significant feature is a layering of black bands of very fine composition and rich in organic matter, found in Fields I, VII, and XIII. They were probably deposits from agricultural plots and threshing floors. Houses of poor quality stood among these plots, and in Field XIII, a roadway paved with small stones ran diagonally across the field. The once powerful city had reverted to the status of an agricultural village.

b. Iron IB–IIA (Strata X–IX). Political stability in the reigns of David and Solomon accelerated the pace of Shechem's recovery. By the time of division of the monarchy, the city had been reestablished. Drawn undoubtedly by Shechem's long tradition as the principal sacred place of the N tribes, Solomon's son Rehoboam went to Shechem to be crowned (1 Kgs 12:1). His brutal rejection of the demands of his prospective subjects led to the establishment of the independent N Kingdom under Jeroboam I. 1 Kgs 12:25 states that Jeroboam "built" Shechem and made it his capital, but whether this refers to the construction of the fortifications *de novo* or to a strengthening of existing structures is not clear.

Unfortunately, the archaeological evidence for the period is sparse and ambiguous. The fortifications were rebuilt along the lines of the LB defenses. The preserved fragments indicate that they were of casemate construction. Building activity went on also at the East Gate where the towers were reconstructed.

By Stratum IX a steep slope ran from the acropolis area downward toward the East Gate. This slope was terraced to facilitate the construction of houses. One of the terraces and fragments of two others ran across Field VII. The remains of the housing constructed on these terraces show an improvement in the economic condition of the city.

Strata X and IX are separated from one another by a destruction level which has been attributed to the invasions of the Egyptian Pharaoh Shishak (ca. 918 B.C.). Stratum IX also ends in a destruction, possibly one of the unhappy events in the recurrent war between Israel and Damascus (e.g., 1 Kings 20).

c. Iron IIB (Strata VIII–VII). Shechem lost some of its status when Jeroboam moved his capital to Tirzah, but the city flourished as capital and tax collection center of the district of Mt. Ephraim. One of the Samaritan ostraca names Shechem as a source of taxes in wine. On the former acropolis area a rectangular building, approximately 18 m wide by 16 m deep, was built on the stumps of the old temple walls. Its lower walls were constructed of unhewn boulders. A corridor ran the width of the building at the front and gave access to three long, narrow storage rooms. The floor was a very thick layer of heavy plaster which lapped up over the base of the walls. The plan of the structure suggests a granary and the flooring may be an early example of rodent-proofing a building. The building probably housed grain collected as revenue from the district.

The terraces and the houses built on them were in use

throughout the period with frequent rebuilding and repair. The middle terrace of Stratum VII supported a fine Israelite courtyard house, almost completely preserved. The open central court was a work area where domestic activities and home industry went on. In the center of the court was a cylindrical stone 90 cm in diameter. Its surface was covered with irregularly spaced, shallow grooves, leading to a deeper circular groove around the edge. A lip allowed liquid collected in the circular groove to run off into a storage jar, set into the ground beside the installation. Abutting it was a stone vat 55 cm deep. A number of large grinding stones were found in the courtyard. The installation was probably an olive press. Some of the supply of olives kept in the vat would be transferred to the flat stone and abraded against the grooves with a grinder. The oil expressed from the fruit would run off into the jar. In a later phase of the building an oval hearth 2 m long, the rim of which was coated with lime, replaced the press. The hearth was most likely a kiln for slaking lime used in the preparation of plaster, although its use as a pottery kiln cannot be ruled out. A saddle quern against the N wall of the court indicates that grain was ground there.

The N and S walls of the courtyard were flanked by two small rooms. Considerable water must have been used in the two S rooms, since they were drained by two stone-filled sumps. A long room with a silo ran the full length of its E side. It seems to have been the main living room of the house, and was connected by a corridor to the kitchen. In a later enlargement of the building, additional rooms were added on the N and S sides.

The destruction which ended Stratum VIII may be attributed to the campaign of Menahem after his successful seizure of the throne from Shallum (2 Kgs 15:13–16). The Assyrian invasion of 724 B.C. brought about the total destruction of Stratum VII. The city was reduced to a heap of ruins, completely covered by debris of fallen brickwork, burned beams and tumbled building stones. The Assyrian destruction of the N cities, of which Shechem is a typical example, made a profound and lasting impression on the people of Judah. Ps 60:6–8 (= Ps 108:7–9) is an obscure oracle of uncertain date which predicts the deliverance of the N regions. Shechem is the first place name mentioned.

d. Iron IIC (Stratum V). The impoverished reoccupation at the end of the Israelite period at Shechem shows a marked decline in every aspect of culture. The Iron II defense system and the East Gate underwent shoddy repairs. Flimsy houses covered the area once occupied by the LB guardrooms. In Fields VII and IX some advantage was taken of existing foundations, but mainly the houses were not much more than shanties. The presence of many imitations of Assyrian vessels in local clay indicates the dominance of the Assyrian overlords.

5. Persian and Hellenistic Periods (Strata V–I). Shechem remained in an impoverished state during the Neo-Babylonian and Persian Periods (Stratum V) and toward their end, had declined to such a degree that the site was abandoned for almost a century and a half. At the beginning of the period a delegation from Shechem and two other N towns came to Jerusalem to mourn the destruction of the Temple, only to be murdered by Ishmael, the assassin of Gedaliah (Jer 41:4–10).

Religious factors brought Shechem back into prominence about 330 B.C. Following their break with the Jewish community, the Samaritans built a temple of their own on Mt. Gerizim. At the foot of the mountain on the ruins of ancient Shechem they designed a city to rival the Holy City of Jerusalem. They constructed a defensive wall on the line of the MB fortifications and laid down a plastered glacis in front of it. The orthostats at the East Gate had long ago been buried in debris, but the Samaritan engineers cleared out the old roadway to form a sunken approach to the gate. A small building, erected over the remains of the LB and Israelite guardrooms housed a wine or olive press.

House construction of the period is of excellent quality. The foundations on which the mudbrick superstructures rested are made of an outer and inner face of dressed stone with a rubble core between. Broad streets separated the blocks of houses. A destruction ended this phase of the city's life.

In the succeeding phase (Stratum III) the concepts of defense and housing remained essentially unaltered. A particularly fine specimen of a Samaritan house came to light in Field II. Its door and window frames were of drafted masonry. The plastered walls were painted a different color in each room. The iron key to an interior room of the house and a clay seal from a papyrus document, showing a kneeling archer, were found in the remains of the building. Judging by the number of loom weights in the debris, a small-scale weaving industry went on in the building. From the remains of a house in Field VII came a small jar which contained a hoard of 35 silver tetradrachmas, minted by the Ptolemaic rulers of Egypt. It was probably left behind by a refugee fleeing the city at the time of the destruction of Stratum III. A possible historical context for this destruction is the wars between the Ptolemies of Egypt and the Seleucids of Damascus for the control of Palestine, which culminated in the victory of the Seleucid Antiochus III at Paneas in 198 B.C.

The development of increasingly efficient siege equipment rendered the defenses of Shechem obsolete. Ballisti could now hurl their missiles into the city from the slopes of Mt. Ebal or Mt. Gerizim. The fortification system was, accordingly abandoned and the walls robbed for building stone. At the foot of the slope below the East Gate a rectangular tower and a narrow screening wall provided a checkpoint at the entrance to the city.

Shechem was already in its final decline when in 107 B.C. Jewish forces, carrying out the expansionist policies of John Hyrcanus, destroyed Shechem completely. This time there was no recovery. In A.D. 72 the Emperor Vespasian built the city of Flavius Neapolis about 1.5 km W of ancient Shechem on the site now occupied by the Arab city of Nablus. Nablus became the urban center of the region, and Shechem remained in ruins, visited on occasion by pilgrims to the nearby traditional locations of Jacob's Well and the Tomb of Joseph.

Bibliography

Anderson, B. W. 1957. The Place of Shechem in the Bible. *BA* 20: 10–19.

Boling, R. G. 1969. Bronze Age Buildings at the Shechem High Place: ASOR Excavations at Tananir. *BA* 32: 81–103.

Bull, R. J. 1960. A Re-examination of the Shechem Temple. *BA* 23: 110–19.
Bull, R. J.; Callaway, J. A.; Ross, J. F.; and Wright, G. E. 1965. The Fifth Campaign at Balâṭah (Shechem). *BASOR* 180: 7–41.
Campbell, E. F. 1960. Excavation at Shechem. *BA* 23: 101–110.
———. 1968. The Shechem Area Survey. *BASOR* 190: 19–41.
Campbell, E. F., and Ross, J. F. 1963. The Excavation of Shechem and the Biblical Tradition. *BA* 26: 1–27.
Campbell, E. F., and Wright, G. E. 1969. Tribal League Shrines in Amman and Shechem. *BA* 32: 104–16.
Campbell, E. F.; Ross, J. F.; and Toombs, L. E. 1971. The Eighth Campaign at Balâṭah (Shechem). *BASOR* 204: 2–17.
Cole, D. P. 1984. *Shechem I.* Winona Lake, IN.
Dever, W. G. 1974. The MB IIC Stratification in the Northwest Gate Area at Shechem. *BASOR* 216: 341–52.
Fowler, M. D. 1983. A Closer Look at the Temple of el-Berith at Shechem. *PEQ* 115: 49–53.
Graesser, C. F. 1972. Standing Stones in Ancient Palestine. *BA* 35: 34–63.
Gregori, B. 1986. Three Entrance Gates of the Middle Bronze Age in Syria and Palestine. *Levant* 18: 83–102.
Harif, A. 1979. Common Architectural Features at Alalak, Megiddo and Shechem. *Levant* 11: 162–67.
Horn, S. H. 1962. Scarabs from Shechem. *JNES* 21: 1–14.
———. 1973. Scarabs and Scarab Impressions from Shechem III. *JNES* 32/3: 281–89.
Jaros, K. 1976. *Sichem. Eine Archäologische und religionsgeschichtliche Studie mit besonderer Berucksichtigung von Jos 24.* Göttingen.
Key, H. C., and Toombs, L. E. 1957. The Second Season of Excavation at Biblical Shechem. *BA* 20: 82–105.
Lapp, N. 1985. The Stratum V Pottery from Balâṭah (Shechem). *BASOR* 257: 19–43.
Lapp, P. W. 1963. Palestine, Known but Mostly Unknown. *BA* 26: 121–34.
Ross, J. F., and Toombs, L. E. 1976. Six Campaigns at Biblical Shechem. Pp. 119–28 in *Archaeological Discoveries in the Holy Land.* New York.
Seger, J. D. 1972. Shechem Field XIII, 1969. *BASOR* 205: 20–35.
———. 1974. The Middle Bronze IIC Date of the East Gate at Shechem. *Levant* 6: 117–30.
———. 1975. The MB II Fortifications at Shechem and Gezer: A Hyksos Retrospective. *EI* 12: 34–45.
Sellin, E. 1926a. Die Ausgrabung von Sichem. *ZDPV* 49: 229–36.
———. 1926b. Die Ausgrabung von Sichem. *ZDPV* 49: 304–20.
———. 1927a. Die Ausgrabung von Sichem. *ZDPV* 50: 205–11.
———. 1927b. Die Ausgrabung von Sichem. *ZDPV* 50: 265–73.
———. 1928. Die Masseben des el-Berit im Sichem. *ZDPV* 51: 119–23.
Sellin, E., and Steckeweh H. 1941. Sichem. *ZDPV* 64: 1–20.
Shiloh, Y. 1970. The Four Room House: Its Situation and Function in the Israelite City. *IEJ* 20: 180–90.
Toombs, L. E. 1972. The Stratigraphy of Tell Balâṭah (Ancient Shechem). *ADAJ* 17: 99–110.
———. 1976. The Stratification of Tell Balâṭah (Shechem). *BASOR* 223: 57–59.
———. 1979. Shechem: Problems of the Early Israelite Era. Pp. 69–83 in *Symposia,* ed. Frank M. Cross. Cambridge, MA.
———. 1985. Temple of Palace: A Reconsideration of the Shechem Courtyard Temple. Pp. 42–58 in *Put Your Future in Ruins,* ed. H. O. Thompson. Bristol.
Toombs, L. E., and Wright, G. E. 1961. The Third Campaign at Balâṭah (Shechem). *BASOR* 161: 11–54.
———. 1963. The Fourth Campaign at Tell Balâṭah (Shechem). *BASOR* 169: 1–60.
Welter, G. 1932. Stand der Ausgrabungen in Sichem. *Archäologischer Anzeiger* 3–4, Cols. 289–314.
Wright, G. E. 1956. The First Campaign at Tell Balâṭah (Shechem). *BASOR* 144: 9–20.
———. 1957a. Shechem. *BA* 20: 2–32.
———. 1957b. The Second Campaign at Tell Balâṭah (Shechem). *BASOR* 148: 11–28.
———. 1962a. Selected Seals from the Excavations at Balâṭah (Shechem). *BASOR* 167: 77–78.
———. 1962b. The Samaritans at Shechem. *HTR* 55: 357–66.
———. 1963. The Biblical Traditions of Shechem's Sacred Area. *BASOR* 160: 27–32.
———. 1965. *Shechem.* New York.
———. 1967. Shechem. Pp. 353–70 in *Archaeology and Old Testament Study,* ed. D. W. Thomas. Oxford.
———. 1978. Shechem. *EAEHL* 4: 1083–94.
Wright, G. R. H. 1968. Temples at Shechem. *ZAW* 80: 1–35.
———. 1970a. The 'Granary' at Shechem and the Underlying Storage Pits. *ZAW* 82: 275–78.
———. 1970b. The Mythology of Pre-Israelite Shechem. *VT* 20: 75–82.
———. 1971. Pre-Israelite Temples in the Land of Canaan. *PEQ* 103/1: 17–32.
———. 1984. The Monumental City Gate in Palestine and Its Foundations. *ZA* 74: 267–89.
———. 1985. The City Gates at Shechem, Simple Reconstruction Drawings. *ZDPV* 101: 1–8.

LAWRENCE E. TOOMBS

SHECHEM, TOWER OF (PLACE) [Heb *migdal-šĕkem*]. Apparently some sort of fortified place in the city of Shechem; together with its stronghold (Heb *ṣĕrîaḥ*) named "the house of El-berith" (Heb *bêt ᵓēl bĕrît*), it was destroyed by Abimelek (Judg 9:46–49). The word "tower" (Heb *migdal*) has a wide range of meanings, the most common of which is a building fortified for military purposes (Gen 11:4–5; 2 Kgs 9:17; 17:9) and a part of a fortification system of a town (Jer 31: 38). Mazar has shown that Migdal may have had a cultic meaning as well, taking into account the origin of the term from the Bronze Age traditions (*EncMiqr* 4: 633–36, in Hebrew). This interpretation is based upon names composed with *migdal,* such as Migdal-El, Migdal-Gad, Migdal-Penuel, etc., places which bore cultic traditions prior to the Israelite period (cf. also names composed with *bêt*: Bethel, Beth-shemesh, Beth-shean, etc.).

During Sellin's 1913–14 and 1926–27 excavations at ancient Shechem (Tel Balatah), a series of four fortified temples were unearthed. These consisted of consecutive stages of buildings (Tower-Temple 1-a to 2-b), dated from "Temenos 6" phase (ca. 1650–1600 B.C.E.) to "Temenos 9" (ca. 1200–1100 B.C.E.). The tower-Temples of Shechem were located in the NW part of the city, approximately 40 m S of the N gate. It was a stone building whose external measurements were 26.3 × 21.2 m. It had very thick walls (5.2 m) and a narrow, straight single entrance with two flanking frontal towers. The single cella contained six column bases and a niche for the god's statue (which was not found). In the different phases an altar and maṣṣebôt were put in the courtyard in front of the temple. This building, unquestionably a temple that was in continuous use for 400 years, has been identified with the Tower of Shechem ever since its discovery. The existence of similar tower-temples at Megiddo, also dating to the LB (strata VIII–VIIb, ca. 1479–1150 B.C.E.) and probably at Hazor (area A) strengthened the opinion that this was a common type of temple in LB Canaan. Taking into account the dating of Gideon's family in the 2d half of the 12th century B.C.E., it seems highly probable that the temple destroyed by Abimelech was Temple 2-b, the last in the series. The excavators dated this destruction to 1150–1100 B.C.E., which correlates well with Abimelech narrative.

But this raises questions about the meaning of the stronghold *(ṣĕrîaḥ)* of the house of El-Berith. The word *ṣĕrîah* can be interpreted as a natural cave rather than part of a fortification (1 Sam 13:6), a meaning also evident in three Nabatean inscriptions from Petra, as well as in Safaitic and modern Arabic. These considerations may associate the Bronze Age Tower-Temple structure excavated at Shechem with the "house of El-Berith," while the whole fortified acropolis of Tel Balatah would be associated with the "tower of Shechem." Nevertheless, this solution seems difficult, since it seems to refute the regular meaning of the term "tower" *(migdal)*.

This led Milik (1959: 560–62) and Naʾaman (1986) to suggest that the Tower of Shechem was not located within the city. Milik supposed that the *ṣerîah* of El-Berith was a cultic cave on the neighboring Mt. Ebal. Naʾaman suggested that the recently discovered Iron I cultic site on Mt. Ebal (Zertal 1986–87) should be identified as the Tower of Shechem, a suggestion based on the fact that the gathering in the Tower of Shechem (Judg 9:46) followed and came after the final destruction of the city by Abimelech (v 45), which might mean a separation between the two. The main obstacles with this hypothesis are that the architectural elements of the Mt. Ebal structure can hardly fit a temple, and the site had never been destroyed and/or burned, a crucial feature of the Abimelech narrative. On the contrary, the Mt. Ebal site was abandoned complete and was deliberately covered by a stone cover, presumably to protect it against secular use.

Bibliography

Milik, J. T. 1959. Notes d'epigraphie et de topographie palestiniennes. *Revue Biblique* 66: 550–75.

Naʾaman, N. 1986. The Tower of Shechem and the House of El Berith. *Zion* 51: 259–80 (in Hebrew).

Zertal, A. 1986–87. An Early Iron Age Cultic Site on Mount Ebal: Excavation Seasons 1982–1987. *TA* 13–14 (2): 105–65.

ADAM ZERTAL

SHEDEUR (PERSON) [*šĕdêʾûr*]. The father of the chief (*nāśîʾ*, Num 2:10) Elizur of the tribe of Reuben. Each of the five times that Shedeur is mentioned in the OT occurs in a tribal list where his mark of distinction is his status as the father of Elizur. Under the leadership of Shedeur's son Elizur, the tribe of Reuben participated in the census of Israelite fighting men carried out by Moses (Num 1:5, 20–21), presented its offerings on the fourth day of the twelve-day celebration of the dedication of the altar (Num 7:30, 35), took its proper place on the south side of the tabernacle in the Israelite camp (Num 2:10–11), and assumed its position in the order of march at the Israelites' departure from Mt. Sinai (Num 10:18).

The name "Shedeur" could mean either "Shaddai is fire" or "Shaddai is light." The Masoretic vocalization favors the former interpretation, where the deity bears the ambiguous character of either warming or destroying those who draw near (cf. Isa 47:14). However, Noth (*IPN*, 168) contends that the original form of the name meant "Shaddai is light," a characterization of the deity which is also found in Ps 27:1. Both interpretations should be maintained in view of Isa 10:17, where "the light of Israel will become a fire and his Holy One a flame."

DALE F. LAUNDERVILLE

SHEEP, SHEPHERD. Shepherding was one of man's earliest occupations. Flocks and herds, always a prominent feature in Palestine and other Near Eastern societies, consisted specifically of cows, sheep, and goats, but could also include horses, asses, and camels; the principal animal, however, owing to size, abundance, and usefulness, was the sheep.

Possession of these animals indicated power and wealth; Job had thousands of sheep, camels, oxen, and she-asses (42:12), and Abraham's flocks, herds, camels, and asses were counted among his blessings (Gen 24:35). At the dedication of the temple, Solomon sacrificed innumerable sheep and oxen (1 Kgs 8:5).

The owner himself was sometimes the shepherd of his flock. Abel was a "keeper of sheep" (Gen 4:2, 3) and Jacob cared for his own flocks (Gen 30:40). God is pictured as a shepherd who seeks out his own scattered sheep (Ezek 34:12). The work might be delegated to the owner's children; Rachel looked after Laban's sheep (Gen 29:6), and David, though the youngest of Jesse's sons, was given this responsibility (1 Sam 16:11; 17:15).

The principal duty of the shepherd was to see that the animals found enough food and water (cf. Psalm 23); and it was important that he guard the sheep, since they were easy prey for wild animals (1 Sam 17:34–35; Amos 3:12). There was also a danger that thieves might sneak among the sheep and carry them off (John 10:1).

The good shepherd was especially concerned for the condition of the flock, careful that the animals not be overdriven (cf. Gen 33:13–14); and would sometimes carry helpless lambs in his arms (cf. Isa 40:11), or on his shoulders (e.g., the Arcadian god Hermes Criophorus, shepherd and protector of livestock). At night, sheep were often kept in simple walled enclosures made from tangled bushes, providing a minimum of protection from weather and enemies (Num 32:16; Judg 5:16; 2 Chr 32:28; Ps 78:70; Zeph 2:6; John 10:1), or caves might have been used, affording the best protection (1 Sam 24:3). The work of the shepherd was essentially to keep the flock intact, counting each animal as it passed under his hand (Jer 33:12–13; Ezek 20:37; cf. Jer 31:10–11; Pss 49:15—Eng v 14; 77: 21—Eng v 20).

From this routine of daily life an extensive and complex stock of shepherd and flock imagery developed throughout the ANE. It was one of man's earliest symbols, and is used repeatedly in the Bible to picture God, or national leaders ruling over their people. It was an ancient figure of speech common in Mesopotamia and Egypt, and the Greeks also used the image for several abstract concepts.

The early church saw Jesus as the great shepherd and the fulfillment of the good shepherd. Even in modern times the image continues in the pastorale, or the eclogue, as a recognized form of poetry, and the picturesque nature of the image has inspired some of the great composers to immortalize in music the idyllic shepherd life.

A. Mesopotamia
B. Egypt
C. Greece
D. The Old Testament
E. The Apocrypha and Pseudepigrapha
F. The New Testament

A. Mesopotamia

Throughout Mesopotamian history the shepherd image was commonly used to designate gods and kings; and as a title for kings this use is attested from practically every period.

The symbol suggests the concept of righteous government and often appears in contexts where the subject of justice is prominent. The king as a shepherd and as a representative of the gods was expected to rule with justice and to show kindness in counseling, protecting, and guiding the people through every difficulty.

The early 3d millennium epic hero Enmerkar, king of Uruk, is called a shepherd when he subjects the distant city of Aratta; and the people of Aratta "bend the knee" before him "like highland sheep." He is also called a "beloved provider" (Kramer 1959: 26). The early king figures Dumuzi, ruler in Bad-tibira; Etana of Kish; and Lugalbanda of Uruk are all called shepherds. The famous Gilgamesh, acting tyrannically over Uruk, was challenged by the people: "Is this our shepherd, Bold, Stately, Wise?" (*ANET,* 73).

The *ensi* of Lagash, Gudea (ca. 2144–2124) was called a "shepherd" who "leads the people with a good religious hand" (Thureau-Dangin 1907: 101); and it is significant that this king's reign is known for its peace, prosperity, and useful pursuits. Ur-Nammu (ca. 2111–2094), whose name is associated with the first known law code in history, was called the shepherd of his people. Lipit-Ishtar of Isin (ca. 1934–1924), known for his law code and his social reforms, is called "humble shepherd of Nippur, the right installed builder (cultivator) of Ur" (Thureau-Dangin 1907: 205). Bur-Sin of Isin (ca. 1895–1874) is "the shepherd who has made the heart of the people happy, the mighty builder of Ur" (Thureau-Dangin 1907: 205). Warad-Sin of Larsa (ca. 1834–1823) and his brother Rim-Sin, also of Larsa (ca. 1822–1763) were each called shepherd (ibid., 213, 215, 217), and the symbol is attested during the time of the Eshnunna kings (from ca. 1840) (Frankfort, Lloyd, and Jacobsen 1940: 138). The great Hammurabi of Babylon is referred to as shepherd in several places in the prologue and epilogue of his law code; he says of himself, "Hammurabi, the shepherd, called by Enlil, am I; the one who makes affluence and plenty abound" (*ANET,* 164). A strong sense of royal responsibility is revealed in this law code, and the need of governing in justice is of paramount concern. The use of the symbol in early Mesopotamia appears to have been an epithet intended to dignify rulership as good, just, and beneficent for the people.

The image was especially significant as a royal name for the Assyrian kings. It appeared early, as a title for Shalmaneser I (ca. 1280), and later kings such as Tukulti-Ninuurta I, Tiglath-pileser I, Assurnasirpal, Shamshi-Adad V, Adad-nirari III, Sargon II, Sennacherib, Esarhaddon, and Assurbanipal were called shepherds (*LAR* 1: 38, 56, 58, 73, 139, 140, 169, 187, 188, 254, 261; *LAR* 2:80, 258, 405; *LAS* 48, 55, 117).

Several Sumerian deities were known as shepherds. The high god Enlil was called the faithful shepherd (*ANET,* 337). The sun god Utu was regarded as a compassionate and kind shepherd (Kramer 1959: 210–11). When ancient Ur was destroyed, a poet compared the city to an abandoned stable and sheepfold; and the goddess Ningal wailed that she herself was like an "unworthy shepherd." The destroyed city was also compared to "an innocent ewe," bereft of its "trustworthy shepherd" and its "shepherd boy" (*ANET,* 456, 457, 458, 459, 461; cf. this terminology to Zeph 11:4–17; Matt 26:15; 27:9, 10).

In the Babylonian creation epic, Marduk is celebrated as the fertility god of the land, and in this role is called faithful shepherd (*ANET,* 69, 71, 72). The epic is also political, elevating Marduk in the Semitic pantheon as shepherd of all the gods. The Semitic sun god Utu/Shamash, the universal judge and guardian of justice, acquired a great following of the Mesopotamian masses and was called the "Shepherd of the lower world, guardian of the upper" (*ANET,* 387–88), and it is from this god that Hammurabi is depicted receiving his law code.

B. Egypt

Here, as in Mesopotamia, the imagery was used to depict gods, kings, and various other figures, and the people were commonly thought of as a herd or flock. Though the imagery occurs early, and probably carried with it political implications of a centralized monarchy, the terminology is rare, but the concept and thought of the king as shepherd is extensive.

Evidence for the symbolic nature of the shepherd figure is found in the widespread use of the simple shepherd's crook as an insignia of kings, princes, and chieftains. The instrument symbolized the ruler's power and eminence, and especially the nature of his rule, the king's obligation to maintain order and justice *(maat)* in the land.

The appearance of the crook-staff in the Late Predynastic period at first signified princely, and later royal, authority, and in historical times the heket-scepter symbolized rulership. The shepherd's crook as a symbol is traceable to the god Osiris, considered the dead ancestor of the kings of Menes' line. Osiris is always depicted with a royal crown, flail, and crook and is sometimes called shepherd. The crook is found on monuments, pillars, pylons, sarcophaguses, and on artifacts from practically every period. It is prominent on Tutankhamen's gold coffin, and a statue of Ramesses II depicts the king holding a crook in his right hand. Some scholars consider the crook, as a symbol of authority, to have originated with a primitive shepherding people who inhabited the E Delta, in the district of Busiris (House of Osiris). The god of this region in early times was Andjeti, who appears with a scepter in one hand.

In the grim years between the Old and Middle Kingdoms (2300–2050 B.C.), Ipuwer insists that the duty and responsibility of the king is to be the "herdsman of all men," and he challenges king Meri-ka-Re to act for the god, for men are "well directed," being the "cattle of the god" (*ANET,* 417). It is significant that during this period of internal crisis the cult of Osiris was revitalized to its highest level.

In the Karnak temple, Amenhotep III (1411–1374) is called "the good shepherd, vigilant for all people" (*ARE* 2: 365–66). An inscription at Redesiyeh calls Seti I (1313–1292) "the good shepherd, who preserves his soldiers alive" (*ARE* 3: 86). At Karnak, an inscription by Merneptah (1225–1215) says "I am the ruler who shepherds you" (*ARE* 3: 243).

Throughout Shechem history, protection, kindness, and even intimate personal feeling by the ruler for his subjects are implied by the use of the image.

C. Greece

The appearance of the figure in the *Iliad* and *Odyssey* demonstrates that it had already acquired an accepted and customary meaning in very early times. The common phrase used in these works, "shepherd of the host," describes various individuals in both the Greek and Trojan military. The metaphor is used technically, and the compassionate features often implied in the Mesopotamian and Egyptian literature are conspicuously absent. The ancestral scepter of Agamemnon, and the scepters of other kings, shows the instrument to be a symbol of rank and authority; it significantly appears in context with the phrase "shepherd of the host" (*Iliad* 2. 75–109; *Odyssey* 3. 156).

Aeschylus calls a storm at sea an "evil shepherd" (*Agamemnon,* 657), and even captains are spoken of as "shepherds of ships" (*The Suppliant Maidens,* 767). Euripides speaks of the Athenian ruler Theseus as a "young and valiant shepherd" (*Suppliants,* 191; cf., *Helen,* 1479–1494), and in a description of a battle scene refers to "shepherds of chariots" (*Suppliants,* 674). In Plato's *Republic* the definitions of justice find analogy in shepherd and flock symbolism, and the inferences suggest that a ruler, who is a "shepherd," should be concerned only with what is good for his subjects (*Republic* 1. 342, 343, 345; cf. 3. 415D, E, 416A; 4. 440D). He uses the symbol in the *Statesman* to show that the work of a ruler was nothing less than royal art, or statecraft, since the best government must have a good and wise leader, who serves only for the interest of the people he governs (*Statesman,* 266–72b).

Greek pastoral literature shows man retreating to nature, resisting the allurements of the city. The heroes of the poetry are herdsmen and shepherds like Daphnis (see von Geisau PW 4: 2141–46), an ancient and archetypal shepherd, and also Thyrsis, Corydon, Tityrus, Lycidas, and Amyntas (Theocritus *The Bucolic Poets, passim;* Virgil, *Eclogues, passim*). Behind the facade of these shepherds and the accompanying stories of summer days and pastoral delights were the poets' attempts to understand the profound issues of life.

D. The Old Testament

The Bible's extensive use of shepherd/flock imagery may be most attributable to Israel's earliest years of nomadic and seminomadic existence, and to some extent, ANE sources, but the shepherd life was so general it is difficult to trace common derivations for the use of the symbol.

1. God as Shepherd. The traditions of Israel's life in the desert seem to have given rise to the thought of God as their shepherd, for it is during the early period that he alone is viewed as shepherd and protector (Gen 48:15; 49:24; cf. Deut 26:5–8; Jer 13:17; Mic 7:14). Though God is seldom called a shepherd, the concept was common and remained a favorite idiom throughout Israelite history (cf. Pss 31:4—Eng v 3; 80:2—Eng v 1). God is pictured carrying in his bosom animals which cannot keep up, and mindful of the sheep which have young, he does not overdrive them (Isa 40:11; cf. Gen 33:13; Ps 28:9).

The symbol was a favorite for depicting the Exodus. In one of Israel's earliest traditions, the Song of Moses, the image of God as a shepherd leading the people to safe pastures is implied (Exod 15:13, 17), and later reflection upon this event shows God as a powerful leader driving out other nations and making room for his own flock (Ps 78:52–55, 70–72). A number of passages use the figure to compare the return from Babylonian exile with the Exodus (Jer 23:1–8; 31:8–14; Isa 40:11; 49:9–13). God's loyalty and devotion to an individual sheep is presented in the classic Shepherd Psalm (23); it is possible, however, that this psalm alludes to the exiled community and is a symbolic expression of their return to Palestine (cf. Isa 49:9–13 and Psalm 121).

The picture of Israel as a flock given into the hands of butchers (the nations) in Ps 44: 12–24—Eng vv 11–23 is a variation on the usual thought of God as Israel's shepherd, for here the psalmist views God as a sleeping shepherd, unmindful for the welfare of the flock (cf. Isa 56:10, 11); and in Ps 74:1, God is an angry shepherd, casting off his flock.

2. Human Leaders as Shepherds. As among other ANE peoples, Israel's leaders were often regarded as shepherds, and even though God was always their principal shepherd, responsible human agents were necessary so that Israel would not be as "sheep without a shepherd" (Num 27:16, 17); and significantly, a charismatic element is said to have rested on such leaders (Num 27:16–21; cf. Isa 11:1–9; 44:28–45:1). God is said to have led the flock Israel through the wilderness by the hand of Moses and Aaron (Ps 77: 21—Eng v 20; Isa 63:11). Although no Israelite king is ever directly called by the title "shepherd," it is implied, since David as prince feeds, or shepherds, Israel (2 Sam 5:2), and when Micaiah predicted the death of Ahab and Israel's defeat, he said the scattered army would be "as sheep which have no shepherd" (1 Kgs 22:17; 2 Chr 18:16; cf. Num 27:16, 17).

In the book of Jeremiah the image includes both religious and political figures of varying rank and authority, showing that by the prophet's time it was a well-established and regular portrait for the ruling nobility (Jer 2:8; 3:15; 10:21; 25:34–38; cf. Ezekiel 34). Even the commanders of the enemy from the north are described as shepherds in a manner reminiscent of Homer's usage (Jer 6:3; 12:10; cf. 13:20).

The symbol receives its most extensive treatment in Ezekiel 34. Here the prophet uses the evil shepherd theme to illustrate selfish and irresponsible leadership (vv 2–3), and to rebuke kingship based on domination and crushing oppression: "With force and harshness you ruled them" (v 4), words which echo the cruel period of Egyptian bondage (cf. Exod 1:13–14; Lev 25:43).

The Persian king Cyrus is anointed as God's servant and chosen as his shepherd to rebuild Jerusalem and the temple (Isa 44:28; cf. Jer 23:1–8).

3. Other Uses of the Image. Even death is personified as a shepherd, from which only God can ransom the psalmist (Ps 49: 15–16—Eng vv 14–15; cf. Hos 13:14). In an ironic application, the wind is called a shepherd which drives away Jerusalem's shepherds (Jer 22:22). The imagery is sometimes equated with an era of peace (cf. Mic 5:2–6; Isa 11:1–9; Ps 23:2); and it is often God himself who leads Israel to an idyllic place (Jer 31:8–10; Pss 1:3; 5:9—Eng v 8; 23:3, 4; 36:9–10—Eng vv 8–9; Isa 41:18–19; 43:19–20; 48:21).

The use of the sleeping shepherd motif implies irresponsible leadership (Isa 56:10–12; Nah 3:18); and such rulers are called "stupid," since they failed to "enquire of the Lord," and as a consequence "their flock is scattered" (Jer 10:21).

Because sheep are passive and defenseless, a prevailing picture associated with this imagery is that of Israel as straying sheep (Isa 53:6; Ps 119:176; cf. Isa 13:14).

The prophet Jeremiah refers to himself as a "lamb led to the slaughter" (11:19), and in vengeance prays that his enemies be taken as sheep for slaughter (12:2–3); but he weeps that "the Lord's flock has been taken captive" (13:17; cf. 13:20).

E. The Apocrypha and Pseudepigrapha

Here the image generally follows the patterns of the OT. God, as the universal shepherd, is a didactic leader who rebukes, trains, and teaches mankind (Sir 18:13, 14; cf. Eccl 12:11). The history of the world and Israel is given, using animal and shepherd metaphors (*1 Enoch* 85–90; cf. 89:13, 20, 36–39 with Ps 77:21—Eng v 20). The Babylonian Holofernes, as conqueror of Jerusalem, is compared to a leader of sheep that have no shepherd, since God had forsaken Israel (Jdt 11:19). A Davidic king will rise to shepherd God's scattered flock *Pss. Sol.* 17:23–46). A kind, spiritual leader shepherds and comforts his suffering and guilty congregation (*Fragments of a Zadokite Work* 16:1–3). See ZADOKITE FRAGMENTS. Shepherds are considered essential for the preservation of the Law, and the evils which fell on Israel were the result of their loss, an apparent reference to prophets and priests (*2 Bar.* 77:13, 15, 16). A future shepherd is presented who takes on messianic proportions (2 Esdr 2:34), and Esdras himself is regarded as a shepherd (2 Esdr 5:17).

F. The New Testament

The OT concepts about the shepherd as a responsible leader were continued by the disciples of Jesus, who used the motif to characterize his role and mission. The description of Jesus as the second David, and as Israel's shepherd, begins when shepherds in the fields near Bethlehem, the city of David, heard that his son was born, and angels announcing "peace" to mankind (Luke 2:8–20). The narrative is reminiscent of the OT declaration that the coming of David would result in a "covenant of peace" (Ezek 34:23–25; cf. also 1 Sam 16:1, 12, 13; Jer 23:1–8; Mic 5:2–4).

Jesus is presented as going to "sheep without a shepherd" (Mark 6:34; Matt 9:35–10:6; 15:24; cf. Luke 19:10). The terminology in Mark appears to be based on Num 27:16, 17, where Joshua is appointed Israel's leader, and also on Ezekiel 34, where the leaderless and scattered sheep await the new David (Ezek 34:1–10; 23–24).

The most developed shepherd and flock imagery of the NT appears in the gospel of John (10:1–18, 22–29), where Jesus' concern for Israel is contrasted with the feigned care of their present leadership. As a compassionate and trustworthy shepherd, his mission and quality of leadership are marked by a willingness to die for the sheep (v 11; cf. 1 Sam 17:34–35). The author has specifically identified the mission and death of Jesus with his role as a shepherd by using ideas which look back to the Davidic shepherd of Ezek 34:11–16, 23–24, and the smitten shepherd of Zech 13:7 was also in view (cf. Mark 14:27). Since Zechariah 9–14 was especially significant for the early disciples and for their interpretation and understanding of Jesus' eschatological program, the statement, "Strike the shepherd that the sheep may be scattered," and the entire dying shepherd passage (Zech 11:4–14; cf. Matt 27:9), formed a core around which their savior's life and death might be interpreted. The context in Zechariah had a pronounced emotional effect on the disciples when they saw their leader arrested and the apostles scattered like helpless sheep. Both Ezekiel 34 and Zechariah 9–13 were especially productive as the source for much reflection on the role of the shepherd in the gospels.

At the end time the nations are to be gathered before the Son of Man like a great flock of sheep and goats (Matt 25:31–33), and the book of Revelation suggests a military shepherd image (2:27; 19:15; cf. Ps 2:8, 9).

Based on the view that Jesus was the great Shepherd and Guardian of souls (1 Pet 2:25; 5:4), the early church used the symbol to describe the work of its leaders, who were expected to pattern their life and work after that of their chief Shepherd (1 Pet 5:1–4; Heb 13:17, 20–21).

Church leaders were instructed to "tend the flock of God" (1 Pet 5:2), and the titles which were applied to them, such as elder *(presbyteros)* and guardian, bishop, or overseer *(episkopos)*, are directly linked to the work of shepherding (cf. Acts 11:30; 14:23; 15:2, 4, 6, 22, 23; 16:4; 20:17, 28–29; 1 Tim 3:2; 4:14; 5:17; Titus 1:5; 1 Pet 5:2–3; and the church was to be sustained by the responsible oversight of these leaders, who were the shepherds over God's flock.

Bibliography

Frankfort, H.; Lloyd, S.; and Jacobsen, T. 1940. *The Gilmilsin Temple and the Palace of the Rulers at Tell Asmar.* Chicago.

Kramer, S. N. 1959. *History Begins at Sumer.* Garden City.

Thureau-Dangin, F. 1907. *Sumerischen und Akkadischen Konigsinschriften.* Leipzig.

JACK W. VANCIL

SHEERAH (PERSON) [Heb *šeʾĕrâ*]. A descendant of Ephraim (1 Chr 7:24). This passage is part of a fragment, vv 21b–24, that interrupts the Ephraimite (Joshua) genealogy, though the Chronicler's reasons for putting it here are unclear. The only other listing of the Ephraimite clan in the OT is Num 26:35–36 and it contains no mention of Sheerah.

Sheerah is Beriah's (v 23) daughter. She is said to be the founder of three cities, two named Beth-horon and one Uzzen-sheerah. The former are located in S Ephraim (Josh 18:13–14) and are traditionally linked to Joshua (*IDB*, 394). Both were the scene of numerous military conflicts (Josh 10:10–11; 1 Sam 13:18). Uzzen-sheerah is not known elsewhere in the OT.

M. STEPHEN DAVIS

SHEHARIAH (PERSON) [Heb *šĕḥaryāh*]. A Benjaminite, the son of Jeroham (1 Chr 8:26). According to the Chronicler, Shehariah was a tribal chief residing in Jerusalem in the postexilic period. The name "Shehariah" occurs only once in the long list of Benjaminites in 1 Chr 8:1–40. The origin and provenance of the name is uncertain. Noth (*IPN*, 169) suggested Shehariah means "Yah is dawning," making reference to the similar idea in Isa 60:2. The almost identical name "Shaharaim," differing only in the vowel pointing and final consonant, occurs earlier in the list (1 Chr 8:8).

TOM WAYNE WILLETT

SHEIKH ABU ZARAD (PLACE). See TAPPUAH (PLACE); TEPHON (PLACE).

SHEKEL [Heb *šeqel*]. "Shekel" is also the RSV rendering of the Gk *statēr*. See COINAGE; WEIGHTS AND MEASURES.

SHELAH (PERSON) [Heb *šelaḥ; šēlâ*]. SHELANITES.
1. Son of Arpachshad and father of Eber (Gen 10:24; 11:12–15). Shelah lived to an age of 433 years. In Genesis 11, Shelah forms part of the line which culminates in Abram; in Luke 3:35, Shelah (Gk *sala*) forms part of the line which culminates in Jesus. The LXX inserts *kainan* in the genealogy of Genesis 5 between Arpachshad and Shelah, and this is reflected in the Lukan genealogy. The name itself is related to the West Semitic root, *šlḥ*, identified variously as a weapon, a canal, or even a divine name (Skinner *Genesis* ICC, 131–32, 232; Driver 1948: 77, 81). A divine name based on *šlḥ* is plausible. Whether or not a Canaanite deity, *Šalaḥ*, was specifically god of the infernal river (Tsevat 1954; Loretz 1975), such a divine name may also have formed part of the personal name "Methuselah." However, this interpretation suffers from the fact that such a deity is unattested outside of personal names. The form *šlḥn* occurs as a personal name in Old South Arabic (RES 2687, 1; cf. Müller 1963: 315).

2. Third son of Judah (*šēlâ;* Gen 38: 5; 1 Chr 1: 18; 4: 21), and ancestor of the Shelanites (Gen 46: 12; Num 26: 20).

Bibliography

Driver, S. R. 1948. *The Book of Genesis with Introduction and Notes.* 15th ed. London.
Loretz, O. 1975. Der Gott *ŠLḤ*, He. *ŠLḤ* I und *ŠLḤ* II. *UF* 7: 584–85.
Müller, W. M. 1963. Altsüdarabische Beiträge zum hebräischen Lexikon. *ZAW* 75:304–16.
Tsevat, M. 1954. The Canaanite God *ŠÄLAḤ*. *VT* 4: 41–49.

RICHARD S. HESS

SHELAH, POOL OF (PLACE) [Heb *bĕrēkat haššelaḥ*]. Name of a pool near the King's Garden in the area of the Fountain Gate, where Shallun under Nehemiah's governorship repaired the city wall of Jerusalem (Neh 3: 15). The LXX reads *tōn kōdiōn* "of the sheepskins" for Shelah. However, Siniaticus and Theodotion read *tou Silōam,* with the Vulgate and the Arabic versions. The pool of Shelah has been related to the Shiloah of Isa 8:4; both names share the same Heb consonants which mean "to send" (with the idea of supplying water; Simons 1952: 109 n. 2, 190). It may be identified with modern Birket el-Hamra, S of the city and outside its wall (Wilkinson 1978: 120–21; Williamson *Ezra-Nehemiah* WBC, 207). The "artificial pool" of Neh 3: 16 may be identified with the King's Pool (Neh 2: 14; Avi-Yonah 1954: 246), the possible remains of which have been excavated on the W side of the Kidron Valley (Adan 1979). If so, then this "artificial pool" would be different from the Pool of Shelah. However, the King's Pool has also been identified with the Pool of Shelah (Ussishkin 1976: 90).

Bibliography

Adan (Bayewitz), D. 1979. The "Fountain of Siloam" and "Solomon's Pool" in First-Century C.E. Jerusalem. *IEJ* 29: 92–100.
Avi-Yonah, M. 1954. The Walls of Nehemiah—A Minimalist View. *IEJ* 4: 239–48.
Simons, J. 1952. *Jerusalem in the Old Testament. Researches and Theories.* Leiden.
Ussishkin, D. 1976. The Original Length of the Siloam Tunnel in Jerusalem. *Levant* 8: 82–95.
Wilkinson, J. 1978. The Pool of Siloam. *Levant* 10: 116–25.

RICHARD S. HESS

SHELEMIAH (PERSON) [Heb *šelemyāh; šelemiyāhû*]. The personal name of some nine individuals, most of whom were in the late Judean or postexilic period.

1. A Judean to whom the cast of the lot fell for the office of high gatekeeper of the Solomonic temple's E gate (1 Chr 26:12–14a). His son Zechariah, a shrewd counselor, obtained the lot for the N gate. In the meagerness of detail one can only speculate that those gatekeepers listed in 1 Chr 26: 1–11 were the ruling body of the concerns to the temple gates: the sacred, ethical, legal, and social judgments affecting the priest-laity relationship. The specific task of Shelemiah appears to have been the executive administrator of the dictates of the governing body. It seems that Shelemiah had six associates in the administration of his office (1 Chr 26:17). He may be identical to SHALLUM #10.

2. The grandfather of Jehudi and son of Cushi, a member of the nobility, a judgment deduced from the four generations recounted, and by the political strata in which Jehudi trafficked (Jer 36:14). That the princes chose to send a member of this family to encourage Baruch to appear before the princes of the realm and to read the provocative words of Jeremiah before them, that Baruch consented to accompany them to the court exhibits a confidence that Baruch must have felt in the delegation, and suggests that the family of Cushi were political moderates and sympathetic to the message of the prophetic party. On the other hand, it was Jehudi that read the scroll of Jeremiah to King Jehoiakim, a thankless and dangerous task which aroused the brazen king to such anger that he degraded the holy scroll by using it as fuel for his brazier (Jer 36:20). That Jehudi functioned in the immediate presence of the king indicates the nobility of his family stature.

3. The son of Abdeel, a noble of the court of Jehoiakim, an intimate and supportive adherent of the policies of the king (Jer 36:26). When Jehudi had finished reading the scroll and when Jehoiakim had burned the entire scroll in the brazier, the king set about to crush, no doubt once and for all, the antithetical proposals of the prophetic party, largely the followers of Jeremiah. He dispatched his own son, the prince Jerahmeel, together with Seraiah the son of Azriel and Shelemiah the son of Abdeel to apprehend Baruch and Jeremiah.

4. The father of Jehucal (Jer 37:3) or Jucal (Jer 38:1), who with the priest Zephaniah, the son of Maaseiah, was sent to implore Jeremiah to pray for the Judeans.

5. The father of Irijah, a Judean sentry stationed at the Benjamin Gate (Jer 37:13). When Jeremiah the prophet sought to finalize a property settlement in his family and to purchase land that appeared destined to fall into the hands of the Babylonians, he was seized by this officer as a deserter to the enemy. The plea of the prophet was preemptorily rejected; he was examined before the enraged militaristic princes, beaten, and imprisoned. That the family is traced to the third generation may suggest a military involvement of its members.

6. A son of Binnui who had contracted a marriage with a foreign wife in the postexilic period (Ezr 10:39; 1 Esdr 9:34). However, he banished his wife (and children?) in accordance with the judgment of Ezra and the majority voice of the Judean community to rid the new national structure of the taint of paganism (Ezra 8–10; 1 Esdr 8:68–9:36).

7. A second son of Binnui, according to the RSV, who had married a foreign wife and submitted to the edict of Ezra endorsed by the Judean community to dissolve the marriages in which a foreign woman and offspring were concerned and to banish them from the community (Ezra 10:41). See BANI.

8. The father of Hananiah, who restored a portion of the ruined wall of Jerusalem (Neh 3:30). The son Hananiah may possibly be the person called an apothecary (Neh 3:8), a member of a guild responsible for the production of incense, sacred ointments, and other apothecary products designed for sacred use (cf. Exod 30:22–38).

9. One of the four treasurers whom Nehemiah appointed to supervise the ministration of funds to the Levites. The choice of these officers was quite varied: Shelemiah was a priest, Zadok was a scribe, Pedaiah was of the Levites, and their assistant Hanan undesignated, were considered responsible personnel who would fulfill their duty to distribute the tithes equitably to the Levites, certainly to correct some of the flagrant abuses that prevailed at the time (Neh 13:10–13).

EDWARD R. DALGLISH

SHELEPH (PERSON) [Heb *šālep*]. A son of Joktan (Gen 10:26; 1 Chr 1:20) whose name appears in the so-called "Table of Nations" (Genesis 10) as a tribal rather than personal name (Westermann 1984: 526–27). It may be identified as the name of a South Arabian tribe. Already in the 19th century, E. Osiander (1857: 153–55) had pointed out that Arab geographers refer to a Yemenite tribe bearing the name *as-Salif* or *as-Sulaf.* Al-Hamdānī (1884: 100.7) mentions *as-Salif* bin Zurʿa, which form a tribal branch of al-Kalāʿ and which resided in the *miḫlāf* as-Saḥūl in the region of present-day Ibb, where a place name *al-Aslāf* (pl. of *Salif*) bears evidence to them. This origin is adduced by the same author in his *Al-Iklīl* (1966: 331–32) as Banū *s-Suluf* (another pl. of *Salif*) bin Zurʿa bin Sabaʾ. A genealogy which is taken over from the Table of Nations in Genesis 10 is to be found in *Al-Iklīl* (Al-Hamdānī 1954: 52.1), where an *as-Sulaf* and a *Sālif* are listed as sons of Qaḥṭān (biblical Joktan). Together with the tribes of ʿAkk and al-Ašʿar in the Yemenite coastal plain, the *Sulaf* are said to have venerated the idol al-Munṭabiq (Ibn Ḥabīb 1942: 318.4). Those *as-Salif* (or *as-Suluf* or *as-Sulaf* respectively) are most probably to be identified with the *slfn* mentioned in the Late Sabean inscription CIH 621.5, where they are listed among the tribal groups which participated in the construction of the stronghold Māwiyat, the present-day Ḥuṣn al-Ghurāb near the ancient harbor of Qanaʾ, where the inscription was found. This identification is supported by the fact that in line 2 of the same inscription the tribe *klʿn* (= *al-Kalāʿ*) is mentioned, a tribe to which the *Salif* belong according to the South Arabian tradition. One of the nine gates of the ancient Himyaritic capital Ẓafār bore the name *bāb al-Aslāf* (al-Hamdānī 1979) which likewise could have been named after the *Salif.*

It is uncertain whether the tribe Radmān *D̲ū-Salifān (rdmn d̲slfn)* in the Sabean inscription CIH 648, 2–3 belongs to the *slfn* in CIH 621; probably they are separate, and the first one might be associated to the land of *Salif* mentioned in al-Hamdānī (1884: 76), which was situated in the region of the Sakāsik near al-Ǧanad, NE of present-day Taʿizz in the S part of Yemen. Other less likely possibilities of an identification of the biblical *šelep* and the Sabean *slfn* with the Yemenite place names *Salafa* or *as-Salf* respectively were considered by H. von Wissmann (1975: 78, n. 1).

The *salapēnoi* in Ptol. *Geog.* 6.7.23, with which the *šelep* were occasionally joined, are to be separated from them; first, they are to be located much farther in the N of the Arabian Peninsula; and second, the correct reading of the name is most probably *alapēnoi.* Attempts to compare the biblical *šelep* with the Arabic nouns *salaf,* "ancestors," or *silf,* "brother-in-law," are certainly also to be rejected.

Bibliography
Hamdānī, al-. 1884. *Ṣifat Ğazīrat al-Arab,* ed. D. H. Müller. Leiden.
———. 1954. *Al-Iklīl,* vol. 1, ed. O. Löfgren. Uppsala.
———. 1966. *Al-Iklīl,* vol. 2, ed. M. al-Akwaᶜ. Cairo.
———. 1979. *Al-Iklīl,* vol. 8, ed. M. al-Akwaᶜ. Damascus.
Ibn Ḥabīb. 1942. *Kitāb al-MuḤabbar.* Hyderabad.
Osiander, E. 1857. Über den Joktaniden Selef *šelep* Genes. 10:26. *ZDMG* 11: 153–55.
Wissmann, H. von. 1975. *Über die frühe Geschichte Arabiens und das Entstehen des Sabäerreichs. Die Geschichte von Saba' I.* SÖAW 301/5. Vienna.

W. W. MÜLLER

SHELESH (PERSON) [Heb *šēleš*]. A descendant of Asher, named in the genealogical list of 1 Chr 7:35. In keeping with his name ("third"), Shelesh is listed as the third son of Helem, who perhaps is to be identified with Hotham (7:32). No other information is given about this figure, either in this genealogy or elsewhere in the Hebrew Bible. His name, however, is similar to that of Shilshah (1 Chr 7:37), and the two have been associated with the lands of Shalishah and Shaalim in Saulide narratives (see Edelman 1985: 86).

Bibliography
Edelman, D. 1985. The "Ashurites" of Eshbaal's State. *PEQ* 117: 85–91.

JULIA M. O'BRIEN

SHELOMI (PERSON) [Heb *šělōmî*]. The father of Ahihud, a leader of the tribe of Asher who was appointed to oversee the distribution of the land to the children of Israel (Num 34:27).

Shelomi is a shortened form of the name "Shelemiah," a theophoric name consisting of the root *šlm,* "to make full," "to complete," and the divine element *yh.* The name "Shelemiah" occurs in texts from the end of the Judahite monarchy (Jer 36:14; 37:3; 38:1) and from the postexilic era (Ezra; Nehemiah; Chronicles). The name "Shelomi" may be translated "the Lord has made full" or "the Lord has made complete." In the LXX, it is rendered *Selemi,* and as *Salomi* in the Vulgate.

The name "Shelomi" has been found in extrabiblical writings from Palestine. On a stamp of unknown provenance, one finds the words *šlmy/ hᶜd,* "Shelomay, the notary (witness)" (Naveh 1971: 29). On an Aramaic ostracon from Arad, dated to the 4th century B.C., the name *šlmy* is found.

Bibliography
Naveh, J. 1971. Hebrew Texts in Aramaic Script in the Persian Period? *BASOR* 203:27–32.

RAPHAEL I. PANITZ

SHELOMITH (PERSON) [Heb *šělōmît*]. Var. SHELOMOTH. The name "Shelomith" is held by five persons in the Hebrew Bible, who range by date from the 10th to the 6th century B.C.E. Shelomith is sometimes confused in the Hebrew text with the very similar name SHELOMOTH. It has been argued by Noth that, where the text refers to a man, the form "Shelomoth" is correct and Shelomith an error (cf. 1 Chr 23:18; 24:22; 1 Chr 26:25–28). Although this may be correct, it is to be noted that the source of confusion between the two names in the Hebrew text lies in the confusion of the similar letters *yod* and *waw.* Whether or not Noth is correct, the problem is compounded by this epigraphic fact.

1. The daughter of Dibri, from the tribe of Dan. During the wanderings in the wilderness (Lev 24:11), she married an Egyptian. Their son cursed the Name (of Yahweh) and was taken before Moses for judgment. He was then stoned to death as punishment.

2. The daughter of Zerubbabel (1 Chr 3:19). This verse lists the first group of Zerubbabel's children, who may have been born before the return to Jerusalem. She is the only woman named in this list of postexilic, Davidic descendants (vv 17–24).

3. A Levite (1 Chr 23:18). He is called the chief of the sons of Izhar. The same person appears in 1 Chr 24:22 as Shelomoth.

4. The child of Rehoboam, king of Judah (932–916 B.C.E.), and Maacah the daughter of Absalom (2 Chr 11:20). The child may have been either a daughter or a son, since the form "Shelomith" is used for either gender. Cf. SHELOMOTH #4.

5. Shelomith is the name given to the head of a father's house who returned to Jerusalem with Ezra (Ezra 8:10). If the reading of 1 Esdr 8:36 is followed, he is of the family of Bani (missing from Ezra 8:10) and the son of Josiphiah. Cf. SHELOMOTH #5.

RUSSELL FULLER

SHELOMOTH (PERSON) [Heb *šělōmôt*]. Var. SHELOMITH. **1.** Son of Shimei, who was of the levitical family of Gershon, son of Levi, or perhaps the son of Ladan, where *běnê šimᶜî* (1 Chr 23:9a) has entered the text as an intrusion. Although there is no textual warrant for this reading, it is the most natural way to solve the difficulty of v 9b, which describes the sons of Shimei as "heads of the fathers for *laᶜdān.*" Shelomoth is named as one of the family "heads" in v 9, whether the son of Shimei or Ladan. The Qere *(šělōmît)* is given in the LXX, Targums, and Vulgate but the Ketib *(šělōmôt)* occurs in the Syriac and Arabic versions. The most common form of the name seems to be "Shelomoth" (cf. SHELOMITH). By etymology, the name is related to the verb *šālam* ("to be complete").

2. Son of Izhar and head of the levitical family made up of Izhar's sons. As such, Shelomoth is mentioned in 1 Chr 23:18 and 24:22. The MT of 23:18 reads Shelomith rather than Shelomoth although the LXX reads Shelomoth (Gk *Salōmōth*). The MT of 24:22 reads Shelomoth. Each time the name "Shelomoth/Shelomith" is used in the Hebrew Bible, its alternate form occurs in the Ketib of the MT or in another important source. The only exception is 24:22, where the name occurs twice without alternate readings. Noth claimed that the form *šlmyt* was taken by later readers as a plural of the feminine *šlmy* and hence emended to read *šlmwt,* which was considered a more proper masculine form (*IPN,* 165). The same Hebrew root does in fact provide the basis for the name "Salome." The individual denoted in the preceding passages was also the father of Jahath.

3. The son of Zichri, who, with his brothers, was responsible for the treasury of dedicated things. He is mentioned in 1 Chr 26:25, 26, and 28. The forms "Shelomoth" and "Shelomith" both occur in this short span of verses. The treasuries he administered consisted of booty captured by Samuel, Saul, and Joab. 2 Sam 8:11 seems to corroborate this, but temple officials are not included in that passage. Elmslie entertained the possibility that 1 Chr 26:20–32 contained "scraps of ancient information" (*IB* 3:429). If this is true, its inclusion in this portion of Chronicles is intended to fill in details on the identity of the officials and their precise duties. This best accounts for the inclusion of this somewhat reduplicative section (compare chaps. 23 and 24). The treasuries were used for temple maintenance.

4. The son of Rehoboam and Maacah, according to 2 Chr 11:20. The man was otherwise undistinguished, since his name occurs only here. The Hebrew text actually has Shelomith, but in keeping with other texts, it is often emended to Shelomoth (cf. SHELOMITH #4). Maacah is not named among the children of Absalom in 2 Sam 14:27; therefore, Shelomoth should not be identified as his grandson. By what seems an odd coincidence, Absalom's mother was also named Maacah (1 Chr 3:2). The interpreter would expect that *bat* was a corruption of *ʾim* (wife), but even if Absalom's mother were not removed by two generations from the time of Rehoboam, there is no textual warrant for such a correction.

5. The son of Josiphiah and head of the house of Bani. Shelomoth was one of the family leaders, named in Ezra 8:10, who accompanied Ezra to Jerusalem. This identification is based on LXX texts rather than the MT (cf. SHELOMITH #5). In the Hebrew Bible, Ezra 8:10 departs from the pattern which first lists family lines, then the returning member who represents the line. In this case, Shelomoth is mentioned as if he were the family namesake, but with no representative mentioned. Consequently, the name *bānî* has been added to match LXX texts. Bani is thus indicated as the name of the lineage, and Shelomoth stands as its representative. The name "Shelomoth" also reflects a textual change: The Hebrew is *šelōmît.* Other occurrences of the name in the MT and LXX texts provide the basis for the change.

DONALD K. BERRY

SHELUMIEL (PERSON) [*šĕlumîʾēl*]. The son of Zurishaddai and the chief (*nāśîʾ*, Num 2:12) of the tribe of Simeon during the wilderness sojourn after the Exodus. He is mentioned only five times in the OT in four different tribal lists. As leader of the tribe of Simeon, he helped Moses conduct a census of the able-bodied fighting men of Israel prior to their departure from Mt. Sinai (Num 1:6), presented the offerings of the tribe of Judah on the fifth day of the twelve-day celebration of the dedication of the altar (Num 7:36, 41), and directed his tribe to its proper place on the south side of the tabernacle in the Israelite camp (Num 2:12) and to its position in the order of march as the Israelites prepared to depart from Mt. Sinai (Num 10:19).

Johnson (*IDB* 4:320) suggests that Shelumiel may be the same person as the one named SALAMIEL (Gk *Salamiēl*), son of Sarasadai, in the genealogy of Judith (Jdt 8:1; note the LXX for Shelumiel is identical to Salamiel). The meaning of the name "Shelumiel" admits of at least three interpretations: (1) "God is peace" (*IPN*, 165), (2) "at peace with God," and (3) "God is friendly" (Gray *Numbers* ICC, 7).

DALE F. LAUNDERVILLE

SHEM (PERSON) [Heb *šēm*]. The name of the eldest son of Noah. It appears in the Hebrew Bible seventeen times (Gen 5:32; 6:10; 7:13; 9:18, 23, 26, 27; 10:1, 21, 22, 31; 11:10, 11; 1 Chr 1:4, 17, 24), once in the NT (Luke 3:36), and once in the Apocrypha (Sir 49:16).

A. The Name

The etymological origin and meaning of the name "Shem" is disputed. It has been suggested that Shem is an abbreviated or corrupted form of a theophoric name such as *Šĕmûʾēl, šem* meaning "son." In this regard, it is thought that the name refers to an ethnic deity, "heros eponymus," not an ethnic or geographic entity. The hypothesis that "Shem" is related to Akkadian *sumu,* "name" or "son," is more plausible. Names are regarded in Semitic culture to have very significant spiritual connotations. In view of this fact, it is conceivable that Shem means "The Name" derived appropriately from the common Semitic base *šVm-* "name." A case can also be made that Shem, as in the South Semitic languages Sabean and Ethiopic, means "appointed one," "honored one," "elevated one," or even "holy one."

B. Biblical Data

Shem is the eldest of Noah's three sons, the brother of Ham and Japhet (Gen 5:32; 6:10). All three sons and their wives joined Noah in the Ark and escaped the Flood (6:9; 7:13–15; 9:1–18). He also shares together with his brothers the divine blessing and covenant (9:1, 17). On Shem's role in the story of Noah's drunkenness (Gen 9:20–27), see HAM (PERSON).

Shem is the father of all Semites, particularly the Hebrews and the Arabs. He had five sons (Elam, Asshur, Arpachshad, Lud, and Aram) and twenty-five descendants (Gen 10:21–32; 1 Chr 1:17, 24). According to the biblical ethnographic conceptions, the descendants of Shem occupy chiefly the lands to the E of Israel (Arabia and Mesopotamia). Some of his descendants, however, may have controlled part of the Horn of Africa. Shem's descendants Asshur, Elam, and Sheba are identified with peoples known from ancient history. Hazarmaveth (Gen 10:26; 1 Chr 1:20) is generally identified with Hadramaut in South Arabia. Joktan is claimed by both Yemenis and Ethiopia to be their ancestor. Albright identifies "Havilah" with N Ethiopia. Others identify Ophir with the Afar in E Ethiopia.

Although Shem does not figure prominently in biblical literature, he is the lineal ancestor of the Jewish people; Abraham is his tenth-generation descendant (Gen 11:10–31). In the Table of Nations his genealogy is given after that of Ham and Japhet, probably to express continuity with the history of the family of Abraham and his descendants that follows.

C. Jewish Tradition

Very few references are made to Shem in the Pseudepigrapha, and hardly any in the published literature of Qumran (*Jub.* 2:64, 69, 72–77, 92, 93; *2 En.* 73:5; *Apoc. Adam* 4:1; *T. Sim.* 6:5; *T Isaac* 3:15; *Ps-Philo* 1:22; 4:1ff). The book of *Jubilees* deals with divine land distribution. See Fig. GEO.05. The *Sibylline Oracles* give the sons of Noah the names of Greek gods, Shem being identified with Cronos (3:110–15). The gnostic Sethian Tractate *Apoc. Adam* (V 5:72, 17; 73:14, 25; 74:11; 76:13, 4) deals with the division of the world and empires among the sons of Noah.

The Tannaitic and Amoraitic teachers considered Shem, or *šēm rabbā,* "Shem the Great" as he is called by some (*b. Sanh.* 108b), Noah's youngest son. They say that in the Bible he is mentioned first among the members of his family because he was the most righteous, wisest, and most important son, not because he was the oldest (*b. Sanh* 69b.; *Gen. Rab.* 26:3; 37:7).

Shem is extolled in various ways: he initiated the covering of his father with a garment and hence even more than his brother Japheth was blessed to have the fringed *tallit* for cover and the Shekinah to dwell in his tent (i.e., Jerusalem; *b. Yoma* 10a; *Gen Rab.* 26:3; 36:6, 8); he was given the choice, middle part of the earth which included the land of Israel (*b. Sanh.* 91a; *Midr. Haggadol* Gen 9:27; *Gen. Rab.* 1:2; *Pirqe R. El.* 24); he is one of the eight righteous persons who lived in his time and who has a place in the world to come (*Midr. Haggadol* Gen 9:18; 11:10; *Tanhuma Yelammedenu,* Noah; *b. Sanh.* 69b); he was born circumcised (*Gen. Rab.* 26:3; *ʾAbot R. Nat* 2); he was a prophet for 400 years and priest *par excellence.* In fact, Adam's priestly garment was inherited by Shem from Noah. When they emerged out of the Ark, Shem fulfilled this priestly obligation by offering the sacrifices on behalf of his father Noah (cf. Gen 8:20), who became unfit after he was mauled by a lion in the ark (*Gen. Rab.* 30:6).

Shem was identified in some traditions with Melchizedek, King of Salem, the "priest of the God Most High" who lived in Salem/Jerusalem and who met Abraham after his victory over the four kings (Gen 14:18–20). Abraham was afraid that Shem/Melchizedek might curse him for having killed his other descendants, the Elamites. So, to demonstrate to Abraham that he was not angry at him, Shem/Melchizedek came out to meet him (*Gen. Rab.* 44:8; *Tanḥuma* Lech Lecha 19). In some instances Abraham is elevated higher than Shem. Thus, according to some teachers, it was Shem/Melchizedek who gave tithes to Abraham, not Abraham to Shem. Furthermore, Jerusalem, the City of the Holy Temple, is so named by combining Salem, the name Shem gave it, with *yirʾeh* (Gen 22:14), the name Abraham gave it. Shem ultimately lost his priestly position because, in his meeting with Abraham, he put the blessing of Abraham ahead of the blessing of the divine name (*B. Ned.* 32b; *Pirqe R. el.* 27). According to another tradition, however, Shem himself, knowing that he had no other worthy descendants, asked divine favor to pass the priestly office to Abraham. At Abraham's funeral, Shem and his great-grandson Eber, walked before his bier and chose a suitable place for the burial (*Gen. Rab.* 62:6; cf. *Yal.* Gen 110).

To Shem is also attributed the founding of the first school (*b. Mak.* 23b; *Gen. Rab.* 36:8; *Tg. Ps.-J.* Gen 9:27; 25:22). Eber also shares this honor with him. Shem received the Hebrew script of the Torah at the time of divine land distribution. At that time, Shem not only received his share of 26 countries and 33 islands, but also 26 of the 72 world languages and 6 (Hebrew, Egyptian, Assyrian, Lybian, Chaldean, and Gutazaki [Sabean? Sanskrit?]) of the 16 international scripts (*Midr. Haggadol* Gen 10:32). The school was not only a place for the study of the Torah but also a law court in which the divine presence dwelt (*B. Mak.* 23b). Jacob was a student in the Shem-Eber school. His brother Esau did not kill him because of the fear of the judgment of that same court. Judah condemned Tamar to death for adultery, following one of the laws the court had promulgated (*b. ʿAbod. Zar.* 36b; *Gen. Rab.* 63:7; 67:8). Inasmuch as the study of the Torah preceded the Sinai revelation and continues after the end of the world, Torah will be studied in heaven in the academy established by Shem and Eber (*Cant. Rab.* 6:2:6; *Qoh. Rab.* 5:11:5).

D. Christian Literature

In the NT Shem is mentioned once in the genealogy of Jesus (Luke 3:36). In the early Christian literature, particularly in Irenaeus of Lyon, Lactantius, Hippolytus of Rome, Clement, Origen, Epiphanius, and Eusibius, the sons of Noah and their generations are often alluded to but without much elaboration.

EPHRAIM ISAAC

SHEM, PARAPHRASE OF (NHC VII,*1*). This enigmatic, gnostic tractate is one of the longest and best preserved in the Nag Hammadi codices. It occupies pp. 1,1–49,9 in Codex VII. Only parts of the bottom lines of a few pages are missing. There is no reason to doubt that *Paraph. Shem* was translated from the Greek. It is written in preclassical Sahidic Coptic. The title is found at the beginning and is supplemented by a subtitle: "The paraphrase which was about the unbegotten Spirit" (1,2–3). Aland understands the word "paraphrase" to refer to a literary genre which tries to achieve insight through a series of variations on a theme, in this case the imprisonment and liberation of the light (1978: 81). To be sure, the work does not follow the expected chronological order of cosmogony and salvation history often found in mythological gnostic texts. Its use of repetitions, expansions, changes in terminology, and obscure symbolism leaves the reader more bewildered than enlightened. The word "paraphrase," however, is used in a stricter sense within the tractate itself (32,26) where it appears to refer to an explanation of the role of mythological beings who were listed earlier (31,4–32,5) and whose names are recited later by Shem on leaving the body for his final ascent (46,4–47,7). The race of Shem are to remember this "testimony" for their escape from the body.

The genre of *Paraph. Shem* is that of an apocalypse. Shem (consistently spelled Seem) is taken out of the body "to the top of the creation" (1,4–16) where Derdekeas, the son of the infinite Light, reveals to him matters pertaining to the three primeval powers—Light, Darkness, and Spirit between them. The center of the myth is the capture of Spirit by Darkness and its rescue by the revealer-redeemer Derdekeas. The revelation ends in 41,20 after which Shem awakens "as from a long sleep." Then follows an eschatological discourse in which Shem describes his ascent at the end of his life (42,11–48,30). Finally, without a proper transition, there is a brief farewell address to Shem, apparently spoken again by Derdekeas (48,30–49,9).

Three issues have crystalized at this early point in the interpretation of *Paraph. Shem.* Still unresolved is its relationship to Hippolytus' account of the teaching of the Sethians based on a writing which he knows as "The Paraphrase of Seth" (*Elenchos* V.19–22). The striking agreement in content leaves no doubt that the two works are related, but the explanation that Hippolytus must have known a Christianized form of *Paraph. Shem* (Wisse 1970: 138) is rejected by some in favor of a more distant relationship (Wisse and Roberge 1988: 341).

Closely related is the question of the possible Christian influence on *Paraph. Shem.* In contrast to some clear allusions to the OT, i.e., the flood (25,11–15; 28,5–14), Sodom (28,34–29,33), and the tower of Babel (25,17–26; 28,9), there is no obvious Christian material. Faith appears to be personified, but its role is obscure. Parallels with the NT are distant. The striking polemic against baptism may include an allusion to the Baptism of Jesus by John the Baptist (30,21–32,17), but this reading is far from compelling. There are some interesting general parallels between the role of Derdekeas and Christ (Wisse 1970: 135), but the differences make dependence of the one on the other unlikely. The question remains whether the enigmatic references in the tractate were intended to be decoded in a Christian way.

The eschatology of *Paraph. Shem* is less controversial but has important consequences for our understanding of Gnosticism. The theme of the ascent of the soul is as expected. The tractate's preoccupation with apocalyptic eschatology, however, was not thought to be characteristic of Gnosticism. The same emphasis is found also in other gnostic writing from Nag Hammadi, such as *On the Origin of the World* (NHC II,*5*) and *The Concept of our Great Power* (NHC VI,*4*). Evidently Gnosticism and Apocalypticism did not essentially differ in their understanding of eschatology.

If Hippolytus knew a Christianized version of *Paraph. Shem*, then its *terminus ad quem* is the first part of the 3d century. The Gk model of the Coptic version could then be dated back to the late 2d century. Nothing in the tractate betrays the identity and provenance of the author.

Bibliography

Aland, B. 1978. Die Paraphrase als form gnostischer Verkündigung. Pp. 75–90 in *Nag Hammadi and Gnosis*, ed. R. McL. Wilson. NHS 14. Leiden.

Fisher, K.-M. 1975. Die Paraphrase des Seem. Pp. 255–67 in *Essays on the Nag Hammadi Texts in Honour of Pahor Labib*, ed. M. Krause. NHS 6. Leiden.

Krause, M. 1973. Die Paraphrase des Seem. Pp. 2–105 in *Christentum am Roten Meer, 2. Band*, ed. G. Altheim and R. Stiehl. Berlin.

Sevrin, J.-M. 1975. A propose de le "Paraphrase de Sem." *Mus* 88: 69–96.

Wisse, F. 1970. The Redeemer Figure in the Paraphrase of Shem. *NovT* 12: 130–40.

Wisse, F., and Roberge, M. 1988. The Paraphrase of Shem (VII,1). *NHL*, 339–361.

Frederik Wisse

SHEM, TREATISE OF. Preserved in only one 15th-century paper manuscript is a Syriac document attributed to Shem, the son of Noah. It is an astrological almanac *(Dodekaeteris Chaldaica)*, whereby the characteristics of the coming year are predicted according to the stars. The original language seems to be Semitic; there are abundant Semitisms that are most likely original and names are identified according to the Semitic alphabet. The provenience is probably Egyptian (Charlesworth *OTP* 1: 473–86; *HJP* 3/1: 369–72); the Nile is frequently mentioned, and the crops noted are characteristically Egyptian (wheat, barley, peas). Irrigation and illnesses due to the winds and desert sands also suggest Egypt. The references to the beneficial effects of the north wind, the numerous comments about the sea and fishing, and the mention of Alexandria may well indicate that the document was composed in Alexandria.

The date of composition is difficult to discern. Mingana (1917) suggested that the pseudepigraphon postdates the Jewish War of 130–135 C.E. Charlesworth is convinced that the document may well date from the latter part of the 1st century B.C.E. Astrological documents found at Qumran and the argument against astrology in *Jubilees* 12 prove that Jewish interest in astrology is not late and medieval, as some scholars have erroneously claimed. The argument that the document must be Christian and late because Jews did not compose such almanacs is dismissed by the recognition that precisely this type of thought is represented in Fragment A from the Cairo Genizah. For example, as Vermes and his colleagues note (in *HJP* 3/1: 369–72), compare *Treat. Shem* 2:1 ("And if the year begins in Taurus: Everyone whose name contains a Beth, or Yudh, or Kaph will become ill. . . .") with Cairo Genizah Fragment A (A/2, 9–12 [ed. Gruenwald] = "He who is born on the third day of the week in the constellation Scorpio of Leo . . . will at the age of nineteen marry a woman whose name begins with He, Yod."). The claim that this genre of astrological writing must be late is disproved by the recognition that Boll (1900: 139–44) drew attention to a *Dodekaeteris Chaldaica* that was composed in Syria during the time of Octavian (who received the name "Augustus" by a decree of the Roman Senate in January, 27 B.C.E.). While it is impossible to be certain, it is conceivable that the *Treatise of Shem* was composed shortly after the famous nonbattle at Actium, in which Octavian "defeated" Anthony and Cleopatra, both of whom fled to Alexandria. Note these interesting excerpts: "And the king of the Romans will not remain in one place . . . a great war and misery (will occur) on all the earth, and especially in the land of Egypt" (1:5–9). "And the king (the Roman Emperor Octavian?) will strive with a king (Anthony?) and will slay him. And Alexandria will be lost. . . . And many ships will be wrecked" (6:13–17). "And the king will stay in one place.

And power will then leave the land" (7:16–17). Perhaps the author was an Alexandrian Jew, who—in reaction to the Roman propaganda over their "victory" at Actium—composed this astrological document to clarify the inexplicable: Anthony and Cleopatra's superior forces lost the so-called battle of Actium.

Bibliography

Boll, F., et al., eds. 1900. *Catalogus Codicum Astrologorum Graecorum* 2:139–44.

Charlesworth, J. H. 1977. Jewish Astrology in the Talmud, Pseudepigrapha, Dead Sea Scrolls, and Early Palestinian Synagogues. *HTR* 70:183–200.

———. 1978. Rylands Syriac MS 44 and a New Addition to the Pseudepigrapha: The Treatise of Shem. *BJRL* 60: 376–403.

———. 1987. Jewish Interest in Astrology during the Hellenistic and Roman Period. *ANRW* 2/20.2:926–50.

Charlesworth, J. H., with Mueller, J. R. 1987. Die "Schrift des Sem": Einführung, Text und Übersetzung. *ANRW* 2/20.2:951–87.

Leaney, A. R. C. 1984. Treatise of Shem. P. 170 in *The Jewish and Christian World: 200 BC to AD 200*. Cambridge and New York.

Mingana, A., ed. 1917. The Book of Shem Son of Noah. Pp. 20–29 and 52–59 in *Some Early Judaeo-Christian Documents in the John Rylands Library: Syriac Texts*. Manchester.

Russell, D. S. 1987. *The Old Testament Pseudepigrapha: Patriarchs & Prophets in Early Judaism*. Philadelphia.

JAMES H. CHARLESWORTH

SHEMA (PERSON) [Heb *šĕmaᶜ*]. Four individuals in the Hebrew Bible bear this name.

1. One of the many descendants of Judah referred to in the Chronicler's genealogical lists (1 Chr 2:43–44). More precisely, Shema appears within the Calebite line as the son of Hebron and the father of Raham. However, the presence of place names within this section of 1 Chronicles has long been noted. Caleb is typically seen, therefore, as the father of a collection of cities rather than individuals. Similarly, Shema was possibly a settlement in the vicinity of Hebron (Braun *1 Chronicles* WBC, 41).

2. One of the descendants of Reuben according to the Chronicler's lists (1 Chr 5:8), he was the son of Joel and the father of Azaz. In 1 Chr 5:4, Joel's descendants include a certain Shemaiah and Shimei. Shema can possibly be equated with one of them.

3. One of the descendants of Benjamin referred to in the Chronicler's lists (1 Chr 8:13), he was the head of a father's house of Aijalon. In 1 Chr 8:21, Shema appears as Shimei.

4. One of the men who stood on Ezra's right hand during the great public reading of the Law (Neh 8:4; 1 Esdr 9:43). Not designated as a Levite, Shema's position at this event suggests that he was an influential or representative member of the Israelite laity.

TERRY L. BRENSINGER

SHEMA (PLACE) [Heb *šĕmaᶜ*]. One of the cities of Judah "in the extreme South, toward the boundary of Edom" (Josh 15:21,26). A place with this name is only explicitly mentioned in this biblical reference. In the list of Simeonite cities (Josh 19:2 ff) however, there is a town named Sheba. Since the two lists in large parts run parallel, it is a quite common suggestion that the name Shema has arisen as a scribal error from Sheba (Cohen *IDB* 4:311). However, it is obvious that the Simeonite list in Joshua 19 is not merely an excerpt from the Judahite list in Joshua 15 (Axelsson 1987: 73–79). The two lists deal with roughly (but not exactly) the same area, but some names occurring in chap. 15 are absent in chap. 19, probably because they never were Simeonite settlements. Thus it is perfectly possible that once a town named Shema existed in S Judah, inhabited not by Simeonites but by some of the groups that joined or constituted the tribe of Judah. This leads us to turn our attention to some Chronistic genealogical passages. There is a Calebite clan (or place?) named Shema (1 Chr 2:43), and we also read of a group of Kenites called Shimeathites (1 Chr 2:55). It is conceivable to see a connection between one or the other of these names and the place named Shema. We probably cannot get much further in our knowledge. The name "Shema" may be just an erroneous variant of Sheba. But it is just as possible that a settlement with the name "Shema" really existed in S Judah. If that is the case, we naturally do not know anything more about its exact location.

Bibliography

Axelsson, L. E. 1987. *The Lord Rose Up from Seir*. ConBOT 25. Stockholm.

LARS E. AXELSSON

SHEMAᶜ, KHIRBET (M.R. 191264). Literally "the ruin of Shammai," possibly to be identified with Galilean Tekoa, is situated just S of ancient Meiron on one of the foothills of Mt. Meiron at a level of 760 m above sea level. Venerated since medieval times by Jewish pilgrims as the holy burial site of Shammai and other Jewish priests and sages, the site is distinguished by the presence of a large mausoleum at the SW extent of the settlement and by a large megalith to the W known by locals as "Elijah's chair." Although known to the explorers of the 19th century, the first excavations were undertaken between 1970–72 by a team headed by E. M. Meyers.

Although excavations focused on a rather large public building that turned out to be a synagogue complex, numerous soundings were also conducted in the village itself and in the necropolis which surrounded the site, primarily on the E and S. The following chronological chart summarizes the main cultural phases of occupation that had clear architectural remains associated with them (table 1):

Stratum	Date	Period
I	ca. 103–37 B.C.E.	Late Hellenistic
Unstratified remains	ca. 37 B.C.E.–180 C.E.	Early-Middle Roman
II	ca. 180–284 C.E.	Middle Roman
III	ca. 284–306 C.E.	Late Roman
IV	ca. 306–419 C.E.	Byzantine 1
V	ca. 419–640 C.E.	Byzantine 2
VI	ca. 640–850 C.E.	Early Arab
(gap)	ca. 850–1150 C.E.	
VII	ca. 1150–1277 C.E.	Medieval

Excavation in the village revealed agriculture to be the main source of livelihood. Several olive presses were uncovered and flotation analysis was conducted on the associated soils, which made it possible to ascertain the high quality of oil from Tekoa and Upper Galilee that is so noted in the Talmud. Several cisterns were revealed and a unique ritual bath that has its own pre-wash facility associated with it was also recovered.

The excavated tombs indicate that secondary burial or ossilegium was a normal manner of inhumation, apparently often without ossuaries since only few fragments of stone ossuaries were found. Similar evidence was found in nearby MEIRON. See BURIALS (ANCIENT JEWISH). The main discovery of the expedition was the broadhouse synagogue that was built over several pre-synagogue installations from Stratum I or II, including a very elaborate ritual bath. The synagogue is the first broadhouse ever excavated in the Galilee and the first one to be found with internal columnation. A broadhouse is a rectangular hall which focuses attention or worship upon a long wall as opposed to a short wall as is the case in a basilica. See SYNAGOGUE. In a synagogue in the Galilee the wall of orientation would be the S wall that faces toward Jerusalem.

The Khirbet Shemaᶜ broadhouse synagogue is founded in Stratum III, measures 18 m by 9 m, and is erected on a basilica-like plan with two rows of four columns oriented on an E-W axis. The principal entrance is on the N, opposite a Stratum IV *bema* or raised platform, used for the reading of Scripture which is attached to the long S wall. The handsome N entryway was crowned with a large lintel piece with a *menorah* carved into its external face. During Stratum III a Torah Shrine or *aedicula* apparently stood on the S wall where a *bema* was constructed in Stratum IV. Another entrance with an eagle incised into a doorjamb is located on top of a monumental stairway on the W. It is necessary to descend several stairs after entering from either direction, a most unusual feature for a house of worship but one which suits the unusual mountain topography of the site. A gallery for additional seating is situated on the W short wall, partially founded on bedrock, and lies above a frescoed room, which might have been used as a storage area for scrolls not in use, or possibly as a scriptorium. A *genizah,* or storage area for scrolls, no longer in use lies under the W stairwell and opens into the frescoed room. Remnants of benches are to be found on all four walls and it may be conjectured that most worshipers either stood, leaned on poles, or simply sat on the floor. Because of the broadhouse plan, however, the view toward the *bema* from many places in the hall was obscured by the columns.

The earthquake of 306 C.E. did great damage at the site in general and destroyed the synagogue almost entirely. It was nonetheless rebuilt soon after in the same broadhouse form in which it was originally erected. Instead of a Torah Shrine on the long S wall, however, a *bema* was constructed, and perhaps in stratum IV the frescoed room came to serve a more integral part in the storage of scrolls for ritual use. Some architectural pieces were reused if they were not too severely damaged, and many of them were simply used as building stones in the E stylolate wall; this wall was built to shore up the E end of the building where bedrock severely dips and where a ritual bath complex had functioned in an earlier period. The second synagogue thus was even more eclectic than the first, with each column capital being different from the other.

Another building to the N was identified by the excavators as a House of Study, or *bêt-midraš.* It could be entered by a stairway off the main N entrance path to the synagogue from this building. Benches line one sector of the large room where it is possible to imagine a group of students studying with their master. The rest of the space might have been utilized as a guest room. Both study and hospitality were important functions of the ancient synagogue and provide much insight into its multipurpose use in antiquity.

The significance of the discoveries at Khirbet Shemaᶜ are twofold. First, they conclusively demonstrate that no rigid typological scheme dictated the norms of synagogue building in the Galilee. This most unusual broadhouse synagogue reveals an eclectic architectual style whose floor plan hearkens back to an old Palestinian temple type. Second, the remoteness of the Upper Galilean mountain hinterland underscores the high level of the achievement of the inhabitants in religious affairs, trade, and other aspects of communal life. A similar, high level of material culture in metal, glass, ceramics, and architecture also indicates how much a part of their contemporary world the inhabitants were, no matter what the extent of their geographical isolation.

Bibliography

Meyers, E. M. 1980. Ancient Synagogues in Galilee: Their Religious and Cultural Setting. *BA* 43: 97–108.

———. 1981. The Synagogue of Ḥorvat Shemaᶜ. Pp. 70–74 in *Ancient Synagogues Revealed,* ed. L. I. Levine. Jerusalem.

———. 1982. Synagogues of Galilee. *Archaeology* 35: 51–58.

Meyers, E. M.; Kraabel, A. T.; and Strange, J. F. 1976. *Ancient Synagogue Excavations at Khirbet Shemaᶜ, Upper Galilee, Israel 1970–72.* AASOR 42. Durham, NC.

ERIC M. MEYERS

SHEMAAH (PERSON) [Heb *šĕmaᶜâ*]. Father of Ahiezer and Joash, two of the Benjaminite warriors who defected from tribal loyalty to Saul in order to join David at Ziklag (1 Chr 12:3). Some Hebrew mss and LXX mss read "son of" instead of "sons of," so that Shemaah would in this case be the father only of Joash. The Chronicler has doubled the list of warriors who supported David (1 Chr 11:41b–12:40) beyond what was contained in the parallel narrative (2 Sam 23:8–39 [= 1 Chr 11:10–41a]). The source for these additional lists can only be a matter of conjecture, though Williamson has provided a convincing argument for the structure of 1 Chronicles 11–12. The long list reflects the Chronicler's concern to show "all Israel" united in support for David, a characteristic theme of the history. Ambidexterity or lefthandedness among Benjaminites is also noted in Judg 3:15; 20:16.

Bibliography

Williamson, H. G. M. 1981. We Are Yours, O David. *OTS* 21: 164–76.

RAYMOND B. DILLARD

SHEMAIAH (PERSON) [Heb *šĕmaʿyāh; šĕmaʿyāhû*]. Shemaiah is a theophoric personal name commonly rendered "Yahweh has heard" (*TPNAH,* 90; *IPN* 184–86). Dahood (1978: 92) translates, "Hear, O Ya," comparing the Ugaritic personal name *šmʿy* ("Hear, O Ya," *UT,* no. 1128: 33) and the Eblaite personal name *sí-mi-na-ià* ("Hear, I pray, O Ya," TM 75.G.336 IV 16; see Pettinato and Matthiae 1976: 4). The name appears in nonbiblical ancient Hebrew in a preexilic papyrus found in a cave in the Wadi Murabbat (Mur. B 4, *TSSI* 1: 32), in the Lachish ostraca (4:6, *TSSI* 1: 41; 19:4, *TSSI* 1: 49), and in a seal (no. 6, *TSSI* 1: 61; see also *TPNAH,* 363).

1. A chief of the tribe of Simeon (1 Chr 4:37).

2. Son of Joel and a chief of the tribe of Reuben (1 Chr 5:4).

3. A chief of the sons of Elizaphan and head of a family of Levites with 200 "brothers" or members of the clan (1 Chr 15:8, 11). David summoned him and other levitical chiefs to transfer the ark of the covenant from the house of Obed-edom (13:14) to the tent in Jerusalem (16:1).

4. Son of Nethanel; the levitical scribe who registered the appointment by lot of the priestly divisions in the presence of the king, the principal officials, Zadok the priest, Ahimelech the son of Abiathar, and the heads of the priestly and levitical families. There were twenty-four divisions, with sixteen being allocated to the sons of Eleazar and eight to the less numerous sons of Ithamar (1 Chr 24:6; cf. Williamson 1979: 257–59).

5. Firstborn son of Obed-edom, eponym of a levitical family responsible for service in the temple. When the Levites were being organized they were allocated by lot responsibility for the S gate of the temple and the storehouses. Shemaiah was the father of several outstanding sons who exercised leadership in the family (1 Chr 26:4, 6–7).

6. A man of God or prophet in the reign of Rehoboam who forbade the king from fighting in order to suppress the revolt of the ten tribes from the house of David after the death of Solomon. All were to return to their homes because the division of the kingdom came from Yahweh. And this the people did (1 Kgs 12:22–24; 2 Chr 11:2–4). Some scholars (e.g., Jones *1 and 2 Kings* NCBC, 255) believe that this tradition is a late creation, for "there was war between Rehoboam and Jeroboam continually" (1 Kgs 14:30). Jones (ibid., 279) argues that the Deuteronomistic editor simply prefers not to elaborate his brief statement in v 30, although he "probably" found details of military engagements in his sources. But this is quite speculative. Gray (*1 and 2 Kings* OTL, 349) points out that the existence of a state of war between the two kings does not necessarily imply actual campaigns. It may have been more an armed truce with both sides fortifying frontier fortresses. Furthermore, prophets frequently functioned in times of war, so that the tradition of Shemaiah's oracle may well be historical (ibid., 309). In any case, Yahweh expressly confirms what has already been announced to Solomon (11:11–13) and Jeroboam (vv 30–39). The LXX has a long insertion after 1 Kgs 12:24, including a brief version of the story of Ahijah the prophet and Jeroboam (11:29–39). In it Samaias (= Shemaiah, see LXX 12:22) the son of Enlami is told by the Lord to take a new garment, not yet washed, and tear it into twelve pieces. He gives ten to Jeroboam and explains, "Thus speaks the Lord about the ten tribes of Israel," i.e., God gives them to Jeroboam. The incident takes place at Shechem, apparently in the presence of Rehoboam (contrast 11:29–31 where Ahijah meets Jeroboam before his flight to Egypt while he is still an official of Solomon). Shemaiah is "indicating that it was the will of Yahweh to condone the disruption," disapproving of Rehoboam rather than approving of Jeroboam (ibid., 311). The historical value of the insertion is doubtful (Gordon 1975: 393).

The name also occurs in 2 Chr 12:5, 7 in a narrative (vv 1–12) which depends, at least in part, on 1 Kgs 14:25–28 (Williamson *1 and 2 Chronicles* NCBC, 245–48). The prophet delivers an oracle to Rehoboam and the principal men of Judah who had assembled in Jerusalem when Shishak king of Egypt invaded the land: "You abandoned me, so I have abandoned you to the power of Shishak" (v 5), the reference being probably to the worship of foreign gods (ibid., 246). King and officials now "humble themselves" and say, "Yahweh is righteous" (v 6), that is, they repent (ibid., 247–48, 225–26). Yahweh then speaks again through Shemaiah: He will quickly deliver them and Jerusalem will be spared, but they will become subject to Shishak (vv 7–8). In the event, Shishak required a heavy indemnity (v 9, cf. 1 Kgs 14:26). The absence of Jerusalem from Shishak's list of conquests suggests that the city was indeed spared (*ANET,* 242). The Chronicler finally mentions a book of events of Rehoboam's reign attributed to Shemaiah the prophet (2 Chr 12:15).

7. One of the nine Levites (2 Chr 17:8) whom King Jehoshaphat in the third year of his reign (ca. 870 B.C.) sent to teach in the cities of Judah (vv 7–9). The Levites, together with two priests, accompanied five lay officials who headed the mission, and they taught from the book of the law, probably a royal law code (Myers *2 Chronicles* AB, 99–100).

8. Son of Jeduthun; a member of one of the three families of levitical singers, and one of the fourteen Levites who are listed as responding with enthusiasm to the command of King Hezekiah to cleanse the temple (2 Chr 29:14).

9. One of the six Levites who, at the command of King Hezekiah and under the directions of Kore, distributed the general priestly and levitical portions of first fruits, tithes, and offerings to those resident in the cities of the priests (2 Chr 31:15).

10. Probably a son of Shecaniah in a list of the descendants of David (1 Chr 3:22) and more specifically of Jehoiachin (Jeconiah) and Zerubbabel (vv 17, 19) but the text is difficult. Myers (*1 Chronicles* AB, 21) dates his birth ca. 495 B.C. He is given five named sons.

11. From Kiriath-jearim, father of Uriah the prophet who was a contemporary of the prophet Jeremiah (Jer 26:20).

12. The Nehelamite, a false prophet in Babylon and contemporary of Jeremiah (Jer 29:24, 31–32). Shemaiah wrote to "all the people," to Zephaniah the son of Maaseiah the priest who was overseer of the temple, and to "all the priests" (v 25). There is no precise date, but the time is after 597 B.C., perhaps in 595/94 B.C. when there was unrest in Babylon (Wiseman 1956: 36, 73) in which deported Jews seem to have been involved (cf. vv 20–23). A summary of this letter is given (vv 26–29), or vv 25b–28 may be a quotation from Shemaiah's letter, vv 24–32 representing "an almost unchanged copy of a letter to Shemaiah written by Jeremiah's secretary" (Dijkstra 1983: 319). Shemaiah blames Zephaniah for not disciplining "Jeremiah of Anathoth" who has foretold a long exile and advised the deported Jews to settle down (cf. vv 1–15). Zephaniah reads this letter in the hearing of Jeremiah, who then delivers an oracle against Shemaiah which is to be sent to the exiles: Yahweh has not sent Shemaiah and yet he has prophesied and led the people to trust in a falsehood. He and his descendants will therefore be punished. None will live to enjoy the prosperity Yahweh is going to bestow on his people. Shemaiah's chief offense was that he had preached rebellion against Yahweh (vv 31–32), which meant rebellion against the king of Babylon. Jeremiah wrote in terms similar to those in which he had addressed Hananiah (cf. 28:15–16). The rejection of Yahweh's word spoken by one of his "servants the prophets" leads to judgment.

13. Father of Delaiah, who was one of the officials who heard Baruch read Jeremiah's oracles from the scroll (Jer 36:12).

14. Son of Hasshub, descendant of Merari (1 Chr 9:14), and one of the seven levitical heads of families who lived in or around Jerusalem in the time of Nehemiah. Shemaiah's family is also listed in Neh 11:15 where, however, "Bunni" replaces "Merari." According to v 16, he was one of those in charge of "the work outside the house of God," which would indicate noncultic duties such as maintenance and the gathering and storing of provisions for the temple (Myers *Ezra, Nehemiah* AB, 187).

15. Descended from Jeduthun, son of Galal and father of Obadiah (1 Chr 9:16), who was the head of a levitical family, living at Netophah near Jerusalem in the time of Nehemiah. Perhaps Shemaiah is identical with Shammua the father of Abda in Neh 11:17, the difference in names being due to abbreviation: "Shammua" for "Shemaiah," "Abda" for "Obadiah."

16. One of the chiefs of the Levites, who gave generously to the Levites for the celebration of the Passover held by King Josiah (2 Chr 35:9).

17. A son of Adonikam and head of a family; one of those who accompanied Ezra from exile in Babylon to Jerusalem (Ezra 8:13; 1 Esdr 8:39).

18. A leading man, one of a delegation sent by Ezra to Iddo at Casiphia to obtain Levites when Ezra discovered on the way that they were absent from the group returning from Babylon (Ezra 8:16; 1 Esdr 8:44).

19. A son of Harim and priest in the list of those who put away their foreign wives and children according to Ezra's reform banning marriage with foreigners (Ezra 10:21, note vv 3–5; 1 Esdr 9:21).

20. A son of Harim and layman in the list of those who put away their foreign wives and children during Ezra's reform (Ezra 10:31; cf. variant SABBAIAS in 1 Esdr 9:32).

21. One of the sons of Ezora listed among the laymen who agreed to put away their foreign wives and children in accordance with the law of the postexilic community (1 Esdr 9:34; Gk *Samatus*).

22. Son of Shecaniah and keeper of the East Gate (of the temple); he led one of eight groups repairing the NE wall of Jerusalem between the Water Gate and the Sheep Gate in the time of Nehemiah (Neh 3:29; cf. Myers *Ezra, Nehemiah* AB, 115).

23. Son of Delaiah and descendant of Mehetabel (Neh 6:10). The context is one of plots against Nehemiah. Sanballat and other Persian officials were opposed to Nehemiah's work of reconstruction, and with the wall now repaired, were making a last desperate effort to stop the work being completed. Nehemiah came to the house of Shemaiah who was "shut up" (*ʿāṣûr*), perhaps physically (LXX *synechomenos,* "confined;" see Myers *Ezra, Nehemiah* AB, 138–39), but certainly in view of what follows, morally (*LHA,* 621b): vv 12–13 show that he had been bribed to prophesy. The expression "shut up" would then be an instance of "delayed identification" (on this literary device, see Watson 1984: 336–38). Shemaiah prophesies to Nehemiah that his enemies are planning to kill him and that he should take refuge in the temple (v 10). This was an attempt to involve Nehemiah in violating religious taboo. It was forbidden for a layman to enter the temple, though he could seek asylum at the altar (Exod 21:13–14; 1 Kgs 1:50–53; 2:28–34) outside the temple proper. Furthermore, Nehemiah was a eunuch so that it would have been doubly offensive for him to enter the temple (Lev 21:17–23; Deut 23:1; cf. Myers *Ezra, Nehemiah* AB, 138–39). He was a courageous man and refused to jeopardize himself and his work by following the counsel of Shemaiah, who was merely a hired prophet (v 12) and who spoke in order to terrorize him (v 13).

24. A priest who set his seal on Nehemiah's covenant (Neh 10:9—Eng v 8), the head of a priestly family who returned from Babylon with Zerubbabel (12:6), and the head of a priestly family in the time of the high priest Joiakim (12:18). The name seems to be that of an old priestly family.

25. A priest (Neh 12:34) in the procession led by Ezra the scribe, which "went to the right," or counterclockwise, toward the Dung Gate (v 31) during the ceremony dedicating the walls of Jerusalem after the repairs were completed.

26. A descendant of Asaph and ancestor of Zechariah (Neh 12:35). Zechariah was one of the priests with trumpets who, during the dedication of the walls of Jerusalem under Nehemiah, went in the counterclockwise procession led by Ezra the scribe.

27. One of the Levite musicians who accompanied the procession led by Ezra the scribe going toward the right in the ceremony dedicating the walls of Jerusalem (Neh 12:36).

28. One of the Levites who accompanied the procession led by Nehemiah going toward the left in the ceremony dedicating the walls of Jerusalem (Neh 12:42).

29. Referred to as "the great Shemaiah" (LXX *Semeios*, Sinaiticus reads *Semelios*), he is the father of Ananias and Jathan, relatives of Tobias (Tob 5:14—Eng v 13).

Bibliography

Dahood, M. 1978. Ebla, Ugarit and the Old Testament. Pp. 81–112 in *Congress Volume: Göttingen 1977,* ed. J. A. Emerton et al. VTSup 29. Leiden.

Dijkstra, M. 1983. Prophecy by Letter (Jeremiah xxix 24–32). *VT* 33: 319–22.

Gordon, R. P. 1975. The Second Septuagint Account of Jeroboam: History or Midrash?. *VT* 25: 368–93.

Pettinato, G., and Matthiae, P. 1976. Aspetti amministrativi e topografici di Ebla nel III millennio av. Cr. *RSO* 50: 1–30.

Pritchard, J. B., ed. 1959. *Hebrew Inscriptions and Stamps from Gibeon.* Museum monographs 5. Philadelphia.

Watson, W. G. E. 1984. *Classical Hebrew Poetry.* JSOTSup 26. Sheffield.

Williamson, H. G. M. 1979. The Origins of the Twenty-four Priestly Courses: A Study of 1 Chronicles xxiii-xxvii. Pp. 251–68 in *Studies in the Historical Books of the Old Testament,* ed. J. A. Emerton. VTSup 30. Leiden.

Wiseman, D. J. 1956. *Chronicles of Chaldaean Kings (626–556 B.C.) in the British Museum.* London.

ROBERT ALTHANN

SHEMARIAH (PERSON) [Heb *šĕmaryāhû; šĕmaryāh*]. **1.** A Benjaminite who defected to David while he was at Ziklag (1 Chr 12:5). The name listed here is the longer form *(šĕmaryāhû),* which means "Yahweh has preserved." Shemariah, along with his companions, is considered an excellent warrior possessing the very desirable quality of being ambidextrous. Because Shemariah and the Benjaminites are "compatriots of Saul" *(ʾaḥê šāʾûl),* their defection to David is very significant; therefore, they are listed first among those who came to Ziklag. The Chronicler uses this as clear evidence of the growing popular preference for David over Saul. The list in which Shemariah's name appears, although put in place by the Chronicler, is probably much older, possibly going back to the Davidic era itself (Williamson *Chronicles* NCBC, 106; cf. Myers *1 Chronicles* AB, 95). Williamson notes that Bealiah (the name preceding Shemariah in the list) contains the element "Baal," indicating a date before strict Yahwism would have excluded such (106). Thus, Shemariah's defection to David may be considered authentic.

2. A son of Rehoboam by his first wife, Mahalath (2 Chr 11:19). The name listed here is the shorter form *šĕmaryāh* (as are the names in #3 and #4 below). Because of certain tensions with other passages from the Chronicler, Williamson believes the list of Rehoboam's children is adopted from an older source (*Chronicles* NCBC, 244). Shemariah's mother was a great-granddaughter of Jesse through both parents and a second cousin of the king. However, Rehoboam favored his second wife, Maacah, and made her first son, Abijah, his royal heir. The king did place his other sons, presumably including Shemariah, in "strategic centers to maintain his position and to guard against disloyalty" (Myers *2 Chronicles* AB, 71).

3. A descendant of Harim and one of the returned exiles who married a foreign woman during the era of Ezra's mission (Ezra 10:32). Shemariah does not appear in the parallel text of 1 Esdr 9:29. Shemariah seems to be a member of a family from which groups of exiles returned with Zerubbabel (Ezra 2:32; Neh 7:35). The three-month investigation (Ezra 10:16–17) culminating in the list in which Shemariah's name appears produced a relatively small number of names, leading some to believe that the list only includes prominant members of the community. Shemariah's position in the community, however, remains a mystery. While it seems probable that Shemariah divorced his foreign wife (note the prior oath taken by the people [Ezra 10:3–5] and the possibly generalizable v 19), that is not certain. The RSV follows 1 Esdr 9:36 in clearly stating that all on the list did indeed divorce their foreign wives and put away their children, but the Hebrew text of Ezra 44b is so corrupt that a definite translation is impossible, leaving the final outcome of the investigation in doubt.

4. Presumably a descendant of Binnui and one of the returned exiles who married a foreign woman during the era of Ezra's mission (Ezra 10:41). The name "Shemiah" appears in the parallel text of 1 Esdr 9:34. However, Noth argues that the name "Machnadebai," which occurs before Shemariah, is a corruption of the phrase "from the sons of" (*IPN,* 249). If that is true, then Shemariah would be a descendant of Shashai. In the parallel text of 1 Esdr 9:34, the phrase "from the sons of" does replace the name "Machnadebai." Assuming Binnui was Shashai's ancestor, Shashai was a member of a family who returned from Babylon with Zerubbabel. (See Neh 7:15; note that Bani replaces Binnui in Ezra 2:10.) For further discussion, see #3 above.

JEFFREY A. FAGER

SHEMEBER (PERSON) [Heb *šemʾēber*]: King of Zeboiim (Gen 14:2); appears simply as the "king of Zeboiim" in v 8. The form of the name ending in *dalet,* as in Sam. Pent. and 1QapGen, is preferable because it means "the name is lost" and belongs to the same type of pejorative names as those of the other kings who rebelled against Chedorlaomer. See also CHEDORLAOMER.

MICHAEL C. ASTOUR

SHEMED (PERSON) [Heb *šemed*]. A Benjaminite, one of the sons of Elpaal who along with Eber and Misham built Ono and Lod (1 Chr 8:12). Many Hebrew mss as well as the LXX, Syriac, and Targums read Shemer for Shemed. The similarity of the Heb *dalet* and *reš* make this a likely option; however, most translators and commentators read Shemed as the most difficult reading. Curtis and Madsen (*Chronicles* ICC, 160) suggested that v 12a, which lists the sons of Elpaal, is a transcriber's blunder since Elpaal's sons are also listed in vv 17–18. If the sons of Elpaal—Eber, Misham, and Shemed—were deleted from v 12a, this would make Elpaal the *one* who built the towns of Ono and Lod. Shemed would then be identified with Ishmerai (v 18).

TOM WAYNE WILLETT

SHEMER (PERSON) [Heb *šemer*]. Var. SHOMER. **1.** The original owner of the hill upon which Samaria was built and after which the city was named (1 Kgs 16:24). Gray (*1 and 2 Kings* OTL, 367) suggested that Shemer was the name of a tribe or clan since the hill was quite large and fertile and the name is of a segholate form. The OT, however, does not elsewhere mention a tribe by the name of Shemer, and Noth (*Könige* BKAT, 353) regarded the connection of Samaria to Shemer as a secondary explanatory gloss, *šōmĕrôn* being the original name of the hill. The name "Samaria" comes from the LXX.

2. A Levite of the clan of Merari (1 Chr 6:31—Eng 6:46). The name "Shemer" (in the pausal form *šāmer*) is found in a genealogical list tracing the ancestry of Ethan, a singer in the Jerusalem temple at the time of David (1 Chr 6:16–33—Eng 6:31–48).

3. A descendant of Asher (1 Chr 7:34). In 1 Chr 7:32 the name appears as Shomer *(šômēr)*; it is generally agreed, however, that it should be read as "Shemer" as in 7:34. The LXX tradition is mixed. Codex Vaticanus reads Shemer in both 7:32 and 7:34. Codex Alexandrinus, however, reads Shomer in both places. See also SHOMER.

Bibliography

Stade B. 1885. Miscellen 7. Der Name der Stadt Samarein und Seine Herkunft. *ZAW* 5: 165–75.

TOM WAYNE WILLETT

SHEMIDA (PERSON) [Heb *šĕmîdāʿ*]. SHEMIDAITE. Shemida's name occurs in three kinds of biblical texts that deal with the tribe of Manasseh: a military census [Num 26:32], a tribal allotment [Josh 17:2], and a genealogy [1 Chr 7:19]), as well as in the Samaria Ostraca. The name appears to derive from the Hebrew words "name" *(šēm)* and "know" *(yādaʿ)* and so may have meant "the Name (= God) knows," although alternative derivations have been proposed (Noth *IPN,* 28, 123; *IDB* 4:323).

Shemida's name first appears in the Bible in Num 26:32, which lists him as the fifth of Gilead's six sons and designates his descendants "Shemidaites." This verse is part of the Manassite section (26:28–34) of a military census. The text exhibits no interest in Shemida's descendants, but directs attention to those of Shemida's brother, Hepher, whose son, Zelophehad, had five daughters. This passage is often accepted as establishing the correct relationship of Shemida to the rest of the tribe of Manasseh (Rudolph *Chronikbücher* HAT, 69–70).

Joshua 17 deals with the allotment of tribal lands to the tribe of Manasseh. The passage notes that Machir was Manasseh's firstborn, that Gilead was the son of Machir, and that the regions of Gilead and Bashan were given to Gilead. Then, however, the passage reports that allotments were given to the rest of the tribe of Manasseh according to their families. The six families or clans (called "sons of Manasseh") that are named are: Abiezer, Helek, Asriel, Shechem, Hepher, and Shemida. It seems likely, therefore, that the writer believed that Manasseh had seven sons, of whom the first was Machir and the seventh Shemida. In addition, Joshua reverses the sequence of the names in Num 26:32 to "Hepher, Shemida." As was the case in Numbers 26, the interest in Joshua 17 is not with Shemida's descendants but with those of Hepher: Zelophehad and his five daughters (17:3–6).

Finally, Shemida is mentioned in 1 Chr 7:19, a genealogical fragment, whose relationship to the rest of the Manassite genealogy (7:14–18) is unclear. The verse records the names of Shemida and his four sons: Ahian, Shechem (the name of Shemida's brother in Num 26:31 and Josh 17:2), Likhi, and Aniam. The verse does not, however, link Shemida and his sons to the Manassites, who appear earlier in 1 Chronicles 7. Consequently, a variety of proposals have arisen in order to fit the verse (7:19) more coherently into its context (7:10–18). Curtis and Madsen (*Chronicles* ICC, 152), for example, have suggested that Shemida was the fourth son of Hammolecheth (7:18). Others, however, regard Shemida as the son of Gilead (cf. Num 26:30–32; Josh 17:1–3), and along the lines of this interpretation, Rudolph (HAT, 69–71) has undertaken a comprehensive emendation of the Manassite genealogy in 1 Chronicles 7 on the basis of Num 26:28-34.

The names of Shemida and other descendants of Manasseh occur in the Samaria Ostraca as clans or territories from which shipments of agricultural produce originated. These documents suggest that in the 8th century B.C.E. the names of Manassite clans (including Abiezer, Helek, Asriel, Shechem, Shemida, and Hepher), were still significant as designations of clan territories (Aharoni *LBHG,* 366–67) or administrative districts in Israel (Albright 1931: 249–51). While the biblical text does not specify the location of Shemida, Cross (1961: 12–14) has proposed that it was situated W of Samaria and N of the Wadi et-Tin.

Bibliography

Albright, W. F. 1931. The Site of Tirzah and the Topography of Western Manasseh. *JPOS* 11: 241–51.
Cross, F. M. 1961. Epigraphic Notes on Hebrew Documents of the Eighth–Sixth Centuries B.C.: I. A New Reading of a Place Name in the Samaria Ostraca. *BASOR* 163: 12–14.

M. PATRICK GRAHAM

SHEMIRAMOTH (PERSON) [Heb *šĕmîrāmôt*]. The name of two different persons mentioned in the OT.

1. One of the Levites of second rank appointed to provide music during David's second effort to move the ark to Jerusalem (1 Chr 15:18, 16:5). For further discussion, see ELIPHELEHU.

2. One of the Levites appointed by Jehoshaphat to teach the law in the cities of Judah (2 Chr 17:8). For teaching as a function of cultic personnel, see Lev 10:11; Deut 33:10; Jer 18:18; Mal 2:7; Hos 4:6; 2 Chr 15:3.

RAYMOND B. DILLARD

SHEMUEL (PERSON) [Heb *šĕmûʾēl*]. Two individuals mentioned in the Hebrew Bible bear this name.

Shemuel is a theophoric name, composed of the term *šm* and the divine element *ʾēl.* In the birth narrative of the prophet Samuel (although the Hebrew spelling of the prophet's name is identical to that of the individuals being discussed here, they should not be confused), Samuel is explained, in the Bible, as "requested from the Lord," or "dedicated to the Lord" (1 Sam 1:20, 27, 28). Many have noted that we should expect the name *šāʾûl* instead of Samuel, if the explanation in the Bible is to be followed, and have suggested that the authors have confused Samuel's birth narrative with that of Saul. The medieval Hebrew grammarian David Kimchi regarded Shemuel as a contraction of *šāʾûl mēʾēl,* "requested of God." Other possible explanations of Shemuel include "the *šēm* is *ʾēl,*" and "the son of El." Note that Shemuel is rendered as *samouēl* in the LXX.

Shemuel has cognates in other Semitic languages. In the Amorite personal names found in the Mari texts, one finds *sumu-la-ilu* and *sumu-li-ili* (*APNM,* 248–49), a Phoenician text has *lsmʾl,* and combinations of *śm* with theophoric elements appear in texts from Amarna and Alalakh, and in Ugaritic.

1. The son of Ammihud, leader of the tribe of Simon who was appointed to oversee the distribution of the land to the children of Israel (Num 34:20).

2. A leader of the clan of Tola of the tribe of Issachar (1 Chr 7:2).

RAPHAEL I. PANITZ

SHENAZZAR (PERSON) [Heb *šenʾaṣṣar*]. The name "Shenazzar" is held by only one person in the Hebrew Bible. In 1 Chr 3:18 Shenazzar is the name of the fourth son of Jehoiachin (= Jeconiah) who was exiled to Babylon by Nebuchadnezzar in 597 B.C. Albright argued that the name "Shenazzar" was one of two Hebrew variants of the Akkadian form *Sin-apla-uṣur* (May Sin protect the son). The other Hebrew variant, he argued, was Sheshbazzar (Ezra 1:8, 11; 5:14, 16). This led to the possibility that the two people who held these names were actually one and the same and that the first return from the Babylonian Exile was led by a descendant of David, Sheshbazzar, the "prince" of Judah.

It has recently been argued (Berger 1971: 98ff.), however, on the basis of an examination of the onomastic evidence, that the name "Sheshbazzar" can in no way be linked with the same Akkadian form which the name "Shenazzar" reflects, but must instead be the Hebrew form of the Akkadian name *shamash-ab(a)-uṣur* although spelled *shash(sh)u-ab-uṣur.* This means that the two names, and the people who held them, are no longer to be considered identical.

Bibliography

Albright, W. F. 1921. The Date and Personality of the Chronicler. *JBL* 40: 108–10.

Berger, P.-R. 1971. Zu den Namen *ššbṣr* und *šnʾṣr. ZAW* 83: 98–100.

RUSSELL FULLER

SHEOL [Heb *šĕʾôl*]. See DEAD, ABODE OF THE.

SHEPHAM (PLACE) [Heb *šĕpām*]. A place located near Riblah on the Upper Orontes, on the NE border of Canaan (Num 34:10–11). The site is completely unknown. Aharoni (*LBHG,* 67) suggests that it was on the SE edge of the Sea of Galilee; however, this would seem to be too far to the S for the description given in the book of Numbers.

SIDNIE ANN WHITE

SHEPHATIAH (PERSON) [Heb *šĕpaṭyāh, šĕpaṭyāhû*]. **1.** The fifth son born to King David at Hebron, by Abital (2 Sam 3:4; 1 Chr 3:3).

2. A Haruphite and one of the twenty-three Benjaminite warriors who joined David at Ziklag (1 Chr 12:6—Eng 12:5).

3. Son of Maacah and, according to 1 Chr 27:16, leader of the tribe of Simeon during the reign of King David.

4. A son of King Jehoshaphat (2 Chr 21:2). Together with five of his brothers, he inherited silver, gold, possessions, and fortified cities upon the death of his father, while the throne went to Jehoshaphat's eldest son, Jehoram. The Chronicler reports that after ascending the throne, Jehoram had his brothers executed (21:3–4).

5. Son of Mattan (Jer 38:1) and one of King Zedekiah's (597–586 B.C.E.) court officials (he was a *śar* [Jer 38:4], a term translated as "prince" in the RSV). During the Babylonian siege of Jerusalem, Shephathiah was one of four (three in the LXX) officials who, representing the pro-Egyptian faction in Judah, demanded that Zedekiah put the prophet Jeremiah to death because of the treasonable nature of his preaching. Jeremiah's message, which centered on the certain fall of Jerusalem and the necessity of submitting to the Babylonians, was demoralizing the Judean troops (lit. "weakening the hands" of those defending the city of Jerusalem; cf. the use of this expression in one of the ostraca [Ostracon 6] found at Lachish [see *ANET,* 322]). Zedekiah is portrayed as being powerless to resist his court official, and Jeremiah is cast into an empty cistern to die (38:2–6). He is later rescued when Ebed-melech acts on his behalf (38:7–13).

6. Founder of one of the lay families which returned with Zerubbabel from exile in Babylonia (Ezra 2:4; Neh 7:9; 1 Esdr 5:9). 372 (472 in 1 Esdr 5:9) members of this family are said to have returned at this time. A further 81 (71 in 1 Esdr 8:34) male members of the family accompanied Ezra (Ezra 8:8).

7. Ancestor of one of the families of "the sons of Solomon's servants" which returned from exile with Zerubbabel (Ezra 2:57; Neh 7:59). These families, the origin of which is uncertain (cf. however 1 Kgs 9:20–21; 2 Chr 8:7–8), are closely linked with the families of temple servitors in Ezra 2:58 and Neh 7:60, where the total number of temple servants and sons of Solomon's servants is reported to have been 392.

8. Father of Meshullam, head of one of the Benjaminites lay families which settled in Jerusalem following the exile (1 Chr 9:8). The Meshullam branch of the Benjaminite line is not mentioned in the similar list contained in Nehemiah 11.

9. Son of Mahalalel and ancestor of Athaiah, head of one of the Judahite lay families which resided in Jerusalem at the time of Nehemiah (Neh 11:4). The family belonged to the Perez line, of which 468 male descendants were reported to have been living in Jerusalem (11:6). The name of Shephatiah does not occur in the genealogy of the Perez line in 1 Chr 9:4.

Bibliography

Migsch, H. 1981. *Gottes Wort über das Ende Jerusalem.* ÖBS 2. Klosterneuburg.

Pohlmann, K.-F. 1978. *Studien zum Jeremiabuch.* FRLANT 118. Göttingen.

JOHN M. BERRIDGE

SHEPHELAH (PLACE) [Heb *šĕpēlâ*]. This regional name is mentioned 20 times in the Hebrew Bible (arguably 21 times if one includes Isa 32:19) where the vowels are slightly different. In all but two cases a region adjacent to the highlands of Judah is intended. It is difficult to translate this regional designation into a generic physiographic term, and it probably would be wise to leave it in a transliterated form, possibly with a qualifier (Judah or Israel) if that distinction is helpful to a reader. The Heb meaning conveys a meaning of lowness, and consequently some translators have referred to the Shephelah region as "lowlands." This "lowness" may, however, represent an ancient bias on the part of Judahites up on the plateau looking down on their own brethren. The area is certainly "lower" (with hills only ranging from 300 to 1300 feet in elevation) whereas the highlands of the plateau have elevations that can reach about 3300 feet. But a more precise physiographic term may be "foothills" or "piedmont." However, even these terms fail to convey the significance of the morphology of this region because the hilly parts of the Shephelah were largely unimportant, except as supply of wood ("as plentiful as the sycomore of the Shephelah" 1 Kgs 10:27). What did matter most about the Shephelah was a N-S valley separating it from the Judean highlands to the E. This valley was a natural moat that acted to isolate and defend the ramparts of Judah. What also mattered about the Shephelah were the E-W trending valleys that transected the foothills and led up to the Judean Plateau. These valleys were natural locations for walled cities because they were at the cross roads of easy transportation routes that led from the coastal plains to the highlands. In these valleys were located Gezer at the entrance to the Aijalon Valley, Beth-shemesh by the Sorek Valley, Azekah and Socoh at the Elah Valley, and Maresha and Lachish farther S in the wadis that led up to Hebron. Control of these routes and the cities that guarded them were critical to the defense of Judah, and equally vital to any nation that wanted dominance over the adjacent coastal plains and its coastal highway. Throughout biblical history (and even into modern times), the Shephelah has been of strategic military significance. An authoritative and comprehensive study of the history of this region during biblical times can be found in a paper by Rainey (1983). An interpretative geographic study of this region can be found in a paper written by Brodsky (1987).

The Shephelah of Judah appears as one of four administrative subdivisions of the territory of Judah (Deut 1:7–8; Josh 10:40; 11:16a; 12:8; Judg 1:9). The identification of the settlements listed in Josh 15:33–34 aid in the exact delineation of the boundaries of the Shephelah. The boundary with the Negeb in the S may perhaps be located in a narrow pass N of Tel Halif. The N boundary was around Gezer and Gimzo. In all, the Shephelah of Judah is no more than about 10 miles wide and about 50 miles long along the NE-SW axis of the Judean plateau. Consequently, the importance of the Shephelah throughout history is largely as a transition zone between the coastal plain to the W, and to the Judean highlands to the E.

In two biblical passages the term "Shephelah" refers to the "Shephelah of Israel": Joshua 11:1–3, and in the second use of the Hebrew word in Joshua 11:16.

Some scholars have placed the N "Shephelah of Israel" in the hilly region between the mountains of Samaria and the coastal plain of the Sharon. But this region is not at all physiographically similar to the Shephelah of Judah. A widely accepted location of the Shephelah of Israel, suggested originally by G. A. Smith, is the low hills that lie between the Samarian hill country and the Carmel range, known today as Ramot Manasseh. However, this location is sandwiched between two mountain ridges whereas the Judean Shephelah lies between the mountains and the coastal plains. Finkelstein (1981) offers another possibility: the N-S foothills of W Galilee extending up to the coastal plain of Tyre in S Lebanon. See GALILEE (PREHELLENISTIC). Here a Shephelah-like physiography lies between mountains and coastal plain. Finkelstein further suggests that this region was well recognized throughout history as distinctive, and consequently was used extensively for administrative purposes, especially during the 19th century, and during Crusader times. He also finds evidence that during talmudic times the "Shephelah of Galilee" was differentiated as a "Land of Gentiles," while the mountains to the E were included in the "Land of Israel." Still earlier in history, the border between the tribes of Asher and Naphtali (Josh 19:24–40) may have corresponded to this morphological division: Asher in the Shephelah and coastal plains, and Naphtali in the mountains. Apparently only in modern times has this physiographic region failed to serve as a basis for a political-administrative subdivision.

Bibliography

Brodsky, H. 1987. Bible Lands: The Shephelah-Guardian of Judea. *BRev* 3/4: 48–52.

Finkelstein, I. 1981. The Shephelah of Israel. *TA* 8: 84–94.

Rainey, A. F. 1983. The Biblical Shephelah of Judah. *BASOR* 251: 1–22.

HAROLD BRODSKY

SHEPHER, MOUNT (PLACE) [Heb *har-šeper*]. One of the camping sites of the Israelites as they journeyed through the wilderness (Num 33:23, 24). Its exact location is unknown, as are the locations of most of these sites. Noth (*Numbers* OTL) suggests that it is part of a "document" of the wilderness camping sites used by the Priestly writer.

SIDNIE ANN WHITE

SHEPHERD. See SHEEP, SHEPHERD.

SHEPHERD OF HERMAS. See HERMAS' THE SHEPHERD.

SHEPHO (PERSON) [Heb *šĕpô*]. Var. SHEPHI. A clan name in the genealogy of Seir the Horite in Gen 36:23. Shepho is listed as the fourth of five sons of the clan chief Shobal, and is thus a grandson of Seir. The name also appears in the parallel genealogy in 1 Chr 1:40. However, it is written Shephi (Heb *šĕpî*). As Horwitz (1973: 70) notes, this may be due to a confusion between the letters *waw* and *yod.* These Horite clans are not to be confused with the

Hurrians of Mesopotamia. They were the original inhabitants of the region of Edom (perhaps as cave dwellers), but they eventually lost control of the area to the encroaching "sons of Esau" (Deut 2:12–22). This conquest of the Horites is paired in the text with the conquest of Canaan by the tribes of Israel.

Bibliography

Horwitz, W. J. 1973. Were There Twelve Horite Tribes? *CBQ* 35: 69–71.

VICTOR H. MATTHEWS

SHEPHUPHAM (PERSON) [Heb *šĕpûpām*]. Var. SHEPHUPHAN. SHUPHAMITES. The fourth of Benjamin's five sons (Num 26:38–40). Although the name "Shephupham" occurs in only one of the Benjaminite genealogies (Num 26:39), what may be corrupt forms of the name are also present in the other genealogies for the tribe (Muppim, Gen 46:21; Shuppim, 1 Chr 7:12, 15; Shephuphan, 1 Chr 8:5). In addition, the name "Shephupham" and its variants usually occur in the company of similar names, which may be variants of a single name, as well: Huppim (Gen 46:21; 1 Chr 7:12, 15), Hupham (Num 26:39), and Huram (1 Chr 8:5). There are numerous differences, however, among these Benjaminite genealogies, and there is no consensus among scholars about which should be used to correct the others. Among the reconstructions that have been proposed, however, Rudolph's preference for that in Numbers 26 (*Chronikbücher* HAT, 70–71) has won much, though not universal, support.

Gen 46:8–27 lists the descendants of Jacob who entered Egypt. In v 21, the MT gives Benjamin ten sons, one of whom was Muppim. The LXX, however, gives Benjamin only three sons, but adds six grandsons, one of whom was Mamphin, and one great-grandson. It may be that Muppim/Mamphin is a corrupted form of Shephupham (Westermann 1986: 153). Commentators usually note that according to Genesis, Benjamin was only about 25 years old at the time that he and his family entered Egypt (cf. Gen 35:16–19; 41: 46, 53; 45:6)—rather young to have had ten sons (or the great-grandson that one finds in the LXX; Westermann 1986: 160). In addition, the MT of Gen 46:21 is incongruent with the list of Benjamin's descendants in Num 26:38–40; the MT of Numbers 26 assigns him five sons (Bela, Ashbel, Ahiram, Shephupham, and Hupham) and two grandsons (Ard and Naaman) through Bela. The LXX of Numbers 26:42–44 omits Hupham from the list and gives variant spellings for each of the other names.

1 Chr 7:6–12 provides a third list of Benjamin's descendants and lists Bela, Becher, and Jediael as the patriarch's three sons. The firstborn (Bela) had five sons (v 7): Ezbon, Uzzi, Uzziel, Jerimoth, and Iri (or Ir, v 12). Iri, in turn, had two sons, Shuppim and Huppim. It may be that the text or tradition of this Benjaminite genealogy is corrupt and this Shuppim was the same person as the Shephupham of Num 26:39. Curtis and Madsen (*Chronicles* ICC, 145–49) proposed that since 1 Chr 7:6–11 is so strikingly different from the Benjaminite genealogy in Numbers 26, it was originally a genealogy for the tribe of Zebulun, and v 12 was a genealogy for Dan. In addition, there is already a genealogy for Benjamin in 1 Chronicles 8 but none in 1 Chronicles 1–9 for Zebulun. However, this suggestion has won little support, since most scholars find it easier to attribute the differences between the two (Benjaminite) genealogies to textual corruption or to intentional changes by those who transmitted the genealogical material (Braun *1 Chronicles* WBC, 106–9).

In 1 Chr 7:15, it is reported that Manasseh's son Machir "took a wife for Huppim and Shuppim." The identity of Shuppim, however, is unclear. Was he a Benjaminite, perhaps the same Shuppim that was met in 1 Chr 7:12, or perhaps his name is a corrupted form of Shephupham (Num 26:39)? Or was he a Manassite, possibly the son of Machir? The LXX, at any rate, gives his name as Mamphin, the same form that occurs in Gen 46:21, where the MT reads Muppim. The genealogy for Manasseh in 1 Chr 7:14–19 presents a number of complex problems which have not been resolved to the satisfaction of most scholars, and so it appears that the identity of Shuppim will remain unknown. The same name occurs in 1 Chr 26:16, where it is reported that when lots were cast to assign the various gatekeepers their posts in Jerusalem, two of the Levites, Shuppim and Hosah, were given charge of Shallecheth, a gate on the W.

Another genealogy for the tribe of Benjamin occurs in 1 Chronicles 8. Among the names there is Shephuphan (v 5), one of the nine sons of Bela the son of Benjamin. This may also be a corrupted form for Shephupham, as the Targum and some Hebrew mss indicate by reading Shephupham.

Therefore, two points remain uncertain: (1) the relationship among the names "Shephupham," "Muppim," "Shuppim," and "Shephuphan" and (2) their relationship(s) to the patriarch Benjamin.

Bibliography

Westermann, C. 1986. *Genesis 37–50*. Minneapolis.

M. PATRICK GRAHAM

SHERD. See POTTERY.

SHEREBIAH (PERSON) [Heb *šērēbyāh*]. The name of several individuals, in which the theophoric element *yāh* is added to a form of *šrb*. Several explanations or derivations of the name have been proposed. Noth (*IPN*, 259) believes it to be a *Piʿel* perfect of a verb *šrb* whose meaning is unknown. A verb stem meaning "parch" is, according to BDB, 1055 and KB, 1010, attested in post-biblical Hebrew, Aramaic, and Syriac. A Heb noun, *šārāb*, is found in Isa 35:7 and 49:10 (where Caspari 1931: 81 believes it refers to a demon) and conveys the sense of "heat." Zadok (*EncMiqr* 8:259) suggests a West Semitic root *šrb* meaning, perhaps, "to go before," and in Piel "to send." The Ar *sariba* carries similar meanings—"flow, run" and "send in groups." (Zadok's bibliography suggests several derivation possibilities.) Combinations of the above have suggested to many "Yahweh has sent burning heat" as a translation of the name. Robinson (1868: 42) points to the Ar *serāb* as denoting a "mirage." Clay (1904: 53) notices the name's similarity to a personal name *Ish-ri-bi-Ia-a-ma* found on a 5th century B.C. cuneiform text from Nippur. The use of the name to refer to family and to individual persons makes it difficult to determine from its eight occurrences in the Hebrew Bible the number of people who bear it. Opperwall (*ISBE* 4:474) is correct in observing the name may be of one, two, or three individuals.

1. One of those (Ezra 8:18) who, with his sons and brothers, was sent by Iddo to Ezra in response to a request for "ministers *(mĕšartîm)* for the house of our God" (v 17) to return from Babylon (v 1) to Jerusalem (v 31) with him. The LXX omits his name reading instead *kai archēn* (a corruption, suggests Bewer [1922: 76], of *kai Sarcheia* = Heb *wšrkyh) ēlthosan.* If the *waw* preceding his name in the MT is an explicative (Rudolph *Esra und Nehemia* HAT, 81; Clines *Ezra Nehemiah, and Esther* NCBC, 110; Williamson *Ezra, Nehemiah* WBC, 113) and is to be rendered "namely," or if, as in 1 Esdr 8:46—Eng 8:47 (where the name is *Asebēbian*), the copula is to be dropped (Bertholet *Esra und Nehemia* HKAT, 36; Bewer 1922: 72), then this Sherebiah is the one "from the sons of Mahli, son of Levi, son of Israel (instead of *bn-yśrʾl* Batten *Ezra and Nehemiah* ICC, reads *brʾšwn* "at the head")—"the man of discretion *(ʾîš śekel).*" If the *waw* preceding the name is a simple conjunction ("and"), the "man of discretion" remains unnamed or is itself the proper name of the Levite (Bertholet, 36; cf. Gunneweg *Esra* KAT, 148).

According to Ezra 8:24, a Sherebiah is one of those among the priests and Levites (v 30) charged by Ezra with conveying "the offering *(tĕrûmāh)* of the house of our God" (v 25) from Babylon to Jerusalem (v 30). The MT places *lĕ* before his name either as a sign of the dative (LXX *tǭ Saraia*) (cf. Bertheau *Esra, Nechemia und Ester* EHAT, 106)—thus Ezra separated twelve leading priests and assigned them to Sherebiah—or as "an error but not accidental" to avoid stating that Sherebiah and Hashabiah were priests (Batten, 328). It is easier to read, with 1 Esdr 8:54 *(kai Eserebian),* the conjunction *we* ("and," "in addition to") before his name (Myers *Ezra-Nehemiah* AB, 65; Williamson, 114; Blenkinsopp *Ezra-Nehemiah* OTL, 168). This would allow for a team of twelve priests and twelve Levites (Bertholet, 37; Blenkinsopp, 169) to perform the assigned task.

It is reasonable to conclude that this Sherebiah who, along with Hashabiah, is charged with bringing the offering to Jerusalem is the same Sherebiah (v 18) who, along with Hashabiah, returns to Jerusalem with Ezra. That he was a Levite is most certain.

2. The third listed of thirteen (Neh 8:7) who "read from the book, from the Torah of God" (v 8). In the LXX only the first three of these names—Jeshua, Bani, and Sherebiah *(Sarabia)*—are recorded and there is no mention of Levites who, in the MT, are represented as "and the Levites *(wĕhalwiyyîm).*" Perhaps the *waw* was affixed by a scribe who took *hlwym* to be the last proper name in the list (Williamson, 278) or by the Chronicler whose partiality for the Levites caused him to add the word (Bertholet, 69) or the entire verse (Rudolph, 147). In 1 Esdr 9:48 (where the name is *Sarabias*), this conjunction is missing. Holmgren (1987: 124) believes the Levites' participation combined the functions of interpretation and translation. Their activity during this liturgical event has been variously explained depending on the interpretation given the verbs in v 8b (see Clines, 184–85 and Blenkinsopp, 288).

According to Neh 9:4, Sherebiah (LXX Codex Vaticanus *Sarabia,* Sinaiticus *Saradia,* Alexandrinus *Sachania* [= Heb *šĕkanyāh*]) was the sixth listed of eight who "stood on the platform of the Levites" and "cried *(wayyizʿăqû)* with a loud voice to the Lord their God." The verb *zʿq,* suggests Williamson (p. 311), refers to a public expression of grief.

In Neh 9:5, Sherebiah (absent from LXX) is the fifth listed of eight Levites who invite the assembly to "stand up, bless the Lord your God," and then intone the prayer psalm (Myers, 166–70). Blenkinsopp (p. 296) and Clines (p. 191) believe the groups in v 4 and v 5 are identical, the differences in lists being attributable to text transmission. Brockington (*Ezra, Nehemia and Esther* Century Bible, 171) disagrees, holding that if they were the same, there would be no need of both.

In Neh 10:13—Eng 10:12, Sherebiah (LXX Codex Vaticanus *Zarabia,* Alexandrinus and the corrector of Sinaiticus *Sarabia,* Sinaiticus *Zatharia*) is listed thirteenth of seventeen (or fifteen if the repetition of Shebaniah and Hodiah are due to scribal error [Blenkinsopp, 313]) levitical signatories of the "firm covenant *(ʾămānā)* made by the community (10:1—Eng 9:38). Brockington (p. 101) suggests Sherebiah is here a family name while Blenkinsopp (p. 313) believes only the first three names are patronymics, the rest appearing to be personal names.

Blenkinsopp's (p. 313) observation that seven, including Sherebiah, of the thirteen in Neh 8:7 and seven or eight, including Sherebiah, of the sixteen in Neh 9:4–5 are listed in Neh 10:10–14—Eng 9–13 lead to the conclusion that the same Sherebiah is meant in all four occurrences. The mention of Hashabiah in 10:12—Eng 10:11 suggests an identity with #1 above (Clines, 203).

3. The fourth listed (Neh 12:8) of eight Levites who returned from exile with Zerubbabel and Jeshua (v 1). Clines (p. 224) discounts the belief that Sherebiah (LXX *Sarabia*) and Judah are here family heads and suggests that Sherebiah was "erroneously introduced into that period from the time of Ezra (Neh 8:7; 9:4f) and Nehemiah (10:12; 12:24)." Myers (p. 196) and Brockington (p. 101) believe this name is a family name while Blenkinsopp (p. 335) believes these names are all patronymics serving here as personal names.

In Neh 12:24 Sherebiah (LXX *Sarabia*) is the second listed of three (or five depending on the reading of the Heb *Vorlage* behind the LXX "and the sons of Kadmiel" as "Binnui/Bani, Kadmiel"—a proposal made by Rudolph, 194; Williamson, 357–358) "heads of the Levites." The list (see Williamson, 361 for an explanation of the literary development of vv 1–26 of which vv 23a, 24–25 is a "list of Levitical heads of families from the time of Johanan") intends to represent the circumstances during the time of Joiakim, Nehemiah, and Ezra (v 26), an improbable combination, suggests Myers (p. 199), since Eliashib was high priest in Nehemiah's time and, suggests Blenkinsopp (p. 335), since Joiakim antedated Ezra (and therefore Sherebiah and Hashabiah).

It is possible, although not clear, that this Sherebiah, a Levite associated with Hashabiah, was identical with #1 above (Williamson, 359).

Bibliography

Bewer, J. A. 1922. *Der Text des Buches Ezra.* Göttingen.
Caspari, W. 1931. Jesaja 34 und 35. *ZAW* 49: 67–86.

Clay, A. T. 1904. *Business Documents of Murashû Sons of Nippur.* Philadelphia.
Holmgren, F. C. 1987. *Israel Alive Again: A Commentary on the Books of Ezra and Nehemiah.* International Theological Commentary. Grand Rapids, MI.
Robinson, E. 1868. *Biblical Researches in Palestine and in the Adjacent Regions.* Vol. 1. Boston.

RODNEY H. SHEARER

SHERESH (PERSON) [Heb *šereš* or *šāreš*]. The Manassite son of Machir and his wife Maacah (1 Chr 7:16), whose name probably meant "clever" or "cunning" (Noth *IPN,* 228). The genealogy of Manasseh in 1 Chr 7:14–19 indicates that his brothers were Peresh and Gilead, and perhaps Huppim and Shuppim as well. In addition, Sheresh had two sons, Ulam and Rakem, although the LXX omits the name of the second (1 Chr 7:16–17). No other biblical text mentions Sheresh.

There are two problems in 1 Chr 7:14–19 that affect the identification of Sheresh. First, Maacah, the mother of Sheresh, is called the wife of Machir in v 16, but his sister in v 15. Moreover, v 14 indicates that Gilead was the brother of Sheresh, but v 17 includes him among the "sons of Gilead." Curtis and Madsen (*Chronicles* ICC, 151–52) attempted to resolve these difficulties by emending "Machir" to "Gilead" (v 16). This made Maacah the sister of Machir and the wife of Gilead (as well as his aunt), and consequently, Sheresh's father was Gilead, rather than Machir. Furthermore, they proposed that the names of Shuppim and Huppim (v 15) were glosses from v 12 (the genealogy of Naphtali) and so could not have been the brothers of Sheresh.

Rudolph (*Chronikbücher* HAT, 68–71), however, has attempted to resolve the difficulties in 1 Chr 7:14–19 by emending the text on the basis of Num 26:29–34. His reconstruction makes Maacah the daughter of Gilead and the mother of Sheresh. The name of Maacah's husband is missing, since it was elided in the course of transmission. Rudolph's suggestions have won more support than those of Curtis and Madsen, but neither has been found completely convincing by interpreters.

M. PATRICK GRAHAM

SHESHAI (PERSON) [Heb *šēšay*]. One of three Anakite clans inhabiting Hebron visited by the twelve Israelite spies (Num 13:22), later driven out of their city by Caleb (Josh 15:14; Judg 1:10). The name is patronymic, i.e., it probably refers to the founder of the tribe rather than to a chieftain of the clan or an individual person living at the time. Although the name has been derived from Hurrian (Blenkinsopp 1972: 18, 113), or as a reduplicated *šin* representing a more complete name (Noth *IPN,* 41), it occurs in Egypt as the name of a Hyksos ruler (Albright *YGC,* 153). Boling and Wright (*Joshua* AB, 374) suggest they were a "pre-Philistine" Sea People who were driven out of the S hill country by the Israelites (Josh 11:21–22).

Bibliography

Blenkinsopp, J. 1972. *Gibeon and Israel.* SOTSMS 2. Cambridge.

KIRK E. LOWERY

SHESHAN (PERSON) [Heb *šēšān*]. A descendant of Judah through Jerahmeel; he is the son of Ishi and father of Ahlai (1 Chr 2:31). However, while v 31 indicates that the son of Sheshan was Ahlai, v 34 states that Sheshan had no sons, only daughters, and gave his daughter to an Egyptian slave Jarha. The identity of Sheshan's issue is a complex and unsolved problem. Several suggestions are possible: (1) v 31 should be read Attai as in v 36; (2) Ahlai (if modified to mean "a brother to me") was a name given to Jarha at the time of his adoption into the family of Sheshan; (3) Ahlai was a son of Sheshan but one born after the marriage of his daughter (however, note v 34); or (4) different sources are reflected in this genealogy. See Williamson (1979: 352) for a recent discussion of sources in this genealogy and the conclusion that 2:25–33 and 42–50a stand as a related unit but that v 34 reflects a different source. See also Curtis and Madsen (*Chronicles* ICC, 83) for an analysis of older, but still debated, theories of genealogical sources. The wording of v 35 "So Sheshan gave his daughter in marriage to Jarha his slave . . ." is considered by some commentators as equivalent to making his servant his heir (Elmslie *Chronicles* CBC, 19), similar to Eliezer's relationship to Abraham (Gen 15:2–3). See also ADOPTION. Some scholars regarded Jarha as an eponymn of Jerahmeel and proceeded to identify Sheshan with Sheshai of Hebron concluding that the genealogy presents a northward movement of this tribe to the area around Hebron.

Locating Sheshan chronologically is difficult. This tenth generation from Judah is often placed shortly before the Exodus (Keil 1872: 67), or in the days of Eli, or nearer the Chronicler's own time (see Braun *1 Chronicles* WBC, 46). Lacking sufficient evidence the question must remain open.

Variant spellings of Sheshan are found in the LXX (A reads *Sōsan,* Lucian reads *Sisan,* and B reads *Sōsam* in v 34). Many scholars consider those genealogies in the LXX corrupt (especially codex Vaticanus), however the genealogies of Jerahmeel in the MT are viewed by most contemporary scholars as being in good order.

The meaning of the name "Sheshan" is obscure although many, such as Mauch (*IDB* 4: 326), follow suggestions of Noth and others that Sheshan is a duplication of an abbreviation expressing endearment (*IPN,* 40–41).

Bibliography

Keil, C. F. 1872. *The Books of Chronicles.* Vol. 3 of *Commentary on the Old Testament.* Grand Rapids. Repr. 1978.
Williamson, H. G. M. 1979. Sources and Redaction in the Chronicler's Genealogy of Judah. *JBL* 98: 351–59.

W. P. STEEGER

SHESHBAZZAR (PERSON) [Heb *šešbaṣṣar*]. A leading Babylonian Jew, "a prince of Judah" (Ezra 1:8), who was commissioned by Cyrus to return the temple vessels to Jerusalem in 538 B.C.E. (Ezra 1:8–11) and a governor responsible for laying the temple foundations (Ezra 5:14–17). As the first Judean governor after the Babylonian exile, Sheshbazzar ushers in a new mode of leadership in an age without monarchy and self-determination. Yet nothing more is known about him. This ephemeral Sheshbazzar, who appears in only these two places, has been the subject of much controversy. His name, identity, role, and activities have all been debated. The ancient sources reflect some confusion concerning Sheshbazzar. 1 Esdras refers to him as Sanabassar, whereas the LXX retains Sasabasar. Josephus equates Sheshbazzar with Shethar-bozenai of Ezra 5:6, and hence considers him a Persian official of foreign origin (*Ant* 11.4 §6). The rabbinic sages equate him with Daniel.

Modern scholars have often identified Sheshbazzar, on the one hand, with Shenazzar of 1 Chr 3:18 and, on the other, with Zerubbabel. Both identifications, however, have recently lost their force. The equation with Shenazzar, son of Jeconiah, grew out of the similarity of the names and Sheshbazzar's titles. The designations "prince of Judah" and "governor" indicate an important personage who would most likely be a Davidic heir; Shenazzar was a Davidic descendant. To some extent, this identification, harks back to an era when continuity between Ezra-Nehemiah and Chronicles was presumed. It may also reflect scholarly discomfort with the fact that the literature is largely silent about so important a figure as the first Judean governor. Although more common a generation ago, this identification has been recently discredited on linguistic grounds (Berger 1971) and proved less compelling with the discovery of several other postexilic Judean governors, some with no clear Davidic ancestry.

The identification of Sheshbazzar with Zerubbabel grew out of a discrepancy among the accounts of temple founding and represents scholars' attempts to reconcile these accounts. Haggai and Zechariah emphatically assert that Zerubbabel was a governor and credit him with laying the temple's foundations in 520 B.C.E. They present this founding as a new and unprecedented act. Ezra-Nehemiah is inconsistent. The narrative first attributes the laying of the foundations to the community as a whole, led by Zerubbabel and Jeshua (Ezra 3:8–13). The later report to the Persian officials at the time of Darius, however (Ezra 5:14–17), claims that Sheshbazzar, whom Cyrus appointed governor, had earlier laid the foundations. The report asserts that the present builders (who, according to Ezra 5:1–2, have been exhorted to build by Haggai and Zechariah) merely continue what had already begun by Sheshbazzar. If Zerubbabel and Sheshbazzar were the same person, some of the contradictions could be eliminated and the mystery of Sheshbazzar's ancestry would be resolved. It has therefore been proposed that Zerubbabel and Sheshbazzar are two different names for the same person, as often happens in the postexilic era (note Daniel's second name). Zerubbabel is thus the governor to whom Cyrus delivers the vessels; he is also, according to this view, the prince of Judah, who laid the foundations according to both Haggai and Zechariah and Ezra-Nehemiah. As a Davidic descendant, he is eminently suitable for such a role.

This view has been discredited as well (Ben Yashar 1981). Scholars now recognize that biblical sources only partially reflect the rich complexities of the postexilic era. Sheshbazzar is no longer the only postexilic governor whose memory has not been adequately preserved. Archeology has identified several such governors (see below). Moreover, equating Sheshbazzar and Zerubbabel does not wholly eliminate the discrepancies: Ezra-Nehemiah still describes two stages that do not directly conform to Haggai and Zechariah. Ezra-Nehemiah maintains that Haggai and Zechariah appear at a later stage of the building process (Ezra 5:1), after the foundations have been set (Ezra 3:8–13). Haggai and Zechariah imply that the events of 520 were brand new, that Haggai has stirred up Zerubbabel, who then proceeded to found the temple. As to the names, although double names are common in the postexilic era, they typically include one Hebrew name and one foreign. Sheshbazzar and Zerubbabel, however, are both Babylonian names. See also Japhet 1982.

The reconstruction of the history of Sheshbazzar, his role in the postexilic era, and his relation to Zerubbabel are best understood as follows: Sheshbazzar has been appointed governor by Cyrus and sent to Jerusalem with the temple vessels. The precise authority of such an appointment and the nature of the Judean province at the time are not clear. Eber Nahara, the Persian name for the larger province of which Judah would have been a part, had undergone administrative reorganization between the time of Cyrus and the stabilization under Darius. Although Sheshbazzar could have been from the house of David, he need not have been. Ezra-Nehemiah's silence about Sheshbazzar's patronym could be either a deliberate attempt to supress Davidic origins (in light of Ezra-Nehemiah's general tendency to defuse the role of the house of David) or a sign that Sheshbazzar's ancestry had been forgotten by the time when Ezra-Nehemiah was written. The title "prince of Judah" obviously indicates a leader but need not designate royalty. Blenkinsopp (*Ezra-Nehemiah* OTL) observes that "prince" is used in Chronicles for a tribal head (e.g. 1 Chr 2:10) or the head of an ancestral house (e.g., 2 Chr 1:2). Williamson (*Ezra, Nehemiah* WBC) links it with other pentateuchal occurrences (e.g., Num 2:3–31) which could echo the exodus motif. In either case, the term does not possess the royal connotations that it has in Ezekiel 40–48 and hence removes the need to assign Davidic origin to Sheshbazzar.

As to the question "Who, then, laid the temple foundations?," the answer is that both Sheshbazzar and Zerubbabel did so at different times and probably to a different extent. Sheshbazzar, as the first governor, began the process. Leading the first return, he must have encountered many obstacles: financial problems because the Persian empire had not yet been well organized fiscally (Meyers *Haggai, Zechariah* AB, xxxiv), harassment by neighbors depicted in Ezra 4, and apathy of the returnees themselves, alluded to in Haggai, all very likely played a role; they contributed to the cessation of building efforts. Such efforts were renewed with the second wave of return during Darius's reign (520), led by Zerubabbel and Jeshua, as reported in Ezra 3. At such time Haggai prompts Zerubbabel to being once more what proves to be the successful founding and completion of the temple.

Ezra-Nehemiah, for its own purpose of emphasizing continuity, combines the first and second return, implying that the journey of Sheshbazzar (Ezra 1:11) is identical with the one in Ezra 2. Indeed, it may be for this reason that Ezra 2:1 names only eleven men at the head of the caravan; Sheshbazzar completes the twelve that symbolically represent the reconstituted Israel.

It should not be surprising that Ezra-Nehemiah, Haggai,

and Zechariah perceive the founding of the temple differently and offer contradictory accounts. Each text presents a distinctive ideology, not simply all the facts that are in its disposal. Ezra-Nehemiah, especially in the report to the Persians who inquire about authority for such building, seeks to emphasize continuity. Practical considerations support its theological stance that all the stages of the building were in essence a single unified response to Cyrus' edict. Haggai and Zechariah, however, prefer to emphasize the newness of the venture, a perspective that is understandable if earlier building efforts were skimpy. As for the ephemeral identity of the governor Sheshbazzar, it has become apparent that other Judean governors have been even more ephemeral since biblical literature does not even mention them. Archeologists have helped reconstruct a plausible list of governors, even as they recognize that the scope of authority granted such persons in the Persian province of Judah is unclear. Sheshbazzar is the first of several governors of Judah, only three of whom (Sheshbazzar, Zerubbabel, and Nehemiah) appear in the Bible. At present a cachet of jar handles and seals have helped construct the following list of governors from Sheshbazzar to Nehemiah: Sheshbazzar (538); Zerubbabel (520–510?); Elnathan (510–490?); Yehoezer (490–470?); Ahzai (470–); Nehemiah (445–433) (see Meyers, 14). Later governors have been preserved in documents such as the Aramaic Papyri from Elephantine. See also Cline *Ezra, Nehemiah, Esther* NCBC.

The silence surrounding the activities and fate of such an important leader as the first Judean governor points to the complexity of the era for which the biblical sources constitute but the tip of the iceberg.

Bibliography

Ben Yashar, M. 1981. On the Problem of Sheshbazzar and Zerubbabel. *Beth Mikra* 27: 46–56 (in Hebrew).

Berger, P.-R. 1971. Zu den Namen *ssbsr* un *sin sr. ZAW* 95: 111–12.

Japhet, S. 1982. Sheshbazzar and Zerubbabel—Against the Background of the Historical and Religious Tendencies of Ezra-Nehemiah. *ZAW* 94: 66–98.

TAMARA C. ESKENAZI

SHETH (PERSON) [Heb *šēt*]. The more phonologically correct name for Seth, the son of Adam. See also SETH. The name is rendered "Sheth" by the KJV at 1 Chr 1:1 and by both the KJV and RSV at Num 24:17. According to Num 24:17, Sheth is the eponymous ancestor of the Moabites against whose descendants Balaam issues his final curse:

> A star shall come forth out of Jacob,
> and a scepter shall rise out of Israel.
> It shall crush the forehead of Moab
> and break down [*qarqar*] all the sons of Sheth.

This text, however, presents several problems, the first of which is textual. A similar ancient ballad is recorded in Num 21:28:

> For fire went forth from Heshbon,
> flame from the city of Sihon.
> It devoured Ar of Moab,
> the lords of the heights of the Arnon.

Owing to their similarity, these two songs were conflated by the oracle against Moab in Jer 48:45, which coupled the first bicolon of Num 21:28 with the second bicolon of Num 24:17, yielding the following mixed reading:

> For a fire has gone forth from Heshbon,
> a flame from the house of Sihon.
> It has destroyed the forehead of Moab,
> the crown [*qodqod*] of the sons of tumult [*šāʾôn*].

The similarities between Num 24:17bβ and Jer 48:45bβ have led many scholars (e.g., Budd *Numbers* WBC, 253) to reconstruct the former text along the lines of the latter. As such, Sheth is read as the noun *šāʾôn,* "strife." Others suggest reading it alternatively as *šēʾt* ("devastation") as at Lam 3:47.

The second question relates to whether or not Israelite tradition understood Adam's son Sheth to be the eponymous ancestor of the nation of Moab. The major tradition, to the contrary, states that the Moabites owe their name to Lot's son Moab, whom Lot fathered by his elder daughter (Gen 19:30–38). The LXX of Gen 19:37 stresses the etymological nature of the story by adding to the phrase "and called his name Moab" the note *legousa ek tou patros mou* ("saying, 'from my father' "). In so doing the LXX clearly understood the etymology of "Moab" to be from Heb *mēʾābi.* This patronymic connection of Moab with Lot is further attested by the note in Deut 2:9 that Ar (i.e., Moab; cf. Num 21:28) had been given to the sons of Lot for a possession.

Third, there is the problem of the suitability of the figure of Sheth to serve as an eponymous ancestor at all. Since every one of the postdeluvial nations was traced back to Sheth (Gen 5:1–32; 10:2–32), it is highly unlikely that Israelite tradition would have made him the eponym of any single nation, such as of Moab. Because of the unsuitability of using Seth as an eponym for any nation, and because that function was fulfilled by Lot and his son, it seems best, therefore, to emend the reading of *šēt* in Num 24:17 to conform more closely to the later tradition in Jer 48:45 or Lam 3:47 as proposed by critical scholarship.

ROD R. HUTTON

SHETHAR (PERSON) [Heb *šētār*]. One of the seven princes of Persia and Media who were the advisers of King Ahaseuros (Esth 1:14). These men were the most prominent at the court (lit. "sat first in the kingdom") and had the privilege of personal audience with the king (lit. "saw the king's face"). That such a council of seven prominent nobles customarily advised the Persian monarch is well known from extrabiblical sources (for references see Paton *Esther* ICC, 153 and esp. Hayden in *ISBE* 3: 971). Although the presumption that the names of these counselors are Persian is reasonable (see the arguments of Millard 1977, who counters the excessive caution of Moore *Esther* AB, XLI–XLIV regarding the reliability of the MT spellings), no name equivalent to this has thus far been found in the extant extrabiblical literature. Recently, however, on the basis of the Aramaic transcription of Old Persian vocables at Persepolis (see Bowman 1970: 64–65), Millard has plausibly suggested an etymology from Old Persian *cica* "bright" (1977: 485). See also Paton *Esther* ICC, 68 and Gehman 1924: 324.

Bibliography

Bowman, R. A. 1970. *Aramaic Ritual Texts from Persepolis.* OIP 21. Chicago.

Gehman, H. S. 1924. Notes on the Persian Words in the Book of Esther. *JBL* 43: 321–28.

Millard, A. R. 1977. The Persian Names in Esther and the Reliability of the Hebrew Text. *JBL* 96: 481–88.

FREDERIC W. BUSH

SHETHAR-BOZENAI (PERSON) [Aram *šětar bôzěnay*]. Var. SATHRABUZANES. Persian official named in conjunction with Tattenai as co-senders of correspondence to Darius I (ruled 521–486 B.C.E.) informing the king of building activity in Jerusalem (Ezra 5:3, 6; 6:6, 13 = 1 Esdr 6:3, 7, 27; 7:1). 1 Esdras renders the name Sathrabuzanes (Gk *Sathrabouzanēs*). The texts are unclear as to the position Shethar-bozenai holds, unlike the mention of Shimshai in the correspondence to Artaxerxes in Ezra 4:8–23, where Shimshai is named second after Rehum the commander, and identified always as "the scribe." Shethar-bozenai is named second after Tattenai in all four instances suggesting that Shethar-bozenai may also be a scribe. The meaning of the name is uncertain. *CAP* 5:16 (p. 11) has a related form *štrzn.* Cheyne (*EncBib* 4: 4462) presents some interesting possibilities, one being that Shethar-bozenai is a Persian official title (e.g., "chief clerk of the chancery"). In this case, one might regard it as a title of Tattenai denoting his role as investigator, rather than the proper name of another person. The context of the Aramaic section of Ezra 4:8–6:18, deals with opposition to the rebuilding of the temple. However, the letter Tattenai sent to Darius does not have the hostile tone apparent in the Aramaic letter to Artaxerxes in Ezra 4:11–16. Darius in turn replies in positive tones and instructs that the Jews are to be assisted in the building.

Bibliography

Bowman, R. A. 1941. An Aramaic Journal Page. *AJSL* 58: 302–13.

DAVID E. SUITER

SHEVA (PERSON) [Heb K *šyʾ;* Q *šěwāʾ*]. **1.** According to 2 Sam 20:25, Sheva was David's secretary. In 2 Sam 8:17, his secretary is called Seraiah, while in the parallel to this at 1 Chr 16:18, his name is given as Shavsha. In 1 Kgs 4:3 a certain Shisha is mentioned as the father of Solomon's secretaries Elihoreph and Ahijah. Most commentators agree that all these forms of the name refer to the same person. If this is correct, however, it is difficult, if not impossible, to determine what the original form of the name was. The various forms found in the LXX may be of some help. For 2 Sam 20:25 the OG has *Sousa* (*Iēsous* in B and *Isous* in A may be explained by the presence of an initial *waw* in the context). Similar variations (*Sousa* [OG] and *Iēsous* [B]) are found at 1 Chr 18:16. For 2 Sam 8:17 OG *Saraias* here agrees with MT while *Asa* in B and *Sasa* in MN reflect the variant *(š)šʾ*. These variations suggest *ššʾ* or *šawšāʾ* as the original Hebrew form. Driver (*NHT,* 283) preferred the former while McCarter (*2 Samuel* AB, 433) opts for the latter.

Marquart (1896: 22) put forth the opinion that Shisha represents a Babylonian name, *Šamšu,* although this has not received recent following. More commonly accepted is de Vaux's suggestion (1939: 397–400) that the name is of Egyptian origin, a possibility that is strengthened by the name "Elihoreph" as one of Shisha's sons (1 Kgs 4:3). That it was in any case a foreign name seems likely from the fact that this person is the only one of David's officers for whom the father's name is not given. Cody (1965: 381–93) suggested that Seraiah was the actual name of David's secretary and *šyšʾ* or something similar was a corrupt form of the Egyptian title *šš šʿ.t* for a scribe. This suggestion, however, has not been widely accepted.

2. According to 1 Chr 2:49, Sheva was one of the sons of Caleb by his concubine Maacah. Sheva was the father of Machbenah and Gibea.

Bibliography

Cody, A. 1965. Le titre égyptien et le nom propre du scribe de David. *RB* 72: 381–93.

Marquart, J. 1896. *Fundamente israelitischer und jüdaischer Geschichte.* Göttingen.

Vaux, R. de. 1939. Titres et fonctionnaires égyptiens à la cour de David et de Salomon. *RB* 48: 394–405.

STEPHEN PISANO

SHIBAH (PLACE) [Heb *šibʿâ*]. The name of a well dug by Isaac's servants (Gen 26:33). News of the well's completion reached Isaac just as he was concluding a treaty by making an oath (*šbʿ*) with Abimelech, the Philistine king from Gerar (Genesis 26). According to the biblical account, the name "Shibah" ("oath") was given in honor of this occasion. The Genesis author identifies the town subsequently built on the site as Beer-sheba, "well of the oath" (v 33). This incident either is a reopening of a well previously named by Abraham (Gen 21:25–31), or an alternative tradition regarding the nomenclature.

Tell Beer-sheba (Tell es-Saba; M.R. 134072) lies 2 miles E of the modern town of Beer-sheba (Bir es-Saba; M.R. 130072). The former only shows occupation during the Israelite period (Aharoni *EAEHL* 1: 160–68). The latter site shows a much longer period of settlement, ranging from the 4th millennium B.C. through the Iron Age and later. Gophna has proposed that the older settlement remained occupied on the traditional site of the wells, while an administrative center was later built at a little distance on the tell (*EAEHL* 1: 159). The site in Genesis would then more likely be identified with Bir es-Saba rather than Tell es-Saba. See BEER-SHEBA.

DAVID W. BAKER

SHIBBOLETH [Heb *šibbōlet*]. Word which occurs 20 times in the Bible, most often meaning "ear of grain," but in several instances also "flowing stream." In one of these occurrences, Judg 12:6, the dialectal form *sibbōlet* appears. This verse, which has come to be known as the shibboleth incident, has been the subject of much debate. Regardless of how one interprets it, however, scholars agree that the passage indicates a certain difference in the pronunciation of Hebrew between Ephraimites and Gileadites. Accordingly, it is an important piece of evidence for establishing the fact that regional dialects of Hebrew, at least in regard to phonology, existed in ancient Israel.

The story of Judg 12:1–6 describes a battle between the tribe of Ephraim and the people of Gilead in Transjordan. The Gileadites were in control of the fords of the Jordan River. When an Ephraimite tried to cross the river to retreat homeward to Cisjordan, the men of Gilead asked him to pronounce the word *šibbōlet.* Typically he was unable to do so and instead said *sibbōlet,* thus revealing his Ephraimite identity.

The simple approach, taking the story at face value, is to assume that at least in some instances the Ephraimites pronounced *š* as [s] (e.g., GKC 17). But few scholars today would hold to this opinion. Instead, numerous theories have been devised with alternative interpretations.

Marquart (1888) believed that the Ephraimite dialect retained the phoneme /ṯ/, but that when the Gileadites heard this it sounded like [s]. Speiser (1942) reversed this hypothesis by suggesting that it was the Gileadite dialect which retained the phoneme /ṯ/, but that the Ephraimites were unable to render it correctly and thus said [s]. Speiser pointed to the existence of an Aramaic word *tūblāʾ* "ear of grain" to posit a proto-Semitic root *ṯbl* for *šibbōlet.*

Subsequently, Marcus (1942) and Kutscher (1967: 173–74), based on the earlier work of Fraenkel (1905), noted that *tūblāʾ* was actually a ghost word, a doctored form attested only once in the vast Aramaic literary corpus, thus greatly weakening Speiser's theory. Kutscher's (1982: 15) final words on the subject represented the common view of about two decades ago: "The riddle remains, therefore, unresolved."

A spate of recent articles has renewed the debate concerning the shibboleth incident. The first two articles concentrated mainly on the problem of the Hebrew *śin,* but also commented on the shibboleth incident. Diem (1974: 242–43) accepted Speiser's interpretation, in spite of Marcus' and Kutscher's objections. Blau (1971: 109) opted to return to the simple interpretation mentioned above. A novel analysis was attempted by Beeston (1979), who proposed that the proto-Semitic root of our word is *sblt,* which the Ephraimites preserved, but that in non-Ephraimite Hebrew the pronunciation shifted to *šblt.*

Swiggers (1981) also accepted Speiser's theory that the Gileadites retained the phoneme /ṯ/, but he alleviated the objection raised by Marcus and Kutscher by proposing to distinguish two roots: *šbl* for "ear of grain" and *ṯbl* for "flowing stream." The former is based on the cognate Ugaritic, Akkadian, Arabic, and South Arabian evidence. The latter, unfortunately, has no Semitic etyma to substantiate it. Moreover, Swiggers noted that in the context of Judg 12:6 only the meaning "flowing stream" pertains. Parallel folk stories show that the password used in such incidents always is related to the context. Since the Ephraimites are crossing the Jordan at this point only "flowing stream" and not "ear of grain" is germane. On the question of how the Ephraimites pronounced the word, Swiggers claimed that they said [*šibbōlet*] as in standard Hebrew, though for graphemic reasons the text of Judg 12:6 uses *sblt.*

Emerton (1985) dismissed the theories which posit a proto-Semitic /ṯ/ as the first root letter based on the failure to find a relevant cognate. Instead, he advanced the working hypothesis that Ephraimites and Gileadites simply articulated the phoneme /š/ slightly differently from one another. The realization of individual phonemes is often subject to minor local variation. Thus, in the Ephraimite dialect, the /š/ sound may have been realized as something closer to [s] than to [š], or in the very least the Gileadites may have heard the Ephraimite /š/ as closer to [s] than to [š].

Lemaire (1985), on the other hand, lent support to the possibility that a root with /ṯ/ is involved. He noted that the Aramaic version of the Tell Fakhariyeh bilingual inscription also represents proto-Semitic /ṯ/ with *s.* According to Lemaire, this situation may not only serve as a parallel to the shibboleth incident, but it even may be related historically since a segment of the Israelites undoubtedly hailed from the general region of Tell Fakhariyeh in Aram Naharayim.

Finally, Rendsburg (1988a; 1988b) demonstrated that Ammonite preserved the phoneme /ṯ/, but that when a Cisjordanian speaker tried to articulate this sound he said [s]. The evidence is the Ammonite royal name *bʿlyšʿ* (the root of the second element in this anthroponym is *yṯʿ*), found on a seal at Tell el-ʿUmeiri, which appears in Jer 40:14 as *bʿlys.* Thus, we have another, and in fact much closer, parallel to the situation Lemaire described. Accordingly, Speiser and Swiggers are correct concerning the Gileadite retention of the phoneme /ṯ/, and we can posit an important phonological feature shared by two neighboring dialects in Transjordan. Swiggers is correct that the Ephraimites generally said [šibbōlet] as in standard Hebrew, but Speiser is correct concerning Judg 12:6 specifically. When asked to pronounce /ṯ/ the Ephraimites were unable to do so and instead articulated an [s]. Swiggers is also justified in differentiating two roots, although it is still true that no cognate to Hebrew *šibbōlet* "flowing stream" (derived from proto-Semitic *ṯbl*) has been found.

Lastly, it should be noted that based on the story in Judges 12, "shibboleth" passed into the English language as a word meaning "password."

Bibliography

Beeston, A. F. L. 1979. Hebrew *Šibbolet* and *Šobel. JSS* 24: 175–77.

Blau, J. 1971. "Weak" Phonetic Change and the Hebrew *Śin. HAR* 1: 67–119.

Diem, W. 1974. Das Problem von *ś* im Althebräischen und die kanaanäische Lautverschiebung. *ZDMG* 124: 221–52.

Emerton, J. A. 1985. Some Comments on the Shibboleth Incident (Judges XII 6). Pp. 150–57 in *Mélanges bibliques et orientaux en l'honneur de M. Mathias Delcor,* ed. A Caquot, S. Légasse, and M. Tardieu. Neukirchen-Vluyn.

Fraenkel, S. 1905. Zu Zeitschrift 58. S. 954, Z. 6. *ZDMG* 54: 252.

Kutscher, E. Y. 1967. Mittelhebräisch und Jüdisch-Aramäisch in neuen Koehler-Baumgartner. Pp. 158–75 in *Hebräische Wort-*

forschung: Festschrift zum 80. Geburtstag von Walter Baumgarten. VTSup 16. Leiden.

———. 1982. *A History of the Hebrew Language.* Jerusalem.

Lemaire, A. 1985. L'incident du *sibbolet* (Jg 12,6). Pp. 275–81 in *Mélanges bibliques et orientaux en l'honneur de M. Mathias Delcor,* ed. A. Caquot, S. Légasse, and M. Tardieu. Neukirchen-Vluyn.

Marcus, R. 1942. The Word *Šibboleth* Again. *BASOR* 87: 39.

Marquart, J. 1888. *Šibbōlet* = ephraimitisch *Sibbōlet* = *Śibbōlet? ZAW* 8: 151–55.

Rendsburg, G. A. 1988a. The Ammonite Phoneme /T̠/. *BASOR* 269: 73–79.

———. 1988b. More on Hebrew *Šibbōlet. JSS* 33: 255–58.

Speiser, E. A. 1942. The Shibboleth Incident (Judges 12:6). *BASOR* 85: 10-13.

Swiggers, P. 1981. The Word Šibbōlet̠ in Jud. XII.6. *JSS* 26: 205–7.

GARY A. RENDSBURG

SHIHOR (PLACE) [Heb *šîḥôr; šiḥôr; šiḥōr*]. A river or body of water in the NE Nile delta region mentioned four times in the Bible (Josh 13:3; Isa 23:3; Jer 2:18; 1 Chr 13:5), the precise identification of which is still uncertain. Shihor was understood by biblical writers as being part of the Nile, if not the Nile itself. If one follows the MT of Isa 23:3, Shihor is in parallelism with the Nile (Heb *yĕʾōr*). In Jer 2:18, Egypt and Shihor (RSV "Nile") are counterpart to Assyria and the Euphrates. Josh 13:3 uses Shihor with the definite article (Heb *haššîḥôr*) and refers to the ideal or actual southernmost boundary between Egypt and the land of Israel, described as opposite or facing Egypt (Heb *pĕnê miṣrayim*]. David assembled all of Israel from Shihor of Egypt to the entrance of Hamath to bring up the ark of God (1 Chr 13:5).

The name "Shihor" seems to reflect the Eg p^{3} *š-ḥr* "The waters of Horus" (see Gardiner 1918: 251; 1947: 201; Köhler 1936: 289–90; Bietak in *LÄ* 5: 623–26). The Hebrew name "Shihor" caused difficulties for the LXX translators. For example, in Josh 13:5, LXX reads *aoikētou* "uninhabited;" Jer 2:18, *gēōn* (see also Gen 2:13 and GIHON); and 1 Chr 13:5, *horiōn* "boundaries." The Greek translation of Isa 23:3 is also problematic (see Wildberger *Jesaja* BKAT, 856 for discussion of MT).

There has been a great deal of discussion among scholars concerning the identification of Shihor. In the light of papyrological and biblical evidence, it has been concluded that Shihor refers to running water, is drinkable, is associated with the city of Pi Rameses (see RAMESES), and empties into the sea at the N coastal town of Pelusium (Gardiner 1918: 251; cf. Bietak 1975: 129–30). It must therefore be identified as part of the Nile (e.g., Gardiner 1918: 250–52; see also 1947: 172, 202). Others (e.g., *GTTOT,* 27, 104; Wilson in *DB* 4: 498–99) have claimed that Shihor refers to the Brook of Egypt (Heb *naḥal miṣrayim*) identified with Wadi el-Arish. Supporting this identification is a parallel between the markings of the N and S boundaries of Israel in the time of David in 1 Chr 13:5 and 1 Kgs 8:65. Where 1 Chr 13:5 reads Shihor, 1 Kgs 8:65 reads *naḥal miṣrayim* (Brook of Egypt). Shihor must therefore be a reference to the river of Egypt. However, some scholars have turned away from identifying Shihor with Wadi el-Arish. Bar-Deroma (1960) equates Shihor with the Brook of Egypt but identifies it with the easternmost (Pelusaic) arm of the Nile (note also Kitchen 1982: 2–3 and *NBD,* 310–12, who identifies the Brook of Egypt with Wadi el-Arish and Shihor with the northernmost portion of the Pelusian branch of the Nile before it enters the sea; cf. also Montet 1968: 49–51).

More recent scholars (e.g., Bietak 1975) have been wrestling with the problem of how Shihor can refer to flowing water and standing water at the same time, as suggested by the ancient Egyptian papyri. Another problem concerns the relationship between Shihor and the "Way of Horus," a road that was used for travel between Egypt and Palestine. It has been suggested that Shihor flows through the NE part of the Nile delta parallel with the Way of Horus. Before Shihor empties into the Mediterranean Sea, it runs into a drainage reservoir also known as the Waters of Horus. Traveling S into Egypt from Palestine on the Way of Horus, it is the first body of water that one encounters (for discussion see Bietak 1975; cf. Naʾaman 1979; 1980).

Bibliography

Bar-Deroma, H. 1960. The River of Egypt (NAḤAL MIZRAIM). *PEQ* 92: 37–56.

Bietak, M. 1975. *Tell el Dab'a II.* Oesterreichische Akademie Der Wissenschaften Denkschriften Der Gesamptakademie 4. Vienna.

Gardiner, A. H. 1918. The Delta Residence of the Ramessides. *JEA* 5: 127–200, 242–71.

———. 1920. The Ancient Military Road between Egypt and Palestine. *JEA* 6: 99–116.

———. 1947. *Ancient Egyptian Onomastica.* Vol. 2. Oxford.

Kitchen, K. 1982. *Pharaoh Triumphant: The Life and Times of Ramesses II.* Warminster.

Köhler, L. 1936. Hebräische Vokabeln I. *ZAW* 13: 287–93.

Lambdin, T. O. 1953. Egyptian Loan Words in the Old Testament. *JAOS* 73: 145–55.

Montet, P. 1968. *Egypt and the Bible.* Trans. L. R. Keylock. Philadelphia.

Naʾaman, N. 1979. The Brook of Egypt and Assyrian Policy on the Border of Egypt. *TA* 6: 68–90.

———. 1980. The Shihor of Egypt and Shur That Is Before Egypt. *TA* 7: 95–110.

ARNOLD BETZ

SHIHOR-LIBNATH (PLACE) [Heb *šîḥôr libnāt*]. A place mentioned in the description of the S border of the territory of the tribe of Asher (Josh 19:26). According to this passage, the S border "on the west touches Carmel and Shihor-libnath." Shihor is derived from the Egyptian *si-hor* (lake/river of the god Horus) (e.g. *ANET,* 471). In the Bible the term *šîḥôr* either refers to the E arm of the Nile/ Delta as the S border of the Holy Land (Josh 13:3; 1 Chr 13:5) or it is used as a synonym for the Nile (Isa 23:3; Jer 2:18). See SHIHOR.

Shihor-libnath must then be a river in the vicinity of the Carmel. Its identification depends, however, on whether or not Mt. Carmel was part of the territory of Asher. Scholars who include the Carmel within Asher's territory identify Shihor-libnath with Naḥal Dāyah or with Haḥal Tanninim to the S of the Carmel. They see a possible connection between the name of the latter ("Crocodile river") and of the town that was located near its estuary,

Crocodilopolis (Strabo *Geog.* 16.2.27; Pliny *HN* 5.17.75) and its Egyptian name "Shihor" (*GP* I: 270–71).

However, the Heb term *āga* ("and touched on") that is used in the border descriptions in Joshua apparently relates to places *outside* the tribal territories themselves, in which case Mt. Carmel is outside the territory of Asher and Shihor-libnath is to be identified with the lower reaches of the Kishon river to the N of the Carmel (Maisler 1942: Map 5; *HGB*, 205). Libnath, the town that gave its name to the river, has been identified with Tell Abu Huwam (M.R. 152245) at the estuary of this river in modern Haifa (*LBHG*, 238).

Bibliography

Maisler (Mazar), B. 1942. *The Graphic Historical Atlas of Palestine-Israel in Biblical Times.* Tel Aviv.

RAFAEL FRANKEL

SHIKKERON (PLACE) [Heb *šikkĕrôn*]. A station on the N border of the tribal allotment of Judah (Josh 15:11), between the better known towns of Ekron (probably Tel Miqne) and Jabneel (probably modern Yavne). Alt (*KlSchr* 1: 193–202) has persuasively argued that the border list of Joshua 15 is derived from an ancient legal document delineating the territorial claims of the tribes during the period of the Judges. It is clear that the boundary in this region generally follows the Sorek Valley, running from the edge of the hill country at Beth-shemesh to the Mediterranean shore near modern Palmahim. A thorough examination of this region led Aharoni (*LBHG*, 384) to propose that Shikkeron be identified with Tell el-Ful (M.R. 132136), a small mound on the N edge of the Sorek Valley approximately 6 km N and slightly W of Tel Miqne, and 8 km SE of Yavne. Although this identification is not certain, the general location is no doubt correct.

WADE R. KOTTER

SHILHI (PERSON) [Heb *šilḥî*]. The father of Azubah, who was wife of Asa and mother of Jehoshaphat, kings of Judah (1 Kgs 22:42). The queen mother (Heb *gĕbîrâ*) was an influential figure in the Judean court, and regnal formulas opening the account of a Judean king's reign almost always mention her name along with that of her father, her provenance, or in late reigns, both. The personal name "Shilhi" is otherwise unknown. Šanda (*1 Kings* EHAT, 502) conjectures that *šlḥy* may not be the name of Azubah's father, but a corruption of the phrase *mn-šlḥym* ("from Shilhim"; see Josh 15:32); the same result can be achieved without emendation by reading *šlḥy* as a gentilic: "(daughter of) a Shilhite."

JEROME T. WALSH

SHILHIM (PLACE) [Heb *šilḥîm*]. An unidentified town in the Judean Negeb (Josh 15:32). In the lists of Simeonite towns incorporated into Judah, its place is taken by Sharuhen (Josh 19:6) and Shaaraim (1 Chr 4:31). Owing to these putative parallels, most scholars view the three towns as one (e.g., Boling and Wright *Joshua* AB, 384). Since Shaaraim is generally dismissed as a late corruption of Sharuhen, the discussion has centered on the respective claims of the names "Shilhim" and "Sharuhen." Albright (1924: 134–35 n. 6) felt that Sharuhen and Shilhim were alternate names for the same place, the former form reflecting Egyptian influence and the latter Canaanite. He further conjectured that the original form of the name was *Šir/lḥōn*. Noth (*Josua* HAT, 88) advocated the primacy of Sharuhen in the context of the biblical text. Recently Na᾿aman (1980: 147–48) has called into question the identification of Egyptian and biblical Sharuhen with each other, thus arguing for an original Shilhim in the Hebrew Bible (possibly also mentioned in Shishak's list). Aḥituv (*CTAED*, 173), on the other hand, has argued that there is no reason to assume that Shilhim, Sharuhen, and Shaaraim refer to the same place, since there are many differences in the three lists that cannot be dismissed as scribal variants. He regards the three lists as representing three different stages in the history of Simeon's inheritance.

Bibliography

Albright, W. F. 1924. Egypt and the Early History of the Negeb. *JPOS* 4: 131–61.
Na᾿aman, N. 1980. The Inheritance of the Sons of Simeon. *ZDPV* 96: 136–52.

CARL S. EHRLICH

SHILLEM (PERSON) [Heb *šillēm*]. SHILLEMITES. The youngest of the four sons of Naphtali (Gen 46:24). Shillem was a grandson of Jacob and Bilhah, the maid whom Laban gave to his daughter Rachel on the occasion of Rachel's marriage to Jacob (Gen 29:29). Shillem was one of the 70 people listed in the genealogical list of Jacob who descended to Egypt with Jacob's family at the time of a severe famine in the land of Canaan (Gen 46:8–27). Little is known about Shillem. According to the genealogical list of Naphtali found in the second census taken by Moses (Numbers 26), Shillem became the father of the Shillemites, one of the clans of Naphtali (Num 26:49). In the Chronicler's enumeration of Naphtali's genealogy (1 Chr 7:13) his name appears as Shallum [Heb *šallûm*]. See SHALLUM #8.

CLAUDE F. MARIOTTINI

SHILOAH, WATERS OF (PLACE) [Heb *šilōaḥ*]. See SILOAM, POOL OF (PLACE).

SHILOH (PLACE) [Heb *šīlōh*]. A place N of Bethel inside the land of Canaan where the Israelites convened sacred assemblies in the days before Solomon established the Jerusalem temple as the major center of Yahwistic worship (Joshua 19:51; Judg 18:31; 21:12–21). The priests who presided at this shrine appear to have been from the lineage of Eli (1 Samuel 1–4; 14:3; 1 Kgs 2:27). At some early time the shrine was apparently abandoned (Jer 7:12–14; 26:6–9; cf. Ps 78:60).

A. The Site

Located in the heart of the Ephraimite hills, Shiloh (Khirbet Seilun, M. R. 177162) occupied a midpoint between the important centers of Bethel and Shechem. See

SEILUN, KHIRBET. The book of Joshua makes Shiloh the first permanent home for the ark after the conquest of Canaan. There, Joshua parceled out land to most of the tribes (Josh 18:1–10; 19:51; 21:2; also 22:9). These traditions are late—Josh 21:2 cites Num 35:1–8, a text from the Priestly source in the Pentateuch (Friedman 1981: 116–18), which was produced sometime in the 7th–6th centuries B.C.E. by a clergy that claimed descent from Aaron. Shiloh's role in the book of Joshua is thus part of a historian's reconstruction. The historian writing in Joshua (presumably the Deuteronomist [DH]) knew of three key premonarchic sanctuaries (Gilgal, Shiloh, Shechem); he therefore traced Israel's use of them to the earliest possible era. The view of Shiloh in this historian's sources, this review will show, was somewhat different.

Two sets of data underlie the historian's deduction: first, tradition located a sanctuary associated with the ark in Shiloh during Eli's time (including Judg 18:31); second, both Ps 78:60 (for the date of which, see Clifford 1981) and Jer 7:12; 26:6–9 reflect a 7th-century conviction, probably widespread and based on the traditions about the Elides (Eissfeldt 1957), that Jerusalem had succeeded Shiloh as YHWH's unique "chosen place."

Possibly, 2 Sam 7:6–7 reflects an earlier Jerusalemite posture. It affirms that YHWH had always "roved in a tent and a tabernacle . . . among all the children of Israel," denying that YHWH had any permanent dwelling before he elected Zion (cf. Psalm 132). But the Deuteronomistic Historian (DH), writing from Josiah's court (Cross, *CMHE,* 278–85), embraces the idea of an election of Shiloh (with Jer 7:12). To avoid contradiction, he therefore interprets 2 Sam 7:6–7 (from a source) to distinguish between a site elected for YHWH's residence and a site elected to house a temple. His formulation, "I never elected a city from among all the tribes of Israel to build a temple for my name to be there" (1 Kgs 8:16), echoes Deut 12:5, which speaks of "the place that YHWH your god will elect from among all your tribes to put his name there, for it to dwell." But it carefully states that no town was elected before Zion *for a temple*—the qualification leaves open the possibility that other towns, such as Shiloh, but not their temples, were previously "chosen places." Again, this is the posture of the Deuteronomistic movement in the late 7th century—the posture reflected in Joshua.

Little can be said with certainty concerning the cultic establishment at Shiloh. Judg 21:18–23 (with a possible oral variant preserved in 21:5–14) implies the existence of a local virginal rite.

Shiloh's eminence is best attested in the era just before the onset of the monarchy. Whether Shiloh had a temple (Eissfeldt 1957: 146) is disputed (Cross 1981: 173–74; Haran 1985: 1998–204). The textual evidence is ambiguous. On the one hand, 1 Sam 1:9 and other nearby texts speak of the establishment in Shiloh as one with regular architectural features: a "nave," a "doorjamb," "doors" (3:15); there are also references to a "house," though whether this always implies an enclosed temple is unsure. On the other hand, as noted above, 2 Sam 7:6–7 denies that YHWH had had a "house of cedar" prior to Solomon's building; he had "roved about in a tent and in a tabernacle" (the parallel in 1 Chr 17:5 is corrupt). Ps 78:60–61 seem to concur: these verses make no mention of a temple. Which is it? Was the Shilonite shrine a temple or an open-air sanctuary?

The passages that imply the presence of a temple in Shiloh certainly stem from the sources used by DH, for as we have seen, he took the opposite view. In this connection, it is noteworthy that neither Ps 78:60 nor Jer 7:12 speaks of a temple at Shiloh, although both affirm that Shiloh was the "chosen place" before Jerusalem. Their concurrence with Dtr suggests a broad consensus among the reform movements of the 7th century: despite Shiloh's election, YHWH commissioned no temple before Solomon's—in accordance with 2 Sam 7:6 and with the Deuteronomistic fixation on "high places." Traditions of a temple in premonarchic Shiloh are probably the older, not the late traditions.

The Deuteronomistic Historian, then, presumably took the references to the Shiloh temple to describe a sanctuary the construction of which had not been divinely ordained—and indeed, no account of its construction is furnished. Too, that the sources of DH placed a temple at Shiloh does not guarantee that a temple was in fact there.

However, one further element favors the sources' view. Recent excavations have disclosed that the Shilonite cult had extensive architectural fixtures (Finkelstein 1985: 169–70). The floruit of the site and of its cultic component can be placed in the first half of the 11th century (Finkelstein 1985: 170; S. Bunimovitz *apud* Finkelstein 1985: 131–38), on the eve of Israel's monarchic revolution, just when the book of Samuel depicts it. See SEILUN, KHIRBET. And all scholars agree, the ark stood at Shiloh—whether in a tent or a temple—until it was captured by Philistines (1 Samuel 4). Indeed, Shiloh sustained a destruction in the mid–11th century, which scholars reasonably and unanimously ascribe to the aftermath of the Philistine victory in 1 Sam 4:10 (see Finkelstein 1985: 173–74). The traditions in Samuel appear reliable, including traditions of a temple.

Texts and archaeology indicate that Shiloh was occupied throughout the Iron Age, and into the exile (1 Kgs 11:29; Jer 7:12–15; 41:5; Finkelstein 1985), though Jer 7:12–15 indicates that the temenos, at least (and thus probably a building), was in ruins in the late 7th century. The Iron I, or more probably, the early Iron II city apparently had a gate complex, with an extended arm, like the gates at Iron II Megiddo and Tel Batashi: from the arm, Eli is said to have awaited news of the battle of Ebenezer; he died by falling backward into the area between the arm and the inner gate passage itself (1 Sam 4:18). Shiloh's continuous occupation had to do primarily with its location, commanding a fertile valley. The sacral tradition, nevertheless, continued. The activity of a Shilonite prophet in the late 10th century (1 Kgs 11:29; 14) suggests that a priestly school remained active on the site.

B. The Priesthood

The priesthood of Shiloh in the premonarchic age had, according to one tradition, charge of YHWH's ark (1 Sam 3:3; 4:3). This icon eventually found its way into Solomon's temple, however, and into the care of its Aaronide priests. The transfer was fully effected with Solomon's ejection of Abiathar, the scion of the Elide line, from the high priesthood (1 Kgs 2:26–27, 35).

Aaronide tradition had it that from the Mosaic era

forward, only Aaronides could minister at the ark (Exod 28:1). Further, two Aaronide lineages had disqualified themselves by a ritual violation (Lev 10:1–2), and the line of Eleazar—the Jerusalemite Aaronide line—had secured a promise of the priesthood by the signal loyalty of Eleazar's son (Num 25:10–13). As a result, late priestly writing associates the Elides with Aaron's son, Ithamar (1 Chr 24:3). When the ark was forfeit for Elide wickedness, thus, the definitive transfer of the priesthood to the line of Eleazar occurred (1 Sam 2:12–36). It is not clear, however, that this was the position adopted by the Shilonites themselves, who continued to minister at the ark until forcibly removed from it (1 Kgs 2:26.35).

Wellhausen argued (*WPHI,* 142–43) that the complaint to Eli in 1 Sam 2:27 presupposed descent from Moses. Through a prophet, YHWH queries, "Did I not reveal myself to the house of your father when they were in Egypt?" The verb used in this passage, "reveal," generally denotes direct discourse with some party (almost always so in older sources). Wellhausen therefore deduced that Moses was the ancestor of Eli's line (and others). There is a problem with this logic, however: Moses was not a "house." The reference could well be to Israel generally, or to the tribe of Levi, or to some other group.

Wellhausen bolstered his analysis with the contention that several old texts represent Levitic orders as descendants of or members of a guild founded by Moses. Judg 18:30 speaks of Jonathan son of Gershom son of Moses (MT, Manasseh), whose descendants presided at the shrine of Dan. And Deut 33:8–11, among other texts depicting Moses in a priestly role, alludes to Moses as the archetypical Levite.

Wellhausen's case was refined and sophisticated by F. M. Cross, who identified pieces of partisan priestly polemic in the Pentateuchal sources. There are pericopes in P (the Jerusalemite Aaronide source in the Pentateuch) whose sole purpose and point is to defame the Levitical orders (as P in Numbers 16, the Korah revolt; Num 25:6:15, perhaps directed also against the cult in Reuben [Cross, *CMHE,* 201–205]). Conversely, E (the Elohistic source in the Pentateuch) and Deuteronomy retail accounts that indict Aaron, and defend Moses' authority. Thus, Numbers 12 underscores the unique character of Moses' relationship with YHWH. More to the point, Exodus 32 damns Aaron as the maker of the golden calf, and the Levites earn priestly status by rising to YHWH's support. This tale probably stems from Shilonite circles (*CMHE,* 198–206; Halpern 1976: 39–42; Friedman 1987: 70–74). Its hero is Moses, and it rejects both Aaron and the golden calf of Jeroboam I at Bethel and Dan (1 Kgs 12:26–33). There are indications of Shilonite assaults on Jeroboam's icon (1 Kings 14), despite the fact that other Mosaic priests serviced the calf at Dan (Judg 18:30). The implication is that Jeroboam refused the Shilonites an exclusive franchise in his royal sanctuaries.

Shilonites are twice depicted as adopting an anti-Solomonic stance: Abiathar supports a rival pretender (1 Kgs 1:7); and Ahijah of Shiloh instigates Jeroboam's coup and the Solomonic schism (1 Kgs 11:26–40). This is one of several indications that the Deuteronomic program was rooted in the Shilonite line. DH charges Solomon with apostasy (1 Kgs 11:1–3), and Josiah acts against his "high places" (2 Kgs 23:13–14). Deuteronomy also recapitulates the charges of Exodus 32 against Aaron, if in a more palatable form (Deut 9:12–21 with 10:1–6). And of course, Deuteronomy makes Moses the font of all authority in Israel. One interesting clue may be present in the Aaronide polemic of 1 Sam 2:27–36: Eli's descendants, says the text, will come begging to the "faithful priest"—the Eleazarites—for an adjunct priesthood. This is just what Deut 18:1–8 enjoins concerning priests from outside Jerusalem: they must be accommodated at the central shrine (= 2 Kgs 23:8–9).

There is one last link between the Deuteronomic program and Shiloh. Jeremiah is the only prophet to mention Shiloh (7:12, 14; 26:6, 9). An avid supporter of Deuteronomic doctrine, Jeremiah had priestly origins, in Anathoth (Jer 1:1), a Levitical city assigned to Aaron. Nevertheless, Jeremiah, who was declared a persona non grata by the Aaronides of the Jerusalem temple, suffered a contretemps with the people of his hometown (Jer 11:21). Some scholars have concluded that Jeremiah was in fact a descendant of Abiathar, banished by Solomon to Anathoth (1 Kgs 2:36). This is at least a strong possibility. Thus, the priesthood of the Shilonite line seems to have shaped much of the literature of the Hebrew Bible, directly or indirectly. Even if Jeremiah was not himself an Elide, his testimony links Shiloh and Deuteronomy.

Bibliography

Clifford, R. J. 1981. In Zion and David a New Beginning: An Interpretation of Psalm 78. Pp. 121–41 in *Traditions in Transformation: Turning-Points in Biblical Faith,* ed. B. Halpern and J. D. Levenson. Winona Lake.

Cross, F. M. 1981. The Priestly Tabernacle in the Light of Recent Research. Pp. 169–80 in *Temples and High Places in Biblical Times,* ed. A. Biran. Jerusalem.

Eissfeldt, O. 1957. Silo und Jerusalem. VTSup 4:138–47.

Finkelstein, I. 1985. Excavations at Shiloh 1981–1984. *Tel Aviv* 12: 123–80.

Friedman, R. E. 1981. *The Exile and Biblical Narrative.* HSM 22. Chico.

———. 1987. *Who Wrote the Bible?* New York.

Halpern, B. 1976. Levitic Participation in the Reform Cult of Jeroboam I. JBL 95: 31–42.

Haran, M. 1985. *Temples and Temple Service in Ancient Israel.* Winona Lake.

BARUCH HALPERN

SHILONITE [Heb *šîlōnî*]. **1.** A description of the prophet Ahijah as somehow associated with the amphictyonic shrine at Shiloh (1 Kgs 11:29). Some scholars argue that the reference to Ahijah as a "Shilonite" suggests that a guild of prophets survived the destruction of both the shrine and the cult at Shiloh (Gray *Kings* OTL, 294).

2. A description given to some of those Judeans who returned to Palestine after the exile (1 Chr 9:5; Neh 11:5). Shiloh, however, is in Ephraim and so most scholars now agree that the text should be vocalized to read "Shelanite," meaning descendant of Shelah, another of the sons of

Judah, mentioned in Num 26:20 (Reed in *IDB* 4: 330; Myers *1 Chronicles* AB; Williamson *Ezra, Nehemiah* WBC, 343).

FREDERICK W. SCHMIDT

SHILSHAH (PERSON) [Heb *šilšâ*]. The ninth son of Zophah, named in the genealogy of Asher in 1 Chr 7:37. While this figure is unknown elsewhere in the Hebrew Bible, his name is similar to that of Shelesh in 7:35, and scholars have associated these figures with the lands of Shalishah and Shaalim in the Saul narratives (Edelman 1985: 86). Such an identification is in keeping with Gray's thesis that most names in the Ahserite genealogy are tribal or geographical rather than personal (Gray 1896: 239).

Bibliography

Edelman, D. 1985. The "Ashurites" of Eshbaal's State. *PEQ* 117: 85–91.
Gray, G. B. 1896. *Studies in Hebrew Proper Names*. London.

JULIA M. O'BRIEN

SHIMEA (PERSON) [Heb *šimʿāʾ*]. Var. SHIMEAH. **1.** Older brother of David, third son of Jesse (1 Chr 2:13). He is called SHAMMAH in 1 Sam 16:9, where he was rejected (along with his other brothers) as God's choice for Israel's king in favor of David, and 1 Sam 17:13, where he was present at the confrontation between David and Goliath. He was the father of Jonadab, who gave devious counsel to Amnon (2 Sam 13:3, 32, where he is called Shimeah [Heb *šimʿâ*]), and the father of Jonathan, who killed a Philistine giant (21:20–21, where he is called SHIMEI; 1 Chr 20:6–8). See SHAMMAH #2.

2. A son of David born in Jerusalem (1 Chr 3:5). His mother was Bathsheba (Bathshua) and he had three full brothers: Shobab, Nathan, and Solomon. He is called SHAMMUA in 2 Sam 5:14 and 1 Chr 14:4. In addition, his father had six sons born in Hebron to six different wives, and nine born in Jerusalem to unnamed wives, as well as many sons born to his concubines in Jerusalem (1 Chr 3:9). See also DAVID, SONS OF.

3. A descendant of Merari, son of Levi (1 Chr 6:15—Eng 6:30), named in the independent levitical genealogy of 6:1–15—Eng 6:16–30).

4. A descendant of Gershom, son of Levi (1 Chr 6:24—Eng 6:39), named in a list of levitical singers appointed by David (6:16–33—Eng 6:31–48).

DAVID M. HOWARD, JR.

SHIMEAH (PERSON) [Heb *šimʿâ; šimʾâ*]. Var. SHIMEAM; SHIMEEAH. **1.** Older brother of David (*šimʿâ;* 2 Sam 13:3, 32). An alternate form of SHIMEA #1.

2. A Benjaminite, son of Mikloth, part of the family of Saul (*šimʾâ;* 1 Chr 8:32). He was descended from Jeiel, founder of Gibeon. It is not clear whether he lived in Gibeon or Jerusalem, although most of those listed in vv 29–40 were Gibeonites (Williamson *1 and 2 Chronicles* NCBC, 85–86). He is called Shimeam (Heb *šimʾām*) in 1 Chr 9:38. In 1 Chr 8:31 the RSV transcribes the name of the son of Mikloth as "Shimeeah."

DAVID M. HOWARD, JR.

SHIMEATH (PERSON) [Heb *šimʿāt*]. Parent of Jozabad (MT), one of two assassins of Joash, king of Judah (2 Kgs 12:22—Eng 12:21). See SHIMRITH. 2 Chr 24:26 explicitly labels her an Ammonitess, making her Jozabad's mother. Note that the RSV reads "Jozacar" accepting a minority reading in order to resolve the problem that the co-conspirators' names are variants of each other. The final *taw* of Shimeath is a marker of a feminine noun, although it is not required to understand a name of a woman, but simply a feminine gender for a masculine name (cf. Gray *Kings* OTL, 591). It would be unusual for a man to be identified by the name of his mother rather than his father, especially as it implies that the father is unknown. 2 Chr 24:26 also has a different variant for the man, "Zabad." Some LXX manuscripts read "Jozacar," making a plausible mistake, interchanging the similar looking *beth* with the *zayin* and the *dalet* with the *reš*.

KIRK E. LOWERY

SHIMEATHITES [Heb *šimʿātîm*]. Part of the Calebite family as well as one of three groups or families of scribes who lived at Jabez (1 Chr 2:55). The verse in which the word "Shimeathites" occurs is not clearly comprehensible (Myers *1 Chronicles* AB, 16). Apart from the fact that Jabez cannot be located, whether the three scribal names designate families or functions is difficult to determine (Curtis and Madsen *Chronicles* ICC, 98). The Vulgate treats the word Shimeathites as *resonantes,* "melody makers," and attributes this activity to the scribes living in Jabez. The Targum of 1 Chronicles interprets the term Shimeathites as disciples of Torah whose task is to proclaim the tradition. From designating a government bureaucrat in the preexilic period, the function of the scribe evolved in postexilic times to indicate someone trained in Mosaic Torah. This postexilic perspective on the scribe's task might be the informing background for why the Targum of 1 Chronicles and the Vulgate interpret the scribal Shimeathites in terms of proclamation and public worship.

Whatever or whoever the Shimeathites were, the Chronicler viewed them as related to the Kenites, who are associated likewise with the Rechabites in v 55. That the latter two were related is not improbable (Curtis and Madsen *Chronicles* ICC, 98) but the exact contours of their relationship cannot be traced.

JAMES M. KENNEDY

SHIMEEAH (PERSON) [Heb *šimĕʾâ*]. See SHIMEAH (PERSON).

SHIMEI (PERSON) [Heb *šimʿî*]. Sixteen men or clans bear this name in the OT. The name is short for such names as Shemaiah and Elishama, "Yah(weh)/God has heard." A seal from the period of the Restoration bears the name Baruch the son of Shimei (Avigad 1976: pls. 8–9).

It should be noted that the consonantal writing *šmʿy*, i.e., Shimei, in 2 Sam 21:21 is an error for *šmᵓ*, Shimea (cf. 2 Sam 13:3, 32; 1 Chr 2:13; 20:7); 1 Sam 16:9 and 17:13 read Shammah. See SHIMEA #1 and SHAMMAH #2.

1. The second son of Gershon the son of Levi, i.e., a subclan of Levites (Exod 6:17; Num 3:18, 21; 1 Chr 6:2—Eng 6:17; 23:7, 10; Zech 12:13). His brother clan is Libni/Ladan. 1 Chr 23:10–11 refers to four families of Shimeites—Jahath, Zina/Zizah, Jeush and Beriah—noting that only the first two were of significance. In 1 Chr 23:9 Shimei is probably an error for one of the sons of Ladan. Curiously, Shimei is called the grandson of Gershon and the son of Jahath in 1 Chr 6:27–28—Eng 6:42–43) and the son of Libni the son of Mahli the son of Merari in 1 Chr 6:14—Eng 6:29).

2. A clan or individual of Simeon (1 Chr 4:27), supposedly the son of Mishma.

3. A clan or individual of Reuben (1 Chr 5:4), supposedly the son of Gog.

4. A clan or individual of Benjamin (1 Chr 8:21), probably an error for Shema (1 Chr 8:13; see SHEMA #3).

5. A cult musician under David (1 Chr 25:17; also v 3 in Greek Version), of the clan of Jeduthun.

6. A man from Ramah, overseer of David's vineyards (1 Chr 27:27).

7. The son of Gera, a Benjaminite kinsman of Saul from Bahurim, who held David responsible for the deaths of the Saulides (2 Sam 16:7–8), as indeed he may have been. David was a vassal of the Philistines when they conquered Saul (1 Samuel 27, 29): An Amalekite anticipated reward for bringing David news of the deaths of Saul and Jonathan (2 Sam 1:1–16) and the head of Saul's son Ishbaal/Ishbosheth was therefore carried to David for an expected bounty (2 Sam 4:8): David allowed the Gibeonites to kill seven sons of Saul (2 Sam 21:1–14), though he spared the crippled Meribbaal/Mephibosheth (2 Sam 21:1–14) who was kept under close supervision in Jerusalem (2 Samuel 9). David thus was and is naturally suspect of harboring malice toward the house of his former liege.

When David is fleeing Jerusalem, which is temporarily under Absalom's control, Shimei casts curses, stones, and dirt at the king and his cohort (2 Sam 16:5–13). Abishai proposes to execute him, but David orders him to be spared, later renewing his amnesty when he returns triumphant to Jerusalem and receives Shimei's submission (2 Sam 19:17–24—Eng 6:16–23). In his deathbed testament to Solomon, however, David revokes his pardon and charges his son to punish Shimei (1 Kgs 2:8–9).

Scholarly supporters of David suppose, not implausibly, that in fact Solomon fabricated these final instructions. Since, however, throughout his reign David's actions toward the Saulides are suspect, despite his protestations of innocence, we perhaps discern David's true colors in his public pardon and secret vengeance. At any rate, Solomon confines Shimei to Jerusalem, presumably to keep an eye on him, and later executes him when he violates the terms of his parole (1 Kgs 2:36–46).

8. A leader who does not support Adonijah's usurpation (1 Kgs 1:8); he may be the same as #9.

9. The son of Ela, Solomon's administrator over Benjamin (1 Kgs 4:18).

10. A Levite of the house of Heman during the reign of Hezekiah (2 Chr 29:14). He may be the same as #11.

11. The assistant overseer of donations and tithes under Hezekiah (2 Chr 31:12–13).

12. The brother of Zerubbabel, the son of Pedaiah (1 Chr 3:19).

13. A Levite who divorces his foreign wife when compelled by Ezra (Ezra 10:23; 1 Esdr 9:23).

14. A member of the family of Hashum forced by Ezra to divorce his foreign wife (Ezra 10:33; 1 Esdr 9:33).

15. A member of the family of either Bani, or, if we emend in Ezra 10:38 (cf. 1 Esdr 9:34) *ûbānî ûbinnûy* to **ûbĕnê binnûy*, Binnui. He divorces his foreign wife at Ezra's behest.

16. An individual through whom Mordechai descends from Kish the Benjaminite (Esth 2:5). He could be the same as #7.

Bibliography

Avigad, N. 1976. *Bûlôt wĕḥôtāmôt mittôk ᵓarkîyôn mamlaktî miymê šîbat ṣiyyôn.* Qedem 4. Jerusalem.

William H. Propp

SHIMEON (PERSON) [Heb *šimʿôn*]. A descendant of Harim and one of the returned exiles who married a foreign woman during the era of Ezra's mission (Ezra 10:31; cf. 1 Esdr 9:32, where the much longer name "Simon Chosomaeus" appears). The Hebrew spelling of the name is the same as that for the patriarch Simeon and means "God has heard" (*IPN,* 38, 60 n. 2, 185). Shimeon seems to be a member of a family from which groups of exiles returned with Zerubbabel (Ezra 2:32; Neh 7:35). The three-month investigation (Ezra 10:16–17) culminating in the list in which Shimeon's name appears produced a relatively small number of names, leading some to believe that the list only includes prominent members of the community. Shimeon's position in the community, however, remains a mystery. While it seems probable that Shimeon divorced his foreign wife (note the prior oath taken by the people [Ezra 10:3–5] and the possibly generalizable v 19), that is not certain. The RSV follows 1 Esdr 9:36 in clearly stating that all on the list did indeed divorce their foreign wives and put away their children, but the Hebrew text of Ezra 44b is so corrupt that a definite translation is impossible, leaving the final outcome of the investigation in doubt.

Jeffrey A. Fager

SHIMON (PERSON) [Heb *šîmôn*]. An individual of the tribe of Judah (1 Chr 4:20).

SHIMRATH (PERSON) [Heb *šimrāt*]. A Benjaminite, a son of Shimei (1 Chr 8:21). According to 1 Chr 8:28,

Shimrath was one of the Benjaminites who dwelt in Jerusalem. Noth (*IPN*, 177) suggested that the name is a long form of Shemer, with the *-at* ending being either Arabic or Akkadian.

TOM WAYNE WILLETT

SHIMRI (PERSON) [Heb *šimrî*]. **1.** A Simeonite, the son of Shemaiah (1 Chr 4:37). His name occurs in one of the most extensive and most recent lists (1 Chr 4:24–43) dealing with the tribe of Simeon (cf. also Josh 19:1–9; 15:26, 28–32, 42), in the third subsection of this list, the portion dealing with thirteen tribal princes and their conquests (1 Chr 4:34–43). For the other two subsections, see 1 Chr 4:24–27 (Simeonite genealogy) and 4:28–33 (Simeonite cities and villages). Because of overpopulation and the need for pasture land, the tribe of Simeon is reported to have conquered and settled toward "Gedor," or as often amended on the basis of the LXX, in a more southwesterly direction, toward "Gerar," in the days of King Hezekiah (1 Chr 4:38–41), as well as in the opposite, southeasterly direction toward Amalek in the region of Mt. Seir (1 Chr 4:42–43). Shimri is mentioned as an ancestor of Ziza, one of the 13 Simeonite princes involved in the initial W expansion. The inclusion of Simeon, a tribe in the Chronicler's day, which had long ceased to be a geographical or political entity, was part of the Chronicler's agenda to present and promote the theme of a unified Israel.

2. The father of Jediael and Joha, two of David's mighty men (1 Chr 11:45). The name occurs in the unparalleled supplement (1 Chr 11:41b–47) to the larger synoptic listing (2 Sam 23:8–39 = 1 Chr 11:10–41a) of key personnel in David's military contingent. These men are representative, for the Chronicler, of the suggestion that all Israel was behind David's rise to kingship (1 Chr 11:10), including individuals from Transjordan, as the only identifiable places in this supplement are locatable there.

3. A Levite, the son of Hosah, descended from Merari (1 Chr 26:10). Although not the firstborn, this Shimri (spelled Simri in the KJV) was designated the foremost of the four Hosah subgroupings, involving a total of 13 men out of a grand total of 93 (1 Chr 26:5, 8, 10–11). As the Chronicler also ascribes to King David the sanctioning of 4000 gatekeepers in all (1 Chr 23:5), these 93 must be intended as leaders. Beside the Merari line of levitical gatekeepers, to which Shimri belonged, the gatekeepers were divided among two other main families: the Kohathite family of Meshelemiah (= Shelemiah ? 1 Chr 26:1–3, 14) and the family of Obed-edom (1 Chr 26:4–8), who, with no stated levitical ties given in the text, if not a Kohathite in view of 1 Chr 26:19, could have been the person from Gath at whose house David deposited the ark for safekeeping for three months after the death of Uzzah (2 Sam 6:10–12; 1 Chr 26:5b; 1 Chr 13:13–14; 15:24–25; 16:38). See OBED-EDOM. Shimri and the other Hosah subgroupings were assigned responsibility for the W gate of the temple, together with the Shallecheth Gate (1 Chr 26:16) on the causeway which probably ascended from the Tyropeon Valley to the W side of the temple (Curtis and Madsen *Chronicles* ICC, 285). By virtue of their location they supplied 6 gatekeepers of the 24 in toto required daily for the temple complex (1 Chr 26:17–18). Such details must have been important to the Chronicler for the temple of his day.

4. A Kohathite Levite, the son of Elizaphan (alternately Elzaphan in Exod 6:22; Lev 10:4) the son of Uzziel, and brother of Jeuel (MT K = RSV) or Jeiel (MT Q = NEB; 2 Chr 29:13; Num 3:30). According to the Chronicler, he was one of 14 representative Levites who answered the call of King Hezekiah at the beginning of his reign to clean and restore the temple for service (2 Chr 29:3–5, 11–19, 35b). As this event is unparalleled in 2 Kings, it is part of the Chronicler's effort to heighten the conscientious role of the Levites in the past as a justification for their continued importance for the postexilic community of his day, as an example for all in ongoing zeal for Yahweh's house and its cultic purity.

ROGER W. UITTI

SHIMRITH (PERSON) [Heb *šimrît*]. Var. SHOMER. Parent of Jehozabad, one of two assassins (see SHIMEATH) of Joash, king of Judah (2 Kgs 12:22—Eng 12:21). The form of the name, which is masculine in 2 Kings 12 (Heb *šōmēr*), changes to a feminine form in 2 Chr 24:26 (Heb *šimrît*), and is identified as Jehozadab's mother, a Moabitess. The change is usually attributed to an alteration of the gender of the name paralleling what was misunderstood by an editor to be a feminine name. However, it is unclear whether the problem is one of textual transmission or one of different sources used by the Chronicler (cf. Gray *Kings* OTL, 591). The name means "guardian" or "steward." See SHOMER.

KIRK E. LOWERY

SHIMRON (PERSON) [Heb *šimrôn*]. SHIMRONITES. The fourth and youngest son of Issachar (Gen 46:13; 1 Chr 7:1) and the grandson of Jacob and Leah. Shimron is listed with other descendants of Jacob who migrated to Egypt with their families at the time of a great famine in Canaan (Gen 46:8–22). Nothing is known about Shimron. According to the second census list of the tribes of Israel mentioned in the book of Numbers, Shimron became the eponymous ancestor of the Shimronites, one of the clans of Issachar (Num 26:24). The name "Shimron" may be related to Shamir (*LBHG*, 244), a village in the tribe of Issachar, located in the hill country of Ephraim and home of Tola, one of the minor judges of Israel (Judg 10:1–2).

CLAUDE F. MARIOTTINI

SHIMRON (PLACE) [Heb *šimrôn*]. A Canaanite royal town (Josh 11:1). Its antiquity is known by the references to it in the Egyptian Execration Texts. It is also mentioned by Thutmose III in his list of Palestinian towns. El Amarna Letters relate how its prince joined the king of Acco to plot and plunder a Babylonian caravan at Hannathon. "Shimron" is written in a variety of ways ranging from Simeon to Samaria, Shimʿon being a well-attested form. In Josh 12:20 the MT reads "Shimron-meron" whereas the LXX reads them separately, which seems to be accurate. The Mishnah and Talmud identify it with Simonia, while Josephus identifies it with Khirbet Sammuniyeh (Tell Shimron; M.R. 170234). The latter is located in the N portion of Esdraelon, N of Megiddo. It is about 5 miles W of Nazareth. According to the book of Joshua, the king of Shimron was defeated by Israel. The Deuteronomistic History mentions it to show that the Lord would unfailingly give powerful royal cities into the hands of Israel if it remained obedient to his commands. Shimron was later allotted to Zebulun (Josh 19:15).

PAUL BENJAMIN

SHIMRON-MERON (PLACE) [Heb *šimrôn mĕrʾôn*]. One of the towns whose king and people were defeated by the Israelites under the leadership of Joshua (Josh 12:20). The name SHIMRON occurs two other times in Joshua (11:1; 19:15). Because Meron appears only in Josh 12:20, modifying Shimron, its occurrence is problematic. However, a comparison of Josh 11:1 and 12:19–20 reveals several possible explanations for the addition of Meron in Josh 12:20. In 11:1, four cities are mentioned: Hazor, Madon, Shimron, and Achshaph. In 12:19–20, the towns are given in the order: Madon (MT, absent in LXX), Hazor, Shimron-meron, and Achshaph. One explanation for the appearance of Meron, on the basis of the order of names in both passages, i.e., Shimron(-meron) and Achshaph, is that Shimron-meron may simply be the full name of Shimron, and hence the names represent identical sites (Boling and Wright *Joshua* AB, 328). Still other explanations may be discernible in the LXX. The LXX renders Madon in Josh 11:1 as *Marrōn.* However, it omits Madon in Josh 12:19, but renders Meron (v 20) as *Marrōn.* In addition, the LXX in Josh 12:20 separates the MT's "Shimron-meron" into "the king of Shimron, the king of Meron." On the one hand, this may represent a tradition that Shimron and Meron were two distinct towns. On the other hand, it is possible that the LXX, confronted with the addition of Meron in Joshua 12 (MT), concluded that Madon and Meron were identical, and hence rendered *Marrōn* for both of them (perhaps compounded by the confusion of the *dalet* in *mdwn* with the *reš* in *mrʾwn*). It might be concluded, however, that the LXX was confused by the situation of Shimron in 11:1 and Shimron-meron in 12:20, trying unsuccessfully to resolve the difference (indeed, note that the LXX also renders Merom in 11:5, 7 with *Marrōn,* thereby increasing the confusion). It therefore seems that the best explanation is to conclude that Shimron and Shimron-meron designate relatively interchangeable referents.

JOHN KUTSKO

While the tradition of a Canaanite king in Shimron is legendary, the existence of an Israelite city during the monarchy is documented. The original name was *šimʿôn* which is still preserved as *Symoōn* in the LXX; this reading is also supported by the Egyptian sources which read *š-mw-ʿ-nw* (Execration Text E 55) or *š-m-ʿ-n* (List of Thutmose III, no. 35), respectively, and by the reading *šamḫuna* of the Amarna Letters. These references show that Shimron must have been an important city during the MB and LB ages. The Masoretic form *šimrôn* still lacks sufficient explanation; the Rabbinic literature (*y. Meg.* 70a) identifies the name with *simônîyāh* which is most probably identical with *Simōnias* mentioned by Josephus (*Life* 24.115). Shimron can be located at Khirbet Sammuniyeh (Tell Shimron, M.R. 170234) close to the NW boundary of the Jezreel Valley; according to surface research this site was occupied from the EB age to the Hellenistic and Roman times.

Bibliography

Fritz, V. 1969. Die sogenannte Liste der besiegten Könige in Josua 12. *ZDPV* 85: 136–61.
Rainey, A. F. 1976. Toponymic Problems. *TA* 3: 57–69.

V. F.

SHIMSHAI (PERSON) [Aram *šimšay*]. A Persian official identified as "the scribe," who in conjunction with Rehum the commander, wrote to Artaxerxes I (ruled from 465–423 B.C.E.) accusing the Jews in Jerusalem of rebellion (Ezra 4:8, 9, 17, 23 = 1 Esdr 2:16, 17, 25, 30). Shimshai's position as scribe (Aram *sāpar*) in this context properly means secretary or recorder. The correspondence is preserved in the Aramaic section of Ezra (Ezra 4:8 to 6:18) which Hensley (1977) considers an authentic official Persian document. The letter is conspicuously hostile in tone, informing Artaxerxes specifically that Jerusalem's walls are being built for the purpose of usurping Persian power in the region. Artaxerxes' rescript (Ezra 4:17–22) ordered a halt to the work; Rehum and Shimshai forcibly executed the king's command (Ezra 4:23). At what time in the reign of Artaxerxes this correspondence was exchanged is not known; the chronological relationship of this episode to the missions of Ezra and Nehemiah varies widely among the reconstructions of the restoration period.

Bibliography

Hensley, L. V. 1977. *The Official Persian Documents in the Book of Ezra.* Diss., Liverpool.

DAVID E. SUITER

SHIN [Heb *šin*]. The twenty-first letter of the Hebrew alphabet.

SHINAB (PERSON) [Heb *šinʾāb*]. King of Admah (Gen 14:2); appears simply as "king of Admah" in the same chapter, v 8. The name has been often explained as a genuine theophoric name: "Sin (the Babylonian Moon-god) is the father" (e.g., Dhorme 1931: 260). Akkadian personal names of this type (with *Sin* spelled *šn*) occur indeed in Aramaic inscriptions and papyri of late neo-Assyrian, neo-Babylonian, and Persian periods (Lidzbarski 1915: 117, 128; *KAI* no. 225:1); cf. also *šenʾaṣṣar* (Shenazzar, a son of Jeconiah) in 1 Chr 3:18. However, in view of the intentionally pejorative meanings of the names of the other kings of this group (e.g., Bera, Birsha, Shemeber, and Zoar), it is more plausible to attribute the name *šinʾāb* to the same category, to read its sibilant as *śin,* and to interpret it as "hater of the father," as this was adumbrated in *Tg. Ps.-J.* and guessed by Rashi (*śôneʾ ʾabîw šebaššāmayîm* "who hated his father in heaven"). In a fragment of an Assyrian tablet relating a legend about a tyrant who cruelly oppressed the Babylonians by corvée labor (King 1902: 1: 220; 2 pl. 73), it is said that he *abi kala ilāni iziru* "hated the father of all gods." Since that text is thematically related to the "Chedorlaomer texts" (see CHEDORLAOMER), it is possible that the compiler of Genesis 14 was inspired by the quoted epithet in choosing the name for the king of Admah (Astour 1966: 75).

Bibliography

Astour, M. C. 1966. Political and Cosmic Symbolism in Genesis 14 and in its Babylonian Sources. Pp. 65–112 in *Biblical Motifs: Origins and Transformations,* ed. A. Altmann. Cambridge, MA.

Dhorme, E. 1931. Abraham dans le cadre de l'histoire. Part IV. *RB* 40: 503–18. Repr. as pp. 256–72 in *Recueil Édovard Dhorme.* Paris, 1951.

King, L. W. 1902. *The Seven Tablets of Creation.* 2 vols. London .

Lidzbarski, M. 1915. *Ephemeris für Semitische Epigraphik.* Vol. 3. Giessen.

MICHAEL C. ASTOUR

SHINAR (PLACE) [Heb *šinʿār*]. A name for the region of Babylonia (Gen 10:10). It can be called either the "land of Shinar" or simply "Shinar." The first mention of the "land of Shinar" (Gen 10:10, in the fragment of the Yahwistic Table of Nations) calls it the mainstay or beginning of the kingdom of Nimrod. In it were found the cities Babel (Babylon), Accad (Agade), Erech (Uruk), and possibly Calneh. According to Gen 11:2 the early human race settled in a valley in the "land of Shinar" and began to build the abortive Tower of Babel. Abraham had a hostile encounter with a coalition of four kings, one of whom was "Amraphel king of Shinar" (Gen 14:1, 9). When the Israelites were thwarted in their conquest of Ai because Achan had stolen some of the "devoted things," one of the items he stole was a (presumably valuable) "cloak of Shinar" (Josh 7:21). An oracle in the book of Isaiah promises that a remnant of Yahweh's people will be returned from many places, including "Shinar" (Isa 11:11). After the Exile the prophet Zechariah saw a vision in which the sin of the people, personified as a woman, is transported to the "land of Shinar" in an ephah (a large container) and set up in a temple there (Zech 5:11). The book of Daniel relates that Nebuchadnezzar, king of Babylon, removed some of the vessels from the temple of God in Jerusalem and took them to the "land of Shinar," where he placed them in the temple treasury of his own god (Dan 1:2).

The meaning of Shinar is clear from the biblical references. It is the area known to the Mesopotamians as "the land of Sumer and Akkad," corresponding to the portion of modern Iraq S of Baghdad. This meaning is confirmed by the LXX, *Targum Onqelos,* and the *Genesis Apocryphon.* All three sometimes translate "Shinar" as Babylon(ia).

The question of the origin of the name "Shinar" is more difficult. It first appears in Egypt in the 15th century B.C.E. as *Sngr.* In cuneiform texts of roughly the same period it is *Šanḫaru.* One suggestion is that Shinar is derived from "Sumer." This identification, however, is phonologically impossible, since it cannot explain the origin of the third consonant (*ʿayin,* original *ġayin*), which never appears in any form of "Sumer." A more plausible etymology has recently been proposed by Ran Zadok (1984). He believes that Shinar derives from cuneiform *Samḫarû,* apparently the name of a Kassite tribe. The Kassites were rulers of Babylon during the period when the term "Shinar" was used in Egyptian and cuneiform sources. There is no strong phonological objection to this etymology, and it may be that peoples W of the Euphrates generalized the name of a familiar Kassite tribe until it became a term for the whole region of Babylonia. Such generalizations are common. For example, the Greeks called themselves "Hellenes," but the Roman word for them was "Greeks," *Graeci, Graii,* after a Hellene tribal name or geographical location.

Bibliography

Zadok, R. 1984. The Origin of the Name Shinar. *ZA* 74: 240–44.

JAMES R. DAVILA

SHION (PLACE) [Heb *šîʾôn*]. A town given by Joshua to Issachar in the allocation of the land following the conquest (Josh 19:19). It has been suggested (Smith 1966: map 2; *GTTOT,* 184; cf. *RAB,* 129) that the town be identified with Ayun es-Shain, 3 miles E of Nazareth. A proposal has been made to read the name as Sirion, reading *reš* for *ʾalep,* an error made by LXX B in the very next verse (v 20) where Abez is read "Rabez," a minor difference between the two letters in the early Hebrew script (*HGB,* 424). This would not then be the same Sirion as Mt. Hermon, since the latter is in Transjordan and far removed from Issachar's holdings. An identification with Sirin, some 10 miles SE at Mt. Tabor has also been suggested (*IDB* 4:333; *HGB,* 424). This latter location places Shion/Sirion firmly in Issachar's territory, while the former proposal places it on Issachar's border with Zebulun. Either location is thus geographically possible, although rereading the text as Sirion is less preferable since there is no evidence for such a reading in any of the ancient textual witnesses.

Bibliography

Smith, G. A. 1966. *The Historical Geography of the Holy Land.* New York.

DAVID W. BAKER

SHIPHI (PERSON) [Heb *šipʿî*]. Son of Allon, a descendant of Simeon (1 Chr 4:37), described as one of the "princes in their families" (1 Chr. 4:38). The name probably means "Yahweh is fulness." In the LXX the name appears as *Sephei.* The name "Shiphi," along with the names of the other Simeonite princes, is not found in any of the genealogies assigned to this patriarch. (Compare the Peshitta where 1 Chr 4:34–41 contains no personal names.) Nevertheless, in view of 1 Chr 4:42, Shiphi and the others were probably part of the tribe of Simeon (Williamson *Chronicles* NCBC, 62).

CRAIG A. EVANS

SHIPHMITE [Heb *šipmî*]. The gentilic identification of Zabdi, one of twelve stewards of royal property appointed by David (1 Chr 27:27). His specific charge was oversight of the produce of the vineyards. The term is not used elsewhere.

RICHARD W. NYSSE

SHIPHRAH (PERSON) [Heb *šiprâ*]. One of the midwives of the Hebrews in Egypt (Exod 1:15). She and her partner Puah were ordered by the Pharaoh to kill all Israelite boys as soon as they were born. Though no reason is given to justify the king's expecting the midwives to do so, perhaps the summons by such a powerful figure was calculated to frighten them (Durham *Exodus* WBC, 11). The midwives, however, feared God and through acts of civil disobedience helped to pave the way for an exodus from Egypt. The prominent role assigned in chaps. 1–2 to these and other women—a group often powerless in ancient societies—makes the eventual victory of the Hebrews all the more striking from the traditional patriarchal point of view (Fox 1986: 14). Most later Jewish legends identify Shiphrah with Jochebed, but at least one declares the midwives to have been proselytes (Ginzberg 1909–38: 2.251; 5.393 n. 17). "Shiphrah" is a good Semitic name of an early type. Albright (1954: 229) found *špr(3)* as the hypocoristic name of a female Asiatic on an Egyptian list of slaves from Dynasty XIII (18th century B.C.) and related it to the Hebrew and Aramaic stem *špr,* "to be fair," and the Ar *sfr,* "to shine." From the same Semitic root comes the Hebrew feminine name *špyrh* in the caves of Murabbaᶜât (Stamm 1967: 323)—Aram form *špyr*ʾ (cf. Sapphira in Acts 5:1).

Bibliography

Albright, W. F. 1954. Northwest-Semitic Names in a List of Egyptian Slaves from the Eighteenth Century B.C. *JAOS* 74: 222–33.
Fox, E. 1986. *Now These Are the Names.* New York.
Ginzberg, L. 1909–38. *The Legends of the Jews.* 7 vols. Philadelphia.
Stamm, J. J. 1967. Hebräische Frauennamen. Pp. 301–39 in *Hebräische Wortforschung,* eds. B. Hartmann et al. VTSup 16. Leiden.

EDWIN C. HOSTETTER

SHIPHTAN (PERSON) [Heb *šipṭān*]. The father of Kemuel, leader of the tribe of Ephraim who was responsible for overseeing the distribution of the land of Canaan to the Israelites (Num 34:24). The name is based on the root *špṭ,* "to judge," "to lead," "to rule," and is similar in form to other biblical names such as Azzan and Zethan. The name is usually defined as "judgment" or "the deity has judged." The name was rendered *Sabatha(n)* in LXX (A) and *Sabathe* in LXX (B). In the Vulgate, *Sephtan* appears.

RAPHAEL I. PANITZ

SHISHA (PERSON) [Heb *šîšāʾ*]. Secretary in King David's administration and father of Elihoreph and Ahijah, secretaries of Solomon's administration. See also SERAIAH #1; SHAVSHA; SHEVA.

SHISHAK (PERSON) [Heb K *šwšq;* Q *šîšaq*]. An Egyptian pharaoh who harbored Jeroboam (1 Kgs 11:40) and advanced against Jerusalem during the reign of Rehoboam (1 Kgs 14:25). The form of the name in MT indicates that its proper pronunciation was uncertain in later biblical tradition. The name derives from Libyan *ššnḳ* and appears in Akkadian as *Susinku* and in Greek as *Sesonchis;* the conventional English spelling is Sheshonk. Shishak (Sheshonk) was the founder of the Egyptian 22d Dynasty, and the first of perhaps five kings to bear the name Sheshonk.

A scion of the seventh generation of a line of chieftains of the Libyan tribe of the Meshwesh, who had settled in Egypt at the end of the New Kingdom, Shishak first came to prominence during the reign of the last king of the 21st Dyn., Psusennes II (ca. 965–931 B.C.), as the commander-in-chief of the Egyptian army. He first appears on a stela from Abydos, dated sometime after Psusennes' 5th year, in which he sets up a mortuary endowment for his father, the great chief Namlot. By the close of the reign he was a mature man with grown children and well connected by marriage. An uncle was high priest of Memphis, a daughter was married to a general, a son was married into an important priestly family of Thebes, and another son, Osorkon, was married to a daughter of Psusennes II himself. Presumably upon the latter's dying without male issue, Shishak took the throne and inaugurated two and a half centuries of Libyan rule.

Shishak's 21-year reign (ca. 931–910 B.C.) represents a brief resurgence of the political and military élan of Egypt in the Near East moving from the erstwhile patrimony of his ancestral house in the city of Herakleopolis, which he left in the charge of his son the general Namlot (II), Shishak took up residence in "Pi-ese-the Great-*Ku*-of-Reharakhty," probably a faubourg of the (now abandoned) Per-Ramesses in the E Delta. From here he inaugurated a major building program in the Delta (Tell Tebillah, Tanis, Bubastis), the Memphite region (his own mortuary Temple), Herakleopolis (the Temple of Arsaphes) and Teudjoy, the headquarters of the governor of Upper Egypt. Thebes had refused to acknowledge his accession to the throne; and perhaps in consequence he terminated the high-priestly family and appointed his son Yewepet to the high priesthood. A monumental gate was erected on the S side of the East-West axis of the Amun Temple at Karnak, and late in his reign Shishak authorized the construction of a large festival court in front of the great Temple. There were disturbances also in the W oases, apparently against Libyan rule; but Shishak was able early to quell this opposition.

Shishak also revived Egypt's active involvement in the political affairs of West Asia. His statue at Byblos seems to indicate suzerainty over this part of the Phoenician coast, and his court became a refuge for dissidents fleeing the regime of his earlier contemporary Solomon (Hadad of Edom: 1 Kings 11:19; Jeroboam: 1 Kings: 11:40). Upon Solomon's death and perhaps spurred on by Israelite expansion into the Negeb and increased trade through Ezion Geber, Shishak construed some minor incident on the frontier—a fragmentary stela localizes it on the Red Sea coast—as a *casus belli,* and marched into Palestine. Whether or not he came as the ostensible champion of his erstwhile protégé Jereboam, both Judah and Israel suffered from the destructive march of the Egyptian army which left numerous levels of destruction in settlements all over the country. The commemorative relief and text of Shishak at Karnak reflects this campaign: the text is banal and devoid of historical content, but lists 154 towns claimed to have been destroyed. A careful study of the list and identification of the toponyms has made possible the reconstruction of the routes of march of the Egyptian forces. These involve the Negeb, the coastal plain and northern hill country, and some names even mark the devastation of a flying column across the Jordan to destroy the foundries and smithies around Mahanain in Transjordan. According to 1 Kgs 14:26, Jerusalem escaped the fate of other cities—and it does not indeed appear in the list—thanks to Rehoboam's pragmatic decision to pay Shishak a substantial indemnity which included the golden shields his father Solomon had made for the guard. Nonetheless, this very act, together with Shishak's setting up a triumphal stela at Megiddo, show that the Egyptian monarch construed his victory as tantamount to the reestablishment of an imperial hegemony over Palestine, a hegemony which his son Osorkon's epithets show continuing in the Egyptian view to the end of the 10th century.

The account of Shishak's incursion into Judea is greatly expanded by the Chronicler (2 Chr 12:2–12), providing a theological rationale for the campaign (v 2), a description of Shishak's forces (v 3), a summary of his conquests (v 4), an account of the role of Shemaiah the prophet in Jerusalem (v 5), the reaction of the Jerusalem nobility (v 6), and a word of deliverance that followed the people's repentance (vv 7–8). (The rest of the account, vv 9–11, follows 1 Kgs 14:25–28, with a summary statement in v 12.)

Shishak died ca. 910–909 B.C. perhaps after a brief coregency with his son and successor, Osorkon I. Recently the latter's excessive donations of gold and silver to the temples, on record in an inscription from Bubastis, have been understood as reflecting Shishak's booty from the Palestine campaign.

Bibliography

Feucht, E. 1978. Zwei Reliefs Scheschongs I. aus el-Hebeh. *SAK* 6: 69–77.

Green, A. R. 1979. Israelite Influence at Shishak's court? *BASOR* 233: 59–62.

Kitchen, K. A. 1973. *The Third Intermediate Period in Egypt.* Warminster.

Malamat, A. 1982. A Political Look at the Kingdom of David and Solomon and Its Relations with Egypt. Pp. 189–204 in *Studies in the Period of David and Solomon,* ed. T. Ishida. Tokyo.

———. 1983. *Das davidische und salomonische Königreich und seine Beziehungen zu Ägypten und Syrien.* Vienna.

Mazar, B. 1957. The Campaign of Pharaoh Shishak to Palestine. *VTSup* 4: 37–66.

Redford, D. B. 1973. Studies in Relations between Palestine and Egypt during the First Millennium B.C., II. The Twenty-second Dynasty. *JAOS* 93: 3–17.

Tresson, P. 1934. L'inscription de Chechanq I[er] au musee de Caire. Pp. 817ff. in *Melanges Maspero* 1. Cairo.

DONALD B. REDFORD

SHITRAI

SHITRAI (PERSON) [Heb *šiṭray*]. A state official; a Sharonite. One of twelve stewards of royal property appointed by David, his specific charge was oversight of the herds which pastured in Sharon (1 Chr 27:29). Of the twelve, he is one of seven identified with a gentilic rather than by paternity, indicating perhaps that he was from outside the tribal structure.

RICHARD W. NYSSE

SHITTAH TREE.

SHITTAH TREE. See FLORA.

SHITTIM

SHITTIM (PLACE) [Heb *šiṭṭîm*]. The encampment site of Israel in the plains of Moab NE of the Dead Sea. Since Shittim was the final encampment of the Israelites before they crossed Jordan, it is notable in the history of Israel. At Shittim, the Israelites fell into the idolatrous and immoral practices of Baal-peor. The men of Israel who had taken Moabite and Midianite wives were smitten with a plague, killing 24,000, because they had engaged in the Baal-peor cult (Num 25:1–9). Final preparation was made at Shittim to enter Canaan: (1) A census was taken of all men (20 years and up) in view of military need and eventual settlement allotments (Num 26); (2) Joshua was publicly announced as Moses' successor (Num 27:12–23); (3) Reuben, Gad, and part of the tribe of Manasseh received their land allotment E of the Jordan after promising to fight with their brethren (Num 32); (4) Moses delivered his final address to the people (Deut 31 ff.); and (5) Joshua sent out spies to Jericho. In addition, the Israelites defeated the Midianites from the base camp of Shittim.

Shittim is probably the same as Abel-shittim of Numbers 33:49, with the abbreviated version being the more popular. According to the biblical text, the location of Abel-shittim was immediately E of the Jordan and N of the Dead Sea. Two sites have been proposed. Originally, Tell el-Kefrein (M.R. 210139), located on a hill overlooking the Plains of Moab, was proposed as the site of Shittim. The location is 6 miles N of the Dead Sea and E of the Jordan, and notable evidence of habitation in OT times contributed to its selection. Potsherds from Iron Ages I and II (12th to 6th centuries B.C.) were recovered from the site. Nelson Glueck, however, proposes the larger site of Tell el-Hamman (M.R. 214138) for Abel-shittim. This tell is located 2 miles farther E on the Wadi el-Kefrein. Here, remains of Iron Age I and II fortresses with 1.2 m thick outer walls have been discovered. The foundations of massive towers at each end and a strong glacis possibly surrounding the wall indicate that Tell el-Hamman held a strategic position in ancient times. The confusion over the identification of the site exists because the biblical name, Abel-shittim, and its Roman name, Abila, no longer exist in the area. While other familiar names survived, Abel-shittim was forgotten. The names "Shittim," meaning "achaias," and Abel-shittim, "stream of the achaias," indicate that the place was in the once-forested hills of Moab.

Bibliography

Glueck, N. 1943. Some Ancient Towns in the Plains of Moab. *BASOR* 91: 13–18.

———. 1948. *Explorations in Eastern Palestine IV.* AASOR 25–28. New Haven.
———. 1968. *The River Jordan.* New York.

JOEL C. SLAYTON

SHIZA (PERSON) [Heb *sîzāʾ*]. The father of Adina who was the leader of a band of Reubenites associated with King David's chief military men (1 Chr 11:42). Adina son of Shiza is the first of a list of sixteen men from the Transjordan in the Chronicler's expansion (1 Chr 11:41b–47) of the parallel lists of David's military elite (1 Chr 11:10–41a = 2 Sam 23:8–39). Linked with the name "Shiza" in v 42 is the ambiguous Heb expression *ʿālāyw šĕlôšîm* (RSV "with him thirty"), which may indicate that Shiza (or Adina?) either was the leader of a unit of thirty warriors or was accompanied by thirty other Reubenites who joined David (cf. the similar expression in 1 Chr 12:4). There is general agreement that these expanded verses were not part of the original list, and Williamson (*1 & 2 Chronicles* NCBC, 104) and others (Mazar 1986: 101–2; Rudolph *Chronikbücher* HAT 1st series, 101) have argued convincingly that the Chronicler or a later redactor did not fabricate these names.

Bibliography

Mazar, B. 1986. The Military Élite of King David. Pp. 83–103 in *The Early Biblical Period: Historical Studies.* Ed. S. Aḥituv and B. Levine. Jerusalem.

RUSSELL FULLER

SHOA (PERSON) [Heb *šôaʿ*]. A people mentioned in a military setting in Ezek 23:23. The context is a prediction of punishment (vv 22–27) in a judgment oracle against Judah, which is described in allegorical terms as the grossly wayward wife of Yahweh ("Oholibah," vv 4, 11, 22). Babylon, the scorned political lover (v 17), was to retaliate, using against Judah the military machismo once so attractive (v 15). The national contingents of its army include Shoa. The preceding name, Pekod, refers to the Aramean tribe of Puqudu located east of the Tigris. Accordingly one expects Shoa to refer to a historical people within the same general area of Babylonian hegemony.

Zadok (1978: 178–79) has compared the listing of ethnic groups in v 23 with that of an inscription of Nebuchadnezzar: the trio of Pekod, Shoa, and Koa correspond to a list of four or six Aramean and other West-Semitic tribes, including the Pukudu, although none of the other names match. The present name is not found elsewhere, and any suggested identification runs into the difficulty of explaining why its form is unique. Thus Zadok declined to equate them with the Sutu, with which generally Shoa is tentatively identified, because of lack of phonetic correspondence. He did note that the grouping of Shoa and Koa sounded onomatopoeic. Oppenheim (*IDB* 3: 48) has compared pairs of names like the Cherethites and the Pelethites. Indeed, one may note the allegorical names of the S and N kingdoms in this chapter, Oholibah and Oholah, which sound like Tweedledum and Tweedledee. Accordingly, there seems to be some focus on this pair of names. Zimmerli (1979: 488) found assonance in the triple grouping, Pekod, Shoa and Koa, in terms of their common "ô" vowel. Eichrodt (*Ezekiel* OTL, 328) has helpfully found wordplay in the three names, Pekod referring to punishment (Heb *pqd;* cf; the wordplay in Jer 50:21) and Shoa to a cry for help (Heb *šwʿ*). See KOA. Then the fate in store for Judah is expressed in a rhetorically forceful fashion. By means of this explanation it is possible to return to the common identification with more confidence, as a deliberate distortion.

The Sutu or Sutians were seminomads who for centuries engaged in raids on Assyrian and Babylonian territory (Brinkman 1968: 285–87). At the end of the 8th century B.C. they supported the Babylonian rebel Merodach-baladan against the Assyrian king Sargon. Here they may feature as mercenaries, if not vassals.

Bibliography

Brinkman, J. A. 1968. *A Political History of Post-Kassite Babylonia 1158–722 B.C.* Rome.
Zadok, R. 1978. West-Semitic Toponyms in Assyrian and Babylonian Sources. Pp. 163–79 in *Studies in Bible and the Ancient Near East,* ed. Y. Avishur. Jerusalem.
Zimmerli, W. 1979. *Ezekiel 1.* Trans. R. E. Clements. Philadelphia.

LESLIE C. ALLEN

SHOBAB (PERSON) [Heb *šôbāb*]. **1.** A son of David born in Jerusalem to Bathsheba (Bathshua; 2 Sam 5:14; 1 Chr 3:5; 14:4). Three full brothers of Shobab's are listed: Shammua (Shimea), Nathan, and Solomon. In addition, David had six sons born in Hebron to six different wives, and nine born in Jerusalem to unnamed wives, as well as many sons born to his concubines in Jerusalem (1 Chr 3:9). See also DAVID, SONS OF.

2. One of three sons of Caleb's daughter Jerioth (1 Chr 2:18). He was a Judahite. His grandfather Caleb (also known as Chelubai; 1 Chr 2:9) was not the famous spy of Joshua's day (Numbers 13). Rather, he lived earlier, and was the great-grandfather of Bezalel (1 Chr 2:19–20), the great Tabernacle craftsman (Exod 31:1; 35:30; etc.).

The text of 1 Chr 2:18 is difficult, and some versions (e.g., RSV, NIV) see Jerioth to be a second wife to Caleb (and not a daughter), since they are both introduced by *ʾet,* the common sign of the direct object. All solutions have some difficulties, however. The present one sees the first *ʾet* as the preposition "with" and the second one as the direct object marker, and reads *ʾištô* ("his wife") for *ʾiššâ w-* ("a wife and . . .") between the two names (or else understands the *waw* as an emphatic). See also Braun *1 Chronicles* WBC, 37.

DAVID M. HOWARD, JR.

SHOBACH (PERSON) [Heb *šōbak*]. Var. SHOPHACH. Aramean army general leading the forces of Hadadezer (2 Sam 10:16 and 18). According to the "Ammonite War Narratives" of 2 Samuel 10 (= 1 Chronicles 19), once Joab defeated the Ammonite-Aramean coalition (2 Sam 10:13–14), Hadadezer mustered his forces from "beyond the river" to fight Israel. Shobach, whom the Chronicler calls Shophach (1 Chr 19:16), was the general in charge of the army for this war, which reportedly took place at Helam, located in the Transjordan. In this battle Shobach suffered a major defeat at the hands of David.

There is much question as to whether the battle described in 2 Sam 10:16–19 is the same as the battle reported in 2 Sam 8:3–8, in which Hadadezer also is defeated and the Arameans are again completely subjugated by David (cf. McCarter *2 Samuel* AB). In that passage, however, Hadadezer is mentioned as being the king and commander of the army and there is no mention of Shobach. Given the different literary emphases of both passages, such as giving the credit for the victory of Yahweh in 2 Sam 8:6, as opposed to giving the credit to David for almost singlehandedly defeating this army (cf. the use of all 3d mas. sing. verbs in 2 Sam 10:18), it is most probable to cite different authors for both passages and to see them as relating to the same battle. See also HADADEZER).

In this case the function of Shobach being mentioned in 2 Sam 10:16 and 18 as both general of the army and as one whom David himself wounded and killed is to demonstrate the military prowess of David. Since the tradition did not record the death of Hadadezer in an Israelite-Aramean war, the introduction of the name of the general into the second narrative suits the purpose of building the status of the Israelite king by having him get close enough to the leader to inflict upon him a mortal wound (Bailey 1989).

Bibliography

Bailey, R. C. 1989. *David in Pursuit of Power: 2 Samuel 10–12 and Its Implications for the so-called Throne Succession Narrative.* Sheffield.

RANDALL C. BAILEY

SHOBAI (PERSON) [Heb *šōbāy*]. The name of a levitical family of temple gatekeepers who returned to Palestine with Zerubbabel shortly after 538 B.C.E., the end of the Babylonian exile. The name appears in Ezra 2:42 in the phrase "the sons of Shobai" (Gk *sabaou/sōbai*), where the Levites are distinguished from the people of Israel, the priests, and the temple servants. The parallel verse Neh 7:45 lists "the sons of Shobai" (Gk *sabi/sabei/sabai/sōbai*) under the Levites, as does the later parallel 1 Esdr 5:28. The different versions of the Apocrypha use three transliterations of this word: *sobai, sabei,* and *tobeis*. These differences do not appear, however, in the Eng versions.

STEVEN R. SWANSON

SHOBAL (PERSON) [Heb *šôbāl*]. **1.** The son of Seir, the Horite (Gen 36:20; 1 Chr 1:38) and the father of Manahath (among other "sons"; Gen 36:23; 1 Chr 1:40).

2. A son of Hur, son of Caleb (1 Chr 2:50) and father of Haroe, "half of the Manahathites" (1 Chr 2:52).

3. A son of Judah, brother of Hur, and father of Reaiah (1 Chr 4:1–2).

According to Gen 36:29, Shobal was a Horite tribe with its own chief. The three "persons" named Shobal listed above are actually personifications of this tribe in various historical circumstances. Shobal #1 represents the tribe as part of the Horite population within the Edomite state in the 7th century B.C. Shobal #2 and #3 presuppose the immigration of Edomite/Idumean tribes and clans into S Judah during the exilic and postexilic period. Those who compiled the statistics of the Judean population in the form of genealogies, which we now read in 1 Chronicles 2 and 4, first linked the immigrants with the Calebites—Shobal (2)—and later directly to Judah—Shobal (3). Here is a primary example for how tribal genealogies, being political in nature, shift with changes in administration and politics. See HORITES; HUR; MANAHATHITES.

As a personal name, *sbl* occurs several times in Safaitic (Harding 1971: 309). It seems, however, that the Edomite/Horite name "Shobal" was primarily a geographical designation which is still preserved: Jebel Sôbala S of Wādī al-Ḥasâ (Musil 1907–08,1: 2, 313), and the name of a ruin, Kh. Sôbal, on its top (Musil 1907–8, 2: 242). Tribal names, especially the names of sedentary tribes, are frequently derived from geographical names (cf. "Judah" and "Ephraim"). Etymologically, one could perhaps connect "Shobal" with Akkadian *šubultu,* Ugaritic *šblt,* Sabaic s_1*blt,* Ethiopic *säbl,* Heb *šibbôlet,* etc., "ear of grain;" the etymology would also point to a geographical name, which referred to the fertility of that particular part of Edom.

Bibliography

Harding, G. L. 1971. *An Index and Concordance of Pre-Islamic Arabian Names and Inscriptions.* Toronto.
Musil, A. 1907–8. *Arabia Petraea II.* Parts 1–2. Vienna.

ERNST AXEL KNAUF

SHOBEK (PERSON) [Heb *šôbēq*]. A leader of the people and a signatory to the covenant established by Ezra (Neh 10:24). The name means "victor," but nothing else is known about him.

FREDERICK W. SCHMIDT

SHOBI (PERSON) [Heb *šōbî*]. Son of Nahash, a ruler of the Ammonites (2 Sam 17:27). Shobi helped David during the revolt of Absalom. When David was on the E side of the Jordan in Mahanaim, preparing for a major battle with Absalom's forces, Shobi, accompanied by Machir and Barzillai, brought supplies to the king's tired and famished troops.

Older scholarship tended to doubt this account of events, feeling that Shobi never existed since his name is not mentioned elsewhere. Shobi's kindness was also difficult to reconcile with David's earlier subjugation of Ammon (2 Samuel 10–12). Consequently, the expression "Shobi son of" was emended from the text in 2 Sam 17:27 and the Ammonite conquest was viewed as occurring later than the revolt of Absalom (Cook 1899–1900: 156–60, cf. McCarter *II Samuel* AB, 274, 394).

Such measures are unnecessary. Shobi's older brother was Hanun, who had succeeded his father, Nahash, to the throne. He had fought unsuccessfully with David (2 Samuel 10–12), and David probably replaced him with his younger brother as the king of the Ammonites. This was a common practice in the ANE.

Bibliography

Cook, S. A. 1899–1900. Notes on the Composition of 2 Samuel. *AJSL* 16: 145–77.

STEPHEN G. DEMPSTER

SHOHAM (PERSON) [Heb *šōham*]. Son of Jaaziah (1 Chr 24:27). Several names appear in 24:20–31 which are lacking in 23:6–24. None of the sons of Jaaziah are included in the previous list of sons of Merari. Apparently, the names were added to the earlier list in order to attest to the authority of Jaaziah's family for levitical service. The passage begins with the introduction, "of the remaining sons of Levi . . . ," which implies an intent to fill out the previous list.

DONALD K. BERRY

SHOMER (PERSON) [Heb *šômēr*]. The son of Heber, listed in the Asherite genealogy in 1 Chr 7:32. This figure receives no further mention by the Chronicler, but a related name—Shemer (pausal form *šāmer*)—appears in 1 Chr 7:34. Because Shemer's father is not mentioned and because his descendants are listed after those of Japhlet, Shomer's brother, scholars have suggested that these two figures are identical.

The genealogy of Heber (1 Chr 7:32–35) is confusing on several points. Not only does Shomer seem equated with Shemer, but also Helem (v 35) appears identified with Hotham (v 32). The names of Shemer's descendants also are unclear: two of the three have been vocalized differently than their consonantal form, by means of a common scribal technique known as *qere/kethib.*

The name "Shomer/Shemer" also appears in 1 Kgs 16:24, 1 Chr 6:31, 2 Kgs 12:21, with no apparent relation to the figure mentioned here. A possible connection, however, has been drawn between Shomer and a descendant of Benjamin in 1 Chr 8:12. Although the MT refers to this latter figure as Shemed, various mss read the name as Shomer/Shemer. Based on the presence of such other Asherite names as Beriah, Serah, Heber in the Benjaminite genealogies, Edelman suggests that the "Ashurites" of 2 Sam 2:9 refer to an Asherite enclave living on the frontiers of Benjamin and Ephraim (Edelman 1985: 85–86).

Bibliography

Edelman, D. 1985. The "Ashurites" of Eshbaal's State. *PEQ* 117: 85–91.

JULIA M. O'BRIEN

SHOPHACH (PERSON) [Heb *šôpak*]. See SHOBACH (PERSON).

SHOVEL [Heb *yāᶜ*]. A cultic utensil mentioned in several lists of objects used in the tabernacle (Exod 27:3; 28:3; Num 4:14) and the temple (1 Kgs 7:40, 45; 2 Kgs 25:14; 2 Chr 4:11, 16; Jer 52:18). The shovels were made of bronze, as was the courtyard altar they serviced; they were used to carry away the ashes of the burnt offerings. So apparently were the temple shovels, which are included in the list of utensils (1 Kgs 7:40) even though, in the 1 Kings temple account, the altar itself is not mentioned. The altar probably did exist, having been erected by David, not Solomon; the presence of "shovels" in the Kings text is indirect evidence of the altar's presence.

Incense shovels are frequently depicted in artistic presentations of the temple or its features in Jewish art of the postbiblical period, as in the mosaic floors of Palestinian synagogues. Such shovels are rectangular in shape, with handles projecting from the narrow side. Ceramic incense shovels, both rectangular and oval in shape, have been recovered from Roman period sites.

Another word for "shovel," *raḥat,* refers to a winnowing tool and is found only in Isa 30:24.

CAROL MEYERS

SHUA (PERSON) [Heb *šûᶜā*ʾ]. A descendant of Asher in the segmented tribal genealogy in 1 Chr 7:30–40. The name appears in v 32 as a third-generation female descendant of the eponymous tribal ancestor Asher, the daughter of Heber and sister of Japhlet, Shomer, and Hotham. The form of the name found in the MT and presupposed by Lucianic LXX derives from the root *šwᶜ* meaning "cry for help." The final *ʾalep* has been explained as an ending with a vocative force that was added to indicate that the name is a shortened form (Noth *IPN,* 38, 154). The LXX has the variant reading Sola, which would reflect an underlying Hebrew consonantal text *šwlh,* in which the *ᶜayin* either was mistaken for a *lamed* or was omitted from transliteration as a silent letter. In the latter case, an original Hebrew text could be restored as *šwᶜlh,* Shualah, a feminine form of the name "Shual."

In light of the intergenerational repetition of other names in the Asherite genealogy, including Zophah, Beriah/Beri, Shelesh/Shilshah and Imnah/Imna/Imrah, it is possible to suggest that Shua is a corrupted reading of Shual in v 36 (Edelman 1988: 21, n. 3). The LXX reading Sola preserves a possible stage of textual transmission that presents the name in v 32 as a feminine form of Shual. Such an alteration between masculine and feminine forms occurs elsewhere in the genealogy with Shelesh/Shilshah. If the Greek evidence is excluded from consideration, the MT form *šwᶜʾ* could have resulted from a copyist's error in which the final *lamed* of a square script was mistakenly read as a final *ʾalep.* Alternately, since the following word begins with *ʾalep,* a scribal eye could have jumped over the *lamed,* writing *ʾalep* instead and then, when appraising the sense of the consonants, reduplicating the *ʾalep* to begin the word *ʾăḥôtām,* "their sister."

Bibliography

Edelman, D. 1988. The Asherite Genealogy in 1 Chr 7:30–40. *BR* 33: 13–23.

DIANA V. EDELMAN

SHUAH (PERSON) [Heb *šûaḥ*]. SHUHITE. A son of Abraham and Keturah (Gen 25:2; 1 Chr 1:32). Like all the sons of Abraham and Keturah, Shuah represents an Arabian or Syrian landscape associated with the incense trade around the middle of the 1st millennium B.C. See KETURAH. Shuah is identical with Akkadian *Sūḫu*, a country (and Assyrian province) on the middle Euphrates. In its strategic position vis-à-vis the main trade routes through the Syrian desert, Sūḫu was preceded by the kingdom of Mari, and followed by Dura Europos. As a country, *Sūḫu* is already mentioned in the Mari archives (Háclár 1983), and in Egyptian topographical lists from the LB Age. The hieroglyphic rendering of the name suggests that the Egyptians learned from the Canaanites (Görg 1989). In this case, it can also be explained why Akkadian *s* became *š* in Hebrew (cf. Knauf 1988: 74; 105). As early as the time of Sargon II, *Sūḫu* was the summer pasture of Arab bedouin tribes (*ABL* 547 = Parpola 1987: 82.13–18). A caravan of Sabeans and people from Tema was intercepted by the governor of *Sūḫu* shortly before the reign of Tiglath-pileser III (see J. Black in Northedge et al. 1988).

The only person from Shuah mentioned in the OT is Job's friend Bildad (Job 2:11). Job's friends seem to come from the extremities of the Arabian peninsula: Eliphaz the Temanite from NW Arabia, Bildad the Shuhite from NE Arabia, and Zophar the Naamathite from S Arabia. See also BILDAD; NAAMATHITE; TEMANITE; UZ.

Bibliography

Görg, M. 1989. ŠWḤ (Schuach)—Wege der Namensüberlieferung. *BN* 47: 7–9.
Háclár, N. 1983. Die Stellung Suḫis in der Geschichte. Eine Zwischenbilanz. *OrAnt* 22: 25–36.
Knauf, E. A. 1988. *Midian*. ADPV. Wiesbaden.
Northedge, A., et al. 1988. *Excavations at ᶜÂna (1981–1982): Excavations at ᶜAna: Qalᶜa Island.* Iraq Archaeological Reports 1. Warminster.
Parpola, S. 1987. *The Correspondence of Sargon II, Part 1.* State Archives of Assyria I. Helsinki.

ERNST AXEL KNAUF

SHUAL (PERSON) [Heb *šûᶜāl*]. A descendant of Asher in the segmented tribal genealogy in 1 Chr 7:30–40. The name appears in v 36 as the son of Zophah, as a fifth-generation descendant of the eponymous tribal ancestor Asher. It derives from the root *šᶜl* and means "fox, jackal."

In the context of the genealogy, Shual appears to be a personal name, but is more likely a clan designation or geographical term. The summary in v 40 would seem to indicate that the information presented in genealogical form derives from administrative lists used for army conscription and possibly also taxation. Recruitment could be done by village, region, or clan rather than by individual name (Mendenhall 1958: 60–65). In addition, Shual appears as the name of a region in S Mt. Ephraim in 1 Sam 13:17 (see SHUAL [PLACE]), which is consistent with the secondary use of a clan name to designate the region belonging to the clan or of a regional name being applied to those who live within its confines, but not with the designation of open country (*ʾereṣ*) by the name of an individual owner. When the reference to the Asherite clan/region is set beside the one in 1 Sam 13:17 and is further combined with similar geographically specific names in the genealogy such as Birzvaith, Shelesh/Shilshah, Zophah, Imnah/Imna, Japhlet, Beriah, Shemer, and Serah/Sheerah, the association of the entire Asherite genealogy in 1 Chr 7:30–40 with the Asherite enclave located in S Mt. Ephraim rather than the Galilean territory of Asher becomes clear (Yeivin 1971: 228; *LBHG*, 244; Edelman 1985: 86; 1989: 48–58). The cumulative evidence favors an equation of the Asherite descendant Shual with the land of Shual in the vicinity of Ophrah.

An equation of Shual with Shua in v 32 of the genealogy has been proposed (Edelman 1988: 21, n. 3). On the understanding that the repetition of the names Zophah, Shelesh/Shishah, Beriah/Beri, and Imna/Imrah within the genealogy is evidence for its composite nature and creation through the combination of three administrative lists detailing the constituents of the enclave at three separate points in time (Edelman 1988: 15–16), Shua becomes an additional possible example of name overlap within the underlying administrative sources that has been obscured through textual corruption.

Bibliography

Edelman, D. 1985. The "Ashurites" of Eshbaal's State (2 Sam. 2:9). *PEQ* 117: 85–91.
———. 1988. The Asherite Genealogy in 1 Chr 7:30–40. *BR* 33: 13–23.
———. 1989. Saul's Journey through Mt. Ephraim and Samuel's Ramah (1 Sam. 9:4–5; 10:2–5). *ZDPV* 104: 44–58.
Mendenhall, G. 1958. The Census Lists of Numbers 1 and 26. *JBL* 77: 52–66.
Yeivin, S. 1971. *The Israelite Conquest of Canaan*. Istanbul.

DIANA V. EDELMAN

SHUAL (PLACE) [Heb *šûᶜāl*]. A region located within the confines of S Mt. Ephraim (1 Sam 13:17). The name derives the root *šᶜl* and means "fox, jackal."

A Philistine raiding party is reported to have been sent out from the Michmash garrison to the land of Shual via the road to Ophrah in the wake of Jonathan's defeat of the Philistine garrison across the Wadi Suweinit at Gibeah (1 Sam 13:3). Ophrah is commonly identified with modern day eṭ-Ṭaiyibe (M.R. 178151) NW of Bethel (i.e. Aharoni *LBHG*, 440). Ophrah would accordingly be the name of the main settlement within the territory of the clan of Shual, in the easternmost portion of the Bethel plateau. The adjoining village at Rammun (M.R. 178148) was probably also part of the Shual region in the Saulide era (Edelman 1989: 53).

Since Shual appears to have been a clan name that was secondarily applied to the region inhabited by that clan, or a regional label that was used to designate villagers living within its borders, one is justified in equating the place name in 1 Sam 13:17 with the Asherite clan/region of Shual listed in 1 Chr 7:36. See SHUAL (PERSON). A careful study of the genealogy reveals that it enumerates clans and villages of the Asherite enclave located in S Mt. Ephraim rather than in the traditional Asherite tribal territory in W Galilee (Edelman 1988). See ASHER; ASHURITES. The genealogical context thus accords well with the geographical indications of 1 Sam 13:17.

It is likely that the land of Shaalim mentioned in 1 Sam 9:4 is to be identified with the land of Shual in 1 Sam 13:17 (Kirkpatrick 1880: 63 n. 2; Smith, *Samuel* ICC, 60;

Albright 1922: 116–17; Kallai 1971: 193; McCarter, *1 Samuel* AB, 174–75, n. 9; Edelman 1989: 53). The singular form *šāʿāl* or *šʿl* would represent an earlier, variant spelling of *šûʿāl* or *šwʿl,* before *waw* became a standard *mater lectionis* for *o*- and *u*-class vowels. The geographical progression of Saul's trek through the four subregions of Mt. Ephraim—the lands of Shalishah, Shaalim, Yimni, and Zuph—is consistent with both the location of the land of Shual around Ophrah and with the appearance of all four regions as clans within the Asherite enclave of S Mt. Ephraim in the genealogy of Asher in 1 Chr 7:30–40 (Edelman 1989: 50–58).

Bibliography

Albright, W. F. 1922. Appendix II. Ramah of Samuel. *AASOR* 4:112–23.

Edelman, D. 1988. The Asherite Genealogy in 1 Chr 7:30–40. *BR* 33: 13–23.

———. 1989. Saul's Journey through Mt. Ephraim and Samuel's Ramah (1 Sam. 9:4–5; 10:2–5). *ZDPV* 104: 44–58.

Kallai, Z. 1971. Baal-Shalisha and Ephraim. Pp. 191–95 in *Bible and Jewish History,* ed. B. Uffenheimer. Tel Aviv (in Hebrew).

Kirkpatrick, A. F. 1880. *The First Book of Samuel.* Cambridge.

DIANA V. EDELMAN

SHUBAEL (PERSON) [Heb *šûbāʾēl*]. See SHEBUEL.

SHUHAH (PERSON) [Heb *šûḥâ*]. The brother of a certain Chelub listed in the genealogy of Judah in the book of Chronicles (1 Chr 4:11).

H. C. LO

SHUHAM (PERSON) [Heb *šûḥām*]. Var. HUSHIM. SHUHAMITES. The only son of Dan according to the second census taken by Moses in the wilderness. He is listed in Num 26:42 as the ancestor of the tribe of the Shuhamites. The LXX (Num 26:46) contains an alternate rendition of this name: *sami.* The parallel genealogy in Genesis 46 also lists only one son for Dan, but gives him the name Hushim (Gen 46:23). It is interesting to note that although Shuham is the only son of Dan, the phraseology of the verse is in the plural. He is introduced by the clause, "These are the sons of Dan." This is due to the desire to keep the form of the genealogy consistent, and should not be taken to suggest that some entries have been lost.

CHRISTINA DE GROOT VAN HOUTEN

SHUHITE. See SHUAH.

SHULAMMITE [Heb *šûlammît*]. A reference to the woman in Cant 7:1—Eng 6:13. Four interpretations occur individually and in combination. The first interprets it as the feminine form of Solomon, which is used to refer to the man in Cant 1:5; 3:7, 11; 8:11, 12 (in addition to the superscription in 1:1). However, the expected feminine form of Solomon is *šĕlōmît* (which occurs in Lev 24:11 and 1 Chr 3:19); in addition, unlike proper names, "Shulammite" is used with the article.

The second regards it as a designation for an inhabitant of the town of SHUNEM (identified with modern Solem). Alteration of liquid sounds is not uncommon, and did occur later with Shunem, as its modern equivalent indicates. However, substitution of *l* for *n* in this name is unattested in biblical times, and the woman of Cant is elsewhere associated with Jerusalem rather than Shunem. In addition, given the strong alliteration of the verse as a whole, it would be surprising for a less alliterative option to be used (*nun* also occurs in *wĕneḥĕzeh* and *hammaḥănāyim; lamed* does not occur elsewhere in the verse). Some proponents of this theory identify the woman of Cant with Abishag, for which there is no clear evidence.

The third interpretation sees Shulammite as a reference to a goddess (Šala or Šulmânîtu), equivalent of Ishtar. This explanation is popular with proponents of the sacred marriage interpretation of Cant.

The fourth interprets it as a noun from the root *šlm,* with meaning "the perfect one." Although there are morphological difficulties, Fox (1985: 157–58) explains the word as a *nisbe* form of the otherwise unknown *šûlam,* perhaps pointed incorrectly.

The first and fourth options are reflected in rabbinic references to the term; LXX B has *hē Soumaneitis,* which probably reflects the second option.

Since none of these explanations has won majority approval, many interpreters choose to transliterate the name rather than attempting to translate. This seems the best option. It is possible that no single explanation is adequate (and in fact a number of commentators combine elements of two theories): the form may well be related to *šlm,* and influenced by the name of Solomon. The *u*-vowel may be affected by the long *u* of *šûbî* to increase the assonance of the verse. Recent thorough discussions may be found in Fox (1985: 157–58) and Pope (*Song of Songs* AB, 600).

Bibliography

Fox, M. V. 1985. *The Song of Songs and Ancient Egyptian Love Poetry.* Madison, WI.

ELIZABETH F. HUWILER

SHUMATHITE [Heb *šūmātî*]. One of the four families that resided in Kiriath-jearim (1 Chr 2:53). They were Judahites if not also Calebites. Shobal, a son of Hur, was the father of Kiriath-jearim—but whether this means he was the founder of the city or the ancestor of its inhabitants is not certain. Williamson (*1–2 Chronicles* NCBC, 55) considers vv 53–55 to be an obscure fragment, attached before the Chronicler's time on account of the link through Kiriath-jearim. The name "Shumathite," which came probably from a proper name **šūmâ,* is of an adjective type designating clans, tribes, or nations. Both of these names could be shortened forms based upon either the word *šmʿ,* "to hear," or the term *šmr,* "to keep." In any case, *šūmātî* is used with the article as a collective noun.

EDWIN C. HOSTETTER

SHUNA (NORTH), TELL ESH- (M.R. 207224). A Neolithic–EB I site located on the NE edge of the Jordan

Valley along the Wadi al-Arab. When first identified during the 1953 Point IV Archaeological Survey, the size of the site was recorded at ca. 1 km in length with a maximum height of 10 m. Since the early 1950s, the villages of Kh. esh-Shuna and Kh. esh-Sheikh Hussein, situated on and around the ancient mound, have grown at the expense of the archaeological material beneath. Today, though the sherd scatter extends throughout the modern town of Tell esh-Shuna Shamaliyeh, only small fragments of the original tell are preserved and/or are accessible for excavation. The best-preserved fragment of the mound is located in the middle of the bus stop. Even this area, measuring only 45 x 50 m with a maximum preserved height of 6 m, was only available for excavation owing to the destruction of the overlying houses in 1967. The accompanying destruction debris and garbage accumulation alone account for up to 1.5 m of the mound's preserved height.

During the 1953 survey, several small probe trenches were excavated by Hasan Abu Awad and J. Mellaart, yielding an occupational sequence dating from the "middle Chalcolithic" through to the EB III (de Contenson 1960a; 1960b; 1961; Mellaart 1962). Tell esh-Shuna North was revisited during the 1975 East Jordan Valley Survey (Ibrahim, Sauer, and Yassine 1976), after which salvage excavations were conducted in 1984 and 1985 (Gustavson-Gaube 1985; 1986; Baird 1987). Based on a 75 m^2 exposure with a maximum 4.3 m depth of occupation, 109 strata were identified which outlined the local development from the "Pottery Neolithic B–related"/late Chalcolithic to the EB I.

Since the basic chronological framework for the N Jordan Valley during 4th millennium remains controversial at best, the emphasis of the 1984 and 1985 excavations was to trace and reconstruct the chronological sequence. Based on the preliminary analysis, Tell esh-Shuna North has yielded three basic artifact assemblages, distinguished primarily by ceramic criteria. Many of the craft traditions characteristic of the early assemblage(s) endured, and the local traditions, though undergoing continual modification, did not yield to abrupt change.

The provisional "early phase" (strata 114–61/55) is characterized by overlapping series of pits and postholes dug into the natural alluvium, rectilinear dwellings with associated courtyards (one dwelling with sunken flooring), and a series of outdoor graveled, cobbled, and clay pavements with a variety of associated pits and burning installations. The ceramic repertoire is predominantly coarse plain ware (ca. 60%). Decorated wares include a simple red-painted coarse ware with clear Pottery Neolithic B affinities and a coarse red-slipped ware (both representing ca. 20% of the sherd total). The three coarse ware series had rare examples of horizontal bands of thumb impressed, pinched, and incised decoration. Nonlocally produced ceramics include a rare simple geometric painted ware and a dark-face slipped and burnished ware, clearly of the N Syrian tradition. Individual parallels to the late Ghassulian traditions point to contemporaniety; however, too many elements of the classical Ghassulian forms, decorations, and manufacturing techniques are absent to posit the Tell esh-Shuna North as an "early phase" within the late Chalcolithic Ghassulian.

The "middle phase" (strata 60/54–23) is characterized by a series of rectilinear and curvilinear dwellings with associated courtyards, large pits and ash lenses, cobbled pavements, and a series of fragmentary wall foundations. Many of the former craft traditions continue into the "middle phase," notably the coarse plain and red-slipped ceramic traditions (representing ca. 60% and 40% respectively). Most of the simple red-painted wares fall out of use although their production is marginally continued and the more regularized multiple parallel band motif appears. The application of impressed or incised horizontal bands to a vessel surface increases. The distinguishing factor of this phase, however, is the inclusion of the black and gray polished "Esdraelon" wares (though representing less than 1% of the sherd total) and the innovations in local ceramic production that the appearance of these wares seems to have provoked.

The latest preserved phase at Tell esh-Shuna North (strata 22–7) yielded a substantial multiphase building complex and a large basalt wall (preserved width ca. 2 m, but with the W face destroyed. With this wall was a chipped stone surface spanning the "late phase" sequence with an intervening series of poorly preserved wall foundations and pits. Small fragments of eroded copper and slag were found in pit debris, implying the presence of local craftsmen working in small-scale metallurgy. The basic ceramic repertoire of the preceding phase continues with slight modifications in the form repertoire. The gray and black polished "Esdraelon" wares end with the introduction of the "grain wash" wares, clearly placing the Tell esh-Shuna "late phase" within the general development of the EB I.

Bibliography

Baird, D. 1987. Analysis of the Chipped Stone from the 1985 Excavations at Tell esh-Shuna North. *ADAJ* 31: 461–80.

Contenson, H. de. 1960a. Three Soundings in the Jordan Valley. *ADAJ* 4/5: 12–98.

———. 1960b. La chronologie relative du niveau le plus ancien de Tell esh-Shuna. *MUSJ* 37: 57–77.

———. 1961. Remarques sur le Chalcolithique Recent de Tell esh-Shuna. *RB* 68: 546–66.

Gustavson-Gaube, C. 1985. Tell esh-Shuna North 1984: A Preliminary Report. *ADAJ* 29: 43–87.

———. 1986. Tell esh-Shuna North 1985: A Preliminary Report. *ADAJ* 30: 69–114.

Ibrahim, M.; Sauer, J.; and Yassine, K. 1976. The East Jordan Valley Survey 1975. *BASOR* 222: 41–46.

Mellaart, J. 1962. Preliminary Report of the Archaeological Survey in the Yarmouk and Jordan Valley. *ADAJ* 6/7: 126–57.

CARRIE GUSTAVSON-GAUBE

SHUNEM (PLACE) [Heb *šûnēm*]. SHUNAMMITE. A town in the hill territory of Issachar (Josh 19:18), at the foot of the hill of Moreh, identified with modern Solem (M.R. 181223). Surface surveys have yielded remains from the MB age to the Islamic period; most historical information is from the LB and Early Iron ages.

Shunem was the site of a Philistine encampment during an Israelite-Philistine battle under Saul (1 Sam 28:4). Abishag, the woman who warmed the aging King David and who was sought in marriage by David's son Adonijah, was a Shunammite (Heb *šûnammî;* 1 Kings 1–2). Elisha visited the town; a Shunammite woman fed and housed him, and he later revived her dead son (2 Kgs 4:8–27).

A Canaanite city-state before the Israelite period, Shunem (*š-n-m* or *š-n-m-i3* in the Egyptian orthography) is mentioned in the conquest list of Pharaoh Thutmose III (15th century B.C.E.; *ANET,* 243; Simon 1937: 214; *CTAED,* 176). It is also referred to (as Shunama) in the 14th-century Amarna Letters (*ANET,* 485). Having been attacked and destroyed by Labʾayu, it was the site of forced labor under the king of Megiddo, who described its inhabitants as recalcitrant. It is also listed in the conquest list of Pharaoh Sheshonk I (Shishak in biblical accounts) in the early days of the divided kingdom (*ANET,* 243; *CTAED,* 176), although the biblical account of his campaign does not mention an invasion of cities in the N kingdom. Some connect Shunem (and at times Abishag) with the SHULAMMITE of the Song of Songs (7:1—Eng 6:13).

Bibliography

Simon, J. 1937. *Handbook for the Study of Egyptian Topographical Lists Relating to Western Asia.* Leiden.

ELIZABETH F. HUWILER

SHUNI (PERSON) [Heb *šûnî*]. SHUNITES. The third of the seven sons of Gad mentioned in the genealogical list of the sons of Jacob (Gen 46:16). Shuni was the grandson of Jacob and Zilpah, the maid whom Laban gave to his daughter Leah on the occasion of her marriage to Jacob (Gen 29:24). His name appears among the seventy people who migrated with Jacob to Egypt at the time of a great famine in the land of Canaan (Gen 46:8–27). Nothing is known about Shuni. According to the second census of Israel mentioned in the book of Numbers, Shuni became the eponymous ancestor of the Shunites, one of the clans of Gad (Num 26:15).

None of the sons of Gad mentioned in the genealogical lists in Genesis and Numbers appear in the enumeration of the other clans of Gad in 1 Chr 5:11–17. Several proposals have been advanced to explain this omission. Some scholars had said that when the Chronicler listed the clans of Gad, he departed from his usual source of information. Others have said that the clans of Gad are implicitly mentioned in 1 Chr 5:11. Curtis and Madsen (*Chronicles* ICC, 122), however, identified Shuni with Guni (1 Chr 5:15). According to the Chronicler, seven of the eleven (or twelve, according to the enumeration of the LXX) clans of Gad traced their genealogical line to Guni. For this reason, some commentators believe that Shuni is a corrupted spelling of Guni.

CLAUDE F. MARIOTTINI

SHUPHAMITES [Heb *šûpāmîm*]. See SHEPHUPHAM.

SHUPPIM (PERSON) [Heb *šuppīm*]. This name occurs three times in the OT.

1. One of the sons of Ir named in 1 Chr 7:12 in a "fragmentary addition" (Williamson *Chronicles* NCBC, 78) to a Benjaminite genealogy (1 Chr 7:6–12). Although it has been proposed that the larger list was originally Zebulunite (Brunet 1953: 485–86), the correspondence of Shuppim and Huppim in v 12 with Shephupham and Hupham in Num 26:38–41 may testify to an original Benjaminite association of 1 Chr 7:12a, at least (Rudolph *Chronikbücher* HAT, 65). If in fact *ʿîr* (Shuppim's "father") is to be read as a personal name, then it might be associated with Iri son of Bela in v 7 (Williamson *Chronicles* NCBC, 78). Others, however, see no patronym for Shuppim here but read *dān* ("Dan") in place of *ʿîr* (Rudolph *Chronikbücher* HAT, 64–66). Verse 12b then represents the vestige of a Danite genealogy rather than a continuation of a Benjaminite fragment.

2. Shuppim occurs again in 1 Chr 7:15 (again with Huppim) where there are considerable textual difficulties. Rudolph (Ibid., 68–71), among many others, considers these names to be corruptions of Shechem and Hepher, sons of Gilead (cf. Num 26:29–34).

3. Shuppim also occurs in 1 Chr 26:16, where it is usually considered a dittograph (Rudolph Ibid., 172). Williamson (*Chronicles* NCBC, 171), however, proposes it might be a copyist's note for erasure indicating damage to the exemplar.

Bibliography

Brunet, A.-M. 1953. Le Chronist et ses Sources. *RB* 60: 481–508.

J. S. ROGERS

SHUQBA CAVE (M.R. 154154). Shuqba cave lies on the right bank of Wadi el-Natuf (from which the Natufian culture derives its name), which is a tributary of the Yarkon River, and descends from the Judean Hills into the coastal plain. The cave is a large chamber with a chimney at the rear part and three small side chambers. The excavations in 1928 by D. Garrod exposed a sequence of Mousterian layers overlaid by a Natufian layer covered by a more recent deposit composed of EB through modern debris.

The Mousterian layers were of two kinds. The lower one (D) was a soft red cave earth, which accumulated to a depth of about 2 m with remains of gray ashes. It contained artifacts and bones. Some of this layer had become consolidated into *breccia.* The overlying layer (C) was a red clay sediment which contained abraded Mousterian artifacts. This accumulation is explained as the results of water activity, such as caused by the presence of a spring inside the cave. The abraded artifacts were extracted from layer (D) and after being washed and worn by the water were redeposited inside the cave and one of the side chambers.

The contents of the *in situ* material of layer D included among others a lithic industry mostly made by Levallois technique with numerous side scrapers, some points, a few disks, and a few bifaces and burins. Among the faunal remains were hippopotamus and rhinoceros. The Mousterian remains appear to correlate with those of the Mt. Carmel sites.

The cave is better known for its Natufian remains, which included typical cultural attributes of this culture, namely, burials and a microlithic stone industry with numerous lunates as well as sickle blades. Among the heavy-duty tools were mortars and pestles. The Natufian lithic assemblage from Shuqba is Late Natufian and the microliths were often shaped without the exploitation of the microburin technique. It therefore resembles some other Late Natufian sites such as Salibiya I in the Lower Jordan Valley. The collection of bone tools consists mainly of points and awls, a few needles, and an engraved rib.

The fauna of the Natufian layer is chiefly represented by abundant gazelle remains, some cattle, deer, and wild cat.

The lack of Upper Paleolithic sediments in Shuqba is hard to explain unless the spring activity lasted, even intermittently, for a very long time. The Natufians settled on an uneven surface, and after abandoning the cave, a rockfall at the entrance and a subsidence in the area of the sinkhole distorted the lower and upper boundaries of this layer.

OFER BAR-YOSEF

SHUR, WILDERNESS OF (PLACE) [Heb *midbar šûr*]. A desert region and perhaps a place located in the N Sinai between the S border of Canaan and the NE border of Egypt (Gen 16:7; 20:1; 25:18; Exodus 15:22; 1 Sam 15:7; 27:8). The designation "Wilderness of Shur" *(midbar šûr)* occurs only once in the Bible, where it refers to one of the seven wildernesses (Shur, Etham, Sin, Sinai, Paran, Zin, and Kadesh) traversed by Moses and the children of Israel in the Exodus. In the Exodus accounts this area is located between the Red Sea and Marah and is the place where Israel murmured for water: "Then Moses led Israel onward from the Red Sea, and they went into the wilderness of Shur; they went three days in the wilderness and found no water" (Exod 15:22). The lack of water was remedied through the miraculous sweetening of the bitter water at Marah and Israel's eventual arrival at the twelve springs of Elim (Exod 15:23–27). In the parallel account in Num 33:8 this same area is designated as the Wilderness of Etham rather than Shur. See ETHAM.

While the general location of this area in the NW part of the Sinai peninsula between borders of Egypt and Palestine is assured, the precise boundaries of this wilderness depend on where the crossing of the Red Sea and the subsequent stopping place at Marah are to be located. There is no scholarly agreement regarding the location of either of these places. See RED SEA. Those who argue the S route to Sinai would place it E of the Red Sea (i.e., E of the Gulf of Suez) while those who argue for the northern route would place it farther N closer to the Mediterranean.

In the patriarchal narratives, Abraham is said to have "dwelt between Kadesh and Shur" before moving to Gerar (Gen 20:1), and it is noted that the descendants of Ishmael lived in an area "from Havilah to Shur, which is opposite Egypt in the direction of Assyria" (Gen 25:18; see also 1 Sam 15:7). Hagar fled to a well between Kadesh "on the way to Shur" (Gen 16:7). Some have suggested the "way of Shur" is a reference to an ancient caravan route Darb el-Shur used by the patriarchs in their journeys to Egypt running along the line Hebron-Beersheba-Khalasa-Quseima-Ismailia (Woolley and Lawrence 1914–15: 39–44; Lipschitz 1978: 51–52). In addition, twice the Amalekites are pursued "as far as Shur, to the land of Egypt" in the wars waged by Saul (1 Sam 15:7) and David (1 Sam 27:8). Several of these references suggest that in addition to the wilderness of Shur, there may be a specific place in this area by the same name (Naʾaman 1980: 100–5).

The word *šûr,* meaning "wall," occurs in the Bible in Hebrew (Gen 49:22; 2 Sam 22:30 = Ps 18:30) as well as in Aramaic (Ezra 4:12–13, 16). Because of this, many have supposed that the designation "Shur" originally referred to a line of individual Egyptian fortresses strategically placed on the E border, approximately along the line of the present-day Suez Canal, forming a "wall" to repel invaders as the "Wall-of-the-Ruler" in the story of Sinuhe (*GP* I: 434; *GTTOT,* 217, 251, 317–18; Lipschitz 1978: 27, 51–52). For arguments against this view, see Mazar 1957: 64. Others maintain that "Shur" was a reference to the range of cliffs E of the Gulf of Suez, extending along the western side of the et-Tih plateau from Wadi Gharandal in the S toward the Mediterranean in the N, which viewed from the W resemble a wall (Palmer 1872: 38–39). There is no consensus as to the meaning or the reference of the designation "Shur."

Bibliography

Lipschitz, O. 1978. *Sinai.* Tel Aviv.
Mazar, B. 1957. The Campaign of Pharaoh Shishak to Palestine. *VTSup* 4: 57–66.
Naʾaman, N. 1980. The Shihor of Egypt and Shur That Is Before Egypt. *Tel Aviv* 7: 95–109.
Palmer, E. H. 1872. *The Desert of the Exodus.* New York.
Woolley, C. L., and Lawrence, T. E. 1914–15. *The Wilderness of Zin.* PEFA 3. London.

DAVID R. SEELY

SHUTHELAH (PERSON) [Heb *šûtelaḥ*]. SHUTHELAHITES. **1.** Shuthelah is the first son of Ephraim according to 1 Chr 7:20. This genealogy of Ephraim lists many descendants including Shuthelah's son Bered, two Tahaths, Zabad, another Shuthelah (v 21), and others. The significance of the 1 Chronicles 7 passage is to point toward Joshua (v 27), an Ephraimite, the hero of the conquest. Braun (*1 Chronicles* WBC, 114) speculates that this genealogy is a combination of two earlier lists owing to the repetition of various names (Shuthelah, Tahath), similarity of others (Bered, v 20, and Zabad, v 21; Eleadah, v 20, and Ladan, v 26; Tahath, v 20, and Tahan, v 25) and length of the genealogy. Hogg (1900–1: 147–49) argues that the 1 Chronicles 7 text is corrupt and suggests that Ephraim's descendants should be reduced to Shuthelah, Tahath (or equivalents), and Eleadah (or equivalents).

Numbers 26:35–36 is the only other OT listing of the Ephraimite clan (except Genesis 46 in the LXX). Based on the Numbers passage, Ephraim had three sons: Shuthelah, Becher, and Tahan. They are described as the heads of clans—the Shuthelahites, the Becherites, and the Tahanites (26:35). Also mentioned in Numbers 26 is an Eran who is a descendant of Shuthelah.

2. Shuthelah is a descendant of Ephraim (1 Chr 7:21). See #1 above. Because the text is confusing, this Shuthelah may simply be a repetition of the earlier name (v 20).

Bibliography

Hogg, H. W. 1900–1. The Ephraimite Genealogy. *JQR* 13: 147–54.

M. STEPHEN DAVIS